THE FOUNDATION DIRECTORY 1991 Edition

13TH EDITION

Compiled by
THE FOUNDATION CENTER

Stan Olson, Editor
Margaret Mary Feczko, Assistant Editor

The Foundation Center

CONTRIBUTING STAFF

Director of Publications	Bill Bartenbach
Director of Information Systems	Martha David
Director of Information Systems Services	Margaret Derrickson
Production Manager	Rick Schoff
Information Control Coordinator	Ted Murphy
Editorial Associates	Alexander Anderson Sonje Berg Gilbert Hennessey Margaret B. Jung Cheryl L. Loe José Santiago Zoe Waldron Mara B. Zeldin
Database Analyst	Virginia Higgins
Search Analyst	M. Lara Brock

The editors gratefully acknowledge the many other Foundation Center staff who contributed support, encouragement, and information which was indispensable to the preparation of this volume. Special mention should also be made of the staff members of the New York, Washington, D.C., Cleveland, and San Francisco libraries who assisted in tracking changes in foundation information. We would like to express our appreciation as well to the many foundations which cooperated fully in updating information prior to the compilation of the *Directory*.

ISBN 0-87954-345-0
ISSN 0071-8092
Printed and bound in the United States of America

CONTENTS

INTRODUCTION

The Foundation Directory is the standard reference work for information about private and community grantmaking foundations in the United States. It is used by fundseekers, foundation and government officials, scholars, journalists, and others generally interested in foundation giving in this country.

THE THIRTEENTH EDITION

The Thirteenth Edition of the *Directory* is the first to be updated on an annual basis. It documents a significantly larger universe of foundations meeting the criteria of at least $1 million in assets or $100,000 in annual giving. Entries for 7,581 private and community foundations are included in this volume, up from 6,615 in the Twelfth Edition. These 7,581 foundations represent fully one-fourth of all active grantmaking foundations in the United States. Together they held over $125 billion or 96 percent of all foundation assets and awarded more than $7 billion or 93 percent of total foundation giving in the latest year of record.

In addition, the Thirteenth Edition includes for the first time an entry describing the Howard Hughes Medical Institute, classified by the IRS as a Medical Research Organization rather than a private foundation. The Hughes Institute closely resembles a private foundation in that it has its own funds from a single source, does not make appeals to the public for donations, and aids charitable purposes through grantmaking in accordance with an IRS payout requirement. For these reasons, an entry for this major philanthropic organization was included; however, the statistical tables and summaries below do not include figures from the Hughes Institute.

FOUNDATIONS NEW TO THE *DIRECTORY*

There are 1,225 foundations in the Thirteenth Edition that were not covered in last year's Twelfth Edition, indicating accelerated growth in the rate at which new and newly qualifying foundations are meeting *Directory* criteria. By comparison, the Twelfth Edition of the *Directory* added 1,713 foundations over a two-year period, an unprecedented increase at that time. Of the foundations new to this edition, 1,086 (88.7 percent) are independent foundations, 81 (6.6 percent) are company-sponsored foundations, 19 (1.6 percent) are community foundations, and 39 (3.2 percent) are operating foundations.

Seventeen of the foundations new to this edition hold assets of $20 million or more (Table 6), but, like the other *Directory* foundations, the majority fall into the $1 million to $5 million asset range. The 1,225 newly qualifying foundations make up 16.2 percent of the 7,581 foundations in this volume, but hold only 2.6 percent of assets ($2.8 billion) and paid only 3.8 percent of grants ($269.6 million). Their share of gifts received, $606 million or 12.7 percent, was much more substantial. Foundations new to the *Directory* can be identified by the symbol ☆ in their descriptive entries. They are also listed separately in the Index of Foundations New to Edition 13.

WHAT'S IN THE *DIRECTORY*?

The *Directory* includes only those organizations which meet the Foundation Center's definition of a community or private grantmaking foundation and which held assets of $1 million or more or gave $100,000 or more in the latest year of record. The Center defines a foundation as a nongovernmental, nonprofit organization with its own funds (usually from a single source, either an individual, family, or corporation) and program managed by its own trustees and directors, which was established to maintain or aid educational, social, charitable, religious, or other activities serving the common welfare primarily by making grants to other nonprofit organizations.

The *Directory* does not include private foundations whose total giving is restricted by charter to one or more specified organizations; foundations which function as endowments for special purposes within and under the governance of a parent institution, such as a college or church; operating foundations which do not maintain active grantmaking programs; organizations which act as associations for industrial or other special groups; and organizations which make general appeals to the public for funds. Lists of private foundations which meet the asset size criteria for the *Directory* but which are excluded from this volume for the reasons cited above are provided in the Appendixes.

TYPES OF FOUNDATIONS

Foundations included in this *Directory*, in addition to meeting the Center's definition, fall into one of four categories:

Independent Foundation: a fund or endowment designated by the Internal Revenue Service as a private foundation under the law, the primary function of which is the making of grants. The assets of most independent foundations are derived from the gift of an individual or family. Some function under the direction of family members and are known as "family foundations." Depending on the range of their giving, independent foundations may also be known as "general purpose" or "special purpose" foundations.

Company-Sponsored Foundation: a private foundation under the tax law deriving its funds from a profit-making company or corporation but independently constituted, the purpose of which is to make grants, usually on a broad basis although not without regard for the business interests of the corporation. Company-sponsored foundations are legally distinct from corporate contributions programs administered within the corporation directly from corporate funds. This *Directory* does not include direct giving programs. The Foundation Center's *National Directory of Corporate Giving*, published in 1989, includes corporate giving profiles on approximately 1,500 companies.

Operating Foundation: a fund or endowment designated under the tax law by the Internal Revenue Service as a private foundation, the primary purpose of which is to operate research, social welfare, or other programs determined by its governing body or charter. Most operating foundations award few or no grants to outside organizations, and therefore do not appear in the *Directory*.

Community Foundation: in its general charitable purpose, a community foundation is much like many private foundations; however, its funds are derived from many donors rather than a single source as is usually the case with private foundations. Further, community foundations are usually classified under the tax law as public charities and are therefore subject to different rules and regulations under the tax law than those which govern private foundations. Public charities other than community foundations are not included in this *Directory*.

SOURCES OF INFORMATION

To identify organizations for inclusion in *The Foundation Directory*, Foundation Center staff monitor IRS information returns for private foundations (Form 990-PF), journal and newspaper articles, press releases and news services related to foundation activities, and foundation publications such as newsletters and annual reports. Entries are prepared from the most recent information available and sent to the individual foundations for verification.

The Thirteenth Edition of *The Foundation Directory* is completely revised and updated using the latest information from the foundations themselves or from public records. In the year since the publication of the Twelfth Edition in 1989, requests for verification were sent to all 7,581 foundations listed in this volume, and 2,765 foundations (36 percent) responded fully. Among the 1,000 largest *Directory* foundations, the response rate was over 72 percent. For those foundations not responding to our mailings, entries were prepared from the most recent IRS information returns available as of June 1990. These entries are indicated in the *Directory* by the symbol ¤ following the foundation name.

This edition includes more current information than ever before. A breakdown of the 7,581 foundations in the *Directory* by fiscal year-end date reveals the following: 48 foundations (0.6 percent) with early 1990 fiscal data; 2,478 foundations (32.7 percent) with 1989 fiscal data; 3,977 foundations (52.5 percent) with 1988 fiscal data; 946 foundations (12.5 percent) with 1987 fiscal data; and 132 foundations (1.7 percent) with 1986 fiscal data. Thus, 1989 or early 1990 fiscal information is reported for 33 percent of all foundations listed. Of the 50 largest foundations, over four-fifths are represented by 1989 or 1990 fiscal data. Addresses, program information, and application procedures are based on the latest updates received by the Center through June 1990, even when more recent financial information was not available.

TABLE 1. AGGREGATE FISCAL DATA BY FOUNDATION TYPE (All dollar figures expressed in thousands)

Foundation Type	Number of Foundations	Percent	Assets	Percent	Gifts Received	Percent	Total Giving*	Percent	Loans
Independent Foundations	6,264	82.6	$107,743,231	85.9	$2,968,949	62.3	$5,245,949	74.1	$67,018
Company-Sponsored Foundations	946	12.5	5,409,730	4.3	1,109,286	23.3	1,334,441	18.9	10,129
Community Foundations	189	2.5	5,896,424	4.7	525,034	11.0	403,500	5.7	5,285
Operating Foundations	182	2.4	6,443,561	5.1	162,045	3.4	92,877	1.3	3,575
Total	7,581	100.0	$125,492,947	100.0	$4,765,314	100.0	$7,076,767	100.0	$86,008

Note: Figures may not add up due to rounding.
*Throughout this introduction, "Total Giving" figures include grants, scholarships, employee matching gifts, and other amounts reported as "Grants and Contributions Paid During the Year" on the 990-PF reporting form. Loan amounts including program-related investments (PRIs) are indicated separately. Total giving does not include all qualifying distributions under the tax law, i.e., loans, PRIs, and program or other administrative expenses.

TABLE 2. AGGREGATE FISCAL DATA FOR FOUNDATIONS NEW TO THE *DIRECTORY* BY FOUNDATION TYPE (All dollar figures expressed in thousands)

Foundation Type	Number of Foundations	Percent	Assets	Percent	Gifts Received	Percent	Total Giving*	Percent	Loans
Independent Foundations	1,086	88.7	$2,484,935	87.8	$541,877	89.4	$223,254	82.8	$1,177
Company-Sponsored Foundations	81	6.6	158,129	5.6	27,154	4.5	24,702	9.2	5
Community Foundations	19	1.6	82,925	2.9	20,629	3.4	6,672	2.5	0
Operating Foundations	39	3.2	103,703	3.7	16,366	2.7	14,971	5.6	0
Total	1,225	100.0	$2,829,691	100.0	$606,026	100.0	$269,599	100.0	$1,182

Note: Figures may not add up due to rounding.
*Throughout this introduction, "Total Giving" figures include grants, scholarships, employee matching gifts, and other amounts reported as "Grants and Contributions Paid During the Year" on the 990-PF reporting form. Loan amounts including program-related investments (PRIs) are indicated separately. Total giving does not include all qualifying distributions under the tax law, i.e., loans, PRIs, and program or other administrative expenses.

TABLE 3. FISCAL DATA OF FOUNDATIONS BY REGION AND STATE (All dollar figures expressed in thousands)

	Number of Foundations	Percent	Assets	Percent	Gifts Received	Percent	Expenditures	Percent	Total Giving	Percent
Middle Atlantic	**2,040**	**26.9**	**$ 43,341,463**	**34.5**	**$ 935,175**	**19.6**	**$2,732,355**	**33.0**	**$2,357,777**	**33.3**
New Jersey	227		4,512,851		95,443		300,041		277,903	
New York	1,428		29,221,921		672,563		1,883,399		1,579,399	
Pennsylvania	385		9,606,692		167,169		548,916		500,475	
East North Central	**1,400**	**18.5**	**27,317,589**	**21.8**	**844,447**	**17.7**	**1,707,007**	**20.6**	**1,450,467**	**20.5**
Illinois	475		7,851,652		252,366		588,786		464,782	
Indiana	122		4,474,186		81,301		177,298		156,037	
Michigan	239		9,206,154		271,970		498,037		445,025	
Ohio	410		4,600,552		180,961		338,814		295,133	
Wisconsin	154		1,185,046		57,849		104,072		89,490	
Pacific	**855**	**11.3**	**15,964,344**	**12.7**	**804,843**	**16.9**	**967,887**	**11.7**	**806,380**	**11.4**
Alaska	4		6,053		1,139		1,389		937	
California	669		14,251,429		733,798		841,594		694,953	
Hawaii	33		332,873		7,296		19,421		17,009	
Oregon	50		595,648		30,037		37,847		33,508	
Washington	99		778,341		32,573		67,635		59,973	
West South Central	**604**	**8.0**	**9,737,384**	**7.8**	**266,864**	**5.6**	**659,011**	**8.0**	**545,974**	**7.7**
Arkansas	34		246,060		14,496		29,054		25,166	
Louisiana	66		374,151		12,496		22,866		17,082	
Oklahoma	80		1,705,217		11,876		93,222		71,280	
Texas	424		7,411,955		227,996		513,869		432,447	
South Atlantic	**1,100**	**14.5**	**13,065,380**	**10.4**	**902,076**	**18.9**	**952,517**	**11.5**	**800,627**	**11.3**
Delaware	58		834,918		4,983		52,388		38,154	
District of Columbia	92		1,479,377		84,384		127,393		83,967	
Florida	303		2,095,061		223,096		192,347		158,075	
Georgia	163		2,479,734		244,728		110,249		105,794	
Maryland	138		1,566,802		187,950		146,338		129,634	
North Carolina	149		2,793,179		85,087		175,800		159,978	
South Carolina	50		277,667		12,703		20,518		16,774	
Virginia	120		1,349,473		50,840		116,142		98,819	
West Virginia	27		189,169		8,305		11,341		9,432	
West North Central	**532**	**7.0**	**6,205,363**	**4.9**	**312,786**	**6.6**	**512,188**	**6.2**	**462,930**	**6.5**
Iowa	60		425,455		12,154		37,141		31,895	
Kansas	64		296,446		8,707		26,689		23,669	
Minnesota	169		3,368,348		146,471		243,956		219,063	
Missouri	182		1,704,455		122,165		164,321		152,655	
Nebraska	46		371,455		15,476		37,277		33,925	
North Dakota	7		23,024		1,838		2,076		1,428	
South Dakota	4		16,179		5,975		729		294	
New England	**616**	**8.1**	**5,331,513**	**4.2**	**222,952**	**4.7**	**443,016**	**5.3**	**391,362**	**5.5**
Connecticut	167		2,113,814		119,371		206,759		177,323	
Maine	16		43,959		3,926		4,179		3,613	
Massachusetts	349		2,375,268		82,269		180,609		164,371	
New Hampshire	30		181,223		7,722		12,025		9,854	
Rhode Island	46		553,733		8,515		35,709		34,184	
Vermont	8		63,516		1,150		3,735		2,019	
Mountain	**225**	**3.0**	**2,974,573**	**2.4**	**408,364**	**8.6**	**180,226**	**2.2**	**153,353**	**2.2**
Arizona	38		414,185		17,449		30,604		24,440	
Colorado	90		1,298,419		106,530		94,134		82,513	
Idaho	12		52,799		637		3,869		3,380	
Montana	11		49,134		4,613		2,990		2,735	
Nevada	19		703,922		246,177		24,688		20,429	
New Mexico	11		152,658		17,721		6,762		4,937	
Utah	32		256,013		13,744		13,775		11,891	
Wyoming	12		47,442		1,493		3,403		3,026	
East South Central	**207**	**2.7**	**1,545,863**	**1.2**	**64,629**	**1.4**	**124,615**	**1.5**	**106,614**	**1.5**
Alabama	64		292,981		9,538		22,060		20,617	
Kentucky	38		373,220		24,879		37,358		30,992	
Mississippi	18		76,679		3,090		8,939		7,787	
Tennessee	87		802,983		27,122		56,257		47,218	
Puerto Rico	**2**	**0.0**	**9,473**	**0.0**	**3,178**	**0.1**	**1,999**	**0.0**	**1,283**	**0.0**
Total	**7,581**	**100.0**	**$125,492,947**	**100.0**	**$4,765,314**	**100.0**	**$8,280,821**	**100.0**	**$7,076,767**	**100.0**

Note: Figures may not add up due to rounding.

TABLE 4. 100 LARGEST FOUNDATIONS BY ASSETS

Name	Assets	Total Giving	Fiscal Date
1. The Ford Foundation	**$5,832,426,000**	$217,669,414	09/30/89
2. W. K. Kellogg Foundation	**4,201,240,259**	106,948,094	08/31/89
3. J. Paul Getty Trust	**3,982,184,662**	12,583,675[1]	06/30/88
4. Lilly Endowment, Inc.	**3,357,904,453**	92,510,387	12/31/89
5. The Pew Charitable Trusts	**3,321,890,529**	137,083,529	12/31/89
6. John D. and Catherine T. MacArthur Foundation	**3,134,508,720**	95,332,920	12/31/88
7. The Robert Wood Johnson Foundation	**2,608,347,000**	98,600,000	12/31/89
8. The Rockefeller Foundation	**2,140,244,924**	65,717,663	12/31/89
9. The Andrew W. Mellon Foundation	**1,832,347,000**	75,501,129	12/31/89
10. The Kresge Foundation	**1,261,100,053**	57,533,000	12/31/89
11. The Duke Endowment	**990,835,850**	45,940,739	12/31/89
12. Charles Stewart Mott Foundation	**961,114,454**	43,795,989	12/31/89
13. The McKnight Foundation	**917,641,548**	31,961,975	12/31/89
14. Carnegie Corporation of New York	**905,106,313**	39,306,029	09/30/89
15. Richard King Mellon Foundation	**878,877,690**	15,431,712	12/31/89
16. The New York Community Trust	**829,783,809**	46,422,562	12/31/89
17. W. M. Keck Foundation	**764,433,113**	35,286,000	12/31/89
18. Robert W. Woodruff Foundation, Inc.	**755,690,077**	8,731,763	12/31/89
19. DeWitt Wallace-Reader's Digest Fund, Inc.	**697,122,307**	17,754,259	12/31/89
20. The William and Flora Hewlett Foundation	**687,664,000**	36,970,028	12/31/89
21. Robert R. McCormick Charitable Trust	**630,994,902**	19,904,476	12/31/89
22. Alfred P. Sloan Foundation	**622,070,457**	17,249,581	12/31/89
23. Houston Endowment, Inc.	**614,658,550**	35,966,333	12/31/88
24. Knight Foundation	**581,138,052**	16,665,311	12/31/89
25. The Annie E. Casey Foundation	**580,000,000**	17,755,391	12/31/89
26. The Cleveland Foundation	**579,897,967**	27,560,926	12/31/89
27. The Harry and Jeanette Weinberg Foundation, Inc.	**560,117,000**	53,706,000	02/28/89
28. Gannett Foundation	**547,540,276**	24,869,119	12/31/88
29. The James Irvine Foundation	**540,000,000**	20,487,000	12/31/89
30. Lila Wallace-Reader's Digest Fund, Inc.	**527,739,800**	11,086,288	12/31/89
31. The J. E. and L. E. Mabee Foundation, Inc.	**494,281,654**	18,664,903	08/31/89
32. Conrad N. Hilton Foundation	**492,092,546**	10,179,630	02/28/90
33. Meadows Foundation, Inc.	**476,217,532**	18,608,011	12/31/89
34. The William Penn Foundation	**470,442,587**	25,417,928	12/31/89
35. The Starr Foundation	**464,860,690**	21,147,022	12/31/88
36. Marin Community Foundation	**456,903,000**	21,385,000	06/30/89
37. The Ahmanson Foundation	**437,995,000**	20,150,353	10/31/89
38. Howard Heinz Endowment	**433,860,577**	15,299,077	12/31/88
39. The Henry Luce Foundation, Inc.	**419,279,061**	19,589,345	12/31/89
40. The Bush Foundation	**417,968,000**	17,387,493	11/30/89
41. The Brown Foundation, Inc.	**413,019,005**	21,090,350	06/30/89
42. The Henry J. Kaiser Family Foundation	**408,513,703**	12,846,314	12/31/89
43. Weingart Foundation	**404,198,697**	18,136,124	06/30/89
44. The Moody Foundation	**396,462,000**	15,460,064	12/31/88
45. The Edna McConnell Clark Foundation	**372,054,687**	18,471,486	09/30/88
46. The Joyce Foundation	**348,286,228**	12,816,299	12/31/89
47. The Samuel Roberts Noble Foundation, Inc.	**345,256,786**	5,041,136	10/31/89
48. The Lynde and Harry Bradley Foundation, Inc.	**339,775,000**	23,040,293	07/31/88
49. Longwood Foundation, Inc.	**336,356,687**	15,117,664	09/30/89
50. Hall Family Foundations	**323,873,343**	4,581,115	12/31/89
51. Arthur S. DeMoss Foundation	**323,687,337**	15,880,682	12/31/87
52. The Chicago Community Trust	**316,431,057**	26,210,194	09/30/89

TABLE 4. (cont.)

Name	Assets	Total Giving	Fiscal Date
53. The Commonwealth Fund	**$ 314,132,587**	$ 10,553,889	06/30/89
54. Surdna Foundation, Inc.	**312,534,326**	18,205,839	06/30/89
55. Joseph B. Whitehead Foundation	**310,191,188**	9,489,695	12/31/89
56. William Randolph Hearst Foundation	**297,000,000**	9,737,500	12/31/89
57. Horace W. Goldsmith Foundation	**290,551,412**	11,155,225	12/31/89
58. The Whitaker Foundation	**287,225,775**	10,527,861	12/31/88
59. Meyer Memorial Trust	**276,842,089**	11,953,746	03/31/90
60. The Robert A. Welch Foundation	**270,041,000**	12,472,645	08/31/89
61. The William K. Warren Foundation	**269,743,325**	15,389,470	12/31/88
62. The Herbert H. and Grace A. Dow Foundation	**266,179,667**	8,391,468	12/31/88
63. F. W. Olin Foundation, Inc.	**263,959,853**	9,290,658	12/31/89
64. Kate B. Reynolds Charitable Trust	**262,596,647**	12,628,574	08/31/89
65. The John A. Hartford Foundation, Inc.	**259,328,174**	7,623,735	12/31/89
66. The George Gund Foundation	**257,234,830**	10,277,060	12/31/88
67. McCune Foundation	**251,109,513**	13,364,994	09/30/89
68. Alcoa Foundation	**250,314,828**	11,403,961	12/31/89
69. El Pomar Foundation	**250,000,000**	10,131,717	12/31/89
70. Sid W. Richardson Foundation	**249,876,981**	6,307,466	12/31/89
71. Smith Richardson Foundation, Inc.	**248,907,833**	15,311,787	12/31/88
72. The David and Lucile Packard Foundation	**245,887,758**	27,675,502	12/31/89
73. The Skillman Foundation	**243,785,298**	10,958,840	12/31/88
74. The Champlin Foundations	**243,569,771**	12,677,323	12/31/89
75. T. L. L. Temple Foundation	**242,162,688**	10,009,877	11/30/89
76. Rockefeller Brothers Fund	**242,120,725**	7,999,659	12/31/88
77. Public Welfare Foundation, Inc.	**236,686,000**	12,331,100	10/31/89
78. William R. Kenan, Jr. Charitable Trust	**234,367,668**	8,630,000	12/31/89
79. The Colorado Trust	**232,899,690**	8,026,412	12/31/89
80. Andersen Foundation	**232,768,426**	8,861,650	12/31/88
81. Northwest Area Foundation	**228,378,768**	12,998,505	02/28/90
82. The Spencer Foundation	**224,871,503**	10,686,022	03/31/89
83. The Boston Foundation, Inc.	**224,313,974**	12,966,006	06/30/89
84. The Clark Foundation	**223,791,850**	7,624,520	06/30/89
85. Lettie Pate Whitehead Foundation, Inc.	**223,365,208**	6,999,333	12/31/89
86. The Morris and Gwendolyn Cafritz Foundation	**222,908,164**	7,377,539	04/30/89
87. M. J. Murdock Charitable Trust	**220,760,817**	11,940,078	12/31/89
88. Z. Smith Reynolds Foundation, Inc.	**220,214,158**	7,392,004	12/31/89
89. Lucille P. Markey Charitable Trust	**215,460,532**	43,115,626	06/30/89
90. Vira I. Heinz Endowment	**212,563,283**	6,913,371	12/31/88
91. Herrick Foundation	**210,459,774**	10,745,750	09/30/88
92. Sarah Scaife Foundation, Inc.	**203,133,504**	8,304,000	12/31/89
93. James Graham Brown Foundation, Inc.	**200,075,499**	8,459,687	12/31/89
94. F. M. Kirby Foundation, Inc.	**200,000,000**	8,000,000	12/31/89
95. Peter Kiewit Foundation	**196,998,982**	16,224,525	06/30/89
96. Connelly Foundation	**196,355,181**	8,500,089	12/31/88
97. Bat Hanadiv Foundation No. 3	**195,644,879**	7,278,280	12/31/88
98. The San Francisco Foundation	**193,526,511**	11,124,714	06/30/89
99. W. Alton Jones Foundation, Inc.	**193,450,890**	11,545,227	12/31/89
100. The Sherman Fairchild Foundation, Inc.	**188,385,412**	10,199,030	12/31/88

[1]J. Paul Getty Trust is an operating foundation and most of its qualifying distributions are paid out for administration of operating programs and not for grants. Total giving includes only grants and grant-related expenses as reported. In 1988, program amounts totaled $136.77 million.

TABLE 5. 100 LARGEST FOUNDATIONS BY TOTAL GIVING

Name	Total Giving	Assets	Fiscal Date
1. The Ford Foundation	**$217,669,414**	$5,832,426,000	09/30/89
2. The Pew Charitable Trusts	**137,083,529**	3,321,890,529	12/31/89
3. W. K. Kellogg Foundation	**106,948,094**	4,201,240,259	08/31/89
4. The Robert Wood Johnson Foundation	**98,600,000**	2,608,347,000	12/31/89
5. John D. and Catherine T. MacArthur Foundation	**95,332,920**	3,134,508,720	12/31/88
6. Lilly Endowment, Inc.	**92,510,387**	3,357,904,453	12/31/89
7. The Andrew W. Mellon Foundation	**75,501,129**	1,832,347,000	12/31/89
8. The Rockefeller Foundation	**65,717,663**	2,140,244,924	12/31/89
9. The Kresge Foundation	**57,533,000**	1,261,100,053	12/31/89
10. The Harry and Jeanette Weinberg Foundation, Inc.	**53,706,000**	560,117,000	02/28/89
11. The New York Community Trust	**46,422,562**	829,783,809	12/31/89
12. The Duke Endowment	**45,940,739**	990,835,850	12/31/89
13. Charles Stewart Mott Foundation	**43,795,989**	961,114,454	12/31/89
14. Lucille P. Markey Charitable Trust	**43,115,626**	215,460,532	06/30/89
15. Carnegie Corporation of New York	**39,306,029**	905,106,313	09/30/89
16. The William and Flora Hewlett Foundation	**36,970,028**	687,664,000	12/31/89
17. Houston Endowment, Inc.	**35,966,333**	614,658,550	12/31/88
18. W. M. Keck Foundation	**35,286,000**	764,433,113	12/31/89
19. The McKnight Foundation	**31,961,975**	917,641,548	12/31/89
20. AT&T Foundation	**30,426,888**	126,766,000	12/31/89
21. The David and Lucile Packard Foundation	**27,675,502**	245,887,758	12/31/89
22. The Cleveland Foundation	**27,560,926**	579,897,967	12/31/89
23. The Chicago Community Trust	**26,210,194**	316,431,057	09/30/89
24. The William Penn Foundation	**25,417,928**	470,442,587	12/31/89
25. General Motors Foundation, Inc.	**25,262,453**	169,056,275	12/31/88
26. Gannett Foundation	**24,869,119**	547,540,276	12/31/88
27. Amoco Foundation, Inc.	**23,991,838**	68,480,472	12/31/89
28. Ford Motor Company Fund	**23,301,862**	82,342,201	12/31/89
29. The Lynde and Harry Bradley Foundation, Inc.	**23,040,293**	339,775,000	07/31/88
30. Orville D. & Ruth A. Merillat Foundation	**22,377,750**	64,695,846	02/28/88
31. Communities Foundation of Texas, Inc.	**21,499,977**	152,028,702	06/30/89
32. Marin Community Foundation	**21,385,000**	456,903,000	06/30/89
33. The Starr Foundation	**21,147,022**	464,860,690	12/31/88
34. The Brown Foundation, Inc.	**21,090,350**	413,019,005	06/30/89
35. The James Irvine Foundation	**20,487,000**	540,000,000	12/31/89
36. The Ahmanson Foundation	**20,150,353**	437,995,000	10/31/89
37. Robert R. McCormick Charitable Trust	**19,904,476**	630,994,902	12/31/89
38. US WEST Foundation	**19,708,234**	6,069,021	12/31/89
39. The Henry Luce Foundation, Inc.	**19,589,345**	419,279,061	12/31/89
40. Arnold and Mabel Beckman Foundation	**19,343,124**	179,263,236	08/31/89
41. General Electric Foundation	**18,834,164**	32,613,000	12/31/89
42. The J. E. and L. E. Mabee Foundation, Inc.	**18,664,903**	494,281,654	08/31/89
43. Meadows Foundation, Inc.	**18,608,011**	476,217,532	12/31/89
44. The Xerox Foundation	**18,500,000**	18,500,000	12/31/89
45. The Edna McConnell Clark Foundation	**18,471,486**	372,054,687	09/30/88
46. Exxon Education Foundation	**18,233,815**	42,621,000	12/31/89
47. Surdna Foundation, Inc.	**18,205,839**	312,534,326	06/30/89
48. Weingart Foundation	**18,136,124**	404,198,697	06/30/89
49. GTE Foundation	**18,043,847**	21,455,383	12/31/89

TABLE 5. (cont.)

Name	Total Giving	Assets	Fiscal Date
50. The Annie E. Casey Foundation	**$17,755,391**	$580,000,000	12/31/89
51. DeWitt Wallace-Reader's Digest Fund, Inc.	**17,754,259**	697,122,307	12/31/89
52. The Bush Foundation	**17,387,493**	417,968,000	11/30/89
53. Alfred P. Sloan Foundation	**17,249,581**	622,070,457	12/31/89
54. Autry Foundation	**17,042,492**	41,119,961	12/31/88
55. Knight Foundation	**16,665,311**	581,138,052	12/31/89
56. Peter Kiewit Foundation	**16,224,525**	196,998,982	06/30/89
57. Arthur S. DeMoss Foundation	**15,880,682**	323,687,337	12/31/87
58. The Aaron Diamond Foundation, Inc.	**15,685,261**	126,198,026	12/31/88
59. Southwestern Bell Foundation	**15,580,000**	42,012,377	12/31/89
60. The Moody Foundation	**15,460,064**	396,462,000	12/31/88
61. Richard King Mellon Foundation	**15,431,712**	878,877,690	12/31/89
62. The William K. Warren Foundation	**15,389,470**	269,743,325	12/31/88
63. Smith Richardson Foundation, Inc.	**15,311,787**	248,907,833	12/31/88
64. Howard Heinz Endowment	**15,299,077**	433,860,577	12/31/88
65. Shell Oil Company Foundation	**15,233,402**	14,067,360	12/31/89
66. Longwood Foundation, Inc.	**15,117,664**	336,356,687	09/30/89
67. John M. Olin Foundation, Inc.	**14,840,000**	90,000,000	12/31/89
68. The Procter & Gamble Fund	**14,622,593**	24,259,320	06/30/89
69. Burlington Northern Foundation	**14,590,777**	18,405,341	12/31/88
70. The Prudential Foundation	**14,386,965**	104,344,000	12/31/89
71. ARCO Foundation	**14,091,746**	3,270,037	12/31/88
72. Mobil Foundation, Inc.	**13,866,911**	13,253,485	12/31/88
73. McCune Foundation	**13,364,994**	251,109,513	09/30/89
74. Northwest Area Foundation	**12,998,505**	228,378,768	02/28/90
75. The Boston Foundation, Inc.	**12,966,006**	224,313,974	06/30/89
76. The Columbus Foundation	**12,882,000**	156,000,000	12/31/89
77. The Henry J. Kaiser Family Foundation	**12,846,314**	408,513,703	12/31/89
78. The Joyce Foundation	**12,816,299**	348,286,228	12/31/89
79. The Champlin Foundations	**12,677,323**	243,569,771	12/31/89
80. Kate B. Reynolds Charitable Trust	**12,628,574**	262,596,647	08/31/89
81. J. Paul Getty Trust	**12,583,675**[1]	3,982,184,662	06/30/88
82. The Robert A. Welch Foundation	**12,472,645**	270,041,000	08/31/89
83. Public Welfare Foundation, Inc.	**12,331,100**	236,686,000	10/31/89
84. James S. McDonnell Foundation	**12,035,472**	103,523,741	12/31/89
85. Meyer Memorial Trust	**11,953,746**	276,842,089	03/31/90
86. M. J. Murdock Charitable Trust	**11,940,078**	220,760,817	12/31/89
87. American Express Foundation	**11,736,028**	1,501,402	12/31/89
88. Chrysler Corporation Fund	**11,656,646**	31,000,000	12/31/89
89. W. Alton Jones Foundation, Inc.	**11,545,227**	193,450,890	12/31/89
90. Dayton Hudson Foundation	**11,452,875**	16,700,000	01/31/90
91. Alcoa Foundation	**11,403,961**	250,314,828	12/31/89
92. Horace W. Goldsmith Foundation	**11,155,225**	290,551,412	12/31/89
93. The San Francisco Foundation	**11,124,714**	193,526,511	06/30/89
94. Lila Wallace-Reader's Digest Fund, Inc.	**11,086,288**	527,739,800	12/31/89
95. Koret Foundation	**11,012,929**	186,660,915	12/31/89
96. The Skillman Foundation	**10,958,840**	243,785,298	12/31/88
97. Herrick Foundation	**10,745,750**	210,459,774	09/30/88
98. Westinghouse Foundation	**10,692,769**	8,373,427	12/31/88
99. The Spencer Foundation	**10,686,022**	224,871,503	03/31/89
100. The Commonwealth Fund	**10,553,889**	314,132,587	06/30/89

[1]J. Paul Getty Trust is an operating foundation and most of its qualifying distributions are paid out for administration of operating programs and not for grants. Total giving includes only grants and grant-related expenses as reported. In 1988, program amounts totaled $136.77 million.

TABLE 6. FOUNDATIONS NEW TO THE *DIRECTORY* WITH ASSETS OVER $20 MILLION (All dollar figures expressed in thousands)

Name	State	Establishment Year	Type of Foundation*	Fiscal Date	Assets	Gifts Received	Total Giving
The Milken Family Foundation	CA	1986	I	11/30/87	$97,537	$105,276	$4,015
John S. Dunn Research Foundation	TX	1985	I	12/31/89	72,320	127	2,950
Milken Family Medical Foundation	CA	1986	I	10/31/88	68,953	50,219	4,524
FHP Foundation	CA	1985	CS	06/30/89	54,830	0	773
The Francis Families Foundation[1]	MO	1989	I	12/31/87	53,668	0	2,453
Christy-Houston Foundation, Inc.	TN	1987	I	04/30/88	45,308	1,741	158
The Ian Woodner Family Collection, Inc.	NY	1986	I	06/30/89	37,495	7,717	262
Clay Foundation, Inc.	WV	1986	I	10/31/88	32,317	17	906
The Tull Charitable Foundation	GA	1952	I	12/31/89	32,000	0	1,490
The Gordon and Mary Cain Foundation	TX	1988	I	12/31/88	29,684	29,186	281
G.P.G. Foundation	CA	1986	I	12/31/88	24,900	0	1,926
The Arcana Foundation, Inc.	DC	1986	I	09/30/89	23,405	0	1,276
Camp Younts Foundation	GA	1955	I	12/31/88	22,556	355	1,366
Robert R. Young Foundation	CT	1958	I	12/31/88	22,282	6,782	986
Hill Crest Foundation, Inc.	AL	1988	I	06/30/89	21,670	0	609
Community Foundation of Greater Memphis	TN	1969	CM	04/30/89	20,633	3,112	2,641
Malcolm Hewitt Wiener Foundation, Inc.	NY	1984	I	12/31/88	20,496	139	1,110

*Type of foundation codes: O = operating foundation; I = independent foundation; CS = company-sponsored foundation; CM = community foundation.
[1]The Francis Families Foundation was established in 1989 from the merger of the Parker B. Francis Foundation and the Parker B. Francis III Foundation. The foundation's fiscal data reflects the combined financial statements of the two absorbed foundations.

TABLE 7. FOUNDATIONS BY ASSET CATEGORIES (All dollar figures expressed in thousands)

Asset Categories	Number of Foundations	Percent	Assets	Percent	Gifts Received	Percent	Total Giving	Percent	Grants*	Percent
$100 million and over	165	2.2	$ 74,929,853	59.7	$1,317,212	27.6	$2,922,459	41.3	$2,819,831	42.1
$50 million-under $100 million	180	2.4	12,711,238	10.1	492,760	10.3	683,627	9.7	653,983	9.8
$25 million-under $50 million	269	3.5	9,461,924	7.5	530,205	11.1	583,267	8.2	552,003	8.2
$10 million-under $25 million	761	10.0	11,867,311	9.5	743,067	15.6	909,511	12.9	853,021	12.7
$5 million-under $10 million	1,002	13.2	7,082,548	5.6	475,572	10.0	590,179	8.3	550,053	8.2
$1 million-under $5 million	4,007	52.9	9,036,741	7.2	871,915	18.3	924,325	13.1	847,933	12.7
Under $1 million	1,197	15.8	403,331	0.3	334,582	7.0	463,400	6.5	426,062	6.4
Total	7,581	100.0	$125,492,947	100.0	$4,765,314	100.0	$7,076,767	100.0	$6,702,886	100.0

Note: Figures may not add up due to rounding.
*"Grants" figures represent grants paid out to organizations.

TABLE 8. FOUNDATIONS NEW TO THE *DIRECTORY* BY ASSET CATEGORIES (All dollar figures expressed in thousands)

Asset Categories	Number of Foundations	Percent	Assets	Percent	Gifts Received	Percent	Total Giving	Percent	Grants*	Percent
$50 million-under $100 million	5	0.4	$ 347,308	12.3	$155,623	25.7	$14,716	5.5	$14,716	5.7
$25 million-under $50 million	5	0.4	176,803	6.2	38,661	6.4	3,098	1.1	3,098	1.2
$10 million-under $25 million	31	2.5	476,083	16.8	43,771	7.2	26,265	9.7	26,243	10.2
$5 million-under $10 million	57	4.7	396,003	14.0	72,184	11.9	21,041	7.8	19,759	7.7
$1 million-under $5 million	727	59.3	1,306,411	46.2	213,731	35.3	95,165	35.3	89,062	34.6
Under $1 million	400	32.7	127,083	4.5	82,058	13.5	109,315	40.5	104,835	40.7
Total	1,225	100.0	$2,829,691	100.0	$606,026	100.0	$269,599	100.0	$257,712	100.0

Note: Figures may not add up due to rounding.
*"Grants" figures represent grants paid out to organizations.

TABLE 9. INDEPENDENT FOUNDATIONS BY ASSET CATEGORIES (All dollar figures expressed in thousands)

Asset Categories	Number of Foundations	Percent	Assets	Percent	Gifts Received	Percent	Total Giving	Percent	Grants*	Percent
$100 million and over	143	2.3	$ 65,860,261	61.1	$1,149,405	38.7	$2,591,068	49.4	$2,501,935	49.7
$50 million-under $100 million	151	2.4	10,685,922	9.9	295,592	10.0	520,159	9.9	498,980	9.9
$25 million-under $50 million	221	3.5	7,759,649	7.2	256,164	8.6	398,527	7.6	389,597	7.7
$10 million-under $25 million	603	9.6	9,426,653	8.7	312,522	10.5	516,112	9.8	498,244	9.9
$5 million-under $10 million	838	13.4	5,920,724	5.5	245,823	8.3	385,659	7.4	368,031	7.3
$1 million-under $5 million	3,507	56.0	7,807,934	7.2	548,742	18.5	591,511	11.3	548,801	10.9
Under $1 million	801	12.8	282,088	0.3	160,703	5.4	242,914	4.6	230,637	4.6
Total	6,264	100.0	$107,743,231	100.0	$2,968,949	100.0	$5,245,949	100.0	$5,036,225	100.0

Note: Figures may not add up due to rounding.
*"Grants" figures represent grants paid out to organizations.

TABLE 10. COMPANY-SPONSORED FOUNDATIONS BY ASSET CATEGORIES (All dollar figures expressed in thousands)

Asset Categories	Number of Foundations	Percent	Assets	Percent	Gifts Received	Percent	Total Giving	Percent	Grants*	Percent
$100 million and over	5	0.5	$ 750,739	13.9	$ 0	0.0	$ 89,883	6.7	$ 81,006	6.8
$50 million-under $100 million	10	1.1	662,236	12.2	46,348	4.2	89,354	6.7	83,745	7.0
$25 million-under $50 million	26	2.7	893,089	16.5	154,097	13.9	148,252	11.1	128,791	10.8
$10 million-under $25 million	95	10.0	1,434,007	26.5	315,826	28.5	331,047	24.8	299,317	25.0
$5 million-under $10 million	104	11.0	733,200	13.6	170,301	15.4	176,915	13.3	156,869	13.1
$1 million-under $5 million	347	36.7	825,551	15.3	261,770	23.6	296,568	22.2	267,123	22.4
Under $1 million	359	37.9	110,909	2.1	160,944	14.5	202,422	15.2	178,188	14.9
Total	946	100.0	$5,409,730	100.0	$1,109,286	100.0	$1,334,441	100.0	$1,195,040	100.0

Note: Figures may not add up due to rounding.
*"Grants" figures represent grants paid out to organizations.

TABLE 11. COMMUNITY FOUNDATIONS BY ASSET CATEGORIES (All dollar figures expressed in thousands)

Asset Categories	Number of Foundations	Percent	Assets	Percent	Gifts Received	Percent	Total Giving	Percent	Grants*	Percent
$100 million and over	12	6.3	$3,386,470	57.4	$165,804	31.6	$207,886	51.5	$204,298	51.9
$50 million-under $100 million	13	6.9	961,325	16.3	100,024	19.1	69,988	17.3	69,525	17.7
$25 million-under $50 million	14	7.4	494,591	8.4	73,873	14.1	33,499	8.3	31,446	8.0
$10 million-under $25 million	37	19.6	598,755	10.2	98,477	18.8	49,289	12.2	46,787	11.9
$5 million-under $10 million	35	18.5	248,092	4.2	41,877	8.0	20,888	5.2	20,157	5.1
$1 million-under $5 million	74	39.2	204,560	3.5	43,174	8.2	20,686	5.1	19,899	5.1
Under $1 million	4	2.1	2,630	0.0	1,805	0.3	1,263	0.3	1,240	0.3
Total	189	100.0	$5,896,424	100.0	$525,034	100.0	$403,500	100.0	$393,352	100.0

Note: Figures may not add up due to rounding.
*"Grants" figures represent grants paid out to organizations.

TABLE 12. *DIRECTORY* OPERATING FOUNDATIONS BY ASSET CATEGORIES (All dollar figures expressed in thousands)

Asset Categories	Number of Foundations	Percent	Assets	Percent	Total Giving*	Percent	Program Amount	Percent
$100 million or more	5	2.7	$4,932,383	76.5	$33,622	36.2	$145,215	75.8
$50 million–under $100 million	6	3.3	401,755	6.2	4,126	4.4	11,740	6.1
$25 million–under $50 million	8	4.4	314,596	4.9	2,989	3.2	6,254	3.3
$10 million–under $25 million	26	14.3	407,896	6.3	13,063	14.1	17,202	9.0
$5 million–under $10 million	25	13.7	180,532	2.8	6,717	7.2	7,013	3.7
$1 million–under $5 million	79	43.4	198,696	3.1	15,560	16.8	3,469	1.8
Under $1 million	33	18.1	7,704	0.1	16,800	18.1	689	0.4
Total	182	100.0	$6,443,561	100.0	$92,877	100.0	$191,581	100.0

Note: Figures may not add up due to rounding.
*Throughout this introduction, "Total Giving" figures include grants, scholarships, employee matching gifts, and other amounts reported as "Grants and Contributions Paid During the Year" on the 990-PF reporting form. Loan amounts including program-related investments (PRIs) are indicated separately. Total giving does not include all qualifying distributions under the tax law, i.e., loans, PRIs, and program or other administrative expenses. For operating foundations the major portion of qualifying distributions are paid out as program amounts.

FIGURE A. GENERAL CHARACTERISTICS OF FOUR TYPES OF FOUNDATIONS

Foundation Type	Description	Source of Funds	Decision-Making Activity	Grantmaking Requirements	Reporting
Independent Foundation	An independent grant-making organization established to aid social, educational, religious, or other charitable activities.	Endowment generally derived from a single source such as an individual, a family, or a group of individuals. Contributions to endowment limited as to tax deductibility.	Decisions may be made by donor or members of donor's family; by an independent board of directors or trustees; or by a bank or trust officer acting on donor's behalf.	Broad discretionary giving allowed but may have specific guidelines and give only in a few specific fields. About 70% limit their giving to local area.	Annual information returns 990-PF filed with IRS must be made available to public. A small percentage issue separately printed annual reports.
Company-sponsored Foundation	Legally an independent grantmaking organization with close ties to the corporation providing funds.	Endowment and annual contributions from a profit-making corporation. May maintain small endowment and pay out most of contributions received annually in grants, or may maintain endowment to cover contributions in years when corporate profits are down.	Decisions made by board of directors often composed of corporate officials, but which may include individuals with no corporate affiliation. Decisions may also be made by local company officials.	Giving tends to be in fields related to corporate activities or in communities where corporation operates. Usually give more grants but in smaller dollar amounts than independent foundations.	Same as above.
Operating Foundations	An organization which uses its resources to conduct research or provide a direct service.	Endowment usually provided from a single source, but eligible for maximum tax deductible contributions from public.	Decisions generally made by independent board of directors.	Makes few, if any, grants. Grants generally related directly to the foundation's program.	Same as above.
Community Foundations	A publicly-sponsored organization which makes grants for social, educational, religious, or other charitable purposes in a specific community or region.	Contributions received from many donors. Usually eligible for maximum tax deductible contributions from public.	Decisions made by board of directors representing the diversity of the community.	Grants generally limited to charitable organizations in local community.	IRS 990 return available to public. Many publish full guidelines or annual reports.

How to Use *The Foundation Directory*

The Foundation Directory is one of the first tools grantseekers should consult to identify foundations that might be interested in funding their project or organization. It provides basic descriptions of the giving interests and current fiscal data for the nation's largest foundations—those with assets of $1 million or more or annual giving of at least $100,000. Indexes help grantseekers to quickly identify foundations which have expressed an interest in a particular subject field or geographic area or which provide the specific type of support needed.

Researchers, journalists, grantmakers, and others interested in philanthropic activities also use the *Directory* to get a broad overview of current foundation activities nationally or within a particular geographic region or to gather basic facts about one or more specific foundations.

In using the *Directory* to identify potential funding sources, be sure to note the limitation statements many foundations have provided to see whether your project falls within the general scope of the foundation's giving program. Some foundations restrict their giving to a particular subject field or geographic area; others are not able to provide certain types of support, such as funds for building and equipment or for general operating funds.

ARRANGEMENT

The *Directory* is arranged alphabetically by state, and foundation descriptions are arranged alphabetically by name within the state in which the foundation maintains its primary offices. Each entry is assigned a sequence number, and references in the indexes which follow the main listings are to entry sequence numbers.

There are 27 basic data elements which could be included in a *Directory* entry. The completeness of an entry varies widely due to the differences in the size and nature of a foundation's program and the availability of information from the foundation. Entries which have been prepared by Foundation Center staff from public records are indicated by the symbol ¤. The specific data elements which could be included are:

1. The full legal **name of the foundation.**
2. The **former name** of the foundation.
3. **Street address, city, and zip code** of the foundation's principal office.
4. **Telephone number** supplied by the foundation.
5. Any **additional address** supplied by the foundation for correspondence or grant applications.
6. **Establishment data,** including the legal form (usually a trust or corporation) and the year and state in which the foundation was established.
7. The **donor(s)** or principal contributor(s) to the foundation, including individuals, families, and corporations. If a donor is deceased, the symbol † follows the name.
8. **Foundation type:** community, company-sponsored, independent, or operating.
9. The **year-end date** of the foundation's accounting period for which financial data is supplied.
10. **Assets:** the total value of the foundation's investments at the end of the accounting period. In a few instances, foundations that act as "pass-throughs" for annual corporate or individual gifts report zero assets.
11. **Asset type:** generally, assets are reported at market value (M) or ledger value (L).
12. **Gifts received:** the total amount of new capital received by the foundation in the year of record.
13. **Expenditures:** total disbursements of the foundation, including overhead expenses (salaries; investment, legal, and other professional fees; interest; rent; etc.) and federal excise taxes, as well as the total amount paid for grants, scholarships, matching gifts, and loans.
14. The dollar value and number of **grants paid** during the year, with the largest grant paid (**high**) and smallest grant paid (**low**). When supplied by the foundation, the average range of grant payments is also indicated. Grant figures do not include commitments for future payment or amounts spent for grants to individuals, employee-matching gifts, loans, or foundation-administered programs.
15. The total amount and number of **grants made directly to or on behalf of individuals,** including scholarships, fellowships, awards, or medical payments. When supplied by the foundation, high, low, and average range are also indicated.
16. The dollar amount and number of **employee matching gifts** awarded, generally by company-sponsored foundations.
17. The total dollars expended for **programs administered by the foundation** and the number of foundation-administered programs. These programs can include museums or other institutions supported exclusively by the foundation, research programs administered by the foundation and conducted either by the foundation staff or at other institutions, etc.
18. The dollar amount and number of **loans** made to nonprofit organizations by the foundation. These can include program-related investments, emergency loans to help nonprofits that are waiting for grants or other income payments, etc. When supplied by the foundation, high, low, and average range are also indicated.

19. The number of **loans to individuals** and the total amount loaned. When supplied by the foundation, high, low, and average range are also indicated.
20. The **purpose and activities,** in general terms, of the foundation. This statement reflects funding interests as expressed by the foundation or, if no foundation statement is available, an analysis of the actual grants awarded by the foundation during the most recent two-year period for which public records exist.
21. The **types of support** (such as endowment funds, support for buildings and equipment, fellowships, etc.) offered by the foundation. Definitions of the terms used to describe the forms of support available are provided at the beginning of the Types of Support Index at the back of this volume.
22. Any stated **limitations** on the foundation's giving program, including geographic preferences, restrictions by subject focus or type of recipient, or specific types of support the foundation cannot provide.
23. **Publications** or other printed materials distributed by the foundation which describe its activities and giving program. These can include annual or multiyear reports, newsletters, corporate giving reports, informational brochures, grant lists, etc. It is also noted if a foundation will send copies of its IRS information return (Form 990-PF) on request.
24. **Application information,** including the name of the contact person, the preferred form of application, the number of copies of proposals requested, application deadlines, frequency and dates of board meetings, and the general amount of time the foundation requires to notify applicants of the board's decision. Some foundations have also indicated that applications are not accepted or that their funds are currently committed to ongoing projects.
25. The names and titles of **officers, principal administrators, trustees or directors,** and members of other governing bodies. An asterisk following the individual's name indicates an officer who is also a trustee or director.
26. The number of professional and support **staff** employed by the foundation, and an indication of part-time or full-time status of these employees, as reported by the foundation.
27. **Employer Identification Number:** the number assigned to the foundation by the Internal Revenue Service for tax purposes. This number can be useful in ordering microfilm or paper copies of the foundation's annual information return, Form 990-PF.

APPENDIXES

Following the Descriptive Directory section are three appendixes. Appendix A lists 278 foundations described in Edition 12 of the *Directory* that are not included in Edition 13 because they have terminated operations, changed their legal status, or no longer meet fiscal criteria for inclusion. Appendix B lists 506 private operating foundations that hold assets of $1 million or more but are excluded from the *Directory* because they do not maintain active grantmaking programs. Appendix C lists 487 private non-operating foundations that are excluded because they contribute only to a few specified beneficiaries or to the support of a single organization or institution.

INDEXES

Six indexes to the descriptive entries are provided at the back of the book.

1. The **Index of Donors, Officers, and Trustees** is an alphabetical listing of individuals and corporations that have made substantial contributions to *Directory* foundations or who serve as officers or members of the governing boards of these foundations. Many grantseekers find this index helpful to learn whether current or prospective members of their own governing boards, alumni of their school, or current contributors are affiliated with any foundations.
2. The **Geographic Index** references foundation entries by the state and city in which the foundation maintains principal offices and includes cross-references to indicate foundations located elsewhere that have made substantial grants to a particular state. Foundations that award grants on a national or regional level are indicated in bold type. The other foundations generally limit their giving to the state or city in which they are located.
3. The **Types of Support Index** indicates entry numbers for foundations that offer specific types of grants and other forms of support, such as consulting services or program-related investments. Definitions of the terms used to describe the types of support offered are provided at the beginning of the index. Under each type of support term, entry references are arranged by the state in which the foundation is located, and foundations that award grants on a national or regional basis are indicated in bold type. In using this index, grantseekers should focus on foundations located in their own state which offer the specific type of support needed or, if their project has national impact, on foundations listed in bold type that are located in other states.
4. The **Subject Index** allows users to identify foundations by the broad giving interests expressed in the "Purpose and Activities" section of their descriptive entry. A list of the subject terms used is provided at the beginning of the index. Like the Types of Support Index, entry references are arranged under each term by the state in which the foundation is

located, and foundations that award grants on a national or regional basis are indicated in bold type. Again, grantseekers should focus on foundations located in their own state that have indicated an interest in their subject field, as well as foundations listed in bold type that are located in other states.

5. The **Index of Foundations New to Edition 13** lists foundations which appear in this edition of the *Directory* but did not appear in the previous edition. The descriptive entries for these foundations are highlighted with a star.
6. The **Foundation Name Index** is an alphabetical list of all foundations appearing in the Descriptive Directory. If a foundation has changed its name since the last *Directory,* the former name is also listed. If the name of a particular foundation does not appear in this index, users should consult the foundation listings in the appendixes to determine whether the foundation has terminated operations or is otherwise ineligible for inclusion in the *Directory.*

RESEARCHING FOUNDATIONS

Foundations receive many thousands of worthy requests each year. Most of these requests are declined because there are never enough funds to go around or because the applications clearly fall outside the foundation's fields of interest. Some of the applications denied are poorly prepared and do not reflect a careful analysis of the applicant organization's needs, its credibility, or its capacity to carry out the proposed project. Sometimes the qualifications of the staff are not well established. The budget or the means of evaluating the project may not be presented convincingly. The organization may not have asked itself if it is especially suited to make a contribution to the solution of the problem or to provide the service proposed or if others are not already effectively engaged in the same activity.

The first step in researching foundation funding support, then, is to analyze your own program and organization to determine the need you plan to address, the audience you will serve, and the amount and type of support you need. Become familiar with the basic facts about foundations and how they operate. Consider other sources of funding, such as individual contributors, government grants, earned income possibilities, and so on. Although foundations are an important source of support for nonprofit organizations, their total giving represents a relatively small percentage of the total private philanthropic dollars contributed annually, and an even smaller percentage of the total support of nonprofit activities when government grants and earned income are included.

Once you have clearly in mind the amount and type of support you need and the reasons why you are seeking foundation support, *The Foundation Directory* can help you to develop an initial list of foundations that might be interested in funding your project. In determining whether or not it is appropriate to approach a particular foundation with a grant request, keep in mind the following questions:

1. Has the foundation demonstrated a real commitment to funding in your subject area?
2. Does it seem likely that the foundation will make a grant in your geographic area?
3. Does the amount of money you are requesting fit within the foundation's grant range?
4. Does the foundation have any policy prohibiting grants for the type of support you are requesting?
5. Does the foundation prefer to make grants to cover the full cost of a project or do they favor projects where other foundations or funding sources share the cost?
6. What type of organizations does the foundation tend to support?
7. Does the foundation have specific application deadlines and procedures or does it review proposals continuously?

Some of these questions can be answered from the information provided in the *Directory,* but grantseekers will almost always want to consult a few additional resources before submitting a request for funding. If the foundation issues an annual report, application guidelines, or other printed materials describing its program, it is advisable to obtain copies and study them carefully before preparing your proposal. The foundation's annual information return (Form 990-PF) includes a list of all grants paid by the foundation, as well as basic data about its finances, officers, and giving policies. Copies of these returns are available for free examination at most of the Foundation Center's cooperating libraries listed later in this volume.

The Foundation Center's quarterly publication, *Source Book Profiles*, describes in detail the 1,000 largest U.S. foundations and, with the exception of publications issued directly by the foundations, is the most complete source of information available on this group. *Directory* foundations which are described more fully in *Source Book Profiles* are indicated by the symbol ▼ next to their entry. The Center also publishes a number of other reference tools which provide information on private foundations, as well as a guidebook on researching foundation funding sources, *Foundation Fundamentals.* Copies of all Center publications, as well as other relevant state and local foundation directories, are available for free examination at the Foundation Center libraries and cooperating collections listed in this volume.

Glossary

The following list includes important terms used by grantmakers and grantseekers. A number of sources have been consulted in compiling this glossary, including *The Handbook on Private Foundations,* by David F. Freeman (Washington, D.C.: Seven Locks Press, 1981); *The Law of Tax-Exempt Organizations,* 5th Edition, by Bruce R. Hopkins (New York: John Wiley & Sons, 1987); *Corporate Philanthropy: Philosophy, Management, Trends, Future, Background* (Washington, D.C.: Council on Foundations, 1982); and a glossary prepared by Caroline McGilvray, former Director of the Foundation Center San Francisco Office, with the Northern California Foundation Group.

Annual Report: A *voluntary* report issued by a foundation or corporate giving program which provides financial data and descriptions of grantmaking activities. Annual reports vary in format from simple typewritten documents listing the year's grants to detailed publications which provide substantial information about the grantmaking program. Perhaps 10 to 15 percent of all *Directory* foundations issue such reports (as distinguished from the publicly available Form 990-PF, below, the annual information return *required* of all private foundations). A current listing of reports issued by private foundations and corporate grantmakers is provided in the Foundation Center's *Foundation Grants Index Bimonthly. Foundation Directory* entries also indicate if an annual report is published.

Assets: The amount of capital or principal—money, stocks, bonds, real estate, or other resources of the foundation or corporation. Generally, assets are invested and the income is used to make grants.

Beneficiary: In philanthropic terms, the donee or grantee receiving funds from a foundation or corporate giving program is the beneficiary, though society benefits as well. Foundations whose legal terms of establishment restrict their giving to one or more named beneficiaries are not included in this *Directory.*

Bricks and Mortar: An informal term for grants for buildings or construction projects.

Capital Support: Funds provided for endowment purposes, buildings, construction, or equipment and including, for example, grants for "bricks and mortar."

Challenge Grant: A grant award that will be paid only if the donee organization is able to raise additional funds from another source(s). Challenge grants are often used to stimulate giving from other donors. (*See also* **Matching Grant**)

Community Fund: An organized community program which makes annual appeals to the general public for funds which are usually not retained in an endowment but are used for the ongoing operational support of local social and health service agencies. (*See also* **Federated Giving Program**)

Community Foundation: A 501(c)(3) organization which makes grants for charitable purposes in a specific community or region. Funds are usually derived from many donors and held in an endowment independently administered; income earned by the endowment is then used to make grants. Although a few community foundations may be classified by the IRS as private foundations, most are classified as public charities eligible for maximum income tax-deductible contributions from the general public. (*See also* **501(c)(3); Public Charity**)

Company-Sponsored Foundation (also referred to as Corporate Foundation): A private foundation whose grant funds are derived primarily from the contributions of a profit-making business organization. The company-sponsored foundation may maintain close ties with the donor company, but it is an independent organization with its own endowment and is subject to the same rules and regulations as other private foundations. (*See also* **Private Foundation**)

Cooperative Venture: A joint effort between or among two or more grantmakers (including foundations, corporations, and government agencies). Partners may share in funding responsibilities or contribute information and technical resources.

Corporate Giving Program: A grantmaking program established and administered within a profit-making company. Corporate giving programs do not have a separate endowment and their annual grant totals are generally more directly related to current profits. They are not subject to the same reporting requirements as private foundations. Some companies make charitable contributions through both a corporate giving program and a company-sponsored foundation. Company-sponsored foundations are included in this *Directory;* corporate giving programs are not.

Distribution Committee: The board responsible for making grant decisions for community foundations. It is intended to be broadly representative of the community served by the foundation.

Donee: The recipient of a grant. (Also known as the grantee or the beneficiary.)

Donor: The individual or organization which makes a grant or contribution. (Also known as the grantor.)

Employee Matching Gift: A contribution to a charitable organization by a corporate employee which is matched by a similar contribution from the employer. Many corporations have employee matching gift programs in higher education that stimulate their employees to give to the college or university of their choice.

Endowment: Funds intended to be kept permanently and invested to provide income for the continued support of an organization.

Expenditure Responsibility: In general, when a private foundation makes a grant to an organization which is not classified by the IRS as a "public charity," the foundation is required by law to provide some assurance that the funds will be used for the intended charitable purposes. Special reports on such grants must be filed with the IRS. Most grantee organizations are public charities and many foundations do not make "expenditure responsibility" grants.

Family Foundation: An independent private foundation whose funds are derived from members of a single family. Family members often serve as officers or board members of the foundation and have a significant role in grantmaking decisions. (*See also* **Private Foundation**)

Federated Giving Program: A joint fundraising effort usually administered by a nonprofit "umbrella" organization which in turn distributes contributed funds to several non-profit agencies. United Way and community chests or funds, United Jewish Appeal and other religious appeals, the United Negro College Fund, and joint arts councils are examples of federated giving programs. (*See also* **Community Fund**)

501(c)(3): The section of the Internal Revenue Code which defines nonprofit, charitable (as broadly defined), tax-exempt organizations. 501(c)(3) organizations are further defined as public charities, private operating foundations, and private non-operating foundations. (*See also* **Operating Foundation; Private Foundation; Public Charity**)

Form 990-PF: The annual information return that all private foundations must submit to the IRS each year and which is also filed with appropriate state officials. The form requires information on the foundation's assets, income, operating expenses, contributions and grants, paid staff and salaries, program funding areas, grantmaking guidelines and restrictions, and grant application procedures. Foundation Center libraries maintain files of 990-PFs for public inspection.

General Purpose Foundation: An independent private foundation which awards grants in many different fields of interest. (*See also* **Special Purpose Foundation**)

General Purpose Grant: A grant made to further the general purpose or work of an organization, rather than for a specific purpose or project. (*See also* **Operating Support Grant**)

Grantee Financial Report: A report detailing how grant funds were used by an organization. Many corporations require this kind of report from grantees. A financial report generally includes a listing of all expenditures from grant funds as well as an overall organizational financial report covering revenue and expenses, assets and liabilities.

Grassroots Fundraising: Efforts to raise money from individuals or groups from the local community on a broad basis. Usually an organization does grassroots fundraising within its own constituency—people who live in the neighborhood served or clients of the agency's services. Grassroots fundraising activities include membership drives, raffles, bake sales, auctions, benefits, dances, and a range of other activities.

Independent Foundation: A grantmaking organization usually classified by the IRS as a private foundation. Independent foundations may also be known as family foundations, general purpose foundations, special purpose foundations, or private non-operating foundations. The Foundation Center defines independent foundations and company-sponsored foundations separately; however, federal law normally classifies both as private, non-operating foundations subject to the same rules and requirements. (*See also* **Private Foundation**)

In-Kind Contributions: A contribution of equipment, supplies, or other property as distinguished from a monetary grant. Some organizations may also donate space or staff time as an in-kind contribution.

Matching Grant: A grant which is made to match funds provided by another donor. (*See also* **Challenge Grant; Employee Matching Gift**)

Operating Foundation: A 501(c)(3) organization classified by the IRS as a private foundation whose primary purpose is to conduct research, social welfare, or other programs determined by its governing body or establishment charter. Some grants may be made, but the sum is generally small relative to the funds used for the foundation's own programs. (*See also* **501(c)(3)**)

Operating Support Grant: A grant to cover the regular personnel, administrative, and other expenses for an existing program or project. (*See also* **General Purpose Grant**)

Payout Requirement: The minimum amount that private foundations are required to expend for charitable purposes (includes grants and, within certain limits, the administrative cost of making grants). In general, a private foundation must meet or exceed an annual payout requirement of 5 percent of the average market value of the foundation's assets.

Private Foundation: A nongovernmental, nonprofit organization with funds (usually from a single source, such as an individual, family, or corporation) and program managed by its own trustees or directors which was established to maintain or aid social, educational, religious or other charitable activities serving the common welfare, primarily through the making of grants. "Private foundation" also means an organization that is tax-exempt under Code section 501(c)(3) and is classified by IRS as a private foundation as defined in the Code. The Code definition usually, but not always, identifies a foundation with the characteristics first described. (*See also* **501(c)(3); Public Charity**)

Program Amount: Funds which are expended to support a particular program. In the *Guide,* this term refers to the total dollars spent to operate programs administered internally by the foundation or the corporate giving program.

Program Officer: A staff member of a foundation who reviews grant proposals and processes applications for the board of trustees. Only a small percentage of foundations have program officers.

Program-Related Investment (PRI): A loan or other investment (as distinguished from a grant) made by a foundation or corporate giving program to another organization (including a business enterprise) for a project related to the grantmaker's stated charitable purpose and interests. Program-related investments are often made from a revolving fund; the foundation or corporation generally expects to receive its money back with interest or some other form of return at less than current market rates, which becomes available for further program-related investments. These investments are currently made by relatively few foundations.

Proposal: A written application often with supporting documents submitted to a foundation or corporation in requesting a grant. Preferred procedures and formats vary. Consult published guidelines.

Public Charity: In general, an organization which is tax-exempt under Code section 501(c)(3) and is classified by IRS as a public charity and not a private foundation. Public charities generally derive their funding or support primarily from the general public in carrying out their social, educational, religious, or other charitable activities serving the common welfare. Some public charities engage in grantmaking activities, though most engage in direct service or other tax-exempt activities. Public charities are eligible for maximum income tax-deductible contributions from the public and are not subject to the same rules and restrictions as private foundations. Some are also referred to as "public foundations" or "publicly supported organizations" and may use the term "foundation" in their names. (*See also* **501(c)(3); Private Foundation**)

Qualifying Distributions: Expenditures of private foundations used to satisfy payout requirement. These can include grants, reasonable administrative expenses, set-asides, loans and program-related investments, and amounts paid to acquire assets used directly in carrying out exempt purposes.

Query Letter: A brief letter outlining an organization's activities and its request for funding sent to a foundation or corporate giving program to determine whether it would be appropriate to submit a full grant proposal. Many grantmakers prefer to be contacted in this way before receiving a full proposal.

RFP: Request For Proposal. When the government issues a new contract or grant program, it sends out RFPs to agencies that might be qualified to participate. The RFP lists project specifications and application procedures. A few foundations occasionally use RFPs in specific fields, but most prefer to consider proposals that are initiated by applicants.

Seed Money: A grant or contribution used to start a new project or organization. Seed grants may cover salaries and other operating expenses of a new project.

Set-Asides: Funds set aside by a foundation for a specific purpose or project which are counted as qualifying distributions toward the foundation's annual payout requirement. Amounts for the project must be paid within five years of the first set-aside.

Special Purpose Foundation: A private foundation which focuses its grantmaking activities in one or a few special areas of interest. For example, a foundation may only award grants in the area of cancer research or child development. (*See also* **General Purpose Foundation**)

Technical Assistance: Operational or management assistance given to nonprofit organizations. It can include fund-raising assistance, budgeting and financial planning, program planning, legal advice, marketing, and other aids to management. Assistance may be offered directly by a foundation or corporate staff member or in the form of a grant to pay for the services of an outside consultant. (*See also* **In-Kind Contribution**)

Trustee: A member of a governing board. A foundation's board of trustees meets to review grant proposals and make decisions. Often also referred to as "director" or "board member."

Publications and Services of The Foundation Center

The Foundation Center is a national service organization founded and supported by foundations to provide a single authoritative source of information on foundation giving. The Center's programs are designed to help grantseekers as they begin to select those foundations which may be most interested in their projects from the over 30,000 active U.S. foundations. Among its primary activities toward this end are publishing reference books on foundations and foundation grants, and disseminating information on foundations through a nationwide public service program.

Publications of the Foundation Center are the primary working tools of every serious grantseeker. They are also used by grantmakers, scholars, journalists, regulators, and legislators—in short, everyone seeking any type of factual information on foundation philanthropy. All private foundations actively engaged in grantmaking, regardless of size or geographic location, are included in one or more of the Center's publications. The publications are of three kinds: directories which describe specific foundations, characterizing their program interests and providing fiscal and personnel data; grants indexes which list and classify by subject recent foundation awards; and guides, brochures, monographs, and bibliographies which introduce the reader to funding research, elements of proposal writing, and nonprofit management issues.

Foundation Center publications may be ordered from the Foundation Center, 79 Fifth Avenue, New York, NY 10003. For more information about any aspect of the Center's program or for the name of the Center's library collection nearest you, call toll-free (800) 424-9836.

GENERAL RESEARCH DIRECTORIES

THE FOUNDATION DIRECTORY, 1991 EDITION

The Foundation Directory has been widely known and respected in the field for 30 years. It includes the latest information on all foundations whose assets exceed $1 million or whose annual grant total is $100,000 or more. The new 1991 Edition is the biggest ever: 7,600 foundations are included, over 1,100 of which are new to this edition, and over 900 of which are corporate foundations. *Directory* foundations hold over $115 billion in assets and award nearly $7 billion in grants annually, accounting for 92% of all U.S. foundation dollars awarded in 1985 and 1986.

Each *Directory* entry now contains more precise information on application procedures, giving limitations, types of support awarded, the publications of each foundation, and foundation staff—all this in addition to such vital data as the grantmakers' giving interests, financial data, grant amounts, addresses and telephone numbers. The Foundation Center works closely with foundations to ensure the accuracy and timeliness of the information provided.

The *Directory* includes indexes by foundation name; subject areas of interest; names of donors, trustees, and officers; geographic location; and the types of support awarded. Also included are analyses of the foundation community by geography, asset and grant size, different types of foundations, trends in foundation establishment, and information on the effects of inflation on the field since 1975.

1991 Edition, Nov. 1990. Published annually.
Paperbound: ISBN 0-87954-345-0 / $140
Hardbound: ISBN 0-87954-344-2 / $165

THE FOUNDATION DIRECTORY, PART 2: A Guide to Grant Programs $25,000–$100,000

Following in the tradition of *The Foundation Directory, Foundation Directory, Part 2* brings you the same thorough coverage for the next largest set of foundations—those with grant programs between $25,000–$100,000. For the first time in print, grantseekers will find directory-level information on mid-sized foundations, an important group of grantmakers responsible for millions in funding annually. Essential data on 4,200 foundations is included along with over 25,000 recently awarded foundation grants which provide an excellent view of the foundations' true giving interests. Immediate access to foundation entries is facilitated by five indexes organized by: city and state; donors, officers, and trustees; types of support; foundation names; and over 200 specific subject areas. A valuable research directory for nonprofits of all sizes and giving interests.

1990–1991 edition. December 1990. Published bienially.
ISBN 0-87954-378-7 / $150

SOURCE BOOK PROFILES

Source Book Profiles is an annual subscription service offering detailed descriptions of the 1,000 largest foundations, analyzing giving patterns by subject area, type of support, and type of recipient. The service operates on a two-year publishing cycle, with each one-year series covering 500 foundations. Each installment includes new profiles as well as information on changes occurring in foundations profiled earlier in the year, including revised information on address, telephone, personnel, and program interests. Also included is a revised cumulative set of indexes to all 1,000 foundations covered in the two-year cycle by name, subject interest, type of grants awarded, and city and state location or concentration of giving.

1991 Subscription (500 Profiles) / $350 /
ISBN 0-87954-383-3
1990 Cumulative Volume (500 Profiles) / $350 /
ISBN 0-87954-335-3
1990–1991 Set (1,000 Profiles) / $650

NATIONAL DATA BOOK OF FOUNDATIONS: A Comprehensive Guide to Grantmaking Foundations, 15th Edition

The *National Data Book of Foundations* gives fast access to vital information on over 30,000 U.S. foundations—the most complete listing of grantmakers ever published. It can help you quickly develop a list of initial funding prospects from the largest national to the smallest local foundations. Each entry features foundation name and address, name of principal officer or contact person, foundation asset amount, total grants paid during the year, total gifts received, and the IRS number to help you locate tax returns, often the only source of public information on family-run foundations. In the introduction, a series of eight statistical tables analyze the entire spectrum of U.S. foundations, contrasting giving by foundation size, by the type of foundation, and by the geographic region and state. *National Data Book* also includes an extensive bibliography. Listed by state, these carefully reviewed entries highlight regional foundation directories for further research on the local level.

January 1991 / ISBN 0-87954-385-X / $125
Published annually.

NATIONAL DIRECTORY OF CORPORATE GIVING

In 1988, corporations donated well over $4 billion to nonprofit organizations and community development projects. To help tap this vital source of funding dollars, the new *National Directory of Corporate Giving* offers authoritative information on over 1,500 corporate foundations and direct corporate giving programs—the best corporate funding opportunities in the United States! Finding accurate information on the programs and interests of these corporations is vital to the success of any corporate fundraising effort, and no printed source offers more thorough and current information than the *National Directory of Corporate Giving*. The directory outlines program policies for both kinds of corporate giving, and covers both cash awards and in-kind gifts such as staff time, products, and real estate. The information in the *National Directory* can be searched through indexes that list names of key personnel, subject areas of funding, geographic locations, types of support preferred, types of business, and names of corporations, their foundations, and their direct giving programs. The editors have also added an introduction commenting on the state of corporate charity today, an extensive bibliography for further research, and a useful guide to corporate fundraising techniques.

December 1989 / ISBN 0-87954-246-2 / $175
Published bienially.

CORPORATE FOUNDATION PROFILES, 6TH EDITION

This newly updated volume includes comprehensive information on corporate direct giving programs and company-sponsored foundations. A total of almost 900 grantmakers with assets of $1 million or annual giving of $100,000 or more are listed with full subject, types of support, and geographic indexes. Detailed profiles of the largest corporate foundations and timely information on foundation policies, guidelines, representative grants, and application procedures are included in the listing. Financial data provides a summary of the size and grantmaking capacity of each foundation and contains a list of assets, gifts or contributions, grants paid, operating programs, expenditures, scholarships, and loans.

6th Edition / Mar. 1990 / ISBN 0-87954-336-1 / $125.
Published biennially.

NEW YORK STATE FOUNDATIONS: A Comprehensive Directory, 2nd Edition

New York State Foundations offers fundraisers complete coverage of independent, corporate and community foundations throughout New York State—all in one comprehensive source. This information-packed volume will help fundraisers to identify the giving interests and funding policies of this very important segment of the foundation world—the over 4,500 foundations which, combined, hold assets of $26 billion and award $1.4 billion annually to thousands of nonprofit organizations throughout New York State. Fundraisers will find carefully researched data on every known New York foundation, small and large, with funding policies that cover a broad range of program areas. Every foundation entry in this directory has been drawn from the most current sources of information available on New York-based foundations, including IRS 990-PF foundation tax returns and, in many cases, foundations themselves. Along with over 4,500 entries, are complete or sample grants lists for over 3,000 foundations; convenient arrangement of foundations by county of origin; close to 100 grantmakers outside of New York State which fund nonprofits in New York State; and critical foundation facts to help fundraisers pinpoint potential funders. Five time-saving indexes offer quick access to foundations according to their fields of interest; types of support awarded; city and county; names of donors, officers, and trustees; and foundation names.

March 1991 / ISBN 0-87954-384-1 / $150. Published biennially.

FOUNDATION GRANTS TO INDIVIDUALS, 7TH EDITION

The only publication devoted entirely to specialized foundation grant opportunities for qualified individual applicants. The 7th Edition provides full descriptions of the programs specifically designated for individuals of over 1,200 foundations. Entries also include foundation addresses and telephone numbers, financial data, giving limitations, and application guidelines. This volume can save individuals seeking grants countless hours of research.

January 1991 / ISBN 0-87954-387-6 / $40 /

SUBJECT DIRECTORIES

THE NATIONAL GUIDE TO FUNDING IN AGING, 2nd Edition

This comprehensive reference is the result of a unique collaborative effort between the Foundation Center, Long Island University, and the Nassau County, New York, Department of Senior Citizen Affairs. Carefully researched, up-to-date, and truly comprehensive, *The National Guide to Funding in Aging, 2nd Edition* is the only funding tool to cover all public and private sources of funding support and technical assistance for programs for the aging. Areas of support categorized are: federal funding programs, with detailed profiles of 124 funding programs in 15 areas of service; 68 state government funding programs, including programs and up-to-date listings for all 50 states and U.S. territories; foundations, covering 495 private and community grantmakers with an expressed interest in the field of the aging, *plus* lists of actual grants made by many foundations in the field of aging; and *Private* Organizations, with 74 profiles of academic, religious, and service agencies offering funding and technical aid.

January 1990 / ISBN 0-87954-333-7 / $75

AIDS FUNDING: A Guide to Giving by Foundations and Charitable Organizations

In the summer of 1987, the Foundation Center surveyed over 500 foundations and discovered 85 funders which had awarded more than 250 grants totaling over $18 million in AIDS-related grants. In this newly updated report on AIDS funding, our researchers have uncovered data on 72 additional foundations with AIDS-related programs and services for a total of nearly 600 grants—a figure up 50% from our 1987 report. In addition to these foundations, public foundations, and an analysis of AIDS grantmaking by charitable organizations outside of the U.S. have been included for the first time. Fundraisers seeking information on foundations awarding grants in this area will find a wealth of information on grantmakers' interests, purposes, and limitations, plus detailed information on the hundreds of AIDS grants awarded.

October 1988 / ISBN 0-87954-243-8 / $38

NATIONAL GUIDE TO FUNDING IN ARTS AND CULTURE

Designed specifically to meet the needs of development professionals in the field of arts and culture, this new subject guide prepares fundraisers for an informed grant search. The Foundation Center's expert staff has performed the first crucial stage of fundraising research, by including in the *National Guide to Funding in Arts and Culture* both foundations and corporate giving programs that have already demonstrated a commitment to funding art colonies, dance companies, museums, theaters, and many other types of arts and culture programs. With over 3,300 listings of grantmakers, five indexes, and two bibliographies, the volume facilitates rapid and accurate research. The volume also lists over 7,000 actual grants recently awarded by foundations, to show the kinds of projects currently receiving support from grantmakers. The *National Guide to Funding in Arts and Culture* affords immediate access to crucial information on the programs that each year award millions of dollars to arts and culture groups.

February 1990 / ISBN 0-87954-248-9 / $125

NATIONAL GUIDE TO FUNDING FOR CHILDREN, YOUTH, AND FAMILIES

The National Guide to Funding for Children, Youth, and Families caters specifically to development professionals for organizations serving the needs of children, youth, and families. With over 2,400 listings of funding sources—from both foundations and corporate direct giving programs—the volume affords immediate access to the programs that award millions of dollars each year to organizations committed to causes involving children, youth, and families. Included are the names, addresses, giving purposes, and guidelines for all funders listed. Grantseekers will also find useful the listing of over 8,300 sample grants recently awarded by many of these foundations. These offer a unique view of funders' actual interests as well as a look at the nonprofit organizations who are receiving these grants. Supplementary information includes an introduction that reviews the larger picture of funding in this field, complete with a series of related statistical tables. Five indexes and a bibliography of other resources also facilitate funding research.

1991–1992 Edition, November 1990. Published biennially. ISBN 0-87954-391-4 / $125

THE NATIONAL GUIDE TO FOUNDATION FUNDING IN HEALTH, 2nd Edition

Now fundraisers seeking foundation support or tracking health giving patterns can have immediate access to information on the top health funders in the nation in one convenient source. The *National Guide to Foundation Funding in Health* contains essential facts on more than 2,500 foundations which have a history of awarding grant dollars to hospitals, universities, research institutes, community-based agencies, and national health associations for a broad range of health-related programs and services. With competition on the rise for the funding of crucial health programs, fundraisers need the best information available about foundations in order to direct their proposals to appropriate funders. Included in this volume is a wealth of information on the programs and policies of more than 2,500 health funders, plus additional information on leading grantmakers who award in health—including actual grants lists. This all-in-one source of essential foundation data includes facts on foundation program interests, contact persons, application guidelines, listings of board members, and much more. And, three indexes help fundraisers find foundation entries easily according to their state, subject interest, or foundation name. A useful bibliography of publications on health issues and philanthropic initiatives in the field is included as a guide to further study.

November 1990 / ISBN 0-87954-379-5 / $125

NATIONAL GUIDE TO FOUNDATION FUNDING IN HIGHER EDUCATION

The *National Guide to Foundation Funding in Higher Education* provides current data on thousands of foundations, all with a proven history of awarding grants to colleges, universities, graduate programs, and research institutes. Each of the 2,905 entries gives a thorough portrait of the foundation, including the foundation address, name of the contact person, financial data, purpose statement, types of support preferred, and geographic limitations. And, to show the type of projects that have already received funding, the book lists every grant for higher education of $5,000 or more awarded by 228 foundations—over 9,500 sample grants in all. To complement the extensive listings of grantmakers, the *National Guide to Foundation Funding in Higher Education* offers two additional features: an introduction reviewing the larger picture of foundation-administered grants in the field, including a table that analyzes foundation grants by subject area, and a selected bibliography to direct further research on higher education and philanthropy.

November 1989 / ISBN 0-87954-290-X / $95

Also in 1991, subject directories covering funding for elementary education, libraries, women's issues and religion. All subject directories are published bienially.

GRANT GUIDES

COMSEARCH PRINTOUTS

This popular series of computer-produced guides to foundation giving derived from the Foundation Center Database is now issued in four separate categories:

COMSEARCH: Broad Topics

This series indexes and analyzes recent foundation grants in 26 broad subject categories. Each listing includes all grants in the particular subject area reported to the Foundation Center during the preceding year, along with an index listing name and geographic location of organizations which have received grants, a geographic index arranged by state of the recipient organization, and a key word index listing descriptive words and phrases which link foundation giving interests with your organization's field. Write for the complete listing of 26 Broad Topics.

Series published annually in September. $55 each

COMSEARCH: Subjects

This series includes 28 specially focused subject listings of grants reported to the Foundation Center during the preceding year. Listings are arranged by the state where the foundatin is located and then by foundation name, and include complete information on the name and location of the grant recipient, the amount awarded, and the purpose of the grant. *COMSEARCH: Subjects* may be purchased as a complete set on microfiche or individually by particular subject area of interest in paper or microfiche form. Write for the complete listing of 28 subject categories.

Series published annually in September. $165 microfiche set; $33 per subject on paper; $11 per subject on microfiche

COMSEARCH: Geographics

This series provides customized listings of grants received by organizations in two cities, eleven states, and seven regions. These listings make it easy to see which major foundations have awarded grants in your area, to which nonprofit organizations, and what each grant was intended to accomplish. Write for the complete listing of geographic locations.

Series published annually in September. $55 each

COMSEARCH: Special Topics

These are three of the most frequently requested special listings from the Center's computer databases. The three special listings are:

- The 1,000 Largest U.S. Foundations by Asset Size
- The 1,000 Largest U.S. Foundations by Annual Grants Total

- The over 2,000 Operating Foundations which Administer Their Own Projects or Programs

Series published annually in September. $33 each

THE FOUNDATION GRANTS INDEX ANNUAL, 1990/1991 EDITION

The Foundation Grants Index Annual lists the grants of $5,000 or more awarded to nonprofit organizations by over 450 foundations. It is the most thorough subject index of actual grants of major U.S. foundations available, and includes the top 100 grantmakers.

The 1990/1991 Edition is the largest annual *Index* ever, with an expanded analytical introduction, an improved and enlarged subject index, and more grant descriptions than ever before—more than 45,000 grants of $5,000 or more made to nonprofit organizations reported to the Center in 1988/1989. The volume is arranged alphabetically by state, then by foundation name. Each entry includes the amount and date of the grant, name and location of the recipient, a description of the grant, and any known limitations of the foundation's giving pattern. The grants are indexed by subject and geographic location, by the names of the recipient organizations, and by a multitude of key words describing all aspects of each grant.

The Foundation Grants Index Annual is the reference used by educators, librarians, fundraisers, medical personnel, and other professionals interested in learning about foundation grants. It shows you what kind of organizations and programs the major foundations have been funding.

1990/1991 Edition, October 1990 / ISBN 0-87954-346-9 / $95. Published annually.

THE FOUNDATION GRANTS INDEX QUARTERLY

This unique subscription service keeps your fundraising program up-to-date, bringing you important new information on foundation funding every three months. Each issue of *The Foundation Grants Index Quarterly* brings you descriptions of over 5,000 recent foundation grants, arranged by state and indexed by subjects and recipients. This enables you to zero in on grants made in your subject area within your geographic region. You can use the *Quarterly* to target potential sources of funding for medical schools in Washington, D.C., for example, modern dance troupes in New York, or any other combination of factors.

The *Quarterly* also contains updates on grantmakers, noting changes in foundation address, personnel, program interests, and application procedures. Also included is a list of grantmakers' publications—annual reports, information brochures, grants lists, and newsletters. *The Foundation Grants Index Quarterly* is a trusted current-awareness tool used by professional fundraisers.

Annual subscription $60 / 4 issues ISSN 0735-2522
Two year subscription $100/Three year subscription $140

GUIDEBOOKS

FOUNDATION FUNDAMENTALS: A Guide for Grantseekers, 4th Edition
Edited by Judith B. Margolin

This comprehensive, easy-to-read guidebook presents the facts you need to understand the world of foundations, and to identify foundation funding sources for your organization. Illustrations take you step-by-step through the funding research process, and worksheets and checklists are provided to help you get started in your search for funding. Comprehensive bibliographies and detailed research examples are also supplied.

Revised edition, March 1991 / ISBN 0-87954-392-2 / $14.95

THE FOUNDATION CENTER'S USER-FRIENDLY GUIDE
Grantseeker's Guide to Resources
Edited by Judith B. Margolin

This helpful book answers the most commonly asked questions about fundraising in an upbeat, easy-to-read style. Specifically designed for novice grantseekers, the *User-Friendly Guide* leads the reader through the maze of unfamiliar jargon and the wide range of research guides used successfully by professional grantseekers every day. Whether a grantseeker needs $100 or $100,000 for a project or organization, this guide offers an excellent first step in the fundraising process.

June 1990 / ISBN 0-87954-342-6 / $7.50

BENCHMARK STUDIES

AGING: The Burden Study on Foundation Grantmaking Trends

This in-depth analysis of foundation funding for programs that benefit the elderly covers private, corporate, and community grantmakers and considers such pertinent topics as: the availability of support for caregivers, the frail elderly, and Alzheimer's patients; a renewed interest in support services and institutional long-term care; and intergenerational programs.

1991 / ISBN 0-87954-389-2 / $40

ALCOHOL AND DRUG ABUSE FUNDING: An Analysis of Foundation Grants 1983–1987

This new report provides an authoritative study of independent, corporate, and community foundation grants awarded between 1983–1987 for drug and alcohol abuse programs. The study presents the complete picture of private funding, as it examines the historical background, present status, and future directions of grantmaking in this critical field. Designed for foundation policymakers, grantseekers, and researchers in the fields of health care and prevention, education, and social service.

August 1989 / ISBN 0-87954-286-1 / $45

CRIME AND JUSTICE: The Burden Study on Foundation Grantmaking Trends

This comprehensive work examines foundation funding for programs involved with crime prevention, juvenile justice, law enforcement, correction facilities, rehabilitation, and victim assistance. *Crime and Justice* looks at significant developments in the criminal justice field, changing public perceptions of crime, and cuts in governmental expenditures. It also documents the remarkable growth of funding for programs combatting spouse and child abuse, and those assisting victims of violence.

1991 / ISBN 0-87954-381-7 / $35

BIBLIOGRAPHIES

THE LITERATURE OF THE NONPROFIT SECTOR: A Bibliography with Abstracts, Volumes I and II

These volumes tap into the vast and growing body of literature on the many aspects of the philanthropic tradition in America. This comprehensive bibliography of philanthropy and voluntarism—recently expanded by nearly 2,000 new titles in Volume II for a combined total of over 6,500 listings—has been designed to help you access the books and articles you need quickly and easily. The entries are divided into twelve broad subject fields, and the books include subject, title, and author indexes to speed your research. Plus, to make thorough research even easier, nearly one-third of the entries in the first volume and well over two-thirds in the second are abstracted to give you a clear idea of the material covered in each work. The titles covered in these two extensive volumes explore many different sides of the nonprofit world.

Whether you are looking for a manual that outlines development strategies for museums, an article that considers rural poverty in the 1970s, or a book that tackles the interplay of federal tax policy and charitable giving, the two volumes of *The Literature of the Nonprofit Sector* will help direct your research.

Volume I, August 1989 / ISBN 0-87954-287-X / $55
Volume II, July 1990 / ISBN 0-87954-343-4 / $45
Volume I and II SET / $75

AUTHORED PUBLICATIONS

AN AGILE SERVANT: Community Leadership by Community Foundations

Editor Richard Magat celebrates the 75th anniversary of the founding of the first community foundation with the publication of *An Agile Servant,* a book that explores the far-reaching impact of this important branch of philanthropy. *An Agile Servant* collects essays from some of the most distinguished men and women in the field, each approaching the unique institution of the community foundation from a different perspective. Drawing on their own experience and research, the authors investigate its origins, historical development, and changing role in society and its ability to combat social ills and encourage progressive change—a point illustrated through sixteen case studies. Richard Magat has organized a study that will fascinate anyone interested in successful philanthropic efforts.

December 1989 / ISBN 0-87954-332-9 / $15.95 / paperbound
ISBN 0-87954-330-2 / $24.95—hardbound

AMERICA'S VOLUNTARY SPIRIT: A Book of Readings

In this thoughtful collection, Brian O'Connell, President of INDEPENDENT SECTOR, brings together 45 selections which celebrate and examine the richness and variety of America's unique voluntary sector. O'Connell researched nearly 1,000 selections spanning over 300 years of writing to identify those speeches, articles, chapters, and papers which best define and characterize the roles that philanthropy and voluntary action play in our society. Contributors as diverse as de Tocqueville, and John D. Rockefeller, Thoreau, and Max Lerner, Erma Bombeck, and Vernon Jordan are unified in a common examination of this unique dimension of American life. The anthology includes a bibliography of over 500 important writings and a detailed subject index.

October 1983 / ISBN 0-87954-079-6 (hardcover) / $19.95

AMERICA'S WEALTHY AND THE FUTURE OF FOUNDATIONS
Edited by Teresa J. Odendahl
Co-sponsored by the Council on Foundations and the Yale University Program on Non-Profit Organizations

Recent studies indicate that the "big foundations" with giant assets and high public profiles are declining in popularity as charitable vehicles of the rich. *America's Wealthy* poses the compelling question: What impact will the declining birthrate of "big foundations" have on the future of philanthropy and the social programs it supports? It also takes us behind the scenes for a first-hand look at the culture of the wealthy and reveals a complex set of attitudes, motivations, economic forces, and policy regulations that offer insight into how and why America's wealthy commit their private resources for the public good. A must-read for all concerned with philanthropy in America.

March 1987 / ISBN 0-87954-194-6 / $24.95 / paperbound
ISBN 0-87954-197-0 / $34.95—hardbound

THE BOARD MEMBER'S BOOK
by Brian O'Connell, President,
INDEPENDENT SECTOR

Based on his extensive experience working with and on the boards of voluntary organizations, Brian O'Connell has developed this practical guide to the essential functions of voluntary boards. O'Connell offers practical advice on how to be a more effective board member and how board members can help their organizations make a difference. This is an invaluable instructional and inspirational tool for anyone who works on or with a voluntary board. Includes an extensive reading list.

May 1985 / ISBN 0-87954-133-4 / $21.95

CAREERS FOR DREAMERS AND DOERS: A Guide to Management Careers in the Nonprofit Sector

Co-authors Lilly Cohen and Dennis Young have written a comprehensive career guide for the nonprofit world. *Careers for Dreamers and Doers* shows how to build a professional career on a foundation of idealism, offering practical advice for starting a job search and strategies tested by successful managers throughout the voluntary sector. The first work of its kind, this informative guide draws on the experience of 27 established professionals, offering profiles of nonprofit C.E.O.s, development officers, and consultants of the "third sector." For those looking for a job in the voluntary sector, a field that the authors predict will become increasingly exciting and remunerative, this book provides an excellent opportunity to learn both the fundamentals and the finer points of the market.

November 1989 / ISBN 0-87954-294-2 / $24.95

THE CHARITABLE IMPULSE: Wealth and Social Conscience in Communities and Cultures Outside the United States
by James A. Joseph

The Charitable Impulse is the product of author James Joseph's life-long interest in how compassionate values are developed, nurtured, and activated. In his quest to identify the motives and personal attributes that lead to a caring society, he has traveled around the world—from South America to South Africa, to England, India, and the Middle East—interviewing men and women who contribute to the public good. *The Charitable Impulse* adds a much-needed international dimension to the growing body of literature on philanthropy and voluntarism, and will be a vital resource for policymakers in the public and private sectors, for political and social scientists, and for all who study or participate in not-for-profit initiatives worldwide.

September 1989 / ISBN 0-87954-301-9 / $19.95—paperbound
ISBN 0-87954-300-0 / $24.95—hardbound

FINANCING A COLLEGE EDUCATION: The Essential Guide for the '90s

Judith B. Margolin has written a comprehensive guide for families anxious about the skyrocketing costs of higher education. In this clearly written book, she navigates obstacles such as the new tax laws and plummeting federal aid by uncovering a range of investment options and pointing out various "bargain" colleges and universities where one can still get an excellent education at an affordable price. *Financing a College Education* offers sound advice for young parents planning for the future as well as for families currently undergoing the rigors of financing a college education.

May 1989 / ISBN 0-306-43071-1 / $24.95

FOUNDATION TRUSTEESHIP: Service in the Public Interest
by John W. Nason

Changing public expectations of foundations and new challenges for foundation board members necessitate a fresh approach and an expert guide through the complexities of foundation trusteeship. John Nason, calling upon his years of experience as a trustee, has identified the probl-term "shadow state" to describe a sector of society composed of technically independent voluntary organizations, a sector that, Wolch contends, is increasingly controlled by the government. *The Shadow State* is a timely and informative piece of scholarship, offering sound advice to voluntary groups that seek to accomplish significant social change: to avoid the compromising power of state control.

March 1990 / ISBN 0-87954-231-0 / $24.95 /

A HISTORIOGRAPHIC REVIEW OF FOUNDATION LITERATURE
by Joseph C. Kiger

An historical overview of literature on the foundation field from 1894 to the present, this book is an excellent resource for anyone interested in foundation history, both in itself and as a guide to further reading.

October 1987 / ISBN 0-87954-233-0 / $7.50

MANAGING FOUNDATION ASSETS: An Analysis of Foundation Investment and Payout Procedures and Performance
by Lester M. Salamon and Kenneth P. Voytek

In their new study, Salamon and Voytek address some of the most critical questions from the foundation community on foundation investing and payout procedures, including: how do foundations manage the immense wealth in their control?, how does the payout requirement affect foundation investment operations?, what impact has the change in the payout requirement of 1981 had on both the investment and payout performance of foundations?

After addressing these questions, Salamon offers insight into key topics: the process foundations use to make their payout decisions and manage their investments, the rate of return they have achieved and the payout rates foundations have adopted.

March 1989 / ISBN 0-87954-283-7 / $19.95

MANAGING FOR PROFIT IN THE NONPROFIT WORLD
by Paul B. Firstenberg

How can service-oriented nonprofits expand their revenue bases? In this title in our series on nonprofit management, author Paul B. Firstenberg shares his view that a vital nonprofit is an entrepreneurial nonprofit. Drawing upon his 14 years of experience as a professional in the nonprofit sector—at the Ford Foundation, Princeton, Tulane, and Yale Universities, and Children's Television Workshop—as well as his extensive for-profit experience, Firstenberg outlines innovative ways in which nonprofit managers can utilize the same state-of-the-art mangement techniques as the most successful for-profit enterprises.

September 1986 / ISBN 0-87954-159-8 / $19.95

MAPPING THE THIRD SECTOR: Voluntarism in a Changing Social Economy
by Jon Van Til

Over 700,000 nonprofit organizations. Over 15 million volunteers. What impact do they have on society today? Professor Jon Van Til, Editor of the *Nonprofit Voluntary Sector Quarterly,* raises this compelling question in his scholarly new work as he sets the stage for a coherent view of the voluntary sector. His review of historical and contemporary models of voluntary action paves the way for one that stresses the need for a new conception of how to preserve, extend, and experience community within the interactive web of modern society.

March 1988 / ISBN 0-87954-240-3 / $24.95

THE NONPROFIT ENTREPRENEUR: Creating Ventures to Earn Income
Edited by Edward Skloot

Nonprofit consultant and entrepreneur Edward Skloot, in a well-organized topic-by-topic analytical approach to nonprofit venturing, demonstrates how nonprofits can launch successful earned income enterprises without compromising their missions. Skloot has compiled a collection of writings by the nation's top practitioners and advisors in nonprofit enterprise. Topics covered include legal issues, marketing techniques, business planning, avoiding the pitfalls of venturing for smaller nonprofits, and a special section on museums and their retail operations.

September 1988 / ISBN 0-87954-239-X / $19.95

PHILANTHROPY IN AN AGE OF TRANSITION
The Essays of Alan Pifer

This is a collection of essays by one of the most respected and well-known individu American history.

Alan Pifer is President Emeritus of Carnegie Corporation of New York where he was President for over seventeen years.

April 1984 / ISBN 0-87954-104-0 / $12.50

PHILANTHROPY AND VOLUNTARISM: An Annotated Bibliography
by Daphne N. Layton
for the Association of American Colleges

Finally, a comprehensive bibliography on philanthropy and voluntarism to aid students, scholars, and the general public in understanding the field. All of the best and most important works can be found here, including over 1,600 books and articles which analyze aspects of the philanthrophic tradition in the U.S. and abroad. Among these are 250 extensively annotated scholarly works particularly useful as texts or background reading for undergraduate study and research in philanthropy.

June 1987 / ISBN 0-87954-198-9 / $18.50

PHILANTHROPY IN ACTION
by Brian O'Connell, President,
INDEPENDENT SECTOR

Goddard's rocketry research. The suffrage and civil rights movements. Salk's polio vaccine. Historic Williamsburg. *Philanthropy in Action* tells the fascinating stories of hundreds of grants which have made a difference, revealing the history, role, and impact of philanthropy in our society. O'Connell captures the remarkable relationships between donors and grantees as he presents philanthropy according to nine roles, including discovering new frontiers of knowledge, supporting and encouraging excellence, relieving human misery, and making communities a better place to live. The stories of the invaluable contributions made by community foundations, cooperative benevolence associations, and corporate giving programs are also narrated. Lively, entertaining, and informative, *Philanthropy in Action* is both an essential resource tool for students, teachers, writers, and scholars of philanthropy, and a collection of great stories, masterfully told.

September 1987 / ISBN 0-87954-231-4 / $19.95 / paperbound
ISBN 0-87954-230-6 / $24.95—hardbound

PROMOTING ISSUES AND IDEAS: A Guide to Public Relations for Nonprofit Organizations by Public Interest, Public Relations, Inc. (PIPR)

PIPR, specialists in promoting the issues and ideas of nonprofit groups, present proven strategies which will put your organization on the map and attract the interest of the people you wish to influence and inform. Included are the "nuts-and-bolts" of advertising, publicity, speechmaking, lobbying, and special events; how to write and produce informational literature that leaps off the page; public relations on a shoestring budget; how to plan and evaluate "pr" efforts, and the use of new communication technologies.

March 1987 / ISBN 0-87954-192-X / $24.95

RAISE MORE MONEY FOR YOUR NONPROFIT ORGANIZATION: A Guide to Evaluating and Improving Your Fundraising by Anne L. New

In *Raise More Money,* Anne New sets guidelines for a fundraising program that will benefit the incipient as well as the established nonprofit organization.

The author divides this new guidebook into three sections: "The Basics," which delineates the necessary steps a nonprofit must take before launching a development campaign; "Fundraising Methods," which encourages organizational self-analysis and points the way to an effective program involving many sources of funding; and "Fundraising Resources," a 20-page bibliography that highlights the most useful research and funding directories available.

October 1990 / ISBN 0-87954-388-4 / $14.95

THE SHADOW STATE: Government and Voluntary Sector in Transition

In this fascinating analysis, Jennifer Wolch explains the dynamics of the unfolding relationship between the voluntary sector and government. The author uses the term "shadow state" to describe a sector of society composed of technically independent voluntary organizations, a sector that, Wolch contends, is increasingly controlled by the government. *The Shadow State* is a timely and informative piece of scholarship, offering sound advice to voluntary groups that seek to accomplish significant social change: to avoid the compromising power of state control.

March 1990 / ISBN 0-87954-231-0 / $24.95

SECURING YOUR ORGANIZATION'S FUTURE: A Complete Guide to Fundraising Strategies by Michael Seltzer

Michael Seltzer, a well-known pioneer in the field of nonprofit management, uses compelling case studies and bottom-line facts to demonstrate how fundraisers—whether beginners or seasoned pros—can help their nonprofit organizations achieve long-term financial well-being. Seltzer uses a step-by-step approach to guide fundraisers through the world of money and shows how to build a network of support from among the wide variety of funding sources available today. Seltzer's work is supplemented with easy-to-follow worksheets and an extensive bibliography of selected readings and resource organizations. Highly recommended for use as a text in nonprofit management programs at colleges and universities.

February 1987 / ISBN 0-87954-190-3 / $24.95

VOLUNTEERS IN ACTION

In *Volunteers in Action,* authors Brian O'Connell and Ann Brown O'Connell illustrate the impact of ordinary citizens and how their dedication to voluntary action enriches their lives and changes their communities, the country, and the world. Using interviews and anecdotes, the authors provide unique insight into the true character of the voluntary sector. The book also serves as a call to action, encouraging citizens to involve themselves in this rewarding form of participatory democracy. The authors of this fascinating study conclude by commending efforts to foster the ethic of volunteerism in young people, suggesting that the betterment of society ultimately depends on the idealism of the young.

September 1989 / ISBN 0-87954-292-6 / $19.95 / paperbound
ISBN 0-87954-291-8 / $24.95—hardbound

WORKING IN FOUNDATIONS: Career Patterns of Women and Men By Teresa Jean Odendahl, Elizabeth Trocolli Boris, and Arlene Kaplan Daniels

This publication is the result of a groundbreaking study of foundation career paths of women and men undertaken by Women and Foundations/Corporate Philanthropy with major funding from the Russell Sage Foundation. This book offers a detailed picture of the roles and responsibilities of foundation staff members, employment opportunities in philanthropy, and the management styles and grantmaking processes within foundations.

April 1985 / ISBN 0-87954-134-2 / $12.95

MEMBERSHIP PROGRAM

ASSOCIATES PROGRAM
"Direct Line to Fundraising Information"

The Associates Program puts important facts and figures on your desk through a toll-free telephone reference service helping you to:

- identify potential sources of foundation funding for your organization,
- gather important information to target and present your proposals most effectively.

Your annual membership in the Associates Program gives you vital information on a timely basis, saving you hundreds of hours of research time.

- Membership in the Associates Program puts important funding information on your desk, including information from:

  —foundation annual reports, information brochures, press releases, grants lists, and other documents

  —IRS 990-PF information returns for all 30,000 U.S. foundations—often the only source of information on small foundations

  —books and periodicals chronicling foundation and philanthropic history and regulations

  —files filled with news clippings about foundations

  —The Foundation Center's own publications: *Foundation Directory, Foundation Grants Index*—annual and quarterly, *Source Book Profiles, Corporate Foundation Profiles, National Data Book, COMSEARCH Printouts, Foundation Fundamentals, Grants to Individuals,* and *Special Topics.*

- The Associates Program puts this vital information on your desk through a *toll-free telephone call.* The annual fee of $475 for the Associates Program grants you *10 free calls, or 2½ hours* worth of answers per month.

- Membership in the Associates Program allows you to request *custom searches of The Foundation Center's computerized databases* which contain information on *all 30,000* active U.S. foundations.

Thousands of professional fundraisers find it extremely cost effective to rely on the Center's Associates Program. Put our staff of experts to work for your fundraising program. For more information call TOLL-FREE 800-424-9836.

FOUNDATION CENTER COMPUTER DATABASES

Foundation and Grants Information Online

As the only nonprofit organization whose sole purpose is to provide information on philanthropic activity, the Foundation Center offers two important databases online. Perhaps the most flexible way to take advantage of the Foundation Center's vast resources, computer access lets you design your own search for the foundations most likely to suport your nonprofit organization. Online retrieval provides vital information on funding sources, philanthropic giving, grant application guidelines, and the financial status of foundations to:

Nonprofit organizations seeking funds
Grantmaking institutions
Corporate contributors
Researchers
Journalists
Legislators

Searches of the Center's databases can provide comprehensive and timely answers to your questions, such as . . .

- Which New York foundations support urban projects? Who are their officers and trustees?
- What are the program interests of the ten largest corporate foundations? Which ones publish annual reports?
- Which foundations have given grants in excess of $100,000 in the past two years for continuing education for women?
- Which foundation would be likely to fund a cancer research project at a California hospital?
- Which are the ten largest foundations in Philadelphia by annual grants amount?
- What are the names and addresses of smaller foundations in the 441 zip code range?

The Center's up-to-date and authoritative data is available online through DIALOG Information Services, and through many online utilities. For further information on accessing the Center's databases directly through DIALOG, contact DIALOG at 415-858-2700. To learn more about which online utilities provide "gateway" access, or for free materials to help you search our files, call the Online Support Staff at the Foundation Center at 212-620-4230.

THE FOUNDATION CENTER COOPERATING COLLECTIONS NETWORK

Free Funding Information Centers

The Foundation Center is an independent national service organization established by foundations to provide an authoritative source of information on private philanthropic giving. The New York, Washington, DC, Cleveland and San Francisco reference collections operated by the Foundation Center offer a wide variety of services and comprehensive collections of information on foundations and grants. Cooperating Collections are libraries, community foundations and other nonprofit agencies that provide a core collection of Foundation Center publications and a variety of supplementary materials and services in areas useful to grantseekers. The core collection consists of:

Foundation Directory
Foundation Fundamentals
Foundation Grants Index
Foundation Grants to Individuals
Literature of the Nonprofit Sector
National Data Book of Foundations
National Directory of Corporate Giving
Source Book Profiles

Many of the network members have sets of private foundation information returns (IRS 990-PF) for their state or region which are available for public use. A complete set of U.S. foundation returns can be found at the New York and Washington, DC offices of the Foundation Center. The Cleveland and San Francisco offices contain IRS 990-PF returns for the midwestern and western states, respectively. Those Cooperating Collections marked with a bullet (•) have sets of private foundation information returns for their state or region.

Because the collections vary in their hours, materials and services, IT IS RECOMMENDED THAT YOU CALL EACH COLLECTION IN ADVANCE. To check on new locations or more current information, call 1-800-424-9836.

Reference Collections Operated by the Foundation Center

The Foundation Center
8th Floor
79 Fifth Avenue
New York, NY 10003
212-620-4230

The Foundation Center
Room 312
312 Sutter Street
San Francisco, CA 94108
415-397-0902

The Foundation Center
1001 Connecticut Avenue, NW
Washington, DC 20036
202-331-1400

The Foundation Center
Kent H. Smith Library
1442 Hanna Building
Cleveland, OH 44115
216-861-1933

ALABAMA

• Birmingham Public Library
Government Documents
2100 Park Place
Birmingham 35203
205-226-3600

Huntsville Public Library
915 Monroe St.
Huntsville 35801
205-532-5940

University of South Alabama
Library Reference Dept.
Mobile 36688
205-460-7025

• Auburn University at Montgomery Library
7300 University Drive
Montgomery 36117-3596
205-244-3649

ALASKA

• University of Alaska
Anchorage Library
3211 Providence Drive
Anchorage 99508
907-786-1848

Juneau Public Library
292 Marine Way
Juneau 99801
907-586-5249

ARIZONA

• Phoenix Public Library
Business & Sciences Dept.
12 East McDowell Road
Phoenix 85004
602-262-4636

• Tucson Public Library
101 N. Stone Ave.
Tucson 85726-7470
602-791-4393

ARKANSAS

• Westark Community College Library
5210 Grand Avenue
Fort Smith 72913
501-785-7000

• Central Arkansas Library System
Reference Services
700 Louisiana Street
Little Rock 72201
501-370-5950

CALIFORNIA

• Peninsula Community Foundation
1204 Burlingame Avenue
Burlingame 94011-0627
415-342-2505

Ventura County Community Foundation
Community Resource Center
1357 Del Norte Road
Camarillo 93010
805-988-0196

• Orange County Community Developmental Council
1695 W. MacArthur Blvd.
Costa Mesa 92626
714-540-9293

• California Community Foundation
Funding Information Center
606 S. Olive St., Suite 2400
Los Angeles 90014
213-413-4042

• Community Foundation for Monterey County
177 Van Buren
Monterey 93942
408-375-9712

Riverside Public Library
3581 7th Street
Riverside 92501
714-782-5201

California State Library
Reference Services, Rm. 301
914 Capitol Mall
Sacramento 95814
916-322-4570

• San Diego Community Foundation
525 "B" Street, Suite 410
San Diego 92101
619-239-8815

• Nonprofit Development Center
1762 Technology Dr., Suite 225
San Jose 95110
408-452-8181

California Community Foundation
Volunteer Center of Orange County
1000 E. Santa Ana Blvd.
Santa Ana 92701
714-953-1655

• Santa Barbara Public Library
40 East Anapamu
Santa Barbara 93101-1603
805-962-7653

Santa Monica Public Library
1343 Sixth Street
Santa Monica 90401-1603
213-458-8859

COLORADO

Pikes Peak Library District
20 North Cascade Avenue
Colorado Springs 80901
719-473-2080

• Denver Public Library
Sociology Division
1357 Broadway
Denver 80203
303-640-8870

CONNECTICUT

Danbury Public Library
170 Main Street
Danbury 06810
203-797-4527

• Hartford Public Library
Reference Department
500 Main Street
Hartford 06103
203-293-6000

D.A.T.A.
70 Audubon St.
New Haven 06510
203-772-1345

DELAWARE

• University of Delaware
Hugh Morris Library
Newark 19717-5267
302-451-2965

FLORIDA

Volusia County Library Center
City Island
Daytona Beach 32014-4484
904-255-3765

• Nova University
Einstein Library—Foundation Resource Collection
3301 College Avenue
Fort Lauderdale 33314
305-475-7497

Indian River Community College
Learning Resources Center
3209 Virginia Avenue
Fort Pierce 34981-5599
407-468-4757

• Jacksonville Public Libraries
Business, Science & Documents
122 North Ocean Street
Jacksonville 32206
904-630-2665

• Miami-Dade Public Library
Humanities Department
101 W. Flagler St.
Miami 33130
305-375-2665

- Orlando Public Library
  Orange County Library System
  101 E. Central Blvd.
  Orlando 32801
  407-425-4694

Selby Public Library
1001 Boulevard of the Arts
Sarasota 34236
813-951-5501

- Leon County Public Library
  Funding Resource Center
  1940 North Monroe Street
  Tallahassee 32303
  904-487-2665

Palm Beach County Community Foundation
324 Datura Street, Suite 340
West Palm Beach 33401
407-659-6800

GEORGIA

- Atlanta-Fulton Public Library
  Foundation Collection—Ivan Allen Department
  1 Margaret Mitchell Square
  Atlanta 30303-1089
  404-730-1900

HAWAII

- Hawaii Community Foundation
  Hawaii Resource Room
  222 Merchant Street
  2nd Floor
  Honolulu 96813
  808-537-6333

University of Hawaii
Thomas Hale Hamilton Library
2550 The Mall
Honolulu 96822
808-948-7214

IDAHO

- Boise Public Library
  715 S. Capitol Blvd.
  Boise 83702
  208-384-4024

- Caldwell Public Library
  1010 Dearborn Street
  Caldwell 83605
  208-459-3242

ILLINOIS

Belleville Public Library
121 East Washington Street
Belleville 62220
618-234-0441

- Donors Forum of Chicago
  53 W. Jackson Blvd., Rm. 430
  Chicago 60604
  312-431-0265

- Evanston Public Library
  1703 Orrington Avenue
  Evanston 60201
  708-866-0305

- Sangamon State University Library
  Shepherd Road
  Springfield 62794-9243
  217-786-6633

INDIANA

- Allen County Public Library
  900 Webster Street
  Fort Wayne 46802
  219-424-7241

Indiana University Northwest Library
3400 Broadway
Gary 46408
219-980-6582

- Indianapolis-Marion County Public Library
  40 East St. Clair Street
  Indianapolis 46206
  317-269-1733

IOWA

- Cedar Rapids Public Library
  Funding Information Center
  500 First Street, SE
  Cedar Rapids 52401
  319-398-5145

- Southwestern Community College
  Learning Resource Center
  1501 W. Townline Rd.
  Creston 50801
  515-782-7081, ext. 262

- Public Library of Des Moines
  100 Locust Street
  Des Moines 50308
  515-283-4152

KANSAS

- Topeka Public Library
  1515 West Tenth Street
  Topeka 66604
  913-233-2040

- Wichita Public Library
  223 South Main
  Wichita 67202
  316-262-0611

KENTUCKY

Western Kentucky University
Helm-Cravens Library
Bowling Green 42101
502-745-6122

- Louisville Free Public Library
  Fourth and York Streets
  Louisville 40203
  502-561-8617

LOUISIANA

- East Baton Rouge Parish Library
  Centroplex Branch
  120 St. Louis Street
  Baton Rouge 70802
  504-389-4960

- New Orleans Public Library
  Business and Science Division
  219 Loyola Avenue
  New Orleans 70140
  504-596-2580

- Shreve Memorial Library
  424 Texas Street
  Shreveport 71120-1523
  318-226-5894

MAINE

- University of Southern Maine
  Office of Sponsored Research
  246 Deering Ave., Rm. 628
  Portland 04103
  207-780-4871

MARYLAND

- Enoch Pratt Free Library
  Social Science and History Department
  400 Cathedral Street
  Baltimore 21201
  301-396-5320

Carroll County Public Library
Government and Funding Information Center
50 E. Main St.
Westminster 21157
301-848-4250

MASSACHUSETTS

- Associated Grantmakers of Massachusetts
  294 Washington Street
  Suite 840
  Boston 02108
  617-426-2608

- Boston Public Library
  666 Boylston St.
  Boston 02117
  617-536-5400

- Western Massachusetts Funding Resource Center
  Campaign for Human Development
  73 Chestnut Street
  Springfield 01103
  413-732-3175

- Worcester Public Library
  Grants Resource Center
  Salem Square
  Worcester 01608
  508-799-1655

MICHIGAN

- Alpena County Library
  211 North First Avenue
  Alpena 49707
  517-356-6188

University of Michigan-Ann Arbor
209 Hatcher Graduate Library
Ann Arbor 48109-1205
313-764-1149

- Battle Creek Community Foundation
  One Riverwalk Centre
  34 W. Jackson St.
  Battle Creek 49017
  616-962-2181

- Henry Ford Centennial Library
  16301 Michigan Avenue
  Dearborn 48126
  313-943-2330

- Wayne State University
  Purdy-Kresge Library
  5265 Cass Avenue
  Detroit 48202
  313-577-6424

- Michigan State University Libraries
  Reference Library
  East Lansing 48824-1048
  517-353-8818

- Farmington Community Library
  32737 West 12 Mile Road
  Farmington Hills 48018
  313-553-0300

- University of Michigan-Flint Library
  Reference Department
  Flint 48502-2186
  313-762-3408

- Grand Rapids Public Library
  Business Dept.
  60 Library Plaza NE
  Grand Rapids 49503-3093
  616-456-3600

- Michigan Technological University Library
  Highway U.S. 41
  Houghton 49931
  906-487-2507

- Sault Ste. Marie Area Public Schools
  Office of Compensatory Education
  460 W. Spruce St.
  Sault Ste. Marie 49783-1874
  906-635-6619

MINNESOTA

- Duluth Public Library
  520 W. Superior Street
  Duluth 55802
  218-723-3802

Southwest State University Library
Marshall 56258
507-537-7278

- Minneapolis Public Library
  Sociology Department
  300 Nicollet Mall
  Minneapolis 55401
  612-372-6555

Rochester Public Library
11 First Street, SE
Rochester 55902-3743
507-285-8002

St. Paul Public Library
90 West Fourth Street
Saint Paul 55102
612-292-6307

MISSISSIPPI

Jackson/Hinds Library System
300 North State Street
Jackson 39201
601-968-5803

MISSOURI

- Clearinghouse for Midcontinent Foundations
  Univ. of Missouri
  Law School, Suite 1-300
  52nd Street and Oak
  Kansas City 64113-0680
  816-276-1176

• Kansas City Public Library
311 East 12th Street
Kansas City 64106
816-221-9650

• Metropolitan Association for Philanthropy, Inc.
5585 Pershing Avenue
Suite 150
St. Louis 63112
314-361-3900

• Springfield-Greene County Library
397 East Central Street
Springfield 65801
417-866-4636

Montana

• Eastern Montana College Library
1500 N. 30th Street
Billings 59101-0298
406-657-1662

• Montana State Library
Reference Department
1515 E. 6th Avenue
Helena 59620
406-444-3004

Nebraska

• University of Nebraska
106 Love Library
14th & R Streets
Lincoln 68588-0410
402-472-2848

• W. Dale Clark Library
Social Sciences Department
215 South 15th Street
Omaha 68102
402-444-4826

Nevada

• Las Vegas-Clark County Library District
1401 East Flamingo Road
Las Vegas 89119-6160
702-733-7810

• Washoe County Library
301 South Center Street
Reno 89501
702-785-4012

New Hampshire

• New Hampshire Charitable Fund
One South Street
Concord 03302-1335
603-225-6641

• Plymouth State College
Herbert H. Lamson Library
Plymouth 03264
603-535-5000

New Jersey

Cumberland County Library
800 E. Commerce Street
Bridgeton 08302-2295
609-453-2210

The Support Center
17 Academy Street, Suite 1101
Newark 07102
201-643-5774

County College of Morris
Masten Learning Resource Center
Route 10 and Center Grove Rd.
Randolph 07869
201-361-5000 ext. 470

• New Jersey State Library
Governmental Reference
185 West State Street
Trenton 08625-0520
609-292-6220

New Mexico

Albuquerque Community Foundation
6400 Uptown Boulevard N.E.
Suite 500-W
Albuquerque 87105
505-883-6240

• New Mexico State Library
325 Don Gaspar Street
Santa Fe 87503
505-827-3827

New York

• New York State Library
Cultural Education Center
Humanities Section
Empire State Plaza
Albany 12230
518-473-4636

Suffolk Cooperative Library System
627 North Sunrise Service Road
Bellport 11713
516-286-1600

New York Public Library
Bronx Reference Center
2556 Bainbridge Avenue
Bronx 10458
212-220-6575

Brooklyn in Touch
One Hanson Place
Room 2504
Brooklyn 11243
718-230-3200

• Buffalo and Erie County Public Library
Lafayette Square
Buffalo 14202
716-858-7103

Huntington Public Library
338 Main Street
Huntington 11743
516-427-5165

Queens Borough Public Library
89-11 Merrick Boulevard
Jamaica 11432
718-990-0700

• Levittown Public Library
One Bluegrass Lane
Levittown 11756
516-731-5728

SUNY/College at Old Westbury Library
223 Store Hill Road
Old Westbury 11568
516-876-3156

• Plattsburgh Public Library
15 Oak Street
Plattsburgh 12901
518-563-0921

Adriance Memorial Library
93 Market Street
Poughkeepsie 12601
914-485-3445

• Rochester Public Library
Business Division
115 South Avenue
Rochester 14604
716-428-7328

Staten Island Council on the Arts
One Edgewater Plaza, Rm. 311
Staten Island 10305
718-447-4485

• Onondaga County Public Library at the Galleries
447 S. Salina Street
Syracuse 13202-2494
315-448-4636

• White Plains Public Library
100 Martine Avenue
White Plains 10601
914-682-4480

North Carolina

• Asheville-Buncomb Technical Community College
Learning Resources Center
340 Victoria Rd.
Asheville 28802
704-254-1921 x300

• The Duke Endowment
200 S. Tryon Street, Ste. 1100
Charlotte 28202
704-376-0291

Durham County Library
300 N. Roxboro Street
Durham 27702
919-560-0100

• North Carolina State Library
109 East Jones Street
Raleigh 27611
919-733-3270

• The Winston-Salem Foundation
229 First Union Bank Building
Winston-Salem 27101
919-725-2382

North Dakota

• North Dakota State University
The Library
Fargo 58105
701-237-8886

Ohio

Stark County District Library
715 Market Avenue North
Canton 44702-1080
216-452-0665

• Public Library of Cincinnati and Hamilton County
Education Department
800 Vine Street
Cincinnati 45202-2071
513-369-6940

Columbus Metropolitan Library
96 S. Grant Avenue
Columbus 43215
614-645-2590

• Dayton and Montgomery County Public Library
Grants Information Center
215 E. Third Street
Dayton 45402-2103
513-227-9500 ext. 211

• Toledo-Lucas County Public Library
Social Science Department
325 Michigan Street
Toledo 43624-1614
419-259-5245

Ohio University-Zanesville
Community Education and Development
1425 Newark Road
Zanesville 43701
614-453-0762

Oklahoma

• Oklahoma City University Library
2501 North Blackwelder
Oklahoma City 73106
405-521-5072

• Tulsa City-County Library System
400 Civic Center
Tulsa 74103
918-596-7944

Oregon

• Pacific Non-Profit Network
Grantsmanship Resource Library
33 N. Central, Ste. 211
Medford 97501
503-779-6044

• Multnomah County Library
Government Documents Room
801 S.W. Tenth Avenue
Portland 97205-2597
503-223-7201

Oregon State Library
State Library Building
Salem 97310
503-378-4274

Pennsylvania

Northampton Community College
Learning Resources Center
3835 Green Pond Road
Bethlehem 18017
215-861-5360

• Erie County Public Library
3 South Perry Square
Erie 16501
814-451-6927

• Dauphin County Library System
101 Walnut Street
Harrisburg 17101
717-234-4961

Lancaster County Public Library
125 North Duke Street
Lancaster 17602
717-394-2651

• The Free Library of Philadelphia
Logan Square
Philadelphia 19103
215-686-5423

• University of Pittsburgh
Hillman Library
Pittsburgh 15260
412-648-7722

Economic Development Council of Northeastern Pennsylvania
1151 Oak Street
Pittston 18640
717-655-5581

RHODE ISLAND

• Providence Public Library
Reference Department
225 Washington St.
Providence 02903
401-455-8000

SOUTH CAROLINA

• Charleston County Library
404 King Street
Charleston 29403
803-723-1645

• South Carolina State Library
Reference Department
1500 Senate Street
Columbia 29211
803-734-8666

SOUTH DAKOTA

• South Dakota State Library
800 Governors Drive
Pierre 57501-2294
605-773-5070
800-592-1841 (SD residents)

Sioux Falls Area Foundation
141 N. Main Ave., Suite 500
Sioux Falls 57102-1134
605-336-7055

TENNESSEE

• Knoxville-Knox County Public Library
500 West Church Avenue
Knoxville 37902
615-544-5750

• Memphis & Shelby County Public Library
1850 Peabody Avenue
Memphis 38104
901-725-8877

• Public Library of Nashville and Davidson County
8th Ave. N. and Union St.
Nashville 37203
615-259-6256

TEXAS

• Community Foundation of Abilene
Funding Information Library
708 NCNB Bldg.
402 Cypress
Abilene 79601
915-676-3883

Amarillo Area Foundation
70 1st National Place I
800 S. Fillmore
Amarillo 79101
806-376-4521

• Hogg Foundation for Mental Health
University of Texas
Austin 78713
512-471-5041

• Corpus Christi State University Library
6300 Ocean Drive
Corpus Christi 78412
512-994-2608

• Dallas Public Library
Grants Information Service
1515 Young Street
Dallas 75201
214-670-1487

• Pan American University
Learning Resource Center
1201 W. University Drive
Edinburg 78539
512-381-3304

• El Paso Community Foundation
1616 Texas Commerce Building
El Paso 79901
915-533-4020

• Texas Christian University Library
Funding Information Center
Ft. Worth 76129
817-921-7664

• Houston Public Library
Bibliographic Information Center
500 McKinney Avenue
Houston 77002
713-236-1313

Lubbock Area Foundation
502 Texas Commerce Bank Building
Lubbock 79401
806-762-8061

• Funding Information Center
507 Brooklyn
San Antonio 78215
512-227-4333

UTAH

• Salt Lake City Public Library
Business and Science Dept.
209 East Fifth South
Salt Lake City 84111
801-363-5733

VERMONT

• Vermont Dept. of Libraries
Reference Services
109 State Street
Montpelier 05602
802-828-3268

VIRGINIA

• Hampton Public Library
Grants Resources Collection
4207 Victoria Blvd.
Hampton 23669
804-727-1154

• Richmond Public Library
Business, Science, & Technology
101 East Franklin Street
Richmond 23219
804-780-8223

• Roanoke City Public Library System
Central Library
706 S. Jefferson Street
Roanoke 24014
703-981-2477

WASHINGTON

• Seattle Public Library
1000 Fourth Avenue
Seattle 98104
206-386-4620

• Spokane Public Library
Funding Information Center
West 906 Main Avenue
Spokane 99201
509-838-3364

WEST VIRGINIA

• Kanawha County Public Library
123 Capital Street
Charleston 25304
304-343-4646

WISCONSIN

• University of Wisconsin-Madison
Memorial Library
728 State Street
Madison 53706
608-262-3242

• Marquette University Memorial Library
1415 West Wisconsin Avenue
Milwaukee 53233
414-288-1515

WYOMING

• Laramie County Community College Library
1400 East College Drive
Cheyenne 82007-3299
307-778-1205

AUSTRALIA

ANZ Executors & Trustees Co. Ltd.
91 William St., 7th floor
Melbourne VIC 3000
03-648-5764

CANADA

Canadian Centre for Philanthropy
1329 Bay St., Suite 200
Toronto, Ontario M5R 2C4
416-368-1138

ENGLAND

Charities Aid Foundation
18 Doughty Street
London WC1N 2PL
01-831-7798

JAPAN

Foundation Center Library of Japan
Elements Shinjuku Bldg. 3F
2-1-14 Shinjuku, Shinjuku-ku
Tokyo 160
03-350-1857

MEXICO

Biblioteca Benjamin Franklin
American Embassy, USICA
Londres 16
Mexico City 6, D.F. 06600
905-211-0042

PUERTO RICO

University of Puerto Rico
Ponce Technological College Library
Box 7186
Ponce 00732
809-844-4150

Universidad Del Sagrado Corazon
M.M.T. Guevarra Library
Correo Calle Loiza
Santurce 00914
809-728-1515 ext. 357

U.S. VIRGIN ISLANDS

University of the Virgin Islands
Paiewonsky Library
Charlotte Amalie
St. Thomas 00802
809-828-3261

THE FOUNDATION CENTER NETWORK

Participants in the Cooperating Collections Network are libraries or nonprofit agencies that provide fundraising information or other funding-related technical assistance in their communities. Cooperating Collections agree to provide free public access to a basic collection of Foundation Center publications during a regular schedule of hours, offering free funding research guidance to all visitors. Many also provide a variety of special services for local nonprofit organizations, using staff or volunteers to prepare special materials, organize workshops, or conduct library orientations.

The Foundation Center welcomes inquiries from agencies interested in providing this type of public information service. If you are interested in establishing a funding information library for the use of nonprofit agencies in your area or in learning more about the program, we would like to hear from you. For more information, please write to: Anne J. Borland, The Foundation Center, 79 Fifth Avenue, New York, NY 10003.

DESCRIPTIVE DIRECTORY

DESCRIPTIVE DIRECTORY

ALABAMA

1
Abroms Charitable Foundation, Inc. ⌑
3132 Guilford Rd.
Birmingham 35223-1217

Established in 1970 in AL.
Donor(s): Harold L. Abroms, Judith E. Abroms.
Foundation type: Independent
Financial data (yr. ended 11/30/88): Assets, $2,591,576 (M); gifts received, $62,000; expenditures, $172,969, including $147,500 for 19 grants (high: $55,000; low: $500).
Purpose and activities: Support primarily for Jewish welfare and secondary and higher education.
Limitations: Giving primarily in AL.
Application information: Contributes only to pre-selected organizations. Applications not accepted.
Officers: Harold L. Abroms, Pres. and Treas.; James M. Abroms, V.P.; Judith E. Abroms, Secy.
Employer Identification Number: 237058629

2
Andalusia Health Services, Inc. ⌑
P.O. Box 1418
Andalusia 36420 (205) 222-6591

Established in 1981 in AL.
Foundation type: Independent
Financial data (yr. ended 6/30/88): Assets, $2,337,038 (M); expenditures, $234,358, including $167,096 for 12 grants (high: $76,250; low: $1,100) and $43,941 for 56 grants to individuals (high: $1,500; low: $250).
Purpose and activities: Giving primarily for community health services; support also for scholarships in a health-related field, such as nursing, medicine, and medical or laboratory technology.
Types of support: Equipment, operating budgets, student aid.
Limitations: Giving primarily in Andalusia, AL, and the surrounding area; scholarships only to residents of Covington County.
Application information: Contributes only to pre-selected organizations; accepts applications only from individuals seeking scholarships; application form required.
Deadline(s): Apr. 15 for scholarships
Write: William H. McWhorter
Officers and Directors:* George H. Proctor,* Pres.; Hugh King,* V.P.; Eiland E. Anthony,* Secy.-Treas.; J. Dige Bishop, Ray Latimer, W.B. McDonald, John S. Merrill, Catherine D. Roland.
Employer Identification Number: 630793474

3
The Baker Foundation ⌑
c/o AmSouth Bank
P.O. Box 11426
Birmingham 35206

Established in 1983 in AL.
Donor(s): Raymon J. Baker.
Foundation type: Independent
Financial data (yr. ended 12/31/87): Assets, $1,844,282 (M); expenditures, $209,313, including $186,951 for 27 grants (high: $100,000; low: $282).
Purpose and activities: Contributes to Christian churches and Christian colleges; support also for education, denominational giving, health, and youth.
Limitations: Giving primarily in AL. No grants to individuals.
Application information: Contributes only to pre-selected organizations. Applications not accepted.
Officers and Directors:* Michael W. Curl,* Pres.; Cindy B. Paler,* Secy.; Becky Baker, Marjorie R. Baker, Raymon J. Baker, G. Ralph Jones, Charles R. Paler.
Employer Identification Number: 630843636

4
George W. Barber, Jr. Foundation ⌑ ☆
36 Barber Court
Birmingham 35209

Established in 1986 in AL.
Donor(s): George W. Barber, Jr.
Foundation type: Independent
Financial data (yr. ended 12/31/88): Assets, $2,001,144 (M); expenditures, $148,735, including $146,850 for 14 grants (high: $100,500; low: $250).
Purpose and activities: Giving primarily for wildlife preservation and animal welfare; support also for nutrition, youth, child welfare, and a community fund.
Limitations: Giving primarily in AL. No grants to individuals.
Application information: Contributes only to pre-selected organizations. Applications not accepted.
Officers: George W. Barber, Chair. and Pres.; Albert E. Geiss, Secy.; B. Austin Cunningham, Treas.
Employer Identification Number: 630941684

5
A. H. Bean Foundation ⌑
c/o First Alabama Bank Trust Dept.
2222 Ninth St.
Tuscaloosa 35401

Established in 1985 in AL.
Donor(s): A.H. Bean.
Foundation type: Independent
Financial data (yr. ended 12/31/88): Assets, $1,479,114 (M); expenditures, $133,656, including $124,186 for 450 grants to individuals (high: $300; low: $146).
Purpose and activities: Awards student aid to Christian individuals who are active members of a church, enrolled in a post-secondary educational institution, and recommended for aid by the church minister.
Types of support: Student aid.
Limitations: Giving primarily in AL.
Application information:
Deadline(s): None
Directors: Billie S. Brown, John R. Hinton, Connie B. Oswalt.
Employer Identification Number: 636134142

6
J. L. Bedsole Foundation ⌑
c/o AmSouth Bank, NA
P.O. Box 1628
Mobile 36621
Application address: P.O. Box 1137, Mobile, AL 36633

Established in 1972.
Foundation type: Independent

Financial data (yr. ended 12/31/88): Assets, $32,348,325 (M); gifts received, $1,532,977; expenditures, $1,708,999, including $1,124,821 for 45 grants (high: $200,000; low: $450).
Purpose and activities: Giving for higher education and social services.
Types of support: Scholarship funds, building funds, special projects.
Limitations: Giving primarily in southwest AL.
Application information: Application form required.
Initial approach: Letter
Deadline(s): None
Write: Mrs. Mabel B. Ward
Officer and Distribution Committee:* T. Massey Bedsole,* Chair.; James A. Bedsole, Jr., M. Palmer Bedsole, Jr.
Trustees: S. Boyd Adams, AmSouth Bank, N.A.
Employer Identification Number: 237225708

7
The Greater Birmingham Foundation
P.O. Box 131027
Birmingham 35213 (205) 933-0753

Established in 1959 in AL by resolution and declaration of trust.
Foundation type: Community
Financial data (yr. ended 12/31/88): Assets, $18,202,738 (M); gifts received, $602,467; qualifying distributions, $1,505,875, including $1,505,875 for grants.
Purpose and activities: To promote the health, welfare, cultural, educational, and social needs of the Birmingham area only.
Limitations: Giving limited to the Birmingham, AL, area. No support for religiously oriented agencies. No grants to individuals, or for endowment funds or operating budgets.
Publications: Annual report.
Application information:
Initial approach: Letter
Board meeting date(s): Quarterly
Write: Mrs. William C. McDonald, Jr., Exec. Dir.
Officer: Mrs. William C. McDonald, Jr., Exec. Dir.
Distribution Committee: William M. Spencer III, Chair.; Houston Blount, Donald Brabston, Frank Dominick, A. Gerow Hodges, Crawford Johnson III, Rosalind Markstein, Richard Russell, James Simpson.
Trustees: AmSouth Bank, N.A., Central Bank of the South, Colonial Bank, First Alabama Bank of Birmingham, SouthTrust Bank of Alabama.
Employer Identification Number: 636019864

8
Mildred Weedon Blount Educational & Charitable Foundation, Inc. ⌑
304 Barnett Blvd.
P.O. Box 26
Tallassee 36078

Established in 1981 in AL.
Donor(s): Mildred W. Blount.†
Foundation type: Independent
Financial data (yr. ended 6/30/87): Assets, $2,077,337 (M); gifts received, $198,946; expenditures, $30,278, including $30,078 for 1 grant.
Purpose and activities: Support for a Catholic church, a hospital, a public library and a scholarship fund for secondary school students.
Officers and Trustees:* Arnold B. Dopson,* Chair.; Daniel P. Wilbanks,* Vice-Chair.; Jerry B. Denton, Carl W. Fuller, O.C. Harden, Jr., Teddy O. Taylor.
Employer Identification Number: 630817472

9
The Blount Foundation, Inc. ⌑
c/o Blount, Inc.
4520 Exec. Park Dr.
Montgomery 36116 (205) 244-4000

Incorporated in 1970 in AL.
Donor(s): Blount, Inc.
Foundation type: Company-sponsored
Financial data (yr. ended 2/29/88): Assets, $112,646 (M); gifts received, $505,000; expenditures, $668,821, including $576,565 for 164 grants (high: $100,000; low: $25) and $90,870 for 486 employee matching gifts.
Purpose and activities: Giving for culture and the arts, higher and secondary education, including an employee matching gift program, civic affairs, and health care.
Types of support: General purposes, building funds, equipment, endowment funds, scholarship funds, matching funds, research, publications, employee matching gifts.
Limitations: No support for certain religious or sectarian groups, governmental or quasi-governmental agencies. No grants to individuals, or for demonstration projects, conferences, seminars, or courtesy advertising; no loans; no in-kind grants.
Publications: Informational brochure (including application guidelines).
Application information: Application form not required.
Initial approach: 2- or 3-page letter
Copies of proposal: 1
Deadline(s): None
Board meeting date(s): As needed
Final notification: 12 weeks after board meets
Write: D. Joseph McInnes, Pres.
Officers: D. Joseph McInnes,* Pres.; W. Houston Blount,* V.P.; Louis A. Griffin, Secy.
Directors:* Winton M. Blount.
Number of staff: 1 full-time professional; 1 full-time support.
Employer Identification Number: 636050260

10
Herman & Emmie Bolden Foundation ⌑
P.O. Box 360028
Birmingham 35236 (205) 252-5356

Established in 1982 in AL.
Donor(s): Herman D. Bolden, Southern Coach Manufacturing Co., Inc.
Foundation type: Independent
Financial data (yr. ended 6/30/87): Assets, $1,207,087 (M); expenditures, $258,332, including $257,110 for 27 grants (high: $155,000; low: $100).
Purpose and activities: Grants primarily for health, hospitals, and denominational giving.
Application information:
Deadline(s): None
Write: Rachel Ziegler, Secy.
Officers: Emmie C. Bolden, Pres.; Herman D. Bolden, V.P.; Rachel M. Ziegler, Secy.
Employer Identification Number: 630828670

11
The Joseph S. Bruno Charitable Foundation ⌑ ☆
P.O. Box 7341-A
Birmingham 35259

Established in 1985.
Foundation type: Independent
Financial data (yr. ended 11/30/88): Assets, $5,612,863 (M); expenditures, $289,737, including $285,000 for 3 grants (high: $250,000; low: $10,000).
Purpose and activities: Giving primarily for cancer research.
Limitations: Giving primarily in AL. No grants to individuals.
Application information: Contributes only to pre-selected organizations. Applications not accepted.
Officers: Joseph S. Bruno, Pres.; Robert A. Sprain, Jr., V.P. and Secy.; Benny M. La Russe, Jr., V.P. and Treas.
Employer Identification Number: 630936234

12
The Angelo J. Bruno Foundation ⌑
4248 Abingdon Trail
Birmingham 35243

Established in 1980 in AL.
Donor(s): Angelo J. Bruno.
Foundation type: Independent
Financial data (yr. ended 11/30/89): Assets, $5,028,609 (M); gifts received, $238,388; expenditures, $189,533, including $178,568 for 22 grants (high: $147,550; low: $30).
Purpose and activities: Support primarily for a university and Catholic giving; support also for indigent individuals.
Types of support: General purposes, grants to individuals.
Limitations: Giving primarily in the Birmingham, AL, area.
Application information: Contributes only to pre-selected organizations. Applications not accepted.
Officers: Angelo J. Bruno, Pres.; Mary Bruno, V.P.; Ann Bruno, Secy.-Treas.
Employer Identification Number: 630819540

13
Central Bank Foundation
701 South 20th St.
Birmingham 35233

Established in l981 in AL.
Donor(s): Central Bank of the South.
Foundation type: Company-sponsored
Financial data (yr. ended 12/31/89): Assets, $57,409 (M); gifts received, $330,893; expenditures, $317,884, including $316,366 for 270 grants (high: $25,000; low: $25).
Purpose and activities: Giving primarily for community funds, business and business education, health, social service and youth agencies, education, civic affairs, and arts and cultural programs.

Types of support: General purposes, annual campaigns, building funds, employee-related scholarships.
Limitations: Giving generally limited to AL-based organizations or those with significant AL connections. No support for religious organizations. No grants to individuals.
Application information:
Copies of proposal: 1
Deadline(s): None
Officers: Terence C. Brannon, Pres.; Jerry W. Powell, Secy.; Michael A. Bean, Treas.
Trustee: Harry B. Brock, Jr., Chair.
Employer Identification Number: 630823545

14
The Chandler Foundation ⌑
304 Government St.
Mobile 36602

Established in 1963 in AL.
Donor(s): Ralph B. Chandler.†
Foundation type: Independent
Financial data (yr. ended 12/31/88): Assets, $7,543,444 (M); expenditures, $380,483, including $303,094 for 7 grants (high: $159,470; low: $1,000).
Purpose and activities: Giving for higher education, a hospital, religious welfare, a community foundation, and a museum.
Types of support: Building funds, capital campaigns.
Limitations: Giving limited to Mobile County, AL.
Application information:
Write: William J. Hearin, Trustee
Trustee: William J. Hearin.
Employer Identification Number: 636075470

15
Child Health Foundation
P.O. Box 530964
Birmingham 35253 (205) 251-9966

Established in 1985 in AL.
Foundation type: Operating
Financial data (yr. ended 12/31/88): Assets, $1,012,686 (M); gifts received, $10,872; expenditures, $137,591, including $66,654 for 1 grant (high: $31,250; low: $5,013) and $50,249 for 4 grants to individuals.
Purpose and activities: A private operating foundation; the foundation's goal is "to reduce illness and disease in the children of the world by transfer of medical information and skills across international boundaries."
Types of support: Fellowships, grants to individuals, research.
Publications: Annual report, application guidelines.
Application information: Application form required.
Initial approach: Letter
Copies of proposal: 3
Deadline(s): Aug. 31
Board meeting date(s): Annually
Final notification: 6 months
Write: Dr. Sergio Stagno
Officer: Dr. Sergio Stagno, Exec. Dir.
Directors: John Trafford, Chair.; Joseph D. Johnson, Carlos Jorquiera, Peter Ryan, Rosa Serrano.
Advisory Board: Donny Harwell, Betty Loeb, Ed Robbins, Alvaro Ronderos, Nancy Wagnon.
Number of staff: 1 part-time professional.
Employer Identification Number: 621248169

16
The Christian Workers Foundation
3038 Bankhead Ave.
Montgomery 36106

Trust established about 1939 in IL.
Donor(s): Herbert J. Taylor,† Stanley S. Kresge,† Thesaurus Foundation.
Foundation type: Independent
Financial data (yr. ended 06/30/89): Assets, $3,031,381 (M); expenditures, $207,612, including $191,408 for 27 grants (high: $85,500; low: $1,000; average: $500-$2,000).
Purpose and activities: To support Christian organizations that are in evangelistic or mission fields of youth work and have close ties to present or former trustees.
Types of support: Program-related investments.
Limitations: No grants to individuals.
Application information: Applications by invitation only. Applications not accepted.
Write: G.R. Lockhart, Trustee
Trustees: Robert Lockhart, Mrs. Robert Lockhart, Allen W. Mathis, Jr., Beverly T. Mathis, Mrs. Herbert J. Taylor.
Number of staff: None.
Employer Identification Number: 362181979

17
The Comer Foundation ⌑
P.O. Box 302
Sylacauga 35150 (205) 249-2962

Incorporated in 1945 in AL.
Donor(s): Avondale Mills, Comer-Avondale Mills, Inc., Cowikee Mills.
Foundation type: Independent
Financial data (yr. ended 12/31/88): Assets, $8,549,171 (M); expenditures, $582,114, including $469,800 for 52 grants (high: $50,000; low: $250).
Purpose and activities: Emphasis on higher education, health, recreation, community funds, and cultural programs.
Limitations: Giving primarily in AL.
Application information:
Initial approach: Letter
Deadline(s): None
Write: R. Larry Edmunds, Secy.-Treas.
Officers: Richard J. Comer,* Chair.; R. Larry Edmunds, Secy.-Treas.
Trustees:* Jane S. Crockard, Herbert C. Ryding, Jr., Jane B. Selfe, William Bew White, Jr.
Number of staff: 1 full-time professional.
Employer Identification Number: 636004424

18
The Daniel Foundation of Alabama ▼ ⌑
200 Office Park Dr., Suite 100
Birmingham 35223 (205) 879-0902

Established in 1978 in AL as partial successor to the Daniel Foundation.
Donor(s): Charles W. Daniel,† R. Hugh Daniel.†
Foundation type: Independent
Financial data (yr. ended 12/31/87): Assets, $19,120,099 (M); expenditures, $1,458,248, including $1,326,840 for 26 grants (high: $270,340; low: $500; average: $5,000-$50,000).
Purpose and activities: Emphasis on health and higher education; support also for cultural programs, social service and youth agencies, and civic affairs.
Limitations: Giving primarily in the southeastern states, especially AL.
Application information: Application form not required.
Initial approach: Letter
Deadline(s): None
Board meeting date(s): Apr. and Oct.
Final notification: Varies
Write: S. Garry Smith, Secy.-Treas.
Officers: M.C. Daniel, Chair.; Harry B. Brock, Jr., Pres.; Charles W. Daniel, V.P.; S. Garry Smith, Secy.-Treas.
Number of staff: 1 part-time professional.
Employer Identification Number: 630736444

19
The Dixon Foundation ☆
1625 Financial Center
Birmingham 35203 (205) 252-2828

Established in 1986.
Foundation type: Operating
Financial data (yr. ended 10/31/89): Assets, $4,062,762 (M); gifts received, $804,030; expenditures, $299,091, including $8,879 for 2 grants (average: $2,000-$3,505) and $215,152 for 62 grants to individuals (average: $200-$25,000).
Purpose and activities: Primarily awards grants to ministers of the United Methodist Church for continuing study and programs; also awards three-year fellowships in pediatrics research and provides support for prescription medicines and health supplies through local welfare department.
Types of support: Grants to individuals, fellowships.
Limitations: Giving primarily in AL.
Application information: Application form required.
Deadline(s): None
Write: Carol D. Dixon, Secy., or Joy Levio
Officers and Directors:* Margaret Y. Dixon,* Pres. and Treas.; David E. Dixon,* V.P.; Edwin M. Dixon,* V.P.; Alice D. Grotnes,* V.P.; Carol D. Dixon, Secy.
Number of staff: None.
Employer Identification Number: 630944809

20
Gunter Dixon Foundation, Inc.
P.O. Drawer 990
Andalusia 36420 (205) 222-3138

Established in 1982 in AL.
Donor(s): Ellie G. Dixon.
Foundation type: Independent
Financial data (yr. ended 04/30/89): Assets, $1,460,822 (M); expenditures, $58,113, including $51,500 for 12 grants (high: $30,000; low: $100).
Purpose and activities: Giving primarily for higher and medical education, medical

research and mental health, and the environment.
Types of support: Building funds, equipment, research, special projects.
Limitations: Giving primarily in AL, with emphasis on Andalusia.
Application information: Contributes only to pre-selected organizations. Applications not accepted.
Write: Gordon S. Jones, Treas.
Officers: Martha B. Dixon, Pres.; T.A. Broughton, Jr., V.P.; Thomas G. Mancuso, Secy.; Gordon S. Jones, Treas.
Number of staff: 1 part-time professional.
Employer Identification Number: 630813623

21
The Solon & Martha Dixon Foundation
P.O. Drawer 990
Andalusia 36420 (205) 222-3138

Established in 1981 in AL.
Donor(s): Solon Dixon.
Foundation type: Independent
Financial data (yr. ended 06/30/88): Assets, $1,387,540 (M); expenditures, $95,342, including $50,100 for 4 grants (high: $25,000; low: $100).
Purpose and activities: Giving for education building funds and a religious educational institution, libraries, computer sciences, community development, crime and law enforcement programs, wildlife protection, and health services, including mental health and medical research.
Types of support: Building funds, special projects, equipment, research.
Limitations: Giving primarily in AL, with emphasis on the city of Andalusia and Covington County.
Application information: Contributes only to pre-selected organizations. Applications not accepted.
Write: Gordon S. Jones, Treas.
Officers: Martha B. Dixon, Pres.; Thomas G. Mancuso, V.P. and Secy.; Gordon S. Jones, Treas.
Number of staff: 1 part-time professional.
Employer Identification Number: 630812726

22
S. E. & Margaret W. Dove Christian Foundation ⌑ ☆
1431 Kinsey Rd.
Dothan 36302

Established in 1982.
Donor(s): S. Earl Dove.
Foundation type: Independent
Financial data (yr. ended 12/31/88): Assets, $370,319 (M); expenditures, $201,453, including $200,501 for 7 grants (high: $150,000; low: $150).
Purpose and activities: Giving primarily to a Baptist church and other religious organizations.
Types of support: General purposes.
Officers: S. Earl Dove, Pres.; Margaret W. Dove, V.P.; Charles E. Coggins, Secy.-Treas.
Employer Identification Number: 630836252

23
David R. Dunlap, Jr. Memorial Trust ⌑ ☆
c/o First Alabama Bank
P.O. Box 2527
Mobile 36601 (205) 690-1419

Foundation type: Independent
Financial data (yr. ended 12/31/88): Assets, $1,177,784 (M); expenditures, $114,049, including $97,698 for 51 grants to individuals (high: $5,250; low: $500).
Purpose and activities: Awards scholarships and student loans for higher education to local residents, employees of trustee bank, and AL Dry Docks & Shipbuilding Co.
Types of support: Employee-related scholarships, student aid, student loans.
Limitations: Giving limited to Mobile County, AL residents.
Application information: Application form required.
Initial approach: Letter
Deadline(s): July
Trustee: First Alabama Bank.
Employer Identification Number: 636020944

24
Durr-Fillauer Medical Foundation ⌑
P.O. Box 951
Montgomery 36192

Established in 1982 in AL.
Donor(s): Durr-Fillauer Medical, Inc.
Foundation type: Company-sponsored
Financial data (yr. ended 12/31/88): Assets, $11,691 (M); gifts received, $110,000; expenditures, $116,160, including $115,368 for 58 grants (high: $15,000; low: $100) and $100 for 1 employee matching gift.
Purpose and activities: Support primarily for higher education, culture, and community funds.
Types of support: Scholarship funds, fellowships, building funds.
Application information:
Deadline(s): None
Trustees: John W. Durr, Charles T. Gross, Richard L. Klein.
Employer Identification Number: 630847294

25
William P. Engel Foundation ⌑
P.O. Box 187
Birmingham 35201 (205) 323-8081

Established in 1972 in AL.
Foundation type: Independent
Financial data (yr. ended 12/31/88): Assets, $1,198,247 (M); expenditures, $88,885, including $70,523 for 27 grants (high: $32,000; low: $100).
Purpose and activities: Emphasis on Jewish welfare funds; support also for cultural programs, health, and education.
Limitations: Giving primarily in AL.
Application information: Application form not required.
Deadline(s): None
Write: Marvin R. Engel, Trustee
Trustees: Marvin R. Engel, Ruth S. Engel, Robert D. Reich, Jr.
Employer Identification Number: 237182007

26
Fig Tree Foundation ⌑ ☆
144 Mountain Brook Park Dr.
Birmingham 35223

Established in 1986 in AL.
Donor(s): Jo Ann Myers.
Foundation type: Independent
Financial data (yr. ended 11/30/88): Assets, $4,283,038 (M); gifts received, $12,510; expenditures, $232,112, including $221,944 for 52 grants (high: $80,000; low: $18).
Purpose and activities: Support primarily for Jewish organizations, including welfare funds.
Limitations: Giving primarily in Birmingham, AL.
Application information:
Initial approach: Letter
Deadline(s): None
Write: Jo Ann Myers, Pres.
Officers: Jo Ann Myers, Pres.; Alan Engel, V.P.; Donald Hess, Secy.-Treas.
Employer Identification Number: 630932247

27
J. Hunter Flack Foundation, Inc. ⌑ ☆
P.O. Box 4479
Montgomery 36103

Established in 1979.
Donor(s): J. Hunter Flack.
Foundation type: Independent
Financial data (yr. ended 1/31/89): Assets, $68,806 (M); gifts received, $43,900; expenditures, $581,883, including $580,532 for 8 grants (high: $572,732; low: $100).
Purpose and activities: Giving for Protestant churches and religious or educational organizations.
Limitations: Giving primarily in AL. No grants to individuals.
Application information: Contributes only to pre-selected organizations. Applications not accepted.
Officer: J. Hunter Flack, Pres.
Directors: Eleanor Flack, Alexander Green.
Employer Identification Number: 636009500

28
The Florence Foundation ☆
P.O. Box 2727
Mobile 36652
Application address: P.O. Box 1403, Mobile, AL 36633; Tel.: (205) 432-0980

Established in 1984 in AL.
Foundation type: Independent
Financial data (yr. ended 12/31/88): Assets, $2,299,633 (M); expenditures, $162,613, including $139,395 for 8 grants (high: $50,000; low: $1,000).
Purpose and activities: Giving primarily for health associations and higher education.
Limitations: Giving primarily in AL. No grants to individuals.
Application information: Application form not required.
Deadline(s): None
Write: Dwain G. Luce, Trustee
Trustees: William C. Bodie, M.D., Dwain G. Luce, G. Sage Lyons.
Number of staff: None.
Employer Identification Number: 630843906

29
E. L. Gibson Foundation
201 South Edwards
Enterprise 36330 (205) 347-0555

Established in 1944.
Foundation type: Independent
Financial data (yr. ended 12/31/88): Assets, $1,938,844 (M); expenditures, $124,392, including $94,327 for grants.
Purpose and activities: Giving for medical and nursing education and scholarships; support also for health agencies and civic affairs.
Types of support: Student aid, conferences and seminars, equipment, lectureships, special projects.
Limitations: Giving limited to Coffee County, AL, and contiguous counties.
Application information: Application form not required.
Initial approach: Letter
Copies of proposal: 1
Deadline(s): None
Board meeting date(s): Quarterly
Write: J.B. Brunson, Mgr.
Officers and Trustees:* J.E. Pittman,* Chair.; Herbert Gibson,* Vice-Chair.; J.B. Brunson,* Mgr.; Frank Bynum, James S. DuBois, Robert Foy, Joe Herod, William Mitchell, Raymond Pappas, Horace Sanders, Roger Williams.
Directors: Whit Armstrong, Ben Henderson, Joe Pittman, Moultrie Sessions.
Number of staff: 1 part-time support.
Employer Identification Number: 630383929

30
Anna & Seymour Gitenstein Foundation ⌑
3815 Interstate Ct.
Montgomery 36109

Established in 1963 in AL.
Donor(s): Seymour Gitenstein.
Foundation type: Independent
Financial data (yr. ended 3/31/88): Assets, $1,220,036 (M); gifts received, $1,847; expenditures, $75,587, including $49,458 for 33 grants (high: $10,000; low: $10).
Purpose and activities: Giving primarily in the area of medical research, especially for Alzheimer's disease; support also for education, including higher education.
Types of support: Research.
Limitations: Giving primarily in the eastern U.S.
Application information: Contributes only to pre-selected organizations. Applications not accepted.
Trustee: Seymour Gitenstein, Chair. and Mgr.
Employer Identification Number: 636045533

31
Estes H. & Florence Parker Hargis Charitable Foundation ⌑
317 20th St. North
P.O. Box 370404
Birmingham 35237 (205) 251-2881

Established in 1966 in AL as Estes Hargis Charitable Foundation, merged with Florence Parker Hargis Charitable Foundation in 1980.
Donor(s): Estes H. Hargis,† Florence Parker Hargis.†
Foundation type: Independent
Financial data (yr. ended 6/30/88): Assets, $2,674,204 (M); expenditures, $414,302, including $395,374 for 7 grants (high: $376,074; low: $300).
Purpose and activities: Giving for health and youth services, Protestant organizations, and for the maintenance of a museum and garden area.
Types of support: Endowment funds.
Limitations: Giving primarily in AL and TN.
Application information: Application form not required.
Copies of proposal: 1
Deadline(s): May 1
Board meeting date(s): Jan., May, Aug., and Nov.
Final notification: June 30
Write: Gerald D. Colvin, Jr., Chair.
Trustees: Gerald D. Colvin, Jr., Chair.; Melvin Bailey, George Crawford, Rosemary Morse, Florence Wade.
Number of staff: None.
Employer Identification Number: 636062967

32
Robert H. Heath Foundation ⌑ ☆
P.O. Box 4452
Huntsville 35815

Established in 1985.
Donor(s): Robert H. Heath.
Foundation type: Independent
Financial data (yr. ended 11/30/88): Assets, $289 (M); gifts received, $101,500; expenditures, $101,262, including $101,000 for 2 grants (high: $100,000; low: $1,000).
Purpose and activities: Support primarily for a local foundation.
Limitations: Giving primarily in Huntsville, AL.
Officers: Robert H. Heath, Pres.; Joe H. Ritch, V.P.; Gerry E. Shannon, Secy.-Treas.
Employer Identification Number: 630911587

33
Ronne & Donald Hess Charitable Foundation ⌑ ☆
2936 Southwood Rd.
Birmingham 35223

Established in 1985 in AL.
Donor(s): Ronne Hess, Donald Hess.
Foundation type: Independent
Financial data (yr. ended 11/30/89): Assets, $3,968,628 (M); expenditures, $523,415, including $418,780 for 39 grants (high: $258,500; low: $200).
Purpose and activities: Giving primarily for Jewish organizations, social services, and performing arts groups.
Limitations: Giving primarily in AL.
Application information:
Initial approach: Letter
Deadline(s): None
Write: Ronne Hess, Pres.
Officers and Directors:* Ronne Hess,* Pres.; Donald Hess, V.P. and Secy.-Treas.; Alan Z. Engel,* V.P.
Employer Identification Number: 630916545

34
Hess Foundation, Inc. ⌑ ☆
200 Research Pkwy.
Birmingham 35211

Foundation type: Independent
Financial data (yr. ended 12/31/88): Assets, $655,877 (M); expenditures, $320,382, including $318,218 for 22 grants (high: $77,000; low: $250).
Purpose and activities: Support for higher education, Jewish organizations, and general charitable activities.
Application information:
Deadline(s): None
Write: Shirley Hess, Secy.
Officers and Directors:* Emil Hess,* Pres.; Donald Hess,* V.P.; Shirley Hess,* Secy.; Joanne Meyers.
Employer Identification Number: 636056717

35
Hill Crest Foundation, Inc. ☆
310 North 19th St.
Bessemer 35020 (205) 425-5800

Established in 1988 in AL.
Foundation type: Independent
Financial data (yr. ended 06/30/89): Assets, $21,670,168 (M); expenditures, $838,154, including $609,223 for 25 grants (high: $100,000; low: $5,000).
Purpose and activities: Giving primarily for higher education, especially the psychiatry department of a university, and health, including mental health services, pharmacology, and hospitals; support also for arts and culture, a community fund, community development, and a youth organization.
Types of support: Endowment funds, capital campaigns, special projects, research, scholarship funds, publications, equipment, building funds, professorships.
Limitations: Giving limited to AL. No grants to individuals.
Publications: 990-PF.
Application information: Application form not required.
Initial approach: Letter
Copies of proposal: 8
Deadline(s): None
Board meeting date(s): Quarterly
Write: Jack G. Paden, Chair.
Officers and Trustees:* Jack G. Paden,* Chair.; Charles R. Terry, Sr.,* Vice-Chair.; F. Brooks Yielding III,* Secy.; J.D. Rosenberger, Jr.,* Treas.; Hugh W. Agricola, Peter G. Cowin, Stanley E. Graham, Willard L. Hurley.
Number of staff: 2 full-time professional.
Employer Identification Number: 630516927

36
Caroline P. and Charles W. Ireland Foundation
(Formerly C Foundation)
c/o AmSouth Bank, N.A.
P.O. Box 11426
Birmingham 35202 (205) 326-5396

Established in 1977 in AL.
Foundation type: Independent
Financial data (yr. ended 12/31/89): Assets, $1,545,815 (M); expenditures, $44,493,

including $28,500 for 6 grants (high: $10,000; low: $1,000).
Purpose and activities: Giving primarily for higher and other education and the arts and cultural programs.
Types of support: Annual campaigns, building funds, capital campaigns, equipment.
Limitations: No grants to individuals.
Application information:
Initial approach: Letter
Deadline(s): None
Write: Kathryn W. Miree, Trust Officer, AmSouth Bank, N.A.
Officer and Directors:* Mrs. Charles Ireland,* Pres.; John Arthur Jones, Cynthia Wilson.
Agent: AmSouth Bank, N.A.
Employer Identification Number: 636106086

37
The Thomas E. Jernigan Foundation ⌑ ☆
Independence Plaza, Suite 908, No. 1
Homewood 35209-2624

Established in 1986 in AL.
Donor(s): Marathon Corp., Thomas E. Jernigan.
Foundation type: Independent
Financial data (yr. ended 3/31/89): Assets, $1,337,569 (M); gifts received, $750,000; expenditures, $96,457, including $94,784 for 21 grants (high: $5,000; low: $50).
Purpose and activities: Giving primarily for higher and other education; support also for a civic center, health associations, a community fund, and social services, especially child welfare and youth programs.
Types of support: Scholarship funds.
Limitations: Giving primarily in AL. No grants to individuals.
Application information: Contributes only to pre-selected organizations. Applications not accepted.
Officers: Thomas E. Jernigan, Pres.; Audrey Wadleigh, Secy.-Treas.
Employer Identification Number: 630935852

38
Martha Annie Jordan Charitable Trust ⌑ ☆
P.O. Box 1389
Chatom 36518 (205) 847-2237

Established in 1986 in AL.
Foundation type: Independent
Financial data (yr. ended 7/31/88): Assets, $1,966,511 (M); expenditures, $72,807, including $8,845 for 7 grants (high: $4,095; low: $500) and $25,597 for 39 grants to individuals (high: $1,800; low: $200; average: $500-$1,500).
Purpose and activities: Awards scholarships to individuals for higher education; minor support also for elementary and secondary education and human services.
Types of support: Student aid.
Limitations: Giving primarily in Washington, Mobile, Clarke, and Choctaw counties, AL.
Application information: Preference for scholarships given to students attending Oral Roberts University in OK or any college or university in AL. Application form required.
Deadline(s): May 1 for scholarships
Write: Michael Onderdonk, Trustee
Trustee: Andrew Michael Onderdonk.
Advisory Committee: James T. Baxter, Jr., Tillman Parker, Edith Wilcox.
Employer Identification Number: 636141960

39
Linn-Henley Charitable Trust ⌑
c/o Central Bank of the South, Trust Dept.
P.O. Box 10566
Birmingham 35296 (205) 558-6717

Trust established in 1965 in AL.
Donor(s): Walter E. Henley.†
Foundation type: Independent
Financial data (yr. ended 3/31/88): Assets, $5,680,095 (M); expenditures, $324,110, including $249,350 for 28 grants (high: $50,000; low: $250).
Purpose and activities: Emphasis on cultural programs and higher education.
Limitations: Giving limited to Jefferson County, AL.
Application information:
Initial approach: Letter
Deadline(s): None
Write: Mitzie Hall
Trustees: John C. Henley III, Central Bank of the South.
Employer Identification Number: 636051833

40
The Ben May Charitable Trust ⌑
P.O. Drawer 1467
Mobile 36621
Application address: P.O. Box 123, Mobile, AL 36601

Established in 1971 in AL.
Foundation type: Independent
Financial data (yr. ended 12/31/87): Assets, $6,495,448 (M); expenditures, $585,877, including $482,664 for 5 grants (high: $371,789; low: $1,000).
Purpose and activities: Support for higher education.
Limitations: Giving primarily in AL.
Application information:
Deadline(s): None
Write: Vivian G. Johnston, Jr.
Trustee: AmSouth Bank, N.A.
Employer Identification Number: 237145009

41
D. W. McMillan Foundation
329 Belleville Ave.
Brewton 36426 (205) 867-4881
Application address: P.O. Box 867, Brewton, AL 36427

Trust established in 1956 in AL.
Donor(s): D.W. McMillan Trust.
Foundation type: Independent
Financial data (yr. ended 12/31/88): Assets, $9,221,134 (M); expenditures, $489,228, including $392,000 for 21 grants (high: $60,000; low: $1,500).
Purpose and activities: Aid to poor and needy people, including welfare and medical aid, through grants to local health and welfare organizations; limited to programs giving direct aid.
Types of support: Emergency funds.
Limitations: Giving limited to Escambia County, AL, and Escambia County, FL. No support for education or medical research.
Application information: Applications accepted only from Escambia County, AL, and Escambia County, FL. Application form not required.
Initial approach: Letter
Copies of proposal: 1
Deadline(s): Dec. 1
Board meeting date(s): Dec. 1
Final notification: Dec. 31
Write: Ed Leigh McMillan, II, Managing Trustee
Trustees: Ed Leigh McMillan II, Managing Trustee; John David Finlay, Jr., M.N. Hoke, Jr., Allison R. Sinrod.
Number of staff: 1 part-time support.
Employer Identification Number: 636044830

42
McWane Foundation
P.O. Box 43327
Birmingham 35243 (205) 991-9888

Established in 1961.
Foundation type: Company-sponsored
Financial data (yr. ended 12/31/88): Assets, $1,762,342 (M); expenditures, $374,266, including $373,400 for 14 grants (high: $100,000; low: $1,000).
Purpose and activities: Emphasis on higher and secondary education and social services.
Limitations: Giving primarily in AL.
Application information: Application form not required.
Initial approach: Letter
Copies of proposal: 1
Deadline(s): None
Write: J.R. McWane, Trustee
Trustees: John McMahon, J.R. McWane.
Employer Identification Number: 636044384

43
George C. Meyer Foundation, Inc. ⌑
P.O. Box 238
Gulf Shores 36542 (205) 968-7128

Established in 1962 in AL.
Donor(s): George C. Meyer.†
Foundation type: Independent
Financial data (yr. ended 10/31/88): Assets, $2,921,864 (M); expenditures, $84,579, including $63,400 for 1 grant.
Purpose and activities: Giving primarily for a town; support also for education.
Limitations: Giving primarily in Gulf Shores, AL, and the Baldwin County area. No grants to individuals.
Application information:
Initial approach: Letter
Deadline(s): None
Write: Joseph Wade Ward, Pres.
Officers: Joseph Wade Ward, Pres.; Myrtle H. Ward, Secy.
Employer Identification Number: 630508176

44
Robert R. Meyer Foundation
c/o AmSouth Bank, N.A., Trust Dept.
P.O. Box 11426
Birmingham 35202 (205) 326-5396

Trust established in 1942 in AL.
Donor(s): Robert R. Meyer,† John E. Meyer.†
Foundation type: Independent
Financial data (yr. ended 12/31/89): Assets, $21,125,396 (M); expenditures, $1,260,206, including $1,139,000 for 36 grants (high: $200,000; low: $3,000).
Purpose and activities: Aid largely to local health and welfare organizations, educational institutions, and cultural organizations selected by an advisory committee.
Types of support: Building funds, equipment, land acquisition, research, scholarship funds.
Limitations: Giving limited to the Birmingham, AL, metropolitan area. No grants to individuals, or for endowment funds or operating budgets.
Publications: Application guidelines.
Application information: Application form not required.
Initial approach: Proposal
Copies of proposal: 7
Deadline(s): Apr. 15 and Oct. 15
Board meeting date(s): June and Dec.
Final notification: 4 weeks
Write: Kathryn W. Miree, V.P. and Trust Officer, AmSouth Bank, N.A.
Grants Committee: Seybourn H. Lynne, William J. Rushton III, William M. Spencer III, Louis J. Willie.
Trustee: AmSouth Bank, N.A.
Number of staff: None.
Employer Identification Number: 636019645

45
Kate Kinloch Middleton Fund ⌑
P.O. Drawer 2527
Mobile 36601

Established in 1957 in AL.
Foundation type: Independent
Financial data (yr. ended 1/31/89): Assets, $1,903,750 (M); gifts received, $8,229; expenditures, $153,621, including $108,286 for 63 grants to individuals (high: $8,094; low: $81) and $4,508 for 1 loan to an individual.
Purpose and activities: Grants to individuals for medical expenses limited to local residents.
Types of support: Grants to individuals.
Limitations: Giving limited to Mobile County, AL.
Application information:
Initial approach: Interview, making disclosure of medical problem and the related financial burden
Deadline(s): None
Write: Joan Sapp
Trustee: First Alabama Bank.
Employer Identification Number: 636018539

46
The Mitchell Foundation, Inc. ⌑
2405 First National Bank Bldg.
P.O. Box 1126
Mobile 36601 (205) 432-1711

Incorporated in 1957 in AL.
Donor(s): A.S. Mitchell,† Mrs. A.S. Mitchell.
Foundation type: Independent
Financial data (yr. ended 1/31/88): Assets, $10,760,792 (M); expenditures, $692,758, including $595,400 for 36 grants (high: $134,200; low: $1,000).
Purpose and activities: Emphasis on secondary and higher education; support also for social service programs, including religious welfare agencies, aid to the handicapped, and youth agencies; hospitals and health associations; and Protestant church support.
Limitations: Giving primarily in AL. No grants to individuals.
Application information:
Initial approach: Letter
Deadline(s): None
Board meeting date(s): Quarterly
Write: M.L. Screven, Jr., Secy.-Treas.
Officers and Directors:* Augustine Meaher, Jr.,* Pres.; Frank B. Vinson, Jr.,* V.P.; M.L. Screven, Jr.,* Secy.-Treas.; William Brevard Hand, Augustine Meaher III.
Employer Identification Number: 630368954

47
Joseph & Rebecca Mitchell Foundation ⌑
P.O. Box 16006
Mobile 36616 (205) 344-3800

Established in 1962 in AL.
Donor(s): The Mitchell Co., Gulf Coast Building & Supply.
Foundation type: Independent
Financial data (yr. ended 06/30/89): Assets, $1,314,445 (M); expenditures, $116,681, including $2,635 for 7 grants (high: $2,000; low: $10).
Purpose and activities: Giving primarily for Jewish welfare funds; support also for medical research, education, and public policy groups.
Types of support: Research.
Limitations: Giving primarily in AL, with emphasis on Mobile. No grants to individuals.
Application information: Contributes only to pre-selected organizations. Applications not accepted.
Write: Mayer Mitchell, Pres.
Officers: Mayer Mitchell, Pres.; Abraham A. Mitchell, V.P.; William A. Lubel, Secy.-Treas.
Employer Identification Number: 636045908

48
The Mobile Community Foundation
100 St. Joseph St., Suite 416
Mobile 36602 (205) 438-5591

Incorporated in 1976 in AL.
Foundation type: Community
Financial data (yr. ended 9/30/89): Assets, $10,167,583 (M); gifts received, $972,063; expenditures, $1,373,548, including $1,371,556 for 139 grants (high: $350,000; low: $100; average: $1,000-$5,000).
Purpose and activities: Giving in the fields of health and human services, education, civic affairs, and culture and the arts.
Types of support: Capital campaigns, endowment funds, general purposes, operating budgets, scholarship funds, special projects.
Limitations: Giving primarily in the Mobile, AL, metropolitan area. No grants to individuals.
Publications: Annual report, informational brochure (including application guidelines), newsletter, 990-PF.
Application information: Application form required.
Initial approach: Letter
Copies of proposal: 8
Deadline(s): Oct. 1
Board meeting date(s): Quarterly
Write: Thomas H. Davis, Jr., Exec. Dir.
Officers and Directors:* Robert J. Williams,* Pres.; William J. Hearin,* V.P.; Arlene Mitchell,* V.P.; Jack C. Smith,* Secy.; G. Porter Brock, Jr., Treas.; Thomas H. Davis, Jr., Exec. Dir.; and 16 additional directors.
Number of staff: 1 full-time professional; 1 part-time support.
Employer Identification Number: 630695166

49
Forrest C. Mobley Foundation ⌑
Route One, Box 169-M
Tallassee 36078 (205) 857-2662

Established in 1985 in AL.
Donor(s): Forrest C. Mobley M-1 Trust.
Foundation type: Independent
Financial data (yr. ended 07/31/89): Assets, $1,011,361 (M); expenditures, $65,508, including $59,575 for 7 grants (high: $55,000; low: $75).
Purpose and activities: Support primarily for Episcopal charitable organizations.
Types of support: General purposes.
Limitations: Giving primarily in AL.
Application information: Application form not required.
Initial approach: Proposal
Deadline(s): None
Final notification: 2 months
Write: Nancy M. Mobley, Trustee
Trustees: Forrest C. Mobley, Jr., Nancy M. Mobley.
Employer Identification Number: 596835987

50
Reese Phifer, Jr. Memorial Foundation Trust ⌑
c/o The First National Bank of Tuskaloosa
P.O. Box 2028
Tuscaloosa 35403

Established in 1967 in AL.
Donor(s): Phifer Wire Products, J. Reese Phifer.
Foundation type: Independent
Financial data (yr. ended 12/31/87): Assets, $1,078,922 (M); gifts received, $100,000; expenditures, $123,339, including $113,083 for 51 grants (high: $25,000; low: $35).
Purpose and activities: Giving primarily for higher education, hospitals and health associations, and youth agencies.
Limitations: Giving primarily in AL.
Officer and Trustees:* Susan Phifer Cork,* Mgr.; Karen P. Brooks, Beverly Phifer, J. Reese Phifer, Sue C. Phifer.
Employer Identification Number: 636061552

51
Randa, Inc. ⌑
P.O. Box 511
Montgomery 36134

Trust established in 1948 in AL.
Donor(s): Adolf Weil, Jr., Robert S. Weil.
Foundation type: Independent
Financial data (yr. ended 12/31/88): Assets, $2,780,356 (M); expenditures, $141,534, including $135,025 for 16 grants (high: $40,000; low: $400).
Purpose and activities: Giving primarily for higher education and community funds; support also for cultural programs.
Application information: Contributes only to pre-selected organizations. Applications not accepted.
Trustee: First Alabama Bank.
Directors: M.J. Rothschild, Adolf Weil, Jr., Robert S. Weil.
Employer Identification Number: 636048966

52
The Rime Companies Charitable Foundation ⌑ ☆
500 Robert Jemison Rd.
Birmingham 35209

Established in 1986 in AL.
Donor(s): Harold W. Ripps, Herbert A. Meisler.
Foundation type: Company-sponsored
Financial data (yr. ended 12/31/88): Assets, $5,818 (M); expenditures, $187,869, including $187,348 for 5 grants (high: $100,000; low: $1,000).
Purpose and activities: Giving primarily for a synagogue; support for other Jewish organizations.
Application information:
Initial approach: Letter
Deadline(s): None
Write: Harold W. Ripps, Dir.
Directors: Samuel A. DiPiazza, Jr., Herbert A. Meisler, Harold W. Ripps.
Employer Identification Number: 630943463

53
Adelia Russell Charitable Foundation ⌑ ☆
One Willow Point Rd.
Alexander City 35010 (705) 329-0835

Established in 1987 in AL.
Foundation type: Independent
Financial data (yr. ended 12/31/87): Assets, $1,221,689 (M); expenditures, $106,681, including $77,646 for 2 grants (high: $75,000; low: $2,646).
Purpose and activities: Initial year of operation, 1987; support for a welfare organization and a library.
Application information:
Initial approach: Proposal
Deadline(s): None
Write: Benjamin Russell, Pres.
Officers: Benjamin Russell, Pres.; Duanne Russell, V.P.; Thomas T. Lambetta, Secy.
Employer Identification Number: 630930330

54
Benjamin and Roberta Russell Educational and Charitable Foundation, Inc. ⌑
P.O. Box 272
Alexander City 35010

Incorporated in 1944 in AL.
Donor(s): Benjamin Russell.†
Foundation type: Independent
Financial data (yr. ended 12/31/87): Assets, $16,344,884 (M); expenditures, $993,252, including $915,917 for 35 grants (high: $163,000; low: $2,000).
Purpose and activities: Giving for higher and public education, health agencies, youth programs, and a hospital.
Types of support: Scholarship funds.
Limitations: Giving limited to AL; scholarship funds limited to Tallapoosa and Coosa counties.
Application information:
Write: James D. Nabors, Secy.-Treas.
Officers and Directors:* Nancy R. Gwaltney,* Pres.; Benjamin Russell,* V.P.; James D. Nabors,* Secy.-Treas.; Roberta A. Baumgardner, James W. Brown, Jr., Julia G. Fuller, Edith L. Russell, Julia W. Russell, Ann R. Skinner.
Employer Identification Number: 630393126

55
Barbara Ingalls Shook Foundation
2800 Old Mill Ln.
Birmingham 35223 (205) 870-0299

Established in 1980.
Foundation type: Independent
Financial data (yr. ended 08/31/89): Assets, $4,885,976 (M); expenditures, $367,088, including $188,873 for 39 grants (high: $50,100; low: $25).
Purpose and activities: Emphasis on hospitals and medical research; support also for higher education and cultural programs.
Types of support: Research.
Limitations: Giving primarily in AL and CO.
Application information: Application form required.
Initial approach: Proposal
Copies of proposal: 1
Deadline(s): None
Final notification: Within 6 months
Write: Barbara Ingalls Shook, Chair.
Officers and Trustees:* Barbara Ingalls Shook,* Chair. and Treas.; Robert P. Shook,* Pres. and Secy.; Adele Shook Merck, Elesabeth Ridgely Shook, Ellen Gregg Shook, William Bew White.
Employer Identification Number: 630792812

56
The Simpson Foundation ⌑
c/o First Alabama Bank
P.O. Box 511
Montgomery 36134

Established in 1985 in AL.
Foundation type: Independent
Financial data (yr. ended 4/30/89): Assets, $2,583,843 (M); expenditures, $106,994, including $63,465 for 15 grants to individuals (high: $6,000; low: $465).
Purpose and activities: Scholarship aid for local area residents.
Types of support: Student aid.
Limitations: Giving limited to residents of Wilcox County, AL.
Application information: Application form required.
Deadline(s): Applications accepted Jan. 1 to Mar. 31
Trustees: Lulu E. Palmer, John R. Stewart, First Alabama Bank.
Employer Identification Number: 630925496

57
Don McQueen Smith 1963 Charitable Trust ⌑
c/o First Alabama Bank of Montgomery
P.O. Box 511
Montgomery 36134

Established in 1963 in AL.
Foundation type: Independent
Financial data (yr. ended 12/31/88): Assets, $1,869,993 (M); expenditures, $174,213, including $153,350 for 12 grants (high: $62,000; low: $200).
Purpose and activities: Giving primarily for youth and social service agencies, including community funds, and education.
Limitations: Giving primarily in AL and FL. No grants to individuals.
Application information: Contributes only to pre-selected organizations. Applications not accepted.
Advisory Director: Don McQueen Smith.
Trustee: First Alabama Bank of Montgomery.
Employer Identification Number: 636049793

58
M. W. Smith, Jr. Foundation ⌑
c/o AmSouth Bank, N.A.
P.O. Drawer 1628
Mobile 36629 (205) 438-8260

Trust established in 1960 in AL.
Donor(s): M.W. Smith, Jr.†
Foundation type: Independent
Financial data (yr. ended 12/31/88): Assets, $1,780,033 (M); expenditures, $35,917, including $17,456 for 5 grants (high: $10,000; low: $1,000).
Purpose and activities: Emphasis on education, cultural organizations, and youth activities.
Types of support: Operating budgets, general purposes, continuing support, annual campaigns, seed money, emergency funds, deficit financing, building funds, equipment, land acquisition, endowment funds, special projects, research, publications, conferences and seminars, scholarship funds, matching funds.
Limitations: Giving primarily in southwest AL. No grants to individuals; no loans.
Application information: Application form not required.
Initial approach: Letter
Copies of proposal: 1
Deadline(s): None
Board meeting date(s): May and Nov.
Final notification: 1 month
Write: Kenneth E. Niemeyer

Distribution Committee: Maida S. Pearson, Chair.; Mary M. Riser, Secy.; Louis M. Finlay, Jr., Sybil H. Lebherz, John H. Martin.
Trustee: AmSouth Bank, N.A.
Number of staff: None.
Employer Identification Number: 636018078

59
The Sonat Foundation Inc. ▼
1900 Fifth Ave., North
P.O. Box 2563
Birmingham 35202 (205) 325-7460

Established in 1982 in AL.
Donor(s): Sonat Inc.
Foundation type: Company-sponsored
Financial data (yr. ended 12/31/89): Assets, $6,200,000 (M); gifts received, $3,000,000; qualifying distributions, $1,556,136, including $1,066,152 for 307 grants (high: $200,000; low: $1,000; average: $5,000), $144,839 for 293 employee matching gifts, $25,000 for 1 foundation-administered program and $320,145 for 34 in-kind gifts.
Purpose and activities: Giving mainly for higher education, including employee-related scholarships, and community funds; some support also for social service and youth agencies, including programs for the aged, women, and minorities; health associations and services; community development and civic affairs; the environment; and cultural programs, including the performing arts.
Types of support: Matching funds, employee-related scholarships, general purposes, operating budgets, building funds, research, employee matching gifts, annual campaigns, capital campaigns, emergency funds, endowment funds, land acquisition, renovation projects, program-related investments, seed money, special projects, technical assistance, lectureships, professorships, in-kind gifts, scholarship funds.
Limitations: Giving primarily in AL, CT, and TX. No grants to individuals (except for employee-related scholarships).
Publications: Application guidelines.
Application information: Application form required.
Initial approach: Letter
Copies of proposal: 1
Deadline(s): None
Board meeting date(s): As necessary
Final notification: Normally within 2 weeks
Write: Darlene Sanders, Secy.
Officers and Directors:* J. Robert Doody,* Pres.; Beverley Krannich,* V.P.; William E. Matthews IV,* V.P.; Sarrah W. Rankin,* V.P.; William A. Smith,* V.P.; Darlene Sanders,* Secy.; Don J. DeMetz, Jr.,* Treas.
Number of staff: 1 full-time professional.
Employer Identification Number: 630830299

60
The William H. and Kate F. Stockham Foundation, Inc. ⌑
c/o Stockham Valves & Fittings, Inc.
4000 North Tenth Ave., P.O. Box 10326
Birmingham 35202

Incorporated in 1948 in AL.
Donor(s): Stockham Valves and Fittings, Inc.
Foundation type: Company-sponsored
Financial data (yr. ended 12/31/88): Assets, $3,635,122 (M); expenditures, $289,220, including $248,900 for 56 grants (high: $65,000; low: $100) and $18,609 for 21 grants to individuals (high: $3,500; low: $225).
Purpose and activities: Emphasis on educational purposes, including higher education and public affairs groups; human services, including community funds and hospitals; Christian religious education and church support; and assistance to employees and former employees of the donor, including scholarships, fellowships, and welfare assistance.
Types of support: Employee-related scholarships, grants to individuals.
Limitations: Giving primarily in AL and the Southeast. No grants to individuals (except for employee-related grants, including scholarships).
Application information:
Initial approach: Letter
Deadline(s): None
Write: Herbert C. Stockham, Chair.
Officer and Trustees:* Herbert C. Stockham,* Chair.; Sam Perry Given, Kate Stockham, Richard J. Stockham, Jr.
Employer Identification Number: 636049787

61
Charles W. & Minnie Temerson Foundation Trust ⌑
P.O. Box 2554
Birmingham 35202-2554

Foundation type: Independent
Financial data (yr. ended 12/31/88): Assets, $503,604 (M); expenditures, $176,500, including $170,563 for 13 grants (high: $49,500; low: $3,625).
Purpose and activities: Giving primarily for Jewish giving and education, including a public library; support also for cultural organizations.
Limitations: Giving primarily in Birmingham, AL.
Trustee: SouthTrust Bank of Alabama.
Employer Identification Number: 636069899

62
Tractor & Equipment Company Foundation ⌑
5336 Airport Hwy.
Birmingham 35212 (205) 591-2131
Scholarship application address: James W. Waitzman, Sr., Pres., Tractor & Equipment Co., P.O. Box 2326, Birmingham, AL 35201

Established in 1977 in AL.
Donor(s): Tractor & Equipment Co.
Foundation type: Company-sponsored
Financial data (yr. ended 12/31/87): Assets, $187,639 (M); gifts received, $152,000; expenditures, $195,125, including $173,574 for 74 grants (high: $35,783; low: $100) and $21,492 for 14 grants to individuals (high: $6,000; low: $150).
Purpose and activities: Support for churches and higher education, including scholarships for employees' children.
Types of support: Employee-related scholarships.
Limitations: Giving limited to AL. No grants to individuals (except for employee-related scholarships).
Application information: Application form required for scholarship.
Deadline(s): Mar. 1; May 20 for scholarships
Write: Benny Winford, Secy.-Treas.
Officers and Directors:* James W. Waitzman, Sr.,* Chair. and Pres.; B.J. Roberts,* V.P.; James W. Waitzman, Jr.,* V.P.; Benny F. Winford,* Secy.-Treas.
Employer Identification Number: 630718825

63
Susan Mott Webb Charitable Trust
c/o AmSouth Bank, N.A.
P.O. Box 11426
Birmingham 35202 (205) 326-5396

Established in 1978 in AL.
Donor(s): Susan Mott Webb.†
Foundation type: Independent
Financial data (yr. ended 12/31/89): Assets, $8,675,261 (M); expenditures, $495,041, including $459,333 for 38 grants (high: $50,000; low: $500).
Purpose and activities: Emphasis on a university and other educational institutions, health services, and cultural programs; support also for religion and civic affairs.
Types of support: Building funds, equipment, special projects, capital campaigns.
Limitations: Giving limited to the greater Birmingham, AL, area. No grants to individuals, or for scholarships or fellowships; no loans.
Application information: Application form not required.
Initial approach: Letter or proposal
Copies of proposal: 6
Deadline(s): Apr. 15 and Oct. 15
Board meeting date(s): June and Dec.
Write: Kathryn W. Miree, V.P. and Trust Officer, AmSouth Bank, N.A.
Trustees: Stewart Dansby, Suzanne Dansby, Charles B. Webb, Jr., William Bew White, Jr., AmSouth Bank, N.A.
Number of staff: None.
Employer Identification Number: 636112593

64
Diane Wendland 1962 Charitable Trust ⌑
c/o First Alabama Bank of Montgomery, Trust Dept.
P.O. Box 511
Montgomery 36134

Established in 1962 in AL.
Foundation type: Independent
Financial data (yr. ended 12/31/88): Assets, $1,408,556 (M); expenditures, $129,254, including $118,250 for 51 grants (high: $30,500; low: $100).
Purpose and activities: Giving primarily for civic affairs, social service and youth agencies, higher and other education, and cultural programs.
Limitations: Giving primarily in AL, with emphasis on Autauga County.
Trustee: First Alabama Bank.
Advisory Committee: Milton Wendland, Mrs. Milton Wendland.
Employer Identification Number: 636019220

ALASKA

65
Alaska Conservation Foundation
430 West Seventh St., Suite 215
Anchorage 99501 (907) 276-1917

Incorporated in 1980 in AK.
Foundation type: Community
Financial data (yr. ended 06/30/89): Assets, $418,694 (M); gifts received, $676,922; expenditures, $666,680, including $442,432 for 160 grants (high: $40,250; low: $150; average: $2,000-$5,000).
Purpose and activities: Giving limited to research and education projects for environmental protection; awards to honor outstanding environmental volunteer activists and professionals.
Types of support: General purposes, continuing support, seed money, emergency funds, equipment, matching funds, consulting services, technical assistance, internships, research, special projects, conferences and seminars, publications, loans, operating budgets.
Limitations: Giving limited to AK. No grants for annual campaigns, deficit financing, building funds, land acquisition, renovation projects, general or special endowments, scholarships, fellowships, professorships, exchange programs, student loans, or program-related investments.
Publications: Annual report, program policy statement, application guidelines, financial statement, grants list, informational brochure.
Application information: Application form required.
Initial approach: Letter or telephone
Copies of proposal: 15
Deadline(s): 6 weeks prior to board meeting
Board meeting date(s): 3 times annually
Write: Denny Wilcher, Pres.
Officers: Denny Wilcher, Pres.; Jim Stratton, V.P.
Trustees: Steve Williams, Chair.; Eric Smith, Vice-Chair.; William Ahearn, Celia Hunter, Matt Kirchhoff, Ken Leghorn, Ellin London, Cindy Marquette-Admas, Ave Thayer, Peg Tileston, Denny Wilcher.
Number of staff: 2 full-time professional; 2 full-time support.
Employer Identification Number: 920061466

66
Arctic Education Foundation ¤
P.O. Box 129
Barrow 99723 (907) 852-8633

Established in 1978 in AK.
Donor(s): Arctic Slope Regional Corp., Chevron U.S.A., Inc., BP Alaska, Shell Oil Co., Amoco Corp., Piqunik Management Corp., UIC Construction.
Foundation type: Company-sponsored
Financial data (yr. ended 06/30/89): Assets, $503 (M); gifts received, $153,448; expenditures, $158,995, including $158,980 for 74 grants to individuals (high: $5,184; low: $50).
Purpose and activities: Scholarships for needy Native Alaskan high school graduates and shareholders of the Arctic Slope Regional Corp.
Types of support: Scholarship funds.
Limitations: Giving primarily in AK.
Publications: Annual report.
Application information: Student may request application form only after being admitted into a higher educational institution. Application form required.
Initial approach: Letter
Deadline(s): None
Board meeting date(s): Aug. and Jan.
Write: Ms. Flossie Andersen
Trustees: Jacob Adams, George Agnassagga, Elizabeth Hollingsworth, Edward E. Hopson, Sr., Brenda Itta, Jeslie Kaleak, Oliver Leavitt, Roosevelt Paneak, Joseph Upiksoun.
Number of staff: 1 full-time professional.
Employer Identification Number: 920068447

67
Atwood Foundation, Inc. ¤
P.O. Box 40
Anchorage 99510

Established in 1965 in AK.
Donor(s): Robert B. Atwood, Anchorage Times Publishing Co.
Foundation type: Independent
Financial data (yr. ended 12/31/88): Assets, $2,873,867 (M); expenditures, $169,642, including $150,000 for 2 grants (high: $100,000; low: $50,000).
Purpose and activities: Support largely for educational, cultural, and civic affairs organizations.
Limitations: Giving primarily in AK.
Officers and Trustees:* Robert B. Atwood,* Pres.; Sara Elaine Atwood,* V.P. and Secy.
Employer Identification Number: 926002571

68
CIRI Foundation
(also known as The Cook Inlet Region, Inc. Foundation)
P.O. Box 93330
Anchorage 99509-3330 (907) 274-8638

Established in 1982 in AK.
Donor(s): Cook Inlet Region, Inc.
Foundation type: Independent
Financial data (yr. ended 12/31/89): Assets, $2,759,862 (M); gifts received, $308,966; expenditures, $393,909, including $14,500 for 5 grants (high: $3,000; low: $500; average: $500-$3,000), $171,036 for grants to individuals (high: $5,000; low: $150; average: $150-$5,000) and $2,378 for 1 in-kind gift.
Purpose and activities: Educational support for enrollees of Cook Inlet Region; giving also for native cultural and heritage projects.
Types of support: Student aid, grants to individuals, internships, fellowships, special projects.
Publications: Informational brochure (including application guidelines), application guidelines.
Application information: Applicant must be an enrollee, or child or spouse of an enrollee, of Cook Inlet Region for individual educational scholarships, grants, internships, and fellowships. Application form required.
Initial approach: Letter requesting application form
Copies of proposal: 2
Deadline(s): For Individual Awards: July 1 and Dec. 15 for scholarships; Mar. 31, June 30, Sept. 30, and Dec. 31 for grants, fellowships and internships. For Organizational Awards for educational and cultural projects: Mar. 31, June 30, and Dec. 31
Board meeting date(s): Quarterly
Final notification: Within 2 weeks of board meeting
Write: Lydia L Hays, Exec. Dir.
Officers and Directors:* Margaret Sagerser-Brown,* Chair.; John Monfor,* Pres.; Don Karabelnikoff,* V.P.; Roy M. Huhndorf,* Secy.-Treas.; Esther Combs, Britton E. Crosly, William English, Bart Garber, Jeff Gonnason, Carol Gore, David Heatwole, Frank Klett, Janie Leask, Edward Rasmuson, Robert Gottstein.
Number of staff: 1 full-time professional; 1 full-time support.
Employer Identification Number: 920087914

ARIZONA

69
A.P.S. Foundation, Inc.
P.O. Box 53999, Station 9930
Phoenix 85072-3999

Established in 1981 in AZ.
Donor(s): Arizona Public Service Co.
Foundation type: Company-sponsored
Financial data (yr. ended 12/31/89): Assets, $8,671,603 (M); expenditures, $746,811, including $738,079 for 185 grants (high: $50,000; low: $25).
Purpose and activities: Grants for education, culture, hospitals, and youth.
Types of support: Operating budgets, matching funds, capital campaigns.
Limitations: Giving primarily in AZ, with emphasis on Phoenix. No grants to individuals.
Application information: Contributes only to pre-selected organizations. Applications not accepted.
Officers: O. Mark De Michele, Pres.; Jaron B. Norberg, Jr., V.P.; William J. Post, V.P.; Nancy C. Loftin, Secy.; William J. Hemelt, Treas.
Directors: Shirley A. Richard, Richard Snell.
Employer Identification Number: 953735903

70
Arizona Community Foundation
4350 East Camelback Rd., Suite 216C
Phoenix 85018 (602) 952-9954

Incorporated in 1978 in AZ.
Donor(s): L. Dilatush, R. Kieckhefer, Bert A. Getz, Newton Rosenzweig, G.R. Herberger.
Foundation type: Community

Financial data (yr. ended 12/31/89): Assets, $23,008,191 (L); gifts received, $3,695,459; expenditures, $2,657,899, including $2,017,865 for 182 grants (average: $1,000-$10,000).
Purpose and activities: Support for children's mental health, youth agencies, health agencies, organizations for the handicapped, and other human services programs, community-based economic development, performing arts, and cultural programs.
Types of support: Seed money, emergency funds, equipment, technical assistance, special projects, operating budgets, continuing support, building funds, matching funds, scholarship funds, special projects, general purposes, conferences and seminars, publications, renovation projects, research.
Limitations: Giving limited to AZ. No support for sectarian religious purposes. No grants to individuals, or for deficit financing, annual campaigns, land acquisition, endowment funds, travel to or support of conferences, consulting services, or capital grants; no loans.
Publications: Annual report, program policy statement, application guidelines, newsletter, financial statement, informational brochure.
Application information: Application form required.
Initial approach: Letter or telephone
Copies of proposal: 6
Deadline(s): Feb. 1, June 1, and Oct.1
Board meeting date(s): Semiannually
Final notification: 60 days
Write: Stephen D. Mittenthal, Pres.
Officers and Directors:* Richard H. Whitney,* Chair.; Barbara J. Polk,* Vice-Chair.; Stephen D. Mittenthal,* Pres. and Exec. Dir.; Joan C. Nastro,* Secy.; F. Lee Jacquette,* Treas.; and 21 other directors.
Number of staff: 4 full-time professional; 1 part-time professional; 1 full-time support.
Employer Identification Number: 860348306

71
BF Foundation
114 North San Francisco St., Suite 107
Flagstaff 86001 (602) 774-1094

Established in 1965 in AZ.
Donor(s): Harvey W. Branigar, Jr.
Foundation type: Independent
Financial data (yr. ended 6/30/89): Assets, $1,163,000 (M); gifts received, $248,723; expenditures, $258,879, including $221,121 for 200 grants to individuals (high: $6,000; low: $300; average: $600-$2,000) and $23,500 for 68 loans to individuals.
Purpose and activities: Awards scholarship grants and loans for college and university undergraduates. Awards made to institutions on behalf of named recipients.
Types of support: Student loans, student aid.
Publications: Informational brochure.
Application information: Initial screening of applicants done by educational institution; final selection made by foundation. Application form required.
Deadline(s): Varies with each institution
Write: Katherin Lee Chase, Pres.
Officers and Directors:* Harvey W. Branigar, Jr.,* Chair.; Katharin Lee Chase,* Pres. and Exec. Dir.; Sarah Lee Branigar,* V.P.; David D. Chase,* Secy.-Treas.
Number of staff: 1 full-time professional; 1 part-time professional.
Employer Identification Number: 366141070

72
Herbert Cummings Charitable Trust
6900 East Camelback Rd., No. 700
Scottsdale 85251-2431 (602) 990-0880

Established in 1984 in AZ.
Donor(s): Herbert K. Cummings.
Foundation type: Independent
Financial data (yr. ended 12/31/89): Assets, $1,287,078 (M); gifts received, $34,600; expenditures, $67,737, including $66,687 for 136 grants (high: $22,000; low: $10).
Purpose and activities: Giving primarily for cultural organizations and institutions, health-related research and services, and Jewish concerns; support also for child welfare and the aged.
Types of support: Annual campaigns, endowment funds, matching funds, research.
Limitations: Giving primarily in AZ. No grants to individuals.
Application information: Applications not accepted.
Write: Herbert K. Cummings, Trustee
Trustees: Diane M. Cummings, Herbert K. Cummings.
Employer Identification Number: 866148404

73
DeGrazia Art & Cultural Foundation, Inc. ⌘
c/o Jennifer Potter, Dir.
6300 North Swan Rd.
Tucson 85718 (602) 299-9191

Established in 1977 in AZ.
Foundation type: Operating
Financial data (yr. ended 06/30/89): Assets, $15,281,396 (M); gifts received, $6,674; expenditures, $484,565, including $80,233 for 23 grants (high: $30,000; low: $48).
Purpose and activities: Support for displaying the art works and artifacts of DeGrazia, promoting the appreciation of art and other cultural interests, perpetuating and maintaining for the benefit of the public the artistic works of DeGrazia, and providing a dignified cultural center for their display.
Types of support: General purposes.
Limitations: Giving primarily in AZ.
Application information:
Initial approach: Letter or proposal
Deadline(s): One month prior to the end of each calendar quarter
Officers and Directors:* Marion DeGrazia,* Pres.; Thomas McCarville,* Secy.-Treas.; Gary Avey, Frank DeGrazia, Lucia DeGrazia, Ira S. Feldman, Harold Grieve, Jennifer Potter.
Employer Identification Number: 860339837

74
Dougherty Foundation, Inc.
3620 N. 3rd St.
Phoenix 85012-2020 (602) 264-3751

Incorporated in 1954 in AZ.
Donor(s): M.J. Dougherty,† Mrs. M.J. Dougherty.†
Foundation type: Independent
Financial data (yr. ended 12/31/88): Assets, $6,759,919 (M); gifts received, $1,310; expenditures, $679,821, including $290,267 for grants to individuals (high: $2,000; low: $250; average: $250-$2,000) and $226,600 for loans to individuals.
Purpose and activities: Student loans and scholarships to needy college students of high academic ability who are AZ residents and U.S. citizens.
Types of support: Student aid, student loans.
Limitations: Giving limited to AZ.
Publications: Program policy statement, application guidelines.
Application information: Application form required.
Initial approach: Letter or telephone
Copies of proposal: 1
Deadline(s): Submit proposal between Jan. and Apr.; no set deadline
Board meeting date(s): Monthly and as required
Write: Mary J. Maffeo, Secy.-Treas.
Officers and Directors:* John A. LaSota, Jr.,* Pres.; Bruce E. Babbitt,* V.P.; Rose Mary Eden,* V.P.; William P. Mahoney, Jr.,* V.P.; Mary Martha Prince,* V.P.; James P. Walsh,* V.P.; Mary J. Maffeo,* Secy.-Treas.
Number of staff: 1 full-time professional; 1 part-time support.
Employer Identification Number: 866051637

75
E. Blois du Bois Foundation, Inc. ⌘
3620 North Third St.
Phoenix 85012 (602) 264-3751
Grant application address: P.O. Box 33426, Phoenix, AZ 85067
Scholarship inquiries: Dir. of Financial Aid at Univ. of Arizona, Arizona State Univ., or any of the Arizona community colleges

Incorporated in 1960 in AZ.
Donor(s): E. Blois du Bois.†
Foundation type: Independent
Financial data (yr. ended 05/31/89): Assets, $12,688,323 (M); expenditures, $743,735, including $471,181 for 14 grants (high: $113,075; low: $250).
Purpose and activities: Grants limited to humane societies and to scholarship funds for students recommended by financial aid officers of universities and community colleges in AZ.
Types of support: Scholarship funds, operating budgets.
Limitations: Giving limited to AZ. No grants to individuals, or for endowment funds.
Application information: Application forms for scholarships avilable at various directors of financial aid offices; no form necessary for other grant requests.
Initial approach: Letter
Copies of proposal: 2
Deadline(s): For scholarships, established by various institutions; none for other awards
Board meeting date(s): As required
Write: Alan du Bois, Pres.
Officers: Alan du Bois,* Pres.; Robert C. Horne,* V.P.; Gail B. Horne,* Secy.-Treas.
Employer Identification Number: 866052886

76
First Interstate Bank of Arizona, N.A. Charitable Foundation ▼ ⌑
P.O. Box 29743
Phoenix 85038-9743 (602) 229-4520

Established in 1976 in AZ.
Donor(s): First Interstate Bank of Arizona, N.A.
Foundation type: Company-sponsored
Financial data (yr. ended 12/31/87): Assets, $6,701,032 (M); gifts received, $2,002,041; expenditures, $1,087,046, including $1,062,853 for 262 grants (high: $189,180; low: $50; average: $500-$10,000).
Purpose and activities: Support for community funds and higher education, community development, hospitals, social service agencies, cultural programs, and youth agencies.
Types of support: Annual campaigns, building funds, continuing support, emergency funds, equipment, general purposes, land acquisition, research, scholarship funds, seed money, capital campaigns, renovation projects, operating budgets, special projects.
Limitations: Giving limited to AZ-based organizations or national organizations which fund programs in AZ. No support for solely religious purposes. No grants to individuals, or for endowment funds or travel; no loans.
Publications: Application guidelines.
Application information: Application form required.
Initial approach: Letter
Copies of proposal: 1
Deadline(s): Submit proposals Jan. through June, Sept., and Oct.
Board meeting date(s): Twice a month
Final notification: 2 months
Write: Mark A. Dinunzio, Chair., Corp. Contribs. Comm.
Trustees: Mark A. Dinunzio, Chair.; William T. Rauch, Dianne E. Stephens.
Number of staff: 2 part-time professional.
Employer Identification Number: 510204372

77
The Flinn Foundation ▼
3300 North Central Ave., Suite 2300
Phoenix 85012 (602) 274-9000

Trust established in 1965 in AZ.
Donor(s): Irene Flinn,† Robert S. Flinn, M.D.†
Foundation type: Independent
Financial data (yr. ended 12/31/89): Assets, $98,893,027 (M); expenditures, $6,006,032, including $4,595,753 for 97 grants (high: $500,000; low: $1,000; average: $20,000-$100,000).
Purpose and activities: The foundation's grantmaking interests, limited to AZ, involve three objectives: 1) to strengthen the capabilities of AZ's institutions in the fields of health, education, and the cultural arts; 2) to develop future leaders in health and education through research fellowship programs for promising students at the high school and college levels; and 3) to increase the availability of basic health care services for the frail elderly, pregnant and parenting teenagers, young children, and persons with AIDS.
Types of support: Special projects, research, seed money.
Limitations: Giving limited to AZ. No grants to individuals, or for matching gifts, emergency funds, land acquisition, renovation projects, annual campaigns, capital or endowment funds, operating or deficit costs, or film projects; no support for equipment, publications, or workshops and conferences that are not an integral part of a larger project.
Publications: Application guidelines, grants list, newsletter, occasional report, biennial report.
Application information: Application form not required.
Initial approach: Letter or telephone
Copies of proposal: 2
Deadline(s): None
Board meeting date(s): 6 times a year
Final notification: Within 12 weeks
Write: John W. Murphy, Exec. Dir.
Officers: Donald K. Buffmire, M.D., Chair. and Pres.; David R. Frazer, V.P. and Treas.; Jay S. Ruffner, Secy.
Directors: John W. Murphy, Exec. Dir.; Robert A. Brooks, M.D., David J. Gullen, M.D., Merlin W. Kampfer, M.D., Edward V. O'Malley, Jr., A.J. Pfister.
Number of staff: 6 full-time professional; 1 part-time professional; 3 full-time support.
Employer Identification Number: 860421476

78
Erwin Fry Foundation ⌑
P.O. Box 610
Sierra Vista 85636-0610 (602) 886-1263

Foundation type: Independent
Financial data (yr. ended 12/31/88): Assets, $1,481,438 (M); expenditures, $131,420, including $90,000 for 1 grant.
Purpose and activities: Giving for scholarships administered by the Cochise College Foundation, Douglas, AZ.
Types of support: Scholarship funds.
Limitations: Giving limited to Cochise County, AZ.
Publications: Application guidelines.
Application information: Contact Conchise College for application guidelines. Application form required.
Final notification: By June 30
Write: A. Jay Busby, Trustee
Trustees: Gaytha L. Bradley, A. Jay Busby, Grace E. Pomeroy.
Employer Identification Number: 860400719

79
Globe Foundation ⌑
3634 Civic Center Plaza
Scottsdale 85251 (602) 947-7888

Established in 1958 in IL.
Donor(s): Bert A. Getz.
Foundation type: Independent
Financial data (yr. ended 12/31/88): Assets, $8,910,852 (M); gifts received, $75,000; expenditures, $556,058, including $492,542 for 59 grants (high: $150,000; low: $25).
Purpose and activities: Giving primarily for publicly supported organizations and institutions, with emphasis on youth, education, and cultural organizations.
Limitations: Giving limited to AZ and IL. No support for privately supported groups. No grants to individuals, or for general operating expenses.
Application information: Contributes only to pre-selected organizations. Applications not accepted.
Write: C.L. Lux, V.P.
Officers and Directors:* George F. Getz, Jr.,* Pres.; C.L. Lux,* V.P. and Treas.; Bert A. Getz,* Secy.; James W. Ashley, Lynn Getz Polite.
Employer Identification Number: 366054050

80
The Greyhound Corporation Fund ⌑ ☆
Greyhound Tower, Suite 1701
Phoenix 85077

Established in 1987 in AZ.
Donor(s): The Greyhound Corporation.
Foundation type: Company-sponsored
Financial data (yr. ended 12/31/88): Assets, $3,820,741 (M); gifts received, $3,700,000; expenditures, $256,559, including $201,450 for 60 grants (high: $25,000; low: $200).
Purpose and activities: Giving primarily for social services, child welfare and youth agencies, and health associations.
Limitations: Giving primarily in AZ. No grants to individuals.
Application information: Contributes only to pre-selected organizations. Applications not accepted.
Officers: John W. Teets, Pres. and C.E.O.; Frederick G. Emerson, V.P. and Secy.; Ronald G. Nelson, V.P. and Treas.; Richard C. Stephen, V.P. and Controller; Armen Ervanian, V.P.; F. Edward Lake, V.P.; L. Gene Lemon, V.P.
Employer Identification Number: 742499884

81
The Hankins Foundation
7812 North El Arroyo Rd.
Paradise Valley 85253 (602) 998-1693

Trust established in 1952 in OH.
Donor(s): Edward R. Hankins,† Ann H. Long,† Jane H. Lockwood,† Ruth L. Hankins.
Foundation type: Independent
Financial data (yr. ended 12/31/88): Assets, $2,848,265 (M); expenditures, $192,091, including $170,471 for 82 grants (high: $27,500; low: $250).
Purpose and activities: Emphasis on higher education, community funds, health agencies and hospitals, youth and social service agencies, and cultural programs.
Limitations: Giving primarily in OH, with emphasis on Cleveland. No grants to individuals; no loans.
Application information: Application form not required.
Initial approach: Proposal
Copies of proposal: 1
Deadline(s): None
Board meeting date(s): As required
Write: Edward G. Lockwood, Trustee
Trustees: Ruth L. Hankins, Richard R. Hollington, Jr., Edward G. Lockwood, Gordon G. Long, Janet L. Tarwater.
Employer Identification Number: 346565426

82
The Hermundslie Foundation ⌑
3762 North Harrison Rd.
Tucson 85749 (602) 749-2982

Established in 1968 in AZ.
Foundation type: Independent
Financial data (yr. ended 12/31/88): Assets, $1,388,405 (M); expenditures, $84,969, including $82,500 for 4 grants (high: $35,250; low: $12,000).
Purpose and activities: Support primarily for health organizations and medical research.
Types of support: Research.
Application information: Application form not required.
Deadline(s): None
Write: Elaine Hermundslie, V.P.
Officers: Gerold Hermundslie, Pres.; Elaine Hermundslie, V.P.; G.D. Engdahl, Treas.
Employer Identification Number: 237001359

83
J. W. Kieckhefer Foundation
116 East Gurley St.
P.O. Box 750
Prescott 86302 (602) 445-4010

Trust established in 1953 in AZ.
Donor(s): John W. Kieckhefer.†
Foundation type: Independent
Financial data (yr. ended 12/31/89): Assets, $13,050,273 (M); expenditures, $693,648, including $674,800 for 42 grants (high: $125,000; low: $1,000; average: $1,000-$10,000).
Purpose and activities: Emphasis on medical research and hospices and health agencies, social services, education, youth and child welfare agencies, conservation, community funds, and cultural programs.
Types of support: Operating budgets, continuing support, annual campaigns, emergency funds, building funds, equipment, land acquisition, endowment funds, matching funds, research, publications, conferences and seminars, special projects.
Limitations: No grants to individuals, or for seed money, deficit financing, scholarships, fellowships, or demonstration projects; no loans.
Publications: 990-PF.
Application information: Application form not required.
Initial approach: Letter
Copies of proposal: 1
Deadline(s): Submit proposal preferably between May and Nov.
Board meeting date(s): Nov., Dec., and as required
Final notification: 6 months
Write: Eugene P. Polk, Trustee
Trustees: John I. Kieckhefer, Robert H. Kieckhefer, Eugene P. Polk.
Number of staff: None.
Employer Identification Number: 866022877

84
Marshall Foundation ⌑
4000 North Scottsdale Rd., Suite 203
Scottsdale 85251 (602) 622-8613

Incorporated in 1930 in AZ.
Donor(s): Louise F. Marshall.†
Foundation type: Independent
Financial data (yr. ended 12/31/88): Assets, $2,027,317 (M); expenditures, $128,151, including $81,745 for 10 grants (high: $10,000; low: $2,000; average: $5,000-$50,000).
Purpose and activities: Emphasis on education, youth and social service agencies, and hospitals.
Limitations: Giving limited to the Tucson, AZ, area. No grants to individuals.
Publications: 990-PF.
Application information: Application form not required.
Initial approach: Letter
Deadline(s): None
Board meeting date(s): Monthly
Officers and Directors:* John F. Molloy,* Pres.; Maxine B. Marshall,* Secy.; David R. Frazer.
Number of staff: 2 full-time professional; 2 full-time support; 1 part-time support.
Employer Identification Number: 860102198

85
The Marshall Fund ☆
4000 North Scottsdale Rd., Suite 203
Scottsdale 85251 (602) 941-5249

Established in 1987 in AZ.
Donor(s): Jonathan Marshall, Maxine B. Marshall.
Foundation type: Independent
Financial data (yr. ended 12/31/88): Assets, $2,027,317 (M); gifts received, $500,000; expenditures, $131,155, including $81,745 for grants (high: $25,000).
Purpose and activities: Giving in the following general areas: 1) Cultural and artistic projects, 2) Civil liberties, 3) Human and social problems, 4) Environmental protection and conservation, and 5) Promotion of world peace and understanding.
Types of support: Exchange programs, matching funds, special projects.
Limitations: Giving primarily in AZ. No support for religious organizations for religious purposes. No grants to individuals, or for building or capital funds, operating budgets, endowments, debt reduction, fundraising events, medical or academic research, annual campaigns, land acquisition, or publications.
Publications: Informational brochure (including application guidelines).
Application information:
Initial approach: Letter
Copies of proposal: 5
Deadline(s): None
Board meeting date(s): Quarterly
Final notification: 4 to 6 months
Write: Maxine Marshall, V.P.
Officers and Directors:* Jonathan Marshall,* Pres.; Maxine B. Marshall,* V.P.; Paul Eckstein, David R. Frazer, Laura Marshall-Sapon.
Number of staff: 1 full-time support.
Employer Identification Number: 742470266

86
Margaret T. Morris Foundation ▼
P.O. Box 592
Prescott 86302 (602) 445-4010

Established in 1967.
Donor(s): Margaret T. Morris.†
Foundation type: Independent
Financial data (yr. ended 12/31/89): Assets, $21,560,064 (M); expenditures, $1,149,679, including $1,078,300 for 60 grants (high: $250,000; low: $1,000).
Purpose and activities: Support for the performing arts and other cultural programs, education, with emphasis on higher education, youth and child welfare, a community foundation, population control, medical research and education, the environment and animal welfare, and social services, primarily those benefitting the handicapped.
Types of support: Land acquisition, general purposes, building funds, scholarship funds, deficit financing, endowment funds, operating budgets.
Limitations: Giving primarily in AZ. No support for religious organizations or their agencies. No grants to individuals; no loans.
Publications: 990-PF.
Application information: Application form not required.
Initial approach: Proposal or letter
Copies of proposal: 1
Deadline(s): Submit proposal preferably in May through Nov.
Board meeting date(s): Aug. and Dec.
Final notification: After board meetings
Write: Eugene P. Polk, Trustee
Trustees: Richard L. Menschel, Eugene P. Polk.
Number of staff: None.
Employer Identification Number: 866057798

87
The Mulcahy Foundation
80 West Franklin St.
Tucson 85701 (602) 623-6416

Incorporated in 1957 in AZ.
Donor(s): John A. Mulcahy,† Mulcahy Lumber Co.
Foundation type: Independent
Financial data (yr. ended 06/30/89): Assets, $1,844,456 (M); expenditures, $145,201, including $120,675 for 23 grants (high: $57,204; low: $200; average: $1,000).
Purpose and activities: Support for higher education, including medical education, youth agencies, and hospitals.
Types of support: General purposes, operating budgets, continuing support, annual campaigns, emergency funds, deficit financing, building funds, equipment, endowment funds, matching funds, scholarship funds, internships, exchange programs, fellowships, research, conferences and seminars, special projects.
Limitations: Giving primarily in AZ, with emphasis on the Tucson area. No grants to individuals, or for land acquisition, demonstration projects, or publications.
Application information: Application form not required.
Initial approach: Letter or telephone
Deadline(s): None
Board meeting date(s): Monthly and as required
Final notification: 1 to 2 months
Write: Linda Lohse, Prog. Officer
Officers: Cliffton E. Bloom, Pres.; Ashby I. Lohse, Secy.-Treas.
Trustee: Florence W. Lohse.
Number of staff: 1
Employer Identification Number: 866053461

88

The Meyer and Aileen Osofsky Foundation ⌑ ☆

9475 East Mariposa Grande St.
Scottsdale 85255

Established in 1968.
Donor(s): Meyer Osofsky, Aileen Osofsky.
Foundation type: Independent
Financial data (yr. ended 12/31/88): Assets, $147,576 (M); gifts received, $75,000; expenditures, $119,183, including $118,928 for 63 grants (high: $70,000; low: $25).
Purpose and activities: Support for Jewish welfare funds and other Jewish organizations, health associations, and cultural programs.
Limitations: Giving primarily in NY and AZ. No grants to individuals.
Application information: Contributes only to pre-selected organizations. Applications not accepted.
Trustees: Aileen Osofsky, Meyer Osofsky.
Employer Identification Number: 136263683

89

Elizabeth Ann Parkman Foundation ⌑

1840 East River Rd., Suite 302
Tucson 85718

Established in 1962 in AZ.
Foundation type: Independent
Financial data (yr. ended 12/31/87): Assets, $1,114,757 (M); expenditures, $57,280, including $53,515 for 43 grants (high: $7,500; low: $10).
Purpose and activities: Grants primarily for Christian institutions, hospitals and medical research, community projects, and education.
Application information:
Initial approach: Letter
Trustees: James M. Murphy, Elizabeth Ann Parkman.
Employer Identification Number: 866022954

90

Milton and Lillian Peck Foundation, Inc. ⌑

c/o Irving Lowe
4729 East Clearwater Pkwy.
Paradise Valley 85253

Established in 1958.
Donor(s): Peck Meat Packing Corp., Emmber Brands, Inc., Gibbon Packing, Inc., Moo-Battue, Inc.
Foundation type: Independent
Financial data (yr. ended 12/31/88): Assets, $2,980,302 (M); gifts received, $743,322; expenditures, $218,697, including $200,000 for 2 grants of $100,000 each.
Purpose and activities: Grants primarily for hospitals and health associations, Jewish welfare funds and temple support, and cultural organizations.
Limitations: Giving primarily in Milwaukee, WI. No grants to individuals.
Application information: Contributes only to pre-selected organizations. Applications not accepted.
Officers and Directors:* Bernard Peck,* Pres. and Treas.; Irving Lowe, V.P. and Secy.; Miriam Lowe, Miriam Peck.
Employer Identification Number: 396051782

91

William L. & Ruth L. Pendleton Memorial Fund ☆

c/o Citibank (Arizona)
P.O. Box 1095
Phoenix 85001 (602) 530-1540

Established in 1987 in AZ.
Foundation type: Independent
Financial data (yr. ended 12/31/88): Assets, $2,590,805 (M); expenditures, $127,803, including $87,800 for 4 grants (high: $25,000; low: $12,800).
Purpose and activities: "To provide services for children and the elderly," including child welfare and development and early childhood education; support also for a diabetes association, a Girl Scout council, and a symphony orchestra.
Types of support: Continuing support, general purposes, special projects.
Limitations: Giving primarily in Phoenix, AZ. No grants to individuals.
Application information: Application form required.
Copies of proposal: 1
Deadline(s): Sept. 30
Write: Maria Moreno, Trust Officer, Citibank (Arizona)
Committee Members: Robert Burt, Mildred May, Polly Miller, Janet Wilson.
Trustee: Citibank (Arizona).
Number of staff: None.
Employer Identification Number: 742475483

92

Phelps Dodge Foundation ▼ ⌑

2600 North Central Ave.
Phoenix 85004-3014 (602) 234-8100

Incorporated in 1953 in NY.
Donor(s): Phelps Dodge Corp., and subsidiaries.
Foundation type: Company-sponsored
Financial data (yr. ended 12/31/87): Assets, $11,418,432 (M); expenditures, $956,013, including $623,259 for grants (high: $25,000) and $208,897 for employee matching gifts.
Purpose and activities: Emphasis on higher education, community funds, health and welfare, civic activities, and cultural programs.
Types of support: Continuing support, annual campaigns, endowment funds, employee matching gifts, scholarship funds, fellowships.
Limitations: Giving primarily in areas of operations of Phelps Dodge Corp. and its subsidiaries. No grants to individuals, or for operating budgets, seed money, emergency funds, deficit financing, research, special projects, publications, or conferences; no loans.
Application information: Application form not required.
Initial approach: Letter or proposal
Copies of proposal: 1
Deadline(s): Oct. to Nov.; budgeting process occurs in Dec.
Board meeting date(s): Apr.
Final notification: 3 to 4 months
Write: William C. Tubman, Pres.
Officers: William C. Tubman, Pres.; Frank W. Longto, V.P. and Treas.; Mary K. Sterling, Secy.
Directors: Cleveland E. Dodge, Jr., G. Robert Durham, George B. Munroe, Edward L. Palmer, John P. Schroeder.
Number of staff: 2 part-time professional; 1 part-time support.
Employer Identification Number: 136077350

93

Raymond Educational Foundation, Inc.

P.O. Box 1423
Flagstaff 86002 (602) 774-8081

Incorporated in 1951 in AZ.
Donor(s): R.O. Raymond.†
Foundation type: Independent
Financial data (yr. ended 04/30/90): Assets, $2,303,420 (M); expenditures, $168,622, including $144,900 for 9 grants (high: $90,300; low: $1,000).
Purpose and activities: Grants limited to institutions within Coconino County, Arizona, principally for scholarship funds; some support for museums and other cultural programs and health services, including hospitals and medical education.
Types of support: Scholarship funds, capital campaigns, continuing support.
Limitations: Giving limited to Coconino County, AZ.
Publications: Program policy statement.
Application information:
Initial approach: Proposal not exceeding 2 pages
Copies of proposal: 9
Deadline(s): Mar. 1
Board meeting date(s): As required
Write: Henry L. Giclas, Pres.
Officers: Henry L. Giclas,* Pres.; Eldon Bills,* Exec. V.P.; Robert E. Gaylord, Secy.; John Stilley,* Treas.
Directors:* Catherine Adel, Valeen T. Avery, Platt C. Cline, Wilfred Killip, Joyce Leamon, Ralph Wheeler.
Number of staff: None.
Employer Identification Number: 866050920

94

Research Corporation ▼

6840 East Broadway Blvd.
Tucson 85710-2815 (602) 296-6771

Incorporated in 1912 in NY.
Donor(s): Frederick Gardner Cottrell,† and others.
Foundation type: Independent
Financial data (yr. ended 12/31/89): Assets, $82,658,029 (M); gifts received, $394,500; expenditures, $4,838,134, including $3,491,812 for 356 grants (high: $55,000; low: $5,500).
Purpose and activities: To advance academic science and technology. The Grants Program, which comprehends the Cottrell College Science Program, Research Opportunity Awards, the Partners In Science Program, and General Foundation Grants, is open to U.S. colleges and universities and supports basic research in the physical sciences (physics, chemistry, and astronomy). The foundation furthers the transfer of useful inventions from universities and other nonprofit research institutions to industry through Research

Corporation Technologies, Inc., an allied, not-for-profit corporation.
Types of support: Research.
Limitations: No grants to individuals directly, or for building or endowment funds, indirect costs, common supplies and services, tuitions, research leave to start new projects, faculty academic year salaries, postdoctoral or graduate student stipends, secretarial assistance, general support, scholarships, fellowships, publications, travel expenses to scientific meetings or to research facilities, or matching gifts; no loans.
Publications: Annual report, application guidelines, newsletter, occasional report.
Application information: The foundation no longer reviews research proposals in biology. Application form required.
Initial approach: Request application
Copies of proposal: 10
Deadline(s): General grants and Cottrell College Science Program, none, target dates May 15 and Nov. 15. Research Opportunity Awards nominations, May 1; Partners In Science, Dec. 1 and Feb. 1
Board meeting date(s): Oct. and Mar.-Apr.
Final notification: 10 months
Write: John P. Schaefer, Pres., or Brian H. Andreen, Grants Coord.
Officers: John P. Schaefer,* Pres.; Helen Day, Secy.; Colin B. Mackay,* Treas.
Directors:* Stuart B. Crampton, Burt N. Dorsett, Michael P. Doyle, John W. Johnstone, Jr., Margaret L.A. MacVicar, Joan Selverstone Valentine, G. King Walters.
Number of staff: 3 full-time professional; 3 part-time professional; 3 full-time support.
Employer Identification Number: 131963407

95
La Nelle Robson Foundation ⌑ ☆
25612 E. J. Robson Blvd.
Sun Lakes 85248 (602) 895-9600

Established in 1987 in AZ.
Foundation type: Independent
Financial data (yr. ended 1/31/89): Assets, $1,986,474 (M); gifts received, $12,300; expenditures, $170,157, including $145,400 for 15 grants (high: $100,000; low: $500).
Purpose and activities: Support for higher education and health.
Limitations: Giving primarily in AZ.
Application information: Application form not required.
Initial approach: Proposal
Deadline(s): None
Write: Steven S. Robson, V.P.
Officers and Directors:* Edward J. Robson,* Pres.; Steven S. Robson,* V.P. and Treas.; Kimberly A. Robson,* V.P.; Mark E. Robson,* V.P.; Robert D. Robson,* V.P.; Lynda Robson Estes,* Secy.; Edward N. Basha, Jr., Roger C. Mitten.
Employer Identification Number: 742461052

96
Security Pacific Bank Arizona Foundation
(Formerly Arizona Bank Charitable Foundation)
101 North First Ave.
Phoenix 85003 (602) 262-4217

Established in 1977.
Donor(s): Security Pacific Bank Arizona.
Foundation type: Company-sponsored
Financial data (yr. ended 12/31/89): Assets, $90,473 (M); expenditures, $697,214, including $695,869 for 239 grants (high: $195,339; low: $25) and $1,345 for 4 employee matching gifts.
Purpose and activities: Emphasis on social services, mainly through the United Way; capital fund drives for hospitals and other medical facilities; early childhood, elementary, and higher education, including scholarship programs for qualified and needy students; cultural programs, especially the fine and performing arts; and civic organizations, especially those concerned with the environment, civic planning, law and order, improving government, and preserving the free enterprise system.
Types of support: Employee matching gifts, continuing support.
Limitations: Giving primarily in AZ. No support for religious denominations and church affiliate schools, fraternal organizations whose programs mainly benefit their own members, or organizations eligible for the United Way, but who refuse membership. No grants to individuals.
Publications: Annual report.
Application information: Application form not required.
Initial approach: Letter
Copies of proposal: 1
Deadline(s): 14 days prior to meeting
Board meeting date(s): Quarterly
Write: Kathi A. Haas, Chair.
Officers and Trustees:* Kathi Haas,* Chair.; Ron Hernandez,* Secy.-Treas.; Robert L. Matthews, James E. Neihart, William S. Thomas, Jr.
Number of staff: None.
Employer Identification Number: 860337807

97
Solheim Foundation
501 West Wakonda Ln.
Phoenix 85023

Established in 1985 in AZ.
Donor(s): Karsten Solheim, Louise C. Solheim.
Foundation type: Independent
Financial data (yr. ended 06/30/89): Assets, $3,423,230 (M); gifts received, $3,000,000; expenditures, $256,075, including $225,000 for 4 grants (high: $100,000; low: $20,000; average: $20,000-$100,000).
Purpose and activities: Giving primarily for Christian education, missions, and other related activities.
Limitations: No grants to individuals.
Application information: Contributes only to pre-selected organizations. Applications not accepted.
Write: Louise C. Solheim, Trustee
Trustees: Allan D. Solheim, John A. Solheim, K. Louis Solheim, Karsten Solheim, Louise C. Solheim.
Number of staff: None.
Employer Identification Number: 742378207

98
Steele Foundation, Inc.
702 East Osborn Rd.
Phoenix 85014-5215

Established in 1980 in AZ.
Donor(s): Horace Steele,† Ethel Steele.
Foundation type: Independent
Financial data (yr. ended 12/31/88): Assets, $17,540,104 (M); gifts received, $475,130; expenditures, $1,067,934, including $838,700 for 28 grants (high: $275,000; low: $200).
Purpose and activities: Support for social and health service organizations, education, and religious welfare.
Types of support: Building funds, general purposes.
Limitations: Giving primarily in Phoenix, AZ.
Application information:
Initial approach: Letter
Officers: Daniel Cracchiolo, Pres.; Joseph F. Anselmo, Secy.; Burt Caldwell, Treas.
Number of staff: 1 full-time support.
Employer Identification Number: 953466880

99
The Tell Foundation ⌑
4020 North 38th Ave.
Phoenix 85019

Incorporated in 1952 in AZ.
Donor(s): Andrew P. Tell,† Mary J. Tell.
Foundation type: Independent
Financial data (yr. ended 6/30/87): Assets, $1,851,674 (M); gifts received, $48,684; expenditures, $126,102, including $81,514 for 67 grants (high: $14,000; low: $25; average: $350).
Purpose and activities: To support Protestant churches and church-related institutions including theological education.
Limitations: Giving primarily in AZ. No grants to individuals.
Application information: Applications not accepted.
Write: Ron L. Lewis, Admin.
Officers and Trustees:* Mary J. Tell,* Pres.; Marilyn P. Hamman,* V.P. and Treas.; Elizabeth P. Hirshberg,* Secy.; Ron L. Lewis,* Admin.
Employer Identification Number: 866050214

100
Tucson Community Foundation
6601 East Grant Rd., Suite 111
Tucson 85715-3847 (602) 722-1707

Established in 1980 in AZ.
Foundation type: Community
Financial data (yr. ended 07/31/89): Assets, $5,650,002 (M); gifts received, $864,059; expenditures, $932,749, including $670,599 for 300 grants (high: $10,000; low: $250) and $50,000 for 30 grants to individuals (high: $25,000; low: $500).
Purpose and activities: Giving primarily for arts and culture, social services, youth, education, health, and the environment.
Types of support: General purposes, equipment, renovation projects, student aid, conferences and seminars, matching funds, seed money, special projects, technical assistance.

Limitations: Giving primarily in the Tucson, AZ, metropolitan area. No support for sectarian organizations. No grants to individuals (except scholarships and art fellowships).
Publications: Annual report, application guidelines, financial statement, informational brochure.
Application information: Application form required.
Initial approach: Telephone call to obtain application guidelines
Copies of proposal: 20
Deadline(s): Feb. and Aug.
Board meeting date(s): Monthly
Write: Donna L. Grant, Exec. Dir.
Officers and Trustees:* Sidney B. Brinckerhoff,* Pres.; John Even,* V.P.; Nancy Kinerk,* Secy.; Jerry Shull,* Treas.; and 24 other trustees.
Staff: Donna L. Grant, Exec. Dir.
Number of staff: 1 full-time professional; 1 part-time professional; 1 full-time support; 2 part-time support.
Employer Identification Number: 942844781

101
Valley Bank Charitable Foundation, Inc. ▼
P.O. Box 71, B633
Phoenix 85001 (602) 221-4613

Incorporated in 1978 in AZ.
Donor(s): Valley National Bank of Arizona.
Foundation type: Company-sponsored
Financial data (yr. ended 12/31/87): Assets, $2,233,646 (M); expenditures, $1,493,613, including $1,483,151 for 162 grants (high: $285,937; low: $200; average: $1,000-$10,000).
Purpose and activities: Emphasis on community funds, cultural programs, including museums and the performing arts, higher education, social services, youth agencies, and hospitals.
Types of support: Annual campaigns, capital campaigns, operating budgets, seed money, continuing support.
Limitations: Giving limited to AZ. No support for religious organizations. No grants to individuals, or for research.
Publications: Informational brochure (including application guidelines).
Application information: Application form required.
Initial approach: Letter
Copies of proposal: 1
Deadline(s): None
Board meeting date(s): Quarterly
Final notification: Following board meetings
Write: Neil H. Christensen, Secy.-Treas.
Officers and Directors:* Robert Whalstrom,* Pres.; James P. Simmons,* V.P.; Neil H. Christensen,* Secy.-Treas.; Richard Lehmann, Harold Mosanko.
Number of staff: 1 full-time professional; 2 full-time support.
Employer Identification Number: 953330232

102
Nellie Kellogg Van Schaick Scholarship Fund
c/o Valley National Bank of Arizona, Trust Dept.
P.O. Box 13779
Tucson 85732 (602) 792-7130

Established in 1975.
Foundation type: Independent
Financial data (yr. ended 05/31/89): Assets, $3,532,145 (M); expenditures, $263,641, including $233,946 for 6 grants (high: $104,246; low: $8,000).
Purpose and activities: Grants limited to undergraduate and graduate scholarship programs in medicine and public health at nonprofit hospitals and universities.
Types of support: Scholarship funds.
Limitations: Giving primarily in the Philippines and other developing East Asian and Western Pacific countries.
Application information: Application form not required.
Initial approach: Proposal
Copies of proposal: 1
Deadline(s): May 1
Write: Mason Borgman
Trustee: Valley National Bank of Arizona.
Employer Identification Number: 866090500

103
The Wallace Foundation
3370 North Hayden Rd., Suite 123-287
Scottsdale 85251 (602) 962-4059

Established in 1977 in AZ.
Foundation type: Operating
Financial data (yr. ended 11/30/89): Assets, $152,936 (L); gifts received, $190,256; expenditures, $203,854, including $184,530 for 28 grants (high: $22,842; low: $3,200).
Purpose and activities: A private operating foundation with emphasis on social welfare services.
Types of support: Seed money, special projects.
Limitations: Giving limited to AZ. No grants for capital or building expenses, annual drives, donations, or scholarships.
Publications: Program policy statement, application guidelines.
Application information: Application form required.
Initial approach: Letter
Copies of proposal: 4
Deadline(s): Mar. 15 and Sept. 15
Final notification: Grants made by June 15 and Dec. 15
Write: Nancy Shaw, Exec. Dir.
Officers: Jane W. Thorne, Pres. and Treas.; Cynthia K. Gillespie, V.P.; Nancy K. Bissel, Secy.; Nancy G. Shaw, Exec. Dir.
Number of staff: 1 full-time professional.
Employer Identification Number: 942400615

104
Del E. Webb Foundation ▼
2023 West Wickenburg Way
P.O. Box 20519
Wickenburg 85358 (602) 684-7223

Incorporated in 1960 in AZ.
Donor(s): Del E. Webb.†
Foundation type: Independent
Financial data (yr. ended 12/31/88): Assets, $38,494,385 (M); expenditures, $2,291,220, including $1,723,057 for 20 grants (high: $500,000; low: $5,000; average: $10,000-$50,000).
Purpose and activities: Giving primarily for medical research and health care.
Limitations: Giving primarily in AZ, NV, and CA. No support for government agencies, sectarian or religious organizations, or pass-through organizations. No grants to individuals, or for deficit financing or indirect costs.
Application information: Application form required.
Initial approach: Letter
Copies of proposal: 4
Deadline(s): Mar. 31 and Oct. 31
Board meeting date(s): May and Dec.
Final notification: Following each meeting
Write: Marjorie Klinefelter, Secy.
Officers: Robert H. Johnson, Pres.; Owen F. Childress, V.P.; Marjorie Klinefelter, Secy.; Del V. Werderman, Treas.
Director: W.D. Milliken.
Number of staff: 1
Employer Identification Number: 866052737

105
Edna Rider Whiteman Foundation
Empire Southwest
P.O. Box 2985
Phoenix 85062 (602) 898-4400
Application address: 1725 South Country Club, Phoenix, AZ 85062

Established in 1961 in AZ.
Donor(s): C.O. Whiteman.†
Foundation type: Independent
Financial data (yr. ended 07/31/89): Assets, $1,850,450 (M); expenditures, $122,436, including $97,016 for 85 grants (high: $12,500; low: $25; average: $1,000-$1,500).
Purpose and activities: Grants for health and social services, arts and culture, youth and education, and civic affairs.
Types of support: Annual campaigns, building funds, capital campaigns, conferences and seminars, continuing support, emergency funds, equipment, general purposes, land acquisition, lectureships, matching funds, operating budgets, publications, renovation projects, research, seed money, special projects, endowment funds.
Limitations: Giving primarily in the Phoenix, AZ, metropolitan area. No support for religious organizations, athletic organizations, fraternal organizations, or organizations that are largely tax-supported. No grants to individuals.
Publications: Informational brochure (including application guidelines).
Application information: Contributes only to pre-selected organizations. Applications not accepted.
Board meeting date(s): 2nd Wed. in Sept., Dec., Mar., and June
Write: Carol DuVal, Exec. Dir.
Officers: Jack W. Whiteman, Pres.; E.R. Strahm, Secy.; John G. Hough, Treas.
Directors: Lynne Denton, Louise Kleinz, Jeffrey Whiteman.
Number of staff: 1 part-time professional.
Employer Identification Number: 866052816

106
Robert T. Wilson Foundation ¤ ☆
Route 4, Box 7378
Flagstaff 86001
Application address: Route 4, Box 712, Flagstaff, AZ 86001; Tel.: (602) 774-5457

Trust established in 1954 in TX; incorporated in 1963.
Donor(s): Richard F. Wilson, Jean H. Wilson, and other family members.
Foundation type: Operating
Financial data (yr. ended 12/31/87): Assets, $753,260 (M); gifts received, $1,382,176; expenditures, $292,136, including $176,364 for grants.
Purpose and activities: A private operating foundation; grants awarded for environmental protection, child welfare, higher education, and international relief.
Types of support: Seed money, emergency funds, special projects, matching funds, scholarship funds.
Limitations: Giving primarily in AZ. No grants to individuals, or for building or endowment funds, or operating budgets; no loans.
Publications: Application guidelines.
Application information: Application form not required.
Initial approach: Letter
Copies of proposal: 1
Deadline(s): Submit proposal preferably in Apr.; deadline May 1
Board meeting date(s): July and as required
Write: Robert W. Koons, Exec. Dir.
Officers and Directors:* Richard F. Wilson,* Pres.; Suzanne Horst,* V.P.; Jean H. Wilson,* Secy.-Treas.; Robert W. Koons,* Exec. Dir.; Winifred W. Hanseth, Soonya Wilson McDavid, Amanda Wilson.
Number of staff: 1 full-time professional; 1 full-time support.
Employer Identification Number: 860264036

ARKANSAS

107
Clarence E. Anthony Charitable Trust ¤
P.O. Box 199
Murfreesboro 71958 (501) 285-3471

Established in 1977 in AR.
Donor(s): Clarence E. Anthony.
Foundation type: Independent
Financial data (yr. ended 12/31/88): Assets, $1,047,829 (M); expenditures, $71,013, including $65,365 for 21 grants (high: $21,000; low: $25).
Purpose and activities: Emphasis on churches, church-supported colleges or universities, church-supported orphanages, and other charities.
Limitations: Giving primarily in Murfreesboro, AR; some support in other parts of the state. No grants to individuals.
Application information:
Initial approach: Proposal
Deadline(s): None
Final notification: Notices of rejection not sent
Write: Clarence E. Anthony, Trustee
Trustee: Clarence E. Anthony.
Employer Identification Number: 716102641

108
The John O. Anthony Charitable Trust ¤
P.O. Box A
Murfreesboro 71958 (501) 285-3471

Established in 1977 in AR.
Donor(s): John O. Anthony.
Foundation type: Independent
Financial data (yr. ended 12/31/88): Assets, $1,407,627 (M); expenditures, $76,704, including $71,000 for 4 grants (high: $35,000; low: $1,500).
Purpose and activities: Preference to established and recognized religious organizations, church-supported colleges or universities, and church-supported orphanages; support also for youth.
Limitations: Giving primarily in AR, with emphasis on Murfreesboro.
Application information:
Initial approach: Letter
Deadline(s): None
Trustee: John O. Anthony.
Employer Identification Number: 716102642

109
Arkansas Community Foundation, Inc.
604 East Sixth St.
Little Rock 72202 (501) 372-1116

Established in 1976 in AR.
Foundation type: Community
Financial data (yr. ended 07/31/89): Assets, $6,743,966 (M); gifts received, $1,270,932; expenditures, $1,239,920, including $958,642 for grants.
Purpose and activities: Grants for social services, cultural programs, health, community development, the environment, and scholarships.
Types of support: Scholarship funds, general purposes, research, seed money, special projects, student loans, student aid.
Limitations: Giving primarily in AR.
Publications: Annual report (including application guidelines), financial statement, newsletter, informational brochure, grants list.
Application information: Application form required.
Initial approach: Letter or telephone
Copies of proposal: 7
Deadline(s): Jan. 1, Apr. 1, July 1, Sept. 1, and Oct. 1
Board meeting date(s): Mar., June, Sept., and Dec.
Write: Martha Ann Jones, Exec. Dir., Bonnie Nickol, Prog. Dir., or Becky Bien, Admin.
Officers and Trustees:* Don Munro,* Pres.; William Dunklin,* lst V.P.; William Fisher,* 2nd V.P.; Betty E. Lile,* Secy.; Bronson Van Wyck,* Treas.; Martha Ann Jones,* Exec. Dir.; Diane Alderson, Bum Atkins, Curtis Bradbury, Thedford Collins, Herman Davenport, Michael Gibson, Janelle Hembree, Carter Hunt, Kent Ingram, Malcolm McNair, Julia Peck Mobley, Sloan Rainwater, John Rush, Charles Scharlau, Larry Wallace, Charles West.
Number of staff: 4 full-time professional; 1 full-time support.
Employer Identification Number: 521055743

110
Bodenhamer Foundation ¤
P.O. Box 7588
Little Rock 72217-7588

Donor(s): Lee Bodenhamer.
Foundation type: Independent
Financial data (yr. ended 11/30/89): Assets, $1,860,145 (M); gifts received, $138,080; expenditures, $88,560, including $85,200 for 17 grants (high: $15,500; low: $200).
Purpose and activities: Support for education, with emphasis on higher education.
Limitations: Giving primarily in AR, KY, and MI.
Application information: Contributes only to pre-selected organizations. Applications not accepted.
Trustee: Lee Bodenhamer.
Employer Identification Number: 752070352

111
Jesse W. Cannon Scholarship Foundation ¤ ☆
c/o First National Bank
P.O. Box 1287
Fayetteville 72702-1287
Application address: 112 South East Ave., Fayetteville, AR 72701; Tel.: (501) 443-4313

Foundation type: Independent
Financial data (yr. ended 7/31/89): Assets, $1,308,180 (M); qualifying distributions, $115,338, including $1,000 for 1 grant and $114,132 for loans to individuals.
Purpose and activities: Awards low-interest educational loans to students attending the University of Arkansas; minor support also for higher education institutions.
Types of support: Student loans.
Limitations: Giving limited to AR.
Application information: Application form required.
Deadline(s): None
Write: Lewis Jones, Trustee
Directors: Lewis D. Jones, Mark Lungaro, Curtis Shipley.
Employer Identification Number: 716099820

112
Elizabeth H. & Stanley E. Evans Foundation ¤
1402 Hendricks Blvd.
Fort Smith 72901

Established in 1965 in AR.
Foundation type: Independent
Financial data (yr. ended 12/31/88): Assets, $1,281,995 (M); expenditures, $114,960, including $103,200 for 20 grants (high: $25,000; low: $200).

Purpose and activities: Giving primarily for hospitals and health services, social service and youth agencies, and higher education.
Limitations: Giving primarily in AR. No grants to individuals.
Application information:
Initial approach: Letter
Deadline(s): None
Trustees: Jim Alexander, King Basham, Jr., Ray Kraus, Bruce Shaw.
Employer Identification Number: 716058375

113
William Thomas & May Pitman Hennessy Foundation ⌑
c/o First National Bank
P.O. Box 7, 602 Garrison
Fort Smith 72902

Established in 1962 in AR.
Foundation type: Independent
Financial data (yr. ended 12/31/88): Assets, $135,677 (M); gifts received, $231,667; expenditures, $120,037, including $119,600 for 20 grants (high: $35,700; low: $500).
Purpose and activities: Giving primarily to hospitals; support also for youth and social services, including shelters.
Limitations: Giving primarily in AR.
Trustee: First National Bank.
Employer Identification Number: 716058272

114
Frank D. Hickingbotham Foundation ⌑
425 West Capitol, Suite 1100
Little Rock 72201

Established in 1984 in AR.
Donor(s): Frank D. Hickingbotham.
Foundation type: Independent
Financial data (yr. ended 11/30/89): Assets, $2,428,200 (M); expenditures, $321,939, including $308,500 for 10 grants (high: $206,000; low: $500).
Purpose and activities: Support for a university, a cancer research center, and various religious groups.
Limitations: No grants to individuals.
Application information:
Initial approach: Proposal
Deadline(s): None
Write: Frank D. Hickingbotham, Trustee
Trustee: Frank D. Hickingbotham.
Employer Identification Number: 716124938

115
The Inglewood Foundation ⌑
P.O. Box 906
Little Rock 72203 (501) 376-0766

Incorporated in 1961 in AR.
Donor(s): Christoph Keller, Jr., Caroline M. Keller, Christoph Keller III, Cynthia K. Davis, Caroline K. Theus, Kathryn K. Timmons, James F. Stutts, and others.
Foundation type: Independent
Financial data (yr. ended 1/31/88): Assets, $1,631,778 (M); gifts received, $209,146; expenditures, $377,395, including $345,953 for 29 grants (high: $105,000; low: $300).
Purpose and activities: Grants largely for projects which tend to build community; not a political entity or geographic area but relationships between diverse groups of people, including support for intercultural relations, public education, and social services.
Types of support: Seed money, emergency funds, matching funds, special projects.
Limitations: No grants to individuals, or for annual campaigns, deficit financing, capital or endowment funds, scholarships, fellowships, or continuing support; no loans.
Publications: Program policy statement, application guidelines.
Application information: Proposals should not exceed 1 page. Application form not required.
Initial approach: Letter
Copies of proposal: 1
Deadline(s): Usually Mar. 15 and Sept. 15
Board meeting date(s): Usually May and Oct.
Final notification: Varies
Write: B. Frank Mackey, Jr., Secy.
Officers and Directors:* Elisabeth K. Bonsey,* Chair.; Cornelia K. Biddle,* Pres.; Cynthia K. Davis,* V.P.; B. Frank Mackey, Jr.,* Secy.; Caroline M. Keller,* Treas.; Craig Biddle, Steven Keller Bonsey, Corwith Davis, Jr., Christoph Keller, Jr., Christoph Keller III, Julie H. Keller, Caroline G. Theus, James G. Theus, Kathryn K. Timmons, R. Randall Timmons.
Number of staff: 1 part-time professional.
Employer Identification Number: 716050419

116
The Harvey and Bernice Jones Foundation ▼
P.O. Box 233
Springdale 72765 (501) 756-0611

Trust established in 1956 in AR.
Donor(s): Harvey Jones, Mrs. Harvey Jones, and their related companies.
Foundation type: Independent
Financial data (yr. ended 11/30/88): Assets, $7,981,722 (M); gifts received, $2,500,000; expenditures, $2,353,796, including $2,300,865 for 62 grants (high: $1,000,000; low: $30; average: $500-$50,000) and $30,080 for 42 grants to individuals.
Purpose and activities: Giving primarily for Protestant church support, hospitals, and education; scholarships restricted to students in the fields of health care and religion.
Types of support: Student aid.
Limitations: Giving primarily in Springdale, AZ.
Application information: Application form required.
Initial approach: Letter
Deadline(s): None
Board meeting date(s): Nov. 30
Write: Mary Sellars, Dir.
Directors: Bernice Jones, Co-Chair.; Harvey Jones, Co-Chair.; H.G. Frost, Jr., Mary Sellers.
Number of staff: 3
Employer Identification Number: 716057141

117
Lyon Foundation, Inc. ⌑
65th and Scott Hamilton Dr.
Little Rock 72204
Mailing address: P.O. Box 4408, Little Rock, AR 72214

Incorporated in 1946 in AR.
Donor(s): Frank Lyon Co., Inc., members of the Lyon family, and others.
Foundation type: Independent
Financial data (yr. ended 12/31/88): Assets, $1,382,002 (M); gifts received, $192,039; expenditures, $428,605, including $390,979 for grants and $35,729 for grants to individuals.
Purpose and activities: Emphasis on higher education, welfare agencies, and Protestant churches and church-related organizations; some assistance for students and individuals in need.
Types of support: Student aid, grants to individuals.
Limitations: Giving primarily in AR.
Application information:
Initial approach: Letter or proposal
Deadline(s): None
Write: Ralph Cotham, Secy.
Officers and Directors:* Frank Lyon,* Pres.; Marion Lyon,* V.P.; Ralph Cotham,* Secy.-Treas.
Employer Identification Number: 716052168

118
Vera & Walter Morris Foundation, Inc. ⌑ ☆
700 East Ninth St., Apt. 13B
Little Rock 72202-3978

Established in 1983.
Donor(s): Walter Morris.
Foundation type: Independent
Financial data (yr. ended 12/31/88): Assets, $1,094,778 (M); gifts received, $40,000; expenditures, $42,867, including $39,331 for 19 grants (high: $6,000; low: $100).
Purpose and activities: Giving for youth organizations, medical research, and social services.
Limitations: No grants to individuals.
Application information: Contributes only to pre-selected organizations. Applications not accepted.
Directors: Jerry Bedford, Edgar Garcia-Rill, Dorothy Morris, Walter S. Morris, Josey Smeaker.
Employer Identification Number: 710597938

119
The Murphy Foundation
200 Jefferson
El Dorado 71730 (501) 862-6411

Incorporated in 1958 in AR.
Donor(s): Members of the Murphy family.
Foundation type: Independent
Financial data (yr. ended 04/30/90): Assets, $9,134,000 (M); expenditures, $580,700, including $566,000 for 25 grants (high: $100,700; low: $200; average: $200-$100,700) and $14,700 for 10 grants to individuals (high: $2,000; low: $1,000; average: $500-$2,000).
Purpose and activities: Emphasis on higher education, including scholarships; grants also for welfare agencies and the arts.
Types of support: Student aid, operating budgets, grants to individuals, annual campaigns, endowment funds, special projects.
Limitations: Giving primarily in AR and LA; scholarships restricted to students from the south AR area.
Application information: Application form required for educational grants to individuals.

Initial approach: Letter
Copies of proposal: 1
Deadline(s): Aug. 1 for educational grants
Board meeting date(s): Semiannually
Write: Lucy A. Ring, Secy.-Treas.
Officers and Directors:* Johnie W. Murphy,* Pres.; Bertie Murphy Deming,* V.P.; Lucy A. Ring,* Secy.-Treas.; John W. Deming, C.H. Murphy, Jr.
Number of staff: None.
Employer Identification Number: 716049826

120
Murphy Foundation of Louisiana ⌑
200 North Jefferson, Suite 400
El Dorado 71730
Application address: 200 Peach St., El Dorado, AR 71730; Tel.: (501) 862-6411

Established in 1958 in LA.
Donor(s): Bertie Murphy Deming, John W. Deming, C.H. Murphy, Jr.
Foundation type: Independent
Financial data (yr. ended 4/30/89): Assets, $1,525,888 (M); expenditures, $66,221, including $64,000 for 7 grants (high: $15,000; low: $1,000).
Purpose and activities: Grants primarily for higher education, culture, social services, and a Presbyterian church.
Limitations: Giving primarily in LA and AR.
Application information:
Initial approach: Letter
Deadline(s): None
Write: Lucy A. Ring, Secy.-Treas.
Officers: Johnie W. Murphy,* Pres.; Bertie Murphy Deming,* V.P.; Lucy A. Ring, Secy.-Treas.
Directors:* John W. Deming, C.H. Murphy, Jr.
Employer Identification Number: 726018262

121
William C. & Theodosia Murphy Nolan Foundation ⌑
200 North Jefferson, Suite 308
El Dorado 71730 (501) 863-7118

Established in 1962 in AR.
Donor(s): Theodosia Murphy Nolan, William C. Nolan.
Foundation type: Independent
Financial data (yr. ended 2/28/88): Assets, $1,169,193 (M); gifts received, $25,000; expenditures, $56,312, including $55,250 for 17 grants (high: $26,000; low: $100).
Purpose and activities: Grants primarily for education, medical research, culture, and historic preservation.
Types of support: Building funds, operating budgets, general purposes, research, scholarship funds.
Application information:
Initial approach: Letter
Deadline(s): None
Write: William C. Nolan, V.P.
Officers: Theodosia Murphy Nolan, Pres.; William C. Nolan, V.P.; William C. Nolan, Jr., Secy.-Treas.
Director: Robert C. Nolan.
Employer Identification Number: 716049791

122
Overstreet Short Mountain Foundation ⌑
1500 South Albert Pike, Unit 29
Fort Smith 72903-3053

Established in 1982 in AR.
Foundation type: Operating
Financial data (yr. ended 5/31/88): Assets, $595,693 (M); expenditures, $243,844, including $229,984 for 4 grants (high: $199,789; low: $205).
Purpose and activities: Support primarily for an agricultural museum; support also for a Presbyterian church.
Application information: Contributes only to pre-selected organizations. Applications not accepted.
Officers: Maudress E. Overstreet, Chair.; Carl E. Hefner, Vice-Chair.; R.C. Taylor, Secy.
Employer Identification Number: 710564702

123
Rebsamen Fund ⌑
P.O. Box 3198
Little Rock 72203

Incorporated in 1944 in AR.
Donor(s): Rebsamen Companies, Inc.
Foundation type: Company-sponsored
Financial data (yr. ended 11/30/88): Assets, $1,118,354 (M); gifts received, $105,930; expenditures, $131,359, including $126,130 for 86 grants (high: $28,000; low: $50).
Purpose and activities: Emphasis on higher education, community funds, health services, civic affairs and recreation, cultural programs, and religion.
Limitations: Giving primarily in AR.
Application information: Application form not required.
Deadline(s): None
Officers and Directors:* Kenneth Pat Wilson,* Pres.; H. Maurice Mitchell,* V.P.; Sam C. Sowell,* V.P.; Patricia Lavender,* Secy.-Treas.
Employer Identification Number: 716053911

124
The Donald W. Reynolds Foundation, Inc. ⌑
920 Rogers Ave.
Fort Smith 72901
Application address: P.O. Box 1359, Fort Smith, AR 72902; Tel.: (501) 785-7810

Incorporated in 1954 in NV.
Donor(s): Donald W. Reynolds, Southwestern Publishing Co., Southwestern Operating Co., and others.
Foundation type: Independent
Financial data (yr. ended 6/30/88): Assets, $12,661,693 (M); gifts received, $6,000,000; expenditures, $399,874, including $226,112 for 88 grants (high: $20,000; low: $100).
Purpose and activities: Grants largely for higher education, community funds, cultural programs, health, social service and youth agencies, civic affairs and community development.
Types of support: Matching funds, scholarship funds.
Limitations: Giving primarily in areas served by Donney Media Group in AR, CA, CO, HI, MO, NM, NV, OK, TX, and WA.
Publications: Application guidelines.
Application information: Application form not required.
Initial approach: Proposal
Deadline(s): June 15, Sept. 15, Dec. 15, and Mar. 15
Board meeting date(s): Quarterly
Officers and Directors:* Donald W. Reynolds,* Pres.; Fred W. Smith,* Exec. V.P.; E.H. Patterson,* Treas.; Don R. Buris, Bob G. Bush, Robert S. Howard, George O. Kleier, Ross Pendergraft, Don E. Pray.
Employer Identification Number: 716053383

125
Riggs Benevolent Fund
c/o Worthen Bank and Trust Co., N.A., Trust Dept.
P.O. Box 1681
Little Rock 72203-1681 (501) 378-1248

Trust established in 1959 in AR.
Donor(s): Members of the Riggs family, Robert G. Cress, J.A. Riggs Tractor Co., Inc.
Foundation type: Independent
Financial data (yr. ended 12/31/88): Assets, $3,132,115 (M); gifts received, $109,275; expenditures, $229,985, including $205,500 for 48 grants (high: $44,200; low: $300).
Purpose and activities: Emphasis on higher education and Protestant church support and church-related organizations; support also for youth agencies, hospitals, and community funds.
Limitations: Giving primarily in AR.
Application information: Unsolicited applications rarely produce a response.
Initial approach: Proposal
Deadline(s): None
Write: Anne Roark
Trustees: Robert G. Cress, John A. Riggs III, Worthen Bank and Trust Co., N.A.
Number of staff: None.
Employer Identification Number: 716050130

126
The Winthrop Rockefeller Foundation ▼
308 East Eighth St.
Little Rock 72202 (501) 376-6854

Incorporated in 1956 in AR as Rockwin Fund, Inc.; renamed in 1974.
Donor(s): Winthrop Rockefeller.†
Foundation type: Independent
Financial data (yr. ended 12/31/88): Assets, $41,227,377 (M); gifts received, $690,000; expenditures, $4,188,292, including $3,044,494 for 389 grants (high: $1,000,000; low: $70; average: $10,000-$40,000) and $273,703 for loans.
Purpose and activities: Emphasis on economic development and education; support for local projects which (a) improve the delivery of services or administrative capacity of institutions; (b) increase the participation of people in the decision-making process; or (c) achieve more productive development and use of human, physical, and fiscal resources. The foundation will fund innovative demonstration projects which improve people's living

standards and the institutions which serve the community; projects which have economic development potential; and community-based projects concerned with organizational planning and fundraising.
Types of support: Special projects, seed money, conferences and seminars, matching funds, technical assistance, consulting services, program-related investments, publications.
Limitations: Giving primarily in AR, or projects that benefit AR. No grants to individuals, or for capital expenditures, endowments, building funds, equipment, annual fund drives, deficit financing, general support, emergency funds, most types of research, trips by community organizations, scholarships, or fellowships.
Publications: Annual report (including application guidelines), occasional report.
Application information: Application form required.
Initial approach: Telephone or letter
Copies of proposal: 2
Deadline(s): Submit proposal preferably by June 1 or Dec. 1
Board meeting date(s): On the 1st weekend in Mar., June, Sept., and Dec.; new projects considered only in Mar. or Sept.
Final notification: 2 weeks after board meeting dates
Write: Mahlon Martin, Pres.
Officers: Mahlon Martin, Pres.; Teresa Hudson, Controller.
Directors: John L. Ward, Chair.; Leslie Lilly, Vice-Chair.; James D. Bernstein, Willard B. Gatewood, Joe Hatcher, Cora D. McHenry, Olly Neal, Robert D. Pugh, Andree Layton Roaf, Winthrop Paul Rockefeller, Thomas B. Shropshire, Martin D. Strange, Kathryn J. Waller.
Number of staff: 5 full-time professional; 2 full-time support; 1 part-time support.
Employer Identification Number: 710285871

127
Winthrop Rockefeller Trust ▼ ⌑
2230 Cottondale Ln., Suite 6
Little Rock 72202 (501) 661-9294

Etablished in 1973 in AR.
Donor(s): Winthrop Rockefeller.†
Foundation type: Independent
Financial data (yr. ended 6/30/88): Assets, $84,359,098 (M); gifts received, $107,170; expenditures, $9,390,391, including $7,837,459 for 19 grants (high: $3,657,000; low: $2,152).
Purpose and activities: Support primarily for an agricultural development institute and an historic preservation foundation.
Types of support: General purposes.
Limitations: No grants to individuals.
Application information: Application form not required.
Deadline(s): None
Write: Marion Burton, Trustee
Trustees: Marion Burton, J. Richardson Dilworth, Donal C. O'Brien, Jr., Winthrop Paul Rockefeller, Robert Schults.
Employer Identification Number: 716082655

128
The Ross Foundation
1039 Henderson St.
Arkadelphia 71923 (501) 246-9881
Application address: P.O. Box 335, Arkadelphia, AR 71923

Established in 1966 in AR.
Donor(s): Esther C. Ross,† Jane Ross.
Foundation type: Independent
Financial data (yr. ended 12/31/89): Assets, $18,276,500 (M); expenditures, $743,792, including $321,046 for 40 grants (high: $100,000; low: $100; average: $1,000-$10,000).
Purpose and activities: Support for higher and public education, youth agencies, mental retardation, conservation of natural resources, and community improvement programs.
Types of support: Seed money, emergency funds, building funds, equipment, endowment funds, matching funds, research, publications, general purposes, special projects, consulting services.
Limitations: Giving limited to Arkadelphia and Clark County, AR. No grants to individuals, or for scholarships or fellowships; no loans.
Publications: Informational brochure (including application guidelines), application guidelines.
Application information: Application form required.
Initial approach: Letter or telephone
Copies of proposal: 4
Deadline(s): Dec. 1
Board meeting date(s): Apr., Aug., and Nov.
Final notification: 30 days
Write: Ross M. Whipple, Pres.
Officers and Trustees:* Jane Ross,* Chair.; Ross M. Whipple,* Pres.; Robert Rhodes,* Secy.; Peggy Clark, Toney D. McMillan.
Number of staff: 3 full-time professional; 1 part-time professional; 1 full-time support; 2 part-time support.
Employer Identification Number: 716060574

129
Harold S. Seabrook Charitable Trust ⌑
c/o National Bank of Commerce, Trust Dept.
P.O. Box 6208
Pine Bluff 71601

Established around 1983 in AR.
Donor(s): Dorothy S. Bennet.
Foundation type: Independent
Financial data (yr. ended 10/31/88): Assets, $1,578,437 (M); expenditures, $107,489, including $89,495 for 25 grants (high: $12,000; low: $1,000).
Purpose and activities: Giving primarily for youth and child welfare, recreation, social services, and higher education.
Types of support: Operating budgets.
Limitations: Giving limited to AR, with emphasis on Pine Bluff.
Application information:
Initial approach: Letter
Deadline(s): Preferably by Oct. 1
Write: Richard Metcalf
Trustees: David S. Fox, Sr., Jack McNulty, Sam Thompson, National Bank of Commerce.
Employer Identification Number: 716119636

130
The Roy and Christine Sturgis Charitable and Educational Trust ⌑
P.O. Box 92
Malvern 72104 (501) 332-3899

Trust established about 1979.
Donor(s): Roy Sturgis,† Christine Sturgis.
Foundation type: Independent
Financial data (yr. ended 12/31/88): Assets, $12,038,034 (M); expenditures, $632,645, including $513,528 for 20 grants (high: $302,500; low: $2,830).
Purpose and activities: Giving for hospitals, youth and social service agencies, education, and church support.
Limitations: Giving primarily in AR. No grants to individuals.
Application information: Application form not required.
Initial approach: Letter
Deadline(s): None
Write: Katie Speer or Barry Findley, Trustees
Trustees: Barry Findley, Katie Speer.
Employer Identification Number: 710495345

131
W. P. Sturgis Foundation ⌑
P.O. Box 394
Arkadelphia 71923-0394 (501) 246-6514

Established in 1958 in AR.
Foundation type: Independent
Financial data (yr. ended 12/31/88): Assets, $1,036,414 (M); expenditures, $116,043, including $42,532 for 3 grants (high: $19,966; low: $2,600) and $64,226 for grants to individuals.
Purpose and activities: Giving primarily for scholarships for higher education; support also for hospitals and child welfare programs.
Types of support: Student aid.
Limitations: Giving primarily in AR.
Application information: Completion of application form required for scholarships.
Initial approach: Letter
Deadline(s): None
Write: June Anthony, Secy.-Treas.
Officers and Directors:* Curtis E. Echols,* Pres.; J. Hugh Lookadoo,* V.P.; June Anthony,* Secy.-Treas.; Harold Echols, Mark Jansen, Larry Whitley.
Trustee: Commercial National Bank.
Employer Identification Number: 716057063

132
Godfrey Thomas Foundation, Inc. ⌑
117 North Adams
DeWitt 72042-2032 (501) 946-3567

Established in 1967 in AR.
Donor(s): Godfrey Thomas.†
Foundation type: Independent
Financial data (yr. ended 12/31/88): Assets, $1,080,681 (M); gifts received, $1,748; expenditures, $90,555, including $5,700 for 5 grants (high: $1,500; low: $200) and $42,755 for 74 grants to individuals.
Purpose and activities: Primarily awards scholarships to individuals for higher education; support also for public education, museums, and community funds.
Types of support: Student aid.
Limitations: Giving primarily in AR.

Application information: Application form required.
Initial approach: Letter or telephone
Deadline(s): July 1 and Dec. 1 for scholarships
Write: Wilbur Botts, Trustee
Trustees: Wilbur Botts, Mary B. Carr, Harry C. Erwin, Harry C. Erwin III, Mildred H. Thomas.
Employer Identification Number: 716065971

133
Alvin S. Tilles Item XX Testamentary Trust ¤
P.O. Box 1392
Fort Smith 72902

Established in 1980 in AR.
Foundation type: Independent
Financial data (yr. ended 12/31/88): Assets, $1,245,120 (M); expenditures, $68,054, including $56,758 for 8 grants (high: $14,189; low: $2,888).
Purpose and activities: Grants for hospitals, Jewish welfare, social services, and education.
Trustees: Bernard Stein, Jeanette G. Stein, Jennings J. Stein.
Employer Identification Number: 716109531

134
Trinity Foundation
P.O. Box 7008
Pine Bluff 71611 (501) 534-7120

Incorporated about 1952 in AR.
Donor(s): Pine Bluff Sand & Gravel Co., McGeorge Contracting Co., Cornerstone Farm & Gin Co., Standard Investment Co., Harvey W. McGeorge.†
Foundation type: Independent
Financial data (yr. ended 09/30/88): Assets, $8,722,589 (M); expenditures, $409,281, including $346,000 for 27 grants (high: $150,000; low: $1,000) and $30,293 for 68 grants to individuals (high: $7,000; low: $250).
Purpose and activities: Emphasis on higher education, including scholarships.
Types of support: Student aid.
Limitations: Giving primarily in AR.
Application information: Scholarship application information available only at guidance offices of public high schools in Pine Bluff, Little Rock, Benton, and Bauxite, AR.
Deadline(s): Apr. 10 of senior year in high school for scholarships
Write: W.K. Atkinson, Secy.
Officers: H. Tyndall Dickinson, Pres.; Haskell L. Dickinson, V.P.; Wallace P. McGeorge, Jr., V.P.; W. Scott McGeorge, V.P.; W.K. Atkinson, Secy.-Treas.
Employer Identification Number: 716050288

135
Tyson Foundation, Inc. ¤
P.O. Drawer E
Springdale 72764 (501) 756-4513

Established in 1970 in AR.
Donor(s): Tyson Foods.
Foundation type: Company-sponsored
Financial data (yr. ended 12/31/88): Assets, $6,850,156 (M); gifts received, $190,500; expenditures, $347,768, including $236,200 for 36 grants (high: $125,000; low: $100) and $96,230 for grants to individuals.
Purpose and activities: Grants for community projects, education, social services, and culture; scholarships also available to individuals.
Types of support: Student aid.
Limitations: Giving limited to the mid-South area.
Application information: Application form required.
Deadline(s): None
Write: Oleta Selman
Trustees: James B. Blair, Harry C. Erwin, Joe F. Starr, Cheryl L. Tyson, John H. Tyson.
Employer Identification Number: 237087948

136
Wal-Mart Foundation ▼ ¤
708 S.W. Eighth St.
Bentonville 72716-0671

Established in 1979 in AR.
Donor(s): Wal-Mart Stores, Inc.
Foundation type: Company-sponsored
Financial data (yr. ended 1/31/88): Assets, $6,065,791 (M); gifts received, $2,537,755; expenditures, $4,445,579, including $4,428,568 for 2,742 grants (high: $500,953; low: $19; average: $350-$3,000) and $4,510 for 10 grants to individuals.
Purpose and activities: Giving for health and welfare, higher education, community funds, and youth. Foundation administers two scholarship programs: (1) to high school seniors graduating from schools in towns that patronize a Wal-Mart store, and (2) to associates of Wal-Mart or their children.
Types of support: Student aid.
Limitations: Giving primarily in areas of company operations.
Application information: Application forms for community scholarships available at high schools, and from local store managers for associate scholarships.
Deadline(s): Mar. 1 for associate scholarship program, Mar. 20 for community scholarship program
Trustees: David Glass, Don Soderquist, Sam R. Walton.
Employer Identification Number: 716107283

137
Walton Foundation ¤
125 West Central, No. 210
Bentonville 72712 (501) 273-5743
Scholarship application address: Walton Scholarship Program, c/o Wal-Mart Stores, Inc., Bentonville, AR 72716

Established in 1974 in AR.
Foundation type: Company-sponsored
Financial data (yr. ended 1/31/89): Assets, $4,928 (M); gifts received, $1,404; expenditures, $613,217, including $449,345 for grants (high: $153,245) and $155,643 for 104 grants to individuals (average: $1,500).
Purpose and activities: Grants primarily for a business council, a public library, higher and other education, and social services; also awards scholarships for higher education to children of Wal-Mart Stores' employees.
Types of support: Employee-related scholarships.
Application information: Application form required for scholarships.
Initial approach: Letter
Write: Jan Ney
Trustees: Alice L. Walton, Helen R. Walton, James C. Walton, John T. Walton, Sam R. Walton.
Employer Identification Number: 716091647

138
The Sam M. & Helen R. Walton Foundation ¤
125 West Central, No. 210
Bentonville 72712 (501) 273-5743

Established in 1977 in AR.
Donor(s): Members of the Walton family.
Foundation type: Independent
Financial data (yr. ended 1/31/89): Assets, $750,100 (M); gifts received, $145,831; expenditures, $468,809, including $440,633 for grants (high: $100,000).
Purpose and activities: Grants for health services, education, youth programs, social services, and religious support.
Limitations: Giving primarily in AR.
Application information:
Initial approach: Letter or proposal
Deadline(s): None
Write: Jan Ney
Trustees: Alice L. Walton, Helen R. Walton, James C. Walton, John T. Walton, S. Robson Walton, Sam M. Walton.
Employer Identification Number: 716091648

139
Bess A. Wilkins Memorial Scholarship Fund ¤
c/o Union National Bank
P.O. Box 1541
Little Rock 72203-1541 (501) 378-4000

Established in 1972 in AR.
Foundation type: Independent
Financial data (yr. ended 12/31/88): Assets, $1,033,807 (M); expenditures, $83,551, including $74,930 for 11 grants.
Purpose and activities: Support primarily for higher education.
Types of support: Scholarship funds.
Limitations: Giving primarily in AR.
Application information:
Initial approach: Letter
Deadline(s): None
Write: William Webster, Trust Officer, Union National Bank
Trustee: Union National Bank.
Employer Identification Number: 716084050

140
The Wrape Family Charitable Trust ¤
P.O. Box 412
Little Rock 72203 (501) 663-1551

Trust established in 1953 in AR.
Donor(s): Regina Sellmeyer,† A.M. Wrape,† and members of the Wrape family.
Foundation type: Independent
Financial data (yr. ended 12/31/88): Assets, $4,150,423 (M); expenditures, $359,915,

including $268,535 for 37 grants (high: $32,250; low: $100).
Purpose and activities: Support primarily for Roman Catholic educational and religious organizations.
Limitations: Giving primarily in AR.
Application information:
Initial approach: Letter
Deadline(s): None
Write: A. J. Wrape, Jr., Trustee
Officer and Trustees:* A.J. Wrape, Jr.,* Mgr.; A.J. Wrape III, Tom Wrape, W.R. Wrape II.
Employer Identification Number: 716050323

CALIFORNIA

141
ABC Foundation ¤
P.O. Box 3809
San Francisco 94119-3809

Donor(s): Nonie B. Ramsay.
Foundation type: Independent
Financial data (yr. ended 12/31/88): Assets, $1,726,425 (M); expenditures, $125,882, including $122,000 for 9 grants (high: $70,000; low: $1,000).
Purpose and activities: Giving primarily for education, cultural programs, and general charities.
Limitations: Giving limited to CA. No grants to individuals.
Application information: Contributes only to pre-selected organizations. Applications not accepted.
Officers: Nonie B. Ramsay,* Pres.; Elizabeth H. Bechtel,* V.P.; A. Barlow Ferguson, Secy.; Theodore J. Van Bebber, Treas.
Directors:* S.D. Bechtel, Jr.
Employer Identification Number: 942415607

142
The Abelard Foundation, Inc.
2530 San Pablo Ave., Suite B
Berkeley 94702 (415) 644-1904
East Coast grant application office: Joint Foundation Support, Inc., 40 West 20th St., 10th Fl., New York, NY 10011; Tel.: (212) 627-7710

Incorporated in 1958 in NY as successor to Albert B. Wells Charitable Trust established in 1950 in MA.
Donor(s): Members of the Wells family.
Foundation type: Independent
Financial data (yr. ended 12/31/88): Assets, $1,741,522 (M); gifts received, $225,000; expenditures, $395,682, including $267,000 for 39 grants (high: $14,000; low: $5,000; average: $6,000-$7,000).
Purpose and activities: Giving especially for seed money to new organizations and model projects, with emphasis on protection of civil rights and civil liberties; support for programs designed to achieve social, political, and economic equality for urban and rural poor, including giving them a voice in decisions about their environment.
Types of support: Operating budgets, seed money, matching funds, technical assistance, special projects, publications.
Limitations: Giving limited to western states, New York, NY, and southern states, including the Appalachia region. No support for medical, educational, or cultural institutions. No grants to individuals, or for building or endowment funds, continuing support, annual campaigns, emergency funds, scholarships, fellowships, or research; no loans.
Publications: Informational brochure (including application guidelines), grants list.
Application information: Application form not required.
Initial approach: Letter, telephone, or proposal
Copies of proposal: 1
Deadline(s): None
Board meeting date(s): Feb., May, and Nov.
Final notification: Immediately following board meeting
Write: Leah Brumer, Exec. Dir. (West Coast); Nanette Falkenberg, Pres., Joint Foundation Support, Inc. (East Coast)
Officers and Directors:* Albert B. Wells II,* Pres.; Kristen Wells Buck,* V.P.; Frances W. Magee,* V.P.; Adele Neufeld,* V.P.; Joel Schreck,* V.P.; Susan Wells,* V.P.; Malcolm J. Edgerton, Jr.,* Secy.; Charles R. Schreck,* Treas.; Michael Bernhard, Nancy Bernhard, Sheryl Bernhard, Steven Bernhard, Randal Buck, Lewis H. Butler, Donald Collins, Susan Collins, Andrew D. Heineman, David B. Magee, Peter Neufeld, Albert Schreck, Christine Schreck, Daniel W. Schreck, Jean Schreck, Thomas A. Schreck, George B. Wells II, Laura Wells, Melissa R. Wells, Ruth D. Wells.
Number of staff: 1 full-time professional; 1 part-time support.
Employer Identification Number: 136064580

143
Aequus Institute
4650 Arrow Hwy., Suite D-6
Montclair 91763-1223 (714) 621-6825

Established in 1983 in NV.
Donor(s): Loran Alan Mansfield.†
Foundation type: Independent
Financial data (yr. ended 12/31/88): Assets, $8,407,905 (M); expenditures, $536,694, including $314,000 for grants.
Purpose and activities: Giving for the promotion of the free market economic system in the U.S. and throughout the world; support also for the teachings of Mary Baker Eddy and the Christian Science Church.
Types of support: Annual campaigns, building funds, capital campaigns, conferences and seminars, fellowships, general purposes, in-kind gifts, internships, publications, research, scholarship funds.
Limitations: No grants to individuals.
Publications: Informational brochure (including application guidelines).
Application information: Proposals for major funding solicited form organizaitons familiar to the board. Application form not required.
Initial approach: Proposal
Copies of proposal: 1
Board meeting date(s): Quarterly
Final notification: Within 6 months of receipt
Write: Larry P. Arnn, Exec. Dir.
Officers: Larry P. Arnn, Exec. Dir.; Edwin Feulner, Jr., Mgr.; David Keyston, Mgr.; Patrick Parker, Mgr.
Number of staff: 1 full-time professional; 1 full-time support; 1 part-time support.
Employer Identification Number: 880191269

144
The Ahmanson Foundation ▼
9215 Wilshire Blvd.
Beverly Hills 90210 (213) 278-0770

Incorporated in 1952 in CA.
Donor(s): Howard F. Ahmanson,† Dorothy G. Sullivan,† William H. Ahmanson, Robert H. Ahmanson.
Foundation type: Independent
Financial data (yr. ended 10/31/89): Assets, $437,995,000 (M); qualifying distributions, $23,015,166, including $20,150,353 for 406 grants (high: $1,850,000; low: $300; average: $10,000-$25,000) and $2,864,813 for 5 in-kind gifts.
Purpose and activities: Emphasis on higher and other education, the arts and humanities, medicine and health, and a broad range of social welfare programs, including youth organizations.
Types of support: Building funds, equipment, land acquisition, endowment funds, matching funds, scholarship funds, special projects, renovation projects, capital campaigns.
Limitations: Giving primarily in southern CA, with emphasis on the Los Angeles area. No grants to individuals, or for continuing support, annual campaigns, deficit financing, professorships, internships, fellowships, film production, underwriting, or exchange programs; no loans.
Publications: Program policy statement, application guidelines, grants list.
Application information: Application form not required.
Initial approach: Proposal or letter
Copies of proposal: 1
Deadline(s): None
Board meeting date(s): 3 to 4 times annually
Final notification: 30 to 60 days
Write: Lee E. Walcott, V.P. and Managing Dir.
Officers: Robert H. Ahmanson,* Pres.; Lee E. Walcott, V.P. and Managing Dir.; William H. Ahmanson,* V.P.; Karen A. Hoffman, Secy.; Donald B. Stark, Treas.
Trustees:* Howard F. Ahmanson, Jr., Daniel N. Belin, Robert M. DeKruif, Robert F. Erburu, Franklin D. Murphy, M.D.
Number of staff: 7 full-time professional; 1 part-time professional.
Employer Identification Number: 956089998

145
The Albertson Foundation ⌑
c/o Robert Sutton
12839 Marlboro St.
Los Angeles 90049-3720 (213) 386-1196

Incorporated in 1964 in CA.
Donor(s): Hazel H. Albertson.†
Foundation type: Independent
Financial data (yr. ended 12/31/86): Assets, $0 (M); expenditures, $1,324,807, including $1,311,850 for 2 grants (high: $1,310,850; low: $1,000; average: $5,000-$10,000).
Purpose and activities: Emphasis on private secondary education, cultural institutions, hospitals, and youth activities.
Types of support: Continuing support, annual campaigns, building funds, equipment, research.
Limitations: Giving primarily in southern CA. No grants to individuals, or for operating budgets, seed money, emergency funds, deficit financing, endowment funds, matching gifts, scholarships, fellowships, special projects, publications, or conferences; no loans.
Application information: Application form not required.
Initial approach: Letter
Copies of proposal: 3
Deadline(s): Submit proposal preferably in Sept. or Oct.; deadline Oct. 31
Board meeting date(s): Nov.
Final notification: 4 weeks
Write: Robert F. O'Neill, Pres.
Officers: Robert F. O'Neill, Pres.; Kay S. Onderdonk, V.P. and Secy.; Jean A. Peck, V.P. and Treas.
Number of staff: 1 part-time professional; 1 part-time support.
Employer Identification Number: 956100378

146
Phil N. Allen Charitable Trust ⌑
c/o Bank of America
P.O. Box 5848
Palo Alto 94305

Established in 1981 in CA.
Donor(s): Phil N. Allen.†
Foundation type: Independent
Financial data (yr. ended 6/30/88): Assets, $4,223,497 (M); expenditures, $345,705, including $192,000 for 6 grants (high: $126,000; low: $4,000).
Purpose and activities: Grants primarily for multiple sclerosis and cancer research.
Types of support: Research.
Limitations: Giving primarily in CA and CT.
Application information: Application form not required.
Deadline(s): None
Trustees: Mayreta V. Allen, Marvin Siegel, Wells Fargo Bank, N.A.
Employer Identification Number: 956766982

147
Winifred & Harry B. Allen Foundation ☆
83 Beach Rd.
Belvedere 94920-2363 (415) 435-4525

Established in 1963.
Foundation type: Independent
Financial data (yr. ended 12/31/88): Assets, $1,083,837 (M); expenditures, $69,327, including $64,730 for 70 grants (high: $6,000; low: $100).
Purpose and activities: Giving primarily for environmental and wildlife conservation; support also for health, the fine and performing arts, and human services.
Types of support: Building funds, endowment funds.
Limitations: Giving primarily in CA. No grants to individuals.
Application information: Application form not required.
Initial approach: Letter
Deadline(s): None
Board meeting date(s): June 15, Sept. 15, Dec. 15, and Apr. 15
Write: David W. Allen, Trustee
Trustees: Andrew E. Allen, David W. Allen, Howard B. Allen, Elizabeth Straus.
Number of staff: 3 part-time support.
Employer Identification Number: 946100550

148
Allequash Foundation ⌑
234 East Colorado Blvd., Rm. 225
Pasadena 91101-2206

Established in 1961 in CA.
Donor(s): Alexander P. Hixon, Midland Investment Co.
Foundation type: Independent
Financial data (yr. ended 12/31/87): Assets, $971,817 (M); gifts received, $979,066; expenditures, $658,931.
Purpose and activities: Grants for higher and secondary education, social services, culture, and a nature conservancy program.
Application information: Contributes only to pre-selected organizations. Applications not accepted.
Directors: Adelaide F. Hixon, Alexander P. Hixon.
Employer Identification Number: 956050003

149
The Alpert & Alpert Foundation ⌑
1820 South Soto St.
Los Angeles 90023

Established in 1974 in CA.
Donor(s): Alpert & Alpert Iron & Metal, Inc., and others.
Foundation type: Independent
Financial data (yr. ended 6/30/88): Assets, $766,686 (M); gifts received, $270,000; expenditures, $166,957.
Purpose and activities: Giving primarily for Jewish welfare funds.
Limitations: Giving primarily in CA.
Officers and Directors: Jake Farber, Pres.; Alan Alpert, V.P.; Howard Farber, V.P.; Raymond Alpert, Secy.-Treas.
Employer Identification Number: 237388729

150
Altos Foundation, Inc. ⌑
76 Adam Way
Atherton 94025

Established in 1982 in CA.
Donor(s): David Jackson, Susan Jackson.
Foundation type: Independent
Financial data (yr. ended 9/30/88): Assets, $2,666,916 (M); gifts received, $1,001,747; expenditures, $446,447, including $421,000 for 46 grants (high: $20,000; low: $1,000).
Purpose and activities: Grants primarily for social services, youth, and child welfare.
Application information: Contributes only to pre-selected organizations. Applications not accepted.
Officers: Susan Jackson, Pres.; Ronald C. Conway, Treas.
Employer Identification Number: 942853627

151
Maurice Amado Foundation ⌑
3600 Wilshire Blvd., Suite 1228
Los Angeles 90020 (213) 381-3622

Incorporated in 1961 in CA.
Donor(s): Maurice Amado.†
Foundation type: Independent
Financial data (yr. ended 11/30/89): Assets, $17,425,794 (M); expenditures, $907,605, including $716,389 for 44 grants (high: $203,745; low: $500).
Purpose and activities: Grants primarily for Sephardic Jewish organizations.
Types of support: Building funds, continuing support, endowment funds, fellowships, general purposes, operating budgets, renovation projects, research, scholarship funds, special projects.
Application information: Application form not required.
Initial approach: Letter
Deadline(s): None
Board meeting date(s): Biannually
Write: Aaron Oliver
Officers and Directors:* Stella A. Lavis,* Pres.; Regina A. Tarica,* V.P.; Bernice Amado,* V.P. and Treas.; Ralph A. Amado, Ralph D. Amado, Renee Kaplan, Victor R. Lavis, Samuel R. Tarica.
Number of staff: 1 part-time professional.
Employer Identification Number: 956041700

152
American Honda Foundation
P.O. Box 2205
Torrance 90509-2205 (213) 781-4090

Established in 1984 in CA.
Donor(s): American Honda Motor Co., Inc.
Foundation type: Company-sponsored
Financial data (yr. ended 06/30/89): Assets, $1,400,000 (M); gifts received, $2,000,000; expenditures, $3,200,000, including $775,000 for 30 grants (high: $81,000; low: $2,500; average: $40,000-$60,000) and $170,000 for 30 employee matching gifts.
Purpose and activities: Support for national organizations working in the areas of youth and scientific education, including private elementary and secondary schools, public and private colleges and universities, adult education programs, scholarship and fellowship programs, and scientific and educational organizations.
Types of support: Scholarship funds, fellowships, special projects, operating budgets, continuing support, research, building funds, equipment, seed money, annual campaigns, professorships, internships, matching funds,

capital campaigns, conferences and seminars, exchange programs, program-related investments.
Limitations: No support for religious, veterans', fraternal, or political organizations, labor groups, or beauty and talent contests. No grants to individuals, or for trips or hospital operating funds.
Publications: Grants list, newsletter, informational brochure (including application guidelines), program policy statement, application guidelines.
Application information: Application form required.
Initial approach: Letter or telephone
Copies of proposal: 1
Deadline(s): Nov. 1, Feb. 1, May 1, and Aug. 1
Board meeting date(s): Jan., Apr., July, and Oct.
Final notification: 2 months
Write: Kathryn A. Carey, Mgr.
Officers and Directors:* S. Iizuka,* Pres.; John Petas,* V.P.; Tak Ageno,* Secy.-Treas.; Kathryn A. Carey, Mgr.; S. Cameron, R. Downing, Y. Yoshida.
Number of staff: 2 full-time professional; 1 full-time support.
Employer Identification Number: 953924667

153
American President Companies Foundation ⌑
1800 Harrison St., 21st Fl.
Oakland 94612-3429 (415) 272-8369

Established in 1984 in CA.
Donor(s): American President Cos., Ltd.
Foundation type: Company-sponsored
Financial data (yr. ended 12/31/87): Assets, $1,005,328 (M); gifts received, $500,000; expenditures, $448,662, including $448,189 for 138 grants (high: $142,100).
Purpose and activities: Giving to health, educational, civic, and cultural programs.
Types of support: General purposes.
Limitations: Giving primarily in the City of Oakland, the San Francisco Bay Area, CA, and company and subsidiary operating locations; support also for national programs. No support for religious, veterans', labor, or fraternal organizations.
Application information: Applications must be submitted in writing using forms provided for this purpose or by means of other documentation acceptable to the foundation.
Initial approach: Letter
Deadline(s): None
Write: Michael T. Maher, V.P.
Officers and Directors:* W.B. Seaton,* Pres.; John E. Flynn,* V.P. and C.F.O.; Richard L. Tavrow,* V.P., Secy., and General Counsel; Joji Hayashi,* V.P.; Michael T. Maher, V.P.; Derek Foote, Treas.; William J. Stuebgen, Controller.
Employer Identification Number: 942955262

154
Ameritec Foundation ⌑ ☆
760 Arrow Grand Circle
Covina 91722 (818) 915-5441

Established in 1987 in CA.
Donor(s): Ameritec Corp.
Foundation type: Company-sponsored
Financial data (yr. ended 12/31/88): Assets, $1,217,741 (M); gifts received, $1,200,000; expenditures, $54,253, including $52,290 for grants to individuals.
Purpose and activities: Awards prizes to individuals to promote medical research toward the goal of finding a cure for spinal cord functional impairment (paralysis).
Types of support: Research.
Application information: Prize not available to individuals conducting clinical research.
Initial approach: Resume and proposal in form suitable for publication in a medical journal
Deadline(s): None
Write: John Watson, Pres.
Officers and Directors: John Watson, Pres.; Michael P. Newman, Secy.; Tom Hollfelder, C.F.O.; Leroy McDaniel, Van Windham.
Employer Identification Number: 954147156

155
Arthur C. and Gertrude H. Anderson Trust ⌑
c/o San Diego Trust & Savings Bank
P.O. Box X-1013
San Diego 92112 (619) 557-3167

Established in 1949 in CA.
Foundation type: Independent
Financial data (yr. ended 12/31/87): Assets, $1,138,229 (M); expenditures, $96,856, including $75,723 for 34 grants (high: $10,000; low: $500).
Purpose and activities: Giving primarily for youth organizations.
Application information:
Initial approach: Letter
Deadline(s): None
Write: Laurie Dick, Trust Officer, San Diego Trust & Savings Bank
Trustee: San Diego Trust & Savings Bank.
Employer Identification Number: 956018486

156
Aplin Foundation ⌑ ☆
122 Pepperwood Court
Danville 94526 (415) 838-2134

Established in 1986 in CA.
Donor(s): Arthur I. Appleton, Linda S. Appleton.
Foundation type: Independent
Financial data (yr. ended 12/31/88): Assets, $87,184 (M); expenditures, $161,944, including $161,062 for 12 grants (high: $86,025; low: $136).
Purpose and activities: Giving primarily for Christian organizations, including churches and a community center; support also for education, recreation, and a women's shelter.
Limitations: No grants to individuals.
Application information: Application form not required.
Initial approach: Letter
Deadline(s): None
Write: Arthur I. Appleton, Pres.
Officers: Arthur I. Appleton, Pres.; Gordon A. Berke, V.P.; Linda S. Appleton, Secy.-Treas.
Employer Identification Number: 943017054

157
Sheldon & Carol Appel Family Foundation ⌑
2924 1/2 Main St.
Santa Monica 90405-5316

Established in 1977 in CA.
Donor(s): Sheldon Appel.
Foundation type: Independent
Financial data (yr. ended 11/30/87): Assets, $703,633 (M); gifts received, $22,500; expenditures, $116,453, including $103,722 for 66 grants (high: $20,000; low: $14).
Purpose and activities: Support for Jewish giving, Jewish welfare, and higher education.
Types of support: General purposes.
Trustees: Carol Appel, Sheldon Appel.
Employer Identification Number: 953190683

158
Apple Valley Foundation ⌑ ☆
P.O. Box 1A
Apple Valley 92507

Established in 1953.
Foundation type: Independent
Financial data (yr. ended 12/31/88): Assets, $1,104,764 (M); expenditures, $129,390, including $125,000 for 2 grants (high: $100,000; low: $25,000).
Purpose and activities: Giving primarily for a stadium foundation and education.
Limitations: Giving primarily in Apple Valley, CA. No grants to individuals.
Application information: Contributes only to pre-selected organizations. Applications not accepted.
Officers: Francis Bass, Pres.; Barbara Davisson, Secy.-Treas.
Employer Identification Number: 956047057

159
K. Arakelian Foundation ⌑
596 West Sierra Ave.
Clovis 93612-0122 (209) 299-8390

Incorporated in 1943 in CA.
Donor(s): Krikor Arakelian.†
Foundation type: Independent
Financial data (yr. ended 12/31/87): Assets, $1,476,211 (M); expenditures, $121,372, including $50,255 for 42 grants (high: $9,000; low: $10).
Purpose and activities: Giving primarily for educational purposes; student loan funds established at five higher educational institutions which administer them; support also for health agencies, the aged, youth agencies, and community funds.
Types of support: General purposes.
Limitations: Giving primarily in CA, particularly in Fresno and Madera counties. No grants to individuals.
Application information: Application form not required.
Write: Aram Arakelian, Pres.
Officers and Directors: Aram Arakelian, Pres.; Mike Garabedian, Jr., V.P.; Gay Arakelian, Secy.-Treas.; Mike Garabedian, Sr., Levon Kirkorian, Queenie Nishkian.
Employer Identification Number: 941095610

160
Arata Brothers Trust ⌑
c/o Renato R. Parenti, Trustee
P.O. Box 430
Sacramento 95802

Trust established in 1976 in CA.
Foundation type: Independent
Financial data (yr. ended 12/31/88): Assets, $3,628,733 (M); expenditures, $354,085, including $330,339 for 47 grants (high: $50,000; low: $1,000).
Purpose and activities: Emphasis on hospitals, education, and religion.
Types of support: General purposes.
Limitations: Giving primarily in CA.
Application information:
Initial approach: Letter
Deadline(s): None
Trustees: Francis B. Dillon, Nellie Lavezzo, Renato R. Parenti.
Employer Identification Number: 237204615

161
ARCO Foundation ▼ ⌑
515 South Flower St.
Los Angeles 90071 (213) 486-3342

Incorporated in 1963 in NY.
Donor(s): Atlantic Richfield Co.
Foundation type: Company-sponsored
Financial data (yr. ended 12/31/88): Assets, $3,270,037 (M); gifts received, $19,724,125; expenditures, $14,091,746, including $12,213,497 for 1,539 grants (high: $103,495; low: $500; average: $2,500-$25,000) and $1,878,249 for 11,125 employee matching gifts.
Purpose and activities: Giving primarily to programs that address the underlying causes of educational, social, and cultural disparity in American life. Early involvement in "root-cause" issues allows the foundation to test innovative models, build leadership and leverage its investments to generate the greatest return to ARCO and the society. Support largely for higher and pre-collegiate education, including minority retention programs in business and science and engineering; community programs, especially for low income groups, including job creation and job training programs, community economic development, neighborhood revitalization, and youth agencies; aging programs; access to the humanities and the arts; public information organizations; and environmental programs.
Types of support: Operating budgets, seed money, equipment, land acquisition, matching funds, employee matching gifts, employee-related scholarships, special projects, technical assistance.
Limitations: Giving primarily in areas of company operations, especially Anchorage, AK, Dallas, TX, and Los Angeles, CA. No support for sectarian religious organizations, professional associations, specialized health organizations, or military or veterans' organizations. No grants to individuals, or for professional schools of art, academic art programs, performances at colleges or universities, university art museums, campus performance halls, individual high school or college performing groups, endowment funds, annual campaigns, deficit financing, hospital or university operating funds, research, publications, building programs (except for economic revitalization in a deteriorating urban neighborhood), or conferences; no loans.
Publications: Annual report (including application guidelines), application guidelines.
Application information: Application form not required.
Initial approach: Proposal limited to 2 pages
Copies of proposal: 1
Deadline(s): None
Board meeting date(s): June and Dec.
Final notification: 4 to 6 months
Write: Eugene R. Wilson, Pres.
Officers: Eugene R. Wilson,* Pres.; L. Marlene Bailey-Whiteside, Secy.; M.C. Recchuite, Treas.
Directors:* Lodwrick M. Cook, Chair.; Ronald J. Arnault, K.R. Dickerson, S.J. Giovanisci, J.S. Middleton, J.S. Morrison, Robert E. Wycoff.
Number of staff: 6 full-time professional; 4 part-time support.
Employer Identification Number: 953222292

162
Argyros Foundation
950 South Coast Dr., Suite 200
Costa Mesa 92626 (714) 241-5000

Established in 1979 in CA.
Donor(s): The Argyros Charitable Trusts.
Foundation type: Independent
Financial data (yr. ended 07/31/89): Assets, $9,903,000 (M); gifts received, $2,272,000; expenditures, $954,000, including $915,000 for 90 grants (high: $145,000; low: $50).
Purpose and activities: Giving for culture, higher and other education, religious giving, social services, recreation, and health services.
Types of support: General purposes.
Limitations: Giving primarily in CA.
Application information:
Initial approach: Proposal
Deadline(s): June 1
Write: Chuck Packard, Trustee
Officers: Julianne Argyros,* Pres.; George L. Argyros,* Secy.; Carol Campbell, Exec. Dir.
Trustees:* Chuck Packard.
Employer Identification Number: 953421867

163
Ben H. and Gladys Arkelian Foundation ⌑
1107 Truxtun Ave.
P.O. Box 1825
Bakersfield 93303 (805) 324-5029

Established in 1959 in CA.
Foundation type: Independent
Financial data (yr. ended 12/31/87): Assets, $2,160,685 (M); expenditures, $132,903.
Purpose and activities: Emphasis on higher education, youth, social services, hospitals, and health agencies.
Limitations: Giving limited to Kern County, CA. No grants to individuals.
Application information:
Initial approach: Letter and request for appearance before Board of Directors
Deadline(s): None
Board meeting date(s): 1st Thursday of each month
Write: Frank I. Ford, Jr., Secy.
Officers and Directors: Henry C. Mack, Pres.; Henry C. Mack, Jr., V.P.; Frank I. Ford, Jr., Secy.-Treas.; D. Bianco, Harvey H. Means.
Employer Identification Number: 956103223

164
Philip D. Armour Foundation ⌑
505 Sansome St., Suite 900
San Francisco 94111

Established in 1949 in CA.
Foundation type: Independent
Financial data (yr. ended 12/31/88): Assets, $1,229,175 (M); expenditures, $79,643, including $66,500 for 39 grants (high: $7,500; low: $250).
Purpose and activities: Giving primarily to theater groups; also supports a wide range of charitable organizations.
Limitations: No grants to individuals.
Application information: Contributes only to pre-selected organizations. Applications not accepted.
Officers and Directors:* John St. John,* Pres.; Julia H. Armour,* V.P.; Donald E. Schlotz,* Secy.; Gillian McDonald,* Treas.
Employer Identification Number: 362407161

165
Arrillaga Foundation ⌑
2560 Mission College Blvd., Rm. 101
Santa Clara 95050

Established around 1978 in CA.
Donor(s): John Arrillaga.
Foundation type: Independent
Financial data (yr. ended 9/30/88): Assets, $6,124,704 (M); gifts received, $135,275; expenditures, $393,638, including $364,255 for 40 grants (high: $154,409; low: $88).
Purpose and activities: Giving for higher and secondary education, and social services.
Limitations: Giving primarily in CA.
Application information:
Initial approach: Proposal
Deadline(s): None
Write: John Arrillaga, Pres.
Officers: John Arrillaga, Pres.; Francis C. Arrillaga, V.P.; John Arrillaga, Jr., Treas.
Director: Richard T. Peery.
Employer Identification Number: 942460896

166
Artevel Foundation ⌑
Crocker Center I
333 South Grand Ave., Suite 4150
Los Angeles 90071

Incorporated in 1966 in CA.
Donor(s): Harm te Velde, Zwaantina te Velde.
Foundation type: Independent
Financial data (yr. ended 12/31/88): Assets, $2,067,582 (M); expenditures, $144,332, including $132,200 for 33 grants (high: $23,000; low: $500).
Purpose and activities: Grants largely for Protestant evangelistic, missionary, and charitable programs.
Types of support: Building funds, general purposes.
Limitations: No grants to individuals.

Application information: Contributes only to pre-selected organizations. Applications not accepted.
Officers and Trustees: Harm te Velde, Pres.; Zwaantina te Velde, V.P.; George R. Phillips, Secy.-Treas.; Shirley A. DeGroot, Harriet Hill, Margaret E. Houtsma, Grace Kreulen, Betty Meyer, John te Velde, Marvin te Velde, Ralph te Velde.
Employer Identification Number: 956136405

167
Associated Foundations, Inc.
100 South Los Robles Ave., Suite 470
Pasadena 91101 (818) 796-3917

Incorporated in 1973 in CA.
Foundation type: Independent
Financial data (yr. ended 8/31/89): Assets, $3,679,189 (M); expenditures, $287,612, including $178,400 for 33 grants (high: $20,000; low: $1,000).
Purpose and activities: Giving for higher education, including achievement scholarships awarded by institutions to undergraduates majoring in business management, engineering, nursing, and agribusiness.
Types of support: Scholarship funds, operating budgets, general purposes, equipment.
Limitations: Giving primarily in CA. No grants to individuals, or for building or endowment funds, research, or matching gifts; no loans.
Application information:
Board meeting date(s): Oct. and as required
Officers: Brenda K. Oddou, Pres.; Marie Colaccechi-Herlihy,* Secy.-Treas.
Trustees:* Katherine S. Burns, Mildred Herlihy, Frederick T. Nelson, William G. Olsen, E. Lee Smith III, Richard Trautwein.
Employer Identification Number: 237324126

168
Atkinson Foundation
Ten West Orange Ave.
South San Francisco 94080 (415) 876-1559

Incorporated in 1939 in CA.
Donor(s): George H. Atkinson,† Mildred M. Atkinson,† and others.
Foundation type: Independent
Financial data (yr. ended 12/31/89): Assets, $16,237,035 (M); expenditures, $922,582, including $779,942 for 110 grants (high: $149,506; low: $865; average: $2,000-$10,000).
Purpose and activities: Broad purposes are to help people reach their highest potential in their spiritual and economic life and to reach self-sufficiency; giving primarily for social services, education, the United Methodist Church and other church activities, and international development and relief.
Types of support: Seed money, operating budgets, emergency funds, scholarship funds, continuing support, equipment, general purposes, technical assistance.
Limitations: Giving primarily in San Mateo County, CA, for social welfare, secondary schools, and colleges; United Methodist churches and church activities in northern CA; and international grantmaking for technical assistance, relief, and population issues. No support for doctoral study or elementary schools. No grants to individuals, or for research or fundraising events; no loans.
Publications: Annual report (including application guidelines), informational brochure (including application guidelines).
Application information: Application form not required.
Initial approach: Telephone, proposal, or letter
Copies of proposal: 1
Deadline(s): None
Board meeting date(s): Feb. or Mar., May or June, Sept., and Dec.
Final notification: 3 months
Write: Norma Arlen, Admin.
Officers and Directors:* Duane E. Atkinson,* Pres.; Ray N. Atkinson,* V.P.; Thomas J. Henderson,* V.P.; Donald K. Grant,* Treas.; Lavina M. Atkinson, Elizabeth H. Curtis, James C. Ingwersen, Robert D. Langford, Lawrence A. Wright.
Number of staff: 1 full-time professional; 1 part-time professional.
Employer Identification Number: 946075613

169
Myrtle L. Atkinson Foundation ▼
P.O. Box 688
La Canada 91011

Incorporated in 1940 in CA.
Donor(s): Guy F. Atkinson,† Rachel C. Atkinson, Elizabeth A. Whitsett, George H. Atkinson.†
Foundation type: Independent
Financial data (yr. ended 12/31/88): Assets, $19,710,911 (M); expenditures, $905,561, including $869,349 for 292 grants (high: $65,000; low: $50; average: $1,000-$10,000).
Purpose and activities: "To teach, promulgate and disseminate the gospel of Jesus Christ throughout the world and also to unite in Christian Fellowship the large number of consecrated Christians in the various evangelical churches...; to encourage and promote religious, scientific, technical and all other kinds of education, enlightenment and research." Giving mainly for capital funds for Christian churches and evangelism; support also for local and international relief and welfare agencies, literacy, hospices, and hunger.
Types of support: Scholarship funds, fellowships, endowment funds, building funds.
Limitations: Giving primarily in southern CA and the West Coast. No support for education, outside of foundation's primary area of interest in Protestant denominational programs. No grants to individuals, or for music groups, research, non-theological scholarships and fellowships, telecommunications, doctoral studies, or continuing programs.
Application information: Application form not required.
Initial approach: Letter (1 page)
Copies of proposal: 1
Deadline(s): Submit proposal preferably in Feb., early May, Aug., or Nov.; no set deadline
Board meeting date(s): Jan., May, Sept., and Dec.
Final notification: 2 months
Write: Elizabeth A. Whitsett, Pres.
Officers and Directors:* Elizabeth A. Whitsett,* Pres.; Rachel C. Atkinson,* V.P.; Myrtle W. Harris,* Secy.; John F. Whitsett,* Treas.; William N. Harris, Virginia L. Hutchinson, Stanley D. Ryals, Kirsten A. Whitsett.
Number of staff: None.
Employer Identification Number: 956047161

170
Autry Foundation ▼
5858 Sunset Blvd.
P.O. Box 710
Los Angeles 90078 (213) 460-5676

Established in 1974 in CA.
Donor(s): Gene Autry.
Foundation type: Independent
Financial data (yr. ended 12/31/88): Assets, $41,119,961 (M); expenditures, $17,114,187, including $17,042,492 for 24 grants (high: $16,821,067; low: $25; average: $500-$7,500).
Purpose and activities: Giving primarily for Gene Autry Western Heritage Museum; support also for the homeless and hungry, hospitals, and youth-related programs.
Limitations: Giving limited to the Los Angeles, CA, area and Riverside and Orange counties, CA. No grants to individuals.
Application information: Applications not accepted.
Write: Maxine Hansen, Secy.
Officers and Directors:* Gene Autry,* Pres.; Jacqueline Autry, V.P.; Maxine Hansen, Secy.; Stanley Schneider,* Treas.; Clyde Tritt.
Number of staff: None.
Employer Identification Number: 237433359

171
Avery-Fuller Children's Center ⌘
251 Kearny St., No. 301
San Francisco 94108 (415) 930-8292

Established in 1914 in CA.
Donor(s): Jean A. McCallum.
Foundation type: Independent
Financial data (yr. ended 6/30/89): Assets, $3,080,917 (M); gifts received, $28,595; expenditures, $205,589, including $151,667 for grants to individuals (average: $1,500).
Purpose and activities: To provide financial assistance to handicapped and disabled children for the purpose of increasing their self-sufficiency; funds to be used for medical services, physical and occupational therapy, psychotherapy, special school or remedial education, prosthetics, appliances, prescriptions, and related services.
Types of support: Grants to individuals.
Limitations: Giving primarily in CA. No support for preliminary evaluations, orthodontia, eye glasses, or routine eye care. No grants for groups of children.
Application information: Rejected applications will be reconsidered once at the next review date, provided applicant requests so in writing. Application form required.
Deadline(s): Feb. 14, May 14, Aug. 14, and Nov. 14
Final notification: Within 4 weeks of deadline
Write: Bonnie Van Manen Pinkel, Exec. Dir.
Officers and Directors: Whiting Welch, Pres.; Mrs. H.A. Richardson, V.P.; Charles N.

Whitehead, V.P.; David Wisnom, Secy.-Treas.; Bonnie Van Manen Pinkel, Exec. Dir.; and 8 additional directors.
Employer Identification Number: 941243657

172
The B.Y. Foundation ☆
132 South Rodeo Dr., Suite 600
Beverly Hills 90212 (213) 274-8111

Established in 1986.
Foundation type: Independent
Financial data (yr. ended 11/30/88): Assets, $9,116 (M); gifts received, $10,000; expenditures, $169,844, including $168,755 for 96 grants (high: $60,800; low: $50).
Purpose and activities: Giving primarily for museums and the arts, Jewish organizations, and health, including AIDS programs.
Limitations: Giving primarily in CA, with emphasis on Los Angeles.
Application information: Application form not required.
Deadline(s): None
Officers and Directors:* Bud Yorkin,* Pres.; Nicole Yorkin,* Secy.; David Yorkin,* C.F.O.
Employer Identification Number: 954068964

173
William Babcock Memorial Endowment
305 San Anselmo Ave., Suite 219
San Anselmo 94960 (415) 453-0901

Trust established in 1954 in CA; incorporated in 1959.
Donor(s): Julia May Babcock.†
Foundation type: Independent
Financial data (yr. ended 02/28/89): Assets, $3,120,888 (M); gifts received, $249,781; expenditures, $540,575, including $407,020 for 480 grants to individuals (high: $10,000; low: $50) and $64,322 for 16 loans to individuals.
Purpose and activities: To meet through grants or loans the exceptional medical, surgical, and hospital expenses of residents of Marin County.
Types of support: Grants to individuals.
Limitations: Giving limited to Marin County, CA. No support for organizations.
Publications: Application guidelines.
Application information: Application form required.
Initial approach: Telephone
Deadline(s): None
Board meeting date(s): Monthly
Write: Alelia Gillin, Exec. Dir.
Officers: James Placak,* Pres.; Galen Foster,* 1st V.P.; Edward Boero, D.D.S.,* 2nd V.P.; Katharine Kirk,* Secy.; Fred Enemakr, Treas.; Alelia Gillin, Exec Dir.
Directors:* Joane Berry, A. Crawford Greene, Jr., Russell R. Klein, M.D., Rex Silvernale.
Number of staff: 1 full-time professional; 2 part-time support.
Employer Identification Number: 941367170

174
The R. C. Baker Foundation ▼
P.O. Box 6150
Orange 92613-6150

Trust established in 1952 in CA.
Donor(s): R.C. Baker, Sr.†
Foundation type: Independent
Financial data (yr. ended 12/31/88): Assets, $16,661,290 (M); gifts received, $394,800; expenditures, $1,186,915, including $1,046,490 for 220 grants (high: $100,000; low: $100; average: $100-$100,000).
Purpose and activities: Emphasis on higher education, including scholarships administered by selected colleges and universities; some support for hospitals and health agencies, cultural programs, and social service and youth agencies.
Types of support: Emergency funds, deficit financing, building funds, equipment, research, operating budgets, scholarship funds, fellowships, exchange programs, general purposes, continuing support, annual campaigns, capital campaigns, renovation projects, special projects.
Limitations: No grants to individuals, or for endowment funds; no loans.
Application information: Application form not required.
Initial approach: Cover letter with proposal
Copies of proposal: 1
Deadline(s): Submit proposal preferably in Apr. or Sept.; deadline May 1 and Oct. 1
Board meeting date(s): June and Nov.
Write: Frank L. Scott, Chair.
Officer and Trustees:* Frank L. Scott,* Chair.; George M. Anderson, K. Dale, J. Shelton, R. Turner, Robert N. Waters, Security Pacific National Bank.
Number of staff: 3
Employer Identification Number: 951742283

175
The Solomon R. and Rebecca D. Baker Foundation, Inc. ⌑
1901 Ave. of the Stars, Suite 1231
Los Angeles 90067 (213) 552-9822

Incorporated in 1952 in DE.
Donor(s): Solomon R. Baker.
Foundation type: Independent
Financial data (yr. ended 4/30/89): Assets, $2,607,085 (M); expenditures, $125,967, including $119,650 for 8 grants (high: $100,000; low: $200).
Purpose and activities: Giving for medical research in autism and related fields and the care and therapy of autistic individuals; support also for education of the disadvantaged, Jewish welfare agencies, and animal welfare.
Limitations: Giving primarily in CA. No grants to individuals.
Application information:
Initial approach: Letter
Deadline(s): None
Write: Solomon R. Baker, Pres.
Officers and Trustees: Solomon R. Baker, Pres.; Rebecca D. Baker, V.P. and Secy.-Treas.; Malcolm F. Baker, Robert J. Plourde.
Employer Identification Number: 237152503

176
Bank of America - Giannini Foundation ⌑
Bank of America Ctr., Dept. 3246
Box 37000
San Francisco 94137 (415) 953-0932

Incorporated in 1945 in CA.
Donor(s): A.P. Giannini.†
Foundation type: Independent
Financial data (yr. ended 12/31/88): Assets, $8,541,571 (M); gifts received, $38,438; expenditures, $532,014, including $169,755 for grants (high: $15,000; low: $1,000) and $302,000 for 18 grants to individuals (high: $20,000; low: $1,700).
Purpose and activities: Medical research fellowships for advanced applicants sponsored by accredited medical schools. Limited number of grants made to support charitable or other educational endeavors, or those pertaining to the advancement of human health and the eradication of disease.
Types of support: Fellowships, research.
Limitations: Giving limited to CA. No grants to individuals (except for research fellowships), or for endowment funds or matching gifts; no loans.
Publications: Application guidelines, annual report, 990-PF.
Application information: Application form required for fellowships only. Application form not required.
Initial approach: Letter, telephone, or proposal
Copies of proposal: 1
Deadline(s): Aug. 1 for grants; Dec. 1 for fellowships
Board meeting date(s): Apr. and Nov.
Write: Caroline O. Boitano, Admin.
Officers: Cheryl Knowles-Sorokin, Secy.; Linda Butterfield, Treas.
Directors: C.J. Medberry, Chair.; Claire Giannini Hoffman, Vice-Chair.; J.A. Carrera, Thomas C. Fitzpatrick, James P. Miscoll, D.A. Mullane, Kyhl S. Smeby, Arthur V. Toupin.
Number of staff: 1
Employer Identification Number: 946089512

177
BankAmerica Foundation ⌑
Bank of America Ctr.
Dept. 3246, P.O. Box 37000
San Francisco 94137 (415) 953-3175

Incorporated in 1968 in CA.
Donor(s): BankAmerica Corp., and subsidiaries.
Foundation type: Company-sponsored
Financial data (yr. ended 12/31/87): Assets, $2,199,459 (M); gifts received, $2,613,458; expenditures, $3,181,783, including $3,172,937 for grants.
Purpose and activities: To fund private, nonprofit, tax-exempt organizations providing services to communities locally, nationally, and internationally in areas where the company operates. Support both through grants and loans in 5 major funding areas: health, human resources, community and economic development, education, and culture and the arts; support also for special programs developed by the foundation to use its resources most effectively.

Types of support: Annual campaigns, building funds, special projects, scholarship funds, employee-related scholarships, matching funds, general purposes, continuing support, capital campaigns, emergency funds.
Limitations: Giving limited to areas of major company operations, including communities in CA, metropolitan areas nationwide, and foreign countries. No support for religious organizations for sectarian purposes, organizations where funding would primarily benefit membership, or government-funded programs. No grants to individuals, or for fundraising events, memorial campaigns, or endowment funds. Generally no grants for research, conferences or seminars, publications, or operating support.
Publications: Program policy statement, application guidelines, 990-PF.
Application information: The employee matching gift program has been discontinued.
Initial approach: Letter
Copies of proposal: 1
Deadline(s): For capital/major campaigns, July 31; all others, none
Board meeting date(s): Annually and as necessary
Final notification: Varies
Write: Caroline O. Boitano, V.P. and Asst. Dir.
Officers: James P. Miscoll,* Chair.; Donald A. Mullane,* Pres. and C.E.O.; Caroline O. Boitano, V.P. and Asst. Dir.; John S. Stephan,* V.P.; James S. Wagele, V.P.; Michael Anderson, Treas.; Judy Granucci, Financial Officer.
Trustees:* Robert N. Beck, Robert W. Frick, Richard Rosenberg.
Number of staff: 1 full-time professional; 1 full-time support.
Employer Identification Number: 941670382

178
Arline & Thomas J. Bannan Foundation ⌑

74-399 Hwy. III, Suite K
Palm Desert 92660
Application address: P.O. Box M, Palm Desert, CA 92261; Tel.: (619) 340-1330

Established in 1958 in CA.
Donor(s): Thomas J. Bannan.
Foundation type: Independent
Financial data (yr. ended 12/31/87): Assets, $1,537,142 (M); expenditures, $83,343, including $76,590 for 45 grants (high: $20,000; low: $25).
Purpose and activities: Support primarily for health agencies and hospitals, and for higher education; support also for religious purposes, child welfare, and social services.
Limitations: Giving primarily in CA and WA.
Application information:
Initial approach: Letter or proposal
Deadline(s): None
Write: Thomas J. Bannan, Pres.
Officers: Thomas J. Bannan, Pres.; J.F. O'Hara, V.P.; N.M. Grossman, Secy.-Treas.
Employer Identification Number: 916029798

179
The William C. Bannerman Foundation

1405 North San Fernando Blvd., Suite 201
Burbank 91504-4150

Established in 1958 in CA.
Foundation type: Independent
Financial data (yr. ended 04/30/89): Assets, $4,600,000 (M); expenditures, $171,000, including $147,575 for 25 grants (high: $52,000; low: $400; average: $400-$52,000).
Purpose and activities: Support primarily for a medical center and a university; support also for health associations, education, the arts, wildlife and the environment, and social services, including the disadvantaged and disabled.
Types of support: Annual campaigns, building funds, matching funds, operating budgets, scholarship funds.
Limitations: Giving primarily in CA, with emphasis on the Los Angeles area.
Application information: Application form not required.
Initial approach: Letter
Deadline(s): Feb. 28
Final notification: Prior to Apr. 30
Write: Ms. E.T. Ponchick, Pres.
Officers: E.T. Ponchick, Pres.; W.F. Pongle, Treas.
Employer Identification Number: 956061353

180
Banyan Tree Foundation ⌑ ☆

1800 Century Park East, No. 300
Los Angeles 90067

Established in CA in 1986.
Donor(s): Peter Ackerman, Joanne Leedom-Ackerman.
Foundation type: Independent
Financial data (yr. ended 11/30/89): Assets, $10,316,720 (M); expenditures, $799,303, including $741,000 for grants.
Purpose and activities: Giving primarily to international development and relief programs and literary journals and centers.
Limitations: No grants to individuals.
Application information: Contributes only to pre-selected organizations. Applications not accepted.
Officers: Joanne Leedom-Ackerman, Pres.; Peter Ackerman, Secy.-Treas.
Employer Identification Number: 954088915

181
The Donald R. Barker Foundation ⌑

P.O. Box 936
Rancho Mirage 92270 (619) 321-2345

Established in 1977 in OR.
Donor(s): Donald R. Barker.
Foundation type: Independent
Financial data (yr. ended 11/30/88): Assets, $3,925,901 (M); expenditures, $229,407, including $190,440 for 24 grants (high: $75,000; low: $1,000).
Purpose and activities: Giving largely to higher education, the handicapped, and hospitals; support also for youth and health agencies, cultural programs, and high school athletic programs.
Types of support: Operating budgets, scholarship funds, building funds, equipment, special projects.
Limitations: Giving primarily in CA and OR. No support for sectarian religious purposes, or for agencies that rely on federal or tax dollars for their principal support. No grants to individuals, or for endowment funds, conferences, or operational deficits.
Publications: Application guidelines.
Application information: Application form required.
Initial approach: Letter
Copies of proposal: 1
Deadline(s): Mar. 1 and Aug. 1
Board meeting date(s): May and Oct.
Final notification: Promptly after decision
Trustees: John R. Lamb, Coeta Barker McGowan, J.R. McGowan, Joseph A. Moore.
Employer Identification Number: 930698411

182
Battistone Foundation

1325 Chapala St., No. 2
P.O. Box 3858
Santa Barbara 93130 (805) 965-2250

Trust established in 1968 in CA.
Donor(s): Sam Battistone, Sr.
Foundation type: Operating
Financial data (yr. ended 12/31/88): Assets, $8,571,525 (M); gifts received, $300,000; expenditures, $728,885, including $2,140 for 15 grants (high: $520; low: $10) and $991,907 for 1 foundation-administered program.
Purpose and activities: A private operating foundation; giving to finance low-income housing for economically disadvantaged senior citizens; grants also to local charitable organizations.
Limitations: Giving primarily in CA. No grants to individuals.
Publications: 990-PF.
Application information: Contributes only to pre-selected organizations. Applications not accepted.
Trustees: Sam Battistone, Sr., Chair.; J. Roger Battistone, Sam D. Battistone.
Number of staff: 6 full-time support.
Employer Identification Number: 956225967

183
The Donald E. and Delia B. Baxter Foundation ⌑

201 South Lake Ave., Suite 602
Pasadena 91101-3091 (818) 577-4955

Incorporated in 1959 in CA.
Donor(s): Delia B. Baxter.
Foundation type: Independent
Financial data (yr. ended 12/31/87): Assets, $15,295,711 (M); expenditures, $911,811, including $450,000 for 6 grants (high: $150,000; low: $20,000).
Purpose and activities: Support for educational and scientific institutions for research and development of medicine, instruments, and fluids for alleviating pain and protecting and prolonging human life.
Types of support: Research, building funds, professorships, fellowships.
Limitations: Giving primarily in CA.

Application information: Grants usually initiated by the foundation's board.
Write: Richard N. Mackay, Pres.
Officers and Directors: Richard N. Mackay, Pres.; Richard H. Haake, V.P.; Adam Y. Bennion, Secy.-Treas.; Donald B. Haake, Martha B. Haake.
Employer Identification Number: 956029555

184
Beaver Foundation ¤
100 Requa Rd.
Piedmont 94611

Established in 1969 in CA.
Donor(s): Wallace W. Knox.†
Foundation type: Independent
Financial data (yr. ended 12/31/88): Assets, $5,185,363 (M); expenditures, $313,495, including $240,000 for 6 grants (high: $125,000; low: $7,813).
Purpose and activities: Giving primarily for population studies and youth; support also for a building fund.
Types of support: Building funds, general purposes, continuing support.
Limitations: Giving limited to Alameda County, CA, excluding Livermore Valley. No grants to individuals.
Application information: Application form not required.
Initial approach: Letter
Copies of proposal: 1
Deadline(s): None
Write: Marjorie J. Beard, Secy.-Treas.
Officers: Charles N. Whitehead, Pres.; Philbrick Bowhay, V.P.; John C. Ricksen, V.P.; William C. Robbins III, V.P.; Marjorie J. Beard, Secy.-Treas.
Employer Identification Number: 941682883

185
Bechtel Foundation ▼ ¤
50 Beale St.
San Francisco 94105 (415) 768-5974

Incorporated in 1953 in CA.
Donor(s): Bechtel Power Corp.
Foundation type: Company-sponsored
Financial data (yr. ended 12/31/88): Assets, $19,557,092 (M); expenditures, $1,730,485, including $1,339,728 for 256 grants (high: $260,000; low: $100; average: $1,000-$20,000) and $134,879 for employee matching gifts.
Purpose and activities: Grants for higher education and community funds, and to organizations related to some aspect of the engineering business and construction. Support also for cultural programs, public interest, health organizations, and social services.
Types of support: Employee matching gifts.
Limitations: No support for religious organizations. No grants to individuals, or for endowment funds or special projects.
Application information:
Initial approach: Letter or proposal
Deadline(s): None
Board meeting date(s): Annually
Final notification: Varies
Write: K.M. Bandarrae, Asst. Secy.
Officers: R.P. Bechtel,* Chair.; C.W. Hull,* Vice-Chair.; John Neerhout, Jr.,* Vice-Chair.; D.M. Slavich,* Pres. and Treas.; W.L. Friend,* Exec. V.P.; D.J. Gunther,* Exec. V.P.; L.G. Hinkelman, Exec. V.P.; J.D. Carter,* Sr. V.P. and Secy.; T.G. Flynn, Sr. V.P.
Directors:* Stephen D. Bechtel, Jr.
Number of staff: 1 full-time professional; 1 part-time professional; 1 full-time support; 1 part-time support.
Employer Identification Number: 946078120

186
S. D. Bechtel, Jr. Foundation ¤
50 Beale St.
San Francisco 94105 (415) 768-7620
Mailing address: P.O. Box 3809, San Francisco, CA 94119

Incorporated in 1957 in CA.
Donor(s): S.D. Bechtel, Jr., Mrs. S.D. Bechtel, Jr.
Foundation type: Independent
Financial data (yr. ended 12/31/86): Assets, $16,577,521 (M); gifts received, $10,168,575; expenditures, $35,777, including $24,500 for 15 grants (high: $5,000; low: $500).
Purpose and activities: Grants restricted to institutions in which the directors have personal involvement, primarily educational institutions and cultural programs.
Limitations: Giving primarily in the San Francisco Bay Area, CA. No grants to individuals.
Application information: Contributes only to pre-selected organizations. Applications not accepted.
Board meeting date(s): As required
Write: Charles J. Spevak, V.P.
Officers and Directors:* S.D. Bechtel, Jr.,* Pres.; A. Barlow Ferguson,* V.P. and Secy.; Charles J. Spevak, V.P. and Treas.; Elizabeth Hogan Bechtel,* V.P.; Thomas G. Flynn, V.P.
Employer Identification Number: 946066138

187
The Newton D. & Rochelle F. Becker Foundation ¤ ☆
15760 Ventura Blvd., Suite 1101
Encino 91436
Application address: 2743 Aqua Verde Circle, Los Angeles, CA 90077

Established in 1986 in CA.
Donor(s): Newton D. Becker.
Foundation type: Independent
Financial data (yr. ended 12/31/88): Assets, $1,203,066 (M); gifts received, $130,000; expenditures, $125,000, including $125,000 for 1 grant.
Purpose and activities: Support primarily for a Jewish welfare fund.
Application information:
Initial approach: Letter
Deadline(s): None
Write: Newton D. Becker, Pres.
Officers and Directors: Newton D. Becker, Pres.; David E. Becker, V.P. and Treas.; David J. Cohen, Secy.; Herbert M. Gelfand, Carl Rheuban.
Employer Identification Number: 954095134

188
Arnold and Mabel Beckman Foundation ▼
c/o Hopper Kaufman & Co.
5140 Campus Dr., Suite 100
Newport Beach 92660 (714) 851-0500

Incorporated in 1977 in CA.
Donor(s): Arnold O. Beckman, Mabel M. Beckman.†
Foundation type: Independent
Financial data (yr. ended 08/31/89): Assets, $179,263,236 (M); expenditures, $19,343,124, including $19,343,124 for 12 grants (high: $7,800,000; low: $2,500).
Purpose and activities: Support for higher education and scientific and medical research; emphasis on research in genetics, biochemistry, chemistry, and human and artificial intelligence.
Types of support: Annual campaigns, conferences and seminars, endowment funds, equipment, matching funds, professorships, research, seed money, building funds.
Limitations: Giving primarily in CA. No grants to individuals; no loans.
Application information: Contributes only to pre-selected organizations. Applications not accepted.
Board meeting date(s): Nov. and July
Write: Arnold O. Beckman, Pres.
Officers and Trustees:* Arnold O. Beckman,* Pres.; Donald A. Strauss, V.P. and Secy.; Harold Brown, Maurice H. Stans.
Number of staff: 1 part-time support.
Employer Identification Number: 953169713

189
Milo W. Bekins Foundation ¤
c/o Wells Fargo Bank, N.A.
525 Market St., 17th Fl.
San Francisco 94163 (213) 253-3183

Trust established in 1953 in CA.
Donor(s): Milo W. Bekins, The Bekins Co.
Foundation type: Independent
Financial data (yr. ended 12/31/88): Assets, $3,432,055 (M); expenditures, $246,648, including $174,000 for 38 grants (high: $16,000; low: $1,000).
Purpose and activities: To assist various charitable and educational institutions, with emphasis on higher education, including support for a scholarship foundation that awards grants to individuals; giving also for hospitals, youth agencies, social services, and community funds.
Application information: Contributes only to pre-selected organizations. Applications not accepted.
Write: Milo W. Bekins, Jr., Trustee
Trustees: Michael Bekins, Milo W. Bekins, Jr., Virginia Bekins Daum.
Agent: Wells Fargo Bank, N.A.
Employer Identification Number: 956039745

190
Bellini Foundation ¤ ☆
400 Estudillo Ave., Suite 200
San Leandro 94577

Established in 1981.
Donor(s): J. Bellini.†
Foundation type: Independent

Financial data (yr. ended 6/30/89): Assets, $2,844,539 (M); gifts received, $14,500; expenditures, $133,601, including $131,000 for 31 grants (high: $10,000; low: $500).
Purpose and activities: Support primarily for hospitals, medical research, elementary and secondary education, youth organizations, and social services.
Limitations: Giving primarily in CA.
Application information:
Initial approach: Letter
Deadline(s): None
Write: B. K. Jayswal, Secy.
Officers: Patrick W. Bellini, Pres.; Michael J. Bellini, V.P.; B.K. Jayswal, Secy.
Employer Identification Number: 942768903

191
Belvedere Scientific Fund ⌑
c/o W.A. Bucci
P.O. Box 2760
Yountville 94599-2760

Established in 1959 in CA.
Foundation type: Independent
Financial data (yr. ended 12/31/87): Assets, $1,094,319 (M); expenditures, $51,945, including $46,600 for 13 grants (high: $15,000; low: $300).
Purpose and activities: Support primarily for higher education and Christian organizations and churches; some support for music and the fine arts.
Application information: Contributes only to pre-selected organizations. Applications not accepted.
Officers and Trustees: Nancy F. Ogg, Pres.; Robert D. Ogg, Secy.; W.A. Bucci, Treas.; David T. Slusser.
Employer Identification Number: 946065257

192
Legler Benbough Foundation ⌑
2550 Fifth Ave., Suite 132
San Diego 92103-6622 (619) 235-8099

Established in 1985 in CA.
Donor(s): Legler Benbough.
Foundation type: Independent
Financial data (yr. ended 12/31/87): Assets, $4,148,540 (M); expenditures, $155,708, including $140,850 for 13 grants (high: $70,000; low: $100).
Purpose and activities: Support primarily for cancer research, museums, and the arts. Some support for community development.
Types of support: General purposes.
Limitations: Giving primarily in the San Diego, CA, area.
Application information:
Initial approach: Letter
Write: Legler Benbough, Pres.
Officers: Legler Benbough, Pres.; Winifred Demming, V.P.; Peter K. Ellsworth, Secy.; Thomas Cisco, Treas.
Employer Identification Number: 330105049

193
H. N. and Frances C. Berger Foundation ⌑
P.O. Box 3064
Arcadia 91006

Incorporated in 1961 in CA.
Donor(s): Frances C. Berger, H.N. Berger.
Foundation type: Independent
Financial data (yr. ended 12/31/88): Assets, $12,392,415 (M); gifts received, $334,064; expenditures, $626,306, including $541,781 for 42 grants (high: $147,251; low: $25).
Purpose and activities: Emphasis on higher education, cultural programs, public health organizations, and hospitals. Committed to long-term support of present donees.
Limitations: Giving primarily in CA. No grants to individuals.
Application information:
Initial approach: Letter
Deadline(s): None
Board meeting date(s): Semiannually and as required
Write: Frances C. Berger, Pres.
Officers and Directors: Frances C. Berger, Pres.; Joan Auen, Secy.; John N. Berger, Treas.; Richard Auen, Robert M. Barton, Harry F. Booth, Jr.
Employer Identification Number: 956048939

194
Bergstrom Foundation, Inc.
149 Hawthorn Dr.
Atherton 94027
Mailing address: P.O. Box 126, Palo Alto, CA 94302-0126; Tel.: (415) 323-0596

Established in 1981 in CA.
Donor(s): Arline Bergstrom Trust, Erik E. Bergstrom.
Foundation type: Independent
Financial data (yr. ended 9/30/88): Assets, $5,950,193 (M); gifts received, $2,848,007; expenditures, $161,006, including $141,000 for 6 grants (high: $50,000; low: $3,000).
Purpose and activities: Support only for programs for the control and/or study of the growth in human populations, including focus on Latin America.
Types of support: General purposes.
Limitations: Giving primarily in Latin America. No grants to individuals.
Publications: 990-PF.
Application information: Applications not accepted.
Initial approach: Letter or proposal
Deadline(s): None
Write: Erik E. Bergstrom, Pres.
Officers and Director:* Erik E. Bergstrom,* Pres. and Mgr.; Helen L. Erd, Secy.-Treas.
Employer Identification Number: 942789679

195
Peter Berkey Foundation ⌑
1260 Coast Village Circle
Santa Barbara 93108
Application address: 840 20th St., No. 13, Santa Monica, CA 90403; Tel.: (213) 453-1334

Incorporated in 1947 in IL.
Donor(s): Peter Berkey.†
Foundation type: Independent
Financial data (yr. ended 12/31/86): Assets, $1,620,387 (M); expenditures, $154,142, including $148,200 for 42 grants (high: $50,000; low: $50; average: $500-$5,000).
Purpose and activities: Emphasis on health agencies, hospitals, youth agencies, and higher education.
Application information: Applications not accepted.
Write: Andrew D. Berkey II, Pres.
Officers and Directors: Andrew D. Berkey II, Pres.; Anne S. Kratz, Secy.; June B. D'Arcy.
Employer Identification Number: 362447326

196
The Lowell Berry Foundation ▼
Four Orinda Way, No. 140B
Orinda 94563-2513 (415) 254-1944

Incorporated in 1950 in CA.
Donor(s): Lowell W. Berry,† Farm Service Co., The Best Fertilizer Co. of Texas.
Foundation type: Independent
Financial data (yr. ended 12/31/89): Assets, $19,928,402 (M); expenditures, $1,122,940, including $1,024,868 for 230 grants (high: $346,000; low: $100; average: $500-$25,000).
Purpose and activities: Support for evangelical Christian religious programs, non-religious grants are focused on social services. Grants also for education, youth agencies, health associations, and cultural programs.
Types of support: Annual campaigns, conferences and seminars, continuing support, emergency funds, endowment funds, general purposes, operating budgets, professorships, scholarship funds, special projects.
Limitations: Giving primarily in Contra Costa and northern Alameda counties, CA. No grants to individuals, or for building or capital funds, equipment, seed money, or land acquisition.
Publications: Application guidelines, program policy statement, grants list.
Application information: Application form not required.
Initial approach: Letter
Copies of proposal: 1
Deadline(s): None
Board meeting date(s): Bimonthly
Final notification: 1 to 2 months for religious grants; 2 to 4 months for secular grants
Write: Susan L. Shira, Admin.; John C. Branagh, Pres. (for religious grants); Barbara Berry Corneille, Dir. (for secular grants)
Officers and Directors:* John C. Branagh,* Pres.; Herbert Funk,* V.P.; Barbara Berry Corneille,* Secy.; Robert Wiley,* Treas.; Patricia Berry Felix, William Stoddard.
Number of staff: 1 full-time professional.
Employer Identification Number: 946108391

197
Winifred M. Best Charitable Trust ⌑ ☆
c/o Security Pacific National Bank
P.O. Box 3189, Terminal Annex
Los Angeles 90051-1189
Application address: 3737 Main St., Riverside, CA 92501; Tel.: (714) 781-1221

Established in 1986 in CA.
Foundation type: Independent

Financial data (yr. ended 7/31/88): Assets, $1,589,244 (M); gifts received, $48,600; expenditures, $156,969, including $132,681 for 9 grants (high: $35,912; low: $681).
Purpose and activities: Support primarily for health associations, including cancer research and heart disease, and a hospital for crippled children.
Application information:
Write: Tammy Fox, Sr. Trust Officer, Security Pacific National Bank
Trustee: Security Pacific National Bank.
Employer Identification Number: 956859661

198
Burton G. Bettingen Corporation
9777 Wilshire Blvd., Suite 611
Beverly Hills 90212 (213) 276-4115

Established in 1984 in CA.
Donor(s): Burton G. Bettingen.†
Foundation type: Independent
Financial data (yr. ended 9/30/88): Assets, $24,200,362 (M); gifts received, $1,482,145; expenditures, $4,689,398, including $4,477,000 for 16 grants (high: $4,000,000; low: $5,000).
Purpose and activities: Support primarily for health, social services, and higher education.
Publications: Application guidelines.
Application information: Application form not required.
Initial approach: Letter
Copies of proposal: 1
Deadline(s): None
Board meeting date(s): Early May
Write: Patricia A. Brown, Secy.
Officers and Directors: Sandra G. Nowicki, Pres.; Stuart P. Tobisman, V.P.; Gyte Van Zyl, V.P.; Patricia A. Brown, Secy. and Admin. Dir.; Jane Van Zyl.
Number of staff: 2 full-time professional; 1 part-time professional.
Employer Identification Number: 953942826

199
The Kathryne Beynon Foundation ⌑
350 West Colorado Blvd., Suite 400
Pasadena 91105-1894

Established in 1967 in CA.
Donor(s): Kathryne Beynon.†
Foundation type: Independent
Financial data (yr. ended 10/31/88): Assets, $5,103,774 (M); expenditures, $299,223, including $215,000 for 20 grants (high: $38,000; low: $1,000).
Purpose and activities: Emphasis on hospitals, youth agencies, child welfare, Catholic church support, and higher education.
Types of support: Building funds, general purposes.
Limitations: Giving primarily in CA.
Application information: Application form not required.
Deadline(s): None
Write: Robert D. Bannon, Trustee
Trustees: Earl J. Bannon, Robert D. Bannon.
Employer Identification Number: 956197328

200
Bialis Family Foundation ⌑
c/o O'Melveny & Meyers
1800 Century Park East, Suite 600
Los Angeles 90067 (213) 553-6700

Established in 1981 in CA.
Donor(s): Gary C. Bialis, Bialis Trading.
Foundation type: Independent
Financial data (yr. ended 06/30/89): Assets, $1,415,212 (M); gifts received, $74,800; expenditures, $222,277, including $203,373 for 38 grants (high: $15,000; low: $500).
Purpose and activities: Grants for social services, education, health services, and Jewish organizations.
Application information: Funds are committed for the foreseeable future. Applications not accepted.
Write: Frederick Richman, Esq., Dir.
Directors and Trustees:* Gary C. Bialis,* Pres.; Ellen Bialis, Frederick A. Richman.
Employer Identification Number: 953646277

201
Bing Fund ⌑
9700 West Pico Blvd.
Los Angeles 90035 (213) 277-5711

Trust established in 1958 in CA.
Donor(s): Anna Bing Arnold, Peter S. Bing.
Foundation type: Independent
Financial data (yr. ended 2/28/89): Assets, $3,579,046 (M); gifts received, $15,378; expenditures, $170,918, including $168,000 for 3 grants (high: $100,000; low: $18,000).
Purpose and activities: Giving for higher education and cultural programs.
Types of support: General purposes.
Limitations: Giving primarily in CA. No grants to individuals.
Application information: Application form not required.
Initial approach: Letter
Copies of proposal: 1
Deadline(s): None
Board meeting date(s): Quarterly
Write: Peter S. Bing, Trustee
Trustees: Anna H. Bing, Peter S. Bing, Robert D. Burch.
Employer Identification Number: 956031105

202
The Bireley Foundation ⌑
144 North Brand Blvd.
Glendale 91203 (818) 500-7755

Incorporated in 1960 in CA.
Donor(s): Frank W. Bireley.†
Foundation type: Independent
Financial data (yr. ended 12/31/88): Assets, $5,918,282 (M); expenditures, $631,667, including $564,030 for 61 grants (high: $50,000; low: $500).
Purpose and activities: Grants mainly to a local medical school and children's hospital for research and treatment of adolescent skin diseases. Support also for local higher education, hospitals, and health agencies.
Limitations: Giving primarily in CA and UT. No grants to individuals.
Application information:
Initial approach: Letter or proposal
Copies of proposal: 2
Deadline(s): Submit proposal preferably between Jan. and June; no set deadline
Board meeting date(s): 6 times a year
Write: Christine Harriet Bireley, Pres.
Officers and Directors: Christine Harriet Bireley,* Pres.; Ernest R. Baldwin,* V.P. and Secy.; Frank W. Bireley,* V.P.; William Robert Bireley, V.P.; Christine Bireley Oliver, V.P.; Leroy M. Gire, Treas.
Number of staff: None.
Employer Identification Number: 956029475

203
Sam & Rie Bloomfield Foundation, Inc. ⌑
P.O. Box 686
200 Dinsmore Dr.
Fortuna 95540

Established in 1958 in KS.
Donor(s): Sam Bloomfield,† Rie Bloomfield.
Foundation type: Independent
Financial data (yr. ended 11/30/87): Assets, $6,836,966 (M); expenditures, $98,943, including $64,500 for 8 grants (high: $26,700; low: $200).
Purpose and activities: Giving primarily for Jewish temple support and higher education; some support also for hospitals and cultural organizations.
Limitations: No grants to individuals.
Application information:
Write: Paul Mahan, Trustee
Officers and Trustees: Rie Bloomfield, Pres.; Vernon McKay, Secy.; Paul D. Mahan, Treas.
Employer Identification Number: 956074613

204
Blume Foundation ☆
85 El Cerrito Ave.
Hillsborough 94010 (415) 343-5585

Established in 1957.
Donor(s): John A. Blume, Ruth C. Blume.†
Foundation type: Independent
Financial data (yr. ended 11/30/89): Assets, $1,090,799 (M); expenditures, $58,112, including $52,675 for 18 grants (high: $46,000; low: $25).
Purpose and activities: Giving primarily for higher education; support also for animal welfare, health, and medical research.
Limitations: Giving primarily in CA. No grants to individuals.
Publications: 990-PF.
Application information: Contributes only to pre-selected organizations. Applications not accepted.
Board meeting date(s): Nov.
Write: Jene Blume, Dir.
Officer and Directors: John A. Blume, Pres.; Jene F. Blume.
Employer Identification Number: 946073163

205
Boeckmann Charitable Foundation ⌑
15505 Roscoe Blvd.
Sepulveda 91343

Established in 1982 in CA.
Donor(s): Herbert F. Boeckmann, Jane Boeckmann.
Foundation type: Independent

Financial data (yr. ended 11/30/88): Assets, $59,836 (L); gifts received, $850,000; expenditures, $894,350, including $847,350 for 45 grants (high: $250,000; low: $500).
Purpose and activities: Giving primarily for religion and youth services.
Limitations: Giving primarily in CA.
Application information: Application form not required.
Initial approach: Letter
Deadline(s): None
Write: The Officers
Officers: Herbert F. Boeckmann II, C.E.O.; Jane Boeckmann, Secy.
Employer Identification Number: 953806976

206
The Bolthouse Foundation ⌑ ☆
7200 East Brundage Ln.
Bakersfield 93307 (805) 366-7205

Established in 1988 in CA.
Donor(s): William Bolthouse Farms, Inc.
Foundation type: Independent
Financial data (yr. ended 12/31/88): Assets, $108,263 (M); gifts received, $226,500; expenditures, $124,516, including $120,310 for 13 grants (high: $13,810; low: $5,000).
Purpose and activities: "To provide financial support or necessary services or activities in support of organizations whose operations and principles are consistent with evangelical Christianity." Recipients include missionary programs and Bible studies.
Limitations: No support for private foundations. No grants to individuals.
Application information: Application form required.
Deadline(s): None
Board meeting date(s): June
Final notification: Within one month
Write: William J. Bolthouse, Pres.
Officers and Trustees: William J. Bolthouse, Chair. and Pres.; Amy Louise Shane, Secy.-Treas.; Kathy J. Bolthouse, Lisa A. Bolthouse, Nora J. Bolthouse, William T. Bolthouse, Michael T. Shane.
Employer Identification Number: 770186343

207
Otis Booth Foundation ⌑
c/o Otis Booth, Jr.
1100 Glendon Ave., Suite 2017
Los Angeles 90024

Established in 1967 in CA.
Donor(s): Berkshire Hathaway Corp.
Foundation type: Independent
Financial data (yr. ended 11/30/86): Assets, $1,798,194 (M); gifts received, $13,484; expenditures, $79,918, including $78,278 for 13 grants (high: $39,748; low: $100).
Purpose and activities: Giving primarily for medicine and education.
Officers and Trustees: Otis Booth, Jr., Pres.; Charles T. Munger, V.P. and Treas.; Richard D. Ebenshade, Secy.
Employer Identification Number: 956140019

208
Albert & Elaine Borchard Foundation ⌑
22055 Clarendon St., Suite 210
Woodland Hills 91367

Established in 1978 in CA.
Foundation type: Independent
Financial data (yr. ended 07/31/89): Assets, $14,201,722 (M); expenditures, $995,278, including $422,949 for 36 grants (high: $60,000; low: $1,000).
Purpose and activities: Giving for social services and higher education, including scholarship funds.
Types of support: Scholarship funds.
Limitations: No grants to individuals.
Application information:
Initial approach: Letter
Deadline(s): None
Directors: Willard A. Beling, Edward D. Spurgeon.
Employer Identification Number: 953294377

209
Anna Borun and Harry Borun Foundation
c/o Wells Fargo Bank, N.A.
333 South Grand Ave.
Los Angeles 90071

Established in 1957 in CA.
Donor(s): Anna Borun,† Harry Borun.†
Foundation type: Independent
Financial data (yr. ended 12/31/88): Assets, $5,541,901 (M); expenditures, $382,191, including $143,000 for 19 grants (high: $200,000; low: $200) and $200,000 for 1 loan.
Purpose and activities: Support largely for Jewish welfare funds, education, and an environmental preservation association.
Limitations: Giving primarily in CA. No grants to individuals.
Application information:
Initial approach: Letter
Deadline(s): None
Write: Sue Boling, Trust Officer, Wells Fargo Bank, N.A.
Trustee: Wells Fargo Bank, N.A.
Number of staff: None.
Employer Identification Number: 956150362

210
The James G. Boswell Foundation ▼ ⌑
4600 Security Pacific Plaza
333 South Hope St.
Los Angeles 90071 (213) 485-1717

Incorporated in 1947 in CA.
Donor(s): James G. Boswell.†
Foundation type: Independent
Financial data (yr. ended 12/31/87): Assets, $47,596,875 (M); expenditures, $2,275,004, including $2,019,250 for 44 grants (high: $1,000,000; low: $500).
Purpose and activities: Giving primarily for education, health, the environment, social services, and public policy organizations.
Types of support: General purposes, annual campaigns, scholarship funds, continuing support.
Limitations: Giving primarily in CA.
Application information:
Initial approach: Letter
Deadline(s): None
Board meeting date(s): Feb. and as required
Final notification: Varies
Write: Greer J. Fearon, Exec. Secy.
Officers and Trustees: James G. Boswell II, Pres.; Rosalind M. Boswell, Secy.-Treas.; Susan W. Dulin.
Number of staff: None.
Employer Identification Number: 956047326

211
The Bothin Foundation
873 Sutter St., Suite B
San Francisco 94109 (415) 771-4300

Incorporated in 1917 in CA.
Donor(s): Henry E. Bothin,† Ellen Chabot Bothin,† Genevieve Bothin de Limur.†
Foundation type: Independent
Financial data (yr. ended 12/31/88): Assets, $16,113,613 (M); expenditures, $933,031, including $644,382 for 84 grants (high: $50,000; low: $25).
Purpose and activities: Giving for youth and cultural programs for youth, community activities, health, the handicapped, social services, minorities, the aged, and the environment.
Types of support: Building funds, equipment, matching funds, technical assistance, capital campaigns.
Limitations: Giving primarily in CA, with emphasis on San Francisco, Marin, Sonoma, and San Mateo counties. No support for religious organizations, educational institutions (except those directly aiding the developmentally disabled), or for production or distribution of films or other documentary presentations. No grants to individuals, or for general operating funds, endowment funds, scholarships, fellowships, or conferences; no loans.
Publications: Biennial report (including application guidelines).
Application information: Application form not required.
Initial approach: Letter containing a brief and comprehensive outline of the project
Copies of proposal: 1
Deadline(s): 8 weeks prior to meeting
Board meeting date(s): Early to mid-Feb., June, and Oct.
Final notification: 2 to 3 months
Write: Lyman H. Casey, Exec. Dir.
Officers: Genevieve di San Faustino,* Pres.; Edmona Lyman Mansell,* V.P.; Frances L. Joyce, Secy.; Lyman H. Casey,* Treas. and Exec. Dir.
Directors:* William W. Budge, A. Michael Casey, William F. Geisler, Benjamin J. Henley, Jr., Stephanie P. MacColl, Rhoda W. Schultz.
Number of staff: 1 full-time professional; 1 full-time support.
Employer Identification Number: 941196182

212
Ethel Wilson Bowles & Robert Bowles Memorial Fund
c/o Emrys J. Ross and Sally A. Terry, et al
301 East Colorado Blvd., No. 900
Pasadena 91101 (818) 796-9123

Trust established in 1974 in CA.

Donor(s): Ethel W. Bowles.†
Foundation type: Independent
Financial data (yr. ended 12/31/88): Assets, $9,430,896 (M); expenditures, $580,028, including $490,440 for 8 grants of $61,305 each.
Purpose and activities: Grants to tax-exempt institutions in the fields of medicine and medical research.
Types of support: Continuing support.
Limitations: Giving primarily in CA. No grants to individuals, or for building or endowment funds.
Application information: Contributes only to pre-selected organizations. Applications not accepted.
Board meeting date(s): As required
Trustees: Emrys J. Ross, Sally A. Terry.
Employer Identification Number: 956481575

213
Herbert & Marigrace Boyer Foundation ⌑
700 Larkspur Landing Circle, Suite 175
Larkspur 94939

Established in 1986 in CA.
Foundation type: Independent
Financial data (yr. ended 12/31/88): Assets, $470,081 (M); expenditures, $519,024, including $505,631 for 1 grant.
Purpose and activities: Giving to a medical school.
Types of support: Building funds.
Limitations: Giving primarily in New Haven, CT.
Application information: Contributes only to pre-selected organizations. Applications not accepted.
Directors: Herbert Boyer, Marigrace Boyer, Robert T. Stenson.
Employer Identification Number: 680118055

214
George and Ruth Bradford Foundation ⌑ ☆
P.O. Box E
San Mateo 94402-0017

Established in 1985 in CA.
Donor(s): Ruth Bradford.
Foundation type: Independent
Financial data (yr. ended 6/30/89): Assets, $2,066,934 (M); gifts received, $1,138; expenditures, $148,635, including $139,186 for 15 grants (high: $29,960; low: $1,000).
Purpose and activities: Giving primarily for higher and other education; support also for human services, including programs for the aged, youth, and mental health.
Types of support: Scholarship funds.
Limitations: Giving primarily in CA. No grants to individuals.
Application information:
Initial approach: Letter
Deadline(s): None
Write: Rebecca Haseleu
Directors: Robert Bradford, Ruth Bradford, Lloyd Haefner, Joan Richardson.
Employer Identification Number: 943015722

215
Braun Foundation ⌑
400 South Hope St.
Los Angeles 90071-2899 (818) 577-7000

Incorporated in 1953 in CA.
Donor(s): Members of the Braun family.
Foundation type: Independent
Financial data (yr. ended 12/31/88): Assets, $1,642,078 (M); gifts received, $895,844; expenditures, $372,585, including $329,500 for 37 grants (high: $50,000; low: $500; average: $2,500-$21,000).
Purpose and activities: Contributions to hospitals, medical research, elementary and secondary schools, higher education, youth agencies, museums, cultural programs, and social services, including support programs for the handicapped.
Limitations: Giving primarily in CA.
Application information:
Deadline(s): None
Board meeting date(s): Oct. or Nov.
Final notification: Varies
Write: Donald R. Spuehler
Officer and Directors: Henry A. Braun, Pres.; C. Allan Braun, John G. Braun.
Number of staff: None.
Employer Identification Number: 956016820

216
Carl F. Braun Trust ⌑
400 South Hope St.
Los Angeles 90071-2899 (818) 577-7000

Trust established in 1955 in CA.
Donor(s): Carl F. Braun.†
Foundation type: Independent
Financial data (yr. ended 12/31/87): Assets, $17,082,855 (M); expenditures, $2,195,354, including $2,105,000 for 4 grants (high: $1,430,000; low: $75,000).
Purpose and activities: Contributions to colleges and universities.
Limitations: Giving limited to CA.
Application information:
Deadline(s): None
Final notification: Varies
Write: Donald R. Spuehler
Trustee: John G. Braun.
Number of staff: None.
Employer Identification Number: 956016828

217
Donald L. Bren Foundation ⌑ ☆
11111 Santa Monica Blvd., Suite 2110
Los Angeles 90025

Established in 1986.
Foundation type: Independent
Financial data (yr. ended 11/30/88): Assets, $3,791,345 (M); expenditures, $416,834, including $410,000 for 3 grants (high: $300,000; low: $10,000).
Purpose and activities: Giving primarily for higher education and an art museum.
Types of support: Endowment funds.
Limitations: Giving primarily in CA.
Application information: Funds currently committed. Applications not accepted.
Officers and Directors: Donald L. Bren, Pres.; Mary Ann Pope, V.P. and Secy.-Treas.; Ashley Ann Bren.
Employer Identification Number: 954094426

218
The Mervyn L. Brenner Foundation, Inc. ⌑
Three Embarcadero Ctr., 21st Fl.
San Francisco 94111 (415) 951-7508

Incorporated in 1961 in CA.
Donor(s): Mervyn L. Brenner.†
Foundation type: Independent
Financial data (yr. ended 8/31/88): Assets, $2,589,142 (M); expenditures, $147,000, including $126,600 for 60 grants (high: $10,000; low: $150).
Purpose and activities: Emphasis on health and hospitals, including medical research, social services and youth agencies, including Jewish welfare funds, cultural organizations, higher education and the fields of law and accounting.
Types of support: Annual campaigns, operating budgets.
Limitations: Giving primarily in CA. No grants to individuals.
Application information: Funds fully committed.
Initial approach: Proposal
Deadline(s): None
Write: John R. Gentry, Pres.
Officers and Directors: John R. Gentry, Pres.; William D. Crawford, V.P.; Marvin T. Tepperman, V.P.; Marc H. Monheimer, Secy.; John T. Seigle, Treas.
Number of staff: None.
Employer Identification Number: 946088679

219
Robert and Alice Bridges Foundation
Two Embarcadero Center, No. 2140
San Francisco 94111 (415) 392-6320

Established in 1957 in CA.
Donor(s): Robert L. Bridges, Alice M. Bridges.
Foundation type: Independent
Financial data (yr. ended 12/31/88): Assets, $1,757,004 (M); gifts received, $37,125; expenditures, $108,227, including $90,860 for 69 grants (high: $10,000; low: $25).
Purpose and activities: Support largely for higher education; grants also for youth agencies, hospitals and health associations, and the arts, including the performing arts.
Types of support: Capital campaigns, continuing support, general purposes.
Limitations: Giving primarily in the San Francisco Bay Area, CA. No grants to individuals for education or for any other purpose.
Publications: Annual report.
Application information: Contributes only to pre-selected organizations. Applications not accepted.
Deadline(s): None
Write: Robert L. Bridges, Pres.
Officers: Robert L. Bridges, Pres.; Alice M. Bridges, V.P.; David M. Bridges, V.P.; James R. Bridges, V.P.; Linda Bridges Ingham, V.P.; Michael L. Mellor, Secy.
Employer Identification Number: 946066355

220
Briggs Foundation ⌑
P.O. Box 1510
Rancho Santa Fe 92067 (619) 756-4875

Established in 1985 in CA.
Donor(s): Blaine A. Briggs, Laverne S. Briggs.
Foundation type: Independent
Financial data (yr. ended 07/31/89): Assets, $1,189,711 (M); gifts received, $6,781; expenditures, $55,342, including $44,589 for 74 grants (high: $9,900; low: $15).
Purpose and activities: Support for churches, hospitals and health centers, social services, and education.
Limitations: Giving primarily in San Diego County, CA.
Application information:
Initial approach: Letter
Deadline(s): None
Write: Robert B. Briggs
Trustees: Blaine A. Briggs, Laverne S. Briggs.
Employer Identification Number: 330119350

221
Bright Family Foundation ⌑
2741 Yosemite Blvd.
Modesto 95380 (209) 526-8242

Established in 1986 in CA.
Donor(s): Calvin Bright, Marjorie Bright.
Foundation type: Independent
Financial data (yr. ended 12/31/88): Assets, $1,736,952 (M); gifts received, $250,000; expenditures, $67,314, including $56,000 for 14 grants (high: $14,000; low: $500).
Purpose and activities: Giving primarily for youth groups, higher education, a Methodist church and health organizations.
Types of support: Operating budgets, renovation projects.
Limitations: Giving primarily in CA.
Application information: Application form required.
Deadline(s): None
Final notification: Dec. 20
Write: Marjorie Bright, V.P.
Officers: Calvin Bright, Pres.; Marjorie Bright, V.P.; Lyn Bright, Secy.-Treas.
Employer Identification Number: 770126942

222
Eli Broad Family Foundation
11601 Wilshire Blvd., 12th Fl.
Los Angeles 90025

Established in 1980 in CA.
Donor(s): Eli Broad.
Foundation type: Operating
Financial data (yr. ended 06/30/89): Assets, $18,386,276 (M); gifts received, $1,451,850; qualifying distributions, $4,007,415, including $67,250 for 13 grants (high: $25,000; low: $500; average: $500-$2,500) and $3,668,088 for 4 foundation-administered programs.
Purpose and activities: A private operating foundation; support primarily for organizations which support the exhibition of contemporary American art.
Types of support: General purposes.
Limitations: Giving primarily in CA.
Application information: Contributes only to pre-selected organizations. Applications not accepted.
Officers: Eli Broad, Pres.; Sharon McQueen, Secy.; Edythe L. Broad, Treas.
Number of staff: 1 full-time professional; 3 full-time support; 1 part-time support.
Employer Identification Number: 953537237

223
Dana & Albert R. Broccoli Charitable Foundation ⌑
2121 Avenue of the Stars, Suite 1240
Los Angeles 90067

Established in 1980 in CA.
Donor(s): Albert R. Broccoli, Dana Broccoli.
Foundation type: Independent
Financial data (yr. ended 12/31/88): Assets, $2,735,099 (M); gifts received, $83,000; expenditures, $151,166, including $148,685 for 23 grants (high: $27,000; low: $1,000).
Purpose and activities: Support for higher education, hospitals and health associations, cultural programs, and youth and family services.
Types of support: General purposes.
Application information: Contributes only to pre-selected organizations. Applications not accepted.
Officers: Albert R. Broccoli, Pres.; Dana Broccoli, V.P.; Michael G. Wilson, C.F.O.
Employer Identification Number: 953502889

224
Brotman Foundation of California ⌑
c/o Robert D. Hartford
433 North Camden Dr., No. 600
Beverly Hills 90210 (213) 271-2910

Established in 1964.
Foundation type: Independent
Financial data (yr. ended 12/31/88): Assets, $6,717,330 (M); expenditures, $452,630, including $302,200 for 36 grants (high: $50,000; low: $500).
Purpose and activities: Giving mainly for children and health; some support for arts and education.
Limitations: Giving primarily in CA.
Application information:
Initial approach: Letter
Deadline(s): None
Officers and Directors:* Michael B. Sherman,* Pres.; Lowell Marks,* Secy.; Robert D. Hartford,* Treas.; Toni Wald.
Employer Identification Number: 956094639

225
The David J. Brown and Virginia L. Brown Foundation ⌑
(Formerly The Brown Foundation)
2290 North First St.
San Jose 95131

Established in 1981 in CA.
Donor(s): David J. Brown.
Foundation type: Independent
Financial data (yr. ended 12/31/86): Assets, $332 (M); gifts received, $223,659; expenditures, $223,771, including $218,183 for 31 grants (high: $37,325; low: $100).
Purpose and activities: Giving primarily for religion and education.
Application information: Contributes only to pre-selected organizations. Applications not accepted.
Officers and Directors: David J. Brown, Pres.; Virginia L. Brown, V.P.; B. Craig Duncan, Secy.-Treas.; Stanley M. Johnson.
Employer Identification Number: 942807836

226
The Robert Brownlee Foundation ⌑ ☆
26050 Kristie Ln.
Los Altos Hills 94022

Established in 1986.
Foundation type: Independent
Financial data (yr. ended 09/30/89): Assets, $1,325,476 (M); expenditures, $51,805, including $34,983 for 4 grants (high: $10,000; low: $7,313).
Purpose and activities: Gives primarily for science and technology, including programs or facilities which develop scientific creativity and/or disseminate knowledge in pre-college use.
Application information: Application form not required.
Deadline(s): None
Write: Robert Brownlee, Pres.
Officers and Directors:* Robert Brownlee,* Pres.; Leonard Simon,* V.P.; Robert Borawski, Secy.-Treas.; Randall Blair,* C.F.O.; Edith Twombley Eddy.
Employer Identification Number: 770131702

227
Buchalter, Nemer, Fields, Chrystie & Younger Charitable Foundation ⌑
700 South Flower St., Suite 700
Los Angeles 90017 (213) 626-6700

Trust established in 1965 in CA.
Donor(s): Buchalter, Nemer, Fields, Chrystie & Younger.
Foundation type: Company-sponsored
Financial data (yr. ended 12/31/87): Assets, $304,435 (M); gifts received, $88,250; expenditures, $146,501, including $138,735 for 93 grants (high: $17,750; low: $25).
Purpose and activities: Emphasis on Jewish welfare funds, hospitals, and educational and cultural programs.
Limitations: Giving primarily in CA. No grants to individuals, or for endowment funds, research, scholarships, or fellowships; no loans.
Application information:
Initial approach: Letter, telephone, or proposal
Copies of proposal: 1
Deadline(s): Submit proposal preferably in Nov. or Dec.; deadline Dec. 31
Board meeting date(s): As required
Trustees: Irwin R. Buchalter, Arthur Chinski, Murray M. Fields, Terrance Nunan, Philip J. Wolman.
Employer Identification Number: 956112980

228
The Henry W. Bull Foundation
c/o Santa Barbara Bank & Trust
P.O. Box 2340
Santa Barbara 93120-2340 (805) 564-6211

Trust established in 1960 in CA.

Donor(s): Maud L. Bull.†
Foundation type: Independent
Financial data (yr. ended 12/31/88): Assets, $4,997,550 (M); expenditures, $262,756, including $223,500 for 76 grants (high: $20,000; low: $500; average: $1,000-$2,500).
Purpose and activities: Grants primarily for higher education, the handicapped, health, and church support.
Limitations: No grants to individuals, or for building or endowment funds.
Application information: Applications not accepted.
Board meeting date(s): Monthly
Write: Gary Newman, Asst. V.P., Santa Barbara Bank & Trust
Trustees: James W.Z. Taylor, Santa Barbara Bank & Trust.
Employer Identification Number: 956062058

229
The Alphonse A. Burnand Medical and Educational Foundation
P.O. Box 59
593 Palm Canyon Dr.
Borrego Springs 92004 (714) 767-5314

Incorporated in 1957 in CA.
Foundation type: Independent
Financial data (yr. ended 12/31/88): Assets, $2,029,509 (M); expenditures, $67,999, including $54,625 for 14 grants (high: $10,000; low: $1,000).
Purpose and activities: Emphasis on higher education, hospitals, youth agencies, and the handicapped.
Limitations: Giving primarily in Borrego Springs and San Diego County, CA. No grants to individuals, or for endowment funds.
Application information: Application form not required.
Initial approach: Letter
Copies of proposal: 1
Deadline(s): Submit proposal in Oct.
Board meeting date(s): As required, at least semiannually
Write: A.A. Burnand III, Pres.
Officers: A.A. Burnand III, Pres.; A.G. Hansen, Secy.; G.J. Kuhrts III, Treas.
Number of staff: 1 part-time support.
Employer Identification Number: 956083677

230
Burnham Foundation ⌑
610 West Ash St.
San Diego 92101

Established in 1980 in CA.
Foundation type: Independent
Financial data (yr. ended 12/31/88): Assets, $3,417,620 (M); expenditures, $376,361, including $348,237 for 56 grants (high: $250,000; low: $25).
Purpose and activities: Giving primarily for higher and other education and medical research.
Limitations: Giving primarily in CA. No grants to individuals.
Application information: Contributes only to pre-selected organizations. Applications not accepted.
Officers: Malin Burnham, Pres.; Roberta Burnham, V.P.; Nina Galloway, Secy.; Louis J. Garday, Treas.
Trustees: Robert Brettbard, Pauline des Granges, Philip M. Klauber.
Employer Identification Number: 953565278

231
Fritz B. Burns Foundation ▼ ⌑
4001 West Alameda Ave., Suite 203
Burbank 91505 (818) 840-8802

Incorporated in 1955 in CA.
Donor(s): Fritz B. Burns.†
Foundation type: Independent
Financial data (yr. ended 9/30/88): Assets, $138,492,443 (M); expenditures, $4,685,160, including $3,164,450 for 82 grants (high: $500,000; low: $300; average: $1,000-$100,000).
Purpose and activities: Grants primarily for education, hospitals and medical research organizations; support also for Roman Catholic religious associations and schools, social welfare agencies, and church support.
Limitations: Giving primarily in the Provo, UT and Los Angeles, CA, areas. No grants to individuals or private foundations.
Application information:
Initial approach: Letter
Deadline(s): None
Board meeting date(s): Feb., May, Aug., and Nov.
Write: Joseph E. Rawlinson, Pres.
Officers and Directors: William Herbert Hannon, Chair.; Joseph E. Rawlinson, Pres.; W.K. Skinner, Exec. V.P. and Secy.-Treas.; Charles S. Casassa, Richard Dunn, Don Freeburg, J. Robert Vaughan.
Number of staff: None.
Employer Identification Number: 956064403

232
Burns-Dunphy Foundation ⌑
c/o Walter M. Gleason
Hearst Bldg., Third & Market Sts., Suite 1200
San Francisco 94103

Foundation established in 1969 in CA.
Donor(s): Walter M. Gleason.
Foundation type: Independent
Financial data (yr. ended 12/31/88): Assets, $1,349,497 (M); gifts received, $90,000; expenditures, $87,878, including $87,000 for 32 grants (high: $10,000; low: $1,000).
Purpose and activities: Grants primarily for Roman Catholic welfare, educational, and missionary services.
Officers and Directors: Walter M. Gleason, Pres., Treas., and Mgr.; Patricia Gleason, V.P.; Cressey H. Nakagawa, Secy.
Employer Identification Number: 237043565

233
C & H Charitable Trust ☆
830 Loring Ave.
Crockett 94525

Established in 1974.
Donor(s): Hawaiian Commercial & Sugar, Hamakua Sugar Co.
Foundation type: Company-sponsored
Financial data (yr. ended 12/31/89): Assets, $31,140 (M); gifts received, $107,972; expenditures, $108,059, including $102,345 for 28 grants (high: $40,000; low: $100) and $5,605 for employee matching gifts.
Purpose and activities: Support for health and welfare, education, culture and the arts, and civic organizations.
Types of support: Employee matching gifts.
Limitations: Giving primarily in the Crockett, CA, area.
Application information:
Write: Cheri Tillotson, Exec. Secy.
Trustees: James M. Burt, Harold R. Somerset, William H. Stewart.
Employer Identification Number: 237410587

234
C.S. Fund ▼
469 Bohemian Hwy.
Freestone 95472 (707) 874-2942

Established in 1981 in CA as "pass through" fund for annual gifts of donors.
Donor(s): Maryanne Mott, Herman E. Warsh.
Foundation type: Operating
Financial data (yr. ended 10/31/89): Assets, $558,438 (M); gifts received, $1,200,000; expenditures, $1,341,342, including $820,000 for 60 grants (high: $50,000; low: $600; average: $5,000-$30,000) and $294,407 for foundation-administered programs.
Purpose and activities: A private operating foundation; giving for programs with national or international impact, in the areas of peace, especially alternative security; toxics, especially source reduction; protection of dissent and diversity, and preservation of biological diversity.
Types of support: Special projects, research, matching funds, publications, continuing support, operating budgets, technical assistance.
Limitations: No grants for endowment funds, capital ventures, emergency requests, or video or film production.
Publications: Annual report (including application guidelines), informational brochure (including application guidelines), financial statement, grants list.
Application information: Application form not required.
Initial approach: Proposal
Copies of proposal: 1
Deadline(s): Jan. 15, May 15, and Sept. 15, or the next Monday if deadline falls on a weekend
Final notification: Approximately 12 weeks after deadline
Officers and Directors:* Maryanne Mott,* Pres.; Herman E. Warsh,* Secy.-Treas.
Number of staff: 4 full-time professional; 1 full-time support; 2 part-time support.
Employer Identification Number: 953607882

235
Caddock Foundation, Inc. ⌑
1793 Chicago Ave.
Riverside 92507
Application address: 1717 Chicago Ave., Riverside, CA 92507; Tel.: (714) 788-1700

Incorporated in 1968 in CA.

Donor(s): Richard E. Caddock, Anne M. Caddock.
Foundation type: Independent
Financial data (yr. ended 12/31/88): Assets, $949,125 (M); expenditures, $335,312, including $332,000 for 31 grants (high: $20,000; low: $1,000).
Purpose and activities: Grants to Protestant religious associations and activities, including Bible studies.
Application information:
Initial approach: Proposal
Deadline(s): None
Write: Richard E. Caddock, Pres.
Officers: Richard E. Caddock, Pres.; Anne M. Caddock, V.P.; Sue E. Brinkman, Secy.; Richard E. Caddock, Jr., Treas.
Employer Identification Number: 952559728

236
The John R. Cahill Foundation ☆
425 California St., Suite 2300
San Francisco 94104 (415) 986-0600

Established in 1983 in CA.
Foundation type: Independent
Financial data (yr. ended 5/31/89): Assets, $3,847,793 (M); gifts received, $3,868,775; expenditures, $127,874, including $120,000 for 1 grant.
Purpose and activities: Giving primarily for youth and vocational education.
Limitations: Giving primarily in San Francisco, CA.
Application information: Applications not accepted.
Write: William R. Cahill, Chair.
Officers and Directors:* William R. Cahill,* Chair. and Pres.; Richard F. Cahill,* Treas.; J. Peter Cahill, John E. Cahill.
Employer Identification Number: 942860339

237
California Community Foundation ▼
606 South Olive St., Suite 2400
Los Angeles 90014 (213) 413-4042
Orange County office: 13252 Garden Grove Blvd., Suite 195, Garden Grove, CA 92643; Tel: (714) 750-7794

Established in 1915 in CA by bank resolution.
Foundation type: Community
Financial data (yr. ended 06/30/89): Assets, $80,053,899 (M); gifts received, $7,902,336; expenditures, $10,176,348, including $8,686,382 for grants (average: $5,000-$25,000).
Purpose and activities: Giving in the areas of arts and culture, civic affairs, education, health and medicine, and human services, with emphasis on children and youth and community development.
Types of support: Matching funds, technical assistance, emergency funds, program-related investments, seed money, special projects.
Limitations: Giving limited to Los Angeles, Orange, Riverside, San Bernadino, and Ventura counties, CA. No support for sectarian purposes. No grants to individuals, or for building funds, annual campaigns, equipment, endowment funds, operating budgets, scholarships, fellowships, films, conferences, dinners, or special events; no loans.
Publications: Annual report, application guidelines, informational brochure, newsletter.
Application information: Application form required.
Initial approach: Proposal
Copies of proposal: 1
Deadline(s): None
Board meeting date(s): Quarterly
Final notification: 3 months after board meets
Write: Jack Shakely, Pres.
Officers: Jack Shakely, Pres.; Paul Vandeventer, Exec. V.P.
Board of Governors: Stephen D. Gavin, Chair.; Caroline L. Ahmanson, Bruce C. Corwin, Hon. John Gavin, Walter B. Gerken, Robert Hurwitz, Hon. Ignacio E. Lozano, Jr., Sr. Marie Madeleine, S.C.L., Paul A. Miller, Bruce M. Ramer, Daniel H. Ridder, Ann Shaw, Hon. William French Smith, Esther Wachtell, Peggy Fouke Wortz.
Trustees: Security Pacific National Bank, City National Bank, First Interstate Bank, Trust Services of America, Wells Fargo Bank, N.A.
Number of staff: 7 full-time professional; 1 part-time professional; 8 full-time support.
Employer Identification Number: 956013179

238
California Educational Initiatives Fund
c/o Bank of America Center-Tax Dept. No. 3246
555 California St., P.O. Box 37000
San Francisco 94137 (415) 953-3175

Established in 1983 in CA as successor to Educational Initiatives Program (EIP) developed by BankAmerica Foundation in 1979.
Donor(s): BankAmerica Foundation, Chevron U.S.A., Inc., Wells Fargo Foundation, First Interstate Bank of California Foundation, Security Pacific Foundation, McKesson Foundation, ARCO Foundation, Union Bank Foundation, McDonnell Douglas West Personnel Community Service, Pacific Telesis Foundation, Ralph M. Parsons Foundation.
Foundation type: Company-sponsored
Financial data (yr. ended 12/31/88): Assets, $293,627 (M); gifts received, $530,481; expenditures, $690,072, including $659,622 for 71 grants (high: $13,580; low: $890; average: $5,000-$15,000).
Purpose and activities: Giving to public school districts that are winners of statewide competition; seeks proposals for innovative programs which address student needs and broaden support for public education; support to improve basic learning skills in the areas of language arts, mathematics, science, and the fine arts, and to encourage effective schools.
Types of support: Special projects.
Limitations: Giving limited to CA. No support for public school foundations, private schools, or university schools of education. No grants to individuals, or for construction or renovation of capital facilities, purchase of computer hardware, or employment of permanent personnel.
Publications: Application guidelines, program policy statement, informational brochure, grants list.
Application information: Send original copy of proposal. Grant requests in the $8,000-$12,000 range are encouraged. Application form required.
Initial approach: Solicitation letter
Copies of proposal: 1
Deadline(s): Mid-Oct.; funding available in Mar. and Apr.
Board meeting date(s): May and Nov.
Final notification: Feb.
Write: Joanne El-Gohary, Admin.
Officers: Donald A. Mullane, Pres.; Ruth Jones-Saxey, V.P.; Tom Donahue, Secy.; Alan Gordon, Treas.; Joanne El-Gohary, Admin.
Number of staff: None.
Employer Identification Number: 953830359

239
California Foundation for Biochemical Research
10901 North Torrey Pines Rd.
La Jolla 92037 (619) 234-6533

Incorporated in 1952 in CA.
Foundation type: Independent
Financial data (yr. ended 04/30/89): Assets, $2,078,302 (M); expenditures, $242,153, including $186,400 for 18 grants (high: $50,000; low: $1,200).
Purpose and activities: To support biochemical research fellowships.
Types of support: Fellowships, research.
Limitations: Giving primarily in southern CA. No grants to individuals.
Application information:
Initial approach: Letter
Deadline(s): Oct.
Board meeting date(s): Semiannually
Write: William Drell, V.P.
Officers: Eugene Roberts,* Pres.; William Drell, V.P.; James Bonner,* Secy.-Treas.
Trustees:* Emil L. Smith, Donald W. Visser.
Employer Identification Number: 956092628

240
California Masonic Foundation ⌘
1111 California St.
San Francisco 94108 (415) 776-7000

Incorporated in 1969 in CA.
Donor(s): Grand Lodge F & AM of California.
Foundation type: Independent
Financial data (yr. ended 6/30/87): Assets, $1,483,769 (M); gifts received, $113,125; expenditures, $97,407, including $81,500 for grants to individuals.
Purpose and activities: Scholarships for full-time undergraduate students residing in CA or HI who are U.S. citizens.
Types of support: Student aid.
Limitations: Giving limited to CA and HI.
Application information: Application form required.
Initial approach: Letter
Deadline(s): None
Board meeting date(s): 5 times yearly
Final notification: 6 months
Officers and Trustees:* Robert J. Valdisera,* Pres.; Richard Pierce,* V.P.; Gerald S. Blackburn, James B. Bouick III, Donald C. Briggs, Clyde Cole, Jr., Robert N. Deter, Maurice L. Hamm, Roy J. Henville, Lloyde Hoffmeister, Glen C. Johnson, Dexter Lum, Haven R. Martin, Thomas J. May, Andrew J. Nocas, George Sluder.
Number of staff: None.

Employer Identification Number: 237013074

241
The Callison Foundation ⌑
1319 Rosita Rd.
Pacifica 941044 (415) 359-2105

Established in 1965 in CA.
Donor(s): Fred W. Callison.
Foundation type: Independent
Financial data (yr. ended 12/31/88): Assets, $4,439,364 (M); expenditures, $386,045, including $300,000 for 32 grants (high: $25,000; low: $5,000).
Purpose and activities: Emphasis on Roman Catholic religious organizations, youth agencies, social welfare, cultural programs, hospitals, aid to the handicapped, and higher education.
Types of support: General purposes.
Limitations: Giving primarily in San Francisco, CA. No grants to individuals.
Application information:
Initial approach: Proposal
Deadline(s): None
Write: Dorothy J. Sola, Secy.
Officers and Directors:* Ward Ingersoll,* Pres.; Chester MacPhee,* V.P.; Dorothy J. Sola,* Secy.; Peter O'Hara,* C.F.O.; Thomas E. Feeney, Frances M. Smith.
Employer Identification Number: 946127962

242
Capital Fund Foundation ▼
(Formerly The Milken Family Foundation)
15250 Ventura Blvd., 2nd Fl.
Sherman Oaks 91403 (818) 784-9224

Established in 1982 in CA.
Donor(s): Michael R. Milken, Lowell J. Milken, Lori A. Milken.
Foundation type: Independent
Financial data (yr. ended 11/30/88): Assets, $178,101,758 (M); gifts received, $50,000; expenditures, $8,657,677, including $8,463,951 for 199 grants (high: $1,000,000; average: $1,000-$175,000).
Purpose and activities: Grants primarily for community services, education, health care and medical research, and human welfare programs.
Limitations: No grants to individuals.
Application information:
Initial approach: Letter or proposal
Write: Julius Lesner, Exec. V.P.
Officers: Lowell J. Milken, Pres.; Julius Lesner, Exec. V.P., C.F.O., and Exec. Dir.; S. Milken, V.P.; E. Sandler, V.P.; Janice L. Shapiro, Secy.
Directors: Ralph Finerman, Mariano Guzman, Lori A. Milken, Michael R. Milken, Richard Riordan, Edward G. Victor.
Employer Identification Number: 953727913

243
Carnation Company Foundation ⌑
5045 Wilshire Blvd.
Los Angeles 90036 (213) 930-5755

Incorporated in 1952 in CA.
Donor(s): Carnation Co.
Foundation type: Company-sponsored
Financial data (yr. ended 12/31/87): Assets, $6,849,812 (M); expenditures, $389,457, including $299,100 for 31 grants (high: $50,000; low: $500).
Purpose and activities: Sustained support for four-year private colleges and universities.
Types of support: Continuing support, operating budgets.
Publications: Annual report (including application guidelines).
Application information: Application form not required.
Initial approach: Proposal
Copies of proposal: 1
Deadline(s): Submit proposal preferably after Aug. 1; deadline Oct. 15
Board meeting date(s): Dec.
Final notification: Jan. 31
Write: Philanthropy Dept.
Officers: J.N. Kvamme,* Pres.; M.S. Adams, V.P.; Paul Devereaux, V.P.; M.W. Malone,* V.P.; J.M. Weller,* V.P.; W.N. Brakensiek, Secy.; P.D. Argentine, Treas.
Directors:* T.F. Crull, R.N. Matthews.
Number of staff: 1 full-time professional.
Employer Identification Number: 956027479

244
Carnation Company Scholarship Foundation
c/o Board of Advisors
5045 Wilshire Blvd.
Los Angeles 90036 (213) 932-6259

Established in 1952 in CA.
Donor(s): Carnation Co.
Foundation type: Company-sponsored
Financial data (yr. ended 12/31/86): Assets, $3,618,912 (M); expenditures, $228,869, including $188,850 for 120 grants to individuals (high: $3,225; low: $750; average: $1,000-$2,000).
Purpose and activities: Giving limited to children of Carnation Co. employees for higher education scholarships only.
Types of support: Employee-related scholarships.
Application information: Application form required.
Deadline(s): Mar. 15
Write: Geraldine M. Manlin
Advisors: Paul Devereaux, T.F. Crull.
Trustee: Seattle-First National Bank.
Employer Identification Number: 956118622

245
Helen M. Carr Charitable Trust ⌑ ☆
12223 Addison St.
North Hollywood 91607-3003

Foundation type: Independent
Financial data (yr. ended 6/30/88): Assets, $504,129 (M); expenditures, $311,519, including $289,675 for 1 grant.
Purpose and activities: Support for a college bible study group.
Application information: Contributes only to pre-selected organizations. Applications not accepted.
Officer and Trustees:* J. Burton Brown,* Mgr.; Walter Blicharz, Emile Herrscher, Stephen Roskiewicz.
Employer Identification Number: 956795779

246
The Carsey Family Foundation ☆
c/o Capell, Coyne & Co.
2121 Ave. of the Stars, Suite 1240
Los Angeles 90067

Established in 1988 in CA.
Donor(s): Marcia L. Carsey, John J. Carsey.
Foundation type: Independent
Financial data (yr. ended 09/30/89): Assets, $1,037,781 (M); gifts received, $2,100; expenditures, $73,025, including $65,000 for 3 grants (high: $50,000; low: $5,000).
Purpose and activities: Support for the fine and performing arts, education, media and communications, and cancer research.
Types of support: Annual campaigns, general purposes, research, special projects.
Officers: Marcia L. Carsey, Pres.; John J. Carsey, V.P.; Frederick Richman, Secy.-Treas.
Number of staff: None.
Employer Identification Number: 954135538

247
John W. Carson Foundation, Inc. ⌑
c/o Ernst & Whinney
1875 Century Park East, Suite 2200
Los Angeles 90067

Established in 1981 in CA.
Donor(s): John W. Carson.
Foundation type: Independent
Financial data (yr. ended 11/30/88): Assets, $1,196,786 (M); expenditures, $721,808, including $657,926 for 45 grants (high: $400,000; low: $100).
Purpose and activities: Giving primarily for child welfare programs; some support also for medical research, cultural programs, and higher education.
Limitations: No grants to individuals.
Application information: Contributes only to pre-selected organizations. Applications not accepted.
Write: John W. Carson, Pres.
Officers: John W. Carson, Chair. and Pres.; Norman R. Marcus, Secy. and C.F.O.
Employer Identification Number: 953714138

248
Carver Foundation ⌑
c/o Anne Martensen
655 Montgomery St., Suite 1730
San Francisco 94111

Established in 1982 in CA.
Donor(s): Carver Grandchildren's Trust, Carver Greatgrandchildren's Trust.
Foundation type: Independent
Financial data (yr. ended 05/31/89): Assets, $91,326 (M); gifts received, $212,156; expenditures, $176,840, including $176,500 for 19 grants (high: $50,000; low: $500).
Purpose and activities: Giving primarily for the arts, including museums and the performing arts.
Limitations: No grants to individuals.
Application information: Contributes only to pre-selected organizations. Applications not accepted.
Officers and Directors:* Ann D. Gralnek, Pres.; Anne Martensen,* Secy.-Treas.; Philae C. Dominick, Pauline C. Duxbury.
Employer Identification Number: 942825557

249
Cedars-Sinai Medical Center Section D Fund ⌘
8700 Beverly Blvd.
Los Angeles 90048

Established in 1984 in CA.
Donor(s): Mark Goodson.
Foundation type: Independent
Financial data (yr. ended 12/31/87): Assets, $3,320,353 (M); expenditures, $701,120, including $666,700 for 47 grants (high: $200,000; low: $500).
Purpose and activities: Grants to Jewish organizations and welfare funds, hospitals and health associations, and film associations.
Limitations: Giving primarily in New York, NY, and Los Angeles, CA. No grants to individuals.
Application information: Contributes only to pre-selected organizations. Applications not accepted.
Trustee: Cedars-Sinai Medical Ctr.
Employer Identification Number: 953918393

250
Hugh Stuart Center Charitable Trust ⌘
152 North Third St., Suite 400
San Jose 95115-0024 (408) 293-0463

Trust established in 1977 in CA.
Donor(s): Hugh Stuart Center.†
Foundation type: Independent
Financial data (yr. ended 12/31/88): Assets, $7,822,482 (M); expenditures, $534,847, including $382,680 for 74 grants (high: $43,250; low: $20).
Purpose and activities: Support largely for higher and secondary education, hospitals, and cultural programs.
Limitations: Giving primarily in San Jose, CA.
Application information: Contributes only to pre-selected organizations. Applications not accepted.
Trustees: Arthur K. Lund, Louis O'Neal.
Employer Identification Number: 942455308

251
Chais Family Foundation ⌘ ☆
611 North Oakhurst Dr.
Beverly Hills 90210-3530

Established in 1985.
Donor(s): Stanley Chais, Pamela Chais.
Foundation type: Independent
Financial data (yr. ended 5/31/88): Assets, $1,155,371 (M); gifts received, $401,850; expenditures, $64,869, including $63,561 for 1 grant.
Purpose and activities: Giving for a Jewish welfare fund supporting an Israel education fund.
Limitations: Giving primarily in CA. No grants to individuals.
Application information: Contributes only to pre-selected organizations. Applications not accepted.
Officers and Directors:* Stanley Chais,* Chair. and Pres.; Emily Chais,* V.P.; Mark Chais,* V.P.; William Chais,* V.P.; Pamela Chais,* Secy. and C.F.O.
Employer Identification Number: 954017323

252
Charis Fund
Box 124
Tahoe City 95730 (916) 583-4348

Trust established in 1938 in CA.
Donor(s): Hugh Trowbridge Dobbins,† Roberta Lloyd Dobbins,† and others.
Foundation type: Independent
Financial data (yr. ended 12/31/87): Assets, $1,049,310 (M); expenditures, $177,490, including $154,565 for 20 grants (high: $31,000; low: $2,000).
Purpose and activities: Emphasis on Protestant church-related organizations, education, and social service agencies.
Types of support: Seed money, special projects.
Limitations: Giving primarily in the San Francisco Bay Area, CA, and in WA and OR. No grants to individuals.
Application information: Funds largely committed; new requests not encouraged. Application form not required.
Initial approach: Letter
Copies of proposal: 6
Deadline(s): None
Board meeting date(s): Spring and fall
Officers and Trustees:* Paul D'Anneo,* Pres.; Elizabeth Dobbins Simmonds,* V.P.; Virginia Chappelle,* Secy.; Robert Dobbins,* Treas.; Andrew H. D'Anneo, Allen Dobbins.
Number of staff: None.
Employer Identification Number: 946077619

253
Chartwell Foundation ⌘ ☆
1901 Ave. of the Stars, Suite 680
Los Angeles 90067 (213) 556-7600

Established in 1986 in CA.
Donor(s): A. Jerrold Perenchio.
Foundation type: Independent
Financial data (yr. ended 11/30/89): Assets, $4,598,824 (M); expenditures, $2,273,028, including $2,181,235 for 366 grants (high: $250,000; low: $500).
Purpose and activities: Giving primarily for cultural programs, including fine and performing arts groups, and higher education; support also for social service and youth agencies and health associations.
Limitations: No grants to individuals.
Application information:
Initial approach: Letter
Deadline(s): None
Officers: A. Jerrold Perenchio, Pres.; Robert V. Cahill, V.P.; John Perenchio, V.P.
Employer Identification Number: 954080111

254
The Christensen Fund ▼
780 Welch Rd., Suite 100
Palo Alto 94304

Incorporated in 1957 in CA.
Donor(s): Allen D. Christensen,† Carmen M. Christensen.
Foundation type: Operating
Financial data (yr. ended 11/30/87): Assets, $41,882,600 (M); gifts received, $25,830,525; expenditures, $2,293,341, including $964,606 for 21 grants (high: $390,962; low: $100; average: $500-$15,000).
Purpose and activities: A private operating foundation supporting natural sciences, medical research, education, and the arts, including the display of art objects in museums and support of educational institutions and programs in the U.S. and abroad; very limited grants.
Types of support: Fellowships, matching funds, publications, research, seed money, special projects.
Limitations: Giving limited to the greater San Francisco Bay Area, CA. No loans.
Publications: Annual report, program policy statement, application guidelines.
Application information: Contributes only to pre-selected organizations. Applications not accepted.
Officers: C. Diane Christensen,* Pres.; Carmen M. Christensen,* V.P.; William R. Benevento,* Secy.
Directors:* Karen K. Christensen Calvin, Rosemary Pratt.
Employer Identification Number: 946055879

255
Chuan Lyu Foundation
(Formerly The Lee Foundation)
132 Isabella Ave.
Atherton 94027

Established in 1986 in GA.
Donor(s): Hwalin Lee.
Foundation type: Independent
Financial data (yr. ended 11/30/89): Assets, $1,380,000 (M); qualifying distributions, $48,000, including $48,000 for 4 grants (high: $20,000; low: $1,000; average: $1,000-$20,000).
Purpose and activities: Support for the study of topics related to Taiwan.
Types of support: Special projects.
Trustee: Hwalin Lee.
Employer Identification Number: 586203563

256
Civitas Fund ⌘
P.O. Box 49951
Los Angeles 90049 (213) 472-2334

Incorporated in 1975 in CA.
Donor(s): Elsie B. Ballantyne.
Foundation type: Independent
Financial data (yr. ended 12/31/88): Assets, $4,137,366 (M); expenditures, $272,123, including $250,000 for 1 grant.
Purpose and activities: Giving for higher education and a senior citizens' center.
Limitations: Giving primarily in CA.
Application information: Application form not required.
Deadline(s): None
Write: Robert B. Ballantyne, Pres.
Officers: Robert B. Ballantyne, Pres.; Mavoureen O'Connor, V.P.; Yvonne S. Dean, Secy.-Treas.; Norman C. Obrow.
Employer Identification Number: 952994948

257
The Clorox Company Foundation ▼
1221 Broadway
Oakland 94612 (415) 271-7747
Mailing address: P.O. Box 24305, Oakland, CA 94623

Incorporated in 1980 in CA.
Donor(s): Clorox Co.
Foundation type: Company-sponsored
Financial data (yr. ended 6/30/88): Assets, $2,056,242 (M); gifts received, $1,500,000; expenditures, $1,309,881, including $1,243,275 for 428 grants (high: $90,000; low: $25; average: $1,000-$10,000) and $44,484 for 110 employee matching gifts.
Purpose and activities: Giving primarily for youth, education, social welfare, civic affairs, arts and culture, and health; some support also for economic development and employment training; and emergency product donations.
Types of support: Building funds, operating budgets, general purposes, employee matching gifts, capital campaigns, matching funds, employee-related scholarships, special projects, technical assistance, scholarship funds.
Limitations: Giving primarily in Oakland, CA, and other areas of company operations. No support for sectarian religious purposes, or for veterans', fraternal, or labor organizations. No grants to individuals, or for goodwill advertising.
Publications: Corporate giving report (including application guidelines), program policy statement, application guidelines.
Application information: Application form required.
Initial approach: Letter requesting application
Copies of proposal: 1
Deadline(s): By 15th of month prior to board meetings
Board meeting date(s): 3rd Fridays of July, Sept.-Nov., Jan., Mar., and May
Final notification: Varies
Write: Carmella Johnson, Contribs. Admin.
Officers: Patricia J. Marino,* Pres.; David L. Goodman,* V.P.; Elizabeth A. Harvey, Secy.; Priscilla Thilmony,* Treas.
Trustees:* Jack J. Calderini, Rita A. Glazer, Roderic A. Lorimer, Ignacio R. Martinez, Patrick M. Meehan, Richard C. Soublet.
Number of staff: 1 full-time professional; 1 part-time professional; 1 full-time support.
Employer Identification Number: 942674980

258
Francis H. Clougherty Charitable Trust ⌑
c/o Patrick F. Collins
P.O. Box 93490
Pasadena 91109-3490

Established in 1984 in CA.
Foundation type: Independent
Financial data (yr. ended 12/31/88): Assets, $5,986,703 (M); expenditures, $396,970, including $386,000 for 9 grants (high: $150,000; low: $2,000).
Purpose and activities: Support primarily for higher and secondary education, Catholic churches, and hospitals.
Types of support: General purposes.
Limitations: Giving primarily in southern CA. No grants to individuals.
Application information: Contributes only to pre-selected organizations. Applications not accepted.
Trustees: Bernard J. Clougherty, Joseph D. Clougherty.
Employer Identification Number: 956818523

259
The Roy E. Coats Fund for the Research and Treatment of Cancer ⌑ ☆
c/o REC Management
333 North Glenoak Blvd., Suite 695
Burbank 91502 (818) 846-5079

Established in 1988 in CA.
Donor(s): Laura R. Coats.
Foundation type: Independent
Financial data (yr. ended 12/31/88): Assets, $1,008,640 (M); gifts received, $1,008,444; expenditures, $0.
Purpose and activities: Initial year of operation, 1988; no grants awarded.
Limitations: No grants to individuals.
Application information: Contributes only to pre-selected organizations. Applications not accepted.
Trustees: Virginia Coats Ashworth, Glenna Cadmus, Laura R. Coats.
Employer Identification Number: 954144621

260
The Colburn Collection ⌑
6311 Romaine St., No. 7111
Los Angeles 90038

Established in 1986 in CA.
Foundation type: Operating
Financial data (yr. ended 12/31/88): Assets, $7,708,722 (M); gifts received, $7,600; expenditures, $243,454, including $200,000 for 1 grant.
Purpose and activities: Support for instruction in the performing arts, including music. Musical instruments are loaned to students of music until they can afford to purchase their own.
Types of support: Endowment funds, building funds.
Limitations: Giving primarily in Los Angeles, CA.
Application information: Application form not required.
Initial approach: Letter
Deadline(s): None
Write: Frances K. Rosen, Mgr.
Officers: Richard W. Colburn,* Pres.; Frances K. Rosen, Mgr. and Secy.; Richard D. Colburn, Carol Colburn Hogel.
Directors:* Keith W. Colburn.
Employer Identification Number: 954021014

261
The Tara and Richard Colburn Fund ⌑
1516 Pontius Ave.
Los Angeles 90025

Established in 1985 in CA.
Donor(s): Richard D. Colburn, Consolidated Electrical Distributors, U.S. Rentals, Inc.
Foundation type: Independent
Financial data (yr. ended 12/31/87): Assets, $1,523,768 (M); gifts received, $1,085,000; expenditures, $577,036, including $576,750 for 26 grants (high: $250,000; low: $100).
Purpose and activities: Giving primarily for music and education.
Application information: Application form not required.
Deadline(s): None
Write: Bernard E. Lyons, Dir.
Directors: Richard D. Colburn, Tara G. Colburn, Bernard E. Lyons.
Employer Identification Number: 954018318

262
Columbia Foundation ▼
Koshland Bldg.
1160 Battery St., Suite 400
San Francisco 94111 (415) 986-5179

Incorporated in 1940 in CA.
Donor(s): Madeleine H. Russell, Christine H. Russell.
Foundation type: Independent
Financial data (yr. ended 05/31/89): Assets, $32,745,444 (M); gifts received, $80,000; expenditures, $1,492,794, including $1,335,533 for 124 grants (high: $291,000; low: $500; average: $1,000-$50,000).
Purpose and activities: Current focus is on projects that address critical issues and offer promise of significant positive impact in the following areas: preservation of the natural environment; enhancement of urban community life and culture; the interdependence of nations and understanding among people from different cultures; reversal of the arms race worldwide; and protection of basic human rights. The foundation focuses its program primarily on projects that seek common ground between the San Francisco community and the shared global concerns facing an interdependent world.
Types of support: Seed money, special projects, research, publications, conferences and seminars.
Limitations: Giving primarily in northern CA, with emphasis on the San Francisco Bay Area. No support for private foundations, institutions supported by federated campaigns or heavily subsidized by government funds, or projects in medicine or religion. No grants to individuals, or for building or endowment funds, scholarships, fellowships, or operating budgets.
Publications: Application guidelines, program policy statement, grants list, annual report (including application guidelines), multi-year report.
Application information: Application form not required.
Initial approach: Letter
Copies of proposal: 1
Deadline(s): None
Board meeting date(s): 4 times per year
Final notification: 2 to 3 months
Write: Susan Clark Silk, Exec. Dir.
Officers and Directors:* Madeleine H. Russell,* Pres.; Charles P. Russell,* V.P.; Alice Russell-Shapiro,* Secy.; Christine H. Russell,* Treas.; Susan Clark Silk, Exec. Dir.
Number of staff: 1 full-time professional; 1 full-time support.
Employer Identification Number: 941196186

263
Columbia Savings Charitable Foundation ⌑
8840 Wilshire Blvd.
Beverly Hills 90211

Established in 1985 in CA.
Foundation type: Independent

Financial data (yr. ended 12/31/87): Assets, $14,988,692 (M); gifts received, $7,145,000; expenditures, $437,877, including $415,991 for 30 grants (high: $145,000; low: $1,000).
Purpose and activities: Giving primarily for Jewish organizations; contributions also for higher education and medical research.
Application information:
Initial approach: Letter
Write: Hillel S. Aronson, V.P.
Officers: Abraham Spiegel, Chair.; Thomas Spiegel, Pres.; Hillel S. Aronson, V.P.; Lee N. Eckel, Secy.; Curtis Webster, Secy.
Employer Identification Number: 954002331

264
Compton Foundation, Inc. ▼
525 Middlefield Rd., Suite 115
Menlo Park 94025 (415) 328-0101

Incorporated in 1972 in NY as successor to The Compton Trust.
Donor(s): Members of the Compton family.
Foundation type: Independent
Financial data (yr. ended 12/31/86): Assets, $48,617,010 (M); gifts received, $10,466,526; expenditures, $2,582,824, including $2,165,756 for 436 grants (high: $135,000; low: $30; average: $200-$60,000).
Purpose and activities: To coordinate the family giving to community, national, and international programs in areas of its special interests, including higher education, peace and world order, population control, the arts, conservation, race relations, and welfare.
Types of support: Endowment funds, fellowships, general purposes, matching funds, scholarship funds, operating budgets, continuing support, annual campaigns, seed money, special projects, consulting services.
Limitations: No grants to individuals, or for capital or building funds; no loans.
Publications: Biennial report.
Application information: Application form not required.
Initial approach: Letter
Deadline(s): None
Board meeting date(s): May and Nov.
Final notification: 6 months, favorable replies only
Write: James R. Compton, Pres.
Officers and Directors:* James R. Compton,* Pres.; Ann C. Stephens,* V.P. and Secy.; Arthur L. Bowen,* Treas.; Jan H. Lewis, Kenneth W. Thompson, Michael P. Todaro.
Number of staff: 1 part-time support.
Employer Identification Number: 237262706

265
Confidence Foundation ▼ ⌑
1260 Huntington Dr., Suite 204
South Pasadena 91030 (213) 259-0484

Established in 1980 in CA.
Donor(s): Paul N. Whittier.†
Foundation type: Independent
Financial data (yr. ended 12/31/87): Assets, $7,051,113 (M); gifts received, $2,112,860; expenditures, $1,625,678, including $1,469,275 for 61 grants (high: $385,000; low: $250; average: $5,000-$150,000).
Purpose and activities: Giving primarily for social services and medical research.
Application information: Contributes only to pre-selected organizations. Applications not accepted.
Write: Linda J. Blinkenberg, Secy.
Officers: Arlo G. Sorensen, Pres.; Steven A. Anderson, V.P.; Linda J. Blinkenberg, Secy.; Robert D. Sellers, Treas.
Number of staff: 1
Employer Identification Number: 953500483

266
Michael J. Connell Foundation ⌑
201 South Lake Ave., Suite 303
Pasadena 91101 (213) 681-8085

Incorporated in 1931 in CA.
Donor(s): Michael J. Connell.†
Foundation type: Independent
Financial data (yr. ended 6/30/89): Assets, $9,938,528 (M); expenditures, $881,684, including $742,588 for 19 grants (high: $250,000; low: $1,000; average: $15,000-$50,000).
Purpose and activities: Giving generally restricted to programs initiated by the foundation in social, cultural, educational, and medical fields.
Types of support: Internships, fellowships, special projects.
Limitations: Giving primarily in southern CA, with emphasis on Los Angeles. No grants to individuals, or for building funds; no loans.
Publications: Financial statement.
Application information: Application form not required.
Initial approach: Letter
Copies of proposal: 1
Deadline(s): None
Board meeting date(s): Quarterly
Final notification: 3 months
Write: Michael J. Connell, Pres.
Officers: Michael J. Connell,* Pres.; Richard A. Wilson,* V.P.; Ruth E. Dodd, Secy.
Directors:* Mary C. Bayless, John Connell.
Number of staff: 1 full-time professional; 1 part-time professional.
Employer Identification Number: 956000904

267
Cook Brothers Educational Fund ⌑
1217 Bel Air Dr.
Santa Barbara 93105

Established about 1980 in CA.
Donor(s): Howard F. Cook.†
Foundation type: Independent
Financial data (yr. ended 12/31/88): Assets, $1,984,616 (M); expenditures, $492,545, including $329,224 for 22 grants (high: $65,140; low: $500).
Purpose and activities: Support for social service agencies, cultural programs, and higher education.
Limitations: No grants to individuals.
Application information: Contributes only to pre-selected organizations. Applications not accepted.
Officers and Trustees:* Susan V. Cook,* Pres.; Kathleen M. Cook,* Secy.; Frank C. Cook,* Grants Admin.; William H. Cook.
Employer Identification Number: 237306457

268
James S. Copley Foundation ▼
7776 Ivanhoe Ave.
P.O. Box 1530
La Jolla 92038-1530 (619) 454-0411

Incorporated in 1953 in CA.
Donor(s): The Copley Press, Inc.
Foundation type: Company-sponsored
Financial data (yr. ended 12/31/89): Assets, $19,541,950 (M); gifts received, $3,014,279; expenditures, $2,196,471, including $2,124,722 for 179 grants (high: $300,000; low: $100; average: $500-$10,000) and $39,860 for 155 employee matching gifts.
Purpose and activities: Support for higher and secondary education, including an employee matching gift program, performing arts groups and other cultural programs, a community fund, journalism, social services, hospices and hospitals, the aged, and youth and child development.
Types of support: Annual campaigns, emergency funds, building funds, equipment, land acquisition, scholarship funds, employee matching gifts, capital campaigns.
Limitations: Giving primarily in circulation areas of company newspapers: San Diego, Torrance, San Pedro, and Santa Monica in CA; and Aurora, Elgin, Wheaton, Joliet, Springfield, Lincoln, and Waukegan in IL. No support for religious, fraternal, or athletic organizations, local chapters of national organizations, or public elementary or secondary schools. No grants to individuals, or for endowment funds, research, publications, conferences, unrestricted purposes, operating budgets, or large campaigns; no loans.
Publications: Informational brochure (including application guidelines).
Application information: Application form not required.
Initial approach: Letter
Copies of proposal: 1
Deadline(s): None
Board meeting date(s): Feb. and as required
Final notification: 2 to 3 weeks
Write: Anita A. Baumgardner, Secy.
Officers and Directors:* Helen K. Copley,* Chair.; David C. Copley,* Pres.; Alex De Bakcsy,* V.P.; Hubert L. Kaltenbach,* V.P.; Anita A. Baumgardner,* Secy.; Charles F. Patrick,* Treas.
Number of staff: None.
Employer Identification Number: 956051770

269
The Corcoran Community Foundation ⌑
P.O. Box 655
Corcoran 93212 (209) 992-5551

Incorporated in 1965 in CA.
Donor(s): W.W. Boswell, Mrs. W.W. Boswell.
Foundation type: Community
Financial data (yr. ended 7/31/86): Assets, $4,138,993 (M); gifts received, $1,284,654; expenditures, $519,164, including $418,164 for 32 grants (high: $259,920; low: $200; average: $5,000).
Purpose and activities: Support for organizations benefiting the inhabitants of Corcoran, CA, and its surrounding area.

Types of support: Operating budgets, continuing support, annual campaigns, emergency funds, building funds, equipment, land acquisition, endowment funds, matching funds, consulting services, technical assistance, program-related investments, loans, special projects, publications, conferences and seminars.
Limitations: Giving primarily in the Corcoran, CA, area. No grants to individuals, or for deficit financing.
Publications: Annual report, application guidelines, newsletter.
Application information: Application form required.
Initial approach: Letter
Copies of proposal: 1
Deadline(s): Submit proposal preferably in the month preceding board meetings
Board meeting date(s): Oct., Dec., Feb., Apr., June, and Aug.
Final notification: After board meeting
Write: Mike Graville, Exec. Dir.
Officers and Trustees:* Mrs. W.W. Boswell, Sr.,* Pres.; James B. Hansen,* V.P.; Charles Gilkey,* Secy.; Robert A. Lyman,* Treas.; Bill Case, Leslie S. Corcoran, Glenda Doan, Leslie J. Doan, George M. Fuller, Jr., Gary Gamble, Ross F. Hall, Robert U. Hansen, Morris Proctor, Eloise Salyer.
Trustee Banks: Security Pacific National Bank, Lloyds Bank.
Number of staff: 1 full-time professional.
Employer Identification Number: 941608857

270
Dorothy and Sherril C. Corwin Foundation ⌑
8727 West Third St.
Los Angeles 90048

Established in 1958 in CA.
Donor(s): Sherrill C. Corwin, Dorothy Corwin, Metropolitan Theatres Corp.
Foundation type: Independent
Financial data (yr. ended 12/31/88): Assets, $782,826 (M); gifts received, $30,000; expenditures, $160,100, including $159,395 for 76 grants (high: $26,250; low: $100).
Purpose and activities: Giving primarily for Jewish welfare, social services, medical research, cultural programs, and temple support.
Application information: Contributes only to pre-selected organizations. Applications not accepted.
Trustees: Martin S. Appel, Bruce C. Corwin, Dorothy Corwin, Bonnie Fuller.
Employer Identification Number: 956061525

271
Cow Hollow Foundation
Two Embarcadero Center, Suite 2900
San Francisco 94111 (415) 956-2424

Established in 1985 in CA.
Donor(s): Sally L. Lilienthal.
Foundation type: Independent
Financial data (yr. ended 07/31/89): Assets, $1,902,278 (M); expenditures, $384,469, including $361,700 for 65 grants (high: $65,000; low: $200).
Purpose and activities: Support primarily for an international political science organization; some support also for higher education.
Types of support: General purposes, special projects.
Limitations: No grants to individuals.
Application information: Contributes only to pre-selected organizations. Applications not accepted.
Write: Sanford P. Lowengart, Jr., Secy.-Treas.
Officers: Sally L. Lilienthal, Pres.; Laurie Cohen, V.P.; Sanford P. Lowengart, Jr., Secy.-Treas.
Employer Identification Number: 942978691

272
S. H. Cowell Foundation ▼
260 California, Suite 501
San Francisco 94111 (415) 397-0285

Trust established in 1955 in CA.
Donor(s): S.H. Cowell.†
Foundation type: Independent
Financial data (yr. ended 12/31/89): Assets, $81,762,725 (M); expenditures, $12,775,509, including $10,407,136 for 152 grants (high: $5,480,577; low: $3,000; average: $20,000-$100,000) and $550,000 for loans.
Purpose and activities: Support for programs aiding the handicapped, educational programs, including preschool and primary public educational programs, community organizations, childcare programs, programs for prevention and treatment of alcohol abuse, family planning projects, youth agencies, including training and employment programs, and a new program to provide affordable housing for the very poor of northern CA.
Types of support: Seed money, building funds, equipment, land acquisition, matching funds, renovation projects, capital campaigns, employee matching gifts, special projects.
Limitations: Giving limited to northern CA. No support for hospitals or sectarian religious purposes. No grants to individuals, or for operating budgets, endowments, media programs, continuing support, annual campaigns, routine program administration, workshops, symposia, deficit financing, fellowships, special projects, medical research or treatment, publications, or conferences.
Publications: Annual report (including application guidelines), grants list.
Application information: The foundation has terminated the Minority Scholarship Program and the Small Arts Program. Application form not required.
Initial approach: Letter
Copies of proposal: 1
Deadline(s): None
Board meeting date(s): Monthly
Final notification: 4 to 5 months
Write: Stephanie Wolf, Exec. Dir.
Officers and Directors:* Max Thelen, Jr.,* Pres.; William P. Murray, Jr.,* V.P.; George A. Hopiak, Secy.-Treas.; Stephanie Wolf, Exec. Dir.; J.D. Erickson, Wells Fargo Bank, N.A.
Number of staff: 5 full-time professional; 1 part-time professional; 3 full-time support.
Employer Identification Number: 941392803

273
Douglas S. Cramer Foundation ⌑
4605 Lankersham Blvd., Suite 714
North Hollywood 91602

Established in 1987 in CA.
Foundation type: Operating
Financial data (yr. ended 4/30/88): Assets, $3,686,717 (M); gifts received, $823,000; expenditures, $136,796, including $33,750 for 5 grants (high: $25,000; low: $250).
Purpose and activities: A private operating foundation; support primarily for a fine arts museum; support also for outside arts organizations.
Types of support: Special projects.
Application information: Contributes only to pre-selected organizations. Applications not accepted.
Write: Paula Kendall-Waxman, Curator
Officers and Directors:* Douglas S. Cramer,* Pres. and Treas.; Douglas S. Cramer, Jr.,* V.P.; Craig W. Johnson,* V.P.
Number of staff: 2
Employer Identification Number: 956358014

274
The Crean Foundation ⌑ ☆
760 West 16th St., Bldg. C
Costa Mesa 92627-4319

Established in 1981.
Donor(s): John C. Crean.
Foundation type: Independent
Financial data (yr. ended 12/31/88): Assets, $547,633 (M); gifts received, $300,000; expenditures, $678,609, including $640,100 for 6 grants (high: $500,000; low: $100).
Purpose and activities: Giving primarily for a Catholic diocese; support also for higher and secondary education.
Types of support: General purposes.
Limitations: Giving primarily in CA. No grants to individuals.
Application information: Contributes only to pre-selected organizations. Applications not accepted.
Officers: John C. Crean, Pres. and Treas.; Johnnie R. Crean, V.P.; Donna C. Crean, Secy.
Employer Identification Number: 953676334

275
The Mary A. Crocker Trust ⌑
233 Post St., 2nd Fl.
San Francisco 94108 (415) 982-0139

Trust established in 1889 in CA.
Donor(s): Mary A. Crocker.†
Foundation type: Independent
Financial data (yr. ended 12/31/88): Assets, $11,513,804 (M); expenditures, $752,520, including $490,080 for 48 grants (high: $50,000; low: $3,000; average: $5,000-$15,000).
Purpose and activities: Support for creative and innovative programs in the areas of child welfare, social services, women's projects, education, health services, and community development.
Types of support: Seed money, emergency funds, equipment, matching funds, publications, special projects, general purposes, renovation projects.

Limitations: Giving primarily in the San Francisco Bay Area, CA. No support for conduit agencies or tax-supported projects. No grants to individuals, or for operating budgets, continuing support, annual campaigns, deficit financing, building or endowment funds, land acquisition, scholarships, fellowships, research, demonstration projects, or conferences; no loans.
Publications: Application guidelines, program policy statement.
Application information: Application form required.
Initial approach: Letter
Copies of proposal: 1
Deadline(s): None
Board meeting date(s): 2 to 3 times a year
Final notification: 3 months
Write: Barbaree Jernigan, Admin.
Officer and Trustees:* Tania W. Stepanian,* Chair. and C.E.O.; Elizabeth Atcheson, Charles Crocker, William H. Crocker, Frederick W. Whitridge.
Number of staff: 1 full-time professional.
Employer Identification Number: 946051917

276
Roy E. Crummer Foundation ⌑
11990 San Vincente Blvd., Suite 340
Los Angeles 90049 (213) 826-0086

Established in 1964 in NV.
Foundation type: Independent
Financial data (yr. ended 12/31/87): Assets, $7,472,550 (M); expenditures, $292,903, including $276,000 for 50 grants (high: $50,000; low: $200).
Purpose and activities: Emphasis on education, social services, hospitals, and animal welfare.
Officers: Jean Crummer Coburn, Pres.; Milton Coburn, V.P.; Margarite Brown, Secy.-Treas.
Employer Identification Number: 886004422

277
John D. Crummey Benevolent Trust II ⌑ ☆
50 Fremont St., Suite 3825
San Francisco 94105-2230

Established in 1947.
Donor(s): Faith C. Davies.
Foundation type: Independent
Financial data (yr. ended 6/30/89): Assets, $1,135,441 (M); gifts received, $19,217; expenditures, $108,359, including $100,650 for grants (high: $25,000).
Purpose and activities: Giving primarily for the fine and performing arts, including a symphony orchestra and museums; support also for hospitals and higher education.
Limitations: Giving primarily in CA. No grants to individuals.
Application information: Contributes only to pre-selected organizations. Applications not accepted.
Trustees: Faith C. Davies, Paul L. Davies, Jr.
Employer Identification Number: 946080075

278
Damien Foundation ⌑
235 Montgomery St., Suite 1010
San Francisco 94104 (415) 421-7555

Established in 1979 in DE.
Donor(s): Kristina Tara Fondaras Charitable Lead Trust.
Foundation type: Independent
Financial data (yr. ended 12/31/88): Assets, $507,744 (M); gifts received, $250,715; expenditures, $171,933, including $105,850 for 8 grants (high: $20,850; low: $5,000; average: $5,000).
Purpose and activities: Giving for innovative contemporary art education, transformative psychology, ecology, and human awareness.
Types of support: General purposes, special projects.
Limitations: Giving limited to the San Francisco Bay Area, CA, and England. No grants to individuals.
Application information: Application form not required.
Initial approach: Letter and proposal
Copies of proposal: 1
Deadline(s): None
Write: Sheila Weintraub, Asst. Secy.
Officers and Director:* Tara Lamont,* Pres.; Thomas Silk, Secy.-Treas.
Number of staff: 2
Employer Identification Number: 133006359

279
The Diana and Robert Davidow Foundation ⌑ ☆
1721 Carlyle Ave.
Santa Monica 90402-2425

Established in 1986 in CA.
Donor(s): Robert A. Davidow, Diana R. Davidow.
Foundation type: Independent
Financial data (yr. ended 10/31/87): Assets, $1,133,866 (M); gifts received, $1,427,980; expenditures, $53,510, including $51,450 for 76 grants (high: $10,800; low: $50).
Purpose and activities: Initial year of operation, fiscal 1987; support for health associations and Jewish organizations.
Limitations: No grants to individuals.
Application information: Contributes only to pre-selected organizations. Applications not accepted.
Officers: Robert A. Davidow, Pres. and C.E.O.; Diana R. Davidow, Secy. and C.F.O.
Employer Identification Number: 330210307

280
Davies Charitable Trust ⌑
c/o Donald D. Crawford, Jr., Northern Trust of California
580 California St., Suite 1800
San Francisco 94104

Trust established in 1974 in CA.
Donor(s): Ralph K. Davies.†
Foundation type: Independent
Financial data (yr. ended 09/30/89): Assets, $3,854,551 (M); expenditures, $237,156, including $209,000 for 34 grants (high: $35,000; low: $500).
Purpose and activities: Emphasis on the cultural programs, including performing arts, and higher and secondary education.
Limitations: Giving primarily in CA and HI. No grants to individuals.
Application information: Contributes only to pre-selected organizations. Applications not accepted.
Trustees: Alicia C. Davies, Maryon Davies Lewis, Northern Trust of California.
Employer Identification Number: 237417287

281
Louise M. Davies Foundation ⌑
580 California St., Suite 1800
San Francisco 94104 (415) 765-2641

Established in 1974 in CA.
Donor(s): Louise M. Davies.
Foundation type: Independent
Financial data (yr. ended 09/30/89): Assets, $1,213,744 (M); gifts received, $70,000; expenditures, $164,929, including $136,900 for 39 grants (high: $25,000; low: $100).
Purpose and activities: Giving primarily for education, youth, and social services.
Types of support: Capital campaigns, scholarship funds, general purposes, endowment funds.
Limitations: No grants to individuals.
Application information: Contributes only to pre-selected organizations. Applications not accepted.
Write: Donald D. Crawford, Jr., Treas.
Officers and Directors:* Louise M. Davies,* Pres.; Chandler Ide,* V.P.; Philip Hudner,* Secy.; Donald D. Crawford, Jr.,* Treas.
Employer Identification Number: 237359841

282
Elizabeth Lloyd Davis Foundation ⌑ ☆
4892 North St.
P.O. Box 840
Somis 93066-0840

Established in 1984 in CA.
Foundation type: Independent
Financial data (yr. ended 12/31/88): Assets, $1,469,207 (M); expenditures, $85,011, including $73,691 for 78 grants (high: $8,150; low: $10).
Purpose and activities: Giving primarily for a museum of cultural history; support also for higher and other education, health associations, and youth.
Limitations: Giving primarily in CA. No grants to individuals.
Application information: Contributes only to pre-selected organizations. Applications not accepted.
Officers and Directors:* Elizabeth L. Davis,* Pres.; Elizabeth D. Rogers,* V.P. and Secy.; William L. Davis,* C.F.O.
Employer Identification Number: 953920286

283
Willametta K. Day Foundation
400 South Hope St., Rm. 500
Los Angeles 90071 (213) 683-4285
Mailing address: P.O. Box 71289, Los Angeles, CA 90071

Trust established in 1954 in CA.

Donor(s): Willametta K. Day.†
Foundation type: Independent
Financial data (yr. ended 12/31/89): Assets, $7,882,169 (M); qualifying distributions, $305,000, including $305,000 for grants (high: $100,000; low: $50; average: $1,000-$5,000).
Purpose and activities: Grants for higher and secondary education, hospitals, religion, and cultural programs.
Types of support: General purposes.
Limitations: Giving primarily in CA. No grants to individuals.
Publications: 990-PF, financial statement.
Application information: Application form not required.
Initial approach: Letter
Copies of proposal: 1
Deadline(s): Apr. and Nov.
Board meeting date(s): Semiannually
Write: Alvin R. Albe, Jr., C.F.O.
Officers: Jerry W. Carlton,* Chair. and Pres.; Steven D. Holzman, Secy.; Alvin R. Albe, Jr., C.F.O. and Treas.
Trustees:* Howard M. Day, Robert A. Day, Jr., Tammis M. Day, Theodore J. Day.
Employer Identification Number: 956092476

284
Christian de Guigne Memorial Foundation
c/o O'Donnell, Waiss, Wall and Meschke
100 Broadway, Third Fl.
San Francisco 94111 (415) 434-3323

Established in 1960 in CA.
Foundation type: Independent
Financial data (yr. ended 12/31/88): Assets, $3,561,606 (M); expenditures, $197,697, including $136,680 for 9 grants (high: $45,000; low: $5,000; average: $5,000-$15,000).
Purpose and activities: Support for higher and secondary education, hospitals, and health agencies; support also for a French medical institution.
Types of support: Equipment, general purposes, research.
Limitations: Giving limited to the San Francisco Bay Area, CA. No grants to individuals, or for building or endowment funds, fellowships, matching gifts, or special projects; no loans.
Application information: Application form not required.
Initial approach: Letter
Copies of proposal: 3
Deadline(s): Submit proposal any time except Nov. or Dec.; deadline Oct. 31
Board meeting date(s): Nov. or Dec.
Final notification: 1 month
Write: John A. Meschke, Secy.-Treas.
Officers and Directors:* France de Sugny Bark,* Pres.; Fredrik S. Waiss,* V.P.; John A. Meschke,* Secy.-Treas.
Number of staff: None.
Employer Identification Number: 946076503

285
Cecil B. DeMille Trust ⌑
223 West Alameda, Suite 101
Burbank 91502 (213) 660-3244

Trust established in 1952 in CA.
Foundation type: Independent
Financial data (yr. ended 12/31/88): Assets, $2,696,653 (M); gifts received, $181,751; expenditures, $350,412, including $245,571 for 28 grants (high: $130,596; low: $50).
Purpose and activities: Emphasis on social services, education, cultural programs, and child welfare.
Limitations: Giving primarily in CA.
Application information:
Initial approach: Letter or proposal
Deadline(s): None
Write: Cecilia DeMille Presley
Trustees: Peter DeMille Calvin, Joseph W. Harper, Jr., Cecilia DeMille Presley.
Employer Identification Number: 951882931

286
The Deutsch Foundation ⌑
c/o The Deutsch Co.
2444 Wilshire Blvd., Suite 600
Santa Monica 90403-5813 (213) 453-0055

Incorporated in 1947 in CA.
Donor(s): The Deutsch Co.
Foundation type: Company-sponsored
Financial data (yr. ended 8/31/87): Assets, $4,618,269 (M); gifts received, $130,000; expenditures, $526,048, including $518,648 for 113 grants (high: $150,000; low: $25).
Purpose and activities: Emphasis on Jewish welfare funds; support also for hospitals, higher education, social welfare, and scientific research.
Limitations: Giving primarily in CA.
Application information:
Initial approach: Letter
Deadline(s): None
Officers and Directors:* Alex Deutsch,* Pres.; Carl Deutsch,* V.P.; Lester Deutsch,* Secy.-Treas.
Employer Identification Number: 956027369

287
Frank C. Diener Foundation
P.O. Box 278
Five Points 93624

Established in 1967 in CA.
Donor(s): Shining D Farms.
Foundation type: Independent
Financial data (yr. ended 06/30/88): Assets, $1,543,859 (M); gifts received, $100,049; expenditures, $88,768, including $82,250 for 9 grants (high: $32,000; low: $1,500).
Purpose and activities: Giving only for Catholic welfare.
Limitations: Giving limited to Fresno County, CA.
Application information: No new applications accepted.
Trustees: Marie C. De Mera, Edward F. Diener, Mary A. Diener.
Employer Identification Number: 946165307

288
The Diller Foundation ⌑ ☆
c/o Breslauer, Jacobson et al
2121 Ave. of the Stars, No. 1700
Los Angeles 90067

Established in 1986 in CA.
Foundation type: Independent
Financial data (yr. ended 12/31/88): Assets, $306,585 (M); expenditures, $315,115, including $314,140 for 26 grants (high: $60,000; low: $1,000).
Purpose and activities: Giving primarily for hospitals and medical research, especially for AIDS, an art institute and a museum for film, and human rights organizations.
Types of support: Research.
Limitations: Giving primarily in CA and NY.
Officers: Barry Diller, Pres.; Gerald Breslauer, V.P. and Treas.; Richard Sherman, Secy.
Employer Identification Number: 954081892

289
The Rene & Veronica DiRosa Foundation ⌑
5200 Sonoma Hwy.
Napa 94558

Established in 1983 in CA.
Donor(s): Rene di Rosa, Maude Conner.
Foundation type: Independent
Financial data (yr. ended 12/31/88): Assets, $3,231,796 (M); expenditures, $141,315, including $79,318 for 53 grants (high: $25,000; low: $10).
Purpose and activities: Giving primarily to environmental organizations, arts programs, and education.
Application information:
Deadline(s): None
Officers: Rene di Rosa, Pres.; Veronica di Rosa, V.P.; Maude Conner, C.F.O.
Employer Identification Number: 942856000

290
Roy Disney Family Foundation ⌑
c/o Shamrock Ctr.
4444 Lakeside Dr., P.O. Box 7774
Burbank 91510-7774

Incorporated in 1969 in CA.
Donor(s): Roy E. Disney, Roy O. Disney,† Edna F. Disney, Redna Inc.
Foundation type: Independent
Financial data (yr. ended 5/31/88): Assets, $10,358,520 (M); expenditures, $847,340, including $782,075 for 11 grants (high: $500,075; low: $5,000).
Purpose and activities: Support primarily for an arts institute and higher education.
Limitations: Giving primarily in CA. No grants to individuals, or for building or endowment funds.
Application information: Contributes only to pre-selected organizations. Applications not accepted.
Board meeting date(s): Annually and as required
Officers: Patricia Ann Disney,* Pres.; Abigail E. Disney,* V.P.; Linda J. Disney,* V.P.; Roy E. Disney,* V.P.; Roy P. Disney,* V.P.; Timothy J. Disney,* V.P.; Susan M. Disney,* Secy.; Marilyn Jackson, Treas.
Directors:* Richard T. Morrow.
Employer Identification Number: 237028399

291
Disney Foundation ▼ ⌑
500 South Buena Vista St.
Burbank 91521 (818) 840-1000

Incorporated in 1951 in CA.
Donor(s): Walt Disney Productions, and its associated companies.
Foundation type: Company-sponsored
Financial data (yr. ended 9/30/87): Assets, $191,250 (M); gifts received, $725,650; expenditures, $608,833, including $440,487 for 80 grants (high: $100,000; low: $100; average: $1,000-$20,000) and $158,685 for 50 grants to individuals.
Purpose and activities: Emphasis on youth and child welfare agencies, health, higher education, cultural programs, and community funds; scholarships for the children of employees.
Types of support: Annual campaigns, continuing support, operating budgets, special projects, scholarship funds, employee-related scholarships, general purposes, capital campaigns.
Limitations: Giving primarily in areas where the company's businesses are located, including central FL, and Los Angeles and Orange County, CA. No grants to individuals (except for scholarships to children of company employees) or for endowment funds.
Publications: Application guidelines.
Application information: Application form not required.
Initial approach: Letter, proposal, or telephone
Copies of proposal: 1
Deadline(s): Oct. 1 for scholarships
Board meeting date(s): Annually between Jan. and May
Final notification: 20 to 30 days
Write: Doris A. Smith, Secy.
Officers: Michael D. Eisner,* Pres.; Roy E. Disney,* V.P.; Jack B. Lindquist,* V.P.; Doris A. Smith, Secy.; Frank G. Wells, Treas.
Number of staff: None.
Employer Identification Number: 956037079

292
The Lillian B. Disney Foundation ⌑
P.O. Box 15159
North Hollywood 91615

Established in 1974 in CA.
Donor(s): Lillian D. Truyens.
Foundation type: Independent
Financial data (yr. ended 12/31/89): Assets, $1,389,439 (M); expenditures, $134,482.
Purpose and activities: Support for cultural programs, civic affairs and youth.
Types of support: General purposes.
Limitations: Giving primarily in CA.
Officers: Lillian B. Disney, Pres.; Sharon D. Lund, V.P.; Diane D. Miller, V.P.; Roy W. McClean, Secy.-Treas.
Employer Identification Number: 237425637

293
The Marguerite Doe Foundation ⌑
202 East Carrillo St., Suite 201
Santa Barbara 93101 (805) 963-3871

Established in 1968 in CA.
Donor(s): Marguerite Doe Ravenscroft.†
Foundation type: Operating
Financial data (yr. ended 12/31/88): Assets, $210,529 (M); gifts received, $124,868; expenditures, $187,722, including $180,000 for 6 grants (high: $50,000; low: $15,000; average: $20-$25,000).
Purpose and activities: To aid organizations operated for the prevention of cruelty to animals, specifically canines; support for humane societies.
Types of support: Building funds, equipment, land acquisition, matching funds, renovation projects, seed money, special projects.
Limitations: No grants to individuals.
Application information:
Initial approach: Letter
Deadline(s): None
Board meeting date(s): As required
Write: Anthony Gunterman, Dir.
Directors: Raymond A. Buelow, Anthony Gunterman, Antonio R. Romasanta.
Number of staff: 1 part-time support.
Employer Identification Number: 956226536

294
Thelma Doelger Charitable Trust ⌑
950 John Daly Blvd., Suite 300
Daly City 94015-3004

Established in 1980 in CA.
Foundation type: Independent
Financial data (yr. ended 06/30/90): Assets, $14,998,876 (M); gifts received, $440,615; expenditures, $589,243, including $394,302 for 17 grants (high: $100,000; low: $100).
Purpose and activities: Support primarily for a zoological society, animal welfare organizations, and a center for the aged.
Types of support: General purposes.
Limitations: Giving primarily in the San Francisco Bay Area, CA. No grants to individuals.
Application information: Application form required.
Deadline(s): None
Trustees: Susan Doelger, Edward M. King, Chester W. Lebsack.
Employer Identification Number: 946500318

295
Carrie Estelle Doheny Foundation ▼
911 Wilshire Blvd., Suite 1750
Los Angeles 90017 (213) 488-1122

Trust established in 1949 in CA.
Donor(s): Mrs. Edward L. Doheny.†
Foundation type: Independent
Financial data (yr. ended 12/31/88): Assets, $75,938,492 (M); expenditures, $3,759,226, including $3,015,849 for 94 grants (high: $1,000,000; low: $750; average: $3,000-$25,000).
Purpose and activities: The foundation was established for the "advancement of education, medicine, religion, science; the improvement of the health and welfare of infants, children, adults, families, and the aged; the help and care of the sick, aged, and incapacitated; and the aid of the needy."
Types of support: General purposes.
Limitations: Giving primarily in the Los Angeles, CA, area. No support for tax-supported organizations or radio or television programs. No grants to individuals, or for endowment funds, publications, travel, advertising, or scholarships.
Publications: Annual report (including application guidelines).
Application information: Application form not required.
Initial approach: Letter
Copies of proposal: 1
Deadline(s): None
Board meeting date(s): Monthly
Final notification: 1 to 2 months
Write: Robert A. Smith III, Pres., Carrie Estelle Doheny Foundation Corp.
Trustee: Carrie Estelle Doheny Foundation Corp.
Corporation Officers: Robert A. Smith III,* Pres.; Arthur E. Thunell, Secy.-Treas.
Corporation Directors:* Sister M. Coughlin, Robert Erburu, Austin F. Gavin, George Gibbs, Joseph Nally, Rev. Francis D. Pansini, C.M.
Number of staff: 1 full-time professional; 1 part-time support.
Employer Identification Number: 952051633

296
Douglas Charitable Foundation ⌑
141 El Camino Dr.
Beverly Hills 90212

Established in 1964 in CA.
Donor(s): Kirk Douglas, Anne Douglas.
Foundation type: Independent
Financial data (yr. ended 12/31/88): Assets, $4,302,117 (M); gifts received, $498,075; expenditures, $109,183, including $90,505 for 42 grants (high: $26,250; low: $100).
Purpose and activities: Giving for Jewish welfare, social services, and the arts.
Limitations: Giving primarily in CA.
Officers: Anne Douglas, Mgr.; Kirk Douglas, Mgr.; Karl Samuelian, Mgr.; John T. Trotter, Mgr.; Jack Valenti, Mgr.
Employer Identification Number: 956096827

297
Dr. Seuss Foundation ⌑
7301 Encelia Dr.
La Jolla 92037 (619) 454-7384

Incorporated in 1958 in CA.
Donor(s): Theodor S. Geisel.
Foundation type: Independent
Financial data (yr. ended 12/31/88): Assets, $1,891,006 (M); expenditures, $171,123, including $125,060 for 88 grants (high: $15,000; low: $50).
Purpose and activities: Support for mental health, hospitals, higher education, youth agencies, cultural programs, and the arts.
Limitations: Giving primarily in CA. No grants to individuals.
Application information:
Deadline(s): None
Write: Theodor S. Geisel, Pres.
Officers and Directors:* Theodor S. Geisel,* Pres.; Robert L. Bernstein,* V.P.; Audrey Geisel,* V.P.; Karl Zobell,* Secy.; Edward Lathem.
Employer Identification Number: 956029752

298
Joseph Drown Foundation ▼ ⌘
10900 Wilshire Blvd., Suite 1200
Los Angeles 90024 (213) 208-2267

Established in 1953 in CA.
Donor(s): Joseph W. Drown.†
Foundation type: Independent
Financial data (yr. ended 3/31/88): Assets, $70,000,000 (M); expenditures, $5,673,700, including $4,975,000 for 150 grants (high: $250,000; low: $1,000; average: $25,000).
Purpose and activities: Grants primarily for education and medical research.
Types of support: General purposes, research, scholarship funds.
Limitations: Giving primarily in CA. No grants to individuals, or for endowments or building funds.
Application information: Application form not required.
Initial approach: 1-page proposal
Copies of proposal: 1
Deadline(s): Jan. 15, Apr. 15, July 15, and Oct. 15
Board meeting date(s): Quarterly
Write: Norman C. Obrow, Pres.
Officers: Milton F. Fillius, Jr.,* Chair.; Norman C. Obrow,* Pres.; Thomas C. Marshall,* V.P.; Philip S. Magaram,* Secy.-Treas.
Directors:* Harry C. Cogen, Benton C. Coit, Elaine Mahoney.
Number of staff: 1 full-time professional; 1 part-time professional; 1 full-time support.
Employer Identification Number: 956093178

299
The Drum Foundation ⌘
c/o Northern Trust of California, N.A.
580 California St., Suite 1800
San Francisco 94104

Incorporated in 1956 in CA.
Donor(s): Frank G. Drum.†
Foundation type: Independent
Financial data (yr. ended 12/31/89): Assets, $5,315,963 (M); expenditures, $355,225, including $303,500 for 42 grants (high: $25,000; low: $500; average: $1,000-$50,000).
Purpose and activities: To aid Roman Catholic church-related educational and charitable organizations, usually limited to the Archdiocese of San Francisco, including those supported by the donor during his lifetime.
Types of support: General purposes, operating budgets, continuing support, annual campaigns, seed money, emergency funds, deficit financing, building funds, equipment, land acquisition, scholarship funds, professorships, internships, exchange programs, fellowships, special projects, research, publications, conferences and seminars, matching funds.
Limitations: Giving primarily in the San Francisco Area, CA. No grants to individuals, or for endowment funds or matching gifts.
Application information: Contributes only to pre-selected organizations. Applications not accepted.
Board meeting date(s): As required
Officers: Philip Hudner, Pres.; Janet Abbott, V.P.; C. Albert Schumante, M.D., V.P.; Donald D. Crawford, Secy.-Treas.
Number of staff: None.
Employer Identification Number: 946067469

300
Ducommun & Gross Foundation ⌘
237 Strada Corta Rd.
Los Angeles 90077-3726 (213) 472-3977

Established in 1968 in CA.
Foundation type: Independent
Financial data (yr. ended 12/31/88): Assets, $1,370,940 (M); expenditures, $113,875, including $102,500 for 13 grants (high: $40,000; low: $1,000).
Purpose and activities: Support primarily for higher education and the arts, including art museums.
Application information:
Initial approach: Letter
Deadline(s): None
Write: Charles E. Ducommun, Pres.
Officers: Charles E. Ducommun, Pres.; Virginia D. Ward, V.P.; Frederick A. Richmond, Secy.
Employer Identification Number: 956210834

301
The Dunning Foundation
P.O. Box 1207
Claremont 91711-1207

Established in 1982 in CA.
Donor(s): George A.V. Dunning.
Foundation type: Independent
Financial data (yr. ended 10/31/89): Assets, $3,309,993 (M); gifts received, $330,000; expenditures, $262,812, including $256,528 for 4 grants of $64,132 each.
Purpose and activities: Support for higher education, community funds, and social services.
Limitations: Giving primarily in CA.
Application information: Applications not accepted.
Directors: George A.V. Dunning, Mrs. Joseph L. Hegener, Michael Preston, Jack Shakely.
Number of staff: None.
Employer Identification Number: 953806262

302
The Durfee Foundation
11444 West Olympic Blvd., Suite 1017
Los Angeles 90064 (213) 312-9543

Incorporated in 1960 in CA.
Donor(s): Ray Stanton Avery, Dorothy Durfee Avery.†
Foundation type: Independent
Financial data (yr. ended 12/31/89): Assets, $15,865,187 (M); expenditures, $506,421, including $353,629 for 24 grants (high: $65,450; low: $750).
Purpose and activities: Support for cultural programs and education. Biannual cash awards of up to $25,000 are made to individuals who have enhanced human dignity through the law.
Types of support: Special projects.
Limitations: Giving primarily in CA. No grants for endowment funds or operating budgets.
Publications: Occasional report, multi-year report.
Application information: Submit grant application at request of foundation only; foundation solicits proposals in areas of interest.
Copies of proposal: 1
Deadline(s): None
Write: Robert S. Macfarlane, Jr., Managing Dir.
Officers and Trustees:* Ray Stanton Avery,* Chair.; Russell D. Avery,* Pres.; Judith A. Newkirk,* V.P. and Treas.; Caroline Newkirk,* Secy.; Robert S. Macfarlane, Jr.,* Managing Dir.; Michael Newkirk.
Number of staff: 1 part-time professional; 1 part-time support.
Employer Identification Number: 952223738

303
Margaret E. Early Medical Research Trust ⌘
c/o Harrington, Foxx, Dubrow, Canter & Keene
611 West Sixth St., 30th Fl.
Los Angeles 90017 (213) 489-3222

Established in 1982.
Foundation type: Independent
Financial data (yr. ended 12/31/88): Assets, $4,668,063 (M); expenditures, $438,438, including $367,830 for 6 grants (high: $75,240; low: $37,130).
Purpose and activities: Giving for cancer research.
Types of support: Research.
Limitations: Giving limited to southern CA.
Application information:
Initial approach: Proposal
Deadline(s): Established annually
Write: Eli B. Dubrow, Trustee
Trustee: Eli B. Dubrow.
Employer Identification Number: 953740506

304
The East Bay Community Foundation
6230 Claremont Ave.
Oakland 94618 (415) 658-5441

Established in 1928 in CA as The Alameda County Community Foundation by resolution and declaration of trust; revised in 1972.
Foundation type: Community
Financial data (yr. ended 12/31/88): Assets, $1,009,943 (M); gifts received, $1,542,484; expenditures, $1,103,911, including $817,115 for 123 grants (high: $101,035; low: $350).
Purpose and activities: Grants for community welfare, youth, the aged, women's programs, health care, arts and culture, and educational programs.
Limitations: Giving limited to Alameda and Contra Costa counties, CA. No support for sectarian religious causes, educational or hospital foundations, public or private educational institutions, or drug and/or alcohol abuse detoxification programs. No grants to individuals, or for building and endowment funds, equipment, annual fund drives, teachers' salaries, capital improvements, scholarships, deficit financing, media production, research projects, matching gifts, travel, or conferences; no loans.
Publications: Annual report, program policy statement, application guidelines.
Application information: Application form not required.
Initial approach: Letter or proposal
Copies of proposal: 1
Deadline(s): Jan. 1, May 1, and Sept. 1
Board meeting date(s): Feb., June, and Oct.
Write: Sandra L. Pyer, Exec. Dir.
Officers: Sandra L. Pyer, Exec. Dir.; Virginia H. Hooper, Secy.-Treas.

Governing Board: Lois De Domenico, Chair.; David L. Cutter, Vice-Chair.; Hon Chew, R. Kenneth Coit, Penny Deleray, Barbara C. Donald, Salvatore V. Giuffre, M.D., Margaret Stuart Graupner, Edwin A. Heafey, Jr., Lucile Lansing Levin, Gregory L. McCoy, Neil W. McDaniel, H.E. Mikkelsen, Charles J. Patterson, Linda C. Roodhouse.
Trustees: First Interstate Bank, Wells Fargo Bank, N.A.
Number of staff: 1 full-time professional; 1 part-time professional; 1 full-time support.
Employer Identification Number: 946070996

305
Lucius & Eva Eastman Fund, Inc. ⌑
24120 Summit Woods Dr.
Los Gatos 95030

Established in 1946 in CA.
Foundation type: Independent
Financial data (yr. ended 12/31/88): Assets, $1,149,964 (M); expenditures, $71,135, including $55,375 for 43 grants (high: $2,500; low: $500).
Purpose and activities: Support for law and justice, including civil and human rights, social services, women, and cultural programs, especially the fine arts.
Application information: Application form not required.
Deadline(s): None
Board meeting date(s): Quarterly
Write: Lucius R. Eastman, Jr., Pres.
Officer: Lucius R. Eastman, Jr., Pres.
Number of staff: None.
Employer Identification Number: 131958483

306
Edwin M. & Gertrude S. Eaton Foundation ⌑ ☆
440 Davis Court, No. 1711
San Francisco 94111

Established in 1979.
Donor(s): Evelyn T. Eaton.
Foundation type: Independent
Financial data (yr. ended 6/30/89): Assets, $105,765 (M); gifts received, $2,683,188; expenditures, $2,766,607, including $2,753,773 for 32 grants (high: $2,657,877; low: $100).
Purpose and activities: Giving primarily for a French social service organization; support also for Catholic organizations, including churches and missions.
Limitations: Giving primarily in CA, with emphasis on San Francisco, and France. No grants to individuals.
Application information: Contributes only to pre-selected organizations. Applications not accepted.
Officer and Trustees:* Evelyn T. Eaton,* Pres.; Geraldine Carrigan, Mary Ellen Dougherty.
Employer Identification Number: 942674856

307
Ebell of Los Angeles Rest Cottage Association ⌑
743 South Lucerne Blvd.
Los Angeles 90005 (213) 931-1277

Established in 1918 in CA.
Foundation type: Independent
Financial data (yr. ended 6/30/88): Assets, $1,737,445 (M); gifts received, $520; expenditures, $125,638, including $90,000 for 3 grants of $30,000 each.
Purpose and activities: Giving for social services to provide medical care for indigent persons.
Limitations: Giving primarily in Los Angeles, CA.
Application information:
Initial approach: Letter
Deadline(s): None
Write: Alberta Burke, Chair.
Officers: Alberta Burke, Chair.; LaRose Alber, Chair. of Finance; Mrs. Albert R. Weigel, Pres.; Mrs. Arthur B. Cecil, V.P.; Mrs. Robert M. Parker, V.P.; Erma L. Schmalzried, V.P.; Mrs. Vincent P. Swackenberg, V.P.; Mrs. George G. Luethye, Recording Secy.; Mrs. Arnold H. Bachmann, Corresponding Secy.; Mrs. Eugene B. Glenn, Treas.
Employer Identification Number: 956102928

308
Ebell of Los Angeles Scholarship Endowment Fund
743 South Lucerne Blvd.
Los Angeles 90005 (213) 931-4336

Established in 1921 in CA.
Foundation type: Independent
Financial data (yr. ended 06/30/88): Assets, $1,641,934 (M); expenditures, $87,723, including $61,949 for 31 grants to individuals (high: $2,000).
Purpose and activities: Scholarships for undergraduate college students who are U.S. citizens, unmarried, registered voters (if 18), and enrolled in colleges in Los Angeles County, CA, with sophomore or better standing, carrying 12 or more units and with GPA's of 3.25 or better.
Types of support: Student aid.
Limitations: Giving limited to Los Angeles County, CA, residents attending Los Angeles County, CA, colleges.
Publications: Application guidelines.
Application information: Application form required.
Deadline(s): June 1 for the following Sept.
Write: Scholarship Chair.
Officers and Directors:* Mrs. Arthur B. Cecil,* Pres.; Mrs. Sylvester M. Scott,* 1st V.P.; Erma L. Schmalzried,* 2nd V.P.; Mrs. Robert M. Parker,* 3rd V.P.; Mrs. Donald E. Dupree,* 4th V.P. and Membership Chair.; Mrs. George G. Luethye,* Recording Secy.; Mrs. Arnold H. Bachmann,* Corresponding Secy.; Mrs. Harold C. Henneberry,* Treas.; LaRose Alber,* Chair. of Finance; Mrs. Daniel Bloxsom, Jr.,* Chair. of Scholarships.
Employer Identification Number: 237049580

309
Paul & Magdalena Ecke Poinsettia Foundation ⌑
P.O. Box 607
Encinitas 92024

Established around 1981 in CA.
Donor(s): Magdalena Ecke.†
Foundation type: Independent
Financial data (yr. ended 05/31/87): Assets, $1,723,805 (M); expenditures, $174,092, including $163,075 for 21 grants (high: $40,000; low: $575).
Purpose and activities: Giving primarily for youth activity and child welfare, and to higher and some secondary education.
Application information:
Initial approach: Letter
Deadline(s): None
Officers and Directors:* Paul Ecke, Sr.,* Chair. and Pres.; Paul Ecke, Jr.,* V.P.; Barbara Ecke Winter,* Secy.; Paul Ecke III.
Employer Identification Number: 953758658

310
Charles C. & Sue K. Edwards Foundation ☆
9351 La Jolla Farms Rd.
La Jolla 92037

Established in 1984 in CA.
Donor(s): Charles C. Edwards, Sue K. Edwards.
Foundation type: Independent
Financial data (yr. ended 11/30/87): Assets, $79,873 (M); gifts received, $100,000; expenditures, $154,252, including $152,872 for 86 grants (high: $73,500; low: $50).
Purpose and activities: Giving primarily for the arts and museums; support also for health associations and social services.
Limitations: Giving primarily in San Diego and La Jolla, CA. No grants to individuals.
Application information: Contributes only to pre-selected organizations. Applications not accepted.
Officers and Directors:* Charles C. Edwards,* Pres.; Sue K. Edwards,* Secy.-Treas.
Employer Identification Number: 330071699

311
Ben B. and Joyce E. Eisenberg Foundation
11999 San Vincente Blvd., Suite 300
Los Angeles 90049 (213) 471-4220

Established in 1986 in CA.
Foundation type: Independent
Financial data (yr. ended 5/31/89): Assets, $11,450,372 (M); expenditures, $683,684, including $677,048 for 46 grants (high: $130,926; low: $25).
Purpose and activities: Support primarily for Jewish education and Jewish giving; support also for medical research and care facilities and civic affairs.
Types of support: Annual campaigns, continuing support, research.
Limitations: Giving primarily in the U.S. and Israel.
Application information: Applications not accepted.
Write: David J. Cohen, V.P.
Officers: Joyce E. Eisenberg, Pres.; David J. Cohen, V.P. and Secy.
Number of staff: 3 full-time support.
Employer Identification Number: 990246427

312
Eldorado Foundation
50 Lupine Ave., Apt. 3
San Francisco 94118 (415) 221-0734

Established in 1964 in CA.
Foundation type: Independent
Financial data (yr. ended 12/31/88): Assets, $1,403,031 (M); expenditures, $76,730, including $72,000 for 30 grants (high: $6,000; low: $500).
Purpose and activities: Giving primarily for cultural programs and conservation; support also for social services, hospitals, education, and religion.
Limitations: Giving primarily in San Francisco, CA. No grants to individuals.
Application information:
Initial approach: Letter
Deadline(s): Apr. 1
Write: Ava Jean Brumbaum, Secy.-Treas.
Officers and Directors:* Helen D. Van Blair,* Pres.; Jack F. Dohrmann,* V.P.; Ava Jean Brumbaum,* Secy.-Treas.; Henry K. Evers, Peggy Merrifield.
Number of staff: None.
Employer Identification Number: 946100642

313
Elks of Los Angeles Foundation Fund ¤
c/o Wells Fargo Bank, N.A.
525 Market St., 17th Fl.
Los Angeles 90005 (213) 387-1136
Application address: 607 South Western Ave., Los Angeles, CA 90004; Tel.: (818) 881-4728

Established in 1929 in CA.
Foundation type: Independent
Financial data (yr. ended 12/31/88): Assets, $1,315,924 (M); gifts received, $38,373; expenditures, $155,854, including $138,161 for 50 grants (high: $7,000; low: $1,000).
Purpose and activities: Giving primarily for youth, child welfare, and health services.
Limitations: Giving primarily in CA, especially Los Angeles.
Application information: Application form required.
Deadline(s): Feb. and Mar.
Write: Frank Lorenzi, Pres.
Officer: Frank Lorenzi, Pres.
Trustee: Wells Fargo Bank, N.A.
Employer Identification Number: 956019849

314
The Erteszek Foundation ¤
918 South Bundy Dr.
Los Angeles 90049 (213) 826-1357

Incorporated in 1984 in CA.
Donor(s): Jan Erteszek,† Olga Erteszek.
Foundation type: Independent
Financial data (yr. ended 12/31/88): Assets, $1,632,507 (M); expenditures, $100,495, including $73,500 for 8 grants (high: $20,000; low: $1,000).
Purpose and activities: Grants for public policy studies, civic affairs, and medical research.
Types of support: Research.
Limitations: Giving primarily in CA and OR.
Application information: Due to funding limitations, the directors of the foundation prefer to initiate grants.
Write: Olga Erteszek, Pres.
Officers: Olga Erteszek, Pres.; Christina Erteszek Johnson, V.P.; George F. Moody, Treas.
Employer Identification Number: 953952646

315
The Essick Foundation, Inc. ¤
609 South Grand Ave., Suite 1217
Los Angeles 90017 (213) 626-6658

Incorporated in 1947 in CA.
Donor(s): Jeanette Marie Essick,† Bryant Essick, Essick Investment Co.
Foundation type: Independent
Financial data (yr. ended 12/31/88): Assets, $3,098,406 (M); expenditures, $114,471, including $103,090 for 82 grants (high: $27,500; low: $45).
Purpose and activities: Giving mainly to local organizations in which the donors are interested, with emphasis on higher education, hospitals, and a community fund.
Limitations: Giving primarily in southern CA. No grants to individuals.
Application information: Grants generally initiated by the donors.
Initial approach: Letter
Deadline(s): None
Write: Bryant Essick, Pres.
Officers and Directors:* Bryant Essick,* Pres.; James H. Essick,* V.P.; Lillian M. Ringe, Secy.; Robert N. Essick,* Treas.
Employer Identification Number: 956048985

316
Max Factor Family Foundation ¤
9777 Wilshire Blvd., Suite 1015
Beverly Hills 90212 (213) 274-8193

Trust established in 1941 in CA.
Donor(s): Members of the Factor family.
Foundation type: Independent
Financial data (yr. ended 12/31/88): Assets, $10,404,174 (M); expenditures, $950,434, including $875,000 for 23 grants (high: $225,000; low: $1,000; average: $1,000-$50,000).
Purpose and activities: Emphasis on Jewish welfare funds, hospitals, medical research, education, care of the aged, and aid to the handicapped.
Types of support: Research, scholarship funds, general purposes, continuing support, operating budgets, building funds.
Limitations: Giving primarily in southern CA. No grants to individuals.
Application information:
Initial approach: Letter
Deadline(s): None
Board meeting date(s): Monthly
Final notification: Varies
Write: Barbara Factor Bentley, Trustee
Trustees: Barbara Factor Bentley, Gerald Factor, Max Factor III.
Number of staff: 3 part-time professional.
Employer Identification Number: 956030779

317
Freeman E. Fairfield Foundation
3610 Long Beach Blvd.
P.O. Box 7798
Long Beach 90807 (213) 427-7219

Established in 1969 in CA.
Donor(s): Freeman E. Fairfield.†
Foundation type: Independent
Financial data (yr. ended 12/31/88): Assets, $4,797,302 (M); expenditures, $457,259, including $378,486 for 20 grants (high: $150,000; low: $1,000; average: $5,000-$20,000).
Purpose and activities: Emphasis on youth agencies, medical centers and clinics, the handicapped, and general social services, including the aged and child welfare and development.
Types of support: Matching funds, equipment, operating budgets, renovation projects, special projects.
Limitations: Giving limited to Long Beach and Signal Hill, CA. No support for religious purposes. No grants to individuals, or for endowment funds, unrestricted operating costs, deficit financing, intermediary funding agencies, or general fundraising drives.
Publications: Program policy statement, application guidelines.
Application information: Application form required.
Initial approach: Proposal
Copies of proposal: 3
Deadline(s): May 1
Board meeting date(s): As required
Final notification: July 1
Write: Edna E. Sellers, Trustee
Trustees: Pierre Auw, Glenn Conway, Edna E. Sellers.
Number of staff: 1 part-time support.
Employer Identification Number: 237055338

318
Elizabeth M. Falk Foundation ¤
c/o S.L. Beckwith
6433 Topanga Canyon Blvd., Suite 414
Canoga Park 91303

Established in 1984 in CA.
Foundation type: Independent
Financial data (yr. ended 8/31/88): Assets, $1,541,163 (M); expenditures, $77,801, including $45,991 for 1 grant and $11,921 for 1 grant to an individual.
Purpose and activities: Support for education and animal welfare.
Application information: Contributes only to pre-selected organizations. Applications not accepted.
Officers and Directors:* Stephen Falk,* Pres.; James E. Beal,* Secy.; Howard O. Wilson,* Treas.
Trustee: City National Bank.
Employer Identification Number: 953950915

319
Isadore and Sunny Familian Family Foundation ¤
906 Loma Vista Dr.
Beverly Hills 90210 (213) 272-0191

Incorporated in 1947 in CA.
Donor(s): The Familian family and others.

Foundation type: Independent
Financial data (yr. ended 12/31/87): Assets, $1,200,542 (M); gifts received, $380,082; expenditures, $144,976, including $122,321 for 75 grants (high: $64,345; low: $18).
Purpose and activities: Support for Jewish welfare funds and religious organizations, higher education, and cultural programs.
Limitations: Giving primarily in CA.
Application information: Contributes only to pre-selected organizations. Applications not accepted.
Write: Isadore Familian, Pres.
Officers: Isadore Familian, Pres. and Treas.; Sondra Smalley, Secy.
Director: Marvin Smalley.
Employer Identification Number: 956027950

320
Zalec Familian Foundation ⌑
P.O. Box 5149
Compton 90224

Established in 1958 in CA.
Donor(s): Zalec Familian,† and others.
Foundation type: Independent
Financial data (yr. ended 3/31/88): Assets, $1,491,535 (M); expenditures, $66,288.
Purpose and activities: Emphasis on higher education, social services, and cultural programs.
Types of support: General purposes.
Limitations: Giving primarily in CA.
Application information: Budget for grants considered late in the calendar year. Application form not required.
Initial approach: Proposal
Write: Robert J. Cannon, Asst. Secy.
Officers: Lilian Levinson, Pres.; Albert T. Galen, V.P.; Albert Levinson, Secy.-Treas.
Employer Identification Number: 956099164

321
Farallon Foundation
P.O. Box 13314, No. 461
Oakland 94661-0314 (415) 339-6501

Established in 1972 in CA.
Donor(s): Nancy M. Ditzler, Hugh W. Ditzler, Jr., Marian Zischke, Peter H. Zischke, John R. Shuman, Josephine R. Shuman, and 10 other contributors.
Foundation type: Independent
Financial data (yr. ended 6/30/88): Assets, $1,576,320 (M); gifts received, $502,882; expenditures, $109,754, including $85,189 for 149 grants (high: $11,402; low: $10).
Purpose and activities: Support for education, social services, including community funds, health, religion, and conservation.
Limitations: No grants to individuals.
Application information: Contributes only to pre-selected organizations. Applications not accepted.
Write: Hugh W. Ditzler, Jr., Chair. and Pres.
Officer and Trustees:* Hugh W. Ditzler, Jr.,* Chair. and Pres.; Kate D. Devereux, Nancy M. Ditzler, Peter H. Zischke.
Number of staff: None.
Employer Identification Number: 237216373

322
Feintech Family Foundation ⌑
321 South Beverly Dr., Suite K
Beverly Hills 90212 (213) 879-3262

Established in 1950 in CA.
Donor(s): Irving Feintech, Norman Feintech.
Foundation type: Independent
Financial data (yr. ended 9/30/88): Assets, $1,977,125 (M); gifts received, $892,500; expenditures, $133,900, including $114,178 for 30 grants (high: $36,125; low: $50).
Purpose and activities: Support primarily for Jewish welfare and concerns, including giving to Jewish universities; support also for the arts and health service organizations.
Limitations: Giving primarily in CA.
Application information:
Initial approach: Letter
Deadline(s): None
Write: Norman Feintech, Pres. or Irving Feintech, V.P.
Officers: Norman Feintech, Pres.; Irving Feintech, V.P.
Director: Celia Littenberg.
Employer Identification Number: 956072287

323
Lorser Feitelson and Helen Lundeberg Feitelson Arts Foundation ⌑
8307 West Third St.
Los Angeles 90048 (213) 655-3245

Established in 1979.
Donor(s): Lorser Feitelson.
Foundation type: Independent
Financial data (yr. ended 11/30/89): Assets, $1,092,572 (M); expenditures, $20,681, including $5,000 for 2 grants to individuals of $2,500 each.
Purpose and activities: Grants and loans in the form of art works by Lorser Feitelson to major universities with prominent art museums and art history departments and to municipal art museums; also individual grants based on need to artists living in southern CA.
Types of support: Grants to individuals.
Limitations: Giving primarily in CA.
Application information:
Initial approach: Letter
Deadline(s): None
Officers and Directors:* Helen L. Feitelson,* Pres.; Josine Ianco-Starrels,* Secy.; Monroe Price,* Treas.
Employer Identification Number: 953451355

324
Leopold & Clara M. Fellner Memorial Foundation ⌑
615 South Flower St., Suite 1700
Los Angeles 90017 (213) 624-7391

Established in 1983 in CA.
Foundation type: Independent
Financial data (yr. ended 12/31/87): Assets, $2,539,098 (M); expenditures, $281,742, including $184,700 for 15 grants (high: $73,000; low: $500).
Purpose and activities: Distributions are to be used for the benefit of Jewish people in or in relation to the State of Israel.
Application information: Application form not required.
Initial approach: Letter
Deadline(s): None
Write: Frederick L. Simmons, Trustee
Trustee: Frederick L. Simmons.
Employer Identification Number: 953859307

325
Femino Foundation
P.O. Box 567
West Covina 91793

Donor(s): James J. Femino, Sue Femino, Dominic Femino.
Foundation type: Independent
Financial data (yr. ended 9/30/89): Assets, $2,314,450 (M); gifts received, $190,000; expenditures, $96,875, including $90,687 for 28 grants (high: $50,000; low: $100).
Purpose and activities: Support primarily for hospitals and health organizations and institutions of medical research and education; support also for higher and other education.
Types of support: Scholarship funds.
Officers: James J. Femino, Pres.; Sue Femino, V.P.; Robert L. Bacon, Secy.; Frank P. Uehle, Treas.
Employer Identification Number: 237423792

326
FHP Foundation ☆
401 East Ocean Blvd., Suite 206
Long Beach 90802-4933 (213) 590-8655

Established in 1985 in CA.
Donor(s): FHP International Corp.
Foundation type: Company-sponsored
Financial data (yr. ended 06/30/89): Assets, $54,829,942 (M); qualifying distributions, $773,064, including $773,064 for 17 grants (high: $89,000; low: $2,911).
Purpose and activities: Support for direct delivery of health care services including health education programs, programs for the elderly and chronically ill, and primary care projects in underserved areas, and for educational and research activities.
Types of support: Research.
Limitations: Giving primarily in southern CA, UT, NM, AZ, and Micronesia. No grants to individuals.
Publications: Biennial report, multi-year report, newsletter, occasional report, informational brochure (including application guidelines), application guidelines.
Application information:
Initial approach: Letter
Deadline(s): Feb. 15, May 15, Aug. 15, and Nov. 15
Board meeting date(s): Mar., June, Sept., Dec.
Final notification: After board meetings
Write: Sandra Lund Gavin, Exec. Dir.
Officer and Directors:* Robert Gumbiner,* Chair.; Paul Carpenter, Stephen Horn, Scott Matheson, Jack W. Peltason, Joseph F. Prevratil, W.W. Price III.
Number of staff: 1 full-time professional; 1 full-time support; 1 part-time support.

327
The Irene C. Finkelstein Foundation ⌑
623 North Camden Dr.
Beverly Hills 90210

Established in 1984 in CA.
Donor(s): Irene C. Finkelstein.
Foundation type: Independent
Financial data (yr. ended 11/30/88): Assets, $1,153,374 (M); expenditures, $64,755, including $60,500 for 9 grants (high: $25,000; low: $1,000).
Purpose and activities: Emphasis on Jewish giving and higher education.
Officers: Irene C. Finkelstein, C.E.O.; Alla Kutz, Secy.; Sid Levine, C.F.O.
Director: Leonard Unger.
Employer Identification Number: 953943474

328
Fireman's Fund Foundation ▼
(Formerly Fireman's Fund Insurance Company Foundation)
777 San Marin Dr.
P.O. Box 777
Novato 94998 (415) 899-2757

Incorporated in 1953 in CA.
Donor(s): Fireman's Fund Insurance Co., and subsidiaries.
Foundation type: Company-sponsored
Financial data (yr. ended 12/31/89): Assets, $106,740 (M); gifts received, $1,500,000; expenditures, $1,469,885, including $1,081,767 for 653 grants (high: $299,250; low: $50; average: $100-$5,000) and $374,978 for 876 employee matching gifts.
Purpose and activities: Giving primarily to assist higher, secondary, and elementary education, including programs for minorities and libraries; human service agencies, including the aged, the handicapped, rehabilitation, and youth groups; and civic and cultural activities. Grants also for United Way campaigns nationwide in cities where principal company offices are located.
Types of support: Annual campaigns, equipment, technical assistance, continuing support, employee matching gifts, matching funds.
Limitations: Giving primarily in the counties of San Francisco, Marin, and Sonoma, CA. No support for religious or national organizations, or other grantmaking bodies. No grants to individuals, or for travel, benefit events, or operating expenses of organizations that receive federated-campaign support; no loans.
Publications: Annual report (including application guidelines).
Application information: Application form not required.
Initial approach: Letter
Copies of proposal: 1
Deadline(s): None
Board meeting date(s): Jan.; distribution committee meets once a month
Final notification: 6 weeks
Write: Mary K. Anderson, Secy. and Dir.
Officers: Morgan W. Davis,* Chair.; Edward T. Laugle,* Pres.; Mary K. Anderson,* Secy.; Robert Marto, Treas.
Directors:* Raymond Barrette, Joseph W. Brown, Jr., Thomas A. Swanson, Lawrence E. Wiesen.
Number of staff: 1 full-time professional; 1 part-time support.
Employer Identification Number: 946078025

329
The Firks Foundation ⌑ ☆
10375 Wilshire Blvd., Suite 109
Los Angeles 90024 (213) 859-8244

Established in 1959.
Foundation type: Independent
Financial data (yr. ended 7/31/88): Assets, $360,369 (M); gifts received, $360,000; expenditures, $416,712, including $414,935 for 42 grants (high: $241,080; low: $15).
Purpose and activities: Giving primarily for art museums; support also for Jewish welfare and educational institutions, hospitals and medical research, and music.
Limitations: No grants to individuals.
Application information: Application form not required.
Deadline(s): None
Write: Geri Firks Brawerman, Pres.
Officers and Directors:* Geri Firks Braverman,* Pres.; Nancy Gamm,* V.P.; Stanley Scherdorf,* Secy.-Treas.; Richard Miller, Raymond C. Sandler.
Employer Identification Number: 956067106

330
First Interstate Bank of California Foundation ▼
1055 Wilshire Blvd., B9-75
Los Angeles 90017 (213) 580-6658
Additional tel.: (213) 580-6666

Established in 1978 in CA.
Donor(s): First Interstate Bank of California.
Foundation type: Company-sponsored
Financial data (yr. ended 12/31/89): Assets, $18,514,611 (M); expenditures, $2,496,312, including $2,342,000 for 287 grants (high: $680,853; low: $500; average: $1,000-$25,000) and $154,312 for 688 employee matching gifts.
Purpose and activities: Giving primarily for community funds, education, the performing arts and cultural programs, hospitals, urban and civic affairs, and social service and youth agencies; employee-related scholarships made through the Citizens' Scholarship Foundation of America.
Types of support: Building funds, land acquisition, endowment funds, matching funds, technical assistance, scholarship funds, employee-related scholarships, special projects, employee matching gifts, annual campaigns, operating budgets, continuing support, capital campaigns, general purposes.
Limitations: Giving limited to CA. No support for religious organizations for religious purposes, agencies supported by the United Way, or private foundations. No grants to individuals, or for research, conferences, or equipment for hospitals; no loans.
Publications: Informational brochure (including application guidelines), annual report.
Application information: Application form required.
Initial approach: Letter, telephone, or proposal
Copies of proposal: 1
Deadline(s): Capital campaigns July 1; for other programs, none
Board meeting date(s): Quarterly
Final notification: 6 weeks to 3 months after board meeting
Write: Ruth Jones-Saxey, Secy.-Treas.
Officers: William E.B. Siart,* Chair.; Gary S. Gertz,* C.F.O.; Ruth Jones-Saxey, Secy.-Treas.
Directors:* Charles J. Buchta, John F. Futcher, Lillian R. Gorman, John Popovich, Alan Thompson.
Number of staff: 2 full-time professional.
Employer Identification Number: 953288932

331
Myrtle V. Fitschen Charitable Trust ⌑
25 Van Ness Ave., Suite 200
San Francisco 94102 (415) 558-4161
Additional address: 380 Eddy St., San Francisco, CA 94102

Established about 1982 in CA.
Foundation type: Independent
Financial data (yr. ended 11/30/88): Assets, $1,248,690 (M); expenditures, $91,842, including $67,650 for 10 grants (high: $10,000; low: $2,400; average: $5,000).
Purpose and activities: Support for health and related services, especially for the elderly, including medical, dental, hospital, psychological, educational, and social assistance.
Limitations: Giving primarily in San Francisco and San Francisco County, CA.
Application information:
Initial approach: Letter
Deadline(s): Sept. 1
Write: Richard Livingston, Exec. Dir.
Directors: Lou Aronian, Allan D. Bonapart, Robert Gamble, Haig G. Mardikian, Barbara Turner.
Employer Identification Number: 946551204

332
Reginald S. & Julia W. Fleet Foundation ⌑ ☆
530 B. St., Suite 1600
San Diego 92101

Established in 1973 in CA.
Donor(s): Julia B. Fleet, Reginald S. Fleet,† Julia W. Fleet.†
Foundation type: Independent
Financial data (yr. ended 03/31/89): Assets, $7,703,474 (M); expenditures, $414,390, including $382,000 for 9 grants (high: $100,000; low: $2,000).
Purpose and activities: Giving for higher, secondary, and elementary education.
Types of support: Scholarship funds.
Limitations: No grants to individuals.
Application information: Contributes only to pre-selected organizations. Applications not accepted.
Officers and Directors:* Julia B. Fleet,* Pres.; John S. Barry,* V.P.; John A. McColl,* V.P.; Harlan F. Harmsen,* Secy.; Irene R. Welch,* Treas.; S. Douglas Fleet, Albert Stoddard.
Employer Identification Number: 237272465

333
Fleishhacker Foundation
One Maritime Plaza, Suite 830
San Francisco 94111 (415) 788-2909

Incorporated in 1947 in CA.
Donor(s): Mortimer Fleishhacker, Sr.,† Janet Fleishhacker Bates.†
Foundation type: Independent
Financial data (yr. ended 12/31/89): Assets, $7,509,000 (M); gifts received, $215,000; qualifying distributions, $879,226, including $672,650 for 112 grants (high: $40,000; low: $500; average: $5,000-$25,000), $47,500 for 6 grants to individuals (high: $15,000; low: $5,000; average: $15,000) and $159,076 for 1 loan.
Purpose and activities: The foundation operates the Eureka Fellowships program for individual artists to spend uninterrupted time pursuing creative work; grants also to literary and performing arts organizations. Support for pre-collegiate education.
Types of support: Operating budgets, special projects, fellowships, general purposes, grants to individuals, publications, seed money, building funds, capital campaigns, conferences and seminars, endowment funds, equipment, technical assistance.
Limitations: Giving limited to northern CA. No grants for annual campaigns, deficit financing, or matching gifts; no loans.
Publications: Application guidelines, program policy statement, grants list.
Application information: Fellowship seekers should contact the foundation for detailed application information. Application form required for certain grant programs.
Initial approach: Letter
Copies of proposal: 1
Deadline(s): Announced in Jan.-Feb. of each year for fellowships
Board meeting date(s): Quarterly
Final notification: 2 to 5 months
Write: Christine Elbel, Exec. Dir.
Officers: David Fleishhacker,* Pres.; Leon Sloss,* V.P.; Lois Gordon,* Secy.; Mortimer Fleishhacker III,* Treas.; Christine Elbel, Exec. Dir.
Directors:* Delia F. Ehrlich, John Stephen Ehrlich, Jr., Laurie Sloss.
Number of staff: 1 full-time professional; 1 part-time professional; 1 part-time support.
Employer Identification Number: 946051048

334
Willis & Jane Fletcher Foundation ⌑
530 Broadway, Suite 1048
San Diego 92101 (619) 239-0481

Established in 1969 in CA.
Foundation type: Independent
Financial data (yr. ended 12/31/88): Assets, $1,470,752 (M); expenditures, $82,667, including $72,826 for 61 grants (high: $19,000; low: $40; average: $1,000-$19,000).
Purpose and activities: Support primarily for education and social services, including child welfare and youth agencies, health and family services, and programs for homelessness and hunger; some support also for arts and culture, conservation, community development, and literacy.
Types of support: Annual campaigns, building funds, endowment funds, equipment, matching funds, seed money.
Limitations: Giving limited to San Diego County, CA. No grants for capital funds other than gifts to the United Way.
Publications: Application guidelines.
Application information: Application form required.
Initial approach: Telephone call or letter
Copies of proposal: 1
Deadline(s): June and Oct.
Board meeting date(s): July and Nov.
Final notification: Aug. and Dec.
Write: Willis H. Fletcher, Pres. or Mary V. Todal, Asst. Secy.
Officers: Willis H. Fletcher, Pres.; Jane C. Fletcher, V.P.; Susan Randerson, Secy.; Mary Harker, Treas.
Number of staff: 1 part-time support.
Employer Identification Number: 952624912

335
The Ebell of Los Angeles/Charles N. Flint Scholarship Endowment Fund
743 South Lucerne Blvd.
Los Angeles 90005-3707 (213) 931-1277

Established in 1927 in CA.
Foundation type: Independent
Financial data (yr. ended 06/30/89): Assets, $1,180,086 (M); expenditures, $74,113, including $69,750 for grants to individuals.
Purpose and activities: Scholarships awarded to eligible, unmarried, local area undergraduates who are enrolled in a Los Angeles County university or college and show a financial need.
Types of support: Student aid.
Limitations: Giving limited to Los Angeles County, CA, residents.
Application information: Applications available from financial aid officer of student's university or college. Application form required.
Deadline(s): June 1 for fall
Write: Mrs. Daniel Bloxsom, Jr., Scholarship Chair.
Officers and Directors:* Mrs. Arthur B. Cecil,* Pres.; Mrs. Sylvester Scott,* 1st V.P.; Erma L. Schmalzried,* Secy.; Mrs. Daniel Bloxsom, Jr.,* Scholarship Chair.; and 11 additional directors.
Employer Identification Number: 956100327

336
Flintridge Foundation ⌑
1100 El Centro St., Suite 103
South Pasadena 91030 (818) 799-4178

Established in 1984 in CA.
Donor(s): Francis Loring Moseley,† Louisa Moseley.†
Foundation type: Independent
Financial data (yr. ended 12/31/88): Assets, $15,844,240 (M); expenditures, $961,866, including $682,640 for 19 grants (high: $250,000; low: $960; average: $30,000).
Purpose and activities: Support for medical and scientific research, conservation, cultural programs, particularly those involving theatre, painting, and sculpture, and social service agencies, with emphasis on combined teenage pregnancy and AIDS education, peer counseling program for seniors, and afterschool latchkey program.
Types of support: Fellowships, matching funds, professorships, research, seed money, special projects.
Limitations: Giving primarily in CA, OR, and WA. No support for religious groups. No grants for endowment funds, annual campaigns, capital funds, deficit financing, or building funds.
Publications: Annual report (including application guidelines), application guidelines.
Application information: Most grants foundation-initiated. Application form not required.
Initial approach: Letter
Board meeting date(s): Feb., May, Aug., and Nov.
Write: Jaylene L. Moseley, Managing Dir.
Officers: Susan A. Addison, Pres.; Ann A. Morris, V.P.; Alexander Moseley, Secy.; Peter Moseley, Treas.
Directors: Jaylene L. Moseley, Mgr.; Joshua D. Addison, Michael Addison, Clea Morris, Joany Mosher, Joan Tanner.
Number of staff: None.
Employer Identification Number: 953926331

337
The Fluor Foundation ▼
3333 Michelson Dr.
Irvine 92730 (714) 975-6797

Incorporated in 1952 in CA.
Donor(s): Fluor Corp.
Foundation type: Company-sponsored
Financial data (yr. ended 10/31/88): Assets, $1,548,425 (M); expenditures, $1,388,951, including $1,388,215 for grants (average: $100-$40,000).
Purpose and activities: Support for higher education, culture and the arts, public and civic affairs, and health and welfare organizations, especially the United Way; scholarships for children of company employees are administered by an independent scholarship corporation.
Types of support: Annual campaigns, building funds, employee matching gifts, operating budgets, technical assistance, employee-related scholarships, general purposes, endowment funds, scholarship funds.
Limitations: Giving primarily in areas where the corporation has permanent offices, with some emphasis on CA, TX, IL, SC, NJ, and PA. No support for medical research, guilds, and sports organizations. No grants to individuals (except for employee-related scholarships).
Publications: Program policy statement, application guidelines.
Application information: Application form not required.
Initial approach: Letter
Copies of proposal: 1
Deadline(s): None
Board meeting date(s): Dec. and June
Final notification: 3-4 months
Write: Suzanne H. Esber, Dir., Comm. Affairs
Officers: J.R. Fluor II,* Pres.; L.N. Fisher, Secy.; V.L. Prechtl, Treas.

Trustees:* David S. Tappan, Jr., Chair.; H.K. Coble, Robert L. Guyett, V.L. Kontny, L.G. McCraw, E.J. Parente, N.A. Peterson.
Number of staff: 1 full-time professional; 1 full-time support.
Employer Identification Number: 510196032

338
The Foothills Foundation ⌑
P.O. Box 3809
San Francisco 94119-3809

Established in 1977 in CA.
Donor(s): Gary Hogan Bechtel.
Foundation type: Independent
Financial data (yr. ended 12/31/88): Assets, $2,689,619 (M); expenditures, $290,941, including $286,500 for 12 grants (high: $140,000; low: $2,000).
Purpose and activities: Support for hospitals and health associations, higher and secondary education, social service and child welfare agencies, cultural programs, and religion.
Types of support: Endowment funds, capital campaigns, annual campaigns.
Limitations: No grants to individuals.
Application information: Contributes only to pre-selected organizations. Applications not accepted.
Officers and Directors:* Gary Hogan Bechtel,* Pres.; Carolyn M. Bechtel,* V.P.; George T. Argyris,* Secy.; Theodore J. Van Bebber, Treas.
Investment Manager: S.D. Bechtel, Jr.
Employer Identification Number: 942412392

339
Robert F. Ford Charitable Foundation ⌑ ☆
P.O. Box 1068
Pebble Beach 93953

Established in 1961.
Foundation type: Independent
Financial data (yr. ended 12/31/88): Assets, $1,032,470 (M); expenditures, $61,519, including $51,750 for 43 grants (high: $4,000; low: $100).
Purpose and activities: Giving primarily for culture, higher and secondary education, and welfare; some support for religious organizations.
Limitations: Giving primarily in CA. No grants to individuals.
Application information: Contributes only to pre-selected organizations. Applications not accepted.
Officers: Freeman A. Ford, Pres.; Mary T. Ford, V.P.; Phyllis L. Krystal, Secy.
Director: Judith Ford Newman.
Employer Identification Number: 956016768

340
Forest Lawn Foundation ⌑
1712 South Glendale Ave.
Glendale 91205

Incorporated in 1951 in CA.
Donor(s): Forest Lawn Co., Hubert Eaton Estate Trust.
Foundation type: Independent
Financial data (yr. ended 12/31/88): Assets, $7,769,429 (M); gifts received, $863,234; expenditures, $327,120, including $295,250 for 53 grants (high: $50,000; low: $250).
Purpose and activities: Grants for higher education, welfare, health, youth agencies, hospitals, and religious institutions.
Limitations: Giving primarily in CA. No grants to individuals, or for endowment funds or special projects.
Application information: Grants generally initiated by the foundation. Applications not accepted.
Board meeting date(s): Quarterly
Write: John Llewellyn, V.P.
Officers and Trustees:* Frederick Llewellyn,* Pres.; John Llewellyn,* V.P. and Secy.; Richard L. Wall,* C.F.O.; Jane Llewellyn, Myron Smith.
Employer Identification Number: 956030792

341
Foundation for Advanced Brain Studies ⌑
10900 Wilshire Blvd., Suite 1600
Los Angeles 90024-6501

Established in 1984 in CA.
Donor(s): David H. Murdock.
Foundation type: Independent
Financial data (yr. ended 12/31/87): Assets, $176 (M); gifts received, $353,000; expenditures, $357,878, including $357,844 for 1 grant.
Purpose and activities: Support primarily for medical research.
Limitations: Giving primarily in Los Angeles, CA.
Application information: Contributes only to pre-selected organizations. Applications not accepted.
Officers: David H. Murdock, Pres.; Jeffrey O. Henley, V.P. and Secy.; William J. Scully, Treas.
Employer Identification Number: 953908070

342
John H. Fox Foundation ⌑
(Formerly Fox Foundation)
c/o Union Bank
P.O. Box 109
San Diego 92112

Established in 1955 in CA.
Foundation type: Independent
Financial data (yr. ended 03/31/89): Assets, $1,528,544 (M); expenditures, $76,860, including $52,750 for 55 grants (high: $3,010; low: $250) and $3,000 for 1 grant to an individual.
Purpose and activities: Emphasis on culture, youth activities, hospitals and health agencies, and social services.
Limitations: Giving limited to San Diego County, CA.
Application information: Application form not required.
Deadline(s): None
Trustees: Mrs. John H. Fox, Union Bank.
Employer Identification Number: 956010288

343
Lawrence L. Frank Foundation ⌑
2950 Los Feliz Blvd., Suite 204
Los Angeles 90039

Established in 1959 in CA.
Donor(s): Richard N. Frank.
Foundation type: Independent
Financial data (yr. ended 11/30/88): Assets, $53,653 (M); gifts received, $128,889; expenditures, $216,692, including $216,291 for 124 grants (high: $100,000; low: $25).
Purpose and activities: Giving primarily for higher and secondary education; support also for social service agencies, including community funds, youth, and Jewish welfare funds, and cultural programs.
Limitations: Giving primarily in CA. No grants for scholarships, fellowships, or prizes; no loans.
Application information:
Deadline(s): None
Officers and Directors:* Richard N. Frank,* Pres.; Susan S. Rosenberg,* V.P. and Secy.; Arthur Wynne,* V.P. and Treas.; Richard R. Frank,* V.P.; Lorraine Petitfils,* V.P.; Stuart Kadison.
Employer Identification Number: 956034851

344
Samuel H. French III and Katharine Weaver French Fund ⌑
c/o Wells Fargo Bank, Private Banking Group
101 West Broadway, Suite 400
San Diego 92101 (619) 238-6504

Established in 1986 in CA.
Foundation type: Independent
Financial data (yr. ended 5/31/88): Assets, $1,170,378 (M); expenditures, $80,251, including $60,000 for 4 grants.
Purpose and activities: Support for a hospital, religious and health organizations, and youth services.
Limitations: No grants to individuals.
Application information: Application form not required.
Deadline(s): None
Write: Rebecca A. Cowlisman
Trustee: Wells Fargo Private Banking Group.
Employer Identification Number: 956855617

345
Fresno Regional Foundation
1551 Van Ness Ave.
Fresno 93721 (209) 233-2016

Established as a Trust in 1966 in CA.
Foundation type: Community
Financial data (yr. ended 12/31/88): Assets, $1,014,236 (M); gifts received, $249,018; expenditures, $294,568, including $242,805 for grants.
Purpose and activities: Interests include health, the arts, alleviation of social problems, education, senior citizens, character building, conservation and beautification, religious institutions, conservation of human and natural resources, and local historical programs.
Types of support: Continuing support, equipment, program-related investments, seed money.
Limitations: Giving primarily in the central San Joaquin Valley, CA, area, especially Fresno, Madera, Merced, Tulane, and Kings counties.

No support for government agencies. No grants to individuals, or for building or endowment funds, operating budgets, annual campaigns, local or national capital fund drives, or research; no loans.
Publications: Annual report, program policy statement, application guidelines, 990-PF.
Application information: Application form required.
Initial approach: Letter or telephone
Deadline(s): Feb. 1
Board meeting date(s): Quarterly
Final notification: Apr.
Write: Robert S. Miner, Exec. Dir.
Officers and Governors:* Paul S. Asperger,* Chair.; Chris Rogers,* Vice-Chair.; Shirley Brinker,* Secy.-Treas.; Robert S. Miner, Exec. Dir.; Glee Ewell.
Trustee Banks: First Interstate Bank, Lloyds Bank California, Wells Fargo Bank, N.A.
Number of staff: 1 part-time professional; 1 part-time support.
Employer Identification Number: 946140207

346
Friedman Brothers Foundation ⌘
801 East Commercial St.
Los Angeles 90012
Application address: 184 Sherwood Pl., Engelwood, NJ 07631

Trust established about 1944 in CA.
Donor(s): Members of the Friedman family, Friedman Bag Co.
Foundation type: Independent
Financial data (yr. ended 12/31/88): Assets, $7,020,100 (M); gifts received, $5,399; expenditures, $471,567, including $416,400 for 43 grants (high: $40,000; low: $1,000).
Purpose and activities: Emphasis on education, including religious education, and Jewish religious and welfare organizations.
Application information:
Initial approach: Letter
Deadline(s): Oct. 31
Write: Leslie Mendelsohn, Trustee
Trustees: William Bernstein, Sam Frank, Albert Friedman, Ephraim Friedman, Harvey Friedman, Rudy Lowy, Leslie Mendelsohn, William S. Stein.
Employer Identification Number: 956072294

347
Friedman Family Foundation
1160 Battery St., Suite 400
San Francisco 94111 (415) 986-7570

Established in 1964 in CA.
Donor(s): Phyllis K. Friedman, Howard Friedman.
Foundation type: Independent
Financial data (yr. ended 02/28/89): Assets, $2,075,399 (M); expenditures, $165,689, including $149,675 for 63 grants (high: $30,000; low: $25).
Purpose and activities: Support primarily for social services and education; some support for culture, Jewish welfare, and women.
Application information:
Deadline(s): None
Write: Phyllis K. Friedman, Pres.
Officers and Directors:* Phyllis K. Friedman,* Pres. and Treas.; Howard A. Friedman,* V.P.; William K. Coblentz,* Secy.
Employer Identification Number: 946109692

348
The Friend Family Foundation
585 Mission St.
San Francisco 94105 (415) 546-0696

Established in 1967 in CA.
Donor(s): Donald A. Friend, Eugene L. Friend, Robert B. Friend.
Foundation type: Independent
Financial data (yr. ended 06/30/89): Assets, $802,266 (M); gifts received, $195,000; expenditures, $216,964, including $214,640 for 95 grants (high: $104,250; low: $20).
Purpose and activities: Grants primarily for Jewish giving, including Jewish welfare funds; support also for cultural programs.
Application information: Application form not required.
Deadline(s): None
Write: Eugene L. Friend, Pres.
Officers and Directors:* Eugene L. Friend,* Pres. and Treas.; Robert B. Friend,* V.P.; Donald A. Friend,* Secy.
Employer Identification Number: 946163916

349
Furth Foundation ⌘
201 Sansome St., No. 1000
San Francisco 94104 (415) 433-2070

Established in 1969 in CA.
Donor(s): Frederick P. Furth.
Foundation type: Independent
Financial data (yr. ended 12/31/88): Assets, $2,439,308 (M); gifts received, $542,984; expenditures, $253,292, including $248,955 for 146 grants (high: $25,000; low: $25).
Purpose and activities: Giving primarily for social services and education; some support for public affairs and culture.
Limitations: No grants to individuals.
Application information:
Deadline(s): None
Write: Frederick P. Furth, Mgr.
Officer and Directors:* Frederick Furth,* Mgr.; Donna Furth, Alison Darby Furth, Peggy Furth.
Employer Identification Number: 237062014

350
Georges and Germaine Fusenot Charity Foundation ⌘
7060 Hollywood Blvd., Suite 912
Hollywood 90028 (213) 462-7702

Trust established in 1967 in CA.
Donor(s): Germaine Fusenot.†
Foundation type: Independent
Financial data (yr. ended 7/31/87): Assets, $4,897,998 (L); expenditures, $290,611, including $213,000 for 66 grants (high: $10,000; low: $500).
Purpose and activities: Emphasis on hospitals, aid to the handicapped, and child welfare.
Types of support: Operating budgets, continuing support, annual campaigns, seed money, building funds, equipment, land acquisition, research, general purposes, capital campaigns, special projects.
Limitations: Giving limited to CA. No grants to individuals, or for emergency or endowment funds, deficit financing, demonstration projects, publications, conferences, scholarships, or fellowships; no loans.
Application information: Application form not required.
Initial approach: Letter
Copies of proposal: 1
Deadline(s): Sept. 30 for consideration in the same year
Board meeting date(s): Oct.
Final notification: Jan.
Write: Richard G. Herlihy, Mgr.
Officer: Richard G. Herlihy, Mgr.
Trustees: Katherine S. Burns, Elizabeth Herlihy, Michael J. Herlihy, Fred W. Hoar, Virginia Markel, Guy Arnold Stone, Patricia H. Stone, Troy E. Stone.
Number of staff: 1 full-time professional.
Employer Identification Number: 956207831

351
G.A.G. Charitable Corporation
50300 Hwy. 245
P.O. Box 52
Badger 93603

Incorporated in 1968 in CA.
Donor(s): Dorothy Salant Garrett, George A. Griesbach.†
Foundation type: Independent
Financial data (yr. ended 12/31/88): Assets, $1,893,221 (M); expenditures, $89,405, including $76,350 for 65 grants (high: $5,000; low: $500).
Purpose and activities: Grants for religious organizations, drug addiction rehabilitation, community funds, Jewish welfare funds, Africa, and the environment.
Types of support: Annual campaigns.
Limitations: Giving primarily in NY and CA. No grants to individuals, or for building or endowment funds, research, scholarships, fellowships, or matching gifts; no loans.
Publications: 990-PF, annual report.
Application information: Contributes only to pre-selected organizations. Applications not accepted.
Board meeting date(s): May
Write: Dorothy Salant Garrett, Pres.
Officers and Director:* Dorothy Salant Garrett,* Pres.; William Rybnick, Secy.; Peter Salant, Treas.
Number of staff: None.
Employer Identification Number: 952568756

352
G.P.G. Foundation ☆
50 California St., Suite 3315
San Francisco 94111

Established in 1986 in CA.
Donor(s): Gordon P. Getty.
Foundation type: Independent
Financial data (yr. ended 12/31/88): Assets, $24,900,305 (M); expenditures, $2,463,445, including $1,926,000 for 4 grants (high: $1,515,000; low: $10,000).

Purpose and activities: Giving primarily for a private foundation; support also for the fine and performing arts.
Limitations: No grants to individuals.
Application information: Applications not accepted.
Officers and Directors:* Gordon P. Getty,* Chair. and Pres.; Marc E. Leland,* V.P.; George E. Stephens, Jr., Secy.; Lawrence J. Chazen,* C.F.O.
Employer Identification Number: 954078344

353
Gallo Foundation ⌑
P.O. Box 1130
Modesto 95353 (209) 579-3204

Incorporated in 1955 in CA.
Foundation type: Company-sponsored
Financial data (yr. ended 10/31/87): Assets, $460,902 (M); gifts received, $600,000; expenditures, $241,093, including $233,600 for 60 grants (high: $50,000; low: $250) and $7,103 for employee matching gifts.
Purpose and activities: Emphasis on education, particularly higher education; some grants also for church support.
Types of support: Employee matching gifts.
Limitations: Giving primarily in CA.
Application information:
Initial approach: Letter
Deadline(s): None
Write: Mrs. Ouida McCullough
Officers and Directors:* Ernest Gallo,* Pres.; Julio R. Gallo,* V.P.; Jack L. Dickman,* Secy.; Jon B. Shastid,* Treas.; David E. Gallo, Robert J. Gallo.
Employer Identification Number: 946061538

354
The Ernest Gallo Foundation ⌑
P.O. Box 1130
Modesto 95353 (209) 521-3091

Incorporated in 1955 in CA.
Donor(s): Members of the Gallo family, E. & J. Gallo Winery.
Foundation type: Independent
Financial data (yr. ended 10/31/88): Assets, $5,409,368 (M); gifts received, $230,000; expenditures, $85,309, including $77,225 for 12 grants (high: $25,000; low: $200).
Purpose and activities: Support for higher and secondary education, religious purposes and general charitable organizations.
Limitations: Giving primarily in CA. No grants to individuals.
Application information: Contributes only to pre-selected organizations. Applications not accepted.
Officers and Directors:* Ernest Gallo,* Pres.; David E. Gallo,* V.P.; Joseph E. Gallo,* V.P.; Jack L. Dickman, Secy.; Dick Beal, Treas.
Employer Identification Number: 946061537

355
The Julio R. Gallo Foundation ⌑
P.O. Box 1130
Modesto 95353 (209) 579-3373

Incorporated in 1955 in CA.
Donor(s): Julio R. Gallo, Robert J. Gallo.
Foundation type: Independent
Financial data (yr. ended 10/31/88): Assets, $5,382,884 (M); gifts received, $350,000; expenditures, $248,016, including $235,500 for 31 grants (high: $66,000; low: $500).
Purpose and activities: Emphasis on education and Roman Catholic church support and religious associations.
Limitations: Giving primarily in CA. No grants to individuals.
Application information:
Initial approach: Letter
Deadline(s): None
Write: Robert J. Gallo, V.P.
Officers and Directors:* Julio R. Gallo,* Pres.; Robert J. Gallo,* V.P.; James E. Coleman,* Secy.; James B. Owens, Treas.
Employer Identification Number: 946061539

356
Gamble Foundation ⌑
P.O. Box 2655
San Francisco 94126

Established in 1968 in CA.
Foundation type: Independent
Financial data (yr. ended 12/31/87): Assets, $1,305,378 (M); gifts received, $12,000; expenditures, $74,781, including $69,800 for 40 grants (high: $11,000; low: $50).
Purpose and activities: Support primarily for a land trust and for environmental conservation organizations; support also for community funds, a hospital, a symphony association, and a fine arts museum.
Application information: Application form not required.
Initial approach: Letter
Deadline(s): None
Officers: Launce E. Gamble, Pres.; George F. Gamble, V.P. and Secy.-Treas.; Mary S. Gamble, V.P.
Employer Identification Number: 941680503

357
The Gap Foundation ⌑
900 Cherry Ave.
San Bruno 94066 (415) 952-4400

Established in 1977 in CA.
Donor(s): The Gap, Inc.
Foundation type: Company-sponsored
Financial data (yr. ended 06/30/89): Assets, $308,089 (M); gifts received, $623,500; expenditures, $396,935, including $327,448 for 98 grants (high: $25,000; low: $100) and $68,131 for employee matching gifts (high: $2,000; low: $25).
Purpose and activities: Support for higher and other education, civic and public affairs, cultural programs, and health and welfare, including youth organizations.
Types of support: Employee matching gifts, capital campaigns, general purposes, operating budgets.
Limitations: Giving primarily in San Francisco and San Mateo, CA. No grants to individuals.
Application information:
Initial approach: Letter
Deadline(s): None
Write: Sherry Reson, Mgr.
Officers: Donald G. Fisher, Chair. and C.E.O.; Dexter C. Tight, Sr. V.P. and Secy.; Robert J. Fisher, V.P.; Sherry Reson, V.P., Admin.; Doris F. Fisher, Treas.
Number of staff: 1 part-time professional.
Employer Identification Number: 942474426

358
John Jewett & H. Chandler Garland Foundation ▼ ⌑
P.O. Box 550
Pasadena 91102-0550

Trust established in 1959 in CA.
Donor(s): Members of the Garland family.
Foundation type: Independent
Financial data (yr. ended 12/31/86): Assets, $162,927 (M); gifts received, $1,025,269; expenditures, $1,305,660, including $1,261,500 for 50 grants (high: $480,000; low: $1,000; average: $5,000-$20,000).
Purpose and activities: Emphasis on cultural and historical programs, secondary and higher education, social services, especially for the elderly, youth agencies, hospitals, and health services.
Limitations: Giving primarily in CA, with emphasis on Los Angeles.
Application information:
Initial approach: Letter
Deadline(s): None
Board meeting date(s): 3 times per year
Final notification: After each meeting
Officer and Trustees:* G.E. Morrow,* Mgr.; Gwendolyn Garland Babcock, Louise Grant Garland.
Number of staff: None.
Employer Identification Number: 956023587

359
The David Geffen Foundation ⌑
2121 Ave. of the Stars, Suite 1700
Los Angeles 90067

Incorporated in 1986 in CA.
Donor(s): David Geffen.
Foundation type: Independent
Financial data (yr. ended 12/31/87): Assets, $1,297,646 (M); expenditures, $161,045, including $160,725 for 61 grants (high: $30,000; low: $100).
Purpose and activities: Support primarily for medical research, international human rights societies and education.
Application information:
Deadline(s): None
Trustees: Eric Eisner, David Geffen, Richard Sherman.
Employer Identification Number: 954085811

360
The Carl Gellert Foundation
2222 19th Ave.
San Francisco 94116 (415) 566-4420

Incorporated in 1958 in CA.
Donor(s): Carl Gellert,† Atlas Realty Co., Pacific Coast Construction Co., Gertrude E. Gellert.†
Foundation type: Independent
Financial data (yr. ended 11/30/89): Assets, $7,535,654 (M); expenditures, $704,103, including $642,990 for 114 grants (high: $100,000; low: $1,000; average: $1,000-$10,000).
Purpose and activities: Support for the aged, medical research, drug abuse programs, and

hospitals; grants also for Roman Catholic church support; higher, secondary, and elementary education, including engineering and scholarship funds; and to community development programs and social service agencies, including family planning.
Types of support: Operating budgets, continuing support, annual campaigns, deficit financing, building funds, equipment, endowment funds, scholarship funds, research, publications, special projects, renovation projects, capital campaigns, general purposes.
Limitations: Giving primarily in the San Francisco Bay Area, CA. No grants to individuals, or for seed money, emergency funds, land acquisition, matching gifts, or conferences; no loans.
Publications: 990-PF, program policy statement, application guidelines.
Application information: Application form not required.
Initial approach: Proposal
Copies of proposal: 5
Deadline(s): Submit proposal preferably in Aug. and Sept.; deadline Oct. 1st
Board meeting date(s): Apr. and Nov.
Final notification: Nov. 30, for recipients only
Write: Peter J. Brusati, Secy.
Officers and Directors:* Fred R. Bahrt,* Pres.; Robert L. Pauly,* V.P.; Peter J. Brusati,* Secy.; Marie Simpson,* Treas.; Celia Berta Gellert.
Number of staff: None.
Employer Identification Number: 946062858

361
Celia Berta Gellert Foundation ☆
2222 19th Ave.
San Francisco 94116-1896 (415) 566-4420

Established in 1970.
Donor(s): Celia Berta Gellert.
Foundation type: Independent
Financial data (yr. ended 11/30/89): Assets, $1,625,613 (M); gifts received, $376,000; expenditures, $148,087, including $134,300 for 28 grants (high: $15,000; low: $1,000; average: $2,000-$5,000).
Purpose and activities: Giving primarily for homes for the aged and other social services, hospitals and medical research, community development, Catholic churches, and higher, secondary, and elementary education.
Types of support: Scholarship funds, general purposes, operating budgets, building funds, renovation projects, endowment funds, annual campaigns, capital campaigns, continuing support, equipment, publications, research, special projects.
Limitations: Giving primarily in the San Francisco, CA, area. No grants to individuals.
Publications: 990-PF, program policy statement, application guidelines.
Application information: Application form not required.
Initial approach: Proposal
Copies of proposal: 5
Deadline(s): Oct. 1
Board meeting date(s): Nov.
Final notification: Nov. 30 for positive responses
Write: Peter J. Brusati, Secy.
Officers and Directors:* Robert L. Pauly,* Chair.; Fred R. Bahrt,* Vice-Chair.; Peter J. Brusati,* Secy. and Mgr.; Andrew A. Cresci,* Treas.; Celia Berta Gellert.
Number of staff: None.
Employer Identification Number: 237083733

362
The Fred Gellert Foundation
1655 Southgate Ave., Suite 203
Daly City 94015 (415) 991-1855

Established in 1958 in CA.
Donor(s): Fred Gellert, Sr.†
Foundation type: Independent
Financial data (yr. ended 11/30/89): Assets, $9,784,256 (M); expenditures, $749,203, including $649,773 for 95 grants (high: $100,000; low: $300; average: $1,000-$5,000).
Purpose and activities: Grants for cultural programs, hospitals, health care programs, programs for the disabled, social service agencies, the environment and ecology, and education, including ophthalmology education.
Types of support: Operating budgets, continuing support, building funds, equipment, research, special projects, general purposes, endowment funds.
Limitations: Giving primarily in San Francisco and San Mateo counties, CA. No grants to individuals, or for annual campaigns; no loans.
Publications: Application guidelines, financial statement.
Application information: Application form not required.
Initial approach: Letter
Copies of proposal: 5
Deadline(s): Submit proposal preferably in May through Aug.; deadline Sept. 15
Board meeting date(s): Nov.
Final notification: 1st week in Dec.
Write: Fred Gellert, Jr., Chair.
Officers and Directors:* Fred Gellert, Jr.,* Chair.; John D. Howard,* Secy.-Treas.; Annette Gellert, James Sargen, Joan Sargen, Marche H. Yoshioka.
Number of staff: 1 part-time professional.
Employer Identification Number: 946062859

363
Wallace Alexander Gerbode Foundation ▼
470 Columbus Ave., Suite 209
San Francisco 94133 (415) 391-0911

Incorporated in 1953 in CA.
Donor(s): Members of the Gerbode family.
Foundation type: Independent
Financial data (yr. ended 12/31/88): Assets, $40,961,000 (M); qualifying distributions, $3,188,439, including $1,938,439 for 150 grants (high: $150,000; low: $475; average: $5,000-$25,000) and $1,250,000 for loans.
Purpose and activities: Support for innovative, positive programs in the arts, education, environment, health, and urban affairs.
Types of support: Consulting services, technical assistance, program-related investments, loans, special projects.
Limitations: Giving primarily to programs directly affecting residents of Alameda, Contra Costa, Marin, San Francisco, and San Mateo counties in CA, and HI. No support for religious purposes. No grants to individuals, or for general or continuing support, direct services, operating budgets, capital or endowment funds, fundraising or annual campaigns, emergency funds, matching gifts, scholarships, fellowships, publications, deficit financing, building funds, equipment or materials, land acquisition, or renovation projects.
Publications: Grants list, annual report (including application guidelines).
Application information: Application form not required.
Initial approach: Letter
Copies of proposal: 1
Deadline(s): None
Board meeting date(s): 6 times a year
Final notification: 2 to 3 months
Write: Thomas C. Layton, Exec. Dir.
Officers and Directors:* Maryanna G. Shaw,* Pres.; Frank A. Gerbode, M.D.,* V.P.; Joan Richardson,* Secy.; Charles M. Stockholm,* Treas.; Thomas C. Layton,* Exec. Dir.
Number of staff: 1 full-time professional; 1 full-time support.
Employer Identification Number: 946065226

364
The Ann and Gordon Getty Foundation ▼
50 California St., Suite 3315
San Francisco 94111 (415) 788-5844

Established in 1986 in CA.
Donor(s): Gordon P. Getty.
Foundation type: Independent
Financial data (yr. ended 12/31/88): Assets, $3,499,509 (M); gifts received, $4,707,500; expenditures, $9,560,650, including $9,380,500 for 300 grants (high: $760,000; low: $250; average: $10,000-$50,000).
Purpose and activities: Support primarily for symphonies, opera companies, and educational institutions.
Types of support: General purposes.
Limitations: Giving primarily in CA, especially the San Francisco Bay Area.
Application information: Contributes only to pre-selected organizations. Applications not accepted.
Board meeting date(s): Annually
Write: Lawrence Chazen, Dir.
Officers: Gordon P. Getty, Pres.; George E. Stephens, Jr., Secy.
Number of staff: 4
Employer Identification Number: 954078340

365
J. Paul Getty Trust ▼ ⌑
401 Wilshire Blvd., Suite 1000
Santa Monica 90401-1455 (213) 393-4244

Operating trust established in 1953 in CA as J. Paul Getty Museum.
Donor(s): J. Paul Getty.†
Foundation type: Operating
Financial data (yr. ended 6/30/88): Assets, $3,982,184,662 (M); gifts received, $13,950; qualifying distributions, $149,143,432, including $11,553,597 for 107 grants (high: $1,500,000; low: $100; average: $10,000-$50,000), $1,030,078 for 56 grants to individuals (high: $73,421; low: $1,394) and $136,771,341 for foundation-administered programs.

Purpose and activities: A private operating foundation. In addition to the Getty Grant Program, there are seven operating entities in the visual arts and related humanities: the J. Paul Getty Museum (a public museum), the Getty Center for the History of Art and the Humanities, the Getty Center for Education in the Arts, the Getty Conservation Institute, the Getty Art History Information Program, the Museum Management Institute, and the Program for Art on Film (a joint venture with the Metropolitan Museum of Art). Through the Getty Grant Program, begun in October l984, support is available for scholarship in the history of art and the humanities (senior research grants, postdoctoral fellowships, centers for advanced research in art history, archival projects, reference tools, and art historical publications); documentation and interpretation of art museum collections; art conservation training, libraries, surveys, treatment, and publications; architectural conservation and related national and international service organizations.
Types of support: Special projects, fellowships, publications, matching funds, research.
Limitations: No grants to individuals (except senior research grants and postdoctoral fellowships). No support for operating or endowment purposes, construction or maintenance of buildings, or acquisition of works of art.
Publications: Informational brochure, biennial report, newsletter, grants list, application guidelines.
Application information: Application form available for publication grant requests, architectural conservation grants, postdoctoral fellowships, and senior research grants.
Initial approach: Letter
Copies of proposal: 3
Deadline(s): For publications grants, 6 months before book goes into production; Nov. 10 for senior research grants and postdoctoral fellowships; for architectural conservation grants, request specific deadline from Grants Program; otherwise, no deadline
Board meeting date(s): As necessary
Final notification: 6 months
Write: The Getty Grant Program
Officers: Harold M. Williams,* Pres. and C.E.O.; Joseph J. Kearns, V.P. and Treas.
Trustees:* Jon B. Lovelace, Chair.; Harold E. Berg, Norris Bramlett, Kenneth N. Dayton, John T. Fey, Gordon P. Getty, Vartan Gregorian, Herbert L. Lucas, Jr., Franklin D. Murphy, Stuart T. Peeler, Rocco C. Siciliano, Jennifer Jones Simon, J. Patrick Whaley, Otto Wittmann.
Employer Identification Number: 951790021

366
William & Marian Ghidotti Foundation
P.O. Box 925
Nevada City 95959 (916) 265-2708

Established in 1969 in Nevada City, CA.
Donor(s): William Ghidotti, Marian Ghidotti.†
Foundation type: Independent
Financial data (yr. ended 12/31/87): Assets, $5,650,384 (M); expenditures, $376,430, including $274,391 for grants.
Purpose and activities: Awards student scholarships to graduating seniors residing in and attending Nevada County, CA, high schools; some support also for schools and educational purposes.
Types of support: Student aid, equipment.
Limitations: Giving limited to Nevada County, CA.
Application information: Application form required.
Deadline(s): Feb. for new scholarships, Aug. for renewals
Write: Erica Erickson, Trustee
Trustees: Mary Bouma, Erica Erickson, Frank Francis, William Toms, Ruth Halls Unger, Bank of America.
Employer Identification Number: 946181833

367
Gildred Foundation ▼
c/o Lomas Sante Fe, Inc.
462 Stevens Ave., Suite 102
Solana Beach 92075 (619) 755-5572

Incorporated in 1965 in CA.
Donor(s): Members of the Gildred family.
Foundation type: Independent
Financial data (yr. ended 05/31/88): Assets, $5,808,266 (M); expenditures, $686,458, including $628,581 for 14 grants (high: $125,000; low: $400).
Purpose and activities: Support mainly for an independent inter-American studies institute housed at the University of California, San Diego.
Limitations: Giving primarily in San Diego County, CA. No grants to individuals.
Application information: Applications not accepted.
Board meeting date(s): Oct. and Apr.
Write: Walter D. Warner, Pres.
Officers and Director:* Walter D. Warner,* Pres.; William P. Shannahan, V.P. and Secy.
Number of staff: None.
Employer Identification Number: 956135592

368
Earl B. Gilmore Foundation ⌑
6301 West Third St.
P.O. Box 480314
Los Angeles 90036

Incorporated in 1958 in CA.
Donor(s): A.F. Gilmore Co., Marie Dent Gilmore.†
Foundation type: Independent
Financial data (yr. ended 12/31/86): Assets, $2,615,755 (M); expenditures, $141,025, including $135,100 for 97 grants (high: $7,500; low: $50).
Purpose and activities: Emphasis on social services; grants also for higher and secondary education, health agencies, hospitals, youth agencies, and Protestant church support.
Limitations: Giving primarily in CA.
Application information: Contributes only to pre-selected organizations. Applications not accepted.
Officers: John B. Gostovich,* Pres.; Henry L. Hilty, Jr.,* V.P. and Secy.; Frank W. Clark, Jr.,* V.P.; Frances Gilmore Hilen,* V.P.; Karl M. Samuelian,* V.P.; Robert Sibert,* V.P.; M.B. Hartman, Treas.
Directors:* Andrew G. Hilen, Sr.
Employer Identification Number: 956029602

369
The William G. Gilmore Foundation
120 Montgomery St., Suite 1880
San Francisco 94104 (415) 546-1400

Incorporated in 1953 in CA.
Donor(s): William G. Gilmore,† Mrs. William G. Gilmore.†
Foundation type: Independent
Financial data (yr. ended 12/31/88): Assets, $11,311,069 (M); expenditures, $870,270, including $766,345 for 132 grants (high: $50,000; low: $200; average: $500-$5,000).
Purpose and activities: Grants largely for community-based organizations, including development and urban affairs, family and social services, child welfare and development, health services, AIDS programs, conservation, and the arts.
Types of support: Annual campaigns, continuing support, emergency funds, general purposes, operating budgets, scholarship funds.
Limitations: Giving primarily in northern CA, OR, and WA. No grants to individuals.
Application information: Application form not required.
Initial approach: Letter of intent
Copies of proposal: 1
Deadline(s): May 1 and Nov. 1
Board meeting date(s): June and Dec.
Final notification: 2 months
Write: Faye Wilson, Secy.
Officers and Trustees:* Robert C. Harris,* Pres.; Lee Emerson,* V.P., and Treas.; William R. Mackey,* V.P.; Faye Wilson, Secy.; Thomas B. Boklund, V. Neil Fulton.
Number of staff: 1 part-time support.
Employer Identification Number: 946079493

370
James Gleason Foundation ⌑
Hearst Bldg., Suite 1200
Third and Market Sts.
San Francisco 94103

Established in 1978.
Donor(s): Ruth M. Gleason, Walter M. Gleason.
Foundation type: Independent
Financial data (yr. ended 12/31/88): Assets, $1,805,584 (M); gifts received, $100,000; expenditures, $86,370, including $85,250 for 19 grants (high: $15,000; low: $1,000).
Purpose and activities: Giving primarily for a university, Catholic welfare agencies, and church support.
Officers and Directors:* Walter M. Gleason,* Pres., Treas., and Mgr.; Patricia Gleason,* V.P.; Cressey H. Nakagawa,* Secy.
Employer Identification Number: 942471399

371
Katherine Gleason Foundation ⌑
Hearst Bldg., Suite 1200
Third and Market Sts.
San Francisco 94103

Incorporated in 1969 in CA.
Donor(s): Walter M. Gleason.
Foundation type: Independent
Financial data (yr. ended 12/31/88): Assets, $3,237,115 (M); expenditures, $225,728,

including $214,000 for 30 grants (high: $25,000; low: $1,000).
Purpose and activities: Giving to Roman Catholic religious and welfare associations, and secondary schools; support also for a college.
Officers and Directors:* Walter M. Gleason,* Pres. and Treas.; Patricia Gleason,* V.P.; Cressey H. Nakagawa,* Secy.
Employer Identification Number: 237043569

372
Glendale Community Foundation ☆
100 North Brand Blvd., Suite 316
Glendale 91203 (818) 241-8040
Mailing Address: P.O. Box 313, Glendale, CA 91209-0313

Community foundation incorporated in 1956 in CA.
Foundation type: Community
Financial data (yr. ended 08/31/89): Assets, $1,259,390 (M); gifts received, $76,753; expenditures, $141,200, including $110,096 for 37 grants (high: $11,380; low: $100).
Purpose and activities: Giving primarily for social services; support also for the performing arts, a medical center, the handicapped, and higher education.
Types of support: Student loans, equipment, matching funds.
Limitations: Giving limited in the Glendale, CA, area, including Montrose, La Crescenta, and La Canada. No grants to individuals.
Publications: 990-PF, informational brochure.
Application information: Application form not required.
Initial approach: Letter
Copies of proposal: 1
Deadline(s): None
Board meeting date(s): 6 times a year
Write: Thomas R. Miller, Exec. Dir.
Officers and Trustees:* Page Whyte,* Pres.; Michael Malone,* 1st V.P.; Clifford Cate,* 2nd V.P.; John M. Lawson, Jr.,* 3rd V.P.; Gwynn Bacon,* 4th V.P.; Lynne Raggio,* Secy.; Frances Doll, Beth Doty, Editha Edwards, Randy Melby, Donald G. Orosz, Donald L. Platz, Jack Quinn, Freda Terrill, Joe Thomson.
Number of staff: 1 full-time professional; 1 part-time support.
Employer Identification Number: 956068137

373
Maxwell H. Gluck Foundation, Inc. ⌑
10375 Wilshire Blvd., Apt. 8-D
Los Angeles 90024

Established in 1955 in NY.
Donor(s): Maxwell H. Gluck.†
Foundation type: Independent
Financial data (yr. ended 2/28/89): Assets, $34,720,796 (M); expenditures, $1,873,363, including $1,809,486 for 70 grants (high: $865,640).
Purpose and activities: Support for higher and other education, Jewish welfare, and the arts.
Application information:
Initial approach: Letter
Deadline(s): None
Write: Muriel Gluck, Dir.
Directors: Muriel Gluck, Leonard Marx, Sr.
Employer Identification Number: 953979100

374
Gold Family Charitable Foundation ⌑ ☆
4444 Lakeside Dr., 2nd Fl.
Burbank 91505 (818) 845-4444

Established in 1986 in CA.
Donor(s): Stanley P. Gold.
Foundation type: Independent
Financial data (yr. ended 7/31/88): Assets, $115,854 (M); gifts received, $235,000; expenditures, $218,016, including $216,375 for 41 grants (high: $110,400; low: $25).
Purpose and activities: Support primarily for Jewish organizations, including education, a welfare fund, and religious support; support also for cultural and educational advancement.
Application information:
Write: Stanley P. Gold, Pres., or Ilene C. Gold, V.P.
Officers: Ilene C. Gold, Pres.; Stanley P. Gold, V.P.
Employer Identification Number: 954076113

375
Richard and Rhoda Goldman Fund
1160 Battery St., Suite 400
San Francisco 94111 (415) 788-1090

Incorporated in 1951 in CA.
Donor(s): Rhoda H. Goldman, Richard N. Goldman.
Foundation type: Independent
Financial data (yr. ended 10/31/89): Assets, $5,856,989 (M); expenditures, $1,001,592, including $773,183 for 82 grants (high: $135,000; low: $300; average: $7,500-$25,000).
Purpose and activities: Giving with emphasis on the elderly, the environment, civic affairs, health, youth, and child welfare.
Types of support: Seed money, special projects.
Limitations: Giving primarily in the San Francisco Bay Area, CA. No grants to individuals, or for deficit budgets, building or endowment funds, general fundraising campaigns, conferences, research, scholarships, fellowships, or matching gifts; no loans.
Publications: Annual report.
Application information: Application form not required.
Initial approach: Letter or telephone
Deadline(s): None
Board meeting date(s): Jan., Apr., July, and Oct.
Write: Duane Silverstein, Exec. Dir.
Officers and Directors:* Richard N. Goldman,* Pres.; Rhoda H. Goldman,* Secy.-Treas.; Duane Silverstein,* Exec. Dir.; Michael C. Gelman, Susan R. Gelman, Douglas E. Goldman, John D. Goldman, Marcia L. Goldman, Susan S. Goldman.
Number of staff: 1 full-time professional; 1 full-time support.
Employer Identification Number: 946064502

376
Goldsmith Family Foundation
400 North Roxbury Dr.
Beverly Hills 90210 (213) 550-5711

Established in 1980 in CA.
Donor(s): Mrs. Bram Goldsmith, Bram Goldsmith.
Foundation type: Independent
Financial data (yr. ended 09/30/88): Assets, $2,150,063 (M); gifts received, $816,400; expenditures, $433,363, including $424,380 for 17 grants (high: $155,000; low: $75).
Purpose and activities: Support for higher education, Jewish giving, and cultural programs.
Types of support: Annual campaigns, building funds, continuing support, endowment funds.
Limitations: Giving primarily in the southern CA area.
Application information: Contributes only to pre-selected organizations. Applications not accepted.
Officers: Bram Goldsmith, Pres.; Elaine Goldsmith, V.P. and Secy.-Treas.
Directors: Bruce L. Goldsmith, Russell Goldsmith.
Number of staff: 1 part-time support.
Employer Identification Number: 953545880

377
The Samuel Goldwyn Foundation
10203 Santa Monica Blvd., Suite 500
Los Angeles 90067 (213) 552-2255

Established in 1947 in CA.
Donor(s): Samuel Goldwyn,† Frances H. Goldwyn.†
Foundation type: Independent
Financial data (yr. ended 12/31/88): Assets, $19,696,611 (M); expenditures, $1,370,722, including $301,512 for 98 grants (high: $24,000; low: $25; average: $1,000-$10,000).
Purpose and activities: To promote community-related activities; grants primarily for a library, higher and other education, cultural programs, youth, child development, medical research and health, and innovative social service programs.
Types of support: Annual campaigns, seed money, scholarship funds, research, special projects.
Limitations: Giving limited to the Los Angeles, CA, metropolitan area. No grants to individuals, or for building funds.
Application information: Application form not required.
Initial approach: Proposal
Copies of proposal: 1
Deadline(s): Mar. 31 for June grants; Sept. 30 for Dec. grants
Board meeting date(s): Quarterly
Final notification: June and Dec.
Officers and Directors:* Samuel Goldwyn, Jr.,* Pres.; Peggy E. Goldwyn,* V.P.; Meyer Gottlieb,* Treas.; Anthony Goldwyn, Francis Goldwyn, John Goldwyn.
Number of staff: 1 full-time professional.
Employer Identification Number: 956006859

378
The Goodman Family Foundation ⌑ ☆
700 South Flower St.
Los Angeles 90017-4101

Established in 1977.
Donor(s): Lawrence M. Goodman, Jr.
Foundation type: Independent
Financial data (yr. ended 06/30/89): Assets, $1,624,617 (M); gifts received, $430,650; expenditures, $140,789, including $136,240 for 82 grants (high: $50,100; low: $25).

Purpose and activities: Giving primarily for health, including a Planned Parenthood chapter; support also for Jewish giving.
Limitations: Giving primarily in Los Angeles, CA.
Application information:
Deadline(s): None
Officers and Trustees:* Lawrence M. Goodman, Jr.,* Pres. and Secy.-Treas.; Muriel F. Goodman,* V.P.; James Durbin.
Employer Identification Number: 953169740

379
Edward & Marion Goodman Foundation ⌑
445 Bayshore Blvd.
San Francisco 94124

Established in 1978 in CA.
Donor(s): Goodman Lumber Co.
Foundation type: Independent
Financial data (yr. ended 12/31/88): Assets, $3,391,121 (M); gifts received, $120,000; expenditures, $158,018, including $152,313 for 22 grants (high: $64,500; low: $100).
Purpose and activities: Support for Jewish giving and Jewish welfare.
Officers: Edward Goodman, Pres. and Treas.; Charles Goodman, Secy.
Employer Identification Number: 942538815

380
I. H. and Anna Grancell Foundation ⌑
1469 Carla Ridge
Beverly Hills 90210 (213) 272-7091

Incorporated in 1957 in CA.
Donor(s): Anna Grancell, Anna Grancell Charitable Trust.
Foundation type: Independent
Financial data (yr. ended 07/31/90): Assets, $608,326 (M); expenditures, $247,488, including $235,180 for 14 grants (high: $81,955; low: $180).
Purpose and activities: Giving for hospitals, temple support, higher education, and cultural programs.
Limitations: Giving primarily in CA. No grants to individuals.
Application information: Application form not required.
Initial approach: Letter
Deadline(s): None
Write: Sherman Grancell, Treas.
Officers: Paul Grancell, Pres.; Morton Bauman, Secy.; Sherman Grancell, Treas.
Employer Identification Number: 956027429

381
Burton E. Green Foundation ⌑
9777 Wilshire Blvd., Suite 618
Beverly Hills 90212

Incorporated in 1960 in CA.
Donor(s): Burton E. Green.†
Foundation type: Independent
Financial data (yr. ended 12/31/88): Assets, $2,039,580 (M); expenditures, $93,146, including $91,000 for 41 grants (high: $15,000; low: $1,000).
Purpose and activities: Support for child welfare, animal care, higher education, hospitals, and a community fund.
Limitations: Giving primarily in CA.
Application information:
Initial approach: Letter
Deadline(s): Nov. 30
Write: Hugh M. Mullen, Treas.
Officers and Trustees:* Gyte Van Zyl,* Pres.; Dorothy Green,* V.P.; Elinor F. Logan, Secy.; Hugh M. Mullen,* Treas.
Number of staff: None.
Employer Identification Number: 956026935

382
Leonard & Emese Green Foundation ⌑ ☆
333 South Grand Ave., Suite 5400
Los Angeles 90071 (213) 625-0005

Established in 1986.
Donor(s): Leonard I. Green, Emese Green.
Foundation type: Independent
Financial data (yr. ended 7/31/88): Assets, $86,457 (M); gifts received, $574,438; expenditures, $575,058.
Purpose and activities: Support primarily for Jewish organizations, performing arts groups, and social services.
Application information:
Deadline(s): None
Write: Leonard I. Green, Trustee
Trustee: Leonard I. Green.
Employer Identification Number: 954084789

383
The Greenville Foundation ⌑
P.O. Box 885
Pacific Palisades 90272 (213) 454-0448

Trust established in 1949 in CA.
Donor(s): William Miles.
Foundation type: Independent
Financial data (yr. ended 12/31/87): Assets, $2,148,972 (M); expenditures, $120,275, including $96,000 for 5 grants (high: $50,000; low: $1,000).
Purpose and activities: Grants primarily for Protestant religious programs and higher education, including studies of world peace and hunger, and experimental or pilot projects; support also for the environment and ecology, and community development.
Types of support: Professorships, general purposes, conferences and seminars, seed money, special projects.
Limitations: No grants to individuals, or for operating budgets.
Application information: Application form not required.
Initial approach: Proposal outline
Copies of proposal: 3
Deadline(s): Oct. 1
Board meeting date(s): Semiannually
Write: William Miles, Jr., Chair.
Officer and Trustees:* William Miles, Jr.,* Chair.; Herbert A. Crew, Jr., L.M. Fish.
Number of staff: None.
Employer Identification Number: 956043258

384
Virginia Greiner Trust ⌑ ☆
c/o Wells Fargo Bank, N.A., Trust Tax Dept.
400 Capitol Mall
Sacramento 95814

Established in 1986 in CA.
Foundation type: Independent
Financial data (yr. ended 07/31/89): Assets, $1,703,576 (M); expenditures, $82,922, including $53,000 for 1 grant.
Purpose and activities: Giving for Catholic organizations.
Limitations: Giving primarily in CA. No grants to individuals.
Application information: Contributes only to pre-selected organizations. Applications not accepted.
Trustees: Robert H. Schwab, Jr., Wells Fargo Bank, N.A.
Employer Identification Number: 956818356

385
Stella B. Gross Charitable Trust
c/o Bank of the West
P.O. Box 1121
San Jose 95108 (408) 998-6856

Trust established in 1966 in CA.
Donor(s): Stella B. Gross.†
Foundation type: Independent
Financial data (yr. ended 06/30/89): Assets, $4,656,003 (M); expenditures, $315,358, including $235,372 for 49 grants (high: $32,707; low: $458; average: $1,000-$10,000).
Purpose and activities: Giving to youth agencies, higher education, aid to the handicapped, and health agencies and hospitals.
Types of support: Continuing support, general purposes, seed money, special projects.
Limitations: Giving limited to Santa Clara County, CA. No grants to individuals.
Publications: Annual report, 990-PF.
Application information: Contributes only to pre-selected organizations. Applications not accepted.
Board meeting date(s): June and Dec.
Write: Lori C. Stentzenmeyer, Trust Administrator, Bank of the West
Trustee: Bank of the West.
Number of staff: None.
Employer Identification Number: 237142181

386
The Grove Foundation ⌑ ☆
c/o Aufmuth, Fox & Baigent
400 Hamilton Ave., Suite 205
Palo Alto 94301

Established in 1986.
Donor(s): Andrew S. Grove, Eva K. Grove.
Foundation type: Independent
Financial data (yr. ended 9/30/88): Assets, $15,040 (M); gifts received, $103,488; expenditures, $111,424, including $106,700 for 21 grants (high: $15,000; low: $200).
Purpose and activities: Giving primarily for family planning and other social services, higher education, Jewish welfare, international refugee assistance, and the performing arts.

Application information: Contributes only to pre-selected organizations. Applications not accepted.
Officers: Andrew S. Grove, Pres.; Eva K. Grove, Secy.
Employer Identification Number: 770108124

387
Miriam and Peter Haas Fund
Levi Plaza, LS/7
1155 Battery St., 7th Fl.
San Francisco 94111 (415) 544-7623

Incorporated in 1953 in CA.
Donor(s): Peter E. Haas.
Foundation type: Independent
Financial data (yr. ended 08/31/88): Assets, $7,327,180 (M); expenditures, $321,383, including $279,783 for 120 grants (high: $53,450; low: $25; average: $250-$1,000).
Purpose and activities: Giving primarily for higher and other education; support also for community funds, youth, and cultural programs, including the fine arts.
Types of support: Operating budgets, continuing support, deficit financing, building funds, equipment, special projects.
Limitations: Giving primarily in northern CA. No grants to individuals.
Application information: Application form not required.
Copies of proposal: 1
Deadline(s): None
Board meeting date(s): As required
Final notification: 1 month
Write: Peter E. Haas, V.P.
Officers: Miriam L. Haas, Pres.; Peter E. Haas, V.P.
Number of staff: None.
Employer Identification Number: 946064551

388
Walter and Elise Haas Fund ▼ ⌑
1160 Battery St., Suite 400
San Francisco 94111 (415) 398-4474

Incorporated in 1952 in CA.
Donor(s): Walter A. Haas,† Elise S. Haas.
Foundation type: Independent
Financial data (yr. ended 12/31/88): Assets, $58,425,000 (M); expenditures, $3,493,600, including $3,218,846 for 150 grants (high: $800,000; low: $500; average: $1,000-$25,000).
Purpose and activities: Support for projects which demonstrate an ability to have a wide impact within their respective fields through enhancing public education and access to information, serving a central organizing role, addressing public policy, demonstrating creative approaches toward meeting human needs, supporting the work of a major institution in the field, or extending the arts and humanities into the community.
Types of support: Operating budgets, continuing support, seed money, emergency funds, building funds, equipment, endowment funds, matching funds, scholarship funds, professorships, fellowships, special projects, capital campaigns, land acquisition.
Limitations: Giving primarily in the San Francisco Bay Area, CA. No grants to individuals, or for deficit financing.
Publications: Multi-year report, program policy statement, application guidelines.
Application information: Application form required.
Initial approach: Letter
Copies of proposal: 1
Deadline(s): None
Board meeting date(s): As required
Final notification: 2 to 4 months
Write: Bruce R. Sievers, Exec. Dir.
Officers and Directors:* Rhoda H. Goldman,* Pres.; Elise S. Haas,* V.P.; Peter E. Haas,* V.P.; Walter A. Haas, Jr.,* V.P.; Bruce R. Sievers, Exec. Dir. and Secy.-Treas.
Number of staff: 2 full-time professional; 1 full-time support; 1 part-time support.
Employer Identification Number: 946068564

389
Evelyn and Walter Haas, Jr. Fund ▼
1160 Battery St., Suite 400
San Francisco 94111 (415) 544-6575

Incorporated in 1953 in CA.
Donor(s): Walter A. Haas, Jr., Evelyn D. Haas.
Foundation type: Independent
Financial data (yr. ended 12/31/89): Assets, $30,441,675 (L); expenditures, $2,092,195, including $1,753,490 for 164 grants (high: $150,000; average: $5,000-$25,000).
Purpose and activities: Giving primarily for alternatives to institutional care for the elderly, selected programs serving the hungry and homeless, higher and other education, the Hispanic community, corporate social responsibility and business ethics, and community development.
Types of support: Seed money, special projects, technical assistance, general purposes.
Limitations: Giving primarily in San Francisco and Alameda counties, CA. No support for private foundations or religious organizations. No grants to individuals, or for deficit financing, workshops, conferences, publications, capital campaigns, films, or research.
Publications: Annual report (including application guidelines).
Application information: Grants in the areas of arts and education are initiated by the trustees. Application form not required.
Initial approach: Letter (1 or 2 pages)
Copies of proposal: 1
Deadline(s): None
Board meeting date(s): 3 times a year
Final notification: Within 90 days
Write: Melissa Bannett, Exec. Dir.
Officers and Trustees:* Walter A. Haas, Jr.,* Pres.; Evelyn D. Haas,* V.P.; Walter J. Haas, Secy.-Treas.
Advisory Trustees: Dyke Brown, Elizabeth Haas Eisenhardt, James C. Gaither, Robert D. Haas, Cecil F. Poole.
Number of staff: 1 full-time professional; 1 full-time support.
Employer Identification Number: 946068932

390
The Hafif Family Foundation ⌑ ☆
Claremont Professional Bldg.
269 West Bonita Ave.
Claremont 91711 (714) 624-1671

Established in 1986.
Donor(s): Herbert Hafif.
Foundation type: Independent
Financial data (yr. ended 12/31/88): Assets, $1,237,279 (M); gifts received, $500,000; expenditures, $128,995, including $118,965 for 24 grants (high: $36,925; low: $40).
Purpose and activities: Giving primarily for welfare, community development, and health, including hospitals and drug abuse programs.
Limitations: Giving primarily in CA.
Application information:
Initial approach: Letter
Deadline(s): None
Director: Herbert Hafif.
Employer Identification Number: 954081964

391
Ernest W. and Jean E. Hahn Foundation ▼ ⌑
P.O. Box 2009
Rancho Santa Fe 92067 (619) 756-2453

Established in 1981 in CA.
Donor(s): Ernest W. Hahn, Jean E. Hahn.
Foundation type: Independent
Financial data (yr. ended 12/31/88): Assets, $12,096 (M); gifts received, $290,000; expenditures, $456,048, including $451,100 for grants.
Purpose and activities: Giving for social services, youth agencies, hospitals and health services, the arts, and conservation.
Limitations: Giving primarily in CA.
Application information:
Initial approach: Letter
Deadline(s): None
Write: Ernest W. Hahn, Pres.
Officers: Ernest W. Hahn, Pres.; Jean E. Hahn, V.P.; Anna M. Renn, Secy.
Employer Identification Number: 953643330

392
Haigh-Scatena Foundation
P.O. Box 4399
Davis 95617-4399 (916) 758-5327

Established in 1967 in CA.
Donor(s): Isabelle Simi Haigh,† Vivien Haigh.†
Foundation type: Independent
Financial data (yr. ended 08/31/89): Assets, $3,187,744 (M); expenditures, $226,827, including $123,724 for 6 grants (high: $36,500; low: $4,800).
Purpose and activities: "Grants awarded to innovative, social impact projects benefitting high risk children and youth. Priority consideration for primary prevention projects targeting very young children. The foundation is interested in preventing (for example) delinquency, school failure, teen pregnancy, and substance abuse before they occur."
Types of support: Research, special projects, technical assistance, loans, seed money, conferences and seminars, emergency funds.
Limitations: Giving limited to northern CA. No grants to individuals, or for capital campaigns, general operating funds, or replacement of other grants.
Publications: Informational brochure (including application guidelines).
Application information: Application materials issued upon receipt of acceptable concept letter. Application form required.

Initial approach: 3-page concept letter
Copies of proposal: 1
Deadline(s): None
Board meeting date(s): Generally bimonthly
Final notification: Within 6 months
Write: Ronald W. Clement, Exec. Dir.

Officers and Directors:* Jean Bacigalupi,* Pres.; Andrew Eber,* V.P.; Jeanette M. Dunckel,* Secy.; H. Bruce Collard,* Treas.; Ronald W. Clement,* Exec. Dir.; Bruce Goldstein, Gloria Hom, Arnold Perkins, Gary Templin, Caroline Tower, Joanna Uribe de Mena.
Number of staff: 1 full-time professional.
Employer Identification Number: 941753746

393
Crescent Porter Hale Foundation
220 Bush St., Suite 1069
San Francisco 94104 (415) 986-5177

Incorporated in 1961 in CA.
Donor(s): Elwyn C. Hale,† M. Eugenie Hale.†
Foundation type: Independent
Financial data (yr. ended 12/31/88): Assets, $17,887,457 (M); expenditures, $861,160, including $773,960 for 72 grants (high: $25,000; low: $1,000; average: $10,000).
Purpose and activities: Emphasis on Roman Catholic organizations, education, including art and music education, specific hospital projects, disadvantaged youth, and the elderly.
Types of support: Special projects, equipment, capital campaigns, operating budgets, scholarship funds.
Limitations: Giving primarily in the San Francisco Bay Area, CA. No grants to individuals.
Publications: Application guidelines, program policy statement.
Application information: Application form not required.
Initial approach: Letter of intent
Copies of proposal: 11
Deadline(s): Feb., July, and Oct.
Board meeting date(s): Apr., Sept., and Dec.
Write: Ulla Davis, Consultant

Officers: L.E. Alford, Pres.; Thomas J. Mellon, Jr., V.P.; A.L. Ballard, Secy.-Treas.
Directors: Eugene E. Bleck, M.D., Rev. Charles Dullea, S.J., Ephraim P. Engleman, M.D., Elfreda Hale, E. William Swanson, Osamu Yamada.
Number of staff: 1 full-time professional; 1 part-time support.
Employer Identification Number: 946093385

394
O. L. Halsell Foundation ⌑
P.O. Box 6300
Santa Ana 92706 (714) 558-3211

Trust established in 1948 in CA.
Donor(s): Oliver L. Halsell.†
Foundation type: Independent
Financial data (yr. ended 12/31/87): Assets, $5,644,545 (M); gifts received, $22,024; expenditures, $220,990, including $113,000 for 12 grants (high: $16,000; low: $8,000).
Purpose and activities: Giving to religious, charitable and youth-oriented organizations.
Limitations: Giving primarily in Orange County, CA. No grants to individuals.
Application information:
Initial approach: Letter
Deadline(s): None
Write: Royce Johnson, Secy.

Officers: George V. Barr, Pres.; William D. Stauffer, V.P.; Phillip Royce Johnson, Secy.
Employer Identification Number: 956027266

395
Florence P. Hamilton Foundation ⌑
c/o Edmund R. Davis, Brobeck, Phleger et al.
440 South Flower St.
Los Angeles 90017

Established about 1969 in CA.
Donor(s): Florence P. Hamilton, William H. Peterson Trust.
Foundation type: Independent
Financial data (yr. ended 12/31/89): Assets, $2,235,126 (M); expenditures, $158,383.
Purpose and activities: Support for cultural programs, social services, and hospitals.
Limitations: No grants to individuals.
Application information: Contributes only to pre-selected organizations. Applications not accepted.
Trustees: F. George Herlihy, Frederick T. Nelson, Charles Price II, Richard Trautwein.
Employer Identification Number: 956235131

396
Edna & Yu-Shan Han Charitable Foundation ⌑
606 South Lucerne Rd.
Los Angeles 90005 (213) 277-0300

Established in 1983 in CA.
Foundation type: Independent
Financial data (yr. ended 12/31/88): Assets, $1,487,275 (M); expenditures, $74,132, including $62,016 for 4 grants (high: $34,000; low: $2,500).
Purpose and activities: Support for scholarship funds to assist needy students in studies of Chinese culture, art, or history; preference given to students of Chinese ancestry to pursue any field of study.
Types of support: Scholarship funds.
Application information: Applications must include financial statement, scholastic record, letter of admission from accredited college or university, and a short essay about applicant's goals.
Deadline(s): None
Write: Robert Sung, Trustee

Trustees: Patsy Sung, Robert Sung.
Employer Identification Number: 953823449

397
The Luke B. Hancock Foundation ▼ ⌑
360 Bryant St.
Palo Alto 94301 (415) 321-5536

Incorporated in 1948 in NV.
Donor(s): Luke B. Hancock.†
Foundation type: Independent
Financial data (yr. ended 4/30/88): Assets, $18,899,069 (M); expenditures, $1,100,938, including $877,216 for 85 grants (high: $50,000; low: $500; average: $1,000-$30,000).
Purpose and activities: Giving primarily for job training and employment for youth. Special project grants include: consortium with other foundations in areas where there is unmet need; some support for technical assistance, emergency funding, music and the arts in education. During I988, primary focus on youth employment.
Types of support: Operating budgets, continuing support, seed money, emergency funds, matching funds, consulting services, technical assistance, conferences and seminars.
Limitations: Giving limited to CA, particularly the six counties of the San Francisco Bay Area. No support for films. No grants to individuals, or for deficit financing, capital or building funds, acquisitions, endowment funds, scholarships, fellowships, personal research, or publications.
Publications: Annual report (including application guidelines).
Application information: Application form not required.
Initial approach: Letter
Copies of proposal: 1
Deadline(s): None
Board meeting date(s): Feb., July, and Oct.
Final notification: 3 to 4 months
Write: Joan H. Wylie, Exec. Dir.

Officers and Directors: Marsha A. Adams,* Chair.; Jane Hancock,* Pres.; Noble Hancock,* V.P.; Janice H. Pettit,* Secy.; Tom Hancock,* Treas.; Joan H. Wylie,* Exec. Dir.; Courtney J. Catron, Linda Catron, Carol E. Hancock, Denise J. Hancock, James Hancock, Lorraine A. Hancock, Marian L. Hancock, Mark Hancock, Wesley Hancock, William Hancock, Susan Hillstrom-Masi, Joseph L. Masi.
Number of staff: 1 full-time professional; 1 part-time support.
Employer Identification Number: 886002013

398
William H. Hannon Foundation ⌑
8055 West Manchester Blvd., No. 400
Playa Del Rey 90293-7990

Established in 1982 in CA.
Donor(s): William Herbert Hannon.
Foundation type: Independent
Financial data (yr. ended 11/30/89): Assets, $2,633,883 (M); gifts received, $5,160; expenditures, $178,219, including $171,596 for 18 grants (high: $156,825; low: $75).
Purpose and activities: Giving primarily for higher education; support also for churches and medical research and hospitals.
Limitations: Giving primarily in the Playa Del Ray, CA, area. No grants to individuals.
Application information:
Initial approach: Letter
Deadline(s): None
Write: William H. Hannon, Pres.

Officers and Directors:* William Herbert Hannon,* Chair. and Pres.; Kathleen Aikenhead,* Secy.-Treas.; Nancy M. Cunningham, Elaine S. Ewen, Patrick H. Hannon, J. Robert Vaughn.
Employer Identification Number: 953847664

399
Marian & Pink Happ Fund ⌑
c/o Wells Fargo Bank, N.A.
525 Market St., 17th Fl.
San Francisco 94163

Established in 1981 in CA.
Foundation type: Independent
Financial data (yr. ended 9/30/88): Assets, $1,305,464 (M); expenditures, $147,787, including $130,000 for 12 grants (high: $15,000; low: $5,000).
Purpose and activities: Support for health, social and youth services, and education, including religious schools.
Trustee: Wells Fargo Bank, N.A.
Employer Identification Number: 956025857

400
Harden Foundation ⌑
P.O. Box 779
Salinas 93902-0779
Application address: 234 Capitol St., Salinas, CA 93902; Tel.: (408)424-7314

Established in 1963 in CA.
Foundation type: Independent
Financial data (yr. ended 2/29/88): Assets, $19,433,302 (M); expenditures, $1,298,946, including $1,069,152 for 32 grants (high: $200,000; low: $950).
Purpose and activities: Support primarily for a hospital; giving also for a college, social services, and youth organizations.
Types of support: Operating budgets, special projects, general purposes, building funds.
Limitations: Giving primarily in the Salinas Valley, CA, area.
Application information: Application form required.
Initial approach: Letter
Deadline(s): May 1 and Nov. 1
Board meeting date(s): June and Dec.
Write: Andrew Church, Secy.
Officers and Directors:* Ralph L. Kokjer,* Pres. and Treas.; Andrew Church,* Secy.; Thomas Merrill, Patricia Tynan-Chapman.
Employer Identification Number: 946098887

401
Harkham Foundation ⌑
1157 South Crocker St.
Los Angeles 90021 (213) 745-6010

Established in 1980 in CA.
Donor(s): Uri P. Harkham, Efrem Harkham.
Foundation type: Independent
Financial data (yr. ended 3/31/88): Assets, $61,978 (M); gifts received, $158,000; expenditures, $295,687, including $277,476 for 43 grants (high: $100,000; low: $250) and $17,673 for 7 grants to individuals (high: $9,923; low: $300).
Purpose and activities: Support for Jewish giving; scholarships awarded through applications submitted to an office in Israel based upon recommendations by school officials.
Limitations: Giving primarily in Los Angeles, CA, and Tel Aviv, Israel.
Application information: Applications not accepted.
Write: Nachum Harkham
Directors: David Harkham, Efrem Harkham, Nachum Harkham, Sally Harkham, Uri P. Harkham.
Employer Identification Number: 953532383

402
Mark H. & Blanche M. Harrington Foundation ⌑
c/o Citizens Commercial Trust and Savings Bank
225 East Colorado Blvd.
Pasadena 91101

Established in 1956 in CA.
Donor(s): Mark H. Harrington, Blanche M. Harrington.
Foundation type: Independent
Financial data (yr. ended 12/31/86): Assets, $5,536,975 (M); expenditures, $203,068, including $174,128 for grants.
Purpose and activities: Giving primarily for hospitals, church support, and education.
Limitations: Giving primarily in CA. No grants to individuals.
Application information: Contributes only to pre-selected organizations. Applications not accepted.
Trustee Bank: Citizens Commercial Trust and Savings Bank.
Employer Identification Number: 956025594

403
Ina & Ray Harris Fund ⌑
110 West A St., Suite 1700
San Diego 92101-8218 (619) 236-1414

Established in 1979 in CA.
Foundation type: Operating
Financial data (yr. ended 12/31/87): Assets, $497,428 (M); expenditures, $126,114, including $113,532 for 100 grants to individuals (high: $2,500; low: $500).
Purpose and activities: Scholarships for secondary schools and higher education.
Types of support: Student aid.
Limitations: Giving limited to residents of San Diego County, CA.
Application information:
Deadline(s): 2 months prior to school term
Write: William A. Yale, Trustee
Trustee: William A. Yale.
Employer Identification Number: 953414419

404
William R. & Virginia Hayden Foundation
(Formerly William R. Hayden Foundation)
110 West Las Tunas Dr., Suite A
San Gabriel 91776

Established in 1960 in CA.
Donor(s): William R. Hayden,† Mrs. William R. Hayden.
Foundation type: Independent
Financial data (yr. ended 12/31/89): Assets, $8,121,674 (M); gifts received, $1,562,500; expenditures, $820,465, including $789,168 for 71 grants (high: $89,000; low: $50).
Purpose and activities: Emphasis on Roman Catholic religious and social service organizations, including support for churches.
Types of support: Building funds, capital campaigns, continuing support.
Limitations: Giving primarily in CA. No grants to individuals.
Application information: Contributes only to pre-selected organizations. Applications not accepted.
Officers and Directors:* Stanley D. Hayden,* Pres.; Patrick F. Collins,* V.P., Secy., and C.F.O.; David S. Aikenhead, C. Richard Bradley, Marcia A. Hayden, Peter J. Vogelsang.
Employer Identification Number: 956055676

405
The John Randolph Haynes and Dora Haynes Foundation ▼
727 West Seventh St., Suite 618
Los Angeles 90017 (213) 623-9151

Trust established in 1926 in CA.
Donor(s): John Randolph Haynes,† Mrs. John Randolph Haynes.†
Foundation type: Independent
Financial data (yr. ended 08/31/89): Assets, $36,225,707 (M); expenditures, $1,724,299, including $1,601,340 for 35 grants (high: $264,000; low: $1,000; average: $5,000-$85,000).
Purpose and activities: "...Promoting the well-being of mankind" by making grants for study and research in the social sciences - economics, history, government, and sociology; provides undergraduate scholarships, graduate fellowships, and fellowships for faculty members in the social sciences in selected colleges and universities. Grants made only through local colleges and universities or other nonprofit institutions.
Types of support: Fellowships, research, scholarship funds, internships.
Limitations: Giving limited to the greater Los Angeles, CA, area. No grants to individuals, or for building or endowment funds or operating budgets.
Publications: Informational brochure (including application guidelines).
Application information: Application form not required.
Initial approach: Letter or telephone
Copies of proposal: 15
Deadline(s): Several weeks before board meetings
Board meeting date(s): Quarterly throughout year
Final notification: 1 to 2 weeks
Write: F. Haynes Lindley, Jr., Pres.
Officers and Trustees:* F. Haynes Lindley, Jr.,* Pres. and Secy.; Robert R. Dockson,* 1st V.P.; Jack K. Horton,* 2nd V.P.; Paul A. Albrecht, R. Stanton Avery, Philip M. Hawley, Chauncey J. Medberry III, Donn B. Miller, Jane G. Pisano.
Number of staff: 1 full-time professional; 1 full-time support.
Employer Identification Number: 951644020

406
Hedco Foundation ▼ ⌑
c/o Fitzgerald, Abbott & Beardsley
1221 Broadway, 21st Fl.
Oakland 94612-1837

Incorporated in 1972 in CA.
Donor(s): Herrick Corp., Catalina Associates.
Foundation type: Independent

Financial data (yr. ended 11/30/88): Assets, $6,699,210 (M); gifts received, $920,000; expenditures, $1,024,890, including $1,019,454 for 23 grants (high: $469,167; low: $500).
Purpose and activities: Giving predominantly to qualified educational and health service institutions; support also for social services, arts and culture, and youth organizations.
Types of support: Building funds, equipment, land acquisition, matching funds, renovation projects.
Limitations: Giving primarily in CA. No grants to individuals, or for general support, operating budgets, endowment funds, scholarships, fellowships, special projects, research, publications, or conferences; no loans.
Application information: Application form not required.
Initial approach: Proposal
Copies of proposal: 1
Deadline(s): None
Board meeting date(s): Nov.
Final notification: 3 to 4 months
Write: Mary A. Goriup, Fdn. Mgr.
Officers and Directors:* Ester M. Dornsife,* Pres.; David H. Dornsife,* V.P.; Harold W. Dornsife,* C.F.O.; Dorothy Jernstedt,* Secy.; Laine Ainsworth, S.G. Herrick, James S. Little, William Picard, J.G. Ross.
Foundation Manager: Mary A. Goriup.
Number of staff: None.
Employer Identification Number: 237259742

407
Heights Foundation ⌑
2465 Mesa Terrace
Upland 91786

Established in 1971 in CA.
Donor(s): Ethel M. Beiseker, Thomas C. Beiseker.
Foundation type: Independent
Financial data (yr. ended 6/30/87): Assets, $35,454 (M); gifts received, $204,600; expenditures, $208,412, including $208,300 for 13 grants (high: $155,000; low: $200).
Purpose and activities: Giving primarily to religious organizations.
Application information: Contributes only to pre-selected organizations. Applications not accepted.
Write: Thomas C. Beiseker, Pres.
Officers: Thomas C. Beiseker, C.E.O. and Pres.; Ethel M. Beiseker, Secy.; Thomas L. Beiseker, C.F.O.
Employer Identification Number: 237104815

408
The Held Foundation ⌑
10866 Wilshire Blvd., No. 800
Los Angeles 90024-4303

Established in 1985 in CA.
Donor(s): Harold Held, Louise Held.
Foundation type: Independent
Financial data (yr. ended 12/31/88): Assets, $182,152 (M); gifts received, $100,000; expenditures, $165,805, including $165,805 for grants (high: $81,445).
Purpose and activities: Giving primarily for Jewish concerns and the arts.
Limitations: No grants to individuals.
Application information: Contributes only to pre-selected organizations. Applications not accepted.
Trustees: Harold Held, Louise Held.
Employer Identification Number: 954016569

409
Heller Charitable and Educational Fund
P.O. Box 336
Kentfield 94914

Established in CA.
Donor(s): Members of the Heller family.
Foundation type: Independent
Financial data (yr. ended 12/31/89): Assets, $1,000,000 (M); expenditures, $100,000, including $100,000 for 18 grants (high: $15,000; low: $1,000; average: $5,000).
Purpose and activities: The fund seeks to promote prison reform, especially programs to develop alternatives to incarceration; support programs for research, litigation, or other means of arresting despoilation of the natural environment; help preserve open space lands for agriculture, wilderness, and recreation through purchase and other means; and support the acquisition of books, periodicals, and other educational materials for libraries.
Limitations: Giving primarily in CA. No grants to individuals, or for capital projects; no loans.
Publications: Application guidelines.
Application information: Application form not required.
Initial approach: Proposal (no longer than 2 pages)
Copies of proposal: 1
Deadline(s): Nov. 1
Board meeting date(s): Dec. 1
Final notification: Dec. or Jan.
Write: Ruth B. Heller, Corresponding Secy.
Officers: F. Jerome Tone IV,* Pres.; Ruth B. Heller,* Corresponding Secy.
Trustees:* Anne E. Heller, Miranda Heller, Rolf Lygren, Olivia Mandell, Peter Mandell.
Number of staff: None.
Employer Identification Number: 946066671

410
Helms Foundation, Inc. ⌑
25765 Quilla Rd.
P.O. Box 55827
Valencia 91355 (805) 253-3485

Incorporated in 1946 in CA.
Donor(s): The Helms family, Helms Bakeries.
Foundation type: Independent
Financial data (yr. ended 06/30/89): Assets, $4,186,537 (M); expenditures, $365,429, including $318,238 for 77 grants (high: $36,000; low: $75).
Purpose and activities: Support primarily for higher and other education, including scholarship funds and religious education; support also for health agencies and hospitals, cultural organizations, and youth and social service agencies.
Limitations: No support for private foundations.
Application information: Application form not required.
Deadline(s): None
Write: William D. Manuel, Asst. Secy.
Officers and Trustees:* Peggy Helms Hurtig,* Pres.; Elizabeth Helms Adams,* V.P. and Secy.-Treas.; John B. Gostovich, Frank J. Kanne, Jr.
Employer Identification Number: 956091335

411
The Herbst Foundation, Inc. ▼
Three Embarcadero Ctr., 21st Fl.
San Francisco 94111 (415) 951-7508

Incorporated in 1961 in CA.
Donor(s): Herman H. Herbst,† Maurice H. Herbst.†
Foundation type: Independent
Financial data (yr. ended 07/31/89): Assets, $41,456,247 (M); gifts received, $1,000; expenditures, $2,100,819, including $1,778,226 for 70 grants (high: $750,000; low: $500).
Purpose and activities: Grants for bricks and mortar projects in areas of educational facilities, recreation for the handicapped, civic improvement of existing city structures owned by public tax-exempt entities, and hospitals and health-care organizations; very small budget per year for broad purposes, which include child development and the disadvantaged.
Types of support: Building funds, renovation projects.
Limitations: Giving limited to the city and county of San Francisco, CA. No grants to individuals, or for endowment funds, scholarships, fellowships, research, or matching gifts; no loans.
Publications: Application guidelines.
Application information: Application form not required.
Initial approach: Letter
Copies of proposal: 1
Deadline(s): None
Board meeting date(s): Usually in Sept., Nov., Feb., and May
Final notification: 30 days after board meeting
Write: John T. Seigle, Pres.
Officer and Directors:* John T. Seigle,* Pres.; William D. Crawford, George D. Hart, Dennis B. King, Melvyn I. Mark, Ralph L. Preston, Haskell Titchell.
Number of staff: 1 full-time support; 2 part-time support.
Employer Identification Number: 946061680

412
Fannie and John Hertz Foundation ▼
Box 5032
Livermore 94551-5032 (415) 373-1642

Incorporated in 1945 in IL.
Donor(s): John D. Hertz,† Fannie K. Hertz.†
Foundation type: Independent
Financial data (yr. ended 6/30/89): Assets, $30,373,751 (M); expenditures, $2,568,501, including $20,000 for 1 grant and $1,987,970 for 160 grants to individuals (high: $26,000; low: $500; average: $500-$26,000).
Purpose and activities: To promote education and the defense of the U.S. through support of fellowships for graduate education for students with outstanding potential in the fields constituting the applied physical sciences at specified nationwide institutions; also provides scholarships to area high school graduates.

Types of support: Fellowships, research.
Limitations: Giving for scholarship program limited to San Francisco Bay Area, CA, high school graduates; competition for fellowship program is nationwide. No grants for general support, capital or endowment funds, matching gifts, program support, research, demonstration projects, publications, or conferences; no loans.
Publications: Informational brochure (including application guidelines).
Application information: No grants for joint Ph.D./professional degree programs, or for biological sciences. Application form required.
Initial approach: Request for application form
Copies of proposal: 2
Deadline(s): Submit application form in Sept. or Oct.; deadline Nov. 1
Board meeting date(s): Mar. and Nov.
Final notification: By Apr.
Write: Dr. Wilson K. Talley, Pres.
Officers and Directors:* Allan B. Hunter,* Chair. and Treas.; Wilson K. Talley,* Pres.; Paul L. Hexter,* V.P.; Peter Strauss,* V.P.; Robert M. Pennoyer,* Secy.; John W. Boyd, Gregory H. Canavan, Robert A. Duffy, Jerome L. Ettelson, Lawrence Goldmuntz, John T. Hayward, Arthur R. Kantrowitz, Hans Mark, Thomas McCann, Richard Miles, Edward Teller, Thomas A. Weaver, Lowell L. Wood.
Number of staff: 1 part-time professional; 2 part-time support.
Employer Identification Number: 362411723

413
Hester Family Foundation ¤
1105 Quail St.
Newport Beach 92660 (714) 883-1560

Established in 1976 in CA.
Donor(s): Charles W. Hester, Nora Hester.
Foundation type: Independent
Financial data (yr. ended 12/31/87): Assets, $999,766 (M); gifts received, $30,000; expenditures, $115,136, including $108,517 for 35 grants (high: $10,000; low: $100).
Purpose and activities: Support for hospitals and health associations, cultural programs, education, and social service and youth agencies.
Application information:
Write: Charles W. Hester, Pres.
Officers: Charles W. Hester, Pres.; Nora Hester, V.P. and Secy.-Treas.
Directors: Marilyn Gianulias, Janet Hamilton, Charlene Immell.
Employer Identification Number: 510189743

414
George E. Hewitt Foundation for Medical Research ¤
137 Jasmine Creek Dr.
Corona del Mar 92625-1422

Established in 1982 in CA.
Donor(s): George E. Hewitt.
Foundation type: Operating
Financial data (yr. ended 12/31/88): Assets, $1,610,989 (M); gifts received, $25,000; expenditures, $91,246, including $83,560 for 6 grants to individuals (high: $20,594; low: $91).
Purpose and activities: A private operating foundation; grants for medical research.
Types of support: Student aid.
Application information:
Initial approach: Letter and resume
Deadline(s): None
Write: George E. Hewitt, Pres.
Officers: George E. Hewitt, Pres.; Roy B. Woolsey, Secy.
Employer Identification Number: 953711123

415
The William and Flora Hewlett Foundation ▼
525 Middlefield Rd., Suite 200
Menlo Park 94025 (415) 329-1070

Incorporated in 1966 in CA.
Donor(s): Flora Lamson Hewlett,† William R. Hewlett.
Foundation type: Independent
Financial data (yr. ended 12/31/89): Assets, $687,664,000 (M); gifts received, $108,682; expenditures, $39,793,733, including $36,947,733 for 269 grants (high: $1,333,000; low: $3,500; average: $20,000-$600,000) and $22,295 for 111 employee matching gifts.
Purpose and activities: Emphasis on conflict resolution, the environment, performing arts, education, especially at the college-university level, population, and regional grants program.
Types of support: General purposes, operating budgets, continuing support, seed money, emergency funds, land acquisition, special projects, matching funds, employee matching gifts, endowment funds.
Limitations: Giving limited to the San Francisco Bay Area, CA, for regional grants program; performing arts limited to the area in part. No support for medicine and health-related projects, law, criminal justice, and related fields, juvenile delinquency, drug and alcohol addiction, problems of the elderly and the handicapped, or television or radio projects. No grants to individuals, or for building funds, basic research, equipment, scholarships, or fellowships; no loans.
Publications: Annual report, program policy statement, application guidelines, informational brochure.
Application information: Application form not required.
Initial approach: Letter
Copies of proposal: 1
Deadline(s): Jan. 1, music; Apr. 1, theater; July 1, dance, film, and video service organizations; no deadlines for other programs
Board meeting date(s): Jan., Apr., July, and Oct.
Final notification: 1 to 2 months
Write: Roger W. Heyns, Pres.
Officers: Roger W. Heyns,* Pres.; Marianne Pallotti, V.P. and Corp. Secy.; William F. Nichols, Treas.
Directors:* William R. Hewlett, Chair.; Walter B. Hewlett, Vice-Chair.; Robert M. Brown, Robert Erburu, Eleanor H. Gimon, Mary H. Jaffe, Herant Katchdourian, M.D., Arjay Miller, Lyle M. Nelson, William D. Ruckelshaus.
Number of staff: 9 full-time professional; 6 full-time support; 3 part-time support.
Employer Identification Number: 941655673

416
Hewlett-Packard Company Foundation
3000 Hanover St., 20AH
Palo Alto 94304 (415) 857-3053
Mailing address: P.O. Box 10301, Palo Alto, CA 94303-0890

Established in 1979.
Donor(s): Hewlett-Packard Co.
Foundation type: Company-sponsored
Financial data (yr. ended 10/31/89): Assets, $2,448,329 (M); gifts received, $1,000,000; expenditures, $328,786, including $326,500 for 3 grants (high: $302,500; low: $2,000).
Purpose and activities: National giving for causes related to higher education in science, engineering, medicine, and business; international giving in countries where Hewlett-Packard has subsidiaries. Support for community service, health, and cultural agencies in locations where the company has major facilities.
Limitations: No grants to individuals, or for conferences, seminars, meetings, or workshops.
Publications: Informational brochure (including application guidelines).
Application information:
Write: Roderick Carlson, Exec. Dir.
Officers: Roderick Carlson, Exec. Dir.; Craig Nordlund, Secy.; Robert P. Wayman, C.F.O.
Directors: Jack Brigham III, Dean O. Morton, John A. Young.
Employer Identification Number: 942618409

417
Ormsby Hill Trust ¤
5039 Angeles Crest Hwy.
La Canada 91011

Foundation type: Operating
Financial data (yr. ended 6/30/88): Assets, $2,228,748 (M); expenditures, $175,631, including $104,377 for 3 grants (high: $48,925; low: $15,452).
Purpose and activities: Giving primarily to religious institutions and childrens health services.
Application information: Contributes only to pre-selected organizations. Applications not accepted.
Officers and Trustees:* Maitland Hardyman,* Pres.; Joe C. Ortega,* Secy.-Treas.; Norman Frank.
Employer Identification Number: 951866004

418
The Edward E. Hills Fund ¤
c/o Pillsbury, Madison and Sutro
225 Bush St., Rm. 1900
San Francisco 94104

Incorporated in 1953 in CA.
Donor(s): Edward E. Hills.†
Foundation type: Independent
Financial data (yr. ended 12/31/87): Assets, $8,576,162 (M); expenditures, $646,713, including $575,000 for 8 grants (high: $100,000; low: $10,000).
Purpose and activities: Grants primarily to the performing arts, a museum, and higher and secondary educational institutions.
Limitations: Giving primarily in CA.
Application information:
Deadline(s): None

Officers: Reuben W. Hills III, Pres.; John B. Bates,* Secy.-Treas.
Directors:* Edmond S. Gillette, Jr.
Employer Identification Number: 946062537

419
Hinz Family Charitable Foundation ☆
c/o Hi Torque Publications
10600 Sepulveda Blvd.
Mission Hills 91345 (818) 365-6831

Established in 1986 in CA.
Donor(s): Lila Hinz, Roland Hinz.
Foundation type: Independent
Financial data (yr. ended 06/30/88): Assets, $433,496 (M); gifts received, $872,000; expenditures, $650,255, including $650,150 for 8 grants (high: $500,000; low: $3,650).
Purpose and activities: Support primarily for a Protestant church, school, and ministry programs; support also for missionaries and religious welfare organizations.
Application information:
Deadline(s): None
Write: Roland Hinz, Trustee
Trustees: Lila Hinz, Roland Hinz.
Employer Identification Number: 954121438

420
Hoag Foundation ▼ ⌑
2029 Century Park East, Suite 4392
Los Angeles 90067 (213) 683-6500

Incorporated in 1940 in CA.
Donor(s): George Grant Hoag,† Grace E. Hoag, George Grant Hoag II.
Foundation type: Independent
Financial data (yr. ended 12/31/87): Assets, $29,190,947 (M); expenditures, $1,488,679, including $1,145,000 for 9 grants (high: $1,000,000; low: $5,000).
Purpose and activities: Emphasis on medical research and health; support also for youth and cultural programs.
Limitations: Giving primarily in Orange County, CA. No support for government agencies, tax-supported projects, or sectarian or religious organizations for the benefit of their own members. No grants to individuals, or for deficit financing, or normal operating expenses.
Application information: Application form required.
Initial approach: Letter not exceeding 2 pages
Deadline(s): Feb. 15 and Sept. 15
Board meeting date(s): Mar. and Oct.
Final notification: Following meeting at which proposal is acted upon
Write: W. Dickerson Milliken, Secy.
Officers and Directors:* John Macnab,* Pres.; George Grant Hoag II,* V.P.; W. Dickerson Milliken,* Secy.; Del V. Werderman,* Treas.; John Curci, Patty Hoag, Gwyn Parry, Melinda Hoag Smith.
Employer Identification Number: 956006885

421
Hoefer Family Foundation ⌑
2180 Sand Hill Rd., Suite 340
Menlo Park 94025
Application address: 100 Pine St., 5th Fl., San Francisco, CA 94111; Tel.: (415) 342-7111

Foundation type: Independent
Financial data (yr. ended 12/31/88): Assets, $1,488,001 (M); expenditures, $65,907, including $54,070 for 66 grants (high: $10,000; low: $20).
Purpose and activities: Support primarily for higher education and general charitable giving.
Limitations: Giving primarily in CA.
Application information: Application form not required.
Initial approach: Letter or proposal
Deadline(s): None
Write: Alan Hoefer, Pres.
Officers: Alan Hoefer, Pres.; Leo A. Hoefer, V.P.; Wanda Hoefer Bingham, Secy.-Treas.
Trustee: Gladys Hoefer.
Employer Identification Number: 366065404

422
The H. Leslie Hoffman and Elaine S. Hoffman Foundation
626 Wilshire Blvd.
Los Angeles 90017 (213) 620-0621

Trust established in 1952 in CA.
Donor(s): H. Leslie Hoffman.†
Foundation type: Independent
Financial data (yr. ended 12/31/88): Assets, $4,656,614 (M); expenditures, $224,885, including $162,109 for 53 grants (high: $50,000; low: $100).
Purpose and activities: Support for higher education, a secondary school, and cancer research; grants also for hospitals and youth.
Types of support: General purposes.
Limitations: Giving primarily in the Los Angeles, CA, area. No grants to individuals.
Application information: Application form not required.
Initial approach: Letter
Copies of proposal: 1
Board meeting date(s): As required
Write: Eugene P. Carver
Trustees: Eugene P. Carver, Herbert S. Hazeltine, Jane H. Popovich.
Employer Identification Number: 956048600

423
The Hofmann Foundation
(Formerly K. H. Hofmann Foundation)
P.O. Box 907
Concord 94522 (415) 687-1826

Established in 1963 in CA.
Donor(s): Alta Mortgage Co., Hofmann Co., New Discovery, Inc., Kenneth H. Hofmann.
Foundation type: Company-sponsored
Financial data (yr. ended 07/31/89): Assets, $10,401,092 (M); gifts received, $3,944,548; expenditures, $891,096, including $743,242 for 90 grants (high: $1,000,000; low: $100; average: $25-$211,800).
Purpose and activities: Support for 1) acquisition, preservation,and conservation of wildlife lands specifically the wetland marshlands that are sanctuaries to waterfowl and related wildlife; 2) education of the community to its needs to preserve wildlife without undermining related sports and recreation; 3) local educational institutions that demonstrate a profound need to challenge and improve the hearts and minds of its students; 4) local cultural organizations, especially those which demonstrate a desire to establish and create long lasting cultural programs and facilities; and 5) to a limited degree, local organizations which address the general citizens' welfare. Some support for local medical and health agencies, as well as nationally recognized medical research agencies.
Types of support: Building funds, research, scholarship funds, special projects, emergency funds, endowment funds, matching funds.
Limitations: Giving primarily in northern CA, with a concentration on Bay Area organizations; limited support for national organizations. No grants for general purposes, capital funding, routine operating expenses, or repayment of indebtedness.
Publications: Annual report (including application guidelines).
Application information: Application form not required.
Initial approach: Inquiry letter of no more than 3 pages
Copies of proposal: 1
Deadline(s): None
Board meeting date(s): Quarterly
Final notification: 3-4 months
Write: Nick Rossi
Officers: Kenneth H. Hofmann, Pres.; Lisa Ann Hofmann-Sechrest, V.P.; Albert T. Shaw, Secy.; Vita Lori Hofmann, Treas.
Number of staff: 4
Employer Identification Number: 946108897

424
Royal Barney Hogan Foundation ⌑
P.O. Box 3809
San Francisco 94119-3809

Established in 1977 in CA.
Donor(s): Riley P. Bechtel.
Foundation type: Independent
Financial data (yr. ended 12/31/88): Assets, $3,254,362 (M); expenditures, $146,637, including $141,167 for 34 grants (high: $36,667; low: $500).
Purpose and activities: Giving for hospitals and health services, education, and museums.
Types of support: Equipment.
Limitations: Giving primarily in CA. No grants to individuals.
Application information: Contributes only to pre-selected organizations. Applications not accepted.
Officers: Riley P. Bechtel,* Pres.; S.D. Bechtel, Jr.,* V.P.; Susan Peters Bechtel,* V.P.; Theodore J. VanBebber, Secy.-Treas.
Directors:* Lauren B. Dachs, Shana B. Johnstone.
Employer Identification Number: 942416417

425
Glen Holden Foundation ⌑
11365 West Olympic Blvd., Suite 444 W
Los Angeles 90064

Established in 1980 in CA.
Donor(s): Glen A. Holden, Sr.
Foundation type: Independent
Financial data (yr. ended 11/30/88): Assets, $455,514 (M); gifts received, $8,200; expenditures, $314,747, including $312,673 for 26 grants (high: $105,000; low: $20).

Purpose and activities: Support for human services, higher education, and cultural programs.
Officers: Glen A. Holden, Sr., Chair.; Gloria A. Holden, Pres.; Georgianne Holden-Stone, V.P. and Secy.; Glen A. Holden, Jr., V.P. and Treas.; Geannie Holden-Sheller, V.P.
Employer Identification Number: 953450000

426
Hollywood Canteen Foundation ¤
c/o Union Bank
P.O. Box 3100
Los Angeles 90051
Application address: Corporate Trust Dept., Union Bank, P.O. Box 2461, Los Angeles, CA 90051

Trust established in 1946 in CA.
Foundation type: Independent
Financial data (yr. ended 2/29/88): Assets, $1,537,035 (M); expenditures, $147,385, including $139,000 for 27 grants (high: $11,500; low: $1,500).
Purpose and activities: To promote the well-being of military personnel and veterans and their families through grants to hospitals, colleges, social service agencies, and other similar institutions.
Limitations: Giving primarily in CA. No grants to individuals.
Application information:
Initial approach: Proposal
Deadline(s): Dec. 1
Write: Bertram L. Linz, Exec. Secy.
Trustees: Lew R. Wasserman, Chair.; Ralph H. Claire, William K. Howard, Sherman Jones, Gerald H. Oppenheimer, Arthur N. Ryan, John te Groen, Union Bank.
Employer Identification Number: 956023639

427
William Knox Holt Foundation
505 Sansome St., Suite 1001
San Francisco 94111 (415) 981-3455

Established in 1967.
Donor(s): William Knox Holt.†
Foundation type: Independent
Financial data (yr. ended 12/31/88): Assets, $8,400,471 (M); expenditures, $728,799, including $620,000 for 11 grants (high: $249,000; low: $2,500; average: $5,000).
Purpose and activities: Giving primarily for higher and secondary education in the field of science; some support also for museums.
Types of support: Building funds, matching funds, research, special projects, scholarship funds, fellowships.
Limitations: Giving primarily in northern CA and southern TX. No grants for general support, operating budgets, continuing support, annual campaigns, emergency funds, deficit financing, equipment, land acquisition, or endowment funds; no loans.
Application information: Application form not required.
Initial approach: Letter
Copies of proposal: 1
Deadline(s): Submit proposal in Jan. or Feb.; deadline Feb. 15
Board meeting date(s): Quarterly
Final notification: 3 months
Write: Stephen W. Veitch, Secy.
Officer and Directors:* Stephen W. Veitch,* Secy.; Stevenson Atherton, George M. Malti, Roberta Plummer.
Employer Identification Number: 746084245

428
The Homeland Foundation
412 North Pacific Coast Hwy., Suite 345
Laguna Beach 92651-1381 (714) 494-5480

Established in 1986 in CA.
Donor(s): The NISA Trust.
Foundation type: Independent
Financial data (yr. ended 12/31/88): Assets, $8,269,804 (M); gifts received, $3,140,514; expenditures, $768,732, including $743,192 for 76 grants (high: $150,000; low: $500).
Purpose and activities: Giving to preserve individual rights to have a safe place to live, and to organizations that work to preserve the earth's natural resources; support also for wildlife and crafts museums.
Limitations: No grants to individuals.
Application information: Application form not required.
Initial approach: Letter or proposal
Deadline(s): Mar. 1, June 1, Sept. 1, and Dec. 1
Board meeting date(s): Quarterly
Officers: John E. Earhart, Pres.; Anne Earhart, Secy.; Oliver Crary, Treas.
Trustee: Kate Raftery.
Number of staff: 1 full-time professional.
Employer Identification Number: 330200133

429
The Margaret W. and Herbert Hoover, Jr. Foundation
200 South Los Robles Ave., Suite 520
Pasadena 91101-2431 (818) 796-4014

Incorporated in 1968 in CA.
Donor(s): Herbert Hoover, Jr.,† Margaret W. Hoover.†
Foundation type: Independent
Financial data (yr. ended 12/31/88): Assets, $13,793,093 (M); expenditures, $922,417, including $858,744 for 23 grants (high: $166,123; low: $600; average: $10,000-$50,000).
Purpose and activities: Giving for medical and scientific research, with particular emphasis on sight and hearing.
Types of support: Continuing support, seed money, emergency funds, equipment, matching funds, research.
Limitations: No support for performing arts. No grants to individuals, or for endowment funds, building funds, renovation projects, operating budgets, annual campaigns, deficit financing, land acquisition, scholarships, or fellowships; no loans.
Publications: Application guidelines.
Application information: Application form not required.
Initial approach: Letter
Copies of proposal: 1
Deadline(s): Submit proposal when requested by the foundation; no set deadline
Board meeting date(s): As required
Final notification: 2 to 3 months
Write: Herbert Hoover III, Pres.
Officers and Trustees:* Herbert Hoover III,* Pres.; Margaret Hoover Brigham,* V.P. and Secy.; Joan Hoover Vowles,* V.P. and Treas.; Sally K. Bond,* V.P.; Robert J. Plourde,* V.P.
Number of staff: 1 part-time professional.
Employer Identification Number: 952560832

430
Lucile Horton Howe and Mitchell B. Howe Foundation
180 South Lake Ave.
Pasadena 91101 (213) 684-2240

Incorporated in 1964 in CA.
Donor(s): Mitchell B. Howe.†
Foundation type: Independent
Financial data (yr. ended 12/31/89): Assets, $1,970,602 (M); expenditures, $158,286, including $151,400 for 49 grants (high: $75,000; low: $100).
Purpose and activities: Giving primarily for youth and social welfare agencies, hospitals, church support, and education, with emphasis on local organizations.
Application information:
Initial approach: Letter
Deadline(s): July 1
Write: Mitchell B. Howe, Jr., Pres.
Officers: Lynne Howe Myers, Chair.; Mitchell B. Howe, Jr., Pres. and Treas.; Martha Taylor, Secy.
Number of staff: None.
Employer Identification Number: 956081945

431
The Humboldt Area Foundation
P.O. Box 632
Eureka 95502 (707) 442-2993

Established in 1972 in CA by declaration of trust.
Donor(s): Vera P. Vietor,† Lynn A. Vietor,† and others.
Foundation type: Community
Financial data (yr. ended 12/31/89): Assets, $9,895,201 (M); gifts received, $1,103,382; expenditures, $699,759, including $562,914 for 154 grants (high: $42,550; low: $100; average: $3,000-$4,000) and $15,201 for 32 grants to individuals (high: $1,000; average: $300-$500).
Purpose and activities: Grants for cultural programs, health, recreation, public safety, education, and human service programs.
Types of support: Special projects, equipment, building funds, continuing support, matching funds, renovation projects, student aid.
Limitations: Giving limited to Humboldt, Del Norte, Siskiyou, and Trinity counties, CA. No grants to individuals (except from donor-designated funds); generally no grants for endowment funds, unspecified emergency purposes, deficit financing, or operating budgets.
Publications: Annual report, application guidelines, informational brochure (including application guidelines).
Application information: Application form required.
Initial approach: Letter or telephone
Copies of proposal: 8
Deadline(s): Feb. 1, May 1, Aug. 1, and Nov. 1

Board meeting date(s): Monthly; applications reviewed quarterly near Jan. 15, Apr. 15, July 15, and Oct. 15
Write: Ellen A. Dusick, Exec. Dir.
Officers and Governors:* Ellen A. Dusick, Exec. Dir.; Dolores Vellutini,* Chair.; Don Albright,* Vice-Chair.; Willis J. Tyson,* Secy.; Sam B. Merryman, Jr., Edward L. Nilsen, John R. Selvage, M. Dale Stanhope, Edythe "Edy" Vaissade.
Trustees: First Interstate Bank, Security Pacific National Bank, Wells Fargo Bank, N.A.
Number of staff: 1 full-time professional; 1 part-time professional; 1 part-time support.
Employer Identification Number: 237310660

432
Jaquelin Hume Foundation
550 Kearny St., Suite 1000
San Francisco 94108 (415) 421-6615

Established in 1962 in CA.
Donor(s): Jaquelin H. Hume, Caroline H. Hume.
Foundation type: Independent
Financial data (yr. ended 12/31/88): Assets, $2,253,840 (M); gifts received, $30,000; expenditures, $211,376, including $194,430 for 68 grants (high: $25,000; low: $30).
Purpose and activities: Support primarily for education, cultural programs, public interest, and civic affairs.
Types of support: Annual campaigns, conferences and seminars, general purposes, operating budgets, special projects.
Limitations: Giving primarily in the San Francisco Bay, CA, area and to organizations with a national impact.
Application information: Application form not required.
Initial approach: Letter
Copies of proposal: 1
Deadline(s): None
Board meeting date(s): Quarterly
Write: Mr. Jaquelin H. Hume, Pres.
Officers and Trustees:* Jaquelin H. Hume,* Pres.; Caroline H. Hume,* Sr. V.P.; George H. Hume,* 1st V.P. and Secy.; William J. Hume,* 2nd V.P. and Treas.; Edward A. Landry, Walter H. Sullivan, Jr.
Number of staff: None.
Employer Identification Number: 946080099

433
Ingraham Memorial Fund ⌘
301 East Colorado Blvd., Suite 900
Pasadena 91101

Established in 1955 in CA.
Foundation type: Independent
Financial data (yr. ended 12/31/88): Assets, $1,187,139 (M); expenditures, $81,201, including $61,425 for 5 grants (high: $49,425; low: $3,000).
Purpose and activities: Supports religious education and higher education.
Types of support: Continuing support, professorships.
Limitations: Giving primarily in Claremont and Pasadena, CA. No grants to individuals.
Application information: Contributes only to pre-selected organizations. Applications not accepted.
Trustee: Emrys J. Ross.
Employer Identification Number: 956017839

434
Audrey & Sydney Irmas Charitable Foundation ⌘
13500 Paxton St.
Pacoima 91331

Established in 1986 in CA.
Foundation type: Independent
Financial data (yr. ended 12/31/87): Assets, $2,800,469 (M); gifts received, $2,275,000; expenditures, $232,680, including $230,490 for 26 grants (high: $115,000; low: $100).
Purpose and activities: Support primarily for a charitable foundation; support also for housing, the arts, and Jewish welfare.
Types of support: General purposes.
Limitations: Giving primarily in Los Angeles, CA.
Application information: Application form not required.
Initial approach: Letter
Deadline(s): None
Write: Sydney Irmas, Mgr.
Employer Identification Number: 954030813

435
The James Irvine Foundation ▼
One Market Plaza
Spear Tower, Suite 1715
San Francisco 94105 (415) 777-2244
Southern CA office: 450 Newport Center Dr., Suite 545, Newport Beach, CA 92660; Tel.: (714) 644-1362

Incorporated in 1937 in CA.
Donor(s): James Irvine.†
Foundation type: Independent
Financial data (yr. ended 12/31/89): Assets, $540,000,000 (M); expenditures, $25,600,000, including $20,487,000 for 273 grants (high: $2,000,000; low: $5,000; average: $25,000-$750,000).
Purpose and activities: Giving for private higher education; health associations and services, including AIDS programs; community social services, including programs for youth and child welfare, drug and alcohol abuse, family planning, housing and homelessness, literacy, and women; and arts and culture, including the fine arts, music, and the performing arts.
Types of support: Seed money, equipment, matching funds, special projects, capital campaigns, renovation projects, technical assistance, program-related investments.
Limitations: Giving limited to CA. No support for primary or secondary schools, agencies receiving substantial government support, films, or sectarian religious activities. No grants to individuals, or for operating budgets, continuing support, annual campaigns, deficit financing, endowment funds, research, scholarships, publications, or conferences; no loans.
Publications: Annual report (including application guidelines), informational brochure (including application guidelines).
Application information: Application form not required.
Initial approach: Letter and/or proposal
Copies of proposal: 1
Deadline(s): Proposals from institutions of higher education are reviewed separately in mid-summer; no other deadlines
Board meeting date(s): Mar., June, Sept., Oct., and Dec.
Final notification: Three to six months
Write: Luz A. Vega, Dir. of Grants Prog.
Officers: Dennis A. Collins, Pres.; Larry R. Fies, Treas. and Corp. Secy.
Directors: Myron Du Bain, Chair.; Samuel H. Armacost, Virginia B. Duncan, Camilla C. Frost, Walter B. Gerken, Roger W. Heyns, Donn B. Miller, Forrest N. Shumway, Kathryn L. Wheeler, Edward Zapanta, M.D.
Number of staff: 9 full-time professional; 1 part-time professional; 6 full-time support; 1 part-time support.
Employer Identification Number: 941236937

436
Irvine Health Foundation
4199 Campus Dr., Suite 550
Irvine 92715 (714) 854-6484

Established in 1985 in CA.
Donor(s): Irvine Medical Center.
Foundation type: Independent
Financial data (yr. ended 06/30/88): Assets, $17,678,871 (M); expenditures, $1,328,557, including $913,441 for 10 grants (high: $300,000; low: $2,500).
Purpose and activities: Emphasis on community health care including support for medical research, research on health care systems and programs, health programs and clinics, including a senior care center and a drug abuse program.
Limitations: Giving limited to Orange County, CA. No support for religious organizations for religious purposes.
Publications: Multi-year report (including application guidelines).
Application information: Application form not required.
Initial approach: Letter
Copies of proposal: 1
Deadline(s): None
Board meeting date(s): Regularly throughout the year
Write: Edward B. Kaie, Exec. Dir.
Officers and Directors:* David G. Sills,* Chair.; Gary H. Hunt,* Secy.; Timothy L. Strader,* Treas.; Edward B. Kaie,* Exec. Dir.; Carol A. Hoffman, John R. Miltner, Gerald B. Sinykin, M.D.
Number of staff: 1 full-time professional; 1 part-time support.
Employer Identification Number: 330141599

437
The William G. Irwin Charity Foundation ▼ ⌘
711 Russ Bldg.
235 Montgomery St.
San Francisco 94104 (415) 362-6954

Trust established in 1919 in CA.
Donor(s): Fannie M. Irwin,† Helene Irwin Fagan.†

Foundation type: Independent
Financial data (yr. ended 12/31/86): Assets, $45,089,029 (M); expenditures, $1,835,134, including $1,465,068 for 30 grants (high: $150,000; low: $7,500; average: $50,000-$150,000).
Purpose and activities: To apply its net income to charitable uses, including medical research and other scientific uses designed to promote or improve the physical condition of mankind; support also for hospitals, cultural programs, education, and social service agencies.
Types of support: Building funds, equipment, general purposes, land acquisition, research.
Limitations: Giving limited to HI and CA.
Application information:
Initial approach: Letter or proposal
Deadline(s): Approximately 3 weeks prior to board meeting
Board meeting date(s): Approximately every 2 months
Write: Michael R. Gorman, Exec. Dir.
Officers: Jane Fagan Olds,* Pres.; Atherton Phleger,* V.P.; Michael R. Gorman, Exec. Dir.
Trustees:* Fred R. Grant, Merl McHenry, William Lee Olds, Jr.
Number of staff: 2 full-time professional.
Employer Identification Number: 946069873

438
The Ishiyama Foundation ⌑
465 California St.
San Francisco 94104 (415) 392-0800

Established in 1968 in CA.
Donor(s): George S. Ishiyama.
Foundation type: Independent
Financial data (yr. ended 12/31/88): Assets, $7,411,655 (M); expenditures, $359,023, including $348,000 for 12 grants (high: $250,000; low: $1,000).
Purpose and activities: Grants to higher and secondary educational institutions in Japan and California.
Types of support: General purposes.
Limitations: Giving primarily in CA and Japan. No grants to individuals.
Application information: Application form not required.
Initial approach: Letter
Deadline(s): None
Final notification: 2 months
Write: George S. Ishiyama, Pres.
Officers and Directors:* George S. Ishiyama,* Pres.; Ralph Bardoff,* V.P.; Joan Ishiyama,* Secy.; Setsuko Ishiyama,* Treas.; Margaret Raffin.
Employer Identification Number: 941659373

439
The Itakura Operating Trust ⌑ ☆
c/o Marie Cannella
135 South Maryland Ave., Suite 201
Glendale 91205

Established in 1982.
Donor(s): Keiichi Itakura.
Foundation type: Operating
Financial data (yr. ended 12/31/88): Assets, $1,163,459 (M); expenditures, $90,465, including $79,500 for 1 grant.
Purpose and activities: A private operating foundation; support for medical research.
Limitations: Giving primarily in Los Angeles, CA.
Trustees: Keiichi Itakura, Yasuko Itakura, Warren F. Ryan.
Employer Identification Number: 953694738

440
Ann Jackson Family Foundation ⌑
P.O. Box 5580
Santa Barbara 93150

Established in 1978.
Donor(s): Ann G. Jackson, The Ann Jackson Family Charitable Trust.
Foundation type: Independent
Financial data (yr. ended 5/31/88): Assets, $8,014,916 (M); gifts received, $1,150,000; expenditures, $1,923,827, including $1,868,900 for 103 grants (high: $500,200; low: $100).
Purpose and activities: Emphasis on secondary education, health, aid to the handicapped, and prevention of cruelty to children and animals.
Types of support: General purposes.
Limitations: Giving primarily in CA. No grants to individuals.
Application information:
Initial approach: Proposal
Deadline(s): None
Write: Palmer G. Jackson, C.F.O.
Officers and Directors:* Flora J. Ramsey,* Pres.; Peter Jackson,* V.P.; Palmer G. Jackson,* C.F.O.
Employer Identification Number: 953367511

441
J. W. and Ida M. Jameson Foundation ⌑
481 West Highland Ave.
P.O. Box 397
Sierra Madre 91024 (818) 355-6973

Incorporated in 1955 in CA.
Donor(s): J.W. Jameson Corp., Ida M. Jameson.†
Foundation type: Independent
Financial data (yr. ended 06/30/89): Assets, $896,368 (M); gifts received, $740,000; expenditures, $742,058, including $727,000 for 62 grants (high: $50,000).
Purpose and activities: Emphasis on higher education, including theological seminaries; hospitals and medical research; cultural programs; and youth agencies; grants also for Protestant church support.
Types of support: Research, general purposes, scholarship funds.
Limitations: Giving primarily in CA.
Application information: Application form not required.
Deadline(s): None
Write: William M. Croxton, V.P.
Officers and Directors:* William M. Croxton,* V.P. and Treas.; Pauline Vetrovec,* Secy.; Bill B. Betz, Fred L. Leydorf, Les M. Huhn,* Pres.
Employer Identification Number: 956031465

442
Elizabeth Bixby Janeway Foundation
2029 Century Park East, Suite 4000
Los Angeles 90067

Established in 1966 in CA.
Donor(s): Elizabeth Bixby Janeway.
Foundation type: Independent
Financial data (yr. ended 9/30/87): Assets, $2,837,271 (M); expenditures, $94,707, including $82,000 for 13 grants (high: $25,000; low: $1,000).
Purpose and activities: Grants primarily for social services, including child welfare, health services, and culture.
Limitations: Giving primarily in southern CA. No grants to individuals.
Application information: Application form not required.
Deadline(s): None
Write: Robert D. Burch, Secy.
Officers and Directors:* Elizabeth Bixby Janeway,* Pres.; Preston B. Hotchkis,* V.P.; Freeman Gates,* 2nd V.P.; Robert D. Burch,* Secy.; R.M. Faletti,* Treas.
Employer Identification Number: 952466561

443
John Percival and Mary C. Jefferson Endowment Fund ⌑
114 East De La Guerra, No. 7
Santa Barbara 93101

Trust established in 1952 in CA.
Donor(s): Mary C. Jefferson.†
Foundation type: Independent
Financial data (yr. ended 3/31/87): Assets, $2,795,714 (M); gifts received, $1,295; expenditures, $158,415, including $21,000 for 3 grants (high: $10,000; low: $1,000; average: $1,000-$3,900) and $71,648 for 31 grants to individuals (high: $7,350; low: $174).
Purpose and activities: Grants mainly to persons of limited means for medical, dental, and living expenses.
Types of support: Grants to individuals.
Limitations: Giving limited to Santa Barbara County, CA.
Application information: Application form required.
Initial approach: Letter
Write: Patricia M. Brouard, Trustee
Trustees: Steven M. Anders, Patricia M. Brouard, Arthur R. Gaudi.
Employer Identification Number: 956005231

444
Jerome Foundation ⌑
4020 Bandini Blvd.
Los Angeles 90023
Application address: 2660 West Woodland Dr., Suite 160, Anaheim, CA 92801; Tel.: (714) 995-1696

Incorporated in 1956 in CA.
Donor(s): Members of the Jerome family, Baker Commodities, Inc., and others.
Foundation type: Independent
Financial data (yr. ended 12/31/88): Assets, $2,770,595 (M); gifts received, $50,000; expenditures, $162,101, including $147,383 for 17 grants (high: $124,533; low: $100).
Purpose and activities: Emphasis on medical research, services for handicapped

children, the blind, hospitals, youth, health agencies, and the Jerome Foundation in the Philippines.
Limitations: Giving primarily in southern CA. No grants to individuals.
Publications: Annual report.
Application information: Application form not required.
Deadline(s): None
Write: Pat Perry
Officers: James M. Andreoli, Pres.; Edward S. Murakami, V.P.; Mitchell Ebright, Secy.-Treas.
Directors: Frank Jerome, Richard Jerome.
Employer Identification Number: 956039063

445
George Frederick Jewett Foundation ▼
One Maritime Plaza, Suite 990
San Francisco 94111 (415) 421-1351

Trust established in 1957 in MA.
Donor(s): George Frederick Jewett.†
Foundation type: Independent
Financial data (yr. ended 12/31/89): Assets, $16,470,748 (M); expenditures, $1,223,297, including $953,597 for 134 grants (high: $25,000; low: $500; average: $1,000-$15,000).
Purpose and activities: To carry on the charitable interests of the donor to stimulate, encourage, and support activities of established, voluntary, nonprofit organizations which are of importance to human welfare. Interests include social welfare; arts and humanities, including the performing arts; conservation of natural resources; higher education; population planning; health care and medical research and services; religion and religious training; and public affairs.
Types of support: General purposes, building funds, equipment, land acquisition, research, matching funds, special projects, operating budgets, seed money, technical assistance.
Limitations: Giving primarily in the Pacific Northwest, with emphasis on northern ID and eastern WA, particularly Spokane, and in San Francisco, CA. No grants to individuals, or for scholarships or fellowships; no loans. No emergency grants, except for disaster relief.
Publications: Annual report (including application guidelines).
Application information: Application form not required.
Initial approach: Letter
Copies of proposal: 1
Deadline(s): Feb. 15, May 15, Aug. 15, and Nov. 1
Board meeting date(s): Mar., June, Sept., and Dec. (for annual distributions)
Final notification: Annually, at the end of the year
Write: Theresa A. Mullen, Prog. Dir.
Officers and Trustees:* George F. Jewett, Jr.,* Chair.; Mary Jewett Gaiser,* Secy.; Margaret Jewett Greer, William Hershey Greer, Jr., Lucille McIntyre Jewett.
Number of staff: 1 full-time professional; 1 full-time support.
Employer Identification Number: 046013832

446
Walter S. Johnson Foundation ▼
525 Middlefield Rd., Suite 110
Menlo Park 94025 (415) 326-0485

Established in 1968 in CA.
Donor(s): Walter S. Johnson.†
Foundation type: Independent
Financial data (yr. ended 12/31/88): Assets, $44,894,000 (M); expenditures, $2,405,283, including $2,131,619 for 25 grants (high: $186,710; low: $8,000; average: $30,000-$60,000) and $100,000 for loans.
Purpose and activities: Giving primarily for public schools and social service agencies concerned with the quality of public education and the social family experiences of children between kindergarten and twelfth grade.
Types of support: Operating budgets, seed money, special projects, research, technical assistance, general purposes.
Limitations: Giving primarily in Alameda, Contra Costa, San Francisco, San Mateo, and Santa Clara counties in CA, and in Washoe County, NV. No support for religious organizations for sectarian purposes, or for private schools. No grants to individuals, or for continuing support, annual campaigns, deficit financing, memorial funds, capital or endowment funds, matching gifts, scholarships, fellowships, publications, or conferences; no loans.
Publications: Annual report.
Application information: Application form not required.
Initial approach: Telephone or letter
Copies of proposal: 4
Deadline(s): Submit proposal 12 weeks before board meeting
Board meeting date(s): Mar., May, July, and Oct.
Final notification: 2 to 4 months
Write: Donna Terman, Exec. Dir.
Officers: Gloria Eddie,* Pres.; Sandra Bruckner,* Secy.; Elio L. Martin, Treas.; Donna Terman, Exec. Dir.
Trustees:* Gloria Jeneal Eddie, Christopher Johnson, Mary Lanigar, Hathily J. Winston.
Number of staff: 1 full-time professional; 1 part-time professional; 1 full-time support.
Employer Identification Number: 237003595

447
The Fletcher Jones Foundation ▼
(Formerly The Jones Foundation)
One Wilshire Bldg., Suite 1210
624 South Grand Ave.
Los Angeles 90017 (213) 689-9292

Established in 1969 in CA.
Donor(s): Fletcher Jones.†
Foundation type: Independent
Financial data (yr. ended 12/31/89): Assets, $88,000,000 (M); expenditures, $4,603,345, including $4,051,076 for 47 grants (high: $1,350,000; low: $5,000; average: $5,000-$100,000).
Purpose and activities: Support primarily for private higher educational institutions; grants also for cultural programs, social services, health and hospitals, and organizations promoting law and justice and citizenship.
Types of support: Seed money, building funds, equipment, professorships, special projects, endowment funds, scholarship funds, renovation projects.
Limitations: Giving primarily in CA. No support for secondary schools. No grants to individuals, or for operating funds, deficit financing, conferences, travel exhibits, surveys, or projects supported by government agencies.
Publications: Annual report (including application guidelines).
Application information: Application form not required.
Initial approach: Letter
Copies of proposal: 1
Deadline(s): One month prior to board meetings
Board meeting date(s): Mar., May, Sept., and Nov.
Final notification: 3 to 6 months
Write: John W. Smythe, Exec. Dir.
Officers: John P. Pollock,* Pres.; Houston Flournoy,* V.P.; Jess C. Wilson, Jr.,* V.P.; Jack Pettker, Secy.; John W. Smythe, Treas. and Exec. Dir.
Trustees:* Robert F. Erburu, Chauncey J. Medberry III, Rudy J. Munzer, Donald E. Nickelson, Dickinson C. Ross.
Number of staff: 1 part-time professional; 1 part-time support.
Employer Identification Number: 237030155

448
Marcellus L. Joslyn Foundation
12857 Camino Emparrado
San Diego 92128 (714) 485-7938

Trust established in 1960 in CA.
Donor(s): Marcellus L. Joslyn.†
Foundation type: Independent
Financial data (yr. ended 09/30/89): Assets, $6,283,719 (M); expenditures, $425,195, including $355,490 for 28 grants (high: $54,000; low: $2,000).
Purpose and activities: Support for hospitals, higher education, and senior citizens centers.
Types of support: Scholarship funds, continuing support, operating budgets.
Limitations: Giving primarily in southern CA.
Publications: Informational brochure.
Application information: Funds presently committed. Future support for maintaining previous recipients. Applications not accepted.
Board meeting date(s): Semiannually in Apr. and Oct.
Write: Remy L. Hudson, Chair.
Trustees: Remy L. Hudson, Chair.; John MacIntosh, Jean Mill.
Number of staff: None.
Employer Identification Number: 952276744

449
Felix & Helen Juda Foundation ⌑
3510 Torrance Blvd., Suite 100
Torrance 90503-5802

Established in 1951 in CA.
Donor(s): Felix M. Juda, Helen Juda.
Foundation type: Independent
Financial data (yr. ended 11/30/89): Assets, $1,257,294 (M); expenditures, $148,223, including $134,650 for 18 grants (high: $47,050; low: $500).

Purpose and activities: Emphasis on cultural programs, social services, and higher education; some support for hospitals.
Types of support: General purposes.
Trustees: Felix M. Juda, Helen Juda, Tom Juda, Patsy Palmer.
Employer Identification Number: 956048035

450
The Henry J. Kaiser Family Foundation ▼
Quadrus
2400 Sand Hill Rd.
Menlo Park 94025 (415) 854-9400

Trust established in 1948 in CA.
Donor(s): Bess F. Kaiser,† Henry J. Kaiser,† Henry J. Kaiser, Jr.,† and others.
Foundation type: Independent
Financial data (yr. ended 12/31/89): Assets, $408,513,703 (M); expenditures, $20,248,860, including $12,733,633 for grants (average: $155,476) and $112,681 for employee matching gifts.
Purpose and activities: Major share of resources devoted to programs in health and medicine.
Types of support: Special projects, research, seed money, fellowships, professorships, scholarship funds, conferences and seminars, publications, matching funds, technical assistance.
Limitations: Giving limited to the San Francisco Bay Area, CA, for the Community Grants Program only; other grants nationwide. No grants to individuals, or for construction, equipment, or capital funds.
Publications: Annual report, informational brochure (including application guidelines).
Application information: For Community Health Promotion Grants Program, contact foundation for brochure. Application form not required.
Initial approach: Letter
Copies of proposal: 3
Deadline(s): None
Board meeting date(s): Mar., July, and Nov.
Final notification: 3 to 6 months
Write: Karen P. Sparks, Proposal and Grants Mgr.
Officers: Alvin R. Tarlov, M.D.,* Pres.; Hugh C. Burroughs, V.P.; Lawrence W. Green, V.P.; Barbara H. Kehrer, V.P.; Sol Levine, V.P.; Bruce W. Madding, V.P.
Trustees:* Hale Champion, Chair.; Joseph A. Califano, Jr., Richard P. Cooley, Daniel J. Evans, Daniel J. Evans, Barbara C. Jordan, Henry M. Kaiser, Kim J. Kaiser, Edwin H. Morgens, June E. Osborn, M.D., Richard Ravitch.
Number of staff: 20 full-time professional; 13 full-time support; 3 part-time support.
Employer Identification Number: 946064808

451
Alice & Julius Kantor Charitable Trust
809 North Bedford Dr.
Beverly Hills 90210 (213) 550-6778

Established in 1977 in CA.
Foundation type: Independent
Financial data (yr. ended 12/31/87): Assets, $1,404,472 (M); expenditures, $72,131, including $52,060 for 20 grants (high: $6,000; low: $200).
Purpose and activities: Giving primarily for medical research, education, and community funds and programs.
Limitations: Giving primarily in the Los Angeles, CA, area.
Application information:
Initial approach: Letter
Deadline(s): Oct. 31
Write: Arnold Seidel, Trustee
Trustee: Arnold Seidel.
Employer Identification Number: 953218378

452
Richard and Elizabeth Kasper Foundation ⌑ ☆
2625 West Alameda, No. 208
Burbank 91505

Established in 1987.
Donor(s): Richard L. Kasper, Elizabeth H. Kasper.
Foundation type: Independent
Financial data (yr. ended 12/31/88): Assets, $90,668 (M); gifts received, $79,000; expenditures, $105,432, including $103,700 for 26 grants (high: $25,000; low: $200).
Purpose and activities: Giving primarily for Christian churches, associations, and missionary programs; support also for Armenian-related organizations and health services and medical sciences.
Limitations: No grants to individuals.
Application information: Contributes only to pre-selected organizations. Applications not accepted.
Trustees: Elizabeth H. Kasper, Richard L. Kasper.
Employer Identification Number: 330265820

453
Kawaguchi-Kihara Memorial Foundation ☆
1324-1327 East 15th St.
Los Angeles 90021

Established in 1979 in CA.
Donor(s): Fishking Processors, Inc.
Foundation type: Independent
Financial data (yr. ended 03/31/89): Assets, $31,181 (M); gifts received, $200,000; expenditures, $172,092, including $168,000 for 36 grants (high: $50,000; low: $1,000).
Purpose and activities: Support for Japanese organizations, including Buddhist churches, education, culture, and human services.
Limitations: Giving primarily in CA. No grants to individuals.
Application information: Application form not required.
Deadline(s): Apr. 1
Write: Mrs. Mitsuko Kawaguchi, Pres.
Officers: Mitsuko Kawaguchi, Pres.; Koichi Kihara, V.P.; Gary Kawaguchi, Secy.; Kivoshi Kawaguchi, Treas.
Number of staff: 1 part-time professional; 1 part-time support.
Employer Identification Number: 953397616

454
Danny Kaye and Sylvia Fine Kaye Foundation ⌑
c/o Manny Flekman & Co.
9171 Wilshire Blvd., No. 530
Beverly Hills 90210

Established in 1983 in CA.
Donor(s): Danny Kaye,† Sylvia Fine Kaye.
Foundation type: Independent
Financial data (yr. ended 12/31/88): Assets, $1,157,099 (M); gifts received, $300,000; expenditures, $62,133, including $52,450 for 13 grants (high: $25,000; low: $250).
Purpose and activities: Giving primarily for culture, with emphasis on the performing arts.
Limitations: Giving primarily in CA and NY.
Application information: Contributes only to pre-selected organizations. Applications not accepted.
Officer and Directors:* Sylvia Fine Kaye,* Pres.; Dena Kaye.
Employer Identification Number: 953864096

455
W. M. Keck Foundation ▼
555 South Flower St., Suite 3230
Los Angeles 90071 (213) 680-3833

Established in 1954 and incorporated in 1959 in DE; sole beneficiary of W.M. Keck Trust.
Donor(s): William M. Keck.†
Foundation type: Independent
Financial data (yr. ended 12/31/89): Assets, $764,433,113 (M); expenditures, $37,996,122, including $35,286,000 for 58 grants (high: $2,500,000; low: $50,000; average: $50,000-$519,000).
Purpose and activities: To strengthen studies and programs in educational institutions of higher learning in the areas of earth science, engineering, general science, medical education and research, and liberal arts. Eligible institutions in these fields are accredited colleges and universities, medical schools, and major independent medical researcth institutions. Some consideration, limited to southern CA, given to organizations and institutions in health care and hospitals, arts and culture, civic and community services, and primary and secondary education.
Types of support: Building funds, seed money, equipment, special projects, research, renovation projects, fellowships, scholarship funds, endowment funds.
Limitations: Giving primarily in southern CA in all categories except higher education, and medical research. No support for conduit organizations. No grants to individuals, or for routine expenses, general endowments, deficit reduction, fundraising events, dinners, mass mailings, conferences, seminars, publications, films, or public policy research.
Publications: Annual report (including application guidelines), informational brochure (including application guidelines).
Application information: Foundation selects applicant institutions to submit a complete proposal. Application form required.
Initial approach: Letter
Copies of proposal: 1
Deadline(s): Mar. 15 and Sept. 15 for complete proposal; initial letters accepted year-round

Board meeting date(s): June and Dec.
Final notification: June and Dec.
Write: Sandra A. Glass for sciences, engineering, and liberal arts, Joan DuBois for medical research, medical education, and Southern California program (arts/culture; civic/community affairs; health care/hospitals; pre-collegiate education)

Officers and Directors:* Howard B. Keck,* Chair., Pres., and C.E.O.; Gregory R. Ryan, V.P. and Secy.; Robert A. Day, Jr.,* V.P.; Walter B. Gerken,* V.P.; W.M. Keck II,* V.P.; Julian O. von Kalinowski,* V.P.; Dorothy A. Harris, Treas.; Norman Barker, Jr., Marsh A. Cooper, Naurice G. Cummings, Howard M. Day, Tammis M. Day, Theodore J. Day, Bob Rawls Dorsey, Thomas P. Ford, Erin A. Keck, Howard B. Keck, Jr., John E. Kolb, Max R. Lents, James Paul Lower, Simon Ramo, Arthur M. Smith, Jr., David A. Thomas, Kerry C. Vaughan, C. William Verity, Jr., Thomas R. Wilcox.
Number of staff: 12
Employer Identification Number: 956092354

456
William M. Keck, Jr. Foundation ⌑
2049 Century Park East, Suite 2500
Los Angeles 90067 (213) 680-3833

Incorporated in 1958 in DE.
Donor(s): William M. Keck, Jr.
Foundation type: Independent
Financial data (yr. ended 12/31/88): Assets, $11,741,273 (M); gifts received, $175,000; expenditures, $720,104, including $600,000 for 13 grants (high: $112,500; low: $10,000).
Purpose and activities: Emphasis on higher and secondary education, hospitals, cultural programs and church support.
Application information: Contributes only to pre-selected organizations. Applications not accepted.
Officers and Directors:* William M. Keck II,* Pres.; Robert E. Westlund,* V.P. and Secy.; V. Thomas Dock,* V.P.; Marie E. Keck,* V.P.; Arthur Logan,* Treas.
Employer Identification Number: 136097874

457
Harry M. Keller Foundation ⌑ ☆
101 South First St., Suite 402
Burbank 91502-1975

Foundation type: Independent
Financial data (yr. ended 12/31/88): Assets, $1,043,820 (L); expenditures, $57,000, including $57,000 for grants to individuals.
Purpose and activities: Awards scholarships and student loans for individuals attending three specified institutions of higher education.
Types of support: Student aid, student loans.
Application information: Application form required.
Deadline(s): Nov. 30
Officers: George W. Humphries, Pres.; Hamer L. Martin, V.P.; Janice Clair Croft, Secy.; Richard C. Manning, Treas.
Employer Identification Number: 956114924

458
The Thomas and Miriam Kendall Foundation ⌑ ☆
141 Emerald Bay
Laguna Beach 92651 (714) 494-7031

Established in 1986.
Donor(s): Thomas W. Kendall, Miriam A. Kendall.
Foundation type: Independent
Financial data (yr. ended 11/30/88): Assets, $1,072,847 (M); expenditures, $38,754, including $37,589 for 7 grants (high: $19,035; low: $630).
Purpose and activities: Giving primarily for higher education.
Types of support: General purposes.
Limitations: Giving primarily in CA.
Application information:
Deadline(s): None
Write: Thomas Kendall, Pres.
Officers: Thomas W. Kendall, Pres.; Miriam A. Kendall, C.F.O.
Trustees: Susan K. Maass, Mark Van Maurick.
Employer Identification Number: 330291184

459
A. H. Kerr Foundation
16661 Ventura Blvd., Suite 826
Encino 91436 (818) 990-2831

Incorporated in 1945 in CA.
Donor(s): Ruth Kerr.†
Foundation type: Independent
Financial data (yr. ended 12/31/88): Assets, $8,450,099 (M); expenditures, $428,902, including $248,938 for 39 grants (high: $83,820; low: $500; average: $1,000-$3,000).
Purpose and activities: Giving primarily for higher education in California and for church support and religious associations, including foreign missions. Support also for hospitals, health agencies, and social services.
Types of support: Operating budgets, continuing support, annual campaigns, emergency funds, building funds, equipment, land acquisition, publications, special projects, capital campaigns.
Limitations: No grants to individuals, or for seed money, deficit financing, or demonstration projects; no loans.
Publications: Program policy statement, application guidelines.
Application information: Application form not required.
Initial approach: Proposal
Copies of proposal: 1
Deadline(s): None
Board meeting date(s): Apr. and Oct.
Final notification: Several months to 2 years
Write: William A. Kerr, V.P.
Officers and Directors:* Alexander H. Kerr, Jr.,* Pres.; William A. Kerr,* V.P. and Treas.; Ruth K. O'Dell,* Secy.
Number of staff: None.
Employer Identification Number: 956085982

460
The Sol and Clara Kest Family Foundation ⌑ ☆
5150 Overland Ave.
Culver City 90230 (213) 204-2050

Established in 1987 in CA.
Donor(s): Clara Kest, Sol Kest, Jona Goldrich, Doretta Goldrich, Michael Kest.
Foundation type: Independent
Financial data (yr. ended 11/30/89): Assets, $58,660 (M); gifts received, $2,100,000; expenditures, $2,155,929, including $2,152,000 for 11 grants (high: $1,000,000; low: $1,000).
Purpose and activities: Support primarily for Jewish organizations, including educational institutions and temples.
Limitations: No grants to individuals.
Application information:
Initial approach: Letter
Deadline(s): None
Write: Sol Kest, Pres.
Officers and Directors:* Sol Kest,* Pres.; Clara Kest,* Secy.; Michael Kest,* C.F.O.; Freada Berkowitz, Benjamin Kest, Ezra Kest.
Employer Identification Number: 954109864

461
Lewis A. Kingsley Foundation ⌑
12365 Lewis St., Suite 201
Garden Grove 92640

Established in 1963 in CA.
Foundation type: Independent
Financial data (yr. ended 5/31/88): Assets, $4,549,237 (M); expenditures, $348,187, including $272,150 for 43 grants (high: $51,000; low: $250).
Purpose and activities: Giving primarily for higher and secondary education.
Types of support: Scholarship funds.
Limitations: Giving primarily in the Los Angeles, CA, area.
Application information: Contributes only to pre-selected organizations. Applications not accepted.
Officers: Michael Polito, Pres.; David R. Streiff, V.P.; Frank J. Cordon, Secy.
Employer Identification Number: 956092364

462
The Karl Kirchgessner Foundation ⌑
1900 Ave. of the Stars, Suite 2100
Los Angeles 90067 (213) 553-3610

Established in 1977 in CA.
Donor(s): Karl Kramer,† Nina Kramer.†
Foundation type: Independent
Financial data (yr. ended 6/30/88): Assets, $8,824,985 (M); gifts received, $463,179; expenditures, $741,756, including $593,524 for 15 grants (high: $176,162; low: $5,000; average: $10,000-$50,000).
Purpose and activities: "For the advancement of medical research and for the provision of medical and clinical services to disadvantaged persons, particularly the elderly, the young and handicapped." Applicants should be involved with research and/or clinical programs connected with eyesight, eye care, or helping the blind and partially-sighted to be more self-sufficient.
Types of support: Research, continuing support, endowment funds, equipment, general purposes, matching funds, operating budgets, professorships, publications, scholarship funds, seed money, special projects, technical assistance.

Limitations: Giving limited to the southern CA area; geographical restriction may be broadened in the future. No grants to individuals, or for fund-raising campaigns.
Publications: Informational brochure, application guidelines.
Application information: Application form not required.
Initial approach: Brief proposal
Copies of proposal: 1
Deadline(s): Jan. 1 for preliminary applications
Board meeting date(s): Grants made once a year, generally on or about June 30
Final notification: Before June 30
Write: Martin H. Webster, Pres.
Officers and Directors:* Martin H. Webster,* Pres.; Amelia Louise Mills,* V.P.; Lewis Whitney,* Secy.; Karl Kramer, Jr., C.F.O.; Rev. Patrick Cahalan.
Number of staff: 2 part-time professional; 1 part-time support.
Employer Identification Number: 953439716

463
Joseph B. Kirshbaum Family Foundation ⌑
P.O. Box 3000
Encino 91316

Established in 1967 in CA.
Foundation type: Independent
Financial data (yr. ended 12/31/87): Assets, $631,110 (M); expenditures, $129,399, including $120,674 for 17 grants (high: $50,000; low: $25).
Purpose and activities: Giving primarily for general charitable organizations, Jewish concerns, medical research, and higher education.
Application information: Contributes only to pre-selected organizations. Applications not accepted.
Officers: Joseph B. Kirshbaum, Pres.; Jacqueline Kirshbaum, V.P.; Ira Kirshbaum, Secy.; Jeffrey D. Kirshbaum, Treas.
Employer Identification Number: 952501233

464
The Tom and Valley Knudsen Foundation
900 Wilshire Blvd., No. 1424
Los Angeles 90017 (213) 614-1940

Incorporated in 1951 in CA.
Donor(s): Th. R. Knudsen,† Valley M. Knudsen.†
Foundation type: Independent
Financial data (yr. ended 12/31/89): Assets, $3,732,565 (M); gifts received, $131,767; expenditures, $746,751, including $672,088 for 28 grants (high: $100,000; low: $1,000; average: $5,000).
Purpose and activities: Emphasis on private higher educational institutions; grants also for cultural institutions.
Types of support: General purposes, annual campaigns.
Limitations: Giving limited to southern CA. No grants to individuals, or for matching gifts, capital or endowment funds, scholarships, fellowships, research, or special projects; no loans.
Publications: Program policy statement, application guidelines.
Application information: Application form not required.
Initial approach: Proposal
Copies of proposal: 1
Deadline(s): Mar. 1 and Sept. 1
Board meeting date(s): Apr. and Oct.
Final notification: 2 months
Write: Helen B. McGrath, Exec. V.P.
Officers and Directors:* J.R. Vaughan,* Pres.; Helen B. McGrath,* Exec. V.P. and Secy.-Treas.; Peter O'Malley,* 1st V.P.; Christian Castenskiold, William W. Escherich, Gene Knudsen Hoffman, Doris Holtz, Robert E. Osborne, Harold Skou.
Number of staff: None.
Employer Identification Number: 956031188

465
Allen D. Kohl Charitable Foundation, Inc. ⌑
450 North Roxbury Dr., Suite 600
Beverly Hills 90210

Incorporated in 1972 in WI.
Donor(s): Allen D. Kohl.
Foundation type: Independent
Financial data (yr. ended 12/31/88): Assets, $6,078,634 (M); gifts received, $59,000; expenditures, $445,088, including $309,050 for 17 grants (high: $100,000; low: $100).
Purpose and activities: Grants for charitable causes of interest to the directors, including support for local Jewish welfare agencies.
Limitations: No grants to individuals.
Application information: Contributes only to pre-selected organizations. Applications not accepted.
Officers and Directors:* Allen D. Kohl,* Pres.; Bonnie A. Kohl,* V.P.; Thomas F. Bickelhaupt,* Secy.-Treas.; Mary Kohl.
Employer Identification Number: 237211587

466
Komes Foundation
1801 Van Ness Ave., Suite 300
San Francisco 94109 (415) 441-6462

Established in 1965 in CA.
Donor(s): Jerome W. Komes, Flora Komes.
Foundation type: Independent
Financial data (yr. ended 12/31/89): Assets, $2,667,000 (M); expenditures, $206,075, including $189,605 for 79 grants (high: $25,000; low: $250; average: $2,394).
Purpose and activities: Emphasis on hospitals and health agencies, higher and other education, cultural programs, the aged, youth agencies, Christian giving and welfare organizations, and law and justice.
Types of support: Building funds, capital campaigns, continuing support, endowment funds, general purposes, operating budgets, program-related investments, research, seed money, annual campaigns, scholarship funds.
Limitations: Giving primarily in northern CA. No support for literary publications. No grants to individuals, or for budget deficits, conferences, or travel.
Publications: Annual report (including application guidelines), occasional report, informational brochure (including application guidelines).
Application information: Application form not required.
Initial approach: Letter
Copies of proposal: 1
Deadline(s): None
Write: J.W. Komes, Pres.
Officers: Jerome W. Komes, Pres.; Flora Komes, V.P.; Michael L. Mellor, Secy.
Employer Identification Number: 941611406

467
Koret Foundation ▼
33 New Montgomery St., Suite 1090
San Francisco 94105 (415) 882-7740

Established in 1966 in CA.
Donor(s): Joseph Koret,† Stephanie Koret.†
Foundation type: Independent
Financial data (yr. ended 12/31/89): Assets, $186,660,915 (M); qualifying distributions, $11,193,429, including $11,012,929 for 317 grants (high: $640,000; low: $1,000) and $180,500 for 1 in-kind gift.
Purpose and activities: To promote the well-being of the general and Jewish communities of the San Francisco Bay Area and to assist the people of Israel through special projects.
Types of support: Operating budgets, continuing support, special projects, building funds, general purposes, consulting services, renovation projects, seed money.
Limitations: Giving limited to the Bay Area counties of San Francisco, Alameda, Contra Costa, Marin, Santa Clara, and San Mateo, CA, and Israel. No support for veterans', fraternal, military, religious, or sectarian organizations whose principal activity is for the benefit of their own membership. No grants to individuals, or for general fundraising campaigns, endowment funds, equipment funds, deficit financing, or emergency funds; no loans.
Publications: Application guidelines, annual report (including application guidelines).
Application information: Consult guidelines for application deadlines. Application form required.
Initial approach: Letter of inquiry
Copies of proposal: 1
Board meeting date(s): 5 times per year
Final notification: 3 months
Officers: Eugene L. Friend,* Pres.; Stephen Dobbs, C.E.O. and Exec. Dir.; Jack R. Curley, Treas.
Directors:* Susan Koret, Chair.; Richard Blum, William K. Coblentz, Richard L. Greene, Stanley Herzstein, Bernard A. Osher, Melvin M. Swig, Thaddeus N. Taube.
Number of staff: 7 full-time professional; 6 full-time support.
Employer Identification Number: 941624987

468
The Koshland Foundation ⌑
3991 Happy Valley Rd.
Lafayette 94549

Established in 1985 in CA.
Donor(s): Marian E. Koshland.
Foundation type: Independent

Financial data (yr. ended 7/31/87): Assets, $1,034,650 (M); expenditures, $96,631, including $74,623 for 4 grants (high: $50,000; low: $2,000).
Purpose and activities: Giving primarily for social service organizations and education.
Application information:
Initial approach: Letter
Deadline(s): None
Write: James M. Koshland, Secy.
Officers: Marian E. Koshland, Pres.; Daniel E. Koshland, Jr., V.P.; Gail F. Koshland, V.P.; James M. Koshland, Secy.-Treas.
Employer Identification Number: 680069874

469
The Trustees of Ivan V. Koulaieff Educational Fund ⌑
651 11th Ave.
San Francisco 94118
Application address: 651 11th Ave., San Francisco, CA 94118

Incorporated in 1930 in CA.
Donor(s): Ivan V. Koulaieff.
Foundation type: Independent
Financial data (yr. ended 12/31/88): Assets, $8,149,380 (M); expenditures, $482,327, including $178,160 for 55 grants (high: $24,000; low: $220) and $166,170 for 29 grants to individuals (high: $33,400; low: $400).
Purpose and activities: Aid to Russian immigrants throughout the world through grants, scholarships, and loans; support also for Russian Orthodox education and churches in the U.S.
Types of support: Student aid, loans, grants to individuals.
Application information:
Write: W.W. Granitow, Secy.
Officers and Directors:* C. Parshooto,* Pres.; W.W. Granitow,* Secy.; A.D. Psiol,* Treas.; R.A. Folkert, Mrs. O.P. Hughes, N.A. Kaliakin, B.J. Koulaieff.
Employer Identification Number: 946088762

470
L.L.W.W. Foundation ⌑
1260 Huntington Dr., Suite 204
South Pasadena 91030-4561 (213) 259-0484

Established in 1980 in CA.
Donor(s): Laura-Lee Whittier Woods.
Foundation type: Independent
Financial data (yr. ended 12/31/87): Assets, $9,086,677 (M); gifts received, $187,968; expenditures, $634,915, including $530,015 for 61 grants (high: $100,000; low: $50).
Purpose and activities: Emphasis on the arts, including museums; giving also for education and social services.
Limitations: Giving primarily in southern CA.
Application information: Contributes only to pre-selected organizations. Applications not accepted.
Write: Linda J. Blinkenberg, Secy.
Officers: Laura-Lee Whittier Woods, Pres.; Arlo G. Sorensen, V.P.; Linda J. Blinkenberg, Secy.; Robert D. Sellers, C.F.O.
Employer Identification Number: 953464689

471
Walter & Francine Laband Foundation ⌑ ☆
3311 East Cameron Ave.
West Covina 91791

Established in 1961.
Foundation type: Independent
Financial data (yr. ended 9/30/88): Assets, $22,107 (M); gifts received, $118,904; expenditures, $123,260, including $122,745 for 64 grants (high: $50,000; low: $10).
Purpose and activities: Giving primarily to Catholic social service and religious organizations; support also for hospitals.
Limitations: Giving primarily in CA.
Application information: Contributes only to pre-selected organizations. Applications not accepted.
Officers: Walter H. Laband, Pres.; Francine Laband, V.P. and Secy.
Employer Identification Number: 956050923

472
Lakeside Foundation ⌑
50 Fremont St., Suite 3825
San Francisco 94105 (415) 768-6022

Incorporated in 1953 in CA.
Donor(s): S.D. Bechtel, Mrs. S.D. Bechtel, S.D. Bechtel, Jr., Mrs. Paul L. Davies, Jr., Bechtel Corp.
Foundation type: Independent
Financial data (yr. ended 12/31/86): Assets, $6,520,167 (M); gifts received, $78,765; expenditures, $238,702, including $211,100 for 63 grants (high: $77,500; low: $250).
Purpose and activities: Emphasis on health care, higher education, including international studies, and cultural programs; support also for religious, scientific, and literary purposes, a community fund, and youth agencies.
Types of support: General purposes, operating budgets, continuing support, building funds.
Limitations: Giving primarily in the San Francisco Bay Area, CA. No grants to individuals, or for endowment funds, scholarships, fellowships, or matching gifts; no loans.
Application information: Contributes only to pre-selected organizations. Applications not accepted.
Board meeting date(s): Annually, usually in the spring
Write: Barbara B. Davies, Pres.
Officers: Barbara B. Davies,* Pres.; D.A. Ruhl, V.P. and Treas.; Laura P. Bechtel,* V.P.; Marlies A. Carver, Secy.
Directors:* S.D. Bechtel, Paul L. Davies, Jr., Paul Lewis Davies III, A. Barlow Ferguson, Laura Davies Mateo.
Number of staff: None.
Employer Identification Number: 946066229

473
Lane Family Charitable Trust ⌑ ☆
500 Almer Rd., No. 301
Burlingame 94010

Established in 1985 in CA.
Donor(s): Joan Lane, Ralph Lane.
Foundation type: Independent
Financial data (yr. ended 6/30/89): Assets, $1,241,070 (M); gifts received, $132,727; expenditures, $120,786, including $108,500 for 14 grants (high: $25,000; low: $1,000).
Purpose and activities: Support primarily for secondary, higher, and other education and a community foundation.
Types of support: General purposes.
Limitations: No grants to individuals.
Application information:
Initial approach: Letter
Deadline(s): None
Write: Ralph Lane and Joan Lane, Trustees
Trustees: Joan Lane, Ralph Lane.
Employer Identification Number: 946585396

474
Stanley S. Langendorf Foundation
c/o Pat Grier & Associates
1674 University Ave.
Berkeley 94703 (415) 649-1300

Established in 1982 in CA.
Donor(s): Stanley S. Langendorf.†
Foundation type: Independent
Financial data (yr. ended 12/31/88): Assets, $9,118,403 (M); gifts received, $1,814,966; expenditures, $552,290, including $450,522 for 27 grants (high: $100,000; low: $2,500).
Purpose and activities: Annual grants for eight specified beneficiaries; additional support for education, youth, social service agencies, and Jewish giving.
Limitations: Giving primarily in CA. No grants to individuals.
Publications: Application guidelines, 990-PF.
Application information: Application form not required.
Initial approach: Letter
Copies of proposal: 1
Deadline(s): None
Write: Patricia Grier, Mgr.
Officers and Trustees:* Richard J. Guggenhime,* Pres.; Ann Wagner,* Secy.; Charles H. Clifford,* C.F.O.; Patricia Grier,* Mgr.
Employer Identification Number: 942861512

475
Lannan Foundation
5401 McConnell Ave.
Los Angeles 90066 (213) 306-1004

Established in 1960 in IL.
Donor(s): J. Patrick Lannan.†
Foundation type: Operating
Financial data (yr. ended 12/31/88): Assets, $116,951,285 (M); expenditures, $4,820,622, including $1,372,029 for 77 grants (high: $900,000; low: $250) and $1,491,035 for foundation-administered programs.
Purpose and activities: A private foundation with grant programs to support the visual and literary arts. The visual arts program has developed 4 programs: grants for varied programs and activities in contemporary art, exhibition and interpretation of the Lannan Foundation collection, and fostering serious scholarship and criticism in contemporary art. The foundation also operates a public gallery. The literary arts program fosters the creation of prose and poetry through grants and projects designed to recognize excellence in English language literature, to widen the audience for serious literature. The foundation makes a

limited number of grants to miscellaneous charitable causes.
Limitations: No grants to individuals.
Publications: Program policy statement.
Application information: Contributes only to pre-selected organizations for its charitable giving program; literary arts program is by invitation only; 5 copies of proposal needed for visual arts program. Application form required.
Initial approach: For visual arts program, telephone or letter
Deadline(s): For visual arts, Feb. 1, May 1, and Oct. 1; none for literary arts
Officers: J. Patrick Lannan, Jr., Pres.; Sharon Ferrill,* 1st V.P.; John R. Lannan, V.P. and Treas.; Barbara A. Dalderis, V.P., Finance and Administration; Frank Lawler,* Secy.
Directors:* Tsheng S. Feng, John J. Lannan, Lawrence Lannan, Jr., Patricia Lawler, Mary M. Plauche.
Number of staff: 12
Employer Identification Number: 366062451

476
Laural Foundation ⌑
P.O. Box 3809
San Francisco 94119-3809

Established in 1977 in CA.
Foundation type: Independent
Financial data (yr. ended 12/31/88): Assets, $1,455,748 (M); expenditures, $46,338, including $44,310 for 15 grants (high: $25,000; low: $100).
Purpose and activities: Giving primarily for education and culture.
Limitations: Giving primarily in San Francisco and Oakland, CA.
Application information: Contributes only to pre-selected organizations. Applications not accepted.
Officers and Directors:* Lauren B. Dachs,* Pres.; Alan M. Dachs,* V.P.; A. Barlow Ferguson,* Secy.; Theodore J. Van Bebber, Treas.
Employer Identification Number: 942417772

477
Layne Foundation
19 Rue Cannes
Newport Beach 92660 (714) 644-6438
Additional tel.: (714) 644-4059

Incorporated in 1927 in CA.
Foundation type: Independent
Financial data (yr. ended 12/31/89): Assets, $6,380,000 (L); qualifying distributions, $1,297,000, including $1,297,000 for 7 loans.
Purpose and activities: Assistance limited to current interest loans given to Christian churches and religious organizations, principally for capital purposes and to those churches ineligible for loans from other sources.
Types of support: Program-related investments, loans.
Limitations: Giving limited to southern CA. No grants to individuals, or for operating budgets, building or endowment funds (except for loans for churches only), scholarships or fellowships, or matching gifts.
Publications: Informational brochure.
Application information: Application form required.
Initial approach: Letter
Copies of proposal: 1
Deadline(s): None
Board meeting date(s): Nov.
Write: Robert H. Mason, Pres.
Officers and Directors:* Robert H. Mason,* Pres.; Harold L. Semans,* V.P.; Wesley M. Mason,* Secy.-Treas.; James W. Hamilton, Larry T. Smith.
Number of staff: 1 part-time professional.
Employer Identification Number: 951765157

478
The Norman Lear Foundation
1800 Century Park East, Suite 200
Los Angeles 90067 (213) 553-3636

Established in 1986 in CA.
Donor(s): Norman Lear.
Foundation type: Independent
Financial data (yr. ended 11/30/88): Assets, $690,647 (M); expenditures, $507,524, including $498,208 for 94 grants (high: $50,000; low: $100).
Purpose and activities: Giving primarily to promote health; support also for the arts, citizenship and public policy, business education, Jewish welfare, women, and conservation.
Limitations: No grants to individuals.
Application information: Contributes only to pre-selected organizations. Applications not accepted.
Write: Betsy Kenny
Officers and Trustees:* Norman Lear,* Pres.; Paul D. Schaeffer,* V.P.; Stuart P. Tobisman,* Secy.; Warren Spector,* Treas.; Betsy Kenny.
Number of staff: 2 part-time support.
Employer Identification Number: 954036197

479
Thomas and Dorothy Leavey Foundation ▼ ⌑
4680 Wilshire Blvd.
Los Angeles 90010 (213) 930-4252

Trust established in 1952 in CA.
Donor(s): Thomas E. Leavey,† Dorothy E. Leavey.
Foundation type: Independent
Financial data (yr. ended 12/31/87): Assets, $85,984,845 (M); expenditures, $7,462,821, including $6,689,480 for 62 grants (high: $1,000,000; average: $10,000-$25,000) and $177,101 for grants to individuals.
Purpose and activities: Giving primarily for hospitals, medical research, higher and secondary education, and Catholic church groups; provides scholarships to children of employees of Farmers Group, Inc.
Types of support: Employee-related scholarships.
Limitations: Giving primarily in southern CA.
Application information:
Initial approach: Letter
Copies of proposal: 1
Deadline(s): None
Board meeting date(s): As required
Write: J. Thomas McCarthy, Trustee
Trustees: E.W. Boland, Dorothy E. Leavey, Joseph James Leavey, J. Thomas McCarthy, Kathleen Leavey McCarthy, Kenneth Tyler.
Number of staff: None.
Employer Identification Number: 956060162

480
Bertha Lebus Trust ⌑
c/o Trust Services of America, Inc.
700 Wilshire Blvd., Suite 420
Los Angeles 90017

Foundation type: Independent
Financial data (yr. ended 12/31/88): Assets, $2,555,252 (M); expenditures, $112,523, including $75,000 for 16 grants (high: $12,000; low: $2,500).
Purpose and activities: Grants primarily for education.
Limitations: No grants to individuals.
Application information: Contributes only to pre-selected organizations. Applications not accepted.
Write: M.D. Blood
Trustee: Trust Services of America, Inc.
Employer Identification Number: 956022085

481
The Ledler Foundation ▼ ⌑
1800 West Magnolia Blvd.
P.O. Box 828
Burbank 91503

Established in 1966 in CA.
Donor(s): Lawrence E. Deutsch,† Lloyd E. Rigler, Adolph's, Ltd., Adolph's Food Products Manufacturing Co.
Foundation type: Independent
Financial data (yr. ended 12/31/88): Assets, $2,268,278 (M); gifts received, $46,706,631; expenditures, $830,454, including $565,182 for 80 grants (high: $200,000; low: $50).
Purpose and activities: Grants mainly for cultural programs in the performing arts.
Limitations: No grants to individuals.
Application information: Application form not required.
Initial approach: Letter
Deadline(s): None
Board meeting date(s): As necessary
Final notification: Varies
Write: Audre Estrin, Asst. Treas.
Officers and Director:* Lloyd E. Rigler,* Pres.; Simon Miller, V.P.; Donald Rigler, Secy.
Number of staff: None.
Employer Identification Number: 956155653

482
The LEF Foundation
1095 Lodi Ln.
St. Helena 94574 (707) 963-9591

Established in 1985 in CA.
Donor(s): Lyda Ebert Trust.
Foundation type: Independent
Financial data (yr. ended 6/30/89): Assets, $5,887,568 (M); gifts received, $146,250; expenditures, $521,424, including $336,933 for 54 grants (high: $34,000; low: $500; average: $5,000-$15,000).
Purpose and activities: Support for intersection of art and environment; giving also for AIDS research.
Types of support: Land acquisition, general purposes, publications, seed money, special projects.
Limitations: Giving primarily in northern CA and New England and proactive in other states.
Publications: Application guidelines, 990-PF, grants list.

Application information: Application form not required.
Initial approach: Letter or telephone
Copies of proposal: 7
Deadline(s): Mar. 1 and Sept. 1
Board meeting date(s): Varies
Write: Marina Drummer, Exec. Dir.
Officers: Marion E. Greene, Pres.; Dean Kuth, V.P.; Lyda Ebert Kuth, Secy. and C.F.O.
Number of staff: 1 full-time professional; 1 part-time support.
Employer Identification Number: 680070194

483
Leonardt Foundation ⌑
1801 Ave. of the Stars, Suite 811
Los Angeles 90067 (213) 556-3932

Incorporated in 1953 in CA.
Donor(s): Amy L. Powell, Clara L. McGinnis.
Foundation type: Independent
Financial data (yr. ended 12/31/88): Assets, $2,730,695 (M); expenditures, $209,685, including $185,550 for 77 grants (high: $26,000; low: $100).
Purpose and activities: Grants primarily for Roman Catholic church support; support also for welfare funds, higher and secondary education, hospitals, and health agencies.
Limitations: No grants to individuals.
Application information:
Initial approach: Letter
Copies of proposal: 1
Write: Felix S. McGinnis, Jr., Pres.
Officers and Directors:* Felix S. McGinnis, Jr.,* Pres.; Carl L. McGinnis,* V.P. and Secy.-Treas.; Barbara J. McGinnis, J. Frank McGinnis.
Employer Identification Number: 956045256

484
Levi Strauss Foundation ▼
1155 Battery St.
P.O. Box 7215
San Francisco 94111 (415) 544-1378

Incorporated in 1941 in CA.
Donor(s): Levi Strauss & Co.
Foundation type: Company-sponsored
Financial data (yr. ended 12/31/88): Assets, $21,503,343 (M); gifts received, $3,800,000; expenditures, $4,960,310, including $2,936,000 for 258 grants (high: $79,600; low: $100) and $100,810 for 886 employee matching gifts.
Purpose and activities: To improve human services through direct grants and encouragement of employee volunteer activities. Focus is on enhancing the economic opportunities of the disadvantaged through job training and job creation. Support also for international economic development.
Types of support: Matching funds, continuing support, seed money, equipment, exchange programs, employee-related scholarships, employee matching gifts, technical assistance, general purposes, special projects, operating budgets.
Limitations: Giving generally limited to areas of company operations in AR, CA, GA, KY, MS, TN, NV, NM, NC, TX, and VA, and abroad. No support for sectarian or religious purposes. No grants to individuals, or for tickets for banquets, or courtesy advertising; research, conferences, films, videos, or publications are considered only if they are a small part of a larger effort being supported.
Publications: Corporate giving report (including application guidelines), grants list, informational brochure.
Application information: Application forms required for scholarships for children of company employees; all other types of scholarships discontinued. Application form not required.
Initial approach: Letter
Copies of proposal: 1
Deadline(s): None
Board meeting date(s): Mar., June, Sept., and Dec.
Final notification: 2 to 3 months
Write: Martha Montag Brown, Dir. of Contribs.; Myra Chow, Mgr. of Contribs. (Bay Area); Herman Davenport (AR, MS, VA, and Centerville, TN); Mario Griffin (TX); Mary Ellen McLoughlin (GA, KY, NC, and TN)
Officers and Directors:* Peter E. Haas,* Pres.; Walter A. Haas, Jr.,* V.P.; Martha Montag Brown, Secy. and Dir. Contribs.; Joseph Maurer, Treas.; Frances K. Geballe, Rhoda H. Goldman, Pete Haas, Jr., Robert D. Haas, George B. James, Madeleine Haas Russell, Thomas W. Tusher.
Number of staff: 13 part-time professional; 6 part-time support.
Employer Identification Number: 946064702

485
Hyman Levine Family Foundation ⌑
9300 Wilshire Blvd., Suite 410
Beverly Hills 90212 (213) 274-5291

Established in 1943 in CA.
Donor(s): Members of the Levine family.
Foundation type: Independent
Financial data (yr. ended 12/31/87): Assets, $1,554,345 (M); gifts received, $66,120; expenditures, $111,235, including $106,080 for 34 grants (high: $45,680; low: $25).
Purpose and activities: Grants primarily for Jewish giving.
Application information:
Initial approach: Letter
Deadline(s): None
Write: Sid B. Levine, Pres.
Officers: Sid B. Levine, Pres.; Ronald Levine, 1st V.P.; Donald Slate, 2nd V.P.; Dana Schechter, Secy.; Malden Levine, Treas.
Employer Identification Number: 956058255

486
The Levitt Foundation ⌑
8484 Wilshire Blvd., Suite 310
Beverly Hills 90211 (213) 852-0744

Incorporated in 1949 in NY.
Donor(s): Levitt and Sons, Inc., Abraham Levitt,† Alfred Levitt,† William Levitt.
Foundation type: Independent
Financial data (yr. ended 4/30/89): Assets, $3,713,714 (M); expenditures, $91,950.
Purpose and activities: Support primarily for higher education, medical research, welfare agencies, and aid to the handicapped.
Limitations: No grants to individuals.
Application information:
Initial approach: Letter
Deadline(s): None
Write: William J. Levitt, Jr., Pres.
Officers and Directors:* William J. Levitt, Jr.,* Pres.; Stephen Mathes,* Secy.; Robert J. Appel, Prudence Brown, Farrell Jones, May W. Newberger.
Employer Identification Number: 136128226

487
Achille Levy Foundation ⌑ ☆
c/o Bank of A. Levy
P.O. Box 2575
Ventura 93002 (805) 487-6541

Established in 1969 in CA.
Donor(s): Bank of A. Levy.
Foundation type: Company-sponsored
Financial data (yr. ended 11/30/88): Assets, $818 (M); gifts received, $305,500; expenditures, $305,500, including $284,250 for 183 grants (high: $45,000; low: $25) and $21,250 for 17 grants to individuals of $1,250 each.
Purpose and activities: Support for higher and secondary education, including scholarships for local area high school students, community funds, social services, culture and the arts, health associations, and youth.
Types of support: Operating budgets, annual campaigns, emergency funds, building funds, equipment, employee matching gifts, scholarship funds, employee-related scholarships.
Limitations: Giving limited to Ventura County, CA, near branch offices. No grants for continuing support, seed money, deficit financing, land acquisition, endowment funds, special projects, research, publications, or conferences; no loans; no scholarships to bank employees or children of bank employees.
Application information: Final selections of scholarship recipients are made by the principals or counselors of the various high schools, along with three officers of the bank. Application form required.
Initial approach: Letter
Copies of proposal: 1
Write: Robert L. Mobley, Vice-Chair.
Officers and Directors:* A.A. Milligan,* Chair.; Robert L. Mobley,* Vice-Chair.; James F. Koenig,* Secy.-Treas.; Walter H. Hoffman.
Number of staff: None.
Employer Identification Number: 956264755

488
Hyman Jebb Levy Foundation ⌑
2222 South Figueroa St.
Los Angeles 90007 (213) 749-9411

Established in 1974.
Donor(s): Hyman Levy, Raymond Mallel.
Foundation type: Independent
Financial data (yr. ended 11/30/88): Assets, $3,195,603 (M); expenditures, $168,710, including $162,450 for 26 grants (high: $20,000; low: $100).
Purpose and activities: Grants primarily for Jewish education and temple support, including support for institutions in Israel; support also for social service agencies.
Limitations: Giving primarily in NY and Los Angeles, CA.

Application information:
Initial approach: Letter
Deadline(s): None
Write: Hyman Levy, Pres.
Officers: Hyman Levy, Pres. and Treas.; Raymond Mallel, Secy.
Employer Identification Number: 237422872

489
Elvirita Lewis Foundation for Geriatric Health and Nutrition ⌑
c/o Small Grant Assistance Program
255 North El Cielo Rd., Suite 144
Palm Springs 92262 (619) 397-4552

Established about 1976 in CA.
Donor(s): Elvirita L. Stafford.†
Foundation type: Operating
Financial data (yr. ended 12/31/87): Assets, $3,302,078 (M); gifts received, $1,025,898; expenditures, $1,900,277, including $325,950 for 45 grants (high: $224,000; low: $150) and $353,210 for foundation-administered programs.
Purpose and activities: An operating foundation which makes grants for organizations aiding the elderly, including those involving self-help programs, networking systems, peer support, intergenerational projects, and volunteer opportunities.
Application information:
Initial approach: 1-page letter
Deadline(s): Sept. 1 for grants in the following calendar year
Write: Lynn Dawson
Officers: Steven W. Brummel, Pres.; Shari M. Reville, Secy.
Directors: Jeffrey R. Barlow, Georgeanne Kerwin, Robert L. Stafford.
Employer Identification Number: 942344734

490
Mabelle McLeod Lewis Memorial Fund ⌑
P.O. Box 3730
Stanford 94305 (415) 723-3903

Trust established in 1968 in CA.
Donor(s): Donald McLeod Lewis.†
Foundation type: Operating
Financial data (yr. ended 3/31/88): Assets, $2,291,310 (M); expenditures, $179,984, including $106,500 for 12 grants to individuals (high: $10,000; low: $2,500).
Purpose and activities: A private operating foundation; awards grants to scholars in the humanities affiliated with northern CA universities and colleges to bring about the completion of a scholarly dissertation. Presently limited to advanced doctoral candidates.
Types of support: Research, fellowships.
Limitations: Giving limited to northern CA. No grants for publication of dissertations.
Publications: Application guidelines, program policy statement.
Application information: Application form required.
Initial approach: Letter
Copies of proposal: 2
Deadline(s): Submit application preferably in Nov. or Dec.; deadline Jan. 15
Board meeting date(s): Feb. or Mar.
Final notification: Mid-Mar.
Write: Ms. Shirleyann Shyne, Exec. Secy.
Officer: Shirleyann Shyne, Exec. Secy.
Trustees: Sheldon G. Cooper, Wells Fargo Bank, N.A.
Number of staff: 1
Employer Identification Number: 237079585

491
Edmund Wattis Littlefield Foundation ⌑
550 California St.
San Francisco 94104-1006

Established in 1958 in CA.
Donor(s): Edmund W. Littlefield.
Foundation type: Independent
Financial data (yr. ended 12/31/88): Assets, $1,413,071 (M); gifts received, $269,274; expenditures, $222,642, including $220,431 for 44 grants (high: $153,781; low: $100).
Purpose and activities: Support primarily for education, with emphasis on higher education, and for youth, cultural, and social service organizations.
Limitations: Giving primarily in CA.
Application information: Contributes only to pre-selected organizations. Applications not accepted.
Officers: Edmund W. Littlefield, Pres. and Treas.; Jeannik M. Littlefield, V.P.; Harry R. Horrow, Secy.
Employer Identification Number: 946074780

492
Foundation of the Litton Industries ▼
360 North Crescent Dr.
Beverly Hills 90210 (213) 859-5423

Incorporated in 1954 in CA.
Donor(s): Litton Industries, Inc., and its subsidiaries.
Foundation type: Company-sponsored
Financial data (yr. ended 04/30/89): Assets, $27,026,005 (M); gifts received, $632,279; expenditures, $1,299,970, including $1,283,360 for 78 grants (high: $315,000; low: $1,000; average: $1,000-$10,000).
Purpose and activities: Grants largely for higher education, including scholarship funds, and community funds; support also for cultural activities; limited employee matching gifts program.
Types of support: Operating budgets, continuing support, seed money, endowment funds, employee matching gifts, scholarship funds.
Limitations: No grants to individuals, or for deficit financing, capital funds, equipment, land acquisition, renovation projects, special projects, publications, dinners, conferences, or purchased research; no loans.
Application information: Application form not required.
Initial approach: Letter
Copies of proposal: 1
Deadline(s): None
Board meeting date(s): As required
Write: Clarence L. Price, Pres.
Officers and Directors:* Clarence L. Price,* Pres.; Virginia S. Young,* V.P. and Secy.; John L. Child, V.P.; Norma E. Nelson,* V.P.; Cynthia M. Stec, Treas.
Number of staff: None.
Employer Identification Number: 956095343

493
Livingston Memorial Foundation
625 North A St.
Oxnard 93030 (805) 983-0561
Mailing address: P.O. Box 1232, Oxnard, CA 93032

Incorporated about 1974 in CA.
Donor(s): Ruth Daily Livingston.†
Foundation type: Independent
Financial data (yr. ended 04/30/89): Assets, $5,326,208 (M); expenditures, $378,756, including $313,750 for 27 grants (high: $165,000; low: $850).
Purpose and activities: Support for health and health-related activities.
Types of support: Matching funds, operating budgets.
Limitations: Giving limited to Ventura County, CA. No grants to individuals.
Publications: Application guidelines, program policy statement.
Application information: Application form required.
Initial approach: Letter
Copies of proposal: 8
Deadline(s): Submit proposal preferably in Dec. or Jan.; deadline Feb. 1
Board meeting date(s): As required
Write: Laura K. McAvoy
Officers and Directors:* Charles M. Hair, M.D.,* Pres.; W.C. Huff, M.D.,* V.P.; Walter W. Hoffman,* Secy.-Treas.; Ralph L. Cormany, James K. Mason, M.D.
Number of staff: None.
Employer Identification Number: 237364623

494
Llagas Foundation ⌑ ☆
50 Fremont St., Suite 3520
San Francisco 94105-2230

Established in 1980.
Donor(s): Members of the Davies family.
Foundation type: Independent
Financial data (yr. ended 06/30/89): Assets, $1,675,033 (M); expenditures, $94,966, including $84,450 for 26 grants (high: $26,000; low: $500).
Purpose and activities: Giving primarily for public affairs, higher education, Protestant churches, and human services; support also for a science museum and wildlife preservation.
Limitations: Giving primarily in CA. No grants to individuals.
Application information: Contributes only to pre-selected organizations. Applications not accepted.
Officers and Directors:* Barbara B. Davies,* Pres.; P.H. Davies,* V.P.; Paul L. Davies, Jr.,* V.P.; Paul Lewis Davies III,* V.P.; Laura Davies Mateo,* V.P.; S. Mateo,* V.P.; A. McDonald, Secy.; D.A. Ruhl, Treas.
Employer Identification Number: 942678807

495
Lockheed Leadership Fund ▼
4500 Park Granada Blvd.
Calabasas 91399-0510 (818) 712-2397

Incorporated in 1953 in CA.
Donor(s): Lockheed Corp.
Foundation type: Company-sponsored

Financial data (yr. ended 12/31/88): Assets, $0 (M); gifts received, $1,500,000; expenditures, $1,500,000, including $1,500,000 for 74 grants (high: $160,000; low: $1,000; average: $1,000-$160,000).
Purpose and activities: Support for higher education through grants, 12 four-year scholarships awarded annually to children of Lockheed employees through the National Merit Scholarship Corporation, two four-year Achievement Scholarships, and two four-year G.I. Forum scholarships for Hispanics annually. Grants principally to support education for engineers, scientists, and managers for aerospace industry.
Types of support: Employee-related scholarships, scholarship funds, annual campaigns, capital campaigns, endowment funds, professorships.
Limitations: Giving primarily in areas where Lockheed facilities are located. No grants to individuals, or for special projects or matching gifts; no loans.
Application information: Selection of recipients are made by the organizations to which the Fund donates. Application form not required.
Initial approach: Letter, telephone, or proposal
Copies of proposal: 1
Deadline(s): Sept.-Oct.
Board meeting date(s): Mar. and as required
Write: Alex J. McCloskey, V.P.
Officers and Directors:* L.J. Barnard,* Pres.; Alex J. McCloskey, V.P.; W.T. Vinson, Secy.; A.G. Van Schaick,* Treas.; K.W. Cannestra, R.P. Caren, S.E. Chaudet, H.I. Fluornoy, D.C. Jones, C.R. Scanlon, J.G. Twomey.
Number of staff: 1 part-time professional; 1 part-time support.
Employer Identification Number: 956066086

496
Mary S. Lowe Trust
c/o Wells Fargo Bank, N.A.
P.O. Box 150
Palo Alto 94302 (415) 855-7674

Established in 1985 in CA.
Donor(s): Mary S. Lowe.
Foundation type: Independent
Financial data (yr. ended 06/30/89): Assets, $1,417,259 (M); expenditures, $92,677, including $74,565 for 3 grants (high: $25,074; low: $24,419).
Purpose and activities: Giving primarily for animal welfare and a social welfare agency.
Application information: Contributes only to pre-selected organizations. Applications not accepted.
Write: Mary Nelson, Trust Officer, Wells Fargo Bank, N.A.
Trustee: Wells Fargo Bank, N.A.
Employer Identification Number: 946576822

497
Richard M. Lucas Cancer Foundation ⌑
Bldg. 3, Suite 210
3000 Sandhill Rd.
Menlo Park 94025

Established in 1982 in CA.
Foundation type: Independent
Financial data (yr. ended 6/30/88): Assets, $5,927,252 (M); expenditures, $779,925, including $600,000 for 2 grants (high: $500,000; low: $100,000).
Purpose and activities: Support for medical, primarily cancer, research.
Types of support: Research.
Limitations: Giving primarily in Stanford, CA.
Directors: Donald L. Lucas, John W. Lucas, Mary G. Lucas, and 4 additional directors.
Employer Identification Number: 942781117

498
Lund Foundation ⌑ ☆
P.O. Box 15159
North Hollywood 91615

Established in 1973.
Donor(s): Sharon D. Lund.
Foundation type: Independent
Financial data (yr. ended 12/31/88): Assets, $2,905,167 (M); expenditures, $198,738, including $191,887 for 8 grants (high: $50,042; low: $1,048).
Purpose and activities: Giving for the arts, and education, including secondary education.
Officers: Sharon D. Lund, Pres.; Roy W. McClean, V.P. and Secy.-Treas.
Employer Identification Number: 237306460

499
Louis R. Lurie Foundation ▼
555 California St., Suite 5100
San Francisco 94104 (415) 392-2470

Incorporated in 1948 in CA.
Donor(s): Louis R. Lurie,† Robert A. Lurie, George S. Lurie.†
Foundation type: Independent
Financial data (yr. ended 12/31/89): Assets, $15,820,721 (M); gifts received, $353,534; expenditures, $1,240,930, including $164,137 for 187 grants (high: $175,000; low: $1,000; average: $5,000-$25,000).
Purpose and activities: Giving primarily for higher and secondary education, Jewish welfare agencies, community services, hospitals and health agencies, and cultural programs.
Types of support: General purposes, matching funds, scholarship funds, special projects, operating budgets.
Limitations: Giving limited to the San Francisco Bay Area, CA, and the Chicago, IL, metropolitan area. No grants to individuals, or for building funds; no loans.
Publications: Application guidelines.
Application information: Application form not required.
Initial approach: Telephone call, followed by letter
Copies of proposal: 1
Deadline(s): Applicants should contact foundation for deadlines
Board meeting date(s): Twice a year, and as needed
Final notification: After board meeting
Write: Robert A. Lurie, Pres.
Officers: Robert A. Lurie,* Pres.; H. Michael Kurzman,* V.P.; Eugene L. Valla,* V.P. and Controller; Charles F. Jonas, Secy.
Directors:* Patricia R. Fay, A.R. Zipf.
Number of staff: None.
Employer Identification Number: 946065488

500
Alfred Lushing Family Foundation ⌑ ☆
2029 Century Park East, Suite 1550
Los Angeles 90067

Established in 1964.
Donor(s): Gerald Lushing.
Foundation type: Independent
Financial data (yr. ended 7/31/89): Assets, $397,094 (M); expenditures, $102,679, including $100,753 for 67 grants (high: $38,893; low: $25).
Purpose and activities: Giving primarily for Jewish organizations, including welfare funds; support also for child welfare and the arts.
Limitations: No grants to individuals.
Application information: Contributes only to pre-selected organizations. Applications not accepted.
Officers: Gerald Lushing, Pres.; Janet Semler, Secy.-Treas.
Employer Identification Number: 956064906

501
Miranda Lux Foundation
57 Post St., Suite 604
San Francisco 94104 (415) 981-2966

Incorporated in 1908 in CA.
Donor(s): Miranda W. Lux.†
Foundation type: Independent
Financial data (yr. ended 6/30/89): Assets, $3,779,325 (M); expenditures, $242,756, including $208,523 for 17 grants (high: $70,000; low: $600).
Purpose and activities: Support to promising proposals for preschool through junior college programs in the fields of prevocational and vocational education and training.
Types of support: Operating budgets, continuing support, seed money, equipment, matching funds, scholarship funds, special projects, fellowships, internships.
Limitations: Giving limited to San Francisco, CA. No grants to individuals, or for annual campaigns, emergency funds, deficit financing, building or endowment funds, land acquisition, renovations, research, publications, or conferences; no loans.
Publications: Annual report, application guidelines, informational brochure, program policy statement.
Application information: Application form not required.
Initial approach: Letter or telephone
Copies of proposal: 6
Deadline(s): Submit proposal 3 weeks prior to board meeting; no set deadline
Board meeting date(s): Jan., Mar., June, Sept., and Nov.
Final notification: 1 week after board meeting
Write: Lawrence I. Kramer, Jr., Exec. Dir.
Officers: Benson B. Roe, M.D., Pres.; David Wisnom, Jr., V.P.; Philip F. Spalding, Secy.-Treas.; Lawrence I. Kramer, Jr., Exec. Dir.
Trustees: Edmond S. Gillette, Jr., Diana Potter Wolfensperger.
Number of staff: None.
Employer Identification Number: 941170404

502
Bertha Russ Lytel Foundation
P.O. Box 893
Ferndale 95536 (707) 786-4682

Established in 1974 in CA.
Donor(s): Bertha Russ Lytel,† L.D. O'Rourke.†
Foundation type: Independent
Financial data (yr. ended 09/30/89): Assets, $11,049,712 (M); expenditures, $589,651, including $486,111 for 45 grants (high: $60,000; low: $300; average: $300-$60,000).
Purpose and activities: Giving primarily to social service agencies for the aged and handicapped, civic and cultural programs, and agricultural and nursing scholarship funds.
Types of support: Operating budgets, seed money, building funds, equipment, scholarship funds, continuing support, matching funds.
Limitations: Giving limited to Humboldt County, CA. No grants to individuals, or for annual campaigns, emergency or endowment funds, deficit financing, land acquisition, renovations, research, demonstration projects, or publications; no loans.
Publications: Application guidelines, 990-PF.
Application information: Application form required.
Initial approach: Letter
Copies of proposal: 8
Deadline(s): 1st Thursday of each month
Board meeting date(s): Monthly
Final notification: 30 to 60 days
Write: George Hindley, Mgr.
Officers and Directors:* Charles M. Lawrence,* Pres.; Carl Carlson, Jr.,* V.P.; James K. Morrison,* Secy.; Doris Nairne,* Treas.; George Hindley, Mgr.; Gerald Becker, Clarence Crane, Jr., Jack Russ.
Number of staff: 1 part-time professional.
Employer Identification Number: 942271250

503
M.E.G. Foundation ¤
7855 Ivanhoe Ave., Suite 420
La Jolla 92037 (619) 454-3237

Established in 1974 in CA.
Donor(s): Lindavista, S.A., Members of the Gildred family.
Foundation type: Independent
Financial data (yr. ended 5/31/87): Assets, $11,093,353 (M); expenditures, $668,409, including $514,000 for 14 grants (high: $120,000; low: $3,000).
Purpose and activities: Emphasis on medical research and hospitals, including buildings and equipment; support also for higher education, social welfare, and cultural programs.
Types of support: Annual campaigns, seed money, building funds, equipment, research, general purposes, matching funds, continuing support, special projects.
Limitations: Giving primarily in San Diego County, CA. No grants to individuals, or for endowment funds or operating budgets.
Application information: Applications for grants presently not invited. Application form not required.
Initial approach: Proposal
Copies of proposal: 1
Deadline(s): None
Board meeting date(s): Oct. and Apr.
Final notification: Up to 7 months
Write: William P. Shannahan, V.P.
Officers: Stuart C. Gildred,* Pres.; William P. Shannahan, V.P. and Secy.
Directors:* Ferdinand T. Fletcher, Helen C. Gildred, Lynne E. Gildred.
Number of staff: 1
Employer Identification Number: 237364942

504
The MacKenzie Foundation ¤
c/o Sanwa Bank California
P.O. Box 439, Tax Dept.
Pasadena 91102
Application address: 400 Hope St., Los Angeles, CA 90012; Tel.: (213) 669-6377

Established about 1978 in CA.
Donor(s): Sophia MacKenzie.†
Foundation type: Independent
Financial data (yr. ended 12/31/86): Assets, $6,321,240 (M); expenditures, $392,951, including $311,000 for 10 grants (high: $38,500; low: $8,500).
Purpose and activities: The principal purpose of the foundation is to make grants for the benefit of students enrolled in medical schools located in the state of CA.
Limitations: Giving limited to CA.
Application information:
Deadline(s): None
Write: Philip D. Irwin
Trustees: H. Vernon Blankenbaker, William G. Corey, Philip D. Irwin, Sanwa Bank California.
Employer Identification Number: 956588350

505
B. N. Maltz Foundation ¤
9100 Wilshire Blvd., Suite 404
Beverly Hills 90212

Incorporated in 1948 in IL.
Donor(s): B.N. Maltz, Medal Distilled Products Co., Inc.
Foundation type: Independent
Financial data (yr. ended 12/31/88): Assets, $2,049,828 (M); expenditures, $534,918, including $524,567 for 88 grants (high: $175,135; low: $50).
Purpose and activities: Grants largely for Jewish welfare funds, hospitals, and health agencies; support also for higher education and social services.
Application information: Contributes only to pre-selected organizations. Applications not accepted.
Officers: B.N. Maltz, Pres.; M.M. Maltz, Treas.
Employer Identification Number: 956034307

506
Margoes Foundation
57 Post St., Suite 604
San Francisco 94104 (415) 981-2966

Established in 1984 in CA.
Donor(s): John A. Margoes.†
Foundation type: Independent
Financial data (yr. ended 02/28/90): Assets, $2,489,518 (M); gifts received, $502,401; expenditures, $165,832, including $151,327 for 14 grants (high: $25,000; low: $500; average: $5,000-$10,000).
Purpose and activities: Giving for cardiac research, and rehabilitation of mentally ill patients; also provides scholarships for minority medical students and fellowships for African nationals studying agriculture in the U.S.
Types of support: Scholarship funds, continuing support, exchange programs, fellowships, operating budgets, research, special projects, matching funds.
Limitations: Giving primarily in CA. No grants to individuals.
Publications: Annual report.
Application information: Application form not required.
Initial approach: Proposal
Deadline(s): None
Write: John S. Blum, Principal Mgr.
Officers and Directors:* A.R. Zipf,* Chair.; Neal L. Peterson,* Secy.; Robert H. Erwin III,* C.F.O.
Employer Identification Number: 942955164

507
Mariani Foundation ¤
20480 Pacific Dr., Suite E
Cupertino 95014

Established about 1981 in CA.
Foundation type: Independent
Financial data (yr. ended 11/30/86): Assets, $1,352,640 (M); expenditures, $82,944, including $68,700 for 18 grants (high: $22,100; low: $200; average: $200-$1,000).
Purpose and activities: Giving primarily to Roman Catholic organizations, including secondary schools, welfare funds, and for higher education.
Types of support: Building funds.
Application information:
Deadline(s): Aug. and Sept.
Board meeting date(s): Oct.
Trustee: Conroy F. Bets.
Employer Identification Number: 946102749

508
Marin Community Foundation
1100 Larkspur Landing Circle, Suite 365
Larkspur 94939 (415) 461-3333

Incorporated in 1986 in CA; the Buck Foundation Trust, its original donor, was established in 1973 and administered by the San Francisco Foundation through 1986.
Donor(s): Leonard Buck,† Beryl Buck.
Foundation type: Community
Financial data (yr. ended 06/30/89): Assets, $456,903,000 (M); gifts received, $6,656,660; expenditures, $23,124,000, including $21,385,000 for grants (average: $50,000).
Purpose and activities: The Marin Community Foundation was established in July 1986 as a nonprofit public benefit corporation to engage in, conduct, and promote charitable, religious, educational scientific, artistic, and philanthropic activities primarily in Marin County, CA. On Jan. 1, 1987, administration of the Buck Trust, created in accordance with the 1973 will of Beryl Buck and valued at approximately $447,000,000, was transferred from the Foundation. To realize its purposes, the Foundation will seek advice and guidance from the community; work as a partner with organizations and individuals; and, encourage the participation of volunteers. Grantmaking for the fiscal year 1987/88 was approximately

$22.3 million. As part of the settlement agreement, three major projects, located in Marin County but intended to be of national and international importance, were selected by the Court. During the fiscal year 1987/88 these three projects received approximately $6,356,882 from the Buck Trust.
Types of support: Continuing support, emergency funds, equipment, land acquisition, loans, matching funds, operating budgets, program-related investments, renovation projects, seed money, special projects, technical assistance.
Limitations: Giving limited to Marin County, CA. No grants to individuals, or for planning initiatives, research, or generally for capital projects (except those meeting criteria specified in the funding guidelines).
Publications: Application guidelines, program policy statement, newsletter, 990-PF.
Application information: Application form required.
Initial approach: Request for funding policies and application guidelines
Copies of proposal: 2
Deadline(s): Nov. 15 for environment and arts and humanities; Dec. 15 for housing and community development; Jan. 15 for integrative approaches; and Feb. 15 for religion
Board meeting date(s): Monthly (except July)
Final notification: 3 months
Write: Berit Ashla, Prog. Asst.
Officers: Douglas X. Patino, Pres. and C.E.O.; Barbara B. Lawson, V.P. of Administration and Finance and Treas.; Lynn Clifford Michals, Secy. and Asst. to Pres.
Trustees: Gary R. Spratling, Chair.; Rev. Douglas K. Huneke, Vice-Chair.; Peter R. Arrigoni, Rita Granados, William L. Hamilton, Shirley A. Thornton, John L. Ziegler, M.D.
Number of staff: 12 full-time professional; 2 part-time professional; 9 full-time support; 1 part-time support.
Employer Identification Number: 943007979

509
Marini Family Trust
c/o Wells Fargo Bank, N.A.
420 Montgomery St., 5th Fl.
San Francisco 94163 (415) 396-3215

Trust established about 1970 in CA.
Donor(s): Frank Marini.†
Foundation type: Independent
Financial data (yr. ended 04/30/89): Assets, $3,496,568 (M); expenditures, $200,700, including $168,500 for 15 grants (high: $48,000; low: $500; average: $5,000-$15,000).
Purpose and activities: Giving for Catholic church support, education, and social services to local charities supported by the donor during his lifetime.
Limitations: Giving limited to the San Francisco Bay Area, CA. No grants to individuals.
Application information: Contributes only to pre-selected organizations. Applications not accepted.
Board meeting date(s): Dec.
Write: Eugene Ranghiasci, V.P., Wells Fargo Bank, N.A.
Trustee: Wells Fargo Bank, N.A.
Number of staff: None.
Employer Identification Number: 946073636

510
The Marshburn Foundation ¤
1201 South Beach Blvd., Suite 105
La Habra 90631

Trust established in 1961 in CA.
Foundation type: Independent
Financial data (yr. ended 10/31/89): Assets, $2,303,905 (M); gifts received, $368,333; expenditures, $171,494, including $159,869 for 21 grants (high: $26,000; low: $319; average: $4,000).
Purpose and activities: Giving for Protestant church support and higher education.
Types of support: Loans.
Limitations: Giving primarily in CA.
Application information: Contributes only to pre-selected organizations. Applications not accepted.
Trustees: T.J. Cummins, D.C. Marshburn, F.K. Marshburn, L.C. Marshburn.
Employer Identification Number: 956049100

511
Della Martin Foundation
c/o Sheppard, Mullin, Richter & Hampton
333 South Hope St., 48th Fl.
Los Angeles 90071 (213) 620-1780

Trust established in 1973 in CA.
Donor(s): Della Martin.†
Foundation type: Independent
Financial data (yr. ended 12/31/89): Assets, $3,916,717 (M); expenditures, $205,715, including $135,518 for 1 grant.
Purpose and activities: To advance the study and discovery of cures for all forms of mental illness through grants for research to publicly supported organizations.
Types of support: Research, endowment funds.
Limitations: Giving primarily in southern CA. No grants to individuals, or for general support, capital funds, scholarships, fellowships, or matching gifts; no loans.
Application information: Application form not required.
Initial approach: Letter
Copies of proposal: 7
Deadline(s): None
Board meeting date(s): Quarterly
Write: Laurence K. Gould, Jr.
Trustees: Edward J. Flynn, Lawrence K. Gould, Jr., Edward Mills, John D. Roberts, Thomas R. Sheppard, Frank Simpson III.
Number of staff: None.
Employer Identification Number: 237444954

512
Maurice J. Masserini Charitable Trust
c/o Wells Fargo Bank, N.A.
101 West Broadway, Suite 400
San Diego 92101

Established in 1984 in CA.
Foundation type: Independent
Financial data (yr. ended 03/31/89): Assets, $3,621,729 (M); expenditures, $204,672, including $175,000 for 14 grants (high: $25,000; low: $2,000).
Purpose and activities: Support primarily for higher education and medical research.
Types of support: Research, scholarship funds, special projects.
Limitations: Giving primarily in CA.
Publications: 990-PF.
Application information: Contributes only to pre-selected organizations. Applications not accepted.
Trustee: Wells Fargo Bank, N.A.
Employer Identification Number: 956812685

513
Mattel Foundation
c/o Mattel Toys
5150 Rosecrans Ave., MS 12012R01
Hawthorne 90250 (213) 978-5477

Foundation established in 1978 in CA.
Donor(s): Mattel, Inc.
Foundation type: Company-sponsored
Financial data (yr. ended 12/31/88): Assets, $395,133 (M); expenditures, $225,104, including $191,367 for 20 grants (high: $50,000; low: $500) and $32,755 for 53 employee matching gifts.
Purpose and activities: Grants largely for care and special education of children in areas of company operations; support also for international programs, including relief projects throughout Asia, Europe, and South America, and for employee matching gifts to higher education.
Types of support: Operating budgets, seed money, employee matching gifts, special projects, emergency funds, general purposes, in-kind gifts, employee-related scholarships.
Limitations: No support for religious, fraternal, athletic, social, veterans', or labor organizations; or for programs receiving substantial financial support from federal, state, or local government agencies. No grants to individuals, or for capital or endowment funds, equipment, land acquisition, renovation projects, research, fundraising activities, or courtesy advertising; no loans.
Publications: Application guidelines, 990-PF, program policy statement.
Application information: Application form not required.
Initial approach: Letter or telephone
Copies of proposal: 1
Write: Janice R. Morimoto, Fdn. Admin.
Officers: John A. Sage, Sr. V.P.; Timothy P. Reames, Secy.; Michael G. McCafferty, Treas.
Directors: Richard J. Riordan, Chair.; Ronald M. Loeb, Edward H. Malone.
Number of staff: 1 full-time professional.
Employer Identification Number: 953263647

514
Max Charitable Foundation
Breslauer, Jacobson, Rutman & Sherman
10345 Olympic Blvd.
Los Angeles 90064

Established in 1985 in CA.
Foundation type: Independent
Financial data (yr. ended 11/30/89): Assets, $7,204,657 (M); expenditures, $2,805,869, including $2,789,000 for grants.

Purpose and activities: Support for Jewish giving; support also for youth and child welfare, education, health associations, environmental organizations, and the arts.
Limitations: No grants to individuals.
Application information: Contributes only to pre-selected organizations. Applications not accepted.
Officers and Directors:* Gerald Breslauer,* Pres.; Michael Rutman,* Secy.-Treas.; Bruce Ramer.
Employer Identification Number: 954016320

515
The Maxfield Foundation
12930 Saratoga Ave., Suite B-3
Saratoga 95070 (408) 253-0723

Established in 1985 in CA.
Donor(s): Robert R. Maxfield.
Foundation type: Independent
Financial data (yr. ended 12/31/89): Assets, $4,722,030 (M); expenditures, $219,614, including $207,500 for 9 grants (high: $80,000; low: $2,000).
Purpose and activities: Support primarily for cancer research, including leukemia; secondary purpose is to give for charitable activities.
Types of support: Research, grants to individuals, seed money, special projects.
Publications: Annual report (including application guidelines).
Application information:
Write: Robert R. Maxfield, Pres.
Officers: Robert R. Maxfield, Pres.; Melinda Maxfield, V.P.; Clarence J. Ferrari, Jr., Secy.
Employer Identification Number: 770099366

516
Maxwell Memorial Foundation ⌑ ☆
c/o Trust Services of America, Inc.
700 Wilshire Blvd., Suite 420
Los Angeles 90017
Application address: 525 University Ave., Suite 32, Palo Alto, CA 94301

Established in 1987 in CA.
Donor(s): Robert W. Maxwell.†
Foundation type: Independent
Financial data (yr. ended 4/30/88): Assets, $1,421,356 (M); gifts received, $1,298,063; expenditures, $78,740.
Purpose and activities: Initial year of operation, fiscal 1988; no grants awarded. Giving limited to graduate science students at the University of California.
Types of support: Student aid.
Limitations: Giving primarily in CA.
Application information:
Write: Dewey J. Panattoni
Trustees: Harry C. Barr, Audrey Maxwell Brown, Trust Savings of America, Inc.
Employer Identification Number: 956878317

517
Wilbur D. May Foundation ▼ ⌑
10738 West Pico Blvd.
Beverly Hills 90064

Incorporated in 1951 in CA.
Donor(s): Wilbur D. May.†
Foundation type: Independent
Financial data (yr. ended 5/31/87): Assets, $30,889,200 (M); expenditures, $1,828,470, including $1,480,500 for 36 grants (high: $850,000; low: $1,000; average: $2,000-$25,000).
Purpose and activities: Grants primarily for hospitals and medical research, a department of parks and recreation, education, a community fund, and youth agencies.
Limitations: Giving primarily in CA and NV. No grants to individuals.
Publications: Application guidelines.
Application information:
Deadline(s): None
Board meeting date(s): Usually in Aug.
Final notification: Immediately after board meeting
Officers: David May II, Chair.; Aaron Clark, V.P.; Arthur J. Crowley, V.P.
Number of staff: None.
Employer Identification Number: 956038298

518
Tom May and David May II Foundation ⌑
c/o Stanley M. Lederman & Co.
9744 Wilshire Blvd., Suite 210
Beverly Hills 90212

Established in 1982 in CA.
Foundation type: Independent
Financial data (yr. ended 05/31/87): Assets, $1,171,603 (M); expenditures, $57,657, including $52,357 for 46 grants (high: $10,000; low: $20).
Purpose and activities: Support primarily for Jewish welfare, education, social services, and a church.
Officers and Directors: Dorothy D. May, Pres.; Donald May II, V.P.; Anita Rosenstein, V.P.; Michael Hong, Kathryn May Paben.
Employer Identification Number: 956021725

519
George Henry Mayr Trust
c/o Wells Fargo Bank, N.A.
P.O. Box 54410
Los Angeles 90054

Trust established in 1949 in CA.
Donor(s): George Henry Mayr.†
Foundation type: Independent
Financial data (yr. ended 07/31/89): Assets, $15,713,813 (M); expenditures, $1,047,338, including $881,000 for 38 grants (high: $55,500; low: $2,500).
Purpose and activities: Grants to California educational institutions for scholarships to students residing in CA for study.
Types of support: Scholarship funds.
Limitations: Giving limited to CA. No support for medical education other than dentistry. No grants to individuals.
Application information: Applications not accepted.
Advisors: Benjamin F. Grier, Chair.; Richard Daum, Donald Leahy.
Trustee: Wells Fargo Bank, N.A.
Number of staff: 1 part-time support.
Employer Identification Number: 956062009

520
MCA Foundation, Ltd. ▼
100 Universal City Plaza
Universal City 91608 (818) 777-1208

Incorporated in 1956 in CA.
Donor(s): MCA, Inc.
Foundation type: Company-sponsored
Financial data (yr. ended 12/31/87): Assets, $11,131,442 (M); expenditures, $920,815, including $867,500 for 81 grants (high: $100,000; low: $1,000).
Purpose and activities: Grants largely for health and welfare, including support for minorities, cultural programs, higher and other education, child and youth agencies, medical research, and leadership development.
Types of support: Annual campaigns, general purposes, research, special projects.
Limitations: Giving primarily in southern CA and NY. No grants to individuals, or for film or video projects.
Publications: Application guidelines.
Application information: Proposal of not more than three pages.
Write: Helen D. Yatsko, Admin.
Officers and Directors:* Sidney J. Sheinberg,* Pres.; Thomas Wertheimer,* V.P.; Michael Samuel, Secy.; Harold M. Hass,* Treas.
Number of staff: 2 full-time professional.
Employer Identification Number: 136096061

521
The Harold McAlister Charitable Foundation ▼
4801 Wilshire Blvd., Suite 232
Los Angeles 90010 (213) 937-0927

Incorporated in 1959 in CA.
Donor(s): Harold McAlister.†
Foundation type: Independent
Financial data (yr. ended 5/31/88): Assets, $19,793,460 (M); gifts received, $50,000; expenditures, $1,109,940, including $928,600 for 51 grants (high: $240,000; low: $100; average: $1,000-$30,000).
Purpose and activities: Support primarily for health and hospitals, education, and social welfare agencies.
Limitations: Giving primarily in the Los Angeles, CA, area. No grants to individuals.
Application information: Applications not accepted.
Board meeting date(s): Monthly
Write: Virginia Gilbert
Officers and Trustees:* Hobart S. McAlister,* Pres.; Fern Smith McAlister,* V.P.; David B. Heyler, Jr., Soni McAlister.
Number of staff: 1 full-time professional.
Employer Identification Number: 956050036

522
Alletta Morris McBean Charitable Trust ⌑
100 California St., Rm. 744
San Francisco 94115

Established in 1986 in CA.
Donor(s): Alletta Morris McBean.†
Foundation type: Independent
Financial data (yr. ended 12/31/89): Assets, $23,131,796 (M); expenditures, $1,288,069, including $1,125,000 for 16 grants (high: $150,000; low: $10,000).

Purpose and activities: Support for a historical preservation society; giving also for education and the environment.
Limitations: Giving primarily in RI. No grants to individuals.
Application information:
Initial approach: Letter
Deadline(s): None
Write: Peter McBean, Trustee
Trustees: Donald Christ, Noreen Drexel, Peter McBean, Elizabeth Morris Smith.
Employer Identification Number: 943019660

523
The Atholl McBean Foundation ⌑
c/o Price Waterhouse
555 California St., Suite 3800
San Francisco 94104

Incorporated in 1955 in CA.
Donor(s): Atholl McBean.†
Foundation type: Independent
Financial data (yr. ended 12/31/89): Assets, $4,183,795 (M); gifts received, $52,493; expenditures, $419,358, including $382,000 for 13 grants (high: $100,000; low: $1,000).
Purpose and activities: Emphasis on hospitals, higher and secondary education, and cultural organizations.
Limitations: Giving primarily in CA. No grants to individuals, or for endowment funds, research, scholarships, or fellowships; no loans.
Application information:
Initial approach: Letter
Copies of proposal: 1
Deadline(s): None
Board meeting date(s): Dec. and as required
Write: Peter McBean, Pres.
Officers: Peter McBean, Pres.; Clark Nelson, Secy.-Treas.
Directors: P. Folger, R. Gwen Follis, Judith McBean Hunt, Edith McBean, H. Newhall.
Employer Identification Number: 946062239

524
The McConnell Foundation
(Formerly Carl R. & Leah F. McConnell Foundation)
P.O. Box 930
Redding 96099 (916) 243-8931

Established in 1964 in CA.
Donor(s): Carl R. McConnell Trust III.
Foundation type: Independent
Financial data (yr. ended 12/31/89): Assets, $43,667,401 (M); expenditures, $2,094,168, including $2,063,570 for 29 grants (high: $250,000; low: $5,000).
Purpose and activities: Giving primarily for high school scholarship funds and community development; support also for arts and culture, the environment, health, recreation, and social services.
Types of support: Scholarship funds, equipment, general purposes, renovation projects, special projects.
Limitations: Giving primarily in Shasta and Siskiyou counties, CA. No support for sectarian religious purposes. No grants to individuals, or for endowment funds.
Publications: Program policy statement, application guidelines, annual report.
Application information: Application form required.
Initial approach: Letter of intent
Copies of proposal: 2
Deadline(s): Feb. 15
Board meeting date(s): Feb., Mar., July, and Oct.
Final notification: July 31
Write: Lee W. Salter, Exec. Dir.
Officers: Leonard B. Nelson, Pres.; William B. Nystrom, V.P.; Samuel Taylor, V.P.; Leah F. McConnell, Secy.-Treas.; Lee W. Salter, Exec. Dir.
Number of staff: 1 part-time professional; 3 part-time support.
Employer Identification Number: 946102700

525
McKesson Foundation, Inc. ▼
One Post St.
San Francisco 94104 (415) 983-8673

Incorporated in 1943 in FL.
Donor(s): McKesson Corp.
Foundation type: Company-sponsored
Financial data (yr. ended 03/31/90): Assets, $10,400,000 (M); expenditures, $2,000,000, including $1,735,532 for 171 grants (high: $115,050; low: $1,000; average: $5,000-$25,000) and $155,000 for employee matching gifts.
Purpose and activities: Giving primarily to programs for junior high school students, and for emergency services such as food and shelter; limited support for other educational, civic, cultural, and human service programs.
Types of support: Continuing support, emergency funds, employee matching gifts, matching funds, operating budgets, seed money, employee-related scholarships, equipment.
Limitations: Giving primarily in the Bay Area of San Francisco, CA, and in other cities where the company has a major presence. No support for religious organizations or political groups. No grants to individuals, or for endowment funds, advertising, or capital fund drives; no loans.
Publications: Annual report, application guidelines.
Application information: Application form not required.
Initial approach: Letter
Copies of proposal: 1
Deadline(s): Submit initial letter preferably between Apr. and Oct.; submit full proposal upon request
Board meeting date(s): Bimonthly beginning in Apr.
Final notification: 60 to 90 days
Write: Marcia M. Argyris, Pres.
Officers: Marcia M. Argyris, Pres.; Douglas L. Thompson,* V.P.; Dena J. Goldberg, Secy.; Garrett A. Scholz,* Treas.
Trustees:* Ronald C. Anderson, Arthur Chong, James S. Cohune, Judie Doherty, Kenneth C. Hicken, James I. Johnston, Marvin L. Krasnansky, Rex R. Malson, Ivan D. Meyerson, Alan Seelenfreund, Gregg Tarr, Susan Weir, John S. Wheaton, Charles Woods.
Number of staff: 1 full-time professional; 1 part-time professional; 1 full-time support; 1 part-time support.
Employer Identification Number: 596144455

526
Giles W. and Elise G. Mead Foundation
P.O. Box 1298
South Pasadena 91030-1298 (213) 799-0070

Incorporated in 1961 in CA.
Donor(s): Elise G. Mead.†
Foundation type: Independent
Financial data (yr. ended 10/31/89): Assets, $9,467,964 (M); expenditures, $469,413, including $314,417 for 9 grants (high: $125,000; low: $100; average: $1,000-$10,000).
Purpose and activities: Giving for the arts, education, natural and medical sciences, the environment, and other activities likely to enhance civilization.
Types of support: Seed money, land acquisition, endowment funds, research, scholarship funds, matching funds, equipment.
Limitations: Giving primarily in CA. No grants to individuals, or for general operating expenses; no loans.
Publications: Application guidelines.
Application information: Application form not required.
Initial approach: Letter
Copies of proposal: 10
Deadline(s): None
Board meeting date(s): Jan., June, and Oct.
Final notification: 2 months
Write: Myrna L. Patrick, V.P.
Officers and Directors:* Giles W. Mead, Jr.,* Pres. and C.E.O.; Daniel E. McArthur,* V.P.; Myrna L. Patrick,* V.P.; Calder M. Mackay,* Secy.-Treas.; Parry Mead Ahmad, Stafford R. Grady, Katherine Cone Keck, Richard N. Mackay, Jane W. Mead.
Number of staff: 1 full-time professional.
Employer Identification Number: 956040921

527
Masud Mehran Foundation ⌑
P.O. Box 640
San Ramon 94583

Established in 1984 in CA.
Donor(s): Masud Mehran.
Foundation type: Independent
Financial data (yr. ended 12/31/88): Assets, $1,015,339 (M); gifts received, $50,000; expenditures, $126,173, including $124,914 for 54 grants (high: $32,000; low: $25).
Purpose and activities: Emphasis on child welfare, higher education, and social service agencies; support also for a museum.
Officer: Masud Mehran, Pres.
Directors: Joseph Claas, Alexander Mehran, Dan L. Shehi.
Employer Identification Number: 680008630

528
Meland Outreach, Inc. ⌑
One Country Oak Ln.
Danville 94526 (415) 820-8441

Established in 1985 in CA.
Donor(s): Dennis Snyder.
Foundation type: Independent
Financial data (yr. ended 12/31/87): Assets, $1,885,964 (M); gifts received, $2,019,547; expenditures, $171,964, including $142,967 for grants (high: $39,530; low: $10).

Purpose and activities: Support primarily for Christian programs.
Limitations: Giving primarily in CA.
Application information:
Initial approach: Letter
Deadline(s): None
Write: Dennis Snyder, Dir.
Officer: Geraldine Snyder, Secy.
Director: Dennis Snyder.
Employer Identification Number: 680072477

529
Menlo Foundation ⌑ ☆
501 South Fairfax Ave.
Los Angeles 90036

Established in 1978.
Donor(s): Sam Menlo, Vera Menlo.
Foundation type: Independent
Financial data (yr. ended 11/30/89): Assets, $3,734 (M); gifts received, $500,000; expenditures, $780,620, including $780,620 for grants.
Purpose and activities: Giving to Jewish organizations, including welfare funds, educational institutions, and temple support.
Application information:
Write: Sam Menlo, Trustee
Trustees: Judith Frankel, Sam Menlo, Vera Menlo.
Employer Identification Number: 953388159

530
Mericos Foundation ▼ ⌑
1260 Huntington Dr., Suite 204
South Pasadena 91030 (213) 259-0484

Established in 1980 in CA.
Donor(s): Donald W. Whittier Charitable Trust.
Foundation type: Independent
Financial data (yr. ended 12/31/88): Assets, $9,812,717 (M); gifts received, $2,778,120; expenditures, $1,798,219, including $1,760,378 for 22 grants (high: $550,000; low: $2,500; average: $10,000-$50,000).
Purpose and activities: Primarily local giving for cultural programs, the aged, and medical research.
Limitations: Giving primarily in CA.
Application information: Grants generally initiated by foundation.
Deadline(s): None
Write: Linda J. Blinkenberg, Secy.
Officers: Joanne W. Blokker, Pres.; Steven A. Anderson, V.P.; Linda J. Blinkenberg, Secy.; Arlo G. Sorensen, Treas.
Number of staff: 1
Employer Identification Number: 953500491

531
Merry Mary Charitable Foundation, Inc. ⌑
c/o Merry Mary Fabrics
19701 Magellan Dr.
Torrance 90502 (213) 217-0066

Incorporated in 1954 in CA.
Donor(s): Merry Mary Fabrics, Inc., Teddi of California, Inc., South Sea Imports, Inc.
Foundation type: Company-sponsored
Financial data (yr. ended 3/31/87): Assets, $714,110 (M); gifts received, $135,000; expenditures, $452,516, including $451,684 for 51 grants (high: $257,775; low: $100; average: $100-$10,000).
Purpose and activities: Grants mainly for Jewish welfare funds and temple support, higher education in Israel, and hospitals.
Application information:
Initial approach: Letter
Deadline(s): None
Write: Albert Mass, V.P.
Officers: Stephen Meadow, Pres.; Albert Mass, V.P.; Samuel Krane, Secy.
Employer Identification Number: 953263582

532
Metropolitan Theatres Foundation ⌑
8727 West Third St.
Los Angeles 90048

Established in 1980 in CA.
Donor(s): Metropolitan Theatres Corp.
Foundation type: Company-sponsored
Financial data (yr. ended 04/30/89): Assets, $4,084 (M); gifts received, $95,200; expenditures, $105,547, including $95,350 for 90 grants (high: $5,700; low: $40) and $10,000 for 1 loan.
Purpose and activities: Support for civic programs, education, health and welfare agencies, Jewish organizations, cultural programs, Hispanic and youth organizations.
Limitations: No grants to individuals.
Application information: Contributes only to pre-selected organizations. Applications not accepted.
Officers: Bruce C. Corwin, C.E.O., Pres. and C.F.O.; Jill Cowan, Secy.
Employer Identification Number: 953520828

533
Milton and Sophie Meyer Fund
c/o Wells Fargo Bank, N.A.
P.O. Box 63002
San Francisco 94163 (415) 396-3895

Established in 1979.
Donor(s): Milton Meyer.†
Foundation type: Independent
Financial data (yr. ended 12/31/89): Assets, $3,006,972 (M); expenditures, $171,764, including $124,500 for 15 grants (high: $15,000; low: $3,500; average: $5,000-$10,000).
Purpose and activities: Grants primarily for Jewish charitable purposes.
Limitations: Giving primarily in the San Francisco Bay Area, CA. No grants to individuals.
Application information: Application form not required.
Initial approach: Letter
Copies of proposal: 1
Deadline(s): None
Board meeting date(s): As required
Final notification: Only successful applicants are contacted
Write: Joseph E. Fanucci, Trust Officer, Wells Fargo Bank, N.A.
Trustee: Wells Fargo Bank, N.A.
Employer Identification Number: 946480997

534
Ida S. Miles Foundation
c/o Herbert A. Crew, Jr.
P.O. Box 853
Pacific Palisades 90272-0853

Foundation type: Independent
Financial data (yr. ended 12/31/89): Assets, $1,435,000 (M); expenditures, $71,100, including $60,600 for 5 grants (high: $25,000; low: $5,000).
Purpose and activities: Support for programs directed toward world hunger, Christian-mission education, a program to rehabilitate disabled employees, a college scholarship fund, and medical research.
Types of support: Scholarship funds, program-related investments, special projects.
Limitations: Giving primarily in WA and CA. No grants to individuals, or for operating budgets.
Application information:
Initial approach: Proposal
Deadline(s): Aug. 31
Write: Herbert A. Crew, Jr., Treas.
Officers: A.S. Fish, Jr., Secy.; Herbert A. Crew, Jr., Treas.
Trustees: L.E. Fish, William Miles, Jr.
Number of staff: None.
Employer Identification Number: 956048943

535
The Milken Family Foundation ☆
c/o Foundations of the Milken Families
15250 Ventura Blvd., 2nd Fl.
Sherman Oaks 91403

Established in 1986 in CA.
Donor(s): Lowell Milken, Michael Milken, L.A. Milken, S.E. Milken.
Foundation type: Independent
Financial data (yr. ended 11/30/87): Assets, $97,536,838 (M); gifts received, $105,276,297; expenditures, $4,073,824, including $4,015,074 for grants (high: $500,000; low: $100).
Purpose and activities: To build human resources through programs in 4 major areas: 1) Education - to reward educational innovators, stimulate creativity among students, involve parents and other citizens in the school system, and offer opportunities to the disadvantaged student; 2) Health Care and Medical Research - to make the benefits of both basic and highly advanced health care available to those who need them; 3) Community Services - to support programs and facilities that meet the essential needs at the neighborhood level; and 4) Human Welfare - to meet the compelling needs of the disadvantaged.
Types of support: Research, conferences and seminars, scholarship funds, building funds, renovation projects, general purposes.
Limitations: Giving primarily in the Los Angeles, CA, area.
Publications: Annual report.
Application information:
Initial approach: Letter or proposal
Deadline(s): None
Write: Dr. Jules Lesner, Exec. Dir.
Officers and Directors:* L.J. Milken,* Pres.; Dr. Jules Lesner,* Exec. V.P. and Exec. Dir.;

S.E. Milken,* V.P.; E. Sandler,* V.P.; J.L. Shapiro,* Secy. and C.F.O.; Ralph Finerman, F. Milken, L.A. Milken, M.R. Milken.
Employer Identification Number: 954073646

536
Milken Family Medical Foundation ☆
c/o Foundations of the Milken Families
15250 Ventura Blvd., 2nd Fl.
Sherman Oaks 91403

Established in 1986 in CA.
Donor(s): Michael R. Milken, Lori A. Milken.
Foundation type: Independent
Financial data (yr. ended 10/31/88): Assets, $68,953,318 (M); gifts received, $50,219,395; expenditures, $4,829,635, including $4,524,310 for 68 grants (high: $950,000; low: $180).
Purpose and activities: To build human resources through programs in 4 major areas: 1) Education - to reward educational innovators, stimulate creativity among students, involve parents and other citizens in the school system, and offer opportunities to the disadvantaged student; 2) Health Care and Medical Research - to make the benefits of both basic and highly advanced health care available to those who need them; 3) Community Services - to support programs and facilities that meet the essential needs at the neighborhood level; and 4) Human Welfare - to meet the compelling needs of the disadvantaged.
Limitations: Giving primarily in the Los Angeles, CA, area. No grants to individuals.
Publications: Annual report.
Application information: Contributes only to pre-selected organizations. Applications not accepted.
Write: Lori Milken, Pres.
Officers and Directors:* Lori A. Milken,* Pres.; E. Sander,* Secy. and C.F.O.; M. Hackel, J. Lesner, Michael R. Milken.
Employer Identification Number: 954078350

537
L. and S. Milken Foundation ☆
c/o Foundations of the Milken Families
15250 Ventura Blvd., 2nd Fl.
Sherman Oaks 91403

Established in 1986 in CA.
Donor(s): L.J. Milken, S.E. Milken.
Foundation type: Independent
Financial data (yr. ended 10/31/88): Assets, $15,485,400 (M); gifts received, $9,732,237; expenditures, $832,627, including $738,000 for 40 grants (high: $150,000; low: $500).
Purpose and activities: To build human resources through programs in 4 major areas: 1) Education - to reward educational innovators, stimulate creativity among students, involve parents and other citizens in the school system, and offer opportunities to the disadvantaged student; 2) Health Care and Medical Research - to make the benefits of both basic and highly advanced health care available to those who need them; 3) Community Services - to support programs and facilities that meet the essential needs at the neighborhood level; and 4) Human Welfare - to meet the compelling needs of the disadvantaged.
Types of support: Research, conferences and seminars, scholarship funds, building funds, renovation projects, general purposes.
Limitations: Giving primarily in the Los Angeles, CA, area. No grants to individuals.
Publications: Annual report.
Application information: Contributes to pre-selected organizations. Applications not accepted.
Write: S. Milken, V.P.
Officers and Directors:* L.J. Milken,* Pres.; S.E. Milken,* V.P.; E. Salka,* V.P.; R.V. Sandler,* Secy. and C.F.O.; J. Lesner.
Employer Identification Number: 954078354

538
The Millard Foundation ⌑
P.O. Box 10408
Oakland 94610
Mailing address: P.O. Box 549 CHRB, Saipan, CNMI 94650

Established in 1982 in CA.
Donor(s): William H. Millard, ComputerLand Corp.
Foundation type: Independent
Financial data (yr. ended 12/31/86): Assets, $592,514 (M); expenditures, $161,067, including $152,601 for 24 grants (high: $51,000; low: $100).
Purpose and activities: Giving primarily for health and social services, international affairs, and the arts.
Limitations: Giving primarily in CA and the Commonwealth of the Northern Mariana Islands.
Application information: Contributes only to pre-selected organizations. Applications not accepted.
Officers: Michael A. Judith,* Pres.; Alton G. Burkhalter, Secy.
Directors:* Elizabeth A. Judith, Michael W. Wichman.
Employer Identification Number: 942894847

539
Arjay R. & Frances F. Miller Foundation ⌑ ☆
225 Mountain Home Rd.
Woodside 94062-2511

Established in 1955.
Foundation type: Independent
Financial data (yr. ended 12/31/88): Assets, $1,324,654 (M); expenditures, $61,677, including $56,030 for 34 grants (high: $11,625; low: $55).
Purpose and activities: Giving primarily for higher education and family planning; support also for museums and other cultural organizations.
Limitations: Giving primarily in CA. No grants to individuals.
Application information:
Deadline(s): None
Officers: Frances F. Miller, Pres.; Kenneth F. Miller, V.P.; Arjay R. Miller, Secy.-Treas.
Employer Identification Number: 386082895

540
Diane D. Miller Foundation ☆
P.O. Box 77732
San Francisco 94107

Established in 1986 in CA.
Donor(s): Diane D. Miller.
Foundation type: Independent
Financial data (yr. ended 11/30/89): Assets, $530,819 (M); expenditures, $478,940, including $470,000 for 8 grants (high: $175,000; low: $10,000).
Purpose and activities: Giving primarily for education of students with learning disabilities and the performing arts; support also for crime and law enforcement and drug abuse-related social services.
Limitations: Giving primarily in Los Angeles CA, and MA. No grants to individuals.
Application information: Contributes only to pre-selected organizations. Applications not accepted.
Trustee: Diane D. Miller.
Employer Identification Number: 954090844

541
Earl B. & Loraine H. Miller Foundation ⌑ ☆
P.O. Box 87
Long Beach 90801-0087
Application address: 444 West Ocean Blvd., Top Fl., Long Beach, CA 90802; Tel.: (213) 435-1191

Established in 1967 in CA.
Foundation type: Independent
Financial data (yr. ended 6/30/89): Assets, $3,809,002 (M); expenditures, $87,610, including $60,000 for 2 grants (high: $50,000; low: $10,000).
Purpose and activities: Funding for a children's health clinic, an educational foundation, and a fine arts museum.
Limitations: Giving primarily in Long Beach, CA. No grants to individuals.
Application information:
Initial approach: Letter
Deadline(s): None
Write: Paul D. McClaughry
Officers: Loraine Miller, Pres.; Larry A. Collins, Jr., V.P.; Paul D. McClaughry, Secy.
Trustees: Donald C. Carner, Richard C. Degolia, M.D., Elsie Rash, Leon L. Wiltse, M.D.
Employer Identification Number: 952500545

542
Edward D. and Anna Mitchell Family Foundation ⌑
6222 Wilshire Blvd., Suite 450
Los Angeles 90010

Established in 1953.
Donor(s): Anna Mitchell,† Edward D. Mitchell,† members of the Mitchell family.
Foundation type: Independent
Financial data (yr. ended 12/31/86): Assets, $10,558,025 (M); gifts received, $8,419,260; expenditures, $398,121, including $333,334 for 50 grants (high: $96,000; low: $35).
Purpose and activities: Giving primarily for Jewish welfare funds, a community fund, and higher education.

Application information: Contributes only to pre-selected organizations. Applications not accepted.
Officers and Directors:* Joseph N. Mitchell,* Pres.; Kayla Mitchell,* V.P.; Jonathan E. Mitchell,* Secy.-Treas.; Daniel R. Attias.
Employer Identification Number: 956027618

543
Community Foundation for Monterey County
P.O. Box 1384
Monterey 93942 (408) 375-9712
Additional tel.: (408) 758-4492

Incorporated in 1945 in CA.
Foundation type: Community
Financial data (yr. ended 12/31/89): Assets, $9,300,000 (M); gifts received, $800,000; expenditures, $600,000, including $450,000 for grants.
Purpose and activities: Giving primarily for social services, education, the environment, the arts, health, and other charitable purposes.
Types of support: Operating budgets, continuing support, seed money, emergency funds, building funds, equipment, land acquisition, matching funds, special projects, research, consulting services, technical assistance, program-related investments, capital campaigns, renovation projects, general purposes.
Limitations: Giving primarily in Monterey County, CA. No grants to individuals, or for annual campaigns, deficit financing, general endowments, or publications.
Publications: Annual report (including application guidelines), 990-PF, application guidelines, informational brochure, newsletter.
Application information: Application form not required.
Initial approach: Telephone or letter
Copies of proposal: 2
Deadline(s): Mar. 15, June 15, Sept. 15, and Dec. 15
Board meeting date(s): 3rd Tuesday of every month
Final notification: 1 day after each quarterly meeting
Write: Todd Lueders, Exec. Dir.
Director: Todd Lueders, Exec. Dir.
Board of Governors: Wilfred Daly, Pres.; Roberta Bialek, V.P.
Number of staff: 3 full-time professional.
Employer Identification Number: 941615897

544
Monterey Peninsula Golf Foundation ⌑ ☆
40 Bonifacio Plaza
Monterey 93940
Application address: P.O. Box 869, Monterey, CA 93942; Tel.: (408) 649-1533

Foundation type: Independent
Financial data (yr. ended 06/30/89): Assets, $400,734 (M); gifts received, $919,400; expenditures, $1,059,063, including $903,448 for 22 grants (high: $517,000; low: $500).
Purpose and activities: Support primarily for youth, human services, health, and other general activities.
Limitations: Giving limited to the Monterey Peninsula, CA, area. No grants to individuals.
Application information:
Initial approach: Letter
Deadline(s): Apr. 1
Write: Louis Russo, Exec. Dir.
Officers and Directors:* William F. Borland,* Pres.; John Zoller,* V.P.; Cindy Zoller, Secy.; Richard Falge, Treas.; Louis A. Russo, Exec. Dir.; and 8 additional directors.
Employer Identification Number: 942541783

545
Montgomery Street Foundation ▼
235 Montgomery St., Suite 1107
San Francisco 94104 (415) 398-0600

Incorporated in 1952 in CA and originally funded by Crown Zellerbach Corp.; later became a totally separate entity from the corporation.
Foundation type: Independent
Financial data (yr. ended 12/31/89): Assets, $21,055,000 (M); expenditures, $1,178,628, including $1,003,000 for 137 grants (high: $25,000; low: $2,500; average: $5,000-$10,000).
Purpose and activities: Grants made selectively to qualified organizations, primarily in the fields of higher education, international understanding, community funds, community welfare, cultural institutions, youth, health, rehabilitation, and related areas.
Types of support: General purposes, annual campaigns, operating budgets, capital campaigns.
Limitations: Giving primarily in CA; limited grants awarded nationally. No grants to individuals; no loans.
Application information: Application form not required.
Initial approach: Concise letter request
Copies of proposal: 1
Deadline(s): Reviewed on ongoing basis
Board meeting date(s): As required
Final notification: Usually within 3 months
Write: Carol K. Elliott, Secy.-Treas.
Officers and Directors:* Charles E. Stine,* Pres.; Carol K. Elliott, Secy.-Treas.; C.S. Cullenbine, C.R. Dahl, R.W. Roth, Richard G. Shephard.
Number of staff: 2 full-time professional.
Employer Identification Number: 941270335

546
Moore Family Foundation ☆
23965 Jabil Ln.
Los Altos Hills 94024

Established in 1986.
Donor(s): Betty I. Moore, Gordon E. Moore.
Foundation type: Independent
Financial data (yr. ended 09/30/89): Assets, $9,126,685 (M); gifts received, $7,843,750; expenditures, $137,544, including $133,833 for 7 grants (high: $50,000; low: $3,000).
Purpose and activities: Support primarily for a hospital foundation; support also for higher education.
Limitations: No grants to individuals.
Application information: Contributes only to pre-selected organizations. Applications not accepted.
Trustees: Betty I. Moore, Gordon E. Moore, Kenneth G. Moore, Steven E. Moore.
Employer Identification Number: 943024440

547
Robert W. Morey & Maura Burke Morey Charitable Trust ⌑
134 Lyford Dr.
Box I
Tiburon 94920 (415) 435-2225

Established in 1983 in CA.
Donor(s): Robert W. Morey, Jr., Maura Morey.
Foundation type: Independent
Financial data (yr. ended 10/31/88): Assets, $777,970 (M); gifts received, $450,000; expenditures, $272,092, including $230,008 for 28 grants (high: $56,850; low: $200).
Purpose and activities: Support primarily for Catholic churches and secondary and higher education.
Limitations: No grants to individuals.
Application information: Contributes only to pre-selected organizations. Applications not accepted.
Board meeting date(s): Oct.
Write: Maura B. Morey
Trustees: Maura Burke Morey, Robert W. Morey, Jr.
Employer Identification Number: 680003873

548
Samuel B. Mosher Foundation ⌑
3278 Loma Riviera Dr.
San Diego 92110 (714) 226-6122

Incorporated in 1951 in CA.
Donor(s): Samuel B. Mosher,† Goodwin J. Pelissero, Deborah S. Pelissero.
Foundation type: Independent
Financial data (yr. ended 8/31/88): Assets, $4,820,707 (M); expenditures, $221,238, including $203,200 for 14 grants (high: $67,500; low: $200; average: $10,000-$15,000).
Purpose and activities: Grants mainly for educational purposes; some support for agencies or organizations benefiting youth and cultural organizations.
Types of support: Building funds, general purposes, operating budgets, program-related investments, scholarship funds.
Limitations: Giving primarily in AZ and CA. No grants to individuals, or for endowment funds, scholarships, fellowships, or matching gifts.
Application information: Application form not required.
Initial approach: Proposal
Copies of proposal: 1
Deadline(s): None
Board meeting date(s): Monthly
Final notification: None
Write: Robert R. Fredrickson, Secy.
Officers and Trustees:* Margaret C. Mosher,* Pres.; Robert R. Fredrickson,* Secy.; Marjorie Chelini, Marilyn I. Fredrickson, Laverne Gates, Lester Maitlan.
Number of staff: None.
Employer Identification Number: 956037266

549
Irving I. Moskowitz Foundation ⌑
4201 Long Beach Blvd.
Long Beach 90807

Established in 1968 in CA.
Donor(s): Irving I. Moskowitz, Cherna Moskowitz.
Foundation type: Independent
Financial data (yr. ended 12/31/86): Assets, $2,971,802 (M); gifts received, $207,550; expenditures, $295,419, including $291,625 for 30 grants (high: $200,000; low: $100).
Purpose and activities: Grants to Jewish organizations, including educational institutions, and to organizations promoting institutions in Israel.
Application information: Contributes only to pre-selected organizations. Applications not accepted.
Write: Irving I. Moskowitz, M.D., Pres.
Officers and Directors:* Irving I. Moskowitz, M.D.,* Pres.; Abraham Moskowitz,* V.P.; Cherna Moskowitz,* Secy.-Treas.
Employer Identification Number: 956201346

550
MSK Foundation ⌑ ☆
100 Shoreline Hwy., Bldg. A, Suite 190
Mill Valley 94941

Established in 1986 in CA.
Foundation type: Independent
Financial data (yr. ended 3/31/89): Assets, $16,041 (M); expenditures, $186,377, including $181,625 for 9 grants (high: $50,000; low: $100).
Purpose and activities: Giving for hospitals and medical research, child welfare, higher education, and a ballet company.
Types of support: General purposes.
Limitations: Giving primarily in CA. No grants to individuals.
Application information: Contributes only to pre-selected organizations. Applications not accepted.
Officers: Michael S. Klein, Pres.; Lauren T. Klein, Secy.
Employer Identification Number: 680114584

551
Muller Foundation ⌑
(Formerly Frank Muller, Sr. Foundation)
7080 Hollywood Blvd., Suite 318
Hollywood 90028 (213) 463-8176

Established in 1965 in CA.
Donor(s): Frank Muller.
Foundation type: Independent
Financial data (yr. ended 7/31/88): Assets, $6,086,560 (M); expenditures, $402,303, including $274,620 for 221 grants (high: $25,000; low: $100).
Purpose and activities: Emphasis on higher and secondary education, social service agencies, Roman Catholic church support, hospitals, and cultural programs.
Limitations: Giving primarily in CA. No grants to individuals.
Application information:
Initial approach: Letter
Deadline(s): None
Write: Walter Muller, Treas.
Officers and Directors:* R.A. Vilmure,* Pres.; Mary M. Thompson,* V.P.; Walter Muller,* Secy.; John Muller,* Treas.; James Muller, Tim Muller.
Employer Identification Number: 956121774

552
Alfred C. Munger Foundation ⌑
355 South Grand Ave., 35th Fl.
Los Angeles 90071-1560

Established in 1965 in CA.
Donor(s): Charles T. Munger, Nancy B. Munger.
Foundation type: Independent
Financial data (yr. ended 11/30/89): Assets, $13,473,343 (M); gifts received, $34,751; expenditures, $699,724, including $699,724 for 44 grants (high: $251,300; low: $100).
Purpose and activities: Grants primarily for higher and secondary education, a hospital, a family planning and population control institute, and health agencies; giving also for Protestant religious organizations.
Application information: Contributes only to pre-selected organizations. Applications not accepted.
Write: Richard D. Ebenshade, V.P.
Officers and Trustees:* Charles T. Munger,* Pres.; Richard D. Ebenshade,* V.P. and Secy.; Nancy B. Munger,* Treas.
Employer Identification Number: 952462103

553
David H. Murdock Foundation ⌑
10900 Wilshire Blvd., Suite 1600
Los Angeles 90024

Established in 1978 in CA.
Donor(s): Murdock Investment Corp.
Foundation type: Independent
Financial data (yr. ended 6/30/87): Assets, $14,026 (M); gifts received, $475,000; expenditures, $569,861, including $569,261 for 22 grants (high: $202,000; low: $250).
Purpose and activities: Support for cultural programs, with emphasis on ballet, and youth.
Application information: Contributes only to pre-selected organizations. Applications not accepted.
Officers: David H. Murdock, Pres.; Lilymae Penton, Secy.; William J. Scully, Treas.
Employer Identification Number: 953367891

554
Murdy Foundation ⌑
335 Centennial Way
Tustin 92680

Established in 1958.
Donor(s): John A. Murdy, Jr., Norma Murdy Trust B.
Foundation type: Independent
Financial data (yr. ended 12/31/87): Assets, $3,251,418 (M); expenditures, $162,035, including $141,555 for 13 grants (high: $41,175; low: $250).
Purpose and activities: Giving primarily for higher education and Protestant church support; support also for cultural programs, social agencies, and conservation.
Limitations: Giving primarily in CA.
Application information: Contributes only to pre-selected charitable organizations. Applications not accepted.
Officers: George E. Trotter, Jr., Pres.; John A. Murdy III, V.P.; Maxine Trotter, Secy.-Treas.
Employer Identification Number: 956082270

555
Lluella Morey Murphey Foundation ⌑
c/o Nossaman, Gunther, et al.
445 South Figueroa St., 31st Fl.
Los Angeles 90071

Established in 1967.
Donor(s): Lluella Morey Murphey.†
Foundation type: Independent
Financial data (yr. ended 11/30/88): Assets, $3,020,568 (M); expenditures, $206,579, including $113,789 for 27 grants (high: $10,000; low: $1,000; average: $1,000-$5,000).
Purpose and activities: Support for higher and secondary education, youth programs, health, and cultural programs.
Types of support: General purposes, building funds, equipment, matching funds, scholarship funds.
Limitations: Giving primarily in CA.
Application information:
Initial approach: Proposal
Deadline(s): None
Write: Harold S. Voegelin, Mgr.
Trustees: Alfred B. Hastings, Jr., James A. Schlinger, Harold S. Voegelin.
Employer Identification Number: 956152669

556
Dan Murphy Foundation ▼ ⌑
800 West Sixth St., Suite 1240
Los Angeles 90017-2715 (213) 623-3120
Mailing address: P.O. Box 76026, Los Angeles, CA 90076

Incorporated in 1957 in CA.
Donor(s): Bernadine Murphy Donohue.†
Foundation type: Independent
Financial data (yr. ended 12/31/87): Assets, $174,061,302 (M); expenditures, $4,682,939, including $4,349,139 for 96 grants (high: $2,544,400; low: $1,000; average: $1,000-$100,000).
Purpose and activities: Giving primarily for support of activities and charities of Roman Catholic Church Archdiocese of Los Angeles, including religious orders, colleges and schools, social service agencies, and medical institutions.
Types of support: Continuing support, special projects, general purposes.
Limitations: Giving primarily in Los Angeles, CA.
Publications: Informational brochure.
Application information: Grants generally initiated by the trustees. Applications not accepted.
Board meeting date(s): As needed
Write: Grace Robinson
Officers and Trustees:* Daniel J. Donohue,* Pres.; Oscar T. Lawler,* V.P.; Richard A. Grant, Jr.,* Secy.-Treas.; Rosemary E. Donohue,* Mgr.; Edward A. Landry, Julia D. Schwartz.
Number of staff: 1
Employer Identification Number: 956046963

557
The Peter & Mary Muth Foundation
335 Centennial Way
Tustin 92680-3786

Established in 1984 in CA.
Foundation type: Independent
Financial data (yr. ended 12/31/87): Assets, $2,135,088 (M); gifts received, $800,000; expenditures, $246,696, including $243,000 for 11 grants (high: $75,000; low: $1,000).
Purpose and activities: Support primarily for a hospital, a museum, secondary education, historic preservation, and a speech and hearing center; support also for various charitable organizations.
Types of support: General purposes.
Limitations: No grants to individuals.
Application information: Contributes only to pre-selected organizations. Applications not accepted.
Officers: Verlyn N. Jensen, Pres.; Joseph P. McCormick, V.P.; Robert Pralle, V.P.; Richard J. Muth, Secy.; Marvin E. Helsley, Treas.
Number of staff: 1 part-time professional.
Employer Identification Number: 330016627

558
The E. Nakamichi Foundation ▼
515 South Figueroa St., Suite 320
Los Angeles 90071 (213) 683-1608

Incorporated in 1982 in CA.
Donor(s): E. Nakamichi.†
Foundation type: Independent
Financial data (yr. ended 12/31/89): Assets, $32,288,108 (M); expenditures, $1,917,920, including $1,569,319 for 32 grants (high: $350,000; low: $3,250; average: $30,000-$50,000).
Purpose and activities: Emphasis on the musical arts (primarily baroque and classical); supports musical performances, television and radio broadcasts, public concert series, and occasional lecture series.
Types of support: Special projects.
Limitations: No grants to individuals, or for capital campaigns, endowments, deficit financing, building funds, or equipment.
Publications: Grants list, occasional report, program policy statement.
Application information: Application form not required.
Initial approach: Letter
Copies of proposal: 1
Deadline(s): None
Board meeting date(s): 3 times annually, generally Mar., June, and Oct.
Final notification: 1 week following board meeting
Write: Les Mitchnick, V.P. and Exec. Dir.
Officers: Yas Yamazaki,* Pres.; Les Mitchnick, V.P., Secy., and Exec. Dir.; Ray Privette,* Treas.
Directors:* Niro Nakamichi, Chair.; Douglas Brengel, Edward Y. Kakita, Takeshi Nakamichi, Ray Privette, Shunji Shinoda, Ted T. Tanaka, Koichi Yamasaki, Yas Yamazaki.
Number of staff: 1 full-time professional; 1 full-time support.
Employer Identification Number: 953847716

559
National Pro-Am Youth Fund
(Formerly Bing Crosby Youth Fund, Inc.)
490 Calla Principal
Monterey 93940 (408) 375-3151
Mailing address: P.O. Box 112, Monterey, CA 93942

Established in 1963 in CA.
Donor(s): Bing Crosby.†
Foundation type: Independent
Financial data (yr. ended 06/30/89): Assets, $440,832 (M); gifts received, $563,237; expenditures, $683,448, including $663,945 for 152 grants (high: $25,000; low: $600).
Purpose and activities: Giving primarily for youth agencies, social services, and higher and secondary education; support also for health services and cultural organizations.
Types of support: Building funds, equipment, scholarship funds, consulting services.
Limitations: Giving primarily in Monterey and Santa Cruz counties, CA. No grants to individuals.
Application information: Application form not required.
Initial approach: Letter
Deadline(s): None
Write: Carmel Martin, Jr., Secy.
Officers: Ted Durein, Pres.; Carmel C. Martin, Jr., Secy.; John Burns, Treas.
Trustees: Marsha Searle Brown, Peter J. Coniglio, Leon E. Edner, Warner Keeley, Frank Thacker, Murray C. Vout.
Employer Identification Number: 946050251

560
National Solar Energy Consortium ⌑
666 Baker St., Suite 405
Costa Mesa 92626 (714) 557-0202
Application address: 17330 Brookhurst St., Suite 350, Fountain Valley, CA 92708; Tel.: (714) 964-0898

Established in 1985 in CA.
Foundation type: Operating
Financial data (yr. ended 3/31/86): Assets, $132,512 (M); expenditures, $300,221, including $223,750 for 165 grants to individuals (high: $3,264; low: $135).
Purpose and activities: A private operating foundation. "To promote energy conservation and the use of renewable energy resouces and to assist, to the extent possible, energy conservation applications in a manner which renders such applications financially viable." The Solar Energy Conservation Assistance Program (SECAP) helps defray costs of a qualified Solar Energy Domestic Hot Water System, providing grants to individuals who purchase and install the system in their home.
Types of support: Grants to individuals.
Limitations: Giving primarily in CA.
Application information:
Write: Barry S. Tabachnick, C.E.O.
Officer and Directors: Barry S. Tabachnick, C.E.O.; Don Glazer, Aaron Goldsmith, Harvey Harms.
Employer Identification Number: 330102171

561
Nelson Family Foundation ⌑ ☆
4801 Wilshire Blvd., Suite 304
Los Angeles 90010-3814 (213) 933-9399

Established in 1985 in CA.
Donor(s): Elizabeth S. Nelson.
Foundation type: Independent
Financial data (yr. ended 8/31/89): Assets, $1,141,309 (M); gifts received, $150,000; expenditures, $163,368, including $161,000 for 5 grants (high: $100,000; low: $1,000).
Purpose and activities: Giving for higher education, youth, and social service organizations.
Types of support: General purposes.
Limitations: Giving primarily in CA. No grants to individuals.
Application information: Contributes only to pre-selected organizations. Applications not accepted.
Trustees: Clarke A. Nelson, Elizabeth S. Nelson.
Employer Identification Number: 953945578

562
Florence Nelson Foundation ☆
120 Montgomery St., Suite 2425
San Francisco 94104-4327 (415) 392-2384

Established in 1952.
Foundation type: Independent
Financial data (yr. ended 09/30/88): Assets, $2,948,233 (M); gifts received, $1,500; expenditures, $44,553, including $25,700 for 16 grants (high: $3,000; low: $500).
Purpose and activities: Giving generally restricted to the handicapped, the elderly, underprivileged youth, and animal welfare.
Types of support: General purposes.
Limitations: Giving limited to Santa Clara County, CA. No grants to individuals.
Application information: Applications not accepted.
Board meeting date(s): As required
Write: Evylyn Pearce
Officers and Directors:* John C. Higgins,* Pres.; Roger W. Ross,* V.P.; Edwina Kump,* Secy.-Treas.; Ray L. Byrne, Yuen T. Gin, P.E. Greenlee, Helen R. Nelson.
Number of staff: 1 part-time professional.
Employer Identification Number: 946092218

563
New Roads Foundation ⌑
c/o Gelfand, Rennert & Feldman
1880 Century Park East, No. 900
Los Angeles 90067

Donor(s): Neil Diamond.
Foundation type: Independent
Financial data (yr. ended 12/31/88): Assets, $1,338,133 (M); gifts received, $17,000; expenditures, $50,734, including $49,065 for 24 grants (high: $16,500; low: $65).
Purpose and activities: Grants for social services, Jewish organizations and welfare funds, and secondary education; some support for music.
Application information: Applications not accepted.
Trustees: David Braun, Neil Diamond, Marshall M. Gelfand.
Employer Identification Number: 136327069

564
The Henry Mayo Newhall Foundation ⌑
Three Embarcadero Ctr., Suite 2100
San Francisco 94111 (415) 951-7509

Incorporated in 1963 in CA.
Donor(s): Alice O'Meara,† The Newhall Land and Farming Co.
Foundation type: Independent
Financial data (yr. ended 12/31/88): Assets, $10,000,000 (M); expenditures, $400,000, including $354,000 for grants.
Purpose and activities: Giving "within the geographic areas that are associated with the career of Henry Mayo Newhall"; support for the Henry Mayo Newhall Hospital and secondary and agricultural education.
Limitations: Giving primarily in CA. No grants to individuals.
Application information:
Initial approach: Letter
Deadline(s): None
Write: Ralph L. Preston, Secy.
Officers: George Newhall,* Pres.; David N. Hill,* V.P.; Jon Newhall,* V.P.; Ralph L. Preston, Secy.
Directors:* Judith Hunt, Peter McBean, Henry K. Newhall, Jane Newhall, Scott Newhall, Prudence Noor, Edwin Newhall Woods.
Number of staff: 1 part-time professional.
Employer Identification Number: 946073084

565
Calvin M. and Raquel H. Newman Charitable Trust ⌑
44 Macondray Ln., Apt. 6W
San Francisco 94133

Established in 1973.
Foundation type: Independent
Financial data (yr. ended 12/31/88): Assets, $2,062,504 (M); expenditures, $183,356, including $144,815 for 35 grants (high: $25,000; low: $18; average: $100-$1,000).
Purpose and activities: Grants primarily for Jewish welfare funds and religious education.
Limitations: No grants to individuals, including scholarships and loans.
Application information: Contributes only to pre-selected organizations. Applications not accepted.
Trustee: Raquel H. Newman.
Employer Identification Number: 476081135

566
Andrew Norman Foundation
10960 Wilshire Blvd., Suite 820
Los Angeles 90024 (213) 478-1213

Incorporated in 1958 in CA.
Donor(s): Andrew Norman.†
Foundation type: Independent
Financial data (yr. ended 06/30/88): Assets, $6,258,630 (M); expenditures, $354,298, including $193,350 for 24 grants (high: $60,000; low: $200; average: $5,000-$25,000).
Purpose and activities: Emphasis on seed money for the environment, medical education, justice and the legal system, and the arts and humanities.
Types of support: Seed money, special projects.
Limitations: Giving primarily in CA, with emphasis on the Los Angeles area. No grants to individuals, or for endowment funds, scholarships, or fellowships.
Application information: Contributes only to pre-selected organizations. Applications not accepted.
Board meeting date(s): May and as required
Write: Dan Olincy, Secy.
Officers and Trustees:* Virginia G. Olincy,* Pres.; Bernice G. Kranson,* V.P.; Dan Olincy,* Secy.-Treas.
Number of staff: None.
Employer Identification Number: 953433781

567
Merle Norman/Nethercutt Foundation ⌑ ☆
15180 Bledsoe St.
Sylmar 91342-2797

Established in 1985 in CA.
Donor(s): Jack B. Nethercutt, Dorothy S. Nethercutt.
Foundation type: Independent
Financial data (yr. ended 12/31/88): Assets, $233,235 (M); gifts received, $100,000; expenditures, $500,104, including $500,000 for 1 grant.
Purpose and activities: Support for hospitals and higher education.
Types of support: Building funds.
Limitations: Giving primarily in CA. No grants to individuals.
Application information: Contributes only to pre-selected organizations. Applications not accepted.
Officers and Directors: Jack B. Nethercutt, Pres.; Dorothy S. Nethercutt, V.P.; Arthur O. Armstrong, Secy.
Employer Identification Number: 954007395

568
The Kenneth T. and Eileen L. Norris Foundation ▼
11 Golden Shore, Suite 440
Long Beach 90802 (213) 435-8444

Trust established in 1963 in CA.
Donor(s): Kenneth T. Norris,† Eileen L. Norris.†
Foundation type: Independent
Financial data (yr. ended 11/30/89): Assets, $79,400,000 (M); expenditures, $3,640,298, including $3,286,800 for 121 grants (high: $625,000; low: $1,000; average: $5,000-$20,000).
Purpose and activities: Emphasis on hospitals, health, higher and other education, medical research, cultural programs, social services, child welfare, and the handicapped.
Types of support: Building funds, equipment, research, scholarship funds, continuing support, endowment funds, professorships, seed money, matching funds, special projects, general purposes.
Limitations: Giving primarily in Los Angeles County, CA. No grants to individuals; no loans.
Application information: Application form not required.
Initial approach: Letter
Copies of proposal: 1
Deadline(s): None
Board meeting date(s): As required
Write: Ronald R. Barnes, Exec. Dir.
Officer and Trustees: Ronald R. Barnes, Exec. Dir.; William G. Corey, George M. Gordon, Harlyne J. Norris, Kenneth T. Norris, Jr.
Number of staff: 1 part-time professional; 4 part-time support.
Employer Identification Number: 956080374

569
The Numata Center for Buddhist Translation and Research ⌑
2620 Warring St.
Berkeley 94704 (415) 843-4128

Established in 1984 in CA.
Donor(s): Ekoji Buddhist Temple.
Foundation type: Independent
Financial data (yr. ended 12/31/88): Assets, $45,452 (M); gifts received, $317,155; expenditures, $300,330, including $123,068 for grants to individuals.
Purpose and activities: Support for major educational institutions with strong faculties in Buddhist studies, and for scholarly Buddhist publications.
Types of support: Publications.
Application information:
Initial approach: Letter
Deadline(s): None
Write: Kiyoshi Yamashita, Pres.
Officer: Rev. Kiyoshi Yamashita, Pres.
Trustees: Archbishop Shocho Hagami, Rev. Kenryu Tsuji, Shigeru Yamamoto, Bishop Seigen Yamaoka.
Employer Identification Number: 942935534

570
The Oak Foundation U.S.A. ⌑ ☆
c/o Price Waterhouse (ITS)
555 California St., Suite 3800
San Francisco 94104

Established in 1986 in NY.
Donor(s): The Oak Trust, The Forest Trust.
Foundation type: Independent
Financial data (yr. ended 12/31/88): Assets, $6,340,671 (M); gifts received, $4,850,000; expenditures, $250,004, including $227,500 for 5 grants (high: $120,000; low: $15,000).
Purpose and activities: Support for higher education and child development.
Limitations: No grants to individuals.
Application information: Contributes only to pre-selected organizations. Applications not accepted.
Officers and Directors: Alan M. Parker, Pres.; Jette Parker, V.P. and Secy.
Employer Identification Number: 133321196

571
The Oakland Athletics Community Fund ⌑
Oakland-Alameda County Coliseum
Oakland 94621
Application address: Oakland-Alameda County Coliseum, Oakland CA 94621

Established in 1981 in CA.
Foundation type: Independent
Financial data (yr. ended 12/31/87): Assets, $38,427 (M); gifts received, $224,308; expenditures, $252,588, including $189,843 for grants (high: $27,500).

Purpose and activities: Giving for charitable purposes; some emphasis on youth and the aged.
Limitations: No grants to individuals.
Application information:
Write: Dave Perron, Trustee
Trustee: Dave Perron.
Employer Identification Number: 942826655

572
Occidental Petroleum Charitable Foundation, Inc. ▼ ⌑
10889 Wilshire Blvd.
Los Angeles 90024 (213) 208-8800

Incorporated in 1959 in NY.
Donor(s): Occidental Petroleum Corp.
Foundation type: Company-sponsored
Financial data (yr. ended 12/31/87): Assets, $1,649,160 (M); gifts received, $1,500,000; expenditures, $1,207,963, including $1,010,797 for 33 grants (high: $100,000; low: $500; average: $5,000-$50,000) and $191,951 for 667 employee matching gifts.
Purpose and activities: Grants primarily for cultural programs and for higher education, including an employee matching gift program, hospitals, and a few national organizations for social betterment on a national basis.
Types of support: Employee matching gifts, scholarship funds, general purposes, building funds, equipment, capital campaigns.
Limitations: No grants to individuals.
Publications: Application guidelines.
Application information:
Initial approach: Proposal of no more than 4 pages
Copies of proposal: 1
Deadline(s): Proposals accepted between Sept. 1 and Nov. 1
Board meeting date(s): Mar., June, Sept., and Dec.
Write: Evelyn S. Wong, Asst. Secy.-Treas.
Officers: Arthur Groman, Pres.; Maurie A. Moss, V.P.; Paul C. Hebner, Secy.-Treas.
Directors: Armand Hammer, Ray R. Irani, Richard Jacobs, Rosemary Tomich.
Employer Identification Number: 166052784

573
Robert Stewart Odell and Helen Pfeiffer Odell Fund ⌑
49 Geary St., Rm. 244
San Francisco 94108 (415) 391-0292

Established in 1967 in CA.
Donor(s): Robert Stewart Odell,† Helen Pfeiffer Odell.
Foundation type: Independent
Financial data (yr. ended 12/31/88): Assets, $20,491,401 (M); expenditures, $986,595, including $774,890 for 89 grants (high: $14,500; low: $750).
Purpose and activities: Emphasis on higher education, social services, youth agencies, the handicapped, and child welfare.
Limitations: Giving primarily in the San Francisco Bay Area, CA. No grants to individuals.
Application information:
Initial approach: Letter
Copies of proposal: 1
Deadline(s): Apr. 15 through Oct. 15
Board meeting date(s): Monthly
Trustees: John P. Collins, Paul B. Fay, Jr., Wells Fargo Bank, N.A.
Employer Identification Number: 946132116

574
Orleton Trust Fund ⌑
40 West Third Ave., No. 904
San Mateo 94402
Additional office: c/o Mrs. Anne Johnston Greene, Co-Trustee, 1101 Runnymede Rd., Dayton, OH 45419

Trust established in 1944 in OH.
Donor(s): Mary E. Johnston.†
Foundation type: Independent
Financial data (yr. ended 12/31/88): Assets, $7,195,072 (M); expenditures, $780,967, including $731,967 for 97 grants (high: $230,000; low: $250; average: $500-$5,000).
Purpose and activities: Support for secondary and higher education, cultural programs, youth and social service agencies, and community funds; grants also for Protestant churches and religious associations, health associations, and ecology and population control groups.
Limitations: Giving primarily in Dayton, OH, and San Mateo County, CA. No grants to individuals.
Application information: Contributes only to pre-selected organizations. Applications not accepted.
Board meeting date(s): As required
Trustees: Anne Johnston Greene, Jean J. Weaver.
Employer Identification Number: 316024543

575
Samuel and Helen Oschin Foundation, Inc. ⌑
P.O. Box 48289
Los Angeles 90048

Established in 1980 in CA.
Donor(s): Samuel Oschin, Helen Oschin.†
Foundation type: Independent
Financial data (yr. ended 09/30/89): Assets, $4,648,733 (M); expenditures, $226,295, including $207,769 for 28 grants (high: $100,000; low: $18).
Purpose and activities: Support primarily for Jewish welfare organizations, higher education, and cultural programs.
Limitations: Giving primarily in CA, particularly Los Angeles. No grants to individuals, or for scholarships.
Application information: Contributes only to pre-selected organizations. Applications not accepted.
Officers: Samuel Oschin, Pres.; William Glikbarg, V.P.; Irving Oschin, Secy.-Treas.
Directors: Barbara Oschin, Michael Oschin.
Employer Identification Number: 953560088

576
Bernard Osher Foundation ▼
220 San Bruno Ave.
San Francisco 94103-5090 (415) 861-5587

Established in 1977 in CA.
Donor(s): Bernard A. Osher.
Foundation type: Independent
Financial data (yr. ended 12/31/88): Assets, $38,808,530 (M); expenditures, $1,361,778, including $1,291,290 for 105 grants (high: $300,000; low: $130).
Purpose and activities: Giving primarily for the arts and humanities, including the fine and performing arts; education, especially higher education; and social services, with emphasis on youth and drug abuse; support also for Jewish organizations.
Types of support: General purposes, special projects.
Limitations: Giving primarily in San Francisco, Alameda, Contra Costa, Marin, and San Mateo counties, CA. No grants to individuals.
Publications: Informational brochure.
Application information: Application form not required.
Initial approach: Letter
Copies of proposal: 1
Deadline(s): None
Board meeting date(s): Six times per year
Write: Patricia Tracy-Nagle, Exec. Admin.
Officers: Barbro Sachs-Osher, Pres.; Patricia Tracy-Nagle, Exec. Admin.
Directors: Frederick Balderston, Reeder Butterfield, Judith E. Ciani, Robert Friend, Ron Kaufman, Bernard A. Osher, Alfred Wilsey.
Number of staff: 1 full-time professional.
Employer Identification Number: 942506257

577
Ottenstein Family Foundation, Inc. ⌑
225 Stevens, Suite 210A
Solana Beach 92075

Established in 1960 in MD and DC.
Donor(s): Members of the Ottenstein family.
Foundation type: Independent
Financial data (yr. ended 4/30/88): Assets, $1,784,316 (M); gifts received, $2,000; expenditures, $136,043, including $113,850 for 31 grants (high: $65,500; low: $50).
Purpose and activities: Giving primarily for Jewish welfare and temple support; support also for cultural programs, social services, health, and education.
Limitations: Giving primarily in CA, particularly San Diego.
Directors: Leonard Glass, Adam S. Ottenstein, Paul F. Ottenstein, S.G. Ottenstein, V.H. Ottenstein.
Employer Identification Number: 526036064

578
The Ovitz Family Foundation ⌑ ☆
1888 Century Park East, 14th Fl.
Los Angeles 90067

Established in 1986 in CA.
Donor(s): Michael S. Ovitz.
Foundation type: Independent
Financial data (yr. ended 12/31/88): Assets, $594,732 (M); expenditures, $425,911, including $424,733 for 19 grants (high: $195,000; low: $200).
Purpose and activities: Giving primarily for health, hospitals, and higher education, including medical education.
Limitations: Giving primarily in CA. No grants to individuals.

Application information: Contributes only to pre-selected organizations. Applications not accepted.
Officers: Michael S. Ovitz, Pres.; Robert Goldman, Secy.; Bruce King, C.F.O.
Employer Identification Number: 521354173

579
Oxnard Foundation
505 Sansome St., Suite 1001
San Francisco 94111 (415) 981-3455

Established in 1973.
Donor(s): Thomas Thornton Oxnard.†
Foundation type: Independent
Financial data (yr. ended 12/31/88): Assets, $4,826,812 (M); expenditures, $400,805, including $321,843 for 8 grants (high: $75,000; low: $20,000).
Purpose and activities: Giving primarily for medical research, with emphasis on cancer and surgical research.
Types of support: Matching funds, professorships, research.
Limitations: Giving primarily in NY, TX, NM, and northern CA. No grants to individuals, or for general support, capital funds, endowments, scholarships, fellowships, special projects, publications, or conferences; no loans.
Application information: Application form not required.
Initial approach: Letter
Deadline(s): Feb. 15
Board meeting date(s): Quarterly
Final notification: 3 months
Write: Stephen W. Veitch, Pres.
Officer and Directors:* Stephen W. Veitch,* Pres.; Caroline Meade, Gary J. Meade, Charles H. Thieriot, Jr., Christopher Veitch.
Employer Identification Number: 237323007

580
The Pacific Endowment ⌑ ☆
7910 Ivanhoe Ave., Suite 436
La Jolla 92037

Established in 1985.
Donor(s): Stephen Schutz, Susan Schutz.
Foundation type: Independent
Financial data (yr. ended 6/30/88): Assets, $1,068,546 (M); gifts received, $210,000; expenditures, $47,288, including $44,000 for 11 grants (high: $10,000; low: $1,000).
Purpose and activities: Support primarily for social services, a day school, and health associations.
Types of support: General purposes.
Limitations: Giving primarily in San Diego and La Jolla, CA.
Application information: Contributes only to pre-selected organizations. Applications not accepted.
Officers: Stephen Schutz, Pres.; Susan Schutz, Secy.-Treas.
Employer Identification Number: 330142633

581
Pacific Mutual Charitable Foundation
700 Newport Center Dr.
Newport Beach 92660 (714) 640-3014

Established in 1984 in CA.
Donor(s): Pacific Mutual Life Insurance Co.
Foundation type: Company-sponsored
Financial data (yr. ended 12/31/88): Assets, $5,544,750 (M); gifts received, $10,513; expenditures, $530,218, including $499,513 for 105 grants (high: $201,385; low: $100; average: $500-$2,000).
Purpose and activities: Grants for health and human services, education, arts and culture, and civic and community services; special emphasis on AIDS education and support programs.
Types of support: Capital campaigns, special projects.
Limitations: Giving primarily in areas of company operations. No support for professional associations, veterans', labor, or fraternal organizations, athletic or social clubs, or sectarian religious groups, except for programs which are available to everyone. No grants to individuals, or for operating expenses of organizations which receive United Way funding, except under special circumstances.
Publications: Corporate giving report (including application guidelines).
Application information: Application form not required.
Initial approach: Proposal
Deadline(s): Sept. 15
Board meeting date(s): Dec.
Final notification: After Jan. 1
Write: Robert G. Haskell, Pres.
Officers: Harry G. Bubb,* Chair.; Robert G. Haskell,* Pres.; Patricia A. Kosky, V.P.; Audrey L. Milfs, Secy.; Harold T. Joanning, C.F.O.
Directors:* Walter B. Gerken, Thomas C. Sutton, Joseph A. Thomas.
Number of staff: 1 full-time professional; 1 full-time support.
Employer Identification Number: 953433806

582
Pacific Telesis Foundation ▼
Pacific Telesis Ctr.
130 Kearney St., Rm. 3351
San Francisco 94108 (415) 394-3693

Established in 1984 in CA.
Donor(s): Pacific Telesis Group.
Foundation type: Company-sponsored
Financial data (yr. ended 12/31/89): Assets, $62,460,587 (M); gifts received, $10,000,000; expenditures, $9,596,767, including $8,022,255 for 350 grants (high: $250,000; low: $500; average: $2,000-$50,000) and $131,088 for 523 employee matching gifts.
Purpose and activities: Support primarily for elementary and secondary education reform, higher education, culture, community funds, and community and civic affairs.
Types of support: Publications, special projects, fellowships, scholarship funds, seed money, employee matching gifts, matching funds, technical assistance.
Limitations: Giving primarily in CA, NV, and other select states where Pacific Telesis Group has business interests. No support for religious organizations for religious purposes, organizations receiving operating support from the United Way, medical clinics, or individual primary or secondary schools or school districts. No grants to individuals, or for general operating purposes, medical research, capital projects or endowments, or goodwill advertising; no loans.
Publications: 990-PF, annual report (including application guidelines).
Application information: Application form not required.
Initial approach: Letter
Copies of proposal: 1
Deadline(s): None
Board meeting date(s): Quarterly
Final notification: 2 months
Write: Thomas S. Donahoe, Pres.
Officers and Directors:* Sam Ginn,* Chair.; Arthur C. Latno, Jr.,* Vice-Chair.; Thomas S. Donahoe,* Pres.; Richard R. Roll,* V.P.; Richard W. Odgers,* Secy.; Lydell L. Christensen,* Treas.; Jim Moberg.
Number of staff: 8 part-time professional; 3 part-time support.
Employer Identification Number: 942950832

583
Pacific Western Foundation ⌑
8344 East Florence, Suite E
Downey 90240

Successor to Western Gear Foundation, incorporated in 1953 in CA; name changed in 1982.
Donor(s): Western Gear Corp.
Foundation type: Independent
Financial data (yr. ended 11/30/89): Assets, $3,563,426 (M); expenditures, $291,084, including $234,450 for 34 grants (high: $80,000; low: $50).
Purpose and activities: Giving for higher and secondary education, Roman Catholic church support, hospitals, and medical research.
Limitations: Giving primarily in CA.
Application information:
Initial approach: Proposal
Deadline(s): None
Write: Charles F. Bannan, Pres.
Officers: Charles F. Bannan, Pres.; Joseph T. Nally, V.P.; M. Patricia Cruden, Secy.; Elmer L. Stone, Treas.
Employer Identification Number: 956097360

584
The David and Lucile Packard Foundation ▼
300 Second St., Suite 200
Los Altos 94022 (415) 948-7658

Incorporated in 1964 in CA.
Donor(s): David Packard, Lucile Packard.†
Foundation type: Independent
Financial data (yr. ended 12/31/89): Assets, $245,887,758 (M); gifts received, $126,789,104; expenditures, $30,219,451, including $27,675,502 for 354 grants (high: $7,500,000; low: $800; average: $5,000-$100,000) and $2,280,000 for 4 loans.
Purpose and activities: Local support for the performing arts, education, youth, homeless children, management assistance, handicapped, and child welfare; national and international giving in areas of conservation, ancient studies, film preservation, and population issues.
Types of support: General purposes, building funds, equipment, land acquisition, research, internships, matching funds, program-related investments, consulting services, technical

assistance, loans, operating budgets, capital campaigns, seed money, renovation projects, fellowships, special projects, emergency funds.
Limitations: Giving for the arts and community development primarily in the San Francisco, and Monterey Bay, CA, areas, with some suport also in the Pueblo area of CO; national giving for child health and education; national and international giving for population and the environment. No support for religious purposes. No grants to individuals; generally no grants for endowment funds.
Publications: Annual report (including application guidelines), grants list, newsletter, occasional report, informational brochure (including application guidelines).
Application information: Application form not required.
Initial approach: Proposal
Copies of proposal: 1
Deadline(s): Jan. 2, Apr. 1, July 1, and Oct. 1
Board meeting date(s): Mar., June, Sept., and Dec.
Final notification: Directly after board meetings
Write: Colburn S. Wilbur, Exec. Dir.
Officers and Trustees:* David Packard,* Chair.; Susan Packard Orr,* Vice-Chair.; David Woodley Packard,* Vice-Chair.; Barbara P. Wright, Secy.; Edwin E. Van Bronkhorst, Treas.; Colburn S. Wilbur, Exec. Dir.; Nancy Packard Burnett, Robin Chandler Duke, Robert Glaser, M.D., Julie E. Packard, Frank Roberts.
Number of staff: 10 full-time professional; 2 part-time professional; 13 full-time support; 4 part-time support.
Employer Identification Number: 942278431

585
George B. Page Foundation ⌑
P.O. Drawer MM
Santa Barbara 93102 (805) 963-1841

Established in 1961 in CA.
Donor(s): Mission Linen Companies, Montecto Mfg. Co.
Foundation type: Independent
Financial data (yr. ended 12/31/86): Assets, $1,861,868 (M); expenditures, $69,202, including $59,640 for 24 grants (high: $10,000; low: $500; average: $500).
Purpose and activities: Giving mainly for youth and child welfare agencies.
Types of support: Operating budgets, continuing support, annual campaigns, seed money, emergency funds, deficit financing, general purposes, special projects.
Limitations: No grants to individuals, or for endowment funds or matching gifts.
Application information: Application form required.
Initial approach: Letter
Deadline(s): Submit proposal preferably from Jan. through June; deadline June 30
Board meeting date(s): Annually
Final notification: 6 months
Write: John R. Erickson, Trustee
Trustees: John R. Erickson, Anthony Gunterman, Wayne Kees, Henry W. Logan, George B. Page, Harold Scollin, Louis Simon.
Number of staff: None.
Employer Identification Number: 956121985

586
Paloheimo Charitable Trust ⌑ ☆
c/o Security Pacific National Bank
P.O. Box 3189, Terminal Annex
Los Angeles 90051
Application address: Security Pacific National Bank, 234 East Colorado Blvd., Pasadena, CA 91101; Tel.: (818) 304-3040

Established in 1980.
Foundation type: Operating
Financial data (yr. ended 6/30/89): Assets, $1,544,345 (M); gifts received, $70,052; expenditures, $61,904.
Purpose and activities: A private operating foundation; support for the preservation and care of the historic and cultural heritage of local properties.
Limitations: Giving primarily in Pasadena, CA, and surrounding communities.
Application information:
Deadline(s): None
Write: Larry Plumer, V.P., Security Pacific National Bank
Trustee: Security Pacific National Bank.
Employer Identification Number: 953643948

587
The Hoyt and Carol Pardee Foundation ⌑
8530 Wilshire Blvd., Suite 407
Beverly Hills 90211

Established in 1986 in CA.
Donor(s): Hoyt S. Pardee, Carol K. Pardee.
Foundation type: Independent
Financial data (yr. ended 12/31/89): Assets, $309,784 (M); gifts received, $300,000; expenditures, $187,742, including $183,299 for 16 grants (high: $127,500; low: $100).
Purpose and activities: Initial year of grantmaking, 1987; general charitable giving with substantial support for a youth organization.
Limitations: Giving primarily in CA. No grants to individuals.
Application information: Contributes only to pre-selected organizations. Applications not accepted.
Officers: Hoyt S. Pardee, Pres.; Raymond C. Sandler, Secy.-Treas.
Employer Identification Number: 954079475

588
The Parker Foundation
1200 Prospect St., Suite 575
La Jolla 92037 (619) 456-3038

Trust established in 1971 in CA; incorporated in 1975.
Donor(s): Gerald T. Parker,† Inez Grant Parker.†
Foundation type: Independent
Financial data (yr. ended 09/30/89): Assets, $13,092,252 (M); expenditures, $795,623, including $713,250 for 62 grants (high: $100,000; low: $1,000; average: $5,000-$15,000).
Purpose and activities: Equal emphasis on cultural programs, health and welfare, including medical support and research, adult services, and youth agencies; grants also for education and community activities. Giving largely in the form of partial seed money and matching or challenge grants; generally no support that would make an organization dependent on the foundation.
Types of support: Seed money, matching funds, operating budgets, annual campaigns, emergency funds, building funds, equipment, land acquisition, research, program-related investments, continuing support, special projects, publications, general purposes, renovation projects.
Limitations: Giving limited to San Diego County, CA. No support for sectarian religious purposes. No grants to individuals, or for endowment funds, scholarships, or fellowships; no loans.
Publications: Annual report, informational brochure (including application guidelines).
Application information: Application form not required.
Initial approach: Letter
Copies of proposal: 6
Deadline(s): None
Board meeting date(s): Monthly
Final notification: 2 months
Write: Robbin C. Powell, Asst. Secy.
Officers and Directors:* Kenneth R. Rearwin,* Pres.; V. DeWitt Shuck,* V.P.; William E. Beamer,* Secy.-Treas.; John F. Borchers, Roy M. Drew, Judy McDonald.
Number of staff: None.
Employer Identification Number: 510141231

589
The Ralph M. Parsons Foundation ▼
1055 Wilshire Blvd., Suite 1701
Los Angeles 90017 (213) 482-3185

Incorporated in 1961 in CA.
Donor(s): Ralph M. Parsons.†
Foundation type: Independent
Financial data (yr. ended 12/31/88): Assets, $142,044,082 (M); expenditures, $7,713,799, including $6,020,765 for 111 grants (high: $465,819; low: $1,000; average: $10,000-$75,000).
Purpose and activities: Giving for higher and secondary education, with emphasis on engineering, technology, law, science and medicine; and for social impact areas, including assistance to children, women, families, and seniors; grants also for cultural and civic projects, and health services for disadvantaged populations.
Types of support: Seed money, equipment, matching funds, special projects, internships, renovation projects, research, scholarship funds, fellowships, operating budgets.
Limitations: Giving limited to Los Angeles County, CA, with the exception of some grants for higher education. No support for sectarian religious or fraternal purposes, or for programs for which substantial support from government or other sources is readily available. No grants to individuals, or for continuing support, annual campaigns, emergency or endowment funds, land acquisition, workshops, exhibits, surveys, or conferences.
Publications: Annual report.
Application information: Application form not required.
Initial approach: Letter
Copies of proposal: 1
Deadline(s): None

Board meeting date(s): Bimonthly beginning in Jan.
Final notification: 4 months
Write: Christine Sisley, Exec. Dir.
Officers: Joseph G. Hurley,* Pres.; Leroy B. Houghton,* V.P. and C.F.O.; Everett B. Laybourne,* V.P.; Christine Sisley, Secy. and Exec. Dir.
Directors:* Ira J. Blanco, Albert A. Dorskind, Robert F. Erburu, Alex Haley, Edgar R. Jackson.
Number of staff: 3 full-time professional; 3 full-time support.
Employer Identification Number: 956085895

590
The Albert Parvin Foundation ⌑
9100 Wilshire Blvd., No. 458
Los Angeles 90212 (213) 858-8890

Incorporated in 1960 in CA.
Donor(s): Albert B. Parvin.
Foundation type: Independent
Financial data (yr. ended 12/31/88): Assets, $5,660,307 (M); expenditures, $575,414, including $471,050 for 21 grants (high: $205,000; low: $500).
Purpose and activities: "... to promote peace, understanding and goodwill among the nations of the world through education, enlightenment and recognition of achievements toward this objective." Supports fellowship programs for young men from new and underdeveloped nations for study at Princeton University and University of California at Los Angeles. Grants also to social agencies, for child welfare services, and medical research.
Types of support: General purposes, fellowships.
Application information: Application form not required.
Initial approach: Letter
Deadline(s): None
Write: Albert B. Parvin, V.P.
Officers and Directors: Robert L. Spencer, Pres.; Albert B. Parvin, V.P.; Phyllis Parvin, Secy.; Henry Jaffe, Joseph Lowitz, Bernard Silbert.
Employer Identification Number: 952158989

591
Pasadena Area Residential Aid A Corporation ⌑
P.O. Box 984
Pasadena 91102 (213) 681-1331

Foundation established in 1948 in CA.
Foundation type: Independent
Financial data (yr. ended 7/31/87): Assets, $2,437,261 (M); gifts received, $3,522,645; expenditures, $2,423,048, including $2,374,503 for 913 grants (high: $331,794; low: $20).
Purpose and activities: Grants largely for higher education, cultural programs, Christian church support, and social services; support also for youth agencies, hospitals, and community funds.
Application information: Contributions initiated by donor/members only. Applications not accepted.
Board meeting date(s): Annually
Write: Linda M. Moore, Asst. Secy.
Officers and Directors:* Joseph D. Messler,* Pres.; Robert R. Huffman,* V.P.; Thomas S. Jones III,* Secy.; James N. Gamble,* Treas.; Kathy L. Golden, Thayer S. Holbrook, George D. Jagels, Mary W. Johnson, Linda M. Moore, Robert F. Niven, Lee G. Paul, Philip V. Swan.
Number of staff: 1 part-time professional.
Employer Identification Number: 952048774

592
Pasadena Foundation
16 North Marengo Ave., Suite 219
Pasadena 91101 (818) 796-2097

Established in 1953 in CA by resolution and declaration of trust.
Donor(s): Louis A. Webb,† Marion L. Webb,† Helen B. Lockett,† Dorothy I. Stewart,† Rebecca R. Anthony,† Lucille Crumb.†
Foundation type: Community
Financial data (yr. ended 12/31/88): Assets, $2,522,337 (M); gifts received, $368,103; expenditures, $480,776, including $441,712 for 168 grants.
Purpose and activities: Grants for capital improvements to established local agencies, with emphasis on child welfare and development, youth agencies, and senior citizen welfare; support also for alcohol and drug abuse programs, family planning and services, the handicapped, hospitals, hospices and health services, mental health, medical research, and museums.
Types of support: Building funds, equipment, matching funds, renovation projects, research.
Limitations: Giving limited to the Pasadena, CA, area. No grants to individuals, or for operating budgets, continuing support, annual campaigns, emergency funds, seed money, deficit financing, land acquisition, endowment funds, research, special projects, publications, conferences, consulting services, scholarships, or fellowships; no loans.
Publications: Annual report, application guidelines, informational brochure, program policy statement.
Application information: Application form required.
Initial approach: Letter
Copies of proposal: 1
Deadline(s): July 1
Board meeting date(s): Apr. and Dec.
Final notification: After Dec. meeting
Write: Josephine L. Stephen, Exec. Dir.
Advisory Board: Albert C. Lowe, Chair.; Fred H. Felberg, Vice-Chair.; Josephine L. Stephen, Exec. Dir. and Secy.; James B. Boyle, Jr., Harriman Cronk, James M. King, Sr., Joel V. Sheldon, David A. Werbelow, Marjorie Wyatt.
Trustees: Bank of America, Citizens Commercial Trust and Savings Bank, Interstate Bank, Security Pacific National Bank.
Number of staff: 1 part-time professional.
Employer Identification Number: 956047660

593
Pattiz Family Foundation ⌑
9304 Civic Center Dr., Suite 5
Beverly Hills 90210

Foundation established in 1953 in CA.
Donor(s): Oscar S. Pattiz.
Foundation type: Independent
Financial data (yr. ended 1/31/89): Assets, $1,395,613 (M); expenditures, $146,172, including $97,544 for 41 grants (high: $40,000; low: $35).
Purpose and activities: Emphasis on education, Jewish welfare funds, and temple support.
Limitations: Giving primarily in CA.
Officers and Directors:* Henry A. Pattiz,* Pres.; Cathy Lee Pattiz,* V.P.; Nancy Ilene Pattiz, Secy.-Treas.
Employer Identification Number: 956029776

594
Norman and Mary Pattiz Foundation
c/o Westwood One
9540 Washington Blvd.
Culver City 90232 (213) 473-2266

Established in 1985 in CA.
Donor(s): Norman Pattiz, Mary Pattiz.
Foundation type: Independent
Financial data (yr. ended 12/31/89): Assets, $1,570 (M); gifts received, $195,000; expenditures, $296,168, including $295,115 for 20 grants (high: $100,000; low: $100; average: $100-$100,000).
Purpose and activities: Support for hospitals, music education, youth and Jewish welfare.
Types of support: Continuing support, general purposes.
Application information: Applications not accepted.
Write: Ralph Goldman
Directors: Mary Pattiz, Norman Pattiz.
Employer Identification Number: 954019729

595
Edwin W. Pauley Foundation
10900 Wilshire Blvd., Suite 521
Los Angeles 90024 (213) 518-7377

Trust established in 1962 in CA.
Donor(s): Edwin W. Pauley,† Barbara Pauley Pagen.
Foundation type: Independent
Financial data (yr. ended 11/30/88): Assets, $6,850,140 (M); gifts received, $4,897,921; expenditures, $286,231, including $265,300 for 13 grants (high: $184,690; low: $110).
Purpose and activities: Grants principally for hospitals, cultural and civic organizations, and educational institutions, especially universities.
Types of support: Building funds, annual campaigns, continuing support, general purposes.
Limitations: Giving primarily in CA.
Application information: Application form not required.
Initial approach: Letter
Deadline(s): None
Write: William R. Pagen and Barbara Pauley Pagen, Trustees
Trustees: Barbara Pauley Pagen, William R. Pagen.
Employer Identification Number: 956039872

596
The PCS Foundation ⌑
2180 Sand Hill Rd., Suite 300
Menlo Park 94025 (415) 845-9080

Established in 1977 in CA.
Donor(s): Members of the Moldaw family.
Foundation type: Independent
Financial data (yr. ended 11/30/88): Assets, $1,769,534 (M); gifts received, $1,249,391; expenditures, $134,273, including $124,895 for 31 grants (high: $25,250; low: $50).
Purpose and activities: Support primarily for Jewish welfare and other social service agencies; grants also for AIDS and other medical research and health associations, foreign policy and international studies, the arts, and race relations.
Limitations: Giving primarily in CA, with emphasis on San Francisco and Stanford.
Application information: Application form not required.
Deadline(s): None
Write: Susan J. Moldaw
Officers: Stuart Moldaw, Pres.; Phyllis Moldaw, V.P. and Treas.
Employer Identification Number: 942450734

597
Peery Foundation ⌑
2560 Mission College Blvd., Suite 101
Santa Clara 95050

Established in 1977.
Donor(s): Richard T. Peery.
Foundation type: Independent
Financial data (yr. ended 9/30/88): Assets, $6,907,708 (M); gifts received, $135,275; expenditures, $395,464, including $363,688 for 33 grants (high: $299,000; low: $88).
Purpose and activities: Grants largely for Mormon religious organizations; some support for youth, education, and civic organizations.
Limitations: No grants to individuals.
Application information:
Initial approach: Letter
Write: Richard T. Peery, Pres.
Officers: Richard T. Peery, Pres.; Mildred D. Peery, V.P.; Dennis Peery, Treas.
Directors: John Arrillaga, Boyd C. Smith.
Employer Identification Number: 942460894

598
Charles Pelletier & Ray Precourt Memorial Foundation ⌑
c/o William T. Barden
P.O. Box 368
Los Alamitos 90720-0368

Established in 1967 in CA.
Foundation type: Independent
Financial data (yr. ended 09/30/89): Assets, $1,083,361 (M); expenditures, $56,967, including $45,000 for 3 grants (high: $35,000; low: $5,000).
Purpose and activities: Grants for social service and youth agencies, cultural programs, higher education, and hospitals.
Types of support: General purposes.
Limitations: Giving primarily in southern CA. No grants to individuals.
Application information: Contributes only to pre-selected organizations. Applications not accepted.
Officers: Leonard J. Pelletier, Chair.; Donalda Pelletier, Pres.; Kurt Shepard, V.P.; Renee P. Shepard, V.P.; Ben J. Little, Secy.-Treas.
Employer Identification Number: 952499281

599
Peninsula Community Foundation ▼
1204 Burlingame Ave.
P.O. Box 627
Burlingame 94011-0627 (415) 342-2477

Established as a trust in 1964 in CA; incorporated about 1982.
Foundation type: Community
Financial data (yr. ended 12/31/89): Assets, $41,848,306 (M); gifts received, $25,605,292; expenditures, $2,688,445, including $2,320,518 for 15 grants (high: $50,000; low: $50; average: $5,000-$20,000).
Purpose and activities: To support local cultural, educational, social service, and health programs; interests include youth, environment, elderly, disabled, civic concerns, and recreation; provides counseling services for local fund seekers. Giving includes grants to individuals as student aid, emergency assistance, and grants to local artists.
Types of support: Operating budgets, continuing support, seed money, emergency funds, equipment, matching funds, consulting services, technical assistance, internships, scholarship funds, special projects, publications, conferences and seminars, general purposes, lectureships, student aid, renovation projects, grants to individuals.
Limitations: Giving limited to San Mateo County and northern Santa Clara County, CA. No grants for endowment funds, annual campaigns, building funds, deficit financing, land acquisition, or research.
Publications: Annual report, application guidelines, informational brochure, newsletter, grants list.
Application information: Application form not required.
Initial approach: Letter
Copies of proposal: 1
Deadline(s): None
Board meeting date(s): Distribution committee meets in Jan., Mar., May, July, Sept., and Nov.
Final notification: 2 months
Write: Bill Somerville, Exec. Dir.
Officer: Bill Somerville, Exec. Dir.
Directors: Marjorie Bolton, Chair.; Rosemary Young, Vice-Chair.; T. Jack Foster, Jr., Bruce Hinchliffe, Albert J. Horn, Esq., Thomas M. Jenkins, Charles B. Johnson, Robert Kirkwood, Ernest A. Mitchell, John P. Renshaw, William Wilson III.
Number of staff: 3 full-time professional; 4 full-time support.
Employer Identification Number: 942746687

600
Penta Corporation
525 Middlefield Rd., Suite 200
Menlo Park 94025 (415) 329-1070
Additional address: c/o Hewlett-Packard Co., Bldg. 3U, P.O. Box 10490, Palo Alto, CA 94303-0971

Incorporated in 1980 in CA.
Donor(s): William R. Hewlett Charitable Trust.
Foundation type: Independent
Financial data (yr. ended 12/31/88): Assets, $26,646 (M); gifts received, $650,000; expenditures, $795,227, including $787,764 for 3 grants (high: $400,000; low: $33,564).
Purpose and activities: Giving for higher education and science.
Limitations: Giving primarily in CA. No grants to individuals.
Application information: Contributes only to pre-selected organizations. Applications not accepted.
Write: Roger W. Heyns, Secy.
Officers: Edwin E. Van Bronkhorst, Pres.; Roger W. Heyns, Secy.-Treas.
Director: William R. Hewlett.
Employer Identification Number: 942682181

601
Ann Peppers Foundation ⌑
199 South Los Robles Ave., Suite 711
Pasadena 91101-2460 (818) 449-1821

Established in 1959 in CA.
Donor(s): Ann Peppers.†
Foundation type: Independent
Financial data (yr. ended 12/31/87): Assets, $5,384,404 (M); expenditures, $397,393, including $304,097 for 65 grants (high: $40,000; low: $500).
Purpose and activities: Emphasis on small private colleges and community organizations with limited resources for fund raising; support also for activities that benefit young people and enhance their moral, educational and social well-being; and activities for senior citizens.
Types of support: Conferences and seminars, special projects, equipment.
Limitations: Giving limited to the Los Angeles, CA, metropolitan area. No grants to individuals, or for endowment funds.
Application information:
Initial approach: Brief letter
Copies of proposal: 1
Deadline(s): None
Board meeting date(s): Quarterly
Write: A.L. Burford, Jr., Secy.
Officers and Directors: W. Paul Colwell, Pres.; Giles S. Hall, V.P.; A.L. Burford, Jr., Secy.; Howard O. Wilson, Treas.
Employer Identification Number: 952114455

602
Walter K. Peterry Foundation, Inc. ⌑
1000 Elysian Park Ave.
Los Angeles 90012-1199

Established in 1967 in CA.
Foundation type: Independent
Financial data (yr. ended 12/31/87): Assets, $1,014,789 (M); expenditures, $73,933, including $64,000 for 16 grants (high: $25,000; low: $500).
Purpose and activities: Giving primarily to Catholic churches and organizations, including universities and secondary schools.
Application information: Applications not accepted.
Officers: Peter O'Malley,* V.P.; Mrs. Roland Seidler, Jr., Secy.-Treas.
Trustees:* Roland Seidler, Jr.
Employer Identification Number: 952484314

603
Leon S. Peters Foundation, Inc. ⌑
4712 North Van Ness Blvd.
Fresno 93704 (209) 227-5901

Established in 1959 in CA.
Donor(s): Leon S. Peters.†
Foundation type: Independent
Financial data (yr. ended 11/30/88): Assets, $9,694,960 (M); expenditures, $470,675, including $446,430 for 65 grants (high: $96,480; low: $100; average: $5,000).
Purpose and activities: Giving for community funds, cultural programs, higher education, youth agencies, museums, and hospitals.
Types of support: Scholarship funds, building funds, operating budgets.
Limitations: Giving primarily in Fresno, CA. No grants to individuals.
Application information: Applications not accepted.
Initial approach: Letter
Copies of proposal: 1
Board meeting date(s): Feb., May, Aug., and Nov.
Officers and Directors: Alice A. Peters, Pres. and Secy.-Treas.; Pete P. Peters, V.P.; Craig Apregan, George Apregan, Darrell Peters, Ronald Peters.
Number of staff: None.
Employer Identification Number: 946064669

604
Pfaffinger Foundation ▼ ⌑
Times Mirror Square
Los Angeles 90053 (213) 237-5743

Incorporated in 1936 in CA.
Donor(s): Frank X. Pfaffinger.†
Foundation type: Independent
Financial data (yr. ended 12/31/87): Assets, $58,094,393 (M); gifts received, $11,132; expenditures, $3,236,143, including $960,819 for 42 grants (high: $130,000; low: $4,769; average: $7,500-$35,000) and $1,740,530 for 390 grants to individuals (high: $40,553; low: $13; average: $1,000-$10,000).
Purpose and activities: Giving primarily to assist employees and former employees of the Times Mirror Company; limited support for educational and charitable institutions in Los Angeles and Orange counties when funds are available.
Types of support: Grants to individuals.
Limitations: Giving limited to Los Angeles and Orange counties, CA, for educational and charitable institutions. No grants to individuals other than company employees; no scholarships.
Application information: Application form required for grants to individuals.
Initial approach: Letter
Copies of proposal: 1
Deadline(s): Submit proposal preferably between July and Sept.; deadline Oct. 1
Board meeting date(s): Dec.
Final notification: Within 1 week of receipt
Write: James C. Kelly, Pres.
Officers: James C. Kelly,* Pres.; William A. Niese,* Secy.; Joyce M. Fields, Treas.
Directors: Charles R. Redmond, Chair.; James D. Boswell, Don Clark, Robert F. Erburu, Tom Johnson, George C. Kuekes, Richard Schlosberg III, Donald F. Wright.
Number of staff: 5 full-time professional; 2 full-time support.
Employer Identification Number: 951661675

605
Gustavus and Louise Pfeiffer Research Foundation
P.O. Box 1153
Redlands 92373-0361 (714) 792-6269

Incorporated in 1942 in NY.
Donor(s): Gustavus A. Pfeiffer.†
Foundation type: Independent
Financial data (yr. ended 12/31/89): Assets, $13,842,215 (M); qualifying distributions, $705,603, including $705,603 for 27 grants (high: $75,000; low: $3,642; average: $3,642-$75,000).
Purpose and activities: The improvement of public health through the advancement of medicine and pharmacy; the foundation's primary area of interest is in medical and pharmacological research.
Types of support: Research, matching funds, seed money.
Limitations: No support for national fundraising organizations or publicly financed projects. No grants to individuals, or for building or endowment funds, scholarships, fellowships, travel, conferences, or general purposes; no loans.
Publications: Biennial report (including application guidelines).
Application information: Application form not required.
Initial approach: Letter
Copies of proposal: 9
Deadline(s): 1 month before board meeting
Board meeting date(s): Annually, usually in the spring, and as required
Final notification: 1 week after annual board meeting
Write: George R. Pfeiffer, Secy.
Officers and Directors:* Matthew G. Herold, Jr.,* Pres.; H. Robert Herold II,* V.P.; George R. Pfeiffer,* Secy.-Treas.; Lise P. Chapman, Patricia Herold Nagle, Paul H. Pfeiffer, M.D., Robert H. Pfeiffer, Milton C. Rose.
Number of staff: 1
Employer Identification Number: 136086299

606
The Stephen Philibosian Foundation
46-930 West El Dorado Dr.
Indian Wells 92210-8649 (619) 568-3920

Trust established in 1969 in PA.
Donor(s): Armenian Missionary Assn. of America.
Foundation type: Independent
Financial data (yr. ended 12/31/88): Assets, $7,047,806 (M); expenditures, $628,337, including $572,702 for 96 grants (high: $194,000; low: $10; average: $100-$5,000).
Purpose and activities: Grants largely for missionary, educational, and social programs of the Armenian-American church, including aid for Armenian schools in the Middle East; support also for child welfare.
Types of support: Continuing support, annual campaigns, endowment funds, scholarship funds.
Limitations: Giving primarily in CA. No grants to individuals, or for operating budgets, seed money, emergency funds, deficit financing, building funds, matching gifts, research, special projects, publications, or conferences; no loans.
Application information: Contributes only to pre-selected organizations. Applications not accepted.
Board meeting date(s): Semiannually in spring and fall
Trustees: Nazar Daghlian, Louise Danelian, Stephanie Landis, Albert Momjian, Joyce Stein.
Number of staff: None.
Employer Identification Number: 237029751

607
The Phillips Foundation ⌑
c/o Security Pacific National Bank
P.O. Box 100
Rancho Mirage 92270

Incorporated in 1951 in CA.
Donor(s): Philip M. Virtue.†
Foundation type: Independent
Financial data (yr. ended 12/31/87): Assets, $1,806,309 (M); expenditures, $93,197, including $71,400 for 14 grants (high: $22,000; low: $1,000).
Purpose and activities: Grants primarily for research in economics and for religious and educational organizations.
Limitations: No grants to individuals.
Application information:
Initial approach: Letter
Deadline(s): None
Write: Tecla M. Virtue, Pres.
Officers: Tecla M. Virtue, Pres.; Lauren W. Breese, Secy.; Donald Breese, C.F.O.
Employer Identification Number: 956042761

608
Phonetic Bible Printing Committee, Inc. ⌑
3915 San Fernando Rd.
Glendale 91204 (818) 245-9424

Established about 1967 in CA.
Foundation type: Independent
Financial data (yr. ended 3/31/87): Assets, $636,342 (M); gifts received, $26,783; expenditures, $145,313, including $104,934 for 6 grants (high: $36,800; low: $5,000).
Purpose and activities: Giving primarily to religious organizations, including churches; support also for other charitable purposes.
Application information: Application form not required.
Write: Jonathan Warner
Officers: Helen Farson, Pres.; Keith Boswell, V.P.; D. Booth, Secy.-Treas.
Employer Identification Number: 951816036

609
Mary Pickford Foundation ⌑
9171 Wilshire Blvd., Suite 512
Beverly Hills 90210 (213) 273-2770

Established in 1968.
Donor(s): Mary Pickford Rogers.†
Foundation type: Independent

Financial data (yr. ended 5/31/88): Assets, $8,914,674 (M); expenditures, $721,745, including $563,910 for 93 grants (high: $70,000; low: $125; average: $1,000-$20,000).
Purpose and activities: Grants largely for scholarship funds at colleges and universities, and for "well-established medical or community service organizations."
Types of support: Scholarship funds, general purposes, endowment funds.
Limitations: Giving primarily in CA. No support for drug rehabilitation. No grants to individuals, or for building funds or land acquisition.
Application information: Application form not required.
Initial approach: Letter or telephone
Deadline(s): None
Write: Edward C. Stotsenberg, Pres.
Officers and Directors: Edward G. Stotsenberg, Pres. and C.E.O.; Sull Lawrence, Secy.; Charles B. Rogers, Treas.
Number of staff: None.
Employer Identification Number: 956093487

610
Pioneer Fund, Inc. ☆
P.O. Box 33
Inverness 94937-0033 (415) 669-1122

Established in 1979 in CA.
Donor(s): Peter F. Sloss, Nancy L. Sloss.
Foundation type: Independent
Financial data (yr. ended 6/30/89): Assets, $1,078,398 (M); expenditures, $74,238, including $53,200 for 21 grants (high: $5,000; low: $200; average: $2,533).
Purpose and activities: The fund has 2 areas of interest: 1) to support emerging documentary filmmakers (a person committed to the craft of making documentaries who has demonstrated that commitment by several years of practical film or video experience); and 2) to support programs that address some significant public policy aspect of public school education and that cannot be funded from conventional sources (including structural, organizational and financial issues, e.g., budgeting and finance, teacher seniority and tenure, collective bargaining, parent and/or student empowerment, etc.).
Types of support: Conferences and seminars, matching funds, publications, research, seed money, special projects.
Limitations: Giving limited to northern CA for public education and the Pacific Coast for film and video. No grants to individuals, or for endowments, building campaigns, accumulated deficits, ordinary operating budgets, instructional or performance documentaries or student film projects, or school site or curriculum enrichment programs.
Publications: Multi-year report, program policy statement, application guidelines.
Application information: Application form required.
Initial approach: Letter
Copies of proposal: 1
Deadline(s): Feb. 1, June 1, and Oct. 1
Board meeting date(s): Late Feb., June, and Oct.
Final notification: Mar. 15, July 15, and Nov. 15
Write: Armin Rosencranz, Secy.
Officers: Peter F. Sloss, Pres.; Nancy L. Sloss, V.P. and Treas.; Armin Rosencranz, Secy. and Exec. Dir.
Director: Ruth Chance.
Number of staff: 1 part-time professional.
Employer Identification Number: 942614215

611
The Adele Morse Platt Foundation
110 East Ninth St., Suite C-663
Los Angeles 90079 (213) 239-9245

Established in 1983 in CA.
Donor(s): Adele Morse Platt.
Foundation type: Independent
Financial data (yr. ended 06/30/89): Assets, $55,507 (M); gifts received, $200,000; expenditures, $354,704, including $354,585 for 70 grants (high: $202,175; low: $50).
Purpose and activities: Support primarily for Jewish welfare and a medical center; giving also for health associations and medical research, including AIDS research, the arts, and social services, including child welfare agencies and programs for the disabled.
Types of support: Building funds, general purposes, research.
Publications: Annual report.
Application information: Application form not required.
Write: Adele Morse Platt, Pres.
Officers and Directors:* Adele Morse Platt,* Pres.; David S. Morse,* V.P.; Majorie Roth,* V.P.; Susan Lee Morse,* Secy.; Lois Barbara Reinis,* C.F.O.
Number of staff: None.
Employer Identification Number: 953885959

612
Plitt Southern Theatres, Inc. Employees Fund ⌑
1801 Century Park East, Suite 1225
Los Angeles 90067

Established in 1945 in TX.
Donor(s): Plitt Southern Theatres.
Foundation type: Company-sponsored
Financial data (yr. ended 12/31/88): Assets, $7,102,515 (M); expenditures, $738,593, including $426,100 for 38 grants (high: $50,000; low: $1,000) and $226,878 for 77 grants to individuals (high: $10,068; low: $199).
Purpose and activities: Giving for medical research and hospitals, the arts, higher education, youth, and mental health; also supports an employee welfare fund, religious organizations, and Israeli defense.
Types of support: Grants to individuals, loans.
Application information: Grants are awarded at the discretion of the trustees. Applications not accepted.
Write: Joe S. Jackson, Pres.
Officers and Trustees: Joe S. Jackson, Pres.; W.R. Curtis, V.P. and Secy.-Treas.; Roy H. Aaron, Raymond C. Fox, Henry G. Plitt.
Employer Identification Number: 756037855

613
Michael H. & Natalie F. Podell Foundation ⌑
1199 Howard Ave., Suite 301
Burlingame 94010-4250 (415) 579-7900

Established in 1963 in CA.
Foundation type: Independent
Financial data (yr. ended 2/29/88): Assets, $1,110,050 (M); expenditures, $45,204, including $39,265 for 23 grants (high: $10,000; low: $25).
Purpose and activities: Support for Jewish organizations, higher education, and the arts.
Application information: Application form not required.
Deadline(s): None
Write: Michael H. Podell, Secy.-Treas.
Officers: Natalie F. Podell, Pres.; Michael H. Podell, Secy.-Treas.
Employer Identification Number: 946096039

614
The Polinsky-Rivkin Family Foundation
836 Prospect, Suite 202
La Jolla 92037-4206

Established in 1985 in CA.
Foundation type: Independent
Financial data (yr. ended 12/31/89): Assets, $1,256,688 (M); expenditures, $752,436, including $727,000 for 12 grants (high: $500,000; low: $1,000).
Purpose and activities: Support primarily for Jewish welfare.
Application information: Application form not required.
Deadline(s): None
Write: Jessie W. Polinsky, Pres.
Officers: Jessie W. Polinsky, Pres.; Arthur L. Rivkin, V.P.; Jeannie P. Rivkin, Secy.-Treas.
Employer Identification Number: 954355247

615
John W. Porter Trust ⌑
c/o Wells Fargo Bank, N.A.
P.O. Box 20160
Long Beach 90801-3160 (213) 491-8109

Foundation type: Independent
Financial data (yr. ended 10/31/87): Assets, $1,263,508 (M); expenditures, $73,338, including $60,980 for grants.
Purpose and activities: Support for social and family services.
Limitations: Giving primarily in CA.
Application information:
Initial approach: Letter
Deadline(s): Oct. 31
Write: Linda Bonazzola, Trust Officer, Wells Fargo Bank, N.A.
Trustee: Wells Fargo Bank, N.A.
Employer Identification Number: 956030315

616
Potlatch Foundation for Higher Education ⌑
P.O. Box 3591
San Francisco 94119 (415) 981-5980

Incorporated in 1952 in DE.
Donor(s): Potlatch Corp.
Foundation type: Company-sponsored

Financial data (yr. ended 12/31/88): Assets, $122,894 (M); gifts received, $275,000; expenditures, $321,089, including $70,500 for 12 grants (high: $10,000; low: $2,000) and $229,500 for 193 grants to individuals (high: $1,200; low: $600).
Purpose and activities: Grants chiefly for scholarships and fellowships.
Types of support: Student aid, fellowships, employee-related scholarships.
Limitations: Giving limited to areas of company operations, primarily in ID, MN, and AR. No grants for general support, building or endowment funds, research, or matching gifts; no loans.
Publications: Annual report, program policy statement, application guidelines.
Application information: Application forms will be mailed to students seeking scholarships. Application form required.
Initial approach: Letter
Deadline(s): Feb. 15 for new applications for scholarships; July 1 for scholarship renewals; students are urged to request application packets no later than Oct. 15 preceding the year for which the scholarship is sought
Board meeting date(s): Apr.
Final notification: May 1 for new applications; by Aug. 31 for renewals
Write: John M. Richards, Pres.
Officers and Trustees: John M. Richards, Pres.; George F. Jewett, Jr., V.P.; Sandra T. Powell, Secy.-Treas.; Albert L. Alford, Jr., Jack A. Buell, John B. Frazer, Jr., Robert W. Gamble, Jack L. Hogan, Sally J. Ihne.
Employer Identification Number: 826005250

617
Potlatch Foundation II ⌑
One Maritime Plaza, Suite 2400
San Francisco 94111 (415) 576-8826

Established in 1985 in CA.
Foundation type: Independent
Financial data (yr. ended 12/31/87): Assets, $1,895,584 (M); gifts received, $2,488,490; expenditures, $593,516, including $593,445 for 219 grants (high: $167,500; low: $10).
Purpose and activities: First year of giving, 1987; support for higher education in the form of matching gifts and grants, health services and business education.
Application information:
Write: George C. Cheek, Pres.
Officers and Trustees: George C. Cheek, Pres.; John M. Richards, V.P.; Sandra T. Powell, Secy.; L. Pendleton Siegel, Treas.; Richard N. Congreve, Frances M. Davis, George F. Jewett, Jr., Richard V. Warner.
Employer Identification Number: 942948030

618
The Charles Lee Powell Foundation ▼ ⌑
7742 Herschel Ave., Suite K
La Jolla 92037 (619) 459-3699

Established in 1954 in CA.
Donor(s): Charles Lee Powell.†
Foundation type: Independent
Financial data (yr. ended 12/31/88): Assets, $32,794,749 (M); expenditures, $3,354,790, including $2,262,000 for 4 grants (high: $705,750; low: $518,750).
Purpose and activities: Grants primarily for research in computer sciences, applied mathematics, biotechnology and engineering sciences.
Types of support: Equipment, research.
Limitations: Giving primarily in CA.
Application information: Application information for scholarships available from universities.
Deadline(s): None
Board meeting date(s): Varies; next meeting date fixed at each board meeting
Write: Herbert Kunzel, Chair.
Officers and Directors:* Herbert Kunzel,* Chair.; Lawrence W. Cox,* Treas.; James L. Focht, William McElroy, Charles W. Rees, Jr.
Number of staff: 2
Employer Identification Number: 237064397

619
Arthur P. Pratt and Jeanette Gladys Pratt Memorial Fund
c/o Union Bank
7807 Girard Ave.
La Jolla 92037 (619) 230-4770
Mailing address: P.O. Box 1907, La Jolla, CA 92038

Established in 1973 in CA.
Donor(s): Jeanette Gladys Pratt.†
Foundation type: Independent
Financial data (yr. ended 4/30/89): Assets, $3,009,980 (M); expenditures, $169,224, including $133,850 for 45 grants (high: $10,000; low: $950; average: $3,281).
Purpose and activities: Support primarily for youth agencies and restoration of buildings in a park.
Types of support: Operating budgets, continuing support, annual campaigns, emergency funds, general purposes, building funds, equipment, land acquisition, renovation projects, research, publications, matching funds, endowment funds.
Limitations: Giving limited to San Diego County, CA. No grants to individuals, or for scholarships or fellowships; no loans.
Application information: Application form not required.
Initial approach: Proposal
Copies of proposal: 1
Deadline(s): Feb. 1
Board meeting date(s): Mar.
Final notification: Immediately after board meeting
Write: R.A. Cameron, V.P., Union Bank
Corporate Trustee: Union Bank.
Number of staff: None.
Employer Identification Number: 956464737

620
Preuss Foundation, Inc. ⌑
c/o Peter G. Preuss, Pres.
P.O. Box 2689
Rancho Santa Fe 92067

Established in 1985 in CA.
Donor(s): Peter G. Preuss.
Foundation type: Independent
Financial data (yr. ended 12/31/87): Assets, $1,845,841 (M); gifts received, $57,708; expenditures, $927,722, including $640,385 for 26 grants (high: $60,000; low: $100).
Purpose and activities: Grants for medical research, including cancer and neurology.
Types of support: Research.
Publications: Annual report.
Application information: Contributes only to pre-selected organizations. Applications not accepted.
Officers: Peter G. Preuss, Pres.; Peggy L. Preuss, Secy.; Howard F. Cox, Stephen A. Hurwitz.
Employer Identification Number: 330085513

621
Price Foundation, Inc. ⌑
c/o George R. Ehrnman
P.O. Box 1730
Ontario 91762-0730
Application address: c/o Emily Smith, 1679 Carmel Circle East, Upland, CA 91786; Tel.: (714) 981-0441
Student loan application address: c/o Barbara Biane, 190 South 14th St., Upland, CA 91786; Tel.: (714) 985-7338

Established in 1955 in CA.
Foundation type: Independent
Financial data (yr. ended 12/31/88): Assets, $970,748 (M); expenditures, $132,943, including $45,627 for 7 grants (high: $33,000; low: $100) and $75,785 for 20 loans to individuals.
Purpose and activities: Support primarily for social services, youth organizations, a dental center, the handicapped, and hospitals; also awards student loans.
Types of support: Student loans.
Application information: Application form required for student loans.
Initial approach: Letter
Deadline(s): None
Officers and Trustees: Gene L. Alair, Chair.; George R. Ehrnman, Vice-Chair. and Treas.; Lillian Torres, Secy.; Edmund Accomazzo, and 18 additional trustees.
Employer Identification Number: 956069011

622
The R & R Foundation
1911 Spruce St.
South Pasadena 91030 (213) 236-2100

Trust established in 1967 in CA.
Donor(s): Charles H. Reeves, Richard J. Riordan, Ralph Richley,† and others.
Foundation type: Independent
Financial data (yr. ended 02/28/89): Assets, $90,536 (M); gifts received, $19,164; expenditures, $458,525, including $446,344 for 164 grants (high: $150,000; low: $25).
Purpose and activities: Grants largely for higher education, social welfare and health agencies, including population control, church support and religious associations, and cultural programs.
Limitations: No grants to individuals.
Application information: Contributes only to pre-selected organizations. Applications not accepted.

Officers and Trustees:* Richard J. Riordan,* Chair.; Charles H. Reeves,* Pres.; Paul T. Guinn, William E. Gunther, Jr.
Number of staff: None.
Employer Identification Number: 956192664

623
R.P. Foundation, Inc. ⌑
4438 Ingraham Blvd.
San Diego 92109

Incorporated in 1966 in CA.
Donor(s): Robert O. Peterson.
Foundation type: Independent
Financial data (yr. ended 11/30/89): Assets, $5,015,782 (M); expenditures, $212,190, including $192,500 for 9 grants (high: $80,000; low: $1,000).
Purpose and activities: Emphasis on cultural programs, including an historic preservation organization; support also for an oceanographic research institute and education.
Limitations: Giving primarily in CA and NY.
Application information:
Initial approach: 1-page letter
Deadline(s): None
Write: Robert O. Peterson, C.E.O.
Officers and Directors:* Robert O. Peterson,* C.E.O.; John J. McCloskey,* Secy.; Maureen F. O'Connor,* C.F.O.
Employer Identification Number: 952536736

624
Radin Foundation ⌑
444 West Shaw Ave.
Fresno 93704 (209) 226-5711

Established in 1971.
Donor(s): Leta H. Radin.†
Foundation type: Independent
Financial data (yr. ended 12/31/88): Assets, $5,858,227 (M); gifts received, $150,674; expenditures, $272,448, including $266,300 for 20 grants (high: $50,000; low: $1,000).
Purpose and activities: Support for hospitals, cultural programs, education, and social services.
Limitations: Giving primarily in Fresno, CA. No grants to individuals.
Application information:
Initial approach: Proposal
Deadline(s): None
Write: H.M. Radin, Pres.
Officers and Directors: H. Marcus Radin, Pres.; Bruce Rosenblatt, V.P.; Lawrence A. Meyer, Secy.-Treas.
Employer Identification Number: 237155525

625
RCM Capital Management Charitable Fund
Four Embarcadero Center, Suite 2900
San Francisco 94111 (415) 954-5474

Established in 1982 in CA.
Donor(s): Partners of RCM General.
Foundation type: Independent
Financial data (yr. ended 08/31/89): Assets, $161,368 (M); gifts received, $164,544; expenditures, $116,416, including $116,200 for 25 grants (high: $10,000; low: $500).
Purpose and activities: Emphasis on health, self help, and general welfare, including youth and child welfare and development; support also for education, including early childhood, elementary, and programs for minorities.
Types of support: Special projects, seed money.
Limitations: Giving limited to the San Francisco Bay Area, CA.
Publications: Application guidelines.
Application information: Application form not required.
Initial approach: Letter or telephone
Copies of proposal: 1
Deadline(s): None
Board meeting date(s): Four times a year
Write: Trish Dehn, Secy.
Officers: Claude N. Rosenberg, Jr., Chair.; G. Thomas Mortensen,* V.P. and C.F.O.; William L. Price, V.P.; Trish Dehn, Secy.
Directors: G. Nicholas Farwell, Craig C. Gordon, Melody L. McDonald, G. Thomas Morzensen, Walter C. Price, Jr., Claude N. Rosenberg, Jr., Robert K. Urquhart.
Number of staff: 1
Employer Identification Number: 942918601

626
The Mabel Wilson Richards Scholarship Fund ⌑
3333 Glendale Blvd., Suite One
Los Angeles 90039 (213) 661-1396

Trust established in 1951 in CA.
Donor(s): Mabel Wilson Richards.†
Foundation type: Independent
Financial data (yr. ended 3/31/87): Assets, $7,847,828 (M); expenditures, $490,194, including $413,924 for 61 grants to individuals (high: $45,898; low: $150; average: $500).
Purpose and activities: Provides scholarships for worthy and needy girls of the Los Angeles area recommended by financial aid offices of selected CA educational institutions. Trustees select recipients; awards paid directly to schools.
Types of support: Student aid.
Limitations: Giving limited to CA. No grants for building or endowment funds, or operating budgets; no scholarships for study abroad.
Publications: Program policy statement, application guidelines.
Application information: Application form submitted by financial aid office of selected CA colleges and universities required for scholarships. Application form required.
Initial approach: Letter
Copies of proposal: 1
Deadline(s): Submit proposal preferably in Sept.; deadline Oct. 15 or Feb. 15
Board meeting date(s): Jan., Apr., July, and Oct.
Write: Trustees
Trustees: Joanie Crown Freckmann, Ruth Walker, Alice Walsh.
Employer Identification Number: 956021322

627
Rincon Foundation ⌑ ☆
595 East Colorado Blvd., Suite 323
Pasadena 91101 (818) 405-8950

Established in 1986 in CA.
Donor(s): Harriet P. Fullerton, James D. Fullerton.
Foundation type: Independent
Financial data (yr. ended 1/31/89): Assets, $227,077 (M); gifts received, $220,000; expenditures, $145,525, including $142,100 for 52 grants (high: $20,000; low: $250).
Purpose and activities: Giving primarily for higher and other education and Christian institutions; support also for general charitable activities.
Types of support: Operating budgets.
Application information: Contributes only to pre-selected organizations. Applications not accepted.
Write: James D. Fullerton, V.P.
Officers and Trustees: Harriet P. Fullerton, Pres.; James D. Fullerton, V.P.
Employer Identification Number: 954076512

628
The Richard & Jill Riordan Foundation
300 South Grand Ave., 29th Fl.
Los Angeles 90071

Established in 1981 in CA.
Donor(s): Richard J. Riordan, Jill Riordan.
Foundation type: Independent
Financial data (yr. ended 11/30/89): Assets, $15,451,011 (M); gifts received, $288,053; expenditures, $2,846,915, including $2,424,985 for 118 grants (high: $204,562; low: $81).
Purpose and activities: Giving primarily for early childhood education, focusing on the prevention of illiteracy starting from the pre-school level.
Types of support: Matching funds, special projects.
Limitations: Giving primarily in CA. No grants to individuals.
Publications: Application guidelines.
Application information: Contributes only to pre-selected organizations. Applications not accepted.
Officers and Directors:* Richard J. Riordan,* Chair.; Jill Riordan,* Pres.; Paul T. Guinn,* Secy.
Number of staff: 2 full-time professional; 1 full-time support.
Employer Identification Number: 953779967

629
Rivendell Stewards' Trust Dated February 23, 1985 ⌑
2661 Tallant Rd., No. 620
Santa Barbara 93105 (805) 969-5856

Established in 1985 in CA.
Foundation type: Independent
Financial data (yr. ended 12/31/88): Assets, $284,761 (M); gifts received, $383,496; expenditures, $276,125.
Purpose and activities: Giving for Christian institutions and missionary efforts and for needy people who work within the Christian church.
Types of support: Grants to individuals.
Application information:
Initial approach: Letter
Deadline(s): Jan.-Apr. for higher education; Sept. 15-Oct. 15 for all other grants
Final notification: Dec. 1
Write: K.N. Hansen, Trustee
Trustees: D.K. Hansen, G.W. Hansen, Jean H. Hansen, K.N. Hansen, D.R. Johnson, J.H.

Johnson, L.A. Kuhnhausen, R.J. Kuhnhausen, C.M. Nelson, V.C. Nelson, D.R. Spurlock, J.H. Spurlock.
Employer Identification Number: 776016389

630
Riverside Community Foundation
6833 Indiana Ave., Suite 102
Riverside 92506 (714) 684-4194

Established as a trust in 1941 in CA.
Foundation type: Community
Financial data (yr. ended 12/31/89): Assets, $9,912,672 (L); gifts received, $1,093,095; expenditures, $667,195, including $576,515 for 47 grants (high: $81,000; low: $1,000; average: $12,800).
Purpose and activities: Grants for educational and welfare purposes.
Types of support: Seed money, emergency funds, building funds, equipment, matching funds, scholarship funds, special projects.
Limitations: Giving limited to the greater Riverside, CA, area. No grants to individuals, or for endowment funds, operating budgets, continuing support, annual campaigns, deficit financing, land acquisition, fellowships, publications, or research; no loans.
Publications: Informational brochure, application guidelines.
Application information: Application form not required.
Initial approach: Telephone, letter, or proposal
Copies of proposal: 10
Deadline(s): Submit proposal preferably in Feb.-Mar., May-Aug., or Oct.-Dec.; deadlines Mar. 31, Aug. 31, or Dec. 31
Board meeting date(s): Apr., Sept., and Jan.
Final notification: 1 month after board meetings
Write: Alger J. Fast, Exec. Dir.
Officers and Distribution Committee:* Robert Jaspan,* Pres.; Robert Fitch,* V.P.; Eileen Ashwal,* Secy.-Treas.; Sandra Bryant, Bernard Clark, Charles Ford, Evelyn Guin, Charles MacBeth.
Trustee Bank: Security Pacific National Bank.
Number of staff: 1 part-time professional; 1 part-time support.
Employer Identification Number: 952031692

631
The Roberts Foundation ⌑
873 Sutter St., Suite B
San Francisco 94109 (415) 771-4300

Established in 1985 in CA.
Donor(s): George R. Roberts.
Foundation type: Independent
Financial data (yr. ended 12/31/87): Assets, $4,577,931 (M); gifts received, $3,321,579; expenditures, $1,547,201, including $1,475,000 for 15 grants (high: $500,000; low: $5,000).
Purpose and activities: Giving primarily for youth, conservation and environmental issues, wildlife preservation, health care, the elderly, Hispanics, public broadcasting, and education; special emphasis on the learning disabled and for innovative programs with an impact on the homeless.
Limitations: Giving limited to CA. No support for medical research, endowment funds, annual or year-end appeals, or for religious organizations. No grants to individuals.
Application information:
Initial approach: Letter
Deadline(s): 60 days prior to a meeting
Board meeting date(s): Feb., June, and Oct.
Write: Lyman H. Casey, Dir.
Officers and Directors:* Leanne B. Roberts,* Pres.; George R. Roberts, V.P. and Secy.; John P. McLoughlin, V.P.; Lyman H. Casey.
Employer Identification Number: 942967074

632
The Robinson Foundation ⌑
700 South Flower St., Suite 1122
Los Angeles 90017 (213) 626-4481

Established in 1981 in CA.
Donor(s): Laura Robinson.
Foundation type: Independent
Financial data (yr. ended 6/30/87): Assets, $1,959,590 (M); gifts received, $200,000; expenditures, $186,077, including $139,049 for 14 grants (high: $54,500; low: $2,000).
Purpose and activities: Grants primarily to the First Church of Christ Scientist in MA or organizations that directly or indirectly promote and extend religion of Christian Science; support also for organizations that "promote man's recognition of his highest selfhood", including education.
Limitations: Giving primarily in MA. No grants to individuals.
Application information: Application form required.
Deadline(s): None
Trustees: C. Grant Gifford, Chair.; Daniel Robinson, Laura Robinson.
Employer Identification Number: 953681443

633
Robinson Foundation for Hearing Disorders, Inc. ⌑ ☆
2107 West Washington Blvd.
Los Angeles 90018

Incorporated in 1986 in CA.
Foundation type: Independent
Financial data (yr. ended 12/31/88): Assets, $30,674 (M); gifts received, $10,000; expenditures, $151,910, including $150,000 for 1 grant.
Purpose and activities: Support limited to hearing and ear research.
Application information: Contributes only to pre-selected organizations. Applications not accepted.
Write: Ray C. Robinson, Dir.
Director: Ray C. Robinson.
Employer Identification Number: 954047622

634
Mary Stuart Rogers Foundation ⌑
c/o Stockton & Sadler
P.O. Box 3153
Modesto 95353

Established in 1985 in CA.
Foundation type: Independent
Financial data (yr. ended 12/31/88): Assets, $3,892,330 (M); gifts received, $1,062,396; expenditures, $95,079, including $85,000 for 5 grants (high: $25,000; low: $10,000).
Purpose and activities: Grants primarily for medical research and animal welfare.
Limitations: Giving primarily in CA.
Application information:
Initial approach: Letter
Deadline(s): None
Write: Cleveland J. Stockton, V.P.
Officers and Directors: Mary Stuart Rogers, Pres.; Cleveland J. Stockton, V.P.
Employer Identification Number: 770099519

635
Rollnick Foundation ⌑
c/o William D. Rollnick
92 Sutherland Dr.
Atherton 94025

Established in 1981 in CA.
Donor(s): William D. Rollnick, Eloise Rollnick.
Foundation type: Independent
Financial data (yr. ended 9/30/88): Assets, $105,218 (M); gifts received, $85,354; expenditures, $245,332, including $232,500 for 24 grants (high: $75,000; low: $200).
Purpose and activities: Giving primarily to Jewish welfare and educational institutions; support also for higher education.
Limitations: Giving primarily in NY and CA and for support of institutions in Israel.
Officer and Directors:* William D. Rollnick,* Pres.; Eloise Rollnick.
Employer Identification Number: 942837777

636
Eli & Mae Rosen Foundation, Inc. ⌑ ☆
507 Polk St.
San Francisco 94102-3344

Established in 1969.
Donor(s): Mae Rosen.†
Foundation type: Independent
Financial data (yr. ended 12/31/87): Assets, $1,150,577 (M); gifts received, $577,500; expenditures, $58,958, including $57,590 for 32 grants (high: $11,000; low: $20).
Purpose and activities: Giving primarily for Jewish organizations, including temple support and social services; minor support for health, education, and the performing arts.
Limitations: Giving primarily in San Francisco, CA.
Officers and Directors: Melvin A. Schiller, Pres. and Treas.; Raymond Bolton, V.P. and Secy.; Lila B. Schiller.
Employer Identification Number: 237045725

637
The Theodore Rosenberg Charitable Foundation ⌑ ☆
333 Fell St.
San Francisco 94102-5146

Donor(s): Theodore Rosenberg.
Foundation type: Independent
Financial data (yr. ended 12/31/88): Assets, $400,886 (M); gifts received, $120,000; expenditures, $129,605, including $129,535 for 82 grants (high: $15,000; low: $10).
Purpose and activities: Support primarily for Jewish organizations, including welfare funds;

grants also for medical research, higher education, and cultural programs.
Types of support: General purposes.
Limitations: No grants to individuals.
Application information: Contributes only to pre-selected organizations. Applications not accepted.
Officers and Directors:* Theodore Rosenberg,* Pres.; Allen M. Singer, Secy.; Neenah Rosenberg,* Treas.
Employer Identification Number: 946097120

638
Rosenberg Foundation ▼
210 Post St.
San Francisco 94108-5172 (415) 421-6105

Incorporated in 1935 in CA.
Donor(s): Max L. Rosenberg,† Charlotte S. Mack.†
Foundation type: Independent
Financial data (yr. ended 12/31/88): Assets, $29,135,983 (M); gifts received, $100; expenditures, $1,875,336, including $1,523,970 for grants (average: $15,000-$50,000).
Purpose and activities: New and innovative programs benefiting children and youth. Priority given to 1) children and their families in poverty in rural and urban areas of CA: activities which reduce dependency, promote self-help, create access to the economic mainstream, or which address the causes of poverty among children and families; and 2) the changing population of CA: activities which promote the full social, economic, and cultural integration of immigrants and other minorities into a pluralistic society.
Types of support: Special projects, research, loans.
Limitations: Giving limited to CA, except for national grants related to the promotion of philanthropy. No grants to individuals, or for endowment, building, or capital funds, operating expenses of established agencies, scholarships, fellowships, continuing support, annual campaigns, emergency funds, deficit financing, matching funds, land acquisition, renovation projects, or conferences and seminars; generally no grants for equipment, films, or publications (except when a necessary part of larger project).
Publications: Multi-year report, program policy statement (including application guidelines).
Application information: Application form not required.
Initial approach: Letter
Copies of proposal: 1
Deadline(s): None
Board meeting date(s): 6 times a year
Final notification: 2 to 3 months
Write: Kirke Wilson, Exec. Dir.
Officers: Cruz Reynoso,* Pres.; Phyllis Cook,* V.P.; Kirke Wilson, Exec. Dir. and Secy.; S. Donley Ritchey,* Treas.
Directors:* Herma Hill Kay, Benton W. Dial, Leslie L. Luttgens, Mary S. Metz, Peter F. Sloss, Norvel L. Smith.
Number of staff: 2 full-time professional.
Employer Identification Number: 941186182

639
The Louise and Claude Rosenberg, Jr., Family Foundation ⌑ ☆
2465 Pacific Ave.
San Francisco 94115 (415) 921-2465

Established in 1986 in CA.
Donor(s): Claude N. Rosenberg, Jr., Louise J. Rosenberg.
Foundation type: Independent
Financial data (yr. ended 10/31/89): Assets, $7,391,283 (M); gifts received, $1,866,133; expenditures, $339,866, including $324,350 for 31 grants (high: $100,000; low: $500).
Purpose and activities: Support primarily for a Jewish welfare fund, a community fund, and cultural programs; support also for secondary education, public affairs, and conservation.
Limitations: Giving primarily in San Francisco, CA. No grants to individuals.
Application information: Application form not required.
Initial approach: Letter or proposal
Deadline(s): None
Write: Claude Rosenberg, Jr., Secy.
Officers and Directors:* Louise J. Rosenberg,* Pres.; Claude N. Rosenberg, Jr.,* Secy.; John P. Levin.
Employer Identification Number: 947023148

640
Gordon Ross Medical Foundation ⌑
1731 Oxley Ave., Apt. A
South Pasadena 91030-3326

Established in 1962 in CA.
Foundation type: Independent
Financial data (yr. ended 12/31/87): Assets, $1,080,866 (M); expenditures, $46,455, including $38,425 for grants (high: $31,000).
Purpose and activities: Giving primarily in medical research to two organizations; some support for welfare.
Officers: S. Gordon Ross, M.D., Pres.; E.C. Newcomer, V.P.
Director: Mrs. Joseph Gatti.
Employer Identification Number: 956044011

641
Roth Family Foundation
12021 Wilshire Blvd., Suite 505
Los Angeles 90025

Established in 1966 in CA.
Donor(s): Louis Roth and Co., Louis Roth,† Fannie Roth,† Harry Roth.†
Foundation type: Independent
Financial data (yr. ended 10/31/89): Assets, $7,152,000 (M); expenditures, $356,000, including $299,700 for grants.
Purpose and activities: Emphasis on cultural organizations, educational programs, and general charitable giving.
Limitations: Giving primarily in CA. No grants to individuals.
Application information: Grants limited to established charities; unsolicited grants are rarely funded.
Initial approach: Brief proposal letter
Write: Sukey Garcetti, Exec. Dir.
Officers and Directors:* Michael Roth,* Pres.; Gilbert Garcetti,* V.P.; Patricia Roth,* V.P.; Susan Roth, V.P.; Sukey Garcetti,* Secy.-Treas. and Exec. Dir.
Number of staff: 1
Employer Identification Number: 237008897

642
Rudin Richman & Appel Charitable Foundation ⌑
9601 Wilshire Blvd.
Beverly Hills 90210 (213) 274-4841

Established in 1983 in CA.
Donor(s): Martin S. Appel, Fredric N. Richman, Milton A. Rudin.
Foundation type: Independent
Financial data (yr. ended 1/31/88): Assets, $13,349 (M); gifts received, $100,000; expenditures, $148,931, including $148,092 for 59 grants (high: $5,000; low: $20) and $800 for 1 grant to an individual.
Purpose and activities: Emphasis on Jewish giving and health organizations; some support for child welfare agencies and cultural programs.
Limitations: Giving primarily in CA.
Application information:
Deadline(s): Letter
Write: Martin S. Appel, Mgr.
Officers: Milton A. Rudin, Pres.; Fredric N. Richman, V.P.; Martin S. Appel, Secy.-Treas. and Mgr.
Employer Identification Number: 953892817

643
David Claude Ryan Foundation ⌑
P.O. Box 6409
San Diego 92106 (619) 291-7311

Established in 1959 in CA.
Donor(s): Jerome D. Ryan, Gladys B. Ryan.
Foundation type: Independent
Financial data (yr. ended 12/31/88): Assets, $2,525,638 (M); gifts received, $80,000; expenditures, $170,408, including $160,942 for 40 grants (high: $50,000; low: $500).
Purpose and activities: Giving primarily for Christian religious organizations, social service and youth agencies, education, and cultural programs.
Types of support: Continuing support.
Limitations: Giving primarily in CA, with emphasis on San Diego. No grants to individuals.
Application information:
Initial approach: Letter
Deadline(s): None
Write: Jerome D. Ryan, Pres.
Officers: Jerome D. Ryan, Pres.; Gladys B. Ryan, V.P. and Secy.-Treas.; Stephen M. Ryan, V.P.
Employer Identification Number: 956051140

644
S.G. Foundation ⌑
7855 Ivanhoe Ave.
La Jolla 92037

Established in 1984 in CA.
Donor(s): F. Javier Alverdo.
Foundation type: Independent
Financial data (yr. ended 12/31/88): Assets, $3,874,603 (M); gifts received, $50,000; expenditures, $176,027, including $115,635 for 10 grants (high: $52,500; low: $400).
Purpose and activities: Support for education and Christian organizations.

Types of support: Endowment funds.
Application information: Application form not required.
Initial approach: Letter
Deadline(s): None
Write: William P. Shannahan, V.P.
Officers: Stuart C. Gildred, Pres.; William P. Shannahan, V.P. and Secy.
Employer Identification Number: 330048410

645
Charles E. Saak Trust ☆
c/o Wells Fargo Bank, Tax Dept.-MAC No. D103-179
P.O. Box 63954
San Francisco 94163
Application address: c/o Wells Fargo Bank, 2222 West Shaw Ave., Suite 11, Fresno, CA 93711 Tel.: (209) 442-6230

Established in 1963.
Foundation type: Independent
Financial data (yr. ended 01/31/89): Assets, $1,010,918 (M); expenditures, $56,376, including $40,935 for 170 grants to individuals (high: $960; low: $67).
Purpose and activities: Provides aid to economically disadvantaged youth under 21 years of age in the form of dental and emergency medical assistance and scholarships for higher education.
Types of support: Grants to individuals, student aid.
Limitations: Giving limited to the Poplar, CA, area.
Application information: Application form required.
Deadline(s): Mar. 31
Trustee: Wells Fargo Bank, N.A.
Employer Identification Number: 946076213

646
Sacramento Regional Foundation ⌑
1420 River Park Dr., Suite 140
Sacramento 95815-4506 (916) 927-2241

Incorporated in 1983 in CA.
Foundation type: Community
Financial data (yr. ended 12/31/88): Assets, $2,810,463 (M); gifts received, $664,522; expenditures, $713,602, including $592,242 for 139 grants (high: $50,300; low: $10) and $4,633 for 5 grants to individuals (high: $1,500; low: $200).
Purpose and activities: Support primarily for education, the arts, conservation, health, and community development.
Types of support: Student aid, conferences and seminars, consulting services, emergency funds, equipment, publications, renovation projects, seed money, technical assistance, scholarship funds.
Limitations: Giving limited to organizations within or those offering services to Sacramento, Yolo, Placer, and El Dorado counties, CA. No grants to individuals (except scholarships), or for annual campaigns, endowments, building funds, continuing support, deficit financing, foundation-managed projects, research, or land acquisition; no loans.
Publications: Annual report (including application guidelines), financial statement.
Application information: Application form not required.
Initial approach: Letter
Copies of proposal: 1
Deadline(s): Jan. 6
Board meeting date(s): Mar. 15, June 15, Sept. 21, and Jan. 18
Write: David F. Hess, Exec. Dir.
Officers: F. Frederick Brown, Pres.; Merrily Wong, V.P.; Jean Runyon Graham, Secy.; A. Alan Post, Treas.; David F. Hess, Exec. Dir.
Number of staff: 1 full-time professional; 1 full-time support.
Employer Identification Number: 942891517

647
Bernard & Gloria Jeanne Salick Foundation
407 North Maple Dr., Suite K
Beverly Hills 90210-3850 (213) 276-0732

Established in 1984 in CA.
Foundation type: Operating
Financial data (yr. ended 12/31/89): Assets, $76,023 (M); gifts received, $166,550; expenditures, $268,604, including $266,917 for 25 grants (high: $100,000; low: $200).
Purpose and activities: Giving primarily for Jewish concerns and medical research.
Types of support: Conferences and seminars, continuing support, general purposes, professorships.
Limitations: Giving primarily in Los Angeles, CA. No grants to individuals.
Application information: Contributes only to pre-selected organizations. Applications not accepted.
Write: Bernard Salick, M.D., Trustee
Trustees: Les F. Bell, Bernard Salick, M.D., Gloria Salick.
Employer Identification Number: 953946003

648
San Diego Community Foundation
525 B St., Suite 410
San Diego 92101 (619) 239-8815

Established in 1975 in CA.
Foundation type: Community
Financial data (yr. ended 06/30/89): Assets, $39,074,744 (M); gifts received, $7,842,742; expenditures, $2,390,838, including $2,045,622 for 373 grants (high: $60,000; low: $250; average: $2,000-$15,000).
Purpose and activities: Giving to religious organizations, social service agencies, cultural activities, education, civic affairs, and recreational activities.
Types of support: Seed money, matching funds, building funds, equipment, general purposes, special projects, publications, renovation projects, technical assistance.
Limitations: Giving limited to San Diego County, CA. No support for political or religious organizations. No grants to individuals, or for operating support, annual or capital fund campaigns, endowment funds, research, conferences, travel, or to underwrite fundraising events and performances; no loans.
Publications: Annual report, informational brochure (including application guidelines).
Application information: Application form required.
Initial approach: Telephone or letter
Copies of proposal: 1
Deadline(s): Bimonthly; call for details
Board meeting date(s): Bimonthly beginning in Jan.
Final notification: 3 months
Write: Helen Monroe, Exec. Dir., or Pamela Hall, Asst. Dir.
Officers and Board of Governors:* Ronald E. Hahn,* Pres.; Sr. Sally Furay,* V.P., Distribs.; Frank H. Ault,* V.P., Finance; Ira R. Katz,* V.P., Marketing; John A. McColl,* Secy.; Maurice T. Watson,* Treas.; and 16 additional governors.
Number of staff: 3 full-time professional; 3 full-time support.
Employer Identification Number: 952942582

649
San Felipe del Rio, Inc. ⌑ ☆
401 West A St., Suite 2000
San Diego 92101
Application address: P.O. Box 21, Oakland, OR 97462; Tel.: (503) 459-4474

Established in 1973.
Donor(s): Philip Y. Hahn Foundation.
Foundation type: Operating
Financial data (yr. ended 6/30/88): Assets, $2,977,677 (M); gifts received, $5,716; expenditures, $230,615, including $48,705 for grants (high: $34,750) and $3,852 for 3 grants to individuals (high: $1,500; low: $1,102).
Purpose and activities: A private operating foundation; "assists in the development of programs providing shelter and care for dependent, neglected, abused, or developmentally disabled children and youth," including minor support through scholarships to individuals.
Types of support: Student aid.
Application information: Application form not required.
Deadline(s): None
Write: Robert P. Conte, Exec. Dir.
Officers: Andrew De Paolo, Pres.; Charles Anderson, V.P.; Peter Frederick, 1st Secy.; June Marsh, 2nd Secy.; Dewayne Mathews, Treas.; Michelle Conte, Exec. Dir.; Robert Conte, Exec. Dir.
Directors: Gilbert L. Brown, Jr., C. Lynn Curran, Mrs. Andrew De Paolo, Sherwood T. Erneweine, Peter C. Marsh.
Employer Identification Number: 237276447

650
The San Francisco Foundation ▼
685 Market St., Suite 910
San Francisco 94105-9716 (415) 543-0223

Established in 1948 in CA by resolution and declaration of trust.
Foundation type: Community
Financial data (yr. ended 06/30/89): Assets, $193,526,511 (M); gifts received, $17,930,715; expenditures, $13,408,151, including $11,124,714 for grants (average: $20,000).
Purpose and activities: Grants principally in five categories: the arts and humanities, community health, education, environment, and urban affairs. Technical assistance grants also made, primarily to current recipients. On

Jan. 1, 1987, the foundation transferred the entire Buck Trust, which is limited to use for charitable purposes in Marin County, CA, to a new and independent foundation, the Marin Community Foundation. The foundation continues to serve five counties of the Bay Area, and in the 12 months ending June 30, 1989, paid out $11 million (excluding Buck Trust funds) in grants to nonprofit agencies.
Types of support: Operating budgets, seed money, loans, technical assistance, special projects.
Limitations: Giving limited to the Bay Area, CA counties of Alameda, Contra Costa, Marin, San Francisco, and San Mateo. No support for religious purposes. No grants to individuals, or for annual campaigns, general fundraising campaigns, emergency or endowment funds, deficit financing, matching gifts, scholarships (except when so designated by donor), or fellowships.
Publications: Annual report, newsletter, application guidelines, program policy statement, informational brochure.
Application information: Application form required.
Initial approach: Letter of intent (not exceeding 3 pages)
Copies of proposal: 1
Deadline(s): Letters reviewed continuously; proposal closing dates available upon request
Board meeting date(s): Monthly except Aug.; applications are reviewed 4-6 times each year
Final notification: 3 to 4 months
Write: Robert M. Fisher, Dir.
Director: Robert M. Fisher.
Board of Trustees: Peter E. Haas, Chair.; Leonard E. Kingsley, Vice-Chair. and Treas.; Lucille S. Abrahamson, Herman Gallegos, John F. Kilmartin, Joan F. Lane, Mary Lee Widener.
Number of staff: 10 full-time professional; 8 full-time support; 2 part-time support.
Employer Identification Number: 941101547

651
George H. Sandy Foundation
P.O. Box 18275
San Francisco 94118

Trust established in 1960 in CA.
Donor(s): George H. Sandy.†
Foundation type: Independent
Financial data (yr. ended 12/31/88): Assets, $11,947,243 (M); expenditures, $785,027, including $599,000 for 120 grants (high: $15,000; low: $1,000; average: $3,000).
Purpose and activities: Charitable and educational purposes, with emphasis on aid to the handicapped and underprivileged.
Types of support: Operating budgets, continuing support, equipment.
Limitations: Giving limited to the San Francisco Bay, CA, area. No support for other private non-operating foundations. No grants to individuals, or for annual campaigns, seed money, emergency funds, deficit financing, capital campaigns, endowment or building funds, matching gifts, scholarships, fellowships, special projects, research, publications, or conferences; no loans.
Application information: Application form not required.
Initial approach: Letter
Copies of proposal: 1
Board meeting date(s): Semiannually
Final notification: 6 months
Write: Chester R. MacPhee, Jr., Trustee
Trustees: Thomas E. Feeney, Chester R. MacPhee, Jr., The Bank of California, N.A.
Number of staff: None.
Employer Identification Number: 946054473

652
Annunziata Sanguinetti Foundation
c/o Wells Fargo Bank, N.A.
420 Montgomery St., 5th Fl.
San Francisco 94163 (415) 396-3215

Trust established in 1958 in CA.
Donor(s): Annunziata Sanguinetti.†
Foundation type: Independent
Financial data (yr. ended 09/30/88): Assets, $3,333,672 (M); expenditures, $225,477, including $181,566 for grants (high: $10,000; average: $11,000-$1,000).
Purpose and activities: Giving for the benefit of sick, needy children; grants for mental health, rehabilitation, welfare, hospitals, youth and social service agencies.
Limitations: Giving limited to San Francisco, CA. No grants to individuals, or for building or endowment funds.
Publications: Application guidelines.
Application information: Application form not required.
Initial approach: Letter and proposal
Copies of proposal: 1
Deadline(s): Submit proposal between July and Oct.; deadline Oct. 31
Board meeting date(s): Nov. or Dec.
Write: Eugene J. Ranghiasci
Trustee: Wells Fargo Bank, N.A.
Employer Identification Number: 946073762

653
Santa Barbara Foundation ▼
15 East Carrillo St.
Santa Barbara 93101 (805) 963-1873

Incorporated in 1928 in CA.
Foundation type: Community
Financial data (yr. ended 12/31/89): Assets, $35,050,273 (M); gifts received, $978,278; expenditures, $2,458,683, including $1,692,087 for 137 grants and $52,223 for 27 loans to individuals.
Purpose and activities: Giving for social services, youth, health services, cultural activities, education, and student aid loans for Santa Barbara County secondary school graduates.
Types of support: Building funds, equipment, land acquisition, matching funds, student loans, renovation projects, publications, technical assistance.
Limitations: Giving limited to Santa Barbara County, CA. No support for religious organizations or schools, colleges, or universities. No grants to individuals (except for student loans for Santa Barbara County secondary school graduates), or for operating budgets, annual campaigns, seed money, deficit financing, endowment funds, scholarships, fellowships, research, publications, or conferences; no loans.
Publications: Annual report, application guidelines, newsletter, informational brochure, 990-PF.
Application information: The foundation considers 30 applications per quarter. Application form required.
Initial approach: Letter or telephone
Copies of proposal: 1
Deadline(s): None
Board meeting date(s): Monthly except July; decisions on grant requests made in Mar., June, Sept. and Dec.
Final notification: 2 months
Write: Edward R. Spaulding, Exec. Dir.
Officers and Trustees:* Patricia Dow,* Pres.; B. Paul Blasingame,* V.P.; Edwin F. Froelich,* V.P.; P. Paul Riparetti, M.D.,* V.P.; Valencia Nelson, Secy.; Warren E. Fenzi, Treas.; Fritz Amacher, Spaulding Birss, William L. Coulson, James J. Giusto, Mrs. Robert Grogan, John Howland, Charles H. Jarvis, Marshall A. Rose, Michael Towbes, Mrs. Howard Vesey.
Fund Managers: Capital Research & Management Co., Crocker National Bank, Security Pacific Investment Mgrs.
Number of staff: 2 full-time professional; 1 part-time professional; 1 full-time support; 1 part-time support.
Employer Identification Number: 951866094

654
Community Foundation of Santa Clara County
960 West Hedding, No. 220
San Jose 95126-1215 (408) 241-2666

Established in 1954 in CA.
Foundation type: Community
Financial data (yr. ended 12/31/89): Assets, $10,088,000 (M); gifts received, $2,594,630; expenditures, $2,076,874, including $1,471,969 for 300 grants (high: $35,000; low: $500; average: $2,500-$15,000).
Purpose and activities: Giving primarily for education, including awards in literature; health and social services, including AIDS programs, youth and child welfare, women and minorities, and employment and housing; the fine and performing arts; community development and urban affairs; and the environment.
Types of support: Seed money, emergency funds, matching funds, consulting services, technical assistance, loans, scholarship funds, special projects.
Limitations: Giving primarily in Santa Clara County, CA. No support for religious organizations for sectarian purposes. No grants for deficit financing or building funds.
Publications: Annual report, newsletter, 990-PF, financial statement, informational brochure, application guidelines.
Application information: Application form not required.
Initial approach: Telephone or letter
Copies of proposal: 1
Deadline(s): 12 weeks prior to board meetings
Board meeting date(s): Varies
Final notification: Within 2 weeks of meetings

Write: Peter Hero, Exec. Dir.
Directors: William F. Scandling, Chair.; Peter Hero, Exec. Dir.; John Black, Phillip Boyce, Marti de Benedetti, Leonard Ely, Bernadine Chuck Fong, John Freidenrich, Robert Joss, Tom Killefer, Sandra Kurtzig, David W. Mitchell, Ernest Renzel, Jr., Tom Rimerman, James Rosse, Barbara Doyle Roupe, Sven Simonsen, Roger Smith, Mrs. C. Barron Swenson, William Terry, John A. Wilson.
Number of staff: 3 full-time professional; 1 part-time professional.
Employer Identification Number: 770066922

655
Greater Santa Cruz County Community Foundation ⌘
820 Bay Ave., Suite 204
Capitola 95010 (408) 662-8290

Incorporated in 1982 in CA.
Foundation type: Community
Financial data (yr. ended 12/31/88): Assets, $2,787,687 (M); gifts received, $1,277,211; expenditures, $285,608, including $178,826 for 148 grants.
Purpose and activities: Giving for social services, health, education, cultural programs, the environment, conservation, and community development programs.
Types of support: General purposes, seed money, operating budgets, emergency funds, equipment, special projects, conferences and seminars, technical assistance, consulting services, matching funds, building funds, continuing support.
Limitations: Giving limited to Santa Cruz County, CA. No grants to individuals, or for continuing support, annual campaigns, deficit financing, building funds, land acquisition, student loans, fellowships, or research.
Publications: Grants list, newsletter, program policy statement, application guidelines, annual report.
Application information: Application form not required.
Initial approach: In person, telephone, or letter
Copies of proposal: 15
Deadline(s): Mar. 31 and Sept. 30
Board meeting date(s): 4th Monday of every other month
Final notification: Within 60 days of each deadline
Write: Grace Jepsen, Exec. Dir.
Officers and Directors: William F. Locke-Paddon, Pres.; Alan Simpkins, V.P.; Gloria Hihn Welsh, Secy.; Donald Starr, Treas.; and 23 other directors.
Number of staff: 1 full-time professional; 1 full-time support.
Employer Identification Number: 942808039

656
William Saroyan Foundation ⌘
1905 Baker St.
San Francisco 94115-2012 (415) 433-9400

Established about 1981 in CA.
Donor(s): William Saroyan.
Foundation type: Independent
Financial data (yr. ended 9/30/88): Assets, $2,211,310 (M); gifts received, $25,435; expenditures, $99,886, including $5,017 for 3 grants (high: $2,697; low: $1,000).
Purpose and activities: Support primarily for a library.
Types of support: General purposes.
Application information:
Initial approach: Proposal
Deadline(s): None
Write: Robert Setrakian, Trustee
Trustees: Anthony Frank, Harold H. Haak, James D. Hart, Cosette Saroyan, Henry Saroyan, Robert Setrakian.
Employer Identification Number: 941657684

657
The Vidal Sassoon Foundation ⌘
c/o Parks, Palmer, Turner & Yemenidjian
1990 South Bundy Dr., Suite 600
Los Angeles 90025

Established in 1979.
Donor(s): Vidal Sassoon.
Foundation type: Independent
Financial data (yr. ended 12/31/86): Assets, $9,419 (M); gifts received, $143,450; expenditures, $148,395, including $145,360 for 34 grants (high: $25,000; low: $50).
Purpose and activities: Support for Jewish organizations and cultural programs, and youth and social service agencies.
Application information: Contributes only to pre-selected organizations. Applications not accepted.
Officers: Vidal Sassoon, Pres.; George Shaw, V.P. and Secy.; Brian Adams, V.P. and Treas.; Linda Turner, V.P.
Employer Identification Number: 953401086

658
The Daniel A. and Edna J. Sattler Beneficial Trust ⌘ ☆
200 East Carrillo St., Suite 400
Santa Barbara 93101

Donor(s): Edna J. Relyea.†
Foundation type: Independent
Financial data (yr. ended 6/30/89): Assets, $2,342,384 (M); gifts received, $195,079; expenditures, $218,890, including $159,402 for grants.
Purpose and activities: Support for cancer research and other health associations, social service organizations, and a community foundation.
Types of support: General purposes.
Limitations: Giving primarily in the Santa Barbara, CA, area. No grants to individuals.
Application information: Contributes only to pre-selected organizations. Applications not accepted.
Trustees: H. Clarke Gaines, Robert M. Jones, Cecil I. Smith.
Employer Identification Number: 237127370

659
Saturno Foundation ⌘
c/o Security Pacific National Bank
P.O. Box 3189, Terminal Annex
Los Angeles 90051 (818) 304-3422

Trust established in 1957 in CA.
Donor(s): Joseph Saturno,† Victor Saturno.
Foundation type: Independent
Financial data (yr. ended 10/31/88): Assets, $5,075,162 (M); expenditures, $74,060, including $17,220 for 1 grant.
Purpose and activities: Grants to organizations in Italy that assist orphaned children.
Limitations: Giving primarily in Italy. No grants to individuals, or for general support, building or endowment funds, research, scholarships, fellowships, or matching gifts; no loans.
Publications: 990-PF.
Application information:
Initial approach: Letter
Copies of proposal: 1
Deadline(s): None
Write: Victor Saturno
Trustee: Security Pacific National Bank.
Employer Identification Number: 946073765

660
Scaife, Northern California Scholarship, and Helen Parmelee Educational Foundations
(Formerly Oakland Scottish Rite Scaife, Oakland Scottish Rite Scholarship, and Parmelee Educational Foundation)
1547 Lakeside Dr.
Oakland 94612 (415) 451-1906

Incorporated in 1927 in CA.
Donor(s): Irene Jones,† Walter B. Scaife,† S. Sidney Morton, Helen Wegman Parmelee.
Foundation type: Independent
Financial data (yr. ended 05/31/89): Assets, $9,340,964 (M); expenditures, $481,386, including $443,100 for 184 grants to individuals (high: $10,000; low: $500).
Purpose and activities: Scholarships for graduates of local public high schools only.
Types of support: Student aid.
Limitations: Giving limited to northern CA.
Publications: Informational brochure, program policy statement, application guidelines.
Application information: Applications sent only to those students recommended by northern CA public high school administrations. Application form required.
Initial approach: Letter
Copies of proposal: 1
Deadline(s): Submit proposal preferably in Mar.; deadline Mar. 17
Board meeting date(s): Jan., Feb., May, and Aug.
Final notification: 1 month
Write: Merv Weiner, Secy.
Officers and Trustees:* David Tucker,* Pres.; Zook Sutton,* V.P.; Merv Weiner,* Secy.; Alden W. Badal, George Bliss, William Kent, D.H. Madsen, Elmer Ross, Norman Shapiro, George Vukasin, Wallace E. York.
Number of staff: 1 part-time professional; 1 part-time support.
Employer Identification Number: 941540333

661
The Stephen Edward Scarff Memorial Foundation ⌘ ☆
601 California St., Suite 1800
San Francisco 94108

Established in 1985.
Donor(s): Nancy V. Scarff.
Foundation type: Independent

Financial data (yr. ended 3/31/88): Assets, $1,160,618 (M); gifts received, $530,335; expenditures, $17,983, including $14,200 for 15 grants (high: $5,000; low: $100).
Purpose and activities: Support primarily for youth clubs; support also for social services and environmental groups.
Types of support: General purposes, capital campaigns, building funds.
Trustee: Nancy V. Scarff.
Distribution Advisor's Committee: Susan Nesmith, Linda Paine, Catherine Scarff.
Employer Identification Number: 942984078

662
Frances Schermer Charitable Trust ⌘
c/o Security Pacific National Bank
P.O. Box 3189, Terminal Annex
Los Angeles 90051
Application addresses: James L. Pazol, Trustee, 21 Wickliffe Circle, Youngstown, OH 44515; Tel.: (216) 792-6033; and Dr. Saul Friedman, Trustee, 3560 Sandburg Dr., Youngstown, OH 44515; Tel.: (216) 793-3570

Trust established in 1980 in CA.
Donor(s): Charles I. Schermer,† Frances Schermer.
Foundation type: Independent
Financial data (yr. ended 06/30/89): Assets, $1,936,663 (M); expenditures, $163,477, including $124,683 for grants.
Purpose and activities: Giving to Jewish welfare funds and Jewish studies, higher education, social service agencies, aid to the handicapped, health agencies, and child welfare.
Limitations: Giving primarily in CA and OH. No support for religious purposes. No grants to individuals.
Application information:
Initial approach: Letter and budget
Deadline(s): None
Trustees: Saul Friedman, James L. Pazol, Security Pacific National Bank.
Employer Identification Number: 956685749

663
Marjorie Mosher Schmidt Foundation
2111 Palomar Airport Rd., Suite 370
Carlsbad 92009
Additional address: P.O. Box 7096, Newport Beach, CA 92660; Tel.: (619) 438-4300

Incorporated in 1956 in CA.
Donor(s): Marjorie Mosher Schmidt.†
Foundation type: Independent
Financial data (yr. ended 12/31/88): Assets, $1,845,735 (M); expenditures, $141,286, including $137,350 for 36 grants (high: $5,000; low: $700; average: $1,000-$5,000).
Purpose and activities: Giving to conservation, health agencies, higher and secondary education, child welfare, aid to the handicapped, and religious organizations.
Types of support: Annual campaigns, building funds, conferences and seminars, continuing support, endowment funds, equipment, general purposes, research, scholarship funds, special projects.
Limitations: Giving primarily in Southern CA. No grants to individuals.
Application information: Grants initiated by board. Applications not accepted.
Board meeting date(s): Nov.
Write: Mark F. Scudder, Pres.
Officers and Directors:* Mark F. Scudder,* Pres.; Richard Charles Cringle,* V.P.; Kent M. Scudder,* V.P.; John H. Scudder,* Secy.; John T. Kearns,* Treas.
Number of staff: 1 part-time professional; 1 part-time support.
Employer Identification Number: 956047798

664
Charles M. Schulz Foundation
One Snoopy Place
Santa Rosa 95401

Established in 1982 in CA.
Donor(s): Charles M. Schulz, Jean F. Schulz, Charles M. and Jean F. Schulz Trust.
Foundation type: Independent
Financial data (yr. ended 12/31/89): Assets, $13,455 (M); gifts received, $134,078; expenditures, $504,083, including $502,424 for 22 grants (high: $334,250; low: $100; average: $500-$2,500).
Purpose and activities: Grants primarily for culture, social services, early childhood education, and ecology.
Types of support: General purposes.
Limitations: Giving primarily in Sonoma County, CA.
Application information:
Initial approach: Proposal (3-6 pages)
Copies of proposal: 1
Deadline(s): None
Officers and Directors:* Craig Schulz,* Pres.; Edwin C. Anderson, Jr.,* Secy.; Ronald A. Nelson,* C.F.O.; Meredith Hodges, Amy Johnson, Charles M. Schulz, Jr., Jill Schulz.
Number of staff: 1 part-time support.
Employer Identification Number: 942715935

665
Virginia Steele Scott Foundation
1151 Oxford Rd.
San Marino 91108 (818) 405-2152

Established in 1974.
Donor(s): Virginia Steele Scott,† Grace C. Steele.†
Foundation type: Independent
Financial data (yr. ended 06/30/89): Assets, $2,736,430 (M); gifts received, $135,141; expenditures, $2,927,793, including $300,500 for grants (high: $263,000; low: $5,000).
Purpose and activities: Giving of works of art to a local art museum, and other fine arts organizations.
Limitations: Giving primarily in Pasadena, CA.
Application information:
Write: Sandra S. Bradner
Officer: Charles Newton,* Pres.
Directors:* Blake R. Nevius, Robert R. Wark.
Employer Identification Number: 237365076

666
The Ellen Browning Scripps Foundation
California First Bank, P.O. Box 1907
La Jolla 92038 (619) 230-4770

Trust established in 1935 in CA.
Donor(s): Ellen Browning Scripps,† Robert Paine Scripps,† Margaret C. Hawkins.
Foundation type: Independent
Financial data (yr. ended 6/30/89): Assets, $13,065,538 (M); expenditures, $1,191,762, including $1,110,000 for 54 grants (high: $80,000; low: $1,000).
Purpose and activities: Emphasis on institutions engaged in medical and oceanographic research, higher education, conservation and recreation, the arts, and youth and child welfare agencies.
Limitations: Giving primarily in San Diego County, CA. No grants to individuals.
Application information: Application form not required.
Initial approach: Proposal
Copies of proposal: 1
Deadline(s): May 1
Board meeting date(s): June
Write: Bettie J. Withem, V.P., California First Bank
Trustees: Ellen Scripps Davis, Deborah Goddard, Edward S. Meanley, John P. Scripps, Paul K. Scripps.
Employer Identification Number: 951644633

667
Richard C. Seaver Charitable Trust ⌘ ☆
350 South Figueroa St., Suite 270
Los Angeles 90071

Established in 1978.
Foundation type: Independent
Financial data (yr. ended 12/31/88): Assets, $3,607,683 (M); expenditures, $199,911, including $187,000 for grants.
Purpose and activities: Giving primarily for Episcopal churches; support also for a museum foundation and education.
Limitations: No grants to individuals.
Application information:
Initial approach: Letter
Deadline(s): None
Write: Myron E. Harpole, Trustee
Trustee: Myron E. Harpole.
Employer Identification Number: 953311102

668
The Seaver Institute ⌘
800 West Sixth St., Suite 1410
Los Angeles 90017 (213) 688-7550

Incorporated in 1955 in CA.
Donor(s): Frank R. Seaver.†
Foundation type: Independent
Financial data (yr. ended 6/30/86): Assets, $31,444,632 (M); expenditures, $1,636,726, including $1,324,659 for 83 grants (high: $150,000; low: $450; average: $1,000-$75,000).
Purpose and activities: Emphasis on education, health, the arts, and the community.
Types of support: Matching funds, special projects, research.
Limitations: Giving primarily in CA, MA, and MN. No grants to individuals, or for operating budgets, continuing support, annual campaigns, emergency or endowment funds, scholarships, fellowships, deficit financing, capital or building funds, equipment, land acquisition, publications, or conferences; no loans.

Publications: Informational brochure (including application guidelines).
Application information: Application form not required.
Initial approach: Telephone
Deadline(s): None
Board meeting date(s): Dec. and June
Final notification: 3 to 6 months
Write: Richard Call, Pres.
Officers and Directors: Blanche Ebert Seaver, Chair.; Richard Seaver, Vice-Chair.; Richard Call, Pres.; John F. Hall, V.P. and Treas.; Christopher Seaver, Secy.; Richard A. Archer, Camron Cooper, Myron E. Harpole, Raymond Jallow, Victoria Seaver.
Number of staff: 2 full-time professional; 3 part-time professional.
Employer Identification Number: 956054764

669
Security Pacific Foundation ▼ ⌘
333 South Hope St.
Los Angeles 90071 (213) 345-6688
Grant application address: P.O. Box 2097, Terminal Annex, Los Angeles, CA 90051

Incorporated in 1977 in CA.
Donor(s): Security Pacific Corp.
Foundation type: Company-sponsored
Financial data (yr. ended 12/31/88): Assets, $6,720,754 (M); expenditures, $5,054,509, including $4,579,425 for 625 grants (high: $1,050,650; low: $100; average: $500-$2,500) and $428,523 for 1,982 employee matching gifts.
Purpose and activities: Support for charitable efforts including higher education, community programs, arts and cultural programs, social services, youth agencies, and civic affairs.
Types of support: Annual campaigns, building funds, continuing support, employee matching gifts, operating budgets, employee-related scholarships, general purposes, capital campaigns.
Limitations: Giving primarily in CA. No support for national agencies, legal defense funds, veterans', military, fraternal, or professional organizations, or churches or religious groups. No grants to individuals (except for employee-related scholarships), or for seed money, emergency funds, deficit financing, land acquisition, equipment, endowments, matching or challenge grants, operational grants for hospitals or health associations, scholarships, fellowships, special projects, research, media projects, or advertising in charitable publications; no loans.
Publications: Annual report, informational brochure, program policy statement, application guidelines.
Application information: Application form not required.
Initial approach: Letter or proposal
Copies of proposal: 1
Deadline(s): July 15 for capital grant requests; none for operating grants
Board meeting date(s): Aug. (for capital grants) and Nov.
Final notification: 4 to 6 weeks; Sept. for capital grants
Write: Mrs. Carol E. Taufer, Pres.
Officers: Carol E. Taufer,* Pres. and C.E.O.; Richard J. Flamson III,* V.P.; Joseph A. Irwin,* V.P.; John F. Kooken,* V.P.; George F. Moody,* V.P.; Richard A. Warner,* V.P.; Howard B. Stevens, Secy.; Kenneth C. Sherman, Treas.
Directors:* Carl E. Hartnack, Chair.; John Mangels, Robert Philipp, Robert H. Smith, Stephen J. Yoder.
Number of staff: 4 full-time professional.
Employer Identification Number: 953195084

670
Charles See Foundation
2222 Ave. of the Stars, Suite 2505
Los Angeles 90067 (213) 879-1182

Incorporated in 1960 in CA.
Donor(s): Charles B. See.
Foundation type: Independent
Financial data (yr. ended 12/31/89): Assets, $1,935,852 (M); expenditures, $96,635, including $78,700 for 23 grants (high: $20,000; low: $200).
Purpose and activities: Emphasis on mental health, education, hospitals, church support, conservation, cultural programs, and international affairs.
Limitations: Giving primarily in CA. No grants to individuals.
Application information:
Initial approach: Letter
Deadline(s): Nov. 14
Board meeting date(s): Around Dec. 1
Write: Charles B. See, Pres.
Officers and Directors:* Charles B. See,* Pres. and Treas.; C.H. Baumhefner, V.P.; Ann R. See,* Secy.; Harry A. See, Richard W. See.
Employer Identification Number: 956038358

671
Frances Seebee Trust ⌘
c/o Wells Fargo Bank, N.A.
525 Market St., 17th Fl.
San Francisco 94163

Established in 1983 in CA.
Foundation type: Independent
Financial data (yr. ended 1/31/89): Assets, $2,405,611 (M); expenditures, $284,219, including $215,389 for 18 grants (high: $32,394; low: $2,500).
Purpose and activities: Giving primarily to wildlife research and animal protection; support also for medical research.
Limitations: No grants to individuals.
Application information: Contributes only to pre-selected organizations. Applications not accepted.
Write: Minh Le, Trust Admin.
Trustee: Wells Fargo Bank, N.A.
Employer Identification Number: 956795278

672
J. W. Sefton Foundation ⌘
P.O. Box 1871
San Diego 92112

Incorporated in 1945 in CA.
Donor(s): J.W. Sefton, Jr.†
Foundation type: Independent
Financial data (yr. ended 12/31/86): Assets, $3,353,047 (M); expenditures, $161,478, including $104,945 for 16 grants (high: $20,000; low: $69).
Purpose and activities: Giving for community development, including grants for the police, museums, and a historical society.
Limitations: Giving primarily in San Diego, CA.
Application information:
Write: Thomas W. Sefton, Pres.
Officers and Trustees: Thomas W. Sefton, Pres.; Donna K. Sefton, V.P.; Gordon T. Frost, Secy.; Gordon E. McNary, Treas.
Employer Identification Number: 951513384

673
Barnet Segal Charitable Trust ⌘
P.O. Box S-1
Carmel 93921

Established in 1986 in CA.
Foundation type: Independent
Financial data (yr. ended 3/31/89): Assets, $11,325,891 (M); gifts received, $11,569; expenditures, $653,400, including $507,270 for 10 grants (high: $400,000; low: $20).
Purpose and activities: Giving primarily for libraries; support also for fine and performing arts groups, housing for senior citizens, family planning, and health education.
Limitations: Giving primarily in Monterey County, CA.
Application information: Contributes only to pre-selected organizations. Applications not accepted.
Trustee: Herbert Berman.
Employer Identification Number: 776024786

674
The Segerstrom Foundation ⌘ ☆
c/o C.J. Segerstrom & Sons
3315 Fairview Rd.
Costa Mesa 92626

Established in 1987 in CA.
Foundation type: Independent
Financial data (yr. ended 12/31/88): Assets, $1,914,000 (M); expenditures, $181,834, including $172,500 for 4 grants (high: $100,000; low: $10,000).
Purpose and activities: Initial year of grantmaking activity, 1988; support primarily for the performing arts.
Limitations: Giving primarily in CA.
Application information: Currently developing application guidelines.
Deadline(s): None
Write: Thomas Santley, Pres.
Officers: Thomas Santley, Pres.; Mark Heim, Secy. and C.F.O.
Directors: Harold T. Segerstrom, Henry T. Segerstrom, Nellie Ruth Segerstrom, Ted Segerstrom.
Employer Identification Number: 330269599

675
Sequoia Trust Fund ⌘
555 California St., 36th Fl.
San Francisco 94104 (415) 393-8552

Established in 1944 in CA.
Foundation type: Independent
Financial data (yr. ended 9/30/88): Assets, $1,363,349 (M); gifts received, $1,225; expenditures, $83,842, including $26,500 for 7 grants (high: $10,000; low: $1,000) and

$31,400 for 4 grants to individuals (high: $12,000; low: $2,400).
Purpose and activities: Support for arts, social service organizations, and aid to needy individuals.
Types of support: Grants to individuals.
Limitations: Giving limited to the San Francisco Bay, CA, area.
Application information: Application form not required.
Initial approach: Letter
Write: Walter M. Baird, Secy.
Officer and Trustees: Walter M. Baird, Secy.; Roy A. Folger, W. Parmer Fuller III, Raymond W. Hackett, Patrick O'Nelveny.
Employer Identification Number: 946065506

676
The Setzer Foundation ⌑
2555 Third St., Suite 200
Sacramento 95818

Trust established in 1965 in CA.
Donor(s): Members of the Setzer family.
Foundation type: Independent
Financial data (yr. ended 03/31/89): Assets, $3,861,856 (M); expenditures, $237,938, including $192,065 for grants (high: $15,000; low: $15).
Purpose and activities: Emphasis on higher education, cultural programs, youth and social service agencies, and hospitals.
Limitations: Giving primarily in CA. No grants to individuals.
Application information: Contributes only to pre-selected organizations. Applications not accepted.
Trustees: G. Cal Setzer, Hardie C. Setzer, Mark Setzer.
Employer Identification Number: 946115578

677
The Seven Springs Foundation
P.O. Box 687
Cupertino 95015-0687

Established in 1979 in CA.
Foundation type: Independent
Financial data (yr. ended 12/31/88): Assets, $2,130,138 (M); gifts received, $2,269; expenditures, $101,651, including $82,700 for 37 grants (high: $10,000; low: $100).
Purpose and activities: Giving for the environment and conservation, women's welfare, cultural organizations, and the media.
Types of support: General purposes, special projects, matching funds.
Limitations: Giving primarily in CA.
Application information: Contributes only to pre-selected organizations. Applications not accepted.
Write: Martha D. Lyddon, Pres.
Officers and Trustees:* Martha D. Lyddon,* Pres.; Alvin T. Levitt,* Secy.-Treas.; John Knight Lyddon.
Employer Identification Number: 942570260

678
The Shalan Foundation, Inc.
82 Second St., Suite 300
San Francisco 94105 (415) 543-4561

Incorporated in 1969 in NY.
Foundation type: Independent
Financial data (yr. ended 9/30/87): Assets, $1,315,691 (M); gifts received, $409,000; expenditures, $376,154, including $287,000 for 23 grants (high: $35,000; low: $5,000; average: $10,000-$15,000).
Purpose and activities: Grants primarily to groups promoting economic policy development to increase social justice and environmental balance.
Types of support: General purposes, continuing support, matching funds, special projects, conferences and seminars, research, seed money, technical assistance.
Limitations: Giving primarily in AZ, CA, ID, MT, NM, NV, OR, UT, TX, WA, WY, and western CO; some national giving. No support for social service programs, projects addressing international issues, or medical, arts, cultural, international, or educational institutions. No grants to individuals, or for capital or endowment funds, renovation projects, media or arts projects, scholarships, or fellowships.
Publications: Annual report (including application guidelines), grants list.
Application information: Application form not required.
Initial approach: Brief description or proposal only; no letters of inquiry
Copies of proposal: 1
Deadline(s): Mar. 1 and July 15
Board meeting date(s): May and Oct.
Final notification: 1 to 3 months
Write: Catherine Lerza, Exec. Dir.
Officer: Catherine Lerza, Exec. Dir.
Number of staff: 3 full-time professional.
Employer Identification Number: 237063923

679
David and Fela Shapell Foundation ⌑ ☆
9401 Wilshire Blvd., Suite 1200
Beverly Hills 90212

Established in 1967.
Donor(s): David Shapell, Fela Shapell.
Foundation type: Independent
Financial data (yr. ended 7/31/87): Assets, $1,153,152 (M); gifts received, $237,766; expenditures, $173,554, including $170,250 for grants.
Purpose and activities: Giving primarily for Jewish welfare funds, temple support, and religious education.
Limitations: Giving primarily in CA, NY, and Israel.
Officers: David Shapell, Pres.; Fela Shapell, V.P. and Secy.; Irvin Sterman, Treas.
Employer Identification Number: 956187271

680
Nathan & Lilly Shapell Foundation ⌑ ☆
8383 Wilshire Blvd., Suite 724
Beverly Hills 90211-2470

Established in 1959.
Donor(s): Nathan Shapell.
Foundation type: Independent
Financial data (yr. ended 5/31/89): Assets, $3,119,471 (M); gifts received, $362,337; expenditures, $94,996, including $48,790 for 5 grants (high: $25,050; low: $100).
Purpose and activities: Support primarily for a secondary school and a Jewish welfare fund; minor giving for health services.
Application information: Application form not required.
Deadline(s): None
Officers: Nathan Shapell, Pres.; Lidy Shapell, Secy.-Treas.
Employer Identification Number: 956047847

681
J. F. Shea Company Foundation ⌑
655 Brea Canyon Rd.
Walnut 91789 (714) 594-9500

Established in 1967.
Donor(s): John F. Shea Co.
Foundation type: Company-sponsored
Financial data (yr. ended 12/31/88): Assets, $1,381,902 (M); expenditures, $158,516, including $153,212 for 32 grants (high: $50,000; low: $100).
Purpose and activities: Emphasis on higher and secondary education, Roman Catholic religious organizations, health, and recreation.
Limitations: Giving primarily in CA. No grants to individuals.
Application information: Contributes only to pre-selected organizations. Applications not accepted.
Officers: John F. Shea, Pres. and Treas.; Edmund H. Shea, Jr., V.P.; Peter O. Shea, V.P.
Employer Identification Number: 952554052

682
The Shea Foundation ⌑
655 Brea Canyon Rd.
Walnut 91789

Incorporated in 1960 in CA.
Donor(s): Members of the Shea family.
Foundation type: Independent
Financial data (yr. ended 11/30/89): Assets, $3,358,824 (M); expenditures, $170,175, including $157,900 for 58 grants (high: $14,000; low: $200).
Purpose and activities: Emphasis on Roman Catholic church support and religious associations; support also for secondary education and the handicapped.
Types of support: Scholarship funds.
Limitations: Giving primarily in CA.
Application information: Application form not required.
Initial approach: Proposal
Copies of proposal: 1
Deadline(s): None
Board meeting date(s): Apr.
Write: Rudy Magallanes
Officers: John F. Shea,* Pres.; Patricia Ann Shea Meek, V.P.; Michael L. Mellor,* Secy.-Treas.
Trustees:* Robert L. Bridges.
Employer Identification Number: 956027824

683
John & Dorothy Shea Foundation ⌑ ☆
655 Brea Canyon Rd.
Walnut 91789

Established in 1986 in CA.
Donor(s): John F. Shea, Dorothy Shea.
Foundation type: Independent
Financial data (yr. ended 12/31/88): Assets, $9,405,892 (M); gifts received, $271,920; expenditures, $598,470, including $553,505 for 40 grants (high: $204,233; low: $50).
Purpose and activities: Giving to Catholic churches and an archdiocese, and secondary education, especially a public school district; support also for higher education.
Limitations: Giving primarily in CA. No grants to individuals.
Application information: Contributes only to pre-selected organizations. Applications not accepted.
Officers: John F. Shea, Pres.; Dorothy Shea, Secy.; John F. Shea, Jr., Treas.
Employer Identification Number: 954084694

684
Shenandoah Foundation ⌑
P.O. Box 3809
San Francisco 94119-3809

Established in 1968 in CA.
Foundation type: Independent
Financial data (yr. ended 12/31/88): Assets, $2,248,769 (M); expenditures, $65,175, including $60,900 for 22 grants (high: $20,000; low: $100).
Purpose and activities: Giving primarily for secondary and higher education.
Limitations: Giving primarily in CA.
Application information: Contributes only to pre-selected organizations. Applications not accepted.
Officers and Directors:* Shana B. Johnstone,* Pres.; Elizabeth H. Bechtel,* V.P.; A. Barlow Ferguson,* Secy.; Theodore J. Van Bebber, Treas.; S.D. Bechtel, Jr., Investment Mgr.
Employer Identification Number: 941675019

685
Milton Shoong Foundation ⌑
929 Market St.
San Francisco 94103 (415) 392-1371

Incorporated in 1941 in CA.
Donor(s): Joe Shoong,† Rose Shoong,† Milton W. Shoong, Betty Shoong Bird, Doris Shoong Lee, National Dollar Stores, Ltd., Richard Tam, Corinne Shoong.
Foundation type: Independent
Financial data (yr. ended 12/31/87): Assets, $6,441,056 (M); expenditures, $738,782, including $503,298 for 118 grants (high: $110,400; low: $100).
Purpose and activities: Originally established as The Joe Shoong School to provide for the maintenance of a school or college in China and scholarships or loans to assist worthy students. Now giving largely to educational, religious, and welfare institutions, including the operation of a community center principally aiding the local Chinese population.
Types of support: Operating budgets, seed money, building funds, equipment, matching funds, scholarship funds, research.
Limitations: Giving primarily in CA. No grants to individuals; no loans.
Application information: Application form not required.
Initial approach: Letter
Copies of proposal: 1
Deadline(s): None
Board meeting date(s): Monthly
Final notification: 30 days
Officers and Directors: Milton W. Shoong, Pres.; Dave E. Quan, V.P. and Secy.-Treas.; Jim Ellis, V.P.; Jerry Fitzpatrick, V.P.; Howard T. Garrigan, V.P.; Paul Godkin, V.P.; Ted Lee, V.P.; Peter Mantegani, V.P.; Charles Pius, V.P.; Dwight Wright, V.P.
Number of staff: None.
Employer Identification Number: 941200291

686
Walter H. and Phyllis J. Shorenstein Foundation ⌑
One California St., Rm. 2900
San Francisco 94111

Established in 1965 in CA.
Donor(s): Phyllis J. Shorenstein, Walter H. Shorenstein.
Foundation type: Independent
Financial data (yr. ended 12/31/88): Assets, $13,251 (M); gifts received, $310,000; expenditures, $380,491, including $380,028 for 26 grants (high: $100,000; low: $100).
Purpose and activities: Giving primarily for cultural programs; support also for Jewish giving and education, with emphasis on medical education.
Limitations: Giving primarily in San Francisco, CA. No grants to individuals.
Application information: Contributes only to pre-selected organizations. Applications not accepted.
Officers: Walter H. Shorenstein, Pres.; Phyllis J. Shorenstein, V.P.; Iona Blampied, Secy.; Douglas W. Shorenstein, Treas.
Employer Identification Number: 946113160

687
The Sierra Foundation ▼
11211 Gold Country Blvd., Suite 101
Rancho Cordova 95670 (916) 635-4755

Established in 1984 in CA.
Donor(s): Foundation Health Plan of Sacramento, Americare Health Corp.
Foundation type: Independent
Financial data (yr. ended 6/30/88): Assets, $80,039,376 (M); expenditures, $3,721,291, including $1,592,162 for 64 grants (high: $168,429; low: $600; average: $20,000-$40,000).
Purpose and activities: Giving for health-related programs that (a) will have a long-term impact on the general health of the population; (b) provide a positive change in health care systems; and (c) may cause a positive change in the use of health care resources. Support also for model projects that may be replicated by others. The foundation has an ongoing significant involvement in prenatal care and AIDS.
Types of support: Matching funds, seed money, special projects, technical assistance, employee matching gifts.
Limitations: Giving limited to the following CA counties: Alpine, Amador, Butte, Calaveras, Colusa, El Dorado, Glenn, Lassen, Modoc, Mono, Nevada, Placer, Plumas, Sacramento, San Joaquin, Shasta, Sierra, Siskiyou, Solano (eastern), Stanislaus, Sutter, Tehama, Trinity, Tuolumne, Yolo, and Yuba. No support for programs or organizations that are not health-related, or for lobbying activities. No grants to individuals, or for endowments or scholarships.
Publications: Grants list, newsletter, application guidelines, informational brochure (including application guidelines), occasional report.
Application information: Application form not required.
Initial approach: Letter of intent
Copies of proposal: 1
Deadline(s): None
Board meeting date(s): Quarterly
Write: Len McCandliss, Pres.
Officers and Directors:* J. Rod Eason,* Chair.; Len McCandliss,* Pres.; Leo McAllister,* Secy.; Byron Demorest, M.D., George Deubel, Wendy Everett-Watson, Albert R. Jonsen, Robert Petersen, Gordon D. Schaber, James Schubert, M.D.
Number of staff: 4 full-time professional; 1 part-time professional; 6 full-time support.
Employer Identification Number: 680050036

688
Sierra Pacific Foundation ⌑ ☆
P.O. Box 1189
Arcata 95521 (707) 443-3111

Established in 1978.
Donor(s): Sierra Pacific Industries.
Foundation type: Company-sponsored
Financial data (yr. ended 6/30/89): Assets, $1,576,064 (M); expenditures, $102,957, including $47,812 for 62 grants (high: $8,322; low: $20) and $50,092 for 60 grants to individuals (high: $2,000; low: $500).
Purpose and activities: Support for higher and secondary education, including libraries; parks and recreational activities for youth; museums and other cultural programs; civic affairs, including citizens' associations and public media; wildlife and environmental preservation; social services, including women's shelters and child welfare; and hospitals, an eye bank, and other health organizations. Scholarships are restricted to dependent children of Sierra Pacific Industries employees.
Types of support: Employee-related scholarships.
Application information: Application form required.
Initial approach: Letter
Board meeting date(s): Mar. 30
Write: R.L. Smith, V.P.
Officers: Ida Emmerson, Pres.; Richard L. Smith, V.P.; Carolyn I. Dietz, Treas.
Employer Identification Number: 942574178

689
Jennifer Jones Simon Foundation
411 West Colorado Blvd.
Pasadena 91105 (818) 449-6840

Established in 1954 in LA.

Donor(s): Norton Simon, Norton Simon, Inc., and its subsidiaries and predecessors, Braun 1981 Charitable Annuity Trust, Norton Simon Charitable Lead Trust.
Foundation type: Independent
Financial data (yr. ended 11/30/89): Assets, $4,424,329 (M); gifts received, $279,982; expenditures, $325,881, including $294,500 for 3 grants (high: $280,000; low: $2,000; average: $2,000-$280,000).
Purpose and activities: Giving primarily to operate a program of mental health workshops and support mental health activities.
Types of support: Annual campaigns.
Limitations: No grants to individuals, or for building or endowment funds, research, scholarships, fellowships, or matching gifts; no loans.
Application information: Grants generally restricted to programs initiated by the foundation; no new scholarships to individuals will be awarded. Application form not required.
Initial approach: Letter
Deadline(s): None
Board meeting date(s): As required
Final notification: 1 month
Write: Walter W. Timoshuk, V.P.
Officers and Trustees:* Jennifer Jones Simon,* Chair.; Norton Simon,* Pres.; Walter W. Timoshuk,* V.P. and Treas.
Number of staff: None.
Employer Identification Number: 953660147

690
The Lucille Ellis Simon Foundation ¤
c/o Hufstedler, Miller, Carlson & Beardsley
355 South Grand Ave., 45th Fl.
Los Angeles 90071

Incorporated in 1960 in CA.
Donor(s): Donald Simon, Lucille Ellis Simon, and other members of the Simon family.
Foundation type: Independent
Financial data (yr. ended 12/31/88): Assets, $1,552,042 (M); expenditures, $149,537, including $128,060 for 60 grants (high: $25,000; low: $35).
Purpose and activities: Giving for Jewish welfare funds, social service agencies, and health services.
Limitations: Giving primarily in CA. No grants to individuals.
Application information: Contributes only to pre-selected organizations. Applications not accepted.
Write: Donald Ellis Simon, Pres.
Officers: Donald Ellis Simon, Pres.; Mrs. Sidney Foorman, V.P.; Jerome Craig, Secy.; Brian E. Lewis, Treas.
Members: David Amsterdam, James R. McDaniel, Douglas Simon, Lucille Ellis Simon, Pamela Simon.
Employer Identification Number: 956035906

691
The Robert Ellis Simon Foundation
152 South Lasky Dr.
Beverly Hills 90212

Trust established in 1961 in CA.
Donor(s): Robert Ellis Simon.†
Foundation type: Independent
Financial data (yr. ended 12/31/87): Assets, $3,251,221 (M); expenditures, $280,772, including $222,674 for 7 grants (high: $58,000; low: $10,000).
Purpose and activities: Grants for "preventive or educational approaches to any of a variety of mental health issues"; support for new, short-term, and innovative programs or demonstration projects and not for long-term funding.
Types of support: Seed money, special projects.
Limitations: Giving limited to Los Angeles County, CA.
Application information: Applications accepted by invitation only; unsolicited applications not accepted.
Initial approach: Letter and 2-page concept proposal; final proposals only at request of foundation
Copies of proposal: 4
Write: Dr. Joan Willens, Trustee
Trustees: Donald Simon, Joan G. Willens, Harold M. Williams.
Employer Identification Number: 956035905

692
Isaac D. and Ruth G. Sinaiko Foundation ¤
P.O. Box 4207
Cerritos 90703-4207

Established in 1968 in CA.
Donor(s): Isaac D. Sinaiko, Ruth G. Sinaiko.
Foundation type: Independent
Financial data (yr. ended 12/31/88): Assets, $139,190 (M); gifts received, $145,000; expenditures, $128,768, including $127,500 for 5 grants (high: $100,000; low: $500).
Purpose and activities: Giving primarily for Jewish welfare funds and religious organizations; minor support also for higher education.
Limitations: No grants to individuals.
Application information: Contributes only to pre-selected organizations. Applications not accepted.
Officers: Ruth G. Sinaiko, Pres.; Edward J. Field, V.P.; Irwin S. Field, Secy.-Treas.
Employer Identification Number: 237010727

693
L. J. Skaggs and Mary C. Skaggs Foundation ▼
1221 Broadway, 21st Fl.
Oakland 94612-1837 (415) 451-3300

Incorporated in 1967 in CA.
Donor(s): L.J. Skaggs,† Mary C. Skaggs.
Foundation type: Independent
Financial data (yr. ended 12/31/89): Assets, $9,005,248 (M); gifts received, $840,000; expenditures, $3,299,658, including $2,436,390 for grants (high: $200,000).
Purpose and activities: Giving for the performing arts, specifically theater, youth programs, ecology programs, and projects of historic interest.
Types of support: Special projects, general purposes, continuing support, publications.
Limitations: Giving limited to northern CA for theater, youth programs, ecology programs, and special projects; giving with national focus limited to projects of historic interest. No support for higher education, residence home programs, halfway houses, or sectarian religious purposes. No grants to individuals, or for capital funds, annual fund drives, budget deficits, scholarships, or fellowships; no loans.
Publications: Annual report (including application guidelines), informational brochure (including application guidelines), grants list.
Application information: Application form not required.
Initial approach: Letter
Copies of proposal: 1
Deadline(s): June 1 for letter of intent, Sept. 1 for invited proposal
Board meeting date(s): Nov.
Final notification: 2 to 3 weeks after board meeting
Write: Philip M. Jelley, Secy., or David G. Knight, Prog. Dir. and Office Mgr.
Officers and Directors:* Mary C. Skaggs,* Pres.; Peter H. Forsham, M.D.,* V.P.; Catherine L. O'Brien,* V.P.; Philip M. Jelley,* Secy. and Fdn. Mgr.; Donald D. Crawford,* Treas.; David Knight, Prog. Dir.
Number of staff: 4 full-time professional.
Employer Identification Number: 946174113

694
The H. Russell Smith Foundation ¤
150 North Orange Grove Blvd.
Pasadena 91103-3596

Established in 1968 in CA.
Donor(s): Kinsmith Financial Corp.
Foundation type: Independent
Financial data (yr. ended 12/31/88): Assets, $18,490 (M); gifts received, $411,250; expenditures, $397,649, including $389,052 for 30 grants (high: $263,100; low: $25).
Purpose and activities: Support primarily for hospitals and medical research; support also for youth education and guidance, community organizations and higher education.
Application information: Contributes only to pre-selected organizations. Applications not accepted.
Officers and Directors: H. Russell Smith, Pres.; Stewart R. Smith, V.P.; Jeanne R. Smith, Secy.-Treas.
Number of staff: None.
Employer Identification Number: 237423945

695
Lon V. Smith Foundation ¤
9440 Santa Monica Blvd., Suite 300
Beverly Hills 90210-4201

Established in 1952 in CA.
Foundation type: Independent
Financial data (yr. ended 12/31/88): Assets, $16,380,866 (M); expenditures, $1,071,892, including $925,400 for 93 grants (high: $200,000; low: $500).
Purpose and activities: Support primarily for higher education, health and medical organizations, social services, and museums.
Types of support: General purposes.
Limitations: Giving primarily in southern CA.
Application information: Contributes only to pre-selected organizations. Applications not accepted.

Officers: W. Layton Stanton, Pres.; Marguerite B. Smith, V.P.; Marguerite M. Murphy, Secy.-Treas.
Director: Stefan A. Kantardjieff.
Employer Identification Number: 956045384

696
The Stanley Smith Horticultural Trust ⌑
49 Geary St., Rm. 244
San Francisco 94108 (415) 391-0292
Application address: Belhaven House, East Lothian, EH 421 NS, Scotland

Trust established in 1970 in CA.
Donor(s): May Smith.
Foundation type: Independent
Financial data (yr. ended 12/31/88): Assets, $6,851,029 (M); expenditures, $361,578, including $331,188 for 20 grants (high: $50,000; low: $1,000).
Purpose and activities: Grants to organizations for horticultural programs, including education and research.
Types of support: Building funds, operating budgets, special projects, research.
Limitations: No grants to individuals, or for endowment funds.
Application information: Application form required.
Initial approach: Proposal
Copies of proposal: 1
Deadline(s): None
Board meeting date(s): As required
Write: Sir George Taylor, Trustee
Trustees: John P. Collins, Barbara de Brye, James R. Gibbs, May Smith, George Taylor.
Employer Identification Number: 946209165

697
The May and Stanley Smith Trust ⌑
49 Geary St., Suite 244
San Francisco 94108 (415) 391-0292

Donor(s): May Smith.
Foundation type: Independent
Financial data (yr. ended 12/31/88): Assets, $3,024,903 (M); expenditures, $150,197, including $144,400 for 30 grants (high: $10,000; low: $1,500).
Purpose and activities: Giving for church support and religious welfare funds, including aid to the handicapped, the aged, and children; support also for other social service agencies.
Types of support: Operating budgets, building funds, general purposes.
Limitations: Giving primarily in the San Francisco, CA, area and in Canada, England, Scotland, and Australia. No grants to individuals.
Application information:
Initial approach: Letter
Deadline(s): Apr. 15 to Sept. 30
Write: John P. Collins, Sr., Trustee
Trustees: John P. Collins, Sr., John P. Collins, Jr., J. Ronald Gibbs.
Employer Identification Number: 946435244

698
Smith-Welsh Foundation ⌑
760 North La Cienega Blvd.
Los Angeles 90069-5279

Established in 1985 in CA.
Donor(s): Omer Smith Marital Trust.
Foundation type: Independent
Financial data (yr. ended 12/31/87): Assets, $1,821,786 (M); gifts received, $788,830; expenditures, $32,674, including $15,250 for 15 grants (high: $2,500; low: $250).
Purpose and activities: Giving for health services, social services, and arts organizations.
Application information: Applications not accepted.
Officers: Nancy S. Welsh, C.E.O.; James E. Welsh, C.F.O. and Secy.
Employer Identification Number: 953958030

699
Elaine H. Snyder Cancer Research Trust ⌑
c/o Mulvey & Mulvey
6255 Sunset Blvd., Suite 714
Los Angeles 90028

Established in 1983 in CA.
Donor(s): Elaine H. Snyder.
Foundation type: Independent
Financial data (yr. ended 12/31/87): Assets, $1,438,587 (M); expenditures, $137,581, including $116,655 for 1 grant.
Purpose and activities: Support for cancer research.
Application information: Contributes only to a pre-selected organization. Applications not accepted.
Trustee: Bernard M. Mulvey.
Employer Identification Number: 956781723

700
Albert Soiland Cancer Foundation ⌑
c/o Meserve, Mumper & Hughes
5190 Campus Dr., P.O. Box 7820
Newport Beach 92660 (714) 752-8995

Incorporated in 1946 in CA.
Donor(s): Albert Soiland, M.D.†
Foundation type: Independent
Financial data (yr. ended 6/30/87): Assets, $1,285,478 (M); expenditures, $267,961, including $208,427 for 1 grant.
Purpose and activities: Care and treatment of needy cancer patients; fellowships in radiological therapy; grants to approved institutions for cancer research.
Types of support: Research, fellowships.
Application information: Application form not required.
Deadline(s): None
Write: J. Robert Meserve, Secy.-Treas.
Officer and Directors: J. Robert Meserve, Secy.-Treas.; Brian Henderson, Stanley van den Noort.
Employer Identification Number: 956027828

701
Richard & Mary Solari Charitable Trust ⌑
527 St. Andrews Dr.
Aptos 95003-5422

Established in 1984 in CA.
Foundation type: Independent
Financial data (yr. ended 9/30/88): Assets, $1,779,125 (M); gifts received, $592,127; expenditures, $64,210, including $56,900 for 9 grants (high: $25,000; low: $100).
Purpose and activities: Giving primarily for community projects, health causes and higher education.
Limitations: No grants to individuals.
Application information: Contributes only to pre-selected organizations. Applications not accepted.
Trustees: Mary C. Solari, Richard C. Solari.
Employer Identification Number: 776012078

702
The Sonoma County Foundation ☆
1260 North Dutton Ave., Suite 280
Santa Rosa 95401 (707) 579-4073

Incorporated in 1983 in CA.
Foundation type: Community
Financial data (yr. ended 12/31/89): Assets, $2,342,326 (M); qualifying distributions, $594,000, including $341,000 for 60 grants (high: $5,000; low: $250; average: $500-$5,000), $10,000 for 10 grants to individuals (high: $1,000) and $243,000 for 2 foundation-administered programs.
Purpose and activities: Grants for the arts and culture, education, the environment, and health and human service programs.
Types of support: Student aid, grants to individuals, renovation projects, building funds, equipment, general purposes, matching funds, publications, scholarship funds, seed money, special projects, technical assistance.
Limitations: Giving limited to Sonoma County, CA. No support for religious purposes or lobbying activities. No grants for annual campaigns, conferences and seminars, deficit financing, endowments, operating budgets, or research.
Publications: Annual report, informational brochure (including application guidelines), 990-PF, program policy statement.
Application information: Application form not required.
Initial approach: Letter
Copies of proposal: 2
Deadline(s): June 1 and Sept. 1
Board meeting date(s): July 16, Oct. 15, and Nov. 19
Final notification: Aug., Nov., and Dec.
Write: Virginia Hubbell, Exec. Dir.
Officers and Trustees:* John Shanahan,* Pres.; Arthur L. Lafranchi,* V.P.; Nancy Henshaw,* Secy.; Edward J. Pisenti,* Treas.; Virginia Hubbell,* Exec. Dir.; and 25 other trustees.
Number of staff: 1 full-time professional; 1 part-time professional; 2 full-time support; 1 part-time support.
Employer Identification Number: 680003212

703
John W. Spencer Trust ⌑ ☆
c/o Mechanics Bank
3170 Hilltop Mall Rd.
Richmond 94806 (415) 262-7300

Foundation type: Independent

Financial data (yr. ended 11/30/89): Assets, $1,380,602 (M); expenditures, $105,818, including $91,385 for 45 grants to individuals (high: $4,500; low: $278).
Purpose and activities: Scholarships for local residents attending the University of California or Leland Stanford Junior University.
Types of support: Student aid.
Limitations: Giving limited to residents of Richmond and El Cerrito, CA.
Application information: Application form required.
Deadline(s): Mar. 1
Write: William H. Reid, Pres.
Trustees: Gene B. Beckel, Henry E. Conell, Jr., William M. Reid.
Employer Identification Number: 946055547

704
Abraham & Edita Spiegel Family Foundation ⌑ ☆
8840 Wilshire Blvd.
Beverly Hills 90211

Established in 1961.
Donor(s): Members of the Spiegel family.
Foundation type: Independent
Financial data (yr. ended 6/30/89): Assets, $784,383 (M); gifts received, $2,500; expenditures, $228,373, including $223,600 for 4 grants (high: $189,900; low: $1,200).
Purpose and activities: Giving primarily for Jewish organizations.
Limitations: No grants to individuals.
Application information: Contributes only to pre-selected organizations. Applications not accepted.
Officers: Abraham Spiegel, Pres.; Thomas Spiegel, V.P. and Secy.; Edita Spiegel, Treas.
Employer Identification Number: 956093034

705
Caryll M. and Norman F. Sprague, Jr. Foundation ⌑
2049 Century Park East, No. 2760
Los Angeles 90067-3202 (213) 387-7311

Trust established in 1957 in CA.
Donor(s): Caryll M. Sprague, Norman F. Sprague, Jr., M.D.
Foundation type: Independent
Financial data (yr. ended 12/31/87): Assets, $3,458,261 (M); expenditures, $192,567, including $174,350 for 32 grants (high: $93,750; low: $250).
Purpose and activities: Emphasis on higher education including medical education, hospitals, secondary education, and museums.
Limitations: Giving primarily in CA. No grants to individuals.
Application information:
Initial approach: Letter or telephone
Board meeting date(s): Annually and as required
Write: Norman F. Sprague, Jr., M.D., Trustee
Trustees: Cynthia S. Connolly, Caryll S. Mingst, Charles T. Munger, Norman F. Sprague, Jr., M.D., Norman F. Sprague III, M.D.
Employer Identification Number: 956021187

706
Springhouse Foundation ☆
1505 Bridgeway, Suite 201
Sausalito 94965 (415) 331-4400

Established in 1986 in MA.
Donor(s): Bruce R. Katz.
Foundation type: Independent
Financial data (yr. ended 11/30/88): Assets, $1,401,317 (M); expenditures, $62,865, including $55,500 for grants.
Purpose and activities: Support for a farm and wilderness camp, education, the arts, and programs for youth and child welfare, housing and homelessness, the disadvantaged and hungry, and women.
Types of support: Building funds, capital campaigns, land acquisition, renovation projects, scholarship funds, seed money, special projects.
Limitations: Giving primarily in the West Coast, especially CA. No grants to individuals.
Application information: Application form not required.
Initial approach: Proposal
Copies of proposal: 1
Board meeting date(s): Oct. 15
Final notification: Nov. 15
Write: Claudia Stroud or Tracy Barbutes
Trustees: Bruce R. Katz, Roger Katz.
Number of staff: None.
Employer Identification Number: 042947276

707
C. J. Stafford & Dot Stafford Memorial Trust
c/o San Diego Trust & Savings Bank
P.O. Box X-1013
San Diego 92112 (619) 557-3167

Established in 1984 in CA.
Donor(s): C.J. Stafford,† Dot Stafford.†
Foundation type: Independent
Financial data (yr. ended 04/30/89): Assets, $1,398,813 (M); expenditures, $131,345, including $102,689 for 25 grants (high: $10,000; low: $500; average: $500-$30,000).
Purpose and activities: Giving primarily for hospitals, youth agencies, community funds, medical research and health associations, social services, education, and the fine and performing arts.
Types of support: Building funds, continuing support, emergency funds, equipment, general purposes, matching funds, operating budgets, renovation projects, special projects, capital campaigns.
Limitations: Giving limited to San Diego County, CA.
Publications: 990-PF, application guidelines.
Application information:
Initial approach: Letter
Copies of proposal: 6
Deadline(s): Apr. 1
Board meeting date(s): Quarterly - varies
Write: Laurie Dick, Asst. V.P., San Diego Trust & Savings Bank
Trustee: San Diego Trust & Savings Bank.
Number of staff: 1 full-time professional; 4 part-time professional; 1 full-time support.
Employer Identification Number: 330085374

708
James L. Stamps Foundation, Inc.
P.O. Box 250
Downey 90241 (213) 861-3112

Incorporated in 1963 in CA.
Donor(s): James L. Stamps.†
Foundation type: Independent
Financial data (yr. ended 12/31/89): Assets, $17,000,000 (M); expenditures, $780,000, including $750,000 for 66 grants (high: $25,000; low: $1,000).
Purpose and activities: Emphasis on Protestant evangelical churches, seminaries, associations, and programs; support also for medical research and hospitals. Capital fund grants restricted to Christian organizations; new equipment grants restricted to Christian organizations and hospitals; camping grants restricted to Christian camps.
Types of support: Operating budgets, continuing support, annual campaigns, seed money, emergency funds, matching funds, special projects, internships, scholarship funds.
Limitations: Giving primarily in southern CA. No grants to individuals, or for endowment funds, deficit financing, scholarships, fellowships, publications, or conferences.
Application information: Application form required.
Initial approach: Letter
Copies of proposal: 1
Deadline(s): 1st of month prior to meeting
Board meeting date(s): Bimonthly beginning in Feb., on the 2nd Tuesday of the month
Final notification: 5 to 10 days after meeting
Write: Jolene Boutault, Mgr.
Officers and Trustees:* E.C. Boutault,* Pres.; Thomas P. Lynch,* V.P.; Kenneth E. Gail,* Secy.-Treas.; I. W. Johnson, Willis R. Leach, Richard Salyer.
Number of staff: 1 full-time support; 1 part-time support.
Employer Identification Number: 956086125

709
The Stans Foundation
350 West Colorado Blvd.
Pasadena 91105 (818) 795-5947

Incorporated in 1945 in IL.
Donor(s): Maurice H. Stans, Kathleen C. Stans.†
Foundation type: Independent
Financial data (yr. ended 12/31/88): Assets, $4,300,000 (M); expenditures, $259,000, including $220,000 for 125 grants (high: $59,000; low: $20; average: $20-$59,000).
Purpose and activities: Emphasis on a restoration project, an historical society, and a museum; grants also for public service organizations, research, higher education, and church support.
Types of support: General purposes, continuing support, annual campaigns, building funds, equipment, research, conferences and seminars, program-related investments.
Limitations: No grants to individuals, or for operating budgets, endowment funds, scholarships, fellowships, or matching gifts; no loans.
Publications: 990-PF.
Application information: Funds fully committed for next 5-7 years. Applications not accepted.

Write: Maurice H. Stans, Chair.
Officers: Maurice H. Stans,* Chair. and Treas.; Steven H. Stans,* Pres.; Maureen Stans Helmick,* V.P.; William Manley,* V.P.; Theodore M. Stans,* V.P.; Mary C. Elia, Secy.
Directors:* Walter Helmick, Terrell Stans Manley, Diane Stans, Susan Stans.
Number of staff: None.
Employer Identification Number: 366008663

710
John Stauffer Charitable Trust ▼ ⌑
Equitable Plaza, Suite 2500
3435 Wilshire Blvd.
Los Angeles 90010 (213) 385-4345

Trust established in 1974 in CA.
Donor(s): John Stauffer.†
Foundation type: Independent
Financial data (yr. ended 5/31/89): Assets, $29,915,885 (M); expenditures, $1,406,150, including $1,083,067 for 16 grants (high: $150,000; low: $17,500; average: $25,000-$50,000).
Purpose and activities: Grants restricted to hospitals and higher education.
Types of support: Building funds, endowment funds, equipment, fellowships, general purposes, matching funds, professorships, scholarship funds.
Limitations: Giving primarily in CA. No grants to individuals, or for research, special projects, conferences, or publications; no loans.
Publications: Application guidelines.
Application information: Application form not required.
Initial approach: Letter
Copies of proposal: 3
Deadline(s): None
Board meeting date(s): Bimonthly beginning in Feb.
Final notification: 6 to 9 months
Write: Stanley C. Lagerlof, Trustee
Trustees: Carl M. Franklin, A. Richard Kimbrough, Stanley C. Lagerlof.
Number of staff: 1 part-time support.
Employer Identification Number: 237434707

711
John and Beverly Stauffer Foundation ⌑
P.O. Box 2246
Los Angeles 90028 (213) 381-3933

Incorporated in 1954 in CA.
Donor(s): John Stauffer,† Beverly Stauffer.†
Foundation type: Independent
Financial data (yr. ended 12/31/88): Assets, $3,322,025 (M); expenditures, $221,403, including $191,647 for 57 grants (high: $20,000; low: $40; average: $1,000-$5,000).
Purpose and activities: Support for higher and secondary education; hospitals and medical research, including cancer research; social service and child welfare agencies, including projects for the homeless, alcoholism, and drug abuse; cultural programs; and Christian religious associations.
Types of support: Continuing support, annual campaigns, building funds, equipment, scholarship funds, general purposes.
Limitations: Giving primarily in the southern CA, area. No grants to individuals, or for endowment funds or operating budgets.
Application information: Application form not required.
Initial approach: Letter
Copies of proposal: 1
Deadline(s): None
Board meeting date(s): 4 times a year
Write: Jack R. Sheridan, Pres.
Officers and Directors: Jack R. Sheridan, Pres.; Felix W. Robertson, V.P.; Mary Ann Frankenhoff, Secy.; Thomas C. Towse, Treas.; Leslie Sheridan Bartleson, Louise Camp, Brooke Sheridan Carnes, Craig Flanaghan, Harriette Hughes, Katherine Stauffer Sheridan.
Employer Identification Number: 952241406

712
Marshall Steel, Sr. Foundation ⌑
P.O. Box 915
Pebble Beach 93953 (408) 624-7341

Trust established in 1957 in CA.
Donor(s): Members of the Steel family and family-related businesses.
Foundation type: Independent
Financial data (yr. ended 12/31/86): Assets, $5,130,000 (M); expenditures, $250,269, including $220,800 for 56 grants (high: $30,000; low: $500).
Purpose and activities: Giving for higher education and science studies, cultural programs and museums, hospitals, social service agencies, and conservation.
Limitations: Giving primarily in CA; no grants outside the U.S. No support for religious purposes. No grants to individuals, or for publications or film making.
Application information:
Initial approach: Letter stating objectives, scope of project, and evidence of local support
Copies of proposal: 1
Deadline(s): None
Board meeting date(s): Usually Oct. and Dec.
Write: Marshall Steel, Jr.
Trustees: Alison Steel, Eric Steel, Gordon Steel, Jane Steel, Lauri Steel, Marshall Steel, Jr.
Number of staff: None.
Employer Identification Number: 946080053

713
The Harry and Grace Steele Foundation ▼
441 Old Newport Blvd., Suite 301
Newport Beach 92663 (714) 631-9158

Incorporated in 1953 in CA.
Donor(s): Grace C. Steele.†
Foundation type: Independent
Financial data (yr. ended 10/31/89): Assets, $45,701,382 (M); expenditures, $8,412,493, including $8,317,646 for 63 grants (high: $2,061,250; low: $1,000; average: $5,000-$250,000).
Purpose and activities: Emphasis on higher and secondary education, including scholarship funds, the fine arts, population control, hospitals and clinics, and youth agencies.
Types of support: Building funds, endowment funds, scholarship funds, matching funds, continuing support, general purposes, special projects, equipment.
Limitations: Giving primarily in Orange County, CA. No support for tax-supported organizations or private foundations. No grants to individuals; no loans.
Publications: Annual report, program policy statement, application guidelines.
Application information: Application form not required.
Initial approach: Letter, followed by proposal
Copies of proposal: 1
Deadline(s): None
Board meeting date(s): Quarterly
Final notification: 6 months
Write: Marie F. Kowert, Asst. Secy.
Officers and Trustees: Audrey Steele Burnand, Pres.; Richard Steele, V.P. and Treas.; Alphonse A. Burnand, Secy.; Marie F. Kowert, Elizabeth R. Steele, Barbara Steele Williams, Nick B. Williams.
Number of staff: 1 full-time support.
Employer Identification Number: 956035879

714
Jules and Doris Stein Foundation ▼
(Formerly Doris Jones Stein Foundation)
P.O. Box 30
Beverly Hills 90213 (213) 276-2101

Established in 1981 in CA.
Donor(s): Doris Jones Stein Family Trust.
Foundation type: Independent
Financial data (yr. ended 12/31/89): Assets, $38,145,000 (M); expenditures, $4,850,000, including $4,666,900 for 262 grants (high: $1,500,000; low: $250; average: $5,000-$20,000).
Purpose and activities: Support for hospitals, health associations, and medical research; higher, medical, and other education; cultural organizations, including museums and the performing and fine arts; computer sciences; and social welfare.
Types of support: General purposes, building funds, continuing support, endowment funds, equipment, matching funds, research, special projects, capital campaigns, fellowships, operating budgets.
Limitations: Giving primarily in the metropolitan areas of Los Angeles, Kansas City, and New York City. No support for political advocacy groups. No grants to individuals.
Publications: Application guidelines, newsletter.
Application information: Application form required.
Initial approach: Letter
Deadline(s): None
Board meeting date(s): Varies
Write: Linda L. Valliant, Secy.
Officers and Directors:* Lew R. Wasserman,* Chair.; Gerald H. Oppenheimer,* Pres.; Gil Shiva,* V.P.; Jean Stein,* V.P.; Linda L. Valliant,* Secy.; Stephen P. Petty,* C.F.O.; Hamilton G. Oppenheimer.
Number of staff: 1 full-time professional; 2 part-time professional; 2 part-time support.
Employer Identification Number: 953708961

715
Sidney Stern Memorial Trust ▼
P.O. Box 893
Pacific Palisades 90272
Additional address: c/o Susan Boling, Asst. V.P. & Trust Officer, Wells Fargo Bank, P.O. Box 54410, Los Angeles, CA 90054; Tel.: (213) 253-3154

Trust established in 1974 in CA.
Donor(s): S. Sidney Stern.†
Foundation type: Independent
Financial data (yr. ended 08/31/87): Assets, $18,368,257 (M); expenditures, $1,188,290, including $1,041,845 for 168 grants (high: $100,500; low: $500; average: $1,000-$15,000).
Purpose and activities: Giving primarily for higher education, social service agencies, including aid to the handicapped; youth and child welfare agencies, health associations, and cultural programs.
Types of support: Operating budgets, annual campaigns, seed money, emergency funds, deficit financing, building funds, equipment, land acquisition, endowment funds, matching funds, scholarship funds, special projects, research.
Limitations: Giving primarily in CA; all funds must be used within the U.S. No grants to individuals, or for continuing support, publications, or conferences; no loans.
Publications: Informational brochure (including application guidelines).
Application information: Application form not required.
Initial approach: Letter or proposal
Copies of proposal: 1
Deadline(s): None
Board meeting date(s): Monthly, except Aug.
Write: Marvin Hoffenberg, Chair.
Board of Advisors: Marvin Hoffenberg, Chair.; Ira E. Bilson, Secy.; Betty Hoffenberg, Peter H. Hoffenberg, Edith Lessler, Howard O. Wilson.
Number of staff: None.
Employer Identification Number: 956495222

716
Laura May Stewart Trust
c/o Wells Fargo Bank
P.O. Box 7980
Newport Beach 92658 (714) 849-5097
Application address: P.O. Box 574, Banning, CA 92220

Trust established in 1975 in CA.
Donor(s): Laura May Stewart.†
Foundation type: Independent
Financial data (yr. ended 5/31/88): Assets, $1,308,426 (M); expenditures, $94,959, including $71,262 for 20 grants (high: $11,000; low: $200).
Purpose and activities: Emphasis on civic affairs and cultural programs.
Limitations: Giving limited to the Banning-Beaumont, CA, area.
Application information: Application form not required.
Initial approach: Letter
Copies of proposal: 1
Deadline(s): None
Board meeting date(s): 4 times a year
Write: Judith Hawkins, Secy. to the Distribution Committee
Trustee: Wells Fargo Private Banking Group.
Number of staff: 1 part-time professional.
Employer Identification Number: 956527634

717
Glen & Dorothy Stillwell Charitable Trust ⌑
3435 Wilshire Blvd., Suite 2500
Los Angeles 90010 (213) 385-4345

Established in 1981 in CA.
Donor(s): Glen Stillwell, Dorothy Stillwell.
Foundation type: Independent
Financial data (yr. ended 11/30/89): Assets, $1,771,021 (M); expenditures, $121,645, including $93,141 for 9 grants (high: $12,500; low: $6,360).
Purpose and activities: "Emphasis on grants to charitable organizations which provide social assistance for the needy, infirm, educationally handicapped, drug and alcohol dependent, blind, hearing impaired, abused, and other disadvantaged persons."
Limitations: Giving limited to Orange County, CA.
Application information:
Initial approach: Letter
Copies of proposal: 1
Deadline(s): None
Write: Stanley C. Lagerlof, Chair.
Officer and Trustees:* Stanley C. Lagerlof,* Chair.; John F. Bradley, H. Jess Senecal.
Employer Identification Number: 956751888

718
Elbridge Stuart Foundation ▼
(also known as Stuart Foundations)
c/o Stuart Foundations
425 Market St., Suite 2835
San Francisco 94105 (415) 495-1144

Trust established in 1937 in CA.
Donor(s): Elbridge A. Stuart.†
Foundation type: Independent
Financial data (yr. ended 12/31/88): Assets, $63,792,356 (M); expenditures, $3,688,720, including $3,443,294 for 122 grants (high: $239,663; low: $2,500; average: $5,000-$30,000).
Purpose and activities: Giving primarily for children and youth, with emphasis on Preventing Child Abuse, Preventing School Failure, Preventing Teen Pregnancy, Making Schools More Effective, Strengthening the Foster Care System, and Increasing Access to Prenatal Care. Some support for health and social services.
Types of support: Operating budgets, seed money, special projects.
Limitations: Giving primarily in CA, although applications from Washington will be considered. No grants to individuals, or generally for endowments, building funds, or annual campaigns.
Publications: Informational brochure (including application guidelines).
Application information: Application should be addressed to Stuart Foundations. Application form not required.
Initial approach: Letter or telephone
Copies of proposal: 1
Deadline(s): 2 months prior to meeting
Board meeting date(s): Mar., June, Sept., and Dec.
Final notification: 2 weeks after meeting
Write: Theodore E. Lobman, Pres.
Officers: Theodore E. Lobman, Pres.
Advisors: Dwight L. Stuart, Dwight L. Stuart, Jr., E. Hadley Stuart, Jr., Elbridge H. Stuart III.
Trustee: Security Pacific National Bank.
Number of staff: 4 full-time professional; 2 part-time professional; 2 full-time support.
Employer Identification Number: 956019876

719
Elbridge and Evelyn Stuart Foundation ⌑
c/o Security Pacific National Bank
333 South Hope St.
Los Angeles 90071 (213) 613-4877

Trust established in 1961 in CA.
Foundation type: Independent
Financial data (yr. ended 12/31/87): Assets, $7,302,522 (M); expenditures, $564,948, including $451,000 for 26 grants (high: $100,000; low: $2,000).
Purpose and activities: Emphasis on higher and secondary education, hospitals, youth agencies, medical research, and church support.
Limitations: Giving primarily in CA.
Application information:
Initial approach: Letter
Deadline(s): None
Write: Bill August, V.P., Security Pacific National Bank
Trustees: Clarke A. Nelson, H.E. Olson, Security Pacific National Bank.
Employer Identification Number: 956014019

720
Elbridge and Mary Stuart Foundation ▼
(also known as Stuart Foundations)
c/o Stuart Foundations
425 Market St., Suite 2835
San Francisco 94105 (415) 495-1144

Trust established in 1941 in CA.
Donor(s): Elbridge A. Stuart.†
Foundation type: Independent
Financial data (yr. ended 12/31/88): Assets, $57,021,854 (M); expenditures, $2,532,783, including $2,364,426 for 44 grants (high: $371,468; low: $3,800; average: $5,000-$30,000).
Purpose and activities: Giving primarily for children and youth, with emphasis on Preventing Child Abuse, Preventing School Failure, Preventing Teen Pregnancy, Making Schools More Effective, Strengthening the Foster Care System, and Increasing Access to Prenatal Care. Some support for health, family and social services, and public policy.
Types of support: Operating budgets, seed money, special projects.
Limitations: Giving primarily in CA; although applications from WA will be considered. No grants to individuals, or generally for endowments, building funds, or annual campaigns.
Publications: Informational brochure (including application guidelines).
Application information: Application should be addressed to Stuart Foundations. Application form not required.
Initial approach: Letter or telephone
Copies of proposal: 1
Deadline(s): 2 months prior to board meeting

Board meeting date(s): Mar., June, Sept., and Dec.
Final notification: Within 2 weeks after board meeting
Write: Theodore E. Lobman, Pres.
Officers: Theodore E. Lobman, Pres.
Advisors: Dwight L. Stuart, Dwight L. Stuart, Jr., E. Hadley Stuart, Jr., Elbridge H. Stuart III.
Trustee: Security Pacific National Bank.
Number of staff: 8
Employer Identification Number: 956019888

721
Mary Horner Stuart Foundation ▼
(also known as Stuart Foundations)
c/o Stuart Foundations
425 Market St., Suite 2835
San Francisco 94105 (415) 495-1144

Trust established in 1941 in WA.
Donor(s): Elbridge H. Stuart.†
Foundation type: Independent
Financial data (yr. ended 12/31/88): Assets, $33,624,012 (M); expenditures, $1,483,614, including $1,368,870 for 46 grants (high: $295,800; low: $2,000; average: $5,000-$30,000).
Purpose and activities: Giving primarily for children and youth with emphasis on Preventing Child Abuse, Preventing School Failure, Preventing Teen Pregnancy, Making Schools More Effective, Strengthening the Foster Care System, and Increasing Access to Prenatal Care. Some support for health, family and social services, and public policy.
Limitations: Giving primarily in CA and WA. No grants to individuals, or generally for endowments, building funds, or annual campaigns.
Publications: Informational brochure.
Application information: Application should be addressed to Stuart Foundations. Application form not required.
Initial approach: Letter or telephone
Copies of proposal: 1
Deadline(s): Two months prior to meeting
Board meeting date(s): Mar., June, Sept., and Dec.
Final notification: Within 2 weeks after meeting
Write: Theodore E. Lobman, Pres.
Officers: Theodore E. Lobman, Pres.
Foundation Advisors: Dwight L. Stuart, Dwight L. Stuart, Jr., E. Hadley Stuart, Jr., Elbridge H. Stuart III.
Trustee: Seattle-First National Bank.
Number of staff: 8
Employer Identification Number: 916037460

722
The Morris Stulsaft Foundation ▼
100 Bush St., Suite 825
San Francisco 94104 (415) 986-7117

Incorporated in 1953 in CA; sole beneficiary of feeder trust created in 1965; assets reflect value of assets of testamentary trust.
Donor(s): The Morris Stulsaft Testamentary Trust.
Foundation type: Independent
Financial data (yr. ended 12/31/89): Assets, $201,846 (M); gifts received, $1,298,656; expenditures, $1,321,844, including $1,170,777 for grants.
Purpose and activities: "To aid and assist needy and deserving children"; giving for youth programs, including recreational, health, educational, cultural, and social service programs.
Types of support: Operating budgets, building funds, equipment, matching funds, renovation projects, research, special projects, seed money.
Limitations: Giving limited to the San Francisco Bay Area, CA: Alameda, Contra Costa, Marin, San Francisco, Santa Clara, and San Mateo counties. No support for sectarian religious projects, or ongoing support for private schools. No grants to individuals, or for emergency funding, annual campaigns, workshops, or conferences.
Publications: Biennial report (including application guidelines).
Application information: Application form required.
Initial approach: Letter or call requesting application form
Copies of proposal: 1
Deadline(s): 7 months prior to meetings
Board meeting date(s): Jan., Mar., May, July, Sept., and Nov.
Final notification: Approximately 7 months
Write: Joan Nelson Dills, Admin.
Officers and Directors:* J. Boatner Chamberlain,* Pres.; Adele Corvin,* V.P.; Raymond A. Marks,* Secy.-Treas.; Roy L. Bouque, Dorothy Corvin, Andrew C. Gaither, Loral Good-Swan, Isadore Pivnick, Yori Wada.
Number of staff: 2 full-time professional.
Employer Identification Number: 946064379

723
Dorothy Grannis Sullivan Foundation
9215 Wilshire Blvd.
Beverly Hills 90210 (213) 278-0770

Foundation type: Independent
Financial data (yr. ended 12/31/88): Assets, $1,415,181 (M); expenditures, $83,450, including $66,001 for 12 grants (high: $25,000; low: $1,000).
Purpose and activities: Support for health organizations and hospitals, and cultural organizations.
Limitations: Giving primarily in CA.
Application information:
Initial approach: Letter or proposal
Deadline(s): None
Write: William H. Ahmanson, Pres.
Officer and Trustee:* William H. Ahmanson,* Pres.
Employer Identification Number: 237010674

724
Sundean Foundation ⌑
927 Hanover St.
Santa Cruz 95060 (408) 425-5927

Donor(s): Harold A. Sundean, Edith P. Sundean.
Foundation type: Independent
Financial data (yr. ended 1/31/86): Assets, $17,784,486 (M); gifts received, $1,000; expenditures, $931,794, including $283,989 for 50 grants (high: $50,000; low: $10).
Purpose and activities: Support primarily for Seventh Day Adventist churches and missionary activities, with some emphasis on Central America.
Application information:
Write: Harold A. Sundean, Pres.
Officers: Harold A. Sundean, Pres.; Harold C. Sundean, V.P.; Raymond Nelson, V.P.; Carol Nelson, Secy.-Treas.
Director: Edith P. Sundean.
Employer Identification Number: 946050302

725
Suzuki Automotive Foundation for Life ⌑
3251 East Imperial Hwy.
Brea 92621 (714) 996-7040

Established in 1986 in CA.
Donor(s): Suzuki of America Automotive.
Foundation type: Company-sponsored
Financial data (yr. ended 3/31/88): Assets, $271,746 (M); gifts received, $125,798; expenditures, $125,798, including $125,798 for 4 grants (high: $50,000; low: $10,000).
Purpose and activities: Giving primarily for children's health care and youth programs.
Types of support: Equipment.
Limitations: No grants to individuals.
Application information:
Initial approach: Proposal
Deadline(s): None
Write: N. Douglas Mazza, V.P.
Officers: Kiyoshi Arai, Pres.; N. Douglas Mazza, V.P.; Duffern H. Helsing, Secy.
Employer Identification Number: 330221552

726
The Swanson Foundation ⌑
P.O. Box 8353
Rancho Santa Fe 92067
Additional address: 122 East 42nd St., New York, NY 10017

Incorporated in 1952 in NY.
Donor(s): Glen E. Swanson.
Foundation type: Independent
Financial data (yr. ended 12/31/88): Assets, $2,914,524 (M); expenditures, $222,238, including $199,850 for 11 grants (high: $59,000; low: $125).
Purpose and activities: Giving for medical research, hospitals, and youth.
Limitations: Giving primarily in southern CA.
Application information:
Initial approach: Letter
Deadline(s): None
Write: Glen E. Swanson, Pres.
Officer and Directors:* Glen E. Swanson,* Pres.; Arthur Richenthal.
Employer Identification Number: 136108509

727
Swift Memorial Health Care Foundation
P.O. Box 7048
Oxnard 93031 (805) 385-3650

Established in 1984 in CA.
Foundation type: Independent
Financial data (yr. ended 06/30/89): Assets, $2,259,688 (M); expenditures, $298,439, including $197,705 for 21 grants (high: $20,000; low: $300; average: $100-$20,000).

Purpose and activities: Support for health organizations, drug and alcohol rehabilitation, and social services.
Types of support: Internships, student loans.
Limitations: Giving primarily in Ventura County, CA.
Publications: Occasional report.
Application information: Application form required.
Copies of proposal: 1
Deadline(s): None
Board meeting date(s): Bimonthly
Write: Emma M. Orr, Chair. of Awards Comm.
Officers: Carl Lowthorp, Jr., Pres.; Emma M. Orr, Secy.
Directors: Jack Erbeck, Lester E. Jacobson, Robert E. Jordan, M.D., Robert Juarez, Frank Leiblein, R. Blinn Maxwell, Ray Swift, Jessica White.
Number of staff: None.
Employer Identification Number: 770132512

728
Mae and Benjamin Swig Charity Foundation
c/o The Swig Foundations
Fairmont Hotel
San Francisco 94106

Established in 1955 in CA.
Foundation type: Independent
Financial data (yr. ended 12/31/88): Assets, $9,575,954 (M); expenditures, $771,978, including $742,669 for 66 grants (high: $13,500; low: $22).
Purpose and activities: Grants primarily for Jewish welfare funds, higher and other education, and the arts.
Limitations: Giving primarily in the San Francisco Bay Area, CA.
Application information:
Initial approach: Letter
Deadline(s): None
Board meeting date(s): Apr., Aug., and Dec.
Final notification: Immediately following board meeting
Write: Nat Starr, Dir.
Trustees: Richard S. Dinner, Melvin M. Swig, Richard L. Swig.
Administrator: Nat Starr, Dir.
Number of staff: 1
Employer Identification Number: 237416746

729
Swig Foundation
c/o The Swig Foundations
Fairmont Hotel
San Francisco 94106 (415) 772-5275

Established in 1957 in CA.
Donor(s): Benjamin H. Swig,† members of the Swig family.
Foundation type: Independent
Financial data (yr. ended 12/31/88): Assets, $15,074,797 (M); expenditures, $1,277,705, including $1,230,960 for 197 grants (high: $250,000; low: $90; average: $1,000-$65,000).
Purpose and activities: Grants for arts and culture, education, community welfare, medical care, and projects in Israel.
Limitations: Giving primarily in the San Francisco Bay Area, CA. No grants to individuals, or for conferences, seminars, or workshops.
Application information: Application form not required.
Initial approach: Letter
Deadline(s): None
Board meeting date(s): Apr., Aug., and Dec.
Final notification: Immediately following board meeting
Write: Nat Starr, Dir.
Trustees: Richard S. Dinner, Melvin M. Swig, Richard L. Swig.
Administrator: Nat Starr, Dir.
Number of staff: 1
Employer Identification Number: 946065205

730
Mr. & Mrs. G. Kirk Swingle Foundation ⌑
c/o Wells Fargo Bank
400 Capital Mall
Sacramento 95814
Application address: Dept. of Animal Sciences, University of California, Davis, CA 95616

Established in 1983 in CA.
Foundation type: Independent
Financial data (yr. ended 12/31/87): Assets, $1,439,206 (M); expenditures, $89,715, including $69,468 for 7 grants of $9,924 each.
Purpose and activities: Support for a fellowship in animal science, and for health associations.
Application information: Fellowship candidates must be a graduate student in Animal Science doing research in sheep production. Application form required.
Deadline(s): None
Write: Professor R.W. Touchberry
Trustee: Wells Fargo Bank, N.A.
Employer Identification Number: 942901783

731
Szekely Foundation for American Volunteers ⌑ ☆
c/o J.H. West
2550 Fifth Ave., Suite 1009
San Diego 92103
Application address: 3335 Reservoir Rd., Washington, DC 20007

Donor(s): Deborah Szekely.
Foundation type: Independent
Financial data (yr. ended 12/31/88): Assets, $320,436 (M); gifts received, $290,500; expenditures, $136,572, including $130,800 for 46 grants (high: $20,000; low: $250).
Purpose and activities: Areas of support include volunteerism, public policy, the performing arts, and general charitable giving.
Application information: Application form not required.
Initial approach: Letter
Deadline(s): None
Write: Deborah Szekely, Pres.
Officers: Deborah Szekely, Pres.; James H. West, Secy.
Employer Identification Number: 953655645

732
Henri & Tomoye Takahashi Foundation ⌑
200 Rhode Island St.
San Francisco 94103

Established in 1985 in CA.
Foundation type: Independent
Financial data (yr. ended 12/31/88): Assets, $1,151,082 (M); expenditures, $43,144, including $40,125 for 10 grants (high: $7,000; low: $1,000).
Purpose and activities: Supports Japanese cultural programs and Japanese-American cross-cultural projects.
Limitations: Giving primarily in CA. No grants to individuals.
Application information: Contributes only to pre-selected organizations. Applications not accepted.
Officers and Directors: Henri Takahashi, Pres.; Martha Suzuki, Secy.; Tomaye Takahashi, Treas.
Employer Identification Number: 942977890

733
The Tang Foundation
c/o Leslie W. Tang
944 Market St., Suite 610
San Francisco 94102-4010

Established in 1984 in CA.
Donor(s): Members of the Tang family.
Foundation type: Independent
Financial data (yr. ended 10/31/88): Assets, $4,302,827 (M); expenditures, $178,093, including $101,655 for 4 grants (high: $100,000; low: $130).
Purpose and activities: Support primarily for higher education and organizations with a focus on Asian concerns.
Limitations: Giving primarily in the San Francisco Bay Area, CA.
Application information: Application form not required.
Deadline(s): None
Officers and Directors:* Jack C.C. Tang,* Pres.; Madeline H. Tang, V.P.; Martin Y. Tang, V.P.; Leslie W. Tang, Secy. and C.F.O.
Employer Identification Number: 942963249

734
Mark Taper Foundation ▼
12011 San Vicente Blvd., Suite 401
Los Angeles 90049 (213) 476-5413

Incorporated in 1952 in CA.
Donor(s): S. Mark Taper.
Foundation type: Independent
Financial data (yr. ended 06/30/89): Assets, $10,596,237 (M); gifts received, $4,100,000; expenditures, $24,779, including $2,800 for 6 grants (high: $1,000; low: $100).
Purpose and activities: Currently undergoing an internal review and assessment in order to chart a course for future grantmaking.
Types of support: Building funds, special projects, general purposes.
Limitations: Giving primarily in CA. No grants to individuals.
Publications: Application guidelines.
Application information: Application form required.
Initial approach: Letter

Deadline(s): None
Board meeting date(s): As required
Final notification: As needed
Write: Raymond F. Reisler, Exec. Dir.
Officers and Directors:* S. Mark Taper,* Pres.; Barry H. Taper,* V.P. and Secy.; Janice Taper Lazarof,* V.P. and Treas.
Number of staff: 2
Employer Identification Number: 956027846

735
S. Mark Taper Foundation ☆
12011 San Vicente Blvd., Suite 401
Los Angeles 90049 (213) 476-5413

Incorporated in 1989 in CA.
Donor(s): S. Mark Taper.
Foundation type: Independent
Financial data (yr. ended 12/31/89): Assets, $2,500,000 (M); expenditures, $0.
Purpose and activities: Initial year of operation, 1989; currently undergoing an internal assessment in order to chart a course for future grantmaking.
Types of support: Building funds, general purposes, special projects.
Limitations: No grants to individuals.
Publications: Application guidelines.
Application information: Application form required.
Initial approach: Letter
Copies of proposal: 1
Deadline(s): None
Board meeting date(s): As required
Final notification: As needed
Write: Raymond F. Reisler, Exec. Dir.
Officers and Directors:* S. Mark Taper,* Chair.; Janice Taper Lazarof,* Pres.
Number of staff: 2
Employer Identification Number: 954245076

736
Taube Family Foundation ⌑
1050 Ralston Ave.
Belmont 94002-2243

Established in 1980 in CA.
Donor(s): Members of the Taube family.
Foundation type: Independent
Financial data (yr. ended 11/30/88): Assets, $7,574,027 (M); gifts received, $2,354,050; expenditures, $238,908, including $237,756 for 56 grants (high: $100,000; low: $75).
Purpose and activities: Support primarily for higher education and Jewish organizations.
Officers: Thaddeus N. Taube,* Pres.; Anita T. Hirsch,* V.P.; Kenneth A. Moline, Secy.-Treas.
Directors:* Robert Hirsch.
Employer Identification Number: 942702180

737
Teledyne Charitable Trust Foundation ▼ ⌑
1901 Ave. of the Stars, Suite 1800
Los Angeles 90067 (213) 277-3311

Trust established in 1966 in PA.
Donor(s): Teledyne, Inc., and its subsidiaries and divisions.
Foundation type: Company-sponsored
Financial data (yr. ended 12/31/88): Assets, $47,446 (M); gifts received, $1,520,298; expenditures, $1,520,298, including $813,400 for 322 grants (high: $50,000; low: $100; average: $200-$20,000) and $706,898 for 440 employee matching gifts.
Purpose and activities: Support for higher and secondary education, community funds, hospitals, social services, and youth agencies.
Types of support: Employee matching gifts.
Limitations: No support for projects directly related to religious activities.
Application information: Applications not accepted.
Write: G.A. Zitterbart, Treas.
Officer and Trustees: G.A. Zitterbart, Treas.; Berkley J. Baker, Jack H. Hamilton, George A. Roberts.
Employer Identification Number: 256074705

738
Thagard Foundation ⌑
215 East Commonwealth Ave., Suite A
P.O. Box 171
Fullerton 92632

Established in 1968 in CA.
Foundation type: Independent
Financial data (yr. ended 4/30/87): Assets, $2,929,866 (M); expenditures, $175,116, including $134,000 for 13 grants (high: $50,000; low: $500).
Purpose and activities: Giving primarily for higher education, medical research, and hospitals.
Limitations: Giving primarily in CA.
Application information: Contributes only to pre-selected organizations. Applications not accepted.
Officers and Trustees: George F. Thagard, Jr., Pres.; Roy Reynolds, V.P.; Raymond G. Thagard, Sr., V.P.; Richard L. O'Connor, Secy.-Treas.; Belle L. Ellis.
Employer Identification Number: 956225425

739
Roy E. Thomas Medical Foundation ⌑
c/o Security Pacific National Bank
P.O. Box 3189 Terminal Annex
Los Angeles 90051 (213) 613-7141
Application address: 333 South Hope St., Los Angeles, CA 90071

Established in 1979.
Donor(s): Roy E. Thomas,† Georgia Seaver Thomas.†
Foundation type: Independent
Financial data (yr. ended 12/31/88): Assets, $1,850,926 (M); expenditures, $125,004, including $100,000 for grants.
Purpose and activities: Giving solely for charitable purposes of a medical nature.
Limitations: Giving primarily in CA.
Application information: Contributes only to pre-selected organizations. Applications not accepted.
Write: Kim E. Wilkinson
Trustees: Seaver T. Page, Richard C. Seaver, Security Pacific National Bank.
Employer Identification Number: 953190677

740
The Thornton Foundation
523 West Sixth St., Suite 636
Los Angeles 90014 (213) 629-3867

Incorporated in 1958 in CA.
Donor(s): Charles B. Thornton,† Flora L. Thornton.
Foundation type: Independent
Financial data (yr. ended 12/31/87): Assets, $6,000,000 (M); gifts received, $90,000; expenditures, $99,000, including $90,000 for 10 grants (high: $50,000; low: $100).
Purpose and activities: Emphasis on higher and secondary education and cultural programs.
Types of support: Operating budgets, continuing support, annual campaigns, building funds, endowment funds, research.
Limitations: Giving primarily in CA. No grants to individuals, or for seed money, emergency funds, deficit financing, equipment, land acquisition, demonstration projects, publications, conferences, scholarships, or fellowships; no loans.
Application information: Application form not required.
Initial approach: Letter
Deadline(s): None
Board meeting date(s): As required
Final notification: 1 month
Write: Charles B. Thornton, Jr., Pres.
Officers and Trustees:* Charles B. Thornton, Jr.,* Pres.; William Laney Thornton,* V.P.; Robert E. Novell, Secy.
Number of staff: 2 part-time professional; 2 part-time support.
Employer Identification Number: 956037178

741
Flora L. Thornton Foundation ⌑
c/o Edward A. Landry
4444 Lakeside Dr., Suite 300
Burbank 91505

Established in 1983 in CA.
Donor(s): Flora L. Thornton.
Foundation type: Independent
Financial data (yr. ended 11/30/88): Assets, $3,941,470 (M); expenditures, $295,230, including $287,870 for 28 grants (high: $100,000; low: $200).
Purpose and activities: Grants primarily for culture, with emphasis on music, and for secondary and higher education; some support for a foundation.
Application information: Application form not required.
Deadline(s): None
Write: Flora L. Thornton, Trustee
Trustees: Edward A. Landry, Glen P. McDaniel, Flora L. Thornton, William Laney Thornton.
Employer Identification Number: 953855595

742
John M. & Sally B. Thornton Foundation ⌑
2125 Evergreen St.
San Diego 92106

Established in 1982 in CA.
Foundation type: Independent
Financial data (yr. ended 9/30/88): Assets, $2,429,874 (M); gifts received, $241,600;

expenditures, $444,296, including $432,684 for 66 grants (high: $190,000; low: $10).
Purpose and activities: Giving primarily for cultural programs, education, and health services; support also for a community foundation.
Types of support: Operating budgets.
Application information: Contributes only to pre-selected organizations. Applications not accepted.
Officers and Directors: Sally B. Thornton, Pres.; John M. Thornton, Secy.; Mark B. Thornton, Steven B. Thornton.
Employer Identification Number: 953800986

743
Ticor Foundation
P.O. Box 92790
Los Angeles 90009 (213) 852-6311

Incorporated in 1952 in CA.
Donor(s): Ticor, and its subsidiaries.
Foundation type: Company-sponsored
Financial data (yr. ended 12/31/89): Assets, $2,752,789 (M); expenditures, $256,219, including $209,960 for 66 grants (high: $75,000; low: $1,000; average: $1,000-$4,000) and $24,085 for 94 employee matching gifts.
Purpose and activities: Emphasis on community funds, the environment and safety, animal welfare and wildlife, private higher education, performing arts groups and other cultural programs, health and hospitals, child welfare and youth agencies, and social services, including AIDS programs, the aged, minorities, women, and the disadvantaged.
Types of support: General purposes, continuing support, annual campaigns, building funds, employee matching gifts, emergency funds.
Limitations: Giving primarily in CA. No support for secondary education. No grants to individuals, or for endowment funds, research, operating grants to organizations receiving money from community funds, scholarships, or fellowships; no loans.
Publications: Annual report, application guidelines.
Application information: Application form not required.
Initial approach: Proposal
Copies of proposal: 1
Deadline(s): Submit proposal preferably in June or Dec.; no set deadline
Board meeting date(s): Feb. and Nov.
Final notification: 3 months
Write: Virginia Veracka, Exec. Dir.
Officers: Winston V. Morrow,* Chair. and Pres.; Virginia Veracka, V.P., Secy.-Treas., and Exec. Dir.; William D. Lang, Jr.,* V.P.; John W. Uhlman,* V.P.; Richard C. White,* V.P.
Trustees:* Ernest J. Loebbecke.
Number of staff: 1 full-time professional.
Employer Identification Number: 956030995

744
The Times Mirror Foundation ▼ ¤
Times Mirror Sq.
Los Angeles 90053 (213) 237-3945

Incorporated in 1962 in CA.
Donor(s): The Times Mirror Co.
Foundation type: Company-sponsored
Financial data (yr. ended 12/31/87): Assets, $10,209,714 (M); gifts received, $6,000,000; expenditures, $5,708,700, including $5,700,844 for 143 grants (high: $600,000; low: $1,500; average: $5,000-$200,000).
Purpose and activities: Giving largely for higher education, including liberal arts, business and communications programs, and arts and culture; support also for health, community service, and civic organizations.
Types of support: Operating budgets, annual campaigns, seed money, building funds, endowment funds, program-related investments, scholarship funds, continuing support, capital campaigns, equipment, general purposes, renovation projects, special projects.
Limitations: Giving primarily in communities served by the company's subsidiaries, with emphasis on southern CA. No support for religious organizations. No grants to individuals, or for publications, conferences, or films; no loans.
Publications: Corporate giving report (including application guidelines).
Application information: Application form not required.
Initial approach: 2-3 page letter
Copies of proposal: 1
Deadline(s): May 1 and Oct. 15
Board meeting date(s): June and Dec.
Final notification: June 30 or Jan. 15
Write: Cassandra Malry, Treas.
Officers: Robert F. Erburu,* Chair.; Charles R. Redmond,* Pres.; Donald S. Kellerman,* V.P.; Stephen C. Meier, Secy.; Cassandra Malry, Treas.
Directors:* Tom Johnson, David Laventhol, Phillip L. Williams, Donald F. Wright.
Number of staff: 1 full-time professional; 1 full-time support.
Employer Identification Number: 956079651

745
Timken-Sturgis Foundation ¤
P.O. Box 1127
La Jolla 92038 (619) 454-2252

Incorporated in 1949 in CA.
Donor(s): The Timken family, Valerie T. Whitney.†
Foundation type: Independent
Financial data (yr. ended 11/30/88): Assets, $1,469,485 (M); expenditures, $103,457, including $91,750 for 21 grants (high: $25,000; low: $250).
Purpose and activities: Giving for education, medical research, and health services; support also for cultural programs.
Types of support: Research, professorships.
Limitations: Giving primarily in southern CA and NV. No grants to individuals, or for general support, capital or endowment funds, or matching gifts; no loans.
Application information: Application form not required.
Initial approach: Letter
Copies of proposal: 1
Deadline(s): None
Board meeting date(s): As required
Final notification: 1 month
Write: Joannie Barrancotto, Treas.
Officers and Trustees: George R. Sturgis, Pres.; Judy Price Sturgis, V.P.; William T. Sturgis, V.P.; Kenneth G. Coveney, Secy.; Joannie Barrancotto, Treas.
Number of staff: None.
Employer Identification Number: 956048871

746
Abigail S. Timme Revocable Trust ¤ ☆
236 Catalina Dr.
San Luis Obispo 93401

Established in 1988 in CA as a successor to the Abigail S. Timme Revocable Trust DTD 2-20-80, a nongrantmaking trust.
Foundation type: Independent
Financial data (yr. ended 9/30/88): Assets, $2,532,693 (M); gifts received, $2,102,870; expenditures, $151,905, including $101,906 for 2 grants.
Purpose and activities: Initial year of operation 1988; support for a hospital and a university.
Application information: Contributes only to pre-selected organizations. Applications not accepted.
Trustees: Robert Enigleben, Clifford Larsen.
Employer Identification Number: 770182900

747
The Grant A. Tinker Foundation ¤ ☆
11940 San Vicente Blvd.
Los Angeles 90049

Established in 1986 in CA.
Donor(s): Grant A. Tinker.
Foundation type: Independent
Financial data (yr. ended 11/30/88): Assets, $892,785 (M); expenditures, $148,332, including $142,400 for 67 grants (high: $50,000; low: $25).
Purpose and activities: Giving primarily for a museum and other cultural programs, support also for social service and youth agencies.
Types of support: Building funds.
Limitations: No grants to individuals.
Application information: Contributes only to pre-selected organizations. Applications not accepted.
Officers: Grant A. Tinker, Pres.; Richard D. Keesling, Secy.; Norton N. Brown, Treas.
Employer Identification Number: 954082632

748
Francis P. Torino Foundation ¤ ☆
24050 Madison St., Suite 110
Torrance 90505-6072

Established in 1986.
Donor(s): Francis P. Torino.
Foundation type: Independent
Financial data (yr. ended 5/31/88): Assets, $4,332 (M); gifts received, $291,000; expenditures, $288,130, including $286,775 for 11 grants (high: $250,000; low: $50).
Purpose and activities: Support primarily to the City of Torrance; minor support for social services.
Limitations: Giving primarily in Torrance, CA. No grants to individuals.
Application information: Contributes only to pre-selected organizations. Applications not accepted.

Officers: Francis P. Torino, Pres.; Brett Torino, V.P.; Courtney Torino, V.P.; Francesca Deaver, Secy.; Robert Schenkman, Treas.
Employer Identification Number: 330219408

749
The Towbes Foundation ⌑ ☆
1270-B Coast Village Circle
Santa Barbara 93108

Established in 1980 in CA.
Donor(s): Michael Towbes, Gail Towbes.
Foundation type: Independent
Financial data (yr. ended 6/30/89): Assets, $18,244 (M); gifts received, $115,000; expenditures, $129,167, including $126,430 for 24 grants (high: $40,475; low: $1,000).
Purpose and activities: Areas of primary interest include: 1) Education; 2) Medical research, especially in the area of neurological disease; 3) Performing arts; and 4) Promotion and preservation of the free enterprise system.
Types of support: Scholarship funds.
Limitations: Giving primarily in CA.
Application information: Foundation generally prefers to initiate grant requests.
Initial approach: Proposal
Copies of proposal: 6
Deadline(s): Apr. 1
Officers: Gail Towbes, Pres.; Carolyn Ferguson, V.P.; Susan S. Sheller, Secy.; Michael Towbes, C.F.O.
Employer Identification Number: 953519577

750
Toyota USA Foundation
19001 South Western Ave.
Torrance 90509 (213) 618-6766

Established in 1987 in CA.
Foundation type: Company-sponsored
Financial data (yr. ended 06/30/89): Assets, $13,193,362 (M); gifts received, $2,000,000; expenditures, $250,072, including $220,000 for 9 grants (high: $45,000; low: $15,000).
Purpose and activities: Support for health and community services, minorities and youth, education programs aiding minorities, elementary and secondary levels of study, and cultural programs.
Types of support: Special projects.
Limitations: No support for religious, fraternal, veterans', or labor groups; or military, political, or lobbying organizations. No grants to individuals, or for trips, tours, seminars, advertising, deficit reduction, or fundraising dinners.
Publications: Annual report, informational brochure, application guidelines.
Application information: Application form not required.
Initial approach: Letter
Deadline(s): Feb. 15, May 15, Aug. 15, and Nov. 15
Write: Kimberly Byron
Officers: Yukiyasu Togo, Pres.; Yale Gieszl, V.P. and Secy.; Yoshio Ishizaka, V.P.; Takao Kawamura, V.P.; Shiro Maruta, Treas.
Director: Robert B. McCurry.
Number of staff: 1 full-time professional; 1 full-time support.
Employer Identification Number: 953255038

751
Perry S. and Stella H. Tracy Scholarship Fund ⌑ ☆
c/o Wells Fargo Bank, N.A.
400 Capitol Mall
Sacramento 95814

Established in 1969.
Donor(s): Perry Tracy, Stella Tracy.
Foundation type: Independent
Financial data (yr. ended 05/31/89): Assets, $1,002,717 (M); expenditures, $72,505, including $50,701 for 128 grants to individuals (high: $950; low: $300).
Purpose and activities: Awards college scholarships to graduates of high schools of El Dorado County, CA.
Types of support: Student aid.
Application information: Application forms available at El Dorado County, CA, high schools. Application form required.
Deadline(s): Apr. 30
Board meeting date(s): May and Aug.
Trustee: Wells Fargo Bank, N.A.
Selection Committee: G.F. Burk, Chair.
Employer Identification Number: 946203372

752
Transamerica Foundation
600 Montgomery St.
San Francisco 94111 (415) 983-4333

Established in 1987 in CA.
Donor(s): Transamerica Airlines, Inc., Transamerica Corp.
Foundation type: Company-sponsored
Financial data (yr. ended 12/31/88): Assets, $22,941,805 (M); gifts received, $5,000,000; expenditures, $1,098,708, including $581,050 for 89 grants (high: $53,000; low: $30; average: $300-$53,000) and $494,093 for 2,330 employee matching gifts.
Purpose and activities: Support for programs involving AIDS, drug abuse, economics, housing, and the homeless.
Types of support: Annual campaigns, capital campaigns, continuing support, matching funds, endowment funds, operating budgets, employee-related scholarships.
Limitations: Giving primarily in the San Francisco Bay Area, CA. No support for political, religious, fraternal, or veterans' organizations. No grants to individuals; no loans.
Application information: Application form not required.
Initial approach: Letter
Copies of proposal: 1
Deadline(s): None
Write: Mae R. Pape, Prog. Dir.
Officers: James R. Harvey,* Chair.; Blair C. Pascoe,* Vice-Chair.; James B. Lockhart,* Pres.; Mae R. Pape, Secy.; Burton E. Broome, Treas.
Directors:* Frank C. Herringer, Richard N. Latzer, Richard J. Olsen, Karen Stevenson.
Number of staff: None.
Employer Identification Number: 943034825

753
Transition Foundation ⌑
One Wilshire Blvd., 18th Fl.
Los Angeles 90017 (213) 629-0349

Established in 1968 in CA.
Donor(s): Frances B. McAllister.
Foundation type: Independent
Financial data (yr. ended 12/31/88): Assets, $2,086 (M); gifts received, $100,000; expenditures, $106,386, including $106,000 for 2 grants (high: $100,000; low: $6,000).
Purpose and activities: Giving primarily for higher education, a horticulture institute, and biological and historical research; support also for the arts and museums.
Limitations: Giving limited to Coconino County, AZ. No grants to individuals.
Application information:
Initial approach: Proposal
Deadline(s): None
Write: John S. Warren, Esq., Secy.-Treas.
Officers and Directors:* Frances B. McAllister,* Pres.; John S. Warren,* Secy.-Treas.; Katherine Chase, Otto Franz, Rayma Sharber.
Employer Identification Number: 952563618

754
Nora Eccles Treadwell Foundation ▼ ⌑
910 Filbert St.
San Francisco 94133 (415) 775-2879
Mailing address: Richard A. Harrison, Chair., 400 Maryland Ave., St. Cloud, FL 32769

Established in 1962 in UT.
Donor(s): Nora Eccles Treadwell Harrison.†
Foundation type: Independent
Financial data (yr. ended 12/31/88): Assets, $1,419,517 (M); gifts received, $2,787,915; expenditures, $2,819,505, including $2,719,874 for 35 grants (high: $800,000; low: $500; average: $500-$125,000).
Purpose and activities: Grants primarily for health and cardiovascular, diabetes, and arthritis research.
Types of support: Professorships, research, general purposes, equipment.
Limitations: Giving limited to UT and CA. No grants to individuals, or for research in areas not related to the cardiovascular system, diabetes, or arthritis.
Application information: Application form not required.
Deadline(s): None
Write: P. Canepa, Pres.
Officers and Directors:* Patricia Canepa,* Pres.; Richard A. Harrison,* V.P.; Alonzo W. Watson, Jr.,* Secy.; Nicholas T. Prepouses,* Treas.; Spencer F. Eccles, William D. Hilger.
Trustee: First Security Bank of Utah, N.A.
Number of staff: 3
Employer Identification Number: 237425351

755
Trefethen Foundation
c/o John Crncich & Co.
300 Lake Side Dr., No. 1086
Oakland 94612

Established in 1980 in CA.
Donor(s): Catherine M. Trefethen, E.E. Trefethen, Jr.

Foundation type: Independent
Financial data (yr. ended 12/31/88): Assets, $168,450 (M); gifts received, $150,000; expenditures, $172,587, including $170,910 for 47 grants (high: $40,000; low: $40).
Purpose and activities: Support primarily for higher education.
Types of support: Annual campaigns, building funds.
Limitations: Giving primarily in CA.
Application information: Contributes only to pre-selected organizations. Applications not accepted.
Officers: E.E. Trefethen, Jr., Pres.; Catherine M. Trefethen, V.P. and Secy.; John V. Trefethen, V.P. and C.F.O.; Carla J. Saunders, V.P.
Number of staff: None.
Employer Identification Number: 942739938

756
Trust Funds, Inc.
100 Broadway, 3rd Fl.
San Francisco 94111 (415) 434-3323

Incorporated in 1934 in CA.
Donor(s): Bartley P. Oliver.
Foundation type: Independent
Financial data (yr. ended 12/31/88): Assets, $3,713,131 (M); expenditures, $239,101, including $203,180 for 48 grants (high: $15,000; low: $300; average: $5,000) and $14,550 for 6 grants to individuals (high: $5,000; low: $300).
Purpose and activities: Grants for Christian religion, education, and social work, primarily through support of institutions and projects related to the Roman Catholic church.
Types of support: General purposes, seed money, emergency funds, research, publications, conferences and seminars, scholarship funds.
Limitations: Giving limited to the San Francisco Bay Area, CA, or to projects of national or global scope. No support for organizations that draw substantial public support. No grants for capital or endowment funds or annual campaigns; no loans. Generally, no grants to individuals.
Publications: Application guidelines, program policy statement.
Application information: Application form not required.
Initial approach: Letter
Copies of proposal: 2
Deadline(s): None
Board meeting date(s): Usually in Jan., Apr., July, and Oct.
Final notification: 2 months
Write: Albert J. Steiss, Pres.
Officers and Directors:* Albert J. Steiss,* Pres.; Rev. James J. Ward,* V.P. and Secy.; James T. Healy,* V.P. and C.F.O.
Number of staff: 1 part-time professional; 1 part-time support.
Employer Identification Number: 946062952

757
Alice Tweed Tuohy Foundation
1006 Santa Barbara St.
Santa Barbara 93101 (805) 963-0675
Mailing address: P.O. Box 2578, Santa Barbara, CA 93120

Incorporated in 1956 in CA.
Donor(s): Alice Tweed Tuohy.†
Foundation type: Independent
Financial data (yr. ended 06/30/89): Assets, $11,688,202 (M); expenditures, $639,275, including $391,165 for 31 grants (high: $83,775; low: $500; average: $1,000-$10,000).
Purpose and activities: Grants for higher education, art as related to higher education, hospital care, patient rehabilitation, and youth programs; substantial support also for the art program at the Duluth campus of the University of Minnesota.
Types of support: Seed money, matching funds, building funds, equipment, land acquisition, scholarship funds, renovation projects.
Limitations: Giving limited to the Santa Barbara, CA, area. No support for private foundations. No grants to individuals, or for operating budgets, national campaigns, research, unrestricted purposes, and rarely for endowment funds; no loans.
Publications: Annual report (including application guidelines).
Application information: Application form not required.
Initial approach: Letter
Copies of proposal: 5
Deadline(s): Submit proposal between July 1 and Sept. 15; proposals received after deadline may be deferred for a year
Board meeting date(s): Apr. or May, and Nov.
Final notification: 2 to 3 months
Write: Harris W. Seed, Pres.
Officers and Directors:* Harris W. Seed,* Pres.; Eleanor Van Cott,* Exec. V.P. and Secy.-Treas.; Lorenzo Dall'Armi, Jr., John R. Mackall, Paul W. Hartloff, Jr.
Number of staff: 2 part-time professional.
Employer Identification Number: 956036471

758
Alice C. Tyler Foundation ⌘
c/o Hoag, Fitzgerald & Robi
11866 Wilshire Blvd., Suite 100
Los Angeles 90025

Established in 1979.
Donor(s): Alice C. Tyler.
Foundation type: Independent
Financial data (yr. ended 11/30/88): Assets, $281,020 (M); gifts received, $265,565; expenditures, $311,747, including $304,885 for 26 grants (high: $195,000; low: $35).
Purpose and activities: Emphasis on higher education, including an ecology-energy fund at a university, hospitals and medical research, religious giving, and child welfare.
Limitations: Giving primarily in Los Angeles, CA.
Application information: Funds fully committed. Applications not accepted.
Officers: Alice C. Tyler, Pres.; Mark Townsend, Secy.
Directors: Frank Clark, Jr., Karl M. Samuelian.
Employer Identification Number: 953432643

759
UCLA Foundation Charitable Fund III ⌘
405 Hilgard Ave.
Los Angeles 90024

Established in 1985 in CA.
Donor(s): Albert B. Glickman, Mrs. Albert B. Glickman.
Foundation type: Independent
Financial data (yr. ended 06/30/89): Assets, $1,151,347 (M); expenditures, $114,226, including $107,490 for 19 grants (high: $25,032; low: $1,000).
Purpose and activities: Support primarily for higher and other education, culture, and a Jewish welfare fund.
Types of support: General purposes.
Limitations: Giving primarily in CA. No grants to individuals.
Publications: 990-PF.
Application information: Contributes only to pre-selected organizations. Applications not accepted.
Officers and Directors:* William Finestone,* Chair.; Bertrand I. Ginsberg,* Pres.; Richard P. Carlsberg,* V.P.; Eugene S. Rosenfeld,* V.P.; Roger A. Meyer, Secy.; Jo Ann Hankin,* C.F.O.
Employer Identification Number: 953975787

760
Union Bank Foundation ⌘
P.O. Box 3100
Los Angeles 90051 (213) 236-5826

Trust established in 1953 in CA.
Donor(s): Union Bank.
Foundation type: Company-sponsored
Financial data (yr. ended 12/31/86): Assets, $23,611 (M); gifts received, $450,000; expenditures, $550,838, including $529,644 for 114 grants (high: $230,000; low: $10) and $21,092 for 109 employee matching gifts.
Purpose and activities: Emphasis on community funds, higher education, hospitals, cultural programs, social services, and youth.
Types of support: General purposes, operating budgets, continuing support, annual campaigns, emergency funds, building funds, equipment, employee matching gifts.
Limitations: Giving primarily in CA, particularly in areas of company operations. No grants to individuals, or for endowment funds, scholarships, fellowships, or research; no loans.
Application information: Application form not required.
Initial approach: Proposal
Copies of proposal: 1
Deadline(s): Submit proposal preferably in Jan.; no set deadline
Board meeting date(s): Monthly
Final notification: 3 months
Trustee: Union Bank.
Number of staff: 3
Employer Identification Number: 956023551

761
Unocal Foundation ▼ ⌘
1201 West Fifth St.
Los Angeles 90017 (213) 977-6172
Mailing address for applications: P.O. Box 7600, Los Angeles, CA 90051

Incorporated in 1962 in CA.
Donor(s): Unocal Corp.

Foundation type: Company-sponsored
Financial data (yr. ended 1/31/88): Assets, $5,481,295 (M); expenditures, $3,054,932, including $2,702,942 for 263 grants (high: $100,000; low: $500; average: $1,000-$20,000) and $325,143 for 1,670 employee matching gifts.
Purpose and activities: Giving primarily for higher education and various national organizations, including those concerned with energy.
Types of support: Annual campaigns, continuing support, employee matching gifts, fellowships, research, scholarship funds, employee-related scholarships, equipment.
Limitations: Giving primarily in areas of parent company operations in CA, IL, and TX. No support for veterans', fraternal, sectarian, social, religious, athletic, choral, band, or similar groups; trade or business associations; political or lobbying organizations; state agencies and departments; or elementary or secondary education. No grants to individuals, or for general purposes, capital funds for education, endowment funds, courtesy advertising, conferences, supplemental operating support to recipients of United Funds, or for trips or tours; no loans.
Publications: Annual report.
Application information: Application form required for employee-related scholarships.
Initial approach: Letter
Copies of proposal: 1
Deadline(s): Sept. 15
Board meeting date(s): As required
Final notification: 6 to 8 weeks
Write: R.P. Van Zandt, V.P.
Officers: Fred L. Hartley,* Pres.; R.P. Van Zandt,* V.P.; R.O. Hedley,* Secy.; E.H. Powell, Treas.
Trustees:* William H. Doheny, Richard J. Stegmeier.
Number of staff: 1 full-time professional; 1 full-time support; 2 part-time support.
Employer Identification Number: 956071812

762
The Upjohn California Fund
P.O. Box 169
Carmel Valley 93924 (408) 659-4662

Incorporated in 1955 in CA.
Foundation type: Independent
Financial data (yr. ended 10/31/89): Assets, $2,400,444 (M); expenditures, $124,140, including $84,750 for 40 grants (high: $11,500; low: $500; average: $1,000-$2,500).
Purpose and activities: Support for hospitals and medical research, education, including secondary schools, civic and cultural affairs, child welfare, youth, and family services.
Limitations: Giving primarily in northern CA. No grants to individuals.
Application information:
Initial approach: Letter, followed by proposal
Copies of proposal: 1
Deadline(s): None
Board meeting date(s): Mar., June, Sept., and Dec.
Write: Eugene C. Wheary, Pres.
Officers and Directors:* Eugene C. Wheary,* Pres.; Ronald Larson,* V.P.; John W. Broad,* Secy.; Cynthia W. Hertlein,* C.F.O.; Edwin W. Macrae.
Employer Identification Number: 946065219

763
Uvas Foundation ⌑ ☆
50 Fremont St., Suite 3825
San Francisco 94105-2230

Established in 1980.
Donor(s): Barbara B. Davies, L.D. Mateo, Paul Lewis Davies III, Paul L. Davies, Jr.
Foundation type: Independent
Financial data (yr. ended 6/30/89): Assets, $1,708,645 (M); expenditures, $72,981, including $62,500 for 23 grants (high: $20,000; low: $500).
Purpose and activities: Giving primarily for higher, secondary, and other education; support also for wildlife preservation and zoological societies.
Types of support: General purposes, endowment funds.
Limitations: Giving primarily in CA. No grants to individuals.
Application information: Contributes only to pre-selected organizations. Applications not accepted.
Officers and Directors:* Paul L. Davies, Jr.,* Pres.; Barbara B. Davies,* V.P.; P.H. Davies,* V.P.; Paul Lewis Davies III,* V.P.; Laura Davies Mateo,* V.P.; S. Mateo,* V.P.; A. McDonald, Secy.; D.A. Ruhl, Treas.
Employer Identification Number: 942678808

764
Wayne & Gladys Valley Foundation
4000 Executive Pkwy., Suite 535
San Ramon 94583 (415) 275-9330

Established in 1977 in CA.
Donor(s): F. Wayne Valley.†
Foundation type: Independent
Financial data (yr. ended 09/30/89): Assets, $70,159,697 (M); gifts received, $31,295,000; expenditures, $2,130,080, including $1,722,176 for 17 grants (high: $500,000; low: $500).
Purpose and activities: Grants for Catholic giving, including Catholic welfare and schools; support also for higher and secondary education, recreation, and hospitals.
Types of support: Building funds, general purposes, matching funds, renovation projects, research.
Limitations: Giving primarily in Alameda, Contra Costa, and Santa Clara counties, CA.
Publications: Informational brochure, application guidelines.
Application information: Application form required.
Initial approach: Letter
Copies of proposal: 1
Deadline(s): None
Write: Paul D. O'Connor, Pres. and Exec. Dir.
Officers and Directors:* Gladys Valley,* Chair.; Paul O'Connor,* Pres. and Exec. Dir.; Charles F. Festo,* V.P.; Richard M. Kingsland,* Treas. and C.F.O.; Robert C. Brown, Stephen M. Chandler, Edwin A. Heafey, Jr., John Stockman, Tamara Valley, Sonya Valley.
Number of staff: 1 full-time professional; 1 part-time professional; 1 part-time support.
Employer Identification Number: 953203014

765
Van Camp Foundation ⌑
8316 Marina Pacifica Dr. North
Long Beach 90803

Trust established in 1975 in CA.
Donor(s): Gilbert C. Van Camp, Sr. Family Trust.
Foundation type: Independent
Financial data (yr. ended 12/31/88): Assets, $6,936,402 (M); expenditures, $399,107, including $385,000 for 6 grants (high: $160,000; low: $5,000).
Purpose and activities: Giving primarily for youth agencies and fine arts groups.
Limitations: Giving primarily in CA.
Application information: Contributes only to pre-selected organizations. Applications not accepted.
Officers: Fred Fox, Jr., Pres. and Treas.; Christine Van Camp Zecca, V.P.; Zane J. Lubin, Secy.
Employer Identification Number: 956039680

766
Ernst D. van Loben Sels-Eleanor Slate van Loben Sels Charitable Foundation
235 Montgomery St., No. 1635
San Francisco 94104 (415) 983-1093
Application address: P.O. Box 7880, Rm. 1635, San Francisco, CA 94120-7880

Incorporated in 1964 in CA.
Donor(s): Ernst D. van Loben Sels.†
Foundation type: Independent
Financial data (yr. ended 12/31/89): Assets, $10,287,000 (M); qualifying distributions, $519,627, including $519,627 for 70 grants (high: $39,000; low: $500; average: $500-$39,000).
Purpose and activities: Priority given to nonrecurring grants in support of projects which will test potentially useful innovations in the areas of education, health, welfare, humanities, and the environment.
Types of support: Seed money, emergency funds, matching funds, special projects, research, publications, conferences and seminars, loans.
Limitations: Giving limited to northern CA. No support for national organizations unless for a specific local project, or to projects requiring medical, scientific, or other technical knowledge for evaluation. No grants to individuals, or for operating budgets of well-established organizations, continuing support, deficit financing, capital or endowment funds, scholarships, or fellowships.
Publications: Annual report, program policy statement, application guidelines.
Application information: Application form not required.
Initial approach: Proposal, letter, or telephone
Copies of proposal: 3
Deadline(s): None

Board meeting date(s): About every 6-8 weeks
Final notification: 3 to 4 weeks
Write: Claude H. Hogan, Pres.
Officers and Directors:* Claude H. Hogan,* Pres.; Edward A. Nathan,* V.P.; Toni Rembe,* Secy.-Treas.
Number of staff: None.
Employer Identification Number: 946109309

767
J. B. and Emily Van Nuys Charities ⌑
1800 Ave. of the Stars, Suite 435
Los Angeles 90067 (213) 552-0175

Incorporated in 1957 in CA.
Donor(s): Emily Van Nuys, J. Benton Van Nuys.
Foundation type: Independent
Financial data (yr. ended 12/31/88): Assets, $438,806 (M); gifts received, $681,001; expenditures, $643,245, including $557,355 for 130 grants (high: $25,000; low: $2,500; average: $5,000).
Purpose and activities: Emphasis on hospitals and health agencies, child welfare, and youth agencies; support also for the handicapped, social service agencies, education, and the environment.
Types of support: General purposes.
Limitations: Giving primarily in southern CA, including the Los Angeles area.
Application information: Application form not required.
Initial approach: Proposal
Deadline(s): None
Board meeting date(s): Quarterly to award grants
Write: Robert Gibson Johnson, Pres.
Officers and Trustees: Robert Gibson Johnson, Pres.; Lawrence Chaffin, V.P.; Franklin F. Moulton, Secy.-Treas.; John M. Heidt, Robert S. Warner.
Employer Identification Number: 956096134

768
I. N. & Susanna H. Van Nuys Foundation ⌑
c/o Security Pacific National Bank
P.O. Box 3189, Terminal Annex
Los Angeles 90051

Established in 1950 in CA.
Foundation type: Independent
Financial data (yr. ended 5/31/87): Assets, $9,525,503 (M); expenditures, $740,107, including $633,827 for 17 grants (high: $333,218; low: $4,000).
Purpose and activities: Support primarily for health services and education.
Limitations: Giving primarily in CA.
Application information:
Initial approach: Letter
Deadline(s): None
Write: Lorraine Tessier, Accountant
Trustees: George A. Bender, Freeman Gates, George H. Whitney, Security Pacific National Bank.
Employer Identification Number: 956006019

769
Frances S. Viele Scholarship Trust
626 Wilshire Blvd., No. 804
Los Angeles 90017

Established in 1977 in CA.
Foundation type: Independent
Financial data (yr. ended 5/31/87): Assets, $1,818,129 (M); expenditures, $97,884, including $72,000 for 28 grants to individuals (high: $4,000; low: $2,500).
Purpose and activities: Scholarship awards given to members of Sigma Phi Society.
Types of support: Student aid.
Limitations: No grants to individuals other than members of Sigma Phi Society.
Application information: Applications not accepted.
Manager: Stevens Weller, Jr.
Employer Identification Number: 953285561

770
The Vinnell Foundation
144 North Brand Blvd.
Glendale 91203-2602 (818) 500-7755

Established in 1959 in CA.
Donor(s): Allan S. Vinnell.
Foundation type: Independent
Financial data (yr. ended 12/31/88): Assets, $1,148,877 (M); expenditures, $91,365, including $81,000 for 12 grants (high: $18,000; low: $1,000).
Purpose and activities: Support primarily for higher education.
Types of support: Scholarship funds.
Limitations: Giving primarily in CA and AZ. No grants to individuals.
Application information: Contributes only to pre-selected organizations. Applications not accepted.
Write: Sandra Franck
Officers: William B. Glassick, Pres.; Don L. McRae, V.P.; Ernest R. Baldwin, Secy.-Treas.
Director: Herbert H. Uyeda.
Number of staff: None.
Employer Identification Number: 956085927

771
Von der Ahe Foundation ⌑
4605 Lankershim Blvd., Suite 707
North Hollywood 91602 (213) 579-1400

Incorporated in 1951 in CA.
Donor(s): Members of the Von der Ahe family, Von's Grocery Co.
Foundation type: Independent
Financial data (yr. ended 12/31/87): Assets, $4,272,737 (M); expenditures, $317,834, including $280,450 for 55 grants (high: $50,000; low: $250).
Purpose and activities: "To promote scientific and charitable causes"; emphasis on Roman Catholic religious institutions and health and welfare services; support also for higher education and a community foundation.
Limitations: Giving primarily in CA. No grants to individuals.
Application information: Due to funding limitations, the trustees prefer to initiate grants.
Board meeting date(s): Apr. and Nov.
Officers and Directors: Wilfred L. Von der Ahe, Pres.; Clyde V. Von der Ahe, M.D., V.P.; Vincent M. Von der Ahe, Secy.-Treas.
Board Members: Charles K. Von der Ahe, Frederick T. Von der Ahe, Thomas R. Von der Ahe.
Employer Identification Number: 956051857

772
Theodore Albert Von der Ahe, Jr. Trust ⌑
3151 Airway Ave., Suite L-1
Costa Mesa 92691 (714) 850-0376

Established in 1978 in CA.
Foundation type: Independent
Financial data (yr. ended 1/31/88): Assets, $4,674,614 (M); expenditures, $290,741.
Purpose and activities: Grants primarily for religious giving, with emphasis on Catholic welfare; support also for international affairs programs.
Application information: Grants initiated by trustees. Application form not required.
Initial approach: Letter
Write: Frederick T. Von der Ahe, Trustee
Trustee: Frederick T. Von der Ahe.
Number of staff: 1 part-time support.
Employer Identification Number: 953371127

773
W.W.W. Foundation ▼ ⌑
1260 Huntington Dr., Suite 204
South Pasadena 91030 (213) 259-0484

Established in 1981 in CA.
Donor(s): Helen W. Woodward.†
Foundation type: Independent
Financial data (yr. ended 7/31/88): Assets, $6,017,600 (M); gifts received, $2,124,731; expenditures, $2,761,865, including $2,610,060 for 18 grants (high: $1,635,000; low: $3,750; average: $5,000-$150,000).
Purpose and activities: Giving primarily for an animal care center; support also for hospitals and civic affiars.
Types of support: Operating budgets, renovation projects, building funds.
Limitations: Giving primarily in CA.
Application information: Contributes only to pre-selected organizations.
Board meeting date(s): Varies
Write: Linda J. Blinkenberg, Secy.
Officers: Winifred W. Rhodes Bea, Pres.; Marcia W. Constance, V.P.; Linda J. Blinkenberg, Secy.; Arlo Sorensen, C.F.O.
Number of staff: 1
Employer Identification Number: 953694741

774
The Elizabeth Firth Wade Endowment Fund ⌑
114 East De la Guerra St., No. 7
Santa Barbara 93101 (805) 963-8822

Trust established in 1961 in CA; incorporated in 1979.
Donor(s): Elizabeth Firth Wade.†
Foundation type: Independent
Financial data (yr. ended 1/31/89): Assets, $2,677,473 (M); expenditures, $222,202, including $108,000 for 11 grants (high: $45,000; low: $1,000).
Purpose and activities: Support for youth agencies, the handicapped, education, and

cultural programs, including performing arts groups.
Application information:
Initial approach: Letter
Deadline(s): None
Write: Patricia M. Brouard, Secy.-Treas.
Officers and Directors: Arthur R. Gaudi, Pres.; Steven M. Anders, V.P.; Patricia M. Brouard, Secy.-Treas.
Employer Identification Number: 953610694

775
T. B. Walker Foundation ¤
P.O. Box 330112
San Francisco 94133

Incorporated in 1925 in MN; reincorporated partially in 1976 in CA.
Donor(s): T.B. Walker,† Gilbert M. Walker.†
Foundation type: Independent
Financial data (yr. ended 9/30/88): Assets, $5,142,422 (M); expenditures, $320,841, including $276,000 for 66 grants (high: $37,000; low: $1,000).
Purpose and activities: Interests primarily in the arts and other cultural and educational programs, with some support for population control, and youth and social agencies.
Types of support: Continuing support, annual campaigns, research, special projects.
Limitations: Giving limited to CA. No grants to individuals.
Application information: Contributes only to pre-selected organizations. Applications not accepted.
Officers and Trustees: John C. Walker, Pres.; Harriet W. Henderson, 2nd V.P.; Colleen Marsh, Secy.; Brooks Walker, Jr., Treas.; Ann M. Hatch, Wellington S. Henderson, Jr., R. Lance Walker, S. Adrian Walker, Jean W. Yeates, Jeffrey L. Yeates.
Number of staff: None.
Employer Identification Number: 521078287

776
Warren Family Foundation ¤
P.O. Box 915
Rancho Santa Fe 92067

Established in 1977 in CA.
Donor(s): Frank R. Warren, Joanne C. Warren.
Foundation type: Independent
Financial data (yr. ended 6/30/87): Assets, $1,106,400 (M); gifts received, $150,750; expenditures, $100,676, including $93,261 for 87 grants (high: $13,300; low: $20).
Purpose and activities: Emphasis on cultural programs and the performing arts, health and social service agencies, and education.
Limitations: Giving primarily in CA.
Officer: Joanne C. Warren, Pres.
Directors: Richard K. Colbourne, Frank R. Warren.
Employer Identification Number: 953201177

777
Warsh-Mott Legacy
469 Bohemian Hwy.
Freestone 95472-9579 (707) 874-2942

Established in 1985 in CA.
Donor(s): Maryanne T. Mott.
Foundation type: Independent
Financial data (yr. ended 09/30/89): Assets, $4,685,365 (M); gifts received, $100,000; expenditures, $270,976, including $167,000 for 10 grants (high: $30,000; low: $5,000) and $50,000 for 1 loan.
Purpose and activities: Support primarily for peace initiatives, arms control, ecology, conservation and the environment, public policy, and civil and human rights.
Types of support: General purposes, continuing support, matching funds, operating budgets, publications, research, special projects, technical assistance.
Limitations: No grants for endowments, capital funds, or video or film production.
Publications: Grants list, informational brochure (including application guidelines).
Application information: Application form not required.
Initial approach: Proposal
Copies of proposal: 1
Deadline(s): Jan. 15, May 15, Sept. 15, or following Monday if deadline falls on a weekend
Final notification: Approximately 12 weeks after deadline
Write: Maryanne T. Mott, Pres.
Officers: Maryanne T. Mott, Pres.; Martin Tietel, V.P. and Exec. Dir.; Herman E. Warsh, Secy. and C.F.O.
Number of staff: 3 full-time professional; 1 full-time support; 1 part-time support.
Employer Identification Number: 680049658

778
Washington Research Institute ¤ ☆
3220 Sacramento St.
San Francisco 94115 (415) 931-2593

Established in 1985 in CA.
Foundation type: Independent
Financial data (yr. ended 12/31/87): Assets, $274,461 (M); gifts received, $45,843; expenditures, $574,979, including $424,722 for 33 grants (high: $90,000; low: $60) and $23,986 for 6 grants to individuals (high: $16,026; low: $443).
Purpose and activities: Support for research and educational projects in the social and natural sciences, especially with regard to Soviet-U.S. relations.
Types of support: Research, grants to individuals.
Limitations: Giving primarily in CA.
Application information:
Initial approach: Proposal
Deadline(s): None
Write: Henry S. Dakin, Pres.
Officers: Henry S. Dakin, Pres. and Treas.; Boris H. Lakusta, Secy.
Employer Identification Number: 942958270

779
Wasserman Foundation ¤
10920 Wilshire Blvd., Suite 1200
Los Angeles 90024-6514

Incorporated in 1956 in CA.
Donor(s): Lew R. Wasserman, Edith Wasserman.
Foundation type: Independent
Financial data (yr. ended 12/31/88): Assets, $23,685,508 (M); gifts received, $119,690; expenditures, $1,082,035, including $1,059,381 for 60 grants (high: $209,375; low: $500).
Purpose and activities: Emphasis on hospitals and medical research, Jewish welfare funds, higher education, public policy groups, and the performing arts.
Types of support: Capital campaigns, endowment funds, research, scholarship funds.
Limitations: Giving primarily in CA.
Application information: Contributes only to pre-selected organizations. Applications not accepted.
Write: William J. Bird, V.P.
Officers and Directors: Lew R. Wasserman, Pres.; Edith Wasserman, V.P., C.F.O. and Secy.; William J. Bird, V.P.; Sidney Jay Sheinberg, V.P.; Allan E. Susman, V.P.; Thomas Wertheimer, V.P.; Carol Ann Leif, Lynne Wasserman.
Employer Identification Number: 956038762

780
Torrey H. and Dorothy K. Webb Educational and Charitable Trust ¤
5966 Abernathy Dr.
Los Angeles 90045 (213) 743-7311

Trust established in 1976 in CA.
Donor(s): Torrey H. Webb.†
Foundation type: Independent
Financial data (yr. ended 12/31/88): Assets, $2,540,519 (M); expenditures, $438,607, including $415,000 for 24 grants (high: $75,000; low: $1,000; average: $9,100).
Purpose and activities: Emphasis on higher education and health agencies.
Types of support: Endowment funds, fellowships.
Limitations: Giving primarily in CA.
Application information: Applications not accepted.
Write: Carl M. Franklin, Trustee
Trustee: Carl M. Franklin.
Number of staff: None.
Employer Identification Number: 510188579

781
The Weiler Foundation ¤
425 Alma St., Suite 410
Palo Alto 94301 (415) 328-7814

Established in 1961 in CA.
Donor(s): Ralph J. Weiler.†
Foundation type: Independent
Financial data (yr. ended 04/30/89): Assets, $7,433,378 (M); expenditures, $418,752, including $248,223 for 46 grants (high: $50,000; low: $100; average: $5,000-$25,000).
Purpose and activities: Emphasis on private education, hospitals, and medical research.
Limitations: Giving primarily in CA. No support for individual churches or religious organizations.
Publications: Application guidelines.
Application information: Application form required.
Initial approach: Proposal
Copies of proposal: 3
Deadline(s): Mar.
Board meeting date(s): Monthly

Write: Bartlett Burnap, Pres.
Officers: Bartlett Burnap, Pres.; William Bullis, V.P.; Elizabeth J. Kelly, Secy.-Treas.
Employer Identification Number: 237418821

782
Adolph and Etta Weinberg Foundation ¤
5355 East Airport Dr.
Ontario 91711
Application address: P.O. Box 4028, Ontario, CA 91761; Tel.: (714) 983-9766

Incorporated in 1952 in CA.
Donor(s): Adolph Weinberg, Coast Grain Co.
Foundation type: Independent
Financial data (yr. ended 9/30/88): Assets, $1,366,316 (M); gifts received, $3,000; expenditures, $212,696, including $165,501 for 39 grants (high: $80,000; low: $45).
Purpose and activities: Grants primarily for Jewish religious organizations and temple support, higher education, and museums.
Limitations: No grants to individuals.
Application information:
Initial approach: Proposal
Copies of proposal: 2
Deadline(s): June 30
Write: Ray Moline, Secy.
Officers: Bob Weinberg, Pres.; Ray Moline, Secy.
Directors: Seiso Kawasaki, George Ogawa.
Number of staff: 1 part-time support.
Employer Identification Number: 956075855

783
Weingart Foundation ▼
1200 Wilshire Blvd., Suite 305
Los Angeles 90017-1984 (213) 482-4343
Mailing address: P.O. Box 17982, Los Angeles, CA 90017-0982

Incorporated in 1951 in CA.
Donor(s): Ben Weingart,† Stella Weingart.†
Foundation type: Independent
Financial data (yr. ended 06/30/89): Assets, $404,198,697 (M); gifts received, $208,562; expenditures, $19,528,815, including $14,694,457 for 174 grants (high: $1,000,000; low: $500; average: $10,000-$250,000) and $3,441,667 for loans.
Purpose and activities: Support for community services, health and medicine, higher education, including a student loan program, and public policy, with emphasis on programs for children and youth.
Types of support: Seed money, building funds, equipment, matching funds, special projects, research, renovation projects, capital campaigns, research.
Limitations: Giving limited to southern CA. No support for environmental, refugee, or religious programs, international concerns, or federated fundraising groups. No grants to individuals, or for endowment funds, normal operating expenses, annual campaigns, emergency funds, deficit financing, land acquisition, scholarships, fellowships, seminars, conferences, publications, workshops, travel, or surveys.
Publications: Annual report (including application guidelines), application guidelines, occasional report, informational brochure (including application guidelines).
Application information: Student loan program limited to 14 private colleges and universities in southern CA. Application form required.
Initial approach: Letter
Copies of proposal: 12
Deadline(s): None
Board meeting date(s): Bimonthly, except July and Aug.
Final notification: 3 to 4 months
Write: Charles W. Jacobson, Pres.
Officers: Charles W. Jacobson, Pres.; Ann Van Dormolen, V.P. and Treas.; Laurence A. Wolfe, V.P.
Directors: Harry J. Volk, Chair.; John T. Gurash, William J. McGill, Sol Price, Dennis Stanfill.
Number of staff: 3 full-time professional; 7 full-time support; 1 part-time support.
Employer Identification Number: 956054814

784
The Frederick R. Weisman Art Foundation
(Formerly The Frederick R. Weisman Collection)
10350 Santa Monica Blvd., Suite 160
Los Angeles 90025 (213) 556-2235

Established in 1982 in CA.
Donor(s): Frederick R. Weisman, Frederick Weisman Co.
Foundation type: Independent
Financial data (yr. ended 01/31/90): Assets, $15,765,734 (M); gifts received, $4,019,971; expenditures, $1,547,432, including $654,556 for 17 grants (high: $600,000; low: $100).
Purpose and activities: Support towards the improvement of the public's understanding of contemporary visual art.
Publications: Occasional report.
Application information: Applications not accepted.
Initial approach: Letter
Deadline(s): None
Write: Mitchell L. Reinschreiber, Exec. V.P. and C.F.O., or Charles E. Castle, Admin.
Officers and Trustees:* Frederick R. Weisman,* Pres.; Mitchell L. Reinschreiber,* Exec. V.P. and C.F.O.; Henry T. Hopkins,* Exec. V.P.; Lee Larssen Romaniello,* Secy.; Billie Milam, Judith Pisar, Edward Ruscha, Marcia S. Weisman, Milton Wexler.
Number of staff: 4 full-time professional; 1 full-time support.
Employer Identification Number: 953767861

785
The David & Sylvia Weisz Foundation ¤
1933 Broadway, Rm. 244
Los Angeles 90007

Established in 1980 in CA.
Foundation type: Independent
Financial data (yr. ended 10/31/88): Assets, $6,894,841 (M); expenditures, $1,054,825, including $665,250 for 82 grants (high: $200,000; low: $100).
Purpose and activities: Support primarily for Jewish welfare, cultural organizations, and social services; some support also for health services and hospitals.
Types of support: General purposes.
Officers and Directors: Sylvia Weisz, Pres.; Richard Miller, Secy.-Treas.; Donald Bean, Jay Grodin, Louis Leviton.
Employer Identification Number: 953551424

786
WELfund, Inc. ¤
152 North Almont Ave.
Los Angeles 90048 (213) 276-6163

Established in 1963 in CA.
Foundation type: Independent
Financial data (yr. ended 12/31/87): Assets, $1,294,357 (M); expenditures, $121,894, including $75,050 for 52 grants (high: $12,000; low: $100).
Purpose and activities: Support primarily for health associations, social service agencies, and the handicapped.
Application information: Application form not required.
Deadline(s): None
Officers and Directors: William E. Lerner, Pres.; Joan A. Merritt, V.P.; Bertha H. Briley, Secy.-Treas.
Employer Identification Number: 956091887

787
Lawrence Welk Foundation
1299 Ocean Ave., Suite 800
Santa Monica 90401 (213) 451-5727

Incorporated in 1960 in CA.
Donor(s): Teleklen Productions, Inc.
Foundation type: Company-sponsored
Financial data (yr. ended 10/31/89): Assets, $1,701,176 (M); gifts received, $80,000; expenditures, $306,509, including $293,800 for 65 grants (high: $50,000; low: $100; average: $5,000).
Purpose and activities: Support for social service agencies, children, and the elderly.
Types of support: Annual campaigns, seed money, building funds, equipment, matching funds, special projects, research, capital campaigns.
Limitations: Giving limited to southern CA. No grants to individuals, or for endowment funds, operating budgets, continuing support, emergency funds, deficit financing, publications, conferences, scholarships, fellowships, or employee matching gifts; no loans.
Publications: Application guidelines.
Application information: Application form required.
Initial approach: Letter
Copies of proposal: 1
Deadline(s): Submit proposal preferably from Jan. through Aug.; deadline Sept. 1
Board meeting date(s): Oct.
Final notification: 1 month
Write: Shirley Fredricks, Exec. Dir.
Officers: Lawrence L. Welk, C.E.O.; Shirley Fredricks,* Pres. and Exec. Dir.; Theodore Lennon, Secy.-Treas.
Directors:* Ronald Gother, Donna Mack.
Number of staff: 1 full-time professional.
Employer Identification Number: 956064646

788
Wells Family Charitable Foundation ⌑
712 North Palm Dr.
Beverly Hills 90210 (213) 274-2884

Established in 1985 in CA.
Foundation type: Independent
Financial data (yr. ended 12/31/87): Assets, $887,203 (M); expenditures, $126,436, including $116,867 for 58 grants (high: $26,000; low: $50).
Purpose and activities: Giving primarily for the arts; support also for health associations.
Application information: Application form not required.
Initial approach: Letter
Deadline(s): None
Write: Frank G. Wells, V.P.
Officers: Luanne Wells, Pres.; Frank G. Wells, V.P. and Secy.-Treas.
Employer Identification Number: 953982216

789
Wells Fargo Foundation ▼ ⌑
420 Montgomery St., MAC 0101-111
San Francisco 94163 (415) 396-3568

Established in 1978 in San Francisco.
Donor(s): Wells Fargo Bank, N.A.
Foundation type: Company-sponsored
Financial data (yr. ended 12/31/87): Assets, $2,711,767 (M); gifts received, $1,445,268; expenditures, $5,789,580, including $4,773,021 for 823 grants (high: $1,500,000; low: $500; average: $1,000-$25,000).
Purpose and activities: Support for art and cultural programs, education, civic affairs organizations, social service agencies, and community funds.
Types of support: Special projects, renovation projects.
Limitations: Giving primarily in CA. No support for government agencies, United Way-supported agencies, hospitals, national health organizations, organizations with multiple chapters, religious activities, political purposes, or secondary schools. No grants to individuals, or for videotapes, films, advertising, publications, endowments, research, conferences, or general operating budgets.
Publications: Corporate giving report, informational brochure.
Application information:
Initial approach: Telephone or letter
Copies of proposal: 1
Deadline(s): 1 month prior to board meeting
Board meeting date(s): Quarterly
Final notification: Varies
Write: Elisa Arevalo Boone, V.P.
Officers: Ronald E. Eadie,* Pres.; Elisa Arevalo Boone, V.P.
Directors:* Regina Chun, Michael J. Dasher, Terri Dial, Stephen A. Enna, Michael Gillfillan, Lois L. Rice.
Number of staff: 2 full-time professional; 3 full-time support.
Employer Identification Number: 942549743

790
Western Cardiac Foundation ⌑
2001 South Barrington Ave., No. 200
Los Angeles 90025
Application address: 436 North Roxbury Dr., No. 222, Beverly Hills, CA 90210; Tel.: (213) 276-2379

Established in 1964 in CA.
Donor(s): Katherine R. Vance.†
Foundation type: Independent
Financial data (yr. ended 12/31/88): Assets, $2,870,335 (M); gifts received, $210,662; expenditures, $218,144, including $187,500 for 3 grants (high: $155,000; low: $7,500).
Purpose and activities: Support for medical research and higher education.
Limitations: No grants to individuals.
Application information: Application form not required.
Initial approach: Letter
Deadline(s): None
Write: Rexford Kennamer, Pres.
Officers: Rexford Kennamer, M.D., Pres.; George Mercader, V.P. & Financial Officer; Gladys Bishop, Secy.
Employer Identification Number: 956116853

791
Westmark Charitable Foundation ⌑ ☆
400 South Hope St., Suite 600
Los Angeles 90071

Established in 1987 in CA.
Donor(s): Vincent F. Martin, Jr., Bruce L. Ludwig, Sol L. Rabin, Roger C. Schultz, Stanton H. Zarrow.
Foundation type: Independent
Financial data (yr. ended 1/31/89): Assets, $113,925 (M); gifts received, $230,619; expenditures, $130,738, including $130,591 for 76 grants (high: $20,000; low: $50).
Purpose and activities: Giving for social services, hospitals, higher education, the performing arts, museums, and historical research.
Limitations: Giving primarily in CA. No support for private foundations. No grants to individuals.
Officers and Directors: Vincent F. Martin, Jr., Pres.; Stanton H. Zarrow, V.P. and Secy.; Bruce L. Ludwig, V.P.; Sol L. Rabin, V.P.; Roger C. Schultz, V.P.
Employer Identification Number: 954107239

792
The Whitelight Foundation ⌑
c/o Ernst & Young
1875 Century Park East, Suite 2200
Los Angeles 90067 (213) 553-2800

Established in 1980.
Donor(s): Betty Freeman.
Foundation type: Independent
Financial data (yr. ended 12/31/88): Assets, $164,636 (M); gifts received, $189,190; expenditures, $159,938, including $154,600 for 49 grants (high: $15,000; low: $500).
Purpose and activities: Giving primarily for music, performing arts and fine arts organizations, and for social service agencies; grants also to established classical musicians in publishing new compositions, copying scores, and performing new compositions in grants generally not exceeding $7,000.
Types of support: Grants to individuals.
Limitations: Giving primarily in southern CA.
Application information: Applications not accepted.
Trustee: Betty Freeman.
Number of staff: None.
Employer Identification Number: 953513930

793
Elia Whittell Trust for Disabled Veterans of Foreign Wars
One Post St., 30th Fl.
San Francisco 94104 (415) 362-6544

Established around 1978 in CA.
Donor(s): Elia Whittell.†
Foundation type: Independent
Financial data (yr. ended 11/30/89): Assets, $2,492,600 (M); expenditures, $174,914, including $135,000 for grants.
Purpose and activities: A private operating foundation established "to provide maintenance and medical support for disabled French veterans not provided by other sources."
Types of support: Continuing support, special projects.
Limitations: Giving limited to France. No grants to individuals.
Application information: Applications not accepted.
Write: Kenneth J. Ashcraft, Trustee
Trustees: Kenneth J. Ashcraft, Edward R. Finch, Jr.
Number of staff: None.
Employer Identification Number: 946449253

794
Whittier Foundation ▼ ⌑
1260 Huntington Dr., Suite 204
South Pasadena 91030 (213) 259-0484

Incorporated in 1955 in CA.
Donor(s): Leland K. Whittier,† and members of the Whittier family.
Foundation type: Independent
Financial data (yr. ended 4/30/87): Assets, $28,802,261 (M); gifts received, $2,553,228; expenditures, $2,949,369, including $2,742,000 for 16 grants (high: $2,000,000; low: $1,000; average: $1,000-$50,000).
Purpose and activities: Emphasis on hospitals and medical research; support also for youth agencies.
Limitations: Giving primarily in CA. No grants to individuals.
Application information:
Initial approach: Proposal
Deadline(s): None
Board meeting date(s): Annually and as necessary
Final notification: Varies
Write: Linda J. Blinkenberg, Secy.
Officers and Directors: Arlo G. Sorensen, Pres.; Laura-Lee Whittier Woods, V.P.; Linda J. Blinkenberg, Secy.; Steven A. Anderson, C.F.O.
Number of staff: 1
Employer Identification Number: 956027493

795
The Wickes Foundation ⌑ ☆
3340 Ocean Park Blvd., Suite 2000
Santa Monica 90405

Established in 1987 in CA.
Foundation type: Independent
Financial data (yr. ended 12/31/88): Assets, $6,607,335 (M); expenditures, $388,367, including $365,050 for 35 grants (high: $50,000; low: $50).
Purpose and activities: Giving primarily for higher education and hospitals; support also for museums, child welfare, Jewish organizations, and a homeless coalition.
Limitations: Giving primarily in southern CA. No grants to individuals.
Application information: Contributes only to pre-selected organizations. Applications not accepted.
Officers and Directors:* James R. Birle,* Pres.; James N. Castleberry, V.P.; Robert S. Fenton,* Secy.; Michael Jamieson, Treas.; Robert B. McKeon.
Employer Identification Number: 954085655

796
Brayton Wilbur Foundation
320 California St., Suite 200
San Francisco 94104 (415) 772-4006

Incorporated in 1947 in CA.
Donor(s): Wilbur-Ellis Co.
Foundation type: Company-sponsored
Financial data (yr. ended 12/31/88): Assets, $3,290,416 (M); gifts received, $75,000; expenditures, $194,409, including $178,500 for 47 grants (high: $35,000; low: $250; average: $1,000-$5,000).
Purpose and activities: Emphasis on the arts and on higher and secondary education; grants also for hospitals and conservation.
Types of support: Annual campaigns, building funds, capital campaigns, continuing support, endowment funds.
Limitations: Giving primarily in San Francisco, CA. No grants to individuals.
Application information: Contributes only to pre-selected organizations. Applications not accepted.
Write: Brayton Wilbur, Jr., Pres.
Officers and Directors:* Brayton Wilbur, Jr.,* Pres.; Carter P. Thacher,* V.P.; Herbert B. Tully,* Secy.-Treas.
Number of staff: None.
Employer Identification Number: 946088667

797
Marguerite Eyer Wilbur Foundation
P.O. Box 3370
Santa Barbara 93130-3370

Established in 1975 in CA.
Donor(s): Marguerite Eyer Wilbur.†
Foundation type: Independent
Financial data (yr. ended 06/30/89): Assets, $2,812,777 (M); expenditures, $196,752, including $55,765 for 13 grants (high: $23,000; low: $500; average: $1,000-$6,000) and $74,000 for 23 grants to individuals (high: $6,000; low: $500).
Purpose and activities: Resident fellowships are provided to writers of promise, to live and work in Mecosta, MI, with preference given to writers in the areas of history, religion, or philosophy. Grants to individuals are provided to those who have demonstrated unique accomplishments or promise in humane literature, particularly in history, religion and philosophy and are personally known to one of the trustees.
Types of support: Operating budgets, seed money, exchange programs, special projects, research, publications, conferences and seminars, fellowships.
Limitations: No support for music or fine arts projects. No grants for continuing support, deficit financing, building or endowment funds, or land acquisition; no loans.
Publications: Program policy statement, application guidelines.
Application information: Application form not required.
Initial approach: Proposal
Copies of proposal: 1
Deadline(s): Sept. 1 through Dec. 31
Board meeting date(s): Feb.
Final notification: Mar.
Write: Gary R. Ricks, C.E.O.
Officers and Trustees:* Gary R. Ricks,* C.E.O.; Russell Kirk,* Pres.; William Longstreth,* V.P.; F. Joseph Frawley,* Secy.
Number of staff: 1 full-time professional; 1 full-time support.
Employer Identification Number: 510168214

798
The Wilsey Foundation
P.O. Box 3532
San Francisco 94119 (415) 391-4150

Established in 1964 in CA.
Donor(s): Alfred S. Wilsey, Wilsey Foods, Inc., Wilsey Bennett Co.
Foundation type: Company-sponsored
Financial data (yr. ended 03/31/88): Assets, $782,991 (M); gifts received, $250,000; expenditures, $153,962, including $150,450 for 84 grants (high: $25,000; low: $100).
Purpose and activities: Grants primarily for secondary and higher education and museums.
Limitations: Giving primarily in the San Francisco Bay Area, CA.
Application information: Application form not required.
Initial approach: Letter; no telephone inquiries
Deadline(s): None
Officers: Alfred S. Wilsey, Pres.; Diane B. Wilsey, V.P.; Michael W. Wilsey, V.P.; Alfred S. Wilsey, Jr., Secy.; Jerome P. Solari, Treas.
Employer Identification Number: 946098720

799
Gary & Karen Winnick Foundation ⌑
150 El Camino Dr., Suite 204
Beverly Hills 90212

Established in 1983 in MD.
Donor(s): Gary Winnick, Karen Winnick, L.P. Pah.
Foundation type: Operating
Financial data (yr. ended 12/31/88): Assets, $57,318 (M); gifts received, $62,500; expenditures, $425,016, including $422,958 for 59 grants (high: $100,325; low: $30).
Purpose and activities: A private operating foundation; support for medical research, a Jewish fund, and higher and secondary education.
Limitations: No grants to individuals.
Application information: Contributes only to pre-selected organizations. Applications not accepted.
Officers and Directors: Gary Winnick, Pres.; Karen Winnick, Secy.; Edward Sanders.
Employer Identification Number: 953855792

800
Bernard E. & Alba Witkin Charitable Trust of 1982 ⌑
2740 Shasta Rd.
Berkeley 94708 (415) 845-3416

Established in 1982 in CA.
Donor(s): B.E. Witkin.
Foundation type: Independent
Financial data (yr. ended 12/31/88): Assets, $246,660 (M); gifts received, $400,000; expenditures, $425,329, including $424,005 for 122 grants (high: $85,000; low: $35).
Purpose and activities: Support primarily for youth activities and child welfare, social services, and an opera company.
Limitations: Giving primarily in CA, with emphasis on the San Francisco Bay area.
Application information: Letter.
Deadline(s): None
Write: Alba Witkin, Trustee
Trustees: Alba Witkin, B.E. Witkin.
Employer Identification Number: 942903377

801
Dean Witter Foundation
57 Post St., Suite 604
San Francisco 94104 (415) 981-2966

Incorporated in 1952 in CA.
Donor(s): Dean Witter,† Mrs. Dean Witter, Dean Witter & Co.
Foundation type: Independent
Financial data (yr. ended 11/30/88): Assets, $6,223,173 (M); gifts received, $9,500; expenditures, $469,687, including $330,122 for 20 grants (high: $61,050; low: $600).
Purpose and activities: Primary purpose is to support postgraduate research in economics and finance, with a secondary purpose to support conservation.
Types of support: Research, publications, special projects, building funds, equipment.
Limitations: Giving for conservation projects limited to northern CA. No grants to individuals, or for endowment funds.
Publications: Annual report (including application guidelines).
Application information: Application form not required.
Initial approach: Letter, telephone, or proposal
Copies of proposal: 6
Deadline(s): Submit proposal 1 month before board meeting
Board meeting date(s): Jan., Apr., July, and Oct.
Write: Lawrence I. Kramer, Jr., Admin. Dir.
Officers: Dean Witter III,* Pres.; James R. Bancroft, V.P.; William D. Witter, Secy.-Treas.

Trustees:* Edmond S. Gillette, Jr., Stephen Nessier, Frank H. Roberts.
Number of staff: None.
Employer Identification Number: 946065150

802
The Wollenberg Foundation ▼ ⌑
235 Montgomery St., Suite 2700
San Francisco 94104 (415) 981-1300

Trust established in 1952 in CA.
Donor(s): H.L. Wollenberg.†
Foundation type: Independent
Financial data (yr. ended 12/31/88): Assets, $33,121,090 (M); expenditures, $857,384, including $838,000 for 21 grants (high: $400,000; low: $2,000; average: $2,000-$20,000).
Purpose and activities: Grants primarily to assist non-tax-supported colleges.
Types of support: Endowment funds, special projects, operating budgets, general purposes.
Limitations: No support for sectarian purposes or religious-affiliated institutions. No grants to individuals; no loans.
Application information: Contributes only to pre-selected organizations. Applications not accepted.
Write: Marc H. Monheimer, Trustee
Trustees: Marc H. Monheimer, J. Roger Wollenberg, Richard P. Wollenberg.
Number of staff: None.
Employer Identification Number: 946072264

803
Wood-Claeyssens Foundation ⌑
P.O. Box 30547
Santa Barbara 93130-0547 (805) 682-4775

Established in 1980.
Donor(s): Ailene B. Claeyssens, Pierre P. Claeyssens.
Foundation type: Independent
Financial data (yr. ended 03/31/89): Assets, $7,507,833 (M); gifts received, $3,000,000; expenditures, $325,516, including $298,000 for 52 grants (high: $50,000; low: $500; average: $500-$2,000).
Purpose and activities: Support for hospitals and health services, and social service and youth agencies.
Limitations: Giving primarily in CA. No grants to individuals.
Application information:
Initial approach: Letter
Deadline(s): Aug. 31
Write: Pierre P. Claeyssens, 1st V.P.
Officers and Directors:* Ailene B. Claeyssens,* Pres.; Pierre P. Claeyssens,* 1st V.P.; Cynthia S. Wood,* 2nd V.P.; James H. Hurley, Jr., Secy.; Charles C. Gray, Treas.
Employer Identification Number: 953514017

804
The Peg Yorkin Foundation
(Formerly The Yorkin Foundation)
2176 Century Hill
Los Angeles 90067

Established in 1979 in CA.
Donor(s): Peg Yorkin.
Foundation type: Independent
Financial data (yr. ended 11/30/88): Assets, $44,124 (M); gifts received, $85,360; expenditures, $189,953, including $182,595 for 189 grants (high: $35,000; low: $100; average: $1,442).
Purpose and activities: Giving for arts and cultural programs, health, Jewish welfare, women's issues, public affairs, and a genetics foundation.
Types of support: Annual campaigns, seed money, emergency funds, special projects, research, conferences and seminars, continuing support.
Limitations: Giving primarily in Los Angeles, CA. No grants to individuals, or for capital or endowment funds, deficit financing, scholarships, fellowships, or matching gifts; no loans.
Application information: Application form not required.
Initial approach: Letter
Copies of proposal: 1
Deadline(s): None
Board meeting date(s): Mar.
Final notification: 2 months
Write: Peg Yorkin, Pres.
Officers and Directors:* Peg Yorkin,* Pres.; Nicole Yorkin,* Secy.; David Yorkin.
Number of staff: None.
Employer Identification Number: 953454331

805
Youth Development Foundation
3355 Via Lido, Suite 235
Newport Beach 92663-3917 (714) 675-6856

Established in 1953 in CA.
Foundation type: Independent
Financial data (yr. ended 11/30/89): Assets, $9,182,638 (M); expenditures, $83,132, including $77,481 for 45 grants (high: $6,700; low: $100).
Purpose and activities: Support primarily for education, child development, the performing arts, the environment, and animal welfare.
Types of support: General purposes, scholarship funds, special projects.
Limitations: Giving primarily in CA.
Application information: Application form required.
Initial approach: Letter
Copies of proposal: 2
Deadline(s): Feb.
Board meeting date(s): Mar.
Write: Frank R. Randall, Trustee
Trustees: Frank R. Randall, Joan P. Randall, Paul S. Randall.
Number of staff: 1 part-time support.
Employer Identification Number: 956087465

806
Takeo Yuki Charitable Trust ⌑ ☆
P.O. Box 567
Los Gatos 95031-0567

Donor(s): Miyoko Yuki.
Foundation type: Operating
Financial data (yr. ended 3/31/89): Assets, $435,725 (M); gifts received, $474,000; expenditures, $123,931, including $123,500 for 8 grants (high: $110,000; low: $500).
Purpose and activities: Giving in the areas of religion and health.
Types of support: Operating budgets, building funds, scholarship funds, endowment funds, general purposes.
Application information:
Initial approach: Letter
Deadline(s): None
Trustees: Herbert T. Yuki, Miyoko Yuki, Thomas M. Yuki.
Employer Identification Number: 942558692

807
Virginia Zanuck Charitable Foundation ⌑
c/o Loeb & Loeb
10100 Santa Monica Blvd., No. 2200
Los Angeles 90067 (213) 282-2061

Established in 1983 in CA.
Donor(s): Richard Zanuck Charitable Trust, Virginia Zanuck Charitable Trust.
Foundation type: Independent
Financial data (yr. ended 08/31/89): Assets, $1,237 (M); gifts received, $192,220; expenditures, $210,036, including $181,860 for 61 grants (high: $50,000; low: $100).
Purpose and activities: Support primarily for higher education, museums, and film-related activities; some support for child welfare, the visually impaired, and health associations.
Limitations: Giving primarily in Los Angeles, CA.
Application information: Application form not required.
Initial approach: Letter
Deadline(s): None
Write: Andrew M. Katzenstein
Officers: Daryl N. Zanuck, Chair.; Richard Zanuck, Pres.; Sybil Brand, V.P. and C.F.O.; Lilli Zanuck, Secy.
Employer Identification Number: 953882409

808
The Zellerbach Family Fund ▼
120 Montgomery St., Suite 2125
San Francisco 94104 (415) 421-2629

Incorporated in 1956 in CA.
Donor(s): Jennie B. Zellerbach.†
Foundation type: Independent
Financial data (yr. ended 12/31/89): Assets, $40,839,011 (M); gifts received, $254,261; expenditures, $2,093,002, including $1,451,466 for grants (average: $5,000-$35,000).
Purpose and activities: Support for direct-service projects in the arts, health, mental health, and social and child welfare.
Types of support: Continuing support, technical assistance, special projects.
Limitations: Giving primarily in the San Francisco Bay Area, CA. No grants to individuals, or for capital or endowment funds, research, scholarships, or fellowships; no loans.
Publications: Annual report (including application guidelines).
Application information: Applications rarely granted; foundation develops most of its own grant proposals. The foundation is currently committed to projects underway and does not expect to make grants to new programs over the next few years. Community arts groups will continue to be funded. Application form not required.

Initial approach: Telephone or proposal (8 copies for arts proposals)
Deadline(s): Submit full art proposal, preferably 2 weeks prior to board meeting
Board meeting date(s): Quarterly
Final notification: 1 week after board meeting for art applications
Write: Edward A. Nathan, Exec. Dir.
Officers and Directors:* William J. Zellerbach,* Pres.; Louis J. Saroni II,* V.P. and Treas.; Robert E. Sinton,* V.P.; Philip S. Ehrlich, Jr.,* Secy.; Edward A. Nathan,* Exec. Dir.; Stewart E. Adams, Nancy Z. Boschwitz, Jeanette M. Dunckel, Lucy Ann Geiselman, George B. James, Verneice Thompson, John W. Zellerbach.
Number of staff: 1 full-time professional; 2 part-time professional; 2 full-time support.
Employer Identification Number: 946069482

809
Zoline Foundation ⌑
624 North Canon Dr.
Beverly Hills 90210

Established in 1954 in CA.
Donor(s): Janice K. Zoline, Joseph T. Zoline.
Foundation type: Independent
Financial data (yr. ended 11/30/89): Assets, $1,320,356 (M); expenditures, $88,863, including $84,070 for 41 grants (high: $20,000; low: $20; average: $25-$20,000).
Purpose and activities: Giving primarily for higher education, health associations, and social services.
Officers: Joseph T. Zoline,* Pres. and Treas.; Janice K. Zoline, Secy.-Treas.
Directors:* James L. Zacharias.
Employer Identification Number: 366083529

COLORADO

810
Airport Business Center Foundation ⌑ ☆
300 East Airport Business Ctr.
Aspen 81611

Established in 1986 in CO.
Donor(s): John P. McBride.
Foundation type: Independent
Financial data (yr. ended 12/31/87): Assets, $344,990 (M); gifts received, $145,500; expenditures, $156,129, including $153,375 for 54 grants (high: $25,000; low: $200).
Purpose and activities: Giving for secondary and higher education, family planning, environmental and conservation groups, animal welfare, and amateur sports organizations.
Limitations: Giving primarily in Aspen, CO, and Washington, DC.
Trustees: John P. McBride, John P. McBride, Jr., Katherine H. McBride, Laura M. McBride, Lester D. Peduora.
Employer Identification Number: 841042661

811
Animal Assistance Foundation ▼
2926 West Jewell Ave.
Denver 80219 (303) 935-6263

Established in 1975 in CO.
Donor(s): Louise C. Harrison.†
Foundation type: Independent
Financial data (yr. ended 7/31/89): Assets, $28,733,758 (M); expenditures, $2,590,813, including $905,032 for grants (high: $554,907; average: $2,000-$100,000) and $753,857 for 3 foundation-administered programs.
Purpose and activities: Giving for animal welfare, especially to prevent cruelty to cats and other small household pets; also operates three spay/neuter clinics.
Types of support: Research, building funds, equipment.
Limitations: Giving primarily in CO.
Publications: Financial statement (including application guidelines).
Application information: Application form not required.
Initial approach: Telephone or letter
Deadline(s): Submit application preferably prior to May meeting; no set deadlines
Board meeting date(s): Monthly
Final notification: Varies
Write: Robert A. Williams, Exec. Dir.
Officer and Directors:* Robert A. Williams,* Exec. Dir.; Charles W. Ennis, Grace Mary B. Greenleaf.
Number of staff: 32 full-time professional; 2 part-time professional.
Employer Identification Number: 840715412

812
The Anschutz Family Foundation ▼
2400 Anaconda Tower
555 17th St.
Denver 80202 (303) 293-2338

Established in 1983 in CO.
Donor(s): Fred B. Anschutz, Antelope Land and Livestock Co., Inc., Medicine Bow Ranch Co., Sue Anschutz Rodgers.
Foundation type: Independent
Financial data (yr. ended 11/30/88): Assets, $6,516,392 (M); gifts received, $200,000; expenditures, $732,595, including $606,900 for 140 grants (high: $55,000; low: $100; average: $5,000-$10,000).
Purpose and activities: Grants for the direct provision of human services, especially for children, the elderly, and the poor, including health services; support also for public policy.
Types of support: Special projects, operating budgets, continuing support, seed money, emergency funds, technical assistance, publications, general purposes.
Limitations: Giving primarily in CO, especially Denver. No support for programs of research organizations. No grants to individuals, or for capital or building funds, deficit financing, endowment funds, scholarships, or fellowships.
Publications: Annual report (including application guidelines).
Application information: Application form not required.
Initial approach: Letter
Copies of proposal: 1
Deadline(s): Submit proposal before Mar. 1 and Sept. 1
Board meeting date(s): Nov.
Final notification: By Nov. 30
Write: Sue Anschutz Rodgers, Pres.
Officers and Directors:* Sue Anschutz Rodgers,* Pres. and Exec. Dir.; Nancy P. Anschutz,* V.P.; Philip F. Anschutz,* V.P.; Hugh C. Braly,* Secy.-Treas.; Fred B. Anschutz, Sarah Anschutz, Melinda A. Couzens, Melissa A. Rodgers, Susan E. Rodgers.
Number of staff: 1 full-time professional; 1 full-time support.
Employer Identification Number: 742132676

813
The Anschutz Foundation
2400 Anaconda Tower
555 17th St.
Denver 80202 (303) 293-2338

Established in 1984 in CO.
Donor(s): Philip F. Anschutz, The Anschutz Corp.
Foundation type: Independent
Financial data (yr. ended 11/30/88): Assets, $1,473,942 (M); expenditures, $435,620, including $335,635 for 34 grants (high: $175,785; low: $500; average: $5,000-$10,000).
Purpose and activities: General purposes; national giving with emphasis on social and cultural organizations which work in areas larger than local communities; support for public policy and traditional family values.
Types of support: General purposes, operating budgets, publications, conferences and seminars.
Limitations: No support for programs within educational or research institutions, or for cultural or arts organizations. No grants to individuals, or for capital campaigns or continuing support.
Publications: 990-PF, application guidelines.
Application information: Application form not required.
Initial approach: Letter of no more than 2 pages
Copies of proposal: 1
Deadline(s): Sept. 1 and Mar. 1
Board meeting date(s): Nov.
Final notification: Oct.
Write: Sue Anschutz Rodgers, Pres.
Officers and Directors:* Philip F. Anschutz,* Chair.; Sue Anschutz Rodgers,* Pres. and Exec. Dir.; Nancy P. Anschutz,* V.P.; Hugh C. Braly,* Secy.-Treas.; Fred B. Anschutz.
Number of staff: 1
Employer Identification Number: 742316617

814
E. L. and Oma Bacon Foundation, Inc.
(Formerly E. L. Bacon Foundation, Inc.)
355 Main St.
Grand Junction 81501 (303) 243-1611
Application address: P.O. Box 908, Grand Junction, CO 81502

Established in 1978 in CO.

Donor(s): E.L. Bacon,† Oma Bacon.†
Foundation type: Independent
Financial data (yr. ended 08/31/88): Assets, $2,050,045 (M); expenditures, $70,105, including $62,270 for 13 grants (high: $20,000; low: $100; average: $2,000-$10,000).
Purpose and activities: Support for health and social services, religion, culture, and community development.
Types of support: General purposes.
Limitations: Giving primarily in CO. No grants to individuals.
Publications: Application guidelines.
Application information: Application form not required.
Initial approach: Letter requesting application guidelines
Copies of proposal: 2
Deadline(s): None
Board meeting date(s): Meets on an on-call basis
Write: Herbert L. Bacon, Pres.
Officers: Herbert L. Bacon, Pres.; Patrick A. Gormley, V.P.; Laura May Bacon, Secy.
Number of staff: None.
Employer Identification Number: 840772667

815
The Hugh Bancroft, Jr. Foundation
1700 Lincoln, Suite 4100
Denver 80203-4541 (303) 861-7000

Established in 1960 in CO.
Donor(s): Jacqueline E. Spencer.
Foundation type: Independent
Financial data (yr. ended 12/31/89): Assets, $6,148,765 (M); gifts received, $1,029,475; qualifying distributions, $100,000, including $100,000 for 2 grants of $50,000 each.
Purpose and activities: In 1988, support for a symphony orchestra and the Boys Club.
Types of support: Continuing support, general purposes.
Limitations: Giving primarily in NM. No grants to individuals.
Application information: Application form not required.
Initial approach: Letter
Deadline(s): None
Write: Paul D. Holleman, Trustee
Officers: A.N. Spencer, Mgr.; Jacqueline E. Spencer, Mgr.
Trustees: Judson W. Detrick, Paul D. Holleman, J. Churchill Owen.
Number of staff: None.
Employer Identification Number: 846020971

816
Dr. Mary E. Bates Trust Fund ⌑ ☆
2201 South Holly St., No. 5
Denver 80222-5613 (303) 757-0147

Established in 1955.
Foundation type: Independent
Financial data (yr. ended 12/31/88): Assets, $1,143,302 (M); expenditures, $48,918, including $39,579 for 7 grants (high: $12,299; low: $1,000) and $3,000 for 3 grants to individuals of $1,000 each.
Purpose and activities: Giving limited to animal humane societies and educational grants to "women in medicine."
Types of support: Student aid.
Limitations: Giving primarily in CO.
Application information:
Initial approach: Letter
Deadline(s): None
Write: Mabel Wolfe, Trustee
Trustees: Marilyn C. Briscoe, Charles Wolfe, Mabel D. Wolfe.
Employer Identification Number: 846028055

817
Boettcher Foundation ▼
1670 Broadway, Suite 3301
Denver 80202 (303) 831-1937

Incorporated in 1937 in CO.
Donor(s): C.K. Boettcher,† Mrs. C.K. Boettcher,† Charles Boettcher,† Fannie Boettcher,† Ruth Boettcher Humphreys.†
Foundation type: Independent
Financial data (yr. ended 12/31/89): Assets, $114,215,000 (M); expenditures, $5,815,595, including $5,252,202 for 246 grants (high: $500,000; low: $500).
Purpose and activities: Grants to educational institutions, with emphasis on scholarships and fellowships; community and social services, including child welfare and women, the disadvantaged and the homeless, and urban and rural development; health, including rehabilitation and drug abuse; and civic and cultural programs, including support for the fine and performing arts.
Types of support: Scholarship funds, operating budgets, seed money, building funds, equipment, land acquisition, matching funds, general purposes, annual campaigns, capital campaigns, renovation projects.
Limitations: Giving limited to CO. No grants to individuals, or for endowment funds.
Publications: Annual report (including application guidelines), informational brochure, application guidelines.
Application information: Application form not required.
Initial approach: Letter
Copies of proposal: 1
Deadline(s): None
Board meeting date(s): Monthly
Final notification: 2 to 3 months
Write: William A. Douglas, Pres.
Officers: Hover T. Lentz,* Chair.; Claudia B. Merthan,* Vice-Chair.; William A. Douglas, Pres. and Exec. Dir.; John C. Mitchell II,* Secy.; George M. Wilfley,* Treas.
Trustees:* Mrs. Charles Boettcher II, E. Atwill Gilman, A. Barry Hirschfeld, Edward Lehman, Harry T. Lewis, Jr.
Number of staff: 2 full-time professional; 2 full-time support.
Employer Identification Number: 840404274

818
Bonfils-Stanton Foundation
1601 Arapahoe St., Suite 5
Denver 80202 (303) 825-3774

Established in 1962 in CO.
Donor(s): Charles E. Stanton.†
Foundation type: Independent
Financial data (yr. ended 06/30/89): Assets, $9,186,569 (M); gifts received, $2,406,832; expenditures, $481,403, including $409,300 for 39 grants (high: $50,000; low: $1,000).
Purpose and activities: Giving in the following major categories of philanthropy: education; scientific, including hospital and health services; civic and cultural; and community and human services. Three annual awards are given to persons in Colorado who have made significant contributions in the fields of arts and humanities, community service, and science and medicine.
Types of support: Capital campaigns, equipment, fellowships, general purposes, land acquisition, lectureships, program-related investments, renovation projects, research, scholarship funds, special projects, technical assistance.
Limitations: Giving limited to CO. No support for religious organizations.
Publications: Annual report (including application guidelines), informational brochure.
Application information: Application form not required.
Initial approach: Proposal
Copies of proposal: 6
Deadline(s): Jan. 1, Apr. 1, July 1, and Oct. 1
Board meeting date(s): Jan., Apr., July, and Sept.
Write: William L. Funk, Exec. Dir.
Officers and Trustees:* Robert E. Stanton,* Pres. and Treas.; Benjamin F. Stapleton,* V.P.; Eileen Greenawalt,* Secy.; William L. Funk,* Exec. Dir.; Louis J. Duman, Flaminia Odescalchi Kelly, Johnston R. Livingston.
Number of staff: 1 full-time professional; 1 full-time support.
Employer Identification Number: 846029014

819
Ruth H. Brown Foundation ⌑
240 St. Paul St., No. 100
Denver 80206-5113 (303) 333-5309

Established in 1959 in CO.
Foundation type: Independent
Financial data (yr. ended 12/31/87): Assets, $1,269,421 (M); expenditures, $67,115, including $58,600 for 28 grants (high: $13,700; low: $50).
Purpose and activities: Support primarily for youth organizations, health services and alcoholism treatment and research.
Types of support: Special projects, operating budgets.
Limitations: Giving primarily in Denver and Aspen, CO.
Application information:
Initial approach: Letter
Deadline(s): None
Write: Ruth H. Brown, Pres.
Officers: Ruth H. Brown, Pres.; David R.C. Brown, V.P.; Darcey B. Kelley, Secy.
Employer Identification Number: 846023395

820
Temple Hoyne Buell Foundation
2700 East Hampden Ave.
Englewood 80110 (303) 761-1717

Incorporated in 1962 in CO.
Donor(s): Temple Hoyne Buell.†
Foundation type: Independent
Financial data (yr. ended 06/30/89): Assets, $31,580,660 (M); expenditures, $1,700,752, including $1,364,500 for 7 grants (high:

$800,000; low: $2,000; average: $1,000-$100,000).
Purpose and activities: Giving primarily for higher education, including architecture, and for charitable organizations.
Types of support: Operating budgets, continuing support, annual campaigns, seed money, building funds, equipment, land acquisition, endowment funds, professorships, scholarship funds.
Limitations: Giving primarily in CO, with emphasis on Denver. No grants to individuals; no loans.
Publications: 990-PF.
Application information: Grant applications will not be reviewed until 1992. Applications not accepted.
Board meeting date(s): Quarterly
Write: Harold E. Williamson, Exec. Dir.
Officers and Trustees:* Jack Kent,* Pres.; Jerome Lindberg,* V.P.; Alexander M. Groos,* Secy.-Treas.; Harold E. Williamson,* Exec. Dir.; George Cannon, Thomas J. Curnes, Eugene E. Dawson.
Number of staff: 1 full-time professional.
Employer Identification Number: 846037604

821
Ralph L. & Florence R. Burgess Trust ⌑
c/o First Interstate Bank of Denver, N.A.
P.O. Box 5825, Terminal Annex
Denver 80217

Established in 1985 in CO.
Foundation type: Independent
Financial data (yr. ended 1/31/88): Assets, $1,606,107 (M); gifts received, $2; expenditures, $104,100, including $88,000 for 5 grants (high: $24,000; low: $1,000).
Purpose and activities: Giving primarily for the arts, especially the performing arts.
Limitations: Giving primarily in Denver, CO.
Application information: Application form not required.
Initial approach: Letter
Deadline(s): None
Trustee: First Interstate Bank of Denver, N.A.
Employer Identification Number: 742383505

822
Franklin L. Burns Foundation ⌑
1625 Broadway Penthouse Dome Tower
Denver 80202-4717 (303) 629-1899

Established in 1951 in CO.
Foundation type: Independent
Financial data (yr. ended 12/31/87): Assets, $700,068 (M); expenditures, $136,039, including $125,086 for 32 grants (high: $82,100; low: $61).
Purpose and activities: Support primarily for youth organizations and services, cultural organizations, colleges and universities and community funds.
Limitations: Giving primarily in Denver, CO.
Application information: Application form not required.
Deadline(s): None
Write: L.E. Canterbury, Secy.
Officers: L.E. Canterbury, Secy. and Mgr.
Employer Identification Number: 846022631

823
The Carroll Foundation ⌑
R.R. 1, Box 159
Franktown 80116

Established in 1978.
Donor(s): International Metals & Machines, Inc., Champion Pneumatic Machinery Co., Inc., Ludlow Industries, Inc., and other companies.
Foundation type: Company-sponsored
Financial data (yr. ended 4/30/87): Assets, $4,788,546 (M); gifts received, $300,520; expenditures, $387,963, including $381,284 for 34 grants (high: $201,000; low: $1,000).
Purpose and activities: Giving primarily for higher education and hospitals; some support also for elementary education.
Limitations: Giving primarily in MA and IL.
Application information:
Initial approach: Letter
Deadline(s): None
Trustees: Barry J. Carroll, Denis H. Carroll, Wallace E. Carroll, Wallace E. Carroll, Jr., Lelia C. Johnson.
Employer Identification Number: 840800849

824
Collins Foundation ⌑ ☆
c/o United Bank of Boulder, N.A.
P.O. Box 299
Boulder 80306-0227 (303) 441-0309

Established in 1982.
Foundation type: Independent
Financial data (yr. ended 8/31/89): Assets, $1,317,736 (M); expenditures, $60,539, including $46,950 for 25 grants (high: $4,000; low: $250).
Purpose and activities: Giving primarily to health services and welfare agencies and youth groups.
Types of support: Operating budgets.
Limitations: Giving primarily in Boulder County, CO.
Application information: Application form required.
Deadline(s): None
Write: Dwight Roberts
Trustee: United Bank of Boulder, N.A.
Employer Identification Number: 742254030

825
Colorado Masons Benevolent Fund Association ⌑
1770 Sherman St.
Denver 80203 (303) 837-0367
Scholarships application address: Scholarship Correspondent, 1130 Panorama Dr., Colorado Springs, CO 80904; Tel.: (719) 471-9589

Incorporated in 1901 in CO.
Foundation type: Operating
Financial data (yr. ended 10/31/88): Assets, $7,787,752 (M); gifts received, $22,077; expenditures, $821,250, including $16,400 for grants, $684,374 for grants to individuals (high: $7,000; low: $1,000), $1,000 for 1 foundation-administered program and $4,500 for loans to individuals.
Purpose and activities: A private operating foundation; grants for worthy, distressed CO Masons and their families; and for scholarships to CO high school seniors planning to attend college in CO; Masonic affiliation not required for scholarships.
Types of support: Student aid, grants to individuals, student loans.
Limitations: Giving limited to CO.
Publications: Annual report.
Application information: Application forms provided for scholarship seekers; applicants are interviewed.
Deadline(s): Feb. 15 for scholarships
Final notification: Apr. for scholarships
Officers and Trustees:* Charles L. Thomson,* Pres.; Milton Brandwein,* V.P.; Arthur J. Carlson, Exec. Secy.; Clarence L. Bartholic,* Secy.; Gaines S. Greene,* Treas.
Employer Identification Number: 840406813

826
Colorado Springs Community Trust Fund ⌑
Holly Sugar Bldg., Suite 1400
Colorado Springs 80903 (719) 475-7730
Application address: Miss Florence Edgerly, Asst. Dir., 1622 North Corona, Colorado Springs, CO 80907

Established in 1928 in CO by declaration of trust.
Foundation type: Community
Financial data (yr. ended 12/31/88): Assets, $2,778,454 (M); expenditures, $170,932, including $135,004 for 20 grants (high: $28,554; low: $100; average: $500-$24,880).
Purpose and activities: Emphasis on community funds, youth agencies, health, and child welfare.
Types of support: Continuing support, annual campaigns, seed money, emergency funds, building funds, equipment.
Limitations: Giving primarily in CO, with emphasis on El Paso County. No grants to individuals, or for operating budgets, deficit financing, endowment funds, matching gifts, scholarships, fellowships, research, demonstration projects, publications, or conferences; no loans.
Publications: Annual report.
Application information: Application form not required.
Initial approach: Letter
Deadline(s): None
Board meeting date(s): 3 or 4 times a year
Final notification: 3 to 4 months
Write: Jack W. Foutch, Dir.
Officer and Trustees:* Jack W. Foutch,* Mgr.; Gary G. Cassell, Richard G. Gillaspie, Gary J. Roberts.
Number of staff: 1 part-time support.
Employer Identification Number: 510217708

827
The Colorado Trust ▼
One Civic Center Plaza
1560 Broadway, Suite 875
Denver 80202-9697 (303) 837-1200

Established in 1985 in CO.
Donor(s): Presbyterian/St. Lukes Health Care Corp.
Foundation type: Independent
Financial data (yr. ended 12/31/89): Assets, $232,899,690 (M); gifts received, $62,867,474; expenditures, $9,103,089,

including $8,026,412 for 124 grants (high: $2,129,373; low: $1,000).
Purpose and activities: Support for institutions and organizations that improve the well-being of the people of CO, with special emphasis on health through six programs: Rural Health Care Initiative, Health Promotion, Indigent Health Policy, Children's Issues, Elderly Issues, and Indian Health; grants also for projects not based in CO that have the potential of broader societal benefit such as health policy research.
Types of support: Equipment, operating budgets, conferences and seminars, special projects.
Limitations: Giving primarily in CO. No support for religious organizations for religious purposes, private foundations, or direct subsidization of care to the medically indigent. No grants to individuals, or for endowments, deficit financing or debt retirement, building funds, real estate acquisition, medical research, fundraising drives and events, testimonial dinners, or advertising.
Publications: Annual report, application guidelines, newsletter.
Application information: Application form not required.
Initial approach: Letter and proposal
Copies of proposal: 3
Deadline(s): None
Board meeting date(s): Monthly
Final notification: Funding decisions announced on even numbered months throughout the year
Write: Judith Anderson, Grants Admin.
Officers and Trustees:* Donald W. Fink, M.D.,* Chair.; Richard F. Walker,* Vice.-Chair.; Bruce M. Rockwell, Pres.; James G. Urban, M.D.,* Secy.; W.R. Alexander,* Treas.; William F. Beattie, Robert G. Boucher, Donald G. Butterfield, M.D., Rev. Kathryn Cone, A. Gordon Rippey.
Number of staff: 6 full-time professional; 3 full-time support.
Employer Identification Number: 840994055

828
Comprecare Foundation, Inc. ☆
P.O. Box 441170
Aurora 80044 (303) 322-1641

Established in 1986 in CO.
Foundation type: Independent
Financial data (yr. ended 12/31/89): Assets, $4,591,030 (M); expenditures, $309,089, including $215,066 for 16 grants (high: $46,000; low: $2,000).
Purpose and activities: "To encourage, aid or assist specific health related programs and to support the actvities of organizations and individuals who advance and promote health care education, the delivery of health care services, and the improvement of community health and welfare."
Types of support: Conferences and seminars, research, seed money, special projects.
Limitations: Giving primarily in CO, with emphasis on front range. No support for private foundations. No grants for operating expenses, debt reduction, land acquisition, fundraising events, or testimonial dinners or promotions.
Publications: Annual report.
Application information: Application form not required.
Initial approach: Letter (1 to 2 pages)
Copies of proposal: 1
Deadline(s): No set deadline, but initial approach should be submitted 2 months prior to board meeting
Board meeting date(s): Monthly
Final notification: Within 10 days following board meeting
Write: J.R. Gilsdorf, Exec. Dir.
Officers and Directors:* Raymond C. Delisle,* Chair.; Harry C. Reese,* Treas.; Marcus B. Bond, M.D., Bradford L. Darling, Ellen J. Mangione, M.D., Joseph P. Natale, Richard F. Negri, M. Eugene Sherman, M.D.
Number of staff: 1 part-time professional; 1 part-time support.
Employer Identification Number: 840641406

829
Adolph Coors Foundation ▼
350-C Clayton St.
Denver 80206 (303) 388-1636

Incorporated in 1975 in CO.
Donor(s): Adolph Coors, Jr.,† Gertrude S. Coors,† Janet Coors.
Foundation type: Independent
Financial data (yr. ended 11/30/89): Assets, $113,519,580 (M); expenditures, $5,979,887, including $4,189,290 for 157 grants (high: $200,000; low: $250; average: $5,000-$20,000).
Purpose and activities: Emphasis on higher and secondary education, public policy, civic affairs, human services, youth, and health.
Types of support: Building funds, general purposes, seed money, operating budgets, special projects.
Limitations: Giving primarily in CO; national giving is limited. No support for pre-schools, daycare centers, nursing homes or other extended care facilities, or tax-supported organizations. Generally, no grants to individuals, or for endowment funds, research, production of films or other media-related projects, capital or program needs of churches, conduit funding, deficits, debt retirement, special benefit programs, or purchase of blocks of tickets.
Publications: Annual report (including application guidelines).
Application information: Application form not required.
Initial approach: Letter
Copies of proposal: 1
Deadline(s): 8 weeks prior to meetings
Board meeting date(s): Jan., Apr., July, and Oct.
Final notification: 3 months
Write: Linda S. Tafoya, Exec. Dir.
Officers: William K. Coors,* Pres.; Peter H. Coors,* V.P.; Linda S. Tafoya, Secy. and Exec. Dir.; Jeffrey H. Coors,* Treas.
Trustees:* Joseph Coors, Robert G. Windsor.
Number of staff: 2 full-time professional; 2 full-time support.
Employer Identification Number: 510172279

830
Ben C. Delatour Foundation ⌑
P.O. Box 2203
Fort Collins 80522-2203
Application address: P.O. Box 96, Fort Collins, CO 80522

Foundation type: Independent
Financial data (yr. ended 12/31/88): Assets, $1,319,575 (M); expenditures, $104,867, including $89,850 for 55 grants (high: $13,000; low: $200).
Purpose and activities: Support for higher education, youth-related activities and organizations, and organizations that serve the handicapped.
Limitations: Giving primarily in CO and NE. No grants to individuals.
Application information:
Deadline(s): None
Write: Leonard F. Banowetz, Trustee
Trustees: Leonard F. Banowetz, Bonnie Delatour Smith, Joy Delatour Smith.
Employer Identification Number: 846076668

831
The Denver Foundation ▼
455 Sherman St., Suite 220
Denver 80203 (303) 778-7587

Established in 1925 in CO by resolution and declaration of trust.
Foundation type: Community
Financial data (yr. ended 12/31/89): Assets, $22,678,189 (M); gifts received, $1,514,745; expenditures, $1,876,690, including $1,516,282 for 126 grants (high: $82,500; low: $75; average: $15,000-$20,000) and $12,500 for 1 loan.
Purpose and activities: To "assist, encourage and promote the well-being of mankind, and primarily the inhabitants of Metropolitan Denver." Grants primarily for education, health and hospitals, social services, and cultural programs.
Types of support: Seed money, renovation projects, technical assistance, special projects, matching funds, scholarship funds.
Limitations: Giving limited to Adams, Denver, Douglas, Jefferson, Arapahoe, and Boulder counties, CO. No support for sectarian programs, or projects supported largely by public funds. No grants to individuals, or for debt liquidation, endowment funds, research, publications, films, travel, or conferences; no loans.
Publications: Annual report, application guidelines, program policy statement.
Application information: Application form not required.
Initial approach: Letter
Copies of proposal: 1
Deadline(s): Mar. 31, June 30, Aug. 31, and Dec. 31
Board meeting date(s): Mar., June, Sept., and Nov.
Final notification: Within 3 months
Write: Robert E. Lee, Exec. Dir.
Officer: Robert E. Lee, Exec. Dir.
Distribution Committee: C. Howard Kast, Chair.; John H. McLagan, Vice-Chair.; Mary Lee Anderson, Donald K. Bain, Sidney Friedman, William H. Hornby, Phyllis Jennings-

Byrd, Virginia P. Rockwell, Darlene Silver, Robert S. Slosky, Julie Smith, Bernard Valdez.
Trustee Banks: Central Bank of Denver, Colorado National Bank, Colorado State Bank, First Bank of Westland, First Interstate Bank of Denver, N.A., First Trust Corp., Guaranty Bank & Trust, Jefferson Bank and Trust, United Bank of Denver, N.A.
Number of staff: 4 full-time professional; 1 part-time professional; 1 full-time support.
Employer Identification Number: 846048381

832
John G. Duncan Trust ⌑
c/o First Interstate Bank of Denver, N.A.
P.O. Box 5825 TA
Denver 80217 (303) 293-5324

Trust established in 1955 in CO.
Donor(s): John G. Duncan.†
Foundation type: Independent
Financial data (yr. ended 12/31/88): Assets, $2,899,092 (M); expenditures, $202,293, including $177,106 for 28 grants (high: $10,000; low: $4,000).
Purpose and activities: Support for hospitals, higher and secondary education, youth agencies, cultural programs, and a community fund.
Types of support: Annual campaigns, building funds, equipment, research, operating budgets, continuing support, seed money, emergency funds, special projects.
Limitations: Giving limited to CO. No grants to individuals, or for endowment funds, scholarships, or fellowships; no loans.
Publications: Application guidelines.
Application information:
Initial approach: Letter or proposal
Copies of proposal: 1
Deadline(s): None
Board meeting date(s): Dec.
Final notification: Dec. 31
Write: Yvonne Baca
Trustee: First Interstate Bank of Denver, N.A.
Number of staff: None.
Employer Identification Number: 846016555

833
El Pomar Foundation ▼
Ten Lake Circle Dr.
P.O. Box 158
Colorado Springs 80906 (719) 633-7733

Incorporated in 1937 in CO.
Donor(s): Spencer Penrose,† Mrs. Spencer Penrose.†
Foundation type: Independent
Financial data (yr. ended 12/31/89): Assets, $250,000,000 (M); expenditures, $11,078,782, including $10,131,717 for 154 grants (high: $1,500,000; low: $1,500; average: $5,000-$100,000).
Purpose and activities: Grants only to nonprofit organizations for public, educational, arts and humanities, health, and welfare purposes, including child welfare, the disadvantaged, and housing; municipalities may request funds for specific projects.
Types of support: Operating budgets, continuing support, emergency funds, building funds, equipment, land acquisition, scholarship funds, special projects, general purposes, capital campaigns, renovation projects.
Limitations: Giving limited to CO. No support for organizations that distribute funds to other grantees, or for camps or seasonal facilities. No grants to individuals, or for annual campaigns, travel, film or other media projects, conferences, deficit financing, endowment funds, research, matching gifts, seed money, or publications; no loans.
Publications: Annual report (including application guidelines), application guidelines, grants list.
Application information: Application form not required.
Initial approach: Letter
Copies of proposal: 1
Deadline(s): None
Board meeting date(s): 7 to 9 times a year
Final notification: 90 days
Write: William J. Hybl, Chair.
Officers: Russell T. Tutt,* Chair., Exec. Committee; William J. Hybl,* Chair and C.E.O.; R. Thayer Tutt, Jr.,* Pres. and C.F.O.; Ben S. Wendelken,* V.P.; Robert J. Hilbert, Secy.-Treas.
Trustees:* Karl E. Eitel.
Number of staff: 3 full-time professional; 6 full-time support; 2 part-time support.
Employer Identification Number: 846002373

834
Freeman E. Fairfield - Meeker Charitable Trust
First Interstate Bank of Denver, N.A.
Terminal Annex Box 5825
Denver 80217 (303) 893-2211

Trust established in 1969 in CO.
Donor(s): Freeman E. Fairfield.†
Foundation type: Independent
Financial data (yr. ended 11/30/89): Assets, $2,539,792 (M); expenditures, $210,105, including $156,842 for 10 grants (high: $110,892; low: $300; average: $500) and $30,750 for 61 grants to individuals (high: $750; low: $500; average: $500-$750).
Purpose and activities: Support for higher educational scholarships to Meeker High School graduates; some support for civic organizations.
Types of support: Student aid.
Limitations: Giving limited to Meeker, CO. No grants for building or endowment funds, research, or matching gifts; no loans.
Publications: 990-PF.
Application information:
Initial approach: Letter
Copies of proposal: 1
Deadline(s): None
Board meeting date(s): As required
Write: Randall C. Rieck, V.P. and Trust Officer, First Interstate Bank of Denver, N.A.
Distribution Committee: K. James Cook, Don Hamilton, Rev. Cope Mitchell, Jerry Oldland, C.J. Wilson.
Trustee: First Interstate Bank of Denver, N.A.
Employer Identification Number: 846068906

835
First Fruit, Inc.
7400 West 20th Ave.
Lakewood 80215 (303) 232-4084

Established in 1976 in CA.
Donor(s): Peter M. Ochs, Gail J. Ochs.
Foundation type: Independent
Financial data (yr. ended 12/31/89): Assets, $9,384,158 (M); gifts received, $2,460,000; expenditures, $694,351, including $642,594 for 23 grants (high: $121,410; low: $3,220).
Purpose and activities: Grants are made only to organizations which engage in advancing the Gospel of Jesus Christ. Preference is given to evangelical ministries, usually with strategic pioneering programs among peoples who have not had repeated contact with the Gospel message.
Types of support: General purposes, special projects.
Limitations: No grants to individuals.
Application information: Application form not required.
Initial approach: Proposal
Copies of proposal: 1
Deadline(s): None
Board meeting date(s): At least quarterly, as determined by the board
Write: Dennis W. Thome, Secy.-Treas.
Officers: Peter M. Ochs,* Pres.; Gail J. Ochs,* V.P.; Dennis W. Thome,* Secy.-Treas.
Board Members:* David W. Bennet.
Number of staff: None.
Employer Identification Number: 953081605

836
First Interstate Bank of Denver Foundation
(Formerly First Interstate Bank Foundation)
633 17th St.
Denver 80270 (303) 293-2211

Established in 1982 in CO.
Donor(s): First Interstate Bank of Denver, N.A.
Foundation type: Company-sponsored
Financial data (yr. ended 09/30/88): Assets, $211,954 (M); gifts received, $219,970; expenditures, $261,802, including $255,520 for 48 grants (high: $200,000; low: $50) and $3,235 for 17 employee matching gifts.
Purpose and activities: Support primarily for higher education and social services.
Types of support: Employee matching gifts.
Limitations: Giving primarily in Denver, CO.
Application information: Application form not required.
Initial approach: Proposal
Copies of proposal: 1
Deadline(s): None
Write: Donn Waage, Sr. V.P.
Trustee: First Interstate Bank of Denver, N.A.
Employer Identification Number: 846169845

837
Harmes C. Fishback Foundation Trust
Eight Village Rd.
Englewood 80110 (303) 789-1753

Trust established in 1972 in CO.
Donor(s): Harmes C. Fishback.†
Foundation type: Independent
Financial data (yr. ended 12/31/88): Assets, $1,698,027 (M); expenditures, $93,937,

including $77,800 for 38 grants (high: $10,000; low: $250).
Purpose and activities: Emphasis on higher education, hospitals, medical research, cultural programs, and youth agencies.
Types of support: Capital campaigns, continuing support, endowment funds, program-related investments, scholarship funds.
Limitations: Giving limited to the metropolitan Denver, CO, area. No grants to individuals.
Application information: Application form not required.
Initial approach: Letter
Copies of proposal: 1
Deadline(s): None
Board meeting date(s): Quarterly
Write: Katharine H. Stapleton, Trustee
Trustee: Katharine H. Stapleton.
Employer Identification Number: 846094542

838
Lulu Frankel Foundation ⌑
2800 South University Blvd., No. 147
Denver 80210

Established in 1955 in CO.
Foundation type: Independent
Financial data (yr. ended 12/31/87): Assets, $1,498,330 (M); expenditures, $90,957, including $59,753 for 33 grants (high: $15,000; low: $25).
Purpose and activities: Giving primarily for Jewish welfare and hospitals.
Application information:
Deadline(s): None
Officers: Eugene J. Weisberg, Pres.; Leona G. Frankel, V.P.; Beth Weisberg, Secy.; Marjorie A. Crane, Treas.
Employer Identification Number: 846034580

839
The Frost Foundation, Ltd. ▼
Cherry Creek Plaza II, Suite 205
650 South Cherry St.
Denver 80222 (303) 388-1687

Incorporated in 1959 in LA.
Donor(s): Virginia C. Frost.†
Foundation type: Independent
Financial data (yr. ended 12/31/89): Assets, $22,880,678 (M); qualifying distributions, $1,818,865, including $1,818,865 for 67 grants (high: $180,000; low: $250; average: $5,000-$15,000).
Purpose and activities: Giving primarily for education, including medical education and business administration; grants also for cultural programs, health associations and hospitals, social service and youth organizations, and denominational giving.
Types of support: Seed money, equipment, endowment funds, matching funds, professorships, internships, scholarship funds, fellowships, special projects, research, publications, conferences and seminars, consulting services, technical assistance.
Limitations: No grants to individuals, or for operating expenses or building funds; no loans.
Publications: Annual report (including application guidelines).
Application information: Application form not required.
Initial approach: Telephone or letter
Copies of proposal: 4
Deadline(s): Dec. 1 and July 1
Board meeting date(s): Feb. and Sept.
Final notification: 7 to 10 days
Write: Theodore R. Kauss, Exec. Dir.
Officers: Edwin F. Whited,* Pres.; Theodore R. Kauss, V.P. and Exec. Dir.; Claude G. Rives III,* V.P.; Mitchell R. Woodard, Treas.
Directors:* Dallas P. Dickinson, J. Luther Jordan, Jr., John A. LeVan, John W. Loftus, Taylor F. Moore, Mary Amelia Whited-Howell.
Number of staff: 1 full-time professional; 1 part-time professional; 1 full-time support.
Employer Identification Number: 720520342

840
Gates Foundation ▼
3200 Cherry Creek South Dr., Suite 630
Denver 80209-3247 (303) 722-1881

Incorporated in 1946 in CO.
Donor(s): Charles Gates,† Hazel Gates,† John Gates.†
Foundation type: Independent
Financial data (yr. ended 12/31/88): Assets, $90,800,000 (M); expenditures, $4,628,000, including $3,911,887 for grants (high: $650,000).
Purpose and activities: To promote the health, welfare, and broad education of mankind whether by means of research, grants, publications, the foundation's own agencies and activities, or through cooperation with agencies and institutions already in existence. Grants primarily for education and youth services, including leadership development; public policy; historic preservation, humanities, and cultural affairs; health care, including cost reduction; and human services.
Types of support: Continuing support, building funds, capital campaigns, endowment funds, matching funds, program-related investments, renovation projects, seed money, special projects, equipment, fellowships, general purposes, land acquisition, publications, technical assistance.
Limitations: Giving limited to CO, especially the Denver area, except for foundation-initiated grants. No support for private foundations. No grants to individuals, or for operating budgets, annual campaigns, emergency funds, deficit financing, purchase of tickets for fundraising dinners, parties, balls, or other social fundraising events, research, or scholarships; no loans.
Publications: Annual report, informational brochure (including application guidelines), program policy statement, grants list.
Application information: Application form not required.
Initial approach: Telephone
Copies of proposal: 1
Deadline(s): Jan. 15, Apr. 15, July 15, and Oct. 15
Board meeting date(s): Approximately Apr. 1, June 15, Oct. 1, and Dec. 15
Final notification: 2 weeks following meetings
Write: F. Charles Froelicher, Exec. Dir.
Officers: Charles C. Gates,* Pres.; Brown W. Cannon, Jr.,* V.P.; F. Charles Froelicher, Secy. and Exec. Dir.; T.J. Gibson, Treas.
Trustees:* George B. Beardsley, William W. Grant III, Diane Gates Wallach, Michael Wilfley.
Number of staff: 4 full-time professional; 2 full-time support.
Employer Identification Number: 840474837

841
General Service Foundation ▼
1445 Pearl St., Suite 201
P.O. Box 4659
Boulder 80302 (303) 447-9541

Incorporated in 1946 in IL.
Donor(s): Clifton R. Musser,† Margaret K. Musser.†
Foundation type: Independent
Financial data (yr. ended 12/31/89): Assets, $28,289,056 (M); expenditures, $1,413,290, including $1,183,000 for grants (average: $10,000-$35,000).
Purpose and activities: Major areas of interest include population, resources, and non-military aspects of international peace. Support for experimental, demonstration, or research projects on a national and international level, particularly in Latin America, Mexico, the Caribbean, and other developing areas.
Types of support: Special projects, research, general purposes, seed money.
Limitations: No support for the arts (except through a small discretionary fund). No grants to individuals, or for capital funds, relief, operating budgets, endowments, scholarships, fellowships, matching gifts, or the annual campaigns of established organizations; no loans.
Publications: Annual report (including application guidelines), grants list.
Application information: Application form not required.
Initial approach: Letter or telephone
Copies of proposal: 1
Deadline(s): Mar. 1 and Sept. 1
Board meeting date(s): May and Nov.
Final notification: 6 months
Write: Robert W. Musser, Pres.
Officers and Directors:* Robert W. Musser,* Pres.; Marcie J. Musser,* V.P. and Treas.; Mary L. Estrin,* V.P.; Ruth C. Dingler,* Secy.; Robert L. Estrin, John W. Gardner, John M. Lloyd, Marion M. Lloyd, Anne Firth Murray, Elizabeth W. Musser, John M. Musser, James E. Palm.
Number of staff: 1 part-time support.
Employer Identification Number: 366018535

842
M. B. & Shana Glassman Foundation ⌑
3773 Cherry Creek Dr. North, No. 575
Denver 80209

Established in 1969 in CO.
Donor(s): M.B. Glassman, Shana Glassman.
Foundation type: Independent
Financial data (yr. ended 12/31/88): Assets, $1,338,581 (M); gifts received, $93,000; expenditures, $62,957, including $58,245 for 32 grants (high: $40,000; low: $15).
Purpose and activities: Support primarily for local Jewish giving.
Limitations: Giving primarily in CO.
Application information: Application form not required.
Initial approach: Letter

Deadline(s): None
Write: M.B. Glassman, Pres.
Officers: M.B. Glassman, Pres.; Ken Jackson, V.P.; Shana Glassman, Secy.-Treas.
Employer Identification Number: 237038717

843
Goodwin Foundation
Box 3806
Grand Junction 81502-3806

Established in 1951 in CO.
Foundation type: Independent
Financial data (yr. ended 10/31/89): Assets, $1,300,798 (M); expenditures, $81,807, including $70,028 for 10 grants (high: $25,000; low: $500; average: $500-$25,000).
Purpose and activities: Support for hospitals, health and social services, the arts, museums, music, community development, medical sciences, and the environment.
Types of support: Building funds.
Limitations: Giving primarily in Grand Junction, CO.
Publications: Annual report.
Application information:
Initial approach: Letter
Copies of proposal: 1
Deadline(s): None
Board meeting date(s): Feb., Apr., Aug., and Oct.
Officer and Trustees:* William M. Ela,* Chair.; Herbert L. Bacon, Ruth H. Gormley.
Number of staff: None.
Employer Identification Number: 846036758

844
Will E. Heginbotham Trust ⌑
P.O. Box 245
Holyoke 80734-0245 (303) 854-2611

Trust established in 1968 in CO.
Donor(s): Will E. Heginbotham.†
Foundation type: Independent
Financial data (yr. ended 12/31/87): Assets, $4,282,469 (M); expenditures, $341,559, including $317,292 for 16 grants (high: $100,660; low: $1,272).
Purpose and activities: Giving for public schools, recreation, hospitals, and community development.
Types of support: Building funds, equipment.
Limitations: Giving primarily in Phillips County, CO.
Application information: Application form not required.
Deadline(s): None
Write: Dave Colver, Trustee
Trustees: Ted Clark, Dave Colver, Josephine McWilliams, Glen E. Stenson.
Employer Identification Number: 846053496

845
Hewit Family Foundation ⌑
621 17th St., Suite 2555
Denver 80293

Established in 1985 in CO.
Donor(s): Members of the Hewit family.
Foundation type: Independent
Financial data (yr. ended 11/30/89): Assets, $1,940,392 (M); gifts received, $600,000; expenditures, $94,340, including $90,000 for 11 grants (high: $10,000; low: $5,000).
Purpose and activities: Support primarily for health, youth organizations, social services, a natural history museum and a zoo.
Limitations: Giving primarily in Denver, CO. No grants to individuals.
Application information:
Initial approach: Letter
Deadline(s): None
Write: William D. Hewit, Pres.
Officers: William D. Hewit, Pres. and Treas.; Betty Ruth Hewit, V.P. and Secy.; Christie F. Hewit, V.P.; William E. Hewit, V.P.
Employer Identification Number: 742397040

846
Hill Foundation ▼
c/o Kutak, Rock & Campbell
2400 Arco Tower, 707 17th St.
Denver 80202 (303) 297-2400
Additional address: First Interstate Bank of Denver, Terminal Annex, Box 5825, Denver, CO 80217

Trust established in 1955 in CO.
Donor(s): Virginia W. Hill.†
Foundation type: Independent
Financial data (yr. ended 4/30/89): Assets, $8,337,908 (M); expenditures, $581,385, including $385,900 for 40 grants (high: $35,000; low: $500; average: $10,000-$15,000).
Purpose and activities: Grants largely for health care for the medically indigent, higher education, services for the elderly, and cultural programs; support also for social service agencies and the disabled.
Types of support: Scholarship funds, matching funds, special projects.
Limitations: Giving primarily in CO and WY. No grants to individuals, or for capital improvements other than equipment acquisition for health care and related purposes.
Publications: Program policy statement.
Application information: Beginning 1988, grants only to qualified charitable organizations from which the foundation will have first requested a proposal or which have been selected by the foundation to carry out one of its specific objectives. Applications not accepted.
Initial approach: Trustees initiate proposals
Write: John R. Moran, Jr., Trustee
Trustees: Francis W. Collopy, John R. Moran, Jr., First Interstate Bank of Denver, N.A.
Number of staff: None.
Employer Identification Number: 846081879

847
Jack Hogan Charitable Foundation ⌑
1780 South Bellaire, Suite 613
Denver 80222 (303) 758-2460

Established in 1978 in CO.
Donor(s): O.T. Hogan Family Foundation.
Foundation type: Independent
Financial data (yr. ended 11/30/89): Assets, $1,426,783 (M); expenditures, $134,069, including $85,000 for 14 grants (high: $75,000; low: $500).
Purpose and activities: Giving for legal systematic strategies relating to at-risk youth.
Types of support: Operating budgets, program-related investments.
Limitations: Giving primarily in the Denver, CO, metropolitan area.
Application information: Application form required.
Deadline(s): July 31
Write: Richard J. Callahan, V.P.
Officers and Directors:* Jack D. Hogan,* Pres. and Treas.; Richard J. Callahan,* V.P. and Secy.; Mary Kaye Hogan,* V.P.
Employer Identification Number: 840776608

848
Mabel Y. Hughes Charitable Trust ⌑
c/o The First Interstate Bank of Denver, N.A.
P.O. Box 5825 TA
Denver 80217 (303) 293-5324

Trust established in 1969 in CO.
Donor(s): Mabel Y. Hughes.†
Foundation type: Independent
Financial data (yr. ended 8/31/88): Assets, $6,475,828 (M); expenditures, $416,934, including $345,246 for 38 grants (high: $40,000; low: $246).
Purpose and activities: Emphasis on hospitals, education, museums, and community funds.
Types of support: Operating budgets, continuing support, annual campaigns, seed money, emergency funds, building funds, equipment, endowment funds, research, special projects.
Limitations: Giving limited to CO, with emphasis on the Denver area. No grants to individuals, or for deficit financing, scholarships, or fellowships; no loans.
Publications: Application guidelines, 990-PF.
Application information: Application form not required.
Initial approach: Letter
Copies of proposal: 1
Deadline(s): None
Board meeting date(s): Dec.
Write: Yvonne J. Baca, V.P., The First Interstate Bank of Denver, N.A.
Trustees: Eugene H. Adams, First Interstate Bank of Denver, N.A.
Number of staff: None.
Employer Identification Number: 846070398

849
The Humphreys Foundation ⌑
555 17th St., Suite 2900
Denver 80202-3929 (303) 295-8065

Established in 1922 in CO.
Foundation type: Independent
Financial data (yr. ended 12/31/88): Assets, $1,180,647 (M); expenditures, $73,273, including $61,500 for 28 grants (high: $13,500; low: $500).
Purpose and activities: Support for educational institutions; health and social services, including an organization involved in family planning; and museums and other cultural programs.
Types of support: Operating budgets, general purposes.
Limitations: Giving primarily in CO.
Application information: Application form not required.
Initial approach: Letter

Copies of proposal: 1
Deadline(s): Oct. 1
Board meeting date(s): Semi-annually
Write: Janet Stork
Officers and Directors: Stephen H. Hart, Pres.; Claude M. Maer, Jr., V.P.; Karen Sweeney, Secy.-Treas.
Number of staff: 1
Employer Identification Number: 846021274

850
A. V. Hunter Trust, Inc.
633 Seventeenth St., Suite 1780
Denver 80202 (303) 292-2048

Trust established in 1927; incorporated in 1937 in CO.
Donor(s): A.V. Hunter.†
Foundation type: Independent
Financial data (yr. ended 12/31/89): Assets, $25,839,696 (M); expenditures, $919,757, including $861,000 for 77 grants (high: $75,000; low: $1,000; average: $5,000-$15,000) and $58,757 for grants to individuals.
Purpose and activities: Distributions to give aid, comfort, support, or assistance to children or aged persons or indigent adults, crippled, maimed or needy, through charitable organizations rendering such aid to persons in the categories named; no direct grants to individuals.
Types of support: General purposes, operating budgets.
Limitations: Giving limited to CO, with emphasis on Denver. No support for tax-supported institutions. No grants for scholarships, capital improvements, or acquisitions; no loans.
Publications: Annual report, informational brochure, application guidelines.
Application information: Application form required for grants to individuals. Application form not required.
Initial approach: Letter
Copies of proposal: 1
Deadline(s): Mar. 1, July 1 and Oct. 1
Board meeting date(s): Apr., Aug., and Nov. and as required
Final notification: Within 20 days after meeting
Write: Sharon Holt, Secy.
Officers: W. Robert Alexander,* Pres.; Allan B. Adams,* V.P.; Sharon Holt, Secy.; Mary Anstine,* Treas.
Trustees:* William K. Coors, George Gibson.
Number of staff: 2 full-time professional.
Employer Identification Number: 840461332

851
Alice N. Jenkins Foundation ⌑
881 Rockway Place
Boulder 80303

Foundation type: Operating
Financial data (yr. ended 9/30/88): Assets, $1,244,443 (M); expenditures, $92,075, including $55,000 for 17 grants (high: $8,000; low: $1,000).
Purpose and activities: To care for and provide shelter for stranded and abandoned domestic and wild animals and fowl, and to protect wildlife.
Limitations: Giving primarily in CO.
Application information:
Initial approach: Letter
Deadline(s): None
Write: Trustees
Trustees: E.W. Gustafson, Betty Lewis, C.M. Reese, W. Reese.
Employer Identification Number: 840811678

852
The JFM Foundation ⌑
P.O. Box 5083
Denver 80217 (303) 832-3131

Established in 1980 in CO.
Donor(s): Frederick R. Mayer.
Foundation type: Independent
Financial data (yr. ended 11/30/89): Assets, $2,956 (M); gifts received, $681,850; expenditures, $723,303, including $711,481 for 31 grants (high: $250,000; low: $300).
Purpose and activities: Support for innovative approaches towards emerging social issues, and towards community service projects focused upon children and youth, and the educational, transportation, and legal systems; grants for the cultural areas of the visual arts, nautical archaeology, and Isthmanian Pre-Columbian art and archaeology.
Types of support: Matching funds, special projects, seed money.
Limitations: Giving limited to CO for community projects and social issues; cultural programs having national or international significance are considered. No support for medical or health-related fields or religious organizations for religious purposes. No grants to individuals, or for endowments, deficit financing, fundraising, or basic research.
Publications: Application guidelines.
Application information:
Initial approach: Letter, and concept paper of no more than 2 pages
Copies of proposal: 3
Deadline(s): None
Write: Loretta Roulier
Officers: Frederick R. Mayer, Pres.; Jan Perry Mayer, V.P. and Secy.-Treas.
Directors: Anthony R. Mayer, Frederick M. Mayer.
Employer Identification Number: 840833163

853
Helen K. and Arthur E. Johnson Foundation ▼
1700 Broadway, Rm. 2302
Denver 80290 (303) 861-4127

Incorporated in 1948 in CO.
Donor(s): Arthur E. Johnson,† Helen K. Johnson.†
Foundation type: Independent
Financial data (yr. ended 12/31/88): Assets, $68,112,202 (M); expenditures, $3,729,012, including $2,897,029 for 111 grants (high: $250,000; low: $100; average: $5,000-$30,000).
Purpose and activities: "To solve human problems and enrich the quality of human life." Emphasis on operational and capital support for community and social services, education, youth, health, and civic and cultural affairs.
Types of support: Operating budgets, building funds, general purposes, equipment, scholarship funds, continuing support, annual campaigns, seed money, land acquisition, research, technical assistance, matching funds, special projects, renovation projects, capital campaigns.
Limitations: Giving limited to CO. No grants to individuals, or for endowment funds, conferences, or purchase of blocks of tickets; no loans.
Publications: Annual report (including application guidelines).
Application information: Application form not required.
Initial approach: Letter or proposal
Copies of proposal: 1
Deadline(s): Jan. 1, Apr. 1, July 1, and Sept. 1
Board meeting date(s): Apr., July, Oct., and Dec.
Final notification: 2 weeks after board meeting
Write: Stan Kamprath, Exec. Dir.
Officers: Mrs. James R. Hartley,* Pres.; David R. Murphy,* V.P. and Treas.; Stan Kamprath, V.P. and Exec. Dir.; Gerald R. Hillyard, Jr.,* Secy.
Trustees:* Lynn H. Campion, Thomas B. Campion, Ralph W. Collins, William H. Kistler, Roger D. Knight, Jr., J. Churchill Owen.
Number of staff: 1 full-time professional; 1 full-time support; 2 part-time support.
Employer Identification Number: 846020702

854
Joslin-Needham Family Foundation ⌑
c/o Farmers State Bank
200 Clayton St.
Brush 80723 (303) 842-5101

Donor(s): Gladys Joslin.†
Foundation type: Independent
Financial data (yr. ended 12/31/88): Assets, $2,854,742 (M); expenditures, $146,125, including $123,650 for 15 grants (high: $60,000; low: $300).
Purpose and activities: Giving for community development and social services; grants also for a library.
Limitations: Giving primarily in the Brush, CO, area.
Application information: Application form not required.
Initial approach: Letter
Deadline(s): None
Write: Judy Gunnon, Exec. Secy.
Officer: Judy Gunnon, Exec. Secy.
Directors: Robert U. Hansen, Robert Petteys, Helen Watrous.
Trustee: Farmers State Bank.
Employer Identification Number: 846038670

855
The Carl W. and Carrie Mae Joslyn Charitable Trust ⌑
c/o First National Bank of Colorado Springs
P.O. Box 1699
Colorado Springs 80942 (719) 471-4990

Trust established in 1971.
Donor(s): Carl W. Joslyn,† Carrie Mae Joslyn.†
Foundation type: Independent

Financial data (yr. ended 12/31/88): Assets, $1,464,494 (M); expenditures, $156,778, including $146,200 for 47 grants (high: $15,900; low: $300; average: $3,000).
Purpose and activities: Emphasis on aid to the elderly and the handicapped, particularly the blind, including education and rehabilitation programs, and on youth agencies.
Types of support: Operating budgets, annual campaigns, building funds, equipment, special projects, endowment funds.
Limitations: Giving limited to El Paso County, CO. No grants to individuals, or for research, scholarships, fellowships, or matching gifts; no loans.
Publications: Application guidelines, 990-PF.
Application information: Application form not required.
Initial approach: Letter
Copies of proposal: 1
Deadline(s): Submit proposal preferably in Apr. or Oct.; deadlines Apr. 30 and Oct. 31
Board meeting date(s): May and Nov.
Final notification: July 1 and Dec. 1
Write: Richard J. Banaszak, V.P., First National Bank of Colorado Springs
Trustee: The First National Bank of Colorado Springs.
Number of staff: None.
Employer Identification Number: 237135817

856
Kejr Foundation, Inc. ⌘
P.O. Box 264
Woodrow 80757
Application address: 6500 Xerxes Ave. South, Minneapolis, MN 55423; Tel.: (612) 920-0574

Incorporated in 1959 in CO.
Donor(s): Joseph Kejr,† Mary Kejr, Kejr Trust, Kejr Family Foundation of Brookville, Kansas, and others.
Foundation type: Independent
Financial data (yr. ended 12/31/88): Assets, $2,064,957 (M); gifts received, $37,437; expenditures, $190,342, including $122,750 for 26 grants (high: $19,750; low: $500) and $48,000 for 2 foundation-administered programs.
Purpose and activities: Support of interdenominational, evangelical religious programs, including radio broadcasting, church extension, and missionary projects. The foundation also sponsors a consultation and evaluation service and a retreat facility for church and educational personnel.
Types of support: Conferences and seminars.
Application information: Application form required.
Deadline(s): None
Write: Spencer Bower, Admin. Asst.
Officers and Trustees: Harry J. Kejr, Pres.; Frank G. Kejr, Secy.-Treas.
Employer Identification Number: 846023358

857
Kitzmiller-Bales Trust
P.O. Box 96
Wray 80758 (303) 332-4824

Established in 1984 in CO.
Donor(s): Edna B. Kitzmiller.†
Foundation type: Independent
Financial data (yr. ended 12/31/88): Assets, $4,803,412 (M); expenditures, $263,982, including $254,698 for 7 grants (high: $150,000; low: $1,752).
Purpose and activities: Giving to civic institutions, including hospitals, and a school district.
Types of support: Building funds, capital campaigns, equipment, matching funds.
Limitations: Giving limited to projects benefiting the area of East Yuma County School District, RJ-2, CO.
Application information: Application form not required.
Initial approach: Letter
Copies of proposal: 1
Deadline(s): None
Board meeting date(s): Monthly
Final notification: Following board meetings
Write: Robert U. Hansen, Trustee
Trustees: Duard Fix, Robert U. Hansen, Farmers State Bank, Brush.
Employer Identification Number: 846178085

858
The Raphael Levy Memorial Foundation, Inc.
401 South Buckley Rd.
Aurora 80017 (303) 695-7979

Incorporated in 1944 in CO.
Donor(s): Edward Levy, Hannah Levy,† Jack H. Levy,† Fashion Bar, Inc.
Foundation type: Independent
Financial data (yr. ended 12/31/88): Assets, $1,507,531 (M); expenditures, $261,497, including $220,625 for 78 grants (high: $50,000; low: $100).
Purpose and activities: Giving for hospitals and Jewish welfare funds; support also for higher education, the environment, health associations, and community funds.
Limitations: Giving primarily in CO.
Application information: Application form not required.
Copies of proposal: 1
Deadline(s): None
Board meeting date(s): As required
Write: Edward Levy, Pres.
Officers and Directors: Edward Levy, Pres.; Robert Levy, V.P.; Barbara Goldburg, Secy.; John Levy, Treas.
Number of staff: 1 full-time support; 1 part-time support.
Employer Identification Number: 846022586

859
Lowe Foundation
Colorado Judicial Ctr.
Two East 14th Ave.
Denver 80203 (303) 837-3750

Incorporated in 1960 in CO.
Donor(s): John G. Lowe,† Edith Eaton Lowe.†
Foundation type: Independent
Financial data (yr. ended 11/30/89): Assets, $3,355,000 (M); expenditures, $135,371, including $129,500 for 22 grants (high: $14,000; low: $1,500; average: $6,000).
Purpose and activities: Grants to organizations involved in the treatment and teaching of the mentally retarded and victims of cerebral palsy and research in these areas.
Types of support: Building funds, equipment, general purposes, operating budgets, program-related investments, seed money.
Limitations: Giving primarily in CO. No grants to individuals, or for endowment funds.
Publications: 990-PF, application guidelines, annual report.
Application information: Application form not required.
Initial approach: Letter
Copies of proposal: 5
Deadline(s): Submit proposal preferably in Jan.; deadline Feb. 1
Board meeting date(s): Mar. and Nov.
Write: Luis D. Rovira, Pres.
Officer and Trustees:* Luis D. Rovira,* Pres.; Donald E. Burton, Robert P. Harvey, Richard I. Kaye.
Number of staff: None.
Employer Identification Number: 846021560

860
Maki Foundation
421D Aspen Airport Business Ctr.
Aspen 81611 (303) 925-3272

Established in 1980 in CO.
Foundation type: Independent
Financial data (yr. ended 12/31/88): Assets, $1,061,375 (M); expenditures, $66,187, including $40,500 for 12 grants (high: $5,000; low: $1,000).
Purpose and activities: Support primarily for environmental protection efforts and conservation education.
Types of support: General purposes, special projects.
Limitations: Giving primarily in the Rocky Mountain region.
Publications: Application guidelines.
Application information: Application form not required.
Initial approach: Letter
Copies of proposal: 1
Deadline(s): June 30
Board meeting date(s): July
Final notification: Aug. 15
Write: Patricia Humphry
Directors: Ruth Adams, Ann Harvey, Constance Harvey.
Number of staff: 1
Employer Identification Number: 840836242

861
Margulf Foundation Inc. ⌘
616 East Hyman Ave., Suite 2-D
Aspen 81611

Established in 1977 in NY and DE.
Donor(s): Martin Flug, James Flug, Robert Flug.
Foundation type: Independent
Financial data (yr. ended 11/30/88): Assets, $2,797,993 (M); gifts received, $126,000; expenditures, $152,148, including $145,000 for 7 grants (high: $50,000; low: $5,000).
Purpose and activities: Grants for higher and secondary education, social services, and culture; support also for Jewish welfare.
Types of support: General purposes.

Application information: Contributes only to pre-selected organizations. Applications not accepted.
Officer and Directors: Martin Flug, Pres.; Ernest Rubenstein.
Employer Identification Number: 132927245

862
The McCoy Foundation ⌑
5040 Lyda Ln.
Colorado Springs 80904

Established in 1979.
Donor(s): Arthur H. McCoy.
Foundation type: Independent
Financial data (yr. ended 11/30/88): Assets, $1,895,573 (M); expenditures, $194,966, including $171,500 for 12 grants (high: $75,000; low: $2,000; average: $5,000-$20,000).
Purpose and activities: Grants for cultural programs, including music, and for hospitals and a university.
Application information: Application form required.
Initial approach: Proposal
Final notification: 2 to 3 months
Write: Arthur H. McCoy, Pres.
Officers: Arthur H. McCoy, Pres. and Treas.; Barbara M. Gartner, V.P.; Craig W. McCoy, V.P.; Virginia G. McCoy, Secy.
Employer Identification Number: 840802889

863
The McHugh Family Foundation ⌑
650 South Cherry St., Suite 1225
Denver 80222 (303) 321-2111

Established in 1980 in CO.
Donor(s): Jerome P. McHugh, Anabel C. McHugh, Kindermac Partnership.
Foundation type: Independent
Financial data (yr. ended 11/30/89): Assets, $1,339,912 (M); gifts received, $107,960; expenditures, $147,968, including $133,900 for 41 grants (high: $25,000; low: $100).
Purpose and activities: Giving primarily for education, including higher education, social services, and cultural programs.
Limitations: Giving primarily in Denver, CO. No grants to individuals.
Application information: Generally does not accept unsolicited applications.
Initial approach: Proposal
Deadline(s): None
Write: Jerome P. McHugh, Pres.
Officers and Directors:* Jerome P. McHugh,* Pres.; Anabel C. McHugh,* V.P.; Paul D. Holleman, Secy.; Jerome P. McHugh, Jr.,* Treas.; June McHugh Fisher, Erin McHugh Gogolak, Hover T. Lentz, Christopher R. McHugh, Malcolm Burke McHugh.
Employer Identification Number: 742131272

864
Milheim Foundation ☆
c/o Colorado National Bank Denver
P.O. Box 5168-TA
Denver 80217 (303) 893-1862

Established in 1987 in CO.
Donor(s): Clara Wheeler.†
Foundation type: Independent
Financial data (yr. ended 12/31/88): Assets, $1,866,141 (M); expenditures, $210,808, including $173,491 for 26 grants to individuals (high: $9,888; low: $1,584).
Purpose and activities: Awards grants for research for the prevention, treatment, or cure of cancer.
Types of support: Grants to individuals.
Limitations: No grants for travel to meetings or presentation of papers.
Application information: Application form required.
Initial approach: Letter
Copies of proposal: 6
Deadline(s): Mar. 15
Board meeting date(s): May
Final notification: May
Write: Margaret Armstrong, Trust Officer, Colorado National Bank Denver
Advisory Board: Norman Aarstad, M.D., John Cohen, M.D., Paul K. Hamilton, Jr., M.D., R. Lee Jennings, M.D., Francis J. Major, M.D., Walden K. Roberts, M.D.
Trustee: Colorado National Bank.
Number of staff: None.
Employer Identification Number: 846018431

865
Monfort Charitable Foundation
804 7th St.
Greeley 80632
Application address: 825 North County Line Rd., Berthoud, CO 80513; Tel.: (303) 352-9469

Established in 1970.
Foundation type: Independent
Financial data (yr. ended 12/31/89): Assets, $11,323,080 (M); gifts received, $2,700,000; expenditures, $414,218, including $395,614 for 31 grants (high: $154,098; low: $200).
Purpose and activities: Giving primarily to community funds, cancer research, and cultural programs, including the performing arts.
Limitations: Giving limited to CO, KS, and NE. No grants to individuals.
Publications: 990-PF.
Application information: Application form not required.
Deadline(s): None
Write: Kaye C. Montera, Secy.-Treas.
Officers: Kenneth W. Monfort, Pres.; Kyle Futo, V.P.; Kaye C. Montera, Secy.-Treas.
Number of staff: None.
Employer Identification Number: 237068253

866
Pauline A. and George R. Morrison Charitable Trust ⌑
1801 York St.
Denver 80206

Established in 1980 in CO.
Donor(s): George R. Morrison.
Foundation type: Independent
Financial data (yr. ended 11/30/89): Assets, $6,457,952 (M); expenditures, $377,026, including $284,261 for 5 grants (high: $100,000; low: $25,000).
Purpose and activities: Support primarily for a natural history museum; support also for parks and recreation.
Types of support: Building funds.
Limitations: Giving primarily in CO. No grants for general operating costs.
Application information:
Initial approach: Proposal
Deadline(s): None
Board meeting date(s): Monthly
Write: Robert D. Ibbotson, Chair.
Officer and Trustees:* Robert D. Ibbotson,* Chair.; Robert W. Findlay, L. Douglas Hoyt, Jerry I. Maine.
Employer Identification Number: 846166335

867
The J. K. Mullen Foundation ⌑
(Formerly The John K. and Catherine S. Mullen Benevolent Corporation)
1640 Logan St.
Denver 80203 (303) 893-3151

Incorporated in 1924 in CO.
Donor(s): John K. Mullen,† Catherine S. Mullen,† The J.K. Mullen Co.
Foundation type: Independent
Financial data (yr. ended 7/31/88): Assets, $3,953,468 (M); expenditures, $296,712, including $252,100 for 36 grants (high: $25,000; low: $2,000).
Purpose and activities: Support primarily for higher and secondary education and hospitals, with emphasis on Roman Catholic church-affiliated organizations.
Limitations: Giving primarily in Denver, CO. No grants to individuals.
Application information:
Initial approach: Letter
Copies of proposal: 1
Deadline(s): Sept. 1
Board meeting date(s): Annually and as required
Write: John F. Malo, Secy.
Officers and Directors: J. Kernan Weckbaugh, Pres.; John K. Weckbaugh, V.P.; John F. Malo, Secy.; Walter S. Weckbaugh, Treas.; Timothy M. O'Connor, Edith M. Roberts, Sheila Sevier.
Employer Identification Number: 846002475

868
The Needmor Fund ▼
1730 15th St.
Boulder 80302 (303) 449-5801

Trust established in 1956 in OH.
Donor(s): Members of the Stranahan family.
Foundation type: Independent
Financial data (yr. ended 12/31/88): Assets, $6,863,287 (M); gifts received, $2,240,624; expenditures, $1,608,166, including $1,390,455 for 283 grants (high: $50,000; low: $100; average: $5,000-$25,000).
Purpose and activities: Primary interest is to assist groups of people working together to overcome problems: those forces and events which have an adverse and profound effect upon their lives as individuals, as families, and as members of a community. Emphasis on grassroots, member-controlled organizations capable of setting out and implementing realistic strategies and goals. There are no specific areas of concern; preference is given to organizations representing traditionally disenfranchised populations.

Types of support: Seed money, technical assistance, general purposes, special projects, operating budgets.
Limitations: No grants to individuals, or for capital or endowment funds, scholarships, fellowships, matching gifts, deficit financing, or operating support for traditional community services, replacement of lost government funding, land acquisition, purchase of buildings or equipment, or publications, media, computer projects or research; no loans.
Publications: Program policy statement, application guidelines, grants list.
Application information: Application form required.
Initial approach: Letter or telephone
Copies of proposal: 1
Deadline(s): Jan. 10 and July 10
Board meeting date(s): May and Nov.
Final notification: 2 weeks after board meeting
Write: Dinny Stranahan, Coord.
Advisory Committee: Mary Bradshaw, Page Howald, Frances W.S. Parry, Scott Parry, Abbot Stranahan, Ann Stranahan, Brie Stranahan, Duane Stranahan, Eileen B. Stranahan, George S. Stranahan, Josh Stranahan, Linda Stranahan, Mary C. Stranahan, Michael Stranahan, Molly Stranahan, Patricia Q. Stranahan, Patrick Stranahan, Sarah S. Stranahan, Stephen Stranahan, Stuart Stranahan, Virginia Stranahan.
Trustee: The Toledo Trust Co.
Number of staff: 4 full-time professional.
Employer Identification Number: 346504812

869
New Early Christian Church-Charities
8840 Coalton Dr.
Louisville 820027
Application address: P.O. Box 8289, Denver, CO 80201

Established in 1981 in CO.
Foundation type: Independent
Financial data (yr. ended 12/31/88): Assets, $1,212,727 (M); expenditures, $68,956, including $52,598 for 6 grants (high: $18,598; low: $2,000).
Purpose and activities: Grants for religious welfare and social services, church support, and youth and child development programs.
Types of support: General purposes.
Limitations: No grants for research, long-term operating budgets, building fund campaigns, endowments, or deficit financing.
Publications: Annual report.
Application information: Application form required.
Initial approach: Proposal
Copies of proposal: 1
Deadline(s): July 1
Board meeting date(s): Fall
Final notification: Fall
Write: Lois A. Gambell, Chair., Grants Comm.
Officers: Peter A. Stelljes, Pres.; Bruce Gambell, V.P.; Ida E. Price, Secy.; Charles Dohnalek, Treas.
Grants Committee: Lois A. Gambell, Chair.; Ellen Ann Dunham, James H. Morris, Susan E. Patterson, Claudia J. Piper, Andrew Price.
Number of staff: None.
Employer Identification Number: 221487262

870
The Aksel Nielsen Foundation ⌑
Three Melody Ln.
Parker 80134-8631

Established in 1956 in CO.
Foundation type: Independent
Financial data (yr. ended 12/31/88): Assets, $1,394,821 (M); expenditures, $89,144, including $70,000 for 14 grants (high: $12,000; low: $500).
Purpose and activities: Support primarily for cultural programs, museums, and general charitable giving.
Application information:
Initial approach: Letter
Deadline(s): None
Write: Virginia N. Muse, Pres.
Officers and Trustees: Virginia N. Muse, Pres.; Judith M. Pemstein, V.P.; Jack M. Muse, Secy.-Treas.
Employer Identification Number: 846025711

871
Carl A. Norgren Foundation
2696 South Colorado Blvd., No. 585
Denver 80222 (303) 758-8393

Incorporated in 1951 in CO.
Donor(s): Carl A. Norgren,† Juliet E. Norgren,† C.A. Norgren Co.
Foundation type: Independent
Financial data (yr. ended 12/31/88): Assets, $3,052,078 (M); expenditures, $267,380, including $225,365 for 94 grants (high: $18,250; low: $90; average: $500-$2,000).
Purpose and activities: Support primarily limited to activities in which the board has a direct interest; support for education, health and hospitals, museums, community funds, and social service and youth agencies.
Types of support: General purposes, annual campaigns, emergency funds, building funds, equipment, land acquisition, matching funds, capital campaigns.
Limitations: Giving limited to the metropolitan Denver, CO, area. No grants to individuals, or for endowment funds, research, scholarships, or fellowships; no loans.
Publications: Annual report (including application guidelines).
Application information: Application form not required.
Initial approach: Letter
Copies of proposal: 1
Deadline(s): None
Board meeting date(s): June and Dec.
Write: Mr. Leigh H. Norgren, Pres.
Officers and Directors:* Leigh H. Norgren,* Pres.; Gene N. Koelbel,* Secy.; C. Neil Norgren, Donald K. Norgren, Vanda N. Werner.
Number of staff: None.
Employer Identification Number: 846034195

872
Nutrition Camp School Foundation, Inc. ⌑
1320 East Cache La Poudre
Colorado Springs 80909 (719) 632-1335

Established in 1963 in CO.
Foundation type: Independent
Financial data (yr. ended 09/30/89): Assets, $1,070,475 (M); gifts received, $6,712; expenditures, $74,044, including $61,335 for 22 grants (high: $7,000; low: $325).
Purpose and activities: Giving primarily to programs that support children's education and health programs.
Limitations: Giving limited to CO, especially the Pikes Peak area.
Application information:
Initial approach: Letter
Deadline(s): None
Write: Karen Reinking, Treas.
Officers and Trustees:* Mrs. Frank Forman,* Pres.; Karen Reinking,* Treas.; Mrs. Peter King, Jr.
Employer Identification Number: 840420204

873
Martin J. and Mary Anne O'Fallon Trust
2800 South University Blvd., Rm. 61
Denver 80210 (303) 753-1727

Trust established in 1951 in CO.
Donor(s): Martin J. O'Fallon.†
Foundation type: Independent
Financial data (yr. ended 12/31/88): Assets, $2,344,372 (M); expenditures, $152,560, including $119,425 for 24 grants (high: $15,000; low: $125; average: $2,000-$5,000).
Purpose and activities: Grants to established organizations and agencies to assist cultural programs and social and educational services; limited support for health.
Types of support: Building funds, equipment, special projects, capital campaigns, technical assistance.
Limitations: Giving limited to CO; priority always given to Denver. No grants to individuals, or for endowment funds, seed money, research, scholarships, travel, fellowships, annual campaigns, or operating support; no loans.
Publications: Annual report (including application guidelines).
Application information: Grant applications from agencies outside CO not accepted. Application form required.
Initial approach: Letter
Copies of proposal: 1
Deadline(s): Submit proposal preferably between May and Aug.
Board meeting date(s): Feb., Aug., Sept., and Nov., and monthly for other trust business
Final notification: Dec.
Write: Alfred O'Meara, Jr., Chair.
Officers and Trustees:* Alfred O'Meara, Jr.,* Chair.; Margaret H. Carey,* Secy.; Patrick E. Purcell,* Treas.; Brian O'Meara.
Number of staff: 1 part-time professional.
Employer Identification Number: 840415830

874
The Jack Petteys Memorial Foundation ⌑
P.O. Box 324
Brush 80723 (303) 573-5860

Established about 1943 in CO.
Foundation type: Independent
Financial data (yr. ended 12/31/88): Assets, $2,532,702 (M); expenditures, $122,354, including $108,889 for 39 grants (high: $12,584; low: $100).

Purpose and activities: Scholarships made to colleges; support also for hospitals, civic projects, and churches.
Types of support: Scholarship funds.
Limitations: Giving limited to northeastern CO.
Application information:
Initial approach: Letter
Copies of proposal: 1
Deadline(s): Submit proposal in Oct. and Nov.; deadline Dec. 1
Board meeting date(s): Monthly
Write: Mrs. Robert Gunnon
Directors: Robert U. Hansen, Robert A. Petteys, Helen C. Watrous.
Trustee: Farmers State Bank.
Employer Identification Number: 846036239

875
Pilot Trust
c/o United Bank of Boulder, N.A., Asset Management Dept.
P.O. Box 227
Boulder 80306 (303) 442-0351

Trust established in 1960 in CO.
Donor(s): Roger Calvert.†
Foundation type: Independent
Financial data (yr. ended 12/31/88): Assets, $3,826,854 (M); expenditures, $230,120, including $179,000 for 11 grants (high: $151,500; low: $1,000).
Purpose and activities: Grants are usually on matching basis for use at foundation's own outdoor educational facility, Cal-Wood Environmental Education Resource Center, which provides opportunities for environmental education for persons generally lacking access to nature and outdoor experiences, and to groups using it.
Types of support: Matching funds.
Limitations: Giving primarily in Boulder County, CO. No grants for any purposes except those stated; no loans.
Application information:
Initial approach: Letter
Copies of proposal: 1
Deadline(s): None
Board meeting date(s): Semiannually
Write: Dr. David M. Knotts, Exec. Dir.
Trustees: Dan Calvert, Richard Meekley, Lawrence M. Wood, United Bank of Boulder, N.A.
Number of staff: 1 full-time professional.
Employer Identification Number: 846030136

876
The Pioneer Fund ⌑
1801 California St., Suite 4500
Denver 80202

Established in 1960 in IL.
Donor(s): Helen M. McLoraine.
Foundation type: Independent
Financial data (yr. ended 12/31/88): Assets, $6,248,105 (M); gifts received, $986,500; expenditures, $13,325, including $4,000 for 5 grants (high: $1,000; low: $500).
Purpose and activities: Support for hospitals, health services, and higher education.
Types of support: General purposes.
Limitations: Giving primarily in IL, with emphasis on Chicago.
Application information: Contributes only to pre-selected organizations. Applications not accepted.
Officers: Helen M. McLoraine, Pres. and Treas.; Robert T. Birdsong, V.P.; Robert Anderson, Secy.
Employer Identification Number: 366108943

877
The Piton Foundation ▼
Kittredge Bldg.
511 16th St., Suite 700
Denver 80202 (303) 825-6246

Incorporated in 1976 in CO.
Donor(s): Samuel Gary, Gary Williams Co.
Foundation type: Independent
Financial data (yr. ended 11/30/89): Assets, $4,395,324 (M); gifts received, $1,490,900; expenditures, $3,018,911, including $1,227,877 for 64 grants (high: $95,000; low: $1,000; average: $100-$95,000), $25,000 for 40 grants to individuals (high: $2,000; low: $300; average: $300-$2,000), $281,491 for 4 foundation-administered programs and $369,000 for loans.
Purpose and activities: To encourage personal effort toward self-realization, to promote the development of strong cooperative relationships between the public and private sectors with emphasis on local involvement, and to improve conditions and opportunities for persons inadequately served by the institutions of society. Almost exclusively local giving, especially for children, youth, families, and community development, especially housing and economic development; support to individual volunteer agencies to encourage improved management and service effectiveness; some giving also for civic, conservation, cultural, educational, and health programs.
Types of support: Operating budgets, seed money, technical assistance, program-related investments, student aid, renovation projects.
Limitations: Giving primarily in CO, with emphasis on the Denver metropolitan area. No grants for basic research, long-range support, debt reduction, building or endowment funds, or media projects.
Publications: Biennial report (including application guidelines), program policy statement.
Application information: Application form not required.
Initial approach: Letter
Copies of proposal: 1
Deadline(s): Jan. 15, Apr. 15, July 15, and Oct. 15 for Community Development Project; none for Grant Program
Board meeting date(s): As required
Final notification: Approximately 4 months for Grant Program; Mar. 1, June 1, Sept. 1, and Dec. 1 for Community Development Project
Write: Phyllis Buchele for Grant Program; Judy Kaufmann or Joe McKeon for Community Development Project
Officer and Directors:* Samuel Gary,* Chair. and Pres.; James E. Bye, Mary Gittings Cronin, Kathryn Gary, Nancy Gary, Ronald W. Williams.
Number of staff: 6 full-time professional; 2 part-time professional; 5 full-time support.
Employer Identification Number: 840719486

878
Harry W. Rabb Foundation ⌑
6242 South Elmira Circle
Englewood 80111 (303) 773-3918

Established in 1960.
Foundation type: Independent
Financial data (yr. ended 6/30/88): Assets, $1,915,004 (M); expenditures, $128,175, including $115,740 for 38 grants (high: $21,000; low: $1,000).
Purpose and activities: Giving for hospitals, Jewish welfare funds, and the aged.
Limitations: Giving primarily in Denver, CO.
Application information:
Write: Richard A. Zarlengo, Secy.-Treas.
Officers and Trustees: Jacob B. Kaufman, Pres.; Myles Dolan, V.P.; Richard A. Zarlengo, Secy.-Treas.
Employer Identification Number: 237236149

879
Waldo E. Rennie Scholarship Fund ⌑
c/o First Interstate Bank of Denver, N.A.
Terminal Annex, Box 5825
Denver 80217 (303) 293-2211

Established in CO in 1985.
Foundation type: Independent
Financial data (yr. ended 09/30/89): Assets, $1,825,942 (M); expenditures, $198,924, including $5,000 for 1 grant and $175,853 for 63 grants to individuals (high: $4,000; low: $975).
Purpose and activities: Awards scholarships for higher education.
Types of support: Student aid.
Limitations: Giving primarily in CO.
Application information:
Initial approach: Letter
Deadline(s): None
Write: Yvonne Baca
Trustee: First Interstate Bank of Denver, N.A.
Employer Identification Number: 846138107

880
Sachs Foundation
101 North Cascade Ave., Suite 430
Colorado Springs 80903 (719) 633-2353

Incorporated in 1931 in CO.
Donor(s): Henry Sachs.†
Foundation type: Independent
Financial data (yr. ended 12/31/88): Assets, $1,473,655 (M); gifts received, $843,798; expenditures, $728,426, including $12,000 for 1 grant and $560,645 for 285 grants to individuals (high: $6,000; low: $182; average: $1,200-$3,000).
Purpose and activities: Giving only to provide graduate and undergraduate scholarships for black residents of CO.
Types of support: Student aid.
Limitations: Giving limited to CO.
Publications: Financial statement, application guidelines.

Application information: Application form required.
Initial approach: Letter
Copies of proposal: 2
Deadline(s): Mar. 1
Board meeting date(s): Jan. and June
Final notification: 3 months after deadline date
Write: Morris A. Esmiol, Jr., Pres.
Officers and Directors:* Morris A. Esmiol, Jr.,* Pres.; Stuart P. Dodge,* V.P.; Ben S. Wendelken,* V.P.; Marjorie Sanchez, Secy.-Treas.
Number of staff: 3 full-time support.
Employer Identification Number: 840500835

881
Schlessman Foundation, Inc.
1301 Pennsylvania St., Suite 800
Denver 80203 (303) 861-8081

Incorporated in 1957 in CO.
Foundation type: Independent
Financial data (yr. ended 03/31/90): Assets, $19,500 (M); expenditures, $866,500, including $866,500 for 60 grants (high: $140,400; low: $100).
Purpose and activities: Support for higher and other education, including theological education and religious schools, cultural programs, youth agencies, aid to the handicapped, and social services.
Types of support: General purposes.
Limitations: Giving limited to CO. No grants to individuals.
Application information: Funds largely committed. Applications not accepted.
Initial approach: Letter
Copies of proposal: 1
Deadline(s): Jan.
Board meeting date(s): Mar., June, Sept., and Dec.
Final notification: Apr. 15
Write: Lee E. Schlessman, Pres.
Officers: Lee E. Schlessman, Pres.; Susan M. Duncan, V.P. and Secy.
Number of staff: 1 part-time support.
Employer Identification Number: 846030309

882
The Schramm Foundation ⌑
8528 West 10th Ave.
Lakewood 80215 (303) 232-1772

Established in 1956.
Foundation type: Independent
Financial data (yr. ended 06/30/89): Assets, $3,855,508 (M); expenditures, $192,402, including $165,338 for 41 grants (high: $20,000; low: $1,000).
Purpose and activities: Giving for hospitals, education, youth activities, social services, and cultural programs.
Types of support: Equipment, general purposes, scholarship funds, operating budgets.
Limitations: Giving primarily in Denver, CO and the surrounding area.
Application information:
Initial approach: Letter
Deadline(s): Aug. 15
Write: Lesley E. Kring, Pres.
Officers: Lesley E. Kring, Pres.; Arnold Tietze, V.P.; Gary S. Kring, Secy.; Joe Heit, Treas.
Number of staff: 4
Employer Identification Number: 846032196

883
Scott Foundation
1700 Lincoln St., No. 3950
Denver 80203 (303) 830-2221

Established in 1979 in CO.
Donor(s): Mary Hugh Scott.
Foundation type: Independent
Financial data (yr. ended 12/31/88): Assets, $1,132,736 (M); expenditures, $103,433, including $100,000 for 1 grant.
Purpose and activities: Support for medical research.
Types of support: General purposes.
Limitations: Giving primarily in Aspen, CO, and Houston, TX. No grants to individuals.
Application information: Contributes only to pre-selected organizations. Applications not accepted.
Write: Russell Scott III, Pres.
Officers and Directors:* Russell Scott III,* Pres.; H. Rex Martin,* Secy.-Treas.; Mary Hugh Scott, Russell Scott, Jr.
Number of staff: None.
Employer Identification Number: 742054301

884
Fay Shwayder Foundation
(Formerly Fay S. Carter Foundation)
6050 West Jewell Ave.
Lakewood 80226

Established in 1964 in CO.
Donor(s): Fay Shwayder.
Foundation type: Independent
Financial data (yr. ended 11/30/89): Assets, $2,860,574 (M); expenditures, $238,480, including $224,590 for 33 grants (high: $71,700; low: $50; average: $100-$25,000).
Purpose and activities: Giving for higher education and cultural programs.
Limitations: Giving primarily in CO.
Application information: Application form not required.
Write: Fay Shwayder, Pres.
Officers: Fay Shwayder,* Pres.; Sydney N. Freidman, Secy.-Treas.
Directors:* Judy Drake, Susan Hedling.
Employer Identification Number: 846041358

885
Galen & Ada Belle Spencer Foundation ⌑ ☆
1600 Colorado National Bldg.
Denver 80202

Established in 1982.
Foundation type: Independent
Financial data (yr. ended 6/30/89): Assets, $1,404,225 (M); expenditures, $82,132, including $60,000 for 23 grants (high: $10,000; low: $750).
Purpose and activities: Giving to cultural programs, including opera companies and museums; support also for hospitals, higher education, museums, and social services.
Limitations: Giving primarily in Denver, CO. No grants to individuals.
Application information: Contributes only to pre-selected organizations. Applications not accepted.
Officers and Directors: Harold A. Norblom, Pres.; Thomas P. Kearns, V.P.; John J. Silver, Secy.; John K. Weckbaugh, Treas.
Employer Identification Number: 742259763

886
The Stauffer Family Foundation ⌑ ☆
P.O. Box 774505
Steamboat Springs 80477-4505

Established in 1987 in CO.
Donor(s): Hope A. Stauffer, Charles W. Stauffer.
Foundation type: Independent
Financial data (yr. ended 12/31/88): Assets, $1,037,322 (M); expenditures, $62,619, including $54,700 for 25 grants (high: $20,000; low: $250).
Purpose and activities: Initial year of grantmaking, 1988; Support primarily for a Methodist church and other religious organizations; giving also for human services.
Limitations: No grants to individuals.
Application information: Contributes only to pre-selected organizations. Applications not accepted.
Officers and Directors:* Hope A. Stauffer,* Pres.; Charles W. Stauffer,* V.P.; Lori A. Stauffer,* Secy.; Jeffrey W. Stauffer,* Treas.; Ann Cranor, Lynne Stauffer, Todd W. Stauffer.
Employer Identification Number: 742483868

887
Sterne-Elder Memorial Trust ⌑
1700 Broadway
Denver 80274-0081

Trust established in 1977 in CO.
Donor(s): Charles S. Sterne.
Foundation type: Independent
Financial data (yr. ended 3/31/88): Assets, $3,971,993 (M); expenditures, $306,916, including $271,250 for 52 grants (high: $50,000; low: $100).
Purpose and activities: Emphasis on the performing arts, health organizations, and social services.
Limitations: Giving primarily in CO.
Director: Dorothy Elder Sterne.
Trustee: United Bank of Denver, N.A.
Employer Identification Number: 846143172

888
H. Chase Stone Trust ⌑ ☆
c/o First National Bank
P.O. Box 1699
Colorado Springs 80901 (719) 471-4990

Foundation type: Independent
Financial data (yr. ended 12/31/88): Assets, $1,942,233 (M); expenditures, $102,534, including $90,411 for 13 grants (high: $12,500; low: $330).
Purpose and activities: Giving primarily for higher and other education, museums, and fine and performing arts.
Types of support: Equipment, annual campaigns, renovation projects.
Limitations: Giving limited to El Paso County, CO. No grants to individuals.

Application information:
Initial approach: Letter
Deadline(s): Apr. 30 and Oct. 31
Trustee: First National Bank.
Employer Identification Number: 846066113

889
Stuart-James Foundation ⌑
8055 East Tuffs Ave. Pkwy., Suite 1200
Denver 80237 (303) 796-8488

Established in 1985 in CO.
Foundation type: Independent
Financial data (yr. ended 11/30/89): Assets, $289,583 (M); gifts received, $361,770; expenditures, $342,827, including $339,627 for 45 grants (high: $750,000; low: $94).
Purpose and activities: Giving primarily for higher education, hospitals and medical research, and the arts.
Application information:
Initial approach: Letter
Deadline(s): None
Write: C. James Padgett, Chair.; or Stuart Graff, Pres.
Officers: C. James Padgett, Chair.; Stuart Graff, Pres.
Employer Identification Number: 742411759

890
The Bal F. and Hilda N. Swan Foundation ⌑
c/o First Interstate Bank of Denver, N.A.
P.O. Box 5825, Terminal Annex
Denver 80217

Established in 1976.
Donor(s): Bal F. Swan.†
Foundation type: Independent
Financial data (yr. ended 12/31/88): Assets, $1,330,838 (M); expenditures, $304,633, including $291,250 for 29 grants (high: $36,800; low: $500).
Purpose and activities: Giving for aid to the handicapped, medical research, child welfare, cultural programs, social agencies, and higher education.
Limitations: Giving primarily in CO.
Application information:
Initial approach: Letter
Deadline(s): None
Write: Julie Ham
Trustees: Anthony F. Zarlengo, First Interstate Bank of Denver, N.A.
Employer Identification Number: 742108775

891
The Ruth and Vernon Taylor Foundation ▼
1670 Denver Club Bldg.
Denver 80202 (303) 893-5284

Trust established in 1950 in TX.
Donor(s): members of the Taylor family.
Foundation type: Independent
Financial data (yr. ended 6/30/89): Assets, $32,468,166 (M); expenditures, $2,065,399, including $977,025 for 134 grants (high: $76,128; low: $100; average: $2,000-$15,000).
Purpose and activities: Support for higher and secondary education, cultural programs, social service and youth agencies, ecology and conservation, and hospitals and medical research.
Types of support: Research, endowment funds, building funds, general purposes.
Limitations: Giving primarily in TX, CO, WY, MT, IL, and the Mid-Atlantic states. No grants to individuals.
Application information: Application form not required.
Initial approach: Proposal
Copies of proposal: 1
Deadline(s): Apr. 30
Board meeting date(s): May and Aug.
Final notification: 30 days
Write: Miss Friday A. Green, Trustee
Trustees: Ruth Taylor Campbell, Friday A. Green, Sara Taylor Swift, Vernon Taylor, Jr.
Number of staff: None.
Employer Identification Number: 846021788

892
The Thatcher Foundation ⌑
P.O. Box 1401
Pueblo 81002
Scholarship application address: Charlene Burkhard, The Thatcher Foundation, Minnequa Bank of Pueblo, Pueblo, CO 81004; Tel.: (719) 545-2345

Established in 1924 in CO.
Foundation type: Independent
Financial data (yr. ended 12/31/88): Assets, $2,965,898 (M); expenditures, $250,474, including $192,895 for 37 grants (high: $40,000; low: $100) and $33,931 for 26 grants to individuals (high: $3,700; low: $575).
Purpose and activities: Giving for higher education, including undergraduate scholarships and a chair in music; a community fund; cultural programs; youth agencies; and health.
Types of support: Student aid.
Limitations: Giving limited to Pueblo County, CO.
Application information: Applications accepted only for scholarships; contributions to organizations are pre-selected.
Deadline(s): Prior to beginning of school year in which assistance is requested
Officers and Trustees: Mahlon T. White, Pres.; Helen T. White, V.P.; Lester L. Ward, Jr., Secy.-Treas.; Adrian Comer, Mahlon T. White II.
Employer Identification Number: 840581724

893
True North Foundation
2190 West Drake, No. 361
Fort Collins 80526
OR Office contact: K.F. Stephens; Tel.: (503) 293-3348

Established in 1986 in CO.
Foundation type: Independent
Financial data (yr. ended 12/31/88): Assets, $6,321,712 (M); expenditures, $349,005, including $301,000 for grants.
Purpose and activities: Support for conservation of wildlife and wilderness areas, environmental projects, family planning and services, and community programs.
Types of support: Equipment, general purposes, research, seed money, special projects.
Limitations: Giving primarily in CA, particularly San Francisco, OR, and for national environmental programs. No support for political activities or religious purposes. No grants to individuals.
Publications: Informational brochure (including application guidelines).
Application information: Application form required.
Initial approach: Letter
Deadline(s): None
Board meeting date(s): Approximately bimonthly
Write: Ms. K. Hoffman
Officer and Directors:* Kerry K. Hoffman,* Pres.; L. Jane Gallup, Kathryn Fong Stephens.
Number of staff: 2 part-time professional.
Employer Identification Number: 742421528

894
US WEST Foundation ▼
(Formerly Mountain Bell Foundation)
7800 East Orchard Rd., Suite 300
Englewood 80111 (303) 793-6661
Application address: Local US WEST Public Relations Office or Community Relations Team

Established in 1985 in CO.
Donor(s): US WEST, and its family of companies.
Foundation type: Company-sponsored
Financial data (yr. ended 12/31/89): Assets, $6,069,021 (M); gifts received, $25,083,744; expenditures, $19,988,390, including $18,266,191 for 3,622 grants (high: $300,000; low: $300; average: $500-$10,000), $74,300 for 21 grants to individuals (high: $5,000; low: $200; average: $200-$5,000) and $1,367,743 for 8,933 employee matching gifts.
Purpose and activities: Giving primarily for health and human services, including programs for minorities and youth; early childhood, elementary, secondary, higher, and other education; rural and community development; and cultural programs.
Types of support: Operating budgets, general purposes, employee matching gifts, special projects, continuing support, matching funds, seed money, technical assistance.
Limitations: Giving limited to the states served by the US WEST calling areas, including AZ, CO, IA, ID, MN, MT, ND, NE, NM, SD, OR, UT, WA, and WY. No support for international organizations, political or religious organizations, or school bands or choral groups. No grants to individuals, or for endowment funds, deficit financing, scholarships, athletic funds, or goodwill advertising.
Publications: Annual report (including application guidelines), grants list.
Application information: Application form not required.
Initial approach: Proposal
Copies of proposal: 1
Deadline(s): None
Board meeting date(s): Feb., May, Aug., and Nov.
Final notification: Most funds disbursed during 4th quarter each year
Write: L.J. Nash, Dir. Administration

Officers: Jack A. MacAllister, Pres.; Jane Prancan, V.P.; Larry DeMuth, Secy.; Howard P. Doerr, Treas.
Number of staff: 8 full-time professional.
Employer Identification Number: 840978668

895
Vinann Foundation ⌑
1817 Welton St.
Denver 80202

Established in CO in 1985.
Donor(s): Vincent J. Duncan.
Foundation type: Independent
Financial data (yr. ended 6/30/87): Assets, $1,352,215 (M); expenditures, $27,113, including $25,000 for 1 grant.
Purpose and activities: First year of grant making 1986-87; support for a secondary school.
Application information: Contributes only to pre-selected organizations. Applications not accepted.
Directors: Vincent J. Duncan, J. James.
Employer Identification Number: 841012090

896
Weckbaugh Foundation, Inc. ⌑ ☆
1636 Logan St., Suite 1
Denver 80203

Incorporated in 1939 in CO.
Donor(s): J. Kernan Weckbaugh, Ella M. Weckbaugh, The J.K. Mullen Co.
Foundation type: Independent
Financial data (yr. ended 12/31/88): Assets, $1,151,718 (M); gifts received, $3,103; expenditures, $80,441, including $60,844 for grants.
Purpose and activities: Support primarily for hospitals, higher and secondary education, cultural programs, and Roman Catholic organizations.
Limitations: No grants to individuals.
Application information:
Initial approach: Letter
Deadline(s): Dec. 1
Officers and Directors: Lawrence K. Weckbaugh, Pres.; John K. Weckbaugh, V.P.; Catherine A. Matthews, Secy.; Walter S. Weckbaugh, Treas.; Anne H. Weckbaugh.
Employer Identification Number: 846029285

897
Eleanore Mullen Weckbaugh Foundation
13064 Parkview Dr.
Aurora 80011 (303) 367-1545
Application address: P.O. Box 31678, Aurora, CO 80041

Established in 1975.
Donor(s): Eleanore Mullen Weckbaugh.†
Foundation type: Independent
Financial data (yr. ended 03/31/90): Assets, $6,251,619 (M); expenditures, $466,181, including $425,080 for 59 grants (high: $30,000; low: $2,000).
Purpose and activities: Emphasis on Roman Catholic church support, welfare funds, education, and missionary programs; grants also for higher and secondary education, the performing arts, hospitals and hospices, health agencies, employment, Latin America, child welfare and development, and women.
Types of support: General purposes.
Limitations: Giving primarily in CO. No grants to individuals.
Publications: 990-PF.
Application information: Application form not required.
Initial approach: Letter
Copies of proposal: 1
Deadline(s): None
Board meeting date(s): Mar., June, Sept., and Dec.
Write: Edward J. Limes, Pres.
Officers and Trustees:* Edward J. Limes,* Pres. and Treas.; Teresa Polakovic,* V.P.; Jean Guyton, Secy.; S.P. Guyton, Michael Polakovic.
Number of staff: 1 full-time professional.
Employer Identification Number: 237437761

898
The Williams Family Foundation ⌑
317 Ensign St.
P.O. Box 597
Fort Morgan 80701 (303) 867-5621

Trust established about 1958 in CO.
Donor(s): A.F. Williams, M.D.,† Mrs. A.F. Williams.†
Foundation type: Independent
Financial data (yr. ended 12/31/88): Assets, $4,915,657 (M); expenditures, $1,242,637, including $1,221,823 for 30 grants (high: $329,642; low: $100).
Purpose and activities: Giving for higher and secondary education, including scholarships for medical-oriented study, hospitals, and civic affairs.
Types of support: Scholarship funds, research.
Limitations: Giving primarily in CO; scholarships for Morgan County high school graduates.
Application information: Scholarship applicants nominated by high schools.
Deadline(s): None
Final notification: Apr. for scholarships
Write: Edward L. Zorn, Trustee
Trustees: Catherine M. Woodward, Paul E. Woodward, Edward L. Zorn.
Employer Identification Number: 846023379

899
Melvin & Elaine Wolf Foundation, Inc. ⌑
1560 Broadway, Suite 1000
Denver 80202 (303) 691-0370

Established in 1978 in CO.
Donor(s): Melvin Wolf, Elaine Wolf.
Foundation type: Independent
Financial data (yr. ended 6/30/89): Assets, $5,844,603 (M); expenditures, $270,032, including $219,230 for 27 grants (high: $100,000; low: $500).
Purpose and activities: Giving primarily for Jewish welfare funds, hospitals and health agencies, and youth programs.
Limitations: Giving primarily in CO. No grants to individuals.
Application information: Contributes only to pre-selected organizations. Applications not accepted.
Officers and Directors: Melvin Wolf, Pres.; Elaine Wolf, V.P.; Henry Reckler, Secy.-Treas.
Employer Identification Number: 840797937

CONNECTICUT

900
Louis H. Aborn Foundation, Inc. ⌑
46 Wilshire Rd.
Greenwich 06830 (203) 661-4046

Established in 1975 in CT.
Donor(s): Louis H. Aborn, Hermine F. Aborn.
Foundation type: Independent
Financial data (yr. ended 12/31/87): Assets, $114,879 (M); gifts received, $50,000; expenditures, $151,073, including $151,000 for 4 grants (high: $90,000; low: $1,000).
Purpose and activities: Giving for public health projects, education, and child welfare.
Application information:
Initial approach: Letter
Write: Louis H. Aborn, Pres.
Officers and Directors: Louis H. Aborn, Pres.; Hermine F. Aborn, V.P.; Nancy Aborn Duffy, Secy.; Sargent L. Aborn, Treas.
Employer Identification Number: 510162063

901
Aetna Foundation, Inc. ▼
(Formerly Aetna Life & Casualty Foundation, Inc.)
151 Farmington Ave.
Hartford 06156 (203) 273-6382

Incorporated in 1972 in CT.
Donor(s): Aetna Life and Casualty Co.
Foundation type: Company-sponsored
Financial data (yr. ended 12/31/89): Assets, $41,827,393 (M); gifts received, $14,991,825; expenditures, $9,044,732, including $8,139,082 for grants (high: $1,163,000; low: $300; average: $500-$25,000) and $837,513 for employee matching gifts.
Purpose and activities: To help preserve a viable society by supporting programs and organizations that can have a real impact on solving social problems and by providing support that will stimulate other donors. Priority areas for giving are problems of urban public education, minority higher education, improving minority youth employment opportunities, urban neighborhood revitalization, and reform of the civil justice system; also support for the arts and social services, with an emphasis on AIDS. The foundation encourages employee participation in community affairs through support for regional grants and FOCUS, foundation initiatives that serve the headquarters city,

Hartford, CT, and cities where Aetna has major field office operations, several international initiatives in countries where the company operates, Dollars-for-Doers, and matching gifts for higher education.
Types of support: Operating budgets, continuing support, seed money, emergency funds, matching funds, employee matching gifts, technical assistance, general purposes, publications, employee-related scholarships, scholarship funds, special projects.
Limitations: Giving limited to organizations in the U.S. No support for religious organizations for religious purposes, or private secondary schools. No grants to individuals, or for endowment funds, medical research, capital or building funds, or renovation projects; or annual operating funds for colleges, universities, social service agencies, secondary schools, museums, hospitals, or other such institutions; no grants for computer hardware; no loans.
Publications: Corporate giving report (including application guidelines), application guidelines, program policy statement, occasional report, informational brochure (including application guidelines).
Application information: Application form required only for FOCUS grants.
Initial approach: Letter with proposal summary
Copies of proposal: 1
Deadline(s): None
Board meeting date(s): Feb., May, July, and Nov.
Final notification: 2 months
Write: Kelly Bedard
Officers and Directors:* William H. Donaldson,* Chair.; Ronald E. Compton,* Pres.; Sanford Cloud, Jr., V.P. and Exec. Dir.; Stephen B. Middlebrook, V.P.; Frederick W. Kingsley, Treas.; Arthur R. Ashe, Jr., Donald G. Conrad, Marian W. Edelman, Barbara Hackman Franklin, Edward K. Hamilton, James T. Lynn, Frank R. O'Keefe.
Number of staff: 10 full-time professional; 6 full-time support.
Employer Identification Number: 237241940

902
AMAX Foundation, Inc. ⌑
Amax Ctr.
Greenwich 06836 (203) 629-6901

Incorporated in 1955 in NY.
Donor(s): AMAX, Inc.
Foundation type: Company-sponsored
Financial data (yr. ended 12/31/87): Assets, $2,753,101 (M); expenditures, $767,416, including $639,101 for 328 grants (high: $25,000; low: $250; average: $500-$2,000), $65,850 for 37 grants to individuals (high: $4,000; low: $500) and $37,876 for 124 employee matching gifts.
Purpose and activities: Grants for higher education, largely in the fields related to mining, metallurgy, geology, geophysics, and geochemistry; employee matching gift program and Amax Earth Sciences Scholarships for children of employees only; health and welfare, especially United Way campaigns; cultural programs; and civic and public affairs.
Types of support: Building funds, continuing support, employee matching gifts, fellowships, general purposes, professorships, research, scholarship funds, employee-related scholarships, matching funds.
Limitations: Giving primarily in areas of company operations. No support for political, fraternal, religious, or sectarian organizations, primary or secondary education, creative arts groups, sports or athletic events, nursing homes, organizations supported by the United Way (unless permission has been granted by the United Way), or governmental or quasi-governmental agencies. No grants to individuals (except company-employee scholarships), or for memorial funds, goodwill advertisements in yearbooks or souvenir programs, charity dinners or special performance events; no support for endowment funds; no loans.
Publications: Application guidelines, program policy statement, informational brochure.
Application information: Application form not required.
Initial approach: Letter
Copies of proposal: 1
Deadline(s): Submit proposal by Mar. 15 for civic and charitable projects and from July 1 to Sept. 1 for educational projects
Board meeting date(s): May, Oct., and as required
Final notification: 60 days
Write: Sonja B. Michaud, Pres.
Officers: Sonja B. Michaud,* Pres.; Malcolm B. Bayliss,* V.P.; Raymond J. Cooke,* Secy.; Dennis Arrouet, Treas.
Directors:* Helen M. Feeney, Charles Toder.
Number of staff: 1 full-time professional; 1 full-time support.
Employer Identification Number: 136111368

903
Ames Foundation, Inc. ⌑
2418 Main St.
Rocky Hill 06067 (203) 563-8234

Incorporated in 1969 in CT.
Donor(s): Ames Department Stores.
Foundation type: Company-sponsored
Financial data (yr. ended 1/31/88): Assets, $17,128 (M); gifts received, $245,000; expenditures, $241,614, including $241,477 for 768 grants (high: $60,000; low: $20).
Purpose and activities: Support primarily for Jewish welfare funds; some support for higher education, health associations, and hospitals.
Limitations: Giving primarily in CT. No grants to individuals, or for endowment funds, scholarships, or fellowships; no loans.
Publications: Annual report.
Application information: Applications not accepted.
Officers and Directors: Herbert Gilman, Pres.; Morris Crosky, V.P.; Earl Spector, Secy.
Employer Identification Number: 237003239

904
The Anthony Trust Association ⌑
c/o The Chase Coggins Memorial Scholarship
5471 Yale Station
New Haven 06520

Established in 1941 in CT.
Foundation type: Operating
Financial data (yr. ended 06/30/88): Assets, $1,928,291 (M); expenditures, $123,812, including $2,000 for 2 grants to individuals.
Purpose and activities: A private operating foundation; support to individuals for wilderness exploration and travel or for artistic or educational intent.
Types of support: Student aid.
Limitations: Giving primarily in CT.
Application information: Application form not required.
Initial approach: Letter
Deadline(s): Mar. 29
Officers: Augustus Kellog, Pres.; Charles Roraback, Treas.
Trustees: Augustus G. Kellogg, Carter Weisman, and 10 additional trustees.
Employer Identification Number: 060245162

905
The Beatrice Fox Auerbach Foundation ▼ ⌑
25 Brookside Blvd.
West Hartford 06107 (203) 232-5854

Incorporated in 1941 by special Act of the CT Legislature.
Donor(s): Beatrice Fox Auerbach,† Fannie F. Samuels, Standard Investment Co.
Foundation type: Independent
Financial data (yr. ended 12/31/88): Assets, $26,178,036 (M); expenditures, $1,572,615, including $1,320,514 for 66 grants (high: $405,000; low: $500; average: $1,000-$50,000).
Purpose and activities: Giving for social service and youth agencies, including a community fund, health and hospitals, Jewish welfare funds, and higher education.
Types of support: Endowment funds, general purposes.
Limitations: Giving primarily in the Hartford, CT, area. No grants to individuals.
Application information: Application form not required.
Initial approach: Proposal
Deadline(s): None
Write: Dorothy A. Schiro, Treas.
Officers and Trustees: Bernard Schiro, Chair.; Richard Koopman, Pres.; Georgette A. Koopman, V.P. and Secy.; Dorothy A. Schiro, Treas.
Number of staff: 1
Employer Identification Number: 066033334

906
Elinor Patterson Baker Foundation ⌑
c/o Putnam Trust Co.
Ten Mason St.
Greenwich 06830 (203) 869-3000

Established in 1984 in CT.
Donor(s): Elinor Patterson Baker.†
Foundation type: Independent
Financial data (yr. ended 5/31/88): Assets, $8,193,891 (M); expenditures, $530,611, including $455,000 for 22 grants (high: $300,000; low: $1,000; average: $1,000-$150,000).
Purpose and activities: Grants for organizations that fulfill the goals of the Humane Society.

Limitations: Giving primarily in CT to organizations exempt from the state succession tax. In the case of organizations incorporated outside of CT, reciprocity must exist between CT and the state of incorporation in order for the organization to qualify for a grant.
Application information:
Deadline(s): None
Write: Donald W. Baker, Trustee
Trustees: Donald W. Baker, Putnam Trust Co.
Employer Identification Number: 066276403

907
The Bannow-Larson Foundation, Inc. ⌑
1976 Post Rd.
Fairfield 06430-5720

Established in 1966 in CT.
Foundation type: Independent
Financial data (yr. ended 07/31/89): Assets, $1,093,389 (M); expenditures, $38,868, including $26,450 for 12 grants (high: $7,800; low: $50).
Purpose and activities: Support primarily for a medical center foundation; support also for cultural programs and a community foundation.
Application information: Contributes only to pre-selected organizations. Applications not accepted.
Officers and Directors:* Gilbert R. Larson,* Pres.; Dorothy B. Larson,* Secy.; Denise L. Lovegrove.
Employer Identification Number: 066084233

908
The Barden Foundation, Inc. ⌑
200 Park Ave.
Danbury 06813-2449 (203) 744-2211

Incorporated in 1959 in DE.
Donor(s): The Barden Corp.
Foundation type: Company-sponsored
Financial data (yr. ended 10/31/89): Assets, $3,023,905 (M); gifts received, $81,000; expenditures, $125,605, including $109,000 for 16 grants (high: $50,000; low: $500) and $15,000 for 10 grants to individuals (high: $3,750; low: $750).
Purpose and activities: Emphasis on higher education, including an employee-related scholarship award program administered through colleges and universities, hospitals and a community fund, the arts, including music, minorities, cancer research, the handicapped; scholarships are restricted to sons and daughters of The Division of The Barden Corp.
Types of support: Employee-related scholarships.
Limitations: Giving primarily in CT.
Publications: Informational brochure.
Application information: Application information for scholarship program available from Scholarship Committee, The Barden Corp. Application form required.
Deadline(s): Apr. 1
Officers and Trustees:* Stanley Noss,* Pres.; Eduard Baruch,* Secy.; R.D. Moore,* Treas.; Donald K. Brush, R.H. Buch, T.R. Hensal.
Employer Identification Number: 066054855

909
The Barnes Foundation, Inc.
P.O. Box 1560
Bristol 06010 (203) 583-7070

Incorporated in 1945 in CT.
Donor(s): Carlyle F. Barnes, Aurelia B. Bristow, Louise B. Adams, Myrtle I. Barnes,† Fuller F. Barnes.†
Foundation type: Independent
Financial data (yr. ended 12/31/89): Assets, $4,698,825 (M); expenditures, $290,608, including $253,000 for 36 grants (high: $20,000; low: $500; average: $5,000-$10,000).
Purpose and activities: Support primarily for secondary school education.
Types of support: Equipment, internships, publications, renovation projects, scholarship funds, seed money, special projects, conferences and seminars, program-related investments.
Limitations: Giving primarily in CT. No grants to individuals, or for endowment funds or operating budgets.
Publications: Annual report (including application guidelines).
Application information:
Initial approach: Letter
Copies of proposal: 1
Deadline(s): Oct. 15 and Mar. 15
Board meeting date(s): Usually in Jan., May, Sept., and Dec.
Write: Carlyle F. Barnes, Pres.
Officers and Trustees:* Carlyle F. Barnes,* Pres.; Aurelia B. Bristow,* V.P.; Sally O'Connor,* Secy. and Exec. Dir.; Louise B. Adams,* Treas.; Fuller F. Barnes II, Elliott B. Bristow.
Number of staff: 1 part-time professional.
Employer Identification Number: 066037160

910
Barnes Group Foundation, Inc. ⌑
123 Main St.
Bristol 06010
Scholarship application address: Citizens' Scholarship Fdn. of America., Inc., 1505 Riverview Rd., P.O. Box 297, St. Peter, MN 56082; Tel.: (603) 627-3870

Incorporated in CT.
Donor(s): Barnes Group, Inc.
Foundation type: Company-sponsored
Financial data (yr. ended 12/31/88): Assets, $114,994 (M); gifts received, $300,000; expenditures, $479,020, including $464,542 for 296 grants (high: $57,225; low: $30).
Purpose and activities: Emphasis on higher education, community funds, and the environment; scholarships only for children of active and retired company employees.
Types of support: Employee-related scholarships.
Application information: Application form required.
Deadline(s): Mar. 1
Officers and Directors:* Wallace Barnes,* Chair.; Carlyle F. Barnes,* Pres.; William R. Fenoglio,* V.P.; John E. Besser, Secy.; George J. Crowley, Treas.
Trustee: United Bank & Trust Co.
Employer Identification Number: 237339727

911
Belgian American Educational Foundation, Inc. ⌑
195 Church St.
New Haven 06510 (203) 777-5765

Incorporated in 1920 in DE.
Donor(s): The Commission for Relief in Belgium.
Foundation type: Independent
Financial data (yr. ended 8/31/87): Assets, $14,098,163 (M); gifts received, $539,734; expenditures, $750,343, including $58,500 for 4 grants (high: $8,200; low: $2,000) and $557,161 for 31 grants to individuals (high: $20,000; low: $8,000).
Purpose and activities: To promote closer relations between Belgium and the United States through graduate exchange fellowships in diverse fields and to assist higher education, scientific research, and the exchange of intellectual ideas.
Types of support: Exchange programs, fellowships, research.
Limitations: No grants for general support, endowment funds, or matching gifts; no fellowships (except for Belgian and American graduate students).
Publications: Financial statement, application guidelines.
Application information: Application form required.
Initial approach: Letter, proposal, or telephone
Copies of proposal: 1
Deadline(s): Submit proposal preferably in Dec.; deadline Dec. 31
Board meeting date(s): Jan., Apr., June, and Oct.
Final notification: Before March 31
Write: Dr. Emile L. Boulpaep, Pres.
Officers and Directors: Emile L. Boulpaep, Chair. and Pres.; William Moody, Secy.; Sherman Gray, Treas.; Gaston Deurinck, Jacques de Groote, John H.F. Haskell, Jr., Andre Jacques, Daniel Janssen, Herman Liebaers, Andre W.G. Newburg, Shelby H. Page, Marshall Robinson, Edward H. Tuck, Hugo van Itallie, Luc Wauters.
Number of staff: 1 full-time support; 1 part-time support.
Employer Identification Number: 131606002

912
Carl and Dorothy Bennett Foundation, Inc. ⌑
28 Windrose Way
Greenwich 06830

Established in 1963.
Donor(s): Caldor, Inc., Carl Bennett, and others.
Foundation type: Independent
Financial data (yr. ended 06/30/89): Assets, $4,017,262 (M); expenditures, $398,332, including $365,975 for 18 grants (high: $100,000; low: $100).
Purpose and activities: Support for Jewish welfare funds and a hospital.
Limitations: Giving primarily in CT.
Application information: Contributes only to pre-selected organizations. Applications not accepted.
Write: Carl Bennett, Pres.

Officers and Directors:* Carl Bennett,* Pres.; Marc Bennett,* V.P.; Malcolm E. Martin,* Secy.; Dorothy Bennett,* Treas.; Bruce Bennett, Robin Bennett Kanarek, Harold Karun, Mathew Manes, Gerald Roth.
Employer Identification Number: 066051371

913
Mr. Bingham's Trust for Charity ▼
21 Ann St.
Old Greenwich 06870 (203) 637-2178
Additional address: R.T.H. Davidson, Trustee, 65 Parker Hill Rd., Killingworth, CT 06417

Trust established in 1934 in NY.
Donor(s): William Bingham II.†
Foundation type: Independent
Financial data (yr. ended 12/31/89): Assets, $33,916,838 (M); expenditures, $1,834,543, including $1,399,000 for 11 grants (high: $300,000; low: $5,000; average: $25,000-$300,000).
Purpose and activities: Grants awarded to invited institutions for projects in the field of writing proficiency in elementary and secondary school, and to institutions which assist psychiatric patients in transition from hospitalization to independent living, excluding programs serving people whose primary problem is substance abuse.
Types of support: Operating budgets, seed money, matching funds, special projects, research, endowment funds, renovation projects.
Limitations: No grants to individuals, or for scholarships or fellowships.
Application information: Applications not accepted.
Board meeting date(s): Quarterly
Write: Robert T. Barr, Trustee
Trustees: Robert T. Barr, Robert T.H. Davidson, U.S. Trust Co. of New York.
Number of staff: 2 part-time professional.
Employer Identification Number: 136069740

914
J. Walton Bissell Foundation ⌘
CityPlace, 25th Fl.
Hartford 06103 (203) 275-0100

Established in 1952 in CT.
Donor(s): J. Walton Bissell.†
Foundation type: Independent
Financial data (yr. ended 12/31/88): Assets, $10,696,374 (M); expenditures, $603,062, including $534,000 for 67 grants (high: $50,000; low: $1,000).
Purpose and activities: Giving for higher and secondary education, including scholarship funds, hospitals, youth and child welfare agencies, care of the aged, Protestant church support, and the arts, including the fine arts, music, and historic preservation.
Types of support: Scholarship funds.
Limitations: Giving primarily in CT, MA, VT, and NH. No grants to individuals; no loans.
Application information:
Initial approach: Letter
Deadline(s): None
Write: J. Danford Anthony, Jr., Trustee
Officer and Trustees:* D.M. Rockwell,* Secy.; J.D. Anthony, Jr., P.R. Reynolds, L. Steiner.
Employer Identification Number: 066035614

915
Henry L. & Nellie E. Blakeslee Trust for Scholarship ⌘
158 Main St.
Thomaston 06787 (203) 283-4141

Established in 1951 in CT.
Foundation type: Independent
Financial data (yr. ended 12/31/87): Assets, $1,134,573 (M); gifts received, $7,586; expenditures, $175,510, including $162,403 for 66 grants to individuals (high: $4,000; low: $217).
Purpose and activities: Support for scholarship grants to individuals attending colleges and universities in Connecticut.
Types of support: Student aid.
Limitations: Giving limited to residents of Thomaston, CT.
Application information:
Write: Rosemary Martini
Trustee: Bank of Boston Connecticut.
Employer Identification Number: 066025519

916
Bodenwein Public Benevolent Foundation
c/o Connecticut National Bank
250 Captain's Walk
New London 06320 (203) 447-6133

Established in 1939 in CT.
Donor(s): The Day Trust, Theodore Bodenwein.†
Foundation type: Independent
Financial data (yr. ended 12/31/89): Assets, $353,119 (M); gifts received, $233,532; expenditures, $229,899, including $219,989 for 36 grants (high: $32,000; low: $663).
Purpose and activities: Giving to social service and health agencies, including AIDS support, the fine and performing arts and other cultural programs, youth and child welfare agencies, civic affairs and community development groups, education, and minority programs.
Types of support: Building funds, capital campaigns, conferences and seminars, consulting services, equipment, matching funds, publications, renovation projects, research, scholarship funds, seed money, special projects.
Limitations: Giving limited to Lyme, Old Lyme, East Lyme, Waterford, New London, Montville, Groton, Ledyard, Stonington, North Stonington, and Salem, CT.
Publications: Informational brochure (including application guidelines).
Application information: Application form required.
Initial approach: Telephone
Copies of proposal: 1
Deadline(s): May 15 and Nov. 15
Board meeting date(s): Jan. and July
Final notification: Feb. 1 and Aug. 1
Write: Mildred E. Devine, V.P., Connecticut National Bank
Trustee: Connecticut National Bank.
Number of staff: None.
Employer Identification Number: 066030548

917
Donald C. Brace Foundation ⌘ ☆
c/o R.A. Beer, Cummings & Lockwood
P.O. Box 120
Stamford 06904-0120
Application address: Seven West 51st St., New York, NY 10019; Tel.: (212) 586-1640

Established in 1987 in CT.
Donor(s): Donna Brace Ogilvie.
Foundation type: Independent
Financial data (yr. ended 12/31/87): Assets, $2,306,250 (M); gifts received, $2,306,250; expenditures, $0.
Purpose and activities: Initial year of operations, 1987; no grants awarded.
Application information:
Initial approach: Letter
Deadline(s): None
Write: Paul Gitlin, Esq., Trustee
Trustees: Paul Gitlin, Donna Brace Ogilvie.
Employer Identification Number: 133442680

918
The Bridgeport Area Foundation, Inc.
280 State St.
Bridgeport 06604 (203) 334-7511

Incorporated in 1967 in CT.
Foundation type: Community
Financial data (yr. ended 12/31/89): Assets, $8,340,000 (M); gifts received, $1,206,205; expenditures, $841,449, including $609,350 for 209 grants (high: $15,000; low: $250; average: $3,000-$5,000).
Purpose and activities: Grants to organizations and for projects that benefit named local communities including support for higher and other education, social service agencies, health, and culture.
Types of support: Continuing support, seed money, emergency funds, consulting services, technical assistance, conferences and seminars, special projects, general purposes, scholarship funds.
Limitations: Giving primarily in Bridgeport, Easton, Fairfield, Milford, Monroe, Shelton, Stratford, Trumbull, and Westport, CT. No grants to individuals, or for operating budgets or deficit financing; no loans.
Publications: Annual report (including application guidelines), newsletter, application guidelines, financial statement, informational brochure (including application guidelines).
Application information: Application form required.
Initial approach: Letter
Copies of proposal: 2
Deadline(s): Feb. 15, May 15, and Sept. 15
Board meeting date(s): Apr. and Oct.; distribution committee meets in Mar., June, and Oct.
Final notification: Nov.
Write: Richard O. Dietrich, Pres. and C.E.O.
Officers and Directors: Richard P. Bodine, Sr., Chair.; Richard F. Freeman, Vice-Chair.; David J. Sullivan, Jr., Vice-Chair.; Richard O. Dietrich, Pres. and C.E.O.; Robert J. Ashkins, Secy.; Henry L. Katz, Treas.; John P. Bassett, Mrs. Gerald C. Baum, Anthony J. Cernera, Frank G. Elliott, Jr., M.D., Michael H. Flynn, Norwick R.G. Goodspeed, John J. Lawrence, M.D., John Marshall Lee, Carmen L. Lopez,* Newman M. Marsilius, Jr., L. Scott Melville,

Robert D. Scinto, Cecil S. Semple, Harold C. Smith, Jack C. Stawarky, Jr., Richard I. Steiber, George F. Taylor, Robert S. Tellalian, Philip Trager, William S. Warner, Ernest A. Wiehl, Jr., Peter Wilkinson, Austin K. Wolf.
Distribution Committee:* Ronald D. Williams, Chair.; Mrs. Leete P. Doty, Assoc. Chair.; Mrs. Henry B. duPont III, William L. Hawkins, Geraldine W. Johnson, Robert C. Lindquist, James E. Marbury, Ronald B. Noren, James F. Tomchik.
Trustees: Citytrust, Connecticut Bank & Trust Co., N.A., Connecticut National Bank, Lafayette Bank & Trust Co., Peoples Bank.
Number of staff: 2 full-time professional.
Employer Identification Number: 066103832

919
John P. & Margaret Mary Brogan Family Foundation ⌑ ☆
289 Greenwich Ave.
Greenwich 06830-6542

Established in 1985 in Ct.
Donor(s): John P. Brogan.
Foundation type: Independent
Financial data (yr. ended 2/28/89): Assets, $389,688 (M); expenditures, $116,967, including $116,300 for 10 grants (high: $25,000; low: $100).
Purpose and activities: Giving primarily for Catholic organizations, including higher educational institutions and a convent.
Limitations: Giving primarily in CT, NY, and MA. No grants to individuals.
Application information: Contributes only to pre-selected organization. Applications not accepted.
Trustees: John P. Brogan, Margaret M. Brogan.
Employer Identification Number: 222592957

920
Elsie A. Brown Fund, Inc. ⌑ ☆
257 Main St., Rm. 301
Norwich 06360

Donor(s): Elsie A. Brown.
Foundation type: Independent
Financial data (yr. ended 12/31/88): Assets, $1,019,298 (M); expenditures, $52,834, including $42,270 for 89 grants (high: $3,000; low: $15).
Purpose and activities: Giving for higher and other education, the arts and museums, health associations, hospitals, and Protestant churches.
Limitations: Giving primarily in New York, NY, and CT.
Application information:
Deadline(s): None
Write: Diogenes P. John, Secy.
Officers: Elsie A. Brown, Pres.; Richard P. John, V.P.; Diogenes P. John, Secy.
Employer Identification Number: 066032102

921
Trustees of the Bulkeley School
c/o Richard Woodworth
Crocker St.
New London 06320
Additional address: P.O. Box 1426, New London, CT 06320

Established in 1852 in CT.
Donor(s): Leonard H. Bulkeley.†
Foundation type: Independent
Financial data (yr. ended 04/30/88): Assets, $1,172,407 (M); expenditures, $92,203, including $67,700 for grants to individuals.
Purpose and activities: Giving only for a scholarship program.
Types of support: Student aid.
Limitations: Giving limited to residents of New London, CT.
Application information: Contact school guidance counselor for application information. Application form required.
Deadline(s): Apr. 1
Board meeting date(s): Apr. 15
Final notification: July 15
Officers: Nathan Belcher, Pres.; Richard Woodworth, Treas.
Number of staff: 1 part-time professional; 1 part-time support.
Employer Identification Number: 066040926

922
Fred R. & Hazel W. Carstensen Memorial Foundation, Inc. ⌑
c/o Tellalian & Tellalian
211 State St.
Bridgeport 06604 (203) 333-5566

Established in 1982 in CT.
Foundation type: Independent
Financial data (yr. ended 06/30/89): Assets, $2,013,372 (M); expenditures, $132,024, including $75,500 for 12 grants (high: $20,000; low: $1,000).
Purpose and activities: Support for churches and church-related activities, cultural programs, including a local symphony, hospitals and health organizations, and a YMCA; some support for education.
Limitations: Giving primarily in CT.
Application information:
Initial approach: Letter
Deadline(s): None
Write: Aram H. Tellalian, Jr., Chair.
Officers and Trustees:* Aram H. Tellalian, Jr.,* Chair. and Pres.; Leo C. O'Loughlin,* V.P. and Treas.; Robert S. Tellalian,* Secy.
Employer Identification Number: 061078756

923
Marjorie Sells Carter Boy Scout Scholarship Fund
c/o Cummings & Lockwood
P.O. Box 120
Stamford 06904
Application address: P.O. Box 527, West Chatham, MA 02669

Established in 1974.
Donor(s): Marjorie Sells Carter.†
Foundation type: Independent
Financial data (yr. ended 8/31/89): Assets, $1,111,702 (M); gifts received, $11,083; expenditures, $163,479, including $128,000 for 128 grants to individuals of $1,000 each.
Purpose and activities: Award undergraduate scholarships to New England high school seniors demonstrating achievement and leadership in the Boy Scouts.
Types of support: Student aid.
Limitations: Giving limited to New England residents.
Application information: Applications must be made through local Boy Scouts council executives. Application form required.
Deadline(s): Apr. 1
Write: Joan Shaffer
Trustees: John P. Hammond, Francis P. Schiaroli, Union Trust Co.
Number of staff: 1 part-time support.
Employer Identification Number: 066174937

924
Arthur H. Carter Scholarship Fund
c/o Cummings & Lockwood
P.O. Box 120
Stamford 06904 (813) 921-7747
Application address: c/o American Accounting Assn., Sarasota, FL 33581

Established in 1974 in CT.
Donor(s): Marjorie Sells Carter.†
Foundation type: Independent
Financial data (yr. ended 8/31/89): Assets, $1,293,471 (M); gifts received, $11,083; expenditures, $148,517, including $115,000 for 46 grants to individuals of $2,500 each.
Purpose and activities: Giving only for a scholarship program for students of accounting.
Types of support: Student aid.
Application information: Application form required.
Deadline(s): Apr. 1
Write: Marie Hamilton
Trustees: John P. Hammond, Francis P. Schiaroli, Union Trust Co.
Employer Identification Number: 066177169

925
The Annie E. Casey Foundation ▼
One Lafayette Place
Greenwich 06830 (203) 661-2773
Fax: (203) 661-5127

Incorporated in 1948 in CA.
Donor(s): Annie E. Casey,† James E. Casey,† and members of the Casey family.
Foundation type: Operating
Financial data (yr. ended 12/31/89): Assets, $580,000,000 (M); gifts received, $1,465,570; expenditures, $25,334,074, including $17,755,391 for 34 grants (high: $2,904,067; low: $1,000; average: $1,000-$2,904,067).
Purpose and activities: "A private operating foundation; activities restricted to the welfare of disadvantaged children, youth, and families. Support for five programs: 1) Casey Family Services: an operating branch of the foundation, is a long-term foster care and permanency planning program; 2) New Futures: a five-year initiative designed to help cities address the interrelated problems of academic failure, dropping out of school, adolescent pregnancy, and youth unemployment; 3) The Child Welfare Reform Initiative: a five year project whose purpose is to change the way state child welfare systems serve children, youth, and families. In particular, the program seeks to prevent unnecessary out-of-home placement, and shifts emphasis to more preventive, developmental supports for families; 4) The Juvenile Justice Program: including the Key Decision Maker Project and other related activities, aims to improve the effectiveness of the nation's juvenile justice systems; and 5)

KIDS COUNT: provides state-by-state information on ten key indcators of children's well-being. The indicators range from rates of infant mortality to the proportion of children living in poverty to per-pupil expenditures. KIDS COUNT is a new five-year project designed to improve the collection and use of national, state, and local data on children and families. Its premise is that bringing this information to the public's attention will heighten awareness of the needs of children and to promote accountability for how they are served."
Limitations: No grants to individuals.
Publications: Informational brochure, 990-PF, occasional report.
Application information: Applications accepted only at invitation of foundation; grantees generally selected by foundation to participate in foundation administered programs. Applications not accepted.
Board meeting date(s): Approximately every other month
Write: Douglas W. Nelson, Exec. Dir.
Officers and Trustees:* Kent C. Nelson,* Chair.; Joseph Moderow,* Secy.; John Alden,* Treas.; James Kelly, Donald W. Layden, Gary E. MacDougal, Jr., Frank J. Middendorf, John W. Rogers, Martin Schwartz, Calvin E. Tyler.
Number of staff: 14 full-time professional; 4 full-time support; 2 part-time support.
Employer Identification Number: 136138589

926
Lucy Pang Yoa Chang Foundation ⌘ ☆
35 Church Ln.
Westport 06880-3589

Donor(s): Edwin C. Whitehead.
Foundation type: Independent
Financial data (yr. ended 10/31/88): Assets, $535,323 (M); gifts received, $500,000; expenditures, $167,540, including $167,000 for 6 grants (high: $125,000; low: $2,000).
Purpose and activities: Giving in the following areas of interest: 1) Hunger and poverty in the U.S.; 2) Mental health in the U.S.; and 3) Education, including the development and support of programs directed to the enhancement of human rights throughout the world.
Limitations: No grants to individuals, or for endowment or building funds or fundraising campaigns.
Application information:
Initial approach: Letter or preliminary proposal
Officers and Governors: Rosalind C. Whitehead, Pres.; Charles Loy Hawley, Secy.; Gladys Brazil, Colin Gunn.
Employer Identification Number: 061190397

927
William H. Chapman Foundation
P.O. Box 1321
New London 06320 (203) 443-2811

Established in 1932 in CT.
Foundation type: Independent
Financial data (yr. ended 03/31/89): Assets, $1,517,843 (M); gifts received, $1,675; expenditures, $90,974, including $65,012 for 84 grants to individuals (high: $925; low: $412; average: $825).
Purpose and activities: Giving only for a post-secondary scholarship program for the residents of New London County, CT.
Types of support: Student aid, endowment funds.
Limitations: Giving limited to New London County, CT, area residents. No support for graduate, secondary, or part-time undergraduate students.
Application information: Application form required.
Initial approach: Letter
Deadline(s): Apr. 1
Officers: John A. McGarry, Pres.; William W. Miner, Secy.; Robert C. Weller, Treas.
Trustees: Donald Bradshaw, Mrs. C. Francis Driscoll, Mrs. Robert Kenyon, Spencer Lancaster, Fedele Mugavero, Wesley W. Stoffel, George Tyropolis.
Employer Identification Number: 066034290

928
The Jane Coffin Childs Memorial Fund for Medical Research ▼
333 Cedar St.
New Haven 06510 (203) 785-4612

Trust established in 1937 in CT.
Donor(s): Alice S. Coffin,† Starling W. Childs.†
Foundation type: Independent
Financial data (yr. ended 06/30/89): Assets, $25,868,911 (M); gifts received, $115,880; expenditures, $1,641,941, including $1,445,026 for 78 grants (high: $24,500; low: $3,167).
Purpose and activities: "Primarily for medical research into the causes, origins and treatment of cancer." Grants to institutions only for support of cancer research fellowships.
Types of support: Fellowships, research.
Limitations: No grants to individuals, or for building or endowment funds, matching gifts, or general purposes; no loans.
Publications: Annual report, program policy statement, application guidelines.
Application information: Application form required.
Initial approach: Letter or telephone
Copies of proposal: 17
Deadline(s): Feb. 1
Board meeting date(s): Oct. or Nov. and Apr. or May
Final notification: Nov. and May
Write: Elizabeth M. Ford, Admin. Dir.
Officers: Frederic M. Richards, Dir.; Alice C. Anderson,* Secy.; William G. Gridley, Jr.,* Treas.
Managers:* John W. Childs, Chair.; H. Allen Mali, Vice-Chair.; James E. Childs, Patrick Crossman, Edgar Koerner, Donald S. Lamm, Starling R. Lawrence.
Number of staff: 1 full-time professional; 1 part-time professional; 1 full-time support.
Employer Identification Number: 066034840

929
Community Cooperative Development Foundation ⌘ ☆
333 State St., Suite 303
Bridgeport 06604-4582 (203) 384-1594

Established in 1985 in CT.
Foundation type: Independent
Financial data (yr. ended 9/30/88): Assets, $3,791,995 (M); qualifying distributions, $866,651, including $8,543 for 3 grants (high: $4,204; low: $150), $47,271 for 19 foundation-administered programs and $773,068 for 1 loan.
Purpose and activities: Support for all aspects of low-income housing, from planning and development to operations, with emphasis on cooperative housing techniques.
Types of support: Renovation projects, program-related investments.
Application information: Applications not accepted.
Write: James N. Dancy, Pres.
Officers and Trustees: James N. Dancy, Pres.; Moshe Lichtman, V.P.; Alfred Reynolds, V.P.; William H. Smoot, V.P.; Bennie E. Whiten, Jr., Secy.; Leroy M. Washington, Treas.; and 7 other trustees.
Employer Identification Number: 061030045

930
The Connecticut Mutual Life Foundation, Inc. ▼
140 Garden St.
Hartford 06154 (203) 727-6500

Established in 1976.
Donor(s): Connecticut Mutual Life Insurance Co.
Foundation type: Company-sponsored
Financial data (yr. ended 12/31/89): Assets, $9,606,297 (M); expenditures, $1,292,429, including $1,071,336 for grants (average: $3,000-$6,000) and $211,461 for employee matching gifts.
Purpose and activities: Giving largely for education, particularly higher education, equal opportunity and employment programs, social services, including housing, civic affairs, health agencies, and cultural programs.
Types of support: Operating budgets, continuing support, seed money, matching funds, employee matching gifts, technical assistance, program-related investments, scholarship funds, special projects, capital campaigns, internships, loans.
Limitations: Giving primarily in the Hartford, CT, area. No support for sectarian groups, political organizations, or federated drives outside the local area. No grants to individuals, or for endowment funds, deficit financing, emergency funds, publications, land acquisition, scholarships, fellowships, capital fund drives outside the local area, or goodwill advertising.
Publications: Corporate giving report, informational brochure (including application guidelines).
Application information: Application form not required.
Initial approach: Letter or proposal
Copies of proposal: 1
Deadline(s): None
Board meeting date(s): Mar. and Nov.

Final notification: 3 months
Write: Astrida R. Olds, Asst. V.P.
Officers and Directors:* Myron P. Curzan,* Pres.; Walter J. Gorski,* V.P.; Katharine K. Miller, Secy.; William J. Sullivan, Treas.; Constance Clayton, William Ellis, Denis Mullane, William C. Steere, Jr.
Number of staff: 2 full-time professional; 1 part-time professional; 1 full-time support.
Employer Identification Number: 510192500

931
Carle C. Conway Scholarship Foundation

c/o Continental Can Co., Inc.
800 Connecticut Ave., P.O. Box 5410
Norwalk 06856 (203) 855-5055
Application address: c/o College Scholarship Service, Sponsored Scholarship Programs, P.O. Box 6731, Princeton, NJ 08541

Established in 1950.
Donor(s): Continental Can Co., Inc.
Foundation type: Company-sponsored
Financial data (yr. ended 06/30/89): Assets, $4,519,261 (M); expenditures, $243,276, including $190,000 for 76 grants (high: $2,500; low: $267; average: $2,500).
Purpose and activities: Grants for scholarships only to children of employees administered by College Scholarship Service.
Types of support: Employee-related scholarships.
Application information: Employees must have at least 6 months of continuous service. Application form required.
Deadline(s): Nov. 15
Board meeting date(s): Usually May of following year
Write: Richard M. Sylte, V.P. and Treas.
Officers: Stephen Bermas, Pres.; Richard M. Sylte, V.P. and Treas.; Robert E. Adams, V.P.; JoAnn Hanson, Secy.
Number of staff: None.
Employer Identification Number: 136088936

932
Charles E. Culpeper Foundation, Inc. ▼

Ten Stamford Forum, 8th Fl.
Stamford 06901 (203) 975-1240

Incorporated in 1940 in CT; in 1955 in NY.
Donor(s): Charles E. Culpeper.†
Foundation type: Independent
Financial data (yr. ended 12/31/89): Assets, $138,290,498 (M); gifts received, $1,762; expenditures, $7,792,537, including $6,461,481 for 227 grants (high: $250,000; low: $500; average: $2,500-$75,000).
Purpose and activities: Grants to organizations concerned with health, education, science and technology, arts and letters, administration of justice, and youth programs.
Types of support: Research, general purposes, special projects.
Limitations: No grants to individuals, or for conferences, conduit organizations, operating budgets, or travel; no loans. Limited support only for endowment or building funds.
Publications: Informational brochure, program policy statement, application guidelines, multi-year report.
Application information: Application form required.
Initial approach: Proposal
Copies of proposal: 1
Deadline(s): None
Board meeting date(s): Quarterly
Write: Linda E. Jacobs, Prog. Dir.
Officers and Directors:* Francis J. McNamara, Jr.,* Chair.; Philip M. Drake,* V.P. and Secy.-Treas.; Michael G. Ulasky, Comptroller; Colin G. Campbell, Joseph F. Fahey, Jr., John A. Huston, Helen D. Johnson, John C. Rose, M.D.
Number of staff: 5 full-time professional; 4 part-time support.
Employer Identification Number: 131956297

933
The Daphne Seybolt Culpeper Memorial Foundation, Inc.

129 Musket Ridge Rd.
Norwalk 06850 (203) 762-3984
Application address: P.O. Box 206, Norwalk, CT 06852

Established in 1983 in DE.
Donor(s): Daphne Seybolt Culpeper.†
Foundation type: Independent
Financial data (yr. ended 12/31/89): Assets, $10,071,717 (M); expenditures, $474,674, including $444,748 for 54 grants (high: $25,000; low: $500).
Purpose and activities: Support primarily for higher education, social services, and a hospital.
Types of support: Annual campaigns, continuing support, equipment, general purposes, matching funds, scholarship funds.
Limitations: No grants to individuals.
Publications: Application guidelines.
Application information: Application form not required.
Initial approach: Letter
Copies of proposal: 1
Deadline(s): None
Write: Nicholas J. Nardi, Secy.-Treas.
Officers: Rodney S. Eielson, Pres.; Nicholas J. Nardi, Secy.-Treas.
Number of staff: 1
Employer Identification Number: 222478755

934
D & L Foundation, Inc. ⌘

227 Main St.
New Britain 06050

Established in 1985 in CT.
Foundation type: Independent
Financial data (yr. ended 04/30/89): Assets, $521,036 (L); gifts received, $250,000; expenditures, $249,469, including $249,024 for 29 grants (high: $90,000; low: $35).
Purpose and activities: Support primarily for Jewish welfare and community funds.
Types of support: General purposes.
Limitations: Giving primarily in CT.
Application information:
Initial approach: Letter
Deadline(s): None
Officers and Directors:* Donald Davidson,* C.E.O. and Co-Chair.; Phillip Davidson,* Co-Chair.; Lawrence Davidson,* Pres. and Treas.; Georgiana Pollowitz,* V.P.; Selma Bernshingle,* Secy.; H. David Leventhal,* Secy.; Karl Kochman, Alix Smullen.
Employer Identification Number: 061126433

935
Nancy Sayles Day Foundation

c/o Union Trust Co.
P.O. Box 1297
Stamford 06904 (203) 348-6211

Trust established in 1964 in CT.
Donor(s): Nancy Sayles Day,† Mrs. Lee Day Gillespie.
Foundation type: Independent
Financial data (yr. ended 9/30/89): Assets, $7,982,852 (M); gifts received, $50,313; expenditures, $369,335, including $324,012 for 31 grants (high: $100,000; low: $1,000).
Purpose and activities: Support for music, the arts, higher and secondary education, family services, and youth agencies.
Types of support: Continuing support, general purposes, operating budgets.
Limitations: Giving primarily in MA. No grants to individuals, or for building or endowment funds, research, or matching gifts; no loans.
Publications: 990-PF.
Application information: Application form not required.
Initial approach: Letter
Copies of proposal: 1
Deadline(s): None
Write: John R. Disbrow, V.P., Union Trust Co.
Trustees: Leonard W. Cronkhite, Jr., M.D., Mrs. Lee Day Gillespie, Union Trust Co.
Number of staff: None.
Employer Identification Number: 066071254

936
The Hazel Dell Foundation ⌘

c/o Carroll & Lane
P.O. Box 771
Norwalk 06852 (203) 853-6565

Incorporated in 1956 in DE.
Donor(s): Harry C. McClarity.†
Foundation type: Independent
Financial data (yr. ended 12/31/88): Assets, $2,474,711 (M); expenditures, $193,454, including $125,000 for 44 grants (high: $12,000; low: $100).
Purpose and activities: Grants largely for hospitals, education, aid to the handicapped, and Roman Catholic church support.
Limitations: No support for individuals.
Application information: Application form not required.
Deadline(s): None
Write: June M. Powers, Pres.
Officers: June M. Powers,* Pres.; Joy S. Dunlop,* Secy.; Thomas F. Ryan, Treas.
Directors:* Gail A. Fallon, Diane Schroeder, William J. Sullivan.
Employer Identification Number: 136161744

937
Marie G. Dennett Foundation ⌘

c/o Badger, Fisher, & Cohen
49 West Putnam Ave., P.O. Box 1189
Greenwich 06836

Incorporated in 1956 in IL.
Donor(s): Marie G. Dennett,† Priscilla D. Ramsey.

Foundation type: Independent
Financial data (yr. ended 08/31/89): Assets, $3,229,325 (M); expenditures, $183,086, including $173,600 for 27 grants (high: $50,000; low: $300).
Purpose and activities: Giving primarily for hospitals, youth, education, conservation, cultural programs, and health agencies.
Limitations: No grants to individuals.
Application information: Application form not required.
Initial approach: Proposal
Deadline(s): Sept. 30
Write: Donat C. Marchand, Esq.
Officers and Trustees:* Priscilla D. Ramsey,* Pres.; Lyle B. Ramsey,* V.P.; Everett Fisher,* Secy.-Treas.; Peter H. Blair, James D. Farley.
Number of staff: None.
Employer Identification Number: 061060970

938
The DeNunzio Foundation ⌑ ☆
Three Bridle Path Ln.
Riverside 06878

Established in 1986 in CT.
Donor(s): Ralph DeNunzio.
Foundation type: Independent
Financial data (yr. ended 12/31/88): Assets, $1,422,197 (M); expenditures, $769,362, including $762,500 for 7 grants (high: $500,000; low: $1,000).
Purpose and activities: Giving primarily for higher, secondary, and elementary education.
Limitations: Giving primarily in NY, NJ, and CT. No grants to individuals.
Application information: Contributes only to pre-selected organizations. Applications not accepted.
Trustees: Jean Ames DeNunzio, Ralph DeNunzio.
Employer Identification Number: 222738275

939
Dexter Corporation Foundation, Inc. ⌑
One Elm St.
Windsor Locks 06096 (203) 627-9051

Established in 1976.
Donor(s): The Dexter Corp.
Foundation type: Company-sponsored
Financial data (yr. ended 12/31/88): Assets, $715,481 (M); gifts received, $1,200,000; expenditures, $553,757, including $453,273 for 254 grants (high: $27,000; low: $20) and $100,077 for 201 employee matching gifts.
Purpose and activities: Grants largely for higher education, including employee matching gifts, and for community funds, public policy organizations, business and professional organizations, health and youth agencies, and cultural and historic programs.
Types of support: Employee matching gifts, annual campaigns, capital campaigns, scholarship funds.
Limitations: Giving primarily in areas of business operations.
Publications: Application guidelines.
Application information:
Initial approach: Letter
Deadline(s): None
Write: David L. Coffin, Chair.
Officers and Directors:* David L. Coffin,* Chair.; Worth Loomis,* Pres.; Robert E. McGill III,* Secy.; James F. Calvert, Walter J. Connolly, Jr., Donald W. Davis, William P. Frankenhoff, John H. Page, Donald R. Roon, Peter L. Scott, George M. Whitesides.
Employer Identification Number: 061013754

940
The Dibner Fund, Inc. ▼ ⌑
c/o Burndy Library
Electra Sq.
Norwalk 06856 (203) 852-6203

Incorporated in 1957 in CT.
Donor(s): Barbara Dibner, Bern Dibner, David Dibner.
Foundation type: Independent
Financial data (yr. ended 12/31/88): Assets, $17,698,951 (M); expenditures, $803,383, including $766,138 for 33 grants (high: $392,875; low: $100; average: $500-$50,000).
Purpose and activities: Support largely for history of science institutions and projects; support also for higher education and cultural programs.
Limitations: Giving primarily in CT, NY, and MA. No grants to individuals, or generally for building or endowment funds, scholarships, fellowships, or matching gifts; no loans.
Application information: Contributes only to pre-selected organizations. Applications not accepted.
Board meeting date(s): May
Officers and Trustees:* David Dibner,* Pres.; Frances K. Dibner,* V.P.; George M. Szabad, Secy.-Treas.
Number of staff: None.
Employer Identification Number: 066038482

941
Dorys McConnell Duberg Charitable Trust
c/o Citytrust
961 Main St.
Bridgeport 06601 (203) 384-5195

Trust established in 1969 in CT.
Foundation type: Independent
Financial data (yr. ended 01/31/89): Assets, $1,130,016 (M); expenditures, $68,005, including $59,200 for 14 grants (high: $12,500; low: $500).
Purpose and activities: Giving for medical education and hospitals; support also for social service agencies and religion.
Application information: Application form not required.
Deadline(s): None
Write: Humphrey T. Nichols II, Sr. V.P., Citytrust
Trustees: H.P.J. Duberg, David Hall Faile, Jr., John B. Faile.
Agent: Citytrust.
Employer Identification Number: 237016974

942
The Sidney and Arthur Eder Foundation, Inc.
P.O. Box 949
New Haven 06504 (203) 934-8381
Scholarship application address: c/o Awards Committee, P.O. Box 949, New Haven, CT 06504

Incorporated in 1954 in CT.
Donor(s): Sidney Eder,† Arthur Eder, Eder Bros., Inc.
Foundation type: Independent
Financial data (yr. ended 12/31/89): Assets, $3,835,434 (M); gifts received, $68,000; expenditures, $340,458, including $290,250 for 66 grants (high: $150,000; low: $50) and $30,500 for 14 grants to individuals (high: $4,000; low: $1,000).
Purpose and activities: Grants primarily to local Jewish welfare funds, hospitals and health services, and educational institutions; awards scholarships for children of present or former employees of Eder Bros., Inc.
Types of support: Operating budgets, continuing support, annual campaigns, seed money, emergency funds, building funds, employee-related scholarships.
Limitations: Giving primarily in CT. No grants for matching gifts; no loans.
Application information: Application form required for scholarships.
Initial approach: Letter
Board meeting date(s): Semiannually
Write: Richard Weiss, Trustee
Officer and Trustees:* Arthur Eder,* Chair.; Andrew J. Eder, Richard M. Weiss.
Number of staff: None.
Employer Identification Number: 066035306

943
The Educational Foundation of America ▼
35 Church Ln.
Westport 06880
Grant application office: 23161 Ventura Blvd., Suite 201, Woodland Hills, CA 91364; Tel.: (818) 999-0921

Trust established in 1959 in NY.
Donor(s): Richard P. Ettinger,† Elsie Ettinger,† Richard P. Ettinger, Jr., Elaine P. Hapgood, Paul R. Andrews,† Virgil P. Ettinger,† Barbara P. Ettinger, John G. Powers.
Foundation type: Independent
Financial data (yr. ended 12/31/89): Assets, $103,339,951 (M); gifts received, $69,214; expenditures, $5,098,247, including $4,050,096 for 72 grants (high: $200,000; low: $1,500; average: $10,000-$50,000).
Purpose and activities: Grants largely for higher education, including education for American Indians, medical education, and medical research; grants also for population control, the environment, children's education, and research in gerontology.
Types of support: General purposes, operating budgets, continuing support, seed money, professorships, internships, scholarship funds, matching funds, special projects, research, publications, fellowships.
Limitations: No grants to individuals, or for capital or endowment funds; no loans.
Publications: Annual report.
Application information: Application form not required.
Initial approach: Letter
Copies of proposal: 1
Deadline(s): None

Board meeting date(s): Mar., June, Aug., and Nov.
Final notification: 2 to 3 months
Write: Richard W. Hansen, Exec. Dir.
Officer: Richard W. Hansen, Exec. Dir.
Directors: Elaine P. Hapgood, Chair.; Lynn P. Babicka, David W. Ehrenfeld, Barbara P. Ettinger, Richard P. Ettinger, Jr., S. Haran Ettinger, Edward E. Harrison, Heidi Landesman, Erica Pifer, John P. Powers, Rosalind C. Whitehead, Paul Windels, Jr.
Number of staff: 2 full-time professional; 4 part-time support.
Employer Identification Number: 136147947

944
EIS Foundation, Inc.
19 West Walk
Clinton 06413 (203) 669-5367
Additional address (Oct. 15 to May 15): c/o 4900 Sanctuary Ln., Boca Raton, FL 33431; Tel.: (407) 368-1074

Incorporated in 1951 in CT.
Donor(s): Joseph W. Gilfix,† C.C. Weiss,† and members of the Weiss and Schwarz families.
Foundation type: Independent
Financial data (yr. ended 12/31/89): Assets, $2,456,000 (M); gifts received, $38,000; expenditures, $160,000, including $133,000 for 55 grants.
Purpose and activities: Grants largely for welfare funds, hospitals, higher education, care of the aged and physically handicapped, temple support, and Israel.
Types of support: Capital campaigns, continuing support, emergency funds, scholarship funds.
Limitations: Giving primarily in CT, NY, and FL. No grants to individuals.
Application information: Applications not accepted.
Board meeting date(s): Quarterly
Write: Maurice L. Schwarz, Pres.
Officers and Directors:* Maurice L. Schwarz,* Pres. and Treas.; Bernard M. Schwarz,* V.P. and Secy.; Michael Schwarz.
Number of staff: None.
Employer Identification Number: 066021896

945
The Ellis Fund ⌘
25 Edgewood Dr.
Greenwich 06830

Established in 1983 in CT.
Donor(s): Charles D. Ellis.
Foundation type: Independent
Financial data (yr. ended 12/31/88): Assets, $2,763,843 (M); gifts received, $441,572; expenditures, $18,305, including $5,000 for 1 grant.
Purpose and activities: Support primarily for higher education.
Limitations: No grants to individuals.
Application information: Contributes only to pre-selected organizations. Applications not accepted.
Write: Charles D. Ellis, Trustee
Trustees: Charles D. Ellis, Steven G. Kurtz.
Employer Identification Number: 222505228

946
Emery Air Freight Educational Foundation, Inc. ⌘
Old Danbury Rd.
Wilton 06897 (203) 762-8601

Incorporated in 1965 in CT.
Donor(s): John C. Emery, Sr.,† Mrs. John C. Emery, Sr.,† Emery Air Freight Corp.
Foundation type: Company-sponsored
Financial data (yr. ended 12/31/88): Assets, $1,523,530 (M); expenditures, $131,722, including $112,100 for 41 grants to individuals (high: $5,000; low: $500).
Purpose and activities: Giving limited to scholarships for eligible children of employees of Emery Air Freight Corp.
Types of support: Employee-related scholarships.
Limitations: Giving primarily in CT. No grants to individuals (except for employee-related scholarships), or for general support, building or endowment funds, research, or matching gifts; no loans.
Publications: Application guidelines.
Application information: Request application from human resource manager or department head. Application form required.
Deadline(s): Submit scholarship application by Jan. 1
Board meeting date(s): Apr. and Oct.
Write: John C. Emery, Jr., Pres.
Officers: John C. Emery, Jr.,* Pres.; Daniel J. McCauley, V.P. and Secy.; Arthur W. DeMelle,* V.P. and Treas.
Trustees:* William F. Souders, John T. Thompson.
Employer Identification Number: 066071565

947
Eno Foundation for Transportation, Inc.
270 Saugatuck Ave.
P.O. Box 2055
Westport 06880 (203) 227-4852

Incorporated in 1921 in CT.
Donor(s): William Phelps Eno.†
Foundation type: Operating
Financial data (yr. ended 12/31/89): Assets, $10,067,410 (M); expenditures, $1,020,199, including $2,174 for grants and $222,054 for foundation-administered programs.
Purpose and activities: A private operating foundation that seeks to help improve transportation in all its aspects through the conduct and encouragement of appropriate research and educational activities and through the publication and distribution of information pertaining to transportation planning, design, operation, and regulation, particularly with support for the publication of "Transportation Quarterly" and "Transportation in America."
Types of support: Endowment funds.
Limitations: No grants to individuals.
Publications: 990-PF, informational brochure.
Application information: Applications not accepted.
Board meeting date(s): Feb., May, Aug., and Oct.
Write: Roland A. Ouellette, Pres.
Officers and Directors:* Wilbur S. Smith,* Chair.; Robert S. Holmes,* Vice-Chair.; Roland A. Ouellette,* Pres.; H. Burr Kelsey,* Secy.-Treas.; Joseph M. Clapp, Lawrence D. Dahms, Mark D. Robeson.
Number of staff: 2 full-time professional; 5 full-time support; 1 part-time support.
Employer Identification Number: 060662124

948
The Ensign-Bickford Foundation, Inc. ⌘
Ten Mill Pond Ln.
Simsbury 06070 (203) 658-4411

Incorporated in 1952 in CT.
Donor(s): Ensign-Bickford Industries, Inc.
Foundation type: Company-sponsored
Financial data (yr. ended 12/31/87): Assets, $271,467 (M); gifts received, $447,000; expenditures, $264,851, including $105,451 for 142 grants (high: $15,000; low: $50), $29,000 for 33 grants to individuals (high: $1,750; low: $500), $79,570 for 462 employee matching gifts and $45,125 for 1 foundation-administered program.
Purpose and activities: Grants for welfare, education, and cultural programs; support also for employee-related scholarships, a summer job program for children of company employees, and for employee matching gifts.
Types of support: Continuing support, annual campaigns, seed money, building funds, equipment, land acquisition, special projects, scholarship funds, internships, research, publications, conferences and seminars, employee-related scholarships, employee matching gifts.
Limitations: Giving primarily in areas of company operations, particularly in the Simsbury and Avon, CT, area. No grants to individuals (except for employee-related scholarships), or for general endowment funds, operating budgets, emergency funds, or deficit financing; no loans.
Application information: Application form not required.
Initial approach: Letter
Deadline(s): None
Board meeting date(s): Approximately every two months
Final notification: 3 months
Write: Linda M. Walsh, Secy.
Officers: Robert E. Darling, Pres.; Thornton B. Morris, V.P.; Linda M. Walsh, Secy.; Jeffrey J. Nelb, Treas.
Directors: David C. Balbon, Austin D. Barney II, John E. Ellsworth, Arnold O. Freas, Sandra Ginnis, Frank S. Wilson.
Number of staff: 1 part-time professional.
Employer Identification Number: 066041097

949
The Ensworth Charitable Foundation ⌘
c/o Connecticut National Bank
777 Main St. - MSN 218
Hartford 06115 (203) 728-2274

Trust established in 1948 in CT.
Donor(s): Antoinette L. Ensworth.†
Foundation type: Independent
Financial data (yr. ended 5/31/88): Assets, $8,671,480 (M); gifts received, $5,000; expenditures, $461,450.
Purpose and activities: Emphasis on health and welfare programs, youth activities,

enjoyment of the natural environment, religion, arts, and education.
Types of support: Continuing support, seed money, emergency funds, matching funds, conferences and seminars.
Limitations: Giving limited to Hartford, CT, and vicinity. No grants to individuals, or for operating budgets, annual campaigns, deficit financing, building or endowment funds, equipment and materials, land acquisition, renovation projects, scholarships, fellowships, research, or publications; no loans.
Publications: 990-PF, program policy statement, application guidelines.
Application information: Application form required.
Initial approach: Letter or full proposal
Copies of proposal: 5
Deadline(s): 18th of month preceding board meetings
Board meeting date(s): Feb., May, Aug., and Nov.
Final notification: 1 month
Write: Maxine R. Dean, Community Action Officer
Advisory Committee: William Brown, Jr., Yasha Escalera, Johanna Murphy.
Trustee: Connecticut National Bank.
Number of staff: 1 full-time professional.
Employer Identification Number: 066026018

950
The Sherman Fairchild Foundation, Inc. ▼ ¤
71 Arch St.
Greenwich 06830 (203) 661-9360

Incorporated in 1955 in NY.
Donor(s): May Fairchild,† Sherman Fairchild.†
Foundation type: Independent
Financial data (yr. ended 12/31/88): Assets, $188,385,412 (M); gifts received, $2,998; expenditures, $12,298,144, including $10,199,030 for 36 grants (high: $1,000,000; low: $11,000; average: $100,000-$800,000).
Purpose and activities: Emphasis on higher education and fine arts and cultural institutions; some support for medical research and social welfare.
Application information:
Initial approach: Proposal
Deadline(s): None
Write: Patricia A. Lydon, V.P.
Officers: Walter Burke,* Pres. and Treas.; Patricia A. Lydon, V.P.; Richard C. Pugh,* Secy.
Directors:* Walter F. Burke III, William Elfers, Lee P. Gagliardi, Robert P. Henderson, Bonnie Himmelman, Paul D. Paganucci, Agnar Pytte.
Number of staff: 1 full-time support; 1 part-time support.
Employer Identification Number: 131951698

951
Fairfield County Cooperative Foundation
Five Landmark Sq.
Stamford 06901 (203) 323-7410

Incorporated in 1982 in CT.
Foundation type: Community
Financial data (yr. ended 12/31/89): Assets, $1,704,717 (M); gifts received, $146,538; expenditures, $1,105,078, including $989,937 for 60 grants (high: $90,000; low: $1,000).
Purpose and activities: Grants for health and social services, arts and culture, education, environment, and government and urban affairs.
Types of support: Scholarship funds, seed money, special projects, conferences and seminars, matching funds, research, consulting services, emergency funds, internships, publications, technical assistance.
Limitations: Giving limited to Fairfield County, CT. No grants to individuals; low priority given to requests for endowments, capital projects, building funds, continuing support, deficit financing, general operating support, fellowships, or annual giving; no loans.
Publications: Grants list, application guidelines, newsletter.
Application information: Application form not required.
Initial approach: Telephone or letter requesting guidelines
Copies of proposal: 1
Deadline(s): 1 month prior to meeting dates
Board meeting date(s): 3rd Friday in Feb., Apr., Aug., and Oct.
Write: Betsy Rich, Exec. Dir.
Officers: Barbara S. Preiskel, Chair.; Lorie A. Slutsky, Pres.; Sidney S. Whelan, Jr., V.P. and Secy.; Karen Metcalf, V.P. and Treas.; Betsy Rich, V.P. and Exec. Dir.; Joyce M. Bove, V.P.
Distribution Committee: Dana Ackerly, Kaye E. Barker, Nancy C. Brown, George F. Carroll, Jr., Karl H. Epple, Edward E. Harrison, Harold Howe, Jr., Sydney C. Kweskin, Violet Manon.
Number of staff: 1 full-time professional; 1 part-time support.
Employer Identification Number: 061083896

952
Fisher Foundation, Inc.
36 Brookside Blvd.
West Hartford 06107 (203) 523-7247

Established in 1959.
Donor(s): Stanley D. Fisher Trust, FIP Corp.
Foundation type: Independent
Financial data (yr. ended 12/31/88): Assets, $21,322 (M); gifts received, $454,291; expenditures, $445,550, including $435,543 for 69 grants (high: $69,000; low: $100).
Purpose and activities: Giving primarily to a Jewish welfare federation, health services, education, the aged, the disadvantaged, employment, and housing.
Limitations: Giving primarily in the greater Hartford, CT, area.
Publications: Application guidelines.
Application information: Application form not required.
Initial approach: Letter or proposal
Copies of proposal: 2
Deadline(s): Feb. 1, May 1, and Oct. 1
Board meeting date(s): Mar., June, and Nov.
Write: Martha Newman, Exec. Dir.
Officers and Directors:* Hinda N. Fisher,* Pres. and Treas.; Diane Fisher Bell,* V.P.; Lois Fisher Ruge,* V.P.; Nancy S. Freeman,* Secy.
Number of staff: 1 part-time professional.
Employer Identification Number: 066039415

953
Maud Glover Folsom Foundation, Inc.
P.O. Box 151
Harwinton 06791 (203) 485-0405

Incorporated in 1957 in NY.
Donor(s): Charles Stuart Folsom.†
Foundation type: Independent
Financial data (yr. ended 07/31/89): Assets, $3,065,953 (M); expenditures, $198,973, including $145,000 for 68 grants to individuals (high: $2,500; low: $1,250).
Purpose and activities: To provide education for selected male students of American ancestry, and of Anglo-Saxon or German descent between the ages of fourteen and twenty, subject to certain conditions; ineligible upon reaching age twenty. Annual grants of $2,500 will contunue, providing grantee maintains a C plus average while persuing his education which could continue through a Doctorate.
Types of support: Student aid.
Publications: Informational brochure (including application guidelines).
Application information: Application form required.
Initial approach: Letter
Board meeting date(s): As required
Write: Leon A. Francisco, Pres.
Officers and Trustees:* Leon A. Francisco,* Pres.; C. Merrill Austin,* Secy.; Barry W. Smith,* Treas.
Number of staff: None.
Employer Identification Number: 111965890

954
Foster-Davis Foundation, Inc. ¤
c/o Cummings & Lockwood
P.O. Box 1669
Greenwich 06836-1669

Donor(s): Charles J.R. Davis,† Alma F. Davis Charitable Lead Trust.
Foundation type: Independent
Financial data (yr. ended 5/31/89): Assets, $3,987,616 (M); gifts received, $960,287; expenditures, $320,237, including $300,309 for 26 grants (high: $150,000; low: $10).
Purpose and activities: Giving primarily for research in biology, recreational facilities, and health associations.
Limitations: No grants to individuals.
Application information: Contributes only to pre-selected organizations. Applications not accepted.
Officers and Directors:* Foster Bam,* Pres.; Edward F. Rodenbach,* V.P. and Secy.; Nancy A. Nelson, Treas.; Howard S. Tuthill.
Employer Identification Number: 060811599

955
Jacob L. & Lewis Fox Foundation Trust ¤
c/o Connecticut National Bank
777 Main St.
Hartford 06115
Scholarship application address: c/o G. William Saxton, Hartford Public Schools, 249 High St., Hartford, CT 06103; Tel.: (203) 722-8725

Trust established about 1951 in CT.
Donor(s): Lewis Fox.†

Foundation type: Independent
Financial data (yr. ended 12/31/88): Assets, $2,894,786 (M); expenditures, $190,728, including $160,451 for 143 grants to individuals (high: $5,430; low: $93).
Purpose and activities: Scholarship awards limited to students graduating from and chosen by Hartford public schools.
Types of support: Student aid.
Limitations: Giving limited to graduates of Hartford, CT, public high schools.
Application information: Scholarship application forms and eligibility requirements provided only through Hartford public schools; applications directly to Trust not accepted. Application form required.
Deadline(s): Usually in late Jan. or early Feb.
Officers and Trustees:* G. William Saxton,* Chair.; Lillian Thomas,* Vice-Chair.; Arthur J. Querido,* Secy.; David W. Parmelee,* Treas.; Amado G. Cruz, Rev. Charles W. Daly, Elizabeth B. Noel, Robert E. Stevens.
Employer Identification Number: 066067700

956
Garden Homes Fund ☆
P.O. Box 4401
29 Knapp St.
Stamford 06907-1799 (203) 348-2200

Established in 1981 in CT.
Foundation type: Independent
Financial data (yr. ended 12/31/89): Assets, $1,500,000 (M); expenditures, $150,000, including $150,000 for grants (average: $50-$10,000).
Purpose and activities: Giving primarily for the United Way and social services; support also for conservation.
Types of support: Annual campaigns, building funds, capital campaigns.
Limitations: No grants to individuals.
Application information: Contributes only to pre-selected organizations. Applications not accepted.
Write: Joel Freedman, Trustee
Trustees and Directors: Deborah Freedman, Jane Freedman, Joel E. Freedman, Naomi K. Freedman, Richard Freedman.
Number of staff: None.
Employer Identification Number: 061043730

957
General Electric Foundation ▼
3135 Easton Tpke.
Fairfield 06431 (203) 373-3216

Trust established in 1952 in NY.
Donor(s): General Electric Co.
Foundation type: Company-sponsored
Financial data (yr. ended 12/31/89): Assets, $32,613,000 (M); gifts received, $12,695,000; expenditures, $24,900,000, including $15,251,328 for 715 grants (high: $575,000; low: $100; average: $5,000-$100,000) and $3,582,836 for employee matching gifts.
Purpose and activities: Institutional grants primarily in support of education, with emphasis on: 1) strengthening specific areas of work in undergraduate education; 2) graduate-level research and teaching; 3) support for disciplinary fields, including the physical sciences, engineering, computer science, mathematics, industrial management, and business administration; 4) support for minority group education programs, with emphasis on engineering and business; and 5) matching educational contributions of employees. Support also for community funds in communities where the company has a significant presence, selected public schools, arts and cultural centers, public issues research and analysis, equal opportunity, international understanding, and other special grants. Grants are directed toward specific programs authorized by the trustees and most are approved in advance of each calendar year.
Types of support: Annual campaigns, continuing support, employee matching gifts, fellowships, general purposes, publications, research, scholarship funds, seed money, special projects.
Limitations: Giving limited to the U.S. and its possessions; grants to community funds limited to areas where the company has a significant presence. No support for religious or sectarian groups. No grants to individuals, or for capital or endowment funds, or other special purpose campaigns, scholarships, or equipment donations; no loans.
Publications: Annual report (including application guidelines), informational brochure.
Application information: Ability to respond to unsolicited requests is extremely limited. Applications for funding is largely by invitation only. Application form not required.
Initial approach: Proposal
Copies of proposal: 1
Deadline(s): None
Board meeting date(s): Quarterly
Final notification: Varies
Write: Clifford V. Smith, Jr., Pres.
Officers: Clifford V. Smith, Jr., Pres.; Michael J. Cosgrove, Treas.; Jane L. Polin, Comptroller.
Trustees: Dennis D. Dammerman, Chair.; James P. Baughman, Frank P. Doyle, Benjamin W. Heineman, Joyce Hergenhan, Jack O. Peiffer, William J. Sheeran.
Number of staff: 7 full-time professional; 4 full-time support.
Employer Identification Number: 146015766

958
General Electric Foundation, Inc.
3135 Easton Turnpike
Fairfield 06431 (203) 373-3216

Established in 1985 in CT.
Donor(s): General Electric Co.
Foundation type: Company-sponsored
Financial data (yr. ended 12/31/89): Assets, $674,000 (M); expenditures, $998,000, including $735,585 for 25 grants (high: $100,000; low: $2,500; average: $5,000-$50,000) and $6,652 for 182 employee matching gifts.
Purpose and activities: Giving primarily to innovative organizations that will play a significant role internationally in advancing charitable, scientific, literary, or educational programs.
Types of support: Special projects, research, employee matching gifts.
Limitations: Giving limited to foreign or domestic organizations whose funds will be spent outside the U.S. and its possessions. No support for religious or sectarian groups. No grants to individuals, or for capital or endowment funds, scholarships, or equipment donations; no loans.
Publications: Annual report (including application guidelines).
Application information: Ability to respond to unsolicited proposals is extremely limited. Applications for funding is largely by invitation only. Application form not required.
Initial approach: Proposal
Copies of proposal: 1
Deadline(s): None
Board meeting date(s): Quarterly
Final notification: Varies
Write: Clifford V. Smith, Jr., Pres.
Officers: Clifford V. Smith, Jr., Pres.; Michael J. Cosgrove, Treas.; Jane L. Polin, Comptroller.
Directors: Dennis D. Dammerman, Chair.; James P. Baughman, Frank P. Doyle, Benjamin W. Heineman, Joyce Hergenhan, Jack O. Peiffer.
Number of staff: 2 full-time professional; 1 full-time support.
Employer Identification Number: 222621967

959
R. S. Gernon Trust
c/o Connecticut National Bank
250 Captain's Walk
New London 06320 (203) 447-6131
Application address for individuals: 161 Water St., Norwich, CT 06360

Established in 1975 in CT.
Foundation type: Independent
Financial data (yr. ended 06/30/89): Assets, $1,221,428 (M); expenditures, $62,496, including $50,779 for 18 grants (high: $6,090; low: $478).
Purpose and activities: Support primarily for cultural programs, health services, youth, and social services, including programs for women.
Types of support: Capital campaigns, conferences and seminars, consulting services, equipment, matching funds, publications, renovation projects, research, scholarship funds, seed money, special projects, technical assistance.
Limitations: Giving primarily in Norwich, CT.
Publications: Program policy statement, application guidelines.
Application information: Application form required.
Copies of proposal: 1
Deadline(s): Feb. 15 and Aug. 15
Final notification: Apr. 1 and Oct. 1
Write: Roger Gross, V.P., Connecticut National Bank
Trustee: Connecticut National Bank.
Employer Identification Number: 066142263

960
Herbert Gilman Family Charitable Foundation ⌑
165 Orchard St.
West Hartford 06117

Established in 1964 in CT.
Foundation type: Independent
Financial data (yr. ended 01/31/89): Assets, $1,123,181 (M); gifts received, $235,003;

expenditures, $240,218, including $238,918 for 32 grants (high: $110,500; low: $18).
Purpose and activities: Support for higher education, health organizations, and the performing arts; some support for Jewish welfare organizations.
Types of support: General purposes.
Application information: Contributes only to pre-selected organizations. Applications not accepted.
Trustees: Morris Crosky, Evelyn Gilman, Herbert Gilman.
Employer Identification Number: 066071321

961
Harry E. Goldfarb Family Foundation, Inc. ⌑ ☆
c/o Blum Shapiro & Co., P.C.
231 Farmington Ave., P.O. Box 900
Farmington 06034

Established in 1980.
Donor(s): Harry E. Goldfarb, Robert B. Goldfarb, William H. Goldfarb.
Foundation type: Independent
Financial data (yr. ended 5/31/89): Assets, $1,305,094 (M); gifts received, $500,000; expenditures, $181,603, including $176,661 for 51 grants (high: $50,000; low: $25).
Purpose and activities: Giving primarily for Jewish organizations, especially welfare funds; support also for higher, legal, and other education.
Types of support: Annual campaigns, building funds, capital campaigns, scholarship funds.
Limitations: Giving primarily in CT. No grants to individuals.
Application information: Contributes only to pre-selected organizations. Applications not accepted.
Officers: Harry E. Goldfarb, Pres.; Robert B. Goldfarb, V.P.; William H. Goldfarb, Secy.-Treas.
Employer Identification Number: 061025623

962
Alexander A. Goldfarb Memorial Trust ⌑ ☆
97 Elm St.
Hartford 06103

Donor(s): Alexander A. Goldfarb.†
Foundation type: Independent
Financial data (yr. ended 12/31/88): Assets, $1,016,725 (M); gifts received, $1,075,000; expenditures, $98,475, including $93,589 for 8 grants (high: $46,539; low: $150).
Purpose and activities: Giving for a municipality, a public radio station, higher education, and the arts.
Types of support: General purposes, capital campaigns, scholarship funds.
Limitations: Giving primarily in CT. No grants to individuals.
Application information:
Initial approach: Letter
Deadline(s): None
Write: James H. Kinsella or A. Carter Pottash, Trustees
Trustees: James H. Kinsella, A. Carter Pottash, M.D.
Employer Identification Number: 066284139

963
Great Northern Nekoosa Foundation, Inc.
P.O. Box 5120
Norwalk 06856-5120 (203) 845-9000

Incorporated in 1974 in CT.
Donor(s): Great Northern Nekoosa Corp.
Foundation type: Company-sponsored
Financial data (yr. ended 12/31/89): Assets, $1,470,000 (M); gifts received, $2,000,000; expenditures, $909,184, including $908,434 for 160 grants (high: $106,136; low: $100; average: $5,000).
Purpose and activities: Giving primarily for hospitals, higher education, and youth agencies; support also for the arts, and civic organizations.
Types of support: Annual campaigns, building funds, capital campaigns, continuing support, general purposes, research, scholarship funds, special projects.
Limitations: Giving primarily in ME, WI, GA, and MS. No support for religious or political organizations.
Application information: Application form not required.
Copies of proposal: 1
Deadline(s): None
Write: Shirley Leopold, Secy.
Officers: William R. Laidig, Pres.; James G. Crump, V.P.; Stephen M. Hill, V.P.; William Laimbeer, V.P.; Victor F. Mattson, V.P.; Arnold M. Nemirow, V.P.; Joseph F. O'Handley, V.P.; Ronald J. Rakowski, V.P.; Raymond H. Taylor, V.P.; Francis G. Walker, V.P.; Shirley Leopold, Secy.; Douglas C. Wright, Treas.
Number of staff: 1 part-time support.
Employer Identification Number: 237424336

964
Maurice Greenberg Family Foundation, Inc. ⌑
c/o Coleco Industries
80 Darling Dr.
Avon 06001-4236

Established in 1963 in CT.
Foundation type: Independent
Financial data (yr. ended 12/31/88): Assets, $101,170 (M); expenditures, $182,736, including $182,008 for 4 grants (high: $130,258; low: $250).
Purpose and activities: Giving primarily for Jewish welfare and the arts.
Limitations: No grants to individuals.
Application information: Contributes only to pre-selected organizations. Applications not accepted.
Officers: Leonard E. Greenberg, Chair. and Secy.; Arnold C. Greenberg, Pres. and Treas.
Employer Identification Number: 066066013

965
Hunter Grubb Foundation, Inc.
P.O. Box 578
Old Lyme 06371

Incorporated in 1968 in FL.
Donor(s): Anna G. Horn,† Martha G. Moore.†
Foundation type: Independent
Financial data (yr. ended 06/30/89): Assets, $1,204,576 (M); gifts received, $11,140; expenditures, $86,813, including $81,300 for 20 grants (high: $10,000; low: $1,000).
Purpose and activities: Giving primarily for scholarships.
Types of support: Scholarship funds.
Limitations: Giving primarily in the northeastern U.S. No grants to individuals.
Application information: Applications not accepted.
Officers and Trustees:* Hunter G. Hannum,* Chair.; Hildegarde Hannum,* Secy.-Treas.; Carl Fulwiler, M.D., Hughes Griffis.
Number of staff: None.
Employer Identification Number: 596202749

966
GTE Foundation ▼
One Stamford Forum
Stamford 06904 (203) 965-3620

Trust established in 1952 in NY as the Sylvania Foundation; renamed in 1960 as General Telephone & Electronics Foundation; renamed again in 1982.
Donor(s): GTE Corp., and subsidiaries.
Foundation type: Company-sponsored
Financial data (yr. ended 12/31/89): Assets, $21,455,383 (M); gifts received, $17,696,375; expenditures, $18,991,288, including $15,262,931 for 1,622 grants (high: $2,300,000; low: $1,000) and $2,780,916 for 5,525 employee matching gifts.
Purpose and activities: Emphasis on higher education in mathematics, science, and technology, and retention of minority students; sponsors an employee-related scholarship program through the College Scholarship Service; support also for community funds, the performing arts, and social service agencies.
Types of support: Emergency funds, scholarship funds, fellowships, employee matching gifts, continuing support, employee-related scholarships, lectureships, operating budgets, special projects, program-related investments.
Limitations: Giving limited to areas of company operations and national organizations deemed to be of broad benefit to GTE companies, employees, shareholders, or customers. No grants to individuals (except for scholarships to the children of GTE employees), or for research; no loans.
Publications: Annual report, application guidelines.
Application information: Application form not required.
Initial approach: Letter or proposal
Copies of proposal: 2
Deadline(s): Fall
Board meeting date(s): Feb., May, Aug., Dec., and as required
Final notification: After Dec. 15
Write: Maureen Gorman, Secy. and Dir., Corporate Social Responsibility
Officer: Maureen Gorman, Secy. and Dir., Corporate Social Responsibility.
Trustees: James L. Johnson, Chair.; Bruce Carswell, Charles R. Lee, Edward Schmults, Nicholas Trivisonno.
Number of staff: 3 full-time professional; 5 full-time support; 2 part-time support.
Employer Identification Number: 136046680

967
Ellen Knowles Harcourt Foundation, Inc. ¤
c/o George Verenes
12 Aspetuck Ave.
New Milford 06776 (203) 355-2631
Application address: c/o Paul B. Altermatt, Pres., 51 Main St., New Milford, CT 06776

Established in 1982 in CT.
Donor(s): Ellen Knowles Harcourt.†
Foundation type: Independent
Financial data (yr. ended 12/31/88): Assets, $1,488,067 (M); expenditures, $94,890, including $76,131 for 26 grants (high: $8,500; low: $500).
Purpose and activities: Support primarily for higher education and music programs.
Limitations: Giving primarily in the New Milford, CT, area.
Application information:
Initial approach: Letter
Deadline(s): None
Officers and Directors: Paul B. Altermatt, Pres.; R. McFarland Tilley, Secy.; George Verenes, Treas.; Adele F. Ghisalbert, Alice McCallister, Leandro Pasqual.
Employer Identification Number: 061068025

968
The Hartford Courant Foundation, Inc.
285 Broad St.
Hartford 06115 (203) 241-6472

Established in 1950 in CT as a corporate foundation; restructured in 1980 as a private, independent foundation.
Foundation type: Independent
Financial data (yr. ended 12/31/89): Assets, $10,551,383 (M); expenditures, $685,575, including $579,340 for 95 grants (high: $65,000; low: $75; average: $4,000-$10,000) and $35,500 for 37 grants to individuals (high: $2,000; low: $500; average: $500-$2,000).
Purpose and activities: Giving primarily for arts and cultural programs, education, health and social service agencies, emerging community needs, and journalism; support also for promotion of excellence in secondary school scholarship aid for Hispanic students through foundation-operated program.
Types of support: Land acquisition, scholarship funds, building funds, capital campaigns, equipment, general purposes, operating budgets, renovation projects, seed money, special projects, student aid, technical assistance, matching funds, publications, scholarship funds.
Limitations: Giving limited to the central CT area. No support for religious organizations (for sectarian purposes), veterans, fraternal, professional, or business associations, political groups, or private schools. No grants to individuals (except secondary school scholarships) or for continuing support, endowment or emergency funds, conferences, performances, or other short-term, one-time events; no loans.
Publications: Annual report, application guidelines, informational brochure (including application guidelines).
Application information: Application form required.
Initial approach: Telephone
Copies of proposal: 1
Deadline(s): Dec. 15, Mar. 15, June 15, and Sept. 15
Board meeting date(s): Feb., May, Sept., and Nov.
Final notification: 3 months
Write: Alexandrina M. Sergio, Exec. Dir.
Officers and Trustees:* Martha S. Newman,* Pres.; Alexandrina M. Sergio, Secy.; Richard H. King, Treas.; William O. Bailey, Michael Davies, Joyce Fields, Elliot F. Gerson, Raymond A. Jansen, Jr., Linda J. Kelly, David Laventhol, Sylvia Levy, Worth Loomis, Millard H. Pryor, Jr., George A. Scott.
Number of staff: 1 full-time professional.
Employer Identification Number: 060759107

969
Hartford Foundation for Public Giving ▼
85 Gillett St.
Hartford 06105 (203) 548-1888

Established in 1925 in CT by resolution and declaration of trust.
Foundation type: Community
Financial data (yr. ended 09/30/89): Assets, $148,444,598 (M); gifts received, $7,455,422; expenditures, $8,518,631, including $7,351,366 for 268 grants (high: $250,000; low: $240; average: $45,000-$55,000) and $141,280 for 3 loans.
Purpose and activities: Giving for demonstration programs and capital purposes, with emphasis on community advancement, educational institutions, youth groups, hospitals, social services, including the aged, and cultural and civic endeavors.
Types of support: Seed money, emergency funds, building funds, equipment, land acquisition, matching funds, scholarship funds, loans, special projects, renovation projects, technical assistance, capital campaigns.
Limitations: Giving limited to the greater Hartford, CT, area. No support for sectarian purposes or tax-supported agencies. No grants to individuals, or for operating budgets, continuing support, annual campaigns, deficit financing, endowment funds, research, publications, or conferences.
Publications: Annual report, application guidelines, program policy statement, newsletter, informational brochure.
Application information: Application form required.
Initial approach: Telephone
Copies of proposal: 3
Deadline(s): Educ. & youth, Jan. 30; Family, children, & early childhood, Mar. 30; Health care, July 30; Housing & economic devel., Sept. 30; Arts & culture, Nov. 30; Sum. prog. & camperships, Jan. 15; and general grants, May 30
Board meeting date(s): Monthly except Aug.
Final notification: 60 to 90 days
Write: Michael R. Bangser, Exec. Dir.
Officers and Distribution Committee: Frederick G. Adams, Chair.; James F. English, Jr., Vice-Chair.; Michael R. Bangser, Secy. and Exec. Dir.; Brewster P. Perkins, Treas.; Maria Borrero, Alan E. Green, George Levine, Jon O. Newman, Sue Ann Shay, Judith S. Wawro, Wilson Wilde.
Trustee Banks: Connecticut Bank & Trust Co., N.A., Connecticut National Bank, United Bank & Trust Co., Society for Savings.
Number of staff: 7 full-time professional; 4 part-time professional; 6 full-time support.
Employer Identification Number: 060699252

970
The Hartford Insurance Group Foundation, Inc. ▼
Hartford Plaza
Hartford 06115 (203) 547-4972
Additional tel.: (203) 547-5816

Incorporated in 1966 in CT.
Donor(s): Hartford Fire Insurance Co., and affiliates.
Foundation type: Company-sponsored
Financial data (yr. ended 12/31/87): Assets, $257,482 (M); gifts received, $2,200,000; expenditures, $1,892,938, including $1,673,175 for grants (high: $420,000; average: $2,000-$25,000), $12,900 for grants to individuals and $200,056 for employee matching gifts.
Purpose and activities: Giving primarily for higher education (including employee-related scholarships through the National Merit Scholarship Corporation and employee matching gifts program), job training, community funds, health, urban and civic affairs, arts and culture, and the aged; also administers a community service fund that supports the efforts of its employees in community programs.
Types of support: Scholarship funds, employee matching gifts, employee-related scholarships, building funds, annual campaigns, special projects.
Limitations: Giving primarily in the Hartford, CT, area, and in communities where the company has a regional office. No support for political or religious purposes, disease-specific health organizations, student group trips or parades, United Way member agencies, public educational organizations (except for matching gifts program), or national fund drives or research programs not having a clear relationship to overall interests of the company and only on an exceptional basis. No grants to individuals, or for endowment funds, conferences, travel, testimonial or fundraising dinners, membership in business, professional and trade associations, courtesy advertising, or capital fund drives outside the greater Hartford area.
Publications: Corporate giving report (including application guidelines), informational brochure.
Application information: Application form required.
Initial approach: Letter
Copies of proposal: 1
Deadline(s): None
Board meeting date(s): Quarterly
Write: Sandra A. Sharr, Dir., Community Affairs
Officers and Director:* Donald R. Frahm,* Pres.; Michael S. Wilder, V.P.; Michael O'Halloran, Secy.; J. Richard Garrett, Treas.
Number of staff: 1 full-time professional; 1 part-time support.
Employer Identification Number: 066079761

971
The Hartley Corporation ⌑
c/o Robert H. Mead
Yale Farm
Norfolk 06058

Established in 1921 in CT.
Foundation type: Independent
Financial data (yr. ended 5/31/88): Assets, $1,262,786 (M); expenditures, $100,000, including $72,000 for 32 grants (high: $33,000; low: $350).
Purpose and activities: Giving primarily for social services.
Application information: Applications not accepted.
Officer: Robert H. Mead, Pres.
Employer Identification Number: 066036296

972
The Hascoe Family Foundation ⌑
35 Mason St.
Greenwich 06830

Foundation type: Independent
Financial data (yr. ended 12/31/88): Assets, $709,229 (M); expenditures, $323,876, including $320,325 for 21 grants (high: $250,000; low: $50).
Purpose and activities: Support primarily for Jewish organizations; support also for research and higher education.
Types of support: General purposes.
Application information: Application form not required.
Initial approach: Letter
Deadline(s): None
Write: Norman Hascoe, Pres.
Officers and Directors:* Norman Hascoe,* Pres.; Suzanne Hascoe,* Secy.; Lloyd Hascoe,* Treas.; Andrew Hascoe, Stephanie Hascoe.
Employer Identification Number: 222529898

973
The Heritage Foundation, Inc. ⌑
572 White Plains Rd.
Trumbull 06611

Incorporated in 1967 in CT.
Donor(s): June C. Anderson, G.W. Aldeen Charitable Trust, Christian Heritage School, Inc.
Foundation type: Independent
Financial data (yr. ended 12/31/88): Assets, $2,145,797 (M); expenditures, $87,878, including $26,920 for 2 grants (high: $17,000; low: $9,920; average: $7,000).
Purpose and activities: Giving primarily for a Protestant church; some support for Christian primary and secondary educational institutions.
Types of support: General purposes, operating budgets, special projects.
Limitations: Giving primarily in CT. No grants to individuals.
Application information: Contributes only to pre-selected organizations. Applications not accepted.
Write: Paul H. Anderson, Pres.
Officers and Directors: Paul H. Anderson, Pres.; Barton P. Anderson, V.P.; Timothy J. Anderson, V.P.; June C. Anderson, Secy.; Bradley S. Anderson, Treas.
Employer Identification Number: 066090012

974
The Carl J. Herzog Foundation, Inc. ▼ ⌑
c/o Bentley, Lane, Mosher, and Babson
970 Summer St.
Stamford 06905 (203) 323-1414

Incorporated in 1952 in CT.
Foundation type: Independent
Financial data (yr. ended 12/31/86): Assets, $20,648,653 (M); expenditures, $912,430, including $825,838 for 72 grants (high: $118,750; low: $6,000; average: $6,000-$60,000).
Purpose and activities: To promote medical research, particularly in the field of dermatology; general support also for hospitals.
Types of support: Research, general purposes.
Application information:
Initial approach: Letter
Deadline(s): None
Write: Peter Bentley, Pres.
Officers and Directors: Peter Bentley, Pres.; Sidney A.W. Cahusac, V.P.; Nancy M. Alcock, Secy.; David F. Babson, Jr., Treas.
Employer Identification Number: 510200524

975
Heublein Foundation, Inc.
P.O. Box 388
Farmington 06032 (203) 677-4061
Application address: Heublein Foundation Scholarship Program, College Scholarship Service, CN 6730, Princeton, NJ 08541

Incorporated in 1960 in DE.
Donor(s): Heublein, Inc., KFC Corp.
Foundation type: Company-sponsored
Financial data (yr. ended 12/31/88): Assets, $322,702 (M); gifts received, $1,200,000; expenditures, $1,040,451, including $827,478 for 89 grants (high: $126,000; low: $500; average: $1,000-$50,000), $36,100 for 20 grants to individuals (high: $5,000; low: $1,000) and $164,478 for employee matching gifts.
Purpose and activities: Emphasis on the arts, community funds, higher education, including employee-related scholarships, hospitals and health services, youth agencies, and hunger.
Types of support: Employee matching gifts, scholarship funds, employee-related scholarships.
Limitations: Giving primarily in Farmington, CT, and areas of company operations. No grants for endowment funds.
Application information: Scholarship program for children of employees of Heublein, Inc. Application form not required.
Initial approach: Letter
Copies of proposal: 1
Deadline(s): Jan. 1 for scholarships
Board meeting date(s): As required
Write: L. Eileen Hall, Treas.
Officers and Directors:* Peter M. Seremet, Pres.; Robert C. Barker, V.P.; Robert M. Furek, V.P.; Richard E. Walton,* Secy.; L. Eileen Hall, Treas.; Chester J. Evans, John A. Powers.
Employer Identification Number: 066051280

976
Annette Heyman Foundation, Inc. ⌑ ☆
Box 7002
Westport 06881-7002

Established in 1960.
Donor(s): Annette Heyman, Samuel J. Heyman.
Foundation type: Independent
Financial data (yr. ended 9/30/88): Assets, $1,383,426 (M); expenditures, $162,995, including $161,935 for 12 grants (high: $150,525; low: $10).
Purpose and activities: Giving primarily for a Jewish university; minor support for other Jewish organizations.
Limitations: Giving primarily in NY. No grants to individuals.
Application information: Contributes only to pre-selected organizations. Applications not accepted.
Officers: Annette Heyman, Pres.; Ronnie Heyman, Secy.; Samuel J. Heyman, Treas.
Employer Identification Number: 066035519

977
Hilltop Foundation, Inc. ⌑ ☆
138 Frogtown Rd.
New Canaan 06840

Established in 1985 in CT.
Donor(s): Austin O. Furst, Jr.
Foundation type: Independent
Financial data (yr. ended 10/31/87): Assets, $1,477,152 (M); expenditures, $156,826, including $156,625 for 14 grants (high: $38,500; low: $1,000).
Purpose and activities: Giving primarily for elementary and secondary education and social services, including a shelter for the homeless and a Methodist home for the aged; support also for higher education and the arts.
Limitations: No grants to individuals.
Application information: Contributes only to pre-selected organizations. Applications not accepted.
Officers and Directors: Leslie Furst, Pres. and Treas.; Klaus Eppler, Secy.; Alan P. Parnes.
Employer Identification Number: 133345688

978
The Howard and Bush Foundation, Inc. ▼
85 Gillett St.
Hartford 06105 (203) 236-8595
Application address for the Troy, NY, area: Deborah Byers, Two Belk Ave., Troy, NY 12180; Tel.: (518) 273-6005

Incorporated in 1961 in CT.
Donor(s): Edith Mason Howard,† Julia Howard Bush.†
Foundation type: Independent
Financial data (yr. ended 12/31/89): Assets, $7,822,626 (M); expenditures, $1,423,024, including $1,346,985 for 77 grants (high: $72,052; low: $3,500; average: $5,000-$25,000).
Purpose and activities: Emphasis on social service and youth agencies, cultural programs, education, civic and urban affairs, and health agencies.
Types of support: Special projects, building funds, equipment, matching funds.

Limitations: Giving primarily in the Hartford, CT, and Troy, NY, areas. No support for government or largely tax-supported agencies, or to colleges, schools, or churches not connected with the founders. No grants to individuals, or for endowment funds, operating budgets, reserve or revolving funds, or deficit financing.
Publications: Annual report, application guidelines.
Application information: Contact staff well before submitting proposal. Application form required.
Initial approach: Letter
Copies of proposal: 10
Deadline(s): Feb. 1, June 1, and Oct. 1
Board meeting date(s): Mar., July, and Nov.
Final notification: Within 10 days after board meeting
Write: Nancy Roberts
Officers and Trustees:* Sara H. Catlin,* Pres.; Thomas S. Melvin,* V.P.; James Lyons,* Secy.; Connecticut Bank & Trust Co., N.A.,* Treas.; David Leith, Margaret Mochan, Ned Paitison, David Parmelee.
Number of staff: 2 part-time professional; 1 part-time support.
Employer Identification Number: 066059063

979
The Harvey Hubbell Foundation
584 Derby-Milford Rd.
P.O. Box 549
Orange 06477-4024 (203) 789-1100

Trust established in 1959 in CT.
Donor(s): Harvey Hubbell, Inc.
Foundation type: Company-sponsored
Financial data (yr. ended 12/31/89): Assets, $407,934 (L); expenditures, $416,680, including $388,230 for 166 grants (high: $40,000; low: $100) and $27,985 for 136 employee matching gifts.
Purpose and activities: Emphasis on community funds, youth agencies, social services, hospitals, higher educational institutions, and health organizations.
Types of support: Employee matching gifts, annual campaigns, building funds, capital campaigns.
Limitations: Giving primarily in areas of company operations. No grants to individuals.
Application information: Applications not accepted.
Write: R.A. McRoberts, Trustee
Trustees: R.W. Davies, Robert A. McRoberts, G. Jackson Ratcliffe.
Number of staff: None.
Employer Identification Number: 066078177

980
The Huisking Foundation, Inc. ⌑
P.O. Box 353
Botsford 06404-0353
Application address: Plumtree Rd. (R.R. No. 1), Newtown, CT 06470

Incorporated in 1946 in NY.
Donor(s): Members of the Huisking family and family-related corporations.
Foundation type: Independent
Financial data (yr. ended 12/31/88): Assets, $4,812,029 (M); gifts received, $6,380; expenditures, $227,943, including $219,100 for 115 grants (high: $55,000; low: $100).
Purpose and activities: Giving for Catholic higher and secondary education, church support and welfare funds, hospitals, and religious associations.
Types of support: Operating budgets, research, special projects.
Limitations: No grants to individuals.
Application information:
Initial approach: Letter
Copies of proposal: 1
Deadline(s): Submit proposal in Feb. and Aug.
Board meeting date(s): Mar. and Oct.
Write: Frank R. Huisking, Treas.
Officers: John E. Haigney,* Pres.; William Huisking, Jr., V.P.; Richard V. Huisking, Jr., Secy.; Frank R. Huisking, Treas.
Directors:* Evelyn F. Daly, Robert P. Daly, Claire F. Hanavan, Taylor W. Hanavan, Richard V. Huisking, Sr., Jean M. Steinschneider, Richard Steinschneider, Jr.
Employer Identification Number: 136117501

981
The ITT Rayonier Foundation
1177 Summer St.
Stamford 06904 (203) 348-7000

Incorporated in 1952 in NY.
Donor(s): ITT Rayonier, Inc.
Foundation type: Company-sponsored
Financial data (yr. ended 12/31/89): Assets, $3,100,000 (M); gifts received, $400,000; expenditures, $402,000, including $304,750 for 213 grants (high: $20,000; low: $25; average: $1,000-$3,000), $57,250 for 45 grants to individuals (high: $2,000; low: $750; average: $1,000-$1,500) and $40,000 for 95 employee matching gifts.
Purpose and activities: Created as a medium to meet civic responsibilities in the areas of company operations and to educational institutions related to ITT Rayonier recruitment or to forest industry specializations. Grants to educational associations for scholarships; to hospitals for buildings and equipment; to health agencies and community funds; for the arts; and to environmental organizations; scholarships to individuals residing in areas of company operations in Nassau County, FL; Wayne County, GA; and Clallam, Mason, and Grays Harbor counties, WA.
Types of support: Scholarship funds, employee-related scholarships, building funds, equipment, operating budgets, continuing support, annual campaigns, seed money, emergency funds, deficit financing, land acquisition, endowment funds, special projects, matching funds, general purposes, capital campaigns, employee matching gifts, in-kind gifts, research.
Limitations: Giving primarily in areas of company operations in FL, GA, and WA. No loans.
Application information: Application form not required.
Initial approach: Letter or proposal
Copies of proposal: 1
Deadline(s): Nov. 30
Board meeting date(s): Feb.
Final notification: 1 month
Write: Jerome D. Gregoire, V.P.
Officers: R.M. Gross,* Chair. and Pres.; Jerome D. Gregoire,* V.P.; C.W. Peacock,* V.P.; J.B. Canning, Secy.; Gerald J. Pollack, Comptroller.
Directors:* W.S. Berry, W.L. Nutter.
Number of staff: None.
Employer Identification Number: 136064462

982
J.J.C. Foundation, Inc.
One Carney Rd.
West Hartford 06110 (203) 246-6531

Incorporated in 1953 in CT.
Donor(s): Florence Carney McGuire,† Helen M. Carney.†
Foundation type: Independent
Financial data (yr. ended 11/30/89): Assets, $1,136,229 (M); expenditures, $69,300, including $60,200 for grants.
Purpose and activities: Support for higher education, health agencies, and community funds.
Types of support: Annual campaigns, continuing support.
Limitations: Giving limited to CT, with emphasis on the Hartford area. No grants to individuals, or for endowment funds, scholarships, fellowships, or matching gifts; no loans.
Publications: Annual report.
Application information:
Initial approach: Letter
Copies of proposal: 1
Board meeting date(s): As required
Write: Grace Carney, Secy.
Officers: Francis X. McGuire, Pres. and Treas.; Grace Carney, Secy.
Number of staff: None.
Employer Identification Number: 066036358

983
The Cyrus W. & Amy F. Jones & Bessie D. Phelps Foundation, Inc. ⌑
c/o Tellalian & Tellalian
211 State St.
Bridgeport 06604

Incorporated in CT.
Donor(s): Amy F. Jones.†
Foundation type: Independent
Financial data (yr. ended 9/30/89): Assets, $2,299,837 (M); expenditures, $128,453, including $71,000 for 15 grants (high: $11,000; low: $1,000).
Purpose and activities: Giving largely for higher education and legal education, cultural programs, religion, and science.
Types of support: Operating budgets.
Limitations: Giving primarily in CT, with emphasis on Bridgeport. No grants to individuals.
Application information:
Initial approach: Letter
Deadline(s): None
Write: Aram H. Tellalian, Jr., Esq., Pres.
Officers and Trustees:* Aram H. Tellalian, Jr.,* Chair., Pres., and Treas.; Alexander R. Nestor,* V.P.; Robert S. Tellalian,* Secy.
Employer Identification Number: 060943204

984
Paul L. Jones Fund ⌑
c/o Meridan Trust & Safe Deposit Co.
P.O. Box 951
Meriden 06450 (202) 235-4456

Established in 1979 in CT.
Foundation type: Independent
Financial data (yr. ended 10/31/89): Assets, $3,094,431 (M); expenditures, $139,450, including $116,000 for 15 grants (high: $18,000; low: $2,000).
Purpose and activities: Giving only for a scholarship program to assist students in medical and health-related fields.
Types of support: Scholarship funds.
Limitations: Giving limited to residents of CT. No support for individuals.
Application information: Contributes only to pre-selected organizations. Applications not accepted.
Trustees: James Kircaldie, Meriden Trust & Safe Deposit Co.
Employer Identification Number: 066222118

985
Charles & Mabel P. Jost Foundation, Inc. ⌑
c/o Nestor, Sarka & Co.
1140 Fairfield Ave.
Bridgeport 06605 (203) 336-0166

Incorporated about 1969.
Foundation type: Independent
Financial data (yr. ended 04/30/89): Assets, $4,979,874 (M); expenditures, $274,901, including $215,000 for 23 grants (high: $25,000; low: $500).
Purpose and activities: Emphasis on aid to the handicapped, hospitals, and higher education.
Types of support: Operating budgets.
Limitations: Giving primarily in CT. No grants for scholarships, fellowships, or prizes; no loans.
Application information:
Initial approach: Letter
Deadline(s): None
Write: Alexander R. Nestor, Chair.
Officers and Trustees:* Alexander R. Nestor,* Chair. and Pres.; Robert S. Tellalian,* V.P.; Aram H. Tellalian, Jr.,* Secy.
Employer Identification Number: 237070398

986
Kohn-Joseloff Fund, Inc. ▼ ⌑
(Formerly Morris Joseloff Foundation, Inc.)
125 La Salle Rd., Rm. 200
West Hartford 06107 (203) 521-7010

Incorporated in 1936 in CT.
Donor(s): Lillian L. Joseloff,† Morris Joseloff Foundation Trust.
Foundation type: Independent
Financial data (yr. ended 12/31/88): Assets, $7,191,522 (M); expenditures, $424,312, including $348,194 for 73 grants (high: $130,000; low: $50; average: $500-$50,000).
Purpose and activities: Giving primarily for Jewish welfare funds, higher and secondary education, and cultural programs.
Limitations: Giving primarily in CT. No grants to individuals.
Application information: Applications not accepted.
Board meeting date(s): 2nd Monday in Jan.
Write: Bernard L. Kohn, Pres.
Officers and Directors:* Bernhard L. Kohn, Sr.,* Pres.; Joan J. Kohn,* V.P. and Secy.-Treas.; Bernhard L. Kohn, Jr.,* V.P.; Kathryn K. Rieger,* V.P.
Number of staff: 2
Employer Identification Number: 136062846

987
The Koopman Fund, Inc.
17 Brookside Blvd.
West Hartford 06107 (203) 232-6406

Incorporated in 1963 in CT.
Donor(s): Richard Koopman,† Georgette Koopman.
Foundation type: Independent
Financial data (yr. ended 12/31/89): Assets, $7,576,433 (M); expenditures, $414,727, including $369,993 for 199 grants (high: $176,050; low: $25).
Purpose and activities: Giving primarily for higher and secondary education, welfare funds, museums, and health organizations.
Types of support: Annual campaigns, building funds, capital campaigns, continuing support, emergency funds, endowment funds, equipment, general purposes, matching funds, publications, scholarship funds.
Limitations: Giving primarily in CT. No grants to individuals.
Application information: Application form not required.
Initial approach: Telephone
Copies of proposal: 1
Deadline(s): None
Board meeting date(s): As required
Write: Georgette Koopman, Pres.
Officer and Trustees:* Georgette Koopman,* Pres.; Beatrice Koopman, Dorothy Koopman, George Koopman, Rena Koopman, Richard Koopman, Jr., Dorothy A. Schiro.
Number of staff: 1
Employer Identification Number: 066050431

988
John & Evelyn Kossak Foundation, Inc.
68 Cross Hwy.
Westport 06880-2147 (203) 259-8779

Established in 1969 in CT.
Donor(s): Evelyn K. Kossak.
Foundation type: Independent
Financial data (yr. ended 12/31/88): Assets, $1,363,152 (M); gifts received, $304,000; expenditures, $292,427, including $288,495 for 24 grants (high: $100,000; low: $50).
Purpose and activities: Support primarily for higher education, health organizations, music, and the fine arts, including an art museum.
Application information:
Deadline(s): None
Write: Evelyn K. Kossak, Pres.
Officers: Evelyn K. Kossak, Pres.; Jeffrey Kossack, V.P.; Steven M. Kossak, Treas.
Employer Identification Number: 237045906

989
The Vernon K. Krieble Foundation, Inc. ⌑
P.O. Box 270
Marlborough 06447

Established in 1985 in CT.
Donor(s): Gladys V.K. Delmas.
Foundation type: Independent
Financial data (yr. ended 12/31/88): Assets, $9,232,871 (M); expenditures, $677,645, including $584,006 for 62 grants (high: $100,000; low: $500).
Purpose and activities: Support primarily for higher education, hospitals, and a historical society.
Application information: Contributes only to pre-selected organizations. Applications not accepted.
Officers: Helen K. Fusscas, Pres.; Frederick B. Krieble, V.P.; Nancy B. Krieble, Secy.; J. Peter Fusscas, Treas.
Employer Identification Number: 222538914

990
Ethel & Abe Lapides Foundation, Inc. ⌑
261 Bradley St.
New Haven 06510 (203) 772-4900

Foundation type: Independent
Financial data (yr. ended 11/30/89): Assets, $1,483,821 (M); expenditures, $114,418, including $91,000 for 81 grants (high: $6,000; low: $250).
Purpose and activities: Grants for higher, medical, and other education, the arts, health agencies and hospitals, and the humanities.
Limitations: Giving primarily in CT.
Application information:
Initial approach: Proposal
Deadline(s): None
Write: Jack H. Evans, V.P.
Officers: Burton Chizzick, Pres.; Jack H. Evans, V.P.; Fred J. Criscuolo, Treas.
Employer Identification Number: 066068567

991
Larrabee Fund Association
c/o Connecticut National Bank
777 Main St., MSN 266
Hartford 06115 (203) 728-2664

Established in 1941.
Donor(s): Larrabee Fund, Willie O. Burr.
Foundation type: Independent
Financial data (yr. ended 10/31/88): Assets, $2,211,278 (M); gifts received, $181,410; expenditures, $245,484, including $203,285 for grants to individuals.
Purpose and activities: Grants to indigent women.
Types of support: Grants to individuals.
Limitations: Giving limited to the Hartford, CT, area.
Application information:
Write: Linda Diberadino, Trust Officer, Connecticut National Bank
Officer: Patricia Walker, Pres.
Number of staff: None.
Employer Identification Number: 066038638

992
Elisha Leavenworth Foundation ⌑ ☆
35 Park Place
Waterbury 06702
Application address: Three Mile Hill, Middlebury, CT 06762; Tel.: (203) 758-1042

Established in 1927.
Foundation type: Independent
Financial data (yr. ended 12/31/87): Assets, $1,108,218 (M); expenditures, $75,651, including $46,805 for 12 grants (high: $27,338; low: $500) and $10,000 for 11 grants to individuals (high: $1,000; low: $500).
Purpose and activities: Giving primarily to youth organizations; also awards scholarships for higher education to local area women.
Types of support: Student aid.
Limitations: Giving primarily in the Waterbury, CT, area.
Application information:
Deadline(s): None
Write: Mrs. E. Donald Rogers, V.P.
Officers: Mrs. Robert N. Whittemore, Pres.; Mrs. E. Donald Rogers, V.P.; Mrs. James C. Hummel, Secy.; Mrs. L.P. Sperry, Jr., Treas.
Trustee: Bank of Boston Connecticut.
Employer Identification Number: 066035206

993
Lender Family Foundation, Inc. ⌑
1764 Litchfield Tpke.
Woodbridge 06525

Established in 1981 in CT.
Donor(s): Lender's Bagel Bakery, Inc.
Foundation type: Independent
Financial data (yr. ended 12/31/88): Assets, $6,412,625 (M); expenditures, $841,821, including $796,257 for 74 grants (high: $381,185).
Purpose and activities: Giving primarily for Jewish welfare and social services.
Limitations: No grants to individuals.
Application information: Contributes only to pre-selected organizations. Applications not accepted.
Officers: Murray Lender, Pres.; Marvin K. Lender, Treas.
Employer Identification Number: 061060037

994
The Frederick H. Leonhardt Foundation, Inc.
c/o Day, Berry & Howard
One Canterbury Green
Stamford 06901 (203) 323-7410
Application address: c/o Fairfield County Cooperative Foundation, Five Landmark Sq., Stamford, CT 06901

Incorporated in 1953 in NY; reorganized in 1989.
Donor(s): Frederick H. Leonhardt.†
Foundation type: Independent
Financial data (yr. ended 7/31/88): Assets, $14,160,332 (M); expenditures, $1,276,021, including $1,031,900 for 52 grants (high: $200,000; low: $1,000).
Purpose and activities: Foundation is newly reorganized with broad purposes. Interests include programs that strengthen the family, education, human services, and the environment.
Types of support: General purposes, matching funds.
Limitations: Giving primarily in CT and NM.
Application information:
Initial approach: Letter
Deadline(s): None
Board meeting date(s): 3 times a year
Write: Betsy Rich, Spec. Advisor
Officers and Directors: Anne S. Leonhardt, Pres. and Secy.; Frederick H. Leonhardt, V.P. and Treas.; Barbara A. Leonhardt, V.P.; Melissa A. Leonhardt, V.P.
Number of staff: None.
Employer Identification Number: 136123271

995
George A. and Grace L. Long Foundation
c/o Connecticut National Bank
777 Main St.
Hartford 06115 (203) 728-4652
Application address: c/o Connecticut National Bank, 65 LaSalle Rd., Suite 200, West Hartford, CT 06107

Trust established in 1960 in CT.
Donor(s): George A. Long, Grace L. Long.†
Foundation type: Independent
Financial data (yr. ended 12/31/88): Assets, $5,096,478 (M); expenditures, $424,707, including $354,950 for 86 grants (high: $20,000; low: $1,000).
Purpose and activities: Emphasis on cultural programs, education, hospitals, social services, and community funds.
Types of support: Scholarship funds, special projects, building funds.
Limitations: Giving primarily in the greater Hartford, CT, area. No grants to individuals, or for operating budgets or endowment funds; no loans.
Application information: Application form required.
Initial approach: Letter
Copies of proposal: 3
Deadline(s): Mar. 15 and Sept. 15
Board meeting date(s): Apr. and Oct.
Write: Amy R. Lynch, Trust Associate, Connecticut National Bank
Trustees: J. Harold Williams, Connecticut National Bank.
Employer Identification Number: 066030953

996
The MacCurdy-Salisbury Educational Foundation, Inc. ⌑
Nine Mansewood Rd.
Old Lyme 06371 (203) 434-2646

Incorporated in 1893 in CT.
Donor(s): Evelyn MacCurdy Salisbury.
Foundation type: Independent
Financial data (yr. ended 05/31/89): Assets, $2,977,281 (M); gifts received, $6,125; expenditures, $135,541, including $101,950 for grants to individuals.
Purpose and activities: Giving to local residents for scholarships.
Types of support: Student aid.
Limitations: Giving limited to Lyme and Old Lyme, CT.
Application information: Application form available in Lyme and Old Lyme high school guidance offices. Application form required.
Deadline(s): Apr. 30 for first semester; Nov. 15 for second semester
Board meeting date(s): Varies
Final notification: July
Write: Ward Bing, Secy.-Treas.
Officer: Ward Bing, Secy.-Treas.
Number of staff: 1 part-time professional.
Employer Identification Number: 066044250

997
The Maguire Foundation, Inc. ⌑
875 Boston Post Rd.
P.O. Box 629
Madison 06443

Incorporated in 1948 in CT.
Foundation type: Independent
Financial data (yr. ended 12/31/87): Assets, $2,996,760 (M); expenditures, $281,746, including $60,397 for 12 grants (high: $16,875; low: $350).
Purpose and activities: Emphasis on higher and secondary education; grants also for a library.
Limitations: Giving primarily in CT.
Application information: Contributes only to pre-selected organizations. Applications not accepted.
Officers: Walter L. Maguire, Sr., Pres. and Treas.; Walter L. Maguire, Jr., V.P. and Secy.
Employer Identification Number: 066039354

998
Main Street Foundation, Inc. ⌑
P.O. Box 58
Southport 06490 (203) 259-7881

Established in 1965.
Foundation type: Independent
Financial data (yr. ended 12/31/88): Assets, $1,097,671 (M); gifts received, $90,476; expenditures, $143,993, including $131,098 for 58 grants (high: $72,032; low: $25).
Purpose and activities: Giving primarily for Protestant churches, and for higher and secondary education.
Types of support: Operating budgets, general purposes, scholarship funds.
Limitations: Giving primarily in CT.
Application information:
Initial approach: Written request
Deadline(s): None
Write: Charles P. Stetson, Pres.
Officers: Charles P. Stetson, Pres. and Treas.; Barbara Stetson, V.P. and Secy.
Director: Charles P. Stetson, Jr.
Employer Identification Number: 066076249

999
The B. L. Manger Foundation, Inc. ⌑
c/o Capossela Cohen, Engelson & Colman
368 Center St.
Southport 06490

Established in 1974 in CT.
Foundation type: Independent
Financial data (yr. ended 04/30/89): Assets, $1,046,058 (M); gifts received, $5,500; expenditures, $62,905, including $60,990 for 37 grants (high: $5,000; low: $200).

Purpose and activities: Support for Jewish agencies, medical research and general charitable giving.
Limitations: Giving primarily in Southport, CT.
Application information:
Initial approach: Letter
Deadline(s): None
Write: Bernard L. Manger, Pres.
Officers: Bernard L. Manger, Pres. and Treas.; Joel Wald, V.P.; I.M. Mackler, Secy.
Employer Identification Number: 237405994

1000
John Jay Mann Foundation, Inc. ⌘
c/o Whitman and Ransom
P.O. Box 2250
Greenwich 06836-2250
Application address: Lucille Dr., Fort Lauderdale, FL 33316

Established in 1973 in CT.
Donor(s): John Jay Mann.
Foundation type: Independent
Financial data (yr. ended 11/30/88): Assets, $1,758,758 (M); expenditures, $94,663, including $85,200 for 23 grants (high: $20,000; low: $100).
Purpose and activities: Support primarily for churches and hospitals.
Application information: Application form not required.
Deadline(s): None
Write: John Jay Mann, Pres.
Officers and Directors: John Jay Mann, Pres. and Treas.; Carol B. Mann, V.P. and Secy.; John Jay Mann, Jr.
Employer Identification Number: 060905078

1001
The Jacob & Ruth Mazer Foundation ⌘
Mooreland Rd.
Greenwich 06830 (203) 661-9733

Established in 1961.
Donor(s): Abraham Mazer Foundation.
Foundation type: Independent
Financial data (yr. ended 12/31/88): Assets, $1,889,779 (M); expenditures, $120,495, including $114,456 for 96 grants (low: $25).
Purpose and activities: Giving primarily for Jewish welfare funds.
Application information:
Initial approach: Letter
Deadline(s): None
Write: David Mazer, V.P.
Officers: Ruth Mazer, Pres.; Richard Mazer, V.P. and Secy.; David Mazer, V.P. and Treas.
Employer Identification Number: 136115875

1002
Meek Foundation ⌘
c/o Connecticut Bank & Trust Co., N.A.
P.O. Box 3334
Hartford 06103

Established in 1947 in CT.
Foundation type: Independent
Financial data (yr. ended 12/31/88): Assets, $1,981,517 (M); expenditures, $104,629, including $64,104 for 197 grants (high: $10,010; low: $10).
Purpose and activities: Giving primarily for Protestant religion, hospital support, and education.
Application information: Contributes only to pre-selected organizations. Applications not accepted.
Trustees: Elizabeth Faber, Samuel E. Meek, Jr., Connecticut Bank & Trust Co., N.A.
Employer Identification Number: 066033662

1003
The Meriden Foundation ⌘
c/o Meriden Trust & Safe Deposit Co.
P.O. Box 951
Meriden 06450 (202) 235-4456

Foundation type: Community
Financial data (yr. ended 12/31/88): Assets, $2,931,223 (M); gifts received, $62,255; expenditures, $172,714, including $93,559 for 35 grants (high: $14,500; low: $100) and $50,968 for 51 grants to individuals (high: $2,250; low: $225).
Purpose and activities: Giving for civic affairs, youth, hospitals, social services, and scholarships to individuals.
Types of support: Student aid.
Limitations: Giving limited to the Meriden-Wallingford, CT, area.
Application information:
Initial approach: Letter
Deadline(s): None
Write: Jeffrey F. Otis, Secy., Distrib. Comm.
Distrib. Comm.: Robert Bailey, Chair.; John F. Peckham, Vice-Chair.; Jeffrey F. Otis, Secy.; Richard S. Boynton, Frederick A. Flatow, Charles H. Hasburg, James P. Rybek, Robert J. Sokolowski.
Trustee: Meriden Trust & Safe Deposit Co.
Employer Identification Number: 066037849

1004
Albert & Helen Meserve Memorial Fund
Union Trust Co.
P.O. Box 404
New Haven 06502 (203) 773-5832
Additional address: Betsy Rich, Exec. Dir., Fairfield County Cooperative Foundation, Three Landmark Sq., Stamford, CT 06904

Established in 1983 in CT; grant program administered through the Fairfield County Cooperative Foundation.
Donor(s): Albert W. Meserve,† Helen C. Meserve.†
Foundation type: Independent
Financial data (yr. ended 08/31/89): Assets, $3,199,636 (M); expenditures, $210,829, including $127,360 for 21 grants (high: $19,350; low: $1,500) and $35,250 for 31 grants to individuals (high: $1,500; low: $750).
Purpose and activities: Support primarily for the arts, education, the environment, health and social services, and urban development.
Types of support: Conferences and seminars, consulting services, matching funds, scholarship funds, seed money, special projects, technical assistance, student aid.
Limitations: Giving primarily in Bethel, Bridgewater, Brookfield, Danbury, New Fairfield, New Milford, Newton, Redding, Ridgefield, and Sherman, CT. No support for religious or sectarian organizations, political activities, or groups desiring to benefit their own membership. No grants for endowment or general fund drives, operating budgets of United Way agencies, or deficit financing.
Publications: Application guidelines, informational brochure, grants list.
Application information: Application form not required.
Initial approach: Proposal
Copies of proposal: 1
Deadline(s): Oct. 15 and Mar. 15
Board meeting date(s): Dec. and June
Write: Eileen M. Wilhem, V.P., Union Trust Co.
Distribution Committee: Karl H. Epple, Chair.; Paul Altermatt, Gino Arconti, Rabbi Jerome R. Malino, Clarice Osiecki.
Number of staff: 2 part-time professional; 1 part-time support.
Employer Identification Number: 066254956

1005
The Morris M. and Helen F. Messing Foundation ⌘
160 Wampus Ln.
Milford 06460

Incorporated in 1957 in NJ.
Donor(s): Morris M. Messing.
Foundation type: Independent
Financial data (yr. ended 12/31/88): Assets, $1,971,155 (M); expenditures, $169,569, including $150,000 for 28 grants (high: $30,000; low: $500).
Purpose and activities: Grants largely for Jewish welfare funds, temple support, medical research, and higher education.
Application information: Contributes only to pre-selected organizations. Applications not accepted.
Trustees: Madeline Levy, Andrew Messing, Gilbert Messing, Robert H. Messing.
Employer Identification Number: 226045391

1006
Marjorie Moore Charitable Foundation
c/o Connecticut National Bank
235 Main St.
New Britain 06050 (203) 224-6466

Trust established in 1958 in CT.
Donor(s): Marjorie Moore.†
Foundation type: Independent
Financial data (yr. ended 07/31/89): Assets, $1,933,393 (M); expenditures, $84,645, including $72,379 for 7 grants (high: $25,379; low: $2,000).
Purpose and activities: To promote local projects of a charitable and civic nature.
Types of support: Operating budgets, continuing support, seed money, building funds, equipment, land acquisition, endowment funds, matching funds, consulting services, special projects.
Limitations: Giving limited to Kensington, CT. No grants to individuals, or for scholarships or fellowships; no loans.
Publications: 990-PF.
Application information: Application form not required.
Initial approach: Telephone or letter
Copies of proposal: 1

Deadline(s): Submit proposal preferably in Aug.
Board meeting date(s): Jan., Apr., July, and Oct.
Final notification: 3 to 6 months
Write: William G. Keeley, V.P., Connecticut National Bank
Trustee: Connecticut National Bank.
Number of staff: None.
Employer Identification Number: 066050196

1007
Emil Mosbacher, Jr. Foundation, Inc. ⌑
c/o The Meridian Bldg.
170 Mason St.
Greenwich 06830 (203) 869-4100

Incorporated in 1974 in NY.
Donor(s): Emil Mosbacher, Jr., Emil Mosbacher III, John D. Mosbacher, R. Bruce Mosbacher.
Foundation type: Independent
Financial data (yr. ended 11/30/88): Assets, $2,484,170 (M); gifts received, $469,781; expenditures, $96,508, including $88,180 for 72 grants (high: $15,000; low: $10).
Purpose and activities: Support primarily for higher education and hospitals.
Limitations: Giving primarily in NY and CT. No grants to individuals.
Application information:
Initial approach: Letter
Deadline(s): None
Write: Emil Mosbacher, Jr., Pres.
Officers: Emil Mosbacher, Jr., Pres. and Treas.; Patricia Mosbacher, V.P. and Secy.
Directors: Emil Mosbacher III, R. Bruce Mosbacher.
Employer Identification Number: 237454106

1008
Leo Nevas Family Foundation, Inc. ☆
246 Post Rd. East
P.O. Box 791
Westport 06881 (203) 226-1211

Established in 1961.
Donor(s): Leo Nevas.
Foundation type: Independent
Financial data (yr. ended 11/30/88): Assets, $1,160,787 (M); expenditures, $95,367, including $90,850 for 33 grants (high: $35,500; low: $100).
Purpose and activities: Giving primarily for Jewish organizations, including some international programs; support also for higher, legal, and other education; a community fund; and international affairs, including a human rights organization.
Limitations: No grants to individuals.
Application information: Applications not accepted.
Write: Leo Nevas, Pres.
Officer: Leo Nevas, Pres.
Number of staff: None.
Employer Identification Number: 066068842

1009
The New Haven Foundation ▼
One State St.
New Haven 06510 (203) 777-2386

Established in 1928 in CT by Resolution and Declaration of Trust.
Foundation type: Community
Financial data (yr. ended 12/31/89): Assets, $93,452,029 (M); gifts received, $2,462,001; expenditures, $5,538,035, including $4,801,002 for grants.
Purpose and activities: Emphasis on social service and youth agencies, hospitals and health agencies, educational institutions, community funds, and the arts.
Types of support: Operating budgets, continuing support, seed money, emergency funds, building funds, equipment, matching funds, consulting services, technical assistance, special projects, loans, scholarship funds, endowment funds.
Limitations: Giving primarily in greater New Haven, CT, and the lower Naugatuck River Valley. No grants to individuals, or for annual campaigns, deficit financing, endowment funds, research, scholarships, or fellowships, or generally for capital projects.
Publications: Annual report, application guidelines, newsletter.
Application information: Application form required.
Initial approach: Telephone or letter
Copies of proposal: 14
Deadline(s): Jan., Apr., Aug., and Oct.
Board meeting date(s): Mar., June, Oct., and Dec.
Final notification: Within 1 week of decision
Write: Helmer N. Ekstrom, Dir.
Distribution Committee: Terry R. Chatfield, Chair.; Theodore F. Hogan, Jr., Vice-Chair.; Richard G. Bell, Richard H. Bowerman, Anne Calabresi, Donald W. Celotto, Jr., Marcella T. Glazer, F. Patrick McFadden, Agnes W. Timpson.
Trustees: Bank of Boston Connecticut, Connecticut Bank & Trust Co., N.A., Connecticut National Bank, New Haven Savings Bank, Peoples Bank, Union Trust Co.
Number of staff: 10 full-time professional; 2 part-time professional; 6 full-time support; 1 part-time support.
Employer Identification Number: 066032106

1010
New York Society for the Advancement of Cutaneous Biology and Medicine, Inc. ⌑ ☆
970 Summer St.
Stamford 06905
Application address: 500 East 62nd St., New York, NY 10021; Tel.: (212) 753-8260

Established in 1987 in NY.
Donor(s): The Carl J. Herzog Foundation, Inc.
Foundation type: Independent
Financial data (yr. ended 12/31/88): Assets, $1,625,606 (M); gifts received, $100,710; expenditures, $690,236, including $510,990 for 2 grants (high: $500,990; low: $10,000).
Purpose and activities: "Grants made primarily in the field of dermatology."
Types of support: Research.
Limitations: Giving primarily in NY.
Application information:
Initial approach: Letter
Deadline(s): None
Write: George W. Hambrick, Jr., M.D., Pres.
Officers and Directors: Peter Bentley, Chair.; George W. Hambrick, Jr., M.D., Pres. and Treas.; D. Martin Carter, M.D., Secy.; Donald G. Calder, Mimi W. Coleman, Arthur J. Mahon, Cecily B. Selby, David D. Thompson, M.D., Rev. Sydney A. Woodd-Cahusac.
Employer Identification Number: 133401320

1011
The O'Meara Foundation, Inc.
Four Grimes Rd.
Rocky Hill 06067 (203) 529-6693

Established in 1944 in CT.
Foundation type: Independent
Financial data (yr. ended 06/30/88): Assets, $1,001,639 (M); expenditures, $49,963, including $40,600 for grants to individuals.
Purpose and activities: Support primarily for scholarships to residents of Hartford County, CT, attending institutions of higher education.
Types of support: Student aid.
Limitations: Giving limited to residents of Hartford County, CT.
Application information: Application form required.
Initial approach: Letter or proposal
Deadline(s): July 1
Board meeting date(s): 3rd week of July
Write: Mrs. John Boyd
Officers: Martin J. O'Meara, Jr., Pres.; Dr. William F. O'Meara, Secy.; Edward L. Storrs, Treas.
Number of staff: 1
Employer Identification Number: 066034580

1012
The Obernauer Foundation, Inc. ⌑
1600 Summer St., Suite 302
Stamford 06905-5125

Incorporated in 1966 in CT as the Marne and Joan Obernauer Foundation.
Donor(s): Marne Obernauer.
Foundation type: Independent
Financial data (yr. ended 12/31/88): Assets, $2,031,466 (M); expenditures, $84,949, including $55,190 for 39 grants (high: $25,000; low: $20).
Purpose and activities: Support for an international community center, Jewish concerns, youth organizations, higher education, and medical research.
Types of support: Annual campaigns, endowment funds, scholarship funds.
Limitations: Giving primarily in PA, CT, and New York, NY. No grants to individuals.
Application information: Contributes only to pre-selected organizations. Applications not accepted.
Officers and Directors:* Marne Obernauer,* Pres.; Joan S. Obernauer,* V.P.; Marne Obernauer, Jr.,* V.P.; June E. Sisson, Secy.
Employer Identification Number: 956149147

1013
Olin Corporation Charitable Trust ▼
120 Long Ridge Rd.
Stamford 06904 (203) 356-3301

Trust established in 1945 in MO.
Donor(s): Olin Corp.
Foundation type: Company-sponsored
Financial data (yr. ended 12/31/89): Assets, $14,671,540 (M); expenditures, $1,950,944,

including $1,560,537 for 537 grants (high: $100,000; low: $50; average: $500-$10,000) and $390,407 for 1,954 employee matching gifts.
Purpose and activities: Emphasis on science and engineering in higher education, business education, environmental studies, conservation programs, community funds, hospitals, youth agencies, and health associations. Support also for a wide variety of programs such as drug abuse, volunteerism, economics, and housing. The trust matches employee gifts to education, arts and culture, and awards scholarships to children of employees through the National Merit Scholarship Corporation.
Types of support: General purposes, operating budgets, continuing support, annual campaigns, seed money, emergency funds, building funds, equipment, land acquisition, special projects, research, publications, conferences and seminars, internships, scholarship funds, employee-related scholarships, fellowships, matching funds, employee matching gifts.
Limitations: Giving primarily in areas of company operations. No grants to individuals, or for endowment funds; no loans.
Application information: Application form not required.
Initial approach: Letter or proposal
Copies of proposal: 1
Deadline(s): Submit proposal preferably between Jan. and Aug.; no set deadline
Board meeting date(s): Dec.
Final notification: 2 to 3 months
Write: Carmella V. Piacentini, Admin.
Trustees: Donald W. Griffin, John W. Johnstone, Jr., Boatmen's Trust Co. of St. Louis.
Number of staff: 1 full-time professional; 1 full-time support; 1 part-time support.
Employer Identification Number: 436022750

1014
The Frank Loomis Palmer Fund
c/o Connecticut National Bank
250 Captain's Walk
New London 06320 (203) 447-6133

Trust established in 1936 in CT.
Donor(s): Virginia Palmer.†
Foundation type: Independent
Financial data (yr. ended 07/31/89): Assets, $13,917,698 (M); expenditures, $850,830, including $774,739 for 57 grants (high: $75,000; low: $915).
Purpose and activities: Grants to encourage new projects and to provide seed money, with emphasis on child welfare and family services, youth agencies, and higher and secondary education; support also for civic groups, cultural programs, social services, churches, and hospitals.
Types of support: Seed money, special projects, capital campaigns, conferences and seminars, consulting services, equipment, matching funds, publications, research, scholarship funds, renovation projects.
Limitations: Giving limited to New London, CT. No grants to individuals, or for endowment funds.
Publications: Informational brochure (including application guidelines).
Application information: Application form required.
Initial approach: Telephone
Copies of proposal: 1
Deadline(s): May 15 and Nov. 15
Board meeting date(s): Jan. and July
Final notification: Feb. 1 and Aug. 1
Write: Mildred E. Devine, V.P., Connecticut National Bank
Trustee: Connecticut National Bank.
Number of staff: None.
Employer Identification Number: 066026043

1015
Lily Palmer-Fry Memorial Trust ⌑
c/o Connecticut Bank & Trust Co., N.A.
P.O. Box 3334
Hartford 06103
Application address: 240 Greenwich Ave., Greenwich, CT 06830; Tel.: (203) 629-4051

Trust established in 1953 in CT.
Donor(s): William Henry Fry.†
Foundation type: Independent
Financial data (yr. ended 12/31/88): Assets, $3,604,311 (M); expenditures, $761,102, including $220,200 for grants (average: $1,500-$20,000).
Purpose and activities: To provide summer vacations for the underprivileged and handicapped through grants to youth agencies and relief and social service agencies, and for Protestant church support.
Limitations: Giving primarily in CT, NY, and NJ.
Application information:
Initial approach: Proposal
Deadline(s): Feb. 1
Board meeting date(s): May
Write: Mrs. Diane Bookmiller
Trustees: Caroline M. Fry, Evelyn Fry Peterson, Connecticut Bank & Trust Co., N.A.
Employer Identification Number: 066033612

1016
Panwy Foundation, Inc. ⌑
Greenwich Office Park
P.O. Box 1800
Greenwich 06836 (203) 661-6616

Trust established in 1943 in NY; incorporated in 1951 in NJ; reincorporated in 1988 in CT.
Donor(s): Olga Resseguier, Henry W. Wyman, Maria Wyman, Ralph M. Wyman, Ruth L. Russell, Pantasote, Inc., and others.
Foundation type: Independent
Financial data (yr. ended 12/31/87): Assets, $582,493 (M); gifts received, $188,634; expenditures, $255,507, including $255,507 for 250 grants (high: $33,000; low: $25).
Purpose and activities: Emphasis on cultural activities, church support, higher and secondary education, and hospitals.
Types of support: Operating budgets, continuing support, annual campaigns, seed money, emergency funds, endowment funds, building funds, research, equipment, conferences and seminars, scholarship funds, capital campaigns, general purposes, loans, renovation projects.
Limitations: No grants for matching gifts.
Application information: Application form not required.
Initial approach: Letter
Copies of proposal: 1
Deadline(s): None
Board meeting date(s): As required
Final notification: 1 month
Write: Ralph M. Wyman, Pres.
Officers and Trustees: Henry W. Wyman, Chair.; Ralph M. Wyman, Pres.; Harry A. Russell, V.P.; Virginia A.W. Meyer, Secy.-Treas.
Number of staff: None.
Employer Identification Number: 136130759

1017
Robert Leet Patterson & Clara Guthrie Patterson Trust
One Landmark Sq.
Stamford 06904-1454 (203) 358-6124

Established in 1981 in CT.
Donor(s): Robert Patterson Trust No. 2, Robert Leet Patterson,† Clara Guthrie Patterson.†
Foundation type: Independent
Financial data (yr. ended 01/31/90): Assets, $10,600,000 (M); qualifying distributions, $600,000, including $600,000 for 15 grants (high: $200,000; low: $10,000; average: $100,000).
Purpose and activities: Giving to hospitals and organizations which are devoted to the advancement of medical science and are engaged in research relating to human diseases.
Types of support: Equipment, matching funds, professorships, research, seed money, special projects.
Limitations: Giving primarily in Continental U.S.; support primarily in CT and other eastern states. No grants to individuals, or for operating budgets, continuing support, annual campaigns, emergency funds, deficit financing, endowment funds, consulting services, technical assistance, demonstration projects, publications, or conferences and seminars; no loans.
Publications: Informational brochure (including application guidelines).
Application information: Application form required.
Initial approach: Letter or proposal
Copies of proposal: 6
Deadline(s): May 1 for June meeting and Nov. 1 for Dec. meeting
Board meeting date(s): June and Dec.
Final notification: 3 months
Write: Peter B. Guenther, V.P., Connecticut National Bank
Trustee: John H. McBride.
Corporate Trustee: Connecticut National Bank.
Number of staff: None.
Employer Identification Number: 066236358

1018
The Pequot Community Foundation, Inc. ⌑
302 Captain's Walk, Rm. 211
P.O. Box 769
New London 06320 (203) 442-3572

Established in 1982 in CT.
Foundation type: Community
Financial data (yr. ended 12/31/88): Assets, $1,814,771 (L); gifts received, $296,450; expenditures, $182,858, including $138,522 for grants.
Purpose and activities: To promote learning, to advance scientific research, to provide care for the needy, sick, aged, or helpless, to secure

the care of children, to encourage historical, literary, and artistic endeavors, and to otherwise contribute to the general welfare.
Types of support: Seed money, emergency funds, equipment, renovation projects, scholarship funds, fellowships, conferences and seminars, publications, general purposes, special projects, student aid.
Limitations: Giving limited to southeastern CT, including East Lyme, Groton, Ledyard, Lyme, Montville, New London, North Stonington, Old Lyme, Salem, Stonington, and Waterford. No support for sectarian or religious programs. No grants to individuals (except for scholarships awarded by nomination only) or for endowment, memorial, or building funds, operating expenses, deficit financing, annual campaigns, or land acquisition; no loans.
Publications: Annual report, application guidelines, informational brochure (including application guidelines), financial statement, grants list, newsletter.
Application information: Application form required.
Initial approach: Letter
Copies of proposal: 2
Deadline(s): 2nd Monday in Jan.
Board meeting date(s): Nov.
Final notification: Grants are distributed in Mar.
Write: Thomas T. Wetmore III, Exec. Dir.
Officers and Trustees:* Stephen Percy,* Pres.; Richard Creviston,* V.P.; Rita Hendel,* Secy.; John O. Zimmerman,* Treas.; Thomas T. Wetmore III, Exec. Dir.; and 35 additional trustees.
Number of staff: 1 part-time professional; 1 part-time support.
Employer Identification Number: 061080097

1019
The Perkin Fund
340 Country Club Rd.
New Canaan 06840 (203) 966-1920
Additional address: c/o Morris & McVeigh, 767 Third Ave., New York, NY 10017

Trust established in 1967 in NY.
Donor(s): Richard S. Perkin.†
Foundation type: Independent
Financial data (yr. ended 12/31/89): Assets, $11,199,359 (M); expenditures, $574,453, including $468,000 for 20 grants (high: $100,000; low: $3,000).
Purpose and activities: Support for advanced education and research, especially in astronomy, biomedicine, and optics.
Limitations: No grants to individuals, or for operating budgets; no loans.
Application information:
Initial approach: Letter
Copies of proposal: 1
Board meeting date(s): May and Nov.
Write: Mrs. Richard S. Perkin, Chair.
Trustees: Mrs. Richard S. Perkin, Chair.; James G. Baker, William F. Close, Winifred P. Gray, John T. Perkin, Richard T. Perkin, Robert S. Perkin, Howard Phipps, Jr., Roderic M. Scott.
Employer Identification Number: 136222498

1020
Pirelli Armstrong Foundation, Inc. ☆
500 Sargent Dr.
P.O. Box 2001
New Haven 06536-0201

Established in 1988 in CT.
Donor(s): Pirelli Armstrong Tire Corp.
Foundation type: Company-sponsored
Financial data (yr. ended 12/31/89): Assets, $22,590 (M); gifts received, $150,000; expenditures, $141,000, including $126,000 for 33 grants (high: $50,000; low: $250), $6,000 for 3 grants to individuals of $2,000 each and $8,695 for 51 employee matching gifts.
Purpose and activities: Giving primarily for the United Fund; support also for education, including an employee matching gift program and community services near company's locations, including child welfare and youth, family services, health, and the performing arts.
Types of support: Annual campaigns, employee matching gifts, equipment, employee-related scholarships.
Limitations: Giving primarily in New Haven, CT; Hanford, CA; Des Moines, IA; Nashville, TN; Little Rock, AR; and Laurel Hill, NC.
Publications: Annual report.
Application information: Application form not required.
Initial approach: Proposal; no calls or appointments
Copies of proposal: 1
Deadline(s): None
Board meeting date(s): Quarterly
Final notification: Following quarterly meetings
Write: Patricia M. Hennessy, Exec. Dir.
Officers and Trustees:* Paul C. James,* Pres.; Harold D. Hoppert,* Secy.; William J. Dunn,* Treas.; Patricia Hennessey,* Exec. Dir.; William C. Bruce, Robert F. Schmalz.
Number of staff: None.
Employer Identification Number: 061263699

1021
Evelyn W. Preston Trust ⌑
c/o Connecticut Bank & Trust Co., N.A.
P.O. Box 3334
Hartford 06115 (203) 244-5000

Trust established in 1978 in CT.
Donor(s): Mary Yale Bettis,† Evelyn Preston.†
Foundation type: Independent
Financial data (yr. ended 12/31/88): Assets, $2,160,147 (M); expenditures, $148,443, including $106,071 for 44 grants (high: $12,965; low: $250) and $15,675 for 10 grants to individuals (high: $4,000; low: $400).
Purpose and activities: Grants for free band and orchestral concerts in the city of Hartford from June through September.
Types of support: General purposes, grants to individuals.
Limitations: Giving limited to Hartford, CT.
Publications: Application guidelines.
Application information: Application form required.
Final notification: 2 months
Trustee: Connecticut Bank & Trust Co., N.A.
Number of staff: None.
Employer Identification Number: 060747389

1022
Lucien B. and Katherine E. Price Foundation, Inc. ⌑
896 Main St.
P.O. Box 790
Manchester 06040 (203) 643-4129

Incorporated in 1922 in CT.
Foundation type: Independent
Financial data (yr. ended 12/31/87): Assets, $2,385,169 (M); expenditures, $161,844, including $105,550 for grants.
Purpose and activities: Emphasis on Roman Catholic church support, religious associations, and church-related schools, colleges, and hospitals.
Application information:
Initial approach: Letter
Write: Rt. Rev. Msgr. Edward J. Reardon, Pres.
Officers and Directors: Rt. Rev. Msgr. Edward J. Reardon, Pres.; Rt. Rev. Msgr. John A. Brown, V.P.; Edward P. Flanagan, Secy.; Morgan P. Ames, Treas.; Most Rev. Joseph L. Federal, Rev. Francis Krukowski.
Employer Identification Number: 066068868

1023
Psychists, Inc. ⌑
72 Cummings Pt. Rd.
Stamford 06902

Incorporated in 1943 in NY.
Donor(s): Richard L. Parish,† American Flange & Manufacturing Co., Inc.
Foundation type: Independent
Financial data (yr. ended 08/31/89): Assets, $3,150,610 (M); expenditures, $132,376, including $117,000 for 37 grants (high: $50,000; low: $500).
Purpose and activities: Grants largely for higher and secondary education, hospitals and health agencies.
Application information: Contributes only to pre-selected organizations. Applications not accepted.
Officers: Richard L. Parish, Jr., Pres. and Treas.; David L. McKissock, V.P. and Secy.
Employer Identification Number: 131869530

1024
The Rich Foundation, Inc. ⌑
One Landmark Sq.
Stamford 06901 (203) 359-2900

Established in 1984 in CT.
Donor(s): F.D. Rich Co., Inc., Members of the Rich family.
Foundation type: Company-sponsored
Financial data (yr. ended 6/30/87): Assets, $848,304 (M); gifts received, $1,643,480; expenditures, $159,041, including $157,450 for 45 grants (high: $25,000; low: $200).
Purpose and activities: Support for educational and cultural institutions, health services and programs, and social service organizations.
Limitations: Giving primarily in lower Fairfield County, CT.
Application information: Applicants are urged to consult with the foundation staff in the development of their proposals.
Initial approach: Proposal
Deadline(s): Aug. 15

Board meeting date(s): Sept. for budgets commencing Oct. 1 and ending Sept. 30 of the following calendar year; Mar. for supplementary budgets requests
Officers: Joseph F. Fahy, Jr., Pres.; Richard G. Bell, Secy.; Harold Spelke, Treas.
Employer Identification Number: 222544173

1025
Edward C. & Ann T. Roberts Foundation, Inc. ⌑
c/o Connecticut Bank & Trust Co., N.A.
P.O. Box 3334
Hartford 06103 (203) 233-0228

Established in 1964 in CT.
Foundation type: Independent
Financial data (yr. ended 12/31/87): Assets, $1,268,851 (M); expenditures, $88,570, including $58,909 for grants (high: $7,500; low: $317).
Purpose and activities: Giving primarily for visual and performing arts.
Limitations: Giving limited to the greater Hartford, CT, area.
Application information: Application form not required.
Initial approach: Letter
Deadline(s): 1st of each month of each calendar quarter
Write: Rosalie B. Lee, Exec. Dir.
Officers: Ann T. Roberts,* Pres.; John H. Riege,* Secy.; John T. Small, Jr.,* Treas.
Directors:* Rosalie Lee, Exec. Dir.; Marshall W. Davenson, William W. Graulty, Donald Harris, Mrs. Christopher Larson.
Employer Identification Number: 066067995

1026
Charles Nelson Robinson Fund ⌑
c/o Connecticut Bank & Trust Co., N.A.
One Constitution Plaza, M08T
Hartford 06115 (203) 244-5826

Trust established in 1928 in CT.
Donor(s): Charles Nelson Robinson.†
Foundation type: Independent
Financial data (yr. ended 06/30/89): Assets, $2,333,329 (M); expenditures, $105,605, including $89,310 for 28 grants (high: $8,000; low: $300).
Purpose and activities: To aid "organized charities having a principal office in the City of Hartford"; support for social service agencies, including aid for the aged and youth, secondary education, and cultural programs.
Limitations: Giving primarily in Hartford, CT. No grants to individuals, or for endowment funds.
Publications: Application guidelines.
Application information: Application form required.
Initial approach: Letter or telephone
Copies of proposal: 5
Deadline(s): Jan. 15, May 15, and Sept. 15
Board meeting date(s): Feb., June, and Oct.
Write: Mrs. Wanda L. Kleinert
Trustee: Connecticut Bank & Trust Co., N.A.
Employer Identification Number: 066029468

1027
Rock Ledge Institute, Inc. ⌑ ☆
31 Ox Ridge Ln.
Darien 06820-2513

Established in 1944.
Foundation type: Independent
Financial data (yr. ended 12/31/88): Assets, $1,021,121 (M); expenditures, $51,977, including $37,500 for 7 grants (high: $10,000; low: $500).
Purpose and activities: Support primarily for social service organizations and medical research.
Limitations: Giving primarily in CT. No grants to individuals.
Application information:
Initial approach: Letter
Deadline(s): None
Write: James H. Rand, IV, Pres.
Officers and Directors: James H. Rand IV, Pres.; D. Seely Hubbard, V.P.; Jane E. Rand, Secy.
Employer Identification Number: 066068946

1028
The Rockfall Foundation
(Formerly Rockfall Corporation)
27 Washington St.
Middletown 06457 (203) 347-0340

Established in 1935 in CT.
Donor(s): Clarence S. Wadsworth,† Katherine F. Wadsworth.†
Foundation type: Independent
Financial data (yr. ended 06/30/89): Assets, $1,747,360 (M); gifts received, $17,680; expenditures, $117,916, including $2,100 for 3 grants (high: $1,100; low: $500), $6,500 for 1 grant to an individual and $84,359 for 5 foundation-administered programs.
Purpose and activities: "To establish, maintain, and care for parks, woodland, wildland, and water bodies and to assist in the development and renewal of urban areas both for the use and enjoyment of the public;" support also for community nonprofit organizations.
Types of support: Internships, special projects, matching funds.
Limitations: Giving limited to Middlesex County, CT.
Publications: Annual report, application guidelines.
Application information: Grant program limited to educational projects having a meaningful impact on the community, with objectives consistent with the foundation's goals, and the balance of conservation, preservation, and development. Application form required.
Initial approach: Written request for application
Copies of proposal: 1
Deadline(s): Mar. 15
Board meeting date(s): Quarterly
Final notification: July 31
Write: Virginia R. Rollefson, Exec. Dir.
Officers and Directors:* John F. Reynolds III,* Pres.; Joan D. Mazzotta,* V.P.; Arthur E. Webster, Jr.,* Secy.; Bruce H. Watrous,* Treas.; and 8 other directors.
Number of staff: 1 part-time professional; 1 full-time support; 1 part-time support.
Employer Identification Number: 066000700

1029
The Rogow Birken Foundation, Inc. ⌑
c/o Rogin, Nassau, Caplan, Lassman & Hirtle
Cityplace
Hartford 06103

Established in 1981 in CT.
Donor(s): Louis B. Rogow.
Foundation type: Independent
Financial data (yr. ended 3/31/88): Assets, $2,283,184 (M); gifts received, $16,338; expenditures, $18,753.
Purpose and activities: Support primarily for Jewish welfare.
Types of support: General purposes.
Application information: Contributes only to pre-selected organizations. Applications not accepted.
Officers and Trustees: Louis B. Rogow, Pres. and Treas.; Herman H. Copelin, Secy.; Edward S. Rogin, Bruce Rogow.
Employer Identification Number: 061051591

1030
The Richard and Hinda Rosenthal Foundation ⌑
High Ridge Park
Stamford 06905 (203) 322-9900

Trust established in 1948 in NY.
Donor(s): Richard L. Rosenthal, and family, associates, and associated interests.
Foundation type: Independent
Financial data (yr. ended 12/31/88): Assets, $9,800,000 (M); gifts received, $14,625; expenditures, $340,000, including $320,000 for 200 grants (high: $46,000; low: $500).
Purpose and activities: To encourage achievement and excellence in the arts, social sciences, medical and scientific research, and clinical medicine. Conceived and annually sponsors the Rosenthal Awards for Fiction and for Painting through the American Academy and National Institute of Arts and Letters; also conceived and sponsors five national awards in clinical medicine through the American College of Physicians, American Heart Association, American Association for Cancer Research, and others. Has sponsored similar "discovery" awards in film.
Types of support: Research, special projects, annual campaigns, capital campaigns, general purposes.
Limitations: No grants to individuals.
Publications: Program policy statement.
Application information:
Initial approach: Letter
Copies of proposal: 1
Deadline(s): Oct. 31
Board meeting date(s): Quarterly and as required
Write: Hinda Gould Rosenthal, Pres.
Officers and Trustees: Richard L. Rosenthal, Chair.; Hinda Gould Rosenthal, Pres.; Richard L. Rosenthal, Jr., V.P.; Jamie G.R. Wolf, V.P.
Number of staff: 3 part-time support.
Employer Identification Number: 136104817

1031
Sachem Fund ⌑
1750 Durham Rd.
Guilford 06437

Trust established in 1969 in CT.
Donor(s): Timothy Mellon.
Foundation type: Independent
Financial data (yr. ended 12/31/88): Assets, $1,059,787 (M); expenditures, $105,892, including $100,000 for 1 grant.
Purpose and activities: Emphasis on innovative social service programs and land management projects.
Limitations: No grants to individuals, or for pure research, capital projects, endowment funds, conferences, film projects, publications, or general operating support.
Publications: Multi-year report.
Application information:
Initial approach: Letter
Deadline(s): None
Board meeting date(s): As required
Officers and Trustees*: Timothy Mellon,* Pres.; Paul Schwendeman, Secy.; Nathan W. Pearson,* Treas.
Employer Identification Number: 066112539

1032
The Helen M. Saunders Charitable Foundation ☆
c/o Shipman & Goodwin
799 Main St.
Hartford 06103 (203) 549-4770

Established in 1985 in CT.
Foundation type: Independent
Financial data (yr. ended 06/30/89): Assets, $2,884,779 (M); expenditures, $177,870, including $146,702 for 23 grants (high: $33,333; low: $150).
Purpose and activities: Giving primarily for hospitals and performing arts groups; support also for education, public broadcasting, and a Protestant church.
Types of support: Annual campaigns, general purposes, matching funds, capital campaigns, endowment funds.
Limitations: Giving primarily in CT, with emphasis on Hartford. No grants to individuals.
Publications: Application guidelines.
Application information:
Initial approach: Letter
Deadline(s): None
Write: Coleman H. Casey, Trustee
Trustee: Coleman H. Casey.
Employer Identification Number: 066284362

1033
The Savin Foundation
P.O. Box 7136
Bloomfield 06002 (203) 242-0800

Incorporated in 1952 in CT.
Donor(s): Marvin S. Savin, Elaine Savin, Stacey S. Chatigny, Nina S. Scott, Sugar S. McCauley, Terri S. Docal, John P. Savin, Savin Bros., Inc.
Foundation type: Independent
Financial data (yr. ended 09/30/88): Assets, $84,291 (M); gifts received, $693,644; expenditures, $649,228, including $648,575 for 9 grants (high: $415,000; low: $100).
Purpose and activities: Giving for Jewish organizations, including a community center and welfare funds.
Limitations: Giving primarily in CT. No grants to individuals.
Application information: Contributes only to pre-selected organizations. Applications not accepted.
Write: Patricia Rankin, Secy.
Officers and Trustees:* Marvin S. Savin,* Pres.; Elaine Savin,* V.P.; Patricia Rankin,* Secy.
Employer Identification Number: 066038483

1034
Schiro Fund, Inc. ⌑
25 Brookside Blvd.
West Hartford 06107 (203) 232-5854

Incorporated in 1963 in CT.
Donor(s): Bernard W. Schiro, Beatrice Fox Auerbach.†
Foundation type: Independent
Financial data (yr. ended 12/31/87): Assets, $5,156,990 (M); expenditures, $336,159, including $246,188 for 203 grants (high: $100,000; low: $10).
Purpose and activities: Emphasis on Jewish welfare funds, higher education, social services, and cultural organizations.
Types of support: General purposes.
Limitations: Giving primarily in CT.
Application information: Application form not required.
Deadline(s): None
Write: Bernard Schiro, Pres., and Dorothy A. Schiro, Secy.
Officers and Trustees: Bernard Schiro, Pres.; Dorothy A. Schiro, Secy.-Treas.; Georgette A. Koopman.
Employer Identification Number: 066056977

1035
Walter Scott Foundation
Three Grand Place
Newtown 06470 (203) 426-4225
Additional mailing address: Chateau Touraine, P.O. Box 147, Scarsdale, NY 10583

Incorporated in 1903 in NY.
Foundation type: Independent
Financial data (yr. ended 09/30/89): Assets, $4,690,370 (M); expenditures, $248,755, including $174,500 for 33 grants (high: $33,000; low: $300; average: $2,000-$5,000).
Purpose and activities: Aid to institutions concerned with handicapped children and adults.
Types of support: Operating budgets, continuing support, annual campaigns, seed money, building funds, equipment, endowment funds, research.
Limitations: Giving primarily in the New York, NY, metropolitan area and lower CT. No grants to individuals, or for matching gifts; no loans.
Application information: Application form not required.
Initial approach: Brief letter
Copies of proposal: 1
Deadline(s): None
Board meeting date(s): Semiannually in the spring and early Sept.
Final notification: 2 to 4 months
Write: Thorpe A. Nickerson, Pres.
Officers and Directors:* Thorpe A. Nickerson,* Pres. and Secy.-Treas.; Hazel P. Nickerson,* V.P.; Norman A. Hill, Brett R. Nickerson, Glendon A. Nickerson, Lisa B. Nickerson.
Number of staff: 1 part-time professional; 2 full-time support.
Employer Identification Number: 135681161

1036
Senior Services of Stamford, Inc.
c/o Union Trust Co.
P.O. Box 863
Shelton 06484 (203) 348-6211
Application address: c/o Union Trust Co., 300 Main St., Stamford, CT 06502

Established in 1909 in CT.
Donor(s): Various individuals.
Foundation type: Independent
Financial data (yr. ended 02/28/90): Assets, $9,533,000 (M); expenditures, $582,710, including $74,475 for 9 grants (high: $32,542; low: $100).
Purpose and activities: Support for social service organizations serving the elderly, allowances to beneficiaries, and payments for medical services.
Limitations: Giving limited to Stamford, CT.
Application information:
Initial approach: Letter
Deadline(s): None
Write: Robert J. Bromfield, Treas.
Officers and Directors: J. Robert Bromley, Pres.; Thomas C. Mayers, V.P.; Steven Ayres, Secy.; Robert J. Bromfield, Treas.; Mrs. Denison Hatch, Mrs. Robert G. Plunkett, Roberta Ratcliffe, William E. Ryan, Hettie Tinsley, Richard B. Tweedy.
Employer Identification Number: 060646916

1037
Smart Family Foundation ▼
15 Benders Dr.
Greenwich 06831 (203) 531-1474

Trust established in 1951 in IL.
Donor(s): David A. Smart,† A.D. Elden,† Vera Elden,† John Smart, Edgar G. Richards, Florence Richards.†
Foundation type: Independent
Financial data (yr. ended 12/31/89): Assets, $51,105,074 (M); expenditures, $2,218,738, including $1,971,899 for 22 grants (high: $500,000; low: $1,500; average: $10,000-$120,000).
Purpose and activities: The foundation is primarily interested in education projects and has, in particular, been focusing on projects that affect primary and secondary school children.
Types of support: Research, seed money.
Application information: Application form not required.
Initial approach: Proposal or letter
Copies of proposal: 1
Deadline(s): 6 weeks prior to meetings
Board meeting date(s): Fall and spring
Final notification: Within 6 weeks after board meetings
Write: Raymond Smart, Pres.

Officers and Directors:* Robert Feitler,* Chair.; Raymond L. Smart,* Pres.; Mary Smart,* Secy.; William Oswald,* Treas.; Joan Feitler, Edgar G. Richards, Ellen Smart, Nancy Smart, Sue Smart Stone.
Number of staff: 2
Employer Identification Number: 061232323

1038
The Society for the Increase of the Ministry
120 Sigourney St.
Hartford 06105

Established in 1857.
Donor(s): Sarah Norton Pardee Trust.
Foundation type: Independent
Financial data (yr. ended 08/31/89): Assets, $2,371,885 (M); gifts received, $30,790; expenditures, $133,599, including $114,815 for 139 grants to individuals (high: $1,780; low: $500; average: $500-$1,780).
Purpose and activities: Grants limited to full-time students preparing for ordination in the Episcopal Church at one of the 11 accredited Episcopal theological seminaries.
Types of support: Student aid.
Limitations: Giving limited to the U.S.
Publications: Application guidelines, informational brochure.
Application information: Contact financial aid officer of each accredited theological seminary of the Episcopal Church. Application form required.
Deadline(s): Mar. 1
Write: Rev. Canon J.S. Zimmerman, Exec. Dir.
Officers: Rev. Borden W. Painter, Pres.; The Very Rev. Stephen H. Gushee, V.P.; Howard W. Bornholm, Treas.; Rev. John Bishop, Secy.
Number of staff: 1 part-time professional; 1 part-time support.
Employer Identification Number: 066053077

1039
Sorenson Family Foundation, Inc. ⌑ ☆
100 Westmont
West Hartford 06117

Established in 1967.
Foundation type: Independent
Financial data (yr. ended 12/31/88): Assets, $2,160,253 (M); expenditures, $114,483, including $108,450 for 70 grants (high: $20,000; low: $100).
Purpose and activities: Support for hospitals and health associations, the performing arts, education, and churches.
Types of support: Endowment funds.
Limitations: Giving primarily in CT. No grants to individuals.
Application information: Contributes only to pre-selected organizations. Applications not accepted.
Officers and Directors: Wendy S. Pearson, Pres.; Hildegarde C. Sorenson, V.P. and Treas.; Richard W. Sorenson, Secy.
Employer Identification Number: 066099725

1040
The Richard W. Sorenson Family Foundation ⌑
60 Johnson Ave.
Plainville 06062

Established in 1984 in CT.
Donor(s): Carlingswitch, Inc.
Foundation type: Operating
Financial data (yr. ended 12/31/88): Assets, $1,570,570 (M); gifts received, $92,000; expenditures, $102,083, including $78,100 for 15 grants (high: $50,000; low: $100).
Purpose and activities: A private operating foundation; support for private schools and a camp.
Application information: Application form required.
Deadline(s): July 1
Write: Richard W. Sorenson, V.P.
Officers and Directors:* Richard W. Sorenson, Pres. and Treas.; Rosalie Sorenson,* Secy.; Edward F. Rosenthal.
Employer Identification Number: 222547323

1041
Martin T. Sosnoff Foundation ⌑ ☆
84 Turtleback Rd.
New Canaan 06840 (203) 972-0795

Established in 1978.
Donor(s): Martin T. Sosnoff.
Foundation type: Independent
Financial data (yr. ended 11/30/88): Assets, $1,591,499 (M); gifts received, $3,460; expenditures, $270,648, including $264,043 for 15 grants (high: $110,000; low: $425).
Purpose and activities: Support primarily for higher and secondary education, including a medical school, hospitals, and a museum.
Limitations: No support for private foundations. No grants to individuals.
Application information:
Initial approach: Letter
Deadline(s): None
Write: Martin T. Sosnoff, Trustee
Trustees: Eugene Sosnoff, Ivor Sosnoff, Martin T. Sosnoff, Toni Sosnoff.
Employer Identification Number: 222231640

1042
The Alix W. Stanley Charitable Foundation, Inc.
235 Main St.
New Britain 06051 (203) 224-6478
Mailing address: P.O. Box 2140, New Britain, CT 06050

Incorporated in 1943 in CT.
Donor(s): Alix W. Stanley.†
Foundation type: Independent
Financial data (yr. ended 12/31/89): Assets, $9,400,000 (M); expenditures, $522,000, including $457,500 for grants (high: $100,000; low: $200).
Purpose and activities: Emphasis on cultural programs, community funds, family and youth agencies, and hospitals.
Types of support: Continuing support, annual campaigns, building funds, capital campaigns, emergency funds, seed money.
Limitations: Giving primarily to organizations benefiting the citizens of New Britain, CT, and surrounding areas. No grants to individuals; no loans.
Application information:
Initial approach: Proposal
Board meeting date(s): Mar., June, Sept., and Dec.
Write: James R. Lemeris, Trust Officer, Connecticut National Bank
Officers: William E. Attwood, Pres.; Timothy Grace, Secy.; Connecticut National Bank, Treas.
Trustees: Donald W. Davis, Marie S. Gustin, Susan Rathgeber, Catherine Rogers, John W. Shumaker, Rev. James A. Simpson, Talcott Stanley.
Employer Identification Number: 060724195

1043
The Stanley Works Foundation ▼
c/o Connecticut Bank & Trust Co., N.A.
P.O. Box 3334
Hartford 06103 (203) 225-5111

Trust established in 1967 in CT.
Donor(s): The Stanley Works.
Foundation type: Company-sponsored
Financial data (yr. ended 12/31/88): Assets, $1,651,173 (M); gifts received, $900,000; expenditures, $1,215,158, including $1,198,847 for 871 grants (high: $75,000; low: $10; average: $2,000-$5,000).
Purpose and activities: Main emphasis on affordable housing, education, including retention programs in elementary and secondary education and higher education; support also for child welfare, health, hospital building funds, engineering, and the environment.
Types of support: Continuing support, annual campaigns, seed money, emergency funds, special projects, research, matching funds, employee matching gifts, building funds, internships.
Limitations: Giving primarily in areas of company operations in CA, CT, GA, MI, OH, OR, PA, RI, SC, TN, and VT. No support for United Way supported organizations. No grants to individuals, or for endowments, operating budgets, deficit financing, equipment, land acquisition, renovation projects, publications, or conferences; no loans.
Publications: Application guidelines.
Application information: Application form required.
Initial approach: Letter
Deadline(s): Jan., Apr., July, and Oct.
Board meeting date(s): Feb., May, Aug., and Nov.
Final notification: One month after board meeting
Write: Ronald F. Gilrain, V.P., Public Affairs
Trustee: Connecticut Bank & Trust Co., N.A.
Number of staff: 1 full-time professional; 1 part-time professional; 1 full-time support.
Employer Identification Number: 066088099

1044
The Stone Foundation, Inc.
25 Ford Road, Suite 200
Westport 06880 (203) 227-2000

Incorporated in 1964 in OH; reincorporated in 1972 in CT.

Donor(s): Marion H. Stone,† Charles Lynn Stone.†
Foundation type: Independent
Financial data (yr. ended 12/31/89): Assets, $8,000,000 (M); expenditures, $371,000, including $231,000 for 6 grants (high: $100,000; low: $700; average: $700-$100,000).
Purpose and activities: Primary interest in seed money for unique projects and programs in medicine, education, and related areas.
Types of support: Seed money, general purposes, building funds, endowment funds.
Limitations: No grants to individuals, or for matching gifts, scholarships, fellowships, or special projects; no loans.
Publications: Program policy statement, application guidelines.
Application information: Funds presently committed; grant requests only from qualified medical schools, colleges, and universities. Application form not required.
Initial approach: Proposal
Copies of proposal: 1
Deadline(s): Submit proposal preferably in Sept.; deadline Oct. 15
Board meeting date(s): Dec.
Final notification: By Jan. 31
Write: Robert B. Milligan, Jr., Secy.-Treas.
Officers and Trustees:* Charles Lynn Stone, Jr.,* Pres.; Edward E. Stone,* V.P.; Robert B. Milligan, Jr.,* Secy.-Treas.; Paul W. Adams, Mary Stone Parsons, Sara S. Stone.
Number of staff: 1 part-time professional.
Employer Identification Number: 237148468

1045
Stratfield Fund ⌑
Ten Middle St., Suite 735
Bridgeport 06604

Trust established in 1955 in CT.
Donor(s): Members of the Hoffman family.
Foundation type: Independent
Financial data (yr. ended 3/31/88): Assets, $1,332,778 (M); gifts received, $1,000; expenditures, $117,906, including $113,752 for 59 grants (high: $30,175; low: $18).
Purpose and activities: Grants primarily for Jewish welfare funds, temple support, and schools and universities; support also for other higher and secondary education.
Trustees: Burton Hoffman, Edna R. Hoffman, Hyacinthe K. Hoffman, Sidney Hoffman, Stephen J. Hoffman.
Manager: Laurence K. Hoffman.
Employer Identification Number: 066046672

1046
Ray H. & Pauline Sullivan Foundation ⌑
c/o Connecticut National Bank
777 Main St.
Hartford 06115
Application address: c/o Connecticut National Bank, 250 Captain's Walk, New London, CT 06320; Tel.: (203) 447-6132

Established in 1972 in CT.
Donor(s): Ray H. Sullivan.†
Foundation type: Independent
Financial data (yr. ended 07/31/89): Assets, $8,541,566 (M); expenditures, $480,888, including $336,935 for 55 grants (high: $20,000; low: $500), $6,750 for 3 grants to individuals (high: $3,000; low: $750) and $78,750 for 102 loans to individuals.
Purpose and activities: Giving limited largely to Roman Catholic charities and educational institutions; some support also for scholarships.
Types of support: Scholarship funds, student aid, student loans.
Limitations: Giving primarily in the diocese of Norwich, CT.
Application information: Application form required.
Deadline(s): May 1
Write: John J. Curtin
Trustees: David C. Cavicke, James McGuire, Msgr. Paul J. St. Onge, Connecticut National Bank.
Employer Identification Number: 066141242

1047
Swindells Charitable Foundation Trust ⌑
c/o Connecticut National Bank
777 Main St.
Hartford 06115 (203) 728-2274

Established in 1936 in CT.
Foundation type: Independent
Financial data (yr. ended 2/29/88): Assets, $1,126,458 (M); expenditures, $64,670, including $54,996 for 8 grants (high: $10,000; low: $2,500).
Purpose and activities: Support primarily for mental health and general health programs, concentrating on children's facilities.
Application information:
Initial approach: Letter
Deadline(s): Feb. 18 and Aug. 18
Write: Maxine Dean
Trustee: Connecticut National Bank.
Employer Identification Number: 066026054

1048
Topsfield Foundation, Inc.
Route 169, Box 203
Pomfret 06258 (203) 928-2616

Established in 1982 in CT.
Donor(s): Paul J. Aicher.
Foundation type: Independent
Financial data (yr. ended 12/31/89): Assets, $3,800,000 (M); gifts received, $2,800,000; expenditures, $415,000, including $71,748 for 26 grants (high: $50,000; low: $100; average: $100-$50,000).
Purpose and activities: In addition to local funding for grassroots organizations working on national security and affordable housing issues, the foundation's resources are devoted to the Study Circles Resource Center project and the International Security News Clipping Service.
Types of support: Operating budgets, seed money, matching funds.
Limitations: Giving primarily in the northeastern region of CT. No grants to individuals.
Publications: Annual report.
Application information: Organizations are funded on the basis of direct involvement of board members. Applications not accepted.
Write: Phyllis Emigh
Officers and Board Members:* Paul J. Aicher,* Chair. and Pres.; Joyce Aicher,* V.P.; V. Duncan Johnson,* Secy.; Peter Aicher, Dennis Landis, Kathryn Wright.
Number of staff: 3
Employer Identification Number: 061074292

1049
The Morris & Sylvia Trachten Family Foundation, Inc. ⌑
33-39 John St.
New Britain 06051 (203) 225-6478

Established in 1984 in CT.
Foundation type: Independent
Financial data (yr. ended 06/30/89): Assets, $203,279 (M); gifts received, $191,859; expenditures, $100,548, including $100,448 for 100 grants (high: $49,100; low: $10).
Purpose and activities: Support primarily for Jewish welfare funds and temples.
Limitations: Giving primarily in the northeastern U.S.
Application information: Application form not required.
Initial approach: Letter
Deadline(s): None
Write: Morris Trachten, Trustee
Trustees: David Trachten, Morris Trachten, Sylvia Trachten.
Employer Identification Number: 222518063

1050
The Travelers Companies Foundation ▼ ⌑
One Tower Sq.
Hartford 06183-1060 (203) 277-2307
Additional tel.: (203) 277-6080

Established about 1984 in CT.
Donor(s): The Travelers Corp., and subsidiaries.
Foundation type: Company-sponsored
Financial data (yr. ended 12/31/88): Assets, $3,667,221 (M); gifts received, $5,015,888; expenditures, $4,535,120, including $4,043,883 for 171 grants (high: $835,000; low: $500; average: $500-$25,000) and $491,237 for 4,229 employee matching gifts.
Purpose and activities: Support primarily for programs that benefit older Americans, youth education, and civil justice reform. Grants also for civic affairs, community development, health and social services, arts and culture, and higher education; support for capital campaigns on a local level only.
Types of support: General purposes, operating budgets, special projects, research, fellowships, technical assistance, capital campaigns, employee matching gifts, seed money.
Limitations: Giving primarily in areas of company operations; giving for capital projects limited to the greater Hartford, CT, area; grants for youth education limited to programs within Hartford, CT, schools. No support for political, fraternal, athletic, social, or veterans' organizations; religious sectarian activities; or for business, professional, or trade associations. No grants to individuals, or for mass mail appeals or testimonial dinners.
Publications: Annual report, informational brochure.
Application information: Application form not required.
Initial approach: Proposal
Copies of proposal: 1

Deadline(s): None
Board meeting date(s): Quarterly
Final notification: Usually within 60 days
Write: Georgina Lucas, Pres. or Janet C. French, Exec. Dir.
Officers: F. Peter Libassi,* Chair.; Georgina I. Lucas, Pres.; Michael S. Smiley, Secy.; John Berthoud,* Treas.; Janet C. French, Exec. Dir.
Directors:* Elliot F. Gerson, Brooks Joslin.
Number of staff: 5 part-time professional; 1 full-time support; 3 part-time support.
Employer Identification Number: 222535386

1051
The UPS Foundation, Inc. ▼ ⌑
Greenwich Office Park 5
Greenwich 06836-3160 (203) 622-6201
Additional tel.: (203) 622-6287

Incorporated in 1951 in DE.
Foundation type: Company-sponsored
Financial data (yr. ended 12/31/88): Assets, $41,988,599 (M); gifts received, $5,007,000; expenditures, $6,678,315, including $6,112,174 for 202 grants (high: $973,390; low: $5,000; average: $2,000-$50,000) and $322,123 for employee matching gifts.
Purpose and activities: Support for any worthy philanthropic project or organization that is tax-exempt under 501(c)(3). Emphasis on human welfare (including programs for families and children in crisis, adult illiteracy and the distribution of food to hungry Americans), economic opportunity for minorities, programs for the handicapped, and community development, medical research and improved health care, and support of higher education (including academic, public policy, and transportation/logistics research).
Types of support: Operating budgets, continuing support, seed money, equipment, matching funds, employee matching gifts, professorships, internships, scholarship funds, employee-related scholarships, fellowships, special projects, research, general purposes.
Limitations: No grants to individuals (except for employee-related scholarships), or for building or endowment funds, annual campaigns, emergency funds, deficit financing, land acquisition, renovation projects, or publications; no loans.
Application information: Letter should address programs, objectives, evaluation, cost and other sources of funding; include IRS letter, budget, and annual report. Application form not required.
Initial approach: Letter, preferably no more than 2 pages
Copies of proposal: 1
Deadline(s): Submit proposal preferably Jan. through Aug.
Board meeting date(s): June and late Nov.
Write: Clement E. Hanrahan, Admin.
Officers: John W. Rogers,* Chair.; Kent C. Nelson,* Vice-Chair. and Treas.; Robert E. Smith,* Secy.; Clem Hanrahan, Admin.
Trustees:* Donald W. Layden, Calvin Tyler.
Number of staff: 2 full-time support.
Employer Identification Number: 136099176

1052
Robert C. Vance Charitable Foundation
21 Winesap Rd.
Kensington 06037-2932

Established in 1960 in CT.
Donor(s): Robert C. Vance.†
Foundation type: Independent
Financial data (yr. ended 1/31/89): Assets, $5,485,102 (M); expenditures, $354,923, including $332,750 for 19 grants (high: $100,000; low: $500).
Purpose and activities: Giving primarily for education, hospitals, civic affairs, the homeless, and youth.
Limitations: Giving limited to the New Britain-Berlin, CT, area. No grants to individuals.
Publications: Application guidelines.
Application information: Application form not required.
Deadline(s): None
Write: Herbert E. Carlson, Jr., Pres.
Officer: Herbert E. Carlson, Jr., Pres.
Trustee Bank: Connecticut National Bank.
Number of staff: None.
Employer Identification Number: 066050188

1053
R. T. Vanderbilt Trust
30 Winfield St.
Norwalk 06855 (203) 853-1400

Trust established in 1951 in CT.
Foundation type: Independent
Financial data (yr. ended 12/31/88): Assets, $6,146,011 (M); expenditures, $350,709, including $300,210 for 118 grants (high: $92,000; low: $50).
Purpose and activities: Emphasis on education and conservation; support also for hospitals, cultural programs, and historic preservation.
Types of support: Building funds, endowment funds, operating budgets, special projects.
Limitations: Giving primarily in CT and NY. No grants to individuals.
Application information: Application form not required.
Initial approach: Proposal
Copies of proposal: 1
Deadline(s): Submit proposal preferably in Nov.
Board meeting date(s): Apr., June, Sept., and Dec.
Write: Hugh B. Vanderbilt, Chair.
Trustees: Hugh B. Vanderbilt, Chair.; Robert T. Vanderbilt, Jr.
Number of staff: 2 part-time support.
Employer Identification Number: 066040981

1054
Hilla Von Rebay Foundation ⌑
c/o Cummings & Lockwood
10 Stamford Forum
Stamford 06904
Application address: P.O. Box 120, Stamford, CT 06904

Established in 1967 in CT.
Foundation type: Independent
Financial data (yr. ended 12/31/87): Assets, $2,863,719 (M); expenditures, $90,709, including $31,028 for 2 grants (high: $26,028; low: $5,000).
Purpose and activities: Support limited to promotion of non-objective painting, particularly to exhibition of the Rebay Collection, and to a nature sanctuary in Westport, CT.
Application information: Application form not required.
Initial approach: Letter or brief proposal
Deadline(s): None
Write: Francis P. Schiaroli
Trustees: Lawrence J. McGrath, Jr., Connecticut Bank & Trust Co., N.A.
Employer Identification Number: 237112973

1055
The Waterbury Foundation
P.O. Box 252
Waterbury 06720 (203) 753-1315

Incorporated in 1923 by special Act of the CT Legislature.
Donor(s): Katherine Pomeroy,† Edith Chase.†
Foundation type: Community
Financial data (yr. ended 12/31/89): Assets, $7,635,000 (M); gifts received, $453,761; expenditures, $451,822, including $269,946 for 45 grants (high: $100,000; low: $45) and $10,450 for 13 grants to individuals (high: $1,000; low: $400).
Purpose and activities: Grants largely for social services, health care, higher and other education, including scholarship funds, youth agencies, community funds, and the arts, with emphasis on providing seed money and venture capital for new projects.
Types of support: Seed money, emergency funds, building funds, equipment, land acquisition, matching funds, research, special projects, publications, conferences and seminars, capital campaigns, consulting services, renovation projects, scholarship funds, technical assistance, student aid.
Limitations: Giving limited to the greater Waterbury, CT, area. No support for sectarian or religious purposes. No grants for deficit financing, continuing support, annual campaigns, endowment funds; no loans.
Publications: Annual report (including application guidelines), program policy statement, newsletter, informational brochure (including application guidelines), application guidelines.
Application information: Application form required.
Initial approach: Telephone or letter
Copies of proposal: 30
Deadline(s): 7 weeks prior to board meetings
Board meeting date(s): Mar., June, and Nov.; Grants Committee meets twice, 6 weeks and 1 week prior to each board meeting
Final notification: 7 weeks
Write: Mrs. Ingrid Manning, Admin.
Officers: Patricia B. Sweet,* Pres.; Charles W. Henry,* V.P.; Ann Y. Smith,* V.P.; N. Patricia Yarborough,* Secy.; Sean T. Egan,* Treas.
Trustees:* Burton Albert, Carol B. Andrews, Dirck Barhydt, Lillian H. Brown, George Frantzis, Robert W. Garthwait, Sr., Sr. Margaret Rosita Kenney, Shiela Largay, Pasquale Palumbo, W. Scott Peterson, M.D., Marie Santopietro, Paul N. Vonckx, Jr.

Trustee Banks: Bank of Boston Connecticut, Citytrust, Connecticut National Bank.
Number of staff: 1 full-time professional; 1 full-time support.
Employer Identification Number: 066038074

1056
Weller Foundation ⌑ ☆
P.O. Box 1145
Woodbury 06798

Established in 1959.
Foundation type: Independent
Financial data (yr. ended 12/31/88): Assets, $1,525,253 (M); expenditures, $72,345, including $18,458 for 33 grants (high: $2,188; low: $300) and $22,433 for 34 grants to individuals (high: $2,500; low: $100).
Purpose and activities: Provides scholarships and awards to high school students in 5 CT communities for higher and vocational education; grants also for health associations, youth organizations, and higher education.
Types of support: Student aid.
Limitations: Giving primarily in Newtown, Monroe, Trumbull, Shelton, and Easton-Redding, CT.
Application information: Contact foundation for application proceedures for the various awards and scholarship programs. Application form required.
Trustees: Robert Swart, Chair.; Michael Zabinski, Vice-Chair.; Alexander Fraser, Secy.; Robert H. Paquette, Treas.; Earle A. Hallstrom, Louis J. LaCroce, Brian E. Skinner, Barton L. Weller.
Employer Identification Number: 066068987

1057
Wilmot Wheeler Foundation, Inc. ⌑
P.O. Box 429
Southport 06490 (203) 259-1615

Incorporated in 1941 in DE.
Donor(s): Wilmot F. Wheeler,† Hulda C. Wheeler.
Foundation type: Independent
Financial data (yr. ended 6/30/88): Assets, $1,582,651 (M); expenditures, $108,705, including $52,140 for 56 grants (high: $8,500; low: $40; average: $100-$1,000).
Purpose and activities: Giving for higher and secondary education, and Protestant church suppport.
Limitations: Giving primarily in CT.
Application information:
Initial approach: Letter
Deadline(s): None
Write: Wilmot F. Wheeler, Jr., Pres.
Officers: Wilmot F. Wheeler, Jr., Pres.; Wilmot F. Wheeler III, V.P. and Treas.; Halsted W. Wheeler, Secy.
Employer Identification Number: 066039119

1058
The Whitehead Charitable Foundation ⌑
15 Valley Dr.
Greenwich 06830 (203) 629-4633

Established in 1976.
Donor(s): Edwin C. Whitehead.
Foundation type: Independent
Financial data (yr. ended 11/30/88): Assets, $3,067,746 (M); gifts received, $1,000,000; expenditures, $587,330, including $571,950 for 19 grants (high: $200,000; low: $100; average: $100,000-$3,600,000).
Purpose and activities: Grants primarily for biomedical research.
Types of support: Research, endowment funds.
Application information: Applications not accepted.
Write: William F. Campbell
Officers and Directors: John J. Whitehead, Pres.; Peter J. Whitehead, V.P.; Rosalind C. Whitehead, Secy.; Arthur W. Brill, Treas.; Susan Whitehead.
Employer Identification Number: 060956618

1059
Widow's Society ⌑
c/o Connecticut National Bank
777 Main St.
Hartford 06115

Established in 1907 in CT.
Donor(s): City of Hartford, Sarah W. Pardee Fund.
Foundation type: Independent
Financial data (yr. ended 8/31/87): Assets, $2,196,041 (M); gifts received, $25,111; expenditures, $121,125, including $102,928 for 115 grants to individuals (high: $4,800; low: $20).
Purpose and activities: Aid to needy individuals, especially women and children.
Types of support: Grants to individuals.
Limitations: Giving primarily in Hartford, CT.
Application information: Applications generally referred through public or private social service agency.
Write: Endowment Admin.
Officers: Jerrine Fiske, Pres.; Mary Hoffer, V.P.; Mrs. John Martin, Secy.
Number of staff: None.
Employer Identification Number: 066026060

1060
Wimpfheimer Foundation, Inc. ⌑ ☆
22 Bayview Ave.
Stonington 06378-1148

Established in 1949.
Donor(s): A. Wimpfheimer & Brothers, Inc., Jacques D. Wimpfheimer.
Foundation type: Independent
Financial data (yr. ended 12/31/87): Assets, $506,063 (M); gifts received, $116,950; expenditures, $167,586, including $165,100 for 52 grants (high: $101,000; low: $100).
Purpose and activities: Support for a public library, cultural programs, and social services.
Limitations: Giving primarily in CT. No grants to individuals.
Application information: Applications not accepted.
Officers: Jacques D. Wimpfheimer, Pres.; Henry Scheibner, Treas.
Employer Identification Number: 066036353

1061
Wiremold Foundation, Inc. ⌑
60 Woodlawn St.
West Hartford 06110 (203) 233-6251

Established in 1967 in CT.
Donor(s): The Wiremold Co.
Foundation type: Company-sponsored
Financial data (yr. ended 12/31/88): Assets, $698,905 (M); gifts received, $72,000; expenditures, $191,101, including $181,350 for 79 grants (high: $53,500; low: $100) and $6,825 for 24 employee matching gifts (high: $1,000; low: $25).
Purpose and activities: Giving primarily for education and cultural activities; support also for social services.
Types of support: Employee matching gifts.
Limitations: Giving primarily in CT. No grants to individuals.
Application information: Preference given to requests for capital and/or start-up funds. Application form not required.
Write: John Davis Murphy, Pres.
Officers: John Davis Murphy, Pres.; Robert H. Murphy, V.P.; Joan L. Johnson, Secy.; Warren C. Packard, Treas.
Employer Identification Number: 066089445

1062
Woman's Seamen's Friend Society of Connecticut
74 Forbes Ave.
New Haven 06502 (203) 467-3887

Established in 1859 in CT.
Donor(s): Betsy Forbes Bradley.†
Foundation type: Independent
Financial data (yr. ended 12/31/87): Assets, $2,148,181 (M); expenditures, $94,929, including $9,400 for 9 grants (high: $4,000; low: $560) and $42,500 for 92 grants to individuals (high: $1,050; low: $250).
Purpose and activities: Scholarship aid for students who are majoring in marine science; support also for public charities which assist needy merchant seamen and their families.
Types of support: Seed money, special projects, research, student aid.
Limitations: Giving limited to CT. No grants to individuals (except scholarships), or for endowment funds; no loans.
Publications: 990-PF.
Application information: Scholarship application available from foundation. Application form required.
Initial approach: Letter
Copies of proposal: 2
Deadline(s): For summer scholarships, Apr. 1; for academic year scholarships, May 15
Board meeting date(s): Feb., Apr., June, Oct., and Dec.
Final notification: 2 or 3 months
Write: The Rev. Henry Burdick, III, Exec. Dir.
Officers and Trustees:* Dorothy Venter,* Pres.; Nancy Pugsley,* 1st V.P.; Kitty Barclay,* 2nd V.P.; Jane Hooker,* Secy.; Floyd Shumway,* Treas.; Nancy Johnstone, Carol Stancliff.
Number of staff: 1 full-time professional; 1 part-time professional.
Employer Identification Number: 060655133

1063
The David, Helen, and Marian Woodward Fund-Watertown
(also known as Marian W. Ottley Trust-Watertown)
Box 817
Watertown 06795

Trust established in 1975 in GA.
Donor(s): Marian W. Ottley.†
Foundation type: Independent
Financial data (yr. ended 5/31/89): Assets, $8,145,021 (M); expenditures, $450,869, including $370,919 for 23 grants (high: $100,000; low: $700; average: $10,000).
Purpose and activities: Giving primarily for higher, secondary, and early childhood education, health services and associations, youth agencies, the environment, church support, and social services. Support for building funds for education and hospitals.
Types of support: Capital campaigns, building funds, endowment funds, scholarship funds.
Limitations: Giving limited to New England (VT, CT, RI, MA, ME, NH) and NY. No grants to individuals.
Application information: Application form not required.
Initial approach: Letter
Copies of proposal: 3
Deadline(s): 30 days prior to board meetings
Board meeting date(s): June and Dec.
Write: E. Edward Thompson, Member, Selection Comm.
Selection Committee: M. Heminway Merriman II, Edith Pelletier, E. Edward Thompson.
Trustee: The First National Bank of Atlanta.
Number of staff: None.
Employer Identification Number: 586222005

1064
The Xerox Foundation ▼
P.O. Box 1600
Stamford 06904 (203) 968-3306

Incorporated in 1978 in DE as successor to Xerox Fund.
Donor(s): Xerox Corp.
Foundation type: Company-sponsored
Financial data (yr. ended 12/31/89): Assets, $18,500,000 (M); gifts received, $18,500,000; expenditures, $18,500,000, including $17,000,000 for 2,940 grants (high: $1,264,000; low: $25; average: $2,000-$20,000) and $1,500,000 for 7,100 employee matching gifts.
Purpose and activities: Broad commitment in support of higher education to prepare qualified men and women for careers in business, government, and education; advance knowledge in science and technology; commitment also to enhance learning opportunities for minorities and the disadvantaged. Also operates employee matching gift program. Support additionally for social, civic, and cultural organizations including the United Way, providing broad-based programs and services in cities where Xerox employees live and work, organizations that foster debate on major national public policy issues, and worldwide, for leadership efforts around major social problems, education, employability, and student exchange.
Types of support: General purposes, operating budgets, annual campaigns, seed money, emergency funds, research, conferences and seminars, scholarship funds, fellowships, professorships, internships, employee-related scholarships, exchange programs, employee matching gifts, program-related investments, consulting services, publications.
Limitations: Giving primarily in areas of company operations. No support for community colleges, organizations supported by United Way, religious organizations, or governmental agencies. No grants to individuals, or for capital or endowment funds; no donations of machines or related services; no loans.
Publications: Application guidelines.
Application information: Application form not required.
Initial approach: Brief proposal
Copies of proposal: 1
Deadline(s): None
Board meeting date(s): Usually in Dec. and as required
Final notification: 3 months
Write: Robert H. Gudger, V.P.
Officers: Douglas M. Reid, Pres.; Robert H. Gudger, V.P.; Martin S. Wagner, Secy.; Allan Z. Senter, Treas.
Trustees: Paul A. Allaire, David T. Kearns, Stuart B. Ross.
Number of staff: 1 full-time professional; 4 full-time support.
Employer Identification Number: 060996443

1065
Robert R. Young Foundation ⌑ ☆
P.O. Box 1423
Greenwich 06830

Donor(s): Anita O.K. Young.†
Foundation type: Independent
Financial data (yr. ended 12/31/88): Assets, $22,281,647 (M); gifts received, $6,782,007; expenditures, $1,029,213, including $986,250 for 24 grants (high: $500,000; low: $500).
Purpose and activities: Giving primarily for higher and other education; support also for Protestant churches, youth, museums, and health and hospitals.
Limitations: Giving primarily in CT and RI.
Application information:
Initial approach: Letter
Deadline(s): None
Final notification: 3 months
Write: David W. Wallace, Pres.
Officer and Trustees: David W. Wallace, Pres.; Jean W. Wallace.
Employer Identification Number: 136131394

1066
The E. Matilda Ziegler Foundation for the Blind, Inc. ⌑
41 Harbor Plaza Dr.
P.O. Box 10128
Stamford 06904-2128 (203) 356-9000

Incorporated in 1928 in NY.
Donor(s): Mrs. William Ziegler.†
Foundation type: Independent
Financial data (yr. ended 12/31/88): Assets, $10,126,356 (M); expenditures, $636,787, including $497,475 for 26 grants (high: $215,000; low: $2,500).
Purpose and activities: Giving for charitable and educational work to ameliorate the condition of the blind; support largely for the monthly publication and free distribution of the Matilda Ziegler Magazine for the Blind.
Types of support: General purposes, continuing support, annual campaigns.
Limitations: No grants to individuals, or for endowment funds, research, scholarships, fellowships, or matching gifts; no loans.
Application information:
Initial approach: Proposal
Copies of proposal: 1
Deadline(s): None
Write: William Ziegler III, Pres.
Officers: William Ziegler III,* Pres.; Helen Z. Steinkraus,* Secy.; Beatrice H. Page, Treas.
Directors:* Lawrence G. Bodkin, Jr., Charles B. Cook, Jr., James J. Marett, Frank K. Sanders, Jr., Eric M. Steinkraus, Cynthia Zeigler-Brighton.
Employer Identification Number: 136086195

DELAWARE

1067
Jack and Mimi Leviton Amsterdam Foundation ⌑
c/o Thomas Sweeney
One Rodney Square, P.O. Box 551
Wilmington 19899 (302) 658-6541

Established in 1977 in DE.
Donor(s): Jack Amsterdam.
Foundation type: Independent
Financial data (yr. ended 12/31/87): Assets, $1,682,693 (M); gifts received, $37,500; expenditures, $54,628, including $47,700 for 13 grants (high: $10,000; low: $200).
Purpose and activities: Giving for medical research, higher education, Jewish organizations in the U.S. and Israel, and the performing arts.
Types of support: Research.
Application information: Contributes only to pre-selected organizations. Applications not accepted.
Officers: Jack Amsterdam, Pres.; Dasha L. Epstein, V.P.
Employer Identification Number: 510220854

1068
Arguild Foundation ⌑
1220 Market St., 10th Fl.
Wilmington 19801 (302) 658-9141

Established in 1959 in DE.
Foundation type: Independent
Financial data (yr. ended 12/31/88): Assets, $1,053,781 (M); gifts received, $25,000; expenditures, $63,316, including $61,050 for 31 grants (high: $5,500; low: $100).

Purpose and activities: Giving for higher and secondary education, welfare funds, and Roman Catholic organizations.
Limitations: No grants to individuals.
Application information:
Initial approach: Letter
Deadline(s): None
Write: Arthur G. Connolly, Sr., Pres.
Officer: Arthur G. Connolly, Sr., Pres.
Employer Identification Number: 516016487

1069
Beneficial Foundation, Inc. ⌑
1100 Carr Rd.
P.O. Box 911
Wilmington 19899 (302) 798-0800

Incorporated in 1951 in DE.
Donor(s): Beneficial Corp., and its subsidiaries, Beneficial New Jersey.
Foundation type: Company-sponsored
Financial data (yr. ended 12/31/87): Assets, $4,805,617 (M); gifts received, $350,000; expenditures, $628,375, including $383,500 for 38 grants (high: $100,000; low: $1,000; average: $1,000-$10,000) and $208,941 for 700 grants to individuals.
Purpose and activities: Grants primarily to educational institutions, hospitals, and for medical research; also a scholarship program for children of employees of Beneficial Corporation or of the Beneficial Finance System. Support also for cultural programs.
Types of support: Employee-related scholarships, research, continuing support, annual campaigns, seed money, building funds, equipment, special projects.
Limitations: Giving primarily in DE, FL, NJ, and NY. No grants for endowment funds; no loans.
Application information: Application form required for scholarship applicants.
Initial approach: Proposal
Copies of proposal: 1
Deadline(s): None
Board meeting date(s): Usually in May and Dec.
Write: John O. Williams, V.P.
Officers: Robert A. Tucker,* Pres.; Finn M.W. Caspersen,* V.P. and Secy.; Kenneth J. Kircher, Treas.
Directors:* Freda R. Caspersen, John O. Williams.
Number of staff: 2 part-time support.
Employer Identification Number: 516011637

1070
Stephen and Mary Birch Foundation, Inc. ⌑
501 Silverside Rd., Suite 13
Wilmington 19809

Incorporated in 1938 in DE.
Donor(s): Stephen Birch.†
Foundation type: Independent
Financial data (yr. ended 12/31/88): Assets, $90,684,987 (M); expenditures, $11,308,433, including $1,695,500 for 8 grants (high: $1,500,000; low: $500).
Purpose and activities: Emphasis on health agencies, hospitals, youth agencies, cultural programs, social services, civic organizations, and the blind.
Application information: Application form not required.
Initial approach: Letter
Copies of proposal: 1
Deadline(s): None
Board meeting date(s): Quarterly
Write: Elfriede Looze
Officers: Patrick J. Patek, Pres.; Christopher Patek, V.P.; Rose B. Patek, Secy-Treas.
Employer Identification Number: 221713022

1071
Edward E. and Lillian H. Bishop Foundation ⌑
c/o Wilmington Trust Co.
Rodney Square North
Wilmington 19890

Trust established in 1953 in DE.
Donor(s): Lillian H. Bishop.
Foundation type: Independent
Financial data (yr. ended 12/31/88): Assets, $2,561,228 (M); expenditures, $113,506, including $105,000 for 39 grants (high: $17,500; low: $100).
Purpose and activities: Emphasis on a museum and planetarium; some support for cultural programs, welfare funds, and care of animals.
Types of support: General purposes.
Limitations: Giving primarily in Manatee County, FL.
Application information:
Deadline(s): None
Trustees: Mary E. Parker, Richard W. Pratt, William D. Sugg, Willett Wentzel, P. Woodrow Young, Wilmington Trust Co.
Employer Identification Number: 516017762

1072
Lillian H. Bishop Trust for the SPCA of Manatee County, Florida ⌑
c/o Wilmington Trust Co.
Rodney Square North
Wilmington 19890

Established in 1973 in DE.
Foundation type: Independent
Financial data (yr. ended 12/31/87): Assets, $6,583,189 (M); expenditures, $397,763, including $315,411 for 8 grants.
Purpose and activities: Grants primarily for animal welfare, with the bulk of support going to the SPCA of Manatee County, FL.
Limitations: Giving primarily in Manatee County, FL.
Manager: Richard W. Pratt.
Trustee: Wilmington Trust Co.
Employer Identification Number: 237334266

1073
Borkee-Hagley Foundation, Inc. ⌑
P.O. Box 230
Wilmington 19899 (302) 652-8616

Incorporated in 1955 in DE.
Foundation type: Independent
Financial data (yr. ended 12/31/87): Assets, $2,064,212 (M); expenditures, $99,291, including $93,200 for 25 grants (high: $15,000; low: $100).
Purpose and activities: Emphasis on organizations benefiting the elderly, and secondary education; support also for housing.
Types of support: Capital campaigns, building funds, general purposes, operating budgets.
Limitations: Giving primarily in DE.
Application information:
Initial approach: Letter
Deadline(s): Nov. 1
Board meeting date(s): Dec.
Write: Henry H. Silliman, Jr., Pres.
Officers: Henry H. Silliman, Jr., Pres.; John E. Silliman, V.P.; Robert M. Silliman, V.P. and Treas.; Eleanor S. Maroney, Secy.
Directors: Thomas F. Husbands, Mariana S. Richards, George A. Sandbach, Henry H. Silliman, Doris S. Stockly.
Employer Identification Number: 516011644

1074
The Carpenter Foundation, Inc. ⌑
Powder Mill Sq., Suite 204
3844 Kennett Pike
Greenville 19807

Incorporated in 1942 in DE.
Donor(s): William K. Carpenter, and members of the Carpenter family.
Foundation type: Independent
Financial data (yr. ended 12/31/88): Assets, $2,218,153 (M); expenditures, $125,123, including $120,000 for grants.
Purpose and activities: Giving for health services, including hospitals, a secondary school, and a conservation association.
Limitations: Giving primarily in DE. No grants to individuals.
Application information: Contributes only to pre-selected organizations. Applications not accepted.
Write: Thomas R. Smith, Pres.
Officers: Thomas R. Smith,* Pres. and Treas.; R.R.M. Carpenter, Jr.,* V.P.; J. Avery Draper,* V.P.; Judith A. Abrego, Secy.
Trustees:* Renee C. Draper.
Employer Identification Number: 516015354

1075
Elizabeth Ewart Casey Perpetual Charitable Trust B ⌑
c/o Wilmington Trust Co.
Rodney Sq. North
Wilmington 19890

Established in 1986 in DE.
Donor(s): R. Elizabeth Ewart Casey.†
Foundation type: Independent
Financial data (yr. ended 7/31/88): Assets, $1,381,686 (M); expenditures, $87,174, including $77,186 for 4 grants (high: $25,729; low: $12,864).
Purpose and activities: Support primarily for Protestant welfare and the Society of Friends.
Application information: Applications not accepted.
Trustee: Wilmington Trust Co.
Employer Identification Number: 516162942

1076
Chichester duPont Foundation, Inc. ▼ ⌑
3120 Kennett Pike
Wilmington 19807-3045 (302) 658-5244

Incorporated in 1946 in DE.
Donor(s): Lydia Chichester duPont,† Mary Chichester duPont Clark,† A. Felix duPont, Jr., Alice du Pont Mills.
Foundation type: Independent
Financial data (yr. ended 12/31/86): Assets, $19,823,423 (M); expenditures, $876,466, including $819,000 for 25 grants (high: $185,000; low: $2,000; average: $15,000-$50,000).
Purpose and activities: Emphasis on child welfare, including support for a camp for handicapped children, education, health, cultural programs, and religion; some support for conservation.
Types of support: Operating budgets, building funds.
Limitations: Giving primarily in the DE, MD, and PA, areas. No grants to individuals.
Application information:
Deadline(s): Oct. 1
Board meeting date(s): Dec.
Final notification: 2 weeks after meeting
Write: Gregory F. Fields, Secy.
Officers: Alice du Pont Mills, Pres.; Gregory F. Fields, Secy.; A. Felix duPont, Jr., Treas.
Trustees: Allaire C. duPont, Caroline J. duPont, Christopher T. duPont, Mary Mills Abel Smith, Phyllis Mills Wyeth.
Number of staff: None.
Employer Identification Number: 516011641

1077
Children's Beach House, Inc.
128A Senatorial Dr., Greenville Place
Wilmington 19807 (302) 655-4288

Established in 1937 in DE.
Foundation type: Operating
Financial data (yr. ended 09/30/89): Assets, $1,680,580 (M); gifts received, $327,662; expenditures, $363,547, including $200 for 1 grant.
Purpose and activities: A private operating foundation; support for a children's home.
Limitations: Giving primarily in DE.
Application information: Applications not accepted.
Write: Harold L. Springer, III, Exec. Dir.
Officers and Trustees:* Henry Rust,* Pres.; Richard A. Dobbs,* Treas.; and 21 additional trustees.
Number of staff: 5 full-time professional; 14 part-time professional; 1 full-time support; 14 part-time support.
Employer Identification Number: 510070966

1078
Melvin S. Cohen Foundation, Inc. ⌑
P.O. Box 2105
Wilmington 19899
Application address: 3925 North Hastings Way, Eau Claire, WI 54703; Tel.: (715) 839-2139

Incorporated in 1963 in WI.
Donor(s): Melvin S. Cohen, Eileen F. Cohen.
Foundation type: Independent
Financial data (yr. ended 12/31/86): Assets, $2,756,027 (M); gifts received, $150,318; expenditures, $211,032, including $196,620 for 19 grants (high: $185,000; low: $10).
Purpose and activities: Emphasis on Jewish welfare funds.
Types of support: Operating budgets, scholarship funds.
Limitations: Giving primarily in northwestern WI, preferably Eau Claire and Chippewa counties.
Application information:
Initial approach: Letter with proposed budget
Deadline(s): None
Write: Eileen F. Cohen, Secy.
Officers: Melvin S. Cohen, Pres.; Maryjo R. Cohen, V.P.; Eileen F. Cohen, Secy.-Treas.
Employer Identification Number: 396075009

1079
The Common Wealth Trust ⌑
c/o Bank of Delaware
222 Delaware Ave.
Wilmington 19899

Established in 1978.
Donor(s): Ralph W. Hayes.†
Foundation type: Independent
Financial data (yr. ended 12/31/88): Assets, $6,247,803 (M); expenditures, $386,784, including $202,573 for 4 grants (high: $188,573; low: $1,000) and $108,000 for 6 grants to individuals of $18,000 each.
Purpose and activities: Support for a historical society and educational purposes; also gives distinguished service awards to prominent individuals in literature, the dramatic arts, and communications.
Types of support: Grants to individuals.
Limitations: Giving primarily in DE.
Application information: Applications not accepted.
Trustee: Bank of Delaware.
Employer Identification Number: 510232187

1080
Copeland Andelot Foundation, Inc. ⌑
1100 DuPont Bldg.
Wilmington 19898

Incorporated in 1953 in DE.
Donor(s): Lammot du Pont Copeland.
Foundation type: Independent
Financial data (yr. ended 12/31/86): Assets, $1,094,743 (M); gifts received, $195,000; expenditures, $16,056.
Purpose and activities: Emphasis on hospitals, cultural institutions, community funds, education, and conservation.
Limitations: Giving limited to Wilmington, DE, and its 50-mile radius.
Application information:
Initial approach: Proposal
Copies of proposal: 5
Deadline(s): None
Write: Blaine T. Phillips, Pres.
Officers: Blaine T. Phillips, Pres.; Gerret van S. Copeland, V.P.; Hugh R. Sharp, Jr., Secy.-Treas.
Employer Identification Number: 516001265

1081
Crestlea Foundation, Inc.
1004 Wilmington Trust Ctr.
Wilmington 19801

Incorporated in 1955 in DE.
Donor(s): Henry B. du Pont.†
Foundation type: Independent
Financial data (yr. ended 12/31/88): Assets, $11,051,791 (M); expenditures, $558,449, including $527,765 for 35 grants (high: $225,565; low: $500; average: $1,000-$25,000).
Purpose and activities: Emphasis on higher and secondary education, housing and urban affairs, health agencies, community funds, welfare agencies, and conservation.
Types of support: Annual campaigns, building funds, capital campaigns, equipment.
Limitations: Giving primarily in DE and CT. No grants to individuals.
Application information:
Initial approach: Letter
Copies of proposal: 1
Board meeting date(s): As required
Write: Stewart E. Poole, Pres.
Officers: Stewart E. Poole,* Pres.; Elizabeth W. Kane, Secy.; Edward B. du Pont,* Treas.
Directors:* Otto C. Fad.
Number of staff: 1 part-time professional; 2 part-time support.
Employer Identification Number: 516015638

1082
Crystal Trust ▼
1088 DuPont Bldg.
Wilmington 19898 (302) 774-8421

Trust established in 1947 in DE.
Donor(s): Irenee du Pont.†
Foundation type: Independent
Financial data (yr. ended 12/31/89): Assets, $60,000,000 (M); expenditures, $2,508,500, including $2,396,025 for 44 grants (high: $250,000; low: $2,150; average: $10,000-$100,000).
Purpose and activities: Giving mainly for higher and secondary education and social and family services, including youth and child welfare agencies, family planning, and programs for the aged, the disadvantaged, and the homeless; support also for the arts and cultural programs and health and hospitals.
Types of support: Seed money, building funds, equipment, land acquisition, program-related investments, renovation projects, capital campaigns, special projects.
Limitations: Giving primarily in DE, especially Wilmington. No grants to individuals, or for endowment funds, research, scholarships, fellowships, or matching gifts; no loans.
Publications: Application guidelines, program policy statement, informational brochure (including application guidelines).
Application information: Application form not required.
Initial approach: Proposal
Copies of proposal: 1
Deadline(s): Oct. 1
Board meeting date(s): Nov.
Final notification: Dec. 15
Write: Burt C. Pratt, Dir.
Director: Burt C. Pratt.

Trustees: Irenee du Pont, Jr., David Greenewalt, Eleanor S. Maroney.
Number of staff: 1 part-time professional; 1 part-time support.
Employer Identification Number: 516015063

1083
Curran Foundation, Inc. ⌑
P.O. Box 1575
Wilmington 19899 (302) 658-4287

Incorporated in 1955 in DE.
Foundation type: Independent
Financial data (yr. ended 12/31/88): Assets, $1,681,229 (M); gifts received, $2,500; expenditures, $80,215, including $68,000 for 10 grants (high: $20,000; low: $1,500).
Purpose and activities: Emphasis on higher education.
Application information:
Initial approach: Letter
Deadline(s): None
Write: Eileen P. Cousineau, Secy.
Officers: Willard A. Speakman III,* Pres.; James C. Stewart,* V.P. and Treas.; Eileen P. Cousineau, Secy.
Trustees:* Edward M. Crane, Jr., E.W. Dykes, Edward C. Kirkpatrick, Charles S. Maddock, John Allen Sparks.
Employer Identification Number: 516017197

1084
The Devonwood Foundation ⌑
c/o Wilmington Trust Co.
Rodney Sq. North
Wilmington 19890

Established in 1968 in DE.
Foundation type: Independent
Financial data (yr. ended 12/31/88): Assets, $2,575,257 (M); gifts received, $788,678; expenditures, $107,608, including $101,500 for 3 grants (high: $51,000; low: $500).
Purpose and activities: Support primarily for a university and a private school.
Application information: Contributes only to pre-selected organizations. Applications not accepted.
Trustee: Wilmington Trust Co.
Employer Identification Number: 516024607

1085
Downs Perpetual Charitable Trust ⌑ ☆
c/o Wilmington Trust Co.
GPM - 21181-0
Wilmington 19890

Foundation type: Independent
Financial data (yr. ended 06/30/89): Assets, $4,122,764 (M); expenditures, $245,006, including $221,664 for 63 grants (high: $22,578; low: $2,578; average: $2,578).
Purpose and activities: Giving primarily for Episcopal organizations, including churches and a school, and higher and other education; support also for civic affairs and community development, health associations, and arts and culture.
Limitations: Giving primarily in DE and PA. No grants to individuals.
Application information: Contributes only to pre-selected organizations. Applications not accepted.
Trustee: Wilmington Trust Co.
Employer Identification Number: 516158138

1086
Ederic Foundation, Inc. ⌑
A-102 Greenville Ctr.
3801 Kennett Pike
Wilmington 19807

Incorporated in 1958 in DE.
Donor(s): John E. Riegel, Natalie R. Weymouth, Richard E. Riegel, Jr., Mrs. G. Burton Pearson, Jr.
Foundation type: Independent
Financial data (yr. ended 12/31/87): Assets, $265 (M); gifts received, $2,855; expenditures, $329,820, including $329,805 for 94 grants (high: $38,000; low: $50).
Purpose and activities: Giving for private elementary and secondary schools, hospitals and health care, community funds, cultural institutions, and higher education; grants also for youth agencies and conservation.
Limitations: Giving primarily in DE.
Application information:
Initial approach: Letter
Deadline(s): None
Write: Harry S. Short, Secy.
Officers: Mrs. G. Burton Pearson, Jr.,* Pres.; Harry S. Short, Secy.-Treas.
Trustees:* Robert C. McCoy, John E. Riegel, Richard E. Riegel, Jr., Philip B. Weymouth, Jr.
Employer Identification Number: 516017927

1087
Fair Play Foundation
350 Delaware Trust Bldg.
Wilmington 19801 (302) 658-6771

Established about 1983 in DE.
Foundation type: Independent
Financial data (yr. ended 12/31/88): Assets, $11,768,788 (M); expenditures, $731,619, including $650,000 for 28 grants (high: $125,000; low: $1,000; average: $20,000-$30,000).
Purpose and activities: Grants for museums, historical preservation, and the environment and wildlife.
Types of support: Renovation projects, equipment, land acquisition.
Application information:
Initial approach: Letter
Deadline(s): None
Board meeting date(s): Dec.
Write: Blaine T. Phillips, Pres.
Officers and Trustees: Blaine T. Phillips, Pres.; James F. Burnett, V.P.; L.E. Grimes, Treas.; George P. Edmonds, D.P. Ross, Jr.
Number of staff: None.
Employer Identification Number: 516017779

1088
Falcon Foundation, Inc. ⌑ ☆
1220 Market Bldg., Suite 804
Wilmington 19801 (302) 429-8436

Established in 1986.
Donor(s): Fred C. Koch Charitable Trust.
Foundation type: Independent
Financial data (yr. ended 12/31/88): Assets, $7,286,669 (M); expenditures, $219,525, including $155,255 for 22 grants (high: $50,000; low: $150).
Purpose and activities: Giving primarily for child welfare, higher education, and environmental conservation; support also for cultural programs.
Limitations: Giving primarily in MA.
Application information:
Initial approach: Letter or proposal
Deadline(s): None
Write: Ronald W. Borders
Officers: William I. Koch,* Pres.; Stephen Wolfberg, Secy.; Zachary Shipley, Treas.
Directors:* Richard P. Callahan.
Employer Identification Number: 222662059

1089
Sumner Gerard Foundation ⌑
1209 Orange St.
Wilmington 19801

Established in 1963 in DE.
Donor(s): Sumner Gerard.†
Foundation type: Independent
Financial data (yr. ended 04/30/89): Assets, $2,021,972 (M); expenditures, $106,849, including $77,650 for 65 grants (high: $11,000; low: $250).
Purpose and activities: Grants primarily for higher and secondary education, hospitals, and church support.
Application information:
Initial approach: Letter
Deadline(s): None
Officers: James W. Gerard, Pres.; C.H. Coster Gerard, V.P.; Sumner Gerard, V.P.; John P. Campbell, Secy.-Treas.
Employer Identification Number: 136155552

1090
Glencoe Foundation, Inc. ⌑
Bldg. C, Suite 300
3801 Kennett Pike
Greenville 19807 (302) 654-9933

Established in 1975 in DE.
Donor(s): Ellice McDonald, Jr., Rosa H. McDonald.
Foundation type: Independent
Financial data (yr. ended 12/31/88): Assets, $1,184,244 (M); gifts received, $526,000; expenditures, $614,500, including $600,600 for 15 grants (high: $270,000; low: $1,000).
Purpose and activities: Grants "exclusively to Scottish and American charitable organizations, such as museums, hospitals, educational institutions, and other publicly-oriented organizations that promote and preserve Scottish-American traditions and culture."
Types of support: Special projects, general purposes, operating budgets, continuing support, seed money, emergency funds, building funds, equipment, land acquisition, publications.
Limitations: Giving limited to the Highlands and islands of Scotland. No grants to individuals, or for scholarships, fellowships, or matching gifts; no loans.
Publications: Application guidelines.
Application information: Application form required.

Initial approach: Proposal
Copies of proposal: 1
Deadline(s): None
Board meeting date(s): Annually and as required
Final notification: 2 to 3 months
Write: Ellice McDonald, Jr., Pres.
Officers: Ellice McDonald, Jr.,* Pres.; Rosa H. McDonald,* V.P.; John C. Milner, Secy.-Treas.
Directors:* Gregory A. Inskip, John F. McDonald, Jr., John P. Sinclair.
Number of staff: None.
Employer Identification Number: 510164761

1091
Good Samaritan, Inc.
One Rodney Sq.
P.O. Box 551
Wilmington 19899 (302) 654-7558

Incorporated in 1938 in DE.
Donor(s): Elias Ahuja.†
Foundation type: Independent
Financial data (yr. ended 12/31/89): Assets, $2,984,889 (M); expenditures, $435,062, including $416,450 for 6 grants (high: $25,000; low: $7,700).
Purpose and activities: Emphasis on higher education, medical research and education, hospitals, and environmental conservation.
Types of support: Endowment funds, operating budgets, special projects, conferences and seminars, professorships.
Limitations: Giving with special attention to projects relating to Spain. No grants to individuals, or for building funds.
Publications: Application guidelines.
Application information: Application form not required.
Initial approach: Proposal
Deadline(s): None
Board meeting date(s): As required
Write: E.N. Carpenter, II, Secy.-Treas.
Officers and Directors:* Henry W. Sherrill,* Pres.; Edmund N. Carpenter II,* Secy.-Treas.
Number of staff: None.
Employer Identification Number: 516000401

1092
George E. Gordy Family Educational Trust Fund
c/o Sussex Trust Co.
P.O. Box 311
Georgetown 19947 (302) 856-4705

Established in 1984 in DE.
Foundation type: Independent
Financial data (yr. ended 06/30/89): Assets, $1,666,982 (M); expenditures, $113,691, including $101,000 for 93 grants to individuals (high: $2,500; low: $250).
Purpose and activities: Awards scholarships for higher education.
Types of support: Student aid.
Limitations: Giving limited to Sussex County, DE, high school graduates.
Application information: Application form required.
Copies of proposal: 5
Deadline(s): Feb. 15
Write: Ms. Connie E. Mears, Trust Officer, Sussex Trust Co.
Directors: John E. Messick, Robert L. Thompson, W. Robert Williams.
Selection Committee: Walter Deakyne, Arthur King, Connie E. Mears, Kuline W. Miller, Ray Stevens.
Employer Identification Number: 222561832

1093
The Gurkha Welfare Trust Foundation U.S.A. ⌑ ☆
Bldg. C, Suite 300
3801 Kennett Pike
Greenville 19807 (302) 654-9933

Established in 1978.
Donor(s): Ellice McDonald, Jr., Rosa H. McDonald.
Foundation type: Independent
Financial data (yr. ended 12/31/88): Assets, $1,005,519 (M); gifts received, $105,100; expenditures, $78,551, including $75,514 for 3 grants (high: $50,000; low: $9,450).
Purpose and activities: Support for "the relief of poverty, suffering, or distress of Gurkhas" and their dependents, including the advancement of education and vocational training in the Kingdom of Nepal areas where Gurkhas live.
Types of support: Endowment funds, renovation projects.
Application information:
Deadline(s): None
Write: Ellice McDonald, Jr., Pres.
Officers: Ellice McDonald, Jr., Pres.; Rosa H. McDonald, Treas.
Trustees: N.L.H. Burian, Christopher G.L. Jones.
Employer Identification Number: 510227053

1094
Albert T. Hanby Trust ⌑
c/o Bank of Delaware, Trust Dept.
300 Delaware Ave.
Wilmington 19899

Established in 1945 in DE.
Foundation type: Operating
Financial data (yr. ended 12/31/87): Assets, $1,807,795 (M); expenditures, $66,009, including $47,881 for 1 grant.
Purpose and activities: Giving for charitable purposes; substantial grant to a youth organization.
Application information: Available funds committed through Jan. 31, 2020. Applications not accepted.
Write: Howard M. Lewis
Trustee: Bank of Delaware.
Employer Identification Number: 516010794

1095
A. Cremieux Israel Foundation, Inc. ⌑
229 South State St.
Dover 19901
Application address: 707 Westchester Ave., White Plains, NY 10604; Tel.: (914) 681-4410

Incorporated in 1967 in DE as successor to the foundation of the same name incorporated in 1946 in NY.
Donor(s): Adrian C. Israel.
Foundation type: Independent
Financial data (yr. ended 12/31/87): Assets, $8,354,105 (M); gifts received, $50,000; expenditures, $394,200, including $312,690 for 23 grants (high: $250,000; low: $100).
Purpose and activities: Giving primarily to higher and secondary education, and hospitals.
Limitations: No grants to individuals.
Application information:
Initial approach: Letter
Deadline(s): None
Write: Barry W. Gray, V.P.
Officers and Directors:* Adrian C. Israel,* Pres.; Barry W. Gray,* V.P.; Jay M. Howard, Secy.; Thomas C. Israel,* Treas.
Employer Identification Number: 516021414

1096
The Laura Julia Foundation, Ltd. ⌑
100 West Tenth St.
Wilmington 19801
Application address: Sempacherstrasse 15, 8032 Zurich, Switzerland; Tel.: (01) 556820

Established in 1956 in DE.
Foundation type: Independent
Financial data (yr. ended 12/31/88): Assets, $4,480,395 (M); expenditures, $295,989, including $208,567 for 3 grants (high: $124,367; low: $34,200).
Purpose and activities: Support for the aged in Israel; some support also for scholarly publications.
Types of support: Publications.
Application information: Contributes only to pre-selected organizations. Applications not accepted.
Write: Veit Wyler, Chair.
Officers: Eric Homburger, Secy.
Trustees: Veit Wyler,* Chair.; Jacob Hirsch, Michael Wyler.
Employer Identification Number: 986001804

1097
The Ada Howe Kent Foundation ⌑
1209 Orange St.
Wilmington 19801

Incorporated in 1962 in DE.
Donor(s): Marjorie K. Kilpatrick.†
Foundation type: Independent
Financial data (yr. ended 9/30/88): Assets, $6,222,524 (M); expenditures, $390,127, including $288,000 for 24 grants (high: $25,000; low: $1,000).
Purpose and activities: Giving for higher education and religious organizations carrying out studies and practical work in comparative religion; grants also for social service agencies.
Application information:
Initial approach: Letter
Deadline(s): None
Write: John P. Campbell, Secy.-Treas.
Officers and Directors: John E. Connelly, Jr., Pres.; Henry P. Renard, V.P.; John P. Campbell, Secy.-Treas.; Virginia Brautigam.
Employer Identification Number: 136066978

1098
Atwater Kent Foundation, Inc.
101 Springer Bldg.
3411 Silverside Rd.
Wilmington 19810 (302) 478-4383

Established in 1919 in DE.
Foundation type: Independent

Financial data (yr. ended 12/31/88): Assets, $1,435,483 (M); expenditures, $81,820, including $72,050 for 67 grants (high: $15,100; low: $100; average: $100-$5,000).
Purpose and activities: Emphasis on museums and historic preservation, higher education, hospitals and health associations, social services, government, and Christian organizations.
Limitations: Giving primarily in the metropolitan Philadelphia, PA, area, ME, and FL, but will consider grants to organizations in other areas. No grants to individuals, or to pass-through organizations.
Application information: Application form not required.
Initial approach: Proposal
Deadline(s): None
Board meeting date(s): Periodically
Write: Hope P. Annan, Pres.
Officers: Hope P. Annan,* Pres. and Treas.; A. Atwater Kent III, V.P.; James R. Weaver, Secy.
Trustees:* Christopher B. Kent.
Employer Identification Number: 510081303

1099
Kent-Lucas Foundation, Inc.
101 Springer Bldg.
3411 Silverside Rd.
Wilmington 19810 (302) 478-4383
Mailing address: P.O. Box 7048, Wilmington, DE 19803

Incorporated in 1968 in DE.
Donor(s): Atwater Kent Foundation, Inc.
Foundation type: Independent
Financial data (yr. ended 12/31/88): Assets, $2,320,668 (M); expenditures, $212,407, including $199,600 for 66 grants (high: $100,000; low: $25; average: $100-$5,000).
Purpose and activities: Grants largely for cultural programs, including historic preservation, hospitals, education, and church support; support also for public information organizations.
Types of support: General purposes, operating budgets, continuing support, building funds.
Limitations: Giving primarily in the Philadelphia, PA, metropolitan area, ME, and FL. No grants to individuals or for endowment funds.
Publications: Application guidelines.
Application information: Application form not required.
Initial approach: Letter
Copies of proposal: 1
Deadline(s): None
Board meeting date(s): As required
Final notification: 1 to 3 months
Write: Elizabeth K. Van Alen, Pres.
Officers: Elizabeth K. Van Alen,* Pres. and Treas.; William L. Van Alen,* V.P.; James R. Weaver, Secy.
Trustees:* James L. Van Alen II, William L. Van Alen, Jr.
Number of staff: 4
Employer Identification Number: 237010084

1100
The Kingsley Foundation ¤
c/o Wilmington Trust Co.
Rodney Sq. North
Wilmington 19890

Established in 1961 in CT.
Donor(s): F.G. Kingsley, Ora K. Smith.
Foundation type: Independent
Financial data (yr. ended 12/31/87): Assets, $3,527,484 (M); gifts received, $118,521; expenditures, $176,329, including $169,938 for 48 grants (high: $90,000; low: $100).
Purpose and activities: Support primarily for health, medical education, social services, and cultural programs.
Application information: Contributes only to pre-selected organizations. Applications not accepted.
Trustees: L. Heagney, Ora Rimes Kingsley, Minot K. Milliken, Roger Milliken, Ora K. Smith.
Employer Identification Number: 066037966

1101
Milton and Hattie Kutz Foundation
101 Garden of Eden Rd.
Wilmington 19803 (302) 478-6200

Established in 1955 in DE.
Donor(s): Milton Kutz, Hattie Kutz.
Foundation type: Independent
Financial data (yr. ended 6/30/89): Assets, $2,329,682 (M); expenditures, $159,077, including $92,250 for grants and $44,500 for grants to individuals.
Purpose and activities: Giving largely for Jewish social service organizations; grants also for child welfare, social services, and higher education, including scholarships to residents of DE who will be college freshmen.
Types of support: Student aid, building funds, capital campaigns, emergency funds, general purposes, operating budgets, grants to individuals, seed money, special projects.
Limitations: Giving primarily in DE.
Publications: Financial statement.
Application information: Scholarship application form required.
Copies of proposal: 1
Deadline(s): Mar. 15 for scholarships
Board meeting date(s): June and Dec.
Final notification: July and Jan.
Write: Robert N. Kerbel, Exec. Secy.
Officers and Directors:* Richard A. Levine, Pres.; Rolf E. Erikson, V.P.; Robert N. Kerbel, Exec. Secy.; Bennett N. Epstein, Secy.; Bernard L. Siegel, Treas.; Martin G. Mand, Irving Morris, Steven J. Rothschild, Jeremiah P. Shea, Henry Topel, William M. Topkis.
Number of staff: 1 part-time professional; 1 part-time support.
Employer Identification Number: 510187055

1102
Laffey-McHugh Foundation ▼
1220 Market Bldg.
P.O. Box 2207
Wilmington 19899 (302) 658-9141

Incorporated in 1959 in DE.
Donor(s): Alice L. McHugh,† Frank A. McHugh, Jr.†
Foundation type: Independent
Financial data (yr. ended 12/31/88): Assets, $38,302,040 (M); expenditures, $2,280,327, including $1,891,215 for 80 grants (high: $183,333; low: $1,000; average: $5,000-$50,000).
Purpose and activities: Grants for Roman Catholic church support and church-related institutions, including schools, welfare agencies, religious associations, child welfare agencies, and a school for the handicapped; support also for a community fund, higher education, and hospitals.
Types of support: Annual campaigns, seed money, emergency funds, building funds, equipment, land acquisition, matching funds, general purposes.
Limitations: Giving primarily in DE, with emphasis on Wilmington. No grants to individuals, or for operating budgets, endowment funds, research, demonstration projects, publications, conferences, professorships, internships, program-related investments, consulting services, technical assistance, scholarships, or fellowships; no loans.
Publications: 990-PF.
Application information: Application form not required.
Initial approach: Letter
Copies of proposal: 1
Deadline(s): Apr. and Oct.
Board meeting date(s): May and Nov.
Final notification: Shortly after meeting
Write: Arthur G. Connolly, Sr., Pres.
Officers and Directors:* Arthur G. Connolly, Sr.,* Pres.; Marie Louise McHugh,* V.P.; Collins J. Seitz,* V.P.; Thomas S. Lodge, Secy.; Arthur G. Connolly, Jr.,* Treas.; Edward J. Goett.
Number of staff: None.
Employer Identification Number: 516015095

1103
The Lalor Foundation
Bldg. B-108
3801 Kennett Pike
Wilmington 19807 (302) 571-1262

Incorporated in 1935 in DE.
Donor(s): Members of the Lalor family, Willard A. Lalor.†
Foundation type: Independent
Financial data (yr. ended 9/30/89): Assets, $6,565,549 (M); gifts received, $50,000; expenditures, $305,040, including $275,230 for 15 grants (high: $20,000; low: $18,770; average: $18,770-$20,000).
Purpose and activities: Support for educational and/or scientific research institutions, for postdoctoral fellowship awards in the field of mammalian reproductive physiology research.
Types of support: Fellowships, research.
Limitations: No grants to individuals, or for operating budgets, capital or endowment funds, continuing support, annual campaigns, seed money, emergency funds, deficit financing, or matching gifts; no loans.
Publications: Informational brochure (including application guidelines).
Application information: Application form required.
Initial approach: Letter or telephone

Copies of proposal: 1
Deadline(s): Submit proposal from Oct. 1 to Jan. 15; deadline Jan. 15
Board meeting date(s): Nov. or Dec.
Final notification: Mar. 1 to 15
Write: Helen L. Colvard, Asst. Secy.
Officers and Trustees: Mrs. James T. Patterson, Pres.; Rodman Ward, Jr., V.P.; Lalor Burdick, Secy.-Treas.; Julian W. Hill, Sally H. Zeckhouser.
Number of staff: 1 part-time support.
Employer Identification Number: 516000153

1104
Morris & Lillie Leibowitz Charitable Trust ⌑
c/o Bank of Delaware
300 Delaware Ave.
Wilmington 19899

Established in 1968 in DE.
Foundation type: Independent
Financial data (yr. ended 12/31/87): Assets, $1,070,063 (M); expenditures, $56,436, including $49,016 for 13 grants (high: $15,000; low: $1,000).
Purpose and activities: Support primarily for the family wing of a congregation and a Jewish community center; support also for medical research, higher education, and cultural institutions.
Limitations: Giving primarily in DE.
Application information:
Initial approach: Letter
Deadline(s): None
Trustee: Bank of Delaware.
Employer Identification Number: 516024643

1105
Longwood Foundation, Inc. ▼
1004 Wilmington Trust Ctr.
Wilmington 19801 (302) 654-2477

Incorporated in 1937 in DE.
Donor(s): Pierre S. du Pont.†
Foundation type: Independent
Financial data (yr. ended 9/30/89): Assets, $336,356,687 (M); expenditures, $16,300,087, including $15,117,664 for 79 grants (high: $5,130,000; low: $2,400; average: $25,000-$250,000).
Purpose and activities: Primary obligation is the support, operation, and development of Longwood Gardens, which is open to the public; limited grants generally to educational institutions, to local hospitals for construction purposes, and to social service and youth agencies, and cultural programs.
Types of support: Annual campaigns, operating budgets, building funds, equipment, land acquisition, endowment funds, research.
Limitations: Giving limited to DE, with emphasis on the greater Wilmington area; some giving in PA. No grants to individuals, or for special projects.
Application information: Application form not required.
Initial approach: Letter
Copies of proposal: 1
Deadline(s): Submit proposal by Apr. 15 or Oct. 1
Board meeting date(s): May and Oct.
Final notification: At time of next board meeting
Write: Endsley P. Fairman, Exec. Secy.
Officers and Trustees: H. Rodney Sharp III, Pres.; Edward B. du Pont, V.P.; Irenee du Pont May, Secy.; Henry H. Silliman, Jr., Treas.; Gerret van S. Copeland, David L. Craven, Pierre S. du Pont IV.
Number of staff: 4 full-time professional.
Employer Identification Number: 510066734

1106
The Lovett Foundation, Inc. ⌑
82 Governor Printz Blvd.
Claymont 19703 (302) 798-6604

Incorporated in 1952 in DE.
Donor(s): Walter L. Morgan.
Foundation type: Independent
Financial data (yr. ended 11/30/89): Assets, $2,925,138 (M); expenditures, $204,582, including $179,340 for 64 grants (high: $20,000; low: $19).
Purpose and activities: Emphasis on church support, hospitals, cultural programs, and civic affairs; grants also for education and social service agencies.
Types of support: General purposes, annual campaigns.
Limitations: Giving primarily in the Wilmington, DE, and Philadelphia, PA, areas. No grants to individuals.
Application information:
Initial approach: Letter
Deadline(s): Submit proposal prior to Mar. 15; no set deadline
Board meeting date(s): Quarterly
Write: Michael J. Robinson III, V.P.
Officers and Trustees:* Walter L. Morgan,* Pres.; Michael J. Robinson III,* V.P.; Leanor H. Silver,* Secy.; Andrew B. Young.
Employer Identification Number: 236253918

1107
John B. Lynch Scholarship Foundation
P.O. Box 4248
Wilmington 19807-0248 (302) 654-3444

Trust established in 1963 in DE.
Donor(s): John B. Lynch,† Katherine C. Lynch.†
Foundation type: Independent
Financial data (yr. ended 12/31/88): Assets, $3,601,200 (M); expenditures, $221,110, including $168,600 for 72 grants to individuals (high: $40,676; low: $600).
Purpose and activities: Scholarships for worthy young persons; grants are paid through the schools for individual students.
Types of support: Student aid.
Limitations: Giving limited to students residing in the immediate, Wilmington, DE, area. No grants for scholarships beyond baccalaureate level.
Publications: Application guidelines.
Application information: Application form required.
Initial approach: Letter
Copies of proposal: 1
Deadline(s): Feb. 15
Board meeting date(s): May
Final notification: After June 10
Write: Winifred Blansfield
Trustees: William Duffy, Charles A. Robinson, Josephine R. Robinson.
Number of staff: 2 part-time support.
Employer Identification Number: 516017041

1108
The Marmot Foundation
1004 Wilmington Trust Ctr.
Wilmington 19801 (302) 654-2477
Application address for FL organizations: P.O. Box 2468, Palm Beach, FL 33480

Established in 1968 in DE.
Donor(s): Margaret F. du Pont Trust.
Foundation type: Independent
Financial data (yr. ended 12/31/89): Assets, $16,316,000 (M); expenditures, $886,000, including $811,000 for 63 grants (high: $65,000; low: $1,000).
Purpose and activities: Support for hospitals, health, higher and secondary education, including libraries, community funds, cultural programs, including museums, youth agencies, social services, literacy programs, and environmental and ecological organizations.
Types of support: Emergency funds, building funds, equipment, research, matching funds, capital campaigns.
Limitations: Giving primarily in DE and FL. No support for religious organizations. No grants to individuals, or for operating budgets or scholarships; no loans.
Application information: Application form not required.
Initial approach: Letter
Copies of proposal: 1
Deadline(s): Submit proposal preferably in Apr. and Oct.
Board meeting date(s): May and Nov.
Final notification: 2 weeks after board meeting
Write: Endsley P. Fairman, Secy. (for DE organizations); Willis H. du Pont, Chair. (for FL organizations)
Officers and Trustees:* Willis H. du Pont,* Chair.; Endsley P. Fairman,* Secy.; Lammot Joseph du Pont, Miren deA. du Pont, George S. Harrington.
Number of staff: 1 part-time professional; 1 full-time support; 1 part-time support.
Employer Identification Number: 516022487

1109
Esther S. Marshall Charitable Trust ⌑
Box 72
Yorklyn 19736-0072 (302) 239-6379

Established in 1980 in DE.
Foundation type: Independent
Financial data (yr. ended 11/30/88): Assets, $709,052 (M); expenditures, $150,324, including $136,100 for 7 grants (high: $45,000; low: $6,100).
Purpose and activities: Support limited to institutions of higher education and museums.
Types of support: Operating budgets.
Limitations: Giving primarily in DE. No grants to individuals.
Application information:
Initial approach: Letter
Deadline(s): None

Write: Thomas C. Marshall, Jr., Trustee
Trustees: Walter W. Anderson, Lindsay Greenplate, Thomas C. Marshall, Jr.
Employer Identification Number: 510256407

1110
The Agnes G. Milliken Foundation ⌑
c/o Wilmington Trust Co.
Rodney Square North
Wilmington 19890

Established in 1954 in DE.
Donor(s): Agnes M. Franchetti, Anne M. Franchetti, Agnes G. Milliken.
Foundation type: Independent
Financial data (yr. ended 12/31/88): Assets, $2,986,480 (M); gifts received, $620,413; expenditures, $376,539, including $371,000 for 12 grants (high: $300,000; low: $1,000).
Purpose and activities: Giving primarily to a hospital corporation; support also for religious organizations and a library.
Types of support: General purposes.
Application information: Contributes only to pre-selected organizations. Applications not accepted.
Officer: Lawrence Heagney, Treas.
Trustees: Sylvia M. Erhart, Gerrish Milliken, Jr., Roger Milliken.
Employer Identification Number: 136103241

1111
The Gerrish H. Milliken Foundation ⌑
c/o Wilmington Trust Co.
Rodney Sq. North
Wilmington 19890

Established in 1962.
Donor(s): Members of the Milliken family.
Foundation type: Independent
Financial data (yr. ended 12/31/87): Assets, $1,520,957 (M); gifts received, $164,282; expenditures, $238,708, including $235,500 for 93 grants (high: $17,000; low: $50; average: $100-$10,000).
Purpose and activities: Giving primarily for higher and secondary education and wildlife; grants also for Protestant church support and child welfare.
Types of support: General purposes.
Application information: Contributes only to pre-selected organizations. Applications not accepted.
Write: Lawrence Heagney, Treas.
Officer: Lawrence Heagney, Treas.
Trustees: Minot K. Milliken, Phoebe Milliken, Roger Milliken.
Employer Identification Number: 066037106

1112
MLKA Foundation ⌑
c/o Corp. Trust Co.
1209 Orange St.
Wilmington 19801-1645

Donor(s): Mossette L. Keyzer-Andre.
Foundation type: Independent
Financial data (yr. ended 12/31/88): Assets, $329,664 (M); gifts received, $378,922; expenditures, $327,478, including $314,262 for 55 grants (high: $200,000; low: $15).
Purpose and activities: Support primarily for medical research foundations and organizations and for higher education.
Limitations: No grants to individuals.
Application information: Contributes only to pre-selected organizations. Applications not accepted.
Officers: Mossette L. Keyzer-Andre, Pres.; Patty B.L. Rome, Secy.; Maurice E. Emswiler, Treas.
Employer Identification Number: 222479420

1113
The Oristano Foundation ⌑ ☆
c/o Prentice Hall Corp.
229 South St.
Dover 19901

Established in 1984 in DE.
Donor(s): Victor Oristano.
Foundation type: Independent
Financial data (yr. ended 5/31/89): Assets, $1,069,526 (M); expenditures, $83,968, including $67,265 for 23 grants (high: $10,000; low: $250).
Purpose and activities: Giving primarily for youth and education; support also for civil rights groups, a community fund, and social services.
Limitations: Giving primarily in NY. No grants to individuals.
Application information: Contributes only to pre-selected organizations. Applications not accepted.
Directors: James Cohen, Joan Oristano, Victor Oristano.
Employer Identification Number: 222471915

1114
Presto Foundation ⌑
P.O. Box 2105
Wilmington 19899
Application address: 3925 North Hastings Way, Eau Claire, WI 54703

Incorporated in 1952 in WI.
Donor(s): National Presto Industries, Inc.
Foundation type: Company-sponsored
Financial data (yr. ended 5/31/87): Assets, $12,917,770 (M); expenditures, $613,936, including $507,045 for 135 grants (high: $100,000; low: $25) and $49,015 for 14 grants to individuals (high: $4,000; low: $1,727).
Purpose and activities: Giving for higher education, including scholarships for employees' children, educational television, local community funds, health, and social service agencies.
Types of support: Employee-related scholarships.
Limitations: Giving primarily in northwestern WI; Eau Claire and Chippewa County preferred.
Application information:
Initial approach: Letter
Deadline(s): None
Write: Harriet Rose
Officers and Trustees: Melvin S. Cohen, Chair. and Pres.; R.J. Alexy, V.P.; Walter Gold, V.P.; William A. Nelson, V.P.; Maryjo R. Cohen, Secy.-Treas.; Eileen Phillips Cohen, Donald Dickson, Kenneth Hansen, Richard Myhers.
Employer Identification Number: 396045769

1115
Quaker City Fund ⌑
P.O. Box 162
North Broad St.
Middletown 19709-1001

Established in 1976 in DE.
Foundation type: Independent
Financial data (yr. ended 12/31/88): Assets, $1,458,970 (M); expenditures, $73,975, including $70,073 for 47 grants (high: $20,000; low: $18).
Purpose and activities: Support primarily for higher education and for hospitals.
Limitations: No grants to individuals.
Application information: Contributes only to pre-selected organizations. Applications not accepted.
Officers: Francis R. Schwarz, Pres.; Scott F. Schumacker, Secy.; John C. Voss, Treas.
Employer Identification Number: 510200152

1116
The Bill Raskob Foundation, Inc.
P.O. Box 4019
Wilmington 19807 (302) 655-4440

Incorporated in 1928 in DE.
Donor(s): John J. Raskob,† Helena S. Raskob Corcoran.†
Foundation type: Independent
Financial data (yr. ended 12/31/89): Assets, $2,299,140 (M); expenditures, $201,200, including $50,000 for 2 loans to organizations and $124,600 for 68 loans to individuals (high: $4,000; low: $500; average: $1,000-$2,000).
Purpose and activities: Giving only for no-interest loans to finance education for American citizens currently enrolled at accredited institutions within the U.S.
Types of support: Student loans.
Limitations: No grants for any purpose except interest-free student loans only.
Publications: Application guidelines, program policy statement.
Application information: The foundation strongly suggests all applicants first apply for government loans or grants. Currently, no applications accepted from incoming students on any level, foreign students, or American students studying abroad. Application form required.
Initial approach: Letter and self-addressed, stamped size 10 envelope
Copies of proposal: 1
Deadline(s): Request application between Jan. 1 and Apr. 1; deadline May 1
Board meeting date(s): Annually
Final notification: Before Sept.
Write: Patricia M. Garey, 1st V.P.
Officers and Directors:* Edward H. Robinson,* Pres.; Patricia M. Garey,* 1st V.P.; Gerard S. Garey,* Secy.; Kathleen D. Smith,* Treas.; Nina B. Bennett, Theodore H. Bremekamp III, Patsy R. Bremer, William S. Bremer, Sister Pat Geuting, Jakob T. Raskob, William F. Raskob III, Anthony L. Robinson, J. Michael Stanton, Jr.
Number of staff: 5
Employer Identification Number: 510110185

1117
Raskob Foundation for Catholic Activities, Inc. ▼
P.O. Box 4019
Wilmington 19807 (302) 655-4440

Incorporated in 1945 in DE.
Donor(s): John J. Raskob.†
Foundation type: Independent
Financial data (yr. ended 12/31/89): Assets, $64,787,954 (M); expenditures, $4,289,902, including $3,572,594 for 575 grants (high: $250,000; low: $100; average: $5,000-$15,000).
Purpose and activities: To support Roman Catholic church organizations and activities worldwide, providing funds to official Catholic organizations for education, training, social services, health, and emergency relief. In order to qualify for consideration for large building or renovation projects, construction must be underway, a signed construction contract must exist, and 50 percent of the total funds needed must already be committed.
Types of support: Operating budgets, seed money, emergency funds, building funds, equipment, land acquisition, matching funds, conferences and seminars, program-related investments, renovation projects, special projects.
Limitations: No grants to individuals, or for continuing support, annual campaigns, deficit financing (except missions), endowment funds, tuition, scholarships, fellowships, individual research, building projects prior to the start or after the completion of construction, after-the-fact requests, or computer projects lacking 50 percent of total cost.
Publications: Biennial report (including application guidelines), application guidelines.
Application information: Application form required.
Initial approach: Letter
Copies of proposal: 1
Deadline(s): Applications accepted for spring meeting from Dec. 15 to Feb. 15, for fall meeting from June 15 to Aug. 15
Board meeting date(s): Spring and fall
Final notification: 6 months
Write: Gerard S. Garey, Pres.
Officers and Trustees:* Anthony W. Raskob,* Chair.; Gerard S. Garey,* Pres.; Peter S. Robinson,* 1st V.P.; Anthony L. Robinson,* 2nd V.P.; Kathleen D. Smith,* Secy.; William F. Raskob III,* Treas.; Helen R. Doordan, John J. Harmon, Eileen D. McGrory, Anthony W. Raskob, Jr., Jakob T. Raskob, Charles R. Robinson, Susan Y. Stanton.
Number of staff: 1
Employer Identification Number: 510070060

1118
Red Clay Reservation, Inc. ⌑
1004 Wilmington Trust Ctr.
Wilmington 19801

Incorporated in 1962 in DE.
Donor(s): Lammot du Pont Copeland, Henry B. du Pont.†
Foundation type: Operating
Financial data (yr. ended 12/31/87): Assets, $6,018,154 (M); gifts received, $552,000; expenditures, $251,629, including $250 for 1 grant.
Purpose and activities: A private operating foundation established to promote the conservation and study of wildlife and game on the North American continent and to maintain wildlife sanctuaries.
Limitations: Giving limited to northern DE. No grants to individuals.
Officers and Trustees: Mrs. Lammot du Pont Copeland, Pres.; Mrs. Henry B. du Pont, V.P.; Lammot du Pont Copeland, Jr., Secy.; Edward B. du Pont, Treas.; Blaine T. Phillips.
Number of staff: 1 part-time professional; 1 full-time support; 1 part-time support.
Employer Identification Number: 516017982

1119
The Bernard Lee Schwartz Foundation, Inc.
P.O. Box 7138
2625 Concord Pike
Wilmington 19803

Incorporated in 1951 in NY.
Donor(s): Bernard L. Schwartz.†
Foundation type: Independent
Financial data (yr. ended 09/30/89): Assets, $12,656,260 (M); gifts received, $190,300; expenditures, $451,307, including $408,280 for 21 grants (high: $295,000; low: $100; average: $100-$30,000).
Purpose and activities: Support largely for higher education, cultural programs, and medical tax-exempt institutions, including hospitals and research facilities.
Types of support: Continuing support, building funds, equipment, endowment funds, internships, fellowships, research.
Limitations: No grants to individuals, or for annual campaigns, seed money, emergency funds, deficit financing, renovation projects, land acquisition, demonstration projects, publications, or conferences; no loans.
Publications: 990-PF.
Application information: Contributes only to pre-selected organizations. Applications not accepted.
Officers and Directors:* Rosalyn R. Schwartz,* Pres.; Tilda R. Orr,* Secy.; Michael L. Schwartz,* Treas.; Eric A. Schwartz.
Number of staff: None.
Employer Identification Number: 136096198

1120
Shandle Foundation ⌑ ☆
P.O. Box 3835
Greenville 19807-2255
Application address: c/o Bank of Delaware, Trust Dept., 222 Delaware Ave., Wilmington, DE 19899

Established in 1981.
Foundation type: Independent
Financial data (yr. ended 6/30/89): Assets, $1,494,011 (M); expenditures, $71,196, including $68,432 for 28 grants (high: $35,350; low: $10).
Purpose and activities: Giving primarily to Jewish organizations, including welfare funds; support also for higher education and a community fund.
Limitations: Giving primarily in Wilmington, DE, and PA.
Application information: Application form not required.
Deadline(s): None
Officer: Irving S. Shapiro, Pres.
Employer Identification Number: 510259146

1121
Ruby R. Vale Foundation ⌑
c/o Bank of Delaware
300 Delaware Ave.
Wilmington 19899

Established in 1960 in DE.
Donor(s): Ruby R. Vale.†
Foundation type: Independent
Financial data (yr. ended 12/31/87): Assets, $2,484,074 (M); expenditures, $200,315, including $180,000 for 13 grants (high: $35,000; low: $2,500).
Purpose and activities: Grants largely for higher education.
Application information:
Deadline(s): Sept. 1
Write: Richard E. Menkiewicz, Sr. Trust Admin., Bank of Delaware
Trustee: Bank of Delaware.
Employer Identification Number: 516018883

1122
Welfare Foundation, Inc. ▼
1004 Wilmington Trust Ctr.
Wilmington 19801 (302) 654-2477

Incorporated in 1930 in DE.
Donor(s): Pierre S. du Pont.†
Foundation type: Independent
Financial data (yr. ended 12/31/89): Assets, $34,954,886 (M); expenditures, $1,773,709, including $1,524,400 for 48 grants (high: $100,000; low: $100; average: $25,000-$50,000).
Purpose and activities: Emphasis on education, hospitals, a community fund, and social service agencies.
Types of support: Building funds, equipment, matching funds, annual campaigns.
Limitations: Giving limited to DE, with emphasis on the greater Wilmington area. No grants to individuals.
Application information: Application form not required.
Initial approach: Letter
Copies of proposal: 1
Deadline(s): Submit proposal preferably in Apr. or Oct.; deadlines Apr. 15 and Nov. 1
Board meeting date(s): May and Dec.
Final notification: 30 to 45 days
Write: Endsley P. Fairman, Exec. Secy.
Officers and Trustees:* Robert H. Bolling, Jr.,* Pres.; J. Simpson Dean, Jr.,* V.P.; Mrs. W. Laird Stabler, Jr.,* Secy.; Edward B. du Pont,* Treas.
Number of staff: 4 part-time professional.
Employer Identification Number: 516015916

1123
Wilmington Trust Company Foundation ⌑
c/o Wilmington Trust Co.
Wilmington 19890

Established in 1966 in DE.
Donor(s): Wilmington Trust Co.

Foundation type: Company-sponsored
Financial data (yr. ended 12/31/87): Assets, $146,912 (M); gifts received, $272,109; expenditures, $325,553, including $324,821 for 74 grants (high: $140,000; low: $100).
Purpose and activities: Grants for community funds, health and social services, culture, and community development.
Types of support: General purposes.
Application information: Contributes only to pre-selected organizations. Applications not accepted.
Trustees: John S. Garrett, Jr., Bernard J. Taylor II.
Agents: Beryl Barmore, Wilmington Trust Co.
Employer Identification Number: 516021540

1124
The Wunsch Americana Foundation ⌑
c/o V.J. Kumar
15 The Strand
New Castle 19720
Application address: 841 63rd St., Brooklyn, NY 11220

Established in 1967 in DE.
Donor(s): Eric M. Wunsch.
Foundation type: Operating
Financial data (yr. ended 12/31/87): Assets, $1,480,856 (M); gifts received, $75,600; expenditures, $68,198, including $67,910 for 2 grants (high: $111,170; low: $15,750).
Purpose and activities: A private operating foundation giving grants primarily for culture, including museums.
Limitations: Giving primarily in NY. No grants to individuals.
Application information:
Initial approach: Letter
Write: Eric M. Wunsch
Officer: Eric M. Wunsch, Pres.
Employer Identification Number: 510106068

DISTRICT OF COLUMBIA

1125
The Alvord Foundation ⌑
918 16th St., N.W., No. 200
Washington 20006 (202) 393-2266

Trust established in 1937 in DC.
Donor(s): Ellsworth C. Alvord.†
Foundation type: Independent
Financial data (yr. ended 12/31/88): Assets, $1,608,923 (M); expenditures, $401,310, including $88,600 for 26 grants (high: $20,000; low: $100).
Purpose and activities: Grants primarily for higher and secondary education, performing arts, and hospitals.
Limitations: Giving primarily in Washington, DC. No grants to individuals.
Publications: 990-PF.
Application information:
Initial approach: Letter
Deadline(s): None
Write: Robert W. Alvord, V.P.
Officers and Trustees: Ellsworth C. Alvord, Jr., Pres.; Robert W. Alvord, V.P.; John H. Doyle, Secy.-Treas.
Employer Identification Number: 526037194

1126
The Appleby Foundation ⌑
c/o Crestar Bank, N.A., Trust Div.
1445 New York Ave., N.W.
Washington 20005 (202) 879-6341

Trust established in 1958 in DC.
Donor(s): Scott B. Appleby.†
Foundation type: Independent
Financial data (yr. ended 12/31/88): Assets, $7,013,029 (M); expenditures, $396,827, including $307,962 for 20 grants.
Purpose and activities: Grants primarily for higher education; giving also for youth agencies, music, Protestant church support, cultural programs, and hospitals.
Types of support: Scholarship funds, general purposes.
Limitations: Giving primarily in Washington, DC, FL, and GA.
Application information:
Initial approach: Letter
Deadline(s): None
Write: Virginia M. Herrin, V.P., Crestar Bank, N.A.
Trustees: F. Jordan Colby, Sarah P. Williams, Crestar Bank, N.A.
Number of staff: 1
Employer Identification Number: 526026971

1127
The Arca Foundation ▼
1425 21st St., N.W.
Washington 20036 (202) 822-9193

Incorporated in 1952 in NY.
Donor(s): Nancy S. Reynolds.†
Foundation type: Independent
Financial data (yr. ended 12/31/88): Assets, $29,720,662 (M); gifts received, $360,000; expenditures, $1,249,434, including $932,096 for 35 grants (high: $225,000; low: $1,000; average: $10,000-$50,000).
Purpose and activities: To promote a reexamination of U.S. foreign policy around the globe, with particular concern for human rights, democratic participation and national sovereignty. Emphasis on public education in the United States. Some support for domestic concerns, particularly those addressing poverty and injustice.
Types of support: Operating budgets, continuing support, seed money, technical assistance, publications, conferences and seminars, special projects.
Limitations: No grants to individuals, or for annual campaigns, emergency funds, capital or endowment funds, deficit financing, matching gifts, scholarships, or fellowships; no loans.
Publications: Annual report.
Application information: Application form not required.
Initial approach: Letter
Copies of proposal: 1
Deadline(s): Submit summary of proposal preferably in Jan., Feb., July, or Aug.; deadlines Feb. 15 and Sept. 15
Board meeting date(s): Apr. and Nov.
Final notification: Up to 4 months
Officers & Directors:* Smith W. Bagley,* Pres.; Mary E. King,* Secy.; Brian Topping,* Treas.; Janet Shenk, Exec. Dir.; Elizabeth Frawley Bagley, Dick Clark, Ellsworth Culver, Margery A. Tabankin.
Number of staff: 1 part-time professional; 1 full-time support; 1 part-time support.
Employer Identification Number: 132751798

1128
The Arcana Foundation, Inc. ☆
901 15th St., N.W., Suite 1000
Washington 20005 (202) 789-7280

Incorporated in 1986 in DC.
Foundation type: Independent
Financial data (yr. ended 09/30/89): Assets, $23,405,303 (M); expenditures, $1,454,003, including $1,276,000 for 30 grants (high: $500,000; low: $1,000; average: $5,000-$50,000).
Purpose and activities: Giving primarily for social services and arts and cultural institutions.
Types of support: General purposes.
Limitations: Giving primarily in the Washington, DC, metropolitan area.
Application information: Applications not accepted.
Officers: Ladislaus von Hoffmann, Pres. and Treas.; Beatrix von Hoffmann, V.P.; Holly Kennedy, Secy.
Number of staff: 1 full-time professional.
Employer Identification Number: 521515952

1129
Bauman Family Foundation, Inc. ☆
1731 Connecticut Ave. N.W., 4th Fl.
Washington 20009-1146 (202) 234-8547

Established in 1982 in NY.
Donor(s): Lionel R. Bauman.†
Foundation type: Independent
Financial data (yr. ended 06/30/88): Assets, $1,026,162 (M); gifts received, $1,300,000; expenditures, $344,536, including $211,348 for 17 grants (high: $50,000; low: $500; average: $15,000-$25,000).
Purpose and activities: Grants to local, state, or national organizations with a clear strategy for translating their projects into nationally applicable ideas.
Types of support: Conferences and seminars, operating budgets, publications, research, seed money, special projects, technical assistance, matching funds.
Limitations: No support for medical or epidemiological research or direct services; generally no support for grassroots organizations. No grants to individuals.
Publications: Grants list, program policy statement, application guidelines.
Application information: Application form not required.
Initial approach: Telephone or brief letter

Copies of proposal: 1
Deadline(s): None
Board meeting date(s): Quarterly
Write: Patricia Bauman or John L. Bryant, Jr.
Officers and Directors:* Patricia Bauman,* Pres. and Treas.; Gail M. Harmon,* Secy.; John L. Bryant, Jr., C. Douglas Lewis, Jr.
Number of staff: 2 full-time professional; 1 full-time support.
Employer Identification Number: 133119290

1130
Beldon Fund ☆
2000 P St., N.W., Suite 410
Washington 20036 (202) 293-1928
Application address for video and film projects: c/o Foundation for Independent Video and Film, 625 Broadway, 9th Fl., New York, NY 10012

Established in 1987 in DC.
Donor(s): John R. Hunting.
Foundation type: Independent
Financial data (yr. ended 11/30/89): Assets, $85,841 (M); gifts received, $1,092,004; expenditures, $1,039,926, including $913,500 for 93 grants (high: $30,000; low: $500; average: $10,000).
Purpose and activities: Primary interest is in strengthening national, regional, and state-wide environmental organizations, including specific areas of hazardous and solid waste, international projects, connecting spirituality with the environment, and ecosystem-wide strategies.
Types of support: Special projects, seed money.
Limitations: No support for historic preservation, direct social service delivery programs, or public or private education. No grants to individuals, or for endowment or capital campaigns, scholarships, or academic research.
Publications: Annual report, application guidelines.
Application information: Application form not required.
Initial approach: Letter or telephone
Copies of proposal: 1
Deadline(s): None
Board meeting date(s): Frequently throughout the year
Write: Judy Donald, Exec. Dir.
Officers: John R. Hunting, Pres.; Judy Donald, Secy.-Treas. and Exec. Dir.
Number of staff: 1
Employer Identification Number: 382786808

1131
Bender Foundation, Inc.
1120 Connecticut Ave., N.W., Suite 1200
Washington 20036 (202) 828-9000

Incorporated in 1958 in DC.
Donor(s): Jack I. Bender.†
Foundation type: Independent
Financial data (yr. ended 2/28/89): Assets, $7,461,631 (M); expenditures, $434,363, including $395,200 for 65 grants (high: $100,000; low: $1,000).
Purpose and activities: Support for higher education, health agencies, Jewish organizations and welfare funds, and social welfare.
Limitations: Giving primarily in Washington, DC, and MD. No grants to individuals.
Application information: Application form not required.
Initial approach: Letter
Copies of proposal: 1
Deadline(s): Nov. 30
Board meeting date(s): Quarterly
Write: Sondra D. Bender, Pres.
Officers: Sondra D. Bender, Pres.; Howard M. Bender, V.P.; Stanley S. Bender, V.P. and Secy.
Directors: Julie Bender Belinkie, Barbara Bender, David S. Bender, Dorothy G. Bender, Eileen Bender Greenberg.
Employer Identification Number: 526054193

1132
Benton Foundation
1710 Rhode Island Ave., N.W., 4th Fl.
Washington 20036 (202) 857-7829

Incorporated in 1948 in NY.
Donor(s): William Benton,† Helen Benton.†
Foundation type: Independent
Financial data (yr. ended 12/31/88): Assets, $11,500,000 (M); expenditures, $846,008, including $445,875 for 50 grants (high: $50,000; low: $500; average: $10,000-$25,000) and $66,300 for 3 foundation-administered programs.
Purpose and activities: Limited number of grants for communications research and education, and media projects.
Types of support: Matching funds, research, special projects, publications, conferences and seminars, consulting services, technical assistance.
Limitations: No grants to individuals, or for general purposes, capital funds, or scholarships; no loans.
Publications: Biennial report, informational brochure (including application guidelines), grants list.
Application information: Application form not required.
Initial approach: Letter
Copies of proposal: 1
Deadline(s): Submit proposal preferably in Dec. or Apr.
Board meeting date(s): Mar., July, and Nov.
Final notification: About 3 weeks after board meetings
Write: Larry Kirkman, Exec. Dir.
Officers and Directors: Charles Benton, Pres. and Chair.; Adrianne Benton, Secy.; Leonard Schrager, Treas. and General Counsel; John Brademas, Dick Clark, Roy Fisher, Richard Neustadt, Michael Pertschuk, Gene Pokorny, Dorothy Ridings, Carolyn Sachs.
Number of staff: 2 full-time professional; 2 full-time support.
Employer Identification Number: 136075750

1133
Leo M. Bernstein Family Foundation ⌑ ☆
600 New Hampshire Ave., N.W., Suite 1155
Washington 20037

Established in 1952.
Foundation type: Independent
Financial data (yr. ended 9/30/88): Assets, $1,178,360 (M); expenditures, $104,341, including $100,378 for 27 grants (high: $15,000; low: $50).
Purpose and activities: Giving primarily for Jewish religious welfare and educational institutions; support also for a museum.
Limitations: Giving primarily in Washington, DC, and Strasburg, VA.
Officers and Directors:* Richard Bernstein,* V.P.; Stuart A. Bernstein,* V.P.; Wilma Bernstein,* Secy.; Leo M. Bernstein,* Pres.
Employer Identification Number: 526041822

1134
Diane & Norman Bernstein Foundation, Inc.
2025 Eye St., N.W., Suite 400
Washington 20006 (202) 331-7500

Established in 1965 in DC.
Foundation type: Independent
Financial data (yr. ended 09/30/89): Assets, $1,660,000 (M); gifts received, $300,000; expenditures, $86,000, including $86,000 for grants (high: $10,000; low: $1,000).
Purpose and activities: Grants primarily to cultural institutions; support also for education, conservation, Jewish welfare, health, AIDS, and the performing arts.
Types of support: General purposes.
Application information: Contributes only to pre-selected organizations. Applications not accepted.
Board meeting date(s): Aug.
Write: Diane and Norman Bernstein, Directors
Directors: Celia Ellen Bernstein, Diane Bernstein, Norman Bernstein, James R. Connell, Marianne Bernstein Kalb.
Number of staff: 1 part-time professional.
Employer Identification Number: 526047356

1135
Walter A. Bloedorn Foundation
c/o Reasoner, Davis & Fox
888 17th St., N.W., Suite 800
Washington 20006 (202) 463-8282

Incorporated in 1966 in DC.
Donor(s): Walter A. Bloedorn.†
Foundation type: Independent
Financial data (yr. ended 12/31/89): Assets, $5,645,210 (M); expenditures, $403,666, including $359,350 for 33 grants (high: $225,000; low: $250; average: $1,000-$4,000).
Purpose and activities: Support for higher and medical education, youth agencies, and medical research and hospitals; support also for civic affairs and a nature conservancy.
Types of support: Continuing support, annual campaigns, endowment funds, professorships.
Limitations: Giving primarily in the Washington, DC, area. No grants to individuals.
Application information: Application form not required.
Initial approach: Proposal
Copies of proposal: 1
Deadline(s): Submit proposal preferably in Jan. and Feb.; should be received by Mar. 31 for consideration at Apr. meeting
Board meeting date(s): Apr.
Final notification: 30 days after board meets

Write: John E. Boice, Jr., Secy.
Officers and Directors: F. Elwood Davis,* Pres.; John E. Boice, Jr.,* Secy.-Treas.; John H. Bloedorn, Jr., Robert E. Davis, Lloyd H. Elliott, J. Hillman Zahn.
Number of staff: None.
Employer Identification Number: 520846147

1136
Walter Brownley Trust ⌑

c/o Security Trust Co., N.A.
15th St. and Pennsylvania Ave., N.W.
Washington 20013

Trust established in 1931.
Foundation type: Independent
Financial data (yr. ended 12/31/88): Assets, $2,747,374 (M); expenditures, $140,023, including $117,000 for 13 grants of $9,000 each.
Purpose and activities: Giving restricted to Washington, DC, hospitals.
Limitations: Giving limited to Washington, DC.
Trustee: Security Trust Co.
Employer Identification Number: 526028605

1137
The Morris and Gwendolyn Cafritz Foundation ▼

1825 K St., N.W., 14th Fl.
Washington 20006 (202) 223-3100

Incorporated in 1948 in DC.
Donor(s): Morris Cafritz,† Gwendolyn D. Cafritz.†
Foundation type: Independent
Financial data (yr. ended 4/30/89): Assets, $222,908,164 (M); gifts received, $38,000; expenditures, $9,348,071, including $7,377,539 for 114 grants (high: $2,500,000; low: $3,000; average: $10,000-$50,000).
Purpose and activities: Giving only for programs of direct assistance, with emphasis on community service, cultural programs, education, and health.
Types of support: Operating budgets, continuing support, annual campaigns, seed money, matching funds, scholarship funds.
Limitations: Giving limited to Washington, DC. No grants to individuals, or for emergency funds, deficit financing, capital, endowment, or building funds, demonstration projects, or conferences; no loans.
Publications: Annual report, application guidelines.
Application information: Application form not required.
Initial approach: Proposal
Copies of proposal: 1
Deadline(s): July 1, Nov. 1, and Mar. 1
Board meeting date(s): May, Oct., and Jan.
Write: Martin Atlas, Pres.
Officers and Directors:* Calvin Cafritz,* Chair. and C.E.O.; Martin Atlas,* Pres. and Treas.; Roger A. Clark, Secy.; Anne Allen, Prog. Dir.; William P. Rogers.
Number of staff: 2 full-time professional; 2 full-time support.
Employer Identification Number: 526036989

1138
Carnegie Endowment for International Peace

2400 N St., N.W.
Washington 20037-1118 (202) 862-7900

Founded in 1910 in DC; incorporated in 1929 in NY.
Donor(s): Andrew Carnegie.†
Foundation type: Operating
Financial data (yr. ended 06/30/89): Assets, $93,184,721 (M); gifts received, $473,523; expenditures, $5,760,115, including $3,852,971 for foundation-administered programs.
Purpose and activities: A private operating (not a grantmaking) foundation that conducts its own programs of research, discussion, publication, and education in international affairs and American foreign policy. Program activities change periodically and cover a broad range of contemporary policy issues - military, political and economic. Publishes the quarterly "Foreign Policy."
Publications: Occasional report, financial statement, informational brochure.
Application information: The endowment does not maintain any grantmaking activities.
Write: Thomas L. Hughes, Pres.
Officers: Thomas L. Hughes,* Pres.; Larry L. Fabian, Secy.; Michael V. O'Hare, Dir. of Finance and Administration.
Trustees:* Charles J. Zwick, Chair.; George N. Lindsay, Vice-Chair.; Charles W. Bailey II, Harry G. Barnes, Jr., Douglas J. Bennet, Jr., Marjorie C. Benton, Robert Carswell, Gregory B. Craig, Richard A. Debs, William H. Donaldson, John W. Douglas, Marion R. Fremont-Smith, James C. Gaither, Robert F. Goheen, Rafael Hernandez-Colon, Shirley Mount Hufstedler, Thomas L. Hughes, Newton N. Minow, Wilbert J. LeMelle, Stephen R. Lewis, Jr., George N. Lindsay, George C. Lodge, William J. Perry, William B. Macomber, Barbara W. Newell, Wesley W. Posvar, Edson W. Spencer, Strobe Talbott.
Number of staff: 33 full-time professional; 2 part-time professional; 21 full-time support; 3 part-time support.
Employer Identification Number: 130552040

1139
Anthony & Anna L. Carozza Foundation ⌑ ☆

c/o Martha Volpe
3027 Davenport St.
Washington 20008

Established in 1963.
Foundation type: Independent
Financial data (yr. ended 4/30/89): Assets, $1,035,948 (M); expenditures, $26,851, including $25,844 for 11 grants (high: $5,000; low: $500).
Purpose and activities: Support primarily for opera and Catholic welfare organizations; also awards scholarships to local area residents.
Types of support: Student aid.
Limitations: Giving primarily in Washington, DC.
Application information: Prefers to award scholarships to residents in metropolitan area of Prince George's County, MD; Washington, DC; and northern VA. Application form required.
Deadline(s): None
Final notification: 3 months
Write: Anna L. Carozza, Pres.
Officers: Anna L. Carozza, Pres.; Sandra Carey, V.P.; Maria C. Volpe, Secy.-Treas.
Employer Identification Number: 520794431

1140
The Manny and Ruth Cohen Foundation, Inc. ⌑

3020 Rodman St., N.W.
Washington 20008 (202) 244-8884

Established in 1986 in CT.
Donor(s): Ruth Cohen.
Foundation type: Independent
Financial data (yr. ended 12/31/88): Assets, $2,006,558 (M); gifts received, $200,000; expenditures, $94,982, including $93,000 for 14 grants (high: $31,000; low: $1,000).
Purpose and activities: Support primarily for higher education, Jewish organizations, the performing arts, and religion.
Limitations: Giving primarily in Washington, DC; Miami, FL; and Philadelphia, PA. No grants to individuals.
Application information: Application form not required.
Deadline(s): None
Write: Alvin Morgenstein, Pres.
Officers: Alvin Morgenstein, Pres.; Steve Morgan, V.P.; Melvin Morgenstein, Secy.; Norman Morgenstein, Treas.
Employer Identification Number: 592744621

1141
Naomi and Nehemiah Cohen Foundation ⌑

(Formerly Cohen-Solomon Family Foundation, Inc.)
P.O. Box 1804
Washington 20013

Incorporated in 1959 in DC.
Donor(s): Naomi Cohen.†
Foundation type: Independent
Financial data (yr. ended 12/31/86): Assets, $12,104,112 (M); gifts received, $6,112,500; expenditures, $223,727, including $100,050 for 30 grants (high: $10,000; low: $200).
Purpose and activities: Grants primarily for Jewish welfare funds, higher education, and medical institutions.
Limitations: Giving primarily in Washington, DC.
Officers and Directors: Lillian Cohen-Solomon, Pres.; Israel Cohen, Secy.-Treas.
Employer Identification Number: 526054166

1142
Cooperative Assistance Fund

(also known as CAF, Inc.)
2100 M St., N.W., Suite 306
Washington 20037 (202) 833-8543

Established in 1968 in DC.
Foundation type: Operating
Financial data (yr. ended 06/30/89): Assets, $4,808,241 (M); gifts received, $41,855; expenditures, $687,237, including $249,669 for foundation-administered programs.
Purpose and activities: A private operating foundation engaged exclusively in making loans

and program-related investments to finance community-based enterprises that can generate jobs, ownership, capital accumulation or other economic and social benefits for minorities and low-income communities.
Types of support: Program-related investments, loans.
Publications: Biennial report, 990-PF, financial statement.
Application information: Application form not required.
Initial approach: Business plan with analysis of company
Copies of proposal: 1
Deadline(s): None
Board meeting date(s): Quarterly
Write: David C. Rice, Exec. V.P.
Officers: Robert L. Bunnen,* Chair.; John G. Simon,* Vice-Chair.; David C. Rice, Exec. V.P. and Treas.
Trustees:* Margaret A. Cheap, Barry Gaberman, Patricia D. Jacobs, John A. Koskinen, Ray B. Loeschner, William F. McCalpin, Ernest L. Osborne, Carl H. Rush, George H. Walker, Louis Winnick.
Number of staff: 3 full-time professional; 2 full-time support.
Employer Identification Number: 136265695

1143
Council on Library Resources, Inc.
1785 Massachusetts Ave., N.W., No. 313
Washington 20036 (202) 483-7474

Incorporated in 1956 in DC.
Donor(s): National Endowment for the Humanities, and private foundations.
Foundation type: Operating
Financial data (yr. ended 6/30/89): Assets, $5,393,068 (M); gifts received, $3,459,755; expenditures, $4,368,191, including $3,168,271 for 68 grants (high: $2,017,000; low: $60; average: $1,500-$25,000).
Purpose and activities: A private operating foundation; grants limited to programs that show promise of helping to provide solutions to problems that affect libraries in general, and academic and research libraries in particular. The council operates programs of its own to serve the same general purpose.
Types of support: Special projects, research, conferences and seminars, grants to individuals.
Limitations: No grants for building construction or improvement, indirect costs, purchase of collections or equipment, normal staffing or operational costs, or programs useful only to the institutions in which they take place.
Publications: Annual report (including application guidelines), newsletter, informational brochure (including application guidelines).
Application information: Application form not required.
Initial approach: Letter
Copies of proposal: 1
Deadline(s): None for general grant applications; deadlines for competitive programs are stated with their announcement
Board meeting date(s): Apr. and Nov.
Write: Warren J. Haas, Pres.
Officers: Warren J. Haas,* Pres.; Mary Agnes Thompson, Secy.-Treas.
Directors:* Maximilian W. Kempner, Chair.; Charles D. Churchwell, Vice-Chair.; Page Ackerman, William O. Baker, Patricia Battin, Laura Bornholdt, Harvey Brooks, James S. Coles, Samuel DuBois Cook, Martin M. Cummings, Ruth M. Davis, Billy E. Frye, Caryl P. Haskins, William N. Hubbard, Jr., Elizabeth T. Kennan, Herman Liebaers, Peter Likens, Basil Stuart-Stubbs, Sidney Verba, Robert Vosper, Frederick H. Wagman, Thomas H. Wright.
Number of staff: 8 full-time professional; 1 part-time professional; 4 full-time support.
Employer Identification Number: 530232831

1144
Marshall B. Coyne Foundation, Inc. ⌑
1156 15th St., N.W., Suite 300
Washington 20005-1704

Foundation type: Independent
Financial data (yr. ended 8/31/88): Assets, $246,916 (M); gifts received, $150,000; expenditures, $173,972, including $173,611 for 63 grants (high: $25,000; low: $25).
Purpose and activities: Support primarily for international studies and secondary and higher education.
Limitations: Giving primarily in Washington, DC, and NY.
Application information: Application form not required.
Deadline(s): None
Write: Marshall B. Coyne, Pres.
Officer: Marshall B. Coyne, Pres.
Employer Identification Number: 526054965

1145
The Charles delMar Foundation
918 16th St., N.W., No. 200
Washington 20006 (202) 393-2494

Trust established in 1957 in DC.
Donor(s): Charles delMar.†
Foundation type: Independent
Financial data (yr. ended 12/31/88): Assets, $2,645,533 (M); expenditures, $127,060, including $94,800 for 90 grants (high: $8,000; low: $100).
Purpose and activities: Special interests include inter-American studies, higher and other education, health and hospitals, underprivileged and crippled youth, the aged, the homeless and housing issues, general welfare organizations, and fine and performing arts.
Types of support: Continuing support, scholarship funds, annual campaigns, seed money.
Limitations: Giving primarily in Washington, DC, Puerto Rico, and Latin America. No grants to individuals, or for building or endowment funds, or matching gifts; no loans.
Application information: Application form not required.
Initial approach: Letter
Copies of proposal: 1
Deadline(s): None
Board meeting date(s): As required
Write: Elizabeth Adams delMar, Pres.
Officers and Trustees:* Elizabeth Adams delMar,* Pres.; Mareen D. Hughes,* V.P.; John H. Doyle,* Secy.; R. Bruce Hughes,* Treas.
Number of staff: None.
Employer Identification Number: 526035345

1146
The Dimick Foundation ⌑
c/o Crestar Bank, N.A.
1445 New York Ave., N.W.
Washington 20005 (202) 879-6345

Established in 1957 in DC.
Donor(s): John Dimick.†
Foundation type: Independent
Financial data (yr. ended 12/31/88): Assets, $4,449,901 (M); expenditures, $513,654, including $464,100 for 59 grants (high: $100,000; low: $1,000).
Purpose and activities: Emphasis on music and other cultural programs, higher education, and social services.
Limitations: Giving primarily in Washington, DC. No grants for student loans.
Application information: Application form not required.
Initial approach: Letter
Deadline(s): None
Write: Joseph R. Riley, Trustee
Trustees: Nancy Cree, John M. Lynham, Jr., Joseph R. Riley, Crestar Bank, N.A.
Employer Identification Number: 526038149

1147
Samuel R. Dweck Foundation ⌑
1730 M St., N.W., Suite 907
Washington 20036

Donor(s): Samuel R. Dweck, and members of the Dweck family, Morris Dweck, Ralph Dweck.
Foundation type: Independent
Financial data (yr. ended 12/31/88): Assets, $4,534,970 (M); gifts received, $236,500; expenditures, $254,251, including $210,221 for 82 grants (high: $54,224; low: $100).
Purpose and activities: Grants primarily for Jewish welfare funds.
Application information: Application form not required.
Deadline(s): None
Directors: Ralph Dweck, Rena Dweck.
Employer Identification Number: 526060826

1148
Families U.S.A. Foundation, Inc. ▼
(Formerly The Villers Foundation, Inc.)
1334 G St., N.W.
Washington 20005 (202) 628-3030
Address for MA applicants: Katherine S. Villers, Exec. Dir., 25 West St., Boston, MA 02111; Tel.: (617) 338-6035

Incorporated in 1981 in MA; qualified as operating foundation in 1987.
Donor(s): Philippe Villers, Katherine S. Villers.
Foundation type: Operating
Financial data (yr. ended 12/31/89): Assets, $18,170,877 (M); gifts received, $49,816; expenditures, $3,914,029, including $2,098,566 for 174 grants (high: $100,000; low: $250; average: $2,000-$50,000), $30,000 for 6 grants to individuals, $1,164,493 for 4 foundation-administered programs and $63,597 for 3 loans.
Purpose and activities: Giving for the purpose of "nurturing a movement of empowerment among elders;" grants primarily for organizations that empower elders through organizing and advocacy to establish and

address the priorities of the aged, particularly those of low income, security and health care; special attention to minority groups and low-income populations.
Types of support: Matching funds, technical assistance, special projects, research, seed money, publications, conferences and seminars.
Limitations: No support for social service models, or biomedical research. No grants for direct services, or building funds.
Publications: Informational brochure, multi-year report, occasional report.
Application information: Award inquiries should be sent to Ronald F. Pollack at DC address. Application form not required.
Initial approach: Proposal, not more than five pages
Deadline(s): None
Board meeting date(s): Mar., June, Sept., and Dec.
Write: Ronald F. Pollack, Exec. Dir.
Officers: Philippe Villers,* Pres. and Treas.; Ronald F. Pollack, V.P. and Exec. Dir.
Directors:* Joseph P. Eaglin, Jr., Judith Feder, Arthur S. Flemming, Douglas A. Fraser, Evelyn F. Murphy, Fernando Torres-Gil, Kip Tiernan, Katherine S. Villers, Roger Wilkins.
Number of staff: 14 full-time professional; 6 full-time support; 4 part-time support.
Employer Identification Number: 042730934

1149
Fannie Mae Foundation
(Formerly Federal National Mortgage Association Foundation)
3900 Wisconsin Ave., N.W.
Washington 20016 (202) 752-6500

Established in 1979 in DC.
Donor(s): Fannie Mae Assn.
Foundation type: Company-sponsored
Financial data (yr. ended 12/31/89): Assets, $4,334,046 (M); gifts received, $1,000,000; expenditures, $1,231,783, including $1,151,567 for 300 grants (high: $50,000; low: $100; average: $500-$2,500) and $73,987 for 542 employee matching gifts.
Purpose and activities: Support primarily awarded for housing and community development programs, cultural and artistic programs, media and communications, youth programs, and health and social concerns.
Types of support: Annual campaigns, building funds, conferences and seminars, employee matching gifts, endowment funds, equipment, general purposes, matching funds, operating budgets, renovation projects, research, seed money, special projects, technical assistance, scholarship funds, capital campaigns.
Limitations: Giving primarily in the Washington, DC, metropolitan area and areas where corporation maintains regional offices in Philadelphia, PA; Atlanta, GA; Chicago, IL; Dallas, TX; and Pasadena, CA. No support for organizations whose fundraising costs are in excess of 20 percent of their contributed support; generally, no support for organizations that benefit from United Way support or for churches and sectarian organizations, though contributions to religious group-sponsored, nondenominational activities are considered. No grants to support charitable activities undertaken outside of the U.S. No grants to individuals; generally no grants to institutions of higher learning or secondary education for general or scholarship support.
Publications: Informational brochure (including application guidelines), grants list, annual report.
Application information: Postcard mailed to confirm receipt of proposal. Application form not required.
Initial approach: Proposal
Copies of proposal: 1
Deadline(s): None
Board meeting date(s): Periodically throughout year
Write: Harriet M. Ivey, Exec. Dir.
Officers and Directors:* David O. Maxwell,* Chair.; Roger E. Birk,* Pres.; Douglas M. Bibby,* V.P.; Michael A. Smilow,* V.P.; Caryl S. Bernstein,* Secy.; Harriet M. Ivey,* Exec. Dir.; Henry C. Cashen II, James A. Johnson, William R. Maloni, Samuel J. Simmons, Mallory Walker, Karen Hastic Williams.
Number of staff: 2 full-time professional.
Employer Identification Number: 521172718

1150
Felburn Foundation ⌑
c/o Robert Philipson & Co.
2000 L St., N.W., Suite 609
Washington 20036

Established in 1978 in VA.
Donor(s): J. Phil Felburn, The Aetna Freight Lines, Inc.
Foundation type: Independent
Financial data (yr. ended 12/31/87): Assets, $2,559,592 (M); expenditures, $44,766, including $2,150 for 3 grants (high: $2,000; low: $25).
Purpose and activities: General charitable purposes.
Limitations: Giving primarily in NC.
Application information: Contributes only to pre-selected organizations. Applications not accepted.
Officers and Directors: J. Phil Felburn, Pres. and Treas.; Charles Freeman, V.P.; Don H. Norman, Secy.
Employer Identification Number: 510234331

1151
FishAmerica Foundation
1010 Massachusetts Ave., N.W., Suite 100
Washington 20001 (202) 898-0869

Established in 1983 in OK.
Donor(s): Zebco Corp., Brunswick Foundation, K Mart Corp., Crappiethon U.S.A., and other donors.
Foundation type: Independent
Financial data (yr. ended 12/31/89): Assets, $257,000 (M); gifts received, $131,716; expenditures, $640,543, including $407,086 for 58 grants (high: $10,000; low: $1,000; average: $1,000-$10,000).
Purpose and activities: Support primarily for projects that enhance fish populations, conserve and enhance waterways and fisheries, promote fish habitat and water quality, and educate private and public sectors on opportunities for becoming involved in key water conservation issues.
Types of support: Special projects.
Limitations: Giving limited to the U.S. and Canada. No grants to individuals, or for research projects, endowments, operating expenses, advertising, or travelling costs; no loans.
Publications: Application guidelines, informational brochure (including application guidelines).
Application information: Application form required.
Initial approach: Proposal
Copies of proposal: 1
Deadline(s): None
Board meeting date(s): Once a year
Write: Tina Berger, Mgr.
Officers: John M. Charvat,* Pres.; Ken Clary, V.P.; Henry G. Kolb, Secy.; Christine Altman, Grants Admin.
Directors:* James C. Hubbard, Admin.; Tina Berger, Mgr.; and 16 other directors.
Number of staff: None.
Employer Identification Number: 363219015

1152
The Folger Fund ⌑
2800 Woodley Rd., N.W.
Washington 20008 (202) 667-2991

Incorporated in 1955 in DC.
Donor(s): Eugenia B. Dulin,† Kathrine Dulin Folger, and others.
Foundation type: Independent
Financial data (yr. ended 8/31/88): Assets, $12,674,214 (M); gifts received, $220,813; expenditures, $668,149, including $638,633 for 103 grants (high: $249,546; low: $25).
Purpose and activities: Giving primarily for the arts, including museums and historic preservation, education, health and hospitals, social services, and church support.
Types of support: General purposes, building funds, capital campaigns.
Limitations: Giving primarily in Washington, DC; Knox County, TN; and Palm Beach County; FL. No grants to individuals.
Publications: Annual report.
Application information: Future funds currently committed. Application form not required.
Initial approach: Proposal
Deadline(s): None
Board meeting date(s): Sept.
Final notification: Usually within 3 months
Write: Kathrine Dulin Folger, Pres.
Officers: Kathrine Dulin Folger, Pres. and Treas.; Lee Merritt Folger, V.P. and Secy.
Trustee: John Dulin Folger.
Employer Identification Number: 520794388

1153
Foundation for Middle East Peace ⌑
555 13th St., N.W.
Washington 20004 (202) 637-6558

Incorporated in 1979 in DC.
Donor(s): Merle Thorpe, Jr.
Foundation type: Independent
Financial data (yr. ended 09/30/89): Assets, $5,383,129 (M); gifts received, $26,611; expenditures, $239,885, including $20,600 for 22 grants (high: $3,000; low: $100) and $205,889 for 3 foundation-administered programs.

Purpose and activities: To assist in an understanding of the Israeli-Palestinian conflict, including the identification of U.S. interests, and to contribute to a just and peaceful resolution of the conflict with security for both peoples. Support directed to elements within the Arab and Jewish communities working for a peaceful resolution of the conflict.
Types of support: Research.
Limitations: No grants to individuals.
Publications: Informational brochure.
Application information: Application form not required.
Initial approach: Letter
Deadline(s): None
Board meeting date(s): As required
Final notification: 30 days
Write: Merle Thorpe, Jr., Pres.
Advisory Committee: Landrum R. Bolling, Stanley Hoffman, Charles W. Yost.
Officers and Trustees:* Merle Thorpe, Jr.,* Pres. and Treas.; Calvin H. Cobb, Jr.,* V.P.; Joan Birdzell,* Secy.; Peter Castelman, Richard S.T. Marsh, Frank Reifsnyder.
Number of staff: 1 full-time professional; 1 full-time support.
Employer Identification Number: 526055574

1154
John Edward Fowler Memorial Foundation ⌑
1725 K Street N.W., Suite 1201
Washington 20006 (202) 728-9080

Incorporated in 1964 in DE.
Donor(s): Pearl Gunn Fowler.†
Foundation type: Independent
Financial data (yr. ended 12/31/88): Assets, $10,006,004 (M); expenditures, $614,575, including $501,000 for 30 grants (high: $70,000; low: $5,000; average: $5,000-$10,000).
Purpose and activities: Giving primarily to small community service organizations without public funding, especially for programs that help the elderly and disabled maintain their independence, and for programs that benefit children and youth.
Types of support: Equipment, general purposes, operating budgets, renovation projects, special projects, matching funds, seed money.
Limitations: Giving primarily in Washington, DC. No grants to individuals, or for research programs; no loans.
Publications: Application guidelines, grants list.
Application information: Application form required.
Initial approach: 2-page letter
Copies of proposal: 1
Deadline(s): None
Board meeting date(s): Periodically
Final notification: 4 months
Write: Richard H. Lee, Pres.
Officers and Trustees: Richard H. Lee, Pres.; Michael P. Bentzen, Secy.; Jeffery P. Capron, Treas.
Number of staff: 1 part-time professional.
Employer Identification Number: 516019469

1155
The Freed Foundation, Inc. ▼
1202 Eton Court, N.W.
Washington 20007 (202) 337-5487

Incorporated in 1954 in DC.
Donor(s): Frances W. Freed,† Gerald A. Freed.†
Foundation type: Independent
Financial data (yr. ended 05/31/89): Assets, $14,314,290 (M); gifts received, $73,340; expenditures, $828,791, including $608,700 for 39 grants (high: $200,000; low: $1,000; average: $100-$20,000).
Purpose and activities: Grants for animal welfare, wildlife and ecology, and AIDS research; grants also to benefit the homeless, the elderly, and the hungry; interests include drug and alcohol abuse and mental illness.
Types of support: General purposes, special projects, annual campaigns, matching funds, continuing support, capital campaigns, equipment, land acquisition.
Limitations: Giving primarily in Washington, DC, and NJ. No support for foreign organizations or international projects. No grants to individuals, or for scholarships, endowment funds, research, or conferences and meetings.
Publications: Annual report (including application guidelines).
Application information: Application form not required.
Initial approach: Letter
Copies of proposal: 1
Deadline(s): None
Board meeting date(s): Feb., May, Aug., and Nov.
Final notification: 3 months
Write: Lorraine Barnhart, Exec. Dir.
Officers and Trustees:* Elizabeth Ann Freed,* Pres. and Treas.; Lloyd J. Derrickson,* Secy.; Joan F. Kahn, Sherwood Monahan.
Number of staff: 1 part-time professional.
Employer Identification Number: 526047591

1156
The Alfred Friendly Foundation ⌑
1645 31st St., N.W.
Washington 20007

Foundation type: Operating
Financial data (yr. ended 6/30/88): Assets, $2,530,280 (M); expenditures, $210,979, including $61,815 for 23 grants to individuals (high: $5,246; low: $648).
Purpose and activities: A fellowship program providing foreign journalists with working experience in the United States; main purposes of the program are to enable the Fellow to gain an understanding of the significance of the free press in American society and to foster continuing working ties between free institutions and journalists in the United States and other countries, particularly developing countries.
Types of support: Fellowships.
Limitations: Giving limited to journalists from countries other than the U.S., especially developing nations.
Application information: Application form required.
Officers: Jean U. Friendly, Pres. and Treas.; Lucinda F. Murphy, 1st V.P.; John G. Murphy, Jr., 2nd V.P.; Alfred Friendly, Jr., Secy.
Directors: Jonathan Friendly, Nicholas Friendly, Victoria F. Maby.
Employer Identification Number: 521307387

1157
GEICO Philanthropic Foundation ⌑
c/o GEICO Corp.
GEICO Plaza
Washington 20076 (301) 986-2055

Established in 1980 in Washington, DC.
Donor(s): Criterion Insurance Co., Government Employees Insurance Co., Government Employees Insurance Co.
Foundation type: Company-sponsored
Financial data (yr. ended 12/31/88): Assets, $3,350,748 (M); gifts received, $2,238,094; expenditures, $787,094, including $765,458 for 275 grants (high: $138,406; low: $25).
Purpose and activities: Grants for higher education, a community fund, health agencies, hospitals, cultural programs, child welfare, and youth and social service agencies.
Application information:
Initial approach: Letter
Deadline(s): None
Write: Carroll R. Franklin
Officers: Donald K. Smith,* Pres.; John M. O'Connor, Secy.; Charles G. Schara, Treas.
Directors:* Louis A. Simpson, Chair.; John J. Krieger, Eugene J. Meyung, David L. Schindler, William B. Snyder, W. Alvon Sparks, Jr., Edward H. Utley.
Employer Identification Number: 521202740

1158
Melvin and Estelle Gelman Foundation ⌑
2120 L St., N.W., Suite 800
Washington 20037

Established in 1963 in DC.
Donor(s): Melvin Gelman,† Towers, Inc.
Foundation type: Independent
Financial data (yr. ended 11/30/87): Assets, $862,074 (M); gifts received, $680,000; expenditures, $371,224, including $368,556 for 187 grants (high: $4,000; low: $10).
Purpose and activities: Support primarily for Jewish welfare, cultural organizations and the arts, and medical research.
Limitations: Giving primarily in Washington, DC.
Officers: Estelle S. Gelman, Pres. and Treas.; Elise G. Lefkowitz, V.P.; Elaine G. Miller, V.P.; Martin Goldstein, Secy.
Employer Identification Number: 526042344

1159
German Marshall Fund of the United States ▼
11 Dupont Circle, N.W., Suite 750
Washington 20036 (202) 745-3950
European reps.: David Kramer, Kaiserstrasse 1c, 5300 Bonn 1, Federal Republic of Germany; Tel.: 0228-210041; Mary Fleming, 20 rue Tournefort, 75005 Paris, France; Tel.: 14-331-8172

Incorporated in 1972 in DC.

Donor(s): Federal Republic of Germany.
Foundation type: Independent
Financial data (yr. ended 05/31/89): Assets, $82,162,833 (M); gifts received, $5,521,062; expenditures, $7,383,701, including $3,323,728 for 145 grants (high: $625,000; low: $550; average: $10,000-$30,000) and $2,154,062 for 271 grants to individuals (high: $30,000; low: $500; average: $500-$30,000).
Purpose and activities: To contribute to the better understanding and resolution of significant common problems of industrial societies, internally and in their relations with each other, by facilitating and supporting sustained working relationships, studies, cooperation, and contacts by and between persons with shared interests and responsibilities in the U.S. and Europe. Fund's program areas include common social/economic problems, international relations, U.S.-German relations, scholarly support, and encouraging media coverage of events in other North Atlantic nations. Sponsors postdoctoral research fellowship program on the problems of industrial societies and several categories of professional fellowships.
Types of support: Seed money, research, fellowships, special projects, publications, conferences and seminars, exchange programs, grants to individuals, continuing support, lectureships, internships.
Limitations: Giving limited to the U.S. and Europe. No support for the arts and humanities, medicine and health, arms control, or diplomatic studies. No grants for capital or endowment funds, or for operating budgets, annual campaigns, emergency funds, deficit financing, medical or scientific research, matching gifts, or graduate or undergraduate studies.
Publications: Newsletter, informational brochure (including application guidelines), grants list, 990-PF, financial statement.
Application information: Application form required for fellowship programs. Application form not required.
Initial approach: Letter, telephone, or proposal
Copies of proposal: 1
Deadline(s): Nov. for research fellowships; Mar. for employment fellowships; other deadlines vary
Board meeting date(s): Feb., May, and Oct.
Final notification: Mar. for research fellowships; 2 to 3 months for all others
Write: Frank E. Loy, Pres.
Officers: Frank E. Loy,* Pres.; Marianne L. Ginsburg, Secy. and Prog. Officer; Peter R. Weitz, Dir. of Progs.
Trustees:* Guido Goldman, Co-Chair.; Richard C. Steadman, Co-Chair.; Harry G. Barnes, Jr., Sandra Feldman, Andrew J. Goodpaster, Larry Jinks, Geri M. Joseph, Marc E. Leland, Paul W. McCracken, Elizabeth Midgley, Neal R. Peirce, Franklin D. Raines, William K. Reilly, Lois Rice, Fritz Stern, Howard R. Swearer, Victoria Tschinkel, William M. Woessner.
Number of staff: 11 full-time professional; 9 full-time support.
Employer Identification Number: 520954751

1160
Bernard and Sarah Gewirz Foundation, Inc. ⌑ ☆
1730 K St., N.W., No. 1204
Washington 20036 (202) 296-7311

Established in 1984 in DC.
Donor(s): Bernard S. Gewirz, Sarah M. Gewirz.
Foundation type: Independent
Financial data (yr. ended 11/30/88): Assets, $1,250,865 (M); gifts received, $139,500; expenditures, $69,885, including $69,535 for grants.
Purpose and activities: Support primarily for cultural programs, Jewish giving, cancer research, and education, including educational research.
Limitations: Giving primarily in the metropolitan Washington, DC, area.
Application information:
Write: Bernard Gewirz, Pres.
Officers and Directors: Bernard S. Gewirz, Pres.; Michael K. Gewirz, V.P.; Sarah M. Gewirz, Secy.; Jonathan K. Gewirz, Steven B. Gewirz.
Employer Identification Number: 521381689

1161
Glen Eagles Foundation ☆
2000 P St., N.W., Suite 410
Washington 20036

Established in 1985 in DC.
Foundation type: Independent
Financial data (yr. ended 12/31/89): Assets, $496,087 (M); gifts received, $600,000; expenditures, $621,870, including $606,405 for 68 grants (high: $50,000; low: $200).
Purpose and activities: Giving primarily to environmental groups and to organizations providing AIDS prevention and education; support also for the arts, education, and social services.
Types of support: General purposes, matching funds, capital campaigns, seed money, conferences and seminars.
Limitations: Giving primarily in Washington, DC. No grants to individuals.
Application information: Contributes only to pre-selected organizations. Applications not accepted.
Officers and Director:* Betsy K. Frampton, Pres.; Susan E. Kaslow,* V.P.; George T. Frampton Jr., Secy.-Treas.
Number of staff: 1
Employer Identification Number: 521451828

1162
Aaron & Cecile Goldman Foundation ⌑
1725 K St., N.W., Suite 907
Washington 20006

Established in 1962 in DC.
Donor(s): Aaron Goldman, Cecile Goldman.
Foundation type: Independent
Financial data (yr. ended 09/30/89): Assets, $2,346,947 (M); expenditures, $117,859, including $96,150 for 94 grants (high: $13,000; low: $100).
Purpose and activities: Giving primarily for Jewish welfare, cultural activities, and education.
Application information: Application form not required.
Deadline(s): None
Write: Aaron Goldman, Trustee
Trustees: Aaron Goldman, Cecile Goldman.
Employer Identification Number: 526037949

1163
Gottesman Fund ⌑
710 O.F.C. Bldg.
1730 Rhode Island Ave., N.W.
Washington 20036

Established in 1965 in DC.
Donor(s): Members of the Gottesman family.
Foundation type: Independent
Financial data (yr. ended 8/31/88): Assets, $13,853,363 (M); gifts received, $2,574,884; expenditures, $446,532, including $366,292 for 81 grants (high: $110,000; low: $50).
Purpose and activities: Support primarily for health associations and hospitals, higher education, and Jewish giving.
Types of support: General purposes.
Limitations: No grants to individuals.
Application information: Contributes only to pre-selected organizations. Applications not accepted.
Officers and Directors: David S. Gottesman, Pres.; Esther Gottesman, V.P.; Ruth L. Gottesman, V.P.; Milton M. Gottesman, Secy.-Treas.; Robert W. Gottesman.
Employer Identification Number: 526061469

1164
The Philip L. Graham Fund ▼
c/o The Washington Post Co.
1150 Fifteenth St., N.W.
Washington 20071 (202) 334-6640

Trust established in 1963 in DC.
Donor(s): Katharine Graham, Frederick S. Beebe,† The Washington Post Co., Newsweek, Inc., Post-Newsweek Stations.
Foundation type: Independent
Financial data (yr. ended 12/31/89): Assets, $72,703,000 (M); expenditures, $2,882,729, including $2,868,000 for 100 grants (high: $200,000; low: $3,000; average: $10,000-$35,000).
Purpose and activities: Support for raising standards of excellence in journalism. Grants also for arts and culture, education, social welfare, with an emphasis on youth agencies, and civic and community affairs.
Types of support: Seed money, building funds, equipment, endowment funds, matching funds, renovation projects, capital campaigns, special projects.
Limitations: Giving primarily in metropolitan Washington, DC. No support for national or international organizations, or for religious organizations for religious purposes. No grants to individuals, or for medical services, research, annual campaigns, operating expenses, conferences, publications, tickets, films, or courtesy advertising; no loans.
Publications: Application guidelines, program policy statement, grants list.
Application information: Application form not required.
Initial approach: Letter, telephone, or proposal
Copies of proposal: 1
Deadline(s): Apr. 1, Aug. 1, and Nov. 1

Board meeting date(s): Spring, summer, and fall
Final notification: 6 months
Write: Mary M. Bellor, Secy.
Officers: Mary M. Bellor, Secy. and Exec. Dir.; Martin Cohen,* Treas.
Trustees:* Donald E. Graham, Katharine Graham, Vincent E. Reed, John W. Sweeterman.
Number of staff: 2 part-time professional; 1 part-time support.
Employer Identification Number: 526051781

1165
The Isadore and Bertha Gudelsky Family Foundation, Inc. ⌑
1503 21st St., N.W.
Washington 20036 (202) 328-0500

Incorporated in 1955 in MD.
Donor(s): Members of the Gudelsky family, Contee Sand & Gravel Co., Inc., and others.
Foundation type: Independent
Financial data (yr. ended 4/30/88): Assets, $10,647,605 (M); expenditures, $860,019, including $754,650 for 26 grants (high: $400,000; low: $1,150).
Purpose and activities: Emphasis on Jewish welfare funds and temple support; grants also for education, hospitals, and youth agencies.
Limitations: Giving primarily in Washington, DC. No grants to individuals.
Application information:
Initial approach: Letter
Deadline(s): None
Write: Philip N. Margolius, Secy.
Officers: Arlene G. Zimmerman, Pres.; Shelley G. Mulitz, V.P.; Philip N. Margolius, Secy.-Treas.
Employer Identification Number: 526036621

1166
Nathan and Sophie Gumenick Foundation ⌑
c/o Robert Philipson & Co.
2000 L St., N.W., Suite 609
Washington 20036

Established in 1954 in DC.
Foundation type: Independent
Financial data (yr. ended 11/30/88): Assets, $4,096,574 (M); gifts received, $300,000; expenditures, $161,279, including $154,975 for 27 grants (high: $50,000; low: $100).
Purpose and activities: Support for higher education; some support for medical education and research.
Limitations: Giving primarily in Richmond, VA, and Miami Beach, FL.
Application information:
Initial approach: Letter
Deadline(s): None
Write: Nathan S. Gumenick, Treas.
Officers: Nathan S. Gumenick, Pres. and Treas.; Sophia Gumenick, V.P.; Harry Grandis, Secy.
Employer Identification Number: 526055611

1167
Hariri Foundation
1020 19th St., N.W., Suite 320
Washington 20036 (202) 659-9200
Application address: Sanayeh Bldg., Beirut, Lebanon

Established in 1985 in Washington, DC.
Donor(s): Rafiq Hariri.
Foundation type: Independent
Financial data (yr. ended 12/31/89): Assets, $3,242,194 (M); gifts received, $16,990,367; expenditures, $16,740,909, including $14,530,094 for loans to individuals.
Purpose and activities: Financial assistance to deserving Lebanese and other Arab students for study at U.S. institutions of higher learning.
Types of support: Student loans.
Limitations: Giving limited to Lebanese and Arab students.
Publications: Multi-year report, informational brochure (including application guidelines), newsletter.
Application information: Initial application must be made in Beirut, Lebanon. Application form required.
Deadline(s): Jan., June and Sept.
Board meeting date(s): Nov.
Write: Rafic A. Bizri, Exec. V.P.
Officers and Directors:* Charles H. Percy,* Chair. and Pres.; Rafic A. Bizri,* Exec. V.P. and Secy.-Treas.; Bahia Hariri, Rafiq Hariri, Fred Herter, Frederick E. Rizk, William Rogers, Bill Schreyer.
Number of staff: 20 full-time professional; 1 part-time professional; 6 full-time support.
Employer Identification Number: 521386338

1168
The M. A. Healy Family Foundation, Inc.
c/o Covington & Burling
P.O. Box 7566, 1201 Pennsylvania Ave., N.W.
Washington 20044

Established in 1984 in MD.
Donor(s): Martha Ann Dumke Healy.
Foundation type: Independent
Financial data (yr. ended 05/31/89): Assets, $2,358,133 (M); gifts received, $299,983; expenditures, $100,290, including $61,000 for 7 grants (high: $30,000; low: $400).
Purpose and activities: Giving primarily to a civic organization and a school; support also for an environmental program and a museum.
Limitations: Giving primarily in the Washington, DC, and Bethesda, MD, areas.
Application information: Contributes only to pre-selected organizations. Applications not accepted.
Officers and Directors:* Martha Ann Dumke Healy,* Pres.; Nancy Healy Schwanfelder,* V.P. and Secy.; Edmund Healy,* V.P.; Doris D. Blazek.
Employer Identification Number: 521313820

1169
Hill-Snowdon Foundation ⌑
888 17th St., N.W., Suite 500
Washington 20006

Donor(s): Arthur B. Hill.†
Foundation type: Independent
Financial data (yr. ended 12/31/88): Assets, $1,939,276 (M); expenditures, $68,462, including $67,765 for 10 grants (high: $20,000; low: $200).
Purpose and activities: Giving for secondary education, the performing arts, including theater, community funds, environmental organizations, and organizations for the blind.
Application information: Contributes only to pre-selected organizations. Applications not accepted.
Write: Richard W. Snowdon, Dir.
Directors: Edward W. Snowdon, Edward W. Snowdon, Jr., Lee Hill Snowdon, Marguerite H. Snowdon, Richard W. Snowdon.
Employer Identification Number: 226081122

1170
Paul and Annetta Himmelfarb Foundation, Inc.
4545 42nd St., Suite 309
Washington 20016 (202) 966-3795

Incorporated in 1947 in DE.
Donor(s): Members of the Himmelfarb family and others.
Foundation type: Independent
Financial data (yr. ended 12/31/88): Assets, $6,135,489 (M); expenditures, $512,252, including $411,550 for 69 grants (high: $50,000; low: $100).
Purpose and activities: Giving for Jewish welfare funds and Israel, education, programs for the elderly, handicapped, and homeless, and health and medical research, including cancer research.
Limitations: Giving primarily in the Washington, DC, area. No grants to individuals.
Application information: Application form not required.
Initial approach: Letter
Write: Lillian N. Kronstadt, Treas. and Exec. Dir.
Officers and Directors:* Ada Naiman,* Pres.; Carol Himmelfarb Parker,* V.P.; Carole Preston,* Secy.; Lillian Kronstadt,* Treas. and Exec. Dir.; Annette Kronstadt.
Employer Identification Number: 520784206

1171
R. David Hirsch Foundation ⌑ ☆
3035 Chain Bridge Rd.
Washington 20016 (202) 466-3430

Established in 1964.
Foundation type: Independent
Financial data (yr. ended 12/31/88): Assets, $1,111,421 (M); expenditures, $38,044, including $34,075 for 40 grants (high: $6,000; low: $50).
Purpose and activities: Giving primarily to social services, Jewish organizations, education, international affairs, health, and cultural programs.
Limitations: No grants to individuals.
Application information:
Initial approach: Letter
Deadline(s): None
Write: Nancy Rubin, Mgr.
Manager: Nancy Rubin.
Trustees: Patrice Feinstein, R. David Hirsch, Peggy Schuloff.
Employer Identification Number: 136107643

1172
The His Right Hand Trust ⌑ ☆
c/o American Security Bank, N.A.
1501 Pennsylvania Ave., N.W.
Washington 20013

Foundation type: Independent
Financial data (yr. ended 12/31/88): Assets, $370,783 (M); expenditures, $128,230, including $122,436 for 9 grants (high: $100,000; low: $215).
Purpose and activities: Support primarily for child welfare and the handicapped; support also for evangelism.
Limitations: No grants to individuals.
Application information: Contributes only to pre-selected organizations. Applications not accepted.
Trustee: American Security Bank, N.A.
Employer Identification Number: 526291132

1173
The Hitachi Foundation
1509 22nd St., N.W.
Washington 20037 (202) 457-0588

Established in 1985 in DC.
Donor(s): Hitachi, Ltd.
Foundation type: Company-sponsored
Financial data (yr. ended 3/31/89): Assets, $22,457,673 (M); gifts received, $2,020,750; expenditures, $1,590,950, including $1,315,093 for 49 grants (high: $114,000; low: $1,500; average: $28,000), $48,500 for employee matching gifts and $49,596 for foundation-administered programs.
Purpose and activities: Giving in 4 areas: 1) Community and economic development - emphasizing leadership skills for individuals and community groups, volunteerism, and help for businesses; 2) Arts and cross-cultural understanding - increasing understanding between Japan and the U.S., making the arts accessible to all segments of society, and encouraging the use of arts to improve education; 3) Education - improving the quality of teaching and learning at all levels, particularly in middle and secondary schools; and 4) Technology and human resource development - enhancing and evaluating the social and economic effects of rapidly changing technology, including its dysfunctional aspects, making it accessible to all segments of society, and the use of new technology in education. The foundation makes awards to individuals for exemplary service to the community.
Types of support: General purposes, program-related investments, seed money, special projects, technical assistance, employee matching gifts.
Limitations: No support for sectarian or denominational religious organizations, health programs, or social organizations. No grants to individuals (except for Yoshiyama Awards for community service), or for fundraising events, building funds, publications, conferences and seminars, endowments, advertising, capital campaigns, or research.
Publications: Annual report (including application guidelines), program policy statement, application guidelines, newsletter.
Application information: Application form not required.
Initial approach: Letter of no more than 3 pages; if project is of interest, a more detailed proposal will be invited
Deadline(s): Feb. 1, June 1, and Oct. 1
Board meeting date(s): Mar., July, and Oct. to review proposal
Write: Felicia B. Lynch, V.P., Progs.
Officers: Delwin A. Roy,* Pres.; Felicia B. Lynch, V.P., Progs.; Soji Teramura, Secy.; Robyn L. James, Treas.
Directors:* Elliot Lee Richardson, Chair.; Katsushige Mita, Honorary Chair.; Patricia Albjerg Graham, Joseph E. Kasputys, Percy A. Pierre, S. Dillon Ripley.
Number of staff: 4 full-time professional; 2 part-time professional; 1 full-time support; 1 part-time support.
Employer Identification Number: 521428862

1174
Institute of Turkish Studies, Inc. ⌑ ☆
2010 Massachusetts Ave., NW
Washington 20036 (202) 296-4502

Established in 1982.
Foundation type: Independent
Financial data (yr. ended 9/30/88): Assets, $111,590 (M); gifts received, $338,962; expenditures, $337,135, including $125,148 for 98 grants (high: $7,000; low: $500) and $78,187 for 48 grants to individuals (high: $6,000; low: $200).
Purpose and activities: Grants for the academic community of U.S. specialists in the field of Turkish studies; support includes awards to individual scholars and to institutions.
Types of support: Research, publications, scholarship funds, fellowships, seed money, conferences and seminars, matching funds, grants to individuals.
Application information: Application form required.
Initial approach: Proposal
Copies of proposal: 4
Deadline(s): Mar. 15
Final notification: Apr. 30
Write: Dr. Heath Lowry, Exec. Dir.
Officers: Sukru Elekdag, Chair.; Parker T. Hart, Vice-Chair.; Ahmed Kafadar, Secy.-Treas.; Heath W. Lowry, Exec. Dir.
Board of Governors: Ahmet Ertegun, Alan W. Fisher, Halil Inalcik, Bernard Lewis, Seymour J. Rubin, Dankwart D. Rustow, Ronald I. Spiers, Rodney B. Wagner.
Employer Identification Number: 521294029

1175
Jerusalem Fund for Education and Community Development
2435 Virginia Ave., N.W.
Washington 20037 (202) 338-1958

Established in 1982 in DC.
Donor(s): Jerusalem Fund.
Foundation type: Independent
Financial data (yr. ended 05/31/88): Assets, $5,240,915 (M); gifts received, $74,637; expenditures, $541,040, including $26,500 for 6 grants (high: $10,000; low: $500) and $280,500 for 557 grants to individuals (high: $2,000; low: $500).
Purpose and activities: Support primarily for emergency aid to Palestinians in the West Bank and Gaza Strip and young people's education and welfare in Palestinian communities in Israel; scholarships, fellowships, and travel and research grants for individuals who reside in those communities.
Types of support: Student aid, student loans, fellowships, research, emergency funds.
Limitations: Giving primarily in Palestinian communities in Israel.
Publications: Financial statement, annual report.
Application information:
Initial approach: Letter
Deadline(s): Aug. 31 and Dec. 15 for individual applicants; none for organizations
Write: Pamela Cadora, Exec. Dir.
Officers and Directors:* Hisham Sharabi,* Chair.; Michael Saah,* Secy.-Treas.; Pamela Cadora,* Exec. Dir.; Raphael Calis, Ziad Deeb, Samih Farsoun, George Hishmeh.
Number of staff: 2 part-time professional; 3 full-time support; 1 part-time support.
Employer Identification Number: 521238142

1176
The James M. Johnston Trust for Charitable and Educational Purposes ▼
1101 Vermont Ave., N.W., Suite 403
Washington 20005 (202) 289-4996

Trust established in 1968 in DC.
Donor(s): James M. Johnston.†
Foundation type: Independent
Financial data (yr. ended 12/31/88): Assets, $53,308,537 (M); expenditures, $2,806,891, including $2,374,150 for 85 grants (high: $520,000; low: $5,000; average: $10,000-$30,000).
Purpose and activities: Grants largely to higher and secondary educational institutions, including support for scholarships and training of nurses.
Types of support: Scholarship funds, continuing support.
Limitations: Giving primarily in NC and Washington, DC. No grants to individuals, or for building or endowment funds, or operating budgets.
Application information: Application form not required.
Initial approach: Letter
Copies of proposal: 1
Deadline(s): None
Board meeting date(s): Monthly
Final notification: 30 days
Write: Betty Frost Hayes, Chair.
Officer and Trustees:* Betty Frost Hayes,* Chair.; Barnum L. Colton, Jr., Wallace Dunbar Gram.
Number of staff: 1 full-time professional.
Employer Identification Number: 237019796

1177
Leonard Kapiloff Foundation ⌑ ☆
3559 Brandywine St., N.W.
Washington 20008 (301) 948-6903

Established in 1987 in DC.
Donor(s): Leonard Kapiloff.
Foundation type: Independent
Financial data (yr. ended 12/31/88): Assets, $2,041,373 (M); gifts received, $1,746,649;

expenditures, $140,552, including $132,972 for 39 grants (high: $49,512; low: $25).
Purpose and activities: Giving primarily for Jewish organizations, including educational institutions and support for Israel.
Limitations: Giving primarily in Washington, DC.
Application information:
Initial approach: Letter
Deadline(s): None
Write: Dr. Leonard Kapiloff, Pres.
Officers: Leonard Kapiloff, Pres. and Treas.; Jonathan Kapiloff,* Secy.
Directors:* Craig A. Emden, William H. Hussman.
Employer Identification Number: 521544512

1178
Charles I. & Mary Kaplan Foundation ⌘
1000 Connecticut Ave., N.W., Suite 1110
Washington 20036-5392 (202) 223-4636

Established in 1956 in DC.
Donor(s): Joan L. Gindes, Edward H. Kaplan.
Foundation type: Independent
Financial data (yr. ended 12/31/87): Assets, $1,725,663 (M); gifts received, $291,667; expenditures, $182,121, including $177,000 for 6 grants (high: $100,000; low: $1,000).
Purpose and activities: Support primarily for Jewish organizations.
Limitations: Giving primarily in Washington, DC.
Application information:
Write: Edward H. Kaplan, Secy.-Treas.
Officers: Jerome Kaplan, Pres.; Joan L. Gindes, V.P.; Edward H. Kaplan, Secy.-Treas.
Employer Identification Number: 526043928

1179
The Joseph P. Kennedy, Jr. Foundation ▼
1350 New York Ave., N.W., Suite 500
Washington 20005-4709 (202) 393-1250

Incorporated in 1946 in DC.
Donor(s): Joseph P. Kennedy,† Mrs. Joseph P. Kennedy.
Foundation type: Independent
Financial data (yr. ended 12/31/88): Assets, $21,931,196 (M); gifts received, $4,105; expenditures, $2,614,990, including $1,625,342 for 27 grants (high: $494,947; low: $500; average: $10,000-$50,000) and $111,257 for 2 grants to individuals (high: $55,671; low: $55,586).
Purpose and activities: The foundation's main objectives are "the prevention of mental retardation by identifying its causes and improving means by which society deals with its mentally retarded citizens." Emphasis on the use of funds in areas where a multiplier effect is possible. Awards scholarships to a one week bioethics course at the Kennedy Institute of Ethics, Georgetown University; fellowships limited to two Kennedy Foundation Public Policy Leadership Fellows.
Types of support: Seed money, research, special projects, conferences and seminars, consulting services, general purposes, technical assistance.
Limitations: No grants for building or endowment funds, equipment, or operating budgets of schools or service organizations.
Publications: Informational brochure, application guidelines.
Application information: Funds are substantially committed to grants initiated by the foundation; however, applications considered for research projects and new models of service for persons with mental retardation and their families. Only proposals in the field of mental retardation are funded. Application form not required.
Initial approach: 2-page letter of intent
Copies of proposal: 1
Deadline(s): Submit letter of intent prior to Oct. 1; deadline for proposals, Nov. 15
Board meeting date(s): Usually Spring
Final notification: 2 weeks to 1 month
Write: Eunice Kennedy Shriver, Exec. V.P.
Officers and Trustees:* Edward M. Kennedy,* Pres.; Eunice Kennedy Shriver,* Exec. V.P.; George A. Zitnay, Secy.; Joseph E. Hakim, Treas.; Patricia Kennedy Lawford, Jean Kennedy Smith.
Number of staff: 3 full-time professional; 3 part-time professional; 4 full-time support.
Employer Identification Number: 136083407

1180
The Kiplinger Foundation ▼
1729 H St., N.W.
Washington 20006 (202) 887-6537

Incorporated in 1948 in MD.
Donor(s): Willard M. Kiplinger.†
Foundation type: Independent
Financial data (yr. ended 12/31/89): Assets, $11,769,782 (M); gifts received, $125,000; expenditures, $971,546, including $802,250 for 115 grants (high: $90,000; low: $1,000; average: $1,000-$10,000) and $68,696 for 83 employee matching gifts.
Purpose and activities: Support primarily for higher education, including journalism programs; grants also for cultural groups, a community fund, social service and youth agencies, and civic affairs groups.
Types of support: Operating budgets, continuing support, annual campaigns, building funds, endowment funds, capital campaigns, matching funds, special projects, employee matching gifts.
Limitations: Giving primarily in the greater Washington, DC, area. No grants to individuals, or for seed money, emergency funds, deficit financing, equipment and materials, land acquisition, renovation projects, publications, conferences, scholarships, or fellowships.
Application information: Application form required for matching gift program.
Initial approach: Letter
Copies of proposal: 1
Deadline(s): None
Board meeting date(s): 4 or 5 times a year
Final notification: 3 to 6 months
Write: Frances Turgeon, Secy.
Officers and Trustees:* Austin H. Kiplinger,* Pres.; Frances Turgeon,* Secy.; James O. Mayo,* Treas.; Knight A. Kiplinger, Todd L. Kiplinger.
Number of staff: 1 part-time support.
Employer Identification Number: 520792570

1181
Helen Sperry Lea Foundation
3534 Fulton St., N.W.
Washington 20007 (202) 337-7339

Established in 1940 in DE and NY.
Donor(s): Helen Sperry Lea.†
Foundation type: Independent
Financial data (yr. ended 12/31/88): Assets, $2,379,522 (M); expenditures, $139,765, including $88,400 for 26 grants (high: $12,000; low: $200).
Purpose and activities: Grants primarily for education and community development organizations.
Types of support: General purposes.
Limitations: Giving generally limited to the Washington, DC, area. No grants to individuals.
Application information: Application form not required.
Initial approach: Letter or telephone
Deadline(s): None
Write: Mr. Sperry Lea, Pres.
Officers and Directors:* Sperry Lea,* Pres. and Treas.; Anna Lea,* V.P.; Helena Lea,* V.P.; R. Brooke Lea II,* V.P.; Carol A. Rhees, Secy.
Employer Identification Number: 136161749

1182
Jacob and Charlotte Lehrman Foundation, Inc.
4801 Massachusetts Ave., N.W., Suite 400
Washington 20016 (202) 363-2700

Incorporated in 1953 in DC.
Donor(s): Jacob J. Lehrman,† Charlotte F. Lehrman.†
Foundation type: Independent
Financial data (yr. ended 10/31/89): Assets, $8,741,120 (M); expenditures, $435,228, including $398,200 for 55 grants (high: $125,000; low: $100).
Purpose and activities: Giving to establish scholarships and fellowships at institutions of learning, and to foster research in medicine and science; grants also for Jewish welfare funds, care of the aged and sick, cancer research, the establishment of trade schools, the fostering of religious observance, museums, and aid to refugees.
Types of support: Scholarship funds, fellowships, research, matching funds.
Limitations: Giving primarily in metropolitan Washington, DC. No grants to individuals; no loans.
Publications: Annual report.
Application information: Application form not required.
Initial approach: Proposal
Copies of proposal: 1
Deadline(s): Submit proposal preferably in May or Sept.; deadline Oct. 15
Board meeting date(s): May and Sept. or Oct.
Write: Robert Lehrman, Pres.
Officers: Robert Lehrman, Pres.; Heidi Berry, V.P.; Fredrica Carmichael, V.P.; Samuel Lehrman, V.P.; Leslie Handler, Secy.; Robert Barry Wertlieb, Treas.
Number of staff: None.
Employer Identification Number: 526035666

1183
William & Nora Lichtenberg Foundation ⌑ ☆
c/o Sachs, Greenebaum & Tayler
1140 Connecticut Ave., N.W.
Washington 20036-4001

Established in 1980 in DC.
Donor(s): Nora Lichtenberg.
Foundation type: Independent
Financial data (yr. ended 10/31/88): Assets, $375,458 (M); gifts received, $61,485; expenditures, $166,282, including $156,700 for 32 grants (high: $27,000; low: $100).
Purpose and activities: Giving primarily for higher and other education and health, including hospitals and health associations; support also for Jewish organizations and fine arts.
Limitations: Giving primarily in Washington, DC.
Application information:
Initial approach: Proposal
Deadline(s): None
Write: Sidney Sachs
Officers and Directors: Nora Lichtenberg, Pres.; Linda Kaplan, Secy.; Louis Kaplan, Treas.
Employer Identification Number: 526036659

1184
Mary and Daniel Loughran Foundation, Inc. ⌑
c/o American Security and Trust Co.
15th St. & Pennsylvania Ave., N.W.
Washington 20013 (202) 624-4283

Incorporated in 1967 in DC.
Donor(s): John Loughran.†
Foundation type: Independent
Financial data (yr. ended 07/31/89): Assets, $14,398,132 (M); expenditures, $1,066,361, including $862,000 for 74 grants (high: $60,000; low: $1,000).
Purpose and activities: Grants largely to religious institutions, youth and social service agencies, and higher educational institutions.
Limitations: Giving primarily in Washington, DC, VA, and MD. No grants to individuals, or for capital or endowment funds; no loans.
Application information:
Initial approach: Proposal
Copies of proposal: 1
Deadline(s): Submit proposal between Jan. and May; deadline June 1
Board meeting date(s): Apr., July, Aug., and Dec.
Write: Tim Talley, Asst. Admin.
Officers and Directors:* Walter R. Fatzinger, Jr.,* Pres.; Richard J.M. Poulson,* V.P.; M. Langhorne Keith,* Secy.; F. William Burke,* Treas. and Admin.; Carl L. Gell, A. Linwood Holton, Jr., Joseph L. Whyte.
Trustee: American Security and Trust Co.
Employer Identification Number: 521095883

1185
The Loyola Foundation, Inc. ▼
308 C St., N.E.
Washington 20002 (202) 546-9400

Incorporated in 1957 in DC.
Donor(s): Members of the Albert Gregory McCarthy, Jr. family.
Foundation type: Independent
Financial data (yr. ended 10/31/89): Assets, $6,368,793 (M); expenditures, $1,541,437, including $1,327,003 for 204 grants (high: $108,600; low: $100; average: $500-$15,000).
Purpose and activities: Grants primarily for basic overseas Roman Catholic missionary work and other Catholic activities of special interest to the trustees. Primary interest in nonrecurring requests for capital improvements in the missionary area, which are self-sustaining after completion; special consideration given to requests where there are matching contributions from the missionary area itself.
Types of support: Building funds, equipment, matching funds, renovation projects, special projects.
Limitations: Giving primarily in developing nations. Grants made in the U.S. only to institutions or organizations of special interest to the trustees. No grants to individuals, or for general or annual budgets, endowment funds, research, continuing support, emergency funds, deficit financing, publications, conferences, scholarships, or fellowships; no loans.
Publications: Biennial report (including application guidelines), informational brochure (including application guidelines).
Application information: Application form required.
Initial approach: Letter
Copies of proposal: 1
Deadline(s): Submit proposal preferably in Apr. or Oct.; deadlines May 1 and Nov. 1
Board meeting date(s): June and Dec.
Final notification: Jan. and July
Write: Albert G. McCarthy, III, Secy.
Officers and Trustees:* Denise M. Hattler,* Pres. and Treas.; Paul R. Dean,* V.P.; Albert Gregory McCarthy III,* Secy.; Daniel J. Altobello, Kathleen D.H. Carr, Ann M. Farrell, Andrea M. Hattler, Hilary A. Hattler, Russell L. Hauser, John N. Malyska, Archbishop Theodore E. McCarrick, Albert Gregory McCarthy IV, Raymond W. Merritt, Rev. Victor R. Yanitelli, S.J.
Number of staff: 1 full-time professional; 1 part-time professional.
Employer Identification Number: 520781255

1186
Marpat Foundation, Inc.
c/o Miller & Chevalier
655 15th St., N.W.
Washington 20005

Incorporated in 1985 in MD.
Donor(s): Marvin Breckinridge Patterson.
Foundation type: Independent
Financial data (yr. ended 12/31/89): Assets, $10,000,000 (M); expenditures, $740,178, including $643,940 for 31 grants (high: $75,000; low: $2,500).
Purpose and activities: "It is anticipated that grants will be made primarily to established charitable organizations whose activities are personally known to the directors. Grants will be made to the following: organizations that advance peace through international understanding, especially through programs involving national and world leaders and future leaders; schools, universities, museums, and libraries for the advancement and diffusion of knowledge; organizations and schools which sponsor programs that advocate and encourage family planning, or which promote or provide health care; organizations promoting or conducting scientific programs and research projects; organizations providing services and/or education designed to preserve natural and historical resources, or advance the knowledge of mankind's history and cultural past; and organizations which promote volunteer participation in, and citizen involvement with, such organizations."
Types of support: Building funds, conferences and seminars, consulting services, equipment, fellowships, program-related investments, special projects.
Limitations: Giving primarily in the mid-Atlantic region. No grants to individuals, or for endowment funds.
Publications: Informational brochure (including application guidelines).
Application information: Application form not required.
Initial approach: Proposal
Copies of proposal: 5
Deadline(s): Oct. 1
Board meeting date(s): Nov.
Final notification: After Dec. 15
Officers and Directors:* Marvin Breckinridge Patterson,* Pres.; Charles T. Akre,* V.P.; Joan F. Koven,* Secy.-Treas.; Isabella B. Dubow, Mrs. John Farr Simons.
Number of staff: None.
Employer Identification Number: 521358159

1187
The J. Willard Marriott Foundation ⌑
One Marriott Dr.
Washington 20058

Established in 1966 in DC.
Donor(s): J. Willard Marriott,† Alice S. Marriott, J. Willard Marriott Charitable Annuity Trust.
Foundation type: Independent
Financial data (yr. ended 12/31/88): Assets, $39,957,031 (M); gifts received, $24,669,949; expenditures, $1,856,603, including $1,668,933 for grants.
Purpose and activities: Grants primarily to local, previously supported charities and a few general scholarship funds.
Types of support: Continuing support, scholarship funds.
Limitations: Giving primarily in Washington, DC. No grants to individuals.
Application information: Contributes only to pre-selected organizations. Applications not accepted.
Trustees: Sterling D. Colton, Alice S. Marriott, J. Willard Marriott, Jr., Richard E. Marriott.
Number of staff: 1 part-time support.
Employer Identification Number: 526068678

1188
Thomas and Frances McGregor Foundation ⌑
c/o Robert Philipson & Co.
2000 L St., N.W., Suite 609
Washington 20036

Incorporated in 1961 in DC.
Donor(s): Thomas W. McGregor, McGregor Printing Corp.

Foundation type: Independent
Financial data (yr. ended 2/28/89): Assets, $3,820,460 (M); expenditures, $203,735, including $193,600 for 63 grants (high: $20,000; low: $100).
Purpose and activities: Emphasis on higher and secondary education, hospitals and health agencies, cultural programs, and support for religious organizations.
Limitations: Giving primarily in Washington, DC.
Application information:
Write: Victor Krakower, Mgr.
Officer: Victor Krakower, Mgr.
Employer Identification Number: 526041498

1189
MCI Foundation ▼
1133 19th St., N.W.
Washington 20036 (202) 887-2175

Established in 1986 in Washington, DC.
Donor(s): MCI Communications Corp.
Foundation type: Company-sponsored
Financial data (yr. ended 12/31/87): Assets, $3,899,287 (M); expenditures, $1,089,881, including $1,080,658 for 55 grants (high: $333,000; low: $625; average: $5,000-$25,000).
Purpose and activities: "The foundation makes donations primarily to support nonprofit organizations and institutions that provide job-related training or education. Priority is given to organizations that offer learning opportunitities to the disadvantaged."
Types of support: Scholarship funds, program-related investments.
Limitations: No support for political, fraternal, or religious organizations or those organizations having the primary purpose of promoting a particular ideological point of view. No grants to individuals, or for capital or endowment campaigns.
Application information: Application form not required.
Initial approach: Proposal
Copies of proposal: 1
Deadline(s): None
Write: Dorothy Olley
Directors: Eugene Eidenberg, Gerald J. Kovach, John R. Worthington.
Number of staff: 1 part-time professional.
Employer Identification Number: 510294683

1190
Robert S. and Margaret C. McNamara Foundation ⌑ ☆
2412 Tracy Pl., N.W.
Washington 20008

Established in 1954 in DC.
Foundation type: Independent
Financial data (yr. ended 11/30/89): Assets, $1,156,847 (M); expenditures, $49,988, including $44,350 for 34 grants (high: $6,000; low: $50).
Purpose and activities: Support for higher education, cultural programs, and international affairs.
Application information: Contributes only to pre-selected organizations. Applications not accepted.
Officer and Directors:* Robert S. McNamara,* Pres. and Treas.; Robert C. Dunham.
Employer Identification Number: 526056486

1191
Eugene and Agnes E. Meyer Foundation ▼
1400 Sixteenth St., N.W., Suite 360
Washington 20036 (202) 483-8294

Incorporated in 1944 in NY.
Donor(s): Eugene Meyer,† Agnes E. Meyer.†
Foundation type: Independent
Financial data (yr. ended 12/31/89): Assets, $53,315,736 (M); expenditures, $2,455,397, including $2,101,862 for 112 grants (high: $100,000; low: $250; average: $10,000-$25,000).
Purpose and activities: To assist in the development of community services and facilities; grants principally for welfare, education, health and mental health, the arts and humanities, and law and justice, preferably to provide new or improved services rather than to support existing programs.
Types of support: Seed money, matching funds, special projects, technical assistance.
Limitations: Giving limited to the metropolitan Washington, DC, area, including VA and MD. No support for sectarian purposes, or for programs that are national or international in scope. No grants to individuals, or for continuing support, annual campaigns, deficit financing, building or endowment funds, equipment, land acquisition, renovations, scholarships, fellowships, research, publications, or conferences; no loans.
Publications: Annual report (including application guidelines).
Application information: Application form not required.
Initial approach: Letter or proposal
Copies of proposal: 3
Deadline(s): Apr. 1, Aug. 1, and Dec. 1
Board meeting date(s): Applications considered only at Feb., June, and Oct. meetings; board meets also in Apr. and Dec.
Final notification: 1 month after meetings
Write: Julie L. Rogers, Pres.
Officers and Directors:* Mallory Walker,* Chair.; Delano E. Lewis,* Vice-Chair.; Julie L. Rogers,* Pres.; Newman T. Halvorson, Jr.,* Secy.-Treas.; Lucy M. Cohen, Theodore C. Lutz, Harry C. McPherson, Peter F. O'Malley, Pearl Rosser, M.D., David W. Rutstein, Carrie Thornhill.
Staff: Irene S. Lee, Prog. Officer.
Number of staff: 2 full-time professional; 1 full-time support; 2 part-time support.
Employer Identification Number: 530241716

1192
The Miller & Chevalier Charitable Foundation ⌑
Miller & Chevalier, Chartered
655 15th St., N.W., Suite 900
Washington 20005 (202) 626-5800

Incorporated in 1929 in DC.
Donor(s): Robert N. Miller.†
Foundation type: Independent
Financial data (yr. ended 12/31/88): Assets, $1,449,083 (M); expenditures, $258,185, including $237,500 for 41 grants (high: $75,000; low: $2,500; average: $2,500).
Purpose and activities: Grants to established charitable organizations working principally in the DC area whose activities are personally known to the directors. Grants also for scholarship funds of schools, particularly law schools.
Types of support: Scholarship funds, general purposes.
Limitations: Giving primarily in Washington, DC. No grants to individuals, or for endowment funds, research, or matching gifts; no loans.
Application information: Application form not required.
Initial approach: Proposal
Copies of proposal: 1
Deadline(s): Oct. 1
Board meeting date(s): Nov. or Dec.
Final notification: By Dec., if action is favorable
Write: John M. Bixler, Pres.
Officers and Directors: John M. Bixler, Pres.; John S. Nolan, V.P.; Ronald D. Aucutt, Secy.-Treas.; Benjamin Lee Bird, Donald B. Craven, Barron K. Grier, David W. Richmond, Numa L. Smith, Jr.
Number of staff: None.
Employer Identification Number: 526035549

1193
National Home Library Foundation
1333 New Hampshire Ave., N.W., Suite 600
Washington 20036 (202) 293-3860

Incorporated in 1932 in DC.
Donor(s): Sherman F. Mittell.†
Foundation type: Independent
Financial data (yr. ended 12/31/88): Assets, $1,040,622 (M); expenditures, $139,847, including $97,723 for 9 grants (high: $34,613; low: $150; average: $3,000-$10,000).
Purpose and activities: To assist in the distribution of books, pamphlets, and documents to libraries and to community groups with limited access to sources of specific areas of information; to encourage new techniques in the operation of libraries of printed and audio-visual materials and to aid in the wider dissemination of information by use of these techniques; and to encourage projects involving radio and television and other technological improvements in the transmission of information relating primarily to literary and cultural topics.
Limitations: No grants to individuals, or for building or endowment funds, operating budgets, scholarships, fellowships, or matching gifts; no loans.
Publications: Biennial report (including application guidelines).
Application information: Application form not required.
Initial approach: Proposal
Copies of proposal: 1
Deadline(s): Submit application 3 weeks prior to board meetings
Board meeting date(s): Mar., June, Sept., and Dec.
Final notification: 3 months

Write: Leonard H. Marks, Pres.
Officers and Directors:* Leonard H. Marks,* Pres.; Alice B. Popkin,* V.P.; Michael R. Gardner,* Secy.-Treas.; Meredith A. Brokaw, Bernard M.W. Knox, Ann Bradford Mathias, Lynda J. Robb.
Number of staff: 1 part-time professional; 1 part-time support.
Employer Identification Number: 526051013

1194
The Ottinger Foundation
1601 Connecticut Ave., N.W., Suite 803
Washington 20009 (202) 232-7333

Incorporated in 1945 in NY.
Donor(s): Lawrence Ottinger.†
Foundation type: Independent
Financial data (yr. ended 12/31/88): Assets, $2,961,933 (M); gifts received, $120,000; expenditures, $259,604, including $213,000 for 28 grants (high: $15,000; low: $2,000).
Purpose and activities: Supports selected projects designed to advance democracy, social justice, civil rights, environmental protection, and peace.
Types of support: Continuing support, seed money, special projects, general purposes, technical assistance.
Limitations: No grants to individuals, or for operating budgets, capital or annual campaigns, deficit financing, building or endowment funds, equipment and materials, land acquisition, publications, scholarships, or fellowships; no loans.
Publications: Application guidelines.
Application information: Application form not required.
Initial approach: Proposal
Copies of proposal: 1
Deadline(s): None
Board meeting date(s): 2 or 3 times a year
Final notification: 1 month after board meeting
Write: Betsy Taylor, Exec. Dir.
Officers: Louise L. Ottinger,* Pres.; Patricia Chernoff,* V.P.; Richard L. Ottinger,* V.P.; William Zabel, Secy.-Treas.
Trustees:* Karen Heath, Jennifer Ottinger, June Godfrey Ottinger, Lawrence Ottinger, LeaAnne Ottinger, Randy Ottinger, Ronald Ottinger, Sharon Kalemkiarian Ottinger.
Number of staff: 2 full-time professional; 1 full-time support.
Employer Identification Number: 136118423

1195
Alicia Patterson Foundation
1001 Pennsylvania Ave., N.W., Rm. 1250
Washington 20004 (301) 393-5995
Additional tel.: (301) 951-8512

Incorporated in 1960 in NY.
Donor(s): Alicia Patterson.†
Foundation type: Operating
Financial data (yr. ended 12/31/89): Assets, $2,943,000 (M); gifts received, $80,000; expenditures, $287,999, including $176,603 for 6 grants to individuals (average: $30,000).
Purpose and activities: Grants one-year fellowships for a small number of print journalists to examine and write about areas or problems of special interest; candidates must be U.S. citizens who have been working professionally as journalists for five years or longer.
Types of support: Fellowships.
Limitations: No grants for fellowships for academic study.
Publications: Annual report, informational brochure, newsletter, application guidelines.
Application information: Application form required.
Initial approach: Letter or telephone
Copies of proposal: 1
Deadline(s): Submit proposal between June and Sept.; deadline Oct. 1
Board meeting date(s): Annually in Dec.
Final notification: Early Dec.
Write: Margaret Engel, Exec. Dir.
Officers and Directors:* Joseph P. Albright,* Chair.; Alice Arlen, Pres.; Adam M. Albright,* V.P.; Blandina Albright,* V.P.; Dorothy J. Holdsworth,* V.P.; Margaret Engel, Secy. and Exec. Dir.; Maria Casale,* Treas.
Number of staff: 1 part-time professional.
Employer Identification Number: 136092124

1196
Pettus-Crowe Foundation, Inc.
1616 P St., N.W., Suite 100
Washington 20036 (202) 328-5186

Incorporated in 1968 in NY.
Donor(s): Irene Pettus-Crowe.
Foundation type: Independent
Financial data (yr. ended 12/31/88): Assets, $1,806,516 (M); expenditures, $97,489, including $77,458 for 30 grants (high: $25,000; low: $5,000).
Purpose and activities: Support for ethical issues and reproductive rights.
Types of support: Conferences and seminars, continuing support, seed money, special projects.
Limitations: Giving primarily in the East Coast and southern U.S. No grants to individuals.
Application information: Contributes only to pre-selected organizations. Applications not accepted.
Write: Dr. Irene Crowe, Pres.
Officers and Directors:* Irene Crowe,* Pres. and Treas.; John R. Young, V.P. and Secy.; Mary Crowe,* V.P.; Phillipa Crowe Neilson,* V.P.; Irene Pettus-Crowe,* V.P.
Number of staff: None.
Employer Identification Number: 237025310

1197
The Marjorie Merriweather Post Foundation
P.O. Box 96202
Washington 20090-6202

Established in 1956.
Donor(s): Marjorie Merriweather Post.†
Foundation type: Independent
Financial data (yr. ended 12/31/89): Assets, $3,708,500 (L); expenditures, $205,500, including $185,500 for 61 grants (high: $7,500; low: $1,000; average: $500-$5,000).
Purpose and activities: Grants primarily for higher and secondary education, cultural programs, international affairs, religious organizations, and social service and health agencies.
Limitations: No grants to individuals.
Application information: Application form not required.
Initial approach: Proposal
Copies of proposal: 1
Deadline(s): May 1 and Nov. 1
Board meeting date(s): June and Dec.
Write: Lois J. Shortell, Secy.
Officers and Trustees:* John A. Logan, Jr.,* Chair.; Spottswood P. Dudley,* Vice-Chair.; Lois J. Shortell,* Secy.; Leonard L. Silverstein,* Treas.; Nina Craig, Henry A. Dudley, Jr., George B. Hertzog, Godfrey T. McHugh.
Number of staff: None.
Employer Identification Number: 526054705

1198
Marjorie Merriweather Post Foundation of D.C. ▼
4155 Linnean Ave., N.W.
Washington 20008 (202) 686-8500

Established in 1967 in DC.
Donor(s): Marjorie Merriweather Post.†
Foundation type: Independent
Financial data (yr. ended 12/31/88): Assets, $69,310,504 (M); gifts received, $5,000; expenditures, $3,131,508, including $1,080,000 for 89 grants (average: $5,000-$10,000).
Purpose and activities: The foundation was formed to perpetuate Hillwood Museum; when an excess of funds is available, grants are utilized for other charitable purposes, including social services, education, hospitals and health associations, and cultural programs.
Types of support: Building funds, capital campaigns, conferences and seminars, continuing support, general purposes, special projects, renovation projects, research, loans, matching funds, operating budgets.
Limitations: Giving primarily in Washington, DC. No grants to individuals.
Publications: Application guidelines.
Application information: Application form not required.
Copies of proposal: 1
Deadline(s): Oct. 1
Board meeting date(s): Dec. and as required
Final notification: Varies
Write: Raymond P. Hunter, Secy.-Treas.
Officers and Directors: Adelaide C. Riggs, Pres.; E. Brevoort MacNeille, V.P.; Nadeenia H. Robertson, V.P.; Raymond P. Hunter, Secy.-Treas.; Ross Barzelay, Antal de Beckessy, Rodion Cantacuzene, David P. Close, Albert G. Perkins, Stanley Rumbough, Douglas R. Smith, Philip L. Smith.
Number of staff: 1 full-time support.
Employer Identification Number: 526080752

1199
Public Welfare Foundation, Inc. ▼
2600 Virginia Ave., N.W., Rm. 505
Washington 20037-1977 (202) 965-1800

Incorporated in 1947 in TX; reincorporated in 1951 in DE.
Donor(s): Charles Edward Marsh.†
Foundation type: Independent
Financial data (yr. ended 10/31/89): Assets, $236,686,000 (M); expenditures, $13,471,000,

including $12,331,100 for 341 grants (high: $240,000; low: $5,000; average: $36,162).
Purpose and activities: Grants primarily to grass roots organizations in the U.S. and abroad, with emphasis on the environment, population, the elderly, youth underclass, and criminal justice; support also for community services, health, and education. Programs must serve low-income populations, with preference to short-term needs.
Types of support: Matching funds, operating budgets, seed money, special projects.
Limitations: No support for religious purposes. No grants to individuals, or for building funds, capital improvements, endowments, scholarships, graduate work, foreign study, conferences, seminars, publications, films, research, workshops, technical assistance, consulting services, annual campaigns, emergency funds, or deficit financing; no loans.
Publications: Annual report (including application guidelines).
Application information: Application form not required.
Initial approach: Proposal with summary sheet
Copies of proposal: 1
Deadline(s): None
Board meeting date(s): Mar., June, Sept., and Dec.
Final notification: 3-4 months
Write: C. Glenn Ihrig, Exec. Dir.
Officers and Directors:* Donald T. Warner, Chair.; C. Glenn Ihrig,* Pres. and Exec. Dir.; Thomas J. Scanlon,* V.P.; Linda J. Leamon, Secy.; Veronica T. Keating,* Treas.; Antoinette M. Haskell, Robert H. Haskell, Robert R. Nathan, Myrtis H. Powell, Thomas W. Scoville, Murat W. Williams.
Number of staff: 8 full-time professional; 4 full-time support.
Employer Identification Number: 540597601

1200
Henry S. and Anne S. Reich Family Foundation ⌑ ☆
1156 15th St., N.W., Suite 329
Washington 20005

Established in 1983.
Donor(s): Anne S. Reich 1983 Charitable Lead Trust No. 1, Anne S. Reich 1983 Charitable Lead Trust No. 2.
Foundation type: Independent
Financial data (yr. ended 5/31/89): Assets, $664,734 (M); gifts received, $176,000; expenditures, $245,018, including $233,850 for 33 grants (high: $75,000; low: $500).
Purpose and activities: Giving for Jewish welfare, temple support, and yeshivas; support also for the performing arts and education.
Limitations: Giving primarily in Washington, DC, and MD. No grants to individuals.
Application information: Application form not required.
Initial approach: Letter
Deadline(s): None
Write: Stephen A. Bodzin, Esq., V.P.
Officers and Directors: Steven M. Reich, Pres.; Stephen A. Bodzin, V.P. and Secy.; Albert Abramson.
Employer Identification Number: 521308578

1201
RJR Nabisco Foundation ▼
1455 Pennsylvania Ave., N.W.
Washington 20004 (202) 626-7200

Established in 1986 in NC.
Donor(s): R.J. Reynolds Tobacco Co., Nabisco Brands, Inc., R.J.R. Nabisco, Inc., Planters Life Savers Co., R.J.R. Tobacco, International, and others.
Foundation type: Company-sponsored
Financial data (yr. ended 12/31/89): Assets, $61,100,000 (M); expenditures, $6,916,674, including $6,806,508 for grants (high: $500,000; low: $500; average: $5,000-$25,000).
Purpose and activities: The foundation is in the process of major restructuring; guidelines and programs are being altered. Support primarily for educational initiatives.
Types of support: Special projects, operating budgets.
Publications: Informational brochure (including application guidelines).
Application information: New guidelines, policies, and procedures will be published. Applications not accepted.
Board meeting date(s): Annually
Write: Jaynie M. Grant, Exec. Dir.
Officers: Louis V. Gerstner, Jr.,* Chair.; Roger D. Semerad,* Pres.; Lawrence R. Ricciardi, Secy.-Treas.; Jaynie M. Grant, Exec. Dir.
Directors:* Richard I. Beattie, David B. Kalis, Henry R. Kravis, George R. Roberts.
Number of staff: 1 full-time professional; 1 full-time support.
Employer Identification Number: 581681920

1202
Walter G. Ross Foundation
c/o ASB Capital Management Inc.
655 15th St., N.W., Suite 800
Washington 20005

Trust established about 1964 in DC.
Foundation type: Independent
Financial data (yr. ended 12/31/88): Assets, $6,865,512 (M); expenditures, $407,379, including $359,528 for grants.
Purpose and activities: Giving generally for higher education, medical research, and care of the sick.
Types of support: Research, general purposes, endowment funds, matching funds.
Limitations: Giving limited to the Washington, DC, area and FL. No grants to individuals, or for scholarships or fellowships; no loans.
Publications: Application guidelines.
Application information: Application form not required.
Initial approach: Letter
Copies of proposal: 1
Deadline(s): Submit proposal preferably in Aug.; deadline Sept. 15
Board meeting date(s): Oct.
Final notification: 1 month after annual meeting
Write: Ian W. Jones, Secy.
Trustees: Lloyd H. Elliott, Chair.; Eugene L. Bernard, Gladys Bludworth, J. Hillman Zahn, First American Bank, N.A, Washington.
Employer Identification Number: 526057560

1203
Sapelo Island Research Foundation, Inc. ⌑
c/o The A.R.C.A. Foundation
1425 21st St., N.W.
Washington 20036 (202) 822-9193

Incorporated in 1949 in GA.
Donor(s): Richard J. Reynolds.†
Foundation type: Operating
Financial data (yr. ended 6/30/88): Assets, $12,829,541 (M); expenditures, $738,348, including $563,738 for 38 grants (high: $175,000; low: $1,000; average: $12,000) and $22,594 for 15 grants to individuals (high: $3,000; low: $500).
Purpose and activities: A private operating foundation; currently supports a marine research laboratory on Sapelo Island through grants to the University of Georgia; some support also for higher education, and social, economic and environmental issues.
Types of support: Operating budgets, continuing support, annual campaigns, seed money, consulting services, technical assistance, scholarship funds, special projects, research, conferences and seminars, student aid.
Limitations: Giving limited to GA. No grants for capital, emergency, or endowment funds, deficit financing, or publications; no loans.
Publications: Annual report, application guidelines.
Application information: Application form not required.
Initial approach: Letter
Board meeting date(s): June and Dec.
Final notification: Up to 6 months
Write: Janet Shenk, Exec. Dir.
Officers and Trustees: Annemarie S. Reynolds, Pres.; William Broker, V.P.; Smith W. Bagley, Treas.; Hubert Humphrey, Katherine B. Mountcastle.
Number of staff: 1 part-time professional; 2 part-time support.
Employer Identification Number: 580827472

1204
Stern Family Fund
(Formerly Philip M. Stern Family Fund)
1601 Connecticut Ave., N.W., Suite 803
Washington 20009 (202) 232-7333

Established in 1959 in DC.
Donor(s): Philip M. Stern, and other members of the Stern family.
Foundation type: Independent
Financial data (yr. ended 06/30/89): Assets, $681,945 (M); gifts received, $597,350; expenditures, $725,900, including $684,482 for 98 grants (high: $28,000; low: $250).
Purpose and activities: Grants for civic affairs, peace, the environment, foreign policy and government, law and justice, minorities, public policy, civil rights, and women.
Types of support: Loans, continuing support, general purposes, matching funds, seed money, special projects, technical assistance.
Limitations: No grants to individuals, or for building or endowment funds, or capital campaigns.
Publications: Application guidelines.
Application information: Application form not required.
Initial approach: Proposal

Copies of proposal: 1
Deadline(s): None
Board meeting date(s): Quarterly
Write: Betsy Taylor, Exec. Dir.
Officers and Directors:* Philip M. Stern, Pres. and Treas.; Walter Slocum,* V.P.; Anne A. Plaster,* Secy.
Number of staff: 2 full-time professional; 1 full-time support.
Employer Identification Number: 526037658

1205
Alexander and Margaret Stewart Trust u/w of the late Helen S. Devore ▼
c/o First American Bank, N.A., Washington
740 15th St., N.W.
Washington 20005 (202) 637-7887

Trust established in 1960 in DC.
Donor(s): Helen S. Devore.†
Foundation type: Independent
Financial data (yr. ended 12/31/88): Assets, $23,916,199 (M); expenditures, $1,301,127, including $1,152,642 for 34 grants (high: $114,038; low: $5,200; average: $25,000).
Purpose and activities: Giving for the prevention and treatment of children's illnesses and for enhancing hospital facilities.
Types of support: Seed money, equipment, continuing support, operating budgets, special projects.
Limitations: Giving primarily in the Washington, DC, area. No grants to individuals, or for endowment funds, annual campaigns, deficit financing, building funds, land acquisition, renovation projects, publications, conferences, research, scholarships, or fellowships; no loans.
Publications: Program policy statement, application guidelines.
Application information: Application form not required.
Initial approach: Letter
Copies of proposal: 1
Deadline(s): None
Board meeting date(s): Mar., June, Sept., Nov., and Dec.
Final notification: Varies
Write: Ruth C. Shaw, V.P., First American Bank, N.A., Washington
Officer: Ruth C. Shaw, Secy.
Trustees: Francis G. Addison III, George E. Hamilton III, First American Bank, N.A., Washington.
Number of staff: None.
Employer Identification Number: 526020271

1206
Alexander and Margaret Stewart Trust u/w of the late Mary E. Stewart ▼
c/o First American Bank, N.A., Washington
740 15th St., N.W.
Washington 20005 (202) 637-7887

Trust established in 1947 in DC.
Donor(s): Mary E. Stewart.†
Foundation type: Independent
Financial data (yr. ended 12/31/88): Assets, $21,498,286 (M); expenditures, $1,135,541, including $993,559 for 15 grants (high: $175,000; low: $20,000; average: $25,000-$100,000).
Purpose and activities: Giving for the prevention of cancer, or the care of those afflicted with cancer.
Types of support: Seed money, equipment, matching funds, continuing support.
Limitations: Giving primarily in the Washington, DC, area. No grants to individuals, or for endowment funds, annual campaigns, deficit financing, building funds, land acquisition, renovation projects, publications, conferences, research, scholarships, or fellowships; no loans.
Publications: Program policy statement, application guidelines.
Application information: Application form not required.
Initial approach: Letter
Copies of proposal: 1
Deadline(s): None
Board meeting date(s): Apr., June, Sept., Nov., and Dec.
Final notification: Upon decision of trustees
Write: Ruth C. Shaw, V.P., First American Bank, N.A., Washington
Officer: Ruth C. Shaw, Secy.
Trustees: Francis G. Addison III, George E. Hamilton III, First American Bank, N.A., Washington.
Number of staff: None.
Employer Identification Number: 526020260

1207
David S. Stone Foundation, Inc.
1140 Connecticut Ave., N.W., Suite 703
Washington 20036 (202) 785-1111

Established in 1978 in DC.
Foundation type: Independent
Financial data (yr. ended 12/31/89): Assets, $2,351,944 (M); expenditures, $173,107, including $145,000 for 6 grants (high: $50,000; low: $5,000).
Purpose and activities: Giving primarily for education, the arts, and Jewish organizations, including community centers and group homes.
Limitations: Giving primarily in Washington, DC; Toledo, OH; and Boca Raton, FL.
Application information: Application form required.
Initial approach: Letter
Copies of proposal: 4
Deadline(s): None
Board meeting date(s): Varies
Write: Shelton Binstock, Pres.
Officers and Directors:* Shelton M. Binstock,* Pres.; Irving Adler,* V.P.; David A. Katz,* V.P.; Ralph Cohen,* Secy.-Treas.
Number of staff: None.
Employer Identification Number: 521120708

1208
The Streisand Foundation ⌘
(Formerly Barbra Streisand Foundation)
P.O. Box 53369
Washington 20009 (202) 331-8776

Established in 1968 in NY.
Donor(s): Barbra Streisand.
Foundation type: Independent
Financial data (yr. ended 12/31/88): Assets, $4,301,218 (M); expenditures, $968,754, including $888,500 for 50 grants (high: $60,000; low: $1,500; average: $10,000-$20,000).
Purpose and activities: Giving primarily for the environment, civil liberties, and voter education.
Types of support: General purposes, operating budgets, seed money, special projects.
Limitations: Giving primarily in Israel and the U.S.
Publications: Annual report (including application guidelines), grants list.
Application information: Application form required.
Deadline(s): Varies
Write: Margery Tabankin, Exec. Dir. or Cooki Collinet, Admin. Dir.
Trustees: Richard Baskin, Alan Bergman, Marilyn Bergman, Gerald Breslauer, Tom Downey, Marvin Goldberger, Patricia Schroeder, Stanley Sheinbaum, Barbra Streisand, Paula Weinstein.
Number of staff: 1 full-time professional; 1 part-time professional.
Employer Identification Number: 132620702

1209
Hattie M. Strong Foundation
Paramont Bldg., Suite 705
1735 I St., N.W.
Washington 20006 (202) 331-1619

Incorporated in 1928 in DC.
Donor(s): Hattie M. Strong.†
Foundation type: Independent
Financial data (yr. ended 8/31/89): Assets, $16,166,117 (M); gifts received, $1,560; expenditures, $1,342,448, including $213,350 for 38 grants (high: $25,000; low: $1,500; average: $5,000-$10,000) and $503,200 for 264 loans to individuals.
Purpose and activities: Non-interest-bearing loans to students who are within one year of their degree in college or graduate school and to students from the metropolitan Washington, DC, area who are enrolled in vocational schools in the Washington area. Maximum loan to vocational school applicants is $2,000; maximum loan to college students is $2,500. Grants program focused primarily on educational programs for the disadvantaged.
Types of support: Student loans.
Limitations: Giving primarily in the Washington, DC, area. No grants to individuals (except for loans), or for building or endowment funds, research, scholarships, or fellowships.
Publications: Annual report.
Application information: Application form required for students. Application form not required.
Initial approach: Letter or telephone
Copies of proposal: 1
Deadline(s): Feb. 1, May. 1, Aug. 1, and Nov. 1 for organizations; Mar. 31 for student aid
Board meeting date(s): Mar., June, Sept., and Dec.
Final notification: Within 1 week
Write: Thelma L. Eichman, Secy.
Officers: Henry Strong,* Chair. and Pres.; Trowbridge Strong,* V.P.; Thelma L. Eichman, Secy.; Barbara B. Cantrell, Treas.

Directors:* Olive W. Covington, Charles H. Fleischer, Richard S.T. Marsh, John A. Nevius, Vincent E. Reed, C. Peter Strong, Henry L. Strong, Bennetta B. Washington.
Number of staff: 2 full-time professional; 3 full-time support; 1 part-time support.
Employer Identification Number: 530237223

1210
The Community Foundation of Greater Washington, Inc. ▼
1002 Wisconsin Ave., N.W.
Washington 20007 (202) 338-8993

Incorporated in 1973 in DC.
Foundation type: Community
Financial data (yr. ended 12/31/88): Assets, $11,036,450 (M); gifts received, $8,617,592; expenditures, $7,368,761, including $5,167,129 for grants (average: $1,000-$100,000).
Purpose and activities: Through its programs and unrestricted funds, the foundation works to establish new coalitions for delivery of public services, develop public-private partnerships of shared resources to meet public needs, catalyze efforts leading to social change, and promote self-help grassroot efforts and increase use of volunteers. Areas of interest include health care for the homeless, substance abuse, community development, newcomers, youth in philanthropy, and ecology.
Types of support: Seed money, emergency funds, technical assistance, special projects, research, publications, general purposes, continuing support.
Limitations: Giving limited to the metropolitan Washington, DC, area. No support for religious purposes. No grants to individuals, or for annual campaigns, endowment funds, equipment, land acquisition, renovation projects, scholarships, fellowships, operating budgets, or matching gifts.
Publications: Annual report (including application guidelines), informational brochure.
Application information: Application form not required.
Initial approach: Letter
Copies of proposal: 1
Deadline(s): May and Oct.
Board meeting date(s): June and Nov.
Final notification: Up to 6 months
Write: Deborah S. McKown, Dir. of Finance
Officers and Directors: John V. Pollack, Chair.; John W. Hechinger, Jr., Vice-Chair.; Haida Sale, Acting Dir.; Stephen J. Slade, Secy.; Jim Adler, Treas.; and 22 additional directors.
Number of staff: 11 full-time professional; 3 full-time support.
Employer Identification Number: 237343119

1211
George Wasserman Foundation, Inc.
3134 Ellicott St., N.W.
Washington 20008-2025 (202) 966-3355

Established in 1948.
Donor(s): George Wasserman.†
Foundation type: Independent
Financial data (yr. ended 12/31/88): Assets, $2,664,838 (M); expenditures, $378,380, including $365,950 for 67 grants (high: $150,000; low: $50).
Purpose and activities: Grants primarily for Jewish welfare funds, theological studies, and temple support; support also for social services and health.
Types of support: Annual campaigns, building funds, continuing support, endowment funds, exchange programs, general purposes, research, scholarship funds, seed money, special projects, technical assistance.
Limitations: No grants to individuals.
Application information:
Initial approach: Letter
Deadline(s): None
Write: Janice W. Goldsten, Pres.
Officers and Directors:* Janice W. Goldsten,* Pres. and Treas.; Carolyn Stopak,* V.P. and Secy.; Lisa Gill,* V.P.
Employer Identification Number: 526035888

1212
Weir Foundation Trust ⌘
c/o American Security and Trust Co.
730 15th St., N.W.
Washington 20013

Trust established in 1953 in DC.
Donor(s): Davis Weir.†
Foundation type: Independent
Financial data (yr. ended 12/31/88): Assets, $2,177,943 (M); expenditures, $111,915, including $106,850 for 66 grants (high: $25,150; low: $100; average: $1,000-$2,000).
Purpose and activities: Giving for higher education, the arts and cultural programs, Protestant church support, and social services.
Types of support: Annual campaigns, building funds, capital campaigns, continuing support, endowment funds, equipment, general purposes, operating budgets, renovation projects, special projects.
Limitations: Giving primarily in Washington, DC, MD, and VA. No grants to individuals.
Publications: 990-PF.
Application information: Applications not accepted.
Write: Charles D. Weir, Trustee
Trustee: Charles D. Weir.
Employer Identification Number: 526029328

1213
The Westport Fund ⌘
1815 Randolph St., N.W.
Washington 20011

Established in 1943.
Donor(s): Milton McGreevy,† and others.
Foundation type: Independent
Financial data (yr. ended 12/31/88): Assets, $2,889,206 (M); expenditures, $134,998, including $124,940 for 68 grants (high: $31,500; low: $250).
Purpose and activities: Giving primarily to cultural organizations, social services, and education, especially higher education.
Types of support: Annual campaigns, building funds, capital campaigns, continuing support, endowment funds, equipment, general purposes, lectureships, operating budgets, publications, research, scholarship funds.
Limitations: Giving primarily in Kansas City, MO. No grants to individuals, or for consulting services, deficit financing, exchange programs, internships, matching funds, land acquisition, renovation projects, seed money, or technical assistance; no loans.
Application information: Contributes only to pre-selected organizations. Applications not accepted.
Officers: Gail McGreevy Harmon, Pres.; Jean McGreevy Green, V.P. and Secy.; Thomas J. McGreevy, V.P.; Ann McGreevy Heller, Treas.
Director: Barbara James McGreevy.
Number of staff: None.
Employer Identification Number: 446007971

1214
Helen Parker Willard Foundation ⌘
c/o Crestar Bank N.A., Trust Dept.
1445 New York Avenue, N.W.
Washington 20005 (202) 879-6337

Established in 1961 in DC.
Foundation type: Independent
Financial data (yr. ended 12/31/87): Assets, $1,928,251 (M); expenditures, $124,052, including $113,500 for 29 grants (high: $13,000; low: $1,000).
Purpose and activities: Giving to health associations and welfare organizations, including those devoted to the blind, youth, and Protestant organizations.
Types of support: Building funds, endowment funds, research, scholarship funds.
Limitations: Giving primarily in Washington, DC. No grants to individuals.
Application information:
Initial approach: Letter
Deadline(s): None
Write: William B. Willard, Pres.
Officers and Directors:* William B. Willard,* Pres.; Sarah Willard Taylor,* V.P.; Henry A. Willard II,* Secy.-Treas.; Annie A. Kirby.
Number of staff: None.
Employer Identification Number: 526036750

1215
The Windom Fund ⌘ ☆
1112 16th St., N.W., No. 750
Washington 20036 (202) 887-1957

Established in 1986 in DC.
Donor(s): Ellen R. Malcolm, Barbara Burnett, Betsy Burnett.
Foundation type: Operating
Financial data (yr. ended 12/31/88): Assets, $26,877 (M); gifts received, $60,352; expenditures, $197,386, including $111,320 for 15 grants (high: $72,025; low: $25).
Purpose and activities: A private operating foundation; giving primarily for human rights organizations and women's coalitions; support also for health, social services, and youth.
Types of support: General purposes.
Limitations: No support for the arts or international affairs. No grants to individuals, or for films or research.
Application information: Application form not required.
Deadline(s): Feb. 15, May 1, and Oct. 15
Write: Ellen Malcolm, Pres.
Officers: Ellen R. Malcolm,* Pres. and Treas.; Gail M. Harmon, Secy.
Directors:* Phillip M. McLaughlin, Jill Strachan.
Employer Identification Number: 521449044

1216
Abe Wouk Foundation, Inc. ⌑
3255 N St., N.W.
Washington 20007

Established in 1954.
Donor(s): Betty Sarah Wouk, Herman Wouk.
Foundation type: Independent
Financial data (yr. ended 12/31/88): Assets, $1,844,786 (M); gifts received, $782,600; expenditures, $179,905, including $173,860 for 58 grants (high: $50,000; low: $100).
Purpose and activities: Grants primarily for higher education, the arts, conservation, and Jewish welfare funds and temple support.
Limitations: Giving primarily in CA, NY, and Washington, DC.
Application information: Application form not required.
Deadline(s): None
Write: Herman Wouk, Pres.
Officers: Herman Wouk,* Pres.; Joseph Wouk, V.P.; Nathaniel Wouk, V.P.; Suzanne Stein, Secy.; Betty Sarah Wouk,* Treas.
Trustees:* Charles Rembar.
Employer Identification Number: 136155699

FLORIDA

1217
Anthony R. Abraham Foundation, Inc. ⌑
6600 S.W. 57th Ave.
Miami 33143 (305) 665-2222

Established in 1978 in FL.
Donor(s): Anthony R. Abraham.
Foundation type: Independent
Financial data (yr. ended 12/31/88): Assets, $5,569,431 (M); gifts received, $42,457; expenditures, $239,762, including $190,415 for 52 grants (high: $25,245; low: $50).
Purpose and activities: Grants for Catholic giving, education, and health and social services.
Types of support: Grants to individuals.
Application information:
Initial approach: Letter
Deadline(s): None
Write: Thomas G. Abraham, Secy.
Officers and Directors: Anthony R. Abraham, Pres.; Thomas G. Abraham, Secy.; Joseph Shaker, Treas.; Robert Fried, Anthony Shaker.
Employer Identification Number: 591837290

1218
Martha & William Adams Scholarship Trust
3001 S.E. Fairway West
Stuart 34997

Incorporated in 1985 in VA.
Donor(s): William B. Adams.†
Foundation type: Independent
Financial data (yr. ended 12/31/88): Assets, $1,120,342 (M); expenditures, $33,933, including $25,000 for 1 grant.
Purpose and activities: Support limited to educational institutions for scholarship and loan assistance to students above the high school level.
Types of support: Scholarship funds.
Limitations: Giving primarily in VA. No grants to individuals.
Application information:
Initial approach: Letter
Deadline(s): None
Write: Betty V. Adams, Trustee
Trustees: Betty V. Adams, Talford H. Kemper.
Employer Identification Number: 521329899

1219
Aegis Foundation, Inc. ⌑ ☆
3200 46th Ave. North
St. Petersburg 33714 (813) 521-2832

Established in 1986.
Donor(s): Marcia Loebel, Terry Loebel.
Foundation type: Independent
Financial data (yr. ended 12/31/88): Assets, $184,594 (M); expenditures, $111,887, including $108,792 for 2 grants (high: $58,792; low: $50,000).
Purpose and activities: Giving for an organization promoting a Native American leadership program and a cancer biomedical research program.
Limitations: No grants to individuals.
Application information: Contributes only to pre-selected organizations. Applications not accepted.
Board meeting date(s): Annually
Write: Marcia Loebel, Pres.
Officers and Directors:* Marcia Loebel,* Pres.; Gregory P. Loebel,* Secy.; Kimberly Loebel, Treas.; Terry Loebel.
Employer Identification Number: 592752648

1220
Ziuta & Joseph James Akston Foundation ☆
444 North Lake Way
Palm Beach 33480
Additional address: 324 Datura St., Suite 300, West Palm Beach, FL 33410; Tel.: (407) 832-1141

Established in 1967.
Donor(s): Ziuta G. Akston.
Foundation type: Independent
Financial data (yr. ended 12/31/88): Assets, $4,043 (M); gifts received, $102,000; expenditures, $104,446, including $104,124 for 73 grants (high: $50,000; low: $20).
Purpose and activities: Giving primarily for a hospice guild; support also for health associations and hospital building funds and cultural programs, including the fine arts, museums, and the performing arts.
Types of support: Annual campaigns.
Limitations: Giving primarily in FL, especially Palm Beach. No grants to individuals.
Application information: Applications not accepted.
Write: Ziuta G. Akston, Pres.
Officers: Ziuta G. Akston, Pres.; Betty G. Marcus, V.P.; Robert P. Marcus, Treas.
Employer Identification Number: 132623634

1221
Norris & Margaret Aldeen Charitable Foundation ⌑
6554 Ridgewood Dr.
Naples 33963

Established in 1965 in IL.
Donor(s): Norris A. Aldeen, Margaret Aldeen.
Foundation type: Independent
Financial data (yr. ended 12/31/88): Assets, $3,203,672 (M); expenditures, $234,910, including $190,500 for 21 grants (high: $36,000; low: $500).
Purpose and activities: Support primarily for Christian education; some support also for churches and hospitals.
Types of support: General purposes.
Limitations: Giving primarily in the Rockford, IL, area.
Application information:
Initial approach: Letter
Deadline(s): None
Write: The Trustees
Trustees: Margaret Aldeen, Norris A. Aldeen.
Employer Identification Number: 366105736

1222
G. W. Aldeen Charity Trust ⌑
6554 Ridgewood Dr.
Naples 33963-2761

Established in 1962 in IL.
Donor(s): Norris A. Aldeen.
Foundation type: Independent
Financial data (yr. ended 05/31/89): Assets, $1,882,824 (M); expenditures, $307,360, including $296,242 for 7 grants (high: $218,242; low: $4,000).
Purpose and activities: Giving to colleges and associations dedicated to the Christian education of young people; support also for churches, hospitals, and community organizations.
Limitations: Giving primarily in Rockford, IL.
Application information:
Initial approach: Letter
Deadline(s): None
Write: Norris A. Aldeen, Trustee
Trustees: Norris A. Aldeen, June C. Anderson.
Employer Identification Number: 366056643

1223
The Amaturo Foundation, Inc. ⌑ ☆
2929 East Commercial Blvd., PH-C
Fort Lauderdale 33308 (305) 776-7815

Established in 1986.
Donor(s): Joseph C. Amaturo.
Foundation type: Independent
Financial data (yr. ended 6/30/88): Assets, $1,000,752 (M); expenditures, $47,046, including $45,285 for 8 grants (high: $23,000; low: $750).
Purpose and activities: Giving primarily for Catholic charities, education, and child welfare; support also for a medical center.
Types of support: Research.
Limitations: Giving primarily in NY and FL.

Application information:
Deadline(s): None
Write: Cara E. Cameron, Mgr.
Officer and Directors: Cara E. Cameron, Mgr.; Douglas Q. Amaturo, Joseph C. Amaturo, Laurence V. Amaturo, Lorna J. Amaturo, Winifred L. Amaturo, Frances A. Arnold, Elizabeth A. Eisenstein, Joseph E. Ferguson, William Ruane.
Employer Identification Number: 592718130

1224
Martin Andersen and Gracia Andersen Foundation, Inc. ⌑
1717 Edgewater Dr.
Orlando 32804

Established in 1953 in FL.
Foundation type: Independent
Financial data (yr. ended 10/31/88): Assets, $1,213,493 (M); expenditures, $23,142, including $11,100 for 27 grants (high: $1,000; low: $25).
Purpose and activities: Grants for health services, education, culture, social services, youth programs, and religious support.
Application information: Applications are accepted by invitation only.
Officers: Gracia B. Andersen, Pres.; Graham Barr, V.P.; A.S. Johnson, Secy.-Treas.
Directors: Robert van Roijen, Richard F. Trismen.
Employer Identification Number: 596166589

1225
Andrews Foundation, Inc. ⌑ ☆
550 South Ocean Blvd.
Palm Beach 33480-4713

Established in 1986 in FL.
Donor(s): Neal L. Andrews, Jr.
Foundation type: Independent
Financial data (yr. ended 12/31/88): Assets, $1,012,471 (M); expenditures, $62,839, including $59,000 for 6 grants (high: $20,000; low: $1,500).
Purpose and activities: Giving primarily for public affairs and a right-to-work organization.
Trustees: Carol L. Andrews, Neal L. Andrews, Jr.
Employer Identification Number: 592765829

1226
Ansin Foundation ⌑ ☆
P.O. Box 610727
North Miami 33161

Established in 1957.
Donor(s): Sunbeam Television Corp.
Foundation type: Independent
Financial data (yr. ended 12/31/88): Assets, $48,005 (M); gifts received, $100,000; expenditures, $116,335, including $115,770 for 21 grants (high: $65,000; low: $25).
Purpose and activities: Support for Jewish welfare funds and higher and other education.
Trustee: Edmund N. Ansin.
Employer Identification Number: 046046113

1227
The Applebaum Foundation, Inc. ⌑
11111 Biscayne Blvd., Suite 883
North Miami 33181

Incorporated in 1949 in NY.
Donor(s): Joseph Applebaum,† Leila Applebaum.
Foundation type: Independent
Financial data (yr. ended 2/28/89): Assets, $8,433,549 (M); gifts received, $41,411; expenditures, $495,313, including $447,781 for 88 grants (high: $195,000; low: $25).
Purpose and activities: Emphasis on higher education, hospitals and medical research, and Jewish organizations, including welfare agencies, schools, and temple support.
Officer: Leila Applebaum, Pres.
Employer Identification Number: 591002714

1228
The Appleman Foundation, Inc. ⌑
c/o Bessemer Trust Co. of FL
249 Royal Palm Way
Palm Beach 33480 (305) 655-4030

Incorporated in 1952 in DE.
Donor(s): Nathan Appleman, and members of the Appleman family.
Foundation type: Independent
Financial data (yr. ended 12/31/88): Assets, $1,369,400 (M); gifts received, $14,448; expenditures, $625,185, including $616,210 for 81 grants (high: $100,000; low: $25).
Purpose and activities: Giving for Jewish welfare funds, higher education, including a Jewish theological seminary, hospitals, social services, and temple support.
Types of support: Research.
Limitations: Giving primarily in NY and in Palm Beach, FL.
Application information:
Initial approach: Letter
Deadline(s): None
Write: Nathan Appleman, Pres.
Officers: Nathan Appleman, Pres.; Jill A. Roberts, V.P.; Susan A. Unterberg, V.P.; Michael F. Page, Secy.-Treas.
Number of staff: None.
Employer Identification Number: 136154978

1229
Arison Foundation, Inc. ▼
100 S.E. 2nd St., 32nd Fl.
Miami 33131-2136 (305) 577-8200

Incorporated in 1981 in FL.
Donor(s): Carnival Cruise Lines, Inc., Festivale Maritime, Inc., Intercon Overseas, Inc.
Foundation type: Independent
Financial data (yr. ended 06/30/89): Assets, $39,406,414 (M); gifts received, $27,860,000; expenditures, $1,134,161, including $1,089,688 for 32 grants (high: $455,000; low: $100).
Purpose and activities: Emphasis on arts and cultural programs; support also for Jewish welfare funds.
Limitations: Giving primarily in FL.
Application information:
Write: Maddy Rosenberg
Officers: Shari Arison, Pres.; Robert B. Sturges, V.P.
Trustee: Marilyn Arison.
Employer Identification Number: 592128429

1230
The Aurora Foundation ▼
P.O. Box 1848
Bradenton 33506 (813) 748-4100

Established in 1969.
Donor(s): Anthony T. Rossi.
Foundation type: Independent
Financial data (yr. ended 6/30/88): Assets, $59,231,775 (M); expenditures, $4,525,283, including $2,944,994 for 60 grants (high: $1,179,954; low: $350; average: $3,000-$65,000), $70,491 for 34 grants to individuals and $1,003,861 for 1 foundation-administered program.
Purpose and activities: Support largely for missionary work; grants also for church support, religious associations, education, scholarships for religious study, social service and youth agencies, also administers and operates the Bradenton Missionary Village, a rent-free housing complex for retired missionaries.
Types of support: Student aid, continuing support.
Limitations: No grants for professorships or building funds of schools and colleges.
Application information: No new requests currently being considered.
Board meeting date(s): Usually mid-Oct.
Write: Anthony T. Rossi, Chair.
Officer and Trustees: Anthony T. Rossi, Chair. and Mgr.; Joseph Aleppo.
Number of staff: 34 full-time support; 4 part-time support.
Employer Identification Number: 237044641

1231
B.C.R. Foundation ⌑ ☆
P.O. Box 13307
Pensacola 32591-3307

Established in 1986.
Foundation type: Independent
Financial data (yr. ended 8/31/88): Assets, $2,148,427 (M); expenditures, $144,424, including $129,000 for 37 grants (high: $37,600; low: $500).
Purpose and activities: Giving primarily for social services, including programs for children and the aged; support also for higher education and conservation.
Limitations: No grants to individuals.
Application information: Contributes only to pre-selected organizations. Applications not accepted.
Officers and Trustees: Crawford Rainwater, Chair.; Betty Gregg Rainwater, Vice-Chair.; Elizabeth R. Woolf, Pres.; Nancy Gregg Rainwater, V.P.; Freddie B. Rainwater, Secy.; Crawford Rainwater, Jr., Treas.; Andrew Sweet, Kenneth Woolf.
Employer Identification Number: 592728836

1232
The George T. Baker Foundation, Inc. ⌑
P.O. Box 6585
Surfside 33154

Incorporated in 1956 in FL.
Donor(s): George T. Baker.†
Foundation type: Independent

Financial data (yr. ended 5/31/89): Assets, $1,701,437 (M); expenditures, $97,286, including $58,639 for grants.
Purpose and activities: Giving for higher education, hospitals, health agencies and medical research; grants also for humane societies, youth agencies, and church support.
Limitations: Giving primarily in Dade County, FL, and Blowing Rock, NC. No grants to individuals.
Application information: Contributes only to pre-selected organizations. Applications not accepted.
Officers and Trustees:* Irma Baker Lyons,* Chair.; Barbara Baker,* Pres.; James F. Lyons, M.D.,* V.P.; Rev. Oscar Wilsen,* V.P.; Elizabeth J. Wright,* Secy.; Patricia A. Corbett.
Employer Identification Number: 596151202

1233
Banyan Foundation, Inc. ☆
4350 West Cypress St., Suite 1000
Tampa 33607 (813) 870-1970

Incorporated in 1985 in FL.
Donor(s): Reese Coppage.
Foundation type: Independent
Financial data (yr. ended 06/30/89): Assets, $1,109,149 (M); gifts received, $200,000; expenditures, $119,464, including $112,237 for 48 grants (high: $50,000; low: $25).
Purpose and activities: Giving "to support research, education, and treatment in the areas of substance abuse, emotional problems, family counseling, trauma-related adjustment problems, stress, and other related mental health problems."
Types of support: Research.
Limitations: No grants to individuals.
Application information: Application form not required.
Initial approach: Proposal
Copies of proposal: 1
Deadline(s): None
Board meeting date(s): Monthly
Write: Reese Coppage, Pres.
Officers: Reese Coppage, Pres.; Martha Ann Coppage, Secy.; Ronald Jaeger, Treas.
Number of staff: None.
Employer Identification Number: 592578626

1234
Barnett Charities, Inc.
100 Laura St.
Jacksonville 32202 (904) 791-5407
Mailing address: P.O. Box 40789, Jacksonville, FL 32203-5407

Established in 1983 in FL as Barnett Foundation, Inc.; re-incorporated with current name in 1987.
Foundation type: Company-sponsored
Financial data (yr. ended 12/31/89): Assets, $233,665 (M); gifts received, $765,204; expenditures, $890,314, including $890,314 for 11 grants (high: $224,114; low: $5,000).
Purpose and activities: Support for culture and the arts, education, fitness, and health and human services.
Types of support: Consulting services, endowment funds, scholarship funds.
Limitations: Giving limited to FL and GA.
Publications: Annual report, grants list.
Application information: Programs which have statewide impact or are beyond the scope of the local banks' markets are submitted to Barnett Charities by the local Barnett Banks. Application form required.
Initial approach: Letter or telephone
Copies of proposal: 1
Deadline(s): None
Board meeting date(s): Weekly on Monday
Final notification: Within 2 weeks of meeting
Write: Beth A. Bollinger, Admin.
Officers: Allen L. Lastinger, Pres.; Jeffrey K. Graf, Secy.
Trustees: Albert D. Ernest, Earl B. Hadlow, Stephen A. Hansel, Hinton Nobles, Charles E. Rice.
Employer Identification Number: 592761362

1235
Barnett Foundation, Inc. ☆
50 North Laura St.
P.O. Box 990
Jacksonville 32231 (904) 791-7427

Established in 1983 in FL.
Foundation type: Independent
Financial data (yr. ended 12/31/88): Assets, $19,788 (M); gifts received, $225,000; expenditures, $223,260, including $221,514 for 88 grants (high: $30,000; low: $25).
Purpose and activities: Contributions for human services, including programs for drug abuse, aid for the disadvantaged, and youth and child welfare agencies; support also for arts and culture, health and hospitals, and education.
Types of support: Annual campaigns, building funds, in-kind gifts.
Limitations: Giving limited to Dural, Clay, and St. John's counties, FL. No grants to individuals.
Application information: Contributes only to pre-selected organizations. Applications not accepted.
Write: Judy Russell, Asst. V.P.
Officers and Trustees:* Hugh H. Jones,* Pres.; Mary Sue Spurlin,* Secy.-Treas.; Judy Russell.
Number of staff: 1 full-time professional; 1 full-time support.
Employer Identification Number: 592444551

1236
John E. and Nellie J. Bastien Memorial Foundation ⌑
150 East Sample Rd.
Pompano Beach 33064

Trust established in 1965 in FL.
Donor(s): Nellie J. Bastien.†
Foundation type: Independent
Financial data (yr. ended 12/31/88): Assets, $8,926,523 (M); expenditures, $667,834, including $459,100 for 100 grants (high: $25,000; low: $200).
Purpose and activities: Giving for higher education, including scholarship funds, medical sciences and hospitals, church support, youth agencies, and general welfare.
Types of support: Scholarship funds.
Limitations: Giving primarily in FL.
Application information:
Deadline(s): None
Write: The Trustees
Trustees: Carol R. Kearns, Gene F. Schneider, J. Wallace Wrightson.
Employer Identification Number: 596160694

1237
The C. Kenneth and Laura Baxter Foundation, Inc. ⌑
c/o Ernst & Whinney
777 South Flagler Dr., West Tower 1200
West Palm Beach 33401

Incorporated in 1986 in FL.
Donor(s): C. Kenneth Baxter, Laura Baxter.
Foundation type: Independent
Financial data (yr. ended 12/31/87): Assets, $1,121,861 (M); gifts received, $500,000; expenditures, $555,528, including $551,179 for 78 grants (high: $500,000; low: $15).
Purpose and activities: First year of grantmaking, 1987; support primarily for a hospital.
Application information: Application form not required.
Deadline(s): None
Directors: C. Kenneth Baxter, Donald K. Baxter, Laura Baxter.
Employer Identification Number: 592706400

1238
The Bay Branch Foundation
c/o Wold Corp.
1515 South Federal Hwy., Suite 201
Boca Raton 33432

Trust established in 1963 in NJ.
Foundation type: Independent
Financial data (yr. ended 12/31/87): Assets, $2,680,484 (M); expenditures, $109,823, including $97,000 for 26 grants (high: $21,000; low: $500).
Purpose and activities: Support primarily for health associations and educational and religious institutions.
Limitations: Giving limited to Palm Beach County, FL.
Application information: Contributes only to pre-selected organizations. Applications not accepted.
Directors: Elaine Wold, Keith C. Wold.
Trustees: Donald E. Baker, Kathleen Besaw, Ray C. Osborne.
Number of staff: None.
Employer Identification Number: 226054888

1239
Cordelia Lee Beattie Foundation Trust
P.O. Box 267
Sarasota 34230 (813) 951-7242

Trust established in 1975 in FL.
Donor(s): Cordelia Lee Beattie.†
Foundation type: Independent
Financial data (yr. ended 10/31/89): Assets, $1,958,270 (M); expenditures, $131,579, including $108,506 for 9 grants (high: $28,000; low: $1,200).
Purpose and activities: Giving for the arts, with emphasis on music.
Types of support: Building funds, equipment, land acquisition, matching funds, scholarship funds, publications.

Limitations: Giving limited to Sarasota County, FL. No grants to individuals, or for general support, endowment funds, special projects, research, or conferences; no loans.
Publications: Application guidelines.
Application information: Application form required.
Initial approach: Letter
Copies of proposal: 3
Deadline(s): Apr. 1 and Oct. 1
Board meeting date(s): May and Nov.
Final notification: May and Nov.
Write: Robert E. Perkins, Admin. Agent
Officer and Trustees:* Jerome A. Jannopoulo,* Chair.; Mrs. Deane Carroll Allyn, Robert A. Kimbrough.
Number of staff: 1 full-time professional; 1 part-time support.
Employer Identification Number: 596540711

1240
Robert R. Bellamy Memorial Foundation, Inc. ⌑
4649 Ponce de Leon Blvd., Suite 303
Coral Gables 33146

Established in 1947 in NC.
Foundation type: Independent
Financial data (yr. ended 12/31/87): Assets, $1,542,751 (M); expenditures, $101,926, including $88,000 for 17 grants (high: $30,000; low: $100).
Purpose and activities: Grants for education, health services, religious support, and social services.
Types of support: General purposes.
Officers and Trustees: Robert B. Bellamy, Pres. and Treas.; Joseph W. Hooper, Jr., V.P.; Cyrus D. Hogue, Jr., Secy.; P.R. Smith, Jr.
Employer Identification Number: 566040601

1241
The Benedict Foundation for Independent Schools
607 Lantana Ln.
Vero Beach 32963 (407) 231-4111

Established in 1983 in DE.
Donor(s): Peter B. Benedict.
Foundation type: Independent
Financial data (yr. ended 12/31/89): Assets, $1,800,560 (M); gifts received, $250,000; expenditures, $67,643, including $59,455 for 5 grants (high: $15,000; low: $6,000).
Purpose and activities: Support primarily for independent secondary schools that are members of the National Association of Independent Schools for ten consecutive years. Challenge grants are preferred for purposes of improving academic programs, scholarship aid, building programs, faculty salaries, faculty summer workshops, or other programs to improve the quality of the school's educational activities.
Types of support: Scholarship funds, building funds, matching funds.
Limitations: No grants to individuals, or for endowment funds, or operating costs; no loans.
Publications: Informational brochure (including application guidelines).
Application information: Application form required.
Initial approach: Proposal
Copies of proposal: 6
Deadline(s): Applications should be received between Jan. 1 and Mar. 31
Board meeting date(s): May
Final notification: June
Write: Mrs. Nancy H. Benedict, V.P.
Officers and Directors:* Peter B. Benedict,* Pres.; Nancy H. Benedict,* V.P.; Christopher C. Angell, Secy.; Louis R. Benzak,* Treas.; Stuart C. Beal.
Number of staff: None.
Employer Identification Number: 592383209

1242
The Edward & Edna Beron Charitable Foundation ⌑ ☆
1800 South Ocean Blvd., Apt. 6F
Boca Raton 33432-8060

Established in 1985 in FL.
Foundation type: Independent
Financial data (yr. ended 12/31/88): Assets, $331,450 (M); gifts received, $151,924; expenditures, $135,011, including $132,850 for 17 grants (high: $41,000; low: $500).
Purpose and activities: Giving primarily for Jewish organizations, including welfare funds; support also for museums, performing arts groups, and hospitals.
Limitations: Giving primarily in FL, NJ, PA, and NY.
Application information: Application form not required.
Deadline(s): None
Write: Edna Beron, Chair.
Officer: Edna Beron, Chair.
Employer Identification Number: 592276327

1243
The Frank Stanley Beveridge Foundation, Inc. ▼
1515 Ringling Blvd., Suite 340
P.O. Box 4097
Sarasota 34230-4097 (813) 955-7575

Trust established in 1947 in MA; incorporated in 1956.
Donor(s): Frank Stanley Beveridge.†
Foundation type: Independent
Financial data (yr. ended 12/31/88): Assets, $32,631,158 (M); expenditures, $2,748,783, including $2,407,802 for 118 grants (high: $125,000; low: $300; average: $1,000-$30,000).
Purpose and activities: A portion of the income designated for maintenance of a local park established by the donor in Westfield, MA; the balance for general local giving, with emphasis on higher and secondary education, social service and youth agencies, community development, culture, and health.
Types of support: Capital campaigns, seed money, general purposes, equipment, building funds, land acquisition, renovation projects, scholarship funds, matching funds, endowment funds, continuing support, special projects, technical assistance.
Limitations: Giving primarily in Hampden and Hamshire counties, MA. No support for tax-supported organizations. No grants to individuals, or for operating funds, scholarships, or fellowships; no loans.
Publications: Informational brochure (including application guidelines), application guidelines.
Application information: Applicants outside the Hampden and Hamshire counties, MA, areas must have support of 1 or more directors; such support must be solicited by the foundation. Application form required.
Initial approach: Letter
Copies of proposal: 1
Deadline(s): Apr. 1, Aug. 1, and Dec. 1
Board meeting date(s): Feb., June, and Oct.
Final notification: 2 weeks after meeting date
Write: Philip Caswell, Pres.
Officers: Philip Caswell,* Pres.; Carole S. Lenhart, Treas.; David F. Woods,* Clerk.
Directors:* Sarah Caswell Bartelt, John Beveridge Caswell, Pamela Everets, John G. Gallup, Joseph Beveridge Palmer, Homer G. Perkins, Evelyn Beveridge Russell, Patsy Palmer Stecher, J. Thomas Touchton.
Number of staff: 1 full-time professional; 1 part-time professional.
Employer Identification Number: 046032164

1244
Bible Alliance, Inc. ⌑
P.O. Box 1894
Bradenton 33506 (813) 748-4100

Established in 1972 in FL.
Donor(s): Anthony T. Rossi, The Aurora Foundation.
Foundation type: Independent
Financial data (yr. ended 6/30/88): Assets, $1,836,995 (M); gifts received, $1,179,959; expenditures, $2,145,120, including $1,716,186 for in-kind gifts.
Purpose and activities: Production and distribution of recorded portions of the Bible and Christian religious messages on cassette tape in various languages for use primarily by the blind and the prison system.
Limitations: Generally no cash grants.
Application information: Certification of blindness required. Application form not required.
Initial approach: Letter
Copies of proposal: 1
Deadline(s): None
Board meeting date(s): Oct. and as required
Write: Anthony T. Rossi, Pres.
Officers and Directors: Anthony T. Rossi, Pres.; Joseph Aleppo, V.P.
Number of staff: 21 full-time support; 2 part-time support.
Employer Identification Number: 237178299

1245
Lydia H. Bickerton Charitable Trust ⌑ ☆
32 Leeward Island
Clearwater 34630

Established in 1986 in FL.
Foundation type: Independent
Financial data (yr. ended 6/30/89): Assets, $1,937,911 (M); expenditures, $123,487, including $83,500 for grants.
Purpose and activities: Giving primarily for religion, higher education, and health and hospitals.
Limitations: Giving primarily in FL and IL.
Application information:
Initial approach: Proposal

Deadline(s): None
Write: Beatrice M. Hurley, Trustee
Trustees: Beatrice M. Hurley, John Hurley.
Employer Identification Number: 592745408

1246
The Bilzerian and Steffen Foundation
(Formerly The Singer Company Foundation)
15438 North Florida Ave., Suite 205
Tampa 33613 (813) 264-7100

Incorporated in 1960 in DE.
Donor(s): The Singer Co.
Foundation type: Company-sponsored
Financial data (yr. ended 12/31/88): Assets, $1,487,995 (M); expenditures, $69,716, including $35,800 for 7 grants (high: $25,000; low: $300; average: $1,000-$25,000), $1,000 for 1 grant to an individual and $23,862 for 62 employee matching gifts (high: $6,990; low: $25).
Purpose and activities: In 1988, the Singer Company was acquired and the foundation is currently reorganizing and redefining its purpose and goals.
Limitations: Giving primarily in areas of major company operations.
Application information:
Initial approach: Telephone, letter, or proposal
Copies of proposal: 1
Board meeting date(s): Annually
Officers: Paul A. Bilzerian, Pres. and Treas.; Terri L. Steffen, Secy.
Number of staff: 1 full-time professional.
Employer Identification Number: 136065363

1247
John Blair Foundation ⌑
c/o Northern Trust Bank of Florida/Naples, N.A.
530 Fifth Ave., South
Naples 33940 (813) 262-8800

Established in 1978 in FL.
Donor(s): E. Blake Blair, Jr. Trust.
Foundation type: Independent
Financial data (yr. ended 12/31/88): Assets, $2,189,791 (M); gifts received, $27,193; expenditures, $120,431, including $105,600 for 48 grants (high: $15,000; low: $150).
Purpose and activities: Support primarily for social services, health associations, and family planning.
Types of support: General purposes.
Limitations: No grants to individuals.
Application information: Application form not required.
Deadline(s): None
Trustees: Dorothy S. Blair, Robert W. Rieman, M.D., Northern Trust Bank of Florida, N.A.
Employer Identification Number: 591831565

1248
Samuel Blank and Family Foundation ⌑
8940 N.W. 24 Terr.
Miami 33172

Trust established in 1943 in FL.
Donor(s): Jerome Blank, and members of the Blank family.
Foundation type: Independent
Financial data (yr. ended 12/31/88): Assets, $5,759,822 (M); expenditures, $289,130, including $265,910 for 49 grants (high: $75,000; low: $50).
Purpose and activities: Emphasis on Jewish welfare funds, hospitals, higher education, and temple support.
Limitations: Giving primarily in FL.
Application information:
Initial approach: Proposal
Deadline(s): None
Write: R.J. Puck
Trustees: Andrew Blank, Jerome Blank, Mark Blank.
Employer Identification Number: 596128978

1249
Norman C. Bradish Trust
NCNB National Bank of Florida
P.O. Box 199
Orlando 32802

Established in 1960 in FL.
Foundation type: Independent
Financial data (yr. ended 06/30/89): Assets, $1,623,117 (M); expenditures, $106,692, including $78,933 for 2 grants (high: $39,717; low: $39,216) and $14,065 for 3 grants to individuals (high: $6,615; low: $2,500).
Purpose and activities: Support primarily for hospitals and scholarships to male graduates of Decorah High School, IA.
Types of support: Student aid.
Application information: Application form not required.
Deadline(s): None
Write: Gladys Backes
Agent: NCNB National Bank of Florida.
Employer Identification Number: 596161559

1250
Breyer Foundation, Inc. ⌑
P.O. Box 3308
Palm Beach 33480

Established in 1940 in NY and DE.
Donor(s): Henry W. Breyer III.
Foundation type: Independent
Financial data (yr. ended 12/31/88): Assets, $1,741,047 (M); expenditures, $129,898, including $115,530 for 55 grants (high: $25,000; low: $100).
Purpose and activities: Support for education, health organizations and hospitals, conservation, social services, religious organizations, culture and performing arts.
Application information:
Initial approach: Letter or proposal
Deadline(s): None
Write: Henry W. Breyer III, Pres.
Officers and Directors:* Henry W. Breyer III,* Pres.; Margaret McKee Breyer,* Secy.; Joanne Breyer.
Employer Identification Number: 236295924

1251
The Briggs Family Foundation
2325 Gordon Dr.
Naples 33940 (813) 261-7625

Incorporated in 1957 in FL.
Donor(s): Stephen F. Briggs,† Beatrice B. Briggs.†
Foundation type: Independent
Financial data (yr. ended 11/30/89): Assets, $4,734,765 (M); expenditures, $174,851, including $154,500 for 24 grants (high: $75,000; low: $100; average: $100-$10,000).
Purpose and activities: Giving for a university, health, education, and conservation.
Types of support: Continuing support, annual campaigns, building funds, equipment, land acquisition, special projects, research, scholarship funds, capital campaigns.
Limitations: Giving primarily in Collier County, FL. No grants to individuals, or for endowment funds or matching gifts; no loans.
Application information: Application form not required.
Initial approach: Letter
Copies of proposal: 1
Deadline(s): Submit proposal in Oct.; deadline Nov. 1
Board meeting date(s): As required
Final notification: 1 month
Write: John N. Briggs, Pres.
Officers: John N. Briggs, Pres.; Josephine Jorstad, Secy.-Treas.
Number of staff: None.
Employer Identification Number: 596130222

1252
The Shepard Broad Foundation, Inc. ⌑
2925 Aventura Blvd., Suite 303
North Miami Beach 33180 (305) 935-2436

Incorporated in 1956 in FL.
Donor(s): Shepard Broad, Ruth K. Broad, Morris N. Broad, and many others.
Foundation type: Independent
Financial data (yr. ended 12/31/88): Assets, $4,046,669 (M); expenditures, $147,529, including $142,752 for 66 grants (high: $30,000; low: $20).
Purpose and activities: Emphasis on higher education, Jewish welfare funds and educational organizations, and health services.
Limitations: Giving primarily in FL. No grants to individuals.
Application information: Application form not required.
Initial approach: Letter
Deadline(s): None
Write: Shepard Broad, Pres.
Officers and Directors: Shepard Broad, Pres.; Ann B. Bussel, V.P. and Secy.; Morris N. Broad, V.P. and Treas.
Employer Identification Number: 590998866

1253
Broward Community Foundation, Inc.
2601 East Oakland Park Blvd., Suite 202
Fort Lauderdale 33306 (305) 563-4483

Incorporated in 1984 in FL.
Foundation type: Community
Financial data (yr. ended 06/30/89): Assets, $1,486,103 (M); gifts received, $639,352; expenditures, $293,392, including $254,171 for 41 grants (high: $25,000; low: $200).
Purpose and activities: Support for social services, the arts, education, health organizations, and the environment.
Types of support: Equipment, matching funds, seed money.

Limitations: Giving primarily in Broward County, FL. No support for religious purposes. No grants to individuals, or for annual campaigns, building funds, consulting services, continuing support, deficit financing, endowment funds, emergency funds, land acquisition, or operating budgets; no loans.
Publications: Annual report (including application guidelines), newsletter, informational brochure.
Application information: Application form not required.
Initial approach: Letter
Copies of proposal: 1
Deadline(s): Sept. 1
Board meeting date(s): Nov.
Final notification: Nov.
Write: Elizabeth C. Deinhardt, Exec. Dir.
Officers and Directors:* Leonard Robbins,* Pres.; Wilson B. Greaton, Jr.,* V.P.; Patricia DuMont,* Secy.; John B. Deinhardt,* Treas.; Elizabeth C. Deinhardt,* Exec. Dir.; W. George Allen, James J. Blosser, Ward J. Curtis, Jr., William D. Horvitz, Marti Huizenga, Chris Mobley, Roy Rogers, George E. Sullivan.
Number of staff: 1 part-time professional; 1 part-time support.
Employer Identification Number: 592477112

1254
Peter D. and Dorothy S. Brown Charitable Trust under agreement dated July 1, 1987 ⌑ ☆
16716 Ironwood Dr.
Delray Beach 33445-7051

Established in 1987 in FL.
Donor(s): Peter Brown, Dorothy S. Brown.
Foundation type: Independent
Financial data (yr. ended 12/31/88): Assets, $1,689,438 (M); gifts received, $465,013; expenditures, $74,872, including $68,743 for 14 grants (high: $38,000; low: $10).
Purpose and activities: Initial year of grantmaking activities fiscal 1988; support for Jewish organizations, with emphasis on welfare funds and social services.
Limitations: No grants to individuals.
Application information:
Initial approach: Letter
Deadline(s): None
Write: Peter D. Brown, Trustee
Trustees: Dorothy S. Brown, Peter D. Brown.
Employer Identification Number: 386517224

1255
Brown Charity Foundation, Inc. ⌑
6515 Collins Ave.
Miami Beach 33141-4693 (305) 866-6511

Established in 1968 in FL.
Foundation type: Independent
Financial data (yr. ended 07/31/88): Assets, $1,097,426 (M); expenditures, $53,058, including $43,100 for 9 grants (high: $12,000; low: $1,000).
Purpose and activities: Support for higher education and Jewish organizations.
Limitations: Giving primarily in FL.
Application information:
Write: Stanley Brown, Treas.
Officers: Jack Brown, Secy.; Stanley Brown, Treas.
Directors: Gary Brown, Steven Brown, Gertrude Weiner.
Employer Identification Number: 596151063

1256
Ford Jeter Brown Foundation ⌑
P.O. Box 9
Fort Lauderdale 33302

Established about 1976 in FL.
Donor(s): William G. Miller, Jr.
Foundation type: Independent
Financial data (yr. ended 12/31/88): Assets, $1,315,042 (M); expenditures, $69,868, including $2,175 for grants.
Purpose and activities: Support primarily for a child development organization.
Types of support: Equipment.
Application information: Contributes only to pre-selected organizations. Applications not accepted.
Officers: William G. Miller, Jr., Pres.; Sharon P. Miller, V.P.; Alicia Zachman, Secy.-Treas.; Rosanne T. Morse, Exec. Dir.
Employer Identification Number: 237125924

1257
Buckingham Smith Benevolent Association ⌑
100 Arricola Ave.
St. Augustine 32084 (904) 824-2881

Established in 1873 in FL.
Foundation type: Independent
Financial data (yr. ended 12/31/88): Assets, $3,929,174 (M); expenditures, $197,496, including $174,835 for 2 grants (high: $95,749; low: $79,086).
Purpose and activities: Giving limited to organizations aiding indigent black persons; aid includes medical care, food, and utilities.
Limitations: Giving limited to St. Augustine, FL.
Application information: Application form not required.
Deadline(s): None
Write: A.J. McGhin, Jr., Secy.-Treas.
Officers: Reuben J. Plant, Pres.; Arthur E. Fisher, V.P.; A.J. McGhin, Jr., Secy.-Treas.
Trustees: Loren Brown, K.C. Bullard, Darrel Poli, C.E. Walker.
Employer Identification Number: 596137514

1258
George N. Bullard Foundation
(Formerly George Newton Bullard Fondation)
P.O. Box 187
Sugarloaf Shores 33044 (305) 296-4567

Established in 1967 in TN; reorganized in 1988 in FL.
Donor(s): Ella Hayes Trust.
Foundation type: Independent
Financial data (yr. ended 12/31/89): Assets, $4,016,160 (M); gifts received, $415,940; qualifying distributions, $150,000, including $150,000 for grants (average: $500-$1,000).
Purpose and activities: Emphasis on spiritual ecology and social justice with an ecological focus.
Types of support: Conferences and seminars, general purposes.
Limitations: Giving primarily in the Southeast.
Publications: 990-PF.
Application information: Application form not required.
Initial approach: Telephone
Deadline(s): None
Board meeting date(s): Monthly
Final notification: Usually monthly
Write: George Bullard, Trustee
Trustee: George N. Bullard, Jr.
Number of staff: None.
Employer Identification Number: 626077171

1259
Edyth Bush Charitable Foundation, Inc. ▼
199 East Welbourne Ave.
P.O. Box 1967
Winter Park 32790-1967 (407) 647-4322

Originally incorporated in 1966 in MN; reincorporated in 1973 in FL.
Donor(s): Edyth Bush.†
Foundation type: Independent
Financial data (yr. ended 08/31/89): Assets, $47,926,494 (M); qualifying distributions, $3,339,460, including $2,260,296 for 58 grants (high: $170,000; low: $4,000; average: $20,000-$75,000), $262,148 for foundation-administered programs and $817,016 for loans.
Purpose and activities: Support for charitable, educational, and health service organizations, with emphasis on human services and health; higher education; the elderly; youth services; the handicapped; and demonstrated nationally-recognized quality arts or cultural programs. Provides limited number of program-related investment loans for construction, land purchase, emergency or similar purposes to organizations otherwise qualified to receive grants. Active programs directly managed and/or financed for able learner education, and for management/volunteer development of nonprofits.
Types of support: Seed money, emergency funds, building funds, equipment, land acquisition, loans, conferences and seminars, matching funds, consulting services, technical assistance, program-related investments, renovation projects, capital campaigns, continuing support.
Limitations: Giving primarily within a 100-mile radius of Winter Park, FL; also AZ and CA if supported by one or more family member directors (normally less than 10% of grants). No support for alcohol or drug abuse projects or organizations, church, denominational, sacramental, or religious facilities or functions; primarily (50% or more) tax-supported institutions; advocacy organizations; foreign organizations; or generally for cultural programs. No grants to individuals, or for scholarships or individual research projects, endowments, fellowships, travel, routine operating expenses, annual campaigns (unless for local United Way), or deficit financing.
Publications: 990-PF, program policy statement, application guidelines, financial statement, grants list, 990-PF (including application guidelines).
Application information: Outline required for applications; see Policy Statement before applying. Application form not required.

Initial approach: Telephone, letter of inquiry, or proposal
Copies of proposal: 2
Deadline(s): Sept. 1 or Jan. 1; May 30 if funds are available for a July meeting
Board meeting date(s): Usually in Oct., Mar., July, and as required
Final notification: 2 weeks after board meetings
Write: H. Clifford Lee, Pres.
Officers: Charlotte H. Forward,* Chair.; H. Clifford Lee,* Pres. and C.E.O.; Herbert W. Holm,* V.P.-Finance and Treas.; David R. Roberts,* Sr. V.P.; Alice J. Rettig, Corp. Secy.; Betty Condon, Controller.
Directors:* Mary Gretchen Belloff, Guy D. Colado, Jerrold S. Trumbower, Milton P. Woodard.
Number of staff: 2 full-time professional; 2 part-time professional; 4 full-time support.
Employer Identification Number: 237318041

1260
C.E. and S. Foundation, Inc. ⌑ ☆
20 North Orange Ave., Suite 1100
Orlando 32801-2499

Established in 1984 in FL.
Foundation type: Independent
Financial data (yr. ended 12/31/88): Assets, $5,818,796 (M); gifts received, $2,000; expenditures, $615,176, including $602,221 for 25 grants (high: $160,000; low: $1,000).
Purpose and activities: Giving primarily for higher education, including a Presbyterian theological seminary.
Types of support: Building funds, renovation projects, endowment funds, capital campaigns.
Limitations: Giving primarily in Louisville, KY.
Application information: Application form required.
Deadline(s): None
Write: Robert Doll, Pres.
Officer: Robert Doll, Pres.
Employer Identification Number: 592466943

1261
William B. Calkins Foundation ⌑
c/o SunBank, N.A.
P.O. Box 3838
Orlando 32802-3631

Foundation type: Independent
Financial data (yr. ended 12/31/87): Assets, $1,032,176 (M); expenditures, $60,341, including $41,700 for 35 grants (high: $6,000; low: $200).
Purpose and activities: Support primarily for higher education and social service organizations.
Limitations: Giving primarily in FL.
Application information:
Initial approach: Letter
Deadline(s): None
Trustee: SunBank, N.A.
Employer Identification Number: 596125154

1262
E. Paul & Patricia P. Casey Foundation ⌑
330 South Beach Rd.
Hobe Sound 33455 (407) 546-9891
Additional address: c/o E. Paul Casey Associates, 76 Lafayette St., Salem, MA 01970-3624

Established in 1964 in MA.
Donor(s): Gertrude Pinkham.
Foundation type: Independent
Financial data (yr. ended 12/31/88): Assets, $1,209,066 (M); expenditures, $97,645, including $87,447 for 126 grants (high: $10,000; low: $25).
Purpose and activities: Support primarily for higher education and hospitals.
Limitations: No grants to individuals.
Application information:
Deadline(s): None
Write: E. Paul Casey, Trustee
Trustee: E. Paul Casey.
Employer Identification Number: 026013556

1263
Raymond H. and Mildred H. Center Foundation, Inc. ⌑ ☆
P.O. Box 3412
Clearwater 34630

Established in 1987 in FL.
Donor(s): Mildred H. Center.
Foundation type: Independent
Financial data (yr. ended 4/30/89): Assets, $673,903 (M); expenditures, $248,932, including $240,000 for 3 grants (high: $140,000; low: $50,000).
Purpose and activities: Giving for a Baptist church, a university, and the Salvation Army.
Types of support: Building funds, renovation projects.
Limitations: Giving primarily in FL. No grants to individuals.
Application information: Contributes only to pre-selected organizations. Applications not accepted.
Officers and Trustees: James H. Center, Pres.; Mildred H. Center, V.P.; Jerry H. Center, Secy.-Treas.; Frank J. Reif III.
Employer Identification Number: 592847124

1264
CenTrust Foundation ⌑ ☆
101 East Flagler St.
Miami 33131

Established in 1986 in FL.
Foundation type: Company-sponsored
Financial data (yr. ended 4/30/89): Assets, $6,776 (M); gifts received, $896,000; expenditures, $892,962, including $892,906 for 35 grants (high: $250,000; low: $500).
Purpose and activities: Support for higher education, civic affairs, the arts, and Jewish welfare.
Limitations: Giving primarily in Miami, FL. No grants to individuals.
Application information: Contributes only to pre-selected organizations. Applications not accepted.
Trustees: Angel Cortina, Jr., Catherine H. Fahringer, Richard H. Judy, Peter K. Moser, David L. Paul.
Employer Identification Number: 592693270

1265
Chadbourne Foundation, Inc. ⌑ ☆
4375 McCoy Dr.
Pensacola 32501 (904) 433-3001

Established in 1980.
Foundation type: Independent
Financial data (yr. ended 11/30/88): Assets, $1,762,574 (M); gifts received, $600,000; expenditures, $64,601, including $61,400 for 37 grants (high: $20,000; low: $150).
Purpose and activities: Giving primarily for Catholic churches and parishes; support also for social services and health associations and services.
Limitations: Giving primarily in Pensacola, FL. No grants to individuals.
Application information: Application form not required.
Initial approach: Letter
Deadline(s): None
Write: Edward M. Chadbourne, Jr., Pres.
Officers: Edward M. Chadbourne, Jr., Pres.; Edward M. Chadbourne III, V.P.; Caroline DeMaria, Secy.-Treas.
Trustee: Ruth Chadbourne.
Employer Identification Number: 592126313

1266
Robert Lee Chastain and Thomas M. Chastain Charitable Foundation ⌑
c/o First Union National Bank of Florida
Drawer G, P.O. Box 190
West Palm Beach 33402

Trust established in 1966 in FL.
Donor(s): Robert Lee Chastain.†
Foundation type: Independent
Financial data (yr. ended 12/31/88): Assets, $2,963,834 (M); expenditures, $154,818, including $121,500 for 10 grants (high: $80,000; low: $1,000).
Purpose and activities: Grants policy confined to community and publicly-managed agencies with emphasis given to public higher education, programs in the humanities and sciences, and environmental resource management projects offering benefits to the general population. A few trustee-initiated contributions may exceed these limits.
Limitations: Giving primarily in the Palm Beach and Martin County, FL, area. No support for church-related groups or national charities. No grants to individuals, or for building or endowment funds or appeals in mass circulation.
Application information:
Initial approach: Proposal with cover letter
Copies of proposal: 2
Board meeting date(s): Quarterly
Write: Thomas M. Chastain, Trustee
Trustees: Thomas M. Chastain, Harry Johnston II, First Union National Bank of Florida.
Employer Identification Number: 596171294

1267
The Chatlos Foundation, Inc. ▼
P.O. Box 915048
Longwood 32791-5048 (407) 862-5077

Incorporated in 1953 in NY.
Donor(s): Bristol Door and Lumber Co., Inc., William F. Chatlos.†
Foundation type: Independent

Financial data (yr. ended 12/31/88): Assets, $72,932,792 (M); expenditures, $3,260,764, including $2,488,325 for 174 grants (high: $100,000; low: $175; average: $5,000-$25,000).
Purpose and activities: Grants for higher education, including religious education, and religious associations; giving also for hospitals, health agencies, social services, international relief, and child welfare.
Types of support: Operating budgets, emergency funds, equipment, land acquisition, matching funds, scholarship funds, special projects, publications, renovation projects.
Limitations: No support for the arts. No grants to individuals, or for seed money, deficit financing, building or endowment funds, research, or conferences; no loans.
Publications: Informational brochure (including application guidelines).
Application information: Only 1 grant to an organization within a 12-month period. Application form not required.
Initial approach: Letter or proposal
Copies of proposal: 1
Deadline(s): None
Board meeting date(s): Feb., May, Aug., and Nov.
Final notification: 30 days after board meeting
Write: William J. Chatlos, Pres.
Officers and Trustees: Alice E. Chatlos, Chair. and Sr. V.P.; Kathryn A. Randle, Vice-Chair.; William J. Chatlos, Pres. and Treas.; Joy E. D'Arata, V.P.; Carol Leongomez, Secy.; Charles O. Morgan, Michele C. Roach.
Number of staff: 6 full-time professional.
Employer Identification Number: 136161425

1268
The Francis and Miranda Childress Foundation, Inc. ⌑
218 West Adams St., Suite 201
Jacksonville 32202

Established in 1963 in FL.
Donor(s): Francis B. Childress.†
Foundation type: Independent
Financial data (yr. ended 12/31/86): Assets, $2,554,213 (M); gifts received, $7,160; expenditures, $225,666, including $197,000 for 19 grants (high: $50,000; low: $1,000).
Purpose and activities: Emphasis on higher and secondary education, Protestant church support, youth agencies, cultural programs, and hospitals.
Limitations: Giving primarily in FL.
Officers and Trustees:* Miranda Y. Childress,* Pres.; Francis Childress Lee,* V.P.; Augusta L. Owens, Secy.; Lewis S. Lee,* Treas.
Employer Identification Number: 591051733

1269
Clabir Corporation Foundation ⌑
5400 118th Ave. North
Clearwater 34620-4315
Application address: P.O. Box 4545, Greenwich, CT 06830

Established in 1977 in CT.
Donor(s): Clabir Corp.
Foundation type: Company-sponsored
Financial data (yr. ended 12/31/87): Assets, $608,986 (M); gifts received, $95,000; expenditures, $454,373, including $444,285 for 39 grants (high: $300,000; low: $250).
Purpose and activities: Support for museums, youth and child welfare, and health.
Application information:
Initial approach: Proposal
Deadline(s): Apr. 30 and Oct. 31
Board meeting date(s): May and Nov.
Write: Henry D. Clarke, Jr., Trustee
Trustees: Donna L. Clarke, Henry D. Clarke, Jr., Robert H. Clarke, Wilmot L. Harris, Jr.
Employer Identification Number: 060972125

1270
Cobb Family Foundation, Inc. ⌑
1575 San Ignacio Ave., Suite 400
Coral Gables 33146 (305) 661-0044

Established in 1984 in FL.
Foundation type: Independent
Financial data (yr. ended 9/30/88): Assets, $4,834,538 (M); gifts received, $1,386,500; expenditures, $147,610, including $112,000 for grants (high: $41,250).
Purpose and activities: Support primarily for higher and secondary education; some support for community development.
Types of support: General purposes.
Limitations: Giving primarily in the Dade County, FL, area.
Application information:
Write: Diane McKay
Trustees: Charles E. Cobb, Jr., Christian M. Cobb, Sue M. Cobb, Tobin T. Cobb.
Employer Identification Number: 592477459

1271
George M. Cohen Foundation, Inc. ⌑
6821 Southpoint Dr., Suite 201
Jacksonville 32216

Established in 1984 in FL.
Foundation type: Independent
Financial data (yr. ended 11/30/88): Assets, $3,192,039 (M); expenditures, $129,788, including $116,870 for 13 grants (high: $50,000; low: $100).
Purpose and activities: Giving primarily for Jewish welfare and a home for the aged.
Limitations: Giving primarily in Jacksonville, FL.
Application information: Contributes only to pre-selected organizations. Applications not accepted.
Officers and Trustees: George M. Cohen, Pres. and Mgr.; Lawrence J. Dubow, Secy.; Samuel R. Shorstein, Treas.
Employer Identification Number: 592469069

1272
Marguerite Cole Foundation, Inc. ⌑
c/o Sarah Quisenberry
19 East Arch Dr.
Lake Worth 33467

Established in 1953 in FL.
Donor(s): Albert Cole.
Foundation type: Independent
Financial data (yr. ended 12/31/88): Assets, $1,215,061 (M); expenditures, $73,433, including $60,130 for 61 grants (high: $20,000; low: $50).
Purpose and activities: Support primarily for youth, community organizations, and churches.
Limitations: Giving primarily in CT and FL.
Application information: Contributes only to pre-selected organizations. Applications not accepted.
Write: Albert Cole, Pres.
Officers: Albert Cole, Pres. and Treas.; Robert Cole, V.P. and Secy.
Trustees: Margaret Jennings, Jean Van Buren.
Employer Identification Number: 066069629

1273
Community Health Association, Inc. ⌑ ☆
45 North Alabama Rd.
Lehigh Acres 33936 (813) 368-7070

Incorporated in 1986 in FL.
Foundation type: Independent
Financial data (yr. ended 6/30/89): Assets, $4,056,131 (M); gifts received, $19,135; expenditures, $172,967, including $31,039 for 17 grants (high: $19,135; low: $25).
Purpose and activities: Support primarily for social services, education, health associations, and a community fund.
Limitations: Giving primarily in Lehigh Acres and Lee County, FL.
Application information:
Initial approach: Letter
Deadline(s): None
Write: Joan Phillips, Admin.
Officers: John J. Foy, Chair.; Rev. Robert B. Doing, Vice-Chair.; Charleen Olliff, Secy.; James Jacob, Treas.
Trustees: Edward J. Heidelmark, Henry P. Manning, Jr., Margaret Petty, Douglas C. Trueman, Larry Turbeville.
Employer Identification Number: 591088536

1274
Conn Memorial Foundation, Inc. ▼ ⌑
220 East Madison St., Suite 822
P.O. Box 229
Tampa 33601 (813) 223-3838

Incorporated in 1954 in FL.
Donor(s): Fred K. Conn,† Edith F. Conn.†
Foundation type: Independent
Financial data (yr. ended 7/31/87): Assets, $15,738,709 (M); expenditures, $950,405, including $778,220 for 49 grants (high: $175,000; low: $1,000; average: $1,000-$20,000).
Purpose and activities: Giving primarily for education, health services and rehabilitation, and charities benefiting youth.
Types of support: Building funds, continuing support, deficit financing, equipment, matching funds, operating budgets, scholarship funds, seed money.
Limitations: Giving limited to the greater Tampa Bay, FL, area. No grants to individuals, or for endowment funds; no loans.
Publications: 990-PF.
Application information: Application form not required.
Initial approach: Letter or proposal
Copies of proposal: 4
Deadline(s): Submit proposal preferably in Nov. or May; deadlines Nov. 30 and May 31

Board meeting date(s): Jan. and July
Final notification: One month after board meeting
Write: David B. Frye, Pres.
Officers: David B. Frye,* Pres. and Treas.; George W. Ericksen,* V.P.; Mary S. Boisselle, Secy.
Directors:* Charles C. Murphy.
Number of staff: 2 full-time professional; 1 part-time professional.
Employer Identification Number: 590978713

1276
The Raymond E. and Ellen F. Crane Foundation ¤
P.O. Box 25427
Tamarac 33320

Trust established in 1949 in PA.
Donor(s): Raymond E. Crane,† Ellen F. Crane.†
Foundation type: Independent
Financial data (yr. ended 12/31/88): Assets, $3,210,246 (M); expenditures, $177,202, including $155,000 for 69 grants (high: $5,000; low: $500).
Purpose and activities: Giving for higher education and community funds; grants also for cultural programs, secondary education, health, and Protestant church support.
Limitations: Giving primarily in the southeastern states. No grants to individuals.
Application information: Contributes only to pre-selected organizations. Applications not accepted.
Officer and Trustees: George A. Owen, Mgr.; Alpo F. Crane, David J. Crane, Jr., Robert F. Crane, Jr., S.R. Crane.
Employer Identification Number: 596139265

1277
Alan H. Cummings Family Foundation ¤ ☆
c/o Bessemer Trust Co. of Florida
249 Royal Palm Way
Palm Beach 33480-4311

Established in 1987 in FL.
Donor(s): Nathan Cummings.†
Foundation type: Independent
Financial data (yr. ended 12/31/88): Assets, $971,402 (M); expenditures, $121,972, including $109,603 for 39 grants (high: $25,000; low: $250).
Purpose and activities: Giving primarily for Jewish organizations; support also for a geriatric center, health associations and medical research, the arts, and higher education.
Limitations: Giving primarily in West Palm Beach, FL.
Application information:
Initial approach: Letter
Deadline(s): None
Officers: Helene C. Gordon, V.P.; Ruth Cummings Sorenson, V.P.
Employer Identification Number: 592635536

1278
Dade Community Foundation
(Formerly Dade Foundation)
200 South Biscayne Blvd., Suite 4970
Miami 33131-2343 (305) 371-2711

Established in 1967 in FL.
Foundation type: Community
Financial data (yr. ended 12/31/89): Assets, $17,947,263 (M); gifts received, $5,902,995; expenditures, $1,601,360, including $1,308,941 for 305 grants (high: $62,147; low: $100).
Purpose and activities: Support for projects which provide an innovative response to a recognized community need but which do not duplicate other efforts; help an organization build internal stability; promise to affect a broad segment of the residents of Dade County; and exert a leverage or multiplier effect in addressing community problems to be solved. Areas of support include health, social services, the homeless and housing, civic affairs, education, and arts and culture.
Types of support: Equipment, land acquisition, seed money, research, general purposes, matching funds, publications, scholarship funds, special projects, technical assistance, annual campaigns, continuing support, endowment funds, internships, operating budgets, renovation projects.
Limitations: Giving limited to Dade County, FL. No grants to individuals, or for building or emergency funds, deficit financing, conferences, or consulting services; no loans.
Publications: Annual report, application guidelines, informational brochure (including application guidelines), newsletter.
Application information: Application form not required.
Initial approach: Letter
Copies of proposal: 1
Deadline(s): Submit proposal preferably in Nov.; deadline Dec. 1
Board meeting date(s): Feb., May, Sept., and Nov.
Final notification: 1st quarter of the year
Write: Ruth Shack, Pres.
Officers: Ruth Shack, Pres.; Frank Scruggs,* Secy.; Stanley Jaffee,* Treas.
Governors:* Sherrill Hudson, Chair.; John E. Porta, Vice-Chair.; and 17 other governors.
Trustee Banks: Barnett Banks Trust Co., N.A., Bessemer Trust Co. of Florida, Florida National Bank of Miami, Northern Trust Bank of Florida, N.A., Southeast Bank, N.A., SunBank Miami, N.A., Trust Co. of the South.
Number of staff: 1 full-time professional; 1 part-time professional; 1 full-time support; 2 part-time support.
Employer Identification Number: 596183655

1279
A. Darius Davis Family - W.D. Charities, Inc. ¤
5050 Edgewood Court
Jacksonville 32205-3699

Established in 1950 in FL.
Donor(s): A. Darius Davis.
Foundation type: Independent
Financial data (yr. ended 12/31/88): Assets, $1,518,871 (M); expenditures, $70,142, including $66,500 for 15 grants (high: $50,000; low: $100).
Purpose and activities: Giving primarily for higher education, tax education, medical research, and hospitals, and Christian institutions.
Limitations: Giving primarily in Jacksonville, FL.
Officers: A. Darius Davis,* Pres.; Robert D. Davis,* V.P.; Thomas W. Bishop, V.P. and Treas.; G.P. Bishop, Jr., Secy.
Directors:* Caroline H. Davis, Lee W. Davis.
Employer Identification Number: 596128575

1280
James E. Davis Family - W.D. Charities, Inc. ¤
5050 Edgewood Court
Jacksonville 32205

Established in 1949 in FL.
Donor(s): James E. Davis.
Foundation type: Independent
Financial data (yr. ended 12/31/88): Assets, $3,764,578 (M); expenditures, $135,654, including $130,650 for 19 grants (high: $50,000; low: $100).
Purpose and activities: Support for higher and other education, medical research, and health services.
Limitations: Giving primarily in FL.
Officers: James E. Davis,* Pres.; Thomas W. Bishop, V.P. and Treas.; A. Dano Davis,* V.P.; Robert D. Davis, V.P.; G.P. Bishop, Jr., Secy.
Directors:* Florence N. Davis, Dorothy D. Smith.
Employer Identification Number: 596128733

1281
M. Austin Davis Family - W.D. Charities, Inc. ¤
5050 Edgewood Court
Jacksonville 32205

Incorporated in 1950 in FL.
Donor(s): Milton Austin Davis.
Foundation type: Independent
Financial data (yr. ended 12/31/88): Assets, $1,034,031 (M); expenditures, $344,422, including $340,500 for 38 grants (high: $150,000; low: $500).
Purpose and activities: Giving primarily to higher education, youth agencies, and a community center.
Officers: Milton Austin Davis,* Pres.; Thomas W. Bishop, V.P. and Treas.; Robert D. Davis, V.P.; G.P. Bishop, Jr., Secy.
Directors:* Alice K. Davis, Charles P. Stephens, Sandra D. Stephens.
Employer Identification Number: 596128871

1282
The Tine W. Davis Family - W.D. Charities, Inc. ¤
4190 Belfort Rd., Suite 240
Jacksonville 32216

Incorporated in 1950 in FL.
Donor(s): Tine W. Davis, and others.
Foundation type: Independent
Financial data (yr. ended 12/31/88): Assets, $14,351,241 (M); expenditures, $1,180,270, including $762,425 for 117 grants (high: $100,000; low: $10; average: $1,000-$5,000).
Purpose and activities: Grants largely for higher education, church support, youth agencies, medical research, and health and social service agencies.
Limitations: Giving primarily in the southeastern U.S. No grants to individuals.
Application information:

Deadline(s): None
Board meeting date(s): 2nd Tuesday in Apr.
Write: Charitable Grants Comm.
Officers: Tine Wayne Davis, Jr., Pres.; Thomas W. Bishop, V.P. and Treas.; Robert D. Davis, V.P.; G.P. Bishop, Jr., Secy.
Director: Eunice Davis McNeil.
Number of staff: None.
Employer Identification Number: 590995388

1283
The Leonard and Sophie Davis Foundation, Inc. ▼
601 Clearwater Park Rd.
West Palm Beach 33401 (407) 832-6466

Incorporated in 1961 in NY.
Donor(s): Leonard Davis, Sophie Davis.
Foundation type: Independent
Financial data (yr. ended 12/31/88): Assets, $19,057,160 (M); gifts received, $4,153,024; expenditures, $1,796,949, including $1,779,250 for 74 grants (high: $350,000; low: $100; average: $1,000-$25,000).
Purpose and activities: Grants primarily for Jewish charitable, religious, and educational organizations, and for higher education; support also for the arts, community services, and health agencies and hospitals; limited giving to public interest groups.
Types of support: Annual campaigns, building funds, conferences and seminars, continuing support.
Limitations: Giving primarily in Palm Beach County, FL, and New York, NY. No grants to individuals.
Application information: Applications not accepted.
Board meeting date(s): As required
Write: Marilyn Hoadley, Pres.
Officers: Marilyn Hoadley, Pres.; Leonard Davis, V.P.; Sophie Davis, V.P.
Number of staff: None.
Employer Identification Number: 136062579

1284
The Arthur Vining Davis Foundations ▼
645 Riverside Ave., Suite 520
Jacksonville 32204 (904) 359-0670

Three trusts established: in 1952 and 1965 in PA; in 1965 in FL.
Donor(s): Arthur Vining Davis.†
Foundation type: Independent
Financial data (yr. ended 12/31/89): Assets, $114,004,000 (M); expenditures, $4,886,000, including $4,443,000 for 59 grants (high: $180,000; low: $1,100; average: $75,000-$125,000).
Purpose and activities: Support largely for private higher education, hospices, medicine, public television, and graduate theological education.
Types of support: Building funds, continuing support, endowment funds, equipment, fellowships, internships, land acquisition, matching funds, professorships, research, scholarship funds, capital campaigns, general purposes, lectureships, operating budgets, publications, renovation projects, special projects, technical assistance.
Limitations: Giving limited to the U.S. and its possessions and territories. No support for community chests, institutions primarily supported by government funds, and projects incurring obligations extending over many years. No grants to individuals; no loans.
Publications: Annual report, informational brochure.
Application information: Application form not required.
Initial approach: Letter
Copies of proposal: 1
Deadline(s): None
Board meeting date(s): Spring, fall, and winter
Final notification: 10 to 15 months for approvals; 8 months for rejections
Write: Max Morris, Exec. Dir.
Officer: Max Morris, Exec. Dir.
Trustees: Nathanael V. Davis, Chair.; Holbrook R. Davis, J.H. Dow Davis, Joel P. Davis, Maynard K. Davis, Atwood Dunwody, Rev. Davis Given, Dorothy Davis Kee, Mrs. John L. Kee, Jr., W.R. Wright, Mellon Bank, N.A., Southeast Bank of Miami.
Number of staff: 3 full-time professional; 2 part-time professional; 3 full-time support.
Employer Identification Number: 256018909

1285
George Delacorte Fund
11556 Turtle Beach Rd.
North Palm Beach 33408

Established about 1977 in NY.
Donor(s): George T. Delacorte, Jr., and others.
Foundation type: Independent
Financial data (yr. ended 12/31/88): Assets, $5,955,475 (M); gifts received, $739,963; expenditures, $115,852, including $26,700 for 38 grants (high: $5,000; low: $50) and $49,992 for foundation-administered programs.
Purpose and activities: Grants for cultural programs, youth, religious organizations, education, and health; program support annually to maintain and build public monuments in New York City.
Limitations: Giving primarily in FL and the New York, NY, area. No grants to individuals.
Application information: Contributes only to pre-selected organizations. Applications not accepted.
Officers: George T. Delacorte, Jr., Pres.; Valerie Delacorte, V.P. and Treas.; Albert P. Delacorte, Secy.
Employer Identification Number: 510202382

1286
Leroy E. Dettman Foundation, Inc.
4401 North Federal Hwy., Suite 201
Boca Raton 33431-5129 (407) 367-9811

Established in 1978 in FL.
Donor(s): Leroy E. Dettman.†
Foundation type: Independent
Financial data (yr. ended 10/31/89): Assets, $2,942,497 (M); expenditures, $226,774, including $78,422 for 109 grants (high: $6,000; low: $25) and $94,700 for 90 grants to individuals (high: $2,500; low: $500).
Purpose and activities: Giving primarily for scholarships to temporary employees of Personnel Pool of America and their children; support also for local charitable institutions.
Types of support: Employee-related scholarships, continuing support, annual campaigns, equipment, endowment funds.
Limitations: No grants for operating budgets, building or emergency funds, seed money, deficit financing, land acquisition, or matching gifts; no loans.
Publications: Application guidelines.
Application information: Application form required.
Initial approach: Letter
Deadline(s): Mar. 15
Board meeting date(s): Quarterly
Write: Gregory L. Dettman, Secy.
Officers: Douglas R. Dettman,* Pres.; Barbara Jane Fleming, V.P.; Gregory L. Dettman,* Secy.; Carolyn Rubin, Treas.
Trustees:* S. Barbara Dettman.
Number of staff: 1 full-time support.
Employer Identification Number: 591784551

1287
P. L. Dodge Foundation, Inc. ⌑
1351 East Tennessee St.
Tallahassee 32308 (904) 878-8780

Established in 1986 in FL.
Foundation type: Independent
Financial data (yr. ended 12/31/88): Assets, $1,500,513 (M); expenditures, $113,904, including $101,350 for 12 grants (high: $35,000; low: $1,750).
Purpose and activities: Support for Christian organizations and child welfare organizations.
Limitations: Giving primarily in FL.
Application information:
Initial approach: Letter
Deadline(s): None
Officers: Rev. Luther Jones, Pres.; Roderick Petrey, V.P.; James O. Plinton, Secy.; Stephen C. O'Connell, Jr., Treas.
Employer Identification Number: 591032805

1288
Elizabeth Ordway Dunn Foundation, Inc.
P.O. Box 016309
Miami 33101-6309 (305) 374-0100
Application addresses: c/o Ann Fowler Wallace, Grants Management Associates, 230 Congress St., Boston, MA 02110; Tel.: (617) 426-7172; c/o Becky Roper Matkov, 11320 S.W. 74th Court, Miami, FL 33156; Tel.: (305) 253-2713

Incorporated in 1983 in FL.
Donor(s): Elizabeth Ordway Dunn Charitable Lead Trust.
Foundation type: Independent
Financial data (yr. ended 12/31/88): Assets, $741,421 (M); gifts received, $496,329; expenditures, $659,062, including $578,700 for 24 grants (high: $47,500; low: $4,500).
Purpose and activities: Giving for conservation, ecology, wildlife, and other environmental concerns; some support for historic preservation.
Types of support: Special projects, seed money.
Limitations: Giving primarily in FL. No support for sectarian religious activities. No grants to individuals, or for capital purposes,

operating budgets, endowments, or deficit financing.
Publications: Informational brochure (including application guidelines), multi-year report, annual report.
Application information: Applicants are urged to submit concept papers to either of the application addresses; if the paper is reviewed favorably, a full proposal will be requested. Application form not required.
Initial approach: Telephone calls to program staff encouraged
Copies of proposal: 3
Deadline(s): Mar. 15 and Sept. 15
Board meeting date(s): May and Nov.
Write: Ann Fowler Wallace or Becky Roper Matkov
Officers and Directors:* Robert W. Jensen,* Pres.; Lynn F. Lummus,* V.P. and Secy.; E. Rodman Titcomb, Jr.,* V.P. and Treas.
Number of staff: 2 part-time professional; 1 part-time support.
Employer Identification Number: 592393843

1289
The Dunspaugh-Dalton Foundation, Inc. ⌑
9040 Sunset Dr., Suite 30
Miami 33173 (305) 596-6951

Incorporated in 1963 in FL.
Donor(s): Ann V. Dalton.†
Foundation type: Independent
Financial data (yr. ended 12/31/87): Assets, $21,751,033 (M); expenditures, $1,131,733, including $749,200 for 82 grants (high: $50,000; low: $300; average: $5,000-$20,000).
Purpose and activities: Grants largely for education, particularly higher education; social service and youth agencies; health organizations and hospitals; cultural programs; and civic groups.
Types of support: General purposes.
Limitations: Giving primarily in Dade County, FL, and Monterey, CA; some giving also in NC. No grants to individuals; no loans.
Publications: 990-PF.
Application information: Application form not required.
Initial approach: Letter
Copies of proposal: 1
Deadline(s): None
Board meeting date(s): Monthly
Write: William A. Lane, Jr., Pres.
Officers and Trustees: William A. Lane, Jr., Pres.; Sarah L. Bonner, V.P.; Thomas H. Wakefield, Secy.-Treas.
Number of staff: 3 part-time professional; 2 part-time support.
Employer Identification Number: 591055300

1290
Alfred I. duPont Foundation ⌑
1550 Prudential Dr., Suite 400
P.O. Box 1380
Jacksonville 32207 (904) 396-6600

Incorporated in 1936 in FL.
Donor(s): Jessie Ball duPont.†
Foundation type: Independent
Financial data (yr. ended 12/31/88): Assets, $14,679,403 (M); gifts received, $168,000; expenditures, $651,920, including $204,699 for 87 grants (high: $25,000; low: $30) and $388,916 for 295 grants to individuals (high: $20,496; low: $150).
Purpose and activities: Giving primarily to elderly adults in distressed situations requiring health, economic, or educational assistance; support also for higher education and medical research.
Types of support: Grants to individuals.
Limitations: Giving primarily in the Southeast.
Application information: Application form required.
Initial approach: Proposal
Copies of proposal: 1
Deadline(s): None
Write: Rosemary Cusimano, Asst. Secy.
Officers and Directors: Braden Ball, Pres.; J.C. Belin, V.P. and Treas.; Lillie S. Land, Secy.; R.E. Nedley.
Employer Identification Number: 591297267

1291
Jessie Ball duPont Religious, Charitable and Educational Fund ▼
225 Water St., Suite 1200
Jacksonville 32202-4424 (904) 353-0890

Trust established in 1976 in FL.
Donor(s): Jessie Ball duPont.†
Foundation type: Independent
Financial data (yr. ended 10/31/89): Assets, $138,051,073 (M); gifts received, $104,782; expenditures, $6,145,678, including $5,034,391 for 109 grants (high: $313,500; low: $500; average: $5,000-$100,000) and $310,000 for 7 loans.
Purpose and activities: Grants limited to those institutions to which the donor contributed personally during the five-year period ending December 31, 1964. Among the 350 institutions eligible to receive funds are higher and secondary education institutions, cultural and historic preservation programs, social service organizations, hospitals, health agencies, churches and church-related organizations, and youth agencies.
Types of support: Seed money, equipment, special projects, research, publications, professorships, scholarship funds, exchange programs, matching funds, general purposes, internships, technical assistance.
Limitations: Giving primarily in the South, especially FL, DE, and VA. No support for organizations other than those awarded gifts by the donor from 1960-1964. No grants to individuals, or, generally, for capital campaigns.
Publications: Annual report (including application guidelines), application guidelines, informational brochure, grants list.
Application information: Applicant must submit proof with initial application that a contribution was received from the donor between 1960 and 1964. Application form required.
Initial approach: Brief proposal
Copies of proposal: 1
Deadline(s): None
Board meeting date(s): Bimonthly beginning in Jan.
Final notification: Approximately 3 to 4 months
Write: George Penick, Exec. Dir.
Officers: George Penick, Exec. Dir.; Jo Ann P. Bennett, Exec. Secy.
Trustees: Mary K. Phillips, Chair.; George C. Bedell, Jean W. Ludlow, Northern Trust Bank of Florida, N.A.
Number of staff: 2 full-time professional; 2 full-time support.
Employer Identification Number: 596368632

1292
Eagles Memorial Foundation, Inc. ⌑
4710 14th St. West
Bradenton 34207

Established in 1946.
Foundation type: Independent
Financial data (yr. ended 5/31/88): Assets, $8,939,089 (M); gifts received, $483,035; expenditures, $687,829, including $539,554 for grants.
Purpose and activities: Grants to organizations through the Golden Eagle Fund, with emphasis on Eagle Village, Inc., the aged, nutrition, and public libraries. Grants to children of deceased Eagle servicemen and women, law officers, and firefighters, for student aid and medical and dental care.
Types of support: Student aid, grants to individuals.
Application information: Application form required.
Officers and Directors: James Bailey, Chair.; Martin Reinhard, Vice-Chair.; Thomas J. McGriff, Exec. Secy.; Russell E. Clark, Secy.; Joe Cook, Jack Crose, Martin Reinhard.
Employer Identification Number: 396126176

1293
Charles & Elizabeth Eaton Charitable Trust ⌑ ☆
c/o Southeast Bank, N.A.
920 Manatee Ave. West
Bradenton 34208 (813) 745-2700

Established in 1969.
Foundation type: Independent
Financial data (yr. ended 12/31/88): Assets, $1,003,463 (M); expenditures, $125,462, including $113,828 for 7 grants (high: $57,658; low: $2,500).
Purpose and activities: Giving primarily for a public library, higher education, and museums.
Types of support: Capital campaigns, building funds, general purposes.
Limitations: Giving primarily in Bradenton, FL. No grants to individuals.
Application information:
Deadline(s): None
Trustee: Southeast Bank, N.A.
Employer Identification Number: 596234709

1294
Horatio B. Ebert Charitable Foundation
P.O. Box 2058
Marco Island 33969

Established in 1985.
Donor(s): Lyda G. Ebert,† Robert O. Ebert.
Foundation type: Independent
Financial data (yr. ended 12/31/88): Assets, $5,812,610 (M); expenditures, $301,440, including $295,000 for 13 grants (high: $90,000; low: $2,000).

Purpose and activities: Support primarily for hospitals, higher education, child welfare, and Christian churches and organizations.
Types of support: Building funds.
Limitations: Giving primarily in NC, OH, KY, and FL.
Application information: Application form not required.
Deadline(s): None
Write: Robert O. Ebert, Trustee
Trustees: Adrienne Ebert, Robert O. Ebert, Viola R. Ebert, Cathy Harkless.
Number of staff: 1 part-time support.
Employer Identification Number: 592602801

1295
James Eblen Trust ⌑ ☆
1150 Eighth Ave., S.W., Suite 2302
Largo 33540

Established in 1973.
Foundation type: Independent
Financial data (yr. ended 05/31/89): Assets, $292,065 (M); expenditures, $348,589, including $340,538 for 8 grants (high: $315,000; low: $500).
Purpose and activities: Giving for higher and medical education.
Types of support: Scholarship funds, professorships.
Limitations: Giving primarily in the South. No grants to individuals.
Application information: Contributes only to pre-selected organizations. Applications not accepted.
Trustee: Frances R. Eblen Allen.
Employer Identification Number: 596562888

1296
The Echlin Foundation ⌑
c/o Engelberg, Cantor & Leone, P.A.
125 Worth Ave.
Palm Beach 33480

Trust established in 1960 in CT.
Donor(s): John E. Echlin, Beryl G. Echlin.
Foundation type: Independent
Financial data (yr. ended 11/30/88): Assets, $3,750,497 (M); expenditures, $207,783, including $202,500 for 15 grants (high: $70,000; low: $500).
Purpose and activities: Grants largely for higher and secondary education and hospitals and health associations.
Application information: Contributes only to pre-selected organizations. Applications not accepted.
Officer and Trustees: John E. Echlin, Dir.; Beryl G. Echlin, John E. Echlin, Jr.
Employer Identification Number: 066037282

1297
Jack Eckerd Corporation Foundation
P.O. Box 4689
Clearwater 34616 (813) 398-8318

Established in 1973 in FL.
Donor(s): Jack Eckerd Corp.
Foundation type: Company-sponsored
Financial data (yr. ended 07/30/89): Assets, $102,158 (M); expenditures, $599,777, including $552,179 for grants and $46,989 for 234 employee matching gifts.
Purpose and activities: Support for higher education, including pharmacy scholarships, health organizations, hospitals, hospices, ophthalmology, community funds, culture, and economics.
Types of support: Operating budgets, continuing support, annual campaigns, emergency funds, building funds, employee matching gifts, scholarship funds, program-related investments, special projects, capital campaigns.
Limitations: Giving primarily in areas with company locations, in AL, DE, FL, GA, LA, MS, NJ, NC, OK, SC, TN, and TX. No grants to individuals, or for endowment funds, deficit financing, equipment, land acquisition, renovation projects, special projects, research, publications, or conferences; no loans.
Publications: Annual report.
Application information: Application form not required.
Initial approach: Letter
Copies of proposal: 1
Deadline(s): None
Board meeting date(s): Quarterly
Final notification: 4 to 6 months
Write: Michael Zagorac, Jr., Chair.
Trustees: Michael Zagorac, Jr., Chair.; Harry W. Lambert, Ronald D. Peterson, James M. Santo.
Number of staff: 1 full-time professional; 1 part-time professional.
Employer Identification Number: 237322099

1298
Emanuel and Klara Edelstein Foundation, Inc. ⌑
3475 Prairie Ave.
Miami Beach 33140
Application address: 201 Alhambra Circle, Coral Gables, FL 33134; Tel.: (305) 446-8188

Established in 1979 in FL.
Donor(s): Emanuel Edelstein.
Foundation type: Independent
Financial data (yr. ended 07/31/89): Assets, $1,874,103 (M); gifts received, $200,000; expenditures, $300,540, including $293,933 for 104 grants (high: $100,000; low: $15).
Purpose and activities: Grants for Jewish organizations, with emphasis on religious education and temple support.
Application information:
Initial approach: Letter
Deadline(s): None
Write: Emanuel Edelstein, Pres.
Officers: Emanuel Edelstein, Pres.; Leopold Edelstein, V.P.; Klara Edelstein, Secy.; Josef Goldberger, Treas.
Employer Identification Number: 591932960

1299
Albert E. & Birdie W. Einstein Fund ⌑
P.O. Box 6794
Hollywood 33081
Application address: 4330 Sheridan St., Bldg. B, Suite 202, Hollywood, FL 33021

Established about 1967 in FL.
Donor(s): Albert E. Einstein,† Birdie W. Einstein.†
Foundation type: Independent
Financial data (yr. ended 6/30/88): Assets, $6,252,291 (M); expenditures, $418,353.
Purpose and activities: Giving primarily for hospitals and medical research, Jewish welfare, and a youth agency.
Limitations: Giving primarily in Broward, Dade, and Palm Beach counties, FL. No grants to individuals.
Application information: Application form required.
Deadline(s): None
Write: Harold Satchell, Pres.
Officers: Harold Satchell, Pres.; R.M. Gardener, V.P.; Joyce Boyer, Secy.-Treas.
Employer Identification Number: 596127412

1300
Ellis Foundation, Inc. ⌑
1201 6th Ave., West, Rm. 319
Bradenton 33505-7428

Established in 1984 in FL.
Donor(s): A.L. Ellis.
Foundation type: Independent
Financial data (yr. ended 6/30/87): Assets, $1,003,507 (M); gifts received, $553,050; expenditures, $533,145, including $78,530 for 14 grants (high: $50,000; low: $30).
Purpose and activities: Support primarily for higher education and a church.
Limitations: Giving primarily in FL. No grants to individuals.
Application information: Contributes only to pre-selected organizations. Applications not accepted.
Officers: E.F. Keen, Jr.,* Chair.; Carol E. Martin,* Pres.; Mary L. Toth, Secy.
Directors:* A.L. Ellis, Stanley G. Gibson, Jr., William Maxfield, M.D.
Employer Identification Number: 592471638

1301
Claudia S. Morse Evans Private Foundation, Inc. ⌑ ☆
c/o Laventhol & Horwath
777 South Flagler Dr., Suite 900W
West Palm Beach 33401

Established in 1987 in FL.
Donor(s): Jeanne and Irwin Levy Foundation, Inc., Claudia S. Morse.
Foundation type: Independent
Financial data (yr. ended 9/30/88): Assets, $916,215 (M); gifts received, $1,119,075; expenditures, $100,036, including $100,000 for 1 grant.
Purpose and activities: Initial year of operation, fiscal 1988; support for a geriatric center.
Limitations: Giving primarily in West Palm Beach, FL.
Application information: Contributes only to pre-selected organizations. Applications not accepted.
Officers: Claudia S. Morse Evans, Pres.; Alan Evans, V.P.; Stanley B. Brenner, Secy.; H. Irwin Levy, Treas.
Employer Identification Number: 592797822

1302
The David Falk Foundation, Inc.
c/o SunBank of Tampa Bay
P.O. Box 1498
Tampa 33601 (813) 224-1877

Incorporated in 1945 in FL.
Donor(s): David A. Falk.†
Foundation type: Independent
Financial data (yr. ended 12/31/88): Assets, $2,015,114 (M); expenditures, $156,995, including $115,031 for 36 grants (high: $10,000; low: $100).
Purpose and activities: Emphasis on child welfare, youth, social service agencies, higher education, hospitals, drug abuse programs, the handicapped, and the aged.
Types of support: Operating budgets, seed money, emergency funds, building funds, equipment, land acquisition, matching funds, publications, general purposes, renovation projects, research, special projects.
Limitations: Giving limited to the Tampa Bay, FL, area. No support for community funds or electoral or political projects. No grants to individuals, or for continuing support, annual campaigns, deficit financing, conferences, scholarships, or fellowships; no loans.
Publications: Program policy statement, application guidelines.
Application information: Application form required.
Initial approach: Full proposal
Copies of proposal: 1
Deadline(s): Submit proposal in Jan., Apr., July, or Oct.; no set deadline
Board meeting date(s): Feb., Apr., June, Sept., Nov., and Dec.
Final notification: 90 days after board meeting
Write: John J. Howley, Secy.-Treas.
Officers: Mary Irene McKay Falk, Chair.; Herbert G. McKay, Pres.; John J. Howley, Secy.-Treas.
Directors: David G. Kerr, John C. Peters, B.G. Smith.
Number of staff: None.
Employer Identification Number: 591055570

1303
Cecelia L. and Victor W. Farris Foundation, Inc. ⌑ ☆
Northbridge Ctr. One, 12th Fl.
West Palm Beach 33401

Established in 1986 in FL.
Donor(s): Cecelia Lipton Farris.
Foundation type: Independent
Financial data (yr. ended 12/31/88): Assets, $615,706 (M); gifts received, $155,000; expenditures, $200,350, including $200,000 for 2 grants of $100,000 each.
Purpose and activities: Support for a center for the arts and a hospital.
Limitations: Giving primarily in West Palm Beach, FL.
Officers and Directors: Cecelia Lipton Farris, Pres.; Elwyn Middleton, Secy.; Stanley Mitchell, Treas.; Aaron Katz, J.E. Morgan, Jr.
Employer Identification Number: 592667398

1304
J. Hugh and Earle W. Fellows Memorial Fund
c/o Beggs and Lane
P.O. Box 12950
Pensacola 32576-2950 (904) 432-2451
Loan application office: c/o The President, Pensacola Junior College, 1000 College Blvd., Pensacola, FL 32504; Tel.: (904) 476-5410

Trust established in 1961 in FL.
Donor(s): Earle W. Fellows-Williamson.†
Foundation type: Independent
Financial data (yr. ended 04/30/88): Assets, $2,524,640 (M); expenditures, $23,742.
Purpose and activities: To provide low-interest-rate loans to students of medicine, theology, nursing, and medical technology who reside in four northwest FL counties and who agree to pursue their professions in this area for five years after graduation.
Types of support: Student loans.
Limitations: Giving primarily in Escambia, Okaloosa, Santa Rosa, and Walton counties, FL.
Publications: Informational brochure (including application guidelines).
Application information:
Initial approach: Letter
Copies of proposal: 1
Deadline(s): Submit proposal preferably in Mar. or Apr.; deadline May 31
Board meeting date(s): Apr. and Dec.
Write: Gary B. Leuchtman
Officers and Trustees:* Rev. LeVan Davis, Chair.; C. Roger Vinson, Secy.; W.C. Payne, Jr., M.D., Milton Rogers, Harold N. Smith.
Employer Identification Number: 596132238

1305
Bert Fish Testamentary Trust ⌑ ☆
P.O. Box 46
Deland 32720

Foundation type: Independent
Financial data (yr. ended 9/30/88): Assets, $7,821,486 (M); gifts received, $9,000; expenditures, $739,711, including $532,502 for 8 grants (high: $213,500; low: $10,000).
Purpose and activities: Giving primarily for a hospital and health services; support also for higher education and social services.
Types of support: Building funds, equipment.
Limitations: No grants to individuals.
Application information: Contributes only to pre-selected organizations. Applications not accepted.
Officers and Trustees: W. Amory Underhill, Chair.; William W. Schildecker, Exec. V.P.; Carl Ward, Secy.; William Cox, Victor E. Fleishel, Frank Ford, Frank Gillingham, John E. Johns, William C. Keebler.
Employer Identification Number: 590588422

1306
Hilda M. Fisher Charitable Trust ⌑ ☆
c/o First National Bank of Palm Beach
255 South County Rd.
Palm Beach 33480

Foundation type: Independent
Financial data (yr. ended 12/31/88): Assets, $1,192,205 (M); expenditures, $9,701.
Purpose and activities: Support primarily for social services and health.
Limitations: Giving primarily in FL, with emphasis on Palm Beach and West Palm Beach.
Application information: Applications not accepted.
Trustee: First National Bank of Palm Beach.
Employer Identification Number: 596686054

1307
Florida Charities Foundation ⌑
Rollins College
Winter Park 32789

Established in 1959 in FL.
Foundation type: Operating
Financial data (yr. ended 7/31/88): Assets, $1,133,553 (M); gifts received, $50,000; expenditures, $38,481, including $26,685 for 39 grants (high: $10,000; low: $20).
Purpose and activities: Giving primarily for the arts and medical facilities.
Limitations: Giving primarily in central FL.
Application information:
Initial approach: Letter
Deadline(s): None
Write: John Tiedke
Trustee: SunBank, N.A.
Employer Identification Number: 596125203

1308
Jefferson Lee Ford III Memorial Foundation, Inc. ⌑
c/o Sun Bank Miami
9600 Collins Ave., P.O. Box 546487
Bal Harbour 33154 (305) 868-2630

Incorporated in 1950 in FL.
Donor(s): Jefferson L. Ford, Jr.†
Foundation type: Independent
Financial data (yr. ended 2/28/89): Assets, $2,198,355 (M); expenditures, $220,440, including $198,500 for 48 grants (high: $15,000; low: $1,000).
Purpose and activities: Support for health agencies, education, medical research, handicapped children, hospitals, and religious institutions.
Limitations: Giving primarily in FL.
Application information:
Initial approach: Letter
Deadline(s): None
Write: Herbert L. Kurras, Sr., Dir.
Officer and Directors: Doris King, V.P.; David P. Catsman, Herbert L. Kurras, Alfonsine Palermo, Anthony Palermo.
Employer Identification Number: 526037179

1309
Hamilton M. & Blanche C. Forman Christian Foundation ⌑
1850 Eller Dr., Suite 503
Fort Lauderdale 33316

Established in 1955 in FL.
Donor(s): Members of the Forman family.
Foundation type: Independent
Financial data (yr. ended 10/31/88): Assets, $1,244,962 (M); expenditures, $215,131, including $167,283 for 79 grants (high: $25,000; low: $25) and $1,750 for 1 grant to an individual.
Purpose and activities: Support for higher and secondary education, religion, youth, and health services.

Types of support: Grants to individuals.
Officers and Directors: Hamilton C. Forman, Pres.; Charles R. Forman, V.P.; Miles A. Forman, Secy.-Treas.; Doris D. Forman, Lucille Forman.
Employer Identification Number: 596131560

1310
Fort Pierce Memorial Hospital Scholarship Foundation ⌑
c/o Lawnwood Medical Center, P.O. Box 188
1700 South 23rd St.
Fort Pierce 33950 (305) 461-4000

Foundation type: Independent
Financial data (yr. ended 9/30/88): Assets, $3,776,680 (M); expenditures, $250,086, including $25,734 for grants and $176,731 for 26 grants to individuals (high: $15,000; low: $1,000).
Purpose and activities: Awards scholarships to local area students following a course of study in the health field.
Types of support: Scholarship funds, student aid.
Limitations: Giving primarily in St. Lucie County, FL.
Application information: Application form required.
Deadline(s): Apr. 15
Officer: David Riley, Secy.
Directors: Bruce Abernathy, John Bahl, C.R. Cambron, Frank H. Fee III, Philip C. Gates, Charles Hayling, Fred Johnston, Basil King, Virginia Sines.
Employer Identification Number: 590651084

1311
The Fortin Foundation of Florida, Inc. ⌑ ☆
c/o First National in Palm Beach Trust Dept.
255 South County Rd.
Palm Beach 33480-4113 (407) 655-9500

Established in 1986.
Foundation type: Independent
Financial data (yr. ended 12/31/88): Assets, $9,400,411 (M); gifts received, $150,000; expenditures, $254,168, including $190,050 for 48 grants (high: $50,000; low: $25).
Purpose and activities: Giving primarily for a college and a hospital; support also for social service and youth agencies, and Catholic churches and a diocese.
Limitations: Giving primarily in FL and MT. No grants to individuals.
Application information:
Initial approach: Letter
Deadline(s): None
Write: Mary Alice Fortin, Pres.
Officers and Directors: Mary Alice Fortin, Pres.; Susan Stockard Rawle, V.P.; L. Frank Chopin, Secy.-Treas.
Employer Identification Number: 592707197

1312
Claiborne and Ned Foulds Foundation
C & S Trust Co.
P.O. Box 927
Fort Myers 33902 (813) 433-6265

Established in 1981 in FL.
Foundation type: Independent
Financial data (yr. ended 7/31/88): Assets, $1,985,817 (M); expenditures, $153,220, including $125,567 for 5 grants (high: $58,000; low: $5,000).
Purpose and activities: Support for a medical research institute, higher education, the arts, social services, and youth.
Types of support: Building funds, equipment, renovation projects.
Limitations: Giving limited to Lee County, FL. No support for churches or religious organizations. No grants to individuals, or for administrative or operational expenses.
Application information: Application form required.
Initial approach: Letter
Copies of proposal: 1
Deadline(s): July 1
Board meeting date(s): 3rd quarter of year
Final notification: Dec. 31
Write: Jim Witte
Trustee: C & S Trust Co.
Number of staff: None.
Employer Identification Number: 596705105

1313
Frankel Family Foundation ⌑
c/o Benjamin Frankel
200 Admiral's Cove Blvd.
Jupiter 33477

Established in 1980 in FL.
Foundation type: Independent
Financial data (yr. ended 11/30/89): Assets, $68,136 (M); gifts received, $75,000; expenditures, $108,799, including $107,500 for 3 grants (high: $70,000; low: $15,000).
Purpose and activities: Support for Jewish concerns and education.
Application information: Contributes only to pre-selected organizations. Applications not accepted.
Trustees: Benjamin Frankel, E.J. Frankel, Leonard Frankel, William Frankel.
Employer Identification Number: 592136612

1314
Free Family Foundation, Inc. ⌑
100 Sunrise Ave.
Palm Beach 33480

Established in 1955 in WI.
Donor(s): Benjamin J. Free.
Foundation type: Independent
Financial data (yr. ended 12/31/87): Assets, $311,460 (M); gifts received, $76,738; expenditures, $154,240, including $151,946 for 84 grants (high: $25,000; low: $50).
Purpose and activities: Grants primarily for Jewish giving.
Limitations: No grants to individuals.
Application information: Contributes only to pre-selected organizations. Applications not accepted.
Officers: Benjamin J. Free, Pres.; Steven Free, V.P.; Florence Free, Secy.-Treas.
Employer Identification Number: 396077346

1315
Robert G. Friedman Foundation ⌑ ☆
76 Isla Bahia Dr.
Fort Lauderdale 33316

Established in 1977.
Donor(s): Robert G. Friedman, Eugenie S. Friedman.
Foundation type: Independent
Financial data (yr. ended 12/31/88): Assets, $1,161,292 (M); expenditures, $71,549, including $57,000 for 13 grants (high: $49,200; low: $100) and $2,000 for 2 grants to individuals of $1,000 each.
Purpose and activities: Giving primarily for an elementary school; minor support for grants to indigent individuals and general charitable activities.
Types of support: Grants to individuals, general purposes.
Application information: Application form not required.
Deadline(s): None
Write: Robert G. Friedman, Pres.
Officers: Robert G. Friedman, Pres.; Eugenie S. Friedman, V.P.
Directors: Jan Aspach, Mary Baske, Jennifer Hillis, Elizabeth O'Connor.
Employer Identification Number: 591726262

1316
A. Friends' Foundation Trust
9100 Hubbard Place
Orlando 32819 (407) 363-4621

Established in 1959 in FL as the Hubbard Foundation; merged in 1985 with A. Friends' Fund, Inc., into A. Friends' Foundation Trust.
Donor(s): Frank M. Hubbard, A Friends' Fund, Inc.
Foundation type: Independent
Financial data (yr. ended 12/31/89): Assets, $5,834,156 (M); gifts received, $49,913; expenditures, $322,421, including $275,000 for 70 grants (high: $120,000; low: $1,000; average: $3,900).
Purpose and activities: Support for private higher education, civic affairs, the arts, youth activities, religion, and health.
Types of support: Annual campaigns, building funds, capital campaigns, conferences and seminars, continuing support, emergency funds, equipment, general purposes, land acquisition, matching funds, operating budgets, renovation projects, special projects.
Limitations: Giving principally in central FL. No grants to individuals, or for endowment funds.
Publications: 990-PF, grants list.
Application information: Emergency funding available at all times. Application form not required.
Initial approach: Letter
Copies of proposal: 1
Deadline(s): Sept.
Board meeting date(s): Varies
Final notification: Oct.
Write: Frank M. Hubbard, Chair.
Officer: Frank M. Hubbard, Chair.
Board Members: L. Evans Hubbard, Ruth C.H. Miller.
Trustee: SunBank, N.A.
Number of staff: None.
Employer Identification Number: 596125247

1317
Charles A. Frueauff Foundation, Inc. ▼
307 East Seventh Ave.
Tallahassee 32303 (904) 561-3508

Incorporated in 1950 in NY.
Donor(s): Charles A. Frueauff.†
Foundation type: Independent
Financial data (yr. ended 12/31/88): Assets, $58,503,204 (M); expenditures, $3,203,877, including $2,824,500 for 195 grants (high: $50,000; low: $1,500).
Purpose and activities: Support for health, including hospitals, mental health, and other health services; welfare purposes, including services to children, the indigent, and the handicapped; and higher education, including student aid.
Types of support: Operating budgets, annual campaigns, emergency funds, building funds, equipment, endowment funds, scholarship funds, matching funds, general purposes, continuing support, capital campaigns, renovation projects.
Limitations: No grants to individuals, or for research; no loans.
Publications: Program policy statement, annual report.
Application information: Application form not required.
Initial approach: Proposal, telephone, or letter
Copies of proposal: 1
Deadline(s): Submit proposal between Sept. and Mar.; deadline Mar. 15
Board meeting date(s): May
Final notification: After annual meeting
Write: David A. Frueauff, Secy.
Officers: A.C. McCully,* Pres.; Harry D. Frueauff,* V.P.; Charles T. Klein,* V.P.; David Frueauff, Secy.
Trustees:* James P. Fallon, Karl P. Fanning, Margaret Perry Fanning.
Number of staff: 1 full-time support; 3 part-time support.
Employer Identification Number: 135605371

1318
The James G. Garner Charitable Trust ⌑
c/o Barnett Banks Trust Co., N.A.
9190 Biscayne Blvd.
Miami Shores 33138

Donor(s): James G. Garner.†
Foundation type: Independent
Financial data (yr. ended 3/31/88): Assets, $6,382,449 (M); expenditures, $322,144, including $212,900 for 44 grants (high: $55,000; low: $500).
Purpose and activities: Support primarily for medical research; grants also to educational and religious organizations.
Limitations: Giving primarily in FL and NC. No grants to individuals.
Application information:
Initial approach: Proposal
Write: Dennis Clum, Sr. Trust Officer, Barnett Banks Trust Co., N.A.
Trustees: John Michael Garner, Beverly Garner Graves, Barnett Banks Trust Co., N.A.
Employer Identification Number: 596824564

1319
General Development Corporation Foundation ⌑ ☆
1111 South Bayshore Dr.
Miami 33131

Established in 1987 in FL.
Donor(s): General Development Corp.
Foundation type: Company-sponsored
Financial data (yr. ended 12/31/88): Assets, $6,436 (M); gifts received, $140,000; expenditures, $134,054, including $134,054 for 88 grants (high: $75,000; low: $50).
Purpose and activities: Giving primarily to community funds; minor support for higher education, social services, health, and youth.
Limitations: Giving primarily in FL. No grants to individuals.
Application information: Contributes only to pre-selected organizations. Applications not accepted.
Officers and Trustees:* David F. Brown,* Chair.; Robert F. Ehrling,* Pres.; Harold W. Fenno, V.P.; David G. Ormsby, Secy.; Gerald A. Stillwell, Treas.
Employer Identification Number: 592769050

1320
Elizabeth Morse Genius Foundation
P.O. Box 40
Winter Park 32790 (407) 644-2900

Established in 1959.
Donor(s): Jeannette G. McKean.†
Foundation type: Independent
Financial data (yr. ended 12/31/88): Assets, $6,083,188 (M); gifts received, $10,408; expenditures, $439,226, including $370,500 for 29 grants (high: $342,000; low: $25; average: $25-$500).
Purpose and activities: Support for education, museums, and wildlife protection.
Types of support: Operating budgets.
Limitations: Giving primarily in Winter Park, FL.
Application information: Contributes only to pre-selected organizations; funds fully committed. Applications not accepted.
Write: Herbert W. Holm, Treas.
Officers: Hugh F. McKean, Pres.; Victor E. Woodman, V.P.; Harold A. Ward III, Secy.; Herbert W. Holm, Treas.
Number of staff: 1 part-time professional; 3 part-time support.
Employer Identification Number: 136115217

1321
B. Milfred Gerson Trust ⌑
c/o Gary R. Gerson
666 71st St.
Miami Beach 33141

Established in 1971 in FL.
Donor(s): Bertram Gerson,† B.M. Gerson Trust.
Foundation type: Independent
Financial data (yr. ended 12/31/88): Assets, $5,742,763 (M); expenditures, $720,607, including $624,290 for 141 grants (high: $133,490; low: $10).
Purpose and activities: Support primarily for Jewish welfare organizations, hospitals and health agencies, and higher education.
Trustees: Irving Cyphen, Gary R. Gerson.
Employer Identification Number: 596473286

1322
Elesabeth Ingalls Gillett Foundation ⌑
159 Via Del Lago
Palm Beach 33480

Established in 1980 in PA.
Donor(s): The Ingalls Foundation, Robert Ingalls Testamentary Trust.
Foundation type: Independent
Financial data (yr. ended 12/31/88): Assets, $5,388,334 (M); gifts received, $3,902; expenditures, $496,893, including $177,402 for 15 grants (high: $64,400; low: $500).
Purpose and activities: Grants largely for hospitals, social services, historic preservation, cultural programs, and higher education.
Limitations: Giving primarily in FL.
Application information: Contributes only to pre-selected organizations. Applications not accepted.
Officers and Director:* Elesabeth I. Gillett,* Chair. and Pres.; F. Warrington Gillett, Jr., Secy.-Treas.
Employer Identification Number: 232142065

1323
Alfred & Ann Goldstein Foundation, Inc. ⌑
682 Mourning Dove Dr.
Sarasota 34236 (813) 366-3833

Established in 1955 in NY.
Donor(s): Joseph I. Lubin.†
Foundation type: Independent
Financial data (yr. ended 12/31/88): Assets, $8,617,530 (M); gifts received, $1,830,000; expenditures, $687,284, including $674,875 for 45 grants (high: $250,000; low: $10).
Purpose and activities: Grants primarily for higher education; support also for health associations.
Limitations: No grants to individuals.
Application information: Application form not required.
Deadline(s): None
Write: Alfred R. Goldstein, Pres.
Officers and Directors: Alfred R. Goldstein, Pres. and Secy.; Ann L. Goldstein, Treas.; Cynthia Goldstein, Richard E. Goldstein, Steven R. Goldstein, Wendy H. Weckstein.
Employer Identification Number: 136033997

1324
The Good Gulfstream Education Foundation, Inc. ⌑ ☆
15310 Amberly Dr., Suite 300
Tampa 33647 (813) 972-5757

Established in 1986 in FL.
Donor(s): Gulfstream Housing Corp., Kenneth M. Good, Sr.
Foundation type: Independent
Financial data (yr. ended 9/30/88): Assets, $9,109,182 (M); gifts received, $102,050; expenditures, $126,123, including $107,750 for 9 grants (high: $100,000; low: $50).
Purpose and activities: Giving restricted to scholarships, endowed chairs, and other purposes of institutions of higher education.
Types of support: Fellowships, matching funds.
Limitations: Giving primarily in FL. No grants to individuals.
Application information: Application form not required.

Initial approach: Telephone or letter
Deadline(s): None
Write: James W. Apthorp, V.P.
Officers and Directors: Kenneth M. Good, Pres.; James W. Apthorp, V.P.; David C.G. Kerr, Secy.-Treas.; Norman Brownstein, Charles L. Knight, J. Larry Rutherford.
Employer Identification Number: 592795158

1325
Leo Goodwin Foundation, Inc. ⌑
c/o Borkson, Simon & Moskowitz
1500 N.W. 49th St., Suite 401
Fort Lauderdale 33309

Established in 1977 in FL.
Donor(s): Leo Goodwin, Jr.†
Foundation type: Independent
Financial data (yr. ended 10/31/89): Assets, $6,534,467 (M); gifts received, $1,400,000; expenditures, $222,814, including $217,000 for 11 grants (high: $100,000; low: $5,000).
Purpose and activities: Support primarily for education and cancer research; some support also for youth groups.
Types of support: General purposes.
Application information: Application form not required.
Initial approach: Proposal
Deadline(s): Allow sufficient time for review before end of fiscal year, Oct. 31
Write: Helen M. Furia, Secy.-Treas.
Officers: Francis B. Goodwin, Pres.; Elliot P. Borkson, V.P.; Helen M. Furia, Secy.-Treas.
Employer Identification Number: 526054098

1326
Gore Family Memorial Foundation
501 East Las Olas Blvd.
Fort Lauderdale 33302

Trust established in 1973 in FL.
Donor(s): R.H. Gore Trust.
Foundation type: Independent
Financial data (yr. ended 01/31/89): Assets, $14,841,836 (M); expenditures, $871,244, including $138,763 for 19 grants (high: $50,000; low: $144) and $584,238 for grants to individuals.
Purpose and activities: Aid to needy and handicapped; aid to needy restricted to Broward County, FL; scholarships restricted to Broward County residents, except for severely handicapped applicants.
Types of support: Student aid, grants to individuals.
Limitations: Giving primarily in FL, especially Broward County. No grants for general programs, capital expenditures, or scholarships for graduate studies (except for the handicapped); no loans.
Publications: 990-PF.
Application information:
Initial approach: Proposal or letter
Deadline(s): None
Trustees: George H. Gore, Robert H. Gore, Jr., Theodore H. Gore, SunBank, N.A.
Number of staff: 2 full-time support.
Employer Identification Number: 596497544

1327
K. W. Grader Foundation, Inc.
1925 Hermosa
Bartow 33830 (813) 533-1048

Established in 1976 in FL.
Donor(s): K.W. Grader.†
Foundation type: Independent
Financial data (yr. ended 10/31/89): Assets, $2,956,852 (M); gifts received, $886,255; expenditures, $296,454, including $292,990 for 67 grants (high: $25,000; low: $250).
Purpose and activities: Grants for health services, higher education, religious giving, and social services, including child welfare.
Types of support: General purposes.
Limitations: No grants to individuals.
Application information: Contributes only to pre-selected organizations. Applications not accepted.
Write: E.L. Grader, V.P.
Officers: E.L. Grader, V.P.; Lynn G. Johnson, Secy.; Richard E. Johnson, Treas.
Number of staff: None.
Employer Identification Number: 591708165

1328
The Greenburg-May Foundation, Inc.
P.O. Box 54-6119
Miami Beach 33154 (305) 864-8639

Incorporated in 1947 in DE.
Donor(s): Harry Greenburg.†
Foundation type: Independent
Financial data (yr. ended 12/31/89): Assets, $3,451,359 (M); expenditures, $170,586, including $151,517 for 53 grants (high: $51,900; low: $50).
Purpose and activities: Grants almost entirely for medical research, primarily in cancer and heart disease; some support also to aging, for hospitals, Jewish welfare funds, and temple support.
Types of support: Operating budgets, continuing support, building funds, research, endowment funds, scholarship funds.
Limitations: Giving primarily in southern FL, IL, and NY. No grants to individuals or for conferences; generally no grants for scholarships or fellowships; no loans.
Application information: Application form not required.
Initial approach: Letter
Copies of proposal: 1
Deadline(s): None
Board meeting date(s): Jan., Apr., July, and Oct.
Final notification: 1 to 2 months
Write: Samuel D. May, Pres.
Officers and Directors: Samuel D. May, Pres. and Treas.; Peter May, V.P.; Linda Sklar, V.P.; Isabel May, Secy.
Number of staff: 2
Employer Identification Number: 136162935

1329
Ben Hill Griffin, Jr. Foundation, Inc. ⌑
P.O. Box 368
Frostproof 33843-0368 (813) 635-2251

Donor(s): Ben Hill Griffin, Jr., Ben Hill Griffin, Inc.
Foundation type: Independent
Financial data (yr. ended 9/30/89): Assets, $191 (M); gifts received, $257,050; expenditures, $257,251, including $255,100 for 81 grants (high: $25,000; low: $100) and $2,014 for 2 grants to individuals (high: $1,800; low: $214).
Purpose and activities: Support for youth, health related organizations and education, including student aid.
Types of support: Scholarship funds.
Application information: Scholarship payments made directly to educational institutions on Aug. 10 and Dec. 10 of each year on behalf of the recipient.
Initial approach: Letter
Deadline(s): June 1 prior to the academic year the scholarship funds are required
Write: Ben Hill Griffin, Jr., Pres.
Officers: Ben Hill Griffin, Jr., Pres.; Ben Hill Griffin III, V.P.; John R. Alexander, Secy.; George W. Harris, Jr., Treas.
Employer Identification Number: 596198076

1330
C. V. Griffin, Sr. Foundation, Inc. ⌑
P.O. Box 126
Howey-in-the-Hills 32737 (904) 324-2881

Established in 1966 in FL.
Donor(s): C.V. Griffin, Sr.†
Foundation type: Independent
Financial data (yr. ended 12/31/87): Assets, $7,216,731 (M); gifts received, $14,500; expenditures, $408,034, including $312,100 for 27 grants (high: $100,000; low: $100).
Purpose and activities: Giving primarily for youth and religion; support also for hospitals.
Limitations: Giving limited to Lake, Polk, Volusia, Orange, and Brevard counties, FL, except grants to hospitals, clinics, and national health organizations represented in the five-county area. No grants to individuals.
Application information: Application form not required.
Initial approach: Proposal
Copies of proposal: 1
Deadline(s): Feb. 1 and Aug. 1
Write: Elsie R. Griffin, Chair.
Officers and Trustees: Elsie R. Griffin, Chair.; Alfred R. Schilling, Secy.; V. Mark Boland, C.E. Davis, W.H. Dial, J.J. McAuliffe, W.C. McGee, C. William Nelson, Charles Nelson, J.J. Parrish.
Employer Identification Number: 596166263

1331
The Griffis Foundation, Inc.
806 Anchor Rode Dr.
Naples 33940 (813) 261-7737

Incorporated in 1943 in NY.
Donor(s): Stanton Griffis,† Nixon Griffis.
Foundation type: Independent
Financial data (yr. ended 12/31/88): Assets, $7,313,308 (M); expenditures, $686,663, including $394,761 for 115 grants (high: $86,000; low: $29; average: $250-$3,000).
Purpose and activities: Emphasis on continuing projects in conservation, education, the humanities, health, and research in oceanographic fields; support also for religious purposes and social services.
Types of support: Operating budgets, continuing support, seed money, deficit

financing, professorships, fellowships, research, publications.
Limitations: Giving primarily in NY, CT, and FL. No grants to individuals, or for capital or endowment funds, annual campaigns, emergency funds, matching gifts, or conferences; no loans.
Publications: Program policy statement, application guidelines.
Application information: Application form not required.
Initial approach: Letter
Copies of proposal: 1
Deadline(s): None
Board meeting date(s): 10 times per year
Final notification: 2 months
Write: Nixon Griffis, Pres.
Officers and Directors:* Nixon Griffis,* Pres.; Heathea Nye,* V.P.; Hughes Griffis,* Secy.-Treas.; William G. Conway.
Number of staff: 1 part-time support.
Employer Identification Number: 135678764

1332
The Griffith Foundation, Inc. ¤
c/o Norman Smith, Esq.
663 N.E. 123rd St.
North Miami 33161

Incorporated in 1985 in GA.
Donor(s): C. Gordon Griffith.
Foundation type: Independent
Financial data (yr. ended 12/31/88): Assets, $1,464,697 (M); expenditures, $161,212, including $143,389 for 1 grant.
Purpose and activities: Support for general charitable activities, including a church and a university.
Types of support: Building funds.
Limitations: Giving primarily in FL. No grants to individuals.
Application information:
Initial approach: Letter or proposal
Deadline(s): The last day of the month preceding each board meeting
Board meeting date(s): Mar., June, Sept., and Dec.
Write: Richard S. Griffith, Sr., Pres.
Officers and Trustees: Richard S. Griffith, Sr., Pres.; Jack S. Griffith, V.P.; Norman B. Smith, Secy.; Robin Griffith, Treas.; C. Gordon Griffith, Donna L. Griffith.
Employer Identification Number: 581654371

1333
Ethel Grobstein Charitable Trust No. 2 ¤ ☆
c/o Northern Trust Bank of Florida, N.A.
700 Brickell Ave.
Miami 33131

Established in 1986.
Donor(s): Ethel Grobstein.†
Foundation type: Independent
Financial data (yr. ended 5/31/88): Assets, $2,067,447 (M); gifts received, $157,735; expenditures, $14,666, including $1,266 for 1 grant.
Purpose and activities: Support for a university.
Application information: Contributes only to pre-selected organizations. Applications not accepted.
Trustees: Stanley B. Richard, Northern Trust Bank of Florida, N.A.
Employer Identification Number: 596884183

1334
J. Erwin Groover Trust ¤
c/o Barnett Banks Trust Co., N.A.
P.O. Box 40200
Jacksonville 32203-0200

Established in 1984 in FL.
Foundation type: Independent
Financial data (yr. ended 9/30/88): Assets, $621,878 (M); gifts received, $77,001; expenditures, $188,172, including $182,500 for 12 grants (high: $30,000; low: $1,000).
Purpose and activities: Giving to agencies for the handicapped and for education and medical research.
Application information:
Deadline(s): None
Trustee: Barnett Banks Trust Co., N.A.
Employer Identification Number: 596781660

1335
Gulf Power Foundation, Inc. ¤ ☆
500 Bayfront Pkwy.
Pensacola 32501
Application address: P.O. Box 1151, Pensacola, Fl 32520-1151; Tel.: (904) 444-6245

Established in 1987 in FL.
Donor(s): Gulf Power Co.
Foundation type: Company-sponsored
Financial data (yr. ended 12/31/88): Assets, $117,320 (M); gifts received, $150,000; expenditures, $150,214, including $149,960 for 77 grants (high: $22,284; low: $350).
Purpose and activities: Support for higher education, cultural programs and a historic preservation society, health associations, and welfare, including a community fund.
Limitations: Giving primarily in FL. No grants to individuals.
Application information: Application form required.
Deadline(s): None
Write: Charles A. Lambert, Chair.
Officers: Charles A. Lambert, Chair.; Arlan E. Scarbrough, Vice-Chair.; Bonnie B. Sprinkle, Secy.; Warren E. Tate, Treas.
Trustees: Jacob F. Horton, Ben F. Kickliter, Earl V. Lee, Earl B. Parsons.
Employer Identification Number: 592817740

1336
Halmos Foundation, Inc. ¤ ☆
6400 N.W. Sixth Way
Fort Lauderdale 33309-6123

Established in 1983.
Donor(s): Peter Halmos, Steven Halmos.
Foundation type: Independent
Financial data (yr. ended 12/31/88): Assets, $2,381,149 (M); expenditures, $121,949, including $115,885 for 24 grants (high: $20,000; low: $70).
Purpose and activities: Support for education and social services.
Limitations: No grants to individuals.
Application information: Contributes only to pre-selected organizations. Applications not accepted.
Trustees: Peter Halmos, Steven Halmos.
Employer Identification Number: 592409780

1337
Harris Foundation
1025 West NASA Blvd.
Melbourne 32919 (305) 727-9378

Incorporated in 1952 in OH.
Donor(s): Harris Corp.
Foundation type: Company-sponsored
Financial data (yr. ended 06/30/89): Assets, $18,172 (M); gifts received, $250,000; expenditures, $273,183, including $23,000 for 5 grants (high: $6,000; low: $2,000) and $250,183 for 2,336 employee matching gifts.
Purpose and activities: Support for higher education, including an employee matching gift program, community funds, cultural programs, youth agencies, and hospitals.
Types of support: General purposes, operating budgets, continuing support, annual campaigns, building funds, research, professorships, scholarship funds, fellowships, employee matching gifts.
Limitations: Giving limited to areas of company operations. No grants to individuals, or for endowment funds; no loans.
Application information: Application form not required.
Initial approach: Proposal
Copies of proposal: 1
Deadline(s): None
Write: R.E. Sullivan, V.P.
Officers and Trustees:* John T. Hartley,* Pres.; R.E. Sullivan,* V.P.; Bryan R. Roub,* Treas.; G.I. Meisel.
Number of staff: None.
Employer Identification Number: 346520425

1338
John H. & Lucile Harris Foundation, Inc. ¤
(Formerly Harris Family Charitable Foundation)
5811 Pelican Bay Blvd., Suite 615
Naples 33963 (813) 597-8687

Donor(s): John H. Harris.
Foundation type: Independent
Financial data (yr. ended 12/31/89): Assets, $2,540,811 (M); expenditures, $244,199, including $210,370 for 74 grants (high: $100,000; low: $10).
Purpose and activities: Giving primarily for higher education, medical research, and religious institutions.
Limitations: No grants to individuals.
Application information:
Initial approach: Letter or proposal
Deadline(s): None
Write: John W. Hoyt, Secy.-Treas.
Officers: John H. Harris, Pres.; Lucile H. Harris, V.P.; John W. Hoyt, Secy.-Treas.
Employer Identification Number: 592600172

1339
Ben F. Harrison Foundation, Inc. ⌑
P.O. Box 1946
Pompano Beach 33061-1946

Established in 1979 in FL.
Donor(s): Harrison Industries, Inc.
Foundation type: Independent
Financial data (yr. ended 8/31/87): Assets, $89,781 (M); gifts received, $150,000; expenditures, $182,100, including $182,100 for 5 grants (high: $100,000; low: $100).
Purpose and activities: Giving primarily to Baptist churches and for higher education.
Officers: B.F. Harrison, Pres.; E.C. McGarity, Jr., Secy.-Treas.
Directors: Carol M. Harrison, Joan Harrison, Elton F. Jones.
Employer Identification Number: 630781485

1340
Nina Haven Charitable Foundation ⌑ ☆
555 Colorado Ave.
Stuart 33497-3013
Application address: c/o Guidance Office, Martin County High School, Stuart, FL 34994

Donor(s): Clyde Fair.†
Foundation type: Independent
Financial data (yr. ended 12/31/88): Assets, $1,667,525 (M); gifts received, $227,056; expenditures, $71,473, including $65,000 for 71 grants to individuals.
Purpose and activities: Giving for scholarships to local area high school students for higher education.
Types of support: Student aid.
Application information: Scholarship recipients must be graduates of Martin County, FL, high school system. Application form required.
Deadline(s): Contact high school guidance counselor for deadlines
Officers: Stuart Tenney, Pres.; Judy Weber, V.P.; Evans Crary, Jr., Secy.; Gordon D. Gaster, Treas.
Employer Identification Number: 136099012

1341
The John T. and Winifred Hayward Foundation Charitable Trust ⌑
c/o First National Bank of Clearwater
P.O. Box 179
Clearwater 33517 (813) 462-1337

Trust established in 1973 in FL.
Donor(s): John T. Hayward,† Winifred M. Hayward.†
Foundation type: Independent
Financial data (yr. ended 12/31/88): Assets, $4,929,971 (M); expenditures, $422,192, including $360,000 for 1 grant.
Purpose and activities: Support for medical research organizations and schools involved in the field of genetics, with emphasis on birth defects and inheritable diseases.
Types of support: Research.
Limitations: No grants to individuals, or for building or endowment funds, or operating budgets.
Publications: Application guidelines.
Application information: Contributes only to pre-selected organizations. Applications not accepted.
Write: L. Bernard Stephenson, V.P., First National Bank of Clearwater
Trustees: William R. LaRosa, M.D., Howard P. Rives, First National Bank of Clearwater.
Employer Identification Number: 237363201

1342
Harry J. Heeb Foundation ⌑ ☆
P.O. Box 3838
Orlando 32802
Application address: Sun Bank, N.A., P.O. Box 8, Leesburg, FL 32749; Tel.: (904) 326-4516

Established in 1977.
Foundation type: Independent
Financial data (yr. ended 5/31/89): Assets, $1,606,364 (M); expenditures, $279,310.
Purpose and activities: Giving primarily for medical and nursing education and youth agencies; support also for the handicapped and a Christian center.
Limitations: No grants to individuals.
Application information:
Initial approach: Letter
Deadline(s): None
Write: Karen Bent, Trust Officer, Sun Bank, N.A.
Trustees: Mabel H. Schwarze, SunBank, N.A.
Employer Identification Number: 596618905

1343
Gordon Henke Family Foundation, Inc. ⌑ ☆
1500 South Ocean Blvd., No. 801
Boca Raton 33432

Incorporated in 1987 in FL.
Donor(s): Gordon G. Henke.
Foundation type: Independent
Financial data (yr. ended 12/31/88): Assets, $1,041,285 (M); expenditures, $9,355, including $6,200 for 8 grants (high: $1,500; low: $250).
Purpose and activities: Support for a hospital, a high school, and Catholic giving, including a church, seminary, and welfare programs.
Limitations: No support for private foundations. No grants to individuals.
Application information:
Initial approach: Letter
Deadline(s): None
Write: Gordon G. Henke, Pres. and Dir.
Officers and Directors:* Gordon G. Henke,* Pres. and Treas.; Brian G. Henke,* V.P.; Mary E. Henke,* Secy.; Frank J. Daily.
Employer Identification Number: 391606928

1344
J. E. & Mildred Hollingsworth Foundation, Inc. ⌑
425 Worth Ave.
Palm Beach 33480

Established in 1966 in FL.
Foundation type: Independent
Financial data (yr. ended 12/31/88): Assets, $1,780,050 (M); expenditures, $113,666, including $92,793 for 51 grants (high: $24,404; low: $18).
Purpose and activities: Giving primarily for higher education, hospitals, and health agencies; support also for a family planning organization.
Limitations: Giving primarily in FL, with emphasis on Palm Beach.
Directors: Mrs. James M. Ballentine, William B. Cudahy, Mildred Hollingsworth, Wyckoff Myers, John Van Ryan.
Employer Identification Number: 596170607

1345
Holmes Foundation, Inc.
3111 Cardinal Dr., Suite B
Vero Beach 32963 (407) 231-6900

Incorporated in 1935 in NY.
Donor(s): Carl Holmes,† Mrs. Christian R. Holmes,† Jay Holmes.†
Foundation type: Independent
Financial data (yr. ended 12/31/88): Assets, $2,346,971 (M); expenditures, $133,751, including $104,500 for 15 grants (high: $40,000; low: $1,000).
Purpose and activities: Emphasis on arts, hospitals, and education.
Types of support: General purposes.
Limitations: Generally no support for exhibitions or one-time events.
Application information: Application form required.
Initial approach: Proposal
Copies of proposal: 1
Deadline(s): Mar. 15 and Sept. 15
Board meeting date(s): Apr. and Nov.
Final notification: Positive replies only
Write: Michael O'Haire, Secy.
Officers: John Peter Holmes,* Pres.; Jacqueline M. Holmes,* V.P.; Michael O'Haire,* Secy.; Richard B. Candler, Treas.
Directors:* Christian R. Holmes, Alvin Ruml.
Employer Identification Number: 131946867

1346
Samuel J. Holtzman Family Foundation, Inc. ⌑
2600 South Ocean Blvd., No. 1015
Palm Beach 33480

Established in 1953 in FL.
Foundation type: Independent
Financial data (yr. ended 12/31/88): Assets, $1,231,491 (M); expenditures, $59,417, including $56,245 for grants.
Purpose and activities: Support primarily for Jewish organizations.
Application information: Application form not required.
Initial approach: Letter
Deadline(s): None
Write: Samuel J. Holtzman, Pres.
Officers: Samuel J. Holtzman, Pres.; Frieda E. Holtzman, V.P.; Joseph A. Holtzman, V.P.
Employer Identification Number: 526036091

1347
Hope Foundation ☆
2335 Tamiami Trail, North, Suite 510
Naples 33940 (813) 262-2131

Donor(s): Philip M. Francoeur.
Foundation type: Independent
Financial data (yr. ended 12/31/88): Assets, $1,015,308 (M); gifts received, $5,000; expenditures, $56,034, including $52,184 for 37 grants (high: $15,500; low: $84).

Purpose and activities: Giving for mental health, higher and other education, social services, and cancer research.
Types of support: Annual campaigns, building funds, capital campaigns, grants to individuals.
Application information:
Initial approach: Letter
Deadline(s): None
Write: Philip M. Francoeur, Trustee
Trustee: Philip M. Francoeur.
Number of staff: None.
Employer Identification Number: 066088319

1348
William & Norma Horvitz Family Foundation, Inc. ☆
One East Broward Blvd., Suite 1101
Fort Lauderdale 33301
Application address: c/o Greenberg, Traurig, Hoffman, Lipoff, Rosen, & Quental, P.A., 1221 Brickell Ave., Miami, FL 33131

Established in 1986.
Donor(s): William D. Horvitz, Norma Horvitz.
Foundation type: Independent
Financial data (yr. ended 08/31/88): Assets, $758,355 (M); gifts received, $672,758; expenditures, $245,162, including $233,500 for 5 grants (high: $200,000; low: $1,000).
Purpose and activities: Giving primarily for a performing arts foundation; support also for social services.
Limitations: Giving primarily in FL.
Application information:
Write: Mr. Norman H. Lipoff
Officer and Trustees:* William D. Horvitz,* Mgr.; Wayne A. Gregory, Jr., Norma Horvitz.
Employer Identification Number: 592722308

1349
May K. Houck Foundation ⌑
c/o Holland & Knight, Attorneys-at-Law
400 North Ashley Dr., Suite 2300
Tampa 33602-4322

Established in 1955 in FL.
Foundation type: Independent
Financial data (yr. ended 4/30/88): Assets, $1,638,718 (M); expenditures, $101,342, including $75,000 for 6 grants (high: $24,000; low: $1,000).
Purpose and activities: Support for education, including early childhood education, social services, and for programs that improve the living conditions of the working poor; support also for a youth organization.
Limitations: Giving primarily in Sarasota, FL, and Rochester, NY.
Application information: Application form required.
Deadline(s): None
Write: John Germany, Esq.
Trustees: Hugh J. Knapp, F. Wesley Moffett, Jr., Earl F. Robison.
Employer Identification Number: 590777857

1350
Hirair and Anna Hovnanian Foundation ⌑ ☆
350 South Ocean Blvd., Apt. 12-B
Boca Raton 33432-6209

Established in 1986 in FL.
Donor(s): Hirair Hovnanian, Anna Hovnanian.
Foundation type: Independent
Financial data (yr. ended 12/31/88): Assets, $4,949,832 (M); expenditures, $405,301, including $384,500 for 8 grants (high: $250,000; low: $500).
Purpose and activities: Giving to a university and for Armenian churches.
Limitations: No grants to individuals.
Application information:
Initial approach: Letter
Deadline(s): None
Officers: Hirair Hovnanian, Chair.; Anna Hovnanian, Pres.; Armen Hovnanian, V.P.; Leela Hovnanian, V.P.; Siran Hovnanian, V.P.; Tanya Hovnanian, Secy.; Edele Hovnanian, Treas.
Employer Identification Number: 592714390

1351
Eric and Jessie Howell Foundation, Inc. ⌑
P.O. Box 5206
Lighthouse Point 33064 (305) 782-9250

Incorporated in 1979 in NY.
Donor(s): Eric Howell.†
Foundation type: Independent
Financial data (yr. ended 12/31/88): Assets, $1,884,990 (M); expenditures, $110,317, including $54,129 for 28 grants (high: $5,364; low: $35).
Purpose and activities: Giving to social service agencies, including programs for the aged.
Limitations: Giving primarily in Tompkins County, NY.
Application information:
Initial approach: Letter or proposal
Deadline(s): None
Write: Manley Thaler, Pres.
Officer: Manley Thaler, Pres.
Employer Identification Number: 161116060

1352
Huizenga Family Foundation ⌑ ☆
901 East Las Olas Blvd.
Fort Lauderdale 33301 (305) 524-8400

Established in 1987 in FL.
Donor(s): H. Wayne Huizenga.
Foundation type: Independent
Financial data (yr. ended 12/31/88): Assets, $1,427,813 (M); gifts received, $509,700; expenditures, $195,407, including $192,500 for 5 grants (high: $100,000; low: $2,500).
Purpose and activities: Giving primarily for social services; support also for a Christian foundation, the performing arts, and a chamber of commerce.
Limitations: Giving primarily in Fort Lauderdale, FL.
Application information:
Deadline(s): None
Write: H. Wayne Huizenga, Pres.
Officers and Directors:* H. Wayne Huizenga,* Pres.; Marti Huizenga,* V.P.; Steven R. Berrard,* Secy.; G. Harry Huizenga,* Treas.
Employer Identification Number: 650018158

1353
Jacksonville Community Foundation
112 West Adams St., No. 902
Jacksonville 32202 (904) 356-4483

Established as a trust in 1979 in FL.
Foundation type: Community
Financial data (yr. ended 12/31/89): Assets, $6,297,746 (M); gifts received, $3,327,077; expenditures, $2,130,132, including $1,874,183 for grants (average: $100-$20,000).
Purpose and activities: General charitable giving.
Types of support: Consulting services, emergency funds, endowment funds, internships, loans, matching funds, program-related investments, seed money, special projects, technical assistance.
Limitations: Giving primarily in northeastern FL.
Publications: Annual report (including application guidelines), newsletter, informational brochure, application guidelines, 990-PF.
Application information: Application form not required.
Initial approach: Letter
Copies of proposal: 1
Deadline(s): Dec. 1, Mar. 1, June 1, and Sept. 1
Board meeting date(s): Feb., May, Aug., and Nov.
Final notification: Feb., May, Aug., and Nov.
Write: L. Andrew Bell III, Pres.
Officers: Robert T. Shircliff,* Chair.; John D. Uible,* Vice-Chair.; L. Andrew Bell III, Pres.
Distribution Committee:* James L. Ade, Guy W. Botts, William K. Hatcher, David M. Hicks, Frances B. Kinne, Max Michael, Jr., Willard Oayne, Jr., Billy J. Walker, Courtenay Wilson.
Number of staff: 3 full-time professional; 2 part-time professional.
Employer Identification Number: 596150746

1354
The Jaharis Family Foundation, Inc. ⌑ ☆
801 Brickell Ave., Suite 1006
Miami 33131 (305) 577-3464

Established in 1986.
Donor(s): Michael Jaharis, Jr.
Foundation type: Independent
Financial data (yr. ended 9/30/88): Assets, $3,211,378 (M); gifts received, $1,500,600; expenditures, $132,247, including $83,277 for 20 grants (high: $30,000; low: $500).
Purpose and activities: Giving primarily for an historic restoration fund; support also to religious organizations, social services, and education.
Types of support: Building funds.
Limitations: No grants to individuals.
Application information:
Write: Michael Jaharis, Jr., Pres.
Officers and Directors:* Michael Jaharis, Jr.,* Pres.; Kathryn Jaharis,* V.P.; Mary Jaharis,* Secy.; Steve Jaharis,* Treas.
Employer Identification Number: 592751110

1355
Janirve Foundation ⌑
c/o First National Bank in Palm Beach, Trustee
255 South County Rd.
Palm Beach 33480
Application address: P.O. Box 2450, Asheville, NC 28802; Tel.: (704) 258-1877

Established in 1964 in FL.
Donor(s): Irving J. Reuter,† Jeannett M. Reuter.†
Foundation type: Independent
Financial data (yr. ended 12/31/88): Assets, $36,242,213 (M); gifts received, $6,029,712; expenditures, $2,045,760, including $1,756,902 for 72 grants (high: $125,000; low: $2,000; average: $25,000-$150,000).
Purpose and activities: Support for youth and child welfare, social services, hospitals and health agencies, and higher education.
Types of support: General purposes.
Limitations: Giving primarily in NC. No grants to individuals, or generally for operating budgets or endowments; no loans.
Application information: Applicants should contact Asheville, NC, office for application procedures. Application form required.
Deadline(s): Dec. 15, Mar. 15, June 15, and Sept. 15
Board meeting date(s): At least monthly
Final notification: Within 4 months
Write: James H. Glenn, Chair.
Advisory Committee: James H. Glenn, Chair.; John W. Erichson, Marion Johnston, Met R. Poston.
Trustee: First National Bank in Palm Beach.
Number of staff: 1 full-time professional.
Employer Identification Number: 596147678

1356
Jenkins Family Foundation, Inc. ⌑
250 Park Ave. South, 6th Fl.
Winter Park 32789

Established in 1985 in FL.
Foundation type: Independent
Financial data (yr. ended 11/30/86): Assets, $201 (M); gifts received, $653,153; expenditures, $657,213, including $653,300 for 3 grants (high: $605,000; low: $2,500).
Purpose and activities: Support primarily for higher education; grants also to an art organization.
Application information: Contributes only to pre-selected organizations. Applications not accepted.
Officers: William S. Jenkins, Pres.; William A. Walker II, Secy.; Alice M. Jenkins, Treas.
Employer Identification Number: 592642034

1357
George W. Jenkins Foundation, Inc. ⌑
P.O. Box 407
Lakeland 33802 (813) 688-1188

Incorporated in 1967 in FL.
Donor(s): George W. Jenkins.
Foundation type: Independent
Financial data (yr. ended 12/31/87): Assets, $10,933,069 (M); expenditures, $372,590, including $342,214 for 95 grants (high: $50,000; low: $200).
Purpose and activities: Emphasis on youth agencies, the handicapped, health, cultural programs, community funds, higher education, and social service agencies.
Types of support: Building funds, operating budgets, special projects.
Limitations: Giving limited to FL. No grants to individuals.
Application information: Application form not required.
Initial approach: Proposal
Copies of proposal: 1
Deadline(s): None
Board meeting date(s): Monthly
Final notification: 2 weeks after first Monday of the month
Write: Barbara Hart Hall, Pres.
Officers and Directors: George W. Jenkins, Chair.; Barbara Hart Hall, Pres.; Charles H. Jenkins, Sr., V.P.; John A. Turner, Secy.-Treas.; Jere W. Annis, Carol Jenkins Barnett, Clayton Hollis, Mark C. Hollis, Charles H. Jenkins, Jr., Howard Jenkins.
Number of staff: None.
Employer Identification Number: 596194119

1358
Alma Jennings Foundation, Inc. ⌑
2222 Ponce de Leon Blvd.
Coral Gables 33134

Established in 1966 in FL.
Foundation type: Independent
Financial data (yr. ended 12/31/88): Assets, $4,312,994 (M); gifts received, $2,054,933; expenditures, $152,013, including $116,375 for 27 grants (high: $15,000; low: $375).
Purpose and activities: Giving primarily for higher education, health, and Catholic support.
Limitations: Giving primarily in FL.
Application information: Applications not accepted.
Directors: Allan T. Abess, Jr., Jeffrey M. Fine, Frank W. Guilford.
Employer Identification Number: 596168955

1359
The D. Mead Johnson Foundation, Inc. ⌑
P.O. Box 549
Palm Beach 33480 (305) 655-8300

Incorporated in 1958 in DE.
Donor(s): D. Mead Johnson.
Foundation type: Independent
Financial data (yr. ended 12/31/87): Assets, $1,353,666 (M); expenditures, $136,211, including $64,535 for 26 grants (high: $36,300; low: $16).
Purpose and activities: Giving for higher education.
Limitations: Giving primarily in FL.
Application information:
Initial approach: Letter
Deadline(s): None
Write: D. Mead Johnson, Pres.
Officer and Director: D. Mead Johnson, Pres.
Employer Identification Number: 356021886

1360
The Calvin K. Kazanjian Economics Foundation, Inc.
220 Indian Harbor Rd.
Vero Beach 32963

Incorporated in 1947 in CT.
Donor(s): Calvin K. Kazanjian.†
Foundation type: Independent
Financial data (yr. ended 12/31/89): Assets, $3,118,740 (M); expenditures, $151,840, including $112,100 for 8 grants (high: $60,000; low: $2,200).
Purpose and activities: To increase man's understanding of economics and to disseminate such knowledge, utilizing various media.
Types of support: Seed money, special projects, conferences and seminars.
Limitations: No grants to individuals, or for capital or endowment funds, operating budgets, continuing support, annual campaigns, emergency funds, deficit financing, matching gifts, scholarships, fellowships, or general purposes; no loans.
Publications: 990-PF, informational brochure.
Application information: Application form not required.
Initial approach: General summary letter; if complex, by proposal
Copies of proposal: 1
Deadline(s): Submit proposal preferably Apr. 1 or Oct. 1; deadline Apr. 15 and Oct. 15
Board meeting date(s): June and Dec.
Final notification: 2 weeks after board meetings
Write: Lloyd W. Elston, Treas.
Officers and Trustees:* Mrs. Lloyd W. Elston,* Pres.; William A. Forbes,* V.P.; David W. Collins,* Secy.; Lloyd W. Elston,* Treas.; Michael A. MacDowell,* Managing Dir.; John Clizbe, Richard L. Elston, Thurston H. Graden, Lynn E. Greaves, Worth Loomis.
Number of staff: None.
Employer Identification Number: 060665174

1361
Keating Family Foundation, Inc. ⌑
4134 Gulf of Mexico Dr., Suite 10
Longboat Key 34228

Incorporated in 1967 in IL.
Donor(s): Edward Keating.
Foundation type: Independent
Financial data (yr. ended 12/31/88): Assets, $3,108,501 (M); expenditures, $135,201, including $98,890 for 99 grants (high: $15,000; low: $50).
Purpose and activities: Emphasis on hospitals, health and mental health agencies, child welfare, higher education, church support, and Jewish welfare funds; support also for a secondary school.
Limitations: Giving primarily in IL.
Application information: Contributes only to pre-selected organizations. Applications not accepted.
Officers and Directors: Edward Keating, Pres.; Arthur E. Keating, V.P.; Lee B. Keating, V.P.; Lucie S. Keating, V.P.; Elaine Mason, V.P.; Alan M. Berry, Secy.-Treas.; Robert Cottle, Joel Mogy.
Employer Identification Number: 366198002

1362
Kelly Foundation, Inc. ⌘
800 East Sugarland Hwy.
Clewiston 33440 (813) 983-8177

Established in 1956 in FL.
Donor(s): Kelly Tractor Co.
Foundation type: Company-sponsored
Financial data (yr. ended 12/31/88): Assets, $1,057,443 (L); gifts received, $27,070; expenditures, $91,030, including $73,350 for 40 grants (high: $12,000; low: $100) and $14,400 for 23 grants to individuals (high: $2,000; low: $250).
Purpose and activities: Support for Protestant churches, higher education, including scholarships, hospitals, and social services.
Types of support: Employee-related scholarships, student aid.
Limitations: Giving primarily in FL.
Application information: Application forms provided for scholarships to individuals; grants to organizations generally pre-selected.
Deadline(s): None for scholarships
Write: Robert Kelly, Pres.
Officers: Robert Kelly, Pres.; Lloyd G. Kelly, V.P.; Lillian V. Kelly, Secy.-Treas.
Directors: Eileen I. Kelly, Marjorie H. Kelly.
Employer Identification Number: 596153269

1363
The Ethel & W. George Kennedy Family Foundation, Inc. ☆
One S.E. 15th Rd.
Miami 33129-1205 (305) 374-2455

Established in 1968 in FL.
Donor(s): W. George Kennedy.†
Foundation type: Independent
Financial data (yr. ended 12/31/89): Assets, $13,000,000 (M); qualifying distributions, $650,000, including $650,000 for grants.
Purpose and activities: Support primarily for organizations which 1) provide or support care, rehabilitation, and welfare for children, both physically and psychologically; 2) conduct or provide services for research, education, and medical equipment in the areas of heart, brain and eye diseases, diabetes, and cancer; and 3) conduct or provide services for the rehabilitation and education of the newly handicapped and their families.
Limitations: Giving limited to Miami, FL. No grants to individuals.
Application information: Application form required.
Initial approach: Proposal
Copies of proposal: 11
Deadline(s): Jan. 1, May 1, and Sept. 1
Board meeting date(s): Jan., June, and Oct.
Write: Wayne G. Kennedy, Pres.
Officers and Directors:* Wayne G. Kennedy,* Pres.; Kathleen P. Kennedy,* Secy.; Kendel Kennedy Dobkin, Karen Kennedy Herterich, William M. Kennedy, Kimberly Kennedy Mulcahy.
Number of staff: None.
Employer Identification Number: 596204880

1364
The Edward & Lucille Kimmel Foundation, Inc. ⌘
625 North Flagler Dr.
West Palm Beach 33401-4024

Established in 1983 in FL.
Foundation type: Independent
Financial data (yr. ended 12/31/88): Assets, $1,406,863 (M); gifts received, $216,666; expenditures, $35,507, including $28,000 for 6 grants (high: $10,000; low: $1,000).
Purpose and activities: Support for the arts, health, education, and Jewish giving.
Limitations: Giving primarily in West Palm Beach, FL, and New York, NY.
Application information: Contributes only to pre-selected organizations. Applications not accepted.
Write: Edward A. Kimmel, Pres.
Officer and Trustees: Edward A. Kimmel, Pres.; Joan K. Eigen, Alan Kimmel, Lucille Kimmel.
Employer Identification Number: 592380662

1365
The Thomas M. and Irene B. Kirbo Charitable Trust ⌘
1111 Barnett Bank Bldg.
Jacksonville 32202 (904) 354-7212

Established in 1959 in GA.
Donor(s): Thomas M. Kirbo,† Irene B. Kirbo.
Foundation type: Independent
Financial data (yr. ended 09/30/89): Assets, $24,460,715 (M); expenditures, $12,743,395, including $1,131,484 for 24 grants (high: $320,390; low: $5,000).
Purpose and activities: Giving primarily for religion, hospitals, universities, and youth.
Limitations: No grants to individuals.
Application information: Application form required.
Deadline(s): None
Write: R. Murray Jenks, Pres.
Officers and Trustees:* Charles H. Kirbo,* Chair.; R. Murray Jenks,* Pres.; John T. Jenks, Bruce W. Kirbo.
Employer Identification Number: 592151720

1366
Klurman Foundation, Inc. ⌘
2745 N.W. 62nd St., Suite A
Fort Lauderdale 33309-1703

Established in 1984 in FL.
Donor(s): Samuel A. Klurman, Ganot Corp.
Foundation type: Independent
Financial data (yr. ended 03/31/89): Assets, $1,043,444 (M); gifts received, $100,000; expenditures, $152,077, including $149,150 for 66 grants (high: $30,000; low: $50).
Purpose and activities: Support primarily for Jewish organizations.
Limitations: No grants to individuals.
Application information: Contributes only to pre-selected organizations. Applications not accepted.
Officers and Directors:* Samuel A. Klurman,* Pres.; Sisel Klurman,* V.P.; Harvey L. Lichtman, Secy.-Treas.; Samuel Oberfest.
Employer Identification Number: 592532272

1367
Koch Foundation, Inc. ▼
2830 N.W. 41st St., Suite H
Gainesville 32606 (904) 373-7491

Incorporated in 1979 in FL.
Donor(s): Carl E. Koch,† Paula Koch.
Foundation type: Independent
Financial data (yr. ended 03/31/89): Assets, $90,184,795 (M); expenditures, $5,076,442, including $4,689,200 for 220 grants (high: $200,000; low: $1,500; average: $4,000-$50,000).
Purpose and activities: Grants only for Roman Catholic religious organizations that propagate the faith.
Types of support: Operating budgets, building funds, equipment, land acquisition, special projects.
Limitations: No grants to individuals, or for endowment funds, deficit financing, emergency funds, or scholarships or fellowships; no loans.
Publications: Annual report, program policy statement, application guidelines.
Application information: Proposals considered at Feb. meeting. Application form required.
Initial approach: Letter
Copies of proposal: 1
Deadline(s): Dec. 1
Board meeting date(s): Sept. and last Wednesday of Feb.
Final notification: 3 months after board meeting
Write: Richard A. DeGraff, Exec. Dir.
Officers and Directors:* Carolyn L. Bomberger,* Chair., Pres., and Treas.; Cletus Humm,* V.P. and Secy.; Paula Koch,* V.P.; Richard A. DeGraff,* Exec. Dir.; Dorothy C. Bomberger, William A. Bomberger, Barbara Humm, Inge Vraney.
Number of staff: 2 full-time professional; 1 part-time support.
Employer Identification Number: 591885997

1368
Koger Foundation ⌘
P.O. Box 4520
Jacksonville 32207 (904) 396-4811

Established in 1977 in FL.
Donor(s): Koger Properties, Inc., The Koger Co.
Foundation type: Independent
Financial data (yr. ended 12/31/88): Assets, $273,973 (M); gifts received, $144,000; expenditures, $557,569, including $557,117 for 120 grants (high: $291,250; low: $25).
Purpose and activities: Support primarily for cultural programs and education.
Limitations: Giving primarily in areas of company operations, including FL, GA, SC, NC, VA, TN, AR, OK, TX, and AL.
Application information: Application form required.
Initial approach: Letter
Copies of proposal: 1
Deadline(s): None
Board meeting date(s): Quarterly
Write: Celeste K. Hampton, Trustee
Trustees: Celeste K. Hampton, Nancy T. Koger, Pamela K. Moore.
Number of staff: None.
Employer Identification Number: 591757872

1369
Sidney Kohl Foundation, Inc. ⌑
304 Royal Poinciana Plaza
Palm Beach 33480

Incorporated in 1972 in WI.
Donor(s): Sidney Kohl.
Foundation type: Independent
Financial data (yr. ended 06/30/89): Assets, $2,784,226 (M); gifts received, $55,500; expenditures, $189,953, including $187,358 for 39 grants (high: $80,000; low: $25).
Purpose and activities: Grants primarily for Jewish welfare funds; some support for other charitable and educational organizations.
Limitations: No grants to individuals.
Publications: 990-PF.
Application information: Contributes only to pre-selected organizations. Applications not accepted.
Officers and Directors:* Sidney Kohl,* Pres.; Mary Kohl,* V.P.; Ian Merritt, Secy.-Treas.; Dorothy Kohl.
Employer Identification Number: 237206459

1370
The William A. Krueger Charitable Trust ⌑ ☆
613 N.E. 17th Terr.
Fort Lauderdale 33304 (305) 462-1660

Foundation type: Independent
Financial data (yr. ended 11/30/88): Assets, $1,703,906 (M); expenditures, $106,140, including $103,000 for 21 grants (high: $50,000; low: $500).
Purpose and activities: Support primarily for hospitals and health, higher education, social services, including a community fund, and Christian organizations.
Limitations: Giving primarily in Fort Lauderdale, FL and NC.
Application information: Contributes only to pre-selected organizations. Applications not accepted.
Write: William A. Krueger, Trustee
Trustees: Evelyn J. Krueger, William A. Krueger.
Employer Identification Number: 596872412

1371
The Kugelman Foundation, Inc. ⌑
4300 Bayou Blvd., Suite 21
Pensacola 32503-2614
Application address: P.O. Box 1630, Pensacola, FL 32597; Tel.: (904) 433-3151

Established in 1961 in FL.
Donor(s): D. Jack Kugelman, Standard Distributing, Inc., United Distributors, Richmond Distributors, Inc.
Foundation type: Independent
Financial data (yr. ended 12/31/88): Assets, $1,590,280 (M); gifts received, $157,628; expenditures, $96,798, including $94,445 for 29 grants (high: $25,000; low: $100).
Purpose and activities: Support for Jewish giving, child development, health organizations, and general charities.
Limitations: Giving primarily in FL.
Application information: Application form not required.
Deadline(s): None
Write: D. Jack Kugelman, Chair.
Officer: D. Jack Kugelman, Chair.
Employer Identification Number: 596177695

1372
The Landegger Charitable Foundation, Inc. ⌑
P.O. Box 1266
New Smyrna Beach 320701266

Established in 1975.
Foundation type: Independent
Financial data (yr. ended 10/31/88): Assets, $7,890,544 (M); expenditures, $384,504, including $332,668 for 39 grants (high: $190,000; low: $200).
Purpose and activities: Grants primarily for higher education and hospitals.
Publications: 990-PF.
Application information: Application form not required.
Deadline(s): None
Write: John F. Bolt, Secy.
Officers and Directors:* Lena Landegger,* Pres.; George Landegger,* V.P.; John F. Bolt, Secy.; Carl Landegger,* Treas.
Employer Identification Number: 510180544

1373
Larsh Foundation Charitable Trust ⌑
15485 Eagle Nest Ln.
Miami Lakes 33014

Established in 1980.
Foundation type: Independent
Financial data (yr. ended 2/28/88): Assets, $3,688,744 (M); expenditures, $145,155.
Purpose and activities: Giving for Protestant religious groups and marine research.
Limitations: Giving primarily in FL.
Officer: Dana P. Brigham, Mgr.
Employer Identification Number: 591946342

1374
Forrest C. Lattner Foundation, Inc. ⌑
1045 East Atlantic Ave.
Delray Beach 33483 (407) 278-3781

Incorporated in 1981 in FL.
Donor(s): Mrs. Forrest C. Lattner, Forrest C. Lattner,† Mrs. Francis Lattner.
Foundation type: Independent
Financial data (yr. ended 12/31/88): Assets, $5,504,542 (M); gifts received, $159,550; expenditures, $249,283, including $225,000 for 28 grants (high: $25,000; low: $1,000).
Purpose and activities: Support for health associations, hospitals, and churches.
Application information: Application form not required.
Deadline(s): None
Write: Susan L. Hollenbeck, Pres.
Officers and Trustees:* Martha L. Connelly, Chair.; Susan L. Hollenbeck, Pres. and Secy.; Bazil J. Zaloom, Exec. Dir. and Treas.
Employer Identification Number: 592147657

1375
Charles A. Lauffer Trust ⌑
P.O. Box 11388
St. Petersburg 33733-1388

Established in 1945 in FL.
Foundation type: Independent
Financial data (yr. ended 08/31/89): Assets, $2,433,746 (M); expenditures, $57,605, including $36,041 for 18 grants (high: $5,432; low: $900).
Purpose and activities: Support primarily for youth, community organizations and social services.
Limitations: Giving primarily in FL.
Application information: Contributes only to pre-selected organizations. Applications not accepted.
Trustees: Richard A. Eagle, Citizens & Southern Trust Co.
Employer Identification Number: 596121126

1376
Robert O. Law Foundation ⌑
8725 East Henderson Terr.
Inverness 32650

Incorporated in 1958 in FL.
Donor(s): Robert O. Law.†
Foundation type: Independent
Financial data (yr. ended 12/31/88): Assets, $2,932,728 (M); gifts received, $364,524; expenditures, $146,911, including $69,700 for 17 grants (high: $10,000; low: $700).
Purpose and activities: Giving for youth, health agencies, and hospitals; some support for education.
Limitations: Giving limited to Broward County, FL. No grants to individuals.
Application information: Contributes only to pre-selected organizations. Applications not accepted.
Write: William A. Thacher, V.P.
Officers and Trustees: Robert O. Law III, Pres.; William A. Thacher, V.P.; William F. Leonard, Secy.-Treas.; Leslie Law Fitzgerald, Mary Jane Law, Mary K. Law.
Employer Identification Number: 590914810

1377
The Charles N. & Eleanor Knight Leigh Foundation, Inc.
c/o Sullivan, Admire & Sullivan
2511 Ponce de Leon Blvd., Suite 320
Coral Gables 33134-6084 (305) 444-6121

Established in 1985 in FL.
Donor(s): Eleanor Knight Leigh.†
Foundation type: Independent
Financial data (yr. ended 04/30/89): Assets, $1,383,094 (M); expenditures, $82,858, including $59,900 for 9 grants (high: $12,500; low: $2,400; average: $2,400-$12,500).
Purpose and activities: Emphasis on youth organizations; support also for a museum of science and technology, child welfare, education, the environment, family planning, the handicapped and disadvantaged, and community development.
Limitations: Giving primarily in Dade County, FL.
Application information: Application form not required.
Initial approach: Proposal
Copies of proposal: 1
Deadline(s): None
Write: Jack G. Admire, Pres.
Officers: Jack G. Admire, Pres.; Marilyn West, V.P.; John C. Sullivan, Jr., Secy.-Treas.
Director: Ruth C. Admire.
Number of staff: 1 part-time support.
Employer Identification Number: 592562596

1378
Harry P. Leu Foundation ⌑
P.O. Box 2869
Orlando 32802 (407) 898-2293

Established in 1953 in FL.
Donor(s): Harry P. Leu.†
Foundation type: Independent
Financial data (yr. ended 10/31/89): Assets, $1,818,341 (M); expenditures, $159,192, including $150,000 for 30 grants (high: $55,000; low: $1,000; average: $1,000-$3,000).
Purpose and activities: Giving primarily for youth agencies, business education, and the arts.
Types of support: Capital campaigns, operating budgets.
Limitations: Giving primarily in central FL. No grants to individuals, or for scholarships, fellowships, or matching gifts; no loans.
Application information:
Initial approach: Letter
Deadline(s): Sept. 15
Board meeting date(s): Oct.
Final notification: Oct.
Write: Joseph P. Stine, Trustee
Trustees: Jon C. Stine, Joseph P. Stine.
Number of staff: None.
Employer Identification Number: 596144721

1379
Linder Family Private Foundation Trust ⌑ ☆
4717 South Florida Ave.
P.O. Box 5330
Lakeland 33807

Donor(s): P. Scott Linder.
Foundation type: Independent
Financial data (yr. ended 12/31/88): Assets, $27,166 (M); gifts received, $179,300; expenditures, $154,169, including $153,475 for 61 grants (high: $17,500; low: $100).
Purpose and activities: Support for Protestant organizations, education, youth, and general charitable giving.
Limitations: Giving primarily in FL.
Trustee: P. Scott Linder.
Employer Identification Number: 591867592

1380
The Link Foundation ⌑
5606 Old Dixie Hwy.
Fort Pierce 34946

Trust established in 1953 in NY.
Donor(s): Edwin A. Link,† Mrs. Edwin A. Link, Link Division of CAE.
Foundation type: Independent
Financial data (yr. ended 6/30/88): Assets, $3,072,310 (M); gifts received, $1,585; expenditures, $222,165, including $185,700 for 15 grants (high: $50,000; low: $3,000).
Purpose and activities: Sponsors research and development of all facets of aviation, space technology, and oceanography, and supports development of energy resources and conservation.
Types of support: Continuing support, fellowships, research, seed money.
Limitations: No grants to individuals.
Publications: Multi-year report, informational brochure (including application guidelines), 990-PF.
Application information: Application form required.
Initial approach: Letter
Copies of proposal: 1
Deadline(s): Nov. 1
Board meeting date(s): June and Jan.
Write: Marilyn C. Link, Secy.-Treas.
Officers and Trustees: Lloyd L. Kelly, Chair.; Marilyn C. Link, Secy.-Treas.; Richard W. Couper, William F. Schmied, Joseph F. Shea.
Technical Assistance Board: William M. Link, J.B. Mooney, Jr., Robert L. Sproull, Brian Thompson.
Number of staff: 1 part-time support.
Employer Identification Number: 536011109

1381
Lost Tree Charitable Foundation, Inc. ☆
11555 Lost Tree Way
North Palm Beach 33408 (407) 622-3780

Incorporated in 1982 in FL.
Foundation type: Independent
Financial data (yr. ended 12/31/89): Assets, $1,598,998 (M); gifts received, $192,811; expenditures, $182,302, including $146,354 for 30 grants (high: $14,546; low: $500).
Purpose and activities: Giving primarily for family and social services, including programs for rehabilitation, alcohol and drug abuse, and the disabled; support also for higher, medical, early childhood, and other education and health services.
Types of support: General purposes.
Limitations: Giving limited to Palm Beach and Martin Counties. No grants to individuals.
Application information: Application form not required.
Initial approach: Letter
Deadline(s): None
Write: Robert C. Porter, Pres., or Pamela M. Rue, Exec. Secy.
Officers: W.W. McCallum, Hon. Chair.; Robert C. Porter, Pres.; Mrs. John T. Connor, V.P.; Selim N. Tideman, Jr., V.P.; William N. Poundstone, Secy.; Robert A. Waidner, Treas.
Number of staff: 1 full-time professional.
Employer Identification Number: 592104920

1382
The Joe and Emily Lowe Foundation, Inc. ▼
249 Royal Palm Way
Palm Beach 33480 (407) 655-7001

Incorporated in 1949 in NY.
Donor(s): Joe Lowe,† Emily Lowe.†
Foundation type: Independent
Financial data (yr. ended 12/31/88): Assets, $16,533,484 (M); expenditures, $1,785,924, including $1,617,207 for 420 grants (high: $100,000; low: $250; average: $1,000-$10,000).
Purpose and activities: Emphasis on Jewish welfare funds and social and religious groups, the arts, museums, higher education, including medical education, hospitals, health services, and medical research; support also for social services, including aid to the handicapped, underprivileged children's organizations, and women's projects.
Types of support: General purposes, building funds, equipment, endowment funds, matching funds, continuing support.
Limitations: Giving primarily in the New York, NY, metropolitan area, including NJ, and in FL, including Palm Beach. No grants to individuals, or for scholarships, fellowships, or prizes; no loans.
Application information: Application form not required.
Initial approach: Letter or brief proposal
Copies of proposal: 1
Deadline(s): None
Board meeting date(s): Feb. and May or June
Final notification: 1 to 3 months
Officers and Trustees:* Helen G. Hauben,* Pres.; David Fogelson,* V.P. and Secy.; Bernard Stern,* V.P. and Treas.
Number of staff: 1 full-time professional.
Employer Identification Number: 136121361

1383
The Sumter and Ivilyn Lowry Charitable Foundation, Inc. ☆
c/o First Florida Bank, N.A.
P.O. Box 1810
Tampa 33601 (813) 251-1607
Application address: P.O. Box 18065, Tampa, FL 33679

Established in 1987 in FL.
Donor(s): Sumter Lowry,† Ivilyn Lowry.†
Foundation type: Independent
Financial data (yr. ended 12/31/88): Assets, $1,267,648 (M); gifts received, $11,352; expenditures, $87,628, including $78,000 for 8 grants (high: $50,000; low: $1,000).
Purpose and activities: Support primarily for a zoological society, a community fund, public affairs, Christian organizations, including religious schools, and social services, including child welfare and development agencies.
Limitations: Giving primarily in Tampa, FL. No grants to individuals.
Application information:
Initial approach: Letter
Deadline(s): None
Write: Florence Murphy
Officers and Directors:* Ann L. Murphey,* Pres.; David R. Murphey III,* V.P.; Helen P. Murphey.
Employer Identification Number: 592824550

1384
E. M. Lynn Foundation
2501 Military Trail
Boca Raton 33431

Established in 1977.
Donor(s): E.M. Lynn, Mrs. E.M. Lynn.
Foundation type: Independent
Financial data (yr. ended 10/31/89): Assets, $16,490,172 (M); gifts received, $2,000,000; expenditures, $834,093, including $814,455 for 74 grants (high: $250,000; low: $25).
Purpose and activities: Giving for higher education, Protestant church support, and community development.
Types of support: General purposes.
Limitations: Giving primarily in FL. No grants to individuals.

Application information: Contributes only to pre-selected organizations. Applications not accepted.
Trustee: E.M. Lynn.
Employer Identification Number: 591788859

1385
MacLeod Stewardship Foundation, Inc. ⌑ ☆
1929 Princess Court
Naples 33942 (813) 566-1806

Established in 1984.
Donor(s): John A. MacLeod.
Foundation type: Independent
Financial data (yr. ended 12/31/88): Assets, $1,718,956 (M); gifts received, $150,000; expenditures, $75,814, including $74,700 for 13 grants (high: $20,500; low: $1,000).
Purpose and activities: Giving primarily for community and private foundations and Christian organizations; support also for low-income housing.
Application information:
Initial approach: Letter
Deadline(s): None
Write: John A. MacLeod, Pres.
Officer and Directors:* John A. MacLeod,* Pres. and Secy.; Monica S. MacLeod, Muriel D. MacLeod, Roderick A. MacLeod, Cynthia MacLeod Quinn.
Employer Identification Number: 592492096

1386
Chesley G. Magruder Foundation, Inc. ⌑
c/o NCNB National Bank
P.O. Box 199
Orlando 32802 (305) 648-2840

Established in 1979 in FL.
Donor(s): Chesley G. Magruder Trust.
Foundation type: Independent
Financial data (yr. ended 06/30/89): Assets, $10,313,217 (M); expenditures, $624,253, including $560,212 for 59 grants (high: $25,000; low: $675).
Purpose and activities: Giving primarily for higher and other education, youth and social services agencies, church support, and cultural programs.
Types of support: General purposes.
Limitations: Giving primarily in FL. No grants to individuals.
Application information: Application form not required.
Initial approach: Proposal
Deadline(s): None
Write: Board of Trustees
Trustee: NCNB National Bank.
Employer Identification Number: 591920736

1387
Lola Mann Memorial Fund
1403 Briarwood Ln.
Lakeland 33803-2305 (813) 688-5501
Application address: P.O. Box 1028, Lakeland, FL 33803

Established in 1947 in FL.
Donor(s): Walter Mann.†
Foundation type: Independent
Financial data (yr. ended 12/31/88): Assets, $1,471,931 (M); expenditures, $74,205, including $48,195 for 34 grants (high: $35,000; low: $25).
Purpose and activities: Support primarily for a chapel; limited giving for social services and cultural programs.
Limitations: Giving primarily in Lakeland, Winter Haven, and Polk County, FL.
Application information:
Initial approach: Letter
Deadline(s): None
Write: Peter Munson, Pres.
Officer and Trustees: Peter Munson, Pres.; Francis Drake, Frances Munson.
Number of staff: 1 part-time professional; 1 part-time support.
Employer Identification Number: 596131211

1388
Lucille P. Markey Charitable Trust ▼
3250 Mary St., Suite 405
Miami 33133 (305) 445-5612

Established in 1983 in FL; set up to distribute entire estate of donor by 1997.
Donor(s): Lucille P. Markey.†
Foundation type: Independent
Financial data (yr. ended 06/30/89): Assets, $215,460,532 (M); gifts received, $114,053,626; expenditures, $46,058,273, including $37,902,856 for 49 grants (high: $4,749,800; low: $5,000; average: $120,000-$3,900,000) and $5,212,770 for 70 grants to individuals (high: $118,800; low: $3,000; average: $27,750-$118,800).
Purpose and activities: Established solely for the purpose of supporting and encouraging basic medical research.
Types of support: Fellowships, research.
Limitations: No grants for endowments, construction, renovation projects, or equipment (except as essential to research project).
Publications: Multi-year report, application guidelines, informational brochure, annual report.
Application information: Nomination information for Scholar Awards in Biomedical Science available from trust office. Nominations must be submitted by the college or university; nominations by individuals are not accepted. Application form not required.
Initial approach: 2- to 3-page outline of proposal with curriculum vitaes of investigators
Copies of proposal: 7
Deadline(s): None
Board meeting date(s): Quarterly
Final notification: Shortly after trustees' decision
Write: Nancy W. Weber, Prog. Coord.
Officers and Trustees:* Louis J. Hector,* Chair.; William P. Sutter,* Pres.; John H. Dickason, V.P., Finance and Administration; Robert J. Glaser, M.D., Dir. for Medical Science; Nancy W. Weber, Prog. Coordinator; Margaret Glass, George L. Shinn.
Number of staff: 4 full-time professional; 2 part-time professional; 4 full-time support; 2 part-time support.
Employer Identification Number: 592276359

1389
The Mary Foundation, Inc. ⌑ ☆
76 Isla Bahia Dr.
Fort Lauderdale 33316

Established in 1968.
Donor(s): Mary Friedman Baske.
Foundation type: Independent
Financial data (yr. ended 12/31/88): Assets, $1,000,444 (M); expenditures, $58,591, including $44,000 for 6 grants (high: $25,300; low: $1,000).
Purpose and activities: Giving primarily for secondary education and a children's museum; support also for health services.
Types of support: General purposes.
Application information: Application form not required.
Initial approach: Letter
Deadline(s): None
Write: Robert G. Friedman, Pres.
Officers: Robert G. Friedman, Pres.; Eugenie S. Friedman, V.P.
Director: Mary Baske.
Employer Identification Number: 346607103

1390
Charles H. & Annetta R. Masland Foundation ⌑ ☆
3223 North Lockwood Ridge Rd., No. D137
Sarasota 34234

Foundation type: Independent
Financial data (yr. ended 11/30/88): Assets, $1,019,155 (M); expenditures, $74,973, including $65,000 for 23 grants (high: $10,000; low: $1,000).
Purpose and activities: Giving primarily for Christian organizations and education; support also for youth and social services.
Types of support: General purposes, scholarship funds.
Limitations: Giving primarily in PA and NY.
Application information: Application form not required.
Initial approach: Letter
Deadline(s): None
Trustees: John D. Bakke, Peter M. Lavin, Frank E. Masland III, David M. McCoy, Walter H. McCoy, Dana G. Stetser, Virginia Stetser.
Employer Identification Number: 236296887

1391
Manuel D. & Rhoda Mayerson Foundation ☆
7584 Rexford Rd.
Boca Raton 33434-5144
Application address: 105 East Fourth St., Suite 1900, Cincinnati, OH 45202; Tel.: (513) 621-7500

Established in 1986 in FL.
Donor(s): Manuel D. Mayerson, Rhoda Mayerson.
Foundation type: Independent
Financial data (yr. ended 10/31/89): Assets, $2,582,339 (M); gifts received, $1,442,745; expenditures, $123,531, including $98,738 for 19 grants (high: $19,500; low: $90).
Purpose and activities: Giving primarily for health; support also for the performing and fine arts, Jewish giving, education, and family and social services, including programs for the aged, the disabled and disadvantaged, the

homeless, hunger, rehabilitation, women, and youth.
Types of support: Building funds, capital campaigns, emergency funds, loans, matching funds, program-related investments, renovation projects, seed money, special projects, technical assistance.
Limitations: Giving primarily in Cincinnati, OH, and South Palm Beach, FL.
Publications: Application guidelines.
Application information: Application form not required.
Initial approach: Telephone or letter
Deadline(s): None
Board meeting date(s): Bimonthly
Final notification: Following meeting
Write: Peter Bloch, Exec. Dir.
Officer: Peter Bloch, Exec. Dir.
Number of staff: 1 full-time professional; 1 part-time support.
Employer Identification Number: 586202977

1392
J. N. McArthur Foundation, Inc. ☆
2800 Biscayne Blvd., Suite 310
Miami 33137 (305) 573-1711

Established in 1959.
Donor(s): J. Neville McArthur.†
Foundation type: Independent
Financial data (yr. ended 12/31/88): Assets, $1,019,310 (M); gifts received, $125,000; expenditures, $67,256, including $62,020 for 41 grants (high: $5,000; low: $300; average: $100-$1,500).
Purpose and activities: Giving for health associations, Christian associations, higher and other education, and social services.
Application information: Application form not required.
Initial approach: Letter
Copies of proposal: 1
Deadline(s): None
Board meeting date(s): Spring and fall
Final notification: Immediately following board meeting
Write: Heidi James
Officer: Jean McArthur Davis, Pres.
Employer Identification Number: 596063228

1393
Robert Earll McConnell Foundation ⌑ ☆
c/o Northern Trust Bank of FL
700 Brickell Ave.
Miami 33131
Application address: 344 South Beach Rd., Hobe Sound, FL 33455

Established in 1936.
Foundation type: Independent
Financial data (yr. ended 12/31/88): Assets, $1,020,423 (M); expenditures, $61,882, including $48,775 for 46 grants (high: $5,000; low: $125).
Purpose and activities: Giving for higher education, social service and youth agencies, and hospitals and health associations.
Limitations: Giving primarily in FL. No grants to individuals.
Application information: Application form not required.
Deadline(s): None
Write: Caryll E. McDonnell
Officers and Trustees:* Elizabeth M. Cayle,* Chair.; James S. Kelly,* Exec. V.P.; Eileen H. Raphel, Secy.; John W. Good, Mildred M. Good, T. Gibbs Kane, Richard E. McConnell, Thomas M. Mettler, Peter Wagner.
Employer Identification Number: 596153509

1394
Ray Sutton McGehee Foundation ⌑
924 Barnett Bank Bldg.
Jacksonville 32202
Application address: 112 West Adams St., Suite 924, Jacksonville, FL 32202; Tel.: (904) 355-4715

Established in 1957 in FL.
Foundation type: Independent
Financial data (yr. ended 12/31/88): Assets, $1,455,537 (M); expenditures, $32,825, including $27,300 for 24 grants (high: $6,250; low: $100).
Purpose and activities: Support primarily for the medical sciences and health associations.
Application information:
Initial approach: Letter or telephone
Deadline(s): None
Write: C. Collier-McGehee, Jr., Secy.-Treas.
Officers and Trustees: C. Graham McGehee, Jr., Chair.; C. Collier-McGehee, Jr., Secy.-Treas.; Ellen M. Cavert, Tillman Cavert, Jr., Berrylin M. Houston.
Employer Identification Number: 596143565

1395
The McIntosh Foundation
215 Fifth St., Suite 100
West Palm Beach 33401 (407) 832-8845

Incorporated in 1949 in NY.
Donor(s): Josephine H. McIntosh.†
Foundation type: Independent
Financial data (yr. ended 12/31/88): Assets, $29,483,326 (M); expenditures, $1,200,638, including $895,350 for 53 grants (high: $60,000; low: $100).
Purpose and activities: Grants limited mainly to the support of lawsuits, primarily environmental, brought by public interest law groups. Some giving to education.
Types of support: General purposes, program-related investments.
Limitations: No grants to individuals, or for building or endowment funds.
Publications: Program policy statement, application guidelines.
Application information: Application form not required.
Initial approach: Letter or proposal
Copies of proposal: 1
Deadline(s): None
Board meeting date(s): Bimonthly
Final notification: 60 to 90 days
Write: Michael A. McIntosh, Pres.
Officers and Directors:* Michael A. McIntosh,* Pres.; Peter H. McIntosh,* V.P. and Treas.; Joan H. McIntosh,* V.P.; Winsome D. McIntosh,* V.P.; Frederick A. Terry, Jr.,* Secy.
Number of staff: 3 full-time professional; 2 full-time support.
Employer Identification Number: 136096459

1396
Father John J. McMahon Charitable Trust Fund ⌑
2730 Southeast 7th Dr.
Pompano Beach 33062

Established in 1961 in VA.
Donor(s): Father John J. McMahon.†
Foundation type: Independent
Financial data (yr. ended 12/31/87): Assets, $2,067,466 (M); expenditures, $91,567, including $80,500 for 36 grants (high: $8,000; low: $500).
Purpose and activities: Giving for scholarships at secondary schools (with emphasis on Catholic schools) and for higher education; support also for denominational giving.
Types of support: Scholarship funds.
Limitations: Giving primarily in VA.
Application information:
Initial approach: Letter
Deadline(s): None
Write: Joseph A. Keating, Mgr.
Officer and Trustees:* Joseph A. Keating,* Mgr.; Robert McMahon, Walter Sullivan.
Employer Identification Number: 526035158

1397
The Philip & Julia Meshberg Foundation, Inc. ⌑ ☆
2500 South Ocean Blvd.
Palm Beach 33480

Established in 1977.
Donor(s): Philip Meshberg, Emil Meshberg, Samuel Meshberg.
Foundation type: Independent
Financial data (yr. ended 12/31/89): Assets, $1,218,123 (M); gifts received, $84,675; expenditures, $176,682, including $164,175 for 57 grants (high: $50,070; low: $10).
Purpose and activities: Giving primarily for Jewish welfare, community, and religious organizations.
Officers: Philip Meshberg, Pres.; Julia Meshberg, Secy.; Emil Meshberg, Treas.
Director: Samuel Meshberg.
Employer Identification Number: 591813108

1398
Metal Industries Foundation, Inc. ⌑
1310 North Hercules Ave.
Clearwater 34625 (813) 441-2651

Donor(s): Metal Industries, Inc.
Foundation type: Company-sponsored
Financial data (yr. ended 10/31/88): Assets, $1,626,024 (M); gifts received, $200,000; expenditures, $85,685, including $77,473 for 40 grants (high: $25,000; low: $50).
Purpose and activities: Support primarily for youth organizations, community development, the arts, Christian churches, and mental health.
Application information: Application form required.
Deadline(s): None
Write: J.L. Fasenmyer
Officers and Trustees: James T. Walker, Jr., Pres.; James T. Walker, V.P.; Jay K. Poppleton.
Employer Identification Number: 237098483

1399
The Baron de Hirsch Meyer Foundation
407 Lincoln Rd., Suite 6J
Miami Beach 33139 (305) 538-2531

Incorporated in 1940 in FL.
Donor(s): Baron de Hirsch Meyer.†
Foundation type: Independent
Financial data (yr. ended 12/31/88): Assets, $2,733,921 (M); expenditures, $207,424, including $144,435 for 39 grants (high: $50,150; low: $30).
Purpose and activities: Support for religious welfare, with emphasis on Jewish welfare funds, hospitals, medical agencies, child welfare, the aged, animal welfare, cancer research, Catholic giving, and the performing arts.
Types of support: Building funds.
Limitations: Giving primarily in FL. No grants to individuals.
Publications: Informational brochure (including application guidelines).
Application information:
Initial approach: Proposal or letter
Copies of proposal: 1
Board meeting date(s): Feb.
Officers and Directors:* Polly de Hirsch Meyer,* Pres. and Treas.; Marie Williams,* V.P.; Martin Steedman,* Secy.
Employer Identification Number: 596129646

1400
Bert & Mary Meyer Foundation, Inc. ⌘ ☆
2913 Corrine Dr.
Orlando 32803
Application address: 1620 Highland Rd., Winter Park, FL 32789; Tel.: (407) 628-1122

Established in 1983.
Foundation type: Independent
Financial data (yr. ended 12/31/88): Assets, $3,471,162 (M); expenditures, $532,092, including $360,565 for 79 grants (high: $26,000; low: $60; average: $2,000-$10,000).
Purpose and activities: Support for "rural self-governing groups, particularly farmworker organizations, whose objectives include: 1) Analyzing their own reality; 2) Appreciating their cultural identity; 3) Creating and executing strategy to affect decisions that control their lives; 4) Networking with like-minded groups with similar objectives; and 5) Grass roots organizing efforts aimed at educating and activating communities on human rights and self-determination issues in Central America."
Limitations: Giving primarily in the rural southeast. No grants to individuals.
Application information: Application form required.
Initial approach: Proposal
Deadline(s): Mar. 1 and Sept. 1
Write: Barbara C. Portee, Pres.
Officers and Trustees:* Hubert Sapp,* Chair.; Patricia Crockett,* Vice-Chair.; Barbara C. Portee, Pres.; Marta Benavides, Gardenia White.
Employer Identification Number: 592348082

1401
C. John and Reva Miller Charitable Foundation, Inc. ⌘
1421 Forrest Court
Marco Island 33937

Established in 1985 in MI.
Donor(s): C. John Miller, Michael J. Miller, Cynthia J. Martin, Sara J. Southwicke, Sally J. Buxton.
Foundation type: Independent
Financial data (yr. ended 09/30/89): Assets, $1,504,531 (M); gifts received, $1,880,000; expenditures, $733,430, including $729,829 for 52 grants (high: $147,525; low: $50).
Purpose and activities: Support for Baptist churches, schools, and missionary programs.
Limitations: Giving primarily in MI. No grants to individuals.
Application information: Contributes only to pre-selected organizations. Applications not accepted.
Officers: C. John Miller, Pres.; Reva Miller, V.P.; Michael Miller, Secy.-Treas.
Employer Identification Number: 382623333

1402
Miller Family Foundation, Inc. ⌘
700 N.W. 107th St., 4th Fl.
Miami 33172

Established in 1984 in FL.
Donor(s): Leonard Miller, Susan Miller.
Foundation type: Independent
Financial data (yr. ended 11/30/88): Assets, $790,425 (M); gifts received, $396,610; expenditures, $550,522, including $549,920 for 23 grants (high: $169,400; low: $200).
Purpose and activities: Support primarily for Jewish organizations; support also for social services, child welfare and performing and fine arts groups.
Limitations: Giving primarily in Miami, FL.
Application information: Contributes only to pre-selected organizations. Applications not accepted.
Directors: Jeffrey Miller, Leonard Miller, Stuart Miller, Susan Miller, Vicki Miller, Leslie Saiontz, Steven Saiontz.
Employer Identification Number: 592474323

1403
Henry L. & Kathryn Mills Charitable Foundation ⌘
4950 N.W. 72nd Ave.
Miami 33166 (305) 887-6631

Established in 1984 in FL.
Donor(s): Kathryn Mills.
Foundation type: Independent
Financial data (yr. ended 06/30/89): Assets, $3,076,298 (M); expenditures, $156,240, including $105,500 for 19 grants (high: $10,000; low: $500).
Purpose and activities: Support for health and medical research, church support, and education.
Types of support: Renovation projects, building funds, emergency funds, scholarship funds, research.
Limitations: Giving primarily in Miami, FL, and the surrounding area. No grants to individuals.
Application information: Contributes only to pre-selected organizations. Applications not accepted.
Write: Debra Mills Grimm, Trustee
Trustees: Kathryn Mills, Managing Trustee; Jacquin D. Bierman, Bonnie Douthitt, Debra Mills Grimm, Northern Trust Bank of Florida, N.A.
Employer Identification Number: 592474884

1404
John Miskoff Foundation ⌘
665 N.E. 58th St.
Miami 33137 (305) 754-5169

Established in 1981 in FL.
Foundation type: Independent
Financial data (yr. ended 6/30/88): Assets, $1,235,631 (M); gifts received, $325,500; expenditures, $347,516, including $6,663 for 2 grants (high: $4,500; low: $2,163) and $34,000 for 7 grants to individuals (high: $7,000; low: $3,450).
Purpose and activities: Scholarship loans for students who have completed their sophomore year of college.
Types of support: Student loans.
Publications: Program policy statement.
Application information: Preliminary screening is done by the college; applicants are then interviewed by the foundation.
Officers: Wilmoth Miskoff, Pres.; Shorme Warn, V.P.
Employer Identification Number: 592193608

1405
Herbert H. & Leonie G. Moffitt Memorial Endowment Fund ⌘
c/o SunBank/South Florida, N.A., Trust Banking Group
303 Royal Poinciana Plaza
Palm Beach 33480

Established in 1978 in FL.
Foundation type: Independent
Financial data (yr. ended 03/31/89): Assets, $1,031,665 (M); expenditures, $92,472, including $79,141 for 1 grant.
Purpose and activities: Support for a public hospital.
Trustee: SunBank/South Florida, N.A.
Employer Identification Number: 596601847

1406
Martha G. Moore Foundation, Inc. ⌘
850 S.E. 7th St., Suite A
Deerfield Beach 33441-4845

Established in 1976 in FL.
Donor(s): Martha G. Moore.†
Foundation type: Independent
Financial data (yr. ended 6/30/88): Assets, $3,309,543 (M); expenditures, $197,621, including $125,000 for 13 grants (high: $28,000; low: $2,000).
Purpose and activities: Support for health and social services.
Limitations: Giving primarily in FL.
Officers and Trustees:* Roger E. Wood,* Chair.; Dean R. Bailey,* Vice-Chair.; Calvin M. Johnson,* Treas.
Employer Identification Number: 510201970

1407
Louie R. and Gertrude Morgan Foundation ⌘
P.O. Box 550
Arcadia 33821

Established in 1960.
Donor(s): Louie R. Morgan,† Mildred Morgan,† Gertrude Morgan, Eleanor Morgan.
Foundation type: Independent
Financial data (yr. ended 12/31/88): Assets, $2,732,041 (M); expenditures, $129,228, including $122,200 for 17 grants (high: $20,000; low: $5,000).
Purpose and activities: Grants primarily for local Protestant churches and a hospital.
Limitations: Giving primarily in FL.
Officers: Robert Summerall, Jr.,* V.P. and Treas.; Jane Weller, Secy.
Directors:* Bobby C. Mixion, Lewis W. Smith.
Employer Identification Number: 596142359

1408
The Allen Morris Foundation ⌘
1000 Brickell Ave., 12th Fl.
Miami 33131 (305) 358-1000

Established in 1962 in FL.
Donor(s): Morris Family Business, and others.
Foundation type: Independent
Financial data (yr. ended 2/28/89): Assets, $817,603 (M); gifts received, $220,025; expenditures, $320,782, including $131,669 for 118 grants (high: $17,500; low: $20; average: $1,000-$5,000) and $54,466 for 1 foundation-administered program.
Purpose and activities: Giving primarily for Evangelical religious groups and a program of religious teaching for adults; support also for educational organizations and social services in the Miami, FL, area.
Types of support: Annual campaigns, conferences and seminars, continuing support, equipment, general purposes, matching funds, operating budgets, seed money, special projects.
Limitations: No grants to individuals.
Application information: Submit applications only in May and Dec. Application form not required.
Initial approach: Proposal with 1-page cover letter
Copies of proposal: 1
Board meeting date(s): Jan. and June
Write: L. Michael Lynch, Exec. V.P.
Officers: W. Allen Morris,* Pres.; Ida A. Morris,* Treas.; L. Michael Lynch, Exec. V.P.
Directors:* L. Allen Morris, Chair.; Ida M. Bell, James F. Bell, Jr., Diane Y. Morris, Gary L. Rupp, Kathryn Morris Rupp.
Number of staff: 1 full-time professional; 1 full-time support.
Employer Identification Number: 596152420

1409
Mote Scientific Foundation, Inc.
580 Spinnaker Ln.
Longboat Key 34228 (813) 383-7802

Incorporated in 1950 in NY.
Donor(s): William R. Mote, T.R. Bartels, Theodore R. Bartels, and others.
Foundation type: Independent
Financial data (yr. ended 11/30/88): Assets, $192,741 (M); gifts received, $30,531; expenditures, $139,038, including $137,933 for 5 grants (high: $103,260; low: $1,000).
Purpose and activities: Giving mainly for oceanography; support primarily for the Mote Marine Laboratory.
Types of support: Research.
Limitations: Giving primarily in FL. No grants to individuals.
Publications: Annual report.
Application information: Contributes only to pre-selected organizations. Applications not accepted.
Officers: William R. Mote, Pres.; Elizabeth Rose, Secy.-Treas.
Number of staff: None.
Employer Identification Number: 136117615

1410
Nadeau Charitable Foundation, Inc.
c/o George F. Hess
333 North New River Dr. East
Fort Lauderdale 33301 (305) 565-7779
Application address: 2600 N.E. Ninth St., Fort Lauderdale, FL 33304

Established in 1985 in FL.
Donor(s): Natalie A. Nadeau.†
Foundation type: Independent
Financial data (yr. ended 08/31/87): Assets, $1,265,710 (M); gifts received, $3,907; expenditures, $3,897.
Purpose and activities: Support for the elderly.
Application information: Application form not required.
Copies of proposal: 1
Board meeting date(s): Quarterly
Write: Dr. Edwin Vasquez, Dir.
Directors: George F. Hess II, Natalie A. Nadeau, Edwin Vasquez, Roger Wagner.
Number of staff: None.
Employer Identification Number: 592583522

1411
Nalith, Inc. ⌘
10923 S.W. 75th Terr.
Miami 33173 (305) 443-4216

Foundation type: Independent
Financial data (yr. ended 12/31/88): Assets, $1,299,783 (M); expenditures, $28,768, including $10,000 for 1 grant.
Purpose and activities: Support for the promotion of research and development of natural organic farming methods and promotion of vegetarianism and vegetarian lifestyles to enhance good health.
Limitations: Giving primarily in Miami, FL. No grants to individuals.
Application information:
Deadline(s): None
Write: Lillian Langer, Director
Officer: Michael Tucker,* Pres.
Directors:* George Eisman, Glen Gilson II, Hiam Karp, Lillian Langer.
Employer Identification Number: 592323680

1412
NAPCO Charitable Foundation ⌘
7800 Bayberry Rd.
Jacksonville 32256

Established in 1979 in OH.
Donor(s): William F. Rein.
Foundation type: Independent
Financial data (yr. ended 12/31/88): Assets, $1,380,021 (M); expenditures, $95,010, including $81,125 for grants (high: $52,000).
Purpose and activities: Grants primarily for Jewish giving, education, and social services.
Types of support: Building funds.
Officer and Trustees:* Robert C. Fullerton,* Treas.; Joan Rein, William F. Rein.
Employer Identification Number: 341296460

1413
National Vulcanized Fibre Company Community Services Trust Fund ⌘
6917 Collins Ave.
Miami Beach 33141

Trust established in 1956 in DE.
Donor(s): National Vulcanized Fibre Co.
Foundation type: Company-sponsored
Financial data (yr. ended 12/31/88): Assets, $1,389,666 (M); expenditures, $6,626, including $3,000 for 2 grants (high: $2,500; low: $500).
Purpose and activities: Giving for higher education, cultural programs, and child welfare.
Limitations: Giving primarily in DE.
Trustees: Jack Coppersmith, Steven Posner, Victor Posner.
Employer Identification Number: 516021550

1414
The Needle's Eye, Inc. ⌘ ☆
c/o Gustave T. Broberg, Jr.
223 Peruvian Ave.
Palm Beach 33480-4635

Established in 1986 in FL.
Donor(s): Mary Barbara Annan.
Foundation type: Independent
Financial data (yr. ended 6/30/89): Assets, $155,728 (M); expenditures, $141,957, including $140,000 for 3 grants (high: $100,000; low: $20,000).
Purpose and activities: Support primarily for education including a medical school, and welfare agencies.
Limitations: Giving primarily in Boston, MA. No grants to individuals.
Application information: Contributes only to pre-selected organizations. Applications not accepted.
Officers and Directors: Ronald V. Albert, Pres. and Treas.; Gustave T. Broberg, Jr., V.P.; Peter S. Broberg, Secy.
Employer Identification Number: 592747299

1415
Helen Kavanagh Nicol Scholarship Foundation ⌘ ☆
c/o SunBank Trust Co.
P.O. Box 14728
Fort Lauderdale 33302
Application address: c/o Lambton Central Collegiate Vocational Institute, Box 5100, Petrolia, Ontario Canada

Established in 1986.
Foundation type: Independent
Financial data (yr. ended 11/30/88): Assets, $1,909,497 (M); gifts received, $969,541; expenditures, $130,332, including $87,261 for grants to individuals.

Purpose and activities: Provides student aid to top 20 percent of senior class of Lambton Central Collegiate Vocational Institute in Canada.
Types of support: Student aid.
Limitations: Giving primarily in Canada.
Application information: Application form required.
Deadline(s): May 1
Write: D.W. Cook
Trustees: Gordon L. Giles, Floyd V. Hull, Jr., SunBank Trust Co.
Employer Identification Number: 596842726

1416
Nuveen Benevolent Trust
c/o Walter R. Sundling, Principal Mgr.
7204 13th Ave. West
Bradenton 34209 (813) 794-0432

Trust established in 1936 in IL.
Donor(s): John Nuveen V,† and others.
Foundation type: Independent
Financial data (yr. ended 12/31/88): Assets, $1,489,544 (M); expenditures, $108,212, including $82,200 for 76 grants (high: $10,000; low: $200; average: $200).
Purpose and activities: Emphasis on higher education and general charitable giving.
Types of support: Continuing support, general purposes, operating budgets.
Limitations: No grants to individuals.
Application information: Contributes only to pre-selected organizations. Applications not accepted.
Trustees: Grace B. Nuveen, Anne Nuveen Reynolds, Walter R. Sundling.
Number of staff: None.
Employer Identification Number: 366069509

1417
Calvin & Flavia Oak Foundation, Inc. ⌑ ☆
1621 Micanopy Ave.
Miami 33133-2509

Established in 1965.
Donor(s): Flavia DeCamp Oak.
Foundation type: Independent
Financial data (yr. ended 11/30/88): Assets, $734,312 (M); gifts received, $148,274; expenditures, $436,546, including $431,375 for 15 grants (high: $120,625; low: $250).
Purpose and activities: Support primarily for hospitals, organizations serving the blind, and medical schools; support also for an Episcopal church.
Limitations: Giving primarily in Miami and Coral Gables, FL.
Application information: Applications not accepted.
Officers and Directors: Flavia DeCamp Oak, Chair.; Tully Dunlap, Pres. and Treas.; Theresa M. Moore, V.P.; Catherine Holloway, Emily M. Romph.
Employer Identification Number: 596192591

1418
Matred Carlton Olliff Foundation ⌑
P.O. Box 385
Wauchula 33873 (813) 773-4131

Established in 1982 in FL.
Donor(s): Matred Carlton Olliff.†
Foundation type: Independent
Financial data (yr. ended 8/31/88): Assets, $4,073,435 (M); expenditures, $219,792, including $134,185 for 45 grants (high: $25,000; low: $100) and $64,243 for 103 grants to individuals (high: $1,400; low: $20).
Purpose and activities: Support primarily for Protestant churches; limited giving for scholarships, hospitals, and health associations.
Types of support: Student aid.
Limitations: Giving primarily in FL.
Application information: Application form not required.
Initial approach: Proposal
Deadline(s): July 1
Write: Doyle E. Carlton, Jr., Trustee
Trustees: Doyle E. Carlton, Jr., Doyle E. Carlton III, Walter S. Farr.
Employer Identification Number: 592241303

1419
Selma Oritt Foundation, Inc. ⌑ ☆
133 Sevilla Ave.
Coral Gables 33134

Established in 1951.
Foundation type: Independent
Financial data (yr. ended 11/30/88): Assets, $1,128,869 (M); expenditures, $61,562, including $55,950 for 44 grants (high: $10,000; low: $100).
Purpose and activities: Support for temples and other Jewish organizations, medical sciences and research, and hospitals.
Limitations: Giving primarily in Miami, FL.
Application information:
Initial approach: Letter
Deadline(s): None
Write: Neil S. Pollnick, Pres.
Officer and Director: Neil S. Pollnick, Pres.
Employer Identification Number: 237416729

1420
The Orlando Sentinel Foundation, Inc.
(Formerly Sentinel Communications Charities, Inc.)
c/o Sentinel Communications Co.
633 North Orange Ave.
Orlando 32801 (407) 420-5591

Established in 1969 in FL.
Donor(s): Sentinel Communications Co.
Foundation type: Company-sponsored
Financial data (yr. ended 12/31/88): Assets, $145,446 (M); gifts received, $344,183; expenditures, $336,984, including $336,604 for 85 grants (high: $67,000; low: $30).
Purpose and activities: Giving for civic affairs, the arts, education, health, and social services.
Types of support: Building funds, capital campaigns, endowment funds, matching funds, renovation projects, special projects.
Limitations: Giving limited to the six-county area of east central FL. No grants to individuals.
Publications: Program policy statement, application guidelines.
Application information: Application form required.
Initial approach: Letter
Copies of proposal: 1
Deadline(s): Mar. 1, June 1, Sept. 1, and Dec. 1
Board meeting date(s): Quarterly
Write: Nancy F. Peed, Community Relations Coord.
Officers and Directors:* Harold R. Lifvendahl,* Pres.; John L. Blexrud,* V.P.; L. John Haile,* V.P.; William E. Steiger,* V.P.; Nancy F. Peed,* Secy.; Richard E. Darden,* Treas.
Number of staff: 1 part-time professional.
Employer Identification Number: 237063917

1421
Overstreet Foundation ⌑
P.O. Box 111
Orlando 32802

Established in 1965 in FL.
Donor(s): Overstreet Investment Co.
Foundation type: Independent
Financial data (yr. ended 12/31/88): Assets, $4,392,864 (M); gifts received, $190,000; expenditures, $382,497, including $379,324 for 69 grants (high: $31,000; low: $150).
Purpose and activities: Support for social services and community funds, higher education, and health services.
Limitations: Giving primarily in FL. No grants to individuals.
Application information: Contributes only to pre-selected organizations. Applications not accepted.
Trustees: Mildred Overstreet, R.T. Overstreet, Robin Sheldon.
Employer Identification Number: 596164658

1422
Palm Beach Community Trust Fund ⌑ ☆
c/o First National Bank of Palm Beach
255 South County Rd.
Palm Beach 33480

Established in 1955.
Donor(s): William Regan.†
Foundation type: Independent
Financial data (yr. ended 12/31/88): Assets, $1,040,538 (M); gifts received, $143,000; expenditures, $84,458, including $75,000 for 25 grants (high: $11,200; low: $1,400; average: $1,400).
Purpose and activities: Giving primarily for health and social services; support also for arts and culture, higher education, and youth organizations.
Limitations: Giving primarily in Palm Beach, FL. No grants to individuals.
Application information: Contributes only to pre-selected organizations. Applications not accepted.
Officer: Wycoff Myers, Mgr.
Employer Identification Number: 510144921

1423
Palm Beach County Community Foundation
324 Datura St., Suite 340
West Palm Beach 33401-5431 (407) 659-6800

Incorporated in 1972 in FL.
Foundation type: Community
Financial data (yr. ended 6/30/89): Assets, $5,831,118 (L); gifts received, $2,441,380; expenditures, $353,411, including $179,658 for 64 grants (high: $43,000; low: $150) and $21,950 for 25 grants to individuals (high: $2,000; low: $500).
Purpose and activities: Support for education including a scholarship program for graduating local high school seniors, the arts, health, social services, and the conservation and preservation of historical and cultural resources.
Types of support: Seed money, student aid, conferences and seminars, emergency funds, equipment, matching funds, special projects, technical assistance, general purposes.
Limitations: Giving primarily in Palm Beach County, FL, and surrounding regions. No grants to individuals (except scholarships), or for operating funds, building campaigns, endowments, or annual campaigns.
Publications: Annual report, newsletter, application guidelines.
Application information: Application form required.
Initial approach: Telephone call followed by proposal
Copies of proposal: 1
Deadline(s): Apr. 1 and Oct. 1
Board meeting date(s): May and Nov.
Final notification: June and Dec.
Officers and Directors:* Dwight L. Allison, Jr.,* Pres.; John B. Dodge,* 1st V.P.; William E. Benjamin II,* 2nd V.P.; Mrs. Max M. Fisher, Secy.; R. Michael Strickland,* Treas.; Shannon G. Sadler, Exec. Dir.; and 17 other directors.
Number of staff: 3 full-time professional; 1 full-time support.
Employer Identification Number: 237181875

1424
The Mary E. Parker Foundation ¤
1215 Manatee Ave. West
Bradenton 33505 (813) 748-3666

Established in 1986 in FL.
Donor(s): Mary E. Parker.
Foundation type: Operating
Financial data (yr. ended 12/31/88): Assets, $5,013,820 (M); expenditures, $283,065, including $200,000 for 38 grants (high: $27,000; low: $1,000).
Purpose and activities: A private operating foundation; support for cultural programs, nursing education, youth and social services, a community fund, animal welfare, and guide dogs for the visually impaired.
Application information:
Initial approach: Letter
Deadline(s): Apr. 30
Write: Richard Pratt, Trustee
Trustees: Robert Blalock, Mary E. Parker, Richard Pratt, W.E. Wentzel, Woodrow Young.
Employer Identification Number: 592708325

1425
Vera Davis Parsons-WD Charities, Inc. ¤
5050 Edgewood Court
Jacksonville 32205

Established in 1967 in FL.
Donor(s): Vera Davis Parsons.
Foundation type: Independent
Financial data (yr. ended 12/31/88): Assets, $17,214,200 (M); expenditures, $1,061,904, including $942,483 for 289 grants (high: $180,000; low: $150).
Purpose and activities: Giving primarily for youth and education; support also for religion, medical research, and health, relief and social agencies.
Limitations: Giving primarily in FL, GA, NC, SC, and AL. No grants to individuals.
Application information:
Write: Thomas W. Bishop, Pres.
Officers: Thomas W. Bishop,* Pres.; Robert D. Davis, V.P. and Treas.; G.P. Bishop, Jr., Secy.
Directors:* R.J. Head, Charles M. Thompson.
Employer Identification Number: 596180346

1426
The Paulucci Family Foundation ¤
250 International Pkwy.
Heathrow 32746

Incorporated in 1966 in MN.
Donor(s): Jeno F. Paulucci.
Foundation type: Independent
Financial data (yr. ended 12/31/88): Assets, $1,893,485 (M); expenditures, $80,318, including $64,850 for 21 grants (high: $24,380; low: $50).
Purpose and activities: Emphasis on higher education, medical research, and support of Italian-American cultural and charitable activities.
Limitations: Giving primarily in MN and FL. No grants to individuals.
Application information:
Initial approach: Letter
Copies of proposal: 1
Board meeting date(s): Annually
Officers and Directors:* Jeno F. Paulucci,* Pres.; Lois M. Paulucci,* V.P.; Michael J. Paulucci,* V.P.; Larry W. Nelson-Heathrow,* Treas.; Gina J. Paulucci, Cynthia Paulucci Soderstrom.
Employer Identification Number: 416054004

1427
Lowell W. Paxson Foundation ¤ ☆
3380 State Rd. 580
Safety Harbor 34695 (813) 726-0202

Established in 1987 in FL.
Foundation type: Independent
Financial data (yr. ended 6/30/88): Assets, $261,450 (M); expenditures, $590,000, including $590,000 for 2 grants (high: $442,500; low: $147,500).
Purpose and activities: Initial year of operation, fiscal 1988; support for Christian organizations.
Application information:
Initial approach: Proposal
Deadline(s): None
Write: Dan Stuecher, Trustee
Trustees: Lynnda L. Speer, Dan Stuecher.
Employer Identification Number: 650037802

1428
Peacock Foundation, Inc. ☆
51 N.W. First St.
Miami 33128 (305) 373-1386

Incorporated in 1947 in FL.
Foundation type: Independent
Financial data (yr. ended 11/30/89): Assets, $1,332,948 (M); gifts received, $85,608; expenditures, $56,301, including $56,202 for 63 grants (high: $10,000; low: $21).
Purpose and activities: Support for health associations.
Limitations: Giving primarily in FL.
Application information: Applications not accepted.
Deadline(s): None
Write: Henry B. Peacock, Jr., Pres.
Officers and Directors:* Henry B. Peacock, Jr.,* Pres. and Treas.; Arthur I. Hemmings,* V.P.; B.A. Rickard,* Secy.
Number of staff: None.
Employer Identification Number: 590999759

1429
Dr. M. Lee Pearce Foundation, Inc. ¤
11880 Bird Rd.
Miami 33175 (305) 477-0222

Established in 1984 in FL.
Donor(s): M. Lee Pearce.
Foundation type: Independent
Financial data (yr. ended 12/31/88): Assets, $5,159,618 (M); expenditures, $228,395, including $226,250 for 10 grants (high: $200,000; low: $300).
Purpose and activities: Giving for social services, higher and other education, and cultural activities; support also for a medical research organization.
Limitations: Giving primarily in FL, with emphasis on Miami.
Application information: Contributes only to pre-selected organizations. Applications not accepted.
Write: A.B. Wiener, Secy.-Treas.
Officers and Directors: M. Lee Pearce, M.D., Pres.; A.B. Wiener, V.P. and Secy.-Treas.; Robert L. Achor, V.P.; Marc H. Bivins, V.P.; John Mudd, V.P.; Nora Lodge Pearce, V.P.
Employer Identification Number: 592424272

1430
A. P. Phillips Foundation, Inc.
P.O. Box 3628
Orlando 32802 (407) 422-8250

Established in 1965.
Foundation type: Independent
Financial data (yr. ended 6/30/88): Assets, $2,362,890 (M); expenditures, $150,890, including $125,250 for 27 grants (high: $15,000; low: $500).
Purpose and activities: Emphasis on youth agencies and child welfare, higher education, and hospitals.
Limitations: Giving primarily in central FL.
Application information:
Initial approach: Proposal
Deadline(s): None
Write: M.W. Wells, Jr., Pres.
Officers and Directors: M.W. Wells, Jr., Pres.; D.K. Wells, V.P.; J.W. Jordan, Secy.; L.A. Wells.
Employer Identification Number: 596165157

1431
The Dr. P. Phillips Foundation
60 West Robinson St.
P.O. Box 3753
Orlando 32802 (305) 422-6105

Incorporated in 1953 in FL.
Donor(s): Della Phillips,† Howard Phillips,† Dr. Phillips, Inc., and others.
Foundation type: Independent
Financial data (yr. ended 05/31/89): Assets, $19,597,180 (M); gifts received, $2,182; expenditures, $386,548, including $195,538 for 42 grants (high: $34,835; low: $25).
Purpose and activities: Emphasis on economic education, child development and youth, and community development, including cultural programs, recreation, and social and family services.
Types of support: Building funds, operating budgets, special projects, capital campaigns, equipment, matching funds, program-related investments.
Limitations: Giving limited to Orange County and the central FL area. No grants to individuals, or for endowment funds.
Publications: Application guidelines.
Application information: Application form not required.
Initial approach: Letter up to 3 pages
Copies of proposal: 1
Board meeting date(s): Semiannually
Final notification: Varies
Write: J.A. Hinson, Pres.
Officers and Directors:* H.E. Johnson,* Chair.; J.A. Hinson,* Pres.; Ben Houston,* V.P.; R.A. Simon,* V.P.
Number of staff: 1 full-time professional.
Employer Identification Number: 596135403

1432
Phipps Florida Foundation
P.O. Box 1351
Tallahassee 32302 (904) 222-2717

Trust established in 1959 in FL.
Foundation type: Independent
Financial data (yr. ended 11/30/89): Assets, $1,106,045 (M); expenditures, $42,776, including $31,750 for 7 grants (high: $14,050; low: $50).
Purpose and activities: Giving for conservation and health.
Types of support: Operating budgets, continuing support, annual campaigns, seed money, emergency funds, building funds, equipment, land acquisition, matching funds, research, publications.
Limitations: Giving primarily in FL. No grants to individuals, or for deficit financing, scholarships, or fellowships; no loans except on an emergency basis.
Application information: Application form not required.
Initial approach: Letter
Board meeting date(s): Monthly except in June, July, and Aug.
Final notification: 2 to 4 months
Write: Benjamin K. Phipps, Secy.
Officer and Trustees: Benjamin K. Phipps, Secy.; Colin S. Phipps, Elizabeth K. Phipps, John E. Phipps.
Number of staff: None.
Employer Identification Number: 596159046

1433
Pinellas County Community Foundation
P.O. Box 205
Clearwater 34617-0205 (813) 462-1130

Established in 1969 in FL by trust agreement.
Foundation type: Community
Financial data (yr. ended 12/31/89): Assets, $3,876,943 (M); expenditures, $265,000, including $260,000 for 29 grants (high: $2,500; low: $1,500; average: $2,000).
Purpose and activities: Support limited to charitable activities in Pinellas County.
Types of support: General purposes, operating budgets.
Limitations: Giving limited to Pinellas County, FL. No grants to individuals (except from donor-designated funds), or for endowment funds, research, scholarships, fellowships, or matching gifts; no loans.
Publications: Application guidelines, 990-PF, annual report.
Application information: Application form required.
Initial approach: Proposal
Copies of proposal: 1
Deadline(s): Nov. 1
Board meeting date(s): Jan.
Final notification: 3 months
Write: Thomas R. Bruckman, Exec. Dir.
Officers and Governors: Dennis P. Thompson, Chair.; J. Fred Campbell, Vice-Chair.; Sandra M. Cassidy, Secy.; Albert Blomquist, Mary Lou Dobbs, Israel Heard, Sherman Pace, Kenneth Webster.
Trustee Banks: Barnett Banks Trust Co., N.A., Citizens & Southern Trust Co., Comerica Trust Co. of Florida, N.A., First Florida Bank, First National Bank of Clearwater, First Union National Bank of Florida, NCNB National Bank of Florida, South Trust Co., Southeast Banks Trust Co., SunBank of Tampa Bay.
Number of staff: 1 part-time professional.
Employer Identification Number: 237113194

1434
Albin Polasek Foundation, Inc. ⌘
P.O. Box 1691
Winter Park 32790

Established in 1963 in FL.
Foundation type: Independent
Financial data (yr. ended 12/31/88): Assets, $1,022,322 (M); expenditures, $78,014, including $12,000 for 3 grants of $4,000 each.
Purpose and activities: Support for educational and arts organizations.
Limitations: Giving primarily in FL.
Officers: Webber B. Haines, Pres.; Kenneth Wacker,* Secy.; John Dem. Haines,* Treas.; Randal L. Knight, William Muska.
Directors:* Roman Hruska.
Employer Identification Number: 591102353

1435
Posnack Family Foundation of Hollywood ☆
c/o Barnett Banks Trust Co., N.A.
P.O. Box 40200
Jacksonville 32203-0200

Established in 1984 in FL.
Foundation type: Independent
Financial data (yr. ended 01/31/89): Assets, $5,152,265 (M); gifts received, $1,477; expenditures, $491,630, including $467,550 for grants.
Purpose and activities: Support for Jewish organizations, including welfare funds and education.
Trustee: Barnett Banks Trust Co., N.A.
Employer Identification Number: 592484512

1436
The Poynter Fund ⌘
490 First Ave. South
P.O. Box 625
St. Petersburg 33731 (813) 893-8111

Incorporated in 1953 in DC.
Donor(s): Henrietta M. Poynter,† Nelson Poynter.†
Foundation type: Independent
Financial data (yr. ended 11/30/88): Assets, $2,597,925 (M); gifts received, $202,000; expenditures, $181,930, including $86,000 for 5 grants (high: $25,000; low: $1,000) and $77,083 for 37 grants to individuals (high: $9,000; low: $500).
Purpose and activities: Scholarships and fellowships to train, assist, and inspire journalists of all media, with emphasis on print journalism, to improve the reporting and the objective interpretation of news of domestic governments; to link the academic study of political science with the practice of journalism and government. Grants also for educational and cultural projects.
Types of support: Fellowships, student aid.
Application information: Applications not accepted.
Write: Catherine Heron, Secy.
Officers: Andrew E. Barnes,* Pres.; John H. O'Hearn,* V.P. and Treas.; Catherine Heron, Secy.
Trustees:* Robert T. Pittman, Marion K. Poynter, George Rahdert.
Employer Identification Number: 596142547

1437
The John E. & Aliese Price Foundation, Inc.
1279 Lavin Ln.
P.O. Box 4607
North Fort Myers 33918-4607 (813) 656-0196

Incorporated in 1961 in FL.
Donor(s): John E. Price,† Aliese Price.†
Foundation type: Independent
Financial data (yr. ended 08/31/89): Assets, $11,654,789 (M); expenditures, $649,016, including $454,220 for 66 grants (high: $151,500; low: $150; average: $1,000-$5,000).
Purpose and activities: Grants primarily for Protestant church support and religious associations, including missionary work; some support also for youth agencies, health agencies, and aid to the handicapped.
Types of support: Continuing support, annual campaigns, building funds, matching funds, scholarship funds, research.
Limitations: Giving primarily in southwest FL. No grants to individuals.
Application information: Application form not required.
Initial approach: Telephone

Deadline(s): Submit proposal preferably in July; no set deadline
Board meeting date(s): Jan. and Sept.
Write: T. Wainwright Miller, Jr., Pres.
Officers and Trustees:* John E. Price, Jr.,* Chair.; T. Wainwright Miller, Jr.,* Pres.; George F. Sanders,* V.P.; Dennis G. Small,* Secy.; Daniel F. Adams, Mavis S. Miller, Mildred Price.
Number of staff: 1 full-time support; 1 part-time support.
Employer Identification Number: 591056841

1438
Pyramid Foundation, Inc. ⌑
P.O. Box 13225
Tampa 33681-3225

Established in 1950 in NY.
Foundation type: Independent
Financial data (yr. ended 12/31/88): Assets, $2,026,840 (L); expenditures, $186,282, including $179,858 for 56 grants (high: $100,000; low: $100).
Purpose and activities: Giving primarily for Jewish welfare and temple support; support also for social services and hospitals.
Limitations: Giving primarily in NY. No grants to individuals.
Application information: Contributes only to pre-selected organizations. Applications not accepted.
Officers: Donald B. Cohen, V.P.; Michael Cohen, Treas.
Employer Identification Number: 136083997

1439
Rainforth Foundation, Inc. ⌑
3001 Ponce de Leon Blvd., Suite 200
Coral Gables 33134 (305) 446-7666

Incorporated in 1949 in FL.
Donor(s): Selden I. Rainforth,† Edith Rainforth,† Continental Equities, Inc.
Foundation type: Independent
Financial data (yr. ended 12/31/88): Assets, $1,523,288 (M); gifts received, $40,000; expenditures, $99,299, including $31,000 for 3 grants (high: $25,000; low: $1,000).
Purpose and activities: Giving for Protestant religious organizations, particularly youth agencies; also publishes and distributes a law review.
Types of support: Seed money.
Limitations: Giving primarily in FL.
Application information: Application form not required.
Deadline(s): None
Write: Tom Maxey, Pres.
Officers and Directors: Tom Maxey, Pres. and Treas.; Wirt T. Maxey, V.P. and Secy.; Eugene M. Short, Jr., V.P.
Number of staff: 2 part-time support.
Employer Identification Number: 592373813

1440
The Norman R. Rales and Ruth Rales Foundation ⌑ ☆
4000 North Federal Hwy., No. 204
Boca Raton 33431

Established in 1986 in FL.
Donor(s): Norman R. Rales.
Foundation type: Independent
Financial data (yr. ended 11/30/88): Assets, $2,360,682 (M); gifts received, $88,300; expenditures, $75,364, including $60,472 for 16 grants (high: $20,000; low: $300).
Purpose and activities: Giving primarily for Jewish welfare and religious organizations, social services, and health associations.
Limitations: Giving primarily in NY and FL. No grants to individuals.
Application information: Contributes only to pre-selected organizations. Applications not accepted.
Trustees: Morris Edelstein, Norman R. Rales, Ruth Rales.
Employer Identification Number: 596874589

1441
The Alexander Rapaport Foundation ⌑
175 Bradley Place
Palm Beach 33480

Established in 1981 in FL.
Foundation type: Independent
Financial data (yr. ended 12/31/88): Assets, $5,211 (L); gifts received, $150,000; expenditures, $153,056, including $153,000 for 3 grants (high: $125,000; low: $3,000).
Purpose and activities: Support primarily for synagogues and hospitals.
Limitations: No grants to individuals.
Application information: Contributes only to pre-selected organizations. Applications not accepted.
Officers: Herbert Marton, Mgr.; Michael S. Rapaport, Mgr.; Robert D. Rapaport, Mgr.
Employer Identification Number: 592161648

1442
Paul E. & Ida Klare Reinhold Foundation, Inc. ☆
112 West Adams St., No. 1725
Jacksonville 32202 (904) 354-2359

Established in 1954.
Donor(s): Paul E. Reinhold.†
Foundation type: Independent
Financial data (yr. ended 12/31/89): Assets, $3,683,927 (M); expenditures, $245,370, including $240,386 for 32 grants (high: $160,200; low: $50).
Purpose and activities: Giving for higher and other education, hospitals and health associations, social services, animal welfare, the arts, religious purposes, and child welfare and youth organizations.
Types of support: Annual campaigns, building funds, capital campaigns, operating budgets.
Limitations: Giving primarily in FL. No grants to individuals.
Publications: Annual report.
Application information: Application form required.
Initial approach: Letter
Copies of proposal: 1
Deadline(s): Apr. 30 and Sept. 30
Board meeting date(s): May and Oct.
Write: June R. Myers, Chair.
Officers: June R. Myers, Chair. and Treas.; Leah B. Giebeig, Secy.
Trustees: Thomas E. Camp III, Ralph H. Martin.
Number of staff: None.
Employer Identification Number: 596140495

1443
The Revere Foundation, Inc. ⌑ ☆
621 Northwest S3, Suite 240
Boca Raton 33487 (407) 241-3911

Established in 1960.
Donor(s): Revere Copper and Brass.
Foundation type: Company-sponsored
Financial data (yr. ended 12/31/88): Assets, $141,597 (M); expenditures, $198,344, including $195,000 for 2 grants (high: $100,000; low: $95,000).
Purpose and activities: Giving for a library and historic preservation.
Application information: Applications not accepted.
Write: Richard Olson, Asst. Treas., Revere Copper and Brass
Employer Identification Number: 136098441

1444
Jacob & Sophie Rice Family Foundation, Inc. ⌑
c/o Hamilton & Co.
P.O. Box 6370
Vero Beach 32961

Incorporated in 1968 in NY.
Donor(s): Mathilde T. Rice.†
Foundation type: Independent
Financial data (yr. ended 12/31/88): Assets, $1,741,326 (M); expenditures, $126,669, including $107,500 for 10 grants (high: $50,000; low: $1,000; average: $2,000-$10,000).
Purpose and activities: Support largely for hospitals and Roman Catholic welfare funds; some grants also for higher education.
Limitations: Giving primarily in NY.
Trustees: Richard G. Keneven, Edwin McMahon Singer.
Employer Identification Number: 136264756

1445
Rinker Companies Foundation, Inc. ⌑
1501 Belvedere Rd.
West Palm Beach 33406 (305) 833-5555

Incorporated in 1957 in FL.
Donor(s): Rinker Materials Corp.
Foundation type: Company-sponsored
Financial data (yr. ended 3/31/89): Assets, $9,216,852 (M); gifts received, $963,304; expenditures, $1,324,831, including $1,045,100 for 8 grants (high: $500,000; low: $100) and $193,612 for 133 grants to individuals (high: $3,000; low: $250).
Purpose and activities: Grants primarily for higher education, including scholarships to individuals who are FL residents with business or construction industry-related majors; support also for Protestant churches.
Types of support: General purposes, student aid.
Limitations: Giving primarily in FL.
Application information: Application form required.
Deadline(s): Apr. 1
Write: Frank S. LaPlaca, Asst. Secy.
Officers and Trustees: M.E. Rinker, Sr., Pres. and Treas.; R.A. Krause, V.P.; J.F. Jackson, Secy.; Frank S. LaPlaca, Admin.; J.F. Kingston, W.J. Payne, D.B. Rinker, J.J. Rinker.
Employer Identification Number: 596139266

1446
River Branch Foundation
1514 Nira St.
Jacksonville 32207 (904) 396-5831

Trust established in 1963 in NJ.
Donor(s): J. Seward Johnson 1951 and 1961 Charitable Trusts, The Atlantic Foundation.
Foundation type: Independent
Financial data (yr. ended 12/31/88): Assets, $4,561,825 (M); expenditures, $184,630, including $146,500 for 12 grants (high: $50,000; low: $500).
Purpose and activities: Giving for youth agencies, education, the environment, the arts, and cultural programs.
Limitations: Giving primarily in the Jacksonville, FL, area. No grants to individuals.
Application information: Contributes only to pre-selected organizations. Applications not accepted.
Write: Walter L. Woolfe, Trustee
Trustees: A.M. Foote, Jr., Nathan J. Travassos, Walter L. Woolfe.
Employer Identification Number: 226054887

1447
Roberts Charitable Trust ⌑
P.O. Box 40200
Jacksonville 32203-0200 (904) 798-1887

Foundation type: Independent
Financial data (yr. ended 8/31/88): Assets, $1,055,115 (M); expenditures, $42,364, including $25,088 for 26 grants (high: $2,100; low: $85; average: $500-$1,000).
Purpose and activities: Support for educational and cultural institutions, and social service and community organizations.
Limitations: Giving primarily in FL.
Application information: Application form not required.
Write: c/o Barnett Banks Trust Co., N.A.
Trustees: Garnet Ashby, T.S. Robert III, Barnett Banks Trust Co., N.A.
Employer Identification Number: 596559688

1448
William Rosenberg Family Foundation
6586 Patio Ln.
Boca Raton 33433 (407) 392-2189

Established in 1986 in FL.
Donor(s): Ann Rosenberg, William Rosenberg.
Foundation type: Independent
Financial data (yr. ended 12/31/89): Assets, $2,578,000 (M); gifts received, $480,000; expenditures, $149,544, including $141,700 for 6 grants (high: $100,000; low: $1,000).
Purpose and activities: Support primarily to a cancer research institute and an umbrella organization that "enables educational institutions to obtain certification in franchising as an academic program." Support also for child development and welfare, social services, Jewish giving, education, the environment, and health.
Types of support: Continuing support, endowment funds, general purposes, professorships, research, seed money.
Limitations: No grants to individuals.
Application information: Application form not required.
Initial approach: Letter
Copies of proposal: 1
Deadline(s): None
Board meeting date(s): First week in Dec.
Final notification: Dec.
Write: Ann Rosenberg, Dir.
Officers and Director:* William Rosenberg, Pres. and Treas.; Ann Rosenberg,* V.P. and Secy.
Number of staff: None.
Employer Identification Number: 592675613

1449
William J. & Tina Rosenberg Foundation
2511 Ponce de Leon Blvd.
Coral Gables 33134 (305) 444-6121

Established in 1970 in FL.
Donor(s): Tina Rosenberg.†
Foundation type: Independent
Financial data (yr. ended 04/30/89): Assets, $2,773,194 (M); expenditures, $168,664, including $134,412 for 10 grants (high: $52,000; low: $5,000).
Purpose and activities: Giving for social service programs for the homeless and disadvantaged, youth and child welfare agencies, education, the environment, museums, and human rights.
Limitations: Giving primarily in Dade County, FL. No grants to individuals.
Publications: Application guidelines.
Application information: Application form not required.
Initial approach: Proposal
Copies of proposal: 2
Deadline(s): None
Board meeting date(s): Monthly
Trustees: Jack G. Admire, Southeast Bank, N.A.
Number of staff: 1 part-time support.
Employer Identification Number: 237088390

1450
Rose & Harry Rosenthal Foundation ⌑ ☆
11 Island Ave., Belle Isle
Miami Beach 33139

Established in 1959.
Donor(s): Harry Rosenthal, Miriam Rosenthal.
Foundation type: Independent
Financial data (yr. ended 12/31/88): Assets, $127,129 (M); gifts received, $27,125; expenditures, $115,498, including $115,340 for 25 grants (high: $103,118; low: $10).
Purpose and activities: Support for Jewish organizations, including welfare funds.
Types of support: General purposes.
Application information:
Initial approach: Letter
Deadline(s): None
Write: Harry Rosenthal, Trustee
Trustee: Harry Rosenthal.
Employer Identification Number: 416034855

1451
Jay B. Rudolph Foundation, Inc. ⌑ ☆
200 South Hoover St., Bldg. No. 205
Tampa 33609-3522

Established in 1969.
Foundation type: Independent
Financial data (yr. ended 12/31/88): Assets, $145,494 (M); gifts received, $130,000; expenditures, $114,457, including $114,304 for 57 grants (high: $21,500; low: $35).
Purpose and activities: Giving primarily for Jewish giving; some support for the arts and higher and other education.
Limitations: Giving primarily in FL. No grants to individuals.
Application information: Contributes only to pre-selected organizations. Applications not accepted.
Officers: Jay B. Rudolph, Pres.; Ronald J. Rudolph, V.P.; Edith B. Rudolph, Secy.; Richard A. Rudolph, Treas.
Employer Identification Number: 237029166

1452
J. H. & F. H. Rumbaugh Foundation ⌑ ☆
1401 Main St.
P.O. Box 3749
Sarasota 34230-3749

Established in 1986 in FL.
Foundation type: Independent
Financial data (yr. ended 3/31/89): Assets, $3,438,813 (M); expenditures, $310,362, including $275,568 for 3 grants of $91,856 each.
Purpose and activities: Giving for higher education.
Types of support: General purposes.
Limitations: Giving primarily in PA. No grants to individuals.
Application information: Contributes only to pre-selected organizations. Applications not accepted.
Trustee: Southeast Bank, N.A.
Employer Identification Number: 596851866

1453
Robert Russell Memorial Foundation ⌑
Northern Trust Bank of Florida, N.A.
700 Brickell Ave.
Miami 33131-2804
Application address: c/o Greenberg, Traurig, et al., 1221 Brickell Ave., Miami, FL 33131

Established in 1984 in FL.
Foundation type: Independent
Financial data (yr. ended 08/31/89): Assets, $13,507,789 (M); gifts received, $8,315,418; expenditures, $545,991, including $482,000 for 14 grants (high: $130,000; low: $10,000).
Purpose and activities: Support primarily for Jewish welfare and higher education.
Types of support: General purposes.
Limitations: Giving primarily in the Dade County, FL, area.
Application information:
Write: Norman H. Lipoff, Trustee
Trustees: Norman H. Lipoff, Simeon D. Spear, Northern Trust Bank of Florida, N.A.
Employer Identification Number: 592486579

1454
The Ryder System Charitable Foundation, Inc. ▼
c/o Ryder System, Inc.
3600 N.W. 82nd Ave.
Miami 33166 (305) 593-3642

Established in 1984 in FL.
Donor(s): Ryder System, Inc.

Foundation type: Company-sponsored
Financial data (yr. ended 12/31/87): Assets, $914,000 (M); gifts received, $1,680,000; expenditures, $1,518,529, including $1,489,922 for 308 grants (high: $150,000; low: $25; average: $1,000-$30,000).
Purpose and activities: Grants for health and human services, educational, cultural, civic, and literary organizations that operate in communities having significant concentrations of Ryder personnel; giving also for the advancement of minorities and disadvantaged groups.
Types of support: Employee matching gifts, annual campaigns, operating budgets, scholarship funds.
Limitations: Giving primarily in areas of company operations.
Publications: Corporate giving report.
Application information:
Initial approach: Letter
Copies of proposal: 1
Deadline(s): 1st half of the calendar year
Board meeting date(s): Annually and as needed
Final notification: Within 4 months
Write: Office of Corp. Progs.
Officers and Directors: M. Anthony Burns, Chair. and Pres.; Edwin A. Huston, V.P.; David R. Parker, V.P.; James M. Herron, Secy.; Wendell R. Beard, Donald W. Estes, Robert G. Lambert, Gail M. McDonald.
Number of staff: 1 full-time professional; 1 full-time support.
Employer Identification Number: 592462315

1455
Saint Gerard Foundation
3041 Braeloch Circle East
Clearwater 34621-2708

Established in 1966 in OH.
Donor(s): Mooney Chemicals, Inc.
Foundation type: Independent
Financial data (yr. ended 12/31/88): Assets, $3,010,097 (M); gifts received, $616,555; expenditures, $693,987, including $686,548 for 280 grants (high: $100,000; low: $10).
Purpose and activities: Giving primarily for conservative public policy organizations and Roman Catholic church support, including groups concerned with social issues; support also for higher and secondary education.
Limitations: No grants to individuals.
Application information: Contributes only to pre-selected organizations. Applications not accepted.
Write: Elizabeth C. Mooney, V.P.
Officers and Trustees:* James B. Mooney,* Pres. and Treas.; Elizabeth C. Mooney,* V.P.; William E. Reichard, Secy.; Rev. Michael X. Mooney.
Number of staff: None.
Employer Identification Number: 346574667

1456
Adrian M. Sample Trust No. 2 ⌑
c/o SunBank/Treasure Coast, N.A.
P.O. Box 8
Fort Pierce 34954 (305) 461-6300
Grant application office: 14050 Fairway Willow Ln., Winter Gardens, FL 32787; Tel.: (407) 877-9901

Trust established in 1972 in FL.
Foundation type: Independent
Financial data (yr. ended 12/31/88): Assets, $1,412,200 (M); expenditures, $106,266, including $82,100 for 81 grants to individuals (high: $4,500; low: $300).
Purpose and activities: Grants for scholarship aid to Protestant students who are unmarried and active church members.
Types of support: Student aid.
Limitations: Giving limited to residents of St. Lucie or Okeechobee counties, FL.
Publications: Program policy statement, application guidelines.
Application information: Application forms available only through churches in St. Lucie or Okeechobee counties. Application form required.
Initial approach: Letter
Copies of proposal: 2
Deadline(s): Apr. 15
Board meeting date(s): May, and as required
Write: Charles W. Sample, Trustee
Trustees: Charles W. Sample, SunBank/Treasure Coast, N.A.
Employer Identification Number: 596490788

1457
The Sarasota County Community Foundation, Inc. ☆
P.O. Box 49587
Sarasota 34230-4958 (813) 955-3000
Office address: 1800 Second St., Suite 753, Sarasota, FL 34236

Incorporated in 1979 in FL.
Foundation type: Community
Financial data (yr. ended 12/31/89): Assets, $459,266 (M); gifts received, $271,809; expenditures, $257,842, including $137,496 for 50 grants (high: $37,500; low: $300; average: $2,000-$5,000), $23,074 for 14 grants to individuals (high: $2,000; low: $1,000; average: $1,000-$5,000), $5,000 for 1 foundation-administered program and $1,000 for 1 in-kind gift.
Purpose and activities: Giving primarily for arts and culture, human services, health care, education, and the environment.
Types of support: Emergency funds, equipment, seed money, special projects.
Limitations: Giving limited to Sarasota County, FL. No support for religious, political, or fraternal organizations. No grants to individuals.
Publications: Informational brochure, annual report, application guidelines, grants list, newsletter, program policy statement.
Application information: Application form required.
Initial approach: Proposal
Copies of proposal: 1
Deadline(s): May 1 and Nov. 1
Board meeting date(s): May and Nov.
Write: Stewart W. Stearns, Exec. Dir.
Officers: Mrs. Michael Gompertz,* Pres.; Kathleen O. Cress,* V.P.; David Steves,* V.P.; Kent Stottlereyer,* Treas.; Stewart W. Stearns, Exec. Dir.
Directors:* Dee Anderson, Gregory M. Colby, Mrs. R.G. Denovan, and 23 other directors.
Number of staff: 1 full-time professional; 1 full-time support.
Employer Identification Number: 591956886

1458
The Saunders Foundation ⌑
c/o First Florida Bank, Trust Dept.
P.O. Box 1810
Tampa 33601 (813) 224-1535

Established in 1970 in FL.
Donor(s): William N. Saunders,† Ruby Lee Saunders.†
Foundation type: Independent
Financial data (yr. ended 12/31/87): Assets, $9,262,389 (M); expenditures, $579,093, including $391,347 for 24 grants.
Purpose and activities: Support for higher education, youth agencies, music, and the fine arts.
Types of support: Scholarship funds, matching funds.
Limitations: Giving primarily in western FL. No support for travel projects or to organizations which promote sports or athletic competition. No grants for fellowships or operating funds.
Publications: Application guidelines.
Application information: Application form required.
Copies of proposal: 2
Deadline(s): None
Board meeting date(s): 1st Wednesday of each month
Write: James M. Kelly, V.P.
Officers and Directors: Herbert G. McKay, Pres.; James M. Kelly, V.P. and Treas.; Michael G. Emmanuel, Secy.; Solon F. O'Neal, Jr.
Number of staff: None.
Employer Identification Number: 596152326

1459
Aaron & Martha Schecter Private Foundation ⌑ ☆
c/o Gene Glasser
P.O. Box 650
Hollywood 33022-0650

Established in 1981.
Foundation type: Independent
Financial data (yr. ended 9/30/88): Assets, $2,082,820 (M); expenditures, $144,311, including $127,050 for 62 grants (high: $25,000; low: $100).
Purpose and activities: Giving to international affairs, public policy groups promoting peace and social responsibilty, and civil rights organizations; support also for education, Jewish giving, Christian organizations, and the arts.
Application information: Contributes only to pre-selected organizations. Applications not accepted.
Trustees: Gene Glasser, Aaron Schecter, Martha Schecter.
Employer Identification Number: 592185762

1460
Schultz Foundation, Inc.
c/o Schultz Bldg.
P.O. Box 1200
Jacksonville 32201 (904) 354-3603

Established in 1964 in FL.
Donor(s): Mae W. Schultz,† Geneive S. Ayers,† Frederick H. Schultz, Nancy R. Schultz.
Foundation type: Independent

Financial data (yr. ended 12/31/89): Assets, $2,423,669 (M); expenditures, $112,852, including $89,191 for 51 grants (high: $10,000; low: $20).
Purpose and activities: Support primarily for community funds; cultural organizations, including the fine arts, music, and dance; social services, including programs for youth and child welfare, drug abuse, and AIDS; educational institutions; and wildlife and the environment.
Types of support: General purposes.
Limitations: Giving primarily in Jacksonville, FL, and GA. No grants to individuals.
Publications: Annual report.
Application information: Application form not required.
Initial approach: Letter; no telephone calls
Deadline(s): None
Write: Clifford G. Schultz II, Pres.
Officers: Clifford G. Schultz II,* Pres.; Nancy R. Schultz,* V.P.; John F. Reilly, Secy.-Treas.
Trustees:* Catherine Kelly, Frederick H. Schultz, Jr., John R. Schultz.
Number of staff: None.
Employer Identification Number: 591055869

1461
William G. Selby and Marie Selby Foundation ▼
Southeast Bank
P.O. Box 267
Sarasota 34230 (813) 951-7241

Trust established in 1955 in FL.
Donor(s): William G. Selby,† Marie M. Selby.†
Foundation type: Independent
Financial data (yr. ended 05/31/89): Assets, $41,474,516 (M); expenditures, $1,963,877, including $1,654,746 for 80 grants (high: $200,000; low: $1,000; average: $10,000-$50,000).
Purpose and activities: Emphasis on scholarships and capital grants for giving directly to Florida colleges and universities; local giving also for the aged, hospitals, social service and youth agencies, and cultural programs.
Types of support: Building funds, equipment, land acquisition, matching funds, scholarship funds, renovation projects.
Limitations: Giving limited to FL, with emphasis on the Sarasota area. No grants to individuals, or for general purposes, continuing support, annual campaigns, deficit financing, seed money, emergency funds, operating budgets, endowment funds, special projects, research, publications, or conferences; no loans.
Publications: Informational brochure, program policy statement, application guidelines.
Application information: Application form required.
Initial approach: Letter
Copies of proposal: 3
Deadline(s): Submit proposal preferably in July and Dec.; deadlines Aug. 1 and Feb. 1
Board meeting date(s): June, Sept., Dec., and Mar.
Final notification: 2 to 6 months
Write: Robert E. Perkins, Exec. Dir.
Trustee: Southeast Banks Trust Co.
Administrative Committee: Jerome A. Jannopoulo, Chair.; Robert E. Perkins, Exec. Dir.; John Davidson, Anthony DeDeyn, Wendel Kent, Martha Marland, Charles E. Stottlemyer.
Number of staff: 1 full-time professional; 1 part-time support.
Employer Identification Number: 596121242

1462
Carl and Ruth Shapiro Foundation ⌑
Two North Breakers Row
Palm Beach 33480

Established originally in MA as Carl Shapiro Foundation.
Foundation type: Independent
Financial data (yr. ended 12/31/88): Assets, $2,274,461 (M); expenditures, $449,956, including $436,750 for 32 grants (high: $126,000; low: $50).
Purpose and activities: Grants primarily for Jewish welfare funds, higher education, hospitals, art organizations, and museums.
Application information: Contributes only to pre-selected organizations. Applications not accepted.
Officers: Carl Shapiro, Pres.; Ruth Shapiro, Secy.
Employer Identification Number: 046135027

1463
The Slotnick Foundation ⌑
7613 Wood Duck Rd.
Boca Raton 33434

Established in 1986 in FL.
Foundation type: Independent
Financial data (yr. ended 12/31/88): Assets, $1,905,108 (M); gifts received, $300,000; expenditures, $107,134, including $93,225 for 9 grants (high: $300,000; low: $225).
Purpose and activities: Support primarily for Jewish welfare, a college, and a symphony orchestra.
Limitations: Giving primarily in FL and Syracuse, NY.
Application information:
Initial approach: Letter
Deadline(s): None
Write: Herbert N. Slotnick, Trustee
Trustee: Herbert N. Slotnick.
Employer Identification Number: 596883622

1464
McGregor Smith Foundation, Inc. ⌑ ☆
Dadeland Towers
9200 Dadeland Blvd., Suite 515
Miami 33156 (305) 662-5852

Established in 1963.
Donor(s): McGregor Smith.†
Foundation type: Independent
Financial data (yr. ended 12/31/88): Assets, $1,125,404 (M); gifts received, $5,852; expenditures, $70,463, including $47,844 for grants.
Purpose and activities: Awards grants and loans to individuals for higher education; limited giving also for Protestant churches and health associations.
Types of support: Student loans.
Application information: Application form required.
Write: Wilson Smith, Esq., Pres.
Officers and Trustees: Wilson Smith, Pres. and Treas.; Elizabeth W. Smith, V.P.; Charles B. Marman, Secy.
Employer Identification Number: 591038572

1465
The Sonderling Foundation, Inc. ⌑ ☆
3050 Biscayne Blvd., Suite 1003
Miami 33137

Established in 1968.
Foundation type: Independent
Financial data (yr. ended 12/31/88): Assets, $16,274 (M); gifts received, $105,000; expenditures, $340,388, including $336,754 for 63 grants (high: $125,000; low: $15).
Purpose and activities: Giving for Jewish welfare and temple support, cancer research and health associations, animal welfare, the performing arts and other cultural programs, churches, and social services.
Limitations: Giving primarily in FL.
Application information:
Initial approach: Letter
Deadline(s): None
Write: Egmont Sonderling, Pres.
Officers: Egmont Sonderling, Pres. and Secy.; Frosene Sonderling, V.P. and Treas.
Employer Identification Number: 237024220

1466
Samuel M. Soref Charitable Trust ⌑
c/o London Witte & Co.
500 Cypress Creek Rd. West, Suite 420
Fort Lauderdale 33309

Trust established in 1969 in FL.
Donor(s): Samuel M. Soref, Helene K. Soref.
Foundation type: Independent
Financial data (yr. ended 12/31/88): Assets, $11,350,944 (M); gifts received, $40,450; expenditures, $528,422, including $516,329 for 23 grants (high: $203,500; low: $100).
Purpose and activities: Emphasis on Jewish welfare funds, temple support, higher education, and social service agencies; some support also for organizations in Israel.
Limitations: Giving primarily in FL. No grants to individuals.
Application information: Contributes only to pre-selected organizations. Applications not accepted.
Officers: Samuel M. Soref, Pres. and Treas.; Helene K. Soref, V.P.; Marvin E. Klitsner, Secy.
Employer Identification Number: 396107640

1467
Samuel M. Soref & Helene K. Soref Foundation ⌑
c/o Citizens & Southern Trust Co.
P.O. Box 5367
Fort Lauderdale 33340-5367

Established in 1983 in FL.
Foundation type: Independent
Financial data (yr. ended 12/31/87): Assets, $2,498,711 (M); gifts received, $489,172; expenditures, $86,100, including $76,321 for 4 grants (high: $35,000; low: $11,321).
Purpose and activities: Support primarily for a Jewish community center; support also for an institute for public research.
Types of support: Building funds, research.

Application information: Contributes only to pre-selected organizations. Applications not accepted.
Trustees: Helene K. Soref, Samuel M. Soref, Citizens & Southern Trust Co.
Employer Identification Number: 592246963

1468
Southeast Banking Corporation Foundation ▼ ⌑
One S.E. Financial Ctr., 22nd Fl.
Miami 33131 (305) 375-7295

Established in 1980 in FL.
Donor(s): Southeast Banking Corp., and its affiliates.
Foundation type: Company-sponsored
Financial data (yr. ended 12/31/88): Assets, $1,030,652 (M); gifts received, $1,556,334; expenditures, $1,475,137, including $1,454,555 for 187 grants (high: $385,000; low: $20; average: $1,500-$35,000).
Purpose and activities: Giving primarily for health and welfare, the United Way, cultural programs, and education.
Types of support: Operating budgets, annual campaigns, seed money, publications, conferences and seminars, scholarship funds, consulting services, technical assistance, general purposes, special projects.
Limitations: Giving primarily in FL. No grants to individuals. Generally no support for capital or endowment funds.
Publications: Annual report (including application guidelines).
Application information: Application form not required.
Initial approach: Telephone, letter, or proposal
Copies of proposal: 3
Deadline(s): None
Board meeting date(s): Quarterly and as required
Final notification: 6 to 8 weeks
Write: Robin Reiter-Faragalli, Exec. Dir.
Officer: Robin Reiter-Faragalli, Exec. Dir.
Trustees: David Aucamp, Rip DuPont, Bill Klich, Tom Woolsey.
Number of staff: 1 full-time professional; 2 full-time support.
Employer Identification Number: 592402225

1469
The Southwest Florida Community Foundation, Inc.
5264 Clayton Court, Suite 1
Fort Myers 33907 (813) 936-3929
Application address: P.O. Box 9326, Fort Myers, FL 33902

Incorporated in 1976 in FL.
Donor(s): Lorraine Blowstine,† Isabel Kirkpatrick,† Leonard Santini.†
Foundation type: Community
Financial data (yr. ended 09/30/89): Assets, $4,929,981 (M); gifts received, $699,000; expenditures, $344,000, including $265,000 for grants (average: $5,000-$15,000) and $14,000 for grants to individuals.
Purpose and activities: Giving locally for charitable purposes with emphasis on education and social services.
Types of support: Seed money, building funds, equipment, matching funds, student aid.
Limitations: Giving limited to Lee County, FL. No grants for operating budgets, continuing support, annual campaigns, emergency funds, deficit financing, land acquisition, endowment funds, research, publications, conferences and seminars, or special programs; no loans.
Publications: Annual report, informational brochure (including application guidelines), 990-PF.
Application information: Application form required.
Initial approach: Telephone, letter, or proposal
Copies of proposal: 22
Deadline(s): Feb. 1, May 1, and Aug. 1
Board meeting date(s): Mar., June, Sept., and Dec.
Final notification: Several days after board meeting
Write: Alan J. Robertson, Exec. Dir.
Officers and Trustees:* Gene R. Solomon,* Pres.; Arnold L. Sarlo,* V.P.; Susan Bennett,* Secy.-Treas.; and 11 additional trustees.
Number of staff: 1 part-time professional; 1 part-time support.
Employer Identification Number: 596580974

1470
St. Joe Foundation, Inc. ⌑ ☆
P.O. Box 1380
Jacksonville 32201 (904) 396-6600

Established in 1986 in FL.
Foundation type: Independent
Financial data (yr. ended 12/31/88): Assets, $803,462 (M); expenditures, $396,181, including $395,500 for 15 grants (high: $250,000; low: $500).
Purpose and activities: Support for higher education, agriculture, and conservation.
Limitations: Giving primarily in FL. No grants to individuals.
Application information:
Initial approach: Letter
Deadline(s): None
Write: Rosemary Cusimano
Officers: J.C. Belin, Pres.; W.L. Thornton, V.P.; S.D. Fraser, Secy.; E.C. Brownlie, Treas.
Employer Identification Number: 592803132

1471
Festus Stacy Foundation II ⌑
c/o McMillan, Unruh & Davis
1941 West Oakland Park Blvd.
Fort Lauderdale 33311-1572

Established in 1980 in FL.
Donor(s): Festus Stacy.
Foundation type: Independent
Financial data (yr. ended 10/31/88): Assets, $3,927,378 (M); gifts received, $1,094,350; expenditures, $141,689, including $127,000 for 26 grants (high: $25,000; low: $1,000).
Purpose and activities: Support primarily for Christian missionary efforts, churches, and social service programs.
Limitations: No grants to individuals.
Application information: Contributes only to pre-selected organizations. Applications not accepted.
Trustees: Festus Stacy, Helen Stacy, Virlee Stacy Stepelton.
Employer Identification Number: 596698852

1472
Emma L. Staley Foundation ⌑
c/o Northern Trust Bank of Florida, N.A.
700 Brickell Ave.
Miami 33131 (305) 372-1000

Trust established in 1957 in IL.
Donor(s): Emma L. Staley.
Foundation type: Independent
Financial data (yr. ended 12/31/87): Assets, $1,810,000 (M); expenditures, $104,612, including $90,000 for 6 grants (high: $50,000; low: $5,000).
Purpose and activities: Emphasis on higher education and hospitals.
Limitations: Giving primarily in IL. No grants to individuals.
Application information: Generally gives to pre-selected organizations.
Write: Barbara Ausick
Trustees: Gigi Carrier, Shirley I. Cowell, Northern Trust Bank of Florida, N.A.
Employer Identification Number: 366023963

1473
Donald A. and Jane C. Stark Charitable Trust ⌑
c/o Southeast Bank, N.A.
P.O. Box 267
Sarasota 34230
Application address: 5036 Willow Leaf Way, Sarasota, FL 34241

Trust established in 1957 in OH.
Foundation type: Independent
Financial data (yr. ended 12/31/88): Assets, $563,370 (M); expenditures, $344,157, including $335,000 for 5 grants (high: $250,000; low: $5,000).
Purpose and activities: Grants primarily for higher education and student aid; support also for botanical gardens and youth organizations.
Types of support: Endowment funds, student aid.
Limitations: Giving primarily in FL and KS.
Application information: Application form not required.
Deadline(s): None
Write: B. Wade White, Trustee
Trustees: Charles E. Manning, Jane C. Stark, B. Wade White, Southeast Bank, N.A.
Employer Identification Number: 346522476

1474
Stein Family Foundation, Inc.
P.O. Drawer U
Jacksonville 32203

Established in 1949 in FL.
Donor(s): David Stein, Martin Stein.
Foundation type: Independent
Financial data (yr. ended 12/31/88): Assets, $215,360 (M); gifts received, $100,000; expenditures, $178,981, including $178,871 for 19 grants (high: $102,250; low: $50).

Purpose and activities: Grants to Jewish community services, youth organizations, and social services.
Limitations: Giving primarily in FL.
Application information: Application form not required.
Initial approach: Letter
Copies of proposal: 1
Officers and Directors:* Lois Chepenik,* Vice-Chair.; David Stein,* Pres. and Secy.; Tracey Stein, Treas.
Employer Identification Number: 596152351

1475
Ida M. Stevens Foundation, Inc. ⌘
P.O. Box 41222
Jacksonville 32203 (904) 359-0922

Established in 1967.
Donor(s): Virgil A. Stevens.†
Foundation type: Operating
Financial data (yr. ended 12/31/87): Assets, $16,027,769 (M); expenditures, $999,496, including $531,885 for 33 grants (high: $122,502; low: $520).
Purpose and activities: A private operating foundation; giving for social services, rent subsidy, and health programs benefiting the elderly.
Limitations: Giving limited to Jacksonville, FL.
Application information:
Initial approach: Proposal
Deadline(s): None
Write: Douglas J. Milne, Trustee
Trustees: C.L. Garnett Ashby, David Lemmel, Douglas J. Milne.
Employer Identification Number: 591746148

1476
Stickelber Charitable Foundation ⌘
P.O. Box 516
Destin 32541 (904) 837-7498

Incorporated in 1969 in MO.
Foundation type: Independent
Financial data (yr. ended 12/31/88): Assets, $1,160,713 (M); expenditures, $104,593, including $14,129 for 18 grants (high: $3,000; low: $25).
Purpose and activities: Grants primarily for social services, hospitals, higher education, church support, and religious associations.
Types of support: General purposes, building funds, equipment, matching funds.
Limitations: Giving primarily in Destin, FL, and Mobile and Baldwin counties, AL. No grants to individuals, or for endowment funds, research, scholarships, or fellowships; no loans.
Application information:
Initial approach: Letter or proposal
Copies of proposal: 1
Deadline(s): None
Board meeting date(s): Apr., July, Nov., and Dec.
Final notification: Dec. 31
Write: Merlin C. Stickelber, Pres.
Officer and Directors:* Merlin C. Stickelber,* Pres.; F.H. Dietz, Frederick G. Helmsing, Jody S. Stickelber.
Number of staff: 5
Employer Identification Number: 237062356

1477
The George B. Storer Foundation, Inc. ▼ ⌘
P.O. Box 1207
Islamorada 33036 (305) 664-8805

Incorporated in 1955 in FL.
Foundation type: Independent
Financial data (yr. ended 12/31/88): Assets, $43,268,708 (M); expenditures, $2,309,907, including $2,017,234 for 69 grants (high: $200,000; low: $1,000; average: $1,000-$50,000).
Purpose and activities: Grants for higher education, social services, particularly for the blind, youth organizations, conservation, hospitals, and cultural programs.
Types of support: Research, general purposes, building funds, matching funds, endowment funds.
Limitations: Giving primarily in FL. No grants for scholarships or fellowships; no loans.
Application information:
Initial approach: Letter and proposal
Copies of proposal: 1
Deadline(s): Nov. 30
Board meeting date(s): Dec.
Write: Peter Storer, Pres.
Officers and Directors: Peter Storer, Pres. and Treas.; William Michaels, V.P.; James P. Storer, Secy.
Employer Identification Number: 596136392

1478
The Edward C. Stuart Foundation, Inc. ⌘
P.O. Box 250
Bartow 33830 (813) 533-4196

Incorporated in 1957 in FL.
Donor(s): William H. Stuart, and family.
Foundation type: Independent
Financial data (yr. ended 5/31/88): Assets, $2,593,431 (M); expenditures, $344,162, including $300,535 for 9 grants.
Purpose and activities: Giving primarily to a Protestant religious organization and scholarship funds.
Types of support: General purposes, continuing support, seed money, scholarship funds, matching funds.
Limitations: No grants to individuals, or for building or endowment funds, or special projects.
Publications: Annual report, application guidelines.
Application information: Application form required.
Initial approach: Letter
Copies of proposal: 1
Deadline(s): None
Board meeting date(s): Monthly, with decisions on grants in late May and Nov.
Write: Margrette M. Stuart, Pres.
Officers and Directors: Margrette M. Stuart, Pres.; William H. Stuart, Jr., V.P.; C.A. Boswell, Secy.-Treas.; Nelle Kennedy Stuart Lane, Nancy S. Stuart, William H. Stuart.
Employer Identification Number: 596142151

1479
SunBank Foundation ⌘
c/o Donations Comm., SunBank, N.A.
P.O. Box 3838
Orlando 32802 (407) 237-4104

Established in 1986 in FL.
Foundation type: Company-sponsored
Financial data (yr. ended 6/30/88): Assets, $1,000,191 (M); expenditures, $318,852, including $305,000 for 2 grants (high: $300,000; low: $5,000).
Purpose and activities: Support for education.
Limitations: Giving limited to FL. No grants to individuals.
Application information:
Initial approach: Letter
Deadline(s): None
Write: Naomi Hodges
Trustee: SunBank, N.A.
Employer Identification Number: 596877429

1480
Sunburst Foundation, Inc. ⌘
c/o Osborne, Hankins, MacLaren & Redgrave
998 South Federal Hwy., Exec. Suite D
Boca Raton 33432 (407) 368-0376

Established in 1986 in FL.
Donor(s): Fred Lieberman.
Foundation type: Independent
Financial data (yr. ended 6/30/88): Assets, $1,970,586 (M); expenditures, $119,885, including $60,900 for 19 grants to individuals (high: $6,500; low: $1,500).
Purpose and activities: Awards scholarships to individuals for study in the physical sciences.
Types of support: Student aid.
Limitations: Giving primarily in Deerfield and Landale, FL.
Application information: Application form required.
Write: James M. Hankins, Pres.
Officers and Trustees: James M. Hankins, Pres.; Paul R. Rugo, Secy.; Donald E. Baker, Treas.
Employer Identification Number: 592637289

1481
Carl S. Swisher Foundation, Inc. ⌘
P.O. Box 14790
Jacksonville 32238-1790 (904) 389-8320

Incorporated in 1949 in FL.
Donor(s): Carl S. Swisher.†
Foundation type: Independent
Financial data (yr. ended 12/31/88): Assets, $6,612,123 (M); expenditures, $368,189, including $340,500 for 85 grants (high: $50,000; low: $500).
Purpose and activities: Support for higher education; grants also for youth agencies, hospitals, and social services.
Types of support: General purposes.
Limitations: Giving primarily in the Jacksonville, FL, area. No grants to individuals; no loans.
Application information:
Initial approach: Letter or proposal
Copies of proposal: 1
Deadline(s): None
Board meeting date(s): Usually quarterly
Write: E.A. Middlebrooks, Jr., Secy.-Treas.

Officers and Trustees: L.D. Hupp, Pres.; George S. Coulter, V.P.; Harold W. Smith, V.P.; E.A. Middlebrooks, Jr., Secy.-Treas.; Kenneth G. Anderson.
Number of staff: 1 part-time professional.
Employer Identification Number: 590998262

1482
Harcourt M. and Virginia W. Sylvester Foundation, Inc. ¤
c/o NCNB National Bank
P.O. Box 407090, EP 2-3
Fort Lauderdale 33340-7090
Application address: NCNB National Bank, Boca Raton, FL 33432

Established in 1980 in FL.
Donor(s): Harcourt M. Sylvester,† Virginia W. Sylvester.†
Foundation type: Independent
Financial data (yr. ended 07/31/89): Assets, $31,184,726 (M); expenditures, $5,716,821, including $5,513,000 for 2 grants (high: $5,500,000; low: $13,000).
Purpose and activities: Giving primarily to a university medical school; support also for social services and a hospital.
Types of support: Endowment funds.
Limitations: Giving primarily in FL. No grants to individuals.
Application information:
Initial approach: Proposal
Deadline(s): None
Write: Nevin B. Gilpatrick
Officer and Directors:* Harcourt M. Sylvester II,* Pres.; Gary King, James J. Linus.
Trustee Bank: NCNB National Bank.
Employer Identification Number: 592018824

1483
Tampa Cable Television Trust ¤
P.O. Box 320265
Tampa 33679 (813) 875-9461

Established in 1982.
Donor(s): Tampa Cable Television.
Foundation type: Independent
Financial data (yr. ended 12/31/88): Assets, $546,272 (M); gifts received, $250,010; expenditures, $267,816, including $242,000 for 36 grants (high: $17,200; low: $1,000; average: $7,500).
Purpose and activities: Giving for higher education, youth and social service agencies, and cultural programs; strong preference for matching funds.
Types of support: Matching funds.
Limitations: Giving limited to the Tampa, FL, community. No support for organizations which limit services to members of any one religious group. No grants to individuals, or for start-up funds, deficit financing, or fundraising events.
Application information: Application form required.
Deadline(s): Varies each year
Write: Homer Tillery, Chair.
Trustees: Homer Tillery, Chair.; T. Terrell Sessums, Secy.; Otis Anthony, Laura Blain, Nick Capitano, Robert L. Cromwell, Joseph Garcia, Rev. Laurence Higgins, Richard S. Hodes, M.D., William R. Klich, J. Leonard Levy, Rev. A. Leon Lowry, J. Benton Stewart, Gilbert E. Turner, Sandra H. Wilson.
Employer Identification Number: 592273947

1484
George G. Tapper Foundation Trust ¤
P.O. Box 280
Port St. Joe 32456 (904) 227-1111
Additional tel.: (902) 227-1112

Established in 1986 in FL.
Foundation type: Independent
Financial data (yr. ended 12/31/88): Assets, $1,166,975 (M); gifts received, $91,437; expenditures, $14,487, including $12,200 for 2 grants (high: $12,000; low: $200).
Purpose and activities: Support for higher education, health, civic affairs, community development, family services, and culture.
Types of support: Scholarship funds, general purposes.
Limitations: Giving primarily in the gulf and Bay County areas of northwest FL.
Application information: Application form required.
Initial approach: Letter
Copies of proposal: 1
Deadline(s): None
Board meeting date(s): Feb.
Write: Amelia G. Tapper, Mgr.
Trustees: David C. Gaskin, Robert McSpadden, Amelia G. Tapper, Patricia M. Tapper.
Number of staff: None.
Employer Identification Number: 592639039

1485
Jack Taylor Family Foundation, Inc. ¤
1111 Kane Concourse, Suite 619
Bay Harbor Islands 33154

Established in 1968.
Donor(s): Taylor Development Corp., Jack Taylor, and other members of the Taylor family.
Foundation type: Independent
Financial data (yr. ended 12/31/88): Assets, $9,062,630 (M); gifts received, $102,200; expenditures, $362,916, including $306,664 for 21 grants (high: $61,000; low: $250).
Purpose and activities: Grants primarily for hospitals and health agencies, higher education, and Jewish welfare funds and temple support.
Application information: Contributes only to pre-selected organizations. Applications not accepted.
Officers: Jack Taylor,* Pres.; Elly Taylor,* V.P.; Mitchell Taylor,* Secy.; Ilene B. Eefting, Treas.
Directors:* Norman A. Arkin, Victor D. Denbrow, Saul S. Silverman, Harold Zinn.
Employer Identification Number: 596205187

1486
C. Herman Terry Foundation ¤
1301 Gulf Life Dr., Suite 2216
Jacksonville 32207

Established in 1982 in FL.
Donor(s): C. Herman Terry.
Foundation type: Independent
Financial data (yr. ended 12/31/86): Assets, $2,110,459 (M); expenditures, $412,525, including $396,727 for 14 grants (high: $303,000; low: $100).
Purpose and activities: Grants for youth, culture, and religious giving; substantial support for an education foundation.
Trustees: Kenneth A. Barnebey, Hugh T. Nelson, C. Herman Terry, Mary Virginia Terry, James H. Winston.
Employer Identification Number: 592241642

1487
Samuel E. & Mary W. Thatcher Foundation, Inc. ¤
3030 N.E. Second Ave.
Miami 33137

Established in 1982 in FL.
Donor(s): John W. Thatcher, Mary W. Thatcher.†
Foundation type: Independent
Financial data (yr. ended 12/31/88): Assets, $10,400,732 (M); gifts received, $2,700,000; expenditures, $358,073, including $293,000 for 22 grants (high: $50,000; low: $500).
Purpose and activities: Support primarily for religious ministries, particularly for youth.
Application information:
Write: John W. Thatcher, Pres. and Treas.
Officers: John W. Thatcher, Pres. and Treas.; William R. Jordan, V.P.; David M. Richardson, Secy.
Employer Identification Number: 592230243

1488
Dorothy Thomas Foundation, Inc. ¤
P.O. Box 3436
Tampa 33601

Incorporated in 1960 in FL.
Donor(s): Wayne Thomas,† Robert Thomas, Port Sutton, Inc.
Foundation type: Independent
Financial data (yr. ended 12/31/88): Assets, $2,377,205 (M); gifts received, $17,286; expenditures, $126,933, including $109,300 for 10 grants (high: $25,000; low: $1,800).
Purpose and activities: Giving primarily for youth, education, and health, including church-sponsored organizations.
Types of support: Continuing support, general purposes.
Limitations: Giving primarily in FL.
Application information: Contributes only to pre-selected organizations. Applications not accepted.
Officers and Trustees:* Michael Thomas,* Chair. and Treas.; Robert Thomas,* Vice-Chair.; Henry Toland, Secy.
Employer Identification Number: 596059765

1489
The Thoresen Foundation ¤
2881 La Concha Dr.
Clearwater 34622

Trust established in 1952 in IL.
Donor(s): William E. Thoresen, Catherine E. Thoresen.
Foundation type: Independent
Financial data (yr. ended 2/29/88): Assets, $4,014,202 (M); gifts received, $75,000; expenditures, $203,221, including $198,525 for grants.
Purpose and activities: Emphasis on higher education; grants also for hospitals, social service agencies, museums, and cultural programs.

Limitations: Giving primarily in FL and IL. No grants to individuals, or for scholarships.
Application information:
Initial approach: Letter
Board meeting date(s): As required
Write: George V. Berger, Trustee
Trustees: George V. Berger, Katherine Culver, Catherine E. Thoresen, William E. Thoresen.
Number of staff: None.
Employer Identification Number: 366102493

1490
Bertha B. Turck Charitable Trust ⌑
c/o Barnett Banks Trust Co., N.A.
P.O. Box 40200
Jacksonville 32203-0200

Established in 1981 in FL.
Foundation type: Independent
Financial data (yr. ended 12/31/88): Assets, $1,535,063 (M); expenditures, $106,771, including $97,153 for 4 grants (high: $24,289; low: $24,288).
Purpose and activities: Support for hospitals.
Application information:
Deadline(s): None
Trustee: Barnett Banks Trust Co., N.A.
Employer Identification Number: 596121061

1491
United States Sugar Corporation Charitable Trust ⌑
c/o United States Sugar Corp.
P.O. Drawer 1207
Clewiston 33440 (813) 983-8121

Trust established in 1952 in FL.
Donor(s): United States Sugar Corp.
Foundation type: Company-sponsored
Financial data (yr. ended 10/31/88): Assets, $2,257,150 (M); expenditures, $375,635, including $349,795 for 66 grants (high: $41,120; low: $500).
Purpose and activities: Giving for private higher education, community improvement, social service agencies, and hospitals.
Limitations: Giving primarily in FL. No grants to individuals, or for scholarships or fellowships; no loans.
Application information:
Initial approach: Proposal
Deadline(s): None
Write: Atwood Dunwody, Trustee
Trustees: Fleming A. Barbour, M.D., Atwood Dunwody, C.S. Harding Mott.
Employer Identification Number: 596142825

1492
Vero Beach Foundation for the Elderly ⌑ ☆
c/o First National Bank
255 South County Rd.
Palm Beach 33480

Established in 1967.
Foundation type: Independent
Financial data (yr. ended 12/31/88): Assets, $1,026,372 (M); expenditures, $50,980, including $37,593 for 43 grants to individuals (high: $3,442; low: $50).
Purpose and activities: Provides relief assistance to indigent individuals for medical and convalescent care, as well as for food and general assistance.
Types of support: Grants to individuals.
Limitations: Giving limited to Vero Beach, FL.
Application information: Assistance payments may be made directly to recipient or to physicians and medical facilities.
Directors: Eugene Searle, J.A. Thompson, Pat Tibbetts.
Trustee: First National Bank of Palm Beach.
Employer Identification Number: 596214870

1493
The Wahlstrom Foundation, Inc.
2855 Ocean Dr., Suite D-4
Vero Beach 32963 (407) 231-0373
Mailing address: P.O. Box 3276, Vero Beach, FL 32964

Incorporated in 1956 in CT.
Donor(s): Magnus Wahlstrom.†
Foundation type: Independent
Financial data (yr. ended 12/31/88): Assets, $4,833,836 (M); gifts received, $20,000; expenditures, $265,988, including $223,220 for 20 grants (high: $63,014; low: $500; average: $5,000).
Purpose and activities: Emphasis on aid to the handicapped, higher education, hospitals, youth agencies, religion, the arts and humanities, the underprivileged, and community priorities.
Types of support: Continuing support, seed money, building funds, equipment, research, special projects, matching funds, capital campaigns, endowment funds, scholarship funds.
Limitations: Giving primarily in Indian River County, FL. No grants to individuals, or for fellowships or operating budgets; no loans.
Publications: Application guidelines.
Application information: Application form required.
Initial approach: Letter
Copies of proposal: 1
Deadline(s): May 1 and Oct. 1
Board meeting date(s): June and Nov.
Final notification: 3 to 6 months
Write: Eleonora W. McCabe, Pres.
Officers and Directors: Eleonora W. McCabe, Pres. and Treas.; Lois J. Hughes, V.P. and Secy.; Bruce R. Johnson, V.P.
Number of staff: 1 part-time support.
Employer Identification Number: 066053378

1494
The I. Waldbaum Family Foundation, Inc. ⌑
16519 Ironwood Dr.
Delray Beach 33445

Incorporated in 1961 in NY.
Donor(s): Bernice Waldbaum, Ira Waldbaum, Waldbaum, Inc.
Foundation type: Independent
Financial data (yr. ended 12/31/88): Assets, $7,527,711 (M); expenditures, $312,344, including $263,755 for 68 grants (high: $150,000; low: $10).
Purpose and activities: Giving primarily to Jewish welfare funds, including temple support, and to cultural programs.
Limitations: Giving primarily in the New York, NY, metropolitan area.
Application information:
Initial approach: Proposal
Write: Lawrence J. Waldman
Officers: Ira Waldbaum, Pres.; Bernice Waldbaum, Treas.
Directors: Randie Malinsky, Julia Waldbaum.
Employer Identification Number: 136145916

1495
Jim Walter Corporation Foundation ⌑
1500 North Dale Mabry Hwy.
P.O. Box 31601
Tampa 33631-3601 (813) 871-4168

Established in 1966 in FL.
Donor(s): Jim Walter Corp., and subsidiaries.
Foundation type: Company-sponsored
Financial data (yr. ended 8/31/88): Assets, $6,298,211 (M); gifts received, $479,328; expenditures, $385,541, including $344,123 for grants.
Purpose and activities: Giving for community funds; support also for higher education, youth and social service agencies, hospitals, and the arts.
Limitations: Giving primarily in FL.
Application information:
Write: W.K. Baker, Trustee
Trustees: W.K. Baker, Joe B. Cordell, J.W. Kynes.
Employer Identification Number: 596205802

1496
Harry E. Ward Foundation ⌑
c/o Harry E. Ward, Jr.
230 South Ocean Ave.
Palm Beach 33480

Established in 1959.
Donor(s): Elizabeth T. Ward,† Harry E. Ward, Jr.
Foundation type: Independent
Financial data (yr. ended 12/31/87): Assets, $1,902,728 (M); gifts received, $30,725; expenditures, $75,782, including $65,000 for 5 grants (high: $35,000; low: $5,000).
Purpose and activities: Grants primarily for higher education and hospitals.
Officers: George H. Sinnoti, Mgr.; Harry E. Ward, Jr., Mgr.
Employer Identification Number: 596169469

1497
The Ware Foundation ▼ ⌑
147 Alhambra Circle, Suite 215
Coral Gables 33134

Trust established in 1950 in PA.
Donor(s): John H. Ware, Jr.†
Foundation type: Independent
Financial data (yr. ended 12/31/88): Assets, $17,063,636 (M); expenditures, $784,668, including $734,500 for 86 grants (high: $70,000; low: $1,000; average: $5,000-$15,000).
Purpose and activities: Giving primarily for Christian schools and higher education; support also for hospitals, historic preservation groups, youth agencies, and Christian organizations.

Limitations: Giving primarily in FL and other southern states. No support for private foundations. No grants to individuals.
Application information:
Initial approach: Letter or proposal; no telephone inquiries
Deadline(s): None
Final notification: Positive responses only
Trustees: Rhoda C. Ware, Chair.; Martha W. Odom, Vice-Chair.; Rhoda W. Cobb, Nancy W. Pascal.
Number of staff: None.
Employer Identification Number: 237286585

1498
The Waterman Foundation, Inc. ⌑ ☆
400 Fifth Ave. South, Suite 304
Naples 33941
Application address: P.O. Box 9170, Naples, FL 33940; Tel.: (813) 261-0576

Donor(s): Arthur H. Waterman.†
Foundation type: Independent
Financial data (yr. ended 7/31/89): Assets, $1,056,812 (M); expenditures, $64,242, including $60,000 for 27 grants (high: $10,000; low: $500).
Purpose and activities: Giving primarily for children's hospitals and health and social services; support also for cancer research and higher education.
Limitations: No grants to individuals.
Application information:
Initial approach: Letter
Deadline(s): None
Write: A. Porter Waterman, Pres.
Officers and Directors: A. Porter Waterman, Pres. and Treas.; Patricia K. Waterman, V.P.; Marian E. Wagner, Secy.
Employer Identification Number: 066042880

1499
Grace Margaret Watterson Trust ⌑
c/o First Union National Bank of Florida
444 Seabreeze Blvd.
Daytona Beach 32018 (904) 254-7288

Established around 1984 in Florida.
Donor(s): Grace Margaret Watterson.†
Foundation type: Independent
Financial data (yr. ended 2/28/89): Assets, $1,619,803 (M); expenditures, $144,086, including $129,767 for grants to individuals.
Purpose and activities: College scholarship support for high school students in the U.S. and Canada.
Types of support: Student aid.
Limitations: Giving primarily in Daytona Beach and Ormond Beach, FL, and in Peterborough, Ontario, Canada.
Application information: Application form required.
Deadline(s): Dec. 31
Final notification: Mar. 31
Write: Arch W. Beard, Trust Officer, First Union National Bank of Florida
Trustee: First Union National Bank of Florida.
Employer Identification Number: 596807104

1500
Joseph Weintraub Family Foundation, Inc. ⌑
(Formerly Weintraub-Landfield Charity Foundation, Inc.)
150 S.E. 3rd Ave., Penthouse
Miami 33131

Established in 1949 in FL.
Donor(s): Joseph Weintraub.
Foundation type: Independent
Financial data (yr. ended 10/31/89): Assets, $4,992,023 (M); expenditures, $275,602, including $263,211 for 28 grants (high: $100,000; low: $25).
Purpose and activities: Support primarily for hospitals and health associations; some support for Jewish organizations and social services.
Application information:
Write: Joseph Weintraub, Pres.
Officers: Joseph Weintraub, Pres.; Hortense Weintraub, Treas.
Employer Identification Number: 590975815

1501
Lillian S. Wells Foundation, Inc. ⌑
600 Sagamore Rd.
Fort Lauderdale 33301 (305) 462-8639
Application address: P.O. Box 14338, Fort Lauderdale, FL 33301

Donor(s): Barbara W. Van Fleet; Preston A. Wells, Jr.
Foundation type: Independent
Financial data (yr. ended 12/31/88): Assets, $5,058,475 (M); expenditures, $228,011, including $226,000 for 6 grants (high: $145,000; low: $3,000).
Purpose and activities: Support for medical research and art education and appreciation.
Limitations: Giving limited to Chicago, IL; Fort Lauderdale, FL; and the Garden County, NE, area.
Application information:
Deadline(s): None
Write: Barbara Van Fleet, Pres.
Officers: Barbara W. Van Fleet, Pres.; Preston A. Wells, Jr., V.P.; Mary B. Moulding, Secy.; Joseph E. Malecek, Treas.
Employer Identification Number: 237433827

1502
Wentworth Foundation, Inc. ⌑ ☆
1667 N.W. 19th Circle
Gainesville 32605-3851 (904) 375-1246

Established in 1968.
Foundation type: Independent
Financial data (yr. ended 12/31/88): Assets, $1,000,991 (M); expenditures, $82,179, including $64,150 for 5 grants (high: $50,500; low: $250).
Purpose and activities: Giving primarily for higher education.
Types of support: Scholarship funds.
Limitations: Giving primarily in FL.
Application information:
Initial approach: Letter
Deadline(s): None
Write: William M. Goza, Pres.
Officer: William M. Goza, Pres.
Employer Identification Number: 596211599

1503
Dr. Herbert A. Wertheim Foundation, Inc. ⌑
4470 S.W. 74th Ave.
Miami 33155 (305) 264-4465

Established in 1977 in FL.
Donor(s): Herbert A. Wertheim.
Foundation type: Independent
Financial data (yr. ended 9/30/88): Assets, $3,351,330 (M); expenditures, $123,141, including $114,574 for 18 grants (high: $85,800; low: $22).
Purpose and activities: Support primarily for the fine arts and medical research.
Types of support: Research.
Limitations: Giving primarily in FL.
Application information:
Initial approach: Letter
Deadline(s): None
Write: Dr. Herbert A. Wertheim, Pres.
Officers and Directors: Herbert A. Wertheim, Pres.; Nicole J. Wertheim, Treas.
Employer Identification Number: 591778605

1504
Whitehall Foundation, Inc. ▼
249 Royal Palm Way, Suite 202
Palm Beach 33480 (407) 655-4474
Application address: P.O. Box 3225, Palm Beach, FL 33480; FAX: (407) 659-4978

Incorporated in 1937 in NJ.
Donor(s): George M. Moffett,† and others.
Foundation type: Independent
Financial data (yr. ended 09/30/89): Assets, $43,349,025 (M); expenditures, $2,349,846, including $1,814,872 for grants (high: $44,495; average: $10,000-$40,000) and $148,875 for grants to individuals.
Purpose and activities: Support for scholarly research in the life sciences, with emphasis on behavioral neuroscience and invertebrate neurophysiology; innovative and imaginative projects preferred. Research grants are paid to sponsoring institutions, rather than directly to individuals. Grants-in-aid are paid to assistant and/or senior professors; research grants are available to Ph.D.'s with established labs. Employee-related scholarships are awarded only through CPC International.
Types of support: Research, seed money, technical assistance, special projects, equipment, publications, employee-related scholarships.
Limitations: No support for investigators who already have, or expect to receive, substantial support from other quarters. No grants for the purchase of major items of permanent equipment; travel, unless to unique field areas essential to the research; salary support; living expenses while working at home; travel to conferences or for consultation; or secretarial services.
Publications: Informational brochure (including application guidelines), grants list.
Application information: Applicant must have Ph.D. before applying. Application form required.
Initial approach: Letter
Copies of proposal: 2
Deadline(s): Mar. l, Sept. l, and Dec. 1 for research grants; Jan. 1, June 1, and Oct. 1 for grants-in-aid

Board meeting date(s): Nov., but votes by mail in Mar., June, and Dec.
Final notification: 4 months
Write: Laurel T. Baker, Secy.
Officers and Trustees:* George M. Moffett II,* Pres. and Treas.; J. Wright Rumbough, Jr.,* V.P.; Laurel T. Baker,* Secy.; Warren S. Adams II, Kenneth S. Beall, Jr., Helen M. Brooks, Van Vetchen Burger, Peter G. Neff.
Number of staff: 2 part-time professional.
Employer Identification Number: 135637595

1505
J. J. Wiggins Memorial Trust ⌘ ☆
P.O. Drawer 1110
Moore Haven 33471 (813) 946-0881

Established in 1987 in FL.
Donor(s): J.J. Wiggins.†
Foundation type: Independent
Financial data (yr. ended 4/30/89): Assets, $3,786,285 (M); gifts received, $2,060,993; expenditures, $77,620, including $5,841 for 4 grants (high: $3,375; low: $950) and $32,500 for 30 grants to individuals (average: $500-$3,000).
Purpose and activities: Primarily awards scholarships to local high school students for higher and vocational education; minor support also for recreation and youth organizations.
Types of support: Student aid, operating budgets, capital campaigns.
Limitations: Giving primarily in Glades County, FL.
Application information: Scholarship applicants must be nominated by high school or college level educators. Application form required.
Deadline(s): May 1
Trustees: John M. Hathaway, John Holbrook, J.C. Sealey, A.E. Wells.
Employer Identification Number: 592675273

1506
The Wilder Foundation ⌘
P.O. Box 99
Key Biscayne 33149

Incorporated in 1945 in LA.
Donor(s): Candace Mossler,† Jacques Mossler.
Foundation type: Independent
Financial data (yr. ended 12/31/88): Assets, $2,444,859 (M); expenditures, $138,107, including $89,576 for 10 grants (high: $87,136; low: $100).
Purpose and activities: Emphasis on a university and secondary education.
Types of support: General purposes, building funds, endowment funds, research, scholarship funds, matching funds.
Limitations: Giving primarily in FL. No grants to individuals; no loans.
Application information:
Initial approach: Proposal
Copies of proposal: 1
Deadline(s): Submit proposal before Sept.
Board meeting date(s): Monthly
Write: Rita Wilder, Pres. or Gary Wilder, V.P.
Officers: Rita Wilder, Pres.; Gary Wilder, V.P.
Number of staff: 1 full-time support.
Employer Identification Number: 746049547

1507
Edna Sproull Williams Foundation ⌘
1500 Independent Sq.
Jacksonville 32202

Donor(s): Edna Sproull Williams.†
Foundation type: Independent
Financial data (yr. ended 12/31/88): Assets, $13,894,291 (M); expenditures, $657,458, including $490,715 for 22 grants (high: $50,000; low: $1,000).
Purpose and activities: Giving for youth agencies, Protestant religious organizations, higher education, hospitals, and social services.
Limitations: Giving primarily in FL.
Application information: Contributes only to pre-selected organizations. Applications not accepted.
Trustees: J.W. Burke, William J. Hamrick, Edward McCarthy, Jr., Charles J. Williams III, Patrick M. Williams.
Employer Identification Number: 510198606

1508
Hugh & Mary Wilson Foundation, Inc.
c/o Wood & Seitl
240 North Washington Blvd., Suite 460
Sarasota 34236-5929 (813) 954-2155

Established in 1984 in FL.
Donor(s): Hugh H. Wilson,† Mary P. Wilson.†
Foundation type: Independent
Financial data (yr. ended 12/31/89): Assets, $4,955,997 (M); expenditures, $326,614, including $238,291 for 26 grants (high: $50,000; low: $1,000; average: $1,000-$50,000).
Purpose and activities: Support for medical and other education, cancer research and health services, the performing arts, and social service issues, including family services, the disadvantaged, the aged, women, and child welfare.
Types of support: Building funds, capital campaigns, conferences and seminars, scholarship funds, equipment, general purposes.
Limitations: Giving limited to the Manatee-Sarasota, FL, area and the Lewisburg-Danville, PA, area. No grants for operating expenses.
Publications: Informational brochure (including application guidelines).
Application information: Application form not required.
Initial approach: Letter or telephone
Copies of proposal: 2
Deadline(s): None
Board meeting date(s): Mar., June, and Sept.
Final notification: Oct.
Write: John R. Wood, Pres.
Officers and Directors:* John R. Wood,* Pres.; Harry Klinger,* V.P.; Sadie L. Wood,* Secy.; George Fraley,* Treas.; Susan Wood.
Number of staff: 1 full-time professional; 1 part-time support.
Employer Identification Number: 592243926

1509
Gertrude R. Wilson Trust ⌘ ☆
c/o Barnett Banks Trust Co., N.A.
P.O. Box 40200
Jacksonville 32203-0200

Established in 1958.
Foundation type: Independent
Financial data (yr. ended 12/31/88): Assets, $1,121,408 (M); expenditures, $88,049, including $75,446 for grants.
Purpose and activities: Giving for a university and general charitable purposes.
Trustee: Barnett Banks Trust Co., N.A.
Employer Identification Number: 596118179

1510
Winn Foundation Trust ⌘ ☆
c/o Florida National Bank
P.O. Box 689
Jacksonville 32201-0689
Application address: c/o Florida National Bank, P.O. Box 790, Gainesville, FL; Tel.: (904) 377-8444

Donor(s): Mary E. Winn.
Foundation type: Independent
Financial data (yr. ended 12/31/88): Assets, $1,073,341 (M); expenditures, $59,810, including $49,066 for 72 grants (high: $5,000; low: $25).
Purpose and activities: Support primarily for wildlife preservation and environmental conservation.
Application information: Application form not required.
Deadline(s): None
Write: Connie Brown, V.P., Florida National Bank
Trustee: Florida National Bank.
Employer Identification Number: 596194105

1511
Winn-Dixie Stores Foundation ▼ ⌘
5050 Edgewood Court
Jacksonville 32205 (904) 783-5000

Incorporated in 1943 in FL.
Donor(s): Winn-Dixie Stores, Inc.
Foundation type: Company-sponsored
Financial data (yr. ended 12/31/88): Assets, $1,775,640 (M); gifts received, $2,000,000; expenditures, $1,801,055, including $691,096 for 421 grants (high: $50,000; low: $50; average: $100-$5,000) and $1,108,618 for 387 employee matching gifts.
Purpose and activities: Functions solely as a conduit through which Winn-Dixie Stores, Inc., in its thirteen-state trade area, makes contributions to local and national welfare agencies, including community funds, youth agencies, educational institutions, scholarship programs, and hospitals.
Types of support: Annual campaigns, building funds, equipment, matching funds, employee matching gifts, research, special projects, conferences and seminars, continuing support, scholarship funds.
Limitations: Giving primarily in the Southeast, in areas of company operations. No grants to individuals.
Application information: Application form not required.
Initial approach: Letter
Deadline(s): None
Board meeting date(s): As required
Final notification: 30 days
Write: Jack P. Jones, Pres.
Officers: Jack P. Jones,* Pres.; A. Dano Davis,* V.P.; Robert D. Davis,* V.P.; F.L.

James,* V.P.; J.S. Bryan, Jr., Secy.; D.H. Bragin,* Treas.
Directors:* A. Darius Davis, James E. Davis, H.S. Wadford.
Number of staff: None.
Employer Identification Number: 590995428

1512
Winter Park Community Trust Fund ⌑
c/o Barnett Banks Trust Co., N.A.
P.O. Box 1000
Winter Park 32790
Application address: 2823 Amber Gate Rd., Winter Park, FL 32789

Trust established in 1951 in FL.
Foundation type: Community
Financial data (yr. ended 11/30/88): Assets, $2,008,064 (M); gifts received, $23,802; expenditures, $96,529, including $68,300 for 35 grants (high: $17,176; low: $29) and $11,950 for 12 grants to individuals (high: $2,000; low: $700).
Purpose and activities: As 90 percent of the fund's income is pre-designated and only 10 percent is for discretionary giving, grantmaking is limited. Emphasis is on health, education, social services, and scholarships for residents of Orange and Seminole counties, FL.
Types of support: Continuing support, student aid, general purposes.
Limitations: Giving limited to Orange and Seminole counties, FL. No grants for building or endowment funds, or matching gifts; no loans.
Application information: Application form not required.
Initial approach: Letter
Copies of proposal: 1
Deadline(s): None
Board meeting date(s): Last Thursday of Jan. and July
Final notification: 1 week
Write: Mary Moody
Trustee: Barnett Banks Trust Co., N.A.
Number of staff: None.
Employer Identification Number: 596126473

1513
Wiseheart Foundation, Inc. ⌑
2840 S.W. Third Ave.
Miami 33129

Incorporated in 1953 in FL.
Donor(s): Malcolm B. Wiseheart,† Dorothy A. Wiseheart.†
Foundation type: Independent
Financial data (yr. ended 12/31/89): Assets, $2,469,789 (M); expenditures, $65,609, including $50,317 for 68 grants (high: $6,667; low: $100).
Purpose and activities: Emphasis on secondary and higher education, Protestant church support and cultural programs, including a local community television foundation.
Limitations: Giving primarily in FL, with a strong preference for the Dade County metropolitan area. No grants to individuals, or for building or endowment funds, or operating budgets.
Application information: Application form not required.
Initial approach: Proposal
Copies of proposal: 2
Deadline(s): Nov. 30
Board meeting date(s): Quarterly
Write: Malcolm B. Wiseheart, Jr., Pres.
Officers and Directors: Malcolm B. Wiseheart, Jr., Pres.; Elizabeth W. Joyce, V.P.; Carolyn W. Milne.
Employer Identification Number: 590992871

1514
The Wolfson Family Foundation, Inc.
P.O. Box 4
Jacksonville 32201 (904) 731-7942

Incorporated in 1951 in FL.
Donor(s): Louis E. Wolfson, Sam W. Wolfson,† Saul Wolfson, Florence M. Wolfson,† Cecil Wolfson.
Foundation type: Independent
Financial data (yr. ended 09/30/89): Assets, $4,573,581 (M); gifts received, $1,150; expenditures, $195,306, including $132,450 for 40 grants (high: $75,000; low: $100).
Purpose and activities: Grants for higher education and hospitals, including buildings and equipment, Jewish welfare funds, community funds, and child welfare.
Types of support: Building funds, equipment.
Limitations: Giving primarily in FL.
Officers: Cecil Wolfson,* Chair.; M.C. Tomberlin,* Secy.; Robert O. Johnson, Treas.
Trustees:* Joe I. Degen, Sylvia W. Degen, Edith W. Edwards, Morris D. Edwards, Rabbi Sidney M. Lefkowitz, Gary L. Wolfson, Nathan Wolfson, Stephen P. Wolfson.
Number of staff: 6
Employer Identification Number: 590995431

1515
Loulyfran Wolfson Foundation, Inc. ⌑
2399 N.E. East 2nd Ave.
Miami 33137-4807

Established in 1967 in FL.
Donor(s): Lynn R. Wolfson.
Foundation type: Independent
Financial data (yr. ended 12/31/89): Assets, $874,500 (M); gifts received, $100,000; expenditures, $140,686, including $137,000 for 12 grants (high: $100,000; low: $1,000).
Purpose and activities: Support primarily for higher education, medical research, and cultural institutions.
Limitations: Giving primarily in Miami, FL.
Officers and Trustees:* Lynn R. Wolfson,* Pres.; J. Bruce Irving, Secy.; Linda Wolfson, Treas.; Louis Wolfson III.
Employer Identification Number: 596196403

1516
The Floyd L. Wray Memorial Foundation, Inc.
3750 Flamingo Rd.
Fort Lauderdale 33330 (305) 473-2955

Incorporated in 1969 in FL.
Donor(s): Jane L. Wray.†
Foundation type: Independent
Financial data (yr. ended 12/31/88): Assets, $8,499,643 (M); gifts received, $50,446; expenditures, $730,282, including $171,000 for 6 grants (high: $50,000; low: $6,000).
Purpose and activities: Giving for Christian Science church support and higher and secondary education; also maintains the Floyd L. Wray Memorial Gardens, botanical display gardens, nature preserve, and zoo.
Limitations: No grants to individuals.
Application information: Contributes only to pre-selected organizations. Applications not accepted.
Board meeting date(s): Nov., May, and as required
Write: Mary Bayuk, Pres.
Officers and Directors: Mary Bayuk, Pres.; Albert Will, V.P.; Glenn Kenngott, Secy.; Stanley Wood, Treas.; Roy L. Aitken, Davie Ledbetter, Edwin P. McDonald.
Number of staff: 5 full-time professional; 1 part-time professional; 12 full-time support; 4 part-time support.
Employer Identification Number: 237112655

1517
Yablick Charities, Inc. ⌑
c/o Jefferson National Bank of Miami
301-41st St.
Miami Beach 33140

Incorporated in 1960 in NJ.
Donor(s): Herman Yablick.†
Foundation type: Independent
Financial data (yr. ended 12/31/86): Assets, $1,175,459 (M); expenditures, $195,518, including $110,678 for 95 grants (high: $13,516; low: $18).
Purpose and activities: Grants largely for higher education, hospitals, and cultural programs.
Limitations: Giving primarily in FL and Israel.
Application information:
Deadline(s): Sept. 30
Write: Jarrold F. Goodman, Pres.
Officers: Jerrold F. Goodman, Pres.; Jane Goodman, V.P.; Ruth Cohen, V.P.
Employer Identification Number: 591411171

1518
Yulman Foundation ⌑
(Formerly Morton & Helen Yulman Trust)
c/o Southeast Bank, N.A.
One S.E. Financial Ctr.
Miami 33131

Established in 1955.
Donor(s): Morton Yulman, Helen Yulman.
Foundation type: Independent
Financial data (yr. ended 12/31/88): Assets, $2,322,603 (M); expenditures, $191,734, including $175,775 for 29 grants (high: $51,500; low: $100).
Purpose and activities: Giving to Jewish welfare organizations, social services, and a college.
Limitations: Giving primarily in upstate NY and FL.
Application information: Contributes only to pre-selected organizations. Applications not accepted.
Trustees: Helen Yulman, Morton Yulman.
Investment Manager: Southeast Bank, N.A.
Number of staff: None.
Employer Identification Number: 146015572

1519
Zeitz Foundation, Inc. ⌑
The Meadows
5657 Pipers Waite
Sarasota 34235 (813) 377-7419

Established in 1943 in FL.
Foundation type: Independent
Financial data (yr. ended 6/30/88): Assets, $1,031,019 (M); expenditures, $64,038, including $50,388 for 103 grants (high: $10,000; low: $10).
Purpose and activities: Support primarily for Jewish organizations; support also for higher education, health services, and cultural institutions.
Application information:
Initial approach: Letter
Deadline(s): June
Write: Robert Z. Rosenthal, V.P.
Officers: Williard Zeitz, Pres.; Wilbur Levin, V.P. and Secy.; Robert Z. Rosenthal, V.P. and Treas.
Director: Daniel Ross.
Employer Identification Number: 116037021

GEORGIA

1520
Francis L. Abreu Charitable Trust u/w of May P. Abreu ⌑ ☆
c/o Trust Co. Bank
P.O. Box 4655
Atlanta 30302-4655

Established in 1977.
Foundation type: Independent
Financial data (yr. ended 9/30/87): Assets, $1,707,282 (M); expenditures, $69,558, including $57,140 for 34 grants (high: $3,000; low: $300).
Purpose and activities: Giving primarily for social service agencies; especially those benefiting women and the young; support also for secondary and higher education, health associations, and cultural programs.
Types of support: Operating budgets.
Limitations: Giving primarily in Atlanta, GA.
Application information:
Initial approach: Letter
Deadline(s): Mar. 15 and Sept. 15
Board meeting date(s): Apr. and Oct.
Write: Brenda Rambeau
Committee members: Peter M. Abreu, Chair.; John A. Wallace, Ray B. Wilhoit.
Trustee: Trust Co. Bank.
Employer Identification Number: 586130937

1521
AEC Trust
c/o First Wachovia Charitable Funds Management, The First National Bank of Atlanta
Two Peachtree St., N.W., Suite 705
Atlanta 30383 (404) 332-6586

Established in 1980 in IL.
Donor(s): Members of the Cofrin family.
Foundation type: Independent
Financial data (yr. ended 11/30/88): Assets, $10,089,295 (M); gifts received, $5,825,000; expenditures, $248,471, including $110,000 for 3 grants (high: $50,000; low: $10,000).
Purpose and activities: Grants primarily for education; some support for a museum.
Application information: Application form not required.
Initial approach: Letter
Copies of proposal: 1
Deadline(s): None
Write: Charles Buchholz
Advisory Committee: David A. Cofrin, Chair.; David H. Cofrin, Edith D. Cofrin, Mary Ann H. Cofrin, Paul G. Schierl.
Trustee: The First National Bank of Atlanta.
Employer Identification Number: 366725987

1522
Allen Foundation, Inc. ⌑
Box 1712
Atlanta 30301 (404) 332-3000

Established in 1956 in GA.
Donor(s): Ivan Allen Co.
Foundation type: Independent
Financial data (yr. ended 2/28/89): Assets, $718,979 (M); gifts received, $265,516; expenditures, $293,589, including $289,066 for 73 grants (high: $47,450; low: $100).
Purpose and activities: Support for education, health services, and cultural programs; scholarship support for dependents of company employees.
Types of support: Employee-related scholarships.
Limitations: Giving primarily in the South, with emphasis on GA. No grants to individuals.
Application information: Application form required.
Deadline(s): June 30
Write: Rodger E. Herndon, Secy.-Treas.
Officers and Trustees: Ivan Allen, Jr., Chair.; Ivan Allen III, Vice-Chair.; Rodger E. Herndon, Secy.-Treas.
Employer Identification Number: 586037237

1523
Anncox Foundation, Inc. ⌑
c/o Dow Lohnes & Albertson
One Ravina Dr., Suite 1300
Atlanta 30346
Application address: 426 West Paces Ferry Rd., Atlanta, GA 30305

Incorporated in 1960 in GA.
Donor(s): Anne Cox Chambers.
Foundation type: Independent
Financial data (yr. ended 12/31/88): Assets, $56,506 (M); gifts received, $417,993; expenditures, $368,868, including $368,868 for 33 grants (high: $100,000; low: $20).
Purpose and activities: Emphasis on educational associations, museums, animal care programs, and cultural programs.
Limitations: Giving primarily in GA.
Application information:
Initial approach: Letter
Deadline(s): None
Write: Anne C. Chambers, Pres.
Officers and Directors: Anne Cox Chambers, Pres. and Treas.; James Cox Chambers, V.P. and Secy.
Employer Identification Number: 586033966

1524
Arnold Fund ⌑
1200 C & S National Bank Bldg.
35 Broad St.
Atlanta 30335 (404) 586-1500

Established in 1952 in GA.
Donor(s): Florence Arnold.
Foundation type: Independent
Financial data (yr. ended 12/31/88): Assets, $3,059,892 (M); expenditures, $155,167, including $148,000 for 9 grants (high: $50,000; low: $1,000).
Purpose and activities: Funds primarily for education; some support for music.
Limitations: Giving primarily in GA.
Application information:
Initial approach: Letter
Deadline(s): None
Write: Arthur Howell, Exec. Dir.
Officer: Arthur Howell, Exec. Dir.
Trustees: Miriam A. Newman, Frank Turner.
Employer Identification Number: 586032079

1525
Metropolitan Atlanta Community Foundation, Inc. ▼
The Hurt Bldg., Suite 449
Atlanta 30303 (404) 688-5525

Incorporated in 1977 as successor to Metropolitan Foundation of Atlanta established in 1951 in GA by bank resolution and declaration of trust.
Foundation type: Community
Financial data (yr. ended 06/30/89): Assets, $81,033,448 (M); gifts received, $11,742,652; expenditures, $6,103,809, including $5,191,271 for 442 grants (high: $123,044; low: $20; average: $3,000-$5,000).
Purpose and activities: Organized for the permanent administration of funds placed in trust by various donors for charitable purposes. Grants, unless designated by the donor, are confined to the metropolitan area of Atlanta, with emphasis on social services, arts and culture, education, health, and civic purposes.
Types of support: Seed money, emergency funds, building funds, equipment, land acquisition, technical assistance, program-related investments, special projects, publications, capital campaigns, matching funds, renovation projects.
Limitations: Giving limited to the metropolitan area of Atlanta, GA, and surrounding regions. No support for religious organizations (except through donor-advised funds). No grants to individuals, or for endowment funds, continuing support, annual campaigns, deficit financing, research, films, conferences,

scholarships, or fellowships; generally no grants for operating budgets or for loans.
Publications: Annual report, program policy statement, application guidelines, newsletter, informational brochure.
Application information: Application form required.
Initial approach: Letter or telephone
Copies of proposal: 1
Deadline(s): Mar. 15, Sept. 15, and Nov. 15
Board meeting date(s): May, Nov., and Jan.
Final notification: 6 weeks
Write: Alicia Philipp, Exec. Dir.
Officers: L.L. Gellerstedt, Jr.,* Pres.; Alicia Philipp, Exec. Dir.
Directors:* Eula Adams, Juanita Baranco, Frank Carter, Cecil D. Conlee, Hon. Clarence Cooper, Marie Dodd, Susie Elson, Robert Guyton, D. Lurton Massee, Jr., William McClatchey, M.D., Mebane M. Pritchett, Raymond D. Riddle, Betty Siegel, Sue Wieland.
Trustees: Bank South, N.A., Citizens & Southern National Bank, First American Bank, The First National Bank of Atlanta, Suntrust, Inc.
Number of staff: 5 full-time professional; 3 full-time support.
Employer Identification Number: 581344646

1526
Atlanta Foundation
c/o The First National Bank of Atlanta
Two Peachtree St., N.W., Suite 1530
Atlanta 30383 (404) 332-6592

Established in 1921 in GA by bank resolution and declaration of trust.
Foundation type: Independent
Financial data (yr. ended 12/31/88): Assets, $6,858,674 (M); gifts received, $116,177; expenditures, $491,812, including $440,520 for 63 grants (high: $35,000; low: $250).
Purpose and activities: Assistance to charitable and educational institutions for promoting education and scientific research and improving local living conditions. Grants chiefly for community funds, hospitals, education, including higher education, cultural programs, and youth agencies.
Types of support: Research, general purposes, seed money, emergency funds, building funds, equipment, land acquisition, endowment funds, renovation projects, special projects.
Limitations: Giving limited to Fulton and DeKalb counties, GA. No grants to individuals, or for scholarships, or fellowships; no loans.
Application information: Application form not required.
Initial approach: Letter
Copies of proposal: 1
Deadline(s): Dec. 1
Board meeting date(s): Jan.
Final notification: 1 week
Write: Joseph Patterson
Distribution Committee: McChesney H. Jeffries, Chair.; Thomas E. Boland, Shirley C. Franklin, Edward C. Harris, D. Raymond Riddle.
Trustee: The First National Bank of Atlanta.
Number of staff: None.
Employer Identification Number: 586026879

1527
Clark and Ruby Baker Foundation ⌑
c/o Bank South, N.A., Personal Trust Dept.
55 Marietta St., N.W., P.O. Box 4956
Atlanta 30302 (404) 529-4627

Established in 1974.
Donor(s): Clark A. Baker.†
Foundation type: Independent
Financial data (yr. ended 12/31/88): Assets, $1,567,250 (M); expenditures, $79,862, including $55,000 for 16 grants (high: $6,000; low: $1,000) and $14,500 for 10 grants to individuals (high: $2,000; low: $500).
Purpose and activities: Emphasis on higher education, including scholarships for study at a college or university operated by or affiliated with the Methodist Church; support also for Protestant welfare funds and pensions for Methodist ministers.
Types of support: Scholarship funds, endowment funds, conferences and seminars, general purposes, grants to individuals, student aid.
Limitations: Giving limited to GA.
Application information:
Initial approach: Letter
Deadline(s): None
Write: Odette Capell, Secy. or Tom Murphy
Officers: Virlyn B. Moore, Jr., Chair.; Odette Capell, Secy.
Trustee: Bank South, N.A.
Employer Identification Number: 581429097

1528
Bank South Charitable Trust ⌑
c/o Bank South, N.A., Personal Trust Dept.
55 Marietta St., N.W., P.O. Box 4956
Atlanta 30302 (404) 529-4627

Trust established in 1960 in GA.
Donor(s): Bank South, N.A.
Foundation type: Company-sponsored
Financial data (yr. ended 12/31/88): Assets, $1,789,208 (M); gifts received, $136,000; expenditures, $291,080, including $284,284 for 108 grants (high: $127,340; low: $25).
Purpose and activities: Giving primarily for community funds and higher education; support also for an art center.
Limitations: Giving primarily in GA.
Application information:
Initial approach: Letter
Deadline(s): None
Write: Odette Capell
Trustee: Bank South, N.A.
Employer Identification Number: 586031447

1529
William N. Banks Foundation ⌑ ☆
c/o William N. Banks, Jr.
Bankshaven
Newnan 30263

Established in 1941.
Donor(s): William N. Banks, Jr.
Foundation type: Independent
Financial data (yr. ended 12/31/88): Assets, $579,217 (M); expenditures, $150,021, including $141,115 for 101 grants (high: $15,000; low: $40).
Purpose and activities: Support primarily for higher and other education, historical societies and other cultural programs, and Protestant churches.
Limitations: No grants to individuals.
Application information: Contributes only to pre-selected organizations. Applications not accepted.
Officer: William N. Banks, Jr., Pres.
Employer Identification Number: 586043761

1530
Lewis H. Beck Foundation ⌑
c/o Trust Co. Bank
P.O. Box 4655
Atlanta 30302 (404) 396-6575

Established in 1954 in GA.
Foundation type: Independent
Financial data (yr. ended 6/30/88): Assets, $1,664,410 (M); expenditures, $95,629, including $75,000 for 9 grants (high: $33,400; low: $5,200).
Purpose and activities: Giving limited to educational institutions, with emphasis on higher education.
Types of support: Scholarship funds.
Limitations: Giving limited to GA.
Application information: Application form not required.
Deadline(s): None
Trustees: Pollard Turman, Chair.; William A. Parker, Vice-Chair.; Clare Ranney, Secy.; Henry L. Bowden, Sr., Hugh M. Dorsey, W. Douglas Ellis, Jr., Thomas Glen II, Kenneth Taratus.
Agent: Trust Co. Bank.
Employer Identification Number: 586025985

1531
BellSouth Foundation ▼
c/o BellSouth Corp.
1155 Peachtree St., N.E., Rm. 7H08
Atlanta 30367-6000 (404) 249-2414
Additional tel.: (404) 249-2429

Established in 1986 in GA.
Donor(s): BellSouth Corp.
Foundation type: Company-sponsored
Financial data (yr. ended 12/31/89): Assets, $36,845,185 (M); expenditures, $3,259,046, including $3,119,146 for 36 grants (high: $390,000; low: $6,000; average: $25,000-$200,000).
Purpose and activities: In elementary and secondary education, to enhance teacher recruitment, education and retention, and to address student motivation, particularly at middle-school age; in higher education, to strengthen the development and retention of faculty, especially in science, engineering and business-related disciplines and to promote excellence in curriculum development and research related to telecommunications.
Types of support: Conferences and seminars, professorships, program-related investments, seed money.
Limitations: Giving primarily in areas of company operations in AL, FL, GA, KY, LA, MS, NC, SC, and TN. No support for programs with local impact only or for non-education-related programs. No grants to individuals, or for capital, building, or general endowment campaigns, operating expenses, scholarships, or fundraising events.

Publications: Multi-year report, application guidelines.
Application information: Application form not required.
Initial approach: Letter of no more than 3 pages
Copies of proposal: 1
Deadline(s): Feb. 1 and Aug. 1
Final notification: Awards are announced in Apr. and Sept.
Write: Patricia L. Willis, Exec. Dir., or Leslie J. Graitcer, Prog. Mgr.
Officers: J.J. Brooks, Pres.; C.W. Shewbridge III, V.P.; Patricia L. Willis, Secy. and Exec. Dir.; K. Patterson, Treas.; P.H. Casey, Comptroller.
Trustees: F.D. Ackerman, Chair.; R.L. McGuire, C.R. Yarbrough.
Number of staff: 3 full-time professional; 1 full-time support.
Employer Identification Number: 581708046

1532
Beloco Foundation, Inc. ⌑
P.O. Box 140
Columbus 31902

Established in 1967 in GA.
Donor(s): Lovick P. Corn, Elizabeth T. Corn.
Foundation type: Independent
Financial data (yr. ended 6/30/88): Assets, $1,545,445 (M); gifts received, $61,000; expenditures, $78,546, including $74,000 for 6 grants (high: $60,000; low: $1,000).
Purpose and activities: Grants for higher education.
Types of support: Capital campaigns.
Limitations: Giving primarily in GA.
Officers and Trustees:* Lovick P. Corn,* Pres.; Elizabeth C. Ogie,* V.P.; Elizabeth T. Corn, Secy.; Polly C. Miller, Treas.
Employer Identification Number: 586065378

1533
The Bibb Foundation, Inc.
237 Coliseum Dr.
Macon 31208 (912) 752-6700

Incorporated in 1930 in GA.
Donor(s): The Bibb Co.
Foundation type: Company-sponsored
Financial data (yr. ended 8/31/89): Assets, $1,538,424 (M); expenditures, $153,926, including $31,682 for 10 grants (average: $100-$8,800) and $113,274 for 190 grants to individuals (average: $200-$2,000).
Purpose and activities: Giving for scholarships for employees or children of employees of The Bibb Co.; also grants for libraries, literacy, colleges and universities, and youth.
Types of support: Employee-related scholarships.
Limitations: Giving primarily in GA, SC, NC, and VA. No grants to individuals (except for employee-related scholarships), or for building or endowment funds or special projects.
Publications: Program policy statement, application guidelines.
Application information: Application form for scholarships required. Application form required.
Initial approach: Proposal
Copies of proposal: 2
Deadline(s): Apr. 30
Board meeting date(s): Aug.
Write: Allan V. Davis, Pres.
Officers and Trustees: Allan V. Davis, Pres.; R.S. Boyter, V.P.; Frank X. Sheehan, V.P.; J. Fletcher Terry, V.P.; L.W. Belk, Secy.
Employer Identification Number: 580566140

1534
R. A. Bowen Trust
P.O. Box 4611
Macon 31208 (912) 742-2565

Established in 1943 in GA.
Foundation type: Independent
Financial data (yr. ended 12/31/88): Assets, $1,409,906 (M); expenditures, $66,571, including $62,992 for 28 grants (high: $18,500; low: $50).
Purpose and activities: Support primarily for scholarships for higher education.
Types of support: Scholarship funds.
Limitations: Giving limited to GA.
Application information: Application form required.
Initial approach: Letter, including transcript and recommendation
Copies of proposal: 1
Deadline(s): May 1
Write: R.A. Bowen, Jr., Trustee
Trustees: R.A. Bowen, Jr., Albert P. Reichert, Charles H. Yates, Jr.
Employer Identification Number: 586032145

1535
Bradley Foundation, Inc. ⌑ ☆
P.O. Box 1408
Savannah 31402-1408

Established in 1946.
Foundation type: Independent
Financial data (yr. ended 11/30/88): Assets, $1,439,478 (M); expenditures, $63,744, including $59,190 for 42 grants (high: $8,500; low: $50).
Purpose and activities: Giving primarily for education, including higher education; support also for Protestant churches, youth, and groups providing shelter and food to the homeless.
Limitations: Giving primarily in Savannah, GA. No grants to individuals.
Application information: Application form not required.
Initial approach: Letter
Deadline(s): None
Officers: W. Waldo Bradley, Pres.; Daniel H. Bradley, V.P.; Clifton R. Jones, V.P.; Jane Bradley Wheeler, V.P.; Henry F. Hobbs, Secy.-Treas.
Employer Identification Number: 586033193

1536
Bradley-Turner Foundation ▼ ⌑
P.O. Box 140
Columbus 31902 (404) 571-6040

Incorporated in 1943 in GA as W.C. and Sarah H. Bradley Foundation; in 1982 absorbed the D.A. and Elizabeth Turner Foundation, Inc., also of GA.
Donor(s): W.C. Bradley,† D.A. Turner, Elizabeth B. Turner.†
Foundation type: Independent
Financial data (yr. ended 12/31/87): Assets, $37,031,428 (M); gifts received, $282,940; expenditures, $2,484,534, including $2,310,516 for 33 grants (high: $1,250,000; low: $400; average: $2,000-$65,000).
Purpose and activities: Giving primarily for higher education, religious associations, a community fund, youth and social service agencies; support also for cultural and health-related programs.
Limitations: Giving primarily in GA, with emphasis on Columbus. No grants to individuals.
Application information: Application form not required.
Initial approach: Letter
Copies of proposal: 2
Deadline(s): None
Board meeting date(s): Quarterly
Final notification: Varies
Write: Stephen T. Butler, Chair.
Officers and Trustees: Stephen T. Butler, Chair.; Lovick P. Corn, Vice-Chair.; R. Neal Gregory, Exec. Secy.; William B. Turner, Treas.; Clarence C. Butler, M.D., Sarah T. Butler, Elizabeth T. Corn, Elizabeth C. Ogie, Sue T. Turner, William B. Turner, Jr.
Number of staff: None.
Employer Identification Number: 586032142

1537
Thomas C. Burke Foundation ⌑
182 Riley Ave., Suite B
Macon 31204 (912) 745-1442

Established in 1965 in GA.
Donor(s): Thomas C. Burke.†
Foundation type: Independent
Financial data (yr. ended 9/30/88): Assets, $3,445,674 (M); gifts received, $8,290; expenditures, $251,366, including $177,200 for grants.
Purpose and activities: Grants primarily to needy individuals who are suffering from disease, particularly cancer; some support also for a local Roman Catholic church and academy.
Types of support: Grants to individuals.
Limitations: Giving limited to GA, with emphasis on Bibb County.
Application information:
Initial approach: By telephone or in person
Deadline(s): None
Write: Carolyn P. Griggers
Advisory Board Members: Mrs. John D. Comer, Donald Rhame, M.D., J. Benham Stewart, M.D.
Trustee: Citizens & Southern National Bank.
Employer Identification Number: 586047627

1538
Dorothy Mustin Buttolph Foundation ⌑
c/o Trust Co. Bank
P.O. Box 927
Augusta 30903

Established in 1983 in GA.
Foundation type: Independent
Financial data (yr. ended 9/30/88): Assets, $1,435,937 (M); expenditures, $77,353, including $67,711 for 10 grants (high: $20,000; low: $100).

Purpose and activities: Giving primarily for educational programs at youth facilities and colleges and universities.
Limitations: Giving primarily in GA.
Application information:
Deadline(s): None
Write: H.C. McGowan, Jr., Trustee
Trustee: H.C. McGowan, Jr.
Employer Identification Number: 586175999

1539
Callaway Foundation, Inc. ▼
209 Broome St.
P.O. Box 790
LaGrange 30241 (404) 884-7348

Incorporated in 1943 in GA.
Donor(s): Textile Benefit Assn., Callaway Mills, Callaway Institute, Inc.
Foundation type: Independent
Financial data (yr. ended 09/30/89): Assets, $145,416,275 (M); expenditures, $7,367,362, including $7,239,308 for 79 grants (high: $3,575,000; low: $200; average: $1,000-$100,000).
Purpose and activities: Giving for elementary, higher, and secondary education, including libraries and buildings and equipment; health and hospitals; community funds; care for the aged; community development; historic preservation; and church support.
Types of support: Continuing support, annual campaigns, general purposes, building funds, equipment, land acquisition, matching funds.
Limitations: Giving primarily in GA, with emphasis on the city of LaGrange and Troup County. No grants to individuals, or for endowment funds, operating expenses, deficit financing, scholarships, or fellowships; no loans.
Publications: Annual report (including application guidelines).
Application information: Application form not required.
Initial approach: Letter
Copies of proposal: 1
Deadline(s): End of month preceding board meetings
Board meeting date(s): Jan., Apr., July, and Oct.
Final notification: 2 months
Write: J.T. Gresham, Pres.
Officers and Trustees:* J.T. Gresham, Pres., General Mgr., and Treas.; Charles D. Hudson,* V.P.; C.L. Pitts, Secy.; Mark Clayton Callaway, Ida Callaway Hudson, James R. Lewis, Fred L. Turner.
Number of staff: 5
Employer Identification Number: 580566147

1540
Fuller E. Callaway Foundation ▼
209 Broome St.
P.O. Box 790
LaGrange 30241 (404) 884-7348

Incorporated in 1917 in GA.
Donor(s): Fuller E. Callaway, Sr.,† and family.
Foundation type: Independent
Financial data (yr. ended 12/31/89): Assets, $27,135,276 (M); expenditures, $1,222,370, including $796,100 for 25 grants (high: $500,000; low: $250; average: $250-$10,000) and $244,500 for 67 grants to individuals (high: $10,000; low: $900; average: $900-$3,000).
Purpose and activities: Grants to religious, charitable, and educational organizations; scholarships for worthy students; modest gifts toward operating expenses of community welfare agencies, including youth programs, and health organizations.
Types of support: Operating budgets, annual campaigns, building funds, equipment, matching funds, general purposes, student aid.
Limitations: Giving primarily in the city of LaGrange and Troup County, GA. No grants for endowment funds; no loans.
Application information: Application form required for scholarship program. Application form not required.
Initial approach: Letter
Copies of proposal: 1
Deadline(s): End of the month preceding board meeting for grants; Feb. 15 for college scholarships; June 30 for law school scholarships
Board meeting date(s): Jan., Apr., July, and Oct.
Final notification: 60 to 90 days
Write: J.T. Gresham, General Mgr.
Officers: J.T. Gresham, Pres., General Mgr., and Treas.; Charles D. Hudson,* V.P.; C.L. Pitts, Secy.
Trustees:* Mark Clayton Callaway, Ida Callaway Hudson, James R. Lewis, Fred L. Turner.
Number of staff: 2 part-time professional; 3 part-time support.
Employer Identification Number: 580566148

1541
Howard Callaway Foundation, Inc. ⌑
1017 First Ave.
P.O. Box 4540
Columbus 31902
Application address: 1900 Grant St., Suite 850, Denver, CO 80203; Tel.: (303) 894-0502

Established in 1951 in GA.
Foundation type: Independent
Financial data (yr. ended 12/31/88): Assets, $1,134,686 (M); expenditures, $126,209, including $114,880 for 28 grants (high: $32,000; low: $100).
Purpose and activities: Support primarily for college foundations and a health association.
Limitations: Giving primarily in CO.
Application information:
Initial approach: Letter
Deadline(s): None
Write: Howard H. Callaway, Pres.
Officers: Howard H. Callaway, Pres.; Elizabeth W. Callaway, V.P.; C.M. Adams, Treas.
Employer Identification Number: 586033829

1542
The Trust for Fuller E. Callaway Professorial Chairs ⌑
c/o Citizens & Southern Trust Co.
150 East Ponce de Leon Ave., Suite 200
Decatur 30030 (404) 377-0781

Trust established in 1968 in GA.
Donor(s): Callaway Foundation, Inc.
Foundation type: Independent
Financial data (yr. ended 6/30/86): Assets, $16,300,000 (M); expenditures, $959,000, including $936,000 for 43 grants (high: $34,000; low: $10,670; average: $21,800).
Purpose and activities: Establishment of professorial chairs at higher educational institutions.
Types of support: Professorships.
Limitations: Giving primarily in GA. No grants to individuals.
Publications: Application guidelines.
Application information: Colleges apply directly to the foundation. Application form required.
Initial approach: Letter
Copies of proposal: 1
Deadline(s): Submit proposal preferably in July; deadline Aug. 30
Board meeting date(s): Feb.
Write: Helen Harkins, Secy.
Officer: Helen Harkins, Secy.
Committee Members: Henry C. Collinsworth, Chair.; James T. Laney, Charles Meredith, H.D. Propst.
Trustee: Citizens & Southern Trust Co.
Employer Identification Number: 586075259

1543
Camp Younts Foundation ⌑ ☆
c/o Trust Co. Bank
P.O. Box 4655
Atlanta 30302-4655

Established in 1955 in GA.
Donor(s): Charles Younts,† Willie Camp Younts.†
Foundation type: Independent
Financial data (yr. ended 12/31/88): Assets, $22,556,019 (M); gifts received, $355,000; expenditures, $1,530,836, including $1,366,000 for 126 grants (high: $50,000; low: $1,000).
Purpose and activities: Giving primarily for education, with emphasis on higher and secondary institutions, and social services; support also for youth, Protestant giving, and health associations and hospitals.
Limitations: Giving primarily in VA, GA, NC, and FL. No grants to individuals.
Application information:
Initial approach: Letter
Deadline(s): None
Trustees: Harold S. Atkinson, John M. Camp, Jr., Phillip L. Hyman, Paul Camp Marks, Harry W. Walker.
Trustee Bank: Trust Co. Bank.
Employer Identification Number: 586026001

1544
J. Bulow Campbell Foundation ▼
1401 Trust Co. Tower
25 Park Place, N.E.
Atlanta 30303 (404) 658-9066

Trust established in 1940 in GA.
Donor(s): J. Bulow Campbell.†
Foundation type: Independent
Financial data (yr. ended 12/31/89): Assets, $123,125,861 (M); qualifying distributions, $6,348,968, including $6,348,968 for 30 grants (high: $500,000; low: $25,000; average: $100,000-$200,000).

Purpose and activities: Broad purposes "including but not limited to privately-supported education, human welfare, youth development, the arts, church-related agencies and agencies of the Presbyterian Church (not congregations) operating within the foundation's giving area. Concern for improving quality of spiritual and intellectual life, with priority to private agencies undertaking work of regional importance, preferably projects of permanent nature or for capital funds. Gives anonymously and requests no publicity."
Types of support: Building funds, endowment funds, equipment, land acquisition, matching funds, renovation projects, capital campaigns.
Limitations: Giving primarily in GA; very limited giving in AL, FL, NC, SC, and TN. No support for local church congregations. No grants to individuals, or for research, scholarships, fellowships, special projects, operating budgets, or recurring items; no loans.
Publications: Informational brochure (including application guidelines).
Application information: Submit 1-page proposal, 3 copies of tax information. Application form not required.
Initial approach: Letter or telephone
Copies of proposal: 1
Deadline(s): Jan. 15, Apr. 15, July 15, and Oct. 15
Board meeting date(s): Jan., Apr., July, and Oct.
Final notification: Within 1 week after board meets
Write: John W. Stephenson, Exec. Dir.
Officer: John W. Stephenson, Exec. Dir.
Trustees: William A. Parker, Jr., Chair.; Richard W. Courts II, Vice-Chair.; John B. Ellis, Langdon S. Flowers, Mark P. Pentecost, Jr., M.D., Lawrence B. Teague.
Number of staff: 1 full-time professional; 1 full-time support.
Employer Identification Number: 580566149

1545
Thalia & Michael C. Carlos Foundation, Inc. ⌘
One National Dr., S.W.
Atlanta 30336

Established in 1980 in GA.
Donor(s): National Distributing Co., Inc., Bay Distributors, Inc., NDC Distributors, Inc., and others.
Foundation type: Independent
Financial data (yr. ended 12/31/88): Assets, $287,924 (M); gifts received, $325,000; expenditures, $293,632, including $274,100 for 15 grants (high: $120,000; low: $100).
Purpose and activities: Support primarily for cultural programs, churches, and higher education.
Limitations: Giving primarily in GA.
Officers: Michael C. Carlos, Pres. and Treas.; Thalia Carlos, Secy.
Employer Identification Number: 581410420

1546
Carter-Menil Human Rights Foundation, Inc. ⌘ ☆
One Copenhill
Atlanta 30307-1405

Established in 1986 in GA.
Donor(s): Dominique de Menil, James E. Carter, Jr.
Foundation type: Operating
Financial data (yr. ended 12/31/88): Assets, $80,308 (M); gifts received, $228,000; expenditures, $228,809, including $143,734 for 3 grants (high: $100,000; low: $2,234) and $29,345 for foundation-administered programs.
Purpose and activities: To promote human rights worldwide by various methods, including the Carter-Menil Human Rights Prize, the Carter International Fellows, and sponsoring conferences between Eastern European and Western societies to protect religious and individual freedoms.
Types of support: Fellowships, conferences and seminars, grants to individuals.
Application information: Contributes only to pre-selected organizations. Applications not accepted.
Officers and Trustees:* James E. Carter, Jr.,* Chair.; Dominique de Menil,* Pres.; Miles Glaser,* Secy.; William Foege, Treas.
Employer Identification Number: 581739971

1547
CB&T Charitable Trust
(also known as Columbus Bank & Trust Company Charitable Trust)
P.O. Box 120
Columbus 31902 (404) 649-2679

Established in 1969.
Donor(s): Columbus Bank and Trust Co., Total System Services, Synovus Financial.
Foundation type: Company-sponsored
Financial data (yr. ended 12/31/88): Assets, $89,255 (M); gifts received, $337,778; expenditures, $410,061, including $408,309 for 44 grants (high: $103,000; low: $25).
Purpose and activities: Emphasis on youth agencies and higher and early childhood education, museums and the arts, historic preservation, health associations, community development, and a library.
Types of support: Annual campaigns, building funds, capital campaigns, endowment funds, general purposes.
Limitations: Giving primarily in the Columbus, GA, area.
Application information:
Write: William Slaughter, Trust Officer
Officer: William Slaughter, Trust Officer.
Employer Identification Number: 237024198

1548
The Chatham Foundation ⌘
P.O. Box 339
Savannah 31402

Trust established in 1953 in GA.
Donor(s): Savannah Foods & Industries, Inc.
Foundation type: Company-sponsored
Financial data (yr. ended 11/30/89): Assets, $10,190,969 (M); expenditures, $76,690, including $47,500 for 7 grants (high: $10,000; low: $2,500).
Purpose and activities: Support primarily for community funds, higher education, and cultural programs.
Limitations: Giving primarily in Savannah, GA. No support for individuals.
Application information: Contributes only to pre-selected organizations. Applications not accepted.
Trustees: Walter C. Scott, John E. Simpson, William W. Sprague, Jr., W.R. Steinhauer.
Corporate Trustee: The C & S National Bank.
Employer Identification Number: 586033047

1549
The Chatham Valley Foundation, Inc. ⌘
1100 Citizens and Southern National Bank Bldg.
Atlanta 30335 (404) 572-6605

Incorporated in 1962 in GA.
Donor(s): A.J. Weinberg,† Elliott Goldstein, W.B. Schwartz, Arthur Jay Schwartz, Robert C. Schwartz.
Foundation type: Independent
Financial data (yr. ended 7/31/88): Assets, $8,570,151 (M); gifts received, $38,250; expenditures, $518,263, including $449,914 for 208 grants (high: $80,000; low: $25).
Purpose and activities: Giving for a local Jewish welfare federation and other Jewish organizations, and broad support for local charitable, educational, cultural and civic activities.
Types of support: Annual campaigns, building funds, capital campaigns.
Limitations: Giving primarily in the metropolitan Atlanta, GA, area.
Application information:
Board meeting date(s): Semiannually
Write: Elliott Goldstein, Secy.
Officers and Trustees: W.B. Schwartz, Jr., Chair.; Harriet Goldstein, Vice-Chair.; Sonia Schwartz, Vice-Chair.; Elliott Goldstein, Secy.-Treas.; Lillian Friedlander, Arthur Jay Schwartz.
Number of staff: 1 part-time support.
Employer Identification Number: 586039344

1550
Cherokee Foundation, Inc. ⌘
P.O. Box 1479
Thomasville 31799
Application address: c/o Sinkola Plantation, Thomasville, GA 31799

Established in 1961 in GA.
Donor(s): H.J. Stringer, Jr.†
Foundation type: Independent
Financial data (yr. ended 12/31/88): Assets, $2,027,152 (M); expenditures, $120,903, including $108,000 for 17 grants (high: $26,850; low: $250).
Purpose and activities: Support for social services, including a United Way chapter, youth, and education.
Limitations: Giving limited to Thomasville and Thomas County, GA. No grants to individuals.
Application information: Usually, applications are acted upon and disbursements made in Dec.
Deadline(s): None
Board meeting date(s): Dec.
Write: Warren Bicknell, III, Pres.
Officers and Trustees: Warren Bicknell III, Pres.; Charles H. Watt, 1st V.P.; Cindy Webster, 2nd V.P.; Thomas H. Vann, Jr., Secy.;

Charles H. Watt III, Treas.; Pamela Firman, Gertrude Olivia, Anna Laura Ragan, Betsy Schafer, L.H. Singletary, T. Heyward Vann.
Number of staff: None.
Employer Identification Number: 580868686

1551
Chipman-Union Foundation ⌑
c/o Union Manufacturing Co.
500 Sibley Ave.
Union Point 30669

Established in 1958 in GA.
Foundation type: Company-sponsored
Financial data (yr. ended 12/31/88): Assets, $629,868 (M); gifts received, $110,000; expenditures, $110,474, including $104,020 for 61 grants (high: $33,500; low: $50) and $5,301 for 8 grants to individuals (high: $1,000; low: $124).
Purpose and activities: Giving primarily for higher education, including scholarships to individuals; support also for churches and community organizations.
Types of support: Student aid.
Application information: Contributes only to pre-selected organizations. Applications not accepted.
Trustees: F. Sibley Bryan, Jr., Carl E. Hagen, John M. Osborne.
Employer Identification Number: 586034848

1552
Churches Homes Foundation, Inc. ⌑
P.O. Box 4956
Atlanta 30302
Application address: 706 West Conway Dr., N.W., Atlanta, GA 30302

Incorporated in 1984 in GA.
Foundation type: Independent
Financial data (yr. ended 03/31/89): Assets, $2,680,382 (M); expenditures, $148,929, including $50,500 for 12 grants (high: $7,500; low: $1,000) and $80,438 for 41 grants to individuals (high: $9,000; low: $300).
Purpose and activities: Awards scholarships to individuals in financial need with satisfactory prior academic performance; support also for youth and social services.
Types of support: Student aid.
Limitations: Giving primarily in GA.
Application information:
Initial approach: Resume and references for scholarships
Deadline(s): None
Write: Duncan G. Peek, Pres.
Officers and Directors:* Duncan G. Peek,* Pres.; George Shell,* V.P.; Robert Threatt,* V.P.; Frances Davis,* Secy.; William P. Clark,* Treas.; and 16 additional directors.
Employer Identification Number: 580568689

1553
The Citizens and Southern Fund ▼ ⌑
c/o Citizens & Southern National Bank
P.O. Box 4899
Atlanta 30302-4899 (404) 581-2496

Trust established in 1956 in GA.
Donor(s): Citizens & Southern National Bank.
Foundation type: Company-sponsored
Financial data (yr. ended 12/31/88): Assets, $1,165,154 (M); gifts received, $769,185; expenditures, $1,349,731, including $1,234,625 for 78 grants (high: $450,000; low: $1,000; average: $5,000-$25,000) and $115,106 for employee matching gifts.
Purpose and activities: Support for education, civic affairs, and art and culture; health and welfare supported through the United Way.
Types of support: Employee matching gifts, annual campaigns, building funds, capital campaigns, seed money.
Limitations: Giving limited to GA, particularly in communities in which the bank operates. No grants to individuals, or for endowment funds.
Publications: Program policy statement, application guidelines.
Application information:
Initial approach: Letter
Copies of proposal: 1
Deadline(s): Sept.
Board meeting date(s): Quarterly
Final notification: Within 3 months
Write: Kirby Thompson, Secy.
Officers and Distribution Committee:* Enoch J. Prow,* Managing Trustee; Kirby Thompson,* Secy.-Treas.; Willard A. Alexander, Hugh M. Chapman, Henry A. Collingsworth, James D. Dixon, John W. McIntyre.
Number of staff: 2 full-time professional.
Employer Identification Number: 586025583

1554
Clinton-Anderson Hospital, Inc. ⌑ ☆
2827 Central Ave.
Augusta 30909 (404) 736-6700

Established in 1933.
Foundation type: Independent
Financial data (yr. ended 12/31/88): Assets, $1,013,994 (M); expenditures, $52,899, including $40,100 for 1 grant.
Purpose and activities: Giving limited to medical organizations which "exist for the use, benefit, and relief of the sick and disabled, particularly those incurable."
Limitations: Giving primarily in Augusta, GA. No grants to individuals.
Application information: Application form not required.
Deadline(s): None
Write: Jeremy M. Coghlan, Secy.-Treas.
Officers: Gardelle Lewis, Jr., Pres.; Maxwell Vallotton, V.P.; Jeremy M. Coghlan, Secy.-Treas.
Employer Identification Number: 510184964

1555
Ty Cobb Educational Fund
P.O. Box 725
Forest Park 30051

Trust established in 1953 in GA.
Donor(s): Tyrus R. Cobb.†
Foundation type: Independent
Financial data (yr. ended 12/31/88): Assets, $5,059,697 (M); expenditures, $284,364, including $216,065 for 107 grants to individuals (high: $19,268; low: $166).
Purpose and activities: Scholarship aid for needy and deserving youth who have completed one year in an accredited institution of higher learning, payable to the institution; graduate school scholarships available to law, medical, or dental students.
Types of support: Student aid.
Limitations: Giving limited to GA residents. No grants for building or endowment funds, operating budgets, special projects, or matching gifts; no loans.
Publications: Application guidelines.
Application information: Application form required.
Initial approach: Letter
Copies of proposal: 1
Deadline(s): June 15
Board meeting date(s): July and Jan.
Write: Rosie Atkins, Secy.
Officer: Rosie Atkins, Secy.
Scholarship Board: Harry S. Downs, Chair.; Merritt E. Hoag, S. Walter Martin, Walter Murphy, Darrell C. Roberts.
Trustee: Trust Co. Bank.
Employer Identification Number: 586026003

1556
The Coca-Cola Foundation, Inc. ▼ ⌑
One Coca-Cola Plaza, N.W.
Atlanta 30313 (404) 676-2568

Incorporated in 1984 in GA.
Donor(s): Coca-Cola Co.
Foundation type: Company-sponsored
Financial data (yr. ended 12/31/88): Assets, $10,534,865 (M); gifts received, $6,808,689; expenditures, $5,144,406, including $5,138,530 for 219 grants (high: $200,000; low: $500; average: $2,500-$50,000).
Purpose and activities: Emphasis on education, arts and cultural programs, health and wellness, civic and community affairs, and social services, including community funds.
Types of support: Annual campaigns, scholarship funds, continuing support, operating budgets, program-related investments, special projects.
Limitations: Giving primarily in Atlanta, GA; Houston, TX; New York, NY; and Los Angeles, CA. No support for religious organizations or religious endeavors, political or veterans' organizations, hospitals, local chapters of national organizations, or legislative or lobbying efforts. No grants to individuals, or for workshops, travel costs, conferences or seminars, building or endowment funds, operating budgets, charitable dinners, fundraising events and related advertising publications, equipment, or land acquisition; generally, no loans.
Publications: Annual report, application guidelines, informational brochure (including application guidelines).
Application information: Application form not required.
Initial approach: Proposal
Deadline(s): None
Board meeting date(s): Feb., May, July, and Nov.
Final notification: 90 to 120 days
Write: Donald R. Greene, Pres.
Officers and Directors: Carl Ware, Chair.; Donald R. Greene, Pres.; Joseph W. Jones, Secy.; Jack L. Stahl, Treas.; William W. Allison, Michelle Beale, Lawrence Coward, Bruce Kirkman.
Number of staff: 7

Employer Identification Number: 581574705

1557
Colonial Foundation, Inc. ⌑
P.O. Box 576
Savannah 31420 (912) 236-1331

Established in 1986 in GA.
Donor(s): Colonial Oil Corp.
Foundation type: Company-sponsored
Financial data (yr. ended 12/31/88): Assets, $1,615,527 (M); gifts received, $266,000; expenditures, $111,450, including $104,875 for 90 grants (high: $12,000; low: $25).
Purpose and activities: Giving for human and social services, including the YMCA, youth, and the United Way.
Limitations: Giving primarily in GA.
Application information:
Deadline(s): None
Write: Beverly E. Leigh, Treas.
Officers: Robert H. Demere, Pres.; Robert H. Demere, Jr., V.P.; Raymond S. Demere, Secy.; Beverly E. Leigh, Treas.
Employer Identification Number: 581693323

1558
Community Welfare Association of Colquitt County ⌑
P.O. Box 38
Moultrie 31776

Established in 1937 in GA.
Donor(s): Lottie T. Vereen,† W.C. Vereen Trust.
Foundation type: Independent
Financial data (yr. ended 12/31/88): Assets, $2,229,527 (M); expenditures, $90,455, including $75,172 for grants and $3,667 for 1 grant to an individual.
Purpose and activities: Grants for education, particularly higher education, social service and youth programs, culture, and denominational giving. Awards 1 scholarship annually to a Colquitt County High School senior.
Types of support: Student aid.
Limitations: Giving limited to GA, with emphasis on Colquitt County.
Application information: Application form required.
Deadline(s): None
Trustees: T.J. Vereen, W.C. Vereen, Jr., W.J. Vereen.
Employer Identification Number: 586032259

1559
Community Enterprises, Inc. ⌑
115 East Main St.
Thomaston 30286 (404) 647-7131

Incorporated in 1944 in GA.
Donor(s): Julian T. Hightower, Thomaston Cotton Mills.
Foundation type: Independent
Financial data (yr. ended 6/30/88): Assets, $7,262,226 (M); expenditures, $229,806, including $202,256 for 36 grants (high: $30,000; low: $100).
Purpose and activities: Giving for higher and secondary education; some support for community development.
Limitations: Giving primarily in Upson County, GA.
Application information:
Initial approach: Letter or proposal
Deadline(s): Dec. 31
Write: William H. Hightower, Jr., Pres.
Officers and Trustees: William H. Hightower, Jr., Pres.; George H. Hightower, V.P.; Neil H. Hightower, Secy.-Treas.
Employer Identification Number: 586043415

1560
The Conboy Foundation ⌑ ☆
1360 Peachtree St.
Two Midtown Plaza, Suite 1450
Atlanta 30309

Established in 1987 in GA.
Donor(s): James J. Conboy, Lynne D. Conboy.
Foundation type: Independent
Financial data (yr. ended 12/31/88): Assets, $1,158,857 (M); gifts received, $153,133; expenditures, $61,763, including $50,000 for 4 grants (high: $25,000; low: $5,000).
Purpose and activities: Giving for social services and Christian organizations.
Limitations: Giving primarily in GA. No grants to individuals.
Application information: Contributes only to pre-selected organizations. Applications not accepted.
Trustees: Opal D. Abbink, James J. Conboy, Lynne D. Conboy.
Employer Identification Number: 581742620

1561
Anne Mays & Charles A. Conklin Trust ⌑
c/o Trust Co. Bank
P.O. Box 4655
Atlanta 30302

Established in 1967 in GA.
Foundation type: Independent
Financial data (yr. ended 12/31/88): Assets, $1,270,429 (M); expenditures, $132,085, including $115,008 for 1 grant.
Purpose and activities: Grants to the Henrietta Egleston Hospital for Children and other religious, educational, and charitable institutions.
Limitations: Giving primarily in GA, especially Decatur.
Application information:
Initial approach: Letter or proposal
Deadline(s): None
Write: Miss Claire Ranney
Officers: Mrs. Elkin G. Alston, Mgr.; Horace Sibley, Mgr.
Trustee: Trust Co. Bank.
Employer Identification Number: 586067206

1562
William F. Cooper Scholarship Trust ☆
c/o Capital Mgmt. Group, First Union National Bank of Savannah
P.O. Box 9947
Savannah 31412

Established in 1984 in GA.
Foundation type: Independent
Financial data (yr. ended 12/31/89): Assets, $1,357,512 (M); expenditures, $91,407, including $80,151 for 34 grants to individuals (high: $15,133; low: $23).
Purpose and activities: Awards scholarships "for the purpose of educating poor, worthy female people of good family, without regard to age."
Types of support: Student aid.
Limitations: Giving primarily to residents of GA, especially Chatham County. No support for the study of theology, law, or medicine.
Application information: Application form required.
Deadline(s): Apr. 15
Write: Elizabeth M. Oxnard, Trust Officer, Capital Management Group
Trustee: First Union National Bank.
Employer Identification Number: 586029952

1563
Courts Foundation, Inc.
50 Hurt Plaza, Suite 1200
Atlanta 30323 (404) 523-6057

Incorporated in 1950 in GA.
Donor(s): Richard W. Courts, Virginia Campbell Courts, Malon C. Courts,† Atlantic Realty Co.
Foundation type: Independent
Financial data (yr. ended 12/31/89): Assets, $5,162,684 (M); expenditures, $259,331, including $250,400 for 39 grants (high: $50,000; low: $1,000; average: $1,000-$6,000).
Purpose and activities: When sufficiently large, corpus to be used to provide a home or clinic for elderly people; grants from income for a home for the retired; smaller amounts to local charities, principally universities, youth agencies, and churches.
Types of support: Capital campaigns, endowment funds, scholarship funds.
Limitations: Giving primarily in GA. No grants to individuals.
Application information: Application form not required.
Initial approach: Letter
Copies of proposal: 1
Deadline(s): None
Board meeting date(s): Mar., June, Sept., and Dec.
Final notification: 1 month
Write: Richard W. Courts II, Pres.
Officers and Trustees:* Richard W. Courts II,* Pres.; Francis J. Heazel, Jr.,* Secy.-Treas.; Richard W. Courts, John B. Ellis, William A. Parker, Jr.
Number of staff: None.
Employer Identification Number: 586036859

1564
The James M. Cox Foundation of Georgia, Inc.
c/o Cox Newspapers
P.O. Box 105720
Atlanta 30348 (404) 843-7912

Incorporated in 1957 in GA.
Donor(s): Cox Enterprises, Inc.
Foundation type: Company-sponsored
Financial data (yr. ended 12/31/89): Assets, $5,917,580 (M); gifts received, $400,000; expenditures, $680,423, including $665,500 for 45 grants (high: $133,000; low: $1,000).
Purpose and activities: Giving primarily for higher, medical, and other education, hospitals and medical research, the fine and performing arts, and social services.

Types of support: Building funds, capital campaigns, endowment funds, renovation projects, research, special projects.
Limitations: Giving limited to areas of company operations. No grants to individuals.
Application information: Applicant should have support of local corporate office for grant requested. Application form not required.
Initial approach: Proposal
Copies of proposal: 1
Deadline(s): None
Board meeting date(s): Quarterly
Write: Leigh Ann Korns
Officers and Trustees:* Barbara Cox Anthony,* Chair.; Anne Cox Chambers,* Pres.; James A. Hatcher, Secy.; John G. Boyette, Treas.; Carl R. Gross, James C. Kennedy.
Number of staff: None.
Employer Identification Number: 586032469

1565
Crawford & Company Foundation, Inc. ⌑ ☆
5620 Glenridge Dr., N.E.
Atlanta 30342-1399
Application address: P.O. Box 5047, Atlanta, GA 30302

Established in 1986 in GA.
Foundation type: Company-sponsored
Financial data (yr. ended 3/31/89): Assets, $255,850 (M); expenditures, $108,728, including $108,259 for 41 grants (high: $38,000; low: $100).
Purpose and activities: Giving primarily for a community fund, higher education, and health associations and services; minor support for the arts and culture.
Limitations: Giving primarily in Atlanta, GA.
Application information:
Write: Tawnya Counts
Officers and Trustees:* F.L. Minix,* Chair.; D.R. Chapman,* V.P.; J.H. Graham,* Secy.; K.R. Stachler, Treas.
Employer Identification Number: 581727529

1566
George E. Crouch Foundation Charitable Trust ⌑
Route 1, Box 703
Louisville 30434
Application address: RFD 2, Louisville, GA 30434; Tel.: (912) 589-7814

Established in 1972 in SC.
Donor(s): George E. Crouch, Jr.
Foundation type: Independent
Financial data (yr. ended 12/31/87): Assets, $1,241,603 (M); expenditures, $25,057, including $11,308 for 9 grants (high: $5,000; low: $100).
Purpose and activities: Support primarily for churches and for higher education.
Application information:
Initial approach: Letter
Deadline(s): None
Write: George E. Crouch, Jr., Trustee
Trustee: George E. Crouch, Jr.
Employer Identification Number: 237238543

1567
The Davis Foundation, Inc. ⌑
One National Dr.
Atlanta 30336

Established in 1960.
Donor(s): Raleigh Linen Service, Inc., National Distributing Co., Inc., and subsidiaries, Truck Rental Co., Alfred M. Davis, ADP Rental Co., Servitex, Inc.
Foundation type: Independent
Financial data (yr. ended 7/31/88): Assets, $111,368 (M); gifts received, $475,000; expenditures, $822,049, including $819,970 for 24 grants (high: $401,000; low: $95).
Purpose and activities: Grants primarily for Jewish welfare funds and temple support in the Atlanta area and for higher education; support also for cultural programs and health services.
Limitations: Giving primarily in Atlanta, GA.
Application information:
Initial approach: Proposal
Deadline(s): None
Write: Alfred A. Davis, Pres.
Officers: Alfred A. Davis, Pres.; Jay M. Davis, V.P.
Employer Identification Number: 586035088

1568
Cecil B. Day Foundation, Inc. ▼
4725 Peachtree Corners Circle, Suite 300
Norcross 30092 (404) 446-1500

Incorporated in 1968 in GA.
Donor(s): Cecil B. Day.†
Foundation type: Independent
Financial data (yr. ended 12/31/88): Assets, $22,556,319 (M); expenditures, $1,412,914, including $1,244,519 for grants (high: $100,000; low: $100; average: $500-$10,000).
Purpose and activities: Grants to Christian churches for evangelism, missions, and discipleships, and for Pastor's Leadership Training.
Types of support: Continuing support, seed money, emergency funds, building funds, land acquisition, matching funds, renovation projects.
Limitations: Giving primarily in the New England states; special consideration for GA, primarily the metropolitan Atlanta area. No grants to individuals, or for deficit financing, endowment funds, scholarships, or fellowships.
Publications: Informational brochure.
Application information: Application form not required.
Initial approach: Letter requesting program brochure
Deadline(s): None
Board meeting date(s): Annually
Write: Edward L. White, Jr., Pres.
Officers: Deen Day Smith, Vice-Chair.; Edward L. White, Jr., Pres.; Ira Q. Craft, V.P.; R.D. Spear, Jr., V.P.; JoAnn F. Dollar, Secy.; Charles A. Sanders, Treas.
Trustees: C. Burke Day, Jr., Clinton M. Day, Lon L. Day, Jr.
Number of staff: 1 full-time professional.
Employer Identification Number: 581030351

1569
Delta Air Lines Foundation
Hartsfield Atlanta International Airport
Atlanta 30320 (404) 765-2795

Established in 1968 in DE.
Donor(s): Delta Air Lines, Inc.
Foundation type: Company-sponsored
Financial data (yr. ended 12/31/88): Assets, $9,355,063 (M); gifts received, $2,281,202; expenditures, $340,045, including $175,500 for 32 grants (high: $25,000; low: $1,000) and $120,688 for 291 employee matching gifts.
Purpose and activities: Giving limited to higher education and educational associations, including employee matching gifts to colleges and universities.
Types of support: Employee matching gifts.
Limitations: No grants to individuals, or for support operations of universities and colleges.
Application information: Application form not required.
Initial approach: Proposal
Copies of proposal: 1
Deadline(s): May 1
Board meeting date(s): June and Nov.
Final notification: July 1
Write: Thomas D. Stone, Asst. Secy.
Officers and Trustees:* R.W. Allen, Jr.,* Pres.; James W. Callison,* Secy.; Frank S. Chew,* Treas.; H.L. Harris, W.W. Hawkins, R.H. Heil, C.J. May, R.A. McClelland, T.J. Roeck, Jr., Thomas D. Stone.
Number of staff: None.
Employer Identification Number: 586073119

1570
Helen and Howard Dobbs Foundation, Inc. ⌑
c/o Life of Georgia Corp. Ctr.
P.O. Box 105006
Atlanta 30348-5006

Foundation type: Independent
Financial data (yr. ended 10/31/88): Assets, $1,337,193 (M); expenditures, $108,553, including $94,000 for 20 grants (high: $25,000; low: $500).
Purpose and activities: Grants primarily for higher and secondary education, health associations and services, and Protestant church support.
Limitations: Giving primarily in the Southeast.
Application information:
Initial approach: Letter
Deadline(s): Aug. 1
Write: Jason Gilliland, Secy.-Treas.
Officers: R. Howard Dobbs, Jr., Chair.; Jason B. Gilliland, Secy.-Treas.
Trustees: Josephine A. Dobbs, E. Cody Laird, Jr.
Employer Identification Number: 586033186

1571
The James Glenwell and Clara May Dodson Foundation
c/o Trust Co. Bank, Trust Dept.
P.O. Box 4655
Atlanta 30302

Trust established in 1967 in GA.
Donor(s): Clara May Dodson.†
Foundation type: Independent
Financial data (yr. ended 12/31/87): Assets, $2,009,960 (M); expenditures, $126,218,

including $120,000 for 20 grants (high: $32,500; low: $500).
Purpose and activities: Giving to benefit underprivileged children; grants largely for homes and hospitals, including medical research; support also for education.
Types of support: Building funds, capital campaigns, equipment, general purposes, special projects.
Limitations: Giving primarily in GA and SC. No grants to individuals.
Publications: Annual report.
Application information: Application form not required.
Initial approach: Typewritten letter
Copies of proposal: 1
Deadline(s): Oct. 1
Board meeting date(s): Nov.
Write: Cathy S. Nix, V.P., Trust Co. Bank
Officers: Robert F. Bryan, Mgr.; Constance G. Chapman, Mgr.; Clara May Godshall, Mgr.; Ellis Godshall, Mgr.; William Reynolds, Mgr.; Elenora Richardson, Mgr.; Edwin L. Sterne, Mgr.
Trustee: Trust Co. Bank.
Employer Identification Number: 586074354

1572
John R. Donnell, Jr. Foundation, Inc. ⌑ ☆
c/o Trust Co. Bank
P.O. Box 4655
Atlanta 30302
Application address: 134 Lindbergh Dr., Atlanta, GA 30305

Established in 1984 in GA.
Donor(s): John R. Donnell, Jr.
Foundation type: Independent
Financial data (yr. ended 12/31/88): Assets, $162,114 (M); gifts received, $71,781; expenditures, $102,976, including $101,500 for 10 grants (high: $30,000; low: $1,000).
Purpose and activities: Giving primarily for youth groups; minor support also for a community fund, a Presbyterian church, social services, and the arts.
Types of support: Operating budgets.
Limitations: No grants to individuals.
Application information:
Initial approach: Letter
Deadline(s): None
Write: John R. Donnell, Jr., Pres.
Officers and Directors: John R. Donnell, Jr., Pres. and Treas.; Marcia G. Donnell, V.P. and Secy.; Thomas B. Donnell, V.P.
Trustee: Trust Co. Bank.
Employer Identification Number: 581594720

1573
John Henry Dorminy Foundation, Inc. ⌑
P.O. Box 870
Fitzgerald 31750

Established in 1962 in GA.
Donor(s): John Henry Dorminy, Jr., and members of the Dorminy family.
Foundation type: Independent
Financial data (yr. ended 12/31/88): Assets, $1,728,341 (M); gifts received, $7,000; expenditures, $170,435, including $88,235 for 61 grants (high: $10,000).
Purpose and activities: Support primarily for hospitals and higher education.
Limitations: No grants to individuals.
Application information: Contributes only to pre-selected organizations. Applications not accepted.
Directors: W.J. Dorminy, Chair. and Pres.; John Henry Dorminy III, Vice-Chair.; Martha Anne D. Verbit, Vice-Chair.
Employer Identification Number: 586033324

1574
Christopher Edwards Foundation Inc. ⌑
One Lemon Ln., N.E.
Atlanta 30307

Established in 1976 in GA.
Donor(s): Carolyn Denise Edwards, Kimberly Lynn Edwards, T.H. Edwards, Edwards Baking Co., Harvey D. Ogletree,† National Christian Charitable Fdn., Inc.
Foundation type: Independent
Financial data (yr. ended 8/31/88): Assets, $1,228,926 (M); gifts received, $225,239; expenditures, $306,396, including $303,700 for 28 grants (high: $79,000; low: $200).
Purpose and activities: Grants primarily for Christian organizations and social services; substantial support also for anti-pornography campaigns.
Application information: Contributes only to pre-selected organizations. Applications not accepted.
Officers and Directors: Thomas J. Edwards, Pres.; Sara Edwards, V.P.; Donald S. Patterson, Julie Tidwell.
Employer Identification Number: 581281737

1575
Nell Warren & William Simpson Elkin Memorial Foundation ⌑
c/o Trust Co. Bank
P.O. Box 4655
Atlanta 30302 (404) 588-8449

Established in 1979 in GA.
Donor(s): Josephine W. Asbury.†
Foundation type: Independent
Financial data (yr. ended 9/30/88): Assets, $2,135,145 (M); expenditures, $146,841, including $118,167 for 12 grants (high: $78,000; low: $500).
Purpose and activities: Support for cancer research, heart associations, Bible study, schools, and churches.
Types of support: Operating budgets, scholarship funds, building funds.
Application information:
Initial approach: Letter and proposal
Deadline(s): None
Write: Clare Ranney
Trustee: Trust Co. Bank.
Advisory Committee: Edward P. Gould, Jesse C. Hall, Clare Ranney.
Employer Identification Number: 581378819

1576
Elson Foundation, Inc. ⌑ ☆
65 Valley Rd., N.W.
Atlanta 30305

Incorporated in 1984 in GA.
Donor(s): Edward E. Elson.
Foundation type: Independent
Financial data (yr. ended 12/31/88): Assets, $1,302,378 (M); expenditures, $291,487, including $286,130 for 35 grants (high: $74,690; low: $25).
Purpose and activities: Support primarily for cultural programs, higher education, and a mental health association, and Jewish organizations, including welfare funds.
Types of support: Operating budgets.
Limitations: No grants to individuals.
Application information: Contributes only to pre-selected organizations. Applications not accepted.
Officers: Edward E. Elson, Chair. and Pres.; Suzanne G. Elson, Secy.-Treas.
Directors: Charles M. Elson, Harry Elson II, Louis G. Elson.
Employer Identification Number: 581595112

1577
EMSA Fund, Inc.
20 Westminster Dr.
Atlanta 30309 (404) 874-8877

Incorporated in 1962 in GA.
Donor(s): Phoebe Weil Lundeen,† and members of the Franklin family.
Foundation type: Independent
Financial data (yr. ended 12/31/88): Assets, $1,610,818 (M); expenditures, $90,875, including $65,037 for 73 grants (high: $30,250; low: $18).
Purpose and activities: Giving primarily for culture, public policy, race relations, rural development, civil rights, community development, and women's programs, particularly for those who have been neglected or hard to reach in the provision of such programs; support also for environmental programs and educational programs for minorities.
Types of support: General purposes, operating budgets, continuing support, annual campaigns, seed money, emergency funds, endowment funds, special projects, capital campaigns.
Limitations: Giving primarily in GA, particularly the Atlanta area, and in CO. No grants to individuals; no loans.
Publications: Grants list.
Application information: Application form not required.
Initial approach: Letter
Copies of proposal: 1
Deadline(s): None
Board meeting date(s): Annually
Final notification: 2 to 4 weeks
Write: Alice Franklin, Pres.
Officers and Trustees:* Andrew D. Franklin,* Chair.; Alice Franklin,* Pres.
Number of staff: None.
Employer Identification Number: 586043282

1578
The Florence C. and Harry L. English Memorial Fund
P.O. Box 4418, MC 041
Atlanta 30302 (404) 588-8246

Established in 1964 in GA.
Donor(s): Florence Cruft English.†
Foundation type: Independent

Financial data (yr. ended 12/31/89): Assets, $8,614,097 (M); expenditures, $509,215, including $442,666 for grants (average: $3,000-$5,000).
Purpose and activities: Grants only for education, health, general welfare, and culture, with emphasis on assisting the aged and chronically ill, the blind, and those persons generally designated as the "underprivileged."
Types of support: Renovation projects, equipment, special projects.
Limitations: Giving limited to the metropolitan Atlanta, GA, area (Fulton and DeKalb counties). No support for veterans' or political organizations, or organizations which have not been operating without a deficit for at least a year. No grants to individuals; no loans.
Publications: Program policy statement, application guidelines.
Application information: Application form required.
Initial approach: Telephone or letter
Copies of proposal: 1
Deadline(s): 1st of month preceding month in which board meeting will be held
Board meeting date(s): Jan., Apr., July, and Oct.
Write: Victor A. Gregory, Secy.
Distribution Committee: E.P. Gould, Chair.; Victor A. Gregory, Secy.; Jesse S. Hall, Robert Strickland.
Trustee: Trust Co. Bank.
Number of staff: 1 full-time professional; 1 full-time support.
Employer Identification Number: 586045781

1579
Equifax Foundation
c/o Equifax Inc.
1600 Peachtree St., N.W.
Atlanta 30309 (404) 885-8301
Mailing address: P.O. Box 4081, Atlanta, GA 30302

Trust established in 1978 in GA.
Donor(s): Equifax, Inc.
Foundation type: Company-sponsored
Financial data (yr. ended 12/31/89): Assets, $0 (L); expenditures, $679,809, including $679,809 for 187 grants (high: $250,000; low: $25; average: $100-$5,000).
Purpose and activities: Giving primarily for higher education, a community fund, and an arts alliance; support also for health and welfare organizations.
Types of support: Operating budgets, continuing support, annual campaigns, seed money, emergency funds, building funds, land acquisition, endowment funds, scholarship funds, special projects, research, conferences and seminars, renovation projects, capital campaigns, general purposes.
Limitations: Giving primarily in GA; increasing support for national organizations. No grants to individuals, or for deficit financing, fellowships, publications, matching gifts, or travel.
Application information: Application form not required.
Initial approach: Proposal
Copies of proposal: 1
Deadline(s): None
Board meeting date(s): Approximately every other month
Final notification: 30 days
Write: Nancy Golonka Rozier, V.P., Corp. Public Affairs
Trustees: Gene Merrigan, Robert Strickland, J.V. White.
Number of staff: 2 part-time professional.
Employer Identification Number: 581296807

1580
Lettie Pate Evans Foundation, Inc. ▼
1400 Peachtree Ctr. Tower
230 Peachtree St., N.W., Suite 1400
Atlanta 30303 (404) 522-6755

Incorporated in 1945 in GA.
Donor(s): Lettie Pate Evans,† Robert W. Woodruff.†
Foundation type: Independent
Financial data (yr. ended 12/31/89): Assets, $87,753,625 (M); expenditures, $3,260,290, including $3,071,000 for 12 grants (high: $500,000; low: $10,000; average: $15,000-$500,000).
Purpose and activities: Grants primarily for higher education; support also for educational institutions and social services. Preference is given to one-time capital projects of established private charitable organizations.
Types of support: Building funds, equipment, land acquisition, seed money, renovation projects, capital campaigns.
Limitations: Giving primarily in the Atlanta, GA, area. No grants to individuals, or generally for operating expenses, research, scholarships, fellowships, or matching gifts; no loans.
Publications: Application guidelines.
Application information: Application form not required.
Initial approach: Letter of inquiry followed by proposal
Copies of proposal: 1
Deadline(s): First of Feb. and Sept.
Board meeting date(s): Apr. and Nov.
Final notification: 30 days after board meeting
Write: Charles H. McTier, Pres.
Officers: Charles H. McTier, Pres.; P. Russell Hardin, Secy.-Treas.
Trustees: J.W. Jones, Chair.; Hughes Spalding, Jr., Vice-Chair.; Roberto C. Goizueta, James M. Sibley, James B. Williams.
Number of staff: 7
Employer Identification Number: 586004644

1581
Exposition Foundation, Inc.
2970 Peachtree Rd., Suite 820
Atlanta 30305 (404) 233-6404

Incorporated in 1950 in GA.
Foundation type: Independent
Financial data (yr. ended 08/31/89): Assets, $2,794,487 (M); expenditures, $151,610, including $131,400 for 29 grants (high: $51,200; low: $500).
Purpose and activities: Giving primarily for cultural programs, including the fine arts, historic preservation, music, and a museum; support also for higher and secondary education, social services and health.
Types of support: Annual campaigns, building funds, capital campaigns, equipment, endowment funds.
Limitations: Giving primarily in GA.
Publications: Annual report.
Application information: Application form not required.
Write: Frank L. Rozelle, Jr., Secy.-Treas.
Officers and Trustees:* Frances F. Cocke,* Pres.; Jane C. Black,* V.P.; Frank L. Rozelle, Jr.,* Secy.-Treas.
Number of staff: None.
Employer Identification Number: 586043273

1582
First Atlanta Foundation, Inc.
c/o First Wachovia Charitable Funds Management, First National Bank of Atlanta
Two Peachtree St., N.W., Suite 705
Atlanta 30383 (404) 332-6586

Incorporated in 1976 in GA.
Donor(s): First Atlanta Corp.
Foundation type: Company-sponsored
Financial data (yr. ended 12/31/88): Assets, $4,737,270 (M); gifts received, $902,134; expenditures, $793,997, including $708,246 for 153 grants (high: $100,000; low: $50) and $66,986 for 550 employee matching gifts.
Purpose and activities: Emphasis on community funds, arts and cultural programs, and youth agencies.
Types of support: Employee matching gifts.
Limitations: Giving primarily in the Atlanta, GA, area.
Application information: Application form not required.
Initial approach: Letter
Deadline(s): 30 days prior to board meetings
Board meeting date(s): Monthly
Final notification: 10 days after board meetings
Write: Charles Buchholz
Officer and Directors: Thomas E. Boland,* Pres.; Arthur Baxter, Secy.-Treas.; George Atkins, D. Raymond Riddle.
Number of staff: None.
Employer Identification Number: 581274979

1583
Foundation for Improvement of Justice, Inc. ☆
P.O. Box 888681
Atlanta 30356-8868 (404) 373-4562

Incorporated in 1985 in GA.
Foundation type: Independent
Financial data (yr. ended 12/31/89): Assets, $1,073,046 (M); expenditures, $123,200, including $49,280 for 4 grants of $12,320 each and $73,920 for 6 grants to individuals of $12,320 each.
Purpose and activities: Confers achievement awards to organizations and individuals for activities which further the cause of justice.
Application information: Applicants must be nominated; self-nominations not accepted. Application form required.
Initial approach: Letter
Copies of proposal: 1
Deadline(s): June 15
Board meeting date(s): Feb. and July
Final notification: Aug.

Officers and Directors:* Paul H. Chapman,* Chair.; Frederick C. McLam,* Pres.; Judith C. Chester,* Secy.; Cilla Chapman,* Treas.; Dorothy Beasley, Shirley Chapman, Paul Chester.
Number of staff: None.
Employer Identification Number: 581593170

1584
The Lawrence & Alfred Fox Foundation, Inc.
3100 Equitable Bldg.
Atlanta 30303 (404) 572-6500
Additional tel.: (404) 572-6311

Foundation type: Independent
Financial data (yr. ended 12/31/88): Assets, $1,149,845 (M); expenditures, $86,676, including $76,550 for 43 grants (high: $25,000; low: $100).
Purpose and activities: Support primarily for Jewish welfare; support also for museums and the fine and other arts, and higher education.
Types of support: Continuing support.
Limitations: Giving primarily in GA.
Application information: Application form not required.
Write: Louis Regenstein, Trustee
Trustees: Ann Abrams, Edward M. Abrams, Louis Regenstein, Alene Uhry.
Number of staff: None.
Employer Identification Number: 586033168

1585
John and Mary Franklin Foundation, Inc. ⌑
c/o Bank South, N.A.
P.O. Box 4956
Atlanta 30302 (404) 529-4614

Incorporated in 1955 in GA.
Donor(s): John Franklin, Mary O. Franklin.†
Foundation type: Independent
Financial data (yr. ended 12/31/86): Assets, $14,956,433 (M); expenditures, $885,918, including $794,300 for 104 grants (high: $65,000; low: $50).
Purpose and activities: Giving for higher and secondary education, youth agencies, hospitals, and cultural programs.
Types of support: General purposes, scholarship funds, building funds.
Limitations: Giving primarily in GA, with emphasis on the metropolitan Atlanta area; special types of grants awarded to institutions in adjoining states.
Publications: Annual report.
Application information:
Initial approach: Letter
Board meeting date(s): Jan. and July, and as needed
Write: Robert B. Rountree, Treas.
Officers and Trustees: W. Kelly Mosley, Chair.; Virlyn B. Moore, Jr., Secy.; Robert B. Rountree, Treas.; George T. Duncan, Frank M. Malone, Marilu H. McCarty, L. Edmund Rast, Alexander W. Smith, Jr., William M. Suttles, Walter O. Walker.
Employer Identification Number: 586036131

1586
The B. I. Friedman Foundation ⌑
Four West State St.
Savannah 31401 (912) 232-4410

Established in 1945 in GA.
Donor(s): Herman K. Friedman, Stanley K. Friedman, Friedman Jewelers, Inc., Stanley Jewelers, Inc.
Foundation type: Independent
Financial data (yr. ended 12/31/88): Assets, $279,436 (M); expenditures, $113,035, including $112,485 for 23 grants (high: $25,660; low: $100).
Purpose and activities: Support for Jewish giving, including Jewish welfare, social services, and community funds.
Limitations: Giving primarily in GA.
Application information:
Initial approach: Letter
Deadline(s): None
Write: Herman K. Friedman, Trustee
Trustees: Herman K. Friedman, Stanley K. Friedman, Zanvly Krieger.
Employer Identification Number: 586043775

1587
J. B. Fuqua Foundation, Inc.
c/o Fuqua National Corp.
4900 Georgia-Pacific Ctr.
Atlanta 30303 (404) 659-5318

Incorporated in 1970 in GA.
Donor(s): J.B. Fuqua.
Foundation type: Independent
Financial data (yr. ended 9/30/88): Assets, $3,159,986 (M); gifts received, $7,500; expenditures, $1,397,512, including $1,342,272 for 41 grants (high: $1,200,000; low: $100).
Purpose and activities: Grants primarily for a botanical garden; support also for higher and secondary education.
Limitations: No grants to individuals.
Publications: Annual report.
Application information: Application form not required.
Deadline(s): None
Write: Mrs. J.B. Fuqua, Secy.
Officers: J.B. Fuqua, Pres.; Rob Draughn, V.P.; Dorothy C. Fuqua, Secy.; J. Rex Fuqua, Treas.
Number of staff: 1 part-time support.
Employer Identification Number: 237122039

1588
Philip and Irene Toll Gage Foundation
c/o Citizens & Southern Trust Co.
P.O. Box 4446
Atlanta 30302 (404) 897-3222

Established in 1985 in GA.
Donor(s): Betty G. Holland.
Foundation type: Independent
Financial data (yr. ended 11/30/89): Assets, $4,545,825 (M); gifts received, $6,000; expenditures, $216,583, including $177,267 for 61 grants (high: $20,000; low: $100).
Purpose and activities: Support for education, culture including the arts and theater, and hospitals and health services; grants also for Protestant giving.
Types of support: Annual campaigns, general purposes.
Limitations: Giving primarily in Atlanta, GA. No grants to individuals, or for endowment programs.
Publications: 990-PF.
Application information: Application form not required.
Initial approach: Proposal
Copies of proposal: 1
Deadline(s): Submit proposals preferably in Aug. and Sept.; deadline Oct. 15
Board meeting date(s): Nov.
Final notification: Within 1 week of annual meeting
Write: Larry B. Hooks, Sr. V.P., Citizens & Southern Trust Co.
Officers: Betty G. Holland, Chair.; William J. Holland, Vice-Chair.; Larry B. Hooks, Secy.
Trustee: Citizens & Southern Trust Co.
Number of staff: None.
Employer Identification Number: 581727394

1589
Allan C. & Lelia J. Garden Foundation ⌑ ☆
c/o Citizens & Southern National Bank
P.O. Box 4007
Macon 31208-4007
Application address: P.O. Box 308, Fitzgerald, GA 31750

Established in 1972.
Foundation type: Independent
Financial data (yr. ended 5/31/89): Assets, $3,392,686 (M); qualifying distributions, $100,929, including $100,096 for 67 loans to individuals (high: $1,600; low: $533).
Purpose and activities: Awards loans to students.
Types of support: Student loans.
Application information: Application form required.
Deadline(s): None
Write: Harvey L. Jay, Trustee
Trustees: Harvey L. Jay, Citizens & Southern Trust Co.
Employer Identification Number: 586103546

1590
Georgia Health Foundation, Inc.
Four Executive Park Dr., Suite 2406
Atlanta 30329 (404) 636-2525

Established in 1985 in GA.
Foundation type: Independent
Financial data (yr. ended 12/31/89): Assets, $6,207,541 (M); expenditures, $280,775, including $245,100 for 8 grants (high: $50,000; low: $6,000).
Purpose and activities: Support primarily for health-related organizations especially medical care and medical research.
Types of support: General purposes, research, scholarship funds, seed money, special projects.
Limitations: Giving primarily in GA.
Publications: Informational brochure (including application guidelines).
Application information:
Initial approach: Proposal
Copies of proposal: 6
Deadline(s): Aug. 1
Board meeting date(s): 4th Monday of Feb., May, Aug., and Dec.
Write: Constance L. Lloyd, Secy.

Officers and Directors:* J. Rhodes Haverty, M.D.,* Chair.; Robert Zwald,* Vice-Chair.; Constance L. Lloyd,* Secy.; Eugene E. Adams,* Treas.; John Borek, E.P. Coverdell, Richard A. Elmer, M.D., Jaquelin Gotlieb, M.D., S. Jarvin Levinson, John T. Maudlin, M.D., Frances Posey, Charles Smithgall III.
Number of staff: 1 part-time professional.
Employer Identification Number: 581352076

1591
Georgia Power Foundation, Inc. ⌑
333 Piedmont Ave., 20th Fl.
Atlanta 30308 (404) 526-6784

Established in 1986 in GA.
Foundation type: Company-sponsored
Financial data (yr. ended 12/31/88): Assets, $12,720,946 (M); expenditures, $2,645,194, including $2,122,949 for 226 grants (high: $652,832; low: $110; average: $1,000-$100,000).
Purpose and activities: Interests include the aged, AIDS, cancer, community development, race relations, education, family services, health, the homeless, rehabilitation, human rights, leadership development, legal services, libraries, medical research, museums, performing arts, theater, historic preservation, and fine arts.
Types of support: Annual campaigns, building funds, capital campaigns, conferences and seminars, endowment funds, equipment, operating budgets, renovation projects, research, scholarship funds, seed money, special projects, deficit financing.
Limitations: Giving primarily in GA. No support for private foundations. No grants to individuals.
Publications: Informational brochure (including application guidelines), 990-PF.
Application information: Application form not required.
Initial approach: Letter with proposal
Copies of proposal: 1
Deadline(s): None
Board meeting date(s): 1st week of each month
Final notification: After board review
Write: Ms. Judy M. Anderson, Exec. Dir.
Officers and Directors: Warren Y. Jobe, Pres.; Judy M. Anderson, Secy.-Treas. and Exec. Dir.; Fred W. Dement, Jr., Carl L. Donaldson, Dwight H. Evans, James W. George, Gene R. Hodges, Ross C. Kist III, Charles W. Whitney.
Number of staff: 2 part-time professional; 1 full-time support; 1 part-time support.
Employer Identification Number: 581709417

1592
Georgia-Pacific Foundation, Inc. ▼ ⌑
133 Peachtree St., N.E.
Atlanta 30303 (404) 521-5228

Incorporated in 1958 in OR.
Donor(s): Georgia-Pacific Corp., and subsidiaries.
Foundation type: Company-sponsored
Financial data (yr. ended 12/31/87): Assets, $2,329,888 (M); gifts received, $2,000,000; expenditures, $1,745,366, including $1,128,971 for 245 grants (high: $100,000; low: $500; average: $1,000-$7,000) and $614,501 for grants to individuals.
Purpose and activities: Giving for higher and other education, including employee-related scholarships to graduating seniors in areas of major company operations; support also for community funds, hospitals and health services, and social services and youth agencies.
Types of support: Employee-related scholarships.
Limitations: Giving limited to areas of company operations, with some emphasis on the Atlanta, GA, area.
Application information:
Deadline(s): None
Board meeting date(s): As required
Write: W.I. Tamblyn, Treas.
Officers and Trustees: Stanley S. Dennison, Chair.; Marion L. Talmadge, Pres.; Diane Durgin, Secy.; W.I. Tamblyn, Treas.
Number of staff: 1 full-time support.
Employer Identification Number: 936023726

1593
Gerson Foundation ⌑ ☆
1801 Peachtree St., N.E., Suite 300
Atlanta 30309-1891

Established in 1954.
Donor(s): Seymour Gerson, Betty Gerson Minsk.
Foundation type: Independent
Financial data (yr. ended 5/31/89): Assets, $768,162 (M); gifts received, $123,700; expenditures, $120,278, including $116,588 for 30 grants (high: $65,000; low: $10).
Purpose and activities: Support for Jewish organizations, including welfare funds, temple support, and Hebrew education.
Limitations: Giving primarily in GA and FL.
Trustees: Seymour Gerson, Alice Gerson Katcher, Betty Gerson Minsk.
Employer Identification Number: 626048350

1594
GFF Educational Foundation, Inc. ⌑
P.O. Box 826
Norcross 30091 (404) 447-4488

Established in 1982 in GA.
Donor(s): Waffle House, Inc.
Foundation type: Independent
Financial data (yr. ended 5/31/86): Assets, $46,000 (M); gifts received, $125,000; expenditures, $120,802, including $78,906 for 35 grants (high: $25,000; low: $100) and $41,604 for 19 grants to individuals (high: $6,444; low: $11).
Purpose and activities: Support for education and health organizations; grants also as scholarship support to individuals.
Types of support: Student aid, grants to individuals.
Application information:
Write: F. Roy Nelson, Secy.-Treas.
Officers: Alice Johnson, Pres.; Joe Renfroe, V.P.; F. Roy Nelson, Secy.-Treas.
Employer Identification Number: 581477023

1595
J. K. Gholston Trust ⌑
c/o Citizens & Southern National Bank
P.O. Box 992
Athens 30613 (404) 549-8700

Trust established in 1967 in GA.
Donor(s): J. Knox Gholston.†
Foundation type: Independent
Financial data (yr. ended 2/29/88): Assets, $3,481,593 (M); expenditures, $261,032, including $232,102 for 79 grants (high: $220,846; low: $100).
Purpose and activities: Support for education, including scholarship funds, and Baptist church support.
Types of support: Scholarship funds.
Limitations: Giving limited to the Comer, GA, area.
Application information: Application form required.
Deadline(s): None
Write: Janey Cooley, Trust Officer
Trustee: Citizens & Southern National Bank.
Employer Identification Number: 586056879

1596
Price Gilbert, Jr. Charitable Trust
c/o First Wachovia Charitable Funds Management, The First National Bank of Atlanta
Two Peachtree St., N.W., Suite 705
Atlanta 30383 (404) 332-6586

Trust established in 1973 in GA.
Donor(s): Price Gilbert, Jr.†
Foundation type: Independent
Financial data (yr. ended 05/31/89): Assets, $7,592,009 (M); expenditures, $229,077, including $168,550 for 12 grants (high: $50,000; low: $1,750; average: $10,000).
Purpose and activities: Emphasis on secondary and higher education, hospitals, a community fund, and youth agencies.
Limitations: Giving limited to metropolitan Atlanta, GA. No grants to individuals.
Application information: Application form not required.
Initial approach: Letter
Copies of proposal: 1
Deadline(s): 30 days before each meeting
Board meeting date(s): 1st week of Jan., Apr., July, and Oct.
Final notification: 1 week
Write: Charles Buchholz
Officers: Richard W. Courts II, Chair. and Secy.; Arthur C. Baxter, Treas.
Trustees: Richard W. Courts, The First National Bank of Atlanta.
Employer Identification Number: 586106959

1597
Lenora and Alfred Glancy Foundation, Inc. ⌑
One Atlantic Ctr., Suite 4200
1201 West Peachtree St.
Atlanta 30309-3424 (404) 881-7000

Incorporated in 1954 in GA.
Donor(s): Alfred R. Glancy, Sr.†
Foundation type: Independent
Financial data (yr. ended 12/31/88): Assets, $4,669,978 (M); expenditures, $243,142, including $200,500 for 47 grants (high: $30,000; low: $500; average: $500-$30,000).

Purpose and activities: Support for higher and secondary education; grants also for hospitals, medical research, cultural programs, and community funds.
Types of support: Operating budgets, continuing support, annual campaigns, seed money, emergency funds, deficit financing, building funds, equipment, land acquisition, endowment funds, general purposes, capital campaigns, conferences and seminars, publications, renovation projects, research, special projects.
Limitations: Giving primarily in Atlanta, GA, and MI. No grants to individuals, or for scholarships or fellowships; no loans.
Publications: Application guidelines, 990-PF.
Application information: Application form not required.
Initial approach: Letter or proposal
Copies of proposal: 1
Deadline(s): Submit proposal before end of Oct.; deadline Nov. 1
Board meeting date(s): Nov. or Dec.
Write: Benjamin T. White, Asst. Secy.
Officers and Directors: Gerry Hull, Chair.; Alfred R. Glancy III, Vice-Chair.; Christopher Brandon, Treas.
Number of staff: None.
Employer Identification Number: 586041425

1598
The Wilbur Fisk Glenn Memorial Foundation, Inc.
c/o Trust Co. Bank
P.O. Box 4655
Atlanta 30302 (404) 588-7442

Incorporated in 1947 in GA.
Foundation type: Independent
Financial data (yr. ended 12/31/88): Assets, $5,237,913 (M); expenditures, $35,559, including $1,000 for 1 grant.
Purpose and activities: Support for a hospital and a Methodist church.
Types of support: Operating budgets.
Limitations: Giving primarily in the Atlanta, GA, area. No grants to individuals.
Application information: Funding limited to organizations to which family has long-term interest. Applications not accepted.
Board meeting date(s): Dec.
Write: Mary Simmons, Admin. Officer, Trust Co. Bank
Officers: Wilbur F. Glenn, Pres.; Jack F. Glenn, V.P.; Thomas K. Glenn II, Secy.-Treas.
Trustee: Trust Co. Bank.
Number of staff: None.
Employer Identification Number: 586026020

1599
W. B. Haley Foundation ⌑
c/o First State Bank and Trust Co.
333 Broad Ave., P.O. Box 8
Albany 31703 (912) 883-4800
Application address: 1612 Orchard Dr., Albany, GA 31707

Established in 1973 in GA.
Donor(s): W.B. Haley, Jr.†
Foundation type: Independent
Financial data (yr. ended 2/29/88): Assets, $2,056,157 (M); expenditures, $115,816, including $96,087 for 13 grants (high: $69,000; low: $500).
Purpose and activities: Emphasis on an art museum; giving also for social services.
Limitations: Giving primarily in Albany, GA.
Application information: Application form not required.
Deadline(s): None
Write: Eloise Haley, Pres.
Officers: Eloise Haley, Pres.; Stuart Watson, Secy.
Directors: Virginia Holman, Emily Jean H. McAfee, Joseph B. Powell, Jr., Harry Willson.
Trustee: First State Bank and Trust Co.
Employer Identification Number: 586113405

1600
Hardaway Foundation, Inc. ⌑ ☆
P.O. Box 1360
Columbus 31993

Foundation type: Independent
Financial data (yr. ended 12/31/88): Assets, $1,006,770 (M); expenditures, $54,833, including $30,181 for 11 grants (high: $15,000; low: $75) and $3,750 for 10 grants to individuals (high: $500; low: $250).
Purpose and activities: Support for community funds, civic affairs groups, youth, and education, including student aid.
Types of support: Student aid, general purposes.
Limitations: Giving primarily in GA.
Application information: Scholarships limited to graduates of Hardaway High School. Application form required.
Deadline(s): Aug. 31
Write: Fred J. Dodelin, Secy.-Treas.
Officers: B.H. Hardaway III, Chair.; Mason H. Lampton, Vice-Chair.; John M. Money, Vice-Chair.; Fred J. Dodelin, Secy.-Treas.
Employer Identification Number: 586033161

1601
John H. and Wilhelmina D. Harland Charitable Foundation, Inc.
Two Piedmont Ctr., Suite 106
Atlanta 30305 (404) 264-9912

Incorporated in 1972 in GA.
Donor(s): John H. Harland.†
Foundation type: Independent
Financial data (yr. ended 12/31/89): Assets, $21,712,601 (M); gifts received, $45,000; expenditures, $1,176,643, including $1,134,500 for 46 grants (high: $200,000; low: $1,500).
Purpose and activities: Support for youth agencies, child welfare, higher education, and community funds. Preference given to projects with little chance of gaining popular support, and which increase long-term effectiveness of the grantee.
Types of support: Operating budgets, annual campaigns, building funds, equipment, endowment funds, professorships, scholarship funds, publications.
Limitations: Giving limited to GA, with emphasis on metropolitan Atlanta. No grants to individuals; no loans.
Publications: Annual report (including application guidelines).
Application information: Application form not required.
Initial approach: Letter or telephone
Copies of proposal: 1
Deadline(s): Mar. 1 and Sept. 1
Board meeting date(s): Apr. 1 and Oct. 1
Final notification: 3 to 4 weeks after board meeting
Write: John A. Conant, Secy.
Officers and Trustees:* Miriam Harland Conant,* Pres.; Margaret C. Butler,* V.P. and Treas.; John A. Conant,* Secy.; James M. Sibley, Allison F. Williams.
Number of staff: 1 part-time professional; 1 part-time support.
Employer Identification Number: 237225012

1602
John H. Harland Company Foundation ⌑
2939 Miller Rd.
Decatur 30035

Incorporated in 1957 in GA.
Donor(s): John H. Harland Co.
Foundation type: Company-sponsored
Financial data (yr. ended 12/31/87): Assets, $2,402,019 (M); gifts received, $253,000; expenditures, $253,320, including $247,996 for grants.
Purpose and activities: Giving for social services, youth agencies, community funds, and higher education.
Types of support: General purposes.
Officers and Directors: J. William Robinson, Pres.; Robert R. Woodson, Secy.; John A. Conant, I. Ward Lang.
Employer Identification Number: 586035073

1603
Health 1st Foundation
100 Colony Sq., Suite 200
Atlanta 30361 (404) 870-9060

Established in 1986 in GA.
Foundation type: Independent
Financial data (yr. ended 06/30/88): Assets, $4,874,563 (M); expenditures, $291,168, including $190,000 for 2 grants (high: $165,000; low: $25,000).
Purpose and activities: Giving primarily for medical education, hospitals, and health associations.
Types of support: Continuing support, operating budgets.
Limitations: Giving limited to GA.
Application information:
Initial approach: Letter
Copies of proposal: 3
Deadline(s): Apr. 1
Write: Joseph Barber, Exec. Dir.
Officer and Directors:* Delutha H. King, Jr., M.D.,* Chair.; Benjamin A. Blackburn II, James Hindy, M. Gerald Hood, James M. Koss, and eight additional directors.
Number of staff: 1 part-time professional.
Employer Identification Number: 581265915

1604
Alonzo F. Herndon and Norris B. Herndon Foundation, Inc. ¤
Herndon Plaza, 100 Auburn Ave., N.E.
Atlanta 30303 (404) 659-2100

Incorporated in 1950 in GA.
Donor(s): Norris B. Herndon.
Foundation type: Independent
Financial data (yr. ended 12/31/88): Assets, $5,601,861 (M); expenditures, $267,758, including $54,200 for 17 grants (high: $15,000; low: $1,000) and $193,250 for 1 foundation-administered program.
Purpose and activities: Emphasis on a museum operated by the foundation, higher education, and social services.
Limitations: Giving primarily in GA. No grants to individuals.
Application information: Contributes only to pre-selected organizations. Applications not accepted.
Officers and Trustees:* Jesse Hill, Jr.,* Pres.; Henry N. Brown,* Secy.; Norris L. Connally,* Treas.; Helen J. Collins, James D. Palmer.
Employer Identification Number: 586036028

1605
Julian T. & Grace L. Hightower Foundation, Inc. ¤
East Main St.
Thomaston 30286

Established in 1947 in GA.
Foundation type: Independent
Financial data (yr. ended 12/31/88): Assets, $2,061,737 (M); expenditures, $25,808, including $24,000 for 4 grants (high: $16,000; low: $500).
Purpose and activities: Support for higher education and general charitable organizations.
Types of support: General purposes.
Officers: Anne H. Plowden, Pres.; Will Best Plowden, V.P.; Elinor P. Boyd, Secy.-Treas.
Employer Identification Number: 586033189

1606
Walter Clay Hill and Family Foundation
c/o Trust Co. Bank
P.O. Box 4655
Atlanta 30302 (404) 588-8197

Trust established in 1967 in GA.
Donor(s): Rebecca Travers Hill.†
Foundation type: Independent
Financial data (yr. ended 08/31/88): Assets, $2,615,217 (M); expenditures, $291,331, including $264,833 for 24 grants (high: $60,000; low: $1,000).
Purpose and activities: Grants for the arts and museums, conservation, and Protestant church support; support also for higher education and an historical association.
Types of support: General purposes, operating budgets, continuing support, annual campaigns, seed money, emergency funds, deficit financing, building funds, equipment, land acquisition, endowment funds, special projects.
Limitations: Giving primarily in the Southeast, particularly in the Atlanta, GA, area. No grants to individuals, or for research, publications, conferences, scholarships, fellowships, or matching gifts; no loans.
Publications: Application guidelines.
Application information: Application form not required.
Initial approach: Proposal
Copies of proposal: 1
Deadline(s): Submit proposal preferably from Jan. through June; no set deadline
Board meeting date(s): July or Oct.
Final notification: Immediately after annual meeting if decision is positive
Write: Ben Harris, Trust Officer, Trust Co. Bank
Trustees: Laura Hill Boland, Walter Clay Hill, Trust Co. Bank.
Number of staff: None.
Employer Identification Number: 586065956

1607
Harold Hirsch Scholarship Fund ¤
c/o Kilpatrick & Cody
100 Peachtree St. N.W., Suite 3100
Atlanta 30043 (404) 572-6500

Foundation type: Independent
Financial data (yr. ended 06/30/89): Assets, $1,221,525 (M); expenditures, $77,286, including $62,625 for 17 grants (high: $10,000; low: $500) and $1,900 for 1 grant to an individual.
Purpose and activities: Support for higher and secondary education; also, scholarship funds to institutions and individuals.
Types of support: Student aid, scholarship funds.
Application information:
Initial approach: Letter
Deadline(s): At least 6 months before the date for which assistance is requested
Write: Anne J. Rivers
Trustees: M.E. Kilpatrick, Jr., E.P. Rogers, Jr., Mary W. Rogers, Ronald W. Rogers.
Employer Identification Number: 586036125

1608
The Hodge Foundation, Inc. ¤
P.O. Box 23559
Savannah 31403

Incorporated in 1962 in GA.
Donor(s): Mrs. Sarah Mills Hodge.†
Foundation type: Independent
Financial data (yr. ended 7/31/88): Assets, $1,865,088 (M); expenditures, $99,589, including $77,971 for 11 grants (high: $24,421; low: $250).
Purpose and activities: Support limited to charitable organizations of special interest to the donor and solely to improve the economic condition of the lower income group; grants largely for youth and family services, particularly those assisting black families, and for scholarship funds at local colleges.
Types of support: Scholarship funds.
Limitations: Giving limited to Chatham County, GA.
Application information: Address scholarship applications to presidents of local Armstrong and Savannah state colleges; scholarships not awarded by foundation directly. Application form not required.
Initial approach: Letter
Copies of proposal: 2
Board meeting date(s): Jan., Apr., July, and Oct.
Write: Abram Minis, Jr., Pres.
Officers and Trustees: Abram Minis, Jr., Pres.; Malcolm Bell, John E. Cay III, J. Wiley Ellis, James E. Hungerpiller.
Employer Identification Number: 580909476

1609
Hollis Foundation, Inc. ¤
P.O. Box 2707
Columbus 31902-2707

Established in 1960 in GA.
Foundation type: Independent
Financial data (yr. ended 12/31/88): Assets, $1,626,471 (M); expenditures, $55,406, including $54,750 for 35 grants (high: $10,000; low: $100).
Purpose and activities: Support for higher and other education, museums and other cultural institutions, and general charitable organizations.
Limitations: Giving primarily in GA. No grants to individuals.
Application information: Contributes only to pre-selected organizations. Applications not accepted.
Officers: Howell Hollis, Pres.; Mary H. Clark, V.P.; Howell Hollis III, Secy.; Dale H. Clark, Treas.
Employer Identification Number: 580870013

1610
The Howell Fund, Inc.
c/o Trust Co. Bank
P.O. Box 4655
Atlanta 30302 (404) 365-3793

Incorporated in 1951 in GA.
Donor(s): Margaret Carr Levings.
Foundation type: Independent
Financial data (yr. ended 12/31/89): Assets, $1,523,598 (M); expenditures, $85,586, including $75,000 for 23 grants (high: $6,000; low: $665).
Purpose and activities: Giving primarily for education, cultural programs, and health associations.
Types of support: Operating budgets.
Limitations: Giving limited to Atlanta, GA.
Publications: Annual report.
Application information: Application form required.
Initial approach: Letter
Copies of proposal: 1
Deadline(s): Oct. 15
Write: Dameron Black, III, Secy.-Treas.
Officer and Directors:* Dameron Black III,* Secy.-Treas.; Clark Howell III, Faye Howell, W. Barrett Howell, Margaret Carr Levings, Ray B. Wilhoit.
Trustee: Trust Co. Bank.
Employer Identification Number: 586026027

1611
John P. and Dorothy S. Illges Foundation, Inc. ¤
c/o 1017 First Ave.
P.O. Box 1673
Columbus 31902

Incorporated in 1947 in GA.
Donor(s): John P. Illges.†
Foundation type: Independent

Financial data (yr. ended 9/30/88): Assets, $3,369,718 (M); expenditures, $157,638, including $140,500 for 11 grants (high: $100,000; low: $1,000; average: $1-$100,000).
Purpose and activities: Giving for education, social services, civic affairs, conservation, and health; support also for a private secondary school and youth agencies.
Types of support: Annual campaigns, building funds, capital campaigns, endowment funds, equipment, operating budgets, professorships, renovation projects, scholarship funds, seed money, special projects.
Limitations: Giving primarily in the areas of west central and Atlanta, GA, and east central AL. No grants to individuals.
Application information: Application form not required.
Initial approach: Letter
Copies of proposal: 1
Deadline(s): Submit proposal between June and Sept.; deadline Sept. 1
Board meeting date(s): June and Sept.
Write: John P. Illges, III, Pres.
Officers: John P. Illges III,* Pres.; Philip A. Badcock,* V.P.; Beth J. Hofstetter, Secy.; Custis G. Illges,* Treas.
Directors:* Emmy Lou P. Illges, Susan I. Lanier, John W. Mayher, Jr.
Number of staff: 1
Employer Identification Number: 580691476

1612
A. and M. L. Illges Memorial Foundation, Inc. ⌑
1224 Peacock Ave.
P.O. Box 103
Columbus 31902 (404) 323-5342

Incorporated in 1947 in GA.
Foundation type: Independent
Financial data (yr. ended 09/30/88): Assets, $2,953,318 (M); expenditures, $144,620, including $110,100 for 45 grants (high: $10,000; low: $100).
Purpose and activities: Emphasis on higher education, including scholarship funds, hospitals, church support, and cultural programs.
Types of support: Operating budgets, endowment funds.
Limitations: Giving primarily in GA.
Application information: Application form not required.
Deadline(s): None
Write: Howell Hollis, Pres.
Officers and Directors: Howell Hollis, Pres. and Treas.; J. Barnett Woodruff, V.P.; John P. Illges III, Secy.; Arthur I. Chenoweth, B.M. Chenoweth, Jr., Martha H. Heinz, A. Illges, Jr.
Employer Identification Number: 586033958

1613
Ruth T. Jinks Foundation ⌑
P.O. Box 375
Colquitt 31737

Established in 1955.
Donor(s): Members of the Jinks family.
Foundation type: Independent
Financial data (yr. ended 11/30/88): Assets, $5,042,372 (M); gifts received, $77,450; expenditures, $97,151, including $90,475 for 50 grants (high: $15,500; low: $100).
Purpose and activities: Giving for Christian religious organizations and churches, higher education, and social services.
Limitations: Giving primarily in GA.
Officers: G.C. Jinks, Sr., Chair. and Pres.; G.C. Jinks, Jr., V.P.
Employer Identification Number: 586043856

1614
Johnson, Lane, Space, Smith Foundation, Inc. ⌑ ☆
101 East Bay St.
Savannah 31401-1287 (912) 236-7101

Incorporated in 1984 in GA.
Donor(s): Johnson, Lane, Space, Smith & Co., Inc.
Foundation type: Company-sponsored
Financial data (yr. ended 12/31/88): Assets, $466,308 (M); expenditures, $129,282, including $126,759 for grants.
Purpose and activities: Giving primarily for community funds and social services; minor support for culture, education, and Jewish organizations.
Limitations: Giving primarily in GA. No grants to individuals.
Application information:
Initial approach: Letter
Deadline(s): None
Write: David T. Johnson or Craig Barrow, Trustees
Trustees: Craig Barrow III, David T. Johnson.
Employer Identification Number: 581550996

1615
Mary Ryan & Henry G. Kuhrt Foundation ⌑
c/o Trust Co. Bank
P.O. Box 4655
Atlanta 30302-4655 (404) 588-7356

Established in 1958 in GA.
Donor(s): Henry G. Kuhrt.
Foundation type: Independent
Financial data (yr. ended 12/31/88): Assets, $1,419,436 (M); expenditures, $90,363, including $75,692 for 23 grants (high: $23,209; low: $1,000).
Purpose and activities: Support primarily for a Catholic hospital, monasteries, convents, and schools.
Types of support: Operating budgets, building funds, capital campaigns, renovation projects, special projects.
Limitations: Giving limited to GA, with emphasis on Atlanta.
Application information:
Initial approach: Letter
Copies of proposal: 1
Deadline(s): Nov. 1
Write: Brenda Rambeau
Officers: Harvey Hill, Mgr.; William H. Izlar, Mgr.; Hughes Spalding, Jr., Mgr.
Trustee: Trust Co. Bank.
Employer Identification Number: 586026031

1616
Mills Bee Lane Memorial Foundation, Inc. ⌑
c/o Citizens & Southern National Bank
P.O. Box 9626
Savannah 31402
Additional mailing address: P.O. Box 2364, Savannah, GA 31402

Incorporated in 1947 in GA.
Donor(s): Members of the Lane family.
Foundation type: Independent
Financial data (yr. ended 12/31/88): Assets, $9,002,239 (M); expenditures, $466,786, including $438,303 for 75 grants (high: $50,000; low: $50).
Purpose and activities: Emphasis on higher and secondary education and cultural programs.
Types of support: Seed money, building funds, equipment, land acquisition, professorships, internships, scholarship funds, exchange programs, fellowships, matching funds, endowment funds.
Limitations: Giving primarily in the Savannah, GA, area. No grants to individuals, or for operating budgets; no loans.
Publications: Application guidelines.
Application information: Application form required.
Initial approach: Letter
Copies of proposal: 1
Deadline(s): Submit proposal in 3 month period prior to each board meeting; deadlines May 15 and Nov. 15
Board meeting date(s): June and Dec.
Final notification: 2 weeks after board meetings
Officers and Trustees: Hugh C. Lane, Jr., Chair.; Mills Lane Morrison, Secy.; Howard Jackson Morrison, Jr., Treas.
Number of staff: None.
Employer Identification Number: 586033043

1617
Lanier Brothers Foundation ⌑
c/o Trust Co. Bank
P.O. Box 4655
Atlanta 30302

Trust established in 1955 in GA.
Donor(s): Members of the Lanier family.
Foundation type: Independent
Financial data (yr. ended 12/31/88): Assets, $7,841,077 (M); expenditures, $424,206, including $345,934 for 96 grants (high: $25,000; low: $500).
Purpose and activities: Emphasis on higher education, community funds, youth agencies, and hospitals; some support for social services.
Limitations: Giving primarily in GA. No grants to individuals.
Application information:
Initial approach: Proposal
Deadline(s): Dec.
Write: Clare Ranney
Officer: H. Spalding Craft, Exec. Dir.
Trustees: Helen S. Lanier, John Reese Lanier, Sartain Lanier, Trust Co. Bank.
Employer Identification Number: 586026033

1618
The Ray M. and Mary Elizabeth Lee Foundation, Inc.
c/o Citizens & Southern Trust Co.
P.O. Box 4446
Atlanta 30302-4899 (404) 897-3222

Incorporated in 1966 in GA.
Donor(s): Ray M. Lee,† Mary Elizabeth Lee.†
Foundation type: Independent
Financial data (yr. ended 09/30/89): Assets, $9,865,000 (M); expenditures, $416,000, including $360,000 for 62 grants (high: $25,000; low: $1,000; average: $6,000).
Purpose and activities: Giving for educational institutions, health agencies, hospitals, religious organizations, and the arts and cultural programs, including theaters.
Types of support: Annual campaigns, building funds, capital campaigns, conferences and seminars, consulting services, continuing support, deficit financing, emergency funds, equipment, exchange programs, fellowships, general purposes, internships, land acquisition, lectureships, matching funds, operating budgets, professorships, program-related investments, publications, renovation projects, research, scholarship funds, seed money, special projects, technical assistance.
Limitations: Giving primarily in Atlanta, GA. No grants to individuals.
Publications: 990-PF, financial statement, grants list.
Application information: Application form not required.
Initial approach: Proposal
Copies of proposal: 1
Deadline(s): Jan. 31, Apr. 30, July 31, Oct. 31
Board meeting date(s): As required
Final notification: Following board meeting
Write: Larry B. Hooks, Admin. Mgr.
Officers and Trustees:* William B. Stark,* Pres. and Treas.; Donald D. Smith,* Secy.; Ronald W. Gann.
Number of staff: None.
Employer Identification Number: 586049441

1619
Livingston Foundation, Inc. ¤
c/o Arnall, Golden & Gregory
55 Park Place, Suite 400
Atlanta 30335 (404) 577-5100

Incorporated in 1964 in GA.
Donor(s): Roy N. Livingston,† Mrs. Leslie Livingston Kellar,† Bess B. Livingston.†
Foundation type: Independent
Financial data (yr. ended 9/30/88): Assets, $6,800,159 (M); expenditures, $666,201, including $545,500 for 23 grants (high: $210,000; low: $1,000).
Purpose and activities: Emphasis on cultural organizations and higher education.
Types of support: Operating budgets, continuing support, annual campaigns.
Limitations: Giving primarily in the Atlanta, GA area. No grants to individuals, or for endowment funds, scholarships, fellowships, or matching gifts; no loans.
Application information: Application form not required.
Initial approach: Letter
Copies of proposal: 1
Deadline(s): None
Board meeting date(s): Quarterly
Final notification: 4 months
Write: Ben W. Brannon, Pres.
Officers: Ben W. Brannon, Pres.; Sol I. Golden, Secy.
Directors: Ellis Arnall, Milton Brannon, Jonathan Golden, C.E. Gregory III, George P. Schmidt.
Number of staff: 1
Employer Identification Number: 586044858

1620
Charles Loridans Foundation, Inc. ¤
c/o Alston & Bird, One Atlantic Ctr.
1201 West Peachtree St., Suite 4200
Atlanta 30309-3424 (404) 881-7000

Incorporated in 1952 in GA.
Donor(s): Charles Loridans,† A.T. Arnold.
Foundation type: Independent
Financial data (yr. ended 12/31/88): Assets, $5,842,256 (M); expenditures, $365,934, including $317,756 for 30 grants (high: $45,000; low: $500; average: $500-$45,000).
Purpose and activities: Support for local educational institutions lacking access to general sources of support.
Types of support: Seed money, emergency funds, building funds, equipment, land acquisition, endowment funds, matching funds, scholarship funds, professorships.
Limitations: Giving primarily in GA, with emphasis on the metropolitan Atlanta area. No grants to individuals, or for operating budgets, continuing support, annual campaigns, deficit financing, special projects, research, publications, or conferences; no loans.
Publications: Annual report, program policy statement, application guidelines.
Application information: Application form not required.
Initial approach: Proposal
Copies of proposal: 1
Board meeting date(s): June and Dec.
Write: Robert G. Edge, Chair.
Trustees: Robert G. Edge, Chair.; Benjamin T. White, Secy.-Treas.; Alex P. Gaines, B. Harvey Hill, Jr., Daniel B. Hodgson, Sidney O. Smith, Jr.
Number of staff: None.
Employer Identification Number: 580871627

1621
Gay and Erskine Love Foundation, Inc. ¤
4335 Wendell Dr., S.W.
Atlanta 30378

Established in 1976 in GA.
Donor(s): Printpack, Inc.
Foundation type: Independent
Financial data (yr. ended 12/31/87): Assets, $4,126,382 (M); gifts received, $396,122; expenditures, $214,863, including $161,000 for 33 grants (high: $25,000; low: $500).
Purpose and activities: Giving primarily for education, especially higher education, and social service and youth agencies; support also for community funds, and cultural programs.
Application information: Contributes only to pre-selected organizations. Applications not accepted.
Officers: Dennis M. Love, Pres.; Gay M. Love, V.P.; R. Michael Hembree, Secy.-Treas.
Director: L. Neil Williams, Jr.
Employer Identification Number: 510198585

1622
Lubo Fund, Inc.
3910 Randall Mill Rd., N.W.
Atlanta 30327

Incorporated in 1958 in GA.
Donor(s): Members of the Bunnen family.
Foundation type: Independent
Financial data (yr. ended 12/31/88): Assets, $1,962,806 (M); expenditures, $119,571, including $93,640 for 206 grants (high: $8,050; low: $20; average: $50-$5,000).
Purpose and activities: Giving for cultural programs, including the performing and visual arts; support also for education.
Types of support: General purposes, special projects, publications, matching funds, annual campaigns, continuing support, seed money, emergency funds.
Limitations: Giving primarily in GA, with emphasis on Atlanta. No grants to individuals, or for land acquisition, renovation projects, endowment funds, scholarships, fellowships, research, or conferences; no loans.
Application information: Application form not required.
Initial approach: Letter or proposal
Copies of proposal: 1
Deadline(s): None
Board meeting date(s): July
Final notification: 1 to 3 months
Write: Lucinda W. Bunnen, Pres.
Officers: Lucinda W. Bunnen, Pres.; Robert L. Bunnen, V.P. and Secy.-Treas.
Number of staff: None.
Employer Identification Number: 586043631

1623
Mattie H. Marshall Foundation ¤
c/o Trust Co. Bank
P.O. Box 4655
Atlanta 30302-4655

Established in 1963 in GA.
Foundation type: Independent
Financial data (yr. ended 12/31/88): Assets, $1,685,736 (M); expenditures, $89,763, including $80,000 for grants.
Purpose and activities: Giving primarily for higher education; support also for churches, hospitals, a clinic, a humane society, and a home for the aged.
Types of support: Operating budgets.
Limitations: Giving primarily in GA.
Application information: Application form not required.
Initial approach: Letter
Deadline(s): None
Officer: Thomas O. Marshall, Chair. and Secy.
Director: Martha M. Dykes.
Employer Identification Number: 586042019

1624
Harriet McDaniel Marshall Trust in Memory of Sanders McDaniel
c/o Trust Co. Bank
P.O. Box 4418; MC 041
Atlanta 30302 (404) 588-8246

Trust established in 1962 in GA.
Donor(s): Harriet McDaniel Marshall.
Foundation type: Independent
Financial data (yr. ended 12/30/89): Assets, $4,166,438 (M); expenditures, $258,625, including $225,337 for grants (average: $3,000-$5,000).
Purpose and activities: Giving for welfare and higher education; support also for the handicapped, the elderly, community funds, and the arts.
Types of support: Building funds, equipment, renovation projects, special projects.
Limitations: Giving primarily in the metropolitan Atlanta, GA, area (Fulton and DeKalb counties). No grants to individuals, or for scholarships or fellowships; no loans.
Publications: Application guidelines, program policy statement.
Application information: Application form required.
Initial approach: Letter
Copies of proposal: 1
Deadline(s): Submit proposal by first of month preceding month in which board meeting will be held
Board meeting date(s): Jan., Apr., July, and Oct.
Write: Victor A. Gregory, Secy.
Distribution Committee: E.P. Gould, Chair.; Victor A. Gregory, Secy.; Jesse S. Hall, Robert Strickland.
Trustee: Trust Co. Bank.
Number of staff: 1 full-time professional; 1 full-time support.
Employer Identification Number: 586089937

1625
Roy C. Moore Foundation ⌑
c/o First National Bank of Gainesville
P.O. Box 937
Gainesville 30503 (404) 535-5561

Established about 1972 in GA.
Foundation type: Independent
Financial data (yr. ended 7/31/88): Assets, $1,711,552 (M); expenditures, $116,896, including $101,967 for 43 grants (high: $16,667; low: $200).
Purpose and activities: Grants for higher and secondary education; some support for youth organizations.
Types of support: Annual campaigns, building funds, capital campaigns, emergency funds, endowment funds, equipment, general purposes, operating budgets, research, scholarship funds, employee-related scholarships, special projects.
Limitations: Giving primarily in GA.
Application information:
Write: J.D. Baumgardner, Group V.P. and Sr. Trust Officer, First National Bank of Gainesville
Trustee: First National Bank of Gainesville.
Employer Identification Number: 586087219

1626
James Starr Moore Memorial Foundation, Inc.
526 East Paces Ferry Rd., N.E.
Atlanta 30305 (404) 262-7134

Incorporated in 1953 in GA.
Foundation type: Independent
Financial data (yr. ended 12/31/89): Assets, $8,505,262 (M); expenditures, $495,404, including $392,862 for 85 grants (high: $80,000; low: $50).
Purpose and activities: Emphasis on the arts and cultural programs, higher education and educational research, Protestant church support, hospitals, and health agencies.
Limitations: Giving primarily in GA. No grants to individuals.
Application information: Applications not accepted.
Initial approach: Letter
Write: Bobbie J. Burnham, Secy.
Officer: Bobbie J. Burnham, Secy.
Trustees: Sara Giles Moore, Chair.; Monroe F. Swilley, Jr., Vice-Chair.; Morton S. Hodgson, Jr., Starr Moore.
Employer Identification Number: 586033190

1627
Katherine John Murphy Foundation ⌑
c/o Trust Co. Bank
P.O. Box 4655
Atlanta 30302 (404) 588-7356

Trust established in 1954 in GA.
Donor(s): Katherine M. Riley.
Foundation type: Independent
Financial data (yr. ended 12/31/88): Assets, $7,315,530 (M); gifts received, $2,404,390; expenditures, $463,197, including $425,100 for 45 grants (high: $100,000; low: $1,000).
Purpose and activities: Emphasis on hospitals, cultural programs, health agencies, higher education, youth agencies, and child welfare.
Types of support: Annual campaigns, building funds, capital campaigns, equipment, general purposes, renovation projects, continuing support, operating budgets, seed money, special projects.
Limitations: Giving primarily in Atlanta, GA. No grants to individuals, or for research, scholarships, fellowships, or matching gifts; no loans.
Application information:
Initial approach: Letter
Copies of proposal: 1
Deadline(s): Mar. 1
Board meeting date(s): Apr., Oct., and as required
Write: Brenda Rambeau, V.P., Trust Co. Bank
Officers: A.D. Boylston, Jr., Chair.; Dameron Black, Mgr.; Martin Gatins, Mgr.
Trustee: Trust Co. Bank.
Employer Identification Number: 586026045

1628
National Service Foundation ⌑
1180 Peachtree St., N.E.
Atlanta 30309

Established about 1969.
Foundation type: Company-sponsored
Financial data (yr. ended 8/31/88): Assets, $2,073 (M); expenditures, $225,551, including $225,139 for 112 grants (high: $59,500; low: $25).
Purpose and activities: Support for culture, education, community funds, and health; some support for social services and Jewish organizations.
Limitations: Giving primarily in GA.
Application information: Contributes only to pre-selected organizations. Applications not accepted.
Trustees: Robert H. Creviston, Mgr.; Henry R. Dressel, Jr., Sidney Kirschner, David Levy, Erwin Zaban.
Employer Identification Number: 586051102

1629
Outreach, Inc. ⌑
P.O. Box 2994
Augusta 30904

Foundation type: Independent
Financial data (yr. ended 12/31/88): Assets, $1,035,216 (L); expenditures, $70,185, including $50,428 for 39 grants (high: $5,000; low: $300).
Purpose and activities: Support for Christian churches, educational institutions, and organizations concerned with child welfare.
Limitations: Giving primarily in the southeastern U.S., including GA, SC, WV, and MD.
Application information:
Initial approach: Letter or proposal
Deadline(s): None
Write: Cecil R. Turner, Pres.
Officers: Cecil R. Turner, Pres.; John L. Mixon III, V.P.; Sammy C. Turner, Secy.
Employer Identification Number: 586043732

1630
Oxford Foundation, Inc. ⌑
222 Piedmont Ave., N.E.
Atlanta 30308

Established in 1963 in GA.
Donor(s): Sartain Lanier.
Foundation type: Independent
Financial data (yr. ended 12/31/88): Assets, $2,215,153 (M); gifts received, $102,020; expenditures, $102,020, including $67,574 for 39 grants (high: $39,188; low: $25).
Purpose and activities: Support for educational institutions, health, and cultural organizations.
Types of support: Operating budgets.
Limitations: Giving primarily in Atlanta, GA.
Application information:
Write: Sartain Lanier, Chair.
Officers: Sartain Lanier, Chair. and Treas.; J. Hicks Lanier, Vice-Chair. and Secy.
Trustee: Mrs. George C. Blount.
Employer Identification Number: 586045056

1631
William A. Parker, Jr. Foundation ⌑ ☆
c/o Trust Co. Bank
P.O. Box 4655
Atlanta 30302

Established in 1987 in GA.
Foundation type: Independent

Financial data (yr. ended 6/30/88): Assets, $1,284,990 (M); gifts received, $964,844; expenditures, $0.
Purpose and activities: Initial year of operation, fiscal 1988; no grants awarded.
Application information:
Initial approach: Letter
Deadline(s): None
Write: Claire Ranney, Trustee
Officers and Trustees: William A. Parker, Jr., Chair.; Nancy Fraser Parker, Vice-Chair.; Richard W. Courts II, Richard Carlyle Parker, William A. Parker III, Trust Co. Bank.
Employer Identification Number: 586212344

1632
Patterson-Barclay Memorial Foundation, Inc.
1020 Spring St., N.W.
Atlanta 30309 (404) 876-1022

Incorporated in 1953 in GA.
Donor(s): Frederick W. Patterson.
Foundation type: Independent
Financial data (yr. ended 12/31/88): Assets, $5,418,358 (M); expenditures, $339,004, including $270,235 for grants (high: $5,000; low: $1,000; average: $1,000-$5,000).
Purpose and activities: Giving for Christian organizations, hospitals, and higher, secondary, and other education; grants also for health, social service and youth agencies, arts and culture, and the environment.
Types of support: Program-related investments, annual campaigns, capital campaigns, continuing support, endowment funds, general purposes.
Limitations: Giving limited to the Atlanta, GA, metropolitan area. No grants to individuals.
Publications: 990-PF.
Application information: Contributes only to pre-selected organizations. Applications not accepted.
Board meeting date(s): 3rd Tuesday in Apr. and Oct.
Write: Mrs. Lee Barclay Patterson Allen, Trustee
Trustees: Jack W. Allen, Mrs. Lee Barclay Patterson Allen, Ross Arnold, Robert F. Bryan.
Number of staff: None.
Employer Identification Number: 580904580

1633
The Pattillo Foundation ⌑
P.O. Box 818
Decatur 30031

Established in 1967.
Foundation type: Independent
Financial data (yr. ended 12/31/88): Assets, $1,315,690 (M); expenditures, $15,475.
Purpose and activities: Giving for higher education and Protestant church support.
Limitations: Giving primarily in GA.
Trustees: D.B. Pattillo, H.G. Pattillo.
Employer Identification Number: 586068757

1634
Pickett & Hatcher Educational Fund, Inc.
1800 Buena Vista Rd.
P.O. Box 8169
Columbus 31908 (404) 327-6586

Incorporated in 1938 in GA.
Donor(s): Claud A. Hatcher.†
Foundation type: Independent
Financial data (yr. ended 9/30/89): Assets, $17,076,725 (M); expenditures, $1,285,042, including $1,193,523 for loans to individuals.
Purpose and activities: Giving in the southeastern U.S. to encourage worthy students to secure a broad liberal education by providing student loans.
Types of support: Student loans.
Limitations: Giving limited to AL, FL, GA, KY, MS, NC, SC, TN, and VA. No support for students planning to enter fields of medicine, law, the ministry, or vocational curricula. No grants for any purpose other than educational loans.
Publications: Informational brochure (including application guidelines).
Application information: Application form required.
Initial approach: Letter or telephone
Deadline(s): May 15 for school year starting in fall; for other periods during the year, 2 months prior to beginning of session in which money will be used
Board meeting date(s): May and Nov.
Final notification: 2 months
Write: Robert E. Bennett, Exec. V.P.
Officers: William K. Hatcher,* Pres.; Robert E. Bennett, Exec. V.P.; Kenneth R. Owens, V.P.; Alice V. Haywood, Secy.
Trustees:* Guy E. Snavely, Jr., Chair.; C. Alex Sears, Jr., Vice-Chair. and Treas.; William B. Hardegree, James W. Key, William T. Miller.
Number of staff: 3 full-time professional; 6 full-time support; 1 part-time support.
Employer Identification Number: 580566216

1635
Pine Mountain Benevolent Foundation, Inc.
P. O. Box 2301
Columbus 31902

Incorporated in 1959 in GA.
Donor(s): Ida Cason Callaway Foundation.
Foundation type: Independent
Financial data (yr. ended 6/30/89): Assets, $1,284,139 (M); expenditures, $288,214, including $263,345 for grants.
Purpose and activities: Support for education and culture; some support for social services.
Limitations: Giving primarily in Harris County, GA. No grants to individuals.
Application information: Applications not accepted.
Initial approach: Letter
Deadline(s): None
Write: Cason J. Callaway, Jr., Dir.
Directors: Cason J. Callaway, Jr., Cason J. Callaway III, Kenneth H. Callaway, Nancy H. Callaway, Virginia H. Callaway.
Employer Identification Number: 586033162

1636
William I. H. and Lula E. Pitts Foundation ⌑
c/o Trust Co. Bank
P.O. Box 4655
Atlanta 30302 (404) 588-8544

Trust established in 1941 in GA.
Donor(s): William I.H. Pitts,† Margaret A. Pitts.
Foundation type: Independent
Financial data (yr. ended 12/31/88): Assets, $13,889,650 (M); gifts received, $30,000; expenditures, $593,889, including $540,725 for 32 grants (high: $47,000; low: $100; average: $5,000-$47,000).
Purpose and activities: Giving almost exclusively to Methodist church-related institutions; emphasis on higher education and care of the aged.
Types of support: Building funds, general purposes, continuing support.
Limitations: Giving limited to GA. No grants to individuals, or for endowment funds, research, scholarships, fellowships, or matching gifts; no loans.
Application information: Application form not required.
Initial approach: Letter
Copies of proposal: 1
Deadline(s): None
Board meeting date(s): Apr. and Nov.
Write: Clare Ranney, Secy.
Officer and Managers: Clare Ranney, Secy.; John H. Boman, Jr., Bishop William R. Cannon, Carroll Payne Jones, Thomas O. Marshall, Walter Y. Murphy, Margaret A. Pitts, Robert M. Strickland, Morris G. Wray.
Trustee: Trust Co. Bank.
Number of staff: None.
Employer Identification Number: 586026047

1637
The Pittulloch Foundation, Inc. ⌑
315 West Ponce De Leon Ave., Suite 843
Decatur 30031

Established in 1985 in GA.
Donor(s): Stone Mountain Industrial Park, Inc., Pattillo Split Interest Trust.
Foundation type: Independent
Financial data (yr. ended 12/31/88): Assets, $6,865,508 (M); gifts received, $2,418,387; expenditures, $61,006, including $48,400 for 10 grants (high: $15,000; low: $200).
Purpose and activities: Support for educational institutions, Christian organizations, and leadership development programs.
Types of support: General purposes.
Limitations: Giving primarily in Atlanta, GA. No grants to individuals.
Application information: Contributes only to pre-selected organizations. Applications not accepted.
Officers and Directors:* H.G. Pattillo,* Chair.; George L. Simpson,* Vice-Chair.; Lynn L. Pattillo,* Pres. and Treas.; John Walter Drake, Secy.; Warren Y. Jobe, Elizabeth M. Pattillo, Robert A. Pattillo.
Employer Identification Number: 581651352

1638
James Hyde Porter Testamentary Trust
c/o Trust Co. Bank of Middle Georgia, N.A.
606 Cherry St., P.O. Box 4248
Macon 31208 (912) 741-2265

Trust established in 1949 in GA.
Donor(s): James Hyde Porter.†
Foundation type: Independent
Financial data (yr. ended 12/31/89): Assets, $6,154,367 (M); expenditures, $334,322, including $289,959 for 24 grants (high: $65,000; low: $1,000).
Purpose and activities: Emphasis on social services, civic affairs, cultural programs, higher education, and health agencies.
Types of support: Building funds, renovation projects, seed money.
Limitations: Giving limited to Bibb and Newton counties, GA. No grants to individuals, or for endowment funds, research programs, scholarships, or fellowships; no loans.
Publications: 990-PF, application guidelines.
Application information: Application form required.
Initial approach: Telephone
Copies of proposal: 7
Deadline(s): Submit proposal preferably in Mar.; deadline Apr. 20
Board meeting date(s): June
Write: Deanna D. Neely, Asst. V.P. and Trust Officer, Trust Co. Bank of Middle Georgia, N.A.
Officers: Rodney Browne, Mgr.; Emory Greene, Mgr.; Rev. Lee Holiday, Mgr.; Kathy Kalish, Mgr.; Lee Robinson, Mgr.; Donald G. Stephenson, Mgr.
Trustee: Trust Co. Bank of Middle Georgia, N.A.
Employer Identification Number: 586034882

1639
Ragan and King Charitable Foundation
c/o First Wachovia Charitable Funds Management, First National Bank of Atlanta
Two Peachtree St., N.W., Suite 705
Atlanta 30383 (404) 332-6586

Established in 1972 in GA.
Donor(s): Carolyn King Ragan.†
Foundation type: Independent
Financial data (yr. ended 9/30/89): Assets, $2,495,374 (M); expenditures, $161,148, including $141,000 for 5 grants (high: $67,000; low: $4,000; average: $15,000).
Purpose and activities: Giving for Baptist organizations only, including churches, religious organizations, and theological seminaries.
Limitations: Giving limited to GA (except for two specific out-of-state beneficiaries). No grants to individuals.
Application information: Application form not required.
Initial approach: Letter
Copies of proposal: 1
Deadline(s): None
Board meeting date(s): Fall
Write: Charles Buchholz
Trustee: The First National Bank of Atlanta.
Number of staff: None.
Employer Identification Number: 586138950

1640
Rainbow Fund ▼ ⌑
P.O. Box 937
Fort Valley 31030

Trust established in 1954 in GA.
Donor(s): Albert L. Luce, Jr., Blue Bird Companies.
Foundation type: Company-sponsored
Financial data (yr. ended 3/31/87): Assets, $481 (M); gifts received, $1,240,220; expenditures, $1,241,615, including $1,240,626 for 178 grants (high: $345,000; low: $250; average: $1,000-$5,000).
Purpose and activities: Emphasis on higher education and Protestant church support, including religious organizations, missionary programs, and theological education.
Application information: Applications not accepted.
Officers: George E. Luce, Chair.; Joseph P. Luce, V.P.; Albert L. Luce, Jr., Treas.
Employer Identification Number: 586043659

1641
Realan Foundation, Inc. ⌑
3060 Peachtree Rd., N.W., Suite 1420
Atlanta 30305

Established in 1985 in GA.
Donor(s): J. Rex Fuqua.
Foundation type: Independent
Financial data (yr. ended 12/31/88): Assets, $1,887,997 (M); expenditures, $109,654, including $93,500 for 23 grants (high: $50,000; low: $300).
Purpose and activities: Support for education, hospitals, and the environment.
Application information: Applications not accepted.
Officers: J. Rex Fuqua,* Pres.; John G. Wright, Secy.-Treas.
Directors:* Thomas V. Chorey, Jr.
Employer Identification Number: 581648407

1642
The Rich Foundation, Inc. ▼
10 Piedmont Ctr., Suite 802
Atlanta 30305 (404) 262-2266

Incorporated in 1942 in GA.
Donor(s): Rich's, Inc., and members of the Rich family.
Foundation type: Independent
Financial data (yr. ended 01/31/89): Assets, $18,459,516 (M); expenditures, $890,698, including $719,600 for 48 grants (high: $175,000; low: $1,000; average: $1,000-$30,000).
Purpose and activities: Giving primarily for a community fund, the performing arts and other cultural programs, higher and secondary education, including private schools, social services, including programs for the homeless and drug abuse, youth agencies, and hospitals.
Types of support: Annual campaigns, building funds, consulting services, continuing support, equipment, operating budgets, technical assistance, research.
Limitations: Giving limited to Atlanta, GA, area. No grants to individuals, or for matching gifts; no loans.
Publications: Application guidelines.
Application information: Application form required.
Initial approach: Letter
Copies of proposal: 1
Deadline(s): Submit proposal 1 month prior to meetings
Board meeting date(s): Feb., May, Aug., and Nov.
Final notification: 2 weeks
Write: Anne Poland Berg, Grant Consultant
Officers and Trustees:* Joel Goldberg,* Pres.; Thomas J. Asher,* V.P.; Michael P. Rich,* Secy.-Treas.; Joseph F. Asher, David S. Baker, Harold Brockey, Joseph K. Heyman.
Number of staff: None.
Employer Identification Number: 586038037

1643
Walter Alan Richards Foundation, Inc. ⌑ ☆
900 Eighth St.
Columbus 31902

Foundation type: Independent
Financial data (yr. ended 8/31/88): Assets, $1,150,347 (M); expenditures, $86,312, including $73,650 for 34 grants (high: $15,000; low: $250).
Purpose and activities: Support for public and private colleges and universities and independent secondary schools.
Limitations: Giving primarily in GA. No grants to individuals.
Application information:
Initial approach: Letter
Deadline(s): None
Officers: J.W. Feighner, Pres.; Thomas B. Black, V.P.; Richard L. Olson, Secy.-Treas.
Employer Identification Number: 586035136

1644
Roxboro Foundation, Inc. ⌑ ☆
156 Morningside Dr.
Cartersville 30120

Established in 1982.
Donor(s): Jon Oscher.
Foundation type: Operating
Financial data (yr. ended 12/31/88): Assets, $909 (M); gifts received, $188,500; expenditures, $204,174, including $204,073 for 2 grants (high: $134,273; low: $69,800).
Purpose and activities: A private operating foundation; giving for an educational foundation providing college and vocational educational opportunities and information; support also for an historical museum.
Limitations: Giving primarily in Cartersville, GA.
Officers and Directors: Jon Oscher, Pres. and Treas.; Harold E. Abrams, Secy.; Herman C. Shiver.
Employer Identification Number: 581484020

1645
Russell Charitable Trust ⌑
P.O. Box 1064
Decatur 30031 (404) 636-0367

Established in 1960 in ME.
Donor(s): H.M. Russell.
Foundation type: Independent
Financial data (yr. ended 7/31/87): Assets, $1,219,263 (M); gifts received, $5,623;

expenditures, $303,082, including $272,600 for 14 grants (high: $200,000; low: $500).
Purpose and activities: Grants primarily to religious-related institutions in higher education (specifically colleges and seminaries), medicine, media communications, and institutions serving youth and the elderly.
Types of support: Capital campaigns, endowment funds, general purposes, seed money.
Application information:
Deadline(s): None
Board meeting date(s): Quarterly
Final notification: Grants are made at the beginning of each calendar quarter
Write: Ernest J. Arnold, Trustee
Trustees: Ernest J. Arnold, Francis P. Arnold, Judy A. Moore.
Employer Identification Number: 016009882

1646
Rutland Foundation, Inc. ⌑
215 Church St.
Decatur 30030

Established in 1976 in GA.
Donor(s): Motor Convoy, Rutland Trusts, Guy W. Rutland, Jr.,† Guy W. Rutland III, Phoenix Enterprises.
Foundation type: Independent
Financial data (yr. ended 12/31/86): Assets, $1,679,041 (M); gifts received, $1,100,000; expenditures, $141,771, including $137,000 for 13 grants (high: $50,000; low: $100).
Purpose and activities: Support primarily for Baptist churches and a university.
Types of support: Building funds, general purposes.
Limitations: Giving primarily in GA.
Officers: Marie Rutland,* Pres.; Guy W. Rutland III,* V.P.; Robert J. Rutland,* V.P.; Elliott Cohen, Secy.-Treas.
Directors:* Susan Rutland McCullar.
Employer Identification Number: 581259085

1647
Savannah Widows' Society ⌑
P.O. Box 3015
Savannah 31410 (912) 232-6312

Foundation type: Operating
Financial data (yr. ended 8/31/88): Assets, $1,337,190 (M); expenditures, $104,138, including $77,388 for 76 grants to individuals (high: $6,000; low: $50).
Purpose and activities: A private operating foundation; giving primarily to single women, 55 or older; also provides aid to seriously disabled or handicapped persons, whose income from other sources is insufficient to provide their care in a reasonably comfortable manner.
Types of support: Grants to individuals.
Limitations: Giving primarily in Chatham County, GA.
Application information: Application form required.
Deadline(s): None
Write: Susanne Thompson, Pres.
Officers: Susanne R. Thompson, Pres.; Margaretha Sterling, 1st V.P.; Becky Trayler, 2nd V.P.; Ellen R. Byck, Recording Secy.; Frances Olsen, Corresponding Secy.; Martha Peeples, Treas.
Employer Identification Number: 580603157

1648
Simon Schwob Foundation, Inc. ⌑
P.O. Box 1014
Columbus 31902 (404) 327-4582

Incorporated in 1949 in GA.
Donor(s): Schwob Manufacturing Co., Schwob Realty Co., Schwob Co. of Florida.
Foundation type: Independent
Financial data (yr. ended 12/31/88): Assets, $2,904,004 (M); expenditures, $163,222, including $135,859 for 21 grants (high: $44,500; low: $100).
Purpose and activities: Giving for higher education, Jewish welfare funds, music, and community funds.
Limitations: Giving primarily in GA.
Application information: Application form not required.
Initial approach: Letter
Copies of proposal: 1
Deadline(s): None
Board meeting date(s): Semiannually
Write: Henry Schwob, Pres.
Officers and Trustees: Henry Schwob, Pres.; Joyce Schwob, V.P.; Hannah Harrison, Secy.-Treas.; Jane Beth Schwob, Simone Schwob.
Employer Identification Number: 586038932

1649
Scott Foundation, Inc. ⌑
21 Laredo Dr.
Scottdale 30079

Established in 1980 in GA.
Donor(s): Milton C. Scott.
Foundation type: Independent
Financial data (yr. ended 5/31/88): Assets, $312,129 (M); expenditures, $120,322, including $117,348 for 2 grants (high: $60,130; low: $57,218).
Purpose and activities: Grants for Protestant missionary programs and churches.
Limitations: Giving primarily in the southern U.S.
Officers and Directors: Milton C. Scott, Pres.; David W. Scott, Secy.; Hansford Sams, Jr., Treas.
Employer Identification Number: 581378681

1650
The Emily W. Scott Foundation ⌑
c/o Trust Co. Bank
P.O. Box 4655
Atlanta 30302

Established in 1985 in GA.
Donor(s): Emily W. Scott.†
Foundation type: Independent
Financial data (yr. ended 4/30/87): Assets, $1,269,366 (M); expenditures, $68,630, including $55,000 for 2 grants (high: $50,000; low: $5,000).
Purpose and activities: Support for an eye clinic and a speech school.
Limitations: Giving primarily in Atlanta, GA.
Application information: Application form not required.
Deadline(s): None
Write: Clare Ranney, Mgr.
Trustee: Trust Co. Bank.
Employer Identification Number: 586184748

1651
Robert B. Scott Trust ⌑
21 Laredo Dr.
Scottdale 30079

Established in 1979 in GA.
Donor(s): Milton C. Scott.
Foundation type: Independent
Financial data (yr. ended 5/31/88): Assets, $575,263 (M); expenditures, $174,243, including $168,637 for 1 grant.
Purpose and activities: Support for the publication of religious articles.
Types of support: Publications.
Trustee: Milton C. Scott.
Employer Identification Number: 581409146

1652
The Selig Foundation ⌑ ☆
1100 Spring St., N.W. Suite 550
Atlanta 30309

Established in 1968.
Foundation type: Independent
Financial data (yr. ended 4/30/88): Assets, $774,559 (M); expenditures, $229,090, including $228,368 for 44 grants (high: $110,000; low: $25).
Purpose and activities: Support primarily for Jewish organizations, including a welfare fund and other social services; support also for the arts.
Limitations: Giving primarily in Atlanta, GA.
Officers: S. Stephen Selig III, Pres.; Cathy S. Fine, Secy.-Treas.; Mercer Granade, Mgr.
Employer Identification Number: 586074209

1653
Warren P. and Ava F. Sewell Foundation
P.O. Drawer 645
Bremen 30110

Trust established in 1948 in GA.
Donor(s): Warren P. Sewell.
Foundation type: Independent
Financial data (yr. ended 1/31/89): Assets, $4,884,165 (M); expenditures, $80,629, including $70,280 for grants (average: $1,000-$10,000).
Purpose and activities: Grants primarily to Protestant churches, secondary and elementary education, health agencies, child development, recreation, and a library.
Types of support: Building funds, capital campaigns.
Limitations: Giving primarily in Haralson and Carroll counties, GA, and Randolph and Cleburne counties, AL.
Application information: Application form not required.
Initial approach: Letter
Copies of proposal: 1
Deadline(s): None
Board meeting date(s): Every 60 days
Write: Guy Darnell
Trustees: Lamar R. Plunkett, Jack Worley.
Number of staff: 2 part-time professional; 2 part-time support.
Employer Identification Number: 586041342

1654
William F. Shallenberger Trust Fund ⌑
c/o Alston & Bird, One Atlantic Ctr.
1201 West Peachtree St., Suite 4200
Atlanta 30309-3424 (404) 881-7000

Established in 1980 in GA.
Foundation type: Independent
Financial data (yr. ended 12/31/88): Assets, $2,019,695 (M); expenditures, $68,333, including $56,147 for 11 grants (high: $9,647; low: $1,000; average: $1,000-$9,647).
Purpose and activities: Emphasis on hospitals, health care, and welfare of senior citizens.
Limitations: Giving primarily in Atlanta, GA.
Application information: Applications not accepted.
Write: Benjamin T. White, Mgr.
Officer: Benjamin T. White, Mgr.
Number of staff: None.
Employer Identification Number: 581403009

1655
Shepherd Foundation, Inc. ⌑ ☆
1800 Briarcliff Rd., N.E.
Atlanta 30329-4096

Established in 1966.
Donor(s): J. Harold Shepherd.
Foundation type: Independent
Financial data (yr. ended 9/30/88): Assets, $1,084,667 (M); gifts received, $125,000; expenditures, $81,800, including $79,218 for 55 grants (high: $26,300; low: $100).
Purpose and activities: Support for medical research, hospitals, health associations, higher education, and Protestant organizations.
Limitations: Giving primarily in Atlanta, GA.
Officers: J. Harold Shepherd, Chair.; W. Clyde Shepherd, Secy.; Dan P. Shepherd, Treas.
Employer Identification Number: 586065260

1656
Ships of the Sea, Inc.
503 East River St.
Savannah 31401

Established in 1965 in GA.
Foundation type: Operating
Financial data (yr. ended 12/31/88): Assets, $2,920,448 (M); expenditures, $225,191.
Purpose and activities: A private operating foundation; support primarily for a historical museum.
Types of support: Renovation projects.
Limitations: Giving primarily in Savannah, GA.
Officers: Mills B. Lane, Chair. and Treas.; Anne W. Lane, Vice-Chair.; Gladys B. Dodd, Secy.; David T. Guernsey, Jr., Exec. Dir.
Employer Identification Number: 580959654

1657
The South Atlantic Foundation, Inc.
428 Bull St.
Savannah 31401 (912) 238-3288

Established in 1953 in GA; Incorporated as a community foundation in 1986.
Foundation type: Community
Financial data (yr. ended 12/31/89): Assets, $2,500,000 (M); gifts received, $628,000; expenditures, $328,000, including $208,000 for 101 grants (high: $20,000; low: $100; average: $100-$20,000).
Purpose and activities: Support primarily for social services, welfare organizations, religious giving, health organizations, medical research, education and cultural programs.
Types of support: Annual campaigns, building funds, conferences and seminars, emergency funds, employee-related scholarships, equipment, endowment funds, land acquisition, operating budgets, professorships, program-related investments, publications, renovation projects, seed money.
Limitations: Giving primarily in GA, SC, and FL. No grants to individuals, or for continuing support, deficit financing, foundation managed projects, matching or challenge grants, program-related investments, operating support, or endowment funds.
Publications: Annual report, informational brochure, application guidelines.
Application information: Application form required.
Initial approach: Telephone
Copies of proposal: 1
Deadline(s): Before end of each quarter
Board meeting date(s): Jan., Apr., July, and Oct.
Write: William W. Byram, Jr., Dir.
Director: William W. Byram, Jr.
Number of staff: 1 full-time professional; 1 full-time support.
Employer Identification Number: 586033468

1658
Albert Steiner Charitable Fund ⌑
3451 Paces Ferry Rd., N.W.
Atlanta 30327 (404) 237-8736

Trust established in 1919 in GA.
Donor(s): Albert Steiner.†
Foundation type: Independent
Financial data (yr. ended 12/31/88): Assets, $1,693,672 (M); expenditures, $195,530, including $166,000 for grants.
Purpose and activities: Grants to institutions to provide hospitalization and medical treatment for the poor.
Types of support: Continuing support, research, general purposes.
Limitations: Giving primarily in Atlanta, GA. No grants to individuals, or for building funds, endowments, scholarships, fellowships, or matching gifts; no loans.
Application information:
Initial approach: Letter
Copies of proposal: 1
Deadline(s): Submit proposal preferably in Oct.
Board meeting date(s): Apr., July, Oct., and Dec.
Write: L.G. Sherman, Jr., Trustee
Trustees: Joyce O. Happ, Bernard L. Lipman, M.D., L.G. Sherman, Jr.
Employer Identification Number: 586030063

1659
Loyd Strickland Foundation, Inc. ⌑
P.O. Box 7181
Chestnut Mountain 30502 (404) 967-6152

Established in 1955 in GA.
Foundation type: Independent
Financial data (yr. ended 12/31/87): Assets, $1,603,510 (M); expenditures, $207,723, including $200,084 for 40 grants (high: $56,400; low: $200).
Purpose and activities: To promote the cause of the Christian faith, education, and human welfare.
Types of support: Operating budgets, building funds, scholarship funds.
Application information:
Initial approach: Letter (2 to 3 pages)
Write: Ben H. Lancaster, Jr., Secy.-Treas.
Officers: Loyd Strickland, Chair.; Diane Strickland, Vice-Chair.; Ben H. Lancaster, Jr., Secy.-Treas.
Trustees: John B. Ellis, Russell F. Lind, Matthew McGowan, Kennedy Smart, Bobby Strickland.
Employer Identification Number: 586038671

1660
Kate and Elwyn Tomlinson Foundation, Inc. ⌑
3000 Habersham Rd., N.W.
Atlanta 30305-2844 (404) 952-2277

Incorporated in 1949 in GA.
Foundation type: Independent
Financial data (yr. ended 12/31/88): Assets, $2,474,850 (M); expenditures, $283,027, including $135,700 for 59 grants (high: $30,000; low: $500).
Purpose and activities: Emphasis on higher and secondary education, arts and culture, hospitals, health agencies, and a community fund.
Limitations: Giving primarily in GA. No grants to individuals.
Application information:
Initial approach: Letter
Deadline(s): None
Write: Kathryn Bridges, Chair.
Officers: Kathryn T. Bridges, Chair.; Mark P. Tomlinson, Vice-Chair.
Employer Identification Number: 580634727

1661
Trust Company of Georgia Foundation ▼
c/o Trust Co. Bank, Atlanta
P.O. Box 4418; MC 041
Atlanta 30302 (404) 588-8246

Trust established in 1959 in GA.
Donor(s): Trust Co. Bank.
Foundation type: Company-sponsored
Financial data (yr. ended 12/31/89): Assets, $10,690,964 (M); gifts received, $3,693,170; expenditures, $1,404,418, including $1,079,857 for grants (average: $3,000-$5,000) and $242,482 for employee matching gifts.
Purpose and activities: Emphasis on local community development and welfare, including a community fund; support also for youth agencies, secondary schools, the fine arts and other cultural groups, and health services, including mental health and programs for the handicapped.
Types of support: Building funds, renovation projects, special projects, employee matching gifts, capital campaigns, equipment.
Limitations: Giving primarily in metropolitan Atlanta, GA (Fulton and DeKalb counties). No support for churches or political organizations. No grants to individuals, or for scholarships,

fellowships, maintenance, or debt service; no loans.
Publications: Application guidelines, program policy statement.
Application information: Application form required.
Initial approach: Letter or telephone
Copies of proposal: 1
Deadline(s): 1st of month preceding month of board meeting
Board meeting date(s): Jan., Apr., July, and Oct.
Final notification: By letter
Write: Victor A. Gregory, Secy.
Distribution Committee: E.P. Gould, Chair.; Victor A. Gregory, Secy.; L.P. Humann, Wade T. Mitchell, John W. Spiegel, Robert Strickland, James B. Williams.
Trustee: Trust Co. Bank.
Number of staff: 1 full-time professional; 1 full-time support.
Employer Identification Number: 586026063

1662
The Tull Charitable Foundation ▼ ☆
230 Peachtree St., N.E., Suite 1502
Atlanta 30303 (404) 659-7079

Trust established in 1952 in GA as The J. M. Tull Foundation; reorganized under current name in 1984 with the I. A. Tull Charitable Foundation.
Donor(s): J.M. Tull,† J.M. Tull Metal and Supply Co., Inc.
Foundation type: Independent
Financial data (yr. ended 12/31/89): Assets, $32,000,000 (M); expenditures, $1,734,774, including $1,490,000 for 41 grants (high: $150,000; low: $5,000; average: $25,000-$75,000).
Purpose and activities: Support for higher and secondary education; grants also for health and human services, youth and child welfare agencies, and culture.
Types of support: Building funds, seed money, endowment funds, capital campaigns, professorships, scholarship funds.
Limitations: Giving limited to GA. No support for projects of religious organizations that primarily benefit their own adherents. No grants to individuals, or for conferences or seminars, scientific research, purchase of tickets to benefit events, or operating support; no loans.
Publications: Informational brochure (including application guidelines).
Application information: Application form not required.
Initial approach: Letter
Copies of proposal: 1
Deadline(s): 1st day of month of meeting
Board meeting date(s): Jan., Apr., July, and Oct.
Final notification: One week after board meeting
Write: Barbara Cleveland, Exec. Dir.
Officers: George E. Smith,* Pres.; Walter J. Thomas,* Secy.-Treas.; Barbara Cleveland, Exec. Dir.
Trustees:* John McIntyre, Larry Prince, L. Edmund Rast, Franklin Skinner, John B. Zellars.
Agent: Trust Co. Bank.
Number of staff: 1 part-time professional; 1 part-time support.
Employer Identification Number: 581687028

1663
Charles M. Walker Foundation, Inc. ☆
416 South Broad St.
Monroe 30655-2122
Application address: 401 Woodland Rd., Monroe, GA 30655; Tel.: (404) 267-3001

Established in 1963.
Foundation type: Independent
Financial data (yr. ended 12/31/88): Assets, $824,456 (M); expenditures, $106,770, including $101,790 for 60 loans to individuals.
Purpose and activities: Giving primarily higher education student loans; minor support for Protestant churches.
Types of support: Student loans.
Limitations: Giving limited to Walton County, GA.
Application information: Completion of application form required for student loans.
Initial approach: Letter or telephone
Deadline(s): Aug. 1
Write: Mrs. Agnes Shackleford, Secy.-Treas.
Officers: Jere Field, Chair.; Mrs. M.T. Sanders, Jr., Vice-Chair.; Agnes Shackleford, Secy.-Treas.
Trustees: George W. Felker III, Dickie Hester, Wilson B. Mitchem, Sr.
Employer Identification Number: 586036759

1664
Gertrude and William C. Wardlaw Fund, Inc. ⌘
c/o Trust Co. Bank
P.O. Box 4655
Atlanta 30302

Trust established in 1936 in GA; incorporated in 1951.
Donor(s): Gertrude Wardlaw, William C. Wardlaw, Jr.†
Foundation type: Independent
Financial data (yr. ended 12/31/88): Assets, $4,356,251 (M); expenditures, $154,165, including $132,000 for 29 grants (high: $17,500; low: $1,000).
Purpose and activities: Emphasis on higher education, youth agencies, cultural programs, a community fund, and hospitals.
Types of support: Operating budgets.
Limitations: Giving primarily in Atlanta, GA. No grants to individuals.
Application information:
Initial approach: Letter
Deadline(s): None
Officers and Trustees: Ednabelle Raine Wardlaw, Chair.; A. Pickney Straughn, Secy.; Victor A. Gregory, William C. Wardlaw III, Trust Co. Bank.
Employer Identification Number: 586026065

1665
Virgil P. Warren Foundation ⌘ ☆
c/o Trust Co. Bank
P.O. Box 4655
Atlanta 30302-4655

Established in 1946.
Donor(s): Virgil P. Warren.†
Foundation type: Independent
Financial data (yr. ended 12/31/88): Assets, $1,003,805 (M); gifts received, $37,000; expenditures, $86,547, including $73,432 for 38 grants (high: $10,000; low: $300).
Purpose and activities: Giving for Protestant churches, higher and other education, hospitals, and youth and child welfare organizations.
Types of support: Operating budgets.
Limitations: Giving primarily in GA. No grants to individuals.
Application information:
Initial approach: Proposal
Deadline(s): Mar. 31 and Sept. 30
Board meeting date(s): Apr. and Oct.
Write: Ben Harris
Trustees: L.C. Warren, Chair.; Darrell Gunby, Joseph L. Harris, W. King Sims, Trust Co. Bank.
Employer Identification Number: 586026067

1666
Watkins Christian Foundation, Inc. ▼ ⌘
1946 Monroe Dr., N.E.
Atlanta 30324

Established in 1983 in GA.
Donor(s): Bill Watkins, Watkins Associated Industries, Inc.
Foundation type: Independent
Financial data (yr. ended 12/31/88): Assets, $3,915,545 (M); gifts received, $725,058; expenditures, $963,635, including $938,327 for 34 grants (high: $50,000; low: $100).
Purpose and activities: Grants for evangelism, churches, ministries, and a variety of religious organizations, including support for human welfare and feeding the hungry.
Application information: Contributes only to pre-selected organizations. Applications not accepted.
Officers: Bill Watkins,* Pres.; George Watkins,* V.P.; George W. Ready, Jr., Secy.-Treas.
Directors:* William A. Freeman.
Employer Identification Number: 581494832

1667
Wehadkee Foundation, Inc. ⌘
P.O. Box 150
West Point 31833

Incorporated in 1952 in AL.
Donor(s): D.A. Turner.
Foundation type: Independent
Financial data (yr. ended 12/31/88): Assets, $1,628,860 (M); expenditures, $112,556, including $110,950 for 36 grants (high: $25,000; low: $150).
Purpose and activities: Giving for education, youth agencies, and social services.
Limitations: Giving primarily in GA.
Application information: Applications not accepted.
Officers: Bruce N. Lanier, Sr., Pres.; Bruce N. Lanier, Jr., V.P.; Ronnie Birchfield, Secy.-Treas.
Trustee: G.P. Barnwell.
Employer Identification Number: 636049784

1668
West Foundation ⌑ ☆
Two Ninth Green Dr.
Roswell 30076

Donor(s): John W. Spiegel, Mrs. John W. Spiegel.
Foundation type: Independent
Financial data (yr. ended 12/31/88): Assets, $288,697 (M); gifts received, $112,300; expenditures, $130,981, including $130,464 for 22 grants (high: $20,000; low: $42).
Purpose and activities: Giving primarily for Christian schools and organizations.
Application information:
Deadline(s): None
Write: John W. Spiegel, Mgr.
Officer and Trustees: John W. Spiegel, Mgr.; Juliet F. Spiegel.
Employer Identification Number: 341233170

1669
The West Foundation ⌑
2845 Amwiler Rd.
Atlanta 30360

Foundation type: Independent
Financial data (yr. ended 12/31/88): Assets, $4,888,829 (M); gifts received, $35,000; expenditures, $140,013, including $102,895 for grants.
Purpose and activities: Support for health organizations, cultural programs, and Protestant churches.
Officers and Directors: Charles B. West, Chair. and Pres.; Charles B. West, Jr., V.P.; Elizabeth D. West, V.P.; G. Vincent West, V.P.; Marian T. West, V.P.; Marjorie E. West, V.P.; Mark C. West, V.P.; Robert Wynne, V.P.; Marjorie West Wynne, Secy.
Employer Identification Number: 586073270

1670
West Point-Pepperell Foundation, Inc. ⌑
West Tenth St.
P.O. Box 342
West Point 31833 (404) 645-4388

Incorporated in 1953 in GA as West Point Foundation, Inc.; merged with Sanford Dunson Foundation, Inc. in 1965.
Donor(s): West Point-Pepperell, Inc.
Foundation type: Company-sponsored
Financial data (yr. ended 12/31/87): Assets, $1,772,818 (M); gifts received, $424,800; expenditures, $757,111, including $674,043 for 252 grants and $30,493 for 160 employee matching gifts.
Purpose and activities: Support for higher and secondary education, hospitals, and health agencies; grants also for youth agencies and community funds.
Types of support: Employee matching gifts.
Limitations: Giving primarily in areas with West Point-Pepperell, Inc. facilities in AL, FL, ME, NC, SC, and TX. No grants to individuals.
Application information: Application form not required.
Initial approach: Letter
Copies of proposal: 1
Board meeting date(s): Varies
Write: H. Hart Cobb, Jr., V.P.
Officers: Joseph L. Lanier, Jr.,* Chair. and Pres.; H. Hart Cobb, Jr., V.P.; C. Powers Dorsett, Secy.; Clayton Sauers, Treas.
Trustees:* Donald J. Keller, Harry M. Philpott, Yetta G. Samford, Jr., C. McKenzie Taylor, C.E. Woodruff.
Number of staff: 2 full-time professional; 2 part-time support.
Employer Identification Number: 580801512

1671
Joseph B. Whitehead Foundation ▼
1400 Peachtree Ctr. Tower
230 Peachtree St., N.W.
Atlanta 30303 (404) 522-6755

Incorporated in 1937 in GA.
Donor(s): Joseph B. Whitehead, Jr.†
Foundation type: Independent
Financial data (yr. ended 12/31/89): Assets, $310,191,188 (M); expenditures, $10,333,655, including $9,489,695 for 35 grants (high: $2,500,000; low: $10,000; average: $10,000-$750,000).
Purpose and activities: Giving primarily for child care and youth programs, education, health, cultural programs, the arts, care of the aged, and civic affairs. Preference is given to one-time capital projects of established private charitable organizations.
Types of support: Seed money, building funds, equipment, land acquisition, special projects, capital campaigns.
Limitations: Giving limited to metropolitan Atlanta, GA. No grants to individuals, or for endowment funds, research, scholarships, fellowships, or matching gifts; no loans; generally no support for operating expenses.
Publications: Application guidelines, informational brochure (including application guidelines), program policy statement.
Application information: Application form not required.
Initial approach: Letter
Copies of proposal: 1
Deadline(s): 1st of Feb. and Sept.
Board meeting date(s): Apr. and Nov.
Final notification: 30 days after board meeting
Write: Charles H. McTier, Pres.
Officers: Charles H. McTier, Pres.; P. Russell Hardin, Secy.-Treas.
Trustees: J.W. Jones, Chair.; James M. Sibley, Vice-Chair.; Roberto C. Goizueta.
Number of staff: 7
Employer Identification Number: 586001954

1672
Lettie Pate Whitehead Foundation, Inc. ▼
1400 Peachtree Ctr. Tower
230 Peachtree St., N.W.
Atlanta 30303 (404) 522-6755

Incorporated in 1946 in GA.
Donor(s): Conkey Pate Whitehead.†
Foundation type: Independent
Financial data (yr. ended 12/31/89): Assets, $223,365,208 (M); expenditures, $7,815,627, including $6,999,333 for 192 grants (high: $220,000; low: $10,000; average: $20,000-$65,000).
Purpose and activities: Grants to institutions for scholarships for the education of poor Christian girls and institutional grants for assistance to poor aged Christian women.
Types of support: Scholarship funds.
Limitations: Giving limited to AL, FL, GA, LA, MS, NC, SC, TN, and VA. No grants to individuals, or for building or endowment funds, or matching gifts; no loans.
Publications: Application guidelines, informational brochure.
Application information: Application form not required.
Initial approach: Letter
Copies of proposal: 1
Deadline(s): Sept. 1
Board meeting date(s): Apr. and Nov.
Final notification: Within 1 year
Write: Charles H. McTier, Pres.
Officers: Charles H. McTier, Pres.; P. Russell Hardin, Secy.-Treas.
Trustees: Hughes Spalding, Jr., Chair.; Herbert A. Claiborne, Jr., M.D., Vice-Chair.; Lyons Gray.
Number of staff: 7
Employer Identification Number: 586012629

1673
John Wieland Family Foundation, Inc. ⌑ ☆
3245 Nancy Creek Rd.
Atlanta 30327 (404) 996-1400

Established in 1986 in GA.
Donor(s): John Wieland.
Foundation type: Independent
Financial data (yr. ended 12/31/88): Assets, $201,421 (M); expenditures, $340,832, including $339,888 for 77 grants (high: $69,880; low: $75).
Purpose and activities: Giving primarily for religion, including churches; support also for higher, elementary, and other education, a community fund, and social services.
Officers and Directors: John Wieland, Pres.; Susan W. Wieland, Secy.; John George Fox Wieland, Jr., Lindsey Gesell Wieland.
Employer Identification Number: 581707424

1674
A. L. Williams, Jr. Family Foundation, Inc. ⌑
3483 Satellite Blvd., Suite 210
Duluth 30186

Established in 1985 in GA.
Donor(s): Arthur L. Williams, Jr., Angela H. Williams, Boe Adams.
Foundation type: Independent
Financial data (yr. ended 12/31/87): Assets, $7,467 (M); gifts received, $795,005; expenditures, $833,274, including $832,639 for 34 grants (high: $258,602; low: $25).
Purpose and activities: Support primarily for religious and social service organizations and educational institutions.
Application information: Contributes only to pre-selected organizations. Applications not accepted.
Officers and Trustees: Angela H. Williams, Pres.; April Ann Williams, V.P.; Arthur L. Williams III, V.P.; Jack Smith, Secy.-Treas.
Employer Identification Number: 581650389

1675
Marguerite N. & Thomas L. Williams, Jr. Foundation, Inc. ¤
Old Monticello Rd.
P.O. Box 378
Thomasville 31799

Established in 1980 in GA.
Donor(s): Diane W. Parker, Marguerite N. Williams, Thomas L. Williams III, Bennie G. Williams.†
Foundation type: Independent
Financial data (yr. ended 11/30/89): Assets, $5,429,511 (M); gifts received, $45,087; expenditures, $375,417, including $321,575 for 40 grants (high: $50,000; low: $250).
Purpose and activities: Support for cultural activities, historic preservation, and higher and secondary education; some support for social services and health.
Limitations: Giving primarily in GA.
Officers and Directors:* Marguerite N. Williams,* Pres.; Diane W. Parker,* Secy.; Bernard Lanigan, Jr.,* Treas.; Joseph E. Beverly, Frederick E. Cooper, Thomas H. Vann, Jr., Thomas L. Williams III.
Employer Identification Number: 581414850

1676
The Frances Wood Wilson Foundation, Inc. ¤
1549 Clairmont Rd., Suite 104
Decatur 30033 (404) 634-3363
Application address: P.O. Box 33188, Decatur, GA 30033

Incorporated in 1954 in GA.
Donor(s): Fred B. Wilson,† Mrs. Frances W. Wilson, St. Louis - San Francisco Railroad.
Foundation type: Independent
Financial data (yr. ended 05/31/89): Assets, $29,458,515 (M); expenditures, $1,800,730, including $859,627 for 36 grants (high: $205,000; low: $500).
Purpose and activities: Grants largely for child welfare, and religious, civic, health, and higher educational organizations; support also for college scholarship funds.
Types of support: General purposes, operating budgets, continuing support, annual campaigns, seed money, emergency funds, building funds, equipment, land acquisition, scholarship funds.
Limitations: Giving limited to GA, except for programs carried on by Chestnut Hill Benevolent Association in Boston, MA. No grants to individuals, or for endowment funds; no loans.
Publications: Application guidelines, program policy statement.
Application information:
Initial approach: Proposal
Copies of proposal: 1
Deadline(s): None
Board meeting date(s): Apr. and Oct.
Write: Emory K. Crenshaw, Pres.
Officers and Trustees:* Emory K. Crenshaw,* Pres.; W.T. Wingfield,* Exec. V.P.; T. Cecil Myers.
Employer Identification Number: 586035441

1677
WinShape Centre, Inc.
5200 Buffington Rd.
Atlanta 30349
Scholarship application address: P.O. Box 9, Mt. Berry, GA 30149; Tel.: (404) 235-8407

Established in 1984 in GA.
Donor(s): Chick-Fil-A, Inc., S. Truett Cathy.
Foundation type: Independent
Financial data (yr. ended 08/31/89): Assets, $1,721,435 (M); gifts received, $1,042,491; expenditures, $651,455, including $129,438 for grants to individuals.
Purpose and activities: Awards scholarships for undergraduate students attending Berry College.
Types of support: Student aid, continuing support.
Limitations: Giving primarily in Rome, GA.
Publications: 990-PF, informational brochure (including application guidelines), application guidelines.
Application information: Application form required.
Initial approach: Letter, recommendation, and list of honors
Deadline(s): Priority given to applications received by Nov. 30 for following academic year
Board meeting date(s): Varies
Final notification: Mar. 31
Write: Terri S. White
Officers: S. Truett Cathy, Pres.; Donald M. Cathy, V.P.; James B. McCabe, Secy.-Treas.
Number of staff: 13 full-time professional.
Employer Identification Number: 581595471

1678
Robert W. Woodruff Foundation, Inc. ▼
(Formerly Trebor Foundation, Inc.)
1400 Peachtree Ctr. Tower
230 Peachtree St., N.W.
Atlanta 30303 (404) 522-6755

Incorporated in 1937 in DE.
Donor(s): Robert W. Woodruff,† The Acmaro Securities Corp., and others.
Foundation type: Independent
Financial data (yr. ended 12/31/89): Assets, $755,690,077 (M); gifts received, $192,765,505; expenditures, $9,750,390, including $8,731,763 for 31 grants (high: $2,500,000; low: $5,000; average: $25,000-$750,000).
Purpose and activities: Interests include expansion and improvement of health and educational facilities, youth and child welfare programs, care of the aged, cultural and civic affairs, and conservation and the environment.
Types of support: Building funds, renovation projects, land acquisition, equipment, general purposes, scholarship funds, capital campaigns.
Limitations: Giving primarily in Atlanta, GA. No grants to individuals, or for endowment funds, operating budgets, research, special projects, publications, conferences and seminars, or operating budgets; no loans.
Publications: Application guidelines.
Application information: Application form not required.
Initial approach: Letter
Copies of proposal: 1
Deadline(s): 1st of Feb. and Sept.
Board meeting date(s): Apr. and Nov.
Final notification: Within 30 days of trustees meeting
Write: Charles H. McTier, Pres.
Officers: Charles H. McTier, Pres.; P. Russell Hardin, Secy.-Treas.
Trustees: Joseph W. Jones, Chair.; James M. Sibley, Vice-Chair.; Ivan Allen, Jr., A.D. Boylston, Jr., James B. Williams.
Number of staff: 7
Employer Identification Number: 581695425

1679
The David, Helen, and Marian Woodward Fund-Atlanta
(also known as Marian W. Ottley Trust-Atlanta)
c/o The First National Bank of Atlanta
Two Peachtree St., N.W., Suite 1530
Atlanta 30383 (404) 332-6592

Trust established in 1975 in GA.
Donor(s): Marian W. Ottley.†
Foundation type: Independent
Financial data (yr. ended 05/31/89): Assets, $24,059,565 (M); expenditures, $1,304,117, including $1,161,584 for 39 grants (high: $100,000; low: $2,000).
Purpose and activities: Support for health associations, social service and youth agencies, arts and cultural programs, and a community fund.
Types of support: Building funds, emergency funds, endowment funds, equipment, operating budgets, special projects.
Limitations: Giving primarily in Atlanta, GA. No grants to individuals.
Application information: Application form not required.
Initial approach: Letter
Copies of proposal: 1
Deadline(s): 30 days prior to board meetings
Board meeting date(s): June and Dec.
Final notification: 10 days after meeting
Write: Joseph Patterson
Distribution Committee: Edward D. Smith, Chair.; William D. Ellis, Jr., Robert L. Foreman, Jr., Joseph H. Hilsman, Horace Sibley.
Trustee: The First National Bank of Atlanta.
Number of staff: None.
Employer Identification Number: 586222004

1680
The Vasser Woolley Foundation, Inc. ¤
c/o Alston & Bird, One Atlantic Ctr.
1201 West Peachtree St., Suite 4200
Atlanta 30309-3424 (404) 881-7000

Incorporated in 1961 in GA.
Donor(s): Vasser Woolley.†
Foundation type: Independent
Financial data (yr. ended 12/31/88): Assets, $5,049,486 (M); expenditures, $245,786, including $196,667 for 13 grants (high: $30,000; low: $5,000; average: $7,500-$25,000).
Purpose and activities: Emphasis on higher education; support also for the arts, youth agencies, community funds, crime prevention, and aid to the handicapped.
Types of support: Seed money, emergency funds, building funds, equipment, land

acquisition, general purposes, professorships, scholarship funds, matching funds.
Limitations: Giving primarily in the metropolitan Atlanta, GA, area. No grants to individuals, or for operating budgets, continuing support, annual campaigns, deficit financing, special projects, research, publications, or conferences; no loans.
Publications: Informational brochure, 990-PF, program policy statement, application guidelines.
Application information: Application form not required.
Initial approach: Letter
Copies of proposal: 1
Board meeting date(s): Jan., Apr., July, and Oct.
Final notification: 3 months
Write: L. Neil Williams, Jr., Chair.
Officers and Trustees: L. Neil Williams, Jr., Chair.; Benjamin T. White, Secy.-Treas.; R. Neal Batson, Alex P. Gaines, G. Conley Ingram, John R. Seydel, Paul V. Seydel.
Number of staff: None.
Employer Identification Number: 586034197

1681
Charm & Goodloe Yancey Foundation ⌑ ☆
P.O. Box 43326
Atlanta 30336

Established in 1980-.
Foundation type: Independent
Financial data (yr. ended 12/31/88): Assets, $1,104,155 (M); expenditures, $59,682, including $43,000 for 16 grants (high: $15,000; low: $500) and $13,334 for 7 grants to individuals (high: $2,000; low: $1,334).
Purpose and activities: Awards scholarships for higher education to children of Yancey Brothers, Inc.; support also for an Episcopal church.
Types of support: Scholarship funds, employee-related scholarships, student aid.
Limitations: Giving primarily in Atlanta, GA.
Application information: Contributes only to pre-selected organizations. Applications not accepted.
Write: Don A. Yancey, Chair.
Officer: Don A. Yancey, Chair.
Trustee: Trust Co. Bank.
Employer Identification Number: 581413050

1682
Zaban Foundation Inc. ⌑
335 Green Glen Way
Atlanta 30327

Established in 1960 in GA.
Donor(s): Erwin Zaban.
Foundation type: Independent
Financial data (yr. ended 06/30/89): Assets, $3,320,955 (M); gifts received, $202,750; expenditures, $454,207, including $449,230 for 8 grants (high: $186,278; low: $1,000).
Purpose and activities: Support primarily for Jewish welfare organizations and temple support; some support for culture and social services.
Limitations: Giving primarily in Atlanta, GA. No grants to individuals.
Application information: Contributes only to pre-selected organizations. Applications not accepted.
Officers: Erwin Zaban, Pres. and Treas.; Marshall Dinerman, Secy.
Employer Identification Number: 586034590

HAWAII

1683
The Barbara Cox Anthony Foundation ⌑
745 Fort St., Suite 1000
Honolulu 96813 (808) 536-1877
Application address: P.O. Box 4316, Honolulu, HI 96813

Incorporated in 1960 in HI.
Donor(s): Barbara Cox Anthony, James M. Cox.†
Foundation type: Independent
Financial data (yr. ended 12/31/88): Assets, $190,969 (M); gifts received, $280,250; expenditures, $199,957, including $199,803 for 50 grants (high: $50,000; low: $80; average: $100-$5,000).
Purpose and activities: Emphasis on higher and secondary education, hospitals, and conservation.
Limitations: Giving primarily in HI.
Application information: Application form not required.
Deadline(s): None
Write: Garner Anthony, V.P.
Officers and Directors:* Barbara Cox Anthony,* Pres.; Garner Anthony,* V.P. and Secy.-Treas.; James Cox Kennedy, Blair Parry-Okeden.
Employer Identification Number: 996005049

1684
Atherton Family Foundation ▼
c/o Hawaiian Trust Co., Ltd.
P.O. Box 3170
Honolulu 96802
Application address: c/o Hawaii Community Foundation, 222 Merchant St., 2nd Fl., Honolulu, HI 96813; Tel. (Grants): (808) 537-6333; Tel. (Scholarships): (808) 536-8839; FAX: (808) 521-6286

Incorporated in 1975 in HI as successor to Juliette M. Atherton Trust established in 1915; F. C. Atherton Trust merged into the Foundation in 1976.
Donor(s): Juliette M. Atherton,† Frank C. Atherton.†
Foundation type: Independent
Financial data (yr. ended 12/31/88): Assets, $42,491,262 (M); expenditures, $3,032,201, including $2,595,900 for 134 grants (high: $200,000; low: $1,000; average: $2,500-$25,000) and $22,800 for 46 grants to individuals (high: $4,000; low: $500; average: $1,000-$3,000).
Purpose and activities: Concerned with education, social welfare, culture and the arts, religion, health, and the environment. Scholarships for the education of Protestant ministers for postgraduate education; Protestant ministers' children for undergraduate study, and for graduate theological education at a Protestant seminary.
Types of support: Operating budgets, building funds, student aid, annual campaigns, consulting services, continuing support, endowment funds, equipment, matching funds, publications, renovation projects, research, seed money, special projects.
Limitations: Giving limited to HI; student aid for HI residents only. No support for private foundations or for organizations engaged in fundraising for the purpose of distributing grants to recipients of their own choosing.
Publications: Annual report, program policy statement, application guidelines.
Application information: Application forms required for scholarships.
Initial approach: Telephone or proposal
Copies of proposal: 6
Deadline(s): 1st day of month preceding board meeting for organizations; Mar. 1 for scholarships
Board meeting date(s): 3rd Wednesday of Feb., Apr., June, Aug., Oct., and Dec.
Final notification: 1 to 2 months
Write: Jeanne Corrigan for grants; Caroline Sherman for scholarships
Officers and Directors:* Alexander S. Atherton,* Pres.; Judith Dawson, V.P. and Secy.; Robert R. Midkiff,* V.P.; James F. Morgan, Jr.,* V.P.; Joan H. Rohlfing,* V.P.; Hawaiian Trust Co., Ltd., Treas.
Number of staff: 7
Employer Identification Number: 510175971

1685
Fred Baldwin Memorial Foundation
P.O. Box 6082
Kahului 96732 (808) 572-8346
Additional address: 222 Merchant St., 2nd Fl., Honolulu, HI 96813; Tel.: (808) 537-6333, FAX: (808) 521-6286

Established in 1910 in HI as the Fred Baldwin Memorial Home.
Foundation type: Independent
Financial data (yr. ended 12/31/88): Assets, $3,302,633 (M); gifts received, $4,374; expenditures, $164,149, including $116,414 for 48 grants (high: $17,050; low: $100).
Purpose and activities: Emphasis on community funds and social services, including youth agencies.
Limitations: Giving limited to HI, with emphasis on Maui County.
Application information: Application form not required.
Initial approach: Proposal
Copies of proposal: 1
Deadline(s): Feb., May or June, and Nov.
Write: Neil H. Swanson, Exec. Dir.
Officers and Trustees: Michael H. Lyons II, Pres.; Shaun L. McKay, V.P.; Neil H. Swanson, Jr., Secy.-Treas.; Bennet M. Baldwin, Douglas B. Cameron, Frances B. Cameron, Joseph P. Cooke, Jr., Mary C. Sanford, Emily Young.

Number of staff: 1 full-time professional.
Employer Identification Number: 990075264

1686
Bancorp Hawaii Charitable Foundation ⌑
c/o Controllers Dept.
P.O. Box 2900
Honolulu 96846

Established in 1981 in HI.
Donor(s): Bank of Hawaii.
Foundation type: Company-sponsored
Financial data (yr. ended 12/31/87): Assets, $1,747,616 (M); expenditures, $73,043, including $70,000 for 6 grants (high: $20,000; low: $5,000).
Purpose and activities: Giving primarily to museums, education, and a church.
Types of support: General purposes, endowment funds, building funds.
Limitations: Giving limited to HI.
Application information: Contributes only to pre-selected organizations. Applications not accepted.
Officers and Directors:* Frank J. Manaut,* Pres.; H. Howard Stephenson,* V.P. and Treas.; Richard J. Dahl, V.P.; Ruth E. Miyashiro, Secy.; and 20 additional directors.
Employer Identification Number: 990210467

1687
C. Brewer Charitable Foundation
827 Fort St.
Honolulu 96813 (808) 536-4461
Mailing address: P.O. Box 1826, Honolulu, HI 96805

Established in 1980 in HI.
Donor(s): C. Brewer and Co., Ltd.
Foundation type: Company-sponsored
Financial data (yr. ended 12/31/88): Assets, $572,829 (M); gifts received, $250,000; expenditures, $255,617, including $251,157 for 67 grants (high: $75,000; low: $82; average: $500-$5,000) and $3,910 for 30 employee matching gifts.
Purpose and activities: Giving for community funds, social services, including youth agencies, education, and the arts.
Types of support: General purposes, equipment, emergency funds, building funds, employee matching gifts, renovation projects, scholarship funds.
Limitations: Giving primarily in HI.
Application information: Application form not required.
Initial approach: Letter
Copies of proposal: 1
Deadline(s): None
Board meeting date(s): Quarterly
Write: James S. Andrasick, Chair.
Officers: James S. Andrasick, Chair. and Pres.; Muliufi F. Hannemann, V.P.; J. Alan Kugle, V.P.; Kim L. Peterson, V.P.; Marlene H. Sasaki, Secy.; Kent T. Lucien, Treas.
Number of staff: None.
Employer Identification Number: 990203743

1688
James & Abigail Campbell Foundation
828 Fort St. Mall, Suite 500
Honolulu 96813 (808) 536-1961

Established in 1980 in HI.
Foundation type: Independent
Financial data (yr. ended 12/31/88): Assets, $1,342,633 (M); gifts received, $92,632; expenditures, $72,961, including $57,738 for 17 grants (high: $14,466; low: $250).
Purpose and activities: Giving for health, education, youth services, environment, recreation, culture and the arts.
Types of support: Scholarship funds, building funds, equipment.
Limitations: Giving limited to HI. No grants to individuals.
Application information: Application form not required.
Initial approach: Letter
Copies of proposal: 1
Deadline(s): None
Board meeting date(s): Monthly
Final notification: 60 days
Write: Theresia Cortez, Mgr., Community Affairs
Officers: Wade H. McVay, Pres.; Fred Trotter, V.P.; Paul R. Cassidy, Secy.; Herbert C. Cornuelle, Treas.
Employer Identification Number: 990203078

1689
Harold K. L. Castle Foundation ⌑
629 Kailua Rd., Rm. 210
Kailua 96734 (808) 262-9413

Incorporated in 1962 in HI.
Donor(s): Harold K.L. Castle,† Mrs. Harold K.L. Castle.†
Foundation type: Independent
Financial data (yr. ended 12/31/88): Assets, $52,078,905 (M); expenditures, $2,752,032, including $2,294,600 for 26 grants (high: $750,000; low: $5,000; average: $25,000-$100,000).
Purpose and activities: Emphasis on education; support also for youth agencies, hospitals, cultural programs, and marine research.
Types of support: Annual campaigns, seed money, emergency funds, building funds, equipment, research, general purposes, continuing support, capital campaigns.
Limitations: Giving primarily in HI. No grants to individuals.
Application information: Application form not required.
Initial approach: Letter
Copies of proposal: 1
Deadline(s): Submit proposal preferably in Jan. or Feb.; deadline Mar. 31
Board meeting date(s): Apr.
Final notification: May
Write: David D. Thoma, V.P.
Officers: James C. Castle,* Pres.; David D. Thoma, V.P. and Treas.; James C. Castle, Jr., V.P.; Carol Conrad, Secy.
Directors:* John C. Baldwin, James C. McIntosh, Peter E. Russell.
Number of staff: 1
Employer Identification Number: 996005445

1690
Samuel N. and Mary Castle Foundation ▼
c/o Hawaii Community Foundation
222 Merchant St., 2nd Fl.
Honolulu 96813 (808) 537-6333
FAX: (808) 521-6286

Incorporated in 1925 in HI; founded as Mary Castle Fund in 1898.
Donor(s): Mary Castle.†
Foundation type: Independent
Financial data (yr. ended 12/31/88): Assets, $18,708,253 (M); expenditures, $1,031,934, including $833,800 for 75 grants (high: $70,000; low: $1,000; average: $3,000-$25,000).
Purpose and activities: Emphasis on higher and secondary education, cultural programs, human service organizations, community funds, and denominational giving; support also for health associations and hospitals and environmental groups; special fund for early childhood education programs. Most grants for direct service activities or capital projects.
Types of support: Special projects, building funds, operating budgets, equipment, seed money, land acquisition, renovation projects, general purposes, capital campaigns.
Limitations: Giving limited to HI. No grants to individuals, or for continuing support, endowment funds, or scholarships; generally no support for research; no loans.
Publications: Annual report, program policy statement, application guidelines.
Application information: 7 copies of an executive summary should be submitted with proposal. Application form not required.
Initial approach: Telephone or proposal
Copies of proposal: 1
Deadline(s): Jan. 1, Apr. 1, July 1, and Oct. 1
Board meeting date(s): 2nd Thursday in Mar., June, Sept., and Dec.
Final notification: 2 or 3 months
Write: Jane R. Smith, Grants Admin.
Officers: W. Donald Castle,* Pres.; James C. Castle,* V.P.; Mark J. O'Donnell, Secy.; Hawaiian Trust Co., Ltd., Managing Agent; Hawaii Community Fdn., Grants Admin.
Trustees:* William E. Aull, Zadoc W. Brown, Alfred L. Castle, Robert R. Midkiff.
Number of staff: 9
Employer Identification Number: 996003321

1691
George P. & Ida Tenney Castle Trust
c/o Hawaiian Trust Co., Ltd.
P.O. Box 3170
Honolulu 96802
Application address: 212 Merchant St., Suite 300, Honolulu, HI 96813; Tel.: (808) 537-6333

Established in 1919 in HI.
Foundation type: Independent
Financial data (yr. ended 09/30/88): Assets, $1,745,634 (M); expenditures, $11,165.
Purpose and activities: Emphasis on youth rehabilitation.
Types of support: Special projects.
Limitations: Giving primarily in HI.
Publications: Application guidelines.
Application information: Application form not required.
Initial approach: Proposal

Copies of proposal: 1
Deadline(s): Prior to board meeting dates
Board meeting date(s): Mar. and Sept.
Final notification: Apr. and Oct.
Write: Suzanne Toguchi
Trustee: Hawaiian Trust Co., Ltd.
Number of staff: 2
Employer Identification Number: 996003320

1692
Cooke Foundation, Ltd. ▼
c/o Hawaii Community Foundation
222 Merchant St., 2nd. Fl.
Honolulu 96813 (808) 537-6333
FAX: (808) 521-6286

Trust established in 1920 in HI; incorporated in 1971.
Donor(s): Anna C. Cooke.†
Foundation type: Independent
Financial data (yr. ended 6/30/88): Assets, $13,447,570 (M); expenditures, $1,189,214, including $1,087,800 for 78 grants (high: $200,000; low: $500; average: $2,500-$25,000).
Purpose and activities: Giving primarily for culture and the arts, education, social services, including programs for youth and the elderly, the humanities, health, and the environment.
Types of support: Special projects, annual campaigns, equipment, research, publications, conferences and seminars, matching funds, operating budgets, renovation projects, seed money.
Limitations: Giving limited to HI or to organizations serving the people of HI. No support for churches or religious organizations, unless the trustees' "missionary forebears" were involved with them. No grants to individuals, or for scholarships or fellowships; no loans.
Publications: Program policy statement, application guidelines, annual report (including application guidelines).
Application information: Application form not required.
Initial approach: Telephone or proposal
Copies of proposal: 7
Deadline(s): 1st week of month preceding each board meeting
Board meeting date(s): 4th Wednesday in Jan., Apr., July, and Oct.
Final notification: 2 weeks after board meeting
Write: Jane R. Smith, Asst. Secy.
Officers: Richard A. Cooke, Jr.,* Pres.; Charles C. Spalding,* 1st V.P.; Samuel A. Cooke,* 2nd V.P.; Dora C. Derby,* Secy.; Hawaiian Trust Co., Ltd., Treas.
Trustees:* Betty P. Dunford, Catherine C. Summers.
Number of staff: 9
Employer Identification Number: 237120804

1693
Theo Davies Foundation
841 Bishop St.
P.O. Box 3020
Honolulu 96802

Established in 1964.
Foundation type: Independent
Financial data (yr. ended 06/30/88): Assets, $1,173,482 (M); gifts received, $190,000; expenditures, $97,925, including $94,263 for 36 grants (high: $30,500; low: $50).
Purpose and activities: Support primarily for higher and secondary education, and a community fund; some support also for cultural programs, youth agencies, and health.
Limitations: Giving primarily in HI.
Application information: Application form not required.
Deadline(s): None
Officers: David A. Heenan, Pres.; Martin J. Jaskot, V.P.
Employer Identification Number: 996009108

1694
First Hawaiian Foundation
165 South King St.
Honolulu 96813 (808) 525-8144

Established in 1975 in HI.
Donor(s): First Hawaiian Bank, and affiliated companies.
Foundation type: Company-sponsored
Financial data (yr. ended 12/31/88): Assets, $5,807,135 (M); gifts received, $1,808,004; expenditures, $741,137, including $733,536 for 50 grants (high: $127,031; low: $177; average: $500-$100,000).
Purpose and activities: Support for social services, education, cultural programs, health services, a church, and a community fund.
Types of support: General purposes, operating budgets, renovation projects, building funds, land acquisition, equipment.
Limitations: Giving primarily in HI.
Application information: Application form not required.
Initial approach: Letter
Deadline(s): None
Board meeting date(s): Minimum once every 2 months
Write: Herbert E. Wolff, Secy.
Officers and Directors:* Walter A. Dods, Jr.,* Pres.; Philip H. Ching,* V.P.; John A. Hoag,* V.P.; Donald G. Horner,* V.P.; Herbert E. Wolff,* Secy.; Howard H. Karr,* Treas.
Employer Identification Number: 237437822

1695
Mary D. and Walter F. Frear Eleemosynary Trust
c/o Bishop Trust Co., Ltd.
1000 Bishop St.
Honolulu 96813 (808) 523-2233
Mailing address: P.O. Box 2390, Honolulu, HI 96804-2390

Trust established in 1936 in HI.
Donor(s): Mary D. Frear,† Walter F. Frear.†
Foundation type: Independent
Financial data (yr. ended 12/31/88): Assets, $9,245,063 (M); gifts received, $18,248; expenditures, $497,741, including $439,325 for 125 grants (high: $10,000; low: $500).
Purpose and activities: Support for health and social welfare, youth development and child welfare, education, and music.
Types of support: Operating budgets, seed money, building funds, equipment, matching funds, scholarship funds, special projects, conferences and seminars, capital campaigns.
Limitations: Giving primarily in HI. No grants to individuals, or for endowment funds, reserve funds, travel, deficit financing, or publications; no loans.
Publications: Annual report (including application guidelines).
Application information: Application form not required.
Initial approach: Proposal
Copies of proposal: 4
Deadline(s): Jan. 15, Apr. 15, July 15, and Oct. 15
Board meeting date(s): Distribution committee meets in Mar., June, Sept., and Dec.; scholarship requests considered at Mar. meeting, capital requests in Dec.
Final notification: 2 to 3 months
Write: Lois C. Loomis, V.P. and Corp. Secy., Bishop Trust Co., Ltd.
Distribution Committee: Sharon McPhee, Chair.; Edwin L. Carter, Howard Hamamoto.
Trustee: Bishop Trust Co., Ltd.
Number of staff: None.
Employer Identification Number: 996002270

1696
The Hawaii Community Foundation
(Formerly The Hawaiian Foundation)
222 Merchant St., 2nd Fl.
Honolulu 96813 (808) 537-6333
FAX: (808) 521-6286

Established in 1916 in HI by trust resolution; incorporated in 1987; reorganizied in 1988.
Foundation type: Community
Financial data (yr. ended 12/31/89): Assets, $91,155,029 (M); gifts received, $2,806,312; expenditures, $1,628,951, including $1,357,149 for 112 grants (high: $200,000; low: $10; average: $500-$50,000) and $271,802 for grants to individuals (high: $8,000; low: $150).
Purpose and activities: To assist charitable, religious, and educational institutions by the distribution of funds, many of which have been restricted for specific purposes and in some instances for specific institutions. General fund priorities are problems of youth, families in crisis, environmental concerns, cultural and historic preservation, and community-based economic development; also provided: one-time only welfare assistance to needy adults or children and partial tuition support for learning disabled children.
Types of support: Operating budgets, seed money, equipment, technical assistance, scholarship funds, student aid, research, special projects, grants to individuals, conferences and seminars, consulting services, renovation projects.
Limitations: Giving limited to HI. No grants for annual campaigns, deficit financing, or land acquisition; no loans.
Publications: Program policy statement, application guidelines, informational brochure, annual report.
Application information: Application procedures vary with foundation's component funds.
Initial approach: Letter requesting applicaiton guidelines
Board meeting date(s): Jan. and July
Write: Jane Renfro Smith, C.E.O.

Officers and Board Members:* Jane Renfro Smith,* C.E.O; James F. Gary,* Pres.; Philip H. Ching,* V.P.; Samuel A. Cooke,* V.P.; Douglas Philpotts,* Secy.; Robert R. Midkiff,* Treas.; and 25 additional board members.
Trustees: Hawaiian Trust Co., Ltd., Bishop Trust Co., Ltd.
Number of staff: 8 full-time professional; 1 part-time professional; 6 full-time support; 1 part-time support.
Employer Identification Number: 990261283

1697
Hawaiian Electric Industries Charitable Foundation
P.O. Box 730
Honolulu 96808 (808) 543-7356

Established in 1984 in HI.
Donor(s): Hawaiian Electric Industries, Inc.
Foundation type: Company-sponsored
Financial data (yr. ended 12/31/89): Assets, $4,129,000 (M); gifts received, $5,000; expenditures, $899,000, including $812,000 for 201 grants (high: $25,000; low: $300; average: $300-$25,000), $25,000 for 15 grants to individuals (high: $1,200; low: $500; average: $500-$1,200) and $10,000 for 78 employee matching gifts.
Purpose and activities: Support for arts and culture, education, health and hospitals, social services and welfare, community development, the disadvantaged, and ecology.
Types of support: Employee matching gifts, capital campaigns, building funds, emergency funds, renovation projects, scholarship funds, conferences and seminars, matching funds, professorships, research, annual campaigns, employee-related scholarships.
Limitations: Giving primarily in HI. No support for political, religious, veterans', or fraternal organizations. No grants for operating budgets or maintenance activities.
Publications: Annual report (including application guidelines).
Application information: Application form not required.
Initial approach: Letter, with project data
Deadline(s): Dec. 1 and June 1
Board meeting date(s): Feb. and Aug.
Write: Ted Souza
Officers and Directors:* C. Dudley Pratt, Jr., Pres.; Robert F. Clarke,* V.P.; George T. Iwahiro, V.P.; Harwood D. Williamson,* V.P.; Betty Ann Splinter,* Secy.; Glenn Hong,* Treas.; John D. Field, Constance Lau, Diane Plotts, Jeffrey Watanabe.
Number of staff: 1 part-time professional; 1 part-time support.
Employer Identification Number: 990230697

1698
Holy Land Charitable Trust ⌑
c/o Elliot H. Loden
737 Bishop St., Suite 2990
Honolulu 96813

Established in 1980.
Foundation type: Independent
Financial data (yr. ended 12/31/88): Assets, $2,324,195 (M); expenditures, $338,932, including $300,000 for 1 grant.
Purpose and activities: Giving to organizations in Israel, and for a synagogue.
Limitations: Giving primarily in HI.
Trustees: Richard F. Behnke, Elliot H. Loden.
Employer Identification Number: 990187302

1699
The May Templeton Hopper Foundation
1412 Whitney St.
Honolulu 96822 (808) 944-2807

Established originally as the King's Daughter's Circle in HI in 1906; incorporated as a private foundation in 1978.
Foundation type: Independent
Financial data (yr. ended 12/31/88): Assets, $7,069,793 (M); gifts received, $23,620; expenditures, $492,234, including $390,024 for grants to individuals (average: $3,000).
Purpose and activities: Medical, housing, and general welfare support for needy, aged individuals who are at least 62 years of age and have been residents of HI for a minimum of 5 years.
Types of support: Grants to individuals, emergency funds, special projects.
Limitations: Giving limited to HI. No support for education. No grants for operating budgets, or for administrative or organizational expenses; no loans.
Publications: Annual report, program policy statement, application guidelines.
Application information: Application form required.
Initial approach: Telephone
Copies of proposal: 2
Deadline(s): 2 weeks before board meeting
Board meeting date(s): Monthly
Final notification: 3rd Thursday of the month
Write: Diana H. Lord, Pres.
Officers: Ethel U. O'Neil,* Chair.; Diana H. Lord, Pres.; Nancy Wright,* 1st V.P.; Esther Temple,* 2nd V.P.; Jeanne E. Taylor, Secy.; First Hawaiian Bank, Treas.
Directors:* Anne Ball, Margaret Blom, Iris Hallaran, Mansel Law, Mary Livingston.
Number of staff: 1 part-time support.
Employer Identification Number: 990073507

1700
Kaiulani Home for Girls Trust
c/o Hawaiian Trust Co., Ltd.
P.O. Box 3170
Honolulu 96802
Application address: c/o Hawaii Community Foundation, 212 Merchant St., Suite 330, Honolulu, HI 96813; Tel.: (808) 537-6333

Established in 1948 in HI.
Foundation type: Independent
Financial data (yr. ended 03/31/89): Assets, $1,390,392 (M); expenditures, $91,806, including $63,675 for 88 grants to individuals (high: $1,500; low: $100; average: $500-$1,150).
Purpose and activities: Scholarships for students who are residents of HI and plan to attend an accredited two- or four-year college.
Types of support: Student aid.
Limitations: Giving limited to HI.
Publications: Program policy statement, application guidelines.
Application information: Application form required.
Deadline(s): Mar. 1
Board meeting date(s): May
Write: Caroline Sharman
Trustees: Cordelia MacLaughlin, Caroline Mee, Hawaiian Trust Co., Ltd.
Number of staff: 3
Employer Identification Number: 996003331

1701
William K. H. Mau Foundation ⌑ ☆
2270 Kalakuaa, Suite 1800
Honolulu 96815

Donor(s): William K.H. Mau.
Foundation type: Independent
Financial data (yr. ended 2/28/89): Assets, $613,262 (M); gifts received, $50,000; expenditures, $305,423, including $302,850 for 14 grants (high: $250,000; low: $250).
Purpose and activities: Giving primarily for secondary and higher education, community services and development.
Limitations: Giving primarily in Honolulu, HI. No grants to individuals.
Application information: Contributes only to pre-selected organizations. Applications not accepted.
Officers and Directors: William K.H. Mau, Pres.; Jean R. Mau, V.P.; Cynthia M. Seu, Secy.; Leighton Mau, Treas.; Letitia S.L. Mau, Lynette L.L. Mau, Milton S.K. Mau.
Employer Identification Number: 990258720

1702
McInerny Foundation ▼
c/o Bishop Trust Co., Ltd.
1000 Bishop St.
Honolulu 96813 (808) 523-2233
Mailing address: P.O. Box 2390, Honolulu, HI 96804-2390

Trust established in 1937 in HI.
Donor(s): William H. McInerny,† James D. McInerny,† Ella McInerny.†
Foundation type: Independent
Financial data (yr. ended 09/30/89): Assets, $30,305,311 (M); expenditures, $2,110,351, including $1,584,981 for 122 grants (high: $100,000; low: $2,000; average: $5,000-$100,000).
Purpose and activities: Emphasis on education, youth and social services, health and rehabilitation, culture and the arts.
Types of support: Operating budgets, continuing support, seed money, building funds, equipment, matching funds, scholarship funds, special projects.
Limitations: Giving limited to HI. No support for religious institutions. No grants to individuals, or for endowment funds, deficit financing, or research; no loans.
Publications: Annual report (including application guidelines).
Application information: Application form required for capital or scholarship funds. Application form not required.
Initial approach: Proposal
Copies of proposal: 7
Deadline(s): Jan. 15 for scholarships; July 15 for capital fund drives; none for others

Board meeting date(s): Distribution committee generally meets monthly
Final notification: 2 months
Write: Mrs. Lois C. Loomis, V.P. and Corp. Secy., Bishop Trust Co., Ltd.
Distribution Committee: Edwin L. Carter, Chair.; Henry B. Clark, Jr., Vice-Chair.; Gerry Ching.
Trustee: Bishop Trust Co., Ltd.
Number of staff: 2
Employer Identification Number: 996002356

1703
The O. L. Moore Foundation ⌑
100 Ridge Rd.
Lahaina, Maui 96761

Established in 1959 in IL.
Donor(s): O.L. Moore.†
Foundation type: Independent
Financial data (yr. ended 12/31/88): Assets, $1,501,170 (M); expenditures, $93,069, including $84,265 for 25 grants (high: $10,000; low: $500).
Purpose and activities: Support for higher education, health associations and services, cultural programs, and Protestant religious organizations.
Types of support: Continuing support.
Limitations: Giving primarily in HI and KY.
Application information: Contributes only to pre-selected organizations. Applications not accepted.
Write: J. Edward Moore, Pres.
Officers and Directors: J. Edward Moore, Pres.; William E. Moore, V.P.; Dee Anne Mahuna, Secy.; Dorothy D. Moore, Treas.; James C. Luckey, Thomas C. Thayer, Howard E. Trent, Jr.
Employer Identification Number: 366101149

1704
Persis Hawaii Foundation ☆
605 Kapiolani Blvd.
Honolulu 96813 (808) 525-8050

Established in 1987.
Donor(s): Persis Corp.
Foundation type: Company-sponsored
Financial data (yr. ended 12/31/89): Assets, $12,333 (M); gifts received, $159,500; expenditures, $139,875, including $138,420 for 30 grants (high: $50,000; low: $500).
Purpose and activities: Giving primarily for the arts; support also for education, a community fund, and social services and youth agencies.
Types of support: General purposes.
Limitations: Giving primarily in HI, with emphasis on Honolulu; Bellevue and Port Angeles, WA; and Knoxville, Maryville, and Nashville, TN.
Application information: Application form not required.
Initial approach: Letter
Deadline(s): None
Board meeting date(s): Dec.
Final notification: Jan.
Write: Kenneth Uemura, Treas.
Officers: Thurston Twigg-Smith, Pres.; David Twigg-Smith, V.P.; Kenneth Uemura, Treas.
Employer Identification Number: 990255225

1705
PRI Foundation ☆
Bishop Trust Co.
P.O. Box 2390
Honolulu 96804 (808) 547-3136
Application address: P.O. Box 3379, Honolulu, HI 96842

Established in 1986 in HI.
Foundation type: Company-sponsored
Financial data (yr. ended 12/31/87): Assets, $166,330 (M); gifts received, $783,797; expenditures, $626,358, including $622,416 for grants.
Purpose and activities: Support for culture and the arts, education, health, religion, social welfare, and youth services.
Types of support: Equipment, renovation projects, capital campaigns.
Limitations: Giving primarily in HI and other areas of company operations. No support for sports. No grants to individuals, or for operating support to Aloha United Way-supported organizations, educational institutions for scholarships, or subsidization of travel.
Publications: Annual report (including application guidelines), application guidelines.
Application information: Application form not required.
Initial approach: Proposal
Copies of proposal: 1
Deadline(s): None
Board meeting date(s): Quarterly
Write: Linda Howe, Secy.
Trustee: Bishop Trust Co., Ltd.
Number of staff: 1 part-time professional; 1 part-time support.
Employer Identification Number: 990248628

1706
Sophie Russell Testamentary Trust
c/o Bishop Trust Co., Ltd.
1000 Bishop St.
Honolulu 96813 (808) 523-2233
Mailing address: P.O. Box 2390, Honolulu, HI 96804-2390

Trust established in 1947 in HI.
Donor(s): Sophie Russell.†
Foundation type: Independent
Financial data (yr. ended 03/31/89): Assets, $1,427,141 (M); expenditures, $81,579, including $70,287 for 10 grants (high: $10,000; low: $2,000; average: $2,000-$10,000).
Purpose and activities: Giving primarily to the Hawaiian Humane Society, and institutions providing nursing care to the physically and mentally handicapped.
Types of support: General purposes, building funds, equipment, operating budgets.
Limitations: Giving limited to HI. No grants to individuals, or for endowment funds, reserve purposes, deficit financing, or travel.
Publications: Annual report (including application guidelines).
Application information: Application form not required.
Initial approach: Letter
Copies of proposal: 4
Deadline(s): Jan. 15
Board meeting date(s): Annually
Final notification: 2 to 3 months
Write: Lois C. Loomis, V.P., Bishop Trust Co., Ltd.
Distribution Committee: Edwin L. Carter, Chair.; Howard Hamamoto.
Trustee: Bishop Trust Co., Ltd.
Number of staff: 1 part-time professional; 1 part-time support.
Employer Identification Number: 996002398

1707
Servco Foundation ⌑ ☆
990 Fort St. Mall, Suite 500
P.O. Box 2788
Honolulu 96803 (808) 521-6511

Established in 1986 in HI.
Donor(s): Servco Pacific, Inc.
Foundation type: Company-sponsored
Financial data (yr. ended 6/30/88): Assets, $1,277,249 (M); gifts received, $721,100; expenditures, $29,834, including $29,000 for grants to individuals.
Purpose and activities: Awards scholarships for higher education to spouses and children of Servco Pacific, Inc. employees.
Types of support: Employee-related scholarships.
Limitations: Giving limited to HI.
Application information: Application form required.
Deadline(s): June 15
Write: Scholarship Selection Committee
Officers and Directors:* George J. Fukunaga,* Chair.; Thomas I. Fukunaga,* Pres.; Gerald K. Harbottle,* V.P.; Jean H. Nakagawa,* V.P.; George S. Sakurai,* V.P.; Edith M. Endo, Secy.; Patrick D. Ching, Treas.
Employer Identification Number: 990248256

1708
Gertrude S. Straub Trust Estate
c/o Hawaiian Trust Co., Ltd.
P.O. Box 3170
Honolulu 96802
Scholarship application address: c/o Hawaii Community Foundation, 212 Merchant St., Suite 330, Honolulu, HI 96813; Tel.: (808) 537-6333

Established in 1966.
Donor(s): Gertrude S. Straub.†
Foundation type: Independent
Financial data (yr. ended 03/31/89): Assets, $3,588,711 (M); expenditures, $224,885, including $176,235 for 72 grants to individuals (high: $4,800; low: $300; average: $500-$4,000).
Purpose and activities: Scholarship grants to HI high school graduates to attend mainland colleges and major in a subject relating to international understanding and cooperation and world peace.
Types of support: Student aid.
Limitations: Giving limited to HI.
Publications: Program policy statement, application guidelines.
Application information: Application form required.
Initial approach: Telephone or letter of inquiry
Copies of proposal: 1
Deadline(s): Submit application preferably between Jan. 1 and Mar. 1; deadline Mar. 1
Board meeting date(s): Apr.

Write: Caroline Sharman, Admin.
Trustee: Hawaiian Trust Co., Ltd.
Number of staff: 3
Employer Identification Number: 996003243

1709
A. & E. Vidinha Charitable Trust ☆
c/o Bishop Trust Co.
Box 2390
Honolulu 96804-2390 (808) 523-2233

Established in 1989 in HI.
Donor(s): Antone Vidinha,† Edene Vidinha.†
Foundation type: Independent
Financial data (yr. ended 06/30/90): Assets, $4,021,116 (M); expenditures, $237,000, including $230,000 for grants.
Purpose and activities: Giving primarily for hospitals and health associations, Protestant churches, and higher education.
Types of support: General purposes, operating budgets, scholarship funds.
Limitations: Giving primarily in HI. No grants to individuals.
Application information: Contributes with preference to pre-selected organizations. Application form not required.
Copies of proposal: 4
Write: Lois C. Loomis, V.P., Bishop Trust Co., Ltd.
Trustee: Bishop Trust Co., Ltd.
Employer Identification Number: 990273993

1710
J. Watumull Estate, Inc. ⌑
c/o First Hawaiian Bank
P.O. Box 3200
Honolulu 96847
Application address: 1341 Kapiolani Blvd., Honolulu, HI 96814; Tel.: (808) 955-1144

Donor(s): Gulab Watumull, Watumull Brothers, Ltd.
Foundation type: Independent
Financial data (yr. ended 12/31/88): Assets, $5,785,813 (M); expenditures, $265,362, including $220,000 for 66 grants (high: $50,000; low: $1,000; average: $1,000-$5,000).
Purpose and activities: Emphasis on education, including higher education, and on an arts academy and museum.
Types of support: Scholarship funds, endowment funds, special projects, building funds, general purposes.
Limitations: Giving primarily in HI.
Application information: Application form required.
Initial approach: Proposal
Deadline(s): None
Final notification: 2 weeks
Write: Gulab Watumull, Pres.
Officers and Directors: Gulab Watumull, Pres.; Khubchand Watumull, V.P.; Clinton R. Ashford, Secy.; Sundri R. Watumull, Treas.
Employer Identification Number: 510205431

1711
Elsie H. Wilcox Foundation ☆
c/o Bishop Trust Co., Ltd.
P.O. Box 2390
Honolulu 96804-2390 (808) 523-2233

Established in 1938 in HI.
Donor(s): Elsie H. Wilcox.†
Foundation type: Independent
Financial data (yr. ended 12/31/89): Assets, $1,062,974 (M); expenditures, $64,615, including $55,800 for 19 grants (high: $5,000; low: $1,500; average: $1,500-$5,000).
Purpose and activities: Giving primarily for education, health associations, and social services, including programs for the handicapped.
Types of support: General purposes, equipment, renovation projects, building funds.
Limitations: Giving primarily in Kauai, HI. No grants to individuals, or for endowments.
Publications: Annual report (including application guidelines).
Application information: Application form not required.
Initial approach: Proposal (2-3 pages)
Copies of proposal: 4
Deadline(s): Oct. 1
Board meeting date(s): Nov.
Final notification: 2 months
Write: Lois C. Loomis, V.P., Bishop Trust Co., Ltd.
Distribution Committtee: Katherine G. Richardson, Chair.; Edwin L. Carter, Aletha Kaohi.
Trustee: Bishop Trust Co., Ltd.
Number of staff: 1 part-time professional; 1 part-time support.
Employer Identification Number: 996002441

1712
G. N. Wilcox Trust
c/o Bishop Trust Co., Ltd.
1000 Bishop St.
Honolulu 96813-2390 (808) 523-2233
Mailing address: P.O. Box 2390, Honolulu, HI 96804-2390

Trust established in 1916 in HI.
Donor(s): George N. Wilcox.†
Foundation type: Independent
Financial data (yr. ended 12/31/89): Assets, $13,646,780 (M); expenditures, $900,902, including $804,377 for 137 grants (high: $50,000; low: $500; average: $1,000-$10,000).
Purpose and activities: Support for education and social service agencies, including child welfare; grants also for arts and culture, care of the sick, health agencies, the aged, community funds, delinquency and crime prevention, family services, and Protestant church support.
Types of support: Seed money, building funds, equipment, matching funds, scholarship funds, general purposes, continuing support, capital campaigns, special projects.
Limitations: Giving limited to HI, particularly the island of Kauai. No support for government agencies or organizations substantially supported by government funds. No grants to individuals, or for endowment funds (except endowments for scholarships), reserve funds, research, publications, or deficit financing; no direct student aid or scholarships; no loans.
Publications: Annual report (including application guidelines).
Application information: Scholarship requests considered at Mar. meeting; capital requests considered at Dec. meeting. Application form not required.
Initial approach: Telephone or proposal
Copies of proposal: 5
Deadline(s): Jan. 15, Apr. 15, July 15, and Oct. 15
Board meeting date(s): Mar., June, Sept., and Dec.
Final notification: 2-3 months
Write: Mrs. Lois C. Loomis, V.P. and Corp. Secy., Bishop Trust Co., Ltd.
Committee on Beneficiaries: Edwin L. Carter, Chair.; Gale Fisher Carswell, Aletha Kaohi.
Trustee: Bishop Trust Co., Ltd.
Number of staff: None.
Employer Identification Number: 996002445

1713
S. W. Wilcox Trust
c/o Bishop Trust Co., Ltd.
1000 Bishop St.
Honolulu 96813 (808) 245-2822
Mailing address: P.O. Box 2096, Puhi-Rural Station, Lihue, HI 96766

Trust established in 1921 in HI.
Donor(s): Samuel Whitney Wilcox.†
Foundation type: Independent
Financial data (yr. ended 12/31/88): Assets, $4,126,104 (M); expenditures, $187,912, including $172,500 for 15 grants (high: $50,000; low: $2,000; average: $1,000-$50,000).
Purpose and activities: Funds presently committed to the support of local health, welfare, and educational organizations.
Types of support: Continuing support, seed money, building funds.
Limitations: Giving limited to Kauai and Big Island, HI. No grants to individuals, or for research programs, scholarships, fellowships, or matching gifts; no loans.
Application information: No unsolicited proposals considered. Applications not accepted.
Board meeting date(s): Dec. and as required
Write: David W. Pratt, Trustee
Trustees: Gale Fisher Carswell, Pam Dohrman, David W. Pratt.
Number of staff: None.
Employer Identification Number: 996002547

1714
C. S. Wo Foundation ⌑ ☆
P.O. Box 1417
Honolulu 96806-1417 (808) 545-5966

Established in 1960.
Donor(s): C.S. Wo & Sons, Inc., James C. Wo, Robert C. Wo.
Foundation type: Independent
Financial data (yr. ended 5/31/89): Assets, $1,210,352 (M); gifts received, $103,000; expenditures, $146,834, including $138,919 for 37 grants (high: $30,000; low: $100).
Purpose and activities: Support primarily for Buddhist and other religious organizations, higher and other education, cultural programs, and social services.

Limitations: Giving primarily in HI. No grants to individuals.
Application information:
Initial approach: Letter
Deadline(s): None
Write: Robert C. Wo, V.P.
Officers and Directors: Bernice Y. Ching, Pres.; Robert C. Wo, V.P.; James C. Wo, Secy.-Treas.; Betty Wo, Juanita Wo.
Employer Identification Number: 996009140

1715
Hans and Clara Davis Zimmerman Foundation
c/o Hawaiian Trust Co., Ltd.
P.O. Box 3170
Honolulu 96802 (808) 537-6333
Application address: c/o Hawaii Community Foundation, 212 Merchant St., Suite 330, Honolulu, HI 96813

Established in 1963.
Donor(s): Hans Zimmerman,† Clara Zimmerman.†
Foundation type: Independent
Financial data (yr. ended 12/31/89): Assets, $6,205,880 (M); expenditures, $437,228, including $336,975 for 158 grants to individuals (high: $3,500; low: $500; average: $100-$1,200).
Purpose and activities: Giving for scholarships, with preference given to students majoring in medicine, nursing, or related health fields.
Types of support: Student aid.
Limitations: Giving primarily in HI.
Publications: Program policy statement, application guidelines.
Application information: Request application forms by Feb. 1. Application form required.
Initial approach: Proposal
Copies of proposal: 1
Deadline(s): Mar. 1
Board meeting date(s): May
Write: Caroline Sharman
Trustee: Hawaiian Trust Co., Ltd.
Scholarship Committee: Jetta M. Zimmerman, Chair.; Mary V. Coyne, Leon Julian, Harold Nicolaus.
Number of staff: 3
Employer Identification Number: 996006669

IDAHO

1716
J. A. & Kathryn Albertson Foundation, Inc. ⌑ ☆
380 East Parkcenter Blvd.
Boise 83706-3962

Established in 1966.
Foundation type: Independent
Financial data (yr. ended 12/31/88): Assets, $796,152 (M); expenditures, $251,095, including $241,798 for 2 grants (high: $238,798; low: $3,000).
Purpose and activities: Support primarily for historic preservation and community development.
Officers and Directors: J.A. Albertson, Pres.; Kathryn Albertson, V.P.; Minnie O. Armstrong, Secy.-Treas.; Everett L. Doty, Barbara Newman, Joseph B. Scott, Robert I. Troxell.
Employer Identification Number: 826012000

1717
Larry Barnes Charitable Foundation ⌑
P.O. Box 2797
Boise 83701-2797

Established in 1977 in ID.
Foundation type: Independent
Financial data (yr. ended 12/31/88): Assets, $1,015,812 (M); gifts received, $633,545; expenditures, $96,487, including $91,899 for 95 grants (high: $12,000; low: $17).
Purpose and activities: Giving primarily for Christian institutions and missionary efforts.
Trustees: Frank B. Barnes, Jon B. Barnes, Larry Barnes.
Employer Identification Number: 820330394

1718
The Leland D. Beckman Foundation ⌑
c/o Holden, Kidwell, Hahn & Crapo
P.O. Box 50130
Idaho Falls 83405-0129 (208) 523-0620

Established in 1965 in ID.
Foundation type: Independent
Financial data (yr. ended 12/31/88): Assets, $1,825,921 (M); expenditures, $70,890, including $50,000 for 11 grants (high: $20,000; low: $1,500).
Purpose and activities: Support primarily for a child development workshop, elementary, secondary and vocational technical educational institutions, and the arts.
Types of support: Equipment, operating budgets.
Limitations: Giving primarily in Idaho Falls, ID.
Application information: Application form not required.
Initial approach: Letter
Deadline(s): None
Write: Stephen E. Martin, Trustee
Trustees: William T. Holden, Stephen E. Martin.
Employer Identification Number: 826009504

1719
CHC Foundation ⌑ ☆
P.O. Box 1644
Idaho Falls 83403

Established in 1984 in ID.
Foundation type: Company-sponsored
Financial data (yr. ended 12/31/88): Assets, $8,320,936 (M); expenditures, $596,217, including $464,531 for 28 grants (high: $219,244; low: $750).
Purpose and activities: Support primarily for a municipality and public libraries.
Limitations: Giving limited to ID. No grants to individuals.
Application information:
Initial approach: Letter or proposal
Deadline(s): None
Write: Gerald Scheid, Exec. Dir.
Officers: Joan Hahn, Pres.; Raymond Pullen, V.P.; Milt Adams, Secy.; Janice Matthews, Treas.; Gerald Scheid, Exec. Dir.
Directors: Donald Bjornson, Joan Chesbro, Ernest Craner, Linda Mortin, Anne Voillegne.
Employer Identification Number: 820211282

1720
Laura Moore Cunningham Foundation, Inc. ⌑
510 Main
Boise 83702-5932

Incorporated in 1964 in ID.
Donor(s): Laura Moore Cunningham.†
Foundation type: Independent
Financial data (yr. ended 08/31/89): Assets, $11,276,605 (M); expenditures, $370,085, including $346,877 for 32 grants (high: $50,000; low: $2,000).
Purpose and activities: Emphasis on higher education, particularly for business scholarship funds; support also for hospitals and child welfare.
Types of support: Building funds, endowment funds, equipment, scholarship funds, special projects.
Limitations: Giving limited to ID. No grants to individuals.
Application information: Application form required.
Copies of proposal: 3
Deadline(s): Feb. 28
Board meeting date(s): Spring
Write: Joan Davidson Carley, Secy.-Treas.
Officers and Directors:* Harry Little Bettis,* Pres.; Marjorie Moore Davidson,* V.P.; Joan Davidson Carley,* Secy.-Treas.
Employer Identification Number: 826008294

1721
Daugherty Foundation ⌑
c/o West One Bank, Idaho, N.A.
P.O. Box 7928
Boise 83707
Application address: P.O. Box 69, Idaho Falls, ID 83402

Established in 1965.
Donor(s): West One Bank, Idaho, N.A.
Foundation type: Independent
Financial data (yr. ended 12/31/88): Assets, $5,236,040 (M); expenditures, $739,783, including $699,948 for 29 grants (high: $135,487; low: $1,000).
Purpose and activities: Giving for hospitals, youth organizations, child welfare, and a historical village.
Types of support: Equipment, matching funds.
Limitations: Giving limited to eastern ID.
Publications: Informational brochure (including application guidelines).
Application information: Application form required.
Initial approach: Letter
Deadline(s): July 31
Write: Hal Peterson, Trust Mgr., West One Bank, Idaho, N.A.
Trustee: West One Bank, Idaho, N.A.
Employer Identification Number: 826010665

1722
The Walter and Leona Dufresne Foundation, Inc. ¤
1150 West State St.
Boise 83702

Incorporated in 1964 in ID.
Donor(s): Walter Dufresne.†
Foundation type: Independent
Financial data (yr. ended 12/31/88): Assets, $1,348,101 (M); expenditures, $92,053, including $76,000 for 7 grants (high: $34,000; low: $2,000).
Purpose and activities: Support primarily for higher education.
Limitations: Giving primarily in ID.
Officers: Jess Hawley, Pres.; John T. Hawley, V.P.; Fred K. O'Brien, Treas.
Employer Identification Number: 820266697

1723
The Kasiska Family Foundation ¤ ☆
P.O. Box 234
Pocatello 83204-0234

Established in 1987 in ID.
Foundation type: Independent
Financial data (yr. ended 12/31/88): Assets, $6,214,295 (M); expenditures, $472,366, including $224,580 for 2 grants (high: $218,000; low: $6,580).
Purpose and activities: Support for a university foundation and a public school district.
Types of support: Scholarship funds, equipment.
Limitations: Giving primarily in Pocatello, ID. No grants to individuals.
Application information: Contributes only to pre-selected organizations. Applications not accepted.
Officers: Wesley F. Merrill, Chair.; Neal A. Jordan, Vice-Chair.; Edward J. Barrett, Secy.
Trustee: Tracy Collins Bank & Trust Co.
Employer Identification Number: 820414752

1724
Harry W. Morrison Foundation, Inc. ¤
P.O. Box 7808
Boise 83729 (208) 345-5000

Incorporated in 1952 in ID.
Donor(s): Harry W. Morrison.†
Foundation type: Independent
Financial data (yr. ended 12/31/88): Assets, $6,638,446 (M); expenditures, $694,432, including $598,635 for grants.
Purpose and activities: Giving primarily for the Morrison Center for the Performing Arts; support also for higher education.
Types of support: Building funds, renovation projects, general purposes.
Limitations: Giving primarily in Boise, ID. No grants to individuals.
Application information:
Initial approach: Proposal
Deadline(s): Mar. 1
Board meeting date(s): Annually in May
Write: Velma V. Morrison, Pres.
Officers: Velma V. Morrison, Pres.; Judith V. Roberts, V.P.; Verna Von Steen, Secy.; Linda Klingner, Treas.
Directors: John J. Hockberger, Edith Miller Klein, Fred Norman.
Number of staff: 1 part-time professional; 1 part-time support.
Employer Identification Number: 826008111

1725
Morrison-Knudsen Employees Foundation, Inc.
One Morrison-Knudsen Plaza
Boise 83729 (208) 386-5000

Established in 1947 in ID.
Foundation type: Company-sponsored
Financial data (yr. ended 12/31/88): Assets, $2,671,009 (M); gifts received, $3,255; expenditures, $155,139, including $35,000 for 5 grants (high: $10,000; low: $5,000) and $117,917 for 26 grants to individuals (high: $9,000; low: $531).
Purpose and activities: Giving primarily in the form of monthly stipends to retired and/or disabled employees of the Morrison-Knudsen Co.; support also for medical research.
Types of support: Grants to individuals.
Application information: Application form required.
Copies of proposal: 1
Deadline(s): None
Write: M.M. Puckett, Secy.-Treas.
Officers: E.J. Gorman,* Pres.; M.J. Shirley,* V.P.; M.M. Puckett, Secy.-Treas.
Directors:* S.G. Hanks.
Number of staff: None.
Employer Identification Number: 826005410

1726
Macauley and Helen Dow Whiting Foundation ¤
P.O. Box 1980
Sun Valley 83353

Incorporated in 1957 in MI.
Foundation type: Independent
Financial data (yr. ended 12/31/88): Assets, $3,953,219 (M); expenditures, $100,309, including $60,828 for 14 grants (high: $15,000; low: $828).
Purpose and activities: Emphasis on higher education and hospitals; support also to environmental and energy conservation organizations; grants only to institutions with which trustees are familiar.
Limitations: No grants to individuals.
Application information: Application form not required.
Initial approach: Letter
Copies of proposal: 1
Deadline(s): None
Board meeting date(s): At least twice a year
Write: Macauley Whiting, Pres.
Officers and Trustees: Macauley Whiting, Pres.; Mary Macauley Whiting, Secy.; Helen Dow Whiting, Treas.; Sara Whiting.
Employer Identification Number: 237418814

1727
Claude R. and Ethel B. Whittenberger Foundation
P.O. Box 1073
Caldwell 83605 (208) 459-0091
Additional tel.: (208) 459-3402

Established in 1970 in ID; commenced grantmaking activities in 1973.
Donor(s): Ethel B. Whittenberger.†
Foundation type: Independent
Financial data (yr. ended 12/31/89): Assets, $3,502,848 (M); expenditures, $229,752, including $183,147 for 34 grants (high: $36,629; low: $625; average: $1,000-$5,000).
Purpose and activities: Giving for youth and children, and higher and secondary education; support also for cultural programs and public libraries.
Types of support: Equipment, scholarship funds.
Limitations: Giving limited to ID. No grants to individuals, or for endowment funds.
Publications: Program policy statement, application guidelines, informational brochure.
Application information: Application form required.
Initial approach: Letter requesting application form
Copies of proposal: 5
Deadline(s): Sept. 1
Board meeting date(s): Apr., July, Sept., and Nov.
Final notification: Dec.
Write: William J. Rankin, Chair., or Margaret Gigray, Vice-Chair.
Officers: William J. Rankin, Chair.; Margaret Gigray, Vice-Chair.; Joe Miller, Secy.
Directors: Robert A. Johnson, D. Whitman Jones.
Employer Identification Number: 237092604

ILLINOIS

1728
The Clara Abbott Foundation ▼
One Abbott Park Rd.
Abbott Park 60064 (312) 937-1091

Established in 1940 in IL.
Donor(s): Wallace Abbott, M.D.,† Mrs. Wallace Abbott.†
Foundation type: Independent
Financial data (yr. ended 12/31/89): Assets, $93,030,000 (M); gifts received, $7,000; expenditures, $3,938,829, including $3,004,387 for 2,047 grants to individuals (high: $44,000; low: $100) and $911,000 for 361 loans to individuals.
Purpose and activities: Grants to individuals for scholarships, and grants and loans to individuals in financial hardship; recipients must be employees or retirees of Abbott Laboratories or members of their families.
Types of support: Employee-related scholarships, grants to individuals, loans.
Application information: Application form required.

Deadline(s): Scholarship application deadline, Mar. 16; for other financial aid, no deadline
Board meeting date(s): Apr. and Dec.
Final notification: Up to 10 working days
Write: David C. Jefferies, Exec. Dir.
Officers: Charles S. Brown,* Pres.; Laurence R. Lee,* V.P.; Eugene L. Worock,* V.P.; Paul E. Roge, Secy.; Barry R. Wojtak, Treas.; David C. Jefferies, Exec. Dir.
Directors:* Patricia Coles, John Condon, Robert Dietmeyer, Lestter E. Hammar, Lucille Heine, John C. Kane, Bernard H. Semler, Dale E. Stavlo, Rudolph Sundberg, Marcia A. Thomas.
Number of staff: 5
Employer Identification Number: 366069632

1729
Abbott Laboratories Fund ▼
Dept. 379, Bldg. 14C
One Abbott Park Rd.
North Chicago 60064-3500 (708) 937-7075
Additional tel.: (708) 937-8686

Incorporated in 1951 in IL.
Donor(s): Abbott Laboratories, and others.
Foundation type: Company-sponsored
Financial data (yr. ended 12/31/88): Assets, $24,684,514 (M); gifts received, $17,000; expenditures, $2,145,917, including $1,651,837 for grants and $463,636 for employee matching gifts.
Purpose and activities: Grants primarily to institutions for higher education, including medicine, pharmacy, and nursing, and for medical research and selected health and welfare causes; also matches contributions of company employees and retirees to higher educational institutions and hospitals.
Types of support: Operating budgets, continuing support, scholarship funds, research, employee matching gifts.
Limitations: Giving primarily in areas of company operations. No support for social organizations, religious institutions, or fundraising events. No grants to individuals, or for deficit financing, land acquisition, internships, employee-related scholarships, exchange programs, fellowships, or publications; no loans.
Publications: Program policy statement.
Application information: Application form not required.
Initial approach: Letter or proposal
Copies of proposal: 1
Deadline(s): None
Board meeting date(s): Apr. and Dec.
Final notification: 6 to 8 weeks
Write: Administrator
Board Members: D.L. Burnham, O.R. Edwards, K.W. Farmer, R.B. Hamilton, J.A. Hanley, R.S. Janicki, John C. Kane, J.G. Kringel, D.A. Thompson.
Number of staff: 1 full-time professional; 1 part-time professional; 1 full-time support; 1 part-time support.
Employer Identification Number: 366069793

1730
Lester S. Abelson Foundation
30 North LaSalle St., Suite 2024
Chicago 60602-2504

Established in 1966 in IL.
Donor(s): Lester S. Abelson,† and members of the Abelson family.
Foundation type: Independent
Financial data (yr. ended 12/31/88): Assets, $1,586,216 (M); gifts received, $36,738; expenditures, $128,109, including $126,160 for 145 grants (high: $40,000; low: $10).
Purpose and activities: Support primarily for cultural programs, including music, theater, and museums and the fine arts; support also for environmental organizations and education.
Limitations: Giving primarily in IL. No grants to individuals.
Application information: Contributes only to pre-selected organizations. Applications not accepted.
Write: Stuart Abelson
Officers: Hope A. Abelson, Pres.; Katherine A. Abelson, V.P.; Stuart R. Abelson, Secy.-Treas.
Employer Identification Number: 366153888

1731
ACP Foundation ⌑
30 Bridlewood Rd.
Northbrook 60062-4702 (312) 272-3034

Established in 1951 in IL.
Foundation type: Independent
Financial data (yr. ended 12/31/87): Assets, $1,094,749 (M); expenditures, $72,037, including $67,654 for grants.
Purpose and activities: Giving primarily for social services and higher education; support also for the fine arts and theaters.
Application information:
Write: A.C. Buehler, Jr.
Officers and Directors: A.C. Buehler, Jr., Pres.; Carl Buehler, V.P.; Pat Buehler, Secy.; A.C. Buehler III, Treas.
Employer Identification Number: 366046903

1732
Adreani Foundation ⌑ ☆
7458 North Harlem Ave.
Chicago 60648

Established in 1978.
Donor(s): Raymond J. Adreani.
Foundation type: Independent
Financial data (yr. ended 11/30/88): Assets, $1,136,682 (M); gifts received, $165,000; expenditures, $63,084, including $55,650 for 73 grants (high: $12,500; low: $50).
Purpose and activities: Giving primarily for hospitals and social services; support also for education, health associations, and Christian churches.
Limitations: Giving primarily in IL.
Director: Raymond J. Adreani.
Employer Identification Number: 363059439

1733
G. J. Aigner Foundation, Inc. ⌑
5617 Dempster St.
Morton Grove 60053 (312) 966-5782

Foundation incorporated in 1957 in IL.
Donor(s): George J. Aigner,† Henrietta Aigner,† A.C. Aigner.
Foundation type: Company-sponsored
Financial data (yr. ended 4/30/88): Assets, $2,008,181 (M); gifts received, $15,000; expenditures, $86,738, including $32,820 for 13 grants (high: $10,000; low: $250), $20,155 for 29 grants to individuals (high: $1,000; low: $300) and $25,000 for loans.
Purpose and activities: Support for innovative programs to equip the disabled and mentally retarded to be self-supporting; therapy programs for families with histories of child abuse and teenagers with conduct disorders; emergency food assistance; and scholarships in business, liberal arts, theology, and for children of company employees.
Types of support: Employee-related scholarships, seed money, special projects, emergency funds.
Publications: Annual report.
Application information: Application forms available upon request. Application form required.
Deadline(s): Apr. 15 for scholarships
Write: Craig P. Colmar, Treas.
Officers and Directors: Rev. Fred Aigner, Pres.; Craig P. Colmar, Treas.; Joyce Aigner Laurence.
Employer Identification Number: 366055199

1734
Allen-Heath Memorial Foundation ⌑
35 West Wacker Dr., Suite 3300
Chicago 60601-1698

Incorporated in 1947 in CA.
Donor(s): Harriet A. Heath,† John E.S. Heath.†
Foundation type: Independent
Financial data (yr. ended 12/31/88): Assets, $2,495,119 (M); expenditures, $170,255, including $145,000 for 14 grants (high: $30,000; low: $2,500).
Purpose and activities: Grants to a limited number of educational institutions, hospitals, museums, air safety organizations, and other charitable institutions.
Limitations: No support for religious or foreign organizations. No grants to individuals; no loans.
Publications: Application guidelines, annual report.
Application information: Contributes only to pre-selected organizations. Applications not accepted.
Board meeting date(s): Nov.
Officers and Directors: Charles K. Heath, Pres.; Ruth R. Hooper, V.P.; Paul E. Hoelschen, Jr., Secy.-Treas.; Nolan Baird.
Number of staff: None.
Employer Identification Number: 363056910

1735
The Allstate Foundation ▼
Allstate Plaza, C06
Northbrook 60062 (708) 402-5502

Incorporated in 1952 in IL.
Donor(s): Allstate Insurance Co.
Foundation type: Company-sponsored
Financial data (yr. ended 12/31/89): Assets, $16,051,937 (M); gifts received, $10,000,000; expenditures, $8,225,197, including

$7,940,396 for 1,645 grants (high: $300,000; low: $500; average: $5,000-$25,000) and $284,801 for 1,556 employee matching gifts.
Purpose and activities: To assist deserving organizations serving the fields of education, including colleges and universities, urban and civic affairs, safety, and health and welfare, including youth agencies and community funds. Particular interest in organizations dedicated to principles of self-help and self-motivation.
Types of support: Employee-related scholarships.
Limitations: No support for fraternal or religious organizations. No grants to individuals (except for employee-related scholarships), or for annual campaigns, deficit financing, building, capital, endowment funds, fund raising events, conferences, films, videotapes or audio productions, or travel funds; no loans.
Publications: Informational brochure (including application guidelines).
Application information: Application guidelines available from the foundation. Application form not required.
Initial approach: Proposal
Copies of proposal: 1
Deadline(s): None
Board meeting date(s): Mar., June, Sept., and Dec.
Final notification: 30 to 90 days
Write: Fred Ramos, Exec. Dir.; Allen Goldhamer, Mgr.; or Debbie Iddings, Admin. Asst.
Officers and Trustees:* Wayne E. Hedien,* Pres.; Robert W. Pike, V.P. and Secy.; Myron J. Resnick,* V.P. and Treas.; Raymond H. Kiefer,* V.P.; John K. O'Loughlin,* V.P.; Lawrence H. Williford, V.P.; Fred Ramos, Exec. Dir.
Number of staff: 2 full-time professional; 1 full-time support; 1 part-time support.
Employer Identification Number: 366116535

1736
The Allyn Foundation, Inc. ⌘
1420 North Sheridan Rd., No. 6C
Wilmette 60091

Foundation type: Independent
Financial data (yr. ended 12/31/88): Assets, $1,628,259 (M); expenditures, $85,715, including $83,000 for 35 grants (high: $5,000; low: $1,000).
Purpose and activities: Giving primarily to health associations and hospitals, secondary and higher education, and youth organizations.
Limitations: Giving primarily in Chicago, IL.
Application information: Contributes only to pre-selected organizations. Applications not accepted.
Officers and Directors: Margaret B. Allyn, Pres.; John W. Allyn, Jr., V.P.; Cynthia A. Stuttley.
Employer Identification Number: 237025589

1737
Leonore & Ernest Alschuler Foundation ⌘ ☆
c/o First National Bank of Chicago
One First National Plaza
Chicago 60670 (312) 732-4283

Foundation type: Independent
Financial data (yr. ended 5/31/88): Assets, $951,424 (M); expenditures, $143,816, including $120,000 for 6 grants (high: $40,000; low: $10,000).
Purpose and activities: Giving primarily for health, including a psychiatric rehabilitation institute, medical research, and hospitals; support also for Jewish organizations.
Limitations: Giving primarily in IL, with emphasis on Chicago.
Application information:
Initial approach: Letter
Deadline(s): None
Write: Helen Johnson
Trustees: Robert S. Jacobs, First National Bank of Chicago.
Employer Identification Number: 366540730

1738
Alsdorf Foundation
301 Woodley Rd.
Winnetka 60093 (708) 501-3335

Incorporated in 1944 in IL.
Donor(s): James W. Alsdorf.†
Foundation type: Independent
Financial data (yr. ended 12/31/88): Assets, $2,084,765 (M); expenditures, $137,679, including $114,773 for 58 grants (high: $64,955; low: $20).
Purpose and activities: Grants largely for the fine arts and higher education.
Limitations: Giving primarily in Chicago, IL. No grants to individuals, or for scholarships, fellowships, or prizes; no loans.
Application information: Application form not required.
Initial approach: Proposal
Copies of proposal: 1
Board meeting date(s): Dec. and as required
Officer and Directors:* Marilynn B. Alsdorf,* V.P. and Secy.; Mary Fujishama.
Employer Identification Number: 366065388

1739
Alton Foundation
Box 1078
Alton 62002 (618) 462-3953

Established in 1947 in IL.
Foundation type: Operating
Financial data (yr. ended 12/31/88): Assets, $2,084,891 (M); gifts received, $46,467; expenditures, $297,295, including $281,969 for grants.
Purpose and activities: Grants awarded for culture, social services, education, women, and youth; some support also for organizations that benefit the handicapped.
Limitations: Giving limited to Madison County, IL, and adjoining counties.
Application information: Application form required.
Initial approach: Letter
Copies of proposal: 1
Deadline(s): None
Write: R.S. Minsker, Secy.
Officers: Carlos Byassee, Chair.; R.S. Minsker, Vice-Chair. and Secy.
Employer Identification Number: 376045370

1740
Alton Woman's Home Association
P.O. Box 552
Alton 62002

Established in 1897 in IL.
Foundation type: Operating
Financial data (yr. ended 12/31/89): Assets, $1,794,000 (M); expenditures, $119,579, including $112,626 for 14 grants (high: $15,500; low: $2,000).
Purpose and activities: A private operating foundation, established to serve local area needy women and children; grants to services for the aged, welfare agencies, and a hospital.
Types of support: Continuing support.
Limitations: Giving limited to Madison County, IL. No support for profit-making organizations. No grants to individuals.
Application information: Application form required.
Initial approach: Letter
Copies of proposal: 1
Deadline(s): Sept. 1
Board meeting date(s): Mar., June, Sept., Nov., and Dec.
Officers and Directors: Dorothy Kelley, Pres.; Mary Grace Utterback, V.P.; Peggy Renshaw, Recording Secy.; June Weinrich, Corresponding Secy.; and 16 additional directors.
Number of staff: None.
Employer Identification Number: 370799839

1741
Altschuler, Melvoin & Glasser Fund ☆
30 South Wacker Dr.
Chicago 60606 (312) 207-2887

Established in 1954 in IL.
Donor(s): Altschuler, Melvoin & Glasser.
Foundation type: Company-sponsored
Financial data (yr. ended 12/31/89): Assets, $85,601 (M); gifts received, $234,856; expenditures, $230,051, including $229,478 for 27 grants (high: $220,903; low: $35).
Purpose and activities: Giving primarily for Jewish organizations, including welfare funds.
Types of support: General purposes.
Limitations: Giving primarily in Chicago, IL. No grants to individuals.
Application information: Contributes only to pre-selected organizations. Applications not accepted.
Write: Bernard L. Hirsh, Secy.
Officers and Directors:* Morris Glasser,* Pres.; Howard L. Stone,* 1st V.P. and Treas.; Harvey Gaffen,* 2nd V.P.; Bernard L. Hirsh, Secy.
Number of staff: None.
Employer Identification Number: 366050988

1742
AMCORE Bank Foundation ⌘
501 7th St.
P.O. Box 1537
Rockford 61110-0037

Established in 1957 in IL.
Foundation type: Company-sponsored
Financial data (yr. ended 11/30/88): Assets, $97,127 (M); expenditures, $134,479, including $134,235 for 41 grants (high: $40,000; low: $100).

Purpose and activities: Support for "organizations whose purpose is to improve the health, well-being and quality of life, both cultural and economic, within the community we serve"; includes support for education, youth activities, social services, civic affairs, and community funds.
Limitations: Giving primarily in Rockford, IL.
Application information:
Initial approach: Proposal
Write: Charles P.A. Frankenthal, V.P.
Officers and Directors: J. Peter Jeffrey, Pres.; Frank Sheley, V.P. and Treas.; Glen Wilson, V.P.; Edward Abegg, Carl J. Dargene, Clayton R. Gaylord, Charlotte Graps, William Nelson.
Employer Identification Number: 366042947

1743
American National Bank and Trust Company of Chicago Foundation
33 North LaSalle St.
Chicago 60690 (312) 661-6115

Trust established in 1955 in IL.
Donor(s): American National Bank & Trust Co. of Chicago.
Foundation type: Company-sponsored
Financial data (yr. ended 12/31/87): Assets, $3,037,731 (M); gifts received, $1,073,535; expenditures, $717,898, including $658,581 for grants (high: $265,000; low: $100; average: $2,500) and $7,736 for employee matching gifts.
Purpose and activities: Emphasis on hospitals, the arts, and elementary and higher education; support also for community organizations, youth agencies, and urban affairs.
Types of support: Employee matching gifts, operating budgets, general purposes, continuing support, annual campaigns, building funds, special projects, capital campaigns.
Limitations: Giving limited to the six-county Chicago, IL, metropolitan area. No support for sectarian religious organizations. No grants to individuals, or for conferences or seminars, land acquisition, endowment funds, fellowships, lectureships, professorships, or scholarships; no loans.
Publications: Application guidelines, program policy statement.
Application information: Application form not required.
Initial approach: Letter; no telephone calls
Copies of proposal: 1
Board meeting date(s): Bimonthly
Final notification: 3 months
Write: Catherine Brown, Administrative Dir.
Trustees: Ronald J. Grayheck, Timothy P. Moen, John F. Reuss, Henry S. Roberts, Robert F. Schnoes, Michael E. Tobin.
Number of staff: 1 full-time professional; 1 part-time support.
Employer Identification Number: 366052269

1744
Ameritech Foundation ▼
30 South Wacker Dr., 34th Fl.
Chicago 60606 (312) 750-5223

Established in 1984 in IL.
Donor(s): American Information Technologies.
Foundation type: Company-sponsored
Financial data (yr. ended 12/31/89): Assets, $67,026,856 (M); expenditures, $4,416,585, including $4,005,526 for 105 grants (high: $250,000; low: $2,000; average: $2,000-$50,000) and $142,745 for 253 employee matching gifts.
Purpose and activities: Grants largely to multi-state organizations for economic revitalization, education, and culture in the Great Lakes region. Support also for research and programs designed to determine ways communications can contribute to the betterment of society, and selected public policy issues which are relevant to the telecommunications industry, health and human services, and to national organizations which address the foundation's stated interests.
Types of support: Employee matching gifts, special projects, conferences and seminars, research.
Limitations: Giving primarily in IL, WI, IN, MI, and OH. No support for religious organizations for sectarian purposes, national or international organizations with limited relationships to local company operations, local chapters of national organizations, veterans' or military organizations, discriminating organizations, political groups, athletics, or health organizations concentrating on research and treatment in one area of human disease. No grants to individuals, or for start-up funds, or advertising.
Publications: Annual report (including application guidelines).
Application information: Application form not required.
Initial approach: Letter
Copies of proposal: 1
Deadline(s): None
Board meeting date(s): Mar., June, Sept., and Dec.
Final notification: 3 months
Write: Michael E. Kuhlin, Dir.
Officers and Directors:* John A. Koten,* Pres.; Carl G. Koch,* C.F.O.; Michael E. Kuhlin,* Secy.; Robert Kolbe, Treas.; James F. Bere, Harry Kalajian, Martha L. Thornton, William L. Weiss.
Number of staff: 1 full-time professional; 1 part-time support.
Employer Identification Number: 363350561

1745
Amoco Foundation, Inc. ▼
200 East Randolph Dr.
Chicago 60601 (312) 856-6306

Incorporated in 1952 in IN.
Donor(s): Amoco Corp.
Foundation type: Company-sponsored
Financial data (yr. ended 12/31/89): Assets, $68,480,472 (M); gifts received, $30,381,523; expenditures, $25,322,937, including $21,826,369 for 1,803 grants (high: $1,100,000; low: $100) and $2,165,469 for employee matching gifts.
Purpose and activities: Grants awarded for higher and precollege education, primarily in science and engineering, and for community organizations, urban programs, and energy conservation, with emphasis on new initiatives; support also for independent public interest research, a limited program in culture and art, a volunteer program, and an employee educational gift matching program. Limited contributions to foreign charitable and educational institutions.
Types of support: Operating budgets, continuing support, annual campaigns, seed money, emergency funds, building funds, equipment, scholarship funds, fellowships, special projects, general purposes, capital campaigns, employee matching gifts.
Limitations: Giving primarily in areas of company representation to assist communities. No support for primary or secondary schools; religious, fraternal, social, or athletic organizations; or, generally, for organizations already receiving operating support through the United Way. No grants to individuals, or for endowment funds, research, publications, or conferences; no loans.
Publications: Annual report (including application guidelines).
Application information: Application form not required.
Initial approach: Letter or proposal
Copies of proposal: 1
Deadline(s): Sept. 1
Board meeting date(s): Mar., June, Sept., and Dec.; contributions committee meets monthly
Final notification: 4 to 6 weeks
Write: Bob L. Arganbright, Exec. Dir.
Officers: R.M. Morrow,* Chair.; H.L. Fuller,* Pres.; F.S. Addy,* V.P.; R.H. Leet, V.P.; B.L. Arganbright, Secy. and Exec. Dir.; J.S. Ruey, Treas.
Directors:* R.W. Anderson, J.H. Bryan, R.D. Cadieux, P.J. Early, W.E. Massey, Arthur E. Rasmussen, G.S. Spindler, L.D. Thomas.
Number of staff: 6 full-time professional; 5 full-time support; 2 part-time support.
Employer Identification Number: 366046879

1746
Amsted Industries Foundation
205 North Michigan Ave., 44th Fl.
Chicago 60601 (312) 645-1700

Trust established in 1953 in IL.
Donor(s): Amsted Industries, Inc.
Foundation type: Company-sponsored
Financial data (yr. ended 09/30/89): Assets, $4,200,000 (M); expenditures, $442,783, including $373,575 for 214 grants (high: $30,000; low: $200; average: $1,000-$2,000) and $50,263 for 100 employee matching gifts.
Purpose and activities: Grants largely for health and human services, education, civic affairs, and cultural activities.
Types of support: Operating budgets, employee matching gifts, building funds, continuing support.
Limitations: Giving limited to areas of company operations: main emphasis on Chicago, IL; support also in KS, AL, MO, MD, IN, NE, DE, VA, CA, PA, DE, CT and Washington, DC. No support for political or religious organizations, or veterans' groups. No grants to individuals, or for endowment funds, scholarships, fellowships, or courtesy advertising; no loans.
Application information: Application form not required.
Initial approach: Letter

Deadline(s): Apr.
Board meeting date(s): Annually
Final notification: 45 days
Write: Jerry W. Gura, Dir., Public Affairs
Officer and Trustees:* Arthur W. Goetschel,* Mgr.; O.J. Sopranos, G.K. Walter, Robert H. Wellington.
Number of staff: 1 part-time professional; 1 part-time support.
Employer Identification Number: 366050609

1747
Arthur Andersen Foundation ⌑
P.O. Box 6
Barrington 60010 (312) 381-8134

Incorporated in 1953 in IL.
Donor(s): Arthur A. Andersen.†
Foundation type: Independent
Financial data (yr. ended 10/31/88): Assets, $2,306,992 (M); gifts received, $4,000; expenditures, $302,518, including $251,500 for 10 grants (high: $100,000; low: $2,000).
Purpose and activities: Grants largely for higher and secondary education, hospitals and medical research, and music and arts.
Application information: Application form not required.
Deadline(s): None
Write: Arthur Andersen III, Pres.
Officers: Arthur E. Andersen III, Pres.; Joan N. Andersen, V.P. and Treas.; John E. Hicks, Secy.
Employer Identification Number: 510175922

1748
Paul Anderson Foundation
1555 North Astor St., Apt. 10 N.E.
Chicago 60610

Established in 1986 in IL.
Foundation type: Independent
Financial data (yr. ended 12/31/88): Assets, $164,630 (M); gifts received, $100,000; expenditures, $201,842, including $200,875 for 8 grants (high: $100,000; low: $375).
Purpose and activities: Giving primarily for higher education, AIDS programs, medical facilities, and a community center.
Application information: Applications not accepted.
Deadline(s): None
Officer and Directors:* Paul Anderson,* Pres. and Secy.-Treas.; Elizabeth Marie Anderson, Allen A. Schuh.
Number of staff: None.
Employer Identification Number: 363461734

1749
The Andreas Foundation ⌑
c/o Archer-Daniels-Midland Co.
P.O. Box 1470
Decatur 62525 (217) 424-5200

Incorporated in 1945 in IA.
Donor(s): Dwayne O. Andreas, Lowell W. Andreas, Glenn A. Andreas, and others.
Foundation type: Independent
Financial data (yr. ended 11/30/88): Assets, $3,935,109 (M); gifts received, $2,434,313; expenditures, $843,235, including $836,812 for 102 grants (high: $195,000; low: $50; average: $500-$5,000).
Purpose and activities: Giving primarily for higher and secondary education, civil rights and economic opportunities for minority groups, and cultural programs; some support for hospitals, public policy research, churches, and youth agencies.
Types of support: Continuing support.
Limitations: No grants to individuals.
Application information: Contributes only to pre-selected organizations. Applications not accepted.
Board meeting date(s): As required
Write: Dwayne O. Andreas, Pres.
Officers and Trustees: Dwayne O. Andreas, Pres.; Lowell W. Andreas, Exec. V.P. and Treas.; Michael D. Andreas, V.P. and Secy.; Dorothy Inez Andreas, Terry Herbert-Burns, Sandra Andreas McMurtrie.
Number of staff: None.
Employer Identification Number: 416017057

1750
Aileen S. Andrew Foundation ▼
10500 West 153rd St.
Orland Park 60462 (312) 349-3300

Incorporated in 1946 in IL.
Foundation type: Independent
Financial data (yr. ended 11/30/88): Assets, $14,453,119 (M); expenditures, $924,444, including $516,415 for 113 grants (high: $91,200; low: $65) and $259,034 for 114 grants to individuals (high: $5,166; low: $660).
Purpose and activities: Giving for higher education, including scholarships for children of Andrew Corporation employees and graduates of a local high school; support also for civic affairs.
Types of support: Employee-related scholarships.
Limitations: Giving primarily in Orland Park, IL.
Application information: Application forms are available for scholarship program.
Deadline(s): Apr. 1 for scholarships
Board meeting date(s): Several times a year
Final notification: May 1 for scholarships
Write: Robert E. Hord, Pres.
Officers and Directors: Robert E. Hord, Pres.; Edward J. Andrew, V.P.; Juanita A. Hord, Secy.; Richard L. Dybala, Treas.; Edith G. Andrew, Robert E. Hord, Jr.
Number of staff: None.
Employer Identification Number: 366049910

1751
Alan & Gail Anixter Family Foundation ⌑ ☆
1111 Turicum
Lake Forest 60045

Established in 1986 in IL.
Donor(s): Alan B. Anixter, Gail A. Anixter.
Foundation type: Independent
Financial data (yr. ended 12/31/88): Assets, $1,169,717 (M); gifts received, $100,000; expenditures, $144,885, including $138,885 for 83 grants (high: $50,000; low: $10).
Purpose and activities: Giving for higher education, Jewish organizations, including welfare funds, health, and hospitals.
Limitations: No grants to individuals.
Application information: Contributes only to pre-selected organizations. Applications not accepted.
Officers and Directors: Alan B. Anixter, Pres.; Gail A. Anixter, V.P.; James R. Anixter, Secy.; Scott C. Anixter, Treas.
Employer Identification Number: 363482639

1752
Edward F. Anixter Family Foundation ⌑
1040 North Lake Shore Dr.
Chicago 60611

Established in 1983 in IL.
Donor(s): Edward Anixter.
Foundation type: Independent
Financial data (yr. ended 1/31/88): Assets, $84,109 (M); gifts received, $50,000; expenditures, $129,805, including $129,160 for 63 grants (high: $37,084; low: $25).
Purpose and activities: Giving primarily for Jewish organizations, museums, hospitals, and medical research.
Application information:
Initial approach: Letter
Deadline(s): None
Write: Edward F. Anixter, Pres.
Officers: Edward Anixter, Pres.; Edith Anixter, V.P.; Jack Ehrlich, Secy.
Employer Identification Number: 363297335

1753
AON Foundation ▼ ⌑
(Formerly Combined International Foundation)
123 North Wacker Dr.
Chicago 60606 (312) 701-3000

Established in 1984 in IL.
Donor(s): Aon Corp., and subsidiaries.
Foundation type: Company-sponsored
Financial data (yr. ended 12/31/88): Assets, $1,316,916 (M); gifts received, $2,365,931; expenditures, $2,078,295, including $1,901,392 for 431 grants (high: $150,000; low: $200; average: $1,000-$10,000) and $140,064 for 172 employee matching gifts.
Purpose and activities: Support for higher and other education, social services, community funds, and hospitals and health associations.
Limitations: No support for the operation of secondary educational institutions or vocational schools.
Application information: Application form not required.
Initial approach: Letter
Deadline(s): None
Board meeting date(s): 4 times a year
Final notification: Varies
Write: Wallace J. Buya, V.P.
Officers: W. Clement Stone,* Chair.; Patrick G. Ryan,* Pres.; Wallace J. Buya, V.P., Secy., and Exec. Dir.; Harvey N. Medvin, Treas.
Directors:* Daniel T. Carroll, Ronald K. Holmberg, Joan D. Manley, Raymond I. Skilling.
Number of staff: 1 part-time professional.
Employer Identification Number: 363337340

1754
Arthur I. Appleton Foundation ⌑
1701 West Wellington Ave.
Chicago 60657-4095

Established in 1951 in IL.
Foundation type: Independent
Financial data (yr. ended 12/31/88): Assets, $1,080,263 (M); expenditures, $62,366, including $38,200 for 31 grants (high: $25,000; low: $50).
Purpose and activities: Giving primarily for a cultural center and higher education.
Trustee: Arthur I. Appleton.
Employer Identification Number: 366062190

1755
Archer-Daniels-Midland Foundation ▼ ⌑
P.O. Box 1470
Decatur 62525 (217) 424-5200

Incorporated in 1953 in MN.
Donor(s): Archer-Daniels-Midland Co.
Foundation type: Company-sponsored
Financial data (yr. ended 6/30/88): Assets, $3,106,807 (M); expenditures, $2,458,805, including $2,387,527 for 467 grants (high: $100,000; low: $25; average: $1,000-$10,000).
Purpose and activities: Grants largely for higher education; support also for minority group development, cultural activities, hospitals, youth agencies, community funds, public policy organizations, and for the prevention of cruelty to animals and children.
Application information:
Initial approach: Letter
Deadline(s): None
Board meeting date(s): As needed
Final notification: Upon acceptance; no notification of negative decision
Write: Richard E. Burket, Mgr.
Officers: Lowell W. Andreas, Pres.; Roy L. Erickson, Secy.; Donald P. Poboisk, Treas.; Richard E. Burket, Mgr.
Employer Identification Number: 416023126

1756
Atwood Foundation
c/o L.B.D. Trust Co.
P.O. Box 5564
Rockford 61125 (815) 398-0907

Incorporated in 1949 in IL.
Donor(s): Atwood Enterprises, Inc., members of the Atwood family.
Foundation type: Independent
Financial data (yr. ended 12/31/89): Assets, $1,930,110 (M); expenditures, $53,635, including $50,930 for 23 grants (high: $10,000; low: $100; average: $100-$10,000).
Purpose and activities: Emphasis on education, hospitals, a community fund, arts and cultural programs, and youth and health agencies.
Types of support: Special projects, capital campaigns.
Limitations: Giving primarily in Rockford, IL. No grants to individuals.
Publications: Informational brochure (including application guidelines).
Application information: Application form not required.
Initial approach: Letter
Copies of proposal: 1
Deadline(s): Sept. 1
Board meeting date(s): Oct. or Nov.
Final notification: Dec.
Write: Bruce T. Atwood, Co-Trustee
Trustees: Bruce T. Atwood, Diane P. Atwood, Seth G. Atwood, Seth L. Atwood, L.B.D. Trust Co.
Number of staff: None.
Employer Identification Number: 366108602

1757
The Aurora Foundation
111 West Downer Place, Suite 312
Aurora 60506-5136 (708) 896-7800

Incorporated in 1948 in IL.
Foundation type: Community
Financial data (yr. ended 9/30/89): Assets, $6,029,269 (M); gifts received, $244,565; expenditures, $2,174,717, including $1,856,272 for grants (high: $1,701,477) and $159,313 for grants to individuals.
Purpose and activities: Grants for higher education, including scholarships and colleges, hospitals, youth activities, and community services.
Types of support: Student aid, matching funds, building funds, equipment, capital campaigns, seed money.
Limitations: Giving limited to the Aurora, IL, area. No grants for operating budgets, research, annual campaigns, or continuing support.
Publications: Annual report, application guidelines, newsletter.
Application information: Application form required.
Initial approach: Telephone
Copies of proposal: 11
Deadline(s): Feb., May, and Sept.
Board meeting date(s): May and Nov.; executive committee meets as required
Write: Sharon Stredde, Exec. Dir.
Officers and Directors: John H. McEachern, Jr., Pres.; Donald A. Schindlbeck, V.P.; Thomas S. Alexander, Treas.; Sharon Stredde, Secy. and Exec. Dir.; and 24 additional directors.
Number of staff: 1 full-time professional; 1 full-time support.
Employer Identification Number: 366086742

1758
Roland G. Balg Charitable Trust ⌑
c/o Continental Illinois National Bank & Trust Co. of Chicago
30 North LaSalle St.
Chicago 60697 (312) 828-1785

Established in 1977 in IL.
Foundation type: Independent
Financial data (yr. ended 8/31/88): Assets, $1,059,419 (M); expenditures, $88,819, including $76,175 for 5 grants of $15,235 each.
Purpose and activities: Support primarily for higher education, hospitals, and a home for the aged.
Limitations: Giving limited to IL and WI.
Application information: Application form not required.
Initial approach: Letter
Deadline(s): None
Write: M.C. Ryan
Trustee: Continental Illinois National Bank & Trust Co. of Chicago.
Employer Identification Number: 366650606

1759
Bates & Rogers Foundation ⌑
40 Skokie Blvd., Suite 615
600 West Jackson Blvd.
Northbrook 60062

Foundation type: Independent
Financial data (yr. ended 10/31/87): Assets, $9,864 (M); expenditures, $169,009, including $166,800 for 6 grants (high: $46,300; low: $500).
Purpose and activities: Support primarily for higher education; giving also for business education for youths.
Limitations: Giving primarily in Madison, WI, and Chicago, IL.
Application information:
Initial approach: Letter
Deadline(s): None
Write: Joseph Gurdak, Treas.
Officers: John W. Rogers, Pres.; Joseph Gurdak, Treas.
Employer Identification Number: 366116458

1760
Alben F. & Clara G. Bates Foundation ⌑
120 Robert T. Palmer Dr.
Elmhurst 60126

Established in 1952 in IL.
Foundation type: Independent
Financial data (yr. ended 12/31/87): Assets, $1,272,767 (M); expenditures, $53,734, including $44,533 for 88 grants (high: $6,000; low: $50).
Purpose and activities: Support primarily for community and youth organizations; support also for hospitals and health organizations.
Application information: Application form not required.
Deadline(s): None
Write: Alben F. Bates, Pres.
Officers and Directors:* Alben F. Bates, Jr.,* Pres. and Secy.; Henry G. Bates, V.P. and Treas.; Carol Bates Edwards,* V.P.
Employer Identification Number: 366081072

1761
Ralph J. Baudhuin Foundation ⌑
501 Seventh St.
Rockford 61101
Application address: 4109 Rural St., Rockford, IL; Tel.: (815) 399-3148

Established in 1959 in IL.
Foundation type: Independent
Financial data (yr. ended 12/31/87): Assets, $1,263,889 (M); expenditures, $81,978, including $68,770 for 23 grants (high: $6,000; low: $100).
Purpose and activities: Support primarily for Catholic churches; giving also to universities and health organizations.
Limitations: Giving primarily in Fort Lauderdale, FL and Rockford, IL.
Application information:
Initial approach: Letter

Deadline(s): None
Write: Fran Baudhuin
Trustee: Lois S. Barton.
Employer Identification Number: 366046399

1762
M. R. Bauer Foundation ▼
208 South LaSalle St., Suite 1750
Chicago 60604 (312) 372-1947

Established in 1955 in IL.
Donor(s): M.R. Bauer,† Evelyn M. Bauer.†
Foundation type: Independent
Financial data (yr. ended 12/31/88): Assets, $38,330,979 (M); expenditures, $2,107,046, including $1,800,000 for 111 grants (high: $200,000; low: $500; average: $2,500-$25,000).
Purpose and activities: Grants primarily for higher education, including medical and legal education, hospitals, cultural programs, and social service and youth agencies.
Types of support: General purposes, operating budgets, professorships, research.
Limitations: Giving primarily in CA and IL. No grants to individuals.
Application information: Contributes only to pre-selected organizations. Applications not accepted.
Board meeting date(s): Irregularly
Write: Kent Lawrence, Treas.
Officers and Directors:* James J. Lawrence,* Pres.; James H. Ackerman,* V.P. and Secy.; Loraine E. Ackerman,* V.P.; Kent Lawrence,* Treas.; Lee James Ackerman, Robert J. Lawrence.
Number of staff: None.
Employer Identification Number: 366052129

1763
The Alvin H. Baum Family Fund ⌑
120 South LaSalle St.
Chicago 60603

Trust established in 1945; incorporated in 1952 in IL.
Donor(s): Members of the Baum family.
Foundation type: Independent
Financial data (yr. ended 12/31/87): Assets, $1,948,395 (M); expenditures, $292,797, including $272,188 for 55 grants (high: $254,428; low: $25).
Purpose and activities: Support largely for higher education, Jewish and Catholic welfare funds, and local temple support.
Limitations: No grants to individuals.
Application information: Applications not accepted.
Board meeting date(s): Annually
Write: Ann F. Baum, Pres.
Officers: Ann F. Baum, Pres. and Treas.; Nathan M. Grossman, V.P. and Secy.
Director: Joel M. Friedman.
Employer Identification Number: 366063093

1764
The Baxter Foundation ▼
(Formerly The Baxter Travenol Foundation)
One Baxter Pkwy.
Deerfield 60015 (312) 948-4604

Established in 1982 in IL.
Donor(s): American Hospital Supply Corp., Baxter Travenol Laboratories, Inc.
Foundation type: Company-sponsored
Financial data (yr. ended 12/31/89): Assets, $9,603,828 (M); expenditures, $3,761,332, including $3,310,994 for 208 grants (high: $333,330; low: $100; average: $2,000-$20,000) and $219,360 for 1,317 employee matching gifts.
Purpose and activities: Supports health care organizations which address a broad national need. Emphasis on research and advocacy efforts that have a broad effect on increasing access to health care services and that provide resources to help hospital managers and medical personnel become more effective. Prize programs include the Foster G. McGraw Prize, the Baxter Health Services Research Award, the Baxter International Faculty Fellowships, the Baxter Fellowships for Innovation in Health Care Management, and the Baxter Foundation Episteme award. Matching gift program for hospitals and education. Scholarships for the children of company employees are paid through the Citizen's Scholarship Foundation of America. The Dollars for Doers program supports organizations in which Baxter employees are active volunteers.
Types of support: Employee matching gifts, employee-related scholarships, special projects, seed money.
Limitations: Giving nationally for health care organizations which address a broad national or regional need. No support for religious organizations, disease-specific organizations, or educational institutions except where grant supports a health care goal. No grants to individuals, or for dinners and special fundraising events.
Publications: Annual report, application guidelines.
Application information: Application form not required.
Initial approach: Letter
Copies of proposal: 1
Deadline(s): One month before meetings
Board meeting date(s): Jan., Apr., July, Oct., and Dec.
Write: Patricia A. Morgan, Exec. Dir.
Officers and Directors:* Wilbur H. Gantz,* Chair.; G. Marshall Abbey,* Pres.; Roger F. Lewis,* Secy.; Barbara Young Morris,* Treas.; William B. Graham, Warren D. Johnson, Wilfred J. Lucas, Robert A. Patterson, Robert J. Simmons.
Number of staff: 1 full-time professional; 1 full-time support.
Employer Identification Number: 363159396

1765
The Beatrice Foundation
Two North LaSalle St.
Chicago 60602 (312) 558-3758

Incorporated in 1953 in IL as the Esmark, Inc. Foundation.
Donor(s): Esmark, Inc., Beatrice Companies, Inc.
Foundation type: Company-sponsored
Financial data (yr. ended 12/31/89): Assets, $17,950,789 (M); expenditures, $2,151,490, including $2,002,353 for 196 grants (high: $50,000; low: $1,000; average: $5,000-$15,000) and $70,663 for 231 employee matching gifts.
Purpose and activities: Giving in two major categories: a nonprofit management program to encourage excellence in nonprofit organizations and a community priorities program to strengthen communities, with special attention to disadvantaged populations. This program also includes support for a community fund; an employee matching gift program for higher education, public media, and performing arts; and scholarships for dependents of company employees.
Types of support: Consulting services, conferences and seminars, equipment, general purposes, operating budgets, capital campaigns, employee matching gifts, employee-related scholarships, research.
Limitations: Giving primarily in the Chicago, IL, metropolitan area. No support for United Way campaigns (other than in Chicago), national health organizations, political, veterans', sectarian, or discriminatory organizations. No grants to individuals, or for advertising or fundraising events.
Publications: Annual report, informational brochure (including application guidelines).
Application information: Contact foundation for new guidelines. Application form required.
Initial approach: Letter
Copies of proposal: 1
Deadline(s): Feb. 1, May 1, Aug. 1, and Nov. 1
Board meeting date(s): Mar., June, Sept., and Dec.
Write: Lynda Robbins, Fdn. Admin.
Officers and Directors:* Lizabeth Sode,* Pres.; William P. Carmichael,* V.P.; Susan Maloney Meyer,* Secy.; Gregg A. Ostrander,* Treas.; Lynda Robbins, Admin.; Barbara Stockton, Matching Gifts Admin.; William Chambers, Floyd W. (Bud) Glisson.
Number of staff: 2 part-time professional; 1 full-time support; 2 part-time support.
Employer Identification Number: 366050467

1766
James F. Beedie Foundation ⌑ ☆
5230 Harvey Ave.
Western Springs 60558 (312) 246-4743

Established in 1987 in IL.
Donor(s): James F. Beedie.
Foundation type: Independent
Financial data (yr. ended 12/31/88): Assets, $110,431 (M); expenditures, $223,975, including $218,565 for 18 grants (high: $70,000; low: $100).
Purpose and activities: Support for higher and theological education and Protestant giving.
Limitations: Giving primarily in IL.
Application information: Contributes only to pre-selected organizations. Applications not accepted.
Write: Albert D. Beedie, Secy.-Treas.
Officers and Directors: James F. Beedie, Pres.; Albert D. Beedie, Secy.-Treas.; Karen Diane Beedie.
Employer Identification Number: 363551641

1767
Francis Beidler Charitable Trust
53 West Jackson Blvd.
Chicago 60604-3608 (312) 922-3792

Trust established in 1935 in IL.
Donor(s): Francis Beidler.†
Foundation type: Independent
Financial data (yr. ended 12/31/88): Assets, $7,099,148 (M); expenditures, $327,834, including $278,075 for 88 grants (high: $23,000; low: $100).
Purpose and activities: To aid public and operating charitable organizations; giving for social services, including care of the aged or crippled, youth agencies, child development and welfare, and education; support also for legal programs and education, the mental and behavioral sciences, international affairs, and the environment. No beneficiary may receive more than one-thirtieth of the net income yearly.
Types of support: Continuing support, operating budgets.
Limitations: Giving primarily in IL. No grants to individuals, or for building funds, research, or matching gifts; no loans.
Application information: Application form not required.
Initial approach: Letter
Copies of proposal: 1
Deadline(s): None
Board meeting date(s): Nov. or Dec.
Write: Rosemarie Smith, Trustee
Trustees: Francis Beidler III, Thomas B. Dorris, Rosemarie Smith.
Number of staff: None.
Employer Identification Number: 362166969

1768
Joseph C. Belden Foundation
1650 East Main St.
St. Charles 60174 (708) 513-5366

Established in 1967 in IL.
Donor(s): J.C. Belden, Jr.
Foundation type: Independent
Financial data (yr. ended 06/30/89): Assets, $1,167,000 (M); expenditures, $183,900, including $138,900 for 58 grants to individuals (high: $3,300).
Purpose and activities: Grants only for the undergraduate education of children of full-time Belden employees.
Types of support: Employee-related scholarships.
Limitations: Giving limited to the education of children of Belden company employees.
Application information: Applications not invited from any sources except children of Belden employees. Application form required.
Deadline(s): Dec. 31 for application; Feb. 1 for related materials
Board meeting date(s): Semiannually
Write: David A. Vanden Brook
Trustees: William Benac, Sarah Jane Camp, James D. Eaton, Albert C. Fifer, Robert G. Greminger, Robert W. Hawkinson, Herbert J. Mayer, Helen D. Nelson, George Schoessling.
Number of staff: 1 part-time professional.
Employer Identification Number: 366209342

1769
Bell & Howell Foundation ⌑
5215 Old Orchard Rd.
Skokie 60077 (312) 470-7100

Incorporated in 1951 in IL.
Donor(s): Bell & Howell Co.
Foundation type: Company-sponsored
Financial data (yr. ended 12/31/87): Assets, $14,419 (M); gifts received, $490,000; expenditures, $479,411, including $432,730 for 93 grants (high: $130,000; low: $135) and $46,591 for employee matching gifts.
Purpose and activities: Support for community funds and education; support also for human services, cultural programs, youth agencies, and social services; scholarships for dependents of employees administered by the National Merit Scholarship Corp.
Types of support: Employee matching gifts, operating budgets, employee-related scholarships.
Limitations: Giving primarily in local plant areas. No support for fraternal, veterans', or labor organizations. No grants to individuals, or for building or endowment funds, research, scholarships, fellowships, or special projects; no loans.
Publications: Application guidelines.
Application information: Application form required for employee-related scholarships.
Initial approach: Proposal
Copies of proposal: 1
Deadline(s): Before Jan. of student's junior year for scholarships
Board meeting date(s): Mar.
Final notification: Mar. of senior year for scholarships
Write: Lois Robinson, Pres., or M.J. Winfield, Scholarship Prog. Dir.
Officers: Lois Robinson,* Pres.; M.D. Phillips, Secy.; Deeon Zadrozny, Treas.
Directors:* Donald N. Frey, J.B. Kambanis, Gerald E. Schultz.
Number of staff: 1 part-time professional; 1 part-time support.
Employer Identification Number: 366095749

1770
Bellebyron Foundation ⌑ ☆
8501 West Higgens Rd.
Chicago 60631

Established in 1983 in IL.
Donor(s): Harold Byron Smith.
Foundation type: Independent
Financial data (yr. ended 12/31/88): Assets, $1,397,068 (M); expenditures, $81,417, including $80,000 for 3 grants (high: $30,000; low: $25,000).
Purpose and activities: General charitable giving, including a library, historic preservation, horticulture, and a hospice.
Limitations: Giving primarily in IL.
Application information:
Initial approach: Letter
Deadline(s): None
Write: Harold Byron Smith, Jr., Secy.
Officers and Directors: Harold Byron Smith, Chair.; Stephen B. Smith, Pres.; Christopher Byron Smith, V.P.; Harold Byron Smith, Jr., Secy.; David Hart Byron Smith, Treas.
Employer Identification Number: 366058056

1771
Beloit Foundation, Inc.
11722 Main St.
Roscoe 61073 (815) 623-6600

Incorporated in 1959 in WI.
Donor(s): Elbert H. Neese.†
Foundation type: Independent
Financial data (yr. ended 12/31/88): Assets, $12,022,955 (M); gifts received, $17,010; qualifying distributions, $1,356,222, including $1,106,222 for 31 grants (high: $500,000; low: $700; average: $700-$500,000) and $250,000 for loans.
Purpose and activities: Giving only to local community organizations for special projects, and new program development: support for education, with emphasis on a local college; family and social services, including youth, minorities, and the homeless; hospital building funds, hospices, and health; recreation; the arts; a community fund; and community development and crime and law enforcement programs.
Types of support: Building funds, matching funds, seed money, special projects, capital campaigns, equipment, renovation projects.
Limitations: Giving limited to local stateline area, including Beloit, WI, and South Beloit, Rockton, and Roscoe, IL. No grants to individuals, or for endowment funds, research, direct scholarships, or fellowships; or for nationally organized fundraising campaigns.
Application information: Application form required.
Initial approach: Letter
Copies of proposal: 1
Deadline(s): Submit proposal in Dec. or June; no set deadline
Board meeting date(s): Feb. and Aug.
Final notification: 3 months
Write: Gary G. Grabowski, Exec. Dir.
Officers and Directors:* Elbert H. Neese,* Pres.; Gary G. Grabowski,* Exec. Dir. and Treas.; Harry C. Moore, Alonzo A. Neese, Jr., Gordon C. Neese, Laura Neese-Malik, Jane Petit-Moore.
Number of staff: 1 part-time professional; 1 part-time support.
Employer Identification Number: 396068763

1772
Bere Foundation, Inc. ⌑
641 South Elm St.
Hinsdale 60521

Established in 1983 in IL.
Donor(s): James F. Bere.
Foundation type: Independent
Financial data (yr. ended 12/31/87): Assets, $4,136,899 (M); gifts received, $286,455; expenditures, $120,157, including $103,700 for 16 grants (high: $31,000; low: $250).
Purpose and activities: Support primarily for churches and religious groups; some support for cultural programs.
Types of support: General purposes.
Limitations: Giving primarily in the greater Chicago, IL, area.
Application information: Contributes only to pre-selected organizations. Applications not accepted.
Write: James F. Bere, Pres.

Officers and Directors: James F. Bere, Pres.; David L. Bere, V.P.; James F. Bere, Jr., V.P.; Robert P. Bere, V.P.; Becky B. Sigfusson, V.P.; Lynn B. Stine, V.P.; Barbara Van Dellen Bere, Secy.-Treas.
Employer Identification Number: 363272779

1773
Albert E. Berger Foundation, Inc. ⌑
c/o Miles Berger
180 North LaSalle St.
Chicago 60601

Established in 1957 in IL.
Donor(s): Members of the Berger family, Berger Investment Co.
Foundation type: Independent
Financial data (yr. ended 12/31/88): Assets, $3,300,592 (M); gifts received, $205,000; expenditures, $410,534, including $169,360 for 94 grants (high: $60,975; low: $25).
Purpose and activities: Giving primarily for Jewish welfare and for cultural organizations; some support for health and social services.
Limitations: No grants to individuals.
Application information: Contributes only to pre-selected organizations. Applications not accepted.
Officers: Miles Berger, Pres.; Robert Berger, Secy.-Treas.
Directors: Ronald Berger, Dorothy Berger Epstein.
Employer Identification Number: 366080617

1774
The Bersted Foundation ⌑
c/o Continental Illinois National Bank & Trust Co. of Chicago
30 North LaSalle St.
Chicago 60697 (312) 828-8026

Established in 1972 in IL.
Donor(s): Alfred Bersted.†
Foundation type: Independent
Financial data (yr. ended 12/31/87): Assets, $8,921,505 (M); expenditures, $415,969, including $336,500 for 19 grants (high: $50,000; low: $2,000).
Purpose and activities: Emphasis on community welfare and family service agencies, aid to the handicapped, conservation, cultural programs, youth agencies, and health care.
Types of support: Building funds, technical assistance, general purposes, operating budgets.
Limitations: Giving limited to Kane, DuPage, DeKalb, and McHenry counties, IL. No support for religious houses of worship or degree-conferring institutions of higher learning. No grants to individuals.
Publications: Multi-year report.
Application information:
Initial approach: Letter
Copies of proposal: 2
Deadline(s): None
Board meeting date(s): Generally in Feb., May, Aug., and Nov.
Write: A.W. Murray
Trustee: Continental Illinois National Bank & Trust Co. of Chicago.
Employer Identification Number: 366493609

1775
Grace A. Bersted Foundation ⌑
Continental Illinois Bank & Trust Co. of Chicago, 6th Fl.
30 North LaSalle
Chicago 60697 (312) 828-1785

Established in 1986 in IL.
Donor(s): Grace A. Bersted.†
Foundation type: Independent
Financial data (yr. ended 12/31/87): Assets, $3,699,113 (M); expenditures, $134,355, including $105,000 for 8 grants (high: $25,000; low: $10,000).
Purpose and activities: Support for youth organizations, social services, wilderness conservation, and culture.
Limitations: Giving limited to DuPage, Kane, Lake and McHenry Counties, IL.
Application information:
Initial approach: Proposal
Deadline(s): None
Write: M.C. Ryan
Trustee: Continental Illinois National Bank & Trust Co. of Chicago.
Employer Identification Number: 366841348

1776
Jacob Best Foundation ⌑ ☆
1129 Romona Rd.
Chicago 60091

Established in 1958.
Donor(s): Jacob H. Best Trust, Thilo M. Best Charitable Trust.
Foundation type: Independent
Financial data (yr. ended 2/28/89): Assets, $1,085,142 (M); gifts received, $24,000; expenditures, $59,610, including $56,750 for 24 grants (high: $5,000; low: $500).
Purpose and activities: Giving primarily for higher and other education; support also for youth and general charitable activities.
Limitations: No grants to individuals.
Application information: Contributes only to pre-selected organizations. Applications not accepted.
Officers and Directors: Jacob H. Best, Jr., Pres.; Thilo H. Best, V.P.; Barbara Bridges, Secy.-Treas.
Employer Identification Number: 366052049

1777
Walter J. and Edith E. Best Foundation
c/o Harris Trust & Savings Bank
111 West Monroe St.
Chicago 60603
Application address: c/o Harris Trust & Savings Bank, P.O. Box 755, Chicago, IL 60690

Established in 1986 in IL.
Donor(s): Edith Best,† Walter Best.†
Foundation type: Independent
Financial data (yr. ended 11/30/88): Assets, $2,913,584 (M); gifts received, $1,613,626; expenditures, $658,797, including $621,641 for 17 grants (high: $167,496; low: $2,500).
Purpose and activities: Giving primarily for hospitals and health associations; support also for child welfare services.
Limitations: Giving primarily in IL. No grants to individuals.
Application information:
Initial approach: Proposal
Deadline(s): None
Write: Ronald F. Tuite, Jr.
Trustees: Robert J. Kuhn, Harris Trust & Savings Bank.
Employer Identification Number: 366857916

1778
The Gary K. and Carlotta J. Bielfeldt Foundation ⌑
124 Southwest Adams St., Suite 340
Peoria 61602 (309) 676-6003

Established in 1985 in IL.
Donor(s): Gary K. Bielfeldt.
Foundation type: Independent
Financial data (yr. ended 12/31/87): Assets, $31,110,732 (M); expenditures, $677,474, including $596,933 for 51 grants (high: $250,000; low: $50; average: $21,000).
Purpose and activities: Support for charitable activities.
Limitations: Giving primarily in Peoria, IL. No grants to individuals.
Publications: Application guidelines.
Application information: Application form required.
Initial approach: Letter
Copies of proposal: 4
Deadline(s): Feb. 15, May 15, Aug. 15, and Nov. 15
Board meeting date(s): End of Mar., June, Oct., and Dec.
Final notification: 1 week after board meetings
Write: Carlotta J. Bielfeldt, V.P.
Officers and Directors: Gary K. Bielfeldt, Pres.; Carlotta J. Bielfeldt, V.P. and Secy.-Treas.; David L. Bielfeldt, Karen J. Bielfeldt, Linda S. Bielfeldt, Bill Blake.
Number of staff: 1
Employer Identification Number: 371188243

1779
Bjorkman Foundation
923 South Bruner St.
Hinsdale 60521 (312) 654-3661

Established in 1959 in IL.
Foundation type: Independent
Financial data (yr. ended 12/31/88): Assets, $1,609,575 (M); gifts received, $374,500; expenditures, $85,501, including $68,000 for 26 grants (high: $20,500; low: $250).
Purpose and activities: Support for denominational giving, including churches, Protestant welfare, and Christian camping; giving also for hospitals, housing, and hunger.
Types of support: Continuing support, general purposes, special projects.
Application information: Applications not accepted.
Deadline(s): None
Write: Glenn Bjorkman
Directors: Adaline E. Bjorkman, Glenn A. Bjorkman, Carol B. Taylor.
Employer Identification Number: 366053641

1780
William Blair and Company Foundation
135 South LaSalle St.
Chicago 60603 (312) 236-1600

Established in 1980 in IL.
Donor(s): William Blair & Co.
Foundation type: Company-sponsored
Financial data (yr. ended 08/31/89): Assets, $1,170,000 (M); gifts received, $125,000; expenditures, $250,797, including $248,500 for 131 grants (high: $25,000; low: $250; average: $500-$4,000).
Purpose and activities: Giving primarily for cultural programs, hospitals and health associations, including cancer research, higher education, social service and youth agencies, civic and public affairs, and Jewish and Catholic giving.
Types of support: Annual campaigns, building funds, capital campaigns, continuing support, endowment funds, fellowships, general purposes, internships, operating budgets.
Limitations: Giving primarily in the metropolitan Chicago, IL, area; the grantee should have significant, but not necessarily exclusive impact on the Chicago metropolitan area.
Application information: Application form not required.
Initial approach: Letter
Copies of proposal: 1
Deadline(s): None
Write: Stephen Campbell, Treas.
Officers: Edgar D. Jannotta, Pres.; E. David Coolidge III, V.P.; James M. McMullan, V.P.; Gregory N. Thomas, Secy.; Stephen Campbell, Treas.
Number of staff: None.
Employer Identification Number: 363092291

1781
The Blowitz-Ridgeway Foundation
2700 River Rd., Suite 300
Des Plaines 60018 (708) 298-2378

Status changed from public charity to private foundation in 1984.
Foundation type: Independent
Financial data (yr. ended 09/30/89): Assets, $15,538,160 (M); expenditures, $927,544, including $700,080 for 32 grants (high: $75,000; low: $5,000).
Purpose and activities: Support for organizations devoted to improving the psychiatric and psychological health and general welfare of juveniles; appropriate research activities may also be considered.
Types of support: Research, continuing support, special projects, capital campaigns.
Limitations: Giving generally limited to IL. No support for government agencies, or for organizations which subsist mainly on 3rd-party funding. No grants to individuals.
Publications: Application guidelines, annual report, grants list, informational brochure (including application guidelines).
Application information: Application form required.
Initial approach: Letter
Copies of proposal: 5
Deadline(s): 60 days prior to final notification dates
Board meeting date(s): Monthly
Final notification: Jan. 10, May 10, and Sept. 10
Write: Rob DiLeonardi, Admin. Asst., preliminary information; and Max Pastin, Pres., applications
Officer and Trustees:* Max Pastin,* Pres.; Arthur Collison, Tony Dean, Rev. J.W. Jackson, Daniel Kline, Joanne Lanigan, Allin Proufoot, Milton Steinberg, Samuel Winston.
Number of staff: 1 full-time professional; 1 part-time support.
Employer Identification Number: 362488355

1782
Harry and Maribel G. Blum Foundation ⌑
919 North Michigan Ave., Suite 2800
Chicago 60611

Established in 1967 in IL.
Donor(s): Harry Blum.†
Foundation type: Independent
Financial data (yr. ended 12/31/87): Assets, $11,429,516 (M); expenditures, $649,111, including $568,550 for 16 grants (high: $310,000; low: $500).
Purpose and activities: Grants primarily for hospitals and health agencies, higher education, temple support, social services, an art institute, and Jewish welfare funds.
Types of support: General purposes.
Limitations: No grants to individuals.
Application information:
Initial approach: Letter or proposal
Deadline(s): None
Board meeting date(s): As required
Officers and Directors: H. Jonathan Kovler, Pres.; H.H. Bregar, Secy.; Peter Kovler.
Employer Identification Number: 366152744

1783
The Nathan and Emily S. Blum Fund ⌑
c/o Harris Bank
111 West Monroe St.
Chicago 60603
Grant application address: c/o Harris Bank, P.O. Box 755, Chicago, IL 60690; Tel.: (312) 461-2613

Established in 1980.
Donor(s): Nathan Blum.†
Foundation type: Independent
Financial data (yr. ended 12/31/88): Assets, $5,617,592 (M); expenditures, $380,542, including $360,000 for 10 grants (high: $102,000; low: $2,000).
Purpose and activities: Giving for hospitals and health and social service agencies, including Jewish welfare funds.
Limitations: Giving primarily in Chicago, IL.
Application information:
Initial approach: Proposal
Deadline(s): None
Write: Ellen A. Bechtold, V.P., Harris Trust and Savings Bank
Trustee: Harris Bank.
Employer Identification Number: 366706638

1784
Blum-Kovler Foundation ▼
500 North Michigan Ave.
Chicago 60611 (312) 828-9777

Incorporated in 1953 in IL.
Donor(s): Harry Blum,† Everett Kovler.
Foundation type: Independent
Financial data (yr. ended 12/31/87): Assets, $25,878,500 (M); expenditures, $1,660,430, including $1,360,850 for 148 grants (high: $310,000; low: $100; average: $500-$5,000).
Purpose and activities: Emphasis on social services, including Jewish welfare funds; higher education; hospitals, health services, and medical research; and cultural programs; support also for youth and child welfare agencies, and public interest and civic affairs groups.
Types of support: General purposes.
Limitations: Giving primarily in the Chicago, IL, area.
Application information:
Initial approach: Written request
Deadline(s): None
Board meeting date(s): As required
Final notification: Varies
Write: H. Jonathan Kovler, Treas.
Officers and Directors: Everett Kovler, Pres.; H.H. Bregar, Secy.; H. Jonathan Kovler, Treas.; Peter Kovler.
Number of staff: 1 full-time support.
Employer Identification Number: 362476143

1785
Mary Wolf Rolfing Bogue Foundation, Inc. ⌑
c/o Joseph D. Ament
200 North LaSalle St., Suite 2100
Chicago 60601-1095

Established in 1980 in IL.
Donor(s): Mary W. Bogue.
Foundation type: Independent
Financial data (yr. ended 10/31/88): Assets, $1,513,579 (M); gifts received, $225,000; expenditures, $79,837, including $76,150 for 66 grants (high: $25,000; low: $150).
Purpose and activities: Support primarily for hospices, churches, community and health organizations, education, social services, Jewish welfare, and youth athletic programs.
Limitations: No grants to individuals.
Application information: Contributes only to pre-selected organizations. Applications not accepted.
Officers and Directors: Mary W. Bogue, Pres.; Joseph D. Ament, Secy.; Verle D. Bogue, Treas.; Mark E. Rolfing, Peter C. Rolfing, Stephen C. Rolfing, Donna Wolf Steigerwaldt.
Employer Identification Number: 363098630

1786
Charles H. and Bertha L. Boothroyd Foundation ⌑
120 West Madison St., Suite 14L
Chicago 60602 (312) 346-8333

Incorporated in 1958 in IL.
Donor(s): Mary T. Palzkill,† Agnes K. McAvoy Trust.
Foundation type: Independent
Financial data (yr. ended 6/30/89): Assets, $3,200,122 (M); gifts received, $17,753;

expenditures, $196,097, including $161,500 for 22 grants (high: $25,000; low: $1,000).
Purpose and activities: Grants to medical schools for research on Parkinson's disease, hospitals, higher education, social services, and cultural institutions.
Types of support: Scholarship funds, research.
Limitations: Giving primarily in IL.
Application information:
Initial approach: Letter
Deadline(s): None
Write: Bruce E. Brown, Pres.
Officers and Trustees: Bruce E. Brown, Pres.; Donald C. Gancer, V.P.; Lorraine Marcus, Secy.
Employer Identification Number: 366047045

1787
Borg-Warner Foundation, Inc. ▼
200 South Michigan Ave.
Chicago 60604 (312) 322-8659

Incorporated in 1953 in IL.
Donor(s): Borg-Warner Corp., and its divisions and subsidiaries.
Foundation type: Company-sponsored
Financial data (yr. ended 12/31/88): Assets, $6,232,702 (M); expenditures, $1,767,226, including $1,295,455 for 150 grants (high: $200,000; low: $500; average: $2,500-$10,000) and $204,445 for employee matching gifts.
Purpose and activities: Support for community funds, educational institutions, culture, neighborhood revitalization, social welfare, health agencies, and civic affairs.
Types of support: General purposes, building funds, equipment, land acquisition, endowment funds, matching funds, professorships, special projects, publications, continuing support, employee matching gifts, seed money, scholarship funds, operating budgets, renovation projects, capital campaigns.
Limitations: Giving primarily in the Chicago, IL, area. No support for sectarian institutions for religious purposes, foreign-based organizations, or medical or academic research. No grants to individuals, or for testimonial dinners, fundraising events, or advertising.
Publications: Annual report, informational brochure (including application guidelines).
Application information: Application form not required.
Initial approach: Letter of intent preferably no longer than 2 pages; RPF details requirements for education
Copies of proposal: 1
Deadline(s): Mar. 1 letter, May 1 proposal
Board meeting date(s): Quarterly
Write: Ellen J. Benjamin, Dir., Corp. Contribs.
Officers and Directors:* James F. Bere,* Chair.; Ellen Benjamin, Pres.; Neal F. Farrell,* V.P. and Secy.; Donald C. Trauscht,* V.P. and Treas.; John D. O'Brien,* V.P.
Number of staff: 1 full-time professional; 1 full-time support.
Employer Identification Number: 366051857

1788
Borwell Charitable Foundation ▼ ⌑
1040 North Lake Shore Dr.
Chicago 60611

Established in 1981 in IL.
Donor(s): Robert C. Borwell, Sr.
Foundation type: Independent
Financial data (yr. ended 10/31/88): Assets, $69,676 (M); gifts received, $736,781; expenditures, $571,160, including $459,100 for 42 grants (high: $222,000; low: $100).
Purpose and activities: Support primarily for higher education, hospitals and health associations, and religious purposes.
Limitations: Giving primarily in IL, with emphasis on Chicago.
Application information: Contributes only to pre-selected organizations. Applications not accepted.
Write: Naomi T. Borwell, Pres.
Officers and Directors: Naomi T. Borwell, Pres.; Robert C. Borwell, Jr., V.P.; Herbert B. Knight, V.P.; Carolyn W. Lodge, Treas.; Robert C. Borwell, Sr.
Number of staff: None.
Employer Identification Number: 363155489

1789
Boulevard Foundation ☆
400-410 North Michigan Ave.
Chicago 60611

Established in 1957.
Donor(s): Boulevard Bank, N.A.
Foundation type: Company-sponsored
Financial data (yr. ended 07/31/89): Assets, $33,902 (M); gifts received, $117,110; expenditures, $101,611, including $101,611 for 51 grants (high: $46,986; low: $100).
Purpose and activities: Giving for education and social services, including programs for youth, and the fine and performing arts.
Limitations: Giving primarily in Chicago, IL. No grants to individuals.
Application information: Contributes only to pre-selected organizations. Applications not accepted.
Trustees: Richard T. Schroeder, Timothy G. Towle, Daniel T. Zapton.
Employer Identification Number: 366068532

1790
The Ambrose and Gladys Bowyer Foundation ⌑
175 West Jackson Blvd., Suite 909
Chicago 60604

Incorporated in 1953 in IL.
Donor(s): Ambrose Bowyer,† Gladys Bowyer.†
Foundation type: Independent
Financial data (yr. ended 12/31/88): Assets, $1,977,518 (M); expenditures, $451,171, including $435,750 for 49 grants (high: $53,000; low: $750).
Purpose and activities: Emphasis on higher education, hospitals, and welfare funds.
Application information: Contributes only to pre-selected organizations. Applications not accepted.
Write: D.T. Hutchison, Pres.
Officers and Directors:* D.T. Hutchison,* Pres.; R.F. Prendergast,* Secy.; E.V. Quinn.
Employer Identification Number: 366091247

1791
Boynton Gillespie Memorial Fund ⌑
Heritage Federal Bldg.
Sparta 62286 (618) 443-2148

Established about 1965.
Donor(s): Bertha Gillespie Boynton,† Charles Otis Boynton.†
Foundation type: Independent
Financial data (yr. ended 12/31/88): Assets, $2,023,595 (M); expenditures, $171,236, including $67,000 for 1 grant and $78,500 for 82 grants to individuals (high: $1,000; low: $500).
Purpose and activities: Grants for a local church and scholarships.
Types of support: Student aid.
Limitations: Giving limited to IL; scholarships limited to undergraduate students residing within a 30-mile radius of Sparta, IL.
Application information: Application form required.
Initial approach: Write for scholarship application
Deadline(s): May 1
Write: John Clendenin, Trustee
Trustees: John Clendenin, John Henderson, Richard Reid.
Employer Identification Number: 376028930

1792
Edwin J. Brach Foundation
664 South Beverly Place
Lake Forest 60045
Application address: 560 Neapolitan Way, Naples, FL 33940; Tel.: (813) 262-8998

Incorporated in 1962 in IL.
Foundation type: Independent
Financial data (yr. ended 10/31/88): Assets, $2,654,958 (M); expenditures, $149,962, including $144,000 for 32 grants (high: $21,000; low: $500).
Purpose and activities: Emphasis on health associations, child welfare, and social services.
Limitations: Giving primarily in IL. No grants to individuals.
Application information:
Initial approach: Letter
Deadline(s): None
Write: E.H. Moore
Officers: Hazel S. Brodie, Pres. and Secy.; Bertram Z. Brodie, V.P. and Treas.
Director: George O'Callaghan.
Employer Identification Number: 366073506

1793
Helen Brach Foundation ▼
55 West Wacker Dr., Suite 701
Chicago 60601 (312) 372-4417

Established in 1974 in IL.
Donor(s): Helen Brach.†
Foundation type: Independent
Financial data (yr. ended 03/31/89): Assets, $32,709,009 (M); expenditures, $1,780,712, including $1,642,737 for 82 grants (high: $100,000; low: $3,500; average: $10,000-$50,000).
Purpose and activities: Support for the prevention of cruelty to animals; programs that test public safety; social and family services, including programs for the prevention of cruelty to children and child welfare, the

homeless and housing, the aged, youth, women, and the disabled and disadvantaged; conservation of the environment; secondary, higher, and other education; the fine arts, including museums; health and hospitals; and law and justice, including legal services.
Types of support: Annual campaigns, building funds, capital campaigns, equipment, general purposes, operating budgets, publications, renovation projects, research, special projects.
Limitations: No grants to individuals.
Publications: Annual report (including application guidelines), application guidelines.
Application information: Application form required.
Initial approach: Letter
Copies of proposal: 7
Deadline(s): Dec. 31
Board meeting date(s): Quarterly
Final notification: Mar.
Write: Raymond F. Simon, Pres.
Officers and Directors:* Charles M. Vorhees,* Chair.; Raymond F. Simon,* Pres.; James J. O'Connor,* V.P.; John J. Sheridan,* Secy.-Treas.; R. Matthew Simon, Charles A. Vorhees.
Number of staff: 1 part-time support.
Employer Identification Number: 237376427

1794
Fred J. Brunner Foundation ⌑
9300 King St.
Franklin Park 60131

Incorporated in 1955 in IL.
Donor(s): Fred J. Brunner.
Foundation type: Independent
Financial data (yr. ended 12/31/87): Assets, $3,888,780 (M); expenditures, $300,931, including $221,540 for grants (high: $20,000; low: $100; average: $1,000-$5,000).
Purpose and activities: Emphasis on education, and social, health, and youth agencies.
Types of support: Continuing support, annual campaigns, seed money, building funds, equipment, research, matching funds, general purposes, operating budgets.
Limitations: Giving primarily in IL. No grants to individuals, or for endowment funds, scholarships, fellowships, or matching gifts; no loans.
Publications: 990-PF.
Application information: Application form not required.
Initial approach: Proposal or letter
Copies of proposal: 1
Deadline(s): Dec. 15
Board meeting date(s): Dec. and as required
Final notification: Dec. 31
Write: A.J. Schwegel, V.P.
Officers and Directors:* Fred J. Brunner,* Pres. and Treas.; Ruth Brunner,* V.P. and Secy.; A.J. Schwegel, V.P. and General Mgr.
Number of staff: 1 part-time professional; 1 part-time support.
Employer Identification Number: 366066471

1795
The Brunswick Foundation, Inc. ▼
One Brunswick Plaza
Skokie 60077 (708) 470-4646

Incorporated in 1957 in IL.
Donor(s): Brunswick Corp.
Foundation type: Company-sponsored
Financial data (yr. ended 12/31/88): Assets, $8,114,516 (M); gifts received, $1,800,000; expenditures, $1,276,386, including $707,113 for 252 grants (high: $57,250; low: $100; average: $1,000-$25,000), $219,375 for 113 grants to individuals (high: $3,000; low: $750) and $289,481 for 872 employee matching gifts.
Purpose and activities: Support primarily for higher education, welfare, civic and health causes, and cultural organizations in areas where there are high concentrations of Brunswick employees, with a preference towards local (plant community) organizations in which employees are personally involved.
Types of support: Employee-related scholarships, employee matching gifts, general purposes, operating budgets, special projects, continuing support.
Limitations: Giving primarily in areas of company operations in CA, FL, MD, MI, NE, OK, TX, TN, VA, WA, WI, AL, AR, AZ, CT, GA, IL, IN, KY, LA, MN, MS, NC, OH, and SC. No support for religious organizations, preschools, primary or secondary schools, fraternal orders, veterans, labor groups, political organizations established to influence legislation, or for trips, tours, tickets or advertising for benefit purposes. No grants to individuals (except for scholarships to children of company employees), or for endowment or capital funds, or company equipment or products; no loans.
Publications: Annual report (including application guidelines).
Application information: Accepts only written requests for application form and guidelines; priority given to organizations that have already generated Brunswick Corp. employee involvement. Application form required.
Initial approach: Letter
Copies of proposal: 1
Deadline(s): None
Board meeting date(s): Annually; Donations Committee meets quarterly
Final notification: Within 90 days
Write: Wendy L. Fuhs, Pres.
Officers and Directors:* Wendy L. Fuhs,* Pres.; Dianne M. Yaconetti,* V.P.; Michael D. Schmitz,* Secy.; Paul Kilius,* Treas.; Jack F. Reichert, Pierre A. Rinfret.
Donations Committee: David Bloomfield, Paul Duvall, Eugene Howard, James Hubbard, John Mikusa, Richard Stone, Robert Teague.
Number of staff: 1 full-time professional.
Employer Identification Number: 366033576

1796
The Buchanan Family Foundation ▼ ⌑
222 East Wisconsin Ave.
Lake Forest 60045

Established in 1967 in IL.
Donor(s): D.W. Buchanan, Sr.,† D.W. Buchanan, Jr.
Foundation type: Independent
Financial data (yr. ended 12/31/87): Assets, $32,442,868 (M); expenditures, $2,144,542, including $2,080,000 for 51 grants (high: $100,000; low: $5,000; average: $5,000-$100,000).
Purpose and activities: Emphasis on cultural programs, hospitals and health associations, education, social service agencies, community funds, and environmental associations.
Limitations: Giving primarily in Chicago, IL.
Application information:
Board meeting date(s): Fall
Write: Huntington Eldridge, Jr., Treas.
Officers: Kenneth H. Buchanan,* Pres.; G.M. Walsh, V.P. and Secy.; Huntington Eldridge, Jr., Treas.
Directors:* Kent Chandler, Jr.
Number of staff: None.
Employer Identification Number: 366160998

1797
A. C. Buehler Foundation ⌑
c/o Continental Illinois National Bank and Trust Co. of Chicago
30 North LaSalle St.
Chicago 60693 (312) 828-1785

Incorporated in 1972 in IL.
Donor(s): Albert C. Buehler.
Foundation type: Independent
Financial data (yr. ended 12/31/87): Assets, $11,925,132 (M); expenditures, $516,450, including $431,000 for 5 grants.
Purpose and activities: Giving for hospitals, health services, medical research, and education.
Limitations: Giving primarily in metropolitan Chicago, IL.
Application information:
Initial approach: Letter
Deadline(s): None
Write: M.C. Ryan
Officer: Fern D. Buehler, Pres.
Directors: A.C. Buehler, Jr., Carl Buehler III, Rose B. Grosse, Dale Park, Jr., Barbara B. Ross, James M. Termondt.
Employer Identification Number: 237166014

1798
Dean L. & Rosemarie Buntrock Foundation ⌑ ☆
3003 Butterfield Rd.
Oak Brook 60521-1107

Established in 1979.
Donor(s): Dean Buntrock.
Foundation type: Independent
Financial data (yr. ended 12/31/87): Assets, $48,747 (M); gifts received, $110,000; expenditures, $110,435, including $100,915 for 52 grants (high: $25,000; low: $25).
Purpose and activities: Support primarily for Lutheran churches and the performing arts, with emphasis on symphony orchestras and opera companies.
Limitations: Giving primarily in Chicago, IL. No grants to individuals.
Application information: Contributes only to pre-selected organizations. Applications not accepted.
Directors: Dean L. Buntrock, Rosemarie Buntrock, Peer Pedersen.
Employer Identification Number: 363001925

1799
The William, Agnes & Elizabeth Burgess Memorial Scholarship Fund ⌘
c/o First National Bank
1515 Charleston
Mattoon 61938 (217) 234-7454

Trust established in 1943 in IL.
Foundation type: Independent
Financial data (yr. ended 3/31/89): Assets, $1,298,250 (M); expenditures, $100,594, including $54,850 for 95 grants to individuals (high: $600; low: $250).
Purpose and activities: Scholarships for graduates of Mattoon, IL, Community High School.
Types of support: Student aid.
Limitations: Giving limited to Mattoon, IL.
Application information: Application forms available at high school. Application form required.
Deadline(s): Mar. 15
Write: Clark W. Brogan, V.P. and Sr. Trust Officer, First National Bank
Trustee: First National Bank.
Employer Identification Number: 376024599

1800
Leo Burnett Company Charitable Foundation ⌘
Prudential Plaza
Chicago 60601

Established in 1985 in IL.
Donor(s): Leo Burnett Co., Inc.
Foundation type: Company-sponsored
Financial data (yr. ended 12/31/87): Assets, $1,816,089 (M); expenditures, $502,163, including $500,405 for 164 grants (high: $70,000; low: $100).
Purpose and activities: Giving to fund research in the field of advertising.
Application information:
Deadline(s): None
Write: Ella Strubel, Secy.
Officers: Theodore Bell, Pres.; William D. Engelbrecht,* V.P.; Ella Strubel, Secy.; Robert S. Minner, Treas.
Managers:* Flinn Dallas, Jr., J. Thompson Ross, Martin H. Snitzer, Hal Weinstein, Carlton Zucker.
Employer Identification Number: 363379336

1801
Burns Family Foundation ⌘
c/o Cottle and Cottle, Ltd.
120 South La Salle St.
Chicago 60603

Incorporated in 1953 in IL.
Donor(s): Arthur E. Keating,† Edward Keating.
Foundation type: Independent
Financial data (yr. ended 12/31/88): Assets, $2,095,426 (M); expenditures, $133,382, including $96,017 for 27 grants (high: $16,000; low: $200).
Purpose and activities: Emphasis on secondary education, youth agencies, conservation, and police organizations.
Limitations: Giving primarily in CA. No grants to individuals.
Application information: Contributes only to pre-selected organizations. Applications not accepted.
Officers and Directors:* Lucy Keating Burns,* Pres.; Donald S. Burns,* V.P. and Treas.; Julie Ann Wrigley,* Secy.
Employer Identification Number: 366051686

1802
George W. & Gladys S. Butler Family Foundation ⌘
1550 Northwest Hwy., Suite 108D
Park Ridge 60068-1482 (312) 294-2244

Established in 1953 in IL.
Foundation type: Independent
Financial data (yr. ended 12/31/87): Assets, $1,641,784 (M); gifts received, $350,301; expenditures, $104,665, including $103,110 for 32 grants (high: $80,000; low: $50).
Purpose and activities: Giving primarily to the Methodist Church and general charitable organizations.
Application information: Application form required.
Initial approach: Letter
Deadline(s): None
Write: Rhett W. Butler, Trustee
Trustees: Gladys A. Butler, Lynne G. Butler, Rhett W. Butler.
Employer Identification Number: 366101775

1803
The Butz Foundation
c/o The Northern Trust Co., Tom Boyden, Admin.
50 South La Salle St.
Chicago 60675 (312) 630-6000

Incorporated in 1951 in IL.
Donor(s): Theodore C. Butz,† Jean Butz James.
Foundation type: Independent
Financial data (yr. ended 12/31/89): Assets, $2,416,700 (M); expenditures, $135,500, including $133,000 for 23 grants (high: $15,000; low: $1,000; average: $10,000-$15,000).
Purpose and activities: Emphasis on medical research; support for insitutions of higher and secondary education, aid to the handicapped, religious associations, and hospitals.
Types of support: Operating budgets, continuing support, equipment, research.
Limitations: Giving primarily in IL. No grants to individuals; no loans.
Application information:
Initial approach: Letter
Copies of proposal: 1
Deadline(s): Submit proposal preferably in first six months of calendar year; deadline Oct. 1
Board meeting date(s): Quarterly
Final notification: 6 months
Write: Jean Butz James, Pres.
Officers and Directors:* Jean Butz James,* Pres.; Barbara Butz,* V.P. and Secy.; Theodore H. Butz,* Treas.; Elvira M. Butz, Herbert K. Butz, Thompson H. Butz.
Number of staff: None.
Employer Identification Number: 366008818

1804
The Charles and Marie Caestecker Foundation
c/o Frank Karaba
Two First National Plaza, Suite 2310
Chicago 60603
Scholarship application address: c/o Guidance Counselor, Green Lake Public High School, Green Lake, WI 54941

Donor(s): Charles E. Caestecker.†
Foundation type: Independent
Financial data (yr. ended 04/30/89): Assets, $6,149,358 (M); gifts received, $1,310,754; expenditures, $400,705, including $366,615 for 12 grants (high: $200,000; low: $215) and $18,897 for 4 grants to individuals (high: $5,000; low: $3,897).
Purpose and activities: Giving primarily for higher education, including scholarships to graduates of Green Lake Public High School, WI.
Types of support: Student aid, operating budgets, scholarship funds.
Limitations: Giving primarily in WI.
Application information: Application form for scholarships.
Deadline(s): Feb. 1 of graduation year for scholarships
Trustees: Thomas E. Caestecker, Frank A. Karaba.
Employer Identification Number: 363154453

1805
Milton H. Callner Foundation ⌘
c/o American National Bank & Trust Co. of Chicago
33 North LaSalle St.
Chicago 60690

Trust established in 1954 in IL.
Donor(s): Members of the Callner family.
Foundation type: Independent
Financial data (yr. ended 1/31/87): Assets, $1,061,768 (M); expenditures, $90,182, including $77,632 for 22 grants (high: $22,232; low: $50).
Purpose and activities: Giving for higher education, Jewish welfare funds, health, and medical research.
Limitations: Giving primarily in Chicago, IL, area.
Application information: Contributes only to pre-selected organizations. Applications not accepted.
Trustee: American National Bank & Trust Co. of Chicago.
Employer Identification Number: 366034633

1806
Apollos Camp and Bennet Humiston Trust ⌘
300 West Washington St.
Pontiac 61764 (815) 844-6155

Trust established in 1925 in IL.
Foundation type: Independent
Financial data (yr. ended 04/30/89): Assets, $4,395,880 (M); expenditures, $368,095, including $196,420 for 9 grants (high: $76,285; low: $1,000).
Purpose and activities: Giving for a municipal park and other community recreational

programs, a youth agency, the aged, and conservation.
Types of support: Operating budgets, equipment, building funds.
Limitations: Giving primarily in Pontiac, IL.
Application information:
Initial approach: Proposal
Write: Neil Bach, Chair.
Officers and Trustees:* Neil C. Bach,* Chair.; William H. Edwards,* Vice-Chair.; David Harding, William C. Harris, Louis Lyons.
Employer Identification Number: 370701044

1807
Carlin Fund ⌑
c/o Nancy Shirmers
8000 Sears Tower
Chicago 60606

Incorporated in 1954 in IL.
Donor(s): Leo J. Carlin, Celia Carlin.
Foundation type: Independent
Financial data (yr. ended 12/31/88): Assets, $1,359,730 (M); expenditures, $77,773, including $69,950 for 70 grants (high: $5,500; low: $200).
Purpose and activities: Giving for higher education, medical research, Jewish welfare funds, temple support, the arts, public policy, and civic affairs.
Limitations: No grants to individuals.
Application information: Contributes only to pre-selected organizations. Applications not accepted.
Officers and Directors:* Jerome E. Carlin,* Pres.; Chester M. Epstein,* V.P.; David C. Epstein,* Secy.; Nicholas Carlin,* Treas.
Employer Identification Number: 366057155

1808
Carson Pirie Scott Foundation ⌑
36 South Wabash St.
Chicago 60603 (312) 641-8055

Incorporated in 1959 in IL.
Donor(s): Carson Pirie Scott & Co., Carson International, Inc.
Foundation type: Company-sponsored
Financial data (yr. ended 12/31/87): Assets, $202,168 (M); gifts received, $340,000; expenditures, $390,637, including $379,115 for 104 grants (high: $185,000; low: $100) and $11,477 for 79 employee matching gifts.
Purpose and activities: Emphasis on community funds; support also for education, the arts, health services, community development, and civic affairs; contributions in proportion to size of company operations.
Types of support: Continuing support, building funds, scholarship funds, equipment.
Limitations: Giving primarily in Chicago, IL, and communities with company operations. No grants to individuals, or for endowment funds, research, or matching gifts; no loans.
Publications: Program policy statement, application guidelines.
Application information:
Initial approach: Letter
Copies of proposal: 1
Deadline(s): None
Board meeting date(s): Feb., May, and Sept.
Final notification: 2 to 3 weeks after meetings

Officers: Peter S. Willmott,* Pres.; Daniel M. Fort, V.P. and Secy.; Charles T. Reice,* V.P. and Treas.
Directors:* Dennis S. Bookshester, Robert P. Bryant, Carroll E. Ebert, Kurt Gasser, Donald J. Gralen, Robert D. Jones, Dean B. McKinney, Robert S. Ruwitch.
Employer Identification Number: 366112629

1809
Cartwright Foundation ⌑
c/o L. Russell Cartwright
One Prudential Plaza, Suite 3800, 130 E. Randolph
Chicago 60601

Established in 1964 in IL.
Donor(s): Levering R. Cartwright.†
Foundation type: Independent
Financial data (yr. ended 12/31/87): Assets, $1,269,628 (M); gifts received, $27,000; expenditures, $82,806, including $60,000 for 17 grants (high: $12,500; low: $125).
Purpose and activities: Support primarily for culture, hospitals, and education.
Application information: Contributes only to pre-selected organizations. Applications not accepted.
Trustees: Cameron Avery, Abigail Cartwright, Janet W. Cartwright, L. Russell Cartwright, Joan M. Hall.
Employer Identification Number: 366101710

1810
Carylon Foundation ⌑
2500 West Arthington St.
Chicago 60612-4108

Established in 1956 in IL.
Foundation type: Independent
Financial data (yr. ended 06/30/89): Assets, $2,524,157 (M); gifts received, $337,350; expenditures, $235,940, including $234,978 for 81 grants (high: $102,000; low: $15).
Purpose and activities: Giving primarily to Jewish welfare groups, health agencies and hospitals, and to a science institute.
Application information:
Initial approach: Letter
Deadline(s): None
Write: Mrs. Marcie Mervis, Dir.
Directors: C. Hemmelstein, Julius Hemmelstein, M. Mervis.
Employer Identification Number: 366033583

1811
Caterpillar Foundation
100 N.E. Adams St.
Peoria 61629-1480

Established in 1952 in IL.
Donor(s): Caterpillar, Inc.
Foundation type: Company-sponsored
Financial data (yr. ended 12/31/87): Assets, $302,994 (M); gifts received, $3,617,000; expenditures, $3,549,462, including $3,122,716 for grants and $419,466 for employee matching gifts.
Purpose and activities: Giving primarily to community funds, higher education, and a youth agency; employee matching gift support for cultural and educational institutions.

Types of support: Employee matching gifts, operating budgets, special projects, capital campaigns.
Limitations: Giving primarily in areas of company operations. No support for fraternal organizations, religious organizations whose services are limited to one sectarian group, or political activities. No grants to individuals, or for general operations or ongoing programs of agencies funded by the United Way, or tickets or advertising for fundraising benefits.
Publications: Corporate giving report.
Application information: Application form not required.
Initial approach: Letter or proposal
Deadline(s): None
Board meeting date(s): Dec. 1
Write: Edward W. Siebert, Mgr.
Officers and Directors:* Peter P. Donis,* Pres.; E.J. Schlegel,* Exec. V.P.; Edward W. Siebert, V.P. and Mgr.; B. DeHaan,* V.P.; H.W. Holling, V.P.; L.A. Kuchan, V.P.; R.R. Thornton, Secy.; A.C. Greer, Treas.
Employer Identification Number: 376022314

1812
CBI Foundation
800 Jorie Blvd.
Oak Brook 60521

Incorporated in 1953 in IL.
Donor(s): Chicago Bridge & Iron Co.
Foundation type: Company-sponsored
Financial data (yr. ended 12/31/89): Assets, $11,479 (M); gifts received, $266,344; expenditures, $223,364, including $223,322 for 58 grants (high: $9,000; low: $30; average: $100-$500).
Purpose and activities: Grants primarily for community funds, the arts, scientific and medical research, health associations and hospitals, child welfare, higher and other education, and civic affairs.
Types of support: Continuing support, annual campaigns, emergency funds, employee matching gifts, scholarship funds, research.
Limitations: Giving primarily in IL. No grants to individuals, or for building or endowment funds; no loans.
Application information: Application form not required.
Initial approach: Letter or proposal
Copies of proposal: 1
Deadline(s): None
Board meeting date(s): As required
Final notification: 45 days after board meets
Write: Susan E. Marks, Secy.
Officers: C.E. Willoughby,* Pres.; C.O. Zeimer,* V.P.; S.E. Marks, Secy.; B.T. Adams, Treas.; F.D. Martell, Admin.
Directors:* J.E. Jones, G.L. Schueppert.
Number of staff: None.
Employer Identification Number: 366050115

1813
Centralia Foundation ⌑ ☆
c/o Old National Bank
235 North Elm St.
Centralia 62801

Established in 1943.
Donor(s): Rollen Robinson, Lecta Rae Robinson.
Foundation type: Operating

Financial data (yr. ended 12/31/88): Assets, $5,117,755 (M); gifts received, $179,580; expenditures, $107,845, including $13,243 for grants.
Purpose and activities: A private operating foundation; giving for civic affairs, churches, and a hospital; also awards interest-free loans for higher education to local students. The foundation operates and maintains a park system and a Carillon Bell Tower.
Limitations: Giving primarily in Centralia, IL.
Trustees: Wendell Lamblin, Chair.; Verle Besant, Vice-Chair.; Lloyd Allen, Bruce Geary, David Harris, John Lackey, Dan Nichols.
Employer Identification Number: 376029269

1814
Community Foundation of Champaign County
c/o Bank of Illinois in Champaign
100 West University Ave., P.O. Box 826
Champaign 61824-0826 (217) 351-6607

Incorporated in 1972 in IL.
Foundation type: Community
Financial data (yr. ended 03/31/89): Assets, $1,643,552 (M); gifts received, $206,929; expenditures, $102,448, including $82,921 for grants.
Purpose and activities: Support for health programs, education, social services, the arts, civic affairs, and the humanities.
Types of support: Student aid, annual campaigns, building funds, consulting services, continuing support, equipment, program-related investments, publications, renovation projects.
Limitations: Giving primarily in Champaign, IL.
Publications: Annual report.
Application information: Application form required.
Copies of proposal: 1
Deadline(s): Feb. 1
Board meeting date(s): Feb. 15
Final notification: Mar. 1
Write: Albert D. Mulliken, Exec. Secy.
Officers: Donald G. Armstrong, Pres.; Richard L. Kirby, V.P.; Marilyn Thies, Secy.; Martin E. Verdick, Treas.
Number of staff: 1 part-time support.
Employer Identification Number: 237176723

1815
Frances Chapin Foundation ⌑
21960 North Harbor Rd.
Barrington 60010

Incorporated in 1966 in NJ.
Donor(s): Frances C. Crook.†
Foundation type: Independent
Financial data (yr. ended 03/31/89): Assets, $3,114,358 (M); expenditures, $151,632, including $140,000 for 20 grants (high: $20,000; low: $1,000).
Purpose and activities: Emphasis on hospitals, hospices and other social services, youth, higher and secondary education, and cultural programs; support also for conservation and historic preservation.
Limitations: Giving primarily in Barrington, IL. No grants to individuals.
Application information: Contributes only to pre-selected organizations. Applications not accepted.
Officer and Director: Thomas O. Maxfield III, Pres.
Employer Identification Number: 226087456

1816
Chapin-May Foundation of Illinois
c/o The Northern Trust Co.
50 South LaSalle St.
Chicago 60675 (312) 630-6000
Application address: c/o Vedder, Price, Kaufman & Kamholz, 222 North LaSalle St., Suite 2600, Chicago, IL, 60601; Tel.: (312) 609-7640

Established in 1944 in IL.
Donor(s): Simeon B. Chapin, Alice Chapin May.†
Foundation type: Independent
Financial data (yr. ended 12/31/87): Assets, $1,511,312 (M); expenditures, $98,809, including $74,500 for grants (average: $800-$6,000).
Purpose and activities: Support primarily for religious organizations, including schools, and higher education; some support for social services and hospitals.
Types of support: Scholarship funds.
Limitations: Giving primarily in the Chicago, IL, area. No grants to individuals.
Application information: Application form not required.
Initial approach: Letter
Copies of proposal: 1
Deadline(s): Mar. and Sept.
Board meeting date(s): Apr. and Oct.
Write: Michael E. Reed, Esq.
Trustee: The Northern Trust Co.
Employer Identification Number: 366039390

1817
Chapman and Cutler Charitable Trust ⌑
111 West Monroe
Chicago 60603

Foundation type: Independent
Financial data (yr. ended 12/31/87): Assets, $2,714 (M); gifts received, $121,168; expenditures, $119,845, including $119,845 for 50 grants (high: $71,985; low: $25).
Purpose and activities: Giving primarily for a community fund; support also for legal services, cultural programs, and youth.
Application information: Contributes only to pre-selected organizations. Applications not accepted.
Trustees: Edwin S. Brown, Richard H. Goss, David G. Williams.
Employer Identification Number: 363125206

1818
Elizabeth F. Cheney Foundation ⌑ ☆
2018 Orrington Ave.
Evanston 60201
Application address: 190 South LaSalle St., Chicago, IL 60604

Established in 1985.
Donor(s): Elizabeth F. Cheney Trust.
Foundation type: Independent
Financial data (yr. ended 5/31/88): Assets, $2,361,554 (M); gifts received, $564,509; expenditures, $368,334, including $281,173 for 19 grants (high: $80,000; low: $500).
Purpose and activities: Support primarily for fine and performing arts groups, historic preservation, and higher education.
Limitations: No grants to individuals.
Application information:
Initial approach: Letter
Deadline(s): None
Write: Howard McCue III, Secy.
Officers and Directors: Lawrence Belles, Pres.; Howard McCue III, Secy.; Allan Drebin, Treas.
Employer Identification Number: 363375377

1819
Chernin's Shoes Foundation ⌑
1001 South Clinton St.
Chicago 60607

Established in 1985 in IL.
Foundation type: Independent
Financial data (yr. ended 12/31/87): Assets, $188,307 (M); gifts received, $100,000; expenditures, $108,384, including $108,303 for 51 grants (high: $35,250; low: $50).
Purpose and activities: Giving primarily to Jewish organizations and youth programs.
Application information:
Initial approach: Letter
Deadline(s): None
Write: Steve B. Larrick, V.P.
Officers: Donald Lord, Pres.; Steven B. Larrick, V.P.; Myrna Lord, Treas.
Employer Identification Number: 363417280

1820
The Chicago Community Trust ▼
222 North LaSalle St., Suite 1400
Chicago 60601 (312) 372-3356

Established in 1915 in IL by bank resolution and declaration of trust.
Donor(s): Albert W. Harris, and members of the Harris family.
Foundation type: Community
Financial data (yr. ended 09/30/89): Assets, $316,431,057 (M); gifts received, $9,199,098; expenditures, $30,115,556, including $26,210,194 for 600 grants (high: $1,000,000; low: $100; average: $10,000-$50,000) and $333,402 for 5 loans.
Purpose and activities: Established "for such charitable purposes as will...best make for the mental, moral, intellectual and physical improvement, assistance and relief of the inhabitants of the County of Cook, State of Illinois." Grants for both general operating support and specific programs and projects in the areas of health and social services, youth agencies, education, particularly higher education, and cultural and civic affairs; awards fellowships to individuals in leadership positions in local community service organizations.
Types of support: Operating budgets, continuing support, emergency funds, building funds, equipment, land acquisition, loans, research, special projects, renovation projects, capital campaigns, general purposes, technical assistance, matching funds, program-related investments, seed money.

Limitations: Giving primarily in Cook County, IL. No support for religious purposes. No grants to individuals, (except for the Community Service Fellowship Program), or for annual campaigns, deficit financing, endowment funds, publications, conferences, or scholarships; no support for the purchase of computer hardware; no general operating support for agencies or institutions whose program activities substantially duplicate those already undertaken by others.
Publications: Annual report, informational brochure, program policy statement, application guidelines, newsletter.
Application information: Application form required for various special programs. Application form not required.
Initial approach: Proposal
Copies of proposal: 2
Deadline(s): Proposals scheduled for next available board meeting; no set deadline
Board meeting date(s): Jan., Mar., June, and Sept.
Final notification: 4-6 months after submission
Write: Ms. Sandy Cheers, Asst. to the Dir. (grants to organizations) and Joan Miller Wood (Community Service Fellowship Program)
Officer: Bruce L. Newman, Exec. Dir.
Executive Committee: James F. Bere, Chair.; Franklin A. Cole, Vice-Chair.; Mrs. Philip D. Block III, James J. Brice, Margaret D. Hartigan, Edgar D. Jannotta, Margaret P. MacKimm, Cordell Reed, Mrs. Patrick G. Ryan, Mrs. Gordon H. Smith, Rev. Dr. Kenneth B. Smith, Arthur R. Velasquez.
Trustees: American National Bank & Trust Co. of Chicago, Boulevard Bank, N.A., Chicago Title and Trust Co., Continental Illinois National Bank & Trust Co. of Chicago, First National Bank of Chicago, Harris Trust & Savings Bank, Heritage Pullman Bank, LaSalle National Bank, The Northern Trust Co.
Number of staff: 18 full-time professional; 1 part-time professional; 13 full-time support; 1 part-time support.
Employer Identification Number: 362167000

1821
Chicago Resource Center ▼ ⌘
53 West Jackson Blvd., Suite 315
Chicago 60604 (312) 461-9333

Established in 1981 in IL.
Donor(s): Thomas A. Dennis, Richard J. Dennis.
Foundation type: Independent
Financial data (yr. ended 12/31/88): Assets, $9,084,810 (M); expenditures, $1,581,129, including $1,322,050 for 228 grants (high: $82,156; low: $1,000; average: $3,000-$10,000).
Purpose and activities: Support for projects dealing with violence against women and families, gay and lesbian issues, and AIDS education.
Types of support: Operating budgets, seed money, equipment, matching funds, continuing support.
Limitations: No grants to individuals, or for annual campaigns, deficit financing, building funds, land acquisition, endowment funds, scholarships, or fellowships; no loans.
Publications: Application guidelines, program policy statement, grants list.
Application information: Application form not required.
Initial approach: Proposal
Copies of proposal: 1
Deadline(s): Mar. 31, June 30, and Sept. 30
Board meeting date(s): Jan., July, and Oct.
Final notification: 4 months
Write: Mary Ann Snyder, Dir.
Officers and Director:* Richard J. Dennis, Pres.; Thomas A. Dennis, V.P.; Mary Ann Snyder,* Secy.-Treas.
Number of staff: 2 full-time professional; 1 full-time support.
Employer Identification Number: 363121813

1822
Chicago Title and Trust Company Foundation ⌘
111 West Washington St.
Chicago 60602 (312) 630-2911

Trust established in 1951 in IL.
Donor(s): Chicago Title and Trust Co.
Foundation type: Company-sponsored
Financial data (yr. ended 12/31/88): Assets, $1,079,986 (M); gifts received, $447,125; expenditures, $405,597, including $391,309 for 331 grants (high: $96,700; low: $25).
Purpose and activities: Emphasis on community funds, social services, higher education, health, hospitals, and culture; support also for community improvement, public policy, and economic understanding and development.
Types of support: Continuing support, employee matching gifts, special projects.
Limitations: Giving primarily in Chicago, IL. No support for United Way member agencies. No grants to individuals, or for operating budgets, annual campaigns, seed money, emergency funds, deficit financing, building funds, equipment, land acquisition, research, scholarships, fellowships, publications, or conferences; no loans.
Publications: Program policy statement, application guidelines.
Application information: Application form required.
Initial approach: Letter
Copies of proposal: 1
Deadline(s): Feb. 1 for culture, May 1 for education, and Aug. 1 for health
Board meeting date(s): Jan., Apr., July, and Oct.
Final notification: 60 days
Write: Ms. Carolyn I. Smith
Trustees: Alvin Behnke, Stuart Bilton, M. Leanne Lachman, Alvin Long, Alan Prince, Richard P. Toft, Lannette Zimmerman.
Number of staff: 2 part-time professional; 1 full-time support.
Employer Identification Number: 366036809

1823
Christiana Foundation, Inc. ⌘
c/o Hinshaw, Culbertson, Moelmann, Hoban and Fuller
222 North LaSalle St., Suite 300
Chicago 60601-1081

Incorporated in 1957 in IL.
Donor(s): Lapham Hickey Steel Co.
Foundation type: Company-sponsored
Financial data (yr. ended 04/30/89): Assets, $1,176,073 (M); expenditures, $108,959, including $105,100 for 51 grants (high: $20,000; low: $250).
Purpose and activities: Emphasis on higher and secondary education, Roman Catholic institutions, health organizations, and social service and youth agencies.
Limitations: Giving primarily in IL. No grants to individuals.
Application information: Application form not required.
Initial approach: Letter
Deadline(s): None
Write: Jerome A. Frazel, Jr., Pres.
Officer and Directors:* Jerome A. Frazel, Jr.,* Pres.; Jerome V. Frazel, Joanne K. Frazel.
Employer Identification Number: 366065745

1824
CLARCOR Foundation
(Formerly Clark Foundation)
2323 Sixth St.
P.O. Box 7007
Rockford 61125 (815) 962-8867

Trust established in 1954 in IL.
Donor(s): CLARCOR.
Foundation type: Company-sponsored
Financial data (yr. ended 12/31/89): Assets, $7,302,078 (M); expenditures, $550,625, including $471,100 for grants (high: $100,000; low: $300) and $17,710 for 31 employee matching gifts.
Purpose and activities: Emphasis on health and hospitals, social services and youth agencies, higher and other education, arts and culture, including museums and the theater, and community funds.
Types of support: Employee matching gifts, continuing support, annual campaigns, emergency funds, building funds, equipment, capital campaigns, operating budgets, renovation projects.
Limitations: Giving primarily in areas of company operations in IL, IN, MD, MI, NE, and PA. No grants to individuals, or for endowment funds, research, scholarships, or fellowships; no loans.
Publications: Program policy statement, application guidelines.
Application information: Application form required.
Initial approach: Letter
Copies of proposal: 1
Deadline(s): None
Board meeting date(s): Jan., Apr., July, and Oct.
Write: W.F. Knese, Chair.
Officers and Trustees:* William F. Knese,* Chair.; Marshall C. Arne, Lawrence E. Gloyd, L.P. Harnois, J.S. Waddell.
Number of staff: None.
Employer Identification Number: 366032573

1825
Alvin & Lorraine Cohn Family Foundation ⌑
1515 North Astor
Chicago 60610

Established in 1982 in IL.
Donor(s): Alvin W. Cohn, Lorraine Cohn.
Foundation type: Independent
Financial data (yr. ended 12/31/88): Assets, $1,560,014 (M); gifts received, $217,250; expenditures, $183,846, including $177,625 for 36 grants (high: $153,000; low: $50).
Purpose and activities: Grants primarily for Jewish welfare funds and other Jewish giving; some support also for hospitals and health associations.
Limitations: Giving primarily in Chicago, IL. No grants to individuals.
Application information: Contributes only to pre-selected organizations. Applications not accepted.
Officers and Directors: Alvin W. Cohn, Pres.; Lee Cohn, V.P.; Bari Michelon, Secy.; Lorraine Cohn, Treas.
Employer Identification Number: 363203303

1826
The Robert & Terri Cohn Family Foundation ⌑
191 Apple Tree Rd.
Winnetka 60093

Established in 1982 in IL.
Donor(s): Robert Cohen.
Foundation type: Independent
Financial data (yr. ended 01/31/89): Assets, $2,219,642 (M); gifts received, $825,000; expenditures, $79,814, including $73,865 for 46 grants (high: $51,000; low: $50).
Purpose and activities: Support primarily for Jewish welfare; support also for hospitals, cultural programs, and health organizations.
Application information:
Deadline(s): None
Officers and Directors: Robert H. Cohn, Pres.; Andrew Cohn, V.P.; Jamie Cohn, V.P.; Jonathan Cohn, V.P.; Lawrence Cohn, V.P.; Terri H. Cohn, Treas.
Employer Identification Number: 363192296

1827
Jacob & Rosaline Cohn Foundation ⌑
c/o Northern Trust Co.
50 South LaSalle St.
Chicago 60675

Established in 1950 in IL.
Foundation type: Independent
Financial data (yr. ended 12/31/87): Assets, $1,589,953 (M); expenditures, $72,421, including $58,045 for 24 grants (high: $21,650; low: $100).
Purpose and activities: Giving primarily to Jewish organizations and higher education.
Limitations: Giving primarily in Chicago, IL.
Application information: Applications not accepted.
Employer Identification Number: 362468452

1828
Cole-Taylor Financial Group Foundation ⌑ ☆
350 East Dundee Rd., Suite 305
Wheeling 60090 (312) 459-1111

Established in 1984 in IL.
Foundation type: Independent
Financial data (yr. ended 12/31/88): Assets, $15,794 (M); gifts received, $9,322; expenditures, $148,682, including $148,335 for 68 grants (high: $80,200; low: $50).
Purpose and activities: Giving primarily for Jewish welfare organizations; support also for higher education, social services, and youth.
Limitations: Giving primarily in Chicago, IL.
Application information: Application form not required.
Deadline(s): None
Write: Sidney J. Taylor, Pres.
Officers and Directors: Sidney J. Taylor, Pres.; Irwin H. Cole, V.P.; Robert I. Logan, Secy.; Frank E. Bauder, Treas.; Bruce Taylor.
Employer Identification Number: 363331558

1829
The Coleman Foundation, Inc. ▼
(Formerly The Coleman/Fannie May Candies Foundation, Inc.)
1137 West Jackson Blvd.
Chicago 60607 (312) 243-2700

Trust established in 1953 in IL.
Donor(s): J.D. Stetson Coleman,† Dorothy W. Coleman,† Fannie May Candy Shops, Inc., Archibald Candy Corp.
Foundation type: Independent
Financial data (yr. ended 12/31/89): Assets, $61,195,768 (M); expenditures, $3,532,330, including $2,797,256 for 106 grants (high: $300,000; low: $500; average: $1,000-$28,000) and $127,200 for 7 foundation-administered programs.
Purpose and activities: Giving for social services and civic affairs; elementary, secondary, entrepreneurial, and other education; and the medical sciences, including hospitals, cancer research, scientific research, rehabilitation, and programs to aid the handicapped.
Types of support: Operating budgets, annual campaigns, general purposes, seed money, special projects, research, publications, conferences and seminars, building funds, equipment, land acquisition, professorships, internships, scholarship funds, fellowships, capital campaigns, renovation projects, endowment funds, emergency funds, continuing support, matching funds, program-related investments.
Limitations: Giving primarily in the Chicago, IL, metropolitan area; support also in Washington, DC, FL, IL, IN, MI, MN, MO, PA, and WI. No grants to individuals (including direct scholarships or fellowships), or for deficit financing, or ticket purchases; no loans.
Publications: Annual report (including application guidelines), financial statement, informational brochure (including application guidelines), program policy statement, application guidelines.
Application information: Submit full proposal only at the request of the foundation. Unsolicited applications not accepted. Application form not required.
Initial approach: Concise letter describing program or institution
Copies of proposal: 1
Deadline(s): Sept. 30 for solicited proposals only
Board meeting date(s): Usually in Jan., Apr., July, and Oct.
Final notification: 3 months; no response to unsolicited proposals
Write: Jean D. Thorne, Exec. Dir.
Officers and Directors:* John E. Hughes,* Pres.; Richard M. Peritz,* Exec. V.P.; C. Hugh Albers,* V.P.; R. Michael Furlong,* V.P.; James H. Jones,* Treas.; Jean D. Thorne,* Exec. Dir.; Trevor C. Davies.
Number of staff: 3 full-time professional; 3 part-time professional; 6 full-time support; 4 part-time support.
Employer Identification Number: 363025967

1830
Earle M. & Virginia M. Combs Foundation ⌑
141 West Jackson Blvd.
Chicago 60604 (312) 922-3900

Established in 1967 in IL.
Donor(s): Earle M. Combs III, Virginia M. Combs.
Foundation type: Independent
Financial data (yr. ended 12/31/88): Assets, $2,615,861 (M); gifts received, $263,132; expenditures, $205,367, including $201,130 for 21 grants (high: $100,000; low: $250).
Purpose and activities: Giving primarily for religious purposes and to youth organizations; some support for higher education and culture.
Types of support: General purposes.
Limitations: No grants to individuals.
Application information: Contributes only to pre-selected organizations. Applications not accepted.
Officers: Earle M. Combs III, Pres.; Virginia M. Combs, Secy.
Directors: B.V. Combs, Earle M. Combs IV, B.F. Etters, Donald F. Miller.
Employer Identification Number: 366168454

1831
The Comer Foundation ⌑ ☆
1325 North Astor
Chicago 60610

Established in 1986 in IL.
Donor(s): Gary C. Comer, Frances Comer.
Foundation type: Independent
Financial data (yr. ended 12/31/88): Assets, $10,999,432 (M); gifts received, $100,000; expenditures, $729,824, including $540,656 for 4 grants (high: $275,000; low: $6,250).
Purpose and activities: Giving primarily for a community pool facility, youth, and education.
Limitations: No grants to individuals.
Application information: Contributes only to pre-selected organizations. Applications not accepted.
Officers and Directors: Gary C. Comer, Pres. and Treas.; Frances Comer, V.P. and Secy.; Nicholas P. Goschi.
Employer Identification Number: 363522486

1832
Continental Bank Foundation
(Formerly Continental Illinois Foundation)
231 South LaSalle St.
Chicago 60697 (312) 923-5114

Incorporated in 1962 in IL.
Donor(s): Continental Illinois Corp.
Foundation type: Company-sponsored
Financial data (yr. ended 12/31/89): Assets, $0 (M); expenditures, $2,374,631, including $1,622,071 for grants (high: $25,000; low: $1,000; average: $2,500-$10,000) and $303,340 for employee matching gifts.
Purpose and activities: Grants primarily for economic development, low- and moderate-income housing, and education of economically disadvantaged youth.
Types of support: Operating budgets, equipment, renovation projects, publications, technical assistance, employee matching gifts, special projects, research, continuing support.
Limitations: Giving limited to the Chicago, IL, metropolitan area. No support for programs designed to influence legislation, or for tax-supported educational institutions; pre-school, elementary, or secondary educational institutions; sectarian or religious organizations supporting any one religious group; or grantmaking foundations. No grants to individuals, or for endowment funds, scholarships, fellowships, trips, advertising, or operating expenses of organizations receiving United Way support; no loans.
Publications: Application guidelines.
Application information: Application form not required.
Initial approach: Proposal
Copies of proposal: 1
Board meeting date(s): Quarterly
Final notification: Varies
Write: Julie Chavez, V.P., or Cynthia Patten
Officers: Kurt Stocker, Pres.; Julie Chavez, V.P. and Treas.; Kevin J. Hallagan, Secy.
Number of staff: 3 full-time support.
Employer Identification Number: 366056976

1833
Continental Charitable Foundation ⌑ ☆
5900 West Howard St.
Skokie 60076

Donor(s): Eugene Witz, Leo Witz, William M. Witz, Continental Electrical Construction Co.
Foundation type: Independent
Financial data (yr. ended 1/31/89): Assets, $632,445 (M); expenditures, $101,200, including $100,550 for 77 grants (high: $15,000; low: $25).
Purpose and activities: Giving primarily for Jewish organizations, including a welfare fund and a Hebrew theological college; support also for health associations and the performing arts, with emphasis on opera companies.
Limitations: Giving primarily in IL and AZ. No grants to individuals.
Application information:
Initial approach: Letter
Deadline(s): None
Officers: William M. Witz, Pres.; Charles L. Witz, Secy.; Neil S. Harris, Treas.
Employer Identification Number: 366047700

1834
Richard H. Cooper Foundation ⌑
611 Enterprise Dr.
Oak Brook 60521

Established in 1969 in IL.
Donor(s): Richard H. Cooper, Cooperfund, Inc.
Foundation type: Independent
Financial data (yr. ended 12/31/88): Assets, $1,713,466 (M); gifts received, $1,208,000; expenditures, $168,630, including $167,900 for 21 grants (high: $31,000; low: $100).
Purpose and activities: Support primarily for youth and community organizations, the performing arts, and museums.
Limitations: Giving primarily in IL. No grants to individuals.
Application information: Contributes only to pre-selected organizations. Applications not accepted.
Officers: Richard H. Cooper,* Pres. and Treas.; Lana S. Cooper,* Secy.
Directors:* Jean Frandsen.
Employer Identification Number: 237024516

1835
Philip H. Corboy Foundation ⌑
30 North LaSalle St.
Chicago 60602

Established in 1983 in IL.
Donor(s): Philip H. Corboy.
Foundation type: Independent
Financial data (yr. ended 12/31/87): Assets, $1,916,120 (M); gifts received, $70,000; expenditures, $101,210, including $98,700 for 51 grants (high: $25,000; low: $100).
Purpose and activities: Grants primarily for health associations and services, religious giving, youth, and education.
Application information: Applications not accepted.
Directors: Philip H. Corboy, Jr., George Costorilos, Thomas Cronin, Thomas T. Durkin.
Employer Identification Number: 363211607

1836
The Cottrell Foundation
c/o Carleton M. Tower & Co.
33 North Dearborn St., Suite 2020
Chicago 60602
Application address: 296 Alexander Palm Rd., Boca Raton, FL 33432

Established in 1965 in IL.
Foundation type: Independent
Financial data (yr. ended 12/31/89): Assets, $1,649,888 (M); gifts received, $50,000; expenditures, $98,300, including $98,300 for 101 grants (high: $10,000; low: $100).
Purpose and activities: Giving primarily for Catholic-affiliated schools, churches, and organizations, including missionaries in Africa and Asia.
Limitations: No grants to individuals.
Application information:
Initial approach: Letter
Deadline(s): None
Write: Joseph J. Cottrell, Sr., Trustee
Trustees: Mary M. Acuff, Joseph J. Cottrell, Sr., Joseph Cottrell, M.D., Mary M. Cottrell.
Number of staff: None.
Employer Identification Number: 166064303

1837
A. G. Cox Charitable Trust ⌑
c/o First National Bank of Chicago
One First National Plaza, Suite 0111
Chicago 60670-0111

Established in 1924 in IL.
Foundation type: Independent
Financial data (yr. ended 12/31/87): Assets, $2,610,506 (M); expenditures, $63,769, including $60,000 for 29 grants (high: $6,000; low: $500).
Purpose and activities: Support primarily for health and social service organizations.
Trustee: First National Bank of Chicago.
Employer Identification Number: 366011498

1838
The Crane Fund ▼ ⌑
327 South LaSalle St., Suite 929
Chicago 60604-3305

Established in 1914.
Foundation type: Independent
Financial data (yr. ended 12/31/88): Assets, $71,043,696 (M); expenditures, $2,001,429, including $1,646,392 for grants to individuals.
Purpose and activities: Grants restricted to indigent and needy former employees of Crane Co. in the U.S. and Great Britain.
Types of support: Grants to individuals.
Limitations: Giving primarily in the U.S. and Great Britain.
Application information:
Deadline(s): None
Write: Fern N. Brodie, Sr. Caseworker
Trustees: W.C. Dackis, E.G. Dalrymple, P.R. Hundt, R.K. Whitley.
Employer Identification Number: 366124341

1839
Crane Fund for Widows and Children ⌑
327 South LaSalle St., Suite 929
Chicago 60604-3305

Established in 1914 in IL.
Foundation type: Independent
Financial data (yr. ended 12/31/88): Assets, $9,694,827 (M); expenditures, $514,957, including $386,759 for 187 grants (high: $32,300; low: $100) and $15,576 for 3 grants to individuals (high: $11,760; low: $1,500).
Purpose and activities: Giving to community funds, hospitals, and for higher education; limited support also to organizations in Canada; assistance to needy and indigent persons, mainly in IL.
Types of support: Grants to individuals.
Limitations: Giving primarily in the U.S. and Canada; grants for needy persons limited to IL.
Application information:
Initial approach: Letter
Deadline(s): None
Write: The Trustees
Officer: K.H. Cardoza, Mgr.
Trustees: J.P. Cronin, E.G. Dalrymple, P.R. Hundt, R.B. Phillips, M.L. Raithel.
Employer Identification Number: 366116543

1840
Crawford Foundation ⌑ ☆
405 North Wabash Ave., Suite 4009
Chicago 60611 (312) 527-4114

Established in 1956.
Donor(s): William F. Crawford.
Foundation type: Independent
Financial data (yr. ended 12/31/88): Assets, $1,105,189 (M); expenditures, $68,322, including $63,600 for 18 grants (high: $35,000; low: $300).
Purpose and activities: Support primarily for higher education, including a military academy.
Limitations: Giving primarily in IL. No grants to individuals.
Application information:
Initial approach: Letter
Deadline(s): Nov. 30
Write: William F. Crawford, Trustee
Trustee: William F. Crawford.
Employer Identification Number: 366111373

1841
Henry P. Crowell and Susan C. Crowell Trust ▼
Lock Box 442
Chicago 60690 (312) 372-5202

Trust established in 1927 in IL.
Donor(s): Henry P. Crowell,† Henry P. Crowell Benevolence and Education Trust, Henry P. and Susan C. Crowell Trust.
Foundation type: Independent
Financial data (yr. ended 12/31/88): Assets, $36,911,401 (M); gifts received, $254,492; expenditures, $2,029,686, including $1,771,500 for 94 grants (high: $350,000; low: $3,000; average: $10,000-$25,000).
Purpose and activities: Created to aid evangelical Christianity by support to organizations having for their purposes its teaching, advancement, and active extension at home and abroad.
Types of support: Matching funds, operating budgets, building funds, equipment, scholarship funds, general purposes.
Limitations: No grants to individuals, or for endowment funds or research; no loans.
Application information: Application form not required.
Initial approach: Proposal or letter
Copies of proposal: 1
Deadline(s): Apr. 1 and Oct. 1
Board meeting date(s): May and Nov.
Final notification: 1 to 2 months
Write: Lowell L. Kline, Exec. Dir.
Officers and Trustees:* LeRoy E. Johnson,* Pres.; Edwin L. Frizen, Jr.,* V.P.; Lowell L. Kline,* Secy. and Exec. Dir.; John T. Bass,* Treas.; John F. Robinson.
Corporate Trustee: Continental Illinois National Bank & Trust Co. of Chicago.
Number of staff: 2 part-time professional.
Employer Identification Number: 366038028

1842
Edward A. Crown Charitable Fund
222 North LaSalle St., Suite 2000
Chicago 60601 (312) 236-6300

Established in 1977 in IL.
Donor(s): Edward A. Crown.†
Foundation type: Independent
Financial data (yr. ended 07/31/89): Assets, $9,149,657 (M); expenditures, $363,264, including $335,000 for 8 grants (high: $100,000; low: $1,000).
Purpose and activities: Grants for higher education and Jewish welfare funds.
Types of support: Continuing support, equipment, endowment funds, matching funds, scholarship funds, fellowships, special projects, research, general purposes.
Limitations: Giving primarily in IL. No grants to individuals; no loans.
Application information: Applications not accepted.
Board meeting date(s): As required
Write: Susan Crown, Trustee
Trustees: Arie Steven Crown, James Schine Crown, Lester Crown, Susan Crown, Charles Goodman, Barbara N. Manilow, Byron S. Miller.
Number of staff: None.
Employer Identification Number: 362996704

1843
Arie and Ida Crown Memorial
222 North LaSalle St.
Chicago 60601 (312) 236-6300

Incorporated in 1947 in IL.
Donor(s): Members of the Crown family.
Foundation type: Independent
Financial data (yr. ended 12/31/88): Assets, $89,697,281 (M); expenditures, $3,923,431, including $3,765,850 for grants (average: $100-$25,000).
Purpose and activities: Broad mandate with focus on "opportunity building"; emphasis on Jewish issues, education, arts and culture, health care, community development, youth agencies, inner city welfare, women, and assistance to the aged and the handicapped.
Types of support: Continuing support, annual campaigns, equipment, endowment funds, matching funds, professorships, research, special projects, general purposes, operating budgets, renovation projects, technical assistance.
Limitations: Giving primarily in the metropolitan Chicago, IL, area or to national organizations with local programs. No support for government-sponsored programs. No grants to individuals, or for consulting services or conferences; no loans.
Application information: Application form not required.
Initial approach: Letter of inquiry (1 page)
Copies of proposal: 1
Deadline(s): Jan. 30, May 31, and Sept. 30
Board meeting date(s): Spring, summer, and fall
Write: Susan Crown, Pres.
Officers and Directors:* Susan Crown,* Pres.; Lester Crown,* V.P. and Treas.; Arie Steven Crown, James Schine Crown, Charles Goodman, Barbara N. Manilow, Byron S. Miller.
Number of staff: 1 full-time professional; 1 part-time professional; 1 full-time support.
Employer Identification Number: 366076088

1844
The Cuneo Foundation
9101 Greenwood Ave., Suite 210
Niles 60648-1466

Incorporated in 1945 in IL.
Donor(s): John F. Cuneo, Milwaukee Golf Development Corp.
Foundation type: Independent
Financial data (yr. ended 12/31/88): Assets, $15,385,335 (M); expenditures, $724,382, including $551,450 for 154 grants (high: $31,413; low: $50).
Purpose and activities: Emphasis on hospitals, Roman Catholic church support, church-related organizations, religious associations, and welfare funds; support also for youth agencies and higher education.
Types of support: General purposes, building funds, equipment, matching funds.
Limitations: Giving primarily in the Chicago, IL, metropolitan area. No grants to individuals, or for scholarships, fellowships, or research projects; no loans.
Application information:
Initial approach: Proposal
Copies of proposal: 1
Deadline(s): None
Board meeting date(s): May and Oct.
Final notification: 2 months
Write: John F. Cuneo, Jr., Pres.
Officers: John F. Cuneo, Jr.,* Pres.; Charles L. McEvoy,* V.P.; Robert F. Routh, Secy.-Treas.
Directors:* Herta Cuneo, Rev. Msgr. Harry C. Koenig, Consuela Cuneo McAlister, Tim McAlister, Rosemary McEvoy.
Number of staff: None.
Employer Identification Number: 362261606

1845
D and R Fund ▼ ⌑
8000 Sears Tower
Chicago 60606

Incorporated in 1951 in IL.
Donor(s): Samuel R. Rosenthal, Marie-Louise Rosenthal, Carolyn S. Dreyfus,† Alice L. Dreyfus.†
Foundation type: Independent
Financial data (yr. ended 12/31/88): Assets, $7,441,286 (M); expenditures, $221,677, including $181,385 for 58 grants (high: $35,000; low: $100; average: $100-$10,000).
Purpose and activities: Grants largely for higher education, hospitals, libraries, cultural institutions, and conservation purposes.
Limitations: No grants to individuals, or for building or endowment funds or operating budgets.
Application information: Contributes only to pre-selected organizations. Applications not accepted.
Board meeting date(s): As necessary
Write: Samuel R. Rosenthal, Pres.
Officers and Directors: Samuel R. Rosenthal, Pres.; Marie-Louise Rosenthal, V.P. and Secy.; Louise R. Glasser, V.P. and Treas.; James J. Glasser, Babette H. Rosenthal, Daniel R. Swet, Anthony G. Zulfer, Jr.
Number of staff: None.
Employer Identification Number: 366057159

1846
The Danielson Foundation ⌘
410 North Michigan Ave., Rm. 590
Chicago 60611-4252

Established in 1964 in IL.
Foundation type: Independent
Financial data (yr. ended 11/30/88): Assets, $889,088 (M); gifts received, $101,000; expenditures, $161,703, including $155,000 for 39 grants (high: $25,000; low: $1,000).
Purpose and activities: Support primarily for cultural and educational organizations; support also for health and civic associations, hospitals, churches, and higher education.
Limitations: Giving primarily in CA and FL. No grants to individuals.
Application information:
Deadline(s): None
Officers and Directors: Richard E. Danielson, Jr., Pres.; Molly Danielson, V.P. and Secy.; Charles E. Schroeder, V.P. and Treas.; Candida D. Burnap, Lee Danielson.
Employer Identification Number: 362540494

1847
James Deering Danielson Foundation ⌘
410 North Michigan Ave., Rm. 590
Chicago 60611

Established in 1969 in IL.
Donor(s): Deering Foundation.
Foundation type: Independent
Financial data (yr. ended 12/31/87): Assets, $790,614 (M); gifts received, $110,000; expenditures, $104,995, including $100,000 for 17 grants (high: $16,000; low: $1,000).
Purpose and activities: Support for higher and other education, religious organizations, particularly Presbyterian churches, and cultural programs.
Types of support: General purposes.
Application information: Contributes only to pre-selected organizations. Applications not accepted.
Officers and Directors: James Deering Danielson, Pres.; Charles E. Schroeder, V.P. and Treas.; Beverly Danielson, Secy.
Employer Identification Number: 237042530

1848
DAO Foundation ⌘ ☆
c/o Rockford Acromatic Products Co.
611 Beacon St.
Rockford 61111-5902

Donor(s): Aircraft Gear Corp., Rockford Acromatic Products Co.
Foundation type: Independent
Financial data (yr. ended 3/31/89): Assets, $1,528,139 (M); gifts received, $20,000; expenditures, $57,700, including $57,000 for 18 grants (high: $10,000; low: $260).
Purpose and activities: Giving primarily for higher and other education; support also for youth and social service agencies.
Limitations: Giving primarily in Rockford, IL. No grants to individuals.
Application information:
Initial approach: Letter
Deadline(s): None
Write: Nobel D. Olson, Trustee
Trustees: Amy Olson, Nancy N. Olson, Nobel D. Olson, Pat Olson.
Employer Identification Number: 366101712

1849
The Davee Foundation ⌘
180 East Pearson St., No. 6503
Chicago 60611 (312) 664-4128

Established in 1964 in IL.
Donor(s): Ken M. Davee.
Foundation type: Independent
Financial data (yr. ended 12/31/88): Assets, $14,349,130 (M); expenditures, $729,216, including $728,230 for 41 grants (high: $500,000; low: $100).
Purpose and activities: Emphasis on the arts, hospitals, and higher education; support also for civil rights organizations.
Types of support: General purposes.
Limitations: Giving primarily in IL.
Application information:
Initial approach: Letter
Deadline(s): None
Write: Ken M. Davee, Pres.
Officer: Ken M. Davee, Pres.
Director: J.W. Dugdale.
Employer Identification Number: 366124598

1850
John Deere Foundation ▼
John Deere Rd.
Moline 61265 (309) 765-4137

Incorporated in 1948 in IL.
Donor(s): Deere & Co.
Foundation type: Company-sponsored
Financial data (yr. ended 10/31/89): Assets, $7,271,233 (M); gifts received, $7,500,000; expenditures, $4,904,122, including $3,707,974 for grants (high: $539,500; low: $500; average: $500-$5,000), $146,704 for 1 foundation-administered program and $300,000 for in-kind gifts.
Purpose and activities: Grants largely for community funds, higher education, agriculture, youth agencies, health services, and cultural programs.
Types of support: Annual campaigns, seed money, building funds, scholarship funds, fellowships, operating budgets, general purposes, continuing support.
Limitations: Giving limited to areas where company employees live and work: IA, IL, and WI. No grants to individuals, or for endowment funds; no loans.
Publications: Corporate giving report (including application guidelines).
Application information: Application form not required.
Initial approach: Letter or telephone
Copies of proposal: 1
Deadline(s): None
Board meeting date(s): As required, usually quarterly
Final notification: 30 days after board review
Write: Donald R. Margenthaler, Pres.
Officers: Joseph W. England, Chair.; Donald R. Margenthaler, Pres.; Hans W. Becherer, V.P.; Robert A. Hanson, V.P.; Sonja Sterling, Secy.; Michael S. Plunkett, Treas.
Number of staff: 1 full-time professional; 1 full-time support.
Employer Identification Number: 366051024

1851
Deering Foundation ⌘
410 North Michigan Ave., Rm. 590
Chicago 60611

Incorporated in 1956 in IL.
Donor(s): Barbara D. Danielson, Richard E. Danielson, Jr., Marion D. Campbell, Miami Corp.
Foundation type: Independent
Financial data (yr. ended 11/30/88): Assets, $6,349,634 (M); expenditures, $485,214, including $460,000 for 15 grants (high: $100,000; low: $5,000).
Purpose and activities: Support for other foundations, hospitals, education, conservation, and museums.
Types of support: General purposes.
Limitations: Giving primarily in IL and MA.
Officers and Directors: Marion D. Campbell, Pres.; James Deering Danielson, V.P.; Richard E. Danielson, Jr., V.P.; Charles E. Schroeder, Secy.-Treas.
Employer Identification Number: 366051876

1852
Edwin F. Deicke Foundation ⌘
P.O. Box 734
Wheaton 60189

Trust established in 1956 in IL.
Donor(s): Edwin F. Deicke, Suburban Casualty Co., Pioneer Insurance Co.
Foundation type: Independent
Financial data (yr. ended 12/31/87): Assets, $1,559,232 (M); expenditures, $240,780, including $221,400 for 24 grants (high: $50,000; low: $100).
Purpose and activities: Support primarily for a performing arts center and an historical museum; support also for youth organizations and higher education.
Limitations: Giving primarily in IL and FL.
Application information:
Initial approach: Letter
Deadline(s): None
Write: Mrs. Edwin F. Deicke, Chair.
Trustees: Mrs. Edwin F. Deicke, Chair.; James D. Anderson, Robert Covert, Lois L. Deicke, Lois D. Martin.
Employer Identification Number: 366053612

1853
DeKalb Genetics Foundation
(Formerly The DeKalb Foundation)
3100 Sycamore Rd.
DeKalb 60115 (815) 758-3461

Incorporated in 1964 in IL.
Donor(s): DeKalb Genetics Corp.
Foundation type: Company-sponsored
Financial data (yr. ended 08/31/89): Assets, $372,000 (M); expenditures, $193,000, including $125,000 for 90 grants (high: $15,000; low: $10; average: $800-$1,000) and $67,000 for 165 employee matching gifts.
Purpose and activities: Grants largely for colleges, civic affairs, social welfare and youth agencies, and community funds in areas of company operations. Educational support limited normally to privately endowed institutions not supported by public tax funds.
Types of support: Continuing support, annual campaigns, seed money, emergency funds,

building funds, equipment, land acquisition, matching funds, special projects, employee matching gifts, publications, general purposes.
Limitations: Giving primarily in areas of company operations. No support for religious or labor organizations, policemen's or firemen's ball activities, or publicly-funded educational institutions. No grants to individuals, or for operating budgets, individual travel, study, or similar purposes; no loans.
Publications: Annual report, application guidelines.
Application information: Application form not required.
Initial approach: Letter
Copies of proposal: 1
Deadline(s): None
Board meeting date(s): Quarterly
Final notification: 2 months
Write: Gregory L. Olson, Secy.
Officers and Directors:* Bruce P. Bickner,* Pres.; Richard O. Ryan,* V.P.; Gregory L. Olson,* Secy.; Alan D. Skouby,* Treas.
Number of staff: None.
Employer Identification Number: 366117737

1854
N. Demos Foundation, Inc.
c/o The Northern Trust Co.
50 South LaSalle St.
Chicago 60675

Incorporated in 1964 in NY.
Donor(s): Nicholas Demos.†
Foundation type: Independent
Financial data (yr. ended 06/30/89): Assets, $3,004,501 (M); expenditures, $178,962, including $150,000 for grants.
Purpose and activities: Grants for education and child welfare.
Types of support: Scholarship funds.
Limitations: Giving limited to Greece. No grants to individuals.
Publications: Application guidelines.
Application information: Application form not required.
Initial approach: Letter
Deadline(s): Sept. 1
Board meeting date(s): Fall
Final notification: Dec. 31
Write: William C. Diebel, Secy.
Officers and Directors:* Gordon H. Smith,* Pres.; William C. Diebel,* Secy.; Robert F. Reusche,* Treas.; Elizabeth R. Gebhard, Charles Gray, Bishop Iakovos, Mrs. Irving Seamen, Jr., Mrs. Theodore D. Tieken.
Number of staff: None.
Employer Identification Number: 366165689

1855
DeSoto Foundation
P.O. Box 5030
1700 South Mt. Prospect Rd.
Des Plaines 60017 (312) 391-9112

Incorporated in 1963 in IL.
Donor(s): DeSoto, Inc.
Foundation type: Company-sponsored
Financial data (yr. ended 12/31/88): Assets, $704,245 (M); gifts received, $250,000; expenditures, $308,660, including $295,265 for 107 grants (high: $40,310; low: $100) and $12,985 for 47 employee matching gifts.
Purpose and activities: Emphasis on community funds, higher education, youth agencies, crime and law enforcement, health agencies, mental health programs, hospitals, and cultural programs.
Types of support: Employee matching gifts.
Limitations: Giving primarily in IL.
Application information: Application form not required.
Initial approach: Letter
Copies of proposal: 1
Deadline(s): Before board meetings
Board meeting date(s): Mar., Aug., and Nov.
Final notification: After meetings
Write: J. Barreiro, V.P.
Officers: R.R. Missar,* Pres.; J. Barreiro,* V.P.; Nicholas A. Vittore, Secy.-Treas.
Directors:* W.L. Lamey, Jr.
Number of staff: 4 part-time professional; 2 part-time support.
Employer Identification Number: 366097563

1856
Dick Family Foundation ⌑
249 Market Sq.
Box 312
Lake Forest 60045

Foundation type: Independent
Financial data (yr. ended 12/31/88): Assets, $2,235,837 (M); expenditures, $83,995, including $65,800 for 44 grants (high: $12,000; low: $200).
Purpose and activities: Support for hospitals, higher and other education, and arts and culture.
Limitations: Giving primarily in IL. No grants to individuals.
Application information: Contributes only to pre-selected organizations. Applications not accepted.
Officers and Directors:* Edison Dick,* Pres.; Albert B. Dick III,* V.P.; John H. Dick,* Secy.-Treas.; Mrs. John O. Cully, Letitia Ellis.
Employer Identification Number: 366057056

1857
Dillon Foundation ▼
2804 West LeFevre Rd.
P.O. Box 537
Sterling 61081 (815) 626-9000

Incorporated in 1953 in IL.
Donor(s): Members of the Dillon family.
Foundation type: Independent
Financial data (yr. ended 10/31/89): Assets, $23,179,465 (M); expenditures, $1,315,409, including $1,046,914 for 83 grants (high: $341,700; low: $75; average: $250-$6,000).
Purpose and activities: Support for community development and civic, urban, and public affairs; vocational, secondary and other education; social services and youth; historic preservation and museums; recreation; and libraries.
Types of support: Continuing support, annual campaigns, seed money, emergency funds, building funds, scholarship funds, general purposes, endowment funds, equipment, land acquisition, matching funds, special projects.
Limitations: Giving primarily in the Sterling, IL, area. No grants to individuals; no loans.
Application information: Application form not required.
Initial approach: Letter
Copies of proposal: 1
Deadline(s): None
Board meeting date(s): Jan.; committee meets quarterly
Final notification: As soon as possible following committee meetings
Write: Peter W. Dillon, Pres.
Officers and Directors:* Peter W. Dillon,* Pres.; John P. Conway,* V.P. and Secy.; James M. Boesen,* Treas.; Margo Dillon, Gale Inglee.
Number of staff: 1 part-time professional.
Employer Identification Number: 366059349

1858
The Distribution Fund ⌑
c/o Klein Gallery
356 West Huron
Chicago 60610

Incorporated in 1965 in CA.
Donor(s): Nora R. Klein,† Robert H. Klein.†
Foundation type: Independent
Financial data (yr. ended 8/31/88): Assets, $1,014,763 (M); expenditures, $298,150, including $290,101 for 19 grants (high: $100,000; low: $500; average: $30-$1,000).
Purpose and activities: Grants largely for agencies primarily serving youth-oriented programs; support also for hospitals and health agencies, welfare, and religious welfare agencies.
Types of support: Continuing support, annual campaigns, seed money, equipment, matching funds, research, special projects.
Limitations: Giving primarily in CA, with emphasis on Menlo Park and the San Francisco Bay Area. No grants to individuals, or for endowment funds, scholarships, or fellowships; no loans.
Application information: Application form not required.
Initial approach: Letter
Copies of proposal: 1
Deadline(s): None
Board meeting date(s): Quarterly
Final notification: 2 months
Write: Paul R. Klein, Pres.
Officers: Paul R. Klein, Pres.; Henry D. Klein, Secy.-Treas.
Number of staff: None.
Employer Identification Number: 946117979

1859
F.B. Doane Foundation ⌑
115 South LaSalle St., Suite 3400
Chicago 60603-3903

Established in 1959 in IL.
Foundation type: Independent
Financial data (yr. ended 12/31/88): Assets, $1,180,356 (M); expenditures, $68,576, including $42,266 for 10 grants (high: $8,000; low: $1,000).
Purpose and activities: Giving to a high school for awards to the highest achieving students and a college for awards to students in the art department; support also for other colleges and art museums.
Limitations: Giving primarily in Bandera, TX. No grants to individuals.

Application information: Contributes only to pre-selected organizations. Applications not accepted.
Officers: S.D. Turk, Pres.; R.W. Calvert, V.P. and Treas.; M.D. Calvert, V.P.; T.P. Healy, Secy.
Employer Identification Number: 746040766

1860
Elliott and Ann Donnelley Foundation ⌘
1121 Ringwood Rd.
Lake Forest 60045

Incorporated in 1954 in IL.
Donor(s): Elliott Donnelley.†
Foundation type: Independent
Financial data (yr. ended 12/31/87): Assets, $2,766,217 (M); expenditures, $202,627, including $200,275 for 67 grants (high: $81,000; low: $25; average: $500-$2,000).
Purpose and activities: Giving for hospitals and education; support also for cultural programs and youth agencies.
Types of support: Continuing support.
Limitations: Giving primarily in IL. No grants to individuals.
Application information: Applications not accepted.
Board meeting date(s): As required
Write: Ann S. Hardy, Pres.
Officers and Director:* Ann S. Hardy,* Pres. and Treas.; Robert Wood Tullis, Secy.
Number of staff: None.
Employer Identification Number: 366066894

1861
Gaylord and Dorothy Donnelley Foundation
350 East 22nd St.
Chicago 60616 (312) 326-7255

Incorporated in 1952 in IL.
Donor(s): Gaylord Donnelley, Dorothy Ranney Donnelley.
Foundation type: Independent
Financial data (yr. ended 12/31/89): Assets, $9,500,000 (M); gifts received, $525,595; expenditures, $744,718, including $681,023 for 125 grants (high: $82,183; low: $500; average: $1,000-$2,000).
Purpose and activities: Support for higher and other education, health, wildlife and conservation, museums and other cultural programs, historic preservation, animal health and welfare, and general welfare institutions, including programs for the homeless.
Types of support: General purposes, operating budgets, special projects.
Limitations: Giving primarily in the Chicago, IL, area and in SC. No support for the performing arts. No grants to individuals, or for emergency funds, pledges, benefits, conferences, meetings, or matching gifts; no loans.
Publications: Application guidelines.
Application information: Application form not required.
Initial approach: 1-page proposal together with more descriptive letter if desired
Copies of proposal: 1
Deadline(s): None
Board meeting date(s): Spring and fall
Write: Mrs. Jane Rishel, Pres.
Officers and Directors:* Gaylord Donnelley,* Chair.; Jane Rishel,* Pres. and Treas.; Dorothy Ranney Donnelley,* V.P.; Elliott R. Donnelley,* V.P.; Laura Donnelley,* V.P.; Strachan Donnelley,* V.P.; Middleton Miller,* Secy.; Larry D. Berning, Robert T. Carter, Robert W. Carton, M.D., C. Bouton McDougal.
Number of staff: 1 full-time professional.
Employer Identification Number: 366108460

1862
Thomas E. Donnelley II Foundation ⌘
255 Overlook Dr.
Lake Forest 60045

Established in 1969 in IL.
Foundation type: Independent
Financial data (yr. ended 12/31/88): Assets, $838 (M); expenditures, $123,987, including $123,250 for 86 grants (high: $15,000; low: $100).
Purpose and activities: General charitable giving, with emphasis on education.
Limitations: Giving primarily in IL. No grants to individuals.
Application information: Contributes only to pre-selected organizations. Applications not accepted.
Officers and Directors: Thomas E. Donnelley II, Pres. and Treas.; Robert Wood Tullis, Secy.; James R. Donnelley.
Employer Identification Number: 362669841

1863
Thomas W. Dower Foundation ⌘ ☆
c/o John M. Hartigan
9730 South Western Ave., Suite 206
Evergreen Park 60642-2814

Established in 1951.
Donor(s): Thomas W. Dower.†
Foundation type: Independent
Financial data (yr. ended 4/30/89): Assets, $3,718,005 (M); gifts received, $926,660; expenditures, $196,109, including $133,021 for 68 grants (high: $35,171; low: $200).
Purpose and activities: Giving primarily for higher and other education; support also for welfare, health and hospitals, and Christian organizations.
Limitations: Giving primarily in IL.
Officer: Daniel J. O'Shaughnessy, Exec. Dir.
Trustee: Mary Hartigan.
Employer Identification Number: 366071665

1864
Dreier-Penrith Family Foundation ⌘
c/o Craig M. Penrith
2401 North Halsted
Chicago 60614

Established in IL.
Donor(s): O.T. Hogan.†
Foundation type: Independent
Financial data (yr. ended 10/31/88): Assets, $1,114,877 (M); expenditures, $266,534, including $239,065 for 31 grants (high: $135,000; low: $50).
Purpose and activities: Giving for religious schools and other educational institutions, hospitals, and other health agencies.
Limitations: Giving primarily in IL and CA.
Application information: Contributes only to pre-selected organizations. Applications not accepted.
Officers: Geraldine I. Dreier, Pres.; Gary L. Penrith, Secy.; Craig M. Penrith, Treas.
Employer Identification Number: 363012144

1865
The Richard H. Driehaus Foundation ⌘
Three First National Plaza, Suite 5315
Chicago 60602

Established in 1983 in IL.
Donor(s): Richard H. Driehaus.
Foundation type: Independent
Financial data (yr. ended 10/31/88): Assets, $5,833,379 (M); expenditures, $346,429, including $280,000 for 8 grants (high: $150,000; low: $10,000).
Purpose and activities: Support for Catholic organizations and associations that aid disadvantaged, handicapped, or terminally ill children.
Types of support: General purposes.
Limitations: Giving primarily in IL.
Application information: Contributes only to pre-selected organizations. Applications not accepted.
Trustees: Margaret F. Driehaus, Joni S. Taylor.
Employer Identification Number: 363261347

1866
The Duchossois Foundation
c/o Lois May
845 Larch Ave.
Elmhurst 60126 (312) 279-3600

Established in 1984 in IL.
Donor(s): Duchossois Industries, Inc.
Foundation type: Company-sponsored
Financial data (yr. ended 12/31/89): Assets, $827,108 (M); expenditures, $635,578, including $613,825 for 45 grants (high: $250,000; low: $100).
Purpose and activities: Support for health programs, community and social services, cultural programs, and elementary education.
Types of support: General purposes, capital campaigns.
Limitations: Giving primarily in the metropolitan Chicago, IL, area.
Publications: Application guidelines.
Application information: Guidelines available upon request. Application form not required.
Initial approach: Letter
Copies of proposal: 1
Deadline(s): None
Board meeting date(s): Every 6 weeks
Write: Kimberly Duchossois Lenczuk, Secy.
Officers and Directors:* Richard L. Duchossois,* Pres.; Craig J. Duchossois,* V.P.; R. Bruce Duchossois,* V.P.; Kimberly Duchossois Lenczuk,* Secy.; Lois B. May,* Treas.
Number of staff: 1 part-time professional.
Employer Identification Number: 363327987

1867
Eades Foundation
Six Dunlap Court
Savoy 61874 (217) 359-7031

Established in 1969 in IL.
Foundation type: Independent
Financial data (yr. ended 12/31/88): Assets, $1,133,729 (M); expenditures, $75,300, including $68,700 for 7 grants (high: $40,000; low: $200).
Purpose and activities: Support primarily for youth organizations; giving also to benefit the handicapped and institutions of higher education.
Types of support: Operating budgets.
Application information: Applications not accepted.
Write: David C. Eades, Trustee
Trustees: David C. Eades, Elizabeth Eades, Jane Y. Eades, Katherine Grill.
Number of staff: None.
Employer Identification Number: 237045810

1868
Education Communications Scholarship Foundation
721 North McKinley Rd.
Lake Forest 60045 (708) 295-6650

Established in 1969 in IL.
Donor(s): Educational Communications, Inc.
Foundation type: Company-sponsored
Financial data (yr. ended 03/31/88): Assets, $72,104 (M); gifts received, $35,000; expenditures, $198,980, including $116,063 for 88 grants (high: $5,750; low: $100).
Purpose and activities: Support primarily for education through awarding approximately 100 higher education scholarships of $1,000 each which are paid through institutions.
Types of support: Student aid, scholarship funds.
Application information: Application form required.
Initial approach: Letter
Deadline(s): June 1
Final notification: Aug. 1
Write: Maureen O'Connor
Directors: Ann Krouse, Paul C. Krouse.
Employer Identification Number: 237032032

1869
Educational Foundation of the National Restaurant Association
(Formerly National Institute for the Food Service Industry)
250 South Wacker Dr., Suite 1400
Chicago 60606 (312) 715-1010
Tel. outside IL: (800) 522-7578

Established in 1971 in IL.
Donor(s): National Restaurant Assn.
Foundation type: Operating
Financial data (yr. ended 06/30/89): Assets, $4,730,613 (M); gifts received, $1,291,843; expenditures, $2,117,798, including $301,523 for grants to individuals.
Purpose and activities: A private operating foundation which "develops courses, programs, and textbooks on topics related to the food service industry." Grants to individuals for scholarships and fellowships for the food service field, as well as work-study grants to teachers and administrators.
Types of support: Student aid, fellowships.
Publications: Application guidelines, program policy statement.
Application information: Application form required.
Deadline(s): Mar. 1 for scholarships; Dec. 31 for work-study grants and Heinz Fellowships
Officers and Trustees:* Jack A. Laughery,* Chair.; Ted Balestreri,* 1st Vice-Chair.; Jim L. Peterson,* 2nd Vice-Chair.; Jon C. Peterson,* Secy.; Michael J. Grisanti,* Treas.; and 22 additional trustees.
Employer Identification Number: 366103388

1870
The George M. Eisenberg Foundation ⌑
4100 West Fullerton Ave.
Chicago 60639

Trust established in 1945 in IL.
Donor(s): George M. Eisenberg, American Decal and Manufacturing Co.
Foundation type: Independent
Financial data (yr. ended 12/31/87): Assets, $2,667,217 (M); gifts received, $525,566; expenditures, $564,373, including $544,975 for 11 grants (high: $500,000; low: $100).
Purpose and activities: Emphasis on hospitals, medical research, and social service agencies, particularly those serving the aged, the handicapped, and youth.
Limitations: Giving primarily in IL.
Trustees: George M. Eisenberg, James L. Pollack, Charles H. Weinman.
Employer Identification Number: 366091694

1871
Epaphroditus Foundation ⌑
650 Devon Ave., Suite 160
Itasca 60143

Established in 1945 in IL.
Foundation type: Independent
Financial data (yr. ended 2/29/88): Assets, $1,814,329 (M); expenditures, $108,158, including $104,000 for 31 grants (high: $15,000; low: $1,000).
Purpose and activities: Giving primarily for religious purposes and for programs aiding the disadvantaged.
Application information: Contributes only to pre-selected organizations. Applications not accepted.
Officers: K.E. Gundersen, Pres.; M.C. Gundersen, V.P. and Treas.; Jane L. Ridder, Secy.
Directors: Fred M. Johnson, R.G. McLennan, Margorie Michaelson, Vernon Mortenson.
Employer Identification Number: 366072198

1872
Eben W. Erickson Charitable Fund ⌑
c/o The Northern Trust Co.
50 South LaSalle St.
Chicago 60675 (312) 630-6000

Established in 1985 in IL.
Donor(s): Eben W. Erickson.
Foundation type: Independent
Financial data (yr. ended 7/31/88): Assets, $7,018,113 (M); expenditures, $386,536, including $348,996 for 85 grants (high: $4,400; low: $3,630).
Purpose and activities: Support for youth and social sevice agencies, higher and other education, including religious education, and churches and other religious organizations.
Application information:
Deadline(s): None
Trustees: Eben W. Erickson, The Northern Trust Co.
Employer Identification Number: 366826316

1873
Dr. Ralph and Marian Falk Medical Research Foundation ⌑
c/o Continental Illinois National Bank and Trust Co. of Chicago
30 North LaSalle St.
Chicago 60693 (312) 828-3666

Established in 1974 in IL.
Donor(s): Marian C. Falk.
Foundation type: Independent
Financial data (yr. ended 12/31/87): Assets, $2,865,739 (M); expenditures, $64,840.
Purpose and activities: Support primarily for medical research.
Limitations: Giving primarily in Chicago, IL.
Application information: Application form not required.
Deadline(s): None
Write: M.J. Termondt, V.P.
Officers and Directors: Marian C. Falk, Pres. and Treas.; Carol C. Fullinwider, V.P.; M.J. Termondt, V.P.; Nicole Kohl, Secy.
Employer Identification Number: 237380541

1874
William F. Farley Foundation ⌑
233 South Wacker Dr., Suite 6300
Chicago 60606 (312) 993-1827

Established about 1979 in IL.
Foundation type: Company-sponsored
Financial data (yr. ended 4/30/88): Assets, $2,717 (M); gifts received, $356,727; expenditures, $392,779, including $392,675 for 208 grants (high: $100,000; low: $25).
Purpose and activities: Grants primarily to community funds and for secondary and higher education; support also for civic and cultural organizations and social service agencies.
Limitations: No grants to individuals.
Application information:
Initial approach: Letter or proposal
Deadline(s): None
Write: Ms. Pamela L. Webber
Officer and Directors: William F. Farley, Pres.; John M. Albertine, Barbara Farley, John F. Farley, Douglas Kinney, Barbara F. Mooney, Maureen Thornton.
Employer Identification Number: 362977029

1875
Joseph and Bessie Feinberg Foundation ⌑
5245 West Lawrence Ave.
Chicago 60630 (312) 777-8600

Established in 1969 in IL.
Donor(s): Ruben Feinberg.

Foundation type: Independent
Financial data (yr. ended 10/31/87): Assets, $34,214,308 (M); gifts received, $21,508,419; expenditures, $331,550, including $278,065 for 38 grants.
Purpose and activities: Giving primarily for Jewish welfare and education; support also for a local television station.
Limitations: Giving primarily in IL.
Application information: Contributes only to pre-selected organizations. Applications not accepted.
Write: June Blossom
Officers and Trustees: Ruben Feinberg, Pres.; Frances Feinberg, Secy.; Beatrice Crain, Barney Goldberg, Louis Goldberg, Paul Goldberg, Evan Maling, Albert Rubenstein, Lauren Rubenstein.
Employer Identification Number: 237028857

1876
Fel-Pro/Mecklenburger Foundation ▼
c/o Fel-Pro Inc.
7450 North McCormick Blvd.
Skokie 60076 (708) 674-7700
Additional tel.: (708) 674-7701, ext. 2411
Fel-Pro Automotive Technicians Scholarship address: c/o Citizens' Scholarship Fdn. of America, P.O. Box 297, St. Peter, MN 56082; Tel.: (507) 931-1682

Incorporated in 1959 in IL.
Donor(s): Fel-Pro Inc., Felt Products Manufacturing Co., Fel-Pro International, Fel-Pro Realty.
Foundation type: Company-sponsored
Financial data (yr. ended 12/31/89): Assets, $5,974,168 (M); gifts received, $500,000; expenditures, $1,135,018, including $1,076,028 for 346 grants (high: $150,000; low: $100; average: $1,000-$10,000) and $29,149 for 314 employee matching gifts.
Purpose and activities: Grants to operating organizations, with emphasis on basic human needs and services, vocational training, corporate social responsibility, minority and inner-city concerns, women's issues, community-based organizations, Israel, Jewish giving and welfare, legal services, civil rights, the disadvantaged, and the environment; scholarships only awarded through a special Automotive Technicians' Scholarship Program.
Types of support: Operating budgets, continuing support, seed money, matching funds, employee matching gifts, special projects.
Limitations: Giving limited to the Chicago, IL, metropolitan area. No grants to individuals, or for emergency, capital, building or endowment funds, deficit financing, equipment, land acquisition, scholarships (except through the Automotive Technicians Scholarship Program), fellowships, research, publications, or conferences; no loans.
Publications: Informational brochure (including application guidelines), 990-PF.
Application information: Scholarship applications available through the Citizens' Scholarship Foundation of America, Inc., which selects recipients, or schools' financial aid offices. Application form not required.
Initial approach: Proposal
Copies of proposal: 1
Deadline(s): None
Board meeting date(s): Bimonthly beginning in Feb.
Final notification: 3 months
Write: Celene Peurye, Dir., Corp. Contrib. Prog.
Officers and Directors:* Paul Lehman,* Pres.; Dennis Kessler,* V.P.; Robert Morris,* V.P.; Sylvia Radov,* Secy.; Frances Lehman,* Treas.; Celene Peurye,* Dir., Corp. Contrib. Prog.
Number of staff: 1 part-time professional.
Employer Identification Number: 366065607

1877
The Field Corporation Fund
333 West Wacker Dr., 30th Fl.
Chicago 60606 (312) 917-1828

Established in 1985 in IL.
Donor(s): Field Corp.
Foundation type: Company-sponsored
Financial data (yr. ended 12/31/89): Assets, $50,523 (M); gifts received, $358,921; expenditures, $361,000, including $257,454 for 69 grants (high: $8,000; low: $500; average: $2,000-$8,000) and $100,257 for 522 employee matching gifts.
Purpose and activities: Support for environmental concerns, and pre-college and adult basic education.
Types of support: Employee matching gifts, operating budgets, general purposes, matching funds, seed money, special projects.
Limitations: Giving primarily in the Chicago, IL, area. No support for religious groups for sectarian purposes, private foundations, political or fraternal organizations, or United Way member agencies for general support. No grants to individuals, or for the purchase of tickets or fundraising benefits.
Publications: Informational brochure (including application guidelines), annual report, grants list.
Application information: Application form not required.
Initial approach: Letter
Copies of proposal: 1
Deadline(s): Dec. 15, Mar. 15, June 15, and Sept. 15
Board meeting date(s): Feb., May, Aug., and Nov.
Write: Iris Krieg, Exec. Dir.
Directors: Iris J. Krieg, Exec. Dir.; Marshall Field, Lee M. Mitchell.
Number of staff: 1 full-time professional; 1 full-time support.
Employer Identification Number: 363308686

1878
Jamee and Marshall Field Foundation ☆
333 West Wacker Dr., 30th Fl.
Chicago 60606-6604 (312) 917-1828

Established in 1982 in IL.
Donor(s): Jamee J. Field, Marshall Field.
Foundation type: Independent
Financial data (yr. ended 09/30/89): Assets, $4,429,602 (M); gifts received, $676,684; expenditures, $326,415, including $323,595 for 63 grants (high: $64,000; low: $200).
Purpose and activities: Giving primarily in the following areas: 1) Conservation and environment, particularly preservation of unique natural areas, wildlife protection, and pollution abatement; 2) Children and youth, particularly programs combatting child abuse by prevention or early intervention or which foster early childhood development among children at risk; and 3) Culture, for selected major cultural institutions.
Types of support: Annual campaigns, capital campaigns, general purposes.
Limitations: Giving primarily in the metropolitan Chicago, IL, area. No support for national health agencies, political or fraternal organizations, or United Way member agencies. No grants to individuals, or for medical or scholarly research, benefits, tickets or advertisements, conferences, meetings, publications, or films or videos.
Application information: Application form not required.
Initial approach: Proposal
Copies of proposal: 1
Deadline(s): Feb. 1, May 1, and Sept. 1
Board meeting date(s): Mar., June, and Oct.
Write: Iris J. Krieg, Exec. Dir.
Officers and Directors:* Marshall Field,* Pres.; Jamee J. Field,* V.P.; Edwin H. Watkins,* Secy.-Treas.; Iris J. Krieg,* Exec. Dir.
Number of staff: 1 full-time professional; 1 full-time support.
Employer Identification Number: 363184245

1879
The Field Foundation of Illinois, Inc. ▼ ⌑
135 South LaSalle St.
Chicago 60603 (312) 263-3211

Incorporated in 1960 in IL.
Donor(s): Marshall Field IV.†
Foundation type: Independent
Financial data (yr. ended 04/30/89): Assets, $29,304,784 (M); expenditures, $2,047,913, including $1,579,109 for 57 grants (high: $97,000; low: $5,000; average: $10,000-$20,000).
Purpose and activities: Giving in the fields of health, community welfare, education, cultural activities, conservation, and urban affairs; grants focused on youth agencies, race relations, and the aged.
Types of support: Building funds, emergency funds, equipment, special projects, land acquisition.
Limitations: Giving primarily in the Chicago, IL, area. No support for member agencies of community funds, national health agencies, neighborhood health clinics, small cultural groups, private schools, or for religious purposes. No grants to individuals, or for endowment funds, continuing operating support, medical research, conferences, operating support of day care centers, fundraising events, advertising, scholarships, or fellowships; no loans.
Publications: Annual report (including application guidelines).
Application information: Application form not required.
Initial approach: Proposal
Copies of proposal: 1
Deadline(s): None
Board meeting date(s): 3 times a year
Write: Handy L. Lindsey, Jr., Exec. Dir.

Officers: E. Leland Webber,* Chair.; Gary H. Kline, Secy.; Handy L. Lindsey, Jr., Exec. Dir. and Treas.
Directors:* Marshall Field, Hanna H. Gray, Philip Wayne Hummer, Arthur F. Quern, George A. Ranney, Jr., Arthur E. Rasmussen.
Number of staff: 1 full-time professional; 1 full-time support.
Employer Identification Number: 366059408

1880
C. W. Finkl Foundation, Inc. ⌑
2011 Southport Ave.
Chicago 60614

Established in 1985 in IL.
Donor(s): Charles W. Finkl.
Foundation type: Independent
Financial data (yr. ended 10/31/88): Assets, $908,049 (M); gifts received, $200,000; expenditures, $210,240, including $203,987 for 28 grants (high: $200,000; low: $24).
Purpose and activities: Support for marine science and vocational education.
Limitations: Giving primarily in Chicago, IL. No grants to individuals.
Application information: Contributes only to pre-selected organizations. Applications not accepted.
Officers and Directors: Charles W. Finkl, Pres.; Sara-Lee Finkl, Secy.-Treas.; Albert Lehman.
Employer Identification Number: 363412118

1881
First Evergreen Foundation ☆
c/o First National Bank of Evergreen Park
3101 West 95th St.
Evergreen Park 60642 (708) 422-6700

Established in 1985 in IL.
Donor(s): First National Bank of Evergreen Park.
Foundation type: Company-sponsored
Financial data (yr. ended 12/31/89): Assets, $2,000,000 (M); gifts received, $500,000; expenditures, $132,500, including $132,500 for 11 grants (high: $25,000; low: $5,000).
Purpose and activities: Giving primarily for hospitals, higher education, and churches.
Limitations: Giving primarily in the southwest Chicago, IL, area. No grants to individuals.
Application information:
Initial approach: Proposal
Deadline(s): None
Write: Kenneth Ozinga, Trustee
Trustees: Alfred E. Bleeker, Jerome J. Cismoski, Kenneth J. Ozinga, Martin Ozinga, Jr.
Employer Identification Number: 363456053

1882
First National Bank of Chicago Foundation ⌑
One First National Plaza
Chicago 60670 (312) 732-6948

Incorporated in 1961 in IL.
Donor(s): First National Bank of Chicago.
Foundation type: Company-sponsored
Financial data (yr. ended 12/31/87): Assets, $893,768 (M); gifts received, $270,000; expenditures, $702,634, including $81,000 for 23 grants (high: $6,500; low: $1,000) and $339,629 for employee matching gifts.
Purpose and activities: Giving to organizations in social welfare, education, community development, culture and the arts, and civic affairs; support also for a local United Way/Crusade of Mercy.
Types of support: Operating budgets, continuing support, annual campaigns, building funds, equipment, endowment funds, matching funds, scholarship funds, fellowships, employee matching gifts, capital campaigns.
Limitations: Giving limited to the metropolitan Chicago, IL, area. No support for fraternal or religious organizations, preschool, elementary, or secondary education, public agencies, or United Way/Crusade of Mercy-supported agencies. No grants to individuals, or for emergency funds, deficit financing, land acquisition, research, publications, conferences, or multi-year operating pledges; no loans.
Publications: Informational brochure (including application guidelines).
Application information: Application form not required.
Initial approach: Letter
Copies of proposal: 1
Deadline(s): None
Board meeting date(s): Mar., June, Sept., and Dec.
Final notification: 3 months
Write: David J. Paulus, Pres.
Officers and Directors:* David J. Paulus,* Pres.; Clark Burrus,* V.P.; Lawrence E. Fox,* V.P.; A.D. Frazier, Jr.,* V.P.; Emile S. Godfrey, Jr., V.P.; William S. Lear,* V.P.; William J. McDonough,* V.P.; Leo F. Mullin,* V.P.; Diane M. Smith,* V.P.; Barry F. Sullivan,* V.P.; Richard L. Thomas,* V.P.; David J. Vitale,* V.P.; Ilona M. Berry, Secy.
Number of staff: 2 full-time professional; 2 full-time support.
Employer Identification Number: 366033828

1883
Father James M. Fitzgerald Scholarship Trust ⌑
c/o Commercial National Bank of Peoria
301 S.W. Adams St.
Peoria 61631 (309) 655-5322

Trust established in 1964 in IL.
Donor(s): Father James M. Fitzgerald.†
Foundation type: Independent
Financial data (yr. ended 12/31/88): Assets, $1,430,753 (M); expenditures, $98,259, including $86,671 for grants to individuals.
Purpose and activities: Grants restricted to priesthood students attending a Catholic university or college, and to the highest ranking boy and girl at St. Mark's Catholic School, Peoria, IL, enrolling in a Catholic high school.
Types of support: Student aid.
Limitations: Giving limited to residents of IL. No grants for general purposes, capital or endowment funds, matching gifts, research, special projects, publications, or conferences; no loans.
Application information: Application form not required.
Initial approach: Letter
Deadline(s): None
Board meeting date(s): As required
Final notification: 30 days
Trustees: Rev. William C. Feeney, Commercial National Bank of Peoria.
Number of staff: None.
Employer Identification Number: 376050189

1884
Fixler Family Foundation ⌑ ☆
c/o Fixler Corp.
400 Skokie Blvd., Suite 590
Skokie 60062

Established in 1985 in IL.
Donor(s): Lowell S. Fixler.
Foundation type: Independent
Financial data (yr. ended 1/31/88): Assets, $832,874 (M); gifts received, $500; expenditures, $124,564, including $112,000 for grants.
Purpose and activities: Support for Jewish welfare funds and general charitable purposes.
Limitations: Giving primarily in Chicago, IL. No grants to individuals.
Application information: Contributes only to pre-selected organizations. Applications not accepted.
Officers and Directors: Lowell S. Fixler, Pres. and Treas.; Michael C. Fixler, V.P.; Kenneth A. Fixler, Secy.
Employer Identification Number: 363411385

1885
FMC Foundation ▼
200 East Randolph Dr.
Chicago 60601 (312) 861-6135

Incorporated in 1953 in CA.
Donor(s): FMC Corp.
Foundation type: Company-sponsored
Financial data (yr. ended 11/30/89): Assets, $636,203 (M); gifts received, $1,350,000; expenditures, $1,816,358, including $1,557,755 for 200 grants (high: $215,900; low: $1,000; average: $2,000-$15,000) and $258,603 for 1,491 employee matching gifts.
Purpose and activities: Giving primarily for higher education and community improvement funds; grants also for public issues, economic education, urban affairs, health and human services, cultural institutions, civic affairs groups, and youth agencies.
Types of support: Building funds, continuing support, employee matching gifts, scholarship funds, special projects, general purposes, employee-related scholarships, capital campaigns, equipment.
Limitations: Giving primarily in areas in which company facilities are located. No support for educational institutions below the college or university level, or state or regional associations of independent colleges, national health agencies, or United Way supported organizations. No grants to individuals, or for endowment funds or hospital operating expenses; no loans.
Publications: Program policy statement, application guidelines.
Application information: Application form not required.
Initial approach: Letter
Copies of proposal: 1
Deadline(s): None
Board meeting date(s): Quarterly
Final notification: 6 weeks

Write: Catherine Johnston, Exec. Dir.
Officers: William R. Jenkins,* Pres.; William J. Kirby,* V.P.; James A. McClung,* V.P.; Daniel N. Schuchardt, Secy.-Treas.
Directors:* Robert N. Burt, Robert H. Malott.
Number of staff: 1 full-time professional; 1 part-time support.
Employer Identification Number: 946063032

1886
Foote, Cone & Belding Foundation ¤
101 East Erie
Chicago 60611 (312) 751-7000

Incorporated in 1947 in IL.
Donor(s): Foote, Cone & Belding Communications, Inc., and subsidiaries.
Foundation type: Company-sponsored
Financial data (yr. ended 12/31/87): Assets, $100,510 (M); expenditures, $250,999, including $250,975 for 50 grants (high: $50,000; low: $100).
Purpose and activities: Emphasis on higher education, community funds, cultural programs, and youth agencies.
Application information:
Initial approach: Letter
Deadline(s): None
Write: Gregory Blaine, Sr. V.P.
Officers and Directors: Willard R. Wirth, Jr., Pres.; Gregory Blaine, Sr. V.P.; David Ofner, V.P.; Thomas F. Randolph, V.P.; Charles H. Gunderson, Jr., Secy.-Treas.
Employer Identification Number: 366116701

1887
The Forest Fund ¤
Route 1, Box 32, St. Mary's Rd.
Libertyville 60048 (312) 362-2994

Incorporated in 1956 in IL.
Donor(s): Marion M. Lloyd.
Foundation type: Independent
Financial data (yr. ended 12/31/88): Assets, $2,687,015 (M); expenditures, $159,313, including $151,050 for 144 grants (high: $5,500; low: $100).
Purpose and activities: Grants primarily for education, health services, and cultural programs.
Limitations: Giving primarily in IL, with emphasis on Chicago. No grants to individuals, or for endowment funds, scholarships, or fellowships; no loans.
Application information: Application form not required.
Initial approach: Proposal
Copies of proposal: 1
Deadline(s): None
Write: Marion M. Lloyd, Pres.
Officers: Marion M. Lloyd, Pres. and Treas.; Louise A. Baker, Secy.
Director: Marianne S. Harper.
Employer Identification Number: 366047859

1888
The Fotsch Foundation ¤
6615 North Leroy Ave.
Lincoln Wood 60646

Established in 1967 in IL.
Foundation type: Independent
Financial data (yr. ended 11/30/88): Assets, $1,343,465 (M); expenditures, $68,715, including $60,250 for 29 grants (high: $5,100; low: $500).
Purpose and activities: Grants primarily for higher education, religious organizations, particularly Roman Catholic institutions, and welfare agencies.
Limitations: Giving primarily in IL.
Application information: Contributes only to pre-selected organizations. Applications not accepted.
Officer: William G. Fotsch, Pres.
Employer Identification Number: 366190007

1889
Foundation for Health Enhancement ¤
c/o Continental Bank, N.A.
30 North LaSalle St.
Chicago 60697 (312) 828-1785

Established in 1979.
Foundation type: Independent
Financial data (yr. ended 12/31/88): Assets, $1,363,407 (M); expenditures, $100,896, including $84,500 for 10 grants (high: $12,000; low: $5,000).
Purpose and activities: To improve medical care in the U.S. with emphasis on smaller qualifying applicants.
Limitations: Giving primarily in the Midwest, with emphasis on the Chicago, IL, area.
Application information:
Initial approach: Proposal
Copies of proposal: 3
Deadline(s): None
Write: M.C. Ryan
Officers and Directors:* Dennis H. Chookaszian,* Pres.; Jae L. Wittlich,* V.P.; Donald M. Lowry,* 2nd V.P. and Secy.; Bernard L. Hergesbaugh,* Treas.; Peter E. Jokiel, Robert M. Kohlenbrener, M.D., Mervin Shalowitz, M.D., William A. Tech.
Employer Identification Number: 363043628

1890
Fraida Foundation ¤ ☆
208 South LaSalle St.
Chicago 60604

Donor(s): Hy Greenhill, Michael L. Greenhill.
Foundation type: Independent
Financial data (yr. ended 4/30/89): Assets, $1,707,248 (M); gifts received, $285,000; expenditures, $110,246, including $105,500 for 4 grants (high: $100,000; low: $1,000).
Purpose and activities: Giving primarily for higher education and medical development in Israel.
Limitations: No grants to individuals.
Application information: Contributes only to pre-selected organizations. Applications not accepted.
Write: Marc Simon, Pres.
Officers: Hy Greenhill, Chair.; Marc S. Simon, Pres.; Michael L. Greenhill, V.P.; Leonard H. Popowcer, V.P.
Employer Identification Number: 363126643

1891
Zollie and Elaine Frank Fund ¤
666 Garland Place
Des Plaines 60016

Incorporated in 1953 in IL.
Donor(s): Zollie S. Frank, Elaine S. Frank, Z. Frank, Inc., Four Wheels, Inc., Wheels, Inc.
Foundation type: Independent
Financial data (yr. ended 12/31/88): Assets, $1,862,086 (M); gifts received, $135,000; expenditures, $230,833, including $225,828 for 143 grants (high: $51,100; low: $10).
Purpose and activities: Emphasis on Jewish welfare funds and temple support; grants also for higher education, hospitals, and organized charities.
Limitations: Giving primarily in IL.
Application information:
Initial approach: Letter
Deadline(s): None
Write: Zollie S. Frank, Pres.
Officers: Zollie S. Frank, Pres.; Elaine S. Frank, V.P.; James S. Frank, Secy.
Employer Identification Number: 366118400

1892
Frankel Foundation ▼ ¤
c/o Harris Trust & Savings Bank
111 West Monroe St.
Chicago 60603
Application address: P.O. Box 755, Chicago, IL 60603

Established in 1959 in IL.
Donor(s): Gerald Frankel,† Gustav Frankel,† Julius N. Frankel.†
Foundation type: Independent
Financial data (yr. ended 10/31/88): Assets, $23,867,327 (M); gifts received, $2,072,309; expenditures, $1,864,106, including $1,655,500 for 37 grants (high: $530,000; low: $3,000).
Purpose and activities: Giving primarily for higher education, hospitals, arts and culture, and social services.
Limitations: Giving primarily in IL. No grants to individuals.
Application information: Application form not required.
Initial approach: Letter
Deadline(s): None
Board meeting date(s): 4 or 5 times a year
Final notification: Immediately following meetings
Write: Ellen A. Bechtold
Trustees: Nelson O. Cornelius, John L. Georgas, Harris Trust & Savings Bank.
Number of staff: None.
Employer Identification Number: 366765844

1893
Norman & Edna Freehling Foundation ¤ ☆
190 South LaSalle St.
Chicago 60603

Established in 1953.
Foundation type: Independent
Financial data (yr. ended 9/30/88): Assets, $1,129,168 (M); expenditures, $79,640, including $55,155 for 109 grants (high: $23,400; low: $10).

Purpose and activities: Giving primarily for Jewish organizations, especially a welfare fund; support also for arts and culture and higher education.
Limitations: Giving primarily in Chicago, IL. No grants to individuals.
Application information: Contributes only to pre-selected organizations. Applications not accepted.
Trustees: Edna Freehling, Norman Freehling.
Employer Identification Number: 366058353

1894
Friedman Family Foundation ⌑ ☆
5005 West Touhy Ave.
Skokie 60077 (312) 982-0400

Established in 1987 in IL.
Donor(s): Michael Friedman, Phillip Friedman.
Foundation type: Independent
Financial data (yr. ended 12/31/88): Assets, $48,321 (M); expenditures, $383,030, including $376,079 for grants (high: $275,000).
Purpose and activities: Giving to Jewish religious and educational institutions.
Limitations: Giving primarily in IL, with emphasis on Chicago. No grants to individuals.
Application information:
Initial approach: Letter
Write: David Friedman, Treas.
Officers: Michael Friedman, Pres.; Phillip Friedman, Secy.; David Friedman, Treas.
Employer Identification Number: 363487475

1895
Lloyd A. Fry Foundation ▼
135 South LaSalle St., Suite 1910
Chicago 60603 (312) 580-0310

Established in 1959 in IL.
Donor(s): Lloyd A. Fry.†
Foundation type: Independent
Financial data (yr. ended 06/30/89): Assets, $63,618,473 (M); expenditures, $3,374,199, including $2,651,460 for 153 grants (high: $115,000; low: $1,000; average: $5,000-$50,000).
Purpose and activities: Emphasis on higher and other education, civic and urban affairs, public policy, minorities and race relations, law and justice, employment, child welfare, the disadvantaged, health and social services, including AIDS programs, and cultural programs, including performing arts.
Types of support: Special projects, seed money, equipment, matching funds, research, publications, conferences and seminars, internships, scholarship funds.
Limitations: Giving primarily in the Chicago, IL, area. No support for governmental bodies or tax-supported educational institutions for services that fall within their responsibilities, or for fund-raising benefits. No grants to individuals, or for continuing support, annual campaigns, emergency funds, general operating budgets, deficit financing, building funds, land acquisition, renovation projects, endowment funds, or employee matching gifts; no loans.
Publications: Application guidelines, annual report (including application guidelines).
Application information: Application form not required.
Initial approach: Letter
Copies of proposal: 1
Deadline(s): None
Board meeting date(s): Feb., May, Aug., and Nov.
Final notification: 3 months
Write: Ben Rothblatt, Exec. Dir.
Officers and Directors:* Edmund A. Stephan,* Chair.; Roger E. Anderson,* Vice-Chair.; Lloyd A. Fry, Jr.,* Pres.; M. James Termondt,* V.P. and Treas.; Howard M. McCue III,* Secy.; Ben Rothblatt, Exec. Dir.
Number of staff: 1 full-time professional; 1 part-time professional; 1 full-time support.
Employer Identification Number: 366108775

1896
Paul A. Funk Foundation ☆
1001 North Main St.
P.O. Box 3488
Bloomington 61702-3488 (309) 828-6241

Established in 1967.
Foundation type: Independent
Financial data (yr. ended 06/30/88): Assets, $1,150,880 (M); expenditures, $52,858, including $48,750 for 33 grants (high: $16,000; low: $100).
Purpose and activities: Giving primarily for higher education; support also for hospitals, social services, and health associations.
Limitations: Giving primarily in McLean County, IL.
Application information: Applications not accepted.
Write: David Dunn, atty.
Trustees: Eugene D. Funk III, Lafayette Funk III, Richard C. Funk, Stephen McCormick, Calvin Rehtmeyer, Eugene D. Roth.
Number of staff: None.
Employer Identification Number: 376075515

1897
Furnas Foundation, Inc. ⌑
1000 McKee St.
Batavia 60510 (312) 879-6000

Incorporated in 1960 in IL.
Donor(s): W.C. Furnas,† Leto M. Furnas.†
Foundation type: Independent
Financial data (yr. ended 12/31/88): Assets, $654,002 (M); gifts received, $300,000; expenditures, $345,947, including $232,589 for 61 grants (high: $100,000; low: $100) and $100,078 for 173 grants to individuals.
Purpose and activities: Emphasis on higher education, including a scholarship program limited to undergraduate study; support also for health and youth agencies, hospitals, and community funds.
Types of support: Annual campaigns, building funds, equipment, matching funds, student aid.
Limitations: Giving primarily in Batavia, IL, and Clarke County, IA. No support for post-graduate students. No grants to individuals (except for scholarships); no loans.
Publications: Informational brochure, program policy statement, application guidelines.
Application information: Application form required for scholarships; request form from Scholarship Committee.
Initial approach: Proposal or letter
Copies of proposal: 1
Deadline(s): Mar. 1 for scholarships
Board meeting date(s): Jan., Apr., July, and Oct.
Final notification: 2 to 3 months
Officer and Directors: Joanne B. Hansen, Pres.; Robert A. Becker, V.P.; Gilbert R. Nary, Treas.; Thomas F. Caughlin, Elizabeth Hall, Richard W. Hansen, William F. Lisman, Dorothy J. Lowe, Robert F. Peterson, Dale F. Willcox.
Number of staff: None.
Employer Identification Number: 366049894

1898
The Galter Foundation
215 East Chicago Ave.
Chicago 60611

Incorporated in 1943 in IL.
Donor(s): Dollie Galter, Jack Galter, Spartus Corp.
Foundation type: Independent
Financial data (yr. ended 12/31/88): Assets, $2,555,415 (M); gifts received, $1,900,000; expenditures, $955,700, including $951,147 for 25 grants (high: $503,000; low: $20).
Purpose and activities: Giving for Jewish welfare funds and temple support, hospitals, and the handicapped.
Officers: Dollie Galter, Mgr.; Jack Galter, Mgr.
Employer Identification Number: 366082419

1899
Robert W. Galvin Foundation ⌑
1303 East Algonquin Rd.
Schaumburg 60196 (312) 576-5300

Incorporated in 1953 in IL.
Donor(s): Robert W. Galvin.
Foundation type: Independent
Financial data (yr. ended 12/31/87): Assets, $7,593,535 (M); gifts received, $643,875; expenditures, $642,507, including $637,797 for 57 grants (high: $100,000; low: $15).
Purpose and activities: Giving largely for higher and secondary education, aid to the handicapped, hospitals, and church support; grants also for child welfare agencies.
Limitations: Giving primarily in IL. No grants to individuals.
Application information: Application form not required.
Initial approach: Letter
Board meeting date(s): Annually
Write: Robert W. Galvin, Pres.
Officers and Directors:* Robert W. Galvin,* Pres.; Christopher B. Galvin,* V.P.; Michael P. Galvin, Secy.; Mary Barnes Galvin,* Treas.
Employer Identification Number: 366065560

1900
Paul V. Galvin Trust ⌑
c/o Harris Trust & Savings Bank
111 West Monroe St.
Chicago 60603
Grant application address: Harris Trust & Savings Bank, 7E, P.O. Box 755, Chicago, IL 60690; Tel.: (312) 461-2613

Donor(s): Paul V. Galvin.†
Foundation type: Independent
Financial data (yr. ended 12/31/87): Assets, $849,761 (M); expenditures, $587,986,

including $567,000 for 8 grants (high: $250,000; low: $2,000).
Purpose and activities: Emphasis on Catholic religious organizations, church support, higher education, and hospitals.
Application information:
Initial approach: Proposal
Deadline(s): None
Write: Lisa R. Curcio
Trustee: Harris Trust & Savings Bank.
Employer Identification Number: 366030329

1901
Anna C. Gamble Foundation ⌑ ☆
c/o William S. Dillon
8026 South Whipple St.
Chicago 60652-2627

Established in 1969.
Donor(s): Anna C. Gamble.†
Foundation type: Independent
Financial data (yr. ended 2/28/89): Assets, $1,228,592 (M); expenditures, $106,313, including $92,700 for 46 grants (high: $20,000; low: $150).
Purpose and activities: Giving primarily for Catholic organizations, including churches, and secondary education; support also for Jewish organizations.
Limitations: No grants to individuals.
Application information: Contributes only to pre-selected organizations. Applications not accepted.
Trustees: William S. Dillon, James E. Elworth.
Employer Identification Number: 366429423

1902
James & Zita Gavin Foundation, Inc. ⌑
161 Thorntree Ln.
Winnetka 60093

Established in 1983 in IL.
Foundation type: Independent
Financial data (yr. ended 12/31/87): Assets, $1,509,060 (M); gifts received, $68,409; expenditures, $30,680, including $29,300 for 13 grants (high: $10,000; low: $250).
Purpose and activities: Support primarily for Catholic charities and for Catholic education.
Application information: Contributes only to pre-selected organizations. Applications not accepted.
Officers: James J. Gavin, Jr., Pres.; Kevin P. Gavin, V.P.; Steven J. Gavin, Secy.; Zita C. Gavin, Treas.
Employer Identification Number: 363256613

1903
Geifman Family Foundation, Inc. ⌑ ☆
2239 29th St.
Rock Island 61201-5025 (309) 788-9531

Established in 1964.
Foundation type: Independent
Financial data (yr. ended 12/31/88): Assets, $1,516,634 (M); expenditures, $78,277, including $76,595 for 67 grants (high: $25,000; low: $50).
Purpose and activities: Giving primarily for Jewish organization and temple support.
Types of support: General purposes, endowment funds.
Limitations: Giving primarily in IL, with some emphsis on Rock Island.
Application information: Application form not required.
Initial approach: Letter
Deadline(s): None
Write: Morris M. Geifman, Pres.
Officers: Morris M. Geifman, Pres. and Treas.; Stephen Geifman, V.P.; Geraldine Geifman, Secy.
Directors: Terri Geifman, Cherie Handler.
Employer Identification Number: 366123096

1904
Generations Fund ⌑
c/o Felt Products Mfg. Co.
7450 North McCormick Blvd.
Skokie 60076 (312) 674-7700

Established in 1977 in IL.
Donor(s): Felt Products Manufacturing Co., Fel-Pro Inc.
Foundation type: Independent
Financial data (yr. ended 12/31/88): Assets, $971,731 (M); gifts received, $20,000; expenditures, $156,195, including $154,110 for 31 grants (high: $58,300; low: $35).
Purpose and activities: Support for Jewish organizations, social services, youth agencies, and cultural programs.
Types of support: General purposes.
Limitations: Giving primarily in Chicago, IL. No grants to individuals.
Application information:
Initial approach: Letter
Deadline(s): None
Write: Robert Morris, V.P.
Officers: Clara Morris, Pres.; Robert Morris, V.P.
Employer Identification Number: 362946589

1905
Geneseo Foundation ⌑
c/o Central Trust & Savings Bank
P.O. Box 89
Geneseo 61254 (309) 944-5601
Additional address: 101 North State St., Geneseo, IL 61254

Established in 1971 in IN.
Donor(s): George B. Dedrick.
Foundation type: Independent
Financial data (yr. ended 3/31/89): Assets, $2,375,728 (M); expenditures, $140,897, including $120,617 for 23 grants (high: $35,000; low: $231) and $9,875 for grants to individuals.
Purpose and activities: Giving for civic organizations, primarily for a community park; support also for social service and youth agencies and scholarships for graduates of Geneseo High School.
Types of support: Student aid.
Application information: Scholarships limited to graduates of Geneseo High School. Application form required.
Deadline(s): 1st week of the month
Board meeting date(s): Monthly
Write: Gary W. Joyner
Directors: Charles Blackenfeld, A. Dean Decker, Bruce Fehlman, John L. Greenwood, Raymond Johnson, Darwin Knudtsen, Eugene Lohman, Todd W. Sieben, Dean D. Urick.
Employer Identification Number: 366079604

1906
Geraldi-Norton Memorial Corporation ⌑
One First National Plaza, Suite 3148
Chicago 60603

Incorporated in 1952 in IL.
Donor(s): Grace Geraldi Norton.†
Foundation type: Independent
Financial data (yr. ended 12/31/87): Assets, $2,524,696 (M); expenditures, $181,562, including $143,275 for 91 grants (high: $15,000; low: $200).
Purpose and activities: Support for higher education, hospitals, cultural programs, and youth agencies.
Limitations: Giving primarily in the Chicago, IL, area. No grants to individuals.
Application information:
Initial approach: Letter
Deadline(s): None
Write: Roger P. Eklund, Pres.
Officers and Directors: Roger P. Eklund, Pres. and Treas.; Dariel Ann Eklund, V.P.; Dariel P. Eklund, V.P.; Sally S. Eklund, Secy.
Employer Identification Number: 366069997

1907
The Max and Lottie Gerber Foundation, Inc. ⌑
4656 West Touhy Ave.
Chicago 60646

Incorporated in 1942 in IL.
Donor(s): Globe Valve Corp., Kokomo Sanitary Pottery Corp.
Foundation type: Independent
Financial data (yr. ended 9/30/88): Assets, $541,137 (M); gifts received, $350,000; expenditures, $290,815, including $290,625 for 56 grants (high: $226,400; low: $100).
Purpose and activities: Giving to Jewish welfare funds and educational organizations; support also for cultural programs.
Limitations: Giving primarily in IL.
Application information: Contributes only to pre-selected organizations. Applications not accepted.
Officers: Harriet G. Lewis, Pres.; Robert C. Luker, Secy.; Ila J. Lewis, Treas.
Employer Identification Number: 366091912

1908
Emma & Oscar Getz Foundation ⌑
30 North LaSalle St., Suite 3210
Chicago 60602

Established in 1966 in IL.
Donor(s): Oscar Getz,† Emma Getz.
Foundation type: Independent
Financial data (yr. ended 12/31/88): Assets, $2,712,720 (M); gifts received, $55,028; expenditures, $253,976, including $243,650 for 35 grants (high: $46,000; low: $400).
Purpose and activities: Grants primarily for higher education in the U.S. and Israel, film and theatre, and Jewish organizations, including welfare funds.
Limitations: No grants to individuals.
Application information: Contributes only to pre-selected organizations. Applications not accepted.
Officers: Emma Getz, Pres.; William Getz, V.P. and Secy.; Ralph P. Silver, Treas.
Employer Identification Number: 366150787

1909
Gianaras Foundation ⌑ ☆
c/o Alex Gianaras
2805 Telegraph Rd.
Deerfield 60015-1564

Established in 1984 in IL.
Foundation type: Independent
Financial data (yr. ended 12/31/87): Assets, $1,107,270 (M); expenditures, $63,902, including $50,274 for 90 grants (high: $7,000; low: $10).
Purpose and activities: Giving to Christian organizations, including Greek churches and associations; support also for social services.
Limitations: No grants to individuals.
Application information: Contributes only to pre-selected organizations. Applications not accepted.
Officers: Alec K. Gianaras, Pres.; Alexander A. Gianaras, V.P.; Maria A. Gianaras, Secy.; Viena P. Gianaras, Treas.
Employer Identification Number: 363283901

1910
Gibbet Hill Foundation ⌑
410 North Michigan Ave., Rm. 590
Chicago 60611

Established in 1976 in IL.
Donor(s): Deering Foundation, Miami Corp.
Foundation type: Independent
Financial data (yr. ended 12/31/87): Assets, $801,029 (M); gifts received, $100,000; expenditures, $148,495, including $100,000 for 20 grants (high: $15,000; low: $2,000).
Purpose and activities: Support for higher and other education, museums, a public library, and conservation groups.
Types of support: General purposes.
Limitations: No grants to individuals; or for scholarships or fellowships; no loans.
Application information: Contributes only to pre-selected organizations determined by foundation's board of directors.
Officers and Directors: Marion D. Campbell, Pres.; Charles E. Schroeder, Secy.-Treas.; Richard Strachan, Stephen M. Strachan.
Employer Identification Number: 510189357

1911
Leo Gluck Charitable Foundation ⌑ ☆
6037 North Monticello
Chicago 60659-1110
Application address: 8121 North Central Park, Skokie, IL 60076; Tel.: (312) 679-1012

Established in 1986 in IL.
Donor(s): Barbara Gluck.
Foundation type: Independent
Financial data (yr. ended 11/30/87): Assets, $1,099 (M); gifts received, $110,500; expenditures, $109,401, including $109,350 for 94 grants (high: $25,000; low: $10).
Purpose and activities: Support primarily for Jewish organizations, including congregations and yeshivas.
Application information: Application form not required.
Deadline(s): None
Write: Bradley Jacobs
Officers and Directors: Barbara Gluck, Pres.; Yisroel Gluck, Secy.; Irving Gluck, Treas.; Robert Gluck.
Employer Identification Number: 363548479

1912
The Milton D. and Madeline L. Goldberg Family Foundation ⌑
(Formerly ISGO Foundation)
8200 West Ogden Ave.
P.O. Box 359
Lyons 60534

Incorporated in 1953 in IL.
Donor(s): ISGO Corp.
Foundation type: Independent
Financial data (yr. ended 05/31/89): Assets, $3,103,078 (M); expenditures, $121,505, including $105,723 for 67 grants (high: $50,185; low: $15).
Purpose and activities: Emphasis on Jewish welfare funds.
Limitations: No grants to individuals.
Application information: Application form not required.
Deadline(s): None
Officers and Directors: Milton D. Goldberg, Pres.; Madeline L. Goldberg, Secy.-Treas.; Irene Swojenski.
Employer Identification Number: 366064876

1913
Max Goldenberg Foundation ⌑
c/o Harris Trust & Savings Bank
111 West Monroe St.
Chicago 60603
Grant application address: P.O. Box 755, Chicago, IL 60690

Trust established in 1946 in IL.
Donor(s): Max Goldenberg.†
Foundation type: Independent
Financial data (yr. ended 12/31/88): Assets, $3,124,385 (M); expenditures, $176,836, including $135,000 for 37 grants (high: $10,000; low: $1,000).
Purpose and activities: Emphasis on medical research and hospitals, higher education, and social services, particularly Jewish charities.
Limitations: Giving primarily in IL.
Publications: Annual report.
Application information:
Initial approach: Proposal
Copies of proposal: 3
Deadline(s): Aug. 31
Board meeting date(s): Oct.
Write: Ellen A. Bechthold
Trustees: Harold J. Baer, Marian Goodman, Harris Trust & Savings Bank.
Employer Identification Number: 362471625

1914
Morris and Rose Goldman Foundation ⌑
845 North Michigan Ave.
Chicago 60611 (312) 337-6435

Established in 1965.
Donor(s): Morris Goldman, Rose Goldman.
Foundation type: Independent
Financial data (yr. ended 12/31/87): Assets, $2,234,179 (M); gifts received, $746,502; expenditures, $302,598, including $284,143 for 128 grants (high: $167,675; low: $15).
Purpose and activities: Giving primarily to Jewish welfare funds, cultural organizations, and social services.
Application information:
Initial approach: Proposal
Deadline(s): None
Write: Rose Goldman, V.P.
Officers: Morris Goldman, Pres.; Rose Goldman, V.P.; Shirley Warshaver, Secy.
Directors: Barbara Pine, Shirley Schnachenberg.
Employer Identification Number: 362615047

1915
Graham Foundation for Advanced Studies in the Fine Arts
Four West Burton Place
Chicago 60610 (312) 787-4071

Incorporated in 1935 in IL.
Donor(s): Ernest R. Graham.†
Foundation type: Independent
Financial data (yr. ended 12/31/89): Assets, $19,027,353 (M); expenditures, $1,132,000, including $662,721 for grants.
Purpose and activities: Grants for advanced research in contemporary architecture, design, and the study of urban planning, principally to Americans working within the U.S. who have demonstrated mature, creative talent and have specific work objectives. Fellows are selected by the trustees on the recommendation of the Director and special advisors. Some support for exhibitions, publications, lectures, and architectural and urban studies.
Types of support: Research, publications, conferences and seminars, fellowships, grants to individuals, special projects, lectureships.
Limitations: No grants for building or endowment funds, scholarships, or matching gifts; no loans.
Publications: Annual report (including application guidelines), application guidelines.
Application information: Application form not required.
Initial approach: Proposal
Copies of proposal: 1
Deadline(s): June 1 and Dec. 1
Board meeting date(s): July and Jan.
Final notification: 1 to 4 months
Write: Carter H. Manny, Jr., Exec. Dir.
Officer: Carter H. Manny, Jr., Exec. Dir.
Number of staff: 2 full-time professional; 1 part-time support.
Employer Identification Number: 362356089

1916
The Grainger Foundation, Inc. ▼
5500 West Howard St.
Skokie 60077 (312) 982-9000

Incorporated in 1967 in IL as successor to the Grainger Charitable Trust established in 1949.
Donor(s): W.W. Grainger,† Hally W. Grainger,† David W. Grainger.
Foundation type: Independent
Financial data (yr. ended 12/31/88): Assets, $56,536,398 (M); expenditures, $5,965,709, including $5,829,188 for 33 grants (high: $2,032,188; low: $1,000).
Purpose and activities: Emphasis on endowments, capital funds, and special program funds for higher education (colleges & universities), cultural and historical institutions (art, symphony, and museums), hospitals, and human service organizations.
Types of support: Continuing support, building funds, equipment, endowment funds, research,

general purposes, renovation projects, special projects, operating budgets.
Limitations: Giving primarily in the Chicago, IL, area. No grants to individuals, or for general operating budgets, seed money, emergency funds, deficit financing, special projects, publications, conferences, scholarships, fellowships, or matching gifts; no loans.
Publications: 990-PF.
Application information: The foundation contributes only to pre-selected charitable organizations as determined by its directors and officers. For this reason, and due to staffing constraints, grant requests received from organizations other than those first contacted by The Grainger Foundation cannot be reviewed or acknowledged.
Board meeting date(s): Periodically
Final notification: Favorable decisions only
Write: Lee J. Flory, V.P.
Officers and Directors: David W. Grainger, Pres. and Treas.; Lee J. Flory, V.P. and Secy.; Juli P. Grainger, V.P.; John S. Chapman.
Number of staff: None.
Employer Identification Number: 366192971

1917
Grant Thornton Foundation
800 One Prudential Plaza
130 East Randolph Dr.
Chicago 60601 (312) 856-0001

Established in 1976 in IL.
Donor(s): Grant Thornton.
Foundation type: Company-sponsored
Financial data (yr. ended 07/31/89): Assets, $0 (M); gifts received, $107,090; expenditures, $107,090, including $53,670 for 82 grants (high: $6,900; low: $25) and $53,420 for employee matching gifts.
Purpose and activities: Grants for higher education.
Types of support: Employee matching gifts.
Application information:
Write: Ken Banet, Trustee
Trustees: Kenneth W. Banet, L.A. Fanchi, Robert Kleckner, Robert Nason, T.J. Thompson.
Employer Identification Number: 510193906

1918
John C. Griswold Foundation
2223 South Martin Luther King Jr. Dr.
Chicago 60616-1471 (312) 326-8188

Established in 1978 in NY.
Donor(s): John C. Griswold.†
Foundation type: Independent
Financial data (yr. ended 11/30/88): Assets, $1,698,656 (M); gifts received, $1,763,281; expenditures, $139,961, including $135,000 for 6 grants (high: $100,000; low: $5,000).
Purpose and activities: Support primarily for higher education; support also for Christian religious organizations and churches.
Types of support: General purposes.
Publications: 990-PF.
Application information: Application form not required.
Initial approach: Letter
Deadline(s): None
Board meeting date(s): Varies
Write: James R. Donnelley, Trustee
Officers and Trustees:* Jacqueline G. Moore,* Pres.; James R. Donnelley,* V.P. and Treas.; Henry W. Hobson, Jr.,* Secy.; Wayne W. Krows.
Employer Identification Number: 132978937

1919
Jessie Griswold Trust ⌑ ☆
White Hall National Bank
White Hall 62092 (217) 374-2181

Foundation type: Independent
Financial data (yr. ended 12/31/88): Assets, $1,783,933 (M); expenditures, $191,181, including $144,756 for 113 loans to individuals (high: $2,250; low: $299).
Purpose and activities: Awards student loans for higher education.
Types of support: Student loans.
Limitations: Giving limited to IL residents.
Application information: Application form required.
Deadline(s): None
Write: Howard Piper, Trustee
Trustee: Howard Piper.
Employer Identification Number: 376105072

1920
The H.B.B. Foundation ⌑
35 East Wacker Dr., Suite 1922
Chicago 60601

Established in 1964 in IL.
Foundation type: Independent
Financial data (yr. ended 12/31/88): Assets, $1,653,666 (M); expenditures, $113,360, including $89,000 for 38 grants (high: $5,000; low: $500).
Purpose and activities: Grants to hospitals, scientific organizations, museums, orchestras, and higher education.
Limitations: Giving primarily in Chicago, IL.
Application information: Contributes only to pre-selected organizations. Applications not accepted.
Officers and Directors: Elizabeth B. Tieken, Pres.; Theodore D. Tieken, Jr., V.P. and Secy.; Mark Stephenitch, Treas.; Theodore D. Tieken, Sr.
Employer Identification Number: 366104969

1921
Haffner Foundation
2223 South Martin Luther King Jr. Dr.
Chicago 60616 (312) 326-8042

Incorporated in 1952 in IL.
Donor(s): Charles C. Haffner, Jr.,† Mrs. Charles C. Haffner, Jr.,† Charles C. Haffner III.
Foundation type: Independent
Financial data (yr. ended 12/31/89): Assets, $2,070,825 (M); expenditures, $122,350, including $118,000 for 44 grants (high: $10,500; low: $500; average: $1,000-$5,000).
Purpose and activities: To contribute to religious, charitable, and educational organizations of whose activities the foundation's officers have personal knowledge. Support largely for higher, business, secondary, elementary, and early childhood education, hospitals and health agencies, social service agencies, cultural activities, including museums and historic preservation, and environmental conservation and ecology.
Types of support: Operating budgets, continuing support, annual campaigns, seed money, emergency funds, building funds, equipment, endowment funds, capital campaigns, general purposes, land acquisition, renovation projects.
Limitations: Giving primarily in IL, MA, and WA. No grants to individuals, or for scholarships, fellowships, or matching gifts; no loans.
Application information: Contributes only to pre-selected organizations. Applications not accepted.
Board meeting date(s): May
Write: Charles C. Haffner III, Pres.
Officers and Directors:* Charles C. Haffner III,* Pres. and Treas.; Clarissa H. Chandler,* V.P. and Secy.; Phoebe H. Andrew, Frances H. Colburn.
Number of staff: None.
Employer Identification Number: 366064770

1922
Hales Charitable Fund, Inc. ⌑
120 West Madison St., Suite 700-E
Chicago 60602 (312) 641-7016

Incorporated in 1939 in IL.
Donor(s): G. Willard Hales,† Burton W. Hales,† William M. Hales.
Foundation type: Independent
Financial data (yr. ended 12/31/88): Assets, $5,847,897 (M); expenditures, $297,092, including $239,475 for 43 grants (high: $150,000; low: $100).
Purpose and activities: Emphasis on higher education, Protestant church organizations, hospitals and health agencies; support also for cultural programs and social agencies.
Types of support: Operating budgets, continuing support, annual campaigns, emergency funds, building funds, endowment funds, scholarship funds, professorships, research.
Limitations: Giving primarily in IL. No grants to individuals, or for seed money, deficit financing, equipment, land acquisition, renovations, matching gifts, demonstration projects, publications, or conferences; no loans.
Application information: The fund has developed a regular schedule of recipient organizations which receive support on a somewhat annual basis. Application form not required.
Board meeting date(s): Annually and as required
Write: William M. Hales, Jr., Pres.
Officers and Directors:* William M. Hales,* Pres.; Burton W. Hales, Jr.,* Secy.-Treas.; Marion J. Hales, Mary C. Hales.
Number of staff: None.
Employer Identification Number: 366060632

1923
Armand Hammer Foundation ▼ ⌑
135 South LaSalle St., Suite 1000
Chicago 60603 (312) 580-1225

Established in 1968 in CA.
Donor(s): Armand Hammer.
Foundation type: Operating

Financial data (yr. ended 12/31/87): Assets, $23,771,555 (M); gifts received, $9,762,000; expenditures, $2,183,224, including $2,054,136 for 62 grants (high: $935,000; low: $15; average: $500-$25,000).
Purpose and activities: Giving primarily for higher education, art museums and galleries, and medical research; support also for the state of Israel.
Limitations: No grants to individuals.
Application information: Application form not required.
Initial approach: Letter
Copies of proposal: 2
Deadline(s): None
Board meeting date(s): Annually and as required
Write: David J. Creagan, Jr.
Directors: Arthur Groman, Armand Hammer.
Number of staff: None.
Employer Identification Number: 237010813

1924
Philip S. Harper Foundation ⌑
c/o Harper-Wyman Co.
930 North York Rd., Suite 204
Hinsdale 60521

Incorporated in 1953 in IL.
Donor(s): Philip S. Harper, Harper-Wyman Co.
Foundation type: Independent
Financial data (yr. ended 11/30/88): Assets, $4,710,435 (M); expenditures, $259,236, including $185,900 for 124 grants (high: $9,000; low: $250).
Purpose and activities: Support for higher education, child welfare, health agencies and medical research, cultural programs, including public broadcasting, social welfare, including youth agencies, and Protestant churches.
Officers: Philip S. Harper, Jr., Pres.; Lamar Harper Williams, V.P.; Charles C. Lamar, Secy.-Treas.
Employer Identification Number: 366049875

1925
Harris Bank Foundation
111 West Monroe St.
P.O. Box 755
Chicago 60690 (312) 461-6660

Incorporated in 1953 in IL.
Donor(s): Harris Trust & Savings Bank.
Foundation type: Company-sponsored
Financial data (yr. ended 12/31/89): Assets, $800,000 (M); expenditures, $1,297,182, including $1,088,375 for 147 grants (high: $335,000; low: $550; average: $2,000-$5,000) and $208,807 for 487 employee matching gifts.
Purpose and activities: Emphasis on community reinvestment and education reform efforts, including an employee matching gifts program; support also for cultural activities, neighborhood development, and social services.
Types of support: Operating budgets, continuing support, annual campaigns, seed money, building funds, equipment, matching funds, technical assistance, scholarship funds, special projects, employee-related scholarships, employee matching gifts, renovation projects.
Limitations: Giving limited to the greater Chicago, IL, metropolitan area, except for matching gifts program. No support for sectarian or religious organizations, fraternal organizations, or political activities. No grants to individuals (except for employee-related scholarships for dependents of Harris Bank employees), or for research, publications, conferences, testimonials, or advertisements; no loans.
Publications: Annual report (including application guidelines), program policy statement.
Application information: Application form not required.
Initial approach: Proposal
Copies of proposal: 1
Deadline(s): Two months prior to each board meeting
Board meeting date(s): Jan., Mar., June, Aug., Oct., and Dec.
Final notification: 2 weeks after board meetings
Write: Diana Nelson, Secy.-Treas.
Officers: Joan M. Baratta,* Pres.; Philip A. Delaney,* V.P.; Diana Nelson, Secy.-Treas.
Directors:* Cecil R. Coleman, David Finch, Donald S. Hunt, Max M. Jacobson, Bruce Osborne, Jamie Thorsen, Edward J. Williams.
Number of staff: 2 full-time professional; 1 full-time support.
Employer Identification Number: 366033888

1926
Harris Family Foundation ⌑
333 Skokie Blvd.
Northbrook 60062 (312) 498-1260

Incorporated in 1957 in IL.
Donor(s): Neison Harris, and family.
Foundation type: Independent
Financial data (yr. ended 2/28/87): Assets, $5,962,465 (M); gifts received, $49,250; expenditures, $621,910, including $604,561 for 133 grants (high: $250,000; low: $25).
Purpose and activities: Emphasis on medical research and health services, Jewish welfare funds, cultural programs, higher and secondary education, community funds, and social service agencies.
Types of support: General purposes, building funds.
Limitations: Giving primarily in the Chicago, IL, area. No grants to individuals.
Application information: Application form not required.
Initial approach: Letter
Copies of proposal: 1
Deadline(s): Submit proposal preferably in May; no set deadline
Board meeting date(s): May and Nov.
Final notification: 30 days
Write: Neison Harris, Pres.
Officers and Directors: Neison Harris, Pres. and Treas.; Bette D. Harris, V.P. and Secy.; Sidney Barrows, Katherine Harris, King W. Harris, Toni H. Paul.
Number of staff: None.
Employer Identification Number: 366054378

1927
Hunt and Diane Harris Family Foundation ⌑
901 46th St.
Moline 61265 (309) 764-0123

Established in 1986 in IL.
Donor(s): Diane B. Harris, John H. Harris II.
Foundation type: Independent
Financial data (yr. ended 12/31/88): Assets, $2,837,188 (M); expenditures, $154,086, including $120,700 for 16 grants (high: $25,000; low: $200).
Purpose and activities: Support for youth, social services, education, a community fund, and a parks department.
Types of support: Operating budgets.
Limitations: Giving primarily in IL and IA. No grants to individuals.
Application information: Application form not required.
Deadline(s): None
Write: John H. Harris II, Dir.
Directors: Diane B. Harris, John H. Harris II, William A. Ratzburg.
Employer Identification Number: 363488560

1928
The Harris Foundation ▼
Two North LaSalle St., Suite 605
Chicago 60602-3703 (312) 621-0566

Incorporated in 1945 in MN.
Donor(s): Members of the Harris family and others.
Foundation type: Independent
Financial data (yr. ended 12/31/89): Assets, $21,456 (M); gifts received, $100,000; expenditures, $2,015,000, including $1,666,077 for 372 grants (high: $300,000; low: $25; average: $100-$10,000).
Purpose and activities: Interests include demonstration and research programs in prevention of family dysfunction: prevention of teenage pregnancy and infant mortality and morbidity; infant mental health and early childhood development; Jewish charities; the arts and educational television.
Types of support: Annual campaigns, seed money, equipment, special projects, research, publications, conferences and seminars, general purposes, operating budgets, scholarship funds.
Limitations: No grants to individuals, or for continuing support, emergency or endowment funds, deficit financing, land acquisition, renovations, scholarships, or fellowships; no loans.
Application information: Application form not required.
Initial approach: Letter
Copies of proposal: 1
Deadline(s): None
Board meeting date(s): Semiannually
Final notification: Following board meeting
Write: Ruth K. Belzer, Exec. Dir.
Officers and Trustees:* Irving B. Harris,* Chair.; William W. Harris,* Vice-Chair.; Benno F. Wolff,* Secy.; Sidney Barrows, Roxanne Harris Frank, Joan W. Harris, Neison Harris, Daniel Meyer, Virginia Harris Polsky.
Staff: Ruth K. Belzer, Exec. Dir.
Number of staff: 1 full-time professional; 1 full-time support.
Employer Identification Number: 366055115

1929
H. H. Harris Foundation ☆
200 West Adams St., Suite 2905
Chicago 60606-5208 (312) 346-7900

Donor(s): Henry Hickman Harris.†
Foundation type: Independent
Financial data (yr. ended 06/30/89): Assets, $2,820,929 (M); expenditures, $105,104, including $61,300 for 22 grants to individuals.
Purpose and activities: Provides scholarships and other forms of educational aid to students and professionals in the metallurgical and casting of metals field.
Types of support: Student aid.
Application information: Application form required.
Deadline(s): June 15
Board meeting date(s): July
Write: John Hough, Mgr.
Officer and Trustees:* John Hough,* Mgr.; Robert J. Dominick, Nicholas P. Milano, William M. O'Neill.
Employer Identification Number: 362615318

1930
J. Ira and Nicki Harris Foundation ⌑
Two North La Salle St., Suite 2205
Chicago 60602

Established in 1965.
Donor(s): J. Ira Harris.
Foundation type: Independent
Financial data (yr. ended 03/31/89): Assets, $6,370,881 (M); expenditures, $215,650, including $163,585 for 76 grants (high: $35,000; low: $100).
Purpose and activities: Grants mainly for Jewish welfare funds and education; support also for a foundation for children with learning disabilities.
Limitations: No grants to individuals.
Application information:
Initial approach: Letter
Deadline(s): None
Write: J. Ira Harris, Pres.
Officers: J. Ira Harris, Pres.; Nicki Harris, V.P.; Newton Minow, Secy.-Treas.
Employer Identification Number: 366122443

1931
Fred G. Harrison Foundation ⌑
101 South Park Ave.
Herrin 62948

Established in 1969 in IL.
Donor(s): Julia Harrison Bruce, Fred G. Harrison.†
Foundation type: Independent
Financial data (yr. ended 12/31/88): Assets, $1,776,237 (M); expenditures, $99,370, including $72,329 for 7 grants (high: $50,000; low: $179) and $2,000 for 4 grants to individuals of $500 each.
Purpose and activities: Support primarily for social services, education, civic improvements, and churches; scholarships awarded to high school seniors.
Types of support: Student aid.
Limitations: Giving primarily in Herrin, Il.
Advisors: Carl Bruce, Julia Harrison Bruce, Mildred Nielsen.
Trustee: Bank of Herrin.
Employer Identification Number: 376085205

1932
Helen M. Harrison Foundation ⌑
One First National Plaza, Suite 5000
Chicago 60603

Established in 1986 in IL.
Donor(s): Helen M. Harrison.
Foundation type: Operating
Financial data (yr. ended 12/31/87): Assets, $1,012,199 (M); expenditures, $93,641, including $85,150 for 11 grants (high: $25,000; low: $1,000).
Purpose and activities: A private operating foundation established in 1986; no grants awarded.
Application information:
Write: Timothy G. Carrol, Trustee
Trustees: George E. Barnes, Philip M. Burnd, Timothy G. Carroll, Helen M. Harrison.
Employer Identification Number: 363475137

1933
Hartmarx Charitable Foundation ⌑
101 North Wacker Dr.
Chicago 60606 (312) 372-6300

Incorporated in 1966 in IL.
Donor(s): Hartmarx Corp.
Foundation type: Company-sponsored
Financial data (yr. ended 11/30/88): Assets, $76,813 (M); expenditures, $760,896, including $737,417 for 344 grants (high: $213,497; low: $60) and $23,479 for 72 employee matching gifts.
Purpose and activities: Grants primarily for community funds, higher education, and cultural, civic and health programs.
Types of support: Employee matching gifts, annual campaigns, building funds, capital campaigns, endowment funds, general purposes, operating budgets, professorships, scholarship funds.
Limitations: Giving primarily in GA, IL, IN, MI, NY, OR, and WA. No grants to individuals.
Application information: Application form not required.
Initial approach: Letter
Copies of proposal: 1
Deadline(s): None
Board meeting date(s): Dec., Mar., June, and Sept.
Write: Kay C. Nalbach, Pres.
Officers: Kay C. Nalbach, Pres.; Wayne H. Ahlberg, V.P.; Jerome Dorf, V.P.; Cary M. Stein, Secy.; J.R. Meinert, Treas.
Employer Identification Number: 366152745

1934
Lynne Cooper Harvey Foundation, Inc. ⌑
1035 Park Ave.
River Forest 60305

Established in 1981 in IL.
Donor(s): Paul Harvey, Lynne Cooper Harvey.
Foundation type: Independent
Financial data (yr. ended 6/30/88): Assets, $1,237,596 (M); gifts received, $167,604; expenditures, $125,112, including $122,200 for 36 grants (high: $15,000; low: $1,000).
Purpose and activities: Support primarily for animal welfare.
Types of support: General purposes.
Limitations: No grants to individuals.
Application information: Contributes only to pre-selected organizations. Applications not accepted.
Officers: Lynne Cooper Harvey, Pres. and Treas.; Paul Harvey, Jr., V.P. and Secy.
Directors: Hal Courson, Joseph J. Maier.
Employer Identification Number: 363148657

1935
John I. Hay Foundation
c/o The Northern Trust Co.
50 South LaSalle St.
Chicago 60675

Incorporated in 1955 in IL.
Donor(s): John I. Hay Trust.
Foundation type: Independent
Financial data (yr. ended 12/31/89): Assets, $3,071,260 (M); expenditures, $198,339, including $194,545 for 5 grants (high: $178,495; low: $1,050).
Purpose and activities: Grants for education and a youth agency.
Types of support: Equipment, general purposes, operating budgets.
Limitations: No grants to individuals.
Application information: Applications not accepted.
Write: John C. Goodall, Jr., Treas.
Officers: Frank P. Markland, Pres.; Arthur H. Vail, V.P.; Robert Sturtevant, Secy.; John C. Goodall, Jr., Treas.
Employer Identification Number: 366103629

1936
Heed Ophthalmic Foundation ⌑
c/o First National Bank of Chicago
One First National Plaza, Suite 0111
Chicago 60670-0111 (312) 732-4266

Trust established in 1946 in IL.
Donor(s): Thomas D. Heed,† Mrs. Thomas D. Heed.†
Foundation type: Independent
Financial data (yr. ended 10/31/88): Assets, $3,277,251 (M); expenditures, $255,288, including $211,200 for 44 grants to individuals of $4,800 each.
Purpose and activities: Fellowships to U.S. citizens who are graduates of medical schools accredited by the American Medical Association, and who show exceptional ability to further their education in the field of diseases of the eye and surgery or to do research in ophthalmology.
Types of support: Fellowships.
Publications: Application guidelines.
Application information: Application form required.
Initial approach: Letter
Copies of proposal: 1
Deadline(s): Nov. 30 for fellowships starting the following academic year
Board meeting date(s): May and Nov.
Write: Margaret Venables
Officers and Directors: Frank W. Newell, M.D., Chair.; David Shoch, M.D., Exec. Secy.
Trustee: First National Bank of Chicago.
Number of staff: 1 full-time support.
Employer Identification Number: 366012426

1937
Walter E. Heller Foundation ⌑
c/o Continental Illinois National Bank and Trust Co. of Chicago, N.A.
30 North LaSalle St., 6th Fl.
Chicago 60693 (312) 828-1785

Incorporated in 1955 in IL.
Donor(s): Walter E. Heller,† Whico, Inc.
Foundation type: Independent
Financial data (yr. ended 12/31/88): Assets, $2,820,184 (M); expenditures, $613,999, including $586,315 for 74 grants (high: $121,000; low: $50).
Purpose and activities: Emphasis on cultural programs, particularly museums and the performing arts; support also for higher education and health organizations.
Limitations: Giving primarily in the Chicago, IL, area.
Application information:
Initial approach: Letter
Deadline(s): None
Write: M.C. Ryan
Officer and Directors:* Alyce H. DeCosta,* Pres.; Edwin J. DeCosta, M.D., Addis E. Hull, M. James Termondt.
Employer Identification Number: 366058986

1938
The Grover Hermann Foundation ▼
c/o Schiff, Hardin & Waite, 7200 Sears Tower
233 South Wacker Dr.
Chicago 60606 (312) 876-1000
Application address for Monterey County, CA, programs: P.O. Box 596, Pebble Beach, CA 93953

Incorporated in 1955 in IL.
Donor(s): Grover M. Hermann.
Foundation type: Independent
Financial data (yr. ended 12/31/88): Assets, $18,855,795 (M); expenditures, $2,861,069, including $2,767,082 for 101 grants (high: $250,000; low: $1,000).
Purpose and activities: Grants largely for higher education, social services, community development, health, public policy organizations, and religion.
Types of support: Renovation projects, equipment, building funds, seed money, endowment funds, annual campaigns, scholarship funds, special projects, general purposes.
Limitations: Giving limited to Chicago, IL, and Monterey County, CA, for social services and community development; other programs funded nationwide. No support for fraternal, athletic, or foreign organizations or private foundations. No grants to individuals; generally no support for operating budgets, except for national health organizations.
Publications: Application guidelines.
Application information: Organizations in Monterey County, CA, should write to the Pebble Beach office, all other inquiries to the Chicago, IL, office. Application form not required.
Initial approach: Letter (telephone inquiries not considered)
Copies of proposal: 1
Deadline(s): None
Board meeting date(s): Quarterly; annual meeting in May
Final notification: From several weeks to 3 or 4 months
Write: Paul K. Rhoads, V.P.
Officers and Directors:* Sarah T. Hermann,* Pres.; Paul K. Rhoads,* V.P.; Harriet R. Thurmond,* Secy.
Number of staff: None.
Employer Identification Number: 366064489

1939
Lawrence & Ada Hickory Foundation ⌑ ☆
615 Woodland Ln.
Northfield 60093

Established in 1985 in IL.
Foundation type: Independent
Financial data (yr. ended 06/30/89): Assets, $1,423,389 (M); expenditures, $187,985, including $185,850 for 35 grants (high: $50,000; low: $100).
Purpose and activities: Giving primarily for Catholic churches and organizations.
Limitations: Giving primarily in IL. No grants to individuals.
Application information: Contributes only to pre-selected organizations. Applications not accepted.
Officers and Directors: Lawrence Hickey, Pres.; L. Mark Hickey, Treas.; Ada Hickey.
Employer Identification Number: 363412793

1940
High Tower Charitable Foundation ⌑
1156 Michigan Ave.
Wilmette 60091 (312) 251-5007

Established in 1980.
Foundation type: Independent
Financial data (yr. ended 12/31/87): Assets, $13,364 (M); gifts received, $914; expenditures, $165,757, including $162,080 for 32 grants (high: $21,580; low: $500).
Purpose and activities: Giving limited to Evangelical Christian religious and welfare organizations.
Application information:
Initial approach: Letter
Deadline(s): None
Write: Amelia J. Radford, Pres.
Officers: Amelia J. Radford, Pres.; Stephen K. Radford, V.P.; Wesley W. Saul, Secy.-Treas.
Employer Identification Number: 363104606

1941
The Himmel Foundation ⌑
205 West Wacker Dr., Suite 1800
Chicago 60606-1214

Established in 1960 in IL.
Donor(s): Jeffrey Himmel, members of the Himmel family.
Foundation type: Independent
Financial data (yr. ended 12/31/87): Assets, $2,528 (M); gifts received, $120,500; expenditures, $119,985, including $119,985 for 36 grants (high: $60,000; low: $25).
Purpose and activities: Support primarily for Jewish organizations, schools, and synagogues.
Application information: Application form not required.
Initial approach: Letter
Deadline(s): None
Write: Jeffrey Himmel, Pres.
Officers: Jeffrey Himmel, Pres.; Ivan Himmel, V.P.; Bernadette Bybicki, Secy.
Employer Identification Number: 366067611

1942
The Hobbs Foundation ☆
c/o M. Rausch
P.O. Box 1107
Jacksonville 62651

Established in 1986 in AL.
Donor(s): The Ioka Fund.
Foundation type: Independent
Financial data (yr. ended 12/31/88): Assets, $3,448,964 (M); gifts received, $3,201,611; expenditures, $161,859, including $154,400 for 43 grants (high: $40,000; low: $50).
Purpose and activities: Support for secondary education, cultural and arts organizations, and churches.
Types of support: Building funds, capital campaigns.
Limitations: Giving primarily in Montgomery, AL.
Application information: Applications not accepted.
Officers and Directors:* Truman M. Hobbs,* Pres. and Treas.; Truman M. Hobbs, Jr.,* V.P. and Secy.; Joyce C. Hobbs.
Employer Identification Number: 630952482

1943
Hochberg Family Foundation ⌑
7233 West Dempster
Niles 60648

Established in 1981 in IL.
Donor(s): Larry J. Hochberg, Joseph Hochberg, Sanford Cantor.
Foundation type: Independent
Financial data (yr. ended 11/30/88): Assets, $398,902 (M); gifts received, $237,000; expenditures, $235,857, including $234,342 for 101 grants (high: $172,774; low: $10).
Purpose and activities: Giving primarily for Jewish organizations, including welfare funds.
Limitations: Giving primarily in Chicago, IL.
Application information:
Initial approach: Letter
Deadline(s): None
Write: Larry Hochberg, Dir.
Directors: Andrew S. Hochberg, Barbara P. Hochberg, Larry J. Hochberg.
Employer Identification Number: 363152002

1944
Hoffer Foundation ⌑
255 Wing Park Blvd.
Elgin 60120 (312) 741-5740
Application address: 500 Collins St., South Elgin, IL 60177

Established in 1966.
Donor(s): Hoffer Plastics Corp., Robert A. Hoffer.
Foundation type: Company-sponsored
Financial data (yr. ended 11/30/88): Assets, $1,278,954 (M); gifts received, $290,000; expenditures, $242,021, including $241,292 for 26 grants (high: $75,000; low: $400).
Purpose and activities: Emphasis on education, civic affairs, and youth.

Limitations: Giving primarily in IL.
Application information:
Initial approach: Letter
Deadline(s): None
Write: Robert A. Hoffer, Pres.
Officer and Trustees: Robert A. Hoffer, Pres.; Helen C. Hoffer, Robert A. Hoffer, Jr.
Employer Identification Number: 366160991

1945
The Dave Hokin Foundation ⌑
875 North Michigan Ave., Rm. 3707
Chicago 60611

Incorporated in 1951 in IL.
Foundation type: Independent
Financial data (yr. ended 10/31/88): Assets, $431,828 (M); gifts received, $127,000; expenditures, $225,744, including $224,382 for 120 grants (high: $4,500; low: $50).
Purpose and activities: Grants for medical research, hospitals, higher education, cultural organizations, and Jewish welfare funds.
Officers: Myron Hokin, Pres.; Carl K. Heyman, Treas.
Employer Identification Number: 366079161

1946
The H. Earl Hoover Foundation ⌑
1801 Green Bay Rd.
P.O. Box 330
Glencoe 60022 (312) 835-3350

Trust established in 1947 in IL.
Donor(s): H. Earl Hoover.
Foundation type: Independent
Financial data (yr. ended 12/31/88): Assets, $2,655,226 (M); expenditures, $248,210, including $231,600 for 58 grants (high: $75,000; low: $250).
Purpose and activities: Giving for youth agencies, hospitals, social and welfare agencies, cultural organizations, and Protestant church support.
Limitations: Giving primarily in IL.
Application information:
Initial approach: Letter
Deadline(s): None
Trustees: Robert L. Foote, Miriam W. Hoover, Michael A. Leppen.
Employer Identification Number: 366063814

1947
Bertrand Hopper Memorial Foundation ⌑
319 West Main Cross
Taylorville 62568 (217) 824-3323

Incorporated in 1956 in IL.
Donor(s): Bertrand C. Hopper, Hopper Paper Co.
Foundation type: Independent
Financial data (yr. ended 12/31/87): Assets, $1,627,859 (M); expenditures, $93,687, including $81,800 for 28 grants (high: $20,700; low: $100).
Purpose and activities: Emphasis on education, including public schools, and youth agencies.
Limitations: Giving primarily in IL. No grants to individuals.
Application information: Application form not required.
Initial approach: Letter or telephone
Deadline(s): None
Write: Bertrand C. Hopper, Pres.
Officer and Directors: Bertrand C. Hopper, Pres.; Frederick C. Hopper, William B. Hopper.
Employer Identification Number: 376026794

1948
Irvin E. Houck Charitable Trust ⌑ ☆
c/o First United Trust Co.
Village Mall Plaza
Oak Park 60301-1194

Established in 1970.
Foundation type: Independent
Financial data (yr. ended 11/30/88): Assets, $1,000,412 (M); expenditures, $74,321, including $63,250 for 46 grants (high: $15,000; low: $100).
Purpose and activities: Giving primarily for churches and other Christian organizations, social welfare, and the environment; support for culture and education.
Limitations: Giving primarily in IL. No grants to individuals.
Application information:
Initial approach: Letter
Deadline(s): None
Trustees: Margaret R. Houck, Richard I. Houck, Mary Houck Olson, Margaret H. Smith, First United Trust Co.
Employer Identification Number: 237128830

1949
Susan Cook House Educational Trust ⌑
Marine Bank of Springfield, Trust Dept.
One Old Capital Plaza East
Springfield 62701 (217) 525-9600

Trust established in 1969 in IL.
Foundation type: Independent
Financial data (yr. ended 11/30/88): Assets, $1,672,217 (M); expenditures, $155,628, including $101,500 for 14 grants (high: $20,000; low: $500) and $15,500 for 21 grants to individuals (high: $1,000; low: $500).
Purpose and activities: Emphasis on higher and secondary education, including a scholarship program; support also for the arts and a social service agency.
Types of support: Student aid.
Limitations: Giving limited to Sangamon County, IL.
Application information:
Initial approach: Letter
Deadline(s): None
Trustee: Marine Bank of Springfield.
Number of staff: None.
Employer Identification Number: 376087675

1950
J. C. Huizenga Foundation ⌑ ☆
200 North LaSalle St., Suite 3000
Chicago 60601-1083
Application address: 105051 Lorraine Dr., Hinsdale, IL 60521; Tel.: (312) 323-6310

Established in 1983 in IL.
Foundation type: Independent
Financial data (yr. ended 12/31/87): Assets, $2,595,424 (M); expenditures, $329,581, including $322,000 for 12 grants (high: $110,000; low: $1,000).
Purpose and activities: Giving limited to organizations "involved in the service of Our Lord Jesus Christ."
Limitations: Giving primarily in IL. No grants to individuals.
Application information:
Initial approach: Letter
Deadline(s): Nov. 1
Write: Mrs. Janet Evenhouse, Pres.
Officers and Directors: Janet Evenhouse, Pres.; June Huiner, Secy.-Treas.; Alyce Jabaay.
Employer Identification Number: 363084430

1951
Hyatt Foundation ⌑
200 West Madison, 38th Fl.
Chicago 60606 (312) 750-8400

Established in 1978 in IL.
Donor(s): Pritzker Foundation.
Foundation type: Independent
Financial data (yr. ended 07/31/88): Assets, $9,618 (M); gifts received, $359,673; expenditures, $350,885, including $100,902 for 2 grants to individuals of $50,451 each.
Purpose and activities: Annual award made to an individual for "significant contribution to humanity through architecture."
Types of support: Grants to individuals.
Application information: No posthumous awards are given. Applications not accepted.
Write: Simon Zunamon
Officers: Jay A. Pritzker, Pres.; Marian Pritzker, V.P.; Thomas J. Pritzker, Secy.; Nicholas J. Pritzker, Treas.
Number of staff: 1 full-time professional; 1 part-time support.
Employer Identification Number: 362981565

1952
I and G Charitable Foundation ⌑
Two North LaSalle St.
Chicago 60603

Incorporated in 1945 in IL.
Donor(s): Members of the Brown family.
Foundation type: Independent
Financial data (yr. ended 12/31/87): Assets, $1,889,330 (M); gifts received, $60,000; expenditures, $241,675, including $218,800 for 51 grants (high: $50,000; low: $400).
Purpose and activities: Giving for Jewish welfare funds, social services, and higher education.
Limitations: Giving primarily in IL. No support for hospitals.
Application information:
Initial approach: 2-page typewritten letter
Deadline(s): None
Write: Roger O. Brown, Pres.
Officers and Directors: Roger O. Brown, Pres. and Treas.; Howard J. Brown, V.P. and Secy.; Barbara E. Brown, Elizabeth K. Brown.
Employer Identification Number: 366069174

1953
Illinois Tool Works Foundation ▼ ⌑
8501 West Higgins Rd.
Chicago 60631 (312) 693-3040

Incorporated in 1954 in IL.
Donor(s): Illinois Tool Works, Inc.
Foundation type: Company-sponsored

Financial data (yr. ended 2/28/87): Assets, $13,595,609 (M); gifts received, $10,461,800; expenditures, $1,204,843, including $601,689 for 156 grants (high: $180,000; low: $100; average: $1,000-$20,000) and $571,650 for 1,809 employee matching gifts.
Purpose and activities: Support for education, health and hospitals, social services, including drug abuse and crime prevention programs, museums and the humanities, the United Way, and technical and public affairs programs.
Types of support: Operating budgets, continuing support, annual campaigns, seed money, building funds, employee-related scholarships, employee matching gifts, capital campaigns.
Limitations: Giving primarily in areas of company operations, particularly Chicago, IL. No grants to individuals, or for endowment funds or research; no loans.
Application information:
Initial approach: Letter
Copies of proposal: 1
Deadline(s): None
Board meeting date(s): Mar., June, Sept., and Dec.
Final notification: Same month as board meeting
Write: Stephen B. Smith, Dir.
Officers and Directors: Harold Byron Smith, Jr., Pres.; Arthur M. Wright, Secy.; Michael J. Robinson, Treas.; W. James Farrell, Michael H. Hudson, John D. Nichols, J. Thomas Schank, Stephen B. Smith.
Number of staff: 1
Employer Identification Number: 366087160

1954
IMC Foundation
2315 Sanders Rd.
Northbrook 60062 (708) 205-2200

Incorporated in 1967 in IL.
Donor(s): International Minerals & Chemical Corp.
Foundation type: Company-sponsored
Financial data (yr. ended 06/30/89): Assets, $669,219 (M); expenditures, $213,733, including $212,125 for 28 grants (high: $45,000; low: $500; average: $1,000-$5,000).
Purpose and activities: Support for youth and family services, the arts and cultural programs, education, and community funds.
Types of support: Annual campaigns, continuing support, operating budgets, special projects.
Limitations: Giving primarily in Chicago, IL; Terre Haute, IN; and St. Louis, MO. No support for religious organizations. No grants to individuals, or for building or endowment funds, scholarships, fellowships, or matching gifts; no loans.
Publications: Annual report (including application guidelines), corporate giving report, informational brochure (including application guidelines), financial statement, grants list.
Application information: Application form required.
Initial approach: Proposal with application form
Copies of proposal: 1
Deadline(s): End of Jan., Apr., July, and Oct.
Board meeting date(s): Feb., May, Aug., and Nov.
Final notification: End of Mar., June, Sept., and Dec.
Write: Colleen D. Keast, Exec. Dir.
Officers: George D. Kennedy,* Pres.; Elizabeth M. Higashi, V.P.; A. Jacqueline Dout, Treas.; Kenneth J. Burns, Secy.
Directors:* Colleen D. Keast, Exec. Dir.; Raymond F. Bentele, John A. Edwardson, M. Blakemon Ingle.
Number of staff: None.
Employer Identification Number: 366162015

1955
Immanuel Bible Foundation
1301 South Fell Ave.
Normal 61761 (309) 452-6710

Incorporated in 1944 in IL.
Donor(s): Keiser-Van Leer Assn. Trust.
Foundation type: Independent
Financial data (yr. ended 12/31/88): Assets, $1,379,504 (M); expenditures, $153,083, including $52,750 for 20 grants (high: $6,400; low: $150).
Purpose and activities: Support for local charities and missions, including family services, youth, welfare, and Christian organizations.
Types of support: General purposes.
Limitations: Giving primarily in IL. No grants to individuals.
Publications: Informational brochure.
Application information: Application form not required.
Initial approach: Letter
Copies of proposal: 1
Deadline(s): None
Board meeting date(s): Feb., Apr., July, and Oct.
Final notification: 2 months
Write: H.W. Stuber, Exec. Dir.
Officer: H.W. Stuber, Exec. Dir.
Number of staff: 1 full-time professional; 1 part-time support.
Employer Identification Number: 370688539

1956
Inland Steel-Ryerson Foundation, Inc.
c/o Inland Steel Industries
30 West Monroe St.
Chicago 60603 (312) 899-3420

Incorporated in 1945 in IL as Inland Steel Foundation, Inc.
Donor(s): Inland Steel Co., its subsidiaries and divisions.
Foundation type: Company-sponsored
Financial data (yr. ended 12/31/88): Assets, $5,342 (M); gifts received, $1,221,400; expenditures, $1,247,477, including $1,231,381 for 160 grants (high: $300,000; low: $500; average: $500-$25,000).
Purpose and activities: Grants to organizations concerned with basic human needs for food and shelter, equal opportunity for minorities, aid to disadvantaged youth, the disabled and handicapped, the aged, and neighborhood development; major interest in higher education with support to carefully chosen colleges and universities, with emphasis on business and engineering. Due to budget cutbacks, the directors have suspended operating support for arts and culture and many civic organizations. New grants will be funded on a limited basis.
Types of support: Operating budgets, special projects, employee-related scholarships, scholarship funds, fellowships, general purposes.
Limitations: Giving primarily in areas of company operations, particularly Chicago, IL, and northwest IN. Generally no grants for sectarian or religious organizations (except churches under the category of social welfare); or political activities. No grants for endowment funds, capital programs, matching grants, publications, conferences, seminars, or benefit affairs. No grants directly to individuals. Scholarships awarded under the All Inland Scholarship Plan and the National Merit and National Achievement Scholarship programs are restricted to children of company employees. Lawndale Community Scholarships are for area high school seniors.
Publications: Application guidelines.
Application information: Application form not required.
Initial approach: Letter or telephone
Copies of proposal: 1
Deadline(s): Submit proposal preferably in 1st 9 months of the year; no set deadline
Board meeting date(s): Dec.
Final notification: 3 to 4 months
Write: James E. Blair, Mgr., Corp. Community Affairs
Officers: David B. Anderson,* Pres.; W. Gordon Kay, V.P.; Earl S. Thompson, Secy.; Jay E. Dittus, Treas.
Directors:* Paul M. Anderson, Judd R. Cool, Joseph D. Corso, Robert J. Darnall, Gordon Kay, Frank W. Luerssen, Robert E. Powell.
Number of staff: 1 part-time professional; 1 part-time support.
Employer Identification Number: 366046944

1957
Interlake Foundation ¤
701 Harger Rd.
Oak Brook 60521 (312) 572-6600

Incorporated in 1951 in IL.
Donor(s): The Interlake Corp.
Foundation type: Company-sponsored
Financial data (yr. ended 12/31/87): Assets, $2,724,000 (M); gifts received, $243,000; expenditures, $555,000, including $445,000 for 164 grants and $52,000 for 195 employee matching gifts.
Purpose and activities: Emphasis on community funds and higher education; support also for youth agencies and cultural programs. The foundation is the main vehicle for giving; a direct corporate contributions program handles requests for fundraisers and other local activities.
Types of support: Employee matching gifts, capital campaigns, continuing support, general purposes, matching funds, research.
Limitations: Giving primarily in Chicago, IL, San Diego, CA, NJ, and CT. No grants to individuals.
Application information:
Initial approach: Letter
Copies of proposal: 1

Deadline(s): Sept. to Dec. is preferred time for applying
Board meeting date(s): Quarterly
Final notification: 3 months
Write: Raymond T. Anderson, Treas.
Officers: Frederick C. Langenberg,* Pres.; Edward D. Hopkins,* V.P.; I.R. MacLeod, Secy.; Raymond T. Anderson, Treas.
Directors:* Edward J. Williams.
Employer Identification Number: 362590617

1958
A. D. Johnson Foundation ⌑
One North LaSalle St., Suite 3000
Chicago 60602 (312) 782-7320

Incorporated in 1965 in IL.
Donor(s): A.D. Johnson.†
Foundation type: Independent
Financial data (yr. ended 12/31/88): Assets, $2,256,175 (M); expenditures, $141,876, including $132,000 for 12 grants (high: $25,000; low: $2,000).
Purpose and activities: Emphasis on medical research, hospitals, education, and agencies for children and youth.
Types of support: General purposes, research.
Limitations: Giving primarily in IL and FL. No grants to individuals.
Application information: Application form not required.
Deadline(s): None
Write: Committee on Charities
Officers: Wayne J. Johnson, Pres. and Treas.; Diane T. Johnson, V.P. and Secy.
Employer Identification Number: 366124270

1959
Albert and Rosemary Joseph Foundation ⌑ ☆
c/o Hunter Publishing Co.
950 Lee St.
Des Plaines 60016-6556

Established in 1985 in IL.
Donor(s): Albert Joseph, and other members of the Joseph family.
Foundation type: Independent
Financial data (yr. ended 12/31/88): Assets, $286,959 (M); gifts received, $25,000; expenditures, $103,101, including $100,296 for 28 grants (high: $38,340; low: $100).
Purpose and activities: Support primarily for Christian organizations, including Greek Orthodox churches.
Limitations: No grants to individuals.
Application information: Contributes only to pre-selected organizations. Applications not accepted.
Directors: Albert Joseph, Janelle M. Joseph, Rochelle T. Joseph, Rosemary Joseph, Rosemarilyn Merriman.
Employer Identification Number: 363377232

1960
The Joyce Foundation ▼
135 South LaSalle St., Suite 4010
Chicago 60603 (312) 782-2464
FAX: (312) 782-4160

Incorporated in 1948 in IL.
Donor(s): Beatrice Joyce Kean.†
Foundation type: Independent
Financial data (yr. ended 12/31/89): Assets, $348,286,228 (M); expenditures, $13,858,798, including $12,786,769 for 443 grants (high: $210,240; low: $100; average: $5,000-$50,000), $4,530 for employee matching gifts and $25,000 for loans.
Purpose and activities: Support for 1) conservation: soil conservation, groundwater protection, reducing atmospheric pollutants, protecting and enhancing the basic qualities of the Great Lakes; 2) culture: encouraging artistic excellence and cultural diversity in the Chicago metropolitan area with special attention given to organizations in early stages of development that have already shown achievement or exceptional promise; 3) economic development: strengthening the economic vitality of the Midwest and expanding opportunities for low-income individuals to fully participate in the economy through projects that work directly with individuals such as training, business development, or testing innovative business structures; 4) education: improving the educational opportunities offered to low-income students in primary, secondary and collegiate institutions by improving the performance of public schools and a limited number of independent and parochial schools that serve low-income students and increasing their access to higher education; emphasis also on strengthening the independent liberal arts colleges; 5) government: encouraging greater citizen participation in the electoral process, strengthening public understanding of and participation in state and local budget making processes.
Types of support: Operating budgets, continuing support, seed money, emergency funds, matching funds, consulting services, technical assistance, program-related investments, scholarship funds, loans, special projects, publications, conferences and seminars, employee matching gifts, general purposes.
Limitations: Giving primarily in the midwestern states, including IL, IN, IA, MI, MN, OH, and WI; limited number of conservation grants made in ND, SD, KS, MO, and NE. No grants to individuals, or for endowment or building funds, annual campaigns, deficit financing, research, or land acquisition.
Publications: Annual report, informational brochure (including application guidelines), financial statement, program policy statement.
Application information: Program policy and grant proposal guidelines reviewed annually in Dec.; completion of questionnaire is required prior to proposal submission in field of higher education; requests should be sent to foundation in Oct. for higher education questionnaire. Application form not required.
Initial approach: Letter
Copies of proposal: 2
Deadline(s): Dec. 15 (for Apr. meeting - Education and Economic Development); Apr. 15 (for Aug. meeting - Conservation); Aug. 15 (for Dec. meeting - Culture and Government)
Board meeting date(s): Apr. or May, Aug. or Sept., and twice in Dec.
Final notification: 3 weeks following meeting
Write: Craig Kennedy, Pres.
Officers: Craig Kennedy,* Pres.; Cushman B. Bissell, Jr.,* V.P., Finance, and Secy.-Treas.; Linda K. Schelinski, V.P., Administration.
Directors:* John T. Anderson, Chair.; Raymond Wearing, Vice-Chair.; Lewis H. Butler, Charles U. Daly, Richard K. Donahue, Roger R. Fross, Carlton L. Guthrie, Marion T. Hall, Jessica T. Mathews, Paula Wolff.
Number of staff: 10 full-time professional; 3 full-time support.
Employer Identification Number: 366079185

1961
Jubilee Foundation ⌑
175 West Jackson, Suite 1800
Chicago 60604

Established in 1984 in IL.
Donor(s): Gary D. Ginter, Gauis Berg, Paul Evans, William Field.
Foundation type: Independent
Financial data (yr. ended 11/30/87): Assets, $5,475 (M); gifts received, $1,374,525; expenditures, $1,389,399, including $1,309,519 for 35 grants (high: $380,303; low: $150).
Purpose and activities: Support for Christian churches, colleges, and religious missions.
Types of support: Operating budgets.
Limitations: Giving primarily in CA, IL, PA, WI, and WA.
Application information:
Initial approach: Proposal
Deadline(s): None
Write: Robin Wainwright
Officers and Directors:* Gary D. Ginter,* Pres.; David Boyce, Secy.; Joanna K. Ginter, Paul Hettinga.
Employer Identification Number: 363412268

1962
Mayer and Morris Kaplan Foundation
191 Waukegan Rd.
Northfield 60093 (708) 441-6630

Incorporated in 1957 in IL.
Donor(s): Alice B. Kaplan, Sealy Mattress Co. of Illinois, Burton B. Kaplan.
Foundation type: Independent
Financial data (yr. ended 10/30/88): Assets, $9,840,659 (M); expenditures, $576,754, including $506,498 for grants.
Purpose and activities: Support primarily for Jewish welfare funds, social services and child welfare, rehabilitation and the handicapped, higher education, and cultural programs, including museums and the performing arts.
Types of support: Operating budgets, continuing support, annual campaigns, endowment funds, employee matching gifts, scholarship funds, professorships, internships, employee-related scholarships, exchange programs, fellowships.
Limitations: Giving primarily in the Chicago, IL, area. No grants to individuals, or for seed money, emergency funds, deficit financing, building funds, equipment or materials, land acquisition, general endowments, matching grants, research, demonstration projects, publications, or conferences and seminars.
Publications: Application guidelines.

Application information: Contributes only to pre-selected organizations. Applications not accepted.
Write: Patricia Tatak
Officers: Morris A. Kaplan, Pres.; Burton B. Kaplan, Treas.
Number of staff: 1
Employer Identification Number: 366099675

1963
Karnes Memorial Fund ⌑
c/o Harvey S. Traub
P.O. Box 8
Fairbury 61739
Scholarship application address: Board of Governors, P.O. Box 2, Fairbury, IL 61739

Established in 1985 in IL.
Foundation type: Independent
Financial data (yr. ended 12/31/86): Assets, $1,075,663 (M); expenditures, $58,626, including $17,000 for 10 grants to individuals of $1,700 each.
Purpose and activities: Established to award scholarships to college students.
Types of support: Student aid.
Limitations: Giving limited to residents of Fairbury, Forrest, and Chatsworth, IL.
Application information: Application form required.
Deadline(s): Mar. 1
Officer and Trustees: Rev. Galen L. Schwartz, Chair.; Roberta Herzog, Janice P. Lancaster, National Bank of Fairbury.
Employer Identification Number: 376243213

1964
Katten, Muchin, & Zavis Foundation, Inc. ⌑
(Formerly Katten, Muchin, Zavis, Pearl & Galler Foundation, Inc.)
525 West Monroe St., Suite 1600
Chicago 60606

Established about 1982 in IL.
Foundation type: Company-sponsored
Financial data (yr. ended 12/31/87): Assets, $152,155 (M); gifts received, $346,220; expenditures, $227,058, including $226,975 for grants.
Purpose and activities: Emphasis on Jewish welfare funds.
Officers and Directors: Michael Zavis, Pres.; Allan Muchin, V.P.; Herbert Wander, Secy.; Melvin Pearl, Treas.; Donald Egan, Melvin Katten, William Kucera, Steven Neumer, Gerald Penner.
Employer Identification Number: 363165216

1965
Leon I. and Sharon Kaufman Foundation ⌑ ☆
1400 Skokie Hwy.
Lake Bluff 60044

Established in 1986 in IL.
Donor(s): Leon I. Kaufman, Sharon Kaufman.
Foundation type: Independent
Financial data (yr. ended 9/30/87): Assets, $1,005,250 (M); gifts received, $1,000,000; expenditures, $39,704, including $19,945 for 15 grants (high: $9,250; low: $100).
Purpose and activities: Support primarily for Jewish giving, including temple support and welfare funds.
Limitations: Giving primarily in IL, with emphasis on Chicago.
Officers and Directors: Leon I. Kaufman, Pres.; Sharon Kaufman, V.P.; Linda Allen, Secy.; Teri Heyden, Treas.
Employer Identification Number: 363480084

1966
Keebler Company Foundation ⌑
One Hollow Tree Ln.
Elmhurst 60126 (312) 833-2900
Application address: 677 Larch Ave., Elmhurst, IL 60126

Established in 1968 in IL.
Donor(s): Keebler Co.
Foundation type: Company-sponsored
Financial data (yr. ended 12/31/87): Assets, $45,394 (M); gifts received, $392,000; expenditures, $360,104, including $359,987 for 239 grants (high: $34,186; low: $10).
Purpose and activities: Emphasis on community funds; support also for minority programs, health and human services, education, culture and the arts, and education, including an employee matching gift program for higher education.
Types of support: Employee matching gifts.
Limitations: Giving primarily in areas where the company has major operations including IL, PA, CO, TX, MI, NC, MN, and IN. No grants to individuals, or for endowment funds, research programs, scholarships, or fellowships; no loans.
Application information:
Initial approach: Letter
Deadline(s): None
Write: A.G. Bland, Treas.
Officers: Thomas M. Garvin,* Pres.; J.J. Kelly,* V.P. and Secy.; A.G. Bland, Treas.
Directors:* C. Allen Gerber.
Employer Identification Number: 362658310

1967
Hattie Hannah Keeney Trust
c/o First National Bank of Chicago
One First National Plaza, Suite 0111
Chicago 60670-0111 (312) 732-4281

Established in 1950 in IL.
Foundation type: Independent
Financial data (yr. ended 12/31/89): Assets, $3,637,643 (M); expenditures, $279,626, including $251,046 for grants.
Purpose and activities: Support for the benefit of crippled children; grants primarily awarded to a hospital.
Limitations: Giving primarily in the Traverse City, MI, area.
Application information:
Initial approach: Letter
Deadline(s): None
Write: A. Gergets
Trustee: First National Bank of Chicago.
Employer Identification Number: 366016171

1968
Kellman Foundation ⌑
208 South LaSalle St., Suite 1860
Chicago 60604

Foundation type: Independent
Financial data (yr. ended 12/31/87): Assets, $1,662 (M); gifts received, $124,000; expenditures, $125,505, including $125,486 for 190 grants (high: $50,000; low: $12).
Purpose and activities: Support primarily for Jewish organizations, youth, and general charitable giving.
Officer: Joseph Kellman, Pres.
Employer Identification Number: 363106842

1969
Kellstadt Foundation
c/o Continental Bank
30 North LaSalle St.
Chicago 60697 (312) 828-1785

Established in 1977 in IL.
Donor(s): Charles Kellstadt Trust.
Foundation type: Independent
Financial data (yr. ended 09/30/89): Assets, $4,257,674 (M); expenditures, $479,682, including $445,000 for 6 grants (high: $100,000; low: $50,000).
Purpose and activities: Grants for private institutions of higher education, with emphasis on graduate schools of business; principal interest in marketing. At least one-half of funds to organizations affiliated with or sponsored by the Roman Catholic Church.
Types of support: Endowment funds, equipment, professorships.
Limitations: Giving primarily in the Midwest and South. No grants to individuals.
Application information: Application form not required.
Initial approach: Letter
Deadline(s): None
Board meeting date(s): Sept.
Write: Emory Williams, Trustee
Trustees: Leo Arnstein, Emory Williams, Continental Bank, N.A.
Number of staff: None.
Employer Identification Number: 362897620

1970
T. Lloyd Kelly Foundation ⌑
c/o Continental Bank
30 North LaSalle St.
Chicago 60693 (312) 828-1785

Incorporated in 1951 in IL.
Donor(s): Mildred Wetten Kelly McDermott.
Foundation type: Independent
Financial data (yr. ended 12/31/87): Assets, $1,864,247 (M); expenditures, $160,834, including $136,010 for 37 grants (high: $49,000; low: $100).
Purpose and activities: Emphasis on family planning; support also for secondary and higher education and hospitals.
Application information:
Write: M.C. Ryan, Treas.
Officers and Directors: Robert A. Malstrom, Pres.; Mildred Wetten Kelly McDermott, V.P.; H. Blair White, Secy.; M.C. Ryan, Treas.; Sally Morris.
Employer Identification Number: 366050341

1971
Kemper Educational and Charitable Fund ⌑
35 East Wacker Dr., Suite 1880
Chicago 60601 (312) 580-1024

Incorporated in 1961 in IL.
Donor(s): James Scott Kemper.†
Foundation type: Independent
Financial data (yr. ended 9/30/88): Assets, $7,836,710 (M); gifts received, $3,362; expenditures, $398,677, including $367,000 for 26 grants (high: $50,000; low: $2,000; average: $5,000).
Purpose and activities: Giving primarily for higher and secondary education; support also for cultural programs and health.
Types of support: Continuing support, equipment, scholarship funds, research.
Limitations: Giving primarily in metropolitan Chicago, IL, area, and adjoining states. No grants to individuals, or for building or endowment funds; no loans.
Publications: Application guidelines.
Application information: Contributes only to pre-selected organizations. Applications not accepted.
Copies of proposal: 1
Deadline(s): None
Board meeting date(s): Annually and as required
Write: Virginia J. Heitz, Secy.-Treas.
Officers: Gertrude Z. Kemper,* Chair.; Peter Van Cleave,* Vice-Chair.; Dale Park, Jr.,* Pres.; Mildred K. Terrill,* V.P.; Virginia J. Heitz, Secy.-Treas.
Trustees:* Margaret M. Archambault, Leslie N. Christensen, Frank D. Stout, John Van Cleave.
Number of staff: 1 part-time professional; 1 part-time support.
Employer Identification Number: 366054499

1972
James S. Kemper Foundation
c/o Kemper Group
Route 22
Long Grove 60047 (312) 540-2846

Incorporated in 1942 in IL.
Donor(s): James Scott Kemper,† and others, Lumbermens Mutual Casualty Co., American Motorists Insurance Co., American Manufacturers Mutual Insurance Co.
Foundation type: Independent
Financial data (yr. ended 07/31/89): Assets, $23,660,266 (M); expenditures, $927,513, including $633,793 for 91 grants (high: $25,000; low: $500; average: $5,000-$10,000).
Purpose and activities: "The foundation concentrates its resources on grants to institutions of higher education and to educational programs of major Chicago-area cultural institutions. Within higher education, priority is given to projects dealing with undergraduate or graduate business education. The Kemper Scholars Grant program is offered in partnership with a small number of colleges and universities. Each institution operates its own selection process."
Types of support: Scholarship funds, fellowships, special projects.
Limitations: No grants to individuals, or for any purposes other than scholarships and fellowships at participating institutions.
Publications: Annual report, application guidelines.
Application information: The Kemper Scholar Grant program is administered by selection committees at participating colleges and universities. The committee on each campus publicizes the program to enrolled freshman students who are oriented toward a career in business and screens the applicants. Application form required.
Initial approach: Letter or telephone
Copies of proposal: 1
Deadline(s): Mid-Oct. for special project grants; varies for scholarships
Board meeting date(s): Nov. and May; other dates vary
Final notification: Feb. for special project grants
Write: John H. Barcroft, Exec. Dir.
Officers: Joseph E. Luecke,* Chair. and Pres.; Walter L. White, Secy.-Treas.; John H. Barcroft, Exec. Dir.
Trustees:* Thomas R. Anderson, J. Reed Coleman, Raymond F. Farley, George D. Kennedy, Dalton L. Knauss, Gerald L. Maatman, David B. Mathis, Richard D. Nordman, Shirley N. Pettis, Kenneth A. Randall, Bernard W. Rogers, Richard N. Rosett, John C. Stetson, Daniel R. Toll.
Number of staff: 1 full-time professional; 2 full-time support.
Employer Identification Number: 366007812

1973
The George R. Kendall Foundation ⌑
c/o NBD Trust Co. of Illinois
1603 Orrington Ave.
Evanston 60201 (312) 491-6000

Trust established in 1969 in IL.
Donor(s): George R. Kendall.†
Foundation type: Independent
Financial data (yr. ended 11/30/88): Assets, $15,740,192 (M); expenditures, $909,278, including $861,850 for 18 grants (high: $258,300; low: $1,000).
Purpose and activities: Emphasis on higher education; giving also for social service and child welfare agencies.
Types of support: General purposes, special projects.
Limitations: Giving primarily in the northern metropolitan Chicago, IL, area. No grants to individuals, or for endowment funds, general operating funds, scholarships, fellowships, or matching gifts; no loans.
Application information: Application form not required.
Initial approach: Proposal
Copies of proposal: 1
Deadline(s): Feb. 1
Board meeting date(s): Apr. and Oct.
Final notification: After Oct. 31; proposals acknowledged only if favorably acted upon; grants paid from Nov. to the end of the year
Write: C. David Howell, V.P. and Trust Officer, NBD Trust Co. of Illinois
Trustees: Helen K. Johnson, G. Preston Kendall, George P. Kendall, Jr., Thomas C. Kendall, NBD Trust Co. of Illinois.
Number of staff: None.
Employer Identification Number: 366403376

1974
Kern Foundation Trust ⌑
c/o The Northern Trust Co.
50 South LaSalle St.
Chicago 60675 (312) 630-6000

Established in 1959 in IL.
Donor(s): Herbert A. Kern.†
Foundation type: Independent
Financial data (yr. ended 12/31/88): Assets, $13,643,199 (M); expenditures, $739,660, including $642,749 for 6 grants (high: $456,743; low: $5,000).
Purpose and activities: "To aid the spiritual enlightenment of as many people as practical by exposing them to the theosophical philosophy," particularly through support of the Theosophical Society in America and the Krotona Institute of Theosophy.
Limitations: No grants to individuals, or for building funds.
Publications: Program policy statement.
Application information: Application form not required.
Deadline(s): None
Trustees: John C. Kern, The Northern Trust Co.
Employer Identification Number: 366107250

1975
Martin & Mary Kilpatrick Educational Fund ⌑ ☆
c/o The Northern Trust Co.
50 South LaSalle St.
Chicago 60675

Established in 1988 in IL.
Donor(s): Martin Kilpatrick.†
Foundation type: Independent
Financial data (yr. ended 07/31/89): Assets, $1,300,614 (M); gifts received, $1,149,425; expenditures, $3,421.
Purpose and activities: Initial year of operation, fiscal 1989; no grants awarded.
Trustee: The Northern Trust Co.
Employer Identification Number: 366914282

1976
Kirkland & Ellis Foundation ⌑
200 East Randolph Dr.
Chicago 60601

Established in 1981 in IL.
Donor(s): Melvin S. Adess, Fred H. Bartlitt, Jr., Francis J. Gerlits, Thomas A. Gottschalk, Glen E. Hess, William R. Jentes, John F. Kirkpatrick, Howard G. Krane, Jack S. Levin, James W. Rankin, Edward W. Warren, and others.
Foundation type: Company-sponsored
Financial data (yr. ended 12/31/88): Assets, $819,461 (M); gifts received, $314,052; expenditures, $691,383, including $450,975 for 55 grants (high: $202,500; low: $62) and $238,626 for 422 employee matching gifts.
Purpose and activities: The foundation serves primarily to provide matching gifts for company employees.
Types of support: Employee matching gifts.
Application information: Applications not accepted.
Officers: James Schink, Pres.; William H. Pratt, Secy.-Treas.
Employer Identification Number: 363160355

1977
R. G. & E. M. Knight Fund ⌑ ☆
105 East Laurel Ave., Suite 201
Lake Forest 60045

Established in 1984 in IL.
Donor(s): R.G. Knight, E.M. Knight.
Foundation type: Independent
Financial data (yr. ended 12/31/88): Assets, $1,012,149 (M); expenditures, $33,806, including $31,895 for 52 grants (high: $2,500; low: $25).
Purpose and activities: Support primarily for higher and other education, Presbyterian churches and other religious organizations, medical research for cancer and other diseases, and social service agencies.
Limitations: Giving primarily in IL, with emphasis on Chicago. No grants to individuals.
Application information: Contributes only to pre-selected organizations. Applications not accepted.
Officers: E.M. Knight, Pres. and Treas.; E.K. Cochran, V.P.; R.G. Knight, Secy.
Employer Identification Number: 366047972

1978
Knowles Foundation ⌑
c/o John W. Hupp, Secy.
200 South Michigan Ave., No. 110
Chicago 60604-2404

Established in 1955 in IL.
Foundation type: Independent
Financial data (yr. ended 9/30/88): Assets, $2,072,881 (M); gifts received, $35,000; expenditures, $144,782, including $111,000 for 8 grants (high: $28,000; low: $4,000).
Purpose and activities: Emphasis on medical research.
Limitations: No grants to individuals.
Application information: Contributions are made only at the discretion of the directors. Applications not accepted.
Officers: Nancy W. Knowles, V.P.; John W. Hupp, Secy.; Robert G. Roth, Treas.
Employer Identification Number: 366051968

1979
Dolores Kohl Education Foundation ⌑
165 Green Bay Rd.
Wilmette 60091

Established in 1972 in IL.
Donor(s): Dolores Kohl Solovy, Ruth Page Fisher.
Foundation type: Operating
Financial data (yr. ended 06/30/88): Assets, $3,270,510 (M); gifts received, $39,784; expenditures, $1,305,824, including $25 for 1 grant, $16,000 for 16 grants to individuals of $1,000 each and $1,262,715 for foundation-administered programs.
Purpose and activities: A private operating foundation which conducts workshops and seminars for teachers, pupils, and parents to improve the education of children; awards to teachers "for exemplary teaching;" some grants for furtherance of education.
Types of support: Grants to individuals.
Application information: Contributes to organizations at the discretion of the directors. Applications not accepted.
Officers: Dolores Kohl Solovy, Pres.; Herbert Kohl, V.P. and Secy.; Allen Kohl, V.P. and Treas.
Employer Identification Number: 237206116

1980
The Koldyke Family Foundation ⌑ ☆
c/o Frontenac Co.
208 South LaSalle St., Rm. 1900
Chicago 60604 (312) 368-0044

Donor(s): Martin J. Koldyke.
Foundation type: Independent
Financial data (yr. ended 7/31/88): Assets, $38,662 (M); gifts received, $18,500; expenditures, $146,106, including $145,363 for 133 grants (high: $40,000; low: $25).
Purpose and activities: Giving primarily for higher education; support also for the handicapped, social services, and cultural programs.
Limitations: Giving primarily in IL, with emphasis on Chicago. No grants to individuals.
Application information:
Initial approach: Proposal
Deadline(s): None
Write: Martin J. Koldyke, Pres.
Officers and Directors: Patricia B. Koldyke, Chair.; Martin J. Koldyke, Pres. and Treas.; Stanford J. Goldblatt, Secy.; Rodney L. Goldstein, Martin Laird Koldyke.
Employer Identification Number: 363482711

1981
Gerald A. & Karen A. Kolschowsky Foundation, Inc. ⌑ ☆
1225 Corporate Blvd.
Aurora 60507-2018

Incorporated in 1986 in IL.
Donor(s): Gerald A. Kolschowsky.
Foundation type: Independent
Financial data (yr. ended 12/31/88): Assets, $1,453,613 (M); gifts received, $100,000; expenditures, $88,957, including $86,600 for 144 grants (high: $32,300; low: $100).
Purpose and activities: Giving primarily for Lutheran churches; support also for health associations and hospitals, and social services, including child welfare.
Limitations: Giving primarily in IL. No grants to individuals.
Application information: Contributes only to pre-selected organizations. Applications not accepted.
Officers and Directors: Karen A. Kolschowsky, Pres.; Michael J. Kolschowsky, V.P.; Timothy J. Kolschowsky, V.P.; Gerald A. Kolschowsky, Secy.-Treas.
Employer Identification Number: 363505302

1982
Kraft General Foods Foundation ▼
(Formerly Kraft Foundation)
Kraft Court
Glenview 60025 (708) 998-7032

Established in 1983 in IL; The General Foods Fund, Inc. merged with Kraft Foundation in 1989 to form Kraft General Foods Foundation.
Donor(s): Kraft, Inc.
Foundation type: Company-sponsored
Financial data (yr. ended 12/26/88): Assets, $55,471,190 (M); gifts received, $5,000,000; expenditures, $10,701,695, including $10,467,687 for grants (average: $25,000-$50,000).
Purpose and activities: Support primarily for innovative "self-help" programs, with emphasis on nutrition and physical fitness, education, and economic and community development; grants also for public policy and cultural programs. Special focus on the needs of minorities, women, and persons with disabilities.
Types of support: Building funds, endowment funds, research, scholarship funds, fellowships, professorships, general purposes, employee matching gifts.
Limitations: Giving to organizations having national impact or which benefit communities where company employees live and work. No support for organizations with a limited constituency, such as fraternal or veterans' groups, and organizations which restrict their services to members of one religious group. No grants to individuals, or for travel, tuition, registration fees, membership dues, or goodwill advertising for benefit purposes; no loans.
Publications: Corporate giving report, application guidelines.
Application information: The foundation requests that applicants do not call or visit. Application form not required.
Initial approach: Proposal
Deadline(s): None
Board meeting date(s): Quarterly
Final notification: 1 to 2 months
Write: Ronald J. Coman, Admin. Dir.
Officers: Margaret P. MacKimm,* Pres.; Gary P. Coughlan,* V.P. and Treas.; William W. Crawford,* V.P.; Thomas J. McHugh, V.P.; Kenneth S. Kirsner, Secy.; Ronald J. Coman, Admin. Dir.
Directors:* Lowell Hoffman, Robert McVicker, John J. Tucker, Joel D. Weiner.
Number of staff: None.
Employer Identification Number: 363222729

1983
Leonard & Ruth Kriser Foundation ⌑
400 Skokie Blvd., Suite 350
Northbrook 60062-2816

Established in 1986 in IL.
Foundation type: Independent
Financial data (yr. ended 12/31/87): Assets, $694,502 (M); gifts received, $85,000; expenditures, $124,005, including $119,950 for 29 grants (high: $60,000; low: $300).
Purpose and activities: Support primarily for Jewish welfare, higher education, and medical facilities.
Application information: Contributes only to pre-selected organizations. Applications not accepted.
Directors: Charles F. Kriser, Daniel C. Kriser, Leonard S. Kriser.
Employer Identification Number: 363457157

1984
Krishna Foundation, Inc. ¤
16443 Kenwood Ave.
South Holland 60473

Established in 1977 in IL.
Donor(s): Kishan Chand Pahuja, Krishna Pahuja.
Foundation type: Operating
Financial data (yr. ended 10/31/88): Assets, $1,183,104 (M); gifts received, $40,000; expenditures, $48,399, including $41,856 for 3 grants (high: $40,356; low: $500).
Purpose and activities: A private operating foundation; giving primarily for an affiliated charitable trust in India; support also for local private secondary schools.
Application information: Applications not accepted.
Officers and Directors: Kishan Chand Pahuja, Pres. and Treas.; Krishna Pahuja, Secy.; Subhash Chander Pahuja.
Employer Identification Number: 362945500

1985
Kugler Foundation ¤ ☆
c/o Fred R. Kugler
7301 North Cicero Ave.
Lincoln Wood 60646-1694

Established in 1965.
Foundation type: Independent
Financial data (yr. ended 10/31/88): Assets, $35,434 (M); gifts received, $118,000; expenditures, $106,247, including $105,700 for 8 grants (high: $27,000; low: $500).
Purpose and activities: Support primarily for higher education, Jewish organizations, including a welfare fund, and medical research.
Types of support: General purposes, research.
Limitations: No grants to individuals.
Application information: Contributes only to pre-selected organizations. Applications not accepted.
Trustees: Eleane H. Kugler, Fred R. Kugler.
Employer Identification Number: 366124171

1986
Landau Family Foundation ¤ ☆
150 North Wacker Dr., Suite 900
Chicago 60606-1611

Established in 1955.
Donor(s): Howard M. Landau.
Foundation type: Independent
Financial data (yr. ended 11/30/88): Assets, $1,002,962 (M); gifts received, $150,000; expenditures, $69,266, including $62,986 for grants (high: $20,000).
Purpose and activities: Support primarily for Jewish organizations, including welfare funds; giving also for higher education.
Limitations: No grants to individuals.
Application information:
Deadline(s): None
Officers: Howard M. Landau, Pres. and Treas.; Herbert H. Heyman, V.P. and Secy.
Employer Identification Number: 366089098

1987
Harry and Sadie Lasky Foundation ¤
30 North Michigan Ave., Suite 1813
Chicago 60602 (312) 782-6515

Incorporated in 1958 in IL.
Donor(s): Mrs. Sadie Lasky.
Foundation type: Independent
Financial data (yr. ended 12/31/88): Assets, $1,822,886 (M); expenditures, $24,905, including $17,500 for 2 grants (high: $15,000; low: $2,500).
Purpose and activities: Giving for Jewish welfare funds and higher education.
Application information: Application form not required.
Deadline(s): None
Write: Mrs. Sadie Lasky, Pres.
Officers and Directors:* Sadie Lasky,* Pres. and Treas.; Norman Handelman,* Secy.; Alex A. Lothorn.
Employer Identification Number: 366105123

1988
The Francis L. Lederer Foundation ¤
c/o Leo H. Arnstein
7500 Sears Tower
Chicago 60606

Established in 1966 in IL.
Foundation type: Independent
Financial data (yr. ended 12/31/88): Assets, $3,793,486 (M); gifts received, $959,062; expenditures, $236,075, including $198,050 for 29 grants (high: $30,000; low: $500).
Purpose and activities: Emphasis on higher and secondary education, medical education and research, Jewish welfare funds, and the arts.
Limitations: Giving primarily in Chicago, IL.
Application information:
Initial approach: Proposal
Deadline(s): None
Officers and Directors:* Francis L. Lederer II,* Pres. and Treas.; Adrienne Lederer,* V.P.; Leo H. Arnstein,* Secy.
Employer Identification Number: 362594937

1989
Otto W. Lehmann Foundation
3240 North Lake Shore Dr., Apt. 7A
Chicago 60657 (312) 929-9851
Mailing address: P.O. Box 11194, Chicago, IL 60611

Incorporated in 1967 in IL.
Donor(s): Otto W. Lehmann.†
Foundation type: Independent
Financial data (yr. ended 07/31/89): Assets, $2,139,056 (M); expenditures, $188,398, including $164,730 for 71 grants (high: $8,000; low: $100; average: $100-$8,000).
Purpose and activities: Emphasis on youth agencies and child welfare, social services, aid for the handicapped, higher and other education, health agencies, medical research, rehabilitation, and cultural organizations, including museums and the performing arts.
Types of support: Annual campaigns, capital campaigns, scholarship funds.
Limitations: Giving limited to the Chicago, IL, area.
Application information: Application form required.
Initial approach: Letter
Copies of proposal: 1
Deadline(s): June 30
Board meeting date(s): July 15
Write: Richard J. Peterson, Managing Trustee
Trustees: Richard J. Peterson, Managing Trustee; James F. Elworth, David W. Peterson, Lucille S. Peterson.
Number of staff: None.
Employer Identification Number: 366160836

1990
Leslie Fund, Inc. ¤
One Northfield Plaza
North Field 60093 (312) 441-2613

Incorporated in 1956 in IL.
Donor(s): Members of the Leslie family.
Foundation type: Independent
Financial data (yr. ended 3/31/88): Assets, $2,949,007 (M); expenditures, $236,886, including $209,275 for 73 grants (high: $50,000; low: $50).
Purpose and activities: Emphasis on cultural programs, aid to the handicapped, education, youth agencies, conservation and social welfare agencies, and hospitals.
Limitations: Giving primarily in IL. No grants to individuals.
Application information: Application form not required.
Initial approach: Letter
Copies of proposal: 1
Deadline(s): None
Board meeting date(s): Jan., Apr., July, and Oct.
Write: John H. Leslie, Pres.
Officers: John H. Leslie,* Pres.; Virginia A. Leslie, V.P.; Barbara Laskin, Secy.-Treas.
Directors:* James W. Leslie, Vicki Leslie, Robert W. Wright.
Number of staff: 1 part-time support.
Employer Identification Number: 366055800

1991
Marcus and Theresa Levie Educational Fund
c/o Jewish Federation of Metropolitan Chicago
One South Franklin St.
Chicago 60606 (312) 346-6700

Trust established in 1959 in IL.
Donor(s): Maude M. Levie,† Jerome M. Levie,† Charles M. Levie.†
Foundation type: Independent
Financial data (yr. ended 7/31/86): Assets, $2,693,811 (M); expenditures, $150,000, including $137,000 for 32 grants to individuals (average: $5,200).
Purpose and activities: Scholarships awarded to Jewish students who are residents of Cook County and who have demonstrated career promise and have financial need to complete their professional or vocational training in the helping professions.
Types of support: Student aid.
Limitations: Giving limited to Cook County, IL. No grants for general support, or for building or endowment funds, research, or matching gifts; no loans.
Publications: Application guidelines, program policy statement.
Application information: Application form required.

Initial approach: Letter or telephone
Copies of proposal: 2
Deadline(s): Submit scholarship application between Nov. and Feb.; deadline Mar. 1
Board meeting date(s): As required, usually in July
Final notification: July or Aug.
Write: Stacy Halpern, Secy.
Officer: Stacy Halpern, Secy.
Distribution Committee: Mrs. David Leavitt, Chair.; Joseph D. Ament, Mrs. Bernard Bagan, Susan Feit, Mrs. Buryl Lazar, Francine F. Levy, Mrs. Maurice L. Lewis, Joy Malkus, Roberta Mann, Mrs. Herbert S. Manning, Mrs. Arnold Newberger, Charlotte Newberger, Rabbi Herman E. Schaalman, Midge Perlman Shafton, Mrs. Lloyd Shefsky, Phyllis Shalowitz.
Trustee: Chicago Title and Trust Co.
Number of staff: 14 part-time professional; 1 full-time support; 1 part-time support.
Employer Identification Number: 366010074

1992
Donald Levin Family Foundation ⌑ ☆
5100 North Ravenswood
Chicago 60640

Established in 1984 in IL.
Donor(s): Donald Levin, DRL Enterprises.
Foundation type: Independent
Financial data (yr. ended 9/30/88): Assets, $1,109,266 (M); gifts received, $300,000; expenditures, $46,379, including $44,450 for 22 grants (high: $15,000; low: $500).
Purpose and activities: Support for secondary and higher education, health services and associations, youth, and welfare.
Limitations: Giving primarily in NC and IL. No grants to individuals.
Application information: Contributes only to pre-selected organizations. Applications not accepted.
Director: Donald Levin.
Employer Identification Number: 363329401

1993
Marilyn & Harry Levinson Foundation ⌑ ☆
739 North Clark St.
Chicago 60610 (312) 337-3720

Established in 1965 in IL.
Donor(s): Harry Levinson, Levinson's, Inc.
Foundation type: Independent
Financial data (yr. ended 4/30/88): Assets, $374,126 (M); gifts received, $145,000; expenditures, $523,429, including $522,365 for 45 grants (high: $400,000; low: $25).
Purpose and activities: Giving primarily to a day school; support also for Jewish welfare, educational, and religious organizations.
Limitations: Giving primarily in Chicago, IL. No grants to individuals.
Application information:
Initial approach: Letter
Deadline(s): None
Write: Harry Levinson, Pres.
Officers and Directors: Harry Levinson, Pres.; Maurice P. Walk, Secy.; Marilyn Levinson, Treas.
Employer Identification Number: 366126293

1994
Joseph & Sarah Levy Family Foundation ⌑ ☆
1603 Orrington St., Suite 1006
Evanston 60201-2675

Established in 1955.
Donor(s): Walton Enterprises, Sarah Levy.†
Foundation type: Independent
Financial data (yr. ended 7/31/89): Assets, $1,155,574 (M); expenditures, $78,016, including $76,382 for 20 grants (high: $50,000; low: $35).
Purpose and activities: Support primarily for a Jewish welfare fund, medical research, and higher education.
Types of support: Scholarship funds.
Limitations: No grants to individuals.
Application information: Contributes only to pre-selected organizations. Applications not accepted.
Officers: Joseph Levy, Jr., Pres.; Jean L. London, Secy.-Treas.
Employer Identification Number: 366130173

1995
Chas and Ruth Levy Foundation
1200 North Branch St.
Chicago 60622 (312) 440-4401

Incorporated in 1959 in IL.
Donor(s): Charles Levy,† Charles Levy Circulating Co., and several other Levy companies.
Foundation type: Independent
Financial data (yr. ended 06/30/89): Assets, $3,233,396 (M); expenditures, $418,408, including $378,500 for 61 grants (high: $130,000; low: $50).
Purpose and activities: Emphasis on Jewish welfare funds, higher education, and performing arts.
Limitations: Giving primarily in IL.
Application information: Contributes only to pre-selected organizations. Applications not accepted.
Write: Barbara Levy Kipper, Pres.
Officer and Directors:* Barbara Levy Kipper,* Pres.; Ruth Levy, Donald Lubin, Ralph Schneider.
Employer Identification Number: 366032324

1996
Frank J. Lewis Foundation ▼ ⌑
Three First National Plaza, Suite 1950
Chicago 60602

Incorporated in 1927 in IL.
Donor(s): Frank J. Lewis.†
Foundation type: Independent
Financial data (yr. ended 12/31/87): Assets, $17,132,707 (M); expenditures, $1,205,294, including $1,060,705 for 92 grants (high: $110,000; low: $100; average: $1,000-$15,000).
Purpose and activities: To foster, preserve, and extend the Roman Catholic faith; grants largely for Roman Catholic educational institutions, churches, social services, religious orders and church-sponsored programs, and hospitals.
Types of support: General purposes.
Limitations: No grants to individuals, or for endowment funds.
Application information: Contributes only to pre-selected organizations. Applications not accepted.
Board meeting date(s): Feb., May, Aug., and Nov.
Officers and Trustees: Edward D. Lewis, Pres.; Philip D. Lewis, V.P.; Victor Hedberg, Treas.; Diana B. Lewis.
Employer Identification Number: 362441931

1997
Marguerite Listeman Foundation ⌑
c/o The Northern Trust Co.
50 South LaSalle St.
Chicago 60675 (312) 630-6000

Trust established in 1958 in WI.
Donor(s): Kurt Listeman.†
Foundation type: Independent
Financial data (yr. ended 12/31/88): Assets, $1,333,091 (M); expenditures, $92,371, including $79,500 for 8 grants (high: $50,000; low: $1,000).
Purpose and activities: Grants primarily for community development, including support for buildings and equipment for parks and recreation areas and cultural facilities.
Types of support: Building funds, equipment.
Limitations: Giving limited to the Clark County-Neillsville, WI, area. No grants to individuals.
Application information: Contributes only to pre-selected organizations. Applications not accepted.
Officer: Mike Krultz, Jr., Secy.
Advisors: Wayne Gross, Bradley Larsen, James Musil, Donald Quicker, Heron Van Gorden.
Trustee: The Northern Trust Co.
Employer Identification Number: 366028439

1998
Michael Littner Charitable Foundation Trust ⌑
180 North Michigan Ave.
Chicago 60601

Established in 1981 in IL.
Foundation type: Independent
Financial data (yr. ended 12/31/87): Assets, $326,777 (M); expenditures, $135,960, including $127,137 for 14 grants (high: $25,000; low: $250).
Purpose and activities: Support for dance companies, theatre companies and productions, and a mental health institute.
Limitations: Giving primarily in Chicago, IL. No grants to individuals.
Application information: Application form not required.
Deadline(s): None
Write: Ner Littner, M.D., Trustee
Trustee: Ner Littner, M.D.
Employer Identification Number: 363235601

1999
Joseph Lizzadro Family Foundation ⌑
2215 York Rd., Suite 304
Oak Brook 60521 (312) 571-7200

Incorporated in 1957 in IL.
Donor(s): Members of the Lizzadro family and others.
Foundation type: Independent

Financial data (yr. ended 12/31/88): Assets, $4,389,573 (M); gifts received, $209,800; expenditures, $71,991, including $51,000 for 11 grants (high: $45,000; low: $500; average: $1,000).
Purpose and activities: Grants primarily for cultural organizations, hospitals, and health agencies.
Limitations: Giving limited to Oak Brook, IL. No grants to individuals, or for endowment funds.
Application information:
Initial approach: Letter
Copies of proposal: 1
Deadline(s): None
Board meeting date(s): Mar. and Dec.
Write: John S. Lizzadro, Treas.
Officers and Directors:* Joseph Lizzadro, Jr.,* Pres.; Angela Anderson,* V.P.; John S. Lizzadro,* Secy.-Treas.; Bonita Hay, Frank C. Lizzadro, Mary Lizzadro, Theresa McPherson, Diane Nicholas.
Employer Identification Number: 366047939

2000
E. J. Logan Foundation ⌑
735 Normandy Ln.
Glenview 60025

Established in 1986 in IL.
Donor(s): M. Joseph Hickey, Jr.
Foundation type: Independent
Financial data (yr. ended 12/31/88): Assets, $1,541,106 (M); gifts received, $1,197,613; expenditures, $194,017, including $193,920 for 11 grants (high: $51,012; low: $1,000).
Purpose and activities: Giving primarily for social services with emphasis on child welfare and the handicapped.
Limitations: Giving primarily in IL. No grants to individuals.
Application information: Contributes only to pre-selected organizations. Applications not accepted.
Trustee: M. Joseph Hickey, Jr.
Employer Identification Number: 363488565

2001
Lord Educational Fund ⌑ ☆
c/o First Trust & Savings Bank
108 West Market St.
Taylorville 62568-0309 (217) 824-4955

Foundation type: Independent
Financial data (yr. ended 9/30/88): Assets, $1,770,136 (M); expenditures, $93,404, including $71,503 for 38 grants to individuals (high: $3,000; low: $503).
Purpose and activities: Scholarships and student loans to local high school graduates for college, vocational, and business school education.
Types of support: Student aid, student loans.
Limitations: Giving primarily in IL, with emphasis on Taylorville and Assumption. No grants for organizations.
Application information: Application form required.
Deadline(s): Apr. 1
Trustee: First Trust & Savings Bank.
Employer Identification Number: 510175613

2002
Michael W. Louis Foundation ⌑ ☆
2840 Sheridan Rd.
Evanston 60201-1796

Established in 1984.
Donor(s): Michael W. Louis.
Foundation type: Independent
Financial data (yr. ended 3/31/89): Assets, $22,162 (M); gifts received, $1,764,000; expenditures, $1,777,274, including $1,746,254 for 16 grants (high: $1,592,504; low: $200).
Purpose and activities: Support primarily for a private college of education; minor support for a junior golf foundation.
Limitations: Giving primarily in Evanston, IL. No grants to individuals.
Application information: Application form not required.
Deadline(s): None
Write: Orley R. Herron, Pres.
Officers: Michael W. Louis, Chair.; Orley R. Herron, Pres.
Directors: Robert L. Moran, Robert C. Whiting.
Employer Identification Number: 363321575

2003
The Lumpkin Foundation
7200 Sears Tower
233 South Wacker Dr.
Chicago 60606 (217) 235-3361
Application address: 121 South 17th St., Mattoon, IL 61938

Incorporated in 1953 in IL.
Donor(s): Besse Adamson Lumpkin,† Richard Adamson Lumpkin,† Illinois Consolidated Telephone Co., Richard Anthony Lumpkin.
Foundation type: Independent
Financial data (yr. ended 12/31/89): Assets, $4,071,623 (M); gifts received, $180,000; expenditures, $166,948, including $133,600 for 43 grants (high: $30,000; low: $100).
Purpose and activities: Grants primarily for higher and secondary education, hospitals, and health agencies; support also for public libraries.
Limitations: Giving primarily in central IL. No grants to individuals.
Application information: Application form not required.
Initial approach: Proposal
Copies of proposal: 1
Deadline(s): Nov. 30
Board meeting date(s): June, Dec., and as required
Write: Richard Anthony Lumpkin, Pres.
Officers and Directors:* Richard Anthony Lumpkin,* Pres.; Mary G. Lumpkin,* V.P.; S.L. Grissom,* Secy.-Treas.
Number of staff: None.
Employer Identification Number: 237423640

2004
Lurie Family Foundation ⌑ ☆
c/o P. Lurie
Two North Riverside Plaza, No. 600
Chicago 60606-2639

Established in 1986 in IL.
Donor(s): Robert Lurie.
Foundation type: Independent
Financial data (yr. ended 12/31/88): Assets, $1,879,167 (M); gifts received, $969,072; expenditures, $91,054, including $83,443 for 22 grants (high: $40,918; low: $50).
Purpose and activities: Support primarily for health, higher education, and youth.
Limitations: Giving primarily in Chicago IL, MI, and IN. No grants to individuals.
Application information: Contributes only to pre-selected organizations. Applications not accepted.
Officers: Robert Lurie, Pres. and Treas.; B. Ann Lurie, V.P.; Sheli P. Rosenberg, Secy.
Employer Identification Number: 363486274

2005
J. Roderick MacArthur Foundation ▼
9333 North Milwaukee Ave.
Niles 60648 (708) 966-0143

Established in 1976 in IL.
Donor(s): J. Roderick MacArthur,† Bradford Exchange AG, Solange D. MacArthur, Bradford Exchange, Ltd.
Foundation type: Independent
Financial data (yr. ended 01/31/90): Assets, $27,385,128 (M); gifts received, $2,243,825; expenditures, $2,737,966, including $2,293,854 for 98 grants (high: $500,000; low: $2,000; average: $2,000-$20,000).
Purpose and activities: The foundation seeks to "aid those who are inequitably or unjustly treated by established institutions" by "protecting and encouraging freedom of expression, human rights, civil liberties, and social justice; and by eliminating political, economic, social, religious, and cultural oppression."
Types of support: Seed money, publications, special projects.
Limitations: No support for ongoing social services, government programs, religious, church-based activities, university or other educational programs, or economic development or training programs. No grants to individuals, or for capital projects, endowments, development campaigns, statues or memorials, annual campaigns, conferences, continuing support, deficit financing, land acquisition, endowments, matching gifts, consulting services, technical assistance, scholarships, internships, fellowships, seminars or benefits; no pass through grants, no support for grassroots organizing or demonstrations; no loans.
Publications: Financial statement, grants list, informational brochure (including application guidelines).
Application information: Application form not required.
Initial approach: Letter
Copies of proposal: 1
Deadline(s): None
Board meeting date(s): Approximately every 2 months
Final notification: 1 to 2 months
Write: Lance E. Lindblom, Pres.
Officers and Directors:* Gregoire C. MacArthur,* Chair.; Solange D. MacArthur,* Vice-Chair.; Lance E. Lindblom, Pres.; John R. MacArthur,* Secy.-Treas.
Number of staff: 4 full-time professional.
Employer Identification Number: 510214450

2006
John D. and Catherine T. MacArthur Foundation ▼
140 South Dearborn St.
Chicago 60603 (312) 726-8000

Incorporated in 1970 in IL.
Donor(s): John D. MacArthur.†
Foundation type: Independent
Financial data (yr. ended 12/31/88): Assets, $3,134,508,720 (M); expenditures, $165,356,267, including $88,132,116 for grants, $7,200,804 for grants to individuals, $28,144,024 for foundation-administered programs and $21,120,000 for loans.
Purpose and activities: Six major initiatives currently authorized: MacArthur Fellows Program, for highly talented individuals in any field of endeavor who are chosen in a foundation-initiated effort (no applications are accepted for this program); the Health Program, for research in mental health and the psychological and behavioral aspects of health and rehabilitation (including designated programs in parasitology and aging); the Special Grants Program for support of cultural and community development in the Chicago metropolitan area (including the Program for Neighborhood Initiatives); the International Peace and Security Program, for support of initiatives which promote and strengthen international security; the World Environment and Resources Program, for support of conservation programs which protect the earth's biological diversity and work to protect tropical ecology; and the Education Program, to focus on the promotion of literacy. Although the foundation has also made grants in such areas as population and mass communications, no formal programs or guidelines have been established to date.
Types of support: Matching funds, general purposes, operating budgets, special projects, research, fellowships.
Limitations: No support for churches or religious programs, political activities or campaigns, or other foundations or institutions. No grants for capital or endowment funds, equipment purchases, plant construction, conferences, publications, media productions, debt retirement, development campaigns, fundraising appeals, scholarships, or fellowships (other than those sponsored by the foundation); no loans.
Publications: Annual report, program policy statement, application guidelines, informational brochure.
Application information: Direct applications for Fellows Program not accepted. Grants increasingly initiated by the board.
Initial approach: Letter
Copies of proposal: 1
Deadline(s): None
Board meeting date(s): Monthly, except Aug.
Final notification: Varies
Write: James M. Furman, Exec. V.P.
Officers and Directors:* William T. Kirby,* Chair.; Adele Simmons,* Pres.; James M. Furman,* Exec. V.P.; William Bevan, V.P. and Dir. of Health Prog.; Lawrence L. Landry, V.P. - Finance; Lawrence G. Martin, V.P.; Nancy B. Ewing, Secy.; Philip M. Grace, Treas.; James T. Griffin, General Counsel; Robert P. Ewing, Murray Gell-Mann, Alan M. Hallene, Paul Harvey, Shirley Mount Hufstedler, Margaret E. Mahoney, Elizabeth Jane McCormack, Jonas Salk, M.D., Jerome B. Wiesner.
Number of staff: 65
Employer Identification Number: 237093598

2007
Nathan Manilow Foundation ⌑
754 North Milwaukee Ave.
Chicago 60622 (312) 829-3655

Incorporated in 1955 in IL.
Donor(s): Nathan Manilow,† Lewis Manilow.
Foundation type: Independent
Financial data (yr. ended 5/31/88): Assets, $4,642,778 (M); expenditures, $326,101, including $241,169 for 43 grants (high: $50,000; low: $250).
Purpose and activities: Emphasis on Jewish welfare funds, culture, and education; grants also for temple support and child welfare.
Limitations: Giving primarily in IL.
Application information: Application form not required.
Initial approach: Letter
Deadline(s): None
Write: Lewis Manilow, Pres.
Officers: Lewis Manilow, Pres. and Treas.; Susan Manilow, Secy.
Director: Norman Altman.
Employer Identification Number: 366079220

2008
Henry & Belle Mann Charitable Foundation ⌑ ☆
990 North Lake Shore Dr., Apt. 26A
Chicago 60611-1353 (312) 332-0800

Established in 1961.
Donor(s): Members of the Mann family.
Foundation type: Independent
Financial data (yr. ended 12/31/88): Assets, $1,394,213 (M); gifts received, $2,000; expenditures, $111,960, including $108,250 for 12 grants (high: $105,000; low: $100).
Purpose and activities: Giving primarily for a Jewish welfare fund; support also for other Jewish organizations.
Limitations: No grants to individuals.
Application information: Applications not accepted.
Initial approach: Letter
Deadline(s): None
Write: Henry Mann, Pres.
Officers: Henry Mann, Pres.; Sheldon Mann, V.P.; Belle Mann, Secy.
Employer Identification Number: 366136141

2009
Albert & Anne Mansfield Foundation ⌑
200 North LaSalle St., Suite 2100
Chicago 60601-1095 (312) 621-1456

Established in 1976.
Donor(s): Albert Mansfield,† Anne Mansfield.
Foundation type: Independent
Financial data (yr. ended 12/31/87): Assets, $1,630,527 (M); expenditures, $96,361, including $69,050 for 9 grants (high: $12,190; low: $3,000).
Purpose and activities: Support for higher education, medicine, and volunteer hospices.
Limitations: Giving primarily in IL, MN, MA, and IN.
Application information: Application form required.
Initial approach: Proposal
Copies of proposal: 3
Board meeting date(s): Nov.
Write: Lawrence Kasakoff, Trustee
Trustees: Marlene Hopmayer, Lawrence Kasakoff, Anne Mansfield, Benetta Mansfield, Seymour Mansfield, Harris Trust & Savings Bank.
Number of staff: None.
Employer Identification Number: 366151176

2010
Bert William Martin Foundation ⌑
c/o The Northern Trust Co.
50 South LaSalle St.
Chicago 60675 (312) 630-6000

Incorporated in 1946 in IL.
Donor(s): Bert W. Martin, Ada La May Martin.
Foundation type: Independent
Financial data (yr. ended 12/31/88): Assets, $3,228,382 (M); expenditures, $185,438, including $147,700 for 23 grants (high: $75,000; low: $300).
Purpose and activities: Grants largely for hospitals and health services.
Limitations: Giving primarily in CA and Mount Vernon, OH. No grants to individuals.
Application information: Contributes only to pre-selected organizations. Applications not accepted.
Officers and Directors:* Winifred M. Warden,* Pres.; Joseph J. Regan,* V.P.; Bert M. Warden,* V.P.; James W. Fisher,* Secy.-Treas.; Winston C. Moore, J. Terrance Murray.
Employer Identification Number: 366060591

2011
Mason Charitable Foundation ⌑
One First National Plaza, Suite 5000
Chicago 60603

Established in 1980 in IL.
Donor(s): Marian Tyler.
Foundation type: Independent
Financial data (yr. ended 1/31/88): Assets, $1,891,088 (M); expenditures, $140,295, including $102,250 for 4 grants (high: $50,000; low: $10,000).
Purpose and activities: Grants primarily for public television and social services; some support for an aquarium.
Application information: Contributes only to pre-selected organizations. Applications not accepted.
Trustees: Katheryn Cowles Douglass, Kingman Scott Douglass, Louise J. Douglass, Robert Dun Douglass, Timothy P. Douglass.
Employer Identification Number: 363101263

2012
Material Service Foundation
222 North LaSalle St.
Chicago 60601

Established about 1952 in IL; incorporated in 1960 in IL.
Donor(s): Material Service Corp., and various subsidiaries of General Dynamics Corp.

Foundation type: Company-sponsored
Financial data (yr. ended 12/31/89): Assets, $322,844 (M); gifts received, $354,000; expenditures, $283,274, including $283,100 for 139 grants (high: $100,000; low: $25; average: $1,000-$2,000).
Purpose and activities: Giving primarily for community funds; grants also for community development, youth agencies, education, health agencies, and cultural activities.
Types of support: Annual campaigns, building funds, capital campaigns, continuing support, operating budgets, seed money, special projects.
Limitations: Giving primarily in IL, with emphasis on Chicago. No grants to individuals.
Publications: Grants list, financial statement.
Application information: Application form not required.
Initial approach: Letter
Copies of proposal: 1
Deadline(s): None
Board meeting date(s): As required
Final notification: Within one month
Write: Louis J. Levy, Admin.
Officer: Lester Crown, Mgr.
Number of staff: None.
Employer Identification Number: 366062106

2013
Oscar G. and Elsa S. Mayer Charitable Trust ⌑
c/o Hugo J. Melvoin
115 South LaSalle St., Rm. 2500
Chicago 60603 (312) 332-3682
Additional application address: c/o Imojean E. Onsrud, One South Pinckney St., Suite 312, Madison, WI 53703; Tel.: (608) 256-3682

Trust established in 1965 in IL.
Donor(s): Oscar G. Mayer, Sr.,† Elsa S. Mayer.†
Foundation type: Independent
Financial data (yr. ended 12/31/88): Assets, $9,201,683 (M); expenditures, $679,319, including $560,000 for 38 grants (high: $50,000; low: $5,000; average: $5,000-$25,000).
Purpose and activities: Grants limited to charitable institutions in which the donors did or their descendants do actively participate, including higher education, hospitals, music, and museums.
Types of support: General purposes.
Limitations: Giving primarily in the Chicago, IL, metropolitan area and in WI. No grants to individuals.
Application information: Application form not required.
Initial approach: Letter
Copies of proposal: 1
Deadline(s): None
Board meeting date(s): As required
Final notification: 2 weeks
Write: Oscar G. Mayer, Managing Trustee
Trustees: Oscar G. Mayer, Managing Trustee; Allan C. Mayer, Harold F. Mayer, Harold M. Mayer.
Number of staff: 1 part-time professional; 1 part-time support.
Employer Identification Number: 366134354

2014
Robert and Beatrice Mayer Foundation ☆
175 East Delaware Place, Apt. 7403
Chicago 60611-1731

Established in 1952.
Donor(s): Robert N. Mayer, Beatrice C. Mayer.
Foundation type: Independent
Financial data (yr. ended 12/31/88): Assets, $1,023,679 (M); expenditures, $62,400, including $50,000 for 1 grant.
Purpose and activities: Giving primarily for an art institute; support also for higher education and museums.
Limitations: Giving primarily in Chicago, IL. No grants to individuals.
Application information: Contributes only to pre-selected organizations. Applications not accepted.
Officers: Beatrice C. Mayer, Pres. and Treas.; Robert N. Mayer, V.P.; Ruth Mayer Durchslag, Secy.
Employer Identification Number: 366051068

2015
Mazza Foundation
225 West Washington St., Suite 1300
Chicago 60606-3405 (312) 444-9300

Incorporated in 1957 in IL.
Donor(s): Leonard M. Lavezzorio,† Louise T. Mazza Trust.
Foundation type: Independent
Financial data (yr. ended 11/30/88): Assets, $37,922,994 (M); gifts received, $925,978; expenditures, $1,049,745, including $967,500 for 40 grants (high: $100,000; low: $500).
Purpose and activities: Giving primarily for churches, religious organizations, social service agencies, and hospitals; support also for education.
Limitations: Giving primarily in Chicago, IL.
Application information: Application form not required.
Deadline(s): None
Write: Joseph O. Rubinelli, Secy.-Treas.
Officers and Directors:* Tina Lavezzorio,* Pres.; Joseph O. Rubinelli,* Secy.-Treas.; Joan F. Lavezzorio, Mary Jane Rubinelli.
Employer Identification Number: 366054751

2016
Robert R. McCormick Charitable Trust
435 North Michigan Ave., Suite 770
Chicago 60611 (312) 222-3510

Trust established in 1955 in IL.
Donor(s): Robert R. McCormick.†
Foundation type: Independent
Financial data (yr. ended 12/31/89): Assets, $630,994,902 (M); expenditures, $21,257,081, including $19,904,476 for 427 grants (high: $4,425,000; low: $500; average: $2,500-$100,000) and $154,000 for 2 loans.
Purpose and activities: Largest contributions for private higher education, health services, including AIDS research and rehabilitation for the physically and mentally handicapped, the performing arts and cultural programs, and human services, including family and legal services, the elderly, the homeless, women, and youth.
Types of support: Building funds, equipment, renovation projects, capital campaigns, operating budgets, technical assistance, land acquisition, matching funds, program-related investments, special projects.
Limitations: Giving primarily in the Chicago, IL, metropolitan area. No grants to individuals, or for endowment funds, research, scholarships, fellowships, or single events; no loans.
Publications: Annual report (including application guidelines), application guidelines.
Application information: Application form not required.
Initial approach: Letter
Copies of proposal: 1
Deadline(s): Feb. 1, May 1, Aug. 1, and Nov. 1
Board meeting date(s): Mar., June, Sept., and Dec.
Final notification: Within 2 weeks
Write: Claude A. Smith, Dir. of Philanthropy
Officers and Trustees:* Stanton R. Cook,* Chair.; Neal Creighton,* Pres. and C.E.O.; Claude A. Smith,* Dir. of Philanthropy; Charles T. Brumback, Jack Fuller, Robert M. Hunt, John W. Madigan.
Number of staff: 5 full-time professional; 2 full-time support.
Employer Identification Number: 366046974

2017
Brooks & Hope B. McCormick Foundation ⌑
410 North Michigan Ave., Rm. 590
Chicago 60611

Established in 1967 in IL.
Donor(s): Brooks McCormick, Hope B. McCormick.
Foundation type: Independent
Financial data (yr. ended 12/31/88): Assets, $547,661 (M); gifts received, $179,000; expenditures, $301,536, including $297,000 for 38 grants (high: $100,000; low: $1,000).
Purpose and activities: Giving for civic, cultural, educational, and health programs; support also for religion and social services.
Types of support: General purposes.
Limitations: No grants to individuals.
Application information: Grants made at the discretion of the board. Applications not accepted.
Write: Brooks McCormick, Chair.
Officers and Directors:* Brooks McCormick,* Chair.; Hope B. McCormick,* Pres.; Charles E. Schroder,* V.P. and Secy.; Martha McCormick Hunt,* V.P. and Treas.; Hilary Hunt.
Employer Identification Number: 366156922

2018
Chauncey and Marion Deering McCormick Foundation ⌑
410 North Michigan Ave., Rm. 590
Chicago 60611 (312) 644-6720

Incorporated in 1957 in IL.
Donor(s): Brooks McCormick, Brooks McCormick Trust, Charles Deering McCormick Trust, Roger McCormick Trust.
Foundation type: Independent
Financial data (yr. ended 7/31/88): Assets, $13,871,559 (M); expenditures, $704,526,

including $492,700 for 20 grants (high: $240,000; low: $1,000).
Purpose and activities: Emphasis on higher and secondary education, hospitals, and cultural institutions, including an art museum; support also for conservation and child welfare.
Types of support: General purposes.
Limitations: Giving primarily in Chicago, IL. No grants to individuals.
Application information: Application form not required.
Officers and Directors: Charles Deering McCormick, Pres.; Brooks McCormick, V.P.; Charles E. Schroeder, Secy.-Treas.; Charlotte McCormick Collins.
Employer Identification Number: 366054815

2019
Roger McCormick Foundation ⌑
410 North Michigan Ave., Rm. 590
Chicago 60611

Established in 1967 in IL.
Foundation type: Independent
Financial data (yr. ended 12/31/87): Assets, $991,721 (M); gifts received, $65,000; expenditures, $130,537, including $125,163 for 18 grants (high: $50,163; low: $2,000).
Purpose and activities: Giving primarily for hospitals, medical research, and museums.
Application information: Contributes only to pre-selected organizations. Applications not accepted.
Officers and Directors: Charlotte McCormick Collins, Pres.; Charles E. Schroeder, Secy.-Treas.; Amy Blair Collins.
Employer Identification Number: 366158862

2020
McFarland Charitable Foundation ⌑
c/o The Havana National Bank
112 South Orange St.
Havana 62644 (309) 543-3361
Scholarship application address: c/o Kathy Tarvin, Dir. of Nursing Service, Mason District Hospital, 520 East Franklin St., Havana, IL 62644; Tel.: (309) 543-4431

Established in 1960 in IL.
Foundation type: Independent
Financial data (yr. ended 12/31/88): Assets, $1,586,676 (M); expenditures, $169,552, including $97,170 for 2 grants (high: $67,570; low: $29,600) and $51,296 for 13 grants to individuals (high: $11,737; low: $391; average: $1,000-$5,000).
Purpose and activities: Scholarships to student nurses for tuition and expenses; recipients must return to Havana, IL, to work a number of years after graduation; support also for the McFarland Medical Trust.
Types of support: Student aid.
Limitations: Giving primarily in Mason County, IL.
Application information: Application is mailed to applicant by Director of Nursing Services. Application form required.
Deadline(s): May 1
Board meeting date(s): June
Write: Linda M. Butler, V.P. and Trust Officer, The Havana National Bank
Trustee: The Havana National Bank.
Number of staff: None.
Employer Identification Number: 376022376

2021
The Foster G. McGaw Educational Foundation ⌑
8300 Sears Tower
233 South Wacker Dr.
Chicago 60606

Donor(s): Foster C. McGraw Living Trust.
Foundation type: Independent
Financial data (yr. ended 12/31/88): Assets, $1,238,883 (M); expenditures, $30,743, including $14,167 for 15 grants to individuals (high: $1,000; low: $500).
Purpose and activities: The goal of the foundation's program is: "Education properly conceived stimulates a kind of ethical questioning that leads to moral integrity."
Types of support: Student aid.
Limitations: Giving limited to the children of employees or retirees of the American Hospital Corp.
Application information: Application form required.
Deadline(s): Feb. 1
Final notification: Mar. 15
Officers and Directors:* James David Vail III,* Pres.; Michael K. Cavanaugh,* Secy.; Hugh A. Solvsberg,* Treas.
Employer Identification Number: 363131160

2022
McGraw Foundation ▼
3436 North Kennicott Dr.
Arlington Heights 60004 (708) 870-8014
Mailing address: P.O. Box 307 B, Wheeling, IL 60090

Incorporated in 1948 in IL.
Donor(s): Alfred Bersted,† Carol Jean Root,† Maxine Elrod,† Donald S. Elrod, Max McGraw,† Richard F. McGraw,† McGraw-Edison Co., and others.
Foundation type: Independent
Financial data (yr. ended 12/31/88): Assets, $14,003,875 (M); expenditures, $1,317,396, including $1,257,180 for 104 grants (high: $40,000; low: $1,000; average: $5,000-$25,000).
Purpose and activities: Giving primarily for higher education, health, civic affairs, social services, science, culture, and the environment.
Types of support: Operating budgets, annual campaigns, building funds, equipment, research, matching funds, seed money, continuing support.
Limitations: Giving primarily in the Chicago, IL, area, and in adjoining states. No grants to individuals.
Publications: Program policy statement, application guidelines.
Application information: Application form not required.
Initial approach: Letter
Copies of proposal: 1
Deadline(s): Submit proposal between Dec. 1 and Feb. 1
Board meeting date(s): June; grant committee meets annually in Mar.
Final notification: 30 days to 1 year
Write: James F. Quilter, V.P.
Officers and Directors:* Raymond H. Giesecke,* Pres.; James F. Quilter,* V.P., Secy.-Treas., and Exec. Dir.; William W. Mauritz,* V.P.; J. Bradley Davis, Scott M. Elrod, Dennis W. Fitzgerald, Jerry D. Jones, Catherine B. Nelson, Bernard B. Rinella, Leah K. Robson.
Number of staff: 1 full-time professional; 1 part-time support.
Employer Identification Number: 362490000

2023
MCH Foundation ⌑
1515 Forest Ave.
River Forest 60305

Established in 1980 in IL.
Foundation type: Independent
Financial data (yr. ended 6/30/88): Assets, $64,454 (M); gifts received, $174,000; expenditures, $142,035, including $135,935 for 324 grants (high: $15,000; low: $20).
Purpose and activities: Support primarily for Jewish organizations, youth and child welfare, education, and health.
Application information: Contributes only to pre-selected organizations. Applications not accepted.
Officers: Harriet Hausman, Pres.; Martin Hausman, V.P.; Barbara Appel, Secy.-Treas.
Employer Identification Number: 363036256

2024
McIntosh Foundation, Inc. ⌑
c/o Salomon Brothers, Inc.
8700 Sears Tower
Chicago 60606

Established in 1985 in IL.
Donor(s): William A. McIntosh.
Foundation type: Independent
Financial data (yr. ended 4/30/88): Assets, $4,726,121 (M); gifts received, $2,000,000; expenditures, $608,035, including $599,398 for 76 grants (high: $150,000; low: $100).
Purpose and activities: Support primarily for programs of the Archdiocese of Chicago and other Catholic parishes, schools, and charities.
Limitations: No grants to individuals.
Application information: Contributes only to pre-selected organizations. Applications not accepted.
Officers and Directors: William A. McIntosh, Pres. and Treas.; Diane H. McIntosh, V.P. and Secy.; Thomas B. McIntosh.
Employer Identification Number: 363358483

2025
Edward Arthur Mellinger Educational Foundation, Inc. ⌑
1025 East Broadway
P.O. Box 278
Monmouth 61462 (309) 734-2419

Incorporated in 1959 in DE.
Donor(s): Mrs. Inez M. Hensleigh.†
Foundation type: Independent
Financial data (yr. ended 12/31/88): Assets, $12,325,307 (M); expenditures, $970,720, including $429,912 for 968 grants to individuals (high: $900; low: $55) and $285,178 for 198 loans to individuals.
Purpose and activities: Scholarships for undergraduate college students and loans primarily to graduate students.
Types of support: Student aid, student loans.
Limitations: Giving limited to students residing or attending college in the Midwest.

Publications: Application guidelines, program policy statement.
Application information: Application form required.
Initial approach: Letter
Deadline(s): June 1 for new applicants, July 1 for renewals
Board meeting date(s): Scholarship committee meets in July
Final notification: 1 month after meeting
Officers and Trustees:* David D. Fleming,* Pres.; Arthur W. Murray II,* V.P.; Merle R. Yontz,* V.P.; Tom Johnson,* Secy.-Treas.; Lloyd C. Stevenson.
Number of staff: 1 full-time professional; 1 part-time professional; 2 full-time support; 2 part-time support.
Employer Identification Number: 362428421

2026
Henry and Louise Mermelstein Charitable Foundation ⌑ ☆
7141 North Kedzie Ave.
Chicago 60645-2847

Established in 1986 in IL.
Donor(s): members of the Mermelstein family.
Foundation type: Independent
Financial data (yr. ended 6/30/88): Assets, $1,234,568 (M); gifts received, $466,631; expenditures, $125,552, including $124,193 for 174 grants (high: $5,480; low: $10).
Purpose and activities: Support for Jewish organizations, including yeshivas and congregations.
Application information: Contributes only to pre-selected organizations. Applications not accepted.
Officer and Directors: Henry Mermelstein, Pres.; Joseph Mermelstein, Louise Mermelstein, Marvin Mermelstein.
Employer Identification Number: 363481731

2027
Merrion Foundation ⌑
10321 South Maplewood
Chicago 60655

Established in 1981 in IL.
Foundation type: Independent
Financial data (yr. ended 12/31/87): Assets, $2,156,288 (M); expenditures, $170,186, including $128,331 for 23 grants (high: $20,000; low: $50).
Purpose and activities: Giving primarily for Catholic organizations, education, and social services.
Application information: Contributes only to pre-selected organizations. Applications not accepted.
Directors: Mary Ann Kennedy, Edwin T. Merrion, John K. Merrion, Mary Ann Merrion, Michael P. Merrion.
Employer Identification Number: 310977268

2028
Mesirow Charitable Foundation ⌑
135 South LaSalle St.
Chicago 60603 (312) 443-5700

Established in 1958 in IL.
Donor(s): Members of the Mesirow family.
Foundation type: Independent
Financial data (yr. ended 12/31/87): Assets, $45,087 (M); gifts received, $94,100; expenditures, $127,975, including $126,665 for 59 grants (high: $106,000; low: $15).
Purpose and activities: Giving primarily to Jewish organizations.
Application information:
Deadline(s): None
Write: Norman Mesirow, Mgr.
Officer: Norman Mesirow, Mgr.
Employer Identification Number: 366060923

2029
The Meyer-Ceco Foundation
c/o The Ceco Corp.
One Tower Ln., Suite 2300
Oak Brook Terrace 60181 (312) 242-2000

Trust established in 1946 in NE.
Donor(s): M.L. Meyer Trust.
Foundation type: Company-sponsored
Financial data (yr. ended 12/31/89): Assets, $4,611,589 (M); expenditures, $243,896, including $225,270 for 123 grants (high: $20,000; low: $25; average: $500-$1,500) and $6,805 for 32 employee matching gifts.
Purpose and activities: Support for higher education, community funds, hospitals, youth agencies, religion, and civic affairs.
Types of support: Continuing support, program-related investments.
Limitations: Giving primarily in the Midwest and Southeast.
Publications: 990-PF.
Application information: Application form not required.
Initial approach: Letter
Copies of proposal: 1
Deadline(s): None
Board meeting date(s): Varies
Write: R.J. Stankus, Asst. Treas., Taxes
Trustees: Alice Meyer Brown, Heidi Hall Jones, Ned A. Ochiltree, Jr.
Number of staff: None.
Employer Identification Number: 366053404

2030
Milbro Charitable Foundation ⌑
100 South Schelter Rd.
Lincolnshire 60069 (312) 634-5713

Established in 1985 in IL.
Donor(s): Harvey L. Miller, Jack Miller, Quill Corp.
Foundation type: Independent
Financial data (yr. ended 12/31/88): Assets, $804,122 (M); gifts received, $336,000; expenditures, $237,449, including $236,986 for 70 grants (high: $50,075; low: $60).
Purpose and activities: Giving primarily for Jewish organizations, especially Jewish welfare funds, and health agencies; some support for social services.
Limitations: Giving primarily in IL.
Application information: Application form not required.
Initial approach: Letter or proposal
Deadline(s): None
Write: Arnold Miller, Treas.
Officers and Directors:* Jack Miller,* Pres.; Arnold Miller,* V.P. and Treas.; Harvey L. Miller,* Secy.
Employer Identification Number: 363390647

2031
Adah K. Millard Charitable Trust
c/o The Northern Trust Co.
50 South LaSalle St.
Chicago 60675 (312) 630-6000

Trust established in 1976 in IL.
Donor(s): Adah K. Millard.†
Foundation type: Independent
Financial data (yr. ended 12/31/89): Assets, $4,824,730 (M); expenditures, $224,121, including $218,127 for 18 grants (high: $54,500; low: $1,000; average: $20,000).
Purpose and activities: Emphasis on local area youth agencies, social welfare groups, and cultural programs.
Types of support: General purposes, continuing support, seed money, building funds, equipment, renovation projects, special projects.
Limitations: Giving limited to Omaha and Douglas counties, NE. No grants to individuals, or for endowment funds, scholarships, or fellowships; generally no grants for operating budgets; no loans.
Publications: Application guidelines.
Application information: Request application form. Application form required.
Copies of proposal: 6
Deadline(s): Apr. 1 and Oct. 1
Board meeting date(s): Apr. and Nov.
Write: John C. Goodall, Jr., V.P.
Trustee: The Northern Trust Co.
Number of staff: None.
Employer Identification Number: 366629069

2032
William Miller Charitable Trust ⌑ ☆
c/o Amcore Bank, N.A.
P.O. Box 1537
Rockford 61110

Foundation type: Independent
Financial data (yr. ended 12/31/88): Assets, $1,094,687 (M); expenditures, $55,786, including $45,300 for 20 grants (high: $8,000; low: $300).
Purpose and activities: Giving primarily for youth development; support also for health care, social services, the arts, education, and a church.
Limitations: Giving primarily in Rockford, IL, area. No grants to individuals.
Application information:
Initial approach: Proposal
Write: Glen W. Wilson
Trustee: Amcore Bank, N.A.
Employer Identification Number: 366581788

2033
James Millikin Trust ⌑
P.O. Box 1278
Decatur 62525 (217) 429-4253
Application address: c/o Milliken National Bank Trust Dept., Decatur, IL 62525

Trust established in 1910 in IL.
Donor(s): James Millikin.†
Foundation type: Independent
Financial data (yr. ended 12/31/87): Assets, $11,456,328 (M); expenditures, $680,264.
Purpose and activities: Grants to a university and a hospital; grants also for a community fund and youth organizations.

Types of support: Operating budgets.
Limitations: Giving primarily in Decatur, IL.
Application information: Application form not required.
Initial approach: Proposal
Deadline(s): None
Board meeting date(s): 3rd Wednesday of each month
Officer: R. Wayne Gill, Secy.
Trustees: Wayne S. Martin, Chair.; G. William Harner, Jack Hunter, James W. Moore, Bernard Wright.
Number of staff: None.
Employer Identification Number: 370661226

2034
Miner-Weisz Charitable Foundation ¤
c/o The Northern Trust Co.
50 South LaSalle St.
Chicago 60675 (312) 630-6000

Established in 1966 in IL.
Foundation type: Independent
Financial data (yr. ended 12/31/87): Assets, $789,956 (M); expenditures, $171,665, including $157,500 for 16 grants (high: $45,000; low: $500).
Purpose and activities: Support primarily for an art institute and for educational foundations; support also for a symphony orchestra, an opera company, and a hospital.
Limitations: Giving primarily in IL.
Application information: Application form not required.
Deadline(s): None
Write: Winifred Date
Trustees: Max E. Meyer, The Northern Trust Co.
Employer Identification Number: 366149589

2035
Bernard & Marjorie Mitchell Family Foundation ¤
c/o Victoria Kohn Trustee
875 North Michigan Ave., Suite 3412
Chicago 60611

Donor(s): Bernard A. Mitchell Trust.
Foundation type: Independent
Financial data (yr. ended 10/31/88): Assets, $2,667,681 (M); gifts received, $10,000; expenditures, $28,111, including $24,950 for 3 grants (high: $20,000; low: $1,250).
Purpose and activities: Support primarily for Jewish welfare; support also for the arts and an art museum, and medical research.
Limitations: Giving primarily in Chicago, IL.
Application information: Contributes only to pre-selected organizations. Applications not accepted.
Trustees: Victoria C. Kohn, Lee H. Mitchell, Marjorie I. Mitchell.
Employer Identification Number: 237007014

2036
Molner Foundation ¤
c/o Morton John Barnard
200 East Randolph Dr., Suite 6900
Chicago 60601-6908

Established in 1980 in IL.
Foundation type: Independent
Financial data (yr. ended 12/31/88): Assets, $1,047,651 (M); expenditures, $98,683, including $79,150 for 52 grants (high: $20,000; low: $100).
Purpose and activities: Support primarily for social services and cultural programs.
Limitations: Giving primarily in IL. No grants to individuals.
Application information: Contributes only to pre-selected organizations. Applications not accepted.
Trustee: Foss, Schuman, Drake & Barnard.
Employer Identification Number: 366702256

2037
Monte and Maxine Monaster Foundation ¤
141 West Jackson Blvd., Suite 1531-A
Chicago 60604
Application address: 125 South LaSalle St., Chicago, IL 60603

Established in 1980 in IL.
Donor(s): Monte Monaster, Maxine Monaster.
Foundation type: Independent
Financial data (yr. ended 12/31/86): Assets, $1,460,842 (M); gifts received, $1,000,000; expenditures, $1,047,179, including $1,045,000 for 9 grants (high: $350,000; low: $25,000).
Purpose and activities: Grants primarily for higher education; some support also for health.
Application information:
Initial approach: Letter
Deadline(s): None
Write: Louis Bernat, Secy.
Officers: Monte Monaster, Pres.; Louis Bernat, Secy.
Employer Identification Number: 363134578

2038
Montgomery Ward Foundation ¤
Montgomery Ward Plaza, 8A
Chicago 60671 (312) 467-7663

Established in 1968 in IL.
Donor(s): Montgomery Ward & Co., Inc.
Foundation type: Company-sponsored
Financial data (yr. ended 12/31/88): Assets, $47,394 (M); gifts received, $850,000; expenditures, $827,545, including $445,305 for 14 grants (high: $377,965; low: $90) and $381,823 for employee matching gifts.
Purpose and activities: Giving currently limited to United Way, arts and cultural programs, and civic and welfare programs in the immediate corporate headquarters' neighborhood; support also for employee matching gifts to higher education, cultural institutions, and public television and radio.
Types of support: Employee matching gifts, emergency funds, continuing support, general purposes.
Limitations: Giving limited to Chicago, IL. No support for hospitals or health-related programs, religious or political organizations, educational funds, organizations with discriminatory policies, or municipal, state, or federal agencies. No grants to individuals, or for building or endowment funds, fund-raising events through sponsorship or merchandise donations, advertising in program booklets, multi-year pledges, or capital campaigns.
Publications: Program policy statement.
Application information: Application form not required.
Initial approach: Letter or telephone
Copies of proposal: 1
Deadline(s): Submit proposal preferably between Jan. and May; deadline Sept.
Board meeting date(s): Mar., June, Sept., and Dec.
Final notification: Up to 7 months
Write: Charles A. Holland, Jr., Secy.
Officers and Directors:* R. Kasenter,* Pres.; Bernard Andrews,* V.P.; Jack Daynard,* V.P.; Spencer Heine,* V.P.; Charles A. Holland, Jr., Secy.
Number of staff: 1 full-time professional.
Employer Identification Number: 362670108

2039
The Monticello College Foundation
The Evergreens
Godfrey 62035 (618) 466-7911

Incorporated in 1843 in IL as Monticello College; reorganized as a foundation in 1971.
Foundation type: Independent
Financial data (yr. ended 06/30/89): Assets, $5,621,540 (M); expenditures, $314,399, including $269,500 for 15 grants (high: $135,000; low: $1,000).
Purpose and activities: Support for programs that assist advancing education for women.
Types of support: Scholarship funds, special projects, fellowships, internships.
Limitations: No support for social service agencies, foreign schools, or foreign-based American schools. No grants to individuals, or for capital funds, operating expenses, endowed chairs, conferences and seminars, or exchange students.
Publications: Annual report (including application guidelines).
Application information: Application form not required.
Initial approach: Proposal
Copies of proposal: 15
Deadline(s): Submit proposal preferably in July or Feb.; deadline 8 weeks before board meeting
Board meeting date(s): Third week of Sept. and Apr.
Final notification: 2 weeks after board meeting
Write: Winifred G. Delano, Exec. Dir.
Officers: Mrs. William J. Barnard,* Chair.; Mrs. Vaughan Morrill,* Secy.; Karl K. Hoagland, Jr.,* Treas.; Winifred G. Delano, Exec. Dir.
Trustees:* Mrs. Glenn L. Allen, Jr., Robert R. Anschuetz, M.D., Mrs. Robert R. Anschuetz, Mrs. Stephen L. Biermann, Mrs. Paul Jones, Mrs. Leland F. Kreid, Nancy C. McCaig, M.D., M. Ryrie Milnor, Alice M. Norton, Mrs. John C. Pritzlaff, Jr., Harry N. Schweppe, Jr., Henry N. Schweppe III.
Number of staff: 1 part-time professional.
Employer Identification Number: 370681538

2040
Moorman Company Fund
1000 North 30th St.
Quincy 62305-3115 (217) 222-7100

Incorporated in 1952 in IL.
Donor(s): Moorman Manufacturing Co.
Foundation type: Company-sponsored
Financial data (yr. ended 12/31/88): Assets, $1,233,122 (M); gifts received, $500,000; expenditures, $435,588, including $381,623 for 118 grants (high: $73,527; low: $100).
Purpose and activities: Emphasis on land-grant universities for agricultural scholarships, and educational associations in the company's market areas; and for local colleges, community funds, youth agencies, health associations, hospitals, and welfare organizations in Adams County, IL.
Types of support: Scholarship funds, operating budgets, general purposes, building funds, equipment.
Limitations: Giving limited to areas of company operations, with emphasis on Adams County, IL. No grants to individuals.
Application information: Application form not required.
Initial approach: Letter
Copies of proposal: 1
Deadline(s): None
Board meeting date(s): 3rd Wednesday of each month
Write: C.F. Bearden, Secy.
Officers: H.C. Eaton,* Pres.; H.D. Hutchinson,* V.P.; C.F. Bearden, Secy.; R.K. McClelland,* Treas.
Directors:* S. Kent Adams, M.J. Foster, Richard L. Jackson, Richard A. Liebig, Thomas L. Shade, R.H. Upper, H.L. Williams.
Number of staff: None.
Employer Identification Number: 376026253

2041
Morton International Foundation
(Formerly Morton Thiokol Foundation)
110 North Wacker Dr.
Chicago 60606

Established in 1984 in IL.
Donor(s): Morton International, Inc.
Foundation type: Company-sponsored
Financial data (yr. ended 6/30/89): Assets, $325,000 (M); gifts received, $200,000; expenditures, $390,614, including $390,614 for 96 grants (high: $121,777; low: $500).
Purpose and activities: Support primarily for health and social services, education, civic affairs, and cultural programs.
Limitations: Giving primarily in areas of company operations.
Publications: Application guidelines.
Application information: Application form not required.
Initial approach: Letter
Copies of proposal: 1
Deadline(s): None
Officers and Directors:* Charles S. Locke,* Pres.; S. Jay Stewart, V.P.; P. Michael Phelps, Secy.
Employer Identification Number: 363282328

2042
Mark Morton Memorial Fund ¤
110 North Wacker Dr.
Chicago 60606

Established in 1951 in IL.
Foundation type: Independent
Financial data (yr. ended 12/31/88): Assets, $10,151,557 (M); expenditures, $619,643, including $484,628 for 229 grants to individuals (high: $17,942; average: $1,820).
Purpose and activities: Grants limited to individuals who are verifable employees of the Morton Salt Co. on or before June 30, 1971, to assist with hospital, medical, and surgical expenses, as well as assistance to the aged, blind, or disabled.
Types of support: Grants to individuals.
Officers and Directors:* Scott Ellwood,* Pres.; Shirley Moolenaar, Secy.; Mildred Cahill, Treas.; F.P.G. Lattner, Davis Roenisch, C.S. Soderstrom, Leonard Zak.
Number of staff: 2
Employer Identification Number: 237181380

2043
Motorola Foundation ▼ ¤
1303 East Algonquin Rd.
Schaumburg 60196 (312) 576-6200

Incorporated in 1953 in IL.
Donor(s): Motorola, Inc.
Foundation type: Company-sponsored
Financial data (yr. ended 12/31/88): Assets, $3,995,519 (M); gifts received, $2,500,000; expenditures, $2,430,053, including $2,099,414 for 327 grants (high: $267,180; low: $200; average: $1,000-$5,000) and $326,152 for 591 employee matching gifts.
Purpose and activities: Giving for higher and other education, including an employee matching gift program, united funds, and hospitals; support also for cultural programs, social services, and youth agencies.
Types of support: Operating budgets, seed money, building funds, scholarship funds, employee matching gifts, fellowships, general purposes, continuing support.
Limitations: Giving primarily in communities where the company has major facilities, with emphasis on Huntsville, AL; Mt. Pleasant, IA; Chicago, IL; Phoenix, AZ; Austin, Fort Worth, and Sequin, TX; and Fort Lauderdale and Boynton Beach, FL. No support for strictly sectarian or denominational religious organizations; national health organizations or their local chapters; or secondary schools, trade schools, or state institutions (except through the employee matching gift program). No grants to individuals, or for university endowment funds, research, courtesy advertising, operating expenses of organizations receiving United Way funding, benefits or capital fund drives of colleges or universities; no loans.
Publications: Application guidelines.
Application information: Application form not required.
Initial approach: Letter, telephone, or proposal
Copies of proposal: 1
Deadline(s): Nov.
Board meeting date(s): Monthly and as required
Final notification: 1 to 2 months
Write: Mrs. Herta Betty Nikolai, Admin.
Officers: Robert W. Galvin,* Pres.; David W.L. Hickie,* V.P. and Exec. Dir.; Donald R. Jones,* V.P.; Victor R. Kopidlansky, Secy.; Garth L. Milne, Treas.
Directors:* William J. Weisz.
Number of staff: 1 full-time professional; 1 full-time support.
Employer Identification Number: 366109323

2044
Mueller Company Foundation ¤
500 West Eldorado St.
Decatur 62525 (217) 423-4471

Established in 1982 in IL.
Donor(s): Mueller Co.
Foundation type: Company-sponsored
Financial data (yr. ended 11/30/86): Assets, $680,010 (M); gifts received, $150,000; expenditures, $212,357, including $211,151 for 98 grants (high: $56,500; low: $25).
Purpose and activities: Grants primarily for secondary and higher education.
Application information:
Deadline(s): None
Write: F.C. Ausnehmer, Pres.
Officers: Fred C. Ausnehmer, Pres.; Allen M. Yurko, V.P.; Robert W. Mallow, Secy.; Lawrence C. Maston, Treas.
Trustee: Citizens National Bank of Decatur.
Employer Identification Number: 371149032

2045
Curtis & Edith Munson Foundation ¤
321 North Clark St.
Chicago 60610 (312) 527-5545

Incorporated in 1982 in FL.
Foundation type: Independent
Financial data (yr. ended 12/31/88): Assets, $20,652,175 (M); expenditures, $1,032,031, including $922,000 for 42 grants (high: $60,000; low: $5,000; average: $20,000-$40,000).
Purpose and activities: Support for conservation of wildlife and natural resources in North America, and U.S. population and immigration issues.
Types of support: Operating budgets, seed money, matching funds, special projects.
Limitations: Giving primarily in FL, IL, and AL. No grants to individuals, or for endowment funds; no loans.
Publications: Annual report, application guidelines.
Application information:
Initial approach: Letter or proposal
Deadline(s): 2 weeks prior to board meeting
Board meeting date(s): 2 to 4 times a year and as required
Final notification: 2 weeks following meeting
Write: C. Wolcott Henry III, Pres.
Officers: C. Wolcott Henry III,* Pres.; Dexter C. Hobbs,* Secy.; Michael C. Rausch, Treas.
Directors:* Truman M. Hobbs.
Employer Identification Number: 592235907

2046
The Nalco Foundation ▼
One Nalco Ctr.
Naperville 60563-1198 (708) 305-1556

Incorporated in 1953 in IL.
Donor(s): Nalco Chemical Co.
Foundation type: Company-sponsored
Financial data (yr. ended 12/31/89): Assets, $2,429,696 (M); gifts received, $1,000,000; expenditures, $1,598,350, including $1,384,090 for 210 grants (high: $75,000; low: $500; average: $2,000-$10,000) and $214,260 for 636 employee matching gifts.
Purpose and activities: Grants largely for private institutions of higher education, educational associations, hospitals, social service and youth agencies, and cultural activities.
Types of support: Operating budgets, continuing support, annual campaigns, seed money, building funds, equipment, land acquisition, capital campaigns, renovation projects, general purposes.
Limitations: Giving primarily in areas where company has manufacturing operations: the metropolitan Chicago area and DuPage County, IL; Carson, CA; Garryville, LA; Jonesboro, GA; Cleveland, OH; Jackson, MI; Paulsboro, NJ; and Sugar Land, TX. No support for state-supported colleges or universities, secondary or elementary schools, churches, or religious education. No grants to individuals, or for endowments, research, scholarships, fellowships, purchase of tickets for fundraising banquets, or matching gifts; no loans.
Publications: Corporate giving report (including application guidelines), application guidelines.
Application information: Application form not required.
Initial approach: Request guidelines
Copies of proposal: 1
Deadline(s): Submit proposal preferably in Jan., Apr., July, or Sept.; deadline Oct. 1
Board meeting date(s): Mar., June, Sept., and Nov.
Final notification: 3 to 6 months
Write: Joanne C. Ford, Pres.
Officers: Joanne C. Ford,* Pres.; Clifford J. Carpenter, V.P. and Treas.; Theresa A. Slaboszewski, Secy.
Directors:* David R. Bertran, James F. Lambe.
Number of staff: 1 full-time professional; 1 full-time support.
Employer Identification Number: 366065864

2047
Navistar Foundation ⌑
401 North Michigan Ave.
Chicago 60611 (312) 836-3034

Incorporated in 1944 in IL.
Donor(s): Navistar International Corp.
Foundation type: Company-sponsored
Financial data (yr. ended 10/31/88): Assets, $292,651 (M); gifts received, $385,000; expenditures, $230,258, including $228,270 for 17 grants (high: $99,850; low: $300).
Purpose and activities: Grants primarily for health care cost containment, community funds, education, and civic and community affairs.
Limitations: Giving primarily in Chicago, IL; Springfield, OH; Fort Wayne and Indianapolis, IN; and Waukesha, WI. No support for strictly sectarian or denominational religious organizations. No grants to individuals, or for scholarships, fellowships, or matching gifts; the foundation does not contribute Navistar International Transportation Corp. equipment or provide funds for special occasions; support for hospitals generally restricted to building programs or equipment additions; no loans.
Application information:
Initial approach: Letter
Copies of proposal: 1
Deadline(s): None
Board meeting date(s): As required
Write: Patricia A. Hays, Exec. Dir.
Officers: Brian B. Whalen,* Pres.; Mary L. Dolan,* V.P.; Patricia A. Hays, Exec. Dir. and Secy.; Robert C. Lannert, Treas.
Directors:* James C. Cotting, Roxanne J. Decyk, Neil A. Springer.
Employer Identification Number: 366058875

2048
The Neese Family Foundation, Inc. ☆
11722 Main St.
Roscoe 61073

Incorporated in 1986 in IL.
Donor(s): Members of the Neese family.
Foundation type: Independent
Financial data (yr. ended 06/30/89): Assets, $2,002,877 (M); gifts received, $79,027; expenditures, $237,681, including $235,800 for 5 grants (high: $100,000; low: $1,000).
Purpose and activities: Giving primarily for a hospital, a college, a historical society, and a community fund.
Types of support: Capital campaigns, scholarship funds, general purposes, annual campaigns.
Limitations: Giving limited to the Beloit, WI, stateline area. No grants to individuals.
Application information: Application form not required.
Initial approach: Letter
Deadline(s): None
Board meeting date(s): Varies
Write: Gary G. Grabowski, Treas.
Officers: Margaret K. Neese, Pres.; Elbert H. Neese, V.P and Secy.; Gary G. Grabowski, Treas. and Exec. Dir.
Number of staff: None.
Employer Identification Number: 363473918

2049
New Horizon Foundation
2302 Orrington Ave.
Evanston 60201
Additional address: 7348 Vista del Mar, La Jolla, CA 92037

Established in 1985 in IL.
Donor(s): Roger R. Revelle, Ellen C. Revelle, William R. Revelle, Eleanor M. Revelle, Piero F. Paci,† Mary Paci, and others.
Foundation type: Operating
Financial data (yr. ended 08/31/89): Assets, $3,683,730 (M); expenditures, $190,202, including $161,100 for 74 grants (high: $40,000; low: $25; average: $100-$1,000).
Purpose and activities: A private operating foundation; giving primarily for higher and other education, social service and youth agencies, public interest groups, and cultural programs.
Types of support: Annual campaigns, building funds, capital campaigns, continuing support, endowment funds, matching funds, operating budgets, research, scholarship funds, seed money.
Publications: Annual report.
Application information: Contributes only to pre-selected organizations. Applications not accepted.
Write: Carolyn Greenslate, Secy.-Treas.
Officers: William R. Revelle,* Pres.; Carolyn Hufbauer,* V.P.; Mary Paci,* V.P.; Carolyn Greenslate, Secy.-Treas.
Directors:* Gary Hufbauer, Eleanor M. Revelle, Ellen C. Revelle, Roger R. Revelle.
Number of staff: 1 part-time professional.
Employer Identification Number: 363406294

2050
New Prospect Foundation
1420 Sheridan Rd., Apt. 9A
Wilmette 60091 (708) 256-3886

Established in 1969 in IL.
Donor(s): Elliot Lehman, Frances Lehman, Fel-Pro Inc.
Foundation type: Independent
Financial data (yr. ended 12/31/89): Assets, $8,200,000 (M); gifts received, $600,000; expenditures, $607,486, including $585,000 for 121 grants (high: $35,000; low: $500; average: $500-$5,000).
Purpose and activities: Support for activities directed toward the improvement of housing, employment, health, welfare, and the economic viability of urban and inner city neighborhoods. Funding priority given to organizations with modest budgets that may not qualify for traditional sources of financial assistance; also supports efforts undertaken in the public interest. Additional areas of interest: pro-choice activities, nuclear disarmament, and Chicago public school reform.
Types of support: General purposes, operating budgets, continuing support, seed money, emergency funds, special projects, matching funds.
Limitations: Giving limited to the Chicago, IL, metropolitan area. Generally no funding for the arts or higher education. No grants to individuals, or for capital or endowment funds, basic research, scholarships, or fellowships; no loans.
Publications: Application guidelines, program policy statement, informational brochure (including application guidelines).
Application information: Application form not required.
Initial approach: Letter, proposal, or telephone
Copies of proposal: 1
Deadline(s): 6 weeks before board meetings
Board meeting date(s): Mar., June, Oct., and Dec.
Final notification: 3 months
Write: Frances Lehman, Pres.
Officer and Directors:* Frances Lehman,* Pres.; Elliot Lehman, Kenneth Lehman, Lucy

Lehman, Paul Lehman, Ronna Stamm Lehman, Kay Schlozman, Stanley Schlozman.
Number of staff: 1 part-time professional.
Employer Identification Number: 237032384

2051
Arthur C. Nielsen, Jr. Charitable Trust
Nielsen Plaza
Northbrook 60062-6210

Established in 1968 in IL.
Donor(s): Arthur C. Nielsen, Jr.
Foundation type: Independent
Financial data (yr. ended 10/31/88): Assets, $466,293 (M); gifts received, $1,347,905; expenditures, $2,192,082, including $2,140,862 for 53 grants (high: $2,010,650; low: $10).
Purpose and activities: Giving primarily for child care and development; support also for media and higher education.
Limitations: Giving primarily in IL. No grants to individuals.
Application information: Contributes only to pre-selected organizations. Applications not accepted.
Officers: Arthur C. Nielsen, Jr., Mgr.; Patricia M. Nielsen, Mgr.
Employer Identification Number: 366224821

2052
Dellora A. & Lester J. Norris Foundation ▼ ⌑
State Bank of St. Charles
One East Main St.
St. Charles 60174 (312) 377-4111

Established in 1979 in IL.
Donor(s): Dellora A. Norris,† Lester J. Norris.†
Foundation type: Independent
Financial data (yr. ended 12/31/87): Assets, $17,784,116 (M); gifts received, $645,033; expenditures, $1,833,729, including $1,514,600 for 93 grants (high: $250,000; low: $500).
Purpose and activities: Giving primarily for hospitals, higher and secondary education, and church support.
Application information:
Initial approach: Letter
Deadline(s): None
Write: Eugene Butler, Treas.
Officers and Directors: Robert C. Norris, Chair.; Joann N. Collins, Pres.; Laverne N. Gaynor, V.P.; Howard S. Tuthill, Secy.; Eugene w. Butler, Treas.; M. James Termondt, Linda Wheeler.
Employer Identification Number: 363054939

2053
The Northern Trust Company Charitable Trust ▼
c/o The Northern Trust Co.
50 South LaSalle St.
Chicago 60675 (312) 444-3538

Trust established in 1966 in IL.
Donor(s): The Northern Trust Co.
Foundation type: Company-sponsored
Financial data (yr. ended 12/31/88): Assets, $259,439 (M); gifts received, $1,200,000; expenditures, $1,182,585, including $1,182,538 for 645 grants (high: $154,000; low: $25; average: $2,000-$5,000).
Purpose and activities: Support for community development, education, hospitals and health services, civic and cultural programs, and social service and youth agencies, including a community fund.
Types of support: Operating budgets, continuing support, annual campaigns, seed money, emergency funds, equipment, land acquisition, employee matching gifts, consulting services, technical assistance, special projects, renovation projects, scholarship funds, matching funds, capital campaigns, general purposes.
Limitations: Giving limited to the metropolitan Chicago, IL, area. No support for national organizations, health organizations concentrating efforts in one area of human disease (except through matching gift program), hospital or college capital campaigns, religious organizations whose services are limited to any one sectarian group, fraternal or political groups, or operating support for United Way agencies. No grants to individuals, or for endowment funds, fellowships, advertising for fundraising benefits, or research; no loans.
Publications: Corporate giving report (including application guidelines), grants list.
Application information: Application form not required.
Initial approach: Telephone or brief proposal
Copies of proposal: 1
Deadline(s): Community Revitalization - Dec. 1 and Aug. 1; Health - Feb. 1; Social Welfare - Feb. 1 and Oct. 1; Arts & Culture - Apr. 1; Education - June 1
Board meeting date(s): Bimonthly
Final notification: 2 months
Write: Marjorie W. Lundy, V.P., The Northern Trust Co.
Contributions Committee: William N. Setterstrom, Chair.; Mary L. Blackett, Sidney R. Bundrage, John S. Darrow, Martin A. Gradman, Robert L. Head, Perry R. Pero, Lorraine M. Reepmeyer, Linda Reising.
Trustee: The Northern Trust Co.
Number of staff: 1 full-time professional; 1 full-time support; 1 part-time support.
Employer Identification Number: 366147253

2054
The Nutrasweet Company Charitable Trust ⌑ ☆
c/o The Northern Trust Co.
50 South LaSalle St.
Chicago 60675
Application address: c/o The Nutrasweet Co., 1751 Lake Cook Rd., Box 730, Deerfield, IL 60015; Tel.: (312) 405-6804

Established in 1987 in IL.
Donor(s): The Nutrasweet Co.
Foundation type: Company-sponsored
Financial data (yr. ended 2/28/89): Assets, $1,142,796 (M); gifts received, $750,000; expenditures, $693,601, including $689,702 for 243 grants (high: $250,000; low: $25).
Purpose and activities: Giving primarily for health associations; support also for education, nutrition, fitness, and hunger.
Limitations: Giving limited to areas where the company is present: the Chicago metropolitan area and University Park, IL; Augusta, GA; and Harbor Beach, MI.
Application information:
Deadline(s): None
Write: Max Downham, V.P.
Committee Members: Robert B. Shapiro, Chair.; Max Downham, Lauren S. Williams.
Trustee: The Northern Trust Co.
Employer Identification Number: 366857049

2055
The Offield Family Foundation ⌑
410 North Michigan Ave., Rm. 942
Chicago 60611

Incorporated in 1940 in IL.
Donor(s): Dorothy Wrigley Offield.
Foundation type: Independent
Financial data (yr. ended 06/30/89): Assets, $32,658,564 (M); expenditures, $1,346,304, including $1,208,122 for 42 grants (high: $200,000; low: $500; average: $1,500-$40,000).
Purpose and activities: Emphasis on hospitals, a population control agency, education, and cultural programs.
Limitations: Giving primarily in the Chicago, IL, area and MI. No grants to individuals.
Application information: Contributes only to pre-selected organizations. Applications not accepted.
Officers and Directors:* Wrigley Offield,* Pres.; Edna Jean Offield,* V.P.; Marie Larson,* Secy.; James E. Elworth,* Treas.; James S. Offield, Paxson H. Offield.
Employer Identification Number: 366066240

2056
The OMC Foundation
(Formerly The Ole Evinrude Foundation)
100 Sea Horse Dr.
Waukegan 60085 (708) 689-5483

Incorporated in 1945 in WI.
Donor(s): Outboard Marine Corp.
Foundation type: Company-sponsored
Financial data (yr. ended 06/30/89): Assets, $1,646,666 (M); gifts received, $1,087,500; expenditures, $312,435, including $255,819 for 51 grants (high: $27,702; low: $1,000) and $44,950 for 45 grants to individuals (high: $2,210; low: $500).
Purpose and activities: Support of private higher education, especially business and engineering, in states in which the company operates, scholarship aid to children of company employees, and capital grants to hospital and cultural building projects in company locations; support also for recreation and environmental programs.
Types of support: Continuing support, annual campaigns, seed money, building funds, equipment, special projects, research, scholarship funds, employee-related scholarships, capital campaigns, employee matching gifts, renovation projects.
Limitations: Giving limited to areas of company operations in GA, IL, NC, TN, WI, SC, MI, TX, FL, MO, OR, IN, AR, and NY. No support for organizations participating in local combined appeals. No grants to individuals (except for employee-related scholarships), or

for endowment funds or operating expenses; no loans.
Application information: Application form not required.
Initial approach: Letter
Copies of proposal: 1
Deadline(s): Submit proposal preferably in Aug.; deadline Sept. 30
Board meeting date(s): Dec.
Final notification: 30 days after annual meeting
Write: Mr. Laurin M. Baker, Dir., Public Affairs
Officers and Directors:* James C. Chapman,* Chair. and Pres.; Thomas J. Beeler,* V.P.; F. James Short,* V.P.; Laurin M. Baker,* Secy.; Michael S. Duffy,* Treas.
Number of staff: None.
Employer Identification Number: 396037139

2057
The Oppenheimer Family Foundation ⌑
P.O. Box 14771
Chicago 60614

Incorporated in 1953 in IL.
Donor(s): Seymour Oppenheimer,† Edward H. Oppenheimer, James K. Oppenheimer, Harry D. Oppenheimer.
Foundation type: Independent
Financial data (yr. ended 12/31/87): Assets, $2,654,236 (M); expenditures, $130,000, including $107,869 for 52 grants (high: $10,000; low: $1,000; average: $2,500).
Purpose and activities: Giving primarily for secondary education, criminal justice, and the environment.
Limitations: Giving primarily in Chicago, IL.
Application information:
Initial approach: Letter
Deadline(s): None
Write: Edward H. Oppenheimer, Pres.
Officers and Directors: Edward H. Oppenheimer, Pres.; Harry D. Oppenheimer, V.P. and Treas.; James K. Oppenheimer, V.P.; William J. Garmisa.
Employer Identification Number: 366054015

2058
Thomas M. & Mary M. Owens Foundation ⌑
10336 Cook Ave.
Oak Lawn 60453 (312) 424-3374

Established in 1986 in IL.
Donor(s): Thomas M. Owens.
Foundation type: Independent
Financial data (yr. ended 12/31/88): Assets, $1,892,696 (M); gifts received, $1,470,000; expenditures, $117,798, including $115,496 for 16 grants (high: $40,000; low: $300).
Purpose and activities: Giving primarily for religious purposes; support also for secondary education and social services.
Application information: Contributes only to pre-selected organizations. Applications not accepted.
Officers and Directors:* Mary M. Owens,* Pres. and Secy.; Thomas M. Owens,* V.P. and Treas.; Julie Owens, Michael Owens, Thomas M. Owens, Jr.
Employer Identification Number: 363429160

2059
James V. and Janet R. Pampinella Foundation ⌑
310 South Michigan Ave., Suite 1900
Chicago 60604

Established in 1986 in IL.
Donor(s): James V. Pampinella, Janet R. Pampinella.
Foundation type: Independent
Financial data (yr. ended 12/31/87): Assets, $129,292 (M); gifts received, $200,000; expenditures, $113,247, including $111,000 for 17 grants (high: $90,000; low: $100).
Purpose and activities: Support primarily for secondary and higher education.
Application information: Contributes only to pre-selected organizations. Applications not accepted.
Trustees: Virginia Munkvold, James V. Pampinella, Janet R. Pampinella.
Employer Identification Number: 366858484

2060
Frank E. Payne and Seba B. Payne Foundation ▼ ⌑
c/o Continental Bank, N.A.
30 North LaSalle St.
Chicago 60697 (312) 828-1785

Trust established in 1962 in IL.
Donor(s): Seba B. Payne.†
Foundation type: Independent
Financial data (yr. ended 6/30/89): Assets, $63,688,219 (M); expenditures, $2,750,545, including $2,488,820 for 44 grants (high: $700,000; low: $2,000; average: $5,000-$50,000).
Purpose and activities: Support for education, hospitals, and cultural programs; support also for child and animal welfare.
Types of support: Equipment, operating budgets, building funds, general purposes.
Limitations: Giving primarily in the metropolitan Chicago, IL, area and PA. No grants to individuals, or for endowment funds, or fellowships; no loans.
Publications: Application guidelines.
Application information: Application form not required.
Initial approach: Proposal
Copies of proposal: 1
Deadline(s): None
Board meeting date(s): May and Nov., and as required
Final notification: 4 months
Write: M.C. Ryan, 2nd V.P., Continental Bank, N.A.
Trustees: Susan Hurd Cummings, George A. Hurd, Sr., Priscilla Payne Hurd, Charles M. Nisen, Continental Bank, N.A.
Number of staff: None.
Employer Identification Number: 237435471

2061
Pepper Family Foundation ⌑ ☆
643 North Orleans St.
Chicago 60610 (312) 266-4703

Established in 1987 in IL.
Donor(s): The Pepper Companies, Inc., Richard S. Pepper, Roxelyn M. Pepper.
Foundation type: Independent
Financial data (yr. ended 12/31/88): Assets, $234,545 (M); gifts received, $250,000; expenditures, $178,020, including $178,000 for 19 grants (high: $50,000; low: $1,000).
Purpose and activities: Giving primarily for higher education; support also for cultural programs and historic preservation.
Types of support: Scholarship funds.
Limitations: Giving primarily in IL. No grants to individuals.
Application information: Contributes only to pre-selected organizations. Applications not accepted.
Officers: Richard S. Pepper,* Pres. and Treas.; Roxelyn M. Pepper,* V.P.; Thomas M. O'Leary, Secy.
Directors:* Lynda Bollman, J. David Pepper, J. Richard Pepper, J. Scot Pepper, J. Stanley Pepper, Lisa Pepper.
Employer Identification Number: 363540747

2062
Edwin E. Perkins Foundation
c/o First National Bank of Chicago
Three First National Plaza, Suite 0111
Chicago 60670-0484 (312) 732-5586

Established in 1961 in IL.
Donor(s): Edwin E. Perkins.†
Foundation type: Independent
Financial data (yr. ended 01/31/89): Assets, $2,039,312 (M); expenditures, $22,153, including $0 for grants.
Purpose and activities: Grants for social services and a hospital.
Application information:
Initial approach: Letter
Deadline(s): None
Write: Jane Williams
Trustees: Richard L. Kahn, Nancy P. O'Neil, First National Bank of Chicago.
Employer Identification Number: 366090223

2063
Kitty M. Perkins Foundation
208 South LaSalle St., Suite 1750
Chicago 60604 (312) 372-1947

Incorporated in 1966 in IL.
Donor(s): Kitty M. Perkins.†
Foundation type: Independent
Financial data (yr. ended 12/31/88): Assets, $6,818,231 (M); expenditures, $350,013, including $326,000 for 20 grants (high: $75,000; low: $1,000; average: $15,000).
Purpose and activities: Grants largely for a hospital and a college; support also for higher education, libraries, medical research, and rural community hospitals.
Types of support: Annual campaigns, building funds, capital campaigns, continuing support, general purposes, operating budgets, professorships, research, special projects, equipment.
Limitations: Giving primarily in NE. No grants to individuals, or for matching gifts; no loans.
Application information: Contributes only to pre-selected organizations. Applications not accepted.
Board meeting date(s): As required
Write: Kent Lawrence, Treas.
Officers and Directors: Ome C. Shoemaker, Pres.; William Shoemaker, V.P.; George

Franklin Shoemaker, Secy.; Kent Lawrence, Treas.; Kathryn Hertmann, Robert J. Lawrence, Don C. Shoemaker, Honor Shoemaker, J. Richard Shoemaker.
Number of staff: None.
Employer Identification Number: 366154399

2064
Harold L. Perlman Foundation ⌑ ☆
33 North Dearborn St., Suite 2020
Chicago 60602-3108 (312) 236-2942

Established in 1964.
Donor(s): Harold L. Perlman.
Foundation type: Independent
Financial data (yr. ended 3/31/89): Assets, $570,794 (M); gifts received, $54,200; expenditures, $154,815, including $154,198 for 51 grants (high: $50,000; low: $25).
Purpose and activities: Giving primarily for a medical research institute and higher education; support also for hospitals and Jewish organizations.
Limitations: Giving primarily in Chicago, IL. No grants to individuals.
Application information:
Initial approach: Letter
Deadline(s): None
Write: Harold L. Perlman, Pres.
Officers: Harold L. Perlman, Pres. and Treas.; Jane Perlman, Secy.
Directors: Sherwyn L. Ehrlich, Marjorie P. Shafton.
Employer Identification Number: 362555314

2065
Pesch Family Foundation ⌑
c/o Richman, Grossman & Friedman
55 East Jackson, Suite 2000
Chicago 60604

Established in 1985 in IL.
Donor(s): Leroy A. Pesch.
Foundation type: Independent
Financial data (yr. ended 03/31/88): Assets, $1,988,493 (M); expenditures, $1,136,774, including $1,049,032 for 21 grants (high: $733,432; low: $25).
Purpose and activities: First year of operation, 1985-86; grants to a church, a child abuse prevention organization, and cultural programs.
Limitations: No grants to individuals.
Application information: Contributes only to pre-selected organizations. Applications not accepted.
Officers and Directors: Leroy A. Pesch, Pres. and Treas.; Brian Pesch, Secy.; Erika G. Eddy, Exec. Dir.; Christopher Kniefel, Linda Kniefel, Alida Pesch, Christopher Pesch, Daniel Pesch, Ellen Pesch, Gerri Pesch.
Employer Identification Number: 363348055

2066
Esper A. Petersen Foundation
1300 Skokie Hwy.
Gurnee 60031 (708) 336-0900

Incorporated in 1944 in IL.
Donor(s): Esper A. Petersen.†
Foundation type: Independent
Financial data (yr. ended 12/31/88): Assets, $5,492,863 (M); expenditures, $245,540, including $235,840 for 40 grants (high: $25,000; low: $100) and $9,700 for grants to individuals.
Purpose and activities: Giving for hospitals, child welfare and youth agencies, and aid to the handicapped.
Types of support: General purposes, research, building funds.
Limitations: Giving primarily in IL and CA.
Publications: Application guidelines.
Application information: The foundation's scholarship program has been discontinued. Application form required.
Initial approach: Letter
Deadline(s): Dec. 1
Board meeting date(s): July and Dec.
Final notification: Dec. 31
Write: Esper A. Petersen, Jr., Dir.
Directors: Daniel H. Foster, Stephen A. Malato, Ann Petersen Pam, Esper A. Petersen, Jr.
Number of staff: None.
Employer Identification Number: 366125570

2067
The Albert Pick, Jr. Fund
30 North Michigan Ave., Suite 819
Chicago 60602 (312) 236-1192

Incorporated in 1947 in IL.
Donor(s): Albert Pick, Jr.†
Foundation type: Independent
Financial data (yr. ended 12/31/89): Assets, $13,739,000 (M); expenditures, $964,099, including $740,423 for 217 grants (high: $30,000; low: $1,000; average: $2,000-$3,000).
Purpose and activities: Giving for cultural programs, education, health and social services, community organizations, and civic affairs.
Types of support: Operating budgets, special projects, continuing support, general purposes, renovation projects, technical assistance.
Limitations: Giving primarily in Chicago, IL. No support for religious purposes. No grants to individuals, or for building or endowment funds, deficit financing, long-term projects, or advertising.
Publications: Program policy statement, application guidelines.
Application information: Application form not required.
Initial approach: Brief proposal
Copies of proposal: 1
Deadline(s): Feb. 1, Apr. 1, July 1, and Oct. 1
Board meeting date(s): Mar. or Apr., June, Sept., Dec., and as required
Write: Nadine Van Sant, V.P.
Officers and Directors:* Alan J. Altheimer,* Pres.; Nadine Van Sant,* V.P. and Secy.; Albert Pick III,* V.P.; Ralph Lewy,* Treas.; Arthur W. Brown, Jr., Burton B. Kaplan, Edward Neisser.
Number of staff: 1 full-time professional; 1 part-time professional.
Employer Identification Number: 366071402

2068
Pilot Foundation ⌑
321 North Clark St., Suite 340
Chicago 60610-4715

Established in 1964 in IL.
Donor(s): Harriet McClure Stuart,† Robert D. Stuart, Anne Stuart Batchelder, Margaret Stuart Hart, Harriet S. Spencer.
Foundation type: Independent
Financial data (yr. ended 6/30/88): Assets, $1,437,638 (M); expenditures, $82,322, including $68,000 for 24 grants (high: $17,000; low: $500).
Purpose and activities: Giving for a historical center; support also for social services including a youth club, community programs, education and religion.
Limitations: Giving primarily in IL. No grants to individuals.
Application information: Contributes only to pre-selected organizations. Applications not accepted.
Officers and Directors: Robert D. Stuart, Jr., Pres.; Margaret Stuart Hart, V.P. and Treas.; James J. McClure, Jr., Secy.
Employer Identification Number: 366087653

2069
Pinkert Charitable Foundation ⌑ ☆
500 Skokie Blvd.
Northbrook 60062-2813 (312) 272-0001

Established in 1974.
Donor(s): Ralph Pinkert.
Foundation type: Independent
Financial data (yr. ended 12/31/88): Assets, $126,612 (M); gifts received, $15,500; expenditures, $108,655, including $107,458 for grants (high: $59,042).
Purpose and activities: Support primarily for Jewish organizations, including Jewish welfare; giving also for cultural programs.
Application information: Application form not required.
Deadline(s): None
Write: Joseph S. Pinkert, Pres.
Officers and Directors: Joseph S. Pinkert, Pres.; Dale R. Pinkert, Secy.; Norman Pinkert, Treas.; Robert Pinkert.
Employer Identification Number: 237444824

2070
Virginia G. Piper Foundation ⌑
Three First National Plaza, Suite 1950
Chicago 60603

Established in 1972 in IL.
Donor(s): Virginia G. Piper.
Foundation type: Independent
Financial data (yr. ended 12/31/88): Assets, $2,106,048 (M); gifts received, $350,000; expenditures, $188,162, including $184,750 for 34 grants (high: $25,000; low: $1,000).
Purpose and activities: Support primarily for social services, the arts, higher education, and hospitals; support also for Catholic churches and religious orders.
Application information: Contributes only to pre-selected organizations. Applications not accepted.
Officer and Directors:* Virginia G. Piper,* Pres.; Carol Critchfield, Raymond Harkrider.
Employer Identification Number: 237230872

2071
Pittway Corporation Charitable Foundation ▼
333 Skokie Blvd.
P.O. Box 3012
Northbrook 60065-3012 (312) 498-1260

Established in 1966 in IL.
Donor(s): Pittway Corp.
Foundation type: Company-sponsored
Financial data (yr. ended 2/29/88): Assets, $4,192,630 (M); gifts received, $1,000,000; expenditures, $1,317,966, including $1,125,461 for 138 grants (high: $225,034; low: $100; average: $500-$25,000) and $183,037 for employee matching gifts.
Purpose and activities: Support for higher education, health associations, community funds, and social service agencies, including child welfare organizations; support also for an early childhood education institute and for cultural organizations, including public radio and television; also gives to primary and secondary schools and supports an employee matching gifts program.
Types of support: Employee matching gifts.
Limitations: Giving primarily in IL. No grants to individuals.
Application information: Application form not required.
Deadline(s): None
Board meeting date(s): Varies
Write: Joseph J. Sclafani, Secy.
Officers: Nelson Harris,* Pres.; King Harris,* V.P.; Joseph J. Sclafani, Secy.; Paul R. Gauvreau, Treas.
Directors:* Irving B. Harris, Chair.; Sidney Barrows, Maurice Fulton, William W. Harris.
Number of staff: None.
Employer Identification Number: 366149938

2072
Polk Bros. Fifty-Five Plus ☆
8311 West North Ave.
Melrose Park 60160 (708) 345-0115

Established in 1984 in IL.
Foundation type: Operating
Financial data (yr. ended 08/31/89): Assets, $3,492,643 (M); expenditures, $232,453, including $209,652 for 683 grants (high: $9,000; low: $60).
Purpose and activities: A private operating foundation; provides group meals for the elderly.
Limitations: Giving limited to the Chicago, IL, area.
Application information:
Initial approach: Letter
Deadline(s): None
Write: Michael A. Crane, Pres.
Officers and Directors:* Michael A. Crane,* Pres.; Paul D. Fischer,* Secy.-Treas.; Warren Arndt, Henry Dembosz, Laurence Weiner.
Number of staff: 1 part-time professional; 2 part-time support.
Employer Identification Number: 363332896

2073
Polk Bros. Foundation, Inc. ⌑
2850 North Central
Chicago 60634 (312) 287-1011

Incorporated in 1957 in IL.
Donor(s): Morris Polk,† and members of the Polk family, Rand Realty and Development Co., Polk Bros., Inc.
Foundation type: Independent
Financial data (yr. ended 12/31/88): Assets, $45,645,546 (M); gifts received, $1,967,700; expenditures, $2,236,938, including $203,452 for 125 grants (high: $20,000; low: $100).
Purpose and activities: Emphasis on social service agencies, including those for the handicapped, Jewish welfare funds and religious organizations, and higher education.
Limitations: Giving primarily in the Chicago, IL, area.
Application information:
Initial approach: Letter
Write: Michael A. Crane, Dir.
Directors: Lester Bachman, Michael A. Crane, Paul Fischer, Howard Polk.
Number of staff: None.
Employer Identification Number: 366108293

2074
The Polk Foundation ⌑
1300 North Waukegan Rd.
Lake Forest 60045

Incorporated in 1942 in OH.
Donor(s): Louis F. Polk, Sr., Louis F. Polk, Jr., Paula Lillard.
Foundation type: Independent
Financial data (yr. ended 12/31/87): Assets, $2,803,839 (M); expenditures, $180,933, including $140,900 for 36 grants (high: $25,000; low: $100).
Purpose and activities: Support primarily for education.
Application information: Contributes only to pre-selected organizations; funds largely committed. Applications not accepted.
Officers and Trustees: Paula Lillard, Pres.; Louis F. Polk, Jr., V.P.
Employer Identification Number: 316028725

2075
Pope Foundation, Inc. ⌑ ☆
c/o The Northern Trust Co.
50 South LaSalle St.
Chicago 60675 (312) 630-6000

Established in 1934.
Foundation type: Independent
Financial data (yr. ended 12/31/88): Assets, $1,145,022 (M); expenditures, $73,144, including $67,400 for 43 grants (high: $13,200; low: $250).
Purpose and activities: Giving primarily for institutions providing health care and conducting medical research, including hospitals, universities, and health and social services.
Types of support: Research.
Limitations: Giving primarily in IL, with emphasis on Chicago.
Application information: Application form not required.
Initial approach: Proposal
Deadline(s): Apr. 1
Officers and Directors: Henry Pope, Jr., Pres.; John W. Pope, V.P. and Secy.; William P. Pope, V.P. and Treas.; Margaret H. Essertier.
Employer Identification Number: 366050134

2076
Abra Prentice Foundation, Inc. ⌑
c/o The Northern Trust Co.
50 South LaSalle St.
Chicago 60675

Established in 1980 in IL.
Donor(s): Abra Prentice Wilkin.
Foundation type: Independent
Financial data (yr. ended 06/30/89): Assets, $4,260,652 (M); expenditures, $388,559, including $356,000 for 9 grants (high: $250,000; low: $10,000).
Purpose and activities: Support for secondary and higher education.
Limitations: No grants to individuals.
Application information: Contributes only to pre-selected organizations. Applications not accepted.
Officers and Directors:* Abra Prentice Wilkin,* Chair. and Pres.; William G. Demas,* Secy.-Treas.; Roy M. Adams, Jere Scott Zenko.
Employer Identification Number: 363092281

2077
Prince Charitable Trusts
Ten South Wacker Dr., Suite 2575
Chicago 60606 (312) 454-9130

Established in 1947 in IL.
Foundation type: Independent
Financial data (yr. ended 12/31/88): Assets, $99,629,783 (M); expenditures, $3,995,270, including $3,623,507 for grants (average: $5,000-$25,000).
Purpose and activities: Support for cultural programs, higher and secondary education, medical research, youth organizations, social services, hospitals, rehabilitation, and ecology.
Types of support: Capital campaigns, continuing support, general purposes, seed money, special projects, technical assistance.
Limitations: Giving limited to Chicago, IL, and RI. No grants to individuals.
Application information: Application form not required.
Initial approach: Letter or proposal
Copies of proposal: 1
Deadline(s): None
Board meeting date(s): Bimonthly
Trustees: William Norman Wood Prince, William Wood Prince, Frederick Henry Prince.
Number of staff: 2 full-time professional; 1 full-time support.
Employer Identification Number: 362411865

2078
Prince Foundation
c/o F.H. Prince & Co.
Ten South Wacker Dr., Suite 2575
Chicago 60606-7401 (312) 454-9130

Incorporated in 1955 in IL.
Donor(s): Central Manufacturing Distributors, Produce Terminal Corp., Union Stock Fund & Transit Co.
Foundation type: Independent

Financial data (yr. ended 12/31/88): Assets, $1,081,923 (M); expenditures, $72,166, including $69,490 for grants.
Purpose and activities: Support primarily for the arts, a chamber of commerce, and a community fund.
Types of support: General purposes.
Limitations: No grants to individuals.
Application information:
Initial approach: Proposal
Deadline(s): None
Write: Trustee
Officers: William Wood Prince,* Pres.; William Norman Wood Prince,* V.P.; Frederick Henry Prince,* V.P.; Thomas S. Tyler,* Secy.; Randall M. Highley, Treas.
Trustees:* Charles S. Potter.
Employer Identification Number: 366116507

2079
The Pritzker Charitable Fund ⌑ ☆
c/o Simon Zunamon, V.P.
200 West Madison Ave., 38th Fl.
Chicago 60606 (312) 750-8400

Established in 1987 in IL.
Donor(s): Members of the Pritzker family.
Foundation type: Independent
Financial data (yr. ended 11/30/88): Assets, $874,165 (M); gifts received, $3,000,000; expenditures, $2,243,815, including $2,243,779 for 192 grants (high: $526,000; low: $15).
Purpose and activities: Support primarily for higher education and Jewish organizations, including a welfare fund; support also for cultural programs.
Limitations: No grants to individuals.
Application information: Contributes to pre-selected organizations. Applications not accepted.
Officers: Jay A. Pritzker, Chair.; Robert A. Pritzker, Pres.; Thomas J. Pritzker, V.P. and Secy.; Simon Zunamon, V.P. and Treas.; Yehuda Ben-Arieh, V.P.; Nicholas J. Pritzker, V.P.
Employer Identification Number: 363554238

2080
Pritzker Foundation ▼ ⌑
c/o Jay Parker
200 West Madison, 38th Fl.
Chicago 60606 (312) 621-4200

Incorporated in 1944 in IL.
Donor(s): Members of the Pritzker family.
Foundation type: Independent
Financial data (yr. ended 12/31/86): Assets, $5,693,979 (M); gifts received, $4,645,374; expenditures, $1,821,774, including $1,802,352 for 255 grants (high: $474,500; low: $25; average: $100-$25,000).
Purpose and activities: Grants largely for higher education, including medical education, and religious welfare funds; giving also for hospitals, temple support, and cultural programs.
Limitations: No grants to individuals.
Application information: Contributes only to pre-selected organizations. Applications not accepted.
Board meeting date(s): Dec. and as required
Write: Simon Zunamon, Asst. Treas.
Officers: Robert A. Pritzker, Chair.; Jay A. Pritzker, Pres.; Nicholas J. Pritzker, V.P. and Secy.; Thomas J. Pritzker, V.P. and Treas.; James N. Pritzker, V.P.
Number of staff: None.
Employer Identification Number: 366058062

2081
George M. Pullman Educational Foundation
5020 South Lake Shore Dr., Suite 307
Chicago 60615 (312) 363-6191

Incorporated in 1949 in IL.
Donor(s): George Mortimer Pullman,† Harriet Sanger Pullman.†
Foundation type: Independent
Financial data (yr. ended 07/31/89): Assets, $12,653,769 (M); expenditures, $9,721,820, including $595,500 for 487 grants to individuals (high: $3,650; low: $250).
Purpose and activities: From 1915 to 1950 the income of this fund was used to operate the Pullman Free School of Manual Training. The foundation, as successor of the School, has focused its resources on college scholarships. Any resident of Cook County, IL, or child or grandchild of graduates of the Pullman Free School of Manual Training is eligible for consideration.
Types of support: Student aid.
Limitations: Giving limited to Cook County, IL.
Publications: Biennial report, informational brochure.
Application information: Application form required.
Deadline(s): Vocational Tech. students, May 18; new upperclassmen, May 1; renewal college students, June 1; freshmen, Jan. 5
Board meeting date(s): Quarterly
Write: John H. Munger, Exec. Dir.
Officers: Phillip Lowden Miller, Pres.; George A. Ranney, Jr., V.P.; Harry M. Oliver, Jr., Secy.; Edward McCormick Blair, Jr., Treas.
Directors: Robert W. Bennett, Edward McCormick Blair, Sr., Robert C. McCormack, Warren Pullman Miller, Mary Nissenson, Rev. Sam A. Portaro, Jr., William Julius Wilson.
Number of staff: 3 full-time professional; 2 part-time professional; 3 full-time support; 2 part-time support.
Employer Identification Number: 362216171

2082
The Quaker Oats Foundation ▼ ⌑
Quaker Tower
321 North Clark St.
Chicago 60610 (312) 222-7033

Incorporated in 1947 in IL.
Donor(s): The Quaker Oats Co.
Foundation type: Company-sponsored
Financial data (yr. ended 6/30/88): Assets, $6,944,335 (M); gifts received, $7,196,702; expenditures, $2,997,287, including $1,593,225 for 456 grants (high: $80,470; low: $100; average: $2,000-$4,000) and $1,033,653 for employee matching gifts.
Purpose and activities: Emphasis on higher education, including scholarships and employee matching gifts programs, and guaranteeing of loans through United Student Aid Funds (USAF); civic affairs, social services, community funds, youth agencies, arts and culture, hospitals, and public policy.
Types of support: General purposes, building funds, equipment, land acquisition, internships, scholarship funds, employee-related scholarships, fellowships, employee matching gifts, operating budgets, special projects, matching funds, annual campaigns, publications, conferences and seminars, continuing support, renovation projects.
Limitations: Giving primarily in areas of company operations, particularly IL. No support for religious organizations. No grants to individuals (except employee-related scholarships), or for advertising; no loans, except for USAF program.
Publications: Corporate giving report (including application guidelines), program policy statement.
Application information: Application form not required.
Initial approach: Proposal
Copies of proposal: 1
Deadline(s): None
Board meeting date(s): Sept., Dec., Mar., and June
Final notification: 6 to 8 weeks
Write: W. Thomas Phillips, Secy.
Officers: William D. Smithburg,* Chair.; Frank J. Morgan,* Pres.; Luther C. McKinney,* V.P.; W. Thomas Phillips, Secy.; Richard D. Jaquith, Treas.
Directors:* Weston R. Christopherson, William J. Kennedy III, Donald E. Meads, Gertrude G. Michelson, William L. Weiss.
Number of staff: 2 full-time professional; 3 full-time support; 1 part-time support.
Employer Identification Number: 366084548

2083
R.F. Foundation ⌑
One First National Plaza, Rm. 4700
Chicago 60603 (815) 758-3461

Incorporated in 1953 in IL.
Donor(s): Thomas H. Roberts, Thomas H. Roberts, Jr., Eleanor T. Roberts, Mary R. Roberts.
Foundation type: Independent
Financial data (yr. ended 12/31/88): Assets, $5,198,848 (M); expenditures, $223,359, including $200,000 for 9 grants (high: $50,000; low: $5,000; average: $8,000-$50,000).
Purpose and activities: Support for social services, with emphasis on a community health center.
Types of support: Operating budgets, continuing support, annual campaigns, building funds, equipment.
Limitations: Giving primarily in limited to the Chicago and DeKalb County, IL, area. No grants to individuals, or for seed money, emergency funds, deficit financing, land acquisition, renovations, endowment funds, matching gifts, scholarships, fellowships, special projects, research, publications, or conferences; no loans.
Application information: Application form not required.
Initial approach: Proposal
Copies of proposal: 1
Deadline(s): None
Board meeting date(s): Sept. and Oct.

Final notification: By Dec. 31
Write: H. Blair White, Pres.
Officers and Directors:* H. Blair White,* Pres.; Mary Eleanor Roberts,* V.P.; Charles C. Roberts,* Secy.-Treas.; Thomas H. Roberts, Jr.,* Treas.
Number of staff: None.
Employer Identification Number: 366069098

2084
James M. Ragen, Jr. Memorial Fund Trust No. 1. ⌑

30 North Michigan Ave.
Chicago 60602-3402

Established in 1973 in IL.
Foundation type: Independent
Financial data (yr. ended 12/31/87): Assets, $2,249,055 (M); expenditures, $202,013, including $180,000 for 29 grants (high: $36,000; low: $1,000).
Purpose and activities: Support primarily for churches, a hospital, social services, and secondary and higher education.
Application information: Application form not required.
Deadline(s): None
Members: Mary Lou Murphy, Francis W. Ragen, Robert E. Ragen, Virginia E. Ragen, Patricia Schaefer.
Trustee: Michigan Avenue National Bank.
Employer Identification Number: 237444822

2085
Reade Industrial Fund

c/o Harris Trust & Savings Bank
P.O. Box 755, 111 West Monroe St.
Chicago 60690 (312) 461-2603

Trust established in 1946 in IL.
Donor(s): Edith M. Reade.†
Foundation type: Independent
Financial data (yr. ended 12/31/88): Assets, $2,360,980 (M); expenditures, $180,158, including $161,939 for 51 grants to individuals (high: $5,000; low: $373).
Purpose and activities: Grants of up to $5,000 are given only to "individuals of good moral character, who are or have been employed in industry in the State of Illinois, and who shall by reason of an emergency beyond their control, such as accidental injury, illness of themselves or family members, inability to obtain any employment, or sudden and involuntary cessation of employment, be unable to care for themselves and their spouse and children and be in need of aid."
Types of support: Grants to individuals.
Limitations: Giving limited to IL residents, particularly to Chicago and its surrounding area.
Application information: Application form required.
Initial approach: Letter
Deadline(s): None
Write: Ronald F. Tuite, Jr.
Trustee: Harris Trust & Savings Bank.
Employer Identification Number: 366048673

2086
Redhill Foundation - Samuel & Jean Rothberg Family Charitable Trust ⌑ ☆

700 Commercial National Bank Bldg.
Peoria 61602-1641

Established in 1987 in IL.
Donor(s): Samuel Rothberg, Lee Patrick Rothberg.
Foundation type: Independent
Financial data (yr. ended 12/31/88): Assets, $794,233 (M); gifts received, $527,450; expenditures, $193,591, including $193,230 for 13 grants (high: $110,000; low: $1,000).
Purpose and activities: Giving primarily for higher education, including a Hebrew university; support also for Jewish giving and hospitals and medical research.
Types of support: Scholarship funds, general purposes, research.
Limitations: Giving primarily in IL and NY.
Trustees: Kathleen M. Barnett, Heidi B. Munday, Jean C. Rothberg, Lee Patrick Rothberg, Michael Rothberg, Samuel Rothberg.
Employer Identification Number: 371217165

2087
The Regenstein Foundation ▼

8600 West Bryn Mawr Ave., Suite 705N
Chicago 60631 (312) 693-6464

Incorporated in 1950 in IL.
Donor(s): Joseph Regenstein,† Helen Regenstein.†
Foundation type: Independent
Financial data (yr. ended 12/31/89): Assets, $82,473,918 (M); expenditures, $5,352,840, including $4,973,172 for 50 grants (high: $1,167,229; low: $500; average: $5,000-$300,000).
Purpose and activities: Giving primarily for music, art, higher and early childhood education, and medical research.
Types of support: Building funds, equipment, research, endowment funds, special projects, renovation projects.
Limitations: Giving primarily in the Chicago, IL, metropolitan area. No grants to individuals, or for scholarships, fellowships, annual campaigns, seed money, emergency funds, deficit financing, land acquisition, publications, conferences, matching gifts, or operating support; no loans.
Publications: Program policy statement, application guidelines.
Application information: Most grants made on the initiative of the trustees. Application form not required.
Initial approach: Letter
Copies of proposal: 1
Deadline(s): None
Board meeting date(s): May and as required
Final notification: 30 days
Write: Joseph Regenstein, Jr., Pres.
Officers and Directors:* Joseph Regenstein, Jr.,* Pres.; Betty R. Hartman,* V.P.; Robert A. Mecca,* V.P.; John Eggum,* Secy.-Treas.
Number of staff: 3 full-time professional.
Employer Identification Number: 363152531

2088
Relations Foundation ⌑

927 Fischer Ln.
Winnetka 60093 (312) 446-4211

Established in 1969 in IL.
Donor(s): Felt Products Manufacturing Co., and others.
Foundation type: Company-sponsored
Financial data (yr. ended 12/31/88): Assets, $3,200,014 (M); gifts received, $420,000; expenditures, $360,750, including $352,389 for grants.
Purpose and activities: Giving primarily to Jewish welfare funds; support also for medical research and social service agencies.
Types of support: Operating budgets.
Limitations: Giving primarily in the Chicago, IL, area. No grants to individuals, or for endowment funds; no loans.
Publications: Application guidelines.
Application information: Application form not required.
Initial approach: Letter
Copies of proposal: 1
Deadline(s): None
Board meeting date(s): Apr., July, and Nov.
Write: Joseph Radov, Pres.
Officers and Directors: Joseph Radov, Pres.; Dennis L. Kessler, V.P.; Sylvia M. Radov, V.P.; Carol Weinberg, V.P.; Daniel C. Weinberg, V.P.; Barbara Kessler, Secy.; David A. Weinberg, Treas.
Employer Identification Number: 237032294

2089
Luther I. Replogle Foundation ⌑ ☆

5744 South Blackstone Ave.
Chicago 60637-1824
Application address: 726 Fifth St. N.E., Washington, DC; Tel.: (202) 544-2355

Foundation type: Independent
Financial data (yr. ended 12/31/88): Assets, $7,276,399 (M); expenditures, $343,187, including $237,733 for 74 grants (high: $31,000; low: $35).
Purpose and activities: Support for museums, churches and other Protestant organizations, hospitals and clinics, and higher education.
Limitations: Giving primarily in Chicago, IL.
Application information: Application form not required.
Initial approach: Letter
Deadline(s): None
Write: Ms. Gwenn Gebhard
Officers: Elizabeth R. Dickie, Pres. and Treas.; James D. Hinchliff, V.P.; William O. Petersen, Secy.
Employer Identification Number: 366141697

2090
The Retirement Research Foundation ▼

1300 West Higgins Rd., Suite 214
Park Ridge 60068 (708) 823-4133

Incorporated in 1950 in MI.
Donor(s): John D. MacArthur.†
Foundation type: Independent
Financial data (yr. ended 12/31/89): Assets, $115,713,942 (M); expenditures, $5,549,285, including $4,131,981 for grants (average: $24,000-$25,000), $30,000 for 14 grants to

individuals (high: $5,000; low: $500; average: $500-$5,000) and $350,000 for 1 loan.
Purpose and activities: Support principally to improve the quality of life of older persons in the U.S. Priority interests are innovative model projects and research designed to: (1) increase the availability and effectiveness of community programs to maintain older persons in independent living environments; (2) improve the quality of nursing home care; (3) provide volunteer and employment opportunities for the elderly; and (4) seek causes and solutions to significant problems of the aged.
Types of support: Seed money, matching funds, research, special projects, employee matching gifts.
Limitations: Giving limited to the Midwest (IL, IN, IA, KY, MI, MO, WI) and FL for service projects not having the potential of national impact. No grants to individuals (except through National Media Awards Program), or for construction, general operating expenses of established organizations, endowment or developmental campaigns, emergency funds, deficit financing, land acquisition, publications, conferences, scholarships, media productions, dissertation research, annual campaigns, or renovation projects; no loans.
Publications: Program policy statement, application guidelines, occasional report, multi-year report (including application guidelines), grants list, informational brochure (including application guidelines).
Application information: Application form not required.
Initial approach: Letter or proposal
Copies of proposal: 3
Deadline(s): Submit proposal preferably in Jan., Apr., or July; deadlines Feb. 1, May 1, and Aug. 1
Board meeting date(s): Jan., Apr., July, and Oct.
Final notification: 3 to 6 months
Write: Marilyn Hennessy, Sr. V.P.
Officers: Edward J. Kelly,* Chair.; Joe L. Parkin,* Pres.; Marilyn Hennessy, Sr. V.P.; Brian F. Hofland, V.P.; Robert P. Ewing,* Secy.; Floyd Caldini, Treas.
Trustees:* Duane Chapman, William T. Kirby, Thomas P. Rogers, John F. Santos, Sister Stella Louise, C.S.F.N., George E. Weaver.
Number of staff: 7
Employer Identification Number: 362429540

2091
Reynolds-Barwick Scholarship Fund ⌑
R.R. One
P.O. Box 129
Sheldon 60966 (815) 429-3921

Established in 1985 in IL.
Foundation type: Independent
Financial data (yr. ended 12/31/88): Assets, $1,166,657 (M); expenditures, $121,055, including $66,530 for 30 grants to individuals (high: $5,503; low: $1,150).
Purpose and activities: Awards college educational scholarships to one high school graduate in each of the ten high schools in Iroquois County, IL.
Types of support: Student aid.
Limitations: Giving limited to graduates from Iroquois County, IL, high schools.
Publications: Application guidelines, informational brochure (including application guidelines).
Application information: Application form required.
Initial approach: Through high school administration
Copies of proposal: 1
Deadline(s): Feb. 15, in year of high school graduation
Board meeting date(s): Varies
Final notification: Apr. 15
Write: Robert W. Reynolds, Trustee
Trustees: Richard W. Reynolds, Robert W. Reynolds, Ronald W. Reynolds.
Number of staff: None.
Employer Identification Number: 376245457

2092
Otto L. and Hazel T. Rhoades Fund ⌑
c/o Harry M. Coffman
6106 North Landers
Chicago 60646 (312) 775-2257

Established in 1978.
Donor(s): Otto L. Rhoades.
Foundation type: Independent
Financial data (yr. ended 12/31/88): Assets, $2,002,744 (M); expenditures, $125,708, including $108,500 for 17 grants (high: $30,000; low: $1,500).
Purpose and activities: Emphasis on religious support, including a Christian communications organization, a Presbyterian church, higher education, health, and social services.
Limitations: Giving primarily in IL.
Officers and Directors:* Hazel T. Rhoades, Pres.; Harry M. Coffman,* V.P.; Julius Lewis,* Secy.
Employer Identification Number: 362994856

2093
Rice Foundation ▼ ⌑
222 Waukegan Rd.
Glenview 60025 (312) 998-6666

Incorporated in 1947 in IL.
Donor(s): Daniel F. Rice,† Ada Rice,† and others.
Foundation type: Independent
Financial data (yr. ended 12/31/88): Assets, $70,621,471 (M); gifts received, $3,581,415; expenditures, $7,584,670, including $7,031,644 for 42 grants (high: $4,000,000; low: $250).
Purpose and activities: Emphasis on higher education, including medical education, hospitals, and youth agencies.
Types of support: General purposes.
Limitations: Giving primarily in IL. No grants to individuals.
Application information:
Initial approach: Proposal
Deadline(s): None
Write: Arthur A. Nolan, Jr., Pres.
Officers and Directors:* Arthur A. Nolan, Jr.,* Pres.; Patricia G. Nolan,* V.P. and Treas.; Beatrice Rice Sheridan,* V.P.; James P. Doherty, Jr.,* Secy.; Donald M. Graham, Peter Nolan, David P. Winchester, Barbara M.J. Wood.
Employer Identification Number: 366043160

2094
Mark and Nancy Ritchie Foundation ⌑ ☆
27220 Darrell Rd.
Wauconda 60084

Established in 1984.
Donor(s): Mark Ritchie.
Foundation type: Independent
Financial data (yr. ended 11/30/87): Assets, $21,814 (M); gifts received, $197,277; expenditures, $199,408, including $199,104 for 21 grants (high: $132,000; low: $10).
Purpose and activities: Support primarily for Christian ministries and other Christian organizations.
Types of support: Operating budgets.
Limitations: Giving primarily in IL, with emphasis on Chicago.
Application information: Applications not accepted.
Trustees: Thomas Novak, Mark Ritchie, Nancy Ritchie.
Employer Identification Number: 363412585

2095
Albert A. Robin Family Foundation ⌑ ☆
1333 North Wells St.
Chicago 60610

Established in 1979.
Donor(s): Robin 1986 Charitable Income Trust.
Foundation type: Independent
Financial data (yr. ended 9/30/88): Assets, $240,469 (M); gifts received, $370,000; expenditures, $424,976, including $414,846 for 53 grants (high: $151,000; low: $100).
Purpose and activities: Giving primarily for higher education, including an art institute; support also for Jewish organizations.
Limitations: No grants to individuals.
Application information: Contributes only to pre-selected organizations. Applications not accepted.
Officers: Albert A. Robin, Pres.; Stephen H. Robin, V.P.; Richard J. Robin, Secy.-Treas.
Directors: Linda Miller, Constance Robin.
Employer Identification Number: 363096033

2096
Robin Scholarship Foundation ⌑
1333 North Wells St.
Chicago 60610 (312) 642-6301

Established in 1982 in IL.
Donor(s): Albert A. Robin.
Foundation type: Independent
Financial data (yr. ended 12/31/88): Assets, $1,073,989 (M); gifts received, $4,200; expenditures, $181,003, including $1,533,155 for 95 grants to individuals (high: $3,750; low: $130).
Purpose and activities: Scholarships for high school seniors of low-income families showing high promise.
Types of support: Student aid.
Limitations: Giving limited to IL, with emphasis on Chicago.
Application information: Application forms available through IL high schools. Application form required.
Deadline(s): Jan.
Officers: Linda Legler, Secy.; Albert Bennett, Admin.; Gayle Mindes, Coord.

Directors: Albert A. Robin, Chair.; Edward Anixter, Martin Binder, Ora McConner, Norman Mesirow, Byron S. Miller, George Olson, Richard Robin, Stephen Robin, Philip Schiller, Chester Schultz, Jerome Stone.
Employer Identification Number: 363204864

2097
The Rockford Community Trust ☆
c/o John Holstrom, Jr., Exec. Dir.
333 East State St., P.O. Box 111
Rockford 61105 (815) 962-2110

Established in 1953 in IL.
Foundation type: Community
Financial data (yr. ended 06/30/89): Assets, $5,596,851 (M); gifts received, $941,731; expenditures, $742,715, including $632,731 for 87 grants (high: $100,000; low: $150).
Purpose and activities: Giving primarily for human and social services; support also for youth and child development, and arts and culture.
Types of support: Equipment, building funds, renovation projects.
Limitations: Giving primarily in the Rockford, IL, metropolitan area, including Winnebago, Boone, Ogle, Stephenson, and Rock counties. No grants to individuals.
Publications: Annual report, application guidelines, program policy statement, 990-PF.
Application information: Application form required.
Initial approach: Proposal
Deadline(s): Dec. 31, Mar. 31, June 30, and Sept. 30
Board meeting date(s): Feb., May, Aug., and Nov.
Write: Gloria Lunden, Asst. Dir.
Officers and Trustees:* James F. Thiede,* Chair.; C. Philip Turner,* Vice-Chair.; Dan G. Loescher,* Treas.; John Holmstrom, Jr., Exec. Dir.; and 13 additional trustees.
Trustee Banks: Amcore Bank-Rockford, N.A., First of America Trust Co. of Rockford, First National Bank and Trust Co. of Rockford, United Bank of Illinois, N.A.
Number of staff: 1 full-time professional; 1 full-time support.
Employer Identification Number: 366076171

2098
Rocque Family Foundation ⌘ ☆
202 Burr Ridge Club
Burr Ridge 60521-5205

Established in 1986 in IL.
Donor(s): Robert E. Rocque, Vivian R. Rocque.
Foundation type: Independent
Financial data (yr. ended 12/31/88): Assets, $851,753 (M); gifts received, $619,201; expenditures, $217,017, including $216,200 for 22 grants (high: $102,000; low: $100).
Purpose and activities: Support primarily for a hospice for terminally ill children and a church; giving also for health associations.
Limitations: No grants to individuals.
Application information:
Initial approach: Letter
Deadline(s): None
Write: Robert E. Rocque, Pres.
Officers: Robert E. Rocque, Pres. and Treas.; Vivian R. Rocque, Secy.
Directors: Beverly G. Fewster, Gregory S. Rocque, Robert A.G. Rocque.
Employer Identification Number: 363480454

2099
Paul and Gabriella Rosenbaum Foundation ▼
1723 South Michigan
Chicago 60616

Established about 1983 in IL.
Donor(s): Gabriella Rosenbaum.
Foundation type: Independent
Financial data (yr. ended 09/30/88): Assets, $634,975 (M); gifts received, $1,028,290; expenditures, $1,262,108, including $1,243,946 for 9 grants (high: $437,941; low: $28,500; average: $1,500-$400,000).
Purpose and activities: Support primarily for cultural programs and the arts, including the theater, mathematics, and social services.
Types of support: Special projects.
Application information: Does not respond to unsolicited proposals. Applications not accepted.
Write: Edith Leonian, Exec. V.P.; or Madge Goldman, Exec. V.P.
Officers: Gabriella Rosenbaum, Chair. and V.P.; Madge Goldman, Exec. V.P. and Treas.; Edith Leonian, Exec. V.P.; Norman R. Liebling, Secy.
Number of staff: None.
Employer Identification Number: 363204862

2100
The Rosenberg Foundation, Inc. ⌘
205 North Michigan Ave., Suite 3909
Chicago 60601

Established in 1957 in IL.
Donor(s): Gary A. Rosenberg.
Foundation type: Independent
Financial data (yr. ended 9/30/88): Assets, $9,698 (M); gifts received, $278,500; expenditures, $298,215, including $296,250 for 15 grants (high: $250,000; low: $100).
Purpose and activities: Support primarily for higher education.
Types of support: Scholarship funds, professorships.
Limitations: Giving primarily in Chicago, IL.
Application information: Application form not required.
Deadline(s): None
Officers: Gary A. Rosenberg, Pres. and Treas.; Richard Sugar, Secy.
Employer Identification Number: 396044473

2101
Benjamin J. Rosenthal Foundation ⌘
36 South State St., Rm. 802
Chicago 60603 (312) 726-6163

Incorporated in 1922 in IL.
Donor(s): Benjamin J. Rosenthal.†
Foundation type: Independent
Financial data (yr. ended 12/31/87): Assets, $2,872,200 (M); expenditures, $181,813, including $128,250 for 219 grants (high: $10,000; low: $50).
Purpose and activities: Support primarily on youth and social service agencies; some support for programs that benefit veterans.
Limitations: Giving primarily in Chicago, IL.
Application information: Application form not required.
Deadline(s): None
Write: Ann Smith
Officers and Directors: Gladys R. Tartiere, Pres.; Elaine R. Moseley, V.P. and Treas.; Melissa Foulke, Secy.
Employer Identification Number: 362523643

2102
Rothman Family Foundation ⌘
208 South LaSalle St., Suite 1408
Chicago 60604 (312) 663-4700

Established in 1986 in IL.
Donor(s): Florence C. Rothman, Hermine C. Rothman, and other members of the Rothman family.
Foundation type: Independent
Financial data (yr. ended 12/31/88): Assets, $1,231,890 (M); expenditures, $64,252, including $52,542 for 21 grants (high: $15,000; low: $50).
Purpose and activities: Giving primarily for the arts and health and medical research.
Limitations: No grants to individuals.
Application information:
Initial approach: Letter or proposal
Deadline(s): None
Final notification: 90 days
Write: Patricia C. Rothman, V.P.
Officers and Directors:* Florence C. Rothman,* Pres.; Patricia C. Rothman,* V.P. and Secy.; Michael C. Rothman,* V.P. and Treas.; Hermine C. Ciancuillo,* V.P.; Gregory C. Rothman,* V.P.; Noel N. Rothman,* V.P.
Employer Identification Number: 363490566

2103
Hulda B. & Maurice L. Rothschild Foundation
c/o First National Bank of Chicago
One First National Plaza, Suite 0101
Chicago 60670-0101 (312) 732-6473

Established in 1981 in IL.
Donor(s): Hulda B. Rothschild.†
Foundation type: Independent
Financial data (yr. ended 12/31/88): Assets, $6,883,821 (M); expenditures, $605,506, including $523,485 for 14 grants (high: $129,668; low: $525; average: $5,000-$10,000).
Purpose and activities: "Giving primarily toward improving the quality of life for older adults in the U.S.; the foundation is particularly interested in innovative projects which develop and/or demonstrate new approaches to the problems of older adults and which have the potential for significant impact."
Types of support: Publications, seed money, special projects.
Limitations: Giving primarily in the Chicago, IL, metropolitan area. No support for political organizations or projects outside the U.S. No grants to individuals, or for general purposes, construction, operating budgets, endowment or development campaigns, or scholarships; no loans.

Publications: Application guidelines.
Application information: Priority given to organizations which have clear objectives, well-defined outcomes or impact, and cost effective approaches. Application form not required.
Initial approach: Letter
Copies of proposal: 1
Deadline(s): None
Final notification: 30-40 days
Write: Donald A. Kress
Officers and Trustees:* Robert N. Mayer,* Pres.; Beatrice Mayer, First National Bank of Chicago.
Number of staff: 1 part-time professional.
Employer Identification Number: 366752787

2104
A. Frank and Dorothy B. Rothschild Fund ⌑
135 South LaSalle St., Rm. 2011
Chicago 60603-4499

Established in 1952 in IL.
Foundation type: Independent
Financial data (yr. ended 12/31/87): Assets, $1,446,986 (M); expenditures, $96,671, including $70,980 for 107 grants (high: $10,000; low: $10).
Purpose and activities: Support primarily for health associations and hospitals, cultural programs, education, Jewish giving, social services, and wildlife and environmental organizations.
Limitations: Giving primarily in IL, NY, and MI.
Application information:
Initial approach: Letter
Deadline(s): None
Write: A. Frank Rothschild, Pres.; or Dorothy B. Rothschild, Secy.-Treas.
Officers and Directors: A. Frank Rothschild, Pres.; Dorothy B. Rothschild, Secy.-Treas.; A. Frank Rothschild, Jr.
Employer Identification Number: 366049231

2105
Tom Russell Charitable Foundation, Inc. ⌑
1315 West 22nd St., Suite 300
Oak Brook 60521

Incorporated in 1960 in IL.
Donor(s): Thomas C. Russell,† Wrap-On Co., Inc., Huron & Orleans Building Corp.
Foundation type: Independent
Financial data (yr. ended 8/31/87): Assets, $3,333,015 (M); gifts received, $198,026; expenditures, $1,140,689, including $147,000 for 43 grants (high: $10,000; low: $500).
Purpose and activities: "To help people to help themselves"; emphasis on higher education; support also for hospitals, health and social service agencies, and youth programs.
Limitations: Giving limited to the metropolitan Chicago, IL, area. No grants to individuals.
Publications: Application guidelines.
Application information: Application form not required.
Initial approach: Proposal
Copies of proposal: 1
Board meeting date(s): Grants are generally made in July and Aug.
Write: Leslie R. Bishop, Secy.
Officers and Directors: Thomas A. Hearn, V.P.; Leslie R. Bishop, Secy.; J. Tod Meserow, Treas.; John Lindquist.
Employer Identification Number: 366082517

2106
Patrick G. & Shirley W. Ryan Foundation ⌑
123 North Wacker Dr., Suite 1190
Chicago 60606

Established in 1984 in IL.
Donor(s): Ryan Holding Corp. of Illinois, Ryan Enterprises Corp.
Foundation type: Independent
Financial data (yr. ended 11/30/87): Assets, $338,457 (M); gifts received, $700,100; expenditures, $719,908, including $719,575 for 66 grants (high: $100,000; low: $50).
Purpose and activities: Support primarily for education, culture, social services, and health.
Limitations: Giving primarily in IL.
Application information: Contributes only to pre-selected organizations. Applications not accepted.
Officers and Directors: Shirley W. Ryan, Pres.; Patrick G. Ryan, V.P.; Glen E. Hess, Secy.
Employer Identification Number: 363305162

2107
The Barry Rymer Foundation ⌑
300 West Washington, Suite 1106
Chicago 60606

Established in 1985 in IL.
Foundation type: Independent
Financial data (yr. ended 12/31/87): Assets, $751,328 (M); expenditures, $267,059, including $259,700 for grants.
Purpose and activities: Grants primarily to Jewish organizations.
Limitations: No grants to individuals.
Application information: Contributes only to pre-selected organizations. Applications not accepted.
Officers and Directors: Barry Rymer, Pres.; Jeffrey Rymer, Secy.; Andrew Rymer, Treas.
Employer Identification Number: 363388569

2108
Alyce F. Salerno Charitable Foundation
c/o Harris Trust & Savings Bank
111 West Monroe St.
Chicago 60603
Application address: c/o Harris Trust and Savings Bank, P.O. Box 755, Chicago, IL 60690; Tel.: (312) 461-2609

Established in 1985 in IL.
Donor(s): Alyce F. Salerno Trust.
Foundation type: Independent
Financial data (yr. ended 12/31/88): Assets, $1,542,277 (M); expenditures, $356,765, including $345,000 for 3 grants (high: $210,000; low: $25,000).
Purpose and activities: Grants primarily to a hospital and an art institute.
Limitations: Giving primarily in IL.
Application information: Application form required.
Initial approach: Letter or telephone
Write: Ronald F. Tuite, Jr.
Trustees: Marian A. Hodgkinson, Marine Holdeiried, Harris Trust & Savings Bank.
Employer Identification Number: 363353261

2109
Salwil Foundation ⌑
400 Skokie Blvd., Suite 675
Northbrook 60062

Established in 1985 in IL.
Donor(s): William L. Searle.
Foundation type: Independent
Financial data (yr. ended 12/31/87): Assets, $2,057,882 (L); expenditures, $98,691, including $96,125 for 19 grants (high: $19,000; low: $1,000).
Purpose and activities: Support primarily for education, wildlife and the environment, health associations and hospitals, and cultural programs.
Application information: Contributes only to pre-selected organizations. Applications not accepted.
Write: William L. Searle, Pres.
Officers: William L. Searle, Pres.; Sally B. Searle, V.P. and Secy.-Treas.
Director: Marianne L. Pohle.
Employer Identification Number: 363377945

2110
Elsie O. and Philip D. Sang Foundation ⌑
180 East Pearson St., Apt. 5805
Chicago 60611

Established in 1954.
Foundation type: Independent
Financial data (yr. ended 10/31/88): Assets, $2,929,481 (M); expenditures, $429,590, including $419,410 for 34 grants (high: $300,000; low: $100).
Purpose and activities: Grants primarily for Jewish welfare funds; support also for hospitals and higher education.
Limitations: Giving primarily in Chicago, IL. No grants to individuals.
Application information: Application form not required.
Initial approach: Letter
Deadline(s): None
Board meeting date(s): As required
Write: Elsie O. Sang, Pres.
Officers: Elsie O. Sang, Pres.; Bernard Sang, Secy.
Number of staff: None.
Employer Identification Number: 366214200

2111
Santa Fe Pacific Foundation ▼
(Formerly Santa Fe Southern Pacific Foundation)
224 South Michigan Ave.
Chicago 60604-2401 (312) 786-6204

Incorporated in 1953 in IL.
Donor(s): Sante Fe Pacific Corp., and subsidiary companies.
Foundation type: Company-sponsored
Financial data (yr. ended 12/31/89): Assets, $1,591,382 (M); gifts received, $2,500,000; expenditures, $2,991,075, including $2,387,874 for 454 grants (high: $180,000;

low: $500; average: $500-$10,000) and $595,319 for 1,361 employee matching gifts.
Purpose and activities: Emphasis on higher education, the performing arts and other cultural programs, civic affairs and public policy, health and human services focusing on the homeless, hungry, children, women, and elderly.
Types of support: Scholarship funds, employee matching gifts, employee-related scholarships, annual campaigns, capital campaigns, continuing support, operating budgets, special projects.
Limitations: Giving limited to areas of company operations in midwestern, southwestern, and western U.S. No support for religious organizations for sectarian purposes; public educational institutions, preschool, primary, and secondary educational institutions; operating funds for organizations already receiving United Way support; political, fraternal, or veterans' organizations; hospitals; national health or cultural organizations; or community and other grantmaking foundations. No grants to individuals, or for conferences, seminars, travel expenses, testimonial dinners, or endowment funds.
Publications: Application guidelines.
Application information: Proposals are accepted and reviewed continuously, except for major requests (over $20,000) which are reviewed annually in the fall. Application form not required.
Initial approach: Proposal
Copies of proposal: 1
Deadline(s): Sept. 1
Board meeting date(s): Feb. and in the fall
Final notification: Varies
Write: Ronald L. Holden, Exec. Dir.
Officers: Robert E. Gehrt,* Pres.; J.F. Kever, V.P. and Treas.; Ronald L. Holden,* V.P. and Exec. Dir.; Sharon M. Gavril, Secy.
Directors:* J.P. Des Barres, R.L. Edwards, M.R. Haverty, J.L. Payne, V.B. Schwartz, R.T. Zitting.
Number of staff: 2 full-time professional.
Employer Identification Number: 366051896

2112
Sara Lee Foundation ▼
Three First National Plaza
Chicago 60602-4260 (312) 558-8448

Incorporated in 1981 in IL.
Donor(s): Sara Lee Corp.
Foundation type: Company-sponsored
Financial data (yr. ended 07/02/89): Assets, $4,694,989 (M); gifts received, $4,224,554; expenditures, $3,753,021, including $2,560,710 for grants (high: $279,500; average: $1,000-$5,000) and $913,017 for 2,502 employee matching gifts.
Purpose and activities: Primary focus is on social service organizations assisting women, the homeless, and the disadvantaged, and arts and cultural organizations.
Types of support: Employee-related scholarships, employee matching gifts, special projects, operating budgets, annual campaigns, continuing support.
Limitations: Giving primarily in the Chicago, IL, area. No support for elementary or secondary schools, religious organizations, disease-specific health organizations, fraternal, political, or veterans' organizations, or national or international organizations with limited relationships to local company operations. No grants to individuals, or for fundraising events, goodwill advertising, endowments, or capital campaigns.
Publications: Corporate giving report, informational brochure (including application guidelines), annual report (including application guidelines).
Application information: Application form required.
Initial approach: Letter or telephone
Copies of proposal: 1
Deadline(s): 1st working day of Mar., June, Sept., or Dec.
Board meeting date(s): 4 to 6 weeks following deadline
Final notification: 1 to 2 weeks after Management Donations Committee meetings
Write: Gretchen Reimel, Exec. Dir.
Officers: Robert L. Lauer,* Pres.; Gordon H. Newman, V.P. and Secy.; Mary Ellen Johnson, Treas.
Directors:* John H. Bryan, Jr., Paul Fulton, Michael E. Murphy.
Staff: Gretchen Reimel, Exec. Dir.; Renee Aten, Grants Admin.
Number of staff: 3 part-time professional; 2 part-time support.
Employer Identification Number: 363150460

2113
Sylvia and Aaron Scheinfeld Foundation ⌑
1040 North Lake Shore Dr., No. 37-A
Chicago 60611

Incorporated in 1955 in IL.
Donor(s): Sylvia R. Scheinfeld, Aaron Scheinfeld.†
Foundation type: Independent
Financial data (yr. ended 12/31/88): Assets, $665,438 (L); gifts received, $110,187; expenditures, $235,179, including $226,286 for 3 grants (high: $89,300; low: $50,313).
Purpose and activities: Support for urban policy research that aims to empower people to control and improve the quality of their lives, largely through experimental programs seeking to meet social needs in housing, job training, employment, neighborhood reinvestment, and ethnic and racial equality; support limited to three major ongoing foundation sponsored projects.
Limitations: Giving limited to the metropolitan Milwaukee, WI, and Chicago, IL, areas. No support for religious activities, medical institutions, government agencies, or fine arts programs. No grants to individuals, or for building or endowment funds, investments, or program advertising; no scholarships or small grants of any kind; no loans.
Publications: Program policy statement.
Application information: Contributes only to pre-selected organizations. Applications not accepted.
Board meeting date(s): 3 times a year
Write: Mrs. Sylvia R. Scheinfeld, Pres.
Officers and Directors:* Sylvia R. Scheinfeld,* Pres.; James D. Scheinfeld,* V.P.; Ruth S. Pollak,* Secy.; Stephen J. Pollak,* Treas.; Daniel R. Scheinfeld, Kathleen M. Scheinfeld, Sandra J.P. Scheinfeld.
Employer Identification Number: 366056338

2114
Schiff Foundation, Inc. ⌑ ☆
200 West Hubbard St.
Chicago 60610-4405

Incorporated in 1986 in IL.
Donor(s): Harold Schiff.
Foundation type: Independent
Financial data (yr. ended 12/31/88): Assets, $282,609 (M); gifts received, $432,006; expenditures, $207,450, including $205,000 for 4 grants (high: $175,000; low: $1,000).
Purpose and activities: Giving primarily for a youth organization; support also for an art institute.
Limitations: Giving primarily in Chicago, IL. No grants to individuals.
Application information: Contributes only to pre-selected organizations. Applications not accepted.
Officers and Directors: Harold Schiff, Pres. and Treas.; Richard C. Halpern, V.P. and Secy.; Mrs. Alan Astrove.
Employer Identification Number: 363485274

2115
Schiff, Hardin & Waite Foundation
233 South Wacker Dr., Suite 7200
Chicago 60606 (312) 876-1000

Established in 1986 in IL.
Foundation type: Company-sponsored
Financial data (yr. ended 11/30/89): Assets, $25,179 (M); gifts received, $384,521; expenditures, $378,774, including $377,931 for 106 grants (high: $259,131; low: $150).
Purpose and activities: Support primarily for legal services agencies and community funds.
Types of support: General purposes.
Limitations: Giving primarily in Chicago, IL.
Application information: Contributes only to pre-selected organizations. Applications not accepted.
Write: Stephen B. Veitch, Admin. Dir.
Officers and Directors:* Burton R. Rissman,* Pres. and Treas.; Allan Horwich,* V.P. and Secy.; Lawrence Block, Joseph P. Collins, Roger Pascal, Peter L. Rossiter, Mark C. Zaander.
Employer Identification Number: 363465740

2116
William E. Schmidt Charitable Foundation ⌑
Two Larkspur
Belleville 62221

Donor(s): William E. Schmidt.
Foundation type: Independent
Financial data (yr. ended 4/30/87): Assets, $4,462,691 (M); gifts received, $1,404,975; expenditures, $110,194, including $105,000 for 23 grants (high: $10,000; low: $1,000).
Purpose and activities: Support primarily for religious organizations, higher education, and health services.

Application information: Contributes only to pre-selected organizations. Applications not accepted.
Directors: Lucille Barton, Robert Lamear, John Schmidt.
Employer Identification Number: 371098426

2117
Arthur J. Schmitt Foundation ▼
Two North LaSalle St., Suite 2010
Chicago 60602 (312) 236-5089

Incorporated in 1941 in IL.
Donor(s): Arthur J. Schmitt.†
Foundation type: Independent
Financial data (yr. ended 06/30/89): Assets, $15,526,204 (M); expenditures, $1,376,877, including $1,124,425 for 68 grants (high: $100,000; low: $100; average: $2,000-$50,000).
Purpose and activities: Giving primarily for scholarships and fellowships established at certain selected universities to aid students in pursuing graduate degrees, with preference given to those engaged or seriously expecting to engage in teaching; grants also to social services and secondary education.
Types of support: Endowment funds, scholarship funds, fellowships, general purposes, continuing support.
Limitations: Giving limited to the Chicago, IL, metropolitan area, except for a few selected colleges and universities. No grants to individuals, or for capital or building funds, research, or matching gifts; no loans.
Publications: Application guidelines.
Application information: Application form not required.
Initial approach: Proposal
Copies of proposal: 3
Deadline(s): Submit proposal preferably in July, Oct., Jan., and Apr.
Board meeting date(s): Sept., Dec., Mar., and June
Final notification: 1 month after board meeting
Write: John A. Donahue, Exec. Dir.
Officers: John J. Gearen, Pres.; Edmund A. Stephan, Secy.; John A. Donahue, Exec. Dir.
Directors: Richard C. Becker, William A. Maloney, Daniel E. Mayworm, Peter J. Wrenn.
Number of staff: 1 part-time professional.
Employer Identification Number: 362217999

2118
Robert E. Schneider Foundation ⌑
150 East Ontario St.
Chicago 60611

Established in 1968 in IL.
Donor(s): Phyllis Schneider, Melvin Schneider.
Foundation type: Independent
Financial data (yr. ended 12/31/88): Assets, $2,389,570 (M); gifts received, $100,050; expenditures, $104,292, including $100,050 for 14 grants (high: $35,000; low: $50).
Purpose and activities: Grants primarily for medical research, hospitals, and higher education.
Application information: Contributes only to pre-selected organizations. Applications not accepted.
Officers and Directors:* Melvin Schneider,* Pres.; Phyllis Schneider,* Secy.-Treas.; Frederic Schneider, Richard Schneider.
Employer Identification Number: 366212061

2119
Schoenstadt Family Foundation ⌑ ☆
232 East Walton St.
Chicago 60611

Established in 1949.
Foundation type: Independent
Financial data (yr. ended 12/31/88): Assets, $1,077,633 (M); gifts received, $61,693; expenditures, $69,128, including $63,550 for 48 grants (high: $6,000; low: $250).
Purpose and activities: Giving primarily for Jewish organizations, including welfare; support also for higher and other education, a community fund, and health and hospitals.
Limitations: No grants to individuals.
Application information: Application form not required.
Initial approach: Letter; no telephone calls
Deadline(s): None
Write: Arthur Schoenstadt, Jr., Pres.
Officers and Directors:* Arthur Schoenstadt, Jr., Pres.; Dennis F. Glass,* Secy.; Ruth Ann Fay,* Treas.; Robert S. Lidenthal.
Employer Identification Number: 366055872

2120
Dr. Scholl Foundation ▼
11 South LaSalle St., Suite 2100
Chicago 60603 (312) 782-5210

Incorporated in 1947 in IL.
Donor(s): William M. Scholl, M.D.†
Foundation type: Independent
Financial data (yr. ended 12/31/89): Assets, $123,247,118 (M); expenditures, $9,302,214, including $7,371,300 for 372 grants (high: $200,000; low: $1,000; average: $5,000-$50,000) and $180,000 for 40 grants to individuals.
Purpose and activities: Support for private education at all levels, including elementary, secondary, and post-secondary schools, colleges and universities, and medical and nursing institutions; general charitable programs, including grants to hospitals, and programs for children, the developmentally disabled, and senior citizens; and civic, cultural, social welfare, economic, and religious activities.
Types of support: Equipment, conferences and seminars, special projects, endowment funds.
Limitations: No support for public education. No grants to individuals, or for building funds, general support, continuing support, operating budgets, deficit financing, or unrestricted purposes.
Publications: Program policy statement, application guidelines.
Application information: The scholarship program for the children of company employees, except for renewals, has been discontinued.
Initial approach: Ask for application form
Copies of proposal: 1
Deadline(s): May 15
Board meeting date(s): Feb., May., Aug., and Oct.
Final notification: Nov.
Write: Jack E. Scholl, Exec. Dir.
Officers: William H. Scholl,* Pres.; Jack E. Scholl,* V.P., Secy., and Exec. Dir.; Leonard J. Knirko, Treas.
Trustees:* George W. Alexander, William T. Branham, Neil Flanagin, William B. Jordan, Charles F. Scholl, Douglas C. Witherspoon.
Number of staff: 2 full-time professional; 2 part-time professional; 3 full-time support.
Employer Identification Number: 366068724

2121
The Seabury Foundation ⌑
c/o The Northern Trust Co.
50 South LaSalle St.
Chicago 60675 (312) 630-6000

Trust established in 1947 in IL.
Donor(s): Charles Ward Seabury,† Louise Lovett Seabury.†
Foundation type: Independent
Financial data (yr. ended 12/31/88): Assets, $15,773,077 (M); expenditures, $674,093, including $605,700 for 138 grants (high: $35,000; low: $500).
Purpose and activities: Emphasis on hospitals, cultural programs, including music, higher and secondary education, aid to the handicapped, youth agencies, and child welfare.
Limitations: Giving primarily in the greater Chicago, IL, area. No grants to individuals; no loans.
Application information: Contributes only to pre-selected organizations. Applications not accepted.
Officers and Trustees:* Clara Seabury Boone,* Exec. Secy.; John Ward Seabury,* Exec. Dir.; Daniel J. Boone, Charles B. Fisk, Elizabeth Seabury Mitchell, Louis Fisk Morris, Charlene B. Seabury, The Northern Trust Co.
Employer Identification Number: 366027398

2122
G. D. Searle & Company Charitable Trust ⌑
c/o G.D. Searle & Co.
P.O. Box 5110
Chicago 60680

Established in 1983 in IL.
Donor(s): G.D. Searle & Co.
Foundation type: Company-sponsored
Financial data (yr. ended 12/31/87): Assets, $41,037 (M); expenditures, $350,196, including $318,649 for 402 grants (high: $55,000; low: $10).
Purpose and activities: Support for charitable and educational purposes. The trust is in the process of reorganizing and is revising its purpose and goals.
Application information:
Initial approach: Letter
Deadline(s): None
Write: William I. Greener, Jr., Sr. V.P., Public Affairs
Committee Members: Peter L. Baron, David R. Bethune, Robert L. Bogomolny, Joseph Davie, Richard U. DeSchutter, Sheldon Gilbore, M.D., William I. Greener.
Trustee: The Northern Trust Co.
Employer Identification Number: 366785886

2123
The Sears-Roebuck Foundation ▼
Sears Tower, Dept. 903--BSC 51-02
Chicago 60684 (312) 875-8337
Additional tel.: (312) 875-7112

Incorporated in 1923 in IL as Sears Agricultural Foundation; re-chartered in 1941.
Donor(s): Sears, Roebuck and Co.
Foundation type: Company-sponsored
Financial data (yr. ended 01/31/90): Assets, $5,808,668 (M); expenditures, $3,696,563, including $3,674,260 for grants (high: $1,423,928; low: $100).
Purpose and activities: Contributions primarily for health and human services, education, arts and culture, and civic and community affairs, reflecting special interest in programs targeted to the foundation's National Focus Priorities. The foundation funds specific national programs related to: older adults, the disabled, health care cost containment, at-risk populations, volunteerism, literacy, early childhood education/day care, teacher excellence, work force readiness and job training, arts education, and neighborhood economic development.
Types of support: Special projects.
Limitations: No support for religious groups for religious purposes, political, fraternal, or labor organizations, or to colleges providing instruction in technology, religion, or a single profession, or whose enrollment is limited by religion. No grants to individuals, or for building or endowment funds, operating budgets, scholarships, fellowships, matching gifts, or advertisements; no loans.
Publications: Corporate giving report (including application guidelines), 990-PF, financial statement.
Application information: Application form not required.
Initial approach: Request guidelines
Deadline(s): None
Board meeting date(s): 4 times annually
Final notification: Proposals and requests are reviewed in a timely manner
Write: Paula A. Banks, Pres.; or Richard K. Hartung, Prog. Mgr.
Officers: Charles J. Ruder,* Chair.; Paula A. Banks,* Pres. and Exec. Dir.; Julie A. Hansen, Secy.; Kathleen A. Mazzarino, Treas.; Philip L. Maughan,* Controller.
Directors:* Edward A. Brennan, Warren F. Cooper, Guy F. Eberhart, Philo K. Holland, Kenneth F. Mountcastle, Jr., Kristine Sandrick, David Shute, Lawrence H. Williford.
Number of staff: 5
Employer Identification Number: 366032266

2124
The Seeley Foundation ⌑
115 South LaSalle St., Rm. 2500
Chicago 60603

Incorporated in 1945 in MI.
Donor(s): Halsted H. Seeley,† Laurel H. Seeley.
Foundation type: Independent
Financial data (yr. ended 12/31/88): Assets, $2,417,776 (M); expenditures, $235,365, including $201,000 for 7 grants (high: $150,000; low: $1,000).
Purpose and activities: Continuing support of fellowship and research funds set up in memory of John Harper Seeley, largely in the field of mental health.
Types of support: Fellowships, research.
Application information:
Initial approach: Letter
Deadline(s): None
Write: Hugo J. Melvoin, Trustee
Trustees: Judith S. Fales, Hugo J. Melvoin, Ellen F. Roberts, Dana M. Seeley, Miles G. Seeley, Miles P. Seeley.
Employer Identification Number: 366049991

2125
Barre Seid Foundation ⌑
334 West Wisconsin Ave.
Chicago 60614 (312) 337-7689

Established in 1985 in IL.
Donor(s): Barre Seid.
Foundation type: Independent
Financial data (yr. ended 12/31/87): Assets, $2,360,645 (M); gifts received, $500,000; expenditures, $162,307, including $158,600 for 11 grants (high: $50,000; low: $100).
Purpose and activities: Support primarily for higher education.
Limitations: Giving primarily in Chicago, IL.
Application information:
Deadline(s): None
Write: Barre Seid, Pres.
Officers and Directors: Barre Seid, Pres. and Treas.; Joyce B. Markle, Secy.; Leonard Schanfield.
Employer Identification Number: 363342443

2126
Selway Foundation ⌑
100 West Willow Rd.
Wheeling 60090 (312) 537-3400

Established about 1959 in IL.
Donor(s): Cresent Cardboard Co.
Foundation type: Independent
Financial data (yr. ended 05/31/89): Assets, $248,550 (M); gifts received, $75,000; expenditures, $166,772, including $166,450 for 71 grants (high: $30,000; low: $100).
Purpose and activities: Support primarily for higher education, religion, health services, and medical research.
Limitations: No grants to individuals.
Application information: Contributes only to pre-selected organizations. Applications not accepted.
Write: P.T. Rooney, V.P. and Secy.-Treas.
Officers and Directors:* D.B. Ozmun,* Pres.; P.T. Rooney,* V.P. and Secy.-Treas.; Terry Boffeli,* V.P.
Employer Identification Number: 366108268

2127
Soretta & Henry Shapiro Family Foundation, Inc. ⌑
1540 North Lake Shore Dr.
Chicago 60610

Established in 1970 in IL.
Donor(s): Isaac and Fannie Shapiro Memorial Foundation.
Foundation type: Independent
Financial data (yr. ended 12/31/88): Assets, $2,510,631 (M); expenditures, $1,805,234, including $339,057 for 134 grants (high: $116,000; low: $25).
Purpose and activities: Support for cultural programs and organizations and for Jewish organizations and schools.
Limitations: Giving primarily in Chicago, IL.
Application information:
Initial approach: Letter or proposal
Deadline(s): None
Write: Henry Shapiro, Trustee
Trustee: Henry Shapiro.
Employer Identification Number: 237063846

2128
Fern Goldstein Shapiro, Morris R. Shapiro, and Charles Shapiro Foundation, Inc. ▼ ⌑
(Formerly Charles and M. R. Shapiro Foundation, Inc.)
330 West Diversey Pkwy., Suite 1801
Chicago 60657 (312) 472-1506

Incorporated in 1958 in IL.
Donor(s): Charles Shapiro,† Mary Shapiro,† Molly Shapiro,† Morris R. Shapiro.
Foundation type: Independent
Financial data (yr. ended 7/31/88): Assets, $14,789,290 (M); expenditures, $1,024,234, including $958,690 for 63 grants (high: $246,900; low: $100).
Purpose and activities: Emphasis on Jewish welfare funds and temple support; grants also for higher education and social services.
Limitations: Giving primarily in Chicago, IL. No grants to individuals.
Application information: Contributes only to pre-selected organizations. Applications not accepted.
Initial approach: Letter
Deadline(s): None
Write: Fern Goldstein Shapiro, Pres.
Officers: Fern Goldstein Shapiro,* Pres.; Andrew Akos, Secy.
Directors:* Joseph L. Muskal, Morris R. Shapiro.
Number of staff: None.
Employer Identification Number: 366109757

2129
Arch W. Shaw Foundation ⌑
135 South LaSalle St.
Chicago 60603 (312) 726-7155

Trust established in 1949 in IL.
Foundation type: Independent
Financial data (yr. ended 12/31/87): Assets, $6,795,612 (M); expenditures, $406,183, including $400,000 for 64 grants (high: $20,000; low: $1,000).
Purpose and activities: Grants for higher education, hospitals, and cultural programs.
Limitations: Giving primarily in IL. No grants to individuals.
Application information:
Initial approach: Letter
Deadline(s): None
Write: John I. Shaw, Trustee
Trustees: William W. Shaw, Arch W. Shaw II, John I. Shaw, Roger D. Shaw.
Employer Identification Number: 366055262

2130
Walden W. & Jean Young Shaw Foundation ⌑
30 North LaSalle St., Suite 3100
Chicago 60602

Established in 1967 in IL.
Donor(s): Walden W. Shaw, Jean Young Shaw.
Foundation type: Independent
Financial data (yr. ended 06/30/88): Assets, $8,341,508 (M); gifts received, $283,495; expenditures, $511,946, including $397,000 for 7 grants (high: $100,000; low: $5,000).
Purpose and activities: Giving primarily for hospitals; support also for educational institutions.
Limitations: No grants to individuals.
Application information: Applications not accepted.
Officers: Newell Carey Iler,* Pres.; Florence Iler, V.P.; Walter Roth, Secy.-Treas.
Directors:* Robert Gordon Iler.
Employer Identification Number: 366162196

2131
Nate H. Sherman Foundation ⌑
919 North Michigan Ave., Suite 2733
Chicago 60611 (312) 787-2373

Established in 1967 in IL.
Donor(s): Nate H. Sherman, Midas-International Corp., Midas-International Corp. Foundation.
Foundation type: Independent
Financial data (yr. ended 12/31/88): Assets, $2,808,506 (M); expenditures, $188,806, including $145,000 for 28 grants (high: $100,000; low: $100).
Purpose and activities: Emphasis on Jewish welfare funds.
Types of support: General purposes.
Limitations: Giving primarily in IL. No grants to individuals.
Application information: Application form not required.
Initial approach: Letter
Deadline(s): None
Write: Sarita Warshawsky, Pres.
Officers and Directors:* Sarita Warshawsky,* Pres. and Treas.; Bette Lou Seidner,* V.P.; Mary Sherman,* Secy.
Employer Identification Number: 366194153

2132
The Shifting Foundation
8000 Sears Tower
Chicago 60606

Established in 1982 in IL.
Foundation type: Independent
Financial data (yr. ended 01/31/89): Assets, $1,912,354 (M); gifts received, $27,436; expenditures, $117,000, including $49,000 for 17 grants (high: $7,500; low: $500; average: $500-$7,500) and $48,000 for 6 grants to individuals (high: $10,000; low: $6,000; average: $4,000-$10,000).
Purpose and activities: Support for grants to individual artists primarily in literature and music, less frequently in visual or multi-media forms; support also for hunger relief, social services, health organizations, human and civil rights, environmental and anti-nuclear interests, and Third World development.
Types of support: General purposes, grants to individuals.
Limitations: No support for work in dance, the behavioral sciences, or for musicians who are mainly performers of traditional, classical or pop music.
Publications: Application guidelines.
Application information: Applications not accpeted from foreign individuals or organizations. Application form required.
Copies of proposal: 1
Deadline(s): None
Final notification: within 4 months
Write: Pat Culver
Number of staff: None.
Employer Identification Number: 366108560

2133
The Russell and Betty Shirk Foundation ⌑
P.O. Box 1549
Bloomington 61702-1549 (309) 827-8580
Application address: 103 North Robinson St., Bloomington, IL 61701

Established in 1968.
Donor(s): Russell O. Shirk, James A. Shirk.
Foundation type: Independent
Financial data (yr. ended 12/31/88): Assets, $5,826,371 (M); expenditures, $233,154, including $224,475 for 47 grants (high: $175,000; low: $100).
Purpose and activities: Support for building funds, with emphasis on higher education, youth agencies, and health.
Types of support: Operating budgets, scholarship funds, building funds.
Limitations: Giving primarily in IL.
Application information:
Initial approach: Letter
Deadline(s): None
Write: James A. Shirk, V.P.
Officers and Directors:* Russell O. Shirk,* Pres.; James A. Shirk,* V.P.; B.J. Shirk, Secy.-Treas.; Merrick C. Hayes.
Employer Identification Number: 237022709

2134
Silver Spring Foundation ⌑
410 North Michigan Ave., Rm. 590
Chicago 60611

Established in 1953 in PA.
Donor(s): Charles Deering McCormick, Miami Corp.
Foundation type: Independent
Financial data (yr. ended 12/31/88): Assets, $4,829,292 (M); gifts received, $110,000; expenditures, $314,448, including $303,000 for 18 grants (high: $50,000; low: $1,000).
Purpose and activities: Emphasis on cultural programs, hospitals, social services, and higher education.
Types of support: General purposes.
Application information: Contributes only to pre-selected organizations. Applications not accepted.
Trustees: Brooks McCormick, Charles Deering McCormick, Charles E. Schroeder.
Employer Identification Number: 236254662

2135
John M. Simpson Foundation ⌑ ☆
33 North Dearborn St., Rm. 1300
Chicago 60602

Established in 1961.
Foundation type: Independent
Financial data (yr. ended 12/31/88): Assets, $1,899,481 (M); gifts received, $519,782; expenditures, $146,681, including $138,050 for 25 grants (high: $22,500; low: $200).
Purpose and activities: Giving primarily for hospitals, clinics, health services, and social services; support also for museums and an aquarium.
Officers: Nancy T. Simpson, Pres.; P.J. Herbert, V.P.; W.J. McDermott, V.P.; J.D. Brown, Secy.; Allison Lang, Treas.
Directors: Patricia S. Okieffe, Howard B. Simpson, William Simpson.
Employer Identification Number: 366071621

2136
The Siragusa Foundation
919 North Michigan, Suite 2701
Chicago 60611 (312) 280-0833

Trust established in 1950 in IL; incorporated in 1980.
Donor(s): Ross D. Siragusa.
Foundation type: Independent
Financial data (yr. ended 12/31/89): Assets, $10,187,540 (M); expenditures, $566,484, including $403,000 for 70 grants (high: $30,000; low: $500; average: $5,757).
Purpose and activities: Emphasis on higher education and medical research; support also for cultural activities, child development programs, education of the handicapped, and care of the elderly.
Types of support: Operating budgets, equipment, matching funds, research, special projects, general purposes, scholarship funds.
Limitations: Giving primarily in in the Midwest, with preference to the Chicago, IL, metropolitan area. No grants to individuals, or for endowment funds; no loans.
Publications: Program policy statement, application guidelines.
Application information: Submit proposal only when invited. Application form not required.
Initial approach: Letter
Copies of proposal: 1
Board meeting date(s): Mar., June, Sept., and Dec.
Final notification: 2 to 3 months
Write: John R. Siragusa, V.P.
Officers and Directors:* Ross D. Siragusa,* Pres.; John R. Siragusa,* V.P. and Secy.-Treas.; Roy M. Adams, George E. Driscoll, Alisa S. Perrotte, Melvyn H. Schneider, Martha P. Siragusa, Richard D. Siragusa, Ross D. Siragusa, Jr., Theodore M. Siragusa, James B. Wilson.
Number of staff: 1 full-time professional; 1 full-time support.
Employer Identification Number: 363100492

2137
Skidmore, Owings & Merrill Foundation ⌘
1365 North Astor St.
Chicago 60610 (312) 951-8006

Established in 1978.
Donor(s): Skidmore, Owings & Merrill.
Foundation type: Company-sponsored
Financial data (yr. ended 8/31/88): Assets, $2,961,846 (M); gifts received, $359,042; expenditures, $386,770, including $43,400 for 9 grants to individuals.
Purpose and activities: Grants "for the purpose of education, research, or publications in or directly related to the fields of architecture or architectural engineering."
Types of support: Fellowships.
Publications: Financial statement.
Application information:
Initial approach: Proposal
Deadline(s): None
Write: Sonia Cooke, Administrative Dir.
Officers and Directors: Bruce J. Graham, Chair.; Marc E. Goldstein, Vice-Chair.; Diane Legge Lohan, Secy.-Treas.; and 13 additional directors.
Employer Identification Number: 362969068

2138
Smail Family Foundation ⌘
1000 North Lakeshore Plaza, Apt. 27A
Chicago 60611

Established in 1965.
Foundation type: Independent
Financial data (yr. ended 6/30/87): Assets, $9,223 (M); gifts received, $194,000; expenditures, $199,840, including $198,990 for 28 grants (high: $150,000; low: $50).
Purpose and activities: "To further the prevention and relief of human suffering"; with emphasis on a medical center, health organizations, hospitals, and social services.
Types of support: General purposes.
Limitations: Giving primarily in Chicago, IL.
Application information: Contributes only to pre-selected organizations. Applications not accepted.
Trustee: Anne W. Smail.
Employer Identification Number: 366136148

2139
Smith Charitable Trust
c/o Gordon Smith
P.O. Box 38
Rockford 61105 (815) 965-0772

Trust established in 1956 in IL.
Donor(s): Smith Oil Corp., Carl A. Smith,† Byron C. Marlowe.
Foundation type: Independent
Financial data (yr. ended 12/31/88): Assets, $3,034,709 (M); gifts received, $32,000; expenditures, $163,700, including $156,575 for grants.
Purpose and activities: Emphasis on hospitals, higher education, and youth and child welfare; grants also for cultural activities and civic affairs.
Types of support: Annual campaigns, building funds, capital campaigns, equipment, scholarship funds, seed money, special projects.
Limitations: Giving limited to IL. No support for churches and schools. No grants to individuals.
Application information: New grant commitments are not being made. Applications not accepted.
Board meeting date(s): Dec. 15
Trustees: Howard Bell, David S. Paddock, C. Gordon Smith.
Number of staff: None.
Employer Identification Number: 366078557

2140
Harry L. & John L. Smysor Memorial Fund ⌘ ☆
c/o First National Bank of Mattoon
1515 Charleston Ave.
Mattoon 61938-3932 (217) 234-7454

Established in 1982.
Donor(s): John L. Smysor.†
Foundation type: Independent
Financial data (yr. ended 5/31/89): Assets, $2,950,664 (M); gifts received, $100,000; expenditures, $120,852, including $3,850 for 6 grants to individuals (high: $2,750; low: $100).
Purpose and activities: Awards scholarships to high school students for higher education.
Types of support: Student aid.
Limitations: Giving primarily in IL.
Application information: Application form available from Windsor, IL, high school or from trustee bank. Application form required.
Write: Clark W. Brogan, Trust Officer, First National Bank of Mattoon
Trustees: Clarence Doehring, Orris Seng, First National Bank of Mattoon.
Employer Identification Number: 371160678

2141
Fred B. Snite Foundation
550 Frontage Rd., Suite 3082
North Field 60093 (312) 446-7705

Incorporated in 1945 in IL.
Donor(s): Fred B. Snite,† Local Loan Co.
Foundation type: Independent
Financial data (yr. ended 06/30/88): Assets, $8,034,473 (M); expenditures, $389,681, including $288,800 for grants.
Purpose and activities: Grants largely for Roman Catholic church support and church-related educational institutions.
Application information:
Initial approach: Proposal
Deadline(s): None
Write: Terrance J. Dillon, Pres.
Officers: Terrance J. Dillon,* Pres.; Mary L. Dillon,* V.P.; Katherine B. Williams,* V.P.; Harry B. Holmes, Jr., Secy.; Allen E. Eliot, Treas.
Directors:* Nicholas Rassas.
Employer Identification Number: 366084839

2142
Soft Sheen Foundation ⌘
1000 East 87th St.
Chicago 60619-6391

Established in 1981 in IL.
Foundation type: Independent
Financial data (yr. ended 2/29/88): Assets, $1,985,537 (M); gifts received, $34,685; expenditures, $96,663, including $67,227 for 1 grant.
Purpose and activities: Support primarily for African-American educational and cultural organizations; support also for a cosmetology association.
Application information:
Deadline(s): None
Directors: Betty A. Gardner, Edward G. Gardner, Robert Martin, Richard McGuire.
Employer Identification Number: 363211525

2143
Solo Cup Foundation
1700 Old Deerfield Rd.
Highland Park 60035

Established in 1959 in IL.
Donor(s): Solo Cup Co.
Foundation type: Company-sponsored
Financial data (yr. ended 03/31/89): Assets, $7,771,305 (M); gifts received, $7,732,473; expenditures, $80,991, including $80,500 for 7 grants (high: $50,000; low: $500).
Purpose and activities: Grants primarily for higher and secondary education and Christian religious organizations.
Application information: Application form not required.
Deadline(s): None
Write: Ronald L. Whaley, Pres.
Employer Identification Number: 366062327

2144
Sarah M. Solomon ⌘ ☆
c/o First National Bank of Chicago
One First National Plaza, Suite 0484
Chicago 60670 (312) 732-5586

Established in 1979.
Foundation type: Independent
Financial data (yr. ended 12/31/88): Assets, $2,658,395 (M); gifts received, $47,451; expenditures, $221,528, including $168,700 for 5 grants (high: $60,500; low: $7,000).
Purpose and activities: Support for higher education.
Limitations: Giving primarily in Chicago, IL. No grants to individuals.
Application information: Contributes only to pre-selected organizations. Applications not accepted.
Write: Jane C. Williams
Trustees: L. Roy Papp, First National Bank of Chicago.
Employer Identification Number: 366613406

2145
Christine and Alfred Sonntag Foundation for Cancer Research ⌘ ☆
2200 East Devon Ave., Suite 220
Des Plaines 60018

Trust established in 1962 in CT.
Donor(s): Alfred Sonntag,† Christine Sonntag.†
Foundation type: Independent
Financial data (yr. ended 9/30/87): Assets, $33,878 (M); expenditures, $136,210, including $136,200 for 6 grants (high: $100,175; low: $25).
Purpose and activities: Support to institutions engaged in basic cancer cell research.
Limitations: No grants to individuals.

Application information: Contributes only to pre-selected organizations. Applications not accepted.
Trustees: Barry J. Carroll, Wallace E. Carroll.
Employer Identification Number: 066050572

2146
The Sophia Fund
53 West Jackson Blvd., Suite 626
Chicago 60604 (312) 663-1552

Established in 1983 in IL; established as a trust in 1985.
Donor(s): Lucia Woods Lindley.
Foundation type: Independent
Financial data (yr. ended 12/31/88): Assets, $24,666 (M); gifts received, $225,131; expenditures, $313,052, including $221,450 for 68 grants (high: $10,000; low: $500; average: $2,000-$5,000).
Purpose and activities: Grants to organizations whose efforts are directed solely or primarily towards women, and who are working in advocacy, community awareness and education, public policy areas, leadership development, the disadvantaged, research, or, on rare occasions, in pilot service projects. Preference is given to social change efforts rather than to social services.
Types of support: Operating budgets, general purposes, special projects, conferences and seminars, continuing support, matching funds, research, seed money, publications.
Limitations: Giving primarily in the Chicago, IL, metropolitan area; some funding for national organizations with national impact. No support for religious organizations for religious purposes, or medical research; grants rarely for social service agencies. No grants to individuals, or for scholarships or fellowships.
Publications: Grants list, informational brochure (including application guidelines).
Application information: Application form not required.
Initial approach: Proposal of not more than five pages
Copies of proposal: 1
Deadline(s): Mar. 1 and Sept. 1
Board meeting date(s): July and Nov.
Final notification: July and Nov.
Write: Sunny Fischer, Exec. Dir.
Officer: Sunny Fischer, Exec. Dir.
Trustee: Lucia Woods Lindley.
Number of staff: 2 full-time professional.
Employer Identification Number: 363395893

2147
Special People In Need ☆
500 West Madison St., Suite 3700
Chicago 60606 (312) 715-5000

Established in 1987.
Donor(s): Josephine M. Thompson, Katherine Morningstar Irrevocable Trust.
Foundation type: Independent
Financial data (yr. ended 12/31/89): Assets, $2,586,641 (M); gifts received, $5,902; expenditures, $116,607, including $92,100 for 14 grants (high: $15,000; low: $1,000) and $6,000 for 1 grant to an individual.
Purpose and activities: "To provide support to financially needy and handicapped persons...and scholarships and fellowships; grants for higher, secondary, and elementary education; the environment and conservation; and a hospital.
Types of support: Grants to individuals, student aid, fellowships, general purposes, scholarship funds, special projects.
Application information: Application form not required.
Initial approach: Proposal
Copies of proposal: 1
Deadline(s): None
Board meeting date(s): Spring and early winter, and as required
Write: Gary H. Kline, Secy.
Officers and Directors:* Molly M. Gerbaz,* Chair.; John M. Morningstar,* Vice-Chair.; Josephine H. Thompson,* Pres.; Larry D. Gerbaz,* V.P.; Leslie H. Morningstar,* V.P.; Gary H. Kline,* Secy.; Thomas A. Polachek,* Treas.; Kent Chandler, Jr.
Employer Identification Number: 581483651

2148
The Spencer Foundation ▼
900 North Michigan Ave., Suite 2800
Chicago 60611 (312) 337-7000

Incorporated in 1962 in IL.
Donor(s): Lyle M. Spencer.†
Foundation type: Independent
Financial data (yr. ended 03/31/89): Assets, $224,871,503 (M); expenditures, $13,533,822, including $10,686,022 for 153 grants (high: $1,880,100; low: $4,800; average: $20,000-$90,000).
Purpose and activities: Supports research in the social and behavioral sciences offering promise of contributing to the improvement of education in one or another of its forms in the U.S. or abroad.
Types of support: Research.
Limitations: No grants to individuals (except those working under the auspices of an institution), or for capital funds, general purposes, operating or continuing support, sabbatical supplements, work in instructional or curriculum development, any kind of training or service program, scholarships, travel fellowships, endowment funds, predoctoral research, or matching gifts; no loans.
Publications: Annual report (including application guidelines), informational brochure, newsletter.
Application information: Submit full proposal only upon request. Application form not required.
Initial approach: Letter or preliminary brief proposal
Copies of proposal: 3
Deadline(s): None
Board meeting date(s): Jan., Apr., July, and Oct.
Final notification: After meetings
Write: Marion M. Faldet, V.P.
Officers: Lawrence A. Cremin,* Pres.; Marion M. Faldet, V.P. and Secy.; Linda M. Schumacher, Treas.
Directors:* David Tatel, Chair.; Catherine M. Spencer, Vice-Chair.; Jacob W. Getzels, Patricia Albjerg Graham, George A. Ranney, Jr., John S. Reed, Donna E. Shalala, William J. Wilson.
Number of staff: 5 full-time professional; 3 part-time professional; 4 full-time support; 1 part-time support.
Employer Identification Number: 366078558

2149
The Otho S. A. Sprague Memorial Institute ⌑
c/o Harris Trust and Savings Bank
190 South LaSalle St., Fourth Fl.
Chicago 60690 (312) 461-7054

Incorporated in 1910 in IL.
Donor(s): Members of the Sprague family.
Foundation type: Independent
Financial data (yr. ended 12/31/88): Assets, $13,028,669 (M); gifts received, $150,000; expenditures, $731,067, including $600,000 for 5 grants (high: $190,000; low: $15,000).
Purpose and activities: To investigate the cause of disease and the prevention and relief of human suffering caused by disease. In accordance with the wishes of the founder, support primarily to the major private, medical teaching and research universities in Chicago.
Types of support: Research, special projects.
Limitations: Giving limited to Chicago, IL. No grants to individuals, or for building or endowment funds, general purposes, scholarships, fellowships, or matching gifts; no loans.
Publications: Annual report.
Application information: Application form not required.
Initial approach: Letter
Copies of proposal: 4
Deadline(s): None
Board meeting date(s): Semiannually in May and Dec.
Write: Thomas E. Macior
Officers and Trustees: Vernon Armour, Pres.; Charles C. Hoffner III, V.P.; Steward S. Dixon, Secy.; Van R. Gathany, Treas.; Harry N. Beaty, M.D., John P. Bent, Charles F. Clark, Jr., Leo M. Henikoff, M.D., Leon O. Jacobson, M.D.
Number of staff: None.
Employer Identification Number: 366068723

2150
Square D Foundation ▼
1415 South Roselle Rd.
Palatine 60067 (312) 397-2600
Application address: Executive Plaza, Palatine, IL 60067

Incorporated in 1956 in MI.
Donor(s): Square D Co.
Foundation type: Company-sponsored
Financial data (yr. ended 12/31/89): Assets, $456,402 (M); gifts received, $1,300,000; qualifying distributions, $1,400,555, including $1,246,521 for 230 grants (high: $50,000; low: $250; average: $500-$5,000) and $154,034 for 552 employee matching gifts.
Purpose and activities: Emphasis on community funds, higher education, and youth; support also for hospitals, health agencies, the arts, and employee-related scholarships administered by National Merit Scholarship Corporation.
Types of support: Building funds, employee-related scholarships, equipment, employee matching gifts, endowment funds, operating

budgets, matching funds, professorships, scholarship funds.
Limitations: Giving primarily in areas of company operations, with emphasis on the Midwest and South. No support for organizations already receiving support through United Way, religious organizations, political groups, or labor unions. No grants to individuals.
Publications: Application guidelines.
Application information:
Initial approach: Letter; no telephone inquiries
Copies of proposal: 1
Deadline(s): None
Board meeting date(s): As necessary
Final notification: 3 months
Write: Charles E. Hutchinson, Secy.
Officers and Directors:* W.W. Kurczewski,* Pres.; Thomas L. Bindley,* V.P. and Treas.; Juris Vikmanis,* V.P. and Treas.; C.E. Hutchinson,* Secy.
Number of staff: 1 part-time support.
Employer Identification Number: 366054195

2151
A. E. Staley, Jr. Foundation ⌑
c/o Citizens National Bank of Decatur
236 North Water St.
Decatur 62525

Trust established in 1955 in IL.
Donor(s): Augustus Eugene Staley, Jr.
Foundation type: Independent
Financial data (yr. ended 12/31/88): Assets, $4,113,219 (M); expenditures, $157,670, including $147,026 for 39 grants (high: $38,469; low: $85).
Purpose and activities: Emphasis on higher education, hospitals, a community fund, and health agencies.
Limitations: Giving primarily in IL.
Application information: Contributes only to pre-selected organizations. Applications not accepted.
Trustee: Citizens National Bank of Decatur.
Employer Identification Number: 376023961

2152
State Farm Companies Foundation ▼
One State Farm Plaza
Bloomington 61710 (309) 766-2039

Incorporated in 1963 in IL.
Donor(s): State Farm Insurance Cos.
Foundation type: Company-sponsored
Financial data (yr. ended 12/31/87): Assets, $4,079,946 (M); gifts received, $4,000,000; expenditures, $1,459,011, including $1,444,950 for grants (high: $178,709; low: $11; average: $500-$10,000).
Purpose and activities: Support for higher education, including scholarships for children of employees, a business fellowship program, exceptional student fellowships, and promotion of educational activities related to the insurance business; grants are generally to national organizations; support also for community funds, hospitals, and a center for automobile safety.
Types of support: Fellowships, scholarship funds, employee-related scholarships, employee matching gifts.
Limitations: No grants to individuals (except for employee-related scholarship programs).
Publications: Annual report, informational brochure.
Application information: Funds largely committed; no direct appeals accepted; scholarship and fellowship recipients must be nominated by their schools. Application form required.
Deadline(s): For scholarships, Dec. 31; for fellowships, Feb. 28; for doctoral program, Mar. 31
Board meeting date(s): Mar., June, Sept., and Dec.
Write: David Polzin, Asst. V.P., Progs.
Officers and Directors:* Edward B. Rust, Jr.,* Chair., Pres., and Treas.; Laura P. Sullivan,* V.P. and Secy.; Robert S. Eckley, Charles O. Galvin, Thomas C. Morrill.
Number of staff: None.
Employer Identification Number: 366110423

2153
Donna Wolf Steigerwaldt Foundation, Inc.
200 North LaSalle St., Suite 2100
Chicago 60601-1095
Application address: 2300 60th St., Kenosha, WI 53140; Tel.: (414) 658-8111, ext. 288

Established in 1980 in IL.
Donor(s): Donna Wolf Steigerwaldt, Jockey International, Inc.
Foundation type: Independent
Financial data (yr. ended 10/31/89): Assets, $1,872,154 (M); gifts received, $10,000; expenditures, $127,676, including $122,121 for 65 grants (high: $12,500; low: $15; average: $100-$1,000).
Purpose and activities: Giving primarily for higher education; support also for musical organizations.
Types of support: Annual campaigns, building funds, continuing support, scholarship funds.
Limitations: Giving primarily in WI, FL, and IL. No grants to individuals.
Application information: Contributes only to pre-selected organizations. Application form not required. Applications not accepted.
Initial approach: Letter
Deadline(s): None
Write: Noreen A. Wilkinson, Secy.
Officers and Directors:* Donna Wolf Steigerwaldt,* Pres. and Treas.; Debra Steigerwaldt Waller,* V.P.; William Steigerwaldt,* V.P.; Noreen A. Wilkinson,* Secy.; Linda Steigerwaldt Davis, Michael R. Shelist.
Employer Identification Number: 363104409

2154
Irvin Stern Foundation ⌑
53 West Jackson Blvd., Suite 930
Chicago 60604 (312) 786-9355

Trust established in 1957 in IL.
Donor(s): Irvin Stern.†
Foundation type: Independent
Financial data (yr. ended 9/30/88): Assets, $7,327,820 (M); expenditures, $564,643, including $491,500 for 57 grants (high: $100,000; low: $1,000; average: $3,000-$20,000).
Purpose and activities: Emphasis on meeting the needs of the Jewish community in the United States and Israel; support for efforts to combat heart disease, mental illness, and cancer; for vocational training and help for the aged; and for improving urban living conditions via neighborhood organizations.
Types of support: Operating budgets, continuing support, seed money, emergency funds, matching funds, conferences and seminars, equipment, internships.
Limitations: Giving primarily in Chicago, IL; New York, NY; and San Diego, CA. No support for religious or political purposes. No grants to individuals, or for endowment funds, deficit financing, or advertising or program books.
Publications: Application guidelines, program policy statement, 990-PF.
Application information: Application form required.
Initial approach: Letter
Deadline(s): Submit proposal preferably in Mar. or Aug.; deadlines Apr. 1 and Sept. 1
Board meeting date(s): Apr. and Oct.
Write: Mrs. Rae W. Epstein, Secy.
Officer: Rae W. Epstein, Secy.
Trustees: E. Allan Epstein, Jeffrey Epstein, Stuart Epstein, Arthur Winter, Dorothy G. Winter, Stanley Winter.
Number of staff: 1 part-time support.
Employer Identification Number: 366047947

2155
Jerome H. Stone Family Foundation ⌑
150 North Michigan Ave.
Chicago 60601

Established in 1963 in IL.
Donor(s): Jerome H. Stone, Cynthia Raskin.
Foundation type: Independent
Financial data (yr. ended 12/31/87): Assets, $3,202,546 (M); gifts received, $87,588; expenditures, $130,434, including $128,297 for 89 grants (high: $16,150; low: $25).
Purpose and activities: Support for Jewish organizations, culture, education, health, and social services.
Application information: Contributes only to pre-selected organizations. Applications not accepted.
Officers: Jerome H. Stone, Pres.; James H. Stone, V.P.; Cynthia Raskin, Secy.
Director: Ellen Stone Belic.
Employer Identification Number: 366061300

2156
Marvin Stone Family Foundation ⌑
c/o Marvin Stone
150 North Michigan Ave.
Chicago 60601

Donor(s): Marvin N. Stone.
Foundation type: Independent
Financial data (yr. ended 12/31/87): Assets, $2,040,816 (M); expenditures, $70,323, including $69,680 for 78 grants (high: $10,000; low: $25).
Purpose and activities: Grants primarily for cultural programs, health services, Jewish welfare, and other Jewish giving.
Limitations: Giving primarily in IL, especially Chicago.

Application information: Contributes only to pre-selected organizations. Applications not accepted.
Officers: Marvin N. Stone, Pres.; Carol Stone, Secy.; Roger W. Stone, Treas.
Director: Avery J. Stone.
Employer Identification Number: 366061303

2157
The Norman H. Stone Family Foundation ⌑
c/o Stone Container Corp.
150 North Michigan Ave.
Chicago 60601

Established in 1963 in IL.
Donor(s): Norman H. Stone,† Ira Stone, Alan Stone.
Foundation type: Independent
Financial data (yr. ended 12/31/88): Assets, $1,905,643 (M); expenditures, $113,069, including $88,938 for 83 grants (high: $30,000; low: $20).
Purpose and activities: Support primarily for health services, Jewish welfare funds and other Jewish giving, and social services.
Limitations: Giving primarily in IL. No grants to individuals.
Application information: Contributes only to pre-selected organizations. Applications not accepted.
Officers and Director:* Alan Stone, Pres.; Ira Stone, V.P. and Secy.; Judi H. Stern, V.P.; Ida F. Stone,* V.P.
Employer Identification Number: 366061301

2158
Roger and Susan Stone Family Foundation ⌑
150 North Michigan Ave.
Chicago 60601-7508

Established in 1969 in IL.
Donor(s): Susan Stone, Roger Stone.
Foundation type: Independent
Financial data (yr. ended 12/31/87): Assets, $169,124 (M); gifts received, $168,261; expenditures, $198,519, including $196,670 for 65 grants (high: $57,300; low: $50).
Purpose and activities: Support for higher education and cultural programs.
Limitations: Giving primarily in Chicago, IL.
Application information: Contributes only to pre-selected organizations. Applications not accepted.
Directors: Roger Stone, Susan Stone.
Employer Identification Number: 237026711

2159
Stone Foundation, Inc. ⌑
150 North Michigan Ave.
Chicago 60601

Incorporated in 1944 in IL.
Donor(s): Stone Container Corp.
Foundation type: Company-sponsored
Financial data (yr. ended 12/31/88): Assets, $1,382,766 (M); gifts received, $1,001,000; expenditures, $736,309, including $691,075 for 71 grants (high: $200,000; low: $40) and $41,750 for 21 grants to individuals (high: $2,000; low: $250).
Purpose and activities: Emphasis on Jewish welfare funds, higher education, hospitals, and cultural activities; scholarships limited to children of employees with two or more years of service.
Types of support: Employee-related scholarships.
Application information: Application form required.
Deadline(s): Apr. 1 for scholarships
Write: Arnold Brookstone, Admin.
Officers and Directors:* Roger W. Stone,* Pres.; Jerome H. Stone,* V.P. and Secy.-Treas.; Marvin N. Stone,* V.P.
Employer Identification Number: 366063761

2160
W. Clement & Jessie V. Stone Foundation
P.O. Box 649
Lake Forest 60045 (708) 615-0228

Incorporated in 1958 in IL.
Donor(s): W. Clement Stone, Jessie V. Stone.
Foundation type: Independent
Financial data (yr. ended 12/31/89): Assets, $2,347,516 (M); gifts received, $775,000; expenditures, $195,000, including $124,200 for 3 grants (high: $70,000; low: $10,000; average: $10,000-$70,000).
Purpose and activities: "Making this world a better place in which to live" through programs which seek to put "Positive Mental Attitude" philosophy into action in the area of homelessness.
Types of support: Technical assistance.
Limitations: Giving limited to Chicago, IL. No grants to individuals, or for building or endowment funds, scholarships, or fellowships.
Publications: Annual report, informational brochure.
Application information: Applications not accepted.
Board meeting date(s): Twice a year
Write: Maree G. Bullock, Exec. Dir.
Officers and Directors:* W. Clement Stone,* Chair.; Norman C. Stone,* Pres.; Steven Stone,* 1st V.P. and Secy.-Treas.; Barbara Stone,* V.P.; Jessie V. Stone,* V.P.; Maree G. Bullock,* Exec. Dir.; Sandra Stone Knecht, James T. Rhind, Linda E. Rupp, Barbara West Stone, Michael Stone, Norah Sharp Stone.
Number of staff: 1 full-time professional.
Employer Identification Number: 362498125

2161
Madeline B. & Henry H. Straus Endowment Fund ⌑ ☆
c/o American National Bank & Trust Co. of Chicago
33 North LaSalle St.
Chicago 60602
Application address: c/o American National Bank & Trust Co. of Chicago, Box DD, Personal Trust Division, Chicago, IL 60690

Established in 1945.
Donor(s): Madeline B. Willner.
Foundation type: Independent
Financial data (yr. ended 12/31/88): Assets, $341,749 (M); gifts received, $52,058; expenditures, $321,718, including $316,146 for 91 grants (high: $250,000; low: $10).
Purpose and activities: Giving primarily for hospitals; support also for secondary and higher education and arts and culture.
Limitations: Giving primarily in Chicago, IL.
Application information: Application form not required.
Initial approach: Letter
Deadline(s): None
Trustee: American National Bank & Trust Co. of Chicago.
Employer Identification Number: 366035112

2162
Robert D. Stuart, Jr. Foundation ⌑ ☆
321 North Clark St., Suite 340
Chicago 60610

Established in 1985 in IL.
Donor(s): Robert D. Stuart, Jr.
Foundation type: Independent
Financial data (yr. ended 11/30/88): Assets, $1,159,399 (M); gifts received, $96,469; expenditures, $55,682, including $53,000 for 26 grants (high: $15,000; low: $500).
Purpose and activities: Giving primarily for arts and culture, education, and intercultural relations.
Limitations: Giving primarily in Chicago, IL. No grants to individuals.
Application information: Contributes only to pre-selected organizations. Applications not accepted.
Officers and Directors: Robert D. Stuart, Jr., Pres.; Barbara E. Stuart, V.P.; Linda Vincent, Secy.-Treas.; Donald C. Pillsbury.
Employer Identification Number: 363422731

2163
Jacob Stump, Jr. and Clara Stump Memorial Scholarship Fund ⌑
c/o Central National Bank of Mattoon
Broadway and Charleston at 14th St.
Mattoon 61938 (217) 234-6434

Trust established in 1967 in IL.
Donor(s): Jacob Stump, Jr.†
Foundation type: Independent
Financial data (yr. ended 7/31/88): Assets, $1,317,894 (M); expenditures, $86,442, including $50,050 for 245 grants to individuals.
Purpose and activities: Scholarships to high school graduates from four local counties.
Types of support: Student aid.
Limitations: Giving limited to high school graduates from Coles, Cumberland, Douglas, and Moultrie counties, IL, attending state-supported colleges and universities in IL.
Application information: Applications available at high schools and bank. Application form required.
Deadline(s): Apr. 1
Write: Malcolm F. O'Neill, Trust Officer, Central National Bank of Mattoon
Trustee: Central National Bank of Mattoon.
Employer Identification Number: 376064295

2164
Sudix Foundation ⌑
c/o Wesley M. Dixon, Jr.
400 Skokie Blvd., Suite 675
Northbrook 60062

Established in 1985 in IL.

Donor(s): Wesley M. Dixon, Jr.
Foundation type: Independent
Financial data (yr. ended 12/31/87): Assets, $3,168,567 (M); expenditures, $153,761, including $150,000 for 7 grants (high: $50,000; low: $5,000).
Purpose and activities: Support primarily for environmental organizations.
Application information: Contributes only to pre-selected organizations. Applications not accepted.
Officers: Wesley M. Dixon, Jr., Pres.; Suzanne S. Dixon, V.P. and Secy.-Treas.
Director: Susan R. Piggott.
Employer Identification Number: 363377946

2165
Sulzer Family Foundation
1940 West Irving Park Rd.
Chicago 60613

Incorporated in 1956 in IL.
Donor(s): Grace E. Sulzer.
Foundation type: Independent
Financial data (yr. ended 12/31/88): Assets, $3,634,546 (M); expenditures, $220,697, including $200,100 for 78 grants (high: $15,000; low: $100).
Purpose and activities: Giving for higher, secondary, and other education; programs for youth and the aged; community development; libraries; and museums.
Types of support: Continuing support, operating budgets, scholarship funds.
Limitations: Giving primarily in IL, particularly the Ravenswood and Lakeview areas of Chicago.
Application information: Application form not required.
Deadline(s): None
Board meeting date(s): Nov.
Officers: John J. Hoellen, Pres.; Rev. George Rice, Secy.; Arthur Teleser, Treas.
Directors: Richard Bjorklund, Robert B. Hoellen, Sherwin Willens.
Number of staff: 1 full-time support.
Employer Identification Number: 362466016

2166
Sundstrand Corporation Foundation ▼
4949 Harrison Ave.
P.O. Box 7003
Rockford 61125 (815) 226-6000

Incorporated in 1952 in IL.
Donor(s): Sundstrand Corp.
Foundation type: Company-sponsored
Financial data (yr. ended 10/31/88): Assets, $1,486,374 (M); expenditures, $1,001,695, including $845,850 for 112 grants (high: $122,000; low: $450) and $144,509 for employee matching gifts.
Purpose and activities: Grants for community funds, education, particularly higher education, hospitals, and youth agencies; support also for the handicapped, social service and health agencies, an employee-related scholarship program and cultural programs.
Types of support: Building funds, equipment, scholarship funds, employee-related scholarships, employee matching gifts, capital campaigns.
Limitations: Giving primarily in areas of company operations. No support for projects of a religious or political nature. No grants to individuals (except for employee-related scholarships), or for operating funds.
Application information: Application form not required.
Initial approach: Letter
Copies of proposal: 1
Deadline(s): None
Board meeting date(s): Mar., June, Sept., and Dec.
Final notification: 2 months
Write: Clarice Kieselburg, Secy.
Officers: Don R. O'Hare,* Pres.; Philip W. Polgreen,* V.P.; Clarice Kieselburg, Secy.; Jim White, Treas.
Directors:* Richard Schilling, Claude Vernon.
Employer Identification Number: 366072477

2167
Supera Family Foundation ⌑
2001 North Halsted
Chicago 60614

Foundation type: Independent
Financial data (yr. ended 11/30/87): Assets, $96,240 (M); gifts received, $197,284; expenditures, $106,458, including $106,458 for grants (high: $69,000).
Purpose and activities: Support primarily to Jewish welfare organizations and general charitable organizations.
Trustee: Michael Supera.
Employer Identification Number: 363013584

2168
Susman and Asher Foundation ⌑
c/o Norman Asher
134 North LaSalle St., Suite 1900
Chicago 60602

Incorporated in 1949 in IL.
Donor(s): Louis Susman, and members of the Asher family.
Foundation type: Independent
Financial data (yr. ended 12/31/87): Assets, $469,288 (M); gifts received, $50,613; expenditures, $287,091, including $270,473 for 39 grants (high: $50,000; low: $100).
Purpose and activities: Emphasis on higher, including religious, education, and Jewish welfare funds.
Application information: Contributes only to pre-selected organizations. Applications not accepted.
Officer and Trustees: Norman Asher, Pres.; Donald Asher, Gilbert Asher, Helen Asher, Robert Asher, Louis Susman.
Employer Identification Number: 366049760

2169
Swiss Benevolent Society of Chicago ⌑
P.O. Box 2137
Chicago 60690

Established in 1872 in IL.
Foundation type: Independent
Financial data (yr. ended 12/31/88): Assets, $1,169,360 (M); gifts received, $6,997; expenditures, $92,653, including $196 for grants and $53,540 for 53 grants to individuals (high: $2,600; low: $250).
Purpose and activities: To aid individuals of Swiss descent; giving includes scholarships for undergraduate study and relief assistance in case of need or emergency; limited support for Swiss organizations in the form of grants or loans.
Types of support: Student aid, grants to individuals, loans.
Limitations: Giving limited to the Midwest, with emphasis on IL.
Application information: Application form required.
Deadline(s): Scholarship applications must be postmarked by Mar. 4
Final notification: No later than May 10 for scholarship winners
Officers: Felix Ganz, Pres.; Erwin H. Bareiss, V.P.; Carla Crosby, Secy.; Werner Gartner, Treas.
Directors: Ernest R. Brauchli, and 10 additional directors.
Employer Identification Number: 366076395

2170
Cyrus Tang Scholarship Foundation ⌑ ☆
1965 Pratt Blvd.
Elk Grove Village 60007
Application address: 10 West 35th St., 19th Fl., Chicago, IL 60616

Donor(s): Tang Industries, Inc.
Foundation type: Independent
Financial data (yr. ended 5/31/89): Assets, $57,728 (M); gifts received, $136,400; expenditures, $122,110, including $105,828 for 7 grants to individuals (high: $15,670; low: $13,650).
Purpose and activities: Awards scholarships in engineering, physics, chemistry, architecture, or business to citizens of the People's Republic of China who intend to return to China after completion of their course of study in the U.S.
Types of support: Student aid.
Application information: Applicants must be member of American Assoc. of Independent Engineering Colleges.
Deadline(s): None
Write: Nora Kyger, Exec. Dir.
Officers and Directors: Nora Kyger, Exec. Dir.; Clyde P. Watkins, Treas.; Paul K. Rhoads, Cecilia Tang, Michael Tang, Michael Zavis.
Employer Identification Number: 363322542

2171
Charles Taveggia Mary Antonini Foundation ⌑ ☆
101 South Park
Herrin 62948-3609 (618) 942-6666

Established in 1981.
Foundation type: Independent
Financial data (yr. ended 4/30/89): Assets, $1,339,211 (M); expenditures, $63,661, including $46,389 for 6 grants (high: $44,182; low: $2,207) and $2,000 for 4 grants to individuals of $500 each.
Purpose and activities: Giving primarily to a Catholic church; also awards grants to local high school seniors.
Types of support: Grants to individuals.
Limitations: Giving primarily in Herrin, IL.
Application information: Application form not required.

Initial approach: Letter
Deadline(s): None
Write: Ed Goodwin, Trustee
Trustees: Herman Colombo, Edward L. Goodwin, Dorothy Mercer, Paul S. Murphy, Bank of Herrin.
Employer Identification Number: 371117154

2172
Mr. & Mrs. George W. Taylor Foundation ⌑
c/o Robert W. Baird & Co.
1700 North Alpine, Suite 302
Rockford 61107

Established in 1984 in IL.
Foundation type: Independent
Financial data (yr. ended 12/31/87): Assets, $182,615 (M); gifts received, $272,319; expenditures, $223,830, including $217,118 for 90 grants (high: $139,753; low: $10).
Purpose and activities: Giving primarily to museums and general charities; also grants scholarships for students at University of Minnesota Institute of Technology.
Types of support: Student aid.
Application information:
Initial approach: Letter
Deadline(s): None
Write: James Thiede, Trustee
Trustees: Stephen R. Hill, James Thiede.
Employer Identification Number: 363321315

2173
Technical Foundation of America
P.O. Box 168
Glen Ellyn 60138
Alternate application address: Eugene Martin, V.P., P.O. Box 1622, San Marcos, TX 78666

Chartered in 1898 in MA as American Technical Society; incorporated in 1980 in IL under current name.
Foundation type: Independent
Financial data (yr. ended 06/30/89): Assets, $4,461,753 (M); expenditures, $295,273, including $178,179 for 19 grants (high: $33,270; low: $600; average: $3,000-$30,000).
Purpose and activities: Grants, technical assistance, and programs to the industrial education community at the national, state, and local levels; interests include evaluating and establishing priorities for critical industrial issues, improving leadership, upgrading industrial education, increasing effectiveness of industrial pilot programs, and raising the public perception of industrial education. In future years, giving will rotate on an annual basis to national and state organizations, local school systems, and colleges and universities.
Types of support: Seed money, matching funds, consulting services, technical assistance, special projects, research, publications, conferences and seminars.
Limitations: No support for cultural, artistic, or religious groups. No grants to individuals, or for general support, operating programs, capital or endowment funds, scholarships, fellowships, continuing support, annual campaigns, emergency funds, or deficit financing; no loans.
Publications: Program policy statement, application guidelines.
Application information: Application form not required.
Initial approach: Letter or proposal
Copies of proposal: 2
Deadline(s): Dec. 1
Board meeting date(s): Quarterly
Final notification: 3 months
Write: David E. Hall, Pres.
Officers and Trustees:* David E. Hall,* Pres.; G. Eugene Martin,* V.P.; John Eames,* Secy.-Treas.
Number of staff: None.
Employer Identification Number: 360730670

2174
The Thorson Foundation ⌑
399 Fullerton Pkwy.
Chicago 60614 (312) 327-2687

Established in 1954 in IL.
Donor(s): Robert D. Thorson,† Reuben Thorson,† Dorothy W. Thorson.
Foundation type: Independent
Financial data (yr. ended 12/31/88): Assets, $1,907,038 (M); expenditures, $76,076, including $71,175 for 56 grants (high: $12,150; low: $50).
Purpose and activities: Grants primarily for higher and other education, cultural programs, health services, hospitals, and medical research; support also for religion and civic affairs.
Types of support: Annual campaigns, capital campaigns, continuing support, fellowships, scholarship funds.
Limitations: No grants to individuals.
Application information: Contributes only to pre-selected organizations. Applications not accepted.
Write: Dorothy W. Thorson, Pres.
Officers and Directors:* Dorothy W. Thorson,* Pres.; Virginia T. Goodall,* V.P. and Treas.; John C. Goodall III,* Secy.
Employer Identification Number: 366051916

2175
Thomas & Gertrude Tibstra Charitable Foundation ⌑
119 South Old Creek Rd.
Palos Park 60464

Foundation type: Independent
Financial data (yr. ended 12/31/88): Assets, $2,853,756 (M); expenditures, $108,409, including $107,000 for 9 grants (high: $20,000; low: $4,000).
Purpose and activities: Support primarily for Christian education and religious programs.
Limitations: Giving primarily in MI and IL. No grants to individuals.
Application information: Contributes only to pre-selected organizations. Applications not accepted.
Officers and Directors: Thomas Tibstra, Pres.; Gertrude Tibstra, Secy.; Larry Tibstra.
Employer Identification Number: 363215222

2176
Tyndale House Foundation ⌑
336 Gundersen Dr., Box 80
Wheaton 60187 (312) 668-8300

Established in 1964 in IL.
Donor(s): Kenneth N. Taylor, Howard A. Elkind, ENB Charitable Trust.
Foundation type: Independent
Financial data (yr. ended 12/31/87): Assets, $199,910 (M); gifts received, $761,697; expenditures, $798,816, including $776,750 for grants (high: $400,000).
Purpose and activities: To promote the gospel through Christian literature projects, Bible translations, and Christian services and activities in the U.S. and abroad.
Types of support: General purposes, special projects, publications, matching funds.
Limitations: No support for libraries. No grants to individuals, or for building or endowment funds, scholarships, fellowships, or personnel support.
Publications: Financial statement, informational brochure (including application guidelines).
Application information: New grants awarded on a limited basis. Application form not required.
Initial approach: Letter or telephone
Copies of proposal: 10
Deadline(s): Middle of Aug.
Board meeting date(s): Early Sept. for grantmaking and as required
Write: Mrs. Mary Kleine Yehling, Exec. Dir.
Officers and Managers: Edwin L. Frizen, Jr., Pres.; Sam F. Wolgemuth, Sr., V.P.; Margaret W. Taylor, Secy.-Treas.; Mary Gieser, Peter Gunther, Wendell C. Hawley, Elizabeth Knighton, Paul Mathews, Kenneth N. Taylor, Mark D. Taylor.
Number of staff: 1 part-time professional.
Employer Identification Number: 362555516

2177
United Airlines Foundation ▼ ⌑
(Formerly UAL Foundation)
P.O. Box 66100
Chicago 60666 (312) 952-5714

Incorporated in 1951 in IL.
Donor(s): United Air Lines, Inc.
Foundation type: Company-sponsored
Financial data (yr. ended 12/31/88): Assets, $7,161,712 (M); gifts received, $5,010,550; expenditures, $1,625,348, including $1,613,345 for 187 grants (high: $234,000; low: $500; average: $2,000-$15,000).
Purpose and activities: Emphasis on programs encompassing education and educational reform, arts and culture, the United Way, and the Friendly Skies program which airlifts terminally and critically ill children to hospitals for treatment.
Types of support: Annual campaigns, operating budgets, research, employee-related scholarships, employee matching gifts.
Limitations: Giving limited to areas of company operations. No support for organizations established to influence legislation, labor unions, fraternal or veterans' organizations, political activities, or propaganda, or for sectarian religious organizations. No grants to individuals, or for endowments, advertising campaigns, purchase

of tickets or tables for fundraising dinners or similar events, club memberships, conferences, or travel; no loans.
Publications: Application guidelines.
Application information: Application form not required.
Initial approach: Proposal
Copies of proposal: 1
Deadline(s): 60 days prior to board meetings
Board meeting date(s): Mar., June, Sept., and Dec.
Final notification: 1 month
Write: Paul G. George, Exec. Dir.
Officers: Stephen M. Wolf,* Pres.; Paul G. George,* V.P. and Exec. Dir.; Eileen M. Younglove,* Secy. and Contribs. Mgr.
Directors:* James M. Guyette, Edward Hoenicke, John C. Pope, John R. Zeeman.
Number of staff: 2
Employer Identification Number: 366109873

2178
United Conveyor Foundation ⌑
300 Wilmot Rd.
Deerfield 60015 (312) 948-0400

Established about 1957 in IL.
Donor(s): United Conveyor Corp.
Foundation type: Company-sponsored
Financial data (yr. ended 12/31/88): Assets, $1,825,656 (M); gifts received, $60,000; expenditures, $99,460, including $82,675 for 42 grants (high: $12,000; low: $100) and $10,000 for 4 grants to individuals of $2,500 each.
Purpose and activities: Giving for youth and child welfare, social services, and higher and precollege education; scholarships for students whose parents have been employed at United Conveyor Corp. for at least three years.
Types of support: Employee-related scholarships.
Application information: Application form required for scholarships.
Deadline(s): July 1 for scholarships
Final notification: Aug. for scholarships
Write: Helen O'Donnell, Mgr.
Managers: Donald N. Basler, David S. Hoyem, Helen D. O'Donnell.
Employer Identification Number: 366033638

2179
Frederick S. Upton Foundation
c/o First National Bank of Chicago
One First National Plaza, Suite 0103
Chicago 60670 (312) 732-4260

Trust established in 1954 in IL.
Donor(s): Frederick S. Upton.†
Foundation type: Independent
Financial data (yr. ended 12/31/88): Assets, $14,196,411 (M); gifts received, $5,000,000; expenditures, $577,491, including $518,440 for 84 grants (high: $70,000; low: $25; average: $2,000-$10,000).
Purpose and activities: Emphasis on higher education; grants also for cultural programs, youth agencies, and church support.
Types of support: Annual campaigns, building funds, capital campaigns, general purposes, operating budgets, renovation projects, special projects.
Limitations: Giving primarily in MI.
Application information: Foundation notifies only those applicants who will receive grants. Application form not required.
Initial approach: Letter
Copies of proposal: 1
Deadline(s): None
Board meeting date(s): Varies
Write: Stephen E. Upton, Trustee
Trustees: Priscilla Upton Byrns, David F. Upton, Stephen E. Upton, Sylvia Upton Wood, First National Bank of Chicago.
Number of staff: 1 part-time support.
Employer Identification Number: 366013317

2180
USG Foundation, Inc. ▼
101 South Wacker Dr.
Chicago 60606 (312) 606-4594

Incorporated in 1978 in IL.
Donor(s): United States Gypsum Co.
Foundation type: Company-sponsored
Financial data (yr. ended 12/31/88): Assets, $1,362,967 (M); expenditures, $766,476, including $474,129 for 98 grants (high: $139,599; low: $30; average: $500-$5,000) and $269,073 for employee matching gifts.
Purpose and activities: Emphasis on higher education and community funds; support also for arts and cultural organizations, hospitals and health, welfare, youth agencies, and public interest organizations. Preference given to supporting appropriate programs in which USG employees actively participate.
Types of support: Continuing support, annual campaigns, building funds, equipment, research, matching funds, employee matching gifts, technical assistance, general purposes, capital campaigns, employee-related scholarships, scholarship funds, renovation projects.
Limitations: Giving primarily in areas of company operations. No support for sectarian organizations that are exclusively religious, or for political parties, offices, or candidates; fraternal or veterans' organizations; primary or secondary schools, or generally organizations receiving funds from united campaigns. No grants to individuals, or for courtesy advertising; no loans.
Publications: Informational brochure, program policy statement, application guidelines.
Application information: Application form not required.
Initial approach: Proposal
Copies of proposal: 1
Deadline(s): None
Board meeting date(s): Quarterly
Final notification: 2 months
Write: Eugene Miller, Pres.
Officers and Directors:* Eugene Miller,* Pres.; Ralph C. Joynes,* V.P.; H.E. Pendexter,* V.P.; Arthur Leisten, Secy.; William K. Hogan, Treas.
Number of staff: 1 full-time professional.
Employer Identification Number: 362984045

2181
Valenti Charitable Foundation ☆
225 Northfield Rd.
Northfield 60093-3311

Established in 1981 in IL.
Donor(s): Joseph E. Valenti, Sr.
Foundation type: Independent
Financial data (yr. ended 11/30/88): Assets, $1,088,358 (M); gifts received, $135,000; expenditures, $28,399, including $26,265 for 68 grants (high: $5,600; low: $15).
Purpose and activities: Support primarily for higher education and hospitals and health associations.
Limitations: Giving primarily in IL. No grants to individuals.
Application information: Application form not required.
Initial approach: Letter
Deadline(s): None
Write: Joseph E. Valenti, Sr., Trustee
Trustees: James Valenti, Joseph E. Valenti, Sr., Joseph E. Valenti, Jr., Thomas Valenti.
Number of staff: None.
Employer Identification Number: 363155159

2182
Everett & Joyce Van Der Molen Foundation
IN 335 Indian Knoll Rd.
West Chicago 60185 (708) 231-3336

Incorporated in 1986 in IL.
Foundation type: Independent
Financial data (yr. ended 11/30/88): Assets, $628,358 (M); gifts received, $3,510; expenditures, $376,032, including $375,098 for 41 grants (high: $262,000; low: $50).
Purpose and activities: Support primarily for Christian ministry; support also for churches and Christian schools.
Types of support: General purposes, capital campaigns, endowment funds.
Limitations: Giving primarily in IL, with emphasis on Chicago. No grants to individuals.
Application information: Contributes only to pre-selected organizations. Applications not accepted.
Write: Everett Van Der Molen, Trustee
Trustees: Everett Van Der Molen, Kathyrn J. Van Der Molen.
Director: Case Hoogendooan.
Number of staff: None.
Employer Identification Number: 363434499

2183
Wadsworth Memorial Fund ⌑ ☆
c/o The Northern Trust Co.
50 South LaSalle St.
Chicago 60675

Foundation type: Independent
Financial data (yr. ended 12/31/88): Assets, $1,201,916 (M); expenditures, $136,873, including $124,000 for 2 grants (high: $106,000; low: $18,000).
Purpose and activities: Giving limited to the field of cancer research.
Types of support: Research.
Limitations: No grants to individuals.

Application information: Contributes only to pre-selected organizations. Applications not accepted.
Trustee: The Northern Trust Co.
Employer Identification Number: 366426753

2184
Walgreen Benefit Fund
200 Wilmot Rd.
Deerfield 60015 (312) 940-2931

Incorporated in 1939 in IL.
Donor(s): Walgreen Co.
Foundation type: Company-sponsored
Financial data (yr. ended 04/30/89): Assets, $10,461,323 (M); expenditures, $558,944, including $321,213 for grants and $213,358 for grants to individuals.
Purpose and activities: Emphasis on a welfare fund for present and former Walgreen employees and their families; balance of income distributed for community organizations, hospitals, minority, women's, and handicapped groups, and social, cultural and youth agencies.
Types of support: Annual campaigns, continuing support, emergency funds, general purposes, grants to individuals, building funds, capital campaigns, equipment, operating budgets, special projects.
Limitations: Giving primarily in areas of Walgreen markets, with emphasis on IL. No support for religious organizations. No grants to individuals (except employees of the company), or for capital or endowment funds, research-related programs, or matching gifts; no loans.
Application information: Application form not required.
Initial approach: Letter or proposal
Copies of proposal: 1
Deadline(s): None
Board meeting date(s): Monthly and as required
Final notification: 30 to 60 days
Write: Edward H. King, V.P.
Officers: Kenneth Weigand,* Pres.; Edward H. King,* V.P.; William G. Thien, V.P.; Nancy Godfrey,* Secy.-Treas.
Directors:* R.E. Engler, Charles D. Hunter, J.A. Rubino, Charles R. Walgreen III.
Number of staff: 1 part-time professional; 1 part-time support.
Employer Identification Number: 366051130

2185
Mary Ann & Charles R. Walgreen, Jr. Fund ⌑
200 Wilmot Rd.
Deerfield 60015
Application address: P.O. Box 138, Deerfield, IL 60015; Tel.: (312) 940-3030

Established in 1952 in IL.
Foundation type: Independent
Financial data (yr. ended 12/31/87): Assets, $1,404,962 (M); expenditures, $175,950, including $168,561 for 35 grants (high: $161,981; low: $30).
Purpose and activities: Support for education, hospitals and health services, youth and child welfare, and cultural programs.
Limitations: Giving primarily in IL. No support for elementary or secondary schools. No grants to individuals.
Application information:
Initial approach: Proposal
Deadline(s): Sept. 30
Write: Charles R. Walgreen, Jr., Pres.
Officers and Directors: Charles R. Walgreen, Jr., Pres. and Treas.; Emily Koulogeorge, V.P. and Secy.; Jean B. Walgreen.
Employer Identification Number: 366051129

2186
The A. Montgomery Ward Foundation ⌑
c/o Continental Bank, N.A., Attn.: M.C. Ryan
30 North LaSalle St.
Chicago 60697 (312) 828-1785

Trust established in 1959 in IL.
Donor(s): Marjorie Montgomery Ward Baker.†
Foundation type: Independent
Financial data (yr. ended 06/30/89): Assets, $9,272,456 (M); expenditures, $621,655, including $520,000 for 22 grants (high: $155,000; low: $2,500).
Purpose and activities: Emphasis on hospitals; support also for higher education, youth agencies, cultural activities, and social agencies.
Types of support: Capital campaigns, scholarship funds, operating budgets.
Limitations: Giving primarily in Chicago, IL, and surrounding metropolitan areas. No grants to individuals.
Publications: Application guidelines.
Application information:
Initial approach: Letter
Copies of proposal: 2
Board meeting date(s): May and Nov.
Trustees: Richard A. Beck, John A. Hutchings, Continental Bank, N.A.
Employer Identification Number: 362417437

2187
Washington Square Health Foundation, Inc.
875 North Michigan Ave., Suite 3516
Chicago 60611 (312) 664-6488

Established in 1985 in IL.
Donor(s): Herotin Hospital.
Foundation type: Independent
Financial data (yr. ended 09/30/89): Assets, $20,235,567 (M); expenditures, $1,135,713, including $812,993 for 36 grants (high: $200,000; low: $1,000; average: $26,000).
Purpose and activities: Emphasis on health services, medical research, and medical education.
Types of support: Research, equipment, scholarship funds, special projects.
Limitations: Giving primarily in the Chicago, IL, area. No support for general operating or administrative expenses. No grants to individuals, or for land acquisition.
Publications: Annual report, application guidelines.
Application information: Application form required.
Initial approach: Pre-application form
Copies of proposal: 4
Deadline(s): June 1 and Dec. 1
Write: Howard Nochumson, Exec. Dir.
Officers and Directors:* James Lutz,* Chair.; Angelo P. Creticos, M.D.,* Vice-Chair.; L.B. Dillehay,* Pres.; Mrs. Arthur M. Wirtz,* V.P.; Arthur L. Margolis,* Secy.; John C. York,* Treas.; Howard Nochumson,* Exec. Dir.; Robert S. Bleier, M.D., William B. Friedeman, Robert S. Kirby, Howard M. McCue III, Bill G. Wiley.
Number of staff: 2 full-time professional.
Employer Identification Number: 361210140

2188
Judd A. & Marjorie Weinberg Family Foundation ⌑ ☆
One First National Plaza, Suite 2740
Chicago 60603

Established in 1977.
Foundation type: Independent
Financial data (yr. ended 12/31/87): Assets, $1,387,269 (M); gifts received, $25,000; expenditures, $156,313, including $150,972 for grants.
Purpose and activities: Giving primarily for Jewish welfare funds and temple support.
Limitations: Giving primarily in IL.
Application information:
Write: Judd A. Weinberg, Pres.
Officers and Directors: Judd A. Weinberg, Pres.; David B. Weinberg, V.P. and Secy.; Marjorie Weinberg, V.P. and Treas.
Employer Identification Number: 362934515

2189
L. A. Weiss Foundation ⌑ ☆
840 North Michigan Ave., Suite 415
Chicago 60611

Donor(s): Jerome H. Hirschmann.
Foundation type: Operating
Financial data (yr. ended 12/31/88): Assets, $526,795 (M); gifts received, $44,500; expenditures, $125,733, including $116,087 for 112 grants (high: $42,949; low: $10).
Purpose and activities: Giving primarily for Jewish welfare services and fine and performing arts groups, especially an opera company; minor support also for health and hospitals.
Limitations: Giving primarily in IL, with emphasis on Chicago. No grants to individuals; no loans or program-related investments.
Application information: Contributes only to pre-selected organizations. Applications not accepted.
Officers: Goldie W. Dworkin, Pres.; Doris W. Hirschmann, V.P.; Robert G. Weiss, V.P.; Jerome H. Hirschmann, Secy.; Howard A. Weiss, Treas.
Employer Identification Number: 237426429

2190
Clara and Spencer Werner Foundation, Inc. ⌑
616 South Jefferson St.
Paris 61944

Incorporated in 1953 in IL.
Donor(s): Clara B. Werner, Spencer Werner, Illinois Cereal Mills, Inc.
Foundation type: Independent
Financial data (yr. ended 06/30/89): Assets, $11,077,807 (M); expenditures, $2,391,646,

including $2,327,360 for 6 grants (high: $2,227,860; low: $4,500).
Purpose and activities: Grants limited to Lutheran programs, including theological education.
Types of support: General purposes, scholarship funds.
Limitations: Giving primarily in IL and surrounding states, including MO and IN. No support for individual churches, congregations, or parochial schools. No grants to individuals.
Application information: Application form not required.
Initial approach: Letter and proposal
Board meeting date(s): Oct. or Nov.
Officers and Directors:* W. Frank Wiggins,* Pres.; Joseph W. Hasler,* Secy.; T. Alan Russell,* Treas.; Robert L. Gibson, Jerry L. Klug.
Employer Identification Number: 376046119

2191
W. P. and H. B. White Foundation
540 Frontage Rd., Suite 332
North Field 60093 (312) 446-1441

Incorporated in 1953 in IL.
Donor(s): William P. White,† Hazel B. White.†
Foundation type: Independent
Financial data (yr. ended 12/31/89): Assets, $20,063,721 (M); expenditures, $1,253,258, including $1,001,975 for 193 grants (high: $25,000; low: $1,000).
Purpose and activities: Support for social services, higher education, hospitals, inner city programs, and community funds.
Types of support: Operating budgets, continuing support, annual campaigns, emergency funds, building funds, professorships, scholarship funds, research, capital campaigns, general purposes, special projects.
Limitations: Giving primarily in metropolitan Chicago, IL. No grants to individuals, or for land acquisition, endowment funds, publications, conferences, deficit financing, or matching gifts; no loans.
Application information: Application form not required.
Initial approach: Letter
Copies of proposal: 1
Deadline(s): None
Board meeting date(s): Mar., June, Sept., and Dec.
Final notification: Several weeks
Write: John H. McCortney, V.P.
Officers and Directors:* Roger B. White,* Pres.; John H. McCortney,* V.P. and Treas.; Steven R. White,* Secy.; Paul E. Plunkett, Paul M. Plunkett, Robert P. White, William P. White, Jr.
Number of staff: 1 full-time professional; 1 full-time support.
Employer Identification Number: 362601558

2192
Wieboldt Foundation
53 West Jackson Blvd., Rm. 930
Chicago 60604 (312) 786-9377

Incorporated in 1921 in IL.
Donor(s): William A. Wieboldt,† Anna Krueger Wieboldt.†
Foundation type: Independent
Financial data (yr. ended 12/31/89): Assets, $15,401,448 (M); expenditures, $782,877, including $536,575 for 74 grants (high: $15,000; low: $500; average: $7,500) and $154,650 for 6 loans.
Purpose and activities: Interest focused on community organizations, resources for community groups, and change-oriented agencies.
Types of support: General purposes, continuing support, operating budgets, program-related investments.
Limitations: Giving limited to the Chicago metropolitan, IL, and IN areas. No support for economic development. No grants to individuals, or for endowment funds, research, capital campaigns, scholarships, fellowships, conferences, or direct service projects.
Publications: Annual report (including application guidelines), grants list.
Application information: Application form not required.
Initial approach: Proposal
Copies of proposal: 1
Deadline(s): End of each month, except Feb., June, and Oct.
Board meeting date(s): Monthly, except Apr., Aug., and Dec.
Final notification: 2 months after receipt of proposal, with exceptions noted above
Write: Anne C. Hallett, Exec. Dir.
Officers and Directors:* Anita S. Darrow,* Pres.; John S. Darrow,* V.P.; Anne C. Hallett,* Secy. and Exec. Dir.; T. Lawrence Doyle,* Treas.; Diane Glenn, Nydra Hoht, Benjamin J. Kendrick, John Kretzmann, Mary Sample, Rita Simo, Dolores J. Smith, Jennifer Straub, John W. Straub, Anne L. Wieboldt, Nancy Wieboldt.
Members: Donald A. Bloom, Cecil C. Butler, Stanley J. Hallett, Robert P. Hohf, Lawrence E. Kennon, Carol W. Larson, John L. McCausland, Joan E. Straub, Robert P. Taylor, Raymond C. Wieboldt, Jr.
Number of staff: 2 full-time professional.
Employer Identification Number: 362167955

2193
Howard L. Willett Foundation, Inc. ⌘
111 West Washington St., Suite 1900
Chicago 60602 (312) 407-7800

Incorporated in 1973 in IL.
Donor(s): Howard L. Willett,† Howard L. Willett, Jr.†
Foundation type: Independent
Financial data (yr. ended 12/31/88): Assets, $4,651,991 (M); expenditures, $1,853,731, including $1,845,050 for 84 grants (high: $521,000; low: $200).
Purpose and activities: Emphasis on higher education, health agencies, support for the aged, secondary education, social services, and cultural organizations.
Limitations: Giving primarily in the Chicago, IL, metropolitan area. No grants to individuals.
Application information: Application form not required.
Initial approach: Letter
Deadline(s): None
Write: John R. Covington, Secy.
Officers and Directors:* Frank C. Rathje,* Pres.; Irwin W. Hart,* V.P. and Treas.; Mrs. Gerald A. Spore,* V.P.; Mrs. Howard L. Willett, Jr.,* V.P.; John R. Covington,* Secy.; Arthur J. Bruen, Jr.
Employer Identification Number: 237311429

2194
Winona Corporation ⌘
c/o Thomas A. Kelly
70 East Cedar St., Apt. 10-W
Chicago 60611

Established in 1965 in IL.
Donor(s): Marjorie M. Kelly.†
Foundation type: Independent
Financial data (yr. ended 12/31/87): Assets, $4,687,294 (M); expenditures, $394,462, including $340,100 for 58 grants (high: $20,000; low: $1,000).
Purpose and activities: Giving for cultural programs, and higher and pre-college education; some support for hospitals and social services.
Limitations: Giving primarily in IL.
Application information:
Initial approach: Proposal
Deadline(s): None
Write: Thomas A. Kelly, Secy.
Officers and Directors: Patricia K. Healy, Pres.; Marjorie K. Webster, V.P. and Treas.; Thomas A. Kelly, Secy.
Employer Identification Number: 366132949

2195
Woods Charitable Fund, Inc. ▼
Three First National Plaza, Suite 2010
Chicago 60602 (312) 782-2698
For applications from Nebraska: Pam Baker, P.O. Box 81309, Lincoln, NE 68501; Tel.: (402) 474-0707

Incorporated in 1941 in NE.
Donor(s): Frank H. Woods,† Nelle C. Woods,† Sahara Coal Co., Inc.
Foundation type: Independent
Financial data (yr. ended 12/31/89): Assets, $43,948,716 (M); expenditures, $2,842,320, including $2,285,807 for 185 grants (high: $100,000; low: $500; average: $10,000-$20,000).
Purpose and activities: Giving primarily to enhance life in Chicago and Lincoln, particularly for the most disadvantaged residents, and largely through citizens' community-based organizations and public interest groups. Interests in both cities include public policy, culture, and education; in Chicago emphasis on community organizing, public school reform, government accountability, and public policy as it affects families; giving in Lincoln for the arts and humanities, the family, historic preservation, and community improvement and leadership.
Types of support: Operating budgets, seed money, matching funds, special projects, research, renovation projects, consulting services, continuing support, technical assistance, general purposes.
Limitations: Giving primarily in the metropolitan Chicago, IL, and Lincoln, NE, areas. No support for medical or scientific research, religious activities, national health, welfare, educational, or cultural organizations or their state or local affiliates, or college or

university programs that do not involve students and/or faculty in projects of benefit to the Chicago or Lincoln areas. In Lincoln, no support for capital projects in health care institutions or for government agencies or projects; in Chicago, no support for residential care, treatment programs, clinics, recreation programs, social services, or health care institutions. No grants to individuals, or for endowments, scholarships, fellowships, fundraising benefits, or program advertising; low priority is given to capital campaigns and capital projects.
Publications: Annual report, program policy statement, application guidelines.
Application information: Capital campaigns and projects considered only at Dec. meeting; Chicago arts proposals considered only at June meeting. Application form not required.
Initial approach: Telephone or letter
Copies of proposal: 1
Deadline(s): Apr. 15, July 15, and Oct. 15 (Chicago); Jan. 15, Apr. 15, July 15, and Oct. 15 (Lincoln)
Board meeting date(s): Mar. (Lincoln proposals only), June, Sept., and Dec.
Final notification: 1 week after board meeting
Write: Jean Rudd, Exec. Dir., Ken Rolling, or Daryl Woods (Chicago area); Pam Baker (Lincoln)
Officers: Lucia Woods Lindley,* Pres.; George Kelm,* V.P.; Thomas C. Woods III,* V.P.; Charles N. Wheatley, Jr., Secy.-Treas.; Jean Rudd, Exec. Dir.
Trustees:* Sheila Griffin, Sokoni Karanja.
Number of staff: 4 full-time professional; 1 full-time support.
Employer Identification Number: 476032847

2196
Woodward Governor Company Charitable Trust
c/o Woodward Governor Co.
5001 North Second St.
Rockford 61101 (815) 877-7441

Trust established in 1947 in IL.
Donor(s): Woodward Governor Co.
Foundation type: Company-sponsored
Financial data (yr. ended 12/31/89): Assets, $9,181,098 (M); expenditures, $715,448, including $688,678 for 80 grants (high: $100,000; low: $200; average: $2,000).
Purpose and activities: Support for community funds; social services, including programs for the homeless, hunger, minorities, the handicapped, and youth; hospitals; higher and other education and literacy programs; and cultural programs, including museums.
Types of support: Continuing support, annual campaigns, seed money, emergency funds, equipment, capital campaigns, operating budgets.
Limitations: Giving primarily in areas of company operations, including Rockford, IL; Fort Collins, CO; and Stevens Point, WI. No grants to individuals, or for endowment funds, research, scholarships, fellowships, special projects, publications, conferences, or matching gifts; no loans.
Application information: Application form not required.
Initial approach: Letter
Copies of proposal: 1
Deadline(s): Submit proposal preferably in Mar. or July; no set deadline
Board meeting date(s): As required
Final notification: 8 weeks
Write: Harry Tallacksen, Chair., Contrib. Comm., Woodward Governor Co.
Trustees: Edward Abegg, Maurice O. Nelson, Leo Powelson, Robert E. Reuterfors, Dick Robbins, Orlo Theon.
Number of staff: None.
Employer Identification Number: 846025403

2197
Wm. Wrigley Jr. Company Foundation ¤
410 North Michigan Ave.
Chicago 60611 (312) 645-3950

Established in 1986 in IL.
Donor(s): Wm. Wrigley Jr. Co.
Foundation type: Company-sponsored
Financial data (yr. ended 12/31/87): Assets, $4,986,199 (M); gifts received, $3,150,000; expenditures, $542,223, including $540,530 for 56 grants (high: $65,900; low: $500).
Purpose and activities: Interest is primarily in national basic health and welfare organizations; support also for community funds, education, and youth organizations.
Limitations: No grants to individuals.
Application information:
Initial approach: Proposal
Deadline(s): Oct. 1
Write: William M. Piet, Pres.
Officers and Directors:* William Wrigley,* Chair.; William M. Piet,* Pres.; William Wrigley, Jr.,* V.P.; Hollis Moyse, Treas.; Mark Monroe, Secy.
Employer Identification Number: 363486958

2198
The Farny R. Wurlitzer Foundation
P.O. Box 387
Sycamore 60178 (815) 895-2923

Established about 1948; incorporated in 1962 in NY.
Donor(s): Farny R. Wurlitzer,† Grace K. Wurlitzer.†
Foundation type: Independent
Financial data (yr. ended 12/31/89): Assets, $2,940,092 (M); expenditures, $145,097, including $130,900 for 36 grants (high: $16,000; low: $500; average: $2,000-$6,000).
Purpose and activities: Support for education, including music education and organizations.
Types of support: Operating budgets, continuing support, annual campaigns, emergency funds, deficit financing, building funds, equipment, land acquisition, endowment funds, special projects, research, capital campaigns, general purposes.
Limitations: Giving primarily in IL and the Midwest. No grants to individuals, or for scholarship funds, fellowships, seed money, publications, or conferences; no loans.
Application information: Application form not required.
Initial approach: Proposal
Copies of proposal: 1
Deadline(s): Submit proposal preferably between Jan. and Mar. or between July and Sept.
Board meeting date(s): May and Nov.
Final notification: 90 days
Write: William A. Rolfing, Pres.
Officers and Directors:* William A. Rolfing,* Pres.; W.S. Turner,* V.P. and Treas.; J.D. Ovitz,* Secy.; H.L. Evans, H.L. Hollingsworth.
Number of staff: None.
Employer Identification Number: 166023172

2199
Wyne Foundation ¤ ☆
c/o Thomas L. Rosenow
17490 Timber Rd.
Sterling 61081-9310

Established in 1964.
Donor(s): Jeanette C. Wyne Trust.
Foundation type: Independent
Financial data (yr. ended 12/31/88): Assets, $1,730,640 (M); gifts received, $9,039; expenditures, $42,981, including $28,690 for 18 grants (high: $5,000; low: $450).
Purpose and activities: Giving primarily for Protestant churches and organizations; some support for recreation and social services.
Limitations: Giving primarily in IL. No grants to individuals.
Application information: Contributes only to pre-selected organizations. Applications not accepted.
Officers and Directors: Thomas L. Rosenow, Pres. and Treas.; Mary V. Rosenow, Secy.; Laura R. Knie.
Employer Identification Number: 366116114

2200
Pauline Yacktman Foundation ¤
2640 Golf Rd.
Glenview 60025

Foundation type: Independent
Financial data (yr. ended 10/31/87): Assets, $1,403,198 (M); gifts received, $400,000; expenditures, $24,570, including $20,000 for 9 grants (high: $10,000; low: $500).
Purpose and activities: Support for recreation programs and general charitable giving.
Types of support: Operating budgets.
Limitations: Giving primarily in NY, IL, and FL.
Application information: Application form not required.
Deadline(s): None
Write: Pauline Yacktman Petre, Trustee
Trustee: Pauline Yacktman Petre.
Employer Identification Number: 363335154

2201
Samuel Zell Foundation ¤ ☆
Two North Riverside Plaza, No. 600
Chicago 60606-2605

Established in 1986.
Donor(s): Samuel Zell.
Foundation type: Independent
Financial data (yr. ended 12/31/88): Assets, $102 (M); gifts received, $150,000; expenditures, $150,030, including $149,068 for 23 grants (high: $40,918; low: $50).

Purpose and activities: Grants primarily to Jewish organizations, higher education, and cultural programs.
Limitations: Giving primarily in Chicago, IL. No grants to individuals.
Application information: Contributes only to pre-selected organizations. Applications not accepted.
Officers: Samuel Zell, Pres.; Robert Lurie, V.P.; Sheli Z. Rosenberg, Secy.; Arthur A. Greenberg, Treas.
Employer Identification Number: 363487811

2202
Eugene and Delores Zemsky Charitable Foundation ⌘ ☆
3919 Fitch
Lincoln Wood 60645 (312) 247-4600

Established in 1974.
Donor(s): Eugene Zemsky.
Foundation type: Independent
Financial data (yr. ended 11/30/88): Assets, $96,969 (M); gifts received, $100,000; expenditures, $129,602, including $129,375 for 16 grants (high: $50,000; low: $50).
Purpose and activities: Giving primarily to Jewish welfare organizations; support also for medical science and research.
Limitations: No grants to individuals.
Application information:
Initial approach: Letter
Deadline(s): None
Write: Eugene M. Zemsky, Trustee
Trustees: Delores Zemsky, Eugene Zemsky.
Employer Identification Number: 237411882

INDIANA

2203
American General Finance, Inc. - Richard E. Meier Foundation, Inc. ⌘
(Formerly Credithrift Financial - Richard E. Meier Foundation, Inc.)
601 Northwest Second St.
Evansville 47708 (812) 429-9322
Scholarship application address: Dir. of Financial Aid, Univ. of Evansville, Evansville, IN 47714

Incorporated in 1958 in IN.
Donor(s): American General Finance, Inc., and subsidiaries.
Foundation type: Company-sponsored
Financial data (yr. ended 12/31/88): Assets, $1,509,854 (M); expenditures, $200,497, including $137,744 for 47 grants (high: $59,707; low: $10; average: $500-$1,000), $45,000 for grants to individuals (average: $1,500) and $14,642 for employee matching gifts.
Purpose and activities: Support for community funds and privately endowed colleges and universities; most grants awarded on pre-established formula to the United Way and state associations of private colleges.
Types of support: Operating budgets, continuing support, annual campaigns, building funds, employee-related scholarships, employee matching gifts.
Limitations: Giving primarily in IN, with emphasis on Evansville, IN. No support for religious organizations for religious purposes or health care organizations. No grants to individuals (except for 4 scholarships to dependents of employees), or for seed money, emergency or endowment funds, deficit financing, equipment, land acquisition, matching gifts, special projects, research, publications, tickets or advertising for benefit purposes, or conferences; no loans.
Publications: Application guidelines.
Application information: Application form required for employee-related scholarships. Application form not required.
Initial approach: Letter
Copies of proposal: 1
Deadline(s): Between Apr. 1 and June 1 for scholarships; no set deadline for grants
Board meeting date(s): Apr.
Final notification: 2 to 3 weeks
Write: Norb Devine, V.P., Systems Control
Officers: John Bolger,* Pres.; G. Jack Downing, Exec. V.P.; Edwin G. Pickett,* Exec. V.P.; Eric H. Krebs, V.P., Taxation; William A. Rotzien, Secy.; George F. Walterhouse,* Treas.
Directors:* Robert F. Floyd, Thomas E. Kleist, Robert P. Plummer, H. Norris Robinson, David C. Seeley.
Number of staff: None.
Employer Identification Number: 356042566

2204
John W. Anderson Foundation ▼
402 Wall St.
Valparaiso 46383 (219) 462-4611

Trust established in 1967 in IN.
Donor(s): John W. Anderson.†
Foundation type: Independent
Financial data (yr. ended 12/31/88): Assets, $85,684,528 (M); expenditures, $3,833,336, including $3,025,286 for 122 grants (high: $633,000; low: $500; average: $5,000-$15,000) and $98,083 for grants to individuals.
Purpose and activities: Emphasis on youth agencies; support also for higher education, legal services, libraries, community funds, aid to the handicapped, and hospitals.
Types of support: Continuing support, special projects, employee-related scholarships, operating budgets.
Limitations: Giving primarily in Lake and Porter counties in northwest IN. No grants to individuals (except for scholarships for children of Anderson Company employees), or for endowment funds, annual campaigns, seed money, deficit financing, scholarship funds, or renovation projects; no loans.
Publications: 990-PF.
Application information: Application form not required.
Initial approach: Letter
Copies of proposal: 5
Deadline(s): None
Board meeting date(s): Feb., Apr., June, Aug., Oct., and Dec.
Final notification: 1 month
Write: Paul G. Wallace, Secy.
Officers and Trustees:* Richard S. Melvin,* Chair.; Wilfred G. Wilkins,* Vice-Chair.; Paul G. Wallace,* Secy.; William Vinovich, Bruce W. Wargo.
Number of staff: 2 part-time professional; 5 full-time support; 1 part-time support.
Employer Identification Number: 356070695

2205
Howard P. Arnold Foundation ⌘ ☆
P.O. Box 110
Fort Wayne 46801-0110

Established in 1987 in IN.
Foundation type: Independent
Financial data (yr. ended 12/31/88): Assets, $1,220,476 (M); expenditures, $6,384, including $5,000 for 4 grants (high: $2,000; low: $1,000).
Purpose and activities: Support for an Episcopal church and health centers.
Limitations: No grants to individuals.
Application information: Contributes only to pre-selected organizations. Applications not accepted.
Directors: William R. O'Dell, Maclyn Parker, Thomas E. Quirk.
Trustee: Fort Wayne National Bank.
Employer Identification Number: 311202969

2206
The Arvin Foundation, Inc.
One Noblitt Plaza, Box 3000
Columbus 47202-3000 (812) 379-3000

Incorporated in 1951 in IN.
Donor(s): Arvin Industries, Inc.
Foundation type: Company-sponsored
Financial data (yr. ended 12/31/89): Assets, $2,352,647 (M); gifts received, $896,134; expenditures, $624,680, including $622,042 for grants.
Purpose and activities: Giving primarily for education and technical training, United Way agencies, youth organizations and youth affiliations, civic and health organizations, and the arts and sciences.
Types of support: General purposes, building funds, operating budgets, continuing support, equipment, special projects.
Limitations: Giving primarily in communities where the company is located. No grants to individuals (except for Outstanding Teacher Awards), or for endowment funds, scholarships, fellowships, or matching gifts; no loans.
Publications: Annual report.
Application information: Application form not required.
Initial approach: 1- or 2-page letter
Copies of proposal: 1
Deadline(s): None
Board meeting date(s): May and Oct.; Contributions Committee meets approximately every 6 weeks
Write: W. Fred Meyer, V.P., Public Affairs; or William Kendall, V.P., Community Relations

Officers and Directors:* James K. Baker,* Chair. and Pres.; William Kendall,* V.P., Community Relations; W. Fred Meyer,* V.P., Public Affairs; Martha J. Schrader,* Secy.; Richard A. Smith,* Treas.; Clyde R. Davis, Loren K. Evans, Richard L. Hendricks, V. William Hunt, J. William Kendall, Charles H. Watson.
Number of staff: None.
Employer Identification Number: 356020798

2207
Ayres Foundation, Inc. ⌑
Two West Washington St., Suite 807
Indianapolis 46204 (317) 633-1506

Incorporated in 1944 in IN.
Donor(s): L.S. Ayres and Co., Theodore B. Griffith,† Mrs. Theodore B. Griffith.†
Foundation type: Company-sponsored
Financial data (yr. ended 12/31/88): Assets, $1,515,177 (M); expenditures, $93,614, including $87,400 for 27 grants (high: $15,000; low: $200; average: $250-$1,000).
Purpose and activities: Giving for community funds, cultural activities, and higher education; also provides relief to needy company employees, former employees, and their dependents.
Types of support: Operating budgets, building funds, grants to individuals.
Limitations: Giving primarily in IN, with emphasis on Indianapolis. No grants to individuals (except for employee-related welfare).
Application information: Application form not required.
Initial approach: Brief proposal including proof of IRS tax-exempt status, financial data, and nature of request
Deadline(s): None
Write: John E.D. Peacock, Pres.
Officers and Directors: John E.D. Peacock, Pres.; Alvin C. Fernandes, Jr., V.P. and Secy.; Daniel F. Evans, V.P. and Treas.; Lyman S. Ayres, William J. Stout, David P. Williams III.
Number of staff: None.
Employer Identification Number: 356018437

2208
Ball Brothers Foundation ▼
222 South Mulberry St.
P.O. Box 1408
Muncie 47308 (317) 741-5500

Incorporated in 1926 in IN.
Donor(s): Edmund B. Ball,† Frank C. Ball,† George A. Ball,† Lucius L. Ball, M.D.,† William A. Ball.†
Foundation type: Independent
Financial data (yr. ended 12/31/89): Assets, $77,478,000 (M); expenditures, $3,384,710, including $3,384,710 for 42 grants (high: $1,500,000; low: $1,000; average: $1,000-$50,000).
Purpose and activities: Support for the humanities and cultural programs, higher and other education, health and medical education, religion, youth, family and social services.
Types of support: Matching funds, professorships, research, publications, conferences and seminars, special projects, annual campaigns, fellowships, internships, operating budgets, renovation projects, seed money, technical assistance.
Limitations: Giving limited to IN. No grants to individuals.
Publications: 990-PF, application guidelines.
Application information: Application form not required.
Initial approach: Letter or proposal
Copies of proposal: 1
Deadline(s): Submit proposal preferably before June; no set deadline
Board meeting date(s): Quarterly and as necessary
Final notification: Varies
Write: Douglas A. Bakken, Exec. Dir.
Officers and Directors: Edmund F. Ball,* Chair.; John W. Fisher,* Pres.; Frank E. Ball,* V.P.; Reed D. Voran,* Secy.; Douglas J. Foy,* Treas.; Douglas A. Bakken, Exec. Dir.; Frank A. Bracken, Lucina B. Moxley, John J. Pruis, Richard M. Ringoen.
Number of staff: 1 full-time professional; 1 part-time professional; 1 full-time support; 1 part-time support.
Employer Identification Number: 350882856

2209
George and Frances Ball Foundation ▼
P.O. Box 1408
Muncie 47308 (317) 741-5500
Additional address: 222 South Mulberry St., Muncie, IN 47305

Incorporated in 1937 in IN.
Donor(s): George A. Ball.†
Foundation type: Independent
Financial data (yr. ended 12/31/89): Assets, $62,450,000 (M); expenditures, $2,784,588, including $2,580,000 for 37 grants (high: $950,000; low: $1,000; average: $10,000-$50,000).
Purpose and activities: Emphasis on higher education.
Types of support: General purposes, equipment, renovation projects, special projects, capital campaigns.
Limitations: Giving primarily in Muncie, IN. No grants to individuals.
Application information: Application form required.
Initial approach: Proposal
Copies of proposal: 1
Deadline(s): None
Board meeting date(s): Quarterly
Final notification: Following board review
Write: Joyce Beck, Admin. Secy.
Officers and Directors:* Alexander M. Bracken,* Chair.; Frank A. Bracken,* Pres.; John J. Pruis,* Exec. V.P.; Reed D. Voran,* Secy.; Douglas J. Foy, Treas.
Number of staff: 1 part-time professional; 1 part-time support.
Employer Identification Number: 356033917

2210
The Beardsley Foundation ⌑
302 East Beardsley Ave.
Elkhart 46514 (219) 264-0330
Additional address: c/o First National Bank Trust Dept., 301 South Main St., Elkhart, IN 46516

Trust established in 1955 in IN.
Donor(s): Walter R. Beardsley.†
Foundation type: Operating
Financial data (yr. ended 12/31/88): Assets, $4,264,520 (M); expenditures, $224,235, including $24,400 for 13 grants (high: $8,400; low: $500).
Purpose and activities: A private operating foundation; giving primarily for a museum, cultural programs, and social services.
Limitations: Giving primarily in IN.
Application information:
Write: Richard C. Spaulding, Treas.
Officers and Directors: Robert B. Beardsley, Chair. and Pres.; John F. Dille, Jr., Vice-Chair. and V.P.; John R. Harman, Secy.; Richard C. Spaulding, Treas.; Dean A. Porter.
Number of staff: 1 full-time professional; 2 full-time support; 10 part-time support.
Employer Identification Number: 351170807

2211
Bierhaus Foundation, Inc. ⌑
P.O. Box 538
Vincennes 47591 (812) 882-0990

Established in 1950 in IN.
Donor(s): Royal Gift Stamps, Inc., R&W Realty Corp.
Foundation type: Independent
Financial data (yr. ended 12/31/89): Assets, $2,068,472 (M); gifts received, $34,444; expenditures, $107,493, including $103,439 for 48 grants (high: $50,100; low: $50).
Purpose and activities: Giving for Protestant churches, higher education, and youth.
Limitations: Giving primarily in IN.
Application information:
Initial approach: Letter or telephone
Deadline(s): None
Write: Robert V. Bierhaus, Jr., Secy.
Officer: Robert V. Bierhaus, Jr., Secy.
Employer Identification Number: 356023894

2212
Edward A. Block Charitable Trust ⌑
1014 Circle Tower Bldg.
Indianapolis 46204

Established in 1982 in IN.
Foundation type: Independent
Financial data (yr. ended 12/31/88): Assets, $1,221,542 (M); expenditures, $69,244, including $55,216 for 2 grants.
Purpose and activities: Supports a congregation and Jewish welfare agency.
Limitations: Giving primarily in Indianapolis, IN.
Application information: Contributes only to pre-selected organizations. Applications not accepted.
Trustees: Maxine T. Bennett, Francis J. Feeney, Jr., Marvin Lasky.
Employer Identification Number: 351502465

2213
Booe-Inlow-d'Arlier Memorial Charitable Foundation ⌑
Three Fountain Square
Covington 47932 (317) 793-3602

Established in 1980 in IN.
Donor(s): George d'Arlier.†
Foundation type: Independent

Financial data (yr. ended 9/30/88): Assets, $2,472,333 (M); expenditures, $99,080, including $79,289 for 18 grants (high: $34,305; low: $80).
Purpose and activities: Support for public libraries, and summer study-abroad programs in France for high school students.
Types of support: Building funds.
Limitations: Giving primarily in Veedersburg, IN, and for benefit of residents or former residents.
Application information:
Initial approach: Letter
Deadline(s): None
Write: Luke White, Trustee
Trustees: Kip White, Luke White, The Fountain Trust Co.
Employer Identification Number: 311001831

2214
Bowker Foundation Trust ¤ ☆
c/o Lincoln National Bank & Trust Co.
116 East Berry St., P.O. Box 960
Fort Wayne 46801-0960

Foundation type: Independent
Financial data (yr. ended 07/31/89): Assets, $1,081,834 (M); expenditures, $49,445, including $41,150 for 7 grants (high: $23,000; low: $400).
Purpose and activities: Giving primarily for organizations benefitting women, including a YWCA and other social services.
Limitations: Giving primarily in Allen County, IN.
Application information:
Initial approach: Letter
Deadline(s): None
Write: Alice Kopfer
Trustee: Lincoln National Bank & Trust Co.
Employer Identification Number: 356072377

2215
The Bowsher-Booher Foundation
First Interstate Bank of Northern IN
112 West Jefferson Blvd.
South Bend 46601 (219) 237-3313

Established in 1980.
Foundation type: Independent
Financial data (yr. ended 5/31/89): Assets, $1,559,076 (M); expenditures, $124,421, including $113,685 for 15 grants (high: $28,000; low: $2,000).
Purpose and activities: Giving primarily for social services.
Limitations: Giving limited to the South Bend area and St. Joseph County, IN.
Application information: Application form not required.
Initial approach: Letter
Copies of proposal: 7
Deadline(s): Apr. 1 for consideration in May; Oct. 1 for consideration in Nov.
Write: Robert R. Cleppe
Trustee: First Interstate Bank of Northern Indiana, N.A.
Employer Identification Number: 310979401

2216
Julia H. Brink Unitrust ¤
P.O. Box 5031
Indianapolis 46255

Established in 1985 in IN.
Foundation type: Independent
Financial data (yr. ended 1/31/89): Assets, $2,744,199 (M); expenditures, $156,196, including $144,000 for 3 grants of $48,000 each.
Purpose and activities: Support for wildlife, medical rehabilitation, a children's hospital, and a zoo.
Limitations: Giving primarily in Indianapolis, IN.
Application information: Contributes only to pre-selected organizations. Applications not accepted.
Trustee: Merchants National Bank & Trust Co.
Employer Identification Number: 356408534

2217
The Sol and Arlene Bronstein Foundation ¤
c/o National City Bank of Evansville
P.O. Box 868
Evansville 47705-0868 (812) 425-6261

Established in 1979 in IN.
Donor(s): Sol Bronstein,† Laketon Asphalt Refining Co.
Foundation type: Independent
Financial data (yr. ended 12/31/89): Assets, $4,060,514 (M); expenditures, $385,749, including $369,912 for 28 grants (high: $117,500; low: $1,000).
Purpose and activities: Giving primarily for Jewish organizations, with emphasis on temple support, Jewish education, and Jewish welfare funds; support also for higher education.
Limitations: Giving primarily in Evansville, IN. No support for non-Jewish-related programs. No grants for capital improvements or endowment funds.
Application information: Application form not required.
Deadline(s): None
Write: Charles Goldman
Trustees: Hubert De Jong,* National City Bank of Evansville.
Advisors:* Rabbi Arthur Abrams, Alfred Gottscalk, M.D., Joel M. Lasker, Leonard Pearson, Howard Treckman.
Number of staff: None.
Employer Identification Number: 356313412

2218
Carmichael Foundation, Inc. ¤
c/o First Source Bank
One First Source Ctr., P.O. Box 1602
South Bend 46601 (219) 236-2790

Incorporated in 1967 in IN.
Foundation type: Independent
Financial data (yr. ended 12/31/88): Assets, $1,222,365 (M); gifts received, $19,840; expenditures, $99,694, including $87,000 for 5 grants (high: $66,000; low: $1,000).
Purpose and activities: Grants mainly for higher and secondary education.
Application information: Application form not required.
Deadline(s): None
Write: Ron Brown
Officers: Mrs. Robert L. Raclin, Chair. and Pres.; C.J. Murphy III, V.P. and Treas.; Ronald J. Jaicomo, Secy.
Trustee: First Source Bank.
Employer Identification Number: 356069904

2219
Central Newspapers Foundation ¤
307 North Pennsylvania St.
Indianapolis 46204-1899

Incorporated in 1935 in IN.
Donor(s): Eugene S. Pulliam, Central Newspapers, Inc., Indianapolis Newspapers, Inc., Phoenix Newspapers, Inc.
Foundation type: Company-sponsored
Financial data (yr. ended 4/30/87): Assets, $179,480 (M); gifts received, $154,000; expenditures, $277,967, including $93,115 for 31 grants (high: $10,000; low: $308) and $102,500 for 57 grants to individuals (high: $2,000; low: $500).
Purpose and activities: Giving primarily to aid the blind of central IN; support for higher education and a scholarship program for children of employees of member newspapers.
Types of support: Employee-related scholarships, scholarship funds.
Limitations: Giving primarily in IN and AZ. No grants to individuals (except scholarships for children of employees).
Application information: Applications not accepted.
Board meeting date(s): Annually
Officer: Marjorie C. Tarplee, Exec. Dir.
Employer Identification Number: 356013720

2220
Central Soya Foundation ¤
P.O. Box 1400
1300 Fort Wayne National Bank Bldg.
Fort Wayne 46801 (219) 425-5100

Trust established in 1954 in IN.
Donor(s): Central Soya Co., Inc.
Foundation type: Company-sponsored
Financial data (yr. ended 8/31/88): Assets, $474,387 (M); gifts received, $400,000; expenditures, $400,452, including $388,364 for 124 grants (high: $43,000; low: $100) and $8,827 for 60 employee matching gifts (high: $1,000; low: $25).
Purpose and activities: Since the company is now privately held, the foundation has been reduced in size and is not endowed; limited grants to fulfil social obligations within communities containing the company's plants and employees. Requests not considered from outside these communities.
Types of support: Employee matching gifts.
Limitations: Giving limited to areas of company operations.
Trustee: Fort Wayne National Bank.
Employer Identification Number: 356020624

2221
The Clowes Fund, Inc. ▼
250 East 38th St.
Indianapolis 46205 (317) 923-3264

Incorporated in 1952 in IN.
Donor(s): Edith W. Clowes,† George H.A. Clowes,† Allen W. Clowes.

Foundation type: Independent
Financial data (yr. ended 12/31/88): Assets, $30,937,099 (M); expenditures, $2,142,861, including $2,038,495 for 38 grants (high: $600,000; low: $2,000; average: $5,000-$50,000).
Purpose and activities: Giving largely for higher and secondary education; the fine and performing arts, including maintenance of the Clowes Collection of Old Master Paintings in Clowes Pavillion; Indianapolis Museum of Art; music; and marine biology; support also for social services.
Types of support: Operating budgets, continuing support, building funds, endowment funds, scholarship funds, special projects, research.
Limitations: Giving primarily in Indianapolis, IN, and Boston, MA. No grants to individuals, or for publications or conferences; no loans.
Application information: Application form not required.
Initial approach: Letter or proposal
Copies of proposal: 2
Deadline(s): Submit proposal between Sept. and Jan.; proposal must be received by the last business day of Jan. of each year
Board meeting date(s): Annually, between Feb. 1 and June 1
Final notification: 1 month after board meeting
Write: Allen W. Clowes, Pres.
Officers and Directors:* Allen W. Clowes,* Pres. and Treas.; Margaret J. Clowes,* V.P.; Thomas M. Lofton,* Secy.; Margaret C. Bowles, Alexander W. Clowes, Byron P. Hollett, William H. Marshall.
Number of staff: 2 full-time professional; 1 part-time support.
Employer Identification Number: 351079679

2222
Olive B. Cole Foundation, Inc. ¤
3242 Mallard Cove Ln.
Fort Wayne 46804 (219) 436-2182

Incorporated in 1954 in IN.
Donor(s): Richard R. Cole,† Olive B. Cole.
Foundation type: Independent
Financial data (yr. ended 3/31/89): Assets, $16,418,203 (M); expenditures, $964,359, including $582,411 for 39 grants (high: $107,000; low: $100; average: $10,400) and $131,559 for 237 grants to individuals (high: $1,000; low: $250; average: $500-$700).
Purpose and activities: Grants largely for education, including student aid for graduates of Noble County high schools, hospitals, civic affairs, youth agencies, and cultural programs.
Types of support: Seed money, building funds, equipment, land acquisition, student aid, matching funds, program-related investments, general purposes, continuing support.
Limitations: Giving limited to the Kendallville, Noble County, area, and to LaGrange, Steuben, and DeKalb counties, IN. No grants for endowment funds or research; no loans.
Publications: Application guidelines, program policy statement.
Application information: Scholarship applications available at all Noble County, IN, secondary schools. Application form required.
Initial approach: Letter
Copies of proposal: 7
Deadline(s): None
Board meeting date(s): Feb., May, Aug., and Nov.
Final notification: 4 months
Write: John E. Hogan, Jr., Exec. V.P.
Officers and Directors:* John N. Pichon, Jr., Pres.; John E. Hogan, Jr., Exec. V.P. and Treas.; Maclyn T. Parker,* Secy.; Robert Borger, Merrill B. Frick, Victor B. Porter, John W. Riemke, Paul Schirmeyer.
Scholarship Administrator: Gwendlyn I. Tipton.*
Number of staff: 1 full-time professional; 1 full-time support.
Employer Identification Number: 356040491

2223
William S. and Lillian R. Coleman Scholarship Trust ¤
c/o Bank One, Indianapolis, N.A.
101 Monument Circle
Indianapolis 46277 (317) 639-7544

Established in 1974 in IN.
Foundation type: Independent
Financial data (yr. ended 6/30/87): Assets, $1,726,255 (M); expenditures, $106,186, including $91,000 for 183 grants to individuals (high: $950; low: $100).
Purpose and activities: Scholarships for post-secondary education.
Types of support: Student aid.
Limitations: Giving limited to Rush County, IN.
Application information: Application form required.
Deadline(s): Apr. 1 or 60 days prior to beginning of a school term
Write: Jackie Weitz, Asst. V.P., Bank One, Indianapolis, N.A.
Corporate Trustee: Bank One, Indianapolis, N.A.
Employer Identification Number: 356279390

2224
CTS Foundation
905 North West Blvd.
Elkhart 46514 (219) 293-7511

Trust established in 1953 in IN.
Donor(s): CTS Corp.
Foundation type: Company-sponsored
Financial data (yr. ended 09/30/89): Assets, $2,317,527 (M); qualifying distributions, $351,250, including $47,900 for 18 grants (high: $15,000; low: $300) and $303,350 for 375 loans to individuals.
Purpose and activities: Principal activity is to make interest-free student loans to employees and children of employees of CTS and its subsidiaries for undergraduate college education. Support also for educational and charitable organizations; some support for community funds.
Types of support: Annual campaigns, student loans.
Limitations: Giving primarily in areas of company operations, primarily in IN, IL, AR, and TX.
Application information: Application form required for student loan program.
Initial approach: Proposal
Copies of proposal: 1
Deadline(s): Before beginning of school term for student loans
Board meeting date(s): Semiannually and as needed
Final notification: Following board meeting
Officers and Trustees:* Duane H. Daering,* Chair.; Charles C. Smith,* Vice-Chair.; Patricia L. Mills, Secy.; David K. Sentman,* Treas.; Joseph DiGirolamo, Clinton W. Hartman.
Number of staff: None.
Employer Identification Number: 356014484

2225
Cummins Engine Foundation ▼ ¤
500 Jackson St.
Columbus 47201 (812) 377-3114
Mailing address: Box 3005, MC 60814, Columbus, IN 47202-3005

Incorporated in 1954 in IN.
Donor(s): Cummins Engine Co., Inc.
Foundation type: Company-sponsored
Financial data (yr. ended 12/31/88): Assets, $2,452,000 (M); expenditures, $3,379,806, including $2,686,774 for grants (high: $315,300), $80,650 for grants to individuals and $296,032 for employee matching gifts.
Purpose and activities: Giving focused primarily on local community needs, youth, civil rights and justice, education, the arts, and public policy, including an employee matching gift program and a company employee scholarship program; selected grants also for national and international needs which combine equal opportunity and excellence and reinforce local programs.
Types of support: Annual campaigns, conferences and seminars, continuing support, emergency funds, endowment funds, matching funds, operating budgets, publications, seed money, technical assistance, employee-related scholarships, special projects, employee matching gifts, general purposes.
Limitations: Giving primarily in areas of company operations, particularly the Columbus, IN, area. No support for denominational religious purposes. No grants to individuals (except scholarships for children of company employees).
Publications: Corporate giving report (including application guidelines).
Application information: Application form not required.
Initial approach: Proposal or letter
Copies of proposal: 1
Deadline(s): None
Board meeting date(s): Feb., July, Sept., and Dec.
Final notification: 1 to 3 months
Write: Adele J. Vincent, Assoc. Dir.
Officers and Directors: Ted L. Marston, Chair.; James A. Henderson, Vice-Chair.; Henry B. Schacht, Vice-Chair.; Richard B. Stoner, Vice-Chair.; Martha D. Lamkin, Pres.; George Fauerbach, Hanna H. Gray, Peter B. Hamilton, James A. Joseph, J. Irwin Miller, Kevin E. Sheehan, Theodore M. Solso, B. Joseph White, Philip E. Wilson.
Number of staff: 2 full-time professional; 1 part-time professional; 1 full-time support; 1 part-time support.
Employer Identification Number: 356042373

2226
Ione C. Davis Trust ⌑
c/o Clinton County Bank and Trust Co.
Two East Washington St.
Frankfort 46041

Established in 1985 in IN.
Foundation type: Independent
Financial data (yr. ended 12/31/88): Assets, $1,746,824 (M); expenditures, $131,452, including $109,746 for 5 grants (high: $43,898; low: $10,975).
Purpose and activities: Support for higher education and social services.
Limitations: No grants to individuals.
Application information: Contributes only to pre-selected organizations. Applications not accepted.
Trustee: Clinton County Bank and Trust Co.
Employer Identification Number: 356413272

2227
Arthur J. Decio Foundation ⌑
c/o Skyline Corp.
2520 By-Pass Rd.
Elkhart 46514

Established in 1970 in IN.
Donor(s): Arthur J. Decio.
Foundation type: Independent
Financial data (yr. ended 9/30/88): Assets, $2,183,272 (M); expenditures, $179,544, including $168,162 for 31 grants (high: $16,500; low: $100).
Purpose and activities: Emphasis on higher and secondary education, cultural programs, and health and social services.
Limitations: Giving primarily in IN.
Application information:
Write: Ronald F. Kloska, Fdn. Mgr.
Trustees: Arthur J. Decio, Patricia C. Decio, Ronald F. Kloska, Andrew McKenna, Richard M. Treckelo.
Employer Identification Number: 237083597

2228
Dekko Foundation, Inc.
P.O. Box 548
Kendallville 46755-0548 (219) 347-1278

Established in 1981 in IN.
Donor(s): Chester E. Dekko.
Foundation type: Independent
Financial data (yr. ended 8/31/89): Assets, $5,997,877 (M); gifts received, $1,250; expenditures, $158,624, including $141,509 for 50 grants (high: $10,000; low: $15).
Purpose and activities: Support primarily for libraries, communications, and education, including early childhood, elementary, and secondary institutions.
Types of support: General purposes, scholarship funds.
Limitations: Giving primarily in Noble, IN, and the surrounding counties. No grants to individuals.
Application information: Application form not required.
Initial approach: Letter
Copies of proposal: 1
Board meeting date(s): Monthly
Write: Linda Speakman, Secy.
Officers: Chester E. Dekko, Pres.; Linda Speakman, Secy.; Chester E. Dekko, Jr., Treas.
Number of staff: 1 part-time professional.
Employer Identification Number: 351528135

2229
Delta Tau Delta Educational Fund ⌑
8250 Haverstick Rd., Suite 155
Indianapolis 46240 (317) 259-1187

Established in 1944 in IN.
Foundation type: Independent
Financial data (yr. ended 07/31/89): Assets, $1,546,068 (M); expenditures, $107,509, including $30,000 for 1 grant, $17,851 for 38 grants to individuals (high: $1,500; low: $10) and $24,200 for loans to individuals.
Purpose and activities: Support for an educational foundation and scholarships and loans for members of Delta Tau Delta.
Types of support: Student loans, student aid.
Application information: Some grants are restricted to a specific chapter or curriculum. Application form required.
Deadline(s): None
Write: Kenneth A. File
Officer: George P. Loomis, Mgr.
Directors: Hoyt D. Gardner, R. Stevens Gilley, David L. Nagel, Thomas S. Sharp, Norval B. Stephens, Jr.
Advisory Committee: Charles R. Cruse, Edwin L. Heminger, Francis M. Hughes, G. Herbert McCracken, John W. Nichols.
Employer Identification Number: 237405401

2230
James R. Duncan Trust ⌑
c/o Citizens National Bank
P.O. Box 719
Evansville 47705-0719

Foundation type: Independent
Financial data (yr. ended 12/31/88): Assets, $2,492,155 (M); expenditures, $185,583, including $165,978 for 30 grants (high: $17,705; low: $500).
Purpose and activities: Support primarily for Protestant and religious welfare organizations, and health associations; giving also for youth organizations and welfare.
Limitations: Giving primarily in Evansville, and the Chicago, IL, area. No grants to individuals.
Application information: Contributes only to pre-selected organizations. Applications not accepted.
Trustee: Citizens National Bank.
Employer Identification Number: 356028034

2231
Sarah E. Durham Trust ⌑
Bank One, Crawfordsville, Drawer 687
Crawfordsville 47933

Established in 1937 in IN.
Foundation type: Independent
Financial data (yr. ended 12/31/88): Assets, $1,518,568 (M); expenditures, $138,455, including $80,503 for 1 grant.
Purpose and activities: Giving primarily to a home for needy persons.
Limitations: Giving limited to Crawfordsville, IN.
Application information: Contributes only to pre-selected organizations. Applications not accepted.
Trustee: Bank One, Crawfordsville.
Employer Identification Number: 356009531

2232
The Harrison Eiteljorg Foundation ⌑ ☆
4567 Cold Spring Rd.
Indianapolis 46208

Established in 1982 in IN.
Donor(s): Harrison Eiteljorg.
Foundation type: Operating
Financial data (yr. ended 10/31/88): Assets, $15,582 (M); gifts received, $2,000; expenditures, $4,940,084, including $4,940,000 for 22 grants (high: $600,000; low: $60,000).
Purpose and activities: A private operating foundation; support primarily for a museum; minor support also for health associations, youth, and welfare to individuals.
Limitations: Giving primarily in Indianapolis, IN.
Application information: Contributes only to pre-selected organizations. Applications not accepted.
Trustee: Harrison Eiteljorg.
Directors: Harrison Eiteljorg II, Jack M. Eiteljorg, Roger S. Eiteljorg, Sonya Eiteljorg, John A. Lienhart.
Employer Identification Number: 311080061

2233
English-Bonter-Mitchell Foundation ▼
900 Fort Wayne National Bank Bldg.
Fort Wayne 46802

Established in 1972 in IN.
Donor(s): Mary Tower English, Louise Bonter, and others.
Foundation type: Independent
Financial data (yr. ended 12/31/87): Assets, $37,416,157 (M); gifts received, $1,756,816; expenditures, $2,163,965, including $2,009,500 for 56 grants (high: $155,000; low: $1,000).
Purpose and activities: Giving primarily for cultural programs and programs for youth; support also for higher education, hospitals, churches and religious organizations, social services, health, and community development.
Limitations: Giving primarily in Fort Wayne, IN.
Officer: Mary E. Mitchell, Board member.
Trustee: Fort Wayne National Bank.
Number of staff: None.
Employer Identification Number: 356247168

2234
First Source Foundation ⌑
c/o First Source Bank
P.O. Box 1602
South Bend 46601 (219) 236-2790

Established in 1952 in IN.
Donor(s): First Source Bank Charitable Trust.
Foundation type: Company-sponsored
Financial data (yr. ended 12/31/88): Assets, $967,472 (M); gifts received, $236,642; expenditures, $112,309, including $104,200 for 22 grants (high: $45,000; low: $250).
Purpose and activities: Support for higher education and social services.

Limitations: Giving primarily in IN.
Application information:
Initial approach: Proposal
Deadline(s): None
Write: Ronald M. Brown, Secy.-Treas.
Officers: E. Blair Warner, Chair.; Ernestine M. Raclin, Pres.; Christopher J. Murphy III, V.P.; Ronald M. Brown, Secy.-Treas.
Trustee: First Source Bank.
Employer Identification Number: 356034211

2235
Foellinger Foundation, Inc. ▼
1125 Lincoln Bank Tower
116 East Berry St.
Fort Wayne 46802 (219) 422-2900

Incorporated in 1958 in IN.
Donor(s): Esther A. Foellinger,† Helene R. Foellinger,† News Publishing Co.
Foundation type: Independent
Financial data (yr. ended 08/31/89): Assets, $101,792,690 (L); gifts received, $15,944,599; expenditures, $3,923,074, including $3,353,044 for 96 grants (high: $375,000; low: $50; average: $10,000-$200,000).
Purpose and activities: Giving primarily for cultural organizations, higher and other education, parks and recreation, social services, including programs for the disadvantaged and youth, and a community fund.
Types of support: Operating budgets, building funds, special projects, capital campaigns, conferences and seminars, consulting services, equipment, general purposes, land acquisition, matching funds, renovation projects, seed money.
Limitations: Giving primarily in the Fort Wayne, IN, area. Generally, no grants for religious groups or pre-college education. No grants to individuals, or generally, for endowments.
Publications: Annual report (including application guidelines).
Application information: Application form not required.
Initial approach: Letter or proposal
Copies of proposal: 1
Deadline(s): 90 days before funds needed
Board meeting date(s): 3rd Thursday of each month
Final notification: Varies, depending on request
Write: Carl D. Rolfsen, Pres.
Officers and Directors:* Ernest E. Williams,* Chair.; Carl D. Rolfsen,* Pres.; Walter P. Helmke,* V.P.; Harry V. Owen,* Treas.; Barbara Burt.
Number of staff: 2 full-time professional; 1 part-time professional.
Employer Identification Number: 356027059

2236
Fort Wayne Community Foundation, Inc.
116 East Wayne St.
Fort Wayne 46802 (219) 426-4083

Incorporated in 1956 in IN.
Foundation type: Community
Financial data (yr. ended 12/31/89): Assets, $7,247,815 (M); gifts received, $551,077; expenditures, $453,077, including $295,837 for 62 grants (high: $18,000; low: $64) and $110,000 for foundation-administered programs.
Purpose and activities: Discretionary grant-making preference given to "projects expected to generate substantial benefits for the greater Fort Wayne area," including capital projects, demonstration projects, and projects promoting effective management, efficient use of community resources or volunteer participation. Areas of interest include social services, education, community development, health services, and the arts.
Types of support: Seed money, emergency funds, building funds, equipment, land acquisition, matching funds, consulting services, conferences and seminars, special projects, renovation projects, research, technical assistance, scholarship funds.
Limitations: Giving primarily in Allen County, IN. No support for religious purposes, hospitals or medical research, or private schools. No grants to individuals, or for operating budgets, continuing support, annual campaigns, deficit financing, endowment funds, fellowships, or publications; no loans.
Publications: Application guidelines, grants list, occasional report, financial statement.
Application information: Application form not required.
Initial approach: Proposal, letter, or telephone
Copies of proposal: 1
Deadline(s): None
Board meeting date(s): Feb., May, Aug., and Nov.
Final notification: 3 months
Write: Mrs. Barbara Burt, Exec. Dir.
Staff: Barbara Burt, Exec. Dir.; Paul Clarke, Dir.-Special Projects; M. Joyce Schlatter, Dir.-Grants.
Number of staff: 1 full-time professional; 1 part-time professional.
Employer Identification Number: 351119450

2237
Frankenthal Family Foundation, Inc. ⌑
P.O. Box 827
5425 Hwy. 31E
Jeffersonville 47131 (812) 283-0734

Incorporated in 1967 in WI.
Donor(s): Members of the Frankenthal family.
Foundation type: Independent
Financial data (yr. ended 8/31/86): Assets, $2,485,899 (M); expenditures, $196,819, including $167,425 for 37 grants (high: $25,200; low: $25).
Purpose and activities: Giving for hospitals, higher education, and Jewish welfare funds; some support for the aged, community funds, and youth agencies.
Types of support: General purposes, building funds, equipment, land acquisition, endowment funds, professorships, scholarship funds, matching funds.
Limitations: Giving primarily in WI and KY. No grants to individuals; no loans.
Application information: Contributes only to pre-selected organizations. Applications not accepted.
Board meeting date(s): Aug.
Write: Betty J. Frankenthal, Pres.
Officers and Directors:* Betty J. Frankenthal,* Pres.; Stuart J. Frankenthal,* V.P.; Howard M. Frankenthal, Secy.; Karola Frankenthal Epstein,* Treas.
Number of staff: 2
Employer Identification Number: 396106541

2238
The Franklin Electric-Edward J. Schaefer and T. W. Kehre Charitable and Educational Foundation, Inc. ⌑ ☆
400 East Spring St.
Bluffton 46714-3798 (219) 824-2900

Established in 1964.
Foundation type: Independent
Financial data (yr. ended 12/31/88): Assets, $271,665 (M); gifts received, $360,950; expenditures, $179,620, including $167,251 for 37 grants (high: $100,000; low: $25) and $12,000 for 10 grants to individuals (high: $1,500; low: $750).
Purpose and activities: Giving primarily for education, including employee-related scholarships; support also for community funds and other social services and civic affairs groups, cutural programs, and health.
Types of support: Employee-related scholarships.
Limitations: Giving primarily in IN.
Application information: Application form required for scholarships.
Deadline(s): Feb. 1 for scholarships
Write: William H. Lawson, Pres.
Officers: William H. Lawson, Pres.; Patricia Schaefer, V.P.; Dean W. Pfister, Treas.
Employer Identification Number: 237399324

2239
The Froderman Foundation, Inc. ⌑
18 South Ninth St.
Terre Haute 47807

Donor(s): Harvey Froderman.†
Foundation type: Independent
Financial data (yr. ended 06/30/89): Assets, $6,980,055 (M); expenditures, $311,559, including $272,519 for 20 grants (high: $70,000; low: $2,000).
Purpose and activities: Grants for church support, medical education, and youth organizations.
Types of support: Building funds, equipment, scholarship funds, operating budgets, publications.
Limitations: Giving primarily in IN.
Application information: Application form required.
Initial approach: Letter
Deadline(s): None
Write: Carl M. Froderman, Pres.
Officer: Carl M. Froderman, Pres.
Employer Identification Number: 356025283

2240
Eugene and Marilyn Glick Foundation Corporation ⌑ ☆
P.O. Box 40177
Indianapolis 46240

Established in 1982.
Donor(s): Eugene B. Glick, Marilyn K. Glick.
Foundation type: Independent

Financial data (yr. ended 11/30/88): Assets, $2,872,448 (M); gifts received, $1,500,000; expenditures, $205,099, including $157,581 for 97 grants (high: $51,643; low: $30).
Purpose and activities: Giving primarily for an employment alliance; support also for sports and youth organizations, social services, and the arts.
Types of support: Operating budgets, special projects, capital campaigns, matching funds, general purposes.
Limitations: Giving primarily in Indianapolis, IN.
Officers: Eugene B. Glick, Pres.; Bernard Landman, Jr., V.P.; Marilyn K. Glick, Secy.-Treas.
Director: Barbara Gunn.
Employer Identification Number: 351549707

2241
The W. C. Griffith Foundation
c/o Merchants National Bank & Trust Co.
P.O. Box 5031
Indianapolis 46255 (317) 267-7281
Application address: 340 Century Bldg., 36 South Pennsylvania St., Indianapolis, IN 46204

Trust established in 1959 in IN.
Donor(s): William C. Griffith,† Ruth Perry Griffith.†
Foundation type: Independent
Financial data (yr. ended 11/30/89): Assets, $5,967,127 (M); expenditures, $305,397, including $274,400 for 71 grants (high: $35,000; low: $500).
Purpose and activities: Support primarily for hospitals and health associations, the arts, including music and museums, community funds, higher, secondary, and other education, medical and cancer research, family planning services, child welfare, the environment, libraries, and Christian religious organizations.
Types of support: Building funds, capital campaigns, continuing support.
Limitations: Giving primarily in Indianapolis, IN. No grants to individuals, or for scholarships and fellowships.
Publications: 990-PF.
Application information: Application form not required.
Initial approach: Letter
Copies of proposal: 1
Deadline(s): None
Board meeting date(s): June and Nov.
Write: Mike Miner, V.P. and Trust Officer
Trustee: Merchants National Bank & Trust Co.
Advisors: Charles P. Griffith, Jr., Ruthelen C. Griffith, W.C. Griffith, Jr., William C. Griffith III, Wendy G. Kortepeter.
Number of staff: 1 part-time support.
Employer Identification Number: 356007742

2242
The Habig Foundation, Inc. ⌑
1600 Royal St.
Jasper 47546
Application address: P.O. Box 460, Jasper, IN 47546; Tel.: (812) 482-1600

Incorporated in 1951 in IN.
Donor(s): Kimball International, Inc.
Foundation type: Company-sponsored
Financial data (yr. ended 6/30/87): Assets, $512,929 (M); gifts received, $222,000; expenditures, $361,736, including $300,636 for 151 grants (high: $60,000; low: $25) and $59,480 for 33 grants to individuals (high: $2,000; low: $1,000).
Purpose and activities: Emphasis on higher education, including scholarships for children of company employees, civic affairs, church support, and cultural programs.
Types of support: Employee-related scholarships.
Limitations: Giving primarily in IN.
Application information: Application form required for scholarships.
Deadline(s): Apr. 1 for scholarships; none for grants
Write: Douglas A. Habig, Treas.
Officers and Directors: Arnold F. Habig, Chair.; Thomas L. Habig, Pres.; Maurice R. Kuper, V.P.; H.E. Thyen, Secy.; Douglas A. Habig, Treas.; Anthony P. Habig, John B. Habig, Leonard B. Marshall, Jr., Patricia H. Snyder, James C. Thyen, Ronald J. Thyen, Jack R. Wentworth.
Employer Identification Number: 356022535

2243
Arnold F. Habig Foundation, Inc. ⌑
1301 St. Charles St.
Jasper 47546
Application address: 1500 Main St., Jasper, IN 47546; Tel.: (812) 634-1010

Established in 1967.
Donor(s): Arnold F. Habig.
Foundation type: Independent
Financial data (yr. ended 12/31/88): Assets, $2,604,533 (M); gifts received, $10,000; expenditures, $184,239, including $164,038 for 106 grants (high: $40,150; low: $10).
Purpose and activities: Grants mainly for education and Roman Catholic religious organizations.
Limitations: Giving primarily in IN. No grants to individuals.
Application information: Application form not required.
Deadline(s): None
Write: Arnold F. Habig, Pres.
Officers: Arnold F. Habig, Pres.; John B. Habig, Secy.; Thomas L. Habig, Treas.
Director: Douglas A. Habig.
Employer Identification Number: 356074146

2244
Hayner Foundation ⌑
c/o Lincoln National Bank and Trust Co.
P.O. Box 9340
Fort Wayne 46899 (219) 461-6451

Established in 1966 in IN.
Donor(s): John F. Hayner.†
Foundation type: Independent
Financial data (yr. ended 12/31/88): Assets, $1,504,903 (M); expenditures, $96,812, including $88,000 for 15 grants (high: $20,000; low: $1,000).
Purpose and activities: Support for education, including health education services, and cultural activities.
Types of support: Operating budgets, continuing support, seed money, equipment, matching funds, general purposes, capital campaigns, renovation projects, scholarship funds.
Limitations: Giving limited to Allen County, IN. No support for religious organizations. No grants to individuals, or for endowment funds, deficit financing, land acquisition, fellowships, research, publications, or conferences; no loans.
Publications: 990-PF.
Application information: Application form not required.
Initial approach: Letter
Deadline(s): None
Board meeting date(s): Monthly
Final notification: 6 weeks
Write: Alice Kopfer, V.P.
Trustee: Lincoln National Bank and Trust Co. of Fort Wayne.
Number of staff: None.
Employer Identification Number: 356064431

2245
Heritage Fund of Bartholomew County, Inc.
P.O. Box 1547
Columbus 47201 (812) 376-7772

Incorporated in 1977 in IN.
Foundation type: Community
Financial data (yr. ended 12/31/89): Assets, $3,944,759 (M); gifts received, $312,059; expenditures, $208,565, including $99,971 for 21 grants (high: $15,000; low: $250), $10,718 for 25 grants to individuals and $11,914 for 3 in-kind gifts.
Purpose and activities: Giving for education, social services, health, hospitals, cultural programs, and civic affairs.
Types of support: Operating budgets, continuing support, seed money, emergency funds, deficit financing, building funds, equipment, land acquisition, matching funds, consulting services, technical assistance, scholarship funds, program-related investments, special projects, research, publications, conferences and seminars, loans, capital campaigns, renovation projects.
Limitations: Giving primarily in Bartholomew County, IN. No support for sectarian religious purposes. No grants to individuals (except for scholarships and special educational programs), or for annual campaigns or endowment funds; no loans.
Publications: Annual report, program policy statement, application guidelines, 990-PF.
Application information: Scholarship payments are made to the educational institutions for the benefit of the individual recipients. Application form not required.
Initial approach: Letter of inquiry
Deadline(s): None
Board meeting date(s): Bimonthly
Write: Edward F. Sullivan, Exec. Dir.
Officers and Directors:* Bobbi Kroot,* Chair. and Pres.; David M. Kirr,* V.P.; Nancy K. King,* Secy.; Thomas C. Bigley, Jr.,* Treas.; Randy Allman, C. Raymond Boll, Carole Bonnell, W. Calvert Brand, Betty F. Brown, Walter Divan, Peter B. Hamilton, V. William Hunt, Ann L. Moeller.
Number of staff: 1 full-time professional; 2 part-time support.
Employer Identification Number: 351343903

2246
Mary Frances Hernandez & Roy E. Smith Scholarship Fund ⌘ ☆
c/o First Citizens Bank, N.A.
P.O. Box 1125
Michigan City 46360
Application address: c/o First Citizens Bank, N.A., 515 Franklin Sq., Box 800, Michigan City, IN 46360; Tel.: (219) 873-2621

Established in 1985 in IN.
Foundation type: Independent
Financial data (yr. ended 12/31/88): Assets, $526,028 (M); expenditures, $112,724, including $107,928 for 26 grants to individuals (high: $12,700; low: $134).
Purpose and activities: Awards scholarships to individuals for higher education.
Types of support: Student aid.
Limitations: Giving primarily in Michigan City, IN.
Application information: Application form required.
Deadline(s): Mar. 1
Trustee: First Citizens Bank, N.A.
Employer Identification Number: 316268745

2247
John A. Hillenbrand Foundation, Inc. ⌘
Hwy. 46 East
Batesville 47006 (812) 934-7000

Incorporated in 1950 in IN.
Donor(s): Hillenbrand Industries, Inc.
Foundation type: Independent
Financial data (yr. ended 11/30/89): Assets, $6,757,559 (M); gifts received, $200,000; expenditures, $197,131, including $153,611 for 28 grants (high: $30,000; low: $1,000).
Purpose and activities: Support for health, social services, youth, education, civic affairs, economics, and religious giving.
Limitations: Giving limited to Batesville, IN, and Ripley County.
Application information:
Initial approach: Letter (typewritten)
Deadline(s): None
Write: Daniel A. Hillenbrand, Pres.
Officers: Daniel A. Hillenbrand, Pres.; W. August Hillenbrand II, V.P. and Secy.-Treas.; John A. Hillenbrand II, V.P.
Directors: George M. Hillenbrand, Ray J. Hillenbrand.
Employer Identification Number: 356042242

2248
William A. and Martha H. Hillenbrand Foundation ⌘ ☆
Hwy. 46
Batesville 47006 (812) 934-7000

Established in 1986 in IN.
Donor(s): Martha H. Hillenbrand.
Foundation type: Independent
Financial data (yr. ended 11/30/88): Assets, $1,118,283 (M); expenditures, $59,591, including $58,027 for 5 grants (high: $25,003; low: $5,040).
Purpose and activities: Giving primarily for secondary education and hospitals; support also for rehabilitation services and higher education.
Limitations: Giving limited to the Batesville, IN, area.
Application information:
Initial approach: Proposal
Deadline(s): None
Write: W. August Hillenbrand, Trustee
Trustees: Martha H. Hillenbrand, W. August Hillenbrand, Catherine H. Kennedy, Martha H. Ragland.
Employer Identification Number: 351707873

2249
Holiday Home Foundation of Evansville, Inc. ⌘
1202 West Buena Vista Rd.
Evansville 47710-3336

Established in 1974 in IN.
Donor(s): Sharon Dunigan, Larry Dunigan, Holiday Home Health Care Corp. of Evansville.
Foundation type: Independent
Financial data (yr. ended 9/30/88): Assets, $1,409,225 (M); gifts received, $144,686; expenditures, $68,928, including $63,524 for grants (high: $27,500).
Purpose and activities: Support primarily for higher education and Christian churches and organizations.
Limitations: Giving primarily in Evansville, IN.
Officers: Larry Dunigan, Pres.; Helen Dunigan, V.P.; Sharon Dunigan, Secy.-Treas.
Employer Identification Number: 237414999

2250
The Honeywell Foundation, Inc. ⌘
P.O. Box 432
275 West Market St.
Wabash 46992 (219) 563-1102

Incorporated in 1941 in IN.
Donor(s): Mark C. Honeywell,† Eugenia H. Honeywell,† Della D. Hubbard,† and others.
Foundation type: Operating
Financial data (yr. ended 9/30/88): Assets, $16,712,713 (M); gifts received, $250,000; expenditures, $618,397, including $48,386 for 14 grants (high: $19,225; low: $48) and $508,400 for 4 foundation-administered programs.
Purpose and activities: A private operating foundation; operates a community center, which includes a variety of educational and cultural programs.
Types of support: General purposes.
Limitations: Giving limited to rural Wabash County, IN. No grants to individuals, or for scholarships or fellowships.
Publications: 990-PF.
Application information: Discretionary grants program is limited to $5,000-$10,000 a year. Application form required.
Initial approach: Telephone
Copies of proposal: 1
Deadline(s): July 1
Board meeting date(s): Monthly; grants are approved in Sept.
Final notification: Oct.
Write: Donald F. Knapp, Exec. Dir.
Officers: Charles R. Tiede,* Pres.; J. Douglas Craig,* V.P.; Donald F. Knapp, Secy. and Exec. Dir.; Kim Clark,* Treas.
Directors:* Larry Curless, Marilyn Ford, Thomas McSpadden.
Number of staff: 2 full-time professional; 10 full-time support; 7 part-time support.
Employer Identification Number: 350390706

2251
Hook Drug Foundation ⌘
2800 Enterprise St.
Indianapolis 46226

Established in 1969 in IN.
Donor(s): Hook Drugs, Inc.
Foundation type: Company-sponsored
Financial data (yr. ended 12/31/87): Assets, $1,022,088 (M); gifts received, $273,001; expenditures, $114,581, including $110,094 for 114 grants (high: $20,000; low: $25).
Purpose and activities: Giving to organizations involved in education, community, cultural, civic and health issues.
Application information:
Initial approach: Varies with nature of request; information available
Deadline(s): None
Write: Newell J. Hall, Pres.
Officers and Directors: Newell J. Hall, Pres.; Kenneth Gaskins, V.P.; Thomas Dingledy, Secy.; John J. Kelly, Treas.; Thomas Cunningham, Gayl W. Doster, James Richter.
Employer Identification Number: 237046664

2252
Walter F. Hulet Trust ⌘
c/o Bank One Crawfordsville
P.O. Drawer 687
Crawfordsville 47933 (317) 362-1100

Established in 1944 in IN.
Foundation type: Independent
Financial data (yr. ended 12/31/88): Assets, $1,002,746 (M); expenditures, $107,092, including $50,693 for 36 grants (high: $5,000; low: $80).
Purpose and activities: Support primarily for social services, higher education, and a church.
Limitations: Giving primarily in IN. No grants to individuals.
Application information:
Initial approach: Letter
Deadline(s): None
Write: Kenneth J. Newnum, Sr., Sr. V.P.
Trustee: Bank One Crawfordsville.
Employer Identification Number: 356009516

2253
Hulman Public Building Trust ⌘
900 Wabash Ave.
Terre Haute 47801 (812) 232-9446

Established about 1960 in IN.
Foundation type: Independent
Financial data (yr. ended 12/31/88): Assets, $1,241,303 (M); expenditures, $56,549, including $55,000 for 1 grant.
Purpose and activities: Giving limited to construction of public buildings and grants for higher education.
Types of support: Building funds.
Limitations: Giving limited to Vigo County, IN.
Application information: Application form not required.
Deadline(s): None
Write: Jeffrey Belskus, Trustee
Trustees: Jeff Belskus, Mari Hulman George, Tony George.
Employer Identification Number: 356013772

2254
Indiana Chemical Trust ⌑
c/o The Merchants National Bank of Terre Haute
701 Wabash Ave.
Terre Haute 47808 (812) 234-5571

Trust established in 1953 in IN.
Donor(s): Indiana Gas and Chemical Corp., Terre Haute Gas Corp., Tribune-Star Publishing Co.
Foundation type: Company-sponsored
Financial data (yr. ended 12/31/88): Assets, $5,171,156 (M); gifts received, $60,500; expenditures, $121,607, including $118,000 for 18 grants (high: $25,000; low: $1,000).
Purpose and activities: Grants primarily to civic, charitable, youth, and educational institutions, with emphasis on an institute of technology; giving also for Catholic church support, including two monasteries.
Types of support: General purposes.
Limitations: Giving primarily in Vigo County, IN.
Application information: Application form not required.
Deadline(s): None
Write: John F. Sweet, Trust Officer, The Merchants National Bank of Terre Haute
Committee Members: Joseph R. Cloutier, Rex R. Detar, Mary F. Hulman.
Trustee: The Merchants National Bank of Terre Haute.
Employer Identification Number: 356024816

2255
Indianapolis A.D.E. Charities, Inc. ⌑
1213 North Arlington Ave., Suite 201
Indianapolis 46219-3238
Application address: P.O. Box 39026, Indianapolis, IN 46239

Established in 1981 in IN.
Donor(s): D. Michael Hockett, CITA, Inc.
Foundation type: Independent
Financial data (yr. ended 12/31/88): Assets, $1,203,487 (M); gifts received, $1,176,900; qualifying distributions, $595,213, including $461,021 for grants (high: $159,810) and $125,000 for foundation-administered programs.
Purpose and activities: Support primarily to organizations that maintain a home for destitute, abandoned, neglected, and dependent children.
Limitations: Giving primarily in the Marion County, IN, area. No grants to individuals.
Application information:
Initial approach: Proposal
Deadline(s): None
Write: D. Michael Hockett, Pres.
Officers and Directors: D. Michael Hockett, Pres.; John Fuller, Secy.-Treas.; Brian Scott Hockett, Judy Hockett.
Employer Identification Number: 311024383

2256
The Indianapolis Foundation ▼
615 North Alabama St., Rm. 119
Indianapolis 46204 (317) 634-7497

Established in 1916 in IN by resolution of trust.
Donor(s): James Proctor,† James E. Roberts,† Delavan Smith,† Charles N. Thompson,† Georgeanna Zumpfe.†
Foundation type: Community
Financial data (yr. ended 12/31/89): Assets, $61,026,115 (M); gifts received, $785,301; expenditures, $3,349,219, including $2,967,065 for 84 grants (high: $246,415; low: $892; average: $4,000-$50,000).
Purpose and activities: Support for the areas of health, welfare, education, character building, and culture through grants for services to youth and children; health, hospitals, and the handicapped; family and neighborhood services; civic and cultural programs; research and community planning; and general education.
Types of support: Matching funds, program-related investments, seed money, general purposes, equipment, special projects, conferences and seminars, annual campaigns, emergency funds, renovation projects, capital campaigns.
Limitations: Giving limited to Indianapolis and Marion County, IN. No support for religious or sectarian purposes, elementary or secondary private schools, or sectarian pre-school or day care centers. No grants to individuals, or for endowment funds; no loans.
Publications: Annual report (including application guidelines), newsletter.
Application information: Application form not required.
Initial approach: Telephone or letter
Copies of proposal: 7
Deadline(s): Submit proposal by last day of Jan., Mar., May, July, Sept., or Nov.
Board meeting date(s): Feb., Apr., June, Aug., Oct., and Dec.
Final notification: Immediately following meetings
Write: Kenneth I. Chapman, Exec. Dir.
Officers and Trustees:* Charles A. Pechette,* Chair.; Matthew E. Welsh,* Vice-Chair.; Howard S. Wilcox,* Secy.; Rexford C. Early, Daniel R. Efroymson, Louis S. Hensley, Jr.
Trustee Banks: Ameritrust National Bank, Bank One, Indianapolis, N.A., First of America Bank, The Huntington National Bank of Indiana, Indiana National Bank, Merchants National Bank & Trust Co., Peoples Bank & Trust Co.
Staff: Kenneth I. Chapman, Exec. Dir.
Number of staff: 2 full-time professional; 2 full-time support.
Employer Identification Number: 350868115

2257
Inland Container Corporation Foundation, Inc.
4030 Vincennes Rd.
Indianapolis 46268-0937 (317) 879-4308

Incorporated in 1951 in IN.
Donor(s): Inland Container Corp., Temple-Inland, Inc.
Foundation type: Company-sponsored
Financial data (yr. ended 12/31/88): Assets, $8,074,400 (M); gifts received, $350,000; expenditures, $648,888, including $445,170 for 380 grants (high: $36,000; low: $100) and $125,025 for 49 grants to individuals.
Purpose and activities: Emphasis on community funds and education, including employee-related scholarships; grants also for cultural programs and youth agencies.
Types of support: Employee-related scholarships, annual campaigns, continuing support, general purposes, operating budgets, special projects.
Limitations: Giving limited to areas of plant locations within IN. No support for religious organizations for sectarian purposes. No grants for building or endowment funds; individual scholarship grants are only for the children of company employees.
Publications: Application guidelines.
Application information: Scholarships limited to children of Inland Container Corp. employees; only eligible applicants should apply. Application form not required.
Initial approach: Letter
Copies of proposal: 1
Deadline(s): Submit proposal in Sept. or Oct.; deadline Oct. 15
Board meeting date(s): June and Dec.
Write: Frank F. Hirschman, Pres.
Officers and Directors:* Frank F. Hirschman,* Pres.; J.M. Areddy,* V.P.; D.J. Harrison,* V.P.; Ben J. Lancashire,* V.P.; P.A. Foley,* Secy.-Treas.
Employer Identification Number: 356014640

2258
Irwin-Sweeney-Miller Foundation ▼
420 Third St.
P.O. Box 808
Columbus 47202 (812) 372-0251

Incorporated in 1952 in IN.
Donor(s): Members of the Irwin, Sweeney, and Miller families.
Foundation type: Independent
Financial data (yr. ended 12/31/89): Assets, $1,682,765 (L); gifts received, $665,861; expenditures, $792,068, including $673,725 for 56 grants (high: $288,715; low: $100; average: $1,000-$5,000).
Purpose and activities: Support for creative programs in social justice, education, religion, the arts, and improving family stability; giving for the disadvantaged, child welfare, social services, and community development.
Types of support: Annual campaigns, conferences and seminars, consulting services, continuing support, emergency funds, general purposes, matching funds, operating budgets, program-related investments, renovation projects, seed money, special projects, technical assistance.
Limitations: Giving primarily in the Columbus, IN, area for new funding. No grants to individuals, or for deficit financing, research, scholarships, or fellowships; no loans.
Publications: Biennial report.
Application information: Application form not required.
Initial approach: Letter with proposal
Copies of proposal: 1
Deadline(s): Mar. 1 and Sept. 1
Board meeting date(s): Apr. and Oct.
Final notification: 1 month
Write: Sarla Kalsi, Exec. Dir.
Officers and Directors:* Clementine M. Tangeman,* Chair.; Richard B. Stoner,* Pres.; Sarla Kalsi,* V.P., Treas., and Exec. Dir.; Susan Ingmire,* Secy. and Prog. Officer; John F.

Dorenbusch, Lynne M. Maguire, Katherine T. McLeod, Robert Alan Melting, Catherine G. Miller, Elizabeth G. Miller, Hugh Thomas Miller, J. Irwin Miller, Margaret I. Miller, William I. Miller, Xenia S. Miller, George W. Newlin, Thomas N. Patch, Jonathan D. Schiller, Carolyn S. Tangeman, John Tangeman.
Number of staff: 1 full-time professional; 1 full-time support.
Employer Identification Number: 356014513

2259
Jenn Foundation ¤
8900 Keystone Crossing, Suite 401
Indianapolis 46240 (317) 848-6944

Established in 1963.
Foundation type: Independent
Financial data (yr. ended 12/31/88): Assets, $1,488,048 (L); expenditures, $113,010, including $109,507 for 37 grants (high: $19,500; low: $100).
Purpose and activities: Giving primarily for higher education, hospitals, youth agencies, and a community fund.
Limitations: Giving primarily in IN.
Application information: Application form not required.
Deadline(s): None
Write: Louis J. Jenn, Pres.
Officers and Directors: Louis J. Jenn, Chair. and Pres.; Gerald R. Jenn, V.P.; Leslie E. Howell, Secy.; Clarence Long, Treas.; George Doyle.
Employer Identification Number: 356037030

2260
Arthur Jordan Foundation
1230 North Delaware St.
Indianapolis 46202 (317) 635-1378

Trust established in 1928 in IN.
Donor(s): Arthur Jordan.†
Foundation type: Independent
Financial data (yr. ended 12/31/89): Assets, $8,758,167 (M); expenditures, $605,866, including $556,750 for 43 grants (high: $155,000; low: $750; average: $5,000-$10,000).
Purpose and activities: Giving primarily for private colleges and universities and fine arts.
Types of support: Operating budgets, general purposes, continuing support, annual campaigns, building funds, matching funds, capital campaigns.
Limitations: Giving limited to Marion County, IN. No support for medical research. No grants to individuals, or for endowment funds, research, scholarships, or fellowships; no loans.
Publications: Application guidelines.
Application information: Application form not required.
Initial approach: Letter
Copies of proposal: 3
Deadline(s): Submit proposal preferably in Apr. or Oct.; deadlines May 1 and Nov. 1
Board meeting date(s): May and Nov.
Final notification: 30 days
Write: Margaret F. Sallee, Admin. Asst.
Officers and Trustees:* Fred C. Tucker, Jr., Chair.; Eugene M. Busche,* Vice-Chair.; Andrew J. Paine, Jr., Secy.; Richard B. DeMars,* Treas.; Margaret F. Sallee, Admin. Asst.; Boris E. Meditch, Frank E. Russell.
Number of staff: 1 part-time professional.
Employer Identification Number: 350428850

2261
Journal Gazette Foundation, Inc. ¤
701 South Clinton
Fort Wayne 46802 (219) 461-8202

Established in 1985 in IN.
Donor(s): Journal-Gazette Co., Richard G. Inskeep.
Foundation type: Company-sponsored
Financial data (yr. ended 12/31/88): Assets, $1,506,738 (M); gifts received, $541,000; expenditures, $317,544, including $316,529 for 80 grants (high: $60,000; low: $15).
Purpose and activities: Support for social services, youth, cultural organizations, and health services.
Types of support: Operating budgets.
Limitations: Giving primarily in northeastern IN.
Application information: Application form required.
Deadline(s): None
Write: Richard G. Inskeep, Pres.
Officers and Directors: Richard G. Inskeep, Pres.; Jerry D. Fox, Secy.-Treas.; Marian F. Abromson, Harriet J. Inskeep, Julia Inskeep Walda.
Employer Identification Number: 311134237

2262
Kelley Foundation, Inc. ¤ ☆
500 East State Blvd.
Fort Wayne 46805 (219) 484-5566

Established in 1986.
Donor(s): Dale Jackson.
Foundation type: Independent
Financial data (yr. ended 12/31/88): Assets, $356,411 (M); gifts received, $14,880; expenditures, $286,466, including $284,964 for 44 grants (high: $100,000; low: $150).
Purpose and activities: Giving primarily for education and a library; support also for civic affairs.
Limitations: Giving primarily in IN.
Application information:
Initial approach: Letter
Deadline(s): None
Write: James E. Kelley, Pres.
Officers: James E. Kelley, Pres.; Thomas W. Kelley, V.P.; Suzanne E. Horten, Secy.-Treas.
Employer Identification Number: 311156904

2263
E. H. Kilbourne Residuary Charitable Trust ¤
c/o Lincoln National Bank Trust Dept.
P.O. Box 9340
Fort Wayne 46899 (219) 461-6451

Trust established in IN.
Donor(s): Edgar Kilbourne.†
Foundation type: Independent
Financial data (yr. ended 1/31/89): Assets, $6,171,177 (M); expenditures, $438,407, including $192,558 for 30 grants (high: $10,600; low: $500) and $196,650 for 133 grants to individuals (high: $19,800; low: $200).
Purpose and activities: Giving for higher education, including scholarships for graduating high school seniors, youth agencies, health and social services, and the arts.
Types of support: Student aid, capital campaigns, equipment, general purposes.
Limitations: Giving limited to Allen County, IN. No grants to individuals (except for scholarships to local, graduating high school seniors), or for endowment funds, research, publications, or conferences; no loans.
Publications: 990-PF, application guidelines.
Application information: Application form required.
Initial approach: Letter
Deadline(s): Apr. 15 for scholarships
Board meeting date(s): May for scholarships; monthly for other grants
Final notification: 6 weeks
Write: Alice Kopfer, V.P.
Trustee: Lincoln National Bank and Trust Co. of Fort Wayne.
Number of staff: None.
Employer Identification Number: 356332820

2264
George Koch Sons Foundation, Inc.
10 South 11th Ave.
Evansville 47744 (812) 426-9600

Incorporated in 1945 in IN.
Donor(s): Gibbs Die Casting Aluminum Corp., George Koch Sons, Inc.
Foundation type: Company-sponsored
Financial data (yr. ended 12/31/88): Assets, $4,929,032 (M); gifts received, $170,000; expenditures, $166,425, including $155,325 for 51 grants (high: $35,000; low: $100).
Purpose and activities: Emphasis on relief for needy families designated by charitable institutions; grants also to cultural and educational institutions, museums, churches, and youth camps, with particular emphasis on underprivileged children; scholarships available to children of company employees.
Types of support: Employee-related scholarships.
Limitations: Giving limited to IN, with emphasis on the Evansville-Vanderburgh County area. No grants to individuals (except for employee-related scholarships).
Application information: Application form not required.
Initial approach: Letter
Deadline(s): None
Write: Robert L. Koch II, Pres.
Officers and Directors: Robert L. Koch II, Pres. and Treas.; James H. Muehlbauer, V.P. and Secy.
Number of staff: None.
Employer Identification Number: 356023372

2265
Kuehn Foundation ¤
P.O. Box 207
Evansville 47702

Established in 1968 in IN.
Foundation type: Independent
Financial data (yr. ended 12/31/88): Assets, $2,882,463 (M); gifts received, $5,075; expenditures, $149,167, including $146,200 for 34 grants (high: $50,000; low: $200).

Purpose and activities: Giving largely for higher and secondary education, museums, cultural affairs, and youth activities.
Limitations: Giving primarily in IN.
Application information: Contributes only to pre-selected organizations. Applications not accepted.
Trustees: Mary Catherine Powell, Chair.; George E. Powell, Jr., Vice-Chair.; Nicholas K. Powell, Secy.; Peter E. Powell, Richardson K. Powell.
Employer Identification Number: 237021199

2266
Charles W. Kuhne Foundation Trust ☆
c/o Lincoln National Bank & Trust Co.
116 East Berry St., P.O. Box 2340
Fort Wayne 46801-0960 (219) 461-6451

Foundation type: Independent
Financial data (yr. ended 07/31/89): Assets, $3,398,402 (M); expenditures, $152,085, including $131,030 for 17 grants (high: $36,000; low: $1,000).
Purpose and activities: Giving primarily for higher education, a library, and the arts, including public television and theater; minor support for community development and social services.
Types of support: Annual campaigns, capital campaigns, special projects.
Limitations: Giving primarily in Fort Wayne, IN. No grants to individuals.
Application information: Application form not required.
Initial approach: Letter
Deadline(s): None
Write: Alice Kopfer, V.P., Lincoln National Bank & Trust Co.
Trustee: Lincoln National Bank & Trust Co.
Employer Identification Number: 356011137

2267
Leighton-Oare Foundation, Inc. ⌑
112 West Jefferson Blvd., Suite 603
South Bend 46601

Incorporated in 1955 in IN.
Donor(s): Mary Morris Leighton.
Foundation type: Independent
Financial data (yr. ended 12/31/88): Assets, $13,325,357 (M); gifts received, $17,442; expenditures, $521,573, including $516,225 for 45 grants (high: $100,000; low: $50).
Purpose and activities: Emphasis on higher education and health; grants also for the arts and community funds.
Types of support: Continuing support.
Limitations: Giving primarily in IN. No grants to individuals, or for capital, endowment or emergency funds, operating budgets, annual campaigns, seed money, deficit financing, matching gifts, scholarships, or fellowships; no loans.
Publications: 990-PF.
Application information: Application form not required.
Initial approach: Letter
Deadline(s): None
Board meeting date(s): Feb., May, Aug., and Nov.
Final notification: 90 to 120 days
Write: Judd C. Leighton, Secy.-Treas.
Officers and Directors: Mary Morris Leighton, Pres.; James F. Thornburg, V.P.; Judd C. Leighton, Secy.-Treas.
Number of staff: None.
Employer Identification Number: 356034243

2268
Liberty Fund, Inc. ⌑
7440 North Shadeland Ave., Suite 100
Indianapolis 46250 (317) 842-0880

Incorporated in 1960 in IN.
Donor(s): Pierre F. Goodrich,† Enid Goodrich, John B. Goodrich.†
Foundation type: Operating
Financial data (yr. ended 4/30/87): Assets, $93,529,320 (M); expenditures, $4,415,133, including $316,000 for 15 grants (high: $70,000; low: $2,000) and $2,605,397 for 1 foundation-administered program.
Purpose and activities: To promote education concerned with human liberty mainly through an operating program.
Types of support: Operating budgets, continuing support, special projects.
Limitations: No grants to individuals, or for annual campaigns, seed money, emergency funds, deficit financing, capital or endowment funds, matching gifts, scholarships and fellowships, research, demonstration projects, publications, or conferences; no loans.
Application information: Application form not required.
Initial approach: Letter or proposal
Copies of proposal: 1
Deadline(s): Apr.
Board meeting date(s): Monthly
Final notification: 1 to 2 weeks if denied; after Apr. meeting if considered further
Write: W.W. Hill, Jr., Chair.
Officers: W.W. Hill, Jr.,* Chair., Pres. and Treas.; Enid Goodrich, Vice-Chair.; J. Charles King, V.P.; Helen W. Garlotte, Secy.
Directors:* Manuel F. Ayau, Ralph W. Husted, Roseda D. Martin, Dr. A. Weil McLeod, Irwin H. Reiss, T. Alan Russell, Richard A. Ware, Don E. Welch.
Number of staff: 8 full-time professional.
Employer Identification Number: 351320021

2269
Eli Lilly and Company Foundation ▼
Lilly Corporate Ctr.
Indianapolis 46285 (317) 276-5342

Incorporated in 1968 in IN.
Donor(s): Eli Lilly and Co.
Foundation type: Company-sponsored
Financial data (yr. ended 12/31/89): Assets, $7,954,230 (M); gifts received, $6,000,000; expenditures, $7,814,907, including $5,850,951 for 199 grants (high: $1,453,956; low: $250; average: $1,000-$100,000) and $1,938,817 for 5,092 employee matching gifts.
Purpose and activities: Giving primarily for health, civic and public affairs, and cultural activities, and education, including higher education, educational programs for minorities, and schools of pharmacy.
Types of support: General purposes, operating budgets, building funds, land acquisition, fellowships, annual campaigns, capital campaigns, employee matching gifts, matching funds.
Limitations: Giving primarily in Indianapolis, IN, and other areas of company operations. No grants to individuals, or for endowment funds, special projects, research, publications, or conferences; no loans.
Application information: Application form not required.
Initial approach: Proposal
Copies of proposal: 1
Deadline(s): None
Board meeting date(s): Quarterly
Final notification: 3 weeks to 3 months
Write: Carol Edgar, Secy.
Officers: Vaughn D. Bryson,* Pres.; Michael S. Hunt, V.P. and Treas.; Carol Edgar, Secy.
Directors:* Vaughn D. Bryon, James M. Cornelius, Earl B. Herr, Jr., Mel Perelman, Eugene L. Step, Richard D. Wood.
Number of staff: 1 full-time professional; 2 full-time support.
Employer Identification Number: 356202479

2270
Lilly Endowment, Inc. ▼
2801 North Meridian St.
P.O. Box 88068
Indianapolis 46208 (317) 924-5471

Incorporated in 1937 in IN.
Donor(s): J.K. Lilly, Sr.,† Eli Lilly,† J.K. Lilly, Jr.†
Foundation type: Independent
Financial data (yr. ended 12/31/89): Assets, $3,357,904,453 (M); expenditures, $100,987,977, including $91,524,113 for grants (high: $12,000,000; low: $1,500; average: $5,000-$75,000), $559,531 for 90 grants to individuals (high: $25,000; low: $4,000; average: $4,000-$6,000) and $426,743 for 282 employee matching gifts.
Purpose and activities: Support for religion, education, and community development, with special concentration on programs that benefit youth, develop leadership, and help develop state-of-the-art fundraising to make nonprofit organizations become more self-sustaining. Giving emphasizes charitable organizations that depend on private support, with a limited number of grants to government institutions and tax-supported programs. Also supports limited grant program in economic education and public policy research.
Types of support: Seed money, research, fellowships, matching funds, special projects, conferences and seminars, employee matching gifts, scholarship funds, student aid.
Limitations: Giving limited to IN, with emphasis on Indianapolis, for community development projects (including the arts, capital building funds, continuing and operating funds, social services), elementary and secondary education, undergraduate scholarship funds, university libraries, and social services; national giving in religion and fund-raising research; higher education programs geographically targeted on a regional or invitational basis; international projects limited to a small number of disaster-relief efforts and public policy programs mostly in the Americas. Generally, no support for health care, biological science projects, endowed chairs, or media grants (other than those few

that deal with the endowment's program interests). No grants to individuals, except for fellowships awarded under a few fellowship or grant programs associated with specific groups of academic institutions. Undergraduate scholarship assistance limited to IN residents attending IN institutions.
Publications: Annual report (including application guidelines), informational brochure (including application guidelines), program policy statement, application guidelines, occasional report.
Application information: Religion, higher education and philanthropy grants primarily national. Most elementary and secondary education/youth grants generally confined to Indiana. Trusteeship/leadership education - research at the national level, education programs primarily limited to Indiana. Community development concentrated chiefly in Indianapolis, then in Indiana. Public policy and economics research generally national in scope. Application form not required.
Initial approach: 1- or 2-page letter
Copies of proposal: 1
Deadline(s): None
Board meeting date(s): Feb., Apr., June, Sept., and Nov.; executive committee considers grant requests of less than $100,000 in Mar., May, July, Oct., and Dec.
Final notification: 3 to 6 months
Write: John M. Mutz, Pres.
Officers: John M. Mutz, Pres.; William C. Bonifield, V.P., Education; Michael A. Carroll, V.P., Community Development; Craig R. Dykstra, V.P., Religion; Charles A. Johnson, V.P., Development; William M. Goodwin, Secy.-Treas.
Directors: Thomas H. Lake, Chair.; Otis R. Bowen, M.D., Rev. William G. Enright, Byron P. Hollett, Eli Lilly II, Eugene F. Ratliff, Margaret Chase Smith, Herman B Wells, Richard D. Wood.
Number of staff: 26 full-time professional; 31 full-time support.
Employer Identification Number: 350868122

2271
The Lincoln National Life Foundation, Inc.
1300 South Clinton St.
P.O. Box 1110
Fort Wayne 46801 (219) 427-3271

Established in 1928; incorporated in 1962 in IN.
Donor(s): Lincoln National Life Insurance Co., Lincoln National Corp.
Foundation type: Company-sponsored
Financial data (yr. ended 12/31/88): Assets, $3,218,807 (M); gifts received, $340,467; qualifying distributions, $335,953, including $10,800 for 2 grants of $5,400 each, $49,267 for 12 grants to individuals (high: $3,698; low: $150) and $166,000 for loans.
Purpose and activities: Maintains the Lincoln Library and Museum and provides scholarships through two programs; one for minority students pursuing business-related studies who are selected by local minority representatives; and one for students of actuarial science; some support for actuarial science programs and loans for local nonprofit organizations.
Types of support: Student aid, loans.
Limitations: Giving limited to the Fort Wayne, IN, area, except for annual actuarial science grants. No grants for building or endowment funds, research, or matching gifts.
Publications: Application guidelines.
Application information: Application forms required for scholarships. Application form not required.
Initial approach: Letter
Copies of proposal: 1
Deadline(s): None
Board meeting date(s): May
Final notification: 45 to 60 days after meeting
Write: C. Suzanne Womack, Dir.
Officers: Ian M. Rolland,* Pres.; C. Suzanne Womack, V.P. and Secy.; Max A. Roesler, Treas.
Directors:* David D. Allen, Robert W. Crispin, P. Kenneth Dunsire, Ladonna Huntley James, Mark E. Neely, Jr., Ian M. Rolland, M. Joyce Schlatter, Thomas M. West, C. Suzanne Womack.
Number of staff: None.
Employer Identification Number: 356042099

2272
Merlin J. Loew Charitable Trust
300 West Third St.
P.O. Box 899
Marion 46925 (317) 664-9041

Established in 1981 in IN.
Donor(s): Merlin S. Loew.†
Foundation type: Independent
Financial data (yr. ended 08/31/89): Assets, $1,687,922 (M); gifts received, $15,950; expenditures, $166,466, including $133,452 for 18 grants (high: $61,579; low: $220; average: $220-$61,579).
Purpose and activities: Support for a world gospel mission, educational institutions, youth and social service agencies, community funds, and the performing arts.
Types of support: Emergency funds, general purposes, operating budgets.
Limitations: Giving limited to charitable organizations in Grant County, IN.
Publications: Annual report.
Application information: Application form not required.
Initial approach: Letter
Copies of proposal: 2
Deadline(s): June 30
Board meeting date(s): July 1
Final notification: Sept.
Write: George P. Osborn, Trustee
Trustees: George P. Osborn, Bank One.
Number of staff: None.
Employer Identification Number: 566223270

2273
Magee-O'Connor Foundation, Inc. ⌑
P.O. Box 11196
Fort Wayne 46856 (219) 461-6280

Established in 1963 in IN.
Foundation type: Independent
Financial data (yr. ended 12/31/88): Assets, $1,744,101 (M); expenditures, $114,653, including $100,100 for 15 grants (high: $75,000; low: $500).
Purpose and activities: Support primarily for a church and a zoological society; grants also for social service organizations.
Limitations: Giving primarily in Fort Wayne, IN.
Application information: Application form not required.
Deadline(s): None
Write: Donald Perrey
Trustee: Lincoln National Bank & Trust Co.
Employer Identification Number: 237087967

2274
The Martin Foundation, Inc. ▼
500 Simpson Ave.
Elkhart 46515 (219) 295-3343

Incorporated in 1953 in IN.
Donor(s): Ross Martin,† Esther Martin,† Lee Martin, Geraldine F. Martin, NIBCO, INC.
Foundation type: Independent
Financial data (yr. ended 06/30/89): Assets, $26,880,063 (M); expenditures, $1,353,443, including $1,121,407 for 89 grants (high: $400,000; low: $100; average: $500-$25,000).
Purpose and activities: Emphasis on education, particularly higher education, and social services, including programs for women, youth, and problems of drug abuse; support also for environmental and conservation organizations, cultural programs, hospitals and hospices, and international development.
Types of support: Capital campaigns, seed money, continuing support, special projects, emergency funds, equipment, general purposes, matching funds, operating budgets, publications, renovation projects.
Limitations: Giving primarily in Elkhart, IN. No grants to individuals.
Application information: Application form not required.
Initial approach: Letter
Deadline(s): None
Board meeting date(s): As required
Final notification: 3 to 6 weeks
Write: Geraldine F. Martin, Pres.
Officers and Directors:* Geraldine F. Martin,* Pres.; Elizabeth Martin,* Secy.; Jennifer Martin,* Treas.; Casper Martin, Lee Martin.
Number of staff: None.
Employer Identification Number: 351070929

2275
McDonald Memorial Fund Trust ⌑
c/o First National Bank of Warsaw
P.O. Box 1447
Warsaw 46580
Application address: Superintendent of the Warsaw Community Schools, Warsaw, IN 46580

Established in 1944 in IN.
Donor(s): Angus C. McDonald.†
Foundation type: Independent
Financial data (yr. ended 12/31/88): Assets, $1,405,997 (M); expenditures, $137,778, including $250 for 1 grant and $109,800 for 144 loans to individuals (high: $11,100; low: $500).
Purpose and activities: Loans for high school, college, or professional studies.
Types of support: Student loans.
Publications: Informational brochure.
Trustee: First National Bank of Warsaw.
Employer Identification Number: 356018326

2276
Frank M. McHale Trust ⌑ ☆
c/o First National Bank
One First National Plaza
Logansport 46947 (219) 722-4111

Established in 1976 in IN.
Foundation type: Independent
Financial data (yr. ended 12/31/88): Assets, $884,093 (M); expenditures, $259,713, including $163,500 for 8 grants (high: $105,000; low: $2,500).
Purpose and activities: Giving primarily for higher education; support also for social services, youth groups, and cultural programs.
Limitations: Giving primarily in IN, with emphasis on Logansport.
Application information: Application form required.
Deadline(s): Aug. 15
Trustee: First National Bank.
Employer Identification Number: 356317208

2277
McMillen Foundation, Inc. ⌑
1302 East Creighton Ave.
Fort Wayne 46803
Application address: 6610 Mutual Dr., Fort Wayne, IN 46825; Tel.: (219) 484-8631

Incorporated in 1947 in IN.
Donor(s): Dale W. McMillen,† members of the McMillen family.
Foundation type: Independent
Financial data (yr. ended 12/31/88): Assets, $11,165,119 (M); expenditures, $736,916, including $537,651 for 23 grants (high: $204,668; low: $1,000).
Purpose and activities: Emphasis on recreation and education; some support for youth agencies and churches.
Limitations: Giving primarily in IN.
Application information:
Initial approach: Letter
Deadline(s): None
Write: John F. McMillen, Pres.
Officers and Directors: John F. McMillen, Pres.; Barry W. McMillen, V.P.; John L. Andreas, Secy.-Treas.; Mary Jane Crowe, Thomas M. Shoaft, Linda Crowe Tate.
Employer Identification Number: 356021003

2278
Dale Jr. & Elizabeth McMillen Foundation ⌑
c/o Fort Wayne National Bank
P.O. Box 110
Fort Wayne 46801-0110 (219) 426-0555

Established in 1962 in IN.
Foundation type: Independent
Financial data (yr. ended 12/31/88): Assets, $1,123,465 (M); expenditures, $56,194, including $50,000 for 4 grants (high: $20,000; low: $10,000).
Purpose and activities: Support primarily for education; support also for a fine arts foundation, a Presbyterian church, a YMCA, and an organization benefiting the handicapped.
Application information:
Initial approach: Letter
Deadline(s): None
Trustee: Fort Wayne National Bank.
Employer Identification Number: 356020615

2279
The Metropolitan Health Council of Indianapolis, Inc. ☆
5638 Professional Circle, Suite 201
P.O. Box 41311
Indianapolis 46241 (317) 247-7276

Established as a private foundation in 1986 in IN.
Foundation type: Independent
Financial data (yr. ended 11/30/89): Assets, $18,597,609 (M); expenditures, $1,063,694, including $847,669 for 30 grants (high: $88,650; low: $2,000).
Purpose and activities: Encourages requests from community-based organizations relating to adolescent health, geriatrics, health education and promotion, mental health, and prenatal care.
Types of support: Building funds, capital campaigns, equipment, matching funds, seed money, special projects.
Limitations: Giving limited to Marion County, IN, and contiguous counties in IN.
Publications: Informational brochure (including application guidelines), application guidelines.
Application information: Application form not required.
Initial approach: Telephone or letter
Copies of proposal: 18
Deadline(s): None
Write: Betty H. Wilson, Exec. Dir.
Officers and Directors:* Martin Radecki,* Pres.; George E. Ludwig,* V.P.; Terence Kahn,* Secy.; G. Scott Olive, Jr.,* Treas.; Betty Wilson, Exec. Dir,; Beverly Baker, Betty A. Conner, Thomas Feeney, Cynthia Holmes, Buford Holt, Elmer Huse, Phillip Love, Robert L. North, Mary O'Donnell, Robert Robinson, M.D., Lawrence M. Ryan, John W. Wall, Reuben L. White.
Number of staff: 1 full-time professional.
Employer Identification Number: 356203550

2280
Edward E. Meyer Educational Trust ⌑ ☆
c/o Citizens National Bank Trust Dept.
P.O. Box 719
Evansville 47705 (812) 464-3400

Foundation type: Independent
Financial data (yr. ended 12/31/88): Assets, $1,082,189 (M); expenditures, $91,043, including $81,257 for 112 grants to individuals (high: $1,000; low: $200; average: $1,000).
Purpose and activities: Awards scholarships for higher education.
Types of support: Student aid.
Limitations: Giving limited to Vanderburgh County, IN, residents.
Application information: Application forms available from Evansville-Vanderburgh School Corporation. Scholarships not available to Indiana University students. Application form required.
Deadline(s): Mar. 1
Trustee: Citizens National Bank.
Employer Identification Number: 356259567

2281
Miles Foundation ⌑
(Formerly Miles Laboratories Foundation)
1127 Myrtle St.
P.O. Box 40
Elkhart 46515 (219) 264-8225

Trust established in 1953 in IN.
Donor(s): Miles, Inc.
Foundation type: Company-sponsored
Financial data (yr. ended 12/31/88): Assets, $5,054,493 (M); gifts received, $2,500,000; expenditures, $573,485, including $511,023 for 113 grants (high: $50,000; low: $100; average: $4,200) and $21,150 for 21 grants to individuals (high: $1,500; low: $200; average: $800).
Purpose and activities: Support for higher education, including scholarship grants, community funds in areas of company operations, and hospitals and health organizations.
Types of support: Annual campaigns, building funds, capital campaigns, continuing support, endowment funds, exchange programs, renovation projects, research, special projects, student aid.
Limitations: Giving primarily in IN, with some support for organizations in other areas of company operations.
Publications: Annual report.
Application information: Application form not required.
Initial approach: Letter
Copies of proposal: 1
Deadline(s): None
Board meeting date(s): Quarterly
Write: Lehman F. Beardsley, Chair.
Officers and Trustees: Lehman F. Beardsley, Chair.; Franklin E. Breckenridge, Secy.; D.L. Cutter, J.A. D'Arco, George Evanega, R.G. Stoll.
Employer Identification Number: 356026510

2282
Ruth M. Minear Educational Trust ⌑
c/o First National Bank in Wabash
202 South Wabash St.
Wabash 46992 (219) 563-1116

Established in 1977.
Foundation type: Independent
Financial data (yr. ended 2/28/89): Assets, $1,524,405 (M); expenditures, $127,074, including $111,526 for grants to individuals.
Purpose and activities: Giving only to graduates of Wabash High School attending accredited post-secondary schools in IN.
Types of support: Student aid.
Limitations: Giving limited to Wabash, IN.
Application information: Submit IN financial aid forms.
Deadline(s): Feb. 14
Write: Allen P. Spring, Sr. V.P.
Trustee: First National Bank in Wabash.
Employer Identification Number: 356335021

2283
Moore Foundation
9100 Keystone Crossing, Suite 390
Indianapolis 46240 (317) 848-2013

Incorporated in 1960 in IN.
Donor(s): Frank M. Moore.†
Foundation type: Independent

Financial data (yr. ended 3/31/89): Assets, $11,821,936 (M); expenditures, $859,304, including $534,500 for 63 grants (high: $77,000; low: $500).
Purpose and activities: Support of the free enterprise system, the development of curriculum at the elementary and secondary school levels, and the support of religious organizations oriented toward youth.
Types of support: Operating budgets, continuing support, matching funds, special projects, conferences and seminars, lectureships, publications.
Limitations: Giving primarily in CA, OH, MI, NJ, CO, AZ, DC, PA, VA, NY, with emphasis on IN. No support for international programs. No grants to individuals, or for capital or endowment funds, seed money, building funds, renovations, emergency funds, deficit financing, scholarships, or fellowships; no loans.
Publications: Program policy statement.
Application information: Application form not required.
Initial approach: Letter, proposal, or telephone
Copies of proposal: 2
Deadline(s): None
Board meeting date(s): May and Nov.; executive committee meets monthly
Final notification: 1 to 2 months
Write: Mrs. Joan R. Barrett, Prog. Coord.
Officers: Martin J. Moore, Pres.; Joan R. Barrett, Prog. Coord.
Directors: Edward C. McKeown, Mark B. Moore, Michael Q. Moore, John M. Rohm.
Number of staff: 3 full-time professional; 1 part-time support.
Employer Identification Number: 356013824

2284
Moriah Fund
445 North Pennsylvania St., Suite 550
Indianapolis 46204
Application address: Two Wisconsin Circle, Suite 700, Chevy Chase, MD 20815

Established in 1985 in IN.
Donor(s): Clarence W. Efroymson,† Robert A. Efroymson,† Gershon Ben-Ephraim Fund, Gustave Aaron Efroymson Fund.
Foundation type: Independent
Financial data (yr. ended 12/31/89): Assets, $130,381,123 (M); gifts received, $39,600,378; expenditures, $3,952,613, including $3,773,650 for 36 grants (high: $767,400; low: $250).
Purpose and activities: Support primarily for pluralism, democracy, agriculture research and education in Israel; for community institutions in IN; and for family planning and conservation of natural resources internationally.
Types of support: Continuing support, matching funds, operating budgets, seed money, special projects.
Limitations: Giving primarily in Indianapolis, IN, Israel, and internationally.
Application information: Contributes only to pre-selected organizations. Applications not accepted.
Write: Mary Ann Efroymson Stein, Pres.
Officers and Directors:* Mary Ann Efroymson Stein,* Pres.; Daniel R. Efroymson,* V.P., Administration and Secy.-Treas.; Shirley G. Efroymson, Frank H. Newman, Robert Jay Stein.
Number of staff: 3 part-time professional; 2 part-time support.
Employer Identification Number: 311129589

2285
Morrill Charitable Foundation, Inc. ⌑ ☆
c/o Fort Wayne National Bank
P.O. Box 110
Fort Wayne 46801-0110 (219) 426-0555

Established in 1983 in IN.
Foundation type: Independent
Financial data (yr. ended 11/30/89): Assets, $2,283,133 (M); expenditures, $98,699, including $91,288 for 11 grants (high: $40,000; low: $2,000).
Purpose and activities: Giving primarily to an organization promoting youth enterprise; support also for education and community projects.
Application information:
Initial approach: Letter
Deadline(s): None
Trustees: Amy B. Morrill, Fort Wayne National Bank.
Employer Identification Number: 351584396

2286
The Community Foundation of Muncie and Delaware County, Inc. ☆
P.O. Box 807
Muncie 47308-0807 (317) 747-7181

Incorporated in 1985 in IN.
Foundation type: Community
Financial data (yr. ended 12/31/89): Assets, $3,761,030 (M); gifts received, $75,007; expenditures, $162,574, including $100,103 for 28 grants (high: $18,000; low: $250).
Purpose and activities: Support for the improvement of the quality of life, including social service, community development, and cultural organizations.
Types of support: Equipment, general purposes.
Limitations: Giving limited to Muncie and Delaware County, IN. No support for religious purposes or public agency projects. No grants to individuals, or for endowment support or budget deficits.
Publications: Annual report, application guidelines.
Application information: Application form required.
Initial approach: Letter
Copies of proposal: 7
Deadline(s): None
Write: Earl Williams, Exec. Dir.
Officers: David Sursa, Pres.; Hamer D. Shafer, V.P.; Jean Drumm, Secy.; William L. Peterson, Treas.; Earl Williams, Exec. Dir.
Number of staff: 1 part-time professional; 1 part-time support.
Employer Identification Number: 351640051

2287
Newman Charitable Foundation, Inc. ⌑
c/o National City Bank, Trust Dept.
P.O. Box 868
Evansville 47705-0868

Foundation type: Independent
Financial data (yr. ended 12/31/88): Assets, $1,062,491 (M); expenditures, $55,880, including $48,690 for 8 grants (high: $20,000; low: $250).
Purpose and activities: Primarily supports health care facilities and programs, an orchestra, and a home for neglected children.
Limitations: Giving primarily in Evansville, IN. No grants to individuals.
Application information: Contributes only to pre-selected organizations. Applications not accepted.
Trustee: National City Bank.
Employer Identification Number: 311018001

2288
John H. Noll Foundation ⌑
c/o Fort Wayne National Bank
P.O. Box 110
Fort Wayne 46801-0110

Established in 1967 in IN.
Foundation type: Independent
Financial data (yr. ended 9/30/88): Assets, $1,524,591 (M); expenditures, $96,266, including $76,088 for 92 grants to individuals (high: $3,000; low: $50).
Purpose and activities: Awards educational grants to graduating seniors from the Fort Wayne, IN, public and parochial high schools as well as Homestead High School.
Types of support: Student aid.
Limitations: Giving primarily in IN.
Application information: Application form required.
Deadline(s): Mar.
Write: Clark Valentine, V.P. and Trust Officer, Fort Wayne National Bank
Trustee: Fort Wayne National Bank.
Employer Identification Number: 237082877

2289
Nicholas H. Noyes, Jr. Memorial Foundation, Inc. ⌑
Lilly Corporate Ctr.
Indianapolis 46285 (317) 276-3171

Incorporated in 1951 in IN.
Donor(s): Nicholas H. Noyes,† Marguerite Lilly Noyes.†
Foundation type: Independent
Financial data (yr. ended 12/31/88): Assets, $15,102,977 (M); expenditures, $841,817, including $801,000 for 56 grants (high: $50,000; low: $500).
Purpose and activities: Giving for higher and secondary education, museums and cultural programs, a community fund, church support, hospitals, and youth agencies.
Types of support: Operating budgets, endowment funds, scholarship funds, matching funds.
Limitations: Giving primarily in IN. No grants to individuals, or for building funds; no loans.
Application information: Application form not required.
Initial approach: Proposal

Copies of proposal: 1
Deadline(s): None
Board meeting date(s): Semiannually
Write: James M. Cornelius, Treas.
Officers: Evan L. Noyes, Jr.,* Pres.; Robert H. Reynolds, V.P.; Frederic M. Ayres,* Secy.; James M. Cornelius, Treas.
Directors:* Janet Noyes Adams, Janet A. Carrington, A. Malcolm McVie, Nicholas S. Noyes.
Employer Identification Number: 351003699

2290
Cornelius and Anna Cook O'Brien Foundation, Inc.
(Formerly Cornelius O'Brien Foundation, Inc.)
One Indiana Sq., No. 631
Indianapolis 46266 (317) 266-6247

Established around 1969 in IN.
Foundation type: Independent
Financial data (yr. ended 11/30/89): Assets, $2,331,458 (M); expenditures, $90,568, including $83,000 for 10 grants (high: $25,000; low: $1,000).
Purpose and activities: Grants primarily for historical societies, historic preservation, college scholarships, and cultural support.
Types of support: Lectureships, scholarship funds.
Limitations: Giving primarily in southeast IN and Washington, DC.
Application information: Applications not accepted.
Board meeting date(s): Oct. and as required
Write: Robert H. Everitt
Officers: Mary O'Brien Gibson, Pres. and Treas.; John Timberlake Gibson, V.P. and Secy.
Directors: Robert A. Edwards, Robert H. Everitt, Cornelius O'Brien Gibson.
Number of staff: None.
Employer Identification Number: 237025303

2291
Hollie & Anna Oakley Foundation, Inc. ⌑
18 South 16th St.
Terre Haute 47807 (812) 232-4437

Established in 1954 in IN.
Donor(s): Hollie N. Oakley.†
Foundation type: Independent
Financial data (yr. ended 12/31/88): Assets, $1,878,440 (M); gifts received, $62,215; expenditures, $58,912, including $48,455 for 34 grants (high: $11,125; low: $30).
Purpose and activities: Emphasis on education, particularly higher education, and a hospital.
Types of support: General purposes.
Limitations: Giving primarily in the Terre Haute, IN, and Winter Park, FL, areas.
Application information:
Initial approach: Letter
Deadline(s): None
Officers and Directors: Alice Oakley Schmidt, Pres.; John G. Schmidt, V.P.; Doris Kiburis, Secy.; Eston L. Perry, Treas.; Alice Ann Perry, Jeffrey J. Perry, Julie Perry.
Employer Identification Number: 237008034

2292
Ober Foundation ⌑ ☆
38 North Pennsylvania St., Rm. 200
Indianapolis 46204

Foundation type: Independent
Financial data (yr. ended 10/31/88): Assets, $1,070,053 (M); gifts received, $79,808; expenditures, $124,160, including $109,024 for 53 grants (high: $40,000; low: $15).
Purpose and activities: Giving primarily for Protestant churches and organizations; support also for higher and secondary education and social services.
Limitations: Giving primarily in IN.
Trustees: C.S. Ober, Mary E. Ober, Mary Ann Wills.
Employer Identification Number: 356036363

2293
Paul Ogle Foundation, Inc. ⌑
Route 1, Box 22
Borden 47106

Established in 1980 in IN.
Donor(s): Paul W. Ogle, Silgas, Inc.
Foundation type: Independent
Financial data (yr. ended 12/31/88): Assets, $34,592,578 (M); gifts received, $42,095; expenditures, $2,134,605, including $1,747,513 for grants.
Purpose and activities: Support for a city. Grants for various churches, schools, and civic affairs; also supports a county foundation for Vevey, Switzerland.
Limitations: Giving primarily in IN.
Officers and Directors: Paul W. Ogle, Pres.; Willis Charles, V.P.; George Lane, V.P.; W.T. Sullivan, V.P.; Robert Lanum, Secy.; Roy Nett, Treas.
Employer Identification Number: 310988988

2294
Old National Bank Charitable Trust ⌑
c/o Old National Bank in Evansville
P.O. Box 207
Evansville 47702 (812) 464-1397

Established in 1957 in IN.
Donor(s): Old National Bank in Evansville.
Foundation type: Company-sponsored
Financial data (yr. ended 12/31/88): Assets, $829,031 (M); gifts received, $97,972; expenditures, $142,021, including $141,398 for 24 grants (high: $63,318; low: $100).
Purpose and activities: Giving for cultural programs, higher and other education, social services, health associations, and hospitals.
Types of support: Capital campaigns.
Limitations: Giving primarily in Evansville, IN.
Application information: Application form not required.
Initial approach: Letter
Copies of proposal: 1
Deadline(s): None
Board meeting date(s): Mar.
Write: M. H. Sunderman
Trustees: Daniel W. Mitchell, Richard A. Schlottman, Old National Bank in Evansville.
Employer Identification Number: 356015583

2295
Oliver Memorial Trust Foundation ⌑
112-114 West Jefferson Blvd.
South Bend 46601 (219) 237-3321

Trust established in 1959 in IN.
Donor(s): C. Frederick Cunningham,† Gertrude Oliver Cunningham, Walter C. Steenburg,† Jane Cunningham Warriner, J. Oliver Cunningham.
Foundation type: Independent
Financial data (yr. ended 12/31/88): Assets, $5,616,567 (M); gifts received, $15,000; expenditures, $276,371, including $244,500 for 26 grants (high: $50,000; low: $300; average: $5,000-$10,000).
Purpose and activities: Emphasis on hospitals, higher education, particularly college endowments, community funds, and youth agencies.
Types of support: Continuing support, annual campaigns, building funds, endowment funds, matching funds, research, capital campaigns, equipment, seed money, special projects.
Limitations: Giving primarily in IN. No grants to individuals, or for equipment and materials, land acquisition, conferences, scholarships, or fellowships; no loans.
Application information: Application form not required.
Initial approach: Letter
Deadline(s): None
Board meeting date(s): Quarterly or as required
Final notification: 9 months to 1 year
Write: William E. Rozycki, V.P., First Interstate Bank of Northern Indiana, N.A.
Officer and Distribution Committee: J. Oliver Cunningham, Chair.; Anne Cunningham McClure, Jane Cunningham Warriner.
Trustee: First Interstate Bank of Northern Indiana, N.A.
Number of staff: None.
Employer Identification Number: 356013076

2296
Marion D. & Eva S. Peeples Foundation ⌑
c/o Bank One, Franklin
P.O. Box 369
Franklin 46131 (317) 736-2498

Established about 1978 in IN.
Foundation type: Independent
Financial data (yr. ended 06/30/89): Assets, $1,203,423 (M); expenditures, $126,712, including $90,550 for 58 grants to individuals (high: $3,000; low: $250).
Purpose and activities: Scholarships for students of nursing, dietetics, and industrial arts education.
Types of support: Student aid.
Limitations: Giving limited to IN residents, with preference given to graduates of Franklin Community High School attending Franklin College.
Application information: Application form required.
Deadline(s): Mar. 20
Final notification: Before June 30
Write: Robert Heuchen, V.P., Bank One, Franklin
Trustee: Bank One, Franklin.
Employer Identification Number: 356306320

2297
The Endowment Fund of Phi Kappa Psi Fraternity, Inc.
510 Lockerbie St.
Indianapolis 46202 (317) 632-5647

Established in 1922 in OH and IL.
Donor(s): George R. Hoffman,† Solon E. Summerfield Foundation, Inc.
Foundation type: Independent
Financial data (yr. ended 05/31/89): Assets, $1,032,520 (M); gifts received, $361,047; expenditures, $562,878, including $143,021 for grants and $125,864 for grants to individuals (high: $2,000; low: $100; average: $100-$2,000).
Purpose and activities: Provides scholarship loans, grants, and awards for higher education to undergraduate and graduate students.
Types of support: Student aid, fellowships, grants to individuals.
Limitations: Giving primarily in the U.S. and Canada.
Publications: Application guidelines.
Application information: Application form required.
Initial approach: Letter or application
Deadline(s): Mar.
Board meeting date(s): Late spring or early summer for next academic year
Final notification: Mid-summer
Write: Admin.
Officer and Trustees:* Eugene A. Conley,* Chair.; Kent H. Buell,* Pres.; David F. Hull, Jr., Jerry Nelson.*
Number of staff: 1 full-time professional; 1 full-time support.
Employer Identification Number: 366130655

2298
The Plumsock Fund ⌑
9292 North Meridian St., Suite 312
Indianapolis 46260 (317) 846-8115

Incorporated in 1959 in IN.
Donor(s): Evelyn L. Lutz,† Herbert B. Lutz, Sarah L. Lutz.
Foundation type: Independent
Financial data (yr. ended 12/31/88): Assets, $3,257,914 (M); gifts received, $406,500; expenditures, $477,750, including $312,800 for 71 grants (high: $130,200; low: $50).
Purpose and activities: Giving for cultural programs, higher and secondary education, anthropology, youth agencies, and welfare and health agencies, with some emphasis on Central America.
Limitations: No grants to individuals, or for scholarships or fellowships; no loans.
Application information:
Initial approach: Letter
Copies of proposal: 3
Deadline(s): None
Board meeting date(s): Annually and as required
Write: John G. Rauch, Jr., Secy.-Treas.
Officers: Edwin Fancher, Pres.; Daniel A. Wolf, V.P.; John G. Rauch, Jr., Secy.-Treas.
Directors: Kenneth Chapman, Christopher H. Lutz.
Employer Identification Number: 356014719

2299
Robert and Elaine Pott Foundation ⌑
c/o Citizens National Bank
P.O. Box 719
Evansville 47705
Application address: c/o Citizens National Bank, 20 N.W. Third St., Evansville, IN 47708

Established in IN.
Foundation type: Independent
Financial data (yr. ended 03/31/89): Assets, $2,858,122 (M); expenditures, $201,548, including $185,000 for 6 grants (high: $95,000; low: $10,000).
Purpose and activities: Giving primarily for secondary and higher education, with emphasis on engineering programs.
Types of support: Scholarship funds.
Limitations: Giving primarily in IN and WI.
Application information: Application form not required.
Deadline(s): Apr. 30
Write: Gordon Maynard, Trust Officer, Citizens National Bank
Trustee: Citizens National Bank.
Employer Identification Number: 356290997

2300
The Prophet Sisters Foundation ⌑ ☆
c/o Fort Wayne National Bank
110 West Berry St.
Fort Wayne 46801-0110 (219) 426-0555

Established in 1983.
Foundation type: Independent
Financial data (yr. ended 10/31/88): Assets, $649,587 (M); expenditures, $156,951, including $150,000 for grants.
Purpose and activities: Support for social services, the handicapped, and women's groups.
Application information:
Initial approach: Proposal
Deadline(s): None
Trustee: Fort Wayne National Bank.
Employer Identification Number: 311087791

2301
M. E. Raker Foundation ⌑
3242 Mallard Cove Lane
Fort Wayne 46804 (219) 436-2182

Established in 1984 in IN.
Donor(s): M.E. Raker.†
Foundation type: Independent
Financial data (yr. ended 06/30/89): Assets, $6,392,330 (M); gifts received, $24,205; expenditures, $371,586, including $269,048 for 32 grants (high: $50,000; low: $500).
Purpose and activities: Support for Catholic secondary and higher education and youth.
Limitations: No support for the arts. No grants to individuals.
Application information: Application form required.
Initial approach: Proposal
Deadline(s): None
Write: John E. Hogan, Pres.
Officer: John E. Hogan, Pres.
Directors: John N. Pichon, Jr., Stephen J. Williams.
Employer Identification Number: 311040474

2302
Ranke Foundation ⌑
c/o Summit Bank, Trust Dept.
P.O. Box 2345
Fort Wayne 46801-2345

Established in 1978 in IN.
Foundation type: Independent
Financial data (yr. ended 12/31/88): Assets, $948,296 (M); expenditures, $130,929, including $123,600 for 30 grants (high: $31,000; low: $100).
Purpose and activities: Grants primarily to Lutheran organizations, including churches, schools, and hospitals.
Limitations: Giving primarily in IN.
Application information: Contributes only to pre-selected organizations. Applications not accepted.
Trustee: Summit Bank.
Employer Identification Number: 356314169

2303
Tom Raper Foundation, Inc. ⌑ ☆
P.O. Box 1365
Richmond 47375

Established in 1980.
Donor(s): Thomas R. Raper.
Foundation type: Independent
Financial data (yr. ended 11/30/89): Assets, $1,658,128 (M); gifts received, $267,548; expenditures, $74,674, including $67,672 for grants and $4,749 for grants to individuals.
Purpose and activities: Grants primarily for Christian ministries; including support for a church and grants to individuals for travel and study related to ministries.
Types of support: Grants to individuals.
Application information: Application form required.
Deadline(s): None
Officers and Directors:* Thomas R. Raper,* Pres.; Ray J. Raper,* V.P. and Secy.; Sally Fares, Mildred Raper, Suzanne D. Raper, Carolyn Runzer.
Employer Identification Number: 310999060

2304
Reilly Foundation ⌑
1510 Market Square Center
151 North Delaware St.
Indianapolis 46204 (317) 638-7531

Trust established in 1962 in IN.
Donor(s): Reilly Tar & Chemical Corp.
Foundation type: Company-sponsored
Financial data (yr. ended 12/31/88): Assets, $659,884 (M); gifts received, $200,000; expenditures, $223,057, including $183,590 for 82 grants (high: $27,000; low: $200) and $38,544 for 79 grants to individuals (high: $920; low: $108).
Purpose and activities: Giving primarily for higher education, community funds, hospitals, and social service agencies; educational grants and scholarships limited to children of company employees.
Types of support: Employee-related scholarships.
Limitations: Giving limited to areas of company operations.
Application information:
Initial approach: Letter

Deadline(s): None
Write: Lorraine D. Schroeder, Trustee
Trustees: Ineva R. Baldwin, Elizabeth B. Reilly, Peter C. Reilly, Lorraine D. Schroeder.
Employer Identification Number: 352061750

2305
Rock Island Refining Foundation ¤
P.O. Box 333
Zionsville 46268 (317) 872-4102

Established in 1973.
Foundation type: Company-sponsored
Financial data (yr. ended 11/30/89): Assets, $1,717,199 (M); expenditures, $119,299, including $104,858 for 28 grants (high: $38,000; low: $100).
Purpose and activities: Emphasis on community funds, health and hospitals, higher education, culture and the arts, and youth agencies.
Limitations: Giving primarily in IN.
Application information: Application form not required.
Initial approach: Letter
Deadline(s): None
Write: Jerry Davis
Trustees: John D. Cochran, Carolyn Kincannon, Dan Sandman, Norma Winkler.
Employer Identification Number: 356264479

2306
Franklin I. Saemann Foundation ¤
c/o Plummer & Co., CPAs
P.O. Box 956
Warsaw 46580

Established in 1983 in IN.
Donor(s): Franklin I. Saemann.
Foundation type: Independent
Financial data (yr. ended 6/30/88): Assets, $6,840,258 (M); expenditures, $692,543, including $212,000 for 12 grants (high: $50,000; low: $3,000).
Purpose and activities: Grants for higher education and social services.
Limitations: Giving primarily in IA.
Application information:
Deadline(s): None
Board meeting date(s): June
Write: Ray E. Plummer or Duane G. Huffer, Trustees
Trustees: B. Inez Feldman, Duane G. Huffer, Ray E. Plummer, Irene L. Saemann.
Employer Identification Number: 626171002

2307
Schurz Communications Foundation, Inc. ¤
225 West Colfax Ave.
South Bend 46626 (219) 287-1001

Incorporated in 1940 in IN.
Donor(s): South Bend Tribune, WSBT.
Foundation type: Company-sponsored
Financial data (yr. ended 12/31/88): Assets, $1,227,757 (M); gifts received, $40,675; expenditures, $128,583, including $117,403 for 30 grants (high: $28,553; low: $500).
Purpose and activities: Giving for higher education and community funds.
Limitations: Giving limited to South Bend, IN.
Application information: Application form not required.
Deadline(s): None
Write: James M. Schurz, Pres.
Officers and Directors: James M. Schurz, Pres.; John J. McGann, V.P.; E. Berry Smith, Secy.-Treas.
Employer Identification Number: 356024357

2308
Clarence L. & Edith B. Schust Foundation ¤
c/o Fort Wayne National Bank
110 West Berry St., P.O. Box 110
Fort Wayne 46801 (219) 426-0555

Established in 1983 in IN.
Foundation type: Independent
Financial data (yr. ended 04/30/89): Assets, $3,287,739 (M); expenditures, $182,529, including $169,728 for 42 grants (high: $16,777; low: $400).
Purpose and activities: Grants primarily for religious giving, hospitals, and youth agencies.
Limitations: Giving primarily in IN and IL.
Application information:
Initial approach: Proposal
Deadline(s): None
Trustee: Fort Wayne National Bank.
Employer Identification Number: 311064803

2309
Sherman Educational Fund ¤ ☆
c/o Sullivan State Bank
32 South Court St.
Sullivan 47882
Application address: c/o Southwest School Corp., North Court St., Sullivan, IN 47882; Tel.: (812) 268-6311

Foundation type: Independent
Financial data (yr. ended 12/31/88): Assets, $2,725,611 (M); expenditures, $157,239, including $128,429 for 115 grants to individuals (high: $3,000; low: $250).
Purpose and activities: Support limited to student aid.
Types of support: Student aid.
Limitations: Giving limited to IN residents.
Application information:
Deadline(s): Apr. 1
Write: Reggie Laconi, Chair., Selection Committee
Selection Committee: Reggie Laconi, Chair.; Paul Asbury, Jim Case, Sarah J. Geitz, Dale Knotts, Rick Walters.
Trustee: Sullivan State Bank.
Employer Identification Number: 356020497

2310
Frank L. and Laura L. Smock Foundation ¤
c/o Lincoln National Bank and Trust Co.
P.O. Box 9340
Fort Wayne 46899 (219) 461-6451

Trust established in 1953 in IN.
Donor(s): Mrs. Laura L. Smock.†
Foundation type: Independent
Financial data (yr. ended 12/31/88): Assets, $7,070,725 (M); expenditures, $259,711, including $96,100 for 12 grants (high: $30,454; low: $140) and $138,325 for 31 grants to individuals (high: $24,783; low: $108).
Purpose and activities: To "promote the health, welfare and happiness of ailing or needy or crippled or blind or elderly and aged men and women of the Presbyterian faith throughout the State of Indiana"; support also for Presbyterian churches and a college.
Types of support: Grants to individuals.
Limitations: Giving limited to IN. No grants for general or operating support, capital campaigns, building or endowment funds, or matching gifts; no loans.
Publications: Application guidelines.
Application information: Application form required.
Initial approach: Letter
Deadline(s): None
Board meeting date(s): Monthly
Final notification: 6 weeks
Write: Alice Kopfer, V.P., Lincoln National Bank and Trust Co.
Advisory Committee: Richard Hutchison, John Walley.
Trustee: Lincoln National Bank and Trust Co. of Fort Wayne.
Number of staff: None.
Employer Identification Number: 356011335

2311
Byron H. Somers Foundation ¤
5814 Reed Rd.
Fort Wayne 46835

Established in 1977.
Foundation type: Independent
Financial data (yr. ended 11/30/88): Assets, $4,010,390 (M); expenditures, $394,504, including $239,000 for 14 grants (high: $115,500; low: $1,000).
Purpose and activities: Emphasis on youth and social service agencies, education, cultural programs, and parks and recreation.
Types of support: Capital campaigns, building funds, matching funds.
Limitations: Giving primarily in Fort Wayne, IN.
Application information: Applications not accepted.
Trustees: Druscilla S. Doehrman, Robert W. Gibson.
Employer Identification Number: 351410969

2312
Eugene & Florence O. Stanley Scholarship Trust ¤
c/o First Source Bank, Trust Dept.
P.O. Box 1602
South Bend 46634
Application address: c/o First Source Bank, P.O. Box 500, Plymouth, IN 46563

Established in 1982 in IN.
Foundation type: Independent
Financial data (yr. ended 12/31/88): Assets, $1,116,219 (M); expenditures, $108,100, including $97,396 for 83 grants to individuals (high: $2,500; low: $147).
Purpose and activities: Support limited to graduates of Plymouth Community School Corp. who will be or who are attending colleges or universities.
Types of support: Student aid.
Limitations: Giving primarily in Plymouth, IN.

Application information: Application form required.
Deadline(s): Mar. 25
Trustee: First Source Bank.
Committee Members: Rosemary Bergman, F. Peter Braasch, Carl Dauler, Charles Glaub, Katherine Kubley, John McNeil, Keith Stewart.
Employer Identification Number: 356375193

2313
Oliver W. Storer Scholarship Foundation ⌑
c/o The Indiana National Bank
One Indiana Sq., Suite 733
Indianapolis 46204-0733
Application address: c/o Beasly, Gilkinson, Retherford & Buckles, 110 East Charles St., Muncie, IN 47305; Tel.: (317) 289-0661

Established in 1952 in IN.
Foundation type: Independent
Financial data (yr. ended 2/28/89): Assets, $3,464,903 (M); expenditures, $251,021, including $224,456 for 117 grants to individuals (high: $6,314; low: $195).
Purpose and activities: Scholarship grants to high school graduates of Delaware County, IN.
Types of support: Student aid.
Limitations: Giving limited to Delaware County, IN.
Application information:
Initial approach: Letter
Deadline(s): 60 days prior to beginning of school year
Write: Charles G. Retherford
Trustee: Indiana National Bank.
Employer Identification Number: 356012044

2314
Thirty Five Twenty, Inc. ⌑
7440 North Shadeland
Indianapolis 46250 (317) 842-0880

Incorporated in 1965 in IN.
Donor(s): Enid Goodrich.
Foundation type: Independent
Financial data (yr. ended 4/30/88): Assets, $1,659,673 (M); expenditures, $85,085, including $57,000 for 7 grants (high: $20,000; low: $3,500).
Purpose and activities: "To further educational activities which concern themselves with human liberty and individual freedom within a free society"; grants largely for higher education and cultural programs.
Types of support: Operating budgets, continuing support, special projects.
Limitations: No grants to individuals, or for annual campaigns, seed money, emergency funds, deficit financing, capital or endowment funds, scholarships, fellowships, matching gifts, research, demonstration projects, publications, or conferences; no loans.
Application information: Application form not required.
Initial approach: Letter
Copies of proposal: 1
Deadline(s): Submit proposal preferably in Mar.; deadline Apr. 1
Board meeting date(s): Apr. and Sept.
Final notification: 1 to 2 weeks if denied; after April meeting if favorable
Write: W.W. Hill, Chair. and C.E.O.
Officers and Directors: W.W. Hill, Pres. and Treas.; Enid Goodrich, Vice-Chair.; Helen W. Garlotte, Secy.; Ruth E. Connolly, Ralph W. Husted, Chris L. Talley.
Number of staff: 2 part-time professional.
Employer Identification Number: 356056960

2315
Jennie Thompson Foundation, Inc. ⌑
P.O. Box 176
Ligonier 46767-0176 (219) 894-3931

Foundation type: Independent
Financial data (yr. ended 12/31/88): Assets, $1,277,887 (M); gifts received, $25,550; expenditures, $76,232, including $59,897 for 5 grants (high: $36,000; low: $1,200).
Purpose and activities: Support primarily for a community center and for community development.
Types of support: General purposes, building funds, capital campaigns.
Limitations: Giving primarily in Ligonier, IN.
Application information: Application form required.
Deadline(s): None
Write: Samuel W. Patton, Jr., Pres.
Officers: Samuel W. Patton, Jr., Pres.; Richard D. Brown, V.P.; Howard K. Heckner, Secy.; Maltha M. Burke, Treas.
Employer Identification Number: 237450325

2316
Thrush-Thompson Foundation, Inc. ⌑
(Formerly H. A. Thrush Foundation, Inc.)
P.O. Box 185
Peru 46970

Incorporated in 1936 in DE.
Donor(s): Homer A. Thrush.†
Foundation type: Independent
Financial data (yr. ended 07/31/89): Assets, $3,422,082 (M); expenditures, $162,181, including $136,231 for 47 grants (high: $23,600; low: $100).
Purpose and activities: Emphasis on higher education, youth agencies, Protestant church support, health agencies, and cultural programs.
Limitations: Giving primarily in IN.
Officers and Directors:* Paul F. Thompson,* Pres. and Treas.; Dean A. Thompson,* V.P.; Jerry T. Thompson,* V.P.; Robert L. Thompson,* Secy.
Employer Identification Number: 356018476

2317
Tokheim Foundation
P.O. Box 360
Fort Wayne 46801 (219) 423-2552

Established in 1954 in IN.
Foundation type: Company-sponsored
Financial data (yr. ended 11/30/88): Assets, $473,173 (M); gifts received, $75,000; expenditures, $194,449, including $194,062 for 51 grants (high: $42,339; low: $100).
Purpose and activities: Support for social services, civic affairs, community funds, education, including religious schools, and youth, including YMCA and religious youth groups.
Limitations: Giving primarily in IN.
Application information: Application form not required.
Initial approach: Letter
Copies of proposal: 1
Deadline(s): None
Write: John E. Overmyer, Trustee
Trustees: Bob F. Jesse, Myron L. Marsh, John E. Overmyer, Thomas M. Shoaff, Randolph J. Straka.
Number of staff: 1 part-time support.
Employer Identification Number: 356043647

2318
Tyson Fund ⌑
One Indiana Sq., No. 733
Indianapolis 46266

Trust established in 1930 in IN.
Donor(s): James H. Tyson.
Foundation type: Independent
Financial data (yr. ended 12/31/88): Assets, $5,588,103 (M); expenditures, $282,617, including $259,878 for grants.
Purpose and activities: Emphasis on education, community services and a library.
Limitations: Giving limited to Versailles, IN.
Application information: Contributes only to pre-selected organizations. Applications not accepted.
Trustee: Indiana National Bank.
Employer Identification Number: 356009973

2319
Vevay-Switzerland County Foundation, Inc. ⌑ ☆
102 West Main St.
P.O. Box 176
Vevay 47043

Incorporated in 1985 in IN.
Donor(s): Paul W. Ogle.
Foundation type: Independent
Financial data (yr. ended 12/31/88): Assets, $5,119,153 (M); gifts received, $1,506,965; expenditures, $783,632, including $229,972 for 6 grants (high: $155,600; low: $319).
Purpose and activities: Support primarily for exterior renovation or restoration of civic and commercial structures.
Types of support: Matching funds, renovation projects.
Limitations: Giving limited to the town of Vevay and Switzerland County, IN.
Application information: Application form required.
Deadline(s): None
Write: Ralph Tilley, Pres.
Officers: Ralph W. Tilley, Pres.; Rick Peters, V.P.; Martha Cole, Secy.; Warren T. Sullivan, Treas.
Employer Identification Number: 351472069

2320
Wayne County, Indiana Foundation, Inc. ☆
600 Promenade
Richmond 47374 (317) 962-1511

Established in 1979 in IN.
Foundation type: Community
Financial data (yr. ended 12/31/89): Assets, $2,652,632 (M); gifts received, $1,478,950; expenditures, $114,232, including $70,778 for

23 grants (high: $10,000; low: $200), $7,690 for 15 grants to individuals (high: $1,717; low: $59) and $2,000 for 3 in-kind gifts.
Purpose and activities: Giving for community and social services, museums and the arts, education and literacy programs, health associations, historic preservation, and youth programs; scholarships to individuals awarded through restricted funds.
Types of support: Publications, scholarship funds, seed money, special projects.
Limitations: Giving primarily in Wayne County, IN. No support for religious organizations for sectarian purposes. No grants to individuals (except through restricted funds), or for annual campaigns, endowment funds, or operating deficits or capital debt reduction.
Publications: Annual report, informational brochure (including application guidelines).
Application information: Application form required.
Initial approach: Letter
Copies of proposal: 16
Deadline(s): Feb. 1 and Aug. 1
Board meeting date(s): 2nd Friday of each month
Final notification: Mar. and Sept.
Write: Ruth J. Wickemeyer, Exec. Dir.
Officers and Directors:* Victor R. Jose,* Pres.; Kenneth D. Bane,* V.P.; Mary C. Sweet,* Secy.; David F. Harper,* Treas.; Ruth J. Wickemeyer,* Exec. Dir.; and 11 other directors.
Number of staff: 1 part-time professional.
Employer Identification Number: 351406033

2321
West Foundation, Inc. ⌑ ☆
4120 North Illinois St.
Indianapolis 46208-4010 (317) 283-5525

Established in 1954.
Donor(s): Stephen R. West.
Foundation type: Independent
Financial data (yr. ended 12/31/88): Assets, $1,700,359 (M); gifts received, $18,400; expenditures, $128,882, including $102,075 for 30 grants (high: $25,000; low: $600).
Purpose and activities: "Emphasis is on international community development and problem-youth agencies and alcohol and drug abuse programs."
Application information: Application form not required.
Deadline(s): None
Write: Stephen R. West, Pres.
Officers: Stephen R. West, Pres. and Treas.; Phyllis West, V.P. and Secy.
Employer Identification Number: 237416727

2322
William H. Willennar Foundation, Inc. ☆
The Auburn State Bank
Auburn 46706
Application address: P.O. Box 229, Auburn, IN 46706; Tel.: (219) 925-3060

Established in 1962.
Foundation type: Independent
Financial data (yr. ended 6/30/89): Assets, $1,850,009 (M); expenditures, $83,194, including $77,550 for 16 grants (high: $19,000; low: $1,000).
Purpose and activities: Giving primarily to a hospital, a municipal parks department, and an organization benefitting handicapped children; support also for civic affairs and a council on aging, a community fund, and an automotive heritage association.
Limitations: Giving primarily in IN, with emphasis on Auburn.
Application information:
Initial approach: Letter
Deadline(s): May 1
Write: M.C. Haggarty, Secy.-Treas.
Trustees: Alice R. Close, Pres.; Donald Allison, V.P.; Michael C. Haggarty, Secy.-Treas.; The Auburn State Bank.
Number of staff: 1 part-time professional.
Employer Identification Number: 356028233

2323
The Winchester Foundation ⌑
100 South Meridian St.
Winchester 47394 (317) 584-3501

Established in 1946 in IN.
Foundation type: Independent
Financial data (yr. ended 12/31/88): Assets, $2,448,542 (M); gifts received, $1,010,835; expenditures, $83,883, including $52,195 for 17 grants (high: $8,500; low: $185; average: $1,000-$5,000) and $11,307 for 7 grants to individuals (high: $6,939; low: $318; average: $500-$2,000).
Purpose and activities: Grants primarily for higher education, educational associations, scholarships, and cultural programs.
Types of support: General purposes, student aid.
Limitations: Giving primarily in IN.
Application information: Candidates for scholarships are pre-selected by a scholarship committee from Winchester Community High School; applications are not accepted by the foundation. Application form not required.
Initial approach: Letter
Deadline(s): Spring for scholarships; no set deadline for grants
Write: Don Welch, Chair.
Officers and Trustees: Don E. Welch, Chair.; Enid Goodrich, Vice-Chair.; Chris L. Talley, Secy.; Helen Garlotte, Robert G. Jones, Terry E. Matchett.
Employer Identification Number: 237422941

2324
Zollner Foundation ⌑
c/o Lincoln National Bank
116 East Berry St.
Fort Wayne 46802
Application address: P.O. Box 960, Fort Wayne, IN 46801; Tel.: (219) 461-6000

Established in 1983 in IN.
Foundation type: Independent
Financial data (yr. ended 12/31/88): Assets, $4,619,105 (M); expenditures, $239,057, including $220,370 for 21 grants (high: $40,000; low: $2,442).
Purpose and activities: Support primarily for liberal arts colleges, hospitals, and youth groups.
Types of support: General purposes.
Limitations: Giving primarily in IN.
Application information:
Initial approach: Letter
Deadline(s): None
Write: Alice Kopfer
Trustee: Lincoln National Bank & Trust Co.
Employer Identification Number: 356381471

IOWA

2325
Aalfs Family Foundation ⌑
300 Commerce Bldg.
P.O. Box 566
Sioux City 51102
Application address: 1006 Fourth St., Sioux City, IA 51102; Tel.: (712) 252-1877

Established in 1980 in IA.
Foundation type: Independent
Financial data (yr. ended 12/31/87): Assets, $968,431 (M); gifts received, $100,000; expenditures, $107,984, including $105,000 for 2 grants (high: $100,000; low: $5,000).
Purpose and activities: Support primarily for a public library and a girls club.
Limitations: Giving primarily in Sioux City, IA.
Application information:
Initial approach: Letter
Deadline(s): None
Write: John W. Aalfs, Pres.
Officers: N. Wilbur Aalfs, Chair.; John W. Aalfs, Pres. and Treas.; William E. Rodawig, Exec. V.P. and Secy.
Employer Identification Number: 421153158

2326
Philip D. & Henrietta B. Adler Foundation Trust ⌑
c/o Davenport Bank & Trust Co.
203 West Third St.
Davenport 52801-1977

Established in 1981 in IA.
Foundation type: Independent
Financial data (yr. ended 12/31/87): Assets, $5,780,772 (M); expenditures, $164,460, including $155,034 for 3 grants (high: $75,034; low: $30,000).
Purpose and activities: Support primarily for a theater and social service agencies.
Application information: Contributes only to pre-selected organizations. Applications not accepted.
Trustees: Henrietta B. Adler, Davenport Bank & Trust Co.
Employer Identification Number: 426262655

2327
Matilda Andres Trust ⌑
(also known as Andres Memorial Trust)
c/o Norwest Bank Des Moines, N.A.
666 Walnut St.
Des Moines 50309 (515) 245-3202

Established in 1985 in IA.

Donor(s): Matilda Andres.†
Foundation type: Independent
Financial data (yr. ended 9/30/88): Assets, $1,568,881 (M); expenditures, $93,597, including $80,000 for 5 grants (high: $20,000; low: $10,000).
Purpose and activities: Charitable giving, including support for municipal organizations.
Limitations: Giving primarily in Floyd County, IA.
Application information: Application form not required.
Initial approach: Letter
Deadline(s): None
Trustee: Norwest Bank Des Moines, N.A.
Employer Identification Number: 426121269

2328
Edith Curtis Armstrong & Florence E. Curtis Foundation ⌑ ☆
2320 North Second St.
Clinton 52732-2494 (319) 242-3440

Established in 1954.
Foundation type: Independent
Financial data (yr. ended 12/31/88): Assets, $1,076,816 (M); expenditures, $85,725, including $77,800 for 19 grants (high: $33,700; low: $50).
Purpose and activities: Giving primarily for social services, higher and other education, and a park commission.
Types of support: General purposes, building funds, equipment.
Limitations: Giving limited to the Clinton, IA, area. No grants to individuals.
Application information: Application form not required.
Initial approach: Proposal
Deadline(s): None
Write: Everett W. Eslinger, Pres.
Officers: Everett W. Eslinger, Pres. and Secy.; David O. Shaff, V.P.; Robert R. Smith, Treas.
Employer Identification Number: 426054969

2329
The Barzillai Foundation ⌑ ☆
Two Ruan Ctr., Suite 1100
601 Locust St.
Des Moines 50309 (515) 283-2076

Established in 1984 in IA.
Donor(s): Stanley J. Vermeer, Alma L. Vermeer.
Foundation type: Independent
Financial data (yr. ended 7/31/88): Assets, $1,684,708 (M); gifts received, $150,000; expenditures, $67,762, including $63,400 for 7 grants (high: $24,100; low: $1,000).
Purpose and activities: Giving primarily for Christian organizations including missionary programs, churches, and evangelism.
Limitations: No grants to individuals.
Application information: Application form required.
Initial approach: Letter
Deadline(s): None
Write: Marvin Winick
Officers: Stanley J. Vermeer, Pres.; Alma L. Vermeer, Secy.-Treas.
Employer Identification Number: 421233554

2330
H. Reimers Bechtel Charitable Remainder Uni-Trust ⌑ ☆
1000 First Bank Ctr.
201 West Second St.
Davenport 52801 (319) 328-3333

Foundation type: Independent
Financial data (yr. ended 8/30/88): Assets, $1,790,535 (M); expenditures, $59,853, including $57,500 for 2 grants (high: $50,000; low: $7,500).
Purpose and activities: Giving for higher education and conservation.
Application information: Application form required.
Initial approach: Letter
Deadline(s): None
Write: R. Richard Bittner, Trustee
Trustee: R. Richard Bittner.
Employer Identification Number: 426342964

2331
Harold R. Bechtel Charitable Remainder Uni-Trust ⌑ ☆
1000 First Bank Ctr.
201 West Second St.
Davenport 52801 (319) 328-333

Established in 1987.
Foundation type: Independent
Financial data (yr. ended 4/30/88): Assets, $4,223,033 (M); expenditures, $6,199, including $2,500 for 1 grant.
Purpose and activities: Giving for civic improvement through the restoration of a local government building.
Types of support: Renovation projects.
Limitations: Giving limited to Scott County, IA.
Application information: Application form required.
Initial approach: Letter
Deadline(s): None
Write: R. Richard Bittner, Trustee
Trustee: R. Richard Bittner.
Employer Identification Number: 426288501

2332
Marie H. Bechtel Charitable Trust ⌑ ☆
1000 First Bank Ctr.
201 West Second St.
Davenport 52801

Established in 1987 in IA.
Foundation type: Independent
Financial data (yr. ended 12/31/88): Assets, $10,466,895 (M); expenditures, $346,658, including $287,000 for 10 grants (high: $75,000; low: $4,500).
Purpose and activities: Giving primarily for community development and higher education; support also for environmental conservation and a YMCA.
Limitations: Giving primarily in Scott County, IA.
Application information: Application form required.
Deadline(s): None
Write: R. Richard Bittner, Trustee
Trustee: R. Richard Bittner.
Employer Identification Number: 426288500

2333
The Myron and Jacqueline Blank Charity Fund ⌑
414 Insurance Exchange Bldg.
505 Fifth Ave.
Des Moines 50309

Incorporated in 1948 in IA.
Donor(s): A.H. Blank, Myron N. Blank, and others.
Foundation type: Independent
Financial data (yr. ended 12/31/88): Assets, $5,268,746 (M); expenditures, $1,244,044, including $1,232,042 for 81 grants (high: $750,000; low: $25).
Purpose and activities: Emphasis on Jewish welfare funds, higher education, and cultural programs.
Limitations: Giving primarily in IA. No grants to individuals.
Application information: Contributions only to pre-selected organizations. Applications not accepted.
Officers and Directors:* Myron N. Blank,* Pres. and Treas.; Jacqueline N. Blank,* V.P. and Secy.; Steven N. Blank.
Employer Identification Number: 237423791

2334
The Bohen Foundation ▼ ⌑
1716 Locust St.
Des Moines 50336 (515) 284-2556

Incorporated in 1958 in IA.
Donor(s): Mildred M. Bohen Charitable Trust, Edna E. Meredith Charitable Trust.
Foundation type: Independent
Financial data (yr. ended 6/30/89): Assets, $8,861,231 (M); gifts received, $1,403,717; expenditures, $2,022,971, including $1,855,700 for 55 grants (high: $305,000; low: $200; average: $5,000-$50,000).
Purpose and activities: Emphasis on higher and secondary education, conservation, and the performing arts.
Types of support: Operating budgets, building funds, annual campaigns, special projects.
Limitations: No grants to individuals.
Application information:
Initial approach: Letter
Copies of proposal: 1
Deadline(s): None
Board meeting date(s): As required
Write: Marilyn J. Dillivan, Treas.
Officers and Directors:* Frederick B. Henry,* Pres.; Linda C. Behr, Secy.; Marilyn J. Dillivan, Treas.
Number of staff: None.
Employer Identification Number: 426054774

2335
Roy J. Carver Charitable Trust
P.O. Box 76
Muscatine 52761 (319) 263-4010

Established in 1982 in IA.
Donor(s): Roy J. Carver, Sr.†
Foundation type: Independent
Financial data (yr. ended 04/30/89): Assets, $127,216,753 (M); expenditures, $7,053,683, including $6,402,565 for 15 grants (high: $2,583,111; low: $500; average: $20,000-$150,000).

Purpose and activities: Support primarily for education, medical research, science and technology, and youth programs.
Types of support: Research, seed money, special projects, scholarship funds.
Limitations: Giving primarily in IA.
Publications: Informational brochure (including application guidelines).
Application information: Application form not required.
Initial approach: Letter
Deadline(s): None
Board meeting date(s): Jan., Apr., July, and Oct.
Write: Roger A. Hughes, Exec. Admin.
Officers and Trustees:* William F. Cory,* Chair.; Roger A. Hughes,* Exec. Admin.; Willard L. Boyd, Lucille A. Carver, Roy J. Carver, Jr., Arthur Dahl, J. Larry Griffith, Clay LeGrand.
Number of staff: 1 full-time professional; 1 full-time support; 1 part-time support.
Employer Identification Number: 421186589

2336
Gardner and Florence Call Cowles Foundation, Inc. ▼
715 Locust St.
Des Moines 50309 (515) 284-8116

Incorporated in 1934 in IA.
Donor(s): Gardner Cowles, Sr.,† Florence C. Cowles.†
Foundation type: Independent
Financial data (yr. ended 12/31/89): Assets, $15,159,230 (M); gifts received, $3,500; expenditures, $4,180,958, including $1,538,000 for 16 grants (high: $649,000; low: $10,000; average: $5,000-$250,000).
Purpose and activities: Grants largely for higher education, with emphasis on 4-year private colleges in IA, including buildings, arts programs, and a civic center.
Types of support: Operating budgets, continuing support, seed money, building funds, endowment funds, matching funds.
Limitations: Giving limited to IA, with emphasis on Des Moines. No grants to individuals, or for scholarships or fellowships; no loans.
Application information: Application form not required.
Initial approach: Proposal or letter
Copies of proposal: 1
Deadline(s): None
Board meeting date(s): Annually and as required
Write: David Kruidenier, Pres.
Officers and Trustees:* David Kruidenier,* Pres.; Kenneth MacDonald,* V.P.; Luther L. Hill, Jr.,* Secy.; Elizabeth S. Kruidenier,* Treas.; Elizabeth Ballantine, Morley Cowles Ballantine, Charles C. Edwards, Jr., Thomas Hutchison, Terry Tinson Saario.
Number of staff: None.
Employer Identification Number: 426054609

2337
E & M Charities ▼ ⌑
2610 Park Ave.
P.O. Box 209
Muscatine 52761 (319) 264-8342

Incorporated in 1979 in IA.
Donor(s): C. Maxwell Stanley,† Elizabeth M. Stanley.
Foundation type: Independent
Financial data (yr. ended 12/31/88): Assets, $23,821,011 (M); gifts received, $752,560; expenditures, $2,224,504, including $2,020,063 for 56 grants (high: $350,000; low: $100; average: $2,000-$50,000) and $101,859 for 1 foundation-administered program.
Purpose and activities: Support for Christian-related projects, churches, church-related independent colleges, the marriage encounter, public education on taxes and government fiscal procedures and principles, the prevention of world hunger, and community charitable and educational projects; support also for the University of Iowa Foundation and the Octagon Place, an historic site located in Muscatine, IA.
Types of support: Endowment funds.
Limitations: No support for private foundations. No grants to individuals, or for research.
Publications: Informational brochure.
Application information: Application form not required.
Initial approach: Letter
Deadline(s): None
Board meeting date(s): Dec.
Final notification: 3 months
Write: Linda A. Thompson, Exec. Secy.
Officers and Directors:* David M. Stanley,* Pres. and Treas.; Elizabeth M. Stanley,* V.P. and Secy.; Jean Leu Stanley,* V.P.; Jane S. Buckles, Jane A. Miller, Richard H. Stanley.
Number of staff: 2 full-time support; 2 part-time support.
Employer Identification Number: 421129959

2338
A. E. Easter Family Charitable Foundation ☆
5320 N.E. 54th Ave.
Altoona 50009 (515) 265-1116

Established in 1983 in IA.
Foundation type: Independent
Financial data (yr. ended 12/31/89): Assets, $624,269 (M); gifts received, $226,912; expenditures, $111,798, including $111,367 for 55 grants (high: $60,000; low: $50).
Purpose and activities: Support primarily for higher education and cultural programs.
Types of support: Annual campaigns, building funds, capital campaigns, special projects.
Limitations: Giving primarily in IA. No grants to individuals.
Application information: Application form not required.
Initial approach: Letter
Deadline(s): Apr. 1
Write: L. Don Easter, Treas.
Officers: Edna Morse, Pres.; L. Don Easter, Treas.
Trustees: Jack Easter, Judith Easter Miller.
Number of staff: None.
Employer Identification Number: 421206865

2339
Engman Foundation ⌑ ☆
P.O. Box 864
Des Moines 50304

Established in 1960.
Donor(s): EMCO Industries, Inc.
Foundation type: Independent
Financial data (yr. ended 2/28/89): Assets, $135,526 (M); gifts received, $141,385; expenditures, $127,861, including $127,529 for 67 grants (high: $33,300; low: $25).
Purpose and activities: Giving primarily for Jewish organizations, including welfare funds, social services, and a synagogue; support also for a community fund and welfare.
Limitations: Giving primarily in IA.
Application information: Application form not required.
Deadline(s): None
Write: Lawrence B. Engman, Dir.
Officers: Gerald Engman, V.P.; Norman Engman, Secy.; Stan Engman, Treas.
Director: Lawrence B. Engman.
Employer Identification Number: 426070926

2340
Fahrney Education Foundation
c/o Union Bank, Trust Dept.
123 East Third St.
Ottumwa 52501 (515) 683-1641

Established in 1979 in IA.
Donor(s): Helen Fahrney.†
Foundation type: Independent
Financial data (yr. ended 02/28/90): Assets, $2,760,786 (M); expenditures, $143,378, including $125,571 for grants to individuals.
Purpose and activities: Support for scholarships for students pursuing a four-year degree at a college or university in IA.
Types of support: Student aid.
Limitations: Giving limited to residents of Wapello County, IA, attending IA schools.
Publications: Application guidelines.
Application information: Application form required.
Deadline(s): Feb. 15
Trustee: Union Bank.
Number of staff: None.
Employer Identification Number: 426295370

2341
Gazette Foundation ⌑ ☆
500 Third Ave., S.E.
Cedar Rapids 52406 (319) 398-2807

Established in 1960 in IA.
Donor(s): The Gazette Co.
Foundation type: Company-sponsored
Financial data (yr. ended 12/31/88): Assets, $218,935 (M); gifts received, $55,000; expenditures, $146,466, including $146,183 for 60 grants (high: $26,000; low: $30).
Purpose and activities: Support for higher education, including programs designed to strengthen the skills of future newspaper and broadcasting professionals, youth agencies, cultural programs, health services, and a community fund. The foundation is also interested in projects designed to improved the environment for persons living and working in the Cedar Rapids community.
Types of support: General purposes.

Limitations: Giving primarily in Cedar Rapids, IA. No grants to individuals.
Publications: Program policy statement.
Application information: Application form required.
Deadline(s): None
Final notification: 3 months
Write: J.F. Hladky III, Pres.
Officers and Directors:* J.F. Hladky III,* Pres.; Ken Slaughter,* V.P.; John L. Donnelly,* Treas.; Elizabeth T. Barry, J.F. Hladky, Jr.
Employer Identification Number: 426075177

2342
Madelyn L. Glazer Foundation ⌑
312 Hubbell Bldg.
Des Moines 50309

Established in 1957.
Donor(s): Madelyn L. Glazer.
Foundation type: Independent
Financial data (yr. ended 12/31/88): Assets, $4,265,878 (M); gifts received, $200,000; expenditures, $337,894, including $326,624 for 36 grants (high: $78,250; low: $25).
Purpose and activities: Giving for higher education, cultural programs, welfare, community funds, and Jewish welfare funds.
Limitations: Giving primarily in Des Moines, IA. No grants to individuals.
Application information: Contributes only to pre-selected organizations. Applications not accepted.
Officers: Madelyn L. Glazer, Pres.; Edward Glazer, V.P.; Lela E. Marker, Secy.-Treas.
Employer Identification Number: 426052426

2343
The Ralph & Sylvia G. Green Charitable Foundation
100 East Grand Ave., Suite 230
Des Moines 50309 (515) 244-5000

Established in 1983 in IA.
Donor(s): Ralph Green.
Foundation type: Independent
Financial data (yr. ended 12/31/88): Assets, $1,183,397 (M); expenditures, $80,178, including $75,275 for 38 grants (high: $25,000; low: $50).
Purpose and activities: Support for higher education, the arts, conservation, and general charitable giving.
Types of support: Operating budgets, endowment funds, program-related investments, seed money.
Limitations: Giving primarily in Des Moines, IA. No grants to individuals.
Application information: Application form not required.
Initial approach: Letter
Deadline(s): None
Board meeting date(s): Quarterly
Final notification: Upon action of the board
Write: Ann G. Anderson, Pres.
Officers and Directors:* Ralph Green,* Chair.; Ann G. Anderson,* Pres. and Secy.; Sigurd Anderson,* V.P. and Treas.
Number of staff: None.
Employer Identification Number: 421208959

2344
The Hall Foundation, Inc. ▼
115 Third St., S.E., No. 803
Cedar Rapids 52401 (319) 362-9079

Incorporated in 1953 in IA.
Donor(s): Members of the Hall family.
Foundation type: Independent
Financial data (yr. ended 12/31/89): Assets, $45,002,073 (M); gifts received, $4,500,100; expenditures, $3,538,799, including $3,395,564 for 35 grants (high: $680,000; low: $500; average: $5,000-$100,000).
Purpose and activities: Support for cultural programs, including fine and performing arts groups, higher education, social service and youth agencies, a community fund, and hospitals and health services.
Types of support: Annual campaigns, seed money, emergency funds, building funds, equipment, land acquisition, special projects, research, capital campaigns, scholarship funds, matching funds.
Limitations: Giving limited to Cedar Rapids, IA, and the immediate trade area. No grants to individuals, or for deficit financing, endowment funds, scholarships, or fellowships; no loans.
Publications: Informational brochure (including application guidelines).
Application information: Application form not required.
Initial approach: Letter
Copies of proposal: 1
Deadline(s): None
Board meeting date(s): Quarterly
Final notification: 3 months
Write: John G. Lidvall, Exec. Dir.
Officers and Directors:* William P. Whipple,* Pres.; John G. Lidvall,* V.P. and Exec. Dir.; George C. Foerstner,* V.P.; Darrel A. Morf,* Secy.; Joseph R. Loufek,* Treas.; Dennis L. Boatman, E.J. Buresh, James E. Coquillette, Jack B. Evans, Carleen Grandon, Alex Meyer, Irene H. Perrine.
Number of staff: 2 part-time professional.
Employer Identification Number: 426057097

2345
The Hanson Foundation
P.O. Box 450
Forest City 50436 (515) 582-2825

Established in 1971 in IA.
Foundation type: Independent
Financial data (yr. ended 12/31/88): Assets, $1,969,790 (M); expenditures, $42,325, including $24,213 for 22 grants (high: $4,000; low: $100).
Purpose and activities: Emphasis on higher education, youth organizations, the arts, community funds, and other charitable activities.
Types of support: Matching funds.
Limitations: Giving primarily in north central IA.
Publications: 990-PF.
Application information: Application form not required.
Initial approach: Letter
Copies of proposal: 1
Deadline(s): None
Write: Linda Johnson
Trustees: Mary Jo Boman, John K. Hanson, John V. Hanson, Luise V. Hanson, Paul D. Hanson.
Number of staff: 1 part-time support.
Employer Identification Number: 237188645

2346
Hawley Foundation ⌑
1530 Financial Ctr.
666 Walnut
Des Moines 50309 (515) 280-7071

Incorporated in 1927 in IA.
Donor(s): Henry B. Hawley,† Mrs. Henry B. Hawley.†
Foundation type: Independent
Financial data (yr. ended 12/31/87): Assets, $1,613,431 (M); expenditures, $94,884, including $73,500 for 16 grants (high: $10,000; low: $1,500).
Purpose and activities: To serve mankind, strengthen family life, and give assistance to organizations without regard to race, religion, or other affiliations; support primarily for youth, child welfare and social service agencies, especially for new projects.
Types of support: Special projects, seed money.
Limitations: Giving primarily in the greater Des Moines, IA, area. No support for individual churches or religious orders. No grants to individuals, or for endowment funds, operating budgets, support drives or membership campaigns, programs directed at specific diseases or disabilities, and rarely for building funds; no loans.
Application information: Application form not required.
Initial approach: Letter or telephone
Copies of proposal: 1
Deadline(s): Submit proposal in Sept. or Oct. if requested by the foundation
Board meeting date(s): Quarterly and as required
Write: Amos C. Pearsall, Jr., Exec. Dir.
Officers and Trustees: Robb B. Kelly, Pres.; Bernard D. Kurtz, Sr., V.P.; Amos C. Pearsall, Jr., Secy. and Exec. Dir.; James W. Hubbell, Jr., Treas.; Daniel F. Crowley, Robert J. Fleming, William Friedman, Jr., Theodore M. Hutchison, William Z. Proctor.
Employer Identification Number: 426056159

2347
Hon Industries Charitable Foundation ⌑
414 East Third St.
Muscatine 52761-4182 (319) 264-7400

Established in 1985 in IA.
Foundation type: Company-sponsored
Financial data (yr. ended 06/30/88): Assets, $989,597 (M); expenditures, $196,815, including $195,645 for 44 grants (high: $32,500; low: $25).
Purpose and activities: Support for higher and other education, social services, youth, science and technology, business, recreation, arts and culture, conservation, and the United Way; scholarships awarded for higher education.
Types of support: Scholarship funds.
Limitations: Giving primarily in areas of company operations in IA, IL, TN, TX, and VA.

Application information: Application form not required.
Deadline(s): None
Write: Raymond E. Lasell, Secy.-Treas.
Officers: Stanley M. Howe, Pres.; R. Michael Derry, V.P.; Russell D. Woodyard, V.P.; Raymond E. Lasell, Secy.-Treas.
Employer Identification Number: 421246787

2348
George S. & Grace A. Jay Memorial Trust ¤
612 1/2 Sheridan Ave.
Shenandoah 51601 (712) 246-3399

Trust established in 1963 in IA.
Foundation type: Independent
Financial data (yr. ended 03/31/89): Assets, $1,508,657 (M); expenditures, $163,739, including $124,850 for 135 loans to individuals (high: $1,350; low: $300).
Purpose and activities: Student loans to graduates of Shenandoah, Essex, and Farragut, IA, high schools, only for higher education at an accredited college, university or trade school; some support also for colleges and universities.
Types of support: Student loans.
Limitations: Giving limited to high school graduates in IA.
Application information: Loan application information available; telephone inquiries accepted on Tuesdays only, during regular business hours. Application form required.
Deadline(s): May 31
Final notification: 1 month
Write: Eileen Dinville
Trustees: Francis Braley, William A. Longman, Robert Read.
Employer Identification Number: 426061515

2349
Kent-Stein Foundation ¤
c/o Grain Processing Corp.
1600 Oregon St.
Muscatine 52761

Established in 1945 in IA.
Donor(s): Grain Processing Corp.
Foundation type: Independent
Financial data (yr. ended 12/31/87): Assets, $2,198,885 (M); gifts received, $500,000; expenditures, $105,453, including $100,000 for 1 grant.
Purpose and activities: Emphasis on higher education, museums and the arts, conservation, libraries, and community funds.
Application information: Contributes only to pre-selected organizations. Applications not accepted.
Trustees: J.H. Kent, J.L. Lamb, S.G. Stein IV.
Employer Identification Number: 426058939

2350
Kinney-Lindstrom Foundation, Inc. ▼ ¤
P.O. Box 520
Mason City 50401 (515) 896-3888

Incorporated in 1957 in IA.
Donor(s): Ida Lindstrom Kinney.†
Foundation type: Independent
Financial data (yr. ended 12/31/87): Assets, $5,832,035 (M); expenditures, $1,083,743, including $886,070 for 45 grants (high: $200,000; low: $100; average: $2,000-$50,000).
Purpose and activities: Grants primarily for building funds for libraries in IA towns; support also for education, cultural programs, social service and youth agencies, health agencies, and civic programs.
Types of support: Building funds.
Limitations: Giving primarily in IA. No grants to individuals, or for endowment funds, operating budgets, or research; no loans.
Application information: Application form not required.
Initial approach: Letter
Copies of proposal: 1
Deadline(s): Mar. 1
Board meeting date(s): 10 times a year
Final notification: 2 weeks after interview
Write: Lowell K. Hall, Secy.
Officer: Lowell K. Hall, Secy.
Trustees: Thor Jenson, Ira Stinson.
Number of staff: 1 full-time professional.
Employer Identification Number: 426037351

2351
Peter H. and E. Lucille Gaass Kuyper Foundation ¤
c/o Rolscreen Co.
Pella 50219 (515) 628-1000

Established in 1970 in IA.
Donor(s): Peter H. Kuyper, E. Lucille Gaass Kuyper.
Foundation type: Independent
Financial data (yr. ended 4/30/88): Assets, $11,196,609 (M); expenditures, $472,710, including $455,220 for 33 grants (high: $250,000; low: $500).
Purpose and activities: Support primarily for a college and for Christian welfare funds, hospitals, and civic affairs.
Limitations: Giving primarily in the Pella, IA area.
Application information: Application form not required.
Deadline(s): None
Write: Joan Kuyper Farver, Pres.
Officer and Directors: Joan Kuyper Farver, Pres.; Suzanne Farver, V.P.; Carol Kuyper Rosenberg, V.P.; Thomas W. Carpenter, Secy.; LeRoy Baughman, Treas.
Employer Identification Number: 237068402

2352
Lee Foundation ¤
130 East Second St.
Davenport 52801

Incorporated in 1962 in IA.
Donor(s): Lee Enterprises.
Foundation type: Company-sponsored
Financial data (yr. ended 9/30/88): Assets, $4,051,743 (M); gifts received, $1,000,000; expenditures, $407,514, including $403,098 for 44 grants (high: $250,000; low: $125).
Purpose and activities: Grants largely for higher education, hospitals, youth agencies, cultural programs, and journalism.
Types of support: Endowment funds, building funds.
Limitations: Giving primarily in areas of company operations in IA, IL, WI, MT, ND, OR, CA, and NE. No support for individuals.
Officers and Directors: Lloyd G. Schermer, Pres.; Richard B. Belkin, V.P.; Richard D. Gottlieb, V.P.; Ronald L. Rickman, V.P.; Richard P. Galligan, Secy.; Michael J. Riley, Treas.
Employer Identification Number: 426057173

2353
Chester P. Luick Memorial Trust
P.O. Box 39
Belmond 50421 (515) 444-3226

Established in 1972 in IA.
Foundation type: Independent
Financial data (yr. ended 12/31/88): Assets, $1,075,000 (M); gifts received, $18,682; expenditures, $55,177, including $44,500 for 9 grants (high: $15,000; low: $500).
Purpose and activities: Giving for civic affairs, education, historic preservation, public administration, and recreation.
Limitations: Giving limited to Belmond, IA, and the surrounding community.
Application information: Application form not required.
Initial approach: Proposal
Deadline(s): None
Board meeting date(s): Monthly
Write: G.S. Hinman, or any other Trustee
Trustees: Merle C. Been, Gary L. Berkland, G.S. Hinman.
Employer Identification Number: 426178601

2354
The Maytag Corporation Foundation
c/o Maytag Corp.
403 West Fourth St., North
Newton 50208 (515) 791-8216

Incorporated in 1952 in IA.
Donor(s): Maytag Corp.
Foundation type: Company-sponsored
Financial data (yr. ended 12/31/89): Assets, $1,187,115 (M); expenditures, $722,665, including $520,581 for grants and $202,084 for 144 grants to individuals (high: $2,800; low: $67).
Purpose and activities: Contributes to worthwhile undertakings to help fulfil the company's role as a responsible corporate citizen. Principal interest in scholarships and career education awards for students in Newton High School and children of company employees, with cost-of-education supplements to colleges attended by scholarship winners; matches company employees' gifts to approved colleges up to $1,000 annually per employee; makes other grants to Iowa College Fund, United Negro College Fund and selected national educational organizations. Supports community betterment, including United Way and cultural organizations in the Newton/Central IA area and other localities where company has plants or offices.
Types of support: Student aid, employee matching gifts, employee-related scholarships, scholarship funds, operating budgets, building funds, annual campaigns, capital campaigns, continuing support, matching funds.

Limitations: Giving for community projects limited to areas of company operations, particularly the Newton/Central IA area. No support for health agencies, churches, religious causes, or international relations. No grants to individuals (except for Maytag Award recipients), or for benefit dinners or complimentary advertising.
Publications: Financial statement, informational brochure.
Application information: Application required for scholarship program and career education awards program.
Initial approach: Letter or telephone inquiry
Copies of proposal: 1
Deadline(s): Feb. 1 for grants to organizations; varies annually for scholarship and career education awards programs
Board meeting date(s): Mar. and as required
Final notification: Varies
Write: Susan J. Martin, Exec. Dir.
Officers: Daniel J. Krumm,* Pres.; Francis C. Miller,* V.P.; Donald C. Byers, Secy.-Treas.; Susan J. Martin, Exec. Dir.
Trustees:* J.C. Enyart, Karl F. Langrock, Jack D. Levin, Donald R. Runger, Jerry A. Schiller, Sterling O. Swanger.
Number of staff: 1 full-time professional; 1 full-time support.
Employer Identification Number: 426055722

2355
The Fred Maytag Family Foundation ▼
200 First St. South
P.O. Box 426
Newton 50208 (515) 792-1800

Trust established in 1945 in IA.
Donor(s): Fred Maytag II,† Members of the Maytag family.
Foundation type: Independent
Financial data (yr. ended 12/31/88): Assets, $26,566,493 (M); expenditures, $1,340,890, including $1,098,673 for 93 grants (high: $150,000; low: $50; average: $1,000-$50,000).
Purpose and activities: Giving for higher and other education, arts and culture, public affairs, social services, and health, including cancer research, the handicapped, and family planning.
Types of support: Operating budgets, continuing support, annual campaigns, seed money, building funds, equipment, land acquisition, matching funds, research, special projects, renovation projects.
Limitations: Giving primarily in Des Moines and Newton, IA. No grants to individuals, or for emergency funds, deficit financing, endowment funds, scholarships, fellowships, demonstration projects, publications, or conferences; no loans.
Application information: Application form not required.
Initial approach: Letter
Copies of proposal: 4
Deadline(s): Submit proposal preferably in Apr. or May; deadline May 31
Board meeting date(s): June or July
Final notification: 30 days after meeting
Write: Francis C. Miller, Secy.
Officer: Francis C. Miller, Secy.
Trustees: Ellen Pray Maytag Madsen, Frederick L. Maytag III, Kenneth P. Maytag.
Number of staff: 2 part-time support.
Employer Identification Number: 426055654

2356
R. J. McElroy Trust ▼
KWWL Bldg.
500 East Fourth St.
Waterloo 50703 (319) 291-1299

Established in 1965 in IA; private foundation status attained in 1984.
Donor(s): R.J. McElroy.
Foundation type: Independent
Financial data (yr. ended 12/31/89): Assets, $29,115,993 (M); expenditures, $1,662,205, including $1,385,178 for 82 grants (high: $125,000; low: $390).
Purpose and activities: Primary emphasis on higher education, especially scholarship and loan programs; public secondary education, particularly for the disadvantaged; early childhood and elementary education and programs for minorities; and youth, including internships. Giving also for the arts, recreation, and the environment; some support through matching gifts, and fellowships for graduate study.
Types of support: Internships, scholarship funds, equipment, matching funds, emergency funds, exchange programs, fellowships, seed money, special projects.
Limitations: Giving primarily in the KWWL viewing area in northeast IA. No grants to individuals (except fellowships).
Publications: Informational brochure (including application guidelines), program policy statement, grants list.
Application information: Application form required.
Copies of proposal: 1
Deadline(s): None
Board meeting date(s): Monthly
Final notification: Monthly
Write: Linda L. Klinger, Exec. Dir.
Officers and Directors:* Robert Buckmaster,* Chair.; Linda L. Klinger, Exec. Dir.; Raleigh D. Buckmaster, Harry G. Slife, James B. Waterbury, Rick Young.
Number of staff: 1 part-time professional; 1 part-time support.
Employer Identification Number: 426173496

2357
Edwin T. Meredith Foundation
1716 Locust St.
Des Moines 50336 (515) 284-2545

Incorporated in 1946 in IA.
Donor(s): Meredith Publishing Co.
Foundation type: Independent
Financial data (yr. ended 12/31/89): Assets, $8,233,622 (M); expenditures, $463,473, including $372,469 for grants.
Purpose and activities: Grants largely for youth agencies, higher education, cultural programs and a historic preservation area; some support for hospitals and health agencies, and conservation.
Types of support: Building funds, capital campaigns, endowment funds.
Limitations: Giving primarily in IA. No grants to individuals.
Application information: Contributes only to pre-selected organizations. Applications not accepted.
Board meeting date(s): June
Write: E.T. Meredith III, Pres.
Officers and Director:* E.T. Meredith III, Pres.; Katherine C. Meredith, V.P.; Gerald Thornton, Secy.; Marilyn J. Dillivan, Treas.
Number of staff: None.
Employer Identification Number: 426059818

2358
Mid-Iowa Health Foundation
550 39th St., Suite 104
Des Moines 50312 (515) 277-6411

Established in 1984 in IA.
Foundation type: Independent
Financial data (yr. ended 12/31/88): Assets, $11,342,086 (M); expenditures, $542,577, including $459,129 for 41 grants (high: $27,345; low: $700; average: $1,000-$50,000).
Purpose and activities: Support limited to health-related service projects, including the areas of drug abuse, the handicapped, mental health, and nutrition.
Types of support: General purposes, equipment, scholarship funds, building funds, matching funds, operating budgets, special projects.
Limitations: Giving limited to Polk County, IA, and seven surrounding counties. No support for hospital capital campaigns. No grants for research.
Publications: 990-PF, informational brochure (including application guidelines), application guidelines.
Application information: Application form required.
Initial approach: Telephone or letter
Copies of proposal: 1
Deadline(s): Feb. 1, May 1, Aug. 1, and Nov. 1
Board meeting date(s): Mar., June, Sept., and Dec.
Final notification: 6 to 8 weeks
Write: Kathryn Bradley
Officers: Ivan Johnson,* Chair.; Bernard Mercer,* Vice-Chair.; Donna Drees, Secy.-Treas.
Directors:* Rex Burns, Simon Casady, Don C. Green, Dale Grunewald, T. Ward Phillips, F.F. Satterlee.
Number of staff: 1 full-time professional.
Employer Identification Number: 421235348

2359
Allison Everett Pearson Foundation ⌘
601 South 3rd St.
Clinton 52732-4313

Established in 1967 in IA.
Foundation type: Independent
Financial data (yr. ended 11/30/87): Assets, $1,038,819 (M); expenditures, $54,821, including $39,820 for 40 grants (high: $7,540; low: $10).
Purpose and activities: Support for scholarship funds to educational institutions and Christian and youth-oriented organizations.
Types of support: Scholarship funds.

Limitations: Giving primarily in IA.
Application information: Scholarship awards are made directly to the educational institution.
Officer and Trustees: Carroll F. Johnson, Mgr.; Lois Burke.
Employer Identification Number: 426122181

2360
Pella Rolscreen Foundation ▼
c/o Rolscreen Co.
102 Main St.
Pella 50219 (515) 628-1000

Trust established in 1952 in IA.
Donor(s): Rolscreen Co.
Foundation type: Company-sponsored
Financial data (yr. ended 12/31/89): Assets, $9,601,114 (M); gifts received, $964,500; expenditures, $959,217, including $614,754 for 116 grants (high: $233,333; low: $100; average: $500-$10,000), $21,875 for 26 grants to individuals (high: $1,000; low: $750; average: $750-$1,000) and $296,555 for 263 employee matching gifts.
Purpose and activities: Emphasis on higher education, cultural programs, and social service agencies; employee gifts matched on one-to-one basis for education, United Way chapters, and tax-exempt organizations.
Types of support: Annual campaigns, building funds, scholarship funds, employee-related scholarships, employee matching gifts.
Limitations: Giving primarily in areas of company operations, with emphasis on Marion, Mahaska, and Carroll counties, IA. No grants to individuals (except for employee-related scholarships), or for endowment funds, research, or matching gifts; no loans.
Publications: Informational brochure, application guidelines.
Application information: Application form not required.
Initial approach: Proposal
Copies of proposal: 1
Deadline(s): None
Board meeting date(s): Quarterly
Final notification: 1 month
Write: William J. Anderson, Admin.
Officers and Directors:* Mary Joan Farver,* Pres.; J. Wayne Bevis,* Secy.-Treas.
Number of staff: 1 part-time support.
Employer Identification Number: 237043881

2361
Frank Pierce Trust ⌑ ☆
102 East Church St.
Marshalltown 50158-2942 (515) 752-4507

Established in 1950.
Donor(s): Frank G. Pierce.†
Foundation type: Independent
Financial data (yr. ended 12/31/88): Assets, $1,266,074 (M); qualifying distributions, $142,678, including $133,752 for 57 loans to individuals (high: $6,000; low: $650).
Purpose and activities: Awards limited to student loans for higher education.
Types of support: Student loans.
Limitations: Giving limited to Marshalltown, IA. No grants for graduate study.
Application information: Application form required.
Deadline(s): May 1 and Nov. 15
Write: Max H. Buck
Officers and Trustees: Otis D. Wolfe, Chair.; Milton K. Schulz, Vice-Chair.; Ronald D. Larson, Treas.; Stanley E. Brown, Floyd P. Harthun.
Employer Identification Number: 420737535

2362
Elmer O. & Ida Preston Educational Trust ⌑
Des Moines Bldg., 11th Fl.
Des Moines 50309 (515) 243-4191

Testamentary trust created in 1958 in IA.
Foundation type: Independent
Financial data (yr. ended 12/31/88): Assets, $1,470,401 (M); expenditures, $96,823, including $73,500 for 39 grants to individuals (high: $3,000; low: $750).
Purpose and activities: Giving is limited to worthy and needy young Protestant men residing in IA pursuing collegiate or professional studies for a career in Christian service.
Types of support: Student aid, student loans.
Limitations: Giving primarily in IA.
Application information: Applicants are interviewed. Application form required.
Deadline(s): None
Final notification: Grant/loan determinations are made in Aug. for ensuing academic year; applicants are notified immediately
Write: Linda Wiedenhoff, Admin. Asst.
Trustees: L.W. Cartwright, Ralph L. Jester, David J.W. Proctor.
Employer Identification Number: 426053621

2363
The Principal Financial Group Foundation
(Formerly The Principal Foundation)
711 High St.
Des Moines 50392-0150 (515) 247-5209

Established in 1987 in IA.
Foundation type: Company-sponsored
Financial data (yr. ended 12/31/89): Assets, $2,340,000 (M); qualifying distributions, $2,238,000, including $1,841,000 for 130 grants (high: $200,000; low: $200; average: $2,500-$5,000), $250,000 for employee matching gifts and $147,000 for in-kind gifts.
Purpose and activities: Support for social services, arts and culture, health, education, civic and community affairs, and the United Way of Central IA.
Types of support: Annual campaigns, building funds, capital campaigns, continuing support, employee matching gifts, operating budgets, special projects, general purposes, in-kind gifts.
Limitations: Giving primarily in IA with emphasis on the Des Moines, IA, area. No support for athletic organizations, fraternal organizations, organizations redistributing funds, private foundations, sectarian, religious, or denominational organizations, social organizations; trade, industrial or professional associations, or veteran's groups. No grants to individuals, or for conference or seminar attendance, goodwill ads, endowments, festival participation, or hospital or health care capital fund drives.
Publications: Informational brochure (including application guidelines).
Application information: Application form not required.
Initial approach: Proposal
Copies of proposal: 1
Deadline(s): 4 to 6 weeks prior to contributions committee meeting
Board meeting date(s): Approximately once a month
Final notification: 6 to 8 weeks
Write: Walter J. Walsh, Pres.
Officer: Walter J. Walsh, Pres. and V.P., Corp. Relations.
Number of staff: None.
Employer Identification Number: 421312301

2364
Pritchard Educational Fund ⌑
c/o Cherokee State Bank
212 West Willow St.
Cherokee 51012 (712) 225-5131

Established in 1931 in IA.
Foundation type: Independent
Financial data (yr. ended 12/31/88): Assets, $2,547,403 (M); expenditures, $133,816, including $98,950 for 149 loans to individuals (high: $1,000; low: $250).
Purpose and activities: Giving limited to student loans for residents of Cherokee County, IA, for high school or college education expenses.
Types of support: Student loans.
Limitations: Giving limited to Cherokee County, IA.
Application information: Application form required.
Deadline(s): None
Write: Leon Klotz, Fdn. Mgr.
Officer: Leon Klotz, Mgr.
Trustee: Cherokee State Bank.
Employer Identification Number: 426051872

2365
Quad City Osteopathic Foundation ☆
c/o ERA Assoc. Counselors
6236 North Brady St.
Davenport 52806 (319) 386-5204

Established in 1984 in IA.
Foundation type: Independent
Financial data (yr. ended 11/30/89): Assets, $4,239,060 (M); gifts received, $8,125; expenditures, $291,146, including $137,414 for 6 grants and $84,000 for 17 grants to individuals (high: $99,665; low: $1,000).
Purpose and activities: Awards scholarships in the field of osteopathy; substantial support for a clinic, health, and medical education.
Types of support: Student aid.
Limitations: Giving primarily in IA and IL.
Publications: Newsletter, annual report.
Application information: Application form required.
Initial approach: Letter
Copies of proposal: 1
Deadline(s): None
Board meeting date(s): 2nd Tuesday of each month
Write: Eugene Holst, Pres.
Officers and Directors:* Michael Roeder,* Chair.; David W. Seitz,* Vice-Chair.; Eugene R. Holst,* Pres.; James D. King,* Secy.; Cal Harnsen,* Treas.; Dennis D. Boekhoff, Gregory

Garvin, Karen Griggs, Margo Hancock, Lydia Jordan-Fellner.
Number of staff: 1 full-time professional.
Employer Identification Number: 420666090

2366
Quarton-McElroy-IRA Foundation ⌑ ☆
c/o Merchants National Bank, Trust Dept.
Second Ave. & Third St., S.E.
Cedar Rapids 52401

Foundation type: Independent
Financial data (yr. ended 05/31/89): Assets, $1,482,254 (M); expenditures, $18,445, including $13,218 for 5 grants (high: $5,000; low: $1,500).
Purpose and activities: Support primarily for higher education in electronic journalism, and to promote and expand the broadcasting industry.
Limitations: Giving primarily in IA.
Application information: Contributes only to pre-selected organizations. Applications not accepted.
Officers: Betty Baudler, Pres.; Bill Williamson, V.P.; Larry Edwards, Secy.; Lew Van Nostrand, Treas.
Directors: Jerry Bretty, Bill Sanders, Jim Waterburg.
Trustee: Merchants National Bank.
Employer Identification Number: 237314096

2367
Hobart A. and Alta V. Ross Family Foundation ⌑
P.O. Box AK
Spirit Lake 51360

Foundation type: Operating
Financial data (yr. ended 12/31/87): Assets, $1,181,749 (M); expenditures, $133,541, including $128,750 for 13 grants (high: $20,000; low: $950).
Purpose and activities: A private operating foundation; support for educational institutions, drug and alcohol treatment programs, youth organizations, and a domestic violence and child abuse program.
Limitations: Giving primarily in Dickinson County, IA, and neighboring counties.
Application information:
Deadline(s): None
Officer: Keith Ross, Pres.
Directors: Robert Ross, Michael Stineman.
Employer Identification Number: 421242755

2368
John Ruan Foundation Trust ⌑
3200 Ruan Ctr.
Des Moines 50304 (515) 245-2555

Trust established in 1955 in IA.
Donor(s): John Ruan.
Foundation type: Independent
Financial data (yr. ended 6/30/88): Assets, $4,068,141 (M); gifts received, $199,842; expenditures, $149,439, including $147,902 for 103 grants (high: $31,250; low: $25).
Purpose and activities: Emphasis on higher education, cultural programs, youth agencies, child welfare, and health agencies.
Limitations: Giving primarily in Des Moines, IA.
Application information: Application form not required.
Deadline(s): None
Write: John Ruan, Trustee
Trustees: Elizabeth J. Ruan, John Ruan.
Employer Identification Number: 426059463

2369
W. A. Sheaffer Memorial Foundation, Inc. ☆
817 Ave. G
Fort Madison 52627-2912

Established in 1952.
Foundation type: Independent
Financial data (yr. ended 02/28/89): Assets, $1,005,116 (M); expenditures, $76,689, including $64,500 for 7 grants (high: $28,000; low: $500).
Purpose and activities: Support primarily for higher and other education; support also for community organizations and social services, including a YMCA.
Limitations: Giving primarily in IA.
Officers and Directors:* Walter A. Sheaffer II,* Pres.; John D. Sheaffer,* V.P.; Robert O. Thomas,* Secy.-Treas.
Number of staff: 2 part-time professional.
Employer Identification Number: 426060302

2370
Mabel E. Sherman Educational Fund ⌑
c/o Citizens First National Bank
Storm Lake 50588 (712) 732-5440

Established in 1977 in IA.
Foundation type: Independent
Financial data (yr. ended 6/30/88): Assets, $1,701,046 (M); expenditures, $64,482, including $45,385 for 4 grants.
Purpose and activities: Grants to Buena Vista College, Cornell College, Morningside College, and Westmar College to finance student loans.
Types of support: Student loans.
Limitations: Giving limited to IA, with preference given to residents of Ida and Cherokee counties.
Publications: Annual report.
Application information: Loan application forms may be obtained from grantee colleges. Application form required.
Copies of proposal: 1
Deadline(s): None
Write: Larry Dugan, Trust Officer, Citizens First National Bank
Trustee: Citizens First National Bank.
Number of staff: 1 part-time professional.
Employer Identification Number: 426278859

2371
Joseph J. Sinek Scholarship Trust ⌑
c/o Citizens State Bank
Pocahontas 50574
Application address: Pocahontas Community School, Pocahontas, IA 50574; Tel.: (712) 335-4848

Established in 1982 in IA.
Foundation type: Independent
Financial data (yr. ended 12/31/88): Assets, $1,138,877 (M); expenditures, $96,262, including $85,764 for 125 grants to individuals (high: $1,080; low: $168).
Purpose and activities: Awards scholarships for higher education to graduates of Pocahontas Community School.
Types of support: Student aid.
Limitations: Giving limited to Pocahontas, IA, area high school graduates.
Application information: Application form required.
Deadline(s): Apr. 1
Write: Martin Jacobsmeier, Guidance Counselor
Trustee: Citizens State Bank.
Employer Identification Number: 426336481

2372
Bertha Stebens Charitable Foundation ⌑ ☆
119 Second St., N.W.
Mason City 50401-3198 (515) 423-1913

Established in 1986 in IA.
Foundation type: Independent
Financial data (yr. ended 7/31/88): Assets, $1,147,610 (M); expenditures, $87,617, including $59,000 for 10 grants (high: $20,000; low: $500).
Purpose and activities: Giving for civic affairs, secondary and other education, a Methodist church, cultural programs, and an organization benefiting the disabled.
Types of support: Scholarship funds, building funds.
Limitations: Giving primarily in Cerro Gordo County, IA. No grants to individuals.
Application information:
Initial approach: Letter
Deadline(s): Dec. 31
Write: Harold R. Winston, Dir.
Directors: Spence Abrams, Sr., Otto C. McDonough, Harold R. Winston.
Employer Identification Number: 421280907

2373
The Van Buren Foundation, Inc. ⌑
c/o Farmers State Bank
Keosauqua 52565 (319) 293-3794

Incorporated in 1959 in IA.
Donor(s): Ralph S. Roberts.†
Foundation type: Independent
Financial data (yr. ended 12/31/88): Assets, $2,393,384 (M); gifts received, $1,206; qualifying distributions, $200,130, including $146,191 for 31 grants (high: $40,000; low: $243), $12,124 for grants to individuals and $41,256 for 2 foundation-administered programs.
Purpose and activities: Grants for local community development, aid for the aged, recreation programs, and education, including student aid; also provides loans to medical and health care students.
Types of support: Special projects, building funds, general purposes, student aid, student loans.
Limitations: Giving limited to Van Buren County, IA.
Application information: Application forms for student aid available from foundation or high school counselors in Van Buren County.
Initial approach: Proposal
Copies of proposal: 1
Deadline(s): None

Board meeting date(s): Apr. to consider educational grants, and as required
Write: For general grants: John A. Manning, Chair.; for educational grants: Arthur P. Ovrom, Treas.
Officers: John A. Manning, Chair.; Norwood Teal, Vice-Chair.; Davis E. Pollock, Pres.; Rex Strait, 1st V.P.; John R. Nickelson, 2nd V.P.; Richard H. Lytle, Secy.; Arthur P. Ovrom, Treas.
Employer Identification Number: 426062589

2374
Vermeer Charitable Foundation, Inc.
c/o Vermeer Manufacturing Co.
P.O. Box 200
Pella 50219 (515) 628-3141

Established in 1977 in IA.
Donor(s): Vermeer Manufacturing Co., Vermeer Sales and Service of Iowa, Vermeer Farms, Inc.
Foundation type: Company-sponsored
Financial data (yr. ended 12/31/89): Assets, $3,686,248 (M); gifts received, $771,212; expenditures, $301,434, including $300,495 for 35 grants (high: $50,000; low: $310; average: $10,000).
Purpose and activities: Giving primarily for Christian religious organizations, higher education, and care of the elderly.
Types of support: Seed money, building funds.
Limitations: Giving primarily in the Pella, IA, area. No grants to individuals, or for endowment funds, scholarships, fellowships, or matching gifts; no loans.
Application information: Application form required.
Initial approach: Letter
Copies of proposal: 2
Board meeting date(s): Dec. and as required
Write: Mary Andringa, Dir.
Directors: Dale Andringa, Mary Andringa, Gary J. Vermeer, Lois J. Vermeer, Matilda Vermeer, Robert L. Vermeer.
Number of staff: 2 part-time professional.
Employer Identification Number: 421087640

2375
Vermeer Foundation Company ⌑
c/o Vermeer Manufacturing Co.
P.O. Box 200
Pella 50219 (515) 628-3141

Trust established in 1958 in IA.
Donor(s): Vermeer Manufacturing Co.
Foundation type: Company-sponsored
Financial data (yr. ended 12/31/87): Assets, $831,569 (M); expenditures, $1,105,658, including $1,101,638 for 63 grants (high: $325,000; low: $250).
Purpose and activities: Emphasis on local church-related institutions, including social service agencies.
Types of support: General purposes, annual campaigns, seed money, building funds, endowment funds.
Limitations: Giving primarily in Pella, IA. No grants to individuals, or for research, scholarships, fellowships, or matching gifts; no loans.
Application information: Applications not invited from any group which does not know a director personally. Application form required.
Initial approach: Letter
Board meeting date(s): Dec. and as required
Final notification: 1 month
Write: Lois J. Vermeer, Secy.
Officers and Directors: Robert L. Vermeer, Pres.; Lois J. Vermeer, Secy.
Number of staff: None.
Employer Identification Number: 426059566

2376
Vermeer Investment Company Foundation ⌑
412 Franklin St.
Pella 50219

Established in 1976 in IA.
Donor(s): Harry G. Vermeer, Michael Vermeer, Marion County State Bank.
Foundation type: Independent
Financial data (yr. ended 12/31/87): Assets, $1,705,871 (M); gifts received, $98,337; expenditures, $129,377, including $128,000 for 8 grants (high: $50,000; low: $500).
Purpose and activities: Limited to Christian giving, including welfare and higher education.
Officers: Harry G. Vermeer, Chair. and Treas.; Michael Vermeer, Vice-Chair.; Bernice Vermeer, Secy.
Employer Identification Number: 510182729

2377
Vogel Charities, Inc. ⌑
Country Rd. P South
Orange City 51041 (712) 737-4993

Established in 1973 in IA.
Donor(s): Vogel Paint & Wax, Marwin Paints.
Foundation type: Independent
Financial data (yr. ended 12/31/87): Assets, $1,101,075 (M); gifts received, $209,000; expenditures, $149,672, including $144,957 for 59 grants (high: $73,500; low: $25).
Purpose and activities: Giving primarily for higher and secondary education, cultural programs, and hospitals and health services.
Types of support: Scholarship funds, building funds.
Application information:
Write: Franklin P. Vogel, Pres.
Officer: Franklin P. Vogel, Pres.
Employer Identification Number: 237169167

2378
Wahlert Foundation
Sixteenth and Sycamore Sts.
Dubuque 52001 (319) 588-5400
Grant application office: c/o FDL Foods, Inc., P.O. Box 898, Dubuque, IA 52001

Incorporated in 1948 in IA.
Donor(s): Dubuque Packing Co., FDL Foods, Inc., H.W. Wahlert,† and officers of the foundation.
Foundation type: Independent
Financial data (yr. ended 11/30/89): Assets, $4,052,257 (M); gifts received, $2,965; expenditures, $275,500, including $272,635 for 16 grants (high: $50,000; low: $500; average: $50-$50,000).
Purpose and activities: Support primarily for higher, secondary, and theological education; grants also for hospitals, social service agencies, cultural activities, including the arts and museums, Catholic welfare, and minorities.
Types of support: Continuing support, annual campaigns, seed money, emergency funds, building funds, equipment, capital campaigns, scholarship funds, special projects.
Limitations: Giving primarily in the Dubuque, IA, metropolitan area. No grants to individuals, publications, conferences, or matching gifts; no loans.
Application information: Application form not required.
Initial approach: Proposal
Copies of proposal: 1
Deadline(s): Nov. 30
Board meeting date(s): Dec.
Final notification: Jan. 30
Write: R.H. Wahlert, Pres. and Treas.
Officers and Trustees:* R.H. Wahlert,* Pres. and Treas.; Al E. Hughes,* Secy.; A.J. Kisting, Donald Strausse, David Wahlert, Donna Wahlert, Jim Wahlert, R.C. Wahlert, R.C. Wahlert III.
Number of staff: None.
Employer Identification Number: 426051124

2379
Waterloo Civic Foundation ☆
P.O. Box 1833
Waterloo 50704 (319) 233-8431

Community foundation incorporated in 1956 in IA.
Foundation type: Community
Financial data (yr. ended 04/30/89): Assets, $838,616 (M); gifts received, $343,916; expenditures, $302,979, including $278,003 for 20 grants (high: $190,024; low: $200).
Purpose and activities: To promote, encourage and aid recreational, benevolent, charitable, medical, scientific, literary, educational and research organizations' projects of work in the city of Waterloo.
Types of support: Continuing support, emergency funds, equipment, publications, research, seed money, professorships, exchange programs, matching funds.
Limitations: Giving limited to Waterloo, IA. No grants to individuals, or for annual campaigns, building funds, operating budgets, renovation projects, or conferences and seminars.
Publications: Application guidelines, 990-PF, financial statement, grants list, informational brochure (including application guidelines).
Application information: Application form not required.
Copies of proposal: 1
Deadline(s): Apr. 15
Board meeting date(s): 1st Monday in June
Write: Robert J. Brown, Pres.
Officers: Robert J. Brown, Pres.; and 24 members of the board.
Number of staff: None.
Employer Identification Number: 426060414

2380
Waverly Community Foundation ⌑
c/o State Bank of Waverly
P.O. Box 58
Waverly 50677 (319) 352-4556

Established in 1958 in IA.

Foundation type: Community
Financial data (yr. ended 12/31/88): Assets, $1,528,374 (M); expenditures, $118,708, including $53,500 for 7 grants (high: $27,000; low: $1,000) and $53,650 for grants to individuals.
Purpose and activities: Support for the aged and scholarships to individuals.
Types of support: Student aid.
Limitations: Giving limited to Bremer County, IA.
Application information:
Initial approach: Letter
Deadline(s): Jan. 1 for grants, Apr. 1 for scholarships
Write: Ruth Rodenbeck
Agent: State Bank of Waverly.
Employer Identification Number: 426058774

2381
Wilson Foundation ⌑ ☆
Conrad 50621

Established in 1967.
Donor(s): Cliff D. Wilson, Jr.
Foundation type: Independent
Financial data (yr. ended 12/31/88): Assets, $131,760 (M); gifts received, $100,000; expenditures, $144,156, including $144,150 for 19 grants (high: $60,000; low: $100).
Purpose and activities: Support primarily for a college and a Baptist theological seminary and Christian religious activities.
Limitations: No grants to individuals.
Application information:
Initial approach: Letter
Deadline(s): None
Write: Cliff D. Wilson, Jr., Chair.
Officers: Cliff D. Wilson, Jr., Chair.; Margaret Wilson, Vice-Chair. and Treas.; Leland Wiseman, Secy.
Employer Identification Number: 420923218

2382
Windsor Charitable Foundation ⌑ ☆
100 Court Ave., No. 600
Des Moines 50309

Established in 1984 in IA.
Donor(s): Mary Belle H. Windsor.
Foundation type: Independent
Financial data (yr. ended 12/31/88): Assets, $187,344 (M); gifts received, $100,000; expenditures, $114,692, including $109,650 for 9 grants (high: $60,000; low: $2,500).
Purpose and activities: Giving primarily for a science center and museums; support also for performing arts and health.
Types of support: Building funds, renovation projects, general purposes.
Limitations: Giving primarily in IA. No grants to individuals.
Application information: Contributes only to pre-selected organizations. Applications not accepted.
Trustees: Herbert W. Montis, Jr., James H. Windsor III, Mary Belle H. Windsor.
Employer Identification Number: 421227965

2383
John H. Witte, Jr. Foundation ⌑
c/o First National Bank
201 Jefferson St., P.O. Box 1088
Burlington 52601 (319) 752-2761

Donor(s): John H. Witte, Jr.†
Foundation type: Independent
Financial data (yr. ended 08/31/89): Assets, $5,810,447 (M); expenditures, $238,009, including $214,114 for 25 grants (high: $35,000; low: $75).
Purpose and activities: Emphasis on social service and youth agencies, education, and a community fund.
Types of support: Special projects, building funds, equipment.
Limitations: Giving primarily in the Burlington, IA, area.
Application information:
Initial approach: Letter
Deadline(s): None
Write: Robert C. Matsch, Sr. V.P., First National Bank
Trustee: First National Bank.
Employer Identification Number: 426297940

2384
Younkers Foundation, Inc. ⌑
c/o Younker Brothers
Seventh and Walnut Sts., Box 1495
Des Moines 50306 (515) 244-1112

Incorporated in 1968 in IA.
Donor(s): Younkers, Inc.
Foundation type: Company-sponsored
Financial data (yr. ended 12/31/87): Assets, $1,438 (M); gifts received, $302,943; expenditures, $301,859, including $301,859 for 48 grants (high: $83,766; low: $25).
Purpose and activities: Grants mainly to community funds; some support also for higher education and cultural activities.
Limitations: Giving limited to areas of company operations in IA. No grants to individuals.
Application information: Applications not accepted.
Officers: William Thomas Gould, Pres.; Jack Prouty, V.P.; Gerry Roth, V.P.; Donald Thomas, V.P.; Carl Ziltz, V.P.; Richard Luse, Secy.-Treas.
Employer Identification Number: 420937873

KANSAS

2385
Jennie G. and Pearl Abell Education Trust
717 Main St.
P.O. Box 487
Ashland 67831 (316) 635-2228

Trust established in 1975 in KS.
Donor(s): P.G. Abell.†
Foundation type: Independent
Financial data (yr. ended 05/31/88): Assets, $1,872,579 (M); expenditures, $205,715, including $174,985 for grants to individuals.
Purpose and activities: Grants only for scholarships for graduates of Clark County, KS, high schools or residents of Clark County, KS.
Types of support: Student aid.
Limitations: Giving limited to Clark County, KS.
Publications: Program policy statement.
Application information: Application form required.
Copies of proposal: 1
Deadline(s): June 15
Board meeting date(s): Monthly
Write: Sarah D. Shattuck, Mgr.
Officer and Trustees:* Sarah D. Shattuck, Mgr.; Juanita Abell Pyle, Roger G. Rankin.
Number of staff: 1 full-time professional; 1 part-time support.
Employer Identification Number: 237454791

2386
Louis W. & Dolpha Baehr Foundation
c/o Miami County National Bank and Trust
Box 369
Paola 66071 (913) 294-4311

Established in 1967 in KS.
Donor(s): L.W. Baehr,† Dolpha Baehr.†
Foundation type: Independent
Financial data (yr. ended 4/30/89): Assets, $2,424,934 (M); expenditures, $196,163, including $178,666 for 13 grants (high: $75,014; low: $600).
Purpose and activities: Emphasis on youth programs, including recreation, education, and hospitals; support also for community development.
Types of support: Building funds, endowment funds, equipment, matching funds, renovation projects, research, seed money, special projects.
Limitations: Giving limited to eastern Kansas, including the greater Kansas City area. No support for sectarian or religious organizations whose services are limited to members of any one religious group, or for agencies operating as chapters of a state or national organization. No grants to individuals, or for advertising; no loans.
Publications: Application guidelines.
Application information: Application form not required.
Initial approach: Proposal
Deadline(s): Dec., Mar., July, and Sept.
Board meeting date(s): Jan., Apr., Aug., and Oct.
Final notification: Within 12 weeks
Write: Carl F. Gump, Chair.
Trustee: Miami County National Bank and Trust.
Number of staff: None.
Employer Identification Number: 486129741

2387
J. H. Baker Trust ⌑
c/o Farmers and Merchants State Bank
Box 280
La Crosse 67548 (913) 222-2537

Established in 1976.

Donor(s): J.H. Baker.†
Foundation type: Independent
Financial data (yr. ended 12/31/87): Assets, $1,102,551 (M); expenditures, $62,966, including $21,375 for 29 loans to individuals.
Purpose and activities: Grants for student loans only.
Types of support: Student loans.
Limitations: Giving limited to Rush, Barton, Ellis, Ness, and Pawnee Counties, KS.
Application information: Application form required.
Deadline(s): None
Write: Tom Dechant, Trustee
Trustees: Tom Dechant, Farmers and Merchants State Bank.
Employer Identification Number: 510210925

2388
Bank IV Charitable Trust ⌑
(Formerly Fourth National Bank of Wichita Charitable Trust)
c/o Bank IV Wichita, N.A.
P.O. Box 1122
Wichita 67201 (316) 261-4361

Trust established in 1952 in KS.
Donor(s): The Fourth National Bank and Trust Co.
Foundation type: Company-sponsored
Financial data (yr. ended 11/30/88): Assets, $1,382,810 (M); expenditures, $495,493, including $490,677 for 101 grants (high: $132,500; low: $120).
Purpose and activities: Emphasis on community funds, youth agencies, higher education, hospitals, health services, including aid to the handicapped, cultural programs, child development, and religious organizations.
Types of support: Building funds, equipment, endowment funds, scholarship funds, capital campaigns, research.
Limitations: Giving primarily in KS, with emphasis on Wichita. No support for political or religious organizations, fraternal groups, or organizations which receive a major portion of their support from government funds. No grants to individuals, or for general support, operating budgets, dinners, travel, annual campaigns, seed money, emergency funds, deficit financing, publications, conferences, or matching gifts; no loans.
Publications: Application guidelines.
Application information: Application form not required.
Initial approach: Letter
Copies of proposal: 1
Deadline(s): None
Board meeting date(s): Mar., June, Sept., and Dec.
Final notification: Up to 3 months
Write: Michael R. Ritchey, Exec. V.P., Bank IV Wichita, N.A.
Trustees: Fred F. Berry, Jr., Wilson K. Cadman, Jordan L. Haines, Mary L. Oliver, Nestor R. Weigand, Bank IV Wichita.
Number of staff: None.
Employer Identification Number: 486103519

2389
Bank IV Topeka Charitable Trust ⌑
P.O. Box 88
Topeka 66601-0088 (913) 925-3432

Established in 1952 in KS.
Foundation type: Company-sponsored
Financial data (yr. ended 12/31/87): Assets, $409,739 (M); expenditures, $120,093, including $119,483 for 18 grants (high: $44,750; low: $800).
Purpose and activities: Support primarily for social services and community funds.
Limitations: Giving primarily in Topeka, KS.
Application information: Application form not required.
Deadline(s): None
Write: S. Kenneth Alexander III
Trustees: Thomas R. Clevenger, Richard O. Shiney, Bank IV Topeka.
Employer Identification Number: 486132391

2390
Baughman Foundation ⌑
112 West Third
P.O. Box 1356
Liberal 67901 (316) 624-1371

Incorporated in 1958 in KS.
Donor(s): Robert W. Baughman,† The John W. Baughman Farms Co.
Foundation type: Independent
Financial data (yr. ended 12/31/88): Assets, $12,936,474 (M); expenditures, $757,831, including $556,020 for 58 grants (high: $81,200; low: $100).
Purpose and activities: Emphasis on higher education, including a community junior college, youth agencies, and civic projects.
Types of support: Building funds, endowment funds, operating budgets, special projects, scholarship funds.
Limitations: Giving primarily in KS, with emphasis on Liberal. No support for private foundations. No grants to individuals.
Application information:
Initial approach: Proposal
Copies of proposal: 3
Deadline(s): Prior to 2nd Wednesday of each month
Board meeting date(s): Monthly
Final notification: 30 days
Write: Eugene W. Slaymaker, Pres.
Officers and Trustees: Eugene W. Slaymaker, Pres.; Oliver S. Brown, V.P.; James R. Yoxall, Secy.-Treas.
Number of staff: None.
Employer Identification Number: 486108797

2391
Beech Aircraft Foundation
9709 East Central Ave.
Wichita 67201 (316) 681-8177

Incorporated in 1966 in KS.
Donor(s): Beech Aircraft Corp.
Foundation type: Company-sponsored
Financial data (yr. ended 12/31/88): Assets, $5,524,033 (M); expenditures, $438,870, including $359,994 for 113 grants, $22,000 for 34 grants to individuals and $25,075 for employee matching gifts.
Purpose and activities: Grants for higher education, community funds, youth agencies, and hospitals; some support for cultural activities, conservation, the handicapped, and the aged.
Types of support: Exchange programs, program-related investments, publications, seed money, employee-related scholarships, employee matching gifts, annual campaigns, capital campaigns, continuing support, matching funds, renovation projects, special projects, building funds.
Limitations: Giving primarily in communities with company facilities, with an emphasis on KS. No grants to individuals (except for employee-related scholarships), or for endowment funds, research, or matching gifts; no loans.
Application information: Application form not required.
Initial approach: Letter
Copies of proposal: 1
Deadline(s): Dec., Mar., June, and Sept.
Board meeting date(s): Jan., Apr., July, and Oct.
Write: Larry E. Lawrence, Secy.-Treas.
Officers: O.A. Beech,* Chair. and Pres.; Wey D. Kenny,* V.P.; Larry E. Lawrence, Secy.-Treas.
Directors:* Max E. Bleck, J.A. Elliot, Lucille Winters.
Employer Identification Number: 486125881

2392
Willard J. and Mary G. Breidenthal Foundation ⌑
c/o Commercial National Bank, Trust Div.
P.O. Box 1400
Kansas City 66117 (913) 371-0035

Trust established in 1962 in KS.
Donor(s): Willard J. Breidenthal,† Mary G. Breidenthal,† and members of the Breidenthal family.
Foundation type: Independent
Financial data (yr. ended 12/31/88): Assets, $2,527,587 (M); expenditures, $157,293, including $145,750 for 37 grants (high: $10,000; low: $500; average: $3,725).
Purpose and activities: Emphasis on higher education and hospitals; support also for agriculture, child welfare, youth agencies, and cultural programs.
Limitations: Giving primarily in the Kansas City, KS, and Kansas City, MO, area. No grants to individuals.
Application information: Application form not required.
Initial approach: Letter
Deadline(s): Submit proposal preferably in Sept. or Oct.; deadline Nov. 1
Board meeting date(s): Nov.
Write: Ruth B. Snyder, Trustee
Trustees: George Gray Breidenthal, Mary Ruth Breidenthal, Ruth B. Snyder, Commercial National Bank.
Number of staff: None.
Employer Identification Number: 486103376

2393
Samuel M. and Laura H. Brown Charitable Trust ⌑
c/o First National Bank in Wichita
P.O. Box One
Wichita 67201 (316) 268-1236

Trust established in 1974 in KS.
Donor(s): S.M. Brown.†
Foundation type: Independent
Financial data (yr. ended 11/30/88): Assets, $1,488,887 (M); expenditures, $129,511, including $116,293 for 25 grants (high: $10,000; low: $500).
Purpose and activities: Emphasis on cultural programs, especially music, higher education, and church support.
Limitations: Giving primarily in Wichita and Sedgwick counties, KS.
Application information: Application form not required.
Deadline(s): None
Write: Steve Woods, V.P. and Trust Officer, First National Bank in Wichita
Trustees: Robert G. Braden, First National Bank in Wichita.
Employer Identification Number: 486193416

2394
Brown Memorial Foundation ⌑
300 North Cedar
P.O. Box 187
Abilene 67410 (913) 263-2351
Scholarship application address: Abilene High School, Abilene, KS; Tel.: (913) 263-1260

Established in 1926 in KS.
Foundation type: Operating
Financial data (yr. ended 12/31/88): Assets, $7,877,269 (M); gifts received, $6,554; expenditures, $396,238, including $24,439 for 16 grants (high: $6,025; low: $24), $10,000 for 20 grants to individuals of $500 each and $320,662 for foundation-administered programs.
Purpose and activities: Support primarily for indigent families ; scholarships awarded to students who have shown evidence of scholastic ability and are in need of financial support.
Types of support: Scholarship funds, grants to individuals.
Application information:
Deadline(s): Mar. for scholarships
Officers and Trustees: Calvin A. Strowig, Pres. and Mgr.; Reilly S. Neil, V.P.; E.L. Fiedler, Secy.-Treas.; Lila B. Clark, William A. Guilfoyle, Kenneth Olson, Paul Veach.
Employer Identification Number: 480573809

2395
Daniel M. Carney Family Charitable Foundation
(also known as Carney Family Charities Foundation)
2024 North Woodlawn, Suite 402
Wichita 67208-1851 (316) 686-7314

Established in 1968 in KS.
Foundation type: Independent
Financial data (yr. ended 12/31/89): Assets, $1,647,545 (M); expenditures, $368,180, including $347,440 for 86 grants (high: $270,940; low: $500).
Purpose and activities: Giving primarily for medical research and general charitable projects.
Limitations: Giving primarily in Wichita, KS. No grants to individuals.
Application information:
Initial approach: Letter
Deadline(s): None
Write: Daniel M. Carney, Mgr.
Officer and Trustees:* Daniel M. Carney,* Mgr.; Beverly A. Carney, Joseph P. Flynn.
Number of staff: None.
Employer Identification Number: 237004875

2396
Cessna Foundation, Inc. ⌑
P.O. Box 7704
Wichita 67277 (316) 946-6000

Incorporated in 1952 in KS.
Donor(s): The Cessna Aircraft Co.
Foundation type: Company-sponsored
Financial data (yr. ended 12/31/88): Assets, $6,387,542 (M); expenditures, $492,181, including $456,882 for 57 grants (high: $67,000; low: $150; average: $500-$1,000) and $19,175 for 45 employee matching gifts.
Purpose and activities: Grants largely for the United Way, higher education, and youth agencies; support also for hospitals and cultural programs, including museums.
Types of support: Employee matching gifts, building funds, annual campaigns, capital campaigns, emergency funds, employee-related scholarships, special projects.
Limitations: Giving primarily in areas of company operations, particularly KS. No grants to individuals.
Application information:
Initial approach: Letter
Copies of proposal: 1
Deadline(s): Submit proposals preferably in Nov.
Board meeting date(s): Feb. and Dec.
Write: H.D. Humphrey, Secy.
Officers and Trustees: Russell W. Meyer, Jr., Pres.; John E. Moore, V.P.; H.D. Humphrey, Secy.-Treas.; Bruce E. Peterman.
Employer Identification Number: 486108801

2397
Coleman Charitable Trust, Inc. ⌑
250 North St. Francis St.
P.O. Box 1762
Wichita 67202 (316) 261-3082

Incorporated in 1944 in KS.
Donor(s): The Coleman Co., Inc.
Foundation type: Company-sponsored
Financial data (yr. ended 12/31/87): Assets, $132,297 (M); gifts received, $240,000; expenditures, $206,306, including $200,550 for 75 grants (high: $58,000; low: $25) and $4,585 for 33 employee matching gifts.
Purpose and activities: Emphasis on a community fund, higher education, and youth and social agencies.
Types of support: Employee matching gifts, operating budgets, scholarship funds, building funds, annual campaigns, special projects, equipment.
Limitations: Giving primarily in Wichita, KS.
Application information:
Initial approach: Letter
Deadline(s): None
Write: Tim Cotter
Officers: Sheldon Coleman, Chair.; Clarence Coleman, V.P.; Frank Shaw, V.P.; R.A. Curry, Treas.
Trustees: Don Berchtold, Richard Smith, Wesley H. Sowers.
Employer Identification Number: 486104738

2398
Edith and Harry Darby Foundation ⌑
333 North Sixth St.
Kansas City 66101 (913) 281-0080

Incorporated in 1961 in KS.
Donor(s): Harry Darby Foundation, and others.
Foundation type: Independent
Financial data (yr. ended 09/30/89): Assets, $1,215,279 (M); expenditures, $531,221, including $513,236 for 101 grants (high: $26,341; low: $50).
Purpose and activities: Emphasis on higher education, hospitals, church support, community development, and cultural programs.
Limitations: Giving primarily in KS and MO.
Application information: Application form not required.
Initial approach: Letter
Deadline(s): None
Write: J.K. Meador, V.P.
Officers: J.K. Meador, Pres.; E.D. Evans, V.P.; L.A. Randall, Secy.-Treas.
Employer Identification Number: 486103395

2399
James A. and Juliet L. Davis Foundation, Inc. ⌑
802 First National Ctr.
P.O. Box 2027
Hutchinson 67504-2027 (316) 663-5021

Incorporated in 1954 in KS.
Foundation type: Independent
Financial data (yr. ended 12/31/88): Assets, $2,388,708 (M); expenditures, $124,112, including $38,543 for 35 grants (high: $8,000; low: $115) and $51,250 for 32 grants to individuals (high: $2,500; low: $750; average: $1,500-$2,500).
Purpose and activities: Support for higher education, including scholarships and awards to educators, cultural programs, and child welfare.
Types of support: Student aid, general purposes, scholarship funds.
Limitations: Giving limited to the Hutchinson, KS, area.
Application information: Scholarships limited to students graduating from Hutchinson High School who will attend college in KS or MO. Application form not required.
Deadline(s): Mar. 15
Board meeting date(s): Third Monday of each month
Final notification: Scholarship awards announced at High School Awards Assembly
Write: William Y. Chalfant, Secy.

Officers and Trustees: Peter M. Macdonald, Pres.; William Y. Chalfant, Secy.; Kent Longenecker, Merl F. Sellers, Carol Shaft.
Number of staff: None.
Employer Identification Number: 486105748

2400
DeVore Foundation, Inc.
P.O. Box 118
Wichita 67201 (316) 267-3211

Incorporated in 1953 in KS.
Donor(s): Floyd DeVore,† Richard A. DeVore, William D. DeVore, and their businesses.
Foundation type: Independent
Financial data (yr. ended 11/30/89): Assets, $2,491,670 (M); gifts received, $7,500; expenditures, $224,561, including $179,559 for 49 grants (high: $135,200; low: $40).
Purpose and activities: Giving to youth agencies, Protestant church support, arts and culture, higher education, and health and social services.
Types of support: Annual campaigns, building funds, capital campaigns, continuing support, endowment funds, equipment, general purposes, operating budgets, renovation projects, seed money, special projects.
Limitations: Giving primarily in Wichita, KS.
Publications: 990-PF, application guidelines, annual report.
Application information: Letter. Application form not required.
Copies of proposal: 1
Deadline(s): None
Write: Richard A. DeVore, Pres.
Officers and Directors: Richard A. DeVore, Pres. and Secy.; William D. DeVore, V.P. and Treas.
Number of staff: None.
Employer Identification Number: 486109754

2401
Stella A. & Ray E. Dillon Foundation, Inc. ¤
One Compound Dr.
Hutchinson 67502 (316) 665-5421

Established in 1980 in KS.
Foundation type: Independent
Financial data (yr. ended 12/31/88): Assets, $1,129,958 (M); expenditures, $76,902, including $71,750 for 21 grants (high: $10,000; low: $250).
Purpose and activities: Support primarily for social services and for youth and community organizations; support also for an historical society.
Limitations: Giving primarily in Reno County, KS.
Application information: Application form not required.
Initial approach: Proposal
Deadline(s): No set deadline; grants usually awarded in May
Write: Ray E. Dillon III, Treas.
Officers: Richard W. Dillon, Pres.; Ray E. Dillon, Jr., V.P.; Brad Dillon, Secy.; Ray E. Dillon III, Treas.
Employer Identification Number: 480913153

2402
The Doskocil Foundation, Inc. ¤
500 North Main
South Hutchinson 67505 (316) 663-1005

Incorporated in 1983 in KS.
Donor(s): Larry D. Doskocil, William L. Rogers, Wendel Strong, Orvin Miller.
Foundation type: Independent
Financial data (yr. ended 12/31/87): Assets, $1,071,005 (M); expenditures, $272,491, including $270,169 for 6 grants (high: $110,500; low: $10,000).
Purpose and activities: Support primarily for college-level Christian education.
Limitations: Giving primarily in KS.
Application information: Contributes only to pre-selected organizations. Applications not accepted.
Initial approach: Letter, personal visit, or telephone
Copies of proposal: 1
Deadline(s): None
Write: Larry D. Doskocil, Pres.
Officers: Larry D. Doskocil, Pres.; Jacquelin Doskocil, V.P.; Ronald Bretches, Secy.-Treas.
Employer Identification Number: 480970383

2403
Leo J. Dreiling & Albina Dreiling Charitable Trust
P.O. Box 1000
Victoria 67671 (913) 735-2204

Established in 1980 in KS.
Donor(s): Leo J. Dreiling.†
Foundation type: Independent
Financial data (yr. ended 09/30/89): Assets, $3,874,455 (M); expenditures, $174,036, including $163,284 for 4 grants (high: $60,266; low: $5,000).
Purpose and activities: Support primarily for education and culture; support also for a rest home.
Types of support: Scholarship funds, building funds, renovation projects.
Limitations: Giving primarily in Ellis County, KS. No grants to individuals.
Application information:
Initial approach: Letter
Deadline(s): None
Write: Joseph A. Hess, Trustee
Trustees: Dennis L. Bieker, John G. Dreiling, Norbert R. Dreiling, Joseph A. Hess.
Number of staff: None.
Employer Identification Number: 480916752

2404
Family Charities Foundation ¤
300 West Douglas, Suite 1000
Wichita 67202

Established in 1960 in KS.
Donor(s): Garvey Foundation, Fink Foundation, Garvey, Inc.
Foundation type: Independent
Financial data (yr. ended 11/30/89): Assets, $160,368 (M); gifts received, $138,000; expenditures, $208,061, including $205,900 for 90 grants (high: $75,000; low: $25).
Purpose and activities: Giving primarily for education, educational associations, and public policy organizations.
Types of support: Operating budgets, building funds, scholarship funds.
Application information: Application form not required.
Initial approach: Letter
Copies of proposal: 1
Deadline(s): None
Officers and Trustees:* Olive W. Garvey,* Pres.; Ruth G. Fink,* V.P.; James S. Garvey,* V.P.; Olivia G. Lincoln,* V.P.; Robert A. Page, V.P.; Willard W. Garvey,* Secy.-Treas.
Employer Identification Number: 486120059

2405
Fink Foundation ¤
800 Bank IV Tower
Topeka 66603 (913) 233-0541

Incorporated in 1962 in KS.
Donor(s): H. Bernerd Fink, Ruth G. Fink.
Foundation type: Independent
Financial data (yr. ended 12/31/88): Assets, $3,233,156 (M); gifts received, $228,152; expenditures, $116,839, including $110,725 for 9 grants (high: $110,000; low: $25).
Purpose and activities: Giving mainly to a local private foundation.
Types of support: Operating budgets, building funds, scholarship funds, annual campaigns.
Limitations: Giving primarily in KS. No grants to individuals.
Application information: Contributes only to pre-selected organizations. Applications not accepted.
Board meeting date(s): May and Dec.
Write: Ruth G. Fink, Pres.
Officers: Ruth G. Fink,* Pres.; H. Bernerd Fink,* V.P.; Jack H. Hamilton, Secy.; Larry D. Riggins, Treas.
Trustees:* Marcia F. Anderson, Bruce G. Cochener.
Employer Identification Number: 486113919

2406
First National Bank in Wichita Charitable Trust ¤
c/o First National Bank in Wichita
P.O. Box One
Wichita 67201

Established in 1952 in KS.
Donor(s): First National Bank in Wichita.
Foundation type: Company-sponsored
Financial data (yr. ended 12/31/88): Assets, $125,106 (M); gifts received, $120,000; expenditures, $119,071, including $119,067 for 16 grants (high: $56,900; low: $500).
Purpose and activities: Giving for higher education, youth agencies, a community fund, and social services.
Types of support: General purposes, building funds.
Limitations: Giving limited to KS, with emphasis on Wichita.
Application information: Application form not required.
Deadline(s): None
Write: E.A. Duguid, Sr. V.P. and Sr. Trust Officer, First National Bank in Wichita
Corporate Trustee: First National Bank in Wichita.

Trustees: William D. Bunten, Charles Q. Chandler, C.O. Chandler IV, R.L. Darmon, E.A. Duguid.
Employer Identification Number: 486102412

2407
Garvey Foundation ▼ ⌑
301 North Main St.
Wichita 67202-1508

Incorporated in 1949 in KS.
Donor(s): Members of the Garvey family and family-related businesses.
Foundation type: Independent
Financial data (yr. ended 12/31/88): Assets, $6,864,058 (M); gifts received, $66,500; expenditures, $635,478, including $542,394 for 104 grants (high: $300,000; low: $10; average: $100-$2,500).
Purpose and activities: Support for higher education, community funds, nutrition research, and aid for the handicapped.
Types of support: Operating budgets, annual campaigns, seed money, building funds, equipment, research, conferences and seminars, scholarship funds, matching funds, continuing support, general purposes.
Limitations: Giving primarily in KS, with emphasis on Wichita. No grants to individuals, or for endowment funds; no loans.
Application information: Application form not required.
Initial approach: Letter
Copies of proposal: 1
Deadline(s): None
Board meeting date(s): Monthly
Final notification: 6 weeks
Write: D. Clifford Allison, Exec. V.P.
Officers and Trustees:* Olive W. Garvey,* Pres.; D. Clifford Allison, Exec. V.P.; Ruth G. Fink,* V.P.; James S. Garvey,* V.P.; Olivia G. Lincoln,* V.P.; Willard W. Garvey,* Secy.-Treas.
Number of staff: None.
Employer Identification Number: 486105223

2408
Garvey Kansas Foundation ⌑
R.H. Garvey Bldg., Suite 1000
300 West Douglas
Wichita 67202 (316) 261-5386

Incorporated in 1964 in KS.
Donor(s): Willard W. Garvey, Jean K. Garvey.
Foundation type: Independent
Financial data (yr. ended 12/31/88): Assets, $5,577,037 (M); gifts received, $830,234; expenditures, $884,516, including $860,185 for 59 grants (high: $726,012; low: $25).
Purpose and activities: Giving primarily for secondary and higher education, and Protestant church support; support also for community funds and legal interest foundations.
Types of support: Operating budgets, building funds, scholarship funds.
Limitations: Giving primarily in KS. No grants to individuals, or for endowment funds; no loans.
Application information: Contributes only to pre-selected organizations. Applications not accepted.
Board meeting date(s): Jan., Apr., July, and Oct.
Write: James H. Childers, Secy.-Treas.
Officers: Jean K. Garvey,* Pres.; Willard W. Garvey,* V.P.; James H. Childers, Secy.-Treas.
Trustees:* Emily Garvey Bonavia, John K. Garvey.
Employer Identification Number: 486115213

2409
Olive White Garvey Trust ⌑
300 West Douglas, Suite 1000
Wichita 67202 (316) 261-5379

Established in 1985 in KS.
Donor(s): Garvey Charitable Trust II.
Foundation type: Independent
Financial data (yr. ended 12/31/88): Assets, $1,422,239 (M); expenditures, $411,154, including $400,000 for 2 grants (high: $350,000; low: $50,000).
Purpose and activities: Giving for medical research, education, and other general charitable purposes.
Types of support: Operating budgets.
Application information: Contributes only to pre-selected organizations. Applications not accepted.
Write: Olive W. Garvey, Trustee
Trustee: Olive W. Garvey.
Employer Identification Number: 486268131

2410
Gault-Hussey Charitable Trust
c/o Bank IV Topeka, N.A., Trust Dept.
P.O. Box 88
Topeka 66601 (913) 295-3463

Established about 1980 in KS.
Foundation type: Independent
Financial data (yr. ended 12/31/89): Assets, $1,735,928 (M); expenditures, $105,829, including $94,500 for 19 grants (high: $14,000; low: $500; average: $500-$10,000).
Purpose and activities: Support for health and social services and education.
Types of support: Building funds, consulting services, endowment funds, equipment, matching funds, operating budgets, seed money, special projects.
Limitations: Giving primarily in the northeast KS, geographical area. No support for individuals.
Application information: Application form not required.
Deadline(s): Jan. 1 or July 1
Board meeting date(s): Semiannually
Write: Rudy Wrenick, Jr., Sr. V.P. & Trust Officer, Bank IV Topeka, N.A.
Trustee: Bank IV Topeka.
Employer Identification Number: 486237061

2411
William L. Graham Charitable Trust ⌑
P.O. Box 780578
Wichita 67278-0578

Established in KS in 1981.
Donor(s): William L. Graham.
Foundation type: Independent
Financial data (yr. ended 3/31/89): Assets, $3,326,328 (M); expenditures, $423,308, including $400,000 for 2 grants (high: $350,000; low: $50,000).
Purpose and activities: Giving to youth organizations; support also for a university.
Types of support: Building funds.
Limitations: Giving primarily in Witchita, KS. No support for private foundations. No grants to individuals.
Application information:
Initial approach: Proposal
Deadline(s): None
Write: Patricia Coyer, Trustee
Trustees: Patricia Coyer, Betty Harrison Graham.
Employer Identification Number: 486244134

2412
Dane G. Hansen Foundation ▼ ⌑
P.O. Box 187
Logan 67646 (913) 689-4832

Incorporated in 1965 in KS.
Donor(s): Dane G. Hansen.†
Foundation type: Independent
Financial data (yr. ended 09/30/89): Assets, $30,607,792 (M); expenditures, $1,655,254, including $932,840 for 74 grants (high: $280,000; low: $100; average: $1,000-$20,000), $162,750 for 107 grants to individuals (high: $4,000; low: $500) and $128,912 for 1 foundation-administered program.
Purpose and activities: Grants largely for higher education, including undergraduate, graduate, theological, and vocational scholarships to individuals, civic affairs and public interest groups, youth agencies, services for the handicapped, and hospitals.
Types of support: Building funds, equipment, operating budgets, publications, general purposes, continuing support, scholarship funds, student aid.
Limitations: Giving primarily in Logan, Phillips County, and northwestern KS; scholarships limited to residents of 26 northwestern KS counties.
Application information: Scholarship seekers should call or write the foundation about eligibility requirements, application forms, and interviews.
Deadline(s): Sept. and Oct. for scholarships
Board meeting date(s): Monthly
Final notification: Within 2 weeks for grants to organizations
Write: Dane G. Bales, Pres.
Officers and Trustees:* Ross Beach,* Pres.; Oscar Belin,* V.P.; W.R. Lappin,* Secy.; Doyle D. Rahjes,* Treas.; Dane G. Bales, Ralph E. Reitz.
Number of staff: 7 full-time support.
Employer Identification Number: 486121156

2413
Frank E. Hedrick Foundation ☆
8150 East Douglas, Suite 30
Wichita 67206-2399

Established in 1966 in KS.
Donor(s): Frank E. Hedrick.†
Foundation type: Independent
Financial data (yr. ended 12/31/88): Assets, $1,436,123 (M); gifts received, $1,000,050; expenditures, $380,661, including $362,715 for 53 grants (high: $259,765; low: $25).

Purpose and activities: Giving primarily to a Methodist church; support also for social services, health associations, youth groups, and programs for the elderly.
Limitations: Giving primarily in Wichita, KS. No grants to individuals.
Publications: Informational brochure (including application guidelines).
Application information: Application form not required.
Initial approach: Letter
Copies of proposal: 1
Deadline(s): None
Board meeting date(s): 4th Tuesday of Apr. and Oct.
Write: Fred Clayton, Pres.
Officers and Trustees:* Harriet E. Hedrick,* Chair.; Fred Clayton,* Pres.; Myrna Clayton,* V.P.; Van E. Fiser,* Treas.; Olive Ann Beech, Mary Ellen Deets, Wey D. Kenny, Kenneth W. Pringle, Ivan M. West.
Employer Identification Number: 486130776

2414
R. L. and Elsa Helvering Trust ⌑
307 South 13th St.
Marysville 66508 (913) 562-3437

Trust established about 1980.
Donor(s): R.L. Helvering,† Elsa Helvering.†
Foundation type: Independent
Financial data (yr. ended 3/31/89): Assets, $1,587,734 (M); expenditures, $74,673, including $61,550 for 3 grants (high: $57,800; low: $3,000) and $4,500 for 6 grants to individuals of $750 each.
Purpose and activities: Giving for civic and community development projects; one four-year scholarship for a KS college or university awarded each year to a graduating senior from a high school in Marshall County, KS.
Types of support: Student aid, building funds.
Limitations: Giving limited to Marshall County and City of Marysville, KS.
Application information: Scholarship application form required.
Deadline(s): May 1
Write: Ira O. Shrock, Trustee
Trustee: Ira O. Shrock.
Employer Identification Number: 480924200

2415
Hesston Foundation, Inc. ⌑
420 West Lincoln Blvd.
Hesston 67062-2094

Incorporated in 1965 in KS.
Donor(s): Hesston Corp., and others.
Foundation type: Company-sponsored
Financial data (yr. ended 12/31/87): Assets, $1,185,135 (L); expenditures, $61,599, including $49,150 for 18 grants (high: $18,500; low: $200; average: $1,000) and $3,672 for 22 employee matching gifts (high: $960; low: $25).
Purpose and activities: Grants are primarily made to causes within the "community of responsibility," with emphasis on higher education, church-supported activities, hospitals, nursing homes and health services, youth agencies, public music and fine arts agencies, and community and general welfare assistance agencies.
Types of support: Operating budgets, continuing support, annual campaigns, seed money, building funds, equipment, matching funds, special projects, research, employee matching gifts.
Limitations: Giving primarily in areas of company operations within KS. No grants to individuals, or for emergency funds, deficit financing, land acquisition, scholarships, or fellowships; no loans.
Application information: Application form not required.
Initial approach: Proposal
Copies of proposal: 1
Deadline(s): Feb. 28, May 31, Aug. 31, and Nov. 30
Board meeting date(s): Mar., June, Sept., and Dec.
Final notification: 2 to 3 weeks after board meetings
Write: Raymond C. Schlichting, Pres.
Officers: Raymond C. Schlichting,* Chair. and Pres.; Harold P. Dyck,* V.P.; Lyle E. Yost,* V.P.; Roberta M. Oliver, Secy.-Treas.
Directors:* Howard L. Brenneman, William L. Friesen, John Siemens, Jr., Kenneth G. Speir.
Number of staff: 1 part-time support.
Employer Identification Number: 480698307

2416
W. J. & Irene Hupfer Foundation ⌑
c/o Russell State Bank
507 Main
Russell 67665

Incorporated in 1986 in KS.
Donor(s): Irene Hupfer.
Foundation type: Independent
Financial data (yr. ended 09/30/89): Assets, $1,279,963 (M); expenditures, $98,990, including $92,587 for 12 grants (high: $18,517; low: $926).
Purpose and activities: Giving primarily for Methodist churches and organizations, higher education, and a senior citizens' center.
Limitations: Giving primarily in the Russell, KS, area. No grants to individuals.
Application information: Contributes only to pre-selected organizations. Applications not accepted.
Trustee: John T. Harrell.
Employer Identification Number: 481025680

2417
Jabara Family Foundation, Inc. ⌑ ☆
4302 East Kellogg
Wichita 67218

Incorporated in 1988 in KS.
Donor(s): Fran Jabara, and other members of the Jabara family.
Foundation type: Independent
Financial data (yr. ended 03/31/89): Assets, $1,441,857 (M); gifts received, $1,397,088; expenditures, $48,231, including $17,120 for 33 grants (high: $4,700; low: $10).
Purpose and activities: Giving primarily for higher education and Protestant churches.
Types of support: Scholarship funds.
Limitations: Giving primarily in Wichita, KS. No grants to individuals.
Application information: Contributes only to pre-selected organizations. Applications not accepted.
Officer and Directors: Robert J. Mobley, Exec. Dir.; F.D. Jabara, Geri Jabara, Harvey Jabara, Leesa Jabara, Lori Jabara.
Employer Identification Number: 481051455

2418
Jellison Benevolent Society, Inc. ⌑ ☆
819 North Washington St.
Junction City 66441 (913) 762-2210
Additional application address: c/o Dean R. Cassity, V.P., 141 Rimrock, P.O. Box 8, Junction City, KS, 66441

Established in 1947.
Foundation type: Independent
Financial data (yr. ended 12/31/88): Assets, $2,045,613 (M); expenditures, $66,347, including $13,354 for 6 grants (high: $11,054; low: $100) and $39,400 for grants to individuals.
Purpose and activities: Support for a YMCA and other social service and youth groups; also awards scholarships to local area students.
Types of support: Student aid, operating budgets.
Limitations: Giving limited to KS, with preference for Greene County residents and/or organizations.
Application information: Completion of application form required for scholarships.
Initial approach: Proposal
Deadline(s): June 1 for fall semester and at least 45 days at other times for scholarships; no set deadline for grants
Write: Robert K. Weary, Pres.
Officers: Robert K. Weary, Pres.; Dorothy J. Cassity, V.P.; Dean R. Cassity, Secy.; Dale J. Weary, Treas.
Trustee: Bank IV.
Employer Identification Number: 486106092

2419
Walter S. and Evan C. Jones Foundation ▼
527 Commercial St., Room 515
Emporia 66801 (316) 342-1714

Established in 1974 in KS.
Donor(s): Walter S. and Evan C. Jones Trust.
Foundation type: Independent
Financial data (yr. ended 03/31/89): Assets, $1,704 (M); gifts received, $925,000; expenditures, $926,753, including $867,927 for 2,625 grants to individuals (high: $6,173; low: $60).
Purpose and activities: Grants only to children of three specified counties who have resided there continuously for one year, for educational and medical expenses.
Types of support: Grants to individuals, student aid.
Limitations: Giving limited to children who have resided continously for one year in Osage, Coffey, or Lyon counties, KS.
Publications: Program policy statement.
Application information: Application form required.
Initial approach: Letter
Deadline(s): Submit application preferably in May

Board meeting date(s): Monthly
Final notification: 2 months
Write: Sharon Brown, General Mgr.
Officers: Kenneth B. Thomas, Pres.; David W. Evans, Jr., Secy.; Ken Calhoun, Treas.; Sharon Brown, General Mgr.
Trustees: Helen Conard, Arnold Graham, Stephen Jones, Max Stewart, Jr.
Number of staff: 1 full-time professional; 2 part-time support.
Employer Identification Number: 237384087

2420
Jordaan Foundation, Inc. ⌑
111 East 8th St.
P.O. Box 360
Larned 67550 (316) 285-3157

Trust established in 1970 in KS.
Donor(s): J.D. Jordaan.†
Foundation type: Independent
Financial data (yr. ended 12/31/88): Assets, $1,627,193 (M); expenditures, $179,404, including $112,806 for 8 grants (high: $31,500; low: $1,500) and $35,000 for 27 grants to individuals (high: $1,750; low: $750).
Purpose and activities: Support for educational and civic development, with emphasis on community programs, museums, an historical society, and scholarships to graduates of a local high school only.
Types of support: General purposes, operating budgets, building funds, equipment, land acquisition, matching funds, consulting services, scholarship funds, special projects, research, publications, conferences and seminars, student aid.
Limitations: Giving limited to organizations and individuals in Pawnee County, KS. No grants for endowment funds; no loans.
Publications: Application guidelines.
Application information: Application form not required.
Initial approach: Telephone or letter
Copies of proposal: 5
Deadline(s): 1st Tuesday of every month
Board meeting date(s): Monthly
Final notification: 2 days
Write: Glee S. Smith, Chair.
Advisory Board: Glee S. Smith, Chair.; Edward B. Boyd, Ned M. Brown, Walter M. Crawford, Reed Peters.
Trustee Bank: First State Bank and Trust Co. of Larned.
Number of staff: None.
Employer Identification Number: 486155003

2421
King Foundation ⌑
P.O. Box 277
Hesston 67062-0277

Established in 1972 in KS.
Foundation type: Independent
Financial data (yr. ended 12/31/87): Assets, $1,061,781 (M); gifts received, $110,000; expenditures, $38,885, including $36,000 for 1 grant.
Purpose and activities: Support primarily for higher education.
Application information: Contributes only to pre-selected organizations. Applications not accepted.
Trustee: Leroy King.
Employer Identification Number: 237175500

2422
Charles G. Koch Charitable Foundation
4111 East 37th St. North
Wichita 67220 (316) 832-5404
Application address: P.O. Box 2256, Wichita, KS 67201; Tel.: (316) 832-5227

Established in 1981 in KS.
Donor(s): Charles G. Koch, Fred C. Koch Foundation, Fred C. Koch Trusts for Charity.
Foundation type: Independent
Financial data (yr. ended 12/31/88): Assets, $12,165,341 (M); expenditures, $638,892, including $618,500 for 23 grants (high: $500,000; low: $1,000).
Purpose and activities: Grants mainly for higher education and research in the social sciences.
Limitations: No grants to individuals.
Application information:
Initial approach: Proposal
Deadline(s): None
Write: George H. Pearson, Admin.
Officers and Directors:* Charles Koch,* Pres.; Elizabeth Koch,* V.P.; George H. Pearson,* Admin. and Secy.; Vonda Holliman, Treas.
Employer Identification Number: 480918408

2423
David H. Koch Charitable Trust ▼
4111 East 37th St., North
Wichita 67220 (316) 832-5227
Application address: P.O. Box 2256, Wichita, KS 67201

Established in 1982 in KS.
Donor(s): David H. Koch, Fred C. Koch Trusts for Charity.
Foundation type: Independent
Financial data (yr. ended 12/31/88): Assets, $4,966,829 (M); expenditures, $3,696,723, including $3,667,236 for 55 grants.
Purpose and activities: Giving for arts, culture, education, public interest, and economics concerns.
Types of support: Annual campaigns, building funds, capital campaigns, conferences and seminars, emergency funds, conferences and seminars, emergency funds, endowment funds, equipment, fellowships, general purposes, internships, lectureships, matching funds, operating budgets, program-related investments, publications, renovation projects, scholarship funds, seed money, special projects, continuing support.
Limitations: No grants to individuals, or for deficit financing, exchange programs, land acquisition, or professorships; no loans.
Application information:
Initial approach: Proposal
Deadline(s): None
Board meeting date(s): As necessary
Final notification: Varies
Write: George Pearson, Admin.
Officers: David H. Koch, Pres.; George H. Pearson, Admin.
Number of staff: None.
Employer Identification Number: 480926946

2424
The Fred C. Koch Foundation, Inc. ⌑
P.O. Box 2256
Wichita 67201 (316) 832-5227

Incorporated in 1955 in KS.
Donor(s): Fred C. Koch,† Mary R. Koch, Koch Industries, Inc.
Foundation type: Independent
Financial data (yr. ended 12/31/88): Assets, $11,099,064 (M); gifts received, $27,000; expenditures, $367,726, including $318,448 for 44 grants (high: $55,417; low: $225) and $27,000 for 27 grants to individuals of $1,000 each.
Purpose and activities: Grants primarily for cultural programs and for services for the mentally and physically handicapped; also supports a scholarship program for dependents of employees of Koch Industries.
Types of support: Employee-related scholarships.
Limitations: Giving primarily in KS. No grants to individuals, except for dependents of Koch Industries employees.
Application information: Application form not required.
Initial approach: Letter
Copies of proposal: 1
Deadline(s): Submit proposal preferably in Feb.
Board meeting date(s): Mar.
Write: George H. Pearson, Pres.
Officers: George H. Pearson, Pres.; Mary R. Koch, V.P.; Donald L. Cordes, Secy.; Vonda Holliman, Treas.
Directors: Charles Koch, David H. Koch.
Employer Identification Number: 486113560

2425
Henry Krause Charitable Foundation ⌑ ☆
305 South Monroe St.
Hutchinson 67504 (316) 663-6161

Incorporated in 1959 in KS.
Donor(s): Krause Plow Corp., Inc.
Foundation type: Independent
Financial data (yr. ended 9/30/88): Assets, $464,547 (M); gifts received, $5,000; expenditures, $136,262, including $134,495 for 31 grants (high: $36,000; low: $20).
Purpose and activities: Giving for higher education, cultural programs, and a community fund.
Types of support: Building funds, capital campaigns, general purposes, operating budgets, research.
Limitations: Giving primarily in KS.
Application information: Application form not required.
Deadline(s): None
Write: Norman L. Krause, Pres.
Officers and Directors: Norman L. Krause, Pres.; Richard T. Parker, Secy.-Treas.; Darrell R. Ames, Joan M. Brunkard, Lila L. Gatlin, Steven L. Krause, Marcia J. Roberts, Patricia D. Rock, John N. Sames.
Employer Identification Number: 486105132

2426
Claude R. Lambe Charitable Foundation ▼
4111 East 37th St., North
Wichita 67220 (316) 832-5404
Application address: P.O. Box 2256, Wichita, KS 67201

Established in 1982 in KS.
Donor(s): Claude R. Lambe.†
Foundation type: Independent
Financial data (yr. ended 12/31/88): Assets, $22,967,791 (M); expenditures, $1,730,745, including $1,575,583 for 13 grants (high: $400,000; low: $2,500; average: $8,000-$300,000).
Purpose and activities: Giving primarily for education; some support also for the arts.
Limitations: No grants to individuals.
Application information:
Initial approach: Proposal
Deadline(s): None
Write: George H. Pearson, Secy.
Officers: George H. Pearson, Secy.; Vonda Holliman, Treas.
Trustee: Charles Koch.
Number of staff: None.
Employer Identification Number: 480935563

2427
The Marley Fund ⌑
1900 Shawnee Mission Pklwy.
Mission Woods 66205 (913) 362-1818
Application address: P.O. Box 2965, Shawnee, KS 66201

Incorporated in 1961 in MO.
Donor(s): The Marley Co.
Foundation type: Company-sponsored
Financial data (yr. ended 04/30/89): Assets, $14,120 (M); gifts received, $285,300; expenditures, $290,544, including $211,854 for 129 grants (high: $66,500; low: $50), $69,085 for 94 grants to individuals (high: $882; low: $375; average: $750) and $9,605 for 55 employee matching gifts.
Purpose and activities: Emphasis on higher education, including scholarships and an employee matching gift program, community funds, health agencies, hospitals, youth and child welfare, and social service agencies.
Types of support: Operating budgets, continuing support, annual campaigns, building funds, equipment, employee matching gifts, employee-related scholarships.
Limitations: Giving limited to areas of company operations. No grants to individuals (except for employee-related scholarships), or for seed money, emergency funds, deficit financing, land acquisition, endowment funds, scholarships, fellowships, special projects, research, publications, or conferences; no loans.
Publications: Application guidelines, program policy statement.
Application information: Application form not required.
Initial approach: Letter
Copies of proposal: 1
Deadline(s): None
Board meeting date(s): Monthly
Final notification: 1 month
Write: Betty L. Paine, V.P.
Officers: Timothy J. Verhagen, Pres.; Betty L. Paine, V.P. and Secy.; Marc G. Naughton, Treas.
Number of staff: None.
Employer Identification Number: 446012343

2428
The Julia J. Mingenback Foundation, Inc. ⌑
One Main Plaza
McPherson 67460
Application address: 112 North Lakeside, McPherson, KS 67460; Tel.: (316) 241-1439

Incorporated in 1959 in KS.
Donor(s): E.C. Mingenback.†
Foundation type: Independent
Financial data (yr. ended 12/31/88): Assets, $3,031,246 (M); expenditures, $292,208, including $226,578 for 10 grants (high: $100,000; low: $500).
Purpose and activities: Emphasis on higher education and cultural programs.
Limitations: Giving primarily in McPherson County, KS.
Application information:
Initial approach: Letter
Deadline(s): None
Write: Willda Coughenour, Pres.
Officers: Willda Coughenour, Pres.; Ruth Lancaster, Treas.
Directors: James Ketcherside, Edwin T. Pyle, Don C. Steffes.
Trustee: McPherson Bank and Trust Co.
Employer Identification Number: 486109567

2429
Muchnic Foundation ⌑
107 North Sixth St., Suite 2
P.O. Box 329
Atchison 66002 (913) 367-4164

Trust established in 1946 in KS.
Donor(s): Valley Co., Inc., Helen Q. Muchnic,† H.E. Muchnic.
Foundation type: Independent
Financial data (yr. ended 11/30/88): Assets, $3,765,698 (M); expenditures, $234,553, including $219,758 for 46 grants (high: $53,758; low: $100).
Purpose and activities: Giving for higher education, health, cultural programs, including museums, and civic affairs.
Limitations: Giving primarily in KS. No grants to individuals.
Application information:
Initial approach: Proposal
Deadline(s): Oct. 31
Board meeting date(s): As required
Write: Roger L. Dennison
Officer and Trustees: E.M. Elicker, William H. Muchnic.
Employer Identification Number: 486102818

2430
Page Foundation ⌑ ☆
58 Via Verde
Wichita 67230-1605

Donor(s): Garvey, Inc.
Foundation type: Independent
Financial data (yr. ended 12/31/88): Assets, $21,092 (M); gifts received, $28,000; expenditures, $242,806, including $240,345 for 16 grants (high: $200,000; low: $20).
Purpose and activities: Giving for welfare funds, medical research, and higher education.
Types of support: General purposes.
Limitations: Giving primarily in KS.
Application information: Contributes only to pre-selected organizations. Applications not accepted.
Officers: Marjorie H. Page, Pres.; Robert A. Page, Secy.-Treas.
Employer Identification Number: 486116606

2431
The Powell Family Foundation ▼ ⌑
10990 Roe Ave.
P.O. Box 7270
Shawnee Mission 66207 (913) 345-3000

Established in 1969 in MO.
Donor(s): George E. Powell, Sr.†
Foundation type: Independent
Financial data (yr. ended 12/31/88): Assets, $56,154,381 (M); expenditures, $2,154,545, including $1,964,507 for 99 grants (high: $707,566; low: $100; average: $1,000-$50,000).
Purpose and activities: Grants for education, religion, civic affairs, and social service and youth agencies; some support also for cultural programs.
Types of support: Operating budgets, annual campaigns, seed money, emergency funds, equipment, program-related investments, scholarship funds, matching funds, general purposes, renovation projects, special projects, continuing support, conferences and seminars.
Limitations: Giving primarily in Kansas City and for projects benefiting residents of the area. No grants to individuals, or for endowment or building funds.
Publications: Annual report (including application guidelines).
Application information: Application form not required.
Initial approach: Proposal (3 to 5 pages)
Copies of proposal: 2
Deadline(s): 30 days preceding board meeting
Board meeting date(s): Usually in Jan., Apr., July, and Oct.
Final notification: 60 days
Write: Marjorie P. Allen, Pres.
Officers and Trustees:* George E. Powell, Jr.,* Chair.; Marjorie P. Allen,* Pres.; Marilyn P. McLeod,* V.P. and Secy.; George E. Powell III,* Treas.; Nicholas K. Powell.
Number of staff: 1 full-time professional; 2 full-time support.
Employer Identification Number: 237023968

2432
Ethel and Raymond F. Rice Foundation ⌑
700 Massachusetts St.
Lawrence 66044 (913) 843-0420

Foundation type: Independent
Financial data (yr. ended 12/31/87): Assets, $6,053,378 (M); gifts received, $22,500; expenditures, $281,123, including $235,885 for 80 grants (high: $16,000; low: $500).

Purpose and activities: Emphasis on higher education, health, youth and social service agencies.
Limitations: Giving limited to the Lawrence, KS, area.
Application information:
Initial approach: Proposal
Deadline(s): Nov. 15
Write: Robert B. Oyler, Pres., or George M. Clem, Treas.
Officers: Robert B. Oyler, Pres.; James W. Paddock, Secy.; George M. Clem, Treas.
Employer Identification Number: 237156608

2433
Ross Foundation
105 South Broadway, Suite 730
Wichita 67202-2009 (316) 264-4981

Established in 1961 in KS.
Donor(s): G. Murray Ross.†
Foundation type: Independent
Financial data (yr. ended 12/31/88): Assets, $2,482,307 (M); expenditures, $127,075, including $103,328 for 12 grants (high: $40,588; low: $250).
Purpose and activities: Support primarily for cultural organizations, including the fine arts, an historical organization, and museums; support also for youth and science and technology.
Limitations: Giving primarily in KS.
Application information: Application form not required.
Deadline(s): None
Board meeting date(s): Early Mar., June, Sept., and Dec.
Write: Hal Ross, V.P.
Officers: Norman Jeter, Pres.; Hal Ross, V.P.; Susan Ross Sheets, Secy.-Treas.
Employer Identification Number: 486125814

2434
Chester Royse Testamentary Trust ⌘
c/o Fidelity State Bank & Trust Co.
510 Second Ave.
Dodge City 67801

Established in 1984 in KS.
Foundation type: Independent
Financial data (yr. ended 12/31/88): Assets, $1,309,574 (M); expenditures, $178,298, including $146,024 for 16 grants (high: $25,000; low: $580).
Purpose and activities: Grants to a children's hospital, Catholic giving, and social service agencies.
Types of support: Matching funds, building funds.
Limitations: Giving primarily in the Dodge City, KS, area.
Application information:
Deadline(s): None
Trustee: Fidelity State Bank & Trust Co.
Selection Committee: Geneva Peppard, Harry Waite, Donald Winfrey.
Employer Identification Number: 486257115

2435
Nicholas M. Salgo Charitable Trust ⌘
300 West Douglas, Suite 1000
Wichita 67202 (316) 261-5364

Established in 1982 in KS.
Donor(s): Nicholas M. Salgo.
Foundation type: Independent
Financial data (yr. ended 11/30/89): Assets, $2,245,806 (M); gifts received, $2,325,883; expenditures, $170,209, including $166,226 for 17 grants (high: $66,276; low: $100).
Purpose and activities: Support primarily for international affairs, including support for an American school and a Hungarian university in Budapest, Hungary, and for higher education in the U.S.
Application information:
Initial approach: Letter
Write: Robert A. Page, Trustee
Trustee: Robert A. Page.
Employer Identification Number: 486250539

2436
The Schowalter Foundation, Inc.
726 Main St.
Newton 67114 (316) 283-3720

Incorporated in 1953 in KS.
Donor(s): J.A. Schowalter.†
Foundation type: Independent
Financial data (yr. ended 12/31/89): Assets, $3,750,000 (M); expenditures, $330,805, including $192,050 for 42 grants (high: $15,000; low: $250; average: $8,000-$10,000).
Purpose and activities: To assist retired ministers and missionaries, theological seminaries and church-related schools (including scholarships); grants also for peace and international cooperation and for technical assistance abroad. Activities related to the Mennonite Church.
Types of support: Technical assistance, scholarship funds, equipment, building funds, special projects, seed money.
Limitations: Giving limited to the Midwest. No grants to individuals, or for endowment funds, fellowships, operating budgets, travel, or matching gifts; no loans.
Publications: Program policy statement, application guidelines.
Application information: Application form not required.
Initial approach: Proposal
Copies of proposal: 1
Deadline(s): Submit proposal preferably in Feb. or Aug.; deadlines Mar. 1 and Sept. 1
Board meeting date(s): Apr. and Oct.
Write: William L. Friesen, Pres.
Officer and Trustees:* William L. Friesen,* Pres.; Howard E. Baumgartner, Allen Becker, Ben T. Ensz, Willis Harder, Howard Hershberger, Elvin D. Yoder.
Number of staff: 1 part-time professional.
Employer Identification Number: 480623544

2437
Arthur E. & Cornelia C. Scroggins Foundation, Inc.
619 Second Ave., Suite 501
Dodge City 67801 (316) 532-5751
Application address: P.O. Box 1112, Dodge City, KS 67801

Established in 1983 in KS.
Foundation type: Independent
Financial data (yr. ended 12/31/88): Assets, $1,601,817 (M); expenditures, $80,279, including $40,300 for 31 grants (high: $5,000; low: $500).
Purpose and activities: Support primarily for medical and other education, child welfare and youth agencies, health associations, community development, and social service agencies.
Types of support: Scholarship funds.
Limitations: Giving primarily in the Dodge City, KS, area. No grants to individuals.
Application information: Application form required.
Deadline(s): None
Write: Stan Simpson, Treas.
Officers: Roderic H. Simpson, Pres.; George Voss, V.P.; Frank Mapel, Secy.; Stanley D. Simpson, Treas.
Directors: Robert Ven John, Fidelity State Bank & Trust Co.
Number of staff: 1 part-time professional.
Employer Identification Number: 480945437

2438
Security Benefit Life Insurance Company Charitable Trust
700 Harrison St.
Topeka 66636 (913) 295-3000

Established in 1976 in KS.
Foundation type: Company-sponsored
Financial data (yr. ended 12/31/88): Assets, $830,774 (M); expenditures, $136,022, including $116,331 for grants (high: $28,000) and $8,407 for employee matching gifts.
Purpose and activities: Giving through grants and employee matching funds for performing and other arts groups, health, higher education, and social services, including programs for women and youth, the disadvantaged, and the homeless.
Types of support: Employee matching gifts, equipment, in-kind gifts, program-related investments.
Limitations: Giving limited to the Topeka, KS, area.
Application information: Application form not required.
Initial approach: Letter
Deadline(s): None
Write: Howard R. Fricke, Trustee
Trustees: Howard R. Fricke, James F. Haake, Security Benefit Trust Co.
Employer Identification Number: 486211612

2439
Kenneth L. & Eva S. Smith Foundation
P.O. Box 25625
Overland Park 66225

Established in 1968 in KS.
Donor(s): Kenneth L. Smith.†
Foundation type: Independent
Financial data (yr. ended 12/31/88): Assets, $4,028,507 (M); expenditures, $189,210, including $180,000 for 4 grants (high: $80,000; low: $10,000).
Purpose and activities: Grants primarily to hospitals.
Types of support: Continuing support.

Limitations: Giving primarily in the greater Kansas City, MO, area. No grants to individuals.
Application information: Contributes only to pre-selected organizations. Applications not accepted.
Write: Thomas K. Jones, Trustee
Trustees: Thomas K. Jones, Eva S. Smith.
Number of staff: None.
Employer Identification Number: 486142517

2440
Smoot Charitable Foundation
710 United Bldg.
P.O. Box 2567
Salina 67402-2567 (913) 825-4674

Established in 1976.
Foundation type: Independent
Financial data (yr. ended 06/30/89): Assets, $6,853,650 (M); expenditures, $408,468, including $342,890 for 14 grants (high: $134,390; low: $1,000).
Purpose and activities: Emphasis on youth agencies and higher education.
Limitations: Giving limited to Saline County, KS. No grants to individuals.
Application information:
Initial approach: Letter
Deadline(s): None
Write: Thomas J. Kennedy, Secy.-Treas.
Officers: Joe C. Cloud, Pres.; Dr. Robert W. Weber, V.P.; Thomas J. Kennedy, Secy.-Treas.
Employer Identification Number: 480851141

2441
The Sosland Foundation ▼
P.O. Box 29155
Shawnee Mission 66201 (913) 236-7300

Incorporated in 1955 in MO.
Donor(s): Members of the Sosland family.
Foundation type: Independent
Financial data (yr. ended 11/30/89): Assets, $20,136,324 (M); expenditures, $1,313,955, including $1,162,966 for 103 grants (high: $352,000; low: $100; average: $1,000-$20,000).
Purpose and activities: Giving to Jewish and social welfare funds, higher and secondary education, the arts, and health organizations.
Types of support: Emergency funds, endowment funds, special projects.
Limitations: Giving primarily in the metropolitan Kansas City, MO, and KS areas. No grants to individuals, or for publications, or conferences; no loans.
Application information: Application form not required.
Initial approach: Letter
Copies of proposal: 1
Deadline(s): None
Board meeting date(s): Mar., June, Sept., and Dec.
Final notification: 3 months
Write: Debbie Sosland-Edelman, Ph.D
Officers and Directors:* Morton I. Sosland,* Pres.; Neil Sosland,* V.P.; H.J. Sosland, Secy.-Treas.
Number of staff: 1 part-time professional.
Employer Identification Number: 446007129

2442
Rose Spurrier Scholarship Fund ⌑
P.O. Box 473
Kingman 67068-0473 (316) 532-3113

Established in 1984 in KS.
Foundation type: Independent
Financial data (yr. ended 12/31/88): Assets, $1,916,200 (M); expenditures, $72,539, including $50,350 for 28 grants to individuals (high: $7,450; low: $125; average: $3,000-$6,000).
Purpose and activities: Awards scholarships for higher education to qualified graduates of Kingman City High School, Kingman, KS; support also for a high school and a library.
Types of support: Student aid.
Limitations: Giving primarily in Kingman, KS.
Application information:
Final notification: Decisions announced at the commencement exercises of Kingman High School
Write: Robert S. Wunsch, Trustee
Trustees: Charles Crouch, D.L. Meisenheimer, Robert S. Wunsch.
Employer Identification Number: 480978238

2443
Stauffer Communications Foundation ⌑
P.O. Box 88
Topeka 66601
Application address: 616 Jefferson, Topeka, KS 66607; Tel.: (913) 295-1111

Foundation type: Independent
Financial data (yr. ended 12/31/87): Assets, $868,400 (M); gifts received, $200,000; expenditures, $123,667, including $120,627 for 78 grants (high: $8,500; low: $25).
Purpose and activities: Support primarily for cultural programs, community development, education, and youth organizations.
Types of support: Building funds, capital campaigns, renovation projects, operating budgets.
Application information:
Deadline(s): None
Write: Stanley H. Stauffer, Chair.
Officers: Stanley H. Stauffer, Chair.; William D. Duckworth, Secy.
Trustee: Bank IV Topeka.
Employer Identification Number: 486212412

2444
Trusler Foundation, Inc. ⌑
P.O. Box 704
Emporia 66801

Established in 1957 in KS.
Foundation type: Independent
Financial data (yr. ended 12/31/88): Assets, $2,492,696 (M); expenditures, $148,398, including $124,000 for 2 grants (high: $114,000; low: $10,000).
Purpose and activities: Grants primarily for religious support and higher education.
Limitations: Giving primarily in Emporia, KS.
Application information: Contributes only to pre-selected organizations. Applications not accepted.
Officers: Michael Turnball, Pres.; S. Richard Mellinger, Secy.; Tom Thomas, Treas.
Employer Identification Number: 486117374

2445
Wellspring Mission Volunteers Foundation ⌑ ☆
7600 State Line Rd., Suite 225
Prairie Village 66208 (913) 383-1778

Established in 1984 in KS.
Donor(s): Harold L. Finch, Peggy D. Finch.
Foundation type: Independent
Financial data (yr. ended 02/29/88): Assets, $34,729 (M); gifts received, $325,030; expenditures, $311,737, including $4,140 for 2 grants (high: $2,640; low: $1,500) and $96,815 for 91 grants to individuals (high: $2,000; low: $123).
Purpose and activities: Primarily awards grants to members of local area Southern Baptist churches conducting international missionary programs.
Types of support: Grants to individuals.
Limitations: Giving primarily in KS and NE.
Application information: Application form required.
Initial approach: Telephone
Deadline(s): None
Write: Pamela Finch, Secy.-Treas.
Officers: Harold L. Finch, Pres.; Peggy D. Finch, V.P.; Pamela R. Finch, Secy.-Treas.
Employer Identification Number: 480985810

2446
Flossie E. West Memorial Trust ⌑ ☆
P.O. Box 607
Augusta 67010 (316) 775-2675

Foundation type: Independent
Financial data (yr. ended 12/31/88): Assets, $1,025,742 (M); expenditures, $61,733, including $54,227 for 1 grant.
Purpose and activities: Support for hospitals, universities, and clinics engaged in cancer research.
Types of support: Research.
Application information:
Initial approach: Letter
Deadline(s): None
Write: Shirley Moon, Trustee
Trustees: Robert Bisagno, Eugene Brooks, Shirley Moon.
Employer Identification Number: 486125209

2447
K. T. Wiedemann Foundation, Inc.
300 Page Court
Wichita 67202 (316) 265-9311

Incorporated in 1959 in KS.
Donor(s): K.T. Wiedemann Trust.
Foundation type: Independent
Financial data (yr. ended 02/28/89): Assets, $1,554 (M); gifts received, $151,200; expenditures, $149,688, including $118,720 for 6 grants (high: $50,000; low: $100; average: $100-$10,000).
Purpose and activities: Emphasis on higher and other education, youth agencies, social service organizations, hospitals, cultural programs, and Protestant church support; giving also for health-related associations.
Types of support: Annual campaigns, seed money, emergency funds, equipment, endowment funds, research, scholarship funds, matching funds, general purposes, continuing support, building funds.

Limitations: Giving primarily in south-central KS, with emphasis on Wichita. No grants to individuals.
Application information: Contributes only to pre-selected organizations. Applications not accepted.
Board meeting date(s): Weekly
Write: Kenneth Pringle, Secy.
Officers and Trustees:* Gladys H.G. Wiedemann,* Pres. and Treas.; Kenneth Pringle,* Secy.; Douglas S. Pringle.
Number of staff: None.
Employer Identification Number: 486117541

2448
Yellow Freight System Foundation ▼
10990 Roe Ave.
Overland Park 66207 (913) 345-3000

Established in 1968 in MO.
Donor(s): Yellow Freight System, Inc.
Foundation type: Company-sponsored
Financial data (yr. ended 12/31/89): Assets, $3,559,969 (M); gifts received, $268,288; qualifying distributions, $1,374,951, including $940,054 for grants and $434,897 for loans.
Purpose and activities: Emphasis on cultural programs, social services, education, and civic affairs.
Types of support: Annual campaigns, capital campaigns, continuing support, general purposes, loans, operating budgets, program-related investments, renovation projects.
Limitations: Giving primarily in the Kansas City, MO, metropolitan area. No grants to individuals.
Application information: Application form not required.
Initial approach: Letter
Copies of proposal: 1
Deadline(s): None
Board meeting date(s): As necessary
Final notification: 45 to 60 days
Write: David A. Wolfram, V.P.
Officers and Directors:* George E. Powell, Jr.,* Pres.; George E. Powell III,* V.P.; David A. Wolfram,* V.P.; P.A. Spangler, Treas.
Number of staff: None.
Employer Identification Number: 237004674

KENTUCKY

2449
The Ashland Oil Foundation, Inc.
1000 Ashland Dr.
Russell 41114 (606) 329-4525
Mailing address: P.O. Box 391, Ashland, KY 41105

Incorporated in 1968 in DE.
Donor(s): Ashland Oil, Inc.
Foundation type: Company-sponsored
Financial data (yr. ended 12/31/89): Assets, $191,104 (M); gifts received, $3,695,000; expenditures, $3,859,143, including $2,526,649 for 269 grants (high: $276,000; low: $500) and $1,327,028 for 802 employee matching gifts.
Purpose and activities: Direct support primarily to educational organizations, mainly colleges and universities; giving also through an employee matching gift program to higher education and community funds.
Types of support: Employee matching gifts, professorships, scholarship funds, fellowships.
Limitations: Giving primarily in KY, OH, PA, and WV. No grants to individuals, or for building or endowment funds.
Application information:
Initial approach: Telephone or letter; form letters are ignored
Deadline(s): None
Board meeting date(s): Feb.
Final notification: Varies
Write: Judy B. Thomas, Pres.
Officers and Trustees:* Harry M. Zachem,* Chair.; Judy B. Thomas,* Pres.; Franklin P. Justice, Jr.,* V.P.; J. Marvin Quin,* V.P.; M. Ray Pace,* Secy.; Gregory W. McKnight,* Treas.; John A. Brothers, John T. Doyle, Walter L. Gooch.
Members: Paul W. Chellgren, Richard W. Spears.
Number of staff: 2 full-time professional; 3 full-time support; 2 part-time support.
Employer Identification Number: 616057900

2450
Bank of Louisville Charities, Inc. ⌑
P.O. Box 1101
Louisville 40201
Application address: 500 West Broadway, Louisville, KY 40202; Tel.: (502) 589-3351

Established in 1973.
Donor(s): Bank of Louisville.
Foundation type: Company-sponsored
Financial data (yr. ended 12/31/88): Assets, $3,458,065 (M); gifts received, $25,000; expenditures, $282,346, including $279,525 for 114 grants (high: $43,500; low: $19).
Purpose and activities: Emphasis on cultural programs, especially in the arts; support also for education, health, civic affairs, and a community fund.
Types of support: Annual campaigns, building funds, continuing support, emergency funds, program-related investments, special projects.
Limitations: Giving primarily in Jefferson County, KY.
Application information:
Initial approach: Letter
Write: Bertram W. Klein, Chair.
Officer: Mary Pfeiffer, Secy.
Directors: Bertram W. Klein, Chair.; Orson Oliver, Thomas L. Weber.
Employer Identification Number: 237423454

2451
James Graham Brown Foundation, Inc. ▼
132 East Gray St.
Louisville 40202 (502) 583-4085

Trust established in 1943 in KY; incorporated in 1954.
Donor(s): J. Graham Brown,† Agnes B. Duggan.†
Foundation type: Independent
Financial data (yr. ended 12/31/89): Assets, $200,075,499 (M); expenditures, $9,984,095, including $8,459,687 for 60 grants (high: $1,500,000; low: $100; average: $5,000-$250,000).
Purpose and activities: Support for higher education, civic organizations, community development, museums, and social service, youth, and health agencies.
Types of support: Annual campaigns, building funds, capital campaigns, conferences and seminars, emergency funds, endowment funds, equipment, matching funds, professorships, renovation projects, research, scholarship funds, special projects, land acquisition.
Limitations: Giving primarily in KY, with emphasis on Louisville. No support for private foundations or the performing arts; no funding for elementary or secondary education. No grants to individuals.
Publications: Grants list, 990-PF.
Application information: Application form required only for larger or more complex requests. Application form not required.
Initial approach: Letter
Copies of proposal: 12
Deadline(s): None
Board meeting date(s): Monthly
Final notification: Grants paid Dec. 31
Write: Mason Rummel, Grants Coord.
Officers and Trustees:* H. Curtis Craig,* Chair.; Joe M. Rodes,* Pres.; Graham B. Loper,* V.P.; Arthur H. Keeney, M.D.,* Secy.; Stanley S. Dickson, Frank B. Hower, Jr., Stanley F. Hugenberg, Jr., Ray E. Loper, Robert L. Royer.
Number of staff: 2 full-time professional; 3 part-time professional; 1 full-time support; 2 part-time support.
Employer Identification Number: 610724060

2452
W. L. Lyons Brown Foundation ⌑
850 Dixie Hwy.
Louisville 40210

Incorporated in 1962 in KY.
Donor(s): W.L. Lyons Brown.†
Foundation type: Independent
Financial data (yr. ended 12/31/88): Assets, $8,171,146 (M); expenditures, $333,619, including $324,483 for 35 grants (high: $40,000; low: $750).
Purpose and activities: Emphasis on education, conservation, cultural activities, and the arts.
Limitations: Giving primarily in KY, with emphasis on the Louisville area.
Application information:
Initial approach: Proposal
Deadline(s): None
Write: Ina H. Brown, Pres.
Officers and Trustees: Ina H. Brown, Pres.; Mrs. W.L. Lyons Brown, Secy.; Owsley Brown II, Treas.; Martin S. Brown, W.L. Lyons Brown, Jr., Earl A. Dorsey, David L. McDonald, Benjamin H. Morris.
Employer Identification Number: 610598511

2453
Citizens Fidelity Foundation, Inc. ▼ ⌑
P.O. Box 33000
Louisville 40296 (502) 581-2016
Application address: Citizens Fidelity Bank and Trust Co., Louisville, KY 40296

Incorporated in 1980 in KY.
Donor(s): Citizens Fidelity Bank and Trust Co.
Foundation type: Company-sponsored
Financial data (yr. ended 12/31/87): Assets, $1,709,870 (M); gifts received, $55,875; expenditures, $1,011,474, including $1,008,035 for 70 grants (high: $200,000; low: $500; average: $1,000-$10,000).
Purpose and activities: Emphasis on cultural programs, education, including higher education, and social services.
Types of support: Building funds, capital campaigns, emergency funds, general purposes, program-related investments, seed money, special projects.
Limitations: Giving primarily in Louisville, KY. No grants to individuals.
Publications: Application guidelines.
Application information: Application form required.
Deadline(s): Mar. 1, June 1, Sept. 1, and Dec. 1
Board meeting date(s): Last Tues. in Jan., Apr., July, and Oct.
Final notification: 2 weeks after board meets
Write: Traci Orman
Officers and Directors: E. Frederick Zopp, Secy.; Mary R. Bush, Treas.; James H. Davis, Warner L. Jones, Jr., Harry LaViers, Jr., Rose L. Rubel, Lawrence L. Smith, Douglas D. Stegner, James Thompson.
Employer Identification Number: 310999030

2454
V. V. Cooke Foundation Corporation
The Summit
4350 Brownsboro Rd., Suite 110
Louisville 40207-1681 (502) 893-4598

Incorporated in 1947 in KY.
Donor(s): V.V. Cooke,† Cooke Chevrolet Co., Cooke Pontiac Co., and others.
Foundation type: Independent
Financial data (yr. ended 8/31/89): Assets, $4,918,711 (M); expenditures, $317,023, including $259,150 for 45 grants (high: $60,000; low: $50; average: $1,983).
Purpose and activities: Emphasis on Baptist church and school support and higher education, including medical education.
Types of support: Continuing support, annual campaigns, emergency funds, building funds, equipment, endowment funds, professorships.
Limitations: Giving primarily in KY. No grants to individuals, or for general endowment funds, research, scholarships, or fellowships; no loans.
Application information: Personal interviews not granted. Application form not required.
Initial approach: Proposal
Copies of proposal: 1
Deadline(s): None
Board meeting date(s): Monthly
Final notification: Following board meeting
Write: John B. Gray, Exec. Dir.
Officers: V.V. Cooke, Jr.,* Pres.; Joe D. Cross,* V.P.; Robert L. Hook,* Secy.; Elva Cooke,* Treas.; John B. Gray, Exec. Dir. and Exec. Secy.
Directors:* Jane C. Cross, June C. Hook.
Number of staff: 1 part-time professional.
Employer Identification Number: 616033714

2455
The Cralle Foundation ⌑
c/o Liberty National Bank & Trust Co. of Louisville
P.O. Box 32500
Louisville 40232 (502) 566-1702

Established in 1984 in KY.
Foundation type: Independent
Financial data (yr. ended 12/31/88): Assets, $4,402,751 (M); gifts received, $172,145; expenditures, $823,206, including $785,833 for 18 grants (high: $300,000; low: $3,500).
Purpose and activities: Support primarily for youth groups, higher education, health services, museums, and community development.
Types of support: General purposes.
Limitations: Giving primarily in KY, with emphasis on Louisville.
Application information: Application form required.
Deadline(s): None
Write: Institutional Trust Dept.
Trustee: Liberty National Bank & Trust Co. of Louisville.
Employer Identification Number: 311070853

2456
John T. and Ada Diederich Educational Trust Fund ⌑ ☆
c/o Third National Bank
P.O. Box 1270
Ashland 41105-1270

Foundation type: Independent
Financial data (yr. ended 12/31/87): Assets, $3,285,126 (M); gifts received, $492,496; expenditures, $68,163, including $32,215 for 20 grants to individuals.
Purpose and activities: Awards scholarships for higher education.
Types of support: Student aid.
Limitations: Giving limited to KY.
Application information: Scholarship forms available from local schools and trustee bank. Application form required.
Deadline(s): May 30
Trustee: Third National Bank.
Employer Identification Number: 316271680

2457
First Kentucky National Charitable Foundation, Inc. ▼
P.O. Box 3600
Louisville 40233 (502) 581-5258

Established in 1981 in KY.
Donor(s): First National Bank of Louisville.
Foundation type: Company-sponsored
Financial data (yr. ended 12/31/88): Assets, $1,200,000 (M); gifts received, $595,829; expenditures, $1,108,320, including $1,105,820 for 81 grants (high: $150,000; low: $1,000; average: $1,000-$10,000).
Purpose and activities: Giving primarily for education, including higher and early childhood education, educational programs for minorities, and educational research; support also for cultural activities, community funds, and social services, including youth and child welfare and development, programs for the homeless, and family services.
Types of support: Continuing support, employee matching gifts, general purposes, special projects.
Limitations: Giving primarily in KY, with emphasis on Louisville. No grants to individuals.
Publications: Occasional report, program policy statement, application guidelines.
Application information: Application form required.
Initial approach: Letter
Copies of proposal: 1
Deadline(s): None
Board meeting date(s): Mar., June, Sept. and Dec.
Final notification: Quarterly, after meetings
Write: Lisa D. Thompson, Secy.
Directors: Morton Boyd, Edward Brandon, W.L. Lyons Brown, Jr., S. Gordon Dabney, Henry F. Frigon, Thomas R. Fuller, Jacob H. Graves III, William H. Harrison, Jr., John B. Holland, George N. King, Sr., Ann Benjamin Levine, A. Stevens Miles, Carl Pollard, Franklin F. Starks, Jr., James W. Stites, Jr., William M. Street.
Number of staff: 2 part-time professional.
Employer Identification Number: 311033629

2458
Foundation for the Tri-State Community
(Formerly Greater Ashland Area Cultural and Economic Development Foundation, Inc.)
P.O. Box 2096
Ashland 41105 (606) 324-3888
FAX: (606) 324-5961

Incorporated in 1972 in KY.
Foundation type: Community
Financial data (yr. ended 12/31/90): Assets, $3,455,316 (M); gifts received, $696,634; expenditures, $848,227, including $177,363 for grants.
Purpose and activities: Giving for charitable, cultural, educational, and scientific purposes.
Types of support: General purposes, special projects, seed money, consulting services, technical assistance.
Limitations: Giving limited to the tri-state area of Ashland, KY, Ironton, OH, and Huntington, WV. No support for religious purposes or medical research. No grants for annual campaigns, deficit financing, operating support, or building or endowment funds.
Publications: Annual report, application guidelines, 990-PF.
Application information: Application form required.
Initial approach: Letter, telephone, or proposal
Copies of proposal: 1
Deadline(s): Sept. 15 for grants from unrestricted funds
Board meeting date(s): Quarterly
Write: Linda L. Ball, Exec. Dir.
Officers and Trustees:* Erland P. Stevens, Jr.,* Pres.; M. Sue Moore,* V.P.; Donald E. McGinnis,* Treas.; Linda L. Ball, Exec. Dir.; Robert J. Arrell, Denise H. Bannister, Darrell J.

Caldwell, Paul W. Chellgren, Philip E. Cline, Bill W. Dingus, Don Edwards, William P. Emrick, Edwin L. Graham, Daniel C. Greer, Frank P. Justice, John H. Mays, Harold D. Miller, Phillip D. Morris, Thomas D. McGinnis, David Osborne, Charles M. Rhodes, Stuart B.A. Webb, James F. Williamson, Hugh M. Wittich.
Number of staff: 1 full-time professional; 1 full-time support.
Employer Identification Number: 610729266

2459
Annie Gardner Foundation ⌑
Sixth and College
Mayfield 42066 (502) 247-5803

Established in 1941 in KY.
Donor(s): Ed Gardner Trust.
Foundation type: Operating
Financial data (yr. ended 5/31/88): Assets, $3,454,211 (M); gifts received, $633,285; qualifying distributions, $817,846, including $389,896 for 3,214 grants and $246,210 for 505 loans to individuals.
Purpose and activities: Support primarily for the disadvantaged, including grants for rent, medical care, clothing, and other necessities; grants also for educational loans, maximum of $2,000 for undergraduates and $3,000 for graduate students.
Types of support: Student loans.
Limitations: Giving limited to Graves County, KY, for student loans.
Application information: Student loan application available from foundation.
Deadline(s): July 1 for student loans
Write: Nancy H. Sparks, Education Dir.
Directors: Nancy H. Sparks, Education Dir.; Thomas McCue.
Trustees: Dal Boyd, George Pickens, Hugh Williams.
Employer Identification Number: 610564889

2460
The Gheens Foundation, Inc. ▼
One Riverfront Plaza, Suite 705
Louisville 40202 (502) 584-4650
FAX: (502) 584-4652

Incorporated in 1957 in KY.
Donor(s): C. Edwin Gheens,† Mary Jo Gheens Hill.†
Foundation type: Independent
Financial data (yr. ended 10/31/88): Assets, $39,460,568 (M); expenditures, $2,384,384, including $1,295,274 for 54 grants (high: $250,000; low: $2,500; average: $5,000-$50,000).
Purpose and activities: Emphasis on higher and secondary education, ongoing teacher education, social service agencies, health associations, programs for the physically and mentally handicapped, and cultural programs.
Types of support: Special projects, building funds, scholarship funds, renovation projects, equipment.
Limitations: Giving primarily in KY, with emphasis on Louisville.
Publications: Application guidelines.
Application information: Application form required.
Initial approach: Letter with 1-to-2 page outline
Deadline(s): None
Board meeting date(s): Quarterly
Final notification: Within 90 days
Write: James N. Davis, Exec. Dir.
Officers: Joseph E. Stopher,* Pres.; Laramie L. Leatherman,* V.P.; Oscar S. Bryant, Jr.,* Secy.; James N. Davis, Treas. and Exec. Dir.
Trustees:* Donald W. Doyle, John M. Smith.
Number of staff: 2 full-time professional; 2 full-time support.
Employer Identification Number: 616031406

2461
Glenmore Foundation, Inc. ⌑ ☆
1700 Citizens Plaza
Louisville 40202-2874 (502) 589-0130

Established in 1980.
Foundation type: Company-sponsored
Financial data (yr. ended 6/30/88): Assets, $244,647 (M); gifts received, $4,080; expenditures, $116,574, including $112,960 for grants.
Purpose and activities: Support for the arts and medical education and research.
Trustee: James Thompson.
Employer Identification Number: 311018779

2462
Claude & Betty Harris Irrevocable Charitable Trust ⌑ ☆
c/o Stock Yards Bank & Trust Co.
1040 East Main St.
Louisville 40206
Application address: P.O. Box 32890, Louisville, KY 40232-2890

Established in 1987.
Foundation type: Independent
Financial data (yr. ended 12/31/89): Assets, $2,023,359 (M); expenditures, $67,727, including $48,700 for 35 grants (high: $3,200; low: $50).
Purpose and activities: Grants for religious welfare, housing for the homeless, and social services.
Application information:
Initial approach: Letter or proposal
Deadline(s): Dec. 31
Write: R. Keith Cullinan, Exec. V.P.
Officers and Advisory Committee:* Theresa Jean Harris Moore,* Chair.; Don Harris,* Vice-Chair.; Paula Harris Stansell,* Secy.; David Harris, Gary Harris, Gayla Harris, Timothy Harris.
Trustee: Stock Yards Bank & Trust.
Employer Identification Number: 616156766

2463
Hayswood Foundation, Inc. ⌑ ☆
c/o John O. Schumacher
One McDonald Pkwy., Suite 2-C
Maysville 41056

Foundation type: Independent
Financial data (yr. ended 6/30/88): Assets, $2,696,627 (M); expenditures, $156,263, including $100,000 for 1 grant.
Purpose and activities: Support for a YMCA.
Limitations: Giving limited to the Maysville, KY, area.
Application information: Application form not required.
Deadline(s): None
Officers and Directors: E.B. Hillenmeyer, Jr., Chair.; Mary V. Clarke, Vice-Chair.; John W. McNeill III, Secy.; Chuck Kirk, Treas.; John C. Schumacher, Robert D. Vance.
Employer Identification Number: 237345996

2464
Blanche and Thomas Hope Memorial Fund
c/o Third National Bank
P.O. Box 1270
Ashland 41105

Established in 1969 in KY.
Donor(s): Blanche Hope,† Thomas Hope.†
Foundation type: Independent
Financial data (yr. ended 12/31/88): Assets, $2,040,976 (M); expenditures, $155,749, including $129,269 for 201 grants to individuals (high: $1,450; low: $50).
Purpose and activities: Funds distributed exclusively as scholarships to individuals graduating from high schools in Boyd and Greenup counties, KY, and Lawrence County, OH.
Types of support: Student aid.
Limitations: Giving limited to Boyd and Greenup counties, KY, and Lawrence County, OH, residents.
Application information: Application form available from high school guidance counselors. Application form required.
Deadline(s): Mar. 1
Selection Committee: Curtis Foutch, Scott Howard, Charles Sinnette, Richard Walton, John W. Woods III.
Number of staff: None.
Employer Identification Number: 616067105

2465
Ervin G. Houchens Foundation, Inc. ⌑
(Formerly Houchens Foundation, Inc.)
900 Church St.
Bowling Green 42101 (502) 843-3252

Incorporated in 1954 in KY.
Donor(s): Houchens Markets, Inc., B.G. Wholesale, Inc.
Foundation type: Independent
Financial data (yr. ended 12/31/88): Assets, $3,685,632 (M); gifts received, $1,000; qualifying distributions, $700,307, including $31,501 for 19 grants (high: $11,562; low: $100) and $668,806 for 35 loans (high: $145,000; low: $125).
Purpose and activities: Support mainly in the form of loans to Baptist and Methodist churches; smaller cash contributions to churches, community funds, youth agencies, health organizations, and education.
Types of support: Loans.
Limitations: Giving limited to southwest KY.
Application information:
Initial approach: Letter with comprehensive details
Deadline(s): None
Write: Ervin D. Houchens, Pres.
Officers and Directors:* Ervin G. Houchens,* Pres.; Lois Lynne,* Secy.; Covella H. Biggers,* Treas.; Gil E. Biggers, Gil M. Biggers, George Suel Houchens, C. Cecil Martin.
Employer Identification Number: 610623087

2466
The Humana Foundation, Inc. ▼ ⌑
The Humana Bldg., 500 West Main St.
P.O. Box 1438
Louisville 40201 (502) 580-3920

Incorporated in 1981 in KY.
Donor(s): Humana, Inc.
Foundation type: Company-sponsored
Financial data (yr. ended 8/31/88): Assets, $15,870,080 (M); gifts received, $6,317,059; expenditures, $8,226,538, including $8,162,032 for grants (high: $1,024,000; low: $100; average: $5,000-$25,000).
Purpose and activities: Support for the performing arts, health organizations, higher and secondary education, community and economic development, and a community center.
Limitations: Giving primarily in KY.
Application information:
Deadline(s): None
Board meeting date(s): Every 2 months
Final notification: Generally, 6 weeks to 2 months
Write: Jay L. Foley, Contribution Mgr.
Officers and Directors:* David A. Jones,* Chair. and C.O.O.; Wendell Cherry,* Pres. and C.O.O.; William C. Ballard, Jr., Exec. V.P., Finance and Administration; Carl F. Pollard,* Exec. V.P.; Thomas J. Flynn, Sr. V.P.; Alice F. Newton, Secy.
Number of staff: None.
Employer Identification Number: 611004763

2467
Kentucky Foundation for Women, Inc. ▼
The Heyburn Bldg., Suite 1215
Louisville 40202 (502) 562-0045

Established in 1985 in KY.
Donor(s): Sallie Bingham.
Foundation type: Independent
Financial data (yr. ended 06/30/88): Assets, $8,047,262 (M); expenditures, $1,039,337, including $213,110 for 14 grants (high: $75,000; low: $25) and $462,740 for 70 grants to individuals (high: $25,000; low: $480).
Purpose and activities: Support primarily for women artists and arts-related organizations, with the goal of improving the status of women in the arts and bringing about social change through the arts; support also for projects relating to the humanities, science, and mathematics, particularly in fields traditionally closed to women.
Types of support: Conferences and seminars, continuing support, fellowships, grants to individuals, research, scholarship funds.
Limitations: Giving primarily in KY and contiguous areas.
Publications: Annual report, application guidelines, informational brochure.
Application information: Application form required.
Initial approach: Letter
Copies of proposal: 2
Deadline(s): Oct. 1
Board meeting date(s): Nov. 1
Final notification: Jan.
Write: Sallie Bingham, Pres.
Officers and Directors: Sallie Bingham, Pres.; Frederick Smock, Secy.; Ann Stewart Anderson, Barry Ellsworth, Camilz Motte.
Number of staff: 1 full-time professional; 1 full-time support; 2 part-time support.
Employer Identification Number: 611070429

2469
The Lake Foundation, Inc. ⌑
P.O. Box 129
Somerset 42501

Incorporated in 1985 in KY.
Foundation type: Independent
Financial data (yr. ended 12/31/88): Assets, $23,445 (M); gifts received, $269,970; expenditures, $284,023, including $283,957 for 32 grants (high: $32,000; low: $105).
Purpose and activities: Giving primarily for Christian institutions and missionary projects; support also for higher education.
Application information: Contributes only to pre-selected organizations. Applications not accepted.
Directors: Jesse T. Correll, Vincent L. Correll, Ward F. Correll.
Employer Identification Number: 611098508

2470
Harry and Maxie LaViers Foundation, Inc. ⌑
P.O. Box 332
Irvine 40336 (606) 723-5111

Established in 1977.
Donor(s): Harry LaViers.†
Foundation type: Independent
Financial data (yr. ended 8/31/88): Assets, $3,234,486 (M); expenditures, $193,685, including $187,700 for 1 grant.
Purpose and activities: Emphasis on Protestant church support, higher education, and medical research.
Types of support: Annual campaigns, building funds, capital campaigns, special projects.
Limitations: Giving primarily in rural eastern KY. No support for national programs. No grants to individuals, or for scholarships.
Application information:
Write: Mrs. Harry LaViers, Jr., Trustee
Officers and Trustees: Harry LaViers, Jr., Pres.; Elizabeth LaViers Owen, V.P.; Barbara P. LaViers, Secy.-Treas.
Number of staff: None.
Employer Identification Number: 310902455

2471
Lexington Orphan Society ⌑
c/o Mrs. Dwight G. Tenney
211 Barrow Rd.
Lexington 40502

Established in 1834 in KY.
Foundation type: Independent
Financial data (yr. ended 12/31/88): Assets, $1,215,319 (M); gifts received, $46,219; expenditures, $67,569, including $53,800 for 14 grants (high: $8,000; low: $300).
Purpose and activities: Giving to child welfare organizations, youth programs, and other social services.
Limitations: Giving limited to Fayette County, KY.
Officer: Mrs. Dwight G. Tenney, Treas.
Employer Identification Number: 610449629

2472
The Lincoln Foundation, Inc. ☆
233 West Broadway, Suite 400
Louisville 40202

Established in 1910.
Donor(s): Lee B. Thomas, Jr.
Foundation type: Operating
Financial data (yr. ended 4/30/89): Assets, $2,920,062 (M); gifts received, $175,849; expenditures, $296,668, including $8,103 for grants (high: $4,000), $229,763 for foundation-administered programs and $8,000 for loans to individuals.
Purpose and activities: A private operating foundation; awards loans to students for higher education; support also for community organizations.
Types of support: Student loans.
Limitations: Giving primarily in KY.
Application information: Application forms available for grants and loans from the Scholarship Committee. Application form required.
Officers: Eleanor Young Love, Pres.; Mrs. Lee B. Thomas, Jr., 1st V.P.; Bettie Johnson, 2nd V.P.; Samuel Robinson, Secy. and Exec. Dir.; Joseph Carrol, Treas.
Trustees: Charles H. Anderson, and 11 other trustees.
Employer Identification Number: 610449631

2473
The Louisville Community Foundation, Inc.
1404 Kentucky Home Life Bldg.
239 South 5th St.
Louisville 40202 (502) 585-4649

Established in 1916 in KY; reorganized in 1984.
Foundation type: Community
Financial data (yr. ended 06/30/89): Assets, $15,711,823 (M); gifts received, $9,799,239; expenditures, $791,932, including $411,701 for 86 grants (high: $30,000; low: $50; average: $50-$30,000) and $89,315 for 144 grants to individuals (high: $4,994; low: $100; average: $100-$4,994).
Purpose and activities: Giving for social services, arts and humanities, education, and environment; support also for scholarships, student loans, and a teacher awards program.
Types of support: Consulting services, seed money, special projects, emergency funds, student loans, equipment, conferences and seminars, deficit financing, matching funds, operating budgets, professorships, publications, research, scholarship funds, endowment funds.
Limitations: Giving limited to Louisville and Jefferson County, KY. No support for sectarian purposes. No grants to individuals (except Teachers Award Recognition), or for continuing support, annual campaigns, capital funds, building funds, internships, land acquistion, renovation projects, or techical assistance.
Publications: Annual report, program policy statement, application guidelines.

Application information: Application form required.
Initial approach: Letter or telephone
Copies of proposal: 10
Deadline(s): Apr. 1
Board meeting date(s): Sept., Dec., Mar., and June
Final notification: June
Write: Darrell L. Murphy, Exec. Dir.
Administrator: Darrell L. Murphy, Exec. Dir.
Officers and Directors: Wilson W. Wyatt, Sr., Chair.; Baylor Landrum, Jr., Pres.; Ina H. Brown, Secy.; John E. Brown, Treas.; and 30 additional directors.
Number of staff: 3 full-time professional; 1 full-time support; 3 part-time support.
Employer Identification Number: 310997017

2474
The Mahan Foundation, Inc. ⌑
P.O. Box 196
Prospect 40059-0196

Foundation type: Independent
Financial data (yr. ended 12/31/88): Assets, $1,071,011 (M); expenditures, $61,212, including $55,800 for 37 grants (high: $4,500; low: $300).
Purpose and activities: Giving primarily for organizations providing aid to children and the elderly.
Limitations: Giving primarily in Oldham County, KY.
Application information:
Initial approach: Letter
Deadline(s): Dec. 1
Write: Ann Smiser, Treas.
Officers: Jack Kimball, Pres.; Raymond Simpson, V.P.; Jennifer Dick, Secy.; Ann Smiser, Treas.
Director: Gene Bottorff.
Employer Identification Number: 311087614

2475
Ralph E. Mills Foundation ⌑
c/o Drawer M
Frankfort 40601

Incorporated in 1947 in KY.
Donor(s): Ralph E. Mills.
Foundation type: Independent
Financial data (yr. ended 12/31/88): Assets, $11,523,687 (M); expenditures, $583,654, including $564,000 for 42 grants (high: $100,000; low: $500).
Purpose and activities: Giving for higher education, hospitals, Christian churches, and social services.
Limitations: Giving primarily in KY. No grants to individuals.
Officers and Directors: Ralph E. Mills, Pres.; John E. Brown, V.P. and Treas.; Charles D. Barnett, Secy.; Travis Bush, Robert M. Hardy, Jr., Zack Saufley, Harry Lee Waterfield.
Employer Identification Number: 610529834

2476
The George W. Norton Foundation, Inc. ⌑
4350 Brownsboro Rd., Suite 133
Louisville 40207 (502) 893-9549

Incorporated in 1958 in KY.
Donor(s): Mrs. George W. Norton.
Foundation type: Independent
Financial data (yr. ended 12/31/88): Assets, $6,131,812 (M); expenditures, $320,707, including $287,335 for 30 grants (high: $46,500; low: $185).
Purpose and activities: Emphasis on education, health, cultural programs, youth agencies, and social services.
Types of support: Operating budgets.
Limitations: Giving primarily in KY. No support for private foundations. No grants to individuals, or for endowment funds.
Application information:
Initial approach: Proposal
Deadline(s): None
Board meeting date(s): Quarterly
Final notification: 90 days
Write: Lucy Crawford
Officers and Directors: Robert W. Dulaney, Pres.; Jane Norton Barrett, V.P.; Mary M. Rodes, Secy.-Treas. and Exec. Dir.
Employer Identification Number: 616024040

2477
The Ogden College Fund ⌑
P.O. Box 930
Bowling Green 42101 (502) 781-2121
Application address: c/o Cooper R. Smith, Jr., 520 Hillwood Dr., Bowling Green, KY 42101

Foundation type: Independent
Financial data (yr. ended 10/31/88): Assets, $2,538,109 (M); gifts received, $10,698; expenditures, $178,263, including $171,287 for grants to individuals.
Purpose and activities: Scholarship grants for students residing in KY and attending Ogden College of Western Kentucky University; limited support also for Western Kentucky University, primarily for equipment.
Types of support: Student aid, equipment, fellowships, matching funds, professorships.
Limitations: Giving limited to KY.
Application information:
Write: Alvis Temple, Exec. Secy.
Officers and Trustees: Cooper R. Smith, Jr., Regent; Alvis Temple, Exec. Secy.; Jerry E. Cohron, Jo Tilden Orendorf, Marvin W. Russell, Herbert J. Smith.
Employer Identification Number: 237078715

2478
E. O. Robinson Mountain Fund ⌑
425 Holiday Rd.
Lexington 40502 (606) 233-0817

Incorporated in 1922 in KY.
Donor(s): Edward O. Robinson.†
Foundation type: Independent
Financial data (yr. ended 6/30/88): Assets, $8,710,214 (M); expenditures, $470,846, including $389,430 for 44 grants (high: $50,000; low: $1,000).
Purpose and activities: To help the people, particularly the youth, of the mountain region of eastern KY improve their living conditions; grants primarily to hospitals and health agencies for medical care and to higher educational institutions for scholarships.
Types of support: Scholarship funds, continuing support, equipment, matching funds, operating budgets, renovation projects.
Limitations: Giving primarily in eastern KY. No grants to individuals.
Application information:
Initial approach: Proposal
Copies of proposal: 11
Deadline(s): Submit proposal 6 months in advance
Board meeting date(s): Every 4 months
Write: Juanita Stollings, Secy.-Treas.
Officers: Lyman V. Ginger,* Pres.; N. Mitchell Meade,* V.P.; Juanita Stollings, Secy.-Treas.; Arthur C. Aumack.
Directors:* J.C. Codell, Jr., William Engle III, Mary P. Fox, M.D., Francis S. Hutchins, Harold H. Mullis, Burl Phillips, Jr., J. Phil Smith, Robert A. Sparks, Jr., Vinson A. Watts.
Number of staff: 1 full-time professional; 2 full-time support.
Employer Identification Number: 610449642

2479
Louis T. Roth Foundation, Inc. ⌑ ☆
2225 Douglas Blvd.
Louisville 40205-1903

Established in 1964.
Donor(s): Louis T. Roth.
Foundation type: Independent
Financial data (yr. ended 4/30/89): Assets, $1,734,829 (M); gifts received, $20,540; expenditures, $111,808, including $102,823 for 50 grants (high: $31,450; low: $25).
Purpose and activities: Support primarily for Jewish organizations, including welfare funds.
Limitations: Giving primarily in Louisville, KY. No grants to individuals.
Application information: Contributes only to pre-selected organizations. Applications not accepted.
Officers and Trustees: Louis T. Roth, Pres.; David M. Roth, Secy.; Bruce J. Roth, Treas.; Lee F. Roth.
Employer Identification Number: 610624305

2480
Rudd Foundation, Inc. ⌑ ☆
4344 Poplar Level Rd.
Louisville 40232 (502) 456-4050

Established in 1978.
Donor(s): Mason C. Rudd.
Foundation type: Independent
Financial data (yr. ended 12/31/88): Assets, $356,515 (M); gifts received, $90,000; expenditures, $130,578, including $129,753 for 9 grants (high: $110,003; low: $100).
Purpose and activities: Support primarily for a Jewish welfare fund and a Jewish community center.
Application information:
Initial approach: Letter
Deadline(s): None
Write: Mason C. Rudd, Pres.
Officers and Directors:* Mason C. Rudd,* Pres.; Mary O. Rudd,* V.P.; Elizabeth R. Bennett, Secy.; Michael D. Rudd,* Treas.
Employer Identification Number: 310945562

2481
Al J. Schneider Foundation Corporation ⌑
3720 Seventh St. Rd.
Louisville 40216

Incorporated in 1957 in KY.
Donor(s): Al J. Schneider.
Foundation type: Independent
Financial data (yr. ended 2/28/89): Assets, $1,387,317 (M); gifts received, $477,000; expenditures, $354,423, including $353,204 for 107 grants (high: $50,000; low: $25).
Purpose and activities: Emphasis on church support, health, cultural programs, youth agencies, and education, particularly higher education.
Limitations: Giving primarily in KY.
Officer and Trustee: Al J. Schneider, Pres.
Employer Identification Number: 610621591

2482
Trover Clinic Foundation, Inc. ⌑
Clinic Dr.
Madisonville 42431

Established in 1956 in KY.
Foundation type: Independent
Financial data (yr. ended 12/31/87): Assets, $1,363,177 (M); gifts received, $700,130; expenditures, $1,358,659, including $800 for 2 grants (high: $750; low: $50) and $100 for 1 grant to an individual.
Purpose and activities: Support for social services; foundation also runs four separate health programs: a family practice residence program, a dialysis center, a respiratory clinic, and a program for developmentally disabled persons.
Limitations: Giving primarily in KY.
Officers: Loman C. Trover, M.D., Pres.; Merle M. Mahr, M.D., V.P.; D.W. Dockrey, Secy.-Treas.
Directors: James L. Beck, M.D., Morton Dickerson, Mark E. Eastin, Jr., Kenneth O. Gibson, Jack L. Hamman, M.D., and 7 additional directors.
Employer Identification Number: 610654587

2483
The Henry Vogt Foundation, Inc.
1000 West Ormsby Ave.
Louisville 40210 (502) 634-1500
Mailing address: P.O. Box 1918, Louisville, KY 40201-1918

Incorporated in 1958 in KY.
Donor(s): Henry Vogt Machine Co.
Foundation type: Company-sponsored
Financial data (yr. ended 06/30/89): Assets, $1,845,136 (M); gifts received, $400,000; expenditures, $179,081, including $176,929 for 23 grants (high: $51,600; low: $100).
Purpose and activities: Emphasis on community development, education, including business and secondary institutions with a focus on improving technical and computer literacy, social services, youth agencies, and a community fund.
Types of support: Renovation projects, continuing support, annual campaigns, building funds, equipment, land acquisition, research.
Limitations: Giving limited to KY, with emphasis on the Jefferson County and Louisville area. No grants to individuals, or for endowment funds, scholarships, fellowships, or matching gifts; no loans.
Application information: Foundation only notifies successful applicants. Application form not required.
Initial approach: Letter
Copies of proposal: 1
Deadline(s): May 1
Board meeting date(s): June 30
Write: Kent Oyler, Mgr.
Officers: Henry V. Heuser, Jr.,* Pres.; Leland D. Schlegel, Jr.,* V.P.; Margaret S. Culver,* Secy.-Treas.; Kent Oyler, Mgr.
Directors:* Henry V. Heuser, David G. White.
Number of staff: None.
Employer Identification Number: 237416717

2484
Fred B. & Opal S. Woosley Foundation, Inc. ⌑ ☆
900 Kentucky Home Life Bldg.
Louisville 40202
Application address: c/o Hilliard Lyons Trust Co., 501 South 4th St., P.O. Box 32760, Louisville, KY 40232

Established in 1986 in KY.
Foundation type: Independent
Financial data (yr. ended 12/31/88): Assets, $1,017,437 (M); expenditures, $58,780, including $50,000 for 17 grants (high: $10,000; low: $1,000).
Purpose and activities: Giving primarily for education, especially institutions for the visually and hearing impaired; support also for welfare and social services.
Limitations: Giving primarily in Louisville, KY. No grants to individuals.
Application information:
Initial approach: Letter
Deadline(s): None
Board meeting date(s): Semi-annually
Final notification: After board meeting
Write: Arthur C. Peter, Dir.
Directors: John McFerran Barr, David A. Bell, Donald E. Meyer, Arthur C. Peter, Opal S. Woosley.
Employer Identification Number: 611104319

2485
W. T. Young Family Foundation, Inc. ⌑ ☆
P.O. Box 1110
Lexington 40589-1110

Established in 1981 in KY.
Donor(s): William T. Young, William T. Young, Jr.
Foundation type: Independent
Financial data (yr. ended 12/31/88): Assets, $726,698 (M); expenditures, $201,855, including $192,366 for 25 grants (high: $40,000; low: $100).
Purpose and activities: Giving primarily for civic affairs, community development, and the arts, including museums; support also for higher and other education.
Limitations: Giving primarily in Louisville and Lexington, KY.
Directors: Lucy M. Young, William T. Young, William T. Young, Jr.
Employer Identification Number: 311020207

2486
John B. & Brownie Young Memorial Fund ⌑
c/o Owensboro National Bank, Trust Dept.
230 Frederica St.
Owensboro 42301

Established in 1961 in KY.
Foundation type: Independent
Financial data (yr. ended 12/31/87): Assets, $2,670,303 (M); gifts received, $141,685; expenditures, $185,111, including $156,850 for 63 grants to individuals (high: $2,500; low: $1,250).
Purpose and activities: Scholarships for students in school districts of Owensboro, Daviess, and McClean counties, KY.
Types of support: Student aid.
Limitations: Giving primarily in Owensboro, Daviess, and McClean counties, KY.
Application information: Application form required.
Deadline(s): None
Trustee: Owensboro National Bank.
Employer Identification Number: 616025137

LOUISIANA

2487
The Azby Fund ⌑
635 Gravier Whitney Bank Bldg., Rm. 1311
New Orleans 70130-2613

Established in 1969 in LA.
Donor(s): Marion W. Harvey,† Herbert J. Harvey, Jr.†
Foundation type: Independent
Financial data (yr. ended 12/31/88): Assets, $9,034,264 (M); gifts received, $1,429,155; expenditures, $721,060, including $255,573 for 31 grants (high: $78,672; low: $100).
Purpose and activities: Support primarily for Catholic giving, higher education, and medical sciences.
Application information: Contributes only to pre-selected organizations. Applications not accepted.
Officers and Directors: Ermine Wadsworth, Pres.; Thomas Lemann, Secy.-Treas.; Michael Liebaert, Managing Dir.; Stewart Farnet, Ann Fitzmorris, Rev. Earl C. Woods.
Employer Identification Number: 726049781

2488
Baton Rouge Area Foundation
One American Place, Suite 1601
Baton Rouge 70825 (504) 387-6126

Incorporated in 1964 in LA.
Foundation type: Community
Financial data (yr. ended 12/31/89): Assets, $7,025,660 (M); gifts received, $605,602;

expenditures, $595,018, including $403,147 for 129 grants (high: $100,000; low: $99).
Purpose and activities: Preference given to those projects which promise to affect a broad segment of the population or which tend to help a segment of the citizenry who are not being adequately served by the community's resources.
Types of support: Seed money, emergency funds, research, equipment, matching funds, special projects, renovation projects.
Limitations: Giving limited to the Baton Rouge, LA, area, including East Baton Rouge, West Baton Rouge, Livingston, Ascension, Iberville, Pointe Coupee, East Feliciana, and West Feliciana parishes. No grants to individuals, or for endowment funds, continuing support, annual campaigns, deficit financing, land acquisition, conferences, scholarships, fellowships, or operating budgets; no loans.
Publications: Annual report, application guidelines, newsletter, informational brochure.
Application information: Application form required.
Initial approach: Telephone, letter, or proposal
Copies of proposal: 1
Deadline(s): Feb. 15, May 15, Aug. 15, and Nov. 15
Board meeting date(s): Mar., June, Sept., and Dec.
Final notification: 1 week after board meeting
Write: John G. Davies, Exec. Dir.
Officers and Directors:* Dudley W. Coates,* Pres.; Gordon A. Pugh,* V.P.; Carolyn W. Carnahan,* Secy.; John C. Gaurreau II,* Treas.; John G. Davies,* Exec. Dir.; and 18 additional directors.
Trustee Banks: Hibernia National Bank, Premier Bank, N.A.
Number of staff: 2 full-time professional; 1 part-time support.
Employer Identification Number: 726030391

2489
Batture Park, Inc. ⌑
Route 1, P.O. Box 217
Braithwaite 70040

Established in 1967 in LA.
Foundation type: Independent
Financial data (yr. ended 09/30/89): Assets, $5,130 (M); gifts received, $555,818; expenditures, $555,818, including $555,818 for 2 grants (high: $555,118; low: $700).
Purpose and activities: Giving to educational and governmental institutions.
Limitations: Giving primarily in St. Bernard Parish, LA.
Application information:
Initial approach: Letter
Deadline(s): None
Write: Lynn Dean, Pres.
Officers: Lynn Dean, Pres.; Nettie Dean, Secy.-Treas.
Employer Identification Number: 726034562

2490
Charles T. Beaird Foundation
P.O. Box 31110
Shreveport 71130 (318) 459-3242

Established in 1960 in LA.
Donor(s): Shreveport Publishing Corp.
Foundation type: Independent
Financial data (yr. ended 12/31/89): Assets, $2,178,724 (M); gifts received, $115,000; expenditures, $99,980, including $83,080 for 26 grants (high: $25,000; low: $200).
Purpose and activities: Support for higher education, including theological seminaries; support also for Protestant welfare, social services for women, and youth organizations.
Types of support: Operating budgets, renovation projects, capital campaigns.
Limitations: Giving primarily in the Shreveport, LA, area.
Application information: Application form not required.
Initial approach: Letter
Deadline(s): June 1, Aug. 15, and Nov. 15
Board meeting date(s): 3 times a year: summer, fall and in Dec.
Final notification: Dec. 31
Write: Charles T. Beaird, Pres.
Officers: Charles T. Beaird, Pres.; Carolyn W. Beaird, V.P.; Edna L. Robinson, Secy.-Treas.
Directors: John B. Beaird, Susan Beaird-Robinson, Marjorie B. Seawell.
Employer Identification Number: 726027212

2491
Nathan Bernstein Scholarship Fund
c/o Louisiana State Univ., School of Medicine, Office of Student Affairs
P.O. Box 33932
Shreveport 71130 (318) 674-6065

Established in 1984 in LA.
Donor(s): Nathan Bernstein,† Mrs. Nathan Bernstein.†
Foundation type: Independent
Financial data (yr. ended 09/30/88): Assets, $1,500,065 (M); expenditures, $51,706, including $39,000 for 26 grants to individuals of $1,500 each.
Purpose and activities: Support primarily for scholarship grants for medical education.
Types of support: Student aid.
Limitations: Giving primarily in Shreveport, LA.
Application information: Application form required.
Deadline(s): June 10
Trustee: Commercial National Bank.
Employer Identification Number: 726103061

2492
Boh Foundation ⌑
730 South Tonti St.
New Orleans 70119

Established in 1975 in LA.
Donor(s): Boh Bros. Construction Co., Inc.
Foundation type: Company-sponsored
Financial data (yr. ended 1/31/89): Assets, $1,231,352 (M); gifts received, $10,000; expenditures, $158,681, including $156,540 for 40 grants (high: $25,000; low: $350).
Purpose and activities: Emphasis on higher education; some support for hospitals and health associations.
Types of support: Building funds.
Limitations: Giving primarily in New Orleans, LA.
Trustees: Robert H. Boh, Chair.; Robert S. Boh, John F. Lipani.
Employer Identification Number: 510167756

2493
The Booth-Bricker Fund ⌑
826 Union St., Suite 300
New Orleans 70112 (504) 581-2430

Established in 1976 in LA.
Donor(s): John F. Bricker, Nina B. Bricker.†
Foundation type: Independent
Financial data (yr. ended 12/31/88): Assets, $15,665,885 (M); gifts received, $1,422; expenditures, $723,583, including $601,635 for 80 grants (high: $50,000; low: $50).
Purpose and activities: Giving primarily for higher and other education, social service and youth agencies, and hospitals.
Types of support: Research.
Limitations: Giving primarily in New Orleans, LA.
Application information: Application form not required.
Initial approach: Letter or proposal
Deadline(s): None
Write: Gray S. Parker, V.P.
Officers and Trustees: John F. Bricker, Chair. and Pres.; Bette P. Minihan, V.P. and Secy.; Gray S. Parker, V.P. and Treas.; N.P. Phillips, Jr., V.P.; Dorothy A. Boyle, Henry N. Kuechler III, Robert L. Goodwin, John B. Waid, H. Hunter White.
Employer Identification Number: 720818077

2494
Joe W. & Dorothy Dorsett Brown Foundation ⌑
1801 Pere Marquette Bldg.
New Orleans 70112 (504) 522-4233

Established in 1959 in LA.
Donor(s): Mrs. Joe W. Brown, Dorothy Dorsett Brown.
Foundation type: Independent
Financial data (yr. ended 12/31/86): Assets, $3,464,187 (L); expenditures, $212,987, including $94,379 for 32 grants (high: $20,000; low: $100) and $46,142 for 8 grants to individuals (high: $11,097; low: $945).
Purpose and activities: Giving for scholarships, hospitals, a community fund, and welfare.
Types of support: Operating budgets, research, student aid.
Limitations: Giving primarily in LA.
Application information:
Initial approach: Proposal
Deadline(s): None
Write: D.P. Spencer, V.P.
Officers: Mrs. Joe W. Brown, Pres.; D.P. Spencer, V.P.; E.K. Hunter, Secy.-Treas.
Employer Identification Number: 726027232

2495
The William T. and Ethel Lewis Burton Foundation ⌑
101 North Huntington St.
Sulphur 70663 (318) 527-5221

Incorporated in 1963 in LA.
Donor(s): William T. Burton, Wm. T. Burton Industries, Inc.
Foundation type: Independent
Financial data (yr. ended 5/31/88): Assets, $3,166,010 (M); expenditures, $128,269, including $25,940 for 12 grants (high: $25,000; low: $240) and $92,556 for 73 grants to individuals (high: $2,000; low: $199).
Purpose and activities: Emphasis on scholarships for southwest LA high school seniors to encourage them to continue their education and to McNeese State University football team; grants also for church support.
Types of support: Student aid.
Limitations: Giving primarily in Sulphur, LA. No grants for endowment funds, or for matching gifts; no loans.
Application information: Scholarship recipients chosen by institutions.
Initial approach: Letter
Copies of proposal: 3
Board meeting date(s): Apr. and Aug.
Write: William B. Lawton, Chair.
Officers and Directors: William B. Lawton, Chair.; Jack E. Lawton, Pres.; Charles W. Carwile, V.P.; Charles M. Drost, Billy Moses, Sam L. Puckett, Allen J. Rhorer.
Employer Identification Number: 726027957

2496
Cahn Family Foundation ⌑
P.O. Box 52005
New Orleans 70152

Incorporated in 1957 in LA.
Donor(s): Dixie Mill Supply Co., Inc.
Foundation type: Independent
Financial data (yr. ended 12/31/88): Assets, $1,909,187 (M); expenditures, $102,461, including $98,400 for 17 grants (high: $50,000; low: $1,000).
Purpose and activities: Emphasis on Jewish welfare funds.
Limitations: Giving primarily in LA.
Application information:
Deadline(s): None
Directors: Emile L. Cahn, Jules L. Cahn.
Employer Identification Number: 726020106

2497
Community Coffee Company, Inc. Foundation ⌑ ☆
4000 South Sherwood Forest Blvd., Suite 502
Baton Rouge 70816

Established in 1988 in LA.
Donor(s): Community Coffee Company, Inc.
Foundation type: Company-sponsored
Financial data (yr. ended 06/30/89): Assets, $25,321 (M); gifts received, $600,000; expenditures, $608,471, including $605,000 for 2 grants (high: $600,000; low: $5,000).
Purpose and activities: Initial year of operation, 1989; support for a university's teacher award program.
Limitations: Giving primarily in LA. No grants to individuals.
Application information: Contributes only to pre-selected organizations. Applications not accepted.
Officers and Trustees: H. Norman Saurage III, Chair.; Robert M. Stuart, Vice-Chair.; Richard S. Dunn, Treas.; Charles E. Lea, Treas.; Wallace F. Armstrong, L. Cary Saurage II.
Employer Identification Number: 721131035

2498
Coughlin-Saunders Foundation, Inc. ⌑
1412 Centre Court, Suite 202
Alexandria 71301-3406 (318) 442-9642

Incorporated in 1950 in LA.
Donor(s): Anne S. Coughlin,† R.R. Saunders, F.H. Coughlin,† J.A. Adams.
Foundation type: Independent
Financial data (yr. ended 11/30/88): Assets, $6,806,326 (M); gifts received, $3,660; expenditures, $472,389, including $463,671 for 43 grants (high: $184,380; low: $50; average: $100-$3,000).
Purpose and activities: Emphasis on higher education and church support; preference given to organizations that have received grants between 1949 and 1983.
Types of support: Professorships, internships, scholarship funds, exchange programs, fellowships, loans, building funds, equipment, emergency funds.
Limitations: Giving primarily in central LA. No grants to individuals, or for matching gifts.
Publications: Application guidelines, program policy statement.
Application information: Application form not required.
Initial approach: Letter
Copies of proposal: 1
Deadline(s): Submit proposal preferably in Jan. or Feb.; deadline Mar. 15
Board meeting date(s): Mar. and Sept.
Final notification: Between Mar. 31 and Oct. 31
Write: R.R. Saunders, Pres.
Officers: R.R. Saunders, Pres.; John Adams, V.P.; Ed Crump, Secy.-Treas.
Directors: Nellie Adams, Homer Adler, Scott Brame, Carolyn Saunders.
Number of staff: None.
Employer Identification Number: 726027641

2499
The M. N. Davidson Foundation ⌑
P.O. Box 1119
Lake Charles 70602-1119

Established in 1948 in TX.
Foundation type: Independent
Financial data (yr. ended 2/29/88): Assets, $1,085,185 (M); gifts received, $1,020; expenditures, $90,404, including $79,179 for 87 grants (high: $30,000; low: $50).
Purpose and activities: Emphasis on Jewish organizations, particularly welfare funds, and higher education.
Application information: Contributes only to pre-selected organizations. Applications not accepted.
Officers and Directors: Simon D. Davidson, Pres.; Melvin T. Davidson, V.P.; Ralph P. Davidson, V.P.; Robert F. Michel, Secy.-Treas.; Gladys S. Brenner, Maurice N. Dannenbaum, Melanie Davidson Rogovein.
Employer Identification Number: 746042120

2500
Thomas B. Favrot Family Fund ☆
400 North Carrollton Ave.
New Orleans 70119-4795 (504) 482-4357

Established in 1985.
Donor(s): Thomas B. Favrot.
Foundation type: Independent
Financial data (yr. ended 12/31/88): Assets, $1,040,451 (M); gifts received, $25,000; expenditures, $50,242, including $46,044 for 53 grants (high: $25,790; low: $15).
Purpose and activities: Giving primarily for schools; minor support also for the community through social services, Presbyterian churches, museums, historic preservation, and other cultural programs.
Limitations: Giving primarily in LA.
Application information: Application form not required.
Copies of proposal: 1
Deadline(s): None
Board meeting date(s): As needed
Write: Thomas B. Favrot, Pres.
Officers: Thomas B. Favrot, Pres.; Aimee F. Favrot, V.P.; Kathryn M. Favrot, V.P.; Michele L. Favrot, V.P.; Kathryn F. Smallpage, V.P.; Julie F. Vickers, V.P.; Lynn Favrot Nolan, Secy.; Thomas B. Favrot, Jr., Treas.
Number of staff: None.
Employer Identification Number: 581611162

2501
Frazier Foundation, Inc. ▼ ⌑
P.O. Box 1175
Minden 71055-1175 (318) 377-0182

Established in 1974 in LA.
Donor(s): J. Walter Frazier.
Foundation type: Independent
Financial data (yr. ended 11/30/88): Assets, $11,706,642 (M); expenditures, $1,481,769, including $1,352,647 for 71 grants (high: $155,500; low: $2,500; average: $5,000-$20,000).
Purpose and activities: Support primarily for the Church of Christ, Christian religious organizations, and educational institutions.
Types of support: Operating budgets.
Limitations: No grants to individuals, or for endowment funds; no loans.
Publications: Application guidelines, 990-PF.
Application information: Application form not required.
Initial approach: Letter or proposal
Copies of proposal: 4
Deadline(s): Submit proposal preferably in Apr. or Oct.; deadlines May 1 and Nov. 1
Board meeting date(s): June and Dec.
Final notification: 2 to 4 weeks
Write: James Walter Frazier, Jr., Pres.
Officers: James Walter Frazier, Jr., Pres.; Rudith A. Drennan, V.P.; Sylvia L. Frazier, Secy.; Altie Don Drennan, Treas.
Number of staff: None.
Employer Identification Number: 720760891

2502
The Ella West Freeman Foundation ⌑
P.O. Box 51299
New Orleans 70151-1299 (504) 568-0378
Additional tel.: (504) 796-9095

Trust established about 1940 in LA.
Donor(s): Richard W. Freeman,† Alfred B. Freeman.†
Foundation type: Independent
Financial data (yr. ended 12/31/88): Assets, $13,672,359 (M); gifts received, $35,393; expenditures, $267,415, including $149,200 for 3 grants (high: $144,000; low: $200).
Purpose and activities: Emphasis on higher education and civic affairs; support also for a museum.
Types of support: Annual campaigns, capital campaigns, endowment funds.
Limitations: Giving primarily in the greater New Orleans, LA, area. No grants to individuals.
Application information: Application form not required.
Initial approach: Proposal
Copies of proposal: 5
Deadline(s): None
Board meeting date(s): Approximately every 4 months beginning in spring
Write: Richard W. Freeman, Jr., Chair.
Trustees: Richard W. Freeman, Jr., Chair.; Louis M. Freeman, Mrs. Montine M. Freeman, Tina F. Woollam.
Number of staff: None.
Employer Identification Number: 726018322

2503
German Protestant Orphan Asylum Association
5342 St. Charles Ave.
New Orleans 70115 (504) 895-2361

Established in 1979 in LA.
Foundation type: Independent
Financial data (yr. ended 11/30/89): Assets, $6,137,599 (M); expenditures, $279,712, including $227,194 for 18 grants (high: $35,931; low: $1,980).
Purpose and activities: Giving for social services, including child welfare, family services, and youth programs; support also for medical purposes.
Types of support: Operating budgets, general purposes, equipment, matching funds, seed money.
Limitations: Giving limited to LA.
Publications: Annual report (including application guidelines).
Application information:
Initial approach: Letter
Copies of proposal: 12
Deadline(s): Dec., Mar., June, and Sept.
Board meeting date(s): Jan., Apr., July, and Sept.
Write: Everett T. Aultman, Exec. Dir.
Officers: George J. Mayer,* Pres.; P.W. Bohne,* V.P.; J. Gary Haller,* Secy.; Robert L. Hattier,* Treas.; Everett T. Aultman, Exec. Dir.
Directors:* Charles Bennett, Albert J. Flettrich, Walter C. Flower III, Charles B. Mayer.
Number of staff: 1 part-time professional; 1 part-time support.
Employer Identification Number: 720423621

2504
Jerome S. Glazer Foundation, Inc. ⌑
P.O. Box 50867
New Orleans 70150

Established in 1961 in LA.
Foundation type: Independent
Financial data (yr. ended 12/31/87): Assets, $1,849,691 (M); expenditures, $86,837, including $83,380 for 54 grants (high: $10,000; low: $100).
Purpose and activities: Emphasis on Jewish organizations, including welfare funds, higher and secondary education, and civic affairs.
Application information: Contributes only to pre-selected organizations. Applications not accepted.
Officers: Jerome S. Glazer, Pres.; Charles Bennett, V.P.; Bradford A. Glazer, Secy.-Treas.
Employer Identification Number: 726020850

2505
Goldring Family Foundation ⌑
809 Jefferson Hwy.
Jefferson 70121

Incorporated in 1955 in LA.
Donor(s): Magnolia Liquor Co., Inc., Sazerac Co., Inc., Great Southern Liquor Co., Inc., N. Goldring Corp.
Foundation type: Independent
Financial data (yr. ended 11/30/88): Assets, $6,198,089 (M); gifts received, $100,000; expenditures, $413,478, including $384,640 for 29 grants (high: $200,000; low: $100).
Purpose and activities: Emphasis on Jewish welfare funds and education; some support also for health agencies and community funds.
Limitations: Giving primarily in LA.
Application information: Application form not required.
Deadline(s): None
Officer: Stephen Goldring, Pres.
Employer Identification Number: 726022666

2506
The Matilda Geddings Gray Foundation ⌑
714 Esplanade Ave.
New Orleans 70116 (504) 581-5396

Established in 1969 in LA.
Donor(s): Matilda Geddings Gray,† Matilda Gray Stream.
Foundation type: Operating
Financial data (yr. ended 10/31/88): Assets, $6,541,733 (M); expenditures, $71,201, including $14,500 for 2 grants (high: $9,500; low: $5,000).
Purpose and activities: A private operating foundation that works with local universities to promote art exhibits and the study of art and art history at educational institutions throughout LA, especially in the fields of graphic, literary, and plastic arts; also supports agricultural education.
Types of support: Professorships.
Limitations: Giving primarily in LA.
Application information: Application form not required.
Initial approach: Letter
Deadline(s): None
Write: Steven Carter
Officers and Trustees: Matilda Gray Stream, Pres.; Harold H. Stream III, Secy.; Edward M. Carmouche, Nolan Miller, Sandra Stream Miller.
Employer Identification Number: 237072892

2507
The Helis Foundation ⌑
912 Whitney Bldg.
New Orleans 70130 (504) 523-1831

Incorporated in 1955 in LA.
Donor(s): Members of the William G. Helis family.
Foundation type: Independent
Financial data (yr. ended 12/31/88): Assets, $10,639,490 (M); expenditures, $520,996, including $500,825 for 40 grants (high: $100,000; low: $500).
Purpose and activities: Giving for music and the arts, community funds, religious associations, civic affairs, youth agencies, and higher education.
Limitations: Giving primarily in LA. No grants to individuals.
Application information:
Initial approach: Letter
Deadline(s): None
Write: David A. Kerstein, V.P.
Officers and Trustees: David A. Kerstein, V.P.; Bettie Conley Helis, Virginia Helis, Esther Helis Henry, Nathan Wallfisch.
Member: Cassandra Marie Helis.
Employer Identification Number: 726020536

2508
Hever Foundation ⌑ ☆
201 St. Charles Ave., Suite 3300
New Orleans 70170

Established in 1981.
Donor(s): Virginia D. Kock.
Foundation type: Independent
Financial data (yr. ended 11/30/88): Assets, $1,458,880 (M); gifts received, $250,943; expenditures, $69,352, including $56,300 for 17 grants (high: $25,000; low: $250).
Purpose and activities: Support for education, a symphony orchestra, a zoo, a wildlife institute, and health.
Limitations: Giving primarily in New Orleans, LA. No grants to individuals.
Application information: Contributes only to pre-selected organizations. Applications not accepted.
Directors: Virginia D. Kock, Thomas B. Lemann, George Montgomery.
Employer Identification Number: 720926451

2509
Heymann Foundation ⌑ ☆
433 Jefferson St.
Lafayette 70501-7013
Application address: P.O. Box 3327, Lafayette, LA 70502; Tel.: (318) 232-4343

Established in 1974.
Donor(s): Jacqueline Cohn.†
Foundation type: Independent
Financial data (yr. ended 5/31/89): Assets, $143,075 (M); gifts received, $134,693; expenditures, $173,479, including $168,329 for 70 grants (high: $47,180; low: $25).

Purpose and activities: Giving primarily to a university; support also for cultural programs, and a community fund.
Types of support: General purposes.
Limitations: Giving primarily in LA. No grants to individuals.
Application information: Application form not required.
Deadline(s): None
Write: Herbert Heymann, Pres.
Officer: Herbert Heymann, Pres.
Employer Identification Number: 237397293

2510
Mr. and Mrs. Jimmy Heymann Special Account ⌑
1201 Canal St.
New Orleans 70112

Incorporated in 1958 in LA.
Donor(s): Jimmy Heymann, Mrs. May H. Wolf.
Foundation type: Independent
Financial data (yr. ended 12/31/88): Assets, $3,109,972 (M); expenditures, $150,685, including $145,741 for 64 grants (high: $37,125; low: $10).
Purpose and activities: Giving for education, a community fund, health services, religious activities, youth activities, and cultural programs.
Limitations: Giving primarily in LA.
Application information: Contributes only to pre-selected organizations. Applications not accepted.
Officers: Janice Heymann, Pres.; Jerry Heymann, V.P. and Secy.-Treas.
Directors: Marion Levy Sontheimer, Maurice Sontheimer.
Employer Identification Number: 726019367

2511
Heymann-Wolf Foundation ⌑
1201 Canal St.
New Orleans 70112

Incorporated in 1947 in LA.
Donor(s): Leon Heymann,† Mrs. Leon Heymann,† Leon M. Wolf,† Mrs. May H. Wolf, Jimmy Heymann, Mrs. Jimmy Heymann, Krauss Co., Ltd.
Foundation type: Independent
Financial data (yr. ended 12/31/88): Assets, $3,190,217 (M); expenditures, $117,388, including $86,800 for 20 grants (high: $28,000; low: $50).
Purpose and activities: Giving for a university, a community fund, hospitals, and cultural programs.
Limitations: Giving primarily in LA.
Application information: Contributes only to pre-selected organizations. Applications not accepted.
Officers: Jerry Heymann, Pres.; Marjorie Heymann, V.P.; Mrs. Jimmy Heymann, Treas.
Employer Identification Number: 726019363

2512
D. H. Holmes Foundation ⌑
3301 Veterans Blvd.
Metairie 70002

Established in 1965.
Donor(s): D.H. Holmes Co., Ltd.
Foundation type: Company-sponsored
Financial data (yr. ended 7/31/88): Assets, $5,390 (M); gifts received, $102,500; expenditures, $102,767, including $102,767 for 16 grants (high: $40,000; low: $1,100).
Purpose and activities: Emphasis on community funds, music, education, and nature centers and parks.
Types of support: Building funds.
Limitations: Giving limited to areas of company trading, including southern LA, Jackson, MS, Mobile, AL and Pensacola, FL.
Application information:
Initial approach: Letter
Deadline(s): None
Write: James E. Ammon, Exec. V.P. - Finance
Officers and Directors: Donald W. Johnston, Chair. and Pres.; James E. Ammon, Exec. V.P. - Finance and Secy.; John F. Bricker, Robert R. Broadbent, Thomas H. Hicks, Alden J. LaBorde, Harry McCall, Jr., Donald J. Nalty, Frank E. Schmidt, Robert G. Sutherland.
Employer Identification Number: 726028216

2513
Huie-Dellmon Trust ⌑
P.O. Box 330
Alexandria 71301

Foundation type: Independent
Financial data (yr. ended 12/31/88): Assets, $1,518,162 (M); expenditures, $72,844, including $64,000 for 17 grants (high: $11,500; low: $500).
Purpose and activities: Emphasis on hospitals, Protestant giving, and secondary education.
Types of support: Operating budgets, building funds, equipment, research.
Limitations: Giving primarily in central LA. No grants to individuals.
Application information: Application form not required.
Initial approach: Letter
Write: Richard L. Crowell, Trustee
Trustee: Richard L. Crowell.
Employer Identification Number: 720809684

2514
Ed E. and Gladys Hurley Foundation
c/o Premier Bank of Shreveport
P.O. Box 21116
Shreveport 71154 (318) 226-2211

Trust established in 1954 in LA.
Donor(s): Ed E. Hurley.†
Foundation type: Independent
Financial data (yr. ended 12/31/88): Assets, $2,721,447 (M); qualifying distributions, $141,491, including $112,536 for loans to individuals.
Purpose and activities: Awards college loans to students residing in AR, LA, and TX.
Types of support: Student loans.
Limitations: Giving limited to LA, AR, and TX.
Application information: Application form required.
Deadline(s): May 31
Write: Alicia T. Jackson
Trustee: Premier Bank of Shreveport.
Employer Identification Number: 726018854

2515
Eugenie and Joseph Jones Family Foundation ⌑
835 Union St., Suite 333
New Orleans 70112 (504) 581-2424

Incorporated in 1955 in LA.
Donor(s): Joseph M. Jones,† Eugenie P. Jones.†
Foundation type: Independent
Financial data (yr. ended 6/30/89): Assets, $6,576,267 (M); expenditures, $298,386, including $226,800 for 36 grants (high: $75,000; low: $100).
Purpose and activities: Giving for higher education; grants also for church support and a community fund.
Types of support: Annual campaigns, building funds, equipment, endowment funds, matching funds, scholarship funds, professorships, fellowships.
Limitations: Giving primarily in LA. No grants to individuals, or for land acquisition, operating budgets, continuing support, special projects, research, publications, conferences, start-up or emergency funds, or deficit financing; no loans.
Application information: Contributes only to pre-selected organizations. Applications not accepted.
Board meeting date(s): July and Dec.
Final notification: 6 months
Officers and Trustees: Eugenie Jones Huger, Pres.; Susan Jones Gundlach, V.P.; Joseph Merrick Jones, Jr., V.P.; Killian L. Huger, Jr., Secy.-Treas.; George Denegre, Elaine Douglass Jones, A.J. Waechter, Jr.
Number of staff: None.
Employer Identification Number: 720507534

2516
Keller Family Foundation ⌑
909 International Bldg.
611 Gravier St.
New Orleans 70130

Trust established in 1949 in LA.
Donor(s): Charles Keller, Jr., Rosa F. Keller.
Foundation type: Independent
Financial data (yr. ended 12/31/86): Assets, $1,586,473 (M); expenditures, $94,827, including $89,210 for 29 grants (high: $16,000; low: $100).
Purpose and activities: Giving for public policy organizations and higher education; support also for cultural programs, community development, a community fund, and a secondary school.
Limitations: Giving primarily in LA.
Trustees: Charles Keller, Jr., Chair.; Julie F. Breitmeyer, Rosa F. Keller, Caroline K. Loughlin, Mary K. Zervigon.
Employer Identification Number: 726027426

2517
LaNasa-Greco Foundation ⌑
3201 Ridgelake Dr.
Metairie 70002-4992 (504) 834-4226

Established in 1961 in LA.
Foundation type: Independent
Financial data (yr. ended 12/31/88): Assets, $1,810,873 (M); expenditures, $102,893, including $80,000 for 5 grants (high: $47,500; low: $7,500).

Purpose and activities: Support primarily for higher education; contributions also for music and health.
Types of support: Scholarship funds.
Limitations: Giving primarily in New Orleans, LA.
Application information: Contributes only to pre-selected organizations. Applications not accepted.
Write: Sarah LaNasa, Pres.
Officers: Sarah LaNasa, Pres.; C. Ellis Henican, V.P.; Sidney M. Rihner, Secy.-Treas.
Employer Identification Number: 726028040

2518
Milton M. Latter Educational and Charitable Foundation ¤
1010 Common St., Suite 3100
New Orleans 70112

Established in 1947 in LA.
Foundation type: Independent
Financial data (yr. ended 12/31/88): Assets, $1,385,577 (M); expenditures, $270,306, including $258,800 for 26 grants (high: $170,000; low: $100).
Purpose and activities: Emphasis on community funds, higher education, Jewish organizations, and hospitals.
Limitations: Giving primarily in New Orleans, LA.
Application information: Contributes only to pre-selected organizations. Applications not accepted.
Officers: Shirley L. Kaufmann, Pres.; L.H. Schlesinger, 1st V.P.; S.R. Rose, V.P.; D.K. Stirton, Secy.-Treas.
Employer Identification Number: 726028027

2519
Libby-Dufour Fund ¤
321 Hibernia Bank Bldg., Suite 202
New Orleans 70112

Incorporated in 1952 in LA.
Donor(s): Edith Libby Dufour.†
Foundation type: Independent
Financial data (yr. ended 5/31/87): Assets, $6,066,559 (M); expenditures, $385,726, including $356,500 for 22 grants (high: $50,000; low: $1,000).
Purpose and activities: Emphasis on Christian charities, including support for churches, church-related education, and Christian welfare funds.
Limitations: Giving limited to the New Orleans, LA, area. No grants to individuals, or for endowment funds, or operating budgets.
Application information:
Initial approach: Proposal
Copies of proposal: 1
Deadline(s): None
Board meeting date(s): Quarterly
Write: Eben Hardie, Pres.
Officers and Trustees: Eben Hardie, Pres.; E. James Kock, Jr., Secy.; Robert P. Lockett, Jr., Treas.; E.T. Colton, Jr., Jackson P. Ducournau.
Employer Identification Number: 726027406

2520
The Louisiana Land and Exploration Company Foundation ¤
P.O. Box 60350
New Orleans 70160

Established in 1979 in LA.
Donor(s): The Louisiana Land and Exploration Co.
Foundation type: Company-sponsored
Financial data (yr. ended 12/31/88): Assets, $3,157,934 (M); expenditures, $637,174, including $509,425 for 93 grants (high: $105,000; low: $125) and $127,178 for 102 employee matching gifts (high: $10,600; low: $50).
Purpose and activities: Support primarily for higher education, including matching gifts and a scholarship program for dependents of LL&E employees administered by selected colleges and universities; support also for community funds, social services, and health agencies.
Types of support: Employee matching gifts, employee-related scholarships.
Limitations: Giving primarily in LA.
Application information: Application form required for scholarships.
Initial approach: Letter
Write: Carolyn Randall, Contribs. Coord.
Officers and Directors: H. Leighton Steward, Pres.; Richard A. Bachmann, V.P. and Secy.-Treas.; John F. Greene.
Employer Identification Number: 720866443

2521
The Lupin Foundation
3715 Prytania St., Suite 403
New Orleans 70115 (504) 897-6125

Incorporated in 1981 in LA.
Foundation type: Independent
Financial data (yr. ended 12/31/88): Assets, $20,091,744 (M); expenditures, $1,311,540, including $833,000 for 58 grants (high: $100,000; low: $400).
Purpose and activities: Giving for education, civic affairs, community funds, religious associations, medical research, and cultural programs.
Types of support: Equipment, research, scholarship funds, special projects, matching funds, continuing support, general purposes, program-related investments, seed money.
Limitations: Giving primarily in LA. No grants to individuals; no loans.
Publications: Application guidelines.
Application information: Application form required.
Initial approach: Brief proposal (not exceeding 6 pages)
Copies of proposal: 1
Deadline(s): 3 weeks before board meetings
Board meeting date(s): 9 times yearly
Final notification: 2 weeks
Write: Lori Wesolowski, Coord.
Officers and Directors: Arnold M. Lupin, M.D., Pres.; Samuel Lupin, M.D., V.P.; Charles C. Mary, Jr., M.D., Secy.; E. Ralph Lupin, M.D., Treas.; Louis Levy II, M.D., Jay S. Lupin, M.D., Louis Lupin, Suzanne Stokar.
Number of staff: 1 full-time support.
Employer Identification Number: 720940770

2522
The Magale Foundation, Inc. ¤
Box 1468
Shreveport 71164 (318) 226-2382
Application address: Premier Bank, N.A., P.O. Box 21116, Shreveport LA 71154

Incorporated in 1957 in LA.
Donor(s): John F. Magale.
Foundation type: Independent
Financial data (yr. ended 11/30/89): Assets, $1,486,325 (M); expenditures, $130,719, including $80,000 for 16 grants (high: $15,000; low: $1,500) and $23,500 for 25 loans to individuals.
Purpose and activities: Grants for higher education, social services, and the performing arts, principally in LA and AR; loans are also made to students who reside in AR, LA, and TX.
Types of support: Student loans.
Limitations: Giving limited to residents of LA, TX, and AR. No grants to individuals.
Application information: Application form required.
Initial approach: Letter
Deadline(s): Apr. 1
Write: Mary J. Fain, V.P. and Trust Officer, Premier Bank, N.A.
Officers and Directors:* Joanna Magale,* Pres.; T.A. Monroe,* V.P.; Mary J. Fain,* Secy.; Premier Bank, N.A.,* Treas.; Nomer Greer, Hugh Lorgino.
Employer Identification Number: 726025096

2523
Agnes T. Maguire Trust ¤
c/o Louisiana Natinoal Bank, Trust Dept.
P.O. Box 1511
Baton Rouge 70821 (504) 389-4251

Established in 1953 in LA.
Foundation type: Independent
Financial data (yr. ended 12/31/87): Assets, $1,298,973 (M); qualifying distributions, $117,300, including $117,300 for loans.
Purpose and activities: Support for education through loans.
Types of support: Loans.
Application information:
Deadline(s): None
Trustees: Fr. John Spriggs, Fr. Frank Uter.
Employer Identification Number: 726021532

2524
Marnie Foundation ¤ ☆
P.O. Box 60600
New Orleans 70160-0600

Established in 1962.
Foundation type: Independent
Financial data (yr. ended 6/30/89): Assets, $160,864 (M); expenditures, $105,037, including $103,000 for 9 grants (high: $20,000; low: $10,000).
Purpose and activities: Giving primarily for Christian organizations, including theological educational institutions; support also for an international agriculture program, hospitals, low-income housing, and higher education.
Limitations: No grants to individuals.

Application information: Contributes only to pre-selected organizations. Applications not accepted.
Officers: Margaret G. Weeks, Pres.; Louise M. Row, V.P.; Violet Weeks Miller, Secy.
Employer Identification Number: 726022310

2525
Leonie & Gus Mayer Foundation ⌑
c/o Whitney National Bank of New Orleans
P.O. Box 61260
New Orleans 70161

Established in 1957 in LA.
Foundation type: Independent
Financial data (yr. ended 3/31/89): Assets, $1,562,942 (M); expenditures, $122,003, including $110,910 for 17 grants (high: $56,560; low: $555).
Purpose and activities: Giving for education, including a university, health agencies, hospitals, and social services.
Limitations: Giving primarily in New Orleans, LA.
Application information: Contributes only to pre-selected organizations. Applications not accepted.
Trustee: Whitney National Bank of New Orleans.
Employer Identification Number: 237418811

2526
J. Edgar Monroe Foundation (1976)
228 St. Charles St., Suite 1402
New Orleans 70130 (504) 529-3539

Established in 1976 in LA.
Donor(s): J. Edgar Monroe.
Foundation type: Independent
Financial data (yr. ended 12/31/89): Assets, $7,500,000 (M); expenditures, $325,000, including $325,000 for 30 grants (high: $75,000; low: $25; average: $25-$1,000).
Purpose and activities: Giving for higher education, social services, Christian organizations, hospitals, hospices, the arts, and historic preservation.
Types of support: Annual campaigns, building funds, capital campaigns, emergency funds, equipment, renovation projects, research.
Limitations: Giving primarily in LA.
Application information:
Write: Robert J. Monroe, Trustee
Officers and Trustees:* J. Edgar Monroe,* Pres.; William F. Finegan,* V.P.; J. Percy Monroe, Jr.,* V.P.; Robert J. Monroe,* Secy.-Treas.
Number of staff: 1 full-time support.
Employer Identification Number: 720784059

2527
The Morgan City Fund ⌑
1316 Federal Ave.
Morgan City 70380

Incorporated in 1955 in LA.
Donor(s): Byrnes M. Young.†
Foundation type: Independent
Financial data (yr. ended 12/31/88): Assets, $6,205,451 (M); gifts received, $90,000; expenditures, $347,447, including $254,500 for 15 grants (high: $123,870; low: $300) and $500 for 2 grants to individuals of $250 each.
Purpose and activities: Emphasis on parks, landscaping, and recreational facilities; support also for a public library, secondary schools, primarily for scholarship programs, and a hospital.
Types of support: Scholarship funds, student aid.
Limitations: Giving limited to Morgan City, LA.
Application information: Contributes only to pre-selected organizations. Applications not accepted.
Officers and Directors: C.R. Brownell, Jr., M.D., Pres.; Eugene B. Garber, V.P.; Anna Pearl Squires, Secy.; Charles F. Sanber, Treas.
Employer Identification Number: 726029365

2528
The Greater New Orleans Foundation
(Formerly The Greater New Orleans Regional Foundation)
2515 Canal St., Suite 401
New Orleans 70119 (504) 822-4906

Established in 1924 in LA, as the Community Chest; became a community foundation in 1983.
Foundation type: Community
Financial data (yr. ended 12/31/89): Assets, $10,462,411 (M); qualifying distributions, $480,210, including $480,210 for grants (average: $500-$10,000).
Purpose and activities: Giving for health, social services, cultural programs, and education.
Types of support: Emergency funds, technical assistance, seed money, special projects, matching funds, equipment.
Limitations: Giving limited to southeast LA, including the greater New Orleans area. No support for religion. No grants to individuals, or for operating budgets, annual fund campaigns, continuing support, endowment funds, building funds, or deficit financing.
Publications: Annual report, application guidelines, program policy statement, newsletter, informational brochure.
Application information: Application form required.
Initial approach: Proposal
Copies of proposal: 2
Deadline(s): None
Board meeting date(s): Quarterly
Write: Patricia C. Mason, Exec. Dir.
Officers: Harry J. Blumenthal, Jr.,* Chair.; Mrs. J. Thomas Lewis,* Vice-Chair.; Mrs. Morris E. Burka, Secy.; William F. Finegan, Treas.; Patricia C. Mason, Exec. Dir.
Trustees:* Ian Arnof, Emmett W. Bashful, M.D., Philip Claverle, David Conroy, Moise Dennery, Thomas J. Egan, D. Blair Favrot, R. Thomas Fetters, Norman Francis, Tina Freeman, Mrs. Ronald French, Mrs. Robert Haspel, Mrs. Francis E. Lauricella, Mrs. P. Roussel Norman, G. Frank Purvis, Mrs. Roger T. Stone, Charles C. Teamer, Sr., Robert Young.
Number of staff: 1 part-time professional; 1 full-time support; 1 part-time support.
Employer Identification Number: 720408921

2529
Parkside Foundation ⌑
201 St. Charles Ave.
New Orleans 70170

Established in 1961 in LA.
Donor(s): Thomas B. Lemann, Stephen B. Lemann.
Foundation type: Independent
Financial data (yr. ended 12/31/88): Assets, $1,312,163 (M); gifts received, $104,375; expenditures, $207,029, including $200,134 for 69 grants (high: $23,000; low: $100).
Purpose and activities: Giving primarily for higher education, cultural programs, and Jewish welfare.
Limitations: Giving primarily in LA, with emphasis on New Orleans.
Application information: Contributes only to pre-selected organizations. Applications not accepted.
Officers: Thomas B. Lemann, Pres.; Stephen B. Lemann, V.P.; Juanita T. Herndon, Secy.-Treas.
Employer Identification Number: 726019058

2530
Willis & Mildred Pellerin Foundation ⌑
c/o A.A. Harman & Co.
311 Baronne St., 1st Fl.
New Orleans 70112 (504) 586-0581

Established in 1975 in LA.
Foundation type: Independent
Financial data (yr. ended 05/31/89): Assets, $1,205,235 (M); expenditures, $65,283, including $54,800 for 86 grants to individuals (high: $600; low: $300).
Purpose and activities: Scholarships for residents of LA who are enrolled in a LA college or university; one-half of the grant to be repaid.
Types of support: Student aid, student loans.
Limitations: Giving limited to LA residents.
Application information: Application form required.
Initial approach: Letter
Deadline(s): 180 days preceding beginning of school term
Write: Trustees
Trustees: Gerald Foret, Paul Larocca, Stanley McDermott, John McGrath, Norvin L. Pellerin, A.W. Walsdorf.
Employer Identification Number: 510166877

2531
Irene W. & C. B. Pennington Foundation ⌑
c/o Robert R. Casey
P.O. Box 1267
Baton Rouge 70821

Established in 1982 in LA.
Donor(s): C.B. Pennington, Irene W. Pennington.
Foundation type: Independent
Financial data (yr. ended 12/31/88): Assets, $10,143,671 (M); gifts received, $6,000,000; expenditures, $214,141, including $205,126 for 17 grants (high: $102,626; low: $500).
Purpose and activities: Giving for a YMCA and other social service and youth organizations.
Types of support: General purposes.

Limitations: Giving primarily in LA, with emphasis on Baton Rouge. No grants to individuals.
Application information: Contributes only to pre-selected organizations. Applications not accepted.
Write: C.B. Pennington, Trustee
Trustees: R.R. Casey, C.B. Pennington, Irene W. Pennington, W.W. Williams, Premier Bank, N.A.
Employer Identification Number: 720938097

2532
Poindexter Foundation, Inc. ⌑
P.O. Box 1692
Shreveport 71165 (318) 226-1040

Established in 1960.
Donor(s): R.D. Poindexter, Superior Iron Works & Supply Co., Inc.
Foundation type: Independent
Financial data (yr. ended 11/30/88): Assets, $1,552,757 (M); expenditures, $86,240, including $75,500 for 44 grants (high: $15,000; low: $500).
Purpose and activities: Giving to youth, health agencies, and higher education.
Types of support: General purposes, building funds.
Limitations: Giving primarily in LA.
Application information:
Initial approach: Letter
Deadline(s): None
Write: Roy W. James, Jr., Secy.-Treas.
Officers: Mrs. R.D. Poindexter, Pres.; John M. Shuey, V.P.; Roy W. James, Jr., Secy.-Treas.
Employer Identification Number: 726019174

2533
Powers Foundation, Inc. ⌑
c/o Heard, McElroy & Vestal
P.O. Box 1607
Shreveport 71165 (318) 221-0151

Established in 1967 in LA.
Donor(s): Gussie N. Power.†
Foundation type: Independent
Financial data (yr. ended 7/31/87): Assets, $2,911,582 (M); expenditures, $175,626, including $151,770 for 20 grants (high: $25,000; low: $1,000).
Purpose and activities: Support for social services and secondary and higher education.
Limitations: Giving limited to Shreveport and Bossier County, LA.
Application information:
Initial approach: Letter or proposal
Deadline(s): None
Write: C. Cody White, Jr., Pres.
Officers: C. Cody White, Jr., Pres.; Judith C. Burt, V.P.; Sara Margaret White, V.P.; Charles E. Vestal, Secy.; James E. Burt III, Treas.
Employer Identification Number: 756080974

2534
Premier Foundation, Inc.
(Formerly First National Bank Foundation)
c/o Premier Bank, N.A.
P.O. Box 21116
Shreveport 71154-0001

Incorporated in 1955 in LA.
Donor(s): Premier Bank, N.A.
Foundation type: Company-sponsored
Financial data (yr. ended 6/30/88): Assets, $664,410 (M); gifts received, $75,000; expenditures, $204,620, including $193,014 for 66 grants (high: $40,624; low: $25).
Purpose and activities: Giving for community development, cultural programs, and a community fund; support also for higher and secondary education, public policy organizations, and health agencies.
Limitations: Giving primarily in Shreveport, LA.
Application information: Application form not required.
Deadline(s): None
Write: Carol Fandefur, Secy.
Officers and Directors: Hugh J. Watson, Pres.; Jerry D. Boughton, V.P.; Don Updegraff, V.P.; Carol Fandefur, Secy.; Joseph M. Cantanese, Treas.
Employer Identification Number: 726022876

2535
Reily Foundation ⌑
640 Magazine St.
New Orleans 70130 (504) 524-6131

Established in 1962.
Donor(s): Wm. B. Reily & Co., Inc.
Foundation type: Company-sponsored
Financial data (yr. ended 12/31/87): Assets, $3,543,348 (M); gifts received, $300,000; expenditures, $359,952, including $354,501 for 39 grants (high: $50,000; low: $250).
Purpose and activities: Giving for higher education and organizations which encourage civic responsibility.
Limitations: Giving primarily in the metropolitan New Orleans, LA, area.
Application information:
Initial approach: Proposal
Deadline(s): None
Write: H. Eustis Reily, Pres.
Officers and Directors:* H. Eustis Reily,* Pres.; Robert D. Reily,* V.P.; Joan Coulter, Secy.-Treas.; William B. Reily III.
Employer Identification Number: 726029179

2536
Edward G. Schlieder Educational Foundation
431 Gravier St., Suite 400
New Orleans 70130 (504) 581-6084

Incorporated in 1945 in LA.
Donor(s): Edward G. Schlieder.†
Foundation type: Independent
Financial data (yr. ended 12/31/88): Assets, $16,179,375 (M); expenditures, $1,033,204, including $916,492 for 17 grants (high: $120,000; low: $18,192; average: $12,000-$30,000).
Purpose and activities: To aid schools, colleges, and universities; grants largely to universities for medical research.
Types of support: Research, equipment, capital campaigns.
Limitations: Giving limited to educational institutions in LA. No grants to individuals, or for general purposes, building or endowment funds, scholarships, fellowships, or operating budgets; no loans.
Publications: Annual report.
Application information: Application form not required.
Initial approach: Letter
Copies of proposal: 3
Deadline(s): Submit proposal preferably in Feb.; no set deadline
Board meeting date(s): As required
Final notification: 30 to 45 days
Write: Blanc A. Parker, Exec. Consultant
Officers: Donald J. Nalty,* Pres.; George G. Westfeldt, Jr.,* Secy.-Treas.; Blanc A. Parker, Exec. Consultant.
Directors:* Morgan L. Shaw, Thomas D. Westfeldt.
Number of staff: 1 part-time professional; 1 part-time support.
Employer Identification Number: 720408974

2537
Scott Foundation, Inc. ⌑
P.O. Box 4948
Monroe 71201

Incorporated in LA.
Foundation type: Independent
Financial data (yr. ended 7/31/88): Assets, $1,815,486 (M); gifts received, $47,000; expenditures, $40,644, including $37,490 for 44 grants (high: $6,963; low: $10).
Purpose and activities: Emphasis on higher education, churches, and youth agencies.
Limitations: Giving limited to northern LA.
Application information: Application form not required.
Deadline(s): None
Write: T.H. Scott, Pres.
Officers: T.H. Scott, Pres.; G.J. Bershen, Secy.-Treas.
Trustees: Betty Scott Cummings, Mayme P. Scott, T.H. Scott, Jr.
Employer Identification Number: 726027563

2538
The Tom B. & Flora Shearman Foundation ⌑ ☆
327 Broad St.
Lake Charles 70602

Donor(s): Thomas B. Shearman, Sr.
Foundation type: Independent
Financial data (yr. ended 3/31/88): Assets, $842,278 (M); expenditures, $225,349, including $221,000 for 3 grants (high: $219,000; low: $1,000).
Purpose and activities: Support primarily for higher education.
Limitations: Giving primarily in Lake Charles and New Orleans, LA. No grants to individuals.
Application information: Contributes only to pre-selected organizations. Applications not accepted.
Trustees: Edwin K. Hunter, Thomas B. Shearman, Sr., Thomas B. Shearman, Jr., W. Hugh Shearman, Maynard Woodhatch, Otray J. Woods, Jr.
Employer Identification Number: 720920599

2539
The Community Foundation of Shreveport-Bossier
401 Edwards St., Suite 1520
Shreveport 71101 (318) 221-0582

Incorporated in 1961 in LA.
Foundation type: Community
Financial data (yr. ended 12/31/88): Assets, $8,499,139 (M); gifts received, $606,241; expenditures, $860,744, including $691,920 for 41 grants (high: $100,000; low: $169).
Purpose and activities: Grants largely to health services, welfare, youth agencies, higher and other education, and cultural programs.
Types of support: Special projects, equipment, building funds, matching funds, scholarship funds, seed money, conferences and seminars, operating budgets, publications, renovation projects, research.
Limitations: Giving limited to the Caddo and Bossier parishes, LA. No grants to individuals.
Publications: Annual report, application guidelines.
Application information: Application form required.
Initial approach: Letter
Copies of proposal: 8
Deadline(s): Mar. 1, June 1, and Sept. 1
Board meeting date(s): Mar., Apr., July, and Oct.
Final notification: Immediately after board meetings
Write: Carol Emanuel, Exec. Dir.
Officers: Margaret W. Kinsey, Chair.; W.C. Raspberry, Jr., Vice-Chair.; Joseph L. Hargrove, Secy.; Charles Ellis Brown, Treas.
Directors: William C. Peatross, Louis C. Pendleton, Donald P. Weiss.
Trustee Banks: Commercial National Bank in Shreveport, First National Bank of Shreveport, Pioneer Bank & Trust Co.
Number of staff: 1 full-time professional; 1 part-time support.
Employer Identification Number: 726022365

2540
Albert & Miriam Sklar Foundation ⌑
2925 Mansfield Rd.
Shreveport 71103-3613

Established in 1957 in LA.
Foundation type: Independent
Financial data (yr. ended 9/30/88): Assets, $1,031,645 (M); expenditures, $54,867, including $52,564 for 21 grants (high: $25,000; low: $200).
Purpose and activities: Giving for Jewish organizations, higher education, and the arts.
Officers: Albert Sklar, Pres.; Howard F. Sklar, V.P.; Miriam M. Sklar, Secy.-Treas.
Employer Identification Number: 726017597

2541
Percival Stern Foundation ⌑
3901 Tulane Ave.
New Orleans 70119

Established in 1946 in LA.
Donor(s): Percival Stern,† Elsie Kahn Stern.
Foundation type: Independent
Financial data (yr. ended 12/31/86): Assets, $3,454,449 (M); expenditures, $317,585, including $80,306 for 5 grants (high: $78,206; low: $100).
Purpose and activities: Giving for higher education.
Officers and Trustees: Walter L. Brown, Jr., Pres.; Perry S. Brown, V.P.; Louis G. Lemle, Secy.-Treas.; Mrs. Walter L. Brown, Clarence Scheps, William Stein, Jr.
Employer Identification Number: 720545551

2542
Erich Sternberg Foundation ☆
1500 Main St.
P.O. Box 91102
Baton Rouge 70821-9102

Foundation type: Independent
Financial data (yr. ended 12/31/88): Assets, $19,601 (M); gifts received, $252,500; expenditures, $256,662, including $256,597 for 161 grants (high: $20,000; low: $10).
Purpose and activities: Giving primarily for Jewish welfare funds and other Jewish organizations; support also for social service and youth agencies, higher and other education, and the arts and other cultural programs.
Limitations: Giving limited to LA and FL. No grants to individuals.
Application information: Contributes to pre-selected organizations. Applications not accepted.
Officers and Trustees:* Mary Ann Sternberg,* Pres.; Insa Abraham,* V.P.; Donna W. Sternberg,* V.P.; Hans J. Sternberg,* V.P.; Josef Sternberg,* V.P.; Donald H. Bell,* Secy.; Brian Kendrick,* Treas.; Thomas Hallin, William Hamblin.
Employer Identification Number: 581731926

2543
Virlane Foundation
1055 St. Charles Ave.
New Orleans 70130

Incorporated in 1958 in LA.
Foundation type: Operating
Financial data (yr. ended 09/30/89): Assets, $4,847,771 (M); expenditures, $100,000, including $85,250 for 18 grants (high: $20,000; low: $250).
Purpose and activities: A private operating foundation; emphasis on maintaining a sculpture plaza to encourage and foster the creation of art and sculpture; grants also for welfare funds, cultural programs, and community funds.
Types of support: Annual campaigns, capital campaigns, continuing support.
Limitations: Giving primarily in LA. No grants to individuals.
Application information: Contributes only to pre-selected organizations. Applications not accepted.
Officers and Directors:* Jac Stich,* Pres.; Virginia F. Besthoff,* Secy.-Treas.
Number of staff: None.
Employer Identification Number: 726019440

2544
West Foundation, Inc. ⌑ ☆
P.O. Box 1336
Minden 71058-1336

Foundation type: Independent
Financial data (yr. ended 12/31/88): Assets, $1,009,919 (M); expenditures, $90,759, including $68,295 for 9 grants (high: $30,000; low: $95).
Purpose and activities: Support for Baptist churches and higher education.
Limitations: Giving primarily in LA.
Application information: Application form not required.
Deadline(s): None
Write: C.O. West, Pres.
Officers and Directors: C.O. West, Pres.; Gladys J. West, V.P.; A. David Evans, Secy.-Treas.; Gloria West Evans, Leatrice David West.
Employer Identification Number: 726018637

2545
Charles & Elizabeth Wetmore Foundation ⌑
226 Carondelet St., Rm. 1007
New Orleans 70130

Established in 1969 LA.
Foundation type: Operating
Financial data (yr. ended 12/31/88): Assets, $1,175,784 (M); gifts received, $143,915; expenditures, $128,369, including $60,000 for foundation-administered programs.
Purpose and activities: Giving primarily to indigent victims of tubercular disease and their immediate families; giving also to local health departments that specialize in the treatment of tuberculosis.
Limitations: Giving limited to the metropolitan New Orleans, LA, area.
Officers: Alvin Johnson, M.D., Pres.; William Shaw, Jr., V.P.; Ted Dampeer, M.D., Secy.; B.B. Wright, Treas.
Trustee: Crestar Bank, N.A.
Employer Identification Number: 237120743

2546
The Wheless Foundation ⌑
c/o Commercial National Bank in Shreveport
P.O. Box 21119
Shreveport 71152 (318) 429-1704

Trust established in 1945 in LA.
Donor(s): N. Hobson Wheless.†
Foundation type: Independent
Financial data (yr. ended 10/31/89): Assets, $2,898,836 (M); expenditures, $148,885, including $116,475 for 55 grants (high: $51,025; low: $100).
Purpose and activities: Emphasis on higher education, church support, community funds, and youth agencies.
Limitations: Giving primarily in LA.
Application information: Application form not required.
Deadline(s): None
Write: Bobby L. Miller, Trust Officer, Commercial National Bank in Shreveport
Board of Control: Elise W. Hogan, Nicholas Hobson Wheless, Jr.
Trustee: Commercial National Bank in Shreveport.
Employer Identification Number: 726017724

2547
Kemper and Leila Williams Foundation
P.O. Box 50580
New Orleans 70150 (504) 523-4162

Incorporated in 1974 in LA.
Donor(s): L. Kemper Williams,† Leila M. Williams,† and others.
Foundation type: Independent
Financial data (yr. ended 03/31/90): Assets, $67,042,359 (M); expenditures, $2,860,611, including $73,771 for 1 grant, $1,587 for 2 grants to individuals and $2,175,811 for foundation-administered programs.
Purpose and activities: Giving primarily to the Historic New Orleans Collection, a museum and research center, and Kemper Williams Park.
Limitations: Giving limited to New Orleans, LA.
Application information: Applications not accepted.
Write: Fred M. Smith, Secy.-Treas.
Officers and Directors:* Benjamin W. Yancey,* Pres.; Mary Lou M. Christovich,* V.P.; Fred M. Smith,* Secy.-Treas.; Francis C. Doyle, G. Henry Person, Jr., John E. Walker.
Number of staff: 1 full-time professional; 1 part-time support.
Employer Identification Number: 237336090

2548
Mary F. Wisdom Foundation ⌑ ☆
c/o Stone, Pigman, Walther, Wittman and Hutchinson
546 Carondelet St.
New Orleans 70130

Established in 1986 in LA.
Foundation type: Independent
Financial data (yr. ended 4/30/89): Assets, $2,381,618 (M); gifts received, $103,858; expenditures, $87,011, including $75,000 for 5 grants (high: $25,000; low: $5,000).
Purpose and activities: Giving primarily for performing arts groups; support also for education, conservation, and social services.
Limitations: Giving primarily in New Orleans, LA.
Application information:
Deadline(s): None
Write: Steven W. Usdin, Trustee
Officers and Trustees: Mary E. Wisdom, Pres.; Adelaide W. Benjamin, Secy.; Helen Wisdom Collins, Treas.; Steven W. Usdin.
Employer Identification Number: 726123208

2549
Dorothy & Malcolm Woldenberg Foundation ⌑
2100 St. Charles Ave., 12-H
New Orleans 70130

Incorporated in 1959 in LA as Woldenberg Charitable and Educational Foundation.
Donor(s): Malcolm Woldenberg, Magnolia Liquor Co., Inc., Sazerac Co., Inc., Great Southern Liquor Co., Inc., Duval Spirits, Inc.
Foundation type: Independent
Financial data (yr. ended 12/31/88): Assets, $2,084,871 (M); gifts received, $803,000; expenditures, $188,645, including $175,450 for 42 grants (high: $50,000; low: $100).
Purpose and activities: Grants largely for Jewish welfare funds, temple support, and higher and secondary educational institutions.
Limitations: Giving primarily in LA and FL. No grants to individuals.
Application information:
Deadline(s): None
Officers: Dorothy Woldenberg, Pres.; Stephen Goldring, V.P.; C. Halpern, Secy.-Treas.
Employer Identification Number: 726022665

2550
William C. Woolf Foundation ⌑
P.O. Box 21119
Shreveport 71152

Incorporated in 1959 in LA.
Donor(s): William C. Woolf,† Geraldine H. Woolf.†
Foundation type: Independent
Financial data (yr. ended 2/28/89): Assets, $3,139,713 (M); expenditures, $182,568, including $137,025 for 39 grants (high: $50,000; low: $250).
Purpose and activities: Giving for church support, higher education, social service and youth agencies, and medical research.
Limitations: Giving primarily in Shreveport, LA.
Application information: Contributes only to pre-selected organizations. Applications not accepted.
Write: Nicholas H. Wheless, Jr., Chair.
Officer: Bobby L. Miller, Secy.
Trustees: Nicholas Hobson Wheless, Jr., Chair.; Claude G. Rives III, C. Lane Sartor.
Employer Identification Number: 726020630

2551
Zemurray Foundation ⌑
1436 Whitney Bldg.
228 St. Charles
New Orleans 70130 (504) 525-0091

Incorporated in 1951 in LA.
Donor(s): Sarah W. Zemurray.
Foundation type: Independent
Financial data (yr. ended 12/31/88): Assets, $38,162,515 (M); expenditures, $2,011,647, including $1,730,420 for 37 grants (high: $640,000; low: $100).
Purpose and activities: Grants primarily for education, particularly higher education, cultural programs, civic affairs, hospitals, and medical research.
Limitations: Giving primarily in New Orleans, LA, and Cambridge, MA. No grants to individuals.
Application information: Contributes only to pre-selected organizations. Applications not accepted.
Board meeting date(s): Usually in Nov.
Write: Walter J. Belsom, Jr., Treas.
Officers and Directors: Doris Z. Stone, Pres.; Samuel Z. Stone, V.P.; Thomas B. Lemann, Secy.; Walter J. Belsom, Jr., Treas.
Employer Identification Number: 720539603

2552
Fred B. and Ruth B. Zigler Foundation
P.O. Box 986
Jennings 70546 (318) 824-2413

Incorporated in 1956 in LA.
Donor(s): Fred B. Zigler,† Ruth B. Zigler.†
Foundation type: Independent
Financial data (yr. ended 12/31/88): Assets, $5,849,926 (M); expenditures, $354,220, including $136,518 for 31 grants (high: $30,000; low: $35; average: $5,000) and $90,325 for grants to individuals.
Purpose and activities: Emphasis on higher and secondary education, including scholarships for local students, and youth agencies; support also for a museum and drug abuse programs.
Types of support: Operating budgets, building funds, general purposes, equipment, student aid, research, endowment funds, matching funds, renovation projects, special projects.
Limitations: Giving primarily in Jefferson Davis Parish, LA. No grants to individuals (except scholarships for graduates of Jefferson Davis Parish high schools).
Publications: Annual report.
Application information: Scholarship application forms available through Parish High Schools. Application form not required.
Initial approach: Proposal or letter
Copies of proposal: 1
Deadline(s): 3 weeks prior to board meetings; scholarship deadline Mar. 10
Board meeting date(s): Bimonthly beginning in Jan.
Write: Margaret Cormier, Secy.-Treas.
Officers: Paul E. Brummett,* Pres.; Margaret Cormier, Secy.-Treas.
Trustees:* Dave Elmore, John Michael Elmore, Mark Fehl, A.J.M. Oustalet, John Pipkin.
Number of staff: 1 full-time professional; 1 part-time professional.
Employer Identification Number: 726019403

MAINE

2553
The Harold Alfond Trust ⌑
c/o Dexter Shoe Co.
P.O. Box 353
Dexter 04930 (207) 924-7341

Trust established in 1950 in ME.
Donor(s): Harold Alfond, Dexter Shoe Co.
Foundation type: Company-sponsored
Financial data (yr. ended 12/31/87): Assets, $12,925,549 (M); gifts received, $1,400,000; expenditures, $400,485.
Purpose and activities: Grants largely for secondary and higher education; giving also for general charitable purposes.
Limitations: Giving primarily in ME and MA.
Application information:
Write: Keith Burden, Mgr.
Trustees: Dorothy Alfond, Harold Alfond, Theodore Alfond.
Employer Identification Number: 016010672

2554
Helen R. Coe Trust ⌑ ☆
400 Congress St.
P.O. Box 3555
Portland 04101-3515
Scholarship application address: c/o Principal, Fryeburg Academy, Fryeburg, ME 04037

Established in 1978.
Foundation type: Independent
Financial data (yr. ended 03/31/89): Assets, $1,239,427 (M); gifts received, $4,338; expenditures, $74,239, including $27,170 for 20 grants (high: $2,000; low: $100) and $35,850 for 27 grants to individuals (high: $1,500; low: $200).
Purpose and activities: Support primarily for higher and other education, including scholarships for graduating seniors of a local academy.
Types of support: Student aid.
Limitations: Giving limited to Lovell, ME.
Application information:
Initial approach: Letter
Distribution Committee: Norman Christopher, Salley Davey, Gladys Littlefield.
Trustee: Maine National Bank.
Employer Identification Number: 010351827

2555
Mabel S. Daveis Trust
One Portland Sq.
Portland 04112 (207) 774-4000

Foundation type: Independent
Financial data (yr. ended 12/31/89): Assets, $1,705,000 (M); expenditures, $112,500, including $101,500 for grants.
Purpose and activities: Giving to the United Way; support also for social services, the arts, youth, and general charitable giving.
Limitations: Giving primarily in the Portland, ME, area. No grants to individuals.
Application information:
Initial approach: Proposal
Deadline(s): Dec.
Final notification: Dec.
Write: Edward F. Dana, Trustee
Trustees: Edward F. Dana, George M. Lord, Alden H. Sawyer, Jr.
Employer Identification Number: 016009342

2556
George P. Davenport Trust Fund ⌑
55 Front St.
Bath 04530 (207) 443-3431

Trust established in 1927 in ME.
Donor(s): George P. Davenport.†
Foundation type: Independent
Financial data (yr. ended 12/31/88): Assets, $4,598,424 (M); expenditures, $303,904, including $166,768 for 26 grants (high: $25,000; low: $400) and $97,498 for 65 loans to individuals.
Purpose and activities: Support for undergraduate scholarships to local students, and for community betterment.
Types of support: Operating budgets, seed money, emergency funds, building funds, matching funds, student loans.
Limitations: Giving limited exclusively to Bath, ME. No grants to individuals (other than student loans to Bath area high school graduates), or for continuing support, annual campaigns, deficit financing, equipment, land acquisition, endowment funds, program support, research, demonstration projects, publications, or conferences.
Publications: 990-PF.
Application information: Application form required for scholarships. Application form not required.
Initial approach: Telephone
Copies of proposal: 1
Deadline(s): 5th of each month for organizations; none for scholarships
Board meeting date(s): Monthly
Final notification: 2 months
Trustees: John W. Coombs, J. Franklin Howe, Leland R. Patton.
Number of staff: 1 part-time support.
Employer Identification Number: 016009246

2557
Guy Gannett Foundation ⌑
390 Congress St.
Portland 04101

Established in 1968 in ME.
Donor(s): Guy Gannett Publishing Co., and subsidiaries.
Foundation type: Company-sponsored
Financial data (yr. ended 12/31/88): Assets, $1,603,711 (M); gifts received, $105,946; expenditures, $210,222, including $188,500 for 27 grants (high: $90,000; low: $500).
Purpose and activities: Giving for community funds, cultural programs, education, and health and social service agencies.
Limitations: Giving primarily in ME. No grants to individuals.
Application information:
Initial approach: Letter
Deadline(s): Mar. 15
Officers and Directors: Jean Gannett Hawley, Pres.; James E. Baker, Treas.; Madeline G. Corson, John R. DiMatteo, John H. Gannett.
Employer Identification Number: 016003797

2558
Kenduskeag Foundation
c/o Dead River Company
One Dana St.
Portland 04101 (207) 773-5841

Established in 1955 in ME.
Donor(s): Dead River Group of Companies, Curtis M. Hutchins.†
Foundation type: Independent
Financial data (yr. ended 12/31/88): Assets, $1,356,058 (M); expenditures, $79,092, including $65,933 for 11 grants (high: $30,000; low: $350).
Purpose and activities: Support for a university, hospital, and local charities.
Types of support: Annual campaigns, building funds, capital campaigns, conferences and seminars, fellowships, program-related investments, special projects.
Limitations: Giving limited to ME.
Application information: Application form not required.
Deadline(s): None
Write: P. Andrews Nixon, Trustee
Trustee: P. Andrews Nixon.
Employer Identification Number: 016018972

2559
The Maine Community Foundation, Inc.
210 Main St.
P.O. Box 148
Ellsworth 04605 (207) 667-9735

Incorporated in 1983 in ME.
Foundation type: Community
Financial data (yr. ended 12/31/89): Assets, $4,165,859 (M); gifts received, $1,649,897; expenditures, $736,375, including $548,222 for 166 grants (high: $40,000; low: $50; average: $500-$5,000), $25,474 for 21 grants to individuals (high: $2,874; low: $400; average: $400-$1,600) and $132,000 for 3 loans.
Purpose and activities: Giving primarily for youth and child welfare, the elderly, environmental conservation, leadership development, the arts, education, and health.
Types of support: Seed money, matching funds, conferences and seminars, general purposes, publications, scholarship funds, special projects, technical assistance, student aid, emergency funds.
Limitations: Giving limited to ME. No support for religious organizations for religious purposes. No grants to individuals (except from donor-designated funds), or for endowment funds, equipment, or annual campaigns for regular operations; grants rarely made for capital campaigns.
Publications: Annual report (including application guidelines), informational brochure, newsletter.
Application information: Application form required.
Initial approach: Letter
Copies of proposal: 1
Deadline(s): Feb. 1, Apr. 1, Aug. 1, and Oct. 1
Board meeting date(s): 4 times a year
Write: Marion Kane, Exec. Dir.
Officers and Directors:* P. Andrews Nixon,* Chair.; Marion Kane,* Exec. Dir.; and 21 additional directors.
Number of staff: 2 full-time professional; 1 part-time professional; 1 part-time support.
Employer Identification Number: 010391479

2560
Market Trust ⌑
c/o Maine National Bank
P.O. Box 3555
Portland 04104 (207) 775-1000

Trust established in 1959 in ME.
Donor(s): Brockton Public Market, Inc., George C. Shaw Co., and subsidiaries.
Foundation type: Company-sponsored
Financial data (yr. ended 12/31/89): Assets, $1,751,814 (M); expenditures, $320,252, including $300,433 for 48 grants (high: $49,700; low: $1,000).
Purpose and activities: Giving for community funds, hospitals, youth agencies, and arts and cultural programs.
Types of support: Annual campaigns, building funds, capital campaigns, emergency funds.
Limitations: Giving primarily in New England. No grants to individuals.

Application information: Applications not accepted.
Write: David MacNichol
Trustee: Maine National Bank.
Employer Identification Number: 016008389

2561
G. G. Monks Foundation ⌑ ☆
45 Exchange St.
Portland 04101

Trust established in 1962 in MA.
Donor(s): Millicent S. Monks, Robert A.G. Monks, and members of the Monks family.
Foundation type: Independent
Financial data (yr. ended 12/31/88): Assets, $1,273 (M); gifts received, $122,487; expenditures, $117,399, including $116,600 for grants.
Purpose and activities: Giving for private charitable foundations, higher and secondary education, and cultural programs.
Types of support: General purposes.
Limitations: Giving primarily in ME.
Application information: Contributes only to pre-selected organizations. Applications not accepted.
Write: Nicholas Higgins
Trustees: Austin D. Higgins, Nicholas Higgins, Robert A.G. Monks.
Number of staff: None.
Employer Identification Number: 046018033

2562
The Clarence E. Mulford Trust ⌑
Eight Portland St.
Fryeburg 04037 (207) 935-2061

Trust established in 1950 in ME.
Donor(s): Clarence E. Mulford.†
Foundation type: Independent
Financial data (yr. ended 12/31/88): Assets, $4,758,263 (M); expenditures, $310,974, including $259,299 for grants (high: $168,676).
Purpose and activities: Support for schools; grants also for church support, community services and welfare programs, libraries, and youth agencies.
Limitations: Giving primarily in Fryeburg, ME, and neighboring towns. No grants to individuals, or for building or endowment funds, scholarships, fellowships, or matching gifts; no loans.
Application information: Application form not required.
Initial approach: Letter
Copies of proposal: 3
Deadline(s): Submit proposal preferably in June or Dec.
Board meeting date(s): Jan. and July
Write: David R. Hastings, II, Trustee
Trustees: David R. Hastings II, Peter G. Hastings.
Employer Identification Number: 010247548

2563
Edith L. & H. Danforth Ross Trust ⌑ ☆
c/o Fleet Bank of Maine
Fleet Ctr., Exchange St.
Bangor 04401

Established in 1986 in ME.
Donor(s): Edith L. Ross.†
Foundation type: Independent
Financial data (yr. ended 8/31/89): Assets, $1,095,723 (M); expenditures, $71,684, including $62,215 for 5 grants (high: $18,664; low: $6,222).
Purpose and activities: Support for hospitals, a Protestant church, a community fund, a YMCA, and a scholarship fund.
Limitations: Giving primarily in ME. No grants to individuals.
Application information: Contributes only to pre-selected organizations. Applications not accepted.
Trustee: Fleet Bank of Maine.
Employer Identification Number: 016075554

2564
Elmina Sewall Foundation ⌑
245 Commercial St.
Portland 04101

Established in 1983 in ME.
Donor(s): Elmina B. Sewall.
Foundation type: Independent
Financial data (yr. ended 09/30/88): Assets, $4,192,641 (M); gifts received, $642,850; expenditures, $259,298, including $234,000 for 72 grants (high: $25,000; low: $500).
Purpose and activities: Giving primarily for animal welfare; support also for social services and youth.
Limitations: No grants to individuals.
Application information: Contributes only to pre-selected organizations. Applications not accepted.
Officers: Elmina B. Sewall, Pres.; Margaret Sewall Barbour, V.P.; Harold E. Woodsum, Jr., Secy.; William E. Curran, Treas.
Employer Identification Number: 010387404

2565
Simmons Foundation, Inc. ⌑
One Canal Plaza
Portland 04101 (207) 774-2635

Established in 1959 in ME.
Foundation type: Independent
Financial data (yr. ended 12/31/88): Assets, $1,309,384 (M); expenditures, $75,493, including $57,950 for 24 grants (high: $7,000; low: $200).
Purpose and activities: Support primarily for social services, health, and community organizations.
Types of support: General purposes.
Limitations: Giving primarily in Portland, ME. No grants to individuals.
Application information: Application form not required.
Initial approach: Letter
Deadline(s): None
Write: Mrs. Elizabeth Woodward, Pres.
Officer and Trustees: Elizabeth Woodward, Pres. and Treas.; Albert Aranson, Audrey Gough, Royden A. Keddy, Suzanne Quirk, H. Travers Smith, Robert F. Woodward, Stephen Woodward.
Employer Identification Number: 010277832

2566
James Striar Family Foundation
c/o Steven Striar
Main St.
Corinna 04928

Trust established in 1952 in ME.
Foundation type: Independent
Financial data (yr. ended 11/30/88): Assets, $10,544 (M); expenditures, $149,305, including $146,779 for grants (high: $31,075).
Purpose and activities: Emphasis on Jewish welfare funds and Jewish-sponsored educational and religious institutions; grants also for hospitals, higher education, and community funds.
Application information: Applications not accepted.
Trustee: Steven Striar.
Employer Identification Number: 016009314

2567
UNUM Charitable Foundation ⌑
2211 Congress St.
Portland 04122 (207) 770-2211
Application address: P.O. Box 9548, Portland, ME 04122

Established in 1969 in ME.
Donor(s): UNUM Life Insurance Co. of America.
Foundation type: Company-sponsored
Financial data (yr. ended 12/31/88): Assets, $863,430 (M); expenditures, $854,526, including $813,833 for 157 grants (high: $208,865; low: $25; average: $15,000) and $36,577 for 144 employee matching gifts.
Purpose and activities: The foundation commits seventy-five percent of annual funds to corporate community grants for health and welfare agencies, arts and cultural programs, education (including employee matching gifts), and civic organizations. The remaining twenty-five percent is targeted for programs in AIDS and aging.
Types of support: Employee matching gifts, capital campaigns, special projects, matching funds, seed money.
Limitations: Giving primarily in ME; capital grants limited to the greater Portland area. No support for religious organizations, fundraising or athletic events, goodwill advertising, or United Way member agencies. No grants to individuals, or for endowments or funds for operating purposes.
Publications: Corporate giving report (including application guidelines), informational brochure (including application guidelines).
Application information: Completion of formal application may be required after review of initial submission. Application form not required.
Initial approach: Letter
Copies of proposal: 1
Deadline(s): For capital grants, June 1; no deadline for other grants
Board meeting date(s): Trustees meet semiannually; grants under $25,000 reviewed by staff on an ongoing basis
Write: Judith Nedeau Harrison, Dir., Corp. Public Involvement
Officers: James F. Orr III,* Pres.; Donna T. Mundy,* V.P.; Judith Nedeau Harrison,* Secy.; Timothy Ludden, Treas.

Trustees:* William Bouman, Terry Cohen, James F. Keenan, James B. Moir, Wendolyn C. Clarke, James S. Orser, Barry W. Larman, Cheryl Stewart, Janet Whitehouse.
Number of staff: 1 full-time professional; 1 part-time professional; 1 part-time support.
Employer Identification Number: 237026979

2568
Warren Memorial Foundation ⌑
645 Hearthside Rd.
North Windham 04062 (207) 892-8832

Incorporated in 1929 in ME.
Donor(s): Susan C. Warren.†
Foundation type: Operating
Financial data (yr. ended 12/31/88): Assets, $2,382,166 (M); expenditures, $103,542, including $8,930 for 5 grants (high: $2,500; low: $700; average: $250-$1,600) and $89,847 for 1 foundation-administered program.
Purpose and activities: A private operating foundation; giving restricted to programs in education and the arts. Giving primarily for cultural and children's programs and secondary education; operates a local public library.
Types of support: Renovation projects, scholarship funds, operating budgets.
Limitations: Giving limited to ME, with emphasis on Westbrook. No grants to individuals, or for endowment funds.
Application information: Application form not required.
Initial approach: Letter
Copies of proposal: 1
Deadline(s): None
Board meeting date(s): Usually monthly
Write: Lawrence B. Abbiati, Treas.
Officers and Directors: Howard C. Reiche, Jr., Pres.; Lawrence B. Abbiati, Treas. and Clerk; Luther B. Francis, Rudolph T. Greep.
Employer Identification Number: 010220759

MARYLAND

2569
The Abell Foundation, Inc. ▼
1116 Fidelity Bldg.
210 North Charles St.
Baltimore 21201-4013 (301) 547-1300

Incorporated in 1953 in MD.
Donor(s): A.S. Abell Co., Harry C. Black,† Gary Black, Sr.†
Foundation type: Independent
Financial data (yr. ended 12/31/89): Assets, $131,950,267 (M); expenditures, $6,605,783, including $5,650,687 for 188 grants (high: $1,250,000; low: $155; average: $1,000-$50,000), $10,920 for 7 grants to individuals of $1,500 each and $66,517 for 60 employee matching gifts.
Purpose and activities: Supports education with emphasis on public education, including early childhood and elementary education, educational research, and minority education; economic development; human services, including programs for child welfare and development and health and family services; arts and culture, including arts preservation; and conservation.
Types of support: Endowment funds, capital campaigns, equipment, land acquisition, matching funds, renovation projects, conferences and seminars, general purposes, scholarship funds, seed money, special projects.
Limitations: Giving limited to MD, with a focus on Baltimore. Generally no support for housing or medical facilities. No grants to individuals, or for operating budgets, sponsorships, memberships, sustaining funds, or deficit financing.
Publications: Annual report (including application guidelines), application guidelines, newsletter, occasional report, program policy statement.
Application information: Detailed information about what to submit with proposal should be requested. Employee-related scholarships have been phased out; previous commitments are being honored. Application form required.
Initial approach: Letter
Copies of proposal: 1
Deadline(s): Jan. 1, Mar. 1, May 1, July 1, Sept. 1, and Nov. 1
Board meeting date(s): Bimonthly
Final notification: Within 1 week of board meetings
Write: Robert C. Embry, Jr., Pres.
Officers and Trustees:* Gary Black, Jr.,* Chair.; Robert C. Embry, Jr.,* Pres.; Anne La Farge Culman, V.P.; Faye V. Auchenpaugh, Secy.; Frances M. Keenan, Treas.; W. Shepherdson Abell, Jr., George L. Bunting, Jr., Robert Garrett, William Jews, Donald H. Patterson, Walter Sondheim, Jr.
Number of staff: 5 full-time professional; 2 part-time professional; 2 full-time support; 2 part-time support.
Employer Identification Number: 526036106

2570
Charles S. Abell Foundation, Inc. ⌑
8401 Connecticut Ave.
Chevy Chase 20815 (301) 652-2224

Established in 1985 in MD.
Donor(s): William S. Abell.
Foundation type: Independent
Financial data (yr. ended 12/31/88): Assets, $6,436,162 (M); expenditures, $315,954, including $238,440 for 16 grants (high: $50,000; low: $5,000).
Purpose and activities: Support for church-related food and shelter centers.
Limitations: Giving primarily in Washington, DC.
Application information: Application form not required.
Deadline(s): None
Officers and Trustees: William S. Abell, Pres.; Patricia O'Callaghan Abell, V.P.; W. Shepherdson Abell, Secy.-Treas.; Anthony F. Abell, Christopher S. Abell, Gregory T. Abell, Kevin O'Callaghan Abell, Marguerite Elaine Abell Nurmi.
Employer Identification Number: 521435573

2571
Abramson Foundation, Inc. ⌑
11501 Huff Court
North Bethesda 20895

Established in 1959 in MD.
Foundation type: Independent
Financial data (yr. ended 12/31/88): Assets, $5,504,006 (M); gifts received, $344,000; expenditures, $313,170, including $311,700 for 31 grants (high: $55,000; low: $100).
Purpose and activities: Support primarily for the performing and fine arts, science and technology, and education.
Types of support: General purposes.
Limitations: Giving primarily in the greater Washington, DC, area.
Application information: Contributes only to pre-selected organizations. Applications not accepted.
Officers: Albert Abramson, Pres.; Gary Abramson, Secy.; Ronald Abramson, Treas.
Employer Identification Number: 526039192

2572
Clayton Baker Trust
c/o John B. Powell, Jr.
250 West Pratt St., 13th Fl.
Baltimore 21201 (301) 539-5541

Established in 1960.
Donor(s): Julia C. Baker.
Foundation type: Independent
Financial data (yr. ended 12/31/89): Assets, $5,289,446 (M); expenditures, $205,051, including $194,060 for 29 grants (high: $25,000; low: $1,000; average: $1,000-$25,000).
Purpose and activities: Giving primarily to aid local area disadvantaged residents; national giving limited to environmental concerns, population control, arms control, and nuclear disarmament.
Types of support: General purposes, operating budgets, seed money, special projects.
Limitations: Giving primarily in Baltimore, MD, for welfare assistance; giving nationally for other specified support. No support for the arts or higher education. No grants to individuals, or for building or endowment funds, or research.
Publications: Application guidelines.
Application information: Application form required.
Initial approach: Letter
Copies of proposal: 1
Deadline(s): Apr. 5, Aug. 5, and Nov. 5
Trustees: Julia C. Baker, William C. Baker, John B. Powell, Jr.
Employer Identification Number: 526054237

2573
The William G. Baker, Jr. Memorial Fund
The Latrobe Bldg.
Two East Read St., 9th Fl.
Baltimore 21202 (301) 332-4171

Established in 1964 in MD.
Foundation type: Independent

Financial data (yr. ended 8/31/88): Assets, $12,928,650 (M); expenditures, $1,070,207, including $1,013,035 for 92 grants (high: $120,000; low: $1,000).
Purpose and activities: Giving primarily for education and community funds; support also for social services and the arts.
Types of support: Operating budgets, seed money, emergency funds, building funds, equipment, land acquisition, endowment funds, capital campaigns, renovation projects, scholarship funds.
Limitations: Giving limited to the Baltimore, MD, metropolitan area. No grants to individuals, or for annual campaigns or deficit financing; no loans.
Publications: Application guidelines.
Application information: Application form not required.
Initial approach: Proposal
Copies of proposal: 6
Deadline(s): Submit proposal 2 months before board meetings
Board meeting date(s): Generally Mar., Sept., June, and Dec.
Final notification: 3 months
Write: Martha K. Johnston, Prog. Officer
Officer and Governors:* Douglas Dodge, Exec. Dir.; Mary Ellen Imboden, John T. King III, Walter Sondheim, Jr., Semmes G. Walsh.
Corporate Trustee: Mercantile-Safe Deposit & Trust Co.
Number of staff: None.
Employer Identification Number: 526057178

2574
Summerfield Baldwin, Jr. Foundation ⌑
c/o Mercantile-Safe Deposit & Trust Co.
P.O. Box 2257, Two Hopkins Plaza
Baltimore 21201 (301) 237-5653

Trust established in 1946 in MD.
Foundation type: Independent
Financial data (yr. ended 12/31/88): Assets, $2,601,830 (M); expenditures, $169,620, including $155,817 for 11 grants (high: $40,000; low: $1,000).
Purpose and activities: Emphasis on Protestant Episcopal church support, church-sponsored secondary schools, higher education, and a hospital.
Limitations: Giving primarily in MD.
Application information:
Initial approach: Letter
Deadline(s): None
Write: J. Michael Miller, V.P., Mercantile-Safe Deposit & Trust Co.
Trustee: Mercantile-Safe Deposit & Trust Co.
Employer Identification Number: 526023112

2575
The Baltimore Community Foundation ▼
(Formerly The Community Foundation of the Greater Baltimore Area, Inc.)
The Latrobe Bldg.
Two East Read St., 9th Fl.
Baltimore 21202 (301) 332-4171

Incorporated in 1972 in MD.
Foundation type: Community
Financial data (yr. ended 12/31/88): Assets, $13,708,214 (M); gifts received, $3,070,552; expenditures, $1,602,260, including $1,280,035 for 141 grants (high: $160,600; average: $1,000-$10,000) and $146,165 for 77 grants to individuals.
Purpose and activities: Giving primarily for educational, civic, cultural, health, welfare, environmental, and other community needs. Grants primarily for pilot projects and to increase organizational effectiveness and self-sufficiency.
Types of support: General purposes, endowment funds, scholarship funds, matching funds, consulting services, technical assistance, seed money, special projects.
Limitations: Giving primarily in the Baltimore, MD, area.
Publications: Annual report, informational brochure (including application guidelines).
Application information:
Initial approach: Letter
Deadline(s): 60 days before meetings
Board meeting date(s): 3 times a year
Final notification: Within 2 weeks after meetings
Write: Timothy D. Armbruster, Exec. Dir.
Officers and Trustees:* Edward K. Dunn, Jr., Chair.; Herbert M. Katzenberg,* Vice-Chair.; Timothy D. Armbruster, Pres. and Exec. Dir.; W. Wallace Lanahan, Jr.,* V.P. and Treas.; and 22 additional trustees.
Number of staff: 2
Employer Identification Number: 237180620

2576
Baltimore Gas and Electric Foundation, Inc. ▼ ⌑
Box 1475
Baltimore 21203 (301) 234-5312

Established in 1986 in MD.
Donor(s): Baltimore Gas and Electric Co.
Foundation type: Company-sponsored
Financial data (yr. ended 12/31/88): Assets, $3,633,103 (M); gifts received, $1,887,500; expenditures, $4,325,003, including $4,321,516 for 230 grants (high: $850,000; low: $1,000; average: $2,500-$75,000).
Purpose and activities: Support for arts and culture, higher and other education, community development, civic and public affairs, health and hospitals, the United Way, and Jewish giving.
Types of support: General purposes, annual campaigns, capital campaigns.
Limitations: Giving primarily in MD, with emphasis on Baltimore.
Application information: Contributes only to pre-selected organizations. Applications not accepted.
Board meeting date(s): 6 times a year
Write: Gary R. Fuhrman
Officers: George V. McGowan,* Pres.; J.M. Files, V.P.; E.A. Crooke, Secy.; C.W. Shivery, Treas.
Directors:* B.C. Trueschler, Chair.; J. Owen Cole, L.B. Disharoon, K. Feeley, Jerome W. Geckle, W. Hackerman, P.G. Miller, G.G. Radcliffe, J.B. Slaughter, H.K. Wells.
Number of staff: 3
Employer Identification Number: 521452037

2577
Helen & Merrill Bank Foundation, Inc. ⌑
c/o Weil, Akman et al.
201 West Padonia Ave.
Timonium 21093
Application address: 1200 Mercantile Bank & Trust Bldg., Two Hopkins Plaza, Baltimore, MD 21201; Tel.: (301) 385-4099

Donor(s): Helen S. Bank, Merrill L. Bank.
Foundation type: Independent
Financial data (yr. ended 6/30/89): Assets, $5,792,172 (M); gifts received, $1,590,120; expenditures, $404,434, including $373,739 for 52 grants (high: $200,000; low: $10).
Purpose and activities: Support for an aquarium, higher education, health organizations, and Jewish welfare.
Limitations: Giving primarily in West Palm Beach and Palm Beach, FL, and Baltimore, MD.
Application information:
Initial approach: Letter or proposal
Deadline(s): None
Write: Irving Cohen, Secy.
Officers: Helen S. Bank, Pres.; Merrill L. Bank, V.P. and Treas.; Irving Cohn, Secy.
Employer Identification Number: 237031791

2578
The Milton A. and Gloria G. Barlow Family Foundation ⌑
5454 Wisconsin Ave., Suite 1650
Chevy Chase 20815

Established in 1986 in MD.
Donor(s): Milton A. Barlow, The Barlow Corp.
Foundation type: Independent
Financial data (yr. ended 2/28/89): Assets, $2,838,803 (M); expenditures, $212,902, including $180,000 for 9 grants (high: $150,000; low: $500).
Purpose and activities: Giving primarily for higher education.
Application information: Applications not accepted.
Officers and Director:* Milton A. Barlow,* Pres.; Gloria G. Barlow, V.P.; Jeannette B. Frederickson, V.P.; Gloria B. Bowman, Secy.; Milton Allan Barlow, Jr., Treas.
Employer Identification Number: 521486741

2579
Fred P. Bergfors Fund ⌑ ☆
6517 80th St.
Cabin John 20818 (301) 229-3503

Foundation type: Independent
Financial data (yr. ended 4/30/89): Assets, $1,049,500 (M); expenditures, $52,522, including $43,000 for 26 grants (high: $8,000; low: $1,000).
Purpose and activities: Giving for the arts and social and human services; support also for hospitals, education, and Protestant churches.
Limitations: Giving primarily in MA, with some emphasis on Quincy. No grants to individuals.
Application information:
Initial approach: Letter
Deadline(s): Jan. 31
Write: Constance B. Rice, Trustee
Trustees: Fred E. Bergfors, Margaret Bergfors, Constance B. Rice.
Employer Identification Number: 046075287

2580
Berman Charitable Trust ⌑ ☆
P.O. Box 86
Laurel 20707

Established in 1984 in MD.
Donor(s): I. Wolford Berman, Melvin J. Berman.
Foundation type: Independent
Financial data (yr. ended 12/31/88): Assets, $1,721,897 (M); gifts received, $973,500; expenditures, $105,444, including $102,096 for 29 grants (high: $30,500; low: $25).
Purpose and activities: Support primarily for Jewish organizations, including welfare funds, community centers, and yeshivas.
Limitations: No grants to individuals.
Application information: Contributes only to pre-selected organizations. Applications not accepted.
Trustees: Dennis Berman, I. Wolford Berman, Melvin J. Berman.
Employer Identification Number: 942940733

2581
The Jacob and Hilda Blaustein Foundation, Inc. ▼
Blaustein Bldg.
P.O. Box 238
Baltimore 21203

Incorporated in 1957 in MD.
Donor(s): Jacob Blaustein.†
Foundation type: Independent
Financial data (yr. ended 12/31/88): Assets, $56,039,166 (M); gifts received, $460,000; expenditures, $3,252,699, including $2,899,976 for 49 grants (high: $540,100; low: $750; average: $1,000-$25,000).
Purpose and activities: Giving primarily for Jewish welfare funds and higher education.
Types of support: General purposes.
Limitations: Giving primarily in MD and NY.
Application information:
Initial approach: Letter
Deadline(s): None
Board meeting date(s): Every 4 to 6 weeks
Final notification: 2 to 3 months
Write: Morton K. Blaustein, Pres.
Officers: Morton K. Blaustein,* Pres.; David Hirschhorn,* V.P.; Henry A. Rosenberg, Jr., V.P.; Louis B. Thalheimer, V.P.; Frank A. Strzelczyk,* Secy.-Treas.
Trustees:* Barbara B. Hirschhorn, Ruth B. Rosenberg, Elizabeth B. Roswell.
Number of staff: None.
Employer Identification Number: 526038382

2582
The Louis and Henrietta Blaustein Foundation, Inc. ⌑
Blaustein Bldg.
P.O. Box 238
Baltimore 21203

Incorporated in 1938 in MD.
Donor(s): Louis Blaustein,† Henrietta Blaustein,† American Trading and Production Corp., and members of the Blaustein family.
Foundation type: Independent
Financial data (yr. ended 12/31/88): Assets, $9,561,145 (M); gifts received, $460,000; expenditures, $852,870, including $773,185 for 29 grants (high: $360,485; low: $500).
Purpose and activities: Giving mainly to recipients already known to the trustees; emphasis on higher and secondary education, Jewish welfare funds, museums, music and the arts, hospitals and health services, and a community fund.
Limitations: Giving primarily in the greater Baltimore, MD, metropolitan area.
Application information:
Initial approach: Letter
Deadline(s): None
Write: Morton K. Blaustein, Pres.
Officers and Trustees:* Ruth B. Rosenberg,* Chair.; Morton K. Blaustein,* Pres.; David Hirschhorn,* V.P.; Henry A. Rosenberg, Jr.,* V.P.; Louis B. Thalheimer,* V.P.; Frank A. Strzelczyk, Secy.-Treas.
Employer Identification Number: 526038381

2583
Lois and Irving Blum Foundation ⌑
100 Garrett Bldg.
Baltimore 21202

Established about 1965 in MD.
Donor(s): Lois Blum-Feinblatt, Irving Blum.†
Foundation type: Independent
Financial data (yr. ended 03/31/89): Assets, $3,430,090 (M); gifts received, $320,879; expenditures, $190,460, including $165,350 for 36 grants (high: $40,000; low: $100).
Purpose and activities: Support for Jewish welfare, education, cultural programs, and social and health services.
Limitations: Giving primarily in MD.
Application information:
Initial approach: Proposal
Deadline(s): None
Write: Lois Blum-Feinblatt, Pres.
Officers: Lois Blum-Feinblatt, Pres.; Jerold C. Hoffberger, V.P.; Lawrence A. Blum, Secy.-Treas.
Number of staff: None.
Employer Identification Number: 526057035

2584
Alex Brown and Sons Charitable Foundation, Inc.
c/o Alex Brown and Sons, Inc.
135 East Baltimore St.
Baltimore 21202 (301) 727-1700

Established in 1954 in MD.
Donor(s): Alex Brown and Sons, Inc., Alex Brown Partners, Alex Brown Investment Management, Alex Brown Management Services, Inc.
Foundation type: Company-sponsored
Financial data (yr. ended 12/31/89): Assets, $4,569,658 (M); gifts received, $62,444; expenditures, $527,381, including $499,150 for 65 grants.
Purpose and activities: Support for cultural programs, higher education, hospitals, social services, and nature conservation.
Types of support: Annual campaigns, building funds, capital campaigns, continuing support, endowment funds, general purposes, operating budgets, scholarship funds, employee-related scholarships.
Limitations: Giving primarily in MD. No grants to individuals.
Publications: Annual report, 990-PF.
Application information: Application form not required.
Copies of proposal: 1
Deadline(s): Fall of year for next year's budget
Board meeting date(s): Mar. of each year
Write: Walter W. Brewster, Secy.
Officers: Jack S. Griswold, Pres.; Truman T. Semans, V.P.; Walter W. Brewster, Secy.; Alvin B. Krongard, Treas.
Trustees: F. Barton Harvey, Jr., Donald B. Webb, Jr.
Number of staff: None.
Employer Identification Number: 526054236

2585
Bruce Ford Brown Charitable Trust ⌑
c/o Mercantile-Safe Deposit & Trust Co.
Two Hopkins Plaza
Baltimore 21201 (301) 237-5653

Established in 1965 in MD.
Donor(s): Donaldson Brown.†
Foundation type: Independent
Financial data (yr. ended 12/31/88): Assets, $1,524,854 (M); expenditures, $81,128, including $72,750 for 23 grants (high: $8,000; low: $1,000).
Purpose and activities: Grants primarily for higher and secondary education; support also for historic preservation.
Limitations: Giving primarily in Baltimore, MD.
Application information:
Initial approach: Letter or proposal
Deadline(s): None
Write: J. Michael Miller, V.P., Mercantile-Safe Deposit & Trust Co.
Trustee: Mercantile-Safe Deposit & Trust Co.
Employer Identification Number: 526063085

2586
H. Barksdale Brown Charitable Trust ⌑
c/o Mercantile-Safe Deposit & Trust Co.
Two Hopkins Plaza
Baltimore 21201 (301) 237-5653

Established in 1965 in MD.
Foundation type: Independent
Financial data (yr. ended 10/31/88): Assets, $1,046,099 (M); expenditures, $142,956, including $137,000 for 10 grants (high: $65,000; low: $1,000).
Purpose and activities: Support primarily for a Protestant church, a hospital, and cultural programs, including the performing arts; grants also for education.
Limitations: Giving primarily in Baltimore, MD.
Application information:
Initial approach: Letter
Deadline(s): None
Write: J. Michael Miller III, V.P., Mercantile-Safe Deposit & Trust Co.
Trustee: Mercantile-Safe Deposit & Trust Co.
Employer Identification Number: 526063083

2587
The Keene C. Brown Charitable Trust ⌑ ☆
c/o Mercantile-Safe Deposit & Trust Co.
Two Hopkins Plaza
Baltimore 21201-2902 (301) 237-5653

Established in 1965.

Foundation type: Independent
Financial data (yr. ended 12/31/88): Assets, $473,249 (M); expenditures, $545,851, including $540,000 for 11 grants (high: $500,000; low: $2,000).
Purpose and activities: Giving primarily for higher education including medical and nursing schools; minor support for hospitals.
Types of support: Endowment funds.
Limitations: Giving primarily in Lynchburg, VA.
Application information:
Initial approach: Letter
Deadline(s): None
Write: J. Michael Miller II, V.P.
Trustee: Mercantile-Safe Deposit & Trust Co.
Employer Identification Number: 526063088

2588
Frank D. Brown, Jr. Charitable Trust ⌑
c/o Mercantile-Safe Deposit & Trust Co.
Two Hopkins Plaza
Baltimore 21201 (301) 237-5653

Established in 1965 in MD.
Foundation type: Independent
Financial data (yr. ended 12/31/88): Assets, $1,592,510 (M); expenditures, $88,980, including $81,000 for 21 grants (high: $10,000; low: $1,000).
Purpose and activities: Support primarily for education, hospitals, and museums.
Application information:
Initial approach: Letter
Deadline(s): None
Write: J. Michael Miller II, V.P., Mercantile-Safe Deposit & Trust Co.
Trustee: Mercantile-Safe Deposit & Trust Co.
Employer Identification Number: 526063084

2589
Buckingham School of Frederick County, Maryland ⌑
1012 Cloverlea Rd.
Baltimore 21204 (301) 828-6557

Established in 1898 in MD.
Foundation type: Independent
Financial data (yr. ended 12/31/87): Assets, $1,009,557 (M); expenditures, $72,326, including $60,984 for 58 grants (high: $17,000; low: $25).
Purpose and activities: Support primarily for higher and secondary education, art museums, and hospitals.
Limitations: Giving limited to MD.
Application information:
Initial approach: Letter
Deadline(s): Apr.
Write: Daniel Baker, Treas.
Officers and Directors: Mrs. Joseph D. Baker, Jr., Pres.; Mrs. A. McGhee Harvey, Secy.; Daniel Baker, Treas.; William F. Fritz.
Employer Identification Number: 526034781

2590
Campbell Foundation, Inc. ⌑
100 West Pennsylvania Ave.
Baltimore 21204

Donor(s): R. McLean Campbell.
Foundation type: Independent
Financial data (yr. ended 12/31/88): Assets, $1,781,209 (M); expenditures, $89,758, including $70,900 for 43 grants (high: $9,500; low: $500).
Purpose and activities: Grants primarily for culture and education; support also for child welfare and health and social services.
Types of support: Building funds, endowment funds.
Limitations: Giving primarily in the greater Baltimore, MD, area. No grants to individuals.
Application information:
Initial approach: Proposal
Deadline(s): None
Write: Bruce S. Campbell III, Secy.
Officers and Trustees: Harry G. Campbell, Jr., Pres.; R. McLean Campbell, V.P.; Bruce S. Campbell, Jr., V.P.; S. James Campbell, V.P. and Treas.; Bruce S. Campbell III, Secy.; William B. Campbell, Margaret C. Worthington.
Employer Identification Number: 520794348

2591
Eugene B. Casey Foundation ⌑
One West Deer Park Dr., Suite 401
Gaithersburg 20877-1701 (301) 948-6505

Established in 1981 in MD.
Foundation type: Independent
Financial data (yr. ended 08/31/89): Assets, $67,575,625 (M); expenditures, $3,749,884, including $2,757,577 for 15 grants (high: $1,327,000; low: $500).
Purpose and activities: Support primarily for higher education and medical research; support also for fine arts and community development.
Types of support: General purposes.
Limitations: Giving primarily in the greater Washington, DC, area.
Application information: Application form not required.
Initial approach: Proposal
Deadline(s): None
Write: Betty Brown Casey, Chair.
Officers and Trustees:* Betty Brown Casey,* Chair. and Pres.; Stephen N. Jones,* 1st V.P.; Nancy Casey Kelly,* 2nd V.P.; Jean K. Motsinger,* Secy.; W. James Price.
Employer Identification Number: 526220316

2592
Children's Fresh Air Society, Inc. ⌑
c/o The Rotunda
711 West 40th St., Suite 317
Baltimore 21211

Foundation type: Independent
Financial data (yr. ended 9/30/88): Assets, $1,125,362 (M); gifts received, $700; expenditures, $74,622, including $55,364 for 12 grants (high: $8,610; low: $2,350).
Purpose and activities: Support primarily for youth, with emphasis on camps and similar outdoor recreational programs; support also for Christian welfare, the handicapped, and health organizations.
Limitations: Giving limited to Baltimore, MD, and surrounding counties.
Application information: Application form not required.
Deadline(s): None
Write: Lynn Lafferty, Pres.
Officers: Lynn Lafferty, Pres.; Walter Hale, V.P.; Helena Hicks, Secy.; Cecil Flamer, Treas.
Employer Identification Number: 520591593

2593
Clark Charitable Foundation, Inc. ⌑ ☆
7500 Old Georgetown Rd.
Bethesda 20814

Incorporated in 1987 in MD.
Donor(s): A. James Clark.
Foundation type: Independent
Financial data (yr. ended 12/31/88): Assets, $3,086,408 (M); gifts received, $2,001,000; expenditures, $33,480, including $32,530 for grants.
Purpose and activities: Giving for higher education, social services, and a community fund.
Limitations: Giving primarily in MD. No grants to individuals.
Application information: Contributes only to pre-selected organizations. Applications not accepted.
Officers: A. James Clark, Pres.; Lawrence C. Nussdoif, V.P.; Courtney C. Pastrick, Secy.
Employer Identification Number: 521512330

2594
Clark-Winchcole Foundation ▼ ⌑
Air Rights Bldg.
4550 Montgomery Ave., Suite 345N
Bethesda 20814 (301) 654-3607

Established in 1964 in DC.
Donor(s): Dorothy C. Winchcole,† Elizabeth G. Clark.†
Foundation type: Independent
Financial data (yr. ended 12/31/88): Assets, $36,747,927 (M); expenditures, $2,280,699, including $1,969,500 for 108 grants (high: $200,000; low: $1,000; average: $50,000-$30,000).
Purpose and activities: Emphasis on higher education, hospitals, health agencies, cultural programs, social service and youth agencies, aid to the handicapped, and Protestant church support.
Types of support: Operating budgets, building funds, general purposes.
Limitations: Giving primarily in the Washington, DC, area.
Application information:
Initial approach: Letter
Deadline(s): Generally, during first 6 months of calendar year
Write: Laura E. Phillips, Pres.
Officers and Trustees:* Laura E. Phillips, Pres.; Vincent E. Burke, Jr.,* V.P.; Joseph H. Riley, V.P.; Thomas C. Thompson, Jr.,* V.P.; E. Marie Lund, Secy.-Treas.
Employer Identification Number: 526058340

2595
The Columbia Foundation
5430 Vantage Point Rd.
Columbia 21044-2624 (301) 730-7840

Incorporated in 1969 in MD.
Foundation type: Community
Financial data (yr. ended 12/31/89): Assets, $913,204 (M); gifts received, $512,729; expenditures, $468,191, including $382,002 for 40 grants (high: $20,000; low: $500; average: $1,000-$15,000).
Purpose and activities: Grants for health and human services, including programs for youth, the aged, and the disabled; arts and culture,

including music, the performing arts, and historic preservation; educational programs; and housing.
Types of support: Seed money, operating budgets, emergency funds, continuing support, equipment, building funds, matching funds, technical assistance, conferences and seminars, consulting services, general purposes, lectureships, special projects.
Limitations: Giving limited to Howard County, MD. No support for medical research, or for projects of a sectarian religious nature. No grants to individuals, or for annual campaigns, deficit financing, land acquisition, or general or special endowments.
Publications: Financial statement, application guidelines, grants list, newsletter, informational brochure (including application guidelines).
Application information: For information on emergency funding, contact the foundation. Project grants are reviewed in Mar. and operational grants in Nov. Application form required.
Initial approach: Telephone
Copies of proposal: 9
Deadline(s): Jan. for project support; Sept. for operating support
Board meeting date(s): 3rd Wednesday of each month
Final notification: 3 months
Write: Barbara K. Lawson, Exec. Dir.
Officers: Jean Moon, Pres.; Dwight Burrill, V.P.; Ronald Schimel, Secy.; Harvey Steinman, Treas.; Barbara K. Lawson, Exec. Dir.
Number of staff: 1 full-time professional; 1 full-time support.
Employer Identification Number: 520937644

2596
Commonweal Foundation, Inc. ☆
10770 Columbia Pike, Suite G100
Silver Spring 20901-1554 (301) 593-5900

Established in 1968 in Washington, DC.
Donor(s): Stewart Bainum, Sr.
Foundation type: Independent
Financial data (yr. ended 12/31/88): Assets, $243,996 (M); gifts received, $185,500; expenditures, $180,258, including $145,486 for 14 grants (high: $45,000; low: $250).
Purpose and activities: Giving primarily to the Washington Institute of Contemporary Issues; support also for elementary, secondary, and higher education, human services, and youth and child welfare organizations.
Types of support: Matching funds.
Limitations: Giving primarily in Washington, DC, and MD. No grants to individuals.
Publications: Application guidelines, program policy statement.
Application information: Request policy statement and guidelines. Application form required.
Copies of proposal: 7
Deadline(s): Apr.1 and Oct. 1
Board meeting date(s): June and Dec.
Final notification: July and Jan.
Officers: Stewart Bainum, Sr.,* Chair.; Les Pitton, Pres.; Barbara Bainum,* Secy.; Christine A. Shreve, Treas.
Directors:* Bruce Bainum, Fenton Froom, Garland P. Moore.
Employer Identification Number: 237000192

2597
J. C. Crothers Foundation, Inc. ⌑
343 North Charles St.
Baltimore 21201-4361 (301) 539-0611

Established in 1969 in MD.
Foundation type: Independent
Financial data (yr. ended 9/30/88): Assets, $1,168,545 (M); expenditures, $61,042, including $46,000 for 26 grants (high: $5,000; low: $500).
Purpose and activities: Support primarily for evangelical Christian organizations.
Application information: Application form not required.
Deadline(s): None
Write: Thomas E. Rosser, Pres.
Officers and Directors: Thomas E. Rosser, Pres.; William D. Smoot, V.P.; P. David Sewell.
Employer Identification Number: 237046562

2598
Crown Central Petroleum Foundation, Inc. ⌑
One North Charles St.
Baltimore 21201 (301) 539-7400

Established in 1981 in MD.
Donor(s): Crown Central Petroleum Corp.
Foundation type: Company-sponsored
Financial data (yr. ended 12/31/88): Assets, $204,199 (M); gifts received, $400,000; expenditures, $250,110, including $195,153 for 89 grants (high: $24,338; low: $50) and $54,957 for employee matching gifts.
Purpose and activities: Support primarily for higher education, community funds, community development, and cultural organizations.
Types of support: General purposes, scholarship funds, special projects, employee matching gifts.
Limitations: Giving primarily in MD and TX.
Application information: Applications not accepted.
Write: W.R. Snyder, Pres.
Officers: W.R. Snyder, Pres.; Ted M. Jackson, V.P. and Treas.; J.G. Yawman, Secy.
Number of staff: 1 part-time support.
Employer Identification Number: 521203348

2599
CSG Foundation, Inc.
8401 Connecticut Ave.
Chevy Chase 20815 (301) 652-6880

Established in 1986 in MD.
Donor(s): Christopher S. Abell, Gregory T. Abell, W. Shepherdson Abell.
Foundation type: Independent
Financial data (yr. ended 12/31/88): Assets, $1,697,058 (M); gifts received, $8,899; expenditures, $50,376, including $45,000 for 1 grant.
Purpose and activities: Support primarily for services to children.
Limitations: Giving primarily in the Washington, DC, area.
Application information: Application form not required.
Copies of proposal: 3
Deadline(s): None
Board meeting date(s): Quarterly
Write: W. Shepherdson Abell, Secy.-Treas.
Officers and Trustees:* Gregory T. Abell,* Pres.; Christopher S. Abell,* V.P.; W. Shepherdson Abell,* Secy.-Treas.
Employer Identification Number: 521488382

2600
Dart Group Foundation, Inc. ⌑ ☆
c/o Dart Group Corp.
3300 75th Ave.
Landover 20785-1599 (301) 731-1200

Established in 1987 in MD.
Foundation type: Company-sponsored
Financial data (yr. ended 12/31/88): Assets, $1,329,256 (M); gifts received, $600,000; expenditures, $170,169, including $169,230 for 67 grants (high: $18,300; low: $100).
Purpose and activities: Support primarily for the performing arts and cultural programs, higher and other education, health associations, and social service and youth organizations.
Limitations: Giving primarily in MD and Washington, DC. No grants to individuals.
Application information:
Initial approach: Letter
Deadline(s): None
Write: Richard J. Koll, Asst. Secy.
Officers and Directors:* Herbert H. Haft,* Chair.; Robert Haft,* Pres.; Gloria G. Haft,* V.P. and Secy.-Treas.; Linda Haft, V.P.
Employer Identification Number: 521497671

2601
Joel Dean Foundation, Inc.
c/o Jurrien Dean
7422 Hampden Ln.
Bethesda 20814

Established in 1957 in NY.
Donor(s): Joel Dean, Joel Dean Associates Corp.
Foundation type: Independent
Financial data (yr. ended 12/31/87): Assets, $2,149,675 (M); expenditures, $136,955, including $94,650 for grants.
Purpose and activities: Grants primarily for higher education and cultural programs.
Types of support: General purposes.
Application information: Applications not accepted.
Officers and Directors:* Jurrien Dean,* Pres.; Gretchen Dean,* V.P.; Gillian Dean, Joel Dean, Jr.
Employer Identification Number: 136097306

2602
Ralph and Dorothy DeChiaro Foundation, Inc. ⌑
700 Fairmount Ave.
Towson 21204

Incorporated in 1958 in MD.
Donor(s): Ralph DeChiaro, Dorothy DeChiaro.
Foundation type: Independent
Financial data (yr. ended 12/31/87): Assets, $848,526 (M); gifts received, $5,000; expenditures, $269,908, including $251,081 for 47 grants (high: $100,000; low: $50).
Purpose and activities: Support primarily for education, with emphasis on higher education.
Application information:
Initial approach: Letter
Deadline(s): None

Write: Ralph DeChiaro, Mgr.
Officers: Dorothy DeChiaro, Pres.; Ralph DeChiaro, Mgr.
Employer Identification Number: 526036672

2603
Community Foundation of the Eastern Shore, Inc.
One Plaza East, Suite 526-528
Salisbury 21801 (301) 742-9911
Additional address: P.O. Box 156, Salisbury, MD 21803

Established in 1984 in MD.
Foundation type: Community
Financial data (yr. ended 08/31/89): Assets, $2,518,892 (M); gifts received, $1,075,669; expenditures, $319,976, including $234,779 for 300 grants (high: $5,000; low: $1,000) and $5,000 for 1 loan.
Purpose and activities: Giving primarily for human services, including youth organizations, the handicapped and homeless, community development, historic preservation, museums, hospices, and drug abuse; support also for higher and other education, including scholarship funds to institutions; and health and hospitals.
Types of support: Scholarship funds, conferences and seminars, consulting services, deficit financing, emergency funds, equipment, endowment funds, matching funds, seed money.
Limitations: Giving within a 50-mile radius of Salisbury, MD. No grants to individuals, or for annual campaigns, building funds, continuing support, foundation-managed projects, land acquisition, operating budgets, program-related investments, student loans, or technical assistance.
Publications: Annual report, application guidelines, financial statement, informational brochure.
Application information: Application form required.
Initial approach: Letter or telephone
Copies of proposal: 2
Deadline(s): Sixty days prior to board meeting
Board meeting date(s): Feb., May, Aug., and Nov.
Final notification: Immediately following board decision
Write: Lucy A. Mohler, Exec. Dir.
Officers and Directors:* Frank H. Morris,* Chair.; W. Thomas Hershey,* Vice-Chair.; Virginia H. Korff,* Secy.-Treas.; Lucy A. Mohler, Exec. Dir.; and 13 other directors.
Number of staff: 1 full-time professional; 1 part-time support.
Employer Identification Number: 521326014

2604
Egenton Home ⌑
109 Old Padonia Rd. East
Cockeysville 21030
Application address: 201 Cedarcroft Rd., Baltimore, MD 21212; Tel.: (301) 572-7809

Foundation type: Independent
Financial data (yr. ended 06/30/89): Assets, $1,886,028 (M); expenditures, $162,008, including $47,000 for 9 grants (high: $10,550; low: $1,250) and $79,180 for 1 foundation-administered program.
Purpose and activities: The foundation owns a home for teenage girls and contributes to organizations that help needy girls.
Limitations: Giving primarily in MD. No grants to individuals.
Application information:
Initial approach: Letter
Deadline(s): Mar. 31
Write: Christine Wallace, Trustee
Officers and Trustees:* Norvell E. Miller III,* Pres.; Richard M. Drought,* Treas.; Kristin Fox, Haswell Franklin, Curtis Janzen, William H. McCormick, George E. Minot II, David Rice, Christine Wallace, David Wallace.
Employer Identification Number: 520600233

2605
The Equitable Bank Foundation, Inc. ⌑
100 South Charles St.
Baltimore 21201 (301) 547-4274

Incorporated in 1964 in MD.
Donor(s): The Equitable Bank.
Foundation type: Company-sponsored
Financial data (yr. ended 12/31/87): Assets, $574,607 (M); gifts received, $468,000; expenditures, $599,161, including $598,282 for 71 grants (high: $175,000; low: $500).
Purpose and activities: Emphasis on community funds, higher education, youth agencies, hospitals, and arts and culture.
Limitations: Giving primarily in the greater Baltimore, MD, area. No grants to individuals.
Application information:
Write: Louis P. Mathews, Secy.
Officers: H. Grant Hathaway, Pres.; Joseph S. Keelty, V.P.; Louis P. Mathews, Secy.; Laura J. Bortle, Treas.
Employer Identification Number: 526060268

2606
Feinberg Foundation, Inc. ⌑
c/o Harab, Kamerow & Assoc., P.C.
11820 Parklawn Dr., Suite 400
Rockville 20852
Application address: Route 1, Box 165, Easton, MD 21601

Established in 1960 in MD.
Foundation type: Independent
Financial data (yr. ended 12/31/88): Assets, $1,184,328 (M); expenditures, $44,102, including $40,750 for 38 grants (high: $25,000; low: $25).
Purpose and activities: Giving primarily for Jewish welfare organizations; support also for cultural programs.
Application information:
Initial approach: Letter
Deadline(s): None
Write: Harry Feinberg, Pres.
Officer: Harry Feinberg, Pres.
Employer Identification Number: 237000380

2607
First Maryland Foundation, Inc.
25 South Charles St.
Baltimore 21201 (301) 244-4907

Incorporated in 1967 in MD.
Donor(s): First National Bank of Maryland.
Foundation type: Company-sponsored
Financial data (yr. ended 12/31/88): Assets, $1,420,481 (M); gifts received, $750,000; expenditures, $854,582, including $851,698 for 228 grants (high: $150,000; low: $25; average: $3,207).
Purpose and activities: Emphasis on community funds; support also for higher education, music, youth agencies, and hospitals.
Types of support: Annual campaigns, general purposes, scholarship funds, employee matching gifts.
Limitations: Giving primarily in the Baltimore, MD, area. No grants to individuals, or for endowment funds, scholarships, or fellowships; no loans.
Publications: 990-PF.
Application information: Application form not required.
Initial approach: Letter
Copies of proposal: 1
Deadline(s): Mar. 31
Board meeting date(s): Mar., June, Sept., and Dec.
Write: Robert W. Schaefer, Secy.
Officers and Trustees:* J. Owen Cole,* Pres.; Charles W. Cole, Jr.,* V.P.; Robert W. Schaefer,* Secy.-Treas.
Employer Identification Number: 526077253

2608
Foundation for Iranian Studies ⌑ ☆
4343 Montgomery Ave., Suite 200
Bethesda 20814-4401

Established in 1987 in MD.
Donor(s): Princess Ashraf Pahlavi.
Foundation type: Independent
Financial data (yr. ended 12/31/88): Assets, $2,210,160 (M); gifts received, $4,100; expenditures, $171,243, including $11,150 for 4 grants (high: $9,000; low: $500) and $1,000 for 1 grant to an individual.
Purpose and activities: Support for research in Iranian studies, including an award for best dissertation.
Types of support: Grants to individuals.
Application information:
Initial approach: Letter
Deadline(s): Feb. 15
Final notification: Apr.
Write: Ms. Mahnaz Afkhami, V.P.
Officers and Directors: Princess Ashraf Pahlavi, Chair.; Mahnaz Afkhami, V.P. and Exec. Dir.; Abdol H. Samiy, Treas.; Amin Alimard, Amad Ghoreishi.
Employer Identification Number: 521238791

2609
The Jacob and Annita France Foundation, Inc. ▼ ⌑
Charles at Woodbrook, Suite 7
6301 North Charles St.
Baltimore 21212 (301) 377-5251

Incorporated in 1959 in MD.
Donor(s): Jacob France,† Annita A. France.†
Foundation type: Independent
Financial data (yr. ended 5/31/88): Assets, $48,956,051 (M); expenditures, $2,520,251, including $2,080,550 for 81 grants (high: $380,000; low: $50; average: $500-$55,000).

Purpose and activities: Giving within five program areas: higher education, social services and health, historic preservation, arts and culture, and conservation and civic projects.
Types of support: General purposes.
Limitations: Giving limited to MD, with emphasis on Baltimore. No grants to individuals.
Publications: Application guidelines.
Application information: Application form not required.
Initial approach: Letter
Copies of proposal: 1
Deadline(s): None
Board meeting date(s): Quarterly
Write: Frederick W. Lafferty, Exec. Dir.
Officers and Directors: Anne M. Pinkard, Pres.; Robert G. Merrick, Jr., V.P.; Frederick W. Lafferty, Exec. Dir.; Vernon T. Pittinger, Donna Silbersack.
Number of staff: 1 full-time professional; 2 full-time support; 1 part-time support.
Employer Identification Number: 520794585

2610
Carl M. Freeman Foundation, Inc.
11325 Seven Locks Rd.
Potomac 20854

Established in 1962.
Donor(s): Carl M. Freeman.
Foundation type: Independent
Financial data (yr. ended 12/31/88): Assets, $2,020,665 (M); gifts received, $102,700; expenditures, $119,237, including $108,500 for 9 grants (high: $25,000; low: $500).
Purpose and activities: Emphasis on arts and culture, child development, and Jewish welfare agencies.
Types of support: Operating budgets, seed money, special projects.
Limitations: Giving primarily in MD and Washington, DC.
Application information: Contributes only to pre-selected organizations. Applications not accepted.
Officers and Trustees:* Carl M. Freeman,* Pres.; Albert E. Arent,* V.P.; Virginia A. Freeman,* Secy.
Number of staff: 1 part-time support.
Employer Identification Number: 526047536

2611
Giant Food Foundation, Inc. ⌑
6300 Sheriff Rd.
Landover 20785 (301) 341-4100
Mailing address: P.O. Box 1804, Washington, DC 20013

Incorporated in 1950 in DC.
Donor(s): Giant Food, Inc.
Foundation type: Company-sponsored
Financial data (yr. ended 1/31/87): Assets, $297,778 (M); gifts received, $200,000; expenditures, $682,706, including $679,022 for 229 grants (high: $300,000; low: $100).
Purpose and activities: Funds largely committed for continuing support in fields of Jewish welfare, community service, community funds, education, culture, and health, including mental health.
Types of support: General purposes, continuing support.
Limitations: Giving primarily in the Baltimore, MD, and Washington, DC, metropolitan areas; normally no grants to programs of national or international scope. No grants to individuals, or for scholarships, fellowships, or matching gifts; no loans.
Application information: Application form not required.
Initial approach: Proposal
Copies of proposal: 1
Deadline(s): None
Board meeting date(s): Monthly
Final notification: 1 month
Write: David Rutstein, Secy.
Officers: Israel Cohen,* Pres.; Samuel Lehrman,* V.P.; David W. Rutstein, Secy.; David B. Sykes,* Treas.
Directors:* John W. Mason, Richard Waxenburg, Millard F. West, Jr., Morton H. Wilner.
Number of staff: None.
Employer Identification Number: 526045041

2612
Ada & Gertrude Goble-Pearl Strickland Foundation ⌑ ☆
850 Sligo Ave., Suite 400
Silver Spring 20910-4703
Application address: 1702 Myrtle Rd., Silver Spring, MD 20902; Tel.: (301) 681-5692

Established in in 1967.
Foundation type: Independent
Financial data (yr. ended 6/30/89): Assets, $1,000,073 (M); expenditures, $54,791, including $30,000 for 5 grants (high: $12,000; low: $1,000).
Purpose and activities: Giving limited to "organizations that promote, provide, or encourage more humane treatment of animals of all kinds."
Application information:
Initial approach: Proposal
Deadline(s): None
Write: Mrs. Doris E. Bucy, Pres.
Officers: Doris E. Bucy, Pres.; Charles Bucy, V.P.; T. Robert Verkouteren, Treas.
Employer Identification Number: 237057130

2613
Morris Goldseker Foundation of Maryland, Inc. ▼
The Latrobe Bldg.
Two East Read St., 9th Fl.
Baltimore 21202 (301) 837-5100

Incorporated in 1973 in MD.
Donor(s): Morris Goldseker.†
Foundation type: Independent
Financial data (yr. ended 12/31/89): Assets, $41,795,606 (M); expenditures, $1,998,346, including $1,527,163 for 34 grants (average: $2,500-$100,000).
Purpose and activities: Grants to nonprofit institutions operating or initiating programs in community affairs, education, housing, medicine and public health, and human services, primarily benefiting economically disadvantaged persons.
Types of support: Seed money, matching funds, technical assistance, special projects.
Limitations: Giving limited to the Baltimore, MD, area. No support for advocacy or political action groups, religious purposes, or for cultural affairs. No grants to individuals, or for building or endowment funds, equipment, land acquisition, renovation projects, deficit financing, annual campaigns, research, or publications.
Publications: Annual report, informational brochure (including application guidelines).
Application information: Submit preliminary letter as early as possible before deadlines. Application form not required.
Initial approach: Letter
Copies of proposal: 1
Deadline(s): Apr. 1, Aug. 1, and Dec. 1
Board meeting date(s): Distribution committee meets 3 times a year in Mar., June, and Oct.
Final notification: After meetings
Write: Timothy D. Armbruster, Pres.
Officers: Sheldon Goldseker,* Chair.; Simon Goldseker,* Vice-Chair.; Timothy D. Armbruster, Pres.; Harry C. Blubaugh, Secy.; Sheila L. Dodson, Treas.
Trustees:* Security Trust Co.
Selection Committee: Darrell Friedman, Earl Richardson, William C. Richardson.
Number of staff: 3 full-time professional.
Employer Identification Number: 520983502

2614
Peggy & Yale Gordon Charitable Trust
Three Church Ln.
Baltimore 21208 (301) 484-6410

Established in 1980 in MD.
Donor(s): Yale Gordon.†
Foundation type: Independent
Financial data (yr. ended 12/31/88): Assets, $8,324,841 (M); gifts received, $8,002; expenditures, $555,602, including $383,023 for 38 grants (high: $60,382; low: $100).
Purpose and activities: Support for Jewish organizations and cultural programs, including music.
Types of support: Continuing support.
Limitations: Giving primarily in Baltimore, MD.
Application information: Application form not required.
Initial approach: Letter
Copies of proposal: 1
Deadline(s): None
Board meeting date(s): As needed
Write: Sidney S. Sherr, Trustee
Trustees: Kenneth Battye, Loraine Bernstein, Sherry B. Gill, Ann Goldberg, Raymond J. Gordon, Sidney S. Sherr, Robert A. Steinberg.
Number of staff: 3 full-time professional; 1 part-time support.
Employer Identification Number: 521174287

2615
Louis H. Gross Foundation, Inc. ⌑
1314 Dulaney Valley Rd.
Baltimore 21204 (301) 821-9171

Established in 1959 in MD.
Donor(s): Frank Sutland, Mrs. Frank Sutland.
Foundation type: Independent
Financial data (yr. ended 12/31/87): Assets, $2,915,777 (M); gifts received, $403,000; expenditures, $30,104, including $28,844 for 9 grants (high: $5,000; low: $100).

Purpose and activities: Support for Jewish welfare, medical research, and child welfare.
Application information:
Write: Dr. and Mrs. Frank V. Sutland
Employer Identification Number: 146018307

2616
The Homer and Martha Gudelsky Family Foundation, Inc. ⌑
11900 Tech Rd.
Silver Spring 20904 (301) 622-0100

Incorporated in 1968 in MD.
Donor(s): Members of the Gudelsky family, Percontee, Inc., Axcorp, Inc.
Foundation type: Independent
Financial data (yr. ended 12/31/88): Assets, $18,016,834 (M); gifts received, $405,449; expenditures, $681,810, including $678,518 for 37 grants (high: $250,000; low: $50).
Purpose and activities: Grants largely for higher education, local temple support, Jewish welfare funds, and a museum for women in the arts.
Limitations: Giving primarily in MD and Washington, DC.
Application information:
Initial approach: Letter or proposal
Deadline(s): None
Write: Medda Gudelsky, Dir.
Officers: Martha Gudelsky,* V.P.; John Gudelsky, Secy.-Treas.
Directors:* Winston T. Brundige, Medda Gudelsky, Jack C. Merriman.
Employer Identification Number: 520885969

2617
Hechinger Foundation ▼
(also known as Sidney L. Hechinger Foundation)
1616 McCormick Dr.
Landover 20785 (301) 341-0999

Incorporated in 1955 in DC.
Donor(s): Hechinger Co., members of the Hechinger family.
Foundation type: Company-sponsored
Financial data (yr. ended 06/30/88): Assets, $3,615,587 (M); gifts received, $1,823,322; expenditures, $1,187,684, including $1,184,297 for 590 grants (high: $188,334; low: $50; average: $500-$10,000).
Purpose and activities: Emphasis on the performing arts, music, and other cultural programs, Jewish welfare funds, higher education, United Way, and youth and social service agencies, including aid to the handicapped.
Types of support: General purposes.
Limitations: Giving limited to areas of company operations in Washington, DC, DE, MD, NJ, NY, NC, OH, PA, SC, UT, and VA. No grants to individuals.
Publications: Application guidelines.
Application information: Application form not required.
Initial approach: Proposal
Copies of proposal: 1
Deadline(s): None
Board meeting date(s): Continuously
Final notification: 8 to 10 weeks if approved
Write: Richard England, Pres.
Managers and Trustees:* Richard England,* Pres.; Lois H. England, John W. Hechinger, Jr., June R. Hechinger.
Number of staff: 1 full-time professional; 1 full-time support; 1 part-time support.
Employer Identification Number: 526054428

2618
The Hecht-Levi Foundation, Inc. ⌑
c/o Mercantile-Safe Deposit & Trust Co.
Two Hopkins Plaza
Baltimore 21201 (301) 237-5521

Incorporated in 1958 in MD.
Donor(s): Alexander Hecht,† Selma H. Hecht,† Robert H. Levi, Ryda H. Levi.
Foundation type: Independent
Financial data (yr. ended 12/31/88): Assets, $6,667,420 (M); expenditures, $427,582, including $362,033 for 64 grants (high: $85,000; low: $250; average: $250-$50,000).
Purpose and activities: Grants primarily for Jewish welfare funds, cultural programs, including music, and higher education.
Limitations: Giving primarily in the Baltimore, MD, metropolitan area. No grants to individuals.
Application information: Application form not required.
Initial approach: Proposal
Copies of proposal: 1
Deadline(s): Submit proposal preferably in Mar. or Sept.
Board meeting date(s): June and Dec.
Write: Patricia Bentz
Officers and Directors: Robert H. Levi, Pres.; Ryda H. Levi, V.P.; Wilbert H. Sirota, Secy.; Sandra L. Gerstung, Frank A. Kaufman, Alexander H. Levi, Richard H. Levi.
Employer Identification Number: 526035023

2619
Corina Higginson Trust
c/o The Accokeek Foundation, Inc.
3400 Bryan Point Rd.
Accokeek 20607 (301) 283-2113

Trust established in 1962 in DC.
Donor(s): Corina Higginson.†
Foundation type: Independent
Financial data (yr. ended 12/31/87): Assets, $2,299,226 (M); expenditures, $115,364, including $88,645 for 22 grants (high: $20,000; low: $500; average: $5,000).
Purpose and activities: Emphasis on education and self-help.
Types of support: Operating budgets, continuing support, seed money, emergency funds, equipment, matching funds, special projects, research, publications, conferences and seminars, exchange programs, general purposes, internships, lectureships.
Limitations: Giving primarily in the Washington, DC, area, including MD and VA. No support for medical or health-related programs or organizations. No grants to individuals, or for endowment funds.
Publications: Application guidelines.
Application information: Application form required.
Initial approach: Proposal, letter, or telephone
Copies of proposal: 5
Deadline(s): Mar. 1 and Sept. 1
Board meeting date(s): Apr. and Oct.
Final notification: 2 months
Write: Dr. Wilton C. Corkern, Jr., Trustee
Trustees: Charles C. Abeles, Wilton C. Corkern, Jr., John Perkins, Jean Sisco, Rev. John P. Whalen.
Number of staff: None.
Employer Identification Number: 526055743

2620
William F. & Caroline Hilgenberg Foundation, Inc. ⌑
c/o Hessey & Hessey, 1311 Fidelity Bldg.
210 North Charles St.
Baltimore 21201 (301) 539-3300

Established in 1951 in MD.
Foundation type: Independent
Financial data (yr. ended 11/30/87): Assets, $663,431 (M); expenditures, $295,560, including $287,000 for 6 grants (high: $255,000; low: $1,000).
Purpose and activities: Support for social services and hospitals.
Limitations: Giving primarily in MD.
Application information:
Initial approach: Letter
Deadline(s): None
Write: Mahlon W. Hessey, Secy.
Officers and Trustees: August Nolte, Pres.; C. David Haacke, V.P.; Mahlon W. Hessey, V.P. and Secy.; William O. Devilbiss, V.P. and Treas.
Employer Identification Number: 526035937

2621
Himmelrich Fund, Inc. ⌑
900 South Eutaw St.
Baltimore 21230-2496

Established in 1968 in MD.
Foundation type: Independent
Financial data (yr. ended 12/31/88): Assets, $19,515 (M); gifts received, $116,600; expenditures, $100,336, including $100,247 for 21 grants (high: $70,000; low: $50).
Purpose and activities: Support primarily for education, Jewish organizations, and the arts.
Limitations: Giving primarily in Baltimore, MD.
Application information: Application form not required.
Deadline(s): None
Officers: Samuel K. Himmelrich, Pres.; Alfred R. Himmelrich, V.P.
Employer Identification Number: 526081812

2622
David and Barbara B. Hirschhorn Foundation, Inc. ⌑ ☆
Blaustein Bldg.
P.O. Box 238
Baltimore 21203

Established in 1986 in MD.
Donor(s): Barbara B. Hirschhorn, David Hirschhorn.
Foundation type: Independent
Financial data (yr. ended 12/31/88): Assets, $1,564,089 (M); gifts received, $135,783; expenditures, $57,522, including $56,750 for 16 grants (high: $50,000; low: $250).
Purpose and activities: Giving primarily for cancer research.

Limitations: Giving primarily in Baltimore, MD.
Application information:
Initial approach: Letter
Write: David Hirschhorn, Pres.
Officers and Trustees:* Barbara B. Hirschhorn,* Chair.; David Hirschhorn,* Pres.; Daniel B. Hirschhorn,* V.P.; Michael J. Hirschhorn,* V.P.; Sarah H. Shapiro,* V.P.; Deborah H. Vogelstein,* V.P.; Frank A. Strzelczyk, Secy.-Treas.
Employer Identification Number: 521489400

2623
The Emmert Hobbs Foundation, Inc. ⌑
c/o Friedman & Friedman
409 Washington Ave., Suite 900
Towson 21204 (301) 494-0100

Incorporated in 1983 in MD.
Donor(s): Emmert Hobbs.†
Foundation type: Independent
Financial data (yr. ended 07/31/89): Assets, $3,044,173 (M); expenditures, $154,610, including $127,500 for 23 grants (high: $50,000; low: $1,000; average: $3,000).
Purpose and activities: Support for health, social services, education, and limited cultural programs.
Types of support: General purposes, scholarship funds, building funds.
Limitations: Giving primarily in the Baltimore, MD, metropolitan area. No support for research. No grants to individuals.
Application information:
Initial approach: Letter
Deadline(s): None
Write: Louis F. Friedman, Dir.
Directors: D. Sylvan Friedman, Louis F. Friedman.
Employer Identification Number: 521285106

2624
Hoffberger Foundation, Inc. ⌑
800 Garrett Bldg.
233 East Redwood St.
Baltimore 21202 (301) 576-4258

Incorporated in 1941 in MD.
Donor(s): The Hoffberger family.
Foundation type: Independent
Financial data (yr. ended 12/31/89): Assets, $12,929,251 (M); expenditures, $871,161, including $834,629 for 68 grants (high: $150,000; low: $250; average: $500-$10,000).
Purpose and activities: Emphasis on local Jewish health and welfare agencies, social services, and higher educational organizations and institutions.
Types of support: Annual campaigns, seed money, building funds, equipment, endowment funds, scholarship funds, fellowships, matching funds, general purposes, continuing support.
Limitations: Giving primarily in Baltimore, MD. No grants to individuals, or for operating budgets; no loans.
Application information: Application form not required.
Initial approach: Proposal
Copies of proposal: 1
Deadline(s): 30 days prior to board meetings
Board meeting date(s): June and Dec.
Final notification: 6 months
Write: LeRoy E. Hoffberger, Pres.
Officers and Directors:* LeRoy E. Hoffberger,* Pres.; Charles H. Hoffberger,* V.P. and Secy.; Jerold C. Hoffberger,* Treas.; Morton J. Hollander, Patti Sparks.
Employer Identification Number: 520794249

2625
Harley W. Howell Charitable Foundation ⌑
c/o Signet Bank of Maryland
Seven Paul St., P.O. Box 17034
Baltimore 21203 (301) 332-5555

Established in 1961 in MD.
Donor(s): Harley W. Howell.
Foundation type: Independent
Financial data (yr. ended 12/31/88): Assets, $1,284,101 (M); expenditures, $110,779, including $100,300 for 33 grants (high: $42,500; low: $300).
Purpose and activities: Support primarily for cultural programs, health services, and medical research.
Types of support: Endowment funds, research, general purposes.
Application information: Application form not required.
Deadline(s): None
Write: Robert C. Rice
Distribution Committee: Geneva E. Howell, H. Thomas Howell, Diane Howell Stewart.
Trustee Bank: Signet Bank of Maryland.
Employer Identification Number: 526033554

2626
The Howard Hughes Medical Institute ☆
6701 Rockledge Dr.
Bethesda 20817 (301) 571-0200

Incorporated in 1953 in DE.
Donor(s): Howard R. Hughes.†
Financial data (yr. ended 08/31/89): Assets, $6,431,979,000 (M); expenditures, $238,448,000, including $39,361,575 for 54 grants (high: $2,000,000; low: $30,000; average: $30,000-$2,000,000), $2,525,425 for 109 grants to individuals (high: $23,000; low: $20,000; average: $20,000-$23,000) and $196,561,000 for 1 foundation-administered program.
Purpose and activities: A nonprofit scientific and philanthropic organization whose principal purpose is the direct conduct of medical research. According to the Institute's charter: "The primary purpose and objective of the Howard Hughes Medical Institute shall be the promotion of human knowledge within the field of the basic sciences (principally the field of medical research and medical education) and the effective application thereof for the benefit of mankind." The Institute is qualified as a medical research organization, not as a private foundation, under the federal tax code. It administers a medical research program for the direct conduct of medical research and a grants program for support of science education.
Types of support: Research, fellowships, special projects.
Limitations: No support for the direct conduct of biomedical research except to scientific investigators employed by the Institute; no grants or fellowships except to individuals or institutions competing under established science education programs.
Publications: Annual report, application guidelines, occasional report, program policy statement.
Application information: Applicants should consult guidelines in the Institute's publication, "Grants for Science Education" prior to application. Fellowships are awarded on the basis of a national and international competition and peer review. Grant proposals to undergraduate institutions are by invitation only. Application form required.
Initial approach: Letter, proposal, or application, depending on program
Copies of proposal: 1
Deadline(s): Grants and Special Programs - varies. Fellowships - Predoctoral in Biological Sciences: early Nov.; Medical Student Research Training: early Dec.; Postdoctoral Research for Physicians: early Mar. Undergraduate invited proposals - 1st week of Jan.
Board meeting date(s): Feb., May, Aug., and Nov.
Final notification: Each graduate and undergraduate program has individual notification date; program brochures and announcements should be consulted
Write: Dr. Joseph G. Perpich, V.P., for general inquiries; Dr. Barbara Filner, Prog. Officer, for graduate programs; Stephen A. Barkanic, Prog. Officer, for undergraduate programs; and David Davis-Van Atta for assessment programs
Officers: Purnell W. Choppin, M.D., Pres.; W. Maxwell Cowan, M.D., V.P. and Chief Scientific Officer; Graham O. Harrison, V.P. and Chief Investment Officer; Joseph G. Perpich, M.D., V.P., Grants and Special Programs; William T. Quillen, V.P. and General Counsel; Robert C. White, V.P. and C.F.O.
Trustees: Irving S. Shapiro, Chair.; Alexander G. Bearn, M.D., Helen K. Copley, Frank William Gay, James H. Gilliam, Jr., Hanna H. Gray, William R. Lummis, George W. Thorn, M.D., James D. Wolfensohn.
Number of staff: 1223 full-time professional; 29 part-time professional; 462 full-time support; 74 part-time support.
Employer Identification Number: 590735717

2627
Israel Family Foundation, Inc. ⌑ ☆
Snug Harbor Farm
P.O. Box 69
Royal Oak 21662 (301) 745-3393

Incorporated in 1986 in MD.
Donor(s): Fred Israel, Lesley Israel.
Foundation type: Independent
Financial data (yr. ended 11/30/88): Assets, $1,056,835 (M); gifts received, $2,076; expenditures, $36,009, including $31,965 for 53 grants (high: $11,500; low: $10).
Purpose and activities: Giving primarily for Jewish organizations.
Limitations: Giving primarily in NY, MD, and Washington, DC.
Application information:
Write: Fred Israel, Pres.
Officers: Fred Israel, Pres.; Lesley Israel, Secy.-Treas.
Employer Identification Number: 521531308

2628
A. S. Kay Foundation, Inc.
5454 Wisconsin Ave., Suite 1300
Chevy Chase 20815 (301) 657-4222

Incorporated in 1948 in MD.
Donor(s): A.S. Kay,† and members of the Kay family.
Foundation type: Independent
Financial data (yr. ended 12/31/89): Assets, $1,097,085 (M); qualifying distributions, $100,790, including $100,790 for 6 grants (high: $50,590; low: $100).
Purpose and activities: Giving primarily for Jewish welfare funds, higher education, and religious schools.
Types of support: Annual campaigns, general purposes, scholarship funds.
Limitations: Giving primarily in MD. No grants to individuals or for endowment funds.
Publications: Annual report, 990-PF.
Application information: Applications not accepted.
Board meeting date(s): Dec.
Write: Louis C. Grossberg, Treas.
Officers: Jack Kay, V.P.; Harold Greenberg, Secy.; Louis C. Grossberg, Treas.
Number of staff: None.
Employer Identification Number: 520794107

2629
The Keelty Foundation, Inc. ¤ ☆
61 East Padonia Rd.
P.O. Box 528
Timonium 21093-0528

Established in 1953 in MD.
Donor(s): James Keelty, Jr.
Foundation type: Independent
Financial data (yr. ended 6/30/89): Assets, $5,716 (M); gifts received, $162,000; expenditures, $169,558, including $169,500 for 8 grants (high: $100,000; low: $1,000).
Purpose and activities: Giving primarily for higher education, especially a law school.
Types of support: Building funds, scholarship funds, general purposes.
Limitations: Giving primarily in MD. No grants to individuals.
Application information: Contributes only to pre-selected organizations. Applications not accepted.
Officers and Directors: James Keelty, Jr., Pres.; James Keelty III, V.P.; Michael Keelty, Secy.; Louise H. Keelty, Treas.
Employer Identification Number: 526035975

2630
Joseph S. Keelty Foundation ¤
61 East Padonia Rd.
P.O. Box 528
Timonium 21093 (301) 252-8600

Established in 1981 in MD.
Donor(s): Joseph S. Keelty.
Foundation type: Independent
Financial data (yr. ended 06/30/88): Assets, $257,578 (M); gifts received, $307,000; expenditures, $249,548, including $249,300 for 19 grants (high: $50,000; low: $800).
Purpose and activities: Emphasis on education; support also for religious organizations.
Limitations: Giving primarily in MD.
Application information: Contributes only to pre-selected organizations. Applications not accepted.
Write: Joseph S. Keelty, Pres.
Officers and Directors:* Joseph S. Keelty,* Pres.; Lucette K. Costa,* V.P.; John B. Howard,* Secy.; James L. Donohue, Treas.
Employer Identification Number: 521218328

2631
Ensign C. Markland Kelly, Jr. Memorial Foundation, Inc.
1406 Fidelity Bldg.
Baltimore 21201 (301) 837-8822

Incorporated in 1946 in MD.
Donor(s): C. Markland Kelly,† Kelly Buick Sales Corp.
Foundation type: Independent
Financial data (yr. ended 12/31/88): Assets, $3,943,923 (M); expenditures, $294,595, including $186,936 for 29 grants (high: $30,439; low: $100).
Purpose and activities: Giving primarily to support elementary and secondary education, youth activities, and civic and cultural organizations.
Types of support: Annual campaigns, building funds, equipment, endowment funds, special projects, scholarship funds, matching funds, capital campaigns.
Limitations: Giving limited to the greater Baltimore, MD, metropolitan area. No grants to individuals, or for operating budgets, research, fellowships, or travel; no loans.
Publications: Informational brochure, program policy statement, application guidelines, occasional report.
Application information: Application form not required.
Initial approach: Proposal
Copies of proposal: 3
Deadline(s): None
Board meeting date(s): Monthly
Final notification: 6 months
Write: Herbert E. Witz, Pres.
Officers and Directors: Herbert E. Witz, Pres.; Bowen P. Weisheit, V.P.; Carol A. Witz, Secy.; Bowen P. Weisheit, Jr., Treas.
Number of staff: 1 part-time professional; 1 part-time support.
Employer Identification Number: 526033330

2632
Kentland Foundation, Inc. ¤
P.O. Box 4689
Rockville 20850 (301) 948-1573

Incorporated about 1966 in MD.
Donor(s): Otis Beall Kent.†
Foundation type: Independent
Financial data (yr. ended 12/31/86): Assets, $4,888,099 (M); expenditures, $621,461, including $184,940 for 36 grants (high: $57,340; low: $100).
Purpose and activities: Primarily local giving for the National Geographic Society and church support.
Limitations: Giving primarily in MD.
Application information: Application form not required.
Deadline(s): None
Write: Helene Walker, Secy.
Officers: Helene D. Kent, Pres.; William Loren, V.P.; Helene Walker, Secy.-Treas.; Thomas Greenland, Sheila Stedman.
Employer Identification Number: 526070323

2633
Knapp Educational Fund, Inc.
P.O. Box O
St. Michaels 21663 (301) 745-5660

Established about 1979 in MD.
Donor(s): The Knapp Foundation, Inc.
Foundation type: Independent
Financial data (yr. ended 12/31/88): Assets, $4,594,630 (M); expenditures, $221,095, including $25,050 for 2 grants (high: $25,000; low: $50) and $137,300 for 62 grants to individuals.
Purpose and activities: Awards scholarships for children of employees of Macmillan, Inc.
Types of support: Employee-related scholarships.
Application information: Applications not accepted.
Write: Robert B. Vojvoda, V.P.
Officers and Trustees:* Antoinette P. Vojvoda,* Pres.; Robert B. Vojvoda,* V.P. and Treas.; Ruth M. Capranica,* Secy.; Frank M. Dahne, Sylvia V. Penny.
Employer Identification Number: 132970128

2634
The Knapp Foundation, Inc.
P.O. Box O
St. Michaels 21663 (301) 745-5660

Incorporated in 1929 in NC.
Donor(s): Joseph Palmer Knapp.†
Foundation type: Independent
Financial data (yr. ended 12/31/88): Assets, $16,118,339 (M); expenditures, $584,795, including $476,709 for 37 grants (high: $100,000; low: $273).
Purpose and activities: Grants primarily for conservation and preservation of wildlife and wildfowl, and for assistance to college and university libraries in the purchasing of reading materials and equipment to improve education.
Types of support: Equipment.
Limitations: Giving primarily in the eastern U.S., including ME, VT, NH, MA, RI, CT, NY, NJ, PA, MD, VA, NC, SC, and FL. No grants to individuals, or for endowment or building funds, operating budgets, scholarships, or fellowships; no loans.
Publications: Application guidelines.
Application information:
Initial approach: Letter
Copies of proposal: 1
Board meeting date(s): Dec.; executive board meets quarterly when necessary
Write: Robert B. Vojvoda, V.P.
Officers and Trustees:* Antoinette P. Vojvoda,* Pres.; Robert B. Vojvoda,* V.P. and Treas.; Ruth M. Capranica,* Secy.; Margaret P. Newcombe, George L. Penny IV, Sylvia V. Penny.
Number of staff: 1 part-time professional.
Employer Identification Number: 136001167

2635
The Marion I. and Henry J. Knott Foundation, Inc.
3904 Hickory Ave.
Baltimore 21211 (301) 235-7068

Established in 1986 in MD as successor to the first Marion I. and Henry J. Knott Foundation, Inc.
Donor(s): Marion I. Knott, Henry J. Knott, Sr.
Foundation type: Independent
Financial data (yr. ended 12/31/89): Assets, $23,496,526 (M); expenditures, $1,425,088, including $611,900 for 37 grants (high: $164,000; low: $1,000; average: $10,000-$30,000).
Purpose and activities: "Giving for Roman Catholic activities and other charitable, cultural, educational, and health and human service organizations."
Types of support: Building funds, capital campaigns, conferences and seminars, continuing support, endowment funds, equipment, general purposes, land acquisition, matching funds, operating budgets, renovation projects, seed money, special projects, technical assistance.
Limitations: Giving limited to the greater Baltimore, MD, metropolitan area. No support for pro-abortion causes and public education. No grants to individuals, or for annual giving or scholarships.
Application information: Application form not required.
Initial approach: Proposal
Copies of proposal: 2
Deadline(s): Feb. 1 and Aug. 1
Board meeting date(s): June and Dec.
Write: Ann von Lossberg, Admin.
Officers and Directors:* Henry J. Knott, Sr.,* Chair.; Marion I. Knott,* Vice-Chair.; Alice K. Voelkel,* Pres.; Patricia K. Smyth,* V.P.; Geralynn D. Smyth,* Secy.; Henry J. Knott, Jr.,* Treas.; Marty Voelkel Hanasen, Carlisle V. Hashim, Carol D. Knott, Francis X. Knott, James F. Knott, John C. Smyth.
Number of staff: 1 full-time professional; 1 full-time support.
Employer Identification Number: 521517876

2636
Fabian Kolker Foundation, Inc. ⌑ ☆
3520 Barton Oaks Rd.
Baltimore 21208-4301

Foundation type: Operating
Financial data (yr. ended 08/31/88): Assets, $34,994 (L); gifts received, $147,125; expenditures, $189,460, including $151,328 for 20 grants (high: $119,500; low: $24).
Purpose and activities: A private operating foundation; giving for Jewish organizations and higher education.
Limitations: Giving primarily in Baltimore, MD.
Application information: Application form not required.
Deadline(s): None
Write: Fabian H. Kolker, Trustee
Trustees: Fabian H. Kolker, Jerome Schuman.
Employer Identification Number: 521275625

2637
The Abraham and Ruth Krieger Family Foundation, Inc. ⌑
(Formerly The Krieger Fund, Inc.)
c/o Wolpoff & Co.
200 St. Paul Place, Suite 2300
Baltimore 21202-2004
Application address: P.O. Box 10493, Baltimore, MD 21209

Incorporated in 1944 in MD.
Donor(s): Abraham Krieger.
Foundation type: Independent
Financial data (yr. ended 12/31/88): Assets, $2,546,860 (M); expenditures, $121,072, including $117,460 for 17 grants (high: $69,610; low: $100).
Purpose and activities: Emphasis on Jewish welfare funds; support also for secondary education and cultural programs.
Limitations: Giving primarily in Baltimore, MD. No grants to individuals.
Application information:
Initial approach: Letter
Deadline(s): None
Board meeting date(s): As required
Write: Jane K. Schapiro, Pres.
Officer: Jane K. Schapiro, Pres.; Joann C. Fruchtman, V.P. and Secy.; Howard K. Cohen, V.P. and Treas.
Employer Identification Number: 526035537

2638
Greta Brown Layton Charitable Trust ⌑
c/o Mercantile-Safe Deposit & Trust Co.
Two Hopkins Plaza
Baltimore 21201 (301) 237-5653

Established in 1965 in MD.
Foundation type: Independent
Financial data (yr. ended 12/31/88): Assets, $1,374,400 (M); expenditures, $132,931, including $126,150 for 49 grants (high: $35,000; low: $200).
Purpose and activities: Grants for education, hospitals, social services, and cultural programs.
Limitations: Giving primarily in DE.
Application information:
Initial approach: Letter
Deadline(s): None
Write: J. Michael Miller, V.P., Mercantile-Safe Deposit & Trust Co.
Trustee: Mercantile-Safe Deposit & Trust Co.
Employer Identification Number: 526063086

2639
John J. Leidy Foundation, Inc. ⌑
c/o Pierson & Pierson
Ten Light St., 30th Fl.
Baltimore 21202 (301) 727-4136

Incorporated in 1957 in MD.
Donor(s): John J. Leidy.†
Foundation type: Independent
Financial data (yr. ended 12/31/87): Assets, $5,091,145 (M); expenditures, $279,662.
Purpose and activities: Emphasis on child welfare, hospitals, higher education, including scholarship funds, and social agencies.
Types of support: Scholarship funds.
Limitations: Giving primarily in MD. No grants to individuals.
Application information:
Initial approach: Proposal
Deadline(s): None
Write: Edward Pierson, Pres.
Officers and Trustees: Edward Pierson, Pres.; W. Michel Pierson, V.P.; Allan H. Fisher, Secy.; Henry E. Pear, Treas.
Employer Identification Number: 526034785

2640
Richard S. Levitt Foundation ⌑
6001 Montrose Rd., Suite 600
Rockville 20852

Established in 1957.
Donor(s): Members of the Levitt Family.
Foundation type: Independent
Financial data (yr. ended 12/31/88): Assets, $4,811,515 (M); gifts received, $1,467,000; expenditures, $273,393, including $263,320 for 63 grants (high: $100,000; low: $10).
Purpose and activities: Giving for higher education, cultural programs, Jewish religious and welfare organizations, and social services.
Limitations: Giving primarily in Des Moines, IA. No grants to individuals.
Application information: Contributes only to pre-selected organizations. Applications not accepted.
Officers: Richard Levitt, Pres. and Treas.; Mark Levitt, V.P.; Randall Levitt, V.P.; Jeanne Levitt, Secy.
Employer Identification Number: 426052427

2641
Life Sciences Research Foundation ▼
115 West University Pkwy.
Baltimore 21210 (301) 467-2597
Application address: c/o Lewis Thomas Laboratories, Princeton University, Princeton, NJ 08544; Tel.: (609) 452-3551

Changed status to a private foudation in 1984 in MD.
Donor(s): Various donors.
Foundation type: Independent
Financial data (yr. ended 5/31/89): Assets, $748,225 (M); gifts received, $1,061,250; expenditures, $1,124,786, including $1,096,250 for 31 grants to individuals (high: $35,000; low: $8,750; average: $22,500-$43,750).
Purpose and activities: Awards postdoctoral research fellowships to graduates of medical schools and graduate schools in the biological sciences.
Types of support: Research, fellowships.
Publications: Annual report, informational brochure, application guidelines.
Application information: Application form required.
Copies of proposal: 3
Deadline(s): Oct. 1; supporting letters must be received by Nov.
Final notification: Mar.
Officers: Donald D. Brown, Pres.; Patricia Englar, Secy.; Roger Redden, Treas.
Directors: David Baltimore, Paul Berg, Konrad Bloch, David Blotsein, Michael S. Brown, Pedro Cuatrecasas, James E. Darnell, Jr., Joseph M. Davie, Donald Frederickson, Arthur Kornberg, Daniel Nathans, Hamilton O. Smith, Lewis Thomas, James Watson, and 20 additional directors.
Employer Identification Number: 521231801

2642
Lime Kiln Valley Foundation, Inc. ⌑ ☆
1800 Cromwell Bridge Rd.
Baltimore 21234-1417
Application address: 1740 East Juppa Rd., Baltimore, MD 21234; Tel.: (301) 661-6886

Established in 1969.
Donor(s): Regina L. Hart.†
Foundation type: Independent
Financial data (yr. ended 12/31/88): Assets, $1,926,321 (M); expenditures, $70,365, including $65,100 for grants.
Purpose and activities: Support primarily for Protestant secondary education and a symphony orchestra.
Application information:
Initial approach: Letter
Deadline(s): None
Write: Daniel S. Sullivan, Jr., Secy.
Officers: William Sebastian Hart, Jr., Pres.; John N. Renneburg, V.P.; Daniel S. Sullivan, Jr., Secy.; Charles A. Bodie, Jr., Treas.
Employer Identification Number: 526075802

2643
Loats Foundation, Inc.
P.O. Box 240
Frederick 21701 (301) 662-2191
Application address: c/o Evangelical Lutheran Church, 35 East Church St., Frederick, MD 21701; Tel.: (301) 663-6361

Established in 1881 in MD.
Donor(s): John Loats.†
Foundation type: Independent
Financial data (yr. ended 5/31/89): Assets, $2,170,566 (M); expenditures, $113,570, including $8,500 for 7 grants (high: $2,500; low: $1,000) and $91,490 for 87 grants to individuals of $2,500 each.
Purpose and activities: To provide for the care and education of needy children and orphans; giving primarily for scholarships.
Types of support: Student aid.
Limitations: Giving limited to Frederick County, MD. No grants for postgraduate scholarships.
Publications: Program policy statement, application guidelines.
Application information: Applications available at all Frederick County High Schools. Application form required.
Deadline(s): Contact Evangelical Lutheran Church office for deadlines
Board meeting date(s): Annually and as required
Write: Glenn E. Biehl, Treas.
Officers: W. Philip Fogarty,* Pres.; Warner L. Brittain, V.P.; Melvin H. Derr,* Secy.; Glenn E. Biehl, Treas.
Trustees:* Marion D. Carmack, Jr., Garland P. Feaga, C. Richard Miller, Jr.
Number of staff: 1 part-time support.
Employer Identification Number: 520610535

2644
The M.E. Foundation ⌑
Two West Rolling Crossroads, Suite 207
Baltimore 21228-6201 (301) 944-8676

Established in 1966 in NY.
Donor(s): Margaret Brown Trimble, Frances Carroll Brown.
Foundation type: Independent
Financial data (yr. ended 12/31/88): Assets, $11,936,972 (M); expenditures, $917,793, including $892,567 for 60 grants (high: $60,000; low: $300).
Purpose and activities: Grants to organizations in the U.S. and abroad for Protestant evangelistic missionary work and Bible studies.
Application information: Application form not required.
Initial approach: Written request
Deadline(s): None
Write: Miss F. Carroll Brown, V.P., or Margaret Brown Trimble, Pres.
Officers and Directors:* Margaret Brown Trimble,* Pres. and Secy.; Frances Carroll Brown,* V.P. and Treas.; Charles W. Colson,* V.P.
Employer Identification Number: 136205356

2645
Morton and Sophia Macht Foundation
ll East Fayette St.
Baltimore 21202 (301) 539-2370

Established in 1956 in MD.
Donor(s): Sophia Macht,† Westland Gardens Co., and others.
Foundation type: Independent
Financial data (yr. ended 04/30/89): Assets, $1,584,730 (M); gifts received, $137,100; expenditures, $184,006, including $161,475 for grants (high: $17,500; low: $25; average: $750).
Purpose and activities: Grants for Jewish giving, higher and other education, community funds, social services, and cultural programs.
Types of support: Annual campaigns, building funds, capital campaigns, consulting services, continuing support, deficit financing, emergency funds, endowment funds, equipment, exchange programs, general purposes, land acquisition, operating budgets, professorships, publications, renovation projects, research, scholarship funds, seed money, special projects, conferences and seminars.
Limitations: Giving primarily in MD. No grants to individuals.
Application information:
Initial approach: Proposal
Deadline(s): None
Write: Bette Cohen, V.P.
Officers and Trustees:* Amy Macht,* Pres.; Robert Gonzales, V.P. and Secy.; Jill Gansler, V.P. and Treas.; Bette Cohen, V.P.; H. William Cohen,* V.P.; Alan Goodhardt,* V.P.; Lee Kaufman,* V.P.; Philip Macht,* V.P.
Number of staff: 1 part-time professional; 1 part-time support.
Employer Identification Number: 526035753

2646
George Preston Marshall Foundation
(also known as Redskin Foundation, Inc.)
5454 Wisconsin Ave., Suite 1455
Chevy Chase 20815 (301) 654-7774

Incorporated in 1972 in DC.
Donor(s): George Preston Marshall.†
Foundation type: Independent
Financial data (yr. ended 12/31/87): Assets, $0 (M); expenditures, $442,504, including $414,640 for 68 grants (high: $27,000; low: $325).
Purpose and activities: "For the health, welfare, education and improvement of conditions of children..."
Types of support: Special projects, equipment, scholarship funds, building funds, capital campaigns, consulting services, general purposes, land acquisition, matching funds, operating budgets, renovation projects, seed money.
Limitations: Giving limited to Washington, DC, MD, and VA. No grants to individuals.
Publications: Annual report, application guidelines, program policy statement.
Application information:
Initial approach: Proposal
Copies of proposal: 1
Deadline(s): Applications accepted throughout year
Board meeting date(s): 5 times per year
Write: Elizabeth B. Frazier, Exec. Dir.
Officers: James C. McKay,* Pres.; William D. Foote,* V.P.; J. Paull Marshall,* Secy.; G. Dewey Arnold, Jr.,* Treas.; Elizabeth B. Frazier, Exec. Dir.
Directors:* John W. Sweeterman.
Number of staff: 1 part-time professional.
Employer Identification Number: 237173302

2647
Martin Marietta Corporation Foundation ▼
6801 Rockledge Dr.
Bethesda 20817 (301) 897-6863

Trust established in 1955 in MD.
Donor(s): Martin Marietta Corp.
Foundation type: Company-sponsored
Financial data (yr. ended 12/31/87): Assets, $4,827,291 (M); gifts received, $9,100,000; expenditures, $4,651,475, including $2,782,695 for 1,186 grants (high: $313,410; low: $25; average: $500-$10,000), $554,325 for grants to individuals and $1,310,000 for employee matching gifts.
Purpose and activities: Primary interest in higher education, particularly through support of scholarships for children of corporation employees; support also for health, cultural, and civic programs.
Types of support: Employee-related scholarships, employee matching gifts, general purposes.
Limitations: Giving primarily in areas of company operations. No support for political or religious groups, or current United Way recipients. No grants to individuals (except for employee-related scholarships).
Publications: Application guidelines.
Application information: Application form not required.
Initial approach: Proposal
Copies of proposal: 1
Deadline(s): Applications accepted throughout the year, with majority of commitments made in the fall
Board meeting date(s): As needed
Final notification: 2 to 3 months
Write: John T. de Viser, Dir., Corporate Affairs

Trustees: Wayne A. Shaner, Peter F. Warren, Jr., A. Thomas Young.
Number of staff: 1
Employer Identification Number: 136161566

2648
George W. McManus Foundation ⌑
3703 Greenway
Baltimore 21218 (301) 243-3703

Established about 1959 in MD.
Foundation type: Operating
Financial data (yr. ended 12/31/87): Assets, $1,666,966 (M); expenditures, $70,668, including $39,821 for 20 grants (high: $25,000; low: $10).
Purpose and activities: A private operating foundation; giving for social services; support also for a scholarship fund.
Types of support: Scholarship funds.
Limitations: No grants to individuals.
Application information: Contributes only to pre-selected organizations. Applications not accepted.
Officers: George W. McManus, Jr., Pres.; T. Ann Miller, V.P. and Secy.; George W. McManus III, Treas.
Trustee: Margaret T. McManus.
Employer Identification Number: 526044928

2649
Morris A. Mechanic Foundation ⌑
P.O. Box 1623
Baltimore 21203

Established in 1942 in MD.
Foundation type: Independent
Financial data (yr. ended 12/31/88): Assets, $2,508,294 (M); expenditures, $91,660, including $70,750 for 28 grants (high: $12,500; low: $250).
Purpose and activities: Support primarily for higher education, hospitals, and music-related organizations.
Limitations: Giving primarily in Baltimore, MD.
Application information: Contributes only to pre-selected organizations. Applications not accepted.
Write: Clarisse B. Mechanic, Pres.
Officers: Clarisse B. Mechanic, Pres.; Blue Barron, Secy.
Employer Identification Number: 526034753

2650
Thomas Meloy Foundation
c/o William W. Wolf
17411 Founders Mill Dr.
Rockville 20855-2508

Foundation type: Independent
Financial data (yr. ended 03/31/89): Assets, $1,062,340 (M); expenditures, $90,505, including $75,500 for 10 grants (high: $50,000; low: $1,000).
Purpose and activities: Support primarily for education, cultural programs, and health and social services.
Types of support: General purposes.
Application information: Contributes only to pre-selected organizations. Applications not accepted.
Officers: Consuelo Nussbaum,* Pres.; J. Pierce Chambers,* V.P.; William W. Wolf, Secy.-Treas.
Directors:* Thomas Stuart Meloy, Lise L. Nussbaum O'Haire.
Employer Identification Number: 521116472

2651
Alfred G. and Ida Mendelson Family Foundation, Inc. ⌑
8300 Pennsylvania Ave.
P.O. Box 398
Forestville 20747-0398

Incorporated in 1970 in DC.
Donor(s): Murry's Steaks, Inc., and subsidiaries.
Foundation type: Independent
Financial data (yr. ended 03/31/89): Assets, $101,019 (M); expenditures, $231,208, including $228,039 for 55 grants (high: $88,584; low: $22).
Purpose and activities: Giving for temple support, Jewish welfare agencies, and social services.
Limitations: Giving primarily in MD and Washington, DC. No grants to individuals.
Application information: Contributes only to pre-selected organizations. Applications not accepted.
Officers: Ida Mendelson, Pres.; David Luftig, V.P.; Murry Mendelson, Secy.
Employer Identification Number: 237068870

2652
Robert G. and Anne M. Merrick Foundation, Inc. ⌑
6301 North Charles St., Suite 7
Baltimore 21212 (301) 377-5251

Established in 1962.
Donor(s): Robert G. Merrick, Sr.,† Anne M. Merrick,† Homewood Holding Co.
Foundation type: Independent
Financial data (yr. ended 05/31/89): Assets, $39,987,787 (M); expenditures, $1,840,425, including $1,474,555 for 89 grants (high: $147,805; low: $500).
Purpose and activities: Emphasis on cultural programs and higher education.
Limitations: Giving primarily in Baltimore, MD. No grants to individuals.
Application information:
Initial approach: Letter
Deadline(s): None
Board meeting date(s): As needed
Write: Frederick W. Lafferty, Exec. Dir.
Officers: Robert G. Merrick, Jr., Pres.; Anne M. Pinkard, V.P.; Frederick W. Lafferty, Exec. Dir.
Directors: Robert M. Pinkard, Vernon T. Pittinger.
Employer Identification Number: 526072964

2653
Robert & Jane Meyerhoff Foundation, Inc.
1025 Cranbrook Rd.
Cockeysville 21030

Established in 1980 in MD.
Donor(s): Robert E. Meyerhoff.
Foundation type: Independent
Financial data (yr. ended 12/31/88): Assets, $741,277 (M); gifts received, $750,000; expenditures, $307,709, including $304,250 for 8 grants (high: $150,000; low: $750).
Purpose and activities: Giving primarily for museums, culture, and higher education.
Limitations: No grants to individuals.
Application information: Contributes only to pre-selected organizations. Applications not accepted.
Directors: David P. Gordon, Rose Ellen Greene, Jane B. Meyerhoff, Neil A. Meyerhoff, Robert E. Meyerhoff.
Employer Identification Number: 521176421

2654
The Joseph Meyerhoff Fund, Inc. ⌑
25 South Charles St.
Baltimore 21201 (301) 727-3200

Incorporated in 1953 in MD.
Donor(s): Joseph Meyerhoff,† Mrs. Joseph Meyerhoff.
Foundation type: Independent
Financial data (yr. ended 12/31/87): Assets, $18,673,291 (M); expenditures, $432,355, including $102,505 for grants (high: $7,500).
Purpose and activities: Giving primarily to support and encourage cultural and higher educational programs and institutions and to facilitate immigration and absorption of new immigrants into Israel.
Types of support: Annual campaigns, seed money, emergency funds, deficit financing, building funds, land acquisition, endowment funds, research, publications, professorships, scholarship funds, matching funds, continuing support.
Limitations: Giving primarily in Baltimore, MD, New York, NY, and to organizations in Israel. No grants to individuals.
Application information: Funds are committed for a 2- or 3-year period beginning in 1986; contributes only to pre-selected organizations. Applications not accepted.
Board meeting date(s): May and Oct. and as required
Write: Louis L. Kaplan, Exec. V.P.
Officers: Harvey M. Meyerhoff, Pres.; Louis L. Kaplan, Exec. V.P.; Lenore P. Meyerhoff, V.P.; Joseph Meyerhoff II, Treas.
Number of staff: 1 part-time professional; 1 part-time support.
Employer Identification Number: 526035997

2655
Middendorf Foundation, Inc.
803 Cathedral St.
Baltimore 21201

Incorporated in 1953 in MD.
Donor(s): J. William Middendorf, Jr.,† Alice C. Middendorf.†
Foundation type: Independent
Financial data (yr. ended 03/31/88): Assets, $13,190,203 (M); expenditures, $564,849, including $419,827 for grants (average: $6,000).
Purpose and activities: Giving primarily for cultural programs, including historic preservation and museums, higher and secondary education, Protestant church support, and conservation; support also for hospitals and the handicapped.
Types of support: Matching funds, endowment funds, professorships.

Limitations: Giving primarily in MD. No grants to individuals.
Application information:
Initial approach: Letter
Copies of proposal: 1
Deadline(s): None
Write: E. Phillips Hathaway, Pres.
Officers and Trustees:* E. Phillips Hathaway,* Pres.; Roger B. Hopkins, Jr.,* V.P.; Theresa N. Knell,* Secy.; Craig Lewis,* Treas.; Forrest F. Bramble, Jr., Phillips Hathaway, Peter B. Middendorf, Robert B. Russell II.
Number of staff: 2 full-time professional.
Employer Identification Number: 526048944

2656
MNC Foundation, Inc.
(Formerly The Maryland National Foundation, Inc.)
P.O. Box 987, MS020330
Baltimore 21203 (301) 244-6784

Incorporated in 1965 in MD.
Donor(s): Maryland National Bank.
Foundation type: Company-sponsored
Financial data (yr. ended 12/31/89): Assets, $6,343,338 (M); gifts received, $6,447,178; expenditures, $3,381,435, including $3,168,298 for 205 grants (high: $325,540; low: $100) and $90,840 for 434 employee matching gifts.
Purpose and activities: To enhance health and welfare in all the communities the foundation serves, and to support those institutions that make communities desirable places to live and work. Emphasis on community funds, education, arts and culture, environmental issues, health and hospitals, and human and community services.
Types of support: Capital campaigns, employee matching gifts, endowment funds, matching funds, special projects.
Limitations: Giving limited to recipient organizations whose activities are principally conducted within the geographic areas in which MNC Financial and its subsidiaries are active, especially MD. No support for strictly sectarian, fraternal, veterans', religious, social, or athletic organizations, or organizations receiving support through the United Way or other federated drives, exclusive of capital funding needs. No grants to individuals, or for fundraising events, trips, conferences, or publications.
Publications: Application guidelines, annual report.
Application information: Application form not required.
Initial approach: Request guidelines from foundation
Copies of proposal: 1
Deadline(s): None
Write: George B.P. Ward, Jr., Secy.-Treas.
Officers: Alan P. Hoblitzell, Jr., Pres.; George B.P. Ward, Jr., Secy.-Treas.
Number of staff: 2 full-time professional.
Employer Identification Number: 526062721

2657
Vincent Mulford Foundation ⌑
c/o Mercantile Safe Deposit & Trust Co.
Two Hopkins Plaza
Baltimore 21201 (301) 237-5416

Trust established in 1951 in NJ.
Donor(s): Vincent S. Mulford,† Edith Mulford.†
Foundation type: Independent
Financial data (yr. ended 12/31/88): Assets, $2,038,120 (M); expenditures, $166,648, including $157,750 for 77 grants (high: $14,000; low: $250).
Purpose and activities: Emphasis on the arts, higher and secondary education, Protestant church support, and social service agencies.
Limitations: Giving primarily in NY, NJ, and CT.
Application information:
Initial approach: Letter or proposal
Deadline(s): None
Write: Lloyd Batzler
Trustees: Walter E. Moor, Donald L. Mulford, Vincent S. Mulford, Jr., Thomas L. Pulling, Christian R. Sonne.
Employer Identification Number: 226043594

2658
The Thomas F. and Clementine L. Mullan Foundation, Inc. ⌑
2330 West Joppa Rd., Suite 210
Lutherville 21093

Incorporated in 1958 in MD.
Donor(s): Thomas F. Mullan, Sr., and his corporations.
Foundation type: Independent
Financial data (yr. ended 11/30/88): Assets, $3,505,731 (M); expenditures, $213,042, including $208,465 for 125 grants (high: $25,200; low: $100).
Purpose and activities: Emphasis on hospitals and health agencies, higher and secondary education, Roman Catholic church support, and social services.
Limitations: Giving primarily in Baltimore, MD.
Application information: Contributes only to pre-selected organizations.
Officers: Thomas F. Mullan, Jr., Pres.; Charles A. Mullan, V.P.; C. Louise Mullan, Secy.; Joseph Mullan, Treas.
Employer Identification Number: 526050776

2659
The Israel & Mollie Myers Foundation, Inc. ⌑ ☆
3635 Old Court Rd., Suite 306
Baltimore 21208 (301) 653-0556

Donor(s): Israel Myers, Jonathan P. Myers, Herschel L. Langenthal.
Foundation type: Independent
Financial data (yr. ended 12/31/88): Assets, $1,452,512 (M); gifts received, $159,970; expenditures, $146,825, including $146,825 for 16 grants (high: $75,900; low: $100).
Purpose and activities: Giving primarily for secondary and higher education, Jewish organizations, including welfare services; support also for the performing arts and services for the blind.
Limitations: Giving primarily in Baltimore, MD.
Application information: Application form not required.
Deadline(s): None
Write: Israel Myers, Pres.
Officers: Israel Myers, Pres.; Jonathan P. Myers, V.P.; Louis Silberstein, Secy.; Herschel L. Langenthal, Treas.
Employer Identification Number: 521314430

2660
Nathan Foundation, Inc. ⌑
c/o Mercantile-Safe Deposit & Trust Co.
Two Hopkins Plaza
Baltimore 21201 (301) 237-5518

Established in 1961 in MD.
Foundation type: Independent
Financial data (yr. ended 12/31/88): Assets, $2,398,901 (M); expenditures, $195,568, including $177,469 for 35 grants (high: $75,000; low: $800).
Purpose and activities: Emphasis on aid to the handicapped and the disadvantaged; support also for education and volunteerism.
Limitations: Giving limited to Dorchester County, MD.
Application information:
Initial approach: Letter
Deadline(s): None
Write: Paul P. Klender, Treas.
Officers and Directors: Edward H. Nabb, Pres.; Russell S. Baker, Jr., V.P.; T. Sewell Hubbard, Secy.; Paul P. Klender, Treas.; Edward Conway, Mrs. J. Dorsey Johnson.
Employer Identification Number: 526033999

2661
NFL Alumni Foundation Fund ⌑
P.O. Box 248
Stevenson 21153-0248 (301) 486-5454

Established in 1969.
Donor(s): NFL Charities, NFL Alumni Assn.
Foundation type: Independent
Financial data (yr. ended 5/31/88): Assets, $144,864 (M); gifts received, $85,000; expenditures, $149,849, including $144,426 for 24 grants to individuals (high: $12,000; low: $2,000).
Purpose and activities: Grants to physically or mentally disabled former National Football League alumni (prior to 1959) who are in financial need; support also for death benefits and medical expenses.
Types of support: Grants to individuals.
Application information:
Initial approach: Letter, including proof of income
Deadline(s): None
Write: Sigmund M. Hyman
Trustees: Pete Rozelle, Chair.; William Bidwell, James Castiglia, William Dudley, Wellington Mara, John Panelli, Arthur Rooney.
Employer Identification Number: 237087489

2662
The Noxell Foundation, Inc. ▼
11050 York Rd.
Hunt Valley 21030-2098 (301) 785-4313

Incorporated in 1951 in MD.
Donor(s): Noxell Corp.
Foundation type: Company-sponsored
Financial data (yr. ended 12/31/88): Assets, $4,251,016 (M); expenditures, $1,520,067, including $1,488,350 for 152 grants (high:

$200,000; low: $300; average: $1,000-$10,000) and $21,458 for employee matching gifts.
Purpose and activities: Emphasis on higher education, social services, hospitals, and the arts, including the performing arts, music, museums, and other cultural programs.
Types of support: Annual campaigns, seed money, emergency funds, building funds, equipment, land acquisition, employee matching gifts, internships, capital campaigns, endowment funds, matching funds, research, scholarship funds.
Limitations: Giving primarily in MD. No grants to individuals, or for operating budgets or deficit financing; no loans.
Application information: Application form not required.
Initial approach: Proposal
Copies of proposal: 1
Deadline(s): None
Board meeting date(s): Quarterly
Final notification: 3 months
Write: William R. McCartin, Treas.
Officers: George L. Bunting, Jr., Pres.; Peter M. Troup, V.P.; Carroll A. Bodie, Secy.; William R. McCartin, Treas.
Number of staff: None.
Employer Identification Number: 526041435

2663
Number Ten Foundation, Inc. ⌑
300 East Lombard St.
Baltimore 21202

Incorporated in 1985 in MD.
Donor(s): Ralph A. Brunn, Simone Brunn.
Foundation type: Independent
Financial data (yr. ended 12/31/89): Assets, $2,529,610 (M); expenditures, $235,163, including $216,024 for 120 grants (high: $120,100; low: $20).
Purpose and activities: Emphasis on Jewish welfare funds; some support for temples.
Application information:
Initial approach: Letter
Deadline(s): None
Write: M. Peter Moser, Secy.
Officers and Directors:* Ralph A. Brunn,* Pres.; Simone Brunn,* V.P.; M. Peter Moser, Secy.
Employer Identification Number: 521400791

2664
The W. O'Neil Foundation ▼ ⌑
5454 Wisconsin Ave., No. 750
Chevy Chase 20815

Incorporated in 1948 in OH.
Donor(s): William O'Neil,† Grace O'Neil,† John J. O'Neil, Grace O'Neil Regan, and others.
Foundation type: Independent
Financial data (yr. ended 12/31/88): Assets, $30,179,730 (M); expenditures, $2,768,354, including $2,559,000 for 58 grants (high: $500,000; low: $3,500; average: $5,000-$12,500).
Purpose and activities: Grants primarily for Roman Catholic church support and church-related institutions, particularly basic necessities programs (food, shelter, basic medical care, basic education).
Application information: Application form not required.
Initial approach: Letter
Copies of proposal: 1
Deadline(s): None
Write: Holly Buchanan, V.P.
Officers: John J. O'Neil, Pres.; Linda Yeager, V.P. and Secy.-Treas.; Holly Buchanan, V.P.; Helene O'Neil Cobb, V.P.; Grace O'Neil Regan, V.P.
Trustee: John Nolan.
Employer Identification Number: 346516969

2665
The Peggy Meyerhoff Pearlstone Foundation, Inc.
Village of Cross Keys
Village Square II, Suite 212
Baltimore 21210 (301) 532-2263

Established in 1975 in MD.
Donor(s): Peggy Meyerhoff Pearlstone.†
Foundation type: Independent
Financial data (yr. ended 02/28/90): Assets, $3,950,000 (M); expenditures, $218,478, including $158,436 for 32 grants (high: $25,000; low: $500).
Purpose and activities: Support mainly for Jewish welfare funds, youth, and the arts, with emphasis on the performing arts.
Types of support: Operating budgets, continuing support, annual campaigns, seed money, emergency funds, deficit financing, building funds, endowment funds, matching funds, publications, special projects, capital campaigns, general purposes, lectureships, renovation projects, scholarship funds.
Limitations: Giving primarily in Baltimore, MD. No grants to individuals; no loans.
Publications: 990-PF.
Application information: Application form not required.
Initial approach: Letter
Copies of proposal: 3
Deadline(s): None
Board meeting date(s): Aug.
Final notification: 60 days
Write: Richard L. Pearlstone, V.P.
Officers: Esther S. Pearlstone, Pres.; Richard L. Pearlstone, V.P. and Secy.-Treas.
Number of staff: None.
Employer Identification Number: 521035731

2666
J. H. Pearlstone, Jr. Charitable Income Trust ▼ ⌑
1200 Sun Life Bldg.
20 South Charles St.
Baltimore 21201

Established in 1982 in MD.
Donor(s): Julius H. Pearlstone, Jr.†
Foundation type: Independent
Financial data (yr. ended 7/31/87): Assets, $14,381,876 (M); expenditures, $2,011,996, including $1,858,475 for 27 grants (high: $170,000; low: $175).
Purpose and activities: Grants primarily for Jewish giving.
Application information:
Initial approach: Letter
Deadline(s): None
Write: Eugene H. Schreiber, Trustee
Trustees: Ann B. Pearlstone, Richard L. Pearlstone, Eugene H. Schreiber.
Employer Identification Number: 526225365

2667
PHH Group Foundation, Inc. ⌑
P.O. Box 2174
Baltimore 21203
Principal office: 11333 McCormick Rd., Hunt Valley, MD 21031

Established in 1962 in MD.
Donor(s): PHH Group, Inc.
Foundation type: Company-sponsored
Financial data (yr. ended 4/30/88): Assets, $521,557 (M); gifts received, $501,000; expenditures, $200,158, including $178,063 for 176 grants (high: $25,000; low: $25) and $21,132 for 106 employee matching gifts.
Purpose and activities: Grants mainly for arts and cultural programs, community funds, higher education, and health.
Types of support: Operating budgets, continuing support, annual campaigns, seed money, emergency funds, building funds, equipment, land acquisition, employee matching gifts, scholarship funds.
Limitations: No support for governmental or religious organizations. No grants to individuals, or for deficit financing, endowment funds, matching or challenge grants, research, special projects, publications, or conferences; no loans.
Publications: Program policy statement, application guidelines.
Application information: Application form required.
Initial approach: Letter
Copies of proposal: 1
Deadline(s): None
Board meeting date(s): June, Sept., Dec., and Mar.
Final notification: 3 months
Write: Jerome W. Geckle, Pres.
Officers: Jerome W. Geckle, Pres.; John T. Connor, Jr., Secy.; Marion Holmes, Treas.
Number of staff: 12 full-time professional; 1 full-time support.
Employer Identification Number: 526040911

2668
Clarence Manger & Audrey Cordero Plitt Trust ⌑
c/o First National Bank of Maryland
25 South Charles St., P.O. Box 1596
Baltimore 21201
Application address: 508 Woodside Rd., Baltimore, MD 21229

Foundation type: Independent
Financial data (yr. ended 10/31/88): Assets, $6,851,224 (M); expenditures, $263,958, including $162,500 for 7 grants (high: $25,000; low: $15,000).
Purpose and activities: Grants to educational institutions for student loans.
Application information:
Initial approach: Letter
Deadline(s): None
Write: Mary E. MacKirgan, Trustee
Trustees: Mary E. MacKirgan, First National Bank of Maryland.
Employer Identification Number: 526195778

2669
Howard and Geraldine Polinger Foundation, Inc. ⌑
5530 Wisconsin Ave., Suite 1000
Chevy Chase 20815 (301) 657-3600

Incorporated in 1968 in MD.
Donor(s): Howard Polinger, Geraldine Polinger.
Foundation type: Independent
Financial data (yr. ended 6/30/87): Assets, $1,758,161 (M); expenditures, $78,247, including $68,500 for 25 grants (high: $10,000; low: $500).
Purpose and activities: Giving for Jewish welfare funds and cultural programs.
Limitations: Giving primarily in the Washington, DC, area. No grants to individuals.
Application information: Application form not required.
Deadline(s): None
Write: Howard Polinger
Officers and Directors: Howard Polinger, Pres.; Jan Polinger Forsgren, V.P.; Arnold Polinger, V.P.; Lorre Beth Polinger, V.P.; Geraldine Polinger, Secy.; David Polinger, Treas.
Number of staff: None.
Employer Identification Number: 526078041

2670
T. Rowe Price Associates Foundation ⌑
100 East Pratt St.
Baltimore 21202 (301) 547-2000

Established in 1982.
Donor(s): T. Rowe Price Associates, Inc.
Foundation type: Company-sponsored
Financial data (yr. ended 12/31/87): Assets, $1,449,808 (M); gifts received, $520,000; expenditures, $438,541, including $430,901 for 215 grants (high: $13,036; low: $25).
Purpose and activities: Giving for higher and secondary education, cultural programs, and social services.
Types of support: General purposes, employee matching gifts.
Limitations: Giving primarily in MD. No grants to individuals.
Publications: Application guidelines.
Application information: Application form not required.
Initial approach: Proposal
Copies of proposal: 1
Deadline(s): None
Write: Albert C. Hubbard, Jr., Chair.
Officers: Albert C. Hubbard, Jr., Chair. and Pres.; M. Jenkins Cromwell, Jr., V.P. and Secy.; Carter O. Hoffman, V.P. and Treas.; Thomas R. Broadus, Jr., V.P.; Patricia O. Goodyear, V.P.
Employer Identification Number: 521231953

2671
Rogers-Wilbur Foundation, Inc. ⌑
Broadwater Way
P.O. Box 46
Gibson Island 21056-0046 (301) 437-5858

Established in 1947 in MD.
Foundation type: Independent
Financial data (yr. ended 12/31/88): Assets, $1,475,212 (M); expenditures, $69,204, including $49,650 for 34 grants (high: $10,000; low: $100).
Purpose and activities: Giving primarily for museums and cultural societies, hospitals and health organizations, and higher education.
Limitations: Giving primarily in MD.
Application information:
Initial approach: Letter
Deadline(s): None
Write: Leroy A. Wilbur, Jr., Pres.
Officers and Directors:* Leroy A. Wilbur, Jr.,* Pres.; Lawrence A. Wilbur,* V.P.; Anne R. Wilbur,* Secy.; Scott E. Wilbur,* Treas.
Employer Identification Number: 136103945

2672
The Rollins-Luetkemeyer Charitable Foundation, Inc.
P.O. Box 10147
17 West Pennsylvania Ave.
Baltimore 21285 (301) 296-4800

Established in 1961 in MD.
Foundation type: Independent
Financial data (yr. ended 12/31/89): Assets, $10,073,429 (M); gifts received, $5,000; expenditures, $437,957, including $412,150 for 84 grants (high: $240,000; low: $50).
Purpose and activities: Support primarily for the arts, cultural programs, education, social services, health, and historic preservation.
Types of support: General purposes.
Limitations: Giving primarily in the Baltimore, MD, area. No grants to individuals.
Application information: Application form not required.
Initial approach: Letter
Deadline(s): None
Write: John A. Luetkemeyer, Sr., Pres.
Officers: John A. Luetkemeyer, Sr.,* Pres.; Robert F. Wilson, V.P. and Treas.; Anne A. Luetkemeyer,* Secy.
Directors:* John A. Luetkemeyer, Jr., Mary E. Rollins, Anne L. Stone.
Employer Identification Number: 526041536

2673
The Henry and Ruth Blaustein Rosenberg Foundation, Inc. ⌑
Blaustein Bldg.
P.O. Box 238
Baltimore 21203

Incorporated in 1959 in MD.
Donor(s): Ruth Blaustein Rosenberg, Henry A. Rosenberg, Jr.
Foundation type: Independent
Financial data (yr. ended 12/31/88): Assets, $7,896,510 (M); gifts received, $330,000; expenditures, $912,151, including $841,800 for 70 grants (high: $298,500; low: $250).
Purpose and activities: Emphasis on secondary and higher education, music and other performing arts, Jewish welfare funds, and health agencies.
Limitations: Giving primarily in the greater Baltimore, MD, area.
Application information:
Initial approach: Letter
Deadline(s): None
Write: Henry A. Rosenberg, Jr., Pres.
Officers: Henry A. Rosenberg, Jr.,* Pres.; Frank A. Strzelczyk, Secy.-Treas.
Trustees:* Ruth Blaustein Rosenberg, Chair.; Judith R. Hoffberger, Ruth R. Marder.
Employer Identification Number: 526038384

2674
Ben & Esther Rosenbloom Foundation, Inc. ⌑
3407 Fielding Rd.
Baltimore 21208-1804

Established in 1982 in MD.
Foundation type: Independent
Financial data (yr. ended 12/31/88): Assets, $1,768,327 (M); gifts received, $80; expenditures, $83,815, including $79,838 for 14 grants (high: $54,000; low: $175).
Purpose and activities: Support primarily for Jewish welfare; grants also for social services and the arts.
Limitations: Giving primarily in Baltimore, MD.
Application information: Application form not required.
Initial approach: Proposal
Deadline(s): None
Officers: Ben Rosenbloom, Pres.; Esther Rosenbloom, V.P.; Howard Rosenbloom, Secy.-Treas.
Employer Identification Number: 521258672

2675
Elizabeth B. and Arthur E. Roswell Foundation, Inc. ⌑ ☆
Blaustein Bldg.
P.O. Box 238
Baltimore 21203-0238

Incorporated in 1986 in MD.
Donor(s): Elizabeth B. Roswell.
Foundation type: Independent
Financial data (yr. ended 12/31/88): Assets, $1,087,655 (M); expenditures, $33,962, including $33,500 for 10 grants (high: $9,000; low: $500).
Purpose and activities: Support for Jewish welfare, housing and other social service organizations, and public policy issues.
Application information:
Initial approach: Letter
Deadline(s): None
Write: Arthur E. Roswell, Pres.
Officers and Trustees:* Elizabeth B. Roswell,* Chair.; Arthur E. Roswell,* Pres.; Judith E. Roswell,* V.P.; Marjorie B. Roswell,* V.P.; Robert A. Roswell,* V.P.; Frank A. Strzelczyk, Secy.-Treas.
Employer Identification Number: 521490498

2676
Rouse Company Foundation, Inc.
c/o John J. Szymanski
Rouse Co. Bldg., Main Level
Columbia 21044 (301) 992-6375
Application address: The Rouse Co., 10275 Little Patuxent Pkwy., Columbia, MD 21044

Established in 1967 in MD.
Donor(s): The Rouse Co.
Foundation type: Company-sponsored
Financial data (yr. ended 12/31/88): Assets, $1,749,807 (M); gifts received, $525,630; expenditures, $73,395, including $62,000 for 5 grants (high: $25,000; low: $2,000).
Purpose and activities: Support for educational research and programs for the disabled.
Types of support: Special projects.

Limitations: Giving primarily in the central MD area. No support for religious programs or political advocacy. No grants to individuals.
Publications: Informational brochure (including application guidelines).
Application information: Application form not required.
Initial approach: Letter or telephone
Copies of proposal: 1
Deadline(s): None
Write: Edwin A. Daniels, Jr., Exec. Dir.
Officers: Mathias J. Devito,* Pres.; Richard G. McCanley,* Secy.-Treas.; Edwin A. Daniels, Jr., Exec. Dir.
Trustees: R. Harwood Beville, Michael D. Spear.
Number of staff: 1 full-time professional.
Employer Identification Number: 526056273

2677
The Ryan Family Charitable Foundation, Inc. ▼
3001 Gillis Falls Rd.
Mount Airy 21771 (301) 795-0266

Incorporated in 1977 in MD.
Donor(s): James P. Ryan.
Foundation type: Independent
Financial data (yr. ended 11/30/89): Assets, $43,755 (L); gifts received, $726,650; expenditures, $1,707,677, including $1,563,432 for 68 grants (high: $440,000; low: $50; average: $2,500-$25,000).
Purpose and activities: Giving primarily for needs of the poor and the developmentally disabled.
Types of support: General purposes, seed money, special projects, matching funds.
Limitations: Giving primarily in Baltimore, MD. No support for the arts. No grants to individuals, or for building or endowment funds, or publications; no loans.
Publications: Program policy statement, application guidelines.
Application information: No funding for new projects in 1989 or 1991. Application form not required.
Initial approach: Letter
Copies of proposal: 1
Deadline(s): None
Board meeting date(s): Quarterly or as necessary
Final notification: Within 1 month after board meeting
Write: Kay W. Martin, Exec. Secy.
Officers: Linda M. Ryan, Pres.; James P. Ryan, V.P.
Directors: George Kalivrentos, Barbara M. Ryan, Daniel M. Ryan, James P. Ryan, Jr., Kathleen C. Ryan, Peter D. Ryan.
Number of staff: 1 part-time professional.
Employer Identification Number: 521102104

2678
Morris Schapiro and Family Foundation ⌑
233 East Redwood St.
Baltimore 21202

Established in 1942 in MD.
Foundation type: Independent
Financial data (yr. ended 12/31/88): Assets, $1,111,553 (M); expenditures, $90,346, including $80,450 for 18 grants (high: $20,000; low: $500).
Purpose and activities: Emphasis on higher education, particularly medical education, youth, and historical associations.
Application information:
Initial approach: Letter
Deadline(s): None
Write: John D. Schapiro, Pres.
Officers: John D. Schapiro, Pres.; Joseph S. Schapiro, V.P.; Eugene M. Feinblatt, Secy.-Treas.
Employer Identification Number: 526025531

2679
J. B. & Maurice C. Shapiro Charitable Trust ⌑
12012 Piney Glen Ln.
Potomac 20854

Established in 1967 in MD.
Donor(s): Maurice C. Shapiro,† Shapiro, Inc.
Foundation type: Company-sponsored
Financial data (yr. ended 7/31/88): Assets, $9,599,974 (M); expenditures, $539,468, including $477,396 for 8 grants (high: $250,000; low: $2,396).
Purpose and activities: Support primarily for hospitals, child welfare, and Jewish welfare.
Types of support: General purposes.
Limitations: Giving primarily in the Washington, DC, area.
Application information: Contributes only to pre-selected organizations. Applications not accepted.
Trustees: Leonard S. Melrod, Gary Roggin, Perry L. Sandler, Dorothy M. Shapiro.
Employer Identification Number: 526073880

2680
Jacob S. Shapiro Foundation ⌑
2545 Wilkens Ave.
Baltimore 21223

Established in 1947 in MD.
Donor(s): Israel D. Shapiro, Bernice S. Levinson, United Iron & Metal Co., Inc.
Foundation type: Independent
Financial data (yr. ended 12/31/87): Assets, $753,912 (M); expenditures, $1,355,856, including $1,331,795 for 14 grants (high: $165,000; low: $90).
Purpose and activities: Support primarily for Jewish organizations.
Limitations: Giving primarily in MD.
Application information: Contributes only to pre-selected organizations. Applications not accepted.
Trustees: Bernice S. Levinson, Israel D. Shapiro, James R. Shapiro.
Employer Identification Number: 526072215

2681
Albert Shapiro Fund, Inc. ⌑
Two Hopkins Plaza, Suite 1200
Baltimore 21201 (301) 385-4099

Established in 1983 in MD.
Foundation type: Independent
Financial data (yr. ended 5/31/88): Assets, $3,332,495 (M); expenditures, $185,475, including $168,150 for 29 grants (high: $90,000; low: $100).
Purpose and activities: Grants primarily for Jewish giving and cultural programs.
Limitations: Giving primarily in Baltimore, MD, and Palm Beach, FL. No grants to individuals.
Application information:
Initial approach: Letter
Deadline(s): None
Write: Irving Cohn, Secy.-Treas.
Officers: Albert Shapiro, Pres.; Eileen Shapiro, V.P.; Irving Cohn, Secy.-Treas.
Employer Identification Number: 521300277

2682
Shawe Family Charitable Foundation, Inc. ⌑ ☆
c/o Sun Life Bldg.
Charles Ctr.
Baltimore 21201

Incorporated in 1986 in MD.
Donor(s): Earle K. Shawe.
Foundation type: Independent
Financial data (yr. ended 6/30/89): Assets, $1,293,314 (M); gifts received, $103,000; expenditures, $74,090, including $42,900 for 17 grants (high: $15,000; low: $100).
Purpose and activities: Giving primarily for higher and other education, the performing and fine arts, civic affairs, and Jewish giving.
Limitations: No grants to individuals.
Application information: Contributes only to pre-selected organizations. Applications not accepted.
Officers: Earle K. Shawe, Pres.; Annette C. Shawe, V.P.; Gail R. Shawe, Secy.; Stephen D. Shawe, Treas.
Employer Identification Number: 521505784

2683
The Thomas B. and Elizabeth M. Sheridan Foundation, Inc.
Executive Plaza II, Suite 604
11350 McCormick Rd.
Hunt Valley 21031 (301) 771-0475

Incorporated in 1962 in MD.
Donor(s): Thomas B. Sheridan,† Elizabeth M. Sheridan.†
Foundation type: Independent
Financial data (yr. ended 12/31/89): Assets, $6,577,564 (M); expenditures, $346,359, including $245,900 for 13 grants (high: $53,000; low: $500).
Purpose and activities: Emphasis on private secondary schools and cultural organizations.
Types of support: Continuing support, annual campaigns, building funds, equipment, endowment funds, scholarship funds, capital campaigns, emergency funds, general purposes, matching funds, operating budgets, program-related investments, seed money, special projects.
Limitations: Giving primarily in the greater Baltimore, MD, area. No grants to individuals, or for matching gifts; no loans.
Publications: Application guidelines, program policy statement.
Application information: Application form required.
Initial approach: Letter
Copies of proposal: 1
Deadline(s): None

Board meeting date(s): Mar., June, Sept., and Dec.
Write: James L. Sinclair, Pres.
Officers and Trustees: James L. Sinclair, Pres.; L. Patrick Deering, V.P.; John B. Sinclair, Secy.; J. Robert Kenealy, Treas.
Number of staff: 1 full-time professional; 1 part-time support.
Employer Identification Number: 526075270

2684
Hanan & Carole Sibel Family Foundation, Inc. ⌑ ☆
2521 North Charles St.
Baltimore 21218 (301) 467-4700

Established in 1986 in MD.
Donor(s): Hanan Y. Sibel.
Foundation type: Independent
Financial data (yr. ended 10/31/88): Assets, $164,688 (M); gifts received, $205,160; expenditures, $103,880, including $103,835 for 12 grants (high: $76,200; low: $10).
Purpose and activities: Support primarily for Jewish organizations, including welfare funds.
Limitations: Giving primarily in Baltimore, MD.
Application information:
Initial approach: Letter
Deadline(s): None
Write: Hanan Y. Sibel, Pres.
Officers: Hanan Y. Sibel, Pres.; Steven J. Sibel, Secy.; Carole C. Sibel, Treas.
Employer Identification Number: 521511976

2685
Gordon V. & Helen C. Smith Foundation ⌑
8716 Crider Brook Way
Potomac 20854 (307) 469-8597

Established in 1986 in MD.
Donor(s): Gordon V. Smith, Helen C. Smith, Miller and Smith, Inc.
Foundation type: Independent
Financial data (yr. ended 12/31/88): Assets, $2,789,327 (M); gifts received, $1,518,254; expenditures, $590,833, including $517,186 for grants (high: $403,000).
Purpose and activities: Grants primarily to a university and a theological school.
Application information: Application form not required.
Deadline(s): None
Write: Gordon V. Smith, Dir.; or Helen C. Smith, Dir.
Directors: Cynthia Skarbek, Bruce G. Smith, Douglas I. Smith, Gordon V. Smith, Helen C. Smith.
Employer Identification Number: 521440846

2686
J. C. Stewart Memorial Trust ⌑
7718 Finns Ln.
Lanham 20706 (301) 459-4200

Trust established in 1973 in MD.
Donor(s): Anna L. Stewart.†
Foundation type: Independent
Financial data (yr. ended 11/30/88): Assets, $6,053,701 (M); qualifying distributions, $231,300, including $10,000 for 1 grant, $6,000 for 3 grants to individuals (high: $3,000; low: $1,500) and $208,300 for loans to individuals.
Purpose and activities: Giving primarily for a legal services agency; support also for student loans and scholarships to MD residents.
Types of support: Student aid, student loans.
Limitations: Giving primarily in MD.
Application information:
Write: Robert S. Hoyert, Trustee
Trustees: Robert S. Hoyert, Bill L. Yoho.
Employer Identification Number: 237357104

2687
The Aaron Straus and Lillie Straus Foundation, Inc. ▼
101 West Mt. Royal Ave.
Baltimore 21201 (301) 539-8308

Incorporated in 1926 in MD.
Donor(s): Aaron Straus,† Lillie Straus.†
Foundation type: Independent
Financial data (yr. ended 12/31/88): Assets, $44,679,788 (M); expenditures, $3,654,527, including $1,809,540 for 70 grants (high: $950,000; low: $250; average: $1,500-$50,000).
Purpose and activities: Emphasis on Jewish welfare funds, family support, and child welfare. The foundation also operates a camp.
Types of support: Seed money, special projects, loans, operating budgets.
Limitations: Giving primarily in the Baltimore, MD, metropolitan area. No grants to individuals, or for endowment funds.
Application information: Application form not required.
Initial approach: Proposal
Copies of proposal: 2
Deadline(s): Feb. 1, May 1, Aug. 1, and Nov. 1
Board meeting date(s): Mar., June, Sept., and Dec.
Final notification: 7 days
Write: Jan Rivitz, Exec. Dir.
Officers: Richard M. Barnett,* Pres.; Henry L. Abraham,* V.P.; Alfred I. Coplan,* Secy.-Treas.; Jan Rivitz, Exec. Dir.
Trustees:* Darrell Friedman, Lewis Hamburger.
Number of staff: 1 full-time professional; 2 part-time support.
Employer Identification Number: 520563083

2688
The Strauss/Hanauer Memorial Fund, Inc. ⌑ ☆
Two Wisconsin Circle, Rm. 540
Chevy Chase 20815

Established in 1936 in MD.
Donor(s): Alice H. Strauss, Lewis H. Strauss.
Foundation type: Independent
Financial data (yr. ended 12/31/88): Assets, $244,424 (M); expenditures, $180,814, including $178,600 for 15 grants (high: $100,000; low: $100).
Purpose and activities: Emphasis organizations "providing research toward the alleviation of world hunger on a broad scope and improving medical facilities available to a substantial mostly rural population."
Types of support: Research, equipment.
Limitations: No grants to individuals.
Application information:
Initial approach: Letter
Deadline(s): None
Write: Lewis H. Strauss, Pres.
Officers and Directors: Lewis H. Strauss, Pres.; Alice H. Strauss, V.P. and Treas.; L.Z. Morris Strauss, V.P.; James W. Horton, Secy.; Jessica Strauss Pittman, Jeremy Strauss Stock, Lewis C. Strauss.
Employer Identification Number: 136089557

2689
Tauber Foundation, Inc. ⌑
5110 Ridgefield Rd.
Bethesda 20816-1424

Established in 1958.
Foundation type: Independent
Financial data (yr. ended 12/31/88): Assets, $7,842,227 (M); gifts received, $21,630; expenditures, $475,538, including $449,834 for 20 grants (high: $150,000; low: $100).
Purpose and activities: Support for Jewish welfare funds.
Types of support: General purposes, building funds.
Application information:
Initial approach: Letter
Deadline(s): Dec. 10
Write: Laszlo N. Tauber, M.D., Pres.
Officers: Laszlo N. Tauber, M.D., Pres.; Alfred I. Tauber, V.P. and Secy.; Ingrid D. Tauber, Treas.
Employer Identification Number: 526054648

2690
The Alvin and Fanny Blaustein Thalheimer Foundation, Inc. ⌑
Blaustein Bldg.
P.O. Box 238
Baltimore 21203 (301) 685-4230

Incorporated in 1958 in MD.
Donor(s): American Trading and Production Corp.
Foundation type: Independent
Financial data (yr. ended 2/28/89): Assets, $9,564,003 (M); gifts received, $240,000; expenditures, $407,599, including $327,715 for 7 grants (high: $252,715; low: $2,500).
Purpose and activities: Support for Jewish welfare funds, art education, and the arts.
Types of support: General purposes.
Limitations: Giving primarily in Baltimore, MD. No grants to individuals.
Application information: Application form not required.
Initial approach: Letter
Deadline(s): None
Board meeting date(s): 6 times a year
Write: Louis B. Thalheimer, Pres.
Officers: Louis B. Thalheimer,* Pres.; Morton K. Blaustein, V.P.; Henry A. Rosenberg, Jr., V.P.; Frank A. Strzelczyk, Secy.-Treas.
Trustees:* Marjorie Thalheimer Coleman, Ruth B. Rosenberg, Elizabeth T. Wachs.
Number of staff: None.
Employer Identification Number: 526038383

2691
G. Frank Thomas Foundation, Inc. ⌑
c/o Mercantile-Safe Deposit & Trust Co.
Two Hopkins Plaza
Baltimore 21201 (301) 347-8242

Established in 1954 in MD.
Foundation type: Independent
Financial data (yr. ended 12/31/88): Assets, $2,136,212 (M); expenditures, $117,780, including $102,500 for 12 grants (high: $30,000; low: $1,000).
Purpose and activities: Support primarily for hospitals, social service organizations, and higher educational institutions.
Limitations: Giving primarily in Frederick County, MD.
Application information: Application form not required.
Initial approach: Letter
Deadline(s): None
Write: Inez H. Winpigler, Pres.
Officers and Directors: Inez H. Winpigler, Pres.; Pamela I. Martin, V.P.; Charles F. Trunk III, Secy.; Helen B. Young, Treas.
Employer Identification Number: 526039803

2692
Columbus W. Thorn, Jr. Foundation
109 East Main St.
Elkton 21921 (301) 398-0611

Established in 1971 in MD.
Donor(s): Columbus W. Thorn.†
Foundation type: Independent
Financial data (yr. ended 12/31/89): Assets, $6,132,363 (M); gifts received, $124,534; expenditures, $220,861, including $206,450 for 98 loans to individuals.
Purpose and activities: Awards educational loans to high school graduates of Cecil County, MD.
Types of support: Student loans.
Limitations: Giving limited to residents of Cecil County, MD.
Application information: Application form required.
Deadline(s): Aug. 15
Write: Trustees
Trustees: Charles L. Scott, Doris P. Scott.
Number of staff: 1 part-time support.
Employer Identification Number: 237153983

2693
Three Swallows Foundation ⌑
8313 Persimmon Tree Rd.
Bethesda 20817-2647

Established in 1981 in VA.
Foundation type: Independent
Financial data (yr. ended 10/31/89): Assets, $5,511,741 (M); expenditures, $1,443,047, including $360,225 for 32 grants (high: $59,500; low: $100).
Purpose and activities: Support for social services, higher education, and religious organizations.
Limitations: No grants to individuals.
Application information: Contributes only to pre-selected organizations. Applications not accepted.
Write: Ross Main, Mgr.
Officers and Directors:* Paul N. Temple,* Pres.; Diane E. Temple,* Secy.; D. Barry Abell,* Treas.; Ross Main, Mgr.; Pamela T. Abell, Steven Greenberg, Logan Kline, Robin T. Kline, Lise Temple-Greenberg, Nancy L. Temple, Thomas D. Temple.
Employer Identification Number: 521234546

2694
Town Creek Foundation, Inc. ▼
P.O. Box 159
Oxford 21654

Established in 1981 in MD.
Donor(s): Edmund A. Stanley, Jr.
Foundation type: Independent
Financial data (yr. ended 12/31/89): Assets, $21,512,321 (M); expenditures, $1,158,058, including $1,056,000 for 79 grants (high: $125,000; low: $2,000; average: $5,000-$25,000).
Purpose and activities: Giving nationally for environmental protection, public radio and television, and conversion from a military to a peace economy; grants also to help the disadvantaged in Talbot County, MD.
Types of support: Operating budgets, continuing support, seed money, special projects.
Limitations: Giving nationally for major programs; support limited to Talbot County, MD, for social services. No support for primary or secondary schools, colleges, hospitals, or religious organizations. No grants to individuals, or for capital campaigns.
Publications: Informational brochure (including application guidelines), application guidelines.
Application information: Application form not required.
Initial approach: Proposal which follows the foundation's guidelines
Deadline(s): Feb. 10, June 10, and Oct. 10
Board meeting date(s): Mar., July, and Nov.
Final notification: 15 days after board meetings
Write: Edmund A. Stanley, Jr., Pres.
Officers and Trustees:* Edmund A. Stanley, Jr.,* Pres. and Exec. Dir.; Jennifer Stanley,* V.P.; Philip E.L. Dietz, Jr.,* Secy.-Treas.; Lisa A. Stanley, Gerald L. Stokes.
Number of staff: None.
Employer Identification Number: 521227030

2695
Marcia Brady Tucker Foundation
11 South Washington St.
Easton 21601 (301) 822-3155

Incorporated in 1941 in NY.
Donor(s): Marcia Brady Tucker.†
Foundation type: Independent
Financial data (yr. ended 12/31/89): Assets, $8,354,869 (M); gifts received, $81,000; expenditures, $521,645, including $455,271 for 94 grants (high: $42,500; low: $150).
Purpose and activities: Support mainly for education, conservation, and medical, welfare, religious, and cultural institutions.
Types of support: Matching funds, capital campaigns, emergency funds, equipment, scholarship funds, seed money, land acquisition.
Limitations: No grants to individuals.
Application information:
Initial approach: Letter or proposal
Deadline(s): None
Write: Luther Tucker, Jr., Pres.
Officers and Directors: Toinette Tucker, Chair.; Luther Tucker, Jr., Pres.; Naomi T. Stoehr, Secy.; Carll Tucker III, Treas.; Marcia T. Boogaard, Anne Draper, Elizabeth Sanders, Gay Tucker, Rev. Luther Tucker, Nicholas Tucker, Stephanie Tucker.
Number of staff: 1 part-time support.
Employer Identification Number: 136161561

2696
The Aber D. Unger Foundation, Inc. ⌑
c/o Gordon, et al.
233 East Redwood St.
Baltimore 21202 (301) 576-4211

Incorporated in 1960 in MD.
Foundation type: Independent
Financial data (yr. ended 2/28/88): Assets, $1,639,001 (M); expenditures, $182,841, including $154,900 for 34 grants (high: $50,000; low: $250).
Purpose and activities: Emphasis on handicapped children, Jewish welfare funds, music, and theatre.
Application information:
Initial approach: Proposal
Deadline(s): None
Write: Eugene M. Feinblatt, Pres.
Officer: Eugene M. Feinblatt, Pres. and Treas.
Directors: John Feinblatt, Marjorie W. Feinblatt, Paul L. Wolman III.
Employer Identification Number: 526034758

2697
The USF&G Foundation, Inc. ▼
100 Light St.
Baltimore 21202 (301) 547-3000

Foundation established in 1980 in MD.
Donor(s): United States Fidelity and Guaranty Co.
Foundation type: Company-sponsored
Financial data (yr. ended 12/31/88): Assets, $14,430,554 (M); gifts received, $7,254,000; expenditures, $2,388,706, including $2,371,786 for 58 grants (high: $450,000; low: $500; average: $1,000-$50,000).
Purpose and activities: Support largely for a community fund, environmental conservation, health and hospitals, child welfare, arts and cultural programs, and higher education.
Types of support: Operating budgets, continuing support, annual campaigns, building funds, equipment, scholarship funds, special projects, endowment funds, capital campaigns, renovation projects.
Limitations: Giving primarily in MD, particularly the Baltimore area. No support for trade and industry associations, political or veterans' organizations, or religious organizations for religious purposes; generally, no grants to primary or secondary schools. No grants to individuals, or for seed money, emergency funds, deficit financing, land acquisition, matching gifts, research, publications, or conferences; no loans.
Publications: Program policy statement, application guidelines.
Application information: Application form required.
Initial approach: Proposal
Copies of proposal: 1

Deadline(s): None
Board meeting date(s): As required
Final notification: 3 to 4 weeks
Write: Jack Moseley, Pres.
Officers and Trustees:* Jack Moseley,* Pres.; Paul J. Scheel,* V.P.; William F. Spliedt, Secy.-Treas.
Number of staff: None.
Employer Identification Number: 521197155

2698
Richard D. Van Lunen Charitable Foundation ⌑
Woodmere I, Suite 400
9881 Broken Land Pkwy.
Columbia 21046

Established in 1985 in MD.
Donor(s): Richard D. Van Lunen.
Foundation type: Independent
Financial data (yr. ended 12/31/88): Assets, $1,376,261 (M); expenditures, $230,468, including $219,750 for 6 grants (high: $198,000; low: $250).
Purpose and activities: Support primarily for a health organization and for a Christian church.
Application information:
Initial approach: Letter
Deadline(s): None
Write: David Abramson, Trustee
Trustees: David Abramson, Gordon Van Der Brug, Richard D. Van Lunen.
Employer Identification Number: 521419025

2699
VBT-HAT Foundation ⌑
8515 Arborwood Rd.
Baltimore 21208 (301) 486-2494
Application address: 343 North Charles St., Baltimore, MD 21201

Incorporated in 1985 in MD.
Foundation type: Independent
Financial data (yr. ended 12/31/89): Assets, $1,191,494 (M); expenditures, $336,675, including $325,000 for 3 grants (high: $150,000; low: $25,000).
Purpose and activities: Support for higher education, particularly in medicine and the sciences; support also for a library restoration fund.
Types of support: Scholarship funds.
Application information:
Initial approach: Letter or proposal
Deadline(s): None
Write: Herbert A. Thaler, V.P.
Officers and Directors:* Vivian B. Thaler,* Pres.; Herbert A. Thaler,* V.P. and Treas.; Herbert A. Thaler, Jr.,* Secy.; David S. Thaler, Miles H. Thaler.
Employer Identification Number: 521409334

2700
E. C. Wareheim Foundation ⌑
c/o First National Bank of Maryland, Trust Dept.
Light and Redwood Sts.
Baltimore 21203
Application address: P.O. Box 3444, Virginia Beach, VA 23454; Tel.: (804) 481-3166

Established in 1956 in MD.
Foundation type: Independent
Financial data (yr. ended 12/31/88): Assets, $6,480,547 (M); gifts received, $17,471; expenditures, $450,647, including $344,682 for 31 grants (high: $50,000; low: $1,000).
Purpose and activities: Support for family services, youth activities and child welfare, and social services.
Application information:
Initial approach: Letter
Deadline(s): None
Write: William L. Mathers, Exec. Dir.
Manager: William L. Mathers, Exec. Dir.
Trustee: First National Bank of Maryland.
Employer Identification Number: 526033212

2701
Anna Emory Warfield Memorial Fund, Inc.
103 West Monument St.
Baltimore 21201 (301) 547-0612

Incorporated in 1928 in MD.
Donor(s): S. Davies Warfield.†
Foundation type: Independent
Financial data (yr. ended 12/31/89): Assets, $3,632,641 (M); gifts received, $22,130; expenditures, $179,138, including $750 for 1 grant and $150,050 for 80 grants to individuals (high: $3,600; low: $325).
Purpose and activities: Organized exclusively to assist aged and dependent women.
Types of support: Grants to individuals.
Limitations: Giving primarily in the Baltimore, MD, metropolitan area. No grants for capital or endowment funds, general support, matching gifts, scholarships, fellowships, or research; no loans.
Publications: Application guidelines.
Application information: Application form required.
Initial approach: Telephone
Copies of proposal: 1
Deadline(s): None
Board meeting date(s): Apr. and Oct.
Final notification: 2 months
Write: Mrs. Thelma K. O'Neal, Secy.
Officers: Charles B. Reeves, Jr.,* Pres.; Braxton D. Mitchell,* V.P.; Thelma K. O'Neal, Secy.; Edward K. Dunn, Jr.,* Treas.
Trustees:* Mrs. W. Page Dame, Jr., Mrs. William E. Grose, Louis W. Hargrave, Mrs. Thomas H. Maddux, Mrs. William F. Schmick, Jr., Mrs. John R. Sherwood, Mrs. Lewis C. Strudwick.
Number of staff: 1 part-time support.
Employer Identification Number: 520785672

2702
The Harry and Jeanette Weinberg Foundation, Inc. ▼
5518 Baltimore National Pike
Baltimore 21228

Incorporated in 1959 in MD.
Donor(s): Harry Weinberg, and various companies.
Foundation type: Independent
Financial data (yr. ended 02/28/89): Assets, $560,117,000 (M); gifts received, $137,473,000; expenditures, $57,640,000, including $53,706,000 for 40 grants (high: $19,330,000; low: $90; average: $100-$100,000).
Purpose and activities: Emphasis on Jewish welfare funds; grants also for temple support, higher education, the homeless, and the elderly.
Types of support: Annual campaigns, building funds, capital campaigns, continuing support, in-kind gifts.
Limitations: Giving primarily in HI, Baltimore, MD, and Scranton, PA. No grants to individuals.
Application information: Contributes only to pre-selected organizations. Applications not accepted.
Board meeting date(s): Annually
Write: Ted Gross, V.P.
Officers: Harry Weinberg,* Pres. and Treas.; Nathan Weinberg,* V.P. and Secy.; Alvin Awaya,* V.P.; Ted Gross, V.P.; Joel Winegarden, V.P.
Directors:* Robert Kelly, William Weinberg.
Number of staff: 1 full-time professional.
Employer Identification Number: 526037034

2703
The Weinglass Foundation, Inc. ⌑
1220 East Joppa Rd.
Towson 21204

Established in 1983 in MD.
Foundation type: Independent
Financial data (yr. ended 12/31/87): Assets, $1,008,829 (M); gifts received, $80,700; expenditures, $81,595, including $62,759 for grants.
Purpose and activities: General charitable giving.
Application information:
Initial approach: Letter
Write: Deborah Layman, Admin. Exec.
Officers: Leonard Weinglass, Pres.; Raymond Altman, V.P.; Alan E. Berkowitz, Secy.-Treas.
Employer Identification Number: 521307628

2704
Jack Wilen Foundation, Inc. ⌑
c/o Sidney M. Friedman
1700 Reisterstown Rd., Suite 222
Baltimore 21208-3815

Foundation type: Independent
Financial data (yr. ended 11/30/88): Assets, $1,233,629 (M); expenditures, $47,243, including $46,622 for 70 grants (high: $12,000; low: $10).
Purpose and activities: Emphasis on Jewish giving; support also for cultural institutions.
Officer and Trustees: Ruth E. Wilen Cooper, Pres.; Elissa Wilen Hellman, Jack Wilen, Jr., James Wilen.
Employer Identification Number: 520794415

2705
Thomas Wilson Sanitarium for Children of Baltimore City
Alex Brown & Sons
135 East Baltimore St.
Baltimore 21202 (301) 727-1700

Trust established in 1879 in MD.
Donor(s): Thomas Wilson.†
Foundation type: Independent
Financial data (yr. ended 01/31/89): Assets, $3,293,856 (M); expenditures, $166,747,

including $130,000 for 13 grants (high: $25,000; low: $5,000).
Purpose and activities: Emphasis on hospitals, medical and educational research, and social services, largely relating to children.
Limitations: Giving limited to Baltimore, MD.
Application information:
Initial approach: Letter
Write: Charles L. Stout, Pres.
Officers and Trustees:* Charles L. Stout,* Pres.; Kinloch N. Yellott III,* V.P.; William C. Trimble, Jr.,* Secy.-Treas.; Perry J. Bolton, Edward K. Dunn, Jr., Nina Gardner, Kenneth Schuberth, Melchijah Spragins, Francis Trimble, Frederick Whitridge, Ralph N. Willis.
Employer Identification Number: 526044885

2706
Wye Institute, Inc. ⌑
Cheston-on-Wye
P.O. Box 50
Queenstown 21658 (301) 827-7401

Incorporated in 1963 in MD.
Donor(s): Arthur A. Houghton, Jr.
Foundation type: Operating
Financial data (yr. ended 12/31/88): Assets, $623,279 (M); expenditures, $800,841, including $675,155 for grants (high: $45,000).
Purpose and activities: A private operating foundation to assist in the advancement of local education, culture, and the economy of the eastern shore of MD.
Types of support: Conferences and seminars, consulting services, publications, seed money, special projects.
Limitations: Giving limited to the eastern shore of MD. No grants to individuals.
Application information: Application form not required.
Initial approach: Letter
Deadline(s): None
Board meeting date(s): Semiannually
Write: James G. Nelson, Pres.
Officers: James G. Nelson, Pres. and Mgr.; Rowland Stebbins III, V.P. and Treas.; Richard Garrett, Secy.
Trustees:* Arthur A. Houghton, Jr., Chair.; Sylvia H. Garrett, Nina R. Houghton, James A. Houston, John R. Kimberly.
Number of staff: None.
Employer Identification Number: 520799244

2707
Mary Byrd Wyman Memorial Association of Baltimore City ⌑
3130 Golf Course Rd. West
Owings Mills 21117

Established in 1884 in MD.
Foundation type: Independent
Financial data (yr. ended 5/31/88): Assets, $1,046,158 (M); expenditures, $74,491, including $42,100 for 27 grants to individuals (high: $2,000; low: $1,300).
Purpose and activities: Awards scholarships for secondary education.
Types of support: Student aid.
Application information:
Deadline(s): Jan. 1
Write: A. Rutherford Holmes, Pres.
Officers: A. Rutherford Holmes, Pres. and Treas.; Gaylord Lee Clark, Jr., Secy.
Employer Identification Number: 520781446

MASSACHUSETTS

2708
The Acushnet Foundation ⌑
P.O. Box 916
New Bedford 02742 (617) 997-2811

Trust established in 1953 in MA.
Donor(s): Acushnet Co.
Foundation type: Company-sponsored
Financial data (yr. ended 06/30/89): Assets, $5,913,343 (M); expenditures, $289,692, including $245,410 for 62 grants (high: $30,610; low: $250; average: $1,000-$5,000).
Purpose and activities: Giving primarily for community funds, hospitals, higher education, and youth agencies.
Types of support: Continuing support, annual campaigns, seed money, emergency funds, building funds, professorships, scholarship funds.
Limitations: Giving generally limited to the greater New Bedford, MA, area. No grants to individuals, or for endowment funds, operating budgets, deficit financing, or matching gifts.
Application information: Application form not required.
Initial approach: Letter
Copies of proposal: 1
Deadline(s): None
Board meeting date(s): As required
Final notification: 4 to 6 weeks
Write: Edward Powers, Mgr.
Trustees: William Bonner, Graeme L. Flanders, Glenn Johnson, John T. Ludes, Ed Powers, Thomas C. Weaver, Richard B. Young.
Number of staff: 1 part-time support.
Employer Identification Number: 046032197

2709
Frank W. and Carl S. Adams Memorial Fund ⌑
(also known as Charles E. & Caroline J. Adams Trust)
c/o First National Bank of Boston
P.O. Box 1861
Boston 02105 (617) 434-5669

Trust established in 1955 in MA.
Donor(s): Charles E. Adams,† Caroline J. Adams.†
Foundation type: Independent
Financial data (yr. ended 5/31/88): Assets, $7,766,673 (M); expenditures, $575,042, including $431,575 for grants (high: $28,348; average: $1,000-$7,500).
Purpose and activities: One half of the net income is distributed for general purposes, in the fields of health, welfare, the humanities, and education; the balance of income is designated to assist needy and deserving students selected by Massachusetts Institute of Technology and the Harvard Medical School.
Types of support: General purposes, building funds, operating budgets, capital campaigns, seed money.
Limitations: Giving limited to the City of Boston, MA. No support for national organizations. No grants for conferences, film production, scholarships, travel, research projects, or publications; no loans.
Application information:
Initial approach: Proposal
Copies of proposal: 1
Deadline(s): First day of month prior to board meetings
Board meeting date(s): Mar., June, Sept., and Dec.
Write: Miss Sharon M. Driscoll, Trust Officer, First National Bank of Boston
Trustee: First National Bank of Boston.
Employer Identification Number: 046011995

2710
Samuel & Adele Ades Charitable Trust ⌑
P.O. Box D-909
New Bedford 02742 (508) 997-1221

Established in 1962 in MA.
Donor(s): Members of the Ades family.
Foundation type: Independent
Financial data (yr. ended 8/30/88): Assets, $1,050,119 (M); gifts received, $182,713; expenditures, $147,297, including $146,273 for 61 grants (high: $50,161; low: $10).
Purpose and activities: Support primarily for Jewish giving, including welfare funds.
Limitations: No grants to individuals.
Application information:
Initial approach: Letter
Deadline(s): None
Write: Samuel Ades, Trustee
Trustees: Adele Ades, Alan Ades, Samuel Ades.
Employer Identification Number: 046059912

2711
Agape Foundation ⌑
49 Forty Acres St.
Wayland 01778 (508) 358-4840

Established in 1985 in MA.
Foundation type: Independent
Financial data (yr. ended 09/30/89): Assets, $1,755,274 (M); expenditures, $102,927, including $67,500 for 5 grants (high: $39,000; low: $1,000).
Purpose and activities: Support for survival education, a school for peace, and wildlife and wilderness conservation.
Application information:
Initial approach: Letter
Deadline(s): None
Write: Alexandra Moses, Trustee
Trustee: Alexandra Moses.
Employer Identification Number: 222690962

2712
The Lassor and Fanny Agoos Charity Fund
48 Wildwood Dr.
Bedford 01730-1138 (617) 275-0120

Established in 1926 in MA.
Foundation type: Independent

Financial data (yr. ended 01/31/89): Assets, $1,493,104 (M); expenditures, $82,523, including $76,000 for 52 grants (high: $22,000; low: $250).
Purpose and activities: Support for Jewish organizations and services, and health and social service organizations.
Types of support: Annual campaigns, building funds, capital campaigns, endowment funds, operating budgets.
Limitations: Giving primarily in NY and MA.
Application information: Application form not required.
Initial approach: Letter and proposal
Copies of proposal: 1
Deadline(s): None
Board meeting date(s): Early summer
Write: Donald B. Bruck, Treas.
Officers: Alan J. Dimond, Pres.; Harriet Finck, Secy.; Donald B. Bruck, Treas.
Number of staff: None.
Employer Identification Number: 046107955

2713
George I. Alden Trust ▼
370 Main St., Suite 1250
Worcester 01608 (508) 798-8621

Trust established in 1912 in MA.
Donor(s): George I. Alden.†
Foundation type: Independent
Financial data (yr. ended 12/31/89): Assets, $76,331,000 (L); expenditures, $3,167,500, including $2,996,000 for 178 grants (high: $400,000; low: $1,000; average: $1,000-$25,000).
Purpose and activities: For the promotion of education in schools, colleges, or other educational institutions, with a preference for industrial, vocational, or professional education; for the promotion of the work carried on by the Young Men's Christian Association, or its successors, either in this country or abroad; and for the benefit of the Worcester Trade Schools and the Worcester Polytechnic Institute; some support also for cultural and historic programs.
Types of support: Seed money, emergency funds, building funds, equipment, land acquisition, research, publications, conferences and seminars, scholarship funds, internships, professorships, matching funds, renovation projects, endowment funds.
Limitations: Giving primarily in the northeast, with emphasis on Worcester, MA. No grants to individuals; no loans.
Publications: Annual report, informational brochure (including application guidelines).
Application information: Application form not required.
Initial approach: Proposal
Copies of proposal: 1
Deadline(s): None
Board meeting date(s): Bimonthly beginning in Feb.
Final notification: 2 months
Write: Francis H. Dewey III, Chair.
Officers and Trustees:* Francis H. Dewey III,* Chair.; Robert G. Hess,* Vice-Chair.; Warner S. Fletcher,* Secy.; Harry G. Bayliss,* Treas.
Number of staff: None.
Employer Identification Number: 046023784

2714
John W. Alden Trust ☆
c/o State St. Bank & Trust Co.
P.O. Box 351
Boston 02101
Application address: 225 Franklin St., Boston, MA 02110; Tel.: (617) 654-3343

Established in 1986 in MA.
Donor(s): Priscilla Alden.†
Foundation type: Independent
Financial data (yr. ended 09/30/89): Assets, $5,026,059 (M); expenditures, $249,602, including $203,100 for 9 grants (high: $26,000; low: $2,100).
Purpose and activities: Grant support directed toward "organizations providing care and administering to the needs of children who are blind, retarded, disabled, or who are either mentally or physically ill ...or organizations engaged in medical and scientific research directed toward the prevention or cure of diseases and disabilities particularly affecting children."
Types of support: Research, seed money, special projects.
Limitations: Giving primarily in MA. No grants to individuals.
Publications: Application guidelines.
Application information: Application form not required.
Initial approach: Letter
Copies of proposal: 2
Deadline(s): None
Board meeting date(s): Feb., May, Aug., and Nov.
Final notification: Within 1 month
Write: William Osgood or Deborah A. Robbins
Trustees: William B. Tyler, State St. Bank & Trust Co.
Number of staff: 1 part-time professional; 1 part-time support.
Employer Identification Number: 222719727

2715
Ansin Foundation ⌑
c/o Charles G. Burke
122 Western Ave.
Lowell 01851

Donor(s): Joan Fabrics Corp.
Foundation type: Independent
Financial data (yr. ended 12/31/88): Assets, $1,532,647 (M); gifts received, $95,125; expenditures, $349,382, including $346,500 for 15 grants (high: $135,000; low: $1,000).
Purpose and activities: Support for health services and hospitals, Jewish giving, and education, with emphasis on higher education.
Limitations: Giving primarily in MA and PA. No grants to individuals.
Application information: Contributes only to pre-selected organizations. Applications not accepted.
Officer: Henry Newell, Mgr.
Trustees: Harold Ansin, Lawrence Ansin.
Employer Identification Number: 046067779

2716
Ronald M. Ansin Private Foundation ⌑
132 Littleton Rd.
Harvard 01451
Application address: One Main St., Leominster, MA 01453

Established in 1984 in MA.
Donor(s): Ronald M. Ansin.
Foundation type: Independent
Financial data (yr. ended 11/30/88): Assets, $2,550,296 (M); gifts received, $600,000; expenditures, $271,674, including $257,811 for 23 grants (high: $115,000; low: $65).
Purpose and activities: Support for Jewish organizations, secondary education, and public policy institutes.
Limitations: Giving primarily in MA. No grants to individuals.
Application information:
Initial approach: Letter
Deadline(s): None
Write: Ronald M. Ansin, Trustee
Trustee: Ronald M. Ansin.
Employer Identification Number: 042786469

2717
Mary Alice Arakelian Foundation ⌑
c/o Institute for Savings
P.O. Box 510
Newburyport 01950
Additional address: P.O. Box 510, Newburyport, MA 01950

Established in 1966 in MA.
Foundation type: Independent
Financial data (yr. ended 12/31/87): Assets, $3,424,454 (M); expenditures, $268,274, including $209,000 for 11 grants (high: $70,000; low: $5,000).
Purpose and activities: Support primarily for higher education, cultural programs, and religious giving.
Application information: Application form not required.
Deadline(s): None
Board meeting date(s): Grants are decided in Oct.
Write: John H. Pramberg, Jr., Pres.
Officer and Directors: John H. Pramberg, Jr., Pres.; Rose M. Marshall, Donald D. Mitchell, Charles P. Richmond, Bank of New England, N.A.
Employer Identification Number: 046155695

2718
Arkwright Foundation, Inc. ⌑ ☆
225 Wyman St.
P.O. Box 9198
Waltham 02254-9198

Established in 1987.
Foundation type: Independent
Financial data (yr. ended 6/30/89): Assets, $825,698 (M); expenditures, $231,286, including $230,991 for 240 grants (high: $89,269; low: $10).
Purpose and activities: Giving primarily to a community fund and higher and other education; support also for fine and performing arts groups and social services.
Limitations: No grants to individuals.

Application information: Contributes only to pre-selected organizations. Applications not accepted.
Officers: Frederick J. Bumpas, Pres.; Michael D. Bank, Treas.
Employer Identification Number: 042996206

2719
Association for the Relief of Aged Women of New Bedford ⌑
27 South Sixth St.
New Bedford 02740

Established in 1866.
Foundation type: Operating
Financial data (yr. ended 3/31/89): Assets, $5,614,977 (M); gifts received, $5,790; expenditures, $259,040, including $225,165 for grants to individuals (high: $38,874).
Purpose and activities: A private operating foundation; grants locally to needy aged women.
Types of support: Grants to individuals.
Limitations: Giving limited to greater New Bedford, MA.
Officers: Mrs. Thornton Klaren, Pres.; Mrs. Frank Marshall, Secy.; Mrs. Ralph Reed, Treas.
Employer Identification Number: 046056367

2720
Trustees of the Ayer Home ⌑ ☆
c/o Barbara Hoar
P.O. Box 1865
Lowell 01853
Application address: Eight Hillcrest Dr., Chelmsford, MA; Tel.: (508) 256-6145

Established in 1898.
Foundation type: Independent
Financial data (yr. ended 12/31/88): Assets, $1,011,740 (M); expenditures, $74,223, including $57,708 for 12 grants (high: $12,000; low: $808).
Purpose and activities: Support for a nursery school, a hospital, a community fund, youth organizations, and higher education.
Limitations: Giving primarily in Lowell, MA. No grants to individuals.
Application information:
Initial approach: Letter
Deadline(s): None
Write: Edward D. Howe, Trustee
Officers and Trustees: Edward D. Howe, Pres.; Jonathan T. Stevens, Secy.; John D. Leggatt, Treas.; Priscilla Clement, Nancy Donahue, Walter B. Reilly, Jr.
Employer Identification Number: 042157061

2721
Alice S. Ayling Scholarship Foundation ⌑ ☆
77 Franklin St.
Boston 02110 (617) 451-0755

Established in MA in 1987.
Donor(s): Alice S. Ayling.
Foundation type: Independent
Financial data (yr. ended 12/31/88): Assets, $8,165,447 (M); gifts received, $5,152,192; expenditures, $188,620, including $74,000 for grants to individuals.
Purpose and activities: Awards scholarships to individuals for higher education, with preference for study in the field of humanities.
Types of support: Student aid.
Application information: Scholarship payments made to recipient's institution. Application form required.
Deadline(s): May 15
Write: Walter S. Robbins, Trustee
Officer: Oliver Andrews, Jr., Exec. Dir.
Trustees: Sumner R. Andrews, Walter S. Robbins.
Employer Identification Number: 222808952

2722
Azadoutioun Foundation ⌑
c/o Mugar Group, Inc.
Two Burlington Woods Dr.
Burlington 01803-4538 (617) 229-2111

Established in 1985 in MA.
Donor(s): Carolyn G. Mugar.
Foundation type: Independent
Financial data (yr. ended 12/31/88): Assets, $1,933,211 (M); gifts received, $10,000; expenditures, $324,849, including $317,750 for 6 grants (high: $200,000; low: $2,750).
Purpose and activities: Support for an ecological organization, an Armenian library and museum, public health and child care organizations.
Limitations: Giving primarily in MA.
Application information: Application form not required.
Deadline(s): None
Write: Laurie A. LeClair, Mgr.
Officer: Laurie A. Le Clair, Mgr.
Trustees: Janet Corpus, Carolyn G. Mugar, Sidney Peck, Sharryn Ross.
Employer Identification Number: 042876245

2723
The Paul and Edith Babson Foundation
c/o Nichols & Pratt
50 Congress St.
Boston 02109 (617) 523-6800

Trust established in 1957 in MA.
Donor(s): Paul T. Babson.†
Foundation type: Independent
Financial data (yr. ended 12/31/88): Assets, $4,770,784 (M); expenditures, $238,904, including $234,000 for 39 grants (high: $40,000; low: $1,000).
Purpose and activities: Giving for education, health, and youth agencies.
Limitations: Giving primarily in MA. No grants to individuals.
Application information:
Initial approach: Letter
Copies of proposal: 1
Deadline(s): Apr. 15 and Oct. 15
Board meeting date(s): May and Nov.
Write: James R. Nichols, Trustee
Trustees: Donald P. Babson, Susan A. Babson, James R. Nichols.
Number of staff: 1 full-time professional; 1 part-time support.
Employer Identification Number: 046037891

2724
Babson-Webber-Mustard Fund ⌑
P.O. Box 559
Sudbury 01776 (617) 443-3972

Established in 1962 in MA.
Foundation type: Independent
Financial data (yr. ended 12/31/87): Assets, $2,367,986 (M); expenditures, $135,904, including $1,000 for 1 grant and $100,000 for 211 grants to individuals (high: $1,000; low: $400).
Purpose and activities: Giving to aid needy individuals.
Types of support: Grants to individuals.
Limitations: Giving primarily in the Wellesley and Gloucester, MA, areas.
Application information:
Write: John O. Rhome, Trustee
Trustees: Robert S. Hoffman, Jr., Jessie M. Putney, John O. Rhome.
Employer Identification Number: 042307820

2725
Charles F. Bacon Trust
c/o Bank of New England, N.A.
28 State St.
Boston 02107 (617) 573-6416

Trust established in 1928 in MA.
Donor(s): Charles F. Bacon.†
Foundation type: Independent
Financial data (yr. ended 12/31/88): Assets, $1,995,397 (M); expenditures, $122,114, including $88,000 for 8 grants (high: $26,000; low: $5,000) and $28,000 for 6 grants to individuals (high: $6,000; low: $2,000; average: $1,000-$5,000).
Purpose and activities: Grants to needy retired employees of Conrad & Chandler Co., to charitable organizations for elderly women, and to other charitable organizations.
Types of support: Grants to individuals, general purposes, seed money, matching funds, building funds, equipment.
Limitations: Giving primarily in MA.
Publications: Application guidelines, 990-PF.
Application information: Application form required.
Initial approach: Letter
Copies of proposal: 1
Deadline(s): Nov. 30
Board meeting date(s): Feb.
Final notification: 2 months
Write: Kerry A. Herlihy, V.P., Bank of New England, N.A.
Trustee: Bank of New England, N.A.
Number of staff: 4 full-time professional; 1 full-time support.
Employer Identification Number: 046024467

2726
L. G. Balfour Foundation
c/o Bank of New England, N.A.
28 State St.
Boston 02107 (617) 573-6415

Established in 1973 in MA.
Donor(s): L.G. Balfour.†
Foundation type: Independent
Financial data (yr. ended 03/31/89): Assets, $48,186,225 (M); expenditures, $5,858,396, including $5,118,197 for 17 grants (high:

$1,000,000; low: $13,588; average: $5,000-$1,000,000).
Purpose and activities: Support primarily for scholarships and "innovative projects designed to eliminate barriers and improve access to education for all potentially qualified students, with a strong emphasis on minority educational programs designed to encourage students to stay in school and eventually attend college."
Types of support: Scholarship funds, fellowships, matching funds, operating budgets, seed money, special projects.
Limitations: Giving primarily in MA and New England. No grants to individuals.
Application information: Application form required.
Initial approach: Query by telephone or letter prior to submitting proposal
Copies of proposal: 1
Deadline(s): Available upon request
Board meeting date(s): As required
Write: John M. Dolan, V.P., Bank of New England, N.A.
Trustee: Bank of New England, N.A.
Number of staff: 5
Employer Identification Number: 046397138

2727
Bank of Boston Corporation Charitable Foundation ▼
c/o Bank of Boston
100 Federal St., Govt. & Community Affairs Dept.
Boston 02106 (617) 434-2171

Trust established in 1961 in MA for First National Bank of Boston Charitable Foundation; absorbed into First National Boston Corporation Foundation in 1983; present name adopted in 1983.
Donor(s): Bank of Boston Corp.
Foundation type: Company-sponsored
Financial data (yr. ended 12/31/88): Assets, $11,314,055 (M); gifts received, $2,119,063; expenditures, $3,727,375, including $3,537,835 for 432 grants (high: $129,968; low: $400; average: $2,500-$7,500).
Purpose and activities: Giving limited to community organizations with programs in education, health and hospitals, social services, arts and culture, and the civic community.
Types of support: Annual campaigns, building funds, general purposes, matching funds, operating budgets, special projects, continuing support, capital campaigns, endowment funds, equipment, scholarship funds, renovation projects.
Limitations: Giving primarily in MA. No support for religious or partisan causes, fundraising events, conferences, forums, or nationally organized health programs. No grants to individuals, or for research or fellowships; no loans.
Publications: Corporate giving report (including application guidelines), grants list, informational brochure.
Application information:
Initial approach: Proposal or letter
Copies of proposal: 1
Deadline(s): At least 6 weeks before meetings
Board meeting date(s): 3rd week of Mar., June, Sept., and Dec.
Final notification: 2 months
Write: Judith Kidd, Mgr., Corp. Contribs.
Trustees: William L. Brown, Ira Stepanian, Eliot N. Vestner, Peter M. Whitman, Jr., Bank of Boston.
Number of staff: 2 full-time professional; 1 full-time support.
Employer Identification Number: 042748070

2728
Barletta Foundation ⌘ ☆
Ten Whipple Ave.
Boston 02131

Established in 1983 in MA.
Foundation type: Independent
Financial data (yr. ended 3/31/89): Assets, $3,189 (M); gifts received, $103,700; expenditures, $103,477, including $103,450 for grants.
Purpose and activities: Giving primarily for education, including higher and secondary educational institutions.
Limitations: Giving primarily in MA.
Application information:
Initial approach: Letter
Write: Vincent Barletta, Trustee
Trustees: Vincent Barletta, William F. DiPesa, Helen Hurlbert.
Employer Identification Number: 237148325

2729
Frank M. Barnard Foundation, Inc.
Three Center Plaza, Suite 800
Boston 02108 (617) 227-9610

Established in 1982 in MA.
Foundation type: Independent
Financial data (yr. ended 12/31/88): Assets, $1,010,209 (M); expenditures, $84,275, including $43,450 for 21 grants (high: $15,000; low: $50).
Purpose and activities: Support for libraries, with emphasis on university collections, higher education, and cultural programs.
Limitations: Giving primarily in New England.
Publications: Application guidelines.
Application information: Application form required.
Deadline(s): None
Write: Dudley A. Weiss, Pres.
Officer: Dudley A. Weiss, Pres. and Treas.
Employer Identification Number: 042767462

2730
The Barrington Foundation, Inc. ⌘
P.O. Box 270
Great Barrington 01230

Established in 1978 in DE.
Donor(s): Samuel A. Strassler,† Gary M. Strassler, R.C.M. Corp., Weston Associates.
Foundation type: Company-sponsored
Financial data (yr. ended 12/31/88): Assets, $1,968,603 (M); gifts received, $303,500; expenditures, $191,154, including $179,250 for 69 grants (high: $100,000; low: $50).
Purpose and activities: Giving primarily for Jewish welfare funds, higher education, and cultural programs.
Application information: Application form not required.
Deadline(s): None
Write: David H. Strassler, Pres.
Officers: David H. Strassler, Pres.; Robert B. Strassler, Secy.-Treas.
Employer Identification Number: 132930849

2731
Adelaide Breed Bayrd Foundation
c/o Russell E. Watts, M.D.
28 Pilgrim Rd.
Melrose 02176

Incorporated in 1927 in MA.
Donor(s): Frank A. Bayrd,† Blanche S. Bayrd.†
Foundation type: Independent
Financial data (yr. ended 12/31/88): Assets, $1,298,409 (M); gifts received, $227,000; expenditures, $282,339, including $244,900 for 61 grants (high: $30,000; low: $150; average: $5,000) and $1,600 for 8 grants to individuals.
Purpose and activities: To aid those causes in which the donor's mother was interested; primarily supports cultural activities. The foundation also grants scholarships to students residing in Malden, MA, and vicinity.
Types of support: Operating budgets, annual campaigns, emergency funds, building funds, equipment, endowment funds, research, special projects, student aid.
Limitations: Giving primarily in the metropolitan Boston, MA, area, with emphasis on Malden. No support for national or out-of-state organizations. No grants to individuals (except for scholarships supplementary to the will of Blanche Bayrd), or for matching or challenge grants, demonstration projects, conferences, or publications; no loans.
Publications: Annual report (including application guidelines).
Application information: Application form not required.
Initial approach: Proposal
Deadline(s): Submit proposal preferably in Dec. or Jan.; deadline Feb. 15
Board meeting date(s): 1st Tuesday in Feb.; special meetings usually held in Mar. or Apr. to consider grant requests
Final notification: Generally in Apr. or May
Write: Russell E. Watts, M.D., Pres.
Officer and Trustees:* Russell E. Watts, M.D.,* Pres.; Florence C. Burns, C. Henry Kezer, Susan C. Mansur, William H. Marshall, Gaynor K. Rutherford, Jean H. Stearns, H. Allen Stevens.
Number of staff: 1 part-time professional; 1 part-time support.
Employer Identification Number: 046051258

2732
Aimee M. L. Becker Foundation ⌘
c/o The Massachusetts Co., Inc.
99 High St.
Boston 02110

Established in 1985 in MA.
Foundation type: Independent
Financial data (yr. ended 12/31/88): Assets, $2,673,971 (M); expenditures, $192,851, including $189,381 for 10 grants (high: $42,085; low: $9,018).
Purpose and activities: Support primarily for Lutheran churches and organizations; some support for higher education.

Limitations: Giving primarily in MO. No grants to individuals.
Application information: Contributes only to pre-selected organizations. Applications not accepted.
Officer: Maurice F. Lesses, V.P.
Trustee: The Massachusetts Co., Inc.
Employer Identification Number: 046082918

2733
Benfamil Charitable Trust ¤
One Financial Ctr.
Boston 02111-2620

Established in 1962 in MA.
Foundation type: Independent
Financial data (yr. ended 12/31/88): Assets, $1,909,495 (M); gifts received, $506,825; expenditures, $160,806, including $156,400 for 21 grants (high: $75,000; low: $100).
Purpose and activities: Support primarily for a theological seminary, higher education and for hospitals.
Limitations: Giving primarily in MA.
Application information: Contributes only to pre-selected organizations.
Trustees: George F. Bennett, Helen F. Bennett, Peter C. Bennett.
Employer Identification Number: 046079101

2734
The Doris L. Benz Trust ¤
c/o Wendell P. Weyland
309 Ipswich Rd.
Boxford 01921
Mailing address: c/o The New Hampshire Charitable Fdn., One South St., Concord, NH 03301

Established in 1984 in NH.
Donor(s): Doris L. Benz.†
Foundation type: Independent
Financial data (yr. ended 6/30/87): Assets, $6,582,059 (M); expenditures, $293,140, including $271,090 for grants (high: $123,447; low: $930).
Purpose and activities: One half of income of trust to be used for student scholarships, and the remaining half to be distributed to charitable organizations.
Types of support: Student aid.
Limitations: Giving primarily in NH and MA; scholarships only to residents of Sandwich, NH, or Carroll County, NH, who have graduated from high schools in these areas. No support for religious purposes.
Application information:
Deadline(s): May 25 for scholarships
Trustee: Wendell P. Weyland.
Employer Identification Number: 046504871

2735
Theodore W. & Evelyn Berenson Charitable Foundation ¤
c/o Goulston & Storrs
400 Atlantic Ave.
Boston 02210-2206 (617) 482-1776

Established in 1953 in MA.
Foundation type: Independent
Financial data (yr. ended 11/30/88): Assets, $1,940,573 (M); expenditures, $438,209, including $251,912 for 32 grants (high: $193,352; low: $10).
Purpose and activities: Support primarily for higher education.
Limitations: Giving primarily in MA.
Application information: Application form not required.
Deadline(s): None
Write: David H. Greenberg, Trustee
Trustees: Evelyn G. Berenson, David H. Greenberg, Thomas Kaplan, Marvin Sparrow.
Employer Identification Number: 046068512

2736
Birmingham Foundation ¤
24-42 Wormwood St.
Boston 02210 (617) 439-9065

Donor(s): John P. Birmingham.†
Foundation type: Independent
Financial data (yr. ended 12/31/88): Assets, $5,210,770 (M); expenditures, $471,416, including $395,000 for 12 grants (high: $150,000; low: $2,000).
Purpose and activities: Giving for Roman Catholic welfare funds, and higher and secondary education; some support also for other social service agencies.
Types of support: Scholarship funds.
Application information:
Initial approach: Letter
Deadline(s): End of 3rd quarter
Write: Paul J. Birmingham, Trustee
Trustees: Paul J. Birmingham, Lois I. Wrightson.
Employer Identification Number: 046050748

2737
Curtis Blake Foundation ¤
c/o Friendly Ice Cream Corp.
33 Mill Rd.
Longmeadow 01106 (413) 567-1574

Established in 1972 in MA.
Donor(s): Curtis L. Blake.
Foundation type: Independent
Financial data (yr. ended 12/31/88): Assets, $1,151,415 (M); expenditures, $139,871, including $125,106 for 19 grants (high: $50,000; low: $900).
Purpose and activities: Emphasis on higher education, culture, and programs for the learning disabled.
Limitations: Giving primarily in MA. No grants to individuals.
Application information: Contributes only to pre-selected organizations. Applications not accepted.
Write: Curtis L. Blake, Trustee
Trustees: Curtis L. Blake, Alfred W. Fuller.
Employer Identification Number: 237204498

2738
S. P. Blake Foundation
666 Bliss Rd.
Longmeadow 01106 (413) 567-9483

Established in 1972 in MA.
Donor(s): S. Prestley Blake.
Foundation type: Independent
Financial data (yr. ended 12/31/87): Assets, $3,276,320 (M); expenditures, $201,405, including $169,102 for 25 grants (high: $125,000; low: $25).
Purpose and activities: Educational purposes with emphasis on higher education and historic preservation, including a museum.
Limitations: Giving primarily in the western MA area. No grants to individuals.
Application information: Application form not required.
Initial approach: Letter
Copies of proposal: 1
Deadline(s): None
Board meeting date(s): Monthly
Final notification: 2 months
Write: S. Prestley Blake, Trustee
Trustees: Benson P. Blake, S. Prestley Blake.
Employer Identification Number: 237185871

2739
Arthur F. Blanchard Trust ¤
c/o Boston Safe Deposit and Trust Co.
One Boston Place
Boston 02108 (617) 722-7340

Trust established in 1943 in MA.
Donor(s): Arthur F. Blanchard.†
Foundation type: Independent
Financial data (yr. ended 08/31/89): Assets, $11,034,653 (M); expenditures, $916,730, including $757,700 for 31 grants (high: $100,000; low: $500) and $17,400 for 30 grants to individuals (high: $1,000; low: $150).
Purpose and activities: Grants principally in the areaas of community development, human services, cultural programs, and higher education, including student aid.
Types of support: General purposes, seed money, emergency funds, equipment, land acquisition, research, special projects, matching funds, capital campaigns, renovation projects, student aid.
Limitations: Giving limited to MA, with emphasis on the Boston metropolitan area. No grants to individuals, or for endowment funds, scholarships, or fellowships; no loans.
Publications: Program policy statement, application guidelines.
Application information:
Initial approach: Proposal
Copies of proposal: 1
Deadline(s): Feb., May., Aug., and Nov.
Board meeting date(s): Mar., June, Sept., and Dec.
Final notification: 3 months
Write: Sylvia Salas, Trust Officer, Boston Safe Deposit and Trust Co.
Trustee: Boston Safe Deposit & Trust Co.
Number of staff: None.
Employer Identification Number: 046093374

2740
John Bolten Charitable Foundation ¤
c/o Hale and Dorr
60 State St.
Boston 02109

Established in 1982 in MA.
Donor(s): Katherine S.A. Bolten.†
Foundation type: Independent
Financial data (yr. ended 12/31/88): Assets, $3,457,715 (M); expenditures, $300,313, including $282,000 for 62 grants (high: $18,750; low: $1,000).

Purpose and activities: Support primarily for Protestant religious organizations and evangelical ministries and programs.
Limitations: No grants to individuals.
Application information: Contributes only to pre-selected organizations. Applications not accepted.
Trustees: John Bolten, Jr., Samuel S. Dennis III, Gisela B. Hogan.
Employer Identification Number: 042767454

2741
Boston Edison Foundation ▼ ⌑
800 Boylston St., P359
Boston 02199 (617) 424-2303

Established in 1981 in MA.
Donor(s): Boston Edison Co.
Foundation type: Company-sponsored
Financial data (yr. ended 12/31/88): Assets, $1,730,608 (M); expenditures, $1,117,084, including $1,073,240 for 97 grants (high: $375,000; low: $500; average: $500-$50,000) and $39,309 for 102 employee matching gifts.
Purpose and activities: Support for higher education, health and welfare organizations, including hospitals and community funds; museums, performing arts groups, and other cultural programs; civic affairs, and community development groups.
Types of support: Employee matching gifts, annual campaigns, building funds, capital campaigns, continuing support, emergency funds, endowment funds, general purposes, renovation projects, research, operating budgets, scholarship funds.
Limitations: Giving primarily in areas of company operations, with emphasis on Boston and eastern MA.
Publications: Application guidelines.
Application information: Application form not required.
Initial approach: Proposal, including proof of 501(c)(3) status, annual report, contributors list, organization and project budget
Deadline(s): Nov. 1
Board meeting date(s): Dec.
Final notification: Within 10 days
Write: Neil F. Doherty, Dir.
Officers: Craig D. Peffer,* Exec. Advisor; Basil G. Pallone, Treas.; Catherine J. Keuthen, Counsel; C.S. Daisy Jao, Tax Advisor.
Trustees:* Stephen J. Sweeney, Chair.; Douglas C. Bauer, Theodora S. Convisser, Eleanor T. Daly, William D. Harrington, Thomas J. May, Bernard W. Reznicek.
Director: Neil F. Doherty.
Number of staff: None.
Employer Identification Number: 042754285

2742
Boston Fatherless & Widows Society
c/o Goodwin, Procter & Hoar
Exchange Place, Rm. 2200
Boston 02109-2881 (617) 570-1130

Established in 1837 in MA.
Foundation type: Independent
Financial data (yr. ended 11/30/89): Assets, $4,246,548 (M); expenditures, $237,306, including $146,075 for grants and $91,231 for 52 grants to individuals.
Purpose and activities: Giving primarily for aid to indigent widows and orphans.
Types of support: Grants to individuals.
Limitations: Giving limited to the Boston, MA, area.
Application information: Application form not required.
Initial approach: Letter
Deadline(s): None
Write: George W. Butterworth III
Officers: Mrs. John S. Clapp, Jr.,* Pres.; Mrs. H. Stephen Kott,* V.P.; Mrs. Vernon S. Dick,* Secy.; Richard Wengren, Treas.
Trustees:* Mrs. Robert B. Bachman, Mrs. Urban H. Eversole, Mrs. John M. Gepson, Mrs. John R. Johnston, Mrs. Clinton H. Shattuck, Mrs. Robert H. Traylor, Margaret S. Welsh.
Employer Identification Number: 046006506

2743
The Boston Foundation, Inc. ▼
60 State St., 6th Fl.
Boston 02109 (617) 723-7415

Established in 1915 in MA by agreement and declaration of trust; incorporated in 1917.
Foundation type: Community
Financial data (yr. ended 06/30/89): Assets, $224,313,974 (M); gifts received, $13,101,437; expenditures, $16,439,583, including $12,966,006 for 1,116 grants (high: $311,000; low: $100; average: $5,000-$75,000).
Purpose and activities: To support local health, welfare, educational, cultural, environmental and housing programs and institutions; grants for start-up expenses of new or experimental programs of both established and new institutions, as well as for capital needs and for coordination and planning projects.
Types of support: Building funds, emergency funds, equipment, land acquisition, matching funds, seed money, special projects, renovation projects.
Limitations: Giving limited to the Boston, MA, metropolitan area. No support for religious purposes, small arts groups, public or private schools, municipalities, or national or international programs. No grants to individuals, or for general operating funds, medical, scientific, or academic research; books or articles; films, radio, or television programs; audio and/or video equipment; travel; scholarships, fellowships, conferences, or multi-million dollar capital campaigns with a national focus; no loans.
Publications: Annual report, application guidelines, newsletter, occasional report.
Application information:
Initial approach: Letter or proposal
Copies of proposal: 1
Deadline(s): 10 weeks prior to board meetings
Board meeting date(s): Mar., June, Sept., and Dec.
Final notification: Within 1 or 2 weeks of board meeting
Write: Anna Faith Jones, Pres.
Officers: Dwight L. Allison, Jr.,* Chair.; Lawrence T. Perera,* Vice-Chair.; Anna Faith Jones, Pres., C.E.O., and Secy.-Treas.
Distribution Committee:* Frieda Garcia, Peter J. Gomes, Daniel A. Hart, Charles Ray Johnson, Martin S. Kaplan, Gael Mahony, David R. Pokross, Sr., David Rockefeller, Jr., John Larkin Thompson.
Trustee Banks: Bank of New England, N.A., Bank of Boston, Boston Safe Deposit & Trust Co., Shawmut Bank, N.A., State Street Bank & Trust Co.
Number of staff: 11 full-time professional; 6 full-time support.
Employer Identification Number: 042104021

2744
The Boston Globe Foundation II, Inc. ⌑ ☆
135 Morrissey Blvd.
Boston 02107 (617) 929-3194

Established in 1987.
Foundation type: Operating
Financial data (yr. ended 6/30/88): Assets, $112,220 (M); gifts received, $4,312,866; expenditures, $4,353,567, including $4,284,715 for 499 grants (high: $340,000; low: $25).
Purpose and activities: Giving primarily for community services, with emphasis on multiservice agencies, handicapped accessibility, housing development, and race relations; support also for culture and the arts, education, science and the environment, hospitals and health care, summer camps, and media business.
Types of support: Employee matching gifts, operating budgets, special projects, building funds, scholarship funds, employee-related scholarships, employee matching gifts, research, renovation projects, emergency funds, endowment funds, internships, publications.
Limitations: Giving primarily in the greater Boston, MA, area.
Publications: Application guidelines.
Application information:
Initial approach: Proposal
Deadline(s): None
Board meeting date(s): Feb., Mar., June, Sept., and Nov.
Final notification: 4 months after submitting proposal
Write: Suzanne Watkin, Exec. Dir.
Officers and Directors: William O. Taylor, Pres.; John P. Guiggio, Treas.; Suzanne Watkin, Exec. Dir.; Dexter Eure, Sr., Catherine E.C. Henn, Benjamin Taylor, William D. Taylor.
Employer Identification Number: 222821421

2745
Managers of Boston Port & Seamen's Aid Society ⌑ ☆
Thompson Sq.
124 Main St.
Boston 02129

Established in 1981 in MA.
Foundation type: Operating
Financial data (yr. ended 12/31/88): Assets, $8,750,504 (M); gifts received, $17,000; expenditures, $516,748, including $26,250 for 4 grants (high: $20,000; low: $250).
Purpose and activities: Giving primarily for a YMCA and a maritime academy.

Types of support: Scholarship funds.
Limitations: Giving primarily in MA. No grants to individuals.
Application information: Contributes only to pre-selected organizations. Applications not accepted.
Officers: Harold F. Lynch, Pres. and Mgr.; Alice Moulton, V.P. and Mgr.; Ralph R. Bagley, Secy.-Treas. and Mgr.; and 22 additional mgrs.
Employer Identification Number: 042104688

2746
John W. Boynton Fund ⌑
c/o State St. Bank and Trust Co.
P.O. Box 351
Boston 02101 (617) 654-3343

Trust established in 1950 in MA.
Donor(s): Dora C. Boynton.†
Foundation type: Independent
Financial data (yr. ended 12/31/88): Assets, $1,999,006 (M); expenditures, $119,116, including $97,221 for 33 grants (high: $7,000; low: $1,000; average: $2,000).
Purpose and activities: Grants principally to organizations serving low-income elderly; special consideration also to the town of Athol, MA. A limited number of other grants are made to groups other than the elderly, including youth agencies.
Types of support: Operating budgets, seed money, building funds, general purposes, equipment, renovation projects.
Limitations: Giving primarily in eastern MA, and in Athol, MA. No grants to individuals, or for endowment funds, research, scholarships, fellowships, or matching gifts; no loans.
Publications: Application guidelines, grants list.
Application information: Application form not required.
Initial approach: Proposal
Copies of proposal: 1
Deadline(s): Mar. 15, June 15, Sept. 15, or Dec. 15
Board meeting date(s): Apr., July, Oct., and Jan.
Final notification: 1 month
Write: Deborah A. Robbins, V.P., State Street Bank and Trust Co.
Trustee: State Street Bank and Trust Co.
Number of staff: 1 part-time professional; 1 part-time support.
Employer Identification Number: 046036706

2747
The Braitmayer Foundation ⌑
c/o North American Management Corp.
28 State St., Suite 3854
Boston 02109

Trust established in 1964 in MA.
Donor(s): Marian S. Braitmayer.
Foundation type: Independent
Financial data (yr. ended 12/31/88): Assets, $2,441,945 (M); expenditures, $128,709, including $104,200 for 13 grants (high: $19,000; low: $2,200).
Purpose and activities: Support primarily for the advancement of higher education, particularly in developing techniques of instruction in the humanities and liberal arts.
Limitations: Giving primarily in New England states. No grants to individuals, or for building or endowment funds, scholarships, fellowships, or matching gifts; no loans.
Application information: Contributes only to pre-selected organizations. Applications not accepted.
Board meeting date(s): Annually and as required
Trustees: John W. Braitmayer, Karen L. Braitmayer, Anne B. Webb, R. Davis Webb, Jr.
Employer Identification Number: 046112131

2748
Robert Brigham Trust ⌑
c/o Rice, Heard & Bigelow, Inc.
294 Washington St.
Boston 02108-4608

Foundation type: Independent
Financial data (yr. ended 12/31/88): Assets, $1,336,540 (M); expenditures, $73,186, including $59,601 for 19 grants (high: $11,462; low: $2,292).
Purpose and activities: Support primarily for hospitals and social services.
Limitations: Giving primarily in MA. No grants to individuals.
Application information: Contributes only to pre-selected organizations. Applications not accepted.
Trustees: Edward S. Heard, Neil W. Rice, George H. Stephenson.
Employer Identification Number: 046094404

2749
Alexander H. Bright Charitable Trust ⌑
c/o Boston Safe Deposit & Trust Co.
One Boston Place
Boston 02106 (617) 722-7336

Established in 1952 in MA.
Donor(s): Alexander H. Bright.†
Foundation type: Independent
Financial data (yr. ended 12/31/88): Assets, $1,547,983 (M); expenditures, $81,156, including $77,400 for 68 grants (high: $10,000; low: $100).
Purpose and activities: Support primarily for wildlife, conservation and environmental organziations; support also for education, social services and youth.
Types of support: General purposes, operating budgets.
Limitations: Giving primarily in MA. No grants to individuals.
Application information: Application form not required.
Initial approach: Proposal
Deadline(s): Feb., May, Aug. and Nov.
Board meeting date(s): Mar., June, Sept. and Dec.
Final notification: Jan.
Write: A. Lyman Parson
Trustee: Edward Weld.
Employer Identification Number: 046013967

2750
Florence Evans Bushee Foundation, Inc.
Palmer & Dodge
One Beacon St., Rm. 2000
Boston 02108 (617) 573-0137

Incorporated in 1953 in MA.
Donor(s): Florence Evans Bushee.†
Foundation type: Independent
Financial data (yr. ended 12/31/88): Assets, $2,000,000 (M); expenditures, $155,313, including $16,400 for 5 grants (high: $7,000; low: $1,000; average: $1,000-$7,000) and $100,000 for 120 grants to individuals (high: $1,600; low: $500; average: $500-$1,600).
Purpose and activities: Grants to charitable institutions of interest to the donor during her lifetime; scholarship grants to college students.
Types of support: Student aid.
Limitations: Giving limited to the Newburyport, MA, area; scholarships for residents of Newburyport only. No grants for building funds, endowment funds, or operating budgets; no loans.
Publications: Informational brochure, application guidelines.
Application information: Application form required for scholarships. Application form required.
Initial approach: Letter
Copies of proposal: 1
Deadline(s): May 1
Board meeting date(s): May, June, and as required
Final notification: Early July
Write: Ann Reidy, Secy.
Officers and Trustees:* Marion Brown,* Pres.; Judith Robertson,* V.P.; Ann Reidy, Secy.; Casimir de Rham,* Treas.
Number of staff: 4 part-time professional; 1 part-time support.
Employer Identification Number: 046035327

2751
Julia B. Buxton Trust ⌑
c/o Shawmut First Bank & Trust Co. of Hampden County
127 State St.
Springfield 01103

Foundation type: Independent
Financial data (yr. ended 12/31/87): Assets, $1,178,853 (M); expenditures, $59,434, including $38,000 for 18 grants (high: $5,000; low: $500).
Purpose and activities: Support primarily for social services, the arts, museums, and public television.
Types of support: General purposes.
Application information:
Initial approach: Proposal
Deadline(s): Aug.
Trustee: Shawmut First Bank & Trust Co. of Hampden County.
Employer Identification Number: 046263415

2752
Cabot Corporation Foundation, Inc. ▼
950 Winter St.
P.O. Box 9073
Waltham 02254-9073 (617) 890-0200

Incorporated in 1953 in MA.
Donor(s): Cabot Corp.
Foundation type: Company-sponsored
Financial data (yr. ended 09/30/89): Assets, $1,047,447 (M); expenditures, $1,000,000, including $511,815 for 80 grants (high: $62,500; low: $750; average: $1,000-$10,000) and $404,772 for 356 employee matching gifts.

Purpose and activities: Emphasis on science and technology, higher and other education, including employee matching gifts, community improvement, and public policy. Support also for community funds and cultural programs; particular interest in strengthening the future scientific and technological capabilities of the nation. As a result, projects, organizations, and activities with a science and technology focus that cut across all program areas receive special attention.
Types of support: Annual campaigns, seed money, building funds, equipment, scholarship funds, fellowships, special projects, matching funds, general purposes, employee matching gifts, capital campaigns.
Limitations: Giving primarily in communities near Cabot corporate installations in TX; Douglas County, IL; St. Mary Parish and Evangeline Parish, LA; Boyertown, PA; and Waltham, MA. No support for political organizations, religious institutions for religious purposes, or fraternal organizations. No grants to individuals, or for advertising or dinner table sponsorship.
Publications: Annual report (including application guidelines), occasional report.
Application information: Application form not required.
Initial approach: Proposal
Copies of proposal: 1
Deadline(s): 1 month prior to meetings
Board meeting date(s): Mar., June, Sept., and Dec.
Final notification: 3 months
Write: Dorothy L. Forbes, Exec. Dir.
Officers: Samuel W. Bodman,* Pres.; John D. Curtain,* V.P. and Treas.; Dorothy L. Forbes,* V.P. and Exec. Dir.; Anthony H. James,* Secy.; Charles D. Gerlinger, Clerk.
Directors:* Louis W. Cabot, Maryellen Cabot, Thomas D. Cabot.
Number of staff: 1 full-time professional; 1 part-time support.
Employer Identification Number: 046035227

2753
Cabot Family Charitable Trust
950 Winter St.
P.O. Box 9073
Boston 02254-9073 (617) 622-3625

Trust established in 1942 in MA.
Donor(s): Godfrey L. Cabot.†
Foundation type: Independent
Financial data (yr. ended 12/31/89): Assets, $12,200,721 (M); expenditures, $601,668, including $568,800 for 39 grants (high: $50,000; low: $3,000; average: $3,000-$15,000).
Purpose and activities: Program interests include urban programs, youth and family services, higher and other education, cultural programs, environmental conservation, and population-related projects.
Types of support: Annual campaigns, seed money, building funds, land acquisition, endowment funds, general purposes, continuing support, capital campaigns, research.
Limitations: No support for computer-related projects, or environmental programs outside the New England area. No grants to individuals, or for medical or scientific research, scholarships, fellowships, or matching gifts; no loans.
Publications: Annual report.
Application information: Application form not required.
Initial approach: Proposal
Copies of proposal: 1
Deadline(s): Aug. and Nov.
Board meeting date(s): Sept. and Dec.
Final notification: 3 to 5 months
Write: Ruth C. Scheer, Exec. Dir.
Trustees: Jane C. Bradley, John Cabot, Louis W. Cabot.
Number of staff: 1 part-time professional; 1 part-time support.
Employer Identification Number: 046036446

2754
Ella Lyman Cabot Trust, Inc.
109 Rockland St.
Holliston 01746 (508) 429-8997

Incorporated in 1939 in MA.
Donor(s): Richard Cabot.†
Foundation type: Independent
Financial data (yr. ended 12/31/88): Assets, $1,374,384 (M); expenditures, $80,239, including $70,211 for 9 grants to individuals (high: $21,000; low: $1,680; average: $4,000-$8,000).
Purpose and activities: Grants for projects involving a departure from one's usual vocation or a creative extension of it, with a promise of good to others. Awards are usually made on a one-year basis and are not renewed.
Types of support: Grants to individuals.
Limitations: No grants for scholarships, fellowships, or research pursued as a regular part of a profession; no grants to organizations.
Publications: Informational brochure, application guidelines.
Application information: Proposals screened before application is issued. Application form required.
Initial approach: Letter and proposal
Copies of proposal: 1
Deadline(s): Feb. 15 and Sept. 15
Board meeting date(s): Nov. and May
Final notification: Usually by May 15 and Nov. 15
Write: Mary Jane Gibson, Exec. Secy.
Officers: Allan L. Friedlich, Chair.; Jeffrey Swope, Treas.; Mary Jane Gibson, Exec. Secy.
Number of staff: 1 part-time professional.
Employer Identification Number: 042111393

2755
Cabot-Saltonstall Charitable Trust ⌑
One Financial Ctr., 38th Fl.
Boston 02111

Trust established in 1936 in MA.
Donor(s): Paul C. Cabot, Virginia C. Cabot, Charles Cabot.†
Foundation type: Independent
Financial data (yr. ended 12/31/88): Assets, $5,033,617 (M); expenditures, $278,842, including $268,260 for 83 grants (high: $50,000; low: $10).
Purpose and activities: Emphasis on higher and secondary education, hospitals, and a community fund.
Limitations: Giving primarily in the Boston, MA, area.
Application information: Applications not accepted.
Trustees: Paul C. Cabot, Paul C. Cabot, Jr., Virginia C. Cabot.
Employer Identification Number: 046042037

2756
Calderwood Charitable Foundation ⌑ ☆
c/o Andrew C. Bailey, Powers & Hall
100 Franklin St.
Boston 02110

Established in 1968.
Donor(s): Stanford M. Calderwood.
Foundation type: Independent
Financial data (yr. ended 12/31/88): Assets, $1,228,328 (M); gifts received, $400,802; expenditures, $85,896, including $85,000 for 4 grants (high: $50,000; low: $5,000).
Purpose and activities: Giving primarily for higher education and a museum.
Limitations: No grants to individuals.
Application information: Contributes only to pre-selected organizations. Applications not accepted.
Trustees: Andrew C. Bailey, Norma J. Calderwood, Stanford M. Calderwood.
Employer Identification Number: 046186166

2757
Cambridge Community Foundation ⌑
(Formerly The Cambridge Foundation)
99 Bishop Allen Dr.
Cambridge 02139 (617) 876-5214

Established in 1916 in MA by declaration of trust.
Foundation type: Community
Financial data (yr. ended 12/31/88): Assets, $2,812,675 (M); qualifying distributions, $181,000, including $181,000 for grants (average: $1,000-$5,000).
Purpose and activities: To promote the mental, moral, and physical welfare of the inhabitants of Cambridge, MA (or elsewhere, if specified by the donor), through grants to community agencies, generally for 1) social services - child welfare and development, emergency aid, employment and job training, legal assistance, and family services; 2) education - elementary and secondary education and ESL/GED programs; 3) health - hospice and home care, mental health and counseling, and substance abuse programs; and 4) housing and shelter - home improvement and repair, housing development, and shelter and transitional housing.
Types of support: Operating budgets, general purposes, special projects, seed money, building funds, equipment.
Limitations: Giving primarily in Cambridge, MA, except as specified by donors. No support for municipal, state, or federal agencies. No grants to individuals, or for scholarships, research studies, conferences, films, or capital fund drives; no loans.
Publications: Annual report, application guidelines, program policy statement.
Application information:
Initial approach: Telephone or letter requesting guidelines

Copies of proposal: 6
Deadline(s): Submit proposal preferably in Feb. through Apr. and Sept. through Oct.; deadline Apr. 15 for June consideration and Oct. 15 for Dec. consideration
Board meeting date(s): Distribution committee meets in June and Dec.
Write: Lynn D'Ambrose, Exec. Dir.
Distribution Committee: Patricia R. Pratt, Pres.; Sybil C. d'Arbeloff, Marion B. Eiseman, Hon. Lawrence F. Feloney, Joan Von Mehren.
Trustees: BayBank Harvard Trust Co., Cambridge Trust Co.
Employer Identification Number: 046012492

2758
Cambridge Mustard Seed Foundation ⌑ ☆
c/o Shawmut Central Tax Unit
P.O. Box 2032
Worcester 01613-2032
Application address: c/o Shawmut Bank, N.A., One Federal Asset St., Boston, MA 02201

Established in 1985 in MA.
Donor(s): Sarah C. Doering, R & T Liquidating Trust.
Foundation type: Independent
Financial data (yr. ended 07/31/88): Assets, $4,319,859 (M); gifts received, $84,000; expenditures, $323,945, including $264,700 for 11 grants (high: $64,700; low: $8,000).
Purpose and activities: Giving primarily for higher and other education; support also for a welfare agency, a music-related media project, and a family planning agency.
Limitations: Giving primarily in MA. No grants to individuals.
Application information:
Initial approach: Letter
Deadline(s): None
Write: David Green, Trust Officer, Shawmut Bank, N.A.
Trustees: Jill Ker Conway, Sarah C. Doering, Gerald E. Fosbroke, Shawmut Bank, N.A.
Employer Identification Number: 046527529

2759
Bushrod H. Campbell and Adah F. Hall Charity Fund
c/o Palmer & Dodge
One Beacon St.
Boston 02108 (617) 573-0100

Trust established in 1956 in MA.
Donor(s): Bushrod H. Campbell,† Adah F. Hall.†
Foundation type: Independent
Financial data (yr. ended 05/31/89): Assets, $8,963,214 (M); gifts received, $177,146; expenditures, $359,155, including $313,050 for 62 grants (high: $40,000; low: $750; average: $3,000-$8,000).
Purpose and activities: Grants limited to organizations devoted to aid the elderly, for population control, special projects in major hospitals, and medical research grants administered through The Medical Foundation. Grants made primarily for services and programs.
Types of support: Operating budgets, continuing support, seed money, building funds, equipment, scholarship funds, fellowships, research, conferences and seminars, special projects, renovation projects.
Limitations: Giving limited to the greater Boston, MA, area. No grants to individuals, or for annual campaigns, emergency funds, deficit financing, land acquisition, publications, or general endowments; no loans.
Publications: Application guidelines.
Application information: Application form required.
Initial approach: Telephone or letter
Copies of proposal: 1
Deadline(s): Feb. 1, May 1, Sept. 1, or Nov. 1
Board meeting date(s): Feb., May, Sept., and Nov.
Final notification: By mail only
Write: Hilary M. Mills, Legal Asst.
Trustees: Donald J. Barker, Casimir de Rham, Jr., Curtis Prout.
Number of staff: 1 part-time professional.
Employer Identification Number: 046013598

2760
Ward M. & Mariam C. Canaday Educational and Charitable Trust ⌑
c/o First National Bank of Boston
P.O. Box 1861
Boston 02105
Application address: P.O. Box 1890, Boston, MA 02106

Trust established in 1945 in OH.
Donor(s): Ward M. Canaday,† Mariam C. Canaday.†
Foundation type: Independent
Financial data (yr. ended 12/31/87): Assets, $10,282,190 (M); gifts received, $567,300; expenditures, $1,010,678, including $928,751 for 5 grants (high: $716,910; low: $25,000).
Purpose and activities: Educational and charitable purposes; grants for higher education.
Application information:
Initial approach: Letter
Deadline(s): None
Board meeting date(s): Quarterly
Write: Robert H. Frey, Dir., Investment Management and Personal Trust
Trustees: George W. Ritter, Doreen Spitzer, Lyman Spitzer, Jr., First National Bank of Boston.
Number of staff: None.
Employer Identification Number: 346523619

2761
CarEth Foundation ⌑
Three Church St.
Cambridge 02138 (617) 354-8343

Incorporated in 1967 in CT.
Donor(s): G. Sterling Grumman.†
Foundation type: Independent
Financial data (yr. ended 12/31/86): Assets, $1,849,326 (M); gifts received, $73,689; expenditures, $126,827, including $100,750 for 38 grants (average: $2,000-$4,000).
Purpose and activities: Grants "only for programs promoting world peace" including religious, educational, and public policy organizations.
Types of support: General purposes, operating budgets, special projects, research.
Limitations: No grants to individuals.
Publications: Application guidelines, program policy statement.
Application information: Application form required.
Initial approach: Letter
Copies of proposal: 2
Deadline(s): July 21
Board meeting date(s): Specific dates decided semiannually
Write: Elizabeth S. Grumman, Secy.
Officers and Directors: Helen Burr Grumman, Pres.; Carol B. Grumman, V.P.; Elizabeth S. Grumman, Secy.; Paul Martin Grumman, Treas.; Ethel G. Ackely, Paul Deats, Jr., Gregory Finger, Sandra Martin Grumman.
Number of staff: 1 part-time professional.
Employer Identification Number: 042433914

2762
Casty-Dunn Families Charitable Foundation ⌑ ☆
400 Eastern Ave.
Chelsea 02150-3197

Established in 1962.
Donor(s): Norman S. Dunn.
Foundation type: Independent
Financial data (yr. ended 11/30/88): Assets, $919,298 (M); gifts received, $100,000; expenditures, $137,554, including $136,229 for 72 grants (high: $45,000; low: $25).
Purpose and activities: Grants for Jewish giving, including welfare funds; support also for health associations and services and hospitals.
Limitations: No grants to individuals.
Application information: Applications not accepted.
Trustees: Arthur Altman, Ronald G. Casty, Norman S. Dunn.
Employer Identification Number: 046074905

2763
Charlesbank Homes ⌑
117 Woodland Rd.
Chestnut Hill 02167 (617) 566-5830

Established in 1911.
Donor(s): Edwin Ginn.†
Foundation type: Independent
Financial data (yr. ended 04/30/89): Assets, $6,846,075 (M); gifts received, $673,371; expenditures, $169,457, including $127,500 for grants.
Purpose and activities: Emphasis on low- and moderate-income housing; support also for youth and social service agencies.
Types of support: Building funds.
Limitations: Giving primarily in the greater Boston, MA, area. No grants to individuals, or for operating budgets.
Application information:
Initial approach: Letter
Deadline(s): None
Board meeting date(s): Annually
Write: Edward D. Rowley, Pres.
Officers and Trustees:* Edward D. Rowley,* Pres. and Secy.; William C. Allison IV,* V.P.; Dudley H. Bradlee II, V.P. y; F. William Andres, Thomas W. Cornu, John B. Kenerson, George Macomber, Mark C. Wheeler.
Employer Identification Number: 042103755

2764
Ida S. Charlton Charity Fund ⌑ ☆
c/o First National Bank of Boston
P.O. Box 1861
Boston 02105

Foundation type: Independent
Financial data (yr. ended 9/30/88): Assets, $1,446,530 (M); expenditures, $108,302, including $82,000 for 5 grants (high: $50,000; low: $1,000).
Purpose and activities: Support for human services through vocational rehabilitation and community funds.
Limitations: Giving primarily in MA, with some emphasis on Fall River.
Trustees: E.P. Charlton II, Alfred W. Fuller, First National Bank of Boston.
Employer Identification Number: 046010540

2765
Earle P. Charlton, Jr. Charitable Trust ⌑
c/o First National Bank of Boston
P.O. Box 1861
Boston 02105 (617) 434-5669

Trust established in 1973 in MA.
Donor(s): Earle P. Charlton, Jr.†
Foundation type: Independent
Financial data (yr. ended 12/31/88): Assets, $4,578,285 (M); expenditures, $264,162, including $209,000 for 5 grants (high: $130,000; low: $4,000).
Purpose and activities: Giving primarily to hospitals.
Limitations: Giving primarily in Boston, MA.
Application information: Contributes only to pre-selected organizations. Applications not accepted.
Write: S. Driscoll, Sr. V.P., First National Bank of Boston
Trustees: Earle P. Charlton II, Afrea Fuller, First National Bank of Boston.
Employer Identification Number: 046334412

2766
Robert A. Charpie Foundation ⌑ ☆
c/o Ampersand Ventures
55 William St., Suite 240
Wellesley 02181

Established in 1984 in MA.
Donor(s): Elizabeth D. Charpie, Robert A. Charpie.
Foundation type: Independent
Financial data (yr. ended 12/31/87): Assets, $588,875 (M); expenditures, $118,915, including $115,250 for 5 grants (high: $35,000; low: $6,500).
Purpose and activities: Giving primarily for higher education; support also for a hospital and a community fund.
Limitations: Giving primarily in MA and PA. No grants to individuals.
Application information: Contributes only to pre-selected organizations. Applications not accepted.
Write: Robert A. Charpie, Trustee
Trustees: Elizabeth D. Charpie, Richard A. Charpie, Robert A. Charpie.
Employer Identification Number: 222589467

2767
The Alfred E. Chase Charity Foundation
c/o Bank of New England, N.A.
28 State St.
Boston 02107 (617) 573-6416

Trust established in 1956 in MA.
Donor(s): Alfred E. Chase.†
Foundation type: Independent
Financial data (yr. ended 10/31/88): Assets, $3,929,462 (M); expenditures, $248,013, including $190,000 for 14 grants (high: $25,000; low: $5,000; average: $10,000-$20,000).
Purpose and activities: Particular interest in social service and welfare organizations and programs for children and youth; support also for hospitals and health services, community development, delinquency programs, the disabled and homeless, and hunger and nutrition.
Types of support: Capital campaigns, operating budgets, building funds, renovation projects, annual campaigns, capital campaigns, equipment, general purposes, operating budgets, renovation projects, special projects.
Limitations: Giving limited to MA, primarily the greater Boston and North Shore areas. No grants to individuals, or for research, scholarships, or fellowships; no loans.
Publications: Application guidelines, 990-PF.
Application information: Application form required.
Initial approach: Proposal
Copies of proposal: 1
Deadline(s): Feb. 28
Board meeting date(s): Apr.
Write: Kerry A. Herlihy, V.P., Bank of New England, N.A.
Trustee: Bank of New England, N.A.
Number of staff: 4 full-time professional; 1 full-time support.
Employer Identification Number: 046026314

2768
Alice P. Chase Trust ⌑
Boston Safe Deposit & Trust Co.
One Boston Place
Boston 02108 (617) 722-7340

Trust established in 1956 in MA.
Donor(s): Alice P. Chase,† Alfred E. Chase.†
Foundation type: Independent
Financial data (yr. ended 8/31/88): Assets, $3,939,220 (M); expenditures, $326,862, including $265,000 for 16 grants (high: $100,000; low: $2,000).
Purpose and activities: Giving for social welfare agencies providing health, educational, recreational, and other support services to mentally, economically, or physically disadvantaged youth and the aged; support also for the arts, especially a museum.
Types of support: Capital campaigns, equipment, general purposes, renovation projects, special projects, technical assistance.
Limitations: Giving primarily in Lynn, MA, and the Boston North Shore area. No grants to individuals, or for matching gifts; no loans.
Publications: Application guidelines.
Application information:
Initial approach: Letter or proposal
Copies of proposal: 1
Deadline(s): Feb. 1, May 1, Aug. 1, and Nov. 1
Board meeting date(s): End of Mar., June, Sept., and Dec.
Write: Ms. Sylvia Salas
Trustee: Boston Safe Deposit & Trust Co.
Employer Identification Number: 046093897

2769
Roberta M. Childs Charitable Foundation
P.O. Box 639
North Andover 01845

Trust established in 1978 in MA.
Donor(s): Roberta M. Childs.†
Foundation type: Independent
Financial data (yr. ended 03/31/88): Assets, $2,434,888 (M); expenditures, $166,602, including $136,000 for 65 grants (high: $5,000; low: $1,000).
Purpose and activities: Emphasis on aid to the indigent, child welfare, education, and the prevention of cruelty to animals.
Types of support: Continuing support, general purposes, operating budgets.
Limitations: Giving primarily in MA. No grants to individuals.
Application information: Application form not required.
Initial approach: Letter
Copies of proposal: 1
Deadline(s): None
Board meeting date(s): Varies
Write: John R.D. McClintock, Trustee
Trustee: John R.D. McClintock.
Number of staff: None.
Employer Identification Number: 042660275

2770
Choss Charitable Trust ⌑ ☆
1000 Main St.
West Barnstable 02668
Application address: Box 1401, Wellfleet, MA 02667; Tel.: (508) 349-9742

Established in 1986.
Foundation type: Operating
Financial data (yr. ended 12/31/88): Assets, $19,242 (M); expenditures, $225,009, including $223,000 for 4 grants (high: $194,500; low: $1,000).
Purpose and activities: A private operating foundation; giving primarily for education; support also for family and social services.
Types of support: Building funds.
Limitations: Giving primarily in MA. No grants to individuals.
Application information:
Initial approach: Letter
Deadline(s): None
Write: George W. Malloy, Trustee
Trustees: Barbara U. Birdsey, David C. Birdsey, George W. Malloy, Marie B. Wetherbee.
Employer Identification Number: 222655511

2771
Clark Charitable Trust
P.O. Box 251
Lincoln 01773

Established in 1937 in MA.
Foundation type: Independent
Financial data (yr. ended 12/31/89): Assets, $1,900,000 (M); expenditures, $86,325, including $73,200 for 33 grants (high: $5,000; low: $350; average: $2,000).
Purpose and activities: Support for basic human needs, preservation of environment, animal welfare, music, and higher education.
Types of support: Annual campaigns, building funds, capital campaigns, endowment funds, equipment, land acquisition, operating budgets, scholarship funds.
Publications: 990-PF, financial statement.
Application information: Application form not required.
Deadline(s): None
Write: Timothy A. Taylor, Trustee
Trustees: Russel T. Kopp, Timothy A. Taylor.
Employer Identification Number: 046037650

2772
Clifford Charitable Foundation, Inc. ⌑ ☆
c/o Gaston & Snow
One Federal St.
Boston 02110-2003

Established in 1980 in MA.
Donor(s): Ellinor B. Clifford.
Foundation type: Independent
Financial data (yr. ended 12/31/88): Assets, $471,837 (M); gifts received, $359,473; expenditures, $245,276, including $239,900 for 41 grants (high: $40,000; low: $100).
Purpose and activities: Giving primarily for higher and other education; support also for hospitals, child welfare, and a community fund.
Limitations: Giving primarily in Boston, MA. No grants to individuals.
Application information: Contributes only to pre-selected organizations. Applications not accepted.
Officers: Stewart A. Clifford, Pres.; Ellinor B. Clifford, Treas.
Director: Frederic M. Clifford.
Employer Identification Number: 042690883

2773
Clipper Ship Foundation, Inc. ⌑ ☆
c/o Hill & Barlow, 100 Oliver St.
One International Place, 20th Fl.
Boston 02110 (617) 439-3555

Established in 1979 in MA.
Donor(s): David Parmely Weatherhead.†
Foundation type: Independent
Financial data (yr. ended 10/31/88): Assets, $12,455,016 (M); expenditures, $700,496, including $537,750 for 97 grants (high: $25,000; low: $1,000).
Purpose and activities: "Priority given to organizations devoted to helping the homeless, the destitute, the handicapped, children and the aged, or supplying the special needs of minority, low-income individuals and families. Special consideration also given to emergency disaster situations."
Types of support: Emergency funds.
Limitations: Giving primarily in the greater Boston, MA, area. No grants to individuals.
Application information:
Initial approach: Proposal
Deadline(s): None
Board meeting date(s): Every 3 months
Officer and Directors: Benjamin H. Lacy, Pres.; John B. Newhall, George F. Pennington.
Employer Identification Number: 042687384

2774
The Ogden Codman Trust
31 Milk St., Suite 620
Boston 02109 (617) 723-4535

Established in 1968 in MA.
Donor(s): Dorothy S.F.M. Codman.†
Foundation type: Independent
Financial data (yr. ended 12/31/89): Assets, $1,703,686 (M); expenditures, $76,121, including $66,000 for 5 grants (high: $26,000; low: $8,000; average: $8,000-$12,000).
Purpose and activities: Giving for educational, recreational, and other community projects.
Types of support: Operating budgets, emergency funds, building funds, equipment, land acquisition, matching funds, renovation projects.
Limitations: Giving limited to Lincoln, MA. No grants to individuals, or for continuing support, annual campaigns, seed money, deficit financing, endowment funds, scholarships, or fellowships; no loans.
Application information: Application form not required.
Initial approach: Telephone
Copies of proposal: 1
Deadline(s): None
Board meeting date(s): 1st week of Mar., June, Sept., and Dec.
Final notification: 2 to 3 weeks
Write: Daniel W. Fawcett, Trustee
Trustees: Daniel W. Fawcett, William B. Tyler, Walter G. Van Dorn.
Number of staff: 1 part-time professional.
Employer Identification Number: 046225360

2775
The James W. Colgan Scholarship Fund
c/o Bank of New England-West, Trust Dept.
P.O. Box 9003
Springfield 01101 (413) 787-8562

Trust established in 1944 in MA.
Donor(s): James W. Colgan.†
Foundation type: Independent
Financial data (yr. ended 12/31/87): Assets, $2,169,038 (M); expenditures, $195,460, including $173,407 for 254 loans to individuals (high: $2,000; low: $20).
Purpose and activities: Student loan program to aid needy, deserving young men and women at the undergraduate level of study.
Types of support: Student loans.
Limitations: Giving limited to residents of MA. No grants for general purposes, capital funds, endowment funds, matching gifts, scholarships, or fellowships.
Publications: Informational brochure (including application guidelines).
Application information: Applicants must be undergraduates under 30 years old. Application form required.
Initial approach: Letter or telephone
Copies of proposal: 1
Deadline(s): June 30
Board meeting date(s): During summer as required
Final notification: Aug. 31
Write: Thea E. Katsounakis, Trust Officer; or Colgan Fund Asst.
Trustee: Bank of New England-West.
Number of staff: None.
Employer Identification Number: 046032781

2776
Connor Foundation, Inc. ⌑
c/o Maiden Trust Co., Trust Dept.
P.O. Box A
Malden 02148-0901 (617) 321-1111

Established in 1978 in MA.
Foundation type: Independent
Financial data (yr. ended 9/30/87): Assets, $1,246,385 (M); expenditures, $73,116, including $63,000 for 20 grants (high: $1,000; low: $6,000).
Purpose and activities: Support primarily for education, youth and community organizations, and medical research.
Limitations: Giving primarily in MA and NH.
Application information:
Initial approach: Letter
Deadline(s): None
Write: Robert M. Wallask, Trust Officer
Officers: Lloyd B. Waring, Pres.; Elmer O. Cappers, Treas.; Gordon H. Miliar.
Employer Identification Number: 042639964

2777
John Brown Cook Foundation, Inc. ⌑
P.O. Box 246
Monument Beach 02553 (617) 759-3188

Incorporated in 1952 in CT.
Donor(s): John Brown Cook,† Marian Miner Cook, Wallace L. Cook,† Whitney Blake Co., Reliable Electric Co.
Foundation type: Independent
Financial data (yr. ended 10/31/89): Assets, $1,564,634 (M); gifts received, $324,898; expenditures, $287,226, including $241,500 for 12 grants (high: $55,000; low: $8,000).
Purpose and activities: Grants to institutions only, including colleges and universities, educational associations, and public policy research organizations relating to preservation of the American economic system and national defense.
Types of support: General purposes, continuing support, seed money, conferences and seminars.
Limitations: No grants to individuals, or for building or endowment funds, scholarships, fellowships, or matching gifts; no loans.
Application information: Application form not required.
Initial approach: Telephone
Copies of proposal: 1
Board meeting date(s): June, Dec., and as required
Write: Harold C. Ripley, Pres.
Officers and Directors:* Marian Miner Cook,* Chair.; Harold C. Ripley,* Pres. and Treas.; Leo C. McKenna,* V.P.; William R. Murphy, Secy.; Gregory M. Cook, Marcia Cook Hart, Boston Safe Deposit & Trust Co.

Number of staff: 1 part-time support.
Employer Identification Number: 066022958

2778
Coolidge Hill Foundation
700 South St.
Pittsfield 01201 (413) 499-4321
Additional address: Judith L. Spencer, Pres., Box 354, Stockbridge, MA 01201

Established in 1917 in MA.
Donor(s): Coolidge Trust.
Foundation type: Independent
Financial data (yr. ended 12/31/89): Assets, $1,350,000 (M); expenditures, $113,600, including $104,250 for 15 grants (high: $40,000; low: $450).
Purpose and activities: Aid for the elderly and the handicapped; support also for child welfare.
Limitations: Giving limited to Berkshire County, MA.
Publications: Application guidelines.
Application information: Details on applications and deadlines available on request.
Initial approach: Letter
Deadline(s): None
Board meeting date(s): 4-5 times per year
Write: Richard M. Sullivan, Secy.
Officers: Judith L. Spencer, Pres.; John C. Donna, V.P.; Howell M. Palmer III, V.P.; Arne McInerny Pinkston, V.P.; Richard M. Sullivan, Secy.; Colin MacFadyen, Treas.
Employer Identification Number: 042121312

2779
The Cove Charitable Trust ⌑
Boston Safe Deposit and Trust Co.
One Boston Place
Boston 02106 (617) 722-7340

Established in 1964 in MA.
Donor(s): Aileen Kelly Pratt,† Edwin H.B. Pratt.†
Foundation type: Independent
Financial data (yr. ended 12/31/88): Assets, $2,140,147 (M); expenditures, $158,707, including $124,800 for 12 grants (high: $33,000; low: $500; average: $1,000-$2,000).
Purpose and activities: Emphasis on child welfare, affordable housing, health care and urban youth programs.
Types of support: General purposes, special projects, operating budgets, continuing support, annual campaigns, seed money, building funds.
Limitations: Giving primarily in MA. No grants to individuals, or for scholarships, fellowships, emergency funds, deficit financing, equipment and materials, land acquisition, renovation projects, endowments, program-related investments, research, publications, or conferences and seminars; no loans.
Application information: Applications not accepted.
Write: Sylvia Salas, Trust Officer, Boston Safe Deposit and Trust Co.
Trustees: Charlotte P. Sudduth, Boston Safe Deposit & Trust Co.
Number of staff: None.
Employer Identification Number: 046118955

2780
The Daniel & Ruth Coven Charitable Foundation ⌑ ☆
665 Cochituate Rd.
Framingham 01701-4649

Established in 1984 in MA.
Donor(s): Ruth Coven, Daniel Coven.
Foundation type: Independent
Financial data (yr. ended 12/31/88): Assets, $394,421 (M); expenditures, $141,766, including $132,650 for 12 grants (high: $85,250; low: $500).
Purpose and activities: Support for Jewish welfare and other Jewish organizations; support also for health, hospitals, and higher education.
Limitations: Giving primarily in MA. No grants to individuals.
Application information: Contributes only to pre-selected organizations. Applications not accepted.
Trustee: Ruth Coven.
Employer Identification Number: 222552913

2781
The Lillian L. and Harry A. Cowan Foundation Corporation
P.O. Box 248
Norwood 02062

Incorporated in 1962 in MA.
Donor(s): Harry A. Cowan.†
Foundation type: Independent
Financial data (yr. ended 04/30/89): Assets, $2,910,203 (M); expenditures, $170,873, including $127,150 for 22 grants (high: $5,000; low: $2,000; average: $1,000-$5,000).
Purpose and activities: To aid the blind and physically and emotionally handicapped children.
Limitations: Giving primarily in the greater Boston, MA, area. No support for umbrella agencies. No grants to individuals, or for capital or annual campaigns, or building funds.
Application information: Application form not required.
Initial approach: Proposal
Copies of proposal: 1
Deadline(s): May 1 and Dec. 1
Board meeting date(s): Semiannually, usually in June and Dec.
Final notification: May 1 and Dec. 1
Officers and Trustees:* Albert Slavin,* Pres. and Treas.; Ellen Glazer,* V.P.; Marjorie Herson,* V.P.; Beatrice Slavin,* Clerk; Donald Glazer.
Number of staff: 1 part-time professional; 1 part-time support.
Employer Identification Number: 046130077

2782
Jessie B. Cox Charitable Trust ▼
c/o Grants Management Associates, Inc.
230 Congress St., 3rd Fl.
Boston 02110 (617) 426-7172

Charitable lead trust established in 1982 in Boston, MA.
Donor(s): Jessie B. Cox.†
Foundation type: Independent
Financial data (yr. ended 12/31/88): Assets, $50,000,000 (M); qualifying distributions, $3,096,286, including $3,096,286 for 73 grants (high: $120,000; low: $3,825; average: $20,000-$100,000).
Purpose and activities: Grants for education, health, the protection of the environment, and the development of philanthropy. The trustees tend to favor organizations which have not received prior grants, and new approaches over those similar to previously funded projects; fixed amount of approximately $3 million to be paid out annually through the life of the trust.
Types of support: Seed money, special projects.
Limitations: Giving primarily in New England. No support for sectarian religious activities, or efforts usually supported by the general public. No grants to individuals, or for capital or building funds, equipment and materials, land acquisition, renovation projects, deficit financing, operating budgets, continuing support, annual campaigns, or general endowments; no loans.
Publications: Annual report, informational brochure (including application guidelines).
Application information: Application form not required.
Initial approach: Brief concept paper
Copies of proposal: 2
Deadline(s): Jan. 16, Apr. 15, July 15, and Oct. 15
Board meeting date(s): Mar., June, Sept., and Dec.
Final notification: Within 3 months of deadline
Write: Administrators
Administrators: Newell Flather, Ala H. Reid, Ann Fowler Wallace.
Trustees: William C. Cox, Jr., Roy A. Hammer, Jane Cox MacElree, George T. Shaw.
Number of staff: 4 part-time professional; 1 full-time support.
Employer Identification Number: 046478024

2783
Cox Foundation, Inc. ⌑
c/o Gaston & Snow
One Federal St.
Boston 02110 (617) 426-4600

Established in 1970.
Donor(s): William C. Cox, Jr.
Foundation type: Independent
Financial data (yr. ended 12/31/87): Assets, $4,358,620 (M); gifts received, $750,000; expenditures, $227,923, including $225,965 for 30 grants (high: $75,000; low: $500).
Purpose and activities: Emphasis on private schools, hospitals and medical research; support also for conservation and the environment, and cultural programs, including museums.
Types of support: Annual campaigns, continuing support, general purposes, land acquisition, operating budgets, research, special projects, capital campaigns.
Limitations: Giving primarily in MA and FL.
Application information: Applications not accepted.
Officers: William C. Cox, Jr., Pres.; David E. Place, Secy.; Martha W. Cox, Treas.
Employer Identification Number: 237068786

2784
Trustees under the Will of Lotta M. Crabtree ⌑
294 Washington St., Rm. 636
Boston 02108 (617) 451-0698

Trust established in 1928; incorporated in 1929 in MA.
Donor(s): Lotta M. Crabtree.†
Foundation type: Independent
Financial data (yr. ended 12/31/86): Assets, $4,807,092 (M); expenditures, $262,907, including $123,421 for grants.
Purpose and activities: Grants distributed from seven funds for musical education at New England Conservatory of Music only, dumb animals, free beds in Boston hospitals, and Christmas gifts; assistance to graduates of the University of Massachusetts, Stockbridge School of Agriculture, College of Food and Natural Resources, or related programs, in order to establish themselves in agriculture; and to needy actors and discharged convicts.
Types of support: Fellowships, grants to individuals, loans.
Limitations: Giving limited to MA.
Application information:
Write: Claire M. McCarthy, Trust Mgr.
Trustees: Thomas F. Donohue, Michael J. Harney, Robert G. Naughton.
Number of staff: 1 full-time professional.
Employer Identification Number: 042105770

2785
Crane & Company Fund ⌑
South St.
Dalton 01226

Established in 1953 in MA.
Donor(s): Crane & Co., Inc., Byron-Weston Co.
Foundation type: Company-sponsored
Financial data (yr. ended 12/31/88): Assets, $154,693 (M); gifts received, $264,500; expenditures, $168,026, including $167,925 for 51 grants (high: $48,000; low: $100).
Purpose and activities: Giving for civic affairs, social services, health, community funding, education and culture.
Application information:
Deadline(s): None
Trustees: Benjamin J. Sullivan, Stephen H. Wismer.
Employer Identification Number: 046057388

2786
Henry H. Crapo Charitable Foundation ⌑
558 Pleasant St.
New Bedford 02740 (617) 999-1351

Established in 1952 in MA.
Foundation type: Independent
Financial data (yr. ended 12/31/88): Assets, $1,734,577 (M); expenditures, $90,875, including $76,000 for 8 grants (high: $35,000; low: $4,000).
Purpose and activities: Support for a community fund, cultural programs, social services, and community development.
Limitations: Giving primarily in New Bedford, MA.
Application information:
Initial approach: Letter
Deadline(s): None
Write: Davis C. Howes, Treas.
Officers: John C. Bullard, Pres.; W. Julian Underwood, V.P.; Davis C. Howes, Treas.
Employer Identification Number: 042270340

2787
The Cricket Foundation ☆
Exchange Place, Suite 2200
Boston 02109-2881 (617) 570-1130

Established in 1978 in MA.
Foundation type: Independent
Financial data (yr. ended 09/30/89): Assets, $1,969,748 (M); expenditures, $100,936, including $70,000 for 20 grants (high: $10,000; low: $1,000).
Purpose and activities: "Current focus of grantmaking is cultural, environmental, and social service projects"; cultural programs include musical associations and museums.
Limitations: Giving primarily in the northeast. No grants to individuals.
Application information: Application form not required.
Initial approach: Letter or proposal
Deadline(s): May 1 and Nov. 1
Board meeting date(s): May and Nov.
Write: A. Joshua Sherman, Trustee
Trustee: A. Joshua Sherman.
Number of staff: 1 part-time professional.
Employer Identification Number: 042655735

2788
Douglas & Isabelle Crocker Foundation
c/o S. F. Chittick
111 Ross St.
Fitchburg 01420 (617) 342-2016

Established in 1954 in MA.
Foundation type: Independent
Financial data (yr. ended 11/30/89): Assets, $1,122,477 (M); expenditures, $70,580, including $56,000 for grants (high: $26,000; low: $2,500).
Purpose and activities: Support primarily for a church and for a youth organization; support also for an art museum.
Limitations: Giving primarily in MA.
Application information: Application form not required.
Deadline(s): None
Write: Stanley F. Chittick, Treas.
Officers and Directors:* Bartow Kelly,* Pres.; Stanley F. Chittick,* Treas.; Donald Crocker.
Employer Identification Number: 046044767

2789
Mary W. B. Curtis Trust ⌑
c/o Welch & Forbes
45 School St.
Boston 02108 (617) 523-1635

Established in 1956 in MA.
Foundation type: Independent
Financial data (yr. ended 12/31/88): Assets, $1,409,884 (M); expenditures, $78,845, including $65,000 for 11 grants (high: $12,000; low: $2,000).
Purpose and activities: Giving to train boys and young men in good citizenship.
Limitations: Giving limited to MA.
Application information:
Initial approach: Letter
Deadline(s): Dec. 31
Write: Guido R. Perera, Jr., Mgr.
Officer: Guido R. Perera, Jr., Mgr.
Trustee: Welch & Forbes.
Employer Identification Number: 046041027

2790
The Fred Harris Daniels Foundation, Inc.
c/o The Mechanics Bank, Trust Dept.
P.O. Box 987
Worcester 01613 (617) 798-6443
Application address: c/o The Mechanics Bank, Trust Dept., 2000 Mechanics Tower, Worcester, MA 01608

Incorporated in 1949 in MA.
Donor(s): Fred H. Daniels,† Riley Stoker Co.
Foundation type: Independent
Financial data (yr. ended 10/31/89): Assets, $8,003,795 (M); expenditures, $402,490, including $389,750 for 65 grants (high: $70,000; low: $500; average: $1,000-$20,000).
Purpose and activities: Grants for the advancement of the sciences and medicine; support for higher education, hospitals, community funds and services, museums, and cultural programs.
Types of support: Operating budgets, continuing support, annual campaigns, emergency funds, building funds, equipment, land acquisition, endowment funds, matching funds, professorships, internships, scholarship funds, fellowships, special projects, capital campaigns, general purposes, renovation projects.
Limitations: Giving primarily in the Worcester, MA, area. No grants to individuals, or for seed money or deficit financing; no loans.
Application information: Application form not required.
Initial approach: Letter
Copies of proposal: 1
Deadline(s): Mar. 1, June 1, Sept. 1 and Dec. 1
Board meeting date(s): Mar., June, Sept., and Dec.
Final notification: 1 to 2 1/2 months
Write: Bruce G. Daniels, Pres.
Officers and Directors:* Bruce G. Daniels,* Pres.; F. Turner Blake, Jr.,* Secy.; William O. Pettit, Jr.,* Treas.; Johnathan D. Blake, Fred H. Daniels II, Janet B. Daniels, Eleanor D. Hodge, Amy B. Morgan, Sarah D. Morse, William S. Nicholson, Meridith D. Wesby.
Number of staff: None.
Employer Identification Number: 046014333

2791
Irene E. and George A. Davis Foundation ⌑
American Saw and Manufacturing Co.
301 Chestnut St.
East Longmeadow 01028 (413) 525-3961

Established in 1970 in MA.
Donor(s): American Saw and Manufacturing Co., Irene E. Davis.
Foundation type: Company-sponsored
Financial data (yr. ended 12/31/88): Assets, $17,185,146 (M); gifts received, $2,000,000; expenditures, $499,668, including $444,040 for 91 grants (high: $55,000; low: $100).

Purpose and activities: Emphasis on higher education and Roman Catholic institutions, including churches; grants also for social services, hospitals, and community funds.
Types of support: Operating budgets, continuing support, annual campaigns, seed money, emergency funds, building funds, land acquisition, general purposes.
Limitations: Giving primarily in MA. No grants to individuals, or for deficit financing, equipment, endowment funds, matching gifts, scholarships and fellowships, research, special projects, publications, or conferences; no loans.
Application information: Contributes only to pre-selected organizations. Applications not accepted.
Board meeting date(s): As required
Write: James E. Davis, Trustee
Trustees: James E. Davis, John H. Davis, Arthur L. Duquette, Robert R. Lepak, David R. Sayles.
Number of staff: None.
Employer Identification Number: 237102734

2792
Dean Foundation for Little Children, Inc. ⌘
c/o Boston Safe Deposit and Trust Co.
One Boston Place
Boston 02108

Established in 1928 in MA.
Foundation type: Independent
Financial data (yr. ended 12/31/88): Assets, $1,484,644 (M); expenditures, $87,640, including $79,750 for 27 grants (high: $5,000; low: $500; average: $3,000).
Purpose and activities: Giving for the care and relief of destitute children; support also for pre-schools, day care, summer camps, and other programs.
Types of support: Operating budgets, special projects, general purposes.
Limitations: Giving limited to MA, with emphasis on Boston. No grants to individuals.
Application information: Application form not required.
Initial approach: Proposal
Deadline(s): Feb., May, Aug., and Nov.
Board meeting date(s): Mar., June, Sept., and Dec.
Write: Ms. Sylvia Salas, Trust Officer, Boston Safe Deposit and Trust Co.
Officers: Arria W. Sands, Pres.; Nancy P. Criscitiello, V.P.; Raymond F. Beaton, Treas.; Jonathan Strong, Clerk.
Trustee Bank: Boston Safe Deposit & Trust Co.
Employer Identification Number: 042210741

2793
Dedham Temporary Home for Women & Children ⌘
c/o Fiduciary Trust Co.
175 Federal St.
Boston 02110-2210 (617) 482-5270

Foundation type: Independent
Financial data (yr. ended 12/31/88): Assets, $1,295,700 (M); gifts received, $17,000; expenditures, $97,759, including $85,000 for 12 grants (high: $14,000; low: $1,000).
Purpose and activities: Support for family service organizations.
Limitations: Giving primarily in MA.
Application information: Application form not required.
Initial approach: Letter
Deadline(s): None
Write: Susan R. Gunderson, Treas.
Officers and Directors:* Ingrid McDonough,* Pres.; Susan R. Gunderson, Treas.; Mrs. Ralph B. Williams, Clerk; and 20 additional directors.
Employer Identification Number: 046012767

2794
Demoulas Foundation ⌘
875 East St.
Tewksbury 01876

Trust established in 1964 in MA.
Donor(s): Demoulas Super Markets, Inc., and members of the Demoulas family.
Foundation type: Company-sponsored
Financial data (yr. ended 12/31/89): Assets, $27,080,448 (M); gifts received, $600,000; expenditures, $1,190,074, including $1,102,961 for grants.
Purpose and activities: Grants largely for the Greek Orthodox Church, higher and secondary education, and youth agencies.
Application information:
Initial approach: Letter
Write: Telemachus A. Demoulas, Trustee
Trustees: A.T. Demoulas, Telemachus A. Demoulas, D. Harold Sullivan.
Employer Identification Number: 042723441

2795
Dennison Foundation, Inc. ⌘
300 Howard St.
Framingham 01701
Application address: 275 Wyman St., Waltham, MA 02254; Tel.: (508) 879-0511

Established in 1954 in MA.
Donor(s): Dennison Manufacturing Co.
Foundation type: Company-sponsored
Financial data (yr. ended 12/31/88): Assets, $236 (M); gifts received, $103,900; expenditures, $171,667, including $171,325 for 38 grants (high: $60,000; low: $250).
Purpose and activities: Support primarily for hospitals and health associations, education, social services, community funds, and youth organizations.
Application information:
Initial approach: Letter
Deadline(s): None
Write: Carolee S. Cain, Clerk
Officers: Nelson S. Gifford,* Pres.; D.J. Sullivan, Treas.; Carolee S. Cain, Clerk.
Trustees:* J.B. Gray, H.R. Lewis.
Employer Identification Number: 046070860

2796
Devonshire Associates ⌘
50 Federal St., 9th Fl.
Boston 02110

Incorporated in 1949 in MA.
Donor(s): Melita S. Howland, Weston Howland III, Thomas Power, Weston Howland, Jr.
Foundation type: Independent
Financial data (yr. ended 12/31/88): Assets, $3,156,615 (M); gifts received, $283,179; expenditures, $213,700, including $176,250 for 13 grants (high: $50,000; low: $500).
Purpose and activities: Emphasis on a college and an aquarium; support also for cultural programs, higher education, and youth agencies.
Limitations: Giving primarily in MA.
Application information: Contributes only to pre-selected organizations. Applications not accepted.
Officers: Weston Howland, Jr., Pres.; William H. MacCrellish, Jr., Secy.; Donald M. DeHart, Treas.
Trustee: Lewis H. Parks.
Employer Identification Number: 046004808

2797
Frances R. Dewing Foundation
c/o Granite State Gas & Electric
36 Washington St., Suite 320
Wellesley Hills 02181 (617) 235-6555

Established in 1976 in MA.
Donor(s): Frances R. Dewing.
Foundation type: Independent
Financial data (yr. ended 12/31/88): Assets, $2,015,582 (M); expenditures, $148,205, including $141,920 for 41 grants (high: $5,000; low: $1,000; average: $3,500).
Purpose and activities: Support for the fine and performing arts and other cultural programs, social services, the handicapped and disadvantaged, conservation and environmental protection, pre-school, elementary, and other education, and youth and child welfare organizations; emphasis on children under twelve.
Types of support: Conferences and seminars, equipment, internships, publications, seed money, special projects.
Limitations: Giving primarily in New England, NY, and CA. No grants to individuals.
Publications: Program policy statement, application guidelines.
Application information: Application form not required.
Initial approach: Letter
Copies of proposal: 5
Deadline(s): Feb. 1, June 1, and Aug. 15
Board meeting date(s): Feb./Mar., June, and Sept.
Write: Margaret Corley, Mgr.
Officer: Margaret Corley, Mgr.
Trustees: Abigail D. Avery, Roger C. Avery, Brenda Ewing, Ruth D. Ewing.
Number of staff: 1
Employer Identification Number: 046114839

2798
Eugene A. Dexter Charitable Fund ⌘
c/o Bernie Stephan, BayBank Valley Trust Co.
P.O. Box 422
Burlington 01803 (617) 273-1700
Grant application address: Community Funds Advisory Comm., 1365 Main St., Springfield, MA 01103

Trust established in 1946 in MA.
Donor(s): Henrietta F. Dexter.†
Foundation type: Independent
Financial data (yr. ended 12/31/88): Assets, $7,566,275 (M); expenditures, $260,217, including $182,932 for 40 grants (high: $25,000; low: $350).

Purpose and activities: Grants for public charitable purposes, including health, welfare, the humanities, and education; emphasis on the physically and mentally handicapped, minorities, youth and child welfare agencies, and health services.
Types of support: Building funds, equipment, land acquisition, conferences and seminars, publications, matching funds, special projects, capital campaigns, seed money, renovation projects.
Limitations: Giving limited to Hampden County, MA, with emphasis on the greater Springfield area. No grants to individuals, or for endowment funds, operating budgets, scholarships, fellowships, or general purposes; no loans.
Publications: Informational brochure (including application guidelines).
Application information: Application form not required.
Initial approach: Telephone, letter, or proposal
Copies of proposal: 12
Deadline(s): 1st Monday in Jan. and May and 1st Tuesday in Sept.
Board meeting date(s): 4th Tuesday of Mar., July, and Nov.
Final notification: Apr., Aug., and Dec.
Trustee: BayBank Valley Trust Co.
Number of staff: 1 part-time professional; 1 part-time support.
Employer Identification Number: 046018698

2799
The Discount Foundation
37 Temple Place, 3rd Fl.
Boston 02111 (617) 426-7471

Established in 1977.
Donor(s): Jeffrey W. Zinsmeyer, Garfield Trust.
Foundation type: Independent
Financial data (yr. ended 09/30/88): Assets, $4,528,173 (M); gifts received, $228,066; expenditures, $213,269, including $150,000 for 16 grants (high: $17,500; low: $7,500; average: $5,000-$20,000).
Purpose and activities: "To support public education and organizational activities to lessen community tensions, alleviate poverty and/or combat neighborhood deterioration by expanding the availability of housing to low-income people through community organizing, citizen empowerment, public policy change and the development of local, regional and national coalitions." Grants mainly for community development.
Types of support: General purposes, operating budgets.
Limitations: Giving limited to the northeastern U.S.: CT, DE, IL, IN, KY, ME, MD, MA, MI, NH, NJ, NY, OH, PA, RI, VT, VA, WV, WI, and Washington, DC. No grants to individuals.
Application information: Application forms available in the fall; grant decisions made in spring. Application form required.
Initial approach: Proposal
Copies of proposal: 1
Deadline(s): Dec. 31
Board meeting date(s): Spring
Write: Susan Chinn, Exec. Dir.
Officers and Directors:* Jeffrey W. Zinsmeyer,* Pres.; Thomas R. Asher,* Secy.-Treas.; Harry Fagan, Margery A. Tabankin, Garland Yates.
Number of staff: 1 part-time professional.
Employer Identification Number: 521095120

2800
Harry Doehla Foundation, Inc. ⌑
c/o Singer and Lusardi
370 Main St.
Worcester 01608 (617) 756-4657

Incorporated in 1950 in DE.
Donor(s): Harry Doehla.†
Foundation type: Independent
Financial data (yr. ended 3/31/89): Assets, $1,264,810 (M); expenditures, $200,641, including $174,000 for 18 grants (high: $35,000; low: $500).
Purpose and activities: Support for higher education and health organizations, including mental health.
Application information:
Initial approach: Letter
Deadline(s): None
Write: Henry Lusardi, Pres.
Officers: Henry Lusardi, Pres.; Philip Straus, V.P.; Paul Singer, Secy.; Philip H. Steckler, Jr., Treas.
Employer Identification Number: 026014132

2801
Oliver S. and Jennie R. Donaldson Charitable Trust ⌑
c/o Durfee Attleboro Bank, Trust Dept.
Ten North Main St.
Fall River 02720 (617) 679-8311

Trust established in 1969 in NY.
Donor(s): Oliver S. Donaldson.†
Foundation type: Independent
Financial data (yr. ended 12/31/87): Assets, $18,695,157 (M); expenditures, $1,087,117, including $858,440 for 37 grants (high: $68,000; low: $1,678).
Purpose and activities: Interests include cancer research and treatment, child welfare and youth agencies, hospitals and health agencies, elementary, secondary, and higher education; support also for wildlife preservation, and the town of Pawling, NY; eleven named institutions are given first consideration.
Limitations: Giving primarily in the Northeast, with emphasis on MA. No grants to individuals.
Publications: Application guidelines.
Application information: Application form required.
Initial approach: Proposal
Copies of proposal: 3
Board meeting date(s): Quarterly
Trustees: William E. Murray, Chair.; Wilson W. Curtis, Vice-Chair.; Marjorie Atwood, Dr. Elizabeth Atwood Lawrence, Durfee Attleboro Bank.
Employer Identification Number: 046229044

2802
The Doyle Charitable Foundation ⌑
c/o First National Bank of Boston
P.O. Box 1861
Boston 02105
Application address: The First National Bank of Boston, P.O. Box 1890, Boston, MA 02105

Foundation type: Independent
Financial data (yr. ended 12/31/88): Assets, $1,542,763 (M); gifts received, $200,000; expenditures, $88,009, including $70,000 for 4 grants (high: $50,000; low: $5,000; average: $2,000-$10,000).
Purpose and activities: Support for hospitals, youth, museums, and an antiquarian society.
Types of support: Capital campaigns, operating budgets, program-related investments.
Limitations: Giving primarily in the greater Boston, MA, area. No support for private foundations, national organizations, or projects requiring multi-year commitment. No grants to individuals, or for conferences, film production, travel, research projects, publications, or scholarships; no loans.
Application information: Only 1 proposal may be submitted per calendar year. Application form not required.
Initial approach: Proposal
Deadline(s): First day of month preceeding board meetings
Board meeting date(s): Mar., July, and Nov.
Write: Sharon M. Driscoll
Trustee: First National Bank of Boston.
Employer Identification Number: 046010367

2803
Drapkin Charitable Foundation
P.O. Box 679
Brookline Village 02147-0679 (617) 731-0700

Established about 1960 in MA.
Foundation type: Independent
Financial data (yr. ended 11/30/88): Assets, $1,467,636 (M); gifts received, $10,000; expenditures, $93,091, including $84,280 for 19 grants (high: $25,000; low: $1,000).
Purpose and activities: Giving for religious organizations, higher education, and social services.
Limitations: Giving primarily in MA.
Trustees: Melvin B. Drapkin, Paul E. Drapkin.
Employer Identification Number: 046109125

2804
Eastern Bank Foundation
270 Union St.
Lynn 01901-1380

Established in 1985 in MA.
Foundation type: Independent
Financial data (yr. ended 10/31/89): Assets, $1,794,763 (M); expenditures, $71,612, including $69,605 for 62 grants (high: $15,000; low: $25).
Purpose and activities: Support primarily for hospitals and health associations, support also for community funds and a business education foundation.
Limitations: Giving primarily in the North Shore of MA.
Application information: "The foundation currently funds numerous projects, and funds available for additional grants are restricted due to existing obligations which presently consume the income generated by the Trust".
Trustees: Douglas F. Allen, Joseph A. Jones, Stanley J. Lukowski, Francis F. Perry, Robert H. Studley.
Employer Identification Number: 222623146

2805
Georgiana Goddard Eaton Memorial Fund
c/o Welch & Forbes
45 School St.
Boston 02108 (617) 523-1635

Trust established in 1917 in MA.
Donor(s): Georgiana Goddard Eaton.†
Foundation type: Independent
Financial data (yr. ended 06/30/89): Assets, $7,198,819 (M); expenditures, $407,451, including $228,000 for 1 grant and $63,180 for 6 grants to individuals (high: $16,800; low: $5,700).
Purpose and activities: Support currently for a rehabilitation agency, including support through pensions to its former employees.
Types of support: General purposes.
Limitations: Giving limited to Boston, MA. No grants to individuals (except former employees of Community Workshops, Inc.), or for endowment funds, or matching gifts; no loans.
Application information: Application form not required.
Initial approach: Brief proposal
Copies of proposal: 1
Deadline(s): None
Board meeting date(s): As required
Write: Kenneth S. Safe, Jr., Trustee
Trustee: Thomas N. Dabney, Kenneth S. Safe, Jr., Welch & Forbes.
Number of staff: None.
Employer Identification Number: 046112820

2806
Harold E. Edgerton Foundation
c/o Hale and Dorr
60 State St.
Boston 02109 (617) 742-9100

Established in 1967 in MA.
Foundation type: Independent
Financial data (yr. ended 12/31/89): Assets, $1,782,612 (M); expenditures, $90,546, including $75,000 for grants.
Purpose and activities: Giving to institutions of higher education for research in electrical engineering.
Types of support: Research.
Limitations: Giving primarily in MA. No grants to individuals.
Application information:
Deadline(s): 180 days after publication of legal notice
Write: Martin S. Kaplan, Trustee
Trustee: Martin S. Kaplan.
Employer Identification Number: 046179458

2807
Edwards Scholarship Fund ¤
Ten Post Office Sq. South, Suite 1230
Boston 02109 (617) 426-4434

Trust established in 1939 in MA.
Donor(s): Grace M. Edwards.†
Foundation type: Independent
Financial data (yr. ended 7/31/89): Assets, $5,306,261 (M); expenditures, $267,591, including $200,950 for 130 loans to individuals (high: $2,500; low: $400).
Purpose and activities: Scholarship loans to students under the age of 25, with preference for undergraduates enrolled in a program leading to a bachelor's or advanced degree at an accredited college or university, for not more than six years. Students to repay loan when financially able.
Types of support: Student loans.
Limitations: Giving limited to students whose families have resided in Boston, MA, since the beginning of the student's junior year of high school. No loans to individuals attending junior colleges, community colleges, or hospital schools of nursing.
Application information: Application form not required.
Deadline(s): Mar. 1
Trustees: Richard Ely, Edward Kirk, Stephen Little.
Number of staff: 1 part-time professional.
Employer Identification Number: 046002496

2808
EG&G Foundation ¤
c/o EG&G, Inc.
45 William St.
Wellesley 02181 (617) 237-5100

Established in 1979 in MA.
Donor(s): EG&G, Inc.
Foundation type: Company-sponsored
Financial data (yr. ended 06/30/89): Assets, $5,350,862 (M); expenditures, $484,364, including $377,200 for 280 grants (high: $25,000; low: $100) and $96,431 for 394 employee matching gifts.
Purpose and activities: Grants primarily for higher education and community funds, including an employee matching gift program.
Types of support: Employee matching gifts.
Application information: Application form required.
Deadline(s): None
Write: Kathleen M. Russo, Trust Admin.
Officer: Kathleen M. Russo, Trust Admin.
Trustees: Donald M. Kerr, John M. Kucharski, Richard F. Murphy, Samuel Rubinovitz.
Employer Identification Number: 042683042

2809
The Ellison Foundation ¤
129 South St.
Boston 02111 (617) 542-0690

Established in 1952 in MA.
Donor(s): Eben H. Ellison.†
Foundation type: Independent
Financial data (yr. ended 12/31/88): Assets, $501,126 (M); expenditures, $175,334, including $175,180 for 20 grants (high: $53,723; low: $200).
Purpose and activities: Emphasis on higher education, hospitals and medical research, a community fund, church support, and cultural programs.
Limitations: Giving primarily in MA. No grants to individuals.
Application information: Contributes only to pre-selected organizations. Applications not accepted.
Write: Wendell R. Freeman, Trustee
Trustees: Elton F. Drew, Alfred W. Fuller, John M. Hall, Maxime F. Leroyer, Harriet E. Rogers.
Employer Identification Number: 046050704

2810
Ruth H. and Warren A. Ellsworth Foundation ¤
370 Main St.
Worcester 01608 (617) 798-8621

Trust established in 1964 in MA.
Donor(s): Ruth H. Ellsworth.†
Foundation type: Independent
Financial data (yr. ended 12/31/87): Assets, $10,481,582 (M); expenditures, $605,681, including $559,650 for 44 grants (high: $150,000; low: $100; average: $7,500).
Purpose and activities: Emphasis on higher education, scientific research, youth agencies, and hospitals.
Types of support: Operating budgets, general purposes, continuing support, annual campaigns, seed money, emergency funds, deficit financing, building funds, equipment, land acquisition, scholarship funds.
Limitations: Giving primarily in the Worcester, MA, area. No grants to individuals, or for endowment funds, scholarships, fellowships, research, publications, conferences, or matching gifts; no loans.
Application information: Application form not required.
Initial approach: Proposal
Copies of proposal: 1
Deadline(s): Submit proposal preferably in June; deadline Nov. 30
Board meeting date(s): July and Dec.
Final notification: By Dec. 28
Write: Sumner B. Tilton, Jr., Trustee
Trustees: David H. Ellsworth, Sumner B. Tilton, Jr., Robert H. Wetzel.
Number of staff: 1 part-time professional.
Employer Identification Number: 046113491

2811
Endowment for Biblical Research, Boston
P.O. Box 993
Boston 02123

Established in 1920 in MA.
Donor(s): Mary Beecher Longyear.†
Foundation type: Independent
Financial data (yr. ended 12/31/89): Assets, $1,695,794 (L); expenditures, $113,258, including $92,655 for 7 grants (high: $25,000; low: $2,000).
Purpose and activities: To facilitate and advance research in the Bible and the history of the Christian church, including archaeological digs, publications, and lecture tours; and maintains the Zion Research Library; prefers seed grants to long-term support.
Types of support: Publications, research, conferences and seminars, seed money, special projects.
Limitations: No support for denominational and non-biblical education.
Publications: Informational brochure (including application guidelines).
Application information: Funds largely committed, but proposals invited.
Board meeting date(s): Apr. and Oct.
Final notification: May and Nov.
Trustees: Merelice K. England, Richard M. Harley, Stephen R. Howard, Virginia B. Stopfel.
Number of staff: 1 part-time professional.
Employer Identification Number: 042104439

2812
ETC Development Corporation ⌑
628-630 Tremont St.
Boston 02118

Established in 1970 in MA.
Foundation type: Independent
Financial data (yr. ended 12/31/88): Assets, $2,166,184 (M); expenditures, $2,226.
Purpose and activities: Support for a welfare organization.
Application information: Contributes only to pre-selected organizations. Applications not accepted.
Officer and Directors: Jose Ruiz,* Pres.; Clara L. Garcia, and 13 other directors.
Employer Identification Number: 237090081

2813
Everett Foundation for Aged Persons, Inc. ⌑
c/o F. H. Boynton & Co.
38 Newbury St.
Boston 02116

Established in 1902 in MA.
Foundation type: Independent
Financial data (yr. ended 12/31/88): Assets, $1,792,317 (M); expenditures, $113,941, including $76,222 for 11 grants (high: $46,424; low: $310).
Purpose and activities: Giving to benefit the aged.
Limitations: No grants to individuals.
Application information: Contributes only to pre-selected organizations. Applications not accepted.
Officers and Directors: Alfred Seaward, Pres.; Caro M. Grace, Treas.; Edwin Ahlin, Barbara Downey, Marie Sapienza, Peter Sapienza, Dana Shattuck, Elizabeth Shattuck.
Employer Identification Number: 042062107

2814
Fall River Women's Union
101 Rock St.
Fall River 02720-3133 (508) 674-8861

Established in 1959 in MA.
Foundation type: Independent
Financial data (yr. ended 12/31/88): Assets, $1,111,914 (M); expenditures, $76,302, including $56,150 for 25 grants (high: $15,000; low: $200).
Purpose and activities: Support primarily for youth and child welfare, health associations, and social service organizations, including hospices, the homeless and disadvantaged, family services, and women.
Types of support: Continuing support.
Limitations: Giving primarily in the greater Fall River, MA, area.
Publications: Annual report, 990-PF.
Application information:
Initial approach: Letter
Deadline(s): Apr. for summer programs; Sept. for other requests
Write: Mrs. John W. Owen, Pres.
Officers: Mrs. John W. Owen, Pres.; Mrs. Benjamin Edmonds, 1st V.P.; Mrs. Gerrit Sanford, 2nd V.P.; Mrs. John J. Bolger, 3rd V.P.; Mrs. Donald A. Bogle, Secy.; Mrs. Donald H. Chace, Treas.
Directors: Mrs. Richard Bowen, and ten additional directors.
Number of staff: 1 part-time support.
Employer Identification Number: 042104051

2815
Charles H. Farnsworth Trust ⌑
c/o State Street Bank & Trust Co.
P.O. Box 351
Boston 02101 (617) 654-3343

Trust established in 1930; became a charitable trust in 1978.
Donor(s): Charles H. Farnsworth.†
Foundation type: Independent
Financial data (yr. ended 9/30/88): Assets, $12,318,489 (M); expenditures, $897,889, including $757,388 for 41 grants (high: $125,000; low: $3,000; average: $20,000).
Purpose and activities: To assist elderly persons to live with dignity and independence. Special focus on services which help prevent premature institutionalization. Grants fostering the development of housing for the elderly are also of special interest.
Types of support: Equipment, general purposes, operating budgets, renovation projects, seed money, building funds.
Limitations: Giving primarily in the greater Boston, MA, area. No grants to individuals.
Publications: Application guidelines, grants list.
Application information: Application form not required.
Initial approach: Letter of intent
Copies of proposal: 1
Deadline(s): Feb. 15, May 15, Aug. 15, and Nov. 15
Board meeting date(s): 3rd Thursday in Mar., June, Sept., and Dec.
Final notification: Within 1 month of meeting
Write: Deborah A. Robbins, V.P., State Street Bank & Trust Co.
Trustee: State Street Bank & Trust Co.
Number of staff: 1 part-time professional; 1 part-time support.
Employer Identification Number: 046096075

2816
Aubert J. Fay Charitable Fund ⌑ ☆
100 Holyrood Ave.
Lowell 01852-3804 (508) 452-6262

Established in 1965.
Foundation type: Independent
Financial data (yr. ended 12/31/88): Assets, $2,026,275 (M); expenditures, $36,026, including $29,475 for 29 grants (high: $3,000; low: $125).
Purpose and activities: Support primarily for Catholic religious and welfare organizations, health and hospitals, youth, and the arts.
Limitations: Giving limited to Lowell, MA.
Application information:
Initial approach: Letter
Deadline(s): None
Write: Gerald F. Donehue, Trustee
Trustees: Gerald F. Donehue, Stephen L. Gervais, Alfred E. Sutherland.
Employer Identification Number: 510203622

2817
The Feldberg Family Foundation ⌑
770 Cochituate Rd.
P.O. Box 910
Framingham 01701 (617) 620-2318

Trust established in 1951 in MA.
Donor(s): Max Feldberg, Morris Feldberg.†
Foundation type: Independent
Financial data (yr. ended 11/30/88): Assets, $6,855,473 (M); gifts received, $208,480; expenditures, $651,472, including $632,000 for grants.
Purpose and activities: Giving for Jewish welfare funds, hospitals, and higher education.
Limitations: Giving primarily in MA. No grants to individuals.
Application information: Contributes only to pre-selected organizations. Applications not accepted.
Board meeting date(s): As required
Trustees: Stanley H. Feldberg, Sumner Feldberg.
Employer Identification Number: 046065393

2818
S. C. Feuerstein Family Foundation ⌑
c/o Malden Knitting Mills, Inc.
46 Stafford Street
Lawrence 01841

Trust established in 1950 in MA.
Foundation type: Independent
Financial data (yr. ended 4/30/89): Assets, $864,865 (M); expenditures, $178,591, including $170,100 for 25 grants (high: $30,000; low: $100).
Purpose and activities: Support primarily for Jewish education and welfare, religious, and youth organizations.
Trustees: Aaron Feuerstein, Felix Feuerstein, Mitzi Feuerstein, Moses Feuerstein.
Employer Identification Number: 046058861

2819
Fidelity Foundation ▼ ⌑
82 Devonshire St.
Boston 02109 (617) 570-6806

Trust established in 1965 in MA.
Donor(s): Fidelity Management & Research Co. (FMR).
Foundation type: Company-sponsored
Financial data (yr. ended 12/31/87): Assets, $18,037,644 (M); gifts received, $3,958,280; expenditures, $7,558,766, including $7,088,450 for 157 grants (high: $5,705,172; low: $30; average: $5,000-$50,000) and $168,422 for employee matching gifts.
Purpose and activities: Giving largely to organizations working in the fields of community development, cultural affairs, education, and health.
Types of support: Building funds, operating budgets, special projects, endowment funds, employee matching gifts.
Limitations: Giving primarily in MA, and in other communities where Fidelity employees live and work. No grants to individuals.
Application information: Application form not required.
Initial approach: Proposal
Copies of proposal: 1
Deadline(s): Mar. 30 and Oct. 30
Board meeting date(s): June and Dec.

Final notification: Immediately following board meeting
Write: Anne-Marie Soulliere, Fdn. Dir.
Trustees: Edward C. Johnson III, Caleb Loring, Jr., Ross E. Sherbrooke.
Number of staff: 1 full-time professional; 1 part-time professional; 1 full-time support; 1 part-time support.
Employer Identification Number: 046131201

2820
Lincoln and Therese Filene Foundation, Inc.
c/o Nutter, McClennen & Fish
One International Place
Boston 02110-2699 (617) 439-2000

Incorporated in 1937 in MA.
Donor(s): Lincoln Filene.†
Foundation type: Independent
Financial data (yr. ended 1/31/89): Assets, $11,658,578 (M); gifts received, $28,408; expenditures, $586,482, including $510,294 for 18 grants (high: $132,000; low: $100; average: $5,000-$100,000).
Purpose and activities: General purposes, including particularly the scientific investigation of the causes of economic distress; grants largely for higher education, music, the performing arts, citizenship, and public policy issues. Funds largely committed to long-term support of existing projects.
Types of support: Continuing support, emergency funds, equipment, matching funds, operating budgets, special projects.
Limitations: No grants to individuals, or for endowment funds, scholarships, or fellowships; no loans.
Application information: Funds largely committed. Application form not required.
Initial approach: Letter
Copies of proposal: 1
Deadline(s): Apr. 1 and Oct. 1
Board meeting date(s): May and Nov.
Final notification: After next semiannual meeting
Write: John K.P. Stone III, Secy.
Officers and Directors: John J. Robertson, Pres.; George E. Ladd III, V.P.; John K.P. Stone III, Secy.-Treas.; G. Michael Ladd, Lincoln F. Ladd, Robert M. Ladd, David A. Robertson, Jr., Catherine F. Shouse, Joan D. Tolley, Benjamin A. Trustman.
Number of staff: None.
Employer Identification Number: 237423946

2821
The Paul and Phyllis Fireman Charitable Foundation ¤
100 Technology Center Dr.
Stoughton 02072 (617) 821-2800

Established in 1985 in MA.
Foundation type: Independent
Financial data (yr. ended 10/31/88): Assets, $16,489,210 (M); expenditures, $2,839,495, including $2,585,736 for 23 grants (high: $1,800,000; low: $10).
Purpose and activities: Giving primarily for private secondary education and Jewish organizations.
Limitations: No grants to individuals.
Application information: Application form not required.
Deadline(s): None
Write: Phyllis Fireman, Trustee
Trustees: Paul Fireman, Phyllis Fireman.
Employer Identification Number: 222677986

2822
First Mutual Foundation ¤
c/o First Mutual of Boston
800 Boylston St.
Boston 02199 (617) 247-6500

Established in 1982 in MA.
Donor(s): Mutual Bank.
Foundation type: Independent
Financial data (yr. ended 12/31/88): Assets, $3,592 (M); gifts received, $135,000; expenditures, $142,055, including $142,000 for 42 grants (high: $30,000; low: $1,000).
Purpose and activities: Support primarily to cultural institutions, social service programs, and a community fund.
Limitations: Giving primarily in areas where bank has branches or investments.
Application information:
Initial approach: Proposal
Deadline(s): 4-6 weeks prior to meeting
Write: Ms. Nancy Hamton, Asst. Secy.
Officer: Joan M. Diver,* Chair.
Trustees:* Cecil W. Cadwell, and nine additional trustees.
Employer Identification Number: 042755093

2823
Fisher Foundation ¤
c/o Boston Safe Deposit and Trust Co.
One Boston Place
Boston 02108

Established in 1969 in MA.
Foundation type: Independent
Financial data (yr. ended 08/31/89): Assets, $1,854,400 (M); expenditures, $123,316, including $98,890 for 10 grants (high: $15,000; low: $2,500).
Purpose and activities: Giving primarily for cultural programs; support also for social services and higher education.
Types of support: Equipment, seed money, general purposes, scholarship funds, fellowships.
Limitations: Giving limited to OH and Buffalo, NY.
Application information: Application form not required.
Initial approach: Proposal
Deadline(s): Feb., May, Aug., and Nov.
Board meeting date(s): Mar., June, Sept., and Dec.
Write: Ms. Sylvia Salas, Sr. Trust Officer, Boston Safe Deposit and Trust Co.
Trustees: John Fisher, Judith Fisher, Gordon A. MacLeod, J. Steven Renkert, Rachel Renkert, Boston Safe Deposit & Trust Co.
Employer Identification Number: 046198798

2824
Flatley Foundation ¤
50 Braintree Hill Office Park
Braintree 02184

Established in 1982 in MA.
Donor(s): Thomas J. Flatley.
Foundation type: Independent
Financial data (yr. ended 12/31/88): Assets, $2,552,196 (M); gifts received, $23,600; expenditures, $644,200, including $626,525 for 74 grants (high: $339,000; low: $100).
Purpose and activities: Giving for hospitals, social services, and education.
Limitations: Giving primarily in MA. No grants to individuals.
Application information: Contributes only to pre-selected organizations. Applications not accepted.
Trustee: Thomas J. Flatley.
Employer Identification Number: 042763837

2825
Fletcher Foundation ¤
c/o Fletcher, Tilton & Whipple, P.C.
370 Main St., Suite 1250
Worcester 01608-1779 (508) 798-8621

Established in 1981 in MA.
Foundation type: Independent
Financial data (yr. ended 12/31/88): Assets, $1,519,426 (M); gifts received, $103,000; expenditures, $88,061, including $81,000 for 24 grants (high: $10,000; low: $1,000).
Purpose and activities: Support primarily for social services and community development.
Types of support: General purposes.
Limitations: Giving primarily in Worcester County, MA. No grants to individuals.
Application information:
Initial approach: Letter
Deadline(s): None
Board meeting date(s): Dec.
Write: Warner S. Fletcher, Treas.
Officers and Trustees: Paris Fletcher, Chair.; Marion S. Fletcher, Vice-Chair.; Allen W. Fletcher, Mary S. Fletcher, Nina M. Fletcher, Patricia A. Fletcher, Warner S. Fletcher.
Employer Identification Number: 046470890

2826
Joseph F. and Clara Ford Foundation ¤
1360 Soldiers Field Rd.
Brighton 02135

Established in 1946 in MA.
Donor(s): Ford Manufacturing, Inc., Clara Ford.
Foundation type: Independent
Financial data (yr. ended 7/31/88): Assets, $2,622,506 (M); gifts received, $4,000; expenditures, $472,821, including $458,378 for 30 grants (high: $80,000; low: $300).
Purpose and activities: Support primarily for Jewish concerns.
Limitations: Giving primarily in MA. No grants to individuals.
Application information: Contributes only to pre-selected organizations. Applications not accepted.
Trustees: Avram J. Goldberg, David Lasty, Joseph M. Linsey, Irving W. Rabb, Norman S. Rabb.
Employer Identification Number: 046111820

2827
Orville W. Forte Charitable Foundation, Inc.
311 Summer St.
Boston 02210 (617) 482-8434

Established in 1952 in MA.
Donor(s): Donald Forte, Jr., Forte Cashmere Corp.
Foundation type: Independent
Financial data (yr. ended 12/31/89): Assets, $1,759,543 (M); gifts received, $27,500; expenditures, $92,714, including $77,650 for 30 grants (high: $10,000; low: $500; average: $1,000-$4,000).
Purpose and activities: Support primarily for organizations working with disadvantaged youth.
Types of support: Building funds, capital campaigns, equipment, general purposes, operating budgets, renovation projects, special projects.
Limitations: Giving limited to the greater Boston, MA, area. No grants to individuals.
Application information: Application form not required.
Initial approach: Proposal
Copies of proposal: 1
Deadline(s): July 31
Board meeting date(s): Sept.
Final notification: Dec.
Write: Cheryl Forte, Exec. Dir.
Officers: Donald Forte,* Pres.; Donald Forte, Jr., Secy.; John H. Forte,* Treas.
Directors:* Cheryl Forte, Richard S. Forte, William R. Forte, David E. Place.
Number of staff: 1
Employer Identification Number: 046017836

2828
Joseph C. and Esther Foster Foundation, Inc. ⌑
122 Buckskin Dr.
Weston 02193 (617) 891-1192

Established in 1961 in MA.
Donor(s): Esther J. Foster, Joseph C. Foster.†
Foundation type: Independent
Financial data (yr. ended 12/31/88): Assets, $2,082,641 (M); expenditures, $242,066, including $227,730 for 27 grants (high: $171,380; low: $250).
Purpose and activities: Grants for higher education and research, Jewish welfare funds, the fine arts and other cultural programs, hospitals and medical research, and minorities and race relations.
Types of support: Annual campaigns, building funds, matching funds.
Application information: Application form not required.
Initial approach: Letter
Deadline(s): None
Write: Marcia J. Scheinbart, Secy.
Officers and Directors:* Leo Scheinbart,* Pres.; Marcia J. Scheinbart, Secy.; Esther J. Foster,* Treas.; Jacob Chatkis, Samuel Rappaporte, Jr.
Number of staff: None.
Employer Identification Number: 046114436

2829
The French Foundation ⌑
c/o Boston Safe Deposit and Trust Co.
One Boston Place
Boston 02106

Established in 1947 in MA.
Foundation type: Independent
Financial data (yr. ended 12/31/88): Assets, $2,121,010 (M); expenditures, $109,873, including $88,350 for 27 grants (high: $10,000; low: $1,000).
Purpose and activities: Giving primarily for conservation and the environment, support also for the arts and social services.
Limitations: No grants to individuals.
Application information: Application form not required.
Initial approach: Letter
Deadline(s): Feb., May, Aug., and Nov.
Board meeting date(s): Mar., June, Sept., and Dec.
Write: Sylvia Salas
Trustees: Catherine L. French, Robert L.V. French, Edward F. Williams, Boston Safe Deposit & Trust Co.
Employer Identification Number: 046053426

2830
Friendship Fund, Inc.
c/o Boston Safe Deposit & Trust Co.
One Boston Place, OBP-2
Boston 02106 (617) 722-7538

Incorporated in 1918 in NY.
Donor(s): Charles R. Crane.†
Foundation type: Independent
Financial data (yr. ended 06/30/87): Assets, $2,887,948 (M); expenditures, $127,468, including $95,813 for 69 grants (high: $14,663; low: $200) and $4,000 for 1 grant to an individual.
Purpose and activities: "For the advancement of the humanities and the sciences and for the welfare of humanity;" emphasis on local giving for environmental protection, social services, and international affairs. Funds largely committed in advance.
Types of support: Seed money, building funds, equipment, land acquisition, publications, special projects, student aid.
Limitations: No grants to individuals (except very limited grants for scholarships).
Application information: Application form not required.
Initial approach: One-page proposal summary and budget
Copies of proposal: 1
Deadline(s): Submit proposal only in May; deadline May 31
Board meeting date(s): Aug.
Final notification: Sept. (positive responses only)
Officers and Trustees:* Josephine DeGive,* Pres.; Sylvia E. Crane,* V.P.; Elizabeth McLane-Bradley,* Secy.; Darby Bradley, Charles R. Crane, Thomas Crane, Mrs. Bruce C. Fisher.
Number of staff: None.
Employer Identification Number: 136089220

2831
George F. and Sybil H. Fuller Foundation ▼
105 Madison St.
Worcester 01610 (508) 756-5111

Trust established in 1955 in MA.
Donor(s): George Freeman Fuller.†
Foundation type: Independent
Financial data (yr. ended 12/31/88): Assets, $58,124,532 (M); expenditures, $3,139,653, including $2,937,276 for 118 grants (average: $2,000-$30,000).
Purpose and activities: Emphasis on higher education, cultural institutions, historic preservation, hospitals, community funds, and youth organizations; support also for social service agencies and schools.
Types of support: Annual campaigns, seed money, emergency funds, general purposes, building funds, endowment funds, research, continuing support, renovation projects.
Limitations: Giving primarily in MA, with emphasis on Worcester. No grants to individuals, or for scholarships, fellowships, or matching gifts; no loans.
Application information: Application form not required.
Initial approach: Proposal
Copies of proposal: 1
Deadline(s): None
Board meeting date(s): Jan.-Mar., June-Aug., and Oct.-Dec.
Final notification: Varies
Write: Russell E. Fuller, Chair.
Officers and Trustees: Russell E. Fuller, Chair. and Treas.; Robert Hallock, Jr., Vice-Chair.; Paris Fletcher, Secy.; Ernest M. Fuller, Mark Fuller, David Hallock.
Number of staff: 1
Employer Identification Number: 046125606

2832
G. Peabody & Rose Gardner Charitable Trust ⌑
c/o Gardner & Preston Moss, Inc.
One Winthrop Sq.
Boston 02110

Established in 1956 in MA.
Foundation type: Independent
Financial data (yr. ended 12/31/88): Assets, $1,986,624 (M); expenditures, $141,133, including $111,000 for 45 grants (high: $13,000; low: $250).
Purpose and activities: Giving for a children's hospital, health-related issues, and social services.
Limitations: Giving primarily in MA. No grants to individuals.
Application information: Application form not required.
Initial approach: Letter
Deadline(s): Nov. 1
Write: John L. Gardner, Trustee
Trustees: George P. Gardner, John L. Gardner, Robert G. Gardner.
Employer Identification Number: 046018072

2833
GenRad Foundation ⌑
300 Baker Ave.
Concord 01742 (617) 369-4400

Trust established in 1934 in MA.
Donor(s): GenRad, Inc., Henry Shaw.†
Foundation type: Company-sponsored
Financial data (yr. ended 12/31/88): Assets, $2,840,773 (M); expenditures, $385,477, including $316,577 for 273 grants (high: $90,052; low: $25) and $22,000 for 22 grants to individuals of $1,000 each.
Purpose and activities: Giving primarily for social services, hospitals, cultural programs, higher and secondary education, and public broadcasting.
Types of support: Employee matching gifts, annual campaigns, building funds, capital campaigns, continuing support, endowment funds, general purposes, operating budgets, renovation projects, seed money, special projects.
Limitations: Giving primarily in MA. No grants to individuals.
Publications: Application guidelines.
Application information: Application form not required.
Initial approach: Telephone for guidelines; proposal limited to 5 pages
Copies of proposal: 1
Deadline(s): None
Board meeting date(s): Bimonthly
Final notification: Within 3 months of receipt of proposal
Write: Linda B. Smoker, Admin.
Officers and Trustees:* Constantine J. Lahanas,* V.P.; Raymond F. McNulty,* Dir.
Number of staff: 1 full-time professional; 1 part-time support.
Employer Identification Number: 046043570

2834
Gerondelis Foundation, Inc.
56 Central Ave.
Lynn 01901 (617) 592-6120

Established in 1966 in MA.
Foundation type: Independent
Financial data (yr. ended 12/31/89): Assets, $3,000,000 (M); expenditures, $338,149, including $228,500 for 34 grants (high: $25,000; low: $1,000).
Purpose and activities: Giving for higher, medical, and other education, child development, hospitals, civic affairs, and Greece.
Types of support: Scholarship funds.
Limitations: Giving primarily in MA.
Application information: Application form not required.
Copies of proposal: 1
Deadline(s): None
Board meeting date(s): 1st Wednesday in Jan., Apr., July, and Oct.
Final notification: Following board meetings
Write: Charles Demakis, Pres.
Members: Charles Demakis,* Pres.; James C. Kaddaras,* Treas.; Louis Demakes, Gregory C. Demakis, Thomas C. Demakis, Benjamin A. Smith II, Nicholas T. Zervas, M.D.
Directors:* Paul C. Demakis, Thomas L. Demakes, Michael Frangos, George J. Marcopoulos, Christopher Scangas.
Number of staff: 1 part-time professional; 1 part-time support.
Employer Identification Number: 046130871

2835
The Goldberg Family Foundation ⌑
(Formerly Avram & Carol Goldberg Charitable Foundation)
P.O. Box 369
Boston 02101

Established in 1961 in MA.
Foundation type: Independent
Financial data (yr. ended 06/30/89): Assets, $5,287,908 (M); expenditures, $211,391, including $179,417 for 133 grants (high: $37,500; low: $10).
Purpose and activities: Giving primarily for higher education and Jewish organizations.
Application information: Application form not required.
Initial approach: Letter
Deadline(s): None
Write: Avram J. Goldberg, Trustee
Trustees: Avram J. Goldberg, Carol R. Goldberg, Deborah Goldberg, Joshua Goldberg.
Employer Identification Number: 046039556

2836
Israel and Matilda Goldberg Family Foundation ⌑
c/o Jomar Co.
209 West Central St., Suite 202
Natick 01760

Trust established in 1952 in MA.
Donor(s): Israel Goldberg, Albert S. Goldberg, Herbert A. Goldberg, and others.
Foundation type: Independent
Financial data (yr. ended 12/31/88): Assets, $3,024,106 (M); expenditures, $135,253, including $112,391 for 128 grants (high: $20,000; low: $10).
Purpose and activities: Emphasis on Jewish welfare funds and temple support.
Limitations: Giving primarily in the Boston, MA, area. No grants to individuals.
Application information: Contributes only to pre-selected organizations. Applications not accepted.
Trustees: Albert S. Goldberg, Herbert A. Goldberg.
Employer Identification Number: 046047066

2837
Gordon Foundation ⌑
c/o Analogic Corp.
Eight Centennial Dr.
Peabody 01961 (617) 246-0300

Established around 1983 in MA.
Donor(s): Frank B. Gordon, Bernard M. Gordon.
Foundation type: Independent
Financial data (yr. ended 12/31/87): Assets, $6,924,882 (M); gifts received, $619,008; expenditures, $20,526, including $4,600 for 3 grants (high: $2,500; low: $100).
Purpose and activities: Giving for charitable purposes.
Application information: Application form not required.
Initial approach: Proposal
Deadline(s): None
Final notification: 2 months
Write: Julian Soshnick, Trustee
Trustees: Gerald P. Bonder, Bernard M. Gordon, Sophia Gordon, Julian Soshnick.
Employer Identification Number: 042794647

2838
Frank B. Gordon Foundation ⌑
111 Devonshire St., Rm. 805
Boston 02109-5407

Established in 1956 in MA.
Foundation type: Independent
Financial data (yr. ended 12/31/88): Assets, $1,034,138 (M); expenditures, $59,992, including $56,385 for 29 grants (high: $25,275; low: $10).
Purpose and activities: Giving primarily for hospitals, Jewish welfare, and higher education.
Limitations: Giving primarily in MA.
Application information: Contributes only to pre-selected organizations. Applications not accepted.
Trustee: Frank B. Gordon.
Employer Identification Number: 046047355

2839
The Nehemias Gorin Foundation
c/o William Gorin
1330 Beacon St.
Brookline 02146 (617) 738-4319

Established in 1964 in MA.
Donor(s): Nehemias Gorin.†
Foundation type: Independent
Financial data (yr. ended 11/30/89): Assets, $2,550,000 (M); gifts received, $8,000; expenditures, $280,000, including $260,000 for 58 grants (high: $60,000; low: $1,000).
Purpose and activities: Support for hospitals, Jewish giving, including welfare funds, Israel, higher education, the handicapped, museums and other cultural programs, community funds, Catholic giving, and health agencies.
Types of support: Annual campaigns.
Limitations: Giving primarily in MA.
Application information: Applications not accepted.
Board meeting date(s): Nov.
Trustees: Bertha G. Fritz, Stephen Goldenberg, William Gorin, Ida G. Leckart.
Number of staff: None.
Employer Identification Number: 046119939

2840
The Grass Foundation ⌑
77 Reservoir Rd.
Quincy 02170 (617) 773-0002

Incorporated in 1955 in MA.
Donor(s): Grass Instrument Co., Albert M. Grass, Ellen R. Grass, Cannon Manufacturing Co., and others.
Foundation type: Independent
Financial data (yr. ended 12/31/88): Assets, $4,787,154 (M); gifts received, $202,000; expenditures, $491,054, including $386,778 for 30 grants (high: $130,590; low: $600).

Purpose and activities: To encourage research in biology, physiology, and neurobiology and allied fields of science and medicine; grants primarily for fellowships for summer study at a marine biological laboratory, lectureships, and for higher education.
Types of support: Fellowships, research, lectureships.
Publications: Application guidelines, program policy statement.
Application information: Application formats and deadlines depend upon type of grant; specific information will be sent upon request.
Write: Mary G. Grass, Secy.
Officers and Directors:* Ellen R. Grass,* Pres.; Albert M. Grass,* V.P.; Mary G. Grass,* Secy.; Richmond B. Woodward,* Treas.; George H. Acheson, M.D., Sidney R. Goldring, M.D., Bernice Gragstein, Henry J. Grass, M.D., Donald B. Lindsley, Fiorindo A. Simeone, M.D., Gary Strichartz, Ph.D., R.R. Young, M.D., Steven J. Zottoli, Ph.D.
Employer Identification Number: 046049529

2841
Grimes-King Foundation for the Elderly, Inc. ¤
c/o Fiduciary Trust Co.
175 Federal St.
Boston 02110
Application address: 36 Beacon St., Boston, MA 02108

Established in 1964 in MA.
Foundation type: Independent
Financial data (yr. ended 11/30/88): Assets, $1,183,287 (M); gifts received, $2,179; expenditures, $66,444, including $55,750 for 4 grants (high: $35,500; low: $6,000).
Purpose and activities: Support primarily for social services and community development, particularly organizations benefitting the elderly Black community.
Types of support: General purposes.
Limitations: Giving limited to Boston, MA. No grants to individuals.
Application information:
Initial approach: Letter
Deadline(s): None
Write: Leonard W. Johnson, Treas.
Officers and Directors: Laura B. Morris, Pres.; Ruth-Arlene W. Howe, Secy.; Leonard W. Johnson, Treas.; and 18 additional directors.
Employer Identification Number: 046070226

2842
The Harold Grinspoon Charitable Foundation ¤ ☆
380 Union St.
West Springfield 01089

Established in 1985 in MA.
Donor(s): Harold Grinspoon.
Foundation type: Independent
Financial data (yr. ended 12/31/87): Assets, $1,080,857 (M); gifts received, $439,407; expenditures, $24,400, including $23,377 for 3 grants (high: $20,015; low: $1,300).
Purpose and activities: Initial year of grantmaking activity 1987; giving to a Jewish welfare fund and a university for Judaic studies. The foundation plans to make grants to individuals for research projects.
Limitations: Giving primarily in Springfield, MA. No grants for scholarships or student aid.
Application information: Applications not accepted.
Trustees: Harold Grinspoon, Jeremy Pava.
Employer Identification Number: 222738277

2843
Grossman Family Trust ¤
14 Federal St.
Nantucket 02554 (617) 228-3650

Trust established in 1938 in MA.
Donor(s): Members of the Grossman family and family-controlled businesses.
Foundation type: Independent
Financial data (yr. ended 12/31/87): Assets, $1,177,581 (M); expenditures, $247,986, including $204,000 for 1 grant.
Purpose and activities: Giving primarily for Jewish welfare funds.
Trustees: Bernard D. Grossman, Everett P. Grossman, Joseph B. Grossman, Joseph B. Grossman II, Maurice Grossman, Morton S. Grossman, Nissie Grossman.
Employer Identification Number: 046041134

2844
Guild of Boston Artists, Inc. ¤
162 Newbury St.
Boston 02116-2889

Established in 1914 in MA.
Foundation type: Independent
Financial data (yr. ended 3/31/88): Assets, $1,189,279 (M); gifts received, $1,610; expenditures, $53,828, including $600 for 5 grants and $800 for 5 grants to individuals (high: $200; low: $150).
Purpose and activities: Support primarily for the arts.
Limitations: Giving primarily in MA.
Application information: Contributes only to pre-selected organizations. Applications not accepted.
Officers: Robert Cormier, Pres.; Marian Williams Steele, Secy.; Roger W. Curtis, Treas.
Employer Identification Number: 042104266

2845
Jon L. Hagler Foundation ¤
c/o Hagler Mastrovita & Hewitt, Inc.
One International Place
Boston 02110

Established in 1984 in MA.
Foundation type: Independent
Financial data (yr. ended 12/31/87): Assets, $2,291,046 (M); expenditures, $64,011, including $61,600 for 14 grants (high: $25,000; low: $100).
Purpose and activities: Support primarily for higher education.
Limitations: Giving primarily in MA.
Application information: Contributes only to pre-selected organizations. Applications not accepted.
Trustee: Jon L. Hagler.
Employer Identification Number: 222600563

2846
Joseph M. Hamilburg Foundation ¤
c/o Plymouth Rubber Co.
104 Revere St.
Canton 02021

Established in 1963.
Donor(s): Daniel M. Hamilburg.
Foundation type: Independent
Financial data (yr. ended 12/31/88): Assets, $1,398,990 (M); expenditures, $73,940, including $57,422 for 89 grants (high: $17,250; low: $20).
Purpose and activities: Giving for health agencies, hospitals, and the performing arts; support also for higher education.
Limitations: Giving primarily in MA. No grants to individuals.
Application information: Contributes only to pre-selected organizations. Applications not accepted.
Trustee: Daniel M. Hamilburg.
Employer Identification Number: 046128210

2847
Francis A. & Jacquelyn H. Harrington Foundation ¤
370 Main St., Suite 1200
Worcester 01608 (617) 798-8621

Trust established in 1965 in MA.
Donor(s): Francis A. Harrington, Charles A. Harrington Foundation.
Foundation type: Independent
Financial data (yr. ended 12/31/87): Assets, $8,043,150 (M); expenditures, $388,449, including $357,350 for 46 grants (high: $25,000; low: $1,000; average: $8,100).
Purpose and activities: Giving primarily for higher and secondary education, a science center, scientific and medical research, and hospitals.
Types of support: Capital campaigns, equipment, general purposes, special projects.
Limitations: Giving primarily in Worcester, MA. No grants to individuals, or for scholarships; no loans.
Application information: Application form not required.
Initial approach: Letter
Copies of proposal: 1
Deadline(s): Dec. 1
Board meeting date(s): Dec. 15
Final notification: December 31
Write: Sumner B. Tilton, Jr., Trustee
Trustees: Francis A. Harrington, Francis A. Harrington, Jr., Jacquelyn H. Harrington, James H. Harrington, Sumner B. Tilton, Jr.
Employer Identification Number: 046125088

2848
George Harrington Trust ¤
c/o Boston Safe Deposit and Trust Co.
One Boston Place
Boston 02108 (617) 722-7340

Trust established in 1936 in MA.
Donor(s): George Harrington.†
Foundation type: Independent
Financial data (yr. ended 08/31/89): Assets, $2,512,300 (M); expenditures, $155,082, including $124,300 for 3 grants (high: $60,000; low: $22,800).

Purpose and activities: "To stimulate major new efforts in the understanding, prevention, and treatment of the mental disorders of adolescents and young adults through the George Harrington Professorship in Clinical and Epidemiologic Psychiatry at Harvard Medical School."
Types of support: Professorships.
Limitations: Giving limited to Cambridge, MA. No grants to individuals.
Publications: 990-PF.
Application information: Application form not required.
Initial approach: Proposal
Deadline(s): Feb., May, Aug., and Nov.
Board meeting date(s): Mar., June, Sept., and Dec.
Write: Sylvia Salas, Trust Officer, Boston Safe Deposit and Trust Co.
Trustees: John M. Cornish, William G. Cornish, William W. Wolbach.
Employer Identification Number: 046037725

2849
Harvard Apparatus Foundation, Inc. ⌑
c/o Palmer & Dodge
One Beacon St.
Boston 02108

Established in 1938.
Foundation type: Independent
Financial data (yr. ended 3/31/88): Assets, $1,690,990 (M); expenditures, $58,092, including $47,749 for 2 grants (high: $37,749; low: $10,000).
Purpose and activities: Grants to promote the teaching of physiology.
Application information: Contributes only to pre-selected organizations. Applications not accepted.
Officers: A. Clifford Barger, Pres.; Nancy S. Milburn, Treas.
Directors: Ranier Beewwkes III, John C.S. Fray, Maurice Goodman, Benjamin Kaminer, Josephus Long.
Employer Identification Number: 042104293

2850
Harvard Musical Association
c/o Chair., Awards Comm.
57A Chestnut St.
Boston 02109-2881 (617) 523-2897

Established in 1837; incorporated in 1845 in MA.
Foundation type: Independent
Financial data (yr. ended 06/30/88): Assets, $3,173,288 (M); expenditures, $80,228, including $21,500 for 20 grants.
Purpose and activities: Supporting grants to musical organizations and commissions to composers for new works; maintains a library of musicology and scores, and practice and concert facilities.
Types of support: Scholarship funds, operating budgets, grants to individuals.
Limitations: Giving limited to the greater Boston, MA, area.
Application information: Application form not required.
Initial approach: Letter
Deadline(s): Apr. 1
Board of Directors: John L. Thorndike, Pres.; Kilmer McCully, V.P.; Ronald G. Sampson, V.P.; George W. Butterworth III, Secy.; Sherwood E. Bain, Treas.; Thomas J. Anderson, Joan T. Bok, Hugh H. Sharpe III.
Number of staff: 1 full-time professional; 1 full-time support.
Employer Identification Number: 042104284

2851
Harvard-Yenching Institute ⌑
Two Divinity Ave.
Cambridge 02138 (617) 495-3369

Incorporated in 1928 in MA.
Donor(s): Trustees of Estate of Charles Martin Hall.
Foundation type: Independent
Financial data (yr. ended 6/30/87): Assets, $57,064,373 (M); qualifying distributions, $1,586,473, including $1,586,473 for 72 grants.
Purpose and activities: To aid the development of higher education in eastern and southern Asia, concentrating on the humanities and social sciences; grants to support teaching, research, and study by Asians in these fields; and to sponsor fellowships for research at Harvard University, or scholarships for graduate study, by younger faculty members of selected Asian institutions; also helps to support East Asian studies at Harvard through publication of the Harvard Journal of Asiatic Studies, and through the Harvard-Yenching Library, which became an integral part of Harvard University as of July 1, 1976. Grants given only for research or study by faculty members of invited universities in East and Southeast Asia.
Types of support: Scholarship funds, research, fellowships.
Limitations: Giving primarily in Asia and Cambridge, MA. No grants to individuals.
Publications: Application guidelines, program policy statement.
Application information: Application form required for scholarships; applicants nominated by participating universities. Application form required.
Initial approach: Letter
Copies of proposal: 1
Deadline(s): Submit proposal in Sept. or Oct. for following autumn; deadlines Oct. 1 for Visiting Scholars; Jan. 10 for Doctoral Scholarships
Board meeting date(s): Usually in Dec. and Apr.
Write: Patrick D. Hanan, Dir.
Officers: Roderick MacDougall, Treas.; Patrick D. Hanan, Dir.
Trustees: Henry Rosovsky, Chair.; T. Jefferson Coolidge, Jr., Bong Hak Hyun, Daniel H.H. Ingalls, Paul T. Lauby, James I. McCord, Nathan M. Pusey, A. Michael Spence, Galen L. Stone.
Number of staff: 1 full-time professional; 1 part-time professional; 2 full-time support; 1 part-time support.
Employer Identification Number: 042062394

2852
Haven Trust ⌑ ☆
50 Congress St., Rm. 800
Boston 02109

Established in 1960.
Donor(s): George Lewis.
Foundation type: Independent
Financial data (yr. ended 12/31/88): Assets, $239,828 (M); gifts received, $200,000; expenditures, $163,495, including $162,350 for 74 grants (high: $50,000; low: $25).
Purpose and activities: Support for primary and secondary education; giving also for museums and conservation groups.
Types of support: Scholarship funds.
Limitations: Giving primarily in MA. No grants to individuals.
Application information: Contributes only to pre-selected organizations. Applications not accepted.
Trustees: George Lewis, W.N. Thorndike.
Employer Identification Number: 046053996

2853
Josiah Willard Hayden Recreation Centre, Inc. ☆
24 Lincoln St.
Lexington 02173 (617) 862-8480

Established in 1937.
Donor(s): William E. Maloney Foundation.
Foundation type: Operating
Financial data (yr. ended 08/31/89): Assets, $13,468,263 (M); gifts received, $8,006; expenditures, $1,406,101, including $22,400 for 46 grants to individuals (high: $1,250; low: $300).
Purpose and activities: A private operating foundation; awards scholarships for college tuition; support also for recreation programs.
Types of support: Student aid.
Limitations: Giving limited to Lexington, MA.
Application information: Application form required.
Deadline(s): Apr.
Officers and Directors:* John P. Chase,* Chair.; Melville T. Hodder,* Pres.; Richard J. Kirk,* V.P. and Mgr.; G. Jean Gilbert,* Exec. Secy.; John W. Maloney,* Treas.; Joseph Crosby, Alan S. Fields, Edwin J. Hodder, David G. Kirk, Anne R. Scigliano.
Employer Identification Number: 042203700

2854
The Heald Foundation ⌑ ☆
c/o Shawmut Worcester County Bank
446 Main St.
Worcester 01613-2032 (508) 793-4552

Established in 1958.
Foundation type: Independent
Financial data (yr. ended 12/31/88): Assets, $1,126,975 (M); expenditures, $58,659, including $50,000 for 16 grants (high: $12,000; low: $1,000).
Purpose and activities: Giving primarily for cultural organizations, including museums and historical preservation; higher and other education; and health associations and services.
Limitations: Giving limited to the Worcester, MA, area. No grants to individuals.
Application information:
Initial approach: Letter

Deadline(s): None
Write: Brian Collins
Trustees: John Adams, Jr., James N. Heald II, Shawmut Worcester County Bank, N.A.
Employer Identification Number: 046028076

2855
Henderson Foundation ⌑
P.O. Box 420
Sudbury 01776 (617) 443-4646

Trust established in 1947 in MA.
Donor(s): Ernest Henderson,† George B. Henderson,† J. Brooks Fenno,† Ernest Henderson III.
Foundation type: Independent
Financial data (yr. ended 12/31/86): Assets, $8,535,618 (M); expenditures, $453,195, including $386,550 for 100 grants (high: $9,900; low: $500).
Purpose and activities: Emphasis on elementary, secondary, and higher education, intercultural relations, health and hospitals, religion, and youth agencies.
Types of support: Continuing support, general purposes.
Limitations: No grants to individuals, or for scholarships or fellowships.
Application information:
Initial approach: Letter
Copies of proposal: 1
Deadline(s): Submit proposal in Oct.
Board meeting date(s): As required
Write: Ernest Henderson III, Trustee
Trustees: Barclay G.S. Henderson, Ernest Henderson III, Joseph Carlton Petrone, Jr.
Employer Identification Number: 046051095

2856
The George B. Henderson Foundation ⌑
c/o Henry R. Guild, Jr.
50 Congress St., Suite 1020
Boston 02109
Application address: c/o Palmer & Dodge, One Beacon St., Boston, MA 02108; Tel.: (617) 573-0100

Established in 1964 in MA.
Donor(s): George B. Henderson.†
Foundation type: Independent
Financial data (yr. ended 12/31/88): Assets, $4,687,398 (M); expenditures, $170,345, including $112,093 for 7 grants (high: $28,000; low: $3,675).
Purpose and activities: Grants for enhancement of the physical appearance of the city of Boston.
Types of support: Renovation projects, special projects.
Limitations: Giving limited to Boston, MA. No grants to individuals, or for endowment funds, maintenance, operating budgets, research, scholarships, fellowships, or general purposes; no loans.
Application information: Application form required.
Initial approach: Letter or proposal
Copies of proposal: 1
Deadline(s): None
Board meeting date(s): As required
Final notification: One to three months
Write: John T. Galvin, Secy., Board of Designators
Trustees: Henry R. Guild, Jr., Ernest Henderson III, Gerard C. Henderson.
Employer Identification Number: 046089310

2857
Nan and Matilda Heydt Fund ⌑
c/o BayBank Valley Trust Co.
1500 Main St.
Springfield 01115 (413) 781-7575
Grant application address: c/o BayBank Valley Trust Co., P.O. Box 422, Burlington, MA 01803; Tel.: (413) 617-2294

Trust established in 1966 in MA.
Donor(s): Matilda L. Heydt.†
Foundation type: Independent
Financial data (yr. ended 12/31/87): Assets, $3,246,138 (M); expenditures, $174,660, including $135,938 for 22 grants (high: $25,000; low: $1,307).
Purpose and activities: Grants for public charitable purposes including health, welfare, the humanities, and education; emphasis on child welfare and youth agencies, community funds, and aid to the handicapped.
Types of support: Capital campaigns, equipment, land acquisition, matching funds, publications, renovation projects, seed money, special projects.
Limitations: Giving limited to Hampden County, MA. No grants to individuals, or for endowment funds, scholarships, fellowships, or operating budgets; no loans.
Publications: Informational brochure (including application guidelines).
Application information: Application form not required.
Initial approach: Telephone, letter, or proposal
Copies of proposal: 12
Deadline(s): Submit proposal preferably in Dec., Apr., or Aug.; deadline 1st Monday in Jan. and May, and 1st Tuesday in Sept.
Board meeting date(s): Mar., July, and Nov.
Final notification: 4 months
Write: Peter Weston, V.P., BayBank Valley Trust Co.
Trustee: Baybank Valley Trust Co.
Number of staff: 1 part-time professional; 1 part-time support.
Employer Identification Number: 046136421

2858
Jacob and Frances Hiatt Foundation, Inc. ⌑
P.O. Box 1657, Station C
Worcester 01607

Incorporated in 1951 in MA.
Donor(s): Jacob Hiatt, Estey Charitable Income Trust, Rand-Whitney Packaging Corp., Frances L. Hiatt.
Foundation type: Independent
Financial data (yr. ended 08/31/88): Assets, $6,129,372 (M); gifts received, $1,382,413; expenditures, $758,897, including $723,123 for grants.
Purpose and activities: Giving primarily for higher education, cultural programs, and Jewish organizations.
Limitations: Giving primarily in Worcester, MA.
Application information: Contributes only to pre-selected organizations. Applications not accepted.
Officer: Jacob Hiatt, Pres. and Treas.
Directors Myra H. Kraft, Robert K. Kraft.
Employer Identification Number: 046050716

2859
Aldus C. Higgins Foundation ⌑
c/o Fiduciary Trust Co.
175 Federal St.
Boston 02110

Trust established in 1946 in MA.
Donor(s): Higgins Trust No. 13, Mary S. Higgins Trust No. 2, and others.
Foundation type: Independent
Financial data (yr. ended 09/30/89): Assets, $2,995,057 (M); expenditures, $158,739, including $133,000 for 19 grants (high: $50,000; low: $500).
Purpose and activities: Giving for higher and secondary education and cultural programs.
Limitations: Giving primarily in the Worcester, MA, area.
Application information:
Initial approach: Letter
Deadline(s): None
Write: Edmund H. Kendrick, Trustee
Trustees: Richard Chapin, Milton P. Higgins, Edmund H. Kendrick.
Employer Identification Number: 046049262

2860
Bradley C. Higgins Foundation ⌑ ☆
370 Main St.
Worcester 01608-1714 (508) 798-8621

Established in 1961.
Donor(s): Bradley C. Higgins.†
Foundation type: Independent
Financial data (yr. ended 12/31/88): Assets, $1,379,004 (M); gifts received, $20,000; expenditures, $65,443, including $55,000 for 3 grants (high: $50,000; low: $1,000).
Purpose and activities: Support for museums and a community fund.
Types of support: General purposes.
Limitations: Giving primarily in Worcester, MA. No grants to individuals.
Application information:
Initial approach: Letter
Deadline(s): None
Write: Sumner B. Tilton, Trustee
Trustees: Lee H. Brejsenback, Gloria M. Lee, Sumner B. Tilton, Jr.
Employer Identification Number: 046027026

2861
John W. & Clara C. Higgins Foundation ⌑
370 Main St., Suite 1250
Worcester 01608 (508) 798-8621

Established in 1956 in MA.
Foundation type: Independent
Financial data (yr. ended 12/31/88): Assets, $1,481,526 (M); expenditures, $92,280, including $74,000 for 32 grants (high: $23,500; low: $50).
Purpose and activities: Giving for the arts, a museum, and education.
Limitations: No grants to individuals.

Application information: Application form not required.
Initial approach: Letter
Deadline(s): None
Write: Sumner B. Tilton, Jr.
Trustees: Richard Higgins, Mary Louise Wilding-White, Philip O. Wilding-White.
Employer Identification Number: 046026914

2862
High Meadow Foundation, Inc.
c/o Country Curtains, Inc.
Main St.
Stockbridge 01262 (413) 298-5565

Established in 1984 in MA.
Donor(s): John H. Fitzpatrick, Jane P. Fitzpatrick, Country Curtains, Inc., Housatonic Curtain Co., Red Lion Inn, Country Curtains Retail.
Foundation type: Independent
Financial data (yr. ended 09/30/89): Assets, $1,036,459 (M); gifts received, $647,487; expenditures, $500,678, including $492,287 for 228 grants (high: $108,525; low: $12) and $1,100 for 2 grants to individuals (high: $1,000; low: $100).
Purpose and activities: Support primarily for the performing arts, especially theater and music, and other cultural organizations; giving also for health, social services, and higher and other education.
Types of support: Annual campaigns, building funds, capital campaigns, continuing support, deficit financing, emergency funds, equipment, matching funds, employee-related scholarships, special projects.
Limitations: Giving primarily in Bershire County, MA.
Application information: Application form not required.
Initial approach: Letter
Deadline(s): None
Write: Mary Ann Snyder
Officers and Directors:* Jane P. Fitzpatrick,* Chair. and Treas.; John H. Fitzpatrick,* Pres.; JoAnn Brown, Nancy J. Fitzpatrick, Mary Ann Snyder, Robert B. Trask.
Number of staff: 1
Employer Identification Number: 222527419

2863
Hinduja Foundation, U.S. ⌑
c/o Ropes & Gray
One International Place
Boston 02110

Established in 1984 in MA.
Donor(s): Hinduja Trust.
Foundation type: Independent
Financial data (yr. ended 12/31/88): Assets, $280,492 (M); gifts received, $526,433; expenditures, $326,738, including $323,795 for 6 grants (high: $200,000; low: $100).
Purpose and activities: Giving primarily to a hospital for medical research.
Types of support: Research.
Limitations: No grants to individuals.
Publications: Newsletter.
Application information: Contributes only to pre-selected organizations. Applications not accepted.
Officer: John E. Lawrence, Pres.
Trustees: G.P. Hinduja, P.P. Hinduja, Srichand P. Hinduja.
Employer Identification Number: 222570780

2864
The Hoche-Scofield Foundation
c/o Shawmut Worcester County Bank, N.A.
446 Main St.
Worcester 01608 (617) 793-4552

Established in 1983 in MA.
Donor(s): William B. Scofield.†
Foundation type: Independent
Financial data (yr. ended 06/30/89): Assets, $10,127,183 (M); expenditures, $621,064, including $536,054 for 74 grants (high: $55,031; low: $250).
Purpose and activities: Grants primarily for community improvement, higher education, cultural organizations, health organizations, and social services, including women, youth and child welfare, and the disadvantaged.
Types of support: Capital campaigns, continuing support, seed money, special projects.
Limitations: Giving primarily in the city and county of Worcester, MA.
Publications: Application guidelines.
Application information: Application form required.
Initial approach: Letter or telephone
Copies of proposal: 4
Deadline(s): Feb. 15, May 15, Aug. 15, and Nov. 15
Board meeting date(s): Mar. 15, June 15, Sept. 15, and Dec. 15
Final notification: Mar. 31, June 30, Sept. 30, and Dec. 30
Write: Norman J. Richardson, Sr. Trust Officer, Shawmut, Worcester County Bank, N.A.
Trustees: Henry B. Dewey, Lois B. Green, Paul S. Morgan, Shawmut Worcester County Bank, N.A.
Employer Identification Number: 222519554

2865
The John Ernest Hoffman Foundation ⌑
c/o Loring, Wolcott & Coolidge Office
230 Congress St.
Boston 02110
Application address: c/o Gaston & Snow, One Federal St., Boston, MA 02110; Tel.: (617) 426-4600

Established in 1985 in MA.
Donor(s): Effe K.D. Hoffman.
Foundation type: Independent
Financial data (yr. ended 12/31/88): Assets, $2,216,325 (M); gifts received, $925,829; expenditures, $73,797, including $61,291 for 3 grants (high: $20,431; low: $20,430).
Purpose and activities: Support for cancer research, a children's hospital, and religious welfare.
Limitations: No grants to individuals.
Application information:
Initial approach: Letter
Deadline(s): None
Write: Roger M. Thomas, Esq., Trustee
Trustees: Effe K.D. Hoffman, Stephen A. Moore, Roger M. Thomas.
Employer Identification Number: 222677966

2866
Home for Aged Men in the City of Brockton ⌑
c/o Creedon & Creedon
One Centre St.
Brockton 02401

Trust established in MA.
Donor(s): Horace Howard.†
Foundation type: Independent
Financial data (yr. ended 3/31/87): Assets, $2,512,180 (M); gifts received, $4,233; expenditures, $104,834, including $22,400 for 3 grants (high: $20,000; low: $400).
Purpose and activities: Grants for homes for the aged and hospitals to encourage development of the facilities' public assistance programs.
Limitations: Giving primarily in MA.
Officers: John Creedon, Pres.; Anthony Froio, Treas.
Employer Identification Number: 042103796

2867
Charles H. Hood Foundation
95 Berkeley St.
Boston 02116 (617) 695-9439

Fund established in 1931; incorporated in 1942 in NH.
Donor(s): Charles H. Hood.†
Foundation type: Independent
Financial data (yr. ended 12/31/88): Assets, $18,722,595 (M); expenditures, $1,158,553, including $1,003,498 for 15 grants (high: $450,000; low: $21,119; average: $20,000-$40,000).
Purpose and activities: Supports projects concerned with child health through its Child Health Advisory Committee; emphasis on the initiation or furtherance of medical research and related projects contributing to a reduction of the health problems and health needs of large numbers of children.
Types of support: Research.
Limitations: Giving limited to New England. No support for nutrition, public health, mental health, education, or social or general welfare. No grants to individuals, or for building or endowment funds, operating budgets, general support, publications, scholarships, fellowships, fundraising campaigns, or matching gifts; no loans.
Publications: Annual report (including application guidelines).
Application information: Application form required.
Initial approach: Letter or telephone
Copies of proposal: 9
Deadline(s): Submit proposal after Feb. 1 for Apr. 15 deadline, and after Aug. 1 for Oct. 15 deadline
Board meeting date(s): Usually in June and Dec.
Final notification: 60 to 70 days
Write: Merle W. Mudd, Exec. Dir.
Officers: Charles H. Hood, 2nd,* Pres. and Treas.; Merle W. Mudd, Secy. and Exec. Dir.
Members:* Roswell M. Boutwell III, John O. Parker, Henry M. Sanders.
Number of staff: 1 part-time professional; 1 part-time support.
Employer Identification Number: 046036790

2868
Charles H. Hood Fund
500 Rutherford Ave.
Boston 02129 (617) 242-0600

Foundation established in 1981.
Foundation type: Independent
Financial data (yr. ended 12/31/88): Assets, $1,950,641 (M); expenditures, $116,900, including $96,350 for grants.
Purpose and activities: Giving limited to scholarships for children of employees of H.P. Hood, Inc. and Agri-Mark, Inc.; awards $3500 per year per student for four years.
Types of support: Employee-related scholarships.
Publications: Application guidelines.
Application information: Application form required.
Deadline(s): Dec. 31 of high school senior year
Write: Prudence M. Dame, Exec. Dir.
Officers: Charles H. Hood,* Chair.; Prudence M. Dame, Exec. Dir. and Secy.; Marius de Vos,* Treas.
Directors:* Barbara N. Tobey.
Members: Warren Donovan, June Fountain, Leonard Wilson.
Employer Identification Number: 046036788

2869
The Hopedale Foundation
43 Hope St.
Hopedale 01747 (508) 473-0820

Trust established in 1946 in MA.
Donor(s): Draper Corp., Thomas H. West,† John D. Gannett.†
Foundation type: Independent
Financial data (yr. ended 10/31/89): Assets, $4,406,459 (M); expenditures, $241,750, including $163,433 for 22 grants (high: $55,000; low: $1,500) and $68,350 for 57 loans to individuals.
Purpose and activities: Emphasis on area community funds and hospitals; support also for museums and other cultural programs, health agencies, youth services, and higher education; student loans limited to local high school graduates. New grants only to organizations having direct impact on the local community.
Types of support: Annual campaigns, capital campaigns, general purposes, student loans.
Limitations: Giving primarily in MA. No grants for endowment funds.
Application information: Application form not required.
Initial approach: Letter
Copies of proposal: 1
Deadline(s): June 1 for student loans; no set deadline for grants
Board meeting date(s): Feb., June, and Oct.
Write: Thad R. Jackson, Treas.
Officers and Trustees:* William B. Gannett,* Chair.; Robert D. Donley,* Secy.; Thad R. Jackson,* Treas.; W. Gregory Burrill, Peter S. Ellis, Alfred H. Sparling, Jr., Thomas H. West, Jr.
Number of staff: 1 part-time professional; 1 part-time support.
Employer Identification Number: 046044779

2870
Henry Hornblower Fund, Inc. ⌑
P.O. Box 2365
Boston 02107 (617) 589-3286

Incorporated in 1945 in MA.
Donor(s): Hornblower & Weeks - Hemphill, Noyes.
Foundation type: Independent
Financial data (yr. ended 12/31/88): Assets, $2,066,689 (M); expenditures, $103,293, including $88,500 for 31 grants (high: $5,000; low: $1,000) and $6,000 for 2 grants to individuals (high: $5,000; low: $1,000).
Purpose and activities: Emphasis on higher and secondary education, hospitals, and cultural programs; support also for needy individuals presently or formerly employed by Hornblower & Weeks.
Types of support: Grants to individuals.
Limitations: Giving primarily in Boston, MA.
Application information: Application form not required.
Initial approach: Letter
Deadline(s): None
Write: Nathan N. Withington, Pres.
Officers and Directors:* Nathan N. Withington,* Pres.; Karl Grace,* Treas.; Jack Beaty, Richard Bloomfield, Dudley H. Bradlee II, Martin J. Carew, George Larson.
Employer Identification Number: 237425285

2871
Mabel A. Horne Trust ⌑
c/o First National Bank of Boston
P.O. Box 1861
Boston 02105 (617) 434-5669

Trust established in 1964 in MA.
Donor(s): Mabel A. Horne.†
Foundation type: Independent
Financial data (yr. ended 9/30/88): Assets, $3,195,512 (M); gifts received, $5,000; expenditures, $206,991, including $159,500 for 15 grants (high: $20,000; low: $3,000).
Purpose and activities: Support primarily for family services and youth agencies and for education.
Limitations: Giving limited to MA, with emphasis on Boston. No grants to individuals.
Publications: Application guidelines.
Application information: Application form required.
Initial approach: Letter
Copies of proposal: 1
Deadline(s): Submit proposal preferably in Dec., May, June, or Sept.; deadline is last day of month prior to meetings
Board meeting date(s): Jan., Apr., July, and Oct.
Write: Miss Sharon M. Driscoll, Trust Officer, First National Bank of Boston
Trustee: First National Bank of Boston.
Employer Identification Number: 046089241

2872
Housen Foundation, Inc. ⌑
c/o Erving Paper Mills
47 East Main St.
Erving 01344 (508) 544-2711

Incorporated in 1968 in MA.
Donor(s): Erving Paper Mills, Brattleboro Paper Products, Inc.
Foundation type: Company-sponsored
Financial data (yr. ended 12/31/88): Assets, $1,329,546 (M); expenditures, $136,036, including $127,921 for 16 grants (high: $50,000; low: $35) and $6,250 for 5 grants to individuals (high: $1,500; low: $250).
Purpose and activities: Emphasis on Jewish welfare funds, community funds, and higher education including scholarships to children of Erving Paper Mill and subsidiary employees.
Types of support: Employee-related scholarships.
Limitations: Giving limited to MA. No grants to individuals (except employee-related scholarships).
Application information: Application form required for scholarship applicants.
Deadline(s): Feb. for scholarships
Board meeting date(s): Jan.
Write: Miss Dawn Williams, V.P.
Officers and Directors:* Charles B. Housen,* Pres.; Dawn M. Williams,* V.P. and Treas.; Morris Housen,* Secy.; Morton Slavin,* Clerk.
Number of staff: None.
Employer Identification Number: 046183673

2873
Howard Benevolent Society ⌑
14 Beacon St., Rm. 507
Boston 02108

Established in 1812.
Donor(s): Elisha V. Ashton.†
Foundation type: Independent
Financial data (yr. ended 9/30/87): Assets, $2,015,052 (M); gifts received, $30,000; expenditures, $143,563, including $101,847 for 125 grants to individuals of $815 each.
Purpose and activities: Giving to aid sick and destitute individuals.
Types of support: Grants to individuals.
Limitations: Giving limited to the Boston, MA, metropolitan area.
Application information:
Initial approach: Letter or telephone
Deadline(s): None
Write: Marcia Burley
Officers: Henry C. Young, Pres.; Richmond W. Bachelder, V.P. and Treas.; Jean C. Nichols, Secy.
Employer Identification Number: 042129132

2874
Humane Society of the Commonwealth of Massachusetts ⌑
177 Milk St.
Boston 02109
Application address: 195 Dedham St., Dover, MA 02030; Tel.: (508) 785-0071

Established in 1785.
Foundation type: Independent
Financial data (yr. ended 3/31/88): Assets, $3,150,851 (M); expenditures, $122,041, including $65,500 for 8 grants (high: $23,000; low: $2,500) and $7,365 for 14 grants to individuals (high: $1,500; low: $65).
Purpose and activities: Giving for medical education and research, and health services.
Types of support: Fellowships.
Limitations: Giving primarily in MA.
Application information:
Initial approach: Letter

Deadline(s): None
Write: Charles F. Adams, Secy.
Officers and Trustees: John E. Lawrence, Pres.; Charles F. Adams, Secy.; Richard M. Cutler, Treas.; Francis H. Burr, Ferdinand Colloredo-Mansfeld, Charles Devens, John H. Finley, George P. Gardner, Jr., Frederick S. Moseley III, Lawrence T. Perera, Curtis Prout, Henry E. Russell.
Employer Identification Number: 042104291

2875
Hurdle Hill Foundation ⌑
c/o Woodstock Service Corp.
18 Tremont St.
Boston 02108

Established in 1960 in MA.
Donor(s): Edith M. Adams, Members of the Phippen family.
Foundation type: Independent
Financial data (yr. ended 12/31/87): Assets, $106,146 (M); gifts received, $217,173; expenditures, $211,478, including $206,200 for 62 grants (high: $20,000; low: $100).
Purpose and activities: Support for higher and secondary education, cultural programs, and health services.
Limitations: Giving primarily in MA.
Application information: Contributes only to pre-selected organizations. Applications not accepted.
Trustees: Nelson J. Darling, Jr., Peter D. Phippen, Richard D. Phippen, Susanne LaCroix Phippen, William LaCroix Phippen.
Employer Identification Number: 046012782

2876
Sarah A. Hyams Fund, Inc.
One Boston Place, 32nd Fl.
Boston 02108 (617) 720-2238

Incorporated in 1929 in MA.
Donor(s): Godfrey M. Hyams Trust.
Foundation type: Independent
Financial data (yr. ended 12/31/89): Assets, $3,096,057 (M); expenditures, $223,313, including $205,000 for 25 grants (high: $25,000; low: $3,500; average: $1,000-$10,000).
Purpose and activities: Giving primarily for operating expenses and capital funds for summer youth programs.
Types of support: Operating budgets, general purposes.
Limitations: Giving primarily in Boston, Cambridge, Chelsea, Lynn, and Somerville, MA. No support for municipal, state or federal agencies, institutions of higher learning for standard educational programs; religious organizations for religious purposes; or national or regional health organizations. No grants to individuals, or for endowment funds, hospitals for capital campaigns, fellowships, publications, conferences, or films or videos.
Publications: Biennial report (including application guidelines).
Application information: Application form required.
Initial approach: Proposal
Copies of proposal: 1
Deadline(s): Submit proposal in Feb. or Mar.; no set deadline
Board meeting date(s): 6 times a year between Sept. and June
Final notification: 1 to 6 months
Write: Elizabeth B. Smith, Exec. Dir.
Officers: John H. Clymer,* Pres. and Treas.; Theresa J. Morse,* Secy.; Elizabeth B. Smith, Exec. Dir.
Trustees:* Lewis H. Spence, William N. Swift, Timothy L. Vaill, Roslyn M. Watson.
Number of staff: 3 full-time professional; 1 part-time professional; 3 full-time support.
Employer Identification Number: 046013680

2877
Godfrey M. Hyams Trust ▼
One Boston Place, 32nd Fl.
Boston 02108 (617) 720-2238

Trust established in 1921 in MA.
Donor(s): Godfrey M. Hyams.†
Foundation type: Independent
Financial data (yr. ended 12/31/89): Assets, $62,605,132 (M); expenditures, $3,455,396, including $2,939,576 for 193 grants (high: $85,000; low: $597; average: $5,000-$20,000).
Purpose and activities: Giving for the benefit of low income residents through support primarily of urban youth agencies and neighborhood centers; support also for other social service and community development purposes, including mental health counseling, services to the handicapped, and health services. Priority program areas initiated since 1984 include housing, refugee services, adolescent pregnancy, and women in prisons.
Types of support: Operating budgets, continuing support, equipment, matching funds, special projects, general purposes.
Limitations: Giving primarily in Boston, Cambridge, Chelsea, Lynn, and Somerville, MA. No support for municipal, state, or federal agencies; institutions of higher learning for standard educational programs; religious organizations for religious purposes; or national or regional health organizations; support for medical research is being phased out. No grants to individuals, or for endowment funds, hospitals for capital campaigns, fellowships, publications, conferences, or films or videos.
Publications: Biennial report (including application guidelines).
Application information: Application form not required.
Initial approach: Proposal
Copies of proposal: 1
Deadline(s): None
Board meeting date(s): 6 times a year regularly from Sept. through June
Final notification: 1 to 6 months
Write: Elizabeth B. Smith, Exec. Dir.
Officer: Elizabeth B. Smith, Exec. Dir.
Trustees: John H. Clymer, Chair.; Theresa J. Morse, Lewis H. Spence, William N. Swift, Roslyn M. Watson, Boston Safe Deposit & Trust Co.
Number of staff: 3 full-time professional; 1 part-time professional; 3 full-time support.
Employer Identification Number: 042214849

2878
Island Foundation, Inc.
589 Mill St.
Marion 02738 (508) 748-2809

Incorporated in 1979 in MA as Ram Island, Inc.; current entity formed in 1986 by merger with Green Island, Inc.
Donor(s): W. Van Alan Clark, Jr.†
Foundation type: Independent
Financial data (yr. ended 12/31/89): Assets, $21,266,657 (M); expenditures, $1,127,170, including $808,947 for grants (average: $3,000-$20,000).
Purpose and activities: Support for education, including environmental education and research, social service agencies for youth, women, and the aged, and land and wildlife conservation.
Types of support: General purposes, operating budgets, special projects, research.
Limitations: Giving primarily in the northeastern U.S. and FL. No support for political campaigns or religious organizations. No grants to individuals.
Publications: Annual report, application guidelines (including application guidelines).
Application information: Application form required.
Initial approach: Telephone or letter
Copies of proposal: 1
Deadline(s): Contact foundation for deadlines
Board meeting date(s): Quarterly
Final notification: After quarterly review
Write: Jenny D. Russell, Exec. Dir.
Officers: Lucy H. Nesbeda, Pres.; Jenny D. Russell, Exec. Dir.
Number of staff: 1 full-time professional; 2 part-time support.
Employer Identification Number: 042670567

2879
Marion Gardner Jackson Charitable Trust ⌑
c/o The First National Bank of Boston
P.O. Box 1861
Boston 02105 (617) 434-5669

Foundation type: Independent
Financial data (yr. ended 12/31/88): Assets, $5,905,984 (M); expenditures, $307,710, including $239,500 for grants.
Purpose and activities: Giving largely in capital funds for youth, social services, health agencies, higher education, and arts and cultural programs.
Types of support: Building funds.
Limitations: Giving primarily in Adams County, IL.
Application information:
Initial approach: Proposal
Deadline(s): Sept. 1
Write: Sharon M. Driscoll, Trust Officer, First National Bank of Boston
Trustee: Bank of Boston.
Employer Identification Number: 046010559

2880
The Howard Johnson Foundation
P.O. Box 235
541 Main St.
South Weymouth 02190 (617) 337-2201

Application address: c/o Howard B. Johnson, 720 Fifth Ave., Suite 1304, New York, NY 10019

Trust established in 1961 in MA.
Donor(s): Howard D. Johnson.†
Foundation type: Independent
Financial data (yr. ended 12/31/89): Assets, $3,023,567 (M); expenditures, $239,101, including $181,000 for 77 grants (high: $25,000; low: $1,000).
Purpose and activities: Giving primarily for higher and secondary education and health and hospitals; support also for museums, churches, religious welfare agencies, and the environment.
Types of support: General purposes.
Limitations: Giving primarily in MA, CT, and NY. No grants to individuals.
Application information: Application form not required.
Initial approach: Letter
Copies of proposal: 1
Deadline(s): Submit proposal early in calendar year
Board meeting date(s): Quarterly
Final notification: 2 months
Write: Eugene J. Durgin, Secy.
Officer: Eugene J. Durgin, Secy.
Trustees: Marissa J. Brock, Dorothy J. Henry, Howard B. Johnson, Howard Bates Johnson, Patricia Bates Johnson, Joshua J. Weeks, William H. Weeks.
Number of staff: 1 part-time support.
Employer Identification Number: 046060965

2881
Edward C. Johnson Fund ⌑
82 Devonshire St.
Boston 02109 (617) 570-6806

Trust established in 1964 in MA.
Donor(s): Edward C. Johnson II,† Edward C. Johnson III.
Foundation type: Independent
Financial data (yr. ended 12/31/88): Assets, $19,568,775 (M); gifts received, $3,289,989; expenditures, $1,961,564, including $1,864,426 for 37 grants (high: $1,187,176; low: $250; average: $500-$40,000).
Purpose and activities: Emphasis on museums, historical societies, institutions of higher education, medical institutions, and some youth programs. Support also for the visual arts, historic preservation, elementary and secondary schools, and environmental organizations.
Types of support: Operating budgets, endowment funds, building funds, special projects.
Limitations: Giving limited to the greater Boston, MA, area. No grants to individuals.
Publications: Application guidelines.
Application information:
Initial approach: Proposal
Deadline(s): Mar. 30 and Oct. 30
Board meeting date(s): June and Dec.
Write: Anne-Marie Soulliere, Foundation Dir.
Officer: Anne-Marie Soulliere, Foundation Dir.
Trustees: Edward C. Johnson III, Caleb Loring, Jr.
Number of staff: 2
Employer Identification Number: 046108344

2882
Clinton O. & Lura Curtis Jones Memorial Trust
c/o Cain, Hibbard, Myers, & Look
66 West St., 3rd Fl.
Pittsfield 01201 (413) 443-4771

Established about 1972 in MA.
Foundation type: Independent
Financial data (yr. ended 12/31/88): Assets, $1,173,815 (M); expenditures, $95,782, including $70,500 for grants to individuals.
Purpose and activities: Giving only for scholarships to individuals for higher education.
Types of support: Student aid.
Limitations: Giving limited to residents of Berkshire County, MA.
Application information: Application form required.
Initial approach: Letter with school transcripts
Deadline(s): Apr. 15
Write: Frederick M. Myers, Trustee
Trustee: Frederick M. Myers.
Employer Identification Number: 046173271

2883
The Kapor Family Foundation ⌑
c/o Foley, Hoag & Eliot
One Post Office Sq.
Boston 02109 (617) 482-1390

Established in 1986 in MA.
Donor(s): Mitchell D. Kapor.
Foundation type: Independent
Financial data (yr. ended 6/30/89): Assets, $7,410,979 (M); expenditures, $707,982, including $688,175 for 4 grants (high: $299,175; low: $39,000).
Purpose and activities: Support primarily for higher education.
Limitations: No grants to individuals.
Application information: Contributes only to pre-selected organizations. Applications not accepted.
Trustees: Mitchell D. Kapor, Ellen M. Poss.
Employer Identification Number: 042943167

2884
Edward Bangs Kelley and Elza Kelley Foundation, Inc.
243 South St.
P.O. Drawer M
Hyannis 02601 (617) 775-3117

Incorporated in 1954 in MA.
Donor(s): Edward Bangs Kelley,† Elza deHorvath Kelley.†
Foundation type: Independent
Financial data (yr. ended 12/31/88): Assets, $2,735,466 (M); expenditures, $154,072, including $83,900 for 22 grants (high: $16,667; low: $1,000) and $37,750 for 34 grants to individuals (high: $3,500; low: $250).
Purpose and activities: To promote health and welfare of inhabitants of Barnstable County, MA; grants for higher education, including scholarships, and particularly for medical and paramedical education; support also for health and hospitals, child development and youth agencies, the elderly, libraries, the environment, and cultural programs, including the fine and performing arts.
Types of support: Operating budgets, seed money, emergency funds, building funds, equipment, matching funds, scholarship funds, special projects, research, student aid, capital campaigns, publications.
Limitations: Giving limited to Barnstable County, MA. No grants to individuals (except for scholarships), or for annual campaigns, deficit financing, land acquisition, endowment funds, exchange programs, fellowships, publications, or conferences; no loans.
Publications: Annual report (including application guidelines).
Application information: Application form required.
Initial approach: Letter, followed by proposal
Copies of proposal: 6
Deadline(s): Apr. 30 for scholarships; no deadline for grants; grants considered Apr. and Oct. if greater than $2,500
Board meeting date(s): Jan., Apr., July, and Oct.
Final notification: 3 weeks
Write: Henry L. Murphy, Jr., Admin. Mgr.
Officers and Directors:* Frank L. Nickerson,* Pres.; Milton L. Penn,* V.P. and Treas.; Katherine A. Leland, M.D.,* Clerk; Henry L. Murphy, Jr., Admin. Mgr.; John F. Aylmer, Palmer Davenport, Frank W. Garran, Jr., M.D., Townsend Hornor, Esther Howes, John M. Kayajan, Kenneth S. MacAffer, Jr., Mary Louise Montgomery, Joshua A. Nickerson, Jr., Thomas S. Olsen.
Number of staff: 1 part-time professional.
Employer Identification Number: 046039660

2885
The Henry P. Kendall Foundation ▼ ⌑
176 Federal St.
Boston 02110 (617) 951-2525

Trust established in 1957 in MA.
Donor(s): Members of the Henry P. Kendell family.
Foundation type: Independent
Financial data (yr. ended 12/31/87): Assets, $48,291,617 (M); gifts received, $1,000; expenditures, $1,301,284, including $842,921 for 7 grants (high: $443,706; low: $5,000).
Purpose and activities: Emphasis on arms control and peace, and matters concerning the natural environment and natural resources; some funding for museums.
Types of support: Operating budgets, seed money, emergency funds, research, special projects, publications, conferences and seminars, loans, continuing support.
Limitations: No grants to individuals, or for capital or endowment funds, scholarships, fellowships, or matching gifts.
Application information: Application form not required.
Initial approach: Brief proposal
Copies of proposal: 1
Deadline(s): Feb. 15, May 15, Aug. 15, and Nov. 15
Board meeting date(s): Mar., June, Sept., and Dec.
Final notification: 2 months
Write: Salvatore F. Battinelli
Officer and Trustees: John P. Kendall, Pres.; Henry W. Kendall, Ann W. Plimpton.
Number of staff: 1 full-time professional.
Employer Identification Number: 046029103

2886
Francis W. Kervick Trust ⌑ ☆
c/o First National Bank of Boston
P.O. Box 1861
Boston 02105

Foundation type: Independent
Financial data (yr. ended 9/30/88): Assets, $1,081 (M); expenditures, $1,225,159, including $1,210,816 for 2 grants of $605,408 each.
Purpose and activities: Support for Roman Catholic dioceses.
Trustee: First National Bank of Boston.
Employer Identification Number: 046054843

2887
Constance Killam Trust ☆
c/o Nutter, McClennen & Fish
One International Place
Boston 02110-2699 (617) 439-2000
Application address: 50 Milk St., Boston, MA 02109

Established in 1977 in MA.
Donor(s): Constance Killam.†
Foundation type: Independent
Financial data (yr. ended 04/30/89): Assets, $2,572,699 (M); gifts received, $99,443; expenditures, $192,964, including $165,000 for 3 grants (high: $100,000; low: $15,000).
Purpose and activities: Support for the Massachusettes Audubon Society regional headquarters; support also for Canadian-related education at universities.
Types of support: Continuing support, professorships, scholarship funds.
Limitations: Giving primarily in MA.
Application information: Application form not required.
Initial approach: Letter
Copies of proposal: 2
Deadline(s): None
Write: John B. Newhall and Nathan Newbury III, Trustees
Trustees: Nathan Newbury III, John B. Newhall.
Employer Identification Number: 046420685

2888
Helen F. Kimball Trust
(also known as The Moses Kimball Fund for the Promotion of Good Citizenship)
c/o Loring, Wolcott and Coolidge
230 Congress St.
Boston 02110 (617) 523-6533

Established in 1925 in MA.
Foundation type: Independent
Financial data (yr. ended 05/31/89): Assets, $1,153,239 (M); expenditures, $35,660, including $30,500 for 5 grants (low: $5,000; average: $5,000-$7,500).
Purpose and activities: Support primarily for community and youth organizations, including leadership development.
Limitations: Giving primarily in Cambridge, MA.
Application information:
Initial approach: Letter
Deadline(s): None
Write: Lawrence Coolidge, Trustee
Trustees: Lawrence Coolidge, Charles K. Cummings III, Walter L. Milne.
Employer Identification Number: 046061028

2889
Charles A. King Trust
c/o Bank of New England, N.A.
28 State St.
Boston 02107 (617) 573-6415

Trust established in 1938 in MA.
Donor(s): Charles A. King.†
Foundation type: Independent
Financial data (yr. ended 12/31/88): Assets, $9,307,507 (M); expenditures, $354,467, including $297,000 for 27 grants (high: $31,000; low: $23,000).
Purpose and activities: To encourage and support medical and surgical research projects carried on by charitable or educational corporations. Grants are awarded soley for postdoctoral research fellowships.
Types of support: Research, fellowships.
Limitations: Giving limited to MA. No grants to individuals.
Publications: Application guidelines.
Application information: Fellowships are paid directly to sponsoring institutions. Application form required.
Initial approach: Telephone
Copies of proposal: 17
Deadline(s): Oct. 15 for projects to start on or after Feb. 1 of following year
Board meeting date(s): Dec.
Final notification: 2 months
Write: John M. Dolan, V.P. Bank of New England, N.A.
Trustees: Edward N. Dane, Richard H. Lovell, Bank of New England, N.A.
Number of staff: 4 full-time professional; 1 full-time support.
Employer Identification Number: 046012742

2890
Norman Knight Charitable Foundation ⌑ ☆
63 Bay State Rd.
Boston 02215-1892 (617) 262-1950

Established in 1959.
Foundation type: Independent
Financial data (yr. ended 12/31/88): Assets, $308,979 (M); expenditures, $241,931, including $241,750 for 146 grants (high: $15,000; low: $100).
Purpose and activities: Support primarily for community development, the performing arts and museums, community funds, hospitals and health associations, higher and other education, and social services and youth organizations; some support also for the Catholic church.
Limitations: Giving primarily in MA, NH, and VT.
Application information:
Initial approach: Letter
Deadline(s): None
Write: Norman Knight, Trustee
Trustees: Norman Knight, N. Scott Knight, Randolph H. Knight.
Employer Identification Number: 046056824

2891
Kraft Foundation ⌑
One Boston Place
Boston 02108 (617) 723-3455

Established in 1973 in MA.
Donor(s): Robert K. Kraft.
Foundation type: Independent
Financial data (yr. ended 11/30/88): Assets, $2,022,225 (M); gifts received, $370,000; expenditures, $332,701, including $328,465 for 79 grants (high: $51,000; low: $50).
Purpose and activities: Support primarily for cultural programs, higher and other education, and Jewish giving.
Limitations: Giving primarily in Boston, MA.
Application information: Application form not required.
Deadline(s): None
Write: Robert K. Kraft, Trustee
Trustees: Richard A. Karelitz, Myra H. Kraft, Robert K. Kraft.
Employer Identification Number: 237326249

2892
The Lacava Foundation, Inc. ⌑
460 Totten Pond Rd.
Waltham 02154 (617) 890-4464

Established in 1983 in MA.
Donor(s): Anthony J. LaCava.
Foundation type: Independent
Financial data (yr. ended 12/31/88): Assets, $1,939,988 (M); expenditures, $176,285, including $176,230 for 7 grants (high: $100,000; low: $30).
Purpose and activities: Support primarily for higher education, including scholarships through local high schools.
Types of support: General purposes, scholarship funds.
Limitations: Giving primarily in MA.
Application information:
Initial approach: Scholarship information available at high schools
Write: Richard B. Ventura, Clerk
Officers: Anthony J. LaCava II, Pres.; Anthony J. LaCava, Treas.; Richard B. Ventura, Clerk.
Employer Identification Number: 042788752

2893
Helen & George Ladd Charitable Corporation ⌑
c/o Notter, McClennen, & Fish
One International Place
Boston 02210-2699 (617) 439-2000

Established in 1984 in MA.
Donor(s): George E. Ladd, Jr. Charitable Trust.
Foundation type: Independent
Financial data (yr. ended 1/31/89): Assets, $1,753,501 (M); gifts received, $545,188; expenditures, $217,478, including $203,507 for 39 grants (high: $34,000; low: $50).
Purpose and activities: Support primarily for colleges and community organizations.
Types of support: General purposes.
Limitations: Giving primarily in ME.
Application information:
Initial approach: Letter
Deadline(s): None
Write: John B. Newhall, Treas.
Officer: John B. Newhall, Treas.
Employer Identification Number: 042767890

2894
Lank Charitable Trust ⌘
Nine Auburn St.
Framingham 01701

Foundation type: Independent
Financial data (yr. ended 12/31/87): Assets, $158,498 (M); expenditures, $100,875, including $100,000 for 1 grant.
Purpose and activities: Support primarily for a research institute.
Application information: Application form not required.
Deadline(s): None
Write: Bertram L. Lank, Trustee
Trustees: Althea B. Lank, Bertram L. Lank.
Employer Identification Number: 222779695

2895
Leclerc Charity Fund ⌘
1045 Oak Hill Rd.
Fitchburg 01420-4819

Established in 1968 in MA.
Donor(s): Raymond Leclerc.
Foundation type: Independent
Financial data (yr. ended 12/31/88): Assets, $1,203,422 (M); gifts received, $25,000; expenditures, $65,927, including $64,991 for 41 grants (high: $15,000; low: $100).
Purpose and activities: Support primarily for Catholic religious organizations and for Catholic churches; support also for schools for the deaf and blind.
Types of support: General purposes.
Application information: Contributes only to pre-selected organizations. Applications not accepted.
Officers: Raymond Leclerc, Mgr.; Francis Wyman, Mgr.
Employer Identification Number: 046183548

2896
Lend A Hand Society ⌘
34 1/2 Beacon St.
Boston 02108

Established in 1870.
Foundation type: Independent
Financial data (yr. ended 12/31/87): Assets, $1,382,675 (M); expenditures, $134,237, including $102,608 for grants.
Purpose and activities: Giving to aid needy individuals, both through agencies and in direct support.
Types of support: Grants to individuals.
Limitations: Giving primarily in Boston, MA.
Application information:
Write: Freda M. Carnes, Exec. Secy.
Officers and Directors: Richard S. Chute, Pres.; Mary Hazard, 1st V.P.; Rhys Williams, 2nd V.P.; Freda M. Carnes, Exec. Secy.; Edward C. Huebner, Treas.; Thomas H. Dahill, Mary Ann Daily, Dana McLean Greeley, Roland D. Grimm, Mrs. George Herrmann, Mrs. James H. Jackson, Henry H. Newell, Harriet Parker, Rev. Carl Seaburg, Thomas B. Williams, Jr.
Employer Identification Number: 042104384

2897
June Rockwell Levy Foundation, Inc. ⌘
One Federal St., 15th Fl.
Boston 02110 (617) 426-4600

Incorporated in 1947 in CT.
Donor(s): Austin T. Levy.†
Foundation type: Independent
Financial data (yr. ended 12/31/88): Assets, $12,881,218 (M); expenditures, $665,115, including $536,300 for 77 grants (high: $50,000; low: $1,000).
Purpose and activities: Grants largely for hospitals, medical research, and higher and secondary education; support also for youth agencies, cultural programs, and the handicapped.
Limitations: Giving primarily in RI. No support for religious purposes.
Application information:
Initial approach: Letter
Deadline(s): None
Write: James W. Noonan, Secy.
Officers: Edward H. Osgood,* Chair. and Pres.; James W. Noonan,* Secy.; Jonathan B. Loring, Treas.
Trustees:* George T. Helm, Winifred H. Thompson.
Employer Identification Number: 046074284

2898
The Lewis Charitable Foundation, Inc. ⌘ ☆
347 Congress St., Suite 6A
Boston 02210 (617) 350-8630

Donor(s): Alan E. Lewis.
Foundation type: Operating
Financial data (yr. ended 09/30/88): Assets, $64 (M); gifts received, $241,800; expenditures, $262,046, including $260,628 for 33 grants (high: $100,000; low: $63).
Purpose and activities: Giving primarily to a health association and a wilderness survival school; support also for Jewish organizations and education.
Application information:
Initial approach: Letter
Deadline(s): None
Write: Alan E. Lewis, Trustee
Trustee: Alan E. Lewis.
Employer Identification Number: 042944450

2899
Linnell Foundation ⌘
75 Second Ave.
Needham 02194

Established in 1977 in MA.
Foundation type: Independent
Financial data (yr. ended 12/31/88): Assets, $7,386,045 (M); expenditures, $257,752, including $213,770 for grants (high: $125,000).
Purpose and activities: Giving for social services and education.
Officer: Arthur G. Carlson, Jr., Exec. Dir.
Trustees: Russell N. Cox, Robert C. Silver.
Employer Identification Number: 042625173

2900
Joseph M. Linsey Foundation ⌘ ☆
189 Wells Ave.
Newton 02159

Established in 1947.
Donor(s): Joseph M. Linsey, Tauton Greyhound Assoc., Burrillville Racing Assoc.
Foundation type: Independent
Financial data (yr. ended 12/31/88): Assets, $399,066 (M); gifts received, $130,000; expenditures, $133,197, including $132,647 for 63 grants (high: $40,650; low: $10).
Purpose and activities: Support for Jewish religious, cultural, and educational organizations and Jewish welfare; support also for a university.
Limitations: No grants to individuals.
Application information: Contributes only to pre-selected organizations. Applications not accepted.
Trustee: Joseph M. Linsey.
Employer Identification Number: 046038331

2901
Fred & Sarah Lipsky Charitable Foundation ⌘
Six Pleasant St., Rm. 510
Malden 02148

Established in 1960 in MA.
Donor(s): Fred Lipsky.†
Foundation type: Independent
Financial data (yr. ended 01/31/89): Assets, $2,122,566 (M); expenditures, $206,422, including $154,400 for 89 grants (high: $25,000; low: $100).
Purpose and activities: Emphasis on Jewish welfare funds and temple support; support also for secondary and other education, including a high school-administered college scholarship program, hospitals, and youth agencies.
Types of support: Scholarship funds.
Limitations: Giving primarily in MA. No grants to individuals.
Application information: Contributes only to pre-selected organizations. Applications not accepted.
Advisory Board: Benjamin L. Cline, Barbara L. Feinberg, Binna L. Golden, Evelyn E. Kosofsky, Jordan E. Patkin.
Trustee: Malden Trust Co.
Employer Identification Number: 046072512

2902
The Arthur D. Little Foundation
25 Acorn Park
Cambridge 02140 (617) 864-5770

Trust established in 1953 in MA.
Donor(s): Arthur D. Little, Inc.
Foundation type: Company-sponsored
Financial data (yr. ended 12/31/88): Assets, $493,342 (M); gifts received, $337,341; expenditures, $315,093, including $308,890 for 92 grants (high: $25,000; low: $100; average: $2,000-$3,000).
Purpose and activities: Grants primarily for education, including higher education, vocational and special projects, and education for minorities and the disadvantaged; scientific and other research; health care; and community charities, with preference to

innovative programs in areas of company operations that benefit the local community.
Types of support: Seed money, research, special projects, conferences and seminars, general purposes, capital campaigns, lectureships, continuing support, fellowships.
Limitations: Giving primarily in areas of company operations, particularly in home-office community, Cambridge, MA. No support for religious, fraternal, or veterans' organizations or national health organizations. No grants to individuals, or for building or endowment funds or matching gifts; no loans.
Publications: Biennial report (including application guidelines), application guidelines.
Application information: Application form not required.
Initial approach: Letter
Copies of proposal: 1
Deadline(s): None
Board meeting date(s): 3-4 times annually
Write: Ann Friedman, Secy.
Officer and Trustees: Ann Friedman, Secy.; Judith C. Harris, Theodore P. Heuchling, D. Reid Weedon, Jr.
Number of staff: 1 part-time professional; 1 part-time support.
Employer Identification Number: 046079132

2903
Mary Friese Lowe Memorial Educational Fund ⌑ ☆
c/o Latanzi, Spaulding & Landreth
P.O. Box 2300, Eight Cardinal Ln.
Orleans 02653

Established in 1980.
Foundation type: Independent
Financial data (yr. ended 06/30/89): Assets, $1,394,600 (M); expenditures, $77,703, including $52,000 for 26 grants to individuals of $2,000 each.
Purpose and activities: Awards educational grants to graduating seniors of local area secondary schools.
Types of support: Student aid.
Limitations: Giving limited to residents of Orleans, MA, and Rye, NY.
Application information: Application form required.
Deadline(s): Apr. 15
Write: Richard J. Barber, Jr., Trustee
Trustee: Richard J. Barber, Jr.
Employer Identification Number: 133040569

2904
Trustee of the Lowell Institute
45 School St.
Boston 02108 (617) 523-1635

Established in 1837.
Donor(s): John Lowell.†
Foundation type: Independent
Financial data (yr. ended 7/31/89): Assets, $18,000 (M); expenditures, $729,108, including $604,903 for 23 grants (high: $175,000; low: $1,000; average: $1,000-$175,000).
Purpose and activities: Grants largely for higher education, cultural programs, religion, and science and technology.
Types of support: Conferences and seminars, lectureships.
Limitations: Giving primarily in MA. No grants to individuals, or for operating budgets, building or endowment funds, scholarships, fellowships, or matching gifts; no loans.
Application information: Contributes only to pre-selected organizations. Applications not accepted.
Write: Mary L. O'Toole, Admin.
Officer and Trustee: John Lowell, Mgr.
Number of staff: 1 part-time support.
Employer Identification Number: 042105771

2905
Stephen C. Luce Charitable Foundation ⌑
c/o Shawmut Central Tax Unit
P.O. Box 2032
Worcester 01613-2032

Established in 1982 in MA.
Foundation type: Independent
Financial data (yr. ended 2/28/87): Assets, $3,061,466 (M); gifts received, $563; expenditures, $183,426, including $152,301 for 12 grants (high: $40,634; low: $2,433).
Purpose and activities: Giving for a library, religion, and a hospital.
Trustee Bank: Shawmut Bank, N.A.
Employer Identification Number: 237105691

2906
William E. Maloney Foundation
P.O. Box 515
Lexington 02173 (617) 862-3400

Established in 1966 in MA.
Donor(s): Margaret A. Maloney,† John W. Maloney.
Foundation type: Independent
Financial data (yr. ended 12/31/88): Assets, $1,212,826 (M); gifts received, $1,000; expenditures, $147,859, including $135,750 for 23 grants (high: $30,000; low: $750) and $12,000 for 3 grants to individuals (high: $5,000; low: $2,000).
Purpose and activities: Giving primarily for youth and hospitals; some support for Christian organizations and scholarship funds and student aid for higher and medical education.
Types of support: Student aid, scholarship funds.
Limitations: Giving primarily in MA.
Application information: Application form available for scholarships. Application form required.
Initial approach: Proposal
Deadline(s): None
Write: John W. Maloney, Trustee
Trustees: David F. Eagle, John W. Maloney, Anthony L. Mancini, Robert F. Sacco.
Number of staff: None.
Employer Identification Number: 046131998

2907
William M. Marcus Family Charitable Trust ⌑ ☆
20 Malia Terr.
Chestnut Hill 02167-1326 (617) 237-6655

Foundation type: Independent
Financial data (yr. ended 03/31/89): Assets, $248,565 (M); expenditures, $147,275, including $140,553 for grants (high: $51,575).
Purpose and activities: Support for cultural programs, Jewish organizations, and general charitable giving.
Types of support: General purposes.
Limitations: Giving primarily in MA.
Application information: Application form not required.
Initial approach: Letter
Deadline(s): None
Write: William M. Marcus, Trustee
Trustee: William M. Marcus.
Employer Identification Number: 046042910

2908
Nancy Lurie Marks Charitable Foundation ⌑
c/o Goulston & Stopps
400 Atlantic Ave.
Boston 02210-2206 (617) 482-1776

Established in 1976 in MA.
Foundation type: Independent
Financial data (yr. ended 10/31/87): Assets, $844,970 (M); gifts received, $335,400; expenditures, $332,076, including $314,649 for 35 grants (high: $60,000; low: $24).
Purpose and activities: Support for educational and cultural institutions, and medical research.
Limitations: No grants to individuals.
Application information:
Initial approach: Letter or proposal
Write: Jay E. Orlin, Trustee
Trustees: Cathy J. Lurie, Jeffrey R. Lurie, Harry L. Marks, Jay E. Orlin.
Employer Identification Number: 042607232

2909
Massachusetts Charitable Mechanic Association
353 Southern Artery
Quincy 02169 (617) 479-1795

Established in 1806.
Foundation type: Independent
Financial data (yr. ended 12/31/88): Assets, $4,495,201 (M); expenditures, $304,129, including $121,212 for 10 grants (high: $21,030; low: $2,000; average: $5,000-$15,000) and $17,350 for 3 grants to individuals (average: $300-$800).
Purpose and activities: Giving for the handicapped, vocational education, and social services.
Types of support: Equipment.
Limitations: Giving primarily in MA.
Application information: Application form not required.
Initial approach: Telephone
Deadline(s): None
Board meeting date(s): Apr. 15
Write: Raymond J. Purdy, Exec. Dir.
Officers: Erling A. Hanson, Jr., Pres.; Almon H. Bridges, Jr., V.P.; Raymond J. Purdy, Exec. Dir.
Trustees: Malcolm S. Burr, David J. Dalzell, Jr., Francis A. Doyle, Charles E. Gale, Wendell R. Hollett, Robert A. Howatt, Francis N. Johnson, William L. Jutila, William F. Lacey, John D. Malcolm, Lester S. McLaughlin, Edmund M. Patey, William P. Stickney.
Number of staff: 1 full-time professional.
Employer Identification Number: 042023566

2910
Massachusetts Maternity & Foundling Hospital Corporation ☆
311 Summer St.
Boston 02210-1779

Established in 1893 in MA.
Foundation type: Independent
Financial data (yr. ended 10/31/89): Assets, $1,109,090 (M); expenditures, $52,594, including $48,000 for 14 grants (high: $6,000; low: $1,000).
Purpose and activities: To provide "care for unwed mothers of limited means and their infant children" through support for hospitals and social services.
Types of support: Endowment funds.
Limitations: Giving limited to the greater Boston, MA, metropolitan area. No grants to individuals.
Application information: Application form not required.
Initial approach: Letter
Deadline(s): July 1
Board meeting date(s): Apr. and Oct.
Write: Donald Forte, Jr., Clerk
Officers and Directors:* John H. Forte,* Pres.; Dexter H. Marsh, Jr.,* V.P.; Warren A. Lewis,* Treas.; Donald Forte, Jr.,* Clerk; Thomas J. Connolly, M.D., Gracelaw S. Durney, Christine R. Robinson, Arthur F. Wilson.
Number of staff: None.
Employer Identification Number: 042628366

2911
Massachusetts Society of the Cincinnati ⌑ ☆
c/o Loring, Wolcott & Coolidge
230 Congress St.
Boston 02110 (617) 523-6531

Established in 1918.
Donor(s): Benjamin Lincoln.†
Foundation type: Independent
Financial data (yr. ended 12/31/88): Assets, $1,293,494 (M); gifts received, $93,380; expenditures, $58,844, including $45,300 for 16 grants (high: $8,500; low: $500).
Purpose and activities: Giving to museums and societies concerned with American history and genealogy; minor assistance also to needy widows of former members of the Massachusetts Society of the Cincinnati.
Types of support: Grants to individuals.
Limitations: Giving primarily in MA.
Application information:
Initial approach: Letter
Deadline(s): None
Write: Samuel H. Wolcott, Jr., Treas.
Officers: William C. Loring, Pres.; Samuel B. Carr, V.P.; Warren M. Little, Secy.; Samuel H. Wolcott, Jr., Treas.
Employer Identification Number: 046046761

2912
Catherine McCarthy Memorial Trust Fund ⌑
P.O. Box 896
Lawrence 01842 (617) 686-6151

Established in 1984 in MA.
Donor(s): John J. McCarthy.†
Foundation type: Independent
Financial data (yr. ended 06/30/89): Assets, $3,360,383 (M); expenditures, $221,022, including $174,105 for 27 grants (high: $34,000; low: $500).
Purpose and activities: Grants for hospitals, higher and secondary education, and social services.
Types of support: Renovation projects, building funds, capital campaigns, equipment, scholarship funds, special projects.
Limitations: Giving primarily in MA and surrounding areas. No support for national health organizations. No grants to individuals, or for annual campaigns or operating funds for standard educational programs.
Application information: Application form not required.
Initial approach: Letter or proposal (maximum of 10 pages)
Copies of proposal: 1
Deadline(s): None
Write: Thomas F. Caffrey, Trustee
Trustees: Thomas F. Caffrey, Shawmut Arlington.
Employer Identification Number: 222549008

2913
Mildred H. McEvoy Foundation ▼
370 Main St.
Worcester 01608 (508) 798-8621

Trust established in 1963 in MA.
Donor(s): Mildred H. McEvoy.†
Foundation type: Independent
Financial data (yr. ended 12/31/87): Assets, $20,194,068 (M); expenditures, $1,100,229, including $1,001,625 for 58 grants (high: $100,000; low: $250; average: $2,500-$35,000).
Purpose and activities: Grants largely for higher education, museums and historic preservation, scientific and medical research, and hospitals.
Limitations: Giving primarily in Worcester, MA, and the Boothbay Harbor, ME, area. No grants to individuals, or for endowment funds.
Application information: Application form not required.
Initial approach: Letter with I.R.S. determination letter
Copies of proposal: 1
Deadline(s): Submit proposal preferably in Apr.; deadline June
Board meeting date(s): Summer and Dec.
Final notification: Dec. 31
Write: Sumner B. Tilton, Jr., Trustee
Trustees: George H. McEvoy, Paul R. Rossley, Sumner B. Tilton, Jr.
Number of staff: None.
Employer Identification Number: 046069958

2914
The David B. Melville Foundation ⌑
30 Colpitts Rd.
Weston 02193

Foundation established in 1980 in MA.
Donor(s): David B. Melville.
Foundation type: Independent
Financial data (yr. ended 06/30/89): Assets, $691,650 (M); expenditures, $142,698, including $141,625 for 8 grants (high: $80,125; low: $500).
Purpose and activities: Giving largely for Christian schools and missionary work.
Limitations: No grants to individuals.
Application information:
Deadline(s): None
Write: E. Christopher Palmer, Trustee
Trustees: Robert C. Hanlon, Aubrey E. Jones, E. Christopher Palmer.
Employer Identification Number: 042680388

2915
Memorial Homes for the Blind ⌑
51 Harvard St.
Worcester 01608 (617) 791-8237

Foundation type: Independent
Financial data (yr. ended 3/31/88): Assets, $2,635,051 (M); gifts received, $8,439; expenditures, $133,869.
Purpose and activities: Support primarily for the care of the visually handicapped.
Limitations: Giving primarily in the Worcester, MA, area.
Application information:
Initial approach: Letter or proposal
Copies of proposal: 1
Deadline(s): None
Write: Alice Taylor, Pres.
Officers and Directors: Alice Taylor, Pres.; Gilbert S. Davis, V.P.; Stephanie Burnett, Treas.; Steve Booth, Elizabeth C. Congdon, Sharon Davis, Carolyn Dik, and 10 other directors.
Employer Identification Number: 041611615

2916
The John Merck Fund ▼
11 Beacon St., Suite 600
Boston 02108 (617) 723-2932

Established in 1970 in NY as a trust.
Donor(s): Serena S. Merck.†
Foundation type: Independent
Financial data (yr. ended 12/31/88): Assets, $49,679,732 (M); expenditures, $2,821,995, including $2,505,261 for 45 grants (high: $250,000; low: $5,000; average: $25,000-$50,000).
Purpose and activities: Grants are made in the following areas: to medical teaching hospitals for research on developmental disabilities in children; to preserve environmental quality in rural New England and globally; to promote alternative defense as a disarmament strategy; to support population control policy and planning initiatives; and to advance international human rights.
Types of support: Research, publications, special projects, operating budgets, fellowships, conferences and seminars.
Limitations: No grants to individuals.
Publications: Grants list, informational brochure.
Application information: Grants usually made at the initiation of the fund. Applications not accepted.
Board meeting date(s): Monthly
Write: Francis W. Hatch, Chair.
Officers and Trustees:* Francis W. Hatch,* Chair.; Richard A. Kimball, Jr.,* Secy.; Huyler

C. Held,* Treas.; Judith M. Buechner, Serena M. Hatch, Arnold Hiatt, Robert M. Pennoyer.
Number of staff: 1 full-time professional; 1 part-time support.
Employer Identification Number: 237082558

2917
The E. F. Merkert Foundation ⌑
c/o Merkert Enterprises
500 Turnpike St.
Canton 02021 (617) 828-4800

Established in 1960.
Donor(s): Merkert Enterprises, Inc., Eugene F. Merkert.
Foundation type: Independent
Financial data (yr. ended 12/31/88): Assets, $599,044 (M); gifts received, $326,000; expenditures, $321,875, including $321,650 for 50 grants (high: $50,000; low: $200).
Purpose and activities: Giving primarily for higher education, social services, and medical organizations, including research and hospitals.
Types of support: Endowment funds, research.
Limitations: Giving primarily in MA.
Application information:
Initial approach: Letter
Deadline(s): None
Write: Eugene F. Merkert, Trustee
Trustee: Eugene F. Merkert.
Employer Identification Number: 046111832

2918
Merlin Foundation ⌑
c/o Loring, Wolcott & Coolidge Office
230 Congress St.
Boston 02110 (617) 523-6531

Foundation type: Independent
Financial data (yr. ended 12/31/88): Assets, $1,101,638 (M); expenditures, $53,354, including $47,500 for 3 grants (high: $35,000; low: $2,500).
Purpose and activities: Support primarily for social services.
Application information:
Write: Peter B. Loring, Trustee
Trustees: Caleb Loring, Jr., Caleb Loring III, Peter B. Loring.
Employer Identification Number: 222765555

2919
Arthur G. B. Metcalf Foundation ⌑
45 Arlington St.
Winchester 01890

Established in 1960 in MA.
Donor(s): Arthur G.B. Metcalf.
Foundation type: Independent
Financial data (yr. ended 12/31/88): Assets, $1,237,576 (M); gifts received, $15,855; expenditures, $16,000, including $14,870 for 14 grants (high: $5,000; low: $20).
Purpose and activities: Grants largely for a national strategic defense institute and the U.S. Air Force; support also for local higher education, church support, and cultural and other charitable organizations.
Limitations: No grants to individuals.
Application information: Contributes only to pre-selected organizations. Applications not accepted.
Write: Richard R. Glendon
Trustee: Arthur G.B. Metcalf.
Employer Identification Number: 046130186

2920
Microwave Associates Charitable Foundation ⌑ ☆
c/o M/A-COM, Inc.
Seven New England Executive Park
Burlington 01803-5003 (617) 272-9600

Established in 1967.
Donor(s): M/A-COM, Inc.
Foundation type: Company-sponsored
Financial data (yr. ended 9/30/88): Assets, $320,944 (M); gifts received, $75,000; expenditures, $109,142, including $108,750 for grants (high: $21,750; low: $100).
Purpose and activities: Giving primarily for higher education, including scholarships for employees' children, and the United Way; support also for youth, culture, health, and hospitals.
Types of support: Scholarship funds, student aid.
Limitations: Giving primarily in MA.
Application information:
Initial approach: Letter
Deadline(s): Mar. 1 for scholarships; no set deadline for grants
Write: Vessario Chigas, Trustee
Officer: Kevin Kietnen, Mgr.
Trustees: Vessario Chigas, Robert Galudel, Howard Hall.
Employer Identification Number: 046169568

2921
Middlecott Foundation
50 Congress St., Suite 800
Boston 02109

Established in 1967 in MA.
Donor(s): Members of the Saltonstall family.
Foundation type: Independent
Financial data (yr. ended 12/31/87): Assets, $610,973 (M); gifts received, $255,243; expenditures, $261,048, including $255,114 for 257 grants (high: $60,000; low: $15; average: $100-$1,000).
Purpose and activities: Support primarily for education, social services, health associations and hospitals, cultural programs, and child and youth agencies.
Application information: Applications not accepted.
Write: William L. Saltonstall, Trustee
Trustees: Robert A. Lawrence, George Lewis, William L. Saltonstall.
Number of staff: 1 part-time support.
Employer Identification Number: 046155699

2922
George H. & Jane A. Mifflin Memorial Fund ☆
c/o Loring, Wolcott & Coolidge
230 Congress St.
Boston 02110 (617) 523-6531

Foundation type: Independent
Financial data (yr. ended 9/30/89): Assets, $6,752,610 (M); expenditures, $282,947, including $264,000 for 19 grants (high: $35,000; low: $1,000).
Purpose and activities: Giving primarily for education, conservation, and welfare, including legal services; support also for museums.
Types of support: Scholarship funds.
Limitations: Giving primarily in MA. No grants to individuals.
Application information:
Deadline(s): None
Write: Lawrence Coolidge, Trustee
Trustees: John C. Brooks, Lawrence Coolidge, Peter B. Loring.
Employer Identification Number: 046384983

2923
The Millipore Foundation ⌑
80 Ashby Rd.
Bedford 01730-2271 (617) 275-9200

Established in 1985 in MA.
Donor(s): Millipore Corp.
Foundation type: Company-sponsored
Financial data (yr. ended 9/30/88): Assets, $406,742 (M); gifts received, $585,000; expenditures, $508,777, including $395,875 for 95 grants (high: $100,000; low: $100) and $105,645 for 821 employee matching gifts.
Purpose and activities: Giving primarily through grants and employee matching gifts program to organizations involved in culture, health, education, educational research, biochemistry research, and social services.
Types of support: Research, general purposes, employee matching gifts.
Limitations: No support for religious programs.
Publications: Annual report, informational brochure (including application guidelines).
Application information: Application form required.
Initial approach: Letter
Copies of proposal: 1
Deadline(s): None
Board meeting date(s): Quarterly
Write: Charleen L. Johnson, Exec. Dir.
Officers: Geoffrey Nunes,* Chair.; Charleen L. Johnson, Exec. Dir.
Trustees:* John A. Gilmartin, Wayne J. Kennedy.
Number of staff: None.
Employer Identification Number: 222583952

2924
John Mirak Foundation ⌑ ☆
1125 Massachusetts Ave.
Arlington 02174

Established in 1972.
Donor(s): John Mirak.
Foundation type: Independent
Financial data (yr. ended 12/31/88): Assets, $541,640 (M); gifts received, $662,362; expenditures, $202,106, including $202,050 for grants (high: $156,000).
Purpose and activities: Support primarily for an Armenian cultural foundation and other Armenian organizations.
Limitations: No grants to individuals.

Application information: Contributes only to pre-selected organizations. Applications not accepted.
Officer: John Mirak, Pres.
Employer Identification Number: 237161662

2925
Morgan-Worcester, Inc. ⌑
15 Belmont St.
Worcester 01605 (508) 755-6111

Incorporated in 1953 in MA.
Donor(s): Morgan Construction Co.
Foundation type: Company-sponsored
Financial data (yr. ended 09/30/89): Assets, $782,452 (M); expenditures, $132,340, including $119,766 for 94 grants (high: $45,000; low: $25).
Purpose and activities: Giving with emphasis on civic affairs, cultural programs, education, health, and community funds.
Types of support: Employee matching gifts, operating budgets, continuing support, annual campaigns, seed money, emergency funds, building funds, equipment, land acquisition.
Limitations: Giving primarily in the greater Worcester, MA, area. No support for religious purposes. No grants to individuals, or for endowment funds, special projects, research, publications, conferences, scholarships, or fellowships; no loans.
Application information: Application form not required.
Initial approach: Letter
Copies of proposal: 1
Deadline(s): None
Board meeting date(s): Quarterly
Final notification: Only in the case of acceptance
Write: Peter S. Morgan, Pres.
Officers and Directors:* Peter S. Morgan,* Pres. and Treas.; Gail M. Wilcox, Clerk; Daniel M. Morgan, Paul B. Morgan, Jr., Paul S. Morgan, Philip R. Morgan, Gavin D. Robertson.
Number of staff: 1 part-time professional.
Employer Identification Number: 046111693

2926
Morse Family Foundation ⌑ ☆
240 Lee St.
Brookline 02146

Established in 1966.
Donor(s): Ruth Morse.†
Foundation type: Independent
Financial data (yr. ended 12/31/88): Assets, $3,101,436 (M); gifts received, $2,040,000; expenditures, $43,606, including $34,156 for 2 grants (high: $19,156; low: $15,000).
Purpose and activities: Giving primarily for the performing arts and museums.
Application information: Applications not accepted.
Trustees: Lester S. Morse, Richard P. Morse.
Employer Identification Number: 046142794

2927
Alfred L. & Annette S. Morse Foundation ⌑
1010 Memorial Dr.
Cambridge 02138

Established in 1962 in MA.
Donor(s): Alfred L. Morse.†
Foundation type: Independent
Financial data (yr. ended 12/31/87): Assets, $1,675,083 (M); expenditures, $59,440, including $57,250 for 11 grants (high: $16,500; low: $250).
Purpose and activities: Support primarily for Jewish welfare, hospitals, and education.
Application information: Contributes only to pre-selected organizations. Applications not accepted.
Employer Identification Number: 046142795

2928
Mugar Foundation ⌑ ☆
Two Burlington Woods Dr.
Burlington 01803-4538 (617) 229-2111

Established in 1951.
Donor(s): David G. Mugar, Carolyn G. Mugar.
Foundation type: Independent
Financial data (yr. ended 12/31/88): Assets, $309,876 (M); gifts received, $30,000; expenditures, $116,327, including $114,870 for 20 grants (high: $55,000; low: $20).
Purpose and activities: Giving primarily for Armenian organizations, including cultural and educational charities; support also for youth.
Limitations: Giving primarily in MA.
Application information: Application form not required.
Deadline(s): None
Write: Carolyn G. Mugar, Trustee
Officer and Trustees: David G. Mugar, Exec. Dir.; Carolyn G. Mugar, John M. Mugar.
Employer Identification Number: 046006717

2929
James Z. Naurison Scholarship Fund
c/o Bank of New England-West, Trust Dept.
P.O. Box 9006
Springfield 01102-9006 (413) 787-8745

Trust established in 1973 in MA.
Donor(s): James Z. Naurison.†
Foundation type: Independent
Financial data (yr. ended 07/31/89): Assets, $6,061,928 (M); expenditures, $408,228, including $342,000 for 371 grants to individuals (high: $2,000; low: $500).
Purpose and activities: Scholarship awards to local students only.
Types of support: Student aid.
Limitations: Giving limited to residents of Hampden, Hampshire, Franklin, and Berkshire counties, MA; and Enfield and Suffield, CT.
Publications: Application guidelines.
Application information: Application form required.
Initial approach: Letter
Deadline(s): Submit application between Dec. and Apr.; deadline Apr. 15
Board meeting date(s): Feb. and June
Final notification: July 1
Write: Thea E. Katsounakis, Assoc. Trust Admin.
Trustee: Bank of New England-West.
Number of staff: None.
Employer Identification Number: 046329627

2930
NEBS Foundation, Inc.
New England Business Service, Inc.
500 Main St.
Groton 01471 (508) 448-6111

Established in 1983 in MA.
Donor(s): New England Business Service, Inc.
Foundation type: Company-sponsored
Financial data (yr. ended 08/31/89): Assets, $107,337 (M); gifts received, $155,000; expenditures, $252,800, including $240,450 for 21 grants (high: $25,000; low: $5,000; average: $5,000-$15,000).
Purpose and activities: Support primarily for education, culture, hospitals and health services, social services, the environment, and civic affairs.
Types of support: Annual campaigns, capital campaigns, equipment, scholarship funds, special projects.
Limitations: Giving primarily in areas where company facilities are located, in AZ, MA, MO, NH, and WI.
Application information: Application form not required.
Copies of proposal: 1
Deadline(s): Mar. 31 and Sept. 30
Board meeting date(s): Apr. and Oct.
Write: Paul F. Robinson, Secy.
Officers and Directors: Jay R. Rhoads, Jr., Pres.; Paul F. Robinson, Secy.; Benjamin H. Lacy, Treas.; Peter A. Brooke.
Number of staff: 1 part-time professional.
Employer Identification Number: 042772172

2931
New England Biolabs Foundation ☆
32 Tozer Rd.
Beverly 01915 (508) 927-2404

Established in 1982 in MA.
Donor(s): Donald G. Comb.
Foundation type: Independent
Financial data (yr. ended 11/30/89): Assets, $2,930,000 (M); expenditures, $221,000, including $134,000 for 29 grants (high: $25,000; low: $50; average: $5,000-$7,000) and $20,000 for 2 foundation-administered programs.
Purpose and activities: Giving primarily for scientific research and programs, education, and environmental, health, and social projects.
Types of support: Research, grants to individuals, matching funds, seed money, special projects.
Limitations: Giving primarily in New England, especially MA, and less-developed countries. No support for religious activities. No grants for capital endowment or building funds, operating costs, fellowships, or projects normally funded by major agencies.
Publications: Informational brochure (including application guidelines).
Application information: Application form not required.
Initial approach: Letter
Deadline(s): Mar. 1, Sept. 1, and Dec. 1
Board meeting date(s): Jan., Apr., and Oct.
Final notification: 4 to 6 weeks after meeting
Write: Martine Kellett, Exec. Dir.
Officer: Martine Kellett, Exec. Dir.

Trustees: Donald G. Comb, Douglas I. Foy, Henry P. Paulus.
Number of staff: 1 full-time professional; 1 part-time support.
Employer Identification Number: 042776213

2932
Newburyport Howard Benevolent Society ⌑ ☆
P.O. Box 9
Newburyport 01950

Foundation type: Independent
Financial data (yr. ended 9/30/89): Assets, $1,342,754 (M); expenditures, $40,444, including $15,800 for 12 grants (high: $2,500; low: $50) and $14,573 for grants to individuals.
Purpose and activities: Giving for welfare and social service organizations and provides welfare assistance to low-income families and individuals.
Types of support: Grants to individuals.
Limitations: Giving limited to Newburyport, MA.
Officers: Robert S. Walters, Pres.; John S. Gove, Secy.; Herb Bean, Treas.
Directors: Rowland Currier, Ralph Johnson, Paul Melitere.
Employer Identification Number: 046041304

2933
Nichols Trust ⌑ ☆
50 Congress St.
Boston 02109
Application address: 16 Pepperell Rd., Hollis, NH 03049

Established in 1957.
Donor(s): Ellen B. Nichols.
Foundation type: Independent
Financial data (yr. ended 4/30/88): Assets, $1,327,665 (M); gifts received, $133,600; expenditures, $94,362, including $88,500 for 46 grants (high: $11,000; low: $100).
Purpose and activities: Giving primarily for higher, secondary, and other education.
Limitations: Giving primarily in Boston, MA, and Hollis, NH. No grants to individuals.
Application information: Application form not required.
Initial approach: Letter
Deadline(s): None
Write: Hollis P. Nichols, Trustee
Trustees: Ernest H. Monrad, Ellen B. Nichols, Frances F. Nichols, Hollis P. Nichols.
Employer Identification Number: 046026880

2934
Deborah Munroe Noonan Memorial Fund u/w Frank Noonan
c/o Bank of New England, N.A.
28 State St.
Boston 02107 (617) 573-6415

Trust established in 1947 in MA.
Donor(s): Frank M. Noonan.†
Foundation type: Independent
Financial data (yr. ended 09/30/89): Assets, $4,549,122 (M); expenditures, $227,038, including $194,923 for 4 grants (high: $65,053; low: $9,689; average: $25,000-$40,000).
Purpose and activities: Grants soley for medical services to handicapped children provided at local hospitals.
Types of support: Special projects.
Limitations: Giving limited to the greater Boston, MA, area. No grants to individuals, or for scholarships or fellowships; no loans.
Publications: Application guidelines.
Application information: Call for deadline information. Application form required.
Initial approach: Telephone
Copies of proposal: 12
Board meeting date(s): Distribution committee meets as required
Final notification: Following annual meeting
Write: John M. Dolan, V.P., Bank of New England, N.A.
Trustee: Bank of New England, N.A.
Number of staff: 4 full-time professional; 1 full-time support.
Employer Identification Number: 046025957

2935
Norton Company Foundation ▼
120 Front St.
Worcester 01608-1446 (508) 795-5334

Trust established in 1953 in MA; incorporated in 1975.
Donor(s): Norton Co.
Foundation type: Company-sponsored
Financial data (yr. ended 12/31/88): Assets, $107,453 (M); gifts received, $1,060,000; expenditures, $1,084,493, including $870,015 for 423 grants (high: $220,000; low: $80; average: $1,000-$10,000) and $214,478 for 1,416 employee matching gifts.
Purpose and activities: Giving primarily for education, social service and youth agencies, and cultural programs.
Types of support: Program-related investments, operating budgets, annual campaigns, seed money, emergency funds, building funds, matching funds, employee matching gifts, continuing support, capital campaigns, general purposes, renovation projects, special projects.
Limitations: Giving primarily in Gainesville, GA; Worcester and Northboro, MA; Milford and Littleton, NH; Wayne, NJ; Akron and Stowe, OH; and Brownsville and Stephenville, TX. Generally no support for national organizations, including national health agencies, religious, veterans', or fraternal organizations, or hospitals for operating support. No grants to individuals, or for endowment funds, scholarships, or fellowships; no loans.
Publications: Application guidelines.
Application information: Application form required.
Initial approach: Telephone or proposal
Copies of proposal: 1
Deadline(s): None
Board meeting date(s): Mar., June, Sept., and Dec.
Final notification: Within 3 weeks
Write: Francis J. Doherty, Jr., Secy. and Clerk
Officers: John M. Nelson,* Pres.; Francis J. Doherty, Jr., Secy. and Clerk; Gilbert A. Fuller, Treas.
Directors:* Thomas J. Hourihan, Bernard F. Meyer.
Number of staff: 1 part-time professional; 1 part-time support.
Employer Identification Number: 237423043

2936
Norwottock Charitable Trust ⌑ ☆
15 Middle St.
Amherst 01002-3009

Established in 1986 in MA.
Donor(s): John L. Simmons, Adele Smith Simmons.
Foundation type: Independent
Financial data (yr. ended 12/31/87): Assets, $145,726 (M); gifts received, $131,657; expenditures, $113,339, including $112,098 for 44 grants (high: $47,688; low: $25).
Purpose and activities: Support primarily for higher education, international affairs and peace associations, and environmental organizations.
Limitations: Giving primarily in MA.
Trustees: Adele Smith Simmons, John L. Simmons.
Employer Identification Number: 046561597

2937
James W. O'Brien Foundation
807 Turnpike St.
North Andover 01845 (617) 686-6112

Established in 1981 in MA.
Foundation type: Independent
Financial data (yr. ended 09/30/88): Assets, $2,765,413 (M); expenditures, $244,548, including $209,000 for 4 grants (high: $140,000; low: $8,000).
Purpose and activities: Giving for scholarship funds of secondary schools; support also for a college.
Types of support: Scholarship funds.
Limitations: Giving primarily in MA. No grants to individuals.
Application information: Scholarships to individuals chosen by school administrators; application forms required by schools. Applications not accepted.
Deadline(s): None
Write: James J. McInnis, Trustee
Trustees: John E. Deegan, Sr. Marie E. Gurry, James J. McInnis, Cecille A. Pineault, Alvin R. Tagney.
Employer Identification Number: 042691136

2938
Olivetti Foundation, Inc.
One Beacon St., Rm. 2000
Boston 02108 (617) 573-0124

Incorporated in 1957 in NY.
Donor(s): Dino Olivetti.†
Foundation type: Independent
Financial data (yr. ended 12/31/88): Assets, $1,338,874 (M); expenditures, $47,334, including $21,000 for 4 grants (high: $12,000; low: $2,000; average: $2,000-$12,000).
Purpose and activities: Emphasis on organizations assisting persons of Italian nationality or Italian-related projects, especially at colleges and universities.

Types of support: Building funds, capital campaigns, fellowships, scholarship funds.
Publications: 990-PF.
Application information: Application form not required.
Initial approach: Letter
Copies of proposal: 1
Deadline(s): Oct. 1
Board meeting date(s): Spring and fall
Final notification: Following board meeting
Write: Casimir de Rham, Jr., Secy.-Treas.
Officers and Directors: Rosamond C. Olivetti, Pres.; Casimir de Rham, Jr., Secy.-Treas.; Alfred C. Olivetti, Philip T. Olivetti.
Number of staff: None.
Employer Identification Number: 046043143

2939
Bessie Pappas Charitable Foundation, Inc.
P.O. Box 318
Belmont 02178 (617) 862-2851

Established in 1984 in MA as successor to the Pappas Family Foundation.
Donor(s): Thomas Anthony Pappas.
Foundation type: Independent
Financial data (yr. ended 12/31/88): Assets, $2,857,177 (M); expenditures, $176,600, including $125,074 for 35 grants (high: $10,000; low: $1,000).
Purpose and activities: Support for the arts, health, education, family and social services, and religious welfare organizations.
Limitations: Giving primarily in MA. No grants to individuals.
Publications: Application guidelines.
Application information:
Deadline(s): Oct. 1
Final notification: Dec. 31
Write: Betsy Pappas, Dir. of Development
Officer and Directors: Charles A. Pappas, Pres. and Treas.; Helen K. Pappas, V.P.; Betsy Z. Pappas, Clerk and Dir. of Development; Sophia Pappas.
Number of staff: 2 full-time professional.
Employer Identification Number: 222540702

2940
Thomas Anthony Pappas Charitable Foundation, Inc.
P.O. Box 463
Belmont 02178 (617) 862-2802

Incorporated in 1975 in MA.
Donor(s): Thomas Anthony Pappas.†
Foundation type: Independent
Financial data (yr. ended 12/31/88): Assets, $15,638,813 (M); expenditures, $977,878, including $744,684 for 57 grants (high: $100,000; low: $1,000; average: $1,000-$100,000).
Purpose and activities: Emphasis on higher education, hospitals, cultural programs, Greek Orthodox church support, religious associations, and youth and social service agencies.
Types of support: Annual campaigns, building funds, endowment funds, research, professorships, scholarship funds, fellowships, continuing support, building funds.
Limitations: Giving primarily in MA. No grants to individuals.
Publications: Program policy statement, application guidelines.
Application information: Application form not required.
Initial approach: Letter or proposal
Deadline(s): Submit proposal preferably in Mar. or Sept.; deadline Sept. 30
Board meeting date(s): Mar., June, Sept., and Dec., and as required
Final notification: Dec. 31
Officers and Directors:* Charles A. Pappas,* Pres. and Treas.; Helen K. Pappas,* Exec. V.P.; Betsy Z. Pappas,* V.P. and Clerk; Sophia Pappas.
Number of staff: 4
Employer Identification Number: 510153284

2941
John C. Pappas Family Charitable Foundation, Inc. ¤
450 Summer St.
Boston 02210

Established in 1984 in MA.
Foundation type: Independent
Financial data (yr. ended 6/30/87): Assets, $375 (M); gifts received, $147,500; expenditures, $150,464, including $147,904 for 52 grants (high: $50,000; low: $50).
Purpose and activities: Support primarily for higher education, health associations, social services, and churches.
Application information: Contributes only to pre-selected organizations.
Officers and Directors: Katherine A. Pappas, Pres.; James A. Pappas, Treas.; Michael S. Sophocles, Clerk; Georgia A. Pappas, T. Peter Pappas.
Employer Identification Number: 042773914

2942
Parker Charitable Foundation ¤ ☆
217 Essex St.
Salem 01970-3728

Established in 1946.
Donor(s): Sally P. Barton.
Foundation type: Independent
Financial data (yr. ended 12/31/88): Assets, $922,659 (M); gifts received, $185,962; expenditures, $608,129, including $600,250 for 26 grants (high: $201,000; low: $350).
Purpose and activities: Giving primarily for hospitals and higher and secondary education; support also for churches and cultural programs.
Limitations: Giving primarily in MA.
Application information:
Initial approach: Letter
Deadline(s): None
Write: Trustees
Trustees: Michael Davenport, Harold G. Macomber, Robert Welch.
Employer Identification Number: 046048065

2943
The Theodore Edson Parker Foundation
c/o Grants Management Associates, Inc.
230 Congress St., 3rd Fl.
Boston 02110 (617) 426-7172

Incorporated in 1944 in MA.
Donor(s): Theodore Edson Parker.†
Foundation type: Independent
Financial data (yr. ended 12/31/89): Assets, $10,000,000 (M); expenditures, $467,000, including $426,200 for 28 grants (high: $60,000; low: $3,000; average: $3,000-$60,000).
Purpose and activities: Giving largely in Lowell, MA, for social services, arts, housing, community development, and the urban environment; with a particular interest in aiding underserved populations, particularly minorities; in Boston, MA, giving for social services and the urban environment.
Types of support: Seed money, building funds, equipment, special projects, renovation projects.
Limitations: Giving limited to the greater Boston and Lowell, MA, area. No grants to individuals, or for operating budgets, continuing support, annual campaigns, emergency funds, deficit financing, matching gifts, scholarships, or fellowships; no loans.
Publications: Program policy statement, application guidelines, grants list.
Application information: Application form not required.
Initial approach: Telephone, proposal, or letter
Copies of proposal: 1
Deadline(s): None
Board meeting date(s): Spring and fall
Final notification: 4 to 5 months
Write: Laura Henze, Admin.
Officers and Trustees:* Newell Flather,* Pres.; Andrew C. Bailey,* Secy.-Treas.; Karen H. Carpenter, Edward L. Emerson, Thomas E. Leggat.
Number of staff: 1 part-time professional; 1 part-time support.
Employer Identification Number: 046036092

2944
Amelia Peabody Charitable Fund ▼
201 Devonshire St.
Boston 02109 (617) 451-6178

Established in 1974.
Donor(s): Amelia Peabody,† Eaton Foundation.
Foundation type: Independent
Financial data (yr. ended 12/31/88): Assets, $87,000,000 (M); expenditures, $5,024,356, including $4,428,000 for 105 grants (high: $1,000,000; low: $500).
Purpose and activities: Grants primarily for higher education; the environment; hospitals, medical research, and health and family services; and culture, including museums and historic preservation.
Types of support: Building funds, endowment funds, capital campaigns, renovation projects, equipment, research.
Limitations: Giving primarily in New England. No support for tax-supported organizations or religious groups. No grants to individuals.
Publications: Application guidelines.
Application information: Application form not required.
Initial approach: Letter
Copies of proposal: 1
Deadline(s): None
Board meeting date(s): Quarterly
Write: Harry F. Rice, Trustee
Trustees: Richard A. Leahy, Harry F. Rice, Patricia E. Rice.
Number of staff: 1 part-time professional.
Employer Identification Number: 237364949

2945
The Peabody Foundation, Inc. ¤
c/o Sherburne, Powers, and Needham
One Beacon St.
Boston 02108

Established in 1894 in MA.
Foundation type: Independent
Financial data (yr. ended 9/30/87): Assets, $9,378,635 (M); gifts received, $28,214; expenditures, $571,558, including $488,493 for 13 grants (high: $126,109; low: $2,000).
Purpose and activities: Grants primarily for medical research relating to handicapped children in the Boston area.
Limitations: Giving primarily in the Boston, MA, area.
Application information:
Deadline(s): None
Write: William V. Tripp III
Officers and Trustees: William V. Tripp III, Pres.; Norman C. Nicholson, Jr., V.P. and Treas.; Harry C. Barr, Dorothy A. Brown, Mrs. Paul F. Burdon, J. Charles Carlson, Edwin F. Cave, Mrs. John L. Damon, Paul W. Hagenburger, M.D., Mrs. Francis B. Haydock, John H. Hewitt, Sally D. Hurlbut, Andrew G. Jessiman, M.D., Mrs. Stephen D. Paine, Mrs. W. Nicholas Thorndike.
Employer Identification Number: 042104767

2946
Amelia Peabody Foundation ▼
c/o Hale and Dore
60 State St.
Boston 02109 (617) 742-9100

Trust established in 1942 in MA; absorbed a share of the assets of The Eaton Foundation, MA, in l985.
Donor(s): Amelia Peabody.†
Foundation type: Independent
Financial data (yr. ended 12/31/88): Assets, $84,467,058 (M); expenditures, $5,581,002, including $5,075,843 for 64 grants (high: $1,367,000; low: $4,000; average: $10,000-$150,000).
Purpose and activities: To assist local charitable and educational organizations, with emphasis on education, hospitals, youth agencies, cultural programs, and conservation.
Limitations: Giving limited to MA. No grants to individuals, or for endowment funds, scholarships, or fellowships; no loans.
Application information:
Initial approach: Letter
Copies of proposal: 1
Deadline(s): None
Board meeting date(s): Quarterly
Final notification: As required
Write: James D. St. Clair, Trustee
Trustees: G. Dana Bill, James D. St. Clair, Margaret N. St. Clair, Bayard D. Waring, Lloyd B. Waring.
Number of staff: 3
Employer Identification Number: 046036558

2947
Joseph Pellegrino Family Foundation ¤
50 Milk St., Suite 1500
Andover 02109

Foundation type: Independent
Financial data (yr. ended 12/31/88): Assets, $1,492,608 (M); expenditures, $156,538, including $114,390 for 22 grants (high: $25,000; low: $100).
Purpose and activities: Support primarily for secondary education; support also for hospitals and health organizations.
Application information: Contributes only to pre-selected organizations. Applications not accepted.
Trustees: Joseph Pellegrino, Joseph P. Pellegrino, Lena Pellegrino.
Employer Identification Number: 046112616

2948
Pellegrino-Realmuto Charitable Foundation, Inc. ¤
50 Milk St., Suite 1500
Boston 02109

Established in 1960 in MA.
Foundation type: Independent
Financial data (yr. ended 12/31/88): Assets, $1,971,865 (M); expenditures, $157,872, including $99,825 for 30 grants (high: $30,000; low: $50).
Purpose and activities: Support for hospitals and medical centers, churches, and higher education.
Application information: Contributes only to pre-selected organizations. Applications not accepted.
Officers and Directors:* Mae Realmuto,* Pres.; Joseph P. Pellegrino,* Secy.; Joseph Pellegrino,* Treas.
Employer Identification Number: 046112614

2949
Perini Memorial Foundation, Inc. ¤
73 Mount Wayte Ave.
Framingham 01701 (617) 875-6171
Scholarship application address: Selection Comm., P.O. Box 31, Framingham, MA 01701

Incorporated in 1953 in MA.
Foundation type: Company-sponsored
Financial data (yr. ended 12/31/88): Assets, $5,648,855 (M); gifts received, $195,012; expenditures, $357,158, including $316,947 for 116 grants (high: $32,500; low: $70) and $32,500 for 9 grants to individuals (high: $4,000; low: $2,000).
Purpose and activities: Emphasis on higher education, Roman Catholic church support and religious associations, and hospitals; also, scholarships granted to children of employees of Perini Corp. and its subsidiaries.
Types of support: Employee-related scholarships.
Limitations: Giving primarily in MA. No grants to individuals (except exmployee-related scholarships), or for research, scholarships, fellowships, or matching gifts; no loans.
Application information:
Initial approach: Letter
Copies of proposal: 1
Write: Bart W. Perini, Treas.
Officers: David B. Perini, Pres.; Charles B. Perini, V.P.; Bart W. Perini, Treas.
Employer Identification Number: 046118587

2950
Joseph Perini Memorial Foundation
73 Mt. Wayte Ave.
Framingham 01701 (508) 875-6171
Application address: P.O. Box 31, Framingham, MA 01701

Incorporated in 1953 in MA.
Donor(s): Joseph R. Perini.†
Foundation type: Independent
Financial data (yr. ended 12/31/88): Assets, $10,262,758 (M); gifts received, $100,000; expenditures, $435,422, including $377,920 for 80 grants (high: $27,905; low: $50; average: $1,000-$4,000) and $32,500 for 12 grants to individuals (high: $4,000; low: $1,000).
Purpose and activities: Giving for education, including scholarships to children of Perini Corp. employees, social services, including family and youth agencies, church support and religious associations; support also for hospices and hospitals.
Types of support: Employee-related scholarships, capital campaigns, endowment funds, matching funds.
Limitations: Giving primarily in MA. No grants to individuals (except for employee-related scholarships), or for research, scholarships, fellowships, or operating budgets; no loans.
Application information: Scholarships available only to sons and daughters of employees of Perini Corp. or its subsidiaries. Application form not required.
Initial approach: Letter
Copies of proposal: 1
Deadline(s): Nov.
Board meeting date(s): Dec.
Write: Joseph R. Perini, Secy.
Officers: Thomas B. Perini, Pres.; Harold Ottobrini, V.P.; Joseph R. Perini, Secy.-Treas.
Number of staff: None.
Employer Identification Number: 046139986

2951
The Perpetual Benevolent Fund
c/o BayBank Middlesex
300 Washington St.
Newton 02158 (617) 894-6500

Charitable trust established in 1932 in MA; activated in 1957.
Donor(s): Nathan P. Cutler,† William H. Cutler,† and others.
Foundation type: Independent
Financial data (yr. ended 08/31/89): Assets, $1,824,236 (M); expenditures, $140,000, including $12,000 for 5 grants (high: $5,000; low: $1,000) and $88,000 for 280 grants to individuals (high: $1,200; low: $74; average: $400-$600).
Purpose and activities: To assist local needy individuals. Individuals are referred by health, welfare, hospitals, or other organizations; support also for child welfare, social services, and the homeless and disadvantaged.
Types of support: Grants to individuals, continuing support.
Limitations: Giving limited to Newton, Waltham, and adjacent communities in MA. No grants for scholarships.
Publications: Application guidelines.
Application information: Application form required.

Initial approach: Telephone or proposal
Copies of proposal: 1
Deadline(s): Nov.-Dec.
Board meeting date(s): Oct.
Final notification: 1 week
Write: Marjorie M. Kelley, Secy.
Officers: Norman E. MacNeil, Chair.; Marjorie M. Kelley, Secy.
Fund Committee: F. Gorham Brigham, Jr., Mrs. Champe A. Fisher, Mrs. Maurice E. Keenan, Giles E. Mosher, Jr., James J. Sidd, M.D., Barry M. Spero.
Trustee: BayBank Middlesex.
Number of staff: 1 full-time professional.
Employer Identification Number: 237011723

2952
Joseph Persky Foundation ⌑
South St. W.
Warren 01092 (413) 436-7704

Incorporated in 1944 in MA.
Donor(s): David Persky, Hardwick Knitted Fabrics, Inc.
Foundation type: Independent
Financial data (yr. ended 12/31/88): Assets, $1,494,981 (M); expenditures, $84,447, including $68,650 for 32 grants (high: $5,000; low: $150).
Purpose and activities: Grants largely for hospitals; support also for higher education, Jewish welfare funds, health agencies, and biological research.
Application information: Contributes only to pre-selected organizations.
Write: David Persky, Pres.
Officers: David Persky, Pres. and Treas.; Suzanne Persky Tompkins, Secy.
Trustees: Marguerite Persky, Warren Persky.
Employer Identification Number: 046057747

2953
Edwin Phillips Trust ⌑
c/o Bank of New England, N.A.
28 State St.
Boston 02107
Application address: 147 Bay State Rd., Boston, MA 02215; Tel.: (617) 353-2200

Established in 1960 in MA.
Donor(s): Edwin Phillips.†
Foundation type: Independent
Financial data (yr. ended 12/31/88): Assets, $5,416,417 (M); expenditures, $634,352, including $365,966 for 11 grants (high: $75,000; low: $7,543).
Purpose and activities: Support limited to providing services to or conducting research pertaining to physically or mentally ill children.
Limitations: Giving primarily in Plymouth County, MA. No grants to individuals.
Application information: Application form not required.
Initial approach: Proposal
Board meeting date(s): As needed
Write: Jon Westling, Asst. to Pres., Boston Univ.
Trustees: Evelyn E. Handler, Joseph G. Lind, John R. Silber, Bank of New England, N.A.
Number of staff: None.
Employer Identification Number: 046025549

2954
Harold Whitworth Pierce Charitable Trust
c/o Nichols and Pratt
50 Congress St.
Boston 02109 (617) 523-6800

Trust established in 1960 in MA.
Donor(s): Harold Whitworth Pierce.†
Foundation type: Independent
Financial data (yr. ended 11/30/88): Assets, $9,849,330 (M); expenditures, $530,513, including $530,513 for 35 grants (high: $25,000; low: $2,000).
Purpose and activities: Emphasis on hospitals and medical research, higher, secondary, and other education, youth agencies, museums and other cultural activities, family planning services, and environmental conservation.
Limitations: Giving primarily in MA.
Application information:
Initial approach: Letter
Deadline(s): Apr. 1 and Oct. 1
Board meeting date(s): May and Nov.
Write: James R. Nichols, Trustee
Trustees: James R. Nichols, Robert U. Ingalls.
Number of staff: 1 part-time professional.
Employer Identification Number: 046019896

2955
The Pilgrim Foundation ⌑
478 Torrey St.
Brockton 02401-4654 (617) 586-6100

Established in 1926 in MA; incorporated in 1927.
Donor(s): Edgar B. Davis.†
Foundation type: Independent
Financial data (yr. ended 12/31/88): Assets, $2,564,778 (M); gifts received, $1,500; expenditures, $82,214, including $3,096 for grants and $51,735 for grants to individuals.
Purpose and activities: Primarily to aid children by assisting needy families through grants to individuals; provides camperships, memberships in character-building organizations, and scholarships for higher education; limited grants to organizations aiding adolescents.
Types of support: Student aid, grants to individuals.
Limitations: Giving limited to Brockton, MA.
Application information: Application form required.
Deadline(s): Apr. 1 for graduating high school students; May 1 for returning college students
Write: Sherry Yuskaitis, Exec. Dir.
Officers and Trustees: Gerald J. Kelleher, Pres.; Richard L. Drew, Secy.; Charles M. Altieri, Treas.; Arthur Ford, Alice Lamond, George J. Thomas, Kenneth Turner.
Employer Identification Number: 042104834

2956
Pittsfield Anti-Tuberculosis Association ⌑
69 Taconic St.
Pittsfield 01201-5150 (413) 499-1611

Established in 1907 in MA.
Foundation type: Independent
Financial data (yr. ended 12/31/88): Assets, $1,274,944 (M); expenditures, $55,939, including $45,544 for 4 grants (high: $20,000; low: $5,794).
Purpose and activities: Support primarily for tuberculosis research; limited support for the arts.
Types of support: General purposes.
Limitations: Giving primarily in NY and Pittsfield, MA.
Application information:
Initial approach: Letter
Deadline(s): None
Write: Richard Power, Pres.
Officers: Richard Power, Pres.; Irving Rubin, V.P.; Patricia Curd, Secy.; Joseph J. Barry, Jr., Treas.
Directors: Louis Bolduc, Clement Curd, George Douglas, Thomas Edwards, Phyllis Lord, Anthony J. Ruberto, Jr., Shirley Rubin.
Employer Identification Number: 042104839

2957
Polaroid Foundation, Inc. ▼
750 Main St., 2M
Cambridge 02139 (617) 577-4035

Incorporated in 1971 in MA.
Donor(s): Polaroid Corp.
Foundation type: Company-sponsored
Financial data (yr. ended 12/31/88): Assets, $15,860 (M); gifts received, $2,241,667; expenditures, $2,251,615, including $1,891,117 for 480 grants (high: $361,000; low: $100; average: $2,000-$10,000), $346,923 for 460 employee matching gifts (high: $20; low: $43,565) and $13,500 for 3 loans.
Purpose and activities: Support for community funds and social service agencies, including programs for the urban poor, and higher education, including matching gifts; grants also to cultural programs, youth agencies, and health services.
Types of support: Matching funds, employee matching gifts, employee-related scholarships, seed money, emergency funds, scholarship funds, exchange programs, fellowships, general purposes, annual campaigns, capital campaigns, continuing support, equipment, loans, operating budgets, publications, renovation projects, special projects.
Limitations: Giving primarily in MA, particularly greater Boston and Cambridge. No grants to individuals (except for employee-related scholarships), or for endowment funds.
Publications: Annual report, application guidelines, program policy statement.
Application information: Application form required.
Initial approach: Proposal
Copies of proposal: 1
Deadline(s): None
Board meeting date(s): Monthly
Final notification: 2 to 3 months after board meeting
Write: Marcia Schiff, Exec. Dir.
Officers: Robert Delahunt, Pres.; Marcia Schiff, Secy. and Exec. Dir.; Ralph Norwood, Treas.
Trustees: I. MacAllister Booth, Sheldon A. Buckler, Richard F. deLima, Milton S. Dietz, Owen J. Gaffney, Peter O. Kliem, Joseph Oldfield, William J. O'Neill, Jr.
Number of staff: 2 full-time professional; 2 full-time support; 1 part-time support.
Employer Identification Number: 237152261

2958
William J. & Lia G. Poorvu Foundation ⌑ ☆
975 Memorial Dr., Apt. 710
Cambridge 02138-5717

Established in 1978.
Donor(s): William J. Poorvu.
Foundation type: Independent
Financial data (yr. ended 12/31/88): Assets, $1,694,444 (M); gifts received, $100,000; expenditures, $91,257, including $71,275 for 21 grants (high: $20,000; low: $500).
Purpose and activities: Giving primarily for higher education; support also for cultural programs.
Limitations: Giving primarily in MA.
Application information:
Write: William Poorvu, Trustee
Trustees: Lia G. Poorvu, William J. Poorvu.
Employer Identification Number: 042651199

2959
Charles G. Pringle Foundation ⌑
c/o Shawmut Bank, N.A., Trust Div. 6-15
P.O. Box 2032
Worcester 01613-2032
Application address: 234 Essex St., Lawrence, MA 01840

Established in 1940 in MA.
Foundation type: Independent
Financial data (yr. ended 10/31/88): Assets, $1,502,008 (M); expenditures, $92,605, including $50,122 for 27 grants (high: $8,000; low: $62) and $17,100 for 24 grants to individuals (high: $3,000; low: $100).
Purpose and activities: Giving primarily for social service and child welfare agencies, hospitals, community funds, and student aid for higher education.
Types of support: Student aid.
Limitations: Giving primarily in Lawrence, MA.
Application information:
Initial approach: Letter
Deadline(s): None
Write: Robert V. O'Sullivan, Jr.
Trustees: John Burke, Margaret Dick, Kevin Sullivan.
Corporate Trustee: Shawmut Bank, N.A.
Employer Identification Number: 046020426

2960
Olive Higgins Prouty Foundation, Inc. ⌑
c/o Bank of New England, N.A.
28 State St.
Boston 02109 (617) 973-1793

Incorporated in 1952 in MA.
Donor(s): Olive Higgins Prouty.†
Foundation type: Independent
Financial data (yr. ended 12/31/88): Assets, $1,707,691 (M); expenditures, $114,596, including $94,000 for 29 grants (high: $18,000; low: $1,000; average: $1,000-$5,000).
Purpose and activities: Giving for hospitals, higher and secondary education, music, and museums.
Types of support: Annual campaigns, building funds, capital campaigns, general purposes, operating budgets, renovation projects, continuing support.
Limitations: Giving primarily in the Greater Worcester, MA, area. No grants to individuals.
Publications: Application guidelines.
Application information: Application form required.
Initial approach: Telephone
Copies of proposal: 1
Deadline(s): Sept. 30
Board meeting date(s): Oct. 31
Final notification: Dec. 31
Write: John M. Dolan, V.P., Bank of New England, N.A.
Officers and Trustees:* Richard Prouty,* Pres.; Jane Prouty Smith,* V.P.; Lewis I. Prouty, Treas.; Kenneth L. Grinnell, Clerk.
Employer Identification Number: 046046475

2961
William Lowell Putnam Prize Fund for the Promotion of Scholarship ⌑ ☆
One Post Office Sq.
Boston 02109

Established in 1936 in MA.
Donor(s): Elizabeth Putman.†
Foundation type: Independent
Financial data (yr. ended 12/31/88): Assets, $3,932,707 (M); expenditures, $177,227, including $100,500 for 6 grants (high: $90,000; low: $500), $6,500 for 26 grants to individuals (high: $500; low: $50) and $46,380 for 1 foundation-administered program.
Purpose and activities: Support for higher education; conducts a mathematics competition under the supervision of the Mathematical Association of America and awards prizes to individuals and their schools.
Types of support: Student aid.
Application information: Applicants must apply through their schools.
Write: George Putnam, Trustee
Trustees: George Putnam III, George Putnam, Jr.
Employer Identification Number: 046130905

2962
Sidney & Esther Rabb Charitable Foundation ⌑
P.O. Box 369
Boston 02101

Established in 1952 in MA.
Donor(s): Sidney R. Rabb.†
Foundation type: Independent
Financial data (yr. ended 12/31/88): Assets, $3,104,020 (M); expenditures, $95,535, including $65,350 for 12 grants (high: $12,500; low: $350).
Purpose and activities: Support for Jewish organizations, higher education, health, and social services.
Limitations: Giving primarily in MA, with emphasis on Boston.
Application information:
Initial approach: Letter
Deadline(s): None
Write: Carol R. Goldberg, Trustee
Trustees: Helene R. Cahners, Carol R. Goldberg.
Employer Identification Number: 046039595

2963
Esther V. & Sidney R. Rabb Family Charitable Trust ⌑ ☆
c/o Boston Safe Deposit & Trust Co.
One Boston Place
Boston 02018
Application address: c/o Harvard Law School, Langdell Hall, Rm. 323W, 1545 Massachusetts Ave., Cambridge, MA 02138

Donor(s): Esther V. Rabb.
Foundation type: Independent
Financial data (yr. ended 8/31/88): Assets, $6,464,629 (M); gifts received, $2,947,141; expenditures, $48,458, including $24,330 for 1 grant.
Purpose and activities: Support for a Jewish congregation's building fund.
Types of support: Building funds.
Limitations: Giving primarily in MA. No grants to individuals.
Application information: Application form not required.
Initial approach: Proposal
Deadline(s): June 30
Board meeting date(s): Aug.
Write: A. James Casner, Trustee
Trustees: Helene R. Cahners, A. James Casner, Carol R. Goldberg, Esther V. Rabb.
Employer Identification Number: 222754563

2964
George A. Ramlose Foundation, Inc. ⌑
c/o Adams and Blinn
43 Thorndike St.
Cambridge 02141 (617) 577-9700

Established in 1956 in NY.
Donor(s): George Ramlose.†
Foundation type: Independent
Financial data (yr. ended 04/30/87): Assets, $1,553,103 (M); expenditures, $58,662, including $40,250 for 19 grants (high: $5,000; low: $250).
Purpose and activities: Giving primarily for higher and medical education, social services, including hospices, health agencies and medical research, and the performing arts and other cultural programs.
Types of support: General purposes, operating budgets, research, special projects.
Application information: Application form not required.
Initial approach: Proposal
Copies of proposal: 7
Deadline(s): May 15 and Oct. 15
Board meeting date(s): June and Nov.; dates vary from year to year
Write: David L. Taylor, Secy.
Officers and Directors: Lloyd W. Moseley, Pres.; James P. Fisher, V.P.; John A. Logan, V.P.; Kenneth Wilson, V.P.; David L. Taylor, Secy.; A. Leavitt Taylor, Treas.; Ernest F. Boyce.
Number of staff: None.
Employer Identification Number: 046048231

2965
A. C. Ratshesky Foundation ⌑
40 Webster Place
Brookline 02146 (617) 277-7426

Incorporated in 1916 in MA.
Donor(s): A.C. Ratshesky,† and family.
Foundation type: Independent

Financial data (yr. ended 12/31/88): Assets, $3,070,577 (M); gifts received, $696,884; expenditures, $203,260, including $164,800 for 83 grants (high: $5,000; low: $1,000; average: $1,000-$5,000).
Purpose and activities: Giving for leagal and other education, the performing arts and other cultural programs, social services, including youth and child welfare and development, vocational education, employment, housing, and programs for the disabled, disadvantaged, minorities, the elderly, and women; some support also for health and hospitals, rehabilitation, community funds and development, and Jewish organizations, including welfare funds.
Types of support: Operating budgets, emergency funds, building funds, equipment, matching funds, technical assistance, scholarship funds, general purposes, renovation projects, special projects.
Limitations: Giving primarily in the greater Boston, MA, area. No support for scientific research. No grants to individuals, or for continuing support, annual campaigns, general endowments, seed money, deficit financing, land acquisition, research, publications, or conferences; no loans.
Publications: Biennial report, application guidelines.
Application information: Application form required.
Initial approach: Proposal
Copies of proposal: 1
Deadline(s): 3 months prior to board meeting
Board meeting date(s): Apr., June, Sept., and Dec.
Final notification: 4 months
Write: Theresa J. Morse, Pres., or Ninon Landaverry Freeman, Exec. Dir.
Officers and Trustees: Theresa J. Morse, Pres.; John Morse, Jr., V.P.; Eric Robert Morse, Secy.; Alan R. Morse, Jr., Treas.; Roberta Morse Levy, Edith Morse Milender, Timothy Morse.
Number of staff: 1 part-time professional.
Employer Identification Number: 046017426

2966
Sumner M. Redstone Charitable Foundation ¤ ☆
c/o Pannell Kerr Forster
100 Summer St.
Boston 02110-2104
Application address: 200 Elm St., Dedham, MA 02026; Tel.: (617) 461-1600

Established in 1986 in MA.
Foundation type: Independent
Financial data (yr. ended 12/31/87): Assets, $834,814 (M); gifts received, $100,000; expenditures, $279,379, including $278,800 for 26 grants (high: $125,000; low: $100).
Purpose and activities: Giving for Jewish organizations, including welfare funds; support also for hospitals and medical centers.
Application information:
Deadline(s): None
Write: Sumner M. Redstone, Trustee
Trustee: Sumner M. Redstone.
Employer Identification Number: 222761621

2967
Reebok Foundation
150 Royall St.
Canton 02021 (617) 821-2800

Established in 1985 in MA.
Donor(s): Reebok International, Ltd.
Foundation type: Company-sponsored
Financial data (yr. ended 12/31/88): Assets, $2,439,600 (M); gifts received, $2,000,000; expenditures, $1,565,628, including $1,519,966 for grants (high: $1,000,000) and $4,759 for employee matching gifts.
Purpose and activities: Support for human and social services; support also for arts and culture, health and medicine, education and religion.
Limitations: No grants to individuals.
Application information: Application form not required.
Deadline(s): None
Write: Jean Mahoney
Trustees: Paul Fireman, William M. Marcus, R. Stephen Rubin.
Employer Identification Number: 222709235

2968
George C. & Evelyn R. Reisman Charitable Trust ¤
c/o Lourie & Cutler
60 State St.
Boston 02109

Established in 1981 in MA.
Donor(s): George C. Reisman, Apparel Retail Corp.
Foundation type: Independent
Financial data (yr. ended 12/31/88): Assets, $8,825,764 (M); expenditures, $591,920, including $507,858 for 31 grants (high: $350,000; low: $100).
Purpose and activities: Giving primarily for education, Jewish welfare, and support for hospitals.
Limitations: Giving limited to Boston, MA. No grants to individuals.
Application information:
Write: David Andelman, Trustee
Trustees: David Andelman, Evelyn R. Reisman, George C. Reisman, Howard Reisman, Robert Reisman, David Rothstein.
Employer Identification Number: 042743096

2969
Eugene J. and Corinne A. Ribakoff Charitable Foundation ¤
c/o Greenberg, Rosenblatt, Kull & Bitsoli, P.C.
306 Main St.
Worcester 01608

Trust established in 1960 in MA.
Donor(s): Auto Rental Corp., Trucklease Corp., Eugene J. Ribakoff.
Foundation type: Independent
Financial data (yr. ended 5/31/87): Assets, $565,637 (M); gifts received, $360,000; expenditures, $156,059, including $154,380 for 76 grants (high: $55,180; low: $25).
Purpose and activities: Giving for Jewish welfare funds and temple support; some support also for hospitals.
Limitations: Giving primarily in Worcester, MA.
Application information: Contributes only to pre-selected organizations. Applications not accepted.
Trustees: Betsy Gordon, Charles K. Ribakoff, Corinne A. Ribakoff, Eugene J. Ribakoff.
Employer Identification Number: 046055498

2970
The Albert W. Rice Charitable Foundation ¤
c/o Shawmut Worcester County Bank, N.A., Trust Dept.
446 Main St.
Worcester 01608 (508) 793-4205

Established in 1959.
Donor(s): Albert W. Rice.†
Foundation type: Independent
Financial data (yr. ended 12/31/88): Assets, $3,525,214 (M); expenditures, $223,356, including $196,845 for 15 grants (high: $30,000; low: $5,000).
Purpose and activities: Giving for historic preservation, higher education, social services, and a community foundation.
Limitations: Giving primarily in Worcester, MA. No grants to individuals.
Application information:
Initial approach: Letter
Deadline(s): Apr. and Oct.
Write: Stephen Fritch, V.P., Shawmut Worcester County Bank, N.A.
Trustee: Shawmut Worcester County Bank, N.A.
Employer Identification Number: 046028085

2971
The Riley Foundation ▼ ¤
230 Congress St., 3rd Fl.
Boston 02110 (617) 426-7172

Foundation established in 1971 in MA as the Mabel Louise Riley Charitable Trust.
Donor(s): Mabel Louise Riley.†
Foundation type: Independent
Financial data (yr. ended 5/31/88): Assets, $28,495,252 (M); expenditures, $1,585,468, including $1,512,468 for 44 grants (high: $105,000; low: $2,700; average: $30,000-$100,000).
Purpose and activities: Interest in new approaches to important problems, with an emphasis on improved social services and race relations; special interest in programs for children and youth; selective support for schools, community and neighborhood development, and for cultural, employment, and housing programs.
Types of support: Seed money, building funds, equipment, land acquisition, special projects, renovation projects, technical assistance, capital campaigns, loans.
Limitations: Giving limited to the greater Boston, MA, area, with emphasis on the city. No grants to individuals, or for operating budgets, continuing support, annual campaigns, emergency funds, deficit financing, research, publications, conferences, professorships, internships, exchange programs, fellowships, or matching gifts; no loans.
Publications: Annual report, application guidelines.

Application information: Application form not required.
Initial approach: Proposal or telephone
Copies of proposal: 1
Deadline(s): Submit proposal preferably in early Feb. or early Aug.; deadlines Feb. 15 and Aug. 15
Board meeting date(s): Apr.-May and Oct.-Nov.
Final notification: 1 month after board meetings
Write: Newell Flather or Naomi Tuchmann, Admin.
Administrators: Newell Flather, Naomi Tuchmann.
Trustees: Josephus Long, Andrew C. Bailey, Douglas Danner, Robert W. Holmes, Jr., Boston Safe Deposit & Trust Co.
Number of staff: 2 part-time professional; 1 part-time support.
Employer Identification Number: 046278857

2972
River Road Charitable Corporation ⌑ ☆
c/o Ropes & Gray
One International Place
Boston 02110-2624

Established in 1968.
Foundation type: Independent
Financial data (yr. ended 12/31/88): Assets, $3,296,922 (M); expenditures, $57,853, including $40,100 for 2 grants (high: $25,000; low: $15,100).
Purpose and activities: Support for higher education.
Limitations: No grants to individuals.
Application information: Contributes only to pre-selected organizations. Applications not accepted.
Write: Carolyn M. Osteen, Esq.
Officers: William A. Coolidge,* Pres.; Angelo C. Luongo, Treas.
Trustees:* Francis H. Burr, Catherine C. Lastavica.
Employer Identification Number: 046169258

2973
Elizabeth Killam Rodgers Trust
c/o Nutter, McClennen & Fish
One International Place
Boston 02110-2699 (617) 439-2000
Application address: 50 Milk St., Boston, MA 02109

Established in 1977.
Donor(s): Elizabeth Killam Rodgers.†
Foundation type: Independent
Financial data (yr. ended 04/30/89): Assets, $4,280,568 (M); expenditures, $422,642, including $394,300 for 7 grants (high: $200,000; low: $5,000).
Purpose and activities: Support for the Massachusetts Audubon Society Regional Headquarters; support also for Canadian-related education at universities.
Types of support: General purposes.
Limitations: Giving primarily in MA.
Application information: Application form not required.
Initial approach: Letter
Copies of proposal: 2
Deadline(s): None
Write: John B. Newhall and Nathan Newbury III, Trustees
Trustees: John B. Newhall, Nathan Newbury III.
Agency: Nutter McClennen and Fish.
Employer Identification Number: 046385523

2974
The Rogers Family Foundation ⌑
P.O. Box 100
Lawrence 01842 (508) 685-1000

Trust established in 1957 in MA.
Donor(s): Irving E. Rogers, Eagle-Tribune Publishing Co., Martha B. Rogers, and others.
Foundation type: Independent
Financial data (yr. ended 12/31/88): Assets, $7,117,643 (M); gifts received, $853,840; expenditures, $313,899, including $301,750 for 49 grants (high: $50,000; low: $300).
Purpose and activities: Support for hospitals, higher and secondary education, Protestant giving, and community funds.
Limitations: Giving limited to the greater Lawrence, MA, area, including Methuen, Andover, and Haverhill, MA, and southeastern NH. No grants to individuals, or for endowment funds, research, scholarships, fellowships, or matching gifts; no loans.
Application information: Funds largely committed.
Initial approach: Proposal
Deadline(s): None
Final notification: Within 2 or 3 months
Write: Irving E. Rogers, Jr., Trustee
Trustees: Irving E. Rogers, Jr., Martha B. Rogers, Richard M. Wyman.
Employer Identification Number: 046063152

2975
Romanow Charitable Trust ⌑
c/o Romanow Enterprises, Inc.
625 Bodwell St. Extension
Avon 02322

Established in 1982 in MA.
Foundation type: Independent
Financial data (yr. ended 9/30/87): Assets, $618,566 (M); expenditures, $219,580, including $217,043 for 99 grants (high: $40,000; low: $25).
Purpose and activities: Grants primarily for Jewish welfare funds, and education, especially Jewish education.
Application information: Contributes only to pre-selected organizations. Applications not accepted.
Trustees: Neal A. Cooper, Martin Gladstone.
Employer Identification Number: 042794666

2976
Sophia F. Romero Trust ⌑
c/o Durfee Attleboro Bank
Ten North Main St.
Fall River 02720

Established in 1953 in MA.
Foundation type: Independent
Financial data (yr. ended 4/30/89): Assets, $1,543,416 (M); expenditures, $92,988, including $77,323 for grants.
Purpose and activities: Support limited to aid the elderly through social services and health care.
Limitations: Giving limited to Bristol County, MA.
Application information:
Initial approach: Letter
Deadline(s): None
Trustee: Durfee Attleboro Bank.
Employer Identification Number: 046029538

2977
Rose Family Charitable Trust Fund ⌑
c/o Robert J. Hurwitz
Eight Portland St.
Worcester 01608 (508) 799-2735

Established in 1967 in MA.
Donor(s): Ralph Rose.
Foundation type: Independent
Financial data (yr. ended 09/30/89): Assets, $1,504,824 (M); expenditures, $80,054, including $74,074 for grants (high: $62,955).
Purpose and activities: Grants for Jewish welfare funds and temple support.
Types of support: General purposes.
Application information: Application form not required.
Deadline(s): None
Trustees: David Rose, Ralph Rose, Sanford Rose, Sidney Rose.
Employer Identification Number: 046147202

2978
Thomas A. Rosse Family Charitable Foundation ⌑ ☆
c/o Rohamanda Corp.
205 Portland St.
Boston 02114

Established in 1978.
Donor(s): Thomas A. Rosse.
Foundation type: Independent
Financial data (yr. ended 11/30/88): Assets, $1,099,290 (M); expenditures, $68,111, including $61,250 for 24 grants (high: $10,000; low: $100).
Purpose and activities: Support primarily for higher and other education, museums, and the performing arts.
Limitations: Giving primarily in MA. No grants to individuals.
Application information: Contributes only to pre-selected organizations. Applications not accepted.
Officer and Directors: Thomas A. Rosse, Pres. and Treas.; Florence M. Rosse.
Employer Identification Number: 042659411

2979
Rowland Foundation, Inc. ▼ ⌑
P.O. Box 13
Cambridge 02238

Incorporated in 1960 in DE.
Donor(s): Edwin H. Land, Helen M. Land.
Foundation type: Independent
Financial data (yr. ended 11/30/88): Assets, $33,809,033 (M); expenditures, $1,895,608, including $1,702,049 for 47 grants (high: $318,000; average: $5,000-$50,000).
Purpose and activities: Grants primarily for education, social services, health, medical research, conservation, and cultural programs, including museums and historical associations.

Types of support: General purposes, professorships, research.
Limitations: Giving primarily in the Boston-Cambridge, MA, area. No grants to individuals, or for capital or endowment funds, or matching gifts; no loans.
Publications: Annual report.
Application information: Application form not required.
Initial approach: Letter
Copies of proposal: 1
Deadline(s): None
Board meeting date(s): As required
Final notification: Varies
Write: Philip DuBois, V.P.
Officers and Trustees:* Edwin H. Land,* Pres.; Helen M. Land,* V.P. and Treas.; Philip DuBois,* V.P.; Julius Silver, Secy.; Jennifer Land DuBois.
Number of staff: None.
Employer Identification Number: 046046756

2980
Lawrence J. and Anne Rubenstein Charitable Foundation
Beacon Hill Capitol Corp.
84 State St., No. 700
Boston 02109

Trust established in 1963 in MA.
Donor(s): Lawrence J. Rubenstein,† Anne C. Rubenstein.
Foundation type: Independent
Financial data (yr. ended 5/31/87): Assets, $7,700,000 (M); expenditures, $500,000, including $500,000 for grants (high: $350,000; low: $10,000).
Purpose and activities: Giving for hospitals, higher and other education, science and technology, medical research and education, with emphasis on medical care and research relating to children's illnesses; support also for programs for the homeless and the performing arts.
Types of support: Annual campaigns, building funds, capital campaigns, emergency funds, endowment funds, equipment, general purposes, professorships, special projects.
Limitations: Giving primarily in MA.
Application information: Application form not required.
Initial approach: Letter
Copies of proposal: 1
Deadline(s): Prior to May 1 of year grant requested
Board meeting date(s): Quarterly
Write: Richard I. Kaner, Trustee
Trustees: Richard I. Kaner, Frank Kopelman, Anne C. Rubenstein.
Number of staff: 1 part-time professional.
Employer Identification Number: 046087371

2981
Cele H. and William B. Rubin Family Fund, Inc. ⌑
32 Monadnock Rd.
Wellesley Hills 02181 (617) 235-1075

Incorporated in 1943 in NY.
Donor(s): Members of the Joseph Rubin family, The Sweets Co. of America, Inc., Joseph Rubin and Sons, Inc., Tootsie Roll Industries, Inc., and others.
Foundation type: Independent
Financial data (yr. ended 12/31/88): Assets, $11,826,184 (M); gifts received, $450,000; expenditures, $620,754, including $544,875 for 66 grants (high: $237,000; low: $100).
Purpose and activities: Grants for higher education (including medical education), secondary schools, and social service agencies, including Jewish welfare funds.
Limitations: Giving primarily in MA and NY.
Application information: Application form not required.
Deadline(s): None
Write: Ellen R. Gordon, Pres.
Officers and Directors:* Ellen R. Gordon,* Pres.; Melvin J. Gordon,* V.P.
Employer Identification Number: 116026235

2982
Josephine G. Russell Trust ⌑
70 East St.
Methuen 01844 (617) 687-0151

Trust established in 1934.
Foundation type: Independent
Financial data (yr. ended 12/31/88): Assets, $5,045,030 (M); expenditures, $217,221, including $187,725 for 21 grants (high: $51,800; low: $25).
Purpose and activities: Giving for hospitals, schools, and a community fund.
Types of support: General purposes, annual campaigns, emergency funds, building funds, equipment, publications, scholarship funds, special projects.
Limitations: Giving limited to the greater Lawrence, MA, area. No grants to individuals, or for matching gifts; no loans.
Publications: 990-PF, application guidelines.
Application information:
Initial approach: Letter or proposal
Copies of proposal: 3
Deadline(s): Jan. 31
Board meeting date(s): Quarterly
Write: Clifford E. Elias, Trustee
Trustees: Archer L. Bolton, Jr., Roger N. Bower, Clifford E. Elias.
Number of staff: 1 part-time professional; 1 part-time support.
Employer Identification Number: 042136910

2983
Sagamore Foundation ⌑
c/o Woodstock Service Corp.
18 Tremont St.
Boston 02108

Trust established in 1947 in MA.
Donor(s): Nelson J. Darling, Jr., members of the LaCroix family.
Foundation type: Independent
Financial data (yr. ended 12/31/87): Assets, $609,700 (M); expenditures, $119,275, including $109,000 for 15 grants (high: $10,000; low: $1,000).
Purpose and activities: Emphasis on higher education, hospitals, arts and cultural programs, particularly museums, and a community fund.
Limitations: Giving primarily in MA.
Application information: Contributes only to pre-selected organizations. Applications not accepted.
Trustees: Bigelow Crocker, Jr., Jeanne LaCroix Crocker, Edith LaCroix Dabney, Nelson J. Darling, Jr., Ruth LaCroix Darling, Richard D. Phippen, Susanne LaCroix Phippen.
Employer Identification Number: 046027799

2984
Sailors' Snug Harbor of Boston
c/o Adams, Harkness and Hill
One Liberty Sq.
Boston 02109 (617) 423-6688

Established in 1852 in MA.
Foundation type: Independent
Financial data (yr. ended 04/30/89): Assets, $3,783,654 (M); expenditures, $271,696, including $221,131 for 27 grants (high: $50,000; low: $2,000).
Purpose and activities: Giving for the health and welfare of the aged, sailors, and others; grants to institutions for the relief and support of aged sailors.
Types of support: Grants to individuals.
Limitations: Giving primarily in the Boston, MA, area. No grants to individuals.
Application information: Application form not required.
Initial approach: Proposal
Deadline(s): In time for approval at board meetings
Board meeting date(s): Nov. 15, Feb. 15, and Apr. 15
Write: Stephen Little, Pres.
Officers and Trustees:* Stephen Little,* Pres.; Charles E. Rogerson II,* Secy.-Treas.; Richard E. Byrd, Charles K. Cobb, Jr., G. Lincoln Dow, Jr., Joseph E. Eaton, Charles R. Eddy, Robert W. Loring, Francis B. Lothrop, Jr., Everett Morse, Jr., John A. Perkins, Thomas Rogerson, G. West Saltonstall, William L. Saltonstall, Henry Wheeler, Benjamin Williams, Thomas B. Williams, Jr.
Employer Identification Number: 042104430

2985
Richard Saltonstall Charitable Foundation
c/o S & Co., Inc.
50 Congress St., Rm. 800
Boston 02109 (617) 227-8660

Established in 1964 in MA.
Foundation type: Independent
Financial data (yr. ended 12/31/88): Assets, $8,734,151 (M); expenditures, $530,329, including $485,000 for 28 grants (high: $80,000; low: $1,000).
Purpose and activities: Giving primarily for cultural programs, hospitals and medical research, and youth organizations.
Limitations: Giving primarily in MA.
Application information: Application form not required.
Initial approach: Letter
Deadline(s): None
Write: Dudley H. Willis or Robert A. Lawrence, Trustees
Trustees: Robert A. Lawrence, Dudley H. Willis.
Employer Identification Number: 046078934

2986
Charles Sanders Trust ⌑
c/o Saltonstall & Co.
50 Congress St., Suite 800
Boston 02109 (617) 227-8660

Foundation type: Independent
Financial data (yr. ended 12/31/86): Assets, $1,951,845 (M); expenditures, $89,787, including $54,500 for 17 grants (high: $7,000; low: $145) and $19,772 for 14 grants to individuals.
Purpose and activities: Support for organizations which aid families in need; support also for youth and women's organizations.
Trustees: George Lewis, William L. Saltonstall, Dudley H. Willis.
Employer Identification Number: 046022091

2987
Sawyer Charitable Foundation ⌑
142 Berkeley St.
Boston 02116 (617) 267-2441

Trust established in 1957 in MA.
Donor(s): Frank Sawyer, William Sawyer, The Brattle Co. Corp., St. Botolph Holding Co., First Franklin Parking Corp., and others.
Foundation type: Independent
Financial data (yr. ended 12/31/88): Assets, $4,575,049 (M); gifts received, $186,150; expenditures, $287,711, including $218,600 for 68 grants (high: $25,000; low: $100).
Purpose and activities: Giving for Jewish and Roman Catholic welfare funds, community funds, health agencies, hospitals, and aid to the handicapped.
Limitations: Giving primarily in the greater New England area. No grants to individuals, or for operating budgets or building funds.
Application information:
Initial approach: Proposal
Deadline(s): Oct. 15
Write: Carol S. Parks, Exec. Dir.
Officer and Trustees: Carol S. Parks, Exec. Dir.; Frank Sawyer, Mildred F. Sawyer.
Employer Identification Number: 046088774

2988
William E. Schrafft and Bertha E. Schrafft Charitable Trust
One Financial Center, 26th Fl.
Boston 02111 (617) 350-6100

Trust established in 1946 in MA.
Donor(s): William E. Schrafft,† Bertha E. Schrafft.†
Foundation type: Independent
Financial data (yr. ended 12/31/89): Assets, $15,317,926 (M); expenditures, $801,886, including $719,180 for 95 grants (high: $75,000; low: $1,000; average: $1,500-$60,000).
Purpose and activities: Grants primarily for hospitals, higher and secondary education, community funds, cultural programs, and youth agencies.
Types of support: General purposes, operating budgets, continuing support, annual campaigns, endowment funds, scholarship funds.
Limitations: Giving limited to MA, with emphasis on the Boston metropolitan area. No grants to individuals, or for matching gifts, seed money, emergency funds, or deficit financing; no loans.
Publications: Annual report, application guidelines.
Application information: Application form not required.
Initial approach: Proposal
Copies of proposal: 4
Deadline(s): Submit proposal preferably from Jan. through July; no set deadline
Board meeting date(s): About 6 times a year
Final notification: 2 months
Write: John M. Wood, Jr., Trustee
Trustees: Robert H. Jewell, Arthur Parker, John M. Wood, Jr.
Number of staff: None.
Employer Identification Number: 046065605

2989
SCOA Foundation, Inc. ⌑
15 Dan Rd.
Canton 02021 (617) 821-1000

Established in 1969 in OH.
Donor(s): SCOA Industries, Inc.
Foundation type: Company-sponsored
Financial data (yr. ended 06/30/87): Assets, $6,300,759 (M); expenditures, $776,719, including $707,475 for 154 grants (high: $100,000; low: $350).
Purpose and activities: Grants primarily for Jewish welfare, child welfare, and community funds. Support also for higher education, hospitals, and cultural activities.
Limitations: Giving primarily in communities where Hills Department Stores are located; in 13 states in the Midwest.
Application information: Contributes only to pre-selected organizations. Applications not accepted.
Write: William K. Friend, Secy.
Officers: William K. Friend, Secy.
Trustees:* Herbert H. Schiff,* Chair.; George R. Friese, Stephen A. Goldberger, Harvey Kruger, Thomas H. Lee, Neil Papiano.
Employer Identification Number: 237002220

2990
Trustees of Sears and Other Funds ⌑
c/o Bank of New England
28 State St.
Boston 02107 (617) 973-1653

Established in 1938 in MA.
Foundation type: Independent
Financial data (yr. ended 02/28/89): Assets, $1,093,970 (M); expenditures, $51,822, including $46,000 for 28 grants (high: $6,000; low: $500).
Purpose and activities: Support for Christian schools and charities, and social service organizations.
Limitations: No grants to individuals.
Application information:
Deadline(s): None
Write: John Bigelow, Treas.
Officers: David S. Lee, Pres.; E. Miles Herter, Secy.; John Bigelow, Treas.
Employer Identification Number: 046040032

2991
Arthur & Bernice Shapiro Charitable Foundation ☆
c/o Charles Broner
826 Boylston St.
Chestnut Hill 02167

Established in 1956.
Donor(s): Arthur H. Shapiro.
Foundation type: Independent
Financial data (yr. ended 9/30/88): Assets, $995,125 (M); gifts received, $1,170,463; expenditures, $244,755, including $121,409 for 11 grants (high: $60,000; low: $10).
Purpose and activities: Support primarily for Jewish organizations, including welfare funds, and rehabilitation and health; support also for a geriatric center.
Limitations: No grants to individuals.
Application information: Contributes only to pre-selected organizations in which the donor has a special interest. Applications not accepted.
Officers and Trustees: Arthur H. Shapiro, Pres.; Bernice D. Shapiro, V.P.; Henry Shapiro, Treas.; Irving F. Cohn.
Employer Identification Number: 046112559

2992
Abraham Shapiro Charity Fund ⌑
65 Sprague St.
Boston 02137 (617) 361-1200

Trust established in 1945 in MA.
Donor(s): Abraham Shapiro, and various companies.
Foundation type: Independent
Financial data (yr. ended 12/31/87): Assets, $5,200,830 (M); expenditures, $300,960, including $274,350 for 15 grants (high: $140,000; low: $100).
Purpose and activities: Giving for Jewish welfare funds, higher education, and hospitals.
Limitations: Giving primarily in MA. No grants to individuals, or for scholarships, fellowships, or matching gifts; no loans.
Application information:
Board meeting date(s): Quarterly
Write: George Shapiro, Trustee
Trustees: Arthur S. Goldberg, George Shapiro, Philip Shir.
Employer Identification Number: 046043588

2993
Gardiner Howland Shaw Foundation
95 Berkeley St., Suite 403
Boston 02116 (617) 451-9206

Trust established in 1959 in MA.
Donor(s): Gardiner Howland Shaw.†
Foundation type: Independent
Financial data (yr. ended 04/30/89): Assets, $9,934,657 (M); expenditures, $539,293, including $359,800 for 43 grants (high: $25,000; low: $600; average: $5,000-$10,000).
Purpose and activities: Giving for the study, prevention, correction, and alleviation of crime and delinquency, and the rehabilitation of adult and juvenile offenders. Awards grants in 3 categories: 1) 50 percent of available funds to programs that expand use of alternative sentencing and dispute resolution in the criminal courts, explore the use of substitutes for confinement, or strengthen the role of the

community in the courts; 2) 30 percent of funds awarded to previous recipients with effective community programs for adult or juvenile offenders; priority to programs serving minority or female offenders and those helping committed adults or juveniles return to the community; and 3) 20 percent of funds awarded to programs that test new ideas or approaches to criminal justice issues and attract new agencies or resources into the criminal justice field. Foundation participates in Emergency Loan Fund.
Types of support: Operating budgets, continuing support, seed money, emergency funds, technical assistance, special projects.
Limitations: Giving limited to MA. No support for drug or mental health programs or the arts. No grants to individuals, or for capital or building funds, equipment, land acquisition, renovations, endowment funds, scholarships, or fellowships.
Publications: Annual report (including application guidelines).
Application information: Application form not required.
Initial approach: Concept paper, proposal, or telephone
Copies of proposal: 1
Deadline(s): Jan. 2, May 1, and Sept. 1
Board meeting date(s): Feb., June, and Oct.
Final notification: 60 days
Write: Thomas Coury, Exec. Dir.
Officer: Thomas Coury, Exec. Dir.
Trustees: James D. Colt, John Lowell, Guido R. Perera, Jr., Kenneth S. Safe, Jr., Welch & Forbes.
Number of staff: 2 full-time professional.
Employer Identification Number: 046111826

2994
Shaw Fund for Mariners' Children ⌑
c/o Russell Brier & Co.
50 Congress St., Rm. 800
Boston 02109
Application address: 64 Concord Ave., Norwood, MA 02062

Incorporated in 1853 in MA.
Donor(s): Robert Gould Shaw.†
Foundation type: Independent
Financial data (yr. ended 12/31/87): Assets, $2,650,651 (M); gifts received, $50; expenditures, $136,401, including $114,727 for grants to individuals.
Purpose and activities: To aid mariners, mariners' wives or widows, and their children who are in distress.
Types of support: Grants to individuals.
Limitations: Giving limited to residents of MA. No grants for building or endowment funds, operating budgets, special projects, research, scholarships, fellowships, or matching gifts; no loans.
Application information:
Initial approach: Letter
Copies of proposal: 1
Deadline(s): None
Write: Claire M. Tolies
Officers and Members: Francis G. Shaw, Pres.; Thomas Whiteside, V.P.; Andrew A. Hunter, Clerk; Norman C. Nicholson, Jr., Treas.; James B. Ames, Walter Amory, Mrs. George B. Blake, Edward D. Cook, Jr., Ingersoll Cunningham, Mrs. Raymond J. Montminy, Paul H. Ockers, Marguerite G. Shaw, S. Parkman Shaw III.
Employer Identification Number: 042104861

2995
The Shawmut Charitable Foundation ▼
Shawmut National Corp.
One Federal St., 35th Fl.
Boston 02211 (617) 292-3748
c/o Maxine Dean, Admin., 777 Main St., Hartford, CT, 06115; Tel.: (203) 728-2274

Trust established in 1961 in MA.
Donor(s): Shawmut National Corp.
Foundation type: Company-sponsored
Financial data (yr. ended 12/31/88): Assets, $48,732 (M); gifts received, $1,090,683; expenditures, $1,125,571, including $1,124,607 for 269 grants (high: $50,000; low: $10; average: $1,000-$10,000).
Purpose and activities: Support for the United Way, community services, education, health, cultural organizations, urban development projects, and programs for youth and the homeless through regional giving programs.
Types of support: Operating budgets, employee matching gifts, capital campaigns.
Limitations: Giving primarily in MA, CT, and RI. No support for national or local medical foundations, or fraternal organizations or religious orders. No grants to individuals, or for research or conferences.
Publications: Program policy statement, application guidelines.
Application information: Send application to local SNC branch or regional office; recommendations are made regionally, within each state. Application form not required.
Initial approach: Telephone or letter
Copies of proposal: 1
Deadline(s): Varies by state
Board meeting date(s): Varies by state
Final notification: Varies by state
Write: Dinah Waldsmith, Admin.
Agent: Shawmut National Corp.
Number of staff: 2 full-time professional; 2 full-time support.
Employer Identification Number: 046023794

2996
Shawmut Worcester County Bank Charitable Foundation, Inc. ⌑
c/o Shawmut Central Tax Unit
P.O. Box 15032
Worcester 01613-0032
Application address: 446 Main St., Worcester, MA 01608; Tel.: (617) 793-4401

Incorporated in 1982 in MA.
Donor(s): Shawmut Worcester County Bank, N.A.
Foundation type: Company-sponsored
Financial data (yr. ended 12/31/88): Assets, $101,275 (M); gifts received, $200,000; expenditures, $301,771, including $301,350 for 52 grants (high: $75,000; low: $500).
Purpose and activities: Giving primarily for community funds and higher education; support also for cultural programs, health and social services, and youth agencies.
Types of support: Annual campaigns, capital campaigns.
Limitations: Giving limited to agencies within the Shawmut Worcester County Bank market area.
Application information:
Initial approach: Letter
Deadline(s): None
Write: Harry I. Spencer, Jr.
Officers and Directors:* F. William Marshall, Jr.,* Pres.; John D. Hunt,* V.P.; John M. Lydon, Secy.-Treas.; Joan M. Bloom, Michael J. Toomey.
Employer Identification Number: 042746775

2997
Sheraton Foundation, Inc.
c/o The Sheraton Corp.
60 State St.
Boston 02109 (617) 367-5454

Incorporated in 1950 in MA.
Donor(s): ITT Sheraton Corp.
Foundation type: Company-sponsored
Financial data (yr. ended 12/31/89): Assets, $3,423,003 (M); expenditures, $257,831, including $189,489 for 29 grants (high: $50,000; low: $50).
Purpose and activities: Support primarily for community funds; some grants to educational institutions, including scholarship funds, health agencies, youth agencies, and hospitals.
Types of support: General purposes, continuing support, annual campaigns, scholarship funds.
Limitations: Giving primarily in the greater Boston, MA, area. No grants to individuals, or for endowment or capital funds, research, or matching gifts; no loans.
Application information: Applicants for scholarship funds must be enrolled in hotel administration and/or restaurant management.
Initial approach: Proposal
Copies of proposal: 1
Board meeting date(s): Apr., July, Sept., and Dec.
Final notification: 6 months
Write: Brenda J. Furlong, Treas.
Officers and Directors:* John Kapioltas,* Pres.; Brenda J. Furlong,* Treas.; William D. Buxton.
Number of staff: 2
Employer Identification Number: 046039510

2998
George and Beatrice Sherman Family Charitable Trust ⌑
c/o Goulston & Storrs
400 Atlantic Ave.
Boston 02110

Trust established in 1969.
Donor(s): George Sherman.†
Foundation type: Independent
Financial data (yr. ended 06/30/89): Assets, $3,222,761 (M); expenditures, $393,518, including $312,300 for 108 grants (high: $50,000; low: $25).
Purpose and activities: Emphasis on Jewish welfare funds, temple support, higher education, and hospitals.

Limitations: Giving primarily in MA.
Trustees: Jacob Lewiton, Alan W. Rottenberg, Norton L. Sherman, Marvin Sparrow.
Employer Identification Number: 046223350

2999
Sholley Foundation, Inc. ⌑
c/o Bank of New England, N.A.
28 State St.
Boston 02107

Established in 1945 in MA.
Foundation type: Independent
Financial data (yr. ended 04/30/89): Assets, $1,261,849 (M); expenditures, $85,421, including $75,284 for grants.
Purpose and activities: Support primarily for education, social services, and youth; some support for health organizations and community development.
Limitations: Giving primarily in MA. No grants to individuals.
Application information: Contributes only to pre-selected organizations. Applications not accepted.
Officers and Trustees:* Peter B. Sholley,* Pres.; William T. Cloney,* Secy.; Charles D. Post,* Treas.; Nancy T. Sholley.
Employer Identification Number: 046014010

3000
Shurtleff Children's Services, Inc. ⌑
c/o BayBank Valley Trust Co.
P.O. Box 422
Burlington 01803
Application address: 10 Elm St., Westfield, MA 01085; Tel.: (413) 568-0914

Established in 1943 in MA.
Foundation type: Independent
Financial data (yr. ended 12/31/88): Assets, $1,531,040 (M); expenditures, $95,425, including $79,535 for 27 grants (high: $6,000; low: $500).
Purpose and activities: Support for youth activities and child welfare organizations, especially for the mentally retarded.
Limitations: Giving primarily in Westfield, MA, and the surrounding areas.
Application information:
Initial approach: In person
Deadline(s): Apr. 1
Write: Donald W. Blair, Treas.
Officers and Trustees: James A. Rogers, Pres.; Constance K. Kellogg, V.P.; Virginia Walthall, Secy.; Donald W. Blair, Treas.; Bernard Cassin, Judith A. Helliwell, Arthur T. Lichtenberger, Lolly Templeton, George S. Wallis, Jr.
Agent: BayBank Valley Trust Co.
Employer Identification Number: 042113268

3001
Siff Charitable Foundation
P.O. Box 70
Webster 01570

Established in 1953 in MA.
Donor(s): B-W Footwear Co., Inc.
Foundation type: Independent
Financial data (yr. ended 12/31/88): Assets, $1,071,822 (M); expenditures, $87,726, including $85,792 for grants (high: $50,250).
Purpose and activities: Support primarily for Jewish welfare; some support for education, health, and medical research.
Types of support: General purposes.
Limitations: Giving primarily in MA. No grants to individuals.
Application information: Contributes only to pre-selected organizations. Applications not accepted.
Trustees: Charlotte E. Siff, Karen Siff, Lawrence Siff, Robert M. Siff, Shirley S. Siff.
Employer Identification Number: 046112346

3002
Joseph F. & Edna Slavik Foundation Charitable Trust ⌑ ☆
17 Maple Ave., No. 3
Cambridge 02139

Established in 1980.
Donor(s): Joseph F. Slavik.
Foundation type: Independent
Financial data (yr. ended 08/31/89): Assets, $1,076,880 (M); expenditures, $78,112, including $54,650 for 12 grants (high: $37,500; low: $500).
Purpose and activities: Giving primarily for Christian organizations; support also for the performing arts.
Limitations: Giving primarily in MI. No grants to individuals.
Application information: Contributes only to pre-selected organizations. Applications not accepted.
Trustees: Berneda Meeks, Edna Slavik, Joseph F. Slavik.
Employer Identification Number: 382330319

3003
Richard and Susan Smith Foundation ⌑
27 Boylston St., Box 1000
Chestnut Hill 02167 (617) 232-8200
To contact only when further clarification of the guidelines is needed: c/o Grants Management Assocs., 100 Franklin St., Boston, MA 02110; Tel.: (617) 357-1514

Trust established in 1970 in MA.
Donor(s): Marian Smith,† Richard A. Smith.
Foundation type: Independent
Financial data (yr. ended 4/30/89): Assets, $3,349,690 (M); gifts received, $1,808,521; expenditures, $803,142, including $735,531 for 62 grants (high: $125,000; low: $100).
Purpose and activities: Grants for health, education, and Jewish organizations serving a worldwide community; the arts are a secondary field of interest. Particularly interested in organizations providing opportunities for economically disadvantaged populations, especially children and youth, and cancer research.
Types of support: General purposes, building funds, capital campaigns, special projects, annual campaigns, fellowships, research.
Limitations: Giving primarily in the greater Boston, MA, area. No support for sectarian religious activities or political causes. No grants to individuals, or for deficit financing, endowment funds, operating budgets, efforts supported by the general public, or efforts in which the foundation may become the sole source of funding.
Publications: 990-PF, application guidelines.
Application information: Application form not required.
Initial approach: Letter
Copies of proposal: 1
Deadline(s): None
Board meeting date(s): Fall and spring
Write: Susan F. Smith, Trustee
Trustees: Amy S. Berylson, Debra S. Knez, Robert A. Smith, Susan F. Smith.
Employer Identification Number: 237090011

3004
Horace Smith Fund
1441 Main St.
Box 3034
Springfield 01101 (413) 739-4222

Established in 1898 in MA.
Donor(s): Horace Smith.
Foundation type: Independent
Financial data (yr. ended 3/31/89): Assets, $5,514,016 (M); expenditures, $468,224, including $401,673 for grants to individuals.
Purpose and activities: Scholarship grants for high school seniors in Agawam, Chicopee, East Longmeadow, Longmeadow, Ludlow, Springfield, West Springfield, and Wilbraham; educational loans for graduates of Hampden County high schools; and fellowships for Hampden County residents.
Types of support: Student loans, student aid, fellowships.
Limitations: Giving limited to Hampden County, MA, residents or high school seniors in 8 specified towns.
Application information: Application form required.
Deadline(s): Feb. 1 for fellowships; June 15 for loans for college students; July 1 for loans for high school seniors; Dec. 31 for scholarships
Write: Philip T. Hart, Exec. Secy.
Officers: Philip T. Hart, Exec. Secy.; Benjamin Bump, Treas.
Trustees: Richard C. Garvey, Richard S. Milstein, Harry Nelson.
Number of staff: 1 part-time professional.
Employer Identification Number: 042235130

3005
Phineas W. Sprague Memorial Foundation ⌑
c/o Tucker Anthony Management Corp.
P.O. Box 1250
Boston 02104

Established in 1956 in MA.
Foundation type: Independent
Financial data (yr. ended 12/31/88): Assets, $1,138,538 (M); expenditures, $63,543, including $49,500 for grants.
Purpose and activities: Giving primarily for a camp and private secondary schools; support also for land and historic preservation.
Limitations: No grants to individuals.
Application information: Contributes only to pre-selected organizations. Applications not accepted.
Officer and Trustees: Henderson Inches, Treas.; Julie Talmadge.
Employer Identification Number: 046043554

3006
The Stare Fund ⌑
c/o Ropes and Gray
One International Place
Boston 02110 (617) 951-7000

Established in 1959 in MA.
Donor(s): Frederick J. Stare.
Foundation type: Independent
Financial data (yr. ended 11/30/88): Assets, $1,718,756 (M); gifts received, $126,563; expenditures, $96,860, including $73,450 for 36 grants (high: $25,000; low: $100).
Purpose and activities: Support for health and nutrition, cultural programs, and higher education.
Application information:
Initial approach: Letter or proposal
Deadline(s): None
Trustees: Harry K. Mansfield, David S. Stare, Fredrick J. Stare, Irene M. Stare, Mary S. Wilkinson.
Employer Identification Number: 046026648

3007
State Street Foundation ▼
c/o State Street Bank and Trust Co.
P.O. Box 351
Boston 02101 (617) 654-3381

Trust established in 1963 in MA.
Donor(s): State Street Bank and Trust Co.
Foundation type: Company-sponsored
Financial data (yr. ended 12/31/87): Assets, $2,987,615 (M); gifts received, $1,378,000; expenditures, $1,115,668, including $1,064,101 for 111 grants (high: $81,250; low: $1,000) and $42,622 for 318 employee matching gifts.
Purpose and activities: Grants to organizations helping to improve the quality of life for residents of the greater Boston area, with emphasis on community funds, neighborhood development, health and human services, public and secondary education, job training, and cultural programs.
Types of support: Annual campaigns, building funds, capital campaigns, conferences and seminars, continuing support, emergency funds, employee matching gifts, endowment funds, equipment, general purposes, land acquisition, lectureships, loans, matching funds, operating budgets, program-related investments, publications, renovation projects, seed money, special projects, technical assistance.
Limitations: Giving primarily in MA. No grants to individuals, or for scholarships.
Publications: Annual report (including application guidelines), 990-PF.
Application information: Application form not required.
Initial approach: Proposal
Copies of proposal: 1
Deadline(s): None
Board meeting date(s): Quarterly
Final notification: 2 weeks after meeting
Write: James J. Darr, V.P., State Street Bank and Trust Co.
Trustee: State Street Bank and Trust Co.
Number of staff: 2 full-time professional; 2 full-time support.
Employer Identification Number: 046401847

3008
Anna B. Stearns Charitable Foundation, Inc. ⌑
c/o Boston Safe Deposit & Trust Co.
One Boston Place
Boston 02108

Established in 1966 in MA.
Foundation type: Independent
Financial data (yr. ended 12/31/88): Assets, $2,180,436 (M); expenditures, $139,201, including $116,500 for 26 grants (high: $10,000; low: $2,000).
Purpose and activities: Giving primarily for community projects, youth programs, and general charitable giving.
Application information:
Initial approach: Letter
Deadline(s): Feb., May, Aug., and Nov.
Board meeting date(s): Mar., June, Sept., and Dec.
Write: Sylvia Salas, Treas.
Officers and Directors:* Ralph B. Hersey, Jr.,* Pres.; Sylvia Salas,* Treas.; Gwen Harper, Joseph R. Watkins, Boston Safe Deposit & Trust Co.
Employer Identification Number: 046144732

3009
Stearns Charitable Trust
66 Commonwealth Ave.
Concord 01742

Trust established in 1947 in MA.
Donor(s): Russell B. Stearns.†
Foundation type: Independent
Financial data (yr. ended 12/31/88): Assets, $2,993,000 (M); expenditures, $157,857, including $135,500 for 32 grants (high: $10,000; low: $1,000).
Purpose and activities: Emphasis on cultural programs, including a science museum; support also for hospitals, education, community funds, the environment, an aquarium corporation, and social services.
Types of support: Annual campaigns, general purposes, endowment funds, special projects.
Limitations: Giving primarily in MA. No grants to individuals.
Application information: Contributes only to pre-selected organizations. Applications not accepted.
Board meeting date(s): As required
Write: Russell S. Beede, Trustee
Trustees: Russell S. Beede, Andree B. Stearns.
Number of staff: None.
Employer Identification Number: 046036697

3010
Artemas W. Stearns Trust ⌑
70 East St.
Methuen 01844 (508) 687-0151

Trust established in 1896 in MA.
Donor(s): Artemas W. Stearns.†
Foundation type: Independent
Financial data (yr. ended 12/31/88): Assets, $2,884,969 (M); expenditures, $192,066, including $161,125 for 24 grants (high: $25,000; low: $750; average: $5,000).
Purpose and activities: Support for organizations which service and benefit the deserving poor and indigent aged people, including hospitals, community projects, and secondary schools.
Types of support: Annual campaigns, building funds, emergency funds, equipment, general purposes, publications, scholarship funds, special projects.
Limitations: Giving limited to the greater Lawrence, MA, area. No grants to individuals, or for endowment funds or matching gifts; no loans.
Publications: 990-PF, application guidelines.
Application information: Contact foundation for addresses to which additional copies of request should be sent.
Initial approach: Letter or proposal
Copies of proposal: 3
Deadline(s): Jan. 31
Board meeting date(s): Quarterly
Write: Clifford E. Elias, Esq., Trustee
Trustees: Clifford E. Elias, Marsha K. Elias, Vincent P. Morton, Jr.
Number of staff: 1 full-time professional; 1 part-time support.
Employer Identification Number: 042137061

3011
Albert Steiger Memorial Fund, Inc.
1477 Main St.
Springfield 01101 (413) 781-4211

Incorporated in 1953 in MA.
Donor(s): Ralph A. Steiger, Chauncey A. Steiger, Albert Steiger, Inc.
Foundation type: Independent
Financial data (yr. ended 12/31/88): Assets, $1,833,294 (M); expenditures, $131,223, including $118,750 for 21 grants (high: $40,000; low: $1,000).
Purpose and activities: Grants recommended by the Community Funds Advisory Committee of the Community Council, primarily for community funds, social service agencies, cultural programs, and higher education.
Types of support: Special projects, building funds, capital campaigns.
Limitations: Giving primarily in Hampden County, MA. No grants to individuals, or for endowment funds or operating budgets.
Application information:
Initial approach: Letter
Copies of proposal: 1
Deadline(s): None
Board meeting date(s): As required
Write: Albert E. Steiger, Jr., Pres.
Officers and Directors:* Albert E. Steiger, Jr.,* Pres.; Ralph A. Steiger, Jr., V.P.; Allen Steiger, Treas.; Richard S. Milstein, Clerk; Albert E. Steiger III, Philip C. Steiger, Jr., Robert K. Steiger.
Employer Identification Number: 046051750

3012
The Abbot and Dorothy H. Stevens Foundation
P.O. Box 111
North Andover 01845 (508) 688-7211

Trust established in 1953 in MA.
Donor(s): Abbot Stevens.†
Foundation type: Independent
Financial data (yr. ended 12/31/89): Assets, $10,897,128 (M); qualifying distributions, $1,174,148, including $627,948 for 90 grants

(high: $100,000; low: $100; average: $2,000-$5,000) and $546,200 for 1 loan.
Purpose and activities: Giving for education, health, welfare, youth organizations, arts and humanities, conservation, and historic preservation.
Types of support: Building funds, capital campaigns, continuing support, endowment funds, equipment, matching funds, operating budgets, renovation projects, seed money, technical assistance.
Limitations: Giving limited to MA, with emphasis on the greater Lawrence area. No support for national organizations, or for state or federal agencies. No grants to individuals, or for annual campaigns, deficit financing, exchange programs, internships, professorships, scholarships, or fellowships; no loans.
Publications: Program policy statement, application guidelines.
Application information: Application form not required.
Initial approach: Proposal
Copies of proposal: 1
Board meeting date(s): Monthly except July and Aug.
Write: Elizabeth A. Beland, Admin.
Trustees: Phebe S. Miner, Christopher W. Rogers, Samuel S. Rogers.
Number of staff: 1
Employer Identification Number: 046107991

3013
The Nathaniel and Elizabeth P. Stevens Foundation
P.O. Box 111
North Andover 01845 (508) 688-7211

Trust established in 1943 in MA.
Donor(s): Nathaniel Stevens.†
Foundation type: Independent
Financial data (yr. ended 12/31/89): Assets, $8,634,397 (M); qualifying distributions, $959,866, including $506,066 for 79 grants (high: $100,000; low: $500; average: $2,000-$10,000) and $453,800 for 1 loan.
Purpose and activities: Giving for education, historic preservation, the arts, social services, health, and conservation.
Types of support: General purposes, seed money, emergency funds, building funds, equipment, land acquisition, endowment funds, special projects, matching funds, capital campaigns, conferences and seminars, consulting services, continuing support, operating budgets, renovation projects, technical assistance.
Limitations: Giving limited to MA, with emphasis on the greater Lawrence area. No support for national organizations, or for state or federal agencies. No grants to individuals, or for deficit financing, exchange programs, internships, lectureships, research, professorships, scholarships, fellowships, or annual campaigns; no loans.
Publications: Application guidelines, program policy statement.
Application information: Application form not required.
Initial approach: Proposal
Copies of proposal: 1
Deadline(s): None
Board meeting date(s): Monthly except July and Aug.
Final notification: 2 months
Write: Elizabeth A. Beland, Admin.
Trustees: Joshua L. Miner IV, Phebe S. Miner, Samuel S. Rogers.
Number of staff: 1
Employer Identification Number: 042236996

3014
The Stoddard Charitable Trust ▼ ⌑
370 Main St., Suite 1250
Worcester 01608 (617) 798-8621

Trust established in 1939 in MA.
Donor(s): Harry G. Stoddard.†
Foundation type: Independent
Financial data (yr. ended 12/31/88): Assets, $51,058,599 (M); gifts received, $515,000; expenditures, $2,896,446, including $2,818,750 for 78 grants (high: $400,000; low: $250; average: $3,000-$50,000).
Purpose and activities: Emphasis on education, cultural programs, historical associations, youth agencies, and a community fund; support also for social service agencies, the environment, and health associations.
Types of support: Annual campaigns, seed money, emergency funds, building funds, equipment, land acquisition, research, scholarship funds, fellowships, professorships, internships, matching funds, general purposes, continuing support, renovation projects.
Limitations: Giving primarily in Worcester, MA. No grants to individuals.
Application information: Application form not required.
Initial approach: Proposal
Copies of proposal: 5
Deadline(s): Submit proposal between Jan. and Nov.; no set deadlines
Board meeting date(s): As required
Final notification: 3 months
Write: Paris Fletcher, Chair.
Officers and Trustees: Paris Fletcher, Chair.; Helen E. Stoddard, Vice-Chair.; Warner S. Fletcher, Secy.-Treas.; Allen W. Fletcher, Marion S. Fletcher, Judith S. King, Valerie S. Loring.
Number of staff: None.
Employer Identification Number: 046023791

3015
The Stone Charitable Foundation, Inc. ⌑
P.O. Box 728
Wareham 02571

Incorporated in 1948 in MA.
Donor(s): Dewey D. Stone,† Stephen A. Stone, Anne A. Stone, Thelma Finn, Jack Finn, Harry K. Stone.†
Foundation type: Independent
Financial data (yr. ended 11/30/88): Assets, $5,236,726 (M); gifts received, $10,000; expenditures, $401,715, including $351,486 for 50 grants (high: $106,486; low: $250).
Purpose and activities: Giving largely for Jewish welfare funds; grants also for hospitals, higher education, and cultural programs.
Types of support: General purposes, research, endowment funds, scholarship funds, building funds, annual campaigns, equipment, capital campaigns.
Limitations: Giving primarily in MA. No grants to individuals.
Application information: Application form not required.
Deadline(s): None
Board meeting date(s): As required
Write: Stephen Stone, Pres.
Officers and Trustees: Stephen A. Stone, Pres.; Theodore Teplow, Secy.; Alfred P. Rudnick, Treas.
Number of staff: None.
Employer Identification Number: 046114683

3016
Albert H. & Reuben S. Stone Fund
c/o Nichols & Stone
232 Logan St.
Gardner 01440 (617) 632-2770

Established in 1948.
Foundation type: Independent
Financial data (yr. ended 12/31/87): Assets, $2,670,756 (M); expenditures, $178,224, including $145,125 for 115 grants to individuals (high: $4,050; low: $200).
Purpose and activities: Giving for scholarships to local residents.
Types of support: Student aid.
Limitations: Giving limited to residents of Gardner, MA.
Application information: Application form required.
Initial approach: Letter
Deadline(s): Early in second semester
Write: Carlton E. Nichols or Carlton E. Nichols, Jr., Trustees
Trustees: James Kenary, Carlton E. Nichols, Sr., Carlton E. Nichols, Jr.
Employer Identification Number: 046050419

3017
Anne and David Stoneman Charitable Foundation, Inc. ⌑
c/o Grants Mgmt. Associates
230 Congress St.
Boston 02110 (617) 426-7172

Incorporated in 1957 in MA.
Donor(s): Anne Stoneman.
Foundation type: Independent
Financial data (yr. ended 7/31/89): Assets, $1,844,806 (M); gifts received, $135,923; expenditures, $359,893, including $357,877 for 73 grants (high: $150,000; low: $25).
Purpose and activities: Giving primarily to Jewish welfare funds, hospitals, and the performing arts; some support also for education.
Limitations: No grants to individuals.
Application information:
Initial approach: Letter
Deadline(s): None
Write: Ala H. Reid, Treas.
Officers: Miriam H. Stoneman, Pres.; Ala H. Reid, Treas.
Trustees: Elizabeth DeKnatel, Jean R. Fitzpatrick, Alan Rottenberg, Robert Smith, Eric Stein, Jane Stein.
Employer Identification Number: 046047379

3018
The Stop & Shop Charitable Foundation ⌑
One Bradley Circle
Braintree 02184 (617) 770-8000

Trust established in 1951 in MA.
Donor(s): Stop & Shop Companies, Inc., and subsidiaries.
Foundation type: Company-sponsored
Financial data (yr. ended 12/31/87): Assets, $4,998,457 (M); gifts received, $999,000; expenditures, $853,528, including $839,089 for 590 grants (high: $175,432; low: $25).
Purpose and activities: Support for community funds, higher education, religious welfare funds, and hospitals.
Types of support: Employee-related scholarships, matching funds.
Limitations: Giving primarily in CT, MA, and RI.
Application information: Application form required for employee-related scholarship program.
Deadline(s): Jan. 31 for scholarship applications
Trustees: Albert F. Frager, Avram J. Goldberg, Carol R. Goldberg, Irving W. Rabb, Norman S. Rabb.
Employer Identification Number: 046039593

3019
Stratford Foundation ▼
c/o Shawmut Bank, N.A.
One Federal St.
Boston 02211-0407 (617) 292-3885

Established in 1983 in MA.
Donor(s): Kenneth H. Olsen.
Foundation type: Independent
Financial data (yr. ended 12/31/89): Assets, $152,542,550 (M); gifts received, $47,800; expenditures, $10,383,771, including $10,375,971 for 57 grants (high: $3,475,000; low: $1,942; average: $30,000-$160,000).
Purpose and activities: In initial years of operation, grants primarily to institutions closely associated with the donor, with emphasis on colleges and universities and religious organizations.
Types of support: General purposes.
Limitations: No grants to individuals.
Publications: Program policy statement.
Application information: Application form required.
Initial approach: Letter
Copies of proposal: 2
Deadline(s): None
Board meeting date(s): Periodically
Write: Peter A. Wilson, Sr. V.P., Shawmut Bank, N.A.
Trustees: Ava Lisa Memmen, Eeva-Liisa Aulikki Olsen, Kenneth H. Olsen.
Trustee Bank: Shawmut Bank, N.A.
Number of staff: None.
Employer Identification Number: 222524023

3020
The Stride Rite Charitable Foundation, Inc. ⌑
c/o The Stride Rite Corp.
Five Cambridge Ctr.
Cambridge 02142 (617) 491-8800

Incorporated in 1953 in MA as J.A. and Bessie Slosberg Charitable Foundation, Inc.
Donor(s): The Stride Rite Corp.
Foundation type: Company-sponsored
Financial data (yr. ended 9/30/88): Assets, $2,640,769 (M); gifts received, $1,600,163; expenditures, $494,829, including $491,628 for 156 grants (high: $175,000; low: $25; average: $1,000-$5,000).
Purpose and activities: Giving primarily for child welfare; support also for cultural programs and community funds.
Types of support: Annual campaigns, continuing support, operating budgets, employee-related scholarships, scholarship funds.
Limitations: Giving limited to MA, with emphasis on the greater Boston area.
Application information: Application form not required.
Deadline(s): None
Write: Vicki Mann
Officer and Director: Arnold Hiatt, Pres.
Employer Identification Number: 046059887

3021
Students House, Inc. ⌑
c/o Sherburne, Powers & Needham
One Beacon St.
Boston 02108-4005

Foundation type: Independent
Financial data (yr. ended 08/31/89): Assets, $1,025,166 (M); expenditures, $60,670, including $48,000 for 4 grants of $12,000 each.
Purpose and activities: Support primarily for higher education.
Limitations: Giving primarily in Boston, MA. No grants to individuals.
Application information: Contributes only to pre-selected organizations. Applications not accepted.
Officers: Mrs. Hiroshi N. Nishino, Pres.; Mrs. Robert H. Hopkins, V.P.; William V. Tripp III, Treas.
Employer Identification Number: 042105949

3022
Sudbury Foundation ⌑
c/o Mechanics Bank Trust Dept.
P.O. Box 987
Worcester 01613 (617) 798-6467

Trust established in 1952 in MA.
Donor(s): Esther M. Atkinson.†
Foundation type: Operating
Financial data (yr. ended 12/31/88): Assets, $13,378,376 (M); expenditures, $362,754, including $174,579 for 14 grants (high: $125,000; low: $300) and $3,500 for 3 grants to individuals (high: $2,000; low: $500).
Purpose and activities: Grants to individuals for student loans; support also for local social services and secondary education.
Types of support: Student loans, student aid, matching funds, seed money.
Limitations: Giving primarily in Sudbury, MA.
Publications: Program policy statement.
Application information: Application form required for student loans.
Initial approach: Letter
Deadline(s): May 1 and Nov. 1 for student loans
Write: John E. Arsenault, V.P. and Trust Officer, Mechanics Bank
Trustees: Richard A. Davison, John E. Taft, Mechanics Bank.
Employer Identification Number: 046037026

3023
The Swasey Fund for Relief of Public School Teachers of Newburyport, Inc. ⌑ ☆
31 Milk St., Rm. 706
Boston 02109 (508) 462-2784

Foundation type: Independent
Financial data (yr. ended 4/30/89): Assets, $2,208,475 (M); expenditures, $109,767, including $7,008 for 2 grants (high: $600; low: $100) and $66,600 for 21 grants to individuals (high: $10,000; low: $100).
Purpose and activities: Provides "financial aid to teachers who have taught in the public schools for at least ten years, if their financial aid conditions require it, and distributions to provide cultural and educational opportunities for current and retired teachers."
Types of support: Grants to individuals.
Application information: Assistance limited to individuals who have taught in Newburyport, MA.
Write: Jean MacDonald, Treas.
Officers: Jean Kirkpatrick, Pres.; Margaret Taranda, Secy.; Jean MacDonald, Treas.
Directors: Irene Grant, Carol Mullen, John H. Pramberg, Jr.
Employer Identification Number: 046044618

3024
Sidney A. Swensrud Charitable Trust ⌑
24 Federal St., Suite 400
Boston 02110

Established in 1955.
Foundation type: Independent
Financial data (yr. ended 12/31/88): Assets, $5,377,027 (M); gifts received, $336,674; expenditures, $320,363, including $296,300 for 29 grants (high: $240,000; low: $100).
Purpose and activities: Giving primarily for population control and public policy organizations.
Limitations: No grants to individuals.
Application information: Application form not required.
Deadline(s): None
Write: Nancy S. Anthony, Trustee
Trustees: Nancy S. Anthony, Stephen B. Swensrud.
Employer Identification Number: 256050238

3025
Tapper Charitable Foundation ⌑
c/o Mintz & Norberg, C.P.A.
340 Main St., Suite 860
Worcester 01608

Established in 1979 in MA.
Foundation type: Independent
Financial data (yr. ended 6/30/88): Assets, $1,560,777 (M); expenditures, $147,258, including $141,171 for 17 grants (high: $110,650; low: $100).

Purpose and activities: Support primarily for Jewish welfare and higher education.
Limitations: Giving primarily in Worcester, MA.
Trustees: Albert Tapper, Charles Tapper.
Employer Identification Number: 042700063

3026
Technical Training Foundation ⌑
c/o BayBank Merrimac Valley
588 Essex St.
Lawrence 01842 (508) 682-1900

Established in 1985 in MA.
Foundation type: Independent
Financial data (yr. ended 08/30/89): Assets, $7,151,855 (M); expenditures, $77,328, including $58,627 for 2 grants (high: $50,000; low: $8,627).
Purpose and activities: Support primarily for scholarship programs at institutions of higher education and technical training.
Types of support: Research, scholarship funds.
Application information:
Initial approach: Letter
Deadline(s): None
Write: Ibrahim Hefni
Trustees: Denis Hamboyan, Ibrahim Hefni, Wensley Hefni.
Employer Identification Number: 042864138

3027
Thermo Electron Foundation, Inc. ⌑ ☆
c/o Thermo Electron Corp.
101 First Ave.
Waltham 02254

Incorporated in 1986 in MA.
Donor(s): Thermo Electron Corp.
Foundation type: Company-sponsored
Financial data (yr. ended 12/31/87): Assets, $473,793 (M); gifts received, $550,000; expenditures, $192,305, including $191,333 for 22 grants (high: $83,000; low: $1,000).
Purpose and activities: Giving primarily for the medical, engineering, and political sciences; support also for arts and culture, including museums.
Limitations: Giving primarily in MA and NY. No grants to individuals.
Application information: Application form not required.
Deadline(s): None
Write: Linda Norberg
Officer: George N. Hatsopoulos, Pres.; Robert C. Howard, V.P.; Paul F. Ferrari, Treas.
Employer Identification Number: 222778152

3028
Thomas Thompson Trust
31 Milk St., Suite 620
Boston 02109 (617) 723-4535

Trust established in 1869 in MA.
Donor(s): Thomas Thompson.†
Foundation type: Independent
Financial data (yr. ended 05/31/89): Assets, $8,036,339 (M); expenditures, $436,288, including $395,938 for 22 grants (high: $100,000; low: $500; average: $2,000-$20,000).
Purpose and activities: To assist poor seamstresses, needlewomen, and shop girls in temporary need. Funds may be distributed "to those charitable organizations...deemed to be directed toward the promotion of health, education, or the general social or civic betterment."
Types of support: Annual campaigns, emergency funds, building funds, equipment, land acquisition, matching funds, special projects, renovation projects.
Limitations: Giving limited to Windham County, VT, particularly in the town of Brattleboro, and to Dutchess County, NY, particularly in the town of Rhinebeck. No grants to individuals, or for operating budgets, continuing support, seed money, deficit financing, endowment funds, scholarships, or fellowships; no loans.
Publications: Occasional report.
Application information: Grants awarded only to organizations that have been in operation for 3 consecutive years. Application form required.
Initial approach: Telephone
Copies of proposal: 1
Deadline(s): None
Board meeting date(s): Monthly except Aug., and as required
Final notification: 6 weeks
Write: Daniel W. Fawcett or William B. Tyler, Trustees
Trustees: Daniel W. Fawcett, William B. Tyler.
Number of staff: 1 part-time professional.
Employer Identification Number: 030179429

3029
Thoracic Foundation ⌑
c/o Robert, Finnegan & Lynah
137 South St.
Boston 02111
Application address: 135 Francis St., Boston, MA 02215; Tel.: (617) 738-7810

Established in 1949 in MA.
Donor(s): Richard H. Overholt, M.D., and others.
Foundation type: Independent
Financial data (yr. ended 12/31/88): Assets, $1,100,357 (M); gifts received, $10,755; expenditures, $145,271, including $116,000 for 6 grants (high: $35,000; low: $1,000).
Purpose and activities: Support for medical research; current contributions to hospitals providing service to thoracic cases.
Types of support: Research, publications, conferences and seminars.
Limitations: Giving primarily in MA.
Application information: Application form not required.
Deadline(s): None
Write: Bradley Cook, Trustee
Trustees: Bradley Cook, R. Willis Leith, Jr., Galen Stone.
Employer Identification Number: 042226641

3030
Willard C. Tilson Foundation ⌑
c/o Hale & Dorr
60 State St.
Boston 02109
Application address: 30 Western Ave., Gloucester, MA 01930; Tel.: (617) 283-0643

Established in 1956 in MA.
Foundation type: Independent
Financial data (yr. ended 12/31/88): Assets, $1,652,429 (M); expenditures, $116,074, including $97,000 for 9 grants (high: $53,000; low: $2,000).
Purpose and activities: Emphasis on secondary and higher education, and youth.
Application information:
Initial approach: Letter
Deadline(s): None
Write: Lloyd B. Waring, Trustee
Trustees: James St. Clair, Lloyd B. Waring.
Employer Identification Number: 046036556

3031
TJX Foundation
(Formerly Zayre Foundation, Inc.)
c/o TJX Cos.
770 Cochituate Rd.
Framingham 01701 (508) 651-8714

Incorporated in 1966 in MA.
Donor(s): Zayre Corp.
Foundation type: Company-sponsored
Financial data (yr. ended 1/30/88): Assets, $362,302 (M); gifts received, $500,000; expenditures, $1,344,990, including $1,269,975 for grants.
Purpose and activities: Giving primarily for health and social service programs, with emphasis on minority groups, the poor, women, the handicapped, and the elderly.
Limitations: Giving limited to areas of company operations. No support for political groups or fraternal organizations. No grants to individuals.
Publications: Annual report.
Application information:
Copies of proposal: 1
Deadline(s): None
Board meeting date(s): Twice a year
Write: Rhonda Boccio
Officers and Directors: Stanley H. Feldberg, Pres.; Stanley Berkovitz, V.P.; Maurice Segall, V.P.; Sumner Feldberg, Treas.
Number of staff: 1 full-time professional; 2 full-time support.
Employer Identification Number: 042399760

3032
Charles Irwin Travelli Fund
c/o Tyler & Reynolds
One Boston Place
Boston 02108

Incorporated in 1914 in MA.
Donor(s): Charles I. Travelli,† Emma R. Travelli.†
Foundation type: Independent
Financial data (yr. ended 11/30/89): Assets, $831,289 (M); gifts received, $598,791; expenditures, $662,426, including $629,650 for 30 grants (high: $80,000; low: $1,000).
Purpose and activities: "...furnishing aid and comfort to the deserving poor; contributes to the support of other MA charitable corporations or associations, and generally for the doing and carrying on of educational, charitable, benevolent and religious work." Grants largely for higher and other education; minor support also for hospitals and social services.
Types of support: Scholarship funds.

Limitations: Giving primarily in the New England area for higher education; grants to other organizations mainly in MA, particularly Boston.
Application information: Scholarship application forms available at participating educational institutions.
Initial approach: Letter
Deadline(s): None
Board meeting date(s): As required
Officers: Sumner R. Andrews, Pres.; Marshall G. Bolster, Treas.; Oliver R. Andrews, Jr., Exec. Dir.
Number of staff: 1 part-time professional.
Employer Identification Number: 042260155

3033
The Tupancy-Harris Foundation of 1986 ☆
Box 1647
Boston 02105-1647
Application address: 175 Federal St., Boston, MA 02110; Tel.: (617) 482-5270

Established in 1986 in MA.
Donor(s): Oswald A. Tupancy.†
Foundation type: Independent
Financial data (yr. ended 12/31/89): Assets, $193,661 (M); gifts received, $670,300; expenditures, $672,267, including $669,632 for 17 grants (high: $361,010; low: $1,000).
Purpose and activities: Support for the activities of the Nantucket Conservation Foundation and the Nantucket Historical Association; grants also for welfare programs, medical research for hospitals, public television, and the University of Michigan.
Limitations: Giving primarily in Nantucket, MA.
Application information: Application form not required.
Initial approach: Letter
Copies of proposal: 1
Deadline(s): None
Write: Robert N. Karelitz, V.P., Fiduciary Trust Co.
Trustee: Fiduciary Trust Co.
Number of staff: None.
Employer Identification Number: 046547989

3034
Urann Foundation
P.O. Box 1788
Brockton 02403 (508) 588-7744

Established in 1963 in MA.
Foundation type: Independent
Financial data (yr. ended 12/31/89): Assets, $2,139,951 (M); expenditures, $141,097, including $47,000 for 2 grants of $23,500 each and $43,780 for 22 grants to individuals (high: $2,600; low: $700).
Purpose and activities: Giving for scholarships and payment of medical bills to members of MA families engaged in cranberry production; remainder of giving to a specified university and hospital.
Types of support: Student aid, grants to individuals.
Limitations: Giving limited to MA and ME.
Application information: Telephone during weekday mornings; scholarship applications also available at guidance offices of high schools; scholarship status decided anew each year; other beneficiaries already specified. Application form required.
Initial approach: Telephone or letter
Deadline(s): Apr. 15 for scholarship; none for medical bill grants
Board meeting date(s): Varies
Write: Howard Whelan, Admin.
Trustees: Balfour Bassett, Reginald T. Cole, Ellen Stillman.
Number of staff: 1 part-time professional.
Employer Identification Number: 046115599

3035
Vingo Trust II ⌘
c/o Ropes & Gray
225 Franklin St.
Boston 02110

Trust established in 1954 in MA as successor to Vingo Trust.
Donor(s): Amory Coolidge,† William A. Coolidge.
Foundation type: Independent
Financial data (yr. ended 12/31/87): Assets, $9,269,924 (M); expenditures, $370,830, including $293,518 for 28 grants (high: $77,032; low: $875; average: $2,000-$25,000).
Purpose and activities: Giving for community-run neighborhood projects in Boston, Cambridge, Somerville, and Chelsea; support for education and religious giving.
Types of support: Operating budgets, special projects, building funds, equipment.
Limitations: Giving limited to Boston, Cambridge, Somerville, and Chelsea, MA. No grants to individuals, or for endowment funds, scholarships, or fellowships; no loans.
Publications: Informational brochure, application guidelines.
Application information: Contributes only to pre-selected organizations. Applications not accepted.
Write: Mary Sargent, Secy.
Officer: Mary Sargent, Secy.
Trustees: Francis H. Burr, William A. Coolidge, George H. Kidder, Catherine C. Lastavica, John Lastavica.
Employer Identification Number: 046027982

3036
The George R. Wallace Foundation ⌘
c/o Boston Safe Deposit & Trust Co.
One Boston Place
Boston 02106 (617) 523-5700
Mailing address: 53 State St., Exchange Place, Boston, MA 02109

Trust established in 1963 in MA.
Donor(s): George R. Wallace.†
Foundation type: Independent
Financial data (yr. ended 12/31/88): Assets, $4,888,058 (M); expenditures, $346,810, including $270,600 for 39 grants (high: $30,500; low: $500).
Purpose and activities: Emphasis on education.
Types of support: General purposes, annual campaigns, seed money, building funds, equipment, land acquisition, endowment funds, matching funds.
Limitations: Giving primarily in MA. No grants to individuals, or for scholarships or fellowships; no loans.
Application information: Application form not required.
Initial approach: Letter
Copies of proposal: 3
Deadline(s): None
Board meeting date(s): Semiannually
Final notification: 6 months
Write: Trustees
Trustees: George R. Wallace III, Chair.; John Grado, Jr., Henry B. Shepard, Jr.
Custodian: Boston Safe Deposit & Trust Co.
Number of staff: None.
Employer Identification Number: 046130518

3037
Blanche M. Walsh Charity Trust
174 Central St., Suite 329
Lowell 01852 (617) 454-5654

Trust established in 1973 in MA.
Foundation type: Independent
Financial data (yr. ended 12/31/88): Assets, $2,532,507 (M); expenditures, $201,460, including $183,165 for 90 grants (high: $11,000; low: $500; average: $2,000).
Purpose and activities: Giving limited to Roman Catholic organizations, including educational institutions and welfare organizations.
Types of support: Operating budgets, seed money, building funds, equipment, scholarship funds, publications, conferences and seminars.
Limitations: No grants to individuals, or for endowment funds, continuing support, annual campaigns, deficit financing, or matching gifts; no loans.
Publications: Application guidelines.
Application information: Application form required.
Initial approach: Letter
Copies of proposal: 1
Deadline(s): Nov. 10
Board meeting date(s): Dec. and as required
Final notification: First week of Jan.
Write: Robert F. Murphy, Jr., Trustee
Trustees: Ruth F. Cowdrey, John E. Leggat, Robert F. Murphy, Jr.
Number of staff: 3 part-time professional.
Employer Identification Number: 046311841

3038
Warren Benevolent Fund, Inc. ⌘ ☆
P.O. Box 46
Ashland 01721 (617) 881-2077

Incorporated in 1953 in MA.
Donor(s): Henry E. Warren.†
Foundation type: Independent
Financial data (yr. ended 12/31/88): Assets, $425,455 (M); expenditures, $140,755, including $2,300 for 2 grants (high: $1,700; low: $600), $10,000 for 2 grants to individuals of $5,000 each and $113,474 for loans to individuals.
Purpose and activities: Primarily awards scholarship loans and grants to Ashland High School students only.
Types of support: Student loans, student aid.
Limitations: Giving primarily in Ashland, MA. No grants for building or endowment funds.
Application information:
Initial approach: Letter
Copies of proposal: 7

Deadline(s): None
Board meeting date(s): Quarterly
Write: Mrs. Ann Thurston, Treas.
Officers: Carl W. Walter, Pres.; James Poitras, V.P.; Ann Thurston, Treas.
Directors: Roy Hayward, William C. Loring, Shirley Morrisette, Finley H. Perry, Erlenge Strano.
Employer Identification Number: 042309470

3039
Leo Wasserman Foundation ⌑ ☆
One Boston Place, 23rd Fl.
Boston 02108 (617) 723-8700

Established in 1951 in MA.
Donor(s): Leo Wasserman.†
Foundation type: Independent
Financial data (yr. ended 12/31/88): Assets, $1,125,479 (M); gifts received, $91,159; expenditures, $69,856, including $43,050 for grants.
Purpose and activities: Support for federated and united funds, particularly Jewish welfare funds, higher education, hospitals, cultural arts, religion, and community development.
Application information:
Write: David R. Pokross, Trustee
Trustees: David R. Pokross, Muriel K. Pokross.
Employer Identification Number: 046014473

3040
Waters Foundation ⌑
1153 Grove St.
Framingham 01701 (508) 877-3791

Trust established in 1958 in MA.
Donor(s): James L. Waters.
Foundation type: Independent
Financial data (yr. ended 12/31/88): Assets, $2,315,248 (M); gifts received, $1,225,000; expenditures, $61,590, including $1,000 for 1 grant.
Purpose and activities: Grants primarily for higher education; support also for cultural programs.
Application information: Seldom contributes to unsolicited applicants.
Initial approach: Letter
Deadline(s): None
Write: James L. Waters, Trustee
Trustees: Faith P. Waters, James L. Waters, Richard C. Waters.
Employer Identification Number: 046115211

3041
The Frederick E. Weber Charities Corporation
34 1/2 Beacon St.
Boston 02108 (617) 523-1455

Incorporated in 1902 in MA.
Donor(s): Frederick E. Weber.†
Foundation type: Independent
Financial data (yr. ended 03/31/89): Assets, $4,201,476 (M); gifts received, $1,394; expenditures, $236,685, including $177,548 for 85 grants to individuals (high: $15,000; low: $100; average: $200-$1,000).
Purpose and activities: Giving primarily to social service agencies for emergency financial assistance to indigent families or individuals.
Types of support: Emergency funds, grants to individuals.
Limitations: Giving primarily in the greater Boston, MA, area. No grants for research, capital projects, or equipment.
Publications: Annual report, program policy statement.
Application information:
Initial approach: Letter
Copies of proposal: 1
Deadline(s): None
Board meeting date(s): Weekly except in Aug.
Final notification: 30 days
Officers and Directors:* Mary Ann Daily,* Pres.; Daniel A. Phillips,* V.P. and Treas.; Janet W. Eustis,* Clerk; Robert H. Baldwin, Lawrence Coolidge, Franklin T. Hammond, Jr., William F. Kehoe, Peter E. Reinhold, Patrick V. Riley, William C. Swan, Daniel P. Wise.
Number of staff: 1 part-time support.
Employer Identification Number: 042133244

3042
Webster Charitable Foundation, Inc. ⌑
c/o Blue Seal Feeds, Inc.
P.O. Box 8
Lawrence 01842 (508) 686-4131

Incorporated in 1951 in MA.
Donor(s): H.K. Webster Co., members of the Webster Family.
Foundation type: Independent
Financial data (yr. ended 12/31/88): Assets, $1,637,991 (M); gifts received, $50,000; expenditures, $96,220, including $80,550 for 52 grants.
Purpose and activities: Emphasis on community funds, education, and hospitals.
Limitations: Giving primarily in the greater Lawrence, MA, area.
Application information:
Initial approach: Letter
Deadline(s): Mar. 1 and Oct. 1
Write: Dean K. Webster, Secy.
Officers and Directors: Walter N. Webster, Pres.; Dean K. Webster, Secy.; Ralph W. Gilman, Treas.; R. Kingman Webster.
Employer Identification Number: 046112387

3043
Edwin S. Webster Foundation
c/o Grants Management Associates, Inc.
230 Congress St., 3rd Fl.
Boston 02110 (617) 426-7172

Trust established in 1948 in MA.
Donor(s): Edwin S. Webster.†
Foundation type: Independent
Financial data (yr. ended 12/31/88): Assets, $15,470,970 (M); expenditures, $775,731, including $701,000 for 52 grants (high: $100,000; low: $2,000).
Purpose and activities: Emphasis on cultural activities, hospitals, medical research, higher and secondary education, youth agencies, community funds, and programs relating to alcoholism, the handicapped, and minorities.
Types of support: Operating budgets, continuing support, annual campaigns, building funds, equipment, land acquisition, endowment funds, matching funds, scholarship funds, professorships, internships, fellowships, special projects, research.
Limitations: Giving primarily in the Northeast, especially MA, NH, and NY. No grants to individuals, or for seed money, emergency funds, deficit financing, publications, or conferences; no loans.
Publications: Grants list, application guidelines.
Application information: Application form not required.
Initial approach: Proposal
Copies of proposal: 1
Deadline(s): Submit proposal preferably in Mar. or Sept.; no set deadline
Board meeting date(s): May or June and Nov. or Dec.
Final notification: 10 days after meetings on grant proposals
Write: Administrator
Officer and Trustees:* Richard Harte, Jr.,* Secy.; Henry U. Harris, Jr., Henry U. Harris III, Edwin W. Hiam.
Number of staff: 2
Employer Identification Number: 046000647

3044
Fred W. Wells Trust Fund ⌑
Bank of New England-West, Trust Dept.
One Federal St.
Greenfield 01301 (413) 772-0281

Donor(s): Fred W. Wells.†
Foundation type: Independent
Financial data (yr. ended 6/30/88): Assets, $2,488,401 (M); expenditures, $135,854, including $40,331 for 10 grants (high: $12,000; low: $800) and $75,375 for 123 grants to individuals (high: $1,600; low: $150).
Purpose and activities: Grants for medical and other health care programs, and agricultural accomplishment prizes; support also for scholarships.
Types of support: Student aid.
Limitations: Giving limited to Franklin County, MA; scholarships limited to residents of Greenfield, Deerfield, Shelburne, Ashfield, Montague, Buckland, Charlemont, Heath, Leyden, Gill, Northfield, Conway, Bernardston, Hawley, Rowe, and Monroe, MA.
Publications: Application guidelines.
Application information: Application form required for education grants.
Initial approach: Letter
Deadline(s): May 1 for education grants
Write: Christopher S. Maniatty, V.P.
Officers and Trustees: Beda A. Langevin, Chair.; Christopher S. Maniatty, V.P.; Ann B. Abbott, Douglas Angelman, Albert W. Charsky, Jean B. Cummings, Laurel Ann Glocheski, Ralph Haskins, Jean Holdsworth, Donald J. LaPierre, Peter C. Mackin, Shelia Moss-White, Theodore Penick, Edward Phelps, Donald Smiaroski.
Employer Identification Number: 046412350

3045
William P. Wharton Trust
c/o Choate, Hall & Stewart
Exchange Place, 34th Fl.
Boston 02109-2808 (617) 227-5020

Established in 1976 in MA.
Foundation type: Independent

Financial data (yr. ended 09/30/89): Assets, $1,609,339 (M); expenditures, $67,073, including $46,155 for 10 grants (high: $9,660; low: $2,000; average: $1,000-$5,000).
Purpose and activities: "To support projects that directly promote the study, conservation, and appreciation of nature. Specific objectives include: bird and forestry research and management, natural areas preservation, and management techniques designed to improve environmental quality and species diversity."
Types of support: Equipment, land acquisition, publications, research, special projects.
Limitations: Giving primarily in MA and New England.
Publications: Informational brochure (including application guidelines).
Application information: Funds limited to no more than $5,000 per application. Application form not required.
Initial approach: Proposal
Copies of proposal: 1
Deadline(s): Apr. 15 and Oct. 15
Board meeting date(s): May and Nov.
Final notification: Within 30 days of board meeting
Write: Rhodes G. Lockwood, Trustee, or Mary A. Willert
Trustees: Peter A. Fine, Rhodes G. Lockwood.
Number of staff: None.
Employer Identification Number: 046407797

3046
Wheelwright Scientific School ⌑
c/o Chase & Lunt
47 State St.
Newburyport 01950 (617) 462-4434

Established in 1882.
Foundation type: Independent
Financial data (yr. ended 6/30/89): Assets, $2,567,305 (M); expenditures, $125,238, including $82,070 for 16 grants to individuals (high: $6,500; low: $2,800).
Purpose and activities: Giving only for scholarships to financially aid young Protestant men of Newburyport in obtaining a scientific education.
Types of support: Student aid.
Limitations: Giving limited to Newburyport, MA, residents.
Application information: Application form required.
Copies of proposal: 1
Board meeting date(s): Apr. and Nov.
Write: Josiah H. Welch, Secy.
Officers and Trustees: Josiah H. Welch, Secy.; Douglas Sloane IV, Treas.; Edward G. Malin, John H. Pramberg, Jr., John W. Pramberg, James A. Zafris, Jr.
Employer Identification Number: 046004390

3047
Thomas J. White Foundation ⌑
One Gateway Ctr.
Newton 02158-2802 (617) 964-0100

Established in 1968 in MA.
Foundation type: Independent
Financial data (yr. ended 1/31/88): Assets, $62,415 (M); gifts received, $360,000; expenditures, $629,908, including $629,854 for grants (high: $150,000).
Purpose and activities: Support primarily for a health organization; support also for a hunger program, missionary work, hospitals, and Catholic welfare.
Application information:
Write: Thomas J. White, Trustee
Trustees: Robert J. Owens, Thomas J. White.
Employer Identification Number: 046121643

3048
White Fund, Inc. ⌑ ☆
c/o Clifford Elias, Managing Trustee
70 East St.
Methuen 01844-4597
Additional application addresses: Archer L. Bolton, Jr., Treas., 102 Millpond, North Andover, MA 01845; Roger N. Bower, Pres., 49 West Parish Dr., Andover, MA 01810

Established in 1852.
Foundation type: Independent
Financial data (yr. ended 3/31/89): Assets, $1,016,112 (M); expenditures, $59,123, including $41,005 for 11 grants (high: $9,500; low: $650).
Purpose and activities: Giving primarily "to sponsor a lecture series and to support the Lawrence Public Library." Support also for youth and hospitals.
Types of support: Equipment, capital campaigns.
Limitations: Giving limited to Lawrence, MA. No grants to individuals.
Application information:
Initial approach: Proposal
Copies of proposal: 4
Deadline(s): Apr. 1
Officers and Trustees: Roger N. Bower, Pres.; Archer L. Bolton, Jr., Treas.; Clifford E. Elias.
Employer Identification Number: 042761754

3049
Widow's Society in Boston ⌑
c/o Bank of New England, N.A.
28 State St.
Boston 02107
Application address: 581 Boylston St., Boston, MA 02116; Tel.: (617) 536-7951

Established in 1916 in MA.
Foundation type: Operating
Financial data (yr. ended 10/31/87): Assets, $2,117,615 (M); expenditures, $157,803, including $107,001 for grants to individuals.
Purpose and activities: A private operating foundation; support for widowed, divorced, or single women who are over 60 years old and in need of financial aid.
Types of support: Grants to individuals.
Limitations: Giving limited to applicants living within 25 miles of the State House in Boston, MA.
Application information: Application form not required.
Initial approach: Referrals from public and social organizations
Deadline(s): None
Write: Jackie Husid
Officers: Mrs. Vincent J. McGugan, Secy.; Richard V. Howe, Treas.
Directors: Ann Beha, Susan G. Loring, Mrs. Samuel E. Shaw II.
Employer Identification Number: 042306840

3050
Arthur Ashley Williams Foundation ⌑
345 Union Ave.
P.O. Box 665
Framingham 01701 (508) 429-1149

Incorporated in 1951 in MA.
Donor(s): Arthur A. Williams.†
Foundation type: Independent
Financial data (yr. ended 12/31/88): Assets, $2,942,125 (M); expenditures, $207,142, including $116,960 for 15 grants (high: $37,500; low: $1,000; average: $5,000-$10,000) and $33,495 for 21 grants to individuals (high: $5,250; low: $722; average: $5,000-$10,000).
Purpose and activities: Grants primarily for churches and social welfare and youth agencies. Financial aid for higher education to students in need.
Types of support: Student aid, scholarship funds.
Publications: Application guidelines.
Application information: Application form required.
Initial approach: Letter
Copies of proposal: 1
Deadline(s): Submit proposal preferably in Dec.; deadline 1 week prior to board meetings
Board meeting date(s): Jan., Apr., July, and Oct.
Write: Frederick Cole, Chair.
Officers and Trustees:* Frederick Cole,* Chair.; Elbert F. Tuttle,* Secy.; Clement T. Lambert,* Treas.; David S. Williams, William Williams, Hayden R. Wood.
Employer Identification Number: 046044714

3051
The Winston Foundation for World Peace ⌑
401 Commonwealth Ave.
Boston 02215 (617) 266-1014

Established in 1984 in MA.
Donor(s): Robert W. Scrivner.†
Foundation type: Operating
Financial data (yr. ended 12/31/88): Assets, $3,556,429 (M); gifts received, $756,905; expenditures, $694,696, including $536,000 for 50 grants (high: $45,000; low: $2,500).
Purpose and activities: A private operating foundation dedicated to the prevention of nuclear war, with primary focus on U.S. public policy; internship program for individuals initiated 1988-89.
Types of support: General purposes, publications, research, seed money, fellowships.
Publications: 990-PF, grants list, occasional report, annual report.
Application information: Application form not required.
Initial approach: Letter
Copies of proposal: 1
Deadline(s): Jan. 15, May 15, and Sept. 15
Board meeting date(s): Feb., June, and Oct.
Final notification: Within 1 month after board meeting
Write: John Tirman, Exec. Dir.
Officers and Directors: Bevis Longstreth, Pres.; William Zabel, V.P. and Secy.; Roy H. Carlin, V.P. and Treas.; John H. Adams, Robert L. Allen, Leslie W. Dunbar, Alice Tepper

Marlin, Karl Mathiasen III, Melinda B. Scrivner, Albert G. Sims.
Number of staff: 1 full-time professional; 1 full-time support.
Employer Identification Number: 133160360

3052
Clara B. Winthrop Trust ⌘ ☆
c/o Welch & Forbes
45 School St.
Boston 02108 (617) 523-1635

Established in 1969.
Foundation type: Independent
Financial data (yr. ended 12/31/87): Assets, $1,512,921 (M); expenditures, $77,166, including $58,550 for 23 grants (high: $5,700; low: $600).
Purpose and activities: Support primarily for museums and other cultural organizations, education, and conservation.
Limitations: Giving primarily in MA. No grants to individuals.
Application information:
Initial approach: Letter
Deadline(s): None
Write: F. Murray Forbes, Jr., Trustee
Trustee: F. Murray Forbes, Jr.
Employer Identification Number: 046039972

3053
Louis E. Wolfson Foundation
c/o Mintz, Levin, et al.
One Financial Ctr.
Boston 02111 (617) 638-4100
Application address: Boston Univ. School of Medicine, 80 East Concord St., Rm. 103, Boston, MA 02118

Trust established in 1951 in MA.
Donor(s): Louis E. Wolfson, M.D.†
Foundation type: Independent
Financial data (yr. ended 06/30/88): Assets, $16,240,984 (M); gifts received, $300,200; expenditures, $1,285,081, including $840,000 for 3 grants of $280,000 each.
Purpose and activities: Two-thirds of income is restricted to the support of student aid endowments at medical schools of Boston University, Harvard University, and Tufts University; remaining grants generally restricted to supporting medical education of M.D. degree candidates at medical schools.
Limitations: No grants to individuals.
Publications: Application guidelines.
Application information: Application form not required.
Initial approach: Letter
Deadline(s): None
Board meeting date(s): Varies; grants paid in late summer and in late Dec. or early Jan.
Final notification: Within 3 months
Write: John I. Sandson, Trustee
Trustees: Henry H. Banks, Allie Cohen, James Cohen, Albert F. Cullen, Jr., Daniel D. Federman, John Penn, John I. Sandson.
Employer Identification Number: 046053295

3054
Greater Worcester Community Foundation, Inc.
44 Front St., Suite 530
Worcester 01608 (508) 755-0980

Incorporated in 1975 in MA.
Foundation type: Community
Financial data (yr. ended 12/31/89): Assets, $23,930,109 (M); gifts received, $1,254,487; expenditures, $1,708,599, including $134,922 for grants (high: $100,000; low: $100; average: $1,000-$4,000).
Purpose and activities: "To help meet the health, educational, social welfare, cultural and civic needs of the people of Greater Worcester, including, but not limited to, assisting charitable and educational institutions; for the needy, sick, aged or helpless; for the care of children; for the betterment of living and working conditions; for recreation for all classes, and for such other public and/or charitable uses and purposes as will best make for mental, moral and physical improvement, or contribute to the public welfare."
Types of support: Seed money, equipment, matching funds, scholarship funds, employee-related scholarships, special projects, technical assistance, student aid, general purposes, operating budgets, program-related investments, renovation projects.
Limitations: Giving limited to the greater Worcester, MA, area.
Publications: Annual report, program policy statement, application guidelines, newsletter.
Application information: Submit 8 copies of Foundation summary sheet plus 2 copies of proposal. Scholarships are for residents of Worcester County, MA or for children of employees of Rotman's Furniture. Application form required.
Initial approach: Telephone or letter
Copies of proposal: 2
Deadline(s): Educational grants, Apr. 1; women and children, June 1; discretionary awards, Dec. 1; and scholarships, Mar. 15
Board meeting date(s): Mar., June, Sept., Nov., and as required
Final notification: 3 1/2 months
Write: Ms. Kay M. Marquet, Exec. Dir.
Officers and Directors:* Michael P. Angelini,* Pres.; John M. Nelson,* 1st V.P.; Martha A. Cowan,* 2nd V.P.; David R. Grenon, Treas.; Helen A. Bowditch, Richard B. Collins, William P. Densmore, Zoila Torres Feldman, Sarah B. Garfield, James H. Harrington, Michael D. Leavitt, Stephen B. Loring, F. William Marshall, John O. Mirick, David A. Persky, J. Robert Seder, Edward D. Simsarian, Polly Traina, David Woodbury.
Distribution Committee: Michael D. Brockelman, Barbara Greenberg, Joseph Hagan, Vincent F. O'Rourke, Jr., David B. Stephens, Corinne C. Turner, Shirley Wright.
Trustee Banks: Bank of New England-Worcester, Mechanics Bank, Shawmut Worcester County Bank, N.A.
Number of staff: 3 full-time professional; 1 part-time professional; 3 part-time support.
Employer Identification Number: 042572276

3055
Wyman-Gordon Foundation ⌘
105 Madison St., Box 789
Worcester 01613-0789 (508) 756-5111

Established in 1966 in DE.
Donor(s): Wyman-Gordon Co.
Foundation type: Company-sponsored
Financial data (yr. ended 12/31/88): Assets, $4,785,863 (M); expenditures, $405,343, including $354,225 for 42 grants (high: $194,500; low: $100) and $9,087 for 76 employee matching gifts.
Purpose and activities: Giving primarily for community funds, cultural programs, higher education, hospitals, and youth agencies.
Types of support: General purposes, operating budgets, continuing support, annual campaigns, seed money, emergency funds, deficit financing, building funds, equipment, land acquisition, employee matching gifts, scholarship funds, employee-related scholarships, fellowships.
Limitations: Giving primarily in MA, with emphasis on the Worcester area, and in plant communities in Danville, IL, Jackson, MI, and South Gate, CA. No grants to individuals, or for endowment funds, special projects, research, publications, or conferences; no loans.
Application information: Application form not required.
Initial approach: Letter or proposal
Copies of proposal: 1
Deadline(s): None
Board meeting date(s): Feb., Apr., June, Aug., Oct., and Dec.
Write: Richard L. Stevens, Secy.-Treas.
Officers and Directors: Joseph R. Carter, Pres.; Henry Dormitzer, V.P.; William S. Hurley, V.P.; James S. Walsh, V.P.; Richard L. Stevens, Secy.-Treas.
Number of staff: 1 part-time professional; 1 part-time support.
Employer Identification Number: 046142600

3056
Yawkey Foundation II ⌘
990 Washington St.
Dedham 02026-6716 (617) 329-7470

Established in 1983 in MA.
Donor(s): Jean R. Yawkey.
Foundation type: Independent
Financial data (yr. ended 6/30/87): Assets, $2,137,610 (M); gifts received, $1,257,643; expenditures, $114,572, including $107,000 for 5 grants (high: $90,000; low: $1,000).
Purpose and activities: Support for youth, education, social services, the arts, wildlife, and amateur athletics.
Limitations: Giving primarily in MA, with emphasis on the greater metropolitan Boston area.
Application information: Primarily supports organizations favored by donor and donor's husband during his lifetime.
Initial approach: Letter
Deadline(s): None
Write: John L. Harrington, Exec. Dir.
Officer and Trustees: William B. Gutfarb, Secy.-Treas.; John L. Harrington, Exec. Dir.; William P. Baldwin, Edward F. Kenney, Jean R. Yawkey.
Employer Identification Number: 042768239

MICHIGAN

3057
Talbert & Leota Abrams Foundation
1000 Michigan National Tower
Lansing 48933

Established in 1960 in MI.
Donor(s): Leota Abrams,† Talbert Abrams.
Foundation type: Independent
Financial data (yr. ended 12/31/89): Assets, $3,078,104 (L); gifts received, $5,000; expenditures, $113,547, including $82,200 for 10 grants (high: $50,000; low: $200).
Purpose and activities: Support primarily for a library and dyslexia institute; giving also for universities and colleges, and community funds.
Types of support: Endowment funds.
Limitations: Giving primarily in central MI. No support for individuals, governmental groups, churches for sectarian use, for political lobbying, operating expenses, athletic activities, or traveling expenses; no loans.
Publications: Annual report.
Application information: Application form not required.
Initial approach: 2 page letter
Copies of proposal: 1
Deadline(s): June 30 for next calendar year
Officers: Barbara J. Brown, Pres.; Joe C. Foster, Jr., Secy.; Robert D. Howard, Treas.
Director: Lyle D. Hepfer.
Number of staff: 1 part-time professional.
Employer Identification Number: 386082194

3058
Americana Foundation ⌑
Solaron Bldg.
28115 Meadowbrook Rd.
Novi 48050 (313) 347-3863

Trust established in 1960 in NY.
Donor(s): Adolph H. Meyer, Ida M. Meyer Charitable Trust.
Foundation type: Independent
Financial data (yr. ended 12/31/87): Assets, $6,347,965 (M); gifts received, $2,338,526; expenditures, $2,055,986, including $1,900,000 for 6 grants (high: $1,500,000; low: $9,000).
Purpose and activities: Emphasis on education related to agricultural and environmental programs.
Types of support: General purposes, equipment, annual campaigns, research.
Limitations: Giving primarily in MI.
Application information:
Write: Thomas F. Ranger, Secy-Treas.
Officers: Gary Rentrop, Pres.; Thomas F. Ranger, Secy.-Treas.
Trustees: Jack Barnes, Barbara Livy, Thomas McMullen, Ernest Morris, Jonathan Thomas.
Employer Identification Number: 382269431

3059
Ann Arbor Area Foundation
121 West Washington, Suite 400
Ann Arbor 48104 (313) 663-0401

Incorporated in 1963 in MI.
Foundation type: Community
Financial data (yr. ended 12/31/89): Assets, $2,731,051 (M); gifts received, $331,825; expenditures, $181,973, including $106,554 for 31 grants (high: $15,000; low: $150).
Purpose and activities: Support for innovative programs and projects encompassing charity, civic affairs, culture, health and human services, ecology, historic preservation, and education.
Types of support: Seed money, emergency funds, building funds, equipment, matching funds, scholarship funds, research, special projects, publications, conferences and seminars.
Limitations: Giving limited to the Ann Arbor, MI, area. No grants to individuals (except for limited scholarship funds), or for operating budgets, continuing support, annual campaigns, deficit financing, fund raising purposes, land acquisition, endowment funds, consulting services, technical assistance, fellowships, or program-related investments; no loans.
Publications: Annual report (including application guidelines), program policy statement, application guidelines.
Application information: Application form required.
Initial approach: Telephone
Copies of proposal: 4
Deadline(s): Feb. 7, June 6, and Oct. 3
Board meeting date(s): Jan., Mar., May, July, Sept., and Nov.
Final notification: 60 days
Write: Terry N. Foster, Pres.
Officers and Trustees:* Charles E. Leahy,* Chair.; Terry N. Foster, Pres.; Charles Reinhart,* Secy.; Pam Horiszny,* Treas.; Charles Borgsdorf, Sandra Campbell, Don Chisholm, Albert Coudron, Stephen B. Dobson, Douglas Freeth, James Frenza, Ruth Hatcher, Henry Landau, Gundar Myran, Michael Radock, Rudolph Reichert, Russell W. Resiter, Norma Sarns.*
Distribution Committee: Barbara Balback, Charles Borgsdorf,* Constance Cress, John Eman, Barbara Grassmuck, James Irwin, Fran Jelinek.
Number of staff: 2 part-time professional; 1 full-time support.
Employer Identification Number: 386087967

3060
ANR Foundation, Inc. ▼ ⌑
One Woodward Ave.
Detroit 48226 (313) 965-1200

Incorporated in 1985 in MI.
Donor(s): American Natural Resources Co., and subsidiaries.
Foundation type: Company-sponsored
Financial data (yr. ended 12/31/88): Assets, $642,827 (M); gifts received, $395,000; expenditures, $1,047,958, including $1,042,945 for 262 grants (high: $89,900; low: $13).
Purpose and activities: Support for health and welfare, culture, education, and community responsibility.
Types of support: Employee matching gifts, operating budgets, general purposes, scholarship funds.
Limitations: No support for organizations supported by the United Way, or for exclusively denominational or sectarian purposes. No grants to individuals, or for fundraising events, conventions, or goodwill advertising.
Application information:
Initial approach: Letter or proposal with annual report
Deadline(s): None
Write: James F. Cordes, Pres.
Officers: James R. Paul,* Chair.; James F. Cordes,* Pres.; Austin M. O'Toole, Secy.; David A. Arledge, Treas.
Directors:* Lawrence P. Doss.
Employer Identification Number: 382602116

3061
Baldwin Foundation ⌑
Old Kent Bank Bldg.
300 Old Kent
Grand Rapids 49503

Trust established in 1964 in MI.
Donor(s): Members of the Baldwin family.
Foundation type: Independent
Financial data (yr. ended 11/30/88): Assets, $2,330,134 (M); expenditures, $153,137, including $135,350 for 45 grants (high: $20,000; low: $250).
Purpose and activities: Giving for arts and cultural programs, higher education, and social service agencies.
Limitations: Giving primarily in western MI.
Application information: Application form not required.
Deadline(s): None
Write: James R. Dice, Secy.-Treas.
Officers: John R. Davies,* Pres.; Ralph B. Baldwin,* V.P.; James R. Dice, Secy.-Treas.
Trustees:* Melvin Dana Baldwin II, Mrs. Ralph B. Baldwin, Carol Curlin, Lemuel Curlin, Dan Heyns, Mrs. Dan Heyns, L.V. Mulnix, Jr., Frances Mulnix, Peter Wolf.
Manager: Old Kent Bank & Trust Co.
Employer Identification Number: 386085641

3062
Theodore and Mina Bargman Foundation ⌑
29201 Telegraph Rd., Suite 500
Southfield 48034

Incorporated in 1954 in MI.
Donor(s): Mina Bargman.†
Foundation type: Independent
Financial data (yr. ended 12/31/87): Assets, $3,141,640 (M); expenditures, $275,208, including $215,775 for 42 grants (high: $45,000; low: $100).
Purpose and activities: Emphasis on Jewish welfare funds, higher education in Israel, and temple support.
Types of support: Continuing support, annual campaigns, general purposes, building funds.

Limitations: No grants for endowment funds, scholarships, fellowships, or matching gifts; no loans.
Application information: Contributes only to pre-selected organizations. Applications not accepted.
Officers and Trustees: Lawrence S. Jackier, V.P.; Bruce R. Mayhew, Treas.; Mark E. Schlussel.
Employer Identification Number: 386087158

3063
The Barstow Foundation ⌑
c/o Chemical Bank and Trust Co.
333 East Main St.
Midland 48640 (517) 631-9200

Trust established in 1967 in MI.
Donor(s): Florence K. Barstow.†
Foundation type: Independent
Financial data (yr. ended 12/31/88): Assets, $4,265,269 (M); expenditures, $208,714, including $197,510 for 17 grants (high: $50,000; low: $510).
Purpose and activities: Primarily to support a specific community center with secondary interest in local organizations and in other charitable organizations engaged in alleviating poverty and hunger on a national or world basis.
Types of support: Operating budgets, annual campaigns, seed money, emergency funds, equipment, endowment funds, matching funds, special projects, technical assistance.
Limitations: Giving primarily in Midland County, MI. No grants to individuals, or for research, continuing support, deficit financing, building funds, scholarships, or fellowships; no loans.
Publications: 990-PF.
Application information: Application form not required.
Initial approach: Proposal
Copies of proposal: 2
Deadline(s): Submit proposal preferably from Aug. through Oct.; deadline Oct. 31
Board meeting date(s): Nov.
Final notification: After annual meeting
Write: Bruce M. Groom, Sr. V.P., Chemical Bank and Trust Co.
Officers and Trustees:* Frederick E. Barstow,* Pres.; Eugene B. Skeebo,* Secy.; Ormond E. Barstow, Ruth B. Dixon, Chemical Bank.
Number of staff: None.
Employer Identification Number: 386151026

3064
Battle Creek Community Foundation
(Formerly Greater Battle Creek Foundation)
One Riverwalk Ctr.
34 West Jackson St.
Battle Creek 49017-3505 (616) 962-2181

Established in 1974 in MI.
Foundation type: Community
Financial data (yr. ended 4/30/89): Assets, $10,398,756 (M); gifts received, $1,131,784; expenditures, $483,069, including $302,067 for 52 grants (high: $31,200; low: $100; average: $4,000) and $25,000 for 18 grants to individuals (high: $2,000; low: $500).
Purpose and activities: Support for charitable, scientific, literary, and educational programs of all kinds that will foster improvement of the physical environment and living, working, and social conditions.
Types of support: Seed money, emergency funds, building funds, equipment, land acquisition, scholarship funds, special projects, publications, conferences and seminars, matching funds.
Limitations: Giving limited to the greater Battle Creek, MI, area. No grants for operating budgets, deficit financing, endowments, or research; no loans.
Publications: Annual report, grants list, newsletter, application guidelines.
Application information: Application form required.
Initial approach: Letter or phone call
Copies of proposal: 1
Deadline(s): Quarterly
Board meeting date(s): Quarterly
Write: James M. Richmond, Pres. and C.E.O.
Officers: Chris T. Christ, Chair.; Theodore E. Sovern, Vice-Chair.; James M. Richmond, Pres. and C.E.O; Lisa Wyatt Knowlton, V.P.; Susan E. Ordway, Secy.; Richard M. Tsoumas, Treas.
Trustees: Ann A. Agnes, Elizabeth H. Binda, Dale G. Griffin, Barbara K. Hill, William E. LaMothe, Robert B. Miller, Sr., Sadie Penn, Charles L. Siefert, M.D., Elizabeth J. Settles, William P. Winslow.
Number of staff: 2 full-time professional; 1 full-time support.
Employer Identification Number: 382045459

3065
Charles M. Bauervic Foundation, Inc. ⌑
R.R. 2, Box 170
Suttons Bay 49682 (313) 356-7890
Additional address: 25154 Acacia Rd., Southfield, MI 48034

Incorporated in 1967 in MI.
Donor(s): Charles M. Bauervic.†
Foundation type: Independent
Financial data (yr. ended 12/31/88): Assets, $3,214,176 (M); expenditures, $188,042, including $131,850 for 27 grants (high: $25,000; low: $500; average: $1,000-$10,000).
Purpose and activities: Giving primarily for private higher, secondary, and elementary education; limited support for hospitals, churches, child welfare and youth development organizations, and cultural organizations.
Limitations: Giving primarily in MI. No grants to individuals.
Application information: Application form required.
Initial approach: Letter
Deadline(s): May 30
Write: Patricia A. Leonard, Pres.
Officers: Patricia A. Leonard, Pres. and Secy.; James P. Leonard,* V.P.; Theodore J. Leonard, Treas.
Directors:* Timothy J. Leonard.
Employer Identification Number: 386146352

3066
Bauervic-Paisley Foundation ⌑
2855 Coolidge Hwy., Suite 103
Troy 48084

Established in 1984 in MI.
Foundation type: Independent
Financial data (yr. ended 12/31/88): Assets, $2,788,877 (M); expenditures, $211,842, including $140,000 for 15 grants (high: $25,500; low: $2,000).
Purpose and activities: Grants primarily for education and social services; support also for cultural programs and religion.
Types of support: Renovation projects, operating budgets, matching funds.
Limitations: No grants to individuals.
Application information: Application form required.
Deadline(s): Oct. 1
Write: The Board of Directors
Officers and Directors: Beverly Paisley, Pres. and Secy.; Peter W. Paisley, Treas.; Rose Bauervic-Wright.
Employer Identification Number: 382494390

3067
Bay Area Community Foundation ☆
809 Saginaw St.
Bay City 48708 (517) 893-4438

Established in 1982 in MI.
Foundation type: Community
Financial data (yr. ended 12/31/88): Assets, $2,228,245 (M); gifts received, $638,129; expenditures, $119,491, including $54,237 for 29 grants (high: $10,822; low: $50) and $14,750 for 30 grants to individuals (high: $1,000; low: $100).
Purpose and activities: Support for "projects that will support and enrich charitable, cultural, artistic, civic, educational, and scientific undertakings."
Types of support: Student aid.
Limitations: Giving limited to Bay City, MI.
Publications: Annual report, application guidelines, informational brochure.
Application information:
Write: Robert D. Sarow, Trustee
Officer and Trustees:* Peggy Rowley,* Exec. Dir.; Robert D. Sarow, and 23 additional directors.
Number of staff: 1 full-time professional; 1 full-time support.
Employer Identification Number: 382418086

3068
Alvin M. Bentley Foundation
P.O. Box 151
Owosso 48867 (517) 723-7464

Incorporated in 1961 in MI.
Donor(s): Alvin M. Bentley,† Arvella D. Bentley.†
Foundation type: Independent
Financial data (yr. ended 12/31/89): Assets, $2,126,962 (M); expenditures, $151,947, including $124,053 for 8 grants (high: $68,104; low: $650).
Purpose and activities: Giving primarily for higher education and community funds.
Types of support: Scholarship funds.
Limitations: Giving primarily in MI. No grants to individuals, or for building or endowment funds, or matching gifts.
Application information: Application form not required.
Initial approach: Letter
Copies of proposal: 1
Deadline(s): Mar. 1

Board meeting date(s): Spring and fall
Write: Jean Koski, Secy.-Treas.
Officers: Paul G. Goebel, Jr.,* Pres.; Jean Koski, Secy.-Treas.
Trustees:* Alvin M. Bentley IV, Clark H. Bentley, Helen Bentley, Michael D. Bentley, Paul Brown, Mary Alice Campbell, Jerry L. Des Jardins, John R. Des Jardins, William J. Edwards, John R. Francis, George W. Hoddy, Ann Bentley Jorgensen, Lawrence Lindemer, Virginia Woodard Matthews.
Number of staff: 1 part-time support.
Employer Identification Number: 386076280

3069
Berrien Community Foundation, Inc. ☆
515 Ship St., Suite A4
St. Joseph 49085 (616) 983-3304
Application address: P.O. Box 92, St. Joseph, MI 49085

Incorporated in 1952 in MI.
Foundation type: Community
Financial data (yr. ended 12/31/89): Assets, $2,957,845 (M); gifts received, $317,943; expenditures, $197,129, including $138,645 for 27 grants.
Purpose and activities: Support for community projects, arts and humanitites, education, health, and human services.
Types of support: Seed money, matching funds, scholarship funds, fellowships, research, conferences and seminars.
Limitations: Giving limited to Berrien County, MI. No support for sectarian religious purposes, political organizations or campaigns, or foundation-managed projects. No grants to individuals, or for consulting services, technical assistance, operating funds, deficit financing, annual fund drives, or program-related investments; no loans.
Publications: Application guidelines, program policy statement, 990-PF, financial statement.
Application information: Application guidelines available on request. Application form required.
Initial approach: Telephone or letter
Deadline(s): Sept. 15 for winter meeting; Mar. 1 for spring meeting
Board meeting date(s): Quarterly
Write: Margaret Poole, Exec. Dir.
Officers: Richard Whiteman, Pres.; Larry Bubb, V.P.; Marthabelle Bowman, Secy.; James P. DeLapa, Treas.; Margaret Poole, Exec. Dir.
Trustees: Merlin Hanson, Lester E. Page, Malcolm S. Ross, John Steimle, Bernice Tiscornia.
Number of staff: 1 full-time professional.
Employer Identification Number: 386057160

3070
Besser Foundation
150-C North State St.
Alpena 49707 (517) 354-4722

Incorporated in 1944 in MI.
Donor(s): J.H. Besser,† Besser Co.
Foundation type: Independent
Financial data (yr. ended 12/31/89): Assets, $12,543,000 (M); expenditures, $650,000, including $525,000 for 57 grants (high: $126,000; low: $200).
Purpose and activities: Grants to local schools and colleges, health and social service agencies, and churches; also full support of Besser Museum, a local historical and art museum.
Types of support: Scholarship funds, matching funds, operating budgets, continuing support, general purposes.
Limitations: Giving limited to the Alpena, MI, area. No support for video projects. No grants to individuals, or for endowment funds or research; no loans.
Publications: Annual report (including application guidelines).
Application information: Application form not required.
Initial approach: Telephone
Copies of proposal: 1
Deadline(s): End of 2nd month in calendar quarter
Board meeting date(s): Quarterly beginning in Mar.
Write: Carl F. Reitz, Secy.-Treas.
Officers and Trustees:* Frederick T. Johnston,* Pres.; J.R. Wilson,* V.P.; Carl F. Reitz,* Secy.-Treas.; Edward Adams, Rev. Robert M. Barksdale, Harold A. Ruemenapp.
Number of staff: 1 part-time support.
Employer Identification Number: 386071938

3071
A. G. Bishop Charitable Trust ⌑
c/o NBD Genesee Merchants Bank & Trust Co.
One East First St.
Flint 48502 (313) 766-8307

Trust established in 1944 in MI.
Donor(s): Arthur Giles Bishop.†
Foundation type: Independent
Financial data (yr. ended 12/31/88): Assets, $4,903,987 (M); expenditures, $249,640, including $227,837 for 49 grants (high: $33,334; low: $750).
Purpose and activities: Emphasis on health agencies and a hospital, a community fund, cultural programs, higher education, and social service and youth agencies.
Types of support: Operating budgets, continuing support, annual campaigns, seed money, emergency funds, deficit financing, building funds, equipment, land acquisition, research.
Limitations: Giving limited to the Flint-Genesee County, MI, community. No grants to individuals, or for endowment funds, scholarships, fellowships, or matching gifts; no loans.
Application information: Application form not required.
Initial approach: Letter
Copies of proposal: 1
Deadline(s): None
Board meeting date(s): Annually in the fall
Final notification: 2 weeks
Write: C. Ann Barton, Trust Officer, NBD Genesee Merchants Bank & Trust Co.
Trustees: Carrie Jane Bellairs, Elizabeth B. Wentworth, NBD Genesee Merchants Bank & Trust Co.
Number of staff: 1 part-time professional.
Employer Identification Number: 386040693

3072
John A. & Marlene L. Boll Foundation ⌑ ☆
930 Lakeshore
Grosse Pointe Shores 48236

Donor(s): John A. Boll, Marlene L. Boll.
Foundation type: Independent
Financial data (yr. ended 12/31/88): Assets, $494,762 (M); gifts received, $200,000; expenditures, $153,123, including $152,104 for 88 grants (high: $25,000; low: $50).
Purpose and activities: Support for general charitable organizations and Christian associations, including missionary programs.
Types of support: General purposes.
Application information: Contributes only to pre-selected organizations. Applications not accepted.
Directors: John A. Boll, Marlene L. Boll, Christian Fenton.
Employer Identification Number: 382708121

3073
Bonisteel Foundation ☆
300 North Fifth Ave., Suite 240
Ann Arbor 48104-7379 (313) 761-5100

Established in 1972 in MI.
Donor(s): Roscoe O. Bonisteel, Sr.,† Lillian Bonisteel.†
Foundation type: Independent
Financial data (yr. ended 12/31/88): Assets, $1,137,670 (M); expenditures, $71,383, including $63,286 for 6 grants (high: $35,436; low: $500).
Purpose and activities: Support in the areas of higher education and Catholic giving.
Types of support: Capital campaigns, building funds, equipment, general purposes.
Limitations: Giving primarily in MI.
Application information: Application form not required.
Initial approach: Letter
Copies of proposal: 5
Deadline(s): None
Board meeting date(s): Dec. 15
Final notification: Dec. 31
Write: Edmund J. Sikorski, Jr.
Officers and Trustees*: Roscoe O. Bonisteel, Jr.,* Pres.; Jean B. Knecht,* V.P.; Frances B. Fisher,* Secy.; Nancy B. Calcutt,* Treas.; Betty B. Johnson.
Employer Identification Number: 237155774

3074
The Borman's, Inc. Fund
18718 Borman Ave.
Detroit 48228 (313) 270-1155
Additional address: P.O. Box 33446, Detroit, MI 48232-5446

Donor(s): Borman's, Inc.
Foundation type: Company-sponsored
Financial data (yr. ended 12/31/88): Assets, $955,807 (M); gifts received, $100,000; expenditures, $432,918, including $430,805 for 58 grants (high: $157,100; low: $100).
Purpose and activities: Giving primarily for Jewish welfare and social services; support also for the arts.
Types of support: Annual campaigns.
Limitations: Giving primarily in southeastern MI.

Publications: Application guidelines.
Application information: Application form not required.
Initial approach: Letter
Copies of proposal: 1
Write: Gilbert Borman, Secy.-Treas.
Officer and Director:* Gilbert Borman,* Secy.-Treas.
Number of staff: 1 part-time support.
Employer Identification Number: 386069267

3075
Arnold and Gertrude Boutell Memorial Fund
c/o Second National Bank of Saginaw
101 North Washington Ave.
Saginaw 48607 (517) 776-7582

Trust established in 1961 in MI.
Donor(s): Arnold Boutell,† Gertrude Boutell.†
Foundation type: Independent
Financial data (yr. ended 03/31/89): Assets, $6,732,791 (M); expenditures, $494,382, including $413,030 for 30 grants (high: $47,500; low: $350; average: $5,000-$20,000).
Purpose and activities: Support largely for a community fund, education, cultural programs, community development, and hospitals.
Limitations: Giving limited to Saginaw County, MI. No grants to individuals, or for endowment funds.
Application information: Application form required.
Initial approach: Letter
Copies of proposal: 1
Deadline(s): None
Board meeting date(s): Bimonthly
Write: Denice McGlaughlin, Trust Admin., Second National Bank of Saginaw
Trustee: Second National Bank of Saginaw.
Employer Identification Number: 386040492

3076
Viola E. Bray Charitable Trust ⌑
c/o NBD Genesee Merchants Bank & Trust Co.
One East First St.
Flint 48502 (313) 766-8307

Trust established in 1961 in MI.
Donor(s): Viola E. Bray.
Foundation type: Independent
Financial data (yr. ended 9/30/88): Assets, $2,534,859 (M); expenditures, $130,594, including $104,231 for 29 grants (high: $23,157; low: $650).
Purpose and activities: Giving for the fine arts.
Types of support: Continuing support, annual campaigns, seed money, emergency funds, building funds, equipment, matching funds.
Limitations: Giving limited to the Flint, MI, area. No grants to individuals, or for research, scholarships, or fellowships; no loans.
Publications: 990-PF, program policy statement, application guidelines.
Application information: Application form not required.
Initial approach: 1-page proposal
Copies of proposal: 3
Deadline(s): None
Board meeting date(s): As required
Final notification: 2 months
Write: C. Ann Barton, Trust Officer, NBD Genesee Merchants Bank & Trust Co.
Trustees: Bertha Bray Richards, Sally Richards Ricker, NBD Genesee Merchants Bank & Trust Co.
Employer Identification Number: 386039741

3077
Wallace and Irene Bronner Family Charitable Trust ☆
625 East Tuscola
Frankenmuth 48734-1717 (517) 652-6723

Established in 1966.
Foundation type: Independent
Financial data (yr. ended 12/31/88): Assets, $1,102,280 (M); gifts received, $125,000; expenditures, $72,076, including $64,500 for 92 grants (high: $11,250; low: $100; average: $100-$1,000).
Purpose and activities: Giving for Lutheran organizations, including churches and a theological institution.
Limitations: Giving primarily in Frankenmuth and Saginaw, MI.
Application information: Applications not accepted.
Write: Wallace J. Bronner, Trustee
Trustee: Wallace J. Bronner.
Number of staff: None.
Employer Identification Number: 386140376

3078
The Bundy Foundation ⌑
12345 East Nine Mile Rd.
Warren 48090 (313) 758-4511

Incorporated in 1952 in MI.
Donor(s): Bundy Corp.
Foundation type: Company-sponsored
Financial data (yr. ended 12/31/88): Assets, $6,564,295 (M); gifts received, $252,575; expenditures, $930,061, including $790,578 for 127 grants (high: $126,000; low: $20).
Purpose and activities: Emphasis on community funds, education, hospitals, and cultural programs.
Types of support: Employee matching gifts, operating budgets.
Limitations: Giving primarily in areas of company operations. No support for organizations currently receiving funds from other organizations which the foundation supports. No grants to individuals.
Application information: Contributes only to pre-selected organizations. Applications not accepted.
Board meeting date(s): As required
Officers and Trustees: Wendell W. Anderson, Jr., Pres.; John W. Anderson II, V.P.; Robert E. Barton, Secy.-Treas.
Employer Identification Number: 386053694

3079
Samuel Higby Camp Foundation ⌑
145 South Jackson
Jackson 49201 (517) 787-4100

Established in 1951 in MI.
Donor(s): Donna Ruth Camp.†
Foundation type: Independent
Financial data (yr. ended 12/31/87): Assets, $1,016,744 (M); expenditures, $60,426, including $48,465 for 18 grants (high: $5,000; low: $1,000; average: $1,000-$5,000).
Purpose and activities: Support for business and medical education, youth and child welfare organizations, community development, public administration, animal welfare, hospices, and cultural programs.
Types of support: Annual campaigns, capital campaigns, deficit financing, lectureships, operating budgets.
Limitations: Giving primarily in Jackson County, MI.
Application information: Application form not required.
Initial approach: Letter or proposal
Copies of proposal: 1
Deadline(s): Aug. 15
Board meeting date(s): As needed
Final notification: Oct. or Nov.
Write: Walter R. Boris, Chair.
Officers: Walter R. Boris, Chair. and Pres.; D.H. Calkins, Secy.; H.E. Spieler, Treas.
Trustees: I.R. Bauer, Nancy J. Ordway.
Employer Identification Number: 381643281

3080
William & Marie Carls Foundation
100 Renaissance Ctr., Suite 1880
Detroit 48243-1062 (313) 259-3070

Established in 1961 in MI.
Foundation type: Independent
Financial data (yr. ended 12/31/88): Assets, $364,993 (M); expenditures, $175,858, including $174,425 for 6 grants (high: $123,000; low: $1,000).
Purpose and activities: Grants primarily for medical and recreational facilities for underprivileged or handicapped children.
Limitations: No grants to individuals.
Application information: Application form not required.
Initial approach: Letter
Copies of proposal: 1
Deadline(s): None
Write: Harold Stieg, V.P.
Officers and Trustees:* William Carls,* Pres. and Treas.; Harold Stieg,* V.P. and Secy.; Arthur Derisley.
Number of staff: None.
Employer Identification Number: 386099935

3081
Gerald W. Chamberlin Foundation, Inc. ⌑
21 Kercheval St., Suite 270
Grosse Pointe 48236

Incorporated in 1955 in MI.
Donor(s): Gerald W. Chamberlin,† Myrtle F. Chamberlin,† Donald F. Chamberlin, Joanne M. Chamberlin, Chamberlin Products.
Foundation type: Independent
Financial data (yr. ended 12/31/88): Assets, $2,314,918 (M); expenditures, $172,419, including $115,400 for 53 grants (high: $10,000; low: $100).
Purpose and activities: Giving for Protestant church support, youth agencies, higher and secondary education, and cultural programs.
Limitations: Giving primarily in MI.

Application information: Contributes only to pre-selected organizations. Applications not accepted.
Officers: Donald F. Chamberlin, Pres.; John W. Butler, V.P.; Joy C. Robbins, Secy.-Treas.
Employer Identification Number: 386055730

3082
Chrysler Corporation Fund ▼
12000 Chrysler Dr.
Highland Park 48288-1919 (313) 956-5194

Incorporated in 1953 in MI.
Donor(s): Chrysler Corp.
Foundation type: Company-sponsored
Financial data (yr. ended 12/31/89): Assets, $31,000,000 (M); expenditures, $11,755,688, including $11,123,161 for 1,156 grants (high: $700,000; low: $325; average: $1,000-$50,000) and $533,485 for 2,620 employee matching gifts.
Purpose and activities: Support for community funds, health and human services, higher education, civic affairs, and cultural programs.
Types of support: Continuing support, annual campaigns, emergency funds, special projects, employee matching gifts, building funds, employee-related scholarships, scholarship funds, operating budgets.
Limitations: Giving primarily in areas where the company has a substantial number of employees. No support for primary or secondary schools, religious organizations for religious purposes, conferences, seminars, veterans' or labor organizations, fraternal associations, athletic groups, social clubs, political organizations or campaigns, or national health organizations, except through the United Way. No grants to individuals (except for scholarships to children of company employees), or for endowment funds, fellowships, deficit financing, equipment and materials, or research; no grants for operating expenses of organizations supported through the United Way; no loans.
Publications: Corporate giving report, program policy statement, application guidelines.
Application information: Application form not required.
Initial approach: Letter
Copies of proposal: 1
Deadline(s): None
Board meeting date(s): As required, usually quarterly; educational grants approved at fall meeting
Final notification: 3 months
Write: Ms. Lynn A. Feldhouse, Mgr.
Officers and Trustees:* T.G. Denomme,* Pres.; Robert S. Miller, Jr.,* V.P. and Treas.; Lynn A. Feldhouse, Secy. and Mgr.; B.E. Bidwell, F.J. Castaing, L. Cutler, R.E. Dauch, F.J. Farmer, M.M. Glusac, W.J. O'Brien III, L.C. Richie, G.E. White.
Number of staff: 3
Employer Identification Number: 386087371

3083
Dorothy U. Dalton Foundation, Inc. ⌑
c/o Old Kent Bank of Kalamazoo
151 East Michigan Ave.
Kalamazoo 49007 (616) 383-6958

Incorporated in 1978 in MI as successor to Dorothy U. Dalton Foundation Trust.
Donor(s): Dorothy U. Dalton.†
Foundation type: Independent
Financial data (yr. ended 12/31/88): Assets, $21,018,236 (M); expenditures, $1,210,751, including $1,072,369 for 58 grants (high: $100,000; low: $100).
Purpose and activities: Emphasis on higher education, mental health, social service and youth agencies, and cultural programs.
Types of support: Operating budgets, continuing support, seed money, emergency funds, deficit financing, building funds, equipment, land acquisition, matching funds, research, special projects, general purposes, capital campaigns, renovation projects.
Limitations: Giving primarily in Kalamazoo County, MI. No grants to individuals, or for religious organizations, annual campaigns, scholarships, fellowships, publications, or conferences; no loans.
Publications: 990-PF.
Application information: Application form not required.
Initial approach: Proposal
Copies of proposal: 5
Deadline(s): Submit proposal preferably in Apr. and Oct.
Board meeting date(s): May and Nov.
Final notification: 30 days after board meetings
Write: Ronald N. Kilgore, Secy.-Treas.
Officers and Trustees: Suzanne D. Parish, Pres.; Howard Kalleward, V.P.; Ronald N. Kilgore, Secy.-Treas.; Thompson Bennett, Arthur F. Homer.
Number of staff: None.
Employer Identification Number: 382240062

3084
Opal Dancey Memorial Foundation ☆
c/o Manufacturers National Bank of Detroit
100 Renaissance Ctr.
Detroit 48243
Application address: 28400 Evergreen Ave., Flat Rock, MI 48134

Established in 1976.
Donor(s): Russell V. Dancey.†
Foundation type: Independent
Financial data (yr. ended 10/31/88): Assets, $1,008,002 (M); expenditures, $49,944, including $35,500 for 7 grants and $500 for 1 grant to an individual.
Purpose and activities: Giving limited to seminaries and schools of theology.
Types of support: Scholarship funds.
Limitations: Giving primarily in the Midwest.
Application information: Application form required.
Deadline(s): June 15
Board meeting date(s): July
Write: Rev. Gary Imms, Chair.
Officers: Rev. Gary Imms, Chair. and Mgr.; Rev. David Boone, Mgr.; Rev. Ken Callis, Mgr.; Rev. Gabe Campbell, Mgr.; Betty J. Goddard, Mgr.
Trustee: Manufacturers National Bank of Detroit.
Number of staff: None.
Employer Identification Number: 386361282

3085
Dart Foundation ⌑
500 Hogsback Rd.
Mason 48854

Established in 1984 in MI.
Donor(s): William A. Dart.
Foundation type: Independent
Financial data (yr. ended 11/30/89): Assets, $9,911,382 (M); expenditures, $415,082, including $395,826 for 9 grants (high: $277,400; low: $600).
Purpose and activities: Support for elementary and secondary education and educational programs; giving also for ecology.
Limitations: No grants to individuals.
Application information: Contributes only to pre-selected organizations. Applications not accepted.
Officers: William A. Dart, Pres.; Claire T. Dart, V.P.; Benjamin O. Schwendener, Jr., Secy.
Director: Thomas J. Dart.
Employer Identification Number: 382562664

3086
M. E. Davenport Foundation
415 East Fulton St.
Grand Rapids 49503 (616) 451-3511

Established in 1986 in MI.
Donor(s): Davenport Schools, Inc.
Foundation type: Independent
Financial data (yr. ended 9/30/89): Assets, $5,798,239 (M); qualifying distributions, $1,636,500, including $111,500 for 3 grants (high: $50,000; low: $16,500; average: $16,500-$50,000) and $1,525,000 for loans.
Purpose and activities: Support primarily for private institutions of higher education.
Types of support: Capital campaigns.
Limitations: Giving primarily in MI.
Application information: Application form not required.
Deadline(s): None
Write: Robert W. Sneden, Pres.
Officers and Directors: Robert W. Sneden,* Pres.; Margaret D. Sneden,* V.P. and Secy.; Tyrus R. Wessell, Treas.
Members:* Kathleen M. Sneden, Marcia A. Sneden, Margaret E. Sneden, Mary P. Sullivan.
Number of staff: None.
Employer Identification Number: 382646809

3087
John R. & M. Margrite Davis Foundation ⌑ ☆
1700 North Woodward, Suite A
Bloomfield Hills 48013
Application address: 1306 Watagua St., Kingsport, TN 37660-4530

Established in 1955.
Foundation type: Independent
Financial data (yr. ended 12/31/88): Assets, $525,848 (M); gifts received, $2,000,000; expenditures, $2,043,401, including $2,037,777 for 26 grants (high: $2,000,000; low: $100).

Purpose and activities: Giving primarily to a cancer research foundation; support also for museums, hospitals, and health associations.
Limitations: Giving primarily in KY, CA, MI, and TN. No grants to individuals.
Application information:
Initial approach: Letter
Deadline(s): None
Write: Raymond C. Cunningham, Jr., Secy.-Treas.
Officers: M. Margrite Davis, Pres.; Susan B. Fisher, V.P.; Raymond C. Cunningham, Jr., Secy.-Treas.
Trustee: James Bradford.
Employer Identification Number: 386058593

3088
Dearborn Cable Communications Fund ⌑
922 South Military
Dearborn 48124 (313) 563-8877
Application address: c/o Cablevision of Dearborn, 15200 Mercantile Dr., Dearborn, MI 48124

Established in 1984 in MI.
Donor(s): Group W Cable, Inc.
Foundation type: Company-sponsored
Financial data (yr. ended 12/31/88): Assets, $1,070,373 (M); expenditures, $63,482, including $52,579 for 5 grants (high: $22,986; low: $1,143).
Purpose and activities: Support for cable television programming of interest to the general community.
Types of support: Equipment, scholarship funds.
Limitations: Giving primarily in the Dearborn, MI, area.
Application information:
Initial approach: Proposal
Deadline(s): None
Final notification: 60 days from receipt of proposal
Write: Dr. Robert T. Pendergrass, Treas.
Officers: Margaret I. Campbell, Pres.; Patricia A. Davis, V.P.; Frank Caddy, Secy.; Robert T. Pendergrass, Treas.
Directors: Thomas Colarossi, Russ Gibb, Jackie Kaiser, Charles Mercado, Elizabeth Rohwer.
Employer Identification Number: 382571195

3089
The Mignon Sherwood DeLano Foundation ⌑
c/o First of America Bank-Michigan, N.A.
108 East Michigan Ave.
Kalamazoo 49007-3931 (616) 388-7021

Incorporated in 1985 in MI.
Donor(s): Mignon Sherwood Delano.†
Foundation type: Independent
Financial data (yr. ended 12/31/88): Assets, $2,603,879 (M); gifts received, $394,823; expenditures, $28,791, including $10,500 for 5 grants (high: $4,500; low: $500).
Purpose and activities: Support primarily for community development, mental health, elementary education, and churches.
Limitations: Giving primarily in Allegan, MI. No grants to individuals.
Application information: Contributes only to pre-selected organizations. Applications not accepted.
Write: David Tichnor, Pres.
Officer and Trustees: David Ticknor, Pres.; Rebecca Burnett, G. Phillip Dietrich, Bernard Riker, Helen Tremble.
Employer Identification Number: 382557743

3090
The Helen L. DeRoy Foundation ⌑
3274 Penobscot Bldg.
Detroit 48226 (313) 961-3814

Incorporated in 1946 in MI.
Donor(s): Helen L. DeRoy.
Foundation type: Independent
Financial data (yr. ended 12/31/88): Assets, $5,133,220 (M); expenditures, $299,518, including $236,947 for 161 grants (high: $25,000; low: $25).
Purpose and activities: Emphasis on Jewish welfare funds and higher education; grants also for child welfare.
Types of support: Operating budgets, general purposes, annual campaigns, research, emergency funds, scholarship funds, building funds, professorships.
Limitations: Giving primarily in MI. No grants to individuals.
Application information:
Deadline(s): None
Write: Arthur Rodecker, Pres., or Leonard H. Weiner, V.P.
Officers and Trustees: Arthur Rodecker, Pres.; Leonard H. Weiner, V.P.; Bernice Michel, Secy.
Employer Identification Number: 386082108

3091
DeRoy Testamentary Foundation ⌑
3274 Penobscot Bldg.
Detroit 48226 (313) 961-3814

Established in 1979 in MI.
Donor(s): Helen L. DeRoy.†
Foundation type: Independent
Financial data (yr. ended 12/31/88): Assets, $14,480,538 (M); expenditures, $851,948, including $629,790 for 67 grants (high: $72,953; low: $560).
Purpose and activities: Emphasis on higher education; support also for arts and culture, Jewish welfare funds, hospitals, and social service and youth agencies.
Types of support: Special projects.
Limitations: Giving primarily in MI. No grants to individuals.
Application information:
Deadline(s): None
Write: Leonard H. Weiner, Pres., or Arthur Rodecker, V.P.
Officers and Trustees: Leonard H. Weiner, Pres.; Arthur Rodecker, V.P.; Bernice Michel, Secy.
Employer Identification Number: 382208833

3092
Deseranno Educational Foundation, Inc. ⌑
4600 Bellevue
Detroit 48207
Application address: Father Taillieu Senior Citizen Home, Inc., 18760 East Thirteen Mile Rd., Roseville, MI 48066

Established in 1968 in MI.
Donor(s): Cold Heading Co., Ajax Metal Processing, Inc.
Foundation type: Independent
Financial data (yr. ended 12/31/88): Assets, $5,497,838 (M); gifts received, $1,214,056; expenditures, $310,860, including $278,900 for 39 grants (high: $60,000; low: $500) and $28,950 for 16 grants to individuals (high: $3,000; low: $850).
Purpose and activities: Support for Catholic organizations and scholarships to a Catholic college.
Types of support: Student aid.
Application information:
Initial approach: Letter
Deadline(s): None
Write: The Right Rev. Ferdinand DeCheudt
Officers and Directors: Aline DeSerrano, Pres.; Don DeSerrano, V.P.; Elizabeth Stevens, V.P.; Carl Morath, Secy.; Paul Morath, Treas.; John Lee.
Employer Identification Number: 237005737

3093
Detroit Edison Foundation ▼
2000 Second Ave., Rm. 1132 WCB
Detroit 48226 (313) 237-8781

Established in 1986 in MI.
Donor(s): Detroit Edison Co.
Foundation type: Company-sponsored
Financial data (yr. ended 12/31/88): Assets, $13,482,385 (M); expenditures, $1,641,248, including $1,621,114 for 449 grants (high: $137,750; low: $10; average: $500-$20,000).
Purpose and activities: Support for higher and other education, and civic, local community, social service, and cultural organizations.
Types of support: Operating budgets, capital campaigns, employee matching gifts.
Limitations: Giving primarily in southeast MI.
Application information:
Initial approach: Letter
Deadline(s): None
Board meeting date(s): 5-6 times a year
Final notification: 60 days
Write: Katherine W. Hunt, Secy.
Officers and Directors: S. Martin Taylor, Pres.; Katherine W. Hunt, Secy.; Leslie L. Loomans, Treas.; Susan M. Beale, Malcolm G. Dade, Jr., Willard R. Holland, Burkhard H. Schneider, B. Ralph Sylvia, Richard M. Thomas, Saul J. Waldman.
Number of staff: 3
Employer Identification Number: 382708636

3094
The Charles DeVlieg Foundation
(Formerly The Charles B. and Charles R. DeVlieg Foundation)
P.O. Box 33010
Bloomfield Hills 48303 (313) 961-0200

Incorporated in 1961 in MI.
Donor(s): Charles B. DeVlieg,† Charles R. DeVlieg, DeVlieg Machine Co., Kathryn S. DeVlieg.
Foundation type: Independent

Financial data (yr. ended 12/31/89): Assets, $3,360,700 (M); expenditures, $229,000, including $188,000 for 28 grants (high: $25,000; low: $500) and $7,000 for grants to individuals.
Purpose and activities: Support largely for higher and other education, including grants to a university for fellowships and a scholarship program for local high school graduates; grants for community funds, hospitals, youth agencies, family planning and services, the arts, environmental organizations, public policy, and science and technology.
Types of support: Fellowships, general purposes, scholarship funds, employee-related scholarships.
Limitations: Giving primarily in southeastern MI. No grants to individuals (except for company-employee scholarships), or for endowment funds, research programs, or matching gifts; no loans.
Application information: Application form required.
Initial approach: Proposal
Copies of proposal: 2
Deadline(s): None
Board meeting date(s): Semiannually
Write: Herbert A. Beyer, Exec. Dir.
Officers and Trustees:* Herbert A. Beyer,* Pres. and Exec. Dir.; Curt DeRoo,* Treas.; Kathryn S. DeVlieg, Richard A. Jerue, Julia DeVlieg O'Neill.
Number of staff: 1 part-time professional.
Employer Identification Number: 386075696

3095
The Richard and Helen DeVos Foundation ▼ ⌑
7575 East Fulton Rd.
Ada 49355 (616) 676-6222

Incorporated in 1969 in MI.
Donor(s): Richard M. DeVos, Helen J. DeVos.
Foundation type: Independent
Financial data (yr. ended 12/31/88): Assets, $18,688,415 (M); gifts received, $6,000,000; expenditures, $1,790,282, including $1,776,214 for 117 grants (high: $316,500; low: $21; average: $1,000-$25,000).
Purpose and activities: Giving largely for religious programs and associations, church support, music, and the performing arts, higher education, and social welfare.
Types of support: General purposes.
Application information:
Write: Richard M. DeVos, Pres.
Officers: Richard M. DeVos, Pres.; Helen J. DeVos, V.P.; Otto Stolz, Secy.; James Rosloniec, Treas.
Employer Identification Number: 237066873

3096
Edward & Ruth Diehl Foundation ⌑
25882 Orchard Lake Rd., No. 204
Farmington Hills 48018-5243

Established in 1948 in MI.
Foundation type: Independent
Financial data (yr. ended 12/31/88): Assets, $1,243,400 (M); expenditures, $74,190, including $60,000 for 10 grants (high: $25,000; low: $1,000).
Purpose and activities: Support primarily for health organizations and the arts.
Application information: Application form not required.
Initial approach: Letter
Deadline(s): None
Write: Gerald W. Diehl, Pres.
Officers: Gerald W. Diehl, Pres.; Charles E. Diehl, V.P.; Gregg A. Diehl, V.P.; Robert W. Wilson, Secy.
Employer Identification Number: 386089393

3097
The Herbert & Junia Doan Foundation
3801 Valley Dr.
Midland 48640-2626 (517) 631-6600

Established in 1964 in MI.
Donor(s): Herbert D. Doan.
Foundation type: Independent
Financial data (yr. ended 12/31/88): Assets, $1,843,116 (M); expenditures, $91,870, including $86,055 for 52 grants (high: $12,800; low: $50).
Purpose and activities: Support primarily for community funds, science, and the arts.
Types of support: General purposes.
Limitations: No grants to individuals.
Application information: Application form not required.
Initial approach: Letter
Deadline(s): Apr. 1
Write: Junia Doan, Exec. V.P.
Officers: Herbert D. Doan, Pres.; Junia Doan, Exec. V.P.; Jeffrey W. Doan, V.P.
Employer Identification Number: 386078714

3098
Domino's Foundation
30 Frank Lloyd Wright Dr.
P.O. Box 2120
Ann Arbor 48106-2120 (313) 930-1855

Established in 1983 in MI.
Donor(s): Domino's Pizza, Inc.
Foundation type: Company-sponsored
Financial data (yr. ended 12/31/88): Assets, $51,486 (M); gifts received, $252,100; expenditures, $245,361, including $244,895 for 49 grants (high: $33,250; low: $50; average: $1,000-$20,000).
Purpose and activities: Giving primarily to promote education; support also for health, religion, and the arts.
Types of support: Special projects.
Limitations: Giving primarily in MI. No grants to individuals.
Publications: Application guidelines, informational brochure (including application guidelines).
Application information: Application form not required.
Initial approach: Letter or telephone
Copies of proposal: 1
Deadline(s): None
Board meeting date(s): Monthly
Final notification: Within 30 to 90 days
Write: Joseph Davis, Prog. Dir.
Officers and Trustees:* Thomas S. Monaghan,* Pres.; Marjorie E. Monaghan,* Secy.; Douglas J. Dawson,* Treas.; Mary Kogelschatz, Tim Kogelschatz, Eugene Power.
Number of staff: 1 full-time professional.
Employer Identification Number: 382514364

3099
The Dow Chemical Company Foundation
1776 Bldg.
Midland 48674 (517) 636-1162

Established in 1979 in MI.
Donor(s): The Dow Chemical Co.
Foundation type: Company-sponsored
Financial data (yr. ended 12/31/88): Assets, $10,583,000 (M); gifts received, $10,000,000; expenditures, $3,809,792, including $3,775,153 for grants (average: $5,000-$15,000).
Purpose and activities: Support for programs at selected schools which encourage outstanding high school graduates to embark on a program leading to a career in chemistry.
Types of support: Scholarship funds, research.
Limitations: No grants to individuals.
Publications: Informational brochure.
Application information:
Initial approach: Brief letter
Deadline(s): None
Board meeting date(s): Usually 4 times a year
Final notification: 2 to 3 months
Write: Theodore E. Tabor, Prog. Mgr.
Officers: F.P. Popoff,* Chair. and Pres.; F.P. Corson, V.P.; A.H. Jenkins, Secy.; Enrique C. Falla,* Treas.
Trustees:* B.B. Butcher, A.J. Butler, J.L. Downey, K.R. McKennon, Paul F. Oreffice, J.G. Temple, Jr.
Number of staff: None.
Employer Identification Number: 382314603

3100
Dow Corning Foundation
2300 West Salzburg Rd.
Midland 48686-0994 (517) 496-6290

Established in 1982 in MI.
Donor(s): Dow Corning Corp.
Foundation type: Company-sponsored
Financial data (yr. ended 12/31/89): Assets, $8,147,683 (M); gifts received, $900,000; expenditures, $461,257, including $428,806 for 7 grants (high: $103,806; low: $25,000; average: $25,000-$50,000).
Purpose and activities: Giving primarily for community projects and higher and other education.
Types of support: Seed money, building funds, capital campaigns, endowment funds, professorships, special projects.
Limitations: Giving primarily in areas of company operations in KY, MI, NC, OR, and TN. No support for veterans', religious, or political organizations. No grants to individuals, or for conferences, dinners, fundraising events, or public advertisements.
Publications: Informational brochure (including application guidelines).
Application information: Application form not required.
Initial approach: Letter and proposal
Copies of proposal: 1
Deadline(s): None
Write: Anne M. DeBoer, Mgr., Corp. Contrib.
Officers: J.K. Campbell,* Pres.; John W. Westcott, V.P. and Treas.; D.G. Deibert, Secy.
Trustees:* J.R. Jenkins, R.L. Johnson, J.S. Ludington, E. Steinhoff.
Number of staff: None.
Employer Identification Number: 382376485

3101
Herbert H. and Barbara C. Dow Foundation ¤
2301 West Sugnet Rd.
Midland 48642

Incorporated in 1957 in MI.
Donor(s): Herbert H. Dow.
Foundation type: Independent
Financial data (yr. ended 12/31/88): Assets, $9,201,813 (M); expenditures, $433,593, including $410,547 for 25 grants (high: $75,031; low: $200).
Purpose and activities: Emphasis on higher education, cultural programs, and community funds.
Types of support: Equipment, continuing support, general purposes.
Limitations: Giving primarily in MI. No grants to individuals.
Application information: Contributes only to pre-selected organizations. Applications not accepted.
Board meeting date(s): Annually
Write: Herbert H. Dow, Pres.
Officers and Trustees: Herbert H. Dow, Pres.; Barbara C. Dow, Secy.-Treas.; Willard H. Dow II.
Employer Identification Number: 386058513

3102
The Herbert H. and Grace A. Dow Foundation ▼
P.O. Box 2184
Midland 48641-2184 (517) 636-2482

Trust established in 1936 in MI.
Donor(s): Grace A. Dow.†
Foundation type: Independent
Financial data (yr. ended 12/31/88): Assets, $266,179,667 (M); gifts received, $32,862; expenditures, $9,682,309, including $8,391,468 for 139 grants (high: $1,428,000; low: $83; average: $100,000-$500,000).
Purpose and activities: "Support of the arts, and especially of the symbiotic relationship between the arts and sciences." Grants largely for education, particularly higher education, community and social services, civic improvement, conservation, scientific research, church support, and cultural programs; maintains a public horticultural garden.
Types of support: General purposes, building funds, equipment, operating budgets, annual campaigns, endowment funds, research, special projects, renovation projects.
Limitations: Giving limited to MI, primarily Midland County. No grants to individuals, or for scholarships, travel, or conferences; no loans.
Publications: Annual report, application guidelines, program policy statement.
Application information: Application form not required.
Initial approach: Proposal
Copies of proposal: 1
Deadline(s): None
Board meeting date(s): Bimonthly
Final notification: 2 months
Write: Herbert H. Dow, Pres.
Officers and Trustees: Herbert H. Dow, Pres. and Treas.; Dorothy D. Arbury, V.P.; Herbert D. Doan, Secy.; Julie Carol Arbury, Michael L. Dow, I. Frank Harlow, Margaret Ann Riecker.
Number of staff: None.
Employer Identification Number: 381437485

3103
Alden & Vada Dow Fund ¤ ☆
315 Post St.
Midland 48640-2658

Donor(s): Vada B. Dow.
Foundation type: Independent
Financial data (yr. ended 12/31/88): Assets, $2,188,879 (M); expenditures, $84,160, including $79,500 for 29 grants (high: $15,000; low: $500).
Purpose and activities: Giving primarily to cultural programs including performing arts groups; support also for higher and other educational institutions, social services, and youth.
Types of support: General purposes.
Limitations: Giving primarily in Midland County, MI.
Application information: Contributes only to pre-selected organizations. Applications not accepted.
Officers: Vada B. Dow, Pres.; Mary Lloyd Mills, Secy.; Michael L. Dow, Treas.
Trustee: Barbara D. Carras.
Employer Identification Number: 386058512

3104
Earhart Foundation ▼
2200 Green Rd., Suite H
Ann Arbor 48105 (313) 761-8592

Incorporated in 1929 in MI.
Donor(s): Harry Boyd Earhart.†
Foundation type: Independent
Financial data (yr. ended 12/31/88): Assets, $41,228,117 (M); expenditures, $2,390,545, including $711,410 for 63 grants (high: $50,000; low: $500; average: $2,000-$15,000) and $1,147,013 for 177 grants to individuals (high: $17,500; low: $475).
Purpose and activities: H.B. Earhart Fellowships awarded through a special nominating process for graduate study, research fellowships awarded upon direct application to faculty members for individual projects in economics, history, international affairs, and political science; grants also to educational and research organizations.
Types of support: Professorships, fellowships, research, publications, conferences and seminars, grants to individuals.
Limitations: No grants for capital, building, or endowment funds, operating budgets, continuing support, annual campaigns, seed money, emergency funds, deficit financing, or matching gifts; no loans.
Publications: Annual report, application guidelines.
Application information: Direct applications from candidates or uninvited sponsors for H.B. Earhart Fellowships are not accepted. Application form not required.
Initial approach: Letter
Copies of proposal: 1
Deadline(s): None
Board meeting date(s): Monthly except in Aug.
Final notification: 90 to 120 days
Write: David B. Kennedy, Pres.
Officers and Trustees:* Dennis L. Bark,* Chair.; William D. Laurie, Jr.,* Vice-Chair.; David B. Kennedy,* Pres.; Anthony T. Sullivan, Secy.; Edward H. Sichler III, Treas.; Thomas J. Bray, Peter B. Clark, Earl I. Heenan, Paul W. McCracken, Robert E. Queller, Richard A. Ware.
Number of staff: 2 full-time professional; 2 full-time support.
Employer Identification Number: 386008273

3105
Earl-Beth Foundation
131 Kercheval Ctr., Suite 311
Grosse Pointe Farms 48236 (313) 882-1577

Incorporated in 1944 in MI.
Donor(s): Earl Holley,† Mrs. Earl Holley,† Holley Carburetor Co.
Foundation type: Independent
Financial data (yr. ended 12/31/89): Assets, $8,752,868 (M); expenditures, $555,199, including $385,342 for 102 grants (high: $50,000; low: $150).
Purpose and activities: "To encourage and support creative programs primarily in the areas of education, health, human social services, and environmental concerns. Focus is to encourage innovative programs to benefit and improve the lives of children and disadvantaged adults with programs that will be beneficial to them and to communities in Detroit."
Types of support: Seed money, special projects.
Limitations: Giving limited to the metropolitan Detroit, MI, area. No grants to individuals, or for endowment funds.
Publications: Application guidelines.
Application information:
Initial approach: Proposal
Copies of proposal: 1
Deadline(s): None
Board meeting date(s): May and Nov.
Final notification: 4 weeks after meeting
Write: Lisa Holley, Pres.
Officers: Lisa C. Holley,* Pres.; Danforth E. Holley,* Exec. V.P.; Theodore H. Oldham, Secy.; Mark Holley,* Treas.
Trustees:* Janie Holley Fleckenstein, Deborah Holley Palms.
Number of staff: 1 full-time professional; 1 part-time support.
Employer Identification Number: 386055542

3106
C. K. Eddy Family Memorial Fund ¤
c/o Second National Bank of Saginaw
101 North Washington Ave.
Saginaw 48607 (517) 776-7582

Trust established in 1925 in MI.
Donor(s): Arthur D. Eddy.†
Foundation type: Independent
Financial data (yr. ended 06/30/89): Assets, $9,169,058 (M); expenditures, $596,685, including $291,173 for 16 grants (high: $170,555; low: $1,000) and $170,555 for loans to individuals.
Purpose and activities: Giving for hospitals, a community fund, musical and cultural activities, and aid to Saginaw public schools.

Types of support: Student loans, special projects, equipment.
Limitations: Giving limited to Saginaw County, MI.
Publications: Application guidelines.
Application information: Application form required.
Deadline(s): For student loans, May 1; for grants under $5,000, the Monday before the weekly Thursday meeting; for grants over $5,000, 2 weeks prior to the bimonthly meeting on the 3rd Wednesday of the month
Write: Denice McGlaughlin (Grants); Marsha Sieggreen (Student Loans)
Trustee: Second National Bank of Saginaw.
Employer Identification Number: 386040506

3107
J. F. Ervin Foundation
3893 Research Park Dr.
P.O. Box 1168
Ann Arbor 48106 (313) 769-4600

Established in 1953 in MI.
Foundation type: Independent
Financial data (yr. ended 12/31/89): Assets, $1,762,080 (M); expenditures, $101,811, including $83,740 for 44 grants (high: $7,000; low: $500; average: $2,000).
Purpose and activities: Giving primarily for health services, the aged, and youth, including child development and welfare.
Types of support: Annual campaigns, continuing support, general purposes, special projects.
Limitations: Giving limited to southeastern MI. No grants for scholarships; no loans.
Publications: Annual report (including application guidelines).
Application information: Application form not required.
Initial approach: Proposal
Deadline(s): None
Board meeting date(s): Quarterly beginning in Mar.-annual meeting in Jan.
Write: H.A. Birch, Secy.
Officers: W.R. Kulenkamp, Pres.; S.K. Lovejoy, V.P.; J.E. Pearson, V.P.; J.E. Stephenson, V.P.; H.A. Birch, Secy.; M.K. Pearson, Treas.
Number of staff: 2 part-time support.
Employer Identification Number: 386053755

3108
H. T. Ewald Foundation
15175 East Jefferson
Grosse Pointe 48230 (313) 821-2000

Established in 1928 in MI.
Donor(s): Henry T. Ewald.†
Foundation type: Independent
Financial data (yr. ended 12/31/88): Assets, $1,733,988 (M); gifts received, $1,500; expenditures, $104,720, including $17,830 for 19 grants (high: $5,000; low: $25; average: $1,500) and $74,070 for 53 grants to individuals (high: $2,550; low: $250; average: $1,400).
Purpose and activities: Giving for four-year scholarships to local area high school seniors and social services.
Types of support: Student aid.
Limitations: Giving limited to Detroit, MI, metropolitan area residents and organizations.
Publications: Informational brochure (including application guidelines).
Application information: Application form required for scholarships.
Initial approach: Letter or telephone
Copies of proposal: 1
Deadline(s): May 1 for scholarships
Final notification: Approximately July 10
Write: H.T. Ewald, Pres.
Officers: Henry T. Ewald, Jr., Pres.; Shirley Pfeifer, V.P.; Carolyn T. Ewald, Secy.-Treas.
Number of staff: None.
Employer Identification Number: 386007837

3109
Fabri-Kal Foundation ⌑ ☆
c/o Fabri-Kal Corp.
Plastics Place
Kalamazoo 49001

Donor(s): Fabri-Kai Corp.
Foundation type: Company-sponsored
Financial data (yr. ended 12/31/88): Assets, $104,289 (M); gifts received, $144,000; expenditures, $129,150, including $70,985 for 22 grants (high: $10,000; low: $500) and $58,099 for 39 grants to individuals (high: $4,994; low: $48).
Purpose and activities: Support for higher education, including scholarships to individuals; support also for community development, a hospital, and social services.
Types of support: Student aid.
Limitations: Giving limited to areas of company operations: Kalamazoo, MI; Hazleton, PA; and Greenville, SC.
Application information:
Initial approach: Letter
Deadline(s): None
Write: R.P. Kittredge, Pres.
Officers: R.P. Kittredge, Pres.; C.W. Wright, Secy.; J.M. Dobrowolski, Treas.
Employer Identification Number: 237003366

3110
Drusilla Farwell Foundation ⌑
c/o Manufacturers National Bank of Detroit
100 Renaissance Ctr.
Detroit 48243

Established in 1937 in MI.
Foundation type: Independent
Financial data (yr. ended 8/31/88): Assets, $1,726,866 (M); expenditures, $91,004, including $69,100 for 100 grants (high: $10,000; low: $100).
Purpose and activities: Giving primarily for Protestant religion, libraries, education, and health, including medical research.
Officers: Hugo Krave, Pres.; Randolph Fields, V.P.; Helmuth Krave, Secy.
Employer Identification Number: 386082430

3111
Federal-Mogul Corporation Charitable Trust Fund ⌑
c/o Federal-Mogul Corp.
P.O. Box 1966
Detroit 48235 (313) 354-9934

Established in 1952 in MI.
Donor(s): Federal-Mogul Corp.
Foundation type: Company-sponsored
Financial data (yr. ended 10/31/88): Assets, $592,484 (M); gifts received, $504,800; expenditures, $595,776, including $589,969 for 293 grants (high: $70,000; low: $25).
Purpose and activities: Support largely for educational and cultural projects, including employee matching gifts.
Types of support: Employee matching gifts, building funds, continuing support, annual campaigns, research, matching funds, general purposes.
Limitations: Giving primarily in Detroit, MI, and other areas where the corporation maintains major manufacturing or distribution facilities. No grants to individuals, or for endowments, scholarships, or fellowships; no loans.
Publications: Application guidelines.
Application information: Application form not required.
Initial approach: Letter
Copies of proposal: 1
Deadline(s): None
Board meeting date(s): May and Nov.
Write: Lonnie Ross, Secy., Corp. Contribs. Comm.
Board of Control: Leonard Gay, C.B. Grant, R.W. Hague, J.J. Zamoyski.
Trustee: National Bank of Detroit.
Employer Identification Number: 386046512

3112
Fibre Converters Foundation, Inc. ⌑ ☆
P.O. Box 117
Three Rivers 49093

Incorporated in 1957 in MI.
Donor(s): Fibre Converters, Inc.
Foundation type: Company-sponsored
Financial data (yr. ended 03/01/89): Assets, $416,730 (M); gifts received, $44,400; expenditures, $268,652, including $267,800 for grants.
Purpose and activities: Grants for community funds, health agencies, and the handicapped.
Officers and Directors:* David T. Stuck,* Pres.; Lois A. Stuck,* Secy.
Employer Identification Number: 386081026

3113
George R. and Elise M. Fink Foundation
20550 Vernier Rd., Suite 101
Harper Woods 48225 (313) 886-5302

Incorporated in 1955 in MI.
Donor(s): George R. Fink.†
Foundation type: Independent
Financial data (yr. ended 11/30/89): Assets, $1,698,001 (M); expenditures, $202,089, including $142,108 for 37 grants (high: $52,000; low: $100; average: $100-$52,000).
Purpose and activities: Grants for secondary and other education, Protestant church support, and church-related institutions.
Types of support: General purposes.
Limitations: Giving primarily in MI. No grants to individuals, or for scholarships or fellowships; no loans.
Publications: Annual report.
Application information: Application form not required.

Initial approach: Proposal
Copies of proposal: 1
Board meeting date(s): Mar., June, Sept., and Dec.
Write: Frank J. Cernak, Secy.
Officers: Elise M. Fink,* Pres. and Treas.; Peter M. Fink,* V.P.; Frank J. Cernak, Secy.
Trustees:* W. Merritt Jones, Jr.
Number of staff: 1
Employer Identification Number: 386059952

3114
Max M. and Marjorie S. Fisher Foundation, Inc.
2700 Fisher Bldg.
Detroit 48202 (313) 871-8000

Established in 1955 in MI.
Donor(s): Max M. Fisher, Martinique Hotel, Inc.
Foundation type: Independent
Financial data (yr. ended 11/30/89): Assets, $489,345 (M); expenditures, $448,902, including $420,854 for 48 grants (high: $175,000; low: $100).
Purpose and activities: Giving primarily for Jewish welfare and education.
Limitations: No grants to individuals.
Application information: Contributes only to pre-selected organizations. Applications not accepted.
Officers and Directors:* Max M. Fisher,* Pres.; Marjorie S. Fisher,* V.P.; Phillip William Fisher,* Secy.-Treas.; Marjorie F. Aronow, Julie Cummings, Mary D. Fisher-Campbell, Jane F. Sherman.
Employer Identification Number: 381784340

3115
Edward I. Fleischman Foundation ⌑
30350 Hunters Dr., Apt. 2
Farmington Hills 48018

Established in 1952 in MI.
Foundation type: Independent
Financial data (yr. ended 12/31/88): Assets, $1,303,017 (M); expenditures, $91,080, including $90,725 for 5 grants (high: $40,000; low: $150).
Purpose and activities: Giving primarily for Jewish welfare.
Application information: Contributes only to pre-selected organizations. Applications not accepted.
Officers: Freda Fleischman, Pres.; Marvin Fleischman, V.P.; Steven Robinson, Secy.; Fannie Robinson, Treas.
Employer Identification Number: 386091812

3116
Community Foundation of Greater Flint
North Bank Ctr., Suite 410
432 North Saginaw St.
Flint 48502-2013 (313) 767-8270

Established in MI in 1978.
Foundation type: Community
Financial data (yr. ended 12/31/89): Assets, $18,611,421 (M); gifts received, $3,907,399; expenditures, $1,246,472, including $970,919 for 115 grants (high: $58,917; low: $278).
Purpose and activities: "To respond to current or emerging needs in the Genesee County, MI, area in conservation and environment, culture and the arts, education, health and human services, and leadership development."
Types of support: Annual campaigns, continuing support, general purposes, program-related investments, special projects.
Limitations: Giving limited to Genesee County, MI. No grants to individuals.
Publications: Annual report, informational brochure (including application guidelines).
Application information: Application form required.
Initial approach: Telephone or personal contact
Deadline(s): Varies
Board meeting date(s): 1st Fri. of even numbered months
Write: David K. Swenson, Exec. V.P.
Officers: Helen Philpott, Chair.; Webb F. Martin, Vice-Chair.; Arthur L. Tuuri, M.D., Pres.; David K. Swenson, Exec. V.P., Administration; H. Halladay Flynn, Exec. V.P., Development; Laura B. Froats, Secy.-Treas.
Number of staff: 2 full-time professional; 1 part-time professional; 1 full-time support.
Employer Identification Number: 382190667

3117
Benson and Edith Ford Fund ⌑
100 Renaissance Ctr., 34th Fl.
Detroit 48243 (313) 259-7777

Incorporated in 1943 in MI as the Hotchkiss Fund.
Donor(s): Benson Ford.†
Foundation type: Independent
Financial data (yr. ended 12/31/88): Assets, $12,463,759 (M); gifts received, $1,111,190; expenditures, $584,683, including $565,500 for 43 grants (high: $103,000; low: $1,000).
Purpose and activities: Giving for education, hospitals, community funds, and the arts; grants also for church support, child welfare, and youth agencies.
Limitations: No grants to individuals.
Application information: Awards generally limited to charities already favorably known to substantial contributors of the foundation.
Initial approach: Letter
Deadline(s): None
Write: P.V. Heftler, Secy.
Officers and Trustees:* Lynn F. Alandt,* Pres.; Pierre V. Heftler,* Secy.; Richard M. Cundiff, Treas.
Employer Identification Number: 386066333

3118
Eleanor and Edsel Ford Fund ⌑
100 Renaissance Ctr., 34th Fl.
Detroit 48243

Incorporated in 1944 in MI.
Donor(s): Eleanor Clay Ford.†
Foundation type: Independent
Financial data (yr. ended 12/31/88): Assets, $17,201,457 (M); expenditures, $951,302, including $935,000 for 9 grants (high: $298,000; low: $10,000; average: $20,000-$100,000).
Purpose and activities: Giving for higher and secondary education, the arts, including museums and an orchestra, a hospital, and a church.
Types of support: Building funds, scholarship funds, general purposes.
Limitations: Giving primarily in MI, with emphasis on Detroit. No grants to individuals.
Application information: Contributes only to pre-selected organizations. Applications not accepted.
Board meeting date(s): Oct. or Nov.
Write: Pierre V. Heftler, Secy.
Officers: William Clay Ford,* Pres.; Pierre V. Heftler,* Secy.; Richard M. Cundiff, Treas.
Trustees:* Josephine F. Ford.
Number of staff: None.
Employer Identification Number: 386066331

3119
Walter and Josephine Ford Fund ⌑
100 Renaissance Ctr., 34th Fl.
Detroit 48243 (313) 259-7777

Incorporated in 1951 in MI.
Donor(s): Josephine F. Ford.
Foundation type: Independent
Financial data (yr. ended 12/31/88): Assets, $6,886,763 (M); gifts received, $1,191,216; expenditures, $683,058, including $663,903 for 137 grants (high: $200,000; low: $50).
Purpose and activities: Giving for education, community funds, the arts, including museums, and hospitals; grants also for Protestant church support, medical research, and youth and social agencies.
Limitations: Giving primarily in MI. No grants to individuals.
Application information: Awards generally limited to charities already favorably known to substantial contributors of the foundation.
Initial approach: Letter
Deadline(s): None
Write: Pierre V. Heftler, Secy.
Officers and Trustees:* Walter B. Ford II,* Pres.; Josephine F. Ford,* V.P.; Pierre V. Heftler,* Secy.; Richard M. Cundiff, Treas.
Employer Identification Number: 386066334

3120
William and Martha Ford Fund ⌑
100 Renaissance Ctr., 34th Fl.
Detroit 48243 (313) 259-7777

Incorporated in 1953 in MI.
Donor(s): William Clay Ford, Martha Firestone Ford.
Foundation type: Independent
Financial data (yr. ended 12/31/88): Assets, $2,392,972 (M); gifts received, $450,400; expenditures, $920,783, including $912,216 for 58 grants (high: $200,000; low: $100).
Purpose and activities: Giving primarily for higher and other education, and hospitals and medical research; support also for community funds, child welfare, church support, the arts, and youth and social service agencies.
Limitations: No grants to individuals.
Application information: Awards generally limited to organizations known to the donors.
Initial approach: Letter
Deadline(s): None
Write: Pierre V. Heftler, Secy.
Officers: William Clay Ford,* Pres.; Pierre V. Heftler,* Secy.; Richard M. Cundiff, Treas.
Trustees:* Martha F. Ford.
Employer Identification Number: 386066335

3121
The Henry Ford II Fund ▼ ⌑
100 Renaissance Ctr., 34th Fl.
Detroit 48243 (313) 259-7777

Incorporated in 1953 in MI.
Donor(s): Henry Ford II.†
Foundation type: Independent
Financial data (yr. ended 12/31/86): Assets, $7,353,375 (M); gifts received, $772,857; expenditures, $1,004,019, including $992,557 for 44 grants (high: $120,000; low: $500; average: $500-$25,000).
Purpose and activities: Grants to cultural programs, education, a community fund, youth and social services, a Jewish welfare fund, civic and public affairs, and hospitals.
Limitations: No grants to individuals.
Application information: Funds presently committed. Applications not accepted.
Board meeting date(s): As needed
Write: Pierre V. Heftler, Secy.
Officers and Trustees: Pierre V. Heftler, Secy.; Richard M. Cundiff, Treas.
Number of staff: None.
Employer Identification Number: 386066332

3122
Ford Motor Company Fund ▼
The American Rd.
Dearborn 48121

Incorporated in 1949 in MI.
Donor(s): Ford Motor Co.
Foundation type: Company-sponsored
Financial data (yr. ended 12/31/89): Assets, $82,342,201 (L); gifts received, $60,575; expenditures, $23,498,004, including $21,048,474 for 1,523 grants (high: $1,200,000; low: $100; average: $13,820) and $2,253,388 for 12,353 employee matching gifts.
Purpose and activities: Support for education, including matching gifts for colleges and universities and basic research grants; community funds and urban affairs; hospitals; and civic and cultural programs.
Types of support: Matching funds, research, annual campaigns, equipment, general purposes, publications, conferences and seminars, employee matching gifts, continuing support, employee-related scholarships.
Limitations: Giving primarily in areas of company operations nation-wide, with special emphasis on Detroit and the rest of MI. No grants to individuals, or for building or endowment funds, scholarships, or fellowships.
Publications: Annual report, application guidelines, informational brochure.
Application information: Application form not required.
Initial approach: Letter
Copies of proposal: 1
Deadline(s): None
Board meeting date(s): Jan., Apr., June, and Oct.
Final notification: 6 months
Write: Leo J. Brennan, Jr., Exec. Dir.
Officer and Trustees:* Harold A. Poling,* Pres.; Philip E. Benton, Allan D. Gilmour, David N. McCammon, Peter J. Pestillo, David Scott, S.A. Seneker.
Number of staff: 6
Employer Identification Number: 381459376

3123
The Fremont Area Foundation ▼
108 South Stewart
Fremont 49412 (616) 924-5350

Incorporated in 1951 in MI.
Foundation type: Community
Financial data (yr. ended 12/31/88): Assets, $33,238,410 (M); gifts received, $420,618; expenditures, $1,508,956, including $1,122,025 for grants (high: $317,905; average: $1,000-$20,000) and $69,029 for 153 grants to individuals (average: $500).
Purpose and activities: "The foundation has established six broad funding categories: 1) Newaygo County Community Services: to sustain operations of this autonomous agency established for the delivery of general social welfare services and educational programs; 2) Civic Responsibilities: to strengthen the municipal activities of villages, cities, governmental units and other related organizations; 3) Education: to augment and promote the special projects of schools, libraries and other organizations for instruction and training and for scholarships to promote higher education and learning in specialized programs; 4) Fine Arts and Culture: to support activities that promote appreciation of and participation in artistic expression such as music, theater, dance, sculpture and painting; 5) Human Services: to foster the delivery of services and the operation of programs to help meet basic human needs and to support the provision of rehabilitative services; and 6) Health and Hospitals: made to health care providers and other related organizations for activities designed to promote optimal well-being to provide health-related education."
Types of support: Operating budgets, seed money, emergency funds, student aid, matching funds, consulting services, equipment, general purposes, renovation projects, special projects.
Limitations: Giving primarily in Newaygo County, MI. No grants to individuals (except for scholarships from specified funds of the foundation), or for endowments, contingencies, reserves, or deficit financing; no loans.
Publications: Annual report, application guidelines, informational brochure, newsletter.
Application information: Application form not required.
Initial approach: Letter or telephone to arrange interview
Copies of proposal: 8
Deadline(s): Oct. 1
Board meeting date(s): Usually in Feb., Apr., July, and Nov.
Final notification: 3 months
Write: Bertram W. Vermeulen, Exec. Dir.
Officers: Kenneth B. Peirce,* Pres.; Maynard DeKryger,* V.P.; Bertram W. Vermeulen, Secy. and Exec. Dir.; Virginia H. Gerber,* Treas.
Trustees:* Stephen R. Clark, Gay G. Cummings, Sally DeShetler, Richard L. Hogancamp, David J. Hoogerwerf, Douglas M. Jeannero, L. Max Lee, Gerald E. Martin, Dean H. Morehouse, Dennis G. Nelson, William A. Rottman, Eric W. Rudert, Ross G. Scott, Philip T. Smith.
Number of staff: 3 full-time professional; 1 full-time support; 1 part-time support.
Employer Identification Number: 381443367

3124
Frey Foundation ⌑
200 Ottowa Ave., N.W.
Grand Rapids 49503 (616) 451-7212

Established in 1974 in MI.
Donor(s): Edward J. Frey, Sr.†
Foundation type: Independent
Financial data (yr. ended 12/31/88): Assets, $16,352,469 (M); gifts received, $16,087,500; expenditures, $71,390, including $64,125 for 21 grants (high: $25,000; low: $25).
Purpose and activities: Giving primarily for the arts, Protestant religion, and social services.
Types of support: General purposes.
Application information: Application form not required.
Deadline(s): None
Write: Mrs. Frances T. Frey, Pres.
Officers and Directors:* Frances T. Frey,* Pres.; Mary Frey Rottschafer,* V.P.; David G. Frey, Secy.-Treas.; Pat Edison, Edward J. Frey, Jr., John M. Frey.
Employer Identification Number: 237094777

3125
The Fruehauf Foundation ⌑
100 Maple Park Blvd., Suite 106
St. Clair Shores 48081-2254 (313) 774-5130

Incorporated in 1968 in MI.
Donor(s): Angela Fruehauf, and others.
Foundation type: Independent
Financial data (yr. ended 12/31/88): Assets, $2,299,899 (M); expenditures, $194,088, including $181,050 for 105 grants (high: $20,000; low: $100).
Purpose and activities: Grants primarily for educational institutions, cultural programs, hospitals, health agencies, welfare, including youth agencies, economic research, and churches and religious programs.
Limitations: Giving primarily in MI. No grants to individuals.
Application information:
Initial approach: Letter
Deadline(s): None; applications reviewed monthly
Board meeting date(s): As required
Write: Elizabeth J. Woods, Asst. Secy.
Officers and Trustees: Harvey C. Fruehauf, Jr., Pres.; Ann F. Bowman, V.P. and Treas.; Barbara F. Bristol, V.P.; Frederick R. Keydel, Secy.
Employer Identification Number: 237015744

3126
Gabooney Foundation ⌑
c/o Michael D. Gibson
2100 Comerica Bldg.
Detroit 48226

Established in 1981 in MI.
Donor(s): David L. Gamble.
Foundation type: Independent
Financial data (yr. ended 3/31/88): Assets, $26,887 (M); gifts received, $106,355; expenditures, $129,032, including $124,039 for 43 grants (high: $56,673; low: $25).
Purpose and activities: Giving primarily for hospitals, social services, and education.
Application information: Contributes only to pre-selected organizations. Applications not accepted.

Officers and Trustees: David L. Gamble, Pres.; Michael D. Gibson, Secy. and Mgr.; Robert B. Deans, Jr., Christopher I. Gamble, David B. Gamble, Kimberly N. Gamble, Richard J. Temkow.
Number of staff: None.
Employer Identification Number: 382382126

3127
General Motors Cancer Research Foundation, Inc. ⌑
13-138 General Motors Bldg.
3044 West Grand Blvd.
Detroit 48202 (313) 556-4260

Established about 1978 in MI.
Donor(s): General Motors Corp.
Foundation type: Company-sponsored
Financial data (yr. ended 12/31/88): Assets, $2,279,382 (M); gifts received, $2,003,985; expenditures, $1,449,765, including $390,000 for 4 grants to individuals (high: $130,000).
Purpose and activities: Awards to individuals for "contributions to the prevention, detection, or treatment of cancer in order to stimulate further research in this field." Candidates for prizes must be nominated by invited proposers.
Types of support: Grants to individuals.
Limitations: No grants for scholarships or fellowships; no loans.
Publications: Application guidelines.
Application information:
Deadline(s): Oct. for prize nominations
Board meeting date(s): Apr. or May
Final notification: June
Write: J.J. Nowicki, Mgr.
Officers and Trustees: Roger B. Smith, Chair.; J.G. Fortner, Pres.; J.W. McNulty, Secy.; R.T. O'Connell, Treas.; W.O. Baker, J.E. Rhoads, L.S. Rockefeller, B.C. Schmidt, R.B. Smith.
Number of staff: 1
Employer Identification Number: 382219731

3128
General Motors Foundation, Inc. ▼
13-145 General Motors Bldg.
3044 West Grand Blvd.
Detroit 48202-3091 (313) 556-4260

Incorporated in 1976 in MI.
Donor(s): General Motors Corp.
Foundation type: Company-sponsored
Financial data (yr. ended 12/31/88): Assets, $169,056,275 (M); expenditures, $25,508,691, including $25,262,453 for grants (high: $2,000,000; low: $100; average: $10,000-$100,000).
Purpose and activities: Grants largely for higher education, community funds, social services, hospitals, health, cancer research, cultural programs, and urban and civic affairs.
Types of support: Operating budgets, continuing support, annual campaigns, seed money, emergency funds, building funds, equipment, land acquisition, research, publications, special projects, capital campaigns, renovation projects, technical assistance.
Limitations: Giving primarily in plant cities where company has significant operations. No support for special interest groups. No grants to individuals, or for deficit financing, endowment funds, or matching gifts; no loans.
Publications: Informational brochure.
Application information: Application form not required.
Initial approach: Letter
Copies of proposal: 1
Deadline(s): None
Board meeting date(s): Contributions committee meets annually
Final notification: 2 months
Write: J.J. Nowicki, Mgr.
Officers: J.E. Mischi, Pres.; W.W. Creek, Secy.; L.J. Krain, Treas.
Trustees: R.T. O'Connell, Chair.; W.E. Hoglund, L.E. Reuss, R.J. Schultz, F. Alan Smith, J.F. Smith, Jr., Robert B. Smith, Robert C. Stempel.
Number of staff: 1 full-time professional; 1 full-time support.
Employer Identification Number: 382132136

3129
The Gerber Companies Foundation
445 State St.
Fremont 49413 (616) 928-2759

Incorporated in 1952 in MI.
Donor(s): Gerber Products Co.
Foundation type: Company-sponsored
Financial data (yr. ended 05/31/89): Assets, $26,095,570 (M); expenditures, $949,818, including $774,966 for grants (high: $50,000; low: $250; average: $100-$5,000), $107,800 for grants to individuals and $47,716 for employee matching gifts.
Purpose and activities: Grants largely for education (including scholarships for company employees or children of employees), and for community funds and hospitals in areas of company operations. Some support for medical education, nursing, public health, family services, research in chemistry, agriculture, and the biological sciences.
Types of support: Operating budgets, continuing support, annual campaigns, building funds, matching funds, scholarship funds, employee-related scholarships, conferences and seminars, employee matching gifts, endowment funds, equipment.
Limitations: Giving limited to cities where company has major operations in AR, MI, NY, NC, PA, SC, TN, and WI. No grants for seed money, emergency funds, deficit financing, land acquisition, renovations, demonstration projects, or publications; no loans.
Publications: Annual report, program policy statement.
Application information: Application form not required.
Initial approach: Telephone or letter
Copies of proposal: 1
Deadline(s): Submit proposal preferably in Dec. or Jan., Feb., or Mar.
Board meeting date(s): Jan., Apr., July, and Oct.
Write: Grace A. Deur, Secy. or Yvonne A. Lee, Pres.
Officers and Trustees:* Yvonne A. Lee,* Pres.; George A. Purvis,* V.P.; Grace A. Deur,* Secy. and Admin.; Richard E. Dunning,* Treas.; Lynn Appleby, Larry Beemer, Stephen Clark, Leonard Griehs, Jay Hartfield, Barbara Ivens, Robert Johnston, L. James Lovejoy, Fred K. Schomer.
Number of staff: None.
Employer Identification Number: 386068090

3130
Charles H. Gershenson Foundation ⌑ ☆
c/o Honigman Miller Schwartz & Cohn
2290 First National Bldg.
Detroit 48226

Established in 1984 in MI.
Foundation type: Independent
Financial data (yr. ended 4/30/89): Assets, $5,228,778 (M); expenditures, $1,082,088, including $1,031,522 for 5 grants (high: $206,305; low: $106,304).
Purpose and activities: Support primarily for higher education, Jewish organizations, and a hospital.
Types of support: Scholarship funds, capital campaigns.
Limitations: Giving primarily in MI. No grants to individuals.
Application information: Contributes only to pre-selected organizations. Applications not accepted.
Trustee: Milton J. Miller.
Employer Identification Number: 386454423

3131
Gerson Family Foundation, Inc. ⌑
30285 Woodside Court
Franklin 48025-1439

Established in 1984 in MI.
Foundation type: Independent
Financial data (yr. ended 4/30/88): Assets, $2,009,079 (M); expenditures, $262,074, including $233,700 for 52 grants (high: $131,000; low: $25).
Purpose and activities: Support primarily for Jewish organizations and Jewish welfare.
Officers: Byron Gerson, Pres.; Mathew Gerson, V.P.; Dorothy Gerson, Secy.; Ralph Gerson, Treas.
Employer Identification Number: 382572982

3132
The Rollin M. Gerstacker Foundation ▼
P.O. Box 1945
Midland 48640 (517) 631-6097

Incorporated in 1957 in MI.
Donor(s): Eda U. Gerstacker,† Carl A. Gerstacker.
Foundation type: Independent
Financial data (yr. ended 12/31/89): Assets, $86,325,247 (M); expenditures, $5,394,707, including $5,240,202 for 93 grants (high: $3,639,906; low: $1,000; average: $5,000-$25,000).
Purpose and activities: To assist community projects, with emphasis on the aged and youth; grants also for higher education (including seminaries), health care, a medical research institute, and a hospital.
Types of support: Annual campaigns, seed money, emergency funds, building funds, equipment, endowment funds, research, matching funds, general purposes, continuing support, land acquisition, capital campaigns.
Limitations: Giving primarily in MI and OH. No grants to individuals, or for scholarships or fellowships; no loans.

Publications: Annual report.
Application information: Application form not required.
Initial approach: Letter
Copies of proposal: 1
Deadline(s): May 15 and Nov. 15
Board meeting date(s): June and Dec.
Final notification: 1 month
Write: E.N. Brandt, V.P.
Officers and Trustees:* Gail E. Allen,* Pres.; E.N. Brandt,* V.P. and Secy.; Carl A. Gerstacker,* V.P. and Treas.; Gilbert A. Currie, Esther S. Gerstacker, Lisa J. Gerstacker, Julius Grosberg, Paul F. Oreffice, Alan W. Ott, Jean Popoff, William D. Schuette.
Number of staff: None.
Employer Identification Number: 386060276

3133
Gilmore Foundation ⌑
c/o Old Kent Bank & Trust Co.
151 East Michigan Ave.
Kalamazoo 49007 (616) 383-6706

Trust established in 1956 in MI.
Donor(s): Irving S. Gilmore.
Foundation type: Independent
Financial data (yr. ended 12/31/88): Assets, $14,206 (M); gifts received, $130,000; expenditures, $166,432, including $17,415 for 2 grants (high: $15,915; low: $1,500) and $144,768 for 66 grants to individuals (high: $6,600; low: $385).
Purpose and activities: Limited primarily to benevolence grants to low-income individuals residing in local area who are unable to care for themselves due to physical limitations or advanced age.
Types of support: Grants to individuals.
Limitations: Giving primarily in the Kalamazoo, MI, area.
Application information: The foundation is curtailing grantmaking activities; no new grants to be awarded. Applications not accepted.
Write: Robert W. Cunningham, Trust Officer, Old Kent Bank & Trust Co.
Trustee: Old Kent Bank & Trust Co.
Disbursing Committee: Robert W. Cunningham, Ted F. McCarty, John C. Schaberg.
Number of staff: None.
Employer Identification Number: 386052803

3134
Gordy Foundation, Inc. ⌑
2648 West Grand Blvd.
Detroit 48208 (313) 867-0991

Established in 1967 in MI.
Donor(s): Jobete Music Co., Inc.
Foundation type: Independent
Financial data (yr. ended 6/30/88): Assets, $1,177,596 (M); gifts received, $25,022; expenditures, $71,692, including $59,050 for 25 grants (high: $20,000; low: $50).
Purpose and activities: Giving primarily for education and community activities; some support for religious and cultural activities.
Types of support: Building funds, scholarship funds, general purposes.
Limitations: Giving primarily in MI and CA. No grants to individuals.
Application information:
Deadline(s): None
Write: Esther Edwards, V.P.
Officers and Directors: Berry Gordy, Pres.; Esther Edwards, V.P. and Secy.; Gwen Fuqua, Treas.
Employer Identification Number: 386149511

3135
Gossett Fund ⌑
505 North Woodward Ave., Suite 3000
Bloomfield Hills 48013-7166

Established in 1955 in MI.
Donor(s): William T. Gossett.
Foundation type: Independent
Financial data (yr. ended 9/30/87): Assets, $1,229,244 (M); expenditures, $65,512, including $62,700 for 24 grants (high: $10,000; low: $100).
Purpose and activities: Giving primarily for higher education; support also for cultural and historical organizations.
Application information: Contributes only to pre-selected organizations. Applications not accepted.
Officers and Trustees: William T. Gossett, Pres. and Treas.; William T. Gossett, Jr., V.P.; Kathryn M. Gossett, Joyce S. Korson.
Employer Identification Number: 386061739

3136
Grand Haven Area Community Foundation, Inc.
One South Harbor
Grand Haven 49417 (616) 842-6378

Incorporated in 1971 in MI.
Foundation type: Community
Financial data (yr. ended 04/30/89): Assets, $4,475,202 (M); gifts received, $787,541; qualifying distributions, $477,076, including $276,397 for 35 grants (high: $36,942; low: $75; average: $1,000-$15,000), $16,675 for 11 grants to individuals (high: $1,500; low: $1,000; average: $500-$1,500) and $184,004 for 95 loans to individuals.
Purpose and activities: Support for education, recreation, culture, social services, civic affairs, community development, and youth.
Types of support: Seed money, matching funds, student loans, capital campaigns, equipment, general purposes, special projects.
Limitations: Giving primarily in the Tri-City and northwest Ottawa County, MI, areas. No grants to individuals (other than scholarships and student loans), or for annual campaigns, emergency or deficit financing, operating costs or ongoing operating support, or endowments.
Publications: Annual report (including application guidelines), informational brochure (including application guidelines), program policy statement, application guidelines, financial statement.
Application information: For student loans, request application form. Application form required.
Initial approach: Proposal, letter, or telephone call
Copies of proposal: 10
Deadline(s): Quarterly
Board meeting date(s): Quarterly
Final notification: 1 week after board meeting
Write: Linda B. Strevy, Dir.
Officers and Trustees:* Nancy Riekse,* Pres.; Bob Swart,* V.P. and Chair., Distrib. Comm.; Mary Jacobson,* Secy.; Kenneth Harestad,* Treas.; Leonard Anderson, George Jackoboice, Doris Van Dam, Michael Volkema, Marcia Witherell.
Number of staff: 1 full-time professional.
Employer Identification Number: 237108776

3137
The Grand Rapids Foundation ▼
209-C Waters Bldg.
161 Ottawa, N.W.
Grand Rapids 49503-2703 (616) 454-1751

Established in 1922 in MI by resolution and declaration of trust.
Foundation type: Community
Financial data (yr. ended 06/30/89): Assets, $43,527,360 (M); gifts received, $4,627,330; expenditures, $2,998,524, including $2,037,565 for 81 grants (high: $195,000; low: $150), $123,309 for 215 grants to individuals (high: $2,500; low: $125; average: $500-$2,500) and $7,500 for 3 loans to individuals.
Purpose and activities: To provide support for projects or causes designed to benefit the people and the quality of life in the Grand Rapids community and its environs, through grants for social welfare, youth agencies, cultural programs, health, recreation, neighborhood development, the environment, and education, including scholarships for Kent County residents to attend selected colleges.
Types of support: Seed money, emergency funds, building funds, equipment, land acquisition, matching funds, scholarship funds, capital campaigns, consulting services, loans, renovation projects, special projects, technical assistance, student aid, employee-related scholarships.
Limitations: Giving limited to Kent County, MI. No grants to individuals (except for scholarships), or for continued operating support, annual campaigns, deficit financing, or endowment funds; no student loans.
Publications: Annual report, informational brochure (including application guidelines), newsletter.
Application information: The student loan program has been discontinued; new loans will not be made. Application form required.
Initial approach: Letter or telephone
Copies of proposal: 12
Deadline(s): Submit scholarship applications between Jan. 1 and Apr. 1; deadline for all other applications is 8 weeks preceding board meeting
Board meeting date(s): Bimonthly beginning in Aug.
Final notification: June 15 for scholarships; 1 month for other requests
Write: Diana R. Sieger, Exec. Dir.
Officer: Diana R. Sieger, Exec. Dir.
Trustees: David B. LaClaire, Chair.; C. Christopher Worfel, Vice-Chair.; Ann M. Cooper, Norman B. DeGraaf, David G. Frey, Benjamin F. Gibson, Shirley Perkins, Herbert L. Vander Mey, David J. Wagner.
Trustee Banks: Michigan National Bank, NBD Grand Rapids, N.A., Old Kent Bank & Trust Co.
Number of staff: 3 full-time professional.
Employer Identification Number: 382877959

3138
Leslie H. & Edith C. Green Charitable Trust ⌑ ☆
c/o Patricia F. Donaldson
525 North Woodward, Suite 1300
Bloomfield Hills 48013

Established in 1975 in MI.
Donor(s): Edith C. Green.†
Foundation type: Independent
Financial data (yr. ended 12/31/88): Assets, $6,064,269 (M); gifts received, $920,294; expenditures, $417,795, including $350,334 for 2 grants (high: $280,267; low: $70,067).
Purpose and activities: Support for a church and a boys' home.
Application information: Contributes only to pre-selected organizations. Applications not accepted.
Trustee: Patricia F. Donaldson.
Employer Identification Number: 386162077

3139
Charles Grosberg Foundation ⌑
987 Arden Ln.
Birmingham 48009-2927
Application address: 201 North Federal Hwy., Suite 207, Drummond Bldg., Deerfield Beach, FL 33441-3696; Tel.: (305) 428-4212

Established in 1948 in MI.
Foundation type: Independent
Financial data (yr. ended 12/31/88): Assets, $1,390,991 (M); expenditures, $93,409, including $82,492 for 24 grants (high: $19,172; low: $20).
Purpose and activities: Giving primarily for Jewish welfare; support also for higher education.
Limitations: Giving limited to MI and FL. No grants to individuals.
Application information:
Write: Merwin Grosberg, Pres.
Officers: Merwin K. Grosberg, Pres.; Samuel Fronkel, V.P.; Joseph Grant, Secy.-Treas.
Employer Identification Number: 386088859

3140
The Grosfeld Foundation ⌑
2290 First National Bldg.
Detroit 48226

Established in 1984 in MI.
Donor(s): Multivest.
Foundation type: Independent
Financial data (yr. ended 11/30/88): Assets, $312,635 (M); gifts received, $100,000; expenditures, $280,641, including $280,403 for 18 grants (high: $144,630; low: $300).
Purpose and activities: Support primarily for Jewish organizations and health associations.
Limitations: No grants to individuals.
Application information: Contributes only to pre-selected organizations. Applications not accepted.
Officers: James Grosfeld, Pres. and Treas.; Nancy Grosfeld, V.P. and Secy.
Employer Identification Number: 382575307

3141
Handleman Charitable Foundation ⌑ ☆
c/o National Bank of Detroit
611 Woodward
Detroit 48232

Established in 1986 in MI.
Foundation type: Company-sponsored
Financial data (yr. ended 4/30/89): Assets, $3,082,164 (M); expenditures, $311,876, including $307,480 for 34 grants (high: $150,000; low: $40).
Purpose and activities: Grants primarily for a Jewish welfare fund; support also for the performing arts and other cultural programs, higher and other education, social services, and a zoological society.
Limitations: Giving primarily in Detroit, MI. No grants to individuals.
Application information: Contributes only to pre-selected organizations. Applications not accepted.
Officers: Frank M. Hennessey, Pres.; Louis Karcos, Treas.; Mark Holowicki, Mgr.
Employer Identification Number: 382736213

3142
Luella Hannan Memorial Home
4750 Woodward Ave.
Detroit 48201 (313) 833-1300

Established in 1925 in MI.
Donor(s): William Hannan,† Luella Hannan.†
Foundation type: Operating
Financial data (yr. ended 11/30/89): Assets, $17,075,388 (M); expenditures, $1,006,970, including $24,222 for grants (high: $500; low: $80; average: $80-$500) and $133,821 for 10 grants to individuals (high: $2,000; low: $250; average: $250-$2,000).
Purpose and activities: A private operating foundation; support for a community fund and welfare assistance to needy individuals 65 and over.
Types of support: Continuing support, grants to individuals.
Limitations: Giving primarily in the city of Detroit and Wayne, Oakland and Macomb counties, MI.
Application information: Applications not accepted.
Write: Ellen Kayrod, Exec. Dir.
Officers: George E. Parker III, Pres.; Zena Baum, V.P.; Gretchen Elston, V.P.; W.C. Osborn, Jr., V.P.; Richard H. Austin, Secy.
Trustees: Kenneth Aird, Harold Berry, Nicholas Hood.
Number of staff: 1 full-time professional; 1 part-time professional; 7 full-time support.
Employer Identification Number: 381358386

3143
Harder Foundation
18301 East Eight Mile Rd., Suite 213
East Detroit 48021 (313) 772-4433
Address for applicants in western states: Harder Foundation Western Office, P.O. Box 7407, Tacoma, WA 98407-7407; Tel.: (206) 756-3256

Incorporated in 1955 in MI.
Donor(s): Delmar S. Harder.†
Foundation type: Independent
Financial data (yr. ended 12/31/88): Assets, $10,005,925 (M); gifts received, $24,000; expenditures, $687,241, including $532,418 for 34 grants (high: $200,000; low: $900).
Purpose and activities: Support for environmental projects only.
Types of support: Operating budgets, continuing support, annual campaigns, seed money, emergency funds, land acquisition, endowment funds, matching funds.
Limitations: No grants to individuals, or for deficit financing, building funds, equipment, renovation projects, scholarships, fellowships, research, publications, or conferences; no loans.
Publications: Annual report, application guidelines.
Application information: Grants considered Feb. through July at western office. Application form required.
Initial approach: Letter, proposal, or telephone
Copies of proposal: 1
Deadline(s): July 31 for western office; no deadline for MI office
Board meeting date(s): July
Final notification: 4 months
Write: Nathan B. Driggers, Pres.; Del N. Langbauer, V.P., for applicants in western states
Officers and Trustees: Nathan B. Driggers, Pres.; Lucille E. Langbauer, V.P. and Treas.; Del N. Langbauer, V.P.; Jay A. Herbst, Secy.; Eldon N. Langbauer, Robert L. Langbauer, William H. Langbauer.
Number of staff: 2 part-time professional; 1 part-time support.
Employer Identification Number: 386048242

3144
Charles Stewart Harding Foundation
1802 Genesee Towers
Flint 48502 (313) 767-0136

Established in 1963 in MI.
Donor(s): C.S. Harding Mott,† C.S. Harding Mott II, Claire Mott White.
Foundation type: Independent
Financial data (yr. ended 12/31/89): Assets, $6,154,440 (M); expenditures, $1,161,599, including $1,142,650 for 42 grants (high: $300,000; low: $250).
Purpose and activities: Support primarily for Christian Scientist organizations and theological education.
Types of support: Annual campaigns, continuing support, operating budgets.
Limitations: No grants to individuals.
Application information: Application form not required.
Initial approach: Letter
Deadline(s): None
Board meeting date(s): Usually Oct.
Write: C. Edward White, Secy.
Officers: C.S. Harding Mott II,* Pres., Treas., and C.E.O.; Claire Mott White,* V.P.; C. Edward White, Secy.
Trustees:* Isabel S. Mott, Paula Kee Mott, William S. White.
Number of staff: None.
Employer Identification Number: 386081208

3145
Harris Foundation ☆
29100 Northwestern Hwy., Suite 370
Southfield 48034 (313) 948-9966

Established in 1983.
Donor(s): Brigitte P. Harris Charitable Lead Trust.
Foundation type: Independent
Financial data (yr. ended 05/31/89): Assets, $150,067 (M); expenditures, $167,776, including $160,657 for 64 grants (high: $60,000; low: $10).
Purpose and activities: Support primarily for religious welfare organizations, including a Jewish welfare fund; support also for health associations and medical research, hospitals, education, and family services.
Limitations: No grants to individuals.
Application information: Contributes only to pre-selected organizations. Applications not accepted.
Write: Morton E. Harris, Trustee
Trustees: Brigitte P. Harris, Morton E. Harris.
Number of staff: None.
Employer Identification Number: 382499405

3146
John and Rose Herman Foundation ⌑
3001 West Big Beaver Rd., Suite 404
Troy 48084 (313) 649-6400

Established in 1967 in MI.
Foundation type: Independent
Financial data (yr. ended 12/31/88): Assets, $2,140,566 (M); expenditures, $288,747, including $273,710 for 95 grants (high: $51,000; low: $100).
Purpose and activities: Grants largely for Jewish welfare funds and temple support; some support also for education and health agencies.
Application information:
Initial approach: Letter
Deadline(s): None
Write: Harold S. Tobias, Secy.
Officers: Rose Herman, Pres.; Hortense Alper, V.P.; Donald L. Herman, V.P.; Harold S. Tobias, Secy.; James E. Fuller, Treas.
Employer Identification Number: 237041624

3147
Herrick Foundation ▼ ⌑
2500 Comerica Bldg.
Detroit 48226 (313) 963-6420

Incorporated in 1949 in MI.
Donor(s): Ray W. Herrick,† Hazel M. Herrick.†
Foundation type: Independent
Financial data (yr. ended 9/30/88): Assets, $210,459,774 (M); expenditures, $11,104,794, including $10,745,750 for 190 grants (high: $1,000,000; low: $500; average: $5,000-$100,000).
Purpose and activities: Emphasis on higher and secondary education, including scholarship and capital funds, Protestant church support, cultural programs, youth agencies, hospitals, and health and welfare agencies.
Types of support: Building funds, equipment, land acquisition, research, scholarship funds, special projects, general purposes.
Limitations: Giving primarily in MI. No grants to individuals.
Application information: Application form not required.
Initial approach: Letter
Deadline(s): None
Board meeting date(s): Every 2 to 3 months
Write: Kenneth G. Herrick, Pres.
Officers: Kenneth G. Herrick,* Chair., Pres., and Treas.; John W. Gelder, V.P. and Secy.; Richard B. Gushee,* V.P.; Todd W. Herrick, V.P.
Trustees:* Catherine R. Cobb.
Number of staff: None.
Employer Identification Number: 386041517

3148
Myrtle E. & William C. Hess Charitable Trust ☆
c/o National Bank of Detroit, Trust Div.
611 Woodward Ave.
Detroit 48226 (313) 225-3124

Established in 1984 in MI.
Donor(s): Myrtle E. Hess.
Foundation type: Independent
Financial data (yr. ended 09/30/89): Assets, $6,908,708 (M); expenditures, $577,338, including $491,736 for 27 grants (high: $115,000; low: $1,000; average: $1,000-$115,000).
Purpose and activities: Giving to Catholic churches, religious orders, and welfare; support also for elementary, secondary, and higher education, including religious schools; social services, including child development and welfare, youth programs, and religious welfare organizations; health, rehabilitation, and hospitals; and a municipal recreation department.
Types of support: General purposes, special projects.
Limitations: Giving primarily in MI.
Publications: 990-PF.
Application information:
Initial approach: Proposal
Deadline(s): None
Board meeting date(s): Jan.
Write: Therese M. Thorn, 2nd V.P., National Bank of Detroit
Trustees: Thomas W. Payne, Therese M. Thorn, National Bank of Detroit.
Number of staff: None.
Employer Identification Number: 382617770

3149
The Clarence and Jack Himmel Foundation ⌑
3000 Town Ctr., Suite 2550
Southfield 48075

Established in 1975 in MI.
Donor(s): Clarence Himmel.†
Foundation type: Independent
Financial data (yr. ended 10/31/88): Assets, $1,494,570 (M); expenditures, $156,145, including $117,250 for 79 grants (high: $10,000; low: $200).
Purpose and activities: Emphasis on family and child welfare services and youth agencies; grants also for hospitals, Jewish welfare funds, health agencies, cultural programs, and the handicapped.
Limitations: Giving primarily in MI.
Application information: Contributes only to pre-selected organizations. Applications not accepted.
Officers and Directors: Robert A. Karbel, Pres. and Secy.; Sidney J. Karbel, V.P.; Ronald A. Rothstein, Treas.
Employer Identification Number: 510140773

3150
James and Lynelle Holden Fund ⌑
1026 Buhl Bldg.
Detroit 48226 (313) 962-4757

Incorporated in 1941 in MI.
Donor(s): James S. Holden,† Lynelle A. Holden.†
Foundation type: Independent
Financial data (yr. ended 12/31/88): Assets, $7,864,558 (M); expenditures, $876,419, including $786,282 for 46 grants (high: $125,000; low: $1,500; average: $2,500-$35,000).
Purpose and activities: Support for medical research, including medical schools and hospitals; aid to youth agencies, minority and underprivileged children, education, and care of the aged; grants also for cultural programs.
Types of support: Annual campaigns, general purposes, building funds, equipment, research, scholarship funds, fellowships, matching funds, continuing support, operating budgets.
Limitations: Giving primarily in MI, with emphasis on Detroit. No grants to individuals, or for endowment funds; no loans.
Application information: Application form not required.
Initial approach: Letter or proposal
Copies of proposal: 1
Deadline(s): None
Board meeting date(s): Jan., Apr., July, and Oct.
Final notification: Several weeks
Write: Joseph Freedman, Pres.
Officers and Trustees: Joseph Freedman, Pres. and Secy.; Louis F. Dahling, V.P.; Herbert J. Wilson, Treas.
Number of staff: 1 full-time professional; 1 part-time professional.
Employer Identification Number: 386052154

3151
The Holley Foundation ⌑
c/o Manufacturers National Bank Detroit
100 Renaissance Ctr., 7th Fl.
Detroit 48243

Established in 1944 in MI.
Foundation type: Independent
Financial data (yr. ended 12/31/88): Assets, $1,820,622 (M); expenditures, $116,391, including $93,600 for 17 grants (high: $20,000; low: $500).
Purpose and activities: Support for hospitals and health associations, including a rehabilitation center, higher and other education, and cultural programs.
Limitations: Giving primarily in MI.
Officers and Trustees:* Margery H. Uihlein,* Chair.; John C. Holley, Sr.,* Pres.; Douglas Rasmussen, Secy.; Edmund R. Sutherland,* Treas.; Margaret Holley, Exec. Dir.; Walker L. Cisler, A.J. Fisher, Barbara K. Frank, David C. Holley, George M. Holley III, John C. Holley, Jr., Philipp Gregg Kuehn, Jr.

Employer Identification Number: 386055168

3152
Honigman Foundation, Inc. ⌑
2290 First National Bldg.
Detroit 48226 (313) 256-7500

Incorporated in 1955 in MI.
Donor(s): Jason L. Honigman, Edith Honigman.
Foundation type: Independent
Financial data (yr. ended 10/31/88): Assets, $4,512,746 (M); expenditures, $218,554, including $194,410 for 46 grants (high: $75,000; low: $15).
Purpose and activities: Emphasis on Jewish welfare funds; grants also for higher and secondary education, including institutions in Israel, and a local cancer research foundation.
Limitations: Giving primarily in MI.
Application information:
Board meeting date(s): First Monday in May
Write: Jason L. Honigman, Pres.
Officers and Trustees: Jason L. Honigman, Pres.; Edith Honigman, V.P.; Daniel M. Honigman, Secy.; Julie R. Levy, Treas.; David M. Honigman, Suzanne Honigman, Kay Honigman-Singer, Edward C. Levy, Jr.
Number of staff: None.
Employer Identification Number: 386059254

3153
Hudson-Webber Foundation ▼
333 West Fort St., Suite 1310
Detroit 48226 (313) 963-7777

Incorporated in 1943 in MI; on Jan. 1, 1984 absorbed The Richard H. and Eloise Jenks Webber Charitable Fund, Inc., and the Eloise and Richard Webber Foundation.
Donor(s): Eloise Webber,† Richard Webber,† The J.L. Hudson Co., The Richard H. and Eloise Jenks Webber Charitable Fund, Eloise and Richard Webber Foundation, and members of the Webber family.
Foundation type: Independent
Financial data (yr. ended 12/31/89): Assets, $84,753,315 (M); expenditures, $4,517,626, including $3,609,400 for grants (high: $400,000; low: $2,000; average: $20,000-$50,000), $78,851 for 92 grants to individuals (high: $2,588; low: $48; average: $400-$1,700), $45,365 for 1 foundation-administered program and $300,000 for loans.
Purpose and activities: Concentrates efforts and resources in support of projects within five program missions, which impact upon the vitality and quality of life of the community: 1) growth and development of the Detroit Medical Center, 2) economic development of southeastern MI, with emphasis on the creation of additional employment opportunities, 3) physical revitalization of downtown Detroit, 4) enhancement of major art and cultural resources in Detroit, and 5) reduction of crime in Detroit. The foundation also provides charitable assistance of J.L. Hudson Co. employees or ex-employees needing help to overcome personal crises and misfortunes.
Types of support: Operating budgets, continuing support, annual campaigns, seed money, building funds, matching funds, special projects, grants to individuals, equipment, consulting services, renovation projects, employee matching gifts, general purposes, program-related investments.
Limitations: Giving primarily in Detroit, MI; limited giving to communities in the Wayne, Oakland, and Macomb tri-county area of southeastern MI. No support for educational institutions or neighborhood organizations, except for projects that fall within current program missions. No grants to individuals (except for J.L. Hudson Co. employees and ex-employees), or for emergency funds, deficit financing, endowment funds, scholarships, fellowships, publications, conferences, fundraising social events, or exhibits; no loans.
Publications: Biennial report (including application guidelines).
Application information: Application form not required.
Initial approach: Proposal
Copies of proposal: 1
Deadline(s): Apr. 15, Aug. 15 (for July and Dec. meetings), and Dec. 15 (for meeting in Apr. of following year)
Board meeting date(s): July, Dec., and Apr.
Final notification: 1 week after board decision
Write: Gilbert Hudson, Pres.
Officers and Trustees:* Joseph L. Hudson, Jr.,* Chair.; Gilbert Hudson,* Pres. and C.E.O.; Hudson Holland, Jr.,* Secy.; Frank M. Hennessey,* Treas.; Lawrence P. Doss, Alfred R. Glancy III, Philip J. Meathe, Theodore H. Mecke, Jr., Mrs. Alan E. Schwartz.
Number of staff: 1 full-time professional; 1 full-time support; 1 part-time support.
Employer Identification Number: 386052131

3154
Edward and Irma Hunter Foundation ⌑
423 Sycamore St., Suite 101
Niles 49120 (616) 684-3248
Additional address: P.O. Box 906, Niles, MI 49120

Established in 1968 in MI.
Donor(s): Edward Hunter,† Irma Hunter.†
Foundation type: Independent
Financial data (yr. ended 12/31/88): Assets, $2,921,273 (M); expenditures, $192,405, including $128,391 for 11 grants (high: $60,000; low: $1,500).
Purpose and activities: Support primarily for economic development and area employment, including support for social services and welfare organizations.
Types of support: Annual campaigns, emergency funds, building funds, equipment, land acquisition, matching funds.
Limitations: Giving limited to the Niles and Buchanan, MI, area. No grants to individuals, or for operating budgets, continuing support, seed money, deficit financing, endowment funds, scholarships, fellowships, program support, research, demonstration projects, publications, or conferences; no loans.
Publications: 990-PF, informational brochure (including application guidelines).
Application information: Application form not required.
Initial approach: Letter
Copies of proposal: 7
Deadline(s): Second week of Feb., May, Aug., and Nov.
Board meeting date(s): Fourth Monday of Feb., May, Aug., and Nov.
Final notification: 1 week
Write: Donald F. Walter, Pres.
Officers and Trustees: Donald F. Walter, Pres.; Philip A. Hadsell, Jr., V.P. and Secy.; Gerald H. Frieling, Jr., Treas.; J. Edward French, Gary G. Gaynor, Paul W. Jedele.
Employer Identification Number: 237065471

3155
The Hurst Foundation
105 East Michigan Ave.
P.O. Box 449
Jackson 49204 (517) 787-6503

Trust established in 1955 in MI.
Donor(s): Peter F. Hurst,† Elizabeth S. Hurst.
Foundation type: Independent
Financial data (yr. ended 12/31/89): Assets, $5,438,489 (M); expenditures, $265,778, including $250,240 for 19 grants (high: $124,500; low: $500; average: $13,250).
Purpose and activities: Emphasis on higher and secondary education, a museum, social services, community development, and youth agencies.
Types of support: Operating budgets, seed money, building funds, equipment, special projects.
Limitations: Giving limited to Jackson County, MI. No grants to individuals, or for endowment funds, scholarships, fellowships, or matching gifts; no loans.
Application information: Application form not required.
Initial approach: Letter
Copies of proposal: 2
Deadline(s): Submit proposal preferably in Oct.; deadline Nov. 10
Board meeting date(s): Dec. and as required
Final notification: 60 days, for favorable decision only
Write: James A. Hildreth
Trustees: Anthony P. Hurst, Elizabeth S. Hurst, Ronald F. Hurst.
Number of staff: None.
Employer Identification Number: 386089457

3156
Stanley Imerman Memorial Foundation ⌑
29201 Telegraph Rd., Suite 500
Southfield 48034

Established in 1971 in MI.
Donor(s): Stanley Imerman.†
Foundation type: Independent
Financial data (yr. ended 12/31/87): Assets, $2,805,566 (M); expenditures, $168,785, including $148,700 for 46 grants (high: $20,000; low: $100).
Purpose and activities: Grants largely for Jewish welfare funds, higher education, and health agencies.
Types of support: Continuing support, annual campaigns, building funds, general purposes.
Limitations: Giving primarily in MI. No grants to individuals, or for endowment funds, scholarships, fellowships, or matching gifts; no loans.

Application information: Contributes only to pre-selected organizations. Applications not accepted.
Officers and Trustees: Lawrence S. Jackier, Pres. and Treas.; Dale G. Rands, V.P.; Ronald H. Ribock, V.P.; Mark E. Schlussel, Secy.
Employer Identification Number: 237152760

3157
India Foundation ⌘
3308 South Cedar, Suite 11
Lansing 48910

Donor(s): Shrikumar Poddar, Mayurika Poddar.
Foundation type: Independent
Financial data (yr. ended 12/31/87): Assets, $1,965,097 (M); gifts received, $40,000; expenditures, $103,654, including $82,566 for 17 grants (high: $23,401; low: $11).
Purpose and activities: Support primarily for East Indian religious and charitable organizations.
Application information:
Initial approach: Letter
Deadline(s): June 30 and Nov. 30
Write: Charles Haynes
Officers: Shrikumar Poddar, Pres.; K.S. Sripada Raju, Secy.
Directors: Eleanor Flinn, Harold Mondol, Mayurika Poddar, Kenneth Smith.
Employer Identification Number: 237300230

3158
The Jackson Foundation
505 Wildwood Ave.
Jackson 49201 (517) 787-1321

Incorporated in 1948 in MI.
Foundation type: Community
Financial data (yr. ended 12/31/89): Assets, $3,201,121 (M); gifts received, $620,958; expenditures, $356,642, including $285,926 for 20 grants (high: $60,000; low: $500; average: $500-$18,000).
Purpose and activities: Support for community improvement and other programs for the benefit of the residents of Jackson County.
Types of support: Seed money, building funds, equipment, land acquisition, matching funds, consulting services, technical assistance, loans, special projects, research, capital campaigns.
Limitations: Giving limited to Jackson County, MI. No support for religious purposes. No grants to individuals, or for endowment funds, scholarships, fellowships, publications, or conferences.
Publications: Annual report (including application guidelines).
Application information: Application form required.
Initial approach: Letter or telephone
Copies of proposal: 1
Deadline(s): Submit proposal preferably in Jan., Apr., July, or Oct.; deadlines Feb. 1, May 1, Aug. 1, and Nov. 1
Board meeting date(s): Mar., June, Sept., and Dec.
Final notification: 6 weeks
Write: Mrs. Jody Bacon, Exec. Dir.
Officers: Douglas L. Burdick,* Pres.; Mark Rosenfeld,* V.P.; Charles H. Aymond,* Secy.-Treas.; Jody Bacon, Exec. Dir.
Trustees:* Robert W. Ballantine, Jerry B. Booth, Donna Hardy, Anthony P. Hurst, Raynard C. Lincoln, Jr., Clara D. Noble, William Sigmund, James Winter, Edward Woods, Susan Wrzesinski.
Number of staff: 1 part-time professional; 1 part-time support.
Employer Identification Number: 386070739

3159
Michael Jeffers Memorial Fund
c/o Second National Bank of Saginaw
101 North Washington Ave.
Saginaw 48607 (517) 776-7353

Established in 1967 in MI.
Donor(s): John Jeffers.†
Foundation type: Independent
Financial data (yr. ended 12/31/88): Assets, $3,184,290 (M); expenditures, $131,132, including $93,053 for loans to individuals (average: $1,000-$2,000).
Purpose and activities: Funds limited solely to educational loans.
Types of support: Student loans.
Limitations: Giving limited to Saginaw County, MI.
Publications: Informational brochure (including application guidelines).
Application information: Applicants must be between 15 and 30 years of age. Application form required.
Deadline(s): June 1
Board meeting date(s): June
Final notification: July
Write: Marcia Sieggreen, Student Loan Admin.
Student Loan Committee: H.M. James, D.H. List, Pauline Lynch, T.R. Niederstadt, R.M. Whiting.
Student Loan Advisory Committee: R. Cook, R. Daniels, J. Finkbeiner, F. Gibbs, H. Karls, Dr. Lawrenz, William Palmer.
Number of staff: 2 full-time support.
Employer Identification Number: 237059762

3160
Jonathan & David Foundation ⌘
801 Monroe N.W.
Grand Rapids 49503

Established in 1982 in MI.
Donor(s): Samuel Butcher, William Biel.
Foundation type: Independent
Financial data (yr. ended 12/31/89): Assets, $501,624 (M); expenditures, $207,363, including $201,450 for 32 grants (high: $25,000; low: $50).
Purpose and activities: Grants for Protestant organizations, including religious education, missionary programs in the U.S. and the Philippines, and church support.
Limitations: Giving primarily in MI.
Application information: Contributes only to pre-selected organizations. Applications not accepted.
Trustees: William Biel, Robert Brummeler.
Employer Identification Number: 382443692

3161
JSJ Foundation
P.O. Box 687
Grand Haven 49417 (616) 842-6350

Established in 1983 in MI.
Donor(s): JSJ Corp.
Foundation type: Company-sponsored
Financial data (yr. ended 12/31/89): Assets, $327,300 (M); gifts received, $50,000; expenditures, $178,600, including $136,517 for grants (high: $25,000) and $25,083 for 104 employee matching gifts.
Purpose and activities: Giving primarily to community funds; some support also for the arts and humanities, civic affairs, education, social service and youth organizations, and health associations.
Types of support: Annual campaigns, building funds, capital campaigns, continuing support, general purposes.
Limitations: Giving primarily in locations where the corporation has facilities. No grants to individuals, or for exchange programs, fellowships, internships, lectureships, or professorships; no loans.
Application information: Application form not required.
Deadline(s): None
Board meeting date(s): Nov.
Write: Donald A. Johnson, Chair.
Officers: Donald A. Johnson,* Chair. and Secy.; Michael D. Metzger, Treas.
Trustees:* Alvin E. Jacobson, Alvin E. Jacobson, Jr., Martin Johnson, Paul A. Johnson, Lynne Sherwood.
Employer Identification Number: 382421508

3162
George W. & Sadie Marie Juhl Scholarship Foundation
c/o Southern Michigan National Bank
51 West Pearl St.
Coldwater 49036 (517) 279-7511

Established in 1983 in MI.
Foundation type: Independent
Financial data (yr. ended 3/31/89): Assets, $1,357,648 (M); expenditures, $72,134, including $62,300 for 44 grants to individuals (high: $2,000; low: $750; average: $1,000-$2,000).
Purpose and activities: Awards scholarships to individuals for education.
Types of support: Student aid.
Limitations: Giving limited to residents of Branch County, MI, attending schools of higher education located in MI.
Application information: Application should be submitted to local high school guidance office. Application form required.
Deadline(s): None
Write: James R. Cole, Sr. V.P. and Trust Officer, Southern Michigan National Bank
Trustees: Elinor Sweet, Southern Michigan National Bank.
Employer Identification Number: 386372257

3163
George W. & Sadie Marie Juhl Scholarship Fund ⌑
c/o Southern Michigan National Bank
51 West Pearl St.
Coldwater 49036 (517) 279-7511

Established in 1983 in MI.
Foundation type: Independent
Financial data (yr. ended 3/31/86): Assets, $1,226,969 (M); expenditures, $66,809, including $60,450 for 40 grants to individuals (high: $2,000; low: $500).
Purpose and activities: Scholarships for Branch County students to attend schools of higher education in MI.
Types of support: Student aid.
Limitations: Giving limited to Branch County, MI, to students attending schools of higher education in MI.
Publications: 990-PF.
Application information: Application form required.
Initial approach: Applications available through Branch County High School counseling offices
Final notification: May
Write: James R. Cole, Sr. V.P. and Trust Officer, Southern Michigan National Bank
Trustees: Elinor Sweet, Southern Michigan National Bank.
Employer Identification Number: 382571129

3164
Kalamazoo Foundation
151 South Rose St., Suite 332
Kalamazoo 49007 (616) 381-4416

Established in 1925; incorporated in 1930 in MI.
Foundation type: Community
Financial data (yr. ended 12/31/89): Assets, $89,248,026 (M); gifts received, $14,265,444; expenditures, $7,203,933, including $6,205,451 for grants (high: $340,000; low: $10).
Purpose and activities: Grants largely for capital purposes for higher and other education, child welfare and youth agencies, music and the arts, a civic auditorium, and hospitals; support also for housing, care of the aged, aid to the handicapped, recreation, public health, and community development.
Types of support: Seed money, building funds, general purposes, emergency funds, matching funds, equipment, scholarship funds.
Limitations: Giving limited to Kalamazoo County, MI. No grants to individuals, or for endowment funds.
Publications: Annual report, informational brochure, application guidelines, newsletter.
Application information: Application form required.
Initial approach: Telephone or letter
Copies of proposal: 9
Deadline(s): Apr. 1, Aug. 1, or Dec. 1
Board meeting date(s): May, Sept., and Jan.
Final notification: 2 months
Write: John E. Hopkins, Exec. Dir.
Officers: Martha G. Parfet,* Pres.; Elizabeth S. Upjohn,* V.P.; John E. Hopkins, Exec. Dir.
Trustees and Distribution Committee:* Joseph J. Dunnigan, David L. Hatfield, William J. Lawrence, Jr.
Trustee Banks: Comerica Bank-Kalamazoo, First of America Bank-Michigan, Old Kent Bank of Kalamazoo.
Number of staff: 3 full-time professional; 2 full-time support.
Employer Identification Number: 386048002

3165
The Kantzler Foundation
900 Center Ave.
Bay City 48708 (517) 892-0591

Incorporated in 1974 in MI.
Donor(s): Leopold J. Kantzler.†
Foundation type: Independent
Financial data (yr. ended 12/31/89): Assets, $3,920,525 (M); expenditures, $199,939, including $182,650 for 12 grants (high: $65,000; low: $1,322).
Purpose and activities: To support projects and capital improvements of charitable, artistic, educational, and cultural organizations.
Types of support: Seed money, building funds, equipment, land acquisition, matching funds, capital campaigns.
Limitations: Giving limited to the greater Bay City, MI, area. No grants to individuals, or for endowment funds, operating budgets, continuing support, annual campaigns, special projects, publications, conferences, emergency funds, deficit financing, research, scholarships, or fellowships; no loans.
Publications: Program policy statement (including application guidelines), financial statement.
Application information: Application form not required.
Initial approach: Proposal
Copies of proposal: 1
Deadline(s): None
Board meeting date(s): Approximately 10 times a year
Final notification: 2 months
Write: Robert D. Sarow, Secy.
Officers: Dominic Monagtiere, Pres.; Clifford C. Van Dyke, V.P.; Robert D. Sarow, Secy.; Arthur E. Hagen, Jr.,* Treas.
Trustees:* Robbie L. Baker, Ruth Jaffe.
Number of staff: None.
Employer Identification Number: 237422733

3166
Louis G. Kaufman Endowment Fund
c/o First National Bank and Trust Co.
P.O. Box 580
Marquette 49855 (906) 228-1244

Trust established in 1927 in MI.
Donor(s): L.G. Kaufman Trust.
Foundation type: Independent
Financial data (yr. ended 12/31/89): Assets, $2,439,000 (M); expenditures, $93,011, including $77,140 for 19 grants (high: $30,000; low: $350).
Purpose and activities: Emphasis on secondary education, community development, family and social services, youth agencies, and recreation.
Types of support: Operating budgets, annual campaigns, seed money, emergency funds, scholarship funds, special projects.
Limitations: Giving primarily in Marquette, MI. No grants to individuals, or for continuing support, deficit financing, land acquisition, endowment funds, matching gifts, research, publications, or conferences; no loans.
Application information: Application form not required.
Initial approach: Letter
Copies of proposal: 7
Deadline(s): May 1
Board meeting date(s): As required
Write: James F. Duranceau, V.P., First National Bank and Trust Co.
Trustee: First National Bank and Trust Co.
Fund Committee: Henry J. Bothwell, Harold N. Herlich, Jr., Ann K. Jordan, Peter Kaufman, Ellwood Mattson, Melvin Rossway.
Employer Identification Number: 386048505

3167
Kaufman Foundation ⌑
716 Nims St.
Muskegon 49443

Established in 1959 in MI.
Foundation type: Independent
Financial data (yr. ended 10/31/87): Assets, $1,251,894 (M); gifts received, $100,000; expenditures, $22,103, including $19,850 for 11 grants (high: $5,000; low: $50).
Purpose and activities: Support for higher education, Jewish institutions, and museums.
Trustees: R.F. Kaufman, Sylvia C. Kaufman.
Employer Identification Number: 386091556

3168
The Chaim, Fanny, Louis, Benjamin and Anne Florence Kaufman Memorial Trust ⌑ ☆
c/o National Bank of Detroit
P.O. Box 222A
Detroit 48232

Established in 1986.
Donor(s): Anne F. Kaufman Trust.
Foundation type: Independent
Financial data (yr. ended 5/31/88): Assets, $1,520,102 (M); gifts received, $119,232; expenditures, $118,398, including $87,500 for 18 grants (high: $15,000; low: $500).
Purpose and activities: Giving primarily to a Jewish welfare fund, performing arts groups, and health and social services.
Types of support: Building funds.
Limitations: Giving primarily in MI.
Trustee: National Bank of Detroit.
Employer Identification Number: 386504432

3169
The Miner S. & Mary Ann Keeler Fund ⌑
220 Monroe, N.W., Suite 440
Grand Rapids 49503

Incorporated in 1985 in MI as successor to the First Keeler Fund established in 1953, which transferred its assets to the new Keeler Fund in 1986.
Donor(s): The Keeler Fund.
Foundation type: Independent
Financial data (yr. ended 7/31/88): Assets, $1,858,767 (M); expenditures, $129,256, including $107,337 for 52 grants (high: $20,000; low: $50).

Purpose and activities: Support for education and arts and culture.
Application information:
Initial approach: Letter
Deadline(s): None
Trustees: Isaac S. Keeler II, Mary Ann Keeler, Miner S. Keeler II.
Employer Identification Number: 382625402

3170
Kellogg Company 25-Year Employees Fund, Inc. ▼
One Kellogg Sq.
P.O. Box 3599
Battle Creek 49016-3599 (616) 961-2000

Established in 1944 in MI.
Donor(s): W.K. Kellogg.†
Foundation type: Company-sponsored
Financial data (yr. ended 12/31/88): Assets, $42,904,864 (M); expenditures, $2,213,778, including $1,205,573 for 17 grants and $892,715 for 128 grants to individuals (high: $300,000; low: $1,750; average: $3,000-$45,000).
Purpose and activities: Grants for living and medical expenses of current and former company employees and their dependents only.
Types of support: Grants to individuals, special projects.
Limitations: Generally, no support for organizations; grants only to Kellogg 25-year employees and their dependents.
Publications: Program policy statement, application guidelines.
Application information: Application form required.
Initial approach: Letter
Copies of proposal: 1
Deadline(s): Submit proposal preferably in Apr.; deadline June 1
Board meeting date(s): Jan., Apr., July, and Oct.
Write: D.E. Kinnisten, Pres.
Officers: D.E. Kinnisten,* Pres.; B.A. Haefner,* V.P.; J.A. Clemence, Secy.; M. Wu, Treas.
Trustees:* C.W. Elliott, S.W. Richards, J.M. Stewart, D.W. Thomason, D.H. Walbridge.
Number of staff: 1 full-time support.
Employer Identification Number: 386039770

3171
W. K. Kellogg Foundation ▼
400 North Ave.
Battle Creek 49017-3398 (616) 968-1611

Incorporated in 1930 in MI.
Donor(s): W.K. Kellogg,† W.K. Kellogg Foundation Trust.
Foundation type: Independent
Financial data (yr. ended 08/31/89): Assets, $4,201,240,259 (M); gifts received, $142,793,625; expenditures, $125,330,807, including $102,400,067 for 653 grants (high: $4,087,131; low: $251) and $4,548,027 for 191 grants to individuals (high: $39,481; low: $33).
Purpose and activities: "To receive and administer funds for educational and charitable purposes." Aid limited to programs concerned with application of existing knowledge rather than research. Supports pilot projects which, if successful, can be continued by initiating organization and emulated by other communities or organizations with similar problems. Current funding priorities include projects designed to improve human well-being through: adult continuing education; problem-focused community-based health services; a wholesome food supply; and broadening leadership capacity of individuals. In MI only, projects are supported for economic development and opportunities for youth. The following areas, which will receive limited funding, may become major interests in the future: the development of rural America, water resources, information management systems, philanthropy and voluntarism in America, science education, and community colleges.
Types of support: Seed money, fellowships.
Limitations: Giving primarily in the U.S., Latin America, the Caribbean and southern African countries; support also for international fellowship programs in other countries. No support for religious purposes. No grants to individuals (except through fellowship programs), or for building or endowment funds, research, development campaigns, films, equipment, publications, conferences, or radio and television programs unless they are an integral part of a project already being funded; no grants for operating budgets, annual campaigns, emergency funds, deficit financing, land acquisition, or renovation projects; no loans.
Publications: Annual report (including application guidelines), informational brochure (including application guidelines), newsletter.
Application information: Proposals must conform to specified program priorities. Application form not required.
Initial approach: Letter
Copies of proposal: 1
Deadline(s): None
Board meeting date(s): Monthly
Final notification: 3 months to 2 years
Write: Nancy A. Sims, Exec. Asst.-Programming
Officers: Russell G. Mawby,* Chair. and C.E.O.; Norman A. Brown,* Pres.; Laura A. Davis, V.P.-Corp. Affairs and Corp. Secy.; William W. Fritz, V.P.-Finance and Treas.; Karen R. Hollenbeck, V.P.-Admin.
Trustees:* Shirley Dunlap Bowser, Chris T. Christ, William N. Hubbard, Jr., Dorothy A. Johnson, Wenda W. Moore, Robert L. Raun, Fred Sherriff, Howard F. Sims, Jonathan T. Walton.
Number of staff: 58 full-time professional; 93 full-time support; 1 part-time support.
Employer Identification Number: 381359264

3172
Elizabeth E. Kennedy Fund
500 City Center Bldg.
Ann Arbor 48104 (313) 761-3780

Incorporated in 1954 in MI.
Donor(s): Elizabeth E. Kennedy.
Foundation type: Independent
Financial data (yr. ended 12/31/89): Assets, $2,840,184 (M); gifts received, $19,000; expenditures, $130,000, including $118,100 for 12 grants (high: $25,000; low: $2,000; average: $1,000-$10,000).
Purpose and activities: Emphasis on higher and other education, the arts, conservation and the environment, health, family planning, medical research, and mental health; preference is to provide seed money.
Types of support: Seed money, operating budgets, renovation projects, capital campaigns, equipment.
Limitations: Giving limited to MI, with emphasis on less populated areas of the state. No grants to individuals.
Publications: Annual report (including application guidelines), 990-PF.
Application information: Application form not required.
Initial approach: Letter
Copies of proposal: 4
Deadline(s): None
Board meeting date(s): Mar. and Sept.
Write: John S. Dobson, Secy.
Officers and Trustees: Elizabeth E. Kennedy, Pres.; John S. Dobson, Secy.; Ann K. Irish, Joan K. Slocum, William W. Slocum.
Number of staff: None.
Employer Identification Number: 386063463

3173
Kogan Foundation ⌑
19901 James Cozens Hwy.
Detroit 48235

Established in 1943 in MI.
Donor(s): Jay M. Kogan.
Foundation type: Independent
Financial data (yr. ended 12/31/86): Assets, $1,756,718 (M); gifts received, $200,000; expenditures, $137,106, including $134,031 for 22 grants (high: $106,150; low: $25).
Purpose and activities: Support primarily for Jewish welfare.
Officers: Jay M. Kogan, Pres.; Douglas S. Mossman, Secy.
Employer Identification Number: 386064802

3174
The Kresge Foundation ▼
3215 West Big Beaver Rd.
P.O. Box 3151
Troy 48007-3151 (313) 643-9630
FAX: (313) 643-0588

Incorporated in 1924 in MI.
Donor(s): Sebastian S. Kresge.†
Foundation type: Independent
Financial data (yr. ended 12/31/89): Assets, $1,261,100,053 (M); expenditures, $62,196,708, including $57,533,000 for 189 grants (high: $2,250,000; low: $25,000).
Purpose and activities: Challenge grants only for building construction or renovation projects, major capital equipment or an integrated system at a cost of at least $75,000 and purchase of real estate; grants generally to tax-exempt institutions involved in higher education (awarding baccalaureate and/or graduate degrees), health and long-term care, social services, science and environment, arts and humanities, and public affairs. Full accreditation is required for higher education and hospital applicants. The foundation does not grant initial funds or total project costs; grants are for a portion of the costs remaining at the time of grant approval. Special Program:

The Kresge Foundation will accept applications for a challenge grant program to upgrade and endow scientific equipment and laboratories in colleges and universities, teaching hospitals, medical schools, and research institutions. Applications may be submitted from Apr. 1, 1988 through Mar. 31, 1990 whether or not a traditional bricks and mortar application has been submitted. For details, request a pamphlet entitled "The Kresge Foundation Science Initiative."
Types of support: Building funds, equipment, land acquisition, matching funds, renovation projects.
Limitations: No support for elementary or secondary schools. No grants to individuals, operating or special project budgets, furnishings, conferences, seminars, church building projects, endowment funds, student aid, scholarships, fellowships, research, debt retirement, completed projects, or general purposes; no loans.
Publications: Annual report, informational brochure (including application guidelines).
Application information: Application form required.
Initial approach: Letter or telephone
Copies of proposal: 1
Deadline(s): None
Board meeting date(s): Monthly
Final notification: Generally within 5 months; grants announced Feb. through June, and Sept. through Dec. for approvals, throughout the year for rejections
Write: Alfred H. Taylor, Jr., Chair.
Officers: Alfred H. Taylor, Jr.,* Chair.; John E. Marshall III, Pres. and Secy.; Thomas W. Herbert, V.P. and Treas.
Trustees:* George E. Cartmill, Jill K. Conway, Bruce A. Kresge, M.D., George D. Langdon, Jr., Edward H. Lerchen, Margaret T. Smith, Richard C. Van Dusen.
Number of staff: 8 full-time professional; 11 full-time support.
Employer Identification Number: 381359217

3175
Kysor Industrial Corporation Foundation ⌑

One Madison Ave.
Cadillac 49601 (616) 779-2200

Established in 1972 in MI.
Donor(s): Kysor Industrial Corp.
Foundation type: Company-sponsored
Financial data (yr. ended 05/31/89): Assets, $1,190,894 (M); expenditures, $209,010, including $95,000 for 159 grants (high: $10,000; low: $50).
Purpose and activities: Support for higher education, health and social welfare, including community funds, civic and community activities, including youth groups, arts and culture, and conservation.
Types of support: Building funds, capital campaigns, continuing support, general purposes, publications, research.
Limitations: Giving primarily in areas of company operations in MI, GA, FL, TX, and IL. No support for political organizations or political campaigns, religious organizations (when exclusively denominational or sectarian in purpose), or national or international organizations not directly serving the foundation's interests. No grants to individuals.
Publications: Application guidelines.
Application information:
Initial approach: Letter no more than 2 pages long
Deadline(s): None
Write: Clayton C. Jesweak, Secy.-Treas.
Officers and Trustees:* George R. Kempton,* Chair. and Pres.; Richard G. DeBoer,* V.P.; Clayton C. Jesweak,* Secy.-Treas.; Raymond A. Weigel.
Employer Identification Number: 237199469

3176
La-Z-Boy Chair Foundation

1284 North Telegraph Rd.
P.O. Box 713
Monroe 48161 (313) 241-4419

Incorporated in 1953 in MI.
Donor(s): E.M. Knabusch,† Edwin J. Shoemaker, H.F. Gertz, La-Z-Boy Chair Co.
Foundation type: Company-sponsored
Financial data (yr. ended 12/31/89): Assets, $8,200,163 (M); expenditures, $683,892, including $583,245 for 186 grants (high: $45,000; low: $100; average: $3,136).
Purpose and activities: Emphasis on community funds, especially the United Way, higher education, human services, culture, and health organizations.
Types of support: Operating budgets, building funds.
Limitations: Giving primarily in communities of company operations in Monroe, MI; Newton and Leland, MS; Redlands, CA; Florence, SC; Neosho, MO; Dayton, TN; Siloam Springs, AR; and Tremonton, UT. No grants to individuals, or for travel, continuing support, annual campaigns, seed money, emergency or endowment funds, deficit financing, equipment, land acquisition, matching gifts, research, special projects, publications, or conferences; no loans.
Publications: Annual report (including application guidelines).
Application information: Application form not required.
Initial approach: Letter
Copies of proposal: 1
Deadline(s): Feb. 15, May 15, Aug. 15, and Nov. 15
Board meeting date(s): Mar., June, Sept., and Dec.
Final notification: 60 days
Write: Donald E. Blohm, Fdn. Admin.
Officers and Directors:* Charles T. Knabusch,* Chair. and Pres.; Edwin J. Shoemaker,* Vice-Chair. and Exec. V.P., Engineering; P.H. Norton,* Sr. V.P.-Sales and Marketing; F.H. Jackson,* V.P.-Finance; G.M. Hardy,* Secy.-Treas.; W.W. Gruber, D.K. Hehl, R.E. Lipford, L.G. Stevens, J.F. Weaver.
Number of staff: 1 part-time support.
Employer Identification Number: 386087673

3177
The Greater Lansing Foundation

c/o First of America Bank-Central
P.O. Box 21007
Lansing 48909 (517) 334-5437

Established as community foundation in 1947 in MI; status changed in 1980 to independent foundation.
Foundation type: Independent
Financial data (yr. ended 12/31/88): Assets, $7,505,404 (M); gifts received, $5,581; expenditures, $667,333, including $521,233 for 108 grants (high: $76,000; low: $96).
Purpose and activities: Support for charitable, public, or educational institutions, including support for health and the handicapped. Grants mainly for capital expenditures.
Types of support: Building funds, equipment, matching funds, seed money, special projects, publications, annual campaigns, conferences and seminars, consulting services, emergency funds, renovation projects, research, scholarship funds.
Limitations: Giving limited to Ingam, Clinton, and Eaton counties, MI. No grants to individuals, or for operating budgets, endowment funds, continuing support, deficit financing, land acquisition, or technical assistance; no loans.
Publications: 990-PF.
Application information: Application form required.
Initial approach: Telephone
Copies of proposal: 6
Deadline(s): Submit application form preferably in Apr.; deadline May 15
Board meeting date(s): June
Write: Dorothy L. Sullivan, Secy.
Officers: Joan Legg, Chair.; Jane White, Vice-Chair.; Dorothy L. Sullivan, Secy.
Distribution Committee: Ralph W. Bonner, Dick Ferris, Robert K. Kinning.
Trustee Bank: First of America Bank-Central.
Number of staff: None.
Employer Identification Number: 386057513

3178
Larson Family Foundation ⌑ ☆

580 Yarboro
Bloomfield Hills 48013

Established in 1987 in MI.
Donor(s): Robert C. Larson.
Foundation type: Independent
Financial data (yr. ended 12/31/88): Assets, $3,123 (M); gifts received, $160,000; expenditures, $157,950, including $157,950 for 14 grants (high: $100,000; low: $200).
Purpose and activities: Support for human services, including urban affairs, health associations, and a hospital; support also for higher education.
Limitations: Giving primarily in MI.
Application information: Application form not required.
Initial approach: Letter
Write: Robert C. Larson, Dir.
Directors: Karen C. Larson, Robert C. Larson.
Employer Identification Number: 382711975

3179
Edward C. Levy Foundation ⌑
8800 Dix Ave.
Detroit 48209

Established in 1973 in MI.
Donor(s): Edward C. Levy Co.
Foundation type: Independent
Financial data (yr. ended 9/30/88): Assets, $2,060,942 (M); gifts received, $460,120; expenditures, $654,210, including $634,372 for 66 grants (high: $251,000; low: $50).
Purpose and activities: Giving primarily to health organizations and Jewish giving, including welfare funds.
Limitations: No grants to individuals.
Trustees: Edward C. Levy, Jr., Joshua J. Stone.
Employer Identification Number: 386091368

3180
Lincoln Health Care Foundation ⌑
70 Hall Place
Grosse Pointe Farms 48236 (313) 882-0597

Foundation type: Independent
Financial data (yr. ended 12/31/88): Assets, $1,730,874 (M); expenditures, $117,760, including $100,000 for 10 grants (high: $25,000; low: $6,000).
Purpose and activities: Emphasis on hospitals and higher education, including medical and health education, and scholarship funds.
Types of support: Scholarship funds.
Limitations: Giving primarily in MI. No grants to individuals.
Application information: Contributes only to pre-selected organizations. Applications not accepted.
Officers: M.B. Landers, M.D., Pres. and Treas.; Stephen Landers, V.P.; Maxine Barr, Secy.
Trustees: Donald Barr, M.B. Landers III, M.D., Virginia V. Landers.
Employer Identification Number: 381359220

3181
The Loutit Foundation
P.O. Box 491
Grand Haven 49417

Incorporated in 1957 in MI.
Donor(s): William R. Loutit.†
Foundation type: Independent
Financial data (yr. ended 12/31/89): Assets, $1,943,000 (M); expenditures, $163,797, including $125,000 for 21 grants (high: $20,000; low: $500).
Purpose and activities: Support for hospitals, public schools and higher education, including buildings and equipment, youth agencies, aid to the handicapped, cultural programs, and community funds.
Types of support: Capital campaigns, annual campaigns, seed money, emergency funds, endowment funds, building funds, equipment, general purposes, land acquisition, matching funds, special projects.
Limitations: Giving limited to MI, with emphasis on the western area of the state. No grants to individuals, or for research; no loans.
Publications: Biennial report.
Application information: Application form not required.
Initial approach: Letter or proposal
Copies of proposal: 6
Deadline(s): 1 week prior to board meeting
Board meeting date(s): Feb., May, Aug., and Nov.
Final notification: 2 weeks after meeting
Write: Paul A. Johnson, Pres.
Officers and Trustees:* Paul A. Johnson,* Pres.; Harvey L. Scholten,* V.P.; C. Christopher Worfel,* Secy.-Treas.; Jon W. Eshleman, Eugene O. Harbeck, Jr.
Number of staff: None.
Employer Identification Number: 386053445

3182
Lyon Foundation, Inc.
1592 Redding
Birmingham 48009-1029

Incorporated in 1951 in MI.
Donor(s): G. Albert Lyon, Sr.
Foundation type: Independent
Financial data (yr. ended 12/31/89): Assets, $1,663,920 (M); expenditures, $100,156, including $82,000 for 44 grants (high: $6,000; low: $250; average: $250-$6,000).
Purpose and activities: Giving for the arts and cultural activities; higher, secondary, elementary, and other education; hospitals, health associations, and nursing; youth agencies and child welfare; and women.
Types of support: Research, operating budgets, general purposes, scholarship funds.
Limitations: Giving primarily in MI. No grants to individuals.
Publications: 990-PF.
Application information: Application form not required.
Initial approach: Proposal
Copies of proposal: 1
Deadline(s): None
Board meeting date(s): Various
Write: A. Randolph Judd, Pres. and Treas.
Officers: A. Randolph Judd, Pres. and Treas.; Alberta L. Judd, V.P.; T. Terrill Judd, Secy.
Agent: National Bank of Detroit.
Number of staff: 1 full-time support.
Employer Identification Number: 386121075

3183
Benard L. Maas Foundation ⌑
28580 Orchard Lake Rd.
Farmington Hills 48018

Established in 1942 in MI.
Donor(s): Benard L. Maas.†
Foundation type: Independent
Financial data (yr. ended 12/31/88): Assets, $6,175,042 (M); expenditures, $509,501, including $393,855 for 136 grants (high: $50,000; low: $35).
Purpose and activities: Giving primarily for Jewish organizations in the U.S. and Israel; grants also for higher education.
Limitations: Giving primarily in MI. No grants to individuals.
Application information: Contributes only to pre-selected organizations. Applications not accepted.
Write: Hiram A. Dorfman, Pres.
Officers: Hiram A. Dorfman, Pres.; David Engelbert, Secy.-Treas.
Trustees: Lucille F. Dorfman, Sol Drachler, Lynn Engelbert, Marvin B. Sheplow.
Employer Identification Number: 386096405

3184
J. Harvey Mallery Trust ⌑
(also known as Mallery Charitable Trust)
c/o Michigan National Bank
519 South Saginaw St.
Flint 48502 (313) 762-5563

Trust established in 1970 in MI.
Donor(s): Harvey J. Mallery.
Foundation type: Independent
Financial data (yr. ended 06/30/89): Assets, $362,722 (M); expenditures, $290,960, including $279,974 for 14 grants (high: $47,000; low: $3,000).
Purpose and activities: Support for education, cultural programs, and recreation, including a youth agency.
Limitations: Giving limited to Genesee County, MI. No grants to individuals, or for endowment funds, scholarships, or fellowships; no loans.
Application information:
Initial approach: Proposal, letter, or telephone
Copies of proposal: 2
Board meeting date(s): Quarterly
Write: Susan K. Piper, Admin.
Officer: Susan K. Piper, Admin.
Trustees: Mary Davis, J. Joseph England, Michigan National Bank.
Employer Identification Number: 386039907

3185
Malpass Foundation
P.O. Box 439
East Jordan 49727-0439

Established in 1953 in MI.
Foundation type: Independent
Financial data (yr. ended 10/31/89): Assets, $74,406 (M); gifts received, $297,000; expenditures, $399,121, including $398,104 for 2 grants (high: $391,259; low: $6,845) and $1,000 for 1 grant to an individual.
Purpose and activities: Support primarily for the construction of a public library and pool.
Types of support: Building funds.
Limitations: Giving primarily in Charlesvoix County, MI. No grants to individuals (except for scholarships).
Application information:
Initial approach: Letter
Deadline(s): None
Write: William J. Lorne
Trustees: Frederick F. Malpass, Tad M. Malpass, Tracy K. Malpass, William E. Malpass.
Employer Identification Number: 386048813

3186
Alex and Marie Manoogian Foundation ▼ ⌑
21001 Van Born Rd.
Taylor 48180 (313) 274-7400

Incorporated in 1942 in MI.
Donor(s): Alex Manoogian, Marie Manoogian.
Foundation type: Independent
Financial data (yr. ended 12/31/88): Assets, $45,010,251 (M); expenditures, $1,696,266, including $1,655,865 for 89 grants (high: $729,425; low: $50; average: $500-$25,000).
Purpose and activities: Support primarily for Armenian welfare funds and religious

institutions, and higher and secondary education; support also for cultural programs.
Types of support: Building funds, equipment, operating budgets, seed money, emergency funds, matching funds, endowment funds, scholarship funds, fellowships, research, continuing support.
Limitations: No grants for annual campaigns, deficit financing, land acquisition, publications, or conferences or seminars.
Application information: Contributes only to pre-selected organizations. Applications not accepted.
Board meeting date(s): Twice a year
Write: Alex Manoogian, Pres.
Officers and Directors:* Alex Manoogian,* Pres.; Richard A. Manoogian,* V.P. and Treas.; Eugene H. Gargaro, Jr.,* Secy.; Louise M. Simone.
Number of staff: None.
Employer Identification Number: 386089952

3187
Maranatha Foundation, Inc. ¤
31625 Franklin Rd.
Franklin 48025

Established about 1965 in MI.
Donor(s): Members of the Pew family.
Foundation type: Independent
Financial data (yr. ended 12/31/88): Assets, $1,362,439 (M); expenditures, $77,187, including $75,557 for 53 grants (high: $24,200; low: $50; average: $500-$2,000).
Purpose and activities: Emphasis on Protestant giving, including missionary programs.
Application information: Contributes only to pre-selected organizations. Applications not accepted.
Officers: William H. Pew, Pres. and Treas.; Margaret E. Pew, V.P. and Secy.
Directors: Robert L. Pew, Ronald K. Pew, William J. Pew.
Employer Identification Number: 386108739

3188
Mardigian Foundation ¤
13920 East Ten Mile Rd.
Warren 48089 (313) 778-4120

Incorporated in 1955 in MI.
Donor(s): Edward S. Mardigian, Helen Mardigian.
Foundation type: Independent
Financial data (yr. ended 12/31/88): Assets, $4,682,442 (M); gifts received, $100,000; expenditures, $419,059, including $394,451 for 100 grants (high: $100,000; low: $10).
Purpose and activities: Grants for Armenian church and cultural support, religious associations, and welfare funds.
Application information: Telephone solicitations not accepted.
Initial approach: Letter
Deadline(s): None
Write: Edward S. Mardigian, Sr., Pres.
Officers and Directors: Edward S. Mardigian, Sr., Pres.; Helen Mardigian, Marilyn Varbedian.
Employer Identification Number: 386048886

3189
Masco Corporation Charitable Trust ¤
(Formerly Masco Screw Products Company Charitable Trust)
c/o Comerica Bank-Detroit, Trust Tax Dept.
Detroit 48275-1022
Application address: 21001 Van Born Rd., Taylor, MI 48180; Tel.: (313) 274-7400

Trust established in 1952 in MI.
Donor(s): Masco Corp.
Foundation type: Company-sponsored
Financial data (yr. ended 12/31/88): Assets, $1,372,629 (M); gifts received, $1,800,000; expenditures, $967,327, including $964,200 for 34 grants (high: $500,000; low: $5,000).
Purpose and activities: Emphasis on the arts, higher education, museums, social services, and church support.
Limitations: Giving primarily in MI. No grants to individuals, or for endowments; no loans.
Application information:
Initial approach: Letter
Deadline(s): None
Write: Karyn L. Wells
Trustee: Comerica Bank-Detroit.
Employer Identification Number: 386043605

3190
McGregor Fund ▼
333 West Fort Bldg., Suite 2090
Detroit 48226 (313) 963-3495

Incorporated in 1925 in MI.
Donor(s): Tracy W. McGregor,† Mrs. Tracy W. McGregor.†
Foundation type: Independent
Financial data (yr. ended 6/30/88): Assets, $69,518,966 (M); expenditures, $4,187,367, including $3,262,889 for 95 grants (high: $102,800; low: $200; average: $10,000-$50,000).
Purpose and activities: A general purpose foundation supporting education, welfare, including health and youth agencies, humanities, and sciences, with emphasis on higher education; grants also to private colleges and universities in MI, OH, and IN.
Types of support: Operating budgets, annual campaigns, building funds, equipment, special projects, capital campaigns, continuing support, general purposes, renovation projects.
Limitations: Giving primarily in Detroit, MI; grants to private colleges and universities limited to IN, MI, and OH. No grants to individuals, or for deficit financing, land acquisition, endowment funds, scholarships, fellowships, research, travel, workshops, publications, or conferences; no loans.
Publications: Annual report (including application guidelines).
Application information: Application form not required.
Initial approach: Proposal
Copies of proposal: 1
Deadline(s): None
Board meeting date(s): Feb., Apr., June, Sept., and Nov.
Final notification: 60 days
Write: W. Calvin Patterson III, Exec. Dir.
Officers: Elliot H. Phillips,* Pres.; Lem W. Bowen,* V.P.; Peter P. Thurber, Secy.; Robert M. Surdam,* Treas.; W. Calvin Patterson III, Exec. Dir.
Trustees:* Carlton M. Higbie, Jr., Eugene Miller, W. Warren Sheldon, Bruce W. Steinhauer, M.D., Peter W. Stroh.
Number of staff: 1 part-time professional; 2 full-time support.
Employer Identification Number: 380808800

3191
B. D. and Jane E. McIntyre Foundation ¤
c/o National Bank of Detroit, Trust Div.
611 Woodward
Detroit 48232 (313) 225-3124

Trust established in 1961 in MI.
Donor(s): Members of the McIntyre family.
Foundation type: Independent
Financial data (yr. ended 11/30/88): Assets, $2,476,930 (M); expenditures, $151,349, including $128,350 for 7 grants (high: $60,000; low: $650; average: $5,000-$10,000).
Purpose and activities: Emphasis on education, Episcopal church support, and a community fund.
Types of support: Continuing support, scholarship funds.
Limitations: Giving primarily in Monroe, MI. No grants to individuals.
Application information: Application form not required.
Initial approach: Letter
Copies of proposal: 1
Deadline(s): Submit proposal preferably in Aug. or Nov.
Board meeting date(s): As required
Final notification: Oct. 31
Write: Therese M. Thorn, 2nd V.P., National Bank of Detroit
Trustees: Rocque E. Lipford, Charles S. McIntyre III.
Managing Trustee: National Bank of Detroit.
Employer Identification Number: 386046718

3192
C. S. and Marion F. McIntyre Foundation ¤
c/o National Bank of Detroit
611 Woodward
Detroit 48232 (313) 225-3124

Trust established in 1961 in MI.
Donor(s): Members of the McIntyre family.
Foundation type: Independent
Financial data (yr. ended 11/30/88): Assets, $1,698,403 (M); expenditures, $46,906, including $30,650 for 2 grants (high: $30,000; low: $650).
Purpose and activities: Support for an historical society and a college.
Types of support: General purposes.
Limitations: Giving primarily in MI, with emphasis on the Monroe, MI, area. No grants to individuals.
Application information:
Initial approach: Letter
Copies of proposal: 1
Deadline(s): Submit proposal between Aug. and Nov.
Board meeting date(s): As required
Final notification: Oct. 31

Write: Therese M. Thorn, 2nd V.P., National Bank of Detroit
Trustees: Rocque E. Lipford, David L. McIntyre.
Managing Trustee: National Bank of Detroit.
Employer Identification Number: 386046733

3193
The Mendel Foundation ⌑
777 Riverview Dr.
Benton Harbor 49022
Application address: P.O. Box 688, Benton Harbor, MI 49022

Established in 1964 in MI.
Donor(s): Herbert D. Mendel.
Foundation type: Independent
Financial data (yr. ended 04/30/89): Assets, $3,651,087 (M); gifts received, $1,000,500; expenditures, $221,606, including $218,300 for 18 grants (high: $100,000; low: $50).
Purpose and activities: Emphasis on Jewish welfare funds, religious associations, and temple support; grants also for the arts and education.
Limitations: Giving primarily in MI.
Application information: Application form not required.
Deadline(s): None
Write: Eleanor Simon
Officers: Herbert D. Mendel, Pres.; Edwin J. Mendel, V.P.
Employer Identification Number: 386099787

3194
Orville D. & Ruth A. Merillat Foundation ▼ ⌑
P.O. Box 1946
Adrian 49221

Established in 1983 in MI.
Donor(s): Orville D. Merillat, Ruth A. Merillat.
Foundation type: Independent
Financial data (yr. ended 2/28/88): Assets, $64,695,846 (M); expenditures, $22,679,807, including $22,377,750 for 52 grants (high: $10,020,000; low: $200; average: $1,000-$100,000).
Purpose and activities: Support primarily for churches and religious welfare.
Types of support: General purposes, building funds, equipment, renovation projects.
Limitations: Giving primarily in MI.
Application information: Contributes only to pre-selected organizations. Applications not accepted.
Officers and Directors:* Orville D. Merillat,* Pres.; Richard D. Merillat,* V.P.; Ruth A. Merillat,* Secy.; John D. Thurman, Treas.
Employer Identification Number: 382476813

3195
Mette Foundation, Inc. ☆
c/o John Snyder, Comerica Bank-Detroit
Comerica Bldg.
Detroit 48275-1032

Donor(s): Norman H. Mette.†
Foundation type: Independent
Financial data (yr. ended 11/30/89): Assets, $2,000,000 (M); qualifying distributions, $60,000, including $60,000 for grants.
Purpose and activities: Support primarily for medical education.
Types of support: Scholarship funds.
Limitations: Giving primarily in MI.
Application information: Contributes only to pre-selected organizations. Applications not accepted.
Officers: John J. Raymond, Pres.; Marilyn Knickerbocker, V.P.; John J. Snyder, Secy.-Treas.
Employer Identification Number: 510177958

3196
MichCon Foundation ⌑
500 Griswold St.
Detroit 48226 (313) 256-5077

Established in 1984 in MI.
Donor(s): MichCon.
Foundation type: Company-sponsored
Financial data (yr. ended 12/31/88): Assets, $11,702,794 (M); gifts received, $1,000,000; expenditures, $785,667, including $747,466 for 214 grants (high: $120,550; low: $25).
Purpose and activities: To enhance the economic vitality and quality of life through support in five areas: 1) economic development, including business development, job training, and neighborhood revitalization; 2) education, including employee matching gifts; 3) United Foundations/United Ways; 4) community services with emphasis on youth and community leadership; and 5) culture and the arts.
Types of support: Employee matching gifts, scholarship funds.
Limitations: Giving primarily in areas of company operations in MI.
Publications: Corporate giving report.
Application information:
Initial approach: Proposal
Deadline(s): Nov. 30
Write: Mary E. Bradish, Secy.
Officers and Directors:* Richard W. Zemmin,* Pres.; Leon H. Atchison,* V.P.; Mary E. Bradish,* Secy.; Peter L. Verardi, Treas.
Employer Identification Number: 382570358

3197
Roy G. Michell Charitable Foundation and Trust ⌑
c/o Janz & Knight
1100 North Woodward
Birmingham 48011 (313) 646-9666

Established in 1963 in MI.
Donor(s): Roy G. Michell.†
Foundation type: Independent
Financial data (yr. ended 4/30/87): Assets, $1,896,514 (M); expenditures, $221,756, including $200,000 for 56 grants (high: $30,000; low: $500).
Purpose and activities: Emphasis on Protestant giving, higher education, and social services, including programs for the handicapped and youth; some support also for hospitals.
Trustees: Frederick C. Janz, Roy G. Michell, Jr., William Michell.
Employer Identification Number: 386071109

3198
Midland Foundation
812 West Main St.
P.O. Box 289
Midland 48640 (517) 839-9661

Established in 1973 in MI.
Foundation type: Community
Financial data (yr. ended 12/31/89): Assets, $17,522,110 (L); gifts received, $5,785,963; expenditures, $2,351,240, including $597,632 for grants (high: $937,482; low: $134; average: $2,000-$4,000) and $33,100 for loans to individuals.
Purpose and activities: "To support the charitable, cultural, educational, and scientific needs of the Midland County, MI, area."
Types of support: Seed money, equipment, matching funds, scholarship funds, student loans, building funds, conferences and seminars, consulting services, land acquisition, renovation projects, technical assistance.
Limitations: Giving limited to Midland County, MI. No grants to individuals, or for operating budgets, continuing support, annual campaigns, deficit financing, or endowment funds.
Publications: Annual report, application guidelines.
Application information: Application form required.
Initial approach: Telephone
Copies of proposal: 1
Deadline(s): None
Board meeting date(s): Feb., Apr., June, Nov., and as required
Final notification: 2 months
Write: M. Gene Arnold, Exec. Dir.
Officers: Eileen C. Starks,* Pres.; Patricia Carbone,* V.P.; William Gibson,* V.P.; Ben Hines,* V.P.; Frank Gerace,* Secy.; Esther S. Gerstacker, Treas.; M. Gene Arnold, Exec. Dir.
Trustees:* Richard Caldwell, Victor Finch, Anita Jenkins, Virginia Morrison, Jean Popoff, Richard Reynolds, Norman C. Rumple, Clark Swayze.
Number of staff: 1 full-time professional; 2 part-time support.
Employer Identification Number: 382023395

3199
Charles & Florence Milan Foundation ⌑ ☆
16500 North Park Dr., Apt. 1708
Southfield 48075

Established in 1953.
Foundation type: Independent
Financial data (yr. ended 10/31/88): Assets, $290,291 (M); expenditures, $106,335, including $105,000 for 1 grant.
Purpose and activities: Support primarily for Jewish organizations and health services, including child welfare.
Officers: Charles Milan, Pres. and Treas.; Florence Milan, V.P.; Robert Rubenstein, Secy.
Employer Identification Number: 386059346

3200
Clyde & Betty Miller Charitable Foundation, Inc. ⌑ ☆
P.O. Box 348
Traverse City 49684
Application address: 2425 118th Ave., Allegan, MI, 49010; Tel.: (616) 673-6336

Established in 1985 in MI.
Donor(s): Clyde E. Miller, Betty E. Miller.
Foundation type: Independent
Financial data (yr. ended 9/30/88): Assets, $157,884 (M); gifts received, $90,500; expenditures, $306,543, including $305,200 for 15 grants (high: $275,000; low: $500).
Purpose and activities: Support primarily for higher education and Baptist giving, including a church and a college; awards scholarships to individuals for higher education.
Types of support: Grants to individuals, student aid, general purposes.
Limitations: Giving primarily in MI.
Application information:
Initial approach: Individuals applying for scholarships: Letter, indicating field of interest, colleges of choice, religious background, scholastic aptitude, and athletic ability
Deadline(s): None
Write: Rev. Ronald Beyer
Officers: C.E. Miller, Pres.; Betty E. Miller, V.P.; Kelly E. Miller, Secy.-Treas.; David A. Miller, Mgr.
Employer Identification Number: 382620981

3201
The Miller Foundation
(Formerly Albert L. and Louise B. Miller Foundation, Inc)
310 WahWahTaySee Way
Battle Creek 49015 (616) 964-2052

Incorporated in 1963 in MI.
Donor(s): Louise B. Miller,† Robert B. Miller.
Foundation type: Independent
Financial data (yr. ended 02/28/90): Assets, $11,137,636 (M); gifts received, $1,056,840; expenditures, $704,831, including $551,284 for 43 grants (high: $200,000; low: $300; average: $500-$10,000).
Purpose and activities: Support for higher education, public schools, and local municipal improvements.
Types of support: Annual campaigns, seed money, emergency funds, building funds, equipment, land acquisition, endowment funds, matching funds, program-related investments, scholarship funds, exchange programs, loans, publications.
Limitations: Giving primarily in the Battle Creek, MI, area. No grants to individuals, or for operating budgets.
Publications: Annual report.
Application information: Application form required.
Initial approach: Letter
Copies of proposal: 10
Deadline(s): None
Board meeting date(s): Bimonthly
Final notification: 2 months
Write: Arthur W. Angood, Exec. V.P. and C.O.O.
Officers and Trustees:* Robert B. Miller,* Chair.; W. James McQuiston,* Pres.; Arthur W. Angood,* Exec. V.P. and C.O.O.; Rebecca A. Engelhardt,* Secy.; Arnold Van Zanten,* Treas.; Barbara L. Comai, Gary E. Costley, Dale G. Griffin, Olive T. Miller, Robert B. Miller, Jr., Fred M. Woodruff, Jr.
Number of staff: 2 part-time professional; 1 part-time support.
Employer Identification Number: 386064925

3202
Howard Miller Foundation ⌑
860 East Main St.
Zeeland 49464

Established in 1976 in MI.
Donor(s): Howard Miller Clock Co.
Foundation type: Independent
Financial data (yr. ended 12/31/88): Assets, $3,324,833 (M); gifts received, $360,200; expenditures, $85,840, including $60,000 for 2 grants (high: $30,000; low: $434) and $2,934 for 6 grants to individuals.
Purpose and activities: Giving primarily for Protestant education and missionary work; also awards college scholarships to residents of Holland, MI.
Types of support: Student aid.
Application information: Contributes only to pre-selected organizations. Applications not accepted.
Officer: Howard C. Miller, Pres.
Directors: Eugene H. Diebold, Jack H. Miller, Philip D. Miller.
Employer Identification Number: 382137226

3203
Frances Goll Mills Fund ⌑
101 North Washington Ave.
Saginaw 48607 (517) 776-7582

Established in 1982 in MI.
Donor(s): Frances Goll Mills.†
Foundation type: Independent
Financial data (yr. ended 9/30/88): Assets, $3,084,295 (M); expenditures, $207,258, including $155,455 for 14 grants (high: $35,000; low: $800).
Purpose and activities: Giving primarily for hospitals, social services, civic organizations, historic preservation, and a church.
Types of support: Operating budgets, continuing support, seed money, emergency funds, building funds, equipment, land acquisition, matching funds, consulting services.
Limitations: Giving primarily in Saginaw County, MI. No grants to individuals, or for annual campaigns, deficit financing, endowments, special programs, scholarships, fellowships, professorships, or internships; no loans.
Publications: Application guidelines.
Application information:
Initial approach: Letter or proposal
Copies of proposal: 1
Deadline(s): None
Board meeting date(s): Bimonthly, beginning in Feb.
Final notification: 1 week after meeting
Write: Denice McGlaughlin
Trustee: Second National Bank of Saginaw.
Number of staff: None.
Employer Identification Number: 382434002

3204
Molloy Foundation, Inc. ⌑
P.O. Box 200
St. Clair Shores 48080

Established in 1962 in MI.
Donor(s): Brian J. Molloy.†
Foundation type: Independent
Financial data (yr. ended 1/31/89): Assets, $1,189,750 (M); expenditures, $155,738, including $125,368 for 50 grants (high: $25,000; low: $100).
Purpose and activities: Support for education, religion, hospitals, and social services.
Limitations: Giving primarily in MI.
Application information:
Initial approach: Letter
Deadline(s): None
Officers: Therese M. Molloy, Pres.; Brian J. Molloy, Jr., V.P.; Thomas C. Molloy, Secy.; Alex G. Bitterman, Treas.
Trustees: Constance M. Kinnear, Mary Alice Molloy, Stephen P. Molloy.
Employer Identification Number: 386061859

3205
David and Miriam Mondry & Ira and Gail Mondry Family Foundation
(Formerly David & Miriam Mondrey Family Foundation)
909 North Sheldon Rd.
Plymouth 48170

Established in 1978 in MI.
Donor(s): David Mondry.
Foundation type: Independent
Financial data (yr. ended 11/30/89): Assets, $885,998 (M); gifts received, $250,000; expenditures, $241,535, including $241,525 for 60 grants (high: $60,000; low: $100).
Purpose and activities: Support primarily for Jewish welfare.
Application information: Contributes only to pre-selected organizations. Applications not accepted.
Officers: David Mondry, Pres.; Miriam Mondry, V.P.; Ira Mondry, Secy.; Gail Mondry, Treas.
Employer Identification Number: 382241543

3206
Monroe-Brown Foundation
229 East Michigan Ave.
Kalamazoo 49007 (616) 381-0055
Mailing address: P.O. Box 987, Kalamazoo, MI 49005

Incorporated in 1983 in MI.
Donor(s): Albertine M. Brown,† Robert J. Brown,† Robert M. Brown, Gail B. Kasdorf, Jane B. Todd.
Foundation type: Independent
Financial data (yr. ended 12/31/88): Assets, $4,693,989 (M); gifts received, $1,487,206; expenditures, $475,460, including $412,825 for 20 grants (high: $160,000; low: $100).
Purpose and activities: Support primarily for an educational foundation and for higher education.
Types of support: Annual campaigns, building funds, capital campaigns, special projects.
Limitations: Giving primarily in MI, with emphasis on Kalamazoo County. No grants to individuals.
Application information: Application form not required.
Initial approach: Letter
Copies of proposal: 5
Deadline(s): Before quarterly meetings
Board meeting date(s): Second Wednesday of Mar., June, Sept., and Dec.
Write: Robert M. Brown, Pres.

Officers: Robert M. Brown,* Pres.; Gail B. Kasdorf,* V.P.; Margaret McLeod, Secy.; Jane B. Todd,* Treas.
Trustees:* John C. Wattles.
Number of staff: 1 full-time support.
Employer Identification Number: 382513263

3207
The C. F. Moore Foundation ⌑
200 South Riverside Ave.
St. Clair 48079 (313) 329-2244

Established in 1954 in MI.
Donor(s): Charles F. Moore.
Foundation type: Independent
Financial data (yr. ended 12/31/87): Assets, $1,789,547 (M); expenditures, $97,873, including $83,050 for 41 grants (high: $10,000; low: $100).
Purpose and activities: Emphasis on health associations, Protestant giving, education, youth, and community funds.
Limitations: Giving primarily in St. Clair County, MI.
Application information: Contributes only to pre-selected organizations. Applications not accepted.
Trustees: Barbara W. Moore, Charles F. Moore, Franklin H. Moore, Jr., Jonathan Moore.
Employer Identification Number: 386055559

3208
Morley Brothers Foundation ⌑
One Tuscola St.
P.O. Box 2485
Saginaw 48605-2485 (517) 792-1427

Incorporated in 1948 in MI.
Donor(s): Ralph Chase Morley, Sr.,† Mrs. Ralph Chase Morley, Sr.†
Foundation type: Independent
Financial data (yr. ended 12/31/88): Assets, $3,677,515 (M); expenditures, $195,023, including $163,601 for 38 grants (high: $25,000; low: $200; average: $200-$12,000).
Purpose and activities: Emphasis on higher and secondary education, community funds, the arts, youth agencies, and hospitals.
Types of support: Operating budgets, continuing support, annual campaigns, seed money, emergency funds, building funds, equipment, scholarship funds, exchange programs, special projects, research, matching funds, employee matching gifts.
Limitations: Giving primarily in the greater Saginaw, MI, area. No grants to individuals, or for endowment funds, deficit financing, land acquisition, renovation projects, publications, or conferences; no loans.
Application information: Application form not required.
Initial approach: Letter
Copies of proposal: 1
Deadline(s): None
Board meeting date(s): Apr., July, Oct., and Dec.
Final notification: 3 months
Write: Edward B. Morley, Jr., Pres.
Officers: Edward B. Morley, Jr.,* Pres.; Lucy M. Thomson,* V.P.; Lois K. Guttowsky, Secy.; Peter B. Morley,* Treas.
Trustees:* Burrows Morley, Burrows Morley, Jr., John D. Morely, Robert S. Morley.
Number of staff: 1 part-time professional.
Employer Identification Number: 386055569

3209
Charles Stewart Mott Foundation ▼
1200 Mott Foundation Bldg.
Flint 48502-1851 (313) 238-5651

Incorporated in 1926 in MI.
Donor(s): Charles Stewart Mott,† and family.
Foundation type: Independent
Financial data (yr. ended 12/31/89): Assets, $961,114,454 (M); expenditures, $47,387,469, including $43,795,989 for 476 grants (high: $9,300,000; low: $2,500; average: $10,000-$100,000).
Purpose and activities: Supports community improvement through grants for expressing individuality; expanding personal horizons; citizenship; volunteer action; counteracting root causes of alienation; community identity and stability; community renewal; environmental management; fostering institutional openness; better delivery of services; and training in and improving practices of leadership. Pioneer in community education concept.
Types of support: Conferences and seminars, continuing support, loans, matching funds, operating budgets, program-related investments, publications, seed money, special projects, technical assistance, general purposes.
Limitations: No grants to individuals, or generally for building or endowment funds, research, scholarships, or fellowships.
Publications: Annual report (including application guidelines), newsletter, financial statement, informational brochure (including application guidelines), program policy statement, occasional report.
Application information: Application form not required.
Initial approach: Letter
Copies of proposal: 1
Deadline(s): None
Board meeting date(s): Mar., June, Sept., and Dec.
Final notification: 60 to 90 days
Write: Judy Samelson, Dir. of Communications
Officers: William S. White,* Chair., Pres. and C.E.O.; William H. Piper,* Vice-Chair.; Richard K. Rappleye, V.P. and Secy.-Treas.; Willard J. Hertz, V.P. for Prog. Planning and Dissemination; Robert E. Swaney, Jr., V.P. for Investments.
Trustees:* Marjorie Powell Allen, Alonzo A. Crim, Charles B. Cumings, Rushworth M. Kidder, C.S. Harding Mott II, Maryanne Mott, Willa B. Player, John W. Porter, Harold P. Rodes, George L. Whyel.
Number of staff: 28 full-time professional; 3 part-time professional; 16 full-time support.
Employer Identification Number: 381211227

3210
Ruth Mott Fund ▼
1726 Genesee Towers
Flint 48502 (313) 232-3180

Incorporated in 1979 in MI.
Donor(s): Ruth R. Mott.
Foundation type: Independent
Financial data (yr. ended 11/30/89): Assets, $1,949,396 (M); gifts received, $2,425,000; expenditures, $2,039,130, including $1,774,880 for 110 grants (high: $50,000; low: $1,000; average: $1,000-$50,000).
Purpose and activities: Support for programs that focus on topics of emerging significance, exemplify originality, and offer the potential for application on a broader scale within four areas: 1) arts and special interests, including arts as a means to a greater educational, humanistic, or social goal, and for arts and beautification in Flint and Genesee County, MI; 2) environment programs focusing on global deforestation, and alternative (sustainable) agriculture; 3) health promotion, with emphasis on preventive programs for low-income sectors of the population that emphasize one or more of the following: improved nutrition, stress control, exercise and fitness, smoking cessation, and reduced alcohol and drug use; the fund realizes that access to health care is a significant problem for low-income Americans and will, from time to time, consider applications which address equity and access concerns about health care for low-income people (proposals encouraged from new or small organizations with budgets of less than $150,000 per year); and 4) national and international security programs which foster public review and discussion of factors that contribute to the security of a nation. In 1990 the fund is especially interested in receiving applications that address the following: a) deepening of examination by the public of national and international security issues in terms of their implications for global security; b) strengthening the process of accountability to the public of national security agencies; c) monitoring the Department of Energy's and the Department of Defense's impacts on the environment and human health; and d) examining the level and quality of expenditures for national security.
Types of support: Operating budgets, continuing support, seed money, matching funds, special projects, general purposes, publications, conferences and seminars.
Limitations: No grants to individuals, or for capital or endowment funds, annual campaigns, emergency funds, major equipment, renovations, films and videos of low-priority, deficit financing, scholarships, or fellowships; no loans.
Publications: Application guidelines, multi-year report (including application guidelines), grants list.
Application information: Application form not required.
Initial approach: Proposal (up to 12 pages)
Copies of proposal: 2
Deadline(s): Nov. 7, Mar. 15, and July 15
Board meeting date(s): Feb., June, and Oct.
Final notification: 3 to 4 weeks after board meeting
Write: Deborah E. Tuck, Exec. Dir.
Officers: George Woodwell,* Chair.; Leslie Dunbar,* Vice-Chair.; Maryanne Mott,* Pres.; Stewart Dansby,* Secy.; Joseph R. Robinson,* Treas.; Deborah E. Tuck, Exec. Dir.
Trustees:* Shelton Davis, Susan Kleinpell, Donna Metcalf, Ruth R. Mott, Melissa Patterson, Herman E. Warsh.

Number of staff: 2 full-time professional; 1 full-time support; 1 part-time support.
Employer Identification Number: 382284264

3211
Muskegon County Community Foundation, Inc.

Frauenthal Ctr., Suite 304
425 West Western Ave.
Muskegon 49440 (616) 722-4538

Incorporated in 1961 in MI.
Donor(s): Harold Frauenthal,† Charles Goodnow.†
Foundation type: Community
Financial data (yr. ended 12/31/89): Assets, $18,444,738 (M); gifts received, $3,007,727; expenditures, $1,087,025, including $518,020 for 53 grants (high: $100,000; low: $100) and $140,171 for 254 grants to individuals (high: $2,500; low: $200; average: $200-$1,000).
Purpose and activities: To assist worthwhile projects, with emphasis on health and human services, the arts and culture, education, and community development and urban affairs. Priority support for pilot projects, seed money, and challenge gifts.
Types of support: Seed money, special projects, matching funds, equipment, scholarship funds, loans, research, publications, conferences and seminars, endowment funds, student aid, consulting services, continuing support, emergency funds, exchange programs, internships, operating budgets, professorships, renovation projects.
Limitations: Giving limited to Muskegon County, MI. No grants to individuals (except for scholarships), or for deficit financing.
Publications: Annual report (including application guidelines), program policy statement, newsletter, financial statement, grants list, informational brochure (including application guidelines), application guidelines.
Application information: Application form required.
Initial approach: Letter or telephone
Copies of proposal: 16
Deadline(s): None
Board meeting date(s): Feb., Apr., June, Aug., Oct., and Dec.
Final notification: 2 to 3 weeks
Write: Patricia B. Johnson, Exec. Dir.
Officers: Robert Jewell,* Pres.; John L. Hilt,* V.P.; Patricia B. Johnson, Secy.-Treas. and Exec. Dir.
Trustees:* Robert Hilleary, Chair.; Josephine F. Anacker, Marilyn V. Andersen, Barbara Andrie, Douglas Bard, George W. Bartlett, Janie Brooks, Robert W. Christie, Bettye Clark-Cannon, Fred C. Culver, Jr., Eugene Fisher, Robert Garrison, John Halmond, Richard G. Johnson, Robert Kersman, John H. Martin, Sherman R. Poppen, Daniel Thill, Robert D. Tuttle.
Trustee Banks: Comerica Bank, First of America Bank, FMB Lumberman's Bank, Old Kent Bank of Grand Haven.
Number of staff: 3 full-time professional; 2 full-time support.
Employer Identification Number: 386114135

3212
National Bank of Detroit Charitable Trust ▼ ⌑

c/o National Bank of Detroit
611 Woodward Ave.
Detroit 48232 (313) 225-3124

Trust established in 1963 in MI.
Donor(s): National Bank of Detroit.
Foundation type: Company-sponsored
Financial data (yr. ended 12/31/88): Assets, $3,535,315 (M); gifts received, $3,695,024; expenditures, $1,880,749, including $1,722,073 for 130 grants (high: $568,000; low: $500; average: $500-$15,000) and $128,716 for employee matching gifts.
Purpose and activities: Emphasis on higher education (including employee matching gifts), cultural programs, and community development; support also for community funds and social services.
Types of support: Employee matching gifts, general purposes.
Limitations: Giving primarily in MI, with emphasis on the Detroit area.
Application information: Application form not required.
Initial approach: Proposal
Deadline(s): None
Board meeting date(s): Every 2 weeks, except July and Aug.
Write: Therese Thorn, Mgr.
Officers: Gerald E. Warren, Chair.; Dennis Kembel, Secy.; Therese Thorn, Mgr.
Board of Control: Bernard Butcher, Charles T. Fischer III, Verne Istock, Thomas Jeffs II, Richard A. Manoogian, James H. McNeal, Irving Rose.
Trustee: National Bank of Detroit.
Number of staff: 2 full-time professional; 1 part-time professional.
Employer Identification Number: 386059088

3213
Northeast Michigan Community Foundation ☆

c/o Alpena Shopping Arcade
150-B North State Ave.
Alpena 49707 (517) 354-2221
Additional address: P.O. Box 282, Alpena, MI 49707

Incorporated in 1974 in MI.
Foundation type: Community
Financial data (yr. ended 12/31/89): Assets, $1,448,611 (M); gifts received, $428,112; expenditures, $154,765, including $137,939 for 35 grants (high: $44,060; low: $200).
Purpose and activities: Support primarily for civic affairs, health, youth, social services, the arts, education, and libraries.
Types of support: Conferences and seminars, continuing support, equipment, land acquisition, matching funds, program-related investments, publications, renovation projects, scholarship funds, seed money.
Limitations: Giving limited to the four-county Alpena, Alcona, Presque Isle, and Montmorency, MI, area and neighboring counties. No support for operating needs or budget deficits. No grants to individuals.
Publications: Annual report, application guidelines, informational brochure.
Application information: Application form required.
Initial approach: Letter or telephone
Copies of proposal: 1
Deadline(s): Feb. 1, May 1, Aug. 1, and Nov. 1
Board meeting date(s): Quarterly
Final notification: Within days of Board meeting
Write: Elizabeth L. Connolly, Exec. Dir.
Officers and Trustees:* Richard Boyce,* Pres.; George Lafleche,* V.P.; Carolynne Wegmeyer,* Secy.; Robert Granum,* Treas.; Kelley Fletcher, Marilyn Frank, Edward Goossens, Gerald Jasinski, Betty Krueger, James Lappan, Jack Leopard, M.D., Lucas Pfeiffenberger, Karl Vogelheim.
Number of staff: 1 part-time professional.
Employer Identification Number: 237384822

3214
Old Kent Charitable Trust ⌑ ☆

300 Old Kent Bldg.
Grand Rapids 49503

Foundation type: Company-sponsored
Financial data (yr. ended 6/30/89): Assets, $1,048,457 (M); expenditures, $148,801, including $142,250 for 26 grants (high: $63,000; low: $500).
Purpose and activities: Support for education, the arts, social services, community funds, and rehabilitation projects for the handicapped.
Limitations: Giving primarily in Grand Rapids, MI.
Application information: Contributes only to pre-selected organizations. Applications not accepted.
Trustee: Old Kent Bank & Trust Co.
Employer Identification Number: 386400384

3215
Oleson Foundation ⌑

729 East Eighth St.
Traverse City 49684 (616) 946-1853

Established in 1959 in MI.
Donor(s): Gerald W. Oleson, Frances M. Oleson.
Foundation type: Independent
Financial data (yr. ended 12/31/88): Assets, $1,599,018 (M); gifts received, $101,300; expenditures, $201,961, including $89,663 for 15 grants (high: $20,056; low: $175).
Purpose and activities: Grants primarily for a college and a maritime heritage league; support also for youth and culture.
Limitations: Giving primarily in the Grand Traverse, MI, area.
Application information:
Initial approach: Letter
Deadline(s): None
Write: Ellen B. Simon
Officers: Gerald W. Oleson, Pres.; John R. Spencer, M.D., V.P.; Harry T. Running, Secy.; Julius H. Beers, Treas.
Trustee: Frances M. Oleson.
Employer Identification Number: 386083080

3216
Louis & Helen Padnos Foundation ⌑ ☆
River Ave. at Bayside Dr.
Holland 49423

Established in 1959.
Donor(s): Louis Padnos Iron & Metal Co.
Foundation type: Independent
Financial data (yr. ended 5/31/89): Assets, $1,897,746 (M); gifts received, $1,126,000; expenditures, $140,628, including $140,615 for grants (high: $50,000).
Purpose and activities: Support primarily for Jewish organizations and a historical trust; minor support also for health, education, and social services.
Limitations: Giving primarily in MI. No grants to individuals.
Application information: Contributes only to pre-selected organizations. Applications not accepted.
Trustees: Seymour K. Padnos, Stuart B. Padnos.
Employer Identification Number: 386053081

3217
William M. and Mary E. Pagel Trust
c/o National Bank of Detroit
611 Woodward Ave.
Detroit 48226 (313) 225-3124
Application address: c/o National Bank of Detroit, P.O. Box 222, Detroit, MI 48232

Established in 1964 in MI.
Donor(s): Mary E. Pagel,† William M. Pagel.†
Foundation type: Independent
Financial data (yr. ended 12/31/89): Assets, $6,720,170 (M); expenditures, $387,230, including $331,750 for 23 grants (high: $45,000; low: $1,000; average: $1,000-$45,000).
Purpose and activities: Emphasis on health and hospitals, the aged, child welfare, rehabilitation and aid to the handicapped, and Protestant church support; support also for a social service agency.
Types of support: Annual campaigns, continuing support, general purposes.
Limitations: Giving primarily in MI, with emphasis on the Detroit metropolitan tri-county area. No grants to individuals.
Application information: Application form not required.
Initial approach: Letter
Copies of proposal: 1
Deadline(s): Oct. 30
Board meeting date(s): Nov. 30
Final notification: Nov. 30
Write: Therese M. Thorn, 2nd V.P., National Bank of Detroit
Trustee: National Bank of Detroit.
Number of staff: None.
Employer Identification Number: 386046204

3218
Elsa U. Pardee Foundation ▼
P.O. Box 1866
Midland 48641-1866 (517) 832-3691

Incorporated in 1944 in MI.
Donor(s): Elsa U. Pardee.†
Foundation type: Independent
Financial data (yr. ended 12/25/89): Assets, $72,450,414 (M); expenditures, $3,016,388, including $2,853,447 for 48 grants (high: $500,000; low: $2,500; average: $30,000-$75,000).
Purpose and activities: To promote the cure and control of cancer; grants to hospitals, universities, and institutes for cancer research and control.
Types of support: Research.
Limitations: No grants to individuals, or for capital, building, or endowment funds, equipment (except when used in a specific project), scholarships, fellowships, general purposes, matching gifts, or fundraising campaigns; no loans.
Publications: Annual report (including application guidelines).
Application information: Application form required.
Initial approach: Letter
Copies of proposal: 7
Deadline(s): None
Board meeting date(s): 3 times a year
Final notification: 4 to 6 months
Write: James A. Kendall, Secy.
Officers and Trustees: Gail E. Allen, Pres.; Carl A. Gerstacker, V.P. and Treas.; James A. Kendall, Secy.; W. James Allen, Lisa J. Gerstacker, Richard J. Kociba, Michael S. Leahy, M.D., Patrick J. Oriel, Alan W. Ott, Norman C. Rumple, William D. Schuette.
Number of staff: 1 part-time support.
Employer Identification Number: 386065799

3219
Mary I. & Robert C. Pew Foundation ⌑ ☆
P.O. Box 1967
Grand Rapids 49501

Established in 1965.
Donor(s): Mary I. Pew, Robert C. Pew.
Foundation type: Independent
Financial data (yr. ended 12/31/88): Assets, $1,203,112 (M); gifts received, $500,000; expenditures, $248,445, including $241,000 for 22 grants (high: $115,000; low: $1,000).
Purpose and activities: Support primarily for youth, welfare, and cultural programs.
Limitations: Giving primarily in Grand Rapids, MI. No grants to individuals.
Trustees: Mary I. Pew, Robert C. Pew.
Employer Identification Number: 386107377

3220
Plym Foundation ⌑
P.O. Box 125
Niles 49120 (616) 683-8300

Incorporated in 1952 in MI.
Donor(s): Mrs. Francis J. Plym.
Foundation type: Independent
Financial data (yr. ended 09/30/90): Assets, $3,444,411 (M); expenditures, $421,078, including $392,637 for 13 grants.
Purpose and activities: Emphasis on education, including a community education center, the arts, and scholarships.
Types of support: Scholarship funds.
Limitations: Giving primarily in MI.
Application information: Application form not required.
Initial approach: Letter
Copies of proposal: 1
Deadline(s): None
Officers: Lawrence J. Plym,* Pres.; J. Eric Plym, V.P.; Rosemary Donnelly, Secy.
Directors:* Sally P. Campbell, Andrew J. Plym.
Employer Identification Number: 386069680

3221
Ralph L. and Winifred E. Polk Foundation ⌑
431 Howard St.
Detroit 48231 (313) 961-9470

Incorporated in 1962 in MI.
Donor(s): Ralph L. Polk.
Foundation type: Independent
Financial data (yr. ended 12/31/88): Assets, $1,900,972 (M); expenditures, $131,953, including $127,000 for 27 grants (high: $25,050; low: $500).
Purpose and activities: Emphasis on welfare funds, Protestant giving, culture, particularly music, hospitals, and youth.
Types of support: General purposes, building funds, capital campaigns.
Limitations: Giving primarily in MI, with emphasis on Detroit. No grants to individuals.
Application information: Contributes only to pre-selected organizations. Applications not accepted.
Officers: Winifred E. Polk,* Pres.; Stephen R. Polk,* V.P. and Treas.; John M. O'Hara, Secy.
Trustees:* Janet P. Read.
Employer Identification Number: 386080075

3222
The Power Foundation ⌑
1201 Old Kent Bank Bldg.
136 East Michigan Ave.
Kalamazoo 49007 (616) 382-5800
Application address: The Plymouth Bldg., 2929 Plymouth Rd., Ann Arbor, MI 48105

Established in 1967 in MI.
Donor(s): Eugene B. Power, Sadye H. Power, Philip H. Power.
Foundation type: Independent
Financial data (yr. ended 12/31/88): Assets, $155,489 (M); gifts received, $190,000; expenditures, $170,536, including $153,504 for 17 grants (high: $40,000; low: $100).
Purpose and activities: Support for a 2-year academic/cultural exchange program providing scholarships to graduates of Cambridge University and University of Michigan; grants also for an Episcopal church.
Types of support: Scholarship funds, exchange programs.
Limitations: Giving primarily in MI, with emphasis on Ann Arbor.
Application information: For Magdalene graduates: The Master, Magdalene College, Cambridge, England CB3 0AG; for New Hall graduates: The President, New Hall, Cambridge, England CB3 0DF; for Michigan graduates: The Director, University of Michigan-LSA Study Abroad, 5208 Angell Hall, Ann Arbor, MI 48104.
Initial approach: Proposal
Write: James S. Hilboldt, Secy.
Officers and Trustees: Eugene B. Power, Pres.; Philip H. Power, V.P.; Sadye H. Power, V.P.; Margaret O. Massialas, Exec. Secy.; James S. Hilboldt, Secy.; Edward M. Hindert, Treas.; James C. Westin.
Employer Identification Number: 386119490

3223
The Meyer and Anna Prentis Family Foundation, Inc.
P.O. Box 7037
Huntington Woods 48070 (313) 398-8415

Incorporated in 1955 in MI.
Donor(s): Members of the Prentis family.
Foundation type: Independent
Financial data (yr. ended 12/31/88): Assets, $4,814,842 (M); expenditures, $4,955,701, including $4,944,278 for 17 grants (high: $3,027,840; low: $500).
Purpose and activities: Giving primarily for medical research, education, the disadvantaged, and cultural programs; support also for Jewish giving, including Jewish welfare funds.
Limitations: Giving primarily in MI. No grants to individuals, or for endowment funds, scholarships, fellowships, or matching gifts; no loans.
Application information:
Initial approach: Letter
Copies of proposal: 1
Board meeting date(s): July and Dec.
Write: Marvin A. Frenkel, Treas.
Officers and Trustees:* Barbara P. Frenkel,* Pres.; Denise L. Brown,* V.P.; Ronald E.P. Frenkel, M.D.,* V.P.; Dale P. Frenkel,* Secy.; Marvin A. Frenkel,* Treas.; Tom P. Frenkel, Cindy Frenkel Kanter, Nelson P. Lande.
Employer Identification Number: 386090332

3224
Prince Foundation ▼ ⌑
1057 South Shore Dr.
Holland 49423

Established in 1977.
Donor(s): Edgar D. Prince, Elsa D. Prince, Prince Corp.
Foundation type: Independent
Financial data (yr. ended 6/30/88): Assets, $9,876,597 (M); gifts received, $5,725,000; expenditures, $3,716,741, including $3,675,340 for 73 grants (high: $1,702,750; low: $150).
Purpose and activities: Giving to Christian organizations, churches, and schools; support also for a senior citizens center.
Types of support: General purposes.
Limitations: Giving primarily in MI.
Officers and Trustees: Edgar D. Prince, Pres.; Elsa D. Prince, V.P. and Secy.; Hannes Meyers, Jr., Treas.
Employer Identification Number: 382190330

3225
Ransom Fidelity Company ⌑
702 Michigan National Tower
Lansing 48933 (517) 482-1538

Incorporated in 1915 in MI.
Donor(s): Ransom E. Olds.†
Foundation type: Independent
Financial data (yr. ended 12/31/88): Assets, $2,759,485 (M); expenditures, $199,953, including $132,500 for 38 grants (high: $25,000; low: $100).
Purpose and activities: Emphasis on higher and secondary education, hospitals, youth agencies, cultural programs, Protestant church support, a conservation organization, and the handicapped.
Limitations: Giving primarily in MI. No grants to individuals.
Application information: Application form required.
Deadline(s): None
Write: R.E. Olds Anderson, Pres.
Officer and Director: R.E. Olds Anderson, Pres.
Employer Identification Number: 381485403

3226
Milton M. Ratner Foundation ⌑
17515 West Nine Mile, Suite 875
Southfield 48075 (313) 424-9373

Incorporated in 1968 in MI.
Donor(s): Milton M. Ratner Trust.
Foundation type: Independent
Financial data (yr. ended 8/31/88): Assets, $5,016,032 (M); expenditures, $248,799, including $190,500 for 41 grants (high: $50,000; low: $200).
Purpose and activities: Giving for higher education, hospitals, and medical research.
Types of support: Building funds, endowment funds, equipment, general purposes, publications, research, scholarship funds, special projects.
Limitations: Giving primarily in MI and GA. No grants to individuals.
Publications: 990-PF.
Application information:
Initial approach: Proposal
Copies of proposal: 1
Deadline(s): Sept. 15
Board meeting date(s): Oct.
Write: Charles R. McDonald, V.P. and Secy.
Officers and Trustees: Mary Jo Ratner Corley, Pres.; Charles R. McDonald, V.P. and Secy.; J. Beverly Langford, Treas.
Agent: National Bank of Detroit.
Employer Identification Number: 386160330

3227
Edward F. Redies Foundation, Inc. ☆
c/o R & B Machine Tool Co.
118 East Michigan Ave.
Saline 48176-1553

Incorporated in 1981 in MI.
Donor(s): R & B Machine Tool Co.
Foundation type: Company-sponsored
Financial data (yr. ended 12/31/88): Assets, $1,727,702 (M); gifts received, $500,000; expenditures, $53,283, including $46,500 for 11 grants (high: $20,000; low: $1,000).
Purpose and activities: Giving for civic affairs, higher education, public schools, social services, and a hospital.
Types of support: Scholarship funds, capital campaigns, equipment.
Limitations: Giving primarily in MI, with emphasis on Saline. No grants to individuals.
Application information: Application form required.
Initial approach: Letter
Deadline(s): Mar. 30
Trustees: Joseph H. Buhr, Wilbur K. Pierpont, Robert D. Redies, Milton E. Stemen.
Employer Identification Number: 382391326

3228
Sigmund and Sophie Rohlik Foundation ⌑
16500 North Park Dr., Apt. 1520
Southfield 48075 (313) 559-1967

Established in 1956 in MI.
Donor(s): Sigmund Rohlik,† Sophie Rohlik.
Foundation type: Independent
Financial data (yr. ended 6/30/88): Assets, $2,045,795 (M); expenditures, $75,091.
Purpose and activities: Giving primarily to a Jewish day school; support also for social service and youth agencies.
Application information: Contributes only to pre-selected organizations. Applications not accepted.
Officers: Sophie Rohlik, Pres. and Treas.; Moe Baumer,* V.P. and Secy.
Directors:* David Hertzberg, Charles Levin, Joseph Levin.
Employer Identification Number: 386056443

3229
May Mitchell Royal Foundation ⌑
c/o Comerica Bank-Midland
201 McDonald St.
Midland 48640
Application address: 2266 Kings Lake Blvd., Naples, FL 33962; Tel.: (813) 774-0420

Established in 1981 in MI.
Donor(s): May Mitchell Royal Trust.
Foundation type: Independent
Financial data (yr. ended 9/30/88): Assets, $1,902,703 (M); expenditures, $120,688, including $103,114 for 10 grants (high: $24,791; low: $665).
Purpose and activities: Giving for hospitals and eye research and treatment; support also for health associations, drug abuse programs, and hospices.
Types of support: Equipment, scholarship funds, research.
Limitations: Giving primarily in MI, FL, and HI.
Application information: Application form required.
Initial approach: Letter
Deadline(s): May 31
Write: Richard O. Hartley, Chair., Grant Comm.
Trustee: Comerica Bank-Midland.
Grant Committee: Richard O. Hartley, Chair.; Tyrone W. Gillespie, Ruth C. Lishman.
Employer Identification Number: 382387140

3230
The Ruffner Foundation ⌑
c/o George H. Meyer
100 West Long Lake Rd., Suite 100
Bloomfield Hills 48013-2731

Established in 1982 in MI.
Foundation type: Independent
Financial data (yr. ended 12/31/88): Assets, $578,518 (L); expenditures, $172,121, including $161,500 for 17 grants (high: $100,000; low: $200).
Purpose and activities: Giving primarily for education and youth; support also for libraries.
Limitations: Giving primarily in FL and MI. No grants to individuals.

Application information: Contributes only to pre-selected organizations. Applications not accepted.
Officers: Frederick G. Ruffner,* Pres.; Alfred R. Reuther, Jr., Secy.
Directors:* Mary E. Ruffner.
Trustees: Frederick G. Ruffner III, Peter E. Ruffner.
Employer Identification Number: 382416462

3231
Sage Foundation ▼
150 West Jefferson, Suite 2500
Detroit 48226 (313) 963-6420

Incorporated in 1954 in MI.
Donor(s): Charles F. Sage,† Effa L. Sage.†
Foundation type: Independent
Financial data (yr. ended 12/31/88): Assets, $51,373,554 (M); gifts received, $3,500; expenditures, $2,288,540, including $2,206,681 for 278 grants (high: $200,000; low: $500; average: $1,000-$15,000).
Purpose and activities: Emphasis on higher and secondary education and hospitals; grants also for aid to the handicapped, Roman Catholic religious and charitable organizations, youth and child welfare agencies, church support, and cultural programs.
Types of support: General purposes, scholarship funds, renovation projects, building funds, operating budgets, research, special projects.
Limitations: Giving primarily in MI.
Publications: Financial statement.
Application information: Application form not required.
Initial approach: Letter
Deadline(s): None
Board meeting date(s): Approximately every 2 weeks
Final notification: 6 to 8 weeks
Write: Dolores deGakeford
Officers: Melissa Sage Booth,* Pres.; John H. Booth, V.P.; John W. Gelder, Secy.
Trustees:* Emmett E. Eagan, Jr., Donato F. Sarapo.
Number of staff: None.
Employer Identification Number: 386041518

3232
The Shirley K. Schlafer Foundation ⌑
228 Lakewood Dr.
Bloomfield Hills 48013

Established in 1985 in MI.
Donor(s): Shirley K. Schlafer.
Foundation type: Independent
Financial data (yr. ended 10/31/88): Assets, $117,313 (M); gifts received, $188,942; expenditures, $181,407, including $181,340 for 67 grants (high: $40,000; low: $10).
Purpose and activities: Support primarily for health associations; giving also to Jewish organizations.
Officers: Shirley K. Schlafer, Pres.; Jeffrey H. Miro, Secy.
Employer Identification Number: 382637259

3233
Lillian H. and Karl W. Scott Foundation ⌑
P.O. Box 699
Utica 48087-0699 (313) 731-3300

Established in 1963 in MI.
Foundation type: Independent
Financial data (yr. ended 10/31/88): Assets, $1,662,636 (M); expenditures, $96,992, including $53,309 for 91 grants (high: $2,500; low: $100).
Purpose and activities: Grants primarily to institutions concerned with the care and education of children and youth; support also for health agencies.
Limitations: Giving primarily in MI.
Officers and Directors: B.A. Chaplow, Pres. and Treas.; Ted Vincent, Secy.; Thomas J. Chaplow.
Employer Identification Number: 386065953

3234
Sebastian Foundation ⌑
2000 Robinson Rd., S.E.
Grand Rapids 49506 (616) 454-7661
Application address: 82 Ionia, N.W., Suite 360, Grand Rapids, MI 49503

Established in 1980.
Donor(s): Audrey M. Sebastian, James R. Sebastian.
Foundation type: Independent
Financial data (yr. ended 8/31/88): Assets, $5,664,850 (M); expenditures, $301,275, including $223,350 for 43 grants (high: $50,000; low: $250).
Purpose and activities: Giving to higher education, community funds, cultural programs, and social services.
Limitations: Giving primarily in the Grand Rapids and Kent County areas, MI. No grants to individuals.
Application information:
Initial approach: Proposal
Deadline(s): None
Write: James R. Sebastian, Trustee
Trustees: Audrey M. Sebastian, David S. Sebastian, James R. Sebastian, John O. Sebastian.
Employer Identification Number: 382340219

3235
Sehn Foundation ⌑
23874 Kean Ave.
Dearborn 48124

Established in 1968 in MI.
Donor(s): Francis J. Sehn, James T. Sehn.
Foundation type: Independent
Financial data (yr. ended 12/31/88): Assets, $3,176,105 (M); gifts received, $162,000; expenditures, $175,384, including $171,448 for 24 grants (high: $110,448; low: $100).
Purpose and activities: Giving for Roman Catholic organizations; some support for health and social service agencies, and education.
Types of support: General purposes.
Limitations: Giving primarily in Detroit, MI.
Application information: Contributes only to pre-selected organizations. Applications not accepted.
Officers: Francis J. Sehn, Pres.; James T. Sehn, V.P.
Employer Identification Number: 386160784

3236
The Thomas Erler Seidman Foundation ⌑
99 Monroe Ave., N.W., Suite 800
Grand Rapids 49503 (616) 453-7719

Trust established in 1950 in MI.
Donor(s): Frank E. Seidman,† Esther L. Seidman.†
Foundation type: Independent
Financial data (yr. ended 12/31/88): Assets, $2,343,899 (M); expenditures, $133,073, including $113,073 for 40 grants (high: $10,000; low: $500).
Purpose and activities: Emphasis on cultural programs and higher education; support also for social service agencies and medical research.
Types of support: General purposes, building funds, endowment funds, annual campaigns, equipment.
Limitations: Giving primarily in MI. No grants to individuals.
Application information: Application form not required.
Deadline(s): None
Write: Augusta Eppinga, Trustee
Trustees: Augusta Eppinga, B. Thomas Seidman, L. William Seidman, Sarah B. Seidman.
Employer Identification Number: 136098204

3237
Seymour and Troester Foundation ⌑
21500 Harper Ave.
St. Clair Shores 48080

Incorporated in 1945 in MI.
Donor(s): Charles E. Troester.†
Foundation type: Independent
Financial data (yr. ended 12/31/88): Assets, $3,150,866 (M); expenditures, $228,956, including $153,000 for 20 grants (high: $37,000; low: $500).
Purpose and activities: Grants largely for higher and secondary educational institutions and Roman Catholic charitable and religious organizations.
Limitations: No grants to individuals.
Application information: Contributes only to pre-selected organizations. Applications not accepted.
Officers and Trustees: Mrs. B.A. Seymour, Sr., Chair.; B.A. Seymour, Jr., Pres. and Treas.; Kathleen Anderson, V.P. and Secy.; Marcella Lilly.
Employer Identification Number: 386062647

3238
The Nate S. and Ruth B. Shapero Foundation
1927 Rosa Parks Blvd.
Detroit 48216-1555

Established in 1949 in MI.
Donor(s): Nate S. Shapero,† Ray A. Shapero.
Foundation type: Independent
Financial data (yr. ended 4/30/87): Assets, $2,368,549 (M); expenditures, $166,239, including $146,420 for 55 grants (high: $80,000; low: $25).
Purpose and activities: Emphasis on Jewish welfare funds, higher education, pharmacology

and nursing, the handicapped, and the arts, including music.
Types of support: General purposes, matching funds.
Limitations: Giving primarily in MI.
Application information: Applications not accepted.
Officers and Trustees: Ray A. Shapero, Chair.; Gloria Stalla, Secy.; J.E. Shapero, Treas.; Alan E. Schwartz, Marianne S. Schwartz.
Employer Identification Number: 386041567

3239
Elizabeth, Allan and Warren Shelden Fund
333 West Fort Bldg., Suite 1870
Detroit 48226 (313) 963-2356

Incorporated in 1937 in MI.
Donor(s): Elizabeth Warren Shelden,† Allan Shelden III,† W. Warren Shelden.
Foundation type: Independent
Financial data (yr. ended 12/31/89): Assets, $3,555,361 (M); expenditures, $247,105, including $240,000 for 21 grants (high: $95,500; low: $500; average: $2,500-$15,000).
Purpose and activities: Support for hospitals, community funds, higher and secondary education, youth agencies, and cultural organizations.
Types of support: Continuing support, annual campaigns, building funds, equipment, endowment funds, research, general purposes, capital campaigns.
Limitations: Giving primarily in MI. No grants to individuals, or for scholarships, fellowships, or matching gifts; no loans.
Publications: 990-PF.
Application information: Application form not required.
Initial approach: Proposal
Copies of proposal: 1
Deadline(s): Submit proposal preferably in Nov.; no set deadline
Board meeting date(s): Dec. or Jan.
Write: W. Warren Shelden, Pres.
Officers: W. Warren Shelden,* Pres.; Virginia D. Shelden,* V.P.; Robert W. Emke, Jr., Secy.; William W. Shelden, Jr.,* Treas.
Trustees:* William G. Butler, Robert M. Surdam.
Number of staff: 1 part-time professional; 1 part-time support.
Employer Identification Number: 386052198

3240
The Shiffman Foundation ⌑
c/o Milton J. Miller
2290 First National Bldg.
Detroit 48226

Incorporated in 1948 in MI.
Donor(s): Abraham Shiffman.
Foundation type: Independent
Financial data (yr. ended 9/30/88): Assets, $1,950,334 (M); expenditures, $141,391, including $121,511 for 36 grants (high: $25,100; low: $100).
Purpose and activities: Emphasis on Jewish welfare funds; giving also for peace issues and community development; some support for higher education in the U.S. and Israel, hospitals, community funds, and temple support.
Limitations: Giving primarily in Detroit, MI. No grants to individuals.
Application information: Contributes only to pre-selected organizations. Applications not accepted.
Officers and Trustees: N. James Levey, Pres.; Robert I. Kohn, Jr., V.P.; Richard Levey, V.P.; Janet S. Kohn, Secy.; Jason L. Honigman, Treas.; Jay Allen, Max M. Fisher, Milton J. Miller, Lester Morris, Victor Shiffman.
Number of staff: 1 part-time professional.
Employer Identification Number: 381396850

3241
Simmons Foundation ⌑
3400 Travis Pointe Rd., Suite A
Ann Arbor 48108

Established in 1961 in MI.
Foundation type: Independent
Financial data (yr. ended 12/31/88): Assets, $1,114,922 (M); expenditures, $68,290, including $65,693 for 53 grants (high: $25,000; low: $10).
Purpose and activities: Support for scholarships at colleges and universities, health care, and Christian organizations and churches.
Types of support: Scholarship funds, equipment.
Limitations: Giving primarily in MI, with emphasis on Ann Arbor. No grants to individuals.
Application information: Contributes only to pre-selected organizations. Applications not accepted.
Officers: Clifford H. Simmons, Pres. and Treas.; Constance M. Simmons, V.P. and Secy.
Trustees: David T. Simmons, Steven M. Simmons.
Employer Identification Number: 386075922

3242
Simone Foundation ⌑
21001 Van Born Rd.
Taylor 48180

Established in 1962 in MI.
Donor(s): Alex Manoogian, Masco Corp.
Foundation type: Independent
Financial data (yr. ended 10/31/88): Assets, $2,537,444 (M); gifts received, $1,121,875; expenditures, $359,082, including $357,725 for 15 grants (high: $171,500; low: $100).
Purpose and activities: Giving for Armenian organizations, including Armenian churches and cultural organizations, and education.
Application information: Contributes only to pre-selected organizations. Applications not accepted.
Officers: Louise Simone, Pres.; Christine Simone, V.P.; David Simone, Secy.-Treas.
Director: Mark Simone.
Employer Identification Number: 381799107

3243
The Simpson Foundation
c/o City Bank & Trust Co.
One Jackson Sq.
Jackson 49201 (517) 788-2780

Established in 1980 in MI.
Donor(s): Robert J. Simpson.†
Foundation type: Independent
Financial data (yr. ended 09/30/89): Assets, $2,794,552 (M); expenditures, $149,678, including $128,276 for 13 grants (high: $30,000; low: $250).
Purpose and activities: Giving for higher, adult, and other education, health and health services, science, religious purposes, child welfare and development, family services, the aged, leadership development, and historic preservation.
Types of support: Seed money, emergency funds, building funds, equipment, matching funds, consulting services, technical assistance, special projects, endowment funds, renovation projects.
Limitations: Giving limited to Hillsdale County or to programs benefiting Hillsdale County, MI. No grants to individuals, or for scholarships or fellowships.
Publications: 990-PF.
Application information: Application form required.
Initial approach: Proposal, letter, or telephone
Copies of proposal: 3
Deadline(s): Submit proposal preferably in Aug.
Board meeting date(s): Oct.
Final notification: 30 to 60 days
Write: Robert E. Carlson, V.P. and Trust Officer, City Bank & Trust Co.
Trustee: City Bank & Trust Co.
Number of staff: None.
Employer Identification Number: 386054058

3244
Simpson Industries Fund ⌑ ☆
32100 Telegraph Rd., Suite 120
Birmingham 48010

Established in 1977 in MI as successor to Simpson Fund.
Donor(s): Simpson Industries, Inc.
Foundation type: Company-sponsored
Financial data (yr. ended 3/31/89): Assets, $307,867 (M); gifts received, $60,000; expenditures, $104,767, including $69,590 for 33 grants (high: $25,000; low: $100), $26,600 for grants to individuals and $4,169 for employee matching gifts.
Purpose and activities: Support for religious, educational, cultural, recreational, civic, and health organizations; support also for an employee matching gift program for education, and college scholarships for employees' children.
Types of support: Employee-related scholarships, employee matching gifts.
Limitations: Giving primarily in MI.
Application information: Application form required.
Deadline(s): Apr. 15 for scholarships
Write: Deborah Baluch
Officer: Robert W. Navarre, Chair.
Director: K.E. Berman.
Trustee: Charles K. Winter.
Employer Identification Number: 382157102

3245
The Skillman Foundation ▼
333 West Fort St., Suite 1350
Detroit 48226 (313) 961-8850

Incorporated in 1960 in MI.
Donor(s): Rose P. Skillman.†
Foundation type: Independent
Financial data (yr. ended 12/31/88): Assets, $243,785,298 (M); gifts received, $738,312; expenditures, $13,561,481, including $10,921,718 for 142 grants (high: $1,000,000; low: $1,000; average: $20,000-$200,000) and $37,122 for employee matching gifts.
Purpose and activities: Giving primarily for children, youth and young persons; education; basic human needs; community-wide collaborative efforts; and culture and arts.
Types of support: Seed money, general purposes, employee matching gifts, special projects.
Limitations: Giving primarily in southeastern MI, with emphasis on metropolitan Detroit, including Wayne, Macomb, and Oakland counties. No support for long-term projects not being aided by other sources, sectarian religious activities, or political lobbying or legislative activities. No grants to individuals, or for endowment funds, annual campaigns, or deficit financing; no loans.
Publications: Annual report, informational brochure (including application guidelines), newsletter.
Application information: Application form not required.
Initial approach: Proposal
Copies of proposal: 1
Deadline(s): Apr. 1 for arts and culture organizations; for other grants no set deadline
Board meeting date(s): Feb., Apr., June, Sept., and Nov.
Final notification: 2 weeks after board meeting
Write: Lisa M. Kaichen, Prog. Officer
Officers: William E. Hoglund,* Chair.; Leonard W. Smith,* Pres. and Secy.; Jean E. Gregory, V.P. and Treas.; Lisa M. Kaichen, Prog. Officer.
Trustees:* James A. Aliber, Lillian Bauder, William M. Brodhead, Bernadine N. Denning, Walter Douglas, Alan Schwartz, Jane R. Thomas.*
Number of staff: 7 full-time professional; 2 full-time support.
Employer Identification Number: 381675780

3246
William E. Slaughter, Jr. Foundation, Inc. ⌑
32949 Bingham Ln.
Birmingham 48010 (313) 666-9300

Incorporated in 1959 in MI.
Donor(s): William E. Slaughter, Jr.
Foundation type: Independent
Financial data (yr. ended 12/31/88): Assets, $1,722,255 (M); expenditures, $129,237, including $115,460 for 54 grants (high: $15,500; low: $60).
Purpose and activities: Grants primarily for youth agencies, higher education, Protestant church support, cultural programs, disease research, and social service agencies.
Limitations: No grants to individuals.
Application information: Contributes only to pre-selected organizations. Applications not accepted.
Officers and Directors: William E. Slaughter, Jr., Pres. and Treas.; William E. Slaughter IV, V.P.; Charles Nida, Secy.; Gloria Slaughter, Kent C. Slaughter.
Employer Identification Number: 386065616

3247
The Snell Foundation Charitable Trust ⌑
918 Rosewood
East Lansing 48823

Established in 1986 in MI.
Donor(s): John Snell, Florence M. Snell.
Foundation type: Independent
Financial data (yr. ended 12/31/87): Assets, $80,642 (M); gifts received, $3,396; expenditures, $326,859, including $323,439 for 1 grant.
Purpose and activities: Support for a social service organization.
Limitations: No grants to individuals.
Application information: Contributes only to pre-selected organizations. Applications not accepted.
Trustee: Florence M. Snell, John Snell.
Employer Identification Number: 382674789

3248
Community Foundation for Southeastern Michigan
333 West Fort St., Suite 2010
Detroit 48226 (313) 961-6675

Established in 1984 in MI.
Foundation type: Community
Financial data (yr. ended 12/31/89): Assets, $22,049,095 (M); gifts received, $4,003,992; expenditures, $2,633,091, including $1,823,727 for 408 grants (high: $200,000; low: $250; average: $10,000), $59,066 for 36 grants to individuals (high: $2,000; low: $25; average: $25-$2,000) and $143,868 for 3 foundation-administered programs.
Purpose and activities: Supports projects in areas of civic affairs, social services, culture, health, and education.
Types of support: Seed money, special projects, employee-related scholarships.
Limitations: Giving limited to southeastern MI. No support for sectarian, religious programs. No grants to individuals, or for capital projects, endowments, annual campaigns, or operating budgets (except in initial years of new ventures).
Publications: Annual report (including application guidelines), application guidelines.
Application information: Application form not required.
Initial approach: Proposal
Copies of proposal: 1
Deadline(s): None
Board meeting date(s): Quarterly
Final notification: Following board meetings
Write: C. David Campbell, Prog. Off.
Officers: Joseph L. Hudson, Jr., Chair.; Wendell W. Anderson, Jr., Vice-Chair.; Max M. Fisher, Vice-Chair.; Frank D. Stella, Vice-Chair.; Mrs. R. Alexander Wrigley, Secy.; Richard H. Austin, Treas.
Number of staff: 3 full-time professional; 2 full-time support.
Employer Identification Number: 382530980

3249
SPX Corporation Foundation
(Formerly Sealed Power Foundation)
700 Terrace Point Dr.
Muskegon 49443 (616) 724-5816

Established in 1984 in MI.
Donor(s): SPX Corp.
Foundation type: Company-sponsored
Financial data (yr. ended 12/31/89): Assets, $132,600 (M); gifts received, $183,496; expenditures, $432,381, including $381,120 for 86 grants (high: $77,000; low: $125) and $35,752 for 230 employee matching gifts.
Purpose and activities: Emphasis on education, community funds, and culture and the arts; some support for employment development.
Types of support: Employee matching gifts, general purposes.
Limitations: Giving primarily in plant communities.
Application information:
Write: John Tyson, Trustee
Officers and Trustees:* J.M. Sheridan,* Pres.; S.A. Lison,* V.P.; D.A. Johnson, D.H. Johnson, R.D. Tuttle, J.D. Tyson, R.B. Werner.
Number of staff: 1 part-time support.
Employer Identification Number: 386058308

3250
Steelcase Foundation ▼
P.O. Box 1967
Grand Rapids 49507 (616) 246-4695

Trust established in 1951 in MI.
Donor(s): Steelcase, Inc.
Foundation type: Company-sponsored
Financial data (yr. ended 11/30/88): Assets, $34,462,334 (M); gifts received, $6,001,133; expenditures, $3,524,804, including $3,393,759 for 104 grants (high: $1,000,000; low: $1,000; average: $2,000-$25,000).
Purpose and activities: Support for human services, including a community fund, health, education, arts, and the environment; particular concerns include helping the disadvantaged, disabled, young, and elderly to improve the quality of their lives.
Types of support: Building funds, general purposes, capital campaigns, special projects, employee-related scholarships.
Limitations: Giving limited to areas of company operations, including Grand Rapids, MI; Orange County, CA; Ashville, NC; Athens, AL; and Toronto, Canada. No support for churches, or programs with substantial religious overtones of a sectarian nature. No grants to individuals, or for endowment funds.
Publications: Annual report (including application guidelines), application guidelines.
Application information: Application form required.
Initial approach: Letter
Copies of proposal: 1
Deadline(s): None

Board meeting date(s): Quarterly and as required
Final notification: At least 90 days
Write: Kate Pew Wolters, Exec. Dir.
Trustees: David D. Hunting, Jr., Roger L. Martin, Frank H. Merlotti, Robert C. Pew, Peter M. Wege, Old Kent Bank & Trust Co.
Number of staff: 1 full-time professional; 1 part-time support.
Employer Identification Number: 386050470

3251
The Edward C. and Hazel L. Stephenson Foundation ⌑
505 Hampton Rd.
Grosse Pointe Woods 48236 (313) 886-2659

Incorporated in 1969 in MI.
Donor(s): Edward C. Stephenson,† Hazel Stephenson.†
Foundation type: Independent
Financial data (yr. ended 12/31/88): Assets, $3,458,370 (M); expenditures, $208,947, including $181,350 for 27 grants (high: $23,000; low: $1,000).
Purpose and activities: Grants to colleges and universities for scholarships to individual students selected by the financial aid officer of the respective institutions.
Types of support: Operating budgets, scholarship funds.
Limitations: Giving limited to MI, IN, OH, and KY; new grants generally only in MI. No grants to individuals, or for capital funds or matching gifts.
Application information: Application form not required.
Initial approach: Letter
Copies of proposal: 1
Deadline(s): Aug. 1
Board meeting date(s): Dec.
Final notification: About 30 days
Write: Ludger A. Beauvais, Pres.
Officers: Ludger A. Beauvais, Pres. and Treas.; Charles R. Kinnaird, V.P. and Secy.; Henry K. Wallstrom, V.P.
Number of staff: None.
Employer Identification Number: 386172669

3252
The Helmut Stern Foundation ☆
P.O. Box 1584
Ann Arbor 48106 (313) 665-4421

Established in 1983 in MI.
Donor(s): Helmut F. Stern.
Foundation type: Independent
Financial data (yr. ended 11/30/89): Assets, $1,513,490 (M); expenditures, $93,773, including $93,773 for 10 grants (high: $25,000; low: $1,420).
Purpose and activities: Giving primarily for higher education; support also for social services, museums, hospitals, and conservation.
Types of support: Scholarship funds, fellowships, land acquisition.
Limitations: Giving primarily in MI.
Application information:
Write: Helmut F. Stern, Pres.
Officer: Helmut F. Stern, Pres.
Employer Identification Number: 579125669

3253
Sarah A. Stewart Foundation
19511 Mack Ave.
Grosse Pointe 48236 (313) 886-0450

Established in 1980 in CA.
Foundation type: Independent
Financial data (yr. ended 09/30/89): Assets, $4,189,281 (M); expenditures, $355,979, including $339,000 for 11 grants (high: $119,000; low: $5,000; average: $5,000-$119,000).
Purpose and activities: Emphasis on education, social and health services, and medical research.
Limitations: Giving primarily in CA. No grants to individuals.
Application information: Contributes only to pre-selected organizations. Applications not accepted.
Write: Richard K. Simonds
Officers: Daniel M. Gibbs, M.D., Pres.; Nancy Richard, V.P.; Mary P. Daniel, Secy.
Number of staff: 1 part-time professional.
Employer Identification Number: 953705192

3254
The Stollman Foundation ⌑
2025 West Long Lake Rd., No. 104
Troy 48098-4109 (313) 643-8810

Incorporated in 1953 in MI.
Donor(s): Phillip Stollman, Max Stollman.
Foundation type: Independent
Financial data (yr. ended 4/30/88): Assets, $145,510 (M); gifts received, $56,000; expenditures, $247,817, including $246,900 for grants (high: $80,000).
Purpose and activities: Grants for education (including religious education and higher education in Israel), temple support, and Jewish welfare.
Types of support: General purposes.
Limitations: Giving primarily in MI and NY.
Application information: Application form not required.
Deadline(s): None
Write: Phillip Stollman, Secy.
Officers and Directors: Max Stollman, Pres.; Bernard H. Stollman, V.P.; Gerald Stollman, V.P.; Phillip Stollman, Secy.-Treas.
Employer Identification Number: 386086417

3255
The Stroh Foundation ⌑
100 River Place
Detroit 48207

Established in 1965 in MI.
Donor(s): Stroh Brewery Co.
Foundation type: Company-sponsored
Financial data (yr. ended 3/31/88): Assets, $46,072 (M); gifts received, $300,000; expenditures, $306,440, including $306,250 for 73 grants (high: $35,000; low: $500).
Purpose and activities: Support for arts and cultural institutions, education (including higher education), social services, health care and research, community development, and conservation and ecology.
Limitations: Giving primarily in MI. No support for religious organizations. No grants to individuals, or for fund raising events.
Officers and Trustees: David V. Van Howe, Pres.; Gari M. Stroh, Jr., Secy.; John W. Stroh, Jr., Treas.; Peter W. Stroh.
Employer Identification Number: 386108732

3256
The Charles J. Strosacker Foundation ▼
P.O. Box 2164
Midland 48641-2164

Incorporated in 1957 in MI.
Donor(s): Charles J. Strosacker.†
Foundation type: Independent
Financial data (yr. ended 12/31/89): Assets, $34,660,000 (M); expenditures, $1,422,000, including $1,380,000 for 49 grants (high: $598,000; low: $100; average: $1,000-$10,000).
Purpose and activities: To assist and benefit political subdivisions of the state of MI and religious, charitable, artistic, or educational organizations.
Types of support: General purposes, fellowships, building funds, operating budgets, special projects, continuing support.
Limitations: Giving primarily in MI, with emphasis on the city of Midland. No grants to individuals, or for matching gifts; no loans.
Publications: Annual report (including application guidelines).
Application information: Application form not required.
Initial approach: Letter
Copies of proposal: 1
Deadline(s): Submit proposal in Oct. of the year preceding the time payment is desired
Board meeting date(s): Mar., July, and Nov.
Write: Patricia E. McKelvey, Secy.
Officers: Eugene C. Yehle,* Chair.; Martha G. Arnold,* Pres.; Patricia E. McKelvey, Secy.; Lawrence E. Burks, Treas.
Trustees:* David J. Arnold, Ralph A. Cole, John S. Ludington, Donna T. Morris, Charles J. Thrune.
Number of staff: 1 part-time professional.
Employer Identification Number: 386062787

3257
The Taubman Charitable Foundation ⌑
200 East Long Lake Rd.
Bloomfield Hills 48303-0200

Established in 1985 in MI.
Donor(s): A. Alfred Taubman.
Foundation type: Independent
Financial data (yr. ended 1/31/87): Assets, $1,919 (M); gifts received, $557,001; expenditures, $557,287, including $550,000 for 7 grants (high: $200,000; low: $10,000).
Purpose and activities: Grants primarily for higher education.
Officers and Trustees: A. Alfred Taubman, Chair., Pres., and Treas.; Jeffrey H. Miro, Secy.
Employer Identification Number: 382590369

3258
Taubman Endowment for the Arts ⌑
200 East Long Lake Rd.
Bloomfield Hills 48303-0200

Established in 1985 in MI.
Donor(s): A. Alfred Taubman.

Foundation type: Independent
Financial data (yr. ended 12/31/87): Assets, $391 (M); gifts received, $140,370; expenditures, $141,446, including $140,329 for 9 grants (high: $34,996; low: $1,000).
Purpose and activities: Giving primarily for the arts.
Officers and Trustees: A. Alfred Taubman, Chair., Pres. and Treas.; Jeffrey H. Miro, Secy.
Employer Identification Number: 382590370

3259
A. Alfred Taubman Foundation ▼ ⌑
P.O. Box 200
200 East Long Lake Rd.
Bloomfield Hills 48303-0200 (313) 258-6800

Established in 1979 in MI.
Donor(s): A. Alfred Taubman.
Foundation type: Independent
Financial data (yr. ended 07/31/89): Assets, $2,064 (M); gifts received, $2,027,912; expenditures, $2,027,981, including $2,027,402 for 143 grants (high: $1,220,050; low: $50; average: $100-$25,000).
Purpose and activities: Giving for education, Jewish welfare funds, and medical research.
Types of support: Operating budgets.
Limitations: Giving primarily in MI, with emphasis on Detroit.
Application information: Application form not required.
Deadline(s): None
Board meeting date(s): As necessary
Final notification: 3 weeks
Write: John Sullivan
Officers and Trustees:* A. Alfred Taubman,* Chair. and Treas.; Max M. Fisher,* Pres.; Jeffrey H. Miro,* Secy.; Gayle T. Kalisman, Dean E. Richardson, Robert S. Taubman, William S. Taubman.
Number of staff: None.
Employer Identification Number: 382219625

3260
W. B. & Candace Thoman Foundation
Dart Management Bldg.
500 Hogsback Rd.
Mason 48854 (517) 676-5137

Established in 1968 in MI.
Donor(s): W.B. Thoman,† Candace Thoman.†
Foundation type: Independent
Financial data (yr. ended 12/31/89): Assets, $2,305,640 (M); gifts received, $37,715; expenditures, $236,177, including $216,450 for 9 grants (high: $72,500; low: $625; average: $4,000-$11,000).
Purpose and activities: Support primarily for "education and the benefit of the young."
Types of support: Continuing support, grants to individuals, matching funds, program-related investments, scholarship funds, seed money, special projects, student aid.
Limitations: Giving primarily in Ingham, Eaton, and Clinton counties, MI. No support for political organizations, churches, or religious organizations or programs.
Publications: Program policy statement, application guidelines.
Application information:
Initial approach: Letter requesting guidelines
Copies of proposal: 3
Deadline(s): 2 weeks prior to board meetings
Board meeting date(s): Quarterly
Write: Benjamin O. Schwendener, Jr., Pres. and Secy.
Officers and Trustees:* Benjamin O. Schwendener,* Pres. and Secy.; John Hannah,* V.P.; Ronald E. Weger,* Treas.; Louis Legg, Jr., Lillian Smuckler.
Number of staff: 1 part-time support.
Employer Identification Number: 237029842

3261
Michael & Nancy Timmis Foundation ⌑
27700 Gratiot Ave.
Roseville 48066-4838

Established in 1984 in MI.
Foundation type: Independent
Financial data (yr. ended 12/31/87): Assets, $37,399 (M); gifts received, $269,000; expenditures, $439,448, including $439,150 for 61 grants (high: $126,000; low: $25).
Purpose and activities: Support primarily for Christian evangelism, missionary work, and religious education; support also for hunger relief.
Types of support: General purposes.
Limitations: Giving primarily in MI.
Application information: Contributes only to pre-selected organizations.
Officers: Michael T. Timmis, Pres. and Treas.; Nancy E. Timmis, V.P.; Wayne C. Inman, Secy.
Employer Identification Number: 382519177

3262
The Tiscornia Foundation, Inc. ⌑
1010 Main St., Suite A
St. Joseph 49085 (616) 926-0812

Incorporated in 1942 in MI.
Donor(s): Auto Specialties Manufacturing Co., Lambert Brake Corp., James W. Tiscornia,† Waldo V. Tiscornia.†
Foundation type: Independent
Financial data (yr. ended 11/30/86): Assets, $3,222,767 (M); gifts received, $1,500; expenditures, $207,977, including $120,925 for 35 grants (high: $51,000; low: $25; average: $1,500) and $15,150 for 9 grants to individuals (high: $2,750; low: $875; average: $2,000).
Purpose and activities: Grants for health, youth, community funds, and higher education.
Types of support: Continuing support, annual campaigns, seed money, emergency funds, building funds, equipment, employee-related scholarships.
Limitations: Giving primarily in MI. No grants to individuals (except for employee-related scholarships), or for endowment funds, research, or matching gifts; no loans.
Publications: 990-PF.
Application information: Scholarships only for Northern Berrien County high school students and children of Auto Specialties Manufacturing Co. employees.
Initial approach: Letter or proposal
Copies of proposal: 1
Deadline(s): Apr. 1 for scholarships; Oct. 1 for general grants
Board meeting date(s): Jan.
Write: Laurianne T. Davis, Secy.
Officers and Trustees: Lester Tiscornia, Pres.; Howard H. Paxson, V.P.; Laurianne T. Davis, Secy.; Henry H. Tippett, Treas.; Bernice Tiscornia, Edward Tiscornia.
Number of staff: 3 part-time support.
Employer Identification Number: 381777343

3263
The Harry A. and Margaret D. Towsley Foundation ▼
670 City Center Bldg.
220 East Huron St.
Ann Arbor 48104 (313) 662-6777

Incorporated in 1959 in MI.
Donor(s): Margaret D. Towsley.
Foundation type: Independent
Financial data (yr. ended 12/31/88): Assets, $38,771,730 (M); expenditures, $1,328,124, including $1,257,963 for 36 grants (high: $150,000; low: $1,000; average: $5,000-$25,000).
Purpose and activities: Support for medical and preschool education, social services, and continuing education and research in the health sciences.
Types of support: Continuing support, annual campaigns, building funds, endowment funds, matching funds, special projects.
Limitations: Giving limited to MI, with emphasis on Ann Arbor and Washtenaw County. No grants to individuals, or for travel, scholarships, fellowships, or conferences; no loans.
Publications: Annual report, application guidelines.
Application information: Application form not required.
Initial approach: Letter and proposal
Copies of proposal: 2
Deadline(s): Submit proposal between Jan. and Mar.; deadline Mar. 31
Board meeting date(s): Apr., July, Sept., and Dec.
Final notification: 60 to 90 days
Write: Margaret Ann Riecker, Pres.
Officers: Harry A. Towsley, M.D.,* Chair.; Margaret Ann Riecker,* Pres.; Margaret D. Towsley,* V.P.; John E. Riecker, Secy.; C. Wendell Dunbar,* Treas.
Trustees:* Judith D. Alexander, Robert L. Bring, Lynn T. Hamblin, Janis T. Poteat, Susan T. Wyland.
Number of staff: None.
Employer Identification Number: 386091798

3264
The Emmet and Frances Tracy Fund ▼ ⌑
400 Renaissance Ctr., 35th Fl.
Detroit 48243

Incorporated in 1951 in MI.
Donor(s): Alma Piston Co., G.P.D., Inc., Snow Manufacturing Co.
Foundation type: Independent
Financial data (yr. ended 11/30/88): Assets, $1,531,669 (M); gifts received, $1,050,000; expenditures, $910,961, including $905,540 for 171 grants (high: $100,000; low: $100; average: $1,000-$30,000).
Purpose and activities: Support for Roman Catholic religious organizations and missionary

groups; grants also for social services, education, and hospitals and health agencies.
Types of support: General purposes.
Limitations: Giving primarily in MI, with emphasis on Detroit.
Application information:
Deadline(s): None
Board meeting date(s): As required
Write: Emmet E. Tracy, Pres.
Officers: Emmet E. Tracy, Pres.; Frances A. Tracy, V.P.; Paul R. Trigg, Jr., Secy.; Emmet E. Tracy, Jr., Treas.
Number of staff: None.
Employer Identification Number: 386057796

3265
The Trico Foundation ⌑ ☆
401 South Woodward, Suite 333
Birmingham 48009

Established in 1986 in MI.
Donor(s): Warren J. Coville, Margot E. Coville.
Foundation type: Company-sponsored
Financial data (yr. ended 6/30/89): Assets, $1,807,063 (M); expenditures, $114,337, including $95,511 for grants (high: $60,000).
Purpose and activities: Giving primarily for Jewish welfare and religious organizations; support also for health associations and arts organizations.
Limitations: Giving primarily in MI. No grants to individuals.
Application information: Contributes only to pre-selected organizations. Applications not accepted.
Officers: Warren J. Coville, Pres.; Margot E. Coville, V.P.; Oscar H. Feldman, Secy.
Trustee: Besty Coville.
Employer Identification Number: 382702725

3266
Triford Foundation
20446 Harper Ave.
Harper Woods 48225 (313) 885-0812

Established in 1968 in MI.
Foundation type: Independent
Financial data (yr. ended 12/31/88): Assets, $2,389,525 (M); expenditures, $155,533, including $126,000 for 70 grants (high: $10,000; low: $100).
Purpose and activities: Emphasis on hospitals, Protestant organizations, and secondary education.
Types of support: Annual campaigns, general purposes.
Limitations: No grants to individuals, or for building funds.
Application information: Funds currently committed. Applications not accepted.
Officers and Trustees:* Frederick S. Ford,* Pres. and Secy.; Horace C. Ford,* V.P. and Treas.; Frederick B. Ford,* V.P. and Mgr.; James W. Ford.
Number of staff: 1 part-time professional; 1 part-time support.
Employer Identification Number: 237003478

3267
The Harold and Grace Upjohn Foundation ⌑
c/o Old Kent Bank of Kalamazoo
151 East Michigan Ave.
Kalamazoo 49007 (616) 383-6957
Mailing address: P.O. Box 4019, Kalamazoo, MI 49003-4019

Incorporated in 1958 in MI.
Donor(s): Grace G. Upjohn.†
Foundation type: Independent
Financial data (yr. ended 10/31/88): Assets, $6,266,953 (M); expenditures, $365,114, including $308,677 for 29 grants (high: $100,000; low: $500).
Purpose and activities: Support for youth agencies, family service agencies, health services, higher education, and population control; grants primarily for specific projects, especially to provide seed money for new projects whose continuing expenses will be met by other sources.
Types of support: Seed money, special projects.
Limitations: Giving primarily in MI. No grants to individuals, or for operating budgets or annual campaigns.
Publications: Annual report, program policy statement, application guidelines.
Application information: Application form available upon request. Application form required.
Initial approach: Call for application form
Copies of proposal: 1
Board meeting date(s): Semiannually as required
Final notification: 30 days after board meeting
Write: Floyd L. Parks, Secy.-Treas.
Officers: Gene R. Conrad,* Pres.; William A. Kirkpatrick,* V.P.; Floyd L. Parks, Secy.-Treas.
Trustees:* Joseph J. Dunnigan, Edwin E. Meader, Mary U. Meader.
Employer Identification Number: 386052963

3268
W. E. Upjohn Unemployment Trustee Corporation
300 South Westnedge Ave.
Kalamazoo 49007 (616) 343-5541

Incorporated in 1932 in MI.
Donor(s): W.E. Upjohn.†
Foundation type: Operating
Financial data (yr. ended 12/31/89): Assets, $53,846,000 (M); expenditures, $3,650,000, including $284,493 for 10 grants (high: $45,000; low: $5,000).
Purpose and activities: A private operating foundation; supports research into the causes, effects, prevention, and alleviation of unemployment; funds used to support W.E. Upjohn Institute for Employment Research.
Types of support: Research.
Limitations: No grants to individuals, or for building or endowment funds, operating budgets, scholarships, or matching gifts; no loans.
Publications: Program policy statement, application guidelines.
Application information: Application form not required.
Initial approach: Letter
Copies of proposal: 2
Deadline(s): None
Board meeting date(s): May and Dec.
Final notification: 90 days
Write: Robert G. Spiegelman, Dir.
Officers and Trustees:* P.S. Parish,* Chair.; J.H. Duncan,* Secy.-Treas.; John T. Bernhard, David Breneman, C.C. Gibbons, Ray T. Parfet, Jr., Robert G. Spiegelman, Paul H. Todd, E. Gifford Upjohn, M.D.
Number of staff: 30 full-time professional; 27 full-time support; 3 part-time support.
Employer Identification Number: 381360419

3269
Jay and Betty VanAndel Foundation ⌑
7186 Windy Hill Rd., S.E.
Grand Rapids 49506

Established in 1963.
Donor(s): Jay VanAndel, Betty VanAndel.
Foundation type: Independent
Financial data (yr. ended 12/31/87): Assets, $8,540,753 (M); gifts received, $400,000; expenditures, $610,758, including $610,410 for 77 grants (high: $125,000; low: $100).
Purpose and activities: Emphasis on Christian religious activities, including higher and secondary education; giving also for hospitals and cultural programs.
Limitations: Giving primarily in MI.
Officers and Trustees: Jay VanAndel, Pres.; Betty VanAndel, V.P.; Otto Stolz, Secy.; James Roslonic, Treas.
Employer Identification Number: 237066716

3270
Frank S. and Mollie S. VanDervoort Memorial Foundation
1784 Hamilton Rd.
Okemos 48864 (517) 349-7232

Established in 1970 in MI.
Donor(s): Frank S. VanDervoort,† Mollie S. VanDervoort.†
Foundation type: Independent
Financial data (yr. ended 06/30/89): Assets, $1,269,659 (M); expenditures, $93,647, including $67,393 for 17 grants (high: $18,500; low: $1,000).
Purpose and activities: To assist worthy indigent older people and crippled children by funding requests through appropriate operating agencies.
Limitations: Giving limited to Ingham County, MI.
Application information:
Initial approach: Proposal
Copies of proposal: 3
Deadline(s): None
Board meeting date(s): Monthly
Write: Ann L. Gessert
Officers: Robert A. Fisher, Pres.; Robert M. Crosser, Secy.; Helen H. Deliyanne.
Agent: Michigan National Bank.
Employer Identification Number: 386190789

3271
Vicksburg Foundation ⌑
c/o First of America Bank
108 East Michigan Ave.
Kalamazoo 49007 (616) 383-9217

Incorporated in 1943 in MI.
Foundation type: Independent
Financial data (yr. ended 12/31/88): Assets, $2,424,159 (M); expenditures, $140,271, including $109,000 for 13 grants (high: $35,000; low: $1,000; average: $650-$30,000) and $3,570 for 3 grants to individuals (high: $1,800; low: $720).
Purpose and activities: To coordinate and unify the charitable and benevolent activities of the incorporators; emphasis on community programs. Provides minor support to indigent individuals.
Types of support: Operating budgets, special projects, grants to individuals.
Limitations: Giving primarily in MI. No grants for endowment funds.
Application information: Application form not required.
Initial approach: Letter or proposal
Copies of proposal: 1
Deadline(s): Submit proposal in Feb., May, Aug., or Nov.
Board meeting date(s): Mar., June, Sept., and Dec.
Write: Nancy L. Grabiak, Secy.
Officers: Maxwell D. Bardeen,* Pres.; Nancy L. Grabiak, Secy.-Treas.
Directors:* Dennis Boyle, Meredith Clark, Gordon Daniels, Warren Lawrence, William Oswalt.
Employer Identification Number: 386065237

3272
Vlasic Foundation ⌑
200 Town Ctr., Suite 900
Southfield 48075

Established in 1958 in MI.
Donor(s): Robert J. Vlasic, Joseph Vlasic.
Foundation type: Independent
Financial data (yr. ended 5/31/87): Assets, $1,656,198 (M); expenditures, $53,362, including $52,350 for 35 grants (high: $20,000; low: $100).
Purpose and activities: Grants primarily for cultural programs, and health agencies and hospitals; some support for social services and Roman Catholic organizations.
Types of support: General purposes.
Application information: Applications not accepted.
Officers and Trustees: Robert J. Vlasic, Pres.; Richard R. Vlasic, V.P.; William J. Vlasic, V.P.; James J. Vlasic, Secy.-Treas.; Michael A. Vlasic.
Employer Identification Number: 386077329

3273
Frederick A. Vollbrecht Foundation ⌑
300 Park St., Suite 360
Birmingham 48009 (313) 646-7440

Incorporated in 1959 in MI.
Donor(s): Frederick A. Vollbrecht.†
Foundation type: Independent
Financial data (yr. ended 12/31/88): Assets, $2,096,803 (M); expenditures, $118,492, including $91,100 for 37 grants (high: $20,000; low: $100; average: $2,500).
Purpose and activities: Giving for higher education; support also for health services, youth and social service agencies, and aid to the handicapped.
Limitations: Giving primarily in MI. No grants to individuals.
Publications: Annual report.
Application information: Application form not required.
Initial approach: Proposal
Copies of proposal: 1
Deadline(s): None
Board meeting date(s): June
Write: Kenneth J. Klebba, Pres.
Officers and Trustees: Kenneth J. Klebba, Pres. and Treas.; Richard E. Mida, V.P. and Secy.
Number of staff: None.
Employer Identification Number: 386056173

3274
L. C. and Margaret Walker Foundation
c/o Comerica Bank-Hackley, N.A.
P.O. Box 1215
Muskegon 49443-1215 (616) 744-5294

Incorporated in 1951 in MI.
Donor(s): Louis Carlisle Walker,† Shaw Walker Co.
Foundation type: Independent
Financial data (yr. ended 12/31/88): Assets, $10,418,124 (M); expenditures, $601,714, including $474,475 for 58 grants (high: $40,000; low: $500).
Purpose and activities: Emphasis on secondary and higher education.
Limitations: No grants to individuals.
Application information: Contributes only to pre-selected organizations. Applications not accepted.
Write: Shaw Walker, Pres.
Officers: Shaw Walker,* Pres.; John S. W. Spofford,* V.P.; Monica Bauman, Secy.; Walker McKinney,* Treas.
Trustees:* Bruce Fox.
Employer Identification Number: 386060045

3275
Wege Foundation ⌑
P.O. Box 6388
Grand Rapids 49506 (616) 957-0480

Established about 1967 in MI.
Donor(s): Peter M. Wege.
Foundation type: Independent
Financial data (yr. ended 12/31/88): Assets, $4,662,519 (M); expenditures, $164,056, including $154,775 for 30 grants (high: $37,500; low: $1,000).
Purpose and activities: Support primarily for youth, social services, and culture; some support for education and community development.
Limitations: Giving primarily in Greater Kent County, MI, with emphasis on the Grand Rapids area. No grants for operating budgets.
Application information:
Initial approach: Proposal
Deadline(s): None
Write: Peter M. Wege, Pres.
Officers: Peter M. Wege, Pres.; Peter M. Wege II, V.P.; Charles Lundstrom, Secy.; Robert A. Risselade, Treas.
Employer Identification Number: 386124363

3276
Henry E. and Consuelo S. Wenger Foundation, Inc. ⌑
P.O. Box 43098
Detroit 48243

Incorporated in 1959 in MI.
Donor(s): Consuelo S. Wenger.
Foundation type: Independent
Financial data (yr. ended 12/31/88): Assets, $6,961,461 (M); expenditures, $680,528, including $664,200 for 83 grants (high: $150,000; low: $100).
Purpose and activities: Support for secondary and higher education, hospitals, and cultural programs.
Limitations: No grants to individuals.
Application information: Contributes only to pre-selected organizations. Applications not accepted.
Officers and Directors: Henry Penn Wenger, Pres.; Diane Wenger Wilson, V.P.; Miles Jaffe, Secy.; William E. Slaughter, Jr., Treas.
Employer Identification Number: 386077419

3277
Samuel L. Westerman Foundation ⌑
1700 North Woodward, Suite A
Bloomfield Hills 48013 (313) 642-5770

Established in 1971 in MI.
Foundation type: Independent
Financial data (yr. ended 01/31/89): Assets, $6,854,970 (M); expenditures, $435,282, including $350,234 for 46 grants (high: $50,234; low: $500).
Purpose and activities: Giving primarily for hospitals and health agencies, social service and youth agencies, religious organizations, including churches, higher education, and cultural programs.
Limitations: No grants to individuals.
Application information:
Initial approach: Letter
Deadline(s): None
Write: James H. LoPrete, Pres.
Officers: James H. LoPrete, Pres.; Ruth H. Cooke, V.P. and Secy.; Keith H. Muir, Treas.
Employer Identification Number: 237108795

3278
Whirlpool Foundation ▼
2000 M-63
Benton Harbor 49022 (616) 926-3461

Incorporated in 1951 in MI.
Donor(s): Whirlpool Corp.
Foundation type: Company-sponsored
Financial data (yr. ended 12/31/89): Assets, $13,854,245 (L); gifts received, $3,100,000; expenditures, $3,587,922, including $2,977,474 for 384 grants (high: $980,000; low: $200; average: $100-$65,000), $325,500 for 121 grants to individuals (high: $3,000; low: $1,500; average: $1,500-$3,000) and $164,731 for employee matching gifts.
Purpose and activities: Giving primarily to community funds, youth and social welfare

agencies, cultural programs, health services, and higher education, including scholarships for children of corporation employees and employee matching gifts.
Types of support: Matching funds, operating budgets, annual campaigns, emergency funds, building funds, equipment, research, employee-related scholarships, continuing support, employee matching gifts, endowment funds.
Limitations: Giving limited to communities where major company units are located: Clyde, Findlay, Greenville, and Marion, OH; Evansville, IN; Fort Smith, AR; Lavergne, TN; Oxford, MS; and Columbia, SC. No grants to individuals (except employee-related scholarships), or for endowment funds; no loans.
Application information: Application form not required.
Initial approach: Letter or telephone
Copies of proposal: 1
Deadline(s): Oct. 1
Board meeting date(s): As required
Final notification: 30 to 60 days
Write: Sharron Krieger, Secy. and Exec. Dir.
Officers and Trustees:* Stephen E. Upton,* Pres.; Sharron Krieger, Secy. and Exec. Dir.; Bradley J. Bell, Treas.; William K. Emery, William D. Marohn, Jay Van Den Berg.
Number of staff: 1 full-time professional; 1 full-time support.
Employer Identification Number: 386077342

3279
The White Foundation
4800 Avondale
Bloomfield Hills 48013 (313) 546-6660

Established in 1945.
Donor(s): Glenn E. White, Ruth White.
Foundation type: Independent
Financial data (yr. ended 12/31/89): Assets, $1,103,000 (M); expenditures, $218,000, including $124,000 for 10 grants (high: $47,000; low: $500).
Purpose and activities: Support for Christian churches, colleges, and missions.
Types of support: General purposes.
Limitations: Giving primarily in MI. No grants to individuals.
Application information: Contributes only to pre-selected organizations. Applications not accepted.
Officers: Edna C. White, Pres.; Glenn E. White, V.P. and Treas.; Louise W. Beardslee, V.P.
Number of staff: 1 full-time professional.
Employer Identification Number: 386054883

3280
The John and Elizabeth Whiteley Foundation ⌑
c/o First of America Bank-Central
101 South Washington Sq.
Lansing 48933 (517) 374-5436

Incorporated in 1955 in MI.
Donor(s): Nellie M. Zimmerman.†
Foundation type: Independent
Financial data (yr. ended 12/31/88): Assets, $1,689,437 (M); expenditures, $104,805, including $50,832 for 7 grants (high: $15,000; low: $2,500) and $15,466 for 23 grants to individuals (high: $1,500; low: $600).
Purpose and activities: Grants largely for business education scholarships to needy and deserving students and for Protestant church support.
Types of support: Student aid.
Limitations: Giving limited to Ingham County, MI.
Application information: Application form required for scholarships.
Deadline(s): None
Write: Joseph A. Caruso
Officers: Richard P. Lyman, Pres.; Richard F. Burmeister, V.P.; Douglas E. Gilman, V.P.; Jonathan R. White, Secy.; Romayne E. Hicks, Treas.
Employer Identification Number: 381558108

3281
The Whiting Foundation ⌑
901 Citizens Bank Bldg.
328 South Saginaw St.
Flint 48502 (313) 767-3600

Incorporated in 1940 in MI.
Donor(s): Members of the Johnson family.
Foundation type: Independent
Financial data (yr. ended 6/30/88): Assets, $10,635,106 (M); gifts received, $133,000; expenditures, $310,220, including $278,850 for 33 grants (high: $59,000; low: $150).
Purpose and activities: Giving to further secular and religious education and research of all kinds; to aid and improve the physical, financial, mental, and moral condition of the poor, the sick, the young, the aged, and the disabled among all classes. Support nationally for cancer research.
Types of support: General purposes, special projects.
Limitations: Giving primarily in MI.
Application information:
Initial approach: Concise proposal
Copies of proposal: 1
Deadline(s): Apr. 30
Write: Donald E. Johnson, Secy.
Officers and Trustees: Donald E. Johnson, Jr., Pres.; Donald E. Johnson, Secy.-Treas.; Mary Alice J. Heaton, John T. Lindholm, Linda W.J. Utley.
Employer Identification Number: 386056693

3282
Henry and Harriet Whiting Memorial Foundation ⌑
200 South Riverside
St. Clair 48079

Established in 1950 in MI.
Donor(s): Harriet Clark Whiting.†
Foundation type: Independent
Financial data (yr. ended 12/31/88): Assets, $1,690,834 (M); expenditures, $104,611, including $86,600 for 24 grants (high: $10,000; low: $750).
Purpose and activities: Giving primarily for youth, social services, and churches.
Types of support: General purposes, building funds, operating budgets.
Limitations: Giving primarily in MI. No grants to individuals.
Application information: Contributes only to pre-selected organizations. Applications not accepted.
Officers: Franklin H. Moore, Jr., Pres. and Treas.; Charles Staiger, Secy.
Trustees: Charles F. Moore, Frederick S. Moore.
Employer Identification Number: 386091633

3283
David M. Whitney Fund ⌑
2500 Comerica Bldg.
Detroit 48226

Established in 1949 in MI.
Foundation type: Independent
Financial data (yr. ended 12/31/88): Assets, $1,720,042 (M); gifts received, $80,532; expenditures, $95,917, including $62,500 for grants.
Purpose and activities: Support for social services, educational institutions, cultural organizations, and child welfare.
Limitations: No grants to individuals.
Application information:
Initial approach: Letter
Deadline(s): None
Write: Peter P. Thurber, Pres.
Officers: Peter P. Thurber, Pres.; George E. Parker III, V.P. and Secy.; Richard B. Gushee, V.P. and Treas.
Employer Identification Number: 386040080

3284
Harvey Randall Wickes Foundation ▼
Plaza North, Suite 472
4800 Fashion Sq. Blvd.
Saginaw 48604 (517) 799-1850

Incorporated in 1945 in MI.
Donor(s): Harvey Randall Wickes,† members of the Wickes family and others.
Foundation type: Independent
Financial data (yr. ended 12/31/88): Assets, $22,139,450 (M); expenditures, $1,141,753, including $1,034,384 for 37 grants (high: $250,000; low: $200; average: $5,000-$60,000).
Purpose and activities: Giving for education, including higher education, social service and youth agencies, a community fund, civic affairs groups, hospitals, and cultural activities.
Types of support: Building funds, equipment, renovation projects, operating budgets.
Limitations: Giving limited to the Saginaw, MI, area. No grants to individuals.
Application information: Application form not required.
Initial approach: Letter followed by proposal; no set deadline
Copies of proposal: 1
Deadline(s): Submit proposal preferably 1 month prior to meeting
Board meeting date(s): Jan., Apr., June, and Oct.
Final notification: After meeting
Write: James V. Finkbeiner, Pres.
Officers and Trustees: Melvin J. Zahnow, Chair.; James V. Finkbeiner, Pres.; H.E. Braun, Jr., V.P. and Secy.; Lloyd J. Yeo, Treas.; F.N.

Andersen, R.G. App, G.A. Barber, F.M. Johnson, William W. Kessel, D.F. Wallace.
Number of staff: 1 full-time professional; 1 part-time support.
Employer Identification Number: 386061470

3285
Wickson-Link Memorial Foundation
P.O. Box 3275
3023 Davenport St.
Saginaw 48605 (519) 793-9830

Donor(s): James Wickson,† Meta Wickson.†
Foundation type: Independent
Financial data (yr. ended 12/31/89): Assets, $3,475,000 (M); expenditures, $160,926, including $129,900 for 31 grants (high: $30,000; low: $350).
Purpose and activities: Support for community funds, youth and cultural organizations and higher education.
Limitations: Giving primarily in Saginaw County, MI.
Application information: Application form not required.
Initial approach: Letter
Copies of proposal: 3
Deadline(s): None
Board meeting date(s): Quarterly
Write: Lloyd J. Yeo, Pres.
Officers: Lloyd J. Yeo, Pres. and Treas.; B.J. Humphreys, V.P. and Secy.
Director: C. Ward Lauderbach.
Number of staff: 1 full-time professional.
Employer Identification Number: 386083931

3286
Wilkinson Foundation ⌑
c/o Comerica Bank
Detroit 48275-1022
Application address: Two Woodland Place, Grosse Pointe, MI 48230

Established in 1986 in MI.
Foundation type: Independent
Financial data (yr. ended 1/31/89): Assets, $1,606,025 (M); expenditures, $73,070, including $58,585 for 41 grants (high: $22,850; low: $25).
Purpose and activities: Giving primarily for historic preservation; grants also for higher and secondary education, churches, and environmental causes.
Limitations: Giving limited to southeast MI.
Application information: Application form not required.
Deadline(s): None
Write: Warren S. Wilkinson, Trustee
Trustees: Guerin Wilkinson, Todd Wilkinson, Warren S. Wilkinson, Comerica Bank.
Number of staff: None.
Employer Identification Number: 386497639

3287
Matilda R. Wilson Fund ▼ ⌑
100 Renaissance Ctr., Suite 3377
Detroit 48243 (313) 259-7777

Incorporated in 1944 in MI.
Donor(s): Matilda R. Wilson,† Alfred G. Wilson.†
Foundation type: Independent
Financial data (yr. ended 12/31/88): Assets, $28,372,728 (M); expenditures, $1,536,807, including $1,241,557 for 45 grants (high: $165,000; low: $2,500; average: $10,000-$50,000).
Purpose and activities: Support for culture and art, youth agencies, higher education, hospitals, and social services.
Types of support: Operating budgets, general purposes, building funds, equipment, endowment funds, research, special projects, scholarship funds, matching funds.
Limitations: Giving primarily in southeast MI. No grants to individuals; no loans.
Application information: Application form not required.
Initial approach: Proposal or letter
Copies of proposal: 1
Deadline(s): None
Board meeting date(s): Jan., Apr., July, and Oct.
Write: Frederick C. Nash, Pres.
Officers and Trustees:* Frederick C. Nash,* Pres.; Pierre V. Heftler,* V.P.; Robert M. Surdam,* Treas.
Employer Identification Number: 386087665

3288
Lula C. Wilson Trust
c/o National Bank of Detroit
1116 West Long Lake Rd.
Bloomfield Hills 48013 (313) 645-7306

Trust established in 1963 in MI.
Donor(s): Lula C. Wilson.†
Foundation type: Independent
Financial data (yr. ended 12/31/89): Assets, $1,811,000 (M); expenditures, $110,850, including $93,550 for 20 grants (high: $15,000; low: $1,000; average: $2,000-$5,000).
Purpose and activities: Grants primarily for higher and secondary education, performing arts groups and other cultural programs, youth agencies and family services, hospices and the handicapped, women, and community service agencies.
Types of support: Operating budgets, continuing support, annual campaigns, seed money, emergency funds, building funds, equipment, renovation projects.
Limitations: Giving limited to Pontiac and Oakland County, MI. No grants to individuals, or for endowment funds, research, deficit financing, land acquisition, special projects, publications, conferences, scholarships, fellowships, or matching gifts; no loans.
Publications: 990-PF.
Application information: Application form not required.
Initial approach: Letter
Copies of proposal: 1
Deadline(s): None
Board meeting date(s): As required
Final notification: 1 month
Write: Frederick H. Gravelle, V.P., National Bank of Detroit
Trustee: National Bank of Detroit.
Number of staff: None.
Employer Identification Number: 386058895

3289
Winship Memorial Scholarship Foundation ⌑
c/o Comerica Bank-Battle Creek, Trust Div.
25 West Michigan Mall
Battle Creek 49016 (616) 966-6340

Established in 1961 in MI.
Foundation type: Independent
Financial data (yr. ended 12/31/88): Assets, $2,210,738 (M); expenditures, $138,016, including $102,425 for 86 grants to individuals (high: $1,700; low: $200; average: $1,300).
Purpose and activities: Scholarships only for graduates of Battle Creek area public high schools.
Types of support: Student aid.
Limitations: Giving limited to Battle Creek, MI.
Publications: Annual report, informational brochure, application guidelines.
Application information: Applications processed through local high schools. Application form required.
Deadline(s): Mar. 1
Board meeting date(s): 3rd Wednesday of Mar.
Write: Frances A. Hanson, Exec. Dir.
Officers: Richard L. Brown,* Pres.; Robert D. McFee,* V.P.; Margo S. Brush, Secy.; Thomas A. Oatsman,* Treas.; Frances A. Hanson, Exec. Dir.
Trustees:* Paul Bauman, Richard L. Brown, Joseph A. Davio, Charles W. Elliott, Arlon Elser, George Lindenburg, Robert D. McFee, Al Murray, Bruce Sellers, Bruce Shurtz, William S. Ticknor, John Wager.
Corporate Trustee: Comerica Bank-Battle Creek.
Employer Identification Number: 386092543

3290
Howard H. & Joan M. Wolfe Family Foundation ⌑ ☆
3023 Davenport St.
Saginaw 48602-3698

Established in 1984 in MI.
Donor(s): Howard H. Wolfe.
Foundation type: Independent
Financial data (yr. ended 4/30/89): Assets, $495,183 (M); gifts received, $115,438; expenditures, $120,743, including $120,043 for 7 grants (high: $89,932; low: $1,000).
Purpose and activities: Giving primarily for Presbyterian churches; some support also for higher education and health associations.
Limitations: Giving primarily in Saginaw, MI, and Fort Lauderdale, FL. No grants to individuals.
Application information: Contributes only to pre-selected organizations. Applications not accepted.
Officers: Howard H. Wolfe, Pres.; C. Christopher Wolfe, V.P.
Trustees: Ann H. Doerfler, Victoria R. Mueller.
Employer Identification Number: 382532527

3291
Word Investments, Inc.
3366 Burton St., S.E.
Grand Rapids 49546

Established in 1984 in MI.
Foundation type: Independent

Financial data (yr. ended 12/31/88): Assets, $6,349,368 (M); gifts received, $30,300; expenditures, $864,735, including $381,517 for grants (high: $44,823).
Purpose and activities: Emphasis on Christian missionary programs; support also for education.
Limitations: Giving primarily in MI. No grants to individuals.
Application information: Applications not accepted.
Write: Mr. Clare De Graaf, Pres.
Officers: Clare De Graaf, Pres. and Treas.; Susan De Graaf, Secy.
Employer Identification Number: 382470907

3292
World Heritage Foundation ⌑
One Sunroof Ctr.
Southgate 48195

Established in 1985 in MI.
Donor(s): Heinz C. Prechter, Heinz C. Prechter Charitable Lead Trust.
Foundation type: Independent
Financial data (yr. ended 12/31/87): Assets, $1,312,633 (M); gifts received, $1,190,600; expenditures, $10,000, including $10,000 for 1 grant.
Purpose and activities: Support primarily for a hospital.
Limitations: Giving primarily in Wyandotte, MI.
Application information: Contributes only to pre-selected organizations. Applications not accepted.
Officers and Directors: Heinz C. Prechter, Chair.; Waltraud Prechter, Pres.; Evangeline Redmer, Secy.-Treas.; Gerald E. Szpotek, Secy.-Treas.
Employer Identification Number: 382640416

3294
The Youth Foundation of America ⌑
300 Park Ave.
Petoskey 49770 (616) 347-4195

Incorporated in 1947 in MI.
Foundation type: Independent
Financial data (yr. ended 12/31/88): Assets, $179,769 (M); gifts received, $191,995; expenditures, $195,197, including $138,700 for 20 grants (high: $18,000; low: $3,000).
Purpose and activities: Support of local summer camps for underprivileged and handicapped children.
Limitations: Giving limited to MI. No grants to individuals.
Application information: Application form not required.
Initial approach: Letter
Copies of proposal: 1
Deadline(s): None
Board meeting date(s): Annually
Write: Paul W. Brown, V.P.
Officers and Trustees: Clarine R. Bales, Pres.; Paul W. Brown, V.P. and Secy.-Treas.; Robert Bales, Jr.
Number of staff: None.
Employer Identification Number: 386090960

3295
Mary and George Herbert Zimmerman Foundation ⌑
220 Bagley, Suite 408
Detroit 48226

Established in 1937 in MI.
Donor(s): Members of the Zimmerman family.
Foundation type: Independent
Financial data (yr. ended 12/31/88): Assets, $1,911,403 (M); expenditures, $78,671, including $75,320 for 30 grants (high: $30,000; low: $250).
Purpose and activities: Support for a hospital, health services, and education.
Limitations: No grants to individuals.
Application information: Contributes only to pre-selected organizations. Applications not accepted.
Officers and Directors: Louis G. Zimmerman, Pres.; Elaine Z. Peck, Exec. V.P.; Sheila Pette, Sr. V.P.; Andrew G. Bato, V.P.; Doris S. Bato, Secy.; G.H. Zimmerman, Treas.
Employer Identification Number: 381685880

MINNESOTA

3296
Norman & Lisette Ackerberg Foundation ⌑ ☆
100 South Fifth St., Suite 1500
Minneapolis 55402 (612) 335-1500

Established in 1984 in MN.
Donor(s): Norman J. Ackerberg, Lisette L. Ackerberg.
Foundation type: Independent
Financial data (yr. ended 12/31/88): Assets, $3,620 (M); gifts received, $271,200; expenditures, $1,315,703, including $1,310,695 for 26 grants (high: $1,289,340).
Purpose and activities: Support for Jewish organizations, including a welfare fund and a school.
Limitations: Giving primarily in MN. No grants to individuals.
Application information:
Initial approach: Letter
Deadline(s): None
Write: Harold D. Field, Jr., V.P.
Officers and Trustees: Norman J. Ackerberg, Pres.; Harold D. Field, Jr., V.P.; Lisette L. Ackerberg.
Employer Identification Number: 411499830

3297
Adams-Mastrovich Family Foundation ⌑
c/o Norwest Bank-Minneapolis, N.A.
Eighth & Marquette
Minneapolis 55479-0063

Established in 1957 in MN.
Donor(s): Mary Adams Balmat.
Foundation type: Independent
Financial data (yr. ended 12/31/87): Assets, $1,317,499 (M); gifts received, $25,833; expenditures, $26,516, including $3,950 for 8 grants (high: $1,000; low: $100).
Purpose and activities: Support primarily for Catholic churches and welfare-related activities; giving also for the performing arts.
Limitations: No grants to individuals.
Application information: Contributes only to pre-selected organizations. Applications not accepted.
Trustee: Northwest Bank-Minneapolis, N.A.
Employer Identification Number: 416014092

3298
AHS Foundation
c/o First Trust Co.
W-555, First National Bank Bldg.
St. Paul 55101 (612) 291-5128

Established in 1968 in MN.
Donor(s): Arthur H. Schubert,† Helen D. Schubert.
Foundation type: Independent
Financial data (yr. ended 06/30/89): Assets, $1,740,201 (M); expenditures, $93,288, including $85,160 for 23 grants (high: $10,000; low: $960; average: $1,000-$5,000).
Purpose and activities: Giving primarily for education, the arts, social services, conservation, health programs and services for the handicapped, and community programs.
Types of support: General purposes, building funds, capital campaigns, operating budgets.
Limitations: No grants to individuals; no loans.
Application information: Application form not required.
Initial approach: Letter
Copies of proposal: 2
Deadline(s): None
Board meeting date(s): July
Final notification: 1 to 3 months
Write: Leland W. Schubert, Jr., Pres.
Officers and Directors: Leland W. Schubert, Jr.,* Pres.; John D. Schubert,* 1st V.P.; Gage A. Schubert, 2nd V.P.; John L. Jerry,* Secy.-Treas.; William Frels.
Members:* Terence N. Doyle, Jane Rehmke, Christopher Schubert, David A. Schubert, Helen D. Schubert, Leland Schubert.
Number of staff: None.
Employer Identification Number: 410944654

3299
Charles and Ellora Alliss Educational Foundation ▼
c/o First Trust, N.A.
Two West, P.O. Box 64704
St. Paul 55164 (612) 291-5132

Trust established in 1958 in MN.
Donor(s): Charles C. Alliss,† Ellora Martha Alliss.†
Foundation type: Independent
Financial data (yr. ended 12/31/88): Assets, $48,403,047 (M); expenditures, $3,268,299, including $3,033,800 for 21 grants (high: $344,100; low: $28,260; average: $40,000-$300,000).
Purpose and activities: To further the education of young people by granting

scholarships, fellowships, gifts, and awards; grants made in lump sums solely to institutions in support of undergraduate aid programs administered by the grantee institutions.
Types of support: Scholarship funds, continuing support.
Limitations: Giving limited to MN educational institutions for scholarship programs. No grants to individuals, or for general purposes, capital funds, endowment funds, research, operating budgets, special projects, or matching gifts; no loans.
Application information: Application form not required.
Initial approach: Letter with background
Copies of proposal: 1
Deadline(s): Submit proposal preferably in Aug. and Sept.; no set deadline
Board meeting date(s): Mar., June, Sept., and Dec.
Final notification: 3 months
Write: Jeffrey T. Peterson, Secy.
Officer: Jeffrey T. Peterson, Secy.
Trustees: Sidney Barrows, John B. Davis, Jr., Frank Hammond, Harry L. Holtz, Frederick T. Weyenhaeuser, First Trust, N.A.
Number of staff: None.
Employer Identification Number: 416011054

3300
Marshall H. and Nellie Alworth Memorial Fund
506 Alworth Bldg.
Duluth 55802 (218) 722-9366

Incorporated in 1949 in MN.
Donor(s): Marshall W. Alworth.†
Foundation type: Independent
Financial data (yr. ended 12/31/89): Assets, $4,337,818 (M); gifts received, $682,725; expenditures, $839,208, including $720,011 for 400 grants to individuals (high: $2,500; low: $667; average: $1,700-$2,500).
Purpose and activities: Awards scholarships for higher education to high school graduates who intend to specialize in the sciences, including chemistry, physics, mathematics, geology, biological sciences, engineering, nursing, and medicine.
Types of support: Student aid.
Limitations: Giving limited to graduates for high schools in 15 northeastern MN counties. No grants for building or endowment funds or matching gifts; no loans.
Publications: Program policy statement, application guidelines.
Application information: Application form available from high schools in northern MN. Application form required.
Initial approach: Letter
Copies of proposal: 1
Deadline(s): Submit proposal preferably in Dec. through Feb.; deadline Mar. 1
Board meeting date(s): May
Final notification: June
Write: Richard H. Carlson, Exec. Dir.
Officers: James Claypool, Pres.; John M. Donovan,* Secy.; Donald B. Crassweller,* Treas.; Richard H. Carlson, Exec. Dir.
Directors:* Carol Fryberger, William E. Jacott, M.D., Peter J. Johnson, Joseph A. Pittel.
Number of staff: 1 full-time professional; 1 full-time support.
Employer Identification Number: 410797340

3301
Andersen Foundation ▼ ⌑
c/o Andersen Corp.
Bayport 55003 (612) 439-5150

Incorporated in 1959 in MN.
Donor(s): Fred C. Andersen.†
Foundation type: Independent
Financial data (yr. ended 12/31/88): Assets, $232,768,426 (M); expenditures, $9,517,144, including $8,861,650 for 98 grants (high: $1,103,000; low: $400).
Purpose and activities: Grants largely for higher education; support also for cultural programs, medical research, hospitals, and civic affairs.
Limitations: No support for state or federally funded colleges or universities. No grants to individuals.
Application information:
Deadline(s): None
Board meeting date(s): 3 or 4 times a year, as required
Final notification: Varies
Write: Lisa Carlstrom, Asst. Secy.
Officers and Directors: Katherine B. Andersen, Pres.; Earl C. Swanson, V.P. and Secy.; Keith R. Clements, Treas.; W.R. Foster.
Number of staff: 1 part-time professional.
Employer Identification Number: 416020920

3302
Elmer L. & Eleanor J. Andersen Foundation
1483 Bussard Court
Arden Hills 55112

Established in 1957 in MN.
Donor(s): Elmer L. Andersen, Eleanor J. Andersen.
Foundation type: Independent
Financial data (yr. ended 11/30/89): Assets, $2,869,556 (M); expenditures, $168,319, including $140,750 for 44 grants (high: $55,000; low: $500; average: $500-$5,000).
Purpose and activities: Giving for higher education, the environment, music and the arts, and community services.
Types of support: Operating budgets, publications, capital campaigns.
Limitations: Giving limited to MN, with emphasis on the St. Paul area. No grants to individuals.
Publications: 990-PF, annual report.
Application information: Application form not required.
Initial approach: Proposal
Deadline(s): Submit proposal in Feb., May, Aug., or Nov.; deadline 1 month before board meetings
Board meeting date(s): First week of Mar., June, Sept., and Dec.
Final notification: 3 months
Write: Philip L. Roe, Exec. Dir.
Officers and Directors:* Elmer L. Andersen,* Pres.; Eleanor J. Andersen, V.P.; Samuel H. Morgan, Secy.; Julian Andersen,* Treas.; Philip L. Roe, Exec. Dir.; Barbara B. Miller.
Number of staff: 1 part-time professional.
Employer Identification Number: 416032984

3303
Hugh J. Andersen Foundation ▼
287 Central Ave.
Bayport 55003 (612) 439-1557

Established in 1962.
Donor(s): Hugh J. Andersen,† Jane K. Andersen,† Katherine B. Andersen.
Foundation type: Independent
Financial data (yr. ended 02/28/89): Assets, $11,963,912 (M); expenditures, $1,608,174, including $1,525,832 for 121 grants (high: $143,400; low: $350; average: $1,500-$20,000).
Purpose and activities: Emphasis on social service and child and youth programs, and health issues.
Types of support: Research, operating budgets, seed money, special projects, capital campaigns, equipment, general purposes, annual campaigns, renovation projects, endowment funds.
Limitations: Giving primarily in MN, especially the Bayport area, St. Paul, and western WI. No grants to individuals, or for scholarships or fellowships; no loans.
Publications: Annual report (including application guidelines).
Application information: Application form required.
Initial approach: Letter or proposal
Copies of proposal: 1
Deadline(s): Apr. 1, July 1, Oct. 1, and Dec. 1
Board meeting date(s): May, Aug., Nov., and Jan.
Final notification: Approximately 3 months
Write: Carol F. Andersen, Pres. or Peggie Scott, Grants Consultant
Officers and Trustees:* Carol F. Andersen,* Pres.; Sarah J. Andersen,* V.P.; Christine E. Andersen,* Treas.
Number of staff: 2
Employer Identification Number: 416020914

3304
Ankeny Foundation ☆
c/o Sargent Management Co.
1300 TCF Tower
Minneapolis 55402

Established in 1963.
Donor(s): DeWalt H. Ankeny, Jr., Sally A. Anson, Kendall A. Mix, Michael H. Ankeny.
Foundation type: Independent
Financial data (yr. ended 03/31/88): Assets, $1,074,272 (M); expenditures, $81,174, including $65,979 for 61 grants (high: $5,000; low: $25).
Purpose and activities: Support for social and human services, higher education, and cultural programs, including the performing arts.
Types of support: Annual campaigns, capital campaigns, endowment funds, operating budgets, special projects.
Limitations: Giving primarily in MN, with emphasis on Minneapolis.
Application information: Written applications not encouraged; grants to new organizations seldom considered. Application form not required.
Write: DeWalt H. Ankeny, Jr., Pres.

Officers and Trustees:* DeWalt H. Ankeny, Jr.,* Pres.; Sally A. Anson,* V.P.; Kendall A. Mix,* Secy.; Michael H. Ankeny,* Treas.
Employer Identification Number: 416024188

3305
Athwin Foundation
1420 Midwest Plaza West
Minneapolis 55402 (612) 340-3618
Application address: 801 Nicollet Mall, Suite 1420, Minneapolis, MN 55402; Tel.: (612) 340-3616

Trust established in 1956 in MN.
Donor(s): Atherton Bean, Winifred W. Bean.
Foundation type: Independent
Financial data (yr. ended 12/31/89): Assets, $3,930,564 (M); gifts received, $15,750; expenditures, $1,009,604, including $985,154 for 65 grants (high: $500,000; low: $35; average: $1,000-$5,000).
Purpose and activities: Support for educational, cultural, religious, and community welfare programs.
Types of support: Operating budgets, special projects.
Limitations: Giving primarily in the Minneapolis-St. Paul, MN, area; some giving also in Phoenix, AZ, and Claremont, CA. No grants to individuals, or for scholarships or fellowships; no loans.
Publications: Annual report.
Application information: Application form not required.
Initial approach: Proposal
Copies of proposal: 5
Deadline(s): None
Board meeting date(s): Quarterly
Final notification: 60 days
Write: Henry H. Nowicki, Managing Dir.
Trustees: Atherton Bean, Bruce W. Bean, Mary F. Bean, Winifred W. Bean, Eleanor Nolan.
Number of staff: 1 part-time support.
Employer Identification Number: 416021773

3306
Baker Foundation ⌑
4900 IDS Center
Minneapolis 55402 (612) 332-7479

Trust established in 1947; incorporated in 1954 in MN.
Donor(s): Morris T. Baker.†
Foundation type: Independent
Financial data (yr. ended 12/31/88): Assets, $3,378,283 (M); expenditures, $214,922, including $189,750 for 50 grants (high: $50,000; low: $100).
Purpose and activities: Emphasis on medical research, higher education, community funds, conservation, youth agencies, and music.
Types of support: Annual campaigns, building funds, capital campaigns, general purposes, operating budgets.
Limitations: Giving primarily in MN. No grants to individuals.
Application information: Application form not required.
Initial approach: Letter
Copies of proposal: 1
Deadline(s): None
Board meeting date(s): As required
Write: William M. Baker, Pres., or James W. Peter, Secy.
Officers and Directors: William M. Baker, Pres.; Roger L. Baker, V.P.; David C. Sherman, V.P.; James W. Peter, Secy.-Treas.; Morris T. Baker III, Doris G. Baker, Nancy W. Baker, Mary Baker-Philbin, Charles C. Pineo III, Linda Baker Pineo, Sandra B. Sherman.
Employer Identification Number: 416022591

3307
Peggy Bauervic Foundation
(Formerly Bauervic-Carroll Foundation)
92 Mississippi River Blvd. North
St. Paul 55104-5613 (612) 293-0326
Application address: 26 East Exchange St., Suite 312, St. Paul, MN 55101

Established in 1984 in MI.
Foundation type: Independent
Financial data (yr. ended 12/31/88): Assets, $2,726,203 (M); expenditures, $333,325, including $255,465 for 18 grants (high: $25,000; low: $150).
Purpose and activities: Giving primarily for education, social services, and medical research.
Limitations: No grants to individuals.
Application information: Application form required.
Initial approach: Letter requesting application
Copies of proposal: 1
Deadline(s): Oct. 1
Write: Peggy Maitland, Pres.
Officers and Directors:* Peggy L. Maitland,* Pres. and Secy.; Lynne M. Carroll,* V.P.; Jane Carroll,* Treas.; Rose Bauervic-Wright, Jeffrey Carroll, Stuart Maitland.
Employer Identification Number: 382494383

3308
Bayport Foundation, Inc. ⌑
287 Central Ave.
Bayport 55003 (612) 439-1557

Incorporated in 1941 in MN.
Donor(s): Andersen Corp.
Foundation type: Independent
Financial data (yr. ended 11/30/88): Assets, $18,639,584 (M); gifts received, $1,000,000; expenditures, $793,425, including $668,411 for 112 grants (high: $71,000; low: $131).
Purpose and activities: Emphasis on medical education, hospitals and medical research, educational programs, community projects, youth agencies, and religious organizations.
Limitations: Giving primarily in MN. No grants to individuals.
Application information:
Deadline(s): None
Write: Katherine B. Andersen, Trustee
Officers: W.A. Wellman, Pres.; Albert D. Hulings, V.P.; Mary Andersen Hulings, V.P.; Harold C. Meissner, V.P.; Loren R. Croone, Secy.-Treas.
Trustees: Katherine B. Andersen, Earl C. Swanson.
Employer Identification Number: 416020912

3309
The Beim Foundation
6750 France Ave. South, No. 149
Minneapolis 55435 (612) 920-1556

Incorporated in 1957 in MN.
Donor(s): N.C. Beim,† Raymond N. Beim.
Foundation type: Independent
Financial data (yr. ended 12/31/88): Assets, $4,418,760 (M); expenditures, $206,513, including $187,000 for 45 grants (high: $15,000; low: $250; average: $1,000-$10,000).
Purpose and activities: General charitable giving.
Types of support: Seed money, building funds, equipment.
Limitations: Giving limited to Minneapolis, MN, and vicinity. No grants to individuals, or for operating budgets, continuing support, annual campaigns, emergency funds, or deficit financing; no loans.
Application information: Application form not required.
Initial approach: Letter
Copies of proposal: 1
Deadline(s): Sept. 30
Board meeting date(s): Oct. and Dec.
Final notification: By Dec. 15th
Write: William H. Beim, Pres.
Officers and Directors: William H. Beim, Pres.; Raymond N. Beim, V.P.; William H. Beim, Jr., Secy.-Treas.; Patricia Arnold, Judith McKim.
Number of staff: None.
Employer Identification Number: 416022529

3310
David Winton Bell Foundation ⌑ ☆
10000 Hwy. 55 West, Suite 450
Minneapolis 55441

Established in 1955 in NY.
Foundation type: Independent
Financial data (yr. ended 12/31/88): Assets, $1,098,693 (M); expenditures, $47,639, including $37,250 for 18 grants (high: $6,500; low: $500).
Purpose and activities: Giving primarily to wildlife and other conservation efforts; support also for medical research and health associations, higher and other education, and the arts, including a natural history museum.
Limitations: Giving primarily in Minneapolis, MN, and Manitoba, Canada.
Application information:
Initial approach: Letter or proposal
Deadline(s): None
Write: Robert O. Mathson, Exec. Secy.
Officer: Robert O. Mathson, Exec. Secy.
Trustees: Charles H. Bell, Lucy W. Bell, John M. Hartwell, Lucy B. Hartwell.
Employer Identification Number: 416023104

3311
James F. Bell Foundation ⌑
10000 Hwy. 55 West, Suite 450
Minneapolis 55441

Trust established in 1955 in MN.
Donor(s): James Ford Bell.†
Foundation type: Independent
Financial data (yr. ended 12/31/88): Assets, $8,456,554 (M); expenditures, $491,884,

including $412,960 for 55 grants (high: $75,000; low: $500).
Purpose and activities: Emphasis on a local university library and cultural programs; support also for wildlife preservation and conservation and youth agencies.
Limitations: Giving primarily in MN.
Application information:
Initial approach: Proposal
Deadline(s): None
Write: Robert O. Mathson, Exec. Secy.
Officer: Robert O. Mathson, Exec. Secy.
Trustees: Ford W. Bell, Samuel H. Bell, Jr., David B. Hartwell.
Employer Identification Number: 341018779

3312
Bemis Company Foundation
800 Northstar Ctr.
Minneapolis 55402 (612) 340-6018

Trust established in 1959 in MO.
Donor(s): Bemis Co., Inc.
Foundation type: Company-sponsored
Financial data (yr. ended 12/31/87): Assets, $2,461,936 (M); expenditures, $563,740, including $474,665 for 185 grants (high: $80,000; low: $25) and $84,677 for 208 employee matching gifts.
Purpose and activities: Grants largely for scholarship programs for children of employees, state associations of independent colleges, an educational institution matching gift program, community funds, hospitals, and cultural and civic affairs programs.
Types of support: Annual campaigns, building funds, employee-related scholarships, employee matching gifts, continuing support.
Limitations: No support for religious or political purposes. No grants to individuals, or for endowment funds, research, educational capital programs, or trips or tours; no loans.
Publications: Corporate giving report, application guidelines.
Application information: Application form not required.
Initial approach: Proposal
Copies of proposal: 1
Deadline(s): None
Board meeting date(s): Mar., June, Sept., and Dec.
Officer and Trustees: Edward J. Dougherty, Exec. Dir.; Benjamin R. Field, L.E. Schwanke.
Number of staff: 2
Employer Identification Number: 416038616

3313
F. R. Bigelow Foundation ▼ ⌑
1120 Norwest Ctr.
St. Paul 55101 (612) 224-5463

Trust established in 1934; incorporated in 1946 in MN.
Donor(s): Frederick Russell Bigelow,† Eileen Bigelow.
Foundation type: Independent
Financial data (yr. ended 12/31/88): Assets, $57,559,323 (M); expenditures, $2,883,341, including $2,363,737 for grants (average: $10,000-$100,000).
Purpose and activities: Support for higher and secondary education, social services, including a community fund, arts and humanities, and health.
Types of support: Seed money, emergency funds, equipment, land acquisition, building funds, scholarship funds, matching funds, special projects, continuing support, renovation projects.
Limitations: Giving limited to the greater St. Paul, MN, metropolitan area. No grants to individuals, or for endowment funds; giving rarely for operating budgets; no loans.
Publications: Annual report (including application guidelines), application guidelines.
Application information: Application form required.
Initial approach: Telephone, letter, or proposal
Copies of proposal: 1
Deadline(s): 3 months prior to board meetings
Board meeting date(s): June, Aug., and Dec.
Final notification: 3 to 4 months
Write: Paul A. Verret, Secy.-Treas.
Officer: Paul A. Verret, Secy.-Treas.
Trustees: Carl B. Drake, Jr., Chair.; Robert S. Davis, Malcolm W. McDonald, Eileen Bigelow McMillan, Kathleen Culman Ridder, Roger B. Shepard, Jr.
Number of staff: None.
Employer Identification Number: 510232651

3314
The Blandin Foundation ▼
(Formerly Charles K. Blandin Foundation)
100 Pokegama Ave. North
Grand Rapids 55744 (218) 326-0523

Incorporated in 1941 in MN.
Donor(s): Charles K. Blandin.†
Foundation type: Independent
Financial data (yr. ended 12/31/89): Assets, $180,804,275 (M); qualifying distributions, $8,172,694, including $4,798,293 for 170 grants (high: $403,070; low: $600; average: $5,000-$50,000), $293,669 for 467 grants to individuals (high: $2,417; low: $167; average: $500-$1,000), $1,055,732 for foundation-administered programs and $2,025,000 for loans.
Purpose and activities: Giving in six priority areas for rural MN: 1) leadership development; 2) economic development; 3) health and human services; 4) arts and humanities; 5) environment; and 6) educational opportunities, including scholarships for undergraduates and vocational study for recent graduates under the age of 22 who attended an Itasca County, Hill City, or Remer, MN, high school.
Types of support: Seed money, matching funds, scholarship funds, program-related investments, special projects, consulting services, technical assistance, student aid.
Limitations: Giving limited to MN, with emphasis on rural areas; scholarships limited to graduates of an Itasca County, Hill City, or Remer high school. No support for religious activities, camping programs, medical research, or travel. No grants to individuals (other than for scholarships), or for operating budgets, continuing support, annual campaigns, deficit financing, capital funds (outside home community), endowments, publications, conferences, or seminars.
Publications: Annual report, program policy statement, grants list, informational brochure (including application guidelines).
Application information: Scholarship applicants should call or write to the foundation for deadlines and other information. Application form not required.
Initial approach: Letter or visit
Copies of proposal: 1
Deadline(s): Feb. 1, May. 1, Aug. 1, and Nov. 1
Board meeting date(s): During the first two weeks of Feb., May, Aug., and Nov.
Final notification: 2 weeks after board meeting
Write: Paul M. Olson, Pres.
Officers: Margaret Matalamaki,* Chair.; Bruce Stender, Vice-Chair.; Paul M. Olson, Pres.; Kathryn Jensen, V.P.; Mary Jo Jess,* Secy.; Russell E. Virden,* Treas.
Trustees:* Robert L. Bullard, Robert L. Comstock, Jr., Henry Doerr, Peter A. Heegaard, James R. Oppenheimer, Steve Shaler, Brian Vergin.
Number of staff: 5 full-time professional; 1 part-time professional; 4 full-time support; 3 part-time support.
Employer Identification Number: 416038619

3315
Boulevard Foundation ⌑ ☆
(Formerly The Gelco Foundation)
4670 Norwest Ctr.
90 South Seventh St.
Minneapolis 55402

Incorporated in 1973 in MN as The Gelco Foundation; name changed in 1988.
Foundation type: Independent
Financial data (yr. ended 06/30/89): Assets, $1,844,346 (M); gifts received, $5,000; expenditures, $185,122, including $182,989 for 259 grants (high: $80,000; low: $100).
Purpose and activities: Giving primarily for the arts, media and communications, higher education, social services, and civic affairs.
Types of support: Annual campaigns, operating budgets, general purposes, special projects.
Limitations: Giving primarily in MN, with emphasis on the Minneapolis-St. Paul area. No support for political or fraternal organizations, or for religious organizations for sectarian purposes. No grants to individuals, or for scholarships, fellowships, fundraising events, medical research, or matching gifts; no loans.
Application information: Application form not required.
Initial approach: Proposal
Copies of proposal: 1
Deadline(s): Apr. 15
Board meeting date(s): Usually in Jan. and June
Write: Larry Waller
Officers: N. Bud Grossman, Pres.; Sidney Barrows, V.P. and Secy.
Employer Identification Number: 237302799

3316
Otto Bremer Foundation ▼
55 East Fifth St., Suite 700
St. Paul 55101 (612) 227-8036

Trust established in 1944 in MN.
Donor(s): Otto Bremer.†
Foundation type: Independent
Financial data (yr. ended 12/31/89): Assets, $82,496,981 (M); expenditures, $5,367,631, including $4,901,150 for 522 grants (high: $100,000; low: $85; average: $1,000-$25,000) and $178,000 for 5 loans.
Purpose and activities: Emphasis on rural poverty and combating racism. Support also for post-secondary education, human services, health, religion, and community affairs.
Types of support: Seed money, emergency funds, building funds, equipment, special projects, matching funds, scholarship funds, conferences and seminars, technical assistance, program-related investments, internships, continuing support, loans, operating budgets.
Limitations: Giving limited to MN, ND, and WI where there are Bremer Bank affiliates, and to organizations addressing poverty in the city of St. Paul. No support for national health organizations. No grants to individuals, or for endowment funds, medical research, or professorships.
Publications: Annual report (including application guidelines).
Application information: Application form not required.
Initial approach: Letter or telephone
Copies of proposal: 1
Deadline(s): Submit proposal at least 3 months before funding decision is desired
Board meeting date(s): Monthly
Final notification: 3 months
Write: John Kostishack, Exec. Dir.
Officer: John Kostishack, Exec. Dir.
Trustees: William H. Lipschultz, Robert J. Reardon, Gordon Shepard.
Number of staff: 3 full-time professional.
Employer Identification Number: 416019050

3317
The Bush Foundation ▼
East 900 First National Bank Bldg.
332 Minnesota St.
St. Paul 55101 (612) 227-0891

Incorporated in 1953 in MN.
Donor(s): Archibald Bush,† Mrs. Archibald Bush.†
Foundation type: Independent
Financial data (yr. ended 11/30/89): Assets, $417,968,000 (M); expenditures, $22,051,493, including $15,546,152 for 216 grants (high: $1,000,000; low: $4,000; average: $20,000-$500,000) and $1,841,341 for grants to individuals.
Purpose and activities: Support largely for education, arts and humanities, delivery of health care, and social service and welfare agencies. Also operates the Bush Leadership Fellows Program in MN, ND, SD, and western WI, the Bush Fellowships for Artists in MN, ND, and SD, and the Bush Clinical Fellows program in rural areas of MN, ND, and SD.
Types of support: Fellowships, matching funds, endowment funds, special projects, seed money, continuing support, capital campaigns, renovation projects.
Limitations: Giving primarily in MN, ND, and SD. No support for other private foundations, research in biomedical and health sciences, or for hospital construction. No grants to individuals (except for fellowships), or for deficit financing; generally no grants for continuing operating support; no loans.
Publications: Annual report, application guidelines, program policy statement, financial statement.
Application information: Application form not required.
Initial approach: Letter or telephone
Copies of proposal: 2
Deadline(s): 3 1/2 months before board meetings
Board meeting date(s): Feb., Apr. (odd-numbered years only), June, and Oct.
Final notification: 10 days after board meetings
Write: Humphrey Doermann, Pres.
Officers: Diana E. Murphy,* Chair.; Beatrix A. Hamburg,* 1st Vice-Chair.; Merlin E. Dewing,* 2nd Vice-Chair.; Humphrey Doermann, Pres.; Hess Kline,* Secy.; Anita M. Pampusch,* Treas.
Directors:* Thomas J. Clifford, Phyllis B. France, Ellen Z. Green, Thomas E. Holloran, Richard D. McFarland, John A. McHugh, John F. Nash, Kennon V. Rothchild, James P. Shannon, Frank B. Wilderson, Jr.
Number of staff: 7 full-time professional; 4 full-time support; 2 part-time support.
Employer Identification Number: 416017815

3318
Business Incentives Foundation ⌑
P.O. Box 1610
Minneapolis 55440

Established in 1979 in MN.
Donor(s): Business Incentives, Inc., Animal Fair, Inc.
Foundation type: Company-sponsored
Financial data (yr. ended 9/30/88): Assets, $34,086 (M); gifts received, $228,000; expenditures, $314,890, including $314,104 for 14 grants (high: $303,000; low: $25).
Purpose and activities: Giving primarily for education and social services.
Application information: Contributes only to pre-selected organizations. Applications not accepted.
Officers: Guy Schoenecker, Pres. and Treas.; Lila M. Johnson, V.P. and Secy.
Director: James E. O'Brien.
Employer Identification Number: 411369001

3319
Patrick and Aimee Butler Family Foundation
E-1420 First National Bank Bldg.
332 Minnesota St.
St. Paul 55101-1369 (612) 222-2565

Incorporated in 1951 in MN.
Donor(s): Patrick Butler,† and family.
Foundation type: Independent
Financial data (yr. ended 12/31/89): Assets, $9,196,484 (M); gifts received, $450,000; expenditures, $748,601, including $714,900 for 100 grants (average: $1,500).
Purpose and activities: Support for Catholic institutions outside the U.S., higher education, chemical dependency, visual arts, museums and other cultural institutions, health, women, social services, human services, and the environment.
Types of support: Continuing support, annual campaigns, building funds, matching funds, special projects, endowment funds.
Limitations: Giving primarily in the St. Paul and Minneapolis, MN, area; and to Catholic missions outside the U.S. No support for criminal justice, secondary and elementary education, medical research, performing arts, employment, vocational programs, or economic education. No grants to individuals; no loans.
Publications: Financial statement, annual report, informational brochure (including application guidelines).
Application information: Application form required.
Initial approach: Letter of intent; call before submitting request for capital campaign or endowment funds
Copies of proposal: 1
Deadline(s): May 1
Board meeting date(s): June and Oct.
Final notification: July 1 and Nov. 1
Write: Sandra K. Butler, Prog. Officer
Officers: Peter M. Butler,* Pres.; Patrick Butler, Jr.,* V.P.; Terence N. Doyle, Secy.; John K. Butler,* Treas.
Trustees:* Patricia Butler, Sandra K. Butler, Hall James Peterson, Kate B. Peterson.
Number of staff: 1 part-time support.
Employer Identification Number: 416009902

3320
The Cargill Foundation ▼
P.O. Box 9300
Minneapolis 55440 (612) 475-6122

Incorporated in 1952 in MN.
Donor(s): Cargill Charitable Trust, Cargill, Inc.
Foundation type: Company-sponsored
Financial data (yr. ended 12/31/89): Assets, $35,700,000 (M); expenditures, $2,462,168, including $2,462,168 for 134 grants (high: $320,000; low: $1,000; average: $1,000-$10,000).
Purpose and activities: Emphasis on education and social service programs; limited support for health, cultural programs, and civic affairs.
Types of support: Operating budgets, continuing support, general purposes, special projects, capital campaigns.
Limitations: Giving primarily in the seven-county Minneapolis-St. Paul, MN, metropolitan area. No support for religious organizations for religious purposes. No grants to individuals, or for endowment funds, matching gifts, research, demonstration projects, publications, films or videos, travel, conferences, or fellowships; no loans.
Publications: Informational brochure (including application guidelines).
Application information: Application form required.
Initial approach: Telephone
Copies of proposal: 1

Deadline(s): Feb. 1 for educational grants; Mar. 1 for health grants; June 1 for social programs; Oct. 1 for cultural programs
Board meeting date(s): Apr., June, Sept., and Dec.
Final notification: 2 weeks to 1 month after board meetings
Write: Audrey Tulberg, Prog. and Admin. Dir.
Officers and Directors:* James R. Cargill,* V.P.; Peter Dorsey,* V.P.; Henry S. Kingman, Jr., V.P.; Cargill MacMillan, Jr.,* V.P.; Walter B. Saunders, V.P.
Number of staff: 1 full-time professional; 1 full-time support; 1 part-time support.
Employer Identification Number: 416020221

3321
The Curtis L. Carlson Foundation ¤
12755 State Hwy. 55
Minneapolis 55441

Incorporated in 1959 in MN.
Donor(s): Curtis L. Carlson.
Foundation type: Independent
Financial data (yr. ended 12/31/88): Assets, $111,061 (M); gifts received, $101,000; expenditures, $256,818, including $254,977 for 81 grants (high: $100,000; low: $20).
Purpose and activities: Giving for music and the arts, social service agencies, higher education and schools, and Scandinavian intercultural organizations.
Limitations: Giving primarily in MN. No grants to individuals, or for endowment funds, conferences, travel, or athletic events.
Application information:
Initial approach: Proposal
Deadline(s): Sept. 1 for end of calendar year
Final notification: 2 to 4 months
Officers: Curtis L. Carlson, Pres. and Treas.; Arleen E. Carlson, V.P.; Rodney M. Wilson, Secy.
Employer Identification Number: 416028973

3322
Carolyn Foundation
1300 TCF Tower
Minneapolis 55402 (612) 339-7101

Trust established in 1964 in MN.
Donor(s): Carolyn McKnight Christian.†
Foundation type: Independent
Financial data (yr. ended 12/31/89): Assets, $22,243,943 (M); expenditures, $1,174,623, including $989,665 for 37 grants (high: $100,000; low: $1,300; average: $4-$20,000).
Purpose and activities: Priorities include education, culture, health and welfare, including child welfare, the environment, women, and the disadvantaged.
Types of support: General purposes.
Limitations: Giving primarily in the metropolitan areas of New Haven, CT, and Minneapolis-St. Paul, MN. No support for political or veterans' groups, fraternal societies, or religious organizations for religious purposes. No grants to individuals, or for endowment funds, annual fund drives, deficit funding, costs of litigation, or continuing support; no loans.
Publications: Annual report (including application guidelines).
Application information: Application form not required.
Initial approach: Letter
Copies of proposal: 1
Deadline(s): Submit proposal Jan. and Feb. for minor grants (under $10,000) and between Jan. and June for major grants ($10,000 and larger); board awards major grants at Dec. meeting; deadlines Mar. 1 for minor grants; July 1 for major grants
Board meeting date(s): June and Dec.
Final notification: June and Dec.
Write: Carol J. Fetzer, Exec. Dir.
Officers and Trustees:* Lucy C. Mitchell,* Chair.; Guido Calabresi,* Vice-Chair.; Carol J. Fetzer,* Secy. and Exec. Dir.; Edwin L. Crosby,* Treas.; Beatrice C. Booth, Benton J. Case, Jr., Eugenie T. Copp, Franklin M. Crosby III, G. Christian Crosby, Sumner McK. Crosby, Jr., Thomas M. Crosby, Jr., Carolyn C. Graham.
Number of staff: None.
Employer Identification Number: 416044416

3323
CENEX Foundation
5600 CENEX Dr.
Inver Grove Heights 55075 (612) 451-5105

Trust established in 1947 in MN.
Donor(s): Central Exchange Agency.
Foundation type: Company-sponsored
Financial data (yr. ended 11/30/88): Assets, $3,124,110 (M); expenditures, $270,173, including $144,375 for 85 grants (high: $10,000; low: $100) and $113,152 for 33 grants to individuals (high: $7,800; low: $800).
Purpose and activities: Grants largely for research and education related to agriculture, including scholarship funds; assistance to needy former employees of affiliated organizations; grants also to youth agencies and community funds.
Types of support: Scholarship funds, grants to individuals.
Limitations: Giving limited to ID, MN, MT, ND, OR, SD, WA, WI, and WY. No grants for endowment funds.
Application information: Application form not required.
Initial approach: Letter
Copies of proposal: 1
Deadline(s): None
Board meeting date(s): Quarterly
Write: Mary Kaste, Mgr.
Officers: Elroy Webster,* Pres.; David Baker, Exec. V.P.; Arnold Weisenbeck, V.P.; Richard Traphagen, Secy.-Treas.; Mary Kaste, Mgr.
Trustees:* Lloyd Allen, John Broste, Aaron Glanzer, Lloyd Kaercher, Joseph Larson, Lawrence Murry, Robert Nixon, Gaylord Olson, Dixie Lee Riddle, Bernard Saul.
Employer Identification Number: 416025858

3324
Central Minnesota Community Foundation ☆
619 St. Germain Mall, Suite 214
P.O. Box 1284
St. Cloud 56302-1284 (612) 253-4380

Established in 1985 in MN.
Foundation type: Community
Financial data (yr. ended 6/30/89): Assets, $4,763,152 (M); gifts received, $3,201,669; expenditures, $226,132, including $82,256 for 26 grants (high: $18,592; low: $500).
Purpose and activities: "To make a continuing relevant contribution to the present and future vitality of Central Minnesota, building the independence and interdependence of people in the development of self-capacity and fullness of life."
Limitations: Giving primarily in Benton, Stearns, and Sherburne counties, MN. No support for religious, political, or fraternal organizations. No grants to individuals, or for medical research.
Publications: Annual report, informational brochure, application guidelines.
Application information: Application form required.
Initial approach: Proposal
Deadline(s): Mar. 1 and Sept. 1 for undesignated funds
Board meeting date(s): 3rd Monday in May and Nov.
Write: Leland Newman, Exec. Dir.
Officers and Directors:* Alex Didier,* Pres.; Andy Hilger,* V.P.; Caroline Boureson,* Secy.; John Weitzel,* Treas.; Leland E. Newman, Exec. Dir.; and 20 additional directors.
Number of staff: 1 full-time professional; 1 full-time support.
Employer Identification Number: 363412544

3325
Chadwick Foundation
4122 IDS Center
Minneapolis 55402

Established in 1967 in MN.
Donor(s): Members of the Dayton family.
Foundation type: Independent
Financial data (yr. ended 12/31/88): Assets, $4,987,124 (M); expenditures, $336,990, including $324,250 for grants.
Purpose and activities: Emphasis on secondary and higher education, community services, cultural programs, conservation, hospitals and medical research, the arts, and Protestant church support.
Types of support: Research, general purposes.
Limitations: Giving primarily in MN. No grants to individuals.
Application information: Contributes only to pre-selected organizations. Applications not accepted.
Officers and Directors:* Lucy J. Dayton,* Pres. and Treas.; Robert J. Dayton,* V.P. and Secy.; Edward N. Dayton,* V.P.; John W. Dayton,* V.P.; Ronald N. Gross.
Number of staff: None.
Employer Identification Number: 416080619

3326
Albert W. Cherne Foundation
(Formerly Cherne Foundation)
P.O. Box 975
Minneapolis 55440 (612) 944-4378

Established in 1968 in MN.
Donor(s): Albert W. Cherne,† Elizabeth B. Cherne.
Foundation type: Independent

Financial data (yr. ended 12/31/88): Assets, $10,266,906 (M); expenditures, $415,015, including $372,953 for 110 grants (high: $50,000; low: $25; average: $1,000-$4,000).
Purpose and activities: Giving for education and literacy programs and social services, including the handicapped and youth.
Types of support: Annual campaigns, continuing support, endowment funds, general purposes, matching funds.
Limitations: Giving primarily in the 7-county metropolitan area of Minneapolis and St. Paul, MN. No support for political, veterans', or labor organizations. No grants to individuals, or for capital improvements outside of MN.
Publications: Annual report (including application guidelines).
Application information: Application form not required.
Initial approach: Letter
Copies of proposal: 3
Deadline(s): 6 weeks before board meeting
Board meeting date(s): Feb. 15, May 15, Aug. 15, and Nov. 15
Final notification: About 2 weeks after board meeting
Write: Sara Ribbens, Pres.
Officers: Sara C. Ribbens, Pres. and Treas.; A. William Cherne, Jr., V.P.; Elizabeth B. Cherne, V.P. and Secy.; Cathy Long.
Number of staff: 1 full-time professional.
Employer Identification Number: 237005356

3327
Pax Christi Foundation ☆
c/o Hutterer & Krenn
7900 Xerxes Ave., South, Suite 928
Minneapolis 55431

Established in 1987 in MN.
Foundation type: Independent
Financial data (yr. ended 06/30/89): Assets, $2,554,454 (M); gifts received, $1,485,000; expenditures, $33,942, including $24,000 for 1 grant.
Purpose and activities: Giving primarily to a center providing food, clothing, and shelter to needy people.
Limitations: Giving primarily in St. Paul, MN. No grants to individuals.
Application information: Contributes only to pre-selected organizations. Applications not accepted.
Officer: Vincent K. Hutterer, C.F.O.
Employer Identification Number: 363550495

3328
The Circle Foundation ⌘
c/o First Trust, N.A.
P.O. Box 64704, W-8 First National Bank Bldg.
St. Paul 55164 (612) 291-5128

Established in 1975.
Donor(s): Ursula Jaeger, Robert Jaeger.
Foundation type: Independent
Financial data (yr. ended 12/31/87): Assets, $1,126,802 (M); expenditures, $141,813, including $133,589 for 10 grants (high: $30,000; low: $5,000).
Purpose and activities: Grants largely for social service agencies, with emphasis on aid to the mentally handicapped.
Types of support: General purposes.
Limitations: Giving limited to western PA. No grants to individuals.
Application information:
Initial approach: Letter
Write: John L. Jerry, Secy.-Treas.
Officers and Directors: Robert Jaeger, Pres.; Ursula Jaeger, V.P.; John L. Jerry, Secy.-Treas.
Employer Identification Number: 510147632

3329
Cooperative Foundation
480 Cedar St., Suite 580
St. Paul 55101 (612) 228-0213

Established in 1946 in MN.
Foundation type: Independent
Financial data (yr. ended 12/31/88): Assets, $1,378,709 (M); gifts received, $38,212; expenditures, $99,087, including $53,009 for 6 grants (high: $21,259; low: $750; average: $750-$21,259).
Purpose and activities: Giving primarily for education; support also for rural development and program-related investments.
Types of support: Program-related investments, research.
Limitations: Giving generally limited to the upper midwest region of the U.S. No support for political campaigns, churches, religious organizations, or needed new programs that already exist in other locations. No grants to individuals, or for operating budgets, annual campaigns, capital funds, equipment, scholarships, or fellowships.
Publications: Application guidelines.
Application information: Application form required.
Initial approach: Letter requesting application
Copies of proposal: 1
Deadline(s): None
Board meeting date(s): Mar., June, and Sept.
Write: Allen Gerber, Pres.
Officers: Rod Nilsestuen, Chair.; Allen Gerber, Pres.; Larry Kallem, V.P.; Jean Jantzen, Secy.
Trustees: Roger Ginder, Robert Nelson, William Nelson, Gary Rohde, William Takala.
Number of staff: 1 part-time professional.
Employer Identification Number: 410809732

3330
Arthur & David Cosgrove Memorial Fund ⌘ ☆
228 South Main St.
Le Sueur 56058

Established in 1946.
Foundation type: Independent
Financial data (yr. ended 12/31/88): Assets, $1,033,440 (M); gifts received, $13,289; expenditures, $77,835, including $33,400 for 13 grants (high: $5,000; low: $100) and $20,500 for 12 loans to individuals.
Purpose and activities: Giving primarily for education, especially through individual student loans; support also for general charitable activities.
Types of support: Student loans.
Limitations: Giving limited to Le Sueur, MN, area.
Application information:
Initial approach: Letter
Deadline(s): None
Write: Neil Morem, Secy.
Officers and Trustees: Mrs. Dale K. Warner, Chair.; Neil R. Morem, Secy.; Dodd Cosgrove, R.C. Cosgrove, Jr., June Curme, Bradley Warner, C.B. Way.
Employer Identification Number: 416022638

3331
Cowles Media Foundation ▼ ⌘
329 Portland Ave.
Minneapolis 55415 (612) 375-7051

Incorporated in 1945 in MN.
Donor(s): Cowles Media Co.
Foundation type: Company-sponsored
Financial data (yr. ended 4/02/88): Assets, $8,087,019 (M); expenditures, $1,124,321, including $962,500 for 37 grants (high: $250,000; low: $5,000).
Purpose and activities: Support of educational, scientific, and charitable organizations, including higher education, civic agencies, and journalism; support also for social service and youth organizations.
Limitations: Giving limited to the Minneapolis, MN, area. No grants to individuals, or for operating budgets or special projects.
Publications: 990-PF, program policy statement, application guidelines.
Application information:
Initial approach: Letter or telephone
Copies of proposal: 1
Deadline(s): None
Write: Janet L. Schwichtenberg
Officers and Directors: David Kruidenier, Chair.; Roger Parkinson, Pres.; James A. Alcott, V.P.; David C. Cox, V.P.; Norton L. Armour, Secy.; John Cole, Treas.; Hazel Reinhardt.
Employer Identification Number: 416031373

3332
Cray Research Foundation
608 Second Ave. South, 12th Fl.
Minneapolis 55402 (612) 333-5889

Established in 1985 in MN.
Donor(s): Cray Research, Inc.
Foundation type: Company-sponsored
Financial data (yr. ended 12/31/88): Assets, $2,500,000 (L); expenditures, $2,277,667, including $2,258,747 for grants (high: $212,449; low: $500) and $18,920 for employee matching gifts.
Purpose and activities: Giving limited to science and engineering education.
Types of support: Employee matching gifts, operating budgets, special projects.
Limitations: Giving primarily in MN and WI.
Publications: Corporate giving report, application guidelines.
Application information: Application form not required.
Initial approach: Letter
Copies of proposal: 1
Deadline(s): None
Board meeting date(s): Quarterly
Write: William C. Linder-Scholer, Exec. Dir.
Number of staff: None.
Employer Identification Number: 411543634

3333
Dain Bosworth/IFG Foundation
(Formerly Inter-Regional Financial Group, Inc., Foundation)
100 Dain Tower
Minneapolis 55402 (612) 371-2765

Incorporated in 1961 in MN.
Donor(s): Dain, Kalman and Quail, Inc., Inter-Regional Financial Group, Inc.
Foundation type: Company-sponsored
Financial data (yr. ended 12/31/89): Assets, $138,742 (M); gifts received, $213,495; expenditures, $379,098, including $350,095 for 510 grants (high: $56,000; low: $25) and $29,003 for 132 employee matching gifts.
Purpose and activities: Giving for economic development, community funds, cultural and civic affairs, health, education, and social services, including family services and child development and welfare.
Types of support: Employee matching gifts, general purposes, continuing support, annual campaigns, seed money, building funds, operating budgets.
Limitations: Giving primarily in areas of company operations in MN. No support for religious or political groups. No grants to individuals, or for endowment funds, research, scholarships, fellowships, travel, tours, conferences, or multi-year pledges; no loans.
Publications: Annual report (including application guidelines).
Application information: Only MN applications accepted by the foundation; other applications should be sent to the nearest branch office. Application form not required.
Initial approach: Letter
Copies of proposal: 1
Deadline(s): Jan. 31 and July 31
Board meeting date(s): Feb., Mar., Aug., and Sept.
Final notification: 2-3 weeks following Mar. and Sept. meetings
Write: Beth James, Exec. Dir.
Officers and Directors:* James Dlugosch,* Chair.; James Morrell,* Treas.; Elizabeth James,* Exec. Dir.; Robert Bemel, Carol Christianson, Judy Gaviser, Paul Gubrud, Lee Kopp, Wayne Larson, Richard McFarland, John Thompson.
Number of staff: 11 part-time professional; 1 part-time support.
Employer Identification Number: 416030639

3334
Edwin W. and Catherine M. Davis Foundation ⌑
2100 First National Bank Bldg.
St. Paul 55101 (612) 228-0935

Incorporated in 1956 in MN.
Donor(s): Samuel S. Davis,† Edwin W. Davis,† Frederick W. Davis.
Foundation type: Independent
Financial data (yr. ended 12/31/88): Assets, $7,132,058 (M); gifts received, $319,442; expenditures, $707,576, including $659,746 for 76 grants (high: $30,000; low: $130; average: $5,000-$20,000).
Purpose and activities: Concerned with "the amelioration of social problems and increasing the opportunities available to disadvantaged people," with particular interest in the fields of education, social welfare, mental health, the arts, and environmental problems. Educational grants primarily for colleges and universities; support also for religious youth groups.
Types of support: Annual campaigns, continuing support, operating budgets, scholarship funds, endowment funds, fellowships, research.
Limitations: No grants to individuals, or for emergency funds, capital outlay, building and equipment, or endowments; no loans.
Publications: Annual report (including application guidelines).
Application information: Application form not required.
Initial approach: Letter
Copies of proposal: 1
Deadline(s): None
Board meeting date(s): May or June and as required
Final notification: 4 to 6 weeks
Write: Frederick W. Davis, Pres.
Officers and Directors:* Frederick W. Davis,* Pres.; Bette D. Moorman,* V.P.; Mary E. Davis,* Secy.; Albert J. Moorman,* Treas.; Joseph S. Micallef.
Number of staff: None.
Employer Identification Number: 416012064

3335
Dayton Hudson Foundation ▼
777 Nicollet Mall
Minneapolis 55402 (612) 370-6555

Incorporated in 1918 in MN.
Donor(s): Dayton Hudson Corp., and operating companies.
Foundation type: Company-sponsored
Financial data (yr. ended 01/31/90): Assets, $16,700,000 (M); gifts received, $12,413,000; expenditures, $12,346,533, including $11,452,875 for 375 grants (high: $762,600; low: $1,000; average: $5,000-$100,000).
Purpose and activities: "The foundation manages the Minneapolis/St. Paul-based giving for the Dayton Hudson Corp. and its Twin Cities-based operating companies, a small national grants program and major funding initiatives with all three operating companies (Target, Mervyn's and Dayton Hudson Department Store Co.). Giving is concentrated on programs that are committed to achieving results and demonstrating leadership. The foundation's priorities are to social action programs that result in the economic and social progress of individuals, and that develop strategies that respond effectively to community, social, and economic concerns, and to arts programs that result in artistic excellence, community leradership in the arts, and increased access to, and use of, the arts as a means of community expression."
Types of support: Operating budgets, continuing support, annual campaigns, matching funds, consulting services, technical assistance, special projects, publications, general purposes.
Limitations: Giving primarily in areas of company operations including MN, especially the Twin Cities metropolitan area, MI, CA, IN, and TX; grants rarely for national organizations or programs. No support for religious organizations for religious purposes; grants rarely made to health organizations, educational institutions, or tax-supported activities. No grants to individuals, or for seed money, emergency funds, land acquisition, scholarships, fellowships, research, or conferences; grants rarely for endowment funds; no loans.
Publications: Corporate giving report, informational brochure (including application guidelines), program policy statement, application guidelines, annual report, grants list.
Application information: Organizations located outside of MN should apply to a Dayton Hudson operating company. The Grant Application Guide explains how and where to apply. Application form not required.
Initial approach: Letter with proposal
Copies of proposal: 1
Deadline(s): None
Board meeting date(s): Mar., June, and Dec.
Final notification: Usually within 60 days, although decisions are generally not made between Jan. 31 and Apr. 15
Write: Cynthia Mayeda, Chair.
Officers and Trustees:* Cynthia Mayeda,* Chair.; William E. Harder, Secy.; Willard C. Shull III, Treas.; Marvin W. Goldstein, Walter T. Rossi, C. George Scala, Robert J. Ulrich, Stephen E. Watson.
Number of staff: 4 full-time professional; 2 full-time support; 1 part-time support.
Employer Identification Number: 416017088

3336
Roger L. and Agnes C. Dell Charitable Trust II ⌑
c/o First Trust, N.A.
Two South First National Bank Bldg., Box 64704
St. Paul 55164-0704 (612) 291-5132

Established in 1970 in MN.
Foundation type: Independent
Financial data (yr. ended 7/31/88): Assets, $1,386,495 (M); expenditures, $84,184, including $69,256 for 17 grants (high: $15,000; low: $181; average: $500-$5,000).
Purpose and activities: Giving primarily for youth, education, and cultural programs.
Types of support: General purposes.
Limitations: Giving limited to Fergus Falls, MN, and the surrounding area. No grants to individuals.
Application information:
Initial approach: Letter
Write: Gerald S. Rufer, Trustee
Trustees: Richard C. Hefte, Gerald S. Rufer, Stephen F. Rufer, First Trust, N.A.
Employer Identification Number: 416059730

3337
Dellwood Foundation, Inc. ⌑
1000 Pioneer Bldg.
St. Paul 55101 (612) 224-1841

Established in 1958 in MN.
Foundation type: Independent
Financial data (yr. ended 12/31/88): Assets, $1,601,784 (M); expenditures, $123,842, including $112,500 for 30 grants (high: $17,500; low: $1,000).
Purpose and activities: Giving to the United Way, the arts, education, and the environment.

Types of support: Annual campaigns, building funds, capital campaigns, continuing support, endowment funds, general purposes, land acquisition, operating budgets, program-related investments, research.
Limitations: Giving primarily in the Twin Cities, MN, area. No grants to individuals.
Application information: Application form not required.
Initial approach: Proposal
Copies of proposal: 1
Deadline(s): None
Board meeting date(s): Varies
Write: J.G. Ordway, Jr., Pres. and Treas.
Officers and Directors: John G. Ordway, Jr., Pres. and Treas.; Margaret M. Ordway, V.P.; J.C. Foote, Secy.; John G. Ordway III, P.W. Ordway.
Number of staff: None.
Employer Identification Number: 416019244

3338
Deluxe Corporation Foundation ▼
(Formerly Deluxe Check Printers Foundation)
1080 West County Rd. "F"
P.O. Box 64399
St. Paul 55164-0399 (612) 483-7842

Incorporated in 1952 in MN.
Donor(s): Deluxe Corp.
Foundation type: Company-sponsored
Financial data (yr. ended 12/31/89): Assets, $27,866,903 (M); gifts received, $28,950,000; expenditures, $3,409,884, including $3,102,365 for 629 grants (high: $100,000; low: $1,000; average: $1,000-$10,000) and $280,649 for 1,287 employee matching gifts.
Purpose and activities: Giving for private higher education, particularly independent college funds, and for youth organizations, social welfare agencies, and cultural organizations.
Types of support: Building funds, equipment, operating budgets, special projects, employee matching gifts, renovation projects, capital campaigns.
Limitations: Giving primarily in areas of company operations. No support for primary or secondary schools, or for religious or political organizations. No grants to individuals, or for annual campaigns or research; no loans.
Publications: Corporate giving report (including application guidelines).
Application information: Application form required.
Initial approach: Letter or telephone
Copies of proposal: 1
Deadline(s): None
Board meeting date(s): Feb.; regional meetings at least twice a year
Final notification: 3 months
Write: Jennifer Anderson, Grants Admin.
Officer and Trustees:* Michael J. Welch,* Pres.; Francis H. Cloutier, William A. Green, Mark T. Gritton, Harold V. Haverty, James T. Nichols, William J. Oliver, Charles M. Osborne, Jerry K. Twogood.
Number of staff: 1
Employer Identification Number: 416034786

3339
The Donaldson Foundation ⌑
c/o Donaldson Co., Inc.
P.O. Box 1299
Minneapolis 55440 (612) 887-3010

Established in 1966 in MN.
Donor(s): Donaldson Co., Inc.
Foundation type: Company-sponsored
Financial data (yr. ended 7/31/88): Assets, $495,656 (M); gifts received, $100,000; expenditures, $348,386, including $338,875 for 98 grants (high: $38,400; low: $300) and $6,850 for 12 employee matching gifts.
Purpose and activities: Support for community funds, youth agencies, arts and cultural organizations, vocational schools, and higher education; grants also for educational associations, environmental protection, community development, and health services.
Types of support: Employee matching gifts.
Limitations: Giving primarily in areas of company operations, including MN, WI, IL, IN, IA, MO, and KY. No support for religious organizations. No grants to individuals.
Publications: Application guidelines, annual report (including application guidelines).
Application information: Application form not required.
Initial approach: Letter
Copies of proposal: 1
Deadline(s): May 1 and Aug. 1
Board meeting date(s): Aug. and May
Write: Raymond Vodovnik, Secy.
Officers: John R. Schweers, Pres. and Treas.; Raymond Vodovnik,* Secy.
Trustees:* F.A. Donaldson, Sandy Donaldson, Sue Gentilini, Gloria Gordon, Dennis Grigal, Rudy Molck-Ude, Robert Schweitzer, William S. West.
Number of staff: None.
Employer Identification Number: 416052950

3340
Douglas Foundation ⌑
620 12th Ave. South
Minneapolis 55415-1799

Established in 1980 in MN.
Donor(s): Douglas Corp.
Foundation type: Company-sponsored
Financial data (yr. ended 9/30/88): Assets, $43,686 (M); gifts received, $129,000; expenditures, $105,592, including $105,450 for grants.
Purpose and activities: General charitable giving, with emphasis on religious and educational institutions.
Limitations: No grants to individuals.
Officers: Douglas R. Skanse, Pres.; C.T. Skanse, V.P.; Norman Kuehne, Secy.
Employer Identification Number: 411385064

3341
Driscoll Foundation ⌑
2100 First National Bank Bldg.
St. Paul 55101 (612) 228-0935

Incorporated in 1962 in MN.
Donor(s): Members of the Driscoll family.
Foundation type: Independent
Financial data (yr. ended 02/28/89): Assets, $5,887,226 (M); gifts received, $561,113; expenditures, $186,738, including $118,500 for 11 grants (high: $32,500; low: $1,000; average: $5,000).
Purpose and activities: Emphasis on higher and secondary education, hospitals, the arts, Protestant church support, conservation, and community funds.
Limitations: Giving primarily in the metropolitan areas of St. Paul-Minneapolis, MN and San Francisco, CA. No grants to individuals, or for conferences, travel, publications, or films.
Publications: Annual report, application guidelines.
Application information: Application form not required.
Initial approach: Letter
Copies of proposal: 1
Deadline(s): None
Board meeting date(s): Annually and as required
Final notification: 3 to 4 weeks
Write: W. John Driscoll, Pres.
Officers: W. John Driscoll,* Pres.; Rudolph W. Driscoll,* V.P.; Joseph S. Micallef, Secy.; Gordon E. Hed, Treas.
Director:* Elizabeth S. Driscoll.
Number of staff: None.
Employer Identification Number: 416012065

3342
Duluth Improvement Trust ⌑
c/o Norwest Bank Duluth N.A., Trust Dept.
230 West Superior St.
Duluth 55802

Established in 1966 in MN.
Foundation type: Independent
Financial data (yr. ended 12/31/87): Assets, $855,130 (M); expenditures, $659,886, including $650,000 for 1 grant.
Purpose and activities: Support for community developement.
Types of support: Building funds.
Limitations: Giving primarily in the Duluth, MN, area.
Application information:
Initial approach: Letter
Deadline(s): None
Trustees: Robert M. Fischer, Arthur C. Josephs, Caroline Marshall, Newell Marshall, Nick Smith, Donald G. Wirtanen.
Employer Identification Number: 416053771

3343
Duluth-Superior Area Community Foundation
316 Missabe Bldg.
Duluth 55802 (218) 726-0232

Established in 1982 in MN.
Foundation type: Community
Financial data (yr. ended 12/31/89): Assets, $5,834,441 (M); gifts received, $741,081; expenditures, $464,037, including $284,216 for 150 grants (high: $5,000; low: $250) and $9,630 for 10 grants to individuals.
Purpose and activities: Support for community development, emergency relief, higher and other education, employment, hunger, shelter, child welfare, peace organizations, and cultural programs, including music and the arts.

Types of support: Equipment, general purposes, renovation projects, emergency funds, operating budgets, research, seed money, special projects, conferences and seminars, consulting services, exchange programs, matching funds, publications, scholarship funds, technical assistance.
Limitations: Giving primarily in the Duluth-Superior area. To a lesser extent, funds are distributed to Douglas and Bayfield counties, WI, and Koochiching, Itasca, St. Louis, Lake, Cook, Carlton, and Aitkin counties in northeastern MN. No support for medical research or direct religious activities. Generally, no grants to individuals, or for capital or annual campaigns, endowments, debt retirement, national fundraising programs, continuing support, deficit financing, or land acquisition; no loans.
Publications: Financial statement, grants list, application guidelines, annual report, newsletter, 990-PF.
Application information: Application form not required.
Initial approach: Telephone or letter
Copies of proposal: 15
Deadline(s): Feb. 1, May 1 and Oct. 1
Board meeting date(s): Quarterly
Write: Bula Hess, Exec. Dir., or Judith Sedin, Admin. Assoc.
Officers: Holly Sampson,* Pres.; Charles A. Russell,* Treas.
Trustees:* Richard R. Burns, Chair.; Edward C. Bonderson, James Claypool, Mary Dougherty, Robert Edwards, Phyllis France, Robert H. Gee, Sr., Virginia Gooch, William C. Kuhlman, David Lingren, Eugene G. McGillis, Donald V. Moline.
Number of staff: 2 full-time professional; 1 full-time support; 1 part-time support.
Employer Identification Number: 411429402

3344
The Dyco Foundation
4670 Norwest Ctr.
90 South 7th St.
Minneapolis 55402 (612) 337-8194

Established in 1977 in MN.
Donor(s): Dyco Petroleum Corp.
Foundation type: Company-sponsored
Financial data (yr. ended 12/31/89): Assets, $1,248,907 (M); gifts received, $11,650; expenditures, $34,249, including $12,935 for 6 grants (high: $4,750; low: $500; average: $1,000-$2,000) and $9,500 for 6 grants to individuals (high: $2,000; low: $1,000; average: $1,000-$2,000).
Purpose and activities: Support for medicine and health, social service agencies, the arts and cultural programs, community development, and youth organizations. Primary focus: self-sufficiency through employment programs targeting the handicapped, minority teens, and long-term unemployed; support also for scholarships for the children of company employees.
Types of support: General purposes, special projects, employee-related scholarships, matching funds, emergency funds.
Limitations: Giving limited to the Minneapolis, MN, area, and Tulsa and Elk City, OK. No support for sectarian organizations for religious purposes. No grants to individuals (except for employee-related scholarships), or for operating budgets, seed money, capital drives, endowment funds, publications, advertising, tickets, or banquets.
Publications: Annual report, grants list.
Application information: Application form not required.
Initial approach: Telephone
Copies of proposal: 1
Deadline(s): Mar. 1, June 15, Sept. 15, and Dec. 1; Mar. 30 for scholarships
Board meeting date(s): Quarterly
Write: Alicia E. Ringstad, Secy.
Officers and Directors:* Jaye F. Dyer,* Pres.; Alicia E. Ringstad,* Secy.; Roxanne Gilje,* Treas.; Betty F. Dyer, John F. West, Lendell Z. Williams.
Number of staff: 1 part-time professional; 1 part-time support.
Employer Identification Number: 411390020

3345
Ecolab Foundation ¤
Ecolab Ctr., 10th Fl.
St. Paul 55102 (612) 293-2222

Established in 1982 in MN.
Foundation type: Company-sponsored
Financial data (yr. ended 12/31/87): Assets, $3,243,963 (M); gifts received, $2,764,272; expenditures, $406,951, including $254,740 for 133 grants (high: $42,000; low: $25), $77,700 for 79 grants to individuals (high: $1,250; low: $250) and $48,550 for 43 loans to individuals.
Purpose and activities: Gives one-year scholarships for tuition and academic fees at accredited colleges or universities, and also at technical community colleges and nursing schools; only for dependents of an employee or retiree; support also for higher education, social service organizations and the arts.
Types of support: Employee-related scholarships, loans.
Limitations: Giving primarily in Garland, TX; Beloit, WI; Minneapolis and St. Paul, MN; Woodbridge, NJ; Joliet, IL; and Columbus, OH.
Publications: Corporate giving report.
Application information: Application form required.
Initial approach: Letter
Copies of proposal: 1
Deadline(s): July 1
Board meeting date(s): Quarterly
Final notification: Mar.
Write: Kristie L. Greve, Dir. Communications and Commun. Relations
Officers and Directors: Jon R. Grunseth, Pres.; D.A. Grocholski, Secy.; Toni L. Hengesteg, Treas.; G.W. Leimer, S.L. Olson, Allan L. Schuman, M.E. Shannon.
Number of staff: None.
Employer Identification Number: 411372157

3346
Edwin H. Eddy Family Foundation ¤
(Formerly Eddy Foundation)
c/o Norwest Bank Duluth
Capital Management and Trust Dept.
Duluth 55802 (218) 723-2773

Established in 1982 in MN.
Donor(s): Edwin H. Eddy, Jr.†
Foundation type: Independent
Financial data (yr. ended 6/30/88): Assets, $2,308,694 (M); expenditures, $144,671, including $98,318 for 10 grants (high: $50,000; low: $440; average: $20,000) and $17,396 for 20 grants to individuals (high: $1,200; low: $400; average: $1,200).
Purpose and activities: Grants for research into and treatment of individuals with speech or hearing disorders. Also awards scholarships for students studying in the field of communication disorders: first priority for Duluth, MN, area residents at the University of Minnesota, Duluth; second priority for area residents at other institutions; and third priority for non-residents at the University of Minnesota, Duluth.
Types of support: Student aid, conferences and seminars, continuing support, grants to individuals, internships, lectureships, matching funds, professorships, research, scholarship funds, technical assistance.
Limitations: Giving limited to the Duluth, MN, area. No grants for capital improvements or salaries.
Publications: Informational brochure (including application guidelines), program policy statement, application guidelines.
Application information: Application form required for scholarships only.
Initial approach: Proposal
Copies of proposal: 8
Deadline(s): Mar. 31 for scholarships only
Board meeting date(s): June 1 for scholarships only
Write: Murray George, Trustee
Trustees: Rodney J. Edwards, Murray George, Eben S. Spencer, Norwest Bank Duluth.
Employer Identification Number: 416242226

3347
Edwards Memorial Trust
c/o First Trust, N.A.
Two West First National Bank Bldg., P.O. Box 64704
St. Paul 55164 (612) 291-5115

Trust established in 1961 in MN.
Donor(s): Ray Edwards.†
Foundation type: Independent
Financial data (yr. ended 12/31/88): Assets, $10,829,130 (M); expenditures, $662,108, including $610,960 for 66 grants (high: $43,000; low: $1,000).
Purpose and activities: Emphasis on public hospitals, including the maintaining of free beds; some support for social services and health agencies, including those benefitting the handicapped.
Types of support: General purposes.
Limitations: Giving primarily in the Minneapolis-St. Paul, MN, area.
Application information: Application form not required.
Initial approach: Letter
Deadline(s): None
Board meeting date(s): May and Nov.
Write: Leonard J. Ilges, V.P., First Trust, N.A.
Trustee: First Trust, N.A.
Employer Identification Number: 416011292

3348
Ferndale Foundation, Inc. ⌘
c/o First Trust, N.A.
First National Bank Bldg., P.O. Box 64704
St. Paul 55164

Incorporated in 1966 in MN.
Donor(s): William H. Lang, Mrs. William H. Lang, Lang-Ferndale Trusts.
Foundation type: Independent
Financial data (yr. ended 10/31/87): Assets, $36,532 (M); gifts received, $140,714; expenditures, $138,482, including $135,900 for 24 grants (high: $50,000; low: $400).
Purpose and activities: Emphasis on hospitals, cultural programs, and a community fund.
Types of support: General purposes, annual campaigns, building funds, scholarship funds, capital campaigns.
Limitations: Giving primarily in MN.
Application information:
Initial approach: Letter or proposal
Deadline(s): None
Write: Paul J. Kelly, Secy.-Treas.
Officers: Theodora H. Lang, Pres.; A. Scheffer Lang, V.P.; Paul J. Kelly, Secy.-Treas.
Director: Barbara Lang Cochran, Andrew Scott.
Employer Identification Number: 416084166

3349
The William I. Fine Charitable Trust ⌘
1916 IDS Ctr.
Minneapolis 55402

Established in 1986 in MN.
Foundation type: Independent
Financial data (yr. ended 12/31/88): Assets, $4,776 (M); expenditures, $419,380, including $413,000 for 5 grants (high: $400,000; low: $500).
Purpose and activities: Support primarily for higher education.
Limitations: Giving primarily in MN. No grants to individuals.
Application information: Contributes only to pre-selected organizations. Applications not accepted.
Trustees: William I. Fine, Melvin R. Mooty.
Employer Identification Number: 363481742

3350
The Fingerhut Family Foundation ▼
5354 Parkdale Dr., No. 310
Minneapolis 55416 (612) 545-3000

Incorporated in 1960 in MN.
Donor(s): Manny Fingerhut, Rose Fingerhut.
Foundation type: Independent
Financial data (yr. ended 12/31/89): Assets, $5,018,211 (M); gifts received, $5,072,420; expenditures, $316,178, including $298,202 for 72 grants (high: $100,000; low: $100; average: $500-$10,000).
Purpose and activities: Emphasis on Jewish welfare funds, social service agencies, and medical research.
Types of support: Operating budgets, annual campaigns, continuing support, emergency funds, general purposes, research, special projects.
Limitations: Giving primarily in MN, especially the Twin Cities. No grants for building funds.
Application information: Application form not required.
Initial approach: Letter and brief proposal
Copies of proposal: 1
Deadline(s): None
Board meeting date(s): As necessary
Final notification: 2 to 4 weeks
Write: Ronald Fingerhut, Pres.
Officers and Directors:* Ronald Fingerhut,* Pres.; Stanley Nemer,* V.P. and Secy.-Treas.; Rose Fingerhut,* V.P.; Beverly Deikel, Manny Fingerhut.
Number of staff: 1 part-time professional; 1 part-time support.
Employer Identification Number: 416030930

3351
First Bank System Foundation ▼
P.O. Box 522, MPFW0105
Minneapolis 55480 (612) 370-5176

Established in 1979.
Donor(s): First Bank System, First Bank Minneapolis Office, First Bank St. Paul Office, and other First Bank offices and trust, leasing, insurance, and mortgage companies.
Foundation type: Company-sponsored
Financial data (yr. ended 12/31/88): Assets, $1,780,302 (M); gifts received, $5,358,369; expenditures, $7,438,448, including $6,410,161 for grants (high: $735,800; low: $100; average: $2,000-$30,000) and $451,982 for 3,334 employee matching gifts.
Purpose and activities: Support for higher and other education, cultural programs, and social service and youth agencies.
Types of support: Operating budgets, continuing support, annual campaigns, emergency funds, employee matching gifts, employee-related scholarships, special projects, renovation projects, matching funds.
Limitations: Giving primarily in trade areas in CO, MN, MT, ND, SD, WI, and WA. No support for religious organizations for religious purposes, camps, medical facilities, or drug or alcohol abuse prevention treatment. No grants to individuals, or for seed money, deficit financing, land acquisition, endowment funds, publications, conferences, trips, tours, or research; no loans.
Publications: Corporate giving report (including application guidelines).
Application information: Application form required for requests of $5,000 or more.
Initial approach: Letter or telephone
Copies of proposal: 1
Deadline(s): 3 months before committee meetings
Board meeting date(s): Quarterly; grant committee meets monthly
Final notification: 1 month after committee meetings
Write: Barbara B. Roy, Exec. Dir.
Officers: Chris L. Mahai,* Pres.; Barbara B. Roy, Exec. Dir.
Directors:* John F. Grundhofer, Chair.; D.G. Knudson, M.W. Sheffert, J.B. Walters.
Number of staff: 2 full-time professional; 1 full-time support.
Employer Identification Number: 411359579

3352
The Jack and Bessie Fiterman Foundation ⌘
5600 North County Rd. 18
Minneapolis 55428

Established in 1966 in MN.
Donor(s): Fidelity File Box, Inc., Liberty Carton Co., Safco Products Co., Shamrock Industries, Inc., FLS Properties.
Foundation type: Company-sponsored
Financial data (yr. ended 5/31/88): Assets, $26,707 (M); gifts received, $120,000; expenditures, $144,824, including $144,785 for 16 grants (high: $76,000; low: $50).
Purpose and activities: Giving primarily for Jewish welfare funds, hospitals, and social services.
Application information: Contributes only to pre-selected organizations. Applications not accepted.
Officers and Directors: Michael Fiterman, Pres.; Sylvia Sorkin, V.P.; Ben Fiterman, Secy.
Employer Identification Number: 416058465

3353
Frenzel Foundation ⌘
c/o Norwest Bank St. Paul, N.A.
55 East Fifth St.
St. Paul 55101-2701

Established in 1959 in MN.
Foundation type: Independent
Financial data (yr. ended 12/31/87): Assets, $1,111,980 (M); expenditures, $224,773, including $186,700 for 22 grants (high: $125,000; low: $1,000).
Purpose and activities: Support primarily for education and culture.
Types of support: Scholarship funds.
Application information: Applications not accepted.
Trustees: Peter M. Frenzel, Robert P. Frenzel, William E. Frenzel.
Employer Identification Number: 416018060

3354
H. B. Fuller Company Foundation
2400 Energy Park Dr.
St. Paul 55108 (612) 647-3617

Established in 1986 in MN.
Donor(s): H.B. Fuller Company.
Foundation type: Company-sponsored
Financial data (yr. ended 11/30/88): Assets, $793,653 (M); gifts received, $452,733; expenditures, $339,422, including $338,910 for grants (average: $1,000-$5,000).
Purpose and activities: Support for arts and humanities, education, the environment, youth, social services, and the United Way; support for higher education mainly through employee matching gifts. Youth grants have two thrusts: to develop self-esteem and literacy and to prevent drug abuse, teen pregnancy, and domestic violence in families.
Types of support: Annual campaigns, emergency funds, employee matching gifts, general purposes, operating budgets.
Limitations: Giving primarily in areas of company operations in MN, NJ, FL, MA, KY, TN, CA, GA, IL, OH, OR, NY, NC, WA, TX, and MO. No support for religious, political, fraternal, or veterans' organizations. No grants

to individuals, or for travel, basic or applied research, advertising, fundraising campaigns, capital campaigns, endowment drives, or multiple-year grants; grants are made for current year programs.
Publications: Corporate giving report (including application guidelines).
Application information: Application form not required.
Initial approach: Telephone
Copies of proposal: 1
Deadline(s): First day of preceding month in which a committee meeting is held
Board meeting date(s): Mar., June, and Oct. for Contributions Committee; Community Affairs Councils meet monthly
Final notification: 2 weeks following committee meetings; Community Affairs Councils will respond within 6 weeks
Write: Karen Muller
Officer and Directors:* Anthony L. Andersen,* Pres.; Reatha Clark King, Walter Kissling, Robert Odom, Gregory Palen, John Ray, David Stanley, Ann Wynia.
Number of staff: 2 full-time professional.
Employer Identification Number: 363500811

3355
The B. C. Gamble and P. W. Skogmo Foundation ▼
821 Marquette Ave., 500 Foshay Tower
Minneapolis 55402 (612) 339-7343

B.C. Gamble Foundation incorporated in MN in 1948; P.W. Skogmo Foundation also incorporated in 1948 in MN and merged with P.W. Skogmo Charitable Trust in 1962; B.C. Gamble Foundation merged with P.W. Skogmo Foundation in 1982 and became supporting organization of The Minneapolis Foundation.
Donor(s): P.W. Skogmo,† B.C. Gamble.†
Foundation type: Independent
Financial data (yr. ended 03/31/89): Assets, $18,926,522 (M); expenditures, $1,830,826, including $1,694,161 for 128 grants (high: $500,000; low: $1,500; average: $5,000-$20,000).
Purpose and activities: Giving for disadvantaged youth and their families, the handicapped, and programs for low-income senior citizens; health care, including research and education; and higher and secondary educational institutions.
Types of support: Building funds, capital campaigns, equipment, general purposes, seed money, operating budgets, special projects.
Limitations: Giving limited to the Minneapolis-St. Paul, MN, metropolitan area. No support for political organizations, veterans' organizations, fraternal societies, national fundraising campaigns, religious organizations for religious purposes, or for membership in civic or trade organizations. No grants to individuals, or for endowment funds, courtesy advertising, conferences, deficit financing, telephone solicitations or general fundraising expenses, or tickets for benefits.
Publications: Annual report (including application guidelines).
Application information: Only 1 copy of proposal is required for requests $10,000 or less for general operating support. Application form required.
Initial approach: Proposal
Copies of proposal: 10
Deadline(s): Apr. 1 and Oct. 1
Board meeting date(s): June and Dec.
Final notification: As soon as possible following board meeting
Write: Patricia A. Cummings, Mgr. of Supporting Organizations
Officers: Philip B. Harris,* Pres.; Georgia S. Bartlett,* V.P.; Donald G. Dreblow,* V.P.; Marion G. Etzwiler, Secy.-Treas.
Trustees:* Robert H. Engels, Timothy G. Johnson, Raymond O. Mithun, Henry T. Rutledge.
Number of staff: 3
Employer Identification Number: 411410675

3356
General Mills Foundation ▼
P.O. Box 1113
Minneapolis 55440 (612) 540-4662

Incorporated in 1954 in MN.
Donor(s): General Mills, Inc.
Foundation type: Company-sponsored
Financial data (yr. ended 05/31/89): Assets, $28,165,270 (L); gifts received, $13,432,000; expenditures, $6,885,549, including $6,338,967 for 587 grants (high: $719,036; low: $500; average: $5,000-$15,000) and $494,812 for 1,336 employee matching gifts.
Purpose and activities: Grants for higher and secondary education, social services, community funds, health, and civic and cultural activities.
Types of support: Operating budgets, employee matching gifts, scholarship funds, employee-related scholarships, special projects.
Limitations: Giving primarily in areas of major parent company operations, with emphasis on the Minneapolis, MN, area. No support for religious purposes, recreation, or national or local campaigns to eliminate or control specific diseases. No grants to individuals, or generally for endowment or capital funds, research, publications, films, conferences, seminars, advertising, athletic events, testimonial dinners, workshops, symposia, travel, fundraising events, or deficit financing; no loans.
Publications: Corporate giving report (including application guidelines).
Application information: Preliminary telephone calls or personal visits discouraged. Application form not required.
Initial approach: Proposal with brief cover letter
Copies of proposal: 1
Deadline(s): None
Board meeting date(s): 4 times a year and as required
Final notification: 4 weeks
Write: Reatha Clark King, Pres.
Officers and Trustees:* H. Brewster Atwater, Jr.,* Chair.; Reatha Clark King,* Pres. and Exec. Dir.; David Nasby, V.P.; Clifford L. Whitehill,* Secy.; Eugene P. Preiss, Treas.; F. Caleb Blodgett, J.R. Lee, T.P. Nelson, S.M. Rothschild, A.R. Schulze, Mark H. Willes.
Number of staff: 2 full-time professional; 2 full-time support; 1 part-time support.
Employer Identification Number: 416018495

3357
Getsch Family Foundation Trust ⌑
(Formerly Dye Family Foundation Trust)
c/o First National Bank of Minneapolis
120 South Sixth St.
Minneapolis 55480 (612) 540-6207

Trust established in 1958 in MN.
Donor(s): Glen M. Dye, Marjorie D. Getsch, Pako Corp.
Foundation type: Independent
Financial data (yr. ended 12/31/88): Assets, $2,366,209 (M); expenditures, $153,555, including $128,212 for 17 grants (high: $55,000; low: $500).
Purpose and activities: General giving, with emphasis on higher education, a secondary school, youth agencies, and Protestant church support.
Limitations: Giving primarily in MN and WI. No grants to individuals, or for endowment funds.
Application information: Applications not accepted.
Write: Paul Schliesman, V.P., First National Bank of Minneapolis
Director: David D. Getsch.
Trustee: First Bank, N.A.
Employer Identification Number: 416016362

3358
Gilligan Foundation ⌑ ☆
4719 Townes Rd.
Minneapolis 55424
Application address: P.O. Box 24735, Edina, MN 55424; Tel.: (612) 922-5922

Established in 1985 in MN.
Donor(s): Peter J. Gilligan.
Foundation type: Independent
Financial data (yr. ended 11/30/88): Assets, $1,054,600 (M); gifts received, $205,000; expenditures, $37,765, including $36,000 for 8 grants (high: $6,000; low: $2,500).
Purpose and activities: Giving primarily for social welfare programs, including Catholic charity agencies and health projects designed to benefit the homeless, poor, and disadvantaged.
Types of support: General purposes, operating budgets.
Limitations: Giving primarily in Minneapolis, MN. No grants to individuals.
Application information: Application form required.
Deadline(s): None
Write: Peter J. Gilligan, Pres.
Officers: Peter J. Gilligan, Pres. and Treas.; Dorothea R. Gilligan, V.P.; Jerome P. Gilligan, Secy.
Employer Identification Number: 363418218

3359
The Graco Foundation
P.O. Box 1441
Minneapolis 55440-1444 (612) 623-6684

Incorporated in 1956 in MN.
Donor(s): Graco, Inc.
Foundation type: Company-sponsored
Financial data (yr. ended 12/31/88): Assets, $1,503,000 (M); gifts received, $700,000; expenditures, $838,000, including $815,784 for 140 grants (high: $297,000; low: $500;

average: $500-$3,000) and $17,500 for 75 employee matching gifts.
Purpose and activities: Support for social and educational programs with emphasis on community funds, youth agencies, higher, secondary, and economic education; interests also include the homeless, hunger, the handicapped, literacy, urban development, and scholarships for dependent children to age 25 of Graco employees. In-kind giving through Graco, Inc. was valued at 15,000 in 1989. Small percentage of grants for civic/community activities and arts organizations.
Types of support: Operating budgets, continuing support, annual campaigns, building funds, equipment, matching funds, employee-related scholarships, research, special projects, employee matching gifts, capital campaigns.
Limitations: Giving primarily in MN, with special emphasis on north and northeast communities in Minneapolis; and in other areas of company operations, including the suburban Chicago, IL, area, the Detroit, MI, area, and Sand City, CA. No support for political or religious purposes. No grants to individuals (except for company-employee scholarships), or for seed money, emergency funds, deficit financing, land acquisition, endowment funds, publications, or conferences; no loans.
Publications: Annual report, informational brochure (including application guidelines).
Application information: Application form not required.
Initial approach: Letter, proposal, or telephone call
Copies of proposal: 1
Deadline(s): Feb. 15, May 15, Aug. 15, and Oct. 31
Board meeting date(s): May., July, Oct., and Dec.
Final notification: 90 days
Write: Elizabeth M. Jaros, Exec. Dir.
Officers and Directors:* David A. Koch,* Pres.; Elizabeth M. Jaros,* Secy. and Exec. Dir.; Maynard B. Hasselquist, Charles F. Murphy.
Number of staff: 1 full-time professional; 1 full-time support.
Employer Identification Number: 416023537

3360
Mary S. Gray Charitable Trust
c/o First National Bank of Minneapolis
120 South Sixth St.
Minneapolis 55480 (612) 370-4632

Established in 1986 in MN.
Donor(s): Mary S. Gray Trust.
Foundation type: Independent
Financial data (yr. ended 03/31/90): Assets, $2,262,000 (M); expenditures, $80,000, including $80,000 for grants.
Purpose and activities: Support primarily for religious welfare and schools and other educational institutions.
Types of support: Continuing support.
Limitations: Giving primarily in MN.
Application information: Applications not accepted.
Write: Paul Schliesman, Fund Admin.
Trustees: Glenn Bartsch, First Bank, N.A.
Employer Identification Number: 416286732

3361
The Greystone Foundation
400 Baker Bldg.
706 Second Ave., South
Minneapolis 55402 (612) 332-2454

Established in 1948 in MN.
Donor(s): Members of the Paul A. Brooks family.
Foundation type: Independent
Financial data (yr. ended 12/31/88): Assets, $1,526,065 (M); gifts received, $68,747; expenditures, $292,141, including $269,427 for 111 grants (high: $54,600; low: $35; average: $1,000-$10,000).
Purpose and activities: Giving for health and medical research, community funds and a community foundation, private secondary education, animal care and preservation, and arts and cultural programs.
Types of support: Operating budgets, continuing support, annual campaigns, seed money, emergency funds, deficit financing, building funds, equipment, land acquisition, special projects, research, publications, conferences and seminars.
Limitations: Giving primarily in MN. No grants to individuals, or for endowment funds, matching gifts, scholarships, or fellowships; no loans.
Application information: Application form not required.
Initial approach: Proposal
Deadline(s): None
Board meeting date(s): As required
Write: John M. Hollern, Trustee
Trustees: John M. Hollern, Michael P. Hollern.
Number of staff: None.
Employer Identification Number: 416027765

3362
Mary Livingston Griggs and Mary Griggs Burke Foundation ⌑
1400 Norwest Center
55 East Fifth St.
St. Paul 55101 (612) 227-7683

Established in 1966 in MN.
Donor(s): Mary L. Griggs.†
Foundation type: Independent
Financial data (yr. ended 06/30/89): Assets, $15,771,914 (M); expenditures, $882,775, including $734,250 for 70 grants (high: $100,000; low: $500; average: $500-$50,000).
Purpose and activities: Support primarily for arts and culture, including museums and an Asian cultural society; support also for conservation, higher and secondary education, and social services.
Types of support: Fellowships, general purposes, operating budgets, annual campaigns, renovation projects, matching funds, building funds, endowment funds.
Limitations: Giving primarily in St. Paul, MN, and New York, NY. No grants to individuals, or for special projects or research.
Application information: Application form not required.
Initial approach: Letter
Copies of proposal: 1
Deadline(s): None
Board meeting date(s): Quarterly
Final notification: 10 days to 3 months
Write: Marvin J. Pertzik, Secy.
Officers and Directors:* Mary Burke,* Pres.; Richard A. Moore,* V.P.; Marvin J. Pertzik,* Secy. and temporary Treas.; Eleanor Griggs, C. Bayliss Griggs.
Number of staff: None.
Employer Identification Number: 416052355

3363
Grotto Foundation, Inc.
West 1050 First National Bank Bldg.
332 Minnesota St.
St. Paul 55101 (612) 224-9431

Incorporated in 1964 in MN.
Donor(s): Louis W. Hill, Jr.
Foundation type: Independent
Financial data (yr. ended 04/30/89): Assets, $4,441,820 (M); gifts received, $78,240; expenditures, $264,421, including $173,497 for 54 grants (high: $40,000; low: $250; average: $3,000-$5,000).
Purpose and activities: Giving for education, especially higher education, cultural programs, welfare, and health; grants also for special projects relating to American Indians and racially mixed families.
Types of support: Seed money, scholarship funds, special projects, research, general purposes.
Limitations: Giving limited to MN, adjoining midwestern states, and, on a lesser basis, to AK. No support for writing projects, government projects, or art programs. No grants to individuals, or for capital or endowment funds, travel, continuing support, operating budgets (except to aid in initiating occasional programs), annual campaigns, deficit financing, student research, publications, or conferences; no loans.
Publications: Annual report (including application guidelines).
Application information: Application form required.
Initial approach: Proposal
Copies of proposal: 1
Deadline(s): 60 days prior to months in which board meets
Board meeting date(s): Mar., June, Sept., and Dec., and as required
Final notification: 2 months
Write: A.A. Heckman, Exec. Dir.
Officers: Louis W. Hill, Jr.,* Pres.; Irving Clark,* V.P.; A.A. Heckman,* Secy. and Exec. Dir.; Jeffrey T. Peterson, Treas.
Directors:* John E. Diehl, Louis F. Hill, Malcolm W. McDonald, William B. Randall.
Number of staff: 1 full-time professional; 1 part-time support.
Employer Identification Number: 416052604

3364
Groves Foundation ⌑
10000 Hwy. 55 West
P.O. Box 1267
Minneapolis 55440 (612) 546-6943

Incorporated in 1952 in MN.
Donor(s): S.J. Groves & Sons Co., Frank M. Groves.†
Foundation type: Company-sponsored
Financial data (yr. ended 9/30/87): Assets, $10,672,513 (M); expenditures, $244,247, including $149,746 for 32 grants (high:

$58,420; low: $50) and $23,000 for 14 grants to individuals (high: $2,000; low: $1,000).
Purpose and activities: Giving for the arts, medical research, and social services; support for education includes employee-related scholarships for dependents of S.S. Groves & Sons Co. and its subsidiaries.
Types of support: Employee-related scholarships, annual campaigns.
Limitations: Giving primarily in the Minneapolis, MN, area. No grants to individuals (except for employee-related scholarships), or for capital or endowment funds or matching gifts; no loans.
Application information: Application form not required.
Initial approach: Letter
Copies of proposal: 1
Deadline(s): None
Board meeting date(s): Nov. and as required
Write: Elfriede M. Lobeck, Exec. Dir.
Officers and Trustees: F.N. Groves, Pres.; C.T. Groves, V.P.; Elfriede M. Lobeck, Exec. Dir.
Number of staff: 1
Employer Identification Number: 416038512

3365
E. W. Hallett Charitable Trust ⌑ ☆
c/o First Bank, N.A.
First National Bank Bldg.
St. Paul 55164-0704
Application address: c/o First Bank, N.A., 120 South 6th St., Minneapolis, MN 55402; Tel.: (612) 370-4632

Established in 1984 in MN.
Foundation type: Independent
Financial data (yr. ended 7/31/88): Assets, $8,833,481 (M); expenditures, $619,616, including $555,028 for 17 grants (high: $85,885; low: $250).
Purpose and activities: Support primarily for higher and theological education, a Presbyterian church, the handicapped, and a library; minor support for conservation.
Limitations: Giving primarily in MN. No grants to individuals.
Application information:
Initial approach: Letter
Deadline(s): None
Write: Paul Schliesman, V.P., First Bank, N.A.
Trustees: N. Jean Rude, Osmond K. Springsted, First Bank, N.A.
Employer Identification Number: 416261160

3366
Hamm Foundation
1120 Norwest Ctr.
St. Paul 55101 (612) 222-3565

Incorporated in 1952 in MN.
Donor(s): Various companies formerly owned by the Hamm family.
Foundation type: Operating
Financial data (yr. ended 6/21/88): Assets, $8,765,373 (M); gifts received, $62,926; expenditures, $778,725, including $55,000 for 1 grant (high: $55,000) and $628,764 for 1 foundation-administered program.
Purpose and activities: A private operating foundation; primarily operates a local charitable out-patient psychiatric clinic; grants are awarded on a limited basis.
Types of support: General purposes.
Limitations: Giving primarily in St. Paul, MN.
Publications: Financial statement.
Application information: Applications not accepted.
Board meeting date(s): Quarterly
Officers: Sally A. Anson,* Pres.; William H. Hamm III,* 1st V.P.; Cynthia K. O'Neill,* 2nd V.P.; Paul A. Verret, Secy.-Treas.
Directors:* DeWalt H. Ankeny, Jr., Chair. and C.E.O.; Marie H. Ankeny, Barbara Lang Cochran, Edward H. Hamm, James E. Kelley, Margaret H. Kelley, A. Scheffer Lang, Sarah F. Lang, Theodora H. Lang, Kendall A. Mix, Phoebe A. Mix, Kelley M. O'Neill.
Number of staff: 5 full-time professional; 4 part-time professional; 2 full-time support; 2 part-time support.
Employer Identification Number: 416008892

3367
Helen Harrington Charitable Trust ⌑
c/o First Bank, N.A.
First National Bank Bldg., P.O. Box 64704
St. Paul 55164
Application address: First Bank, N.A., 120 South 6th St., Minneapolis, MN 55480

Established in 1984 in MN.
Foundation type: Independent
Financial data (yr. ended 12/31/87): Assets, $1,880,260 (M); expenditures, $102,240, including $74,401 for 8 grants (high: $17,856; low: $744).
Purpose and activities: Support primarily for secondary and higher education and social services.
Application information:
Write: Tom Tarbox
Trustee: First Bank, N.A.
Employer Identification Number: 416094797

3368
Harvest States Foundation ⌑
1667 Snelling Ave., North
P.O. Box 64594
St. Paul 55164 (612) 646-9433

Incorporated in 1947 in MN.
Donor(s): The Terminal Agency, Inc.
Foundation type: Company-sponsored
Financial data (yr. ended 5/31/87): Assets, $3,375,893 (M); expenditures, $229,975, including $218,635 for 73 grants (high: $35,000; low: $100) and $1,650 for 2 grants to individuals (high: $1,200; low: $450).
Purpose and activities: Grants largely for higher education, particularly in agriculture, with preference given to scholarship funds for studies in agricultural vocations in land-grant colleges; support also for youth organizations and community funds; assistance to needy employees or former employees of Harvest State Cooperatives.
Types of support: Scholarship funds, grants to individuals.
Limitations: Giving primarily in MN, IA, ID, MT, ND, SD, and WA.
Application information:
Initial approach: Letter
Copies of proposal: 1
Write: T.F. Baker, Asst. Treas.
Officers: Donald F. Giffey,* Chair.; Philip Testerman,* 1st Vice-Chair.; Allen D. Hanson, 2nd Vice-Chair.; Joanne Burmeister, Secy.; R.L. Zabel,* Treas.
Trustees:* Steven Burnett, Russell Christiansen, Milo Dunn, Edward Ellison, Sheldon Haaland, Marv Hanson, Edward Hereford, Myron Just, Gerald Kuster, Gordon H. Matheson, Raymond Neuhauser, Gerald G. Redlin, William J. Zarak, Jr.
Employer Identification Number: 416039613

3369
Menahem Heilicher Charitable Foundation ⌑
850 Decatur Ave. North
Minneapolis 55427

Incorporated in 1963 in MN.
Donor(s): Amos Heilicher, Daniel Heilicher, Advance Carter Co.
Foundation type: Independent
Financial data (yr. ended 9/30/88): Assets, $1,946,815 (M); gifts received, $115,000; expenditures, $259,944, including $251,208 for 32 grants (high: $210,000; low: $20).
Purpose and activities: Emphasis on Jewish welfare funds and religious education, health services, the arts, and a hospital.
Limitations: Giving primarily in MN.
Application information: Contributes only to pre-selected organizations. Applications not accepted.
Officers: Amos Heilicher, Pres.; Daniel Heilicher, V.P. and Treas.; Marvin Borman, Secy.; Elissa Kane, Secy.
Employer Identification Number: 416043457

3370
Hersey Foundation ⌑
408 St. Peter St., Rm. 440
St. Paul 55102

Established about 1968 in MN.
Donor(s): William Hamm, Jr.†
Foundation type: Independent
Financial data (yr. ended 12/31/88): Assets, $5,011,460 (M); expenditures, $242,591, including $229,000 for 21 grants (high: $59,600; low: $100).
Purpose and activities: Emphasis on historic preservation, youth agencies, and urban affairs.
Limitations: Giving primarily in MN.
Officers: Edward H. Hamm, Pres. and Treas.; Austin Chapman, V.P.; Joseph A. Maun, Secy.
Employer Identification Number: 237001771

3371
Hiawatha Education Foundation ⌑ ☆
2001 Theurer Blvd.
Winona 55987 (507) 454-5374

Established in 1987 in MN.
Foundation type: Independent
Financial data (yr. ended 12/31/88): Assets, $8,039,718 (M); expenditures, $158,038, including $109,140 for 13 grants (high: $92,277; low: $200).
Purpose and activities: Support primarily for Catholic schools.
Limitations: Giving primarily in the Winona and Rochester, MN, areas.

Application information:
Write: Robert Kierlin, Pres.
Officers: Robert Kierlin, Pres.; Stephen Slaggie, Treas.
Directors: Michael Gostomski, Van McConnon, Jack Remick.
Employer Identification Number: 363537959

3372
Honeywell Foundation ▼
Honeywell Plaza
Minneapolis 55408 (612) 870-6821
Grant application address for local agencies: send proposals to nearest company manufacturing facility

Incorporated in 1958 in MN.
Donor(s): Honeywell, Inc.
Foundation type: Company-sponsored
Financial data (yr. ended 12/31/89): Assets, $13,800,000 (M); gifts received, $7,500,000; expenditures, $7,674,444, including $6,798,614 for 1,043 grants (high: $682,500; low: $150; average: $1,500-$35,000) and $415,776 for 919 employee matching gifts.
Purpose and activities: Grants primarily for higher education, community funds, cultural programs, and youth agencies. Additional charitable support through direct corporate contributions.
Types of support: Operating budgets, continuing support, annual campaigns, seed money, building funds, employee matching gifts, scholarship funds, fellowships, special projects.
Limitations: Giving limited to cities where company has major facilities, with emphasis on Minneapolis, MN; support also in AZ, FL, WA, CO, CA, and MA. No grants to individuals, or for general endowment funds, deficit financing, land acquisition, matching or challenge grants, research, demonstration projects, or conferences; no loans.
Publications: Corporate giving report, application guidelines, grants list.
Application information: Application form not required.
Initial approach: Proposal
Copies of proposal: 1
Deadline(s): 15th of month preceding board meetings
Board meeting date(s): Jan., Apr., July, and Oct.
Final notification: 2 to 3 weeks
Write: M. Patricia Hoven, Dir.
Officers and Foundation Board:* Ronald K. Speed,* Pres.; M. Patricia Hoven,* Managing Dir.; Karen Bachman, M. Bonsignore, Richard J. Boyle, J.E. Chenoweth, M.L. Jackson, Kenneth J. Jenson, C.O. Larson, J.J. Meyer, D.L. Moore.
Number of staff: 3 full-time professional; 1 full-time support; 6 part-time support.
Employer Identification Number: 416023933

3373
George A. Hormel Testamentary Trust ⌑
501 16th Ave., N.E.
Austin 55912 (507) 437-5663

Trust established in 1946 in MN.
Donor(s): George A. Hormel.†
Foundation type: Independent
Financial data (yr. ended 12/31/88): Assets, $1,192,953 (M); expenditures, $88,388, including $83,930 for 12 grants (high: $50,000; low: $500).
Purpose and activities: Emphasis on building maintenance of youth agencies, especially the YMCA and YWCA.
Types of support: Operating budgets, continuing support, annual campaigns, seed money, emergency funds, building funds, equipment, lectureships, special projects.
Limitations: Giving limited to Mower County, MN, with emphasis on Austin. No grants to individuals, or for endowment funds, research, fellowships, deficit financing, land acquisition, publications, or conferences; no loans.
Publications: 990-PF.
Application information: Application form not required.
Initial approach: Letter
Copies of proposal: 1
Deadline(s): Sept. 1
Board meeting date(s): Monthly
Final notification: 1 month
Write: R.J. Thatcher, Treas.
Officers and Directors: I.J. Holton,* Chair.; R.B. Ondov,* Vice-Chair.; K.F. Hoversten,* Secy.; R.J. Thatcher, Treas.; J.A. Anfinson, J.A. Birney, D.R. Brezicka, J. Dibble, J.G. Huntting, Jr., R.L. Knowlton, J.R. Mueller, C.D. Nyberg, N.A. Perry, P. Richardson, H.O. Scmid.
Trustees:* The Hormel Foundation.
Number of staff: None.
Employer Identification Number: 416026834

3374
W. R. Hotchkiss Foundation
1080 West County Rd. F
St. Paul 55126 (612) 483-7842

Established in 1959.
Donor(s): Agnes M. Gates,† Lillian Hotchkiss Austin.
Foundation type: Independent
Financial data (yr. ended 06/30/89): Assets, $7,254,505 (M); gifts received, $706,328; expenditures, $422,520, including $47,210 for 2 grants (high: $45,000; low: $2,210) and $359,250 for 110 grants to individuals (high: $4,500; low: $2,000; average: $2,000-$4,500).
Purpose and activities: Scholarships only for children of employees and retirees of Deluxe Corp.
Types of support: Employee-related scholarships.
Application information: Applications not accepted.
Deadline(s): Jan. 31 for scholarships
Write: Jennifer Anderson
Officers and Trustees:* M.J. Welch,* Pres.; Francis H. Cloutier,* V.P. and Treas.; S.L. Peterson,* Secy.; H.R. Newland, T.J. Quigley.
Number of staff: 3
Employer Identification Number: 416038562

3375
The Emma B. Howe Memorial Foundation ▼
500 Foshay Tower
821 Marquette Ave.
Minneapolis 55402 (612) 339-7343

Incorporated in 1985 in MN.
Donor(s): Emma B. Howe.†
Foundation type: Independent
Financial data (yr. ended 3/31/89): Assets, $30,668,565 (M); expenditures, $1,626,518, including $1,305,360 for grants (average: $10,000-$50,000).
Purpose and activities: Giving to organizations which serve the poor and disadvantaged, children, the handicapped, and victims of discrimination by (1) addressing the underlying causes of problems in the community rather than those which deal with only the symptoms of those problems; (2) focusing on the reduction of poverty by fostering individual and family self-sufficiency; (3) working to combat racism, sexism, and other forms of discrimination; (4) focusing on education of children and adults; (5) providing medical research or health services dealing with the prevention, diagnosis, and treatment of chronic diseases of children, in particular, heart and circulatory diseases and cancer; and (6) conducting research or policy analysis on the conditions that underlie poverty, in order to foster innovative approaches designed to improve the quality of life for disadvantaged groups.
Types of support: Seed money, special projects.
Limitations: Giving primarily in MN. No support for religious organizations for religious purposes, or political, veterans', or fraternal organizations. No grants to individuals, or for capital or federated fund drives, annual contributions to general operating budgets, endowments, scholarships, conferences, deficit financing, memberships in civic or trade associations, courtesy advertising, tickets, or national fundraising efforts.
Publications: Annual report (including application guidelines).
Application information:
Initial approach: Letter; if project is of interest, proposal will be requested
Copies of proposal: 10
Deadline(s): Jan. 15 and July 15
Board meeting date(s): Mar. and Sept.
Write: Patricia A. Cummings, Mgr. - Support Orgs.
Officers and Trustees:* Richard O. Hanson,* Pres.; Hoover Grimsby, V.P.; Marion G. Etzwiler, Secy.-Treas.; John Brown, Rosalie Clark, Halsey Halls, Robert Henson, Michele Keith.
Number of staff: 4

3376
The Hubbard Foundation ⌑
3415 University Ave.
St. Paul 55114

Incorporated in 1958 in MN.
Donor(s): Stanley E. Hubbard, KSTP, Inc., Hubbard Broadcasting, Inc.
Foundation type: Company-sponsored
Financial data (yr. ended 11/30/88): Assets, $6,384,601 (M); expenditures, $108,069, including $103,035 for 29 grants (high: $35,000; low: $100).
Purpose and activities: Emphasis on youth agencies, recreation, community funds,

hospitals, higher and secondary education, cultural programs, and health associations.
Types of support: Operating budgets, building funds.
Limitations: Giving primarily in MN.
Application information: Contributes only to pre-selected organizations. Applications not accepted.
Officers: Stanley E. Hubbard,* Pres.; Stanley S. Hubbard,* V.P. and Treas.; Karen H. Hubbard,* V.P.; Gerald D. Deeney, Secy.
Trustees:* Phillip A. Dufrene, Constance L. Eckert.
Employer Identification Number: 416022291

3377
Ingram Foundation ⌑
c/o First Trust, N.A.
W-555 First National Bank Bldg., P.O. Box 64704
St. Paul 55164-0367

Established in 1955 in MN.
Foundation type: Independent
Financial data (yr. ended 10/31/87): Assets, $1,073,639 (M); expenditures, $59,076, including $53,350 for 34 grants (high: $5,000; low: $100).
Purpose and activities: Support primarily for private secondary schools and colleges, cultural programs, and health.
Types of support: General purposes.
Limitations: Giving primarily in FL and TN.
Application information:
Initial approach: Letter
Deadline(s): None
Final notification: Within 3 months of receipt of request
Write: E. Bronson Ingram, Chair.
Officers and Trustees: E. Bronson Ingram, Chair.; Frederic B. Ingram, Vice-Chair.; Martha R. Ingram, Secy.; John L. Jerry, J.R. Oppenheimer.
Employer Identification Number: 416011520

3378
International Multifoods Charitable Foundation ⌑
Multifoods Tower, Box 2942
Minneapolis 55402 (612) 340-3485

Incorporated in 1970 in DE.
Donor(s): International Multifoods.
Foundation type: Company-sponsored
Financial data (yr. ended 02/28/89): Assets, $222,684 (M); gifts received, $282,900; expenditures, $276,867, including $215,428 for 53 grants (high: $18,000; low: $500; average: $1,000-$3,000) and $60,626 for 73 employee matching gifts.
Purpose and activities: Support for higher education and programs for minorities; welfare and youth agencies; health programs for nutrition; community and rural development; and the arts, including museums.
Types of support: Operating budgets, annual campaigns, employee matching gifts, capital campaigns, program-related investments, special projects.
Limitations: Giving primarily to programs and agencies operating in or directly benefiting communities in which company facilities are located. No support for religious purposes or political campaigns. No grants to individuals, or for deficit financing, equipment, fundraising drives, land acquisition, endowment funds, scholarships, fellowships, research, demonstration projects, publications, advertisements, or conferences.
Publications: Annual report, application guidelines.
Application information: Application form required.
Initial approach: Letter
Copies of proposal: 1
Deadline(s): None
Board meeting date(s): Quarterly or as required
Final notification: Within 90 days
Write: Sayre Carlson, Mgr. Community Affairs, V.P., Corp. Comm.
Officers and Directors: Andre Gillet, Chair.; Anthony Luiso, Pres.; K. Marvin Eberts, Jr.
Number of staff: None.
Employer Identification Number: 237064628

3379
J.N.M. 1966 Gift Trust ⌑
c/o Norwest Bank Duluth, Trust Dept.
Duluth 55802

Trust established in 1966 in MN as successor to J.N.M. Gift Trust established in 1949.
Donor(s): Newell Marshall.
Foundation type: Independent
Financial data (yr. ended 12/31/88): Assets, $893,627 (M); expenditures, $208,003, including $198,947 for 27 grants (high: $34,000; low: $65).
Purpose and activities: Emphasis on higher education and cultural programs; support also for international cooperation and conservation.
Limitations: Giving primarily in MN.
Application information:
Initial approach: Proposal
Deadline(s): None
Trustees: Caroline Marshall, Newell Marshall.
Employer Identification Number: 416050249

3380
Jerome Foundation ▼
West 1050 First National Bank Bldg.
332 Minnesota St.
St. Paul 55101 (612) 224-9431

Incorporated in 1964 in MN.
Donor(s): J. Jerome Hill.†
Foundation type: Independent
Financial data (yr. ended 04/30/89): Assets, $34,291,412 (M); gifts received, $120,738; expenditures, $1,979,575, including $1,287,530 for 90 grants (high: $96,000; low: $200; average: $200-$130,000), $227,488 for grants to individuals (high: $20,000), $112,950 for 3 foundation-administered programs and $1,844 for 2 in-kind gifts.
Purpose and activities: Support for arts and humanities programs only, including dance, film and video, literature, music, theater, performance art, visual arts, and selected areas of the humanities, especially arts criticism. The foundation is concerned primarily with providing financial assistance to emerging creative artists of promise, including choreographers, film and video artists, composers, literary and visual artists, and playwrights through the Film and Video Program and the Travel and Study Grant Program.
Types of support: Special projects, general purposes, fellowships, operating budgets, grants to individuals.
Limitations: Giving limited to New York, NY, and MN. Generally no support for crafts or for educational programs in the arts and humanities. No grants to individuals (except for New York City Film and Video Program and Twin Cities Travel and Study Grant Program), or for undergraduate or graduate student research projects, capital or endowment funds, equipment, scholarships, or matching gifts.
Publications: Annual report, informational brochure (including application guidelines).
Application information: Application form not required.
Initial approach: Letter or proposal
Copies of proposal: 1
Deadline(s): Apr. 1 and Oct. 1 for travel and study grants; none for other grants
Board meeting date(s): Bimonthly
Final notification: 3 to 4 months
Write: Cynthia Gehrig, Pres.
Officers and Directors:* A.A. Heckman,* Chair. and Treas.; Irving Clark,* Vice-Chair.; Cynthia Gehrig, Pres. and Secy.; H. Yvonne Cheek, John B. Davis, Thelma E. Hunter, Archibald Leyasmeyer.
Number of staff: 2 full-time professional; 2 full-time support.
Employer Identification Number: 416035163

3381
E. F. Johnson Company Foundation
299 Johnson Ave.
Waseca 56093 (507) 835-6222

Established in 1964 in MN.
Foundation type: Company-sponsored
Financial data (yr. ended 12/31/89): Assets, $1,178,232 (M); expenditures, $62,780, including $61,450 for 30 grants (high: $10,000; low: $200) and $1,330 for 23 employee matching gifts.
Purpose and activities: Giving primarily for higher education, including programs with scientific and technological focus and career awareness. Support also for arts and culture, social services, welfare, rehabilitation, and recreation.
Types of support: Operating budgets, scholarship funds, special projects, employee matching gifts, continuing support, emergency funds.
Limitations: Giving primarily in MN. No support for religious organizations for religious purposes. No grants to individuals, health fund drives (except as part of United Way), national fundraising campaigns, ticket sales, or fundraising dinners.
Publications: Annual report (including application guidelines).
Application information: Application form not required.
Initial approach: Letter
Copies of proposal: 1
Deadline(s): Dec. 1, Mar. 1, June 1, and Sept. 1
Board meeting date(s): Feb., May, Aug., and Nov.

Write: R. Gary Cornell, Administrator
Officers and Directors:* John D. Somrock,* Pres.; Robert E. Cavins,* V.P.; Joseph M. Eastman,* Secy.-Treas.
Number of staff: None.
Employer Identification Number: 416043126

3382
The Jostens Foundation, Inc. ▼
5501 Norman Center Dr.
Minneapolis 55437 (612) 830-8461
Scholarship application address: Citizens' Scholarship Fdn. of America, P.O. Box 297, St. Peter, MN 56082; Tel.: (507) 931-1682

Established in 1976 in MN.
Donor(s): Jostens, Inc.
Foundation type: Company-sponsored
Financial data (yr. ended 06/30/89): Assets, $952,183 (M); gifts received, $1,300,000; expenditures, $1,281,497, including $941,505 for grants and $272,603 for employee matching gifts.
Purpose and activities: Emphasis on organizations primarily serving and benefitting youth; support also for cultural programs, a scholarship program conducted by Citizens' Scholarship Foundation of America, and an employee matching gift program.
Types of support: Employee matching gifts, employee-related scholarships, capital campaigns, general purposes, operating budgets, special projects.
Limitations: Giving primarily in MN, particularly the Twin Cities area and other Jostens manufacturing locations; matching gift programs have a national scope. No support for religious or political organizations, public or private educational institutions, school districts, or organizations covered by the United Way. No grants to individuals, or for endowment funds; no loans.
Publications: Annual report (including application guidelines), program policy statement, application guidelines.
Application information: Application form not required.
Initial approach: Telephone or proposal
Copies of proposal: 1
Deadline(s): Last day of the month preceding board meeting; Nov. 15 for Leader Scholarship Program
Board meeting date(s): Bimonthly beginning in Jan.
Final notification: Within 10 days of board meeting
Write: Ellis F. Bullock, Jr., Exec. Dir.
Officers and Directors: H. William Lurton, Chair.; Don C. Lein, Pres.; Orville E. Fisher, Jr., Secy.; Barbara Thompson, Treas.; Ellis F. Bullock, Jr., Exec. Dir.; Fred Biork, Larry Bradford, Gary Buckmiller, Roger Peters, Bruce Pratt.
Number of staff: None.
Employer Identification Number: 411280587

3383
Kasal Charitable Trust ⌑
c/o Minnesota Trust Co.
107 West Oakland Ave., P.O. Box 463
Austin 55912 (507) 437-3231

Trust established in 1963 in MN.
Foundation type: Independent
Financial data (yr. ended 12/31/88): Assets, $1,630,301 (M); expenditures, $126,404, including $99,054 for grants (high: $10,000; low: $500; average: $1,000).
Purpose and activities: Support for Catholic charities in the U.S. and for education of young men and women for religious life.
Types of support: Matching funds, scholarship funds.
Limitations: No support for education below the college level. No grants to individuals, or for building or endowment funds, or research; no loans.
Publications: Annual report (including application guidelines), program policy statement, application guidelines, 990-PF, informational brochure.
Application information: Application form required.
Initial approach: Letter
Copies of proposal: 2
Deadline(s): Submit proposal preferably in Jan., Apr., or July; deadline 10th of month in which board meets
Board meeting date(s): Jan., Apr., July, Oct., and Nov.
Final notification: 6 months
Write: Warren F. Plunkett, Pres.
Officers and Trustees:* Warren F. Plunkett,* Pres.; Mary Matuska,* Secy.; Rt. Rev. Msgr. B.P. Mangan,* Treas.
Corporate Trustee: Minnesota Trust Co.
Number of staff: None.
Employer Identification Number: 416031334

3384
Margaret H. and James E. Kelley Foundation Inc. ⌑
425 Hamm Bldg.
St. Paul 55102

Established in 1982 in MN.
Foundation type: Independent
Financial data (yr. ended 11/30/88): Assets, $1,439,122 (M); expenditures, $101,586, including $70,475 for 70 grants (high: $10,000; low: $100).
Purpose and activities: Support for education, the arts, health, and social services.
Limitations: Giving primarily in MN.
Application information:
Initial approach: Letter
Deadline(s): Nov. 30
Write: James E. Kelley, Treas.
Officer: James E. Kelley, Treas.
Employer Identification Number: 416017973

3385
Anna M. Kuhl Scholarship Trust ⌑
c/o Norwest Bank St. Paul, N.A., Capital Mgmt. & Trust
55 East Fifth St.
St. Paul 55101-2701

Established in 1956 in MN.
Foundation type: Independent
Financial data (yr. ended 12/31/87): Assets, $918,277 (M); expenditures, $189,106, including $172,725 for grants to individuals.
Purpose and activities: Scholarships to needy full-time students who attend a university in Minneapolis or St. Paul, MN.
Types of support: Student aid.
Limitations: Giving primarily in Minneapolis and St. Paul, MN.
Application information:
Initial approach: Letter
Trustee: Norwest Bank St. Paul, N.A.
Employer Identification Number: 416045981

3386
Helen Lang Charitable Trust ⌑
c/o First Trust, N.A.
W-555 First National Bank Bldg.
St. Paul 55101 (612) 291-5130

Established in 1980.
Donor(s): Helen Lang.†
Foundation type: Independent
Financial data (yr. ended 8/31/88): Assets, $1,467,139 (M); expenditures, $137,733, including $125,000 for 6 grants (high: $50,000; low: $5,000).
Purpose and activities: Support largely for education, conservation, and hospitals.
Types of support: Research, general purposes.
Limitations: Giving primarily in MN.
Application information:
Initial approach: Written form only
Deadline(s): None
Write: Rod Thein
Trustees: Andrew Scott, First Trust, N.A.
Employer Identification Number: 416231202

3387
The Lieberman-Okinow Foundation
9549 Penn Ave. South
Minneapolis 55431 (612) 887-5200

Incorporated in 1961 in MN.
Donor(s): Carousel Snack Bars of Minnesota, Inc., Lieberman Enterprises, Inc.
Foundation type: Company-sponsored
Financial data (yr. ended 09/30/88): Assets, $1,823 (M); gifts received, $378,416; expenditures, $386,872, including $386,840 for 136 grants (high: $220,000; low: $10; average: $100-$1,000).
Purpose and activities: Giving primarily for Jewish welfare funds; some support for community funds and higher education.
Limitations: Giving primarily in MN.
Application information: Contributes only to pre-selected organizations. Applications not accepted.
Write: David Lieberman, V.P.
Officers and Directors:* Adele Lieberman,* Pres.; David Lieberman,* V.P.; Stephen Lieberman,* Secy.; Harold Okinow,* Treas.
Employer Identification Number: 416036200

3388
Richard Coyle Lilly Foundation
c/o First Trust, N.A.
Two West First National Bank Bldg., P.O. Box 64704
St. Paul 55164 (612) 291-5132

Incorporated in 1941 in MN.
Donor(s): Richard C. Lilly.†
Foundation type: Independent
Financial data (yr. ended 12/31/86): Assets, $5,138,609 (M); expenditures, $260,039, including $179,500 for 54 grants (high: $50,000; low: $250).

Purpose and activities: Emphasis on higher and environmental education, culture, youth, social services, and community support organizations.
Types of support: General purposes, continuing support, annual campaigns, seed money, building funds, equipment, land acquisition, endowment funds, research, special projects, publications, matching funds.
Limitations: Giving primarily in St. Paul, MN. No grants to individuals, or for fellowships or scholarships; no loans.
Publications: 990-PF.
Application information: Application form not required.
Initial approach: Proposal or letter
Copies of proposal: 1
Deadline(s): Nov. 15
Board meeting date(s): Dec.
Final notification: 6 weeks
Write: Jeffrey T. Peterson
Officers and Directors:* David M. Lilly, Pres.; Elizabeth M. Lilly, V.P.; David M. Lilly, Jr., Secy.; Susanne Lilly Hutcheson, Bruce A. Lilly.
Employer Identification Number: 416038717

3389
Lutheran Brotherhood Foundation ⌑
625 Fourth Ave. South
Minneapolis 55415 (612) 340-5821

Established in 1982 in MN.
Donor(s): Lutheran Brotherhood, Lutheran Brotherhood Research Corp.
Foundation type: Independent
Financial data (yr. ended 12/31/88): Assets, $31,256,000 (M); gifts received, $8,000,000; expenditures, $900,000, including $736,376 for 34 grants (high: $80,000; low: $2,000; average: $25,000-$35,000).
Purpose and activities: Grants for Lutheran churches, schools, and other religious organizations only; emphasis on innovative projects which are beyond the operational ongoing resources of the recipient organization. The foundation is also establishing a Reformation research library and sponsors conferences on Lutheranism.
Types of support: Seed money, matching funds, special projects.
Limitations: No grants to individuals, or for operating budgets, continuing support, annual campaigns, emergency funds, deficit financing, building funds, equipment and materials, land acquisition, renovation projects, endowments, scholarships, fellowships, program support, research, or publications; no loans.
Publications: Informational brochure (including application guidelines).
Application information: Application form required.
Initial approach: Telephone or letter of not more than 3 typewritten pages
Copies of proposal: 1
Deadline(s): None
Board meeting date(s): Quarterly
Final notification: 3 months after deadlines
Write: Turi Whiting
Officers: Robert P. Gandrud,* Pres.; Paul R. Ramseth,* V.P., Treas. and Exec. Dir.; David J. Larson, Secy. and Legal Counsel.
Trustees:* Arlen R. Bjella, William R. Halling, Mary Ellen Schmider, Stanford Tostengard.
Number of staff: 1 full-time professional.
Employer Identification Number: 411449680

3390
The Mahadh Foundation ▼
287 Central Ave.
Bayport 55003 (612) 439-1557

Established in 1962.
Donor(s): Mary Andersen Hulings, Fred C. Andersen,† Katherine B. Andersen.
Foundation type: Independent
Financial data (yr. ended 02/28/89): Assets, $7,232,291 (M); expenditures, $2,524,810, including $2,468,731 for 112 grants (high: $325,000; low: $250; average: $1,000-$20,000).
Purpose and activities: Emphasis on education, music, medical research and health agencies, and youth and social services, including the disadvantaged and housing programs for the homeless.
Types of support: General purposes, operating budgets, seed money, research, capital campaigns, equipment, special projects, endowment funds.
Limitations: Giving primarily in MN, with emphasis on the Bayport area and St. Paul, and in western WI. No grants to individuals, or for scholarships or fellowships,; no loans.
Publications: Annual report (including application guidelines).
Application information: Application form required.
Initial approach: Letter or proposal
Copies of proposal: 1
Deadline(s): Submit proposal preferably in Mar., June, Sept., or Dec.; no set deadline
Board meeting date(s): Generally May, Aug., Nov., and Jan.
Final notification: 3 months
Write: Mary Andersen Hulings, Pres., or Peggie Scott, Grants Consultant
Officers and Directors:* Mary Andersen Hulings,* Pres.; Albert D. Hulings,* V.P.; Martha H. Kaemmer,* V.P.; Mary H. Rice,* V.P. ; Kathleen R. Conley,* Secy.; William J. Begin,* Treas.
Number of staff: 2
Employer Identification Number: 416020911

3391
Mankato Citizens Telephone Company Foundation ⌑
221 East Hickory
Mankato 56001

Established in 1963 in MN.
Foundation type: Company-sponsored
Financial data (yr. ended 2/28/88): Assets, $1,267,748 (M); gifts received, $300,000; expenditures, $106,094, including $104,935 for 35 grants (high: $34,000; low: $50).
Purpose and activities: Support for education, social services, and general charitable giving.
Limitations: Giving primarily in the areas of company operations.
Application information:
Initial approach: Letter or proposal
Deadline(s): None
Write: David R. Lindenberg, Pres.
Officers: David R. Lindenberg, Pres.; Thomas R. Borchert, V.P.; David A. Christensen, Secy.-Treas.
Employer Identification Number: 416034001

3392
Ted Mann Foundation
704 Hennepin Ave., Rm.202
Minneapolis 55403 (612) 333-2520

Established in 1984 in CA.
Donor(s): Ted Mann.
Foundation type: Independent
Financial data (yr. ended 11/30/89): Assets, $43,396,049 (M); gifts received, $7,432,885; expenditures, $1,302,754, including $1,170,914 for 48 grants (high: $237,500; low: $200).
Purpose and activities: Support primarily for religious and medical purposes; giving also for education.
Types of support: Annual campaigns.
Limitations: No grants to individuals.
Application information: Contributes only to pre-selected organizations. Applications not accepted.
Write: Ted Mann, Pres.
Officers: Ted Mann, Pres.; Marvin Mann, V.P.; Esther Bergman, Secy.-Treas.
Number of staff: 1 part-time professional; 1 part-time support.
Employer Identification Number: 953952657

3393
Marbrook Foundation
400 Baker Bldg.
Minneapolis 55402 (612) 332-2454

Trust established in 1948 in MN.
Donor(s): Edward Brooks,† Markell C. Brooks,† Markell C. Brooks Charitable Trust.
Foundation type: Independent
Financial data (yr. ended 12/31/89): Assets, $6,400,028 (M); expenditures, $302,225, including $260,000 for 58 grants (high: $20,000; low: $750).
Purpose and activities: Support for education, visual and performing arts, social welfare, physical and mental health, and conservation and preservation.
Types of support: Operating budgets, continuing support, annual campaigns, seed money, emergency funds, building funds, endowment funds, matching funds, professorships, internships, research, conferences and seminars, special projects, capital campaigns, equipment, renovation projects.
Limitations: Giving limited to the Minneapolis-St. Paul, MN, area. No support for religious purposes. No grants to individuals, or for deficit financing, equipment, scholarships, fellowships, demonstration projects, or publications.
Publications: Annual report (including application guidelines).
Application information: Application form not required.
Initial approach: Proposal
Copies of proposal: 1
Deadline(s): Submit proposal preferably in Mar. or Sept.; deadlines May 15 and Oct. 15

Board meeting date(s): May and Nov.
Final notification: 3 weeks after meeting
Write: Conley Brooks, Jr., Exec. Dir.
Trustees: Conley Brooks, Jr., Exec. Dir.; John E. Andrus III, Conley Brooks, William R. Humphrey, Jr.
Number of staff: None.
Employer Identification Number: 416019899

3394
Mardag Foundation ▼ ⌑
1120 Norwest Ctr.
St. Paul 55101 (612) 224-5463

Trust established in 1969 in MN.
Donor(s): Agnes E. Ober.†
Foundation type: Independent
Financial data (yr. ended 12/31/88): Assets, $21,494,494 (M); expenditures, $1,172,773, including $946,818 for 68 grants (high: $50,000; low: $1,770).
Purpose and activities: Giving for social service agencies, conservation, programs to benefit senior citizens, arts and cultural programs, and education.
Types of support: Special projects, building funds, research, seed money, deficit financing, matching funds, equipment, emergency funds, general purposes, renovation projects.
Limitations: Giving limited to MN. No support for sectarian religious programs. No grants to individuals, or for annual campaigns, endowment funds, scholarships, fellowships, or generally for continuing support.
Publications: Annual report, 990-PF, program policy statement, application guidelines.
Application information: Application form not required.
Initial approach: Letter or proposal
Copies of proposal: 1
Deadline(s): None
Board meeting date(s): Quarterly and as required
Final notification: 90 days
Write: Paul A. Verret, Secy.
Officers: Thomas G. Mairs,* Principal Officer; Stephen S. Ober,* Financial Officer; Paul A. Verret, Secy.
Trustees:* James E. Davidson, Virginia G. Davidson, Constance M. Levi, Gayle M. Ober, James C. Otis.
Number of staff: None.
Employer Identification Number: 237022429

3395
Maslon Foundation ⌑ ☆
1800 Midwest Plaza Bldg.
Minneapolis 55402

Established in 1955.
Donor(s): James I. Maslon, Patricia J. Maslon.
Foundation type: Independent
Financial data (yr. ended 12/31/88): Assets, $1,028,275 (M); gifts received, $107,753; expenditures, $38,822, including $35,996 for 51 grants (high: $7,701; low: $25).
Purpose and activities: Giving primarily for arts and culture, especially museums; support also for civic affairs, health, education, and Jewish organizations.
Limitations: Giving primarily in CA, NY, and MN. No grants for scholarships, fellowships, or prizes; no loans.
Officers: Luella R. Maslon, Pres.; James I. Maslon, V.P. and Treas.; Enid M. Starr, V.P.; Florence S. Sigal, Secy.
Employer Identification Number: 416021701

3396
The McKnight Endowment Fund for Neuroscience ☆
410 Peavey Bldg.
Minneapolis 55402 (612) 333-4220

Established in 1987 in MN.
Donor(s): The McKnight Foundation.
Foundation type: Independent
Financial data (yr. ended 12/31/89): Assets, $25,036 (M); gifts received, $1,710,000; expenditures, $1,750,976, including $1,668,334 for 42 grants to individuals (high: $50,000; low: $30,000).
Purpose and activities: Awards grants for neuroscience research, especially as it pertains to memory and to a clearer understanding of diseases affecting memory and its biological substrates.
Types of support: Grants to individuals, research.
Limitations: Giving limited to U.S. citizens or permanent residents.
Application information: Applications for Developmental Research Project Awards solicited by invitation only following nominating process. Application form required.
Initial approach: Letter
Deadline(s): Jan. 1 for Scholars Awards
Board meeting date(s): Mar.
Final notification: Apr. 1 for Scholars Awards
Write: Marilyn J. Pidany, Administrator
Officers and Directors:* Samuel H. Barondes, M.D.,* Pres.; Ann M. Graybiel,* V.P.; Michael O'Keefe,* Secy.-Treas.; Cynthia Boynton, Corey S. Goodman, Eric Kandel, M.D., Charles F. Stevens, M.D.
Employer Identification Number: 411563321

3397
The McKnight Foundation ▼
410 Peavey Bldg.
Minneapolis 55402 (612) 333-4220

Incorporated in 1953 in MN.
Donor(s): William L. McKnight,† Maude L. McKnight,† Virginia M. Binger, James H. Binger.
Foundation type: Independent
Financial data (yr. ended 12/31/89): Assets, $917,641,548 (M); expenditures, $33,820,243, including $31,911,975 for 215 grants (high: $2,000,000; low: $1,500; average: $1,500-$2,000,000) and $50,000 for 10 grants to individuals of $5,000 each.
Purpose and activities: Emphasis on grantmaking in the areas of human and social services; has multi-year comprehensive program in the arts, housing, and aid to families in poverty; has multi-year program for support of projects in non-metropolitan areas of MN; supports nationwide scientific research programs in areas of (1) neuroscience, particularly for research in memory and diseases affecting memory, and (2) basic plant biology (applications for these programs are solicited periodically through announcements in scientific journals and directly to institutions carrying out research programs).
Types of support: Research, operating budgets, building funds, seed money, equipment, matching funds, capital campaigns, general purposes, renovation projects, special projects.
Limitations: Giving limited to organizations in MN, especially the seven county Twin Cities , MN, area, except for special programs initiated by the board of directors. No support for religious organizations for religious purposes or biomedical research. No grants to individuals (except for the Human Service Awards), or for basic research in academic disciplines (except for stated programs in plant biology research), endowment funds, scholarships, fellowships, national fundraising campaigns, ticket sales, or conferences; no loans.
Publications: Annual report (including application guidelines), grants list, occasional report.
Application information: Human Service Awards are restricted to MN residents; nominations must be received by Oct. 1. Application form not required.
Initial approach: Letter
Deadline(s): Mar. 8, June 8, Sept. 10, and Dec. 10
Board meeting date(s): June, Sept., Dec., and Mar.
Final notification: 2 and 1/2 months
Write: Michael O'Keefe, Exec. V.P.
Officers: Cynthia Boynton,* Pres.; Michael O'Keefe, Exec. V.P.; James M. Binger,* V.P. and Treas.; Marilyn Pidany, Secy.
Directors:* James H. Binger, Patricia S. Binger, Virginia M. Binger.
Number of staff: 5 full-time professional; 1 part-time professional; 4 full-time support.
Employer Identification Number: 410754835

3398
The Sumner T. McKnight Foundation ⌑
c/o Norwest Bank Minneapolis, Trust Tax Dept.
6th and Marquette Ave.
Minneapolis 55479-0063
Application address: 4555 Nathan Ln., No. 311, Plymouth, MN 55441; Tel.: (612) 577-9421

Incorporated in 1956 in MN.
Donor(s): Sumner T. McKnight,† H. Turney McKnight.
Foundation type: Independent
Financial data (yr. ended 12/31/88): Assets, $3,981,641 (M); gifts received, $25,000; expenditures, $344,031, including $292,833 for 32 grants (high: $40,000; low: $1,000).
Purpose and activities: Emphasis on music, fine arts, conservation and recreation, historical societies, higher and secondary education, inner-city programs, and community funds.
Limitations: Giving primarily in MN; some support also in MD. No support for religion. No grants to individuals, or for endowment or capital funds, or trips or tours.
Application information: Application form not required.
Initial approach: Proposal
Deadline(s): Well in advance of board meeting
Board meeting date(s): Jan.
Write: Iva Kroeger

Officers and Directors:* H. Turney McKnight, Pres.; Sumner T. McKnight II,* V.P.; John T. Westrom,* Secy.-Treas.; Christina McKnight Kippen.
Employer Identification Number: 416022360

3399
The McNeely Foundation
444 Pine St.
St. Paul 55101 (612) 228-4444

Established in 1981 in MN.
Donor(s): Lee and Rose Warner Foundation.
Foundation type: Independent
Financial data (yr. ended 12/31/88): Assets, $2,664,715 (M); gifts received, $20,808; expenditures, $76,067, including $9,793 for 6 grants (high: $3,968; low: $75; average: $3,000-$5,000) and $62,510 for employee matching gifts.
Purpose and activities: Support primarily for economics and business education; grants also for gifts and selected community projects.
Types of support: Matching funds, employee matching gifts.
Limitations: Giving primarily in the St. Paul-Minneapolis, MN, area.
Application information: Application form not required.
Initial approach: Letter
Copies of proposal: 1
Deadline(s): Submit proposal preferably in Sept. or Dec.
Board meeting date(s): As determined by trustees
Write: Malcolm W. McDonald, Trustee
Trustees: W.E. Barness, Frank A. Koscielack, Malcolm W. McDonald, Gregory McNeely, Harry G. McNeely, Jr., Harry G. McNeeley III, Shannon McNeely Whitaker.
Number of staff: None.
Employer Identification Number: 411392221

3400
McVay Foundation
10201 Wayzata Blvd.
Minnetonka 55343

Established in 1984 in MN.
Donor(s): M.D. McVay.
Foundation type: Independent
Financial data (yr. ended 12/31/89): Assets, $3,100,000 (M); qualifying distributions, $170,000, including $170,000 for grants.
Purpose and activities: Support for education, particularly higher and early childhood education, cultural programs, and youth and social service agencies.
Types of support: General purposes.
Application information: Applications not accepted.
Officers: M.D. McVay, Pres.; Danita Greene, V.P.; T. Todd McKay, V.P.; R. Thomas Green, Secy.; Mary McVay, Treas.
Number of staff: None.
Employer Identification Number: 363311833

3401
Meadowood Foundation ⌑
4122 IDS Center
Minneapolis 55402

Established in 1968.
Foundation type: Independent
Financial data (yr. ended 12/31/88): Assets, $5,651,133 (M); expenditures, $369,402, including $303,000 for 10 grants (high: $50,000; low: $5,000).
Purpose and activities: Giving for education, cultural programs, conservation, and youth.
Types of support: General purposes, building funds.
Limitations: Giving primarily in MN. No grants to individuals.
Application information: Contributes only to pre-selected organizations. Applications not accepted.
Officers and Directors:* Douglas J. Dayton,* Pres. and Treas.; Shirley D. Dayton,* V.P.; Ronald N. Gross,* Secy.; Bruce C. Dayton, David D. Dayton, Steven J. Melander-Dayton.
Employer Identification Number: 410943749

3402
The Medtronic Foundation ▼
7000 Central Ave., N.E.
Minneapolis 55432 (612) 574-3024

Established in 1979 in MN.
Donor(s): Medtronic, Inc.
Foundation type: Company-sponsored
Financial data (yr. ended 04/30/89): Assets, $1,303,962 (M); gifts received, $300,000; expenditures, $1,179,348, including $1,086,440 for 78 grants (high: $262,625; low: $1,000; average: $1,000-$20,000) and $87,320 for 315 employee matching gifts.
Purpose and activities: Emphasis on physical health promotion, biomedical engineering, the elderly, higher, secondary, and elementary education, arts and culture, civil rights, social service agencies, and community funds.
Types of support: Operating budgets, continuing support, annual campaigns, seed money, matching funds, scholarship funds, fellowships, special projects, employee matching gifts, endowment funds.
Limitations: Giving primarily in areas of company operations, including Phoenix and Tempe, AZ; Minneapolis, Brooklyn Center, Coon Rapids, Fridley, and Milaca, MN; Irvine, Anaheim, and San Diego, CA; Haverhill, Danvers, and Wellesley, MA; Forest Hills, NY; Canton, OH; and PR, or to national organizations having an effect on these areas. No support for United Way member agencies, primarily social organizations, religious, political, or fraternal activities, primary health care, or health research. No grants to individuals, or for deficit financing, research, travel, fundraising events, advertising, conferences, operating support for smaller arts groups, or multiple-year commitments; grants seldom for capital or endowment funds.
Publications: Annual report, application guidelines.
Application information: Requests from the Twin Cities to be sent to MN address; requests from other Medtronic communities to be sent to local manager who will forward them to headquarters with an assessment of the request. Application form not required.
Initial approach: Proposal with letter
Copies of proposal: 1
Deadline(s): Submit proposal between Aug. and Mar.; no set deadline; most decisions made in Oct., Dec., and Apr.
Board meeting date(s): June, Aug., Oct., Dec., and Apr.
Final notification: At least 60 days
Write: Jan Schwarz, Mgr.
Officers and Directors:* Paul Citron,* Chair.; William W. Chorske,* Vice-Chair.; Celia Barnes,* Secy.; Lester J. Swenson,* Treas.; Janet Fiola, Ron Lund, Daniel R. Luthringshauser, Glen D. Nelson, M.D.
Number of staff: 1 part-time professional; 1 part-time support.
Employer Identification Number: 411306950

3403
The Melamed Foundation ⌑
100 Washington Sq., Suite 1650
Minneapolis 55401 (612) 473-2588
Application address: 2445 M St., N.W., Washington, DC 20037; Tel.: (202) 663-6736

Incorporated in 1947 in MN.
Donor(s): Members of the Melamed family.
Foundation type: Independent
Financial data (yr. ended 12/31/87): Assets, $540,118 (M); expenditures, $222,485, including $215,080 for 21 grants (high: $119,843; low: $22).
Purpose and activities: Emphasis on Jewish welfare funds; grants also for higher education, cultural organizations, temple support, and hospitals.
Application information:
Deadline(s): None
Write: Arthur Douglas Melamed, V.P.
Officers and Trustees: Ruth H. Melamed, Pres. and Secy.; Arthur Douglas Melamed, V.P. and Treas.; Barbara McConagha, V.P.; Robert L. Melamed, V.P.; William L. Melamed, V.P.
Employer Identification Number: 416019581

3404
The Gladys and Rudolph Miller Foundation
5112 IDS Ctr.
Minneapolis 55402 (612) 332-9147

Established in 1980.
Donor(s): Rudolph W. Miller, Miller Felpax Corp.
Foundation type: Independent
Financial data (yr. ended 11/30/89): Assets, $842,807 (M); gifts received, $40,000; expenditures, $191,581, including $181,509 for 6 grants (high: $151,509; low: $500; average: $8,000).
Purpose and activities: Grants primarily as continuing support for medical organizations, Jewish giving, and the performing arts.
Types of support: Annual campaigns, continuing support, research, special projects.
Limitations: Giving primarily in MN, with emphasis on the Twin Cities.
Application information: Grants largely at the initiative of the donor. Application form not required.
Initial approach: Letter

Deadline(s): None
Write: Rudolph W. Miller, Pres.
Officers and Directors:* Rudolph W. Miller,* Pres. and Treas.; Sidney Loyber,* V.P. and Secy.; Sidney Barrows.
Employer Identification Number: 411388774

3405
The Minneapolis Foundation ▼
500 Foshay Tower
821 Marquette Ave. South
Minneapolis 55402 (612) 339-7343
Application address for the Minnesota Nonprofits Assistance Fund: Susan Kenny Stevens, Admin., Colonial Office Park Bldg., 2700 University Ave. West, Suite 70, St. Paul, MN 55114; Tel.: (612) 647-0013

Incorporated in 1915 in MN.
Foundation type: Community
Financial data (yr. ended 03/31/89): Assets, $112,720,434 (M); gifts received, $9,015,620; expenditures, $11,112,794, including $9,096,654 for 1,224 grants (average: $7,500-$35,000) and $1,200,000 for loans.
Purpose and activities: "To attract and mobilize community and philanthropic assets to promote equal access to resources needed for every individual, family and community in MN to reach full potential. The foundation carries forward this mission in the following ways: As Grantmaker, providing direct financial resources to programs that target immediate or emerging community issues; as a Catalyst, mobilizing community leaders and constituencies; as a Community Resource, providing services to donors, nonprofit organizations, and the community at large; as a Resource Developer, building a permanent unrestricted endowment; and as a Steward, receiving and distributing community resources."
Types of support: Seed money, emergency funds, equipment, technical assistance, loans, special projects, continuing support, general purposes, operating budgets.
Limitations: Giving primarily in MN, with emphasis on the Minneapolis-St. Paul, seven-county metropolitan area. No support for national campaigns, religious organizations for religious purposes, veterans' or fraternal organizations, or organizations within umbrella organizations. No grants to individuals, or for annual campaigns, deficit financing, building or endowment funds, land acquisition, matching gifts, scholarships, fellowships, research, publications, conferences, courtesy advertising, benefit tickets, telephone solicitations, or memberships.
Publications: Annual report, newsletter, 990-PF, application guidelines.
Application information: Undesignated funds considered in May and Nov.; requests to the McKnight-Neighborhood Self-Help Initiatives Program and Emma B. Howe Memorial Fdn. reviewed in Mar. and Sept.; Minnesota Women's Fund considered in July and Jan.; B.C. Gamble and P.W. Skogmo Fdn., June and Dec. Application form required.
Initial approach: Applicant should request guidelines for the appropriate fund
Copies of proposal: 17
Deadline(s): Undesignated grants, Mar. 1 and Sept. 1; MNSHIP grants, Jan. 10 and July 10; Emma B. Howe Memorial Fdn. grants, June 1 and Dec. 1; Minnesota Women's Fund, May 15 and Nov. 15; B.C. Gamble and P.W. Skogmo Fdn., Apr. 1 and Oct. 1
Board meeting date(s): Quarterly; distribution committee meets 8 times a year
Write: Marion G. Etzwiler, Pres.
Officers and Trustees:* David P. Crosby,* Chair.; Richard Green, Vice-Chair.; Richard W. Schoenke, Vice-Chair.; Marion G. Etzwiler, Pres.; Conley Brooks, Jr.,* Secy.; Clinton A. Schroeder,* Treas.; and 19 additional trustees.
Trustee Banks: First Bank Minneapolis, Norwest Bank Minneapolis.
Number of staff: 17 full-time professional.
Employer Identification Number: 416029402

3406
Minnesota Foundation
1120 Norwest Ctr.
St. Paul 55101 (612) 224-5463

Incorporated in 1949 in MN; in 1984 became a supporting organization of the Saint Paul Foundation.
Foundation type: Independent
Financial data (yr. ended 12/31/87): Assets, $8,025,244 (M); gifts received, $1,042,675; expenditures, $793,056, including $558,192 for grants (high: $160,000; low: $500; average: $600-$20,000), $2,240 for 1 grant to an individual and $10,093 for 7 foundation-administered programs.
Purpose and activities: Giving primarily for the humanities and social services.
Types of support: Grants to individuals, operating budgets, continuing support, scholarship funds.
Limitations: Giving primarily in MN.
Publications: Annual report, occasional report.
Application information:
Deadline(s): Varies
Board meeting date(s): Quarterly or as required
Final notification: Varies
Write: Judith K. Healey, Pres.
Officers: Judith K. Healey, Pres.; Paul A. Verret, Secy.; Robert S. Davis,* Treas.
Trustees:* Frank Hammond, Chair.; Emily Anne Staples, Vice-Chair.; Robert L. Bullard, Richard A. Moore, Nancy N. Weyerhaeuser, Leonard H. Wilkening.
Number of staff: 2
Employer Identification Number: 410832480

3407
Minnesota Mining and Manufacturing Foundation, Inc. ▼
(also known as 3M Foundation, Inc.)
3M Center, Bldg. 521-11-01
St. Paul 55144-1000 (612) 736-3781

Incorporated in 1953 in MN.
Donor(s): Minnesota Mining & Manufacturing Co.
Foundation type: Company-sponsored
Financial data (yr. ended 12/31/88): Assets, $42,173,581 (M); expenditures, $9,919,552, including $8,688,302 for grants (high: $750,000; low: $500; average: $500-$10,000) and $721,991 for 2,713 employee matching gifts.
Purpose and activities: Support for community funds, higher education, the arts, human services, including programs for alcohol and drug abuse, the disabled and disadvantaged, women and youth, rehabilitation, civic involvement, and preventive health care.
Types of support: Operating budgets, continuing support, annual campaigns, emergency funds, matching funds, employee matching gifts, scholarship funds, professorships, internships, fellowships, special projects, research.
Limitations: Giving primarily in areas where the company has facilities in AL, AK, CA, CO, FL, GA, HI, IL, IN, IA, KY, MD, MA, MI, MN, MS, MO, NE, NJ, NY, NC, ND, OH, OK, OR, PA, SC, SD, TX, UT, VA, WA, WV, and WI. No support for projects of specific religious denominations or sects, athletic events, or conduit agencies. No grants to individuals, or for capital or endowment funds, loans or investments, propaganda and lobbying efforts, fundraising events and associated advertising, travel, publications unrelated to foundation-funded projects, seed money, deficit financing, or conferences; no loans.
Publications: Corporate giving report (including application guidelines), informational brochure (including application guidelines), grants list.
Application information: Application form required.
Initial approach: Letter or personal visit by appointment
Copies of proposal: 1
Deadline(s): At least 8 weeks prior to month in which board meets
Board meeting date(s): Mar., Aug., and Dec.
Final notification: 3 months
Write: Eugene W. Steele, Secy.
Officers and Directors:* Donald W. Larson,* Pres.; Stanley W. Thiele,* V.P.; Eugene W. Steele,* Secy.; Dwight W. Peterson,* Treas.; William E. Coyne, Livio D. DeSimone, Donald H. Frenette, Harry A. Hammerly, Allen F. Jacobson, Lester C. Krogh, Manuel J. Monteiro, Thomas J. Scheuerman, L. James Schoenwetter, Thomas P. Skoog, Christopher J. Wheeler.
Number of staff: 2 full-time professional; 2 full-time support; 2 part-time support.
Employer Identification Number: 416038262

3408
Oscar Mitchell, Jr. Trust ⌑ ☆
c/o Norwest Bank Duluth, N.A.
230 West Superior St.
Duluth 55802-1916

Established in 1983 in MN.
Foundation type: Independent
Financial data (yr. ended 6/30/89): Assets, $1,978,928 (M); expenditures, $127,665, including $105,025 for 42 grants to individuals (high: $2,501; low: $2,500; average: $2,500).
Purpose and activities: Scholarships for local area high school students for higher education.
Types of support: Student aid.
Limitations: Giving limited to Duluth, Carlton, Cloquet, Esko, Hermantown, Proctor, Two Harbors, and Wrenshall, MN, residents.

Application information: Application forms available from guidance department of local high schools. Application form required.
Trustee: William P. Van Evera.
Scholarship Committee: Joe R. Berini, James Bovis, Richard Carlson, Bruce Potter, Jean Sederberg, Maurie Seitz.
Employer Identification Number: 416148927

3409
MSI Foundation ⌑ ☆
Two Pine Tree Dr.
Arden Hills 55112-3715 (612) 631-4862

Established in 1980.
Foundation type: Independent
Financial data (yr. ended 12/31/88): Assets, $1,679,749 (M); expenditures, $167,641, including $160,860 for 83 grants (high: $42,518; low: $50).
Purpose and activities: Support primarily for education, medical research, community affairs, safety, and youth.
Limitations: Giving primarily in the Minneapolis-St. Paul, MN, area.
Application information: Application form required.
Initial approach: Proposal
Deadline(s): None
Write: Richard Cowles, V.P.
Officers: Gordon Lindquist, Pres.; Richard Cowles, V.P. and Treas.; Chester A. Zinn, Jr., Secy.; Richard Rosel, Treas.
Directors: Bruce G. Anderson, and 10 additional directors.
Employer Identification Number: 411392947

3410
MWVE Fund
807 Lonsdale Bldg.
Duluth 55802 (218) 722-4757

Established in 1968 in MN.
Donor(s): Mary C. Van Evera, William P. Van Evera, other members of the Van Evera family.
Foundation type: Independent
Financial data (yr. ended 12/31/88): Assets, $103,127 (M); gifts received, $81,971; expenditures, $102,791, including $100,721 for 134 grants (high: $14,300; low: $10).
Purpose and activities: Aid to indigent persons, higher education, fine arts, public health and medical research, churches, public information, and public policy organizations.
Types of support: General purposes.
Limitations: Giving primarily in northeastern MN, with emphasis on the city of Duluth. No grants to individuals.
Application information:
Initial approach: Proposal
Deadline(s): None
Final notification: Within 1 month
Write: William P. Van Evera or Mary C. Van Evera, Trustees
Trustees: Mary C. Van Evera, William P. Van Evera.
Employer Identification Number: 416081875

3411
Nash Foundation
c/o Norwest Capital Advisers
5300 Norwest Ctr., 620 Marquette
Minneapolis 55479-2049

Established in 1922 in MN.
Foundation type: Independent
Financial data (yr. ended 12/31/89): Assets, $2,393,469 (M); expenditures, $86,000, including $70,650 for 53 grants (high: $7,500; low: $500).
Purpose and activities: Support for education, programs for the handicapped, social service and youth agencies, and cultural programs.
Types of support: Annual campaigns, capital campaigns, continuing support, general purposes, special projects.
Limitations: Giving primarily in the midwestern states, with emphasis on MN.
Publications: Application guidelines.
Application information: Foundation is not actively seeking additional requests for contributions.
Deadline(s): Jan. 15
Board meeting date(s): May
Final notification: June
Write: John M. Nash, Pres.
Officers and Trustees:* John M. Nash,* Pres.; Nicholas Nash,* V.P.; Nanette D. Schoeder,* Secy.; Charles H. Nash,* Treas.; Henry K. Atwood, Mary Anna Dyar, Kathleen L. Nash, Mary A. Nash, Jeffrey Norton.
Number of staff: 1 part-time professional.
Employer Identification Number: 416019142

3412
George W. Neilson Foundation
c/o Norwest Capitol Advisors
5300 Norwest Ctr.
Minneapolis 55479-2049 (612) 667-1771

Trust established in 1962 in MN.
Donor(s): George W. Neilson.†
Foundation type: Independent
Financial data (yr. ended 12/31/89): Assets, $2,895,031 (M); gifts received, $170,438; expenditures, $126,008, including $103,000 for 11 grants (high: $70,000; low: $475).
Purpose and activities: Emphasis on matching funds for community needs, leadership, theater and the arts, and rural and economic development.
Types of support: Annual campaigns, conferences and seminars, matching funds.
Limitations: Giving primarily in the Bemidji, MN, area. No support for religious activities or governmental services. No grants to individuals, or for endowment funds, scholarships, fellowships, or basic research.
Application information: Application form not required.
Initial approach: Letter
Copies of proposal: 1
Deadline(s): May 1
Board meeting date(s): July or Aug.
Write: Jack Randall, Treas.
Officers: Katharine Neilson Cram, Pres.; Edward M. Arundel, Secy.; Jack Randall, Treas.
Number of staff: None.
Employer Identification Number: 416022186

3413
North Star Research Foundation
625 Second Ave. South, Suite 404
Minneapolis 55402 (612) 339-8101

Established in 1982 in MN.
Foundation type: Independent
Financial data (yr. ended 12/31/89): Assets, $1,800,000 (L); expenditures, $82,000, including $56,000 for 1 loan.
Purpose and activities: Grants to businesses or individuals in the form of loans (program-related investments) to produce or retain jobs to strengthen the region.
Types of support: Program-related investments, loans.
Limitations: Giving limited to MN and surrounding states. No loans or grants where other funds are likely to become available, or for building, construction or marketing costs.
Publications: Application guidelines.
Application information: Application form not required.
Initial approach: Telephone or letter
Deadline(s): None
Board meeting date(s): Apr., July, and Oct.
Final notification: Within 120 days if possible
Write: Henry Doerr, Consultant
Officers and Directors:* Donald Brown,* Pres.; Ettore Infante,* V.P.; John E. Haaland,* Secy.; Harold Chucker,* Treas.; and 20 additional directors.
Number of staff: None.
Employer Identification Number: 411408469

3414
Northern Star Foundation ⌑
440 Hamm Bldg.
408 St. Peter St.
St. Paul 55102

Incorporated in 1960 in MN.
Donor(s): Members of the Hamm family.
Foundation type: Independent
Financial data (yr. ended 10/31/88): Assets, $3,071,402 (M); expenditures, $157,175, including $142,000 for 65 grants (high: $25,000; low: $10).
Purpose and activities: Emphasis on secondary and higher education, including scholarship funds, cultural programs, youth agencies, and a community fund.
Types of support: Scholarship funds.
Limitations: Giving primarily in MN and CA.
Application information: Contributes only to pre-selected organizations. Applications not accepted.
Officers and Directors:* William H. Hamm,* Pres.; Edward H. Hamm,* V.P. and Treas.; Candace S. Hamm, V.P.; Joseph A. Mann, Secy.
Employer Identification Number: 416030832

3415
Northwest Area Foundation ▼
West 975 First National Bank Bldg.
St. Paul 55101-1373 (612) 224-9635

Incorporated in 1934 in MN as Lexington Foundation; name changed to Louis W. and Maud Hill Family Foundation in 1950; present name adopted 1975.
Donor(s): Louis W. Hill, Sr.,† and other members of the Hill family.
Foundation type: Independent

Financial data (yr. ended 02/28/90): Assets, $228,378,768 (M); expenditures, $14,167,259, including $12,998,505 for 115 grants (high: $500,000; low: $3,600; average: $56,515-$113,030) and $125,000 for 1 loan.
Purpose and activities: Program directions include 1) regional economic development; 2) basic human needs; 3) natural resource conservation and management; and 4) the arts.
Types of support: Special projects, research, consulting services, technical assistance, program-related investments, seed money.
Limitations: Giving primarily in ID, IA, MN, MT, ND, OR, SD, and WA. No support for religious programs or propaganda. No grants to individuals, or for scholarships, fellowships, endowment or capital funds, films, travel, overhead, physical plants, equipment, publications, operating budgets, continuing support, annual campaigns, emergency funds, deficit financing, building funds, land acquisition, renovation projects, or conferences.
Publications: Annual report, newsletter, application guidelines.
Application information: Application form required.
Initial approach: Letter
Copies of proposal: 1
Deadline(s): None
Board meeting date(s): Bimonthly beginning in Feb.
Final notification: 3 to 4 months
Write: Terry Tinson Saario, Pres.
Officers: Roger R. Conant,* Chair. and Treas.; Marcia J. Bystrom,* Vice-Chair.; Terry Tinson Saario, Pres. and Secy.; Karl N. Stauber, V.P.
Trustees: Irving Clark, W. John Driscoll, Sheila ffolliot, Louis W. Hill, Jr., Maud Hill Schroll.
Directors:* Nina M. Archabal, W.E. Bye Barsness, Steven L. Belton, Worth Bruntjen, David F. Hickok, M.D., David A. Lanegran, Richard S. Levitt, Carlos Luis.
Number of staff: 7 full-time professional; 7 full-time support.
Employer Identification Number: 410719221

3416
Norwest Foundation ▼
Norwest Ctr.
Seventh and Marquette
Minneapolis 55479-1055 (612) 667-7860

Established in 1979 in MN.
Donor(s): Norwest Corp., and affiliated banks.
Foundation type: Company-sponsored
Financial data (yr. ended 12/31/87): Assets, $99,003 (M); gifts received, $1,559,000; expenditures, $2,831,840, including $2,735,731 for 308 grants (high: $585,000; low: $250; average: $1,000-$60,000) and $91,075 for 464 employee matching gifts.
Purpose and activities: Giving for community funds, higher education, cultural programs (including performing arts and theater), social service and youth agencies, and economic development.
Types of support: Annual campaigns, building funds, capital campaigns, continuing support, employee matching gifts, equipment, operating budgets, employee-related scholarships, seed money, special projects.
Limitations: Giving primarily in areas of company operations, including MN, IA, NE, ND, SD, MT, and WI. No support for religious organizations for religious purposes, or for fraternal organizations. No grants to individuals, or for conferences, tickets, or travel; no loans.
Publications: Annual report (including application guidelines).
Application information: Application form not required.
Initial approach: Letter
Copies of proposal: 1
Deadline(s): None
Board meeting date(s): Varies; usually every 2 months
Final notification: 2 weeks after meeting
Write: Diane P. Lilly, Pres.
Officers: Diane P. Lilly,* Pres.; Stanley S. Stroup, Secy.; Carolyn H. Gabanski, Treas.
Directors:* Lloyd P. Johnson, Richard M. Kovacevich.
Number of staff: 1 full-time professional; 1 part-time professional; 1 full-time support.
Employer Identification Number: 411367441

3417
Numero-Steinfeldt Foundation ⌑ ☆
314 West 90th St.
Minneapolis 55420 (612) 926-7714

Donor(s): J.A. Numero.
Foundation type: Independent
Financial data (yr. ended 12/31/88): Assets, $392,518 (M); gifts received, $7,500; expenditures, $114,104, including $105,880 for 46 grants (high: $79,000; low: $20).
Purpose and activities: Giving primarily to Jewish organizations, including federated funds and temple support; some grants also for health and hospitals.
Limitations: Giving primarily in MN. No grants to individuals.
Application information:
Initial approach: Letter
Deadline(s): None
Write: J.A. Numero, Pres.
Officers: J.A. Numero, Pres.; B.M. Numero, V.P.; O.J. Steinfeldt, V.P.; S.J. Steinfeldt, Secy.
Employer Identification Number: 416025897

3418
Alice M. O'Brien Foundation ⌑
324 Forest
Mahtomedi 55115 (612) 426-2143

Incorporated in 1951 in MN.
Donor(s): Alice M. O'Brien.†
Foundation type: Independent
Financial data (yr. ended 12/31/88): Assets, $2,475,554 (M); expenditures, $186,441, including $158,650 for 23 grants (high: $50,000; low: $150).
Purpose and activities: Emphasis on secondary and higher education, including medical education and research; some support for social services and cultural programs.
Types of support: Operating budgets, annual campaigns, seed money, building funds, equipment, research.
Limitations: Giving primarily in MN. No grants to individuals, or for endowment funds, scholarships, fellowships, or matching gifts; no loans.
Application information: Application form not required.
Initial approach: Proposal
Copies of proposal: 1
Deadline(s): May 1 and Nov. 15
Board meeting date(s): June and Dec.
Final notification: 6 months
Write: Julia O'Brien Wilcox, Pres.
Officers and Directors: Julia O'Brien Wilcox, Pres.; Thomond R. O'Brien, Treas.; Eleanor M. O'Brien, Terrance G. O'Brien.
Number of staff: None.
Employer Identification Number: 416018991

3419
The Casey Albert T. O'Neil Foundation
c/o First Trust, N.A.
P.O. Box 64704
St. Paul 55164-0704 (612) 291-6240
Application address: c/o First Trust, N.A., First National Bank Bldg., St. Paul, MN 55101

Trust established in 1965 in MN.
Donor(s): Albert T. O'Neil.†
Foundation type: Independent
Financial data (yr. ended 06/30/89): Assets, $8,374,354 (M); expenditures, $630,605, including $617,742 for 99 grants (high: $35,000; low: $500; average: $2,000-$20,000).
Purpose and activities: Emphasis on Roman Catholic religious associations and missions, health agencies, and aid to handicapped children.
Types of support: Operating budgets, continuing support, annual campaigns, seed money, emergency funds.
Limitations: Giving primarily in St. Paul, MN. No grants to individuals, or for deficit financing, capital campaigns, endowment or scholarship funds, matching gifts, research, special projects, publications, or conferences; no loans.
Application information: Application form not required.
Initial approach: Proposal
Deadline(s): None
Board meeting date(s): As required
Final notification: 3 months
Write: Sally A. Mullen
Trustees: Thomas J. Dwight, John F. Kelly, Casey A.T. O'Neil, First Trust, N.A.
Number of staff: None.
Employer Identification Number: 416044079

3420
I. A. O'Shaughnessy Foundation, Inc. ▼ ⌑
c/o First Trust, N.A.
P.O. Box 64704
St. Paul 55164 (612) 222-2323

Incorporated in 1941 in MN.
Donor(s): I.A. O'Shaughnessy,† John F. O'Shaughnessy, Globe Oil and Refining Companies, Lario Oil and Gas Co.
Foundation type: Independent
Financial data (yr. ended 12/31/86): Assets, $33,919,021 (M); gifts received, $5,255,159; expenditures, $1,653,776, including $1,551,588 for 47 grants (high: $200,000; low: $1,000; average: $5,000-$50,000).
Purpose and activities: Giving for cultural programs, secondary and higher education,

social services, medical research, and Roman Catholic religious organizations.
Types of support: Annual campaigns, building funds, equipment, endowment funds, research, general purposes, continuing support.
Limitations: Giving limited to the U.S., with emphasis on MN, IL, KS, and TX. No support for religious missions or individual parishes. No grants to individuals; no loans.
Publications: Application guidelines.
Application information: Grants usually initiated by the directors. Application form not required.
Initial approach: Letter
Copies of proposal: 1
Deadline(s): None
Board meeting date(s): June and Nov.
Final notification: 6 months
Write: Paul J. Kelly, Secy.-Treas.
Officers and Directors:* John F. O'Shaughnessy,* Pres.; Charles E. Lyman IV,* V.P.; Donald E. O'Shaughnessy,* V.P.; Eileen O'Shaughnessy,* V.P.; Lawrence O'Shaughnessy,* V.P.; Paul J. Kelly, Secy.-Treas.
Employer Identification Number: 416011524

3421
Oakleaf Foundation ⌑
4122 IDS Ctr.
Minneapolis 55402

Established in 1967 in MN.
Donor(s): K.N. Dayton, Julia W. Dayton.
Foundation type: Independent
Financial data (yr. ended 12/31/88): Assets, $177,831 (M); expenditures, $2,371,228, including $2,345,200 for 4 grants (high: $2,300,000; low: $200).
Purpose and activities: Emphasis on cultural programs; support also for philanthropic associations.
Types of support: General purposes.
Limitations: Giving primarily in the Minneapolis and St. Paul, MN, area. No grants to individuals.
Application information: Contributes only to pre-selected organizations. Applications not accepted.
Officers and Directors: K.N. Dayton, Pres. and Treas.; Julia W. Dayton, V.P. and Secy.; Duncan N. Dayton, Judson M. Dayton.
Employer Identification Number: 416080485

3422
Onan Family Foundation
310 Interchange Plaza West
435 Ford Rd.
Minneapolis 55426 (612) 544-4702

Incorporated in 1942 in MN.
Donor(s): Members of the Onan family.
Foundation type: Independent
Financial data (yr. ended 12/31/89): Assets, $4,997,434 (M); expenditures, $276,666, including $208,060 for 32 grants (high: $28,000; low: $1,500; average: $1,500-$10,000).
Purpose and activities: To improve the physical, cultural, and educational condition of mankind; giving primarily to Protestant churches, social welfare agencies, cultural and civic organizations, and educational institutions.
Types of support: Continuing support, emergency funds, general purposes, operating budgets, seed money, special projects.
Limitations: Giving primarily in the Twin Cities, MN, metropolitan area. No grants to individuals, or for capital or endowment funds, research, scholarships, fellowships, trips, political campaigns, or matching gifts; no loans.
Publications: Annual report (including application guidelines).
Application information: Application form not required.
Initial approach: Letter
Copies of proposal: 1
Deadline(s): Submit proposal in Apr. or Sept.
Board meeting date(s): May and Nov.
Write: David W. Onan, II, Pres.
Officers and Trustees:* David W. Onan II,* Pres. and Treas.; Bruce R. Smith,* Secy.; David W. Onan III, Lois C. Onan.
Staff: Susan J. Smith, Exec. Dir.
Number of staff: 1 part-time professional.
Employer Identification Number: 416033631

3423
Ordean Foundation ▼
501 Ordean Bldg.
Duluth 55802 (218) 726-4785

Incorporated in 1933 in MN.
Donor(s): Albert L. Ordean,† Louise Ordean.†
Foundation type: Independent
Financial data (yr. ended 12/31/89): Assets, $21,254,255 (M); expenditures, $1,580,534, including $993,666 for 52 grants (high: $166,500; low: $200; average: $500-$50,000), $103,399 for 1 foundation-administered program and $265,150 for loans.
Purpose and activities: To administer and furnish relief and charity for the local poor; to make grants to local organizations performing services or providing facilities in certain areas of health and youth activities.
Types of support: Building funds, scholarship funds, loans, operating budgets, matching funds, program-related investments, equipment, continuing support, renovation projects, special projects.
Limitations: Giving limited to Duluth and contiguous cities and townships in St. Louis County, MN. No support for national fundraising campaigns or direct religious purposes. No grants to individuals, or for endowment funds, travel, conferences or workshops, benefits, or research, including biomedical research.
Publications: Annual report (including application guidelines), grants list.
Application information: Application form required.
Initial approach: Telephone, letter, or proposal
Copies of proposal: 12
Deadline(s): 15th of each month
Board meeting date(s): Monthly
Final notification: Within 10 days of board meeting
Write: Antoinette Poupore-Haats, Exec. Dir.
Officers and Directors:* Arthur C. Josephs,* Pres.; Charles M. Bell,* V.P.; Antoinette Poupore-Haats,* Secy.-Treas. and Exec. Dir.; Cynthia Albright, Roger M. Bowman, Howard P. Clarke, Robert M. Fischer, Rita D. Hutchens, Arend J. Sandbulte, Donald G. Wirtanen.
Number of staff: 2 full-time professional; 2 part-time support.
Employer Identification Number: 410711611

3424
George M. Palmer Foundation ⌑ ☆
P.O. Box 8500
Mankato 56002-8500 (612) 625-1882

Established in 1959.
Donor(s): Hubbard Milling Co.
Foundation type: Company-sponsored
Financial data (yr. ended 4/30/89): Assets, $45,622 (M); gifts received, $152,730; expenditures, $167,848, including $163,584 for 57 grants (high: $33,333; low: $50) and $4,160 for employee matching gifts.
Purpose and activities: Giving primarily for community funds and higher education, including an employee matching gift program; support also for youth development.
Types of support: Scholarship funds, building funds, employee matching gifts, general purposes.
Limitations: Giving primarily in MN.
Application information: Application form required.
Initial approach: Forms available upon request
Deadline(s): May 10
Write: Ogden W. Confer, Pres.
Officers and Directors: Ogden W. Confer, Pres.; Mary C. Koehler, V.P.; Richard P. Confer, Secy.; Ruth K. Bergerson, George D. McClintock.
Employer Identification Number: 410853757

3425
Persephone Foundation ⌑ ☆
1535 Dain Tower
Minneapolis 55402

Established in 1985 in MN.
Foundation type: Independent
Financial data (yr. ended 12/31/88): Assets, $360,348 (M); expenditures, $151,726, including $144,000 for 3 grants (high: $135,000; low: $2,000).
Purpose and activities: Support primarily for an art center's endowment fund; minor support for environmental conservation and general charitable organizations.
Types of support: Endowment funds, general purposes.
Limitations: Giving primarily in Minneapolis, MN.
Application information:
Initial approach: Proposal
Deadline(s): None
Write: Jane K. Maner, Asst. Secy.-Treas.
Officers and Directors: Benson K. Whitney, Pres. and Treas.; Michael F. Gron, Secy.; Pennell W. Ballentine, Joseph H. Whitney, Wheelock Whitney III.
Employer Identification Number: 366064005

3426
The Jay and Rose Phillips Family Foundation ▼ ¤
(Formerly The Phillips Foundation)
100 Washington Sq., Suite 1650
Minneapolis 55401
Mailing address: 2345 N.E. Kennedy St., Minneapolis, MN 55413; Tel.: (612) 331-6230

Incorporated in 1944 in MN.
Donor(s): Jay Phillips, and members of the Phillips family.
Foundation type: Independent
Financial data (yr. ended 12/31/86): Assets, $56,774,301 (M); expenditures, $2,494,290, including $2,173,337 for 231 grants (high: $537,967; low: $15; average: $1,000-$36,000).
Purpose and activities: Giving primarily for hospitals and medical research, Jewish religious organizations and welfare funds, higher education, social services, and cultural programs.
Types of support: Building funds, equipment, research, scholarship funds, fellowships, professorships, matching funds, loans, lectureships.
Limitations: Giving primarily in MN and the Midwest. No support for religious organizations for sectarian purposes. No grants to individuals, or for endowment funds.
Publications: Application guidelines.
Application information: Application form not required.
Initial approach: Letter
Copies of proposal: 1
Deadline(s): None
Board meeting date(s): As required
Final notification: 30 days
Write: Thomas P. Cook, Exec. Dir.
Officers and Trustees: Jay Phillips, Pres.; Rose Phillips, V.P.; Morton B. Phillips, Treas.; Thomas P. Cook, Exec. Dir.; Paula Bernstein, William Bernstein, Jack I. Levin, Pauline Phillips.
Number of staff: 3 full-time professional; 1 part-time professional.
Employer Identification Number: 416019578

3427
William H. Phipps Foundation
c/o First Trust, N.A.
Two West First National Bank Bldg., Box 64704
St. Paul 55164-0704 (612) 291-5132
Application address: P.O. Box 106, Hudson, WI 54016; Tel.: (715) 386-5848

Incorporated in 1946 in WI.
Donor(s): Helen Clark Phipps,† Stephen C. Phipps.†
Foundation type: Independent
Financial data (yr. ended 04/30/89): Assets, $11,425,320 (M); gifts received, $3,500; expenditures, $1,220,001, including $1,102,350 for 20 grants (high: $33,000; low: $850; average: $100-$25,000).
Purpose and activities: Support for a hospital, an arts center, a church group, and civic organizations.
Limitations: Giving limited to the St. Croix River Valley of WI and MN. No grants to individuals.
Application information: Application form not required.
Initial approach: Proposal
Copies of proposal: 1
Deadline(s): None
Final notification: 3 months
Write: Hugh F. Gwin, Secy.-Treas.
Officers and Directors:* Hugh G. Bryce,* Pres.; Frederick E. Nagel,* V.P.; Hugh F. Gwin,* Secy.-Treas.; Gordon Anderson, Marie B. Blakeman.
Employer Identification Number: 396043312

3428
The Pillsbury Foundation ▼
(Formerly The Pillsbury Company Foundation)
Mail Station 37X5
200 South Sixth St.
Minneapolis 55402-1464 (612) 330-5434

Incorporated in 1957 in MN.
Donor(s): Pillsbury, Inc.
Foundation type: Company-sponsored
Financial data (yr. ended 05/31/89): Assets, $10,815,216 (M); gifts received, $4,207,624; expenditures, $4,727,832, including $4,518,347 for grants.
Purpose and activities: The foundation focuses on prevention programs for disadvantaged children and youth, including support for exceptional programs in the communities of company operations and a limited number of national grants. In addition to focused giving, the foundation also supports a limited number of broader efforts in headquarters and plant communities that reduce or eliminate underlying causes of child poverty and contribute toward the full development of disadvantaged children and youth. Support also for health and welfare, mainly through the United Way, job scholarships through the Citizen's Scholarship Foundation of America and matching gifts, culture and art, and civic affairs and community development. Support for scholarship funds only at pre-selected institutions.
Types of support: Annual campaigns, scholarship funds, employee-related scholarships, matching funds, employee matching gifts, seed money, technical assistance, operating budgets, special projects.
Limitations: Giving primarily in areas where the company has plants and subsidiaries in the U.S. No support for religious denominations or sects or for health organizations. No grants to individuals, or for capital or endowment campaigns, fundraising, or travel; no loans; no product donations except through the Second Harvest Food Bank Network.
Publications: Corporate giving report (including application guidelines), informational brochure (including application guidelines).
Application information: Application form not required.
Initial approach: Letter
Copies of proposal: 1
Deadline(s): None
Board meeting date(s): Bimonthly
Final notification: 1-4 months
Write: Dianne Brennan, Exec. Dir.
Officers: Ian A. Martin,* Pres.; Dianne Brennan, Exec. Dir.
Contributions Committee:* James R. Behnke, Edna Brazaitais, and 10 additional members.
Number of staff: 2 full-time professional; 2 full-time support.
Employer Identification Number: 416021373

3429
The Elizabeth C. Quinlan Foundation, Inc. ¤
1205 Foshay Tower
Minneapolis 55402 (612) 333-8084

Incorporated in 1945 in MN.
Donor(s): Elizabeth C. Quinlan.†
Foundation type: Independent
Financial data (yr. ended 12/31/88): Assets, $2,150,135 (M); expenditures, $191,880, including $127,625 for 46 grants (high: $20,000; low: $100).
Purpose and activities: Grants largely for Roman Catholic institutions, higher and secondary education, cultural programs, health agencies, and social services.
Types of support: Operating budgets, continuing support, annual campaigns, seed money, emergency funds, deficit financing, building funds, equipment, land acquisition, endowment funds, research, scholarship funds, matching funds, general purposes, special projects.
Limitations: Giving limited to MN. No grants to individuals; no loans.
Publications: Annual report (including application guidelines).
Application information: Application form not required.
Initial approach: Letter
Copies of proposal: 1
Deadline(s): Submit proposal preferably in May or June; deadline Sept. 1
Board meeting date(s): Oct.
Final notification: Dec. 1
Write: Richard A. Klein, Pres.
Officers: Richard A. Klein, Pres. and Treas.; Lucia L. Crane, V.P.; Mary Elizabeth Lahiff, Secy.
Trustees: Eileen L. Grundman, Anne L. Klein, Eugene P. McCahill.
Number of staff: 2 part-time support.
Employer Identification Number: 410706125

3430
Gerald Rauenhorst Family Foundation
3434 Norwest Ctr.
Minneapolis 55402 (612) 333-7600

Incorporated in 1965 in MN.
Donor(s): Gerald A. Rauenhorst, Henrietta Rauenhorst, Rauenhorst Corp.
Foundation type: Independent
Financial data (yr. ended 12/31/88): Assets, $13,271,616 (M); gifts received, $494,500; expenditures, $610,738, including $531,000 for 17 grants (high: $100,000; low: $1,000).
Purpose and activities: Giving for higher education, Roman Catholic church support and church-related institutions, and chemical dependency programs.
Limitations: Giving primarily in MN. No grants to individuals.
Application information: Contributes only to pre-selected organizations. Applications not accepted.
Write: John H. Agee, V.P.
Officers and Directors:* Gerald A. Rauenhorst,* Pres.; Henrietta Rauenhorst,* Exec. V.P.; John H. Agee, V.P. and Managing Dir.
Employer Identification Number: 410080773

3431
Red Wing Shoe Company Foundation ⌑
314 Main St.
Red Wing 55066 (612) 388-8211

Incorporated in 1955 in MN.
Donor(s): Red Wing Shoe Co., Inc.
Foundation type: Company-sponsored
Financial data (yr. ended 12/31/87): Assets, $445,912 (M); gifts received, $300,000; expenditures, $277,407, including $277,200 for 36 grants (high: $104,000; low: $50).
Purpose and activities: Emphasis on youth agencies; support also for environmental education, higher and secondary education, civic affairs, and health agencies.
Types of support: Annual campaigns, building funds, capital campaigns, exchange programs, general purposes, lectureships, matching funds, renovation projects, research, scholarship funds, seed money, special projects, continuing support.
Limitations: Giving primarily in the Red Wing, MN, area. No support for individuals.
Publications: Annual report.
Application information:
Initial approach: Letter
Deadline(s): None
Write: Joseph P. Goggin, Secy.-Treas.
Officers: W.D. Sweasy, Pres.; W.J. Sweasy, V.P.; Joseph P. Goggin, Secy.-Treas.
Number of staff: None.
Employer Identification Number: 416020177

3432
The Regis Foundation ⌑
5000 Normandale Rd.
Minneapolis 55436

Established in 1981 in MN.
Foundation type: Company-sponsored
Financial data (yr. ended 6/30/88): Assets, $0 (M); gifts received, $572,085; expenditures, $572,085, including $572,025 for 14 grants (high: $233,425; low: $100).
Purpose and activities: Emphasis on Jewish welfare, culture and the arts, and education.
Application information:
Initial approach: Letter
Write: Myron Kunin, Pres.
Officers: Myron Kunin, Pres. and Treas.; Frank Evangelist, Secy.
Employer Identification Number: 411410790

3433
Margaret Rivers Fund ⌑
c/o First National Bank of Stillwater
213 East Chestnut St.
Stillwater 55082

Incorporated in 1948 in MN.
Donor(s): Robert E. Slaughter.†
Foundation type: Operating
Financial data (yr. ended 12/31/87): Assets, $14,573,453 (M); expenditures, $698,246, including $585,250 for 211 grants (high: $50,000; low: $300).
Purpose and activities: A private operating foundation; grants primarily for hospitals, church support, youth agencies, aid to the handicapped, and care of the aged; grants also for cultural programs and conservation.
Limitations: Giving primarily in MN.
Application information:
Initial approach: Letter
Deadline(s): None
Write: William Klapp, Pres.
Officers and Trustees:* William D. Klapp,* Pres.; Helen Moelter, Secy.; Robert G. Briggs, Treas.; David Pohl.
Employer Identification Number: 416017102

3434
RMT Foundation ⌑
12001 Technology Dr.
Eden Prairie 55344

Established in 1982 in MN.
Donor(s): Rosemount, Inc.
Foundation type: Independent
Financial data (yr. ended 11/30/88): Assets, $621,848 (M); gifts received, $316,349; expenditures, $335,649, including $334,800 for 36 grants (high: $115,000; low: $500).
Purpose and activities: Support for educational institutions, and cultural and social service organizations.
Limitations: Giving primarily in St. Paul and Minneapolis, MN.
Officers: Vernon H. Heath, Pres.; John R. Duxbury, V.P.; Bonnie Smith, Secy.; Robert M. Cox, Treas.
Employer Identification Number: 411433607

3435
Rochester Area Foundation
220 South Broadway, Suite 112
Rochester 55904 (507) 282-0203

Established in 1944 in MN by resolution of trust.
Foundation type: Community
Financial data (yr. ended 12/31/89): Assets, $3,453,967 (M); gifts received, $962,615; qualifying distributions, $122,737, including $122,737 for 11 grants (high: $42,000; low: $875).
Purpose and activities: To help launch new projects which represent innovative approaches to community needs, support special purposes of established organizations, promote volunteer and citizen involvement in community, respond to current human needs in community, and support projects without other sources of support; giving in areas of health, education, human services, and development and assistance of community affairs.
Types of support: Seed money, emergency funds, matching funds, technical assistance, program-related investments, consulting services.
Limitations: Giving limited to Olmsted County, MN. No support for religious organizations for sectarian purposes. No grants to individuals, or for endowment funds, annual campaigns, operating budgets, continuing support, land acquisition, deficit financing, scholarships, fellowships, or research.
Publications: Program policy statement, application guidelines, newsletter, informational brochure.
Application information: Application form required.
Initial approach: Letter
Copies of proposal: 10
Deadline(s): Jan. 1, Apr. 1, July 1, and Oct. 1
Board meeting date(s): Feb., May, Aug., and Nov.
Final notification: 1 week
Write: Joan E. Kark, Exec. Dir.
Trustees: Ann N. Ferguson, Chair.; Charles W. Pappas, Vice-Chair.; Donald M. Sudor, Vice-Chair.; Isabel C. Huizenga, Secy.; Jean H. Freeman, Treas.; William C. Boyne, Dorothy Callahan, Rick Colvin, Lance Davenport, David Griffin, Rev. Lester J. Horntvedt, Jennings O. Johnson, Michael D. Klampe, Anna McGee, Bruce Qualey, Marilyn Stewart, James L. Talen, Alan Tuntland.
Number of staff: 1 full-time professional; 1 full-time support.
Employer Identification Number: 416017740

3436
The Rodman Foundation ⌑
2100 First National Bank Bldg.
St. Paul 55101 (612) 228-0935

Established in 1969 in MN.
Donor(s): Members of the Titcomb family.
Foundation type: Independent
Financial data (yr. ended 12/31/88): Assets, $1,562,725 (M); gifts received, $87,500; expenditures, $205,295, including $167,550 for 36 grants (high: $50,000; low: $100; average: $500-$3,000).
Purpose and activities: Emphasis on higher and secondary education, historic preservation, and a science museum; grants also for cultural programs, hospitals, community funds, and youth agencies.
Types of support: Operating budgets, building funds, scholarship funds.
Limitations: Giving primarily in MN. No grants to individuals.
Application information: Application form not required.
Initial approach: Letter
Copies of proposal: 1
Deadline(s): None
Board meeting date(s): As required
Final notification: 2 to 3 weeks
Write: E. Rodman Titcomb, Jr., Pres.
Officers: E. Rodman Titcomb, Jr.,* Pres.; Julie C. Titcomb,* V.P.; Joseph S. Micallef, Secy.; Gordon E. Hed, Treas.
Directors:* Edward R. Titcomb.
Number of staff: None.
Employer Identification Number: 237025570

3437
Patrick & Alice Rogers Charitable Foundation ⌑
6400 Barrie Rd., No. 1504
Edina 55435-2342 (612) 926-0790

Established in 1985 in MN.
Donor(s): Patrick W. Rogers.
Foundation type: Independent
Financial data (yr. ended 12/31/87): Assets, $1,140,105 (M); gifts received, $150,469; expenditures, $79,476, including $67,960 for 23 grants (high: $30,000; low: $25).
Purpose and activities: Support primarily for Catholic organizations, including welfare agencies, and colleges and universities.
Limitations: Giving primarily in Minneapolis and St. Paul, MN.

Application information: Application form not required.
Initial approach: Letter
Deadline(s): None
Write: Patrick W. Rogers, Pres.
Officers: Patrick W. Rogers, Pres.; Alice Rogers, Secy.
Employer Identification Number: 363381910

3438
The Saint Paul Foundation ▼
1120 Norwest Ctr.
St. Paul 55101 (612) 224-5463

Established in 1940 in MN by adoption of a plan; incorporated in 1964.
Foundation type: Community
Financial data (yr. ended 12/31/88): Assets, $107,730,130 (M); gifts received, $11,197,471; expenditures, $8,691,033, including $6,378,729 for 1,144 grants and $87,617 for 91 grants to individuals.
Purpose and activities: Support for educational, charitable, cultural, or benevolent purposes of a public nature. Grants largely to cultural, educational, health, and welfare agencies.
Types of support: Seed money, emergency funds, building funds, equipment, research, matching funds, special projects, scholarship funds, fellowships, program-related investments, employee-related scholarships, renovation projects, loans, capital campaigns, technical assistance, annual campaigns, conferences and seminars, consulting services, deficit financing.
Limitations: Giving limited to Ramsey, Washington, and Dakota counties and to the St. Paul, MN, metropolitan area. No support for sectarian religious programs, except from designated funds. No grants for operating budgets, land acquisition, publications, endowment funds (except through designated funds) or generally, for continuing support; no student loans.
Publications: Annual report, application guidelines.
Application information: Grants to individuals made from designated funds; applications not accepted. Application form not required.
Initial approach: Proposal
Copies of proposal: 1
Deadline(s): 3 months before next board meeting
Board meeting date(s): Quarterly
Final notification: Within 1 month
Write: Paul A. Verret, Pres.
Officers: Frederick T. Weyerhaeuser,* Chair.; Virginia D. Brooks,* Vice-Chair.; Paul A. Verret, Pres. and Secy.; Jean E. Hart, V.P.; John D. Healey, Jr.,* Treas.
Board of Directors:* David M. Craig, M.D., Patrick J. Donovan, Willis M. Forman, Marice L. Halper, Reatha Clark King, Joseph R. Kingman III, Richard H. Kyle, Thomas W. McKeown, Joseph T. O'Neill, Barbara B. Roy, Jon A. Theobald.
Corporate Trustees: American National Bank & Trust Co., First Trust, N.A., Norwest Bank St. Paul, N.A.
Number of staff: 9 full-time professional; 10 full-time support; 1 part-time support.
Employer Identification Number: 416031510

3439
Carl and Verna Schmidt Foundation ⌑
Route 4, Box 8
St. Peter 56082-9804 (507) 931-2388

Established in 1958 in MN.
Donor(s): Carl Schmidt, Verna Schmidt.
Foundation type: Independent
Financial data (yr. ended 11/30/88): Assets, $1,418,431 (M); expenditures, $73,792, including $63,915 for 17 grants (high: $25,000; low: $20).
Purpose and activities: Support for higher education, hospitals and health associations, and conservation.
Application information:
Initial approach: Letter or proposal
Deadline(s): None
Write: Carl Schmidt, Trustee
Trustees: Alan C. Anderson, Carl Schmidt.
Employer Identification Number: 237423942

3440
The Fred M. Seed Foundation ⌑
1235 Yale Place, No. 1702
Minneapolis 55403

Established in 1960 in MN.
Donor(s): Fred M. Seed,† Fred M. Seed Living Trust.
Foundation type: Independent
Financial data (yr. ended 12/31/87): Assets, $1,117,800 (M); gifts received, $633,858; expenditures, $198,749, including $192,517 for 84 grants (high: $80,100; low: $15).
Purpose and activities: Support primarily for higher and secondary education; limited giving to cultural programs, social services, and civic affairs.
Application information: Contributes only to pre-selected organizations. Applications not accepted.
Officers: Grace M. Seed, Pres.; John C. Seed, V.P.; James M. Seed, Secy.
Employer Identification Number: 416029620

3441
Sexton Foundation ⌑
14973 95th Ave. North
Maple Grove 55369 (612) 440-4505

Donor(s): American Trailers, Inc.
Foundation type: Independent
Financial data (yr. ended 11/30/88): Assets, $1,620,050 (M); expenditures, $75,905, including $60,500 for 16 grants (high: $10,000; low: $1,000).
Purpose and activities: Support primarily for Catholic churches and colleges.
Limitations: Giving primarily in the St. Cloud, MN, and Lewisville, TX, areas. No grants to individuals.
Application information: Application form not required.
Deadline(s): None
Write: Thomas D. Sexton, V.P.
Officers: M. Yvonne Sexton, Pres.; Thomas D. Sexton, V.P.; Phyllis W. Christenson, Secy.; James Sexton, Treas.
Employer Identification Number: 411312086

3442
Sit Investment Associates Foundation ⌑
4600 Norwest Ctr.
90 South Seventh St.
Minneapolis 55402-4130

Donor(s): Sit Investment Associates, Inc.
Foundation type: Company-sponsored
Financial data (yr. ended 12/31/88): Assets, $1,508,356 (M); gifts received, $300,000; expenditures, $97,051, including $93,600 for 66 grants (high: $12,500; low: $100).
Purpose and activities: Giving primarily for social service agencies, especially those concerned with housing; support also for higher education.
Limitations: Giving limited to MN. No grants to individuals.
Application information: Contributes only to pre-selected organizations. Applications not accepted.
Trustees: Douglas C. Jones, Peter L. Mitchelson, Eugene C. Sit, Gloria A. Westlake.
Employer Identification Number: 411468021

3443
Somerset Foundation, Inc.
322 Minnesota St.
P.O. Box 64704
St. Paul 55164-0704

Established in 1960 in MN.
Donor(s): Norman B. Mears.†
Foundation type: Independent
Financial data (yr. ended 12/31/89): Assets, $1,501,331 (M); expenditures, $148,223, including $136,500 for 17 grants (high: $50,000; low: $250).
Purpose and activities: Giving for cultural programs, including performing arts groups and arts councils; support also for education and educational research and community affairs.
Types of support: General purposes.
Limitations: Giving primarily in MN.
Application information: Application form not required.
Initial approach: Letter
Copies of proposal: 1
Deadline(s): None
Write: Thomas H. Patterson, Secy.-Treas.
Officers and Trustees:* Hella L. Mears Hueg,* Pres.; William F. Hueg, Jr.,* V.P.; Thomas H. Patterson, Secy.-Treas.
Employer Identification Number: 416029569

3444
The Southways Foundation
c/o Sargent Management Co.
1300 TCF Tower
Minneapolis 55402 (612) 338-3871

Incorporated in 1950 in MN.
Donor(s): John S. Pillsbury,† and family.
Foundation type: Independent
Financial data (yr. ended 12/31/89): Assets, $6,043,540 (M); expenditures, $770,309, including $721,198 for 130 grants (high: $50,000; low: $100; average: $2,000).
Purpose and activities: Emphasis on secondary and higher education, the fine arts and other cultural activities, and community funds.
Types of support: Annual campaigns, building funds, capital campaigns, endowment funds.

Limitations: Giving primarily in MN.
Application information: Application form not required.
Initial approach: Formal proposal
Deadline(s): None
Write: Carol J. Fetzer, Asst. Secy.
Officers: John S. Pillsbury, Jr.,* Pres.; Donald K. Morrison, V.P. and Treas.; John S. Pillsbury III,* V.P.; George S. Pillsbury,* Secy.
Trustees:* Ella P. Crosby, Lucy C. Mitchell, Mrs. John S. Pillsbury, Jane P. Resor.
Number of staff: None.
Employer Identification Number: 416018502

3445
St. Croix Foundation
c/o First Trust, N.A.
Two West First National Bank Bldg., P.O. Box 64704
St. Paul 55164 (612) 291-5132

Established in 1950 in MN.
Donor(s): Ianthe B. Hardenbergh, I. Hardenbergh Charitable Annuity Trust, Gabrielle Hardenbergh.
Foundation type: Independent
Financial data (yr. ended 12/31/88): Assets, $1,975,947 (M); gifts received, $270,000; expenditures, $290,407, including $273,450 for 62 grants (high: $25,000; low: $300).
Purpose and activities: Giving for health organizations and hospitals, cultural programs, social service and youth agencies, and education, particulary higher education; support also for churches.
Types of support: General purposes, operating budgets.
Limitations: Giving limited to the Stillwater and St. Paul, MN, areas.
Application information: Application form not required.
Initial approach: Proposal
Copies of proposal: 1
Deadline(s): Nov. 15
Board meeting date(s): Dec.
Final notification: 3-4 weeks
Write: Jeffrey T. Peterson
Officers and Directors:* Robert S. Davis,* Pres.; Quentin O. Heimerman,* V.P.; Gabrielle Hardenbergh,* Secy.; Edgerton Bronson,* Treas.; Raymond A. Reister.
Number of staff: None.
Employer Identification Number: 416011826

3446
Sundet Foundation ¤ ☆
2791 Pheasant Rd.
Excelsior 55331-9572
Scholarship application address: c/o Steve Erbstoesser, 9231 Penn Ave. South, Minneapolis, MN 55431

Established in 1980.
Donor(s): Century Manufacturing Co., Fountain Industries Co., Goodall Manufacturing Co.
Foundation type: Independent
Financial data (yr. ended 12/31/88): Assets, $2,504,588 (M); gifts received, $673,241; expenditures, $144,392, including $139,865 for 68 grants (high: $15,800; low: $100) and $2,450 for 4 grants to individuals (high: $800; low: $350).
Purpose and activities: Giving primarily for community and social services, including community funds and youth development; higher and secondary education, including scholarships to children of Century Manufacturing Co. employees; Protestant churches and organizations; and medical research.
Types of support: Employee-related scholarships.
Limitations: Giving primarily in MN.
Application information: Completion of application form required for scholarships.
Deadline(s): Jan. 15 for grants; Feb. 28 for scholarships
Officers and Directors: Leland N. Sundet, Pres.; Louise C. Sundet, V.P.; Scott A. Sundet, Secy.-Treas.
Employer Identification Number: 411378654

3447
Charles B. Sweatt Foundation ¤ ☆
c/o Norwest Bank Minnesota, N.A., Trust Tax Div.
Norwest Ctr.
Minneapolis 55479-0063

Established in 1968.
Donor(s): Margaret L. Sweatt.
Foundation type: Independent
Financial data (yr. ended 2/28/89): Assets, $1,450,743 (M); gifts received, $20,000; expenditures, $69,458, including $58,000 for 26 grants (high: $10,000; low: $100).
Purpose and activities: Giving for higher and secondary education, Protestant churches, the arts, and health associations.
Application information: Applications not accepted.
Trustees: Charles B. Sweatt, Jr., Henry L. Sweatt, Margaret L. Sweatt.
Employer Identification Number: 416075853

3448
The Harold W. Sweatt Foundation ¤
1500 Bracketts Point Rd.
Wayzata 55391 (612) 473-9200

Trust established in 1968 in MN as successor in part to The Sweatt Foundation established in 1951.
Donor(s): Harold W. Sweatt.†
Foundation type: Independent
Financial data (yr. ended 02/28/89): Assets, $1,973,251 (M); expenditures, $128,333, including $105,263 for 104 grants (high: $15,000; low: $10).
Purpose and activities: Emphasis on higher and secondary education, health and social services, religious organizations, and the arts.
Application information: Application form not required.
Deadline(s): None
Write: Karen McGlynn
Trustees: A. Lachlan Reed, Harold S. Reed, Martha S. Reed, William S. Reed.
Employer Identification Number: 416075860

3449
Tennant Company Foundation
701 North Lilac Dr.
P.O. Box 1452
Minneapolis 55440 (612) 540-1207

Established in 1973 in MN.
Donor(s): Tennant Co.
Foundation type: Company-sponsored
Financial data (yr. ended 12/31/89): Assets, $85,638 (M); expenditures, $380,900, including $338,382 for 128 grants (high: $17,000; low: $500) and $22,626 for 191 employee matching gifts.
Purpose and activities: Giving for community funds, social service and youth agencies, higher education, and cultural programs including the arts and public broadcasting; limited support for conservation and health; employee-related scholarships paid through the Citizens' Scholarship Foundation of America.
Types of support: Employee-related scholarships, employee matching gifts, capital campaigns, operating budgets.
Limitations: Giving primarily in areas where Tennant Co. employees live and work; support depends on the extent to which the applicant offers its services to Tennant Co. communities in Minneapolis and the Hennepin County, MN, area. No support for agencies funded through umbrella organizations, or for religious organizations for religious purposes. No grants to individuals, or for travel, benefit tickets, or courtesy advertising.
Publications: Annual report (including application guidelines).
Application information: Application form not required.
Initial approach: Proposal or telephone
Copies of proposal: 1
Deadline(s): 4 weeks prior to board meetings
Board meeting date(s): Feb., May, Sept., and Dec.
Final notification: 4 weeks
Write: Donna Anderson, Admin., or Paul E. Brunelle, Pres.
Officers: Paul E. Brunelle, Pres.; Donna W. Anderson, Secy.; Joseph A. Shaw,* Treas.
Directors:* Chandlee M. Barksdale, Roger L. Hale, George T. Pennock.
Number of staff: 1 part-time professional; 1 part-time support.
Employer Identification Number: 237297045

3450
James R. Thorpe Foundation ¤
8085 Wayzata Blvd.
Minneapolis 55426 (612) 545-1111

Incorporated in 1974 in MN.
Donor(s): James R. Thorpe.†
Foundation type: Independent
Financial data (yr. ended 11/30/88): Assets, $6,393,030 (M); expenditures, $339,176, including $323,700 for 84 grants (high: $18,000; low: $1,000; average: $3,000-$5,000).
Purpose and activities: Giving primarily for social service agencies, especially those addressing the needs of youth, the elderly, and the disadvantaged, arts and cultural programs, and higher and secondary education; support also for community health care and medical research, and religious organizations.

Types of support: Operating budgets, annual campaigns, seed money, building funds, equipment, scholarship funds, capital campaigns, general purposes, internships, research, special projects.
Limitations: Giving primarily in MN, with emphasis on Minneapolis and St. Paul. No grants to individuals, or for continuing support, emergency or endowment funds, deficit financing, land acquisition, matching gifts, publications, seminars, benefits, or conferences; no loans.
Publications: Biennial report.
Application information: Application form not required.
Initial approach: Letter outlining proposal
Copies of proposal: 1
Deadline(s): Mar. 1 and Sept. 1
Board meeting date(s): May and Nov.
Final notification: 1 week
Write: Mrs. Edith D. Thorpe, Pres.
Officers and Directors: Edith D. Thorpe, Pres.; Leonard M. Addington, V.P.; Samuel A. Cote, V.P.; Elizabeth A. Kelly, V.P.; Mary C. Boos, Secy.; Samuel S. Thorpe III, Treas.
Number of staff: 1
Employer Identification Number: 416175293

3451
Tozer Foundation, Inc.
c/o First Trust, N.A.
First National Bank Bldg., P.O. Box 64704
St. Paul 55164 (612) 291-5134

Incorporated in 1946 in MN.
Donor(s): David Tozer.†
Foundation type: Independent
Financial data (yr. ended 10/31/89): Assets, $16,614,506 (M); expenditures, $848,686, including $259,398 for 46 grants (high: $38,000; low: $100; average: $1,000-$20,000) and $491,963 for 377 grants to individuals (high: $1,400; low: $1,200).
Purpose and activities: Giving primarily for scholarships to graduating high school students as well as undergraduate scholarships in various colleges; support also for educational projects, cultural programs, community funds, and aid to the handicapped.
Types of support: Student aid, general purposes.
Limitations: Giving primarily in MN.
Publications: 990-PF.
Application information: Candidates must apply for scholarships through selected high schools. Application form not required.
Initial approach: Letter
Copies of proposal: 1
Deadline(s): None
Board meeting date(s): 6-7 times per year
Final notification: Immediately after board meeting
Write: Grant T. Waldref, Pres.
Officers and Directors: Grant T. Waldref, Pres.; Robert S. Davis, V.P.; James R. Oppenheimer, J. Thomas Simonet, Earl C. Swanson, Jon Theobald, John F. Thoreen.
Number of staff: None.
Employer Identification Number: 416011518

3452
The Valspar Foundation ☆
1101 South Third St.
Minneapolis 55415 (612) 375-7706
Scholarship application address: Valspar Scholarship Comm., Personnel Dept., P.O. Box 1461, Minneapolis, MN 55440

Established in 1979.
Donor(s): The Valspar Corp.
Foundation type: Company-sponsored
Financial data (yr. ended 09/30/89): Assets, $47,955 (M); gifts received, $340,000; expenditures, $321,437, including $291,360 for 139 grants (high: $10,000; low: $100) and $30,000 for 30 grants to individuals of $1,000 each.
Purpose and activities: Giving for the United Way and community restoration; scholarship funds limited to children of Valspar Corp. employees entering as full-time students in post-secondary educational institutions.
Types of support: Employee-related scholarships.
Limitations: Giving limited to Minneapolis, MN and plant locations.
Publications: Application guidelines.
Application information: Application form required.
Initial approach: Telephone
Deadline(s): June 1
Board meeting date(s): As needed
Write: S. Guerrera, V.P.
Officers: C.A. Wurtele, Pres.; D. Olfe, V.P. and Secy.; S. Guerrera, V.P. and Treas.
Employer Identification Number: 411363847

3453
Dewitt & Caroline Van Evera Foundation
(Formerly Dewitt Van Evera Foundation)
29710 Kipper Rd.
St. Joseph 56374 (612) 363-8388

Established in 1959 in UT.
Donor(s): Dewitt Van Evera,† Caroline Irene Van Evera.†
Foundation type: Independent
Financial data (yr. ended 12/31/88): Assets, $2,138,719 (M); gifts received, $404,150; expenditures, $107,685, including $96,000 for 8 grants (high: $30,000; low: $1,000).
Purpose and activities: Grants for higher and secondary education, and projects to aid youth, the arts, and the disadvantaged. Almost all funding distributed on a continuing basis to ongoing projects which have been selected by the foundation's advisors.
Types of support: Continuing support, general purposes, building funds, endowment funds, scholarship funds, lectureships, operating budgets.
Limitations: Giving primarily in MN, WI, and UT. No grants to individuals, or for matching gifts; no loans.
Application information: Application form not required.
Initial approach: Letter
Copies of proposal: 1
Deadline(s): Submit proposal preferably in Sept. through Dec.
Board meeting date(s): Feb.
Write: Laura Jane V.E. La Fond, Advisor
Advisors: Laura Jane V.E. La Fond, Robert W. Van Evera, William P. Van Evera.
Trustee: First Interstate Bank of Utah.
Number of staff: None.
Employer Identification Number: 876117907

3454
Archie D. and Bertha H. Walker Foundation
1121 Hennepin Ave.
Minneapolis 55403 (612) 332-3556

Incorporated in 1953 in MN.
Donor(s): Archie D. Walker,† Bertha H. Walker.†
Foundation type: Independent
Financial data (yr. ended 12/31/89): Assets, $4,753,883 (M); expenditures, $349,757, including $273,275 for 47 grants (high: $43,500; low: $500).
Purpose and activities: Support for programs dealing with chemical dependency (chiefly alcoholism); grants also for organizations that combat white racism in the white community.
Types of support: Special projects, building funds, research, annual campaigns, conferences and seminars, operating budgets.
Limitations: Giving primarily in the seven-county Minneapolis-St. Paul, MN, metropolitan area. No support for private foundations. No grants to individuals, or for endowment funds.
Publications: Annual report (including application guidelines).
Application information: Application form required.
Initial approach: Proposal
Copies of proposal: 1
Deadline(s): Submit proposal by Dec. 1
Board meeting date(s): Annually in Mar. and as required
Final notification: June
Write: David H. Griffith, Pres.
Officers and Trustees:* David H. Griffith,* Pres.; Louise Walker McCannel,* V.P.; Berta Walker,* V.P.; Walter W. Walker,* V.P.; Teri M. Lamb,* Secy.; Harriet W. Fitts,* Treas.; Louise W. Davy, Katherine W. Griffith, Dana D. McCannel, Laurie H. McCannel, Abigail M. Walker, Amy C. Walker, Archie D. Walker, Jr., Archie D. Walker III, Elaine B. Walker, Patricia Walker, Lita W. West.
Number of staff: 2 part-time professional.
Employer Identification Number: 416022758

3455
Lee and Rose Warner Foundation
444 Pine St.
St. Paul 55101 (612) 228-4444

Incorporated in 1959 in MN.
Donor(s): Rose Warner.†
Foundation type: Independent
Financial data (yr. ended 12/31/88): Assets, $5,535,035 (M); expenditures, $295,702, including $287,648 for grants.
Purpose and activities: Support for higher education, religion, health, and social services.
Limitations: Giving primarily in MN. No grants to individuals, or for endowment funds, research programs, scholarships, or fellowships; no loans.
Application information: Application form not required.

Initial approach: Letter
Copies of proposal: 1
Deadline(s): None
Board meeting date(s): Sept. and Dec.
Write: Malcolm W. McDonald
Trustees: Donald G. McNeely, Kevin McNeely, Kevin Richey, S.W. Richey.
Number of staff: None.
Employer Identification Number: 416011523

3456
The Wasie Foundation
909 Foshay Tower
Minneapolis 55402 (612) 332-3883

Incorporated in 1966 in MN as Stan Don Mar Foundation.
Donor(s): Donald A. Wasie,† Stanley L. Wasie,† Marie F. Wasie.
Foundation type: Independent
Financial data (yr. ended 12/31/88): Assets, $11,677,969 (M); expenditures, $521,771, including $311,982 for 28 grants (high: $100,000; low: $50; average: $3,000-$5,000).
Purpose and activities: Giving primarily for higher education, including scholarship funds at selected institutions for qualified students of Polish ancestry; and support also for Roman Catholic religious associations, health organizations, mental health, the handicapped, and issues involving children and the family.
Types of support: Operating budgets, continuing support, seed money, emergency funds, building funds, equipment, land acquisition, endowment funds, special projects, research, publications, conferences and seminars, fellowships, general purposes, capital campaigns.
Limitations: Giving limited to the metropolitan area of Minneapolis and St. Paul. No grants to individuals; no loans.
Publications: Application guidelines, grants list, program policy statement.
Application information: Scholarship information available from the foundation or a participating institution. Application form required.
Initial approach: Telephone
Copies of proposal: 1
Deadline(s): Varies
Board meeting date(s): As required
Final notification: 2 weeks after board meetings
Write: Gregg D. Sjoquist, V.P.
Officers and Directors:* Marie F. Wasie,* Pres. and Treas.; J.J. Choromanski,* V.P. and Secy.; Gregg D. Sjoquist, V.P.; David A. Odahowski,* Exec. Dir.; Andrew J. Leemhuis,* Medical Dir.; Thelma G. Haynes, Ina N. Reed.
Number of staff: 2 full-time professional; 1 part-time professional; 1 full-time support.
Employer Identification Number: 410911636

3457
Wedum Foundation
4721 Spring Circle
Minnetonka 55345 (612) 476-6717

Established in 1959 in MN.
Donor(s): Maynard C. Wedum,† John A. Wedum.†
Foundation type: Independent
Financial data (yr. ended 12/31/88): Assets, $6,288,012 (M); expenditures, $316,427, including $196,012 for 13 grants (high: $75,000; low: $320) and $13,420 for 83 grants to individuals (high: $1,200; low: $50).
Purpose and activities: Giving primarily for social services, including aid for the aged, business and other education, including student aid, and health associations.
Types of support: Student aid, conferences and seminars, land acquisition, matching funds, program-related investments, seed money.
Limitations: Giving primarily in the Alexandria, MN, area.
Publications: 990-PF.
Application information: Student aid support beyond existing programs available through local "Dollars for Scholars" units. Application form required.
Copies of proposal: 1
Deadline(s): None
Board meeting date(s): Fall
Final notification: Late fall
Write: Mayo Johnson, Pres.
Officers: Mayo Johnson, Pres. and Treas.; Gary Slette, V.P.; John A. Wedum, V.P.; Mary Beth Wedum, Secy.
Number of staff: 1 part-time professional; 1 part-time support.
Employer Identification Number: 416025661

3458
Louis F. and Florence H. Weyand 1977 Charitable Trust
c/o First Trust, N.A.
First National Bank Bldg., P.O. Box 64704
St. Paul 55164-0704 (612) 291-6236

Established in 1977.
Donor(s): Louis F. Weyand,† Florence H. Weyand.
Foundation type: Independent
Financial data (yr. ended 09/30/88): Assets, $1,284,901 (M); expenditures, $97,575, including $86,145 for 42 grants (high: $13,000; low: $100; average: $1,000-$10,000).
Purpose and activities: Giving primarily for museums and the arts, including the performing arts; support also for higher and other education, and social services.
Limitations: Giving limited to MI, FL, and CA.
Application information:
Initial approach: Letter
Write: Thomas W. Murray
Trustees: Lois Bachman, Carolyn Yorkston, First Trust, N.A.
Employer Identification Number: 942473421

3459
Weyerhaeuser Family Foundation, Inc. ⌑
(Formerly Weyerhaeuser Foundation)
2100 First National Bank Bldg.
St. Paul 55101 (612) 228-0935

Incorporated in 1950 in MN.
Donor(s): Members of the Weyerhaeuser family.
Foundation type: Independent
Financial data (yr. ended 12/31/88): Assets, $8,146,710 (M); gifts received, $139,702; expenditures, $464,572, including $371,438 for 23 grants (high: $29,938; average: $10,000).
Purpose and activities: Grants restricted to support of national and international programs and services; emphasis on education for members of minority races, conservation, population control, self-help programs, and the promotion of world cooperation and understanding.
Types of support: Seed money, special projects.
Limitations: No support for elementary or secondary education. No grants to individuals, or for building or endowment funds, annual campaigns, operating budgets, equipment, scholarships, fellowships, travel or matching gifts; no loans.
Publications: Annual report (including application guidelines).
Application information: Application form required.
Initial approach: Letter
Copies of proposal: 1
Deadline(s): Submit proposal from Jan. through May; deadline June 1
Board meeting date(s): Program committee meets annually in late summer to review proposals; board meets usually in Nov.
Write: Nancy N. Weyerhaeuser, Pres.
Officers and Trustees:* Nancy N. Weyerhaeuser,* Pres.; George F. Jewett, Jr.,* V.P.; Elizabeth S. Driscoll,* Secy.; Walter S. Rosenberry III,* Treas.; Lynn Weyerhaeuser Day, Rudolph W. Driscoll, Jr., Margaret R. King, W. Howard Meadowcraft, Bette D. Moorman, Catherine W. Morley, Lynn W. Piasecki, Julie C. Titcomb, Charles A. Weyerhaeuser, Ginnie Weyerhaeuser, Nancy N. Wyerhaeuser, William T. Weyerhaeuser.
Number of staff: 1 part-time professional.
Employer Identification Number: 416012062

3460
F.K. and Vivian O'Gara Weyerhaeuser Foundation ⌑
2100 First National Bank Bldg.
St. Paul 55101 (612) 228-0935

Established in 1966 in MN.
Donor(s): F.K. Weyerhaeuser, Lynn Weyerhaeuser Day, Stanley R. Day.
Foundation type: Independent
Financial data (yr. ended 12/31/87): Assets, $1,759,308 (M); gifts received, $42,250; expenditures, $321,258, including $286,650 for 7 grants (high: $218,000; low: $1,000).
Purpose and activities: Giving primarily for cultural programs, higher and secondary education, and conservation.
Application information: Applications considered throughout the year. Application form not required.
Initial approach: Proposal
Deadline(s): None
Write: Vivian W. Piasecki, Pres.
Officers and Directors: Vivian Weyerhaeuser Piasecki, Pres.; Lynn Weyerhaeuser Day, V.P.; Frank N. Piasecki, Secy.; Stanley R. Day, Treas.
Employer Identification Number: 416054303

3461
The Frederick and Margaret L. Weyerhaeuser Foundation ¤
2100 First National Bank Bldg.
St. Paul 55101 (612) 228-0935

Incorporated in 1963 in MN.
Donor(s): Margaret Weyerhaeuser Harmon.
Foundation type: Independent
Financial data (yr. ended 6/30/88): Assets, $1,925,304 (M); gifts received, $189,033; expenditures, $581,154, including $561,200 for 24 grants (high: $200,000; low: $500; average: $1,000-$5,000).
Purpose and activities: Giving primarily for a local college library building fund, a theological seminary, and religious welfare; support also for cultural programs and higher education.
Types of support: Annual campaigns, renovation projects, special projects, general purposes, capital campaigns.
Limitations: Giving primarily in MN. No grants to individuals.
Publications: 990-PF.
Application information: Application form not required.
Initial approach: Letter
Copies of proposal: 1
Deadline(s): None
Board meeting date(s): June
Final notification: 4 to 5 weeks
Write: Frederick T. Weyerhaeuser, Pres.
Officers and Directors:* Frederick T. Weyerhaeuser,* Pres.; Charles L. Weyerhaeuser, V.P.; Joseph S. Micallef,* Secy.; Gordon E. Hed,* Treas.
Number of staff: None.
Employer Identification Number: 416029036

3462
The Charles A. Weyerhaeuser Memorial Foundation ¤
2100 First National Bank Bldg.
St. Paul 55101 (612) 228-0935

Incorporated in 1959 in MN.
Donor(s): Carl A. Weyerhaeuser Trusts, Sarah-Maud W. Sivertsen Trusts.
Foundation type: Independent
Financial data (yr. ended 02/28/89): Assets, $3,269,740 (M); gifts received, $43,045; expenditures, $325,476, including $296,850 for 13 grants (high: $100,000; low: $2,000; average: $1,000-$5,000).
Purpose and activities: Grants primarily for art, music, higher education, and community funds.
Types of support: Annual campaigns, continuing support, special projects.
Limitations: Giving primarily in MN. No grants to individuals.
Publications: 990-PF.
Application information: Application form not required.
Initial approach: Letter
Copies of proposal: 1
Deadline(s): None
Board meeting date(s): As required
Final notification: 5 to 6 weeks
Write: Lucy R. McCarthy, Pres.
Officers and Directors:* Lucy R. McCarthy,* Pres.; Robert J. Sivertsen,* V.P.; Joseph S. Micallef,* Secy.-Treas.; Elise R. Donohue, Gordon E. Hed, Walter S. Rosenberry III.
Employer Identification Number: 416012063

3463
Robert B. and Sophia Whiteside Scholarship Fund ¤
c/o First Bank, N.A.
130 West Superior St.
Duluth 55801 (218) 723-2888

Established in 1976.
Foundation type: Independent
Financial data (yr. ended 12/31/88): Assets, $2,105,603 (M); expenditures, $498,091, including $436,900 for 157 grants to individuals (high: $4,800; low: $500).
Purpose and activities: Scholarships to individuals from the top ten percent of high school graduating classes of Duluth.
Types of support: Student aid.
Limitations: Giving limited to Duluth, MN.
Application information: Applications are submitted to local high school counselors. Application form required.
Deadline(s): None
Write: C.F. Baker
Trustees: First Bank, N.A., Fryberger, Buchanan, Smith & Frederic.
Number of staff: 1
Employer Identification Number: 411288761

3464
Whitney Foundation
1535 Dain Tower
Minneapolis 55402

Established in 1959 in MN.
Donor(s): Wheelock Whitney, J. Kimball Whitney, and members of the Whitney family.
Foundation type: Independent
Financial data (yr. ended 12/31/89): Assets, $1,336,602 (M); gifts received, $86,684; expenditures, $218,675, including $205,567 for 224 grants (high: $15,000; low: $15; average: $200-$1,000).
Purpose and activities: Support for the arts, education, social service and youth agencies, and programs concerned with alcoholism, drug abuse, and AIDS.
Types of support: Annual campaigns, capital campaigns, continuing support.
Limitations: Giving primarily in Hennepin and Ramsey counties, MN. No grants to individuals, or for publications, video productions, or trips.
Application information: The foundation currently is not accepting any new applications for funds.
Write: Gladys Green
Officers: Wheelock Whitney, Pres.; J. Kimball Whitney, V.P. and Treas.; Joseph H. Whitney, Secy.
Number of staff: 2 part-time support.
Employer Identification Number: 416022514

MISSISSIPPI

3465
William Robert Baird Charitable Trust ¤
c/o Citizens National Bank
512 22nd Ave., Box 911
Meridian 39302 (601) 693-1331

Established in 1980 in MS.
Donor(s): William Robert Baird.†
Foundation type: Independent
Financial data (yr. ended 3/31/87): Assets, $1,853,541 (M); expenditures, $82,175, including $73,500 for 14 grants (high: $11,000; low: $1,500).
Purpose and activities: Grants for the benefit of the disadvantaged, including children.
Limitations: Giving limited to LA and MS.
Application information: Application form not required.
Deadline(s): None
Write: Archie R. McDonnell
Trustee: Citizens National Bank.
Employer Identification Number: 646170042

3466
The Community Foundation, Inc. ¤
P.O. Box 924
Jackson 39205-0924 (601) 372-2227

Incorporated in 1963 in MS.
Donor(s): W.K. Paine.
Foundation type: Independent
Financial data (yr. ended 12/31/88): Assets, $4,476,902 (M); expenditures, $222,779, including $217,500 for 12 grants (high: $50,000; low: $1,000).
Purpose and activities: Emphasis on Protestant religious associations, higher education, and social service agencies.
Limitations: Giving primarily in MS. No grants to individuals.
Application information: Contributes only to pre-selected organizations. Applications not accepted.
Write: W.K. Paine, Pres.
Officers: W.K. Paine, Pres. and Treas.; Carolyn P. Davis, V.P.; Werdna McClurkin, Secy.
Employer Identification Number: 237033813

3467
Carl and Virginia Johnson Day Trust ¤
108 West Madison St.
Yazoo City 39194 (601) 746-4901

Trust established in 1948 in MS.
Donor(s): Carl Day, M.D.†
Foundation type: Independent
Financial data (yr. ended 12/31/88): Assets, $2,626,228 (M); gifts received, $1,000; expenditures, $247,490, including $216,000 for 190 loans to individuals (high: $2,400; low: $500).
Purpose and activities: Loans to residents of MS who attend MS schools.
Types of support: Student loans.
Limitations: Giving limited to MS.
Application information:
Initial approach: Letter
Deadline(s): Dec. 15 and Aug. 15
Write: J.C. Lamkin, Mgr.
Officer: J.C. Lamkin, Mgr.
Trustees: W.R. Bridgforth, Hugh M. Love, Sr., R.J. Parks, Jr., F.M. Patty, Jr., B. Seward.
Employer Identification Number: 640386095

3468
Deposit Guaranty Foundation ⌘
One Deposit Guaranty Plaza
P.O. Box 1200
Jackson 39215-1200 (601) 354-8114

Incorporated in 1962 in MS.
Donor(s): Deposit Guaranty National Bank.
Foundation type: Company-sponsored
Financial data (yr. ended 1/31/88): Assets, $14,896 (M); gifts received, $255,000; expenditures, $366,191, including $351,406 for 72 grants (high: $111,352; low: $10) and $14,500 for employee matching gifts.
Purpose and activities: Emphasis on higher education and a community fund; support also for youth and social service agencies, hospitals, and the arts.
Types of support: Annual campaigns, capital campaigns, employee matching gifts, operating budgets, program-related investments, employee-related scholarships, scholarship funds.
Limitations: Giving limited to MS. No grants to individuals.
Application information:
Initial approach: Letter
Copies of proposal: 1
Board meeting date(s): Annually
Write: William M. Jones, Sr. V.P., Deposit Guaranty National Bank
Officers and Directors: E.B. Robinson, Jr., Pres.; Robert G. Barnett, Secy.; Arlen McDonald, Treas.; Howard L. McMillan, Jr.
Employer Identification Number: 646026793

3469
Feild Co-Operative Association, Inc. ⌘
P.O. Box 5054
Jackson 39216 (601) 939-9295

Incorporated in 1919 in TN.
Donor(s): Sons of the late Dr. and Mrs. Monfort Jones.
Foundation type: Independent
Financial data (yr. ended 12/31/88): Assets, $7,300,674 (M); expenditures, $1,297,258, including $82,125 for 18 grants (high: $60,000; low: $25) and $708,224 for loans to individuals.
Purpose and activities: Support for interest-bearing student loans to MS residents who are juniors or seniors in college, graduate and professional students, or students in special fields; some grants to local hospitals and social service agencies.
Types of support: Student loans.
Limitations: Giving limited to MS residents. No grants for building or endowment funds, operating budgets, or special projects.
Publications: Informational brochure, application guidelines.
Application information: Application form and personal interview required for student loans.
Initial approach: Letter
Copies of proposal: 1
Deadline(s): Submit proposal any time of the year
Board meeting date(s): Semiannually
Final notification: 4-6 weeks after applying
Write: Mrs. Ann Stephenson
Officers and Directors: Bernard B. Jones II, Chair.; Hobson C. McGehee, Jr., Pres.; B. Bryan Jones III, 1st V.P.; William M. Link, 2nd V.P.; Mrs. Glenn Pate, Kenneth Wills.
Number of staff: 3
Employer Identification Number: 640155700

3470
First Mississippi Corporation Foundation, Inc. ⌘
700 North St.
P.O. Box 1249
Jackson 39215-1249 (601) 948-7550

Incorporated in 1975 in MS.
Donor(s): First Mississippi Corp.
Foundation type: Company-sponsored
Financial data (yr. ended 6/30/88): Assets, $638,327 (L); gifts received, $125,004; expenditures, $258,820, including $204,572 for 45 grants (high: $20,000; low: $100; average: $5,000-$6,000), $15,800 for 26 grants to individuals (high: $1,200; low: $500) and $37,471 for 64 employee matching gifts.
Purpose and activities: Emphasis on higher education, including scholarships limited to valedictorians of local high schools, and employee matching gifts, community funds, excellence awards to workers (chosen by peer committee) in experimental agriculture programs, and youth agencies.
Types of support: Operating budgets, continuing support, annual campaigns, emergency funds, building funds, equipment, land acquisition, endowment funds, matching funds, employee matching gifts, scholarship funds, special projects, research, student aid.
Limitations: Giving primarily in MS, in areas of company operations. No support for health or church-related programs. No grants for seed money, deficit financing, publications, or conferences; no loans.
Application information: Application form not required.
Initial approach: Letter
Copies of proposal: 1
Deadline(s): Submit education proposals preferably between Feb. and July and all others between Aug. and Jan.; deadline 1 month prior to board meetings
Board meeting date(s): Feb. and Aug.
Final notification: 2 weeks after meetings
Write: Bonnie H. Kelley, Admin. Asst.
Officers: J. Kelley Williams,* Chair. and C.E.O.; Charles R. Gibson,* V.P.; C.M. McAuley, V.P.; R. Michael Summerford, V.P.
Trustees:* R.P. Anderson, Paul A. Becker, James W. Crook, Robert P. Guyton, Charles P. Moreton, Paul W. Murrill, William A. Percy II, Maurice T. Reed, Jr., Frank G. Smith, Jr., Leland R. Speed, R.G. Turner.
Number of staff: None.
Employer Identification Number: 510152783

3471
Phil Hardin Foundation
c/o Citizens National Bank
P.O. Box 911
Meridian 39302 (601) 483-4282
Application address: P.O. Box 3429, Meridian, MS 39302

Incorporated in 1964 in MS.
Donor(s): Philip Bernard Hardin,† Hardin's Bakeries Corp.
Foundation type: Independent
Financial data (yr. ended 12/31/89): Assets, $22,774,836 (M); qualifying distributions, $1,547,261, including $825,868 for 27 grants (high: $250,000; low: $929), $33,133 for 6 foundation-administered programs, $500,000 for loans to organizations and $7,987 for loans to individuals.
Purpose and activities: Grants primarily to schools, institutions of higher education, museums, and other educational institutions and programs. Support is for educational programs only; student loans limited to residents of MS.
Types of support: Operating budgets, continuing support, seed money, building funds, equipment, endowment funds, matching funds, program-related investments, professorships, scholarship funds, fellowships, special projects, research, publications, conferences and seminars, student loans.
Limitations: Giving primarily in MS, but also to out-of-state organizations for programs and projects benefiting the education of Mississippians. No grants to individuals (except for student loans), or for deficit financing or land acquisition.
Publications: Application guidelines, program policy statement.
Application information: Application form provided for student loans.
Initial approach: Telephone, letter, or proposal
Copies of proposal: 2
Deadline(s): None
Board meeting date(s): As required, usually at least every 2 months
Final notification: 3 months
Write: Mr. C. Thompson Wacaster, V.P.
Officers and Directors:* S.A. Rosenbaum,* Pres.; Mark M. Porter,* V.P.; C. Thompson Wacaster, V.P. for Educational Progs.; R.B. Deen, Jr.,* Secy.; Archie R. McDonnell,* Treas.; Joe S. Covington, M.D., William B. Crooks, Jr., Edwin E. Downer, Stephen O. Moore, Robert F. Ward.
Number of staff: 1 full-time professional; 1 part-time professional; 1 part-time support.
Employer Identification Number: 646024940

3472
Robert L. Howell Foundation ⌘
P.O. Box 1071
Greenwood 38930 (601) 453-3331

Established in 1962 in MS.
Foundation type: Independent
Financial data (yr. ended 12/31/88): Assets, $2,716,130 (M); expenditures, $238,132, including $25,318 for 14 grants (high: $15,000; low: $25) and $81,500 for 64 loans to individuals.
Purpose and activities: Support for undergraduate education primarily through student loans; support also for a medical organization.
Types of support: Student loans.
Limitations: Giving primarily in MS.
Application information: Application forms for student loans provided.
Deadline(s): None
Write: R.C. Wingate, Trustee
Trustees: Ellett Lawrence, J.W. Russell, Jr., R.C. Wingate.
Employer Identification Number: 646024550

3473
Elizabeth M. Irby Foundation ¤
P.O. Box 1819
Jackson 39215-1819 (601) 969-1811

Incorporated in 1952 in MS.
Donor(s): Irby Construction Co., Stuart C. Irby Co.
Foundation type: Independent
Financial data (yr. ended 12/31/87): Assets, $1,601,717 (M); gifts received, $176,265; expenditures, $300,657, including $291,104 for 103 grants (high: $38,000; low: $50; average: $1,000).
Purpose and activities: Grants primarily for higher education, including a theological seminary, and Protestant church support and religious organizations.
Types of support: Annual campaigns, building funds, capital campaigns, continuing support, emergency funds, endowment funds, general purposes, matching funds, operating budgets, research, scholarship funds, special projects.
Limitations: Giving primarily in MS. No grants to individuals.
Application information:
Initial approach: Letter
Deadline(s): None
Write: Stuart M. Irby, V.P.
Officers: Stuart C. Irby, Jr.,* Pres.; Stuart M. Irby,* V.P.; William D. Nutt, Secy.-Treas.
Trustees:* Charles L. Irby, Margaret L. Irby, Elizabeth J. Milam.
Number of staff: None.
Employer Identification Number: 646020278

3474
S. H. & D. W. Kyle Educational Trust ¤
c/o Ellis & Hirsberg
P.O. Box 400
Clarksdale 38614-0400

Foundation type: Independent
Financial data (yr. ended 11/30/88): Assets, $1,906,123 (M); expenditures, $11,310.
Purpose and activities: Support for higher education.
Limitations: Giving primarily in MS.
Application information: Application form required.
Deadline(s): 1 week prior to beginning of college semester
Write: Mrs. Bonnie Williams
Trustees: Elsie Joe Askew, George Butler, Elizabeth Eason, B.H. Hirsberg, Alyce Williams.
Employer Identification Number: 646027589

3475
The Luckyday Foundation ¤
c/o Trustmark National Bank
248 East Capitol St.
Jackson 39201

Established in 1978 in MS.
Donor(s): Frank R. Day.
Foundation type: Independent
Financial data (yr. ended 12/31/88): Assets, $1,966,486 (M); gifts received, $100,000; expenditures, $103,951, including $92,868 for 8 grants (high: $28,000; low: $1,000).
Purpose and activities: Support primarily for youth, religion, and higher education.
Limitations: Giving primarily in MS, with emphasis on Jackson.
Officers: Frank R. Day, Mgr.; Dean M. Miller, Mgr.; William Neville, Mgr.
Employer Identification Number: 640617746

3476
Magnolia State Foundation ¤
4155 Industrial Dr.
Jackson 39209-2794 (601) 948-8600

Donor(s): Missco Corp. of Jackson.
Foundation type: Independent
Financial data (yr. ended 12/31/88): Assets, $4,046 (M); gifts received, $133,000; expenditures, $133,654, including $133,000 for 69 grants (high: $20,000; low: $100).
Purpose and activities: Support primarily for higher education, community funds, and youth organizations.
Application information:
Initial approach: Letter
Deadline(s): None
Write: Mark Sorgenfrei, Trustee
Officers: J.B. Campbell, Pres.; R.D. Peets, V.P.; Pat Jeffreys, Secy.
Trustee: Mark Sorgenfrei.
Employer Identification Number: 646025337

3477
McRae Foundation, Inc. ¤
P.O. Box 20080
Jackson 39209 (601) 968-4400

Established in 1965 in MS.
Donor(s): McRae's.
Foundation type: Independent
Financial data (yr. ended 1/31/89): Assets, $6,218,623 (M); expenditures, $329,149, including $289,521 for 48 grants (high: $150,000; low: $20).
Purpose and activities: Grants primarily for social services, religion, and education, especially higher education; some support for cultural programs.
Application information:
Initial approach: Letter
Deadline(s): None
Write: Richard D. McRae, Sr., Pres.
Officers: Richard D. McRae, Sr.,* Pres.; Jim Glasscock, Secy.; Vaughan W. McRae,* Treas.
Directors:* D. Carl Black, Richard D. McRae, Jr.
Employer Identification Number: 646026795

3478
Mississippi Power Foundation, Inc.
2992 West Beach Blvd.
Gulfport 39501-4079 (601) 435-6075

Established in 1984 in MS.
Donor(s): Mississippi Power Co.
Foundation type: Company-sponsored
Financial data (yr. ended 12/31/88): Assets, $1,275,100 (M); gifts received, $300,050; expenditures, $146,406, including $128,562 for 57 grants (high: $8,600; low: $165).
Purpose and activities: Dedicated to the improvement and enhancement of education in MS, from kindergarten to graduate school.
Types of support: Conferences and seminars, equipment, grants to individuals, matching funds, research, special projects.
Limitations: Giving limited to MS.
Publications: Informational brochure (including application guidelines).
Application information: Application form required.
Initial approach: Letter
Copies of proposal: 10
Deadline(s): None
Board meeting date(s): Generally 3rd Tuesday of each month
Final notification: 2 months
Write: Frances Turnage, Secy.
Officers: Huntley H. Biggs, Chair.; Charles H. Ball, Vice-Chair.; Frances Turnage, Secy.; William C. Browning, Treas.
Trustees: Donald Cotten, Tom C. Maynor, Jamie Morris, Dorothy Myles.
Number of staff: None.
Employer Identification Number: 640707536

3479
Ottilie Schillig Trust ▼ ¤
P.O. Box 22683
Jackson 39205

Established in 1983 in MS.
Donor(s): Ottilie Schillig.†
Foundation type: Independent
Financial data (yr. ended 6/30/88): Assets, $2,886,263 (M); expenditures, $983,842, including $939,313 for 4 grants (high: $500,000; low: $25,000).
Purpose and activities: Support for higher education and a medical center.
Trustee: James T. Baird.
Employer Identification Number: 640673508

3480
Vicksburg Hospital Medical Foundation ☆
P.O. Box 1578
Vicksburg 39180-1578 (601) 636-5514

Established in 1956 in MS.
Foundation type: Independent
Financial data (yr. ended 12/31/89): Assets, $8,118,570 (M); expenditures, $458,611, including $365,000 for grants (average: $20,000-$75,000).
Purpose and activities: Giving primarily for medical education, nursing, and medical research.
Types of support: Scholarship funds, endowment funds.
Limitations: Giving primarily in MS and GA. No grants to individuals.
Application information:
Initial approach: Letter
Deadline(s): None
Board meeting date(s): Quarterly
Write: Dr. W.K. Purks, Pres.
Officers: W.K. Purks, M.D., Pres.; I.C. Knox, Jr., V.P.; Philip Watson, Jr., Secy.-Treas.
Trustees: H.D. Andrews, H.N. Gage, Jr., P.K. Watson.
Employer Identification Number: 646025312

3481
W. E. Walker Foundation ▼ ⌑
1675 Lakeland Dr.
Riverhill Tower, Suite 400
Jackson 39216 (601) 362-9895

Established in 1972 in MS.
Donor(s): W.E. Walker, Jr., W.E. Walker Stores, Inc.
Foundation type: Independent
Financial data (yr. ended 12/31/88): Assets, $8,199,004 (M); expenditures, $2,685,270, including $2,639,275 for 56 grants (high: $2,000,000; low: $100; average: $1,000-$15,000) and $8,500 for 4 grants to individuals (high: $3,500; low: $1,500).
Purpose and activities: Giving for independent schools, Protestant churches, higher education, and youth agencies; grants also for cultural programs, health, and welfare agencies, and scholarships to local residents attending graduate school, with a focus on theology and human service.
Types of support: General purposes, student aid.
Limitations: Giving primarily in MS.
Application information: Application form required for scholarships.
Deadline(s): None
Board meeting date(s): As needed
Write: W.E. Walker, Jr., Trustee
Trustees: Edmund L. Brunini, Baker Duncan, Justina W. McLean, Gloria M. Walker, W.E. Walker, Jr.
Number of staff: 1
Employer Identification Number: 237279902

3482
Walker Wildlife Conservation Foundation ⌑ ☆
1675 Lakeland Dr., Suite 400
Jackson 39216

Established in 1986 in MS.
Donor(s): W.E. Walker Foundation.
Foundation type: Independent
Financial data (yr. ended 12/31/88): Assets, $2,101,650 (M); gifts received, $2,000,000; expenditures, $27,408, including $12,671 for 7 grants (high: $5,000; low: $20).
Purpose and activities: Support for wildlife conservation.
Application information:
Deadline(s): None
Write: W.E. Walker, Jr., Trustee
Trustees: Edmund L. Brunini, Justina W. McLean, Gloria M. Walker, W.E. Walker, Jr.
Employer Identification Number: 640697006

MISSOURI

3483
Adler-Rosecan Foundation ⌑
1015 Locust St., Suite 530
St. Louis 63101

Established in 1959 in MO.
Foundation type: Independent
Financial data (yr. ended 12/31/88): Assets, $806,232 (M); expenditures, $110,947, including $109,400 for 22 grants (high: $22,500; low: $250).
Purpose and activities: Giving primarily for higher and secondary education; support also for Jewish welfare, medical research, and Christian religion.
Application information: Contributes only to pre-selected organizations. Applications not accepted.
Directors and Trustees:* Evelyn B. Goldberg, Harold E. Goldberg,* Mary C. Rosecan, Mortimer A. Rosecan.*
Employer Identification Number: 436048911

3484
Anheuser-Busch Charitable Trust ▼ ⌑
c/o Anheuser-Busch Companies, Inc.
One Busch Place
St. Louis 63118 (314) 577-7368

Trust established in 1951 in MO.
Donor(s): August A. Busch, Jr., Alice Busch,† Anheuser-Busch, Inc., August A. Busch & Co. of Massachusetts, Inc.
Foundation type: Company-sponsored
Financial data (yr. ended 9/30/88): Assets, $4,512,038 (M); expenditures, $3,625,538, including $3,602,167 for 52 grants (high: $721,000; low: $2,000).
Purpose and activities: Support for higher education, cultural programs, programs for minorities and youth, health organizations and hospitals, and environmental protection groups.
Types of support: Building funds, equipment, professorships, capital campaigns, renovation projects.
Limitations: Giving primarily in areas of company operations, with emphasis on the St. Louis, MO, area. No support for political, religious, social, fraternal, or athletic organizations, or for hospital operating budgets. No grants to individuals; no loans.
Publications: Application guidelines.
Application information: Application form required.
Initial approach: Proposal
Copies of proposal: 1
Deadline(s): None
Board meeting date(s): As required
Final notification: 6 to 8 weeks
Write: Cynthia M. Garrone, Contrib. Admin.
Board of Control: August A. Busch, Jr., August A. Busch III, Jerry E. Ritter.
Trustee: Boatmen's Trust Co. of St. Louis.
Number of staff: None.
Employer Identification Number: 436023453

3485
Anheuser-Busch Foundation ▼
c/o Anheuser-Busch Companies, Inc.
One Busch Place
St. Louis 63118 (314) 577-7368

Established in 1975 in MO.
Donor(s): Anheuser-Busch, Inc.
Foundation type: Company-sponsored
Financial data (yr. ended 12/31/87): Assets, $44,903,583 (M); gifts received, $14,000,025; expenditures, $3,518,149, including $3,288,853 for 138 grants (high: $665,600; low: $150; average: $3,500-$30,000) and $43,240 for 295 employee matching gifts.
Purpose and activities: Giving primarily for United Way agencies and for higher education; support also for youth, community development, the arts, and health agencies.
Types of support: Building funds, capital campaigns, continuing support, employee matching gifts, matching funds.
Limitations: Giving primarily in areas of company operations. No support for political organizations, organizations whose activities are primarily religious in nature, social or fraternal groups, or athletic organizations. No grants to individuals, or for hospital operating budgets.
Publications: Application guidelines.
Application information: Application form required.
Initial approach: Letter
Copies of proposal: 1
Deadline(s): None
Board meeting date(s): Approximately every 2 months
Final notification: Following board meetings
Write: Cynthia M. Garrone, Contribs. Admin.
Trustees: August A. Busch III, John L. Hayward, Jerry E. Ritter.
Trustee Bank: Boatmen's National Bank of St. Louis.
Employer Identification Number: 510168084

3486
J. B. Arthur Foundation ⌑
c/o Boatmen's National Bank of St. Louis
P.O. Box 7365
St. Louis 63177 (314) 425-7711

Established in 1959 in MO.
Foundation type: Independent
Financial data (yr. ended 8/31/88): Assets, $1,146,267 (M); expenditures, $77,873, including $64,310 for 9 grants (high: $10,110; low: $4,800).
Purpose and activities: Grants primarily for health organizations and college funds.
Limitations: Giving primarily in MO.
Application information: Application form not required.
Deadline(s): None
Write: John L. Phillips, Jr.
Trustees: Bettie Arthur Black, Chair.; Dorothy Arthur Bachmann, Secy.; Carl H. Bachman, C.L. Black, Barbara S. Hook, Boatmen's National Bank of St. Louis.
Employer Identification Number: 436028342

3487
Bakers National Educational Foundation
14 West Tenth St., Box 38
Kansas City 64183 (414) 764-5500
Application address: 2520 Commerce Tower, 911 Main St., Kansas City, MO 64105; Tel.: (816) 221-2700

Foundation type: Independent

Financial data (yr. ended 09/30/89): Assets, $1,123,849 (M); expenditures, $72,874, including $65,000 for 1 grant.
Purpose and activities: Giving limited to support for the higher educational areas of the baking industry.
Application information: Application form not required.
Deadline(s): None
Final notification: 2 months
Write: Steven B. Smith, Secy.-Treas.
Officers and Directors:* Robert W. Bracken,* Pres.; Dennis O'Connor,* V.P.; Steven B. Smith,* Secy.-Treas.
Employer Identification Number: 436042834

3488
Donald L. Barnes Foundation ⌑
7800 Bonhomme
St. Louis 63105 (314) 863-0600

Established in 1948 in MO.
Foundation type: Independent
Financial data (yr. ended 12/31/88): Assets, $1,065,888 (M); expenditures, $59,551, including $44,350 for 30 grants (high: $12,000; low: $100).
Purpose and activities: Support for education, services for the disadvantaged, especially handicapped children, medical research, and social service programs.
Types of support: Research, scholarship funds.
Limitations: No grants to individuals.
Application information: Contributes only to pre-selected organizations. Applications not accepted.
Write: Thomas E. Phelps, Mgr.
Officer and Trustee: Thomas E. Phelps, Mgr.
Employer Identification Number: 436029643

3489
Geraldine & R. A. Barrows Foundation ⌑ ☆
United Missouri Bank Bldg.
1010 Grand Ave., 3rd Fl.
Kansas City 64106
Application address: c/o United Missouri Bank of Kansas City, N.A., Trust Dept., P.O. Box 419226, Kansas City, MO 64141; Tel.: (816) 556-7711

Established in 1979 in MO.
Foundation type: Independent
Financial data (yr. ended 2/28/89): Assets, $5,185,308 (M); gifts received, $69,307; expenditures, $254,716, including $243,100 for 26 grants (high: $40,000; low: $1,000).
Purpose and activities: Giving primarily for underpriviledged children and cancer research; support also for the performing arts and a Methodist church.
Limitations: Giving primarily in Kansas City, MO.
Application information:
Initial approach: Letter
Deadline(s): None
Write: Stephen J. Campbell
Trustee: United Missouri Bank of Kansas City, N.A.
Employer Identification Number: 431184875

3490
The Bellwether Foundation, Inc. ☆
c/o Univ. Club Tower
1034 South Brentwood, Suite 1900
St. Louis 63117-1223 (314) 862-1150

Established in 1985.
Donor(s): Robert B. Smith, Nancy M. Smith.
Foundation type: Independent
Financial data (yr. ended 12/31/87): Assets, $1,016,926 (M); gifts received, $38,619; expenditures, $72,221, including $58,600 for 18 grants (high: $40,000; low: $500).
Purpose and activities: Support primarily for a botanical garden and a community fund.
Limitations: Giving primarily in St. Louis, MO, and MI. No grants to individuals.
Application information: Applications not accepted.
Write: Mary Frances Balmer, Secy.-Treas.
Officers: Robert B. Smith, Chair. and C.E.O.; Sally Duffield, Pres. and C.O.O.; Robert B. Smith II, V.P.; Mary Francis Balmer, Secy.-Treas.
Employer Identification Number: 222635309

3491
The Henry W. and Marion H. Bloch Foundation
4410 Main St.
Kansas City 64111 (816) 753-6900

Established in 1983 in MO.
Donor(s): Henry W. Bloch, Marion H. Bloch.
Foundation type: Independent
Financial data (yr. ended 12/31/89): Assets, $7,586,986 (M); expenditures, $300,736, including $262,028 for 73 grants (high: $50,000; low: $15).
Purpose and activities: Emphasis on the arts, including museums, theater, ballet, and music, and hospitals; some support also for temples, community funds, and business education.
Types of support: Building funds, capital campaigns, special projects.
Limitations: Giving limited to the 50-mile area around Kansas City, MO, including KS. No grants to individuals.
Application information: Contributes only to pre-selected organizations. Applications not accepted.
Board meeting date(s): Dec.
Write: Robert L. Bloch, V.P.
Officers and Directors: Henry W. Bloch, Pres. and C.E.O.; Marion H. Bloch, V.P. and Secy.; Robert L. Bloch, V.P. and Treas.; Thomas M. Bloch, Mary Jo Brown, Edward A. Smith, Elizabeth Bloch Uhlmann.
Number of staff: 1 full-time professional; 1 part-time professional.
Employer Identification Number: 431329803

3492
The H & R Block Foundation
4410 Main St.
Kansas City 64111 (816) 753-6900

Incorporated in 1974 in MO.
Donor(s): H & R Block, Inc.
Foundation type: Company-sponsored
Financial data (yr. ended 12/31/89): Assets, $14,007,026 (M); gifts received, $1,616,000; expenditures, $1,514,387, including $958,751 for 246 grants and $62,000 for 31 grants to individuals.
Purpose and activities: Giving primarily for education, arts and culture, United Way, youth, the elderly, neighborhood development, health, including AIDS programs and mental health, and civic endeavors; scholarships for children of company employees only.
Types of support: General purposes, building funds, equipment, land acquisition, matching funds, employee matching gifts, program-related investments, employee-related scholarships, operating budgets, continuing support, annual campaigns, seed money, emergency funds, capital campaigns, special projects.
Limitations: Giving limited to the 50-mile area around Kansas City, MO, including KS. No support for religious purposes, single-disease agencies, or historic preservation projects. No grants to individuals (except for scholarships to children of company employees), or for endowment funds, travel, telethons, research, demonstration projects, publications, or conferences; no loans.
Publications: Informational brochure (including application guidelines), annual report.
Application information: Application form not required.
Initial approach: 1-2 page letter
Copies of proposal: 1
Deadline(s): 45 days prior to meetings
Board meeting date(s): Mar., June, Sept., and Dec.
Final notification: 2 weeks after board meeting
Write: Terrence R. Ward, Pres.
Officers and Directors:* Henry W. Bloch,* Chair. and Treas.; Edward A. Smith,* Vice-Chair.; Terrence R. Ward, Pres.; Barbara Allmon, V.P., Prog(s).; Charles E. Curran, Morton I. Sosland.
Number of staff: 4 full-time professional; 2 full-time support.
Employer Identification Number: 237378232

3493
Boatmen's Bancshares, Inc. Charitable Trust ▼
P.O. Box 7365
St. Louis 63177 (314) 425-7711

Foundation type: Company-sponsored
Financial data (yr. ended 12/31/87): Assets, $1,545,329 (M); gifts received, $1,181,440; expenditures, $1,436,536, including $1,420,145 for 179 grants (high: $245,640; low: $260; average: $1,000-$20,000).
Purpose and activities: Giving primarily for the arts, including museums; support also for community organizations, social services, and higher education.
Limitations: Giving primarily in MO.
Application information:
Deadline(s): None
Board meeting date(s): Monthly
Write: John L. Phillips, Jr.
Trustee: Boatmen's National Bank of St. Louis.
Number of staff: 1
Employer Identification Number: 431363004

3494
Boatmen's Trust Company Charitable Trust ⌑
(Formerly Centerre Trust Company Charitable Trust Fund)
510 Locust St.
P.O. Box 14737
St. Louis 63178 (314) 436-9228

Established in 1948 in MO.
Foundation type: Independent
Financial data (yr. ended 12/31/88): Assets, $453,896 (M); gifts received, $167,000; expenditures, $172,035, including $170,984 for 12 grants (high: $93,942; low: $1,000).
Purpose and activities: Support for the arts and social services; also awards scholarships to individuals.
Types of support: Student aid.
Limitations: Giving primarily in the greater St. Louis, MO, area.
Application information:
Initial approach: Letter
Deadline(s): None
Write: Martin E. Galt III, Exec. V.P.
Trustees: Donald C. Danforth, Jr., John Peters MacCarthy, Eugene F. Williams, Jr.
Agent: Boatmen's Trust Co. of St. Louis.
Employer Identification Number: 436023132

3495
Boone County Community Trust ⌑
c/o Boone County National Bank
P.O. Box 678
Columbia 65205 (314) 874-8100
Additional tel.: (314) 449-4576

Established in 1976 in MO.
Donor(s): R.B. Price, Jr.,† Noma S. Brown,† Sam Waiton.
Foundation type: Independent
Financial data (yr. ended 5/31/88): Assets, $1,312,137 (M); expenditures, $126,136, including $114,212 for 16 grants (high: $53,826; low: $250).
Purpose and activities: Giving for education, social services, and cultural programs.
Types of support: Equipment, general purposes, seed money, emergency funds, building funds, land acquisition, professorships, internships, scholarship funds, exchange programs, fellowships, special projects, research, publications, conferences and seminars.
Limitations: Giving limited to Boone County, MO. No grants to individuals, or for operating budgets, continuing support, annual campaigns, deficit financing, endowment funds, or matching gifts; no loans.
Publications: Application guidelines, program policy statement.
Application information: Application form not required.
Initial approach: Telephone or letter
Copies of proposal: 1
Deadline(s): None
Board meeting date(s): As needed
Final notification: 6 weeks
Write: Jerry Epple, Trust Admin.
Trustee: Boone County National Bank.
Selection Committee: W.H. Bates, John Epple, Jr., David Knight, A.M. Price, Hazel Riback.
Number of staff: None.
Employer Identification Number: 436182354

3496
Boswell Foundation, Inc. ⌑
1078 South Jefferson
Lebanon 65536

Established in 1985 in MO.
Donor(s): John J. Boswell, Lois Boswell.
Foundation type: Independent
Financial data (yr. ended 11/30/87): Assets, $10,017 (M); gifts received, $280,100; expenditures, $273,483, including $272,750 for 19 grants (high: $145,000; low: $50).
Purpose and activities: Support primarily for community development and education with emphasis on secondary education.
Types of support: Building funds.
Limitations: Giving primarily in Lebanon, MO. No grants to individuals.
Application information: Contributes only to pre-selected organizations.
Officers and Directors: John J. Boswell, Pres. and Treas.; Tifany R. Boswell, V.P.; Paul Walker, Secy.
Employer Identification Number: 431409051

3497
Ella Frances Brisley & Noma Brisley Phillips Scholarship Loan Fund ⌑
c/o Third National Bank
P.O. Box 351
Sedalia 65301 (816) 827-3333

Established in 1984 in MO.
Foundation type: Independent
Financial data (yr. ended 2/29/88): Assets, $1,580,747 (M); expenditures, $50,620, including $611 for 2 grants (high: $361; low: $250) and $40,151 for 29 grants to individuals (high: $2,800; low: $467).
Purpose and activities: Scholarships limited to needy medical and nursing students attending accredited schools and to deserving and needy students attending Methodist colleges.
Types of support: Student aid.
Limitations: Giving primarily in KS and MO.
Application information:
Write: Carol Scrimager, V.P., Third National Bank
Trustee: Third National Bank.
Employer Identification Number: 431343600

3498
Guy I. Bromley Residuary Trust
c/o Boatmen's First National Bank of Kansas City
14 West 10th St.
Kansas City 64183 (816) 691-7481

Established in 1964 in MO.
Donor(s): Guy I. Bromley.
Foundation type: Independent
Financial data (yr. ended 12/31/89): Assets, $2,906,542 (M); expenditures, $124,963, including $121,384 for 12 grants (high: $50,000; low: $100; average: $5,000-$10,000).
Purpose and activities: Giving primarily for education, with emphasis on higher education; support also for social service and youth agencies, and cultural programs.
Types of support: Seed money, special projects.
Limitations: Giving primarily in the metropolitan Kansas City, MO, area and KS.
Publications: 990-PF.
Application information: Application form not required.
Initial approach: Letter not exceeding 3 pages
Deadline(s): None
Final notification: 2 months
Write: David Ross, Sr. V.P., Boatmen's First National Bank of Kansas City
Trustee: Boatmen's First National Bank of Kansas City.
Employer Identification Number: 436157236

3499
George Warren Brown Foundation ⌑
8400 Maryland Ave.
St. Louis 63105 (314) 854-4400

Trust established in 1921 in MO.
Donor(s): George Warren Brown.†
Foundation type: Independent
Financial data (yr. ended 12/31/88): Assets, $2,732,480 (M); expenditures, $212,885, including $174,115 for 21 grants (high: $50,000; low: $1,000; average: $4,000-$8,000) and $37,620 for 18 grants to individuals (high: $275; low: $75; average: $75-$275).
Purpose and activities: Grants largely to provide pensions for Brown Group, Inc. employees; support also for colleges, universities, and youth agencies.
Types of support: General purposes, operating budgets, continuing support, annual campaigns, emergency funds, building funds, equipment, land acquisition, scholarship funds, capital campaigns.
Limitations: Giving primarily in areas of company operations in MO, TN, IL, and AR. No support for hospitals. No grants for endowment funds, matching gifts, program support, research, special projects, publications, or conferences; no loans.
Application information: Application form not required.
Initial approach: Proposal
Copies of proposal: 1
Deadline(s): None
Board meeting date(s): Jan., Mar., June, Sept., Oct., and Dec.
Final notification: 1 to 2 months
Write: David L. Bowman, Treas.
Trustees: B.A. Bridgewater, Jr., Chair.; Richard L. Anderson, Joseph L. Bower, W.L. Hadley Griffin, Joan F. Lane, William E. Maritz, Harry E. Rich, Richard W. Schomaker, Warren McK. Shapleigh, Morton I. Sosland, Daniel R. Toll.
Number of staff: None.
Employer Identification Number: 436027798

3500
Maurice L. & Virginia L. Brown Foundation ⌑
5049 Wornall, Apt. 7AB
Kansas City 64112

Established in 1980 in MO.
Donor(s): Maurice L. Brown, Virginia L. Brown.
Foundation type: Independent
Financial data (yr. ended 9/30/88): Assets, $1,258,298 (M); expenditures, $109,174, including $87,216 for 82 grants (high: $40,000; low: $10).

Purpose and activities: Support primarily for a hospital and health agencies, Jewish welfare funds, and cultural programs.
Limitations: No grants to individuals.
Application information: Contributes only to pre-selected organizations. Applications not accepted.
Trustees: Maurice L. Brown, Virginia L. Brown.
Employer Identification Number: 431213063

3501
Brown Group, Inc. Charitable Trust ▼ ⌑
8400 Maryland Ave.
Clayton 63166 (314) 854-4120

Trust established in 1951 in MO.
Donor(s): Brown Group, Inc.
Foundation type: Company-sponsored
Financial data (yr. ended 10/28/88): Assets, $6,180,337 (M); gifts received, $800,000; qualifying distributions, $1,681,585, including $1,134,284 for 106 grants (high: $300,000; low: $50; average: $100-$20,000), $145,082 for 469 employee matching gifts and $402,219 for in-kind gifts.
Purpose and activities: Giving primarily for community funds, hospitals, higher education, the arts, and youth agencies.
Types of support: General purposes, operating budgets, continuing support, annual campaigns, emergency funds, building funds, equipment, land acquisition, employee matching gifts, scholarship funds, renovation projects.
Limitations: Giving limited to areas of company's major operations, with emphasis on St. Louis, MO. No grants to individuals, or for endowment funds, special projects, research, publications, or conferences; no loans.
Application information: Application form not required.
Initial approach: Proposal
Copies of proposal: 1
Deadline(s): None
Board meeting date(s): As needed
Final notification: 1 to 3 months
Write: Harry E. Rich, C.F.O., Brown Group, Inc.
Control Committee and Trustees:* David L. Bowman, Secy.; Richard Lee Anderson,* Member; B.A. Bridgewater, Jr., Member; W.L. Hadley Griffin, Member; Ben Peck, Member; Harry E. Rich,* Member; Richard W. Shomaker,* Member.
Trustee Bank: Boatmen's Trust Co. of St. Louis.
Number of staff: 2
Employer Identification Number: 237443082

3502
Butler Manufacturing Company Foundation
BMA Tower, P.O. Box 419917
Penn Valley Park
Kansas City 64141-0917 (816) 968-3208

Incorporated in 1952 in MO.
Donor(s): Butler Manufacturing Co.
Foundation type: Company-sponsored
Financial data (yr. ended 12/31/89): Assets, $3,356,638 (M); expenditures, $442,388, including $376,204 for 180 grants (high: $50,000; low: $25; average: $3,000), $10,650 for 3 grants to individuals (high: $8,000; low: $650; average: $500-$2,000) and $34,126 for 84 employee matching gifts.
Purpose and activities: Support for youth programs, minority development, neighborhoods, and non-residential building programs using the company's products; scholarships for children of employees and grants to colleges and universities serving locations where employees reside and the community's principal arts organizations.
Types of support: Annual campaigns, employee matching gifts, employee-related scholarships.
Limitations: Giving primarily in cities where major plants are located: Kansas City, MO; Galesberg, IL; Garland, and San Marcos, TX. No grants for endowment funds; no loans.
Publications: Annual report, informational brochure, application guidelines.
Application information: Application form not required.
Initial approach: Letter
Copies of proposal: 1
Deadline(s): Submit proposal preferably 2 months prior to board meeting
Board meeting date(s): Mar., June, Sept., and Dec.
Final notification: 6 months
Write: Barbara Lee Fay, Fdn. Admin.
Officers: Robert H. West,* Pres.; Donald H. Pratt,* V.P.; Richard O. Ballentine,* Secy.; Larry C. Miller, Treas.
Trustees:* George C. Dillon, John W. Huey, T. Michael Lewis.
Number of staff: None.
Employer Identification Number: 440663648

3503
Ina Calkins Board
c/o Boatmen's First National Bank of Kansas City
14 West 10th St.
Kansas City 64105 (816) 691-7481

Established in 1930 in MO.
Donor(s): Ina Calkins Trust.
Foundation type: Independent
Financial data (yr. ended 12/31/89): Assets, $129,628 (M); gifts received, $213,602; expenditures, $212,260, including $186,000 for 3 grants (high: $180,000; low: $3,000; average: $3,000-$180,000) and $25,450 for 47 grants to individuals (high: $75; low: $20; average: $20-$50).
Purpose and activities: Emphasis on a social service agency; grants also for youth agencies and child welfare.
Types of support: Grants to individuals.
Limitations: Giving limited to Kansas City, MO.
Publications: 990-PF, program policy statement, application guidelines.
Application information:
Initial approach: Telephone or letter
Copies of proposal: 1
Deadline(s): Submit proposal 1 month before board meets
Board meeting date(s): Jan., Apr., July, and Oct.
Write: David P. Ross, Secy.-Treas.
Officers: Betsy Fletcher, Pres.; David P. Ross, Secy.-Treas.
Trustee: Boatmen's First National Bank of Kansas City.
Number of staff: 1
Employer Identification Number: 446088022

3504
The Chance Foundation ⌑
123 North Rollins St.
Centralia 65240 (314) 682-5511

Trust established in 1947 in MO.
Donor(s): A.B. Chance Co., F. Gano Chance,† Nathan A. Toalson.
Foundation type: Independent
Financial data (yr. ended 12/31/88): Assets, $1,903,141 (M); expenditures, $110,210, including $44,376 for 25 grants (high: $10,000; low: $200).
Purpose and activities: Emphasis on higher education, church support, religious associations, and youth agencies.
Limitations: No grants to individuals.
Application information: Contributes only to pre-selected organizations. Applications not accepted.
Trustees: Arthur H. Allen, Managing Trustee; Joseph M. Arndt, James T. Ausmus, John H. Chance, Phillip G. Chance, N.S. Green, L.C. Hansen, M.J. Johnson, William A. Toalson.
Employer Identification Number: 436028959

3505
Chiefs Childrens Fund ⌑
One Arrowhead Dr.
Kansas City 64129

Established in 1983 in MO.
Foundation type: Independent
Financial data (yr. ended 1/31/88): Assets, $24,197 (M); gifts received, $102,952; expenditures, $112,303, including $89,768 for 20 grants (high: $6,000; low: $100) and $20,603 for 15 grants to individuals (high: $1,937; low: $102).
Purpose and activities: Support primarily for youth organizations and scholarships to individuals for higher education.
Types of support: Student aid.
Limitations: Giving primarily in the greater Kansas City, MO, area.
Application information:
Initial approach: Proposal
Deadline(s): None
Write: Donald W. Steadman, V.P.
Officers: Jack W. Steadman, Pres.; Donald W. Steadman, V.P.; James J. Seigfried, Secy.; Robert M. Tamasi, Treas.
Employer Identification Number: 431299453

3506
The Commerce Foundation
P.O. Box 13686
Kansas City 64199

Incorporated in 1952 in MO.
Donor(s): Commerce Bank of Kansas City.
Foundation type: Company-sponsored
Financial data (yr. ended 12/31/88): Assets, $4,428,587 (M); gifts received, $249,061; expenditures, $526,753, including $500,122 for 210 grants (high: $20,000; low: $100).

Purpose and activities: Emphasis on community funds, the performing arts, higher education, music, youth agencies, and hospitals.
Types of support: Continuing support, annual campaigns, seed money, building funds, endowment funds, special projects, professorships, general purposes.
Limitations: Giving primarily in MO. No grants to individuals, or for operating budgets or matching gifts; no loans.
Application information:
Initial approach: Letter
Copies of proposal: 1
Deadline(s): None
Board meeting date(s): As required
Write: Warren W. Weaver, Pres.
Officers: Warren W. Weaver,* Pres.; Charles E. Templer, V.P. and Treas.; T. Alan Peschka,* Secy.
Directors:* David W. Kemper, James M. Kemper, Jr.
Number of staff: None.
Employer Identification Number: 446012453

3507
Community Foundation, Inc.
(Formerly Community Foundation of Greene County, Inc.)
901 St. Louis St., Suite 303
Springfield 65806 (417) 864-6199

Incorporated as a community foundation in 1973 in MO.
Foundation type: Community
Financial data (yr. ended 06/30/89): Assets, $2,024,467 (M); gifts received, $196,613; expenditures, $159,615, including $115,518 for 42 grants (high: $7,632; low: $250; average: $250-$7,632) and $5,800 for 3 grants to individuals (high: $1,700; low: $625; average: $625-$1,700).
Purpose and activities: Support primarily for higher and secondary education, the performing arts and museums, health, recreation, community projects, youth organizations, and social services, including family services, child welfare, alcohol abuse prevention, leadership development, and programs for the aged and the homeless.
Types of support: Conferences and seminars, emergency funds, matching funds, renovation projects, scholarship funds, seed money.
Limitations: Giving primarily in southwest MO. No grants for capital campaigns or operating expenses.
Publications: Annual report, newsletter, application guidelines.
Application information: Application form required.
Initial approach: Letter (one page)
Copies of proposal: 10
Deadline(s): Mar. and Sept.
Board meeting date(s): 4th Tuesday of most months
Final notification: Late May and late Nov.
Write: Jan Horton, Exec. Dir.
Officers: Donald G. Martin, Sr., Pres.; Mary Kay Meek, V.P.; Pat Walker, Secy.; Sam Gardner, Treas.
Number of staff: 1 full-time professional; 1 full-time support.
Employer Identification Number: 237290968

3508
James and Mary Ida Compton Foundation ⌑
c/o United Missouri Bank of Kansas City
P.O. Box 226
Kansas City 64141

Established in 1983 in MO.
Foundation type: Independent
Financial data (yr. ended 04/30/89): Assets, $1,352,237 (M); expenditures, $82,225, including $72,347 for 6 grants (high: $34,674; low: $1,000).
Purpose and activities: Support for higher education and animal welfare.
Application information: Contributes only to pre-selected organizations. Applications not accepted.
Trustee: United Missouri Bank of Kansas City, N.A.
Employer Identification Number: 436271842

3509
Louetta M. Cowden Foundation
c/o Boatmen's First National Bank of Kansas City
14 West Tenth St.
Kansas City 64105 (816) 691-7481
Mailing address: P.O. Box 419038, Kansas City, MO 64183

Trust established in 1964 in MO.
Donor(s): Louetta M. Cowden.†
Foundation type: Independent
Financial data (yr. ended 12/31/89): Assets, $6,134,000 (M); expenditures, $183,955, including $177,500 for 7 grants (high: $50,000; low: $4,000; average: $10,000-$50,000).
Purpose and activities: Support for children's welfare and hospitals, with emphasis on capital fund grants.
Types of support: Building funds, equipment, land acquisition, seed money, emergency funds, capital campaigns, special projects.
Limitations: Giving limited to the metropolitan Kansas City, MO, area. No grants to individuals, or for endowment funds, scholarships, fellowships, or matching gifts; no loans.
Publications: 990-PF, application guidelines.
Application information: Application form not required.
Initial approach: Telephone or letter (no more than 3 pages)
Copies of proposal: 1
Deadline(s): None
Board meeting date(s): Mar., June, Sept., and Dec.
Final notification: 2 months
Write: David P. Ross, Sr. V.P., Boatmen's First National Bank of Kansas City
Trustees: Menefee D. Blackwell, Arthur H. Bowen, Jr., Boatmen's First National Bank of Kansas City.
Number of staff: 1 full-time professional.
Employer Identification Number: 436052617

3510
CPI Corporation Philanthropic Trust
1706 Washington Ave.
St. Louis 63103 (314) 231-1575

Established in 1984 in MO.
Donor(s): CPI Corp.
Foundation type: Company-sponsored
Financial data (yr. ended 01/31/89): Assets, $829,562 (M); gifts received, $700,000; qualifying distributions, $420,792, including $209,992 for 70 grants (high: $57,480; low: $25), $23,900 for 89 grants to individuals (high: $500), $21,300 for 324 employee matching gifts and $165,600 for in-kind gifts.
Purpose and activities: Support primarily for cultural programs; early childhood, higher, and other education; social services, including child welfare and development; and Jewish organizations.
Types of support: Building funds, capital campaigns, employee matching gifts, equipment, in-kind gifts, operating budgets, employee-related scholarships.
Limitations: Giving limited to areas of company operations.
Application information: Application form required.
Copies of proposal: 1
Deadline(s): Oct. 15
Write: Fran Scheper
Trustees: Sander Coovert, Alyn Essman.
Number of staff: 1 part-time professional.
Employer Identification Number: 431334012

3511
The E. L. Craig Foundation, Inc. ⌑
P.O. Box 1404
Joplin 64802 (417) 624-6644

Incorporated in 1960 in MO.
Donor(s): Tamko Asphalt Products, Inc., Royal Brand Roofing, Inc.
Foundation type: Independent
Financial data (yr. ended 7/31/88): Assets, $4,205,490 (M); gifts received, $100,000; expenditures, $186,106, including $174,167 for 18 grants (high: $100,000; low: $100).
Purpose and activities: Interests include higher education, economics, freedom-liberty programs, youth agencies, hospitals, and cancer research.
Limitations: Giving primarily in Joplin, MO. No grants to individuals.
Application information: Contributes only to pre-selected organizations. Applications not accepted.
Write: J.P. Humphreys, Pres.
Officers and Directors: J.P. Humphreys, Pres.; David Craig Humphreys, V.P.; Ethel Mae Craig Humphreys, Secy.-Treas.
Employer Identification Number: 446015127

3512
Cloud L. Cray Foundation
800 West 47th St., Suite 711
Kansas City 64112 (816) 756-0600

Donor(s): Cloud L. Cray.†
Foundation type: Independent
Financial data (yr. ended 12/31/88): Assets, $6,810,185 (M); gifts received, $5,000; expenditures, $336,379, including $254,594 for 29 grants (high: $53,245; low: $500).
Purpose and activities: Giving primarily for business education and economics programs.
Types of support: Endowment funds.
Limitations: Giving primarily in MO and KS. No grants to individuals.

Application information: Contributes only to pre-selected organizations. Applications not accepted.
Write: Richard B. Cray, Trustee
Trustees: Cloud L. Cray, Jr., Richard B. Cray.
Trustee Banks: Boatmen's First National Bank of Kansas City, United Missouri Bank of Kansas City, N.A.
Employer Identification Number: 436077249

3513
The Cross Foundation, Inc.
106 East 31 Terr., Rm. 206
Kansas City 64111 (816) 753-7119

Incorporated in 1955 in MO.
Donor(s): Annette Cross Murphy.†
Foundation type: Independent
Financial data (yr. ended 12/31/88): Assets, $174,661 (M); expenditures, $175,005, including $139,800 for 11 grants (high: $62,500; low: $300).
Purpose and activities: Grants largely for health-related programs, youth, the arts, and education.
Types of support: Operating budgets, endowment funds, special projects, matching funds.
Limitations: Giving primarily in Kansas City, MO.
Application information: Application form not required.
Initial approach: Proposal
Copies of proposal: 1
Deadline(s): Applications are reviewed between Apr. 1 and Dec. 31 for approval for the following year
Board meeting date(s): Mar.
Write: Mrs. Martha O. Lever, Exec. Dir.
Officers: Robert R. Cross,* Pres.; Lyman Field,* V.P. and Secy.; Martha O. Lever, Exec. Dir. and Treas.
Directors:* Michael R. Cross, David Oliver, Gertrude F. Oliver.
Number of staff: 1 full-time professional.
Employer Identification Number: 440613382

3514
The Danforth Foundation ▼
231 South Bemiston Ave., Suite 580
St. Louis 63105-1903 (314) 862-6200

Incorporated in 1927 in MO.
Donor(s): William H. Danforth,† Mrs. William H. Danforth.†
Foundation type: Independent
Financial data (yr. ended 05/31/89): Assets, $150,378,296 (M); expenditures, $6,483,504, including $4,296,457 for 127 grants (high: $333,700; low: $220; average: $10,000-$50,000), $86,354 for 66 employee matching gifts and $1,224,262 for 7 foundation-administered programs.
Purpose and activities: Dedicated to enhancing the humane dimensions of life through activities which emphasize the theme of improving the quality of teaching and learning. Serves precollegiate education through grantmaking and program activities, particularly those in support of administrators and legislators who are formulating public policy on elementary and secondary public education.
Types of support: Consulting services, technical assistance, special projects.
Limitations: No support for colleges and universities (except for projects in elementary and secondary education). No grants to individuals, or for building or endowment funds, or operating budgets; no loans.
Publications: Annual report, informational brochure (including application guidelines), financial statement, grants list.
Application information: Grant proposals for higher education not accepted; fellowship applications available only through participating universities. Application form not required.
Initial approach: Letter
Copies of proposal: 1
Deadline(s): None
Board meeting date(s): May and Nov., and as required
Final notification: 4 weeks
Write: Dr. Bruce J. Anderson, Acting Pres.
Officers: William H. Danforth,* Chair.; James R. Compton,* Vice-Chair. and Secy.; Bruce J. Anderson, Acting Pres.; Donn William Gresso, V.P.; Melvin C. Bahle, Treas.; Katharyn Nelson, Prog. Dir.
Trustees:* John H. Biggs, Virginia S. Brown, Donald C. Danforth, Jr., Charles Guggenheim, George E. Pake, P. Roy Vagelos.
Number of staff: 4 full-time professional; 1 part-time professional; 4 full-time support.
Employer Identification Number: 430653297

3515
Deer Creek Foundation
818 Olive St., Suite 949
St. Louis 63101 (314) 241-3228

Established in 1964 in MO.
Donor(s): Aaron Fischer.
Foundation type: Independent
Financial data (yr. ended 12/31/88): Assets, $5,107,460 (M); gifts received, $400,000; expenditures, $709,749, including $520,700 for 44 grants (high: $25,000; low: $500; average: $500-$25,000).
Purpose and activities: Support primarily for programs to preserve and advance majority rule in this society and government accountability, with protections provided for minorities by the Constitution and the Bill of Rights; grants primarily to "action programs" with promise of making a significant national or regional impact; some preference to projects in MO.
Types of support: Special projects.
Limitations: Giving is national, with some preference to MO organizations. No grants to individuals, or for building or endowment funds, equipment, or operating budgets.
Publications: Application guidelines, program policy statement.
Application information: Application form not required.
Initial approach: Proposal
Copies of proposal: 1
Deadline(s): Jan. 15, Apr. 15, July 15, and Oct. 15
Board meeting date(s): Mar., June, Sept., and Dec.
Final notification: Within 10 days after board meeting
Write: Mary Stake Hawker, Admin.
Trustees: Lattie F. Coor, Aaron Fischer, M. Peter Fischer, Teresa M. Fischer, James C. Kautz, Philip B. Kurland.
Number of staff: 1 full-time professional; 1 part-time support.
Employer Identification Number: 436052774

3516
The Dreiseszun Family Fund ⌑
260 N.E. Barry Rd.
Kansas City 64155-2722 (816) 436-2996

Established in 1985 in MO.
Donor(s): Sherman Dreiseszun.
Foundation type: Independent
Financial data (yr. ended 11/30/88): Assets, $1,470,228 (M); expenditures, $95,032, including $70,300 for 5 grants (high: $65,000; low: $800).
Purpose and activities: Support for Jewish organizations and Jewish welfare.
Limitations: Giving primarily in MO and KS. No grants to individuals.
Application information:
Initial approach: Letter
Deadline(s): Nov. 30
Write: Sherman Dreiseszun, Trustee
Trustees: Helene Abrahams, Irene Dreiseszun, Richard J. Dreiseszun, Sherman Dreiseszun.
Employer Identification Number: 481021776

3517
Ebsworth Foundation ⌑ ☆
7711 Bonhomme Ave.
Clayton 63105-1908

Established in 1982 in MO.
Donor(s): Windsor, Inc.
Foundation type: Independent
Financial data (yr. ended 12/31/88): Assets, $1,624 (M); gifts received, $214,500; expenditures, $212,977, including $212,650 for 16 grants (high: $200,600; low: $100).
Purpose and activities: Giving primarily for the arts, especially for a fine arts museum and an art academy.
Types of support: General purposes.
Limitations: Giving primarily in St. Louis, MO. No grants to individuals.
Application information: Contributes only to pre-selected organizations. Applications not accepted.
Trustees: Barney A. Ebsworth, Patricia A. Ebsworth, S.N. Roseberry.
Employer Identification Number: 431284515

3518
Mr. & Mrs. Barney A. Ebsworth Foundation ⌑
7711 Bonhomme Ave.
St. Louis 63105

Established in 1986 in MO.
Foundation type: Operating
Financial data (yr. ended 12/31/87): Assets, $3,049,025 (M); gifts received, $42,732; expenditures, $17,433, including $15,800 for 1 grant.
Purpose and activities: A private operating foundation; support primarily for an exhibition at an art museum.
Types of support: Special projects.

Application information: Contributes only to pre-selected organizations. Applications not accepted.
Officers: Barney A. Ebsworth, Pres.; Patricia A. Ebsworth, V.P.; Daniel A. Puricelli, Secy.-Treas.
Employer Identification Number: 431397651

3519
Edison Brothers Stores Foundation ⌑
501 North Broadway
St. Louis 63102

Incorporated in 1956 in MO.
Donor(s): Members of the Edison family, Edison Brothers Stores, Inc., and its subsidiaries.
Foundation type: Company-sponsored
Financial data (yr. ended 5/31/88): Assets, $1,957,112 (M); expenditures, $425,963, including $423,470 for 26 grants (high: $140,000; low: $120).
Purpose and activities: Support for community and Jewish welfare funds, higher education, and cultural organizations.
Limitations: Giving primarily in St. Louis, MO. No grants to individuals.
Officers and Directors: Bernard Edison, Pres.; Eric P. Newman, V.P. and Secy.; Lee G. Weeks, V.P. and Treas.; Julian Edison, V.P.; Andrew E. Newman, V.P.
Employer Identification Number: 436047207

3520
Harry Edison Foundation ▼ ⌑
501 North Broadway
St. Louis 63102 (314) 331-6540

Incorporated in 1949 in IL.
Donor(s): Harry Edison.†
Foundation type: Independent
Financial data (yr. ended 12/31/87): Assets, $22,509,365 (M); expenditures, $1,289,515, including $927,500 for 87 grants (high: $300,000; low: $100; average: $100-$10,000).
Purpose and activities: Emphasis on higher education, Jewish welfare funds, children's services, social services, cultural programs, hospitals, and medical research.
Types of support: Professorships, building funds, annual campaigns.
Limitations: Giving primarily in St. Louis, MO. No grants to individuals.
Application information: Contributes only to pre-selected organizations. Applications not accepted.
Board meeting date(s): As required
Write: Eric P. Newman, Pres.
Officers and Directors: Eric P. Newman, Pres.; Bernard Edison, V.P. and Secy.; Henry Kohn.
Number of staff: None.
Employer Identification Number: 436027017

3521
Irving and Beatrice C. Edison Foundation, Inc. ⌑ ☆
501 North Broadway
St. Louis 63102-2102 (314) 331-6502

Established in 1961.
Donor(s): Irving Edison, Bernard Edison.
Foundation type: Independent
Financial data (yr. ended 7/31/89): Assets, $1,731,852 (M); expenditures, $52,818, including $42,675 for 19 grants (high: $16,000; low: $50).
Purpose and activities: Giving primarily to higher and other education and hospitals; support also for Jewish organizations and a community fund.
Limitations: No grants to individuals.
Application information: Contributes only to pre-selected organizations. Applications not accepted.
Write: Bernard Edison, Pres.
Officers and Directors: Bernard Edison, Pres.; Marilyn Edison, V.P.; Peter A. Edison, Secy.
Employer Identification Number: 436027018

3522
Emerson Charitable Trust ▼ ⌑
c/o Emerson Electric Co.
8000 West Florissant, P.O. Box 4100
St. Louis 63136 (314) 553-2000

Established in 1944 in MO as Emerson Electric Manufacturing Company Charitable Trust; present name adopted in 1981.
Donor(s): Emerson Electric Co.
Foundation type: Company-sponsored
Financial data (yr. ended 9/30/88): Assets, $7,411,012 (M); gifts received, $5,500,000; expenditures, $6,588,359, including $6,188,765 for 1,741 grants (high: $600,000; low: $25; average: $100-$10,000) and $131,875 for 211 grants to individuals.
Purpose and activities: Grants for community funds, higher education, cultural programs, hospitals and health agencies, public policy organizations, and youth agencies.
Types of support: Employee matching gifts, employee-related scholarships.
Limitations: Giving primarily in areas of company operations. No grants to individuals.
Application information: Application form required.
Initial approach: Letter
Deadline(s): None
Board meeting date(s): Distribution committee meets 3 times a year
Write: R.W. Staley, Chair.
Officer: R.W. Staley, Chair. and Exec. V.P.
Trustee: Boatmen's Trust Co. of St. Louis.
Number of staff: None.
Employer Identification Number: 526200123

3523
Emerson Directors and Officers Charitable Trust ⌑ ☆
c/o Boatmen's Trust Co. of St. Louis
510 Locust St., P.O. Box 14737
St. Louis 63101-1845
Application address: 8000 West Florissant Ave., P.O. Box 4100, St. Louis, MO; Tel.: (314) 553-2000

Established in 1986 in MO.
Foundation type: Independent
Financial data (yr. ended 12/31/88): Assets, $534,659 (M); gifts received, $79,835; expenditures, $378,097, including $368,480 for 154 grants (high: $100,000; low: $25).
Purpose and activities: Giving primarily for higher and other education; support also for youth, including recreational activities.
Application information: Application form required.
Deadline(s): None
Write: R.W. Staley, Exec. V.P.
Officer and Trustees: Robert W. Staley, Exec. V.P.; and 16 additonal trustees.
Trustee Bank: Boatmen's Trust Co. of St. Louis.
Employer Identification Number: 436316003

3524
Emphraim Block Family Foundation ☆
c/o Mercantile Bank of St. Louis, N.A.
P.O. Box 387
St. Louis 63166 (314) 425-1783

Established in 1987 in MO.
Foundation type: Independent
Financial data (yr. ended 06/30/89): Assets, $3,535,558 (M); expenditures, $191,979, including $100,000 for 2 grants of $50,000 each.
Purpose and activities: Support for organizations providing welfare to indigent Jewish people.
Limitations: No grants to individuals.
Application information: Applications not accepted.
Write: Ms. Gail Yeager, Trust Officer, Mercantile Bank of St. Louis, N.A.
Trustees: Sarah Rosenburg, Mercantile Bank of St. Louis, N.A.
Employer Identification Number: 436331011

3525
Enright Foundation, Inc. ⌑
7508 Main
Kansas City 64114

Established in 1965.
Donor(s): Joseph J. Enright.
Foundation type: Independent
Financial data (yr. ended 3/31/88): Assets, $3,036,872 (M); expenditures, $191,381.
Purpose and activities: Giving for Roman Catholic religious organizations, hospitals, child welfare, and social service agencies.
Limitations: Giving primarily in MO. No grants for scholarships or awards.
Application information: Contributes only to pre-selected organizations. Applications not accepted.
Officers: Anna M. Cassidy, Pres.; John J. Conron, V.P.; Thomas E. King, Secy.; L.J. Cassidy, Treas.
Employer Identification Number: 436067639

3526
Enterprise Leasing Foundation ⌑
35 Hunter Ave.
St. Louis 63124 (314) 863-7000

Established in 1982 in MO.
Donor(s): Enterprise Leasing Co., Jack C. Taylor.
Foundation type: Company-sponsored
Financial data (yr. ended 7/31/88): Assets, $1,064,195 (M); gifts received, $601,200; expenditures, $350,940, including $348,738 for 90 grants (high: $29,920; low: $213).
Purpose and activities: Support primarily for education and community funds; grants also for social service and youth programs, including services for handicapped children.
Types of support: Scholarship funds, building funds, general purposes, endowment funds, equipment.

Application information:
Initial approach: Proposal
Deadline(s): None
Final notification: 3 months
Write: Van Lear Black III, Secy.
Officers: Jack C. Taylor, Pres.; Jo Ann Kindle, Exec. V.P.; Andrew C. Taylor, V.P. and Treas.; Van Lear Black III, Secy.
Directors: Monti Dowling, Ruby Garrison, Marianne Knaup, Bruce Kruenegel.
Employer Identification Number: 431262762

3527
Milton W. Feld Charitable Trust
P.O. Box 418200
Kansas City 64141 (816) 474-6460

Established in 1980 in MO.
Donor(s): Milton W. Feld.†
Foundation type: Independent
Financial data (yr. ended 08/31/88): Assets, $1,568,973 (M); expenditures, $543,741, including $459,600 for 25 grants (high: $300,000; low: $500; average: $1,000-$50,000).
Purpose and activities: Emphasis on hospitals, medicine, and AIDS research; higher education and educational programs for minorities; Jewish welfare organizations; cultural programs, including music; and social service agencies, including family services, drug abuse programs, and child welfare agencies.
Types of support: Special projects, capital campaigns, continuing support, matching funds, operating budgets, scholarship funds.
Limitations: Giving primarily in Kansas City and St. Louis, MO. No grants to individuals, or for travel, conferences, or telethons.
Application information: Application form not required.
Initial approach: Proposal
Deadline(s): None
Board meeting date(s): As necessary
Write: Abraham E. Margolin, Trustee
Trustees: Selma S. Feld, Abraham E. Margolin, Irving Selber.
Number of staff: None.
Employer Identification Number: 431155236

3528
Charles and Jennie Fermaturo Charitable Foundation
c/o The Merchants Bank
1125 Grand Ave.
Kansas City 64106 (816) 531-8000
Additional address: P.O. Box 412496, Kansas City, MO 64141

Established in 1978 in MO.
Foundation type: Independent
Financial data (yr. ended 12/31/89): Assets, $1,162,452 (M); expenditures, $61,084, including $52,331 for 21 grants (high: $18,981; low: $100; average: $1,000-$5,000).
Purpose and activities: Support limited to organizations that perform medical research, including hospitals.
Limitations: Giving primarily in Kansas City, MO, area.
Application information: Application form not required.
Initial approach: Letter
Copies of proposal: 1
Deadline(s): 15th of each month
Board meeting date(s): Monthly
Write: Gena Dysart, Asst. V.P. and Trust Officer, The Merchants Bank
Trustee: The Merchants Bank.
Employer Identification Number: 436213510

3529
Fischer-Bauer-Knirps Foundation ¤
c/o Commerce Bank of St. Louis, N.A.
P.O. Box 11356
Clayton 63105
Application address: P.O. Box 19882, Brentwood Station, Brentwood, MO 63144

Incorporated in 1959 in IL.
Foundation type: Independent
Financial data (yr. ended 12/31/88): Assets, $1,487,574 (M); expenditures, $91,897, including $70,000 for 100 grants (high: $2,000; low: $300).
Purpose and activities: Emphasis on hospitals, higher education, church support, and health agencies.
Limitations: Giving primarily in MO. No grants to individuals.
Application information: Application form not required.
Deadline(s): None
Write: Katherine Gebhard, Pres.
Officers: Katherine Gebhard, Pres.; Richard E. Fister, Secy.
Directors: Dorothy Anderson, Carl Bauer Gebhard, Fritz Gebhard.
Employer Identification Number: 436036524

3530
Gramma Fisher Foundation
c/o The Jasper Corp.
The Bullitt House
Easton 21601 (301) 822-8450

Incorporated in 1957 in IA.
Donor(s): J. William Fisher.
Foundation type: Independent
Financial data (yr. ended 12/31/88): Assets, $8,444,405 (M); expenditures, $818,989, including $785,000 for 6 grants (high: $300,000; low: $2,000).
Purpose and activities: Grants mainly for support and sponsorship of opera.
Limitations: No grants to individuals.
Application information: Application form not required.
Deadline(s): None
Board meeting date(s): As necessary
Write: Christine F. Hunter, Co-Chair.
Officers and Trustees: J. William Fisher, Co-Chair.; Christine F. Hunter, Co-Chair.; William T. Hunter, Jr., Secy.-Treas.
Number of staff: None.
Employer Identification Number: 426068755

3531
Louis and Elizabeth Flarsheim Charitable Foundation
c/o Boatmen's First National Bank of Kansas City
14 West Tenth St.
Kansas City 64183 (816) 691-7481
Application address: Boatmen's First National Bank of Kansas City, P.O. Box 419038, Kansas City, MO 64183

Donor(s): Louis Flarsheim, Elizabeth Flarsheim.
Foundation type: Independent
Financial data (yr. ended 11/30/89): Assets, $2,683,979 (M); expenditures, $133,095, including $130,027 for 6 grants (high: $40,000; low: $5,000; average: $5,000-$50,000).
Purpose and activities: Grants primarily for the performing and visual arts; support also for youth agencies and volunteer and welfare organizations.
Types of support: Seed money, special projects.
Limitations: Giving primarily in the Kansas City, MO, area.
Publications: 990-PF.
Application information: Application form not required.
Initial approach: Letter of no more than 3 pages
Copies of proposal: 1
Deadline(s): None
Write: David P. Ross, Sr. V.P., Boatmen's First National Bank of Kansas City
Trustee: Boatmen's First National Bank of Kansas City.
Number of staff: 1 full-time professional.
Employer Identification Number: 436223957

3532
Forster-Powers Charitable Trust ¤
4635 Wyandotte, Suite 206
Kansas City 64112

Foundation type: Independent
Financial data (yr. ended 12/31/87): Assets, $2,190,471 (M); gifts received, $194,961; expenditures, $49,981, including $46,500 for 24 grants (high: $5,000; low: $1,000).
Purpose and activities: Giving primarily for higher and secondary education; support also for churches and social services.
Trustees: Joseph Doran, Roger Fogelsong, Gerard Meiners, Robert E. Turgeon.
Employer Identification Number: 436110478

3533
The Francis Families Foundation ☆
800 West 47th St., Suite 604
Kansas City 64112 (816) 531-0077
Application address: Donald F. Tierney, M.D., Dir. of Fellowship Program, Dept. of Medicine, UCLA, Los Angeles, CA 90024-1690; Tel.: (213) 825-5316

Established in 1989 in MO from the merger of the Parker B. Francis Foundation (established in 1951 in MO) and the Parker B. Francis III Foundation (established in 1962 in MO).
Donor(s): Parker B. Francis,† Mary B. Francis,† Parker B. Francis III.†
Foundation type: Independent
Financial data (yr. ended 12/31/87): Assets, $53,667,838 (M); expenditures, $3,116,340, including $2,452,688 for 83 grants (high: $300,000; low: $500).
Purpose and activities: Giving primarily to fund medical fellowships in pulmonary medicine and anesthesiology, and to support educational and cultural institutions within the greater Kansas City, MO, metropolitan area.
Types of support: Fellowships, capital campaigns, special projects.

Limitations: Giving limited to the U.S. and Canada for fellowships, and to the greater Kansas City, MO, metropolitan area for educational and cultural institutions.
Application information:
Deadline(s): Sept. 15 for fellowships; May and Dec. for grants
Write: Linda K. French, Asst. Secy.-Treas.
Officers and Directors: John B. Francis, Pres.; Mary Harris Francis, V.P.; Mary Shaw Branton, Secy.-Treas.; C.M. Carson, J. Scott Francis, Thomas A. Reed, James P. Sunderland, Donald F. Tierney, M.D.
Employer Identification Number: 431492132

3534
James H. Fullbright & Monroe L. Swyers Foundation ⌑
c/o Boatmen's Trust Co. of St. Louis
510 Locust St., P.O. Box 14737
St. Louis 63178 (314) 436-9048

Established in 1981 in MO.
Foundation type: Independent
Financial data (yr. ended 9/30/88): Assets, $2,524,187 (M); expenditures, $197,576, including $149,872 for 84 grants to individuals.
Purpose and activities: Awards scholarships to individuals for higher education.
Types of support: Student aid.
Limitations: Giving limited to MO.
Application information: Application form required.
Deadline(s): Apr. 1
Write: Gary M. Rau, Trust Officer, Boatmen's Trust Co. of St. Louis
Trustees: Clifford P. McKinney, Jr., Boatmen's Trust Co. of St. Louis.
Employer Identification Number: 436252766

3535
Edward Chase Garvey Memorial Foundation
c/o Commerce Bank of St. Louis, N.A.
P.O. Box 11356
Clayton 63105 (314) 726-2255

Trust established in 1970 in MO.
Donor(s): Edward C. Garvey.†
Foundation type: Independent
Financial data (yr. ended 09/30/88): Assets, $2,181,646 (M); expenditures, $98,471, including $79,000 for 19 grants (high: $10,000; low: $1,000).
Purpose and activities: Giving for higher and secondary education, music and the performing arts, and youth agencies.
Limitations: Giving primarily in St. Louis, MO. No grants to individuals.
Application information:
Initial approach: Proposal
Copies of proposal: 1
Deadline(s): None
Board meeting date(s): Annually, in the summer
Write: John W. North, V.P., Commerce Bank of St. Louis, N.A.
Trustees: Bliss Lewis Sands, Commerce Bank of St. Louis, N.A.
Employer Identification Number: 436132744

3536
The Catherine Manley Gaylord Foundation
314 North Broadway, Rm. 1230
St. Louis 63102 (314) 421-0181

Trust established about 1959 in MO.
Donor(s): Catherine M. Gaylord.†
Foundation type: Independent
Financial data (yr. ended 06/30/89): Assets, $4,521,725 (M); expenditures, $367,453, including $275,800 for 72 grants (high: $40,000; low: $100; average: $4,000).
Purpose and activities: Emphasis on private higher education, Protestant and Roman Catholic church support, youth and child welfare agencies, civic affairs, social services, and music and art.
Types of support: Operating budgets, continuing support, annual campaigns, seed money, emergency funds, deficit financing, building funds, equipment, endowment funds, matching funds, scholarship funds, special projects, publications, conferences and seminars.
Limitations: Giving primarily in the St. Louis, MO, metropolitan community. No grants to individuals; no loans.
Publications: Annual report, program policy statement, application guidelines.
Application information: Application form not required.
Initial approach: Letter
Copies of proposal: 1
Deadline(s): None
Board meeting date(s): Monthly
Final notification: 30 days
Write: Donald E. Fahey, Trustee
Trustees: Donald E. Fahey, Leigh Gerdine, Glen K. Robbins II.
Number of staff: 1 full-time professional; 1 part-time support.
Employer Identification Number: 436029174

3537
Clifford Willard Gaylord Foundation ⌑
c/o Boatmen's National Bank of St. Louis
P.O. Box 7365, Main Post Office
St. Louis 63166 (314) 425-7714

Trust established in 1948 in MO.
Donor(s): Clifford W. Gaylord.†
Foundation type: Independent
Financial data (yr. ended 12/31/87): Assets, $6,057,843 (M); expenditures, $502,115, including $451,250 for 76 grants (high: $65,000; low: $1,000).
Purpose and activities: Giving for higher education, hospitals, social service and youth agencies, child welfare, health agencies, and cultural programs.
Limitations: Giving primarily in St. Louis, MO. No grants to individuals.
Application information: Application form not required.
Deadline(s): None
Write: George H. Halpin, Jr.
Trustees: H. Sam Priest, Pres.; Frances M. Barnes III, Clair S. Cullinbine, Gaylord Fauntleroy, Robert G.H. Hoester, Barbara P. Lawton.
Agent for Trustees: Boatmen's National Bank of St. Louis.
Employer Identification Number: 436027517

3538
The Goppert Foundation ⌑
9201 Ward Pkwy., Suite 310
Kansas City 64114 (816) 333-0110

Incorporated in 1958 in MO.
Donor(s): Clarence H. Goppert.
Foundation type: Independent
Financial data (yr. ended 10/31/88): Assets, $3,390,813 (M); expenditures, $205,649, including $197,000 for 7 grants (high: $70,000; low: $2,000).
Purpose and activities: Emphasis on education, especially for the disadvantaged, and hospitals.
Types of support: Research, equipment, matching funds, building funds, general purposes.
Limitations: Giving primarily in western MO and eastern KS. No grants to individuals.
Application information: Application form required.
Deadline(s): None
Write: Thomas A. Goppert, Secy.-Treas.
Officers: Vita M. Goppert,* Pres.; M. Charles Kellog, V.P.; Thomas A. Goppert, Secy.-Treas.
Directors:* Clarence H. Goppert, Chair.; Richard D. Goppert, Vice-Chair.; Porter C. Jeffries, Leon G. Kusnetzky, Madeline Regan.
Employer Identification Number: 446013933

3539
William T. & Frances D. Grant Charitable Trust & Foundation ⌑ ☆
c/o United Missouri Bank of Kansas City, N.A.
P.O. Box 226
Kansas City 64141

Established in 1960.
Donor(s): William T. Grant II, Frances Grant Peterson.
Foundation type: Independent
Financial data (yr. ended 12/31/88): Assets, $1,226,744 (M); gifts received, $123,325; expenditures, $41,477, including $38,511 for 17 grants (high: $8,450; low: $500).
Purpose and activities: Giving primarily for higher education and health associations and hospitals.
Limitations: Giving primarily in MO, with emphasis on Kansas City. No grants to individuals.
Application information: Contributes only to pre-selected organizations. Applications not accepted.
Trustee: United Missouri Bank of Kansas City, N.A.
Employer Identification Number: 446010325

3540
Elberth R. & Gladys F. Grant Charitable Trust ☆
c/o Commerce Bank of St. Louis, N.A.
P.O. Box 11356
Clayton 63105
Application address: c/o Commerce Bank of St. Louis, N.A., 8000 Forsyth Blvd., Clayton, MO 63105; Tel.: (314) 854-7220

Established in 1987.
Donor(s): Gladys Flora Grant,† Elberth R. Grant.†
Foundation type: Independent

Financial data (yr. ended 07/31/89): Assets, $2,514,903 (M); gifts received, $1,867,999; expenditures, $106,374, including $100,000 for 1 grant.
Purpose and activities: Giving for higher education.
Types of support: Capital campaigns.
Limitations: Giving primarily in St. Louis, MO.
Application information:
Initial approach: Letter
Deadline(s): July 31
Write: John W. North, V.P., Commerce Bank of St. Louis, N.A.
Trustees: Bertram W. Tremayne, Commerce Bank of St. Louis, N.A.
Employer Identification Number: 436332172

3541
Graybar Foundation ⌑
c/o Graybar Electric Co., Inc.
34 North Meramec Ave.
Clayton 63105 (314) 727-3900

Established in 1984 in MO.
Donor(s): Graybar Electric Co., Inc.
Foundation type: Company-sponsored
Financial data (yr. ended 10/31/88): Assets, $518,715 (M); expenditures, $184,730, including $169,833 for 55 grants (high: $15,000; low: $100) and $14,897 for employee matching gifts.
Purpose and activities: Support for social sciences and cultural programs, including the performing arts.
Types of support: Employee matching gifts, annual campaigns, general purposes, special projects.
Limitations: Giving primarily in MO and in other areas of company operations all over the U.S.
Application information: Applications not accepted.
Officers and Directors: J.L. Hoagland, Pres.; E.A. McGrath, Exec. V.P.; L.C. Owen, Jr., V.P. and Treas.; G.H. Booth, J.R. Seaton, G.S. Tulloch, Jr., J.F. van Pelt, D.H. Whittington.
Trustee: Mercantile Trust Co.
Employer Identification Number: 431301419

3542
Allen P. & Josephine B. Green Foundation
P.O. Box 523
Mexico 65265 (314) 581-5568

Trust established in 1941 in MO.
Donor(s): Allen P. Green,† Mrs. Allen P. Green.†
Foundation type: Independent
Financial data (yr. ended 12/31/88): Assets, $9,265,298 (M); expenditures, $585,100, including $500,600 for 47 grants (high: $30,000; low: $1,000).
Purpose and activities: Giving for health care and educational programs for children and youth, social services, the arts and other cultural programs, and historic preservation projects; giving also for the aged, higher education, and the environment.
Types of support: Seed money, emergency funds, building funds, equipment, endowment funds, scholarship funds, special projects, conferences and seminars, matching funds, capital campaigns, fellowships, renovation projects.
Limitations: Giving primarily in the Mexico, MO, area; no giving outside the continental U.S. No grants to individuals, or for operating budgets; no loans.
Publications: Annual report.
Application information: Application form not required.
Initial approach: Letter
Copies of proposal: 1
Deadline(s): Apr. 1 or Oct. 1
Board meeting date(s): May and Nov.
Final notification: 1 month
Write: Walter G. Staley, Secy.-Treas.
Officers and Directors:* James F. McHenry,* Pres.; Walter G. Staley,* Secy.-Treas.; A.D. Bond III,* Christopher S. Bond, Robert R. Collins, Susan Green Foote, Martha S. Marks, Homer E. Sayad, Walter G. Staley, Jr., George C. Willson III, Robert A. Wood.
Number of staff: 1 part-time support.
Employer Identification Number: 436030135

3543
Group Health Plan Foundation of Greater St. Louis ⌑
3556 Caroline St.
St. Louis 63104 (314) 577-8105

Established in 1986 in MO.
Foundation type: Independent
Financial data (yr. ended 10/31/88): Assets, $3,260,965 (M); expenditures, $257,000, including $204,975 for 8 grants (high: $55,000; low: $15,000).
Purpose and activities: Support primarily for health agencies and health services.
Types of support: Conferences and seminars, equipment, fellowships, lectureships, program-related investments, research, scholarship funds, seed money, special projects.
Limitations: Giving primarily in St. Louis, MO.
Publications: Corporate giving report, informational brochure (including application guidelines).
Application information: Application form not required.
Initial approach: Letter
Copies of proposal: 5
Deadline(s): None
Board meeting date(s): Feb., May, Aug., and Nov.
Write: Robert M. Swanson, Secy.
Directors: Stephen M. Ayres, M.D., and 9 additional directors.
Number of staff: None.
Employer Identification Number: 431141117

3544
Hall Family Foundations ▼
Charitable & Crown Investment - 323
P.O. Box 419580
Kansas City 64141-6580 (816) 274-8516

Hallmark Educational Foundation incorporated in 1943 in MO; Hallmark Education Foundation of KS incorporated in 1954 in KS; combined funds formerly known as Hallmark Educational Foundations.
Donor(s): Hallmark Cards, Inc., Joyce C. Hall,† E.A. Hall,† R.B. Hall.†
Foundation type: Independent
Financial data (yr. ended 12/31/89): Assets, $323,873,343 (M); gifts received, $27,000,000; expenditures, $5,772,606, including $4,309,000 for 50 grants (high: $1,000,000; low: $5,000; average: $30,000-$70,000), $272,115 for grants to individuals (high: $11,978; low: $1,100; average: $1,500-$3,000) and $586,000 for 2 loans.
Purpose and activities: Giving within four main areas of interest: 1) the performing and visual arts; 2) youth, especially education, including student aid for the children of Hallmark employees, and programs that promote social welfare, health and character building of young people; 3) economic development, including programs for the homeless; and 4) the elderly.
Types of support: Seed money, emergency funds, building funds, equipment, special projects, matching funds, general purposes, employee-related scholarships, renovation projects, program-related investments.
Limitations: Giving limited to MO and KS, in the Kansas City area. No support for international or religious organizations or for political purposes. No grants to individuals (except for emergency aid to Hallmark Cards employees, and scholarships for their children and close relatives only), or for endowment funds, travel, operating deficits, conferences, scholarly research, or fundraising campaigns such as telethons.
Publications: Annual report, informational brochure (including application guidelines).
Application information: Scholarships are for the children and close relatives of Hallmark Cards employees only. Only eligible applicants should apply. Application form not required.
Initial approach: Letter
Copies of proposal: 1
Deadline(s): 6 weeks before board meetings
Board meeting date(s): Mar., June, Sept., and Dec.
Final notification: 4 to 6 weeks
Write: Margaret H. Pence, Dir.; Wendy Burcham, Peggy Collins, or John Laney, Prog. Officers
Officers: William A. Hall, Pres.; John A. McDonald, V.P. and Treas.; Eleanor Angelbeck, Secy.
Directors: Donald J. Hall, Chair.; Paul H. Henson, Irvine O. Hockaday, Jr., David H. Hughes, Robert A. Kipp, John P. Mascotte, Margaret H. Pence, Morton I. Sosland.
Number of staff: 2 full-time professional; 7 part-time professional; 4 part-time support.
Employer Identification Number: 446006291

3545
Hallmark Corporate Foundation
P.O. Box 419580, Dept. 323
Kansas City 64141-6580 (816) 274-8515

Established in 1983 in MO.
Donor(s): Hallmark Cards, Inc.
Foundation type: Company-sponsored
Financial data (yr. ended 12/31/88): Assets, $31,007,047 (M); expenditures, $3,456,330, including $3,249,456 for 713 grants (high: $490,000; low: $25) and $53,555 for 103 employee matching gifts.
Purpose and activities: Support for a wide range of programs, including AIDS,

employment, journalism, literacy, urban affairs, youth (including the problem of delinquency), and higher and pre-college education; also provides in-kind giving.
Types of support: In-kind gifts, annual campaigns, building funds, continuing support, employee matching gifts, equipment, internships, matching funds, program-related investments, seed money, technical assistance, special projects.
Limitations: Giving limited to Kansas City, MO, and cities where Hallmark facilities are located.
Publications: Application guidelines.
Application information: Application form not required.
Initial approach: Written proposal
Copies of proposal: 1
Deadline(s): None
Board meeting date(s): Periodic
Final notification: Within 6 weeks
Write: Jeanne Bates, Secy.-Treas.
Officers: Donald J. Hall,* Chair.; William A. Hall, Pres.; Jeanne Bates, Secy.-Treas.
Directors:* Irvine O. Hockaday, Jr., David H. Hughs, Robert L. Stark.
Number of staff: 2 full-time professional; 1 full-time support.
Employer Identification Number: 431303258

3546
Helzberg Foundation ⌑
1600 Baltimore
Kansas City 64108

Established in 1982 in MO.
Donor(s): Barnett C. Helzberg, Jr.
Foundation type: Independent
Financial data (yr. ended 02/28/89): Assets, $3,219,387 (M); expenditures, $224,461, including $213,012 for 120 grants (high: $40,000; low: $15).
Purpose and activities: Support for Jewish welfare organizations and social services.
Limitations: No grants to individuals.
Application information: Contributes to pre-selected organizations only. Applications not accepted.
Officers: Barnett C. Helzberg, Jr., Pres.; Shirley Bush Helzberg, V.P. and Treas.; Ralph G. Wrobley, Secy.
Employer Identification Number: 431265367

3547
Herschend Family Foundation ☆
Silver Dollar City Inc.
Marvel Cave Park 65616 (417) 338-2611

Established in 1985 in MO.
Donor(s): Jack R. Herschend.
Foundation type: Independent
Financial data (yr. ended 12/31/88): Assets, $2,247,671 (M); gifts received, $952,500; expenditures, $255,225, including $239,097 for 32 grants (high: $25,000; low: $2,500) and $11,338 for 9 grants to individuals (average: $2,000).
Purpose and activities: Giving primarily for Protestant organizations, including churches and ministries; support also for family and social services, including child welfare and development and welfare assistance to individuals.
Types of support: Grants to individuals.
Limitations: Giving primarily in MO.
Application information: Application form not required.
Initial approach: Letter
Copies of proposal: 1
Deadline(s): None
Board meeting date(s): 3rd Tuesday of Jan. and Sept.
Write: Jack R. Herschend, Dir.
Directors: Bruce Herschend, Jack R. Herschend, James R. Herschend, Kelly Herschend, Peggy L. Herschend, Ronald J. Herschend, Sherry J. Herschend.
Number of staff: None.
Employer Identification Number: 431391940

3548
Herschend Foundation ☆
2512 South Campbell
Springfield 65807 (417) 883-9970

Established in 1985 in MO.
Donor(s): Peter F. Herschend, JoDee Herschend, John J. Herschend, Sarah Herschend, Chris Herschend.
Foundation type: Independent
Financial data (yr. ended 04/30/89): Assets, $1,491,375 (M); gifts received, $1,460,174; expenditures, $249,294, including $243,280 for 31 grants (high: $43,080; low: $500).
Purpose and activities: Support primarily for Christian projects, including missions and Episcopal churches.
Limitations: No grants to individuals, or for medical expenses.
Application information:
Initial approach: Proposal
Copies of proposal: 1
Deadline(s): None
Board meeting date(s): Annually
Write: Don G. Smillie, Mgr.
Officer: Don G. Smillie, Mgr.
Directors: JoDee Herschend, Jonn J. Herschend, Peter F. Herschend.
Number of staff: None.
Employer Identification Number: 431410633

3549
Oscar C. Hirsch Foundation ⌑
P.O. Box 611
Cape Girardeau 63702-0611 (314) 334-2555

Established in 1964 in MO.
Foundation type: Independent
Financial data (yr. ended 12/31/88): Assets, $1,054,997 (M); expenditures, $65,861, including $63,700 for 16 grants (high: $15,100; low: $200).
Purpose and activities: Grants primarily for Protestant church support; some giving for youth programs, education, and social service agencies.
Types of support: General purposes.
Application information:
Initial approach: Letter
Deadline(s): None
Write: James F. Hirsch, Trustee
Trustees: Keith Deimund, Marjorie H. Deimund, Beverly S. Hirsch, Geraldine Hirsch, James F. Hirsch, Oscar C. Hirsch, Robert O. Hirsch.
Employer Identification Number: 436052895

3550
Charles & Ethel Hughes Foundation, Inc. ⌑
P.O. Box 370
206 North Jefferson
Lebanon 65536-0370 (417) 532-3151

Established in 1978 in MO.
Foundation type: Operating
Financial data (yr. ended 12/31/87): Assets, $2,376,765 (M); expenditures, $322,395, including $250,065 for 1 grant.
Purpose and activities: A private operating foundation which maintains a senior citizens' center.
Types of support: Building funds.
Application information: Application form not required.
Initial approach: Letter
Deadline(s): None
Write: John A. Honssinger, Dir.
Directors: Margeret Burtin, Howard Carrington, Ervin Engsberg, John A. Honssinger, Karen Myers.
Employer Identification Number: 431134135

3551
David Craig Humphreys Foundation, Inc. ⌑ ☆
P.O. Box 1404
Joplin 64802-1404

Incorporated in 1981 in MO.
Foundation type: Independent
Financial data (yr. ended 7/31/88): Assets, $1,054,238 (M); expenditures, $55,878, including $51,749 for 3 grants (high: $50,000; low: $249).
Purpose and activities: Giving primarily for a right-to-work organization and economic education and policy.
Limitations: No grants to individuals.
Application information: Contributes only to pre-selected organizations. Applications not accepted.
Officers: J.P. Humphreys, Pres.; David Craig Humphreys, V.P.; Ethelmae Humphreys, Secy.-Treas.
Employer Identification Number: 431223500

3552
Ethelmae Craig Humphreys Foundation, Inc. ⌑ ☆
P.O. Box 1404
Joplin 64802-1404

Established in 1981.
Foundation type: Independent
Financial data (yr. ended 7/31/89): Assets, $1,124,801 (M); expenditures, $26,758, including $25,000 for 1 grant.
Purpose and activities: Support for a YMCA and public affairs groups.
Types of support: General purposes.
Application information: Contributes only to pre-selected organizations. Applications not accepted.
Officers: J.P. Humphreys, Pres.; Sarah Jane Humphreys, V.P.; Ethelmae Humphreys, Secy.-Treas.
Employer Identification Number: 431223499

3553
John Patrick Humphreys Foundation, Inc. ⌑ ☆
P.O. Box 1404
Joplin 64802-1404

Established in 1981.
Foundation type: Independent
Financial data (yr. ended 7/31/89): Assets, $1,083,241 (M); expenditures, $27,343, including $25,000 for 1 grant.
Purpose and activities: Giving primarily for the study of economics at universities and public policy organizations.
Limitations: No grants to individuals.
Application information: Contributes only to pre-selected organizations. Applications not accepted.
Officers: J.P. Humphreys, Pres.; John Patrick Humphreys, V.P.; Ethelmae Humphreys, Secy.-Treas.
Employer Identification Number: 431223486

3554
Sarah Jane Humphreys Foundation, Inc. ⌑ ☆
P.O. Box 1404
Joplin 64802-1404

Established in 1981.
Foundation type: Independent
Financial data (yr. ended 7/31/88): Assets, $1,033,874 (M); expenditures, $55,878, including $51,749 for 3 grants (high: $50,000; low: $249).
Purpose and activities: Giving primarily for a right-to-work organization.
Limitations: No grants to individuals.
Application information: Contributes only to pre-selected organizations. Applications not accepted.
Officers: J.P. Humphreys, Pres.; Sarah Jane Humphreys, V.P.; Ethelmae Humphreys, Secy.-Treas.
Employer Identification Number: 431223480

3555
May H. Ilgenfritz Testamentary Trust ⌑
108 West Pacific
Sedalia 65301 (816) 826-3310

Trust established in 1941 in MO.
Foundation type: Independent
Financial data (yr. ended 12/31/88): Assets, $2,510,285 (M); expenditures, $110,940, including $35,000 for 1 grant and $59,200 for 70 grants to individuals (high: $1,800; low: $75).
Purpose and activities: Emphasis on scholarships to individuals and a rehabilitation center for handicapped children.
Types of support: Student aid, operating budgets.
Limitations: Giving primarily in MO; scholarship recipients must reside in Sedalia.
Application information: Application form required for scholarships.
Deadline(s): None
Write: John Pelham, Trustee
Trustees: John Pelham, Third National Bank.
Employer Identification Number: 440663403

3556
Joe Ingram Trust
c/o Boatman's Trust Co.
1130 Walnut, P.O. Box 419666
Kansas City 64141 (816) 388-5676
Grant application address: Joe W. Ingram Trust "B" Comm., 111 West Third St., Salisbury, MO 65281; Tel.: (816) 388-5555

Trust established in 1960 in MO.
Donor(s): Joe Ingram.†
Foundation type: Independent
Financial data (yr. ended 12/31/88): Assets, $7,456,513 (M); expenditures, $539,792, including $5,750 for 2 grants (high: $5,000; low: $750), $4,000 for 4 grants to individuals of $1,000 each and $448,491 for 114 loans to individuals.
Purpose and activities: Giving primarily for student loans to local area residents; some support for local civic projects and valedictorian awards.
Types of support: Grants to individuals, student loans.
Limitations: Giving limited to Chariton County, MO.
Application information: Application forms provided for student loans. Application form required.
Initial approach: Letter
Deadline(s): May 1 for fall, winter, and summer term; Dec. 1 to Mar. 1 for spring term
Board meeting date(s): 2nd Thursday of each month
Write: Sandra K. Scheiderer
Trustee: Boatmen's Trust Co. of St. Louis.
Trust Fund Committee: Elmer Arnsperger, Elmer E. Bills, Jr., Thomas H. Ehrhardt, Shirley Hickerson, David McAllister, Joann Ousley, Barbara Pressley, John Ratliff, Eugene Smith, David Sturn, Robert H. Sweeney, George S. Thompson.
Number of staff: 1 part-time professional; 1 part-time support.
Employer Identification Number: 446006475

3557
Interco, Inc. Charitable Trust ▼ ⌑
P.O. Box 387
St. Louis 63166 (314) 863-1100
Application address: Interco, Inc., 101 South Hanley Rd., Clayton, MO 63105

Trust established in 1944 in MO.
Donor(s): Interco, Inc., and subsidiaries.
Foundation type: Company-sponsored
Financial data (yr. ended 12/31/87): Assets, $21,672,844 (M); gifts received, $512,072; expenditures, $1,367,030, including $1,175,333 for 76 grants (high: $305,000; low: $300; average: $1,000-$10,000).
Purpose and activities: Emphasis on a community fund, higher education, and cultural programs; support also for hospitals, and social service and youth agencies.
Limitations: Giving primarily in St. Louis, MO.
Application information:
Deadline(s): None
Board meeting date(s): As required
Write: Robert T. Hensley, Jr., Trustee
Trustees: Robert T. Hensley, Jr., Mercantile Bank, N.A.
Number of staff: None.
Employer Identification Number: 436020530

3558
The Jackes Foundation ⌑
c/o Boatmen's Trust Co. of St. Louis
510 Locust St., P.O. Box 14737
St. Louis 63178 (314) 436-9228

Established in 1967 in MO.
Donor(s): Dorothy J. Miller,† Stanley F. Jackes, Margaret F. Jackes.
Foundation type: Independent
Financial data (yr. ended 12/31/87): Assets, $1,547,413 (M); expenditures, $169,273, including $151,500 for 51 grants (high: $44,650; low: $50).
Purpose and activities: Support for education, cultural programs, social services, religious giving, health associations, and hospitals.
Limitations: Giving primarily in the St. Louis, MO, area.
Application information: Application form not required.
Deadline(s): None
Write: Martin E. Galt III, Trustee
Trustees: Martin E. Galt III, Margaret F. Jackes, Stanley F. Jackes.
Employer Identification Number: 436074447

3559
Mary Ranken Jordan and Ettie A. Jordan Charitable Foundation ⌑
c/o Mercantile Bank, N.A.
P.O. Box 387
St. Louis 63166 (314) 231-7626

Trust established in 1957 in MO.
Donor(s): Mrs. Mary Ranken Jordan.†
Foundation type: Independent
Financial data (yr. ended 12/31/87): Assets, $14,242,095 (M); expenditures, $779,951, including $623,090 for 63 grants (high: $75,000; low: $1,000).
Purpose and activities: Giving limited to charitable and eleemosynary institutions with emphasis on higher education and cultural programs; grants also for social services, secondary education, and hospitals and health services.
Types of support: Building funds, operating budgets, special projects, continuing support.
Limitations: Giving limited to MO, with emphasis on St. Louis. No grants to individuals, or for endowment funds.
Publications: Application guidelines.
Application information: Application form not required.
Initial approach: Letter
Copies of proposal: 3
Deadline(s): None
Board meeting date(s): Jan.
Final notification: After Jan. 15
Write: Jill Fivecoat, Asst. V.P., Mercantile Bank, N.A.
Trustee: Mercantile Bank, N.A.
Number of staff: None.
Employer Identification Number: 436020554

3560
The Greater Kansas City Community Foundation and Its Affiliated Trusts ▼
127 West 10th St., Suite 406
Kansas City 64105 (816) 842-0944

Established in 1978 in MO.

Foundation type: Community
Financial data (yr. ended 01/31/90): Assets, $36,070,782 (M); gifts received, $8,145,333; expenditures, $7,292,659, including $6,699,249 for grants.
Purpose and activities: Giving primarily to improve the quality of life in the metropolitan area in the fields of arts and culture, health, welfare, community action, and education; giving also for matching and challenge grants.
Types of support: Seed money, matching funds, general purposes, lectureships, program-related investments, renovation projects, scholarship funds, special projects.
Limitations: Giving primarily in five-county greater Kansas City, MO, area. No grants to individuals (except through designated scholarship funds), or for deficit financing, endowments, capital or annual campaigns, or operating expenses.
Publications: Annual report, application guidelines, newsletter, informational brochure.
Application information: Application form not required.
Initial approach: Proposal or letter
Copies of proposal: 1
Deadline(s): None
Board meeting date(s): Mar., June, Sept., and Dec.
Final notification: Within 2 weeks of board meeting
Write: Janice C. Kreamer, Pres.
Officers and Directors:* James P. Sunderland,* Chair.; Edward A. Smith,* Vice-Chair.; Janice C. Kreamer,* Pres.; George S. Bittner, V.P., Finance; Dalene D. Bradford, V.P., Program; Marion C. Kreamer, Secy.; Charles A. Duboc,* Treas.; and 22 additional directors.
Number of staff: 8 full-time professional; 4 full-time support.
Employer Identification Number: 431152398

3561
Ewing Marion Kauffman Foundation ☆
922 Walnut St., Suite 1100
Kansas City 64106 (816) 966-4000
Application address: 9300 Ward Pkwy., P.O. Box 8480, Kansas City, MO 64114

Established in 1966.
Donor(s): Ewing M. Kauffman.
Foundation type: Independent
Financial data (yr. ended 06/30/89): Assets, $2,362,273 (M); expenditures, $679,819, including $201,639 for 20 grants (high: $75,000; low: $50) and $478,180 for 3 foundation-administered programs.
Purpose and activities: Support mainly for health agencies, including a foundation-administered program for drug abuse and prevention seminars and training; giving also for child development, early childhood education, family services, and the disadvantaged.
Limitations: Giving primarily in KS and MO.
Application information: Funds primarily disbursed through foundation-administered programs; few grants awarded. Application form not required.
Initial approach: Brief concept paper; no proposals
Copies of proposal: 1
Deadline(s): None
Board meeting date(s): Sept. and Feb.
Write: Carl Mitchell, Treas.
Officers and Directors:* Ewing M. Kauffman,* Chair.; Robert Rogers,* Pres.; Charles L. Hughes,* Secy.; Carl Mitchell, Treas.; Carl Bobkoski.
Number of staff: 11 full-time professional; 13 full-time support; 6 part-time support.
Employer Identification Number: 436064859

3562
Kellwood Foundation ⌑
P.O. Box 14080
St. Louis 63178 (314) 576-3350
Application address: 600 Kellwood Pkwy., St. Louis, MO 63017

Established in 1965 in MO.
Donor(s): Kellwood Co.
Foundation type: Company-sponsored
Financial data (yr. ended 4/30/88): Assets, $277,123 (M); gifts received, $61,244; expenditures, $126,365, including $125,310 for 66 grants (high: $17,000; low: $100).
Purpose and activities: Support for health associations, higher education, community programs, social and welfare services, and youth organizations.
Types of support: Matching funds, general purposes.
Limitations: Giving primarily in St. Louis, MO.
Application information:
Initial approach: Letter
Deadline(s): Nov. 15
Write: Jane Campbell
Officers and Directors: Fred W. Wenzel, Pres.; Robert A. Maddocks, Secy.
Employer Identification Number: 366141441

3563
R. C. Kemper Charitable Trust & Foundation ⌑
c/o United Missouri Bank of Kansas City, N.A.
Tenth & Grand Ave.
Kansas City 64141

Trust established in 1953 in MO.
Donor(s): R. Crosby Kemper, Sr.†
Foundation type: Independent
Financial data (yr. ended 12/31/88): Assets, $12,353,719 (M); expenditures, $653,611, including $595,730 for 16 grants (high: $250,000; low: $50).
Purpose and activities: Emphasis on cultural activities, higher education, including scholarship funds, and youth agencies.
Limitations: Giving primarily in MO.
Application information: Contributes only to pre-selected organizations. Applications not accepted.
Trustees: Mary S. Kemper, R. Crosby Kemper, Jr., United Missouri Bank of Kansas City, N.A.
Employer Identification Number: 446010318

3564
Enid and Crosby Kemper Foundation ⌑
c/o United Missouri Bank of Kansas City, N.A.
Tenth St. and Grand Ave., P.O. Box 226
Kansas City 64141 (816) 556-7722

Established in 1972 in MO.
Donor(s): Enid J. Kemper, R. Crosby Kemper, Sr.†
Foundation type: Independent
Financial data (yr. ended 12/31/86): Assets, $28,394,777 (M); expenditures, $4,050,965, including $3,850,833 for 60 grants (high: $1,589,500; low: $50; average: $500-$5,000).
Purpose and activities: Emphasis on secondary education and cultural programs, including museums and the performing arts; some support also for health and higher education.
Types of support: General purposes.
Limitations: Giving primarily in KS and MO. No support for medical institutions. No grants for capital funds.
Application information: Contributes only to pre-selected organizations. Applications not accepted.
Board meeting date(s): Quarterly and as needed
Write: Melanie Alm
Trustees: Malcolm M. Aslin, Mary S. Kemper, R. Crosby Kemper, Jr., Richard C. King, United Missouri Bank of Kansas City, N.A.
Employer Identification Number: 237279896

3565
The David Woods Kemper Memorial Foundation ⌑
1800 Commerce Bank Bldg.
P.O. Box 419248
Kansas City 64199 (816) 234-2346

Incorporated in 1946 in MO.
Donor(s): James M. Kemper, James M. Kemper, Jr.
Foundation type: Independent
Financial data (yr. ended 12/31/87): Assets, $4,478,986 (M); expenditures, $377,877, including $357,901 for 108 grants (high: $200,000; low: $25).
Purpose and activities: Support for cultural programs, higher and secondary education, population control, Protestant church support, youth agencies, and community funds.
Limitations: Giving primarily in Kansas City, MO.
Application information: Application form not required.
Deadline(s): None
Write: James M. Kemper, Jr., Pres.
Officers and Directors: James M. Kemper, Jr., Pres.; Laura Kemper Fields, V.P. and Treas.
Number of staff: None.
Employer Identification Number: 446012535

3566
Ray & Mary Klapmeyer Charitable Foundation ⌑
c/o United Missouri Bank of Kansas City, N.A.
P.O. Box 226
Kansas City 64141

Established in 1973 in MO.
Foundation type: Independent
Financial data (yr. ended 8/31/88): Assets, $2,349,531 (M); expenditures, $151,855, including $130,523 for 6 grants (high: $43,503; low: $10,873).
Purpose and activities: Support for child welfare and social services.

Application information: Contributes only to pre-selected organizations. Applications not accepted.
Trustees: Coye Wilson, United Missouri Bank of Kansas City, N.A.
Employer Identification Number: 237381612

3567
Laclede Gas Charitable Trust ⌑
720 Olive St., Rm. 1525
St. Louis 63101 (314) 342-0506

Trust established in 1966 in MO.
Donor(s): Laclede Gas Co.
Foundation type: Company-sponsored
Financial data (yr. ended 9/30/88): Assets, $5,851,376 (M); gifts received, $25,000; expenditures, $603,614, including $553,099 for 127 grants (high: $188,125; low: $10) and $24,465 for 62 employee matching gifts.
Purpose and activities: Support of public charitable organizations with emphasis on community funds, higher and secondary education, the arts, hospitals, family services, public policy, and youth agencies.
Types of support: Annual campaigns, endowment funds, general purposes, matching funds, employee-related scholarships, employee matching gifts, operating budgets, scholarship funds, building funds, equipment, emergency funds, conferences and seminars, special projects.
Limitations: Giving primarily in areas of company operations. No support for religious or sectarian organizations, political organizations, or veterans' groups. No grants to individuals.
Publications: Informational brochure.
Application information: Application form not required.
Initial approach: Proposal
Copies of proposal: 1
Deadline(s): None
Board meeting date(s): Mar., June, Sept., and Dec.
Write: David L. Gardner, Trustee
Trustees: David L. Gardner, Lee M. Liberman, D.A. Novatny.
Number of staff: None.
Employer Identification Number: 436068197

3568
The Lantz Welch Charitable Foundation ⌑
1200 Main St., Suite 3500
Kansas City 64105
Application address: P.O. Box 26250, Kansas City, MO 64196

Established in 1985 in MO.
Donor(s): Lantz Welch.
Foundation type: Independent
Financial data (yr. ended 12/31/87): Assets, $1,228,442 (M); gifts received, $21,955; expenditures, $106,159, including $99,309 for 40 grants (high: $15,000; low: $50).
Purpose and activities: Support primarily for health associations, cultural programs, and youth agencies.
Application information:
Initial approach: Proposal
Deadline(s): Apr. 1 and Oct. 1
Board meeting date(s): Twice a year
Write: Lantz Welch, Pres.
Officers and Directors: Lantz Welch, Pres. and Treas.; James Bartimus, V.P.; Laura Gault, Secy.
Employer Identification Number: 431388861

3569
George A. and Dolly F. LaRue Trust
c/o The Greater Kansas City Community Foundation
127 West 10th St., Suite 406
Kansas City 64105 (816) 842-0944

Trust established in 1973 in MO.
Donor(s): George A. LaRue,† Dolly F. LaRue.†
Foundation type: Independent
Financial data (yr. ended 12/31/89): Assets, $2,742,428 (M); expenditures, $83,824, including $70,175 for grants.
Purpose and activities: Grants for the arts and cultural organizations, education and social services.
Types of support: Special projects.
Limitations: Giving primarily in MO, with emphasis on Kansas City.
Publications: Application guidelines.
Application information: Application form required.
Initial approach: Letter or proposal
Copies of proposal: 1
Deadline(s): 4 to 6 months prior to board meetings
Board meeting date(s): Mar., June, Sept., and Dec.
Final notification: Within 2 weeks of board meetings
Write: Janice C. Kreamer, Pres., The Greater Kansas City Community Foundation
Trustee: Commerce Bank of Kansas City.
Number of staff: None.
Employer Identification Number: 436122865

3570
The Leader Foundation
7711 Carondelet Ave., 10th Fl.
St. Louis 63105 (314) 725-7300

Established in 1944.
Foundation type: Independent
Financial data (yr. ended 02/01/89): Assets, $2,485,264 (M); expenditures, $181,547, including $89,000 for 6 grants (high: $33,000; low: $5,000) and $76,308 for 23 grants to individuals (high: $6,660; low: $600).
Purpose and activities: Giving primarily to individuals for pensions and health organizations and family services.
Types of support: Grants to individuals, continuing support, special projects.
Limitations: Giving primarily in St. Louis, MO.
Application information: Application form not required.
Initial approach: Letter
Copies of proposal: 1
Deadline(s): None
Board meeting date(s): May and Nov.
Write: Edwin G. Shifrin, V.P.
Officers: Donald E. Ray, Pres.; J.A. Baer II, V.P.; Edwin G. Shifrin, V.P.; Steven M. Rafsky, Secy.-Treas.
Directors: Philip Marlo, Patricia Reaves.
Number of staff: None.
Employer Identification Number: 436036864

3571
David B. Lichtenstein Foundation ⌑
P.O. Box 19740
St. Louis 63144

Established in 1947 in MO.
Donor(s): David Lichtenstein.†
Foundation type: Independent
Financial data (yr. ended 12/31/88): Assets, $6,130,274 (M); gifts received, $1,813,742; expenditures, $156,116, including $138,300 for 12 grants (high: $55,140; low: $100).
Purpose and activities: Giving primarily to Protestant religious and charitable organizations.
Limitations: Giving limited to MO.
Application information: Application form not required.
Deadline(s): None
Write: Daniel B. Lichtenstein, Mgr.
Officer and Trustees:* Daniel B. Lichtenstein,* Mgr.; Ken Cohen, Sheldon Cohen, David B. Lichtenstein, Jr., Mary Lichtenstein, Barney Reiss, John Straub.
Employer Identification Number: 436033786

3572
R. A. Long Foundation ⌑
127 West Tenth St., Suite 500
Kansas City 64105 (816) 842-2315

Incorporated in 1958 in MO.
Donor(s): Loula Long Combs,† Sally Long Ellis.†
Foundation type: Independent
Financial data (yr. ended 11/30/88): Assets, $3,252,390 (M); expenditures, $174,283, including $134,550 for 36 grants (high: $10,000; low: $300).
Purpose and activities: Giving largely for services for youth, including child welfare, recreation, rehabilitation, and education.
Types of support: Capital campaigns, consulting services, operating budgets, renovation projects.
Limitations: Giving primarily in KS and MO. No grants to individuals, or for endowment funds, research programs, scholarships, or fellowships; no loans.
Publications: Application guidelines.
Application information: Application form not required.
Initial approach: Letter
Copies of proposal: 1
Deadline(s): None
Board meeting date(s): May and Nov.
Write: James H. Bernard, Treas.
Officers: R.A. Long Ellis,* Pres.; Hayne Ellis III,* V.P.; Jack B. O'Hara,* V.P.; James R. Mueller, Secy.; James H. Bernard,* Treas.
Directors:* Linna Place, Ann J. Thompson.
Number of staff: None.
Employer Identification Number: 446014081

3573
Carrie J. Loose Trust
c/o The Greater Kansas City Community Foundation
127 West 10th St., Suite 406
Kansas City 64105 (816) 842-0944

Trust established in 1927 in MO.
Donor(s): Harry Wilson Loose,† Carrie J. Loose.†
Foundation type: Independent

Financial data (yr. ended 12/31/89): Assets, $8,622,000 (M); expenditures, $575,738, including $489,155 for 19 grants (high: $60,000; low: $5,000).
Purpose and activities: Grants to established local educational, health, and welfare institutions; support for research into the community's social and cultural needs and for experimental and demonstration projects. A member trust of the Kansas City Association of Trusts and Foundations.
Types of support: Special projects.
Limitations: Giving limited to Kansas City, MO. No grants to individuals, or for building funds, matching gifts, endowment funds, deficit financing, annual or capital campaigns, general support, scholarships, or fellowships; no loans.
Publications: Application guidelines.
Application information: Application form not required.
Initial approach: Letter or proposal
Copies of proposal: 1
Deadline(s): 4 to 6 months prior to board meetings
Board meeting date(s): Mar., June, Sept., and Dec.
Final notification: Within two weeks of the board meetings
Write: Janice C. Kreamer, Pres., The Greater Kansas City Community Foundation
Officers and Directors:* James P. Sunderland,* Chair.; Edward A. Smith,* Vice-Chair.; Janice C. Kreamer, Pres.; George S. Bittner, V.P., Finance; Dalene D. Bradford, V.P., Prog.; Marion E. Kreamer,* Secy.; Charles A. Duboc,* Treas.; and 20 additional directors.
Trustee: Boatmen's First National Bank of Kansas City.
Number of staff: 12
Employer Identification Number: 446009246

3574
Harry Wilson Loose Trust
c/o The Greater Kansas City Community Foundation
127 West 10th St., Suite 406
Kansas City 64105 (816) 842-0944

Trust established in 1927 in MO.
Donor(s): Harry Wilson Loose.†
Foundation type: Independent
Financial data (yr. ended 12/31/89): Assets, $3,504,000 (M); expenditures, $235,620, including $197,528 for 11 grants (high: $50,000; low: $5,000).
Purpose and activities: Emphasis on civic and community development in Kansas City, including grants for health, social services, and the arts and cultural programs. A member trust of the Kansas City Association of Trusts and Foundations.
Types of support: Research, special projects.
Limitations: Giving limited to Kansas City, MO. No grants to individuals, or for endowment funds, general support, building funds, matching gifts, scholarships, or fellowships; no loans.
Publications: Annual report, application guidelines.
Application information: Application form not required.
Initial approach: Letter or proposal
Copies of proposal: 1
Deadline(s): 4 months prior to full board meetings
Board meeting date(s): Mar., June, Sept., and Dec.
Final notification: Within 2 weeks of the full board meeting
Write: Janice C. Kreamer, Pres., The Greater Kansas City Community Foundation
Officers: James P. Sunderland, Chair.; Edward A. Smith, Vice-Chair.; Janice C. Kreamer, Pres.; George S. Bittner, V.P.; Dalene D. Bradford, V.P.; Marion E. Kreamer, Secy.; Charles A. Duboc, Treas.
Trustees: Donald H. Chisolm, Robert T.H. Davidson, Boatmen's First National Bank of Kansas City.
Number of staff: None.
Employer Identification Number: 446009245

3575
Stanley and Lucy Lopata Foundation ⌑
c/o Lopata Partnership
130 South Bemiston, 8th Fl.
St. Louis 63105

Established in 1968.
Donor(s): Stanley Lopata, Lucy Lopata.
Foundation type: Independent
Financial data (yr. ended 12/31/88): Assets, $3,224,469 (M); gifts received, $50,400; expenditures, $263,623, including $255,813 for 175 grants (high: $50,000; low: $10).
Purpose and activities: Giving primarily for Jewish welfare funds and temple support.
Limitations: Giving primarily in St. Louis, MO. No grants to individuals.
Application information: Contributes only to pre-selected organizations. Applications not accepted.
Officer: Stanley Lopata, Mgr.
Trustees: Lucy Lopata, Monte L. Lopata.
Employer Identification Number: 436099972

3576
John Allan Love Charitable Foundation ⌑
c/o Edgar G. Buedecker, Ziercher & Hocker
130 South Bemiston, 4th Fl.
St. Louis 63105 (314) 863-6900

Established in 1966 in MO.
Donor(s): John Allan Love Trusts.
Foundation type: Independent
Financial data (yr. ended 12/31/88): Assets, $2,481,571 (M); expenditures, $131,307, including $111,300 for 29 grants (high: $20,000; low: $100).
Purpose and activities: Grants for medical research concerning the handicapped, cultural programs, education, community funds, and the promotion of good citizenship.
Limitations: Giving primarily in MO.
Officers: Rumsey Ewing, Pres.; W. Anderson Payne, V.P.; James G. Forsyth, Treas.
Directors: John McKinney, John J. Owen, Jackson C. Parriott.
Employer Identification Number: 436066121

3577
Lowenstein Brothers Foundation ⌑
400 East Red Bridge Rd., Suite 206
Kansas City 64131 (816) 842-0223

Trust established in 1956 in MO.
Foundation type: Independent
Financial data (yr. ended 10/31/88): Assets, $3,608,024 (M); gifts received, $36,956; expenditures, $177,738, including $157,000 for 42 grants (high: $50,000; low: $100).
Purpose and activities: Support for education, health, youth, and social services, with emphasis on Jewish agencies.
Limitations: Giving primarily in MO.
Application information:
Initial approach: Letter
Deadline(s): None
Write: William B. Lowenstein, Trustee
Trustees: Marjorie Sue Kaplan, Sharon Lowenstein, William B. Lowenstein.
Employer Identification Number: 436055404

3578
The Mag Foundation
c/o Boatmen's First National Bank of Kansas City
14 West Tenth St., P.O. Box 419038
Kansas City 64183 (816) 691-7481

Established in 1954 in MO.
Foundation type: Independent
Financial data (yr. ended 12/31/89): Assets, $1,426,387 (M); expenditures, $61,693, including $60,000 for 2 grants (high: $50,000; low: $10,000; average: $10,000-$50,000).
Purpose and activities: Support primarily for a local public university, hunger programs, and women.
Types of support: Building funds, seed money, special projects.
Limitations: Giving primarily in the metropolitan Kansas City, MO, area.
Application information: Application form not required.
Initial approach: Letter
Deadline(s): None
Final notification: 2 months after receipt of letter
Write: David P. Ross, Sr. V.P., Boatmen's First National Bank of Kansas City
Trustees: Donald N. Chisholm, Myron Ellison, Mrs. Oliver Wolcott, Boatmen's First National Bank of Kansas City.
Number of staff: 1
Employer Identification Number: 446012324

3579
Edward Mallinckrodt, Jr. Foundation ⌑
611 Olive, Suite 1400
St. Louis 63101
Application address: One North Jefferson, St. Louis, MO 63103

Incorporated in 1953 in MO.
Donor(s): Edward Mallinckrodt, Jr.†
Foundation type: Independent
Financial data (yr. ended 9/30/88): Assets, $14,229,285 (M); expenditures, $891,791, including $732,433 for 13 grants (high: $130,000; low: $10,000).
Purpose and activities: Grants largely for biomedical education and research, including

grants to individual researchers under the Scholar Program.
Types of support: Research, grants to individuals.
Publications: Annual report, 990-PF.
Application information:
Deadline(s): None
Write: Oliver M. Langenberg, Pres.
Officers and Directors: Oliver M. Langenberg, Pres. and Treas.; Tom Cori, V.P.; Charles C. Allen, Jr., Secy.; Eugene H. Bricker, Juan Traveras.
Number of staff: None.
Employer Identification Number: 436030295

3580
Massman Foundation ⌑
P.O. Box 8458
Kansas City 64114 (816) 523-1000

Established in 1962 in MO.
Donor(s): Land Equipment Co., and others.
Foundation type: Independent
Financial data (yr. ended 12/31/88): Assets, $1,407,988 (M); gifts received, $10,000; expenditures, $60,316, including $55,400 for 16 grants (high: $12,500; low: $100).
Purpose and activities: Giving primarily for education; grants also for hospitals, social services, and the performing arts.
Limitations: Giving primarily in MO.
Application information:
Initial approach: Letter
Deadline(s): None
Write: H.J. Massman IV, Pres.
Officers: H.J. Massman IV,* Pres.; H.W. Martin,* Secy.; J.T. Kopp, Treas.
Directors:* Abraham E. Margolin, P.M. Massman.
Employer Identification Number: 436045266

3581
The Mathews Foundation ⌑
c/o Boatmen's First National Bank
P.O. Box 419038
Kansas City 64183
Application addresses: M. Mathews Jenks, Trustee, P.O. Box 19769, Brentwood, MO 63144; Harry B. Mathews III, Trustee, c/o John D. Schaperkotter, Bryan, Cave, McPheeters, & McRoberts, 500 North Broadway, Suite 2000, St. Louis, MO 63102

Trust established in 1959 in IL.
Donor(s): Harry B. Mathews, Jr. Trust.
Foundation type: Independent
Financial data (yr. ended 11/30/88): Assets, $1,868,803 (M); gifts received, $403,550; expenditures, $76,556, including $44,000 for 3 grants (high: $20,000; low: $10,000).
Purpose and activities: Giving for Protestant church support, including church-related higher and secondary education; support also for cultural programs and historic preservation, hospitals, the handicapped, and social service agencies.
Types of support: Building funds, endowment funds, operating budgets, renovation projects, scholarship funds.
Limitations: Giving primarily in the St. Louis, MO, and Phoenix, AZ, areas.
Publications: 990-PF.
Application information:
Initial approach: Proposal
Deadline(s): None
Trustees: M. Mathews Jenks, George A. Jensen, Harry B. Mathews III, John D. Schaperkotter.
Employer Identification Number: 376040862

3582
The May Stores Foundation, Inc. ⌑
Sixth and Olive Sts.
St. Louis 63101

Incorporated in 1945 in NY.
Donor(s): May Department Stores Co.
Foundation type: Company-sponsored
Financial data (yr. ended 12/31/88): Assets, $21,967,898 (M); gifts received, $7,213,000; expenditures, $9,243,414, including $9,021,907 for grants.
Purpose and activities: Grants to charitable and educational institutions throughout the country, with emphasis on community funds in areas of company operations; support also for cultural programs, hospitals and health care, and civic affairs.
Limitations: Giving primarily in areas of company operations.
Application information: Contributes only to pre-selected organizations. Applications not accepted.
Officers and Directors:* Jerome T. Loeb,* Pres.; Jan R. Kniffen,* V.P. and Secy.-Treas.; David C. Farrell,* V.P.; Thomas A. Hays,* V.P.; Robert F. Cerulli.
Number of staff: None.
Employer Identification Number: 436028949

3583
Flora S. McCourtney Trust ☆
c/o Boatmen's Trust Co.
100 North Broadway, P.O. Box 14737
St. Louis 63102 (314) 466-3409

Established in 1953 in IL.
Donor(s): Plato McCourtney,† Flora McCourtney.†
Foundation type: Independent
Financial data (yr. ended 09/30/88): Assets, $3,351,169 (M); expenditures, $225,530, including $186,650 for 153 grants to individuals (high: $2,000; low: $500).
Purpose and activities: Awards scholarships to graduates of local area high schools.
Types of support: Student aid.
Limitations: Giving limited to Sangamon County, IL.
Application information: Application form available at qualifying high schools. Application form required.
Deadline(s): Mar. 1
Board meeting date(s): Early Apr.
Final notification: May
Write: Christine Secorsky
Trustee: Boatmen's Trust Co. of St. Louis.
Number of staff: None.
Employer Identification Number: 436023586

3584
G. N. and Edna McDavid Dental Education Trust ⌑
c/o Mercantile Bank, N.A.
P.O. Box 387, Main Post Office
St. Louis 63166 (314) 425-2672
Application addresses: Washington University Dental School, 4559 Scott Ave., St. Louis, MO 63110; Tel.: (314) 454-0300; or University of Missouri-Kansas City, 4825 Troost Ave., Kansas City, MO 64110; Tel.: (816) 932-4422

Established in 1975.
Foundation type: Independent
Financial data (yr. ended 12/31/88): Assets, $1,540,806 (M); expenditures, $124,709, including $109,975 for 31 loans to individuals (high: $5,100; low: $2,200; average: $2,500).
Purpose and activities: Loans to students at two accredited dental schools.
Types of support: Student loans.
Limitations: Giving limited to MO, with preference to residents of Madison County.
Application information:
Initial approach: Contact financial aid office of dental school
Deadline(s): None
Write: Ms. Jill Fivecoat, Asst. V.P.
Trustee: Mercantile Bank, N.A.
Employer Identification Number: 436192984

3585
McDonnell Douglas Foundation ▼
c/o McDonnell Douglas Corp.
P.O. Box 516, Mail Code 1001440
St. Louis 63166 (314) 232-8464

Incorporated in 1977 as successor to McDonnell Aerospace Foundation, a trust established in 1963 in MO.
Donor(s): McDonnell Douglas Corp.
Foundation type: Company-sponsored
Financial data (yr. ended 12/31/89): Assets, $69,355,321 (M); expenditures, $8,311,037, including $7,527,265 for 505 grants (high: $1,334,410; low: $25; average: $5,000-$10,000) and $684,925 for 3,731 employee matching gifts.
Purpose and activities: Emphasis on higher and other education and community funds; support also for aerospace and aviation organizations, engineering, the environment, and public, civic, and cultural affairs.
Types of support: General purposes, special projects, employee matching gifts, annual campaigns, building funds, capital campaigns, operating budgets.
Limitations: Giving primarily in AZ, CA, FL, MO, OK, and TX.
Publications: Informational brochure (including application guidelines).
Application information: Application form not required.
Copies of proposal: 1
Deadline(s): None
Board meeting date(s): Bimonthly
Write: Walter E. Diggs, Jr., Pres.
Officers: John F. McDonnell, Chair.; Walter E. Diggs, Jr., Pres.; Gerald A. Johnston,* V.P.; Douglas R. Daniels, Treas.
Directors:* James H. MacDonell, James S. McDonnell III.
Number of staff: None.
Employer Identification Number: 431128093

3586
James S. McDonnell Foundation ▼
1034 South Brentwood Blvd., Suite 1610
St. Louis 63117 (314) 721-1532

Incorporated in 1950 in MO.
Donor(s): James S. McDonnell,† James S. McDonnell III, John F. McDonnell.
Foundation type: Independent
Financial data (yr. ended 12/31/89): Assets, $103,523,741 (M); gifts received, $5,802,692; expenditures, $12,035,472, including $12,035,472 for 69 grants (high: $2,000,000; low: $500; average: $50,000-$200,000).
Purpose and activities: Giving for biomedical research, research and innovation in education, and research on issues related to global understanding; support also for cultural and educational activities in the St. Louis metropolitan area.
Types of support: Special projects, research, conferences and seminars.
Limitations: No grants to individuals, or generally for endowment funds, capital campaigns, building funds, renovations, scholarships, or general purposes.
Publications: Informational brochure (including application guidelines), annual report (including application guidelines).
Application information: Application form not required.
Initial approach: Letter
Copies of proposal: 1
Deadline(s): None
Board meeting date(s): As needed
Final notification: Varies
Write: John T. Bruer, Pres.
Officers and Directors:* John T. Bruer, Pres.; James S. McDonnell III,* V.P. and Secy.; John F. McDonnell,* Treas.; Michael Witunski.
Number of staff: 1 full-time professional; 1 full-time support.
Employer Identification Number: 436030988

3587
Sanford N. McDonnell Foundation, Inc. ¤
1034 South Brentwood, Suite 1916
St. Louis 63117

Established in 1977 in MO.
Foundation type: Independent
Financial data (yr. ended 12/31/88): Assets, $1,634,023 (M); gifts received, $495,300; expenditures, $217,619, including $205,130 for 59 grants (high: $83,500; low: $25).
Purpose and activities: Support for cultural organizations, education, and Christian organizations and churches.
Limitations: No grants to individuals.
Application information: Contributes only to pre-selected organizations. Applications not accepted.
Officers and Directors: Sanford N. McDonnell, Pres.; Priscilla R. McDonnell, V.P.; William R. McDonnell, Secy.-Treas.; Robbin M. MacVittie.
Employer Identification Number: 431104889

3588
The McGee Foundation
4900 Main St., Suite 717
Kansas City 64112-2644 (816) 931-1515

Incorporated in 1951 in MO.
Donor(s): Joseph J. McGee,† Mrs. Joseph J. McGee,† Frank McGee,† Mrs. Frank McGee, Louis B. McGee,† Old American Insurance Co., Thomas McGee and Sons, Joseph J. McGee, Jr.
Foundation type: Independent
Financial data (yr. ended 12/31/89): Assets, $5,905,823 (M); expenditures, $310,750, including $281,163 for 39 grants (high: $50,000; low: $500; average: $7,209).
Purpose and activities: Giving primarily in four areas: "1) to care for the sick, aged, and helpless; 2) to encourage and provide means for the development and advancement of education and educational facilities; 3) to encourage and provide means and facilities for education and training of persons that their lives may be more useful to themselves and others; and 4) to make gifts to other benevolent, charitable, religious, scientific or educational institutions either for specific purposes for their general support."
Types of support: General purposes, operating budgets, continuing support, annual campaigns, building funds, equipment, capital campaigns, scholarship funds, special projects.
Limitations: Giving limited to the greater Kansas City, MO, area. No support for the visual or performing arts, historic preservation, community development or rehabilitation, public information programs, united appeals, or telethons or national organizations with wide support. No grants to individuals, or for endowment funds, matching gifts, research, publications, or conferences; no loans.
Publications: Annual report (including application guidelines).
Application information: Application form not required.
Initial approach: Letter
Copies of proposal: 1
Deadline(s): None
Board meeting date(s): Feb., May, Aug., and Nov.
Final notification: 1 1/2 months
Write: Joseph J. McGee, Jr., Chair.
Officers and Directors:* Joseph J. McGee, Jr.,* Chair. and Member; Thomas F. McGee,* Vice-Chair. and Member; Edward J. Reardon,* Secy. and Member; Thomas R. McGee,* Treas. and Member.
Members: Mrs. Bernard J. Duffy, Jr., Robert A. Long, Thomas R. McGee, Jr.
Number of staff: None.
Employer Identification Number: 446006285

3589
Mercantile Trust Company Charitable Trust ¤
c/o Mercantile Bank, N.A.
P.O. Box 387
St. Louis 63166 (314) 425-2672

Trust established in 1952 in MO.
Donor(s): Mercantile Trust Co.
Foundation type: Company-sponsored
Financial data (yr. ended 02/28/89): Assets, $2,580,434 (M); expenditures, $548,525, including $548,450 for 53 grants (high: $80,000; low: $100; average: $1,000-$7,000).
Purpose and activities: Emphasis on higher education, hospitals, and cultural programs; support also for youth agencies, and community development.
Limitations: Giving primarily in MO.
Application information: Application form not required.
Initial approach: Letter
Copies of proposal: 1
Deadline(s): None
Write: Ms. H. Jill Fivecoat
Trustees: Donald E. Lasater, Mercantile Bank, N.A.
Employer Identification Number: 436020630

3590
Roswell Messing, Jr. Charitable Foundation ¤
No. 30 Westwood Country Club Grounds
St. Louis 63131 (314) 432-8898

Established in 1961 in MO.
Donor(s): Roswell Messing, Jr., Mrs. Roswell Messing, Jr.
Foundation type: Independent
Financial data (yr. ended 12/31/88): Assets, $1,718,523 (M); expenditures, $131,485, including $123,940 for 97 grants (high: $35,000; low: $10) and $1,360 for 3 grants to individuals (high: $1,090; low: $10).
Purpose and activities: Support primarily for hospitals and medical research; grants also for education and Jewish giving.
Types of support: Research, student aid.
Limitations: Giving primarily in St. Louis, MO.
Application information: Application form not required.
Deadline(s): None
Write: Wilma E. Messing, Trustee
Trustees: Harold Goodman, Noel M. Hefty, Terrance Hefty, Roswell Messing III, Wilma E. Messing, Arlene M. Naschke.
Employer Identification Number: 436034863

3591
MFA Foundation ¤
615 Locust
Columbia 65201 (314) 876-5395

Established in 1958.
Donor(s): MFA, Inc., MFA Oil Co.
Foundation type: Company-sponsored
Financial data (yr. ended 6/30/87): Assets, $3,410,297 (M); gifts received, $59,246; expenditures, $250,022, including $58,440 for 16 grants (high: $8,696; low: $500) and $179,261 for 202 grants to individuals (high: $1,800; low: $210).
Purpose and activities: Giving in areas of company operations for scholarships; some support also for higher education and youth organizations.
Types of support: Employee-related scholarships.
Limitations: Giving primarily in MO, and in areas of company operations.
Publications: Informational brochure (including application guidelines), financial statement.
Application information: Application form required.
Deadline(s): Apr. 15

Board meeting date(s): June
Write: Ormal C. Creach, Pres.
Officers: Ormal C. Creach,* Pres.; R.A. Young,* V.P.; Mary F. Gonnerman, Secy.-Treas.
Directors:* Hilton Bracey, Dale Creach, James Cunningham, B.L. Frew, James L. Halsey, Alfred Hoffman, Gene Hoover, David Jobe, Fred Koenig, Phil Perkins.
Employer Identification Number: 436026877

3592
Miller-Mellor Association ¤
708 East 47th St.
Kansas City 64110 (816) 561-4307

Established in 1950 in MO.
Foundation type: Independent
Financial data (yr. ended 06/30/89): Assets, $1,813,914 (M); expenditures, $78,176, including $65,248 for 57 grants (high: $7,000; low: $13).
Purpose and activities: Grants for Catholic church support, higher education, cultural programs, and health services.
Limitations: Giving primarily in Kansas City, MO.
Application information: Application form not required.
Initial approach: Letter or proposal
Deadline(s): None
Write: James L. Miller, Secy.-Treas.
Officers: Jozach Miller IV, Pres.; Helena Miller Norquist, V.P.; James Ludlow Miller, Secy.-Treas.
Employer Identification Number: 446011906

3593
Millstone Foundation
8510 Eager Rd.
St. Louis 63144 (314) 961-8500

Incorporated in 1955 in MO.
Donor(s): I.E. Millstone, Goldie G. Millstone.
Foundation type: Independent
Financial data (yr. ended 5/31/88): Assets, $1,945,403 (M); gifts received, $50,000; expenditures, $274,151, including $265,784 for 84 grants (high: $69,160; low: $60).
Purpose and activities: Grants primarily for higher and other education, Jewish organizations, including Jewish welfare, and Israel.
Types of support: General purposes, operating budgets, continuing support, annual campaigns, emergency funds, deficit financing, research.
Limitations: Giving primarily in St. Louis, MO. No grants to individuals; no loans.
Application information: Application form not required.
Initial approach: Letter
Copies of proposal: 1
Deadline(s): None
Board meeting date(s): Monthly
Final notification: 1 month
Write: I.E. Millstone, Pres.
Officers and Directors:* I.E. Millstone,* Chair. and Pres.; David S. Millstone,* V.P.; Robert Millstone,* V.P.; Goldie G. Millstone,* Secy.; Harry Hammerman,* Treas.
Number of staff: 1 part-time professional.
Employer Identification Number: 436027373

3594
Monsanto Fund ▼
800 North Lindbergh Blvd.
St. Louis 63167 (314) 694-4596

Incorporated in 1964 in MO as successor to Monsanto Charitable Trust.
Donor(s): Monsanto Co.
Foundation type: Company-sponsored
Financial data (yr. ended 12/31/88): Assets, $3,087,287 (M); expenditures, $9,356,571, including $8,285,748 for grants (high: $1,112,000; low: $100; average: $100-$5,000) and $1,019,417 for employee matching gifts.
Purpose and activities: Giving primarily for education, specifically science and math, and community funds; support also for hospitals and health services, cultural programs and the arts, social services, and youth.
Types of support: General purposes, building funds, equipment, operating budgets, annual campaigns, seed money, fellowships, special projects, employee matching gifts, continuing support, employee-related scholarships.
Limitations: Giving primarily in areas of company operations in AL, CA, FL, GA, ID, IL, MA, MI, MO, NJ, NC, OH, SC, TX, and WV, with emphasis on St. Louis, MO. No support for religious institutions. No grants to individuals, or for endowment funds.
Application information:
Initial approach: Proposal
Copies of proposal: 1
Deadline(s): None
Board meeting date(s): 4 to 6 times a year
Final notification: 2 to 4 months
Write: John L. Mason, Pres.
Officers: John L. Mason, Pres.; Richard W. Duesenberg,* V.P.; J. Russell Bley, Secy.; Juanita H. Hinshaw, Treas.
Directors:* Francis A. Stroble, Chair.; Peter Clarke, Norma J. Curby, Robert E. Flynn, Robert J. Mason, Daniel J. Mickelson, Michael E. Miller, Fred L. Thompson.
Number of staff: 2 full-time professional; 2 full-time support.
Employer Identification Number: 436044736

3595
Pearl C. Moorman Charitable Trust ¤ ☆
c/o United Missouri Bank of Kansas City
P.O. Box 419226
Kansas City 64141

Foundation type: Independent
Financial data (yr. ended 9/30/88): Assets, $575,501 (M); expenditures, $117,105, including $105,520 for grants.
Purpose and activities: Support for a hospital.
Limitations: Giving primarily in MO. No grants to individuals.
Application information: Contributes only to pre-selected organizations. Applications not accepted.
Trustee: United Bank of Kansas City.
Employer Identification Number: 436194465

3596
The Morgan Family Fund ¤
260 N.E. Barry Rd.
Kansas City 64155 (816) 436-2996

Incorporated in 1985 in MO.
Donor(s): Frank Morgan.
Foundation type: Independent
Financial data (yr. ended 11/30/88): Assets, $1,457,032 (M); gifts received, $2,500; expenditures, $105,328, including $80,135 for 16 grants (high: $40,000; low: $50).
Purpose and activities: Support primarily for Jewish organizations.
Limitations: Giving primarily in Kansas City, MO, and Overland Park, KS. No grants to individuals.
Application information:
Initial approach: Letter
Deadline(s): Nov. 30 for next fiscal year
Write: Frank Morgan, Trustee
Trustees: Marilyn J. Feingold, Frank Morgan, Mark A. Morgan, Michael B. Morgan, Thomas S. Morgan.
Employer Identification Number: 481024615

3597
Finis M. Moss Charitable Trust ¤ ☆
108 West Walnut
P.O. Box J
Nevada 64772-2339 (417) 667-5076

Established in 1975 in MO.
Donor(s): Finis M. Moss.†
Foundation type: Independent
Financial data (yr. ended 3/31/88): Assets, $5,448,089 (M); gifts received, $3,088,745; expenditures, $216,072, including $95,384 for 27 grants (high: $32,609; low: $200).
Purpose and activities: Support primarily for an ambulance service, civic affairs, and community development, including conservation concerns; giving also for social services and education.
Types of support: Operating budgets, capital campaigns.
Limitations: Giving primarily in Nevada, MO.
Application information: Application form required.
Deadline(s): Between Dec. 31 and Jan. 31
Final notification: Feb.
Write: Donald Russell, Trustee
Trustees: Lee Gilbert, Robert Lasley, Donald B. Russell.
Employer Identification Number: 237451729

3598
Nichols Company Charitable Trust ¤
310 Ward Pkwy.
Kansas City 64112

Trust established in 1952 in MO.
Donor(s): J.C. Nichols Co., and members of the Nichols family.
Foundation type: Company-sponsored
Financial data (yr. ended 12/31/88): Assets, $875,877 (M); gifts received, $164,500; expenditures, $164,789, including $163,897 for 58 grants (high: $50,000; low: $100).
Purpose and activities: Emphasis on the performing arts and higher and secondary education; grants also for a community fund, youth agencies, and hospitals.
Types of support: Annual campaigns, building funds, capital campaigns, continuing support, endowment funds, general purposes, special projects.
Limitations: Giving primarily in MO. No grants to individuals.
Publications: Annual report.

Application information: Contributes only to pre-selected organizations. Applications not accepted.
Trustees: Lee Fowler, Lynn L. McCarthy, Miller Nichols.
Employer Identification Number: 446015538

3599
Miller Nichols Foundation ¤
310 Ward Pkwy.
Kansas City 64112

Established in 1960.
Donor(s): Miller Nichols.
Foundation type: Independent
Financial data (yr. ended 12/31/88): Assets, $2,106,485 (M); gifts received, $175,000; expenditures, $302,544, including $300,842 for 65 grants (high: $100,000; low: $25).
Purpose and activities: Emphasis on civic and cultural organizations and education.
Limitations: Giving primarily in Kansas City, MO.
Application information: Contributes only to pre-selected organizations. Applications not accepted.
Trustees: Kay Nichols Callison, Walter C. Janes, Jeannette Nichols, Miller Nichols.
Employer Identification Number: 446015540

3600
John M. Olin Charitable Trust ¤
c/o Boatmen's Trust Co. of St. Louis
P.O. 14737
St. Louis 63178 (314) 436-9263

Trust established in 1945 in MO.
Donor(s): John M. Olin.†
Foundation type: Independent
Financial data (yr. ended 12/31/87): Assets, $1,621,548 (M); expenditures, $126,364, including $115,000 for 13 grants (high: $20,000; low: $5,000).
Purpose and activities: Grants primarily for medical research, hospitals, museums, cultural programs, and youth agencies.
Limitations: No grants to individuals, or for building funds, endowment funds, or special projects.
Application information:
Initial approach: Letter
Deadline(s): None
Write: Robert Brummet, V.P., Boatmen's Trust Co. of St. Louis
Trustees: Constance B. Josse, Boatmen's Trust Co. of St. Louis.
Employer Identification Number: 436022769

3601
Spencer T. and Ann W. Olin Foundation ▼
Pierre Laclede Bldg.
7701 Forsyth Blvd.
St. Louis 63105 (314) 727-6202

Incorporated in 1957 in DE.
Donor(s): Spencer T. Olin, Ann W. Olin.†
Foundation type: Independent
Financial data (yr. ended 12/31/89): Assets, $38,926,375 (M); gifts received, $765,080; expenditures, $5,704,024, including $5,454,050 for 23 grants (high: $1,500,000; low: $750; average: $1,000-$100,000).
Purpose and activities: Giving primarily for higher education, medical education, research, and health services; support also for community service agencies.
Types of support: Annual campaigns, research, general purposes.
Limitations: Giving primarily in the St. Louis, MO, area. No support for national health or welfare organizations, religious groups, or generally for secondary education, or projects which are substantially financed by public tax funds. No grants to individuals, or for building or endowment funds, deficit financing, operating budgets, conferences, travel, exhibits, scholarships, fellowships, or matching gifts; no loans.
Publications: Annual report (including application guidelines).
Application information: Application form not required.
Initial approach: Letter
Copies of proposal: 1
Deadline(s): None
Board meeting date(s): Usually in Apr.
Final notification: 2 weeks
Write: Warren M. Shapleigh, Pres.
Officers and Trustees:* Warren M. Shapleigh,* Pres.; J. Lester Willemetz, Treas. and Exec. Dir.; Eunice Olin Higgins, William W. Higgins, Rolla J. Mottaz, John C. Pritzlaff, Jr., Mary Olin Pritzlaff, Barbara Olin Taylor, F. Morgan Taylor, Jr.
Number of staff: 2 part-time professional; 1 part-time support.
Employer Identification Number: 376044148

3602
Oppenstein Brothers Foundation
118 West 47th St., Suite 206
Kansas City 64112 (816) 753-6955

Trust established in 1975 in MO.
Donor(s): Michael Oppenstein.†
Foundation type: Independent
Financial data (yr. ended 03/31/90): Assets, $16,951,704 (M); expenditures, $1,001,315, including $914,924 for 93 grants (high: $80,000; low: $1,000).
Purpose and activities: Grants primarily for social services and education, emphasizing the prevention of illness and abuse, and programs which enhance the ability of individuals to remain or become self-sufficient; some support for community development and arts education.
Types of support: Operating budgets, general purposes, seed money, emergency funds, special projects, matching funds, renovation projects, consulting services, lectureships, conferences and seminars.
Limitations: Giving primarily in the Kansas City, MO, metropolitan area. No support for medical research. No grants to individuals, or for annual campaigns, building funds or expansion, scholarships, fellowships, technology, equipment, or generally for endowment funds; limited operating funds for United Way or Jewish Federation supported agencies; no loans.
Publications: Multi-year report (including application guidelines), informational brochure (including application guidelines).
Application information: Application form not required.
Initial approach: Telephone or letter
Copies of proposal: 2
Deadline(s): Submit proposal with complete information 2 weeks preceding board meetings; no set deadline
Board meeting date(s): Usually bimonthly
Final notification: 2 to 4 months
Write: Candace L. Fowler, Prog. Officer
Officer: Candace L. Fowler, Prog. Officer.
Disbursement Committee: John Morgan, Chair.; Mary Bloch, Laura Fields, Roger Hurwitz, Estelle Sosland.
Trustee: Commerce Bank of Kansas City.
Number of staff: 1 part-time professional.
Employer Identification Number: 436203035

3603
Orchard Foundation ¤
1154 Reco Dr.
St. Louis 63126 (314) 822-3880

Established in 1962 in MO.
Donor(s): Orchard Corp. of America.
Foundation type: Company-sponsored
Financial data (yr. ended 12/31/87): Assets, $4,820 (M); gifts received, $213,488; expenditures, $214,118, including $198,480 for 33 grants (high: $100,000; low: $10).
Purpose and activities: Giving primarily for culture and education.
Limitations: No grants to individuals.
Application information: Application form not required.
Write: Robert H. Orchard, Trustee
Trustee: Robert H. Orchard.
Employer Identification Number: 436049376

3604
Orscheln Industries Foundation, Inc.
P.O. Box 280
Moberly 65270 (816) 263-4900
Scholarship application address: William L. Orscheln, Treas., Orscheln Industries Fdn. Scholarship Comm., P.O. Box 266, Moberly, MO 65270; Tel.: (816) 263-4900

Established in 1968 in MO.
Donor(s): Orscheln Industries, and its subsidiaries.
Foundation type: Company-sponsored
Financial data (yr. ended 09/30/88): Assets, $9,235,448 (M); gifts received, $2,006,324; expenditures, $738,205, including $655,919 for grants (high: $253,621; low: $1,000).
Purpose and activities: Emphasis on Roman Catholic church support and religious organizations, community funds, and higher education, including scholarships for those seeking degrees in accounting, engineering, drafting, computer science, business administration, and other business-related areas as approved by the foundation.
Types of support: Employee-related scholarships, annual campaigns, building funds, continuing support.
Limitations: Giving primarily in MO; scholarships restricted to graduates of Cairo, Higbee, Moberly, and Westran high schools, in Randolph County.
Publications: Informational brochure, application guidelines, program policy statement.

Application information: Application form and informational brochure available for scholarship applicants.
Deadline(s): Apr. 1 for scholarships
Officers: G.A. Orscheln, Pres.; Phillip A. Orscheln, V.P.; D.W. Orscheln, Secy.; William L. Orscheln, Treas.
Employer Identification Number: 237115623

3605
The Pendergast-Weyer Foundation ¤
3434 West Coleman Rd.
Kansas City 64111 (816) 561-3002
Application address: c/o Grant Selection Committee, P.O. Box 413245, Kansas City, MO 64141; Tel.: (816) 561-6340

Established about 1976 in MO.
Donor(s): Mary Louise Weyer Pendergast,† Thomas J. Pendergast, Jr.
Foundation type: Independent
Financial data (yr. ended 06/30/89): Assets, $3,855,358 (M); expenditures, $175,178, including $150,000 for 20 grants (high: $30,000; low: $2,000; average: $1,000-$10,000).
Purpose and activities: Support primarily for Roman Catholic church-related day care centers, pre-schools, elementary schools, high schools, and religious organizations. A minimum of 80 percent of all grants must go to Catholic institutions with a maximum of 20 percent available for institutions of other religious denominations.
Types of support: Operating budgets, continuing support, emergency funds, equipment, general purposes, renovation projects, special projects.
Limitations: Giving limited to towns or cities in MO with populations under 100,000. No support for clergymen, chanceries, or church foundations. No grants to individuals, or for annual campaigns, seed money, building funds, land acquisition, endowment funds, matching gifts, research, publications, conferences; no loans.
Publications: Program policy statement, application guidelines.
Application information: Application form required.
Initial approach: Telephone
Copies of proposal: 1
Deadline(s): Submit proposal in Apr. or Sept.; deadlines, Apr. 10 and Sept. 10
Board meeting date(s): Nov. and May
Final notification: Nov. 30 and May 30
Write: Beverly B. Pendergast, Pres.
Officers and Directors:* Thomas J. Pendergast, Jr.,* Chair. and Secy.-Treas.; Beverly B. Pendergast,* Pres.; Taylor L. Bowen, Beverly Brayman, Kennet Burnett.
Number of staff: None.
Employer Identification Number: 431070676

3606
Pet Incorporated Community Support Foundation ¤
400 South Fourth St.
St. Louis 63166 (314) 621-5400

Established in 1959.
Donor(s): Pet, Inc.
Foundation type: Company-sponsored
Financial data (yr. ended 12/31/88): Assets, $296,616 (M); gifts received, $338,000; expenditures, $389,102, including $388,250 for 34 grants (high: $145,000; low: $500).
Purpose and activities: Giving primarily for education, youth, cultural programs, health and welfare, and a community fund.
Types of support: General purposes, operating budgets, equipment, scholarship funds.
Limitations: Giving primarily in MO.
Application information:
Initial approach: Letter and proposal
Deadline(s): None
Write: Thomas R. Pellett, Pres.
Officers: Thomas R. Pellett,* Pres.; Anthony C. Knizel, V.P. and Treas.; Myron W. Sheets, V.P.; James A. Wescott, V.P.; Phyllis P. Vogt, Secy.
Trustees:* A.J. Matson, Ray Morris, Larry D. Umlauf.
Employer Identification Number: 436046149

3607
James T. Pettus, Jr. Foundation
c/o The Guaranty Trust Co. of Missouri
7701 Forsyth, Suite 1200
Clayton 63105 (314) 725-9055
Additional mailing address: P.O. Box 16260, Clayton, MO 63105

Established in 1960 in MO.
Foundation type: Independent
Financial data (yr. ended 12/31/89): Assets, $2,308,000 (M); gifts received, $100,000; expenditures, $113,909, including $100,500 for 41 grants (high: $8,000; low: $500; average: $2,000-$5,000).
Purpose and activities: Grants for social service agencies, education, health associations, youth programs, and community funds.
Types of support: Annual campaigns, continuing support, general purposes.
Limitations: Giving primarily in HI.
Application information: Rarely funds new applicants; all new applications limited to HI.
Initial approach: Letter
Deadline(s): None
Final notification: Within 60 days
Write: James A. Finch III, Trustee
Trustees: James A. Finch III, Betty Pettus, James T. Pettus, Jr., Guaranty Trust Co. of Missouri.
Employer Identification Number: 436029569

3608
The Pillsbury Foundation ▼
Six Oakleigh Ln.
St. Louis 63124

Incorporated in 1944 in MO.
Donor(s): Edwin S. Pillsbury,† Harriette Brown Pillsbury.†
Foundation type: Independent
Financial data (yr. ended 12/31/86): Assets, $16,044,673 (M); gifts received, $84,500; expenditures, $1,059,252, including $820,191 for 67 grants (high: $281,790; low: $100; average: $100-$10,000).
Purpose and activities: Emphasis on higher and other education, Baptist church support and religious associations, and social service agencies.
Limitations: Giving primarily in MO, with emphasis on St. Louis. No grants to individuals; no loans.
Application information: Applications not accepted.
Board meeting date(s): As necessary
Write: Mr. Joyce S. Pillsbury, Pres.
Officers: Joyce S. Pillsbury, Pres.; Linda Pillsbury Roos, V.P.; William E. Pillsbury, Secy.-Treas.
Number of staff: None.
Employer Identification Number: 436030335

3609
Pitzman Fund ¤
c/o Boatmen's Trust Co. of St. Louis
510 Locust St., P.O. Box 14737
St. Louis 63178 (314) 436-9042

Established in 1944.
Donor(s): Frederick Pitzman.†
Foundation type: Independent
Financial data (yr. ended 12/31/88): Assets, $1,980,317 (M); expenditures, $168,796, including $154,700 for 103 grants (high: $10,000; low: $500; average: $500-$1,500).
Purpose and activities: Giving for education, cultural programs, Protestant church support, social services, and youth agencies.
Types of support: Annual campaigns, continuing support, general purposes.
Limitations: Giving primarily in St. Louis, MO.
Application information: Application form not required.
Copies of proposal: 1
Deadline(s): None
Write: Roy T. Blair
Trustees: Pauline S. Eades, Robert H. McRoberts, Boatmen's Trust Co. of St. Louis.
Number of staff: None.
Employer Identification Number: 436023901

3610
Robert W. Plaster Foundation, Inc. ¤
P.O. Box 129
Lebanon 65536-0129

Established in 1983 in MO.
Donor(s): Robert W. Plaster.
Foundation type: Independent
Financial data (yr. ended 11/30/88): Assets, $2,996,352 (M); gifts received, $525,000; expenditures, $39,821, including $30,000 for 3 grants (high: $15,000; low: $5,000).
Purpose and activities: Support primarily for Protestant organizations, including churches and educational institutions.
Types of support: General purposes.
Limitations: Giving primarily in MO. No grants to individuals.
Application information: Contributes only to pre-selected organizations. Applications not accepted.
Officers and Directors: Robert W. Plaster, Pres. and Treas.; Stephen R. Plaster, V.P. and Secy.; Dolly Frances, Lynn C. Hoover, Tammy Plaster, Cheryl J. Schaefer.
Employer Identification Number: 431369856

3611
PMJ Foundation ⌑ ☆
720 Olive St., 24th Fl.
St. Louis 63101

Established in 1986 in MO.
Foundation type: Independent
Financial data (yr. ended 7/31/89): Assets, $395,819 (M); gifts received, $5,637; expenditures, $243,711, including $242,154 for 50 grants (high: $78,116; low: $35).
Purpose and activities: Support primarily for ministries, churches, and other Christian organizations; support also for social services and higher education.
Types of support: General purposes.
Limitations: No grants to individuals.
Application information: Contributes only to pre-selected organizations. Applications not accepted.
Officers: Paul G. Griesemer, Pres.; Douglas L. Kelly, V.P.; Warren R. Maichel, Secy.
Employer Identification Number: 431418697

3612
Herman T. & Phenie R. Pott Foundation
1034 South Brentwood, Suite 1480
St. Louis 63117 (314) 725-8477

Trust established in 1963 in MO.
Foundation type: Independent
Financial data (yr. ended 12/31/89): Assets, $13,622,000 (M); expenditures, $778,800, including $683,000 for 91 grants (high: $47,500; low: $500).
Purpose and activities: Support for a community fund, health agencies, and social service and youth agencies.
Limitations: Giving primarily in MO, particularly the St. Louis area. No grants to individuals.
Application information: Application form not required.
Initial approach: Letter
Copies of proposal: 1
Deadline(s): None
Board meeting date(s): Quarterly
Write: John P. Fechter, Exec. Dir.
Trustee: Mercantile Bank, N.A.
Advisory Committee: James Collins, Roy Collins, Richard Conerly, John P. Fechter, Mary Greco, William Guerri, Jane Murphy, Phenie Pott.
Number of staff: 1 part-time professional.
Employer Identification Number: 436041541

3613
Precious Moments Foundation ⌑
(Formerly Timothy Donald Foundation)
P.O. Box 802
Carthage 64836
Scholarship application address: 99 Monroe Ave. N.W., Grand Rapids, MI 49503; Tel.: (616) 454-8656

Established in 1985 in MO.
Donor(s): Samuel J. Butcher, David E. Hathaway.
Foundation type: Independent
Financial data (yr. ended 7/31/88): Assets, $1,269,306 (M); gifts received, $650,863; expenditures, $300,534, including $187,272 for 26 grants (high: $40,000; low: $10) and $66,436 for grants to individuals.
Purpose and activities: Support for Christian missions, associations and Protestant churches, educational institutions, youth organizations and agencies devoted to child welfare and protection, and scholarships for higher education and welfare assistance to individuals. A major portion of funding allocated to organizations and individuals in the Philippines.
Types of support: Operating budgets, loans, scholarship funds, student aid, building funds, grants to individuals.
Application information: Application form required for scholarships.
Deadline(s): None
Write: David E. Hathaway, Secy.
Officers and Directors:* Samuel J. Butcher,* Pres.; Philip Butcher, V.P.; David E. Hathaway, Secy.; Deborah Pursley,* Treas.; Steve Wiersma.
Employer Identification Number: 431403707

3614
Pulitzer Publishing Company Foundation ⌑
900 North Tucker Blvd.
St. Louis 63101 (314) 622-7000

Incorporated in 1963 in MO.
Donor(s): The Pulitzer Publishing Co.
Foundation type: Company-sponsored
Financial data (yr. ended 12/31/87): Assets, $684,414 (M); gifts received, $544,405; expenditures, $541,236, including $540,315 for 90 grants (high: $100,000; low: $100).
Purpose and activities: Giving primarily for music, cultural programs, a community fund, and higher education, including a scholarship fund to the University of Missouri Journalism School for black students residing in the St. Louis area.
Types of support: Scholarship funds, annual campaigns, building funds, capital campaigns, endowment funds, equipment, general purposes, operating budgets, professorships, research.
Limitations: Giving primarily in MO, with emphasis on the St. Louis area.
Application information: Application form required.
Deadline(s): Mar. 1 for scholarships only
Board meeting date(s): Varies
Officers and Directors: Joseph Pulitzer, Jr., Chair.; Michael E. Pulitzer, Vice-Chair. and Pres.; Ronald H. Ridgway, Secy.-Treas.; David Lipman, Nicholas Penniman, William Woo.
Employer Identification Number: 436052854

3615
Ralston Purina Trust Fund ▼ ⌑
Checkerboard Sq.
St. Louis 63164 (314) 982-3230

Trust established in 1951 in MO.
Donor(s): Ralston Purina Co.
Foundation type: Company-sponsored
Financial data (yr. ended 8/31/88): Assets, $15,320,640 (M); gifts received, $5,015,000; expenditures, $2,182,544, including $2,128,105 for 75 grants (high: $605,688; low: $1,000; average: $2,000-$20,000).
Purpose and activities: Grants principally to community funds; support also for higher education, health, education and human service agencies. Foundation support represents about one-half of the company's charitable giving, which includes funds for an employee matching gift program and employee-related scholarships.
Types of support: General purposes, building funds, capital campaigns, emergency funds, endowment funds.
Limitations: Giving limited to areas of company facilities, especially St. Louis, MO. No support for religious, or politically partisan purposes. No grants to individuals, or for investment funds, advertisements, research which is not action-oriented, underwriting of deficits or post-event funding; no loans.
Publications: Application guidelines.
Application information:
Initial approach: Proposal
Copies of proposal: 1
Deadline(s): None
Board meeting date(s): Quarterly
Final notification: 6-8 weeks
Write: Fred H. Perabo, Dir., Community Affairs
Trustee: Boatmen's National Bank of St. Louis.
Number of staff: 1 part-time professional; 1 part-time support.
Employer Identification Number: 431209652

3616
The J. B. Reynolds Foundation ⌑
3520 Broadway
Kansas City 64111 (816) 753-7000

Incorporated in 1961 in MO.
Donor(s): Walter Edwin Bixby, Sr., Pearl G. Reynolds.†
Foundation type: Independent
Financial data (yr. ended 12/31/87): Assets, $8,726,399 (M); expenditures, $449,529, including $407,300 for 73 grants (high: $30,000; low: $100; average: $1,000-$20,000).
Purpose and activities: Grants for higher education, medical research, social service and youth agencies, and community projects; support also for cultural programs.
Types of support: Annual campaigns, seed money, emergency funds, building funds, equipment, land acquisition, research, publications, conferences and seminars, continuing support.
Limitations: Giving primarily in a 150-mile radius of Kansas City, MO. No grants to individuals.
Application information: Contributes only to pre-selected organizations. Applications not accepted.
Board meeting date(s): Apr. and Dec.
Write: Walter E. Bixby, V.P.
Officers: Joseph Reynolds Bixby,* Pres.; Walter E. Bixby,* V.P. and Treas.; Richard L. Finn, Secy.
Trustees:* Kathryn Bixby, Ann Bixby Oxler.
Employer Identification Number: 446014359

3617
Elmer C. Rhoden Charitable Foundation ⌑ ☆
P.O. Box 322
Grandview 64030

Established in 1986 in MO.
Foundation type: Independent

Financial data (yr. ended 7/31/89): Assets, $4,270,177 (M); expenditures, $247,011, including $223,500 for 8 grants (high: $70,000; low: $5,000).
Purpose and activities: Support primarily for education and social services, including Protestant welfare programs; giving also for a state department of natural resources.
Types of support: Scholarship funds, building funds, equipment.
Limitations: Giving primarily in KS.
Application information: Contributes only to pre-selected organizations. Applications not accepted.
Officers and Directors: Janet E. Rhoden, Pres.; Marilyn A. Rhoden, V.P.; Lois D. Lacy, Secy.-Treas.
Employer Identification Number: 431337876

3618
Joseph H. and Florence A. Roblee Foundation ⌑
c/o Boatmen's Trust Co. of St. Louis
510 Locust St., P.O. Box 14737
St. Louis 63178

Trust established in 1970 in MO.
Donor(s): Louise Roblee McCarthy,† Florence Roblee Trust.
Foundation type: Independent
Financial data (yr. ended 12/31/88): Assets, $8,877,014 (M); expenditures, $447,766, including $366,725 for 90 grants (high: $10,000; low: $1,000; average: $500-$15,000).
Purpose and activities: Emphasis on ecumenical projects, educational projects generally outside the academic area (such as intercultural global understanding, citizen education, and leadership development), health (primarily mental health), and pressing social problems.
Types of support: Seed money, building funds, equipment, endowment funds, scholarship funds, exchange programs, capital campaigns, emergency funds, special projects.
Limitations: Giving primarily in MO, CA, FL, NC, NY, and TX. No grants to individuals, or for research programs; no loans.
Application information: Application form not required.
Initial approach: Proposal
Copies of proposal: 4
Deadline(s): Submit proposal preferably in Mar. or Aug.; deadlines Mar. 15 and Sept. 1
Board meeting date(s): June and Oct.
Final notification: July 1 and Dec. 1
Write: Carol M. Duhme, Pres., or Roy Blair, Trust Officer
Officer and Trustees:* Carol M. Duhme,* Pres.; Marjorie M. Robins, Boatmen's Trust Co. of St. Louis.
Board Members: Warren Duhme, Barbara Foorman, Roblee McCarthy, Jr., Nancy Richardson, Carol R. von Arx, Ann Welker.
Number of staff: 1 part-time professional.
Employer Identification Number: 436109579

3619
Henry and Sadie Rott Foundation ⌑
416 East Lockwood Ave.
St. Louis 63119 (314) 962-8340

Established in 1965 in MO.
Foundation type: Independent
Financial data (yr. ended 9/30/88): Assets, $1,085,341 (M); expenditures, $60,257, including $51,045 for 17 grants (high: $14,812; low: $554).
Purpose and activities: Support for members of the Missouri Conference of the United Church of Christ.
Limitations: Giving primarily in MO.
Application information: Application form required.
Initial approach: Letter
Deadline(s): None
Write: Rev. Reuben P. Koehler
Trustee: Commerce Bank of St. Louis, N.A.
Employer Identification Number: 436128263

3620
Sachs Fund ⌑
400 Chesterfield Ctr., Suite 600
Chesterfield 63017 (314) 537-1000

Trust established in 1957 in MO.
Donor(s): Samuel C. Sachs, Sachs Electric Corp., and others.
Foundation type: Independent
Financial data (yr. ended 04/30/89): Assets, $2,328,534 (M); gifts received, $50,000; expenditures, $1,196,552, including $1,162,382 for 23 grants (high: $1,000,000; low: $100).
Purpose and activities: Emphasis on Jewish welfare funds, community funds, higher education, cultural programs, and hospitals.
Limitations: Giving primarily in MO. No grants to individuals.
Application information: Contributes only to pre-selected organizations. Applications not accepted.
Write: Louis S. Sachs, Trustee
Trustees: Lewis H. Sachs, Louis S. Sachs, Jerome W. Sandweiss.
Employer Identification Number: 436032385

3621
A. J. Schwartze Community Foundation ⌑ ☆
c/o Central Trust Bank
238 Madison
Jefferson City 65101-3254

Established in 1976 in MO.
Donor(s): A.J. Schwartze.
Foundation type: Independent
Financial data (yr. ended 11/30/88): Assets, $1,176,627 (M); gifts received, $100,873; expenditures, $58,779, including $48,364 for 25 grants (high: $5,000; low: $500).
Purpose and activities: Giving for community and civic affairs groups, including volunteer fire departments; support also for Catholic schools.
Types of support: General purposes.
Limitations: Giving primarily in MO.
Distribution Committee: Clyde Angle, Marion Armentrout, Gilbert Hilkemeyer, A.J. Schwartze, Emil Schwartze.
Trustee: Central Trust Bank.
Employer Identification Number: 431092255

3622
Share Foundation ⌑
11901 Grandview Rd.
Grandview 64030

Established in 1965 in MO.
Donor(s): House of Lloyd, Inc., Harry J. Lloyd.
Foundation type: Independent
Financial data (yr. ended 12/31/88): Assets, $13,045,066 (M); expenditures, $732,512, including $715,890 for 146 grants (high: $180,000; low: $50).
Purpose and activities: Giving primarily for religious organizations and church support.
Officers: Harry J. Lloyd, Pres. and Treas.; Patricia A. Lloyd, V.P. and Secy.
Employer Identification Number: 436054985

3623
Shelter Insurance Foundation ⌑
1817 West Broadway
Columbia 65218 (314) 874-4290

Established in 1981 in MO.
Foundation type: Company-sponsored
Financial data (yr. ended 6/30/88): Assets, $1,138,581 (M); gifts received, $229,919; expenditures, $123,667, including $119,022 for 9 grants (high: $99,042; low: $230) and $3,000 for 3 grants to individuals (high: $2,000; low: $250).
Purpose and activities: Support primarily for higher education, including scholarships to individuals, cancer research, and general charitable giving.
Types of support: Research, student aid, scholarship funds.
Limitations: Giving primarily in AR, CO, IL, IN, IA, KS, KY, LA, MS, MO, NE, OK and TN.
Application information:
Initial approach: Proposal
Deadline(s): None
Write: Raymond E. Jones, Secy.
Officers: Gustav J. Lehr, Pres.; Robert W. Maupin, V.P.; Raymond E. Jones, Secy.; J. Donald Duello, Treas.
Employer Identification Number: 431224155

3624
Shoenberg Foundation, Inc.
200 North Broadway, Suite 1475
St. Louis 63102 (314) 421-2247

Incorporated in 1955 in MO.
Donor(s): Sydney M. Shoenberg.†
Foundation type: Independent
Financial data (yr. ended 12/31/88): Assets, $4,757,959 (M); expenditures, $482,954, including $475,100 for 38 grants (high: $100,000; low: $100).
Purpose and activities: Giving for hospitals, community funds, Jewish welfare funds, the arts, medical research, and speech pathology.
Types of support: Annual campaigns, capital campaigns, continuing support.
Limitations: Giving primarily in MO. No grants to individuals.
Application information: Contributes only to pre-selected organizations. Applications not accepted.
Write: William W. Ross, Secy.-Treas.
Officers and Directors:* Sydney M. Shoenberg, Jr.,* Chair.; Robert H. Shoenberg,* Pres.; E.L. Langenberg,* V.P.; William W. Ross,* Secy.-Treas.

Number of staff: None.
Employer Identification Number: 436028764

3625
Shughart, Thomson & Kilroy Charitable Foundation Trust ☆
Shughart, Thomson & Kilroy, P.C.
120 West 12th St., Suite 1700
Kansas City 64105 (816) 421-3355

Established in 1983 in MO.
Donor(s): Shughart, Thomson & Kilroy, P.C., and company members and employees.
Foundation type: Company-sponsored
Financial data (yr. ended 12/31/88): Assets, $131,138 (M); gifts received, $47,953; expenditures, $154,796, including $154,540 for 46 grants (high: $50,000; low: $25; average: $250-$3,000).
Purpose and activities: Giving primarily for higher education; support also for the fine and performing arts, medical research and hospitals, civic affairs, and child welfare.
Types of support: Endowment funds, general purposes.
Limitations: Giving primarily in the greater Kansas City, MO, area.
Application information:
Initial approach: Letter
Deadline(s): None
Board meeting date(s): Monthly
Write: Don Shughart, Trustee
Trustees: Jack L. Campbell, W. Terrence Kilroy, George E. Leonard, William V. North, Joel Pelofsky, William E. Quirk, Donald L. Shughart.
Number of staff: None.
Employer Identification Number: 431273591

3626
Siteman Charitable Foundation ⌑
7755 Carondelet Ave.
St. Louis 63105-3360 (314) 725-4321

Established in 1961 in MO.
Donor(s): Flash Oil Corp.
Foundation type: Company-sponsored
Financial data (yr. ended 3/31/88): Assets, $54,837 (M); gifts received, $50,000; expenditures, $100,888, including $100,800 for 35 grants (high: $85,000; low: $100).
Purpose and activities: Support primarily for Jewish organizations, including welfare funds.
Application information:
Initial approach: Letter or proposal
Trustees: Leonard Adrean, Alvin Siteman.
Employer Identification Number: 436031118

3627
Lindon Q. Skidmore Charitable Foundation
c/o Boatmen's First National Bank of Kansas City
14 West 10th St.
Kansas City 64183 (816) 691-7481

Established in 1977 in MO.
Foundation type: Independent
Financial data (yr. ended 12/31/89): Assets, $1,694,630 (M); expenditures, $92,255, including $89,600 for 7 grants (high: $29,600; low: $10,000; average: $2,000-$20,000).
Purpose and activities: Support for youth organizations, historical societies, and museums.
Limitations: Giving primarily in Henry County, MO.
Publications: 990-PF.
Application information: Application form not required.
Initial approach: Letter
Copies of proposal: 1
Deadline(s): None
Board meeting date(s): 2 months
Write: David P. Ross, Sr. V.P., Boatmen's First National Bank of Kansas City
Trustees: William V. Sisney, Boatmen's First National Bank of Kansas City.
Number of staff: 1
Employer Identification Number: 431119922

3628
Ralph L. Smith Foundation
c/o Boatmen's First National Bank of Kansas City
14 West Tenth St.
Kansas City 64105 (816) 691-2800
Mailing address: P.O. Box 38, Kansas City, MO 64183

Trust established in 1952 in MO.
Donor(s): Harriet T. Smith,† Ralph L. Smith.†
Foundation type: Independent
Financial data (yr. ended 12/31/89): Assets, $7,569,998 (M); expenditures, $309,893, including $296,500 for 74 grants (high: $20,000; low: $500; average: $5,000-$30,000).
Purpose and activities: Grants largely for education, medical research, youth agencies, women's concerns, and conservation.
Limitations: Giving primarily in the Kansas City, MO, metropolitan area. No grants to individuals.
Publications: 990-PF.
Application information: Applications for grants will not be acknowledged.
Initial approach: Telephone followed by 3-page letter
Copies of proposal: 1
Deadline(s): None
Board meeting date(s): Quarterly
Final notification: 2 months
Write: David P. Ross, Sr. V.P., Boatmen's First National Bank of Kansas City
Managers: Harriet Denison, Anne S. Douthat, Ralph L. Smith, Jr.
Trustee: Boatmen's First National Bank of Kansas City.
Employer Identification Number: 446008508

3629
Sidney W. and Sylvia N. Souers Charitable Trust ⌑
c/o Boatmen's Trust Co.
510 Locust St., P.O. Box 14737
St. Louis 63178 (314) 436-9263

Trust established in 1955 in MO.
Donor(s): Sylvia N. Souers.
Foundation type: Independent
Financial data (yr. ended 12/31/88): Assets, $10,659,865 (M); expenditures, $588,221, including $547,000 for 25 grants (high: $100,000; low: $1,000).
Purpose and activities: Emphasis on higher education and hospitals.
Limitations: Giving primarily in MO and Washington, DC.
Application information:
Initial approach: Letter
Deadline(s): None
Grantor: Sylvia N. Souers.
Trustee: Boatmen's Trust Co. of St. Louis.
Employer Identification Number: 436079817

3630
Southern Foundation, Inc. ⌑
114 West 11th St.
Kansas City 64105

Established in MO in 1966.
Foundation type: Independent
Financial data (yr. ended 12/31/88): Assets, $1,306,054 (M); gifts received, $139,063; expenditures, $75,552, including $72,000 for 6 grants (high: $60,000; low: $500).
Purpose and activities: Support for wildlife organizations, education, social services, and health.
Limitations: Giving primarily in MO.
Application information:
Initial approach: Letter
Deadline(s): None
Write: William N. Deramus IV, V.P.
Officers and Directors: Patricia W. Deramus, Pres.; William N. Deramus IV, V.P. and Secy.; Jill D. Dean, V.P.; William N. Deramus III, V.P.; Patricia N. Fogel, V.P.; Jean D. Wagner, Treas.
Employer Identification Number: 436066776

3631
Southwestern Bell Foundation ▼
One Bell Ctr., Rm. 36-P-1
St. Louis 63101 (314) 235-7040

Established in 1984 in MO.
Donor(s): Southwestern Bell Corp.
Foundation type: Company-sponsored
Financial data (yr. ended 12/31/89): Assets, $42,012,377 (M); gifts received, $16,000,000; expenditures, $15,580,000, including $14,830,000 for 2,600 grants (high: $720,000; low: $100) and $750,000 for 5,650 employee matching gifts.
Purpose and activities: Giving largely for education; support also for health, welfare, the arts, and civic affairs.
Types of support: Conferences and seminars, employee matching gifts, lectureships, matching funds, research, seed money, special projects, technical assistance.
Limitations: Giving primarily in KS, MO, DC, TX, AR, and NY. No support for political activities, religious organizations, fraternal, veterans', or labor groups. No grants to individuals, or for operating funds for hospitals, capital funds, operating funds for United Way-supported organizations, special advertising, or ticket/dinner purchases.
Publications: Annual report (including application guidelines), informational brochure (including application guidelines).
Application information: Unsuccessful applicants may not reapply in same calendar year. Application form not required.
Initial approach: Letter
Copies of proposal: 1
Deadline(s): None
Final notification: Four to six weeks

Write: Charles DeRiemer, Exec. Dir.
Officers and Directors:* Gerald Blatherwick,* Pres.; Robert Pope,* V.P. and Treas.; James Ellis,* V.P. and Secy.; Charles DeRiemer,* Exec. Dir.
Number of staff: 3 full-time professional; 2 full-time support.
Employer Identification Number: 431353948

3632
Victor E. Speas Foundation ▼
c/o Boatmen's First National Bank of Kansas City
14 West Tenth St.
Kansas City 64183 (816) 691-7481

Trust established in 1947 in MO.
Donor(s): Effie E. Speas,† Victor E. Speas,† Speas Co.
Foundation type: Independent
Financial data (yr. ended 12/31/89): Assets, $21,843,991 (M); gifts received, $6,163; expenditures, $1,283,261, including $1,262,212 for 38 grants (high: $172,000; low: $1,500; average: $5,000-$50,000).
Purpose and activities: Giving restricted to improving the quality of health care in the Kansas City, MO, area. Support mainly for medically-related higher education, including loans for medical students at the University of Missouri at Kansas City, preventive health care, and medical research; grants also for agencies serving the health care needs of the elderly, youth, and the handicapped.
Types of support: Seed money, emergency funds, equipment, research, special projects, renovation projects, capital campaigns, matching funds, operating budgets, student loans.
Limitations: Giving limited to Jackson, Clay, Platte, and Cass counties in MO. No grants for endowment funds; no loans or scholarships except to medical students at the University of Missouri at Kansas City.
Publications: 990-PF, program policy statement, application guidelines.
Application information: Application form not required.
Initial approach: Telephone
Copies of proposal: 1
Deadline(s): None
Board meeting date(s): Bimonthly
Final notification: 2 months
Write: David P. Ross, Sr. V.P., Boatmen's First National Bank of Kansas City
Trustee: Boatmen's First National Bank of Kansas City.
Number of staff: 1 full-time professional.
Employer Identification Number: 446008340

3633
John W. and Effie E. Speas Memorial Trust ▼
c/o Boatmen's First National Bank of Kansas City
14 West Tenth St.
Kansas City 64183 (816) 691-7481
Application address: Boatmen's First National Bank of Kansas City, P.O. Box 419038, Kansas City, MO 64183

Trust established in 1947 in MO.
Donor(s): Effie E. Speas,† Victor E. Speas,† Speas Co.
Foundation type: Independent
Financial data (yr. ended 12/31/89): Assets, $21,725,953 (M); expenditures, $1,207,883, including $1,189,129 for 28 grants (high: $152,000; low: $5,000; average: $5,000-$100,000).
Purpose and activities: Giving primarily for hospitals and health services, including support for the aged and mentally disabled, higher education in the health professions, and medical research.
Types of support: Special projects, equipment, research, general purposes, operating budgets, seed money.
Limitations: Giving limited to the greater Kansas City metropolitan area.
Publications: 990-PF.
Application information: Application form not required.
Initial approach: Letter of 3 pages or less
Copies of proposal: 1
Deadline(s): None
Board meeting date(s): Biweekly
Final notification: 2 months
Write: David P. Ross, Sr. V.P., Boatmen's First National Bank of Kansas City
Trustee: Boatmen's First National Bank of Kansas City.
Number of staff: 1 full-time professional.
Employer Identification Number: 446008249

3634
St. Louis Community Foundation
818 Olive St., Suite 737
St. Louis 63101 (314) 241-2703

Established in 1915 in MO.
Foundation type: Community
Financial data (yr. ended 12/31/89): Assets, $11,398,779 (M); gifts received, $2,798,452; expenditures, $974,386, including $844,231 for 249 grants (high: $200,000; low: $100; average: $1,000-$7,500) and $2,500 for 2 grants to individuals of $1,250 each.
Purpose and activities: Purposes include, but are not limited to, the promotion of education, social and scientific research, the care of the sick, aged, infirm, and handicapped, the care of children, the improvement of living, working, recreation, and environmental conditions or facilities, cultural programs, and such other charitable, educational, and social purposes that will assist the betterment of the mental, moral, social, and physical conditions of the inhabitants of the St. Louis metropolitan area.
Types of support: Research, seed money, scholarship funds, operating budgets, emergency funds, special projects, renovation projects, equipment, employee-related scholarships.
Limitations: Giving primarily in the St. Louis, MO, metropolitan area and IL. No support for sectarian religious programs, or private elementary or secondary schools. No grants to individuals, or for deficit financing, or endowment or building funds; grants for operating expenses only during an organization's start-up.
Publications: Annual report (including application guidelines), newsletter, informational brochure.
Application information: Application form not required.
Initial approach: Proposal
Copies of proposal: 1
Deadline(s): Jan. 15, Apr. 15, July 15, and Oct. 15
Board meeting date(s): Quarterly
Final notification: Usually within 1 week of board meetings
Write: Mary Brucker, Exec. Dir.
Officers: Henry O. Johnston,* Treas.; Mary Brucker, Exec. Dir.
Directors:* Walter F. Gray, Chair.; Marguerite Ross Barnett, Vincent J. Cannella, F.J. Cornwell, Jr., Mark A. Dow, W. Lynton Edwards III, Eugene J. Gabianelli, James D. Hoagland, Robert Kresko, Stanley L. Lopata, William B. McMillan, Susan B. Musgrave, Kathryn Nelson, Donald H. Streett, Ann Daly Tretter, Franklin F. Wallis.
Trustee Banks: Boatmen's National Bank of St. Louis, Commerce Bank of St. Louis, N.A., Guaranty Trust Co. of Missouri, Mercantile Bank, N.A.
Number of staff: 1 full-time professional; 1 part-time support.
Employer Identification Number: 436023126

3635
Kent D. & Mary L. Steadley Memorial Trust ⌑
c/o Boatmen's Bank of Carthage
231 South Main
Carthage 64836 (417) 358-9011

Established in 1970.
Foundation type: Independent
Financial data (yr. ended 12/31/87): Assets, $5,062,376 (M); gifts received, $211,405; expenditures, $265,207, including $254,800 for 2 grants (high: $250,000; low: $4,800).
Purpose and activities: Giving for community development.
Limitations: Giving limited to Carthage, MO.
Application information: Application form required.
Deadline(s): None
Final notification: Usually within 2 months
Write: Linda M. Hodge
Trustee: Boatmen's Bank of Carthage.
Employer Identification Number: 436120866

3636
Richard J. Stern Foundation for the Arts ☆
c/o Commerce Bank of Kansas City, N.A.
P.O. Box 419248
Kansas City 64141-6248
Application address: 118 West 47th St., Kansas City, MO 64112

Established in 1986 in MO.
Foundation type: Independent
Financial data (yr. ended 06/30/89): Assets, $3,901,239 (M); expenditures, $327,560, including $300,150 for 5 grants (high: $147,650; low: $2,500).
Purpose and activities: Giving for organizations "engaged in supporting the arts," including the performing arts and art education.
Limitations: Giving limited to the greater Kansas City, MO, area. No support for private foundations. No grants to individuals.

Application information:
Initial approach: Letter
Deadline(s): None
Write: Christopher Blair
Trustees: Richard J. Stern, Commerce Bank of Kansas City.
Employer Identification Number: 436313811

3637
Stupp Brothers Bridge & Iron Company Foundation ⌑
P.O. Box 6600
St. Louis 63125 (314) 638-5000

Trust established about 1952 in MO.
Donor(s): Stupp Bros. Bridge & Iron Co.
Foundation type: Company-sponsored
Financial data (yr. ended 10/31/88): Assets, $5,949,747 (M); expenditures, $321,039, including $309,605 for 171 grants (high: $44,000; low: $50).
Purpose and activities: Giving to hospitals, community funds, and higher education and educational associations; support also for cultural, health, and welfare programs.
Limitations: Giving primarily in MO.
Application information: Contributes only to pre-selected organizations. Applications not accepted.
Trustees: Erwin P. Stupp, Jr., John P. Stupp, Robert P. Stupp.
Employer Identification Number: 237412437

3638
Norman J. Stupp Foundation
c/o Commerce Bank of St. Louis, N.A.
8000 Forsyth
St. Louis 63105
Mailing address: P.O. Box 11356, St. Louis, MO 63105

Established in 1952 in MO.
Donor(s): Norman J. Stupp.†
Foundation type: Independent
Financial data (yr. ended 6/30/89): Assets, $10,746,817 (M); expenditures, $534,211, including $457,333 for 44 grants (high: $100,000; low: $1,000).
Purpose and activities: Giving to hospitals and medical research facilities, youth agencies, social services, and education.
Types of support: Capital campaigns, endowment funds, operating budgets, research, scholarship funds, special projects.
Limitations: Giving primarily in St. Louis, MO.
Publications: 990-PF.
Application information: Application form required.
Board meeting date(s): Semiannually
Write: John W. North, V.P. and Trust Officer, Commerce Bank of St. Louis, N.A.
Trustee: Commerce Bank of St. Louis, N.A.
Employer Identification Number: 436027433

3639
Lester T. Sunderland Foundation
9233 Ward Pkwy., Suite 395
Kansas City 64114 (913) 451-8900

Incorporated in 1945 in MO.
Donor(s): Lester T. Sunderland.†
Foundation type: Independent
Financial data (yr. ended 12/31/89): Assets, $14,491,360 (M); expenditures, $634,513, including $613,637 for 102 grants (high: $50,000; low: $50).
Purpose and activities: Emphasis on building funds for higher education; support also for youth agencies, hospitals, and community funds.
Types of support: Operating budgets, continuing support, annual campaigns, seed money, emergency funds, deficit financing, building funds, equipment, land acquisition, endowment funds.
Limitations: Giving primarily in MO, KS, NE, and AR. No grants to individuals; no loans.
Publications: 990-PF.
Application information: Application form not required.
Initial approach: Letter
Copies of proposal: 1
Board meeting date(s): As required
Write: James P. Sunderland, V.P.
Officers and Trustees: Paul Sunderland, Pres.; James P. Sunderland, V.P. and Secy.; Robert Sunderland, V.P. and Treas.; Charles Sunderland, Whitney P. Sunderland.
Number of staff: None.
Employer Identification Number: 446011082

3640
Sunmark Foundation ⌑
1600 South Brentwood Blvd., Suite 1770
St. Louis 63144

Established in 1964.
Donor(s): Sunmark, Inc.
Foundation type: Company-sponsored
Financial data (yr. ended 1/31/88): Assets, $561,796 (M); gifts received, $200,000; expenditures, $297,785, including $296,000 for 36 grants (high: $30,000; low: $1,000).
Purpose and activities: Support for conservative public policy organizations, including labor policy groups; grants also for civic affairs, social services, and economic and higher education; emphasis on education and research.
Application information: Organization's most recent annual report and tax-exempt notice must be sent.
Trustees: Frank H. McCracken, John J. Reed, Menlo F. Smith.
Employer Identification Number: 436061564

3641
Sunnen Foundation ▼
7910 Manchester Ave.
St. Louis 63143 (314) 781-2100

Incorporated in 1953 in MO.
Donor(s): Joseph Sunnen.†
Foundation type: Independent
Financial data (yr. ended 12/31/88): Assets, $14,353,777 (M); expenditures, $922,428, including $811,972 for 36 grants (high: $150,000; low: $100; average: $500-$100,000).
Purpose and activities: Grants for specific goal-oriented activities, education, and litigation, the purpose of which is to protect individual freedom of association; freedom of choice in religious beliefs, particularly contraception and pregnancy termination; freedom from censorship (especially textbooks); freedom from union violence, coercion, and compulsory membership; separation of church and state; separation of church and schools; and economic education. Projects should have an overall impact on the field of concern involved.
Types of support: Seed money, emergency funds, equipment, matching funds, special projects, renovation projects, operating budgets, continuing support.
Limitations: No support for religious bodies, educational institutions, environmental organizations, hospitals, medical charities, or the arts (except for specific projects related to the foundation's area of concern); generally no support for charities with broad-based public appeal. No grants to individuals, or for building or endowment funds, scholarships, fellowships, annual campaigns, land acquisition, research, or conferences; no loans.
Publications: Program policy statement, application guidelines.
Application information: Funds fully committed; no new applications will be considered for at least 2 to 3 years. Application form not required.
Deadline(s): None
Board meeting date(s): Generally in June and Dec.; grants committee meets continuously
Write: Samuel G. Landfather, Chair., Grants Comm.
Officers: Robert M. Sunnen,* Pres.; James K. Berthold,* V.P.; C. Diane Kates, Secy.; Samuel G. Landfather,* Treas. and Exec. Dir.
Directors:* Esther S. Kreider, Helen S. Sly.
Number of staff: 1 part-time professional; 1 part-time support.
Employer Identification Number: 436029156

3642
Sverdrup and Parcel, Inc. Charitable Trust ⌑
c/o Boatmen's Trust Co. of St. Louis
510 Locust St., P.O. Box 14737
St. Louis 63178 (314) 436-7600
Application address: 801 North Eleventh, St. Louis, MO 63101

Established in 1951 in MO.
Donor(s): Sverdrup & Parcel, Inc., Aro, Inc.
Foundation type: Independent
Financial data (yr. ended 12/31/87): Assets, $1,008,967 (M); gifts received, $250,000; expenditures, $181,305, including $174,050 for 70 grants (high: $37,000; low: $50).
Purpose and activities: Support primarily for community funds, education, and culture; grants also for youth and social services.
Application information:
Initial approach: Proposal
Deadline(s): None
Write: Thomas E. Wehrle
Members: E.S. Davis, W.F. Knapp, B.R. Smith, Jr.
Trustee: Boatmen's Trust Co. of St. Louis.
Employer Identification Number: 436023499

3643
John S. Swift Company Charitable Trust, Inc. ⌑
c/o Mercantile Bank, N.A.
P.O. Box 387
St. Louis 63166

Application address: 1248 Research Dr., St. Louis, MO 63132; Tel.: (314) 991-4300

Trust established in 1952 in MO.
Donor(s): John S. Swift Co., Inc.
Foundation type: Company-sponsored
Financial data (yr. ended 12/31/87): Assets, $1,338,200 (M); expenditures, $81,806, including $73,555 for 53 grants (high: $37,500; low: $25).
Purpose and activities: Grants for higher and secondary education, cultural programs, including museums, and hospitals.
Limitations: Giving primarily in MO and IL.
Application information:
Initial approach: Letter
Deadline(s): None
Write: Ben Heckel, Trustee
Trustees: Ben Heckel, Hampden M. Swift, Mercantile Bank, N.A.
Employer Identification Number: 436020812

3644
Edward F. Swinney Trust ⌘
406 Board of Trade Bldg.
Tenth and Wyandotte Sts.
Kansas City 64105 (816) 842-0944

Trust established in 1946 in MO; member of the Kansas City Association of Trusts and Foundations.
Donor(s): Edward F. Swinney.†
Foundation type: Independent
Financial data (yr. ended 12/31/87): Assets, $10,758,738 (M); expenditures, $755,291, including $521,250 for 25 grants (high: $75,000; low: $3,289).
Purpose and activities: To further and develop local charitable and educational purposes; grants for mental health, higher education, hospitals, rehabilitation, and other health and welfare and community action programs; support for consolidation and monitoring of present arts and humanities projects. Giving for demonstration and experimental projects, extension and improvement of human services, with preference in the voluntary sector, planning and cooperation among voluntary agencies and between public and private agencies, and for education and training in community service.
Types of support: Operating budgets, seed money, emergency funds, consulting services, technical assistance, special projects, research, publications, conferences and seminars.
Limitations: Giving limited to Kansas City, MO. No grants to individuals, or for building or endowment funds, annual campaigns, scholarships, fellowships, or matching gifts; generally no grants for base support or deficit financing; no loans.
Publications: Annual report, application guidelines, program policy statement.
Application information: Application form not required.
Initial approach: Letter or proposal
Copies of proposal: 1
Deadline(s): Nov. 3, Feb. 3, June 1, and Aug. 31
Board meeting date(s): Jan., Apr., Aug., and Nov.
Final notification: Within 2 weeks after board meetings
Write: Dalene Bradford, V.P. Program; or Terry Henrichs, Program Secy.
Officers: Dalene D. Bradford, V.P., Program; Terry Henrichs, Program Secy.
Trustee: Boatmen's First National Bank of Kansas City.
Number of staff: 3 full-time professional; 2 full-time support; 1 part-time support.
Employer Identification Number: 446009264

3645
Sycamore Tree Trust ▼
c/o A.G. Edwards Trust Co.
One North Jefferson St., 6th Fl.
St. Louis 63103 (314) 289-4200

Trust established about 1953 in MO.
Foundation type: Independent
Financial data (yr. ended 12/31/88): Assets, $408,751 (M); gifts received, $203,448; expenditures, $761,219, including $754,911 for 116 grants (high: $40,500; low: $25; average: $350-$10,000).
Purpose and activities: Giving for Roman Catholic church support and religious associations; support also for the arts and cultural programs, higher education, and a community fund; some support also for international affairs organizations.
Limitations: Giving primarily in MO. No grants to individuals, or for scholarships or fellowships; no loans.
Application information: Contributes only to pre-selected organizations. Applications not accepted.
Board meeting date(s): Monthly
Write: Joseph C. Morris, Assoc. V.P., A.G. Edwards Trust Co.
Trustee: A.G. Edwards Trust Co.
Number of staff: None.
Employer Identification Number: 436026719

3646
The Ten-Ten Foundation ⌘ ☆
1200 Main, Suite 3500
Kansas City 64105 (816) 474-6180

Established in 1964.
Foundation type: Independent
Financial data (yr. ended 12/31/88): Assets, $1,101,862 (M); gifts received, $63,562; expenditures, $54,736, including $52,387 for 70 grants (high: $10,500; low: $50).
Purpose and activities: Giving primarily for higher education; support also for Jewish organizations and health.
Limitations: Giving limited to Kansas City, MO. No grants to individuals.
Application information: Application form not required.
Initial approach: Letter
Deadline(s): None
Write: Edward A. Smith, Pres.
Officers and Directors: Edward A. Smith, Pres. and Treas.; Beth K. Smith, V.P. and Secy.; Thomas Gill.
Employer Identification Number: 436055675

3647
Tension Envelope Foundation ⌘
819 East 19th St., 5th Fl.
Kansas City 64108 (816) 471-3800

Incorporated in 1954 in MO.
Donor(s): Tension Envelope Corp.
Foundation type: Company-sponsored
Financial data (yr. ended 11/30/88): Assets, $2,887,824 (M); gifts received, $100,000; expenditures, $301,581, including $268,834 for 153 grants (high: $30,094; low: $225).
Purpose and activities: Emphasis on Jewish welfare funds; support also for community funds, higher education, health, civic affairs, culture and the arts, and youth.
Limitations: Giving primarily in areas of company operations. No grants to individuals.
Application information: Application form not required.
Initial approach: Letter
Deadline(s): None
Write: Eliot S. Berkley, Secy.
Officers: Richard L. Berkley,* Pres.; Walter L. Hiersteiner, V.P.; Eliot S. Berkley,* Secy.; E. Bertram Berkley,* Treas.
Directors:* William Berkley, Abraham E. Margolin.
Employer Identification Number: 446012554

3648
Rosalie Tilles Nonsectarian Charity Fund ⌘
c/o Mercantile Bank, N.A.
P.O. Box 387
St. Louis 63166 (314) 425-2672

Trust established in 1926 in MO.
Donor(s): Cap Andrew Tilles.
Foundation type: Independent
Financial data (yr. ended 6/30/89): Assets, $2,263,192 (M); expenditures, $89,948, including $1,000 for 2 grants (high: $600; low: $400) and $62,386 for 48 grants to individuals (high: $4,150; low: $111).
Purpose and activities: To aid deserving girls and boys who are in need of physical or educational help; scholarships provided for students to attend any of the 5 participating higher education institutions: St. Louis University; University of Missouri's Columbia, Rolla, and St. Louis campuses; and Washington University; bus fare for needy high school students also provided.
Types of support: Student aid, grants to individuals.
Limitations: Giving limited to St. Louis City and St. Louis County, MO.
Publications: Application guidelines.
Application information: Application guidelines issued for University Scholarship Program; applications for transportation aid accepted only through authorized social service case workers. Application form not required.
Deadline(s): Mar. 1
Board meeting date(s): University scholarships approved by the trustees at June meeting
Final notification: July
Write: H. Jill Fivecoat, V.P., Mercantile Bank, N.A.
Trustees: Richard W. Braun, Archbishop John L. May, Rabbi Mark L. Shook, Paul P. Weil, Mercantile Bank, N.A.
Employer Identification Number: 436020833

3649
Bess Spiva Timmons Foundation
c/o Duane Lawellin
First National Bank
Joplin 64801 (417) 624-1234
Application address: 5212 East Red Rock Dr., Phoenix, AZ 85018

Established in 1967 in MO.
Donor(s): Bess Spiva Timmons.†
Foundation type: Independent
Financial data (yr. ended 12/31/89): Assets, $2,933,366 (M); expenditures, $132,209, including $118,354 for 20 grants (high: $14,750; low: $1,000).
Purpose and activities: Giving primarily for wildlife, hospitals and health services, higher education, youth activities, and child welfare organizations.
Types of support: Equipment, scholarship funds, special projects.
Publications: Annual report, 990-PF.
Application information: Application form not required.
Initial approach: Proposal
Deadline(s): Apr. 15
Board meeting date(s): 1st weekend in June
Final notification: June 30
Write: George S. Timmons, Pres.
Officers and Directors:* George S. Timmons,* Pres.; Robert Timmons,* V.P. and Secy.; Judith Spears,* Treas.; Duane D. Lawellin,* Financial Adv.; Harry A. Morris,* Legal Counsel; JoAnn Kimball, Joe L. Spears, Monita K. Timmons, Patricia P. Timmons.
Number of staff: None.
Employer Identification Number: 436075014

3650
Courtney S. Turner Charitable Trust
c/o Boatmen's First National Bank of Kansas City
P.O. Box 419038
Kansas City 64183 (816) 691-7481

Established in 1986 in MO.
Donor(s): Courtney S. Turner.
Foundation type: Independent
Financial data (yr. ended 12/31/89): Assets, $15,869,065 (M); expenditures, $1,099,941, including $1,079,776 for 37 grants (high: $252,000; low: $5,000; average: $5,000-$100,000).
Purpose and activities: Support for youth organizations, higher education, and cultural programs.
Types of support: Matching funds, seed money, special projects, capital campaigns.
Limitations: Giving primarily in Atchison, KS.
Publications: 990-PF.
Application information: Application form not required.
Deadline(s): None
Write: David P. Ross, Trust Officer, Boatmen's First National Bank of Kansas City
Trustees: Daniel C. Weary, Boatmen's First National Bank of Kansas City.
Number of staff: 1
Employer Identification Number: 436316904

3651
Union Electric Company Charitable Trust
1901 Chouteau St.
P.O. Box 149
St. Louis 63166 (314) 621-3222

Trust established in 1944 in MO.
Donor(s): Union Electric Co.
Foundation type: Company-sponsored
Financial data (yr. ended 12/31/89): Assets, $4,150,833 (M); gifts received, $2,100,000; expenditures, $1,551,536, including $1,470,380 for 50 grants (high: $405,000; low: $3,000; average: $5,000-$25,000) and $61,741 for 640 employee matching gifts.
Purpose and activities: Giving largely for community funds and education, especially higher education; support also for social service agencies, youth and the aged, cultural programs, including music and dance, community development, and public policy; employee-related scholarships administered by the National Merit Scholarship Corporation.
Types of support: Annual campaigns, building funds, emergency funds, employee matching gifts, equipment, general purposes, land acquisition, operating budgets, employee-related scholarships, scholarship funds, fellowships, capital campaigns, matching funds, renovation projects, special projects, continuing support, research.
Limitations: Giving limited to company locations in IA, IL, and MO. No grants to individuals, or for endowment funds or research-related programs; no loans.
Publications: Application guidelines.
Application information: Application form not required.
Initial approach: Letter
Copies of proposal: 1
Deadline(s): None
Board meeting date(s): 2 or 3 times a year
Final notification: 60 to 90 days
Write: Ms. Patricia Barrett, Mgr., Community Services
Trustees: William E. Cornelius, Boatmen's Trust Co. of St. Louis.
Number of staff: 1 full-time professional; 2 part-time professional; 1 part-time support.
Employer Identification Number: 436022693

3652
Walter and Jean Voelkerding Charitable Trust ⌑
P.O. Box 81
Dutzow 63342

Trust established in 1968 in MO.
Donor(s): Walter J. Voelkerding.†
Foundation type: Independent
Financial data (yr. ended 2/28/87): Assets, $3,456,896 (M); expenditures, $104,448, including $55,000 for 3 grants (high: $30,000; low: $1,000).
Purpose and activities: Support for churches and religious welfare organizations.
Limitations: Giving limited to Warren County, MO.
Application information: Application form not required.
Initial approach: Letter
Deadline(s): None
Trustees: William Marquart, Steven J. Maune, David J. Voelkerding, William J. Zollmann III.
Employer Identification Number: 237015780

3653
The George Herbert Walker Foundation
c/o Stifel, Nicoluas & Co., Inc.
500 North Broadway, Suite 1700
St. Louis 63102 (314) 342-2112

Trust established in 1954 in NY.
Donor(s): G.H. Walker, Jr., George H. Walker III.
Foundation type: Independent
Financial data (yr. ended 12/31/89): Assets, $1,461,131 (M); gifts received, $3,942; expenditures, $118,706, including $110,700 for 24 grants (high: $20,000; low: $250).
Purpose and activities: Grants primarily for higher and secondary education and Protestant church support.
Limitations: Giving primarily in MO and CT. No grants to individuals.
Application information: Contributes only to pre-selected organizations. Applications not accepted.
Write: George H. Walker, III, Trustee
Trustees: John J. Goebel, George H. Walker III, Mary Carter Walker.
Number of staff: 1 part-time support.
Employer Identification Number: 136084806

3654
Louis L. and Adelaide C. Ward Foundation
1000 Walnut St.
Kansas City 64106

Established in 1966 in MO.
Donor(s): Louis L. Ward, Adelaide C. Ward.
Foundation type: Independent
Financial data (yr. ended 12/31/88): Assets, $4,491,364 (M); expenditures, $149,225, including $143,901 for 30 grants (high: $100,500; low: $25; average: $5,000).
Purpose and activities: Support primarily for health and culture; some support for education.
Types of support: Annual campaigns, building funds, capital campaigns, general purposes, scholarship funds, endowment funds.
Limitations: Giving primarily in KS, MO, MT, and OH.
Application information:
Initial approach: Letter
Deadline(s): Dec. 31
Write: Louis L. Ward, Pres.
Officers: Louis L. Ward, Pres.; Adelaide C. Ward, V.P. and Treas.; Scott Howard, Secy.
Employer Identification Number: 436064548

3655
Webb Foundation
232 Kingshighway, Suite 205
St. Louis 63108 (314) 367-0232

Established in 1969 in MO.
Donor(s): Francis M. Webb,† Pearl M. Webb.†
Foundation type: Independent
Financial data (yr. ended 12/31/89): Assets, $6,268,701 (M); expenditures, $411,800, including $407,000 for 68 grants (high:

$20,000; low: $1,000; average: $3,000-$15,000).
Purpose and activities: Support primarily for the welfare and education of children, particularly the indigent and handicapped; support also for social service agencies, especially those contributing to the improvement of society or for the care and support of disadvantaged people, higher and secondary education, and health and hospitals.
Types of support: Operating budgets, continuing support, annual campaigns, seed money, building funds, equipment, scholarship funds, fellowships, research.
Limitations: Giving limited to the Midwest. No grants to individuals, or for emergency funds, deficit financing, land acquisition, endowment funds, matching gifts, special projects, publications, or conferences; no loans.
Publications: Informational brochure (including application guidelines).
Application information: Application form not required.
Initial approach: Letter, proposal, or telephone
Copies of proposal: 2
Deadline(s): Submit proposal preferably in Apr. or Sept.; deadlines end of May and Oct.
Board meeting date(s): June and Nov.
Final notification: After board meetings
Write: Richard E. Fister, Secy.
Officer, Advisory Committee and Trustees:* Richard E. Fister,* Secy.; Virginia M. Fister, Bernice Hock, Donald D. McDonald, Evelyn M. McDonald.
Number of staff: None.
Employer Identification Number: 237028768

3656
Western Philanthropies, Inc. ⌑
c/o Commerce Tower, 911 Main St., Suite 1402
P.O. Box 13503
Kansas City 64199

Established in 1956 in MO.
Donor(s): Charles A. Duboc.
Foundation type: Independent
Financial data (yr. ended 12/31/87): Assets, $1,196,156 (M); gifts received, $246,733; expenditures, $64,010, including $60,000 for 6 grants (high: $31,750; low: $1,000).
Purpose and activities: Support primarily for higher education and cultural organizations.
Limitations: Giving primarily in KS and MO.
Application information: Applications not accepted.
Officers and Directors: Charles A. Duboc, Pres.; Charles M. Duboc, V.P.; Barbara D. Duboc, Secy.-Treas.; Robert M. Duboc.
Number of staff: None.
Employer Identification Number: 446011936

3657
James L. & Nellie M. Westlake Scholarship Fund ▼ ⌑
c/o Mercantile Bank, N.A.
P.O. Box 387
St. Louis 63166
Application address: 111 South Bemiston Ave., Suite 412, Clayton, MO 63105-1954; Tel.: (314) 725-6410

Established in 1981 in MO.
Donor(s): James L. Westlake.†
Foundation type: Independent
Financial data (yr. ended 6/30/88): Assets, $12,622,381 (M); expenditures, $968,060, including $758,650 for 1,140 grants to individuals (high: $1,000; low: $250; average: $300-$900).
Purpose and activities: Giving for higher education scholarships.
Types of support: Student aid.
Limitations: Giving limited to high school graduates who are residents of MO.
Publications: Informational brochure (including application guidelines).
Application information: Application form required.
Deadline(s): Mar. 1
Final notification: May
Selection Committee: Ronald L. Jackson, Chair.; Newell S. Knight, Jr., Vice-Chair.; Emily F. Ullman, Secy.; Gary D. Clark, Amy B. Murphy, Lincoln Scott.
Trustee: Mercantile Bank, N.A.
Number of staff: 1 full-time professional; 1 part-time professional; 1 full-time support; 6 part-time support.
Employer Identification Number: 436248269

3658
Lyndon C. Whitaker Charitable Foundation ⌑ ☆
120 South Central St., Suite 1722
Clayton 63105-1717 (314) 726-8534

Established in 1975.
Foundation type: Independent
Financial data (yr. ended 04/30/89): Assets, $18,398,380 (M); expenditures, $981,040, including $767,625 for 73 grants (high: $155,000; low: $200).
Purpose and activities: Giving primarily for the fine and performing arts, especially an opera company and a symphony; support also for medical education and research, the arts, higher education, and a historical society.
Types of support: Endowment funds, general purposes, research.
Limitations: Giving primarily in St. Louis, MO. No grants to individuals.
Application information:
Initial approach: Proposal
Deadline(s): None
Write: Urban C. Bergbauer, Jr., Trustee
Trustee: Urban C. Bergbauer, Jr.
Employer Identification Number: 510173109

3659
Mr. and Mrs. Lyndon C. Whitaker Charitable Foundation ⌑
c/o Urban C. Bergbauer, Jr.
120 South Central St.
St. Louis 63105

Trust established in 1975 in MO.
Donor(s): Mae M. Whitaker.†
Foundation type: Independent
Financial data (yr. ended 4/30/88): Assets, $15,983,930 (M); expenditures, $1,230,711, including $993,377 for 65 grants (high: $73,600; low: $60; average: $2,000-$25,000).
Purpose and activities: Emphasis on handicapped children, medical research, cultural programs, including music, historic preservation, and hospitals; grants also for youth and social service agencies and education.
Limitations: Giving primarily in St. Louis, MO.
Application information:
Initial approach: Letter or proposal
Deadline(s): None
Trustee: Urban C. Bergbauer, Jr.
Advisory Board: Cyril J. Costello, James D. Cullen, George T. Guernsey, James C. Thompson, Jr., Anita D. Vincel.
Employer Identification Number: 510173108

3660
The John M. Wolff Foundation
c/o Commerce Bank of St. Louis, N.A.
8000 Forsyth, P.O. Box 11356
Clayton 63105 (314) 726-3600

Trust established in 1956 in MO.
Donor(s): John M. Wolff.†
Foundation type: Independent
Financial data (yr. ended 12/31/88): Assets, $2,136,610 (M); expenditures, $130,136, including $108,500 for 21 grants (high: $10,000; low: $1,000).
Purpose and activities: Emphasis on hospitals, higher and other education, the performing arts, and social service agencies.
Types of support: Capital campaigns, general purposes, operating budgets, research.
Limitations: Giving primarily in St. Louis, MO.
Publications: 990-PF.
Application information: Application form not required.
Initial approach: Letter
Deadline(s): Oct. 1
Board meeting date(s): Sept.
Write: John W. North, V.P. and Trust Officer
Trustees: John M. Wolff III, Commerce Bank of St. Louis, N.A.
Employer Identification Number: 436026247

3661
James H. Woods Foundation ⌑
c/o Boatmen's Trust Co. of St. Louis
510 Locust St., P.O. Box 14737
St. Louis 63178
Application address: 1228 South Mason Rd., St. Louis, MO 63131; Tel.: (314) 436-9048

Trust established in 1958 in MO.
Donor(s): James H. Woods.†
Foundation type: Independent
Financial data (yr. ended 11/30/88): Assets, $8,050,140 (M); expenditures, $475,107, including $389,500 for 39 grants (high: $75,000; low: $500).
Purpose and activities: Giving for secondary and higher education, conservation, youth agencies, and church support.
Types of support: Building funds, endowment funds, general purposes, operating budgets, scholarship funds, seed money.
Limitations: Giving primarily in the midwestern states.
Application information: Application form not required.
Deadline(s): None
Write: James H. Woods, Jr., Trustee

Trustees: Elizabeth W. Bradbury, David L. Woods, James H. Woods, Jr., John R. Woods, Boatmen's Trust Co. of St. Louis.
Number of staff: None.
Employer Identification Number: 436024866

3662
Kearney Wornall Charitable Trust & Foundation ⌑
P.O. Box 419226
Kansas City 64141

Established in 1954 in MO.
Donor(s): Kearney Wornall.†
Foundation type: Independent
Financial data (yr. ended 09/30/89): Assets, $3,906,721 (M); gifts received, $2,752,653; expenditures, $104,209, including $85,350 for 29 grants (high: $10,000; low: $350).
Purpose and activities: Support primarily for cultural programs, hospitals, historical societies, and religious welfare.
Types of support: General purposes.
Limitations: Giving primarily in the Kansas City, MO, area. No grants to individuals.
Application information: Contributes only to pre-selected organizations. Applications not accepted.
Trustee: United Missouri Bank of Kansas City, N.A.
Employer Identification Number: 446013874

3663
Henry E. Wurst Family Foundation
1331 Saline St.
North Kansas City 64116 (816) 842-3113

Established in 1967 in MO.
Donor(s): Members of the Wurst family.
Foundation type: Independent
Financial data (yr. ended 12/31/88): Assets, $1,184,808 (M); gifts received, $74,697; expenditures, $79,646, including $70,660 for 95 grants (high: $4,826; low: $25).
Purpose and activities: Giving primarily to welfare agencies and youth organizations; support also for higher education.
Limitations: Giving primarily in the Kansas City, MO, area.
Application information: Application form not required.
Initial approach: Proposal
Copies of proposal: 1
Deadline(s): None
Write: Margaret S. Wurst, Secy.
Officers: John C. Wurst, Chair.; Margaret S. Wurst, Secy.
Employer Identification Number: 486107464

3664
Judson Young Memorial Educational Foundation, Inc. ⌑
101 West Fourth St.
Salem 65560 (314) 729-3137

Established in 1963 in MO.
Foundation type: Independent
Financial data (yr. ended 12/31/88): Assets, $1,387,479 (M); expenditures, $69,227, including $47,000 for 30 loans to individuals.
Purpose and activities: Student loans primarily to graduates of Salem High School, MO.
Types of support: Student loans.
Limitations: Giving primarily in Salem, MO.
Application information: Application form required.
Copies of proposal: 2
Deadline(s): Aug. 15 for fall term; Dec. 15 for winter term; May 15 for summer term
Write: Max J. Coffman, Pres.
Officers: Max J. Coffman, Pres.; Sanborn N. Ball II, V.P.; J.F. Homeyer, V.P.; Susan C. Ball, Mgr.
Employer Identification Number: 436061841

MONTANA

3665
Charles M. Bair Memorial Trust ⌑
c/o First Trust Co. of Montana
P.O. Box 30678
Billings 59115 (406) 657-8122

Established in 1978.
Donor(s): Marguerite B. Lamb.†
Foundation type: Independent
Financial data (yr. ended 1/31/89): Assets, $18,847,092 (M); expenditures, $963,242, including $825,000 for 5 grants (high: $300,000; low: $10,000) and $103,559 for 26 grants to individuals (high: $9,159; low: $1,369).
Purpose and activities: Giving primarily for hospitals and Protestant churches; scholarships limited to graduates or seniors of Harlowton and White Sulphur Springs high schools, and to graduates or seniors of high schools in Meagher and Wheatland counties in MT.
Types of support: Student aid, general purposes.
Limitations: Giving primarily in MT.
Application information: Application form required.
Deadline(s): Set yearly, but normally falls in Apr.
Trustees: Alberta M. Bair, First Trust Co. of Montana.
Employer Identification Number: 810370774

3666
The Cinnabar Foundation ⌑ ☆
c/o Sargent Ranch
Corwin Springs 59021
Application address: 1200 University, Helena, MT 59601

Donor(s): Leonard Sargent.
Foundation type: Independent
Financial data (yr. ended 12/31/88): Assets, $1,288,519 (M); gifts received, $10,700; expenditures, $86,119, including $74,900 for 15 grants (high: $9,000; low: $1,000) and $3,000 for 2 grants to individuals of $1,500 each.
Purpose and activities: Support primarily for environmental protection and wildlife conservation.
Limitations: Giving limited to MT.
Application information:
Initial approach: Letter
Deadline(s): None
Write: James Poscwitz, Secy.
Officers: Leonard Sargent, Pres.; Phil Tawney, V.P.; James Poscwitz, Secy.; Ernest Turner, Treas.
Employer Identification Number: 810415045

3667
Dufresne Foundation
P.O. Box 1484
Great Falls 59403 (406) 452-9414

Established about 1958 in MT.
Donor(s): Fred Dufresne,† Bertha Dufresne.†
Foundation type: Independent
Financial data (yr. ended 12/31/89): Assets, $1,302,648 (M); expenditures, $67,119, including $53,825 for grants (high: $2,500; average: $1,000).
Purpose and activities: Giving primarily for education, especially higher education, and social service and youth agencies; some support for cultural programs.
Types of support: Scholarship funds, special projects, operating budgets.
Limitations: Giving primarily in MT, and the Great Falls Track area.
Publications: Program policy statement.
Application information: Application form not required.
Copies of proposal: 1
Deadline(s): None
Board meeting date(s): As required
Write: Clair A. Willits, Jr., Pres.
Officers and Directors: Clair A. Willits, Jr., Pres.; Dan C. Ewen, V.P.; William M. Scott, Secy.; Clarence D. Misfeldt, Treas.; Milo F. Dean, S.F. Meyer.
Number of staff: None.
Employer Identification Number: 810301465

3668
Haynes Foundation
501 South Tracy St.
Bozeman 59715 (406) 442-5520

Incorporated in 1958 in MT.
Donor(s): J.E. Haynes.†
Foundation type: Independent
Financial data (yr. ended 03/31/89): Assets, $2,247,109 (M); gifts received, $36,000; expenditures, $231,113, including $201,000 for 7 grants (high: $135,000; low: $11,000).
Purpose and activities: Giving to universities for scholarships.
Types of support: Scholarship funds.
Limitations: Giving primarily in MT.
Application information: Application should be made through universities. Applications not accepted.
Write: Margaret Woo Showen, Trustee
Officers and Trustees:* I.M. Haynes,* Pres.; John R. Kline,* V.P.; Margaret Woo Showen.
Employer Identification Number: 816013577

3669
The Heisey Foundation ⌑
c/o First Bank
P.O. Box 5000
Great Falls 59401 (406) 761-7200

Established about 1940 in MT.
Donor(s): Charles E. Heisey.†
Foundation type: Independent
Financial data (yr. ended 12/31/88): Assets, $2,671,087 (M); expenditures, $146,650, including $114,000 for 7 grants (high: $28,500; low: $4,600) and $15,650 for 313 grants to individuals.
Purpose and activities: Support for a high school awards program for students attending specific schools located in the foundation's trade area who have the greatest possibility of improvement in effort, scholarship, and citizenship and who make the improvement within their ability; and for scholarship funds at local colleges and universities.
Types of support: Scholarship funds, student aid.
Limitations: Giving limited to the Great Falls, MT, trade area.
Publications: Application guidelines, program policy statement.
Application information: Trustees designate eligible schools; students are recommended by their schools.
Deadline(s): Oct. 5 for high schools to provide necessary information for awards to foundation
Board meeting date(s): Annually
Trustees: Daniel C. Ewen, Myra Norman, John D. Stephenson.
Employer Identification Number: 816009624

3670
Gladys E. Knowles Charitable Memorial Trust ⌑
c/o First Trust Co. of Montana
P.O. Box 30678
Billings 59115

Established in 1983 in MT.
Foundation type: Independent
Financial data (yr. ended 12/31/87): Assets, $1,571,836 (M); expenditures, $119,247, including $106,285 for 6 grants (high: $26,571; low: $8,503).
Purpose and activities: Support primarily for a hospital, an Episcopal church, and a nursing home.
Application information: Contributes only to pre-selected organizations. Applications not accepted.
Trustees: First Trust Co. of Montana.
Employer Identification Number: 810423029

3671
Lee Endowment Foundation ⌑
c/o First Trust Co. of Montana
P.O. Box 30678
Billings 59115
Application address for Elizabeth Muse Norris Charitable Fund and Lorraine and Ray Rorick Fund: c/o John Van Streonck, Chair., Charitable Fund Screening Committee, Globe-Gazette, Mason City, IA 50401; Tel.: (515) 423-4270
Application address for Will F. Muse Scholarship Fund: c/o Dr. David L. Buettner, Chair., Nominating Committee, North Iowa Area Community College, 500 College Dr., Mason City, IA 50401; Tel.: (515) 421-4399

Established in 1978 in IA.
Donor(s): Elizabeth Norris.†
Foundation type: Independent
Financial data (yr. ended 12/31/88): Assets, $13,815,962 (M); expenditures, $613,608, including $483,301 for 37 grants (high: $51,700; low: $1,000) and $115,870 for grants to individuals (average: $1,300).
Purpose and activities: Support for community development, higher education, health and social services, and for scholarships.
Types of support: Student aid.
Limitations: Giving primarily in Mason City and Cerro Gordo County, IA, for scholarships; in north central IA for other grants.
Application information: Application form required for scholarships.
Deadline(s): Mar. 1 for scholarships; no deadline for charitable fund applications
Officers: Strand Hilleboe, Pres. and Secy.-Treas.; Donald G. Harrer, V.P.; Henry B. Hook, V.P.; Tom L. Williams, V.P.
Employer Identification Number: 421074052

3672
Montana Community Foundation ☆
Power Block Bldg., Suite 4-I
Seven West Sixth Ave.
Helena 59601 (406) 443-8313

Incorporated in 1988 in MT.
Foundation type: Community
Financial data (yr. ended 12/31/89): Assets, $3,500,000 (M); gifts received, $3,000,000; expenditures, $285,000, including $180,000 for 75 grants (high: $36,000; low: $100; average: $100-$36,000) and $2,400 for 2 grants to individuals of $1,200 each.
Purpose and activities: Support for human and social services, including programs for the aged, the handicapped, minorities, women, family services, and youth and child welfare; community organizations, including community funds and rural programs; hospitals and health services; higher and other education; wildlife and environmental preservation; and the fine and performing arts and other cultural programs.
Types of support: Annual campaigns, consulting services, continuing support, emergency funds, equipment, endowment funds, matching funds, operating budgets, renovation projects, research, scholarship funds, seed money, conferences and seminars, general purposes, special projects.
Limitations: Giving limited to MT. No grants for building funds, deficit financing, land acquisition, or publications.
Publications: Annual report, 990-PF, occasional report, informational brochure (including application guidelines), program policy statement, application guidelines.
Application information: Application form required.
Initial approach: Letter
Copies of proposal: 15
Deadline(s): June 1
Board meeting date(s): Quarterly
Final notification: Oct. 15
Write: Raymond E. Dore, Exec. Dir.
Officer: Raymond E. Dore, Exec. Dir.
Number of staff: 2 full-time professional; 1 full-time support.
Employer Identification Number: 810450150

3673
MPCo/Entech Foundation, Inc.
c/o The M-P-Co.
40 East Broadway
Butte 59701 (406) 723-5421

Established in 1985 in MT.
Donor(s): MT Power Co., Entech, Inc.
Foundation type: Company-sponsored
Financial data (yr. ended 12/31/88): Assets, $96,602 (M); gifts received, $258,506; expenditures, $325,408, including $310,159 for 34 grants (high: $76,034; low: $50) and $12,633 for employee matching gifts.
Purpose and activities: Grants primarily for human service and youth organizations, health associations, and hospitals; grants also for higher and other education, including economic education. Support for an employee matching gift program for colleges and universities.
Types of support: Building funds, scholarship funds, employee matching gifts, capital campaigns, continuing support, equipment, general purposes.
Limitations: Giving primarily in areas of company operations. No support for United Way umbrella organizations (except for capital funds), or for preschool, primary, or secondary education, or fraternal, veterans', or similar organizations. No grants to individuals, or for operating funds (except for organizations such as the United Way).
Publications: Annual report (including application guidelines).
Application information: Application form required.
Copies of proposal: 1
Deadline(s): None
Board meeting date(s): Quarterly
Write: John Carl, V.P.
Directors: D.T. Berube, John J. Burke, Alan Cain, R.P. Gannon, Shag Miller, Warren Paul Schmechel, Frank V. Woy.
Number of staff: 1 part-time support.
Employer Identification Number: 810432484

3674
Sample Foundation, Inc. ⌑
14 North 24th St.
P.O. Box 279
Billings 59103 (406) 256-5667

Incorporated in 1956 in FL.
Donor(s): Helen S. Sample.
Foundation type: Independent
Financial data (yr. ended 10/31/88): Assets, $2,589,015 (M); gifts received, $132,817; expenditures, $144,441, including $130,830 for 23 grants (high: $50,000; low: $500).
Purpose and activities: Grants for higher education, museums, social services, youth agencies, hospitals, and community funds.
Limitations: Giving primarily in MT and Collier County, FL. No support for religious organizations or any group with political affiliations. No grants to individuals.

Publications: Application guidelines.
Application information:
Initial approach: Letter
Board meeting date(s): Oct. 1
Write: Miriam T. Sample, V.P.
Officers: Joseph S. Sample, Pres.; Michael S. Sample, V.P.; Miriam T. Sample, V.P.; T.A. Cox, Secy.-Treas.
Number of staff: None.
Employer Identification Number: 596138602

3675
Rudy Suden Scholarship Trust Fund ⌑ ☆
425 First Ave., North
P.O. Box 5010
Great Falls 59403
Application addresses: c/o Michael M. Smith, Superintendent, Denton School District No. 84, P.O. Box 1048, Denton, MT 59430; Tel.: (406) 567-2270; or c/o Larry Biere, Superintendent, Stanford School District No. 12, P.O. Box 506, Stanford MT 59479; Tel.: (406) 566-2265

Established in 1988 in MT.
Donor(s): Rudolph E. Suden.†
Foundation type: Independent
Financial data (yr. ended 03/31/89): Assets, $1,204,028 (M); gifts received, $1,174,655; expenditures, $7,841.
Purpose and activities: Initial year of operation, fiscal 1989; no grants awarded. Intends to award scholarships for higher education to local area high school students.
Types of support: Student aid.
Limitations: Giving limited to MT.
Application information: Application form required.
Deadline(s): Apr. 1
Scholarship Selection Committee: Larry Biere, Bruce Myllmaki, Lloyd Schmitt, Mike Zacher, and 10 additional members.
Trustee Bank: First Interstate Bank of Great Falls.
Employer Identification Number: 816063733

NEBRASKA

3676
The Abel Foundation ⌑ ☆
P.O. Box 80268
Lincoln 68501 (402) 476-1212

Trust established in 1951.
Donor(s): Abel Construction Co.
Foundation type: Company-sponsored
Financial data (yr. ended 12/31/88): Assets, $731,558 (M); gifts received, $110,500; expenditures, $194,887, including $192,410 for grants.
Purpose and activities: Emphasis on higher education, community development programs, community funds, and Protestant religious organizations.
Types of support: Building funds.
Limitations: Giving limited to NE, particularly Lincoln.
Application information:
Write: C.W. Hansen, Secy.-Treas.
Officers: George P. Abel, Pres.; Gene Tallman, V.P.; C.W. Hansen, Secy.-Treas.
Directors: Alice Abel, Elizabeth Abel, Ann Bradbeer.
Employer Identification Number: 476041771

3677
Ameritas Charitable Foundation ⌑
(Formerly BLN Charitable Foundation)
5900 "O" St.
Lincoln 68510 (402) 467-1122

Established in 1985 in NE.
Donor(s): Ameritas Life Insurance Corp.
Foundation type: Company-sponsored
Financial data (yr. ended 12/31/88): Assets, $1,340,250 (M); gifts received, $295,925; expenditures, $96,593, including $92,475 for 34 grants (high: $20,000; low: $100; average: $1,000-$10,000).
Purpose and activities: Giving for charitable purposes.
Types of support: Annual campaigns, capital campaigns, continuing support, general purposes, professorships, research, special projects.
Limitations: Giving primarily in NE. No grants to individuals or organizations that require a major portion of budget for administration and solicitation.
Application information: Applications not accepted.
Board meeting date(s): Varies
Write: Neal E. Tyner, Secy.-Treas.
Officers and Directors: Harry P. Seward, Pres.; Neal E. Tyner, Secy.-Treas.; Lawrence J. Arth.
Number of staff: None.
Employer Identification Number: 363428705

3678
Alan and Marcia Baer Foundation ⌑
5015 Underwood Ave.
Omaha 68132 (402) 556-0464

Established in 1950 in NE.
Donor(s): E. John Brandeis.†
Foundation type: Independent
Financial data (yr. ended 06/30/88): Assets, $2,826,626 (M); expenditures, $206,026, including $177,414 for 146 grants (high: $29,500; low: $10).
Purpose and activities: Giving for health associations and services, youth, culture, and religious giving; substantial support for the Baer Indigent Fund which disburses grants to various charitable organizations.
Limitations: Giving primarily in Omaha, NE.
Application information:
Initial approach: Letter
Deadline(s): At least 30 days before grant is required
Write: Alan Baer, Pres.
Officers: Alan Baer, Pres.; Marcia Baer, V.P. and Secy.; George Krauss, V.P. and Treas.
Employer Identification Number: 476032560

3679
The Theodore G. Baldwin Foundation
P.O. Box 922
Kearney 68848-0922 (308) 234-9889

Established in 1982 in NE.
Donor(s): Ellen W. Craig.
Foundation type: Independent
Financial data (yr. ended 12/31/89): Assets, $1,252,979 (M); expenditures, $87,456, including $85,900 for 7 grants (high: $20,000; low: $4,200).
Purpose and activities: Giving for an opera and a symphony; support also for local arts organization.
Types of support: General purposes, matching funds.
Limitations: Giving primarily in NE. No grants to individuals.
Publications: 990-PF, application guidelines.
Application information: Application form required.
Initial approach: Letter
Copies of proposal: 1
Deadline(s): Sept. 30
Board meeting date(s): 4th quarter of each calendar year
Final notification: Dec. 31
Write: Michael W. Baldwin, Treas.
Officers: Ellen W. Craig,* Pres.; Juli Baldwin Brown,* V.P.; Robert R. Craig, Secy.; Michael W. Baldwin,* Treas.
Directors:* Charles P. Curtiss, James A. McKenzie.
Number of staff: None.
Employer Identification Number: 470641432

3680
The Clifton B. and Anne Stuart Batchelder Foundation ⌑ ☆
500 Energy Plaza
409 South 17th St.
Omaha 68102

Established in 1987 in NE.
Donor(s): Clifton B. Batchelder, Anne Stuart Batchelder.
Foundation type: Independent
Financial data (yr. ended 12/31/88): Assets, $2,359 (M); gifts received, $132,500; expenditures, $131,619, including $127,000 for 14 grants (high: $40,000; low: $500).
Purpose and activities: Giving primarily for higher education, youth clubs, and a Presbyterian church; support also for hospitals.
Limitations: Giving primarily in NE. No grants to individuals.
Application information: Contributes only to pre-selected organizations. Applications not accepted.
Trustees: Anne Stuart Batchelder, Clifton B. Batchelder, John K. Boyer, FirsTier Bank Omaha.
Employer Identification Number: 363584984

3681
Blumkin Foundation, Inc. ⌑
7001 Farnam St.
Omaha 68132

Incorporated in 1956 in Omaha, NE.
Donor(s): Louie Blumkin, Rose Blumkin, Nebraska Furniture Mart, Inc.
Foundation type: Independent

Financial data (yr. ended 11/30/88): Assets, $1,172,643 (M); gifts received, $100,000; expenditures, $296,005, including $278,733 for 39 grants (high: $75,000; low: $50).
Purpose and activities: Giving primarily for Jewish religious groups and welfare funds, higher education, and cultural programs.
Limitations: Giving primarily in NE.
Application information: Application form not required.
Deadline(s): None
Write: Norman B. Batt, Pres.
Officers: Rose Blumkin, Chair.; Norman B. Batt, Pres.; Louie Blumkin, V.P.; Frances V. Blumkin, Secy.; Frances Batt, Treas.
Employer Identification Number: 476030726

3682
Thomas D. Buckley Trust
P.O. Box 647
Chappell 69129 (308) 874-2212

Established about 1980 in NE.
Donor(s): Thomas D. Buckley.†
Foundation type: Independent
Financial data (yr. ended 05/31/89): Assets, $7,815,520 (M); expenditures, $325,590, including $266,736 for 58 grants (high: $35,000; low: $250; average: $500-$10,000).
Purpose and activities: Emphasis on community development programs, Christian churches, civic affairs, hospitals and health services, computer sciences, and elementary and other education.
Types of support: General purposes.
Limitations: Giving primarily in NE, particularly Chappell, and CO. No grants to individuals.
Application information: Application form required.
Initial approach: Letter requesting application form
Copies of proposal: 1
Deadline(s): None
Board meeting date(s): 2nd Wednesday of each month
Write: Dwight E. Smith
Trustees: Bill M. Hughes, D.F. Kripal, Walter W. Peterson.
Number of staff: 1 part-time professional; 1 part-time support.
Employer Identification Number: 476121041

3683
The Buffett Foundation ▼
222 Kiewit Plaza
Omaha 68131 (402) 345-9168

Incorporated in 1964 in NE.
Donor(s): Warren E. Buffett, Berkshire Hathaway, Inc.
Foundation type: Independent
Financial data (yr. ended 6/30/89): Assets, $13,192,715 (M); gifts received, $2,561,545; expenditures, $1,636,677, including $1,368,278 for 56 grants (high: $200,000; low: $500; average: $1,000-$10,000) and $150,000 for 15 grants to individuals of $10,000 each.
Purpose and activities: Grants primarily for family planning programs.
Types of support: General purposes, grants to individuals.
Application information: Applications not accepted.
Write: Allen Greenberg
Officers: Susan T. Buffett, Pres.; Warren E. Buffett, V.P. and Treas.; Gladys Kaiser, Secy.
Directors: Susan Greenberg, Carol Loomis, Thomas S. Murphy.
Number of staff: 1 full-time professional.
Employer Identification Number: 476032365

3684
ConAgra Charitable Foundation, Inc. ⌑
c/o ConAgra, Inc.
One Central Park Plaza
Omaha 68102 (402) 978-4160

Donor(s): ConAgra, Inc.
Foundation type: Company-sponsored
Financial data (yr. ended 5/25/88): Assets, $1,206,967 (M); gifts received, $500,000; expenditures, $822,761, including $821,722 for 196 grants (high: $73,025; low: $50).
Purpose and activities: Emphasis on higher education, youth agencies, community funds, and cultural programs.
Limitations: Giving primarily in Omaha, NE. No grants to individuals.
Application information: Grants are generally pre-selected.
Initial approach: Proposal
Deadline(s): None
Write: M.G. Colladay, V.P.
Officers: Charles M. Harper,* Pres.; M.G. Colladay,* V.P. and Secy.; J.P. O'Donnell, Treas.
Directors:* Robert B. Daugherty.
Employer Identification Number: 362899320

3685
Cooper Foundation
304 Cooper Plaza
211 North 12th St.
Lincoln 68508 (402) 434-2810

Incorporated in 1934 in NE.
Donor(s): Joseph H. Cooper.†
Foundation type: Independent
Financial data (yr. ended 12/31/89): Assets, $10,736,217 (M); expenditures, $774,793, including $461,690 for 93 grants (high: $30,000; low: $100; average: $500-$5,000).
Purpose and activities: Grants largely for programs benefiting children and young people, primarily in education, the arts, and social services.
Types of support: Annual campaigns, seed money, emergency funds, research, scholarship funds, matching funds, consulting services.
Limitations: Giving primarily in NE, with emphasis on Lincoln and Lancaster County. No grants to individuals, or for endowment funds; no loans.
Publications: Biennial report (including application guidelines), informational brochure (including application guidelines).
Application information: Application form required.
Initial approach: Proposal
Copies of proposal: 1
Deadline(s): Last day of month, for consideration at following monthly meeting
Board meeting date(s): Monthly
Final notification: 1 month
Write: Art Thompson, Pres.
Officers and Trustees:* W.W. Nuernberger,* Chair.; E. Arthur Thompson,* Pres.; Jack Campbell,* V.P.; Peg Huff,* Secy.; Kathryn Druliner,* Treas.; Richard Knudsen,* Counsel; Robert Dobson, E.J. Faulkner, John Olsson, Bill Smith, Jack Thompson, Norton E. Warner.
Number of staff: 3 full-time professional.
Employer Identification Number: 470401230

3686
Dr. C. C. and Mabel L. Criss Memorial Foundation ▼ ⌑
c/o FirsTier Bank Omaha
17th and Farnam St.
Omaha 68102

Trust established in 1978 in NE.
Donor(s): C.C. Criss, M.D.,† Mabel L. Criss.†
Foundation type: Independent
Financial data (yr. ended 2/28/87): Assets, $30,016,676 (M); expenditures, $2,321,941, including $1,981,126 for 23 grants (high: $1,170,000; low: $1,000; average: $10,000-$100,000).
Purpose and activities: Educational and scientific purposes; primarily to meet the needs of Creighton University's medical center; support also for education, including higher education, cultural agencies, youth and social service agencies, and a hospital.
Limitations: Giving primarily in NE.
Application information: Contributes only to pre-selected organizations. Applications not accepted.
Write: Joseph J. Vinardi, Trustee
Trustees: M. Thomas Crummer, Richard L. Daly, Gale E. Davis, Joseph J. Vinardi, FirsTier Bank Omaha.
Employer Identification Number: 470601105

3687
The Faith Charitable Trust ⌑
10315 Rockbrook Rd.
Omaha 68124

Established in 1974 in NE.
Donor(s): Marshall E. Faith.
Foundation type: Independent
Financial data (yr. ended 12/31/87): Assets, $1,670,984 (M); gifts received, $1,657,162; expenditures, $181,605, including $180,797 for grants (high: $81,588).
Purpose and activities: Support for Christian organizations and churches and higher education.
Limitations: Giving primarily in Omaha, NE.
Application information: Contributes only to pre-selected organizations. Applications not accepted.
Officer: Marshall E. Faith, Mgr.
Trustees: Mona Faith, Lynda Schwemmer, Louise Van Court.
Employer Identification Number: 476085423

3688
Frank M. and Alice M. Farr Trust ⌑
1101 12th St.
Aurora 68818 (402) 694-3136

Established in 1985 in NE.
Foundation type: Independent
Financial data (yr. ended 12/31/87): Assets, $3,497,360 (M); expenditures, $315,680,

including $200,792 for 7 grants (high: $100,000; low: $2,500).
Purpose and activities: Support for cultural programs and civic affairs.
Limitations: Giving limited to Hamilton County, NE.
Application information: Application form required.
Deadline(s): Feb. 1
Write: James E. Koepke, Trustee
Trustees: James E. Koepke, First National Bank and Trust Co.
Employer Identification Number: 476144457

3689
FirsTier Bank, N.A., Omaha Charitable Foundation ¤
(Formerly Omaha National Bank Charitable Trust)
c/o FirsTier Bank Omaha
17th and Farnam St.
Omaha 68102

Trust established in 1962 in NE.
Donor(s): FirsTier Bank Omaha.
Foundation type: Company-sponsored
Financial data (yr. ended 12/31/87): Assets, $1,478,258 (M); gifts received, $47,420; expenditures, $571,891, including $566,146 for 91 grants (high: $100,500; low: $50).
Purpose and activities: Emphasis on a community fund, higher education, cultural programs, and youth agencies.
Limitations: Giving primarily in Omaha, NE.
Application information: Contributes only to pre-selected organizations. Applications not accepted.
Trustee: FirsTier Bank Omaha.
Employer Identification Number: 476020716

3690
Carl Frohm Memorial Foundation ¤
c/o FirsTier Bank Omaha
17th and Farnam St.
Omaha 68102

Established about 1980 in NE.
Donor(s): Carl Frohm Insurance Trust.
Foundation type: Independent
Financial data (yr. ended 12/31/88): Assets, $1,512,333 (M); expenditures, $121,660, including $103,570 for 12 grants (high: $26,070; low: $1,500).
Purpose and activities: Giving primarily for Jewish welfare funds and temple support.
Limitations: Giving limited to Omaha, NE.
Application information: Contributes only to pre-selected organizations. Applications not accepted.
Write: Donald W. Engdahl
Trustee: Lawrence M. Mann, FirsTier Bank Omaha.
Employer Identification Number: 470607603

3691
FVB Foundation, Inc. ¤ ☆
c/o Wolfgram Accounting
10907 Cottonlane Ln.
Omaha 68164
Application address: 7011 Farnam St., Omaha, NE 68132

Incorporated in 1988 in NE.
Donor(s): Frances V. Blumkin.
Foundation type: Independent
Financial data (yr. ended 11/30/88): Assets, $91,841 (M); gifts received, $200,000; expenditures, $114,859, including $114,851 for 99 grants (high: $25,000; low: $15).
Purpose and activities: Giving primarily for Jewish organizations, including welfare funds.
Types of support: Building funds.
Application information:
Deadline(s): None
Write: Frances Blumkin, Pres.
Officers: Frances V. Blumkin, Pres.; Louie Blumkin, V.P. and Secy.; Norman Veitzer, Treas.
Employer Identification Number: 470712873

3692
Gallagher Foundation ¤
P.O. Box 3128
Omaha 68103-0128

Established in 1948 in NE.
Foundation type: Independent
Financial data (yr. ended 12/31/87): Assets, $1,187,449 (M); expenditures, $46,336, including $33,000 for 23 grants (high: $7,500; low: $500).
Purpose and activities: Giving primarily to educational institutions, health and social service agencies.
Application information: Applications not accepted.
Trustee: First National Bank of Omaha.
Employer Identification Number: 476021511

3693
Gifford Foundation ¤
c/o First National Bank of Omaha, Trust Dept.
P.O. Box 3128
Omaha 68102 (402) 341-0500

Established in 1964 in NE.
Foundation type: Independent
Financial data (yr. ended 12/31/88): Assets, $1,053,235 (M); expenditures, $67,008, including $56,242 for grants.
Purpose and activities: Support for cultural programs, higher education, and conservation.
Limitations: No grants to individuals.
Application information: Application form not required.
Deadline(s): None
Write: Harold Gifford, Pres.
Officers and Directors: Harold Gifford, Pres.; Mary Elizabeth Gifford, V.P. and Treas.; Alfred G. Ellick, Secy.; Charles A. Gifford, Harold M. Gifford, Glenn H. Le Dioyt, Jessica Shestack.
Employer Identification Number: 476025084

3694
Paul and Oscar Giger Foundation, Inc. ¤
c/o Fraser, Stryker Law Firm
500 Electric Bldg.
Omaha 68102 (402) 341-6000

Established in 1985 in NE.
Donor(s): Ruth Giger.†
Foundation type: Independent
Financial data (yr. ended 12/31/88): Assets, $1,693,841 (M); expenditures, $86,822, including $43,504 for 9 grants (high: $17,000; low: $500).
Purpose and activities: Support primarily for music, natural resources, Protestant organizations, and the aged.
Limitations: Giving limited to the Omaha, NE, area. No grants to individuals.
Application information: Application form required.
Copies of proposal: 4
Deadline(s): May 15 and Oct. 1
Board meeting date(s): Quarterly
Write: Amy S. Bones
Officers: Frank A. Blazek, Pres.; Beverly Ingram, V.P.; Janet Acker, Secy.
Employer Identification Number: 470682708

3695
Gilbert M. and Martha H. Hitchcock Foundation
Kennedy Holland Bldg.
10306 Regency Pkwy. Dr.
Omaha 68114 (402) 397-0203

Incorporated in 1943 in NE.
Donor(s): Martha H. Hitchcock.†
Foundation type: Independent
Financial data (yr. ended 12/31/89): Assets, $9,390,357 (M); qualifying distributions, $490,046, including $490,046 for 47 grants (high: $50,000; low: $500; average: $1,000-$15,000).
Purpose and activities: Support for private secondary and higher education; support also for cultural programs and youth and social service agencies; sponsors scholarship program for newspaper carriers.
Types of support: Annual campaigns, building funds, endowment funds, matching funds, general purposes, scholarship funds.
Limitations: Giving limited to NE and western IA, with emphasis on Omaha. No grants to individuals, or for research-related programs.
Publications: Application guidelines.
Application information:
Initial approach: Proposal or letter
Copies of proposal: 4
Deadline(s): Dec. 1
Board meeting date(s): Jan. and as required
Final notification: After Jan. board meeting
Write: Thomas R. Burke, Secy.
Officers: Denman Kountze,* Pres.; Neely Kountze,* V.P.; Thomas R. Burke, Secy.; Tyler B. Gaines,* Treas.
Trustees:* Mary Jennings, Charles Kountze, Ronald R. Ruh, Paul Shirley, Jr.
Number of staff: None.
Employer Identification Number: 476025723

3696
The IBP Foundation, Inc. ¤
P.O. Box 515
Dakota City 68731 (402) 494-2061

Established in 1979 in NE.
Donor(s): IBP, Inc.
Foundation type: Company-sponsored
Financial data (yr. ended 12/31/88): Assets, $2,124,432 (M); gifts received, $500,000; expenditures, $221,632, including $219,916 for grants.
Purpose and activities: Grants primarily for community development, including community

funds, business associations, agricultural organizations, and education; some support for health services.
Limitations: Giving limited to Boise, ID; Columbus Junction, Council Bluffs, Denison, Sioux City, and Storm Lake, IA; Joslin, IL; Emporia and Garden City, KS; Luverne, MN; Dakota City, Madison, South Sioux City, and West Point, NE; Amarillo, TX; and Pasco, WA.
Application information: Application form required.
Deadline(s): None
Write: George S. Spencer, Chair.
Officers: George S. Spencer,* Chair.; Richard A. Jochum, Secy.; Leon O. Trautwein, Treas.
Directors:* Lonnie O. Grigsby, David J. LaFleur, Eugene D. Leman.
Employer Identification Number: 476014039

3697
Hazel R. Keene Trust ⌑
c/o Fremont National Bank Trust, Trust Dept.
152 East 6th St.
Fremont 68025 (402) 721-1050

Established in 1986 in NE.
Donor(s): Hazel Keene.
Foundation type: Independent
Financial data (yr. ended 6/30/88): Assets, $2,203,553 (M); expenditures, $169,314, including $83,000 for 12 grants (high: $41,500; low: $1,500).
Purpose and activities: Giving primarily for social services, including programs for the aged, child welfare, and youth; support also for education, health, the arts, and historic preservation.
Types of support: Building funds, capital campaigns, general purposes, lectureships, matching funds, scholarship funds.
Limitations: Giving primarily in Fremont, NE.
Application information: Application form required.
Copies of proposal: 2
Deadline(s): May 1
Final notification: June 30
Write: Joe Twidwell
Trustee: Fremont National Bank Trust.
Number of staff: None.
Employer Identification Number: 476144486

3698
Peter Kiewit Foundation ▼
Woodmen Tower, Suite 900
17th and Farnam St.
Omaha 68102 (402) 344-7890

Established in 1975 in NE.
Donor(s): Peter Kiewit.†
Foundation type: Independent
Financial data (yr. ended 06/30/89): Assets, $196,998,982 (M); expenditures, $17,926,060, including $15,868,656 for 43 grants (high: $4,500,000; low: $2,557; average: $10,000-$100,000) and $355,869 for 91 grants to individuals.
Purpose and activities: Giving primarily for cultural programs, including the arts, civic affairs, community development, higher and other education, health and social service agencies, and youth programs. Contributions almost always made as challenge or matching grants.
Types of support: Matching funds, student aid, capital campaigns, equipment, general purposes, land acquisition, program-related investments, renovation projects, seed money, special projects.
Limitations: Giving limited to NE and western IA; Sheridan, WY; and Rancho Mirage, CA; college scholarships available to high school students in the Omaha, NE--Council Bluffs, IA, area only. No support for elementary or secondary schools, churches, or religious groups. No grants to individuals (except for scholarships), or for endowment funds or annual campaigns.
Publications: Annual report, informational brochure (including application guidelines), application guidelines.
Application information: For scholarships, request application form from foundation office. Application form required.
Initial approach: Letter or telephone
Copies of proposal: 3
Deadline(s): June 30, Sept. 30, Dec. 31, and Mar. 31 for organizations; Mar. 1 for scholarships
Board meeting date(s): Sept., Dec., Mar., and June
Final notification: Within 30 days of board meeting
Write: Lyn Wallin Ziegenbein, Exec. Dir.
Officer: Lyn Wallin Ziegenbein, Exec. Dir. and Secy.
Trustees: Richard L. Coyne, Chair.; Robert B. Daugherty, Vice-Chair.; Ray L. Daniel, Jr., Marjorie B. Kiewit, Peter Kiewit, Jr., FirsTier Bank Omaha.
Number of staff: 3 full-time professional; 2 full-time support.
Employer Identification Number: 476098282

3699
The Peter Kiewit Sons, Inc. Foundation ▼ ⌑
1000 Kiewit Plaza
Omaha 68131 (402) 342-2052

Established in 1963 in NE.
Donor(s): Peter Kiewit Sons Co., Wytana, Inc., Big Horn Coal Co.
Foundation type: Company-sponsored
Financial data (yr. ended 12/31/87): Assets, $12,600,016 (M); gifts received, $1,000,000; expenditures, $1,628,620, including $1,581,711 for 136 grants (high: $250,000; low: $25; average: $500-$10,000).
Purpose and activities: Grants largely for higher education, the arts, community development, and social service agencies.
Limitations: Giving primarily in NE and the northwestern states, or in areas where the company has permanent operations; in education, preference given to areas where the company recruits. No support for elementary or secondary schools, individual churches or similar religious groups. No grants to individuals, or for endowment funds.
Application information: Application form not required.
Deadline(s): None
Board meeting date(s): As needed
Final notification: Varies
Write: Michael L. Faust
Trustee: FirsTier Bank Omaha.
Number of staff: None.
Employer Identification Number: 476029996

3700
Komarek Charitable Trust ⌑
c/o Norwest Bank Nebraska
P.O. Box 3959
Omaha 68103 (402) 536-2470

Established in 1984 in NE.
Donor(s): Joseph C. Komarek, P. Komarek.
Foundation type: Independent
Financial data (yr. ended 5/31/87): Assets, $1,322,394 (M); expenditures, $124,130, including $94,183 for 33 grants (high: $51,475; low: $300) and $21,500 for 22 grants to individuals (high: $1,800; low: $437).
Purpose and activities: Scholarships for students pursuing careers in the ministry of the Presbyterian and Methodist faiths and for students at the College of Medicine at the University of NE; grants also for church support and social services.
Types of support: Student aid.
Limitations: Giving limited to western IA and eastern NE for churches; other support primarily in NE.
Application information: Ministry students must be nominated by delegates of the Presbyterian and Methodist ministries of Omaha, NE; medical students must be nominated by the University of NE. Charities other than churches must apply through the Rebekah Assembly of the Independent Order of Good Fellows. Direct applications are accepted only from Presbyterian and Methodist churches. Application form required.
Copies of proposal: 4
Deadline(s): Within a reasonable time after May 31
Trustee: Norwest Bank Nebraska.
Employer Identification Number: 476141512

3701
Winthrop and Frances Lane Foundation ⌑
c/o FirsTier Bank Omaha
17th and Farnam St.
Omaha 68102 (402) 348-6350

Established in 1976.
Foundation type: Independent
Financial data (yr. ended 12/31/88): Assets, $2,122,021 (M); expenditures, $132,512, including $23,085 for 5 grants (high: $7,500; low: $2,585) and $84,000 for 53 grants to individuals (high: $5,000; low: $800).
Purpose and activities: Giving limited to students enrolled at Creighton School of Law, the University of Nebraska College of Law, and for educational programs at these institutions.
Types of support: Student aid, research, conferences and seminars.
Limitations: Giving limited to Omaha and Lincoln, NE.
Application information: Application form required.
Deadline(s): None
Trustee: FirsTier Bank Omaha.
Employer Identification Number: 470581778

3702
Leu Foundation, Inc. ⌑
221 West 2nd St.
North Platte 69101
Application address: 2409 Abbott Martin Rd., Nashville, TN 37315

Established in 1976 in NE.
Donor(s): Frank Leu, Marjorie Skala.
Foundation type: Independent
Financial data (yr. ended 12/31/88): Assets, $1,624,247 (M); gifts received, $35,000; expenditures, $80,250, including $32,000 for 12 grants (high: $5,000) and $28,000 for 30 grants to individuals.
Purpose and activities: Support primarily for higher education, including student aid; support also for religion and culture.
Types of support: Student aid.
Limitations: Giving for scholarships primarily in North Platte, NE.
Application information: Completion of application form required for scholarships.
Deadline(s): None
Write: Frank Leu, Pres.
Officers and Trustees: Frank Leu, Pres. and Mgr.; Dennis Barkley, Treas.; Cynthia Leu, Edna Nelson, Marjorie Skala.
Employer Identification Number: 470576937

3703
Lied Foundation Trust ⌑
10050 Regency Circle, Suite 200
Omaha 68114
Application address: 3965 West Charleston Blvd., Las Vegas, NV 89104; Tel.: (702) 878-1559

Established in 1972 in NE.
Donor(s): Ernst F. Lied.†
Foundation type: Independent
Financial data (yr. ended 12/31/87): Assets, $1,920,171 (M); gifts received, $5,000,000; expenditures, $3,371,671, including $3,370,436 for 4 grants (high: $2,000,000; low: $6,000).
Purpose and activities: Giving primarily to youth organizations and higher education.
Limitations: Giving primarily in Las Vegas, NV, and NE.
Application information: Application form not required.
Deadline(s): None
Write: Christina M. Hixson, Trustee
Trustee: Christina M. Hixson.
Employer Identification Number: 237282946

3704
Lincoln Family Foundation ⌑
P.O. Box 80269
Lincoln 68501

Established in 1963 in KS.
Foundation type: Independent
Financial data (yr. ended 12/31/87): Assets, $2,031,991 (M); gifts received, $279,703; expenditures, $215,839, including $170,225 for 36 grants (high: $125,000; low: $25).
Purpose and activities: Grants for higher education, Protestant church support, a charitable foundation, and a youth agency.
Limitations: Giving primarily in NE and KS. No loans.
Officers and Trustees:* George A. Lincoln,* Pres.; Olivia G. Lincoln,* V.P.; Ardean A. Arndt, Secy.; Bill C. Macy, Treas.; Margaret L. Donlan.
Employer Identification Number: 476034708

3705
Lincoln Foundation, Inc.
215 Centennial Mall South, Rm. 200
Lincoln 68508 (402) 474-2345

Incorporated in 1955 in NE.
Foundation type: Community
Financial data (yr. ended 12/31/88): Assets, $16,013,462 (M); gifts received, $13,251; expenditures, $1,035,511, including $794,082 for 137 grants (high: $190,000).
Purpose and activities: To promote the mental, moral, intellectual, and physical improvement, assistance, and relief of the inhabitants of Lincoln and Lancaster County in particular, and elsewhere in the U.S. where funds are available; giving mainly in the areas of civic and community affairs, cultural programs, health and welfare, and higher education.
Types of support: Scholarship funds, seed money, emergency funds, research, matching funds, special projects.
Limitations: Giving primarily in Lincoln and Lancaster County, NE. No grants to individuals, or for building or endowment funds or operating budgets.
Publications: Annual report, program policy statement, application guidelines, newsletter.
Application information: Application form required.
Initial approach: Telephone
Copies of proposal: 12
Deadline(s): 8 weeks prior to board meetings
Board meeting date(s): Jan., Apr., July, and Oct.
Write: Phil Heckman, Pres.
Officers and Directors:* Glenn Clements,* Chair.; Virginia Johnson,* Vice-Chair.; Philip Heckman, Pres.; Otis Young,* Secy.; Jo Kinsey,* Treas.; and 18 additional directors.
Number of staff: 3 full-time professional; 1 part-time professional; 2 full-time support; 1 part-time support.
Employer Identification Number: 470458128

3706
The Milton S. and Corinne N. Livingston Foundation, Inc.
1125 South 103rd St., Suite 600
Omaha 68124-1071 (402) 558-1112

Incorporated in 1948 in NE.
Donor(s): Milton S. Livingston.†
Foundation type: Independent
Financial data (yr. ended 12/31/88): Assets, $3,204,219 (M); expenditures, $397,348, including $361,522 for 64 grants (high: $100,000; low: $100; average: $2,500).
Purpose and activities: Grants largely for local Jewish welfare funds and temple support, higher education, culture, and health services.
Types of support: Continuing support, building funds, general purposes.
Limitations: Giving primarily in NE. No grants to individuals.
Application information: Application form not required.
Initial approach: Letter
Copies of proposal: 1
Deadline(s): None
Board meeting date(s): May and Oct.
Write: Yale Richards, Exec. Dir.
Officers and Trustees: Jule M. Newman, Pres.; Morton A. Richards, V.P.; Robert I. Kully, Secy.; Stanley J. Slosburg, Treas.; Murray H. Newman.
Employer Identification Number: 476027670

3707
Omaha Community Foundation ☆
Two Central Park Plaza
222 South 15th St.
Omaha 68102 (402) 342-3458

Established in 1982 in NE.
Foundation type: Community
Financial data (yr. ended 12/31/89): Assets, $4,053,436 (M); gifts received, $415,115; expenditures, $528,763, including $417,808 for 64 grants (high: $250,000; low: $75).
Purpose and activities: Grants primarily for charitable purposes in the areas of civic, culture, health, education, and social services.
Types of support: Building funds, conferences and seminars, continuing support, emergency funds, matching funds, publications, renovation projects, seed money, equipment, special projects, technical assistance.
Limitations: Giving limited to the metropolitan Omaha, NE, area. No grants to individuals.
Publications: Annual report (including application guidelines), 990-PF, program policy statement, application guidelines, grants list, newsletter, informational brochure.
Application information: Application form required.
Copies of proposal: 7
Deadline(s): Apr. 1 and Oct. 1
Board meeting date(s): June and Dec.
Final notification: June and Dec.
Write: W. Earl Taylor, Exec. Dir.
Officer: W. Earl Taylor, Exec. Dir.
Number of staff: 1 full-time professional; 1 part-time professional; 1 full-time support.
Employer Identification Number: 470645958

3708
The Omaha World-Herald Foundation ▼
c/o Omaha World-Herald Co.
14th and Dodge Sts.
Omaha 68102 (402) 444-1000

Trust established in 1968 in NE.
Donor(s): Omaha World-Herald Co.
Foundation type: Company-sponsored
Financial data (yr. ended 12/31/89): Assets, $527,375 (M); expenditures, $913,047, including $903,585 for grants.
Purpose and activities: Giving primarily for education, cultural programs including historic preservation, social service and youth agencies, civic affairs, the media, and conservation.
Types of support: Seed money, building funds, internships, scholarship funds, matching funds, special projects, continuing support, equipment.

Limitations: Giving limited to the Omaha, NE, area. No grants to individuals, or for operating endowments, research, seminars, or dinners.
Publications: 990-PF.
Application information: Application form not required.
Initial approach: Proposal
Copies of proposal: 1
Deadline(s): None
Board meeting date(s): As required
Final notification: 2 months
Write: John Gottschalk, Pres.
Distribution Committee: Harold W. Andersen, John Gottschalk, G. Woodson Howe.
Trustee: Norwest Capital Management and Trust Co. Nebraska.
Number of staff: None.
Employer Identification Number: 476058691

3709
The Owen Foundation
One Owen Pkwy.
2200 Abbott Dr.
Carter Lake 51510

Incorporated in 1959 in NE.
Donor(s): Paxton & Vierling Steel Co., Missouri Valley Steel Co., Northern Plains Steel Co.
Foundation type: Company-sponsored
Financial data (yr. ended 11/30/88): Assets, $37,366 (M); gifts received, $85,000; expenditures, $140,262, including $139,167 for 10 grants (high: $75,000; low: $250).
Purpose and activities: Emphasis on a zoological society and a state wildlife department; grants also for higher education, cultural programs, and social service agencies.
Limitations: Giving primarily in NE.
Officer: Sam R. Bower, Secy.-Treas.
Trustees: Margaret Owen Gray, Dolores C. Owen, Richard F. Owen, Robert E. Owen.
Employer Identification Number: 476025298

3710
Phelps County Community Foundation, Inc.
701 Fourth Ave., Suite 8
Holdrege 68949 (308) 995-6847

Incorporated in 1976 in NE.
Foundation type: Community
Financial data (yr. ended 06/30/88): Assets, $1,983,264 (M); gifts received, $76,650; expenditures, $65,095, including $15,347 for 10 grants (high: $10,000; low: $100), $2,000 for 5 grants to individuals of $400 each and $15,853 for 6 loans to individuals.
Purpose and activities: Giving for charitable and educational purposes; scholarship grants and loans to residents of Phelps County.
Types of support: Seed money, emergency funds, building funds, equipment, matching funds, student loans, student aid, continuing support, publications, special projects, operating budgets, renovation projects.
Limitations: Giving limited to NE, particularly Phelps County. No grants for annual campaigns, deficit financing, land acquisition, endowments, program support, research, demonstration projects, or conferences and seminars.
Publications: Application guidelines, newsletter, grants list, financial statement, 990-PF.
Application information: Application form required.
Initial approach: Letter
Copies of proposal: 1
Deadline(s): May 15 and Nov. 15 for loans
Board meeting date(s): 1st Thursday each month
Write: Janice L. Layton, Exec. Dir.
Officers: Robert J. Linder, Chair. and Pres.; Michael C. Klein, V.P.; Lynn S. Embury, Secy.; Clinton C. Carlson, Treas.; Janice L. Layton, Exec. Dir.
Number of staff: 1 full-time professional; 1 part-time support.
Employer Identification Number: 510189077

3711
Quivey-Bay State Foundation ⌑
1515 East 20th St.
Scottsbluff 69361 (308) 632-2168

Established in 1948 in NE.
Donor(s): M.B. Quivey, Mrs. M.B. Quivey.
Foundation type: Independent
Financial data (yr. ended 1/31/88): Assets, $2,039,899 (M); expenditures, $143,279, including $133,232 for 60 grants (high: $15,000; low: $100).
Purpose and activities: Emphasis on higher education, church support, and youth and child welfare agencies; support also for historic preservation.
Limitations: Giving primarily in NE. No grants to individuals, or for endowment funds.
Application information:
Initial approach: Letter
Copies of proposal: 1
Deadline(s): Submit proposal in Sept.; deadline Oct. 15
Board meeting date(s): Oct. and Nov.
Write: Ted Cannon, Secy.-Treas.
Officers and Trustees: Earl R. Cherry, Pres.; Ted Cannon, Secy.-Treas.
Employer Identification Number: 476024159

3712
Edgar Reynolds Foundation, Inc. ⌑
204 North Walnut St.
Grand Island 68801 (308) 384-0957

Established in 1977.
Donor(s): Edgar Reynolds.†
Foundation type: Independent
Financial data (yr. ended 12/31/87): Assets, $3,772,082 (M); expenditures, $146,002, including $138,189 for 13 grants (high: $30,000; low: $2,000).
Purpose and activities: Grants primarily to hospitals, youth agencies, and welfare programs.
Types of support: Building funds, research, scholarship funds.
Limitations: Giving primarily in NE.
Publications: Application guidelines.
Application information: Application form required.
Initial approach: Letter
Write: Fred M. Glade, Jr., Chair.
Officers and Directors: Fred M. Glade, Jr., Chair.; William Marshall, Jr., Vice-Chair.; Frances Reynolds, Secy.-Treas.; Jon F. Luebs.
Employer Identification Number: 470589941

3713
Rogers Foundation ⌑
1311 M St., Suite A
Lincoln 68508 (402) 477-3725

Established in 1954 in NE.
Donor(s): Richard H. Rogers.†
Foundation type: Independent
Financial data (yr. ended 12/31/87): Assets, $4,655,866 (M); expenditures, $227,173.
Purpose and activities: Emphasis on support for cultural programs, civic affairs, youth and health agencies, and education.
Limitations: Giving primarily in Lincoln and Lancaster County, NE. No support for religious activities, national organizations, or organizations supported by government agencies. No grants to individuals, or for fundraising benefits, program advertising, endowments, or continuing support; no loans.
Publications: Application guidelines.
Application information:
Initial approach: Proposal
Write: Richard W. Agee, Pres.
Officers and Directors: Richard W. Agee, Pres.; Eloise R. Agee, V.P.; Richard R. Agee.
Employer Identification Number: 476026897

3714
Philip Schrager Foundation ⌑ ☆
3217 South 101st St.
Omaha 68124-2628

Established in 1972 in NE.
Donor(s): The Pacesetter Corp.
Foundation type: Independent
Financial data (yr. ended 9/30/88): Assets, $253,632 (M); gifts received, $1,000; expenditures, $141,892.
Purpose and activities: Giving primarily to Jewish organizations and a private affiliated foundation; support also for youth and a community fund.
Limitations: Giving primarily in Omaha, NE. No grants to individuals.
Application information: Applications not accepted.
Officers: Phillip G. Schrager, Pres.; Terri Lynn Schrager, V.P. and Secy.; Allan Lozier, Treas.
Employer Identification Number: 237184025

3715
Walter Scott, Jr. Charitable Foundation ⌑
c/o FirsTier Bank Omaha, N.A., Estate & Trust Dept.
17th and Farnam St.
Omaha 68102

Established in 1965 in NE.
Donor(s): Walter Scott, Jr.
Foundation type: Independent
Financial data (yr. ended 12/31/88): Assets, $4,876,443 (M); gifts received, $2,000,000; expenditures, $245,846, including $238,050 for 22 grants (high: $104,000; low: $100).
Purpose and activities: Support primarily for a zoological foundation, educational institutions, youth organizations, and wilderness and wildlife conservation.
Limitations: Giving primarily in Omaha, NE. No grants to individuals.

Application information: Contributes only to pre-selected organizations. Applications not accepted.
Trustee: Walter Scott, Jr.
Employer Identification Number: 476038363

3716
The Steinhart Foundation, Inc. ⌑
Box 661
Nebraska City 68410 (402) 873-3285

Incorporated in 1954 in NE.
Donor(s): Morton Steinhart,† Ella S. Steinhart.
Foundation type: Independent
Financial data (yr. ended 12/31/87): Assets, $4,722,255 (M); expenditures, $196,895, including $136,725 for 20 grants (high: $25,000; low: $100).
Purpose and activities: Support for civic projects.
Limitations: Giving primarily in Nebraska City, NE, and the immediate surrounding area.
Application information: Funds presently committed. Application form not required.
Copies of proposal: 1
Deadline(s): None
Board meeting date(s): Annually
Write: Byrl Thostesen, Trustee
Officers and Trustees: Byrl Thostesen, Pres. and Treas.; Gladys Wenzel, V.P.; George T. Blazek, Secy.; Gary Ailes, Mary Ellen Bosworth, Deroy Harshman, John H. Nelson, Mrs. Karl H. Nelson, Henry Schwake.
Employer Identification Number: 476025185

3717
Robert Herman Storz Foundation ⌑
Kiewit Plaza, 8th Fl.
Omaha 68131

Established in 1957.
Donor(s): Robert Herman Storz.
Foundation type: Independent
Financial data (yr. ended 12/31/87): Assets, $5,645,509 (M); gifts received, $250,000; expenditures, $194,346, including $34,355 for 16 grants (high: $9,700; low: $100).
Purpose and activities: Support for hospitals, higher education, and cultural programs.
Limitations: Giving primarily in NE.
Application information: Contributes only to pre-selected organizations. Applications not accepted.
Trustees: Susan Storz Butler, Robert Herman Storz.
Employer Identification Number: 476025980

3718
Stuart Foundation ⌑
852 NBC Ctr.
Lincoln 68508 (402) 475-4204

Established in 1948 in NE.
Foundation type: Independent
Financial data (yr. ended 12/31/87): Assets, $1,187,897 (M); expenditures, $68,094, including $53,276 for 42 grants (high: $23,507; low: $10).
Purpose and activities: Support for Christian organizations, education, and nature conservation.
Types of support: Scholarship funds, research, operating budgets.
Application information:
Deadline(s): None
Final notification: 2 months
Write: James Stuart, Pres.
Officers and Trustees: Helen C. Stuart, Chair.; James Stuart, Pres.; Catherine S. Schmoker, V.P.; Richard C. Schmoker, V.P.; Scott Stuart, Secy.; James Stuart, Jr., Treas.
Employer Identification Number: 476024642

3719
The Valmont Foundation ⌑
c/o Valmont Industries, Inc.
Valley 68064

Established in 1976.
Donor(s): Valmont Industries, Inc.
Foundation type: Company-sponsored
Financial data (yr. ended 2/28/88): Assets, $22,585 (M); gifts received, $215,000; expenditures, $201,678, including $201,663 for 67 grants (high: $31,850; low: $100).
Purpose and activities: Giving primarily for higher education, youth agencies, community funds, and cultural programs.
Limitations: Giving primarily in NE.
Officers: Robert B. Daugherty, Pres.; Paul F. Linemann, Secy.; Terry J. McClain, Treas.
Director: Mel Bannister.
Employer Identification Number: 362895245

3720
Weller Foundation, Inc. ⌑
East Hwy. 20
P.O. Box 636
Atkinson 68713 (402) 925-2803

Incorporated in 1979 in NE.
Donor(s): E.C. Weller, Frances W. Weller.
Foundation type: Independent
Financial data (yr. ended 10/31/88): Assets, $3,496,819 (M); expenditures, $243,309, including $178,400 for 274 grants to individuals (high: $1,500; low: $250).
Purpose and activities: Scholarships for students attending one of the technical community colleges in NE or pursuing other vocational education, such as nursing.
Types of support: Student aid.
Limitations: Giving limited to NE, with primary consideration for residents of Holt, Boyd, Brown, Rock, Keya Paha, and Garfield counties. No grants for scholarships for education toward a Bachelor's degree.
Publications: Application guidelines.
Application information: Application form required.
Deadline(s): June 1 for the fall semester and Nov. 1 for the spring semester
Final notification: Within 30 days of the deadlines
Officers: Ernest J. Gottschalk, Pres.; Robert Clifford, V.P.; Dean Fleming, Secy.-Treas.
Directors: Clayton Goeke, Paul Possnecker, Robert Randall, Frances W. Weller.
Employer Identification Number: 470611350

3721
Wenger Foundation ⌑
141 South 14th St.
Lincoln 68508
Application address: P.O. Box 130, Sabetha, KS; Tel.: (913) 284-2183

Established in 1964 in NE.
Donor(s): Members of the Wenger family.
Foundation type: Independent
Financial data (yr. ended 12/31/87): Assets, $144,958 (M); expenditures, $118,322, including $116,950 for 5 grants (high: $109,000; low: $700).
Purpose and activities: Support primarily for a home for the aged; support also for religious organizations and health services.
Application information: Application form not required.
Initial approach: Letter
Deadline(s): None
Write: Louis Wenger, Pres.
Officers: Louis Wenger, Pres.; Lavon Wenger, V.P.; Don Wenger, Secy.
Employer Identification Number: 476034000

NEVADA

3722
Bing Fund, Inc. ⌑
1155 West 4th St., Suite 210
Reno 89503
Application address: 9700 West Pico Blvd., Los Angeles, CA 90035; Tel.: (213) 277-3222

Incorporated in 1977 in NV as partial successor to Bing Fund, Inc., incorporated in NY.
Donor(s): Leo S. Bing,† Anna Bing Arnold, Peter S. Bing.
Foundation type: Independent
Financial data (yr. ended 5/31/87): Assets, $2,769,793 (M); gifts received, $1,134,713; expenditures, $72,569, including $68,000 for 4 grants (high: $53,000; low: $5,000).
Purpose and activities: Emphasis on medical education and youth agencies.
Limitations: Giving primarily in NV.
Application information: Application form not required.
Deadline(s): None
Write: Dr. Peter S. Bing, Pres.
Officers and Trustees: Peter S. Bing, Pres. and Treas.; Margaret Churn, V.P. and Secy.; Robert D. Burch, V.P. and Secy.
Employer Identification Number: 942496050

3723
Bing Fund Corporation ▼ ⌑
302 East Carson Ave., Suite 617
Las Vegas 89101 (702) 386-6183
Application address: 9700 West Pico Blvd., Los Angeles, CA 90035; Tel.: (213) 277-3222

Incorporated in 1977 in NV as partial successor to Bing Fund, Inc., incorporated in NY.
Donor(s): Leo S. Bing,† Anna Bing Arnold, Peter S. Bing.
Foundation type: Independent
Financial data (yr. ended 5/31/88): Assets, $34,610,348 (M); gifts received, $225,000; expenditures, $1,110,952, including $1,030,350 for 127 grants (high: $155,000; low: $200).
Purpose and activities: Giving primarily for higher education, museums, the arts, secondary education, hospitals, and population control.
Limitations: Giving primarily in southern CA.
Application information: Application form not required.
Deadline(s): None
Write: Peter S. Bing, V.P.
Officers: Anna H. Bing, Pres.; Peter S. Bing, V.P. and Treas.; Robert D. Burch, Secy.
Employer Identification Number: 942476169

3724
Constance H. Bishop Foundation ⌑
3710 Grant Dr., Suite A
Reno 89509 (702) 826-9104

Established in 1966 in NV.
Foundation type: Independent
Financial data (yr. ended 12/31/88): Assets, $1,540,841 (M); expenditures, $89,556, including $72,317 for 10 grants (high: $60,000; low: $125).
Purpose and activities: Emphasis on secondary and higher education and youth organizations; also support for wildlife conservation.
Limitations: Giving primarily in NV and CA.
Application information: Application form not required.
Deadline(s): None
Write: Leonard H. McIntosh, Pres.
Officers: Leonard H. McIntosh, Pres.; H.P. McIntosh IV, V.P.; Frances Lopez, Secy.-Treas.
Employer Identification Number: 886006804

3725
Carol Franc Buck Foundation
(Formerly Carol Buck Sells Foundation)
P.O. Drawer CE
Incline Village 89450 (702) 831-6366

Foundation incorporated in 1979 in NV.
Donor(s): Carol B. Sells, John E. Sells.
Foundation type: Independent
Financial data (yr. ended 11/30/89): Assets, $7,060,180 (M); gifts received, $5,436; expenditures, $339,884, including $223,480 for grants (high: $70,000).
Purpose and activities: Support for the performing arts, especially music.
Types of support: Continuing support, annual campaigns, matching funds, endowment funds, special projects.
Limitations: Giving primarily in the western U.S. No grants to individuals, or for emergency funds, deficit financing, capital campaigns, equipment, land acquisition, renovations, scholarships, fellowships, research, publications, or conferences; no loans.
Application information: Application form not required.
Initial approach: Letter or telephone
Copies of proposal: 1
Deadline(s): Mar. 31 and Sept. 31
Board meeting date(s): Jan., Apr., July, and Oct.
Final notification: 3 months
Write: Marya A. Beam, Admin. Asst., or Carol B. Plummer, Pres.
Officers and Trustees:* Carol B. Plummer,* Pres. and Secy.; Christian P. Erdman,* V.P. and Treas.; Helen O'Hanlon.
Number of staff: 1 full-time professional.
Employer Identification Number: 880163505

3726
The Cord Foundation ⌑
200 Court St.
Reno 89501

Established in 1962 in NV.
Donor(s): E.L. Cord.†
Foundation type: Independent
Financial data (yr. ended 12/31/87): Assets, $38,336,500 (M); gifts received, $10,506,564; expenditures, $1,198,751, including $976,486 for 21 grants (high: $150,000; low: $7,500).
Purpose and activities: Support primarily for secondary and higher education, social services and youth organizations.
Trustees: William O. Bradley, Thomas P. Ford, Edward D. Neuhoff.
Employer Identification Number: 366072793

3727
First Interstate Bank of Nevada Foundation
One East First St.
P.O. Box 11007
Reno 89501 (702) 784-3844

Established in 1983 in NV.
Donor(s): First Interstate Bank of Nevada.
Foundation type: Company-sponsored
Financial data (yr. ended 12/31/89): Assets, $590,368 (M); gifts received, $550,000; expenditures, $476,295, including $474,195 for 61 grants (high: $100,000; low: $1,000; average: $8,000-$9,000), $2,100 for 8 employee matching gifts and $50,000 for 20 in-kind gifts.
Purpose and activities: Emphasis on community funds, rural development, higher education, arts and cultural programs, and social service agencies.
Types of support: Capital campaigns, continuing support, employee matching gifts, equipment, general purposes, matching funds, operating budgets, renovation projects.
Limitations: Giving limited to NV. No support for religious organizations or United Way recipients. No grants to individuals.
Publications: Informational brochure (including application guidelines), annual report, corporate giving report.
Application information: Application form required.
Initial approach: Letter
Copies of proposal: 1
Deadline(s): 10th of each month
Board meeting date(s): 3rd Tuesday of each month
Final notification: Immediately after board meeting
Write: Kevin Day, Pres.
Officers: Kevin Day, Pres.; Larry Tuntland, V.P.; Ronald Zurek, Secy.; Kevin J. Sullivan, Treas.
Trustees: Karen Galatz, Don Snyder.
Number of staff: 1 part-time professional.
Employer Identification Number: 942831988

3728
Gabelli Foundation, Inc. ⌑
c/o Avansino & Melarkey
165 West Liberty St.
Reno 89501

Established in 1985 in NV.
Donor(s): Mario J. Gabelli.
Foundation type: Independent
Financial data (yr. ended 3/31/89): Assets, $2,253,916 (M); gifts received, $286,425; expenditures, $74,414, including $54,700 for 7 grants (high: $20,000; low: $200).
Purpose and activities: Giving primarily for higher education.
Types of support: Scholarship funds.
Application information:
Initial approach: Letter
Deadline(s): None
Officers: Mario J. Gabelli, Pres.; John Gabelli, V.P.; Mary Gabelli Mazzolla, Secy.
Employer Identification Number: 942975159

3729
Golden Nugget Scholarship Fund, Inc.
P.O. Box 7777
129 East Fremont St.
Las Vegas 89177 (702) 791-7131

Established in 1981 in NV.
Donor(s): Golden Nugget, Inc.
Foundation type: Company-sponsored
Financial data (yr. ended 05/31/89): Assets, $2,809,597 (M); expenditures, $410,157, including $395,500 for 146 grants to individuals (high: $8,100; low: $500; average: $2,700).
Purpose and activities: Scholarships for college studies at accredited public or private institutions located in the U.S. for graduates of NV high schools.
Types of support: Student aid.
Limitations: Giving limited to graduates of NV high schools.
Application information: Scholarship applicants must be nominated by their high schools; direct applications from individuals not accepted. Application form required.
Deadline(s): Mar. 10
Write: Elaine Wynn, Vice-Chair.
Officers and Trustees:* Mike O'Callaghan,* Chair. and Pres.; Elaine Wynn,* Vice-Chair. and Treas.; Arthur Nathan, Kevin Wynn, Stephen A. Wynn.
Employer Identification Number: 942768861

3730
Robert Z. Hawkins Foundation ⌑
One East Liberty St., Suite 509
Reno 89505 (702) 786-4646

Established in 1980.
Foundation type: Independent
Financial data (yr. ended 12/31/87): Assets, $9,043,525 (M); expenditures, $663,121,

including $519,365 for 70 grants (high: $89,427; low: $166).
Purpose and activities: Emphasis on education, including a university, youth agencies and child welfare, church support, and a museum.
Types of support: Special projects.
Limitations: Giving limited to NV. No grants to individuals.
Application information: Awards are limited to $20,000 a year per organization.
Deadline(s): None
Write: Paul O. Wiig, Chair.
Trustees: Paul O. Wiig, Chair.; Kathryn A. Hawkins, Robert M. Hawkins, Bill A. Ligon, Security Bank of Nevada.
Employer Identification Number: 880162645

3731
Conrad N. Hilton Foundation ▼
100 West Liberty St., Suite 840
Reno 89501 (702) 323-4221

Trust established in 1944; incorporated in 1950 in CA.
Donor(s): Conrad N. Hilton.†
Foundation type: Independent
Financial data (yr. ended 02/28/90): Assets, $492,092,546 (M); gifts received, $231,630,125; expenditures, $12,853,867, including $10,179,630 for 86 grants (high: $2,235,000; low: $500; average: $5,000-$50,000).
Purpose and activities: The greater part of the foundation's giving is devoted to several major long-term projects, including the areas of drug abuse prevention, hotel administration education, and Catholic welfare; funding for smaller scale miscellaneous grants very limited.
Types of support: Building funds, endowment funds, equipment, operating budgets, publications, scholarship funds, seed money, technical assistance, continuing support.
Limitations: No support for religious organizations for the benefit of their own membership, medical research, the arts, the elderly, political lobbying or legislative activities, or local branches of national charities. No grants to individuals, or for general fundraising events, exhibits, travel, or surveys; no loans.
Publications: Annual report (including application guidelines), application guidelines.
Application information: The foundation accepts applications primarily from its specified beneficiaries. Application form not required.
Initial approach: Letter
Copies of proposal: 1
Deadline(s): None
Board meeting date(s): Quarterly
Final notification: Within 30 days
Write: Donald H. Hubbs, Pres.
Officers and Directors:* Donald H. Hubbs,* Pres.; Vernon Herndon,* V.P.; Steven M. Hilton,* V.P.; Patrick Modugno, V.P.; Jean Van Sickle, Secy.; Deborah Kerr, Treas.; Robert Buckley, M.D., William H. Edwards, James R. Galbraith, Robert A. Groves, Barron Hilton, Eric M. Hilton.
Number of staff: 7 full-time professional; 2 full-time support.
Employer Identification Number: 956038817

3732
The Murray Petersen Foundation ¤
2900 Las Vegas Blvd. South
Las Vegas 89109

Established in 1976 in NV.
Donor(s): Dean Petersen, Faye Petersen Johnson.
Foundation type: Independent
Financial data (yr. ended 12/31/87): Assets, $93,592 (M); gifts received, $107,707; expenditures, $113,691, including $113,637 for 21 grants (high: $25,000; low: $64).
Purpose and activities: Emphasis on higher education, educational broadcasting, youth agencies, recreation, social agencies, child welfare, and cultural programs. Support also for health agencies and medical research.
Limitations: Giving primarily in NV.
Application information: Contributes only to pre-selected organizations. Applications not accepted.
Trustees: Faye Petersen Johnson, Ralph Johnson, Dean Petersen, Mary Petersen.
Employer Identification Number: 880138035

3733
Porsche Foundation
c/o Martha McKinley, Public Relations
P.O. Box 30911
Reno 89520-3911

Established in 1986 in NV.
Foundation type: Company-sponsored
Financial data (yr. ended 12/31/87): Assets, $477,848 (M); gifts received, $100,000; expenditures, $105,328, including $104,951 for grants.
Purpose and activities: Support for cultural programs and general charities.
Limitations: Giving primarily in Reno, NV, and Charleston, SC.
Application information: Application form not required.
Employer Identification Number: 943024854

3734
Nell J. Redfield Foundation ¤
P.O. Box 61
Reno 89504 (702) 323-1373

Established in 1982 in NV.
Foundation type: Independent
Financial data (yr. ended 12/31/88): Assets, $3,968,049 (M); expenditures, $420,123, including $373,193 for 24 grants (high: $50,000; low: $2,000).
Purpose and activities: Support primarily for the advancement of health care, medical research, and the care of handicapped children; support also for the aged, education, and religion.
Types of support: Building funds, equipment, scholarship funds.
Limitations: Giving primarily in Reno, NV.
Application information: Application form required.
Initial approach: Letter
Deadline(s): Jan. 15 through June 1
Write: Gerald C. Smith, Dir.
Directors: Iris G. Brewerton, Betty Alyce Jones, Helen Jeane Jones, Gerald C. Smith, Kenneth G. Walker.
Trustee: Farmers & Merchants Trust.
Employer Identification Number: 237399910

3735
Abraham and Sonia Rochlin Foundation ¤
275 Hill St., Suite 25
Reno 89501

Established in 1969 in CA.
Donor(s): Abraham Rochlin,† Sonia Rochlin.
Foundation type: Independent
Financial data (yr. ended 12/31/88): Assets, $21,482,375 (M); expenditures, $1,563,847, including $1,331,525 for 37 grants (high: $425,000; low: $25; average: $3,000-$50,000).
Purpose and activities: Grants primarily for Jewish religious organizations, welfare funds, and higher education.
Publications: Annual report.
Application information: Contributes only to pre-selected organizations. Applications not accepted.
Write: Larry Rochlin, Pres.
Officers: Larry Rochlin, Pres.; Franz L. Boschwitz, V.P.; Anne Boschwitz, Secy.-Treas.
Number of staff: None.
Employer Identification Number: 941696244

3736
SDB Foundation, Inc. ¤
P.O. Box 247
Boulder City 89005-0772
Application address: P.O. Box 926, Fallbrook, CA 92028; Tel.: (619) 728-4390

Established in 1985 in NV.
Donor(s): Sarah D. Barder.
Foundation type: Independent
Financial data (yr. ended 7/31/88): Assets, $3,491,710 (M); gifts received, $1,500,000; expenditures, $109,401, including $72,723 for 3 grants (high: $66,271; low: $2,952).
Purpose and activities: Giving primarily to secondary schools with an emphasis on gifted student programs.
Types of support: Matching funds, scholarship funds, seed money, special projects.
Limitations: Giving primarily in CA, NV, AZ, and UT.
Publications: Informational brochure (including application guidelines).
Application information: Application form required.
Initial approach: Letter
Copies of proposal: 3
Deadline(s): None
Board meeting date(s): Apr. and Oct.
Write: Elois Veltman, Secy.
Officers: Sarah D. Barder, Pres.; Elois Veltman, Secy.; John W. Duncan, Treas.
Number of staff: 3
Employer Identification Number: 942973293

3737
The Southwest Gas Foundation ¤
P.O. Box 98510
Las Vegas 89193-8510 (702) 876-7222

Established in 1985 in NV.
Donor(s): Southwest Gas Corp.
Foundation type: Company-sponsored
Financial data (yr. ended 12/31/88): Assets, $410,006 (M); gifts received, $100,000; expenditures, $364,856, including $363,295 for 385 grants (high: $25,000; low: $25).

Purpose and activities: Emphasis on higher education, art associations and museums, the United Way, health associations, and services for the handicapped.
Types of support: General purposes, employee matching gifts.
Limitations: Giving primarily in NV, AZ, and San Bernardino County, CA.
Application information: Application form required.
Initial approach: Letter
Write: Dennis M. Hetherington, V.P., Corp. Communications (Fdn. Mgr.)
Officer: Dennis M. Hetherington, Mgr.
Directors: Fred W. Cover, Kenny C. Guinn, Micheal O. Maffie.
Number of staff: None.
Employer Identification Number: 942988564

3738
Stearns-Blodgett Trust ⌑
c/o First Interstate Bank of Nevada
P.O. Box 30100
Reno 89520 (702) 784-3316

Established in 1979 in NV.
Donor(s): Edith Miller Blodgett.†
Foundation type: Independent
Financial data (yr. ended 1/31/89): Assets, $1,012,176 (M); expenditures, $165,516, including $148,876 for 38 grants to individuals (high: $12,069; low: $145).
Purpose and activities: To aid and assist indigent persons in need of ophthalmologic care.
Types of support: Grants to individuals.
Limitations: Giving limited to NV and northern CA.
Publications: Application guidelines.
Application information: Occasional grants to institutions initiated by the administrators. Application form required.
Trustee: First Interstate Bank of Nevada.
Administrative Committee: John Webster Brown, Leo J. Humphries, Clarence Jones.
Employer Identification Number: 886033781

3739
Marion G. Thompson Charitable Foundation ⌑
50 West Liberty St., Suite 800
Reno 89501

Established in 1985 in NV.
Foundation type: Independent
Financial data (yr. ended 3/31/89): Assets, $2,412,456 (M); expenditures, $248,737, including $225,000 for 10 grants (high: $35,000; low: $10,000).
Purpose and activities: Support for the welfare and education of children.
Limitations: Giving primarily in NV and CA.
Application information: Contributes only to pre-selected organizations. Applications not accepted.
Trustee: Lowell C. Bernard.
Employer Identification Number: 886042564

3740
E. L. Wiegand Foundation ▼
Wiegand Ctr.
165 West Liberty St.
Reno 89501 (702) 333-0310

Established in 1982 in NV.
Donor(s): Ann K. Wiegand,† Edwin L. Wiegand.†
Foundation type: Independent
Financial data (yr. ended 10/31/89): Assets, $79,466,446 (M); gifts received, $31,235; expenditures, $4,306,535, including $3,700,120 for 111 grants (high: $100,000; low: $2,000; average: $10,000-$70,000).
Purpose and activities: Grants primarily for education, health and medical research; also for public affairs, civic and community affairs, and arts and cultural affairs; emphasis on Roman Catholic institutions.
Types of support: Equipment, matching funds, special projects, renovation projects.
Limitations: Giving primarily in NV and adjoining western states, including CA, AZ, OR, ID, and UT; Public Affairs grants giving primarily in CA, Washington, DC, and New York, NY. No support for organizations receiving significant support from public tax funds; organizations with beneficiaries of their own choosing; or federal, state, or local government agencies or institutions. No grants to individuals, or for endowment funds, fundraising campaigns, or operating funds.
Publications: Informational brochure (including application guidelines).
Application information: Application form required.
Initial approach: Letter
Copies of proposal: 1
Deadline(s): None
Board meeting date(s): Feb., June, and Oct.
Write: Raymond C. Avansino, Jr., Chair. and Pres.
Officers and Trustees:* Raymond C. Avansino, Jr.,* Chair. and Pres.; Michael J. Melarkey, V.P. and Secy.; Kristen A. Avansino, V.P., California Grants; Joann C. Hildahl, V.P., Grants Prog.; Norbert F. Stanny,* V.P.; James T. Carrico, Treas.; Harvey C. Fruehauf, Jr.
Number of staff: None.
Employer Identification Number: 942839372

NEW HAMPSHIRE

3741
Herbert G. Abbot Testamentary Trust ☆
c/o Bank of New Hampshire, N.A.
P.O. Box 477
Concord 03302-0477

Established in 1947.
Foundation type: Independent
Financial data (yr. ended 07/31/89): Assets, $1,167,327 (M); expenditures, $72,124, including $62,281 for 3 grants (high: $31,141; low: $15,570).
Purpose and activities: Giving to a hospital, a youth center, and a social service society.
Limitations: Giving primarily in Concord, NH. No grants to individuals.
Application information: Funding is limited to various charitable organizations at trustee's discretion. Applications not accepted.
Trustee: Bank of New Hampshire, N.A.
Employer Identification Number: 026004792

3742
The Barker Foundation, Inc. ⌑
P.O. Box 328
Nashua 03061 (603) 889-1763

Incorporated in 1954 in ME.
Donor(s): Walter Barker,† Irene L. Barker.
Foundation type: Independent
Financial data (yr. ended 12/31/87): Assets, $2,722,053 (M); expenditures, $146,713, including $72,700 for 48 grants (high: $40,800; low: $250) and $43,300 for grants to individuals.
Purpose and activities: Giving for hospitals and health associations, higher education, including scholarships, church support, and youth agencies.
Types of support: Student aid.
Limitations: Giving primarily in NH.
Application information: Application form not required.
Write: Allan M. Barker, Pres.
Officers and Trustees: Allan M. Barker, Pres.; Elizabeth M. Bucknam, V.P.; Susan B. Moran, V.P.; Gilbert Bucknam, Treas.; Dorothy A. Barker, Edward P. Moran, Jr.
Employer Identification Number: 026005885

3743
Norwin S. and Elizabeth N. Bean Foundation
c/o New Hampshire Charitable Fund
One South St., P.O. Box 1335
Concord 03302-1335 (603) 225-6641

Trust established in 1957 in NH; later became an affiliated trust of the New Hampshire Charitable Fund.
Donor(s): Norwin S. Bean,† Elizabeth N. Bean.†
Foundation type: Independent
Financial data (yr. ended 12/31/89): Assets, $8,373,048 (M); expenditures, $539,970, including $339,970 for 45 grants (high: $30,000; low: $750) and $200,000 for 1 loan.
Purpose and activities: Giving primarily for social and human services including low-income housing programs, child welfare, and youth; support also for education, health associations, and the performing arts.
Types of support: General purposes, seed money, emergency funds, building funds, equipment, land acquisition, special projects, conferences and seminars, matching funds, loans, program-related investments, consulting services, scholarship funds.
Limitations: Giving limited to Amherst and Manchester, NH. No grants to individuals, or

for scholarships, fellowships, operating budgets, deficit financing, or endowment funds.
Publications: Annual report, informational brochure (including application guidelines).
Application information: Application form not required.
Initial approach: Letter or telephone
Copies of proposal: 1
Deadline(s): Feb. 1, May 1, Aug. 1, and Nov. 1
Board meeting date(s): Mar., June, Sept., and Dec.
Write: Deborah Cowan, Prog. Dir.
Officer and Trustees:* Angie Whidden, R.S.M.,* Chair.; Christy H. Belvin, John H. Hoben, John R. McLane, Jr., James A. Shanahan, Jr.
Number of staff: 5
Employer Identification Number: 026013381

3744
Cogswell Benevolent Trust ⌑
875 Elm St.
Manchester 03101 (603) 622-4013

Trust established in 1929 in NH.
Donor(s): Leander A. Cogswell.†
Foundation type: Independent
Financial data (yr. ended 12/31/88): Assets, $10,484,000 (M); expenditures, $501,083, including $364,925 for grants (high: $30,000; average: $1,000-$15,000).
Purpose and activities: Grants primarily for higher education, youth agencies, the performing arts, health associations, community funds, hospitals, and church support.
Limitations: Giving primarily in NH. No grants to individuals, or for endowment funds or operating budgets.
Application information: The foundation no longer gives scholarships or loans to individuals; scholarship funds have been donated to the New Hampshire Charitable Fund-Student Aid Program, One South St., Concord, NH 03301.
Initial approach: Letter
Copies of proposal: 1
Deadline(s): None
Board meeting date(s): Usually weekly and as required
Final notification: 30 days
Write: David P. Goodwin, Trustee
Trustees: David P. Goodwin, Mark Northridge, Theodore Wadleigh.
Number of staff: 1
Employer Identification Number: 020235690

3745
Alexander Eastman Foundation
c/o New Hampshire Charitable Fund
One South St., P.O. Box 1335
Concord 03302-1335 (603) 225-6641

Established in 1983 in NH.
Foundation type: Independent
Financial data (yr. ended 09/30/89): Assets, $4,546,669 (M); expenditures, $177,232, including $125,806 for 13 grants (high: $30,000; low: $2,425; average: $2,000-$10,000).
Purpose and activities: Awards grants to improve the quality and availability of health care and to promote good health and well-being for residents of the greater Derry, NH, area; giving also includes scholarship assistance for area residents working in the health care field.
Types of support: Employee-related scholarships, conferences and seminars, consulting services, operating budgets, technical assistance.
Limitations: Giving primarily in Derry, Londonderry, Windham, Chester, Hampstead, and Sandown, NH.
Publications: Informational brochure (including application guidelines).
Application information: Application form not required.
Initial approach: Letter or telephone
Copies of proposal: 1
Deadline(s): Feb. 1, May 1, Aug. 1, and Nov. 1
Board meeting date(s): Mar., June, Sept., and Dec.
Write: Deborah Cowan, Prog. Dir.
Trustees: Giacomo Agati, Roger R. Beliveau, Craig Bulkley, Richard Buckley, Clark E. Campbell, Rose Colby, Janet Conroy, Margaret Dekedon, James Gratton, John A. Korbey, Antonia Kropp, Frank Lukosius, James Reinhart.
Number of staff: 1 full-time professional; 1 part-time professional; 1 full-time support.
Employer Identification Number: 020222124

3746
Foundation for Seacoast Health
P.O. Box 4606
Portsmouth 03801 (603) 433-4001

Incorporated in 1984 in NH as the Portsmouth Hospital Foundation; name changed in 1986 to Foundation for Seacoast Health.
Foundation type: Independent
Financial data (yr. ended 12/31/89): Assets, $15,799,061 (L); gifts received, $19,161; expenditures, $843,541, including $634,808 for 39 grants (high: $125,000; low: $500) and $93,811 for 32 grants to individuals (high: $5,000; low: $1,000).
Purpose and activities: To support, develop, and promote health care in five areas: infants/children; adolescents; the elderly; through the discretionary fund for research and development, and health education and information; and through scholarships for local students pursuing health-related fields of study.
Types of support: Student aid, matching funds, seed money, special projects, technical assistance.
Limitations: Giving limited to Portsmouth, Rye, New Castle, Greenland, Newington, and North Hampton, NH; and Kittery, Eliot, and York, ME. No grants to individuals (except through the foundation scholarship program), or for operating expenses, deficit financing, or travels.
Publications: Annual report (including application guidelines), newsletter, application guidelines, occasional report.
Application information: Application form not required.
Initial approach: Letter, not more than 2 pages
Deadline(s): Feb. 15 for scholarships; last day of month for discretionary fund; Mar. 1 for infant/child health; June 1 for adolescent health; Sept. 1 for elderly health; and Dec. 1 for medical financial assistance
Board meeting date(s): 1st Tuesday of Mar., May, Aug., and Nov.; annual meeting, 3rd Tuesday in Apr.
Final notification: Apr. for scholarships; 1 month for discretionary funds; May for infant/child health; Aug. for adolescent health; Nov. for elderly health; Mar. for medical financial assistance
Officers and Trustees: Rodney G. Brock, Pres.; Robert A. Allard, V.P.; John H. Rodgers, Treas.; Ferris G. Bavicchi, Marie Downing, Eileen D. Foley, Thomas M. Keane, Terry L. Morton, C. Peter Rasmussen, G. Warren Wilder.
Number of staff: 1 full-time professional; 1 full-time support.
Employer Identification Number: 020386319

3747
Walter Henry Freygang Foundation
P.O. Box 768
Wolfeboro 03894 (603) 569-3025

Incorporated in 1949 in NJ.
Donor(s): Walter Henry Freygang,† Marie A. Freygang,† and others.
Foundation type: Independent
Financial data (yr. ended 8/31/89): Assets, $5,069,858 (M); expenditures, $238,861, including $213,958 for 46 grants (high: $22,000; low: $418).
Purpose and activities: Grants primarily for higher education, medical research, and hospitals; some support also for social services.
Limitations: No grants to individuals.
Application information: Contributions are made once a year after trustees' meeting; trustees prefer charities previously funded; hence applications are not encouraged. Application form not required.
Initial approach: Letter
Deadline(s): None
Board meeting date(s): Oct.
Write: Gustav G. Freygang, Jr., Pres.
Officers: Gustav G. Freygang, Jr., Pres. and Treas.; Dorothea F. Drennan, V.P.; Dale G. Freygang,* Secy.
Trustees:* Joseph A. Drennan, David B. Freygang, Katherine A. Freygang, W. Nicholas Freygang.
Number of staff: None.
Employer Identification Number: 226027952

3748
The Fuller Foundation, Inc.
Box 461
Rye Beach 03871 (603) 964-6998

Incorporated in 1936 in MA.
Donor(s): Alvan T. Fuller, Sr.†
Foundation type: Independent
Financial data (yr. ended 12/31/88): Assets, $8,050,884 (M); expenditures, $487,746, including $379,756 for 142 grants (high: $103,900; low: $40; average: $1,000-$3,500).
Purpose and activities: Giving to medical research, education, and drug abuse programs.
Types of support: Operating budgets, continuing support, annual campaigns, matching funds, special projects, research.
Limitations: Giving primarily in Boston, MA, and the immediate seacoast area of NH. No

grants to individuals, or for seed money, publications, or conferences; no loans.
Publications: Application guidelines.
Application information: Application form not required.
Initial approach: Proposal
Copies of proposal: 1
Deadline(s): Mar. 15, July 15, and Dec. 15
Board meeting date(s): Feb., May, and Sept.
Final notification: 1 to 6 months
Write: John T. Bottomley, Exec. Dir.
Officers and Trustees:* Peter Fuller,* Pres.; Lydia Fuller Bottomley,* Treas.; John T. Bottomley,* Exec. Dir.; Miranda Fuller Bocko, Stephen D. Bottomley, Ann Fuller Donovan, Peter D. Fuller, Jr., James D. Henderson, Hope Halsey Swasey, Samuel S. Talbot, Melinda F. Van den Heuvel.
Number of staff: 1 full-time professional; 1 full-time support.
Employer Identification Number: 042241130

3749
The Greenspan Foundation ¤
c/o Devine, Millimet, Stahl & Branch Prof. Assoc.
111 Amherst St.
Manchester 03101

Incorporated in 1962 in NH.
Foundation type: Independent
Financial data (yr. ended 5/31/89): Assets, $1,786,694 (M); expenditures, $70,355, including $65,495 for grants.
Purpose and activities: Support primarily for Jewish organizations; grants also for higher education.
Limitations: Giving primarily in NH.
Officers: Saul Greenspan, Pres.; Ethel Greenspan, V.P.
Employer Identification Number: 026008379

3750
Grimshaw-Gudewicz Memorial Charitable Trust ¤ ☆
59 Pine St.
Peterborough 03458

Donor(s): George E. Grimshaw.
Foundation type: Independent
Financial data (yr. ended 4/30/89): Assets, $179,208 (M); gifts received, $50,084; expenditures, $138,507, including $138,115 for 40 grants (high: $100,000; low: $25).
Purpose and activities: Giving primarily for cultural programs, including a historical society and performing arts groups; support also for health and medical research.
Limitations: Giving primarily in MA and NH. No grants to individuals.
Application information: Contributes only to pre-selected organizations. Applications not accepted.
Trustees: Benjamin M. Gottlieb, George E. Grimshaw.
Employer Identification Number: 222533951

3751
Hubbard Farms Charitable Foundation ¤
P.O. Box 505
Walpole 03608 (603) 756-3311

Donor(s): Hubbard Farms, Inc.
Foundation type: Independent
Financial data (yr. ended 12/31/88): Assets, $1,025,388 (M); gifts received, $50,000; expenditures, $107,750, including $86,800 for grants.
Purpose and activities: Support for education, including scholarships, youth agencies, and social services.
Types of support: Scholarship funds.
Application information:
Initial approach: Letter
Deadline(s): Apr. 1 and Oct. 1
Write: Jane F. Kelly, Clerk
Officers and Trustees:* Carl R. Weston,* Chair.; Richard I. Stark,* Vice-Chair.; Paul T. Ledell,* Treas.; Jane F. Kelly,* Clerk; J.B. Barnes, Dr. Ira F. Carter.
Employer Identification Number: 026015114

3752
Samuel P. Hunt Foundation
c/o First NH Investment Services Corp.
P.O. Box 267
Manchester 03105 (603) 668-5000

Trust established in 1951 in NH.
Donor(s): Samuel P. Hunt.†
Foundation type: Independent
Financial data (yr. ended 09/30/89): Assets, $6,948,818 (M); expenditures, $166,304, including $144,310 for 19 grants (high: $25,000; low: $1,000).
Purpose and activities: Giving primarily for education, including higher education, the arts, and programs for the aged.
Types of support: Continuing support, annual campaigns, seed money, emergency funds, building funds, equipment, land acquisition, publications, conferences and seminars, matching funds, special projects, capital campaigns, endowment funds, general purposes, renovation projects, research.
Limitations: Giving limited to NH. No grants to individuals, or for operating budgets, scholarships, or fellowships; no loans.
Publications: Program policy statement, application guidelines.
Application information: Application form not required.
Initial approach: Letter or proposal
Copies of proposal: 3
Deadline(s): Mar. 1 and Sept. 1
Board meeting date(s): Mar. and Sept.
Final notification: 2 weeks after meeting
Write: Therese A. Benoit, V.P., First NH Investment Services Corp.
Trustee: First NH Bank, N.A.
Number of staff: None.
Employer Identification Number: 026004471

3753
Institute of Current World Affairs, Inc.
(also known as The Crane-Rogers Foundation)
Four West Wheelock St.
Hanover 03755 (603) 643-5548

Incorporated in 1925 in NY.
Donor(s): Charles R. Crane, and family.
Foundation type: Operating
Financial data (yr. ended 02/28/89): Assets, $1,847,867 (M); gifts received, $324,717; expenditures, $431,035, including $148,675 for 9 grants to individuals (high: $35,761; low: $1,481) and $39,092 for 2 foundation-administered programs.
Purpose and activities: A private operating foundation; provides full support for a limited number of long-term fellowships to persons of exceptional ability to enable them to work in and write about foreign areas of significance to the U.S.
Types of support: Fellowships.
Limitations: Giving limited to fellowships conducted outside the U.S. No support for formal education or research projects.
Publications: Informational brochure, application guidelines.
Application information: Write for brochure listing current areas of interest. Application form not required.
Initial approach: Letter
Board meeting date(s): June and Dec.
Write: Peter Bird Martin, Exec. Dir.
Officers and Trustees:* John Spencer,* Chair.; Geraldine Kunstadter,* Vice-Chair.; Samuel Levy,* Secy.; Edmond H. Sutton,* Treas.; Joseph Battat, Kimberley Conroy, Thomas Crane, Gary Hartshorn, Peter Bird Martin, Richard Morse, Paul Rahe, Albert Ravenholt, Roger Reynolds, Warren Unna, Woodward Wickham.
Number of staff: 1 part-time professional; 1 full-time support.
Employer Identification Number: 131621044

3754
Oleonda Jameson Trust ¤
One Eagle Sq.
P.O. Box 709
Concord 03302-0709 (603) 224-2381

Established in 1977 in NH.
Foundation type: Independent
Financial data (yr. ended 12/31/88): Assets, $2,591,669 (M); expenditures, $143,433, including $128,880 for 38 grants (high: $16,000; low: $500).
Purpose and activities: Giving primarily for higher education, community funds, social service agencies, hospitals, and cultural programs.
Limitations: Giving limited to NH, with emphasis in Concord. No grants for capital improvements, construction, or endowment funds.
Application information:
Initial approach: Letter
Deadline(s): None
Write: Malcolm McLane, Trustee
Trustees: Malcolm McLane, Dudley W. Orr, Robert H. Reno.
Employer Identification Number: 026048930

3755
Kingsbury Fund ¤
c/o Kingsbury Machine Tool Corp.
80 Laurel St.
Keene 03431 (603) 352-5212

Trust established in 1952 in NH.

Donor(s): Kingsbury Machine Tool Corp., Kingsbury Manufacturing Co., Fitchburg Foundry, Inc.
Foundation type: Company-sponsored
Financial data (yr. ended 12/31/88): Assets, $2,348,037 (M); expenditures, $180,365, including $150,706 for 167 grants (high: $20,000; low: $25; average: $1,000) and $5,059 for 29 employee matching gifts.
Purpose and activities: Giving for higher education, including scholarships for children of employees; support also for youth agencies, and social services.
Types of support: Special projects, employee-related scholarships, employee matching gifts, capital campaigns, equipment, matching funds, seed money.
Limitations: Giving limited to Keene, Chesire County, and the Monadnock region of NH.
Application information: Application form for scholarships only.
Deadline(s): Mar. 30 for scholarships
Write: James E. O'Neil, Jr., Exec. Trustee
Trustees: James E. O'Neil, Jr., Exec. Trustee; John S. Cookson, Priscilla K. Frechette, Charles J. Hanrahan, James L. Koontz.
Employer Identification Number: 026004465

3756
Koehring Foundation ⌑ ☆
c/o AMCA International Corp.
Dartmouth National Bank Bldg.
Hanover 03755

Incorporated in 1952 in WI.
Donor(s): Koehring Co.
Foundation type: Company-sponsored
Financial data (yr. ended 12/31/87): Assets, $249,113 (M); expenditures, $219,020, including $214,040 for grants.
Purpose and activities: Grants primarily for community funds, hospitals, youth agencies, and higher education, including employee matching gifts.
Types of support: Employee matching gifts.
Limitations: Giving primarily in in areas of company operations.
Application information:
Write: Don Reed, Pres.
Officers and Directors:* Donald E. Reed,* Pres.; James R. Moore,* V.P.; Gary Noel, V.P.; Peter Stange,* Secy.; Daniel Jaszi, Treas.
Employer Identification Number: 396044275

3757
Agnes M. Lindsay Trust ▼ ⌑
95 Market St.
Manchester 03101 (603) 669-4140

Trust established in 1938 in NH.
Donor(s): Agnes M. Lindsay.†
Foundation type: Independent
Financial data (yr. ended 12/31/88): Assets, $22,020,533 (M); expenditures, $1,066,449, including $863,771 for 191 grants (high: $15,000; low: $500; average: $1,000-$10,000).
Purpose and activities: Giving for child welfare and the education of poor and deserving students from rural areas; support largely for higher education, health agencies, agencies for the handicapped, and welfare institutions.
Types of support: Scholarship funds, building funds, equipment, special projects, operating budgets, deficit financing, matching funds, general purposes.
Limitations: Giving limited to ME, MA, NH, and VT. No grants to individuals.
Application information:
Initial approach: Proposal
Deadline(s): None
Board meeting date(s): Monthly
Final notification: 2 months
Write: Robert L. Chiesa, Trustee
Trustees: Robert L. Chiesa, Ernest E. Dion, Franklin D. Jerome.
Number of staff: None.
Employer Identification Number: 026004971

3758
Henry C. Lord Scholarship Fund Trust ⌑
c/o Amoskeag Bank
875 Elm St.
Manchester 03105 (603) 647-3200

Trust established in 1978 in NH.
Donor(s): Henry C. Lord.†
Foundation type: Independent
Financial data (yr. ended 06/30/89): Assets, $7,484,360 (M); expenditures, $385,812, including $60,000 for 1 grant and $233,878 for 138 grants to individuals (high: $3,000; low: $250).
Purpose and activities: Awards scholarships for needy local residents.
Types of support: Student aid.
Limitations: Giving limited to residents of Peterborough, NH, and contiguous towns. No grants for general support, capital or endowment funds, or matching gifts; no loans.
Application information: Application form required.
Initial approach: Letter
Deadline(s): Apr. 30 for first-time applicants and June 15 each year thereafter
Write: Suzette Fontaine Collins, Trust Admin.
Trustee: Amoskeag Bank.
Employer Identification Number: 026051741

3759
Mascoma Savings Bank Foundation ☆
c/o Mascoma Savings Bank
67 North Park St.
Lebanon 03766-1317 (603) 448-3650
Application address: P.O. Box 435, Lebanon, NH 03766-0435

Established in 1988 in NH.
Donor(s): Mascoma Savings Bank.
Foundation type: Company-sponsored
Financial data (yr. ended 12/31/89): Assets, $1,102,943 (M); expenditures, $52,648, including $49,560 for 24 grants (high: $15,000; low: $300).
Purpose and activities: Grants for a community land trust and a medical center; support also for programs for the aged and homeless, hospices, community development, adult education, and animal welfare.
Types of support: Annual campaigns, building funds, continuing support, endowment funds, equipment, general purposes, land acquisition, renovation projects, seed money, special projects.
Limitations: Giving primarily in Lebanon, West Lebanon, Enfield, Canaan, Hanover, Meriden, Plainfield, and Lyme, NH. No grants to individuals.
Publications: Grants list, application guidelines.
Application information:
Initial approach: Letter (no telephone calls)
Copies of proposal: 1
Deadline(s): Apr. 1 and Oct. 1
Board meeting date(s): Varies
Final notification: 10 weeks
Write: Jean Kennedy, Chair.
Officers and Trustees:* Jean Kennedy,* Chair.; Reuben D. Cole,* Secy.; Clark Griffiths, Richard L. Patch.
Number of staff: None.
Employer Identification Number: 222816632

3760
McIninch Foundation ⌑ ☆
One Hampshire Plaza
Manchester 03101

Established in 1961.
Donor(s): Ralph McIninch.
Foundation type: Independent
Financial data (yr. ended 12/31/88): Assets, $1,604,014 (M); expenditures, $22,017, including $20,761 for 13 grants (high: $10,000; low: $50).
Purpose and activities: Giving primarily for education including higher education; support also for conservation and a Protestant church.
Types of support: Operating budgets.
Limitations: Giving primarily in NH. No grants to individuals.
Application information: Contributes only to pre-selected organizations. Applications not accepted.
Officer and Trustees: Ralph McIninch, Pres. and Treas.; Douglas McIninch, James A. Shanahan, Jr.
Employer Identification Number: 026006053

3761
Nash Foundation, Inc. ⌑ ☆
40 Temple St.
Nashua 03060-3484

Incorporated in 1986 in NH.
Foundation type: Independent
Financial data (yr. ended 6/30/88): Assets, $1,972,563 (M); expenditures, $38,865, including $28,114 for 24 grants (high: $5,000; low: $50).
Purpose and activities: Support primarily for suicide prevention, health services, youth clubs, local police and fire departments, and a private college.
Limitations: Giving primarily in NH, with emphasis on Nashua. No grants to individuals.
Application information:
Initial approach: Letter
Deadline(s): None
Write: Debra A. Nash, Pres.
Officers and Directors: Debra A. Nash, Pres. and Treas.; David E. Tulley, Secy.; Q. Peter Nash.
Employer Identification Number: 020406835

3762
The New Hampshire Charitable Fund ▼
One South St.
P.O. Box 1335
Concord 03302-1335 (603) 225-6641

Incorporated in 1962 in NH.
Foundation type: Community
Financial data (yr. ended 12/31/89): Assets, $49,504,886 (M); gifts received, $7,128,336; expenditures, $4,388,780, including $2,413,729 for 634 grants (high: $50,000; low: $100; average: $1,000-$5,000), $697,545 for 599 grants to individuals (high: $3,000; low: $500; average: $500-$1,000), $296,200 for loans to organizations and $271,413 for 232 loans to individuals.
Purpose and activities: Giving for charitable and educational purposes including the arts, humanities, the environment and conservation, health, and social and community services; grants primarily to inaugurate new programs and strengthen existing charitable organizations, with emphasis on programs rather than capital needs; support also for college scholarships.
Types of support: Seed money, loans, student aid, scholarship funds, general purposes, special projects, student loans, consulting services, technical assistance.
Limitations: Giving limited to NH. No grants to individuals (except for student aid); generally no grants for building funds, endowments, operating support, or deficit financing.
Publications: Annual report, program policy statement, informational brochure (including application guidelines).
Application information: Application form not required.
Initial approach: Telephone or letter
Copies of proposal: 1
Deadline(s): Feb. 1, May 1, Aug. 1, and Nov. 1; May 2 for student aid applicants for upcoming school year
Board meeting date(s): Mar., June, Sept., and Dec.
Final notification: 4 to 6 weeks
Write: Deborah Cowan, Assoc. Dir.
Officers: Hollis E. Harrington, Jr.,* Chair.; Lewis Feldstein,* Pres.; Linda McGoldrick,* Secy.; Martin L. Gross,* Treas.
Directors:* Ferris G. Bavicchi, Kendra Stearns O'Donnell, Walter Peterson, John F. Weeks, Jr., Kimon S. Zachos.
Number of staff: 6 full-time professional; 1 part-time professional; 4 full-time support; 1 part-time support.
Employer Identification Number: 026005625

3763
Ellis L. Phillips Foundation
13 Dartmouth College Hwy.
Lyme 03768 (603) 795-2790

Incorporated in 1930 in NY.
Donor(s): Ellis L. Phillips.†
Foundation type: Independent
Financial data (yr. ended 06/30/89): Assets, $5,121,557 (M); expenditures, $323,065, including $255,550 for 38 grants (high: $50,000; low: $600; average: $1,000-$10,000).
Purpose and activities: Grants to organizations emerging on the regional or national scene seeking to develop programs and attract wider suppport. Grants made for education on public issues, religion, education, the arts, preservation/conservation, social services and health care.
Types of support: Annual campaigns, conferences and seminars, continuing support, endowment funds, seed money.
Limitations: Giving primarily in northern New England. No support for medical research. No grants to individuals, or for scholarships, fellowships, or matching gifts; no loans.
Publications: Annual report (including application guidelines).
Application information: Application form not required.
Initial approach: Letter of 1 to 3 pages
Copies of proposal: 1
Board meeting date(s): Oct., Feb., and May
Write: Patricia A. Cate, Exec. Dir.
Officers and Directors:* Ellis L. Phillips, Jr.,* Pres.; Ellis L. Phillips III,* V.P.; Elise Phillips Watts,* Secy.; George C. Thompson,* Treas.; Patricia A. Cate,* Exec. Dir.; David L. Grumman, George E. McCully, John W. Oelsner, Walter C. Paine, Marion G. Phillips.
Number of staff: 1 part-time professional.
Employer Identification Number: 135677691

3764
Putnam Foundation ⌑
150 Congress St.
Keene 03431 (603) 352-1130
Additional address: P.O. Box 323, Keene, NH 03431

Trust established in 1952 in NH.
Donor(s): David F. Putnam.
Foundation type: Independent
Financial data (yr. ended 10/31/88): Assets, $3,879,884 (M); expenditures, $322,898, including $283,858 for 44 grants (high: $48,000; low: $250; average: $5,000).
Purpose and activities: Emphasis on civic affairs, cultural programs, historic preservation, ecological maintenance, youth agencies, education, and conservation.
Limitations: Giving limited to NH.
Application information:
Initial approach: Letter
Deadline(s): None
Write: David F. Putnam, Trustee
Officer: Thomas P. Putnam, Secy.
Trustees: David F. Putnam, James A. Putnam, Rosamund P. Putnam.
Employer Identification Number: 026011388

3765
Lou and Lutza Smith Charitable Foundation
c/o New Hampshire Charitable Fund
One South St., P.O. Box 1335
Concord 03302-1335 (603) 225-6641

Established in 1971 in NH.
Donor(s): Lutza Smith,† Louis Smith Marital Trust.
Foundation type: Independent
Financial data (yr. ended 12/31/88): Assets, $3,746,631 (M); expenditures, $484,149, including $431,351 for 28 grants (high: $100,000; low: $3,000; average: $5,000-$10,000).
Purpose and activities: Giving for education, health, social services, and child welfare, as well as programs related to the conduct and operation of horse racing.
Types of support: Building funds, capital campaigns, special projects.
Limitations: Giving primarily in NH, and to organizations providing services to NH residents. No support for religious organizations, except for programs of general social service. No grants to individuals, or for operating expenses for extended periods.
Publications: Informational brochure (including application guidelines).
Application information: Application form not required.
Initial approach: Letter or telephone
Copies of proposal: 1
Deadline(s): Feb. 1, May 1, Aug. 1, Nov. 1
Board meeting date(s): Mar., June, Sept., and Dec.
Write: Deborah Cowan, Prog. Dir.
Trustees: Charles A. DeGrandpre, Kenneth F. Graf, Louise K. Newman.
Number of staff: 1 full-time professional; 1 part-time professional; 1 full-time support.
Employer Identification Number: 237162940

3766
Marion C. Smyth Trust
875 Elm St., Rm. 615
Manchester 03101 (603) 623-3420

Established in 1946 in NH.
Donor(s): Marion C. Smyth.†
Foundation type: Independent
Financial data (yr. ended 12/31/89): Assets, $4,333,830 (M); qualifying distributions, $180,928, including $180,928 for 51 grants (high: $11,500; low: $400).
Purpose and activities: To establish and maintain the Frederick Smyth Institute of music; giving also for musical education, including scholarships in the city of Manchester (a) for the cultural benefit of the citizens of Manchester and the state of New Hampshire and (b) to aid and encourage deserving youth of Manchester and adjacent towns to increase their knowledge of the field of music.
Types of support: Continuing support, equipment, scholarship funds.
Limitations: Giving limited to NH, primarily Manchester.
Application information: Application form required for student scholarships.
Initial approach: Letter
Copies of proposal: 1
Board meeting date(s): As required
Write: John H. Giffin, Jr., Chair.
Officer and Trustees:* John H. Giffin, Jr.,* Chair.; Alan C. Areson, T. William Bigelow.
Number of staff: 1 part-time support.
Employer Identification Number: 026005793

3767
Jason C. Somerville Trust ⌑
P.O. Box 352
Bethlehem 03574-0352

Established in 1972 in NH.
Foundation type: Independent
Financial data (yr. ended 12/31/88): Assets, $1,274,226 (M); expenditures, $105,532,

including $92,100 for 54 grants to individuals (high: $3,700; low: $700).
Purpose and activities: Support for scholarships to individuals residing in Bethlehem, NH.
Types of support: Student aid.
Limitations: Giving primarily in Bethlehem, NH.
Trustees: John Stevenson, Nancy Stevenson.
Employer Identification Number: 026033716

3768
Standex International Foundation ⌑
Six Manor Pkwy.
Salem 03079

Established in 1954 in NH.
Foundation type: Company-sponsored
Financial data (yr. ended 12/31/88): Assets, $53,492 (M); gifts received, $150,000; expenditures, $103,098, including $103,098 for grants (high: $10,500).
Purpose and activities: Support primarily for community funds, hospitals and health services, and education; grants also through a matching gift program.
Types of support: Employee matching gifts.
Limitations: Giving primarily in Salem, NH.
Application information: Application form required.
Deadline(s): None
Write: Jack Wall, V.P. for Industrial Rel., Standex Intl. Corp.
Officers and Trustees:* Thomas L. King,* Pres. and Treas.; Thomas DeWitt,* V.P. and Secy.; Lindsay M. Sedwick,* Treas.
Employer Identification Number: 046173127

3769
The Tamposi Foundation, Inc. ☆
402 Amherst St.
Nashua 03063 (603) 883-2000

Established in 1986.
Foundation type: Independent
Financial data (yr. ended 06/30/89): Assets, $1,966,238 (M); expenditures, $77,630, including $72,996 for 48 grants (high: $20,000; low: $40).
Purpose and activities: Giving primarily for youth organizations and higher and other education; support also for hospitals and social services.
Types of support: General purposes, equipment.
Limitations: Giving primarily in Manchester and Nashua, NH.
Application information:
Initial approach: Letter
Deadline(s): None
Write: Samuel A. Tamposi, Jr., Pres.
Officers and Directors:* Samuel A. Tamposi, Jr.,* Pres.; Celina A. Tamposi,* V.P.; Elizabeth M. Tamposi,* V.P.; David E. Tully,* Secy.; Stephen A. Tamposi,* Treas.
Employer Identification Number: 020406826

3770
Edward Wagner and George Hosser Scholarship Fund Trust ⌑
c/o Amoskeag Bank
875 Elm St.
Manchester 03105 (603) 647-3614

Trust established in 1964 in NH.
Donor(s): Ottilie Wagner Hosser.†
Foundation type: Independent
Financial data (yr. ended 6/30/89): Assets, $3,968,184 (M); expenditures, $190,127, including $142,466 for 93 grants to individuals (high: $2,000; low: $500).
Purpose and activities: Scholarship grants for college or professional education to worthy boys and young men.
Types of support: Student aid.
Limitations: Giving limited to Manchester, NH, residents.
Application information: Application form required.
Deadline(s): Apr. 30
Write: Suzette Fontaine Collins, Trust Admin., Amoskeag Bank
Trustee: Amoskeag Bank.
Employer Identification Number: 026005491

NEW JERSEY

3771
A-P-A Transport Educational Foundation ⌑ ☆
2100 88th St.
North Bergen 07047-4773 (201) 869-6600

Established in 1983 in NJ.
Donor(s): A-P-A Transport Corp.
Foundation type: Independent
Financial data (yr. ended 12/31/87): Assets, $574,430 (M); gifts received, $100,000; expenditures, $146,534, including $122,500 for 87 grants.
Purpose and activities: Awards scholarships or loans to children of A-P-A Transport Corp. employees and certain affiliates.
Types of support: Employee-related scholarships, student loans.
Application information: Application form required.
Initial approach: Letter
Write: Percy E. Clifton, Admin.
Officers: Arthur E. Imperatore, Chair.; George E. Imperatore, V.P.; Armand Pohan, V.P.; George Bauman, Admin.; Percy E. Clifton, Admin.; Burton C. Trebour, Admin.
Scholarship Selection Committee: William Oates, Elmer Pader, M.D., Frank Raimondo, Rosanne L. Wille, Rev. Victor R. Yanitelli.
Employer Identification Number: 222423866

3772
Abrams Foundation ⌑
P.O. Box 6458
Lawrenceville 08648-0458

Established about 1953 in NJ.
Foundation type: Independent
Financial data (yr. ended 11/30/88): Assets, $1,885,364 (M); expenditures, $107,718, including $84,575 for 46 grants (high: $26,500; low: $50).
Purpose and activities: Support for Jewish religious and educational organizations.
Limitations: Giving primarily in NJ.
Application information: Contributes only to pre-selected organizations. Applications not accepted.
Trustees: J. Melvin Kushner, Maynard Weber.
Employer Identification Number: 216016470

3773
Abramson-Clayman Foundation, Inc. ⌑ ☆
c/o Hannoch Weisman
Four Becker Farm Rd.
Roseland 07068-1734

Incorporated in 1984 in NJ.
Donor(s): Edith Abramson Clayman, Melvin Clayman.
Foundation type: Independent
Financial data (yr. ended 4/30/89): Assets, $1,709,740 (M); gifts received, $200,000; expenditures, $92,396, including $82,582 for 44 grants (high: $22,000; low: $25).
Purpose and activities: Giving for Jewish welfare and temple support.
Limitations: No grants to individuals.
Application information:
Initial approach: Letter
Deadline(s): Jan. 31
Final notification: Apr. 30
Write: Dr. Melvin Clayman, V.P., and Mrs. Melvin Clayman, Pres.
Officers and Trustees: Edith Abramson Clayman, Pres. and Treas.; Melvin Clayman, V.P. and Secy.; Andrew Abramson, Richard Abramson, Caryn Clayman.
Employer Identification Number: 222641108

3774
Allied Educational Foundation Fund B ⌑
467 Sylvan Ave.
Englewood Cliffs 07632 (201) 569-8180
Additional tel.: (212) 695-7791

Established about 1981.
Foundation type: Independent
Financial data (yr. ended 12/31/88): Assets, $7,426,102 (M); gifts received, $268,259; expenditures, $770,771, including $66,362 for 60 grants to individuals (high: $2,000; low: $1,000).
Purpose and activities: Scholarship grants to graduating high school seniors, limited to families of Union members.
Types of support: Employee-related scholarships.
Application information:
Initial approach: Letter
Deadline(s): Mar. 15
Write: Gerald Herskowitz, Trustee
Trustees: Morris Aarons, Gerald Herskowitz, Hyman Platnick, Martin Rackmore.
Employer Identification Number: 136202432

3775
Allied-Signal Foundation ▼
(Formerly Allied Corporation Foundation)
Columbia Rd. and Park Ave.
P.O. Box 2245R
Morristown 07962 (201) 455-5876

Incorporated in 1963 in NY; in 1982 absorbed Bunker Ramo Foundation; in 1984 absorbed Bendix Foundation; merged and incorporated in 1982 in NJ as Allied Corporation Foundation; in 1987 name changed to Allied-Signal Foundation.
Donor(s): Allied-Signal, Inc.
Foundation type: Company-sponsored
Financial data (yr. ended 12/31/88): Assets, $111,748 (M); gifts received, $9,085,956; expenditures, $8,676,254, including $7,363,725 for 600 grants (high: $500,000; low: $1,000; average: $2,000-$15,000) and $1,312,529 for 7,007 employee matching gifts.
Purpose and activities: Support primarily for higher education, including fellowship and scholarship programs, and community funds; grants also for health, aging, human services, youth agencies, urban affairs, and cultural programs.
Types of support: Operating budgets, continuing support, annual campaigns, seed money, building funds, equipment, employee matching gifts, fellowships, employee-related scholarships, scholarship funds, renovation projects.
Limitations: Giving primarily in areas of company operations. No support for church-related programs. No grants to individuals, or for endowment funds; no loans.
Application information: Application form not required.
Initial approach: Letter
Copies of proposal: 1
Deadline(s): Submit proposal preferably in July and Aug.; no set deadline
Board meeting date(s): Feb.
Final notification: Only if approved
Write: Alan S. Painter, V.P. and Exec. Dir.
Officers: David G. Powell,* Pres.; Alan S. Painter, V.P. and Exec. Dir.; Brian D. Forrow,* V.P.; Heather M. Mullett, Secy.; G. Peter D'Aloria, Treas.
Directors:* Edward L. Hennessy, Jr., Chair.; John W. Barter, Alan Belzer, John L. Day, Roy H. Ekrom, Mary L. Good, Robert L. Kirk, Edwin M. Halkyard, Fred M. Poses.
Number of staff: None.
Employer Identification Number: 222416651

3776
Anderson Foundation ⌑
31 Roebling Rd.
Bernardsville 07924

Established in 1981 in NJ.
Donor(s): Thomas Anderson, Bear Stearns & Co.
Foundation type: Independent
Financial data (yr. ended 11/30/88): Assets, $4,759,228 (M); gifts received, $1,231,250; expenditures, $152,682, including $120,000 for 3 grants (high: $50,000; low: $20,000).
Purpose and activities: Grants primarily for church support and a right to life organization.
Application information: Contributes only to pre-selected organizations. Applications not accepted.
Trustee: Thomas Anderson.
Employer Identification Number: 222393971

3777
Armco Foundation
300 Interpace Pkwy.
Parsippany 07054-0324 (201) 316-5274

Incorporated in 1951 in OH.
Donor(s): Armco, Inc.
Foundation type: Company-sponsored
Financial data (yr. ended 12/31/89): Assets, $8,872,152 (M); expenditures, $733,472, including $576,957 for 112 grants (high: $35,000; low: $400; average: $100-$5,000) and $156,515 for 1,397 employee matching gifts.
Purpose and activities: Grants for health and hospitals, welfare, and higher education, including a scholarship program for the children of active company employees administered by the College Scholarship Service; support also for public affairs and a matching gift program for higher educational and cultural institutions.
Types of support: Continuing support, seed money, equipment, matching funds, employee-related scholarships, employee matching gifts, special projects, capital campaigns.
Limitations: Giving primarily in areas of company operations. No support for religious organizations. No grants to individuals (except for employee-related scholarships), or for operating budgets, deficit financing, land acquisition, endowment funds, fellowships, demonstration projects, or publications; no loans.
Application information: Funds presently committed. Applications not accepted.
Board meeting date(s): Mar. and Dec.
Write: Ms. Loyce A. Martin, Fdn. Admin.
Officers: Robert E. Boni,* Pres.; John M. Bilich, Exec. V.P.; Robert W. Kent, V.P. and Secy.; James L. Bertsch, Treas.
Trustees:* Brage Golding, Chair.; Wallace B. Askins, Frederick B. Dent, Harry Holiday, Jr., John W. Ladish, Robert L. Purdum.
Number of staff: 1 full-time professional; 1 part-time support.
Employer Identification Number: 316026565

3778
The Armour Family Foundation ⌑
c/o Schotz Simon Miller & Co.
One Mack Centre Dr.
Paramus 07652-3905

Established in 1981.
Donor(s): George and Frances Armour Foundation, Inc.
Foundation type: Independent
Financial data (yr. ended 3/31/88): Assets, $1,406,275 (M); expenditures, $133,037.
Purpose and activities: Emphasis on Jewish sociological areas, medical research and hospitals, cultural programs and higher education; some support also for social service agencies.
Application information: Contributes only to pre-selected organizations.
Officers and Directors: Robert N. Armour, Pres.; Joan Armour, Secy.; David Armour, Frederick Sudekum.
Number of staff: 1 part-time professional.
Employer Identification Number: 510257055

3779
The Atlantic Foundation ▼
16 Farber Rd.
Princeton 08540 (609) 799-8530

Incorporated in 1964 in NJ.
Donor(s): J. Seward Johnson.†
Foundation type: Independent
Financial data (yr. ended 12/31/88): Assets, $90,547,472 (M); expenditures, $4,981,614, including $3,080,000 for 2 grants (high: $3,000,000; low: $80,000).
Purpose and activities: Support for marine science research and education.
Types of support: Research.
Limitations: Giving for marine research off the coast of FL.
Application information: Funds presently committed. Application form not required.
Deadline(s): None
Board meeting date(s): 1st Thurs. in Dec.
Write: Fred W. Nichterlein, Secy.
Officers: J. Seward Johnson, Jr., Chair., Pres., and Treas.; Carl Schafer,* V.P.; Fred W. Nichterlein, Secy.
Trustees and Directors:* Charles H. Bussmann, Garrett M. Heher, James L. Johnson, Marilyn C. Link.
Number of staff: 18
Employer Identification Number: 226054882

3780
Banc Fund ⌑
R.D. 1, White Oak Ln.
Bedminster 07921 (201) 234-2177

Established in 1961 in NJ.
Foundation type: Independent
Financial data (yr. ended 12/31/88): Assets, $1,124,739 (M); expenditures, $60,894, including $53,254 for 58 grants (high: $10,000; low: $25).
Purpose and activities: Giving for education, especially higher education, and youth organizations.
Limitations: No grants to individuals.
Application information:
Initial approach: Proposal
Deadline(s): None
Write: J. Colin Campbell, Trustee
Trustees: Charles E. Campbell, J. Colin Campbell, Mary Ellen Campbell.
Employer Identification Number: 226056517

3781
Elsie E. & Joseph W. Beck Foundation ⌑
c/o John Keegan
1129 Broad St.
Shrewsbury 07701 (201) 389-0330

Established in 1973 in NY.
Donor(s): Elsie Beck.†
Foundation type: Independent
Financial data (yr. ended 12/31/87): Assets, $3,764,858 (M); expenditures, $246,650,

including $200,000 for 23 grants (high: $30,000; low: $1,000).
Purpose and activities: Support primarily for Catholic higher education.
Types of support: Scholarship funds.
Limitations: Giving primarily in NJ. No grants to individuals.
Application information:
Initial approach: Letter
Deadline(s): None
Officers: Frank E. Walsh, Jr., Pres.; Joseph W. Walsh, V.P.; John P. Keegan, Secy.; C. Nelson Winget, Treas.
Employer Identification Number: 237246078

3782
Charles and Els Bendheim Foundation ⌘
One Parker Plaza
Fort Lee 07204

Incorporated in 1947 in NY.
Donor(s): Nannette Bendheim,† and others.
Foundation type: Independent
Financial data (yr. ended 1/31/87): Assets, $294,283 (M); gifts received, $154,496; expenditures, $193,092, including $192,455 for 166 grants (high: $30,000; low: $10).
Purpose and activities: Grants primarily to Jewish-sponsored religious and educational institutions and Jewish welfare funds.
Officers: Charles H. Bendheim, Pres. and Mgr.; Els Bendheim, Mgr.
Employer Identification Number: 136103769

3783
Frank and Lydia Bergen Foundation
c/o First Fidelity Bank
55 Madison Ave.
Morristown 07960 (201) 829-7111

Incorporated in 1983 in NJ.
Donor(s): Charlotte V. Bergen.†
Foundation type: Independent
Financial data (yr. ended 12/31/88): Assets, $5,434,611 (M); expenditures, $378,040, including $298,971 for 36 grants (high: $41,275; low: $1,500).
Purpose and activities: For the benefit of the musical arts; support for educational out-reach activity of performing arts agencies; aid for worthy students of music through institutions; support for the development of music skills; and increased recognition, training, and conducting opportunities for American conductors.
Types of support: Conferences and seminars, consulting services, matching funds, scholarship funds, special projects, continuing support.
Limitations: Giving primarily in the NJ area, except for young American conductor projects of nationwide impact. No grants for annual campaigns, deficit financing, land acquisition, renovation projects; no loans.
Publications: Annual report, informational brochure (including application guidelines), application guidelines.
Application information: Application form not required.
Initial approach: Letter or telephone
Copies of proposal: 1
Deadline(s): 15th of Feb., May, Aug., and Nov.
Board meeting date(s): Apr., July, Oct., and Jan.
Write: Jane Donnelly, Exec. Dir.
Officers and Trustee Committee: A. Daniel D'Ambrosio, Chair.; Peter T. Lillard, Vice-Chair.; Bryant K. Alford, Secy.; Marie Carlone, Treas.; Jane Donnelly, Exec. Dir.
Trustee: First Fidelity Bank.
Number of staff: 1 full-time professional.
Employer Identification Number: 226359304

3784
Sol and Margaret Berger Foundation ⌘
140 Hepburn Rd.
P.O. Box 1222
Clifton 07012 (201) 777-1400

Trust established in 1962 in NY.
Donor(s): Sol Berger.
Foundation type: Independent
Financial data (yr. ended 4/30/88): Assets, $1,511,432 (M); expenditures, $95,130, including $69,867 for 86 grants (high: $30,042; low: $10).
Purpose and activities: Emphasis on medical education, youth agencies, Jewish welfare, and health agencies.
Limitations: Giving primarily in NJ and NY.
Application information:
Initial approach: Letter
Deadline(s): None
Write: Sol Berger, Trustee
Trustees: Sandye Berger Aidner, Margaret Berger, Renee Berger, Sol Berger.
Employer Identification Number: 136118516

3785
Bernstein Development Foundation ⌘ ☆
c/o Raphael Bernstein
25 North Murray Ave.
Ridgewood 07450

Established in 1968.
Donor(s): Raphael Bernstein.
Foundation type: Independent
Financial data (yr. ended 12/31/87): Assets, $1,035,793 (M); gifts received, $80,000; expenditures, $113,348, including $111,020 for 4 grants (high: $55,000; low: $1,000).
Purpose and activities: Support for higher education and the fine and performing arts.
Officers and Trustees: Raphael Bernstein, Pres.; Jane Bernstein, V.P. and Treas.; Robert Anthoine, Secy.; Elizabeth Greene, Jeanette Neal.
Employer Identification Number: 231705459

3786
The Russell Berrie Foundation ⌘
111 Bauer Dr.
Oakland 07436-3192

Established in 1985 in NJ.
Donor(s): Russell Berrie.
Foundation type: Independent
Financial data (yr. ended 10/31/89): Assets, $1,959,463 (M); qualifying distributions, $622,203, including $622,372 for 31 grants (high: $205,864; low: $100).
Purpose and activities: Giving primarily for higher education and Jewish welfare; support also for the arts.
Application information:
Initial approach: Letter
Deadline(s): None
Write: Russell Berrie, Pres.
Officer and Trustees:* Russell Berrie,* Pres.; Leslie Berrie, Myron Rosner, Norman Seiden.
Employer Identification Number: 222620908

3787
Adele & Leonard Block Foundation, Inc. ⌘
257 Cornelison Ave.
Jersey City 07302-3116

Established in 1945 in NJ.
Foundation type: Independent
Financial data (yr. ended 11/30/88): Assets, $8,227 (M); gifts received, $580,000; expenditures, $577,049, including $577,000 for 12 grants (high: $538,933; low: $200).
Purpose and activities: Giving primarily for the arts, higher education, and a school of medicine.
Officers and Directors:* Leonard Block,* Pres.; Thomas Block,* V.P. and Treas.; Adele G. Block,* V.P.; Peggy Danziger,* V.P.; John E. Peters, Secy.
Employer Identification Number: 226026000

3788
The Corella & Bertram Bonner Foundation, Inc.
22 Chambers St., Box 712
Princeton 08542

Established in 1981 in NJ; reactivated in 1989.
Foundation type: Independent
Financial data (yr. ended 06/30/89): Assets, $25,240 (M); gifts received, $350,000; expenditures, $334,484, including $253,037 for 16 grants (high: $50,000; low: $1,000).
Purpose and activities: Support primarily for higher and other education, including educational programs for minorities; Christian religious organizations, including those operating missionary programs, schools, and welfare programs; social services and hunger programs; and hospitals, the handicapped, medical research, and ophthamology.
Types of support: Annual campaigns, general purposes, matching funds, scholarship funds, special projects.
Limitations: Giving limited to domestic programs in the U.S. No grants to individuals.
Publications: Program policy statement, application guidelines.
Application information: Application form required.
Initial approach: Letter (no more than 2 pages)
Copies of proposal: 1
Deadline(s): Jan. 15, May 15, and Oct. 1
Officers and Trustees:* Bertram F. Bonner,* Pres.; Corella A. Bonner,* V.P.
Number of staff: 3 full-time professional; 2 full-time support.
Employer Identification Number: 222316452

3789
Alonzo F. & Jennie W. Bonsal Foundation, Inc. ⌑ ☆
Two Hudson Pl.
Hoboken 07030

Established in 1943.
Foundation type: Independent
Financial data (yr. ended 12/31/88): Assets, $1,095,328 (M); expenditures, $91,581, including $80,500 for 17 grants (high: $31,000; low: $1,000).
Purpose and activities: Giving primarily for a hospital and higher education, including scholarship funds.
Types of support: Scholarship funds.
Limitations: Giving primarily in NJ.
Application information:
Initial approach: Letter
Write: Richard I. Bonsal, Pres.
Officers: Richard I. Bonsal, Pres. and Treas.; Carol Johnson Bald, V.P.; Julia L. Bonsal, V.P.; Margaret B. Soleau, V.P.; Robert C. Mahnken, Secy.
Employer Identification Number: 136089295

3790
The Mary Owen Borden Memorial Foundation
160 Hodge Rd.
Princeton 08540 (609) 924-3637

Incorporated in 1934 in NJ.
Donor(s): Bertram H. Borden,† Victory Memorial Park Foundation.
Foundation type: Independent
Financial data (yr. ended 12/31/88): Assets, $7,529,338 (M); expenditures, $435,525, including $366,158 for 46 grants (high: $27,056; low: $100; average: $7,960).
Purpose and activities: Grants for programs focusing on special needs of youth which include: family planning counselling to teenagers; assistance to unwed, teenage mothers; day care centers for young, disadvantaged parents; assistance to families where instability prevails; assistance to institutions or programs aiding delinquent youth; and innovative or alternative forms of criminal justice for youthful offenders. Support also for human services, the arts, conservation and the environment, nuclear disarmament, and substance abuse. Emphasis on grants for new and innovative projects and preference for support to organizations that are new, or established organizations undertaking new projects.
Types of support: Seed money, matching funds, special projects, general purposes, operating budgets, capital campaigns.
Limitations: Giving primarily in Monmouth and Mercer counties, NJ. No grants to individuals, or for scholarships or fellowships; no loans.
Publications: Annual report (including application guidelines), application guidelines.
Application information: Application form required.
Initial approach: Write for form if request meets foundation guidelines
Copies of proposal: 1
Deadline(s): Jan. 1, Apr. 1, and Sept. 1
Board meeting date(s): Feb., May, and Oct.
Final notification: 2 weeks
Write: John C. Borden, Jr., Exec. Dir.
Officers: Mrs. Q.A. Shaw McKean, Jr.,* Pres.; Mrs. Marvin Broder,* V.P.; Mary L. Miles, Secy.; Joseph Lord, Treas.; John C. Borden, Jr.,* Exec. Dir.
Trustees:* Thomas A. Borden, Rev. Daphne Hawkes, Gordon Litwin, Dorothy Ransom, Stuart A. Young, Jr.
Number of staff: 1 part-time professional; 1 part-time support.
Employer Identification Number: 136137137

3791
Brady Foundation
P.O. Box 351
Gladstone 07934 (201) 234-1900

Incorporated in 1953 in NJ.
Donor(s): Helen M. Cutting,† Nicholas Brady.
Foundation type: Independent
Financial data (yr. ended 12/31/89): Assets, $4,383,000 (M); expenditures, $302,500, including $171,500 for 34 grants (high: $20,000; low: $1,000; average: $5,000).
Purpose and activities: Emphasis on hospitals, youth agencies, museums, and religious organizations.
Limitations: Giving primarily in NJ.
Application information: Application form not required.
Initial approach: Letter
Deadline(s): None
Board meeting date(s): Quarterly
Write: Joseph A. Gaunt, Secy.
Officers: James C. Brady, Jr.,* Pres. and Treas.; Joseph A. Gaunt, Secy.
Trustees:* N.F. Brady, Anderson Fowler.
Number of staff: None.
Employer Identification Number: 136167209

3792
Robert E. Brennan Foundation, Inc. ⌑ ☆
c/o Mortenson, Fleming, et al
340 North Ave.
Cranford 07016-2435

Incorporated in 1984 in NJ.
Donor(s): Robert E. Brennan.
Foundation type: Independent
Financial data (yr. ended 12/31/88): Assets, $8,013,822 (M); gifts received, $2,500; expenditures, $943,737, including $932,459 for 20 grants (high: $295,000; low: $100).
Purpose and activities: Giving primarily to a university for a recreation center; support also for Christian churches and a priory, and health associations, especially cancer therapy and medical care for children.
Types of support: Capital campaigns, general purposes, scholarship funds, building funds.
Limitations: Giving primarily in NJ. No grants to individuals.
Application information: Contributes only to pre-selected organizations. Applications not accepted.
Officers and Trusteess:* Robert E. Brennan,* Pres.; Patricia A. Brennan,* V.P.; Nora Aquilon, Secy.; Ronald J. Riccio,* Treas.
Employer Identification Number: 222550509

3793
Frances Brody Foundation ⌑
2114 Arrowood Dr.
Scotch Plains 07076

Established in 1965 in NJ.
Donor(s): Frances Brody.
Foundation type: Independent
Financial data (yr. ended 3/31/89): Assets, $2,226,671 (M); expenditures, $89,169, including $61,321 for 61 grants (high: $14,000; low: $10).
Purpose and activities: Support primarily for higher education and Jewish welfare.
Limitations: No grants to individuals.
Application information: Contributes only to pre-selected organizations. Applications not accepted.
Trustees: Andrew Brody, Frances Brody, Patti Lehrolf, Wendy Keil, Susan Rosengarten.
Employer Identification Number: 226075222

3794
The Brook Fund, Inc. ⌑ ☆
17 Franklin Tpke.
Mahwah 07430-1398 (201) 529-3666

Incorporated in 1984 in NJ.
Donor(s): Barnet Rukin, Shortline Terminal Agency, Chenanar Valley Bus Lines.
Foundation type: Independent
Financial data (yr. ended 12/31/88): Assets, $18,054 (M); gifts received, $90,000; expenditures, $127,650, including $127,535 for 34 grants (high: $60,000; low: $10).
Purpose and activities: Support primarily for Jewish giving, including welfare funds and a YMHA; minor support also for higher and other education.
Types of support: General purposes.
Application information:
Deadline(s): None
Write: Julius Eisen, Secy.-Treas.
Officers: Irwin Flateman, Pres.; Barnet Rukin, V.P.; Julius Eisen, Secy.-Treas.
Employer Identification Number: 222561995

3795
Brown Foundation ⌑
545 Cedar Ln.
Teaneck 07666

Established in 1985 in NJ.
Donor(s): David M. Brown.
Foundation type: Independent
Financial data (yr. ended 11/30/88): Assets, $1,305,516 (M); gifts received, $165,500; expenditures, $57,770, including $49,650 for 17 grants (high: $27,500; low: $150).
Purpose and activities: Giving primarily to cancer research in Israel; support also for Jewish organizations and education.
Limitations: Giving primarily in NY and NJ. No grants to individuals.
Application information: Contributes only to pre-selected organizations. Applications not accepted.
Trustees: Adam Brown, David M. Brown, Nikki Mintz Brown.
Employer Identification Number: 222663141

3796
The Brown Foundation ⌑
71 West Park Ave.
Vineland 08360

Established in 1966 in NJ.
Foundation type: Independent
Financial data (yr. ended 4/30/88): Assets, $1,353,752 (M); gifts received, $140,000; expenditures, $79,064, including $74,080 for 14 grants (high: $25,000; low: $230).
Purpose and activities: Giving primarily for Jewish organizations.
Application information: Contributes only to pre-selected organizations. Applications not accepted.
Officer and Trustees:* Bernard A. Brown,* Pres.; Irwin J. Brown, Jeffrey S. Brown, Shirley G. Brown, Sydney R. Brown, Ann E. Koons.
Employer Identification Number: 226083927

3797
Charles E. and Edna T. Brundage Charitable, Scientific and Wild Life Conservation Foundation ⌑
c/o Thomas L. Morrissey, V.P.
100 Mulberry St.
Newark 07102

Established in 1955 in NJ.
Donor(s): Edna T. Brundage.
Foundation type: Independent
Financial data (yr. ended 12/31/88): Assets, $1,519,550 (M); gifts received, $20,000; expenditures, $95,652, including $73,800 for 34 grants (high: $5,000; low: $500).
Purpose and activities: Giving for cultural activities, including historical preservation, and for social services.
Types of support: General purposes.
Limitations: Giving primarily in NJ. No grants to individuals.
Application information: Contributes only to pre-selected organizations. Applications not accepted.
Officers and Trustees:* Samuel C. Williams, Jr.,* Pres.; Thomas L. Morrissey,* V.P. and Secy.; William B. Cater,* V.P. and Treas.; Edna T. Brundage, Charles B. Cater, June B. Cater, William B. Cater, Jr., Susan Jukowsky.
Employer Identification Number: 226050185

3798
Brunetti Foundation ⌑ ☆
1655 U.S. Hwy. 9
Old Bridge 08857 (201) 727-3300

Established in 1974.
Donor(s): Aldercrest Development Corp.
Foundation type: Independent
Financial data (yr. ended 12/31/88): Assets, $1,529,492 (M); gifts received, $300,000; expenditures, $64,006, including $57,900 for 49 grants (high: $10,500; low: $100).
Purpose and activities: Support primarily for a military academy, higher education, medical research, and hospitals; minor support for Catholic churches.
Types of support: Research, endowment funds, scholarship funds.
Limitations: Giving primarily in NJ, NY, and FL. No grants to individuals.
Application information: Application form not required.
Deadline(s): None
Write: John J. Brunetti, Pres.
Officers: John J. Brunetti,* Pres.; John J. Brunetti, Jr., V.P. and Secy.
Directors:* Anna G. Brunetti.
Employer Identification Number: 237346205

3799
Emil Buehler Foundation, Inc. ⌑
c/o Rhein Management Corp.
60 Route 17 South
Paramus 07652 (201) 843-1333

Incorporated in 1953 in NJ.
Donor(s): Buehler, Inc., Emil Buehler,† Embu, Inc., E. Buehler Trust.
Foundation type: Independent
Financial data (yr. ended 11/30/88): Assets, $1,655,187 (M); expenditures, $45,538, including $11,498 for 4 grants (high: $5,500; low: $750).
Purpose and activities: Giving for biochemical research and for a mental health program; support also for research, museum displays, and television programs promoting aviation.
Types of support: Continuing support, equipment, exchange programs, internships, operating budgets, research, scholarship funds.
Limitations: Giving primarily in FL and NJ. No grants to individuals.
Publications: 990-PF, financial statement.
Application information: Application form required.
Initial approach: Letter
Deadline(s): None
Write: Anneliese Gillespie, Secy.-Treas.
Officers and Trustees: M. Ray Berberian, Pres.; John H. Payne, V.P.; Anneliese Gillespie, Secy.-Treas.; Edwin T. Boyle, Porter E. Hartman, George W. Weaver.
Number of staff: 1 full-time professional; 1 part-time support.
Employer Identification Number: 226058664

3800
The Bunbury Company, Inc.
169 Nassau St.
Princeton 08542 (609) 683-1414

Incorporated in 1952 in NY.
Donor(s): Dean Mathey.†
Foundation type: Independent
Financial data (yr. ended 12/31/89): Assets, $11,162,091 (M); expenditures, $817,845, including $578,700 for 70 grants (high: $160,000; low: $50; average: $50-$10,000).
Purpose and activities: Grants primarily for higher and secondary education, youth agencies, health and family services, the fine arts and cultural organizations, environment and ecology, and organizations benefiting women.
Types of support: General purposes.
Limitations: Giving primarily in NJ. No grants to individuals, or for building funds, fellowships, or matching gifts; no loans.
Publications: Annual report (including application guidelines).
Application information:
Initial approach: Proposal
Copies of proposal: 1
Deadline(s): 1 month before board meetings
Board meeting date(s): Feb., May, July, and Oct.
Final notification: 1 to 2 weeks after board meeting
Write: Samuel W. Lambert, III, Pres.; or Barbara L. Ruppert, Asst. Secy.
Officers and Directors:* Samuel W. Lambert III,* Pres.; Edward J. Toohey,* V.P.; Charles C. Townsend, Jr.,* Secy.; James R. Cogan,* Treas.; Charles B. Atwater, Stephan A. Morse, Robert M. Olmsted, William B. Wright, Edward R. Zuccaro.
Number of staff: 9 part-time professional; 2 part-time support.
Employer Identification Number: 136066172

3801
The Burstyn Family Foundation, Inc. ⌑ ☆
2029 Morris Ave., Suite 4
Union 07083 (201) 687-3200

Established in 1986 in NJ.
Foundation type: Independent
Financial data (yr. ended 12/31/88): Assets, $305,719 (M); gifts received, $95,000; expenditures, $257,155, including $248,660 for grants (high: $81,000).
Purpose and activities: Giving primarily for Jewish organizations, including welfare agencies and education.
Limitations: Giving primarily in NJ and NY.
Application information:
Initial approach: Letter
Deadline(s): None
Write: Jacob Burstyn, Trustee
Trustees: Ernestine Burstyn, Jacob Burstyn.
Employer Identification Number: 222770867

3802
Campbell Soup Fund ▼
Campbell Place
Camden 08103 (609) 342-6431

Incorporated in 1953 in NJ.
Donor(s): Campbell Soup Co.
Foundation type: Company-sponsored
Financial data (yr. ended 06/30/89): Assets, $10,168,611 (M); gifts received, $1,600,000; expenditures, $1,869,800, including $1,869,800 for 106 grants (high: $200,000; low: $1,300; average: $5,000-$35,000).
Purpose and activities: Capital grants to private institutions of higher education and hospitals and other health care facilities; support also for cultural programs, social service and youth agencies, community funds, and public interest groups.
Types of support: Building funds, renovation projects, capital campaigns.
Limitations: Giving primarily in areas of company operations, with emphasis on the Camden, NJ, and Philadelphia, PA, areas. No grants to individuals, or for operating budgets, continuing support, annual campaigns, seed money, emergency funds, deficit financing, land acquisition, endowment funds, matching gifts, equipment, or scholarships or fellowships; no loans.
Publications: Corporate giving report.
Application information: Application form not required.
Initial approach: Letter

Copies of proposal: 1
Deadline(s): None
Board meeting date(s): As required
Final notification: 4 to 8 weeks
Write: Frank G. Moore, Vice-Chair.
Officers: J.J. Furey, Secy.; D.H. Springer,* Treas.; R.J. Land, Controller.
Trustees:* R.L. Baker, Chair.; Frank G. Moore, Vice-Chair.; J.F. O'Brien, Vice-Chair.; A.A. Austin, J.J. Baldwin, R.S. Page, C.S. Rombach.
Number of staff: 2 full-time professional; 2 part-time professional; 2 part-time support.
Employer Identification Number: 216019196

3803
Cape Branch Foundation
c/o Danser, Balaam & Frank
Five Independence Way
Princeton 08540 (609) 987-0300

Established in 1964 in NJ.
Foundation type: Independent
Financial data (yr. ended 12/31/89): Assets, $3,726,844 (M); expenditures, $246,597, including $210,000 for 3 grants (high: $175,000; low: $10,000; average: $40,000).
Purpose and activities: Support for secondary education, conservation, museums, and a university.
Types of support: Research, building funds, land acquisition, general purposes.
Limitations: Giving primarily in NJ. No grants to individuals.
Publications: 990-PF.
Application information:
Initial approach: Brief letter
Deadline(s): None
Board meeting date(s): Annually
Write: Dorothy Frank
Directors: Gretchen W. Johnson,* James L. Johnson.
Trustees:* G.O. Danser, John R. Wittenborn.
Number of staff: None.
Employer Identification Number: 226054886

3804
Emil Capita Charitable Trust ⌘
7020 Kennedy Blvd.
North Bergen 07047 (201) 869-7112

Established in 1984 in NJ.
Donor(s): Emil R. Capita.
Foundation type: Independent
Financial data (yr. ended 09/30/89): Assets, $2,199,130 (M); expenditures, $165,437, including $160,000 for 1 grant.
Purpose and activities: Support for hearing research.
Types of support: Research.
Application information: Applicant organizations must be affiliated with Columbia Univ.
Write: Denise Meroni, Secy.
Officers: Anthony Del Spina, Pres.; Robert Capita, V.P.; Denise Meroni, Secy.; Roy A. Cohen, Treas.
Trustees: John Mach, Jules G. Walther.
Employer Identification Number: 222669043

3805
Joseph L. Carley Foundation ⌘ ☆
c/o Corporation Trust Ctr.
Two North High St.
Millville 08332-4244 (609) 327-0934

Established in 1981.
Donor(s): Joseph L. Carley.
Foundation type: Independent
Financial data (yr. ended 4/30/89): Assets, $1,431,986 (M); gifts received, $150,000; expenditures, $40,776, including $33,133 for 5 grants (high: $25,000; low: $200).
Purpose and activities: Giving primarily for welfare, especially for the handicapped; support also for health, family services, and a Presbyterian church.
Types of support: Equipment, building funds.
Limitations: Giving primarily in NJ and PA. No grants to individuals.
Application information:
Initial approach: Letter
Deadline(s): None
Write: Joseph L. Carley, Pres.
Officers and Directors: Joseph L. Carley, Pres.; Marie Carley, V.P.; James M. Draper.
Employer Identification Number: 222617552

3806
The Carnegie Foundation for the Advancement of Teaching
Five Ivy Ln.
Princeton 08540 (609) 452-1780

Established in 1905 under NY State charter; incorporated in 1906 under an Act of Congress.
Donor(s): Andrew Carnegie.†
Foundation type: Operating
Financial data (yr. ended 6/30/88): Assets, $49,083,130 (M); gifts received, $431,760; expenditures, $3,042,504, including $1,309,275 for foundation-administered programs.
Purpose and activities: A private operating foundation established to provide retirement allowances for teachers of universities, colleges, and technical schools in the United States and Canada; and in general, to do all things necessary to encourage, uphold, and dignify the profession of teaching and the cause of higher education in the United States and Canada. Present emphasis is on education policy studies.
Types of support: Technical assistance, research, consulting services.
Limitations: No grants to individuals (except for retirement allowances for teachers), or for general support, capital or endowment funds, matching gifts, scholarships, fellowships, special projects, publications, or conferences; no loans.
Publications: Annual report.
Application information: Grants usually initiated by the foundation. Applications not accepted.
Deadline(s): None
Board meeting date(s): Apr. and Nov.
Final notification: 90 days
Write: David Walter, Treas.
Officers: Ernest L. Boyer,* Pres.; Vito Perrone, V.P.; Verne A. Stadtman, V.P. - General Services; Jean Van Gorden, Secy.-Treas.; Shirley Strum Kenny.
Trustees:* David H. Hornbeck, Chair.; Norman Francis, Vice-Chair.; Terrel H. Bell, Martha E. Church, Constance E. Clayton, Eugene Cola-Robles, Donald R. Fronzaglia, Patricia A. Graham, F. Sheldon Hackney, Stanley O. Ikenberry, Nannerl O. Keohane, Reatha Clark King, Walter Leonard, Donald D. O'Dowd, Robert M. O'Neil, Dale Parnell, Jack W. Peltason, David E. Rogers, M.D., Rev. William J. Sullivan, Alexander Tomlinson, Daniel Yankelovich.
Number of staff: 7 full-time professional; 11 full-time support.
Employer Identification Number: 131623924

3807
O. W. Caspersen Foundation for Aid to Health and Education, Inc.
c/o Westby Mgmt. Inc.
P.O. Box 800
Andover 07821 (201) 786-5354

Incorporated in 1964 in DE.
Donor(s): O.W. Caspersen.†
Foundation type: Independent
Financial data (yr. ended 12/31/89): Assets, $2,803,306 (M); expenditures, $180,044, including $180,000 for 6 grants (high: $50,000; low: $5,000).
Purpose and activities: Support for education, including higher and secondary education, and health and hospitals. Present policy to make grants only to those educational and health-oriented institutions with which the foundation has had extensive previous experience.
Types of support: Operating budgets, continuing support, annual campaigns, emergency funds, building funds, equipment, land acquisition, research.
Limitations: Giving primarily in the eastern coastal states. No grants to individuals, or for seed money, scholarships, fellowships, or matching gifts; no loans.
Application information: Application form not required.
Copies of proposal: 1
Deadline(s): None
Board meeting date(s): Jan. and July
Write: Finn M.W. Caspersen, V.P.
Officers and Directors:* Freda R. Caspersen,* Pres.; Finn M.W. Caspersen,* V.P.; John O. Williams,* Secy.; Barbara M. Caspersen,* Treas.
Number of staff: None.
Employer Identification Number: 510101350

3808
Chubb Foundation ⌘
15 Mountain View Rd.
P.O. Box 1615
Warren 07061-1615 (201) 580-3570

Established in 1954 in NJ.
Donor(s): Chubb Group Insurance Co.
Foundation type: Company-sponsored
Financial data (yr. ended 12/31/87): Assets, $7,639,111 (M); expenditures, $409,878, including $340,700 for 67 grants to individuals (high: $5,000; low: $250).
Purpose and activities: Support for employee-related academic scholarships.
Types of support: Employee-related scholarships.
Application information: Application information available from all branches and affiliated companies. Application form required.

Deadline(s): Dec. 15 for return of formal application
Write: Alice Billick, Secy.
Officers: Robert C. Reiss, Pres.; Arthur O. Birkenstock, V.P.; Donald P. Bush, Jr., V.P.; Alice Billick, Secy.; Robert A. Marzocchi, Treas.
Trustees:* Karen O. Burkhardt, John C.K. Chu, Robert B. Fiske, Jr., Brigid Shanley Lamb, William N. Wilson.
Employer Identification Number: 226058567

3809
Liz Claiborne Foundation ⌑
One Claiborne Ave.
North Bergen 07047 (201) 662-6000

Established in 1981 in NY.
Donor(s): Liz Claiborne, Inc.
Foundation type: Company-sponsored
Financial data (yr. ended 12/31/87): Assets, $5,376,223 (M); gifts received, $2,500,000; expenditures, $942,567, including $936,851 for 94 grants (high: $263,050; low: $500).
Purpose and activities: Grants primarily for health, culture, education, including higher education, and Jewish community funds; support also for a public television station.
Application information:
Write: Melanie Lyons
Trustees: Leonard Boxer, Jerome A. Chazen, Arthur Ortenberg, Elisabeth Claiborne Ortenberg.
Employer Identification Number: 133060673

3810
Russell Colgate Fund, Inc. ⌑
15 Exchange Place
Jersey City 07302 (201) 434-7464

Established in 1943 in NJ.
Foundation type: Independent
Financial data (yr. ended 12/31/88): Assets, $1,937,638 (M); expenditures, $74,170, including $61,400 for 64 grants (high: $5,000; low: $25).
Purpose and activities: Support primarily for higher education, social services, and cultural programs.
Application information:
Initial approach: Letter
Deadline(s): None
Officers: John K. Colgate, Jr., Pres.; Josephine Wilkinson, V.P.
Employer Identification Number: 221713065

3811
Colton Family Foundation, Inc. ⌑
232 Hartshorn Dr.
Short Hills 07078 (201) 467-9360

Established in 1983 in NJ.
Donor(s): Judith S. Colton, Stewart M. Colton.
Foundation type: Independent
Financial data (yr. ended 11/30/87): Assets, $215,710 (M); gifts received, $215,200; expenditures, $544,735, including $541,280 for grants (high: $500,000).
Purpose and activities: Grants for higher education in the U.S. and Israel, cultural activities and a Jewish welfare fund.
Limitations: No support for private foundations. No grants to individuals.
Application information:
Initial approach: Letter and proposal
Deadline(s): None
Write: Stewart M. Colton, Mgr.
Officers: Judith S. Colton, Mgr.; Stewart M. Colton, Mgr.; Irving C. Marcus, Mgr.
Employer Identification Number: 222520918

3812
The Corson Family Foundation ⌑
c/o Ben Corson
P.O. Box 397
Delair 08110-3215
Application address: 9000 River Rd., Delair, NJ 08110; Tel.: (609) 662-5500

Established in 1983 in NJ.
Foundation type: Independent
Financial data (yr. ended 09/30/89): Assets, $324,812 (M); gifts received, $30,000; expenditures, $202,631, including $202,160 for 50 grants (high: $92,500; low: $100).
Purpose and activities: Support primarily for Jewish giving, including Jewish welfare organizations; support also for health associations.
Application information:
Initial approach: Letter
Deadline(s): None
Write: Isadore Ressler, Mgr.
Officer: Isadore Ressler, Mgr.
Trustee: Ben Corson, Marie Corson, Stephen Kendell.
Employer Identification Number: 222479269

3813
CPC Educational Foundation ⌑
International Plaza
P.O. Box 8000
Englewood Cliffs 07632 (201) 894-2249

Established in 1961.
Donor(s): CPC International, Inc., Frank K. Greenwall.
Foundation type: Company-sponsored
Financial data (yr. ended 11/30/88): Assets, $2,963,443 (M); gifts received, $50,750; expenditures, $147,483, including $134,595 for 63 grants to individuals (high: $8,000; low: $200).
Purpose and activities: Giving for college scholarships only to children of past and present CPC International, Inc. employees.
Types of support: Employee-related scholarships.
Publications: Application guidelines, program policy statement.
Application information: Application form required.
Deadline(s): Submit application between Aug. 30 and Nov. 30
Write: Ms. Linda Salcito
Officers and Directors:* Richard P. Bergeman,* Pres.; Luis Schuchinski,* V.P.; Clifford B. Storms,* V.P.; John B. Meagher, Secy.; Angelo S. Abdela,* Treas.; Philip Braverman, General Counsel.
Employer Identification Number: 136103949

3814
Crum & Forster Foundation, Inc.
211 Mt. Airy Rd.
Basking Ridge 07920 (201) 204-3540

Incorporated in 1953 in CA as the Industrial Indemnity Foundation; the foundation is registered in CA and NJ.
Donor(s): Crum & Forster Corp., and affiliated companies.
Foundation type: Company-sponsored
Financial data (yr. ended 12/31/87): Assets, $28,425 (L); gifts received, $741,101; expenditures, $712,676, including $650,766 for 454 grants (high: $40,200; low: $100; average: $500-$3,000) and $61,863 for 470 employee matching gifts.
Purpose and activities: Giving primarily for youth agencies, health agencies, higher and secondary education, hospitals, safety, culture and the arts, and civic affairs.
Types of support: Operating budgets, annual campaigns, seed money, emergency funds, equipment, building funds, scholarship funds, exchange programs, continuing support, capital campaigns, employee matching gifts, general purposes.
Limitations: No support for political organizations or candidates, or religious organizations or activities. No grants to individuals; no loans.
Application information: Application form not required.
Initial approach: Letter or proposal
Copies of proposal: 1
Deadline(s): Submit proposal preferably from Sept. through Nov.; deadline Nov. 30
Board meeting date(s): Mar. and as required
Write: Ruth G. Goodell, Contribs. Admin.
Officers and Directors:* Robert J. Vairo,* Chair., Pres., and C.E.O.; Robert A. Zito, V.P.; Antoinette C. Bentley,* Secy.; Dennis J. Hammer, Treas.; Anthony R. Biele, James J. Cutro, Melvin Howard, George J. Rachmiel.
Number of staff: 1 full-time professional.
Employer Identification Number: 946065476

3815
D'Olier Foundation ⌑
611 Medford Leas
Medford 08055 (609) 953-1481

Established in 1964 in NJ.
Foundation type: Independent
Financial data (yr. ended 12/31/88): Assets, $1,218,570 (M); expenditures, $65,809, including $51,800 for 10 grants (high: $32,300; low: $500).
Purpose and activities: Support primarily for the Society of Friends; support also for education and social services.
Limitations: Giving primarily in NJ.
Application information:
Initial approach: Letter
Deadline(s): Sept. 30
Write: James D. Hull, Jr.
Trustees: James D. Hull, Jr., Louis R. Matlack, Grace R. Walton.
Employer Identification Number: 226075471

3816
Darby Foundation ⌑
c/o Somerset Trust Co.
P.O. Box 837
Somerville 08876

Established in 1966 in NJ.
Donor(s): Nicholas F. Brady.
Foundation type: Independent
Financial data (yr. ended 12/31/88): Assets, $1,867,110 (M); expenditures, $96,702, including $90,075 for 69 grants (high: $10,000; low: $100).
Purpose and activities: Supports medical research, community programs and a wide range of charitable organizations.
Application information:
Initial approach: Letter
Deadline(s): None
Trustees: Katherine D. Brady, Nicholas F. Brady.
Employer Identification Number: 136212178

3817
The Diabetes Research & Education Foundation, Inc. ▼
P.O. Box 6168
Bridgewater 08807-9998 (201) 658-9322

Established in 1984 in NJ.
Donor(s): Hoechst-Roussel Pharmaceuticals, Inc.
Foundation type: Independent
Financial data (yr. ended 12/31/88): Assets, $165,418 (M); gifts received, $1,000,000; expenditures, $1,260,178, including $1,192,295 for 99 grants to individuals (high: $20,000; low: $1,575).
Purpose and activities: Awards grants to individuals for diabetes research and education initiatives that would seldom be considered for funding by traditional research foundations; the foundation underwrites projects in basic and clinical research and education.
Types of support: Grants to individuals, research.
Publications: Annual report.
Application information: Application form required.
Initial approach: Proposal
Copies of proposal: 6
Deadline(s): Semiannually
Board meeting date(s): May and Nov.
Final notification: Approximately 2 weeks after board meetings
Write: Herbert C. Rosenkilde, M.D., Exec. Dir.
Officer: Leo P. Krall, M.D., Chair. and Pres.
Directors: Herbert C. Rosenkilde, M.D., Exec. Dir.; R. Keith Campbell, Donnell D. Etzwiler, M.D., Rachmiel Levine, M.D., Rita Nemchik.
Number of staff: 1
Employer Identification Number: 222561975

3818
Geraldine R. Dodge Foundation, Inc. ▼
95 Madison Ave.
P.O. Box 1239
Morristown 07962-1239 (201) 540-8442

Incorporated in 1974 in NJ.
Donor(s): Geraldine R. Dodge.†
Foundation type: Independent
Financial data (yr. ended 12/31/89): Assets, $143,777,546 (M); expenditures, $10,001,554, including $8,998,260 for 296 grants (high: $225,051; low: $100; average: $15,000-$25,000) and $233,276 for 2 foundation-administered programs.
Purpose and activities: Grant-making emphasis in NJ on secondary education, performing and visual arts and other cultural activities, projects in population, environment, energy, and other critical areas, and programs in the public interest, including development of volunteerism, communications, and public issues. Interest in independent secondary schools in New England and Middle Atlantic states and in projects on the national level that are likely to lead to significant advances in secondary education. Projects that have implications beyond the school itself are of special interest. Support also for projects in welfare of animals on a national and local level which explore the human/animal bond, promote humane education, and address issues of cruelty, pet overpopulation, the protection of wildlife, farm animal abuse, and animal exploitation in laboratories.
Types of support: Seed money, conferences and seminars, matching funds, special projects, publications, continuing support, research, operating budgets.
Limitations: Giving primarily in NJ, with support for the arts and local humane groups limited to NJ, and support for other local projects limited to the Morristown-Madison area; some giving in the other Middle Atlantic states and New England, and to national organizations. No support for religion, higher education, health, or conduit organizations. No grants for capital projects, endowment funds, deficit financing, or scholarships.
Publications: Annual report (including application guidelines).
Application information: Application form not required.
Initial approach: Letter or proposal
Copies of proposal: 1
Deadline(s): Submit proposal preferably in Mar., June, Sept., or Dec.; deadlines Dec. 15 for welfare of animals and local projects; Mar. 1 for secondary education; June 15 for the arts; and Sept. 15 for public issues
Board meeting date(s): Mar., June, Sept., and Dec.
Final notification: End of months in which board meets
Write: Scott McVay, Exec. Dir.
Officers: Robert H.B. Baldwin,* Chair.; Robert LeBuhn,* Pres.; Scott McVay, Exec. Dir.
Trustees:* Barbara Knowles Debs, Henry U. Harder, John Lloyd Huck, Nancy D. Lindsay, Walter J. Neppl, Paul J. O'Donnell.
Number of staff: 5 full-time professional; 5 full-time support; 1 part-time support.
Employer Identification Number: 237406010

3819
The Dow Jones Newspaper Fund, Inc. ☆
P.O. Box 300
Princeton 08543-0300 (609) 452-2820

Incorporated in 1958 in DE.
Donor(s): Dow Jones & Co., Inc., and other news companies.
Foundation type: Company-sponsored
Financial data (yr. ended 12/31/88): Assets, $401,775 (M); gifts received, $460,650; expenditures, $453,439, including $239,991 for 33 grants (high: $22,862; low: $2,950; average: $5,000-$20,000), $95,940 for 141 grants to individuals (high: $1,500; low: $350; average: $350-$1,500) and $74,381 for foundation-administered programs.
Purpose and activities: Major effort devoted to practical newspaper experience for college students and journalism training for minority high school students, high school teachers of journalism, and high school publications advisors. Scholarships for about 10 minority college sophomores, 40 juniors, and 10 minority seniors completing summer work on a newspaper. Names National High School Journalism Teacher of the Year. Sponsors a journalism career information program.
Types of support: Fellowships, special projects, student aid, internships.
Limitations: No grants for building or endowment funds, research, publications, or conferences and seminars; no loans.
Publications: Annual report, application guidelines, newsletter, 990-PF.
Application information: Grant application guidelines available for minority high school programs. Application form required.
Initial approach: Letter
Copies of proposal: 1
Deadline(s): Submit proposal preferably in Sept.; deadline Oct. 1
Board meeting date(s): May and Nov.
Final notification: Dec. 1
Write: Thomas E. Engleman, Exec. Dir.
Officers and Directors:* Laurence G. O'Donnell,* Pres.; Everett Groseclose,* V.P. and Secy.; Warren H. Phillips,* V.P.; Thomas Sullivan,* Treas.; Thomas E. Engleman,* Exec. Dir.; Donnel E. Carter, Frank del Olmo, Betty Duval, Jay Harris, Sharon Murphy, Paul S. Swensson, Frederick Taylor.
Number of staff: 3 full-time professional; 1 full-time support.
Employer Identification Number: 136021439

3820
The Edyth and Dean Dowling Foundation ⌑
60 Abbett Ave.
Morristown 07960

Established in 1961 in NJ.
Donor(s): Edythe Dowling, Dean Dowling.
Foundation type: Independent
Financial data (yr. ended 09/30/89): Assets, $5,278 (M); gifts received, $23,000; expenditures, $163,614, including $162,982 for 4 grants (high: $108,507; low: $4,375).
Purpose and activities: Support primarily for higher and other education, libraries, and hospitals.
Application information:
Deadline(s): None
Officer and Directors:* Dean Dowling,* Pres.; Edythe Dowling.
Employer Identification Number: 226058303

3821
David Dreman Foundation ⌑ ☆
30 Montgomery St.
Jersey City 07302

Established in 1986 in NY.
Donor(s): David N. Dreman.
Foundation type: Independent
Financial data (yr. ended 11/30/88): Assets, $2,592,317 (M); expenditures, $85,338, including $72,220 for 62 grants (high: $10,000; low: $35).
Purpose and activities: Giving primarily for higher and other education, Jewish welfare, health associations, a day care center and other youth services.
Limitations: Giving primarily in Monmouth, NJ.
Application information: Contributes only to pre-selected organizations. Applications not accepted.
Officers: David N. Dreman, Pres.; Holly Dreman, V.P.; Milton Raymond, Secy.; Charles E. Schafer, Jr., Treas.
Trustee: Sherrill Hershberg.
Employer Identification Number: 222764782

3822
Alice & Leonard Dreyfuss Foundation ⌑ ☆
c/o Mrs. William Y. Dear, Jr.
Blue Mill Rd.
Morristown 07960-6713

Established in 1952 in NJ.
Foundation type: Independent
Financial data (yr. ended 12/31/88): Assets, $1,092,395 (M); expenditures, $57,002, including $50,400 for 53 grants (high: $8,000; low: $100).
Purpose and activities: Support primarily for museums, health, education, churches, and civic affairs groups.
Limitations: Giving primarily in NY and NJ. No grants to individuals.
Application information: Contributes only to pre-selected organizations. Applications not accepted.
Officers and Trustees: Thelma T. Dear, Pres.; Standish F. Medina, Secy.; Wesley A. Luschenat, Treas.; Allan H. McAlpin, Susan D. Ross.
Employer Identification Number: 226028752

3823
The Doris Duke Foundation, Inc. ⌑
Duke Farms
P.O. Box 2030
Somerville 08876

Incorporated in 1934 in DE.
Donor(s): Doris Duke.
Foundation type: Independent
Financial data (yr. ended 12/31/87): Assets, $5,126,092 (M); expenditures, $253,166, including $82,850 for 14 grants (high: $20,000; low: $300).
Purpose and activities: Grants to charitable institutions on an annual basis, including support for social service programs, improved services for the aging, child welfare and aid to agencies giving relief and medical care; support also for cultural organizations.
Limitations: Giving primarily in NJ, NY, and CA. No support for religious organizations for sectarian purposes. No grants to individuals, or for building or capital funds, publications, or general operating expenses.
Application information: Contributes only to pre-selected organizations. Applications not accepted.
Officer and Directors: Doris Duke, Pres.; Lloyd A. Pantages.
Employer Identification Number: 131655241

3824
Charles Edison Fund ⌑
101 South Harrison St.
East Orange 07018 (201) 675-9000

Incorporated in 1948 in DE.
Donor(s): Charles Edison,† and others.
Foundation type: Independent
Financial data (yr. ended 12/31/88): Assets, $21,372,204 (M); gifts received, $5,116; qualifying distributions, $839,504, including $399,107 for 33 grants (high: $175,000; low: $100) and $118,762 for foundation-administered programs.
Purpose and activities: Grants largely for historic preservation, with emphasis on the homes of Thomas Alva Edison, and for education, medical research, and hospitals. Support also for foundation-sponsored exhibits at over 80 museums throughout the U.S., for science education teaching kits in over 20,000 classrooms, and for cassette re-recording of antique phonograph records for schools and museums.
Types of support: Operating budgets, continuing support, seed money, special projects, research, equipment.
Limitations: No grants to individuals, or for building or endowment funds, scholarships, fellowships, or matching gifts; no loans.
Publications: Informational brochure (including application guidelines).
Application information: Application form not required.
Initial approach: Letter or proposal
Copies of proposal: 1
Deadline(s): 30 days prior to board meetings
Board meeting date(s): Mar., June, Sept., and Dec.
Write: Paul J. Christiansen, Pres.
Officers and Trustees:* Paul J. Christiansen,* Pres.; John P. Keegan,* V.P.; David O. Schantz,* Secy.-Treas.; William M. Henderson, James E. Howe, Nancy M. Milligan, Robert E. Murray, John N. Schullinger, M.D., J. Thomas Smoot, Jr., John D. Venable.
Number of staff: 2 full-time professional; 1 part-time professional; 1 full-time support; 2 part-time support.
Employer Identification Number: 221514861

3825
The Elizabeth Foundation ⌑
c/o Lum, Hoens, Abeles, Conant & Danzes
103 Eisenhower Pkwy., 4th Fl.
Roseland 07068-1049 (201) 622-2300

Incorporated in 1974 in NJ.
Donor(s): The Fund for New Jersey.
Foundation type: Independent
Financial data (yr. ended 3/31/88): Assets, $3,137,223 (M); expenditures, $180,743, including $146,733 for 14 grants (high: $33,233; low: $2,000).
Purpose and activities: Emphasis on aid to the aged, youth, and minorities; grants also for hospitals, education, and social service agencies.
Limitations: Giving primarily in SC and other southern states.
Application information:
Initial approach: Letter
Write: William B. Lum, Treas.
Officers: Melinda G. Atwood, Pres.; Marcelle Skepelhorn, Secy.; William B. Lum, Treas. and Exec. Dir.
Employer Identification Number: 237379321

3826
Engel Family Foundation, Inc. ⌑ ☆
48 Hook Rd.
Bayonne 07002

Established in 1985 in DE.
Donor(s): Barry Engel, Andre S. Engel.
Foundation type: Independent
Financial data (yr. ended 5/31/88): Assets, $1,182 (M); gifts received, $139,000; expenditures, $144,883, including $142,208 for grants (high: $32,457).
Purpose and activities: "Preference is given to organizations engaged in religious education"; giving primarily for Jewish congregations and yeshivas.
Limitations: Giving primarily in Brooklyn, NY. No grants to individuals.
Application information:
Initial approach: Letter
Deadline(s): None
Write: Barry Engel, Trustee
Trustees: Andre S. Engel, Barry Engel, Margaret Fishman.
Employer Identification Number: 133327931

3827
The Charles Engelhard Foundation ▼
P.O. Box 427
Far Hills 07931 (201) 766-7224

Incorporated in 1940 in NJ.
Donor(s): Charles Engelhard,† Engelhard Hanovia, Inc., and others.
Foundation type: Independent
Financial data (yr. ended 12/31/88): Assets, $71,024,437 (M); expenditures, $6,434,489, including $6,045,276 for 199 grants (high: $1,072,500; low: $500; average: $1,000-$100,000).
Purpose and activities: Emphasis on higher and secondary education, and cultural, medical, religious, wildlife, and conservation organizations.
Types of support: General purposes, special projects, continuing support, operating budgets.
Limitations: No grants to individuals, or for building funds.
Publications: Application guidelines.
Application information: Giving only to organizations known to the trustees. Application form not required.
Initial approach: Proposal
Copies of proposal: 1
Deadline(s): None
Board meeting date(s): Quarterly
Final notification: Varies

Write: Elaine Catterall, Secy.
Officers: Jane B. Engelhard,* Pres.; Elaine Catterall, Secy.; Edward G. Beimfohr,* Treas.
Trustees:* Sophie Engelhard Craighead, Charlene B. Engelhard, Susan O'Connor, Sally E. Pingree, Anne E. Reed.
Number of staff: 1 full-time professional.
Employer Identification Number: 226063032

3828
Essex Fells Welfare Foundation ⌑ ☆
P.O. Box 373
New Vernon 07976

Established in 1933.
Donor(s): Gordon McShane.
Foundation type: Independent
Financial data (yr. ended 12/31/88): Assets, $1,172,069 (M); expenditures, $40,207, including $33,586 for 36 grants (high: $7,750; low: $50).
Purpose and activities: Support primarily for churches and other Christian organizations, community funds, and health services; some support for education.
Officer: Gordon McShane, Mgr.
Employer Identification Number: 226042684

3829
Exxon Education Foundation ▼
P.O. Box 101
Florham Park 07932 (201) 765-3004

Incorporated in 1955 in NJ as Esso Education Foundation; name changed in 1972.
Donor(s): Exxon Corp., and affiliated companies.
Foundation type: Company-sponsored
Financial data (yr. ended 12/31/89): Assets, $42,621,000 (M); gifts received, $5,287,000; expenditures, $20,375,000, including $9,532,172 for 459 grants (high: $783,371; low: $1,000; average: $39,245) and $8,701,643 for 8,866 employee matching gifts.
Purpose and activities: "To aid education in the U.S. (a) by matching gifts made by Exxon employees and retirees to colleges and universities; (b) by supporting college and university schools, programs, and departments making outstanding educational contributions in areas of science, technology, and business; (c) by aiding organizations and associations serving significant segments of the educational community; (d) through project-oriented programs concerned with mathematics education from kindergarten through the post-doctoral level; undergraduate general education; undergraduate remedial education; elementary and secondary school restructuring and teacher education reform, particularly as they relate to enhancing the success of the educational system with disadvantaged minority students."
Types of support: Employee matching gifts, general purposes, special projects.
Limitations: No grants to individuals, or for institutional scholarship or fellowship programs, capital or building funds, land acquisition, equipment, renovation projects, or endowment purposes; no loans.
Publications: Annual report, application guidelines.
Application information: Prospective applicants should write to the foundation for detailed program information and guidelines.
Write: Dr. Donald L. Guertin, Exec. Dir.
Officers and Trustees:* Elliot R. Cattarulla,* Chair. and Pres.; J.K. Kansas, V.P.; C.G. Korshin, Secy.; J.E. Bayne, Treas.; Donald L. Guertin, Exec. Dir.; L.S. Berlin, Controller; R.J. Kruizenga, U.J. LeGrange, T.J. McDonagh, F.A. Risch, Edgar A. Robinson, F.B. Sprow.
Number of staff: 5 full-time professional; 3 full-time support.
Employer Identification Number: 136082357

3830
Fanwood Foundation ⌑
c/o King, King & Goldsack
450 Somerset St., P.O. Box 1106
North Plainfield 07061-1106 (201) 756-7804

Trust established in 1940 in NJ.
Donor(s): Dorothy W. Stevens.
Foundation type: Independent
Financial data (yr. ended 12/31/88): Assets, $10,693,748 (M); expenditures, $473,094, including $470,200 for 87 grants (high: $100,000; low: $500).
Purpose and activities: Support primarily for secondary, business, and other education, including educational programs for minorities; support also for museums, the performing arts, and other cultural programs, hospitals and medical research, Christian organizations, wildlife and environmental conservation, economics and public policy, community development, and programs benefiting women, youth, Native Americans, and the disabled.
Types of support: Annual campaigns, endowment funds, operating budgets.
Application information: Contributes only to pre-selected organizations. Applications not accepted.
Deadline(s): None
Write: Victor R. King, Trustee
Officer and Trustees: Whitney Stevens, Mgr.; Victor R. King, Robert T. Stevens, Jr.
Number of staff: None.
Employer Identification Number: 136051922

3831
Fox Foundation ⌑
Railroad Blvd.
Newfield 08344 (609) 692-4400

Established in 1956 in NJ.
Foundation type: Independent
Financial data (yr. ended 12/31/88): Assets, $1,101,699 (M); expenditures, $57,000, including $55,724 for 120 grants (high: $5,000; low: $50).
Purpose and activities: Supports a wide range of charities with an emphasis on Christian institutions and youth programs.
Limitations: Giving primarily in NJ. No grants to individuals.
Application information:
Initial approach: Letter
Deadline(s): None
Write: Ralph J. Fox and Rex S. Fox, Trustees
Trustees: Ralph T. Fox, Jr., Rex S. Fox.
Employer Identification Number: 226057667

3832
Isaac Franco & Sons Foundation, Inc. ⌑ ☆
Two Whitehall Ave.
Deal 07723-1322

Established in 1969.
Donor(s): Harry Franco, Morris Franco, Soundesign Corp.
Foundation type: Independent
Financial data (yr. ended 6/30/89): Assets, $1,108,057 (M); gifts received, $6,200; expenditures, $343,511, including $341,043 for 31 grants (high: $85,024; low: $150).
Purpose and activities: Support for Jewish religious, educational, and cultural organizations.
Limitations: No grants to individuals.
Application information:
Initial approach: Letter
Deadline(s): None
Officers: Harry Franco, Pres.; Morris Franco, Secy.-Treas.
Employer Identification Number: 237028051

3833
The Frelinghuysen Foundation ⌑
P.O. Box 726
Far Hills 07931 (201) 439-3499

Incorporated in 1950 in NJ.
Donor(s): Frelinghuysen family, The.
Foundation type: Independent
Financial data (yr. ended 12/31/88): Assets, $1,752,368 (M); expenditures, $281,116, including $259,937 for 49 grants (high: $100,000; low: $1,000).
Purpose and activities: Emphasis on higher and secondary education, cultural programs, and hospitals.
Types of support: General purposes, fellowships, internships, capital campaigns, equipment.
Limitations: Giving primarily in NJ and NY.
Application information:
Initial approach: Letter
Deadline(s): None
Write: H.O.H. Frelinghuysen, Pres.
Officers: H.O.H. Frelinghuysen, Pres.; George L.K. Frelinghuysen, V.P. and Treas.; John F. Szczepanski, Secy.
Employer Identification Number: 221723755

3834
Samuel Friedland Family Foundation ⌑
c/o Nancy Simpson
32 Mercer St.
Hackensack 07601

Incorporated in 1953 in NJ.
Donor(s): Samuel Friedland, Hasam Realty Corp.
Foundation type: Independent
Financial data (yr. ended 09/30/89): Assets, $1,935,363 (M); expenditures, $127,131, including $121,275 for 11 grants (high: $60,000; low: $125).
Purpose and activities: Grants primarily for Jewish welfare funds, temple support, and higher education, including religious education; support also for hospitals and health associations.
Limitations: No grants to individuals.

Application information: Contributes only to pre-selected organizations. Applications not accepted.
Officers and Trustees:* Leonard Friedland,* Pres.; Marjorie Cowan,* V.P. and Secy.; Jack Friedland,* V.P. and Treas.; Harold Friedland,* V.P.; Nancy Simpson,* Mgr.
Employer Identification Number: 236296545

3835
The Fund for New Jersey ▼
57 Washington St.
East Orange 07017 (201) 676-5905

Incorporated in 1969 in NJ as successor to The Florence Murray Wallace Fund established in 1958.
Donor(s): Charles F. Wallace,† and members of his family.
Foundation type: Independent
Financial data (yr. ended 12/31/89): Assets, $25,703,794 (M); expenditures, $1,140,689, including $732,643 for grants (average: $20,000).
Purpose and activities: Emphasis on projects which provide the basis for public action on state or local problems by way of research, litigation, citizen action, or supervision of government.
Types of support: Seed money, research, special projects, publications, conferences and seminars, matching funds, general purposes, continuing support.
Limitations: Giving primarily in NJ or to regional programs that benefit NJ. No support for recreation, day care centers, drug treatment programs, health care delivery, or curricular changes in educational institutions. No grants to individuals, or for capital projects, equipment, endowment funds, scholarships, or fellowships.
Publications: Annual report (including application guidelines).
Application information: Application form not required.
Initial approach: Letter
Copies of proposal: 1
Deadline(s): None
Board meeting date(s): Mar., June, Sept., and Dec.
Final notification: 2 weeks after board meeting
Write: Mark M. Murphy, Exec. Dir.
Officers: Joseph C. Cornwall,* Chair. and Treas.; Richard J. Sullivan,* Pres.; Mark M. Murphy, Exec. Dir.
Trustees:* William O. Baker, John W. Cornwall, Dickinson R. Debevoise, John J. Gibbons, Gustav Heningburg, Leonard Lieberman, Mary S. Strong, Jane W. Thorne.
Number of staff: 3
Employer Identification Number: 221895028

3836
Lewis M. Gabbe Foundation, Inc.
c/o Mortenson & Pomeroy
155 Morris Ave.
Springfield 07081 (201) 467-9600

Established in 1976 in NJ.
Foundation type: Independent
Financial data (yr. ended 09/29/90): Assets, $1,288,030 (M); expenditures, $70,820, including $65,500 for 25 grants (high: $7,500; low: $200).
Purpose and activities: Support primarily for hospitals and higher education.
Application information: Application form not required.
Deadline(s): None
Write: Robert S. Mortenson, Trustee
Trustees: James G. Mortenson, Robert S. Mortenson.
Employer Identification Number: 222130042

3837
The Herbert & Betty Gallen Foundation ⌑ ☆
165 Polito Ave.
Lyndhurst 07071

Established in 1985 in NJ.
Donor(s): Betty Gallen, Herbert Gallen.
Foundation type: Independent
Financial data (yr. ended 12/31/88): Assets, $302,983 (M); gifts received, $150,000; expenditures, $115,219, including $115,000 for 2 grants (high: $100,000; low: $15,000).
Purpose and activities: Support for Jewish organizations, including welfare funds.
Limitations: No grants to individuals.
Application information: Contributes only to pre-selected organizations. Applications not accepted.
Officers and Trustees: Herbert Gallen, Pres. and Treas.; Betty Gallen, V.P.; Joan Gallen Megibow, V.P.; Nancy Gallen Scheriff, V.P.
Employer Identification Number: 222664537

3838
The Garfield Foundation ⌑
306 Carter Rd.
Princeton 08540

Foundation type: Operating
Financial data (yr. ended 11/30/88): Assets, $1,059,446 (M); gifts received, $136,000; expenditures, $258,082, including $175,000 for 2 grants (high: $100,000; low: $75,000).
Purpose and activities: Support primarily for urban, regional and environmental research; support also for research on energy and arms control.
Limitations: Giving primarily in Princeton, NJ.
Application information: Contributes only to pre-selected organizations. Applications not accepted.
Officers and Trustees:* George Garfield,* Pres.; Ronald Berman, V.P.; Elizabeth Garfield, Secy.; Eberhard Rosenblad.
Employer Identification Number: 222285358

3839
Gindi Associates Foundation, Inc. ⌑
311 Park Ave.
Oakhurst 07755

Established in 1982 in NJ.
Donor(s): Century 21, Inc.
Foundation type: Independent
Financial data (yr. ended 5/31/89): Assets, $1,745,791 (M); gifts received, $200,000; expenditures, $354,332, including $351,560 for grants (high: $118,000).
Purpose and activities: Support for Jewish religious institutions and Jewish welfare.
Application information: Contributes only to pre-selected organizations. Applications not accepted.
Trustees: Abraham Gindi, Ralph I. Gindi, Sam Gindi.
Employer Identification Number: 222412138

3840
Salvatore Giordano Foundation, Inc. ⌑ ☆
154-4 Mountview Ln.
Bernardsville 07924

Donor(s): Salvatore Giordano, Salvatore Giordano, Jr., Joseph Giordano.
Foundation type: Independent
Financial data (yr. ended 7/31/89): Assets, $1,240,880 (M); expenditures, $22,953, including $21,250 for 11 grants (high: $8,000; low: $500).
Purpose and activities: Support primarily for health and hospitals, a diocese, and social services.
Limitations: No grants to individuals.
Application information: Contributes only to pre-selected organizations. Applications not accepted.
Officers and Directors: Salvatore Giordano, Pres. and Treas.; Joseph Giordano, V.P.; Salvatore Giordano, Jr., V.P.
Employer Identification Number: 116003606

3841
Morris & Lydia Goldfarb Foundation ⌑
Ten Woodbridge Center Dr.
Woodbridge 07095

Established in 1969 in NJ.
Foundation type: Independent
Financial data (yr. ended 12/31/89): Assets, $1,058,122 (M); gifts received, $67,691; expenditures, $83,891, including $79,500 for 11 grants (high: $40,000; low: $500).
Purpose and activities: Support primarily for Jewish community centers and homes for the aged.
Limitations: Giving primarily in NJ.
Application information: Applications not accepted.
Trustees: David Kaplowitz, Norman Tanzman, Warren Wilentz.
Employer Identification Number: 237014201

3842
The Grand Marnier Foundation ⌑
Glenpointe Centre West
Teaneck 07666-6897 (201) 836-7799

Established in 1985 in NY.
Donor(s): Carillon Importers, Ltd.
Foundation type: Independent
Financial data (yr. ended 12/31/87): Assets, $5,323,461 (M); gifts received, $2,046,787; expenditures, $283,827, including $202,500 for 1 grant.
Purpose and activities: Support for a Jewish welfare fund, cultural programs, and education.
Application information:
Initial approach: Letter
Deadline(s): None
Write: Jerry Ciraulo, Treas.
Officers and Directors: Michel Roux, Pres.; Joel Buchman, Secy.; Jerry Ciraulo, Treas.
Employer Identification Number: 133258414

3843
E. J. Grassmann Trust ▼
P.O. Box 4470
Warren 07060 (201) 753-2440

Trust established in 1979 in NJ.
Donor(s): Edward J. Grassmann.†
Foundation type: Independent
Financial data (yr. ended 12/31/89): Assets, $28,225,088 (M); gifts received, $8,846; expenditures, $2,485,807, including $2,237,900 for 154 grants (high: $145,000; low: $1,500; average: $5,000-$30,000).
Purpose and activities: Grants for higher and secondary education, hospitals and health organizations, historical associations, environmental conservation, and social welfare organizations, particularly those helping children. Preference given to organizations with low administration costs, and which show efforts to achieve a broad funding base.
Types of support: Endowment funds, scholarship funds, building funds, equipment, land acquisition, capital campaigns.
Limitations: Giving primarily in NJ, particularly Union County; and in GA, primarily middle GA. No grants to individuals, or for operating expenses.
Publications: Application guidelines.
Application information: Application form not required.
Initial approach: Letter
Copies of proposal: 1
Deadline(s): Apr. 20 and Oct. 15
Board meeting date(s): May or June and Nov.
Final notification: After May or June meeting by July 31; after Nov. meeting by Dec. 31
Write: William V. Engel, Exec. Dir.
Officer: William V. Engel,* Exec. Dir.
Trustees:* Charles Danzig, Edward G. Engel, John B. Harris, Jr., Haydn H. Murray.
Number of staff: 1 part-time professional; 2 part-time support.
Employer Identification Number: 226326539

3844
Gulton Foundation, Inc. ⌑
c/o A. P. Bersohn & Co.
17 Arcadian Ave., Suite 108
Paramus 07652-1203

Incorporated in 1961 in NY.
Donor(s): Leslie K. Gulton,† Marian G. Malcolm.
Foundation type: Independent
Financial data (yr. ended 10/31/89): Assets, $7,994,873 (M); expenditures, $342,061, including $316,000 for grants (high: $78,100).
Purpose and activities: Grants for higher education and mental health services; support also for scientific and medical research; some giving in Israel.
Limitations: No grants to individuals.
Application information: Contributes only to pre-selected organizations. Applications not accepted.
Write: Edith Gulton, Pres.
Officers: Edith Gulton, Pres.; Marian G. Malcolm, V.P. and Treas.; Daniel Malcolm, Secy.
Employer Identification Number: 136105207

3845
The Hackett Foundation, Inc.
33 Second St.
Raritan 08869 (201) 231-8252

Incorporated in 1975 in NY.
Donor(s): William J. Hackett.†
Foundation type: Independent
Financial data (yr. ended 12/31/89): Assets, $13,422,323 (M); expenditures, $832,618, including $520,681 for 37 grants (high: $43,131; low: $2,700; average: $1,000-$20,000).
Purpose and activities: Grants primarily to Catholic missions; also giving to Catholic health and social service agencies.
Types of support: Equipment.
Limitations: Giving primarily in NJ, NY, PA. No grants to individuals, or for land acquisition, endowment funds, matching gifts, scholarships, fellowships, research, demonstration projects, publications, or conferences; no loans.
Publications: Annual report, application guidelines.
Application information: Application form required.
Initial approach: Letter
Copies of proposal: 1
Deadline(s): 10th of every month
Board meeting date(s): 3rd Monday of every month
Final notification: 60 days
Write: Ms. Alice T. Hackett, Chair., Grant Comm.
Officers: R. Kevin Hackett, Pres. and Treas.; Denis Hackett, V.P.; Alice T. Hackett, Secy.
Trustees: Rev. Denis P. Hackett, Sr. Patricia Mary Hackett.
Number of staff: 2 full-time professional.
Employer Identification Number: 132840750

3846
Michael and Gertrude Hancouski Foundation ⌑
Three Cobblewood Rd.
Livingston 07039 (201) 994-4175

Incorporated in 1979 in NJ.
Donor(s): Michael Hancouski.†
Foundation type: Independent
Financial data (yr. ended 09/30/88): Assets, $2,928,000 (M); expenditures, $162,299, including $111,000 for 7 grants (high: $20,000; low: $2,000).
Purpose and activities: Awards scholarships paid through institutions.
Types of support: Scholarship funds.
Application information:
Initial approach: Letter
Write: Stephen E. Lampf, Trustee
Trustees: A. William Ferrance, Carolann Lampf, Stephen E. Lampf.
Employer Identification Number: 222487245

3847
The Hanes Foundation ⌑
c/o DiFranco & Co.
2333 Morris Ave.
Union 07083
Application address: P.O. Box 5116 FDR Station, New York, NY 10150; Tel.: (212) 758-7418

Incorporated in 1952 in NY.
Donor(s): John W. Hanes, Sr., Hope Y. Hanes.
Foundation type: Independent
Financial data (yr. ended 12/31/88): Assets, $312,517 (M); gifts received, $118,000; expenditures, $105,432, including $102,100 for 14 grants (high: $50,000; low: $100).
Purpose and activities: Contributes to cultural organizations, conservation programs, and educational institutions.
Application information: Application form not required.
Initial approach: Proposal
Deadline(s): None
Write: David G. Hanes, Secy.
Officers and Directors: John W. Hanes, Jr., Pres.; David G. Hanes, Secy.; John W. Hanes, Sr., Treas.; Mrs. John W. Hanes, Mrs. Ormsby H. Matthiessen, Agnes H. McKnight.
Employer Identification Number: 136087828

3848
Harbourton Foundation ⌑
33 Witherspoon St.
Princeton 08542-3298

Established in 1982 in NJ.
Foundation type: Independent
Financial data (yr. ended 6/30/87): Assets, $1,463,728 (M); expenditures, $36,218, including $24,000 for grants.
Purpose and activities: Support primarily for medical research and for a theater.
Types of support: General purposes.
Application information: Contributes only to pre-selected organizations. Applications not accepted.
Officers and Directors: James S. Regan, Pres. and Treas.; Amy H. Regan, V.P.; Kathleen Dalzell.
Employer Identification Number: 223027014

3849
Harris Brothers Foundation ⌑
Stonewyck 156B Sutton Rd.
Lebanon 08833 (201) 832-2761

Established in 1956 in DE.
Donor(s): Members of the Harris family.
Foundation type: Independent
Financial data (yr. ended 12/31/88): Assets, $1,796,029 (M); expenditures, $95,543, including $91,000 for 23 grants (high: $15,000; low: $2,000).
Purpose and activities: Giving primarily for local Protestant church support.
Limitations: Giving primarily in NJ.
Application information:
Deadline(s): None
Write: Barbara L. Harris, Secy.-Treas.
Officers: Walter I. Harris, Pres.; George W. Harris, V.P.; O.H. Hewit III, V.P.; Frederick Scheidig, V.P.; Barbara L. Harris, Secy.-Treas.
Employer Identification Number: 136167230

3850
Sydney J. Harris Charitable Trust ⌑ ☆
c/o National State Bank
One Maple St.
Summit 07901

Established in 1988 in NJ.
Foundation type: Independent

Financial data (yr. ended 07/31/89): Assets, $1,364,231 (M); gifts received, $1,311,406; expenditures, $69,650, including $65,000 for 5 grants (high: $25,000; low: $5,000).
Purpose and activities: Giving for Jewish organizations, including social services and a congregation; support also for a health care foundation.
Types of support: Renovation projects.
Limitations: Giving primarily in NJ.
Application information:
Write: Robert C. Brandt, V.P., National State Bank
Trustee: National State Bank.
Employer Identification Number: 236455160

3851
O. W. Havens Foundation ⌑
P.O. Box 106
Lakewood 08701

Established in 1978 in NJ.
Foundation type: Independent
Financial data (yr. ended 12/31/88): Assets, $3,508,389 (M); expenditures, $142,108, including $106,000 for 24 grants (high: $5,000; low: $1,000).
Purpose and activities: Emphasis on hospitals and youth; aid also for indigents through religious organizations.
Limitations: Giving primarily in Lakewood, NJ.
Application information: Contributes only to pre-selected organizations. Applications not accepted.
Officers: Mabel E. Curtis, Pres.; Herman Winkelmann, V.P.; James Grandinetti, Secy.-Treas.
Trustee: Florian Lombardi, Edward Rothstein.
Employer Identification Number: 222175726

3852
William T. & Marie J. Henderson Foundation, Inc. ⌑
179 Charlton Ave.
South Orange 07079

Established in 1968 in NJ.
Foundation type: Operating
Financial data (yr. ended 11/30/88): Assets, $1,855,043 (M); expenditures, $71,250, including $67,900 for 62 grants (high: $10,000; low: $100).
Purpose and activities: A private operating foundation; giving to higher education and religious organizations.
Application information: Application form not required.
Initial approach: Proposal
Deadline(s): None
Write: Marie J. Henderson, Pres.
Officers: Marie J. Henderson, Pres.; William Henderson, John T. Magnier, Marie J. Magnier.
Employer Identification Number: 226033693

3853
The Sandy Hill Foundation ⌑
c/o Wesray Corp.
330 South St.
Morristown 07960 (201) 540-9020

Incorporated in 1985 in NJ.
Donor(s): Frank E. Walsh, Jr.
Foundation type: Independent
Financial data (yr. ended 7/31/88): Assets, $3,930,304 (M); gifts received, $2,727,995; expenditures, $467,138, including $454,650 for 38 grants (high: $110,000; low: $100).
Purpose and activities: Support primarily for higher education.
Limitations: Giving primarily in NY, NJ and PA.
Application information: Application form not required.
Deadline(s): None
Write: Rose Bruttaniti
Officers and Directors: Frank E. Walsh, Jr., Pres.; Mary Walsh, Secy.; Jeffrey R. Walsh, Mgr.
Employer Identification Number: 222668774

3854
Historical Research Foundation, Inc. ⌑ ☆
700 South Fourth St.
Harrison 07029 (201) 481-4800

Established in 1958 in NY.
Donor(s): Lawrence Fertig,† Walten Judd Foundation.
Foundation type: Independent
Financial data (yr. ended 12/31/88): Assets, $850,718 (M); gifts received, $88,247; expenditures, $118,147, including $44,750 for 4 grants (high: $25,000; low: $10,000) and $60,000 for 12 grants to individuals (high: $7,500; low: $1,000).
Purpose and activities: Grants to individuals and organizations for scholarly research and studies in the social sciences, including historic or philosophic analysis.
Types of support: Grants to individuals, research.
Application information:
Initial approach: Proposal
Deadline(s): None
Write: Arthur J. Anderson, Pres.
Officers and Trustees: Arthur J. Anderson, Pres. and Treas.; William Buckley, Jr., V.P.; Jeffrey Hart, Secy.; John Chamberlain, Ruth I. Matthews.
Employer Identification Number: 136059836

3855
Hoechst Celanese Foundation, Inc. ☆
Rte. 202-206 North
P.O. Box 2500
Somerville 08876-1258 (201) 231-2880

Established in 1984 in NJ.
Donor(s): Hoechst Celanese Corp.
Foundation type: Company-sponsored
Financial data (yr. ended 12/31/89): Assets, $1,003,148 (M); expenditures, $620,800, including $580,500 for 21 grants (high: $50,000; low: $1,000).
Purpose and activities: Giving for education, particularly the sciences; health and hospitals; and welfare and youth organizations. Support also for civic and public affairs, museums and other cultural programs, and the environment. Grants are based on an organization's influence on the community, its potential of increasing public awareness of Hoechst Celanese, and the level of Hoechst employee involvement.
Types of support: Capital campaigns, operating budgets, research, special projects, in-kind gifts, continuing support, employee matching gifts, employee-related scholarships.
Limitations: Giving primarily in headquarters city and national operating locations; national organizations also considered. No support for religious or fraternal organizations. No grants to individuals, or for operating expenses of United Way recipients; no commitments for more than five years; special projects of hospitals have low priority.
Application information: Application form not required.
Initial approach: Letter
Copies of proposal: 1
Deadline(s): None
Write: Lewis Alpaugh, V.P.
Officers: W.E. Steel, Chair.; Lewis F. Alpaugh, V.P. and Exec. Dir.; E. Collins, Secy.; J. Zeitun, Treas.
Number of staff: 1 full-time professional; 1 part-time professional.
Employer Identification Number: 222577170

3856
The Hoffmann-La Roche Foundation
P.O. Box 278
Nutley 07110 (201) 235-3797

Trust established in 1945 in NJ.
Donor(s): Hoffmann-La Roche, Inc.
Foundation type: Company-sponsored
Financial data (yr. ended 12/31/88): Assets, $28 (M); gifts received, $693,496; expenditures, $693,507, including $693,496 for 26 grants (high: $100,000; low: $1,500; average: $1,500-$100,000).
Purpose and activities: Giving for medical and scientific research at leading universities and teaching hospitals and for general support of education programs in health, science and math; support also for teachers in communities where company has sites or employee populations.
Types of support: Research, fellowships.
Limitations: Giving primarily in the northeastern states, with emphasis on NY and NJ. No grants to individuals, or for general support, operating budgets, capital or endowment funds, matching gifts, special projects, publications, or conferences; no loans.
Application information: Application form not required.
Initial approach: Letter
Copies of proposal: 1
Board meeting date(s): As required
Final notification: 4 to 6 weeks
Write: Rosemary Bruner, Admin. Dir.
Officer: H.F. Boardman, Secy.
Trustees: R.G. Kuntzman, I. Lerner, Martin F. Stadler.
Number of staff: None.
Employer Identification Number: 226063790

3857
Richard H. Holzer Memorial Foundation ⌑
120 Sylvan Ave.
Englewood Cliffs 07632 (201) 947-8810

Established in 1969 in NJ.
Donor(s): Erich Holzer.
Foundation type: Independent
Financial data (yr. ended 06/30/89): Assets, $2,237,538 (M); gifts received, $115,500;

expenditures, $289,936, including $280,615 for 35 grants (high: $57,500; low: $100).
Purpose and activities: Giving primarily for Jewish organizations and welfare funds and for cultural activities, particularly music.
Application information:
Initial approach: Letter
Officers: Eva Holzer, Pres.; Erich Holzer, Secy.-Treas.
Employer Identification Number: 237014880

3858
The Hoyt Foundation ⌑
Half Acre Rd.
Cranbury 08512 (609) 655-6000

Incorporated in 1957 in DE.
Foundation type: Operating
Financial data (yr. ended 06/30/89): Assets, $3,063,992 (M); expenditures, $154,402, including $147,000 for 13 grants (high: $38,000; low: $1,000).
Purpose and activities: Grants primarily for higher and secondary education, with emphasis on medical education and research; support also for health agencies and hospitals, the handicapped, and music.
Limitations: Giving primarily in NJ and NY. No grants to individuals.
Application information:
Initial approach: Letter
Deadline(s): None
Write: Charles O. Hoyt, Pres.
Officers: Charles O. Hoyt, Pres.; Frank M. Berger, M.D., V.P.; Suzanne H. Garcia, Secy.; Henry H. Hoyt, Jr., Treas.
Employer Identification Number: 136110857

3859
The Huber Foundation ▼
P.O. Box 277
Rumson 07760 (201) 872-2322

Incorporated in 1949 in NJ.
Donor(s): members of the Huber and Mertens families, and others.
Foundation type: Independent
Financial data (yr. ended 12/31/88): Assets, $18,900,558 (M); expenditures, $1,212,986, including $1,012,200 for 41 grants (high: $150,000; low: $1,500; average: $5,000-$50,000).
Purpose and activities: Grants primarily to organizations working in the areas of family planning, reproductive freedom, and population control.
Types of support: Annual campaigns, matching funds, operating budgets, seed money, special projects, publications.
Limitations: No support for foreign organizations or international projects. No grants to individuals, or for scholarships, fellowships, research, or building or endowment funds; no loans.
Publications: Annual report (including application guidelines).
Application information: Application form not required.
Initial approach: Letter
Copies of proposal: 1
Deadline(s): None
Board meeting date(s): 4 times a year; dates not fixed
Final notification: 3 months
Write: Lorraine Barnhart, Exec. Dir.
Officers and Trustees:* Hans A. Huber,* Pres.; David G. Huber,* V.P.; Michael W. Huber,* Secy.; Julia Ann Nagy, Treas.; Gertrude H. Mertens, Christopher W. Seely.
Number of staff: 1 part-time professional.
Employer Identification Number: 210737062

3860
The Hyde and Watson Foundation ▼
437 Southern Blvd.
Chatham Township 07928 (201) 966-6024

The Lillia Babbitt Hyde Foundation incorporated in 1924 in NY; The John Jay and Eliza Jane Watson Foundation incorporated in 1949; consolidation of two foundations into Hyde and Watson Foundation in 1983.
Donor(s): Lillia Babbitt Hyde,† Eliza Jane Watson.†
Foundation type: Independent
Financial data (yr. ended 12/31/89): Assets, $53,342,898 (M); expenditures, $2,976,650, including $2,349,270 for 187 grants (high: $100,000; low: $900; average: $3,000-$20,000).
Purpose and activities: "Support primarily for capital projects of lasting value which tend to increase quality, capacity or efficiency of a grantee's programs or services, such as purchase or relocation of facilities, facilities improvements, capital equipment, instructive materials development, and certain medical research areas. Broad fields include health, education, religion, social services, arts, and humanities. A substantial proportion of grant funds each year will be allocated to projects for which the foundation's support makes a major contribution."
Types of support: Building funds, equipment, land acquisition, matching funds, research, seed money, emergency funds, renovation projects, capital campaigns.
Limitations: Giving primarily in the NY-northern NJ metropolitan area. No grants to individuals, or generally for operating budgets, continuing support, annual campaigns, general endowments, deficit financing, scholarships, or fellowships.
Publications: Annual report (including application guidelines).
Application information: Application format required if proposal is considered by grants committee. Application form required.
Initial approach: Letter
Copies of proposal: 1
Deadline(s): Submit preliminary letter of appeal by Feb. 15 for spring meeting and by Sept. 15 for fall meeting
Board meeting date(s): Apr./May and Nov./Dec.
Final notification: After board meeting
Write: Robert W. Parsons, Jr., Pres.
Officers and Trustees:* John G. MacKechnie,* Chair.; Robert W. Parsons, Jr.,* Pres.; Roger B. Parsons,* V.P. and Secy.; Hunter W. Corbin,* V.P.; John W. Holman, Jr.,* Treas.; H. Corbin Day, William V. Engel, David G. Ferguson, G. Morrison Hubbard, Jr., Richard W. KixMiller.
Number of staff: 7 full-time professional.
Employer Identification Number: 222425725

3861
I.J.J. Foundation, Inc. ⌑ ☆
116 Truman Dr.
Edison 08817

Incorporated in 1985 in NJ.
Foundation type: Independent
Financial data (yr. ended 12/31/88): Assets, $90,862 (M); expenditures, $117,456, including $117,200 for 9 grants (high: $80,000; low: $50).
Purpose and activities: Giving for a Jewish welfare fund and for higher education.
Limitations: Giving primarily in NJ. No grants to individuals.
Application information: Contributes only to pre-selected organizations. Applications not accepted.
Officers and Trustees: S. Irving Sherr, Pres.; Julius Kapik, V.P.; Joel Goldschein, Secy.-Treas.
Employer Identification Number: 222634485

3862
Innovating Worthy Projects Foundation
426 Shore Rd., Suite E
Somers Point 08244 (609) 926-1111

Foundation type: Independent
Financial data (yr. ended 08/31/89): Assets, $5,222,063 (M); expenditures, $350,677, including $177,222 for 25 grants (high: $75,000; low: $100) and $322 for 2 grants to individuals (high: $215; low: $107).
Purpose and activities: Support primarily for the education, service or care of the handicapped; programs to help the aged, and preschool medical programs.
Types of support: Seed money, special projects.
Application information: Application form required.
Initial approach: Letter or telephone
Copies of proposal: 6
Deadline(s): None
Board meeting date(s): June, Sept., and Dec.
Final notification: 90 days
Write: Dr. Irving W. Packer, Chair.
Officers and Trustees:* Irving W. Packer,* Chair; John McAfee,* Pres.; Stephen Weiss,* Secy.; Richard Culbertson, Treas.; David Crabtree, Edward E. Packer, Estelle Packer.
Number of staff: 2 full-time professional; 1 full-time support.
Employer Identification Number: 226083636

3863
The International Foundation
c/o John D. Carrico & Associates, P.A.
Ten Park Place, P.O. Box 88
Butler 07405 (201) 838-4664
Additional tel.: (615) 598-0894

Incorporated in 1948 in DE.
Foundation type: Independent
Financial data (yr. ended 12/31/89): Assets, $18,790,995 (M); expenditures, $1,061,674, including $830,000 for 47 grants (high: $50,000; low: $5,000; average: $5,000-$50,000).
Purpose and activities: Giving "to help people of developing nations in their endeavors to solve some of their problems, to attain a better standard of living, and to obtain a reasonable degree of self-sufficiency. Grants are made in

four general areas: 1) Agriculture--research and production, 2) Health--medical, nutrition, and water, 3) Education--formal at all levels and research, and 4) Social Development--cultural, economic, community, and entreprenurial activity. Some aid to refugees and grants for population planning are given."
Types of support: Seed money, building funds, equipment, publications, conferences and seminars, emergency funds, special projects.
Limitations: No grants to individuals, or for endowment funds, operating budgets, scholarships, fellowships, or matching gifts; no loans.
Publications: Informational brochure (including application guidelines).
Application information: Application form not required.
Initial approach: Letter
Copies of proposal: 2
Deadline(s): Submit proposal preferably from Nov. to Mar.
Board meeting date(s): Jan., Apr., July, and Oct.
Final notification: 6 months; grants awarded Nov. 30
Write: Dr. Edward A. Holmes, Grants Chair.
Officers and Trustees:* Frank Madden,* Pres.; David S. Bate,* V.P.; John D. Carrico, Secy.-Treas.; Edward A. Holmes,* Grants Chair.; John D. Carrico, Duncan W. Clark, M.D., J. Carter Hammel.
Number of staff: 1 part-time support.
Employer Identification Number: 131962255

3864
The Ix Foundation ⌑
c/o Frank Ix and Sons, Inc.
3300 Hudson Ave.
Union City 07087 (201) 865-2111

Incorporated in 1948 in NJ.
Donor(s): Franklin Ix and Sons.
Foundation type: Company-sponsored
Financial data (yr. ended 12/31/88): Assets, $1,134,284 (M); expenditures, $163,227, including $139,100 for 66 grants (high: $25,000; low: $100).
Purpose and activities: Grants for higher and secondary education, Roman Catholic church support, hospitals, and community development.
Limitations: Giving primarily in NJ, and in other areas of company operations in New York, NY; Lexington, NC; and Charlottesville, VA.
Application information: Apply to local personnel manager. Application form required.
Deadline(s): None
Trustees: Mary Catherine Gaynor, Alexander F. Ix, Jr., Douglas E. Ix, Barbara E. Leis.
Employer Identification Number: 221713050

3865
Janet Memorial Foundation ⌑
24-52 Rahway Ave.
Elizabeth 07202 (201) 527-9393

Foundation type: Independent
Financial data (yr. ended 12/31/88): Assets, $1,147,486 (M); gifts received, $25,040; expenditures, $160,844, including $100,000 for 20 grants (high: $10,500; low: $200).
Purpose and activities: Support primarily for youth and child welfare programs, including health associations, social services, and educational support.
Limitations: Giving primarily in Union County, NJ.
Application information:
Initial approach: Letter
Deadline(s): Sept. 15
Write: Alvin W. Taylor, Exec. Dir.
Officers and Trustees: Mrs. Michael Bizon, Pres.; Kenneth Benson, V.P.; R. Daniel DiSalvi, Recording Secy.; Janet Kniss, Treas.; Alvin W. Taylor, Exec. Dir.; and 7 additional trustees.
Employer Identification Number: 221487216

3866
Jaqua Foundation ⌑
One Garrett Mountain Plaza
West Paterson 07424 (201) 278-9790

Donor(s): George R. Jaqua.†
Foundation type: Independent
Financial data (yr. ended 12/31/88): Assets, $6,594,851 (M); gifts received, $7,347; expenditures, $336,384, including $264,900 for 23 grants (high: $35,000; low: $2,500).
Purpose and activities: Grants primarily for higher education, hospitals, and health services.
Limitations: No support for private foundations. No grants to individuals.
Application information:
Initial approach: Letter
Deadline(s): None
Write: Eli Hoffman, Chair.
Officers: Eli Hoffman, Chair.; John Minnema, V.P.; Samuel Pollock, V.P.; Evans, Hand, Allabogh & Amoresano, Secy.
Employer Identification Number: 222086399

3867
Clara L. D. Jeffery Charitable Residuary Trust
c/o Summit Trust Co.
367 Springfield Ave.
Summit 07901

Trust established in 1969.
Donor(s): Clara L.D. Jeffery.†
Foundation type: Independent
Financial data (yr. ended 12/31/89): Assets, $6,644,717 (M); qualifying distributions, $278,250, including $278,250 for grants.
Purpose and activities: Grants largely for the prevention of cruelty to animals and for higher education.
Application information:
Write: Coleman Burke, Trustee
Trustees: Coleman Burke, Mary B. Partridge, Summit Trust Co.
Employer Identification Number: 226138410

3868
The Jockey Hollow Foundation, Inc.
P.O. Box 462
Bernardsville 07924

Incorporated in 1960 in NJ.
Donor(s): Carl Shirley, Mrs. Carl Shirley.
Foundation type: Independent
Financial data (yr. ended 03/31/89): Assets, $9,578,177 (M); gifts received, $206,000; expenditures, $690,604, including $596,500 for 48 grants (high: $220,000; low: $1,000).
Purpose and activities: Support for conservation, hospitals, and cultural programs.
Types of support: Scholarship funds.
Limitations: Giving primarily in NJ and MA. No grants to individuals.
Application information:
Initial approach: Proposal
Deadline(s): None
Write: Betsy S. Michel, Pres.
Officers and Trustees:* Betsy S. Michel,* Pres. and Secy.; Joanne S. Forkner,* V.P.; Carl Shirley,* V.P.; Clifford L. Michel,* Treas.; Virginia L. Hartmann, Betsy B. Shirley.
Employer Identification Number: 221724138

3869
Johnson & Johnson Family of Companies Contribution Fund ▼
One Johnson & Johnson Plaza
New Brunswick 08933 (201) 524-3255

Incorporated in 1953 in NJ.
Donor(s): Johnson and Johnson, and subsidiary companies.
Foundation type: Company-sponsored
Financial data (yr. ended 12/31/89): Assets, $3,145,000 (M); gifts received, $7,907,250; expenditures, $8,839,489, including $6,344,825 for 300 grants (high: $1,000,000; low: $200; average: $1,000-$25,000) and $2,441,538 for 4,000 employee matching gifts.
Purpose and activities: Grants for projects or organizations which advance the science of medicine. Support also for higher education, arts and cultural programs, civic affairs and public interest organizations, social welfare agencies, including community funds, and an employee matching gift program.
Types of support: Operating budgets, continuing support, annual campaigns, emergency funds, matching funds, fellowships, research, technical assistance, special projects, employee matching gifts, general purposes, scholarship funds.
Limitations: Giving primarily in areas where company has facilities, to both national and local organizations. No grants to individuals, or for deficit financing, capital or endowment funds, or publications; no loans.
Publications: Application guidelines, program policy statement.
Application information: Application form not required.
Initial approach: Telephone or letter
Copies of proposal: 1
Deadline(s): None
Board meeting date(s): Mar., June, Sept., and Dec.
Final notification: 2 months
Write: Herbert T. Nelson, V.P.
Officers and Trustees:* John J. Heldrich,* Pres.; F.A. Bolden,* V.P. and Secy.; Herbert T. Nelson,* V.P.; Andrew J. Markey,* Treas.
Number of staff: 2 full-time professional; 2 full-time support.
Employer Identification Number: 226062811

3870
Barbara Piasecka Johnson Foundation ▼ ⌑
Eight Lawrenceville Rd.
Princeton 08540 (609) 921-1200

Established in 1976 in DE.
Donor(s): J. Seward Johnson, Sr.,† Barbara Piasecka Johnson.
Foundation type: Independent
Financial data (yr. ended 12/31/88): Assets, $2,561,754 (M); expenditures, $1,337,335, including $1,005,392 for 13 grants (high: $500,000; low: $2,000; average: $2,000-$50,000) and $172,717 for 24 grants to individuals (high: $17,100; low: $1,500).
Purpose and activities: To support institutions which promote human rights in Poland, promote institutions of Polish character in the U.S. and abroad, and support artists and scientists, primarily those who are Polish or of Polish extraction, and institutions which support such individuals.
Types of support: Grants to individuals, conferences and seminars, fellowships, publications, research, special projects, student aid.
Publications: Application guidelines.
Application information: Grants to pre-selected organizations only; scholarships and fellowships are for graduate, Doctoral and post-graduate education only; no undergraduate program considered. Application form required.
Initial approach: Letter or telephone
Copies of proposal: 1
Deadline(s): Mar. 30 and Sept. 1; all considered within three-month basis
Board meeting date(s): July
Write: Beata P. Bulaj, Secy.
Officers and Trustees:* Barbara Piasecka Johnson,* Chair.; Beata Bulaj,* Secy.; John M. Peach,* Treas.; Gregory Gorzynski, Christopher Piasecki, Grzegorz Piasecki, Wojciech Piasecki.
Number of staff: 1 part-time professional; 1 part-time support.
Employer Identification Number: 510201795

3871
The Robert Wood Johnson Foundation ▼
P.O. Box 2316
Princeton 08543-2316 (609) 452-8701

Incorporated in 1936 in NJ.
Donor(s): Robert Wood Johnson.†
Foundation type: Independent
Financial data (yr. ended 12/31/89): Assets, $2,608,347,000 (M); expenditures, $106,030,000, including $98,600,000 for 412 grants.
Purpose and activities: Improvement of health services in the U.S., with emphasis on projects to improve access to personal health care for the most underserved population groups; to make health care arrangements more effective and affordable; and to help people maintain or regain maximum attainable function in their everyday lives. Within these areas, support provided for the development and testing of previously untried approaches; demonstrations to assess objectively the operational effectiveness of approaches shown to be effective in more limited settings; and the broader diffusion of programs objectively shown to improve health status or make health care more affordable.
Types of support: Seed money, research, special projects, fellowships, program-related investments.
Limitations: Giving limited to the U.S. No support for international activities; programs or institutions concerned solely with a specific disease; or basic biomedical research or broad public health problems, except as they might relate to the foundation's areas of interest. No grants to individuals, or for ongoing general operating expenses; endowment funds; capital costs, including construction, renovation, or equipment; conferences or symposia; publications or media projects; or research on unapproved drug therapies or devices.
Publications: Annual report (including application guidelines), informational brochure, program policy statement, application guidelines, occasional report, newsletter.
Application information: Application form not required.
Initial approach: Letter
Copies of proposal: 1
Deadline(s): None
Board meeting date(s): Quarterly
Final notification: 6 to 12 months
Write: Edward H. Robbins, Proposal Mgr.
Officers and Trustees:* Sydney F. Wentz,* Chair. and C.E.O.; Steven A. Schroeder, M.D.,* Pres.; Richard C. Reynolds, M.D., Exec. V.P.; William R. Walsh, Jr.,* Exec. V.P. for Finance and Treas.; J. Warren Wood III, V.P. and Secy.; Thomas P. Gore, V.P. for Communications; Alan B. Cohen, V.P.; Ruby P. Hearn, V.P.; Jeffrey C. Merrill, V.P.; Edward C. Andrews, Jr., M.D., James Burke, Edward R. Eberle, Lawrence G. Foster, Leonard F. Hill, Frank J. Hoenemeyer, John J. Horan, Jack W. Owen, Norman Rosenberg, M.D., Richard B. Sellars, Foster B. Whitlock.
Number of staff: 35 full-time professional; 55 full-time support; 2 part-time support.
Employer Identification Number: 226029397

3872
Blanche and George Jones Fund, Inc. ⌑
Box 306M
Morristown 07960 (201) 766-5763

Established in 1981 in NJ.
Foundation type: Independent
Financial data (yr. ended 2/28/88): Assets, $1,831,140 (M); expenditures, $79,336, including $60,000 for 25 grants (high: $5,000; low: $1,000).
Purpose and activities: Support primarily for hospitals and health organizations, higher and other education, religious organizations, and youth and child welfare programs.
Application information:
Initial approach: Letter
Write: Phyllis J. Stitzer, Pres.
Officers and Trustees: Phyllis J. Stitzer, Pres.; Barbara J. Foreman, V.P.; William E. Bardusch, Jr., Secy.-Treas.
Employer Identification Number: 136028786

3873
Kaplen Foundation ⌑
100 Huguenot Ave.
Englewood 07631 (201) 568-6700

Foundation type: Independent
Financial data (yr. ended 07/31/89): Assets, $6,314,647 (M); gifts received, $1,002,000; expenditures, $212,463, including $197,186 for 62 grants (high: $137,985; low: $25).
Purpose and activities: Contributes to Jewish organizations; support also for general charitable giving.
Application information:
Initial approach: Letter
Deadline(s): None
Write: Wilson R. Kaplen, Trustee
Trustees: Alexander Kaplen, Lawrence Kaplen, Michael L. Kaplen, Wilson R. Kaplen, Andrew V. Schnurr.
Employer Identification Number: 226048152

3874
Harry Katz Memorial Fund ⌑
c/o First Fidelity Bank, N.A., NJ
765 Broad St.
Newark 07101

Foundation type: Independent
Financial data (yr. ended 12/31/87): Assets, $1,210,186 (M); expenditures, $74,370, including $58,000 for 8 grants (high: $10,380; low: $2,500).
Purpose and activities: Support primarily for Jewish education and community and family services.
Application information:
Initial approach: Letter or proposal
Deadline(s): None
Trustees: Florence K. Bernstein, First Fidelity Bank, N.A., NJ.
Employer Identification Number: 510171174

3875
Peter & Cynthia K. Kellogg Foundation ⌑
39 Stewart Rd.
Short Hills 07078

Established in 1983 in NJ.
Donor(s): Peter R. Kellogg, Charles K. Kellogg, Lee I. Kellogg, IAT Syndicate, Inc.
Foundation type: Independent
Financial data (yr. ended 6/30/88): Assets, $2,169,189 (M); gifts received, $383,500; expenditures, $115,673, including $32,000 for 12 grants (high: $10,000; low: $500).
Purpose and activities: Support for education, with emphasis on higher education, and for health and social services.
Limitations: No grants to individuals.
Application information: Contributes only to pre-selected organizations. Applications not accepted.
Officers: Peter R. Kellogg, Pres.; Cynthia K. Kellogg, Secy.; Marguerite Gorman, Treas.
Employer Identification Number: 222472914

3876
The John R. Kennedy Foundation, Inc. ⌑
75 Chestnut Ridge Rd.
Montvale 07645

Incorporated in 1951 in DE.
Donor(s): John R. Kennedy, Sr., Luke A. Mulligan.†
Foundation type: Independent
Financial data (yr. ended 12/31/88): Assets, $3,521,745 (M); expenditures, $302,424, including $286,720 for 14 grants (high: $200,000; low: $1,000).
Purpose and activities: Grants largely for higher education, Roman Catholic church-related programs, social services, and hospitals.
Limitations: No grants to individuals.
Application information:
Initial approach: Letter
Deadline(s): None
Write: John R. Kennedy III, V.P.
Officers: John R. Kennedy, Jr., Pres.; James W. Kennedy, V.P. and Secy.; John R. Kennedy III, V.P.
Directors: Elizabeth Kennedy, Paula Kennedy.
Employer Identification Number: 221714822

3877
Quentin J. Kennedy Foundation ⌑
20 Olds Smith Rd.
Tenafly 07670
Application address: 75 Chestnut Ridge Rd., Montvale, NJ 07645; Tel.: (201) 391-1776

Established in 1986 in NJ.
Foundation type: Independent
Financial data (yr. ended 12/31/88): Assets, $3,893,982 (M); gifts received, $20,000; expenditures, $150,979, including $149,800 for 18 grants (high: $50,550; low: $250).
Purpose and activities: Support primarily for Catholic giving, including welfare; support also for hospitals and for higher education.
Limitations: No grants to individuals.
Application information: Application form not required.
Initial approach: Letter
Deadline(s): None
Write: Quentin J. Kennedy, Pres.
Officers: Quentin J. Kennedy, Pres. and Treas.; Mary Elizabeth Kennedy, V.P.
Employer Identification Number: 222653050

3878
The James Kerney Foundation ⌑
c/o Kerney, Kuser, Drinker, et al.
One Palmer Sq., P.O. Box 627
Princeton 08542

Incorporated in 1934 in NJ.
Donor(s): Members of the Kerney family.
Foundation type: Independent
Financial data (yr. ended 12/31/88): Assets, $2,201,931 (M); gifts received, $25,000; expenditures, $151,223, including $134,694 for 14 grants (high: $50,000; low: $1,000).
Purpose and activities: Giving primarily for hospitals, youth agencies, higher education, and Roman Catholic church support.
Types of support: Scholarship funds, building funds.
Limitations: Giving limited to Trenton, NJ, and its surrounding area. No grants to individuals, or for operating budgets.
Application information:
Write: Albert B. Kahn, Jr., Secy.
Officers: Joseph P. Comley III, Pres.; Albert B. Kahn, Jr., Secy.; J. Regan Kearney, Treas.
Trustees: Richard Bilotti, T. Lincoln Kerney II, Edward L. Meara III, Sheila McNeil Priory.
Employer Identification Number: 226055884

3879
KIHI Foundation ⌑
(Formerly GFI/Knoll International Foundation)
c/o M. Schwartzbard & Associates
354 Eisenhower Pkwy.
Livingston 07039

Established in New York around 1983.
Donor(s): General Felt Industries, Inc.
Foundation type: Company-sponsored
Financial data (yr. ended 12/31/88): Assets, $116,160 (M); gifts received, $1,850,000; expenditures, $1,264,242, including $1,264,056 for grants (high: $256,296).
Purpose and activities: Giving for higher education with emphasis on government, and for cultural affairs, Jewish welfare, organizations in Israel, and secondary education.
Types of support: General purposes.
Limitations: Giving primarily in New York, NY. No grants to individuals.
Application information: Application form not required.
Initial approach: Proposal
Deadline(s): None
Officers: Rocco A. Barbieri, Pres.; Robert Condon, Jr., V.P.; Gary A. Schonwald, Secy.
Director: Marshall S. Cogan.
Employer Identification Number: 222518739

3880
F. M. Kirby Foundation, Inc. ▼
17 DeHart St.
P.O. Box 151
Morristown 07963-0151 (201) 538-4800
Additional tel.: (212) 732-2265; IRS filing state: DE

Incorporated in 1931 in DE.
Donor(s): F.M. Kirby,† Allan P. Kirby, Sr.,† F.M. Kirby.
Foundation type: Independent
Financial data (yr. ended 12/31/89): Assets, $200,000,000 (M); expenditures, $9,000,000, including $8,000,000 for 600 grants (high: $570,000; low: $150; average: $15,000-$25,000).
Purpose and activities: Support for higher and secondary education, health and hospitals, community funds, historic preservation, church support and church-related organizations, social services, conservation, public policy organizations, and population control. Grants almost entirely limited to organizations associated with personal interests of present or former foundation directors.
Types of support: Operating budgets, special projects, general purposes, equipment, renovation projects, research, scholarship funds, seed money, annual campaigns, continuing support.
Limitations: Giving primarily in NY, NJ, PA, and VA. No grants to individuals, or for fundraising campaigns; no loans or pledges.
Publications: Informational brochure.
Application information: Application form not required.
Initial approach: Proposal with cover letter; no telephone solicitations accepted
Copies of proposal: 1
Deadline(s): Proposals considered throughout the year; deadline Oct. 31
Board meeting date(s): Quarterly; proposals are acted on in June and Dec.
Final notification: By Dec. 31 for positive responses only
Write: F.M. Kirby, Pres.
Officers and Director:* F.M. Kirby,* Pres.; Paul B. Mott, Jr., Exec. Dir.
Number of staff: 2 part-time professional; 2 part-time support.
Employer Identification Number: 516017929

3881
Ernest Christian Klipstein Foundation ⌑
Village Rd.
New Vernon 07967

Established in 1954 in NJ.
Donor(s): Kenneth H. Klipstein.
Foundation type: Independent
Financial data (yr. ended 12/31/86): Assets, $1,593,296 (M); expenditures, $65,715, including $52,555 for 91 grants (high: $5,000; low: $25).
Purpose and activities: Grants for higher education, cultural programs, and conservation.
Officers: Kenneth H. Klipstein, Pres.; David H. Klipstein, V.P. and Treas.; Marion C. White, Secy.
Employer Identification Number: 226028529

3882
Fanny and Svante Knistrom Foundation
c/o Richard Wayne Stickel
229 Main St.
Chatham 07928
Mailing address: Three Holbrook Rd., Wayland, MA 01778

Established in 1972 in NJ.
Donor(s): Svante Knistrom,† Fanny Knistrom.†
Foundation type: Independent
Financial data (yr. ended 5/31/89): Assets, $5,695,032 (M); expenditures, $277,544, including $204,270 for 21 grants (high: $30,000; low: $5,000).
Purpose and activities: Emphasis on health, education, and human rights, especially of marginal groups such as battered women, homeless families, and disabled persons; support also for programs for Native Americans primarily in New England.
Limitations: Giving primarily in CA, FL, MA, NH, and NJ; for Native American programs, primarily in New England. No support for political or religious purposes. No grants to individuals.
Application information: Application form not required.
Initial approach: Letter
Copies of proposal: 1
Deadline(s): May 1 and Oct. 1
Board meeting date(s): May and Oct.

Write: Jean Buesing
Officers and Trustees:* Virginia Kreuzberger,* Pres.; Gregory P. Buesing,* V.P. and Treas.; Ann Buesing,* Secy.; Guy K. Buesing, Carl A. Frann, Donald Kreuzberger, Douglas Kreuzberger.
Employer Identification Number: 222011417

3883
The KPMG Peat Marwick Foundation ▼
(Formerly The Peat Marwick Foundation)
Three Chestnut Ridge Rd.
Montvale 07645 (201) 307-7151

Trust established in 1968 in NY.
Donor(s): KPMG Peat Marwick, and its partners and employees.
Foundation type: Company-sponsored
Financial data (yr. ended 06/30/89): Assets, $5,644,111 (L); gifts received, $6,227,588; expenditures, $6,690,497, including $3,119,674 for grants (high: $50,000; low: $500; average: $1,000-$25,000) and $3,479,994 for employee matching gifts.
Purpose and activities: To assist the company in providing outstanding service to the profession by conducting programs to strengthen the profession's educational and research resources; grants restricted to educational purposes related to the company's functional areas of practice - accounting, auditing, taxation, management consulting - and middle market services, including the Research Opportunities in Auditing Program (ROA), Tax Research Opportunities (TRO) and Research Opportunities in International Business Information (ROIBI).
Types of support: Employee matching gifts, scholarship funds, special projects, lectureships, research, professorships, conferences and seminars, endowment funds, fellowships, publications, annual campaigns, building funds, capital campaigns, matching funds.
Limitations: No support for intercollegiate athletics. No grants to individuals, with the exception of the foundation competitive programs.
Publications: Annual report, informational brochure (including application guidelines).
Application information: Application form not required.
Initial approach: Contact operating office first; then submit proposal
Copies of proposal: 1
Deadline(s): ROA, TRO, and ROIBI - Oct. 31
Board meeting date(s): Jan. and Aug.
Final notification: Immediately after meeting
Write: Elizabeth Ernst, Foundation Administrator
Officers and Trustees:* F. David Fowler,* Chair.; J.J. Loughlin,* Secy.; Anthony P. Dolanski, T.E. Hanson, James E. Windlinger.
Number of staff: 2 full-time support; 1 part-time support.
Employer Identification Number: 136262199

3884
The Harold and Adeline Kramer Family Foundation, Inc. ⌑ ☆
85 Central Ave.
Clifton 07011-2309

Established in 1985.
Donor(s): Adeline Kramer, Harold Kramer.
Foundation type: Independent
Financial data (yr. ended 5/31/89): Assets, $972,797 (M); expenditures, $141,379, including $138,040 for 19 grants (high: $30,000; low: $500).
Purpose and activities: Giving primarily for Jewish organizations, including temple support and a seminary; support also for higher education and medical research and hospitals.
Types of support: General purposes.
Limitations: No grants to individuals.
Application information: Contributes only to pre-selected organizations. Applications not accepted.
Officers and Trustees: Harold Kramer, Pres. and Mgr.; Frederick Kramer, V.P.; George Kramer, V.P.; Adeline Kramer, Secy.; Arthur Kramer, Treas.
Employer Identification Number: 222615764

3885
Selma & Raymond Kramer Foundation, Inc. ⌑ ☆
P.O. Box 31
Hawthorne 07507-0031

Established in 1967.
Foundation type: Independent
Financial data (yr. ended 12/31/88): Assets, $958,350 (M); expenditures, $114,501, including $108,205 for 45 grants (high: $52,050; low: $10).
Purpose and activities: Giving primarily for Jewish organizations, including welfare funds.
Limitations: No grants to individuals.
Application information: Contributes only to pre-selected organizations. Applications not accepted.
Officers: Selma Kramer, Pres.; Elizabeth Kramer Penn, V.P.; Paul Kramer, Secy.-Treas.
Directors: Garret Kramer, Robert Kramer.
Employer Identification Number: 136256916

3886
KSM Foundation ⌑ ☆
c/o Kings Super Markets, Inc.
Two Dedrick Place
West Caldwell 07006 (201) 575-3320

Established in 1983 in NJ.
Donor(s): Kings Super Markets, Inc.
Foundation type: Company-sponsored
Financial data (yr. ended 6/30/88): Assets, $1,743,576 (M); gifts received, $214,167; expenditures, $223,906, including $215,000 for 1 grant.
Purpose and activities: Giving primarily for Jewish welfare funds; support also for the arts.
Limitations: Giving primarily in NJ. No support for private foundations. No grants to individuals.
Application information:
Initial approach: Letter
Deadline(s): None
Write: Allen I. Bildner, Pres.
Officers: Allen I. Bildner, Pres.; Joan L. Bildner, V.P.; James L. Bildner, Secy.; Robert L. Bildner, Treas.
Employer Identification Number: 222541254

3887
Fred & Esther Kucklinsky Foundation ⌑ ☆
Seven Holden Ln.
Madison 07940-2614

Foundation type: Independent
Financial data (yr. ended 12/31/87): Assets, $973,230 (M); expenditures, $170,244, including $155,900 for 20 grants (high: $65,000; low: $200).
Purpose and activities: Support for higher and other education, human services, and historic preservation and other cultural programs.
Limitations: Giving primarily in NJ. No grants to individuals.
Application information: Application form not required.
Initial approach: Letter
Deadline(s): None
Write: Fred H. Rohn, Pres.
Officer: Fred H. Rohn, Pres.
Trustees: Richard W. Davis, Philip T. Ruegger.
Employer Identification Number: 226071177

3888
The Stefano La Sala Foundation, Inc.
One Bridge Plaza, Suite 105
Fort Lee 07024 (201) 947-9580

Incorporated in 1956 in NY.
Donor(s): Members of the La Sala family, La Sala Contracting Co., Inc., and others.
Foundation type: Independent
Financial data (yr. ended 11/30/88): Assets, $2,238,658 (M); expenditures, $90,329, including $83,018 for grants.
Purpose and activities: Emphasis on higher and secondary education and hospitals; grants also for Roman Catholic church support, and social service agencies.
Limitations: Giving primarily in the New York, NY, area. No support for private foundations. No grants to individuals.
Publications: Newsletter.
Application information: Application form not required.
Initial approach: Letter
Deadline(s): None
Write: A. Stephen La Sala, Dir.
Directors: A. Stephen La Sala, Andrew J. La Sala, Anthony La Sala, Frank La Sala.
Number of staff: 1 part-time professional; 1 part-time support.
Employer Identification Number: 136110920

3889
Langworthy Foundation ⌑ ☆
c/o Princeton Trust Co.
65 Madison Ave., CN-1969
Morristown 07960-5262
Application address: 18 West 11th St., New York, NY 10011

Foundation type: Independent
Financial data (yr. ended 12/31/88): Assets, $1,053,977 (M); expenditures, $70,783,

including $63,100 for 43 grants (high: $15,000; low: $100).
Purpose and activities: Giving for higher and other education, a nautical archaelogy institute, and culture and the performing arts; some support for health associations.
Limitations: No grants to individuals.
Application information: Application form not required.
Deadline(s): None
Write: D.C. Langworthy, Chair.
Committee Members: D.C. Langworthy, Chair.; H.B. Langworthy, H.D. Ribley.
Trustee: Princeton Trust Co.
Employer Identification Number: 236207359

3890
The Large Foundation ⌑
c/o Large, Scammell & Danziger
117 Main St.
Flemington 08822

Incorporated in 1957 in NJ.
Donor(s): George K. Large,† and members of the Large family.
Foundation type: Independent
Financial data (yr. ended 12/31/88): Assets, $5,805,889 (M); expenditures, $420,054, including $378,000 for 39 grants (high: $125,000; low: $500).
Purpose and activities: Emphasis on health agencies; grants also for social service and youth agencies, and historic preservation.
Limitations: Giving primarily in NJ, particularly Hunterdon County.
Application information:
Initial approach: Letter
Deadline(s): Prior to the annual meeting
Board meeting date(s): Oct.
Officers and Trustees:* Edwin K. Large, Jr.,* Pres.; Lloyd B. Wescott,* V.P.; Robert F. Danziger,* Secy.; Charles W. Fouts,* Treas.; Alfred R. Dorf, Benjamin B. Kirkland, Catherine L. O'Shea, Deborah J. Scammell, H. Seely Thomas, Jr.
Employer Identification Number: 226049246

3891
Lasky Company Foundation ⌑
67 East Willow St.
Millburn 07041

Established in 1964 in NJ.
Donor(s): Lasky Co., Sherwood A. Barnhard, Seymour J. Weissman.
Foundation type: Company-sponsored
Financial data (yr. ended 09/30/88): Assets, $47,738 (M); gifts received, $188,850; expenditures, $178,404, including $177,359 for 79 grants (high: $126,550; low: $10).
Purpose and activities: Giving primarily for Jewish welfare funds and organizations; support also for hospitals, arts and culture, youth, and civic affairs.
Limitations: Giving primarily in NJ and NY.
Application information: Contributes only to pre-selected organizations. Applications not accepted.
Officers: Sherwood A. Barnhard, Pres.; Seymour J. Weissman, V.P. and Secy.
Employer Identification Number: 226059928

3892
Blanche & Irving Laurie Foundation, Inc. ⌑
1280 North Broad St.
Hillside 07205-2480 (201) 289-6644

Established in 1983 in NJ.
Foundation type: Independent
Financial data (yr. ended 09/30/88): Assets, $1,186,450 (M); gifts received, $1,314,275; expenditures, $79,030, including $60,000 for 3 grants (high: $25,000; low: $10,000).
Purpose and activities: Giving primarily for child welfare, Jewish community projects and higher education.
Types of support: Annual campaigns.
Application information: Applications not accepted.
Initial approach: Letter
Deadline(s): None
Write: Albert Rich, Treas.
Officers: Irving Laurie, Pres.; Charles Sloane, V.P.; Stanley Sloane, V.P.; Milton H. Stern, Secy.; Albert Rich, Treas.
Employer Identification Number: 222489725

3893
The Lautenberg Foundation ⌑
P.O. Box 816
Newark 07102

Established in 1967 in NJ.
Donor(s): Frank R. Lautenberg Charitable Trusts.
Foundation type: Independent
Financial data (yr. ended 12/31/88): Assets, $3,133,700 (M); expenditures, $577,454, including $554,850 for 81 grants (high: $185,000; low: $100).
Purpose and activities: Grants largely for Jewish welfare funds, education, and cultural programs locally; support also for educational and cultural institutions in Israel.
Limitations: Giving primarily in the NJ and NY area, and Israel. No grants to individuals.
Application information: Contributes only to pre-selected organizations. Applications not accepted.
Officers: Frank R. Lautenberg, Pres.; Lois Lautenberg, V.P.; Fred S. Lafer, Secy.
Employer Identification Number: 226102734

3894
The Lazarus Charitable Trust ⌑
c/o Toys 'R' Us
395 West Passaic St.
Rochelle Park 07662

Established in 1986 in NJ.
Donor(s): Charles Lazarus.
Foundation type: Independent
Financial data (yr. ended 5/31/88): Assets, $1,682,397 (M); expenditures, $90,746.
Purpose and activities: Support for health, including a foundation, medical research, hospitals, educational institutions, and Jewish concerns.
Limitations: Giving primarily in NY and Washington, DC.
Application information:
Initial approach: Letter
Deadline(s): None
Write: Charles Lazarus, Pres.
Officer: Charles Lazarus, Pres.
Employer Identification Number: 133360876

3895
The Leavens Foundation ⌑ ☆
Llewellyn Park
West Orange 07052-4942

Established in 1959.
Donor(s): William B. Leavens, Jr.†
Foundation type: Independent
Financial data (yr. ended 12/31/88): Assets, $2,584,989 (M); gifts received, $683,672; expenditures, $25,703, including $25,125 for 56 grants (high: $3,000; low: $100; average: $100-$600).
Purpose and activities: Giving for the arts, a community fund, hospitals, health associations, and higher education.
Limitations: Giving primarily in NJ. No grants to individuals.
Application information: Contributes only to pre-selected organizations. Applications not accepted.
Trustees: William B. Leavens III, Mgr.; Margaret Leavens, Nancy Wright.
Employer Identification Number: 226063089

3896
Lebersfeld Family Charitable Foundation ⌑ ☆
365 Route 10
East Hanover 07936

Established in 1985 in NJ.
Donor(s): Max Lebersfeld, Herman Lebersfeld.
Foundation type: Independent
Financial data (yr. ended 8/31/89): Assets, $224,301 (M); expenditures, $114,712, including $114,642 for 91 grants (high: $52,650; low: $50).
Purpose and activities: Giving primarily for Jewish organizations, including synagogues, education, and welfare funds; support also for cultural programs and higher education.
Limitations: Giving primarily in NJ and NY. No grants to individuals.
Application information: Contributes only to pre-selected organizations. Applications not accepted.
Officers and Directors: Herman Lebersfeld, Pres.; Max Lebersfeld, V.P. and Secy.-Treas.; Arthur Lebersfeld.
Employer Identification Number: 222710646

3897
Lester Foundation ⌑ ☆
8 Brayton Rd.
Livingston 07039-5813

Established in 1946.
Foundation type: Independent
Financial data (yr. ended 4/30/89): Assets, $144,181 (M); expenditures, $102,378, including $101,510 for grants (high: $53,101).
Purpose and activities: Giving primarily to Jewish organizations, including welfare funds, temple support, and community services.
Limitations: Giving primarily in NY and NJ. No grants to individuals.
Application information: Contributes only to pre-selected organizations. Applications not accepted.
Officers: William M. Lester, Pres.; Betty L. Lester, V.P.
Employer Identification Number: 226063176

3898
Alan Levin Foundation ⌑
70 Undercliff Terr.
West Orange 07052

Foundation type: Independent
Financial data (yr. ended 8/31/88): Assets, $1,074,348 (M); expenditures, $84,978, including $81,625 for 31 grants (high: $31,365; low: $15).
Purpose and activities: Support primarily for Jewish welfare organizations and art museums.
Officer: Martin Levin, Mgr.
Employer Identification Number: 221711646

3899
The Philip & Janice Levin Foundation ⌑
893 Route 22
North Plainfield 07060

Incorporated in 1963 in NJ.
Donor(s): Philip J. Levin.†
Foundation type: Independent
Financial data (yr. ended 08/31/89): Assets, $7,560,479 (M); gifts received, $1,028,200; expenditures, $365,502, including $346,000 for 16 grants (high: $120,000; low: $1,000).
Purpose and activities: Emphasis on higher education, Jewish welfare funds, and the arts.
Limitations: Giving primarily in NJ and New York, NY.
Application information: Application form not required.
Officer and Trustees:* Janice H. Levin,* Pres. and Treas.; William A. Farber, Paul Skloiersky.
Employer Identification Number: 226075837

3900
Lichtman Foundation ⌑ ☆
Lackawanna Plaza
Millburn 07041-1619

Established in 1954.
Foundation type: Independent
Financial data (yr. ended 12/31/88): Assets, $1,093,967 (M); expenditures, $52,544, including $39,350 for 6 grants (high: $18,000; low: $100).
Purpose and activities: Giving primarily for Jewish welfare and social service organizations; support also for a hospital.
Limitations: Giving primarily in NJ.
Officers and Trustees: Jules Lichtman, Pres. and Treas.; Cecil Lichtman, V.P. and Secy.; Doris Lichtman, John Lichtman, Paul Lichtman, Shirley Lichtman.
Employer Identification Number: 226034110

3901
The Lindberg Foundation ⌑
c/o General Drafting Co., Inc.
Canfield Rd.
Convent Station 07961 (201) 538-7600

Incorporated in 1961 in NJ.
Donor(s): Otto G. Lindberg.†
Foundation type: Independent
Financial data (yr. ended 12/31/86): Assets, $1,439,177 (M); expenditures, $74,644, including $71,750 for 60 grants (high: $7,000; low: $500; average: $500-$1,000).
Purpose and activities: Emphasis on higher education, hospitals, community funds, youth agencies, and health agencies.
Types of support: Building funds, equipment.
Limitations: Giving primarily in Morris County and northern NJ. No grants to individuals, or for endowment funds, scholarships and fellowships, or matching gifts; no loans.
Publications: 990-PF, application guidelines.
Application information:
Initial approach: Letter
Copies of proposal: 1
Deadline(s): Oct.
Board meeting date(s): Mar. and Dec.
Final notification: Jan.
Write: M.B. Bennett, Trustee
Officers and Trustees: Richard E. Scully, Pres.; Margaret M. Murray, V.P.; M.B. Bennett, Secy.-Treas.; Charles J. Gaffney, Edward H. Hein, D.J. Kovar, J.J. Leuchs.
Number of staff: None.
Employer Identification Number: 226058169

3902
Belda & Marcel Lindenbaum Charitable Foundation ⌑ ☆
P.O. Box 2429
Secaucus 07094-1029 (201) 348-1700

Established in 1977.
Donor(s): Marcel Lindenbaum, Belda Lindenbaum.
Foundation type: Independent
Financial data (yr. ended 6/30/89): Assets, $75,973 (M); gifts received, $130,000; expenditures, $201,098, including $200,972 for 103 grants (high: $33,637; low: $18).
Purpose and activities: Giving primarily for Jewish organizations, including synagogues and yeshivas; support also for higher education.
Limitations: Giving primarily in New York, NY.
Application information:
Initial approach: Letter
Deadline(s): None
Write: Marcel Lindenbaum, Pres.
Officers: Marcel Lindenbaum, Pres.; Belda Lindenbaum, Secy.
Employer Identification Number: 222192230

3903
Thomas J. Lipton Foundation, Inc. ⌑
c/o Thomas J. Lipton, Inc.
800 Sylvan Ave.
Englewood Cliffs 07632

Incorporated in 1952 in DE.
Donor(s): Thomas J. Lipton, Inc.
Foundation type: Company-sponsored
Financial data (yr. ended 12/31/88): Assets, $755,646 (M); gifts received, $135,000; expenditures, $886,155, including $855,965 for 244 grants (high: $100,000; low: $200) and $29,729 for employee matching gifts.
Purpose and activities: Emphasis on research in nutrition, community funds, higher education, including scholarship aid, hospitals, cultural programs, social services, and youth agencies.
Types of support: Research, scholarship funds, employee matching gifts.
Application information: Application form required.
Deadline(s): None
Write: Helen Siegle, Grant Coord.
Officers: H.M. Tibbetts, Pres.; D.W. St. Clair, V.P. and Secy.; D.E. Grein, V.P. and Treas.; W.J. Sellitti, V.P. and Controller; J.N. Byrne, V.P.; C.B. Fuller, V.P.; W.K. Godfrey, V.P.; B.R. Hess, V.P.
Employer Identification Number: 226063094

3904
The Magowan Family Foundation, Inc. ⌑
c/o Merrill Lynch
100 Union Ave.
Cresskill 07626
Application address: c/o Mary Ann Chapin, 2100 Washington St., San Francisco, CA 94109; Tel.: (415) 563-5581

Incorporated in 1954 in NY.
Donor(s): Charles E. Merrill,† Robert A. Magowan,† Doris M. Magowan, Merrill L. Magowan, Robert A. Magowan, Jr.
Foundation type: Independent
Financial data (yr. ended 10/31/89): Assets, $5,651,037 (M); expenditures, $448,919, including $395,500 for 155 grants (high: $33,000; low: $500).
Purpose and activities: Grants for higher and secondary education, hospitals, church support, and cultural programs.
Limitations: Giving primarily in NY, CA, and FL. No grants to individuals.
Application information:
Initial approach: Letter
Deadline(s): None
Officers: Peter A. Magowan, Pres.; Doris M. Magowan, V.P.; Mark E. Magowan, V.P.; Merrill L. Magowan, V.P.; Stephen C. Magowan, V.P.; Bernat Rosner, Secy.; Thomas J. Lombardi, Treas.
Employer Identification Number: 136085999

3905
Mamiye Foundation, Inc. ⌑
300 Mac Ln.
Keasbey 08832-0909

Incorporated in 1982 in NJ.
Donor(s): Mamiye Brothers, Inc.
Foundation type: Company-sponsored
Financial data (yr. ended 12/31/87): Assets, $4,005 (M); gifts received, $511,101; expenditures, $508,200, including $508,159 for 60 grants (high: $200,000; low: $15).
Purpose and activities: Grants mainly for Jewish education and social service agencies.
Application information:
Initial approach: Letter and proposal
Deadline(s): None
Officers: Jack C. Mamiye, Pres.; Charles Mamiye, V.P.; Michael Mamiye, V.P.; David Mamiye, Secy.
Employer Identification Number: 222405277

3906
Maneely Fund, Inc. ⌑
900 Haddon Ave., Suite 432
Collingswood 08108 (609) 854-5400

Incorporated in 1952 in PA.
Donor(s): Edward F. Maneely.†
Foundation type: Independent
Financial data (yr. ended 12/31/88): Assets, $2,560,405 (M); expenditures, $137,991, including $82,971 for 72 grants (high: $10,000; low: $25).

Purpose and activities: Grants largely for higher education, hospitals, and community funds.
Limitations: No grants to individuals.
Application information: Application form not required.
Initial approach: Letter
Deadline(s): None
Write: James E. O'Donnell, Pres.
Officer: James E. O'Donnell, Pres. and Treas.
Employer Identification Number: 231569917

3907
The McCutchen Foundation ¤
209 West Second St.
Plainfield 07060 (201) 756-0042

Trust established in 1956 in NJ.
Donor(s): Brunson S. McCutchen, Charles W. McCutchen, Margaret W. McCutchen.
Foundation type: Independent
Financial data (yr. ended 12/31/88): Assets, $2,196,455 (M); expenditures, $107,938, including $101,500 for 10 grants (high: $55,000; low: $500).
Purpose and activities: Giving for religious welfare funds, with emphasis on a home maintained by the Religious Society of Friends; support also for education.
Limitations: Giving primarily in NJ.
Application information:
Initial approach: Letter
Deadline(s): Dec. 1
Write: Charles W. McCutchen, Trustee
Trustees: Marilyn R. Jaeger, Charles W. McCutchen.
Employer Identification Number: 226050116

3908
The Curtis W. McGraw Foundation
c/o Drinker, Biddle & Reath
P.O. Box 627
Princeton 08542 (609) 921-6336

Established in 1964 in NJ.
Donor(s): Elizabeth McGraw Webster.
Foundation type: Independent
Financial data (yr. ended 12/31/89): Assets, $12,771,744 (M); expenditures, $789,073, including $771,056 for 79 grants (high: $69,056; low: $1,000; average: $31,000).
Purpose and activities: Support primarily for hospitals, mental health, educational institutions, the arts, social services, and churches. Grants usually made to charities which are of interest to the officers.
Types of support: Annual campaigns, continuing support.
Limitations: Giving limited to the Princeton, NJ, Vail, CO, and Sun Valley, ID, areas. No grants to individuals, or for endowment funds, research, scholarships, fellowships, or matching gifts; no loans.
Publications: 990-PF.
Application information: Application form not required.
Initial approach: Letter or proposal
Copies of proposal: 1
Deadline(s): Oct. 15
Board meeting date(s): Nov. or Dec., and as required
Write: Samuel W. Lambert III, Secy.
Officers and Trustees:* Elizabeth McGraw Webster,* Pres.; Curtis M. Webster,* Exec. V.P.; Lisette S. Edmond,* V.P.; Marian S. Maricich,* V.P.; John L. McGraw,* V.P.; Dorothy H. Peyton,* V.P.; Samuel W. Lambert III,* Secy.
Number of staff: None.
Employer Identification Number: 221761678

3909
The MCJ Foundation ¤
330 South St., CN-1975
Morristown 07960 (201) 540-9020

Established in 1983 in NJ.
Donor(s): Raymond G. Chambers.
Foundation type: Independent
Financial data (yr. ended 11/30/88): Assets, $16,163,039 (M); gifts received, $6,364,481; expenditures, $579,154, including $495,270 for 18 grants (high: $300,000; low: $500).
Purpose and activities: Support primarily for education, hospitals, health associations, and child welfare.
Limitations: Giving primarily in NJ and NY. No grants to individuals.
Application information: Application form not required.
Deadline(s): None
Write: Gary L. Moore, V.P.
Officers: Raymond G. Chambers, Pres.; Gary L. Moore, V.P.
Directors:* Christine Chambers, Jennifer Chambers, Michael Chambers, Patricia Chambers.
Employer Identification Number: 222497895

3910
McMurray-Bennett Foundation, Inc. ¤
3601 Hwy. 66
Box 1550
Neptune 07754

Established in 1982 in NJ.
Donor(s): Wayne D. McMurray,† Helen Bennett McMurray.
Foundation type: Independent
Financial data (yr. ended 12/31/88): Assets, $1,884,560 (M); expenditures, $228,413, including $192,552 for 15 grants (high: $160,851; low: $500).
Purpose and activities: Support primarily for youth activities and higher education.
Types of support: General purposes, scholarship funds.
Limitations: Giving primarily in NJ, with emphasis on the Monmouth area. No grants to individuals.
Application information:
Initial approach: Letter
Deadline(s): None
Board meeting date(s): Quarterly
Write: Robert E. Murphy, Pres.
Officers: Robert E. Murphy, Pres. and Treas.; Steven G. Siegel, V.P. and Secy.; James Ciavaglia, V.P.
Employer Identification Number: 226083934

3911
Dr. Haroutune & Shake Mekhjian Foundation ¤
Timberline Dr.
P.O. Box 355
Alpine 07620
Application address: c/o Diamant, Katz, Kahn, & Co., 365 West Passaic St., Rochelle Park, NJ 07662

Donor(s): Haroutune Mekhjian, Shake Mekhjian.
Foundation type: Independent
Financial data (yr. ended 09/30/89): Assets, $1,008,633 (M); gifts received, $50,000; expenditures, $136,551, including $134,357 for 31 grants (high: $45,800; low: $10).
Purpose and activities: Support primarily for Christian organizations and hospitals.
Application information:
Initial approach: Letter
Deadline(s): None
Write: Dr. Haroutune Mekhjian, Pres.
Officers: Haroutune Mekhjian, Pres.; Shake Mekhjian, V.P.; Lonnie Wollin, Secy.-Treas.
Employer Identification Number: 222494780

3912
The Merck Company Foundation ▼
P.O. Box 2000
Rahway 07065-0900 (201) 855-2042

Incorporated in 1957 in NJ.
Donor(s): Merck & Co., Inc.
Foundation type: Company-sponsored
Financial data (yr. ended 12/31/89): Assets, $40,477,998 (M); gifts received, $288,536; expenditures, $7,924,403, including $6,655,875 for 279 grants (high: $261,950; low: $350; average: $1,000-$25,000), $254,592 for 8 grants to individuals and $988,324 for 5,356 employee matching gifts.
Purpose and activities: Support of education, primarily medical, and including the Merck Sharp & Dohme International Fellowships in Clinical Pharmacology; community programs, hospitals, medical, biological, and physical sciences, health agencies, public and civic organizations, and colleges in localities where the company has major operations; and an employee matching gift program for colleges, secondary schools, hospitals, public broadcasting and public libraries.
Types of support: Seed money, special projects, equipment, employee matching gifts, fellowships, publications.
Limitations: Giving primarily in areas of company operations, including NJ, PA, GA, VA, and CA. No grants to individuals (except for fellowships in clinical pharmacology), or for operating budgets, continuing support, annual campaigns, emergency or endowment funds, deficit financing, land acquisition, research, travel, or conferences; no loans.
Publications: Corporate giving report.
Application information: Grants usually made at the initiative of the foundation. Application form not required.
Initial approach: Proposal
Copies of proposal: 1
Deadline(s): Aug. 31 for fellowships in clinical pharmacology; no set deadline for other grants

Board meeting date(s): Semiannually and as required
Final notification: 2 months
Write: Charles R. Hogen, Jr., Exec. V.P.
Officers: Albert D. Angel,* Pres.; Charles R. Hogen, Jr., Exec. V.P.; Shuang Ruy Huang, V.P.; Clarence A. Abramson, Secy.; Larry W. Saufley, Treas.
Trustees:* P. Roy Vagelos, M.D., Chair.; H. Brewster Atwater, Jr., William G. Bowen, Frank T. Cary, Carolyne K. Davis, Lloyd C. Elam, Charles E. Exley, Jr., Jacques Genest, Marian S. Heiskell, John J. Horan, John E. Lyons, Albert W. Merck, Ruben F. Mettler, Paul G. Rogers, Richard S. Ross, Dennis Weatherstone.
Number of staff: 4 full-time professional; 4 full-time support.
Employer Identification Number: 226028476

3913
Aaron and Rachel Meyer Memorial Foundation, Inc. ¤
340 North Ave.
Cranford 07016 (201) 272-7000

Incorporated in 1964 in NJ.
Donor(s): Bertram Meyer.†
Foundation type: Independent
Financial data (yr. ended 3/31/88): Assets, $4,591,522 (M); expenditures, $359,841, including $266,250 for grants.
Purpose and activities: Grants largely for hospitals and youth agencies.
Limitations: Giving primarily in Passaic County, NJ. No grants to individuals.
Application information:
Board meeting date(s): 7 or 8 times a year
Write: Robert S. Mortenson, Secy.
Officers and Trustees: Philip B. Lowy, Pres.; A.L. Levine, V.P.; Ruth Samuels, V.P.; Robert S. Mortenson, Secy.
Employer Identification Number: 226063514

3914
Midlantic South Foundation ¤
(Formerly Heritage Bank Foundation)
c/o Midlantic National Bank
P.O. Box 600
Edison 08818 (609) 778-2335

Established in 1958 in NJ.
Donor(s): Midlantic National Bank.
Foundation type: Company-sponsored
Financial data (yr. ended 11/30/88): Assets, $47,672 (M); gifts received, $120,500; expenditures, $156,842, including $154,415 for 35 grants (high: $50,000; low: $315).
Purpose and activities: Support primarily for community funds and hospitals and health services.
Limitations: Giving primarily in NJ. No grants to individuals.
Application information:
Initial approach: Letter
Deadline(s): None
Write: John C. Watson, V.P. and Trust Officer, Midlantic National Bank
Trustee: Midlantic National Bank.
Employer Identification Number: 216011208

3915
Jay R. Monroe Memorial Foundation
44 Main St.
Millburn 07041-1399

Established in 1959 in NJ.
Donor(s): Malcolm Monroe,† Ethlyn Monroe.†
Foundation type: Independent
Financial data (yr. ended 12/31/88): Assets, $1,209,132 (M); gifts received, $150,000; expenditures, $100,126, including $95,350 for 154 grants (high: $25,000; low: $100).
Purpose and activities: Support for the arts and historic preservation, secondary and early childhood education, social services, child welfare and youth programs, health organizations, hospitals, health services, community development, and associations concerned with environmental conservation, ecology and wildlife.
Types of support: Annual campaigns, building funds, capital campaigns, continuing support.
Application information: Contributes only to pre-selected organizations. Applications not accepted.
Officers and Trustees:* Jay R. Monroe V,* Pres.; D.W. Monroe,* V.P.; M.M. Morrow,* V.P.; J.M. McEvoy,* Secy.; C.M. Byrne,* Treas.
Number of staff: None.
Employer Identification Number: 226050156

3916
Nabisco Foundation ▼
(also known as The National Biscuit Company Foundation Trust)
Nabisco Brands Plaza
Parsippany 07054 (201) 682-7098

Incorporated in 1953 in NJ.
Donor(s): Nabisco Brands, Inc.
Foundation type: Company-sponsored
Financial data (yr. ended 12/31/89): Assets, $12,290,922 (M); expenditures, $1,674,173, including $840,640 for 18 grants (high: $500,000; low: $1,000; average: $1,000-$20,000) and $765,685 for 1,332 employee matching gifts.
Purpose and activities: Giving largely for higher education and united funds; support also for education, the aged, handicapped, the homeless, hospitals, youth agencies, and cultural programs, including the performing arts.
Types of support: Building funds, scholarship funds, employee matching gifts, capital campaigns, emergency funds, employee-related scholarships.
Limitations: No grants to individuals.
Application information: Application form not required.
Copies of proposal: 1
Deadline(s): None
Board meeting date(s): As needed
Final notification: Varies
Write: Henry A. Sandbach, V.P., Public Relations
Administrative Committee: John F. Manfredi, Sr. V.P., Corporate Affairs; Henry A. Sandbach, V.P., Public Relations; Robert K. DeVries.
Trustee: Bankers Trust Co.
Employer Identification Number: 136042595

3917
National Starch and Chemical Foundation, Inc. ¤
Ten Finderne Ave.
Bridgewater 08807 (201) 685-5013
Scholarship application address: Charles Jacot, National Merit Scholarship Corp., One American Plaza, Evanston, IL 60621; Tel.: (312) 866-5118

Incorporated in 1968 in NY.
Donor(s): National Starch & Chemical Corp.
Foundation type: Company-sponsored
Financial data (yr. ended 12/31/88): Assets, $678,178 (M); gifts received, $1,213,501; expenditures, $1,099,165, including $1,035,847 for grants.
Purpose and activities: Giving for higher education, hospitals, community funds, and youth agencies; employee-related scholarships disbursed through National Merit Scholarship Corp.
Types of support: Employee-related scholarships, employee matching gifts.
Limitations: Giving primarily in areas of company operations.
Application information:
Deadline(s): Dec. 31 for scholarships
Write: Joyce Stark
Officers: R.B. Hennessey, Pres.; H.J. Baumgarten, Secy.; Robert B. Albert,* Treas.
Directors:* C.G. Caldwell, N.G. Marotta.
Employer Identification Number: 237010264

3918
Community Foundation of New Jersey
P.O. Box 317
Knox Hill Rd.
Morristown 07963-0317 (201) 267-5533

Incorporated in 1979 in NJ.
Foundation type: Community
Financial data (yr. ended 06/30/89): Assets, $5,891,434 (M); gifts received, $1,304,012; expenditures, $835,997, including $597,868 for 109 grants (high: $121,884; low: $50).
Purpose and activities: Support "for innovative programs which can exert a multiplier effect or which through research may contribute to the solution or easing of important community problems." Areas of interest include cultural programs, education, environment and conservation, health, religion, and social services.
Types of support: Seed money, matching funds, technical assistance, special projects, conferences and seminars, program-related investments.
Limitations: Giving limited to NJ. No support for sectarian religious programs. No grants for capital or endowment funds, operating budgets, continuing support, annual campaigns, emergency funds, deficit financing, or fellowships.
Publications: Annual report, application guidelines, newsletter, informational brochure.
Application information: Application form required.
Initial approach: Telephone
Copies of proposal: 1
Write: Sheila C. Williamson, Exec. Dir.
Officers: William Simon, Chair.; John L. Kidde,* Pres.; John D. Mack,* V.P.; Tilly-Jo B.

Emerson,* Secy.; S. Jervis Brinton, Jr.,* Treas.; Sheila C. Williamson, Exec. Dir.
Trustees:* George L. Bielitz, Jr., Barbara M. Caspersen, Raymond G. Chambers, Robert P. Corman, Peter Dawkins, Adrian M. Foley, Jr., Robert M. Gardner, Henry Henderson, Hilda Hidalgo, Frederick G. Meissner, Jr., Herbert F. Moore, Robert B. O'Brien, Jr., Dillard H. Robinson, Richard W. Roper, E. Burke Ross, Jr., Christine T. Whitman.
Number of staff: 3 full-time professional; 2 part-time professional; 1 part-time support.
Employer Identification Number: 222281783

3919
New Jersey Neighborhood Housing Services Foundation, Inc. ⌑
141 South Harrison St., 7th fl.
East Orange 07018

Established in 1980 in NJ.
Foundation type: Independent
Financial data (yr. ended 12/31/86): Assets, $20,959 (M); expenditures, $125,817, including $105,000 for 3 grants of $35,000 each.
Purpose and activities: Support for housing services in four communities.
Limitations: Giving limited to NJ.
Officers: Mary Dehaven Myers, Pres.; Ernest E. Basquette, Jr., Secy.-Treas.
Employer Identification Number: 222310042

3920
The Charlotte W. Newcombe Foundation ▼
35 Park Place
Princeton 08542 (609) 924-7022
Fellowship application address: Newcombe Fellowships, Woodrow Wilson National Fellowship Foundation, P.O. Box 642, Princeton, NJ 08542; Tel.: (609)924-4666

Trust established in 1979 in PA.
Donor(s): Charlotte W. Newcombe.†
Foundation type: Independent
Financial data (yr. ended 12/31/89): Assets, $33,401,498 (M); expenditures, $2,036,636, including $1,531,083 for 65 grants (high: $545,133; low: $1,250; average: $1,000-$41,000).
Purpose and activities: Grants available to colleges and universities for scholarship or fellowship aid only in four programs: 1) doctoral dissertation fellowships awarded annually for degree candidates in the humanities and social sciences whose work focuses on ethics and religion (national selection process administered by Woodrow Wilson National Fellowship Foundation); 2) scholarships for physically disabled students, restricted to private four-year colleges and universities in PA, NJ, New York, NY, MD, DE, and Washington, DC; 3) scholarships for mature second-career women in the same states with no grants made in this program to two-year colleges, professional schools, or theological seminaries; 4) scholarships for economically disadvantaged or minority students attending colleges affiliated with the Presbyterian Church (U.S.A.). Scholarships for undergraduate and graduate students only; no aid available for post-doctoral fellowships. Selection of student recipients and scholarship administration are the responsibility of the academic institution.
Types of support: Scholarship funds, fellowships.
Limitations: No support for colleges except for scholarship and fellowship programs; within the scholarships for physically disabled students, no grants to publicly-supported two-year colleges. No grants to individuals, or for staffing, program development, or building funds; scholarships to institutions only; no loans.
Publications: Annual report (including application guidelines).
Application information: Application materials available from mid-June through mid-Oct. for physically disabled students and mature women students; Presbyterian college scholarships have no application materials--colleges should inquire to the foundation regarding these scholarships; fellowship applicants should request applications by Nov. 30 from the Woodrow Wilson National Fellowship Foundation at address given above. Application form required.
Initial approach: Letter or telephone
Copies of proposal: 5
Deadline(s): Nov. 1 for scholarship programs; Nov. 15 for fellowships
Board meeting date(s): Feb., Apr., June, Sept., and Dec.
Final notification: Apr. for fellowships beginning in June; May for scholarships beginning in July
Write: Janet A. Fearon, Exec. Dir.
Trustees: Robert M. Adams, K. Roald Bergethon, Janet A. Fearon, Aaron E. Gast, Thomas P. Glassmoyer.
Number of staff: 2 full-time professional; 1 part-time support.
Employer Identification Number: 232120614

3921
Theresa and Edward O'Toole Foundation ⌑
Eight Church Court
Closter 07624

Established in 1971.
Donor(s): Theresa O'Toole.†
Foundation type: Independent
Financial data (yr. ended 6/30/88): Assets, $16,892,062 (M); expenditures, $880,469, including $704,482 for 168 grants (high: $100,000; low: $500).
Purpose and activities: Grants primarily for Roman Catholic churches and welfare funds, hospitals, and higher education.
Types of support: Continuing support, annual campaigns, emergency funds, building funds, special projects, research, matching funds, general purposes.
Limitations: Giving primarily in NY, NJ, and FL. No grants to individuals, or for endowment funds, scholarships, or fellowships; no loans.
Application information:
Initial approach: Letter
Deadline(s): None
Final notification: 1 month
Write: Daniel McCarthy, Trust Officer
Trustees: Chris Degheri, The Bank of New York.
Employer Identification Number: 136350175

3922
George A. Ohl, Jr. Trust
c/o First Fidelity Bank, N.A., NJ
765 Broad St.
Newark 07102 (201) 430-4237

Trust established in 1947 in NJ.
Donor(s): George A. Ohl, Jr.†
Foundation type: Independent
Financial data (yr. ended 12/31/89): Assets, $3,581,272 (M); expenditures, $308,434, including $278,751 for 38 grants (high: $93,651; low: $500).
Purpose and activities: Emphasis on hospitals and health agencies, youth projects, and organizations that provide care for the homeless, the aged, and the economically disadvantaged. Support also for youth recreational activities and projects at the secondary school level.
Types of support: Seed money, equipment, research, publications, scholarship funds, matching funds, capital campaigns, program-related investments, renovation projects, special projects.
Limitations: Giving limited to NJ. No grants to individuals; no loans.
Publications: 990-PF, application guidelines.
Application information: Progress report due 9 months after funding. Application form not required.
Initial approach: Proposal
Copies of proposal: 1
Deadline(s): Feb. 15 and Aug. 15
Board meeting date(s): Mar. and Sept.
Final notification: 1 month after board meets
Write: James S. Hohn, V.P., First Fidelity Bank, N.A., NJ
Trustee: First Fidelity Bank, N.A., NJ.
Employer Identification Number: 226024900

3923
The Orange Orphan Society ⌑
Llewellyn Park
West Orange 07052

Established in 1855 in NJ.
Foundation type: Independent
Financial data (yr. ended 12/31/88): Assets, $4,700,805 (M); expenditures, $295,839, including $228,200 for 17 grants (high: $43,000; low: $1,800).
Purpose and activities: Grants to child welfare and youth agencies.
Types of support: Operating budgets.
Limitations: Giving limited to the Orange, NJ, area. No grants to individuals.
Application information: Contributes only to pre-selected organizations. Applications not accepted.
Officers and Trustees: Charles F. Robbins, Jr., Pres.; Betty Wilder, Treas.; and 16 additional trustees.
Employer Identification Number: 221711513

3924
Henry and Carolyn Sue Orenstein Foundation, Inc. ⌑ ☆
1140 Bloomfield Ave.
West Caldwell 07006-7126 (201) 882-9488

Established in 1986.
Donor(s): Henry Orenstein, Carolyn Sue Orenstein.

Foundation type: Independent
Financial data (yr. ended 12/31/87): Assets, $387,316 (M); gifts received, $20,651; expenditures, $103,518, including $103,000 for 13 grants (high: $38,000; low: $200).
Purpose and activities: Grants primarily for Jewish organizations, including educational activities; giving also for medical research.
Limitations: Giving primarily in New York, NY.
Application information:
Write: Henry Orenstein, Trustee
Trustees: Carolyn Sue Orenstein, Frederick Orenstein, Henry Orenstein.
Employer Identification Number: 222806030

3925
Panasonic Foundation
(Formerly Matsushita Foundation)
One Panasonic Way 3G-7C
Secaucus 07094 (201) 392-4132

Established in 1984 in DE.
Donor(s): Matsushita Electric Corp. of America.
Foundation type: Company-sponsored
Financial data (yr. ended 12/31/89): Assets, $12,590,224 (M); expenditures, $1,149,870, including $374,675 for 20 grants (high: $100,000; low: $3,000) and $667,696 for 10 foundation-administered programs.
Purpose and activities: In elementary and secondary education: to promote excellence and equity through providing technical assistance and seed money to school systems to bring about school-based whole-school reform in public education.
Types of support: General purposes, seed money, technical assistance.
Limitations: Giving limited to the U.S., including Puerto Rico. No grants to individuals, or for annual campaigns, emergency funds, deficit financing, building funds, land acquisition, endowment funds, matching gifts, publications, cultural performances or exhibitions (except as related to the foundation's program areas), or regular conferences of professional organizations; support for operating budgets and renovation projects only in unusual circumstances; no loans.
Publications: 990-PF, grants list, informational brochure (including application guidelines).
Application information: Applications not accepted.
Board meeting date(s): 3 to 4 times annually
Write: Sophie Sa, Exec. Dir.
Officers: Ira Perlman,* Pres.; Seth Waller, Secy.; Ralph Pagano, Treas.; Sophie Sa, Exec. Dir.
Trustees:* Masaharu Matsushita, Honorary Chair.; Robert S. Ingersoll, Chair.; Akiya Imura, Richard Kraft, Martin Meyerson, Jack Pluckhan.
Number of staff: 1 full-time professional; 1 full-time support.
Employer Identification Number: 222548639

3926
Paragano Family Foundation, Inc. ⌑ ☆
636 Morris Tpke.
Short Hills 07078-2608 (201) 376-1010

Incorporated in 1983 in NJ.
Donor(s): Nazario Paragano.
Foundation type: Independent
Financial data (yr. ended 12/31/88): Assets, $1,122,790 (M); gifts received, $652,422; expenditures, $58,265, including $58,000 for 10 grants (high: $25,000; low: $1,000).
Purpose and activities: Giving primarily for Catholic churches and religious orders; minor support also for hospitals, Jewish welfare, and higher education.
Types of support: General purposes.
Application information:
Write: Nazario Paragano, Trustee
Trustee: Nazario Paragano.
Employer Identification Number: 222483286

3927
Albert Penick Fund ⌑
c/o Horizon Trust Co.
65 Madison Ave., CN 1969
Morristown 07960

Trust established in 1951 in NY.
Donor(s): A.D. Penick,† Mrs. Albert D. Penick.
Foundation type: Independent
Financial data (yr. ended 12/31/87): Assets, $1,691,709 (M); expenditures, $148,744, including $126,500 for 36 grants (high: $50,000; low: $1,000).
Purpose and activities: Grants largely for higher and secondary education, hospitals, animal welfare, conservation, youth programs, and cultural organizations.
Application information:
Initial approach: Letter
Deadline(s): None
Trustees: Nancy P. Corcoran, K. Philip Dresdner, V. Susan Penick, Horizon Trust Co.
Employer Identification Number: 136161137

3928
F. Mason Perkins Trust ⌑
P.O. Box 547
Hackensack 07602

Established in 1971.
Donor(s): F. Mason Perkins.†
Foundation type: Independent
Financial data (yr. ended 12/31/87): Assets, $2,045,930 (M); expenditures, $175,961, including $161,918 for 12 grants (high: $60,000; low: $4,000; average: $12,000).
Purpose and activities: Giving exclusively in Italy for aid to the poor and handicapped, particularly children and the aged, and for the protection of animals; 50 per cent of giving to six organizations specified by court order.
Types of support: Continuing support.
Limitations: Giving limited to Italy, with emphasis on Assisi and Rome.
Application information: Application form not required.
Initial approach: Letter and proposal
Copies of proposal: 1
Trustee: United Jersey Bank.
Employer Identification Number: 226040411

3929
Petrie Foundation ⌑ ☆
70 Enterprise Ave.
Secaucus 07094-2567

Established in 1945 in NJ.
Donor(s): Milton Petrie.
Foundation type: Independent
Financial data (yr. ended 12/31/87): Assets, $692,537 (M); gifts received, $1,000,000; expenditures, $759,140, including $758,170 for 67 grants (high: $108,500; low: $100).
Purpose and activities: Giving primarily for cultural programs, including museums, the performing arts, a historic preservation group, and intercultural institutions; support also for an association promoting international religious freedom and hospitals and health services, including physical rehabilitation.
Officers and Directors:* Joseph Flom,* V.P.; Bernard Petrie,* V.P.; Peter Left, Secy.-Treas.; H. Kirschenbaum Gerstein, Milton Petrie, D. Fink Stern.
Employer Identification Number: 136108716

3930
Howard Phipps Foundation ▼ ⌑
c/o Bessemer Trust Co.
100 Woodbridge Center Dr.
Woodbridge 07095-0903

Established in 1967 in NJ.
Donor(s): Harriet Phipps.†
Foundation type: Independent
Financial data (yr. ended 06/30/88): Assets, $5,927,759 (M); gifts received, $1,528,545; expenditures, $1,184,828, including $1,059,500 for 46 grants (high: $100,000; low: $5,000; average: $5,000-$50,000).
Purpose and activities: Support for conservation and cultural programs.
Limitations: Giving primarily in New York, NY.
Application information:
Initial approach: Letter
Deadline(s): None
Write: Austin J. Power, Jr.
Trustees: Howard Phipps, Jr., Anne P. Sidamon-Eristoff, Bessemer Trust Co., N.A.
Employer Identification Number: 226095226

3931
The Prudential Foundation ▼
15 Prudential Plaza
Newark 07101 (201) 802-7354

Incorporated in 1977 in NJ.
Donor(s): Prudential Insurance Co. of America, Prudential Property & Casualty Co.
Foundation type: Company-sponsored
Financial data (yr. ended 12/31/89): Assets, $104,344,000 (M); qualifying distributions, $14,876,965, including $12,239,950 for 777 grants (high: $212,000; low: $1,000; average: $5,000-$10,000), $2,147,015 for employee matching gifts and $490,000 for in-kind gifts.
Purpose and activities: Program interests include education, public affairs, urban and community affairs, health and human services, including AIDS programs, arts and culture, and conservation and ecology; support also for United Way drives in areas of company operations.
Types of support: Operating budgets, continuing support, annual campaigns, seed money, emergency funds, deficit financing, building funds, equipment, matching funds, employee matching gifts, consulting services, technical assistance, employee-related scholarships, research, special projects, capital campaigns, conferences and seminars, general purposes.

Limitations: Giving primarily in areas of company operations, especially Newark, NJ, and in CA, FL, MN, and PA. No support for labor, religious or athletic groups, or single-disease health organizations seeking funds independently of federated drives. No grants to individuals, or for endowment funds; no loans.
Publications: Annual report (including application guidelines).
Application information: Additional information will be requested as needed. Application form not required.
Initial approach: Letter with brief description of program
Copies of proposal: 1
Deadline(s): None
Board meeting date(s): Apr., Aug., and Dec.
Final notification: 4 to 6 weeks
Write: Elisa D. Puzzuoli, Secy.
Officers: Peter B. Goldberg, Pres.; Paul S. Lambdin, V.P.; Paul G. O'Leary, V.P.; Elisa D. Puzzuoli, Secy.; Linda Dougherty, Treas.; Eugene M. O'Hara, Comptroller.
Trustees: William H. Tremayne, Chair.; Lisle C. Carter, Jr., Adrian M. Foley, Jr., James R. Gillen, Helen S. Meyner, Donald E. Procknow, Robert C. Winters, Edward D. Zinbarg.
Number of staff: 8 full-time professional; 8 full-time support.
Employer Identification Number: 222175290

3932
The Quaker Hill Foundation ¤
c/o King, King & Goldsack
120 West 7th St.
Plainfield 07060

Trust established in 1948 in NJ.
Donor(s): Edith S. Stevens, John P. Stevens, Jr.†
Foundation type: Independent
Financial data (yr. ended 12/31/88): Assets, $2,125,143 (M); gifts received, $114,972; expenditures, $106,777, including $75,800 for 7 grants (high: $50,000; low: $1,500) and $17,176 for 45 employee matching gifts.
Purpose and activities: Charitable and educational purposes; grants restricted to organizations in which trustees have an active interest, especially for higher and secondary education.
Limitations: No grants to individuals.
Application information: Contributes only to pre-selected organizations. Applications not accepted.
Trustees: Phoebe S. Miner, Edith S. Sheldon, Edith Stevens, John P. Stevens III.
Employer Identification Number: 136088786

3933
The Charles L. Read Foundation
374 Millburn Ave.
P.O. Box 599
Millburn 07041

Trust established in 1954 in NJ.
Donor(s): Charles L. Read.
Foundation type: Independent
Financial data (yr. ended 12/31/88): Assets, $2,553,510 (M); expenditures, $186,899, including $136,300 for 74 grants (high: $21,550; low: $250).
Purpose and activities: Grants for education, hospitals, and religious welfare funds.
Limitations: Giving primarily in NJ and NY.
Application information: Contributes only to pre-selected organizations. Applications not accepted.
Officers: Fred Herrigel III, Pres.; Richard Eisenberg, V.P.; Rodger Herrigel, Secy.; Saul Eisenberg, Treas.
Employer Identification Number: 226053510

3934
Kurt P. Reimann Foundation, Inc. ¤
138 Sunset Ln.
Tenafly 07670 (201) 569-9387

Established in 1971.
Donor(s): Auguste Reimann,† Kurt P. Reimann, Mrs. Kurt P. Reimann.
Foundation type: Independent
Financial data (yr. ended 11/30/88): Assets, $671,140 (M); gifts received, $40,500; expenditures, $188,211, including $184,000 for 10 grants (high: $60,000; low: $2,000).
Purpose and activities: Grants mainly for cultural programs, with emphasis on music and the performing arts; support also for a college.
Limitations: No grants to individuals.
Application information:
Initial approach: Proposal
Deadline(s): None
Write: Reimer Koch-Weser, Pres.
Officers and Directors: Reimer Koch-Weser, Pres.; Anna Elisath, V.P.; J. Nicholas Suhr, Secy.; Benjamin Nadel, Treas.; Carl H. Ficke, Elizabeth Thompson.
Employer Identification Number: 221712688

3935
Fannie E. Rippel Foundation ▼
The Concourse at Beaverbrook
P.O. Box 569
Annandale 08801-0569 (201) 735-0990

Incorporated in 1953 in NJ.
Donor(s): Julius S. Rippel.†
Foundation type: Independent
Financial data (yr. ended 4/30/89): Assets, $57,409,731 (M); expenditures, $3,196,441, including $2,420,064 for 22 grants (high: $500,000; low: $43,558; average: $100,000-$200,000).
Purpose and activities: Restricted to aid hospitals, organizations for the relief and care of aged women, and organizations for treatment of and/or research concerning heart disease and cancer.
Types of support: Equipment, research, renovation projects, special projects.
Limitations: Giving primarily in the eastern seaboard states, particularly NJ and New York, NY. No grants to individuals, or for general purposes, operating budgets, continuing support, annual campaigns, deficit financing, scholarships, fellowships, endowment or building funds, or matching gifts; no loans.
Publications: Annual report, application guidelines.
Application information: Application form not required.
Initial approach: Letter, telephone, or proposal
Copies of proposal: 1
Deadline(s): None
Board meeting date(s): Approximately 6 times a year
Final notification: Varies
Write: Edward W. Probert, V.P. and Secy.
Officers: Eric R. Rippel,* Pres.; Edward W. Probert, V.P. and Secy.; Janet E. Luther, Treas.
Trustees:* Julius A. Rippel, Chair.; Bruce N. Bensley, S. Jervis Brinton, Jr., G. Frederick Hockenjos.
Number of staff: 4 full-time professional; 2 part-time professional; 1 full-time support; 1 part-time support.
Employer Identification Number: 221559427

3936
The Sarah and Matthew Rosenhaus Peace Foundation, Inc. ¤
Picatinny Rd.
Morristown 07960 (201) 267-6583

Incorporated in 1959 in NY.
Donor(s): Sarah Rosenhaus,† Matthew B. Rosenhaus.†
Foundation type: Independent
Financial data (yr. ended 7/31/87): Assets, $10,516,204 (M); gifts received, $235,447; expenditures, $781,117, including $678,000 for 39 grants (high: $100,000; low: $200; average: $1,000-$25,000).
Purpose and activities: To promote world peace and understanding, with emphasis on medical research and health services, Jewish organizations, higher education, including theological education and international peace organizations; some support for social service agencies and cultural programs.
Limitations: Giving primarily in NJ and NY. No grants to individuals.
Application information: Contributes only to pre-selected organizations. Applications not accepted.
Write: Irving Rosenhaus, Managing Dir.
Officers and Directors: Alice Fetro, Secy.; Robert Bobrow, Treas.; Irving R. Rosenhaus, Managing Dir.; Anetra Chester, Jerome Cossman, Harriet Grosc, Albert Rosenhaus, Lawrence Rosenhaus, Gila Rosenhaus Weiner.
Number of staff: 1
Employer Identification Number: 136136983

3937
Eric F. Ross Foundation ¤ ☆
206 Crestwood Dr.
South Orange 07079-1115

Established in 1986 in NJ.
Donor(s): Eric F. Ross.
Foundation type: Independent
Financial data (yr. ended 12/31/88): Assets, $645,456 (M); gifts received, $332,302; expenditures, $164,557, including $164,000 for 4 grants (high: $150,000; low: $1,500).
Purpose and activities: Giving primarily for Jewish organizations, especially a welfare fund.
Application information: Contributes only to pre-selected organizations. Applications not accepted.
Trustees: Eric F. Ross, Lore Ross.
Employer Identification Number: 133383843

3938
Irene Herbert & Harper Grant Ross Foundation ⌑ ☆
390 George St.
New Brunswick 08901-2069 (201) 545-2250

Established in 1952.
Foundation type: Independent
Financial data (yr. ended 12/31/88): Assets, $1,359,895 (M); expenditures, $73,191, including $56,400 for 23 grants (high: $10,000; low: $300).
Purpose and activities: Giving primarily for higher education; support also for Protestant churches and organizations, hospitals, and community funds.
Limitations: Giving primarily in NJ and CT. No grants to individuals.
Application information:
Initial approach: Telephone or letter
Deadline(s): None
Write: A. Dudley Watson
Officer: Millicent R. Wheatley, Pres.
Employer Identification Number: 226058004

3939
E. Burke Ross, Jr. Charitable Foundation, Inc. ⌑ ☆
c/o Stryker, Tams & Dill
33 Washington St.
Newark 07102

Incorporated in 1987 in NJ.
Donor(s): E. Burke Ross, Jr.
Foundation type: Independent
Financial data (yr. ended 11/30/88): Assets, $480,800 (M); gifts received, $980,838; expenditures, $566,220, including $566,050 for 21 grants (high: $250,000; low: $250).
Purpose and activities: Giving primarily to a community foundation; support also for higher and other education and hospitals.
Limitations: Giving primarily in NJ. No grants to individuals.
Application information: Contributes only to pre-selected organizations. Applications not accepted.
Officers and Trustees: E. Burke Ross, Jr., Pres.; Benson T. Ross, V.P.; Andrea C. Ross, Secy.; Amory L. Ross, Treas.
Employer Identification Number: 521578961

3940
Roxiticus Fund
P.O. Box 326
Mendham 07945 (201) 543-4833

Established in 1961 in NJ.
Foundation type: Independent
Financial data (yr. ended 12/31/88): Assets, $1,164,562 (M); expenditures, $87,622, including $86,650 for 166 grants (high: $10,000; low: $50).
Purpose and activities: Support for education, health associations and hospitals, conservation, social service organizations, the arts, and international affairs groups promoting peace activism.
Limitations: Giving primarily in NJ and NY. No grants for scholarships or fellowships; no loans.
Application information: Contributes only to pre-selected organizations. Applications not accepted.
Write: Hugo De Neufville, Trustee
Trustees: Hugo De Neufville, Margaret Wade De Neufville.
Employer Identification Number: 226041443

3941
David and Eleanore Rukin Philanthropic Foundation ⌑
17 Franklin Tpke.
Mahwah 07430 (201) 529-3666

Established in 1951 in NJ.
Donor(s): David Rukin, Eleanore Rukin, Barnett Rukin, Susan Eisen.
Foundation type: Independent
Financial data (yr. ended 12/31/88): Assets, $2,189,501 (M); expenditures, $360,926, including $345,810 for grants (high: $85,000; low: $10).
Purpose and activities: Giving primarily for Jewish welfare and education; some support also for other education, health and hospitals, and culture.
Application information: Application form not required.
Deadline(s): None
Write: Julius Eisen, Dir.
Directors: Julius Eisen, Susan Eisen, Barnett Rukin, Eleanore Rukin.
Employer Identification Number: 221715380

3942
Sadinoff Family Foundation ⌑ ☆
411 Alfred Ave.
Teaneck 07666

Established in 1985 in NJ.
Donor(s): Seymour Sadinoff.
Foundation type: Independent
Financial data (yr. ended 9/30/88): Assets, $1,671,394 (M); expenditures, $101,600, including $79,024 for 64 grants (high: $37,500; low: $30).
Purpose and activities: Support for an elementary school and Jewish organizations.
Limitations: Giving primarily in NJ. No grants to individuals.
Application information: Contributes only to pre-selected organizations. Applications not accepted.
Officers: Seymour Sadinoff, Pres. and Treas.; Trudy Rubin Sadinoff, Secy.
Employer Identification Number: 222669655

3943
Sagamore Foundation ⌑
c/o Martin S. Fox
570 Broad St.
Newark 07102

Established in 1967 in NJ.
Foundation type: Independent
Financial data (yr. ended 11/30/88): Assets, $2,622,279 (M); gifts received, $214,694; expenditures, $460,072, including $450,315 for 2 grants (high: $323,956; low: $126,359).
Purpose and activities: Support for a private foundation and a medical center for vascular research.
Limitations: Giving primarily in NJ. No grants to individuals.
Application information: Contributes only to pre-selected organizations. Applications not accepted.
Officers: Victor Parsonnet, Pres.; Isaac Gielchinsky, V.P.; J. Mansoor Hussain, V.P.; Alexander Shapiro, V.P.; Martin S. Fox, Secy.-Treas.
Employer Identification Number: 221825723

3944
Saibel Foundation, Inc. ⌑ ☆
835 Bloomfield Ave.
Clifton 07012-1117

Established in 1945.
Foundation type: Independent
Financial data (yr. ended 5/31/89): Assets, $1,074,036 (M); expenditures, $61,533, including $47,449 for 58 grants (high: $7,300; low: $25).
Purpose and activities: Giving primarily for Jewish organizations, including synagogues, welfare funds, and family and social services; support also for health and hospitals.
Limitations: Giving primarily in NJ and NY. No grants to individuals.
Application information: Contributes only to pre-selected organizations. Applications not accepted.
Officers: Roy H. Aibel, Pres.; Frederic Aibel, Treas.
Employer Identification Number: 226064734

3945
The Milton Schamach Foundation, Inc. ⌑
810 Belmont Ave.
North Haledon 07508

Incorporated in 1969 in NJ.
Donor(s): Milton Schamach.†
Foundation type: Independent
Financial data (yr. ended 8/31/88): Assets, $2,090,021 (M); expenditures, $197,797, including $157,286 for 29 grants (high: $24,000; low: $1,000).
Purpose and activities: Giving for medical research and hospitals; support also for health agencies and Jewish welfare funds.
Types of support: Equipment, research.
Limitations: Giving primarily in NJ. No grants to individuals.
Application information: Application form not required.
Initial approach: Letter
Deadline(s): May 31
Board meeting date(s): 3 or 4 times a year as required
Final notification: 3 to 4 months
Write: Jack Goodman, Secy.-Treas.
Officers and Trustees: Gene Schamach, Pres.; Jack Goodman, Secy.-Treas.; Andrew E.R. Frommelt, Jr., Alvin Goodman, Jay Rubenstein, Howard Schamach, Rhoda Schamach, Robert Schamach.
Number of staff: 2
Employer Identification Number: 237051147

3946
L. P. Schenck Fund
c/o Midlantic National Bank, Trust Dept.
One Engle St.
Englewood 07631 (201) 894-4825

Trust established in 1960 in NJ.
Donor(s): Lillian Pitkin Schenck.†
Foundation type: Independent
Financial data (yr. ended 8/31/89): Assets, $7,668,742 (M); expenditures, $364,549, including $312,215 for 25 grants (high: $50,000; low: $1,000).
Purpose and activities: Grants restricted to institutions in the immediate local area, including support for youth and social service agencies, and cultural programs.
Types of support: General purposes, operating budgets, special projects, building funds.
Limitations: Giving limited to the Englewood, NJ, area. No grants to individuals, or for endowment funds.
Application information:
Initial approach: Proposal
Copies of proposal: 3
Deadline(s): Aug. 1
Board meeting date(s): Sept.
Write: Norman E. Smyth, V.P., Midlantic National Bank
Trustees: Mary Lou Heath, Mary P. Oenslager, Elizabeth N. Thatcher, Midlantic National Bank.
Employer Identification Number: 226040581

3947
Schering-Plough Foundation, Inc. ▼
One Giralda Farms
P.O. Box 1000
Madison 07940-1000 (201) 822-7412

Incorporated in 1955 in DE.
Donor(s): Schering Corp., The Plough Foundation, Schering-Plough Corp.
Foundation type: Company-sponsored
Financial data (yr. ended 12/31/89): Assets, $16,407,334 (M); expenditures, $2,761,093, including $2,305,555 for 101 grants (high: $100,000; low: $1,000; average: $20-$25,000) and $365,678 for 1,076 employee matching gifts.
Purpose and activities: Primary objective is support of institutional activities devoted to improving the quality and delivery of health care, through medical and allied education. Selective support to higher education, hospitals, health care programs, and cultural organizations in those communities where the corporation has major facilities. Grants made both directly and through national granting groups. Matching gift plan includes accredited higher and secondary educational institutions, and hospitals.
Types of support: Employee matching gifts, annual campaigns, seed money, building funds, equipment, internships, fellowships, general purposes, professorships, continuing support, operating budgets, scholarship funds, capital campaigns, endowment funds, renovation projects, employee-related scholarships, special projects.
Limitations: Giving primarily in areas where corporate sponsor has major facilities, especially NJ and TN. No grants to individuals, or for deficit financing, publications, or conferences; no loans.
Publications: Annual report (including application guidelines).
Application information: Funds fully committed through 1991. Application form not required. Applications not accepted.
Initial approach: Letter
Copies of proposal: 1
Deadline(s): Feb. 1 and Sept. 1
Board meeting date(s): Spring and Fall
Final notification: 6 months
Write: Rita Sacco, Asst. Secy.
Officers and Trustees:* Allan S. Kushen,* Pres.; Richard J. Kinney, Secy.; J. Martin Comey, Treas.; David E. Collins, Donald R. Conklin, Hugh A. D'Andrade, Harold R. Hiser, Jr., Richard J. Kogan, Robert P. Luciano.
Number of staff: 1 full-time professional; 1 part-time professional; 1 part-time support.
Employer Identification Number: 221711047

3948
The Schimmel Foundation ⌑
c/o J.H. Cohn & Co.
75 Eisenhower Pkwy.
Roseland 07068-1697 (201) 228-3500

Incorporated 1n 1960 in NY.
Donor(s): Norbert Schimmel.
Foundation type: Independent
Financial data (yr. ended 12/31/88): Assets, $984,212 (M); expenditures, $133,676, including $124,545 for grants.
Purpose and activities: Giving primarily to art museums, including donations of works of art; support also for Jewish organizations.
Limitations: No support for non-operating private foundations. No grants to individuals.
Application information:
Initial approach: Letter
Deadline(s): None
Write: Stephen Schimmel, Mgr.
Officer: Stephen Schimmel, Mgr.
Trustees: Alan Bloom, Norbert Schimmel.
Employer Identification Number: 136145185

3949
The Schultz Foundation
1037 Route 46 East, Suite 207
Clifton 07013 (201) 614-8880

Incorporated in 1966 in DE; merged in 1987 with The William Lightfoot Schultz Foundation, which was incorporated in 1952.
Donor(s): Mabel L. Schultz,† and other members of the Schultz family.
Foundation type: Independent
Financial data (yr. ended 06/30/89): Assets, $16,284,047 (M); expenditures, $669,575, including $589,753 for 35 grants (high: $151,164; low: $100; average: $100-$151,164).
Purpose and activities: Emphasis on medical research.
Types of support: General purposes, operating budgets, continuing support, seed money, building funds, matching funds, scholarship funds, internships, fellowships, research, special projects.
Limitations: Giving primarily in north central NJ. No grants to individuals, or for endowment funds, deficit financing, equipment, or land acquisition; no loans.
Application information: Application form not required.
Initial approach: Telephone or letter
Copies of proposal: 1
Deadline(s): None
Board meeting date(s): Board meets upon call
Final notification: within 6 months
Write: William L.S. Rigg, Exec. Dir.
Officers and Trustees:* George L. Schultz,* Pres. and Treas.; Elizabeth Schultz Rigg,* V.P.; Margaret F. Schultz,* Secy.; John K. Bangs, John Barker, Margaret Schultz Bilotti, Marilyn Schultz Blackwell, Katharine Schultz Fieldhouse, Douglas C. Rigg, Geoffrey B. Rigg, William L.S. Rigg, Elizabeth Schultz Vanderlinde.
Number of staff: 1 part-time professional; 1 part-time support.
Employer Identification Number: 226103387

3950
The Florence and John Schumann Foundation
33 Park St.
Montclair 07042 (201) 783-6660

Incorporated in 1961 in NJ.
Donor(s): Florence F. Schumann, John J. Schumann, Jr.†
Foundation type: Independent
Financial data (yr. ended 12/31/89): Assets, $61,822,313 (M); expenditures, $2,495,746, including $2,079,300 for 70 grants (high: $250,000; low: $1,000; average: $10,000-$50,000).
Purpose and activities: Grants in effective governance, the environment, and international relations.
Types of support: Operating budgets, continuing support, seed money, matching funds.
Limitations: No grants to individuals, or for annual campaigns, deficit financing, equipment and materials, land acquisition, or endowment funds; no loans.
Publications: Annual report (including application guidelines).
Application information: Application form not required.
Initial approach: Letter
Copies of proposal: 1
Deadline(s): Jan. 15, Apr. 15, Aug. 15, and Oct. 15
Board meeting date(s): Feb., June, Sept., and Dec.
Final notification: 2 to 3 months
Write: Bill Moyers, Pres.
Officers and Trustees:* Robert F. Schumann,* Chair.; Bill Moyers,* Pres.; Howard D. Brundage,* V.P., Finance; Caroline S. Mark,* V.P.; W. Ford Schumann,* V.P.; David S. Bate,* Secy.-Treas.; Edwin D. Etherington, John C. Whitehead.
Staff: Patricia A. McCarthy, Admin. Officer.
Number of staff: 2 full-time professional; 2 part-time support.
Employer Identification Number: 226044214

3951
The Arnold A. Schwartz Foundation ⌑
c/o Kunzman, Coley, Yospin & Bernstein
15 Mountain Blvd.
Warren 07060 (201) 757-7927

Incorporated in 1953 in NJ.
Donor(s): Arnold A. Schwartz.†
Foundation type: Independent
Financial data (yr. ended 11/30/89): Assets, $3,528,031 (M); expenditures, $183,309, including $152,500 for 52 grants (high: $15,000; low: $500).
Purpose and activities: Emphasis on elementary and secondary schools, community services, youth agencies, hospitals, and child welfare.
Limitations: Giving primarily in northern NJ. No support for religious purposes. No grants to individuals, or for endowment funds; no loans.
Application information:
Initial approach: Letter
Copies of proposal: 2
Deadline(s): Sept. 30
Board meeting date(s): Feb., June, Sept., and Nov.
Write: Edwin D. Kunzman, Pres.
Officers: Edwin D. Kunzman, Pres.; Louis Harding, V.P.; Steven Kunzman, Secy.-Treas.
Trustees: Victor DiLeo, David Lackland, Robert Shapiro, Kenneth Turnbull.
Employer Identification Number: 226034152

3952
Schwarz Foundation ⌑ ☆
1163 Route 22 East
Mountainside 07092

Established in 1982.
Donor(s): Steven Schwarz, Henryk Schwarz.
Foundation type: Independent
Financial data (yr. ended 6/30/89): Assets, $1,213,190 (M); gifts received, $150,000; expenditures, $53,015, including $52,700 for 10 grants (high: $22,000; low: $200).
Purpose and activities: Support for Jewish welfare and Jewish giving, including organizations supporting Israel.
Limitations: No grants to individuals.
Application information: Contributes only to pre-selected organizations. Applications not accepted.
Officers: Steven Schwarz, Pres.; Henryk Schwarz, Secy.
Employer Identification Number: 222430208

3953
Hattie and Arnold Segal Foundation, Inc. ⌑ ☆
185 Valley St.
South Orange 07079-2801

Established in 1984 in NJ.
Donor(s): Arnold Segal, Hattie Segal.
Foundation type: Independent
Financial data (yr. ended 12/31/88): Assets, $411,944 (M); expenditures, $310,303, including $310,150 for 13 grants (high: $252,000; low: $500).
Purpose and activities: Giving primarily for Jewish organizations, including those providing welfare; minor support for peace and foreign policy institutions.
Limitations: No grants to individuals.
Application information: Contributes only to pre-selected organizations. Applications not accepted.
Officers and Trustees: Arnold Segal, Pres. and Treas.; Hattie Segal, Secy.; Richard Segal.
Employer Identification Number: 222612583

3954
Norman and Barbara Seiden Foundation ⌑
20 Oxford Dr.
South Brunswick 08810-1600 (201) 585-0770

Established in 1973 in NJ.
Donor(s): Norman Seiden, Barbara Seiden.
Foundation type: Independent
Financial data (yr. ended 12/31/87): Assets, $1,173,481 (M); gifts received, $126,650; expenditures, $304,051, including $290,725 for 64 grants (high: $175,000; low: $10).
Purpose and activities: Support primarily for Jewish welfare and Jewish organizations.
Application information:
Initial approach: Letter
Deadline(s): None
Officers and Trustees: Norman Seiden, Pres. and Treas.; Barbara Seiden, V.P.; Mark Seiden, V.P.; Stephen Seiden, Secy.; Charles Klatskin, Pearl Newman.
Employer Identification Number: 237351938

3955
Sy Sims Foundation ⌑ ☆
Syms Way
Secaucus 07094

Established in 1985 in NJ.
Donor(s): Sy Syms.
Foundation type: Independent
Financial data (yr. ended 4/30/89): Assets, $3,058 (M); gifts received, $125,000; expenditures, $124,218, including $124,000 for 23 grants (high: $25,000; low: $500).
Purpose and activities: Support for Jewish welfare and other Jewish organizations; grants also for higher education.
Types of support: Scholarship funds.
Limitations: No grants to individuals.
Application information: Contributes only to pre-selected organizations. Applications not accepted.
Trustees: Marcy Syms Merns, Sy Syms.
Employer Identification Number: 222617727

3956
The Harold B. and Dorothy A. Snyder Foundation
P.O. Box 671
Moorestown 08057 (609) 273-9745

Established in 1971 in NJ as a trust; incorporated in 1981 in NJ.
Donor(s): Harold B. Snyder, Sr.†
Foundation type: Independent
Financial data (yr. ended 09/30/89): Assets, $5,520,840 (M); gifts received, $322,948; expenditures, $449,604, including $164,763 for 27 grants (high: $35,000; low: $200; average: $200-$35,000) and $15,163 for 7 grants to individuals (high: $3,478; low: $454).
Purpose and activities: Support for social service programs in Union County, NJ, and scholarships for NJ residents entering the Presbyterian or other Protestant ministries, nursing, and the building construction industry; for nuns and priests who wish to further their secular education; and for NJ rabbinical students studying at the Jewish Theological Seminary of America.
Types of support: Continuing support, equipment, general purposes, operating budgets, publications, student aid, matching funds, renovation projects, seed money, special projects, loans, program-related investments, student loans.
Limitations: Giving primarily in the Union County, NJ, area. No grants to individuals directly; generally no capital campaigns.
Application information: Scholarships paid through institutions only. Application form not required.
Initial approach: Letter or telephone
Copies of proposal: 5
Deadline(s): None
Board meeting date(s): Bimonthly or quarterly
Final notification: Aug.
Write: Audrey Snyder, Exec. Dir
Trustees: Ethelyn Allison, Arline Snyder Cortese, Robert G. Longaker, Audrey Snyder, Phyllis Johnson Snyder.
Number of staff: 1 full-time professional.
Employer Identification Number: 222316043

3957
The South Branch Foundation ⌑
c/o Gillen & Johnson
P.O. Box 477
Somerville 08876 (201) 722-6400

Trust established in 1960 in NJ.
Donor(s): J. Seward Johnson, The J. Seward Johnson Charitable Trust.
Foundation type: Independent
Financial data (yr. ended 12/31/88): Assets, $7,978,014 (M); expenditures, $545,933, including $440,500 for 26 grants (high: $80,000; low: $1,000; average: $2,000-$100,000).
Purpose and activities: Emphasis on civil rights, education, conservation, protection of animals, cultural programs, social services, and health.
Types of support: Continuing support, fellowships, research, scholarship funds, special projects.
Limitations: Giving primarily in NY, NJ, and MA. No grants to individuals, or for building funds.
Application information: Application form not required.
Initial approach: Proposal
Copies of proposal: 1
Deadline(s): Submit proposal preferably in Nov. or Dec.; deadline Dec. 31
Board meeting date(s): Jan.
Final notification: 45 days
Write: Peter S. Johnson
Director: Jennifer U. Johnson Duke.
Trustees: Esther U. Johnson, James L. Johnson, John D. Mack.
Number of staff: None.
Employer Identification Number: 226029434

3958
Standish Foundation
P.O. Box 4470
Warren 07060-0470 (201) 753-2440

Established in 1968 in NJ.
Donor(s): Grace H. Smith.†
Foundation type: Independent
Financial data (yr. ended 12/31/88): Assets, $1,021,397 (M); expenditures, $60,825, including $52,941 for 34 grants (high: $5,300; low: $500; average: $500-$3,500).
Purpose and activities: Support primarily for hospitals, education, social services, and community organizataions.
Types of support: Building funds, capital campaigns, equipment, general purposes.
Limitations: Giving primarily in the Westfield, NJ, area. No grants to individuals.
Application information: Application form not required.
Initial approach: Letter
Copies of proposal: 1
Deadline(s): Nov. 15
Board meeting date(s): Dec.
Final notification: Dec. 31
Write: William V. Engel, Pres.
Officers: William V. Engel, Pres.; Jane D. Engel, V.P.; Virginia L. Cavanaugh, Secy.; Thomas H. Campbell, Treas.
Trustees: Joseph G. Engel, Robert J. Engel.
Number of staff: 1 part-time professional; 2 part-time support.
Employer Identification Number: 226102990

3959
The Judy and Michael Steinhardt Foundation ¤ ☆
2333 Morris Ave.
Union 07083 (201) 851-2300

Established in 1986 in NY.
Foundation type: Independent
Financial data (yr. ended 9/30/87): Assets, $4,539,597 (M); gifts received, $5,001,636; expenditures, $476,042, including $463,499 for 24 grants (high: $150,000; low: $150).
Purpose and activities: Support for Jewish giving and Jewish welfare, including organizations supporting Israel; support also for higher and other education and a botanical garden.
Application information: Applications not accepted.
Trustees: Judith Steinhardt, Michael Steinhardt.
Employer Identification Number: 133357500

3960
Max Stern Foundation, Inc. ¤
c/o Richard Stearn
P.O Box 1411
Secaucus 07096

Incorporated in 1945 in DE.
Donor(s): Max Stern,† Stanley Stern.
Foundation type: Independent
Financial data (yr. ended 09/30/89): Assets, $2,976,376 (M); expenditures, $509,035, including $497,905 for 78 grants (high: $125,000; low: $25).
Purpose and activities: Grants largely for higher and secondary education (including religious education), Jewish welfare funds, and organizations in Israel, particularly a hospital.
Types of support: Continuing support.
Application information: Contributes only to pre-selected organizations. Applications not accepted.
Officers and Directors: Leonard N. Stern,* Pres. and V.P.; Armand Lindenbaum,* Secy.; Ronald Catalina, Treas.; Ghity Stern.
Employer Identification Number: 136161280

3961
Howard G. Strauss Foundation ¤
Nine Broadmoor Dr.
Rumson 07760

Established about 1944 in NY.
Foundation type: Independent
Financial data (yr. ended 06/30/89): Assets, $1,098,895 (M); expenditures, $26,671, including $25,391 for 31 grants (high: $8,000; low: $21).
Purpose and activities: Giving primarily for Jewish welfare; support also for health and animal welfare.
Application information:
Initial approach: Letter
Deadline(s): Sept. 1
Write: Howard E. Strauss, Pres.
Officers: Howard E. Strauss, Pres.; Judith A. Strauss, V.P. and Treas.; Robert L. Klein, Secy.
Employer Identification Number: 136161012

3962
Subaru of America Foundation
Subaru Plaza
P.O. Box 6000
Cherry Hill 08034-6000 (609) 488-5099

Established in 1984 in NJ.
Donor(s): Subaru of America, Inc.
Foundation type: Company-sponsored
Financial data (yr. ended 10/31/89): Assets, $1,246,778 (M); gifts received, $100,000; expenditures, $400,581, including $360,034 for grants (high: $15,000; low: $50; average: $2,000-$3,000) and $38,359 for 264 employee matching gifts.
Purpose and activities: Giving for cultural programs, health and hospitals, social services, youth, education, and civic organizations.
Types of support: Operating budgets, continuing support, annual campaigns, seed money, emergency funds, building funds, equipment, employee matching gifts, special projects, general purposes, matching funds, technical assistance.
Limitations: Giving limited to areas of company operations, primarily in the Cherry Hill, NJ, area, and immediate regional office communities in Addison, IL; Portland, OR; San Antonio, TX; Savage, MD; West Palm Beach, FL; and Garden Grove and Irvine, CA. No support for religious, fraternal, or veterans' groups. No grants to individuals, or for land acquisition, endowment funds, scholarships, fellowships, research, publications, conferences and seminars, or vehicle donations; no loans.
Publications: Annual report (including application guidelines).
Application information: Application form not required.
Initial approach: Letter, telephone, or proposal
Copies of proposal: 1
Deadline(s): Dec. 1, Mar. 1, June 1, and Sept. 1
Board meeting date(s): Jan., Apr., July, and Oct.
Final notification: Up to 5 months, depending on cycle
Write: Denise L. Schwartz, Mgr.
Officers and Trustees:* Thomas R. Gibson,* Pres.; Marvin S. Riesenbach,* Exec. V.P. and C.F.O.; Frank T. Aspell, V.P.; Harvey H. Lamm,* C.E.O.
Contributions Committee: Rick L. Crosson, Chair.; Robert A. Brodeur, Deborah D. Donat, Cynthia M. D'Orazio, Sandra M. Foglia, Lee D. Goldring, Ellen Patton, Allan Phelps, Betty Y. Wenger.
Staff: Denise L. Schwartz, Mgr.
Number of staff: 1 full-time professional; 2 full-time support.
Employer Identification Number: 222531774

3963
The Stuart and Anita Subotnick Foundation ¤ ☆
c/o Metromedia Co.
One Harmon Plaza
Secaucus 07094-2803

Established in 1986 in NJ.
Donor(s): Stuart Subotnick, Anita Subotnick.
Foundation type: Independent
Financial data (yr. ended 6/30/88): Assets, $48,656 (M); gifts received, $140,000; expenditures, $130,044, including $128,132 for 10 grants (high: $75,000; low: $45).
Purpose and activities: Giving primarily to a university and a law school.
Limitations: Giving primarily in NY and PA.
Application information: Applications not accepted.
Officers and Directors: Stuart Subotnick, Pres.; Anita Subotnick, V.P.
Employer Identification Number: 222833166

3964
The Samuel and Claire Sudler Charitable Trust ¤ ☆
75 Eisenhower Pkwy.
Roseland 07068 (201) 228-5400

Established in 1986 in NJ.
Donor(s): Samuel Sudler.
Foundation type: Independent
Financial data (yr. ended 12/31/88): Assets, $523,595 (M); expenditures, $257,200, including $255,500 for 13 grants (high: $150,000; low: $1,000).
Purpose and activities: Giving for Jewish welfare and temple support; giving also for higher education and social services.
Limitations: No support for private foundations. No grants to individuals.
Application information:
Initial approach: Letter
Deadline(s): None
Write: Samuel Sudler, Trustee
Trustees: Samuel Sudler, Claire Sudler.
Employer Identification Number: 226423710

3965
The Algernon Sydney Sullivan Foundation ⌑
Box 306M
Morristown 07960 (201) 267-8856

Incorporated in 1930 in NY.
Donor(s): Mrs. Algernon Sydney Sullivan,† George Hammond Sullivan,† Zilph P. Devereaux,† and others.
Foundation type: Independent
Financial data (yr. ended 12/31/88): Assets, $8,369,203 (M); gifts received, $10,000; expenditures, $455,627, including $354,350 for 51 grants (high: $21,500; low: $250; average: $1,000-$10,000).
Purpose and activities: Grants primarily to colleges and universities for scholarship funds.
Types of support: Scholarship funds.
Limitations: Giving primarily in the Southeast. No grants to individuals, or for capital construction.
Application information:
Initial approach: Proposal
Copies of proposal: 1
Deadline(s): None
Board meeting date(s): May and Nov.
Write: William E. Bardusch, Jr., Pres.
Officers and Trustees: William E. Bardusch, Jr., Pres.; John S. Chapman, Jr., V.P.; Charles W. Cook, Secy.; Frederick L. Redpath, Treas.; Walter G. Dunnington, Jr., Hiram B. Ely, Jr., R. Bruce McBratney, Myles C. Morrison IV, Gray Williams, Jr., Emmett Wright, Jr.
Employer Identification Number: 136084596

3966
The Sutton Foundation ⌑ ☆
855 Garfield Ave.
Jersey City 07305-4497

Established in 1974.
Donor(s): Elie S. Sutton, Ralph S. Sutton, Joseph S. Sutton.
Foundation type: Independent
Financial data (yr. ended 7/31/89): Assets, $1,897,357 (M); gifts received, $979,220; expenditures, $323,300, including $323,300 for grants.
Purpose and activities: Support primarily for Jewish welfare and other Jewish organizations, including yeshivas and synagogues.
Officers: Elie S. Sutton, Pres.; Joseph S. Sutton, V.P.; Ralph S. Sutton, Secy.; Altoon Sutton, Treas.
Employer Identification Number: 237387217

3967
The Tal Charitable Trust ⌑ ☆
c/o Bessemer Trust Co.
100 Woodbridge Center Dr.
Woodbridge 07095-0983 (212) 688-4500
Application address: 444 Madison Ave., New York, NY 10022

Established in 1983 in NY.
Donor(s): William M. Lese.
Foundation type: Independent
Financial data (yr. ended 11/30/87): Assets, $441,561 (M); gifts received, $119,600; expenditures, $129,454, including $126,375 for 56 grants (high: $25,000; low: $75).
Purpose and activities: Giving primarily for secondary education, the performing arts, and museums; support also for higher education and Jewish giving, including welfare funds and Israel.
Limitations: Giving primarily in New York, NY, and Windsor, CT.
Application information: Application form not required.
Initial approach: Letter
Deadline(s): None
Write: William M. Lese, Trustee
Trustees: William M. Lese, Bessemer Trust Co., N.A.
Employer Identification Number: 226373268

3968
Ann Earle Talcott Fund
c/o First Fidelity Bank, N.A., NJ
765 Broad St.
Newark 07102 (201) 430-4533

Trust established in 1972 in NJ.
Donor(s): Ann Earle Talcott.†
Foundation type: Independent
Financial data (yr. ended 10/31/89): Assets, $1,733,967 (M); expenditures, $87,856, including $76,000 for 9 grants (high: $25,000; low: $2,500; average: $2,500-$25,000).
Purpose and activities: Emphasis on aid to the indigent, large-scale community service projects, and youth projects at the primary school level. Support also for the prevention of cruelty to animals and children, and testing for public safety.
Types of support: Program-related investments, seed money, special projects.
Limitations: No grants to individuals; no loans.
Publications: 990-PF, application guidelines.
Application information: Progress report due 9 months after funding. Application form not required.
Initial approach: Proposal
Copies of proposal: 1
Deadline(s): Feb. 15 and Aug. 15
Board meeting date(s): Mar. and Sept.
Final notification: 1 month after board meeting
Write: James S. Hohn, V.P., First Fidelity Bank, N.A., NJ
Trustee: First Fidelity Bank, N.A., NJ.
Employer Identification Number: 226203894

3969
Tall Spruce Foundation ⌑
c/o Vincent Murphy
RD 1, Box 96B
Far Hills 07931

Established in 1978 in NJ.
Donor(s): Vincent B. Murphy, Jr.
Foundation type: Independent
Financial data (yr. ended 06/30/89): Assets, $86,241 (M); gifts received, $210,275; expenditures, $165,137, including $162,050 for 26 grants (high: $25,000; low: $250).
Purpose and activities: Funds for education and denominational purposes; support also for equestrian activities.
Limitations: Giving primarily in New York, NY, and NJ. No grants to individuals.
Application information: Contributes only to pre-selected organizations. Applications not accepted.
Officers: Vincent B. Murphy, Jr., Pres. and Treas.; Patricia Murphy, V.P. and Secy.
Director: Vincent B. Murphy III.
Employer Identification Number: 132997573

3970
The Henry and Marilyn Taub Foundation ▼ ⌑
c/o Wiss & Co.
354 Eisenhower Pkwy.
Livingston 07039

Established in 1967 in DE.
Donor(s): Henry Taub.
Foundation type: Independent
Financial data (yr. ended 12/31/87): Assets, $13,278,550 (M); gifts received, $6,006,730; expenditures, $1,006,423, including $945,245 for 89 grants (high: $261,425; low: $20; average: $100-$20,000).
Purpose and activities: Grants largely for Jewish welfare funds; some support for higher and other education, social service and youth agencies, and hospitals.
Limitations: Giving primarily in NJ.
Application information: Contributes only to pre-selected organizations. Applications not accepted.
Officers and Directors:* Henry Taub,* Pres.; Fred S. Lafer, Secy.; Marilyn Taub,* Treas.
Employer Identification Number: 226100525

3971
Joseph and Arlene Taub Foundation ⌑
c/o Wiss & Co.
354 Eisenhower Pkwy.
Livingston 07039

Established in 1968 in DE.
Donor(s): Joseph Taub.
Foundation type: Independent
Financial data (yr. ended 12/31/88): Assets, $2,867,083 (M); gifts received, $355,128; expenditures, $241,148, including $217,674 for 42 grants (high: $61,000; low: $25).
Purpose and activities: Grants for Jewish welfare funds, temple support, education, and the handicapped.
Application information: Contributes only to pre-selected organizations. Applications not accepted.
Officers and Directors:* Joseph Taub,* Pres.; Fred S. Lafer,* Secy.; Arlene Taub,* Treas.; Abraham H. Nechemie.
Employer Identification Number: 226104545

3972
Terner Foundation, Inc. ⌑
P.O. Box 340
Oakhurst 07755

Established in 1953.
Donor(s): Emmanuel M. Terner, Mathilda Terner.
Foundation type: Independent
Financial data (yr. ended 7/31/88): Assets, $2,701,774 (M); expenditures, $222,744, including $202,000 for 80 grants (high: $25,000; low: $100).
Purpose and activities: Giving primarily for Jewish welfare funds and temple support, higher and secondary education, and hospitals.
Application information:

Initial approach: Proposal
Deadline(s): June 30
Write: E.M. Terner, Chair.
Officers and Directors: Emmanuel M. Terner, Chair.; Mathilda Terner, Pres. and Treas.; Elaine Cooper, V.P. and Secy.; Nancy Behrman, V.P.; Carol Lederman, V.P.; Winifred A. Packard, V.P.
Employer Identification Number: 221605265

3973
The Thomas & Betts Charitable Trust ⌑
1001 Frontier Rd.
Bridgewater 08807-2941 (201) 685-1600

Trust established in 1948 in NJ.
Donor(s): Thomas & Betts Corp.
Foundation type: Company-sponsored
Financial data (yr. ended 12/31/88): Assets, $347,788 (M); gifts received, $400,000; expenditures, $421,563, including $420,206 for 93 grants (high: $42,000; low: $100) and $25,895 for employee matching gifts.
Purpose and activities: Grants for higher education, community funds, health services, hospitals, and youth agencies.
Types of support: Employee matching gifts.
Limitations: Giving primarily in the area of company operations in Raritan, NJ. No grants to individuals, or for endowment funds, research, scholarships, or fellowships; no loans.
Publications: Annual report, application guidelines, informational brochure.
Application information:
Initial approach: Letter
Copies of proposal: 1
Deadline(s): Oct. 1
Board meeting date(s): Oct. and Dec. and as required
Write: Janice H. Way, Trust Admin.
Trustees: R.V. Berry, J. David Parkinson, Janice H. Way.
Employer Identification Number: 226032533

3974
W. Parsons Todd Foundation, Inc. ⌑
c/o Shanley & Fisher
131 Madison Ave.
Morristown 07960

Incorporated in 1949 in NJ.
Donor(s): W. Parsons Todd.
Foundation type: Operating
Financial data (yr. ended 12/31/88): Assets, $3,123,379 (M); expenditures, $158,415, including $144,720 for 7 grants (high: $139,620; low: $200).
Purpose and activities: Emphasis on an historical museum; grants also for church support.
Types of support: Operating budgets.
Limitations: Giving limited to the Morris County, NJ, and Houghton County, MI, areas. No grants to individuals.
Application information: Contributes only to pre-selected organizations. Applications not accepted.
Officers and Trustees:* Mortimer J. Propp,* Pres.; H.T. Todd,* V.P.; Seymour Propp.
Employer Identification Number: 136116488

3975
Turrell Fund ▼
111 Northfield Ave.
West Orange 07052 (201) 325-5108

Incorporated in 1935 in NJ.
Donor(s): Herbert Turrell,† Margaret Turrell.†
Foundation type: Independent
Financial data (yr. ended 12/31/89): Assets, $87,033,575 (M); gifts received, $4,575; expenditures, $4,659,104, including $3,682,694 for 200 grants (high: $102,000; low: $500; average: $5,000-$50,000) and $347,960 for 1 foundation-administered program.
Purpose and activities: Grants to organizations dedicated to service to or care of children and youth under 18 years of age, with emphasis on the needy, the socially maladjusted, and the disadvantaged.
Types of support: Operating budgets, seed money, emergency funds, building funds, equipment, land acquisition, matching funds, scholarship funds, renovation projects, general purposes, special projects.
Limitations: Giving limited to NJ, particularly the northern urban areas centered in Essex County, and to VT. No support for advocacy work, most hospital work, or health delivery services; generally no support for cultural activities. No grants to individuals, or for endowment funds, publications, conferences, or research; no loans.
Publications: Annual report (including application guidelines).
Application information: Application form not required.
Initial approach: Letter
Copies of proposal: 1
Deadline(s): Submit proposal preferably in Jan. or Feb. or between June and Sept.; deadlines Feb. 14 and Sept. 15 for first-time applicants; Mar. 1 and Oct. 1 for others
Board meeting date(s): May and Nov. and/or Dec.
Final notification: 3 months after deadlines
Write: E. Belvin Williams, Exec. Dir.
Officers: S. Whitney Landon, Chair.; Frank J. Hoenemeyer, Pres.; E. Belvin Williams,* Secy.-Treas. and Exec. Dir.
Trustees:* Paul J. Christiansen, Ann G. Dinse, Carl Fjellman, Robert H. Grasmere, Richard R. Hough, Frank A. Hutson, Jr., Larry Prendergast, Vivian Shapiro.
Number of staff: 2 full-time professional; 1 part-time professional; 3 full-time support.
Employer Identification Number: 221551936

3976
Union Camp Charitable Trust
c/o Union Camp Corp.
1600 Valley Rd.
Wayne 07470 (201) 628-2248

Trust established in 1951 in NY.
Donor(s): Union Camp Corp.
Foundation type: Company-sponsored
Financial data (yr. ended 12/31/88): Assets, $1,792,295 (M); gifts received, $2,500,000; expenditures, $1,736,779, including $1,728,075 for grants (average: $200-$5,000).
Purpose and activities: Grants largely for community funds, higher and other education, including employee-related scholarships and matching gifts, hospitals and health services, social services, youth and women, civic affairs and public interest, civil rights and law and justice, Jewish giving and Protestant welfare, and cultural programs.
Types of support: Employee matching gifts, employee-related scholarships, operating budgets, continuing support, annual campaigns, building funds, equipment, special projects, research, capital campaigns, consulting services, emergency funds, endowment funds, fellowships, matching funds, renovation projects, scholarship funds, seed money.
Limitations: Giving primarily in areas of company operations and to national organizations (generally east of the Mason-Dixon line). No grants to individuals (except employee-related scholarships); no loans.
Application information: Application form not required.
Initial approach: Proposal
Copies of proposal: 1
Deadline(s): Submit proposal preferably from Jan. through Aug.
Board meeting date(s): Nov.
Final notification: By Jan. 1
Write: Sydney N. Phin, Dir., Human Resources
Trustees: R.W. Boekenheide, R.E. Cartledge, J.M. Reed, Morgan Guaranty Trust Co. of New York.
Number of staff: 2 part-time professional.
Employer Identification Number: 136034666

3977
Union Foundation
31C Mountain Blvd.
P.O. Box 4470
Warren 07060 (201) 753-2440

Incorporated in 1951 in NJ.
Donor(s): Edward J. Grassmann,† and others.
Foundation type: Independent
Financial data (yr. ended 11/30/89): Assets, $9,451,993 (M); expenditures, $707,540, including $656,500 for 82 grants (high: $45,000; low: $600; average: $3,000-$15,000).
Purpose and activities: Grants largely for hospitals and health agencies, social service and youth agencies, privately-supported higher and secondary education, and conservation.
Types of support: Endowment funds, building funds, equipment.
Limitations: Giving primarily in Union County, NJ. No grants to individuals, or for operating budgets.
Publications: Application guidelines.
Application information: Application form not required.
Initial approach: Proposal
Copies of proposal: 1
Deadline(s): Oct. 15
Board meeting date(s): Nov.
Final notification: Dec. 15
Write: William V. Engel, Pres.
Officers: William V. Engel, Pres.; Edward G. Engel, V.P.; Suzanne B. Engel, Secy.; Thomas H. Campbell, Treas.
Trustees: Cynthia Fuller, Haydn H. Murray, William O. Wuester, M.D.
Number of staff: 1 part-time professional; 2 part-time support.
Employer Identification Number: 226046454

3978
United Counties Trust Foundation ⌑ ☆
Four Commerce Dr.
Cranford 07016

Established in 1964.
Foundation type: Independent
Financial data (yr. ended 12/31/88): Assets, $390,907 (M); gifts received, $75,000; expenditures, $118,378, including $118,000 for grants.
Purpose and activities: Support for a community fund, youth organizations, social services, and hospitals.
Officers: William C. Johnson, Jr., Chair.; Joseph B. Crossan, Vice-Chair.
Advisory Committee: Eugene Bauer, Robert W. Dowens, Sr., Donald S. Nowicki.
Employer Identification Number: 226071110

3979
Lucy and Eleanor S. Upton Charitable Foundation ⌑
100 Mulberry St.
Newark 07102

Established in 1965.
Donor(s): Eleanor S. Upton.†
Foundation type: Independent
Financial data (yr. ended 12/31/88): Assets, $4,353,153 (M); expenditures, $273,844, including $222,000 for 10 grants (high: $75,000; low: $3,000).
Purpose and activities: Support primarily for an educational institution; giving also to hospitals and cultural programs.
Types of support: General purposes, research, fellowships.
Limitations: Giving primarily in NJ.
Application information: Contributes only to pre-selected organizations. Applications not accepted.
Trustees: William B. Cater, Thomas L. Morrissey, Samuel C. Williams, Jr.
Employer Identification Number: 226074947

3980
The Edward W. and Stella C. Van Houten Charitable Trust ☆
c/o First Fidelity Bank, N.A., NJ
765 Broad St.
Newark 07102 (201) 430-4533

Established in 1979 in NJ.
Foundation type: Independent
Financial data (yr. ended 11/30/89): Assets, $13,214,819 (M); qualifying distributions, $1,000,000, including $1,000,000 for grants (average: $10,000-$100,000).
Purpose and activities: Giving primarily for human services, including the disabled and the elderly, with special interest in orphaned children; health care and hospitals, with preference given to pediatrics and associated services; and higher education, primarily through support for medical schools and nursing institutions.
Types of support: Capital campaigns, equipment, matching funds, scholarship funds, special projects, seed money.
Limitations: Giving primarily in Bergen and Passaic counties, NJ. No support for churches or political organizations. No grants to individuals, or for general operating support, endowments, fundraising dinners, or athletic events; no loans.
Publications: 990-PF, application guidelines.
Application information: Application form not required.
Initial approach: Proposal
Copies of proposal: 1
Deadline(s): Feb. 15, May 15, Aug. 15, and Nov. 15
Board meeting date(s): Mar., June, Sept., and Dec.
Write: James S. Hohn, Asst. V.P., First Fidelity Bank, N.A., NJ
Trustee: First Fidelity Bank, N.A., NJ.
Employer Identification Number: 226311438

3981
Van Pelt Foundation ⌑
P.O. Box 823
Westwood 07675

Established in 1977 in NJ.
Donor(s): Edwin Van Pelt.
Foundation type: Independent
Financial data (yr. ended 9/30/89): Assets, $43,533 (M); expenditures, $282,005, including $278,310 for 42 grants (high: $50,000; low: $200).
Purpose and activities: Support for smaller organizations who have been hurt by cutbacks in federal monies and/or individual contributions; support primarily for hospitals and AIDS programs, social services and child welfare agencies, and cultural organizations.
Types of support: Building funds, capital campaigns, continuing support, employee matching gifts, equipment, general purposes.
Application information: Application form not required.
Initial approach: Proposal
Copies of proposal: 5
Deadline(s): Before board meetings
Board meeting date(s): June 1 and Dec. 1
Officers and Trustees: Lawrence D. Bass, Pres.; Henry Gerke, V.P.; Robert DuBois, Secy.; Henry Bass, Treas.; Meredith Van Pelt.
Employer Identification Number: 222188141

3982
Victoria Foundation, Inc. ▼
40 South Fullerton Ave.
Montclair 07042 (201) 783-4450

Incorporated in 1924 in NJ.
Donor(s): Hendon Chubb.†
Foundation type: Independent
Financial data (yr. ended 12/31/89): Assets, $106,204,872 (M); qualifying distributions, $4,754,819, including $4,754,819 for 115 grants (high: $100,000; low: $10,000; average: $20,000-$50,000).
Purpose and activities: Grants primarily for welfare and education programs, including urban problems, neighborhood development, youth agencies, and behavioral rehabilitation; support also for certain statewide environmental projects.
Types of support: Operating budgets, continuing support, seed money, emergency funds, deficit financing, building funds, matching funds, scholarship funds, special projects, research, consulting services, technical assistance, general purposes, renovation projects.
Limitations: Giving limited to Essex County, NJ, with emphasis on the greater Newark area; environmental grants limited to NJ. No support for organizations dealing with specific diseases or afflictions, geriatric needs, or day care. No grants to individuals, or for publications or conferences; no loans.
Publications: Annual report (including application guidelines), application guidelines.
Application information: Application form required.
Initial approach: Proposal or 2-page letter of introduction
Copies of proposal: 1
Deadline(s): Submit proposal Jan. 1 through Mar. 1 or June 1 through Sept. 1
Board meeting date(s): May and Dec.
Final notification: Within 3 weeks after board meeting if accepted
Write: Catherine M. McFarland, Exec. Officer
Officers: Percy Chubb III,* Pres.; Margaret H. Parker,* V.P.; Catherine M. McFarland, Secy.; Kevin Shanley,* Treas.
Trustees:* Matthew G. Carter, Charles Chapin, Corinne A. Chubb, Sally Chubb, Mary Coggeshall, Robert Curvin, Haliburton Fales II, Jean Felker, Gordon A. Millspaugh, Jr., Bernard M. Shanley, William Turnbull.
Number of staff: 2 full-time professional; 1 full-time support.
Employer Identification Number: 221554541

3983
Frank Visceglia Foundation ⌑
300 Raritan Center Pkwy.
Edison 08871

Foundation type: Independent
Financial data (yr. ended 12/31/88): Assets, $1,789,887 (M); gifts received, $191,667; expenditures, $128,116, including $127,188 for 226 grants (high: $10,000; low: $25).
Purpose and activities: Support primarily for Catholic schools, colleges, churches and religious orders.
Application information: Contributes only to pre-selected organizations. Applications not accepted.
Officer: Frank D. Visceglia, Mgr.
Employer Identification Number: 510174975

3984
Visceglia-Summit Associates Foundation ⌑
Raritan Plaza I
Raritan Ctr.
Edison 08818 (201) 225-2900

Incorporated in 1953 in NJ.
Donor(s): Vincent Visceglia, Diego R. Visceglia, John B. Visceglia.
Foundation type: Independent
Financial data (yr. ended 3/31/88): Assets, $1,877,437 (M); gifts received, $17,115; expenditures, $226,989, including $200,112 for 207 grants (high: $24,305; low: $15) and $5,900 for 4 grants to individuals (high: $5,000; low: $300).
Purpose and activities: Support for hospitals, higher education, church support, and religious associations; some support also for community

funds, music, opera, ballet, and other performing arts, and youth agencies.
Types of support: Student aid.
Limitations: Giving primarily in Essex and Middlesex counties, NJ.
Publications: Financial statement.
Application information: Contributes only to pre-selected organizations. Applications not accepted.
Officers: Diego R. Visceglia, Pres.; Vincent Visceglia, V.P.; John B. Visceglia, Secy.
Employer Identification Number: 226041608

3985
Vollmer Foundation, Inc.
217 Gravel Hill Rd.
Kinnelon 07405 (201) 492-2309
Additional address: P.O. Box 704, Butler, NJ 07405

Incorporated in 1965 in NY.
Donor(s): Alberto F. Vollmer.†
Foundation type: Independent
Financial data (yr. ended 12/31/89): Assets, $10,721,939 (M); gifts received, $724,138; expenditures, $221,462, including $184,240 for 10 grants (high: $62,862; low: $1,046; average: $2,000-$30,000).
Purpose and activities: Emphasis on health, youth, social services, and higher and other education; support also for the Catholic church in Venezuela.
Types of support: Annual campaigns, seed money, research, general purposes, continuing support.
Limitations: Giving limited to Venezuela. No grants to individuals, or for building funds or matching gifts; no loans.
Publications: Application guidelines.
Application information: Application form not required.
Initial approach: Letter
Copies of proposal: 2
Deadline(s): Submit proposal preferably between Dec. and Mar.
Board meeting date(s): As required
Final notification: 2 to 3 months
Write: Albert L. Ennist, Asst. Secy.
Officers and Directors:* Gustavo J. Vollmer, Pres.; Eugenio A. Estrada,* V.P. and Treas.; Carolina V. de Eseverri, Secy.; Ana M. de Estrada, Gustavo A. Vollmer.
Number of staff: 1 full-time professional; 2 part-time support.
Employer Identification Number: 132620718

3986
W & N Foundation, Inc. ⌑
413 Mt. Prospect Ave.
Newark 07104 (201) 642-6670

Established in 1981 in NJ.
Foundation type: Independent
Financial data (yr. ended 12/31/87): Assets, $1,263,559 (M); gifts received, $1,263,993; expenditures, $13,205, including $12,600 for 2 grants (high: $10,000; low: $2,600).
Purpose and activities: Support for basic and applied research in science and engineering. Preference given to junior faculty proposals for work in food science, production agriculture, and post harvest handling of fruits and vegetables.
Application information: Application form required.
Initial approach: Letter
Deadline(s): None
Write: Karl R. Huber, Pres.
Officers: Karl R. Huber, Pres.; E.R. Huber, Secy.
Employer Identification Number: 226063583

3987
The Warner-Lambert Foundation ▼ ⌑
201 Tabor Rd.
Morris Plains 07950 (201) 540-2243

Incorporated in 1969 in DE.
Donor(s): Warner-Lambert Co.
Foundation type: Company-sponsored
Financial data (yr. ended 12/31/87): Assets, $473,285 (M); gifts received, $2,185,000; expenditures, $6,069,500, including $6,069,250 for grants (high: $600,000; average: $1,500-$40,000).
Purpose and activities: Emphasis on higher education, medical research and education, pharmacology, and community funds; some support for hospitals, civil rights, and social welfare and youth agencies.
Types of support: Annual campaigns, building funds, continuing support, emergency funds, equipment, matching funds, operating budgets, professorships, seed money, research.
Limitations: Giving primarily in communities where company plants are located. No grants to individuals, or for endowment funds, demonstration projects, research (other than medical research), or conferences; no loans.
Application information: Application form not required.
Initial approach: Letter
Copies of proposal: 1
Deadline(s): Submit proposal preferably between July and Sept.; deadline Sept.
Board meeting date(s): Quarterly
Write: Evelyn Self, Asst. Secy.
Officers: Richard Keelty,* Pres.; David Alton, 1st V.P.; Raymond Fino,* 2nd V.P.; Donald E. O'Neill, 3rd V.P.; Ewart V. Thomas, Secy.-Treas.
Directors:* Ronald E. Zier, Chair.; Paul Gerhart.
Number of staff: 1 full-time professional; 1 part-time professional; 1 part-time support.
Employer Identification Number: 237038078

3988
M. Weiner Foundation ⌑ ☆
c/o Krugman, Chapnick & Grimshaw
Park 80 West, Plaza II, 6th Fl.
Saddle Brook 07662 (201) 845-3434

Established in 1944 in NJ.
Foundation type: Independent
Financial data (yr. ended 12/31/88): Assets, $1,043,581 (M); expenditures, $134,962, including $125,675 for 10 grants (high: $101,000; low: $100).
Purpose and activities: Giving for an opera company, educational broadcasting, hospitals, and higher education.
Limitations: Giving primarily in New York, NY, and NJ.
Application information:
Initial approach: Proposal
Deadline(s): None
Write: Sanfurd G. Bluestein, Mgr.
Officer: Sanfurd G. Bluestein, Mgr.
Employer Identification Number: 222236786

3989
Joseph and Yetta Weisberger Fund for the Aged Poor and Needy ⌑
c/o M. Schuhalter & Co.
188 Route 10
East Hanover 07936

Established in 1965 in NJ.
Foundation type: Independent
Financial data (yr. ended 03/31/89): Assets, $1,519,802 (M); expenditures, $141,222, including $84,375 for 23 grants (high: $15,000; low: $500).
Purpose and activities: Giving primarily for Jewish welfare; support also for social services and health agencies.
Limitations: No grants to individuals.
Application information:
Deadline(s): None
Write: Melvin Eisenberg, Mgr.
Officer: Melvin Eisenberg, Mgr.
Trustees: Kenneth Fast, Sheldon Fast, Suzanne Fast, Anthony V. Salerno, Murray Schuhalter.
Employer Identification Number: 226070831

3990
The Westfield Foundation
301 North Ave. W.
P.O. Box 2295
Westfield 07091 (201) 233-2177

Incorporated in 1975 in NJ.
Foundation type: Community
Financial data (yr. ended 12/31/89): Assets, $2,101,655 (M); gifts received, $240,828; expenditures, $152,753, including $139,012 for 35 grants.
Purpose and activities: Charitable giving to programs that benefit the local community.
Types of support: Equipment, matching funds, scholarship funds, emergency funds, loans, publications, renovation projects, special projects, student aid, annual campaigns, capital campaigns, building funds, endowment funds.
Limitations: Giving limited to Westfield, NJ. No support for churches or religious programs. Generally, no grants to individuals (except for limited scholarships from restricted funds), or for annual giving, operating expenses, or endowments, unless suggested by the donor of a particular fund.
Publications: Annual report, informational brochure, application guidelines.
Application information: Application form required.
Initial approach: Letter
Copies of proposal: 2
Deadline(s): Jan. 1, Apr. 1, July 1, and Oct. 1
Board meeting date(s): Feb., May, Aug., and Nov.
Final notification: 1 week after board meeting
Write: Jeremiah A. Lott, Exec. Dir.
Officers and Trustees:* William S. Jeremiah II,* Pres.; Allen R. Malcolm, V.P.; Jeremiah A. Lott,* Secy. and Exec. Dir.; Leo J. Senus,* Treas.; and 11 additional trustees.
Number of staff: None.
Employer Identification Number: 222155896

3991
The Harold Wetterberg Foundation ⌑
c/o Hannoch & Weisman
Four Becker Farm Rd.
Roseland 07068 (201) 535-5300

Incorporated in 1961 in NJ.
Donor(s): Harold Wetterberg.†
Foundation type: Independent
Financial data (yr. ended 11/30/88): Assets, $1,579,299 (M); expenditures, $123,070, including $87,867 for 7 grants (high: $19,588; low: $4,250).
Purpose and activities: Grants primarily to higher educational institutions and a science organization, with emphasis on research programs in the veterinary sciences.
Types of support: Research.
Application information: Application form required.
Deadline(s): None
Write: Gene R. Korf, Esq., Trustee
Officers and Trustees: Albert G. Besser, Pres.; Norbert R. Murphy, Secy.-Treas.; Gene R. Korf.
Employer Identification Number: 226042915

3992
Wicks Chapin, Inc. ⌑
855 Centennial Ave.
Piscataway 08854

Established in 1985 in NJ.
Foundation type: Independent
Financial data (yr. ended 12/31/88): Assets, $1,132,063 (M); expenditures, $62,275, including $54,000 for 27 grants (high: $20,000; low: $100).
Purpose and activities: Giving primarily for private secondary education, higher education, and an adolescent health clinic.
Officers and Trustees: E.J. Foley, Jr., Pres. and Treas.; Joan P. Foley, V.P. and Secy.; E.J. Foley III.
Employer Identification Number: 222691706

3993
The Wight Foundation, Inc. ⌑ ☆
189 Mill Rd.
Saddle River 07458

Incorporated in 1986 in NJ.
Donor(s): Russell Wight Jr.
Foundation type: Independent
Financial data (yr. ended 12/31/88): Assets, $101,601 (M); gifts received, $350,200; expenditures, $328,017, including $241,831 for 29 grants to individuals (high: $20,943; low: $3,570).
Purpose and activities: Awards scholarships for higher education.
Types of support: Student aid.
Application information: Names submitted to foundation committee from various private schools. Applications not accepted.
Write: Russell Wight, Jr., Pres.
Officers: Russell Wight, Jr., Pres.; Russell Wight, Sr., V.P.; Elke Wight, Secy.
Employer Identification Number: 222743349

3994
Wilf Family Foundation ⌑
1640 Vauxhall Rd.
Union 07083 (201) 964-1930

Established in 1964.
Donor(s): Harry Wilf, Joseph Wilf.
Foundation type: Independent
Financial data (yr. ended 10/31/89): Assets, $18,534,540 (M); gifts received, $4,205,905; expenditures, $821,197, including $788,352 for 81 grants (high: $189,300; low: $50).
Purpose and activities: Grants for Jewish welfare funds, including educational programs, and temple support; giving also for educational institutions.
Application information: Contributes only to pre-selected organizations. Applications not accepted.
Officers: Harry Wilf, Pres.; Joseph Wilf, Secy.
Trustees: Elizabeth Wilf, Judith Wilf.
Employer Identification Number: 226075840

3995
The Willits Foundation ⌑
731 Central Ave.
Murray Hill 07974 (201) 277-8259

Incorporated in 1963 in NJ.
Donor(s): Members of the Willits family.
Foundation type: Independent
Financial data (yr. ended 11/30/87): Assets, $4,179,851 (M); gifts received, $175; expenditures, $297,924, including $278,665 for 88 grants (high: $10,000; low: $200).
Purpose and activities: Emphasis on grants to higher educational institutions for scholarships, and on Protestant church support and religious activities, schools, social service agencies, and hospitals.
Types of support: Scholarship funds, general purposes.
Limitations: Giving primarily in NJ. No grants to individuals.
Application information:
Initial approach: Proposal
Copies of proposal: 1
Deadline(s): Submit proposal preferably between Aug. and Oct.
Board meeting date(s): Nov. and as required
Write: Emily D. Lawrence, Secy.-Treas.
Officers: Harris L. Willits, Pres.; Barbara W. Evans, V.P.; Emily D. Lawrence, Secy.-Treas.
Trustees: John H. Evans, Rev. William H. Felmeth, Itto A. Willits, John F. Willits.
Employer Identification Number: 226063106

3996
Windie Foundation ☆
c/o Drinker Biddle & Reath
P.O. Box 627
Princeton 08542-3712 (609) 921-6336

Established in 1987 in NJ.
Donor(s): J.D. Winslow.†
Foundation type: Operating
Financial data (yr. ended 12/31/88): Assets, $1,475,033 (M); expenditures, $110,400, including $100,000 for 1 grant.
Purpose and activities: Giving "to resident homes for the purpose of assisting women alcoholics"; support also for ecology and the environment.
Types of support: Continuing support.
Limitations: Giving primarily in NJ.
Application information: Application form not required.
Initial approach: Letter
Deadline(s): None
Write: Samuel W. Lambert III, Trustee
Trustees: Leila Cannon, Samuel W. Lambert III, L.V. Silvester, Jr., Wren Winslow Wirth.
Number of staff: None.
Employer Identification Number: 222778703

3997
Philip Zinman Foundation ⌑
900 Haddon Ave., Suite 300
Collingswood 08108

Established in 1951 in NJ.
Foundation type: Independent
Financial data (yr. ended 09/30/89): Assets, $1,141,982 (M); expenditures, $211,641, including $180,743 for 41 grants (high: $75,000; low: $10).
Purpose and activities: Support primarily for higher education.
Application information: Application form not required.
Deadline(s): None
Officers and Trustees:* Philip Zinman,* Pres.; Elizabeth Zinman,* V.P.; Sara Lea Rothman,* Treas.
Employer Identification Number: 216015665

NEW MEXICO

3998
Albuquerque Community Foundation
6400 Uptown Blvd. N.E., Suite 500 West
Albuquerque 87110 (505) 883-6240

Established in 1981 in NM.
Foundation type: Community
Financial data (yr. ended 6/30/89): Assets, $3,384,064 (M); gifts received, $2,507,501; expenditures, $471,040, including $299,509 for 86 grants (high: $25,000; low: $100) and $1,000 for 2 grants to individuals.
Purpose and activities: Support for cultural programs, including music, historic preservation, and the fine and performing arts; education; health services; conservation; and social services, including child welfare, leadership development, and programs for the homeless.
Types of support: Exchange programs, fellowships, publications, research, scholarship funds, seed money, special projects, student aid, technical assistance, consulting services, emergency funds, loans.
Limitations: Giving primarily in the greater Albuquerque, NM, area. No support for religious, political, or grant-making organizations. No grants to individuals; or for

purchase of equipment, debt requirement, or interest or tax payments.
Publications: Annual report (including application guidelines), newsletter, occasional report, informational brochure (including application guidelines).
Application information: Selection is by invitation based on letter of intent. Application form not required.
Initial approach: Letter by Mar. 1; proposal by May 1
Copies of proposal: 1
Board meeting date(s): Quarterly
Final notification: annually in Sept.
Write: Laura E. Threet, Exec. Dir.
Officers and Trustees:* John T. Ackerman,* Pres.; Robert J. Stamm,* V.P.; Gloria G. Mallory,* Secy.; Ray Zimmer,* Treas.; Laura E. Threet, Exec. Dir.; and 15 other trustees.
Number of staff: 1 full-time professional; 2 part-time support.
Employer Identification Number: 850295444

3999
William and Nancy Anixter Family Foundation ¤
c/o Chama Resources Inc.
3700 Rio Grande, N.W.
Albuquerque 87107

Established in 1986 in IL.
Donor(s): William R. Anixter.
Foundation type: Independent
Financial data (yr. ended 12/31/88): Assets, $1,154,529 (M); expenditures, $58,263, including $53,166 for 12 grants (high: $13,466; low: $1,000).
Purpose and activities: Support for the aged, higher education, health associations, and cultural organizations.
Limitations: Giving primarily in IL and NM. No grants to individuals.
Application information: Contributes only to pre-selected organizations. Applications not accepted.
Officers and Directors: William R. Anixter, Pres. and Treas.; Nancy A. Anixter, V.P. and Secy.; Gregory Anixter.
Employer Identification Number: 363482640

4000
Dale J. Bellamah Foundation ¤
P.O. Box 36600, Station D
Albuquerque 87176 (505) 293-1098

Established around 1972 in NM.
Donor(s): Dale J. Bellamah.†
Foundation type: Independent
Financial data (yr. ended 12/31/88): Assets, $20,285,069 (M); expenditures, $1,115,112, including $803,217 for 11 grants (high: $100,000; low: $25,000).
Purpose and activities: Giving for higher education, health, and social services, including youth agencies and an organization providing care for the mentally retarded.
Types of support: Scholarship funds, equipment, general purposes, capital campaigns, special projects, research.
Limitations: No grants to individuals.
Application information: Application form not required.
Initial approach: Letter
Deadline(s): None
Board meeting date(s): As necessary
Write: A.F. Potenziani, Chair. and Pres.
Officers and Directors: A.F. Potenziani, Chair. and Pres.; Frank A. Potenziani, V.P.; William Potenziani, Secy.-Treas.; Kathleen Guggimio, Martha M. Potenziani.
Number of staff: None.
Employer Identification Number: 237177691

4001
The Witter Bynner Foundation for Poetry, Inc.
660 East Garcia
P.O. Box 2188
Santa Fe 87504 (505) 988-3251

Incorporated in 1972 in NM.
Donor(s): Witter Bynner.†
Foundation type: Independent
Financial data (yr. ended 05/31/89): Assets, $3,385,660 (M); gifts received, $266,750; expenditures, $175,192, including $57,597 for 12 grants (high: $20,000; low: $1,000).
Purpose and activities: To make grants, particularly as seed money, in support of poetry and poetry translation to nonprofit organizations and institutions.
Types of support: Seed money, matching funds, special projects, research, conferences and seminars.
Limitations: No support for poetry readings. No grants for building or endowment funds, publications, continuing support, or operating expenses; no loans.
Publications: Annual report, application guidelines, program policy statement, informational brochure, grants list.
Application information: Application form required.
Initial approach: Letter or telephone
Copies of proposal: 3
Deadline(s): Feb. 1
Board meeting date(s): Apr. or May
Final notification: 2 weeks after annual meeting
Write: Steven Schwartz, Exec. Dir.
Officer and Trustees:* Douglas W. Schwartz,* Pres.; Thomas B. Catron III, Art Gallaher, Jr., Vera Zorina Lieberson.
Number of staff: 4 part-time professional.
Employer Identification Number: 237169999

4002
Carlsbad Foundation, Inc.
116 South Canyon St.
Carlsbad 88220 (505) 887-1131

Incorporated in 1977 in NM.
Foundation type: Community
Financial data (yr. ended 6/30/88): Assets, $3,731,179 (M); gifts received, $81,715; expenditures, $570,645, including $437,491 for grants.
Purpose and activities: Student loans to medical and paramedical students and grants to local scholars; support also for civic groups and charitable organizations.
Types of support: Student loans, operating budgets, seed money, emergency funds, building funds, equipment, matching funds, renovation projects, student aid, continuing support, consulting services, technical assistance, scholarship funds, program-related investments, special projects, publications, conferences and seminars.
Limitations: Giving limited to South Eddy County, NM. No grants for annual campaigns.
Publications: Annual report (including application guidelines), newsletter.
Application information: Application form not required.
Initial approach: Letter
Copies of proposal: 1
Deadline(s): 1 week in advance of board meetings
Board meeting date(s): Monthly
Write: John Mills, Exec. Dir.
Officers: Barbara Webber,* Pres.; Linda Aycock,* V.P.; W.R. Williamson, Jr.,* Secy.; Wesley Kelley,* Treas.; John Mills, Exec. Dir.
Directors:* Nancy Beard, Sherry Griffin, Jere K. Reid, Jim Walls, Marvin L. Watts.
Number of staff: 1 full-time professional; 3 part-time support.
Employer Identification Number: 850206472

4003
Max and Anna Levinson Foundation
430 West San Francisco St.
Santa Fe 87501 (505) 586-1681

Incorporated in 1956 in DE.
Donor(s): Max Levinson,† Carl A. Levinson.
Foundation type: Independent
Financial data (yr. ended 09/30/89): Assets, $4,384,729 (M); expenditures, $1,406,187, including $703,225 for 114 grants (high: $20,000; low: $500; average: $5,000-$20,000).
Purpose and activities: Support for the development of a more humane and rewarding democratic society, in which people have greater ability and opportunity to determine directions for the future. Seeks to encourage projects that are concerned with promoting social change and social justice, either by developing and testing alternatives or by responsibly modifying existing systems, institutions, conditions and attitudes that block promising innovation. Grants mainly for projects of national and international impact in the areas of world peace, arms control, energy, environment, civil liberties, human rights, and the Jewish community.
Types of support: Seed money, program-related investments, special projects, research, publications.
Limitations: No grants to individuals, or for capital and endowment funds, building programs, travel, projects of primarily local community significance, expansion of existing services, matching gifts, scholarships, or fellowships; no loans.
Publications: Informational brochure (including application guidelines).
Application information: Application form not required.
Initial approach: Proposal
Copies of proposal: 1
Deadline(s): Varies depending on meeting dates
Board meeting date(s): May and Nov.
Final notification: 2 weeks after board meeting
Write: Ms. Jutta von Gontard, Exec. Dir.

Officers and Directors:* Carl A. Levinson,* Pres. and Treas.; Carol A. Doroshow,* V.P.; Jutta von Gontard,* Secy.; Donald Bean, Sandy Close, Helen L. Doroshow, James E. Doroshow, William Doroshow, Anna B. Levinson, Charlotte J. Levinson, Gordon Levinson, Julian Levinson, Lynda B. Levinson.
Number of staff: 1 full-time professional; 1 full-time support.
Employer Identification Number: 236282844

4004
J. F. Maddox Foundation ▼
P.O. Box 5410
Hobbs 88241 (505) 393-6338

Established in 1963 in NM.
Donor(s): J.F. Maddox,† Mabel S. Maddox.†
Foundation type: Independent
Financial data (yr. ended 06/30/89): Assets, $68,464,901 (M); gifts received, $14,772,299; expenditures, $1,924,849, including $1,810,635 for 85 grants (high: $668,614; low: $250; average: $1,000-$25,000) and $90,138 for loans to individuals.
Purpose and activities: Giving for community projects where self-help is evident, activities benefiting the elderly, youth education and development programs, the arts, and higher education, including student loans.
Types of support: Student loans, building funds, equipment, general purposes, matching funds, seed money, special projects, renovation projects.
Limitations: Giving primarily in NM and western TX; student loans limited to Lea County, NM, residents. No support for private foundations. No grants to individuals, or for operating budgets, or endowment funds.
Publications: Application guidelines.
Application information: Application form required for student loans. Application form not required.
Initial approach: Letter
Copies of proposal: 1
Deadline(s): None
Board meeting date(s): As needed
Final notification: Varies
Write: Robert D. Socolofsky, Exec. Dir.
Officers and Directors:* Donovan Maddox,* Pres.; Don Maddox,* V.P.; James M. Maddox,* Secy.-Treas.; Harry H. Lynch.
Number of staff: 1 full-time professional; 2 part-time professional; 1 full-time support.
Employer Identification Number: 756023767

4005
Waite and Genevieve Phillips Foundation ⌑
P.O. Box 5726
Santa Fe 87502

Established in 1986 in NM.
Donor(s): Waite and Genevieve Phillips Charitable Trust.
Foundation type: Independent
Financial data (yr. ended 5/31/87): Assets, $39,287,303 (M); expenditures, $758,018, including $650,125 for 31 grants (high: $452,625; low: $500).
Purpose and activities: Giving primarily to the arts, cultural organizations, and education.
Application information: Contributes only to pre-selected organizations. Applications not accepted.
Officers and Directors: Elliott W. Phillips, Pres.; John Phillips, V.P.; Julie Puckett, V.P.; Virginia Phillips, Secy.-Treas.
Employer Identification Number: 850335071

4006
PNM Foundation, Inc.
Alvarado Sq.
Albuquerque 87158 (505) 768-6613

Incorporated in 1983 in NM.
Donor(s): Public Service Co. of New Mexico.
Foundation type: Company-sponsored
Financial data (yr. ended 12/31/88): Assets, $3,358,563 (M); gifts received, $91,806; expenditures, $115,299, including $58,185 for 13 grants (high: $10,000; low: $800) and $8,505 for 42 employee matching gifts (high: $1,000; low: $25).
Purpose and activities: Giving to keep at-risk students in school. Support also for higher education through an educator award program, chair endowments, and an employee matching gift program.
Types of support: Employee matching gifts, endowment funds, matching funds, renovation projects, seed money, special projects, building funds.
Limitations: Giving primarily in NM.
Publications: Informational brochure (including application guidelines).
Application information: Application form required.
Board meeting date(s): Quarterly
Write: Michael Kroth
Officers and Directors:* James B. Mulcock,* Pres.; Joellyn Murphy,* V.P.; John Von Rusten,* Secy.-Treas.; John Ackerman, William Eglinton.
Employer Identification Number: 850309005

4007
Luther A. Sizemore Foundation ⌑
6010 Lomas Blvd., NE
Albuquerque 87110

Established in 1977.
Foundation type: Independent
Financial data (yr. ended 12/31/88): Assets, $1,093,568 (M); expenditures, $65,699, including $43,915 for 27 grants.
Purpose and activities: Giving for higher education, Christian religious organizations, and cultural programs, with emphasis on a natural history museum.
Limitations: Giving primarily in Albuquerque, NM.
Application information: Application form not required.
Deadline(s): None
Officers: Marcial Rey, Pres.; Wilfred Padilla, V.P.; Clinton N. Abel, Secy.-Treas.
Employer Identification Number: 510206540

4008
The Helene Wurlitzer Foundation of New Mexico
P.O. Box 545
Taos 87571 (505) 758-2413

Incorporated in 1956 in NM.
Donor(s): Mrs. Howard E. Wurlitzer.†
Foundation type: Operating
Financial data (yr. ended 03/31/88): Assets, $4,128,899 (M); gifts received, $1,025; expenditures, $102,093, including $1,378 for 13 grants (high: $250; low: $15) and $19,837 for 19 grants to individuals (high: $3,469; low: $311).
Purpose and activities: A private operating foundation established to encourage and stimulate creative work in the humanities, arts, and allied fields through the provision of rent-free and utilities-free housing in Taos, NM.
Types of support: Grants to individuals, internships.
Application information: Application form required.
Initial approach: Letter
Deadline(s): None
Board meeting date(s): As required
Final notification: Several weeks
Write: Henry A. Sauerwein, Jr., Pres.
Officers and Trustees:* Henry A. Sauerwein, Jr.,* Pres. and Exec. Dir.; Burton Phillips,* V.P. and Treas.; Kenneth Peterson, Secy.; Sumner S. Koch, Mrs. Toni Tarleton.
Number of staff: 1 part-time professional; 1 full-time support; 1 part-time support.
Employer Identification Number: 850128634

NEW YORK

4009
Joseph & Sophia Abeles Foundation, Inc. ⌑
1055 Bedford Rd.
Pleasantville 10570-3907 (914) 769-0781

Established in 1960 in NY.
Foundation type: Independent
Financial data (yr. ended 12/31/88): Assets, $2,091,252 (M); expenditures, $103,198, including $97,668 for 73 grants (high: $12,500; low: $100).
Purpose and activities: Giving primarily for higher education, including a scholarship fund, cultural programs, and social services.
Types of support: Scholarship funds.
Application information:
Initial approach: Letter
Deadline(s): None
Write: Mrs. Sophia Abeles, Treas.
Officers: Joseph C. Abeles, Pres. and V.P.; David Teitelbaum, Secy.; Sophia Abeles, Treas.
Employer Identification Number: 136259577

4010
Abelson Family Foundation, Inc. ⌑ ☆
545 Madison Ave.
New York 10022-4296 (212) 371-2525

Established in 1985 in NY.
Donor(s): Sanford E. Abelson, Albert Abelson.
Foundation type: Independent
Financial data (yr. ended 12/31/88): Assets, $640 (M); gifts received, $127,000; expenditures, $127,716, including $127,685 for 63 grants (high: $25,000; low: $10).
Purpose and activities: Support primarily for Jewish welfare funds, hospitals, and health associations.
Limitations: Giving primarily in NY.
Application information:
Initial approach: Letter
Deadline(s): None
Write: Sanford E. Abelson, Pres.
Officers and Directors: Sanford E. Abelson, Pres.; Frances W. Abelson, V.P.; Carol Nancy Posen, Secy.; Kenneth Frank Abelson, Treas.
Employer Identification Number: 133300042

4011
The Abraham Foundation, Inc. ⌑ ☆
c/o Barry M. Strauss Assoc.
245 Fifth Ave., Suite 1102
New York 10016-8775

Established in 1945.
Donor(s): Alexander Abraham.
Foundation type: Independent
Financial data (yr. ended 9/30/88): Assets, $1,537,695 (M); expenditures, $23,920, including $12,320 for 28 grants (high: $2,000; low: $15).
Purpose and activities: Giving for health associations, animal welfare, museums and other cultural programs, higher education, and social services.
Application information:
Initial approach: Letter
Deadline(s): None
Write: Alexander Abraham, Pres.
Officers: Alexander Abraham, Pres.; Nancy Abraham, V.P.; Helene Abraham, Secy.; James Abraham, Treas.
Employer Identification Number: 136065944

4012
Benjamin and Elizabeth Abrams Foundation, Inc. ⌑
645 Madison Ave.
New York 10022

Incorporated in 1943 in NY.
Donor(s): Benjamin Abrams,† Elizabeth Abrams Kramer.
Foundation type: Independent
Financial data (yr. ended 12/31/87): Assets, $1,955,628 (M); expenditures, $105,332, including $63,650 for 40 grants (high: $14,000; low: $200).
Purpose and activities: Emphasis on higher education, including medical education, hospitals, Jewish welfare funds, and cultural programs.
Limitations: Giving primarily in NY and in Palm Beach County, FL.
Application information: Contributes only to pre-selected organizations. Applications not accepted.
Officers and Directors: Elizabeth Abrams Kramer, Pres. and Treas.; Marjorie A. Hyman, V.P.; Geraldine A. Kory, Secy.; Cynthia Bernstein.
Employer Identification Number: 136092960

4013
Louis and Anne Abrons Foundation, Inc. ▼
c/o First Manhattan Co.
437 Madison Ave.
New York 10017 (212) 832-4376

Incorporated in 1950 in NY.
Donor(s): Anne S. Abrons,† Louis Abrons.†
Foundation type: Independent
Financial data (yr. ended 12/31/89): Assets, $32,000,000 (M); expenditures, $2,850,000, including $2,800,000 for 160 grants (high: $165,000; low: $500; average: $5,000-$50,000).
Purpose and activities: Giving primarily to social welfare agencies, Jewish charities, major New York City institutions, civic improvement programs, education, and environmental and cultural projects.
Types of support: Operating budgets, continuing support, annual campaigns, seed money, general purposes, special projects, scholarship funds, research, technical assistance, building funds, consulting services.
Limitations: Giving primarily in the New York, NY, metropolitan area. No grants to individuals.
Application information: Contributes primarily to pre-selected organizations. Application form not required.
Copies of proposal: 1
Board meeting date(s): Jan., Apr., June, and Sept.
Final notification: 2 weeks after board meeting
Write: Richard Abrons, Pres.
Officers and Directors:* Richard Abrons,* Pres.; Herbert L. Abrons,* V.P.; Rita Aranow,* V.P.; Edward Aranow, Secy.-Treas.; Alix Abrons, Anne Abrons, Henry Abrons, Peter Abrons, Vicki Klein.
Number of staff: None.
Employer Identification Number: 136061329

4014
The Achelis Foundation ▼
c/o Morris & McVeigh
767 Third Ave.
New York 10017 (212) 418-0588

Incorporated in 1940 in NY.
Donor(s): Elizabeth Achelis.†
Foundation type: Independent
Financial data (yr. ended 12/31/89): Assets, $20,986,418 (M); expenditures, $937,516, including $770,000 for 53 grants (high: $30,000; low: $10,000; average: $10,000-$25,000).
Purpose and activities: Support for youth and social service agencies, education, health and hospitals, the arts, and cultural programs.
Types of support: Building funds, general purposes, operating budgets, matching funds, equipment, land acquisition, annual campaigns, capital campaigns, endowment funds, renovation projects, research, fellowships.
Limitations: Giving primarily in the NY area. No grants to individuals, or for experimental projects, films, travel, publications, or conferences; no loans.
Publications: Biennial report (including application guidelines), financial statement.
Application information: Application form not required.
Initial approach: Letter or proposal
Copies of proposal: 1
Deadline(s): None
Board meeting date(s): Usually in May, July, and Dec.
Write: Mary E. Caslin, Secy. and Exec. Dir.
Officers and Trustees: Guy G. Rutherfurd, Pres.; Peter Frelinghuysen, V.P. and Treas.; Mary E. Caslin, Secy. and Exec. Dir.; Harry W. Albright, Jr., Mary B. Braga, Anthony Drexel Duke, John N. Irwin III, Marguerite Sykes Nichols, Russel Pennoyer, Mary S. Phipps.
Number of staff: 2 full-time professional.
Employer Identification Number: 136022018

4015
The Acorn Foundation ⌑
c/o Anna G.B. Vietor
620 Park Ave.
New York 10021

Etablished in 1955 in NY.
Donor(s): Anna Glen Butler Vietor.
Foundation type: Independent
Financial data (yr. ended 12/31/88): Assets, $1,352,584 (M); gifts received, $25,950; expenditures, $259,347, including $228,182 for 75 grants (high: $26,100; low: $100).
Purpose and activities: Support primarily for historic preservation, culture, and education.
Limitations: No grants to individuals.
Application information: Contributes only to pre-selected organizations. Applications not accepted.
Officer and Directors:* Anna Glen Butler Vietor,* Pres.; Pauline V. Sheehan, Robert W. Sheehan.
Employer Identification Number: 136098172

4016
Emma J. Adams Memorial Fund, Inc.
518 Fifth Ave., 7th Fl.
New York 10036 (212) 944-0077

Incorporated in 1932 in NY.
Donor(s): Emma J. Adams.†
Foundation type: Independent
Financial data (yr. ended 12/31/87): Assets, $2,603,000 (M); gifts received, $6,000; expenditures, $135,000, including $70,000 for grants (high: $10,000; low: $100; average: $750) and $18,000 for grants to individuals (high: $7,000; low: $100; average: $750).
Purpose and activities: Giving primarily to aid the elderly and indigent through church-sponsored meals program and ecumenical medical care; also very limited grants to needy individuals on a non-recurring basis, and where agency-sponsored, medically sponsored, or professionally sponsored.
Types of support: Emergency funds, grants to individuals.
Limitations: Giving primarily in the greater New York, NY, metropolitan area. No grants for operating budgets, annual campaigns,

administrative expenses, building funds, special projects, endowments, or scholarships; no loans.
Application information: Application form required.
Initial approach: Letter
Copies of proposal: 1
Deadline(s): None
Board meeting date(s): May 1 and Oct. 1
Final notification: Usually within 60 days
Write: Edward R. Finch, Jr., Pres.
Officer: Edward R. Finch, Jr., Pres.
Directors: Pauline Swayze Finch, Col. F.W. Haskell, Mary D.F. Haskell, Trumbull Higgins, Rev. Elizabeth Jacks, Donald W. Scholle, Harold L. Suttle, Henry Weldon.
Number of staff: 1 part-time professional; 2 part-time support.
Employer Identification Number: 136116503

4017
The Joseph & Rachel Ades Foundation, Inc. ▼ ⌑
(Formerly Ades Foundation, Inc.)
240 Madison Ave.
New York 10016

Incorporated in 1945 in NY.
Donor(s): Joseph Ades, Isaac Ades, Irving Baron, Barney Bernstein, Joseph Karp.
Foundation type: Independent
Financial data (yr. ended 12/31/88): Assets, $313,109 (M); gifts received, $275,000; expenditures, $349,542, including $342,965 for 65 grants (high: $50,000; low: $20; average: $550-$20,000).
Purpose and activities: Grants largely for Jewish welfare funds, temple support, education, and youth agencies.
Application information: Contributes only to pre-selected organizations. Applications not accepted.
Officers: Joseph Ades, Pres.; Robert Ades, Secy.; Albert Ades, Treas.
Employer Identification Number: 136077369

4018
Jack Adjmi & Family Foundation, Inc. ⌑
112 West 34th St.
New York 10001 (212) 594-5511

Established in 1983 in NY.
Donor(s): Popsicle Playwear, Ltd., Dreamsicle Sportswear, Inc., Mark Adjmi, Ronald Adjmi.
Foundation type: Independent
Financial data (yr. ended 11/30/88): Assets, $2,761 (M); gifts received, $180,000; expenditures, $266,001, including $265,110 for grants (high: $26,000).
Purpose and activities: Giving primarily for Jewish concerns.
Application information: Application form not required.
Initial approach: Proposal
Deadline(s): None
Write: Jack Adjmi, Dir.
Directors: Eric Adjmi, Jack Adjmi, Rachel Adjmi.
Employer Identification Number: 133202295

4019
Max A. Adler Charitable Foundation ⌑
1010 Times Square Bldg.
Rochester 14614 (716) 232-7290

Established in 1969 in NY.
Donor(s): Max A. Adler.†
Foundation type: Independent
Financial data (yr. ended 12/31/86): Assets, $5 (M); gifts received, $150,000; expenditures, $150,000, including $146,028 for 22 grants (high: $46,128; low: $500).
Purpose and activities: Giving primarily for Jewish welfare and higher education.
Limitations: Giving primarily in Monroe County, NY. No grants to individuals.
Application information: Application form not required.
Initial approach: Letter and proposal
Deadline(s): None
Write: David M. Gray, Mgr.
Officers: Philip M. Liebschutz, Pres.; David M. Gray, Secy. and Mgr.; Beatrice Schonfeld Rapoport, Treas.
Employer Identification Number: 160961112

4020
Adler Foundation, Inc. ⌑
Purchase Ln.
Rye 10580 (914) 967-3335

Incorporated in 1951 in NY.
Donor(s): Morton M. Adler, Helen R. Adler, Harry Rosenthal.†
Foundation type: Independent
Financial data (yr. ended 09/30/89): Assets, $4,988,201 (M); expenditures, $237,028, including $190,460 for 27 grants (high: $60,000; low: $15).
Purpose and activities: Grants chiefly for medical education and for medical research in diabetes and ophthalmology.
Types of support: Research.
Limitations: No grants to individuals.
Application information: Application form not required.
Initial approach: Letter
Copies of proposal: 2
Deadline(s): None
Board meeting date(s): Apr.
Write: John M. Adler, Pres.
Officers and Trustees:* Morton M. Adler,* Chair.; John Adler,* Pres.; Joel J. Berson,* Secy.; Helen R. Adler,* Treas.; Katherine A. Astrove.
Number of staff: None.
Employer Identification Number: 136087869

4021
Frederick R. Adler Foundation, Inc. ⌑
c/o Fulbright Jaworski & Reavis McGrath
345 Park Ave.
New York 10154

Established in 1983 in NY.
Donor(s): Frederick R. Adler.
Foundation type: Independent
Financial data (yr. ended 11/30/88): Assets, $1,366,006 (M); expenditures, $302,284, including $299,425 for 26 grants (high: $273,750; low: $35).
Purpose and activities: Support primarily for health and medical research.
Application information: Contributes only to pre-selected organizations. Applications not accepted.
Trustees: Frederick R. Adler, William Bush, Carl E. Kaplan.
Employer Identification Number: 133157738

4022
J. & L. Adler Foundation ⌑ ☆
12 Mountain Ave.
Monsey 10952-2944

Established in 1985 in NY.
Donor(s): Joseph Adler, Lillian Adler.
Foundation type: Independent
Financial data (yr. ended 12/31/88): Assets, $472,363 (M); gifts received, $400,000; expenditures, $339,255, including $338,385 for 37 grants (high: $243,636; low: $10).
Purpose and activities: Support for Jewish organizations, especially yeshivas and congregations.
Types of support: Building funds.
Application information:
Initial approach: Letter
Deadline(s): None
Write: Joseph Adler, Chair.
Officers: Joseph Adler, Chair.; Lillian Adler, Secy.
Employer Identification Number: 132737530

4023
Louis and Bessie Adler Foundation, Inc. ⌑
c/o Robert Liberman
654 Madison Ave.
New York 10021

Incorporated in 1946 in NY.
Donor(s): Louis Adler,† Louis Adler Realty Co., Inc.
Foundation type: Independent
Financial data (yr. ended 12/31/88): Assets, $3,782,823 (M); expenditures, $436,908, including $397,500 for 32 grants (high: $100,000; low: $500).
Purpose and activities: Support for Jewish welfare funds, higher and secondary education, hospitals, youth agencies, and museums.
Limitations: Giving primarily in NY. No grants to individuals.
Application information: Contributes only to pre-selected organizations. Applications not accepted.
Officers: Seymour M. Klein, Chair. and Pres.; Robert Liberman, Treas.
Employer Identification Number: 131880122

4024
The Aeroflex Foundation ⌑
c/o Berman and Hecht
10 East 40th St., Rm. 710
New York 10016 (212) 696-4235

Established in 1964 in NY.
Donor(s): The Aeroflex Corp.
Foundation type: Company-sponsored
Financial data (yr. ended 9/30/88): Assets, $3,421,341 (M); expenditures, $246,251, including $156,000 for 9 grants (high: $30,000; low: $5,000).
Purpose and activities: Emphasis on cultural programs and higher education.

Limitations: No grants to individuals.
Application information:
Initial approach: Letter
Copies of proposal: 1
Deadline(s): None
Board meeting date(s): Quarterly
Trustees: Kay Knight Clarke, Derrick Hussey, William A. Perlmuth.
Employer Identification Number: 136168635

4025
Agway Foundation
333 Butternut Dr.
P.O. Box 4933
Syracuse 13221 (315) 449-6506

Established in 1967 in NY.
Donor(s): Agway, Inc.
Foundation type: Company-sponsored
Financial data (yr. ended 06/30/89): Assets, $2,302,880 (M); expenditures, $215,950, including $202,650 for 88 grants (high: $44,100; low: $100).
Purpose and activities: Emphasis on areas of interest to its farmer-members, including statewide and regional agricultural organizations, health, and rural youth organizations.
Types of support: Continuing support, annual campaigns, seed money, emergency funds, building funds, equipment, endowment funds, lectureships.
Limitations: Giving primarily in the Northeast. No support for educational, religious, or political organizations. No grants to individuals, or for operating budgets.
Publications: Application guidelines.
Application information: Application form not required.
Initial approach: Letter and proposal
Copies of proposal: 1
Deadline(s): None
Board meeting date(s): Every 6 to 8 weeks
Write: Arthur J. Fogerty, Chair.
Officers and Trustees:* Arthur J. Fogerty,* Chair.; Peter J. O'Neill,* Secy.-Treas.; Arnon C. Greif.
Number of staff: 1 part-time professional; 1 part-time support.
Employer Identification Number: 166089932

4026
Irving J. Aibel Foundation, Inc. ⌑
c/o Tabb & Co.
200 Madison Ave.
New York 10016

Established about 1944 in NY.
Foundation type: Independent
Financial data (yr. ended 12/31/88): Assets, $1,446,109 (M); gifts received, $2,000; expenditures, $43,571, including $31,700 for 64 grants (high: $17,555; low: $10).
Purpose and activities: Giving primarily for Jewish welfare funds and other Jewish organizations.
Limitations: No grants to individuals.
Application information: Contributes only to pre-selected organizations. Applications not accepted.
Officers: Benjamin Aibel, Pres.; Bertha G. Aibel, Treas.
Trustees: James H. Aibel, Judy Brickman, Robert Todd Lang.
Employer Identification Number: 136090013

4027
AKC Fund, Inc.
165 East 72nd St., Suite 1B
New York 10021 (212) 737-1011

Incorporated in 1955 in NY.
Donor(s): Members of the Childs and Lawrence families.
Foundation type: Independent
Financial data (yr. ended 12/31/89): Assets, $2,481,810 (M); expenditures, $171,677, including $147,000 for 50 grants (high: $20,000; low: $500; average: $750-$5,000).
Purpose and activities: Grants largely for secondary and higher education; support also for conservation, hospitals, and the arts.
Types of support: Annual campaigns, capital campaigns, continuing support, general purposes, lectureships, professorships.
Limitations: No grants to individuals.
Publications: Annual report.
Application information: Currently supporting trustee-sponsored projects only.
Write: Ann Brownell Sloane, Admin.
Officers and Directors: Barbara Childs Lawrence, Pres.; Edward C. Childs, V.P.; Richard S. Childs, Jr., Secy.; John W. Childs, Treas.; Hope S. Childs, Starling W. Childs II, Anne Childs Collins, Barbara L. Garside, Jane L. Mali.
Number of staff: 1 full-time professional; 1 full-time support; 2 part-time support.
Employer Identification Number: 136091321

4028
The Akzo American Foundation ⌑
111 West 40th St., 3rd Fl.
New York 10018 (212) 382-5582

Trust established in 1952 in NC.
Donor(s): Akzo America.
Foundation type: Company-sponsored
Financial data (yr. ended 12/31/88): Assets, $535,642 (M); expenditures, $227,814, including $195,852 for 38 grants (high: $17,700; low: $50) and $31,264 for employee matching gifts.
Purpose and activities: Giving primarily for scholarships, fellowships, and matching contributions of employees to accredited colleges, universities, and preparatory schools; support also for community funds, health organizations, and youth agencies.
Types of support: Employee matching gifts, scholarship funds, fellowships, building funds.
Limitations: Giving primarily in NC and in other areas of company operations including IL, TN, NY, PA, OH, and NJ. No grants to individuals.
Application information: Application form not required.
Initial approach: Letter
Copies of proposal: 1
Deadline(s): Submit proposal in Oct.
Board meeting date(s): Dec.
Write: Mortimer Ryon, Secy.
Officer: Mortimer Ryon, Secy.
Trustees: Allan R. Dragone, Peter S. Gold, Hugh W. Morrell.
Number of staff: 1 part-time professional; 1 part-time support.
Employer Identification Number: 566061194

4029
Albany's Hospital for Incurables
P.O. Box 3628, Executive Park
Albany 12203 (518) 459-7711

Established in 1974 in NY.
Foundation type: Independent
Financial data (yr. ended 12/31/89): Assets, $2,603,000 (M); expenditures, $264,000, including $249,000 for 17 grants (high: $30,000; low: $3,000; average: $15,000).
Purpose and activities: Grants to facilitate the development of better health care; support for hospitals, nursing homes, hospices, medical colleges, community health centers, and regional health planning groups.
Types of support: General purposes, building funds, equipment, matching funds, renovation projects, seed money, continuing support, special projects.
Limitations: Giving limited to Albany, Schenectady, Rensselaer, and Saratoga counties, NY. No grants to individuals, or for deficit financing, endowment funds, scholarships, or fellowships.
Publications: Program policy statement, application guidelines, multi-year report.
Application information: Application form required.
Initial approach: Telephone, letter, or proposal
Copies of proposal: 1
Deadline(s): 30 days before board meetings
Board meeting date(s): Jan., Apr., June, and Sept.
Final notification: 5 days after board meets
Write: Arnold Cogswell, Pres.
Officers and Trustees: Arnold Cogswell, Pres. and Treas.; Albert Hessberg II, Secy.; William Barnet II, Mrs. Lewis Muhlfelder, Mrs. Freeman T. Putney, Jr., Robert H. Randles, M.D., Richard F. Sonneborn, Mrs. Dorann Zimicki.
Number of staff: None.
Employer Identification Number: 141364443

4030
Joseph Alexander Foundation
400 Madison Ave., Suite 906
New York 10017 (212) 355-3688

Established in 1960 in NY.
Donor(s): Joseph Alexander.†
Foundation type: Independent
Financial data (yr. ended 10/31/89): Assets, $12,696,628 (M); expenditures, $832,054, including $651,250 for 67 grants (high: $50,000; low: $1,000).
Purpose and activities: Giving primarily for higher and other education, medical research, AIDS programs, hospices, scientific organizations, health and hospitals, museums and other arts groups, Israel, and Jewish welfare and religious organizations.
Types of support: General purposes, operating budgets, building funds, equipment, research, conferences and seminars, annual campaigns, capital campaigns, endowment funds,

lectureships, renovation projects, scholarship funds, special projects, exchange programs.
Limitations: Giving primarily in Israel and the continental U.S., with emphasis on New York, NY. No grants to individuals.
Publications: Financial statement.
Application information: Application form not required.
Initial approach: Proposal
Copies of proposal: 1
Deadline(s): Submit proposal preferably in Feb. through Aug.
Board meeting date(s): Jan., Apr., July, and Oct.
Write: Alfred Mackler, Treas.
Officers and Directors:* Robert M. Weintraub,* Pres.; Arthur S. Alfert,* V.P.; Helen Mackler,* Secy.; Alfred Mackler,* Treas.; Harvey A. Mackler.
Employer Identification Number: 510175951

4031
Allade, Inc. ⌑
c/o Arthur D. Emil
599 Lexington Ave.
New York 10022

Established in 1956 in NY.
Donor(s): Kate S. Emil.
Foundation type: Independent
Financial data (yr. ended 12/31/88): Assets, $1,947,260 (M); expenditures, $167,199, including $134,457 for 109 grants (high: $35,476; low: $25).
Purpose and activities: Giving primarily for Jewish welfare, temple support, social services, and general charitable contributions.
Limitations: Giving primarily in NY. No grants to individuals.
Application information: Contributes only to pre-selected organizations. Applications not accepted.
Trustees: Arthur D. Emil, Judy E. Tenney.
Employer Identification Number: 136097697

4032
Allen Brothers Foundation ⌑
711 Fifth Ave.
New York 10022

Established about 1983 in NY.
Foundation type: Independent
Financial data (yr. ended 12/31/88): Assets, $2,406,538 (M); expenditures, $117,315, including $115,000 for 7 grants (high: $25,000; low: $5,000).
Purpose and activities: Support for two churches and a hospital.
Limitations: Giving primarily in NY. No grants to individuals.
Application information: Application form not required.
Deadline(s): None
Write: Thomas F. Devine, Treas.
Officers: Herbert A. Allen, Pres.; Paul A. Gould, V.P.; Irwin H. Kramer, V.P.; Robert H. Werbel, Secy.; Thomas F. Devine, Treas.
Employer Identification Number: 133202281

4033
Frances Allen Foundation ⌑
711 Fifth Ave.
New York 10022 (212) 832-8000

Trust established in 1959 in NY.
Donor(s): Members of the Allen family, Allen & Co., Inc.
Foundation type: Independent
Financial data (yr. ended 12/31/88): Assets, $2,940,237 (M); expenditures, $195,550, including $175,850 for 57 grants (high: $12,000; low: $100).
Purpose and activities: Giving for medical research and youth agencies; interests also include higher education, social services, hospitals, and health organizations.
Limitations: Giving primarily in NY. No grants to individuals.
Application information:
Initial approach: Proposal
Copies of proposal: 1
Deadline(s): None
Board meeting date(s): Monthly
Write: Charles Allen, Jr., Trustee
Trustees: C. Robert Allen III, Charles Allen, Jr., Herbert Allen, Herbert Anthony Allen.
Employer Identification Number: 136104670

4034
Rita Allen Foundation, Inc. ⌑
550 Park Ave.
New York 10021

Incorporated in 1953 in NY.
Donor(s): Rita Allen Cassel.†
Foundation type: Independent
Financial data (yr. ended 12/31/88): Assets, $9,875,214 (M); expenditures, $607,006, including $489,240 for 42 grants (high: $90,000; low: $100).
Purpose and activities: Primarily medical grants, with emphasis on research in the fields of cancer, multiple sclerosis, cerebral palsy, and euphorics and analgesics related to the terminally ill; some support for recognized welfare and religious organizations.
Limitations: No grants to individuals (except university research scientists), or for building funds, or operating budgets.
Application information:
Copies of proposal: 1
Deadline(s): Jan. 15
Board meeting date(s): Annually and as required
Write: Milton E. Cassel, Pres.
Officers and Directors: Milton E. Cassel, Pres. and Treas.; Moore Gates, Jr., Secy.; George S. Johnston.
Number of staff: None.
Employer Identification Number: 136116429

4035
The Allyn Foundation, Inc.
P.O. Box 22
Skaneateles 13152
Grant application address: RD No. 1, Cayuga, NY 13034; Tel.: (315) 252-7618

Incorporated in 1956 in NY.
Donor(s): William N. Allyn,† William Allyn, Inc.
Foundation type: Independent
Financial data (yr. ended 12/31/89): Assets, $4,056,615 (M); gifts received, $100,000; expenditures, $195,320, including $190,900 for 52 grants (high: $22,000; low: $250).
Purpose and activities: Emphasis on higher and other education, including medical education; support also for general charitable purposes, youth and social service agencies, arts and culture, hospitals, and community development.
Types of support: Building funds, equipment, fellowships, renovation projects, research, scholarship funds.
Limitations: Giving primarily in Skaneateles and the Onondaga and Cayuga counties, NY, area. No support for religious programs. No grants to individuals, or for endowment funds; no loans.
Publications: Application guidelines.
Application information: Application form not required.
Initial approach: Letter
Copies of proposal: 1
Deadline(s): None
Board meeting date(s): 4 times per year
Write: Mrs. Marie Infanger, Exec. Dir.
Officers and Directors:* William G. Allyn,* Pres.; Lew F. Allyn,* V.P.; William F. Allyn,* V.P.; Marie Infanger,* Secy.-Treas. and Exec. Dir.; Dawn Allyn, Janet J. Allyn, Sonya Allyn, Tasha Falcone, Robert C. Heaviside, Rev. Stephen A. Kish, Ruth C. Penchoen, Elsa A. Soderberg, Peter Soderberg, Robert C. Soderberg.
Number of staff: 1 part-time professional.
Employer Identification Number: 156017723

4036
Alpern Family Foundation, Inc. ⌑ ☆
c/o Weitzman & Rubin, P.C.
400 Jericho Tpke., Suite 205
Jericho 11753

Established in 1952.
Donor(s): Bernard E. Alpern.
Foundation type: Independent
Financial data (yr. ended 12/31/88): Assets, $62,691 (M); gifts received, $100,000; expenditures, $103,634, including $100,000 for 1 grant.
Purpose and activities: Support for medical research, including cancer and cerebral palsy.
Types of support: Research.
Limitations: Giving primarily in NY and MA. No grants to individuals.
Application information: Contributes only to pre-selected organizations. Applications not accepted.
Officers and Directors: Bernard E. Alpern, Pres. and Treas.; Jacob J. Alpern, V.P. and Secy.; Edward M. Alpern, Lloyd J. Alpern, Harry J. Halperin, Laura F. Pinzur, Steven I. Rubin.
Employer Identification Number: 136100302

4037
Altman Foundation ▼
220 East 42nd St., Suite 411
New York 10017 (212) 682-0970

Incorporated in 1913 in NY.
Donor(s): Benjamin Altman,† Col. Michael Friedsam.†
Foundation type: Independent

Financial data (yr. ended 12/31/89): Assets, $120,683,129 (M); expenditures, $5,805,810, including $4,678,725 for 147 grants (high: $300,000; low: $2,500; average: $5,000-$100,000).
Purpose and activities: Support primarily for education, particularly programs benefitting talented underprivileged youth; private voluntary hospitals and health centers to extend medical services to the underserved; artistic and cultural institutions for outreach projects; and social welfare programs providing long-term solutions for the needs of the disadvantaged.
Types of support: Special projects.
Limitations: Giving limited to NY, with emphasis on the New York City metropolitan area. No grants to individuals.
Publications: Application guidelines.
Application information: Application form not required.
Initial approach: Letter
Copies of proposal: 1
Deadline(s): None
Board meeting date(s): 6 times a year
Write: John S. Burke, Pres.
Officers and Trustees:* John S. Burke,* Pres.; Marion C. Baer, Secy.; Thomas C. Burke,* Treas.; Bernard Finkelstein, Jane B. O'Connell, Maurice A. Selinger, Jr., Julia V. Shea, John W. Townsend IV, Victor D. Ziminsky, Jr.
Number of staff: 3 full-time professional; 4 full-time support.
Employer Identification Number: 131623879

4038
The Altschul Foundation ⌑
342 Madison Ave., Suite 1002
New York 10017 (212) 697-3525

Incorporated in 1941 in NY.
Donor(s): Louis Altschul,† Jeanette Cohen Altschul.†
Foundation type: Independent
Financial data (yr. ended 06/30/88): Assets, $7,504,196 (M); expenditures, $977,300, including $636,546 for 74 grants (high: $250,000; low: $30).
Purpose and activities: Emphasis on Jewish welfare funds; support also for higher education, community funds, health agencies, youth agencies, social services, and hospitals.
Limitations: Giving primarily in New York City, NY.
Application information:
Initial approach: Letter
Deadline(s): None
Board meeting date(s): June and Sept.
Write: Leonard Rodney
Officers and Trustees:* Phyllis Rothstein,* Pres.; Louis Rothstein,* V.P.; Vivian Reichman,* Secy.-Treas.; Valerie Aspinwall, William Rothstein.
Number of staff: None.
Employer Identification Number: 136400009

4039
AmBase Foundation, Inc.
(Formerly The Home Group Foundation)
59 Maiden Ln.
New York 10038 (212) 530-6208

Incorporated in 1963 in MO.
Foundation type: Company-sponsored
Financial data (yr. ended 12/31/88): Assets, $4,334,166 (M); expenditures, $733,050, including $720,375 for 92 grants (high: $50,000; low: $500).
Purpose and activities: Support primarily for higher education, hospitals, medical research; youth and civic agencies, cultural programs, and health associations.
Application information: The foundation has currently discontinued its employee-related scholarship program. Applications not accepted.
Officers and Directors:* George T. Scharffenberger,* Chair.; Robert L. Woodrum,* V.P.; Christine Werner, Secy.; Eben W. Pyne.
Number of staff: 1 part-time professional; 1 part-time support.
Employer Identification Number: 133246657

4040
American Academy & Institute of Arts and Letters
633 West 155th St.
New York 10032 (212) 368-5900

Established in 1976 as a result of a merger between the National Institute of Arts and Letters, founded in 1898, and the American Academy of Arts and Letters, founded in 1904.
Donor(s): Mildred B. Strauss,† Channing Pollock,† and others, Archer M. Huntington.
Foundation type: Operating
Financial data (yr. ended 12/31/88): Assets, $20,963,723 (M); gifts received, $274,234; expenditures, $1,519,904, including $192,746 for 17 grants (high: $65,000; low: $1,800), $352,875 for 65 grants to individuals (high: $50,000; low: $300) and $2,550 for 1 loan to an individual.
Purpose and activities: A private operating foundation; arts and letters awards, fellowships, and scholarships to individuals showing promise and/or achievement in literature, music, and the arts. Childe Hassam Fund and Eugene Speicher awards for the purchase of works of contemporary art for distribution to museums.
Types of support: Grants to individuals, emergency funds, fellowships.
Limitations: No support for the performing arts, or for photography.
Publications: Informational brochure.
Application information: Applications for awards or financial assistance not accepted, with the exception of the Richard Rodgers Production Award for the Musical Theatre (for off-Broadway productions).
Write: Jeanie Kim, Asst. to the Exec. Dir.
Officers and Directors:* Hugo Weisgall,* Pres.; Jacob Druckman,* V.P.; John Hawkes,* V.P.; Kevin Roche,* V.P.; William Styron, Secy. of Academy; C. Vann Woodward, Secy. of Institute; Jack Beeson, Treas.; Virginia Dajani, Exec. Dir.; John Updike, Chancellor; Milton Babbitt, Vice-Chancellor; Ralph Ellison, Vice-Chancellor; Jack Levine, Vice-Chancellor.
Number of staff: 4 full-time professional; 2 full-time support.
Employer Identification Number: 130429640

4041
American Chai Trust ☆
c/o Bernard Perlman
470 Park Ave. South, 12th Fl.
New York 10016 (212) 889-0575

Established in 1968 in NY.
Foundation type: Independent
Financial data (yr. ended 2/28/89): Assets, $1,012,802 (M); expenditures, $55,715, including $49,000 for grants (high: $2,000; low: $50; average: $300-$2,000).
Purpose and activities: Support for human services, including child and religious welfare, the aged, the handicapped, and aid for the indigent; and health, including AIDS, mental health, alcoholism, drug abuse, and cancer care; support also for culture.
Types of support: Emergency funds, general purposes.
Limitations: No grants for building funds.
Application information: Application form not required.
Initial approach: Letter
Deadline(s): None
Board meeting date(s): 6-8 times a year
Trustees: Pauline Doynon, Seymour Lang, Julie Mitchell, Bernard Perlman, Walter Stern.
Number of staff: None.
Employer Identification Number: 136130992

4042
American Conservation Association, Inc. ▼
30 Rockefeller Plaza, Rm. 5402
New York 10112 (212) 649-5822

Incorporated in 1958 in NY.
Donor(s): Laurance S. Rockefeller, Laurance Rockefeller, Rockefeller Brothers Fund, Jackson Hole Preserve, Inc.
Foundation type: Operating
Financial data (yr. ended 12/31/89): Assets, $1,803,448 (M); gifts received, $2,000,000; expenditures, $2,250,229, including $1,870,500 for 57 grants (high: $150,000; low: $5,000; average: $20,000-$50,000).
Purpose and activities: A private operating foundation organized to advance knowledge and understanding of conservation; to preserve the beauty of the landscape and the natural and living resources in areas of the U.S. and elsewhere; and to educate the public in the proper use of such areas.
Types of support: Consulting services, continuing support, general purposes, operating budgets, publications, special projects, technical assistance.
Limitations: No grants to individuals, or for building funds, endowments, scholarships, or fellowships; no loans.
Application information: Application form not required.
Initial approach: Letter or proposal
Copies of proposal: 1
Deadline(s): Submit proposal preferably early in the spring
Board meeting date(s): Sept. or Oct.; executive committee meets as needed
Final notification: Varies
Write: George R. Lamb, Exec. V.P.
Officers: Laurance Rockefeller,* Chair.; George R. Lamb,* Exec. V.P.; Gene W. Setzer,* V.P.;

Franklin E. Parker,* Secy.; Ruth C. Haupert, Treas.
Trustees:* John H. Adams, Frances G. Beinecke, Nash Castro, Charles H. Clusen, William G. Conway, Dana S. Creel, Henry L. Diamond, Mrs. Lyndon B. Johnson, Fred I. Kent III, W. Barnabas McHenry, Patrick F. Noonan, Story Clark Resor, David S. Sampson, Cathleen Douglas Stone, Russell E. Train, William H. Whyte, Jr., Conrad L. Wirth.
Number of staff: 2 part-time professional; 2 part-time support.
Employer Identification Number: 131874023

4043
American Express Foundation ▼
c/o American Express Co.
American Express Tower, World Financial Ctr.
New York 10285-4710 (212) 640-5661

Incorporated in 1954 in NY.
Donor(s): American Express Co., and its subsidiaries.
Foundation type: Company-sponsored
Financial data (yr. ended 12/31/89): Assets, $1,501,402 (M); gifts received, $12,479,374; expenditures, $11,741,833, including $10,600,429 for 1,018 grants (high: $480,000; low: $1,000; average: $10,000-$20,000) and $1,135,599 for 2,560 employee matching gifts.
Purpose and activities: The foundation's philanthropic activities focus on three strategic themes: community service, education and employment, and cultural programs.
Types of support: Special projects, employee-related scholarships, employee matching gifts, seed money, general purposes.
Limitations: Giving primarily in AZ, CA, CO, FL, GA, IL, MN, NC, NE, NY, TX, UT, MA, PA, and Washington, DC. International Committees include Asia/Pacific, Canada, Europe, Latin America, and Japan. No support for religious, political or fraternal organizations; sporting events or athletic programs; legislative or lobbying efforts; umbrella organizations with active grantmaking programs; or professional, trade, or marketing associations. No grants to individuals, or for endowments; capital campaigns; advertising in journal or yearbooks; publication of books, magazines or articles in professional journals; or medical research.
Publications: Corporate giving report, grants list, informational brochure (including application guidelines).
Application information: Application form not required.
Initial approach: Letter or proposal
Copies of proposal: 1
Deadline(s): None
Board meeting date(s): Biannually
Final notification: 3 to 4 months
Write: Mary Beth Salerno V.P., Philanthropic Prog. (Domestic Prog.), or Cornelia W. Higginson, V.P., Philanthropic Prog. (Intl. Prog.)
Senior Staff: Cornelia Higginson, V.P., Intl. Prog.; Mary Beth Salerno, V.P., Domestic Prog.
Trustees: Harvey Golub, Aldo Papone, James D. Robinson III, Ken Roman.
Number of staff: 7 full-time professional; 7 full-time support.
Employer Identification Number: 136123529

4044
American Friends of Bet El Yeshiva Center ☆
1174 East 22nd St.
Brooklyn 11210-4515 (718) 253-3465

Donor(s): Martin M. Segal.
Foundation type: Independent
Financial data (yr. ended 12/31/87): Assets, $5,703 (M); gifts received, $516,351; expenditures, $537,177, including $458,000 for 1 grant.
Purpose and activities: Giving to a Jewish center for education.
Application information: Applications not accepted.
Board meeting date(s): Semi-annual
Write: Martin M. Segal, Trustee
Trustee: Martin M. Segal.
Employer Identification Number: 112586564

4045
American Friends of Israel ⌑
c/o Alexander J. Katz
23 Beachway
Port Washington 11050

Established in 1948.
Foundation type: Independent
Financial data (yr. ended 12/31/88): Assets, $1,743,309 (M); expenditures, $52,933, including $48,500 for 5 grants (high: $25,000; low: $1,000).
Purpose and activities: Emphasis on higher and other education in Israel, primarily through U.S. organizations.
Limitations: Giving primarily in NY. No grants to individuals.
Application information: Contributes only to pre-selected organizations. Applications not accepted.
Officers: Samuel Rothberg, Pres.; Cary Schwartz, V.P.; Alexander J. Katz, Secy.; Julian B. Venezky, Treas.
Employer Identification Number: 136113746

4046
American Philanthropic Foundation ⌑
122 East 42nd St., 24th Fl.
New York 10168 (212) 697-2420

Incorporated in 1929 in IL.
Donor(s): Nina Rosenwald.
Foundation type: Independent
Financial data (yr. ended 12/31/88): Assets, $1,094,566 (M); gifts received, $14,928; expenditures, $38,029, including $26,295 for 18 grants (high: $5,000; low: $100).
Purpose and activities: Support for Jewish organizations; grants also for higher education, hospitals, and cultural organizations.
Limitations: Giving primarily in New York, NY; support also in FL, CT, and Chicago, IL.
Application information: Application form not required.
Deadline(s): None
Write: David P. Steinmann, Secy.
Officers and Directors:* William Rosenwald, Pres. and Treas.; Nina Rosenwald,* V.P.; Alice R. Sigelman,* V.P.; Elizabeth R. Varet,* V.P.; David P. Steinmann, Secy.; and 5 additional directors.
Employer Identification Number: 136088097

4047
American Society of the French Legion of Honor, Inc. ⌑
22 East 60th St.
New York 10021 (212) 751-8537

Foundation type: Independent
Financial data (yr. ended 12/31/88): Assets, $3,033,626 (M); gifts received, $1,500; expenditures, $177,200, including $76,000 for 6 grants (high: $40,000; low: $3,500) and $31,408 for 1 foundation-administered program.
Purpose and activities: Grants to promote friendship through education and literature between France and the U.S. The society publishes a magazine.
Application information: Application form not required.
Initial approach: Proposal
Deadline(s): None
Write: Odile Duff
Officers and Directors: Raymond J. Picard, Chair.; Christian A. Chapman, Pres.; George M. Gudefin, Exec. V.P. and Treas.; Edward R. Finch, Jr., V.P. and Secy.; and 19 additional directors.
Employer Identification Number: 130434237

4048
American-Standard Foundation
40 West 40th St.
New York 10018 (212) 703-5100

Trust established in 1952 in PA as Westinghouse Air Brake Foundation; name changed in 1977.
Donor(s): American-Standard, Inc.
Foundation type: Company-sponsored
Financial data (yr. ended 12/31/89): Assets, $11,835,000 (M); expenditures, $1,385,350, including $1,056,350 for 46 grants (high: $100,000; low: $35; average: $35-$94,000) and $315,000 for 193 employee matching gifts.
Purpose and activities: Matches employee gifts to the United Way and educational institutions; employee-related scholarships through the National Merit Scholarship Corp.
Types of support: Employee matching gifts, employee-related scholarships.
Limitations: Giving primarily in areas of significant company operations.
Publications: Program policy statement.
Application information: No application process. Employee matching gifts only. Applications not accepted.
Write: Richard Schultz, Pres., Corp. Contribs. Committee
Officer and Trustees:* Richard Schultz,* Pres.; Fred A. Allardyce.
Number of staff: None.
Employer Identification Number: 256018911

4049
AMEV Foundation
One World Trade Ctr., Suite 5001
New York 10048 (212) 323-9800

Established in 1982 in NY.
Donor(s): Time Insurance Co., AMEV Holdings, Inc.
Foundation type: Company-sponsored
Financial data (yr. ended 06/30/89): Assets, $411,983 (M); expenditures, $206,948, including $144,574 for 76 grants (high:

$10,600; low: $100), $46,150 for 43 grants to individuals (high: $4,000; low: $1,000) and $8,580 for 51 employee matching gifts.
Purpose and activities: Support primarily for higher education through employee-related scholarships. Support also for child welfare and development and the homeless; community development; museums; and health organizations, including drug abuse programs and AIDS research.
Types of support: Employee-related scholarships, employee matching gifts.
Limitations: Giving primarily in NY for social programs; national support for health-related organizations.
Application information: Application form required for scholarships.
Write: Jaqueline Gentile
Officer and Trustees:* Allen R. Freedman,* Pres.; W.D. Greiter, F.L. Maddox.
Employer Identification Number: 133156497

4050
Amicus Foundation, Inc. ¤
c/o Sherman Epstein
342 Madison Ave.
New York 10017

Foundation type: Independent
Financial data (yr. ended 10/31/88): Assets, $1,189,092 (M); expenditures, $79,333, including $58,500 for 7 grants (high: $20,000; low: $500).
Purpose and activities: Giving primarily to art and education.
Limitations: No grants to individuals.
Application information: Contributes only to pre-selected organizations. Applications not accepted.
Officers and Directors: Leigh R. Weiner, Pres.; Sharyn Weiner, V.P.; Barbara R. Reynolds, Secy.; Gregory Reynolds, Treas.
Employer Identification Number: 136075489

4051
Douglas G. Anderson - Leigh R. Evans Foundation ¤
1420 College Ave.
Elmira 14903 (607) 734-2281

Incorporated in 1960 in NY.
Donor(s): Hardinge Brothers, Inc.
Foundation type: Independent
Financial data (yr. ended 10/31/88): Assets, $1,301,265 (M); gifts received, $170,000; expenditures, $288,355, including $281,320 for 34 grants (high: $50,000; low: $400).
Purpose and activities: Giving for higher education, hospitals, community funds, and the performing arts.
Types of support: General purposes, building funds, equipment.
Limitations: Giving primarily in Elmira, NY. No grants to individuals.
Application information:
Initial approach: Proposal
Copies of proposal: 1
Board meeting date(s): Semiannually and as required
Write: Robert G. Prochnow, Pres.
Officers: Robert C. Prochnow,* Pres.; Bertha A. Greenlee,* V.P.; Bela C. Tifft,* Secy.; Malcolm L. Gibson, Treas.
Trustees:* Robert E. Agan, James L. Flynn, E. Martin Gibson, Douglas A. Greenlee, Joseph C. Littleton, Boyd McDowell.
Employer Identification Number: 166024690

4052
The Anderson Foundation, Inc. ¤
c/o Chemung Canal Trust Co.
P.O. Box 1522
Elmira 14902

Incorporated in 1960 in NY.
Donor(s): Jane G. Anderson, Douglas G. Anderson.†
Foundation type: Independent
Financial data (yr. ended 4/30/88): Assets, $2,469,905 (M); expenditures, $240,065, including $232,344 for 22 grants (high: $88,444; low: $1,820).
Purpose and activities: Emphasis on cultural programs and social service agencies.
Types of support: Scholarship funds, operating budgets, deficit financing, equipment, general purposes.
Limitations: Giving primarily in Elmira, NY.
Officers and Trustees: Bertha A. Greenlee, Pres. and Treas.; Charles A. Winding, V.P.; Ethel A. Whittaker, V.P.; Bela C. Tifft, Secy.; Robert T. Jones, Jane G. Joralemon, Charles M. Streetcar, E. William Whittaker.
Employer Identification Number: 166024689

4053
Harry & Bina Appleman Family Foundation, Inc. ¤ ☆
51 Carlton Rd.
Monsey 10952

Donor(s): Freda Aranoff, Shera Aranoff, Jonathan Aranoff, Gaya Bernstein.
Foundation type: Independent
Financial data (yr. ended 08/31/89): Assets, $624,490 (M); gifts received, $5,800; expenditures, $119,664, including $118,645 for 18 grants (high: $100,600; low: $72).
Purpose and activities: Support for education and Jewish organizations.
Limitations: No grants to individuals.
Application information: Contributes only to pre-selected organizations. Applications not accepted.
Officers: Joseph Appleman, Pres.; Hana Goldberg, V.P.; Toby Weingarten, Secy.; Freda Aranoff, Treas.
Employer Identification Number: 116027145

4054
The Aquidneck Foundation ¤ ☆
c/o Goldman, Sachs & Co., Tax Dept.
85 Broad St.
New York 10004-2408

Established in 1981 in NY.
Donor(s): Stephen B. Kay.
Foundation type: Independent
Financial data (yr. ended 2/28/89): Assets, $1,484,749 (M); gifts received, $100,000; expenditures, $100,517, including $85,785 for 54 grants.
Purpose and activities: Giving primarily for Jewish organizations and education, including universities; support also for cancer research.
Limitations: Giving primarily in New York, NY, and Boston, MA. No grants to individuals.
Application information: Contributes only to pre-selected organizations. Applications not accepted.
Trustee: Stephen B. Kay.
Employer Identification Number: 133102904

4055
Adrian & Jessie Archbold Charitable Trust
Seven East 60th St.
New York 10022 (212) 371-1152

Trust established in 1976 in NY.
Donor(s): Mrs. Adrian Archbold.†
Foundation type: Independent
Financial data (yr. ended 11/30/89): Assets, $17,055,011 (M); expenditures, $921,471, including $735,000 for 58 grants (high: $200,000; low: $500; average: $5,000-$10,000).
Purpose and activities: Grants primarily for the medical sciences, especially biology; hospitals and health-related organizations, child welfare and youth programs, and social service agencies.
Types of support: General purposes, continuing support, conferences and seminars.
Limitations: No grants to individuals, or for endowment funds, scholarships, fellowships, or building funds; no loans.
Publications: Program policy statement.
Application information: Unsolicited proposals not encouraged. Application form not required.
Initial approach: Letter
Copies of proposal: 1
Deadline(s): None
Board meeting date(s): As required
Final notification: 3 to 6 months
Write: William G. O'Reilly, Dir.
Trustees: Arthur J. Mahon, Chemical Bank.
Director: William G. O'Reilly.
Number of staff: 2 part-time professional.
Employer Identification Number: 510179829

4056
The Arell Foundation, Inc.
c/o Listowel, Inc.
Two Park Ave., Suite 1525
New York 10016-5790 (212) 683-8660

Established in 1978 in NY.
Foundation type: Independent
Financial data (yr. ended 12/31/88): Assets, $2,104,104 (M); expenditures, $453,922, including $445,000 for 3 grants (high: $315,000; low: $5,000).
Purpose and activities: Giving limited to institutions of higher education.
Limitations: No grants to individuals.
Application information: Contributes only to pre-selected organizations. Applications not accepted.
Officers: George V. Merrill, Pres.; Robert I. Edelson, V.P.; Thomas G. Gillespie, Jr., V.P.; Saul Klein, Secy.
Employer Identification Number: 132943420

4057
Arkell Hall Foundation, Inc.
66 Montgomery St.
Canajoharie 13317 (518) 673-5417

Incorporated in 1948 in NY.
Donor(s): Mrs. F.E. Barbour,† and others.
Foundation type: Independent
Financial data (yr. ended 11/30/89): Assets, $30,546,240 (M); expenditures, $1,545,319, including $618,764 for 78 grants (high: $73,664; low: $500; average: $5,000-$10,000).
Purpose and activities: Maintains a residence and home for needy elderly women who are residents of Montgomery County; also general local giving, with emphasis on higher education, including scholarship funds, hospitals, and health and social services, including youth agencies.
Types of support: Scholarship funds, building funds, equipment.
Limitations: Giving limited to the Canajoharie, NY, area. No grants to individuals, or for multi-year commitments, travel, conferences or other personal expenses; no loans.
Application information: Application form not required.
Initial approach: Proposal
Copies of proposal: 1
Deadline(s): Sept. 15
Board meeting date(s): Feb., May, Aug., and Oct.
Final notification: Dec. 1
Write: Joseph A. Santangelo, Admin.
Officers and Trustees:* Edward W. Shineman, Jr.,* Pres.; William B. Mackenzie,* V.P.; Ferdinand C. Kaiser,* Secy.; Robert H. Wille,* Treas.; Joseph A. Santangelo,* Admin.; James R. Dern, Frances L. Howard, William T. Martin.
Number of staff: 1 full-time professional; 1 part-time professional; 1 full-time support; 1 part-time support.
Employer Identification Number: 141343077

4058
J. Aron Charitable Foundation, Inc. ▼
126 East 56th St., Suite 2300
New York 10022 (212) 832-3405

Incorporated in 1934 in NY.
Donor(s): Members of the Aron family.
Foundation type: Independent
Financial data (yr. ended 12/31/88): Assets, $26,859,983 (M); expenditures, $1,819,389, including $1,499,978 for 252 grants (high: $300,000; low: $100; average: $500-$25,000).
Purpose and activities: Giving primarily for hospitals and health associations, cultural programs, social service and youth agencies, Jewish welfare funds, and education, including medical schools.
Types of support: Annual campaigns, building funds, capital campaigns, general purposes, research, special projects.
Limitations: Giving primarily in New York, NY, and New Orleans, LA. No grants to individuals.
Application information: Application form not required.
Initial approach: Proposal
Copies of proposal: 1
Deadline(s): None
Board meeting date(s): Apr., July, Sept., and Dec.
Write: Peter A. Aron, Exec. Dir.
Officers and Directors:* Jack R. Aron,* Pres.; Robert Aron,* V.P.; Hans P. Jepson,* Secy.-Treas.; Peter A. Aron,* V.P. and Exec. Dir.; Jacqueline A. Morrison, Ronald J. Stein.
Number of staff: 2 full-time professional; 1 full-time support; 1 part-time support.
Employer Identification Number: 136068230

4059
Art Matters, Inc.
131 West 24th St.
New York 10011 (212) 929-7190
Application address: P.O. Box 1428, New York, NY 10011

Established in 1985 in NY.
Donor(s): Laura Donnelley.
Foundation type: Independent
Financial data (yr. ended 12/31/88): Assets, $1,713,042 (M); gifts received, $462,282; expenditures, $468,303, including $102,000 for 54 grants (high: $4,000; low: $1,000; average: $1,000-$4,000) and $248,400 for 147 grants to individuals (high: $5,000; low: $900; average: $1,000-$4,000).
Purpose and activities: Grants and fellowships to fund individual experimental work in the arts, including experimental theater, performance art, film, video, painting, and sculpture.
Types of support: Fellowships.
Limitations: No support for organizations or individuals working in dance or music, or for individual art studies. No grants for publications.
Publications: Grants list, application guidelines, informational brochure.
Application information: Art students, writers, dancers and musicians are ineligible to receive funding. The foundation no longer funds arts organizations. Application form required.
Initial approach: Letter
Copies of proposal: 2
Deadline(s): Fall and spring
Board meeting date(s): 3 months after deadline
Final notification: 1 month after meeting
Write: Philip Yenawine, V.P. or Marianne Weems, Secy.
Officers and Board Members:* Laura Donnelley,* Pres.; Philip Yenawine,* V.P.; Marianne Weems,* Secy.; Laurence Miller,* Treas.; Mary Beebe, Cee Brown.
Number of staff: 1 full-time professional; 2 part-time support.
Employer Identification Number: 133271577

4060
Artists Fellowship, Inc. ⌑ ☆
c/o Salmagundi Club
47 Fifth Ave.
New York 10003

Established in 1925.
Foundation type: Independent
Financial data (yr. ended 12/31/88): Assets, $1,207,992 (M); gifts received, $7,199; expenditures, $70,589, including $53,899 for grants to individuals.
Purpose and activities: Grants for emergency aid to visual artists and their families.
Types of support: Grants to individuals.
Application information: Application form required.
Deadline(s): None
Write: Hughie Lee Smith, V.P.
Officers: Fay Moore, Pres.; Hughie Lee Smith, V.P.; Robert J. Riedinger, Corresponding Secy.; Moses Worthman, Recording Secy.; John R. McCarthy, Treas.
Trustees: Raoul Carranza, Ethel Edwards, Frank E. Field, Mark Freeman, Betty Holiday, Richard Plonk, Pamela Singleton, Joseph Solman, Leon Weiss.
Employer Identification Number: 136122134

4061
ASARCO Foundation ⌑ ☆
180 Maiden Ln.
New York 10038 (212) 510-2000

Incorporated in 1956 in NY.
Donor(s): ASARCO, Inc.
Foundation type: Company-sponsored
Financial data (yr. ended 12/31/88): Assets, $1,201,343 (M); gifts received, $840,000; expenditures, $88,957, including $87,267 for 63 grants (high: $12,000; low: $200; average: $500-$1,000).
Purpose and activities: A limited program, including support for community funds, scholarship programs of colleges and universities with emphasis on mineral technology and engineering, hospitals, and cultural activities.
Types of support: Scholarship funds, fellowships, general purposes, continuing support, employee matching gifts.
Limitations: Giving limited to areas of company operations. No grants to individuals, or for endowment funds, research, or operating budgets; no loans.
Publications: Program policy statement, application guidelines.
Application information: Application form not required.
Initial approach: Letter
Deadline(s): None
Board meeting date(s): As required
Final notification: 2 to 3 months
Write: D.M. Noyes, V.P.
Officers and Directors:* Robert J. Muth, Pres.; J.R. Corbett,* V.P.; Francis R. McAllister,* V.P.; D.M. Noyes, V.P.; K.A. Dockry, Secy.; Stephen P. McCandless,* Treas.; George W. Anderson, R.J. Bothwell, Alexander J. Gillespie, Jr., Richard J. Osborne, T.C. Osborne.
Number of staff: 1 part-time support.
Employer Identification Number: 136089860

4062
The Vincent Astor Foundation ▼
405 Park Ave.
New York 10022 (212) 758-4110

Incorporated in 1948 in NY; reincorporated in 1974 in DE.
Donor(s): Vincent Astor.†
Foundation type: Independent
Financial data (yr. ended 12/31/89): Assets, $25,481,318 (M); expenditures, $4,623,329, including $2,600,500 for 96 grants (average: $1,000-$25,000).

Purpose and activities: Increased support for programs alleviating the problems of homelessness and illiteracy; support for programs which promote the preservation of open space and the thoughtful development of the urban environment; to a lesser extent support for certain cultural institutions, parks and landmark preservation, and neighborhood revitalization projects.
Types of support: Operating budgets, continuing support, seed money, building funds, equipment, endowment funds, matching funds, capital campaigns, general purposes, renovation projects, special projects.
Limitations: Giving primarily in New York, NY. No support for the performing arts, medicine, mental health, or private schools. No grants to individuals, or for annual campaigns, deficit financing, research, film production, publications, or conferences; no loans.
Publications: Annual report (including application guidelines).
Application information: Average range of grants will be reduced to $1,000-$25,000. Application form not required.
Initial approach: Letter or telephone
Copies of proposal: 1
Deadline(s): None
Board meeting date(s): May, Oct., and Dec.
Final notification: 6 months
Write: Linda L. Gillies, Dir.
Officers: Mrs. Vincent Astor,* Pres.; Anthony D. Marshall,* V.P.; Peter P. McN. Gates, Secy.; Fergus Reid III,* Treas.; Linda L. Gillies,* Dir.
Trustees:* Thomas R. Coolidge, Henry N. Ess III, Howard Phipps, Jr., John Pierrepont.
Advisory Trustees: Peter S. Paine, David W. Peck, Richard S. Perkins.
Number of staff: 1 full-time professional; 1 full-time support; 2 part-time support.
Employer Identification Number: 237167124

4063
AT&T Foundation ▼
550 Madison Ave.
New York 10022-3297 (212) 605-6734
Address for application guidelines: P.O. Box 1430, Wall, NJ 07719

Established in 1984 in NY.
Donor(s): American Telephone & Telegraph Co., Western Electric Fund.
Foundation type: Company-sponsored
Financial data (yr. ended 12/31/89): Assets, $126,766,000 (M); expenditures, $30,426,888, including $25,974,595 for 849 grants (high: $800,000; low: $1,000; average: $24,400) and $4,452,293 for 27,226.
Purpose and activities: Principal source of philanthropy for AT&T and its subsidiaries; scope is national, emphasizing support of private higher education, and institutions and projects in the areas of health care, social action, and the arts.
Types of support: Building funds, equipment, matching funds, employee matching gifts, special projects, research, annual campaigns, endowment funds, operating budgets, renovation projects, seed money, technical assistance, capital campaigns, scholarship funds.
Limitations: No support for religious organizations for sectarian purposes; local chapters of national organizations; secondary schools, social sciences or health sciences programs, medical or nursing schools, or junior and community colleges; industrial affiliate programs or technical trade associations; medical research projects, disease-related health associations, or for operating expenses or capital campaigns of local health or human service agencies other than hospitals; or sports, teams, or athletic competitions. No grants to individuals, or for emergency funds, deficit financing, land acquisition, fellowships, publications, or conferences; does not purchase advertisements or donate equipment.
Publications: Program policy statement, biennial report, informational brochure (including application guidelines).
Application information: Detailed program limitations provided in guidelines and addresses of regional Contributions Managers. Application form not required.
Initial approach: Letter and proposal
Copies of proposal: 1
Deadline(s): None
Board meeting date(s): Mar., June, Sept., and Dec.
Final notification: 90 days
Write: Sam A. Gronner, Secy.
Officers: Reynold Levy,* Pres.; Jane Redfern, Sr. V.P.; Anne Alexander, V.P., Education Programs; Tim McClimon, V.P., Cultural Programs; Gina Warren, V.P., Health and Social Action Programs; Sam A. Gronner, Secy.; Sarah Jepsen, Exec. Dir.
Trustees:* Marilyn Laurie, Chair.; John A. Blanchard, W. Frank Blount, John Bucter, Harold Burlingame, Curtis J. Crawford, M.J. Eisen, John C. Guerra, Jr., John A. Hinds, Reynold Levy, Judith A. Maynes, C. Kumar Patel, John C. Petrillo, Yvonne M. Shepard, Frederic S. Topor, Doreen S. Yochum.
Number of staff: 9 full-time professional; 3 part-time professional; 1 full-time support; 3 part-time support.
Employer Identification Number: 133166495

4064
Atalanta/Sosnoff Charitable Foundation, Inc. ⌑ ☆
499 Park Ave.
New York 10022 (212) 755-2800

Established in 1986.
Donor(s): Atlanta Sosnoff Capital Corp.
Foundation type: Independent
Financial data (yr. ended 12/31/87): Assets, $828 (M); gifts received, $279,000; expenditures, $318,418, including $318,075 for 86 grants (high: $48,800; low: $250).
Purpose and activities: Giving to hospitals, religion, education, and social services.
Limitations: No grants to individuals.
Application information:
Initial approach: Letter
Deadline(s): None
Write: Martin T. Sosnoff, Chair.
Trustees: Martin T. Sosnoff, Chair.; Shepard D. Osheron, Harvey Siegel.
Employer Identification Number: 133356184

4065
Atran Foundation, Inc.
23-25 East 21st St., 3rd Fl.
New York 10010 (212) 505-9677

Incorporated in 1945 in NY.
Donor(s): Frank Z. Atran.†
Foundation type: Independent
Financial data (yr. ended 11/30/89): Assets, $14,766,358 (M); expenditures, $746,629, including $631,900 for 50 grants (high: $150,000; low: $250).
Purpose and activities: Support for research relating to labor and labor relations, art, science, literature, economics, and sociology; support of publications furthering these purposes; and endowment for chairs of learning in these fields.
Types of support: Continuing support, annual campaigns, seed money, emergency funds, endowment funds, research, publications, conferences and seminars, scholarship funds, professorships, exchange programs, matching funds, special projects, fellowships, general purposes.
Limitations: No grants to individuals.
Publications: Application guidelines.
Application information: Application form not required.
Initial approach: Proposal
Copies of proposal: 4
Deadline(s): Sept. 30
Board meeting date(s): Between Nov. and Feb. and as required
Write: Diane Fischer, Corp. Secy.
Officers and Directors: Max Atran, Pres.; William Stern, V.P.; Diane Fischer, Corp. Secy.
Employer Identification Number: 135566548

4066
Herman Auerbach Memorial Trust Fund No. 2
Bankers Trust Co.
280 Park Ave., 7 East
New York 10017 (212) 850-2329

Established in 1960 in NY.
Foundation type: Independent
Financial data (yr. ended 12/31/87): Assets, $1,605,878 (M); expenditures, $104,615, including $78,900 for 14 grants (high: $17,000; low: $1,000).
Purpose and activities: Grants primarily for Jewish welfare funds and scientific and educational programs; some support also for youth agencies and health and hospitals.
Application information:
Write: George Ricci, V.P., Bankers Trust Co.
Trustees: Murray Jacobs, Seymour Smallberg, Bankers Trust Co.
Employer Identification Number: 136307278

4067
AVI CHAI - A Philanthropic Foundation
509 Madison Ave., Suite 1100
New York 10022 (212) 371-5948

Established in 1984 in NY.
Donor(s): Zalman Chaim Bernstein.
Foundation type: Independent
Financial data (yr. ended 05/31/89): Assets, $21,865,107 (M); gifts received, $3,054,875; expenditures, $1,295,519, including $768,819 for 31 grants (high: $87,000; low: $2,500).

Purpose and activities: To encourage those of the Jewish faith towards a more traditional form of Jewish observance and lifestyle and to encourage mutual understanding and sensitivity among Jews of various backgrounds.
Types of support: Conferences and seminars, lectureships, research, special projects.
Limitations: No support for youth programs. No grants for building projects or deficits.
Publications: Informational brochure, program policy statement.
Application information: Solicits proposals only in the context of self-initiated projects. Applications not accepted.
Board meeting date(s): Three yearly
Write: Bernie D. Kastner, Assoc. Dir.
Officers: Zalman Chaim Bernstein,* Chair., Pres., and Treas.; Avraham Y. HaCohen, Exec. Dir.
Trustees:* Arthur W. Fried, Samuel J. Silberman, Henry Taub, David R. Weiss.
Number of staff: 2 full-time professional; 1 part-time professional; 2 full-time support.
Employer Identification Number: 133252800

4068
Avon Products Foundation, Inc. ▼ ⌑
Nine West 57th St.
New York 10019 (212) 546-6731

Incorporated in 1955 in NY.
Donor(s): Avon Products, Inc.
Foundation type: Company-sponsored
Financial data (yr. ended 12/31/88): Assets, $205,089 (M); gifts received, $1,700,000; expenditures, $1,764,744, including $1,436,409 for grants (high: $140,000; average: $2,000-$15,000), $191,614 for 77 grants to individuals (high: $6,000; low: $80) and $113,131 for employee matching gifts.
Purpose and activities: Support for social services, including institutions and agencies whose main focus is on individuals, particularly youth, women, minorities and the disadvantaged; support also for hospitals, education (including employee-related scholarships and matching gifts), community funds, cultural organizations, urban programs, and civic projects.
Types of support: General purposes, operating budgets, employee-related scholarships, technical assistance, special projects, employee matching gifts, capital campaigns, scholarship funds, continuing support.
Limitations: Giving limited to areas immediately surrounding company operations in New York City, Rye, and Suffern, NY; Newark, DE; Atlanta, GA; Springdale, OH; Pasadena, CA; and Morton Grove, IL. No support for individual member agencies of United Way and United Fund, or national health and welfare organizations. No grants to individuals (except for scholarships for children of company employees), or for capital or endowment funds; no loans.
Publications: Annual report, application guidelines, informational brochure (including application guidelines).
Application information: Application form required for scholarships only. The foundation has declared a moratorium on active grantmaking activities for 1989 and 1990. Application form not required.
Initial approach: Letter
Copies of proposal: 1
Deadline(s): Sept. 15
Board meeting date(s): 3 times yearly
Final notification: Oct. 15
Write: Glenn S. Clarke, Pres.
Officers and Directors:* Glenn S. Clarke,* Pres.; Donna Blackwell,* V.P.; Phyllis B. Davis,* V.P.; James E. Preston,* V.P.; John F. Cox,* Secy.; Margro R. Long,* Treas.
Number of staff: 1 full-time professional; 1 full-time support.
Employer Identification Number: 136128447

4069
Axe-Houghton Foundation
875 Third Ave., 23rd Fl.
New York 10022 (212) 866-0564

Incorporated in 1965 in NY.
Donor(s): Emerson W. Axe.†
Foundation type: Independent
Financial data (yr. ended 02/28/89): Assets, $4,286,772 (M); expenditures, $233,304, including $166,850 for 38 grants (high: $10,000; low: $1,000; average: $1,000-$10,000).
Purpose and activities: To encourage the improvement of spoken English in all its manifestations, including remedial speech, scientific research pertaining to speech, public speaking, and speaking as an art form.
Types of support: Seed money, research, special projects, conferences and seminars.
Limitations: No grants to individuals, or for operating budgets, general purposes, continuing support, annual campaigns, emergency funds, deficit financing, capital funds, endowment funds, matching gifts, scholarships, fellowships, or publications; no loans.
Publications: Program policy statement, application guidelines.
Application information: Application form not required.
Initial approach: Letter
Copies of proposal: 1
Deadline(s): Submit proposal preferably in Sept.; deadline Oct. 1
Board meeting date(s): May and Nov.
Final notification: 2 months
Write: Remington P. Patterson, Pres.
Officers: Remington P. Patterson,* Pres.; Robert B. von Mehren,* V.P.; Beth Ann Wahl, Secy.; Thomas J. McDonald, Treas.
Directors:* Alfred Berman, William A. Hance, John B. Oakes, Suzanne Schwartz.
Number of staff: 1 part-time professional.
Employer Identification Number: 136200200

4070
N. W. Ayer Foundation, Inc. ⌑
c/o N.W. Ayer, Inc.
1345 Ave. of the Americas
New York 10105 (212) 708-5000

Foundation type: Company-sponsored
Financial data (yr. ended 12/31/88): Assets, $1,007,623 (M); expenditures, $115,736, including $100,000 for 20 grants to individuals of $5,000 each.
Purpose and activities: Scholarships awarded to unmarried children of current full-time regular employees of N.W. Ayers, Inc.
Types of support: Employee-related scholarships.
Application information: Application form required.
Initial approach: Letter
Deadline(s): Jan. 1
Write: Walter Lance, Secy.-Treas.
Officers: Neal W. O'Connor, Pres.; Louis T. Hagopian, V.P.; Walter Lance, Secy.-Treas.
Directors: George Eversman, Jerry Jordan, David Means, John B. Roedig, Marcella Rosen, Earl Shorris, Jerry J. Siano, Roger Smith.
Employer Identification Number: 236296499

4071
The Bachmann Foundation, Inc. ⌑
c/o Danziger, Bangser & Klipstein
230 Park Ave., Rm. 2525
New York 10169 (212) 867-6500

Incorporated in 1949 in NY.
Donor(s): Louis Bachmann, Thomas W. Strauss.
Foundation type: Independent
Financial data (yr. ended 12/31/88): Assets, $4,387,959 (M); gifts received, $207,600; expenditures, $525,280, including $505,400 for 120 grants (high: $91,000; low: $50).
Purpose and activities: Emphasis on Jewish welfare funds, higher and secondary education, hospitals, and child welfare and development programs.
Limitations: Giving primarily in NY. No grants to individuals.
Application information: Contributes only to pre-selected organizations. Applications not accepted.
Write: Louis Bachmann, Pres.
Officers and Directors: Louis Bachmann, Pres.; Barbara Bachmann Strauss, V.P.; Richard M. Danziger, Secy.; Thomas W. Strauss, Treas.
Employer Identification Number: 136043497

4072
Rose M. Badgeley Residuary Charitable Trust
c/o Marine Midland Bank, N.A.
250 Park Ave.
New York 10177 (212) 503-2773

Trust established about 1977 in NY.
Donor(s): Rose Badgeley.†
Foundation type: Independent
Financial data (yr. ended 1/31/89): Assets, $11,931,550 (M); gifts received, $45,575; expenditures, $742,767, including $633,000 for 28 grants (high: $100,000; low: $5,000; average: $5,000-$25,000).
Purpose and activities: Emphasis on hospitals and health associations, particularly those concerned with medical research; higher education, cultural programs, and social service and youth agencies.
Types of support: Annual campaigns, building funds, equipment, general purposes, renovation projects, research, special projects, continuing support.
Limitations: Giving primarily in the five boroughs of New York, NY, and the greater metropolitan area. No grants to individuals.
Application information: Application form not required.
Initial approach: Full written proposal
Copies of proposal: 1

Deadline(s): Submit proposal postmarked no earlier than Dec. 1 and no later than Mar. 15
Board meeting date(s): Late Apr. or early May
Final notification: Usually within a month after grant committee meeting if approved
Write: Mr. Loren R. Sattinger, V.P., Marine Midland Bank, N.A.
Trustees: John J. Duffy, Marine Midland Bank, N.A.
Number of staff: None.
Employer Identification Number: 136744781

4073
The Bagby Foundation for the Musical Arts, Inc. ⌑
501 Fifth Ave.
New York 10017

Established in 1925 in NY.
Donor(s): Eugene M. Grant, John H. Steinway.
Foundation type: Independent
Financial data (yr. ended 12/31/87): Assets, $1,095,897 (M); gifts received, $6,454; expenditures, $82,308, including $10,500 for 8 grants (high: $1,500; low: $1,000) and $23,155 for 19 grants to individuals (high: $2,700; low: $100).
Purpose and activities: Support primarily for aged, needy individuals who have aided the world of music and who are in need of financial support; some support for music schools, societies, and study grants.
Types of support: Grants to individuals, scholarship funds.
Application information:
Initial approach: Letter
Deadline(s): None
Write: Eleanor C. Mark, Exec. Dir.
Officers and Trustees: Rose Bampton, Chair.; F. Malcolm Graff, Jr., Pres.; Jarmila Packard, V.P. and Treas.; William Mayo Sullivan, V.P.; and 10 other trustees.
Employer Identification Number: 131873289

4074
Marie Baier Foundation, Inc. ⌑
Six East 87th St.
New York 10128 (212) 410-2130

Donor(s): John F. Baier.†
Foundation type: Independent
Financial data (yr. ended 1/31/88): Assets, $8,578,197 (M); expenditures, $534,446, including $464,000 for 21 grants (high: $55,000; low: $4,000).
Purpose and activities: Grants primarily for higher and secondary education, cultural programs, and youth agencies; support also for German-American organizations, and a home for the aged.
Limitations: No grants to individuals.
Application information:
Initial approach: Letter
Deadline(s): None
Write: Berteline Dale-Baier, Pres.
Officers: Berteline Dale-Baier,* Pres.; John F. Baier, Jr.,* V.P.; Ida Schuller, Secy.; Erich H. Markel,* Treas.
Directors:* Carl H. Ficke, Guenter F. Metsch, Sidney Sirkin.
Employer Identification Number: 136267032

4075
The Baird Foundation ▼
122 Huntington Ct.
P.O. Box 514
Williamsville 14221 (716) 633-5588

Trust established in 1947 in NY.
Donor(s): Flora M. Baird,† Frank B. Baird, Jr.,† Cameron Baird,† William C. Baird.†
Foundation type: Independent
Financial data (yr. ended 12/31/88): Assets, $5,836,844 (M); expenditures, $202,287, including $178,287 for 72 grants (high: $14,000; low: $500; average: $1,000-$2,000).
Purpose and activities: Emphasis on higher education, church support, cultural programs, hospitals, medical research, and the environment.
Types of support: Research, matching funds, general purposes, capital campaigns.
Limitations: Giving primarily in Erie County, NY. No grants to individuals; no loans.
Application information: Application form not required.
Initial approach: Letter
Copies of proposal: 1
Deadline(s): Between Jan. 1 and Dec. 31
Board meeting date(s): About 4 times a year
Final notification: 3 months
Write: Carl E. Gruber, Mgr.
Officer: Carl E. Gruber, Mgr.
Trustees: Arthur W. Cryer, Robert J.A. Irwin, William Baird Irwin.
Number of staff: 1 full-time professional; 1 part-time professional.
Employer Identification Number: 166023080

4076
The Cameron Baird Foundation ▼ ⌑
Box 564
Hamburg 14075

Trust established in 1960 in NY.
Donor(s): Members of the family of Cameron Baird.
Foundation type: Independent
Financial data (yr. ended 12/31/87): Assets, $11,301,145 (M); expenditures, $1,077,558, including $1,029,533 for 49 grants (high: $55,000; low: $133).
Purpose and activities: Emphasis on music and cultural programs, higher and secondary education, social services, population control, conservation, and civil rights.
Limitations: Giving primarily in the Buffalo, NY, area. No support for religious organizations. No grants to individuals.
Application information: Generally contributes to pre-selected organizations. Application form not required.
Initial approach: Letter
Copies of proposal: 1
Deadline(s): Submit proposal in the fall; most grants are made in Dec.
Board meeting date(s): Annually
Write: Brian D. Baird, Trustee
Trustees: Brian D. Baird, Bridget B. Baird, Bruce C. Baird, Jane D. Baird, Bronwyn Baird Clauson, Brenda Baird Senturia.
Number of staff: None.
Employer Identification Number: 166029481

4077
Jessie H. Baker Education Fund
c/o Marine Midland Bank, N.A., Trust Div.
P.O. Box 719
Binghamton 13902 (607) 772-5521

Established in 1984 in NY.
Foundation type: Independent
Financial data (yr. ended 08/31/88): Assets, $1,315,575 (M); expenditures, $111,251, including $103,450 for 273 grants to individuals (high: $1,000; low: $50; average: $50-$1,000).
Purpose and activities: Awards scholarships only to Broome County high school students.
Types of support: Student aid.
Limitations: Giving limited to residents of Broome County, NY.
Application information: Applicants should contact Broome County high schools for information. Foundation distributes funds to pre-selected individuals only. Application form required.
Copies of proposal: 2
Deadline(s): Apr. 1
Board meeting date(s): May 15
Final notification: June 20
Write: Douglas F. Bissonette, V.P.
Trustees: Vincent A. Sgueglia, Marine Midland Bank, N.A.
Number of staff: None.
Employer Identification Number: 222478098

4078
The Baker Foundation ☆
20 Alpine Ln.
Chappaqua 10514-1615
Application address: 485 Washington Ave., Pleasantville, NY 10570

Established in 1986 in NY.
Foundation type: Independent
Financial data (yr. ended 12/31/88): Assets, $1,420,059 (M); expenditures, $46,012, including $43,000 for 16 grants (high: $10,000; low: $500).
Purpose and activities: Giving primarily to Catholic organizations, including churches, a seminary, child and other welfare agencies, and housing and homelessness.
Limitations: Giving primarily in the New York, NY, and Los Angeles, CA, metropolitan areas.
Application information: Application form not required.
Initial approach: Letter
Write: Marcus D. Baker, Treas.
Officers and Trustees:* Lucelle D. Baker,* Chair.; Marcus D. Baker,* Treas.; M. Catherine Baker.
Number of staff: None.
Employer Identification Number: 133405090

4079
The George F. Baker Trust ▼
767 Fifth Ave., Suite 2850
New York 10153 (212) 755-1890

Trust established in 1937 in NY.
Donor(s): George F. Baker.†
Foundation type: Independent
Financial data (yr. ended 12/31/88): Assets, $24,336,295 (L); expenditures, $2,558,936, including $2,150,166 for 56 grants (high:

$500,000; low: $1,000; average: $1,000-$50,000).
Purpose and activities: Giving primarily for higher and secondary education, hospitals, youth agencies, and conservation.
Types of support: Matching funds, general purposes.
Limitations: Giving primarily in the eastern U.S., with some emphasis on the New York, NY, area. No grants to individuals, or for scholarships; no loans.
Publications: Annual report.
Application information: Application form not required.
Initial approach: Letter with brief outline of proposal
Deadline(s): None
Board meeting date(s): June and Nov.
Final notification: Up to 6 months
Write: Miss Rocio Suarez, Exec. Dir.
Officer: Rocio Suarez, Exec. Dir.
Trustees: Anthony K. Baker, George F. Baker III, Kane K. Baker, Citibank, N.A.
Number of staff: 1 full-time professional.
Employer Identification Number: 136056818

4080
The David M. and Barbara Baldwin Foundation, Inc. ⌑ ☆
c/o McGrath, Doyle, & Phair
150 Broadway
New York 10038
Application address: 20 Broad St., New York, NY 10005

Established in 1986.
Donor(s): David M. Baldwin.
Foundation type: Independent
Financial data (yr. ended 11/30/88): Assets, $2,247,723 (M); gifts received, $1,300,000; expenditures, $47,216, including $43,500 for 20 grants (high: $16,000; low: $100).
Purpose and activities: Giving primarily to higher education and a church; support also for the arts, health, and youth.
Application information:
Initial approach: Letter
Deadline(s): None
Write: David M. Baldwin, Pres.
Officers and Trustees: David M. Baldwin, Pres.; Barbara Baldwin, V.P. and Secy.; Nicholas Jacangelo, Treas.
Employer Identification Number: 133391384

4081
The Harriet and Charles Ballon Foundation, Inc. ☆
40 West 57th St.
New York 10019-4001

Established in 1963.
Donor(s): Charles Ballon, Harriet Ballon.
Foundation type: Independent
Financial data (yr. ended 12/31/88): Assets, $355,350 (M); expenditures, $105,730, including $102,250 for 109 grants (high: $25,000; low: $10).
Purpose and activities: Support for Jewish organizations, including welfare funds and synagogues; grants also for higher education and general charitable giving.
Limitations: Giving primarily in New York, NY. No grants to individuals.
Application information: Contributes only to pre-selected organizations. Applications not accepted.
Officers and Directors:* Charles Ballon,* Pres.; Hilary Ballon-Kramer,* V.P.; Harriet Ballon,* Secy.; Howard Ballon,* Treas.; Carla Gorrell.
Employer Identification Number: 136144787

4082
Banbury Fund, Inc. ▼
c/o Tardino & Stewart
101 Park Ave., 35th Fl.
New York 10178

Incorporated in 1946 in NY.
Donor(s): Marie H. Robertson,† Charles S. Robertson.†
Foundation type: Independent
Financial data (yr. ended 12/31/87): Assets, $26,947,151 (M); expenditures, $1,211,121, including $1,045,256 for 77 grants (high: $223,281; low: $425; average: $3,000-$15,000).
Purpose and activities: Giving primarily for scientific research, including marine science, secondary and higher education, including international studies, and health and welfare agencies.
Types of support: Annual campaigns, building funds, capital campaigns, continuing support, deficit financing, emergency funds, endowment funds, equipment, research, seed money.
Limitations: Giving primarily in NY. No grants to individuals.
Application information:
Initial approach: Letter
Copies of proposal: 3
Deadline(s): None
Board meeting date(s): July and Jan.
Write: William S. Robertson, Pres.
Officers and Directors:* William S. Robertson,* Pres.; Katherine R. Ernst,* V.P. and Secy.; Anne R. Meier,* V.P. and Treas.; Robert Ernst,* V.P.; Townsend J. Knight,* V.P.; Walter C. Meier,* V.P.; John L. Robertson,* V.P.
Number of staff: 1 part-time professional.
Employer Identification Number: 136062463

4083
The Banfi Vintners Foundation ▼ ⌑
(Formerly The Villa Banfi Foundation)
1111 Cedar Swamp Rd.
Old Brookville 11545

Established in 1982 in NY.
Donor(s): Banfi Products Corp.
Foundation type: Independent
Financial data (yr. ended 12/31/88): Assets, $11,534,870 (M); expenditures, $673,084, including $492,745 for 33 grants (high: $400,000; low: $200; average: $500-$20,000).
Purpose and activities: Giving primarily for higher education.
Application information: Funds committed until 1992.
Board meeting date(s): Nov.
Write: John G. Troiano, Exec. Dir.
Officers: Lydia K. Taylor, Secy.; Vincent Aprigliano, Treas.; John G. Troiano,* Exec. Dir.
Directors:* Harry F. Mariani, John Mariani.
Number of staff: 1 part-time professional; 1 part-time support.
Employer Identification Number: 112622792

4084
The Mitchell Barash Foundation, Inc. ⌑
95 Hickory Dr.
Roslyn 11576-2321

Established in 1964 in NY.
Donor(s): Mitchell Barash.
Foundation type: Independent
Financial data (yr. ended 12/31/88): Assets, $1,118,963 (M); gifts received, $7,068; expenditures, $70,365, including $67,138 for 35 grants (high: $17,400; low: $25).
Purpose and activities: Support primarily for Jewish giving and Jewish welfare organizations; support also for education.
Limitations: No grants to individuals.
Application information: Contributes only to pre-selected organizations. Applications not accepted.
Officers and Directors:* Mitchell Barash,* Pres.; Roslyn Barash,* Secy.-Treas.
Employer Identification Number: 112062341

4085
J. M. R. Barker Foundation ⌑
630 Fifth Ave.
New York 10111 (212) 541-6970

Established in 1968 in NY.
Donor(s): James M. Barker,† Margaret R. Barker,† Robert R. Barker.
Foundation type: Independent
Financial data (yr. ended 12/31/88): Assets, $9,246,213 (M); expenditures, $412,609, including $289,000 for 45 grants (high: $30,000; low: $500).
Purpose and activities: Support primarily for organizations that are well known to one or more directors, with some emphasis on the areas of higher education, cultural programs, and scientific research.
Types of support: Operating budgets, continuing support, annual campaigns, seed money, general purposes, building funds, endowment funds, special projects, research.
Limitations: Giving primarily in the greater New York, NY, area, and the greater Boston, MA, area. No grants to individuals, or for scholarships, fellowships, or matching gifts; no loans.
Application information: Application form not required.
Copies of proposal: 1
Deadline(s): Submit proposal in May or Oct.
Board meeting date(s): June and Dec.
Final notification: 3 months
Write: Robert R. Barker, Pres.
Officers: Robert R. Barker,* Pres.; Elizabeth S. Barker,* V.P.; James R. Barker,* V.P.; Dwight E. Lee,* V.P.; Maureen A. Hopkins, Secy.and Admin; Robert P. Connor,* Treas.
Directors:* Margaret W. Barker, W.B. Barker, John W. Holman, Jr., Richard D. Kahn, Ann B. Kolvig.
Number of staff: 1 part-time professional.
Employer Identification Number: 136268289

4086
The Barker Welfare Foundation ▼
P.O. Box 2
Glen Head 11545 (516) 759-5592
Application address for Chicago agencies: c/o Philip D. Block III, One First National Plaza,

Suite 2544, Chicago, IL 60603; Treasurer's Office: c/o Charles C. Hickox, 26 Broadway, New York, NY 10004

Incorporated in 1934 in IL.
Donor(s): Mrs. Charles V. Hickox.†
Foundation type: Independent
Financial data (yr. ended 09/30/89): Assets, $33,018,803 (M); expenditures, $2,134,745, including $1,582,000 for 200 grants (high: $50,000; low: $1,000; average: $3,000-$9,000).
Purpose and activities: Grants to established organizations and charitable institutions, with emphasis on arts and culture, including museums and the fine and performing arts, child welfare and youth agencies, health services and rehabilitation, welfare, aid to the handicapped, family planning, libraries, the environment, and recreation.
Types of support: Operating budgets, continuing support, building funds, equipment, land acquisition, matching funds, special projects, renovation projects, annual campaigns.
Limitations: Giving primarily in Chicago, IL, Michigan City, IN, and New York, NY. No support for private elementary and secondary schools or for higher education. No grants to individuals, or for endowment funds, seed money, emergency funds, deficit financing, scholarships, fellowships, medical or scientific research, or conferences; no loans.
Publications: Program policy statement, application guidelines.
Application information: Proposals must be completed according to the foundation's guidelines to be considered for funding. Application form not required.
Initial approach: Letter or telephone
Copies of proposal: 1
Deadline(s): Submit proposal preferably between Sept. and Dec.; deadline Feb. 1 for completed proposal
Board meeting date(s): May
Final notification: After annual meeting for positive response; from Sept. to May for negative response
Write: Mrs. Walter L. Ross II, Pres. (NY and national agencies); Philip D. Block III (Chicago agencies)
Officers and Directors:* Mrs. Walter L. Ross II,* Pres.; Charles J. Becker,* V.P. and Secy.; Mrs. John A. Garrettson,* V.P.; Charles C. Hickox,* Treas.; Philip D. Block III, Diane Curtis, James R. Donnelley, John A. Garrettson, Mrs. Edward A. Hansen, Mrs. Charles C. Hickox, John B. Hickox, Alline Matheson, Alexander B. Ross.
Number of staff: 1 part-time professional; 1 full-time support.
Employer Identification Number: 366018526

4087
J. Patrick & Christine R. Barrett Charitable Foundation ⌑ ☆
7578 Hunt Ln.
Fayetteville 13066

Established in 1987 in NY.
Donor(s): J. Patrick Barrett, Christine R. Barrett.
Foundation type: Independent
Financial data (yr. ended 12/31/87): Assets, $2,000,000 (M); gifts received, $2,000,000; expenditures, $0.
Purpose and activities: Initial year of operation, 1987; no grants awarded.
Directors: Christine R. Barrett, J. Patrick Barrett, Robert C. Paltz.
Employer Identification Number: 161319333

4088
Chuck Barris Foundation ⌑
c/o Mason & Co.
400 Park Ave.
New York 10022 (213) 278-9550
Application address: 9537 Charleyville Blvd., Beverly Hills, CA 90213

Established in 1984 in CA.
Donor(s): Charles H. Barris.
Foundation type: Independent
Financial data (yr. ended 09/30/89): Assets, $1,004,305 (M); expenditures, $133,419, including $126,938 for 24 grants (high: $41,500; low: $10).
Purpose and activities: Support for cultural programs and social services, including child welfare.
Application information:
Write: Charles Barris, Pres.
Officers and Directors:* Charles H. Barris,* Pres.; David Gotterer,* Secy.-Treas.; Robin Barris.
Employer Identification Number: 953954357

4089
The Theodore H. Barth Foundation, Inc. ⌑
1211 Ave. of the Americas
New York 10036 (212) 840-6000

Incorporated in 1953 in DE.
Donor(s): Theodore H. Barth.†
Foundation type: Independent
Financial data (yr. ended 12/31/87): Assets, $9,766,347 (M); expenditures, $640,995, including $478,700 for 51 grants (high: $75,000; low: $100; average: $1,000-$10,000) and $42,819 for 26 grants to individuals (high: $5,000; low: $454).
Purpose and activities: Grants for higher education, including scholarships, hospitals, religion, the arts and cultural organizations, health agencies, and social services; support also for civic affairs, aid to the handicapped, and conservation.
Types of support: Student aid.
Application information: Application form not required.
Initial approach: Letter
Deadline(s): None
Write: Irving P. Berelson, Pres.
Officers and Directors: Irving P. Berelson, Pres.; Charlton T. Barth, Thelma D. Berelson.
Employer Identification Number: 136103401

4090
Ruth Bartsch Memorial Trust ⌑
c/o Chase Manhattan Bank, N.A.
1211 Ave. of the Americas, 36th Fl.
New York 10036 (212) 730-3244

Established in 1983 in NY.
Donor(s): Ruth Bartsch.†
Foundation type: Independent
Financial data (yr. ended 11/30/88): Assets, $4,539,779 (M); expenditures, $145,649, including $87,300 for 6 grants (high: $35,000; low: $7,600).
Purpose and activities: Support for health associations; substantial grants to a school and a social service organization.
Application information:
Initial approach: Letter
Deadline(s): None
Write: Joyce Schwartz
Trustees: Theodore Norman Richard, Sr., The Chase Manhattan Bank, N.A.
Employer Identification Number: 133188775

4091
Ralph & Jean Baruch Charitable Foundation ⌑ ☆
784 Park Ave.
New York 10021

Established in 1986 in NY.
Donor(s): Ralph Baruch, Jean Baruch.
Foundation type: Independent
Financial data (yr. ended 6/30/88): Assets, $277,544 (M); gifts received, $102,600; expenditures, $134,350, including $132,505 for 37 grants (high: $39,500; low: $15).
Purpose and activities: Giving primarily for an international relief organization and cultural programs, including museums and the performing arts; support also for health associations and hospitals.
Limitations: Giving primarily in NY.
Application information:
Initial approach: Letter
Deadline(s): None
Write: Ralph Baruch, Chair.
Officer and Trustees:* Ralph Baruch,* Chair.; Jean Baruch, Sondra Shalman.
Employer Identification Number: 133392139

4092
The Belle W. Baruch Foundation ⌑
90 Park Ave.
New York 10016

Trust established in 1964 in NY.
Donor(s): Belle W. Baruch.†
Foundation type: Operating
Financial data (yr. ended 12/31/87): Assets, $41,531,643 (M); gifts received, $10,925; expenditures, $718,119, including $657,448 for foundation-administered programs.
Purpose and activities: A private operating foundation promoting education and research in the conservation of natural resources, with special emphasis on forestry, marine biology, the care and propagation of wildlife and flora and fauna; grants to be implemented only through SC universities and colleges; to develop Hobcaw Center in Georgetown, SC, for research and education in ecology.
Limitations: Giving primarily in SC.
Application information:
Write: Donald Vail
Trustees: H.M. Arthur, Nelson A. Buhler, James E. Halpin, Leonard T. Scully, Ella A. Severin.
Employer Identification Number: 570564080

4093
The Sandra Atlas Bass & Edythe & Sol G. Atlas Fund, Inc. ▼ ⌑
185 Great Neck Rd.
Great Neck 11021 (516) 487-9030

Established in 1962 in NY.
Donor(s): Sol G. Atlas.
Foundation type: Independent
Financial data (yr. ended 12/31/87): Assets, $11,101,769 (M); gifts received, $2,496,908; expenditures, $1,423,991, including $1,351,831 for 110 grants (high: $104,000; low: $7; average: $1,000-$15,000).
Purpose and activities: Giving primarily for social services, animal welfare, and Jewish welfare.
Limitations: Giving primarily in the New York, NY, metropolitan area, with emphasis on Long Island.
Application information: Application form not required.
Initial approach: Letter
Deadline(s): None
Write: Sandra Atlas Bass, Mgr.
Officer and Trustees:* Sandra Atlas Bass,* Mgr.; Morton M. Bass, Richard Cunningham, Robert Zabelle.
Employer Identification Number: 116036928

4094
Bat Hanadiv Foundation No. 3 ▼ ⌑
c/o Carter, Ledyard & Milburn
Two Wall St.
New York 10005 (212) 732-3200
Application address outside Israel: Mr. M. Rowe, Trustee, 5 Rue Pedro Mevlan, Geneva, Switzerland; In Israel: Mr. A. Fried, 16 Ibn Gvirol St., Jerusalem 92430

Established in 1981.
Donor(s): Bat Hanadiv Foundation, Bat Hanadiv Foundation No. 2.
Foundation type: Independent
Financial data (yr. ended 12/31/88): Assets, $195,644,879 (M); expenditures, $8,267,989, including $7,278,280 for 57 grants (high: $1,313,629; low: $5,500; average: $10,000-$85,000).
Purpose and activities: Grants primarily for higher and other education; support also for conservation, youth and social service agencies, and cultural programs.
Types of support: Operating budgets, equipment, special projects.
Limitations: Giving primarily in Israel. No grants to individuals.
Application information:
Initial approach: Letter
Deadline(s): None
Write: Jerome Caulfield
Trustee: Doder Trust, Ltd.
Number of staff: None.
Employer Identification Number: 133091620

4095
Bausch & Lomb Foundation, Inc. ⌑ ☆
One Lincoln First Sq.
P.O. Box 54
Rochester 14601-0054

Incorporated in 1927 in NY.
Donor(s): Bausch & Lomb, Inc., and others.
Foundation type: Company-sponsored
Financial data (yr. ended 12/31/88): Assets, $1,031,511 (M); gifts received, $235,702; expenditures, $28,297, including $25,000 for grants.
Purpose and activities: Emphasis on higher education, community funds, cultural programs, civic and community activities, health, and social welfare.
Limitations: Giving primarily in Rochester, NY.
Application information:
Initial approach: Proposal
Write: Barbara M. Kelley, Dir.
Officers and Directors: Daniel E. Gill, Pres.; Thomas C. McDermott, V.P.; Stanley W. Merrell, V.P.; Jay T. Holmes, Secy.; Alan H. Resnick, Treas.; Franklin T. Jepson, Barbara M. Kelley.
Employer Identification Number: 166039442

4096
The Bay Foundation, Inc.
(Formerly Charles Ulrick and Josephine Bay Foundation, Inc.)
666 Fifth Ave., 31st Fl.
New York 10103 (212) 468-4670

Incorporated in 1950 in NY.
Donor(s): Charles Ulrick Bay,† Josephine Bay.†
Foundation type: Independent
Financial data (yr. ended 12/31/89): Assets, $10,500,000 (M); expenditures, $830,000, including $640,000 for 77 grants (high: $300,000; low: $500; average: $2,000-$6,000).
Purpose and activities: Support primarily for art museum conservation, early childhood and other education, with emphasis on pre-college children's projects, animal welfare and wildlife, and veterinary medicine.
Types of support: Operating budgets, seed money, research, scholarship funds, matching funds, general purposes.
Limitations: Giving nationally, with emphasis on: NY, VT, NH, CO, CA, MA, CT, MN, NM, NJ, AZ, FL, AL, MS, and Washington, DC. No support for the performing arts, or for other than publicly supported charities. No grants to individuals, or for capital or endowment funds; no loans.
Publications: Biennial report (including application guidelines).
Application information: Application form not required.
Initial approach: Proposal
Copies of proposal: 1
Deadline(s): Submit proposal by Feb. 1 or Sept. 1
Board meeting date(s): Mar. and Oct.
Final notification: 3 months
Write: Robert W. Ashton, Exec. Dir.
Officers and Directors:* Frederick Bay,* Chair.; Synnova B. Hayes,* Pres.; Robert W. Ashton,* Exec. Dir.; Daniel A. Demarest, Hans A. Ege.
Number of staff: 2 part-time professional.
Employer Identification Number: 135646283

4097
The Howard Bayne Fund
c/o Simpson Thacher & Bartlett
One Battery Park Plaza
New York 10004

Incorporated in 1960 in NY.
Donor(s): Louise Van Beuren Bayne Trust.
Foundation type: Independent
Financial data (yr. ended 12/31/88): Assets, $7,023,705 (M); expenditures, $415,907, including $297,900 for 66 grants (high: $10,000; low: $700; average: $1,000-$2,000).
Purpose and activities: Emphasis on music, cultural programs, education, conservation, and hospitals.
Types of support: Annual campaigns, building funds, endowment funds, equipment, general purposes, renovation projects, research, seed money.
Limitations: Giving primarily in NY.
Publications: 990-PF.
Application information: Contributes only to pre-selected organizations. Applications not accepted.
Write: Kathy Foer
Officers: Gurdon B. Wattles,* Pres.; Daphne B. Shih,* V.P.; Thomas J. McGrath, Secy.-Treas.
Directors:* Diana de Vegh, Pierre J. de Vegh, Elizabeth B. Shields.
Employer Identification Number: 136100680

4098
Beck Foundation ⌑
Six East 43rd St.
New York 10017 (212) 661-2640

Established in 1954 in NY.
Donor(s): T. Edmund Beck.
Foundation type: Independent
Financial data (yr. ended 12/31/88): Assets, $2,814,991 (M); gifts received, $223,410; expenditures, $213,835, including $203,153 for 58 grants (high: $60,000; low: $10).
Purpose and activities: Grants primarily for higher, secondary, and other education; social services, including child welfare, alcohol abuse programs, and organizations benefitting minorities, the elderly, and the disabled; the arts, including historic preservation and museums; health and medical research; animal welfare; and religious giving.
Application information:
Initial approach: Letter
Deadline(s): None
Write: T. Edmund Beck, Pres.
Officers and Trustees:* T. Edmund Beck,* Pres.; John C. Beck, Madeline C. Beck, T.E. Beck, Jr., Susan Beck Wasch.
Number of staff: None.
Employer Identification Number: 136082501

4099
The Bedford Fund, Inc. ⌑
c/o Marjorie E. Brody
Two Overhill Rd.
Scarsdale 10583 (914) 725-3591

Incorporated in 1919 in CT.
Donor(s): Edward T. Bedford.†
Foundation type: Independent
Financial data (yr. ended 06/30/89): Assets, $5,721,740 (M); expenditures, $519,095, including $481,000 for 19 grants (high: $100,000; low: $1,000).
Purpose and activities: Giving largely for hospitals, a youth agency, community funds, and the handicapped; support also for secondary education and conservation.

Limitations: Giving limited to the local area surrounding Westport, CT. No grants to individuals.
Application information: Contributes only to pre-selected organizations. Applications not accepted.
Officers: Ruth T. Bedford,* Pres. and Mgr.; Edward B. Lloyd,* V.P.; Marjorie E. Brody, Secy.; John Fearnley,* Treas.
Trustees:* Mariana L. Clark, William B. Lloyd, Helen B. McCashin.
Employer Identification Number: 066032006

4100
The Bedminster Fund, Inc.
1270 Ave. of the Americas, Rm. 2300
New York 10020 (212) 315-8300

Incorporated in 1948 in NY.
Foundation type: Independent
Financial data (yr. ended 06/30/89): Assets, $3,936,973 (M); expenditures, $129,687, including $103,800 for 12 grants (high: $40,000; low: $800; average: $1,000-$100,000).
Purpose and activities: Emphasis on education, hospitals, the arts, and welfare agencies. Grants only to present beneficiary organizations and to special proposals developed by the directors; additional requests seldom considered.
Types of support: General purposes.
Limitations: No grants to individuals; no loans.
Application information: Applications not accepted.
Board meeting date(s): Nov. and as required
Officers: Dorothy Dillon Eweson,* Pres.; Philip D. Allen,* V.P.; David H. Peipers,* V.P.; Joan Waldron, Secy.; Robert F. Quick, Treas.
Directors:* Christine Allen, Douglas E. Allen, Judith S. Leonard, Anne D. Zetterberg.
Number of staff: None.
Employer Identification Number: 136083684

4101
The Beinecke Foundation, Inc. ▼ ⌑
c/o John R. Robinson
14-16 Elm Place
Rye 10580 (914) 967-2385

Incorporated in 1966 in NY as The Kerry Foundation, Inc.; absorbed Edwin J. Beinecke Trust, NY, in Apr., 1985; new name for combined foundations adopted in Dec., 1985.
Donor(s): Sylvia B. Robinson.
Foundation type: Independent
Financial data (yr. ended 12/31/88): Assets, $35,325,555 (M); expenditures, $2,066,438, including $1,560,700 for 93 grants (high: $500,000; low: $100; average: $100-$30,000).
Purpose and activities: Giving primarily for secondary and higher education, conservation, and Protestant church support.
Types of support: General purposes.
Limitations: Giving primarily in NY-CT area. No grants to individuals; no loans.
Publications: Annual report.
Application information: Contributes only to pre-selected organizations. Applications not accepted.
Board meeting date(s): Spring and fall
Final notification: 30 days
Officers and Trustees:* John R. Robinson,* Pres. and Treas.; Sylvia B. Robinson, V.P.; Theodore H. Ashford, William O. Beers.
Number of staff: 2 full-time professional; 1 full-time support.
Employer Identification Number: 136201175

4102
The Beir Foundation
110 East 59th St.
New York 10022 (212) 355-7733

Incorporated in 1944 in NY.
Donor(s): Members of the Beir family.
Foundation type: Independent
Financial data (yr. ended 12/31/88): Assets, $3,353,617 (M); expenditures, $310,125, including $280,160 for 50 grants (high: $150,000; low: $10).
Purpose and activities: Support for elementary, secondary, and higher education; Jewish welfare funds; hospitals; and social service agencies.
Limitations: Giving primarily in the New York, NY, area.
Application information: Applications not accepted.
Write: Robert L. Beir, Pres.
Officers and Directors: Robert L. Beir, Pres.; Joan S. Beir, V.P. and Secy.; James H. Mathias, Treas.
Employer Identification Number: 136084093

4103
The Belfer Foundation, Inc. ⌑
One Dag Hammarskjold Plaza
New York 10017 (212) 644-2257

Incorporated in 1951 in NY.
Donor(s): Members of the Belfer family, Belfer Corp.
Foundation type: Independent
Financial data (yr. ended 12/31/88): Assets, $21,498,909 (M); expenditures, $1,197,638, including $1,086,693 for 177 grants (high: $202,375; low: $5).
Purpose and activities: Emphasis on health agencies, higher education, and Jewish welfare funds and religious organizations.
Limitations: Giving primarily in NY. No grants to individuals.
Application information: Applications not accepted.
Write: Arthur B. Belfer, Pres.
Officers: Arthur B. Belfer, Pres.; Lawrence Ruben, V.P.; Robert A. Belfer, Secy.; Jack Saltz, Treas.
Employer Identification Number: 136086711

4104
The Ben & Jerry's Foundation ☆
Clinton Hall
108 North Cayuga St.
Ithaca 14850 (607) 272-1813

Established in 1985 in NY.
Donor(s): Ben & Jerry's Homemade, Inc.
Foundation type: Company-sponsored
Financial data (yr. ended 12/31/88): Assets, $730,413 (M); gifts received, $332,096; expenditures, $324,763, including $298,757 for 106 grants (high: $14,800; low: $100; average: $500-$10,000).
Purpose and activities: Support for projects which facilitate progressive social change in the following areas: AIDS programs, homelessness and housing, race relations and educational programs for minorities, women and youth, children and families, disadvantaged groups, and the environment.
Limitations: No support for state agencies or religious projects. No grants to individuals.
Publications: Application guidelines, grants list.
Application information: Preliminary application must be submitted 8 weeks prior to any deadline to be considered for that deadline. Application form required.
Initial approach: Preliminary application
Copies of proposal: 4
Deadline(s): Jan. 1, Apr. 1, July 1, and Oct. 1 for full application
Final notification: Approximately 10 weeks
Write: Annie L. Sherman, Admin.
Officers and Directors:* Jerry Greenfield,* Pres.; Naomi Tannen,* Secy.; Jeffrey Furman,* Treas.
Number of staff: 1 full-time professional.
Employer Identification Number: 030300865

4105
The Benaid Foundation ⌑
c/o A. Stanley Gluck
One Rockefeller Plaza
New York 10020-2001

Foundation type: Independent
Financial data (yr. ended 12/31/87): Assets, $1,411,242 (M); expenditures, $122,552, including $110,250 for grants.
Purpose and activities: Support primarily for Jewish giving.
Limitations: Giving primarily in New York, NY. No grants to individuals.
Application information: Contributes only to pre-selected organizations. Applications not accepted.
Officers and Directors: A. Stanley Gluck, Pres.; Isaac Stern, V.P.; Ann Begley, V.P.; Robert de Rothschild, Secy.
Employer Identification Number: 237169525

4106
The Morris S. & Florence H. Bender Foundation, Inc. ⌑
c/o Summit Rovins & Feldesman
445 Park Ave.
New York 10022

Established in 1978 in NY.
Foundation type: Independent
Financial data (yr. ended 06/30/89): Assets, $1,184,116 (M); expenditures, $154,373, including $128,660 for 34 grants (high: $25,000; low: $500).
Purpose and activities: Giving primarily for Jewish welfare, hospitals and medicine, and cultural activities.
Limitations: No grants to individuals.
Application information:
Initial approach: Proposal
Deadline(s): None
Write: Howard L. Klein, Pres.
Officers and Directors:* Howard L. Klein,* Pres.; Lenore Klein,* V.P.; Ralph M. Engel,* Secy.; Stephen A. Goldstein,* Treas.
Employer Identification Number: 132951469

4107
Frances & Benjamin Benenson Foundation, Inc.
708 Third Ave., 28th Fl.
New York 10017 (212) 867-0990

Established in 1983 in NY.
Donor(s): Charles B. Benenson.
Foundation type: Independent
Financial data (yr. ended 11/30/89): Assets, $158,850,000 (M); gifts received, $2,900,000; expenditures, $597,000, including $579,000 for 34 grants (high: $150,000; low: $1,000; average: $1,000-$150,000).
Purpose and activities: Support primarily for Jewish welfare, secondary and other education, the arts and museums, and health.
Application information: Contributes only to pre-selected organizations. Applications not accepted.
Write: Anthony J. DiNome
Officers: Charles B. Benenson, Pres.; Emanuel Labin, V.P.
Employer Identification Number: 133267113

4108
The James Gordon Bennett Memorial Corporation ⌘
c/o Daily News
220 East 42nd St.
New York 10017
Scholarship application address: Eleanor H. Keil, New York Univ., P.O. Box 908, Madison Square Station, New York, NY 10159; Tel.: (212) 481-5905

Incorporated in 1919 in NY.
Donor(s): James Gordon Bennett.†
Foundation type: Independent
Financial data (yr. ended 12/31/87): Assets, $3,458,628 (M); expenditures, $165,380, including $142,704 for 110 grants to individuals (high: $5,700; low: $150).
Purpose and activities: Direct aid to journalists unable to provide for themselves because of old age, infirmity, or lack of means; limited to employees for ten years or more of a daily newspaper published in New York City, with preference for employees of newspapers in Manhattan; if funds are sufficient, employees of daily newspapers in any borough are eligible, together with their immediate families; any surplus funds to be applied to scholarship aid to children of these persons.
Types of support: Grants to individuals, student aid.
Limitations: Giving limited to employees (and their immediate families) of New York City dailies. No grants for building or endowment funds, operating budgets, or special projects.
Publications: Program policy statement, application guidelines.
Application information: Application form required.
Initial approach: Letter
Deadline(s): Mar. 1 for scholarships
Board meeting date(s): May and Dec.
Write: Denise Houseman
Officers and Directors: Michael Clendenin, Chair.; James F. Crain, Secy.-Treas.; John R. Campbell, Admin.
Employer Identification Number: 136150414

4109
The Berger Mittlemann Family Foundation ⌘ ☆
414 East 59th St.
New York 10022 (212) 758-1111

Established in 1983.
Donor(s): Marion W. Berger, Josef Mittleman.
Foundation type: Independent
Financial data (yr. ended 8/31/88): Assets, $274,122 (M); gifts received, $374,000; expenditures, $307,194, including $306,992 for grants (high: $277,670).
Purpose and activities: Giving primarily for a YM/YWHA and a campground; support also for Jewish welfare, and higher and other education.
Limitations: Giving primarily in NY.
Officers: Josef Mittlemann, Principal Mgr.; Richard W. Berger, Mgr.; Marsy B. Mittlemann, Mgr.; Marion W. Berger, Secy.
Employer Identification Number: 133158539

4110
David & Minnie Berk Foundation, Inc. ⌘
315 West 70th St., Rm. 8I
New York 10023-3504
Application address: c/o 1055 Franklin Ave., Suite 300, Garden City, NY 11530

Established in 1961 in NY.
Donor(s): Members of the Berk family.
Foundation type: Independent
Financial data (yr. ended 10/31/88): Assets, $1,296,032 (M); gifts received, $6,420; expenditures, $68,451, including $47,066 for 2 grants (high: $44,000; low: $3,066).
Purpose and activities: Giving primarily for the aged and social services; support also for education and the arts.
Types of support: General purposes.
Application information: Application form not required.
Initial approach: Letter
Copies of proposal: 10
Deadline(s): None
Write: David Green, Pres.
Officers: David Green, Pres.; Ronald Berk, 1st V.P.; Alan Grossman, 2nd V.P.; Joy Levien, Secy.; Nancy Goodman, Treas.
Number of staff: None.
Employer Identification Number: 116038062

4111
Louis Berkowitz Family Foundation, Inc.
51 Lexington Ave.
New York 10010 (212) 683-6342

Established in 1983 in NY.
Donor(s): Louis Berkowitz.†
Foundation type: Independent
Financial data (yr. ended 12/31/89): Assets, $5,873,567 (M); expenditures, $189,578, including $184,464 for 10 grants (high: $100,000).
Purpose and activities: Giving primarily for hospitals and education; support also for Jewish organizations.
Types of support: Equipment, research, special projects.
Limitations: Giving primarily in the New York, NY, metropolitan area.
Application information:
Initial approach: Letter
Deadline(s): None
Write: John E. Tuchler, Pres.
Officers and Directors: John E. Tuchler, Pres.; Mollie Auerbach, V.P.; Herbert Cohen, V.P.; Paul Heiling, V.P.; Ruth Martin, V.P.; Frederick Siegmund, Secy.; Louis Katz, Treas.
Number of staff: None.
Employer Identification Number: 133190334

4112
Berlex Foundation, Inc. ☆
530 Fifth Ave., 25th Fl.
New York 10036 (212) 719-5613
Application address: CBC, 80 West Madison Ave., Dumont, NJ 07628; Tel.: (201) 385-8080

Incorporated in 1986 in NY.
Donor(s): Berlex Laboratories, Inc.
Foundation type: Independent
Financial data (yr. ended 12/31/88): Assets, $212,212 (M); gifts received, $500,000; expenditures, $514,467, including $266,158 for grants to individuals.
Purpose and activities: Awards research grants to licensed physicians affiliated with a university or laboratory institution.
Types of support: Grants to individuals.
Publications: Newsletter, informational brochure (including application guidelines), application guidelines.
Application information: Application form not required.
Initial approach: Proposal
Copies of proposal: 5
Deadline(s): Oct. 15
Write: S. Lisanti
Officers: Robert S. Cohen, Pres.; Robert S. Chabora, Secy.; Howard W. Robin, Treas.
Employer Identification Number: 133359746

4113
Irving Berlin Charitable Fund, Inc. ⌘
29 West 46th St.
New York 10036

Incorporated in 1947 in NY.
Donor(s): Irving Berlin.†
Foundation type: Independent
Financial data (yr. ended 12/31/88): Assets, $1,968,341 (M); gifts received, $76,718; expenditures, $75,653, including $68,050 for 11 grants (high: $42,000; low: $250).
Purpose and activities: Giving primarily to a music school, an opera association, and to Jewish welfare funds.
Limitations: Giving primarily in NY. No grants to individuals.
Application information: Contributes only to pre-selected organizations. Applications not accepted.
Director: Norman J. Stone.
Employer Identification Number: 136092592

4114
Rhonie & George Berlinger Foundation, Inc. ⌘
1120 Park Ave.
New York 10128

Incorporated in 1958 in NY.
Donor(s): George F. Berlinger, Rhonie H. Berlinger.

Foundation type: Independent
Financial data (yr. ended 05/31/89): Assets, $58,996 (M); gifts received, $69,758; expenditures, $142,149, including $138,663 for 99 grants (high: $25,000; low: $45).
Purpose and activities: Emphasis on health agencies, children, cultural programs, education, and Jewish welfare funds.
Application information: Contributes only to pre-selected organizations. Applications not accepted.
Officers: Rhonie H. Berlinger, Pres.; Nancy K. Stone, Secy.-Treas.
Employer Identification Number: 136084411

4115
The Bernhill Fund
40 West 20th St., Rm. 1022
New York 10011 (212) 627-7710

Incorporated in 1977 in NY as partial successor to the Bernhard Foundation, Inc.
Donor(s): The Bernhard Foundation, Inc.
Foundation type: Independent
Financial data (yr. ended 10/31/89): Assets, $1,020,120 (M); expenditures, $177,590, including $148,725 for 99 grants (high: $25,000; low: $100; average: $100-$25,000).
Purpose and activities: Grants to urban community organizations and service delivery projects; support also for institutions of particular interest to the trustees, including the fine and performing arts, higher and other education, the environment and ecology, wildlife and animal welfare, the homeless, hospices, and AIDS programs.
Types of support: Operating budgets, continuing support, seed money, special projects.
Limitations: Giving primarily in New York, NY. No grants to individuals, or for annual campaigns, emergency funds, deficit financing, matching gifts, scholarships, fellowships, demonstration projects, publications, or conferences; no loans.
Publications: 990-PF.
Application information: Application form not required.
Initial approach: One-page proposal
Deadline(s): None
Board meeting date(s): As required
Officers and Directors:* William L. Bernhard,* Pres.; Catherine G. Cahill, V.P. and Secy.; William C. Breed III,* Treas.
Number of staff: None.
Employer Identification Number: 132988599

4116
Sanford C. Bernstein & Company Foundation, Inc. ⌘
767 Fifth Ave.
New York 10153-0001

Established in 1968 in NY.
Donor(s): Zalman Chaim Bernstein, Sanford C. Bernstein & Co., Inc.
Foundation type: Company-sponsored
Financial data (yr. ended 12/31/88): Assets, $1,789,335 (M); gifts received, $850,000; expenditures, $528,702, including $523,349 for 114 grants (high: $79,888; low: $75).
Purpose and activities: Support primarily for Jewish giving, education, and general charitable purposes.
Limitations: Giving primarily in New York, NY. No grants to individuals.
Application information: Contributes only to pre-selected organizations. Applications not accepted.
Trustees: Zalman C. Bernstein, Kevin R. Brine, Joseph P. Greeley, Roger Hertog, Stuart K. Nelson, Lewis A. Sanders, Andrew Adelson.
Employer Identification Number: 136277976

4117
Bezalel Foundation, Inc.
The Clock Tower Bldg.
Two Madison Ave.
Larchmont 10538 (914) 833-0425
Mailing address: 110 North Chatsworth Ave., Larchmont, NY 10538

Incorporated in 1940 in MD; in 1981 merged with Ferdinand W. Breth Foundation.
Donor(s): Henry Sonneborn III, Rudolf G. Sonneborn,† Gustave Schindler.†
Foundation type: Independent
Financial data (yr. ended 6/30/89): Assets, $1,399,624 (M); gifts received, $23,358; expenditures, $126,760, including $111,250 for 94 grants (high: $28,200; low: $25).
Purpose and activities: Emphasis on Jewish welfare funds and higher education, including institutions in Israel; support also for hospitals, music, and museums.
Limitations: No grants to individuals.
Application information: Funds are fully committed. Applications not accepted.
Write: Henry Sonneborn III, Pres.
Officers and Directors: Henry Sonneborn III, Pres.; Clara L. Sonneborn, Secy.; Amalie S. Katz, Mark D. Neumann, Hans Schindler.
Employer Identification Number: 136066999

4118
Margaret T. Biddle Foundation ⌘
c/o Cusack & Stiles
61 Broadway, Rm. 2912
New York 10006

Incorporated in 1952 in NY.
Donor(s): Margaret T. Biddle.†
Foundation type: Independent
Financial data (yr. ended 12/31/88): Assets, $3,129,932 (M); expenditures, $110,013, including $95,000 for 4 grants (high: $50,000; low: $10,000).
Purpose and activities: Emphasis on research in plant diseases, social services, cancer research and treatment, the handicapped, and health agencies.
Limitations: No grants to individuals.
Application information: Contributes only to pre-selected organizations. Applications not accepted.
Officers and Directors:* Christian Hohenlohe,* Pres.; Richard A. Smith,* V.P. and Secy.; Catherine H. Jacobus,* V.P.; Peter Boyce Schulze,* V.P.; James F. O'Brien, Treas.
Employer Identification Number: 131936016

4119
The Siegfried & Josephine Bieber Foundation, Inc. ⌘
505 Park Ave., 9th Fl.
New York 10022

Incorporated in 1960 in NY.
Donor(s): Siegfried Bieber,† Josephine Bieber.†
Foundation type: Independent
Financial data (yr. ended 12/31/88): Assets, $560,993 (M); expenditures, $205,909, including $181,500 for 49 grants (high: $30,000; low: $500).
Purpose and activities: Emphasis on religious welfare funds, social services, hospitals and medical research, the performing arts, education, and museums.
Limitations: Giving primarily in NY. No grants to individuals.
Application information: Contributes only to pre-selected organizations. Applications not accepted.
Write: Rene Loeb, Pres.
Officers and Directors:* Rene Loeb,* Pres.; Leonard Wacksman,* Secy.; Stephen Connolly, Stephen M. Kellen.
Employer Identification Number: 136162556

4120
William Bingham 2nd Betterment Fund ⌘
c/o U.S. Trust Co. of New York
45 Wall St.
New York 10005
Application address: 330 Madison Ave., Rm. 3500, New York, NY 10017

Foundation type: Independent
Financial data (yr. ended 12/31/88): Assets, $20,659,385 (M); expenditures, $1,179,341, including $832,410 for 26 grants (high: $302,400; low: $5,000).
Purpose and activities: Giving primarily to educational institutions, health and hospitals, and general charitable purposes.
Limitations: Giving limited to ME. No grants to individuals.
Application information:
Initial approach: Letter
Deadline(s): None
Trustees: William M. Troop, Jr., William B. Windship, Carolyn S. Wollen, U.S. Trust Co. of New York.
Employer Identification Number: 136072625

4121
John and Marsha Bisgrove Charitable Trust ⌘ ☆
R.D. 2 Swantout Rd.
Auburn 13021

Established in 1987.
Foundation type: Independent
Financial data (yr. ended 12/31/88): Assets, $90,510 (M); expenditures, $393,986, including $390,000 for 1 grant.
Purpose and activities: Giving primarily for a university, a monastery, and other Christian organizations.
Application information:
Initial approach: Letter
Deadline(s): None

Write: John Bisgrove, Jr., Trustee
Trustees: John Bisgrove, Jr., Marsha Bisgrove, John P. Doyle, Jr.
Employer Identification Number: 222794788

4122
Mona Bismarck Charitable Trust ⌑ ☆
30 Rockefeller Plaza, Suite 3500
New York 10112
Application address: 261 rue Saint Honore, Paris, France 75001

Established in 1986 in NY.
Donor(s): Russell M. Porter.
Foundation type: Independent
Financial data (yr. ended 12/31/88): Assets, $7,040,712 (M); expenditures, $342,431, including $273,000 for 6 grants (high: $235,000; low: $500).
Purpose and activities: Giving primarily to an affiliated private foundation; some support for higher education and cultural institutions.
Limitations: No grants to individuals.
Application information:
Initial approach: Letter
Deadline(s): None
Final notification: Only if grant is awarded
Write: Russell M. Porter, Trustee
Trustee: Russell M. Porter.
Employer Identification Number: 133244269

4123
H. S. Black & A. Fuller Fund ⌑ ☆
c/o U.S. Trust Co. of New York
45 Wall St.
New York 10005

Foundation type: Independent
Financial data (yr. ended 12/31/88): Assets, $1,326,011 (M); expenditures, $63,323, including $47,000 for 7 grants (high: $14,100; low: $4,700).
Purpose and activities: Support primarily for higher education, hospitals and medical centers, and child welfare.
Limitations: Giving limited to Chicago, IL, and New York, NY. No grants to individuals.
Application information: Contributes only to pre-selected organizations. Applications not accepted.
Trustee: U.S. Trust Co. of New York.
Employer Identification Number: 136072632

4124
Henry M. Blackmer Foundation, Inc. ⌑
c/o White & Case
1155 Ave. of the Americas
New York 10036

Incorporated in 1952 in DE.
Donor(s): Henry M. Blackmer.†
Foundation type: Independent
Financial data (yr. ended 12/31/87): Assets, $2,044,506 (M); expenditures, $187,665, including $143,500 for 30 grants (high: $15,000; low: $500).
Purpose and activities: Support for education, hospitals, cultural programs, and a zoological foundation; grants generally limited to a small list of institutional donees who have received grants from the Foundation in the past.
Application information: Contributes only to pre-selected organizations. Applications not accepted.
Officers and Trustees: Morton Moskin, Pres.; W. Perry Neff, V.P.; David W. Swanson, Secy.-Treas.; Henry M. Blackmer II.
Employer Identification Number: 136097357

4125
Blackstone Corporate Trust Lenna Fund ⌑ ☆
c/o Marine Midland Bank, N.A.
P.O. Box 4203
Buffalo 14240

Foundation type: Independent
Financial data (yr. ended 09/30/89): Assets, $1,140,044 (M); expenditures, $53,560, including $47,430 for 26 grants.
Purpose and activities: Support for higher education, cultural organizations, and social services.
Limitations: Giving primarily in NY.
Application information: Contributes only to pre-selected organizations. Applications not accepted.
Trustee: Marine Midland Bank, N.A.
Employer Identification Number: 166021893

4126
Jacob Bleibtreu Foundation, Inc. ⌑
c/o Spicer & Oppenheim
Seven World Trade Center
New York 10048

Incorporated in 1945 in NY.
Donor(s): Helen R. Bleibtreu, Jacob Bleibtreu.†
Foundation type: Independent
Financial data (yr. ended 9/30/88): Assets, $5,217,244 (M); expenditures, $158,632, including $137,000 for 7 grants (high: $50,000; low: $2,000).
Purpose and activities: Giving to hospitals and a Jewish welfare fund.
Limitations: Giving primarily in NY. No grants to individuals.
Application information: Contributes only to pre-selected organizations. Applications not accepted.
Officers: Alexander Abraham, Pres.; George H. Heyman, Jr., V.P.; John N. Bleibtreu, Secy.-Treas.
Employer Identification Number: 136065942

4127
Blinken Foundation, Inc. ⌑
466 Lexington Ave.
New York 10017

Established in 1965 in NY.
Foundation type: Independent
Financial data (yr. ended 12/31/88): Assets, $2,099,450 (M); gifts received, $17,397; expenditures, $124,824, including $123,098 for 49 grants (high: $16,573; low: $100; average: $500-$5,000).
Purpose and activities: Giving for cultural activities, scientific research, and Jewish welfare funds.
Types of support: Annual campaigns, fellowships, general purposes, internships, scholarship funds.
Application information: Contributes only to pre-selected organizations. Applications not accepted.
Officers and Directors: Donald M. Blinken, Pres. and Treas.; Robert J. Blinken, V.P. and Secy.; Alan J. Blinken, V.P.
Number of staff: None.
Employer Identification Number: 136190153

4128
Cornelius N. Bliss Memorial Fund ⌑
c/o U.S. Trust Co. of NY, Tax Dept.
45 Wall St.
New York 10005

Incorporated in 1917 in NY.
Donor(s): Cornelius N. Bliss,† Elizabeth M. Bliss, Lizzie P. Bliss, William B. Markell.
Foundation type: Independent
Financial data (yr. ended 12/31/88): Assets, $1,572,630 (M); gifts received, $2,421; expenditures, $88,190, including $67,500 for 19 grants (high: $12,500; low: $250).
Purpose and activities: Giving primarily to cultural programs, hospitals, and secondary education.
Limitations: Giving primarily in NY. No grants to individuals.
Application information:
Initial approach: Letter
Deadline(s): None
Write: Cornelius N. Bliss, Jr., Pres.
Officers and Directors: Cornelius N. Bliss, Jr., Pres.; Elizabeth B. Parkinson, V.P.; Anthony A. Bliss, Secy.-Treas.; Cornelius N. Bliss III, John Parkinson.
Employer Identification Number: 136400075

4129
Samuel J. Bloomingdale Foundation ⌑
641 Lexington Ave., 29th Fl.
New York 10022 (212) 838-0211

Incorporated in 1951 in NY.
Donor(s): Samuel J. Bloomingdale,† Rita G. Bloomingdale,† Richard C. Ernst, Susan B. Ernst,† Edgar M. Cullman, Louise B. Cullman.
Foundation type: Independent
Financial data (yr. ended 12/31/86): Assets, $1,065,478 (M); gifts received, $18,975; expenditures, $681,182, including $659,150 for 9 grants (high: $257,500; low: $150).
Purpose and activities: Emphasis on Jewish welfare funds, education, and a wildlife fund.
Limitations: Giving primarily in NY.
Application information: Application form required.
Deadline(s): None
Write: Edgar M. Cullman, Pres.
Officer and Directors: Edgar M. Cullman, Pres.; Louise B. Cullman.
Employer Identification Number: 136099790

4130
The Blue Ridge Foundation, Inc. ⌑ ☆
635 Madison Ave.
New York 10022

Established in 1985 in NY.
Donor(s): Walter Scheurer,† and members of the Scheuer family.
Foundation type: Independent

Financial data (yr. ended 10/31/88): Assets, $186,058 (M); gifts received, $107,228; expenditures, $321,845, including $312,895 for 45 grants (high: $115,000; low: $50).
Purpose and activities: Giving primarily for the performing arts and other cultural programs and higher education.
Limitations: Giving primarily in NY. No grants to individuals.
Application information: Contributes only to pre-selected organizations. Applications not accepted.
Directors: Edwin Robbins, David A. Scheuer, Jeffrey J. Scheuer, Judith Scheuer, Marge P. Scheuer, Susan Scheuer.
Employer Identification Number: 133282554

4131
Jacob Bluestein Foundation ⌑
c/o I.H. Finklestein
245 East 19th St., Apt. 6-D
New York 10003

Established in 1958 in NY.
Donor(s): Allan I. Bluestein.†
Foundation type: Independent
Financial data (yr. ended 4/30/88): Assets, $1,331,887 (M); expenditures, $87,611, including $71,300 for 6 grants (high: $40,000; low: $500).
Purpose and activities: Giving primarily for Jewish welfare funds and health agencies.
Limitations: No grants to individuals.
Application information: Contributes only to pre-selected organizations. Applications not accepted.
Write: Milton J. Bluestein, Pres.
Officers: Milton J. Bluestein, Pres.; Gabrielle Bluestein, V.P.; Marian Galison, Secy.-Treas.
Directors: Gerald Galison, Peter Galison.
Employer Identification Number: 136116536

4132
Charles G. & Yvette Bluhdorn Charitable Trust
c/o Reminick, Aarons & Co.
220 East 42nd St.
New York 10017 (212) 333-4300

Established in 1967 in NY.
Foundation type: Independent
Financial data (yr. ended 12/31/88): Assets, $5,587,413 (M); gifts received, $110,000; expenditures, $415,015, including $374,752 for 42 grants (high: $134,710; low: $1,000).
Purpose and activities: Giving for social services, arts and culture, education, the environment, and hospitals and medical research, including AIDS research.
Types of support: General purposes, scholarship funds, special projects.
Application information: Application form not required.
Initial approach: Letter
Copies of proposal: 1
Deadline(s): None
Write: Dominique Bluhdorn, Trustee
Trustees: Dominique Bluhdorn, Paul Bluhdorn, Yvette Bluhdorn.
Number of staff: 1 full-time professional.
Employer Identification Number: 136256769

4133
Edith C. Blum Foundation ⌑
300 Park Ave.
New York 10022

Trust established in 1976 in NY.
Donor(s): Albert Blum,† Edith C. Blum.†
Foundation type: Independent
Financial data (yr. ended 9/30/88): Assets, $10,426,531 (M); expenditures, $673,893, including $524,825 for 117 grants (high: $95,000; low: $100).
Purpose and activities: Emphasis on higher education, including legal education; cultural programs, including the performing arts and museums; and public interest organizations.
Limitations: Giving primarily in New York, NY. No grants to individuals.
Application information: Application form not required.
Deadline(s): None
Write: Wilbur H. Friedman, Trustee
Trustees: Frances M. Friedman, Wilbur H. Friedman.
Employer Identification Number: 132871362

4134
Blythmour Corporation ⌑
c/o Breed, Abbott & Morgan
153 East 53rd St.
New York 10022 (212) 888-0800

Established in 1951 in NY.
Donor(s): Lloyd S. Gilmour.
Foundation type: Independent
Financial data (yr. ended 12/31/88): Assets, $1,485,008 (M); expenditures, $86,892, including $78,700 for 29 grants (high: $10,000; low: $700).
Purpose and activities: Grants primarily for medical research, hospitals, and youth agencies.
Limitations: Giving primarily in NY. No grants to individuals.
Application information: Contributes only to pre-selected organizations. Applications not accepted.
Officers and Directors:* Margery B. Gilmour,* Pres.; Lloyd S. Gilmour, Jr.,* V.P.; Blyth G. Patel,* V.P.; David F. Kroenlein, Secy.-Treas.
Employer Identification Number: 136157750

4135
The Elmer and Mamdouha Bobst Foundation, Inc. ▼ ⌑
c/o The Elmer Holmes Bobst Library, New York Univ.
70 Washington Square South
New York 10012

Incorporated in 1968 in NY.
Donor(s): Elmer H. Bobst.†
Foundation type: Independent
Financial data (yr. ended 12/31/88): Assets, $25,304,511 (M); expenditures, $1,260,528, including $1,135,800 for 42 grants (high: $400,000; low: $25; average: $1,000-$100,000).
Purpose and activities: Emphasis on the promotion of health and medical research services, higher education, cultural programs, youth agencies, and national and international Islamic organizations.
Publications: Annual report, informational brochure (including application guidelines).
Application information:
Initial approach: Letter
Deadline(s): None
Write: Mamdouha S. Bobst, Pres.
Officers & Directors:* Mamdouha S. Bobst,* Pres. and Treas.; Arthur J. Mahon, Secy.; Farouk as-Sayid, Raja Kabbani, Mary Rockefeller, Milton C. Rose.
Employer Identification Number: 132616114

4136
The Bodman Foundation ▼
c/o Morris & McVeigh
767 Third Ave., 22nd Fl.
New York 10017-2023 (212) 418-0500

Incorporated in 1945 in NJ.
Donor(s): George M. Bodman,† Louise C. Bodman.†
Foundation type: Independent
Financial data (yr. ended 12/31/89): Assets, $36,910,740 (M); expenditures, $2,489,475, including $2,230,000 for 65 grants (high: $100,000; low: $10,000; average: $10,000-$75,000).
Purpose and activities: Support largely for youth, the aged, and social service agencies, educational institutions, cultural programs, and health, including hospitals and rehabilitation programs.
Types of support: Building funds, equipment, annual campaigns, capital campaigns, general purposes, land acquisition, matching funds, operating budgets, research.
Limitations: Giving primarily in the New York, NY, area. Generally, no support for colleges or universities, performing arts groups, museums, or national health or mental health organizations. No grants to individuals, or for conferences, publications, travel, or film; no loans.
Publications: Biennial report (including application guidelines), program policy statement.
Application information: Application form not required.
Initial approach: Letter and proposal
Copies of proposal: 1
Deadline(s): None
Board meeting date(s): May, Sept., Dec., and as needed
Final notification: Only when requested
Write: Mary E. Caslin, Secy. and Exec. Dir.
Officers: Guy G. Rutherfurd,* Pres. and Treas.; Marguerite Sykes Nichols,* V.P.; Mary E. Caslin, Secy. and Exec. Dir.
Trustees:* Harry W. Albright, Jr., Mary B. Braga, Anthony Drexel Duke, Peter Frelinghuysen, John N. Irwin III, Russel Pennoyer, Mary S. Phipps.
Number of staff: 2 full-time professional.
Employer Identification Number: 136022016

4137
The Boehm Foundation
500 Fifth Ave., Suite 2107
New York 10110-0296 (212) 354-9292

Trust established in 1963 in NY.
Donor(s): Robert L. Boehm, Frances Boehm.
Foundation type: Independent

Financial data (yr. ended 12/31/89): Assets, $1,822,076 (M); gifts received, $200,000; expenditures, $628,238, including $588,934 for 100 grants (high: $100,000; low: $500; average: $3,000-$4,000).
Purpose and activities: Emphasis on promoting human rights and peace.
Types of support: Seed money, emergency funds, matching funds, special projects, operating budgets.
Limitations: No grants to individuals, or for capital and endowment funds, publications, film and video projects, or individual research projects.
Publications: Application guidelines, annual report, financial statement, grants list.
Application information: Application form not required.
Initial approach: Letter or brief proposal
Copies of proposal: 1
Deadline(s): None
Board meeting date(s): Bimonthly
Final notification: 6-8 weeks
Write: Judy Austermiller, Exec. Dir.
Officers and Trustees:* Robert L. Boehm,* Pres.; Judy Austermiller,* Exec. Dir.; W. Haywood Burns, Nancy L. Coster, Bernard D. Fischman, Joseph Rosenblatt.
Number of staff: 1 part-time professional.
Employer Identification Number: 136145943

4138
The Boisi Family Foundation ⌘
c/o Goldman, Sachs & Co.
85 Broad St., 30th Fl.
New York 10004-2408

Donor(s): Geoffrey T. Boisi.
Foundation type: Independent
Financial data (yr. ended 2/28/88): Assets, $688,903 (M); gifts received, $570,000; expenditures, $328,699, including $328,050 for 40 grants (high: $200,000; low: $100).
Purpose and activities: Giving primarily for higher education.
Limitations: No grants to individuals, or for scholarships and gifts; no loans.
Application information: Applications not accepted.
Trustees: Geoffrey T. Boisi, Norine I. Boisi, Willard J. Overlock, Jr.
Employer Identification Number: 133165815

4139
Booth Ferris Foundation ▼ ⌘
30 Broad St.
New York 10004 (212) 269-3850

Trusts established in 1957 and 1958 in NY; merged in 1964.
Donor(s): Chancie Ferris Booth,† Willis H. Booth.†
Foundation type: Independent
Financial data (yr. ended 12/31/87): Assets, $100,984,048 (M); expenditures, $6,098,830, including $4,893,434 for 88 grants (high: $250,000; low: $5,000; average: $15,000-$100,000).
Purpose and activities: Grants primarily for private education, especially theological education, smaller colleges, and independent secondary schools; limited support also for urban programs, social service agencies, and cultural activities.
Types of support: Continuing support, annual campaigns, seed money, emergency funds, building funds, equipment, renovation projects, endowment funds, matching funds, capital campaigns, general purposes.
Limitations: Giving limited to the New York, NY, metropolitan area for social service agencies and cultural organizations. No support for federated campaigns, community chests, or for work with specific diseases or disabilities. No grants to individuals, or for research; generally no grants to educational institutions for scholarships, fellowships, or unrestricted endowments; no loans.
Publications: Annual report (including application guidelines).
Application information: Application form not required.
Initial approach: Telephone, letter, or proposal
Copies of proposal: 1
Deadline(s): None
Board meeting date(s): Bimonthly
Final notification: 4 months
Write: Robert J. Murtagh, Trustee
Trustees: Robert J. Murtagh, Morgan Guaranty Trust Co. of New York.
Number of staff: 3 part-time professional.
Employer Identification Number: 136170340

4140
The Albert C. Bostwick Foundation ⌘
Hillside Ave. and Bacon Rd.
P.O. Box A
Old Westbury 11568 (516) 334-5566

Trust established in 1958 in NY.
Donor(s): Albert C. Bostwick.†
Foundation type: Independent
Financial data (yr. ended 12/31/88): Assets, $2,100,553 (M); expenditures, $130,586, including $114,450 for 46 grants (high: $25,000; low: $150).
Purpose and activities: Support for hospitals, youth agencies, aid to the handicapped, health agencies, and medical research.
Limitations: Giving primarily in NY. No grants to individuals.
Application information:
Initial approach: Letter
Deadline(s): None
Board meeting date(s): Annually
Write: Eleanor P. Bostwick, Trustee
Trustees: Albert C. Bostwick, Jr., Eleanor P. Bostwick, Andrew G.C. Sage III.
Employer Identification Number: 116003740

4141
Botwinick-Wolfensohn Foundation, Inc.
599 Lexington Ave.
New York 10022 (212) 909-8100

Established in 1952.
Donor(s): James D. Wolfensohn, Benjamin Botwinick, Edward Botwinick.
Foundation type: Independent
Financial data (yr. ended 12/31/88): Assets, $5,176,823 (M); gifts received, $1,523,608; expenditures, $1,226,758, including $1,198,912 for 225 grants (high: $125,300; low: $10; average: $1,000-$5,000).
Purpose and activities: Emphasis on Israeli and Jewish interests, Australia, music education, minority education, medical research, and the homeless.
Types of support: Annual campaigns, building funds, capital campaigns, continuing support, general purposes, research, scholarship funds, seed money, special projects.
Limitations: Giving primarily in New York, NY. No grants to individuals.
Publications: 990-PF.
Application information: Application form not required.
Initial approach: Letter or telephone
Deadline(s): None
Final notification: 3 to 6 months
Write: James D. Wolfensohn, Chair.
Officers: James D. Wolfensohn, Chair.; Benjamin Botwinick, Pres.; Edward Botwinick, V.P.; Elaine Wolfensohn, Secy.; Bessie Botwinick, Treas.; Jamie Carroll, Exec. Dir.
Number of staff: 1 full-time professional; 1 full-time support.
Employer Identification Number: 136111833

4142
The Robert Bowne Foundation, Inc.
345 Hudson St.
New York 10014 (212) 924-5500

Incorporated in 1968 in NY.
Donor(s): Edmund A. Stanley, Jr., Bowne & Co., Inc., and members of the Stanley family.
Foundation type: Company-sponsored
Financial data (yr. ended 12/31/89): Assets, $7,128,076 (M); gifts received, $75,000; expenditures, $459,681, including $389,750 for 26 grants (high: $30,000; low: $750; average: $1,000-$35,000).
Purpose and activities: Support for literacy programs that reach disadvantaged youth. Priority given to programs that provide young people with a variety of reading and writing experiences. Funding also available for advocacy, technical assistance, staff development, evaluation, and job training related to the youth literacy issue.
Types of support: Operating budgets, seed money, special projects, technical assistance, consulting services, continuing support, general purposes, matching funds, conferences and seminars, research.
Limitations: Giving limited to New York, NY, especially the boroughs outside Manhattan. No support for religious organizations, primary or secondary schools, colleges, or universities, except when some aspect of their work is an integral part of a program supported by the foundation. No grants to individuals, or for capital campaigns or endowments.
Publications: Informational brochure (including application guidelines).
Application information: Application form not required.
Initial approach: Letter
Copies of proposal: 1
Deadline(s): None
Board meeting date(s): Varies
Final notification: 3 months
Write: Dianne Kangisser, V.P.
Officers and Trustees:* Edmund A. Stanley, Jr.,* Pres.; Dianne Kangisser,* V.P. and Exec. Dir.; Jennifer Stanley,* V.P.; Franz von

Ziegesar,* V.P.; Douglas F. Bauer,* Secy.-Treas.; Suzanne Carothers, Richard H. Koontz, Carl R. Pite, Thomas O. Stanley.
Number of staff: 1 part-time professional.
Employer Identification Number: 132620393

4143
The Boxer Foundation ⌑ ☆
666 Fifth Ave.
New York 10103

Established in 1985.
Foundation type: Independent
Financial data (yr. ended 11/30/88): Assets, $215,101 (M); expenditures, $221,751, including $206,267 for 48 grants (high: $150,000; low: $10).
Purpose and activities: Giving primarily for health associations and hospitals; support also for higher education, with emphasis on health sciences.
Types of support: General purposes.
Limitations: No grants to individuals.
Application information: Contributes only to pre-selected organizations. Applications not accepted.
Manager: Leonard Boxer.
Employer Identification Number: 133345823

4144
The Martha and Regina Brand Foundation, Inc. ⌑
521 Fifth Ave., Rm. 1805
New York 10175 (212) 687-3505

Established in 1962 in NY.
Donor(s): Martha Brand.†
Foundation type: Independent
Financial data (yr. ended 12/31/88): Assets, $1,963,229 (M); expenditures, $131,694, including $93,450 for 32 grants (high: $25,000; low: $50).
Purpose and activities: Emphasis on Jewish welfare funds, temple support, and a theological seminary; support also for a museum; also grants for Jewish and other organizations whose general purpose relates to the betterment of parent/child relations.
Limitations: Giving primarily in NY, NJ, and CA.
Application information:
Initial approach: Letter
Deadline(s): None
Write: Marjorie D. Kogan, Pres.
Officers: Marjorie D. Kogan, Pres.; Michael S. Kogan, V.P. and Secy.; Barton Kogan, V.P. and Treas.
Employer Identification Number: 136159106

4145
Branta Foundation, Inc. ⌑
c/o Perelson Johnson & Rones
560 Lexington Ave.
New York 10022

Established in 1955 in NY.
Donor(s): Harvey Picker.
Foundation type: Independent
Financial data (yr. ended 5/31/89): Assets, $2,127,059 (M); gifts received, $250,758; expenditures, $221,185, including $191,500 for 24 grants (high: $51,000; low: $1,000).
Purpose and activities: Support primarily for higher education, culture, and international affairs.
Limitations: No grants to individuals.
Application information: Contributes only to pre-selected organizations. Applications not accepted.
Officers and Directors: Jean Picker, Pres. and Treas.; Harvey Picker, V.P. and Secy.; Christine Beshar.
Employer Identification Number: 136130955

4146
The Ludwig Bravmann Foundation, Inc. ⌑
c/o Ludwig Bravmann
3333B Henry Hudson Pkwy., Apt. 6E
Riverdale 10463

Established in 1964 in NY.
Donor(s): Ludwig Bravmann.
Foundation type: Independent
Financial data (yr. ended 6/30/89): Assets, $1,678,115 (M); expenditures, $79,089, including $67,780 for 84 grants (high: $25,000; low: $10).
Purpose and activities: Giving primarily for Jewish welfare and Jewish concerns; support also for higher education.
Limitations: Giving primarily in New York, NY. No grants to individuals.
Application information: Contributes only to pre-selected organizations. Applications not accepted.
Officers and Directors: Ludwig Bravmann, Pres.; Lotte Bravmann, Secy.-Treas.; Arthur Aeder, Judith E. Kaufthal, Carol Lipner, Mathew Maryles, Jack Nash.
Employer Identification Number: 136168525

4147
The Brecher Fund ⌑
48 Concord Dr.
Monsey 10952

Established in 1985 in NY.
Donor(s): Harvey Brecher.
Foundation type: Independent
Financial data (yr. ended 05/31/89): Assets, $57,439 (M); gifts received, $349,792; expenditures, $346,506, including $343,898 for grants.
Purpose and activities: Grants for Jewish giving.
Limitations: No grants to individuals.
Application information: Contributes only to pre-selected organizations. Applications not accepted.
Officers and Directors:* Harvey Brecher,* Pres. and Treas.; Miriam Brecher,* V.P. and Secy.; Eli S. Garber.
Employer Identification Number: 133288971

4148
Brencanda Foundation ▼ ⌑
358 Fifth Ave., Suite 1103
New York 10001 (212) 736-2727

Established in 1979.
Donor(s): Members of the Brenninkmeyer family and affiliated entities.
Foundation type: Independent
Financial data (yr. ended 12/31/88): Assets, $1,060,547 (M); gifts received, $1,825,000; expenditures, $1,736,350, including $1,581,863 for 92 grants (high: $149,288; low: $1,200; average: $5,000-$20,000).
Purpose and activities: Grants largely for Roman Catholic organizations and service agencies.
Types of support: Special projects, conferences and seminars, consulting services, continuing support, emergency funds, equipment, general purposes, matching funds, operating budgets, seed money, technical assistance.
Limitations: Giving limited to the U.S. No support for education or stewardship. No grants to individuals, or for scholarships, or endowments, or large capital campaigns.
Publications: Application guidelines, program policy statement.
Application information: Application form not required.
Initial approach: Letter
Copies of proposal: 1
Deadline(s): Jan. 15, Apr. 15, July 15, and Oct. 15
Board meeting date(s): Apr., June, Sept., and Dec.
Write: Peter S. Robinson, Exec. V.P.
Officers: Anthony Brenninkmeyer,* Pres.; Peter S. Robinson, Exec. V.P.; Miles P. Fischer, V.P. and Secy.; Kenneth R. Allex, V.P. and Treas.
Directors:* C. Mark Brenninkmeyer, Dominic Brenninkmeyer, Roland M. Brenninkmeyer, H.J.H. Cloudt.
Number of staff: 2 full-time professional; 1 full-time support; 2 part-time support.
Employer Identification Number: 133005012

4149
Deborah L. Brice Foundation ⌑ ☆
c/o Loeb Partners Corp.
61 Broadway
New York 10006

Donor(s): Deborah L. Brice.
Foundation type: Independent
Financial data (yr. ended 12/31/88): Assets, $1,193,399 (M); expenditures, $11,244, including $10,000 for 1 grant.
Purpose and activities: Support primarily for a museum.
Limitations: Giving primarily in New York, NY. No grants to individuals.
Application information: Contributes only to pre-selected organizations. Applications not accepted.
Officers: Deborah L. Brice, Pres.; John L. Loeb, V.P.; Frances L. Loeb, Secy.-Treas.
Employer Identification Number: 237065499

4150
The Bristol-Myers Squibb Foundation, Inc. ▼
(Formerly The Bristol-Myers Fund, Inc.)
345 Park Ave., 43rd Fl.
New York 10154 (212) 546-4331

Trust established in 1953 in NY; successor fund incorporated in 1982 in FL as Bristol-Myers Fund, Inc.

Donor(s): Bristol-Myers Squibb Co., divisions and subsidiaries.
Foundation type: Company-sponsored
Financial data (yr. ended 12/31/88): Assets, $7,932,409 (M); gifts received, $3,000,000; expenditures, $5,766,479, including $5,346,739 for grants (high: $265,000; average: $5,000-$35,000) and $416,585 for employee matching gifts.
Purpose and activities: Giving for medical research, community funds, higher and other education (including employee-related scholarships administered by the National Merit Scholarship Corporation and matching gifts), and health care; support also for civic affairs and community services, minority and women's organizations, youth agencies, international affairs, and arts and culture.
Types of support: Annual campaigns, research, employee-related scholarships, fellowships, scholarship funds, general purposes, employee matching gifts.
Limitations: Giving limited to areas of company operations, and to national organizations. No support for political, fraternal, social, or veterans' organizations; religious or sectarian organizations not engaged in a significant project benefiting the entire community; specific public broadcast programs or films; or organizations receiving support through federated campaigns. No grants to individuals, or for endowment funds; no loans.
Publications: Informational brochure.
Application information: Application form not required.
Initial approach: Proposal
Copies of proposal: 1
Deadline(s): Submit proposal preferably between Feb. and Sept.; deadline Oct. 1
Board meeting date(s): Dec. and as needed
Final notification: 2 to 3 months
Write: Marilyn L. Gruber, V.P., or Nancy Arnst Taussig, Mgr.
Officers: Patrick F. Crossman,* Pres.; Marilyn L. Gruber, V.P.; J. Richard Edmondson, Secy.; Jonathan B. Morris, Treas.; Nancy Arnot Taussig, Mgr.
Directors:* Richard L. Gelb, William R. Miller.
Number of staff: 3 full-time professional; 1 part-time professional; 3 full-time support.
Employer Identification Number: 133127947

4151
The Carolyn & Kenneth D. Brody Foundation ⌑
(Formerly Kenneth D. Brody Foundation)
c/o Goldman Sachs & Co.
85 Broad St., Tax Dept.
New York 10004-2408

Established in 1980 in NY.
Donor(s): Kenneth D. Brody.
Foundation type: Independent
Financial data (yr. ended 09/30/89): Assets, $1,514,765 (M); gifts received, $603,801; expenditures, $251,813, including $247,838 for 99 grants (high: $25,000; low: $15).
Purpose and activities: Support primarily for higher education, cultural programs, health services, and hospitals.
Limitations: Giving primarily in New York, NY. No grants to individuals, or for scholarships; no loans.
Application information: Contributes only to pre-selected organizations. Applications not accepted.
Trustees: Kenneth D. Brody, Donald R. Gant, H. Frederick Krimendahl II.
Employer Identification Number: 133050750

4152
Ann L. Bronfman Foundation ⌑
c/o Peat Marwick Main & Co.
599 Lexington Ave.
New York 10022

Established in 1958.
Donor(s): Ann L. Bronfman.
Foundation type: Independent
Financial data (yr. ended 07/31/89): Assets, $152,196 (M); expenditures, $112,720, including $112,709 for 7 grants (high: $60,000; low: $1,200).
Purpose and activities: Giving primarily for cultural programs and groups working to better international relations.
Types of support: General purposes.
Limitations: No grants to individuals.
Application information: Contributes only to pre-selected organizations. Applications not accepted.
Write: L. Foster
Officers: Ann L. Bronfman, Pres.; Ronald J. Stein, Secy.; John L. Loeb, Treas.
Employer Identification Number: 136085595

4153
The Samuel Bronfman Foundation, Inc. ▼ ⌑
375 Park Ave..
New York 10152-0192

Incorporated in 1951 in DE.
Donor(s): Joseph E. Seagram and Sons, Inc.
Foundation type: Company-sponsored
Financial data (yr. ended 12/31/88): Assets, $12,271,352 (M); gifts received, $8,000,000; expenditures, $6,131,225, including $6,084,578 for 26 grants (high: $2,023,500).
Purpose and activities: To perpetuate the ideals of American democracy; finances research programs for the study of democratic business enterprise by means of fellowships and professorships in colleges and universities; grants also for Jewish welfare funds and medical education.
Types of support: General purposes, professorships, fellowships.
Limitations: No grants to individuals, or for building or endowment funds, or operating budgets.
Application information: Application form not required.
Initial approach: Proposal
Copies of proposal: 1
Deadline(s): None
Board meeting date(s): Jan., Apr., July, and Oct.
Final notification: 6 to 8 weeks
Write: William K. Friedman, V.P.
Officers and Trustees:* Edgar M. Bronfman,* Pres.; William K. Friedman, V.P.; Claire Cullen, Secy.; Richard Karl Goeltz,* Treas.; Samuel Bronfman II, David G. Sacks.
Employer Identification Number: 136084708

4154
The Brookdale Foundation
126 East 56th St.
New York 10022 (212) 308-7355

Incorporated in 1950 in NY.
Donor(s): Henry L. Schwartz,† and his brothers.
Foundation type: Independent
Financial data (yr. ended 06/30/89): Assets, $7,824,422 (M); expenditures, $1,409,533, including $960,142 for 15 grants (high: $200,000; low: $2,000).
Purpose and activities: Support for gerontological and geriatric research and innovative service programs; giving also for higher education and youth.
Types of support: Seed money, matching funds, scholarship funds, fellowships, professorships, internships, conferences and seminars, publications, special projects, research.
Limitations: Giving primarily in the metropolitan New York, NY, and NJ area. No grants to individuals, or for operating budgets, continuing support, or annual campaigns; no loans.
Publications: Multi-year report, program policy statement, newsletter.
Application information: Application form not required.
Initial approach: Letter of intent
Copies of proposal: 1
Deadline(s): None
Board meeting date(s): Monthly
Write: Stephen Schwartz, Pres., or call Danylle Rudin, Asst. V.P.
Officers: Stephen L. Schwartz,* Pres.; Mary Ann Van Clief, V.P. and Secy.-Treas.
Directors:* Stanley Epstein, Lois Juliber, John Winthrop, Roy Zuckerberg.
Number of staff: 2 full-time professional; 1 part-time professional; 2 part-time support.
Employer Identification Number: 136076863

4155
Brooklyn Benevolent Society ⌑
84 Amity St.
Brooklyn 11201 (718) 624-0176

Incorporated in 1845 in NY.
Donor(s): Cornelius Heaney.†
Foundation type: Independent
Financial data (yr. ended 12/31/88): Assets, $2,256,444 (M); expenditures, $175,506, including $109,030 for 46 grants (high: $5,350; low: $500).
Purpose and activities: For the support, maintenance, and education of poor orphan children and for supplying clothing, shoes, and fuel to poor persons. Grants primarily to agencies of the Roman Catholic Diocese of Brooklyn.
Limitations: Giving primarily in New York, NY, with emphasis on the borough of Brooklyn.
Application information:
Initial approach: Proposal
Deadline(s): Oct. 30
Write: Dominic J. Pantone, Trustee
Officers: Cornelius A. Heaney, Sr., Secy.; Thomas C. Powers, Treas.
Trustees: James J. Daly, and 13 additional trustees.
Employer Identification Number: 111661344

4156
Brooklyn Home for Aged Men
9701 Shore Rd.
Brooklyn 11209 (718) 745-1638
Mailing address: Box 62, Dyker Heights Station, Brooklyn, NY 11228-0002

Established in 1878 in NY.
Foundation type: Independent
Financial data (yr. ended 12/31/88): Assets, $1,008,572 (M); gifts received, $20,228; expenditures, $172,540, including $100,000 for 5 grants (high: $30,000; low: $1,500).
Purpose and activities: Support for homes for the aged.
Types of support: Continuing support.
Limitations: Giving primarily in NY. No grants to individuals.
Publications: Informational brochure.
Application information: Contributes only to pre-selected organizations. Applications not accepted.
Write: George Schaefer, Secy.-Treas.
Officers and Directors:* Nancy Munson,* Pres.; Dorothy Beckmann,* V.P.; Kenneth Heiberg,* V.P.; George Schaefer,* Secy.-Treas.; Elsa Ciulla, Robert W. Ciulla, Eleanor M. Kaufmann, Constance Olsen, George Olsen, Jean Weber.
Number of staff: 2 part-time professional.
Employer Identification Number: 111630754

4157
Gladys Brooks Foundation ▼
90 Broad St.
New York 10004 (212) 943-3217

Established in 1981 in NY.
Donor(s): Gladys Brooks Thayer.†
Foundation type: Independent
Financial data (yr. ended 12/31/87): Assets, $18,826,109 (M); expenditures, $1,206,735, including $936,150 for 23 grants (high: $100,000; low: $2,000; average: $5,000-$100,000).
Purpose and activities: Grants largely for libraries, higher education, and hospitals and clinics.
Types of support: Endowment funds, building funds, equipment, scholarship funds.
Limitations: Giving limited to the Northeast, including NY, MA, CT, NH, VT, PA, ME, NJ, RI, and DE. No grants to individuals, or for research.
Publications: Annual report (including application guidelines), program policy statement.
Application information: Application form required.
Copies of proposal: 2
Deadline(s): May 31
Board meeting date(s): Bimonthly
Final notification: Dec.
Write: Ms. Jessica L. Rutledge, Admin. Asst.
Board of Governors and Trustees: James J. Daly, Harman Hawkins, Robert E. Hill, U.S. Trust Co. of New York.
Number of staff: 1 full-time professional.
Employer Identification Number: 132955337

4158
The Brothers Ashkenazi Foundation ⌑
c/o Summit Rovins & Feldesman
445 Park Ave.
New York 10022

Established in 1962 in NY.
Donor(s): Members of the Ashkenazi family.
Foundation type: Independent
Financial data (yr. ended 2/28/89): Assets, $304,603 (M); gifts received, $575,000; expenditures, $649,670, including $649,190 for 321 grants (high: $52,000; low: $10).
Purpose and activities: Grants for Jewish giving, including yeshivas and temple support.
Application information:
Deadline(s): None
Write: Ely Ashkenazi, Pres.
Officers: Ely E. Ashkenazi, Pres.; Ezra E. Ashkenazi, V.P.; Ronald Ashkenazi, Secy.; Isaac Ashkenazi, Treas.
Employer Identification Number: 136129359

4159
The Brown Family Charitable Fund ⌑
One State St. Plaza, 27th Fl.
New York 10004

Incorporated in 1958 in NY.
Donor(s): Harry Brown.
Foundation type: Independent
Financial data (yr. ended 12/31/88): Assets, $1,057,155 (M); expenditures, $91,136, including $87,410 for 39 grants (high: $61,000; low: $10).
Purpose and activities: Support primarily for Jewish welfare organizations.
Limitations: Giving primarily in the Chicago, IL, area. No grants to individuals.
Application information: Contributes only to pre-selected organizations. Applications not accepted.
Officers and Directors:* Anthony Lee Brown,* Pres.; Alice L. Brown,* V.P.; Angie Astrin,* Secy.; Francine Brown,* Treas.
Employer Identification Number: 136088815

4160
Richard D. Brown Trust B ⌑ ☆
c/o Chemical Bank
30 Rockefeller Plaza
New York 10112 (212) 621-2143

Foundation type: Independent
Financial data (yr. ended 12/31/88): Assets, $1,441,526 (M); expenditures, $20,165, including $10,722 for 4 loans to individuals (high: $7,802; low: $500).
Purpose and activities: Awards loans to employees of Chemical Bank to provide financial assistance.
Types of support: Grants to individuals.
Application information:
Deadline(s): None
Write: Mrs. B. Strohmeier
Trustee: Chemical Bank.
Employer Identification Number: 136030429

4161
Bruner Foundation, Inc.
244 Fifth Ave.
New York 10001 (212) 889-5366

Incorporated in 1967 in NY.
Donor(s): Rudy Bruner,† Martha Bruner.†
Foundation type: Independent
Financial data (yr. ended 12/31/89): Assets, $6,750,000 (M); expenditures, $681,949, including $447,882 for 12 grants (high: $185,344; low: $2,000).
Purpose and activities: Support primarily for evaluation of New York public schools; support nationally for efforts in educational reform; also gives the Rudy Bruner Award for Urban Excellence.
Types of support: Special projects, research.
Limitations: No grants to individuals, or for general support, building or endowment funds, scholarships, or fellowships.
Publications: Informational brochure (including application guidelines).
Application information: Application form required for Rudy Bruner Award for Excellence in the Urban Environment. Application form not required.
Initial approach: Letter and brief outline of proposal, including budget
Copies of proposal: 1
Deadline(s): Jan. 1 for Rudy Bruner Award; no deadline for other grants
Board meeting date(s): As required
Final notification: 1 month
Write: Janet Carter, Exec. Dir.
Officers and Trustees:* Joshua E. Bruner,* Pres.; R. Simeon Bruner,* Treas.; Martin Barell, Richard J.L. Herson, Jerome S. Katzin.
Number of staff: 1 full-time professional; 2 full-time support.
Employer Identification Number: 136180803

4162
The Robert Brunner Foundation ⌑
c/o Capromont, Ltd.
63 Wall St.
New York 10005 (212) 344-0050

Incorporated in 1949 in NY.
Donor(s): Robert Brunner.†
Foundation type: Independent
Financial data (yr. ended 12/31/88): Assets, $5,185,597 (M); expenditures, $281,549, including $230,500 for 6 grants (high: $128,000; low: $4,000).
Purpose and activities: Grants for Roman Catholic institutions in the U.S. and Belgium, but principally for educational and religious organizations founded by the donor.
Limitations: Giving primarily in the U.S. and Belgium. No grants to individuals, or for building or endowment funds.
Application information:
Initial approach: Letter
Board meeting date(s): May and Dec.
Write: John M. Bruderman, Sr., Treas.
Officers and Directors: Eugene F. Rowan, Pres.; William F. Ray, V.P.; John C. Donnelly, Secy.; John M. Bruderman, Sr., Treas.; Patrick Bonnewyn, Michael Kraynak.
Employer Identification Number: 136067212

4163
BT Foundation ▼ ⌑
280 Park Ave.
New York 10015 (212) 850-3500
Application address: P.O. Box 318, Church St. Station, New York, NY 10012

Established in 1986 in NY.
Donor(s): BT Capital Corp.
Foundation type: Company-sponsored
Financial data (yr. ended 11/30/88): Assets, $30,682 (M); gifts received, $1,648,406; expenditures, $2,034,437, including $787,007 for 48 grants (high: $125,000; low: $1,000; average: $3,000-$20,000) and $1,186,440 for 1,042 employee matching gifts (high: $45,660; low: $50).
Purpose and activities: Support for arts and culture, economic development, with emphasis on community development and housing, social and public services, and urban amenities.
Types of support: General purposes, operating budgets, employee matching gifts, capital campaigns, continuing support.
Limitations: Giving primarily in NY. No support for religious purposes, veterans' and fraternal organizations, or United Way agencies unless they provide a fundraising waiver. No grants to individuals.
Application information: Application form not required.
Initial approach: Proposal
Deadline(s): None
Write: Nancy S. Ticktin, Pres.
Officers and Directors: Nancy S. Ticktin, Pres.; Maureen S. Bateman, V.P.; James J. Baechle, Page Chapman III.
Number of staff: 2 full-time professional; 3 full-time support.
Employer Identification Number: 133321736

4164
The Buffalo Foundation ▼
1601 Main-Seneca Bldg.
237 Main St.
Buffalo 14203-2781 (716) 852-2857

Established in 1919 in NY by resolution and declaration of trust.
Foundation type: Community
Financial data (yr. ended 12/31/89): Assets, $32,896,351 (M); gifts received, $918,500; expenditures, $2,320,782, including $1,859,852 for grants (high: $100,000; low: $1,000).
Purpose and activities: To administer trust funds for charitable, educational, and civic purposes. Grants for educational institutions, scholarships, family and child welfare, health services and hospitals, the arts, and community development.
Types of support: Operating budgets, seed money, emergency funds, building funds, equipment, land acquisition, special projects, matching funds, consulting services, technical assistance, research, publications, conferences and seminars, general purposes, renovation projects, student aid, exchange programs, endowment funds, internships, professorships.
Limitations: Giving limited to Erie County, NY; scholarships awarded to local residents only. No grants for annual campaigns or deficit financing; no loans.
Publications: Annual report (including application guidelines), application guidelines, informational brochure, newsletter, program policy statement, 990-PF.
Application information: Application forms required only for scholarships, and must be requested between Mar. 1 and May 10. Application form not required.
Initial approach: Proposal
Copies of proposal: 1
Deadline(s): Last business day of Mar., June, Sept., and Dec.; May 10 for scholarships
Board meeting date(s): 1st Wednesday of Feb., May, Aug., and Nov.
Final notification: 1st meeting after submission
Write: William L. Van Schoonhoven, Dir.
Officers: Richard B. McCormick, Chair.; Mrs. Warren W. Lane, Vice-Chair; William L. Van Schoonhoven, Dir. and Secy.
Governing Committee: Ronald J. Anthony, Mrs. Robert S. Grantham, Edwin Polokoff, John T. Smythe, Paul A. Willax.
Trustee Banks: Key Trust Co., Manufacturers and Traders Trust Co., Marine Bank West, Norstar Bank, N.A.
Number of staff: 2 full-time professional; 2 part-time professional; 2 full-time support; 1 part-time support.
Employer Identification Number: 160743935

4165
Henrietta B. & Frederick H. Bugher Foundation
c/o Davis, Polk & Wardwell
One Chase Manhattan Plaza, 39th Fl.
New York 10022

Established in 1961 in DC.
Donor(s): Frederick McLean Bugher.†
Foundation type: Independent
Financial data (yr. ended 12/31/88): Assets, $21,042,173 (M); expenditures, $1,358,842, including $1,157,959 for 3 grants (high: $581,530; low: $5,000).
Purpose and activities: Giving limited to cardiovascular research.
Types of support: Research.
Application information:
Initial approach: Letter
Deadline(s): None
Write: D. Nelson Adams, Trustee
Trustees: D. Nelson Adams, Daniel N. Adams, Jr., Robert A. Robinson, Douglas R. Smith.
Agent: Crestar Bank, N.A.
Number of staff: None.
Employer Identification Number: 526034266

4166
Bulova Fund, Inc. ⌑
c/o Maurice Silberman
Two Park Ave.
New York 10016

Incorporated in 1955 in NY.
Donor(s): Members of the Bulova family.
Foundation type: Independent
Financial data (yr. ended 12/31/88): Assets, $7,091,171 (M); expenditures, $525,333, including $480,000 for 1 grant.
Purpose and activities: Giving for a school of watchmaking; some support also for higher education.
Limitations: Giving primarily in the New York, NY, metropolitan area. No grants to individuals.
Application information: Contributes only to pre-selected organizations. Applications not accepted.
Officers and Directors: Harry Henshel, Pres.; Peter Gale, V.P.; Edward Gale, Secy.; Joy Henshel, Treas.; Paul B. Guilden, Dayle Henshel, Dr. Martin Moed.
Employer Identification Number: 131974650

4167
The Arde Bulova Memorial Fund, Inc. ⌑
1081 Palmer Ave.
Larchmont 10538

Established in 1962.
Donor(s): Louise B. Guilden.
Foundation type: Independent
Financial data (yr. ended 12/31/88): Assets, $1,500,178 (M); expenditures, $71,707, including $65,000 for 4 grants (high: $18,750; low: $13,750).
Purpose and activities: Giving primarily for higher education and the handicapped.
Types of support: Operating budgets, research, special projects.
Limitations: Giving primarily in NY. No grants to individuals.
Application information:
Initial approach: Letter or proposal
Final notification: Notification only for postive response
Write: Joseph P. Catera, Secy.
Officers and Directors: Paul B. Guilden, Pres.; Edward M. Gale, V.P.; Joseph P. Catera, Secy.; Peter Gale, Treas.; Joan G. Gale, Ben Lipton.
Employer Identification Number: 136117194

4168
Charles E. Burchfield Foundation, Inc.
210 Convention Tower
Buffalo 14202 (716) 853-7338

Incorporated in 1966 in NY.
Donor(s): Charles E. Burchfield.†
Foundation type: Independent
Financial data (yr. ended 12/31/88): Assets, $2,317,220 (M); expenditures, $178,051, including $130,000 for 10 grants (high: $100,000; low: $500; average: $2,500-$20,000).
Purpose and activities: Support for Lutheran religious and charitable organizations, including a local program for disadvantaged youth and international programs for relief and medical assistance.
Types of support: Operating budgets, continuing support, building funds, matching funds.
Limitations: Giving primarily in NY, CA, and DE.
Publications: Annual report.
Application information:
Initial approach: Letter
Deadline(s): None
Board meeting date(s): Spring and fall
Write: Robert J. Schutrum, Sr., Treas.
Officers and Trustees: C. Arthur Burchfield, Pres.; Sally Hill, V.P.; Robert D. Mustain, Secy.;

Robert J. Schutrum, Sr., Treas.; Violet Burchfield, George Hill.
Number of staff: 1 full-time professional; 2 part-time professional.
Employer Identification Number: 166073522

4169
Florence V. Burden Foundation
630 Fifth Ave., Suite 2900
New York 10111 (212) 332-1150

Incorporated in 1967 in NY.
Donor(s): Florence V. Burden,† and members of her family.
Foundation type: Independent
Financial data (yr. ended 12/31/89): Assets, $12,681,030 (M); expenditures, $994,535, including $635,193 for grants (average: $5,000-$50,000).
Purpose and activities: Support primarily in two fields of concentration: 1) Aging: family caregivers, employment, and voluntarism and 2) Crime and justice: violence prevention for young children, elder abuse, and children of incarcerated women.
Types of support: Seed money, special projects, research.
Limitations: No grants to individuals, or for capital or endowment funds, operating expenses, annual campaigns, emergency funds, deficit financing, scholarships, fellowships, or matching gifts; no loans.
Publications: Annual report (including application guidelines).
Application information: Proposals accepted for crime and justice and aging programs only.
Initial approach: Letter stating concept briefly (maximum 5 pages)
Copies of proposal: 1
Board meeting date(s): 3 times annually
Write: Barbara R. Greenberg, Exec. Dir.
Officers and Directors:* Marvin Bower, Chair.; Edward P.H. Burden,* Secy.; Margaret B. Urden,* Treas.; Barbara R. Greenberg,* Exec. Dir.; Robert R. Barker, Carter Burden, Margaret L. Burden, Ordway P. Burden, Susan L. Burden, Robert F. Higgins, John W. Holman, Jr., Florence C. Macdonald, William L. Musser, Jr., Stephen R. Petschek, John H. Watts III.
Number of staff: None.
Employer Identification Number: 136224125

4170
Alfred G. Burnham Donor Fund, Inc. ⌑
c/o Schlossberg Natale & Ahrenstein
41 East 42nd St.
New York 10017-5201

Incorporated in 1953 in NY.
Donor(s): Alfred G. Burnham,† Rae O. Burnham.
Foundation type: Independent
Financial data (yr. ended 10/31/88): Assets, $3,348,247 (M); expenditures, $178,853, including $168,000 for 37 grants (high: $17,500; low: $500).
Purpose and activities: Grants largely for higher education, medical research, Jewish welfare funds, and population control. Grants only to established charities.
Limitations: No grants to individuals, or for building or endowment funds, or special projects.
Application information:
Initial approach: Letter
Board meeting date(s): Sept. or Oct.
Officers and Directors: Rae O. Burnham, Pres.; Patrick J. James, V.P.; John Oppenheimer, Secy.-Treas.; Elizabeth P. Nevins, Alicia B. Winslow.
Employer Identification Number: 136097278

4171
The Charitable Foundation of the Burns Family, Inc. ⌑
c/o Allen & Brown
295 Madison Ave., Suite 1228
New York 10017

Established in 1962 in NY.
Donor(s): Randal B. Borough.
Foundation type: Independent
Financial data (yr. ended 11/30/88): Assets, $1,947,355 (M); expenditures, $135,947, including $74,650 for 39 grants (high: $10,000; low: $500).
Purpose and activities: Support for education, religious giving, hospitals, and social services.
Types of support: Building funds.
Limitations: No grants to individuals.
Application information:
Initial approach: Letter
Deadline(s): None
Write: Randal B. Borough, Pres.
Officers: Randal B. Borough, Pres.; William J. Burns, V.P.; William J. Ennis, Secy.; Jeremiah E. Brown, Treas.
Directors: D. Bruce Burns, George E.B. King.
Employer Identification Number: 136114052

4172
Jacob Burns Foundation, Inc. ⌑
c/o Jacob Burns
60 East 42nd St.
New York 10165 (212) 867-0949

Incorporated in 1957 in NY.
Donor(s): Mary Elizabeth Hood,† Jacob Burns, Rosalie A. Goldberg.
Foundation type: Independent
Financial data (yr. ended 12/31/88): Assets, $10,252,109 (M); gifts received, $360,517; expenditures, $740,571, including $663,022 for 69 grants (high: $190,840; low: $100).
Purpose and activities: Giving primarily for education, Jewish organizations, law and civil rights organizations, cultural programs, and hospitals and medical research.
Limitations: Giving primarily in NY. No grants to individuals.
Application information: Contributes only to pre-selected organizations. Applications not accepted.
Officers: Jacob Burns, Pres. and Treas.; Rosalie A. Goldberg, V.P. and Secy.
Employer Identification Number: 136114245

4173
The Burrows Foundation, Inc. ⌑ ☆
Ten Rockefeller Plaza, Suite 710
New York 10020

Established in 1954.
Donor(s): Real Estate Industrials, Inc., Sam Spatt Foundation, Inc.
Foundation type: Independent
Financial data (yr. ended 5/31/89): Assets, $22,912 (M); gifts received, $120,036; expenditures, $115,856, including $114,938 for 54 grants (high: $43,153; low: $50).
Purpose and activities: Support primarily for hospitals and medical research, Jewish welfare funds and temples, education, and cultural programs, including museums.
Limitations: No grants to individuals.
Application information: Contributes only to pre-selected organizations. Applications not accepted.
Officers: Selig S. Burrows, Pres.; Jonathan L. Burrows, V.P.; Kenneth D. Burrows, V.P.; Gladys Burrows, Treas.
Employer Identification Number: 132709563

4174
Edward H. Butler Foundation ⌑
161 Marine Dr., Apt. 5D
Buffalo 14202-4213

Established in 1957 in NY.
Donor(s): Kate Butler Wallis.
Foundation type: Independent
Financial data (yr. ended 12/31/87): Assets, $1,186,584 (M); expenditures, $86,921, including $70,000 for 24 grants (high: $10,000; low: $500).
Purpose and activities: Support primarily for higher and secondary education; support also for hospitals.
Limitations: Giving primarily in NY.
Application information: Contributes only to pre-selected organizations. Applications not accepted.
Write: Kate Butler Wallis, Trustee
Trustees: Kate R. Gardner, Edward B. Righter, Paul S. Schoellkopf, Kate Butler Wallis.
Employer Identification Number: 166019785

4175
J. E. & Z. B. Butler Foundation, Inc. ⌑ ☆
c/o Jack E. Butler
888 Park Ave.
New York 10021

Established in 1958.
Donor(s): Zella Butler.
Foundation type: Independent
Financial data (yr. ended 12/31/87): Assets, $1,415,281 (M); gifts received, $172,313; expenditures, $71,368, including $63,202 for 128 grants (high: $9,000; low: $25).
Purpose and activities: Giving primarily for health and hospitals, higher and other education, arts and culture, and Jewish organizations.
Limitations: Giving primarily in New York, NY.
Application information: Contributes only to pre-selected organizations. Applications not accepted.
Officers: Jack E. Butler, Pres.; Zella Butler, Treas.
Employer Identification Number: 136082916

4176
J. Homer Butler Foundation
P.O. Box 1841
Old Chelsea Station
New York 10011 (212) 242-7340
Additional tel.: (718) 209-2254

Incorporated in 1961 in NY.
Donor(s): Mabel A. Tod.†
Foundation type: Independent
Financial data (yr. ended 12/31/89): Assets, $3,202,558 (M); expenditures, $195,540, including $144,250 for 56 grants (high: $10,100; low: $600; average: $2,500).
Purpose and activities: Grants to Roman Catholic missions and religious orders to help improve the quality of life for the sick in the missions, especially those afflicted with leprosy.
Types of support: Continuing support, emergency funds, equipment, general purposes, scholarship funds, special projects.
Publications: Informational brochure (including application guidelines).
Application information: Application form required.
Initial approach: Letter
Copies of proposal: 1
Deadline(s): June 30 and Dec. 31
Board meeting date(s): 1st Tuesday in Mar.
Write: Geraldine Fremer, Secy.-Treas.
Officers and Directors:* Rev. Joseph J. Walter, S.J.,* Pres.; Robert T. Ross,* V.P.; Geraldine Fremer,* Secy.-Treas.; Rev. Edwin J. Brooks, S.J., Daniel H. Coleman, M.D., Martha S. Collin, Rev. Timothy A. Curtin, S.J., Peter F. DeGaetano, Sr. Ann Edgar, Fausto Gonzalez, William F. Hibberd, Rev. James F. Keenan, Joan MacLean, F. Patrick Rogers, Rev. Henry J. Zenorini, S.J.
Number of staff: None.
Employer Identification Number: 136126669

4177
The Bydale Foundation ⌑
299 Park Ave., 17th Fl.
New York 10171 (212) 207-1968

Incorporated in 1965 in DE.
Donor(s): James P. Warburg.†
Foundation type: Independent
Financial data (yr. ended 12/31/88): Assets, $8,721,881 (M); expenditures, $624,327, including $514,750 for 61 grants (high: $50,000; low: $500; average: $2,500-$15,000).
Purpose and activities: Emphasis on international understanding, public policy research, environmental quality, cultural programs, the law and civil rights, social services, higher education, and economics.
Types of support: Operating budgets, continuing support, seed money, matching funds, research, publications, conferences and seminars, special projects, general purposes.
Limitations: No grants to individuals, or for annual campaigns, emergency funds, deficit financing, endowment funds, demonstration projects, capital funds, scholarships, or fellowships; no loans.
Application information: Application form not required.
Initial approach: Letter or proposal
Copies of proposal: 1
Deadline(s): Submit proposal preferably in July or Aug.; deadline Nov. 1
Board meeting date(s): June, Nov., and Dec.
Final notification: 2 or 3 weeks
Write: Milton D. Solomon, V.P.
Officers: Joan M. Warburg,* Pres.; Milton D. Solomon,* V.P. and Secy.; Frank J. Kick, Treas.
Trustees:* Sarah W. Bliumis, James P. Warburg, Jr., Jenny Warburg, Philip N. Warburg.
Number of staff: 1 part-time professional.
Employer Identification Number: 136195286

4178
The C.I.T. Foundation, Inc. ⌑
c/o The C.I.T. Group Holding, Inc.
135 West 50th St.
New York 10020 (212) 408-6000

Incorporated in 1955 in NY.
Donor(s): C.I.T. Financial Corp., and its subsidiaries.
Foundation type: Company-sponsored
Financial data (yr. ended 12/31/88): Assets, $132,227 (M); gifts received, $150,000; expenditures, $207,551, including $199,279 for 128 grants (high: $6,550; low: $25) and $7,500 for 3 employee matching gifts of $2,500 each.
Purpose and activities: Support largely for community funds and education.
Types of support: Employee matching gifts.
Limitations: Giving limited to areas of company operations. No grants to individuals.
Application information:
Initial approach: Letter
Deadline(s): None
Write: Jay Simons, Asst. Secy.
Officers: Albert R. Gamper, Jr., Pres. and C.E.O.; J.A. Pollicino, Exec. V.P.; John J. Carroll, V.P. and Treas.; W. Baranoff, V.P.; H.A. Ittleson, V.P.; W.M. O'Grady, V.P.; T.J. O'Rourke, V.P.
Number of staff: 1 part-time professional; 1 part-time support.
Employer Identification Number: 136083856

4180
The Louis Calder Foundation ▼
230 Park Ave., Rm. 1530
New York 10169 (212) 687-1680

Trust established in 1951 in NY.
Donor(s): Louis Calder.†
Foundation type: Independent
Financial data (yr. ended 10/31/89): Assets, $103,739,111 (M); expenditures, $5,495,395, including $4,483,500 for 166 grants (high: $200,000; low: $2,000; average: $15,000-$50,000).
Purpose and activities: To support mainly those programs deemed best calculated to promote health, education, and welfare of New York City residents through grants to established organizations. Current programs are designed to enhance the potential and increase self-sufficiency of children, youth, and their families.
Types of support: Operating budgets, equipment, special projects, research, scholarship funds, general purposes.
Limitations: Giving primarily in New York, NY. No support for publicly-operated educational or medical institutions, private foundations, or governmental organizations; cultural grants only to well-known and established institutions. No grants to individuals; generally no grants for building or endowment funds, capital development, or continuing support.
Publications: Annual report (including application guidelines).
Application information: Application form not required.
Initial approach: Letter to the attention of the Trustees (one- to three-pages)
Copies of proposal: 1
Deadline(s): Submit proposal between Nov. 1 and Mar. 31; deadline five months prior to end of organization's fiscal year or Apr. 1, whichever is earliest
Board meeting date(s): As required
Final notification: July 31
Write: The Trustees
Trustees: Paul R. Brenner, Peter D. Calder, Manufacturers Hanover Trust Co.
Number of staff: 2 full-time support.
Employer Identification Number: 136015562

4181
The Ed Lee and Jean Campe Foundation, Inc. ⌑
c/o U.S. Trust Co. of New York
114 West 47th St.
New York 10036-1532

Incorporated in 1944 in NY.
Donor(s): Ed Lee Campe,† Jean Campe.†
Foundation type: Independent
Financial data (yr. ended 12/31/86): Assets, $1,395,858 (M); expenditures, $136,398, including $123,260 for grants (high: $15,000; average: $100-$5,000).
Purpose and activities: Giving largely for higher education, including scholarship funds and musical education, community funds, Jewish welfare funds, and youth and social service agencies.
Types of support: Scholarship funds, general purposes, continuing support, building funds, endowment funds, special projects.
Limitations: Giving primarily in NY. No grants to individuals, or for matching gifts; no loans.
Application information: Application form not required.
Initial approach: Letter
Copies of proposal: 1
Deadline(s): Submit proposal between Jan. and Mar.
Board meeting date(s): Apr.
Write: Henry Kohn, Pres.
Officers and Directors: Henry Kohn, Pres.; Anne F. Kohn, V.P.; Herbert A. Schneider, Secy.
Number of staff: None.
Employer Identification Number: 136123939

4182
B. G. Cantor Art Foundation
One World Trade Ctr., Suite 10500
New York 10048

Established in 1967 in NY.
Donor(s): B.G. Cantor, Iris Cantor.
Foundation type: Operating
Financial data (yr. ended 4/30/88): Assets, $4,190,920 (M); gifts received, $1,171,645; expenditures, $2,936,146, including $2,703,224 for grants.
Purpose and activities: Support for exhibits and studies of the work of Rodin.
Application information: Contributes only to pre-selected organizations. Applications not accepted.

Officers: B.G. Cantor,* Pres. and Treas.; Harry Needleman, Secy.
Trustees:* Peter Bing, Iris Cantor, Michele Labozzetta, Michael Spero.
Employer Identification Number: 136227347

4183
Iris & B. Gerald Cantor Foundation ⌑ ☆
c/o Joel Rothstein
One World Trade Ctr., Suite 10500
New York 10048

Established in 1959 in CA.
Donor(s): B. Gerald Cantor, Iris Cantor.
Foundation type: Independent
Financial data (yr. ended 11/30/88): Assets, $1,193,204 (M); gifts received, $1,300,000; expenditures, $1,559,469, including $1,559,002 for 45 grants (high: $550,877; low: $25).
Purpose and activities: Support for hospitals and clinics, including a cancer care center; support also for Jewish welfare organizations, higher education, and health associations.
Application information: Contributes only to pre-selected organizations. Applications not accepted.
Officers: Iris Cantor,* Pres.; B. Gerald Cantor,* V.P.; Harry Needleman, Secy.; Suzanne Fisher,* Treas.
Trustees:* Michael Spero.
Employer Identification Number: 956038007

4184
Cantor, Fitzgerald Foundation ⌑
One World Trade Ctr., Suite 10500
New York 10048

Established in 1982 in NY.
Donor(s): Cantor Fitzgerald Securities Corp.
Foundation type: Company-sponsored
Financial data (yr. ended 12/31/88): Assets, $570,567 (M); gifts received, $200,000; expenditures, $154,360, including $153,915 for 71 grants (high: $25,000; low: $100).
Purpose and activities: Emphasis on Jewish organizations, including charities, cultural and community affairs, and the arts.
Limitations: Giving primarily in NY and CA.
Officers: B. Gerald Cantor,* Pres.; Harry Needleman, Secy.; Joel Rothstein, Treas.
Directors:* James M. Avena, Rod Fisher.
Employer Identification Number: 133117872

4185
Capital Cities/ABC Foundation, Inc. ▼ ⌑
77 West 66th St., Rm. 16-15
New York 10023 (212) 456-7498

Incorporated in 1974 in DE.
Donor(s): Capital Cities Communications, Inc.
Foundation type: Company-sponsored
Financial data (yr. ended 01/01/89): Assets, $1,699,604 (M); gifts received, $1,800,000; expenditures, $1,686,937, including $1,684,125 for 222 grants (high: $100,000; low: $325; average: $1,000-$20,000).
Purpose and activities: Grants for higher education, hospitals, health agencies, and local minority development; some support for social service agencies, civic affairs, communications, cultural programs, and youth agencies.
Limitations: Giving primarily in areas where company properties are located. No grants to individuals, or for building funds.
Application information: Contributes only to pre-selected organizations. Applications not accepted.
Board meeting date(s): Quarterly
Write: Bernadette Longford-Williams, Contribs. Admin.
Officers: Thomas S. Murphy, Pres.; Daniel B. Burke, V.P. and Treas.; Andrew E. Jackson, V.P.
Employer Identification Number: 237443020

4186
Carbonel Foundation
c/o White & Case
1115 Ave. of the Americas
New York 10036
Application address: c/o Joint Foundation Support, 40 West 20th St., 10th Fl., New York, NY 10011; Tel.: (212) 627-7710

Established in 1979 in NY and DE.
Foundation type: Independent
Financial data (yr. ended 12/31/88): Assets, $256,842 (M); gifts received, $179,465; expenditures, $195,156, including $151,660 for 17 grants (high: $12,660; low: $6,000; average: $6,000-$10,000).
Purpose and activities: Areas of giving limited to advocacy projects in three categories: families in crisis, U.S. foreign policy in Central America, and disarmament and human needs.
Types of support: General purposes.
Limitations: No grants to individuals, or for research.
Publications: Biennial report.
Application information: Application form not required.
Initial approach: Letter
Deadline(s): None
Write: Nanette Falkenberg, Pres., Joint Foundation Support
Officer: C. Sims Farr, V.P.
Employer Identification Number: 133006358

4187
Carnahan-Jackson Foundation
Fourth and Pine Bldg.
Jamestown 14701 (716) 483-1015
Additional address: P.O. Box 3326, Jamestown, NY 14702-3326

Trust established in 1972 in NY.
Donor(s): Katharine J. Carnahan.†
Foundation type: Independent
Financial data (yr. ended 7/31/89): Assets, $9,408,883 (M); expenditures, $585,335, including $506,672 for 35 grants (high: $100,000; low: $1,000).
Purpose and activities: Grants for higher and other education, hospitals and the handicapped, ecology, housing, youth agencies, community development, and church support; some support for certain prior interests of the donor.
Types of support: Annual campaigns, building funds, capital campaigns, continuing support, equipment, general purposes, lectureships, matching funds, scholarship funds, seed money, special projects.
Limitations: Giving primarily in western NY, particularly Chautauqua County. No grants to individuals.
Publications: Application guidelines, grants list.
Application information: Application form required.
Initial approach: Letter outlining needs and use of grant
Copies of proposal: 2
Deadline(s): Apr. 30 and Sept. 30
Board meeting date(s): June and Nov.
Write: David H. Carnahan, Exec. Secy.
Advisory Committee: David H. Carnahan,* Exec. Secy.; John D. Hamilton, Samuel P. Price, Rebecca Robbins, Carole W. Sellstrom.
Trustees:* Chase Lincoln First Bank, N.A.
Number of staff: 1 part-time professional; 1 part-time support.
Employer Identification Number: 166151608

4188
Carnegie Corporation of New York ▼
437 Madison Ave.
New York 10022 (212) 371-3200

Incorporated in 1911 in NY.
Donor(s): Andrew Carnegie.†
Foundation type: Independent
Financial data (yr. ended 09/30/89): Assets, $905,106,313 (M); expenditures, $47,587,022, including $37,087,461 for grants and $2,218,568 for foundation-administered programs.
Purpose and activities: The advancement and diffusion of knowledge and understanding among the peoples of the U.S. and of certain countries that are or have been members of the British overseas Commonwealth. In 1984 the foundation announced four program goals: 1) The avoidance of nuclear war and improvement in U.S.-Soviet relations through support for science-based analyses of ways in which the risk of nuclear war can be diminished and for efforts to ensure that the results of such analyses are widely known and understood. This program emphasizes the mobilization of the best possible intellectual, technical, and moral resources to work toward this objective. 2) The education of all Americans, especially youth, for a scientifically and technologically based economy, linking the movement for education reform to changes in society and the economy. This program draws upon the Corporation's past interests in the education of children, youth, and adults and particularly its commitment to equity for women and members of minority groups. 3) The prevention of damage to children from birth through early adolescence. This program focuses on ways to prevent the development of serious problems for children and young teenagers, primarily school failure and school-age pregnancy and secondarily childhood injury and substance abuse. It continues the foundation's interests in early education and child care. 4) Strengthening human resources in developing countries. This program aims to engage the scientific and scholarly communities in the U.S. and developing countries in this effort and to heighten American understanding of Third World development. Giving primarily to academic and research institutions.

Types of support: Operating budgets, continuing support, seed money, program-related investments, special projects, research, publications, conferences and seminars, exchange programs, general purposes, fellowships.
Limitations: Giving primarily in the U.S. Some grants in Sub-Saharan Africa, South Africa, and the Caribbean. No support for the arts, operating budgets of educational institutions or day care centers, or general support for social service agencies. No grants for annual campaigns, deficit financing, capital, building, or endowment funds, scholarships, or matching gifts.
Publications: Annual report, informational brochure, newsletter, grants list, occasional report.
Application information: Application form not required.
Initial approach: Telephone or letter
Deadline(s): None
Board meeting date(s): Oct., Jan., Apr., and June
Final notification: 6 months
Write: Dorothy W. Knapp, Secy.
Officers: David A. Hamburg,* Pres.; Barbara D. Finberg, Exec. V.P. and Prog. Chair., Special Projects; Dorothy W. Knapp, Secy.; Cynthia E. Merritt, Asst. Secy.; Jeanmarie C. Grisi, Assoc. Treas.
Trustees:* Warren Christopher, Chair.; Fred M. Hechinger, Vice-Chair.; Richard I. Beattie, James P. Comer, Eugene H. Cota-Robles, Richard B. Fisher, James Lowell Gibbs, Jr., Joshua Lederberg, Ray Marshall, Mary Patterson McPherson, Newton N. Minow, Robert E. Rubin, Laurence A. Tisch, Thomas A. Troyer, John C. Whitehead, Sheila E. Widnall.
Number of staff: 56 full-time professional; 6 part-time professional; 17 full-time support; 1 part-time support.
Employer Identification Number: 131628151

4189
The Carter-Wallace Foundation ⌑
767 Fifth Ave.
New York 10153 (212) 758-4500

Established in 1986 in NY.
Donor(s): Carter-Wallace, Inc.
Foundation type: Company-sponsored
Financial data (yr. ended 3/31/89): Assets, $1,657,371 (M); gifts received, $1,380,000; expenditures, $882,050, including $881,360 for 154 grants (high: $46,000; low: $20).
Purpose and activities: Support primarily for the arts, health and hospitals, welfare, and higher education.
Types of support: General purposes, capital campaigns, endowment funds, annual campaigns.
Limitations: Giving primarily in NY and NJ. No grants to individuals.
Application information: Contributes only to pre-selected organizations. Applications not accepted.
Officers: Henry H. Hoyt, Jr., Pres.; Charles O. Hoyt, Secy.; Daniel J. Black, Treas.; James L. Wagar, Mgr.
Employer Identification Number: 133359226

4190
The Thomas & Agnes Carvel Foundation ⌑
201 Saw Mill River Rd.
Yonkers 10701 (914) 969-7200

Established in 1976 in NY.
Donor(s): Thomas Carvel, Agnes Carvel.
Foundation type: Independent
Financial data (yr. ended 11/30/88): Assets, $10,645,034 (M); expenditures, $500,288, including $455,000 for 40 grants (high: $100,000; low: $1,000).
Purpose and activities: Support for general charitable purposes, including nutrition research, youth programs, and Protestant churches.
Application information:
Initial approach: Letter
Deadline(s): Oct. 1
Write: Mildred Arcadipane, Secy.
Officers and Directors: Thomas Carvel, Pres.; Mildred Arcadipane, Secy.; Agnes Carvel, Robert Davis, Robert Ettlinger.
Employer Identification Number: 132879673

4191
Mary Flagler Cary Charitable Trust ▼
350 Fifth Ave., Rm. 6622
New York 10118 (212) 563-6860

Trust established in 1968 in NY.
Donor(s): Mary Flagler Cary.†
Foundation type: Independent
Financial data (yr. ended 06/30/89): Assets, $108,730,334 (M); expenditures, $7,527,950, including $6,359,191 for 85 grants (high: $2,387,796; low: $3,000; average: $15,000-$50,000).
Purpose and activities: "The trust entertains grant proposals in three areas: 1) for music in New York City (including institutional support for the performance, commissioning, and recording of contemporary music and support for community music schools and other institutions which provide basic music training for children and young people); 2) for the conservation of natural resources on the Atlantic and Gulf coastlines (particularly the preservation of coastal barrier islands and associated wetlands, with grant funds directed toward land acquisition, legal defense, and citizen action); and 3) for urban environmental programs in New York City (support for community initiatives and to help develop local leadership to work on environmental problems within low-income neighborhoods of the city). The balance of the trust's grant budget is devoted primarily to support for The Mary Flagler Cary Arboretum and its Institute of Ecosystem Studies in Millbrook, NY."
Types of support: Operating budgets, continuing support, land acquisition, matching funds, special projects, program-related investments, general purposes.
Limitations: Giving limited to New York, NY, for music and the urban environment, and the eastern coastal states for conservation. No support for private foundations, hospitals, religious organizations, primary or secondary schools, colleges and universities, libraries, or museums. No grants to individuals, or for scholarships, fellowships, capital funds, annual campaigns, seed money, emergency funds, deficit financing, or endowment funds; no loans to individuals.
Publications: Multi-year report, informational brochure (including application guidelines), grants list.
Application information: Application form not required.
Initial approach: Letter with brief proposal
Copies of proposal: 1
Deadline(s): None
Board meeting date(s): Monthly
Final notification: 2 months
Write: Edward A. Ames, Trustee
Trustees: Edward A. Ames, William R. Grant, Phyllis J. Mills.
Number of staff: 2 full-time professional; 1 full-time support.
Employer Identification Number: 136266964

4192
Sophia & William Casey Foundation ⌑ ☆
c/o Steven T. Rosenberg
201 Moreland Rd., Suite 10
Hauppauge 11788

Established in 1974.
Donor(s): William J. Casey.†
Foundation type: Independent
Financial data (yr. ended 11/30/88): Assets, $562,243 (M); expenditures, $185,776, including $176,500 for 38 grants (high: $50,000; low: $500).
Purpose and activities: Support for a home for unwed mothers, Catholic organizations, and international affairs.
Limitations: No grants to individuals.
Officers: Sophia Casey, Pres. and Treas.; Bernadette Casey Smith, V.P. and Secy.
Employer Identification Number: 510153218

4193
CBS Foundation Inc.
c/o CBS Inc.
51 West 52nd St.
New York 10019 (212) 975-5791

Incorporated in 1953 in NY.
Donor(s): CBS Inc.
Foundation type: Company-sponsored
Financial data (yr. ended 12/31/89): Assets, $7,394,500 (M); gifts received, $819,600; expenditures, $204,600, including $195,500 for 3 grants (high: $100,000; low: $3,500; average: $10,000-$50,000).
Purpose and activities: Grants primarily for education, including higher education, education for minorities, and libraries; cultural affairs, especially the performing and fine arts; civic affairs; and journalism.
Types of support: Annual campaigns, continuing support, general purposes, operating budgets, research.
Limitations: Giving primarily in areas of company operations and for national programs, including New York, NY; Philadelphia, PA; Los Angeles, CA; Chicago, IL; Miami, FL; and St. Louis, MO. No grants to individuals, or for building or endowment funds, or matching gifts; no loans.
Application information: Application form not required.
Initial approach: Letter

Copies of proposal: 1
Deadline(s): None
Board meeting date(s): Quarterly and as required
Final notification: 4-6 months
Write: Helen M. Brown, Pres. and Exec. Dir.
Officers: Helen M. Brown, Pres. and Exec. Dir.; Joseph Castellano, Secy.; Louis J. Rauchenberger, Treas.
Directors: Newton H. Minow, Chair.; Michel C. Bergerac, Walter L. Cronkite, Roswell L. Gilpatric, Franklin A. Thomas, Preston R. Tisch.
Number of staff: None.
Employer Identification Number: 136099759

4194
Centennial Foundation ¤
c/o Joel E. Sammet & Co.
19 Rector St.
New York 10006

Incorporated in 1965 in NY.
Donor(s): Henry H. Arnhold, Arnold S. Bleienroeder, and others.
Foundation type: Independent
Financial data (yr. ended 12/31/87): Assets, $1,622,625 (M); gifts received, $219,989; expenditures, $194,575, including $187,410 for 125 grants (high: $25,000; low: $100).
Purpose and activities: Giving for hospitals and health agencies, international relations, community development, the performing arts, and education.
Limitations: Giving primarily in New York, NY.
Application information: Contributes only to pre-selected organizations. Applications not accepted.
Officers: Stephen M. Kellen, Chair.; Henry H. Arnhold,* Pres.
Trustees:* Michael Kellen, Gilbert Kerlin.
Employer Identification Number: 136189397

4195
The Central National-Gottesman Foundation ¤
100 Park Ave.
New York 10017
Scholarship application address: Harold R. Doughty, Central National-Gottesman Foundation, P.O. Box 909, Cooper Station, New York, NY 10276

Established in 1981 in NY.
Donor(s): Central National Corp., Gottesman & Co., Inc.
Foundation type: Company-sponsored
Financial data (yr. ended 12/31/87): Assets, $3,093,665 (M); expenditures, $141,533, including $58,850 for 12 grants (high: $33,000; low: $300) and $50,207 for 9 grants to individuals (high: $11,750; low: $1,012).
Purpose and activities: Emphasis on research and higher education in the fields of paper and pulp, and forestry. Some giving also to Jewish organizations and to international organizations, particularly the United Nations. Also supports a scholarship program for children of company employees only.
Types of support: Employee-related scholarships.
Application information: Scholarship application form required; applicants must be children of employees.
Deadline(s): Scholarship deadlines vary with academic year
Officers: James G. Wallach, Pres.; Edgar Wachenheim III, Exec. V.P.; Peter C. Siegfried, Secy.; Benjamin Glowatz, Treas.
Employer Identification Number: 133047546

4196
Central New York Community Foundation, Inc. ▼
500 South Salina St., Suite 428
Syracuse 13202 (315) 422-9538

Incorporated in 1927 in NY; reorganized in 1951.
Foundation type: Community
Financial data (yr. ended 03/31/90): Assets, $14,849,546 (M); gifts received, $2,821,544; expenditures, $3,193,602, including $2,512,360 for 324 grants (average: $200-$15,000).
Purpose and activities: Grants primarily to existing agencies for health, welfare, educational, recreational, or cultural purposes.
Types of support: Seed money, building funds, equipment, special projects, matching funds, capital campaigns, technical assistance, renovation projects, consulting services, land acquisition, publications, research, scholarship funds.
Limitations: Giving limited to Onondaga and Madison counties, NY for general grants; giving in a wider area for donor-advised funds. No support for religious purposes. No grants to individuals, or for conferences and seminars, deficit financing, consulting services, endowment funds, fellowships, operating budgets, or travel expenses; no loans.
Publications: Annual report, application guidelines, newsletter, 990-PF.
Application information: Application form required.
Initial approach: Letter or telephone
Copies of proposal: 12
Deadline(s): 6 weeks before board meetings
Board meeting date(s): Mar., May, Sept., and Dec.
Final notification: Immediately following board meetings
Write: Margaret G. Ogden, Pres.
Officers: Margaret G. Ogden, Pres. and C.E.O.; Richard A. Russell,* Treas.
Directors:* Edward S. Green, Chair.; David J. Connor, 1st Vice-Chair.; Richard D. Horowitz, 2nd Vice-Chair.; Mary O. Cooper, Noreen R. Falcone, Maceo Felton, Burnett D. Haylor, Robert J. Hughes, Clarence L. Jordan, Theodore H. Northrup, Henry A. Panasci, Jr., Michael E. Rulison, Robert B. Salisbury, Miriam Swift, M.D., Jay W. Wason, Samuel W. Williams, Peggy Wood.
Number of staff: 2 full-time professional; 1 part-time professional; 1 full-time support.
Employer Identification Number: 150626910

4197
Dorothy Jordan Chadwick Fund ¤
c/o U.S. Trust Co. of New York
114 West 47th St.
New York 10036-1532 (212) 852-1000
Application address: Davidson Dawson & Clark, P.O. Box 298, New Canaan, CT 06840

Trust established in 1957 in NY.
Donor(s): Dorothy J. Chadwick,† Dorothy R. Kidder.
Foundation type: Independent
Financial data (yr. ended 5/31/88): Assets, $7,194,115 (M); gifts received, $198,000; expenditures, $533,989, including $462,038 for 32 grants (high: $158,000; low: $38).
Purpose and activities: Grants largely for the arts, including the performing arts; support also for higher education.
Limitations: Giving primarily in New York, NY, and Washington, DC.
Application information:
Initial approach: Letter
Copies of proposal: 1
Deadline(s): None
Board meeting date(s): As required
Write: Berkley D. Johnson, Jr., Trustee
Trustees: Berkley D. Johnson, Jr., U.S. Trust Co. of New York.
Employer Identification Number: 136069950

4198
The Sara Chait Memorial Foundation, Inc. ¤
860 Fifth Ave.
New York 10021 (212) 734-7894

Incorporated in 1959 in NY.
Donor(s): Abraham Chait,† Murray Backer,† Burton D. Chait, Marilyn Chait, and others.
Foundation type: Independent
Financial data (yr. ended 12/31/88): Assets, $2,142,118 (M); expenditures, $229,176, including $216,060 for 16 grants (high: $50,000; low: $500).
Purpose and activities: Grants to higher educational institutions to aid worthy students training primarily for careers in medicine; support also for medical research.
Limitations: Giving primarily in NY.
Application information:
Initial approach: Letter
Deadline(s): None
Write: Marilyn Chait, Secy.
Officers: Seymour Sobel, Pres.; Richard May, V.P.; Marilyn Chait, Secy.-Treas.
Employer Identification Number: 136121596

4199
Charina Foundation, Inc.
85 Broad St.
New York 10004

Incorporated in 1980 in NY.
Donor(s): Richard L. Menschel, The Menschel Foundation.
Foundation type: Independent
Financial data (yr. ended 8/31/89): Assets, $11,576,054 (M); expenditures, $532,915, including $504,602 for 244 grants (high: $85,000; low: $100; average: $500-$5,000).
Purpose and activities: Emphasis on arts and culture, including museums; support also for health services, medical research, and hospitals; higher and other education; Jewish organizations, including welfare funds; recreation; and community development.
Types of support: Annual campaigns, building funds, capital campaigns, endowment funds, matching funds, seed money.

Limitations: Giving primarily in NY. No grants to individuals.
Application information: Foundation depends almost exclusively on self-initiated grants. Applications not accepted.
Write: Richard L. Menschel, Pres.
Officers and Directors: Richard L. Menschel, Pres. and Treas.; Ronay Menschel, Secy.; Eugene P. Polk.
Number of staff: None.
Employer Identification Number: 133050294

4200
The Chase Manhattan Foundation ▼
c/o The Chase Manhattan Bank, N.A.
Two Chase Manhattan Plaza, 29th Fl.
New York 10081 (212) 552-8205

Incorporated in 1969 in NY.
Donor(s): The Chase Manhattan Bank, N.A.
Foundation type: Company-sponsored
Financial data (yr. ended 12/31/89): Assets, $2,900,492 (M); gifts received, $2,703,000; expenditures, $327,096, including $239,500 for 22 grants (high: $25,000; low: $2,500; average: $5,000-$10,000) and $67,056 for grants to individuals.
Purpose and activities: Grants primarily for child welfare, health care, hunger and disaster relief, education, and for community, economic, and human resource development by organizations that operate largely outside the continental U.S.; also funds an employee-related scholarship program.
Types of support: Operating budgets, continuing support, annual campaigns, seed money, emergency funds, general purposes, employee-related scholarships, special projects.
Limitations: Giving primarily for projects outside the U.S. in countries where the company has an office. No grants to individuals (except for scholarships to children of company employees), or for deficit financing, equipment, land acquisition, endowment funds, or matching gifts; no loans.
Publications: Annual report.
Application information: U.S. (except upstate NY) and foreign applicants: Philanthropic Activities Dept., Chase Manhattan Bank, N.A., 44 Wall St., 14th Fl., New York, NY 10005; Tel.: (212) 676-5081. Upstate NY applicants: Government Relations, Philanthropic Activities, Chase Lincoln First Bank, N.A., One Lincoln First Sq., Rochester, NY 14643; Tel.: (716) 258-5600. Application form required.
Initial approach: Letter or proposal
Copies of proposal: 1
Deadline(s): Submit proposal preferably in Jan. or June; deadline Oct. 1
Board meeting date(s): 3 times a year
Final notification: 6 months
Write: David S. Ford
Officers and Trustees:* Willard C. Butcher,* Pres.; Donald L. Boudreau,* V.P.; Thomas G. LaBrecque,* V.P.; Fraser P. Seitel,* V.P.; Francis X. Stankard,* V.P.; Elaine R. Bond, Richard J. Boyle, Robert R. Douglass, A. Wright Elliott, Michael P. Esposito, Jr., Joseph J. Harkins, Thomas C. Lynch, Arthur F. Ryan, John V. Scicutella, L. Edward Shaw, Jr., Charles A. Smith, Deborah L. Talbot, Michael Urkowitz, J. Richard Zecher.
Number of staff: None.
Employer Identification Number: 237049738

4201
Chautauqua Region Community Foundation, Inc.
104 Hotel Jamestown Mezzanine
Jamestown 14701 (716) 661-3390

Incorporated in 1978 in NY.
Foundation type: Community
Financial data (yr. ended 12/31/89): Assets, $11,038,733 (M); gifts received, $2,513,664; expenditures, $721,769, including $280,245 for 66 grants (high: $44,000; low: $200; average: $2,500-$12,000) and $264,759 for 300 grants to individuals (high: $3,000; low: $100; average: $800-$1,500).
Purpose and activities: Giving for cultural, educational, civic, and charitable projects; scholarships mainly for undergraduate study.
Types of support: Operating budgets, continuing support, seed money, emergency funds, equipment, publications, conferences and seminars, student aid, general purposes, renovation projects.
Limitations: Giving limited to the Chautauqua County, NY, area. No support for religious or sectarian purposes. No grants to individuals (except for scholarship grants); no loans.
Publications: Annual report (including application guidelines), informational brochure, newsletter, application guidelines.
Application information: 1 copy of proposal required for scholarships. Application form required.
Initial approach: Letter
Copies of proposal: 11
Deadline(s): Apr. 30 for scholarships; Nov. 30 for other grants
Board meeting date(s): Feb. for grants; July for scholarships
Final notification: Late Feb. for grants; late July for scholarships
Write: Francis E. Wakely, Exec. Dir.
Officers: Gregory L. Peterson,* Pres.; Marion Panzarella,* V.P.; Elizabeth S. Lenna,* Secy.; R. Michael Goldman,* Treas.; Francis E. Wakely, Exec. Dir.
Directors:* Craig P. Colburn, Russell L. Diethrick, Betty Erickson, Marilyn Gruel, Kenneth W. Strickler, Tyler C. Swanson.
Number of staff: 1 full-time professional; 1 part-time professional; 1 full-time support; 4 part-time support.
Employer Identification Number: 161116837

4202
The Chazen Foundation
543 North Broadway
Upper Nyack 10960

Established in 1985 in NY.
Donor(s): Jerome A. Chazen.
Foundation type: Independent
Financial data (yr. ended 12/31/88): Assets, $2,963,298 (M); expenditures, $560,638, including $519,947 for grants (high: $101,100) and $30,400 for 4 grants to individuals (high: $15,000; low: $5,000).
Purpose and activities: Giving primarily for Jewish welfare funds and other Jewish organizations; support also for social services, higher education, music, museums, and hospital building funds.
Types of support: Student aid.
Application information:
Initial approach: Letter
Deadline(s): None
Trustees: Jerome A. Chazen, Simona A. Chazen.
Number of staff: None.
Employer Identification Number: 133229474

4203
Owen Cheatham Foundation
540 Madison Ave.
New York 10022 (212) 753-4733

Incorporated in 1957 in NY as successor to Owen R. Cheatham Foundation, a trust established in 1934 in GA.
Donor(s): Owen Robertson Cheatham,† Celeste W. Cheatham.†
Foundation type: Independent
Financial data (yr. ended 12/31/88): Assets, $5,519,377 (M); expenditures, $388,145, including $198,295 for 52 grants (high: $37,500; low: $25; average: $1,000-$5,000).
Purpose and activities: Support primarily to assist programs that might not otherwise be achieved; grants mainly for education, health, the arts, and welfare.
Officers and Directors:* Celeste C. Weisglass,* Pres.; Stephen S. Weisglass,* V.P. and Treas.; Ilse C. Meckauer, Secy.; MacDonald Budd.
Employer Identification Number: 136097798

4204
Chehebar Family Foundation, Inc. ⌑
c/o Skiva International
1370 Broadway
New York 10018 (212) 736-9520

Donor(s): Albert Chehebar, Isaac Shehebar, Jack Chehebar, Rainbow Store, Inc.
Foundation type: Independent
Financial data (yr. ended 8/31/88): Assets, $316,555 (M); gifts received, $191,000; expenditures, $273,079, including $272,689 for 618 grants (high: $20,000; low: $10).
Purpose and activities: Giving primarily to Jewish organizations.
Application information: Contributes only to pre-selected organizations. Applications not accepted.
Write: Jack Chehebar, Dir.
Directors: Albert Chehebar, Jack Chehebar, Joseph Chehebar, Isaac Shehebar.
Employer Identification Number: 133178015

4205
Chemical New York Foundation ⌑
c/o Chemical Bank, Admin. Serv. Dept.
30 Rockefeller Plaza
New York 10112 (212) 621-2148

Established in 1982 in NY.
Foundation type: Company-sponsored
Financial data (yr. ended 12/31/88): Assets, $1,255,483 (M); gifts received, $175,000; expenditures, $51,145, including $50,000 for 3 grants (high: $25,000; low: $5,000).
Purpose and activities: Giving for a community center, a nursing home, and a health center.
Limitations: Giving primarily in New York, NY, area.

Application information:
Initial approach: Letter
Deadline(s): None
Write: Mrs. B. Strohmeier, Trust Officer, Chemical Bank
Trustee: Chemical Bank.
Employer Identification Number: 133039012

4206
I. Chera & Sons Foundation, Inc. ⌑
One Hoyt St.
Brooklyn 11201 (718) 643-2550

Established in 1985 in NY.
Donor(s): Issac Chera, Stanley Chera, Morris Chera.
Foundation type: Independent
Financial data (yr. ended 12/31/88): Assets, $2,047,694 (M); gifts received, $306,412; expenditures, $313,610, including $312,284 for 68 grants (high: $715,550; low: $36).
Purpose and activities: Support primarily for Jewish giving and Jewish welfare; support also for health agencies.
Application information:
Initial approach: Proposal
Deadline(s): None
Write: Issac Chera, Pres.
Officers: Issac Chera, Pres.; Stanley Chera, V.P.; Morris Chera, Secy.-Treas.
Employer Identification Number: 112721393

4207
Raymond Chera Family Foundation ⌑ ☆
617 West 181st St.
New York 10033

Established in 1988 in NY.
Donor(s): Charles Chera, Steven Chera, Arco Distributing, Inc.
Foundation type: Independent
Financial data (yr. ended 12/31/88): Assets, $2,032 (M); gifts received, $105,000; expenditures, $102,968, including $102,817 for 8 grants (high: $70,015; low: $52).
Purpose and activities: Support for Jewish giving, including temples and yeshivas.
Limitations: Giving limited to metropolitan New York, NY, area. No grants to individuals.
Application information: Contributes only to pre-selected organizations. Applications not accepted.
Directors: Charles Chera, Michael Chera, Raymond Chera, Steven Chera, Victor Chera.
Employer Identification Number: 117342002

4208
Chernoff Family Foundation, Inc. ⌑ ☆
90 Overlook Rd.
New Rochelle 10804

Established in 1986 in NY.
Donor(s): Edward Chernoff.
Foundation type: Independent
Financial data (yr. ended 12/31/88): Assets, $150,756 (M); gifts received, $280,000; expenditures, $325,471, including $325,270 for 86 grants (high: $116,765; low: $65).
Purpose and activities: Giving primarily for Jewish organizations, including welfare funds and educational institutions.
Limitations: Giving primarily in NY. No grants to individuals.
Application information: Contributes only to pre-selected organizations. Applications not accepted.
Officers: Edward Chernoff, Co-Pres.; Phyllis Chernoff, Co-Pres.
Employer Identification Number: 133384434

4209
Michael Chernow Trust f/b/o Charity Dated 3/13/75 ⌑
c/o Schapiro, Wisan & Krassner
122 East 42nd St.
New York 10168-0057

Trust established in 1975.
Foundation type: Independent
Financial data (yr. ended 6/30/88): Assets, $3,368,447 (M); expenditures, $255,859, including $201,000 for 11 grants (high: $50,000; low: $1,000).
Purpose and activities: Giving primarily for Jewish welfare funds, higher education, and health and medical research.
Application information: Application form not required.
Deadline(s): None
Trustees: Morris I. Chernofsky, Martin P. Krassner, Lynn A. Streim.
Employer Identification Number: 136758226

4210
Michael Chernow Trust for the Benefit of Charity Dated 4/16/68 ⌑
c/o Schapiro, Wisan & Krassner
122 East 42nd St.
New York 10168-0057

Trust established in 1968 in NY.
Foundation type: Independent
Financial data (yr. ended 6/30/89): Assets, $1,556,451 (M); expenditures, $173,600, including $134,834 for 13 grants (high: $50,000; low: $1,000).
Purpose and activities: Giving for Jewish welfare funds, medical education and research, including AIDS research, and a blood bank.
Limitations: Giving primarily in NY.
Application information: Application form not required.
Deadline(s): None
Trustees: Morris I. Chernofsky, Albert Krassner, Martin P. Krassner.
Employer Identification Number: 136758228

4211
Children's Foundation of Erie County, Inc. ⌑
c/o Lewis F. Hazel
292 Northwood Dr.
Buffalo 14223
Application address: 55 Rankin Rd., Snyder, NY 14226; Tel.: (716) 839-1095

Incorporated in 1836 in NY.
Foundation type: Independent
Financial data (yr. ended 12/31/88): Assets, $1,913,160 (M); expenditures, $117,160, including $107,950 for 34 grants (high: $7,500; low: $655).
Purpose and activities: Giving for needy children; grants for health services, clothing, camperships, day care, and disabled children.
Limitations: Giving limited to Erie County, NY. No grants to individuals.
Application information: Application form not required.
Initial approach: Proposal
Deadline(s): Jan. 15
Write: Mrs. Mary Howland, Grants Chair.
Officers: Calvin J. Haller, Pres.; Kevin I. Sullivan, V.P.; Charles J. Hahn, Secy.; Lewis F. Hazel, Treas.
Employer Identification Number: 166000171

4212
The China Medical Board of New York, Inc. ▼
750 Third Ave., 23rd Fl.
New York 10017 (212) 682-8000

Incorporated in 1928 in NY.
Donor(s): The Rockefeller Foundation.
Foundation type: Independent
Financial data (yr. ended 06/30/89): Assets, $114,318,982 (M); expenditures, $5,599,415, including $4,555,055 for 52 grants (high: $350,000; low: $10,000; average: $10,000-$350,000).
Purpose and activities: "To extend financial aid to the Peking Union Medical College and/or like institutions in the Far East or the United States of America." The Board's activities are: 1) to assist institutions in improving the health levels and services in Asian societies, and 2) to assist institutions in improving the quality and increasing the numbers of appropriate health practitioners in these societies. Supports programs in medical research, staff development, cooperative planning, and library endowment only at designated national medical schools, nursing schools, and schools of public health in Hong Kong, Indonesia, Korea, Malaysia, the Philippines, Singapore, Taiwan, Thailand, and the People's Republic of China.
Types of support: Conferences and seminars, research, fellowships, endowment funds, publications, scholarship funds, special projects, technical assistance.
Limitations: Giving limited to East and Southeast Asia, including the People's Republic of China, Hong Kong, Indonesia, Korea, Malaysia, the Philippines, Singapore, Taiwan, and Thailand. No support for governments, professional societies, or research institutes not directly under medical school control. No grants to individuals, or for capital funds, operating budgets for medical care, special projects, or the basic equipping of medical schools, nursing schools, or schools of public health that are the responsibility of various governments or universities; no loans.
Publications: Annual report.
Application information: Submit request through dean's office of Asian institution in which foundation has a program of support. Application form not required.
Deadline(s): None
Board meeting date(s): June and Dec.
Final notification: Immediately following board meetings
Write: William D. Sawyer, M.D., Pres.
Officers: William D. Sawyer, M.D.,* Pres.; Mary Ann Cramer, Secy.; Walter G. Ehlers,* Treas.

Trustees:* J. Robert Buchanan, M.D., Chair.; Mary Brown Bullock, Loring Catlin, Molly Joel Coye, John R. Hogness, M.D., Tom Kessinger, Bayless A. Manning, Gloria H. Spivak, W. Clarke Wescoe, M.D.
Number of staff: 1 full-time professional; 5 full-time support.
Employer Identification Number: 131659619

4213
China Times Cultural Foundation ☒ ☆
43-27 36th St.
Long Island City 11101 (718) 392-0995

Established in 1986 in CA.
Foundation type: Independent
Financial data (yr. ended 12/31/88): Assets, $3,066,198 (M); expenditures, $191,375, including $25,500 for 5 grants (high: $15,000; low: $2,000) and $67,000 for 61 grants to individuals (high: $3,000; low: $500).
Purpose and activities: "Preference is given to awards for the purpose of promoting Chinese culture, improvement in Chinese communities throughout the world, Sino-American cultural exchanges, Chinese language education, scholarly discourse relating to Chinese studies, and other similar cultural and educational projects." Support includes scholarships to individuals for undergraduate, graduate, and Chinese language studies.
Types of support: Student aid.
Application information: Application form required.
Deadline(s): July 1
Final notification: Oct.
Write: Jame N. Tu
Officers: Chi-Chung Yu, Pres.; Norman C.C. Fu, V.P.; Chao Sung Huang, Secy.; Louisa Wong, Treas.
Employer Identification Number: 222711422

4214
The Chisholm Foundation ☒
c/o U.S. Trust Co. of New York
114 West 47th St.
New York 10036-1532

Established in 1960 in MS.
Donor(s): A.F. Chisholm.†
Foundation type: Independent
Financial data (yr. ended 12/31/88): Assets, $5,669,279 (M); expenditures, $353,971, including $266,500 for 15 grants (high: $60,000; low: $1,625).
Purpose and activities: Giving for education and Protestant organizations; support also for health, cultural programs, youth, and community funds.
Types of support: General purposes.
Limitations: Giving primarily in MS and New York, NY. No grants to individuals.
Application information: Contributes only to pre-selected organizations. Applications not accepted.
Officers: Jean C. Lindsey, Pres.; Cynthia C. Saint-Amand, Secy.; Margaret A. Chisholm, Treas.
Director: Nathan E. Saint-Amand.
Employer Identification Number: 646014272

4215
Christodora, Inc.
666 Broadway, Suite 515
New York 10012 (212) 529-6868

Established in 1897 as Christodora House, NY; operated as a grantmaker since 1981.
Foundation type: Independent
Financial data (yr. ended 09/30/89): Assets, $4,179,423 (M); gifts received, $7,454; expenditures, $347,324, including $127,539 for 14 grants (high: $15,000; low: $500; average: $10,000-$15,000).
Purpose and activities: Support primarily for environmental education for disadvantaged youth.
Types of support: Special projects.
Limitations: Giving primarily in New York, NY. No grants to individuals.
Publications: Informational brochure, application guidelines.
Application information: Contact foundation for current brochure and guidelines.
Deadline(s): None
Write: Robert J. Finkelstein, Exec. Dir.
Officers: Thomas N. McCarter III,* Chair.; Edward S. Elliman, Pres.; Russell C. Wilkinson, V.P.; Mrs. Henry U. Harder, Secy.; Arthur S. Penn, Treas.; Robert J. Finkelstein, Exec. Dir.
Trustees:* Edward H. Elliman, Christopher Fischer, Jack Flanagan, George W. Gowen, Pamela Manice, Barbara McKelvey, Hugh D. Robertson, Stephen Slobadin.
Number of staff: 3 full-time professional.
Employer Identification Number: 135562192

4216
Cintas Foundation, Inc. ☒
c/o William B. Warren
140 Broadway, Rm. 4500
New York 10005
Fellowship application address: Institute of International Education, 809 United Nations Plaza, New York, NY 10017; Tel.: (212) 984-5564

Incorporated in 1957 in NY as Cuban Art Foundation, Inc.
Donor(s): Oscar B. Cintas.†
Foundation type: Independent
Financial data (yr. ended 8/31/88): Assets, $3,129,060 (M); expenditures, $170,634, including $8,400 for 2 grants (high: $5,000; low: $3,400) and $100,000 for 10 grants to individuals of $10,000 each.
Purpose and activities: To foster and encourage art within Cuba and art created by persons of Cuban citizenship or lineage within or outside of Cuba. Present activities restricted to fostering art and granting fellowships to those in the above categories living outside of Cuba who show professional achievement in music, literature, or the arts; students pursuing academic programs are not eligible.
Types of support: Fellowships.
Limitations: No grants for building or endowment funds, operating budgets, or special projects.
Publications: Application guidelines.
Application information: Application form required.
Initial approach: Letter
Deadline(s): Mar. 1 for fellowships beginning Sept. 1
Board meeting date(s): May or June, late Oct. or Nov., and as required
Final notification: 4 to 5 months
Write: Rebecca Abrams
Officers and Directors: William B. Warren, Pres.; Maria Heilbron Richter, Secy.; Hortensia Sampedro, Treas.; Margarita Cano, Riva Castleman, Ulises Giberga, Marta Gutierrez, Daniel Serra-Badue, Roger D. Stone.
Number of staff: None.
Employer Identification Number: 131980389

4217
Liz Claiborne & Art Ortenberg Foundation ☒
(Formerly The Ortenberg Foundation)
c/o Nathan Berkman & Co.
29 Broadway
New York 10006

Established in 1984 in NY.
Donor(s): Arthur Ortenberg, Elisabeth Claiborne Ortenberg.
Foundation type: Independent
Financial data (yr. ended 1/31/89): Assets, $10,387,914 (M); gifts received, $4,240,000; expenditures, $653,395, including $578,280 for grants (high: $150,000).
Purpose and activities: Support primarily for a historic preservation society, environmental organizations, public policy groups, and health and social service agencies.
Application information:
Initial approach: Letter
Deadline(s): None
Trustees: Arthur Ortenberg, Elisabeth Claiborne Ortenberg.
Employer Identification Number: 133200329

4218
David C. Clapp Foundation ☒
c/o Goldman, Sachs & Co.
85 Broad St., Tax Dept.
New York 10004

Established in 1985 in NY.
Donor(s): David C. Clapp.
Foundation type: Independent
Financial data (yr. ended 06/30/89): Assets, $336,656 (M); gifts received, $348,761; expenditures, $176,409, including $174,965 for 50 grants (high: $50,000; low: $100).
Purpose and activities: Giving primarily for higher and secondary education; support also for cultural programs, including museums.
Limitations: Giving primarily in NY. No grants to individuals.
Application information: Applications not accepted.
Trustees: David C. Clapp, Francis X. Coleman, Jr., Frederic B. Garonzik.
Employer Identification Number: 133318134

4219
Frank E. Clark Charitable Trust
c/o Manufacturers Hanover Trust Co.
270 Park Ave.
New York 10017

Trust established in 1936 in NY.
Donor(s): Frank E. Clark.†
Foundation type: Independent

Financial data (yr. ended 12/31/89): Assets, $3,670,000 (M); expenditures, $217,259, including $197,000 for 33 grants (high: $15,750; low: $2,500).
Purpose and activities: Income distributed to the parent body of major religious denominations for aid to needy churches; support also for health, welfare, and other charitable organizations.
Limitations: Giving primarily in the New York, NY, metropolitan area.
Application information:
Initial approach: Proposal
Copies of proposal: 1
Deadline(s): Sept. 31
Board meeting date(s): Dec.
Write: J.L. McKechnie, V.P., Manufacturers Hanover Trust Co.
Trustee: Manufacturers Hanover Trust Co.
Employer Identification Number: 136049032

4220
The Clark Foundation ▼
30 Wall St.
New York 10005 (212) 269-1833

Incorporated in 1931 in NY; merged with Scriven Foundation, Inc. in 1973.
Donor(s): Members of the Clark family.
Foundation type: Independent
Financial data (yr. ended 06/30/89): Assets, $223,791,850 (M); gifts received, $200,926; expenditures, $9,685,418, including $5,727,217 for 125 grants (high: $275,000; low: $1,000; average: $5,000-$150,000), $1,897,303 for 680 grants to individuals (average: $500-$3,000) and $742,064 for 1 foundation-administered program.
Purpose and activities: Support for a hospital and museums in Cooperstown, NY; grants also for charitable, welfare, and educational purposes, including undergraduate scholarships to students residing in the Cooperstown area. Support also for health, educational, youth, cultural, environmental, and community welfare organizations and institutions and for medical and convalescence care of needy individuals.
Types of support: Operating budgets, continuing support, annual campaigns, seed money, emergency funds, building funds, equipment, special projects, student aid, general purposes, grants to individuals, capital campaigns.
Limitations: Giving primarily in upstate NY and New York City; scholarships restricted to students residing in the Cooperstown, NY, area. No grants for deficit financing or matching gifts; no loans.
Publications: Program policy statement, application guidelines.
Application information: Application form not required.
Initial approach: Letter
Copies of proposal: 1
Deadline(s): None
Board meeting date(s): Oct. and May
Final notification: 2 to 6 months
Write: Edward W. Stack, Secy.
Officers: Stephen C. Clark, Jr.,* Pres.; Michael A. Nicolais,* V.P.; Edward W. Stack, Secy.; John J. Burkly, Treas.
Directors:* Alfred C. Clark, Jane F. Clark II, William M. Evarts, Jr., Gates Helms Hawn, Archie F. MacAllaster, Mrs. Edward B. McMenamin, John Hoyt Stookey, A. Pennington Whitehead, Malcolm Wilson.
Number of staff: 4 full-time professional; 3 part-time professional; 43 full-time support; 20 part-time support.
Employer Identification Number: 135616528

4221
The Edna McConnell Clark Foundation ▼
250 Park Ave., Rm. 900
New York 10017 (212) 986-7050

Incorporated in 1950 in NY and 1969 in DE; the NY corporation merged into the DE corporation in 1974.
Donor(s): Edna McConnell Clark,† W. Van Alan Clark.†
Foundation type: Independent
Financial data (yr. ended 9/30/88): Assets, $372,054,687 (M); gifts received, $2,030; expenditures, $23,257,094, including $18,471,486 for 170 grants (high: $855,000; low: $50; average: $78,500).
Purpose and activities: Programs presently narrowly defined and directed toward five specific areas: 1) reducing unnecessary removal of children from troubled families by establishing better family preservation policies and services, supporting courts, agencies, and advocates in implementation of specific foster care and adoption reforms; 2) improving the educational opportunities of disadvantaged young people by designing intervention programs for the middle school years; 3) seeking a more rational, humane, and effective criminal justice system by establishing constitutional conditions in adult and juvenile correctional institutions, encouraging community-based sanctions for adults as alternatives to incarceration, and helping to dismantle large state training schools in favor of community-based programs for juveniles; 4) reducing the debilitating and deadly burden of illness in the poorest countries of the developing world through a targeted research program aimed at controlling the tropical diseases schistosomiasis, trachoma, and onchocerciasis; 5) seeking to assist families in New York City to move out of emergency shelters and hotels into permanent housing by supporting projects to assess and plan for the needs of families before and immediately after they leave the shelters; supporting programs aimed at forming tenants associations and other mechanisms that give families a stake in their communties; and supporting efforts to create, improve, and expand public and social services in neighborhoods receiving large numbers of previously homeless families. The foundation also maintains a program of Special Projects which primarily focuses on projects serving the poor and disadvantaged in New York City outside the established program areas that reflect our basic mission.
Types of support: Consulting services, continuing support, research, seed money, technical assistance, special projects.
Limitations: Giving primarily in New York City, NY, for special projects; nationally for other programs. No grants to individuals, or for capital funds, construction and equipment, endowments, scholarships, fellowships, annual appeals, deficit financing, or matching gifts; no loans to individuals.
Publications: Annual report, informational brochure (including application guidelines), grants list, occasional report.
Application information: Action-oriented projects preferred; research support primarily in Tropical Disease Program. Application form not required.
Initial approach: Letter
Copies of proposal: 1
Deadline(s): None
Board meeting date(s): Feb., Apr., June, Sept., and Dec.
Final notification: 1 month for declination; 2-3 months for positive action
Write: Peter D. Bell, Pres.
Officers: James M. Clark,* Chair. and Treas.; Peter D. Bell,* Pres.; Patricia Carry Stewart, V.P. and Secy.; Peter W. Forsythe, V.P.
Trustees:* Hays Clark, Drew S. Days III, Eleanor T. Elliott, John M. Emery, Lucy H. Nesbeda, Walter N. Rothschild, Jr., Sidney J. Weinberg, Jr., O. Meredith Wilson.
Number of staff: 11 full-time professional; 9 full-time support; 3 part-time support.
Employer Identification Number: 237047034

4222
Robert Sterling Clark Foundation, Inc. ▼
112 East 64th St.
New York 10021 (212) 308-0411

Incorporated in 1952 in NY.
Donor(s): Robert Sterling Clark.†
Foundation type: Independent
Financial data (yr. ended 10/31/89): Assets, $61,813,703 (M); expenditures, $2,668,696, including $2,003,800 for 76 grants (high: $100,000; low: $2,000).
Purpose and activities: The foundation supports projects that: 1) strengthen the management of cultural institutions in New York City and the greater metropolitan area; 2) ensure the effectiveness and accountability of public agencies in New York City and State; and 3) protect reproductive freedom and access to family planning services.
Types of support: Special projects, research, consulting services, continuing support, general purposes, research, special projects.
Limitations: Giving primarily in NY, with emphasis on New York City; giving nationally for reproductive freedom projects. No grants to individuals, or for operating budgets, annual campaigns, seed money, emergency funds, deficit financing, capital or endowment funds, matching gifts, scholarships, fellowships, conferences, or films.
Publications: Annual report, application guidelines.
Application information: Application form not required.
Initial approach: Proposal
Copies of proposal: 1
Deadline(s): None
Board meeting date(s): Jan., Apr., July, and Oct.
Final notification: 1 to 6 months

Write: Margaret C. Ayers, Exec. Dir.
Officers: Winslow M. Lovejoy, Jr.,* Pres. and Treas.; Miner D. Crary, Jr.,* Secy.; Margaret C. Ayers, Exec. Dir.
Directors:* Raymond D. Horton, Charles G. Meyer, Jr., Winthrop R. Munyan, Richardson Pratt, Jr., John N. Romans, Philip Svigals.
Number of staff: 3 full-time professional; 1 part-time professional; 1 full-time support.
Employer Identification Number: 131957792

4223
Hazel C. Clarke Memorial Trust ☒
c/o Marine Midland Bank, N.A., Trust Oper. Ctr.
P.O. Box 4203, 17th Fl.
Buffalo 14240

Established in 1974 in NY.
Donor(s): Hazel C. Clarke.†
Foundation type: Independent
Financial data (yr. ended 07/31/89): Assets, $1,223,205 (M); expenditures, $220,813, including $215,472 for 30 grants (high: $43,000; low: $596).
Purpose and activities: Support primarly for youth and social services, and to community funds.
Limitations: Giving primarily in Chautauqua County, NY.
Application information: Contributes only to pre-selected organizations. Applications not accepted.
Trustee: Marine Midland Bank, N.A.
Employer Identification Number: 166177336

4224
Cleft of the Rock Foundation, Inc. ☒ ☆
16 Mystic Ln.
Northport 11768

Foundation type: Independent
Financial data (yr. ended 12/31/88): Assets, $826,646 (M); gifts received, $190,000; expenditures, $117,175, including $106,301 for 18 grants (high: $25,000; low: $60).
Purpose and activities: Support for Christian organizations and youth.
Limitations: No grants to individuals.
Application information: Contributes only to pre-selected organizations. Applications not accepted.
Officers: Mark O. Andre, Pres.; James D. Trump, Secy.; Diane E. Andre, Treas.
Employer Identification Number: 112631834

4225
The Clover Foundation ☒ ☆
455 Main St., Suite 104
New Rochelle 10801-6418 (914) 632-3778

Established in 1986.
Donor(s): Alberto Pacheco, Educational Aid Fund.
Foundation type: Independent
Financial data (yr. ended 12/31/87): Assets, $2,441,219 (M); gifts received, $995,000; expenditures, $102,340, including $100,000 for 1 grant.
Purpose and activities: Support for a cultural interchange association.
Application information: Application form required.
Deadline(s): None
Write: Theodore Wills
Officers and Directors: Francisco Gomez Franco, Pres.; Alberto Pacheco, V.P.; James Snow, Secy.; Thomas Kane, Treas.
Employer Identification Number: 742390003

4226
The Phyllis and Lee Coffey Foundation, Inc. ☒
355 Lexington Ave.
New York 10017-6603

Established in 1952 in NY.
Donor(s): Lee W. Coffey.
Foundation type: Independent
Financial data (yr. ended 12/31/88): Assets, $1,380,662 (M); gifts received, $65,249; expenditures, $70,443, including $64,650 for 13 grants (high: $55,500; low: $50).
Purpose and activities: Support for health services, social services, religious giving and cultural activities.
Limitations: Giving primarily in NY. No grants to individuals.
Application information: Contributes only to pre-selected organizations. Applications not accepted.
Officer: Lee W. Coffey, Pres. and Treas.; Phyllis C. Coffey, V.P. and Secy.
Director: Daniel Cowin.
Employer Identification Number: 116014056

4227
The Cohen Family Foundation, Inc. ☒ ☆
World Financial Ctr., 19th Fl.
New York 10285

Incorporated in 1986 in NY.
Donor(s): Peter A. Cohen, and other members of the Cohen family.
Foundation type: Independent
Financial data (yr. ended 12/31/88): Assets, $419,042 (M); gifts received, $145,409; expenditures, $112,724, including $111,735 for 37 grants (high: $17,850; low: $20).
Purpose and activities: Giving primarily for Jewish organizations, hospitals, higher and other education, and museums.
Limitations: Giving primarily in New York, NY. No grants to individuals.
Application information: Contributes only to pre-selected organizations. Applications not accepted.
Officer: Peter A. Cohen, Mgr.
Employer Identification Number: 133183001

4228
Saul Z. & Amy Scheuer Cohen Family Foundation, Inc. ☒ ☆
c/o 61 Associates
350 Fifth Ave., Suite 3410
New York 10118

Established in 1979 in NY.
Donor(s): Amy Scheuer Cohen.
Foundation type: Independent
Financial data (yr. ended 11/30/89): Assets, $804,668 (M); gifts received, $1,277,434; expenditures, $2,580,289, including $2,543,067 for 106 grants (high: $1,000,000; low: $50).
Purpose and activities: Giving for higher and other education, culture, Jewish giving, and health services, including mental health.
Types of support: General purposes.
Limitations: Giving primarily in NY.
Application information: Contributes only to pre-selected organizations. Applications not accepted.
Officers: Saul Z. Cohen, Pres.; Amy Scheuer Cohen, Secy.-Treas.
Trustee: Thomas M. Cohen.
Employer Identification Number: 133032459

4229
Abraham D. & Annette Cohen Foundation ☒
49-29 30th Place
Long Island City 11101-3192

Donor(s): Abraham D. Cohen.
Foundation type: Independent
Financial data (yr. ended 10/31/88): Assets, $98,351 (M); gifts received, $50,000; expenditures, $123,726, including $123,440 for 15 grants (high: $111,702; low: $18).
Purpose and activities: Support primarily for Jewish giving.
Application information: Applications not accepted.
Officers and Directors: Abraham D. Cohen, Pres.; David A. Cohen, V.P.; Joseph A. Cohen, Secy.-Treas.
Employer Identification Number: 112715279

4230
The Alan N. & Joan M. Cohen Foundation, Inc. ☒ ☆
c/o Paul, Weiss, Rifkind, Wharton & Garrison
1285 Ave. of the Americas
New York 10019 (212) 373-3380

Established in 1985.
Donor(s): Alan N. Cohen.
Foundation type: Independent
Financial data (yr. ended 11/30/88): Assets, $425,344 (M); gifts received, $77,000; expenditures, $108,953, including $105,825 for 37 grants (high: $51,000; low: $50).
Purpose and activities: Support primarily for a Jewish welfare fund and other Jewish organizations and higher education.
Limitations: Giving primarily in New York, NY.
Application information:
Initial approach: Letter
Deadline(s): None
Directors: Alan N. Cohen, Gordon Geoffrey Cohen, Joan M. Cohen, Laurie Elizabeth Cohen.
Employer Identification Number: 133296783

4231
Eli D. Cohen Foundation ☒
c/o Eli D. Cohen
49-29 30th Place
Long Island City 11101-3192

Donor(s): Duane Reade, Eli D. Cohen.
Foundation type: Independent
Financial data (yr. ended 10/31/88): Assets, $220,616 (M); gifts received, $100,000; expenditures, $233,909, including $233,116 for 12 grants (high: $105,000; low: $300).
Purpose and activities: Support primarily for Jewish organizations.

Limitations: No grants to individuals.
Application information: Applications not accepted.
Officers and Directors: Eli D. Cohen, Pres.; Esther Cohen, V.P.; Leon E. Cohen, Secy.; David E. Cohen, Treas.
Employer Identification Number: 112715273

4232
Elias A. Cohen Foundation, Inc. ⌘
45 John St., Rm. 704
New York 10038 (212) 425-1313

Incorporated in 1951 in NY.
Donor(s): Elias A. Cohen,† David Schlang, Joseph Schlang, Maurice H. Schlang, Cohen Family Fund.
Foundation type: Independent
Financial data (yr. ended 12/31/88): Assets, $1,860,956 (M); expenditures, $85,954, including $73,500 for 4 grants (high: $25,000; low: $2,500).
Purpose and activities: Giving for a camp; grants also for higher education, temple support, and Jewish welfare funds.
Limitations: Giving primarily in NY. No grants to individuals.
Application information: Application form not required.
Initial approach: Proposal
Copies of proposal: 1
Deadline(s): None
Board meeting date(s): Quarterly
Write: Joseph Schlang, Treas.
Officers: Pearl Miller, Pres.; Seymor Cohn, V.P.; Maurice H. Schlang, Secy.; Joseph Schlang, Treas.
Employer Identification Number: 136113003

4233
Jack D. Cohen Foundation ⌘ ☆
49-29 30th Place
Long Island City 11101-3192

Established in 1984 in NY.
Foundation type: Independent
Financial data (yr. ended 10/31/89): Assets, $121,245 (M); expenditures, $168,962, including $168,500 for 3 grants (high: $143,000; low: $500).
Purpose and activities: Support for Jewish organizations.
Limitations: No grants to individuals.
Application information: Applications not accepted.
Officers: Jack D. Cohen,* Pres.; Eli D. Cohen,* V.P.; Joseph A. Cohen,* Secy.
Directors:* Abraham D. Cohen.
Employer Identification Number: 112715275

4234
The Marilyn B. & Stanley L. Cohen Foundation, Inc. ⌘
c/o Spicer & Oppenheim
Seven World Trade Ctr.
New York 10048

Established in 1977 in NY.
Donor(s): Stanley L. Cohen.
Foundation type: Independent
Financial data (yr. ended 6/30/87): Assets, $282,349 (M); gifts received, $300,000; expenditures, $153,354, including $150,274 for 122 grants (high: $50,000; low: $10).
Purpose and activities: Support for youth organizations, cultural programs, and Jewish organizations.
Limitations: Giving primarily in New York, NY. No grants to individuals.
Application information: Contributes only to pre-selected organizations. Applications not accepted.
Officers and Directors: Stanley L. Cohen, Pres. and Treas.; Marilyn B. Cohen, V.P. and Secy.; Jacob Cohen, Edward Small, William J. Voute.
Employer Identification Number: 132930968

4235
Sherman & Edward Baron Cohen Foundation, Inc. ⌘
805 Third Ave., 14th Fl.
New York 10022

Established in 1979.
Donor(s): Edward Baron Cohen, Sherman Cohen.
Foundation type: Operating
Financial data (yr. ended 12/31/88): Assets, $1,624 (M); gifts received, $156,000; expenditures, $155,195, including $155,000 for 2 grants (high: $150,000; low: $5,000).
Purpose and activities: A private operating foundation; support primarily for a Jewish welfare fund.
Limitations: No grants to individuals.
Application information: Contributes only to pre-selected organizations. Applications not accepted.
Officers: Sherman Cohen, Pres.; Edward Baron Cohen, Secy.-Treas.
Employer Identification Number: 132994580

4236
Wilfred P. Cohen Foundation, Inc. ⌘
60 East 42nd St., Suite 3016
New York 10165

Incorporated in 1956 in NY.
Donor(s): Wilfred P. Cohen.
Foundation type: Independent
Financial data (yr. ended 3/31/88): Assets, $4,249,821 (M); expenditures, $233,027, including $224,910 for 20 grants (high: $90,000; low: $35).
Purpose and activities: Emphasis on Jewish welfare funds; grants also for temple support, community funds, higher education, and aid to the handicapped.
Limitations: Giving primarily in the New York, NY, metropolitan area.
Application information:
Initial approach: Letter
Deadline(s): None
Write: Wilfred P. Cohen, Pres.
Officers and Directors: Wilfred P. Cohen, Pres.; Jack Greenberg, Secy.; Rose J. Cohen, Treas.
Employer Identification Number: 136108635

4237
Max B. Cohn Family Foundation
c/o Milton Cohn
445 Park Ave.
New York 10022

Established in 1952 in NY.
Donor(s): Milton Cohn.
Foundation type: Independent
Financial data (yr. ended 5/31/89): Assets, $1,165,498 (M); expenditures, $148,251, including $145,203 for 148 grants (high: $27,500; low: $15).
Purpose and activities: Grants for health, Jewish giving, social services, and education.
Limitations: Giving primarily in the greater New York, NY, area. No grants to individuals.
Application information: Contributes only to pre-selected organizations. Applications not accepted.
Officers: Dorothy Cohn, Pres.; Melvin Roth, V.P.; Milton Cohn, Secy.-Treas.
Employer Identification Number: 116005709

4238
Herman & Terese Cohn Foundation ⌘
c/o Chase Lincoln First Bank, N.A.
P.O. Box 1412
Rochester 14603 (716) 258-5175

Trust established in 1954 in NY.
Donor(s): Herman M. Cohn.†
Foundation type: Independent
Financial data (yr. ended 12/31/88): Assets, $4,409,388 (M); expenditures, $226,970, including $195,000 for 6 grants (high: $75,000; low: $10,000).
Purpose and activities: Giving for a musuem, an educational fund, family and youth services, and educational television.
Limitations: Giving primarily in NY. No grants to individuals.
Application information: Contributes only to pre-selected organizations. Applications not accepted.
Write: Patricia C. Bonawitz
Trustee: Chase Lincoln First Bank, N.A.
Employer Identification Number: 166015300

4239
Peter A. and Elizabeth S. Cohn Foundation, Inc. ⌘
c/o Dammann, Edelman & Engel
60 East 42nd St.
New York 10165

Established in 1955 in NY.
Donor(s): Peter A. Cohn.
Foundation type: Independent
Financial data (yr. ended 6/30/88): Assets, $1,755,891 (M); expenditures, $104,948, including $93,600 for 19 grants (high: $44,000; low: $500).
Purpose and activities: Giving for hospitals, Jewish welfare agencies, and higher education.
Limitations: Giving primarily in New York, NY.
Application information:
Initial approach: Letter
Deadline(s): None
Write: Peter A. Cohn, Pres.
Officers and Directors: Peter A. Cohn, Pres.; Elizabeth S. Cohn, V.P. and Treas.; Lillian Schlossberg, Secy.
Employer Identification Number: 136117647

4240
The Coleman Foundation ⌘
551 Fifth Ave.
New York 10176 (212) 986-9753

Trust established in 1962 in NY.
Donor(s): Janet M. Coleman, Martin S. Coleman.
Foundation type: Independent
Financial data (yr. ended 11/30/88): Assets, $2,038,678 (M); gifts received, $33,525; expenditures, $166,489, including $119,205 for 52 grants (high: $50,000; low: $25).
Purpose and activities: Support for Jewish welfare funds and other Jewish organizations, social service agencies, hospitals, and health agencies.
Limitations: Giving primarily in NY. No grants to individuals, or for endowment funds.
Application information: Contributes only to pre-selected organizations. Applications not accepted.
Board meeting date(s): Semiannually
Trustees: Janet M. Coleman, Martin S. Coleman.
Employer Identification Number: 136126040

4241
Sylvan C. Coleman Foundation ⌘
c/o The Bank of New York, Tax Dept.
48 Wall St.
New York 10015 (212) 536-4710

Established about 1956.
Donor(s): Sylvan C. Coleman.
Foundation type: Independent
Financial data (yr. ended 11/30/88): Assets, $1,580,363 (M); expenditures, $86,326, including $69,500 for 20 grants (high: $17,000; low: $500).
Purpose and activities: Giving primarily for higher education, cultural programs, health, social services, and Jewish welfare funds.
Application information:
Initial approach: Letter
Deadline(s): None
Write: Kevin Monahan
Trustees: Clarence B. Coleman, Joan F. Coleman.
Employer Identification Number: 136091160

4242
George E. Coleman, Jr. Foundation ⌘
c/o Neville, Rodie & Shaw, Inc.
200 Madison Ave.
New York 10016 (212) 725-1440

Established in 1979 in NY.
Donor(s): George E. Coleman, Jr.†
Foundation type: Independent
Financial data (yr. ended 12/31/88): Assets, $4,728,518 (M); expenditures, $346,334, including $298,075 for 49 grants (high: $35,000; low: $75).
Purpose and activities: Grants largely for educational institutions and associations, historic preservation, cultural organizations, and conservation.
Types of support: Research.
Application information: Application form not required.
Deadline(s): None
Write: Denis Loncto, Trustee
Trustees: Denis Loncto, Louise Oliver.
Employer Identification Number: 133025258

4243
Coles Family Foundation
c/o Goldman, Sachs & Co.
85 Broad St.
New York 10004

Established in 1980 in NY.
Donor(s): Michael H. Coles, Joan C. Coles.
Foundation type: Independent
Financial data (yr. ended 03/31/89): Assets, $2,470,927 (M); expenditures, $231,554, including $227,677 for 91 grants (high: $33,300; low: $25).
Purpose and activities: Grants for Catholic giving, child welfare, higher and other education, cultural programs, and foreign policy.
Types of support: Endowment funds, general purposes.
Limitations: Giving primarily in NY. No grants to individuals.
Application information: Applications not accepted.
Trustees: Alison Aldredge, Isobel Coles, Joan C. Coles, Michael H. Coles, Richard Coles, Caroline Scudder, Roy C. Smith.
Number of staff: 1 part-time support.
Employer Identification Number: 133050747

4244
Simon & Eve Colin Foundation, Inc. ⌘
500 Old Country Rd.
Garden City 11530-1901
Application address: Eight Hickory Hill, Roslyn Estates, NY 11576

Donor(s): Fred Colin, Stephen Colin.
Foundation type: Independent
Financial data (yr. ended 10/31/88): Assets, $1,354,246 (M); gifts received, $90,000; expenditures, $61,873, including $59,405 for 45 grants (high: $25,100; low: $20).
Purpose and activities: Support for higher education, health, and general charitable giving.
Limitations: Giving primarily in NY.
Application information:
Deadline(s): None
Write: Fred Colin, Dir.
Directors: Barbara Colin, Fred Colin, Stephen Colin.
Employer Identification Number: 112676434

4245
Joseph Collins Foundation ⌘
One Citicorp Ctr.
153 East 53rd St.
New York 10022

Incorporated in 1951 in NY.
Donor(s): Joseph Collins, M.D.†
Foundation type: Independent
Financial data (yr. ended 6/30/89): Assets, $9,870,142 (M); expenditures, $437,518, including $390,250 for 172 grants to individuals (high: $4,000; low: $1,000).
Purpose and activities: Grants ranging from $1,000-$2,500 for tuition and/or subsistence to needy undergraduate medical students on the recommendation of medical school authorities.
Types of support: Fellowships, student aid.
Limitations: No support for pre-medical or post-graduate medical students.
Publications: Annual report, program policy statement, application guidelines.
Application information: Application form should be obtained from medical school.
Initial approach: Full proposal
Copies of proposal: 1
Deadline(s): Submit proposal between Jan. and Mar. 1
Board meeting date(s): Nov. and as required
Write: Mrs. Augusta L. Packer, Secy.-Treas.
Officers and Trustees: Mark F. Hughes, Pres.; W. Graham Knox, M.D., V.P.; Jack H. Nusbaum, V.P.; Chester J. Straub, M.D., V.P.; Augusta L. Packer, Secy.-Treas.
Number of staff: None.
Employer Identification Number: 136404527

4246
James J. Colt Foundation, Inc. ⌘
375 Park Ave., Suite 3806
New York 10152 (212) 371-1110

Incorporated in 1952 in NY.
Donor(s): James J. Colt.†
Foundation type: Independent
Financial data (yr. ended 12/31/88): Assets, $2,159,063 (M); expenditures, $168,393, including $156,497 for 39 grants (high: $25,000; low: $10).
Purpose and activities: Giving for medical education, hospitals, Jewish welfare funds, health agencies, and Protestant church support.
Limitations: Giving primarily in NY.
Application information:
Initial approach: Letter
Deadline(s): None
Write: Anita C. Heard, Pres.
Officers and Directors: Anita C. Heard, Pres.; Thomas H. Heard, V.P.; Vaughn Durbin, Secy.-Treas.; Donald Oresman.
Employer Identification Number: 136112997

4247
Colt Industries Charitable Foundation, Inc. ⌘
c/o Colt Industries, Inc.
430 Park Ave.
New York 10022 (212) 940-0410

Incorporated in 1963 in DE.
Donor(s): Colt Industries, Inc.
Foundation type: Company-sponsored
Financial data (yr. ended 6/30/87): Assets, $3,535 (M); expenditures, $118,702, including $118,271 for 48 grants (high: $20,000; low: $250; average: $2,000-$3,000).
Purpose and activities: Giving for community funds, higher education, hospitals, cultural programs, and youth agencies; support also for civic affairs and public interest groups.
Types of support: Building funds, operating budgets.
Limitations: Giving primarily in areas of company operations. No grants to individuals.
Application information: Application form not required.
Initial approach: Letter
Copies of proposal: 1
Deadline(s): Submit proposal preferably in Sept. or Oct.
Board meeting date(s): Quarterly
Final notification: 3 months
Write: Andrew C. Hilton, Exec. V.P.
Officers and Directors: David I. Margolis, Pres.; Andrew C. Hilton, Exec. V.P.; Anthony J.

di Buono, V.P. and Secy.; Salvatore J. Cozzolino, V.P. and Treas.
Number of staff: 2 part-time support.
Employer Identification Number: 256057849

4248
The Common Giving Fund ▼
666 Broadway, 5th Fl.
New York 10012-2317

Established in 1984 in NY.
Donor(s): Norman Lear, Frances Lear.
Foundation type: Independent
Financial data (yr. ended 4/30/88): Assets, $10,117,859 (M); expenditures, $1,246,905, including $1,097,500 for 9 grants (high: $500,000; low: $25,000; average: $40,000-$200,000).
Purpose and activities: Giving primarily for public policy organizations; some support for hospitals and a university.
Types of support: General purposes, operating budgets.
Application information: Contributes only to donor-designated organizations. Applications not accepted.
Directors: Margie Fine, Pres.; Rosalie Sassano, V.P.; June Makela, Secy.-Treas.
Number of staff: None.
Employer Identification Number: 133269301

4249
The Commonwealth Fund ▼
One East 75th St.
New York 10021-2692 (212) 535-0400

Incorporated in 1918 in NY.
Donor(s): Mrs. Stephen V. Harkness,† Edward S. Harkness,† Mrs. Edward S. Harkness.†
Foundation type: Independent
Financial data (yr. ended 06/30/89): Assets, $314,132,587 (M); expenditures, $15,551,028, including $9,622,513 for grants (high: $595,000; low: $1,000; average: $100,000), $931,376 for grants to individuals and $453,052 for foundation-administered programs.
Purpose and activities: Supports new opportunities to improve Americans' health and well-being and to assist specific groups of Americans who have serious and neglected problems. The Fund's five major programs aim to improve health care services, to advance the well-being of elderly people, particularly those living alone, to develop the capacities of high school students, to promote healthier lifestyles, and to improve the health of minorities. Grants also for related projects supporting these themes, including programs for minority medical students seeking careers in academic medicine and for nurses seeking to obtain advanced management training. Grants are provided to nonprofit institutions to generate service, educational, and research activities. Harkness Fellowships are awarded by selection committees in each country to potential leaders from the United Kingdom, Australia, and New Zealand for study and research in the U.S.; applicants must be citizens of the United Kingdom, Australia, or New Zealand. Requirements and length of fellowship vary depending upon the country of origin.
Types of support: Research, special projects.
Limitations: No grants to individuals (except for Harkness Fellowships), or for building or endowment funds, general support, capital funds, construction or renovation of facilities, purchase of equipment, or assistance with operating budgets or deficits of established programs or institutions, scholarships, or matching gifts; no loans.
Publications: Annual report.
Application information: Application form not required.
Initial approach: Letter or proposal
Copies of proposal: 3
Deadline(s): None
Board meeting date(s): Apr., July, and Nov.
Final notification: Immediately following board meeting
Write: Adrienne A. Fisher, Grants Mgr.
Officers: Margaret E. Mahoney,* Pres.; Thomas W. Moloney, Sr. V.P.; John Craig, V.P. and Treas.; Joseph Peri, Secy.
Directors:* C. Sims Farr, Chair.; Harriet B. Belin, Lawrence S. Huntington, R.L. Ireland III, Helene Kaplan, Robert M. O'Neil, Roswell B. Perkins, Charles A. Sanders, M.D., Alfred R. Stern, Blenda J. Wilson.
Number of staff: 19 full-time professional; 14 full-time support; 4 part-time support.
Employer Identification Number: 131635260

4250
Comstock Memorial Scholarship Trust ⌑
(Formerly James A. Comstock Memorial Scholarship Trust)
c/o Norstar Trust Co.
One East Ave.
Rochester 14638
Scholarship application address: c/o Norstar Trust Co., Wellsville, NY 14895; Tel.: (716) 593-2650

Established in 1981 in NY.
Donor(s): James A. Comstock,† Louise Comstock.
Foundation type: Independent
Financial data (yr. ended 5/31/89): Assets, $1,883,364 (M); gifts received, $210,000; expenditures, $180,342, including $85,000 for 21 grants (high: $8,700; low: $1,010) and $81,850 for 38 grants to individuals (high: $5,500; low: $1,000).
Purpose and activities: Support for higher education, including scholarships to children of employees of Acme Electric Co.
Types of support: Employee-related scholarships.
Application information: Application form required.
Deadline(s): Jan. 31
Write: Trust Officer, Norstar Trust Co.
Trustee: Norstar Trust Co.
Employer Identification Number: 222327403

4251
Congel-Pyramid Trust ⌑ ☆
Four Clinton Sq., Suite 106
Syracuse 13202 (315) 476-0532

Established in 1986 in NY.
Donor(s): Robert J. Congel.
Foundation type: Independent
Financial data (yr. ended 9/30/88): Assets, $1,314 (M); gifts received, $247,000; expenditures, $246,572, including $245,000 for 2 grants (high: $235,000; low: $10,000).
Purpose and activities: Giving primarily for a welfare agency providing emergency aid; some support for a museum.
Limitations: Giving primarily in Syracuse, NY. No grants to individuals.
Application information:
Initial approach: Letter
Deadline(s): None
Write: Robert V. Hunter, Trustee
Trustees: Robert J. Congel, Suzanne M. Congel, Robert V. Hunter, Leonard Leveen, George J. Schunck.
Employer Identification Number: 166291475

4252
Constans Culver Foundation
270 Park Ave.
New York 10017 (212) 270-9107

Trust established in 1965 in NY.
Donor(s): Erne Constans Culver.†
Foundation type: Independent
Financial data (yr. ended 12/31/89): Assets, $4,748,879 (M); expenditures, $345,409, including $287,000 for 122 grants (high: $22,500; low: $500; average: $1,500-$2,500).
Purpose and activities: Emphasis on church support, civic and cultural organizations, higher and insurance education, the disadvantaged, and housing issues.
Types of support: Annual campaigns, continuing support, general purposes.
Limitations: Giving primarily in NY. No grants to individuals, or for endowment funds.
Application information:
Initial approach: Letter
Copies of proposal: 1
Deadline(s): Submit proposal preferably in Sept.
Board meeting date(s): Oct. and as required
Write: Robert Rosenthal, V.P., Manufacturers Hanover Trust Co.
Trustees: Pauline Hoffmann Herd, Pauline May Herd, Victoria Prescott Herd, Manufacturers Hanover Trust Co.
Number of staff: 5
Employer Identification Number: 136048059

4253
Consumer Farmer Foundation, Inc.
121 Ave. of the Americas, Suite 501
New York 10013 (212) 431-9700

Established in 1970 in NY.
Foundation type: Independent
Financial data (yr. ended 12/31/89): Assets, $4,495,127 (M); gifts received, $555,000; qualifying distributions, $1,338,618, including $5,895 for 3 grants (high: $2,500; low: $50), $89,134 for 47 grants to individuals (average: $400-$4,000), $1,117,439 for loans to organizations and $126,150 for 47 loans to individuals.
Purpose and activities: Support for low-income housing efforts, with emphasis on assistance to senior citizens, including forgivable loans to at-risk senior citizen homeowners.

Types of support: Loans, grants to individuals, seed money.
Limitations: Giving limited to New York, NY.
Publications: Annual report, 990-PF, informational brochure, application guidelines.
Application information: Application form required.
Initial approach: Letter
Deadline(s): None
Write: Harold DeRienzo, V.P. and C.E.O.
Officer and Directors:* Harold DeRienzo,* V.P. and C.E.O.; Lisa Kaplan, Meyer Parodneck.
Number of staff: 5
Employer Identification Number: 112229635

4254
The Continental Corporation Foundation ▼ ⌑
180 Maiden Ln.
New York 10038 (212) 440-7729

Incorporated in 1957 in NY.
Donor(s): The Continental Corp.
Foundation type: Company-sponsored
Financial data (yr. ended 12/31/87): Assets, $25,379,209 (M); gifts received, $4,999,995; expenditures, $1,831,002, including $1,414,978 for 687 grants (high: $51,500; low: $25).
Purpose and activities: Grants largely for community funds and colleges and universities, including matching gifts and college scholarship programs for children of Continental Corporation employees, and for health and social welfare.
Types of support: General purposes, building funds, employee-related scholarships, employee matching gifts, scholarship funds.
Limitations: No support for religious, political, or professional groups. No grants to individuals, or for research, courtesy advertising, or endowment funds; no loans.
Publications: Informational brochure (including application guidelines).
Application information: Application form not required.
Initial approach: Letter
Copies of proposal: 1
Deadline(s): Submit proposal preferably between Sept. and Nov.
Board meeting date(s): Mar., June, Sept., and Dec.
Write: David J. Vidal, Asst. V.P., Corp. Affairs
Officers: John P. Mascotte,* Chair. and Pres.; William S. Gibson, V.P. and Secy.; Edward J. Harvey, V.P. and Treas.; William F. Gleason, Jr., V.P.; John H. Loynes, V.P.; Charles A. Parker, V.P.
Trustees:* Ivan A. Burns, L. Edwin Smart, Harold W. Sonn, Michael Weintraub.
Number of staff: 1 full-time professional; 1 full-time support.
Employer Identification Number: 136090280

4255
Robert M. & Lois Conway Foundation ⌑
c/o Goldman Sachs & Co., Tax Dept.
85 Broad St., 30th Fl.
New York 10004-2106

Established in 1982 in NY.
Donor(s): Robert M. Conway.
Foundation type: Independent
Financial data (yr. ended 09/30/89): Assets, $835,083 (M); gifts received, $463,550; expenditures, $419,134, including $417,060 for 13 grants (high: $110,000; low: $100).
Purpose and activities: Support primarily for higher education.
Limitations: No grants to individuals, or for scholarships; no loans.
Application information: Applications not accepted.
Trustees: Lois Conway, Robert M. Conway, Robert J. Hurst.
Employer Identification Number: 133153721

4256
The Cook Foundation ⌑
c/o Goldman, Sachs & Co.
85 Broad St.
New York 10004 (212) 902-6897

Established in 1981 in NY.
Donor(s): Daniel W. Cook III.
Foundation type: Independent
Financial data (yr. ended 1/31/89): Assets, $1,207,837 (M); gifts received, $583,599; expenditures, $636,328, including $635,663 for grants.
Purpose and activities: Support primarily for education, cultural programs, and social services.
Limitations: Giving primarily in Dallas, TX.
Trustees: Daniel W. Cook III, Gail B. Cook, Stephen Friedman.
Employer Identification Number: 133102939

4257
Peter C. Cornell Trust
1000 Cathedral Place
298 Main St.
Buffalo 14202-4096 (716) 856-5500

Established in 1949 in NY.
Donor(s): Peter C. Cornell, M.D.†
Foundation type: Independent
Financial data (yr. ended 09/30/89): Assets, $4,688,952 (M); expenditures, $474,407, including $446,696 for 77 grants (high: $35,000; low: $100; average: $3,000-$5,000).
Purpose and activities: Support for local eleemosynary, social, education, and health needs; some grants to national agencies in those fields.
Types of support: Operating budgets, continuing support, annual campaigns, seed money, emergency funds, building funds, equipment, land acquisition, matching funds, capital campaigns.
Limitations: Giving primarily in Buffalo and Erie County, NY. No grants to individuals, or for program support, research, demonstration projects, publications, or conferences; no loans.
Publications: Application guidelines.
Application information: Application form not required.
Initial approach: Proposal
Copies of proposal: 3
Deadline(s): Oct. 1
Board meeting date(s): May and Nov.
Final notification: 6 months
Write: Joseph H. Morey, Jr., Trustee
Trustees: Alice K. Busch, S. Douglas Cornell, Joseph H. Morey, Jr.
Number of staff: None.
Employer Identification Number: 951660344

4258
Corning Incorporated Foundation ▼
(Formerly Corning Glass Works Foundation)
MP-LB-02-1
Corning 14831 (607) 974-8719

Incorporated in 1952 in NY.
Donor(s): Corning Incorporated.
Foundation type: Company-sponsored
Financial data (yr. ended 12/31/89): Assets, $2,585,117 (M); gifts received, $2,215,188; expenditures, $2,359,023, including $1,712,433 for 238 grants (high: $183,700; low: $100; average: $500-$2,500) and $524,999 for 3,999 employee matching gifts.
Purpose and activities: Support of educational, civic, cultural, health and social service institutions; scholarships and fellowships in selected educational fields at selected institutions.
Types of support: Seed money, equipment, employee matching gifts, scholarship funds, fellowships, special projects.
Limitations: Giving primarily in communities where Corning Incorporated has manufacturing operations. No support for elementary or secondary schools outside of school systems in plant communities, or for veterans' organizations, political parties, labor groups, or religious organizations. No grants to individuals; no loans.
Publications: Annual report (including application guidelines).
Application information: Application form not required.
Initial approach: Letter
Copies of proposal: 1
Deadline(s): None
Board meeting date(s): Mar., June, Sept., and Dec.
Final notification: 2 months
Write: Kristin A. Swain, Pres.
Officers and Trustees:* David N. Van Allen,* Chair.; Kristin A. Swain,* Pres.; James L. Flynn,* V.P.; A. John Peck, Jr., Secy.; Richard B. Klein, Treas.; Roger G. Ackerman, Thomas S. Buechner, Van C. Campbell, David A. Duke, Richard Dulude, E. Martin Gibson, James R. Houghton, Richard E. Rahill, James E. Riesbeck, William C. Ughetta.
Number of staff: 2 full-time professional; 2 full-time support.
Employer Identification Number: 166051394

4259
Jon & Joanne Corzine Foundation ⌑ ☆
c/o Goldman, Sachs & Co., Tax Dept.
85 Broad St.
New York 10004

Established in 1981.
Donor(s): Jon S. Corzine.
Foundation type: Independent
Financial data (yr. ended 1/31/89): Assets, $1,162,676 (M); gifts received, $435,842; expenditures, $229,053, including $228,089 for 76 grants (high: $100,000; low: $10).

Purpose and activities: Giving primarily for family and social services, health, education, and Protestant churches.
Types of support: Building funds.
Limitations: Giving primarily in NY and NJ. No grants to individuals.
Application information: Contributes only to pre-selected organizations. Applications not accepted.
Trustees: Joanne Corzine, Jon S. Corzine, Robert A. Friedman.
Employer Identification Number: 133103160

4260
The Cowles Charitable Trust
630 Fifth Ave., Suite 1612
New York 10111-0144 (212) 765-6262

Trust established in 1948 in NY.
Donor(s): Gardner Cowles.†
Foundation type: Independent
Financial data (yr. ended 12/31/88): Assets, $13,835,228 (M); gifts received, $1,133,136; expenditures, $1,453,820, including $1,238,540 for grants (high: $200,000).
Purpose and activities: Grants largely for arts and culture, including museums and the performing arts; higher and secondary education; hospitals and AIDS programs; community funds; and social services and youth.
Types of support: Operating budgets, continuing support, annual campaigns, seed money, emergency funds, building funds, equipment, endowment funds, matching funds, capital campaigns, general purposes, renovation projects, special projects, professorships.
Limitations: Giving primarily in NY and FL. No grants to individuals; no loans.
Publications: Annual report (including application guidelines), application guidelines.
Application information: Application form not required.
Initial approach: Proposal or letter
Copies of proposal: 7
Deadline(s): 6 weeks before board meeting
Board meeting date(s): Jan., Apr., July, and Oct.
Write: Martha Roby Stephens, Secy.
Officers: Gardner Cowles III,* Pres.; Martha Roby Stephens,* Secy.; Mary Croft, Treas.
Trustees:* Charles Cowles, Jan Cowles, Lois Cowles Harrison, Virginia Cowles Kurtis, Kate Cowles Nichols.
Number of staff: 2 part-time professional.
Employer Identification Number: 136090295

4261
Herbert and Jeanine Coyne Foundation ⌑
230 Park Ave.
New York 10169 (212) 692-4830

Established in 1983 in NY.
Donor(s): Herbert J. Coyne, Jeanine Coyne.
Foundation type: Independent
Financial data (yr. ended 12/31/88): Assets, $495,910 (M); gifts received, $20,000; expenditures, $213,242, including $211,668 for 46 grants (high: $43,958; low: $250).
Purpose and activities: Emphasis on arts and cultural institutions, including a crafts organization, museums, and dance; some support also for the aged, higher education, social services and hospitals.
Limitations: Giving primarily in FL, New York, NY, and MA. No grants to individuals.
Application information: Contributes only to pre-selected organizations. Applications not accepted.
Officers: Herbert J. Coyne, Pres. and Treas.; Jeanine Coyne, V.P. and Secy.
Director: Robert Pelz.
Employer Identification Number: 133206423

4262
The Craigmyle Foundation ⌑
275 Madison Ave., Suite 1414
New York 10016

Trust established in 1951 in NY.
Donor(s): Ronald M. Craigmyle.
Foundation type: Independent
Financial data (yr. ended 12/31/88): Assets, $1,603,512 (M); expenditures, $99,393, including $82,900 for 30 grants (high: $25,000; low: $100).
Purpose and activities: Giving for higher and secondary education, Protestant church support, youth agencies, and hospitals.
Limitations: Giving primarily in NY. No grants to individuals.
Application information: Contributes only to pre-selected organizations. Applications not accepted.
Trustees: William C. Blind, Louise Craigmyle, Ronald M. Craigmyle, Jr.
Employer Identification Number: 136109205

4263
The Crane Foundation ⌑
(Formerly UniDynamics Foundation, Inc.)
c/o Crane Co.
757 Third Ave.
New York 10017 (212) 415-7275

Incorporated in 1937 in DE; in 1951 in MO.
Donor(s): UMC Industries, Inc.
Foundation type: Company-sponsored
Financial data (yr. ended 12/31/88): Assets, $2,249,894 (M); expenditures, $98,500, including $78,490 for 38 grants (high: $17,000; low: $100).
Purpose and activities: Emphasis on community funds, higher education, the performing arts, youth agencies, and hospitals.
Types of support: General purposes, continuing support, annual campaigns, scholarship funds.
Limitations: No grants to individuals, or for endowment funds, capital funds, or research; no loans.
Application information:
Initial approach: Letter
Deadline(s): None
Board meeting date(s): As required
Write: R.K. Whitley, V.P.
Officers and Directors:* R.S. Evans,* Chair. and Pres.; P.R. Hundt,* Exec. V.P. and Secy.; J.P. Cronin,* Exec. V.P. and Treas.; R. Phillips,* Exec. V.P.
Employer Identification Number: 436051752

4264
Josephine B. Crane Foundation ⌑
781 Fifth Ave.
New York 10022

Incorporated in 1955 in NY.
Donor(s): Josephine B. Crane.†
Foundation type: Independent
Financial data (yr. ended 12/31/88): Assets, $1,836,761 (M); expenditures, $69,834, including $56,000 for 9 grants (high: $12,500; low: $2,500).
Purpose and activities: Emphasis on social and cultural advancement.
Limitations: Giving primarily in NY and MA. No grants to individuals.
Application information: Contributes only to pre-selected organizations. Applications not accepted.
Write: Lawrence E. Brinn, Treas.
Officers and Directors:* Louise B. Crane,* Pres.; Peter F. De Gaetano,* Secy.; Lawrence E. Brinn,* Treas.
Employer Identification Number: 136156264

4265
Cranshaw Corporation ⌑
c/o White and Case
1155 Ave. of the Americas
New York 10036 (212) 819-8200

Incorporated in 1954 in DE.
Donor(s): Helen Babbott Sanders.†
Foundation type: Independent
Financial data (yr. ended 12/31/88): Assets, $2,023,517 (M); expenditures, $134,874, including $115,000 for 14 grants (high: $28,000; low: $1,000).
Purpose and activities: Giving for education, including secondary and higher institutions, and art education.
Limitations: Giving primarily in NY. No grants to individuals.
Application information: Contributes only to pre-selected organizations. Applications not accepted.
Write: Edward F. Rover, V.P.
Officers and Directors: Robert MacDonald, Pres.; Edward F. Rover, V.P. and Secy.-Treas.
Employer Identification Number: 136110555

4266
Bruce L. Crary Foundation, Inc.
Hand House, River St.
P.O. Box 396
Elizabethtown 12932 (518) 873-6496

Incorporated in 1973 in NY.
Donor(s): Crary Public Trust, Bruce L. Crary.†
Foundation type: Independent
Financial data (yr. ended 06/30/89): Assets, $5,465,346 (M); expenditures, $241,326, including $8,695 for 13 grants (high: $2,500; low: $100; average: $750), $190,690 for 410 grants to individuals (high: $800; low: $100; average: $500) and $11,322 for 1 foundation-administered program.
Purpose and activities: Emphasis on scholarship aid for post-secondary education, limited to residents of five specified counties; some support for educational and social service agencies, in Essex County only. Recently, the foundation initiated a "Citizen Information Service" at its headquarters in Elizabethtown

patterned after the British "Citizen Advice Bureaux."
Types of support: Student aid.
Limitations: Giving limited to Clinton, Essex, Franklin, Hamilton, and Warren counties, NY, for higher education scholarships, and to Essex County, NY, for educational and social service agencies.
Application information: Application form required for scholarships is available through high school guidance offices in Clinton, Essex, Franklin, Hamilton and Warren counties, NY. Application form required.
Initial approach: Letter or telephone
Copies of proposal: 1
Deadline(s): Mar. 31 for scholarships
Board meeting date(s): Monthly
Final notification: 30 to 60 days for grants; scholarships awarded in early July
Write: Richard W. Lawrence, Jr., Pres.
Officers and Governors:* Richard W. Lawrence, Jr.,* Pres.; G. Gordon Davis,* V.P. and Secy.; Arthur V. Savage,* V.P. and Treas.; Janet Decker, Euphemia V. Hall, John W. Nason, Meredith Prime, Charles O. Warren.
Number of staff: 2 full-time professional.
Employer Identification Number: 237366844

4267
William Nelson Cromwell Foundation for the Research of the Law and Legal History of the Colonial Period of the U.S.A. ⌑
c/o Sullivan & Cromwell
125 Broad St.
New York 10004
Application address: 250 Park Ave., New York, NY 10177; Tel.: (212) 558-3929

Established in 1930 in NY.
Foundation type: Independent
Financial data (yr. ended 11/30/88): Assets, $1,633,993 (M); expenditures, $80,690, including $48,000 for 4 grants (high: $25,000; low: $3,000) and $13,500 for 3 grants to individuals (high: $10,000; low: $500).
Purpose and activities: Support for historical research on the Colonial and early Federal periods of American legal history.
Types of support: Publications, grants to individuals.
Application information:
Initial approach: Letter
Deadline(s): Nov. 15
Write: Henry N. Ess, Trustee
Officers and Trustees: David W. Peck, Chair.; Henry N. Ess III, Secy.-Treas.; Dudley B. Bonsal, Charles D. Breitel, Merrell E. Clark, Jr., Eli Whitney Debevoise, Robert B. Fiske, J. Edward Lumbard, Jr., Robert McKay, Leon Silverman, Harold A. Stevens, Harold R. Tyler, Jr., Jo L. Wachtler, Edward Walsh, Bethuel M. Webster.
Employer Identification Number: 136068485

4268
Crosswicks Foundation, Ltd. ⌑
924 West End Ave.
New York 10025 (203) 491-3676

Established in 1972 in NY.
Foundation type: Independent
Financial data (yr. ended 11/30/88): Assets, $1,594,027 (M); expenditures, $100,981, including $80,000 for 24 grants (high: $10,000; low: $500).
Purpose and activities: Grants for church support, social services, cultural organizations, hospitals, and education.
Types of support: Continuing support, scholarship funds.
Limitations: No grants to individuals.
Application information:
Initial approach: Letter
Deadline(s): Nov. 1
Officers: Madeleine L'Engle Franklin, Pres.; Josephine Jones, V.P.; Laurie Franklin, Secy.; Bion B. Franklin, Treas.
Employer Identification Number: 132732197

4269
Lewis B. & Dorothy Cullman Foundation, Inc. ⌑
c/o Lewis B. Cullman
767 Third Ave.
New York 10017

Established in 1958 in NY.
Donor(s): Lewis B. Cullman, Dorothy F. Cullman.
Foundation type: Independent
Financial data (yr. ended 11/30/89): Assets, $391,575 (M); gifts received, $526,775; expenditures, $315,832, including $307,701 for 103 grants (high: $40,000; low: $25).
Purpose and activities: Emphasis on cultural programs; support also for a Jewish welfare organization.
Limitations: Giving primarily in New York, NY. No grants to individuals.
Application information: Contributes only to pre-selected organizations. Applications not accepted.
Officers and Directors:* Lewis B. Cullman,* Pres. and Treas.; Dorothy F. Cullman,* V.P.; Mildred F. Eisenmayer,* Secy.
Employer Identification Number: 510243747

4270
Louise B. & Edgar M. Cullman Foundation ⌑
641 Lexington Ave., 29th Fl.
New York 10022-4599 (212) 838-0211

Established in 1956 in NY.
Foundation type: Independent
Financial data (yr. ended 12/31/88): Assets, $708,162 (M); gifts received, $343,463; expenditures, $243,870, including $234,800 for 25 grants (average: $25-$80,000).
Purpose and activities: Support for education, including medical education, health, the performing arts and other cultural programs, and wildlife preservation.
Types of support: Annual campaigns, building funds, endowment funds.
Application information: Application form required.
Copies of proposal: 1
Deadline(s): None
Board meeting date(s): Dec.
Write: Edgar M. Cullman, Pres.
Officers: Edgar M. Cullman, Pres.; Louise B. Cullman, V.P.; John C. Emmert, Secy.
Number of staff: 1 part-time professional; 1 part-time support.
Employer Identification Number: 136100041

4271
The Daphne Seybolt Culpeper Foundation, Inc. ⌑
261 Madison Ave., 26th Fl.
New York 10017

Established in 1973 in NY.
Foundation type: Independent
Financial data (yr. ended 10/31/89): Assets, $1,749,882 (M); expenditures, $85,527, including $59,500 for 35 grants (high: $16,000; low: $250).
Purpose and activities: Grants primarily for social service and health organizations, higher and other education, and public policy programs.
Limitations: No grants to individuals.
Application information: Contributes only to pre-selected organizations. Applications not accepted.
Write: Kalman I. Nulman, Esq., Mgr.
Officer: Kalman I. Nulman, Mgr.
Employer Identification Number: 237227846

4272
James H. Cummings Foundation, Inc.
1807 Elmwood Ave., Rm. 112
Buffalo 14207 (716) 874-0040

Incorporated in 1962 in NY.
Donor(s): James H. Cummings.†
Foundation type: Independent
Financial data (yr. ended 05/31/89): Assets, $13,787,672 (M); expenditures, $754,706, including $608,756 for 25 grants (high: $100,000; low: $279).
Purpose and activities: Exclusively for charitable purposes in advancing medical science, research, and education in the U.S. and Canada and for charitable work among underprivileged boys and girls and aged and infirm persons in designated areas.
Types of support: Building funds, seed money, equipment, land acquisition, matching funds, consulting services, research.
Limitations: Giving limited to the vicinity of the cities of Buffalo, NY; Hendersonville, NC; and Toronto, Ontario. No support for national health organizations. No grants to individuals, or for annual campaigns, program support, endowment funds, operating budgets, emergency funds, deficit financing, scholarships, fellowships, publications, conferences, or continuing support; no loans.
Publications: Annual report (including application guidelines).
Application information: Application form not required.
Initial approach: Letter of not more than 2 pages or by telephone
Copies of proposal: 7
Deadline(s): Feb. 1, May 1, Aug. 1, and Nov. 1
Board meeting date(s): Mar., June, Sept., and Dec.
Final notification: 4 to 8 weeks
Write: Robert J. Lyle, Exec. Dir.

Officers: William G. Gisel,* Pres.; Kenneth M. Alford, M.D.,* V.P.; Robert J. Lyle, Secy. and Exec. Dir.; Robert J.A. Irwin,* Treas.
Directors:* John Naughton, M.D., Robert S. Scheu, John N. Walsh, Jr.
Number of staff: 1 full-time professional; 1 part-time support.
Employer Identification Number: 160864200

4273
The Nathan Cummings Foundation, Inc. ▼
885 Third Ave., Suite 3160
New York 10022 (212) 230-3377

Established in 1949 in NY.
Donor(s): Nathan Cummings.†
Foundation type: Independent
Financial data (yr. ended 12/31/88): Assets, $54,120,204 (M); expenditures, $3,022,541, including $2,565,685 for 53 grants (high: $1,000,000; low: $1,000; average: $5,000-$50,000).
Purpose and activities: The foundation is currently undergoing a review of grantmaking activities. Grants will focus on improving the environment on a global scale, supporting multi-cultural arts projects and making the arts more accessible to more people, improving the health-delivery system for the poor, and enhancing understanding between Jews and non-Jews.
Types of support: Annual campaigns, building funds, capital campaigns, consulting services, general purposes, lectureships, special projects.
Application information: Guidelines are currently undergoing review.
Board meeting date(s): 4 times a year
Write: Annette Ensley
Officers and Directors: Beatrice Cummings Mayer, Chair.; Herbert K. Cummings, Vice-Chair.; Ruth Cummings Sorensen, Vice-Chair.; Charles R. Halpern, Pres.; Daniel G. Ross, Secy.; Jay Levy, Treas.; James K. Cummings, Michael A. Cummings, Robert N. Mayer.
Number of staff: 15
Employer Identification Number: 237093201

4274
The Frances L. & Edwin L. Cummings Memorial Fund ▼ ⌑
501 Fifth Ave., Suite 1208
New York 10017-1602 (212) 286-1778

Established in 1982 in NY.
Donor(s): Edwin L. Cummings,† Frances L. Cummings.†
Foundation type: Independent
Financial data (yr. ended 7/31/88): Assets, $25,556,007 (M); expenditures, $2,131,627, including $1,793,124 for 47 grants (high: $280,000; low: $5,000).
Purpose and activities: Support for medical and disease research, specifically on the problems of aging and cancer, rehabilitation and education of the physically and/or mentally handicapped, medical equipment for health care institutions demonstrating special needs, campaigns to build endowments through establishment of challenge grants, youth and child welfare concerns, especially child-abuse prevention, and higher education, particularly as it relates to student populations from disadvantaged backgrounds.
Types of support: Research, consulting services, endowment funds, professorships, scholarship funds, seed money, special projects, equipment, matching funds, publications.
Limitations: Giving primarily in the New York City metropolitan area, including NJ and CT. No support for the cultural arts or private foundations, or for alcoholism or drug prevention. No grants to individuals (except for scientific research projects which have been pre-screened by qualified scientific advisory committee), or for capital building campaigns, general operating expenses, or annual fundraising campaigns.
Publications: Biennial report (including application guidelines).
Application information:
Initial approach: Letter, preferably 7 pages or less
Copies of proposal: 8
Deadline(s): Apr. 1 or Oct. 1
Board meeting date(s): June and Dec.
Final notification: 10 days after board meeting
Write: J. Andrew Lark
Trustees: J. Andrew Lark, Irving Trust Co.
Directors: Lawrence J. Denson, Chair.; William Bricker, Fred J. Brotherton, Fairleigh Dickinson, Jr., Anne Nordeman, Irving S. Wright.
Number of staff: 1 full-time professional; 1 full-time support.
Employer Identification Number: 136814491

4275
Curtice-Burns/Pro-Fac Foundation
P.O. Box 681
Rochester 14603 (716) 383-1850

Trust established in 1966 in NY.
Donor(s): Curtice-Burns Foods, Inc.
Foundation type: Company-sponsored
Financial data (yr. ended 06/30/89): Assets, $622,958 (L); gifts received, $300,000; expenditures, $450,384, including $446,497 for 239 grants (high: $30,000; low: $100; average: $1,000).
Purpose and activities: Emphasis on higher and other education, including scholarship funds, health and hospitals, agriculture, community funds, the handicapped, the disadvantaged, child welfare, and youth agencies.
Types of support: General purposes, operating budgets, annual campaigns, building funds, equipment, endowment funds, scholarship funds, fellowships, professorships, special projects, research, conferences and seminars, capital campaigns, continuing support, renovation projects.
Limitations: Giving primarily in areas of company operations. No support for religious organizations. No grants to individuals, or for seed money, emergency funds, deficit financing, land acquisition, matching gifts, or publications; no loans.
Application information: Application form not required.
Initial approach: Proposal
Copies of proposal: 1
Deadline(s): None
Board meeting date(s): Usually in Jan., Mar., May, Aug., Oct., and Dec.
Final notification: 2 months
Write: Marilyn T. Helmer, V.P.
Officer: Marilyn T. Helmer, V.P.
Trustees: Robert Call, Betty E. Hawthorne, Marilyn T. Hellmer, Roger J. Vallecorsse.
Number of staff: 1 part-time support.
Employer Identification Number: 166071142

4276
The D.T. Foundation, Inc. ⌑
280 Park Ave., #2700 West Bldg.
New York 10017

Established in 1985 in NY.
Donor(s): David Tendler.
Foundation type: Independent
Financial data (yr. ended 6/30/87): Assets, $180,496 (M); gifts received, $78,750; expenditures, $172,762, including $165,500 for 14 grants (high: $50,000; low: $500).
Purpose and activities: Support primarily for Jewish organizations, including Hebrew education.
Limitations: No grants to individuals.
Application information: Contributes only to pre-selected organizations. Applications not accepted.
Officers: Joseph Levine, Beatrice Tendler, David Tendler, Karen Tendler, Pearl Tendler.
Employer Identification Number: 133315585

4277
Dadourian Foundation ☆
168 Canal St., Suite 207
New York 10013

Established in 1961 in NY.
Donor(s): Dadour Dadourian.
Foundation type: Independent
Financial data (yr. ended 04/30/89): Assets, $1,754,432 (M); gifts received, $93,000; expenditures, $90,101, including $88,529 for 52 grants (high: $31,305; low: $20).
Purpose and activities: Support for Armenian organizations, including churches and schools.
Limitations: Giving primarily in the New York, NY, metropolitan area.
Officers: Dadour Dadourian, Pres.; Alex Dadourian, V.P.; Haig Dadourian, Secy.-Treas.
Employer Identification Number: 136125022

4278
Daily News Foundation, Inc. ⌑
220 East 42nd St.
New York 10017 (212) 210-6320

Incorporated in 1958 in NY.
Donor(s): New York News, Inc.
Foundation type: Company-sponsored
Financial data (yr. ended 12/31/88): Assets, $3,643,460 (M); expenditures, $251,116, including $238,915 for 75 grants (high: $65,000; low: $500).
Purpose and activities: Emphasis on a community fund, higher education, urban affairs, cultural activities, and youth agencies.
Limitations: Giving primarily in the five boroughs of New York City.
Application information:
Initial approach: Letter

Deadline(s): No later than the 1st of the month preceding the month meeting is held
Board meeting date(s): Quarterly
Write: Lucius P. Gregg, Asst. Secy.
Officers and Directors:* James F. Hoge,* Pres.; F. Gilman Spencer,* V.P.; J.C. Mason,* Secy.; R.K. Brown,* Treas.; L.L. Bloom, J. Campi, R. Herbert, M. Pankenham, A.W. Zaeske.
Employer Identification Number: 136161525

4279
Fred L. Dake Trust ⌑
c/o Norstar Trust Co.
One East Ave.
Rochester 14638

Established in 1984 in NY.
Donor(s): Dorothy V. Dake Trust.
Foundation type: Independent
Financial data (yr. ended 3/31/86): Assets, $1,706,193 (M); gifts received, $69,146; expenditures, $151,371, including $125,840 for 13 grants (high: $18,877; low: $6,292).
Purpose and activities: Giving primarily for social services.
Types of support: General purposes.
Limitations: Giving primarily in the Nunda, NY, area.
Trustee Bank: Norstar Trust Co.
Employer Identification Number: 166282450

4280
The Dammann Fund, Inc. ⌑
60 East 42nd St., Suite 3014
New York 10165 (212) 687-0880

Incorporated in 1946 in NY.
Donor(s): Members of the Dammann family.
Foundation type: Independent
Financial data (yr. ended 11/30/88): Assets, $9,895,414 (M); expenditures, $627,318, including $525,640 for 249 grants (high: $58,150; low: $10).
Purpose and activities: Grants to hospitals, health and welfare agencies, and religious and educational institutions.
Types of support: Continuing support, annual campaigns, seed money, building funds, endowment funds, general purposes, special projects.
Limitations: No grants to individuals, or for scholarships, fellowships, or matching gifts; no loans.
Application information:
Initial approach: Letter
Copies of proposal: 1
Deadline(s): None
Board meeting date(s): Mar., June, Sept., and Dec.
Write: Margaret D. Eisner, V.P.
Officer and Director: Margaret D. Eisner, V.P.
Number of staff: 2 part-time support.
Employer Identification Number: 136089896

4281
Eleanor Naylor Dana Charitable Trust ▼
375 Park Ave. 38th Fl.
New York 10152 (212) 754-2890

Established in 1979 in CT.
Donor(s): Eleanor Naylor Dana.†
Foundation type: Independent
Financial data (yr. ended 05/31/88): Assets, $10,651,701 (M); expenditures, $4,911,255, including $4,476,446 for 102 grants (high: $200,000; low: $888; average: $5,000-$100,000).
Purpose and activities: Grants are given mainly to foster and finance progress and the pursuit of excellence in two areas: (1) biomedical research, "to support clinical investigations by established scientists in qualified institutions in the U.S., to pursue innovative projects designed to improve medical practice or prevent disease," and (2) the performing arts, to assist the various performing arts fields in ways that could be of substantial import to the grantees and the artists and the public which they serve.
Types of support: Research, special projects.
Limitations: Giving primarily in areas east of the Mississippi River. No grants to individuals, or for instrumentation other than that required for a specific project, large scale field studies of a therapeutic or epidemiological nature, or conferences (in biomedical research); or for deficit financing, exhibits, publications, or conclaves (in the arts).
Publications: Informational brochure.
Application information: Application form not required.
Initial approach: Letter of intent under 1,000 words
Copies of proposal: 6
Deadline(s): Feb. 1, May 1, Sept. 1, and Nov. 1
Board meeting date(s): Mar., June, Oct., and Dec.
Final notification: After meetings
Write: The Trustees
Officers and Trustees:* David Mahony,* Chair.; A.J. Signorile,* Treas.; Robert A. Good, M.D., Carlos Moseley, Robert E. Wise, M.D.
Number of staff: 1 full-time professional.
Employer Identification Number: 132992855

4282
The Charles A. Dana Foundation, Inc. ▼
150 East 52nd St., 23rd Fl.
New York 10022 (212) 223-4040

Incorporated in 1950 in CT.
Donor(s): Charles A. Dana,† Eleanor Naylor Dana.†
Foundation type: Independent
Financial data (yr. ended 12/31/89): Assets, $185,072,368 (M); expenditures, $10,352,957, including $7,555,873 for 144 grants (high: $400,000; low: $2,000; average: $50,000-$200,000) and $150,000 for 4 grants to individuals (high: $50,000; low: $25,000; average: $25,000-$50,000).
Purpose and activities: Principal interests in private higher education at four-year liberal arts colleges and the protection of human health and prevention of disease through grants to major academic medical centers, as well as a program instituted in 1986, the Charles A. Dana Awards for Pioneering Achievements in Health and Higher Education; support also for cultural and civic programs and the Dana-Farber Cancer Institute.
Types of support: Matching funds, scholarship funds, professorships, internships, research.
Limitations: Giving primarily in the eastern U.S.; support of cultural and civic programs principally in the greater New York, NY area. No support for professional organizations. No grants to individuals (except for the Charles A. Dana Awards), or for capital or endowment funds, operating budgets, continuing support, annual campaigns, building or emergency funds, deficit financing, publications, conferences, demonstration projects, or colloquia; no loans.
Publications: Annual report (including application guidelines), newsletter.
Application information: Applications for the Charles A. Dana Awards by nomination only; guidelines available. Application form not required.
Initial approach: Letter
Deadline(s): None
Board meeting date(s): Apr., June, Oct., and Dec.
Final notification: 2 to 3 months
Write: Robert N. Kreidler, Pres.; Marilyn A. Baldwin, Prog. Officer (higher education); Stephen A. Foster, Prog. Officer (health); or Margo Viscusi, Prog. Officer (Dana Awards)
Officers and Directors: David J. Mahoney, Chair.; Robert N. Kreidler, Pres.; Walter G. Corcoran, V.P.; Clark M. Whittemore, Jr., Secy.-Treas.; Edward C. Andrews, Jr., Wallace L. Cook, Charles A. Dana, Jr., Donald B. Marron, Carlos Moseley, L. Guy Palmer II, Donald C. Platten.
Number of staff: 6 full-time professional; 1 part-time professional; 3 full-time support.
Employer Identification Number: 066036761

4283
Gerard & Ruth Daniel Foundation, Inc. ⌑
Polly Park Rd.
Rye 10580

Donor(s): Gerard Daniel & Co.
Foundation type: Independent
Financial data (yr. ended 12/31/88): Assets, $2,997,705 (M); expenditures, $145,674, including $140,450 for 22 grants (high: $56,400; low: $50).
Purpose and activities: Grants primarily for Jewish welfare funds, cultural and educational organizations, and temple support; support also for museums.
Application information: Contributes only to pre-selected organizations. Applications not accepted.
Officers: Gerard Daniel, Pres.; Ruth Daniel, V.P.
Employer Identification Number: 136207879

4284
Jessie Smith Darrah Charitable Trust ⌑
20 Exchange Place
New York 10043

Donor(s): Jessie S. Darrah.†
Foundation type: Independent
Financial data (yr. ended 12/31/88): Assets, $2,054,465 (M); expenditures, $127,662,

including $99,055 for 15 grants (high: $20,000; low: $500).
Purpose and activities: Giving primarily for youth agencies, child welfare, and Methodist church support.
Limitations: Giving primarily in Chautauqua County, NY. No grants to individuals.
Application information: Contributes only to pre-selected organizations. Applications not accepted.
Trustees: Howard A. Johnson, Wesley H. Nord, Charles H. Price, Richard F. Reading, Richard L. Swanson, Citibank, N.A.
Employer Identification Number: 136129875

4285
The Davenport-Hatch Foundation, Inc.
c/o Norstar Trust Co.
One East Ave.
Rochester 14638

Incorporated in 1952 in NY.
Donor(s): Augustus Hatch.†
Foundation type: Independent
Financial data (yr. ended 5/31/89): Assets, $16,767,906 (M); expenditures, $856,598, including $794,250 for 89 grants (high: $50,000; low: $100).
Purpose and activities: Giving for community development; higher, secondary, and elementary education; museums and the fine and performing arts; welfare, including programs for the aged, women and youth; hospitals and health services, and church support.
Types of support: Continuing support, equipment, renovation projects, building funds, capital campaigns.
Limitations: Giving primarily in the Rochester, NY, area. No grants to individuals.
Application information: Contributes only to pre-selected organizations. Applications not accepted.
Board meeting date(s): Approximately the 15th of Apr., June, Sept., and Dec.
Officers and Directors:* Austin E. Hildebrandt,* Pres.; David H. Taylor,* V.P.; Helen H. Heller,* Secy.-Treas.; Earl W. Brinkman, Robert J. Brinkman, J. Wallace Ely, William L. Ely, A. Thomas Hildebrandt, Elizabeth H. Hildebrandt, Douglas F. Taylor, Hart Taylor.
Number of staff: None.
Employer Identification Number: 166027105

4286
The Michel David-Weill Foundation ▼ ⌑
c/o Lazard Freres and Co.
One Rockefeller Plaza
New York 10020 (212) 489-6600

Established in 1984 in NY.
Donor(s): Michel David-Weill.
Foundation type: Independent
Financial data (yr. ended 6/30/88): Assets, $2,073,713 (M); gifts received, $500,000; expenditures, $1,539,074.
Purpose and activities: Support for cultural programs and Jewish welfare funds.
Limitations: Giving primarily in the New York, NY, area.
Application information:
Initial approach: Letter
Deadline(s): None
Write: Thomas R.X. Mullarkey, Secy.
Officers: Michel David-Weill, Pres.; Eliane David-Weill, V.P.; Thomas F.X. Mullarkey, Secy.-Treas.
Number of staff: 2
Employer Identification Number: 133240809

4287
The Marvin H. Davidson Foundation, Inc.
c/o M.H. Davidson & Co.
174 East 64th St.
New York 10021-7478

Established in 1967 in NY.
Donor(s): Marvin H. Davidson.
Foundation type: Independent
Financial data (yr. ended 12/31/88): Assets, $1,413,882 (M); expenditures, $203,678, including $194,550 for 36 grants (high: $42,300; low: $100).
Purpose and activities: Giving primarily to Jewish organizations and to educational institutions.
Limitations: Giving primarily in NY. No grants to individuals.
Application information: Contributes only to pre-selected organizations. Applications not accepted.
Officers: Marvin H. Davidson,* Pres.; Sally Davidson, V.P. and Secy.-Treas.
Directors:* Scott Davidson, Seymour Hertz.
Employer Identification Number: 136217756

4288
The Davidson-Krueger Foundation, Inc. ⌑
5002 Second Ave.
Brooklyn 11232 (718) 439-6300

Incorporated in 1955 in NY.
Donor(s): Philip Davidson, Davidson Pipe Co., Inc., and others.
Foundation type: Independent
Financial data (yr. ended 11/30/88): Assets, $1,005,681 (M); expenditures, $88,669, including $85,127 for 24 grants (high: $18,071; low: $100) and $2,008 for 4 grants to individuals (high: $960; low: $40).
Purpose and activities: Giving primarily for higher education, including scholarships to individuals that cover tuition, room, and board; support also for Jewish welfare funds, hospitals, and education in Israel.
Types of support: Student aid.
Limitations: Giving primarily in NY.
Application information:
Initial approach: Letter
Deadline(s): Mar. 15
Write: Board of Trustees
Officers: H. Peter Davidson, Pres.; Stuart Krueger, Secy.-Treas.
Employer Identification Number: 116005674

4289
Shelby Cullom Davis Foundation ▼
70 Pine St.
New York 10270 (212) 425-3212

Incorporated in 1962 in NY.
Donor(s): Shelby Cullom Davis.
Foundation type: Independent
Financial data (yr. ended 11/30/89): Assets, $53,259,704 (M); gifts received, $6,192,451; expenditures, $2,003,196, including $1,465,658 for 73 grants (high: $600,000; low: $25; average: $100-$10,000).
Purpose and activities: Giving primarily in higher education, and public policy; some support for cultural programs and economic research.
Application information: Contributes only to pre-selected organizations. Applications not accepted.
Write: Shelby Cullom Davis, Chair.
Officer: Shelby Cullom Davis, Chair.
Employer Identification Number: 136165382

4290
Simon and Annie Davis Foundation ⌑
1740 Broadway, 3rd Fl.
New York 10019

Incorporated in 1946 in NY.
Donor(s): Abraham M. Davis,† Meyer Davis,† Ruth Davis.
Foundation type: Independent
Financial data (yr. ended 12/31/88): Assets, $2,389,177 (M); expenditures, $401,428, including $388,500 for 16 grants (high: $254,000; low: $1,000).
Purpose and activities: Giving primarily for Jewish welfare funds and higher education.
Limitations: Giving primarily in NY and Israel.
Application information: Contributes only to pre-selected organizations. Applications not accepted.
Officers and Directors:* Paul B. Gibney, Jr.,* Pres. and Treas.; Leonard Schwartz,* Secy.
Employer Identification Number: 136069454

4291
Day Family Foundation ⌑
c/o Goldman, Sachs & Co.
85 Broad St., Tax Dept.
New York 10004

Established in 1979 in NY.
Donor(s): H. Corbin Day.
Foundation type: Independent
Financial data (yr. ended 7/31/88): Assets, $2,739,450 (M); gifts received, $50,000; expenditures, $295,476.
Purpose and activities: Support primarily for higher and secondary education, youth programs, and hospitals and health organizations.
Limitations: No grants to individuals.
Application information: Applications not accepted.
Trustees: Dorothy J. Day, H. Corbin Day, Stephen Friedman.
Employer Identification Number: 133025969

4292
The Baron de Hirsch Fund ⌑
c/o Federation of Jewish Philanthropies
130 East 59th St.
New York 10022 (212) 980-1000
Fellowship application address: Fellowship Comm., Ministry of Agriculture, Tel Aviv, Israel

Incorporated in 1891 in NY.

Donor(s): Baron Maurice de Hirsch,† Baroness Clara de Hirsch.†
Foundation type: Independent
Financial data (yr. ended 8/31/88): Assets, $5,430,995 (M); expenditures, $486,561, including $349,200 for 21 grants (high: $30,000; low: $5,000).
Purpose and activities: To assist in the economic assimilation of Jewish immigrants in the U.S. and Israel, their instruction in trades and agriculture, and promotion of agriculture among them; aids other agencies that work to obtain education and jobs for immigrants.
Types of support: Operating budgets, continuing support, seed money, emergency funds, exchange programs, special projects, research.
Limitations: Giving primarily in the New York City, NY, area and Israel. No grants to individuals, or for annual campaigns, deficit financing, capital or endowment funds, matching gifts, or publications.
Publications: Application guidelines.
Application information: Application form not required.
Initial approach: Letter
Copies of proposal: 1
Deadline(s): Aug. 1
Board meeting date(s): Oct.
Final notification: 2 weeks after board meeting
Write: Lauren Katzowitz
Officers and Trustees: Francis F. Rosenbaum, Jr.,* Pres.; Martin Blumenthal, V.P.; Arthur Sporn, V.P.; Gail B. Chasin, Secy.; Christopher C. Schwabacher, Treas.; James A. Block, Thomas A. Frank, Jerome W. Gottesman, William M. Heineman, William H. Heyman, Ezra P. Mager, Jennie Morgenthau, George W. Naumburg, Jr., Elizabeth Perle, Steven K. Rosenbaum, Edwin H. Stern III, Seymour Zises.
Number of staff: 2 part-time professional; 1 full-time support; 1 part-time support.
Employer Identification Number: 135562971

4293
Harry De Jur Foundation, Inc. ⌑
c/o Pavia & Harcourt
600 Madison Ave.
New York 10022 (212) 980-3500

Incorporated in 1958 in NY.
Donor(s): Harry De Jur.†
Foundation type: Independent
Financial data (yr. ended 11/30/88): Assets, $1,372,435 (M); expenditures, $129,141, including $114,340 for grants.
Purpose and activities: Emphasis on education, both in Israel and the U.S., social and health agencies, Jewish social and charitable organizations, and cultural programs.
Limitations: Giving primarily in NY.
Application information: Application form not required.
Deadline(s): None
Write: David Botwinik, Secy.
Officers: Robert Greenberg, Pres.; Marian De Jur, V.P.; Benjamin Neuwirth, V.P.; David Botwinik, Secy.
Employer Identification Number: 136110844

4294
The de Kay Foundation ⌑
c/o Manufacturers Hanover Trust Co.
600 Fifth Ave.
New York 10020 (212) 957-1668

Trust established in 1967 in CT.
Donor(s): Helen M. de Kay.†
Foundation type: Independent
Financial data (yr. ended 2/28/89): Assets, $16,760,498 (M); expenditures, $1,017,739, including $669,720 for 3 grants (high: $330,576; low: $169,572) and $202,540 for 83 grants to individuals (high: $7,150; low: $350; average: $1,000-$5,000).
Purpose and activities: To encourage and promote the well-doing and well-being of men and women of culture or refined heritage who are in real need of financial assistance, particularly sick, old, or disabled persons who are not being otherwise properly cared for; after distribution of two-thirds of the income to specified institutions, balance is allocated for above purpose.
Types of support: Continuing support, grants to individuals.
Limitations: Giving limited to NY, NJ, and CT. No grants for building or endowment funds, scholarships, fellowships, or matching gifts; no loans.
Application information: Application form required.
Initial approach: Letter
Copies of proposal: 1
Board meeting date(s): Quarterly
Final notification: 1 or 2 months
Write: Lloyd Saltus, II, V.P., Manufacturers Hanover Trust Co.
Advisory Committee: Howard S. Tuthill, Chair.; Betsy Devecchi, Robert F. Longley, Rev. Hays Rockwell, Lloyd Saltus II, Jerome Shaw.
Trustees: Manufacturers Hanover Trust Co., Morgan Guaranty Trust Co. of New York.
Number of staff: None.
Employer Identification Number: 136203234

4295
The Edmond de Rothschild Foundation ⌑
c/o Proskauer, Rose, Goetz & Mendelsohn
300 Park Ave., Rm. 2100
New York 10022 (212) 909-7724

Incorporated in 1963 in NY.
Donor(s): Edmond de Rothschild.
Foundation type: Independent
Financial data (yr. ended 2/28/89): Assets, $25,935,266 (M); gifts received, $1,400,000; expenditures, $1,196,622, including $989,380 for 48 grants (high: $107,983; low: $500).
Purpose and activities: Grants largely for Jewish welfare funds, higher education, and organizations concerned with Israeli affairs in the U.S. and abroad; support also for cultural programs, hospitals, and scientific research.
Types of support: General purposes.
Limitations: Giving primarily in New York, NY, and in France; some giving in Israel. No grants to individuals.
Application information: Application form not required.
Initial approach: Letter
Copies of proposal: 1
Deadline(s): None
Board meeting date(s): As required
Final notification: Varies
Write: Paul H. Epstein, Secy.-Treas.
Officers and Directors: Edmond de Rothschild, Chair.; George M. Shapiro, Pres.; Georges C. Karlweis, V.P.; Paul H. Epstein, Secy.-Treas.; Benjamin de Rothschild, Bernard Esambert, Stanley Komaroff.
Number of staff: None.
Employer Identification Number: 136119422

4296
B. de Rothschild Foundation for the Advancement of Science in Israel ⌑
One Rockefeller Plaza, 29th Fl.
New York 10020

Incorporated in 1958 in NY.
Donor(s): Mrs. Bethsabee de Rothschild.
Foundation type: Independent
Financial data (yr. ended 5/31/88): Assets, $1,660,642 (M); expenditures, $101,061, including $49,000 for grants.
Purpose and activities: Grants for seminars on scientific research in Israel.
Types of support: Conferences and seminars.
Limitations: Giving limited to Israel.
Application information: Contributes only to pre-selected organizations. Applications not accepted.
Officers: Bethsabee de Rothschild,* Pres.; Joram Piatigorsky,* V.P.; G. Peter Fleck, Secy.
Directors:* Michael A. Varet.
Employer Identification Number: 136075582

4297
The Ira W. DeCamp Foundation ▼ ⌑
c/o Mudge Rose Guthrie Alexander & Ferdon
180 Maiden Ln.
New York 10038 (212) 510-7558

Trust established in 1975 in NY.
Donor(s): Elizabeth DeCamp McInerny.†
Foundation type: Independent
Financial data (yr. ended 10/31/88): Assets, $45,709,430 (M); expenditures, $4,086,592, including $3,242,267 for 46 grants.
Purpose and activities: Grants for health care facilities and equipment and for medical research and education.
Types of support: Building funds, equipment, seed money, research, special projects.
Limitations: No support for government-affiliated organizations. No grants to individuals, or for general support, land acquisition, publications, conferences, endowment funds, operating budgets, continuing support, annual campaigns, emergency funds, or deficit financing; no support for research on live animals other than rats and mice; no loans.
Application information: Application form not required.
Initial approach: Letter
Copies of proposal: 3
Deadline(s): None
Board meeting date(s): Quarterly
Final notification: 3 months
Write: William J. Kramer
Trustees: Herbert H. Faber, Manufacturers Hanover Trust Co.
Number of staff: None.
Employer Identification Number: 510138577

4298
Dr. G. Clifford & Florence B. Decker Foundation
Galleria
Eight Hawley St.
Binghamton 13901 (607) 722-0211

Established in 1979 in NY.
Donor(s): Clifford Decker.†
Foundation type: Independent
Financial data (yr. ended 12/31/87): Assets, $1,056,915 (M); gifts received, $196,500; expenditures, $47,608, including $33,500 for 11 grants (high: $10,000; low: $500).
Purpose and activities: Support for education and general charitable giving.
Types of support: Capital campaigns, seed money, special projects.
Limitations: Giving primarily in Broome County, NY, area.
Publications: Annual report, informational brochure (including application guidelines).
Application information: Application form required.
Copies of proposal: 2
Deadline(s): Mar. 1, May 1, July 1, Sept. 1, and Nov. 1
Board meeting date(s): Apr., June, Aug., Oct., and Dec.
Write: Donna Bechdel, Exec. Dir.
Officers: Ferris G. Akel, Chair.; William S. Chittenden, Vice-Chair.; Eugene E. Peckham, Secy.; Douglas R. Johnson, Treas.; Donna Bechdel, Exec. Dir.
Number of staff: 1 full-time professional; 1 part-time professional.
Employer Identification Number: 161131704

4299
Margarita Victoria Delacorte Foundation ⌑ ☆
c/o U.S. Trust Co. of New York
114 West 47th St.
New York 10036-1532

Donor(s): Marguerita V. Delacorte.
Foundation type: Independent
Financial data (yr. ended 12/31/88): Assets, $322,524 (M); gifts received, $220,019; expenditures, $105,478, including $102,000 for 44 grants (high: $20,000; low: $250).
Purpose and activities: Support for higher and secondary education and religious associations.
Limitations: Giving primarily in New York, NY.
Application information:
Initial approach: Letter
Deadline(s): None
Write: Marguerita V. Delacorte
Trustee: U.S. Trust Co. of New York.
Employer Identification Number: 136197777

4300
Beatrice P. Delany Charitable Trust ▼ ⌑
c/o The Chase Manhattan Bank, N.A.
1211 Ave. of the Americas
New York 10036 (212) 730-5883

Trust established about 1977 in NY.
Donor(s): Beatrice P. Delany.†
Foundation type: Independent
Financial data (yr. ended 10/31/87): Assets, $74,236,515 (M); expenditures, $1,506,960, including $1,357,000 for 51 grants (high: $110,000; low: $500; average: $1,000-$20,000).
Purpose and activities: Giving largely for education, especially higher education, hospitals, health organizations, and religion.
Types of support: General purposes.
Limitations: Giving primarily in the Chicago, IL, metropolitan area.
Application information: Applications not accepted.
Write: Howard Serrell, Jr.
Trust Committee: Thomas A. Reynolds, Jr., Mrs. Thomas A. Reynolds, Jr., Andrew Thomson, M.D.
Trustee: The Chase Manhattan Bank, N.A.
Number of staff: None.
Employer Identification Number: 136748171

4301
Nelson B. Delavan Foundation ⌑ ☆
c/o Chase Lincoln First Bank, N.A.
P.O. Box 1412
Rochester 14603-1412
Application address: c/o Chase Lincoln First Bank, N.A., Five Seneca St., Geneva, NY 14456; Tel.: (315) 781-0280

Established in 1983 in NY.
Foundation type: Independent
Financial data (yr. ended 3/31/89): Assets, $3,292,534 (M); expenditures, $187,560, including $174,810 for 43 grants (high: $10,000; low: $500).
Purpose and activities: Giving primarily for cultural programs and animal welfare, including wildlife preservation; support also for hospitals, health, and social services.
Types of support: Operating budgets.
Limitations: Giving primarily in NY, with preference for the Seneca Falls region. No grants to individuals.
Application information:
Initial approach: Letter
Deadline(s): None
Write: Gary Shultz
Trustee: Chase Lincoln First Bank, N.A.
Employer Identification Number: 166260274

4302
The Gladys Krieble Delmas Foundation
c/o Reid and Priest
40 West 57th St., 27th Fl.
New York 10019 (212) 603-2302

Established in 1976 in NY.
Donor(s): Gladys Krieble Delmas.
Foundation type: Independent
Financial data (yr. ended 12/31/88): Assets, $1,309,280 (M); expenditures, $168,560, including $51,000 for 3 grants (high: $45,000; low: $3,000) and $89,217 for 23 grants to individuals (high: $8,000; low: $954; average: $500-$10,000).
Purpose and activities: Grants limited to pre-doctoral and post-doctoral candidates for research in Venice, Italy, and for travel; support also for a local library.
Types of support: Research, fellowships.
Limitations: No grants for general support, building or endowment funds, or matching gifts; no loans.
Publications: Program policy statement, application guidelines.
Application information: Application form not required.
Initial approach: Proposal
Copies of proposal: 8
Deadline(s): Submit proposal preferably in Oct. or Nov.; deadline Dec. 15
Board meeting date(s): Mar.
Final notification: Apr. 1
Write: Joseph C. Mitchell, Trustee
Trustees: Gladys Krieble Delmas, Patricia LaBalme, Joseph C. Mitchell, David H. Stam.
Number of staff: 1
Employer Identification Number: 510193884

4303
Deloitte Haskins & Sells Foundation ⌑
1114 Ave. of the Americas
New York 10036 (212) 790-0588

Incorporated in 1928 in NY.
Donor(s): Charles Stewart Ludlam,† Charles C. Croggon,† Weldon Powell,† Haskins & Sells.
Foundation type: Company-sponsored
Financial data (yr. ended 8/31/88): Assets, $3,497,385 (M); gifts received, $26,935; expenditures, $1,423,582, including $475,250 for 13 grants (high: $300,000; low: $1,000), $187,500 for 36 grants to individuals and $722,608 for employee matching gifts.
Purpose and activities: To further accounting education in the U.S., including faculty development grants and research in accounting through support of the Doctoral Fellowship Program and the Graduate Research Assistant Program.
Types of support: Employee matching gifts, scholarship funds, fellowships, research, conferences and seminars.
Limitations: No grants for general support, capital campaigns, endowment or matching funds, special programs, or publications; no loans.
Publications: Informational brochure.
Application information: Application form required for Doctoral Fellowship Program only.
Initial approach: Letter
Copies of proposal: 1
Deadline(s): Oct. 15 for Doctoral Fellowship Program; other grants, none
Board meeting date(s): Annually
Final notification: Dec. 1 for Doctoral Fellowship Program
Write: Lester M. Sussman, Pres.
Officers and Directors: J. Michael Cook, Chair.; Lester M. Sussman, Pres.; John T. Cardis, V.P. and Secy.; Jerry W. Kolb, V.P. and Treas.; James Quigley, V.P.
Number of staff: None.
Employer Identification Number: 136400341

4304
Harry Dent Family Foundation, Inc.
P.O. Box 506
Lewiston 14092 (716) 754-8276

Incorporated in 1954 in NY.
Donor(s): Harry M. Dent.†
Foundation type: Independent
Financial data (yr. ended 10/31/89): Assets, $4,732,352 (M); expenditures, $254,017, including $186,000 for 5 grants (high: $150,000; low: $2,000).

Purpose and activities: Grants principally for medical research purposes, with emphasis on a neurological institute; some support for community funds.
Limitations: Giving limited to western NY. No grants to individuals.
Application information: Funds presently committed.
Board meeting date(s): Semiannually
Write: Miss Jane E. Gailey, Secy.
Officers and Directors:* Lucy Dent,* Chair.; Gloria G. Dent,* Pres.; Graham Wood Smith,* V.P.; Jane E. Gailey,* Secy.; Harry M. Dent III,* Treas.; Heidi D. Arthurs, Max Becker, Jr., Benjamin N. Hewitt, L. Nelson Hopkins, Jr., Susan L. Kimberly, Helen Dent Lenahan, Gilbert J. Pedersen.
Employer Identification Number: 160849923

4305
Derby Foundation ⌑
c/o White & Case
1155 Ave. of the Americas
New York 10036-2711
Application address: c/o Peter M. Kennedy, 90 Broad St., New York, NY 10004

Established in 1980 in DE.
Donor(s): John S. Kennedy, Peter M. Kennedy.
Foundation type: Independent
Financial data (yr. ended 11/30/88): Assets, $399,552 (M); gifts received, $100,075; expenditures, $108,652, including $104,652 for 46 grants (high: $21,641; low: $20).
Purpose and activities: Giving for education and Catholic organizations, including Catholic welfare and missionary programs.
Types of support: Annual campaigns, capital campaigns, general purposes.
Application information:
Initial approach: Letter
Deadline(s): None
Write: John J. Kennedy, V.P.
Officers and Directors:* Peter M. Kennedy,* Pres.; John J. Kennedy,* V.P.; John S. Kennedy, V.P.; Marie E. Kennedy,* V.P.; Paul L. Kennedy, V.P.; Peter M. Kennedy III, V.P.; Carol Lawrence,* Secy.
Employer Identification Number: 133066903

4306
Ernst & Paula Deutsch Foundation, Inc. ⌑
c/o Tenzer, Greenblatt, Fallon & Kaplan
405 Lexington Ave.
New York 10174

Established in 1954 in NY.
Foundation type: Independent
Financial data (yr. ended 12/31/88): Assets, $1,352,545 (M); expenditures, $107,548, including $60,000 for 7 grants (high: $25,000; low: $2,500).
Purpose and activities: Support primarily for Jewish giving, including welfare; support also for a medical center in Haifa, Israel, and medical education.
Application information: Application form not required.
Deadline(s): None
Write: Lawrence Rogers, Pres., or Herbert Tenzer, V.P.
Officers and Directors: Lawrence Rogers, Pres.; Herbert Tenzer, V.P.; Erika Hershey, Secy.-Treas.; John D. Cohen.
Employer Identification Number: 136112579

4307
The Dewar Foundation, Inc. ▼ ⌑
c/o Rutson R. Henderson
16 Dietz St.
Oneonta 13820 (607) 432-3530

Incorporated in 1947 in NY.
Donor(s): Jessie Smith Dewar.†
Foundation type: Independent
Financial data (yr. ended 12/31/88): Assets, $14,112,012 (M); expenditures, $1,019,693, including $963,475 for 62 grants (high: $335,000; low: $500; average: $2,000-$10,000).
Purpose and activities: Giving for civic and charitable organizations, including support for cultural organizations, Protestant churches, education, and child welfare and youth agencies.
Limitations: Giving primarily in the greater Oneonta, NY, area. No grants to individuals.
Application information: Application form not required.
Initial approach: Letter
Deadline(s): None
Write: Frank W. Getman, Pres.
Officers: Frank W. Getman, Pres.; Richard T. Applebaugh, V.P.; Nancy A. Lynch, Secy.-Treas.
Employer Identification Number: 166054329

4308
The Aaron Diamond Foundation, Inc. ▼
1270 Ave. of the Americas, Suite 2624
New York 10020 (212) 757-7680

Established in 1955 in NY.
Donor(s): Aaron Diamond.†
Foundation type: Independent
Financial data (yr. ended 12/31/88): Assets, $126,198,026 (M); gifts received, $11,752,372; expenditures, $17,703,264, including $15,685,261 for 333 grants (high: $500,000; low: $500; average: $10,000-$100,000).
Purpose and activities: Grants primarily for medical research, including AIDS research, minority education, and cultural programs.
Types of support: General purposes, research, continuing support, operating budgets, special projects.
Limitations: Giving limited to New York City, NY. No support for theater projects. No grants to individuals, or for building funds, endowments, or other capital expenditures; no loans.
Publications: Annual report (including application guidelines), informational brochure (including application guidelines).
Application information: Application form not required.
Initial approach: Letter and proposal
Deadline(s): None
Board meeting date(s): Quarterly
Write: Vincent McGee, Exec. Dir.
Officers and Directors:* Irene Diamond,* Pres.; Robert L. Bernstein,* V.P.; Charles L. Mandelstam, Secy.; Peter Kimmelman,* Treas.; Vincent McGee,* Exec. Dir.; Adrian W. DeWind, Peggy Dulany, Alfred Gellhorn, Lewis Thomas.
Number of staff: 4 full-time professional; 3 part-time professional; 4 full-time support; 1 part-time support.
Employer Identification Number: 132678431

4309
Harriet Ford Dickenson Foundation
c/o Manufacturers Hanover Trust Co.
270 Park Ave., 21st Fl.
New York 10017

Established about 1958 in NY.
Donor(s): Harriet Ford Dickenson.
Foundation type: Independent
Financial data (yr. ended 12/31/89): Assets, $1,681,768 (M); expenditures, $79,706, including $79,000 for 4 grants (high: $50,000; low: $4,000).
Purpose and activities: Giving primarily for social services, health services, a hospital, higher education, and religion.
Limitations: Giving limited to Broome County, NY. No grants to individuals.
Application information:
Initial approach: Letter
Deadline(s): None
Write: G. Haubner, V.P., Manufacturers Hanover Trust Co.
Trustee: Manufacturers Hanover Trust Co.
Employer Identification Number: 136047225

4310
Fairleigh S. Dickinson, Jr., Foundation, Inc. ⌑
c/o BDO & Seidman
15 Columbus Circle
New York 10023
Application address: c/o Toner, DiBenedetto and Schiffenhaus, Three Becker Farm Rd., P.O. Box 26, Roseland, NJ 07068

Incorporated in 1981 in NY.
Foundation type: Independent
Financial data (yr. ended 09/30/89): Assets, $162,128 (M); gifts received, $307,299; expenditures, $327,272, including $277,100 for 35 grants (high: $42,500; low: $500).
Purpose and activities: Giving primarily for higher and secondary education.
Application information: Application form not required.
Deadline(s): None
Officers: Jack King, Chair.; Jerome Lipper, Vice-Chair.; Roger Toner, Secy.-Treas.
Employer Identification Number: 133118384

4311
The Diebold Foundation, Inc. ⌑ ☆
c/o Bessemer Trust Co., N.A.
630 Fifth Ave.
New York 10111
Application address: 900 Main St. South, 24 South Village, Southbury, CT 06488

Established in 1963.
Foundation type: Independent
Financial data (yr. ended 10/31/88): Assets, $718,304 (M); expenditures, $164,933, including $134,200 for 17 grants (high: $30,000; low: $100).

Purpose and activities: Giving primarily for a university and other educational institutions, Christian organizations, hospitals, and civic affairs.
Application information:
Initial approach: Letter
Deadline(s): None
Write: Olive Simpson
Officers: A. Richard Diebold,* Pres.; Dorothy R. Diebold, V.P.; Andrew W. Bissett,* Secy.-Treas.
Directors:* A. Richard Diebold, Jr., Dudley G. Diebold, Diane Terni.
Employer Identification Number: 136146478

4312
Clarence and Anne Dillon Dunwalke Trust
1270 Ave. of the Americas, Rm. 2300
New York 10020 (212) 315-8343

Trust established in 1969 in NY.
Donor(s): Clarence Dillon.†
Foundation type: Independent
Financial data (yr. ended 06/30/89): Assets, $16,826,145 (M); expenditures, $713,876, including $630,794 for 31 grants (high: $250,000; low: $1,000).
Purpose and activities: Emphasis on hospitals, education, public affairs, the arts, and community funds. Grants primarily to present beneficiary organizations and for special proposals developed by the trustees.
Types of support: Fellowships, endowment funds, equipment, research, annual campaigns, operating budgets, building funds, special projects, general purposes.
Limitations: Giving primarily in NJ and NY. No grants to individuals; no loans.
Application information: New requests seldom considered. Application form not required.
Deadline(s): None
Board meeting date(s): Nov. and as required
Write: Crosby R. Smith, Trustee
Trustees: Philip D. Allen, Joan M. Bryan, Mark M. Collins, Jr., Phyllis Dillon Collins, C. Douglas Dillon, Dorothy Dillon Eweson, David H. Peipers, Crosby R. Smith, Frances C. Stillman.
Number of staff: 1 part-time professional.
Employer Identification Number: 237043773

4313
The Dillon Fund ▼
1270 Ave. of the Americas, Rm. 2300
New York 10020 (212) 315-8343

Incorporated in 1922 in NY.
Donor(s): Clarence Dillon,† C. Douglas Dillon.
Foundation type: Independent
Financial data (yr. ended 12/31/89): Assets, $2,061,302 (M); gifts received, $4,534,209; expenditures, $2,941,348, including $2,882,335 for 84 grants (high: $1,400,000; low: $1,000; average: $1,000-$50,000).
Purpose and activities: Emphasis on education and the arts.
Types of support: Continuing support, annual campaigns, building funds, operating budgets, publications, endowment funds, general purposes, renovation projects.
Limitations: No grants to individuals; no loans.
Application information: New applications seldom considered; giving only to present beneficiaries and for special proposals developed by the directors.
Deadline(s): None
Board meeting date(s): May and as required
Write: Crosby R. Smith, Pres.
Officers: Crosby R. Smith,* Pres.; Robert F. Quick, V.P. and Treas.; Allan Comrie,* V.P.; Shirley Ondrick, Secy.
Directors:* Joan M. Bryan, Mark M. Collins, Jr., Phyllis Dillon Collins, Susan S. Dillon.
Number of staff: 1 part-time professional.
Employer Identification Number: 136400226

4314
Discount Corporation of New York Foundation ⌑ ☆
58 Pine St.
New York 10005-1519

Established in 1986 in NY.
Donor(s): Discount Corp. of New York.
Foundation type: Independent
Financial data (yr. ended 12/31/88): Assets, $54,035 (M); gifts received, $150,000; expenditures, $198,395, including $198,370 for 149 grants (high: $10,000; low: $120; average: $500-$2,000).
Purpose and activities: Giving primarily for health associations and hospitals, welfare, higher and other education, and minor support for a community fund and Protestant churches.
Limitations: Giving primarily in NY, NJ, and Chicago, IL. No grants to individuals.
Application information: Contributes only to pre-selected organizations. Applications not accepted.
Officers: Ralph F. Peters,* Chair.; Rodney T. Bird,* Pres.; Peter E. Gall, Sr. V.P. and Treas.; Edward J. Sawicz,* Sr. V.P.; Phebe C. Miller, V.P. and Secy.; James G. Mannix, V.P. and Comptroller; John A. Magee, V.P.; Kenneth G. Rehm, V.P.
Directors:* Donald G. Brodie, James P. Coughlin.
Employer Identification Number: 133389920

4315
The DLJ Foundation ⌑
c/o DLJ, Inc., Tax Dept.
140 Broadway
New York 10005-1103 (212) 504-3277

Established in 1967 in NY.
Foundation type: Company-sponsored
Financial data (yr. ended 06/30/88): Assets, $258,276 (M); gifts received, $195,700; expenditures, $161,270, including $95,289 for 84 grants (high: $11,815; low: $50) and $65,020 for 192 employee matching gifts.
Purpose and activities: Giving primarily for higher and secondary education through grants and an employee matching gift program.
Types of support: Employee matching gifts.
Application information: Application form not required.
Write: Mary Brannigan, Assoc.
Officers and Directors:* Gerald B. Rigg, Chair. and Pres.; Michael Boyd,* V.P.; Thomas Siegler,* V.P.; Anthony F. Daddino, Secy.-Treas.
Number of staff: 1 part-time support.
Employer Identification Number: 136259415

4316
The Dobson Foundation, Inc. ⌑
Four East 66th St., Suite 1E
New York 10021

Incorporated in 1961 in NY.
Donor(s): Walter M. Jeffords, Jr.†
Foundation type: Independent
Financial data (yr. ended 12/31/88): Assets, $3,980,361 (M); expenditures, $273,286, including $257,005 for 48 grants (high: $185,000; low: $20).
Purpose and activities: Emphasis on conservation; support also for hospitals, higher education, sports museums, and Catholic church support.
Limitations: Giving primarily in NY and ME. No grants to individuals.
Application information: Contributes only to pre-selected organizations. Applications not accepted.
Officers: Walter Jeffords, Pres.; Kathleen McLaughlin Jeffords, V.P.
Employer Identification Number: 136168259

4317
Cleveland H. Dodge Foundation, Inc.
670 West 247th St.
Riverdale 10471 (212) 543-1220

Incorporated in 1917 in NY.
Donor(s): Cleveland H. Dodge.†
Foundation type: Independent
Financial data (yr. ended 12/31/88): Assets, $20,209,310 (M); expenditures, $1,030,947, including $802,930 for grants (high: $125,000).
Purpose and activities: "To promote the well-being of mankind throughout the world." Grants for a selected list of international organizations in the Near East; grants also to a selected few national agencies in the U.S. The balance directed to organizations located in New York City. Most grants in the U.S. for higher and secondary education, youth agencies and child welfare, and cultural programs.
Types of support: Building funds, equipment, endowment funds, matching funds.
Limitations: Giving primarily in New York, NY, the Near East, and national organizations. No support for health care or medical research. No grants to individuals, or for general purposes, research, scholarships, or fellowships; no loans.
Publications: Annual report, program policy statement.
Application information: Application form not required.
Initial approach: Letter
Copies of proposal: 1
Deadline(s): Submit letter prior to the 15th of Jan., Apr., or Oct.
Board meeting date(s): 3 times a year
Final notification: Within 3 months of submitting the proposal
Write: Phyllis M. Criscuoli, Admin. Dir.
Officers: Cleveland E. Dodge, Jr.,* Pres.; Alfred H. Howell,* V.P.; Gilbert Kerlin,* Secy.; Phyllis M. Criscuoli, Admin. Dir. and Treas.
Directors:* David S. Dodge, Margaret Dodge Garrett, Robert Garrett, William Dodge Rueckert, Ingrid R. Warren, Mary Rea Weidlein.
Number of staff: 1 full-time professional.
Employer Identification Number: 136015087

4318
Beryl H. Doft Foundation, Inc. ⌑
124 Fulton St.
Lawrence 11559

Established in 1947 in NY.
Donor(s): Members of the Doft family and others.
Foundation type: Independent
Financial data (yr. ended 12/31/88): Assets, $880,205 (M); gifts received, $19,628; expenditures, $126,611, including $124,870 for 298 grants (high: $12,500; low: $10).
Purpose and activities: Giving primarily for Jewish religious organizations, temple support, and education.
Limitations: Giving primarily in NY and Israel. No grants to individuals.
Application information: Contributes only to pre-selected organizations. Applications not accepted.
Officers: Emanuel Doft, Pres.; Alan Doft, V.P.; Avrom Doft, V.P.; Barry Escott, Secy.; Pauline Doft, Treas.
Employer Identification Number: 116035628

4319
The Henry L. and Grace Doherty Charitable Foundation, Inc.
150 Broadway, Rm. 1703
New York 10038 (212) 406-1990

Incorporated in 1947 in DE.
Donor(s): Mrs. Henry L. Doherty,† Helen Lee Lassen.†
Foundation type: Independent
Financial data (yr. ended 12/31/88): Assets, $6,469,187 (M); expenditures, $307,979, including $215,865 for 41 grants (high: $106,000; low: $15).
Purpose and activities: Primarily to promote research in the marine sciences and to assist institutions engaged in oceanographic activities. Only limited expansion of activities is anticipated in the foreseeable future.
Types of support: Research.
Limitations: No grants to individuals.
Application information: Available funds presently committed. Application form not required.
Initial approach: Letter
Copies of proposal: 1
Deadline(s): None
Board meeting date(s): As required
Write: James R. Billingsley, V.P.
Officers: Walter R. Brown,* Pres.; James R. Billingsley,* V.P. and Treas.; Dorothy R. McCall,* V.P.; George G. Vest,* V.P.; Joan B. Cadmus, Secy.
Trustees:* Helen Lee Billingsley, Kiyoko O. Brown.
Number of staff: 1 part-time support.
Employer Identification Number: 136401292

4320
Ruth W. Dolen Foundation ⌑ ☆
c/o Carter, Ledyard & Milburn
Two Wall St.
New York 10005-1702

Established in 1974.
Foundation type: Independent
Financial data (yr. ended 9/30/88): Assets, $544,700 (M); expenditures, $126,422, including $116,000 for 8 grants (high: $60,000; low: $1,000).
Purpose and activities: Giving primarily for higher education and hospitals; support also for a library, family planning services, and organizations providing relief services in Israel.
Limitations: Giving primarily in New York, NY. No grants to individuals.
Application information: Contributes only to pre-selected organizations. Applications not accepted.
Officers and Directors: Milton W. Hamolsky, Pres.; Ralph E. Hansmann, V.P. and Treas.; Victor Brudney, Secy.; Sandra Z. Hamolsky, John O. Lipkin, Mack Lipkin, Mack Lipkin, Jr.
Employer Identification Number: 237359005

4321
Henri & Eugenia Doll Foundation, Inc.
Four East 66th St.
New York 10021-6548 (212) 769-2157

Established in 1954 in TX.
Donor(s): Henri G. Doll.
Foundation type: Independent
Financial data (yr. ended 12/31/88): Assets, $122,981 (M); gifts received, $100,000; expenditures, $111,673, including $111,400 for 30 grants (high: $15,000; low: $250).
Purpose and activities: Grants primarily to the performing arts, including dance.
Limitations: Giving primarily in New York, NY. No grants to individuals.
Application information: Contributes only to pre-selected organizations; new grants not being considered. Applications not accepted.
Write: Mrs. Eugenia Doll, Pres.
Officer: Eugenia Doll, Pres.
Employer Identification Number: 746036663

4322
The William H. Donner Foundation, Inc. ▼
500 Fifth Ave., Suite 1230
New York 10110 (212) 719-9290

Incorporated in 1961 in DC.
Donor(s): William H. Donner.†
Foundation type: Independent
Financial data (yr. ended 10/31/88): Assets, $42,300,901 (M); expenditures, $3,087,425, including $2,146,409 for 42 grants (high: $175,000; low: $11,000; average: $25,000-$75,000).
Purpose and activities: Concerned with U.S.-Canadian relations; to promote deeper understanding of the common interests which bind, and the issues which vex the two countries; support also for experimental grants in education, public affairs, and other fields.
Types of support: Seed money, matching funds, research, conferences and seminars, publications.
Limitations: No grants to individuals, or for operating budgets, continuing support, annual campaigns, emergency, capital, or endowment funds; deficit financing, charitable drives, scholarships, fellowships, or special projects; no loans. The foundation does not provide consulting services or technical assistance.
Publications: Annual report (including application guidelines).
Application information: Application form not required.
Initial approach: Prefer letter of inquiry before full proposal is sent; telephone also acceptable
Copies of proposal: 1
Deadline(s): 2 months before board meeting
Board meeting date(s): Feb., June, and Oct.
Final notification: Immediately after board meetings
Write: James V. Capua, Pres.
Officers and Trustees:* James V. Capua, Pres.; Robert Donner, Jr.,* V.P.; Curtin Winsor, Jr.,* Secy.; William D. Roosevelt,* Treas.; James Balog, Caroline McMullen, Jeremiah Milbank III, Wilcomb E. Washburn.
Number of staff: 3 full-time professional; 1 full-time support.
Employer Identification Number: 231611346

4323
Donovan Leisure Newton & Irvine Foundation, Inc. ⌑
30 Rockefeller Plaza
New York 10112

Established in 1977.
Donor(s): Donovan Leisure Newton & Irvine.
Foundation type: Company-sponsored
Financial data (yr. ended 5/31/88): Assets, $312,553 (M); gifts received, $155,000; expenditures, $171,948, including $162,725 for 28 grants (high: $42,000; low: $100) and $8,150 for 24 employee matching gifts.
Purpose and activities: Grants largely for programs in law and justice and civil rights; supports an employee matching gifts program, primarily to law schools; support also for a community fund.
Types of support: Employee matching gifts, annual campaigns.
Application information: Contributes only to pre-selected organizations. Applications not accepted.
Write: Kenneth N. Hart, Pres.
Officer and Directors: Kenneth N. Hart, Pres.; George S. Leisure, Jr., Louis C. Lustenberger, Jr., Thomas A. Melfe, Gordon C. Osmond, Stuart B. Peerce.
Number of staff: None.
Employer Identification Number: 132900457

4324
Dorot Foundation ▼ ⌑
100 Park Ave.
New York 10017

Incorporated in 1958 in NY as Joy and Samuel Ungerleider Foundation.
Donor(s): Joy G. Mayerson, D.S. and R.H. Gottesman Foundation.
Foundation type: Independent
Financial data (yr. ended 3/31/89): Assets, $20,492,484 (M); gifts received, $1,259,750; expenditures, $844,981, including $650,597 for 61 grants (high: $124,083; low: $83; average: $2,000-$30,000).
Purpose and activities: Grants primarily for Jewish organizations; support also for higher education and educational organizations.
Limitations: Giving primarily in the U.S. and Israel. No grants to individuals.

Application information: Contributes only to pre-selected organizations. Applications not accepted.
Officers: Joy G. Ungerleider-Mayerson,* Pres.; Philip Mayerson,* V.P.; Edgar Wachenheim III, V.P.; Peter C. Siegfried, Secy.; Benjamin Glowatz, Treas.
Directors:* Milton M. Gottesman.
Employer Identification Number: 136116927

4325
Dorr Foundation
P.O. Box 281
Bedford 10506 (914) 234-3573

Trust established in 1940 in CT.
Donor(s): John Dorr.
Foundation type: Independent
Financial data (yr. ended 12/31/89): Assets, $3,513,174 (M); expenditures, $169,752, including $143,069 for 10 grants (high: $28,000; low: $3,000; average: $5,000-$30,000).
Purpose and activities: Grants primarily for conservation of natural areas and wildlife organizations and to promote research and disseminate information on chemical, metallurgical, and sanitation engineering; support also for educational projects for youth relating to all of the above areas.
Types of support: Seed money, emergency funds, land acquisition, special projects, research, publications, capital campaigns, deficit financing, exchange programs, internships, operating budgets, program-related investments, renovation projects, scholarship funds, equipment.
Limitations: Giving primarily in the northeastern U.S.; selective national and international grants. No grants to individuals, or for annual campaigns, building or matching funds, conferences and seminars, or fellowships; no loans.
Application information: Foundation does not respond to requests for guidelines or other publications. Application form not required.
Initial approach: Brief proposal, including a 1-to-2 page summary
Copies of proposal: 7
Deadline(s): None
Board meeting date(s): Dec.
Final notification: 1 month
Write: Hugh McMillan, Chair.
Officers and Trustees: Hugh McMillan, Chair. and Treas.; Allen Hardon, Secy.; Roger Hardon, Virginia Maxwell, William Phillips, Shirley M. Punzeit, Perry D. Trafford.
Number of staff: None.
Employer Identification Number: 136017294

4326
Paul P. Dosberg Foundation, Inc. ⌑ ☆
c/o M. Lewis, Esq.
1010 Times Square Bldg.
Rochester 14614

Established in 1956.
Donor(s): Paul P. Dosberg.†
Foundation type: Independent
Financial data (yr. ended 12/31/87): Assets, $1,314,627 (M); gifts received, $700,000; expenditures, $28,665, including $23,000 for 4 grants (high: $10,000; low: $3,000).
Purpose and activities: Support for Jewish organizations and higher education.
Limitations: Giving primarily in NY and PA.
Application information:
Initial approach: Letter
Deadline(s): Sept. 1
Write: Myron S. Lewis, Secy.
Officer and Trustees: Myron S. Lewis, Secy.; Charlotte Kramer.
Employer Identification Number: 166030605

4327
Doty Family Foundation
85 Broad St., Tax Dept.
New York 10004

Established in 1977 in NY.
Donor(s): George E. Doty.
Foundation type: Independent
Financial data (yr. ended 02/28/89): Assets, $9,717,144 (M); expenditures, $242,853, including $223,002 for 64 grants (high: $110,000; low: $150).
Purpose and activities: Grants primarily for Catholic giving, including churches and educational organizations; support also for higher and other education and a Korean relief organization.
Limitations: Giving primarily in New York, NY, and Baltimore, MD. No grants to individuals.
Application information: Priority given to charities in which Doty family members are actively involved. Applications not accepted.
Officer and Trustees:* George E. Doty,* Secy.; George E. Doty, Jr., Marie J. Doty, William W. Doty, Sheldon Seevak, Anne Marie Wert.
Number of staff: None.
Employer Identification Number: 132921496

4328
Dow Jones Foundation ▼
200 Liberty St.
New York 10281 (212) 416-2000

Trust established in 1954 in NY.
Donor(s): Dow Jones & Co., Inc.
Foundation type: Company-sponsored
Financial data (yr. ended 12/31/89): Assets, $4,766,336 (M); gifts received, $1,000,000; expenditures, $1,571,411, including $1,543,134 for grants (high: $350,000; low: $100; average: $2,000-$30,000).
Purpose and activities: Giving primarily for community funds, journalism, and higher education.
Types of support: Continuing support, annual campaigns, employee-related scholarships, endowment funds, lectureships, operating budgets, general purposes.
Limitations: Giving primarily in areas of company operations. No support for medical or scientific research, or cultural activities. No grants to individuals (except for employee-related scholarships).
Publications: Application guidelines.
Application information: Application form not required.
Initial approach: Proposal
Copies of proposal: 1
Deadline(s): Submit proposal preferably in Aug. or Sept.; deadline Nov. 1
Board meeting date(s): Usually in the last quarter
Final notification: As soon as decided
Write: Leonard E. Doherty, Admin. Officer
Advisory Committee: Jane B. Cook, Chair.; Frank C. Breese III, Leonard E. Doherty, Bettina Bancroft Klink, Warren H. Phillips.
Trustee: U.S. Trust Co. of New York.
Number of staff: None.
Employer Identification Number: 136070158

4329
Downe Foundation ⌑ ☆
c/o S. Heinberg
Ten East 40th St., Suite 805
New York 10016

Established in 1968.
Donor(s): Edward R. Downe, Jr.
Foundation type: Operating
Financial data (yr. ended 11/30/88): Assets, $7,462 (L); gifts received, $109,675; expenditures, $109,650, including $109,610 for grants.
Purpose and activities: A private operating foundation; support for museums and other cultural programs, social services, and hospitals.
Limitations: No grants to individuals.
Application information: Contributes only to pre-selected organizations. Applications not accepted.
Officer and Directors: Edward R. Downe, Jr., Pres. and Secy.; J. Wingate Brown.
Employer Identification Number: 237005623

4330
The Dreitzer Foundation, Inc.
488 Madison Ave.
New York 10022 (212) 935-5500

Established in 1958 in NY.
Foundation type: Independent
Financial data (yr. ended 12/31/88): Assets, $5,251,081 (M); expenditures, $299,588, including $236,500 for 21 grants (high: $100,000; low: $750).
Purpose and activities: Support primarily for Jewish concerns, social services, and health.
Application information:
Write: Leonard Franklin, Pres.
Officers: Leonard Franklin, Pres.; David B. Goldfarb, Secy.-Treas.
Trustees: Shirley Dreitzer, Judith Wallach.
Employer Identification Number: 136162509

4331
The Camille and Henry Dreyfus Foundation, Inc. ▼
445 Park Ave.
New York 10022 (212) 753-1760

Incorporated in 1946 in NY.
Donor(s): Camille Dreyfus.†
Foundation type: Independent
Financial data (yr. ended 12/31/89): Assets, $53,634,952 (M); expenditures, $1,560,598, including $1,140,736 for grants (high: $50,000; low: $1,000; average: $10,000-$50,000).
Purpose and activities: "To advance the sciences of chemistry, biochemistry, chemical engineering, and related sciences as a means of improving human relations and circumstances throughout the world"; assists organizations

which afford facilities for the production, collection, or dissemination of scientific information; support mainly for post-secondary academic institutions through sponsorship of Dreyfus New Faculty in Chemistry Program, the Dreyfus Teacher-Scholar Awards Program, and the new grant program, Chemistry in Liberal Arts Colleges.
Types of support: Seed money, equipment, research, special projects.
Limitations: No support for health, medicine, biology, or specific research projects. No grants to individuals who are not sponsored or nominated by a non-profit or educational institution, or for continuing support, emergency funds, deficit financing, land acquisition, conferences, capital construction, renovation, or travel (except in the context of existing programs); no loans.
Publications: Biennial report, informational brochure (including application guidelines).
Application information: Candidates for awards must be nominated by applying academic institution; individual applications not accepted; nomination forms required for Teacher-Scholar and New Faculty Programs.
Copies of proposal: 5
Deadline(s): Dec. 15 for Teacher-Scholar Awards Program, May 15 for New Faculty Awards Program, June 30 for Chemistry in Liberal Arts Colleges Program, and Sept. 15 for Special Grant Program in the Chemical Sciences
Board meeting date(s): Jan., Apr., July, and Oct.
Final notification: 4 months
Write: Robert L. Lichter, Exec. Dir.
Officers: Jean Dreyfus Boissevain,* Pres.; Dorothy Dinsmoor,* V.P.; Edward A. Reilly,* Secy.-Treas.; Robert L. Lichter, Exec. Dir.
Directors:* John R.H. Blum, Elizabeth A. Guthrie, Henry B. Guthrie, Joshua Lederberg, Robert L. Mitchell, H. Marshall Schwarz, Reiner G. Stoll, Henry C. Walter.
Number of staff: 1 full-time professional; 1 full-time support.
Employer Identification Number: 135570117

4332
Jean and Louis Dreyfus Foundation, Inc. ⌑
c/o Decker, Hubbard and Welden
30 Rockefeller Plaza
New York 10112 (212) 581-7575

Incorporated about 1978 in NY.
Donor(s): Louis Dreyfus.†
Foundation type: Independent
Financial data (yr. ended 12/31/88): Assets, $12,707,875 (M); gifts received, $875,000; expenditures, $713,000, including $606,500 for 71 grants (high: $32,500; low: $1,000; average: $5,000-$10,000).
Purpose and activities: Grants primarily to established institutions of the arts and medical research; some support also for health and hospitals, and social services, including hospices, youth agencies, literacy, and programs for drug abuse.
Limitations: Giving primarily in the New York, NY, area.
Application information: Application form not required.
Initial approach: Proposal
Copies of proposal: 2
Board meeting date(s): Spring and Fall
Write: Edmee de Montmollin, Prog. Dir.
Officers: Valli V. Dreyfus Firth, Pres.; Thomas J. Sweeney, V.P. and Treas.; Nicholas L.D. Firth, V.P.; Thomas J. Hubbard, Secy.
Number of staff: 1 part-time professional.
Employer Identification Number: 132947180

4333
The Max and Victoria Dreyfus Foundation, Inc. ▼
575 Madison Ave.
New York 10022 (212) 605-0354

Incorporated in 1965 in NY.
Donor(s): Victoria Dreyfus,† Max Dreyfus.†
Foundation type: Independent
Financial data (yr. ended 12/31/88): Assets, $37,425,550 (M); expenditures, $2,078,840, including $1,547,416 for 225 grants (high: $30,000; low: $1,000; average: $1,000-$10,000).
Purpose and activities: Support for hospitals, medical research, education, health and social services, with emphasis on youth and aid to the aged and handicapped, and cultural programs.
Types of support: Research, special projects.
Limitations: No grants to individuals.
Application information: Submit proposal upon request of the foundation only.
Initial approach: Letter (not exceeding 5 pages)
Deadline(s): 10 weeks prior to board meeting dates
Board meeting date(s): Usually in mid-Feb., June, and Oct.
Final notification: 2 weeks following board meetings
Write: Ms. Lucy Gioia, Admin. Asst.
Officers and Directors:* David J. Oppenheim,* Pres.; Nancy E. Oddo,* V.P.; Norman S. Portenoy,* V.P.; Winifred Riggs Portenoy,* Secy.-Treas.
Number of staff: 1 full-time support; 1 part-time support.
Employer Identification Number: 131687573

4334
Dreyfus Medical Foundation ⌑
767 Fifth Ave., 43rd Fl.
New York 10022

Established in 1961 in NY.
Donor(s): Jack J. Dreyfus, Jr., John Dreyfus, Joan D. Blout.
Foundation type: Operating
Financial data (yr. ended 12/31/88): Assets, $10,592,317 (M); gifts received, $1,000,000; expenditures, $8,229,219, including $1,516,000 for 4 grants (high: $1,000,000; low: $1,000) and $6,567,226 for foundation-administered programs.
Purpose and activities: Support primarily for medical research.
Types of support: Research.
Limitations: Giving primarily in NY. No grants to individuals.
Application information: Contributes only to pre-selected organizations. Applications not accepted.
Officers and Directors:* Jack J. Dreyfus, Jr.,* Pres.; Barry H. Smith, V.P.; Helen C. Raudonat,* V.P. and Secy.; Arnold D. Friedman,* Treas.; John Dreyfus.
Employer Identification Number: 136086089

4335
The Caleb C. and Julia W. Dula Educational and Charitable Foundation
c/o Manufacturers Hanover Trust Co.
270 Park Ave., 21st Fl.
New York 10017 (212) 270-9066

Trust established in 1939 in NY.
Donor(s): Julia W. Dula.†
Foundation type: Independent
Financial data (yr. ended 12/31/89): Assets, $20,800,000 (M); qualifying distributions, $897,000, including $897,000 for 95 grants (high: $100,000; low: $1,000).
Purpose and activities: Grants to charities which the Dulas supported during their lifetime, with emphasis on higher and secondary education, hospitals, libraries, social service agencies, child welfare, church support, cultural programs, and historic preservation.
Types of support: Operating budgets.
Limitations: No grants to individuals; no loans.
Application information: Application form not required.
Copies of proposal: 1
Deadline(s): None
Board meeting date(s): Usually spring and fall
Write: Sarita A. Grau, Trust Officer, Manufacturers Hanover Trust Co.
Trustees: Margaret C. Taylor, Julia P. Wightman, Orrin S. Wightman III, Manufacturers Hanover Trust Co.
Employer Identification Number: 136045790

4336
The Dun & Bradstreet Corporation Foundation ▼ ⌑
299 Park Ave.
New York 10171 (212) 593-6736

Incorporated in 1953 in DE.
Donor(s): The Dun & Bradstreet Group.
Foundation type: Company-sponsored
Financial data (yr. ended 12/31/89): Assets, $17,731,782 (M); expenditures, $2,817,747, including $906,475 for 271 grants (high: $105,125; low: $50; average: $200-$15,000) and $1,891,453 for 569 employee matching gifts.
Purpose and activities: To assist charitable and educational institutions, with emphasis on cultural programs, community funds, higher education, health and welfare, and youth agencies.
Types of support: Operating budgets, continuing support, annual campaigns, general purposes, employee-related scholarships, employee matching gifts.
Limitations: No grants to individuals (except for employee-related scholarships), or for building or endowment funds, or research; no loans.
Application information: Application form not required.
Initial approach: Letter or proposal
Copies of proposal: 1

Deadline(s): Submit proposal preferably in Sept. or Oct.; no set deadline
Board meeting date(s): Semiannually
Final notification: 4 weeks
Write: Juliann Gill, Admin.
Officers and Trustees:* Charles W. Moritz,* Pres.; David S. Fehr, V.P.; Manny A. Fernandez, V.P.; William O. Frohlich, V.P.; Virginia Simone, Secy.; Steven G. Klein, Treas.; Edwin A. Bescherer, Jr., Robert E. Weissman.
Number of staff: 2
Employer Identification Number: 136148188

4337
The Durst Foundation, Inc. ⌑
1133 Ave. of the Americas
New York 10036

Established in 1944 in NY.
Donor(s): Durst Partners.
Foundation type: Independent
Financial data (yr. ended 12/31/88): Assets, $749,419 (M); gifts received, $196,200; expenditures, $338,908, including $336,783 for 69 grants (high: $200,100; low: $50).
Purpose and activities: Grants primarily for Jewish organizations and higher education.
Officers and Directors:* Seymour B. Durst,* Pres.; David Durst,* V.P.; Douglas Durst, V.P.; Peter Durst, V.P.; Robert Durst, V.P.; Royal Durst,* V.P.; Irene Forman, Secy.; Irving Frankel, Treas.
Employer Identification Number: 131656537

4338
The Area Fund of Dutchess County ☆
Nine Vassar St.
Poughkeepsie 12601 (914) 452-3077

Established in 1969 in NY.
Donor(s): McCann Foundation, Lester Freer,† and others.
Foundation type: Community
Financial data (yr. ended 12/31/89): Assets, $1,604,229 (M); expenditures, $96,449, including $65,118 for 56 grants (high: $9,849; low: $40) and $15,003 for 34 grants to individuals (high: $1,000; low: $91).
Purpose and activities: Emergency and special grants, particularly as "seed money," to non-profit organizations for charitable, cultural, and educational purposes. The Area Fund Partnershship in Education Grants are awarded to classroom teachers in Dutchess County of pre-kindergarten to twelfth grade for professional development or special projects with their classes. Limited funds available for grantmaking as bulk of assets is in non-income producing properties.
Types of support: Seed money, emergency funds, equipment, scholarship funds, special projects, research, publications, conferences and seminars, grants to individuals.
Limitations: Giving primarily in Dutchess County, NY. No grants to individuals (except through the Area Fund Partnership in Education Grants program), or for endowment funds, capital campaigns, building funds, land acquisition, matching gifts, deficit financing, operating budgets, or where amount of grant will not make a significant impact on a project; no loans.
Publications: Annual report, application guidelines.
Application information: Application form not required.
Initial approach: Letter or telephone
Copies of proposal: 1
Deadline(s): Submit proposal one and a half months before board meetings; no set deadlines
Board meeting date(s): Feb., May, Sept., and Nov.
Final notification: 3 months
Write: Patricia A. Wright, Exec. Dir.
Officers and Trustees:* William E. McLean,* Pres.; William R. Gregg,* V.P.; Richard A. Mitchell,* Secy.; Owen T. Clarke, Jr.,* Treas.; and 21 additional trustees.
Number of staff: 1 full-time professional; 1 full-time support.
Employer Identification Number: 237026859

4339
Dyson Foundation ▼
230 Park Ave., Rm. 659
New York 10169 (212) 661-4600

Trust established in 1949 in NY; incorporated in 1958 in DE.
Donor(s): Charles H. Dyson, Margaret M. Dyson, The Dyson-Kissner-Moran Corp.
Foundation type: Independent
Financial data (yr. ended 12/31/87): Assets, $646,649 (M); gifts received, $1,560,100; expenditures, $1,418,320, including $1,415,875 for 97 grants (high: $100,000; low: $100; average: $1,000-$50,000).
Purpose and activities: Grants primarily for cultural affairs, and for medical research and education, with emphasis on pediatrics; support also for higher and early childhood education and organizations benefitting the disadvantaged.
Types of support: Building funds, endowment funds.
Limitations: Giving limited to the New England states, with emphasis on the greater New York, NY, metropolitan area and Dutchess County, NY. No grants to individuals.
Publications: Annual report.
Application information: Board solicits most proposals. Application form not required.
Initial approach: Proposal
Copies of proposal: 1
Deadline(s): None
Board meeting date(s): Quarterly
Write: Anne E. Dyson, M.D., Pres.
Officers: Anne E. Dyson, M.D.,* Pres.; Ernest H. Lorch,* V.P.; John H. FitzSimons, Secy.; Robert R. Dyson,* Treas.
Trustees:* Charles H. Dyson, Margaret M. Dyson, Joseph V. Mariner, Jr., John A. Moran.
Number of staff: 1 part-time professional; 1 full-time support; 1 part-time support.
Employer Identification Number: 136084888

4340
Eastman Kodak Charitable Trust ▼
c/o Eastman Kodak Company
343 State St.
Rochester 14650-0316 (716) 724-3127

Trust established in 1952 in NY.
Donor(s): Eastman Kodak Co.
Foundation type: Company-sponsored
Financial data (yr. ended 12/31/89): Assets, $6,412,924 (M); gifts received, $8,817,724; expenditures, $8,817,724, including $8,817,724 for 235 grants (high: $3,350,000; low: $150).
Purpose and activities: Support for community funds, higher education, health, human services, civic affairs, community activities, arts and culture, and conservation and environmental affairs.
Types of support: Annual campaigns, general purposes, continuing support.
Limitations: Giving primarily in high employment locations, including Rochester, NY; Kingsport, TN; Windsor, CO; Columbia, SC; and Longview, TX. Giving nationally only for higher education. No grants to individuals, or for matching gifts; no loans; low priority given to building or endowment funds.
Publications: Corporate giving report.
Application information: Contributes only to pre-selected organizations. Applications not accepted.
Board meeting date(s): Monthly
Write: Stanley C. Wright, Dir., Corp. Contribs.
Trustee: Chase Lincoln First Bank, N.A.
Number of staff: None.
Employer Identification Number: 166015274

4341
Samuel & Rae Eckman Charitable Foundation
c/o Baer, Marks & Upham
805 Third Ave.
New York 10022

Established in 1970 in NY.
Donor(s): Rae Eckman,† Samuel Eckman.†
Foundation type: Independent
Financial data (yr. ended 12/31/89): Assets, $2,035,155 (M); expenditures, $185,800, including $152,500 for 15 grants (high: $25,000; low: $1,000; average: $5,000-$10,000).
Purpose and activities: Support for medical research in cancer and allied diseases, homes for the aged, and education of indigent or underprivileged children.
Limitations: Giving primarily in New York, NY.
Application information: Application form not required.
Initial approach: Proposal
Copies of proposal: 1
Deadline(s): None
Board meeting date(s): Quarterly
Write: William E. Friedman, Pres.
Officers and Directors:* William E. Friedman,* Pres. and Treas.; Abraham J. Briloff,* V.P.; Stephen F. Selig,* Secy.; Theodore Harris, William B. Norden.
Number of staff: None.
Employer Identification Number: 237051411

4342
The Edlow Family Fund, Inc. ⌑
c/o Kenneth L. Edlow, The Bear Stearns Companies, Inc.
245 Park Ave., 2nd Fl.
New York 10167

Donor(s): Kenneth Lewis Edlow.
Foundation type: Independent

Financial data (yr. ended 11/30/88): Assets, $1,628,020 (M); expenditures, $90,813, including $87,900 for 19 grants (high: $32,000; low: $100).
Purpose and activities: Support for Jewish welfare and other Jewish concerns; support also for education.
Limitations: Giving primarily in New York, NY. No grants to individuals.
Application information: Contributes only to pre-selected organizations. Applications not accepted.
Officers and Directors: Mary Edlow, Pres. and Treas.; Kenneth Lewis Edlow, V.P. and Secy.; Donald William Edlow.
Employer Identification Number: 133190911

4343
Dean S. Edmonds Foundation ⌑
c/o The Bank of New York
48 Wall St.
New York 10015 (212) 536-4828

Established in 1959 in NY.
Foundation type: Independent
Financial data (yr. ended 12/31/88): Assets, $1,724,989 (M); expenditures, $106,060, including $82,000 for 51 grants (high: $6,000; low: $500).
Purpose and activities: Giving for higher and secondary education and cultural programs.
Application information:
Initial approach: Letter
Deadline(s): None
Write: Marjorie Thompson
Trustees: Dean S. Edmonds III, The Bank of New York.
Employer Identification Number: 136161381

4344
The Edouard Foundation, Inc. ⌑ ☆
40 West 57th St., 32nd Fl.
New York 10019-4001

Established in 1987 in NY.
Donor(s): Lyliane D. Finch.
Foundation type: Independent
Financial data (yr. ended 12/31/88): Assets, $1,527,080 (M); gifts received, $1,750,000; expenditures, $482,321, including $482,000 for 29 grants (high: $50,000; low: $1,000).
Purpose and activities: Giving primarily for health, including hospitals, health associations, services, and AIDS research; support also for domestic and international human services, including youth, child welfare, social services, international relief, and human rights.
Application information: Contributes only to pre-selected organizations. Applications not accepted.
Officers and Directors:* Lyliane D. Finch,* Pres.; Edwin A. Margolius, Secy.; Gerald Meyer, Treas.; Arnold Finch, Beatrice Phillipe.
Employer Identification Number: 133446831

4345
O. P. and W. E. Edwards Foundation, Inc.
P.O. Box 1197
Port Ewen 12466 (914) 338-6388

Incorporated in 1962 in NY.
Donor(s): William E. Edwards,† J.N. Edwards,† Harriet E. Gamper.
Foundation type: Independent
Financial data (yr. ended 08/31/89): Assets, $2,999,384 (M); qualifying distributions, $381,953, including $306,953 for 46 grants (high: $50,000; low: $500; average: $5,000-$10,000) and $75,000 for loans.
Purpose and activities: Major interest in programs helping economically disadvantaged young people become able to survive and thrive on their own, with preference to smaller, comprehensive programs that are integral parts of their communities' networks of services.
Types of support: Operating budgets, continuing support, seed money, emergency funds, deficit financing, matching funds, program-related investments, scholarship funds, loans, special projects, general purposes.
Limitations: No support for organizations with national affiliations or operating budgets above $200,000. No grants to individuals, or for capital or endowment funds.
Publications: Program policy statement, application guidelines.
Application information: Application form not required.
Initial approach: Letter
Copies of proposal: 1
Deadline(s): Feb. 1 and Aug. 1
Board meeting date(s): As required
Final notification: 1 to 2 months
Write: David E. Gamper, Pres.
Officers and Directors:* David E. Gamper,* Pres. and Treas.; Jo Ann Eder,* V.P.; Harriet E. Gamper,* Secy.
Number of staff: None.
Employer Identification Number: 136100965

4346
The Fred and Susan Ehrman Foundation ⌑
63 Wall St.
New York 10005

Established in 1968 in NY.
Foundation type: Independent
Financial data (yr. ended 12/31/87): Assets, $2,482,428 (M); gifts received, $700,000; expenditures, $320,987, including $314,508 for 105 grants (high: $140,000; low: $18).
Purpose and activities: Support primarily for Jewish giving.
Application information: Contributes only to pre-selected organizations. Applications not accepted.
Officers and Directors: Fred Ehrman, Pres. and Treas.; Susan Ehrman, V.P.; Lawrence Kobrin.
Employer Identification Number: 136271584

4347
Seymour Eisenberg Memorial Foundation ⌑
c/o Goldman, Sachs & Co., Tax Dept.
85 Broad St.
New York 10004-2408

Established in 1979 in NY.
Donor(s): Lewis M. Eisenberg.
Foundation type: Independent
Financial data (yr. ended 7/31/88): Assets, $1,374,062 (M); gifts received, $630,658; expenditures, $224,474, including $224,015 for 82 grants (high: $40,000; low: $55).
Purpose and activities: Giving primarily for Jewish welfare funds and other Jewish organizations; support also for health associations, youth, medical research, and higher education.
Limitations: Giving primarily in New York, NY. No grants to individuals.
Application information: Applications not accepted.
Trustees: Judith Ann Eisenberg, Lewis M. Eisenberg, Eugene Mercy, Jr.
Employer Identification Number: 133001003

4348
W. H. Ellworth Trust for Hawthorne-Cedar Knolls School, et al. ⌑
c/o United States Trust Co. of New York
45 Wall St.
New York 10005

Foundation type: Independent
Financial data (yr. ended 1/31/88): Assets, $2,105,079 (M); expenditures, $108,669, including $82,995 for 21 grants of $3,952 each.
Purpose and activities: Giving for social sciences, education, health, and religious organizations.
Application information: Contributes only to pre-selected organizations. Applications not accepted.
Trustee: U.S. Trust Co. of New York.
Employer Identification Number: 136073049

4349
Elsmere Foundation, Inc. ⌑
c/o L.T. Rothschild
222 Broadway, 10th Fl.
New York 10038

Incorporated in 1955 in NY.
Donor(s): Kate S. Heming, Henry L. Heming, Henry A. Cohn, Abraham S. Platt, Richard H. Baer, Walter W. Hess, Jr., Herbert H. Weitsman,† Chester Viale, Stephen Kovacs.
Foundation type: Independent
Financial data (yr. ended 12/31/88): Assets, $709,100 (M); gifts received, $45,000; expenditures, $117,015, including $114,565 for 84 grants (high: $55,000; low: $15).
Purpose and activities: Giving for Jewish welfare funds, social service agencies, cultural programs, and hospitals.
Limitations: Giving primarily in NY. No grants to individuals.
Application information: Contributes only to pre-selected organizations. Applications not accepted.
Write: Walter W. Hess, Jr., Pres.
Officers and Directors: Walter W. Hess, Jr., Pres.; Stephen Kovacs, 1st V.P.; Alexander Bing III, 2nd V.P.; Robert Schoenthal, Treas.; Anny M. Baer, Helen Cohn, Daniel Kampel, Chester Viale.
Employer Identification Number: 136061343

4350
Elyachar Welfare Corporation ⌑
Eight East 48th St.
New York 10017

Established about 1951 in NY.
Donor(s): Gerel Corp., Timston Corp., Ruradan Corp., and others.
Foundation type: Independent
Financial data (yr. ended 12/31/88): Assets, $101,132 (M); gifts received, $43,000; expenditures, $115,337, including $115,000 for 5 grants (high: $50,000; low: $10,000).
Purpose and activities: Giving to Jewish organizations in the U.S. and Israel, including universities.
Limitations: Giving primarily in the U.S. and Israel. No grants to individuals.
Application information: Contributes only to pre-selected organizations. Applications not accepted.
Trustee: J.R. Elyachar.
Employer Identification Number: 136161372

4351
Fred L. Emerson Foundation, Inc.
63 Genesee St.
P.O. Box 276
Auburn 13021 (315) 253-9621

Incorporated in 1932 in DE.
Donor(s): Fred L. Emerson.†
Foundation type: Independent
Financial data (yr. ended 12/31/88): Assets, $43,737,753 (M); expenditures, $2,274,387, including $1,732,022 for 42 grants (high: $350,000; low: $200).
Purpose and activities: Giving to private colleges and universities, community funds, and a library; grants also for youth and social service agencies and cultural programs.
Types of support: Building funds, matching funds, annual campaigns, emergency funds, equipment, endowment funds, scholarship funds, special projects, research, renovation projects, capital campaigns.
Limitations: Giving primarily in the central NY area. No grants to individuals, or for deficit financing; no loans. Support for operating budgets is discouraged.
Publications: Program policy statement, application guidelines.
Application information: Application form not required.
Initial approach: Letter, telephone, or proposal
Copies of proposal: 1
Deadline(s): 2 months prior to board meetings
Board meeting date(s): June and Dec.
Final notification: 2 to 3 weeks after board meetings (positive replies only)
Write: Ronald D. West, Exec. Dir.
Officers and Directors: William V. Emerson, Pres.; Peter J. Emerson, V.P.; Ronald D. West, Exec. Dir. and Secy.; Thomas S. Tallman, Treas.; William F. Allyn, David L. Emerson, W. Gary Emerson, E. Paul Flynn, Anthony D. Franceschelli, J. David Hammond, Richard B. Secrest.
Number of staff: 1 full-time professional; 1 full-time support; 1 part-time support.
Employer Identification Number: 156017650

4352
Blanche T. Enders Charitable Trust ⌑
c/o Chemical Bank, Admin. Serv. Dept.
30 Rockefeller Plaza
New York 10112 (212) 621-2143

Foundation type: Independent
Financial data (yr. ended 12/31/88): Assets, $2,418,280 (M); expenditures, $122,040, including $104,000 for 16 grants (high: $15,000; low: $2,500).
Purpose and activities: Support primarily for child welfare and social services, Catholic religious and welfare institutions, education, animal welfare, and health associations and hospitals.
Limitations: Giving primarily in NY. No grants to individuals.
Application information: Application form not required.
Deadline(s): None
Write: Mrs. B. Strohmeier
Trustee: Chemical Bank.
Employer Identification Number: 136164229

4353
The Eppley Foundation for Research, Inc.
c/o Turk, Marsh, Kelly & Hoare
575 Lexington Ave.
New York 10022 (212) 371-1660

Established in 1947 in RI.
Donor(s): Marion Eppley.†
Foundation type: Independent
Financial data (yr. ended 12/31/88): Assets, $756,158 (M); gifts received, $93,447; expenditures, $170,249, including $141,212 for 10 grants to individuals (high: $30,000; low: $6,657; average: $10,000-$25,000).
Purpose and activities: Support for post-doctoral research in the physical and biological sciences; funds are administered by institutions sponsoring the individual grant recipients.
Types of support: Research.
Limitations: No support for social sciences, computer sciences, or educational programs.
Publications: Program policy statement, application guidelines.
Application information: Funding unavailable for independent research; applicant must be affiliated with recognized institution. Application form required.
Initial approach: Letter; no telephone calls
Copies of proposal: 2
Deadline(s): Feb. 1, May 1, Aug. 1, and Nov. 1
Final notification: 3 months
Write: Huyler C. Held, Secy.-Treas.
Officers and Directors:* Rivington R. Winant,* Pres.; Huyler C. Held,* Secy.-Treas.; Timothy Seldes, Joan O'Meara Winant.
Number of staff: 1 part-time professional.
Employer Identification Number: 050258857

4354
Sander/Ray Epstein Charitable Foundation ⌑
c/o A. Kanis
One West 34th St.
New York 10001

Established in 1962 in NY.
Foundation type: Independent
Financial data (yr. ended 12/31/88): Assets, $1,487,718 (M); expenditures, $50,710, including $48,170 for grants.
Purpose and activities: Giving primarily for Jewish welfare funds and hospitals.
Limitations: Giving primarily in New York, NY.
Application information: Application form not required.
Deadline(s): None
Write: Seymour Epstein, Pres.
Officers and Directors:* Seymour Epstein,* Pres.; Harry Schneider,* V.P.; Alan Kanis,* Secy.
Employer Identification Number: 136218324

4355
The Equitable Foundation, Inc.
787 Seventh Ave., 7th Fl.
New York 10019 (212) 554-3475

Established in 1986 in New York.
Donor(s): The Equitable Financial Cos.
Foundation type: Company-sponsored
Financial data (yr. ended 9/30/88): Assets, $683,715 (M); gifts received, $4,594,546; expenditures, $5,351,816, including $1,238,400 for 54 grants (high: $125,000; low: $3,000; average: $5,000-$25,000), $78,000 for 37 grants to individuals (high: $4,000; low: $750; average: $750-$4,000) and $3,751,775 for employee matching gifts.
Purpose and activities: Giving primarily for minority education, arts and community services, AIDS, and equal opportunity programs.
Types of support: Employee matching gifts, continuing support, general purposes, operating budgets, employee matching gifts, scholarship funds, special projects.
Limitations: Giving primarily in New York City, NY. No support for political, religious, or international purposes. No grants to individuals (other than employee-related scholarships).
Publications: Application guidelines.
Application information: Application form not required.
Initial approach: Letter
Copies of proposal: 1
Deadline(s): None
Board meeting date(s): Quarterly
Write: Nancy H. Green, Pres.
Officers: Nancy H. Green,* Pres.; William T. McCaffrey, V.P.; Patricia A. Kelly, Secy.; Paul H. Olsavsky, Treas.
Directors:* Robert W. Barth, David H. Harris, Benjamin D. Holloway, Eleanor Sheldon.
Number of staff: 4 full-time professional; 3 full-time support.
Employer Identification Number: 133340512

4356
The Armand G. Erpf Fund, Inc. ⌑
c/o Peat Marwick (MMP)
345 Park Ave.
New York 10154
Application address: 640 Park Ave., New York, NY 10021

Incorporated in 1951 in NY.
Donor(s): Armand G. Erpf.†
Foundation type: Independent
Financial data (yr. ended 11/30/88): Assets, $5,395,650 (M); gifts received, $455,191;

expenditures, $528,606, including $421,714 for 98 grants (high: $77,300).
Purpose and activities: Support for environment and conservation, education, and cultural programs.
Limitations: Giving primarily in NY. No grants to individuals, or for endowment funds.
Application information: Application form not required.
Initial approach: Proposal
Copies of proposal: 1
Deadline(s): None
Board meeting date(s): Quarterly
Write: Gerrit P. Van de Bovenkamp, Exec. V.P.
Officers and Trustees:* Sue Erpf Van de Bovenkamp,* Pres.; Gerrit P. Van de Bovenkamp,* Exec. V.P.; John G. Clancy,* Secy.; Carl L. Kempner,* Treas.; Douglas Campbell, Henry B. Hyde, Roger D. Stone.
Employer Identification Number: 136085594

4357
Essel Foundation, Inc. ⌑ ☆
550 Mamaroneck Ave.
Harrison 10528

Established in 1966.
Donor(s): Stephen Lieber, Constance Lieber.
Foundation type: Independent
Financial data (yr. ended 11/30/88): Assets, $5,849,139 (M); gifts received, $1,984,338; expenditures, $434,731, including $364,000 for 10 grants (high: $206,000; low: $1,000).
Purpose and activities: Support for Jewish organizations and higher education.
Limitations: No grants to individuals.
Application information: Contributes only to pre-selected organizations. Applications not accepted.
Officers: Constance Lieber, Pres.; Samuel Lieber, V.P.; Stephen Lieber, Secy.-Treas.
Employer Identification Number: 136191234

4358
The Ettinger Foundation, Inc. ⌑
665 Fifth Ave., No. 200
New York 10022-5305

Incorporated in 1949 in DE.
Donor(s): Members of the Ettinger family.
Foundation type: Independent
Financial data (yr. ended 12/31/87): Assets, $9,824,933 (M); expenditures, $468,767.
Purpose and activities: Giving for higher and secondary education, including scholarships for the children of Prentice-Hall employees; grants also for community funds, health, and youth agencies.
Types of support: Employee-related scholarships, scholarship funds.
Limitations: No grants to individuals (except for employee-related scholarships), or for general support, or building or endowment funds; no loans.
Publications: 990-PF.
Application information:
Initial approach: Letter
Copies of proposal: 1
Deadline(s): None
Board meeting date(s): Feb., May, Aug., and Nov.
Write: Richard P. Ettinger, Jr., Pres.
Officers and Trustee:* Richard P. Ettinger, Jr., Pres.; Elaine P. Hapgood,* V.P.; Ralph F. Anthony, Secy.; Rocco Landesman, Treas.
Number of staff: None.
Employer Identification Number: 066038938

4359
Charles Evans Foundation, Inc. ⌑
745 Fifth Ave., Rm. 1604
New York 10151 (212) 755-0443

Established in 1961 in NY.
Donor(s): Charles Evans.
Foundation type: Independent
Financial data (yr. ended 12/31/88): Assets, $1,279,731 (M); gifts received, $300,000; expenditures, $104,079, including $102,835 for 36 grants (high: $45,000; low: $15).
Purpose and activities: Emphasis on higher education, social service and youth agencies, and health associations.
Limitations: No grants to individuals.
Application information: Contributes only to pre-selected organizations. Applications not accepted.
Write: Charles Evans, Trustee
Trustee: Charles Evans.
Employer Identification Number: 136211837

4360
The T. M. Evans Foundation, Inc.
250 Park Ave.
New York 10177 (212) 557-5575

Incorporated in 1951 in DE.
Donor(s): Thomas Mellon Evans.
Foundation type: Independent
Financial data (yr. ended 12/31/89): Assets, $5,295,308 (M); expenditures, $309,320, including $252,800 for 38 grants (high: $80,000; low: $100; average: $1,000).
Purpose and activities: Grants primarily for museums and historic preservation, higher education, hospitals, medical research, music, religion, youth guidance services, and literary activities.
Types of support: Annual campaigns, building funds, capital campaigns, continuing support, emergency funds, equipment, general purposes, matching funds, operating budgets, renovation projects, research.
Limitations: Giving primarily in NY. No grants to individuals, or for scholarships or fellowships; no loans.
Application information: Application form not required.
Initial approach: Proposal
Copies of proposal: 1
Deadline(s): None
Board meeting date(s): Dec.
Write: L.F. Cerrone, Asst. Secy.
Officers and Trustees:* Thomas Mellon Evans,* Pres.; James H. Fraser,* Secy.-Treas.; Betty B. Evans, Edward P. Evans, Thomas M. Evans, Jr.
Number of staff: 1 part-time support.
Employer Identification Number: 256012086

4361
The David Everett Foundation, Inc. ⌑
150 East 69th St.
New York 10021

Incorporated in 1957 in NY.
Donor(s): Henry Everett, Edith B. Everett.
Foundation type: Independent
Financial data (yr. ended 12/31/88): Assets, $4,040,800 (M); gifts received, $1,000,000; expenditures, $262,664, including $254,989 for 120 grants (high: $60,000; low: $10).
Purpose and activities: Giving primarily for Jewish welfare organizations, including those in Israel; support also for museums, historic preservation, and other cultural programs; higher and other education; the disadvantaged, including issues of employment, hunger, youth opportunities, and housing for the homeless; and citizenship and civic affairs groups.
Limitations: Giving primarily in the New York, NY, metropolitan area. No grants to individuals.
Application information: Application form required.
Initial approach: Letter
Copies of proposal: 1
Write: Edith B. Everett, V.P.
Officers: Henry Everett, Pres. and Treas.; Edith B. Everett, V.P. and Secy.
Employer Identification Number: 116038040

4362
Everitt Charitable Trust ☆
c/o Norstar Trust Co.
One East Ave.
Rochester 14638 (315) 253-2731
Application address: c/o Norstar Trust Co., 120 Genesee St., Auburn, NY 13201

Established in 1957.
Foundation type: Independent
Financial data (yr. ended 12/31/89): Assets, $1,809,457 (M); expenditures, $127,756, including $117,255 for 17 grants (high: $58,627; low: $500).
Purpose and activities: Giving for community funds, higher education, a Presbyterian church, a YMCA, hospitals, and the arts, including performing arts and museums.
Types of support: Scholarship funds.
Limitations: Giving primarily in Cayuga County, NY.
Application information: Application form not required.
Initial approach: Letter
Copies of proposal: 1
Deadline(s): Nov. 1
Board meeting date(s): Late Nov. or early Dec.
Write: Walter M. Lowe
Trustee: Norstar Trust Co.
Employer Identification Number: 156018093

4363
Faith Home Foundation ⌑
57 Willoughby St.
Brooklyn 11201 (718) 875-3500

Incorporated in 1878 in NY.
Foundation type: Independent
Financial data (yr. ended 11/30/88): Assets, $2,053,989 (M); gifts received, $86,155; expenditures, $105,087, including $69,800 for grants.

Purpose and activities: Giving for the aged and child welfare agencies.
Limitations: Giving primarily in NY.
Application information: Contributes only to pre-selected organizations. Applications not accepted.
Write: George Schaefer, Treas.
Officers and Trustees: Owen E. Brooks, Pres.; Gordon M. Brown, V.P.; Charles H. Heinlein, V.P.; William F. deNeergaard, Secy.; George C. Schaefer, Treas.; David W. Alvey, Henry A. Braun, Kenneth S. Heiberg, Elwin S. Larson, George E. Lawrence, Alexander Pearson, William P. Tucker.
Employer Identification Number: 111776032

4364
Michael David Falk Foundation, Inc. ⌑
569 Broadway
New York 10012

Established in 1968.
Donor(s): Isidore Falk.
Foundation type: Independent
Financial data (yr. ended 12/31/88): Assets, $4,043,582 (M); expenditures, $172,635, including $160,225 for 3 grants (high: $160,000; low: $50).
Purpose and activities: Grants largely for higher education and Jewish welfare funds.
Officers: Isidore Falk, Mgr.; Maurice Falk, Mgr.
Employer Identification Number: 136265854

4365
Max M. and Marian M. Farash Foundation ⌑
919 Winton Rd. South
Rochester 14618-1633

Established in 1980 in NY.
Donor(s): Max M. Farash.
Foundation type: Independent
Financial data (yr. ended 8/31/88): Assets, $1,677,636 (M); expenditures, $106,848, including $89,445 for 28 grants (high: $25,000; low: $100).
Purpose and activities: Giving towards Jewish and other welfare; support also for education.
Types of support: Building funds.
Application information:
Deadline(s): Mar. 1
Write: Max M. Farash, Trustee
Trustees: Marian M. Farash, Max M. Farash, Michael W. Farash, Eric R. Fox, Lynn F. Tarbox.
Employer Identification Number: 222340023

4366
Chas. D. Farber Memorial Foundation, Inc. ⌑
c/o National Bank of New York
38th Ave. and 138th St.
Flushing 11354 (718) 358-4400

Established in 1969 in NY.
Donor(s): Jack Farber, Lafayette College.
Foundation type: Independent
Financial data (yr. ended 12/31/87): Assets, $1,096,514 (M); gifts received, $115,213; expenditures, $60,898, including $60,488 for 43 grants (high: $25,050; low: $20).
Purpose and activities: Support primarily for Jewish welfare.
Limitations: Giving primarily in FL and NY. No grants to individuals.
Application information: Contributes only to pre-selected organizations. Applications not accepted.
Write: Jack Farber, Dir.
Director: Jack Farber.
Trustees: Gail Farber, Richard Gelman.
Employer Identification Number: 237017599

4367
Marianne Gaillard Faulkner Trust ⌑
c/o Manufacturers Hanover Trust Co.
600 Fifth Ave.
New York 10020 (212) 957-1595

Trust established in 1959 in VT.
Donor(s): Marianne Gaillard Faulkner.†
Foundation type: Independent
Financial data (yr. ended 12/31/88): Assets, $5,232,070 (M); expenditures, $308,269, including $276,064 for 8 grants (high: $138,170; low: $2,000).
Purpose and activities: Grants for a recreation center and other community development projects.
Types of support: Matching funds, operating budgets, general purposes.
Limitations: Giving primarily in the Northeast, with emphasis on VT. No grants to individuals, or for endowment funds.
Application information: Prefer matching or one-time grants.
Initial approach: Proposal
Copies of proposal: 4
Deadline(s): None
Board meeting date(s): As required
Write: J.J. Kindred III, V.P., Manufacturers Hanover Trust Co.
Trustee: Manufacturers Hanover Trust Co.
Employer Identification Number: 136047458

4368
Fay's Foundation, Inc.
7245 Henry Clay Blvd.
Liverpool 13088 (315) 451-8000

Established in 1981 in NY.
Donor(s): Fay's, Inc.
Foundation type: Company-sponsored
Financial data (yr. ended 01/31/90): Assets, $587,911 (M); gifts received, $130,000; expenditures, $152,327, including $147,412 for 300 grants (high: $13,000; low: $10).
Purpose and activities: Grants for hospitals and health services, community funds, culture, social services, and community development.
Types of support: General purposes.
Limitations: Giving primarily in the Northeast, with emphasis on NY and PA.
Application information: Application form not required.
Initial approach: Proposal
Copies of proposal: 1
Deadline(s): None
Board meeting date(s): 1st Friday of each month
Write: Gillian M. McAuliffe, Pres.
Officers and Directors:* Gillian M. McAuliffe,* Pres.; Donald R. Bregande,* V.P.; Joseph LaLonde,* V.P.; David Panasci,* V.P.; James F. Poole, Jr.,* V.P.; Allan Travis,* V.P.; Warren D. Wolfson,* Secy.-Treas.
Number of staff: None.
Employer Identification Number: 222353455

4369
Louis & Gertrude Feil Foundation, Inc. ⌑
370 Seventh Ave., Suite 618
New York 10001

Established in 1977 in NY.
Donor(s): Louis Feil.
Foundation type: Independent
Financial data (yr. ended 06/30/89): Assets, $4,690,960 (M); expenditures, $248,646, including $245,495 for 69 grants (high: $50,000; low: $25).
Purpose and activities: Support primarily for Jewish organizations and hospitals.
Application information:
Deadline(s): None
Officers and Directors:* Gertrude Feil,* Pres.; Jeffrey Feil,* V.P.; Louis Feil,* Secy.-Treas.; Stanley Barry.
Employer Identification Number: 132958414

4370
Fein Foundation ⌑
P.O. Box 99
Scarsdale 10583

Established in 1954 in NY.
Donor(s): Bernard Fein.
Foundation type: Independent
Financial data (yr. ended 12/31/88): Assets, $2,547,063 (M); expenditures, $99,882, including $95,899 for 89 grants (high: $50,000; low: $15).
Purpose and activities: Giving primarily for education, youth programs, and health agencies.
Limitations: Giving primarily in the New York, NY, metropolitan area.
Application information: Contributes only to pre-selected organizations. Applications not accepted.
Trustees: Kathy Bierman, Bernard Fein, David Fein.
Number of staff: None.
Employer Identification Number: 136161610

4371
The Eugene and Estelle Ferkauf Foundation
67 Allenwood Rd.
Great Neck 11021 (516) 773-3269

Established in 1967 in NY.
Donor(s): Eugene Ferkauf, Estelle Ferkauf.
Foundation type: Independent
Financial data (yr. ended 12/31/88): Assets, $3,161,734 (M); expenditures, $527,876, including $413,100 for 56 grants (high: $25,000; low: $200; average: $10,350).
Purpose and activities: Grants primarily for education, the fine and performing arts, medical facilities, and medical research.
Types of support: Research, building funds, continuing support.
Limitations: No grants to individuals.
Publications: Application guidelines.
Application information: Application form not required.
Initial approach: Letter
Copies of proposal: 1

Deadline(s): Submit proposal preferably in Jan., July, or Dec.
Board meeting date(s): As required
Write: The Trustees
Trustees: Lenore Bronstein, Robert Bronstein, Richard M. Dicke, Barbara Dor, Benny Dor, Estelle Ferkauf, Eugene Ferkauf, Amy Shapira, Israel Shapira.
Number of staff: 1
Employer Identification Number: 132621094

4372
The Donald M. Feuerstein Foundation ⌘
(Formerly The Feuerstein-Dryfoos Foundation, Inc.)
c/o Salomon Brothers, Inc.
One New York Plaza
New York 10004 (212) 747-7843

Established in 1975 in NY.
Donor(s): Donald M. Feuerstein.
Foundation type: Independent
Financial data (yr. ended 06/30/89): Assets, $335,138 (M); gifts received, $500,043; expenditures, $292,725, including $290,800 for 39 grants (high: $80,000; low: $100).
Purpose and activities: Giving for cultural programs, secondary and higher education, and health agencies.
Limitations: Giving primarily in the New York, NY, metropolitan area.
Application information: Contributes only to pre-selected organizations. Applications not accepted.
Officers: Donald M. Feuerstein, Pres. and Treas.; Martin Lipton, V.P. and Secy.
Employer Identification Number: 132838464

4373
FFHS&J Fund, Inc. ⌘
One New York Plaza, 28th Fl.
New York 10004

Incorporated in 1982 in NY.
Donor(s): Fried, Harris, Shriver & Jacobson firm members.
Foundation type: Independent
Financial data (yr. ended 12/31/88): Assets, $612,213 (M); gifts received, $446,940; expenditures, $986,794, including $983,194 for 94 grants (high: $425,000; low: $200).
Purpose and activities: Giving primarily for Jewish welfare funds, public interest law and civil rights associations, and law schools; also supports a community fund.
Limitations: Giving primarily in New York, NY, and Washington, DC.
Application information: Applications not accepted.
Officer and Trustees: Robert H. Preiskel, Co-Chair.; Leon Silverman, Co-Chair.; William Josephson, Pres.; Pamela Jarvis, V.P.; Richard Sauber, V.P.; Ann F. Thomas, V.P.; Herbert Hirsch, Secy.-Treas.
Employer Identification Number: 133111495

4374
Elias and Bertha Fife Foundation, Inc. ⌘
Standard Motor Products, Inc.
37-18 Northern Blvd.
Long Island City 11101 (718) 392-0200

Incorporated in 1959 in NY.
Donor(s): Members of the Fife family, Standard Motor Products, Inc.
Foundation type: Independent
Financial data (yr. ended 04/30/89): Assets, $3,675,592 (M); gifts received, $100,000; expenditures, $197,530, including $196,950 for 120 grants (high: $95,500; low: $100).
Purpose and activities: Support for Jewish welfare funds, health and welfare agencies, and cultural programs.
Application information:
Initial approach: Letter
Deadline(s): None
Write: Bernard Fife, Pres.
Officers and Directors:* Bernard Fife,* Pres.; Nathaniel L. Sills,* Secy.-Treas.; Arlene Fife, Ruth Sills.
Employer Identification Number: 116035634

4375
Allan H. Fine Foundation, Inc. ⌘
c/o Anchin Block & Anchin
1375 Broadway
New York 10018

Established in 1974 in NY.
Donor(s): Allan H. Fine.
Foundation type: Independent
Financial data (yr. ended 6/30/88): Assets, $949,531 (M); gifts received, $25,000; expenditures, $213,938, including $198,205 for 54 grants (high: $25,500; low: $30).
Purpose and activities: Support for health services and cancer research.
Limitations: Giving primarily in NY. No grants to individuals.
Application information: Contributes only to pre-selected organizations. Applications not accepted.
Officers: Allan H. Fine, Pres. and Treas.; Morris Ohit, Secy.
Employer Identification Number: 237411125

4376
Fink Foundation, Inc. ⌘
304 Park Ave. South, Suite 211
New York 10010 (212) 529-6410

Incorporated in 1956 in NY.
Donor(s): David Fink, Nathan Fink.
Foundation type: Independent
Financial data (yr. ended 12/31/88): Assets, $3,221,093 (M); expenditures, $171,933, including $138,200 for 52 grants (high: $10,000; low: $250).
Purpose and activities: Grants largely to Jewish-sponsored organizations, with emphasis on education and welfare.
Application information:
Deadline(s): None
Final notification: 2 months
Write: Romie Shapiro, Pres.
Officers: Romie Shapiro, Pres.; David M. Levitan, V.P.
Employer Identification Number: 136135438

4377
The First Boston Foundation Trust ⌘
c/o Maria Lilly
12 East 49th St.
New York 10017 (212) 909-4575

Trust established in 1959 in MA.
Donor(s): The First Boston Corp.
Foundation type: Company-sponsored
Financial data (yr. ended 12/31/88): Assets, $366,184 (M); gifts received, $1,528,865; expenditures, $1,459,292, including $949,713 for 98 grants (high: $219,613; low: $200) and $504,399 for 404 employee matching gifts.
Purpose and activities: Emphasis on community funds and higher education; support also for cultural programs, community development, and groups seeking to improve international relations.
Types of support: Employee matching gifts.
Limitations: No grants to individuals.
Application information:
Initial approach: Proposal
Deadline(s): None
Write: Michael Raoul-Duval, Chair.
Trustees: Michael Raoul-Duval, Chair.; Robert K. deVeer, Jr., William E. Mayer, Michael G. Zeiss.
Employer Identification Number: 046059692

4378
Fischbach Foundation, Inc. ⌘
Timber Trail
Rye 10580

Incorporated in 1944 in NY.
Donor(s): Members of the Fischbach family.
Foundation type: Independent
Financial data (yr. ended 12/31/87): Assets, $1,876,623 (M); gifts received, $1,500; expenditures, $173,003, including $170,650 for 44 grants (high: $100,000; low: $100).
Purpose and activities: To aid the health, welfare, and education of poor and needy people; giving primarily for higher education, including education in Israel, and hospitals; some support for Jewish welfare funds.
Limitations: Giving primarily in NY; some giving in Israel.
Application information:
Initial approach: Letter
Deadline(s): None
Write: Jerome Fischbach, Pres.
Officers: Jerome Fischbach, Pres.; Beatrice Levinson, Secy.
Employer Identification Number: 237416874

4379
Harry and Jane Fischel Foundation ⌘
310 Madison Ave., Suite 1711
New York 10017 (212) 599-2828

Incorporated in 1932 in NY.
Donor(s): Harry Fischel.†
Foundation type: Independent
Financial data (yr. ended 12/31/89): Assets, $7,361,719 (M); expenditures, $623,391, including $345,084 for grants (high: $271,000).
Purpose and activities: Organized to develop Talmudic research to aid Jewish knowledge and present the Orthodox Jewish contributions to civilization. Grants largely to two educational institutions initiated by the donor.
Limitations: No grants to individuals.

Application information: Contributes only to pre-selected organizations. Applications not accepted.
Write: Michael D. Jaspan, Exec. Dir.
Officers and Directors:* Rabbi O. Asher Reichel,* Chair.; Gabriel F. Goldstein,* Pres.; Michael D. Jaspan,* V.P. and Exec. Dir.; Ronald Jaspan,* Secy.; Frederic S. Goldstein,* Treas.; Rabbi Shear Yashuv Cohen, Seth M. Goldstein, Simeon H.F. Goldstein, Harry Grossman, Norman Jaspan, Rabbi Aaron I. Reichel, Jay Stepelman.
Number of staff: 1 full-time professional; 2 part-time support.
Employer Identification Number: 135677832

4380
Vain and Harry Fish Foundation, Inc. ⌘
66 East 79th St.
New York 10021 (212) 879-2520

Incorporated in 1972 in NY.
Donor(s): Vain B. Fish,† Harry Fish.†
Foundation type: Independent
Financial data (yr. ended 12/31/88): Assets, $3,239,609 (M); expenditures, $238,516, including $182,700 for 53 grants (high: $30,000; low: $500).
Purpose and activities: Grants for higher education and hospitals; grants also for cultural activities, youth agencies, the handicapped, and church support.
Types of support: Endowment funds, seed money.
Limitations: Giving primarily in NY. No grants to individuals.
Application information:
Initial approach: Letter
Deadline(s): None
Write: Alexander W. Gentleman, Pres.
Officers: Alexander W. Gentleman, Pres.; Vivian F. Gentleman, V.P. and Secy.; Bernard Leegant, Treas.
Employer Identification Number: 132723211

4381
The Fisher Brothers Foundation, Inc. ⌘
c/o Fisher Brothers
299 Park Ave.
New York 10017

Established in 1981 in NY.
Donor(s): Fisher Park Ave. Co., Fisher Capital Assets, and other Fisher Brothers affiliates.
Foundation type: Company-sponsored
Financial data (yr. ended 12/31/88): Assets, $55,246 (M); gifts received, $664,550; expenditures, $639,047, including $631,007 for 57 grants (high: $366,666; low: $250).
Purpose and activities: Support primarly for Jewish welfare and concerns, and general charitable giving.
Limitations: Giving primarily in NY. No grants to individuals.
Application information: Contributes only to pre-selected organizations. Applications not accepted.
Directors: Arnold Fisher, Larry Fisher, Richard Fisher, Zachary Fisher.
Employer Identification Number: 133118286

4382
Louis R. & Nettie Fisher Foundation, Inc. ⌘ ☆
c/o Martin A. Rothenberg
90 Broad St.
New York 10004-2205
Application Address: 441 Summit St., Englewood Cliffs, NJ 07632; Tel.: (201) 568-5743

Established in 1968.
Foundation type: Independent
Financial data (yr. ended 12/31/88): Assets, $464,735 (M); expenditures, $133,008, including $127,050 for 46 grants (high: $10,000; low: $50).
Purpose and activities: Giving for Jewish welfare, medical research and health associations, social services, higher and other education, and civil rights.
Types of support: Research.
Limitations: Giving primarily in New York, NY.
Application information: Application form not required.
Deadline(s): None
Write: Bernard Feder, Secy.-Treas.
Officers: Seymour Fisher, Pres.; Bernard Bressler, V.P.; Barnett R. Fisher, V.P.; Bernard Feder, Secy.-Treas.
Employer Identification Number: 136274501

4383
The Fisher Fund
85 Broad St., 2nd Fl.
New York 10004

Established in 1985 in NY.
Donor(s): Pieter A. Fisher.
Foundation type: Independent
Financial data (yr. ended 05/31/89): Assets, $1,454,313 (M); gifts received, $1,586; expenditures, $197,991, including $196,000 for 24 grants (high: $25,000; low: $500).
Purpose and activities: Grants for higher education, hospitals and health, the fine arts and other cultural programs, the environment and wildlife preservation, and international affairs.
Types of support: General purposes, exchange programs, fellowships.
Limitations: No grants to individuals, or for scholarships; no loans.
Application information: Applications not accepted.
Trustees: Geoffrey T. Boisi, M. Helen Fisher, Pieter A. Fisher.
Employer Identification Number: 133318154

4384
The Fisher Landau Foundation ⌘
c/o Fisher Brothers
299 Park Ave.
New York 10017

Established in 1983 in NY.
Donor(s): Emily Landau.
Foundation type: Independent
Financial data (yr. ended 6/30/88): Assets, $166 (M); gifts received, $488,872; expenditures, $490,805, including $453,016 for 3 grants (high: $200,016; low: $80,000).
Purpose and activities: Support primarily for two private elementary and secondary schools.
Limitations: Giving primarily in New York, NY. No grants to individuals.
Application information: Contributes only to pre-selected organizations. Applications not accepted.
Trustees: Joseph Curry, M. Anthony Fisher, Emily Landau.
Employer Identification Number: 133267201

4385
Fishoff Family Foundation ⌘ ☆
1140 Ave. of the Americas
New York 10036

Donor(s): Benjamin Fishoff, Marilyn Fishoff, Donald Fishoff, Interocean Industries, Inc.
Foundation type: Independent
Financial data (yr. ended 07/31/89): Assets, $6,349,647 (M); gifts received, $2,607,480; expenditures, $587,555, including $475,175 for grants.
Purpose and activities: Support primarily for Jewish concerns, including welfare funds; support also for education.
Limitations: Giving primarily in New York, NY.
Application information:
Initial approach: Letter
Deadline(s): None
Write: Benjamin Fishoff, Dir.
Director: Benjamin Fishoff.
Employer Identification Number: 133076576

4386
John J. Flemm Foundation, Inc.
c/o Sidney Horn
190 Willis Ave., Suite 240
Mineola 11501

Established in 1974.
Donor(s): John J. Flemm.†
Foundation type: Independent
Financial data (yr. ended 01/31/90): Assets, $2,612,165 (M); expenditures, $210,518, including $172,433 for 134 grants (high: $12,100; low: $50).
Purpose and activities: Giving for cultural, educational, environmental, health, religious, and other charitable organizations.
Application information: Applications not accepted.
Write: Edward Owen Adler, Counsel
Officers, Directors, and Trustees:* Daniel Harris,* Pres.; Judith Post,* V.P.; Robert Post,* Secy.; Michael Harris,* Treas.; Avery Harris, Leona Post.
Employer Identification Number: 237348789

4387
Shalom and Rebecca Fogel Foundation, Inc. ⌘ ☆
18 Lord Ave.
Lawrence 11559-1322

Established in 1971 in NY.
Donor(s): Shalom Fogel.
Foundation type: Independent
Financial data (yr. ended 5/31/89): Assets, $2,762,939 (M); gifts received, $644,000; expenditures, $239,835, including $237,410 for grants (high: $36,000).
Purpose and activities: Support for Jewish organizations, including yeshivas, a theological institute, and congregations.

Limitations: Giving primarily in Brooklyn, NY.
Application information: Application form not required.
Deadline(s): None
Officers: Shalom Fogel, Pres.; Rebecca Fogel, V.P. and Secy.
Employer Identification Number: 237323166

4388
William T. Foley Foundation, Inc. ⌑
46 Summit Ave.
Bronxville 10708 (914) 779-1691

Established in 1962 in NY.
Foundation type: Independent
Financial data (yr. ended 06/30/89): Assets, $1,456,220 (M); gifts received, $8,725; expenditures, $97,757, including $31,850 for 11 grants (high: $30,000; low: $250).
Purpose and activities: Support primarily for higher education, with emphasis on medical education, and for hospitals and health services.
Limitations: Giving primarily in New York City, NY.
Application information: Rarely funds new recipients. Application form not required.
Initial approach: Letter; telephone inquiries not considered
Deadline(s): None
Final notification: Two weeks
Write: John L. Cady, Secy.
Officers: William T. Foley, Pres.; John L. Cady, Secy.-Treas.
Employer Identification Number: 136161354

4389
Herman Forbes Charitable Trust ⌑
c/o The Chase Manhattan Bank, N.A., Tax Dept.
1211 Ave. of the Americas
New York 10036 (212) 730-3350

Incorporated in 1982 in NY.
Donor(s): Herman Forbes.†
Foundation type: Independent
Financial data (yr. ended 03/31/89): Assets, $4,784,532 (M); expenditures, $172,181, including $100,000 for 28 grants (high: $17,000; low: $500).
Purpose and activities: Emphasis on Jewish giving, including temple support, education, child welfare, and social service agencies.
Application information:
Initial approach: Proposal
Deadline(s): None
Write: Elizabeth W. Eagleson, 2nd V.P., Chase Manhattan Bank
Trustees: Sidney Richman, Jacob Silverman, The Chase Manhattan Bank, N.A.
Employer Identification Number: 136814404

4390
Forbes Foundation ▼ ⌑
c/o Forbes Inc.
60 Fifth Ave.
New York 10011 (212) 620-2248

Established in 1979 in NJ.
Donor(s): Forbes, Inc.
Foundation type: Company-sponsored
Financial data (yr. ended 12/31/88): Assets, $528,381 (M); gifts received, $1,491,368; expenditures, $1,490,516, including $1,490,516 for 470 grants (high: $250,000; low: $20; average: $100-$10,000).
Purpose and activities: Support for higher and secondary education, hospitals, cultural programs and museums, and welfare funds.
Types of support: General purposes, building funds, endowment funds.
Limitations: No grants to individuals, or for matching gifts; no loans.
Publications: 990-PF.
Application information: Contributes only to pre-selected organizations. Applications not accepted.
Board meeting date(s): As required
Write: Leonard H. Yablon, Secy.-Treas.
Officers: Malcolm S. Forbes, Jr., V.P.; Leonard H. Yablon, Secy.-Treas.
Number of staff: None.
Employer Identification Number: 237037319

4391
The Forchheimer Foundation ▼ ⌑
c/o Weitzner, Levine & Hamburg
230 Park Ave.
New York 10169 (212) 661-3140

Established in NY.
Donor(s): Leo Forchheimer.†
Foundation type: Independent
Financial data (yr. ended 12/31/88): Assets, $7,434,731 (M); expenditures, $732,147, including $675,000 for 10 grants (high: $250,000; low: $10,000; average: $10,000-$50,000).
Purpose and activities: Giving primarily for hospitals, health agencies, higher education, including medical and technical education, Jewish welfare funds, museums, and social services.
Limitations: Giving primarily in Israel and New York, NY.
Application information:
Deadline(s): None
Officers: Julia Forchheimer,* Pres.; Ludwig Jesselson, V.P. and Treas.; Rudolph Forchheimer,* Secy.
Directors:* Joseph Levine.
Employer Identification Number: 136075112

4392
The Ford Foundation ▼
320 East 43rd St.
New York 10017 (212) 573-5000

Incorporated in 1936 in MI.
Donor(s): Henry Ford,† Edsel Ford.†
Foundation type: Independent
Financial data (yr. ended 09/30/89): Assets, $5,832,426,000 (M); gifts received, $65,703; expenditures, $284,128,000, including $211,769,514 for 1,542 grants (high: $4,600,000; low: $3,000; average: $25,000-$1,500,000), $5,899,900 for 464 grants to individuals (high: $70,000; low: $500; average: $2,000-$20,000), $2,712,180 for 26 foundation-administered programs and $11,172,580 for 15 loans.
Purpose and activities: To advance the public well-being by identifying and contributing to the solution of problems of national and international importance. Grants primarily to institutions for experimental, demonstration, and developmental efforts that are likely to produce significant advances within the foundation's six major fields of interest: Urban Poverty and the Disadvantaged--including community and neighborhood self-help initiatives, housing rehabilitation, educational and employment programs for disadvantaged youth and for welfare recipients, early childhood education, maternal and child health and nutrition, and research on urban problems; 2) Rural Poverty and Resources--including community-based rural development, national policy planning, income-generating projects, improvement of opportunities for women, the landless, and migrants, management of land and water resources, and environmental problems in the Soviet Union and Eastern Europe; 3) Human Rights and Social Justice--including human rights in the Soviet Union, civil rights, sex discrimination, the rights of refugees and migrants, freedom of expression and opinion, and legal services to the poor; 4) Governance and Public Policy--including projects to strengthen democratic processes and institutions, to promote civic participation, improve state and local governments, and to enhance the vitality of the nonprofit sector; 5) Education and Culture--support for excellence and equity in urban and rural public schools, artistic creativity, and cultural preservation in developing countries; and 6) International Affairs--research, analysis, and public education on international peace, security and arms control, international economics, international economic problems in the Soviet Union and Eastern Europe, international refugees and migration, international organizations and law, and foreign-area studies. In both the U.S. and the developing world the foundation supports efforts to improve women's lives and promote the survival and healthy development of their children. Assistance is provided to programs to strengthen reproductive health, including family planning services, contraceptive safety, and the treatment of gynecological infections and sexually transmitted diseases. A second focus of the foundation's population activity is research that informs policy makers and the public about the consequences of population change.
Types of support: Conferences and seminars, consulting services, exchange programs, general purposes, matching funds, professorships, program-related investments, publications, research, seed money, special projects, technical assistance, continuing support, endowment funds, fellowships, grants to individuals.
Limitations: No support for programs for which substantial support from government or other sources is readily available, or for religious activities as such. No grants for routine operating costs, construction or maintenance of buildings, or undergraduate scholarships; graduate fellowships generally channeled through grants to universities or other organizations; no grants for purely personal or local needs.
Publications: Annual report, newsletter, program policy statement (including application guidelines), occasional report.
Application information: Foreign applicants should contact foundation for addresses of its

overseas offices, through which they must apply. Application form not required.
Initial approach: Letter, proposal or telephone
Copies of proposal: 1
Deadline(s): None
Board meeting date(s): Dec., Mar., June, and Sept.
Final notification: Initial indication as to whether proposal falls within program interests within 1 month
Write: Barron M. Tenny, Secy.
Officers: Franklin A. Thomas,* Pres.; Barron M. Tenny, V.P., General Counsel, and Secy.; Susan V. Berresford, V.P.; John W. English, V.P.; Nancy Feller, Assoc. Gen. Counsel and Dir., Legal Services; John Koprowski, Treas.; Barry D. Gaberman, Deputy V.P.; Diane Galloway-May, Asst. Secy.
Trustees:* Edson W. Spencer, Chair.; Yvonne Braithwaite Burke, Frances D. Fergusson, Sir Christopher Hogg, Vernon E. Jordan, Jr., David T. Kearns, Donald F. McHenry, Paul F. Miller, Jr., William G. Milliken, Gen. Olusegun Obasanjo, Barbara Scott Preiskel, Dorothy S. Ridings, Henry B. Schacht, M.S. Swaminathan, Thomas H. Wyman.
Number of staff: 220 full-time professional; 2 part-time professional; 331 full-time support; 8 part-time support.
Employer Identification Number: 131684331

4393
The John H. Foster Foundation ⌑ ☆
c/o Haythe & Curley
437 Madison Ave.
New York 10022-7001

Established in 1984.
Foundation type: Independent
Financial data (yr. ended 6/30/88): Assets, $1,943,757 (M); gifts received, $635,000; expenditures, $85,036, including $79,462 for 26 grants (high: $28,037; low: $25).
Purpose and activities: Giving primarily for religion and higher and secondary education; support also for a youth club and cultural programs.
Limitations: Giving primarily in NY and CT.
Application information: Contributes only to pre-selected organizations. Applications not accepted.
Officers and Directors: John Foster, Pres.; Lynn A. Foster, V.P.; Nathan Hale, Secy.; Stephen C. Curley, Treas.
Employer Identification Number: 133249353

4394
Foundation for Celebration 33, Inc. ⌑ ☆
888 Seventh Ave., 43rd Fl.
New York 10106 (212) 621-4500

Incorporated in 1980 in DE.
Foundation type: Independent
Financial data (yr. ended 10/31/88): Assets, $313,910 (M); expenditures, $470,410, including $461,644 for 1 grant.
Purpose and activities: "Giving for organizations which benefit educational facilities located in the state of Israel."
Application information: Application form not required.
Initial approach: Letter
Deadline(s): None
Write: Simona Ackerman, Pres.
Officers and Directors: Simona Ackerman, Pres.; Arnold Broser, Secy.; Avigdor Schwartzstein, Treas.
Employer Identification Number: 133054239

4395
Foundation for Child Development ▼
345 East 46th St., Rm. 700
New York 10017 (212) 697-3150

Incorporated as a voluntary agency in NY in 1900 and established as the Association for the Aid of Crippled Children in 1908; current name adopted in 1972, affirming a broader focus on children at risk.
Donor(s): Milo M. Belding,† Annie K. Belding,† and others.
Foundation type: Independent
Financial data (yr. ended 3/31/89): Assets, $47,939,737 (M); gifts received, $401,239; expenditures, $2,559,943, including $1,434,547 for 57 grants (high: $153,916; low: $2,125; average: $5,000-$100,000) and $164,494 for foundation-administered programs.
Purpose and activities: Support is currently focused on children and their families at economic and social risk, with particular attention to families on AFDC who are affected by the Family Support Act of 1988. The foundation makes grants for research, policy and advocacy, and supports a small group of direct-service initiatives in New York City.
Types of support: Continuing support, fellowships, special projects, research, publications, general purposes.
Limitations: Giving limited to New York City, for direct service projects; no other geographic limitations. No grants to individuals, or for capital funds.
Publications: Annual report (including application guidelines), grants list, 990-PF.
Application information: Application form not required.
Initial approach: Proposal
Copies of proposal: 1
Deadline(s): None
Board meeting date(s): June, Sept., Dec., and Mar.
Final notification: 1 to 3 weeks for unfavorable replies; 2 to 4 months for favorable replies
Write: Jane Dustan, V.P.
Officers: John J. Hobbs,* Chair.; E. Mavis Hetherington,* Vice-Chair.; Barbara B. Blum,* Pres.; Jane Dustan, V.P.; Barbara Paul Robinson,* Secy.; Karen N. Gerard,* Treas.
Directors:* Mary L. Bundy, Lindsay Chase-Lansdale, Eleanor T. Elliott, Frank F. Furstenberg, Jr., Sara L. Lightfoot, Julius B. Richmond, Henry W. Riecken, Lisbeth B. Schorr, Gilbert Y. Steiner.
Number of staff: 2 full-time professional; 2 part-time professional; 6 full-time support; 1 part-time support.
Employer Identification Number: 131623901

4396
Foundation for Microbiology
300 East 54th St., Apt. 5-K
New York 10022 (212) 759-8729

Incorporated in 1951 in NJ.
Donor(s): Selman A. Waksman,† Deborah B. Waksman.†
Foundation type: Independent
Financial data (yr. ended 12/31/89): Assets, $1,378,282 (M); expenditures, $104,754, including $84,903 for 13 grants (high: $33,700; low: $500; average: $2,000-$12,000).
Purpose and activities: Grants for lectureships, courses, meetings, unusual projects, and publication of monographs in microbiological sciences.
Types of support: Special projects, publications, conferences and seminars, professorships, exchange programs, lectureships.
Limitations: No grants to individuals, or for fellowships, conventional research projects, travel, general or operating support, or capital or endowment funds; no loans.
Publications: Annual report, 990-PF, multi-year report.
Application information: Application form not required.
Initial approach: Letter
Copies of proposal: 1
Deadline(s): None
Board meeting date(s): May or June
Final notification: 3 to 6 months
Write: Byron H. Waksman, M.D., Pres.
Officers and Trustees:* Byron H. Waksman, M.D.,* Pres.; Alice S. Huang,* V.P.; R. Edward Townsend, Jr.,* Secy.; Nan Schanbacher,* Treas.; Keith A. Bostian, Jean E. Brenchley, Arnold Demain, J. Oliver Lampen, Jonathan G. Seidman, Kenneth V. Thimann.
Number of staff: 1 part-time professional.
Employer Identification Number: 226057913

4397
Foundation for the Needs of Others, Inc. ⌑
c/o Patterson, Belknap, Webb & Tyler
30 Rockefeller Plaza, Suite 3500
New York 10112 (212) 541-4000

Incorporated in 1953 in NY.
Donor(s): Helen W. Buckner, Walker G. Buckner, Thomas W. Buckner.
Foundation type: Independent
Financial data (yr. ended 12/31/87): Assets, $4,771,142 (M); expenditures, $339,200, including $306,500 for 32 grants (high: $40,000; low: $1,000).
Purpose and activities: Emphasis on conservation, higher and elementary education, and cultural programs; grants also for social service agencies and international relief.
Limitations: Giving primarily in New York, NY. No grants to individuals.
Publications: 990-PF.
Application information:
Initial approach: Letter
Deadline(s): None
Write: Mimi Kaplansky
Officers and Trustees: Helen W. Buckner, Pres.; Elizabeth B. Buckner, V.P.; Walker G. Buckner, Jr., V.P.; Thomas W. Buckner, Secy.-Treas.
Employer Identification Number: 136119874

4398
David Franco Foundation, Inc. ⌑
c/o Franco Manufacturing Co., Inc.
309 Fifth Ave.
New York 10016 (212) 481-5400

Established in 1968 in NY.
Donor(s): Franco Manufacturing Co.
Foundation type: Independent
Financial data (yr. ended 12/31/88): Assets, $712,419 (M); expenditures, $287,244, including $285,729 for 134 grants (high: $100,000; low: $36).
Purpose and activities: Support primarily for Jewish organizations, including Jewish welfare funds.
Application information: Application form not required.
Deadline(s): None
Write: Jack Franco, Dir.
Directors: Jack Franco, Louis Franco, Morris Franco.
Employer Identification Number: 136267004

4399
Ernst & Elfriede Frank Foundation ⌑
85-19 Abingdon Rd.
Kew Gardens 11415

Foundation type: Independent
Financial data (yr. ended 08/31/89): Assets, $4,583,766 (M); expenditures, $182,632, including $180,394 for 103 grants (high: $24,000; low: $50).
Purpose and activities: Giving for social services and cultural programs.
Limitations: Giving primarily in NY.
Application information: Contributes only to pre-selected organizations. Applications not accepted.
Officers: Ernest L. Frank, Pres.; Sybil Ann Brennan, V.P.; Ernest H. Frank, V.P.; Eva Maria Tausig, V.P.
Employer Identification Number: 136106471

4400
George and Elizabeth F. Frankel Foundation, Inc. ⌑
60 East 42nd St.
New York 10017

Incorporated in 1945 in NY.
Donor(s): George Frankel,† Elizabeth F. Frankel,† G. David Frankel, Charles Korn.
Foundation type: Independent
Financial data (yr. ended 3/31/88): Assets, $5,686,116 (M); gifts received, $5,000; expenditures, $963,019, including $635,674 for 162 grants (high: $344,030; low: $50).
Purpose and activities: Giving for medical education, health and medical research agencies, and Jewish welfare funds.
Limitations: Giving primarily in NY. No grants to individuals.
Application information: Contributes only to pre-selected organizations. Applications not accepted.
Officers and Trustees: G. David Frankel, Pres.; Doris F. Tulcin, Secy.; Elizabeth F. Bock, Charles Korn, Geraldine F. Merksamer.
Employer Identification Number: 136126076

4401
The Nina Franklin Foundation ⌑ ☆
Archer Road
Harrison 10528

Established 1986.
Donor(s): Roland A.E. Franklin.
Foundation type: Independent
Financial data (yr. ended 12/31/88): Assets, $1,503,639 (M); expenditures, $412,537, including $405,395 for 24 grants (high: $124,000; low: $50).
Purpose and activities: Giving primarily for Jewish organizations, including a welfare fund, and performing arts groups.
Limitations: Giving primarily in NY. No grants to individuals.
Application information: Contributes only to pre-selected organizations. Applications not accepted.
Directors: Nina G. Franklin, Roland A.E. Franklin, Rabbi Norton Shargel.
Employer Identification Number: 133386459

4402
Franklin Fund ⌑
345 East 46th St.
New York 10017

Foundation type: Independent
Financial data (yr. ended 6/30/88): Assets, $866,245 (M); expenditures, $184,609, including $163,822 for grants.
Purpose and activities: Support primarily for international affairs and foreign policy organizations; support also for the arts.
Application information: Application form not required.
Initial approach: Letter
Deadline(s): None
Write: George S. Franklin, Trustee
Trustees: George S. Franklin, Helena Franklin.
Employer Identification Number: 136160092

4403
Herman Frasch Foundation for Chemical Research u/w Elizabeth B. Frasch
c/o U.S. Trust Co. of New York
114 West 47th St.
New York 10036-1532 (212) 852-3683
Mailing address for application forms: c/o Dr. Joseph Rogers, Head, Dept. of Research Grants and Awards, American Chemical Society, 1155 16th St., N.W., Washington, DC 20036; Tel.: (202) 872-4487

Trust established in 1924 in NY.
Donor(s): Elizabeth Blee Frasch.†
Foundation type: Independent
Financial data (yr. ended 12/31/89): Assets, $5,800,000 (M); expenditures, $257,000, including $207,300 for 18 grants (high: $2,750; low: $2,500).
Purpose and activities: Grants for research in agricultural chemistry made for five-year periods to nonprofit incorporated institutions in the U.S. selected with the advice of the American Chemical Society as well as Frasch committee members.
Types of support: Research.
Limitations: No grants to individuals, or for endowment funds, building funds, operating budgets, scholarships, fellowships, or matching gifts; no loans.
Publications: Application guidelines, program policy statement.
Application information: Next application period Apr. 1, 1991 to Aug. 1, 1991; for final notification write Dr. Joseph E. Rogers. Application form required.
Initial approach: Letter or telephone
Copies of proposal: 7
Board meeting date(s): Every 5 years in Nov.
Write: Anne L. Smith-Ganey, Asst. V.P., U.S. Trust Co. of New York
Trustee: U.S. Trust Co. of New York.
Employer Identification Number: 136073145

4404
Fraydun Foundation, Inc. ⌑ ☆
475 Park Ave. South
New York 10016-6901

Established in 1981.
Donor(s): Fraydun Manocherian.
Foundation type: Independent
Financial data (yr. ended 12/31/88): Assets, $1,009,280 (M); gifts received, $52,500; expenditures, $84,458, including $80,100 for 19 grants (high: $50,000; low: $100).
Purpose and activities: Giving for health associations, social services, higher education, community development, and hospitals.
Application information: Application form not required.
Deadline(s): None
Write: Fraydun Manocherian, Dir.
Directors: Fraydun Manocherian, Jennifer Manocherian, Kimberly Manocherian.
Employer Identification Number: 133185696

4405
Samuel Freeman Charitable Trust ⌑
c/o U.S. Trust Co. of New York
114 West 47th St.
New York 10036-1532 (212) 852-1000

Established in 1981 in NY.
Donor(s): Samuel Freeman.†
Foundation type: Independent
Financial data (yr. ended 12/31/87): Assets, $19,298,716 (M); gifts received, $23,195; expenditures, $1,169,013, including $954,748 for 87 grants (high: $100,000; low: $103).
Purpose and activities: Giving primarily for health and education.
Limitations: Giving primarily in New York, NY.
Application information:
Initial approach: Proposal of not more than 2 pages
Deadline(s): None
Write: Anne L. Smith Ganey
Trustees: U.S. Trust Co. of New York, William E. Murray.
Employer Identification Number: 136803465

4406
D. E. French Foundation, Inc. ⌑
120 Genesee St., Rm. 602
Auburn 13021 (315) 253-9321

Incorporated in 1955 in NY.
Donor(s): Clara M. French,† D.E. French.†
Foundation type: Independent

Financial data (yr. ended 12/31/88): Assets, $2,663,940 (M); expenditures, $184,122, including $153,018 for 54 grants (high: $15,000; low: $15).
Purpose and activities: Giving primarily for Protestant church support, youth agencies, health services, and education.
Types of support: Equipment, annual campaigns, building funds, capital campaigns, continuing support, endowment funds, general purposes, matching funds, renovation projects, scholarship funds.
Limitations: Giving primarily in Auburn, NY.
Application information: Application form not required.
Deadline(s): None
Write: J. Douglas Pedley, Pres.
Officers and Directors: J. Douglas Pedley, Pres.; Ronald D. West, V.P. and Treas.; Madeline M. Schneider, Secy.; Frederick J. Atkins, John Y. Critchley, Burke W.W. Drummond.
Employer Identification Number: 166052246

4407
Arnold D. Frese Foundation, Inc. ▼ ⌑
30 Rockefeller Plaza, Suite 1938
New York 10112

Established in 1966.
Donor(s): Arnold D. Frese.†
Foundation type: Independent
Financial data (yr. ended 12/31/88): Assets, $13,489,702 (M); expenditures, $1,919,569, including $1,112,500 for 46 grants (high: $300,000; low: $1,000; average: $1,000-$35,000).
Purpose and activities: Support for hospitals, cultural programs, especially an opera company, and higher education.
Limitations: Giving primarily in New York, NY, and Greenwich, CT.
Application information:
Deadline(s): None
Board meeting date(s): Quarterly
Final notification: 3 to 4 months
Write: E. Gayle Fisher, Exec. Dir.
Officers: James S. Smith, Pres. and Treas.; Hector G. Dowd, Secy.; E. Gayle Fisher, Exec. Dir.
Trustees: Ines Frese, Chair.; Henry D. Mercer, Jr., Emil Mosbacher, Jr.
Number of staff: 1 full-time professional.
Employer Identification Number: 136212507

4408
Fribourg Foundation, Inc. ⌑
277 Park Ave., 48th Fl.
New York 10172 (212) 207-5571

Incorporated in 1953 in NY.
Donor(s): Michel Fribourg, Lucienne Fribourg, Arrow Steamship Co., Inc., Continental Grain Co.
Foundation type: Independent
Financial data (yr. ended 12/31/88): Assets, $2,071,286 (M); gifts received, $25,000; expenditures, $298,396, including $286,995 for 109 grants (high: $45,000; low: $100).
Purpose and activities: Emphasis on higher and secondary education, cultural relations with France and Israel, and Jewish welfare funds; some support for community funds and the performing arts.
Limitations: Giving primarily in New York, NY.
Application information:
Initial approach: Letter
Deadline(s): None
Write: Dwight C. Coffin, Secy.
Officers: Michel Fribourg,* Pres.; Sheldon L. Berens,* V.P.; Dwight C. Coffin, Secy.; Hendrick J. Laverge, Treas.
Directors:* Mary Ann Fribourg, Bernard Steinweg.
Employer Identification Number: 136159195

4409
Eugen Friedlaender Foundation, Inc. ⌑
c/o Bernard E. Brandes
Seven Hanover Sq.
New York 10004

Established in 1953 in NY.
Donor(s): Helmut N. Friedlaender, Edith S.E. Bondi.
Foundation type: Independent
Financial data (yr. ended 12/31/87): Assets, $1,255,175 (M); expenditures, $120,130, including $94,263 for 52 grants (high: $5,250; low: $50).
Purpose and activities: Emphasis on cultural programs, health, higher education, and ecology programs; support also for law and justice programs.
Types of support: General purposes.
Limitations: Giving primarily in NY. No grants to individuals.
Application information: Application form not required.
Deadline(s): None
Officers and Directors: Helmut N. Friedlaender, Pres.; Judith G. Friedlaender, Secy.; Jane Lury, Treas.; Edith S.E. Bondi, Bernard E. Brandes, John R. Menke, Ronald J. Stein.
Employer Identification Number: 136077311

4410
Friedman Family Foundation ⌑ ☆
225 West 37th St.
New York 10018-5793 (212) 354-8537

Established 1983.
Foundation type: Independent
Financial data (yr. ended 12/31/88): Assets, $1,014,506 (M); gifts received, $250,000; expenditures, $43,175, including $41,900 for 11 grants (high: $7,800; low: $1,000).
Purpose and activities: Giving for Jewish organizations, including welfare funds, youth groups, and educational programs.
Application information: Application form not required.
Initial approach: Letter or telephone
Deadline(s): None
Write: Israel Friedman, Pres.
Officers and Directors: Israel Friedman, Pres.; Maralya Friedman, V.P.; Mark Friedman, V.P.; Gary H. Friedman, Paul A. Friedman, Robin Friedman Klatt.
Employer Identification Number: 133181247

4411
Stephen & Barbara Friedman Foundation ⌑
c/o Goldman, Sachs & Co.
85 Broad St.
New York 10004

Established in 1979 in NY.
Donor(s): Stephen Friedman.
Foundation type: Independent
Financial data (yr. ended 07/31/89): Assets, $2,957,421 (M); gifts received, $1,200,000; expenditures, $674,326, including $670,835 for 85 grants (high: $50,000; low: $100).
Purpose and activities: Giving for Jewish organizations, cultural programs, and higher education.
Limitations: Giving primarily in New York, NY. No grants to individuals.
Application information: Contributes only to pre-selected organizations. Applications not accepted.
Trustees: H. Corbin Day, Barbara Friedman, Stephen Friedman.
Employer Identification Number: 133025979

4412
Ludwig W. Frohlich Charitable Trust ⌑
c/o Chadbourne & Parke
30 Rockefeller Plaza
New York 10112

Trust established in 1969 in NY.
Donor(s): Ludwig W. Frohlich.†
Foundation type: Independent
Financial data (yr. ended 12/31/88): Assets, $6,696,944 (M); expenditures, $643,136, including $486,500 for 37 grants (high: $100,000; low: $500).
Purpose and activities: Giving for hospitals, medical research, cultural programs, and social service and youth agencies.
Limitations: Giving primarily in New York, NY.
Application information: Contributes only to pre-selected organizations. Applications not accepted.
Trustees: Kathleen B. Buddenhagen, Ingrid Lilly Burns, Thomas R. Burns, Richard B. Leather.
Employer Identification Number: 136288404

4413
The Alex & Ruth Fruchthandler Foundation, Inc. ⌑ ☆
111 Broadway, 20th Fl.
New York 10006

Established in 1945.
Donor(s): Olympia & York Financial Co., Fruchthandler Bros. Enterprises.
Foundation type: Independent
Financial data (yr. ended 12/31/88): Assets, $1,265,965 (M); gifts received, $1,521,673; expenditures, $1,350,762, including $1,349,601 for 182 grants (high: $250,000; low: $50).
Purpose and activities: Support primarily for Jewish organizations, especially yeshivas.
Limitations: No grants to individuals.
Application information: Contributes only to pre-selected organizations. Applications not accepted.
Officer: Abraham Fruchthandler, Pres.
Employer Identification Number: 136156031

4414
Fuchsberg Family Foundation, Inc. ⌑
500 Fifth Ave., 45th Fl.
New York 10110 (212) 869-3500

Incorporated in 1954 in NY.
Donor(s): Jacob D. Fuchsberg, Abraham Fuchsberg, Shirley Fuchsberg, Fuchsberg & Fuchsberg.
Foundation type: Independent
Financial data (yr. ended 12/31/87): Assets, $6,642,962 (M); gifts received, $250,000; expenditures, $373,295, including $364,135 for 31 grants (high: $200,000; low: $25).
Purpose and activities: To engage in research and promote the study, analysis, and interpretation of legal systems and concepts in order to improve the judicial procedures and techniques of trials in the courts of New York State and of the U.S.; support also for Jewish welfare funds and higher education.
Limitations: No grants to individuals.
Application information: Application form not required.
Initial approach: Proposal
Deadline(s): None
Write: Jacob D. Fuchsberg, Chair.
Officers: Jacob D. Fuchsberg, Chair.; Meyer Fuchsberg, Pres. and Treas.; Seymour Fuchsberg,* V.P.
Directors:* Frances Fuchsberg.
Employer Identification Number: 136165600

4415
Abraham Fuchsberg Family Foundation, Inc. ⌑
100 Church St., 18th Fl.
New York 10007 (212) 962-2800

Established in 1978.
Donor(s): Abraham Fuchsberg, Fuchsberg & Fuchsberg, Fuchsberg Family Foundation.
Foundation type: Independent
Financial data (yr. ended 10/31/88): Assets, $3,244,923 (M); gifts received, $132,725; expenditures, $158,341, including $152,998 for 37 grants (high: $25,000; low: $13).
Purpose and activities: Giving primarily for Jewish welfare funds; support also for public interest groups.
Application information: Application form not required.
Initial approach: Proposal
Deadline(s): Submit proposal between Jan. and June
Write: Abraham Fuchsberg, Pres.
Officers: Abraham Fuchsberg, Pres.; Seymour Fuchsberg, Secy.; Meyer Fuchsberg, Treas.
Employer Identification Number: 132966385

4416
Elizabeth & Richard S. Fuld Foundation ⌑ ☆
c/o Proskauer, Rose, Goetz & Mendelsohn
300 Park Ave.
New York 10022-7402

Foundation type: Independent
Financial data (yr. ended 09/30/89): Assets, $41,261 (M); gifts received, $69,025; expenditures, $104,276, including $102,671 for 61 grants (high: $30,100; low: $25).
Purpose and activities: Giving for education, medical research, and Jewish organizations.
Limitations: Giving primarily in NY. No grants to individuals.
Application information:
Deadline(s): None
Write: Richard S. Fuld, Pres.
Officers: Richard S. Fuld, Pres. and Treas.; Richard S. Fuld, Jr., V.P. and Secy.
Employer Identification Number: 133139002

4417
Helene Fuld Health Trust ▼
c/o Townley & Updike
405 Lexington Ave.
New York 10174 (212) 973-6859

Trust established in 1951 in NJ; activated in 1969 as successor to Helene Fuld Health Foundation incorporated in 1935.
Donor(s): Leonhard Felix Fuld,† Florentine M. Fuld.†
Foundation type: Independent
Financial data (yr. ended 09/30/89): Assets, $83,042,110 (M); expenditures, $5,122,049, including $4,193,189 for 128 grants (high: $138,035; low: $4,870; average: $15,000-$75,000).
Purpose and activities: Grants to state-accredited nursing schools affiliated with accredited hospitals to promote the health, education, and welfare of enrolled student nurses who are being taught to care for the sick and injured at bedside.
Types of support: Equipment, publications, special projects.
Limitations: No grants to individuals, or for endowment funds, operating expenses, matching gifts, or general purposes; no loans.
Publications: Annual report (including application guidelines), application guidelines.
Application information: Applications received by Oct. 31 deadline reviewed in spring of following year. Application form required.
Initial approach: Letter requesting application
Copies of proposal: 1
Deadline(s): Oct. 31
Board meeting date(s): Mar., June, Sept., and Dec.
Final notification: 6 months
Write: Robert C. Miller, Counsel; or Arlene J. Kennare, Grants Office Admin.
Trustee: Marine Midland Bank, N.A.
Number of staff: 1 full-time professional; 4 part-time professional.
Employer Identification Number: 136309307

4418
Fund for the City of New York, Inc.
121 Ave. of the Americas
New York 10013 (212) 925-6675

Incorporated in 1968 in NY.
Donor(s): The Ford Foundation, The Aaron Diamond Foundation, Inc., Helena Rubinstein Foundation, Inc.
Foundation type: Operating
Financial data (yr. ended 09/30/89): Assets, $6,181,433 (M); gifts received, $4,868,691; qualifying distributions, $6,415,277, including $307,441 for 46 grants (high: $40,000; low: $500; average: $5,000-$10,000), $35,000 for 7 grants to individuals of $5,000 each, $2,561,200 for 220 foundation-administered programs and $3,511,636 for 49 loans.
Purpose and activities: An operating foundation and public charity supporting public and private projects designed to improve the management and effectiveness of government and the quality of life in New York City, with particular emphasis on public service productivity, accountability, performance monitoring, and computer assistance; operates a program of assistance to public and nonprofit managers; also runs a cash flow loan program against governmental grants and contracts.
Types of support: Technical assistance, loans, exchange programs, consulting services, special projects, grants to individuals, general purposes, seed money.
Limitations: Giving limited to New York City, NY. No grants to individuals (except for public service awards), or for ongoing service programs, academic research, building or endowment funds, scholarships, fellowships, matching gifts, or studies that do not show promise of leading directly to policy or program improvement.
Publications: Multi-year report (including application guidelines), financial statement, grants list, informational brochure, occasional report, application guidelines.
Application information: Application form not required.
Initial approach: Proposal
Copies of proposal: 1
Deadline(s): None
Board meeting date(s): Approximately 5 times a year in Feb., Apr., June, Oct., and Dec.
Write: Anita Nager, Grants Admin.
Officers: Frederick A.O. Schwarz, Jr.,* Chair.; Stephen Lefkowitz,* Vice-Chair.; R. Palmer Baker,* Secy.; Paul Gibson,* Treas.; Gregory R. Farrell, Exec. Dir.
Directors:* Roscoe Brown, Jr., Carolyn Chin, Nathan Quinones, Suzanne Schwerin, Vaughn Williams.
Number of staff: 19 full-time professional; 3 part-time professional; 8 full-time support; 2 part-time support.
Employer Identification Number: 132612524

4419
Sol and Hilda Furst Foundation ⌑
One Old Country Rd.
Carle Place 11514

Incorporated in 1951 in NY.
Donor(s): Sol Furst.†
Foundation type: Independent
Financial data (yr. ended 4/30/89): Assets, $1,364,095 (M); expenditures, $188,030, including $168,181 for 118 grants (high: $50,000; low: $10).
Purpose and activities: Emphasis on higher education, Jewish religious, educational, and welfare organizations, and hospitals.
Limitations: Giving primarily in NY. No grants to individuals.
Application information: Contributes only to pre-selected organizations. Applications not accepted.
Officers and Directors: Gerald Furst, Pres.; Violet Furst, V.P.; Ronald A. Furst, Secy.-Treas.
Employer Identification Number: 136107416

4420
Gadsby Fund, Inc. ⌑ ☆
c/o Greenstein, Newberger & Orlin
1440 Broadway, Rm. 2259
New York 10018

Established in 1946.
Donor(s): Gad Bernstein.†
Foundation type: Independent
Financial data (yr. ended 12/31/87): Assets, $1,108,945 (M); expenditures, $83,789, including $63,068 for 120 grants (high: $35,000; low: $10).
Purpose and activities: Support primarily for Jewish welfare funds and other Jewish organizations.
Application information:
Initial approach: Letter
Deadline(s): None
Officers: Florence Bernstein, Pres.; David Bernstein, V.P. and Secy.; Geoffrey Giddings, 2nd V.P.; Ellen J. Bernstein Leach, Treas.
Employer Identification Number: 136141484

4421
The Catherine and Henry J. Gaisman Foundation ⌑
P.O. Box 277
Hartsdale 10530-0277

Incorporated in 1934 in DE.
Donor(s): Henry J. Gaisman.†
Foundation type: Independent
Financial data (yr. ended 12/31/88): Assets, $7,119,411 (M); expenditures, $322,796, including $315,500 for 16 grants (high: $150,000; low: $50).
Purpose and activities: Giving for hospitals, including ophthalmologic and respiratory research, and Catholic church support.
Limitations: Giving primarily in NY. No grants to individuals.
Application information: Contributes only to pre-selected organizations. Applications not accepted.
Officer and Directors: Catherine V. Gaisman, Pres.; Robert Arias, Leon Ginzburg, M.D., Eric W. Waldman.
Employer Identification Number: 136129464

4422
The Ganlee Fund ☆
201 East 69th St., No. 11S
New York 10021

Established in 1966.
Foundation type: Independent
Financial data (yr. ended 12/31/88): Assets, $1,023,662 (M); expenditures, $77,180, including $76,800 for 52 grants (high: $45,000; low: $50; average: $500-$2,000).
Purpose and activities: Giving for higher and other education, social services, health, and civic affairs.
Limitations: Giving primarily in NY.
Application information: Applications not accepted.
Trustee: Mabel S. Ingalls.
Number of staff: 1 part-time professional; 1 part-time support.
Employer Identification Number: 136069298

4423
Donald R. & Jane T. Gant Foundation ⌑ ☆
c/o Goldman Sachs & Co., Tax Dept.
85 Broad St., 30th Fl.
New York 10004-2106

Established in 1968.
Donor(s): Donald R. Gant.
Foundation type: Independent
Financial data (yr. ended 5/31/89): Assets, $1,358,347 (M); expenditures, $56,962, including $55,290 for 25 grants (high: $25,000; low: $70).
Purpose and activities: Giving for a Presbyterian church, higher and other education, and a community trust.
Limitations: Giving primarily in NY. No grants to individuals.
Application information: Contributes only to pre-selected organizations. Applications not accepted.
Trustees: Donald R. Gant, Jane T. Gant, James S. Marcus.
Employer Identification Number: 237015091

4424
Garfinkle Family Charitable Trust ⌑ ☆
c/o U.S. Trust Co. of New York
114 West 47th St.
New York 10036-1532

Established in 1987 in NY.
Donor(s): Sandor A. Garfinkle, Lorraine Garfinkle.
Foundation type: Independent
Financial data (yr. ended 12/31/88): Assets, $2,669,117 (M); expenditures, $197,740, including $192,980 for 20 grants (high: $70,000; low: $100).
Purpose and activities: Giving primarily for Jewish welfare and other Jewish organizations; support also for foreign policy.
Limitations: Giving primarily in NJ and NY.
Application information: Applications not accepted.
Trustees: Lorraine Garfinkle, Sandor A. Garfinkle.
Employer Identification Number: 133411139

4425
Gebbie Foundation, Inc. ▼
Hotel Jamestown Bldg., Rm. 308
Jamestown 14701 (716) 487-1062

Incorporated in 1963 in NY.
Donor(s): Marion B. Gebbie,† Geraldine G. Bellinger.†
Foundation type: Independent
Financial data (yr. ended 09/30/89): Assets, $55,839,972 (M); expenditures, $3,638,596, including $3,404,376 for 49 grants (high: $1,419,755; low: $1,000) and $37,000 for loans.
Purpose and activities: Grants primarily for local organizations such as hospitals, libraries, youth agencies, cultural programs, social service agencies, and the United Way. Giving also to organizations that have shown an interest in medical and scientific research related to metabolic diseases of the bone and in detection of deafness in children and their education.
Types of support: Annual campaigns, seed money, building funds, equipment, matching funds, general purposes, loans, scholarship funds.
Limitations: Giving primarily in Chautauqua County and, secondly, in neighboring areas of western NY; giving in other areas only when the project is consonant with program objectives that cannot be developed locally. No support for sectarian or religious organizations or for higher education, except to institutions that were recipients of lifetime contributions of the donor. No grants to individuals, or for endowment funds.
Publications: Annual report.
Application information: Application form not required.
Initial approach: Letter
Copies of proposal: 10
Deadline(s): Mar. 1, Aug. 1, and Oct. 1
Board meeting date(s): Apr., Sept., and Nov.
Final notification: 1 to 4 months
Write: John D. Hamilton, Pres.
Officers and Directors:* John D. Hamilton,* Pres.; Myron B. Franks,* V.P.; William I. Parker, Secy.; Gerald E. Hunt,* Treas.; Charles T. Hall, Kay Johnson, Lillian V. Ney, Geraldine Parker, Paul W. Sandberg.
Number of staff: 1 full-time professional; 2 part-time professional.
Employer Identification Number: 166050287

4426
The Geist Foundation
560 Lexington Ave., 17th Fl.
New York 10022 (212) 758-4999

Incorporated about 1959 in NJ.
Donor(s): Irving Geist.†
Foundation type: Independent
Financial data (yr. ended 09/30/89): Assets, $2,288,458 (M); expenditures, $205,254, including $193,452 for 52 grants (high: $68,000; low: $110).
Purpose and activities: Grants for Jewish welfare funds; support also for higher education and medical research.
Limitations: Giving primarily in NJ and NY. No grants to individuals.
Publications: 990-PF.
Application information:
Initial approach: Letter
Copies of proposal: 1
Deadline(s): None
Board meeting date(s): As required
Write: Steven Rones, Trustee
Officers and Trustees:* Louis Rones,* Pres.; Steven Rones,* V.P.; Benjamin Alpert,* Secy.-Treas.
Number of staff: None.
Employer Identification Number: 226059859

4427
Lawrence M. Gelb Foundation, Inc.
300 Park Ave., Rm. 2100
New York 10022
Application address: 345 Park Ave., New York, NY 10154

Established in 1957 in NY.
Donor(s): Lawrence M. Gelb,† Richard L. Gelb, Bruce S. Gelb.
Foundation type: Independent

Financial data (yr. ended 12/31/88): Assets, $6,663,918 (M); gifts received, $1,193,750; expenditures, $1,158,593, including $1,113,800 for 55 grants (high: $150,000; low: $500).
Purpose and activities: Support primarily for private secondary and higher education; some support also for cultural programs.
Limitations: No grants to individuals.
Application information: Application form not required.
Initial approach: Letter
Deadline(s): None
Write: Robert M. Kaufman, Asst. Secy.
Officers and Directors:* Richard L. Gelb,* Chair.; Wilbur H. Friedman,* Secy.; John T. Gelb, Lawrence N. Gelb, Robert M. Kaufman.
Employer Identification Number: 136113586

4428
The Laurent and Alberta Gerschel Foundation, Inc. ⌑
c/o NCTV
One Madison Ave., 21st Fl.
New York 10010

Donor(s): Laurent Gerschel.
Foundation type: Independent
Financial data (yr. ended 12/31/88): Assets, $7,273,055 (M); expenditures, $413,315, including $39,135 for 19 grants (high: $17,675; low: $100) and $300,000 for 1 foundation-administered program.
Purpose and activities: Support primarily for education, health, and the arts.
Application information:
Initial approach: Proposal
Deadline(s): None
Write: Laurent Gerschel, Pres.
Officers: Laurent Gerschel, Pres.; Alberta Gerschel, V.P.; Monica Hoffman, Secy.-Treas.
Employer Identification Number: 133098507

4429
Patrick A. Gerschel Foundation ⌑
122 East 42nd St.
New York 10168 (212) 490-4995

Established in 1986 in NY.
Foundation type: Independent
Financial data (yr. ended 12/31/88): Assets, $6,562,796 (M); expenditures, $523,404, including $471,700 for 50 grants (high: $100,000; low: $100).
Purpose and activities: Support primarily for an Asian cultural institution; support also for the arts, medical research, community development, and higher and secondary education.
Types of support: Grants to individuals, research.
Limitations: Giving primarily in NY.
Application information:
Write: Patrick A. Gerschel, Pres.
Officers: Patrick A. Gerschel, Chair. and Pres.; Geoffrey Handler, Secy.; Charles H. Richter, Treas.
Employer Identification Number: 133317180

4430
Gibbs Brothers Foundation ⌑
c/o Morgan Guaranty Trust Co. of New York
Nine West 57th St.
New York 10019 (212) 826-7607

Trust established in 1957 in NY.
Donor(s): Gibbs & Cox, Inc.
Foundation type: Company-sponsored
Financial data (yr. ended 12/31/89): Assets, $1,913,450 (M); expenditures, $1,072,725, including $1,043,750 for 60 grants (high: $250,000; low: $250).
Purpose and activities: Grants largely for continuing support of organizations including maritime museums and seamen's institutes, hospitals, colleges and universities, naval engineering societies, and legal organizations.
Types of support: Operating budgets, research.
Limitations: No grants to individuals, or for annual campaigns, seed money, emergency funds, deficit financing, capital and endowment funds, matching gifts, scholarships, fellowships, program support, demonstration projects, publications, or conferences; no loans.
Application information: Application form not required.
Initial approach: Letter with financial information
Copies of proposal: 1
Deadline(s): None
Board meeting date(s): May
Write: Richard Ehrlich
Advisory Committee: M. Bernard Aidinoff, Richard M. Ehrlich, Walter Malmstrom, Edward J. Willi.
Trustee: Morgan Guaranty Trust Co. of New York.
Number of staff: None.
Employer Identification Number: 136037653

4431
Gibraltar Foundation ⌑ ☆
2545 Walden Ave.
Buffalo 14225-4737 (716) 684-1020

Donor(s): Gibraltar Steel.
Foundation type: Company-sponsored
Financial data (yr. ended 12/31/89): Assets, $511,093 (M); expenditures, $151,614, including $149,283 for 19 grants (high: $40,000; low: $50).
Purpose and activities: Support for historical preservation, civic affairs, culture, religious charities, and higher education.
Limitations: Giving primarily in Buffalo, NY. No grants to individuals.
Application information: Contributes only to pre-selected organizations. Applications not accepted.
Write: Ken Lipke
Trustee: Ken E. Lipke.
Employer Identification Number: 510176074

4432
The Rosamond Gifford Charitable Corporation ⌑
731 James St., Rm. 404
Syracuse 13203 (315) 474-2489

Incorporated in 1954 in NY.
Donor(s): Rosamond Gifford.†
Foundation type: Independent
Financial data (yr. ended 12/31/88): Assets, $13,627,203 (M); expenditures, $819,664, including $683,090 for 28 grants (high: $120,000; low: $2,000; average: $4,000-$40,000).
Purpose and activities: Emphasis on urban problems, higher and secondary education, medical research, hospital construction and equipment, youth agencies, rehabilitation of alcoholics, the aged, general welfare, a community fund, and cultural programs.
Types of support: Operating budgets, annual campaigns, seed money, emergency funds, building funds, equipment, research, renovation projects.
Limitations: Giving limited to organizations serving the residents of Syracuse and Onondaga County, NY. No grants to individuals, or for endowment funds, continuing support, deficit financing, land aquisition, special projects, matching gifts, scholarships, or fellowships; no loans.
Publications: Program policy statement, application guidelines, multi-year report.
Application information: Application form not required.
Initial approach: Letter or telephone
Copies of proposal: 2
Deadline(s): None
Board meeting date(s): Monthly
Final notification: 2 months
Write: Dean A. Lesinski, Exec. Dir.
Officers: Virginia Z. Lynch,* Pres.; Roger L. MacDonald,* V.P. and Treas.; Charles J. Miller,* Secy.; Dean A. Lesinski, Exec. Dir.
Directors:* John H. Lynch, Donald M. Mills.
Number of staff: 2 full-time professional; 1 part-time support.
Employer Identification Number: 150572881

4433
Gilder Foundation, Inc.
1775 Broadway, 26th Fl.
New York 10019

Established in 1965 in NY.
Donor(s): Richard Gilder, Jr.
Foundation type: Independent
Financial data (yr. ended 12/31/88): Assets, $3,015,428 (M); gifts received, $712,500; expenditures, $1,132,462, including $1,066,726 for 109 grants (high: $250,000; low: $50).
Purpose and activities: Giving primarily to organizations with programs focusing on the U.S. Civil War period and the history of the Antarctic.
Limitations: No grants to individuals.
Application information: Contributes only to pre-selected organizations. Applications not accepted.
Officer: Richard Gilder, Jr., Pres.
Employer Identification Number: 136176041

4434
John D. Gilliam Foundation ⌑ ☆
c/o Goldman Sachs & Co., Tax Dept.
85 Broad St., 30th Fl.
New York 10004-2106

Established in 1978.
Donor(s): John D. Gilliam.
Foundation type: Independent

Financial data (yr. ended 3/31/89): Assets, $1,167,031 (M); gifts received, $38,625; expenditures, $139,899, including $135,981 for 29 grants (high: $45,625; low: $30).
Purpose and activities: Giving primarily for higher education and the performing arts; support also for hospitals.
Trustees: John D. Gilliam, Peter M. Fahey.
Employer Identification Number: 132967490

4435
The Howard Gilman Foundation, Inc.
111 West 50th St.
New York 10020 (212) 246-3300

Incorporated in 1981 in DE.
Donor(s): Gilman Investment Co., Gilman Paper Co.
Foundation type: Independent
Financial data (yr. ended 04/30/89): Assets, $17,880,661 (M); gifts received, $3,153,000; expenditures, $1,028,021, including $813,317 for 95 grants (high: $157,340; low: $50; average: $50-$157,340).
Purpose and activities: Giving for AIDS programs and hospitals, medical and other higher education, the fine and performing arts and other cultural programs, religious organizations and support for Israel, social services, conservation, and wildlife preservation and animal welfare.
Limitations: Giving primarily in New York, NY.
Application information: Applications not accepted.
Write: Howard Gilman, Pres.
Officer and Directors:* Howard Gilman,* Pres.; Bernard D. Bergreen, Sylvia P. Gilman.
Number of staff: 1 full-time professional; 1 part-time professional.
Employer Identification Number: 133097486

4436
Gilman Paper Company Foundation, Inc.
111 West 50th St.
New York 10020 (212) 246-3300

Established in 1982 in DE.
Donor(s): Gilman Paper Co.
Foundation type: Company-sponsored
Financial data (yr. ended 12/31/88): Assets, $1,466 (M); gifts received, $134,149; expenditures, $136,160, including $67,786 for 175 grants and $64,000 for 16 grants to individuals (high: $24,248; low: $25; average: $25-$2,500).
Purpose and activities: The foundation administers a matching gift program for company employees and awards college scholarships to their children; support also for higher education, culture, health, and animal welfare.
Types of support: Employee matching gifts, employee-related scholarships.
Limitations: Giving primarily in NY. No grants to individuals other than children of company employees.
Publications: Informational brochure.
Application information: Applications not accepted from non-employees.
Write: Bradford A. Warner
Officer: Howard Gilman, Chair. and Pres.
Number of staff: None.
Employer Identification Number: 133134047

4437
Bernard F. and Alva B. Gimbel Foundation, Inc. ⌘
c/o Carol Lebworth
784 Park Ave.
New York 10021 (212) 879-4119

Incorporated in 1943 in NY.
Donor(s): Bernard F. Gimbel,† Alva B. Gimbel.†
Foundation type: Independent
Financial data (yr. ended 12/31/88): Assets, $4,000,000 (M); expenditures, $165,750, including $109,500 for 13 grants (high: $25,000; low: $1,000).
Purpose and activities: Support for social services, hospitals, child welfare, hospices, the environment, and family services, including family planning; support also for rehabilitation programs and organizations that benefit the disadvantaged.
Types of support: Continuing support, special projects.
Limitations: Giving primarily in NY and CT. No grants for scholarships, fellowships, or matching gifts; no loans.
Application information:
Initial approach: Letter
Copies of proposal: 1
Deadline(s): None
Board meeting date(s): Nov.
Officers and Directors: Caral G. Lebworth, Co-Pres.; Hope G. Solinger, Co-Pres.
Employer Identification Number: 136090843

4438
Moses Ginsberg Family Foundation, Inc. ⌘
625 Madison Ave.
New York 10022

Incorporated in 1946 in NY.
Donor(s): Moses Ginsberg.†
Foundation type: Independent
Financial data (yr. ended 12/31/88): Assets, $2,310,304 (M); gifts received, $380,000; expenditures, $458,825, including $457,150 for 11 grants (high: $150,000; low: $150).
Purpose and activities: Support primarily for Jewish welfare funds.
Limitations: Giving primarily in NY.
Application information: Contributes only to pre-selected organizations. Applications not accepted.
Officers: Calmon J. Ginsberg, Pres.; Daniel R. Ginsberg, V.P.; Donald C. Ginsberg, V.P.; Morris Ginsberg, Secy.; Simon C. Wolkenbrod, Treas.
Employer Identification Number: 237418806

4439
The Glanville Family Foundation ⌘ ☆
c/o Lazard Freres & Co.
One Rockefeller Plaza
New York 10020

Established in 1985 in NY.
Donor(s): James W. Glenville, Nancy H. Glanville.
Foundation type: Independent
Financial data (yr. ended 06/30/90): Assets, $336,484 (M); gifts received, $232,341; expenditures, $498,091, including $497,900 for 50 grants (high: $158,000; low: $350).
Purpose and activities: Giving primarily for higher education.
Application information:
Initial approach: Letter
Deadline(s): None
Write: James W. Glanville, Pres.
Officers: James W. Glanville, Pres.; Nancy H. Glanville, V.P.; Howard Sontag, Secy.-Treas.
Employer Identification Number: 133284981

4440
Gleason Fund, Inc. ⌘
1000 University Ave.
P.O. Box 22970
Rochester 14692-2970 (716) 473-1000

Established in 1934 in NY.
Foundation type: Company-sponsored
Financial data (yr. ended 12/31/88): Assets, $11,366,718 (M); expenditures, $601,858, including $479,712 for 5 grants (high: $457,000; low: $1,399) and $37,475 for 41 grants to individuals (high: $2,250; low: $20).
Purpose and activities: Giving limited to former Gleason Corp. employees in poverty and distress; grants awarded for medical bills, house repairs, and new furniture.
Types of support: Grants to individuals.
Limitations: Giving primarily in NY.
Application information:
Initial approach: Letter
Deadline(s): None
Write: James M. Weltzer, Pres.
Officers and Directors:* James M. Weltzer,* Pres. and V.P.; Ralph E. Harper,* Secy.; James R. Spawton, Treas.; James S. Gleason, Royden J. Smith.
Employer Identification Number: 166023234

4441
Gleason Memorial Fund, Inc. ▼
30 Corporate Woods
P.O. Box 22856
Rochester 14692-2856 (716) 272-6005

Incorporated in 1959 in NY.
Donor(s): Miriam B. Gleason.†
Foundation type: Independent
Financial data (yr. ended 12/31/89): Assets, $48,652,310 (M); gifts received, $457,000; expenditures, $2,817,040, including $2,530,097 for grants (high: $915,000; average: $2,500-$15,000).
Purpose and activities: Emphasis on higher education, including research and technology; support also for community funds, youth and social service agencies, public interest and civic affairs groups, and cultural activities.
Types of support: Operating budgets.
Limitations: Giving primarily in Rochester, NY. No support for United Way-supported agencies. No grants to individuals.
Publications: Application guidelines.
Application information: Application form required.
Initial approach: Proposal
Deadline(s): None
Board meeting date(s): Quarterly
Final notification: After board meetings
Write: John B. Kodweis, V.P. for Administration
Officers: Sterling L. Weaver,* Chair.; James S. Gleason,* Pres.; John B. Kodweis,* V.P. for

Administration; Ralph E. Harper,* Secy.; Edward C. Berlinski, Treas.
Directors:* Janis F. Gleason, Albert W. Moore.
Employer Identification Number: 166023235

4442
Paul F. Glenn Foundation for Medical Research, Inc.
72 Virginia Dr.
Manhasset 11030
Application address: 109 East de la Guerra, Santa Barbara, CA 93101; Tel.: (805) 965-8328

Established in 1965.
Foundation type: Independent
Financial data (yr. ended 09/30/89): Assets, $3,152,591 (M); expenditures, $269,292, including $151,552 for 20 grants (high: $50,000; low: $300).
Purpose and activities: Grants to 1) encourage and accelerate research on the biology of aging; 2) assist those engaged in research on mechanisms of the aging process, with the objective of delaying or preventing the onset of senility and prolonging the human life span; 3) increase the stature of the field of gerontology; 4) broaden scientific understanding of aging; and 5) advance the field of biogerontology through special award programs.
Types of support: Research, fellowships.
Limitations: No support for sociological, as opposed to biological, aging projects.
Application information: The foundation does not accept unsolicited grant applications or fellowship nominations.
Initial approach: Proposal
Copies of proposal: 3
Deadline(s): None
Write: Mark R. Collins, Exec. V.P.
Officers and Directors:* Paul F. Glenn,* Chair., Pres., and Treas.; Mark R. Collins, Exec. V.P.; Barbara Boyd,* V.P. and Secy.; Gary S. Kledzik, V.P.; Mary E. Ruth.
Number of staff: 3 part-time professional.
Employer Identification Number: 136191732

4443
The Glens Falls Foundation
237 Glen St.
Glens Falls 12801 (518) 792-1151
Mailing address: P.O. Box 311, Glens Falls, NY 12801

Established in 1939 in NY by declaration of trust.
Foundation type: Community
Financial data (yr. ended 12/31/88): Assets, $2,282,093 (L); gifts received, $445,674; expenditures, $223,462, including $152,064 for 64 grants (average: $1,000-$5,000) and $34,158 for 24 grants to individuals.
Purpose and activities: Giving primarily to promote the mental, moral, and physical improvement of the people of Glens Falls and environs. Grants to graduating seniors from area high schools, and for assistance with medical expenses not covered by government programs or insurance.
Types of support: Seed money, emergency funds, building funds, equipment, research, publications, conferences and seminars, special projects, matching funds, consulting services, technical assistance, grants to individuals, student aid, land acquisition, renovation projects, deficit financing, exchange programs, operating budgets.
Limitations: Giving limited to Warren, Washington, and Saratoga counties, NY. No grants for annual campaigns, continuing support, or endowment funds; no loans.
Publications: Annual report, application guidelines.
Application information: Application form not required.
Initial approach: Letter, telephone, or proposal
Copies of proposal: 8
Deadline(s): Submit proposal by last day of Mar., June, Sept., or Dec.
Board meeting date(s): 2nd Wednesday in Jan., Apr., July, and Oct.
Final notification: 2 days after quarterly meetings
Write: G. Nelson Lowe, Admin.
Officer: G. Nelson Lowe, Admin.
Distribution Committee: John V. Hallett, Chair.; Katherine M. Barton, Marilyn Cohen, Burt M. Keene, Donald A. Metivier, Daniel F. O'Keefe, M.D., Floyd H. Rourke.
Trustee: First National Bank of Glens Falls.
Number of staff: None.
Employer Identification Number: 146036930

4444
The Glickenhaus Foundation ⌑
Six East 43rd St.
New York 10017 (212) 953-7800
Application address: 100 Dorchester Rd., Scarsdale, NY 10583

Incorporated in 1960 in NY.
Donor(s): Glickenhaus & Co., Seth Glickenhaus.
Foundation type: Company-sponsored
Financial data (yr. ended 11/30/88): Assets, $2,663,694 (M); gifts received, $641,375; expenditures, $471,696, including $433,392 for 222 grants (high: $100,000; low: $16).
Purpose and activities: Grants primarily for social welfare, health services, and international peace organizations.
Types of support: Emergency funds, endowment funds, research.
Publications: 990-PF.
Application information:
Initial approach: Proposal
Deadline(s): None
Officers: Nancy G. Pier, Pres.; Alfred Feinman, V.P.; James Glickenhaus, V.P.
Employer Identification Number: 136160941

4445
The Fred C. Gloeckner Foundation, Inc. ⌑
15 East 26th St.
New York 10010 (212) 481-0920

Incorporated in 1960 in NY.
Donor(s): Frederick C. Gloeckner.
Foundation type: Independent
Financial data (yr. ended 10/31/87): Assets, $1,618,352 (M); gifts received, $65,850; expenditures, $131,221, including $126,020 for 21 grants (high: $8,800; low: $3,000).
Purpose and activities: To further research in floriculture and related fields through fellowships; grants to higher educational and agricultural research institutions.
Types of support: Fellowships, equipment.
Publications: Annual report.
Application information:
Initial approach: Proposal
Copies of proposal: 9
Deadline(s): May 1 and Nov. 1
Board meeting date(s): Semiannually in June and Dec.; grants paid in Aug.
Officers and Directors: Frederick C. Gloeckner, Pres.; Gustav H. Poesch, V.P.; Joseph A. Simone, Secy.; Martin D. Kortjohn, Treas.; Paul L. Daum, Douglas K. Dillon, Phillip J. Kurlich, Roy Larson, John G. Seeley.
Employer Identification Number: 136124190

4446
Glyndebourne Association America, Inc. ⌑ ☆
c/o Haythe & Curley
437 Madison Ave.
New York 10022

Established in 1971.
Foundation type: Independent
Financial data (yr. ended 12/31/88): Assets, $238,806 (M); gifts received, $30,550; expenditures, $156,083, including $146,675 for 3 grants (high: $90,675; low: $11,000).
Purpose and activities: Giving for the arts, especially opera; support also for a cultural exchange with the Soviet Union.
Limitations: Giving primarily in Sussex, England. No grants to individuals.
Application information: Contributes only to pre-selected organizations. Applications not accepted.
Officers and Trustees: George Christee, Pres.; Nathan Hale, V.P. and Treas.; Thomas S. Brush, Lily Polk Guest, Roger H. Lloyd, Robert M. Scott, Robert Tobin, John Walker.
Employer Identification Number: 237174079

4447
Henry L. Goldberg Foundation ⌑
20 Broad St.
New York 10005

Established in 1958 in NY.
Donor(s): Henry L. Goldberg.
Foundation type: Independent
Financial data (yr. ended 12/31/87): Assets, $511,190 (M); gifts received, $86,438; expenditures, $115,597, including $109,347 for 42 grants (high: $50,000; low: $25).
Purpose and activities: Grants primarily for Jewish giving; support also for health associations.
Application information: Contributes only to pre-selected organizations. Applications not accepted.
Trustees: William Friedman, Henry L. Goldberg.
Employer Identification Number: 136061341

4448
Goldberg-Rhapsody Foundation, Inc. ⌑ ☆
c/o Rhapsody Blouse
1370 Broadway
New York 10018-7302 (212) 594-5240

Established in 1980.

Donor(s): Murray Goldberg.
Foundation type: Independent
Financial data (yr. ended 9/30/88): Assets, $1,177,868 (M); gifts received, $250,000; expenditures, $81,871, including $81,795 for 30 grants (high: $25,000; low: $25).
Purpose and activities: Support primarily for Jewish welfare, hospitals, and health services, including medical research.
Limitations: Giving primarily in NY. No grants to individuals.
Application information: Contributes only to pre-selected organizations. Applications not accepted.
Officers: Murray Goldberg, Pres.; Charlotte Goldberg, V.P.; Alan Goldberg, Secy.
Employer Identification Number: 133013026

4449
Edward and Marjorie Goldberger Foundation ⌑
126 East 56th St.
New York 10022 (212) 371-8077

Established in 1957 in NY.
Donor(s): Marjorie Goldberger.
Foundation type: Independent
Financial data (yr. ended 12/31/88): Assets, $1,637,174 (M); expenditures, $60,458, including $52,665 for 92 grants (high: $10,000; low: $15).
Purpose and activities: Support primarily for Jewish giving, education, and culture.
Limitations: No grants to individuals.
Application information: Contributes only to pre-selected organizations. Applications not accepted.
Officers and Directors:* Edward Goldberger,* Pres.; Marjorie Goldberger,* Secy.-Treas.; Susan Jacoby, Ann Jurdem, Sarah Siegel.
Employer Identification Number: 136084528

4450
Golden Family Foundation
40 Wall St., Rm. 4201
New York 10005 (212) 425-0333

Incorporated in 1952 in NY.
Donor(s): William T. Golden, Sibyl L. Golden.†
Foundation type: Independent
Financial data (yr. ended 12/31/89): Assets, $30,142,567 (M); gifts received, $1,750,033; qualifying distributions, $2,750,849, including $2,550,849 for 156 grants (high: $688,450; low: $100; average: $100-$7,000) and $200,000 for loans.
Purpose and activities: Support for a broad range of programs in higher education, science, public affairs, and cultural areas.
Types of support: General purposes, building funds.
Limitations: No grants to individuals.
Application information: Contributes only to pre-selected organizations. Applications not accepted.
Board meeting date(s): Jan. and as required
Write: William T. Golden, Pres.
Officers and Directors:* William T. Golden,* Pres.; Sibyl R. Golden,* V.P.; Helene L. Kaplan,* Secy.; Ralph E. Hansmann,* Treas.; Pamela P. Golden.
Number of staff: None.
Employer Identification Number: 237423802

4451
John Golden Fund, Inc. ⌑
c/o Milton Rindler & Co.
36 West 44th St., Suite 707
New York 10036-8102

Incorporated in 1944 in NY.
Donor(s): John Golden.†
Foundation type: Independent
Financial data (yr. ended 12/31/88): Assets, $1,526,552 (M); expenditures, $98,403, including $88,400 for 23 grants (high: $20,000; low: $100; average: $2,000).
Purpose and activities: For the advancement of playwriting for the American legitimate theater or of the individuals in any way associated with it, through improvement of the teaching of drama in universities and colleges, and through other organizations and workshops, prize awards to playwrights engaged in, or in training for, dramatic playwriting in colleges, and promotion of theatrical productions for young people; all grants through organizations only.
Types of support: Special projects.
Limitations: Giving primarily in CT, MA, and NY. No grants to individuals, or for building or endowment funds, research programs, or matching gifts.
Application information:
Initial approach: Proposal
Copies of proposal: 1
Deadline(s): None
Board meeting date(s): May and Nov.
Write: Mrs. Zilla Lippmann, Pres.
Officers and Directors:* Zilla Lippmann,* Pres.; Norman J. Stone,* Treas.; Jean Dalrymple.
Number of staff: None.
Employer Identification Number: 136065978

4452
The Goldie-Anna Charitable Trust ⌑
c/o Greenfield, Eisenberg, Stein & Senior
99 Park Ave., 10th Fl.
New York 10016 (212) 818-9600

Established about 1977 in NY.
Foundation type: Independent
Financial data (yr. ended 12/31/88): Assets, $9,401,537 (M); expenditures, $329,265, including $258,575 for 47 grants (high: $185,825; low: $500).
Purpose and activities: Emphasis on higher education, including some support in Israel, medical research, hospitals, and Jewish giving.
Types of support: Scholarship funds, endowment funds.
Limitations: Giving primarily in the New York, NY, metropolitan area.
Application information:
Initial approach: Proposal
Deadline(s): Nov. 30
Trustees: Julius Greenfield, Kenneth L. Stein.
Employer Identification Number: 132897474

4453
Faith Golding Foundation, Inc.
900 Third Ave., 35th Fl.
New York 10022

Established in 1984 in NY.
Donor(s): First Sterling Corp.
Foundation type: Independent
Financial data (yr. ended 11/30/89): Assets, $374,505 (M); gifts received, $155,000; expenditures, $340,270, including $340,270 for 52 grants (high: $110,300; low: $30).
Purpose and activities: Support for a hospital, education, cultural organizations, and general charitable giving.
Application information: Contributes only to pre-selected organizations. Applications not accepted.
Trustees: Faith Golding, Bernard Greene, Ira W. Krauss.
Employer Identification Number: 133260491

4454
Jerrold R. & Shirley Golding Foundation, Inc. ⌑
1290 Ave. of the Americas, Suite 960
New York 10104

Established in 1969 in NY.
Donor(s): Montvale Imperial, Inc.
Foundation type: Independent
Financial data (yr. ended 12/31/87): Assets, $657,907 (M); gifts received, $350,000; expenditures, $197,959, including $195,750 for 18 grants (high: $100,000; low: $200).
Purpose and activities: Support primarily for higher education, health services, and cultural organizations.
Limitations: Giving primarily in NY.
Application information: Contributes only to pre-selected organizations. Applications not accepted.
Officers: Joseph J. Marcheso, Pres. and Treas.; Harriet G. Levy, V.P.; Morton J. Schlossberg, Secy.
Employer Identification Number: 237046427

4455
The William P. Goldman and Brothers Foundation, Inc. ⌑
1270 Ave. of the Americas, Rm. 1801
New York 10020 (212) 489-9700

Incorporated in 1951 in NY.
Donor(s): William P. Goldman,† William P. Goldman & Bros., Inc.
Foundation type: Independent
Financial data (yr. ended 12/31/88): Assets, $2,781,514 (M); expenditures, $190,564, including $184,250 for 56 grants (high: $25,000; low: $100).
Purpose and activities: Giving for Jewish welfare funds and temple support; support also for hospitals and medical research.
Limitations: Giving primarily in NY.
Application information: Application form not required.
Initial approach: Letter
Deadline(s): None
Write: Sidney Kraines, Pres.
Officers: Sidney Kraines, Pres. and Secy.; Byron Goldman, V.P.; Merrill Kraines, Treas.
Employer Identification Number: 136163100

4456
Herman Goldman Foundation ▼
61 Broadway, 18th Fl.
New York 10006 (212) 797-9090

Incorporated in 1943 in NY.
Donor(s): Herman Goldman.†

Foundation type: Independent
Financial data (yr. ended 2/28/89): Assets, $26,433,377 (M); expenditures, $2,564,852, including $2,076,780 for 108 grants (high: $150,000; low: $500; average: $10,000-$100,000).
Purpose and activities: Emphasis on aiding economically and socially deprived persons through innovative grants in four main areas: Health - to achieve effective delivery of physical and mental health care services; Social Justice - to develop organizational, social, and legal approaches to aid deprived or handicapped people; Education - for new or improved counseling for effective pre-school, vocational and paraprofessional training; and the Arts - to increase opportunities for talented youth to receive training and for less affluent individuals to attend quality presentations; some aid for programs relating to nation-wide problems.
Types of support: Continuing support.
Limitations: Giving primarily in the New York, NY, metropolitan area. No support for religious organizations. No grants to individuals.
Publications: Annual report (including application guidelines).
Application information: Application form not required.
Initial approach: Proposal
Copies of proposal: 1
Deadline(s): Middle of month preceding board meeting
Board meeting date(s): Monthly; grants considered every other month beginning in Apr.
Final notification: 1 to 2 months
Write: Richard K. Baron, Exec. Dir.
Officers: Michael L. Goldstein, Pres.; Stanley M. Klein, V.P.; David A. Brauner, Secy. and Treas.; Richard K. Baron, Exec. Dir.
Directors:* Jules M. Baron, Raymond S. Baron, Paul Bauman, Robert N. Davies, Emanuel Goldstein, Seymour H. Kligler, Elias Rosenzweig, Howard A. Scribner, Jr., Norman H. Sparber.
Number of staff: 2 full-time professional; 1 part-time professional.
Employer Identification Number: 136066039

4457
Goldman Sachs Fund ¤
c/o Goldman Sachs & Co., Tax Dept.
85 Broad St., 30th Fl.
New York 10004

Established in 1968 in NY.
Donor(s): Goldman Sachs & Co., Robert E. Rubin.
Foundation type: Company-sponsored
Financial data (yr. ended 6/30/87): Assets, $5,980,823 (M); gifts received, $1,011,531; expenditures, $696,901, including $625,373 for 1,010 grants (high: $16,262; low: $25) and $65,500 for 32 grants to individuals (high: $5,000; low: $500).
Purpose and activities: Grants for education, including scholarships for the spouses and children of Goldman Sachs & Co. employees.
Types of support: Employee-related scholarships.
Officers: John L. Weinberg,* Chair. and Pres.; H. Frederick Krimendahl II,* Secy.
Directors:* Jonathan C. Cohen, Robert A. Friedman, Stephen Friedman, James P. Gorter, Richard L. Menschel, Robert E. Mnuchin, Robert E. Rubin, Frank P. Smeal.
Employer Identification Number: 237000346

4458
Goldome Foundation ¤
c/o Goldome Tax Dept.
One Fountain Plaza
Buffalo 14203 (716) 847-5800

Established in 1969 in NY.
Donor(s): Goldome F.S.B.
Foundation type: Company-sponsored
Financial data (yr. ended 12/31/87): Assets, $1,156,757 (M); gifts received, $321,170; expenditures, $419,728, including $403,282 for 287 grants (high: $19,350; low: $10) and $16,121 for 190 employee matching gifts.
Purpose and activities: Support for urban affairs, youth agencies, hospitals, educational organizations, social services, community development, culture and the arts; also sponsors an employee matching gift program primarily for higher education.
Types of support: Operating budgets, continuing support, annual campaigns, building funds, employee matching gifts.
Limitations: Giving limited to NY state, with emphasis on western NY (Buffalo, Syracuse, and Rochester); some support also in the New York metropolitan area. No grants to individuals, or for seed money, emergency funds, deficit financing, equipment, land acquisition, renovations, endowment funds, scholarships, fellowships, special projects, research, publications, or conferences; no loans.
Application information: Contributes only to pre-selected organizations. Applications not accepted.
Officers: Robert C. Carroll, Pres.; James J. Batt, V.P.; Mary Ellen Beres, V.P.; Peter Bevins, V.P.; Maureen A. Owens, V.P.; Terry L. Poppleton, V.P.; Jeanette Shaw, V.P.; Robert M. Edwards, Secy.; Richard M. Hessinger, Treas.
Directors: Thomas Bilbao, Edward K. Duch, Jr., Ross B. Kenzie, H. Eugene Richards, E. Peter Ruddy, Jr.
Number of staff: None.
Employer Identification Number: 237029266

4459
The Joseph G. Goldring Foundation
100 Crossways Park West, Rm. 306
Woodbury 11797

Established about 1970 in NY.
Donor(s): Overseas Military Sales Corp., Military Car Sales, Inc., Chrysler Military Sales Corp.
Foundation type: Independent
Financial data (yr. ended 06/30/89): Assets, $20,314 (M); gifts received, $50,000; expenditures, $206,855, including $206,772 for 70 grants (high: $70,000; low: $25).
Purpose and activities: Giving primarily to Jewish welfare funds, museums, and a medical center.
Limitations: Giving primarily in the New York, NY, metropolitan area, including the North Shore of Long Island. No grants to individuals.
Application information: Contributes only to pre-selected organizations. Applications not accepted.
Officers: Allen A. Goldring, Pres.; Lola A. Goldring, V.P.; Bernard Frey, Secy.; Rita G. Frey, Treas.
Employer Identification Number: 116084103

4460
Horace W. Goldsmith Foundation ▼
c/o White & Case
1155 Ave. of the Americas
New York 10036 (212) 819-8580

Incorporated in 1955 in NY.
Donor(s): Horace Goldsmith.†
Foundation type: Independent
Financial data (yr. ended 12/31/89): Assets, $290,551,412 (M); expenditures, $11,950,686, including $11,155,225 for 266 grants (high: $300,000; low: $8,333; average: $25,000-$100,000).
Purpose and activities: Support for cultural programs, including the performing arts and museums; Jewish welfare funds and temple support; hospitals and a geriatric center; and education, especially higher education.
Types of support: Operating budgets, endowment funds, building funds, matching funds, general purposes, capital campaigns, scholarship funds, seed money.
Limitations: Giving primarily in New York, NY, MA, and AZ. No grants to individuals.
Application information: Foundation depends virtually exclusively on self-initiated grants. Applications not accepted.
Board meeting date(s): 8 times a year
Write: Robert R. Slaughter, Chief Exec.
Officers and Directors:* Grace R. Goldsmith,* Chair. (Emeritus); Robert R. Slaughter,* Chief Exec.; Richard Menschel, Robert B. Menschel, James C. Slaughter, William A. Slaughter.
Number of staff: None.
Employer Identification Number: 136107758

4461
Goldsmith-Perry Philanthropies, Inc. ¤
c/o Yohalem Gillman & Co.
477 Madison Ave.
New York 10022-5802

Established in 1969 in NY.
Donor(s): Barbara Lubin Perry Charitable Trust, Joseph I. Lubin.†
Foundation type: Independent
Financial data (yr. ended 12/31/87): Assets, $5,667,481 (M); gifts received, $915,000; expenditures, $685,300, including $574,755 for grants.
Purpose and activities: Support primarily for Jewish giving, higher education, and cultural programs.
Limitations: Giving primarily in New York, NY.
Officers and Directors: Barbara L. Goldsmith, Pres.; Frank Perry, Secy.
Employer Identification Number: 237031986

4462
The Leslie & Roslyn Goldstein Foundation ⌑ ☆
c/o Nathan Berkman & Co.
29 Broadway, Rm. 2800
New York 10006-3103

Established in 1980.
Donor(s): Leslie Goldstein.
Foundation type: Independent
Financial data (yr. ended 11/30/88): Assets, $1,925,585 (M); expenditures, $126,096, including $90,317 for grants (high: $48,650).
Purpose and activities: Giving for Jewish welfare funds and other Jewish organizations.
Application information:
Initial approach: Letter
Deadline(s): None
Trustees: Leslie Goldstein, Roslyn Goldstein.
Employer Identification Number: 061035614

4463
N. S. Goldstein Foundation, Inc. ⌑
650 Park Ave.
New York 10021

Incorporated in 1956 in NY.
Donor(s): Nathan S. Goldstein,† Rosalie W. Goldstein.
Foundation type: Independent
Financial data (yr. ended 10/31/88): Assets, $1,841,940 (M); expenditures, $80,375, including $70,535 for 43 grants (high: $10,000; low: $50).
Purpose and activities: Emphasis on higher education (including scholarship funds), and Jewish welfare funds and other Jewish organizations.
Types of support: Scholarship funds.
Limitations: No grants to individuals.
Application information:
Initial approach: Letter
Deadline(s): None
Write: Rosalie W. Goldstein, Pres.
Officers and Directors: Rosalie W. Goldstein, Pres. and Treas.; Marjorie Doniger, V.P. and Secy.; Burt J. Goldstein, V.P.
Number of staff: None.
Employer Identification Number: 136127750

4464
Goldstone Fund, Inc. ⌑
c/o Wertheim Schroder Holdings, Inc., Tax Dept.
787 Seventh Ave., 6th Fl.
New York 10019-6016 (212) 578-0200

Established in 1959 in NY.
Foundation type: Independent
Financial data (yr. ended 5/31/88): Assets, $1,090,182 (M); expenditures, $56,885, including $52,000 for 13 grants (high: $20,000; low: $500).
Purpose and activities: Support primarily for health, higher education, and Jewish concerns.
Application information:
Initial approach: Letter
Deadline(s): None
Write: Herbert A. Goldstone, Pres.
Officers and Directors: Herbert A. Goldstone, Pres.; Anne S. Goldstone, V.P.; Arthur H. Goldstone, Secy.; Philip P. Goodkin, Treas.; Edwin E. Jedeikin.
Employer Identification Number: 136028782

4465
The Golub Foundation ⌑
501 Duanesburg Rd.
Schenectady 12306 (518) 356-9450
Scholarship application address: c/o Golub Corp., Scholarship Comm., P.O. Box 1074, Schenectady, NY 12301

Established in 1981 in NY.
Donor(s): Golub Corp., Jane Golub, Neil M. Golub.
Foundation type: Company-sponsored
Financial data (yr. ended 3/31/88): Assets, $12,196 (M); gifts received, $401,200; expenditures, $432,917, including $405,037 for 345 grants (high: $34,000; low: $10) and $17,624 for 22 grants to individuals (high: $1,000; low: $180).
Purpose and activities: Support for the United Way, arts, health, and higher education; and scholarship awards to high school graduates in areas served by the company.
Types of support: Student aid.
Limitations: Giving limited to the Price Chopper Supermarket marketing area: the counties of Berkshire, Hampden, and Hampshire counties, MA; Lackawanna, Luzerne, Susquehanna, Wayne, and Wyoming, PA; Bennington, VT; and Albany, Broom, Clinton, Columbia, Delaware, Essex, Franklin, Fulton, Greene, Hamilton, Herkimer, Jefferson, Madison, Montgomery, Oneida, Onondaga, Oswego, Otsego, Rensselaer, Saratoga, Schenectady, Schoharie, Warren, and Washington, NY.
Publications: Informational brochure.
Application information: Application form required for scholarships.
Deadline(s): Mar. 14 for full application packet for scholarships
Write: Mary Lou Sennes, Admin. Golub Foundation
Trustees: A. Susan Gabriel, Frank Lorch, Sue Ann Ritchko.
Employer Identification Number: 222341421

4466
Good Neighbor Foundation, Inc.
777 Third Ave.
New York 10017 (212) 546-2000

Incorporated in 1952 in NY.
Foundation type: Independent
Financial data (yr. ended 12/31/89): Assets, $680,808 (M); expenditures, $340,825, including $340,825 for 80 grants (high: $80,000; low: $50).
Purpose and activities: Giving primarily to Jewish welfare funds, community funds, health associations, AIDS programs, higher and medical education, and cultural programs, including the performing arts, film, museums, and music.
Types of support: General purposes, operating budgets.
Limitations: Giving primarily in New York, NY, and CA.
Application information: Applications not accepted.
Write: Lucille Caserio
Officers: Edward H. Meyer, Pres.; Robert L. Berenson, V.P.; Lucille Caserio, Secy.; Steven G. Felsher, Treas.
Number of staff: None.
Employer Identification Number: 136161259

4467
Mae Stone Goode Trust ⌑
c/o Marine Midland Bank, N.A.
P.O. Box 4203, 17th Fl.
Buffalo 14240

Foundation type: Independent
Financial data (yr. ended 9/30/88): Assets, $2,788,092 (M); expenditures, $171,208, including $119,473 for 8 grants (high: $21,250; low: $5,964) and $24,380 for 2 grants to individuals (high: $12,380; low: $12,000).
Purpose and activities: Support primarily for medical research.
Types of support: Grants to individuals, research.
Limitations: Giving primarily in Buffalo and Rochester, NY.
Application information: Contributes only to pre-selected individuals and organizations. Applications not accepted.
Trustee: Marine Midland Bank, N.A.
Employer Identification Number: 237175053

4468
The Goodman Family Foundation ⌑
c/o Roy M. Goodman
1035 Fifth Ave.
New York 10028 (212) 288-9067

Trust established in 1970 in NY as one of two successor trusts to the Matz Foundation.
Donor(s): Israel Matz.†
Foundation type: Independent
Financial data (yr. ended 06/30/89): Assets, $2,828,146 (M); expenditures, $160,261, including $135,955 for 144 grants (high: $20,000; low: $100).
Purpose and activities: Giving for higher education and Jewish welfare funds; grants also for temple and church support, social service agencies, and arts organizations.
Limitations: Giving primarily in New York, NY.
Application information: Application form not required.
Initial approach: Letter
Deadline(s): None
Trustees: Barbara F. Goodman, Roy M. Goodman.
Employer Identification Number: 136355553

4469
Joseph C. and Clare F. Goodman Memorial Foundation, Inc. ⌑
230 Park Ave., Rm. 2300
New York 10017

Incorporated in 1969 in NY.
Donor(s): Clare F. Goodman.†
Foundation type: Independent
Financial data (yr. ended 9/30/88): Assets, $2,311,021 (M); expenditures, $113,182, including $84,000 for 8 grants (high: $32,000; low: $1,000).
Purpose and activities: Grants for the handicapped, hospitals, and education.
Limitations: Giving primarily in NY. No grants to individuals.
Application information: Contributes only to pre-selected organizations. Applications not accepted.
Officers: Joseph E. Seminara, Pres.; Joyce N. Eichenberg, V.P.; Sheldon Engelhardt, Treas.
Employer Identification Number: 237039999

4470
David Goodstein Family Foundation, Inc. ¤
Ten West 20th St.
New York 10011 (212) 929-2500

Incorporated in 1944 in NY.
Donor(s): Members of the Goodstein family and family-related businesses.
Foundation type: Independent
Financial data (yr. ended 02/28/89): Assets, $4,383,052 (M); expenditures, $272,536, including $252,171 for 54 grants (high: $50,000; low: $100).
Purpose and activities: Emphasis on Jewish welfare funds, hospitals, and higher education, including medical education.
Types of support: General purposes, continuing support, annual campaigns, emergency funds, building funds, equipment, scholarship funds.
Limitations: Giving primarily in NY. No grants to individuals, or for matching gifts; no loans.
Application information:
Initial approach: Proposal
Deadline(s): None
Board meeting date(s): Quarterly
Write: Robert Goodstein, V.P.
Officer: Robert Goodstein, V.P.
Directors: Carol Goodstein, Marilyn Kushner, Gertrude Raabin.
Employer Identification Number: 136094685

4471
Josephine Goodyear Foundation ¤
1920 Liberty Bldg.
Buffalo 14202 (716) 856-2112

Incorporated in 1913 in NY.
Donor(s): Josephine L. Goodyear.
Foundation type: Independent
Financial data (yr. ended 12/31/88): Assets, $2,812,087 (M); expenditures, $179,104, including $156,176 for 34 grants (high: $25,000; low: $500).
Purpose and activities: Giving to promote the health and welfare of indigent women and children, particularly to provide for their physical needs; emphasis on hospitals, child welfare, youth agencies, and community funds.
Types of support: Seed money, emergency funds, building funds, equipment, land acquisition, matching funds, employee matching gifts, capital campaigns, research, special projects.
Limitations: Giving limited to the Buffalo, NY, area. No grants to individuals, or for continuing support, annual campaigns, deficit financing, endowment funds, scholarships, or fellowships; no loans.
Application information: Application form not required.
Initial approach: Letter
Copies of proposal: 7
Deadline(s): Feb. 1, May 1, Sept. 1, and Dec. 1
Board meeting date(s): May, Sept., and Dec.
Final notification: 3 to 6 months
Write: E.W. Dann Stevens, Secy.
Officers and Directors: Clinton R. Wyckoff, Jr., Pres.; Robert M. Goodyear, V.P.; E.W. Dann Stevens, Secy.; Jean G. Bowen, Treas.; Emma L.D. Churchill, Frank H. Goodyear, Stanley A. Tirrell, Edward F. Walsh, Jr., Dorothy G. Wyckoff.
Number of staff: None.
Employer Identification Number: 160755234

4472
Isaac Gordon Foundation, Inc. ¤
c/o Robert Gordon
210 Reynolds Arcade Bldg.
Rochester 14614

Incorporated in 1951 in NY.
Foundation type: Independent
Financial data (yr. ended 09/30/89): Assets, $1,979,062 (M); expenditures, $278,526, including $266,125 for 27 grants (high: $180,000; low: $25).
Purpose and activities: Emphasis on Jewish giving, including Jewish welfare funds and a nursing home; some support for secondary education.
Limitations: Giving primarily in NY.
Application information: Contributes only to pre-selected organizations. Applications not accepted.
Officers: Robert Gordon, Pres.; Robert Clark, V.P.; Beryl Nusbaum, Secy.
Employer Identification Number: 237425361

4473
Gordon Fund ▼ ¤
20 Exchange Place, 8th Fl.
New York 10005-3201

Trust established in 1954 in NY.
Donor(s): Members of the Gordon family.
Foundation type: Independent
Financial data (yr. ended 12/31/88): Assets, $602,696 (M); gifts received, $645,750; expenditures, $202,114, including $185,450 for 63 grants (high: $40,000; low: $250; average: $1,000-$10,000).
Purpose and activities: Giving for elementary, secondary, and higher education; support also for youth agencies, religious organizations, and hospitals.
Types of support: Capital campaigns, continuing support.
Limitations: No grants to individuals.
Application information:
Initial approach: Letter
Deadline(s): None
Board meeting date(s): As necessary
Write: William N. Loverd, Trustee
Trustees: Albert F. Gordon, William N. Loverd.
Number of staff: None.
Employer Identification Number: 136085919

4474
Gordon/Rousmaniere/Roberts Fund ¤ ☆
20 Exchange Place, 8th Fl.
New York 10005-3201

Established in 1985 in NY.
Donor(s): Albert H. Gordon.
Foundation type: Independent
Financial data (yr. ended 12/31/88): Assets, $17,248,172 (M); gifts received, $2,800,000; expenditures, $4,087,936, including $3,915,500 for 111 grants (high: $500,000; low: $200).
Purpose and activities: Giving primarily for higher, secondary, and elementary education, including theological education; support also for a medical center and health associations, cultural programs and a historic preservation foundation, international relations, and environmental programs.
Limitations: Giving primarily in NY, MA, CA, and CT. No grants to individuals.
Application information:
Initial approach: Proposal
Deadline(s): None
Write: William N. Loverd
Trustee: Mary G. Roberts.
Employer Identification Number: 133257793

4475
D. S. and R. H. Gottesman Foundation ¤
100 Park Ave.
New York 10017 (212) 532-7300

Incorporated in 1941 in NY.
Donor(s): D. Samuel Gottesman.†
Foundation type: Independent
Financial data (yr. ended 10/31/88): Assets, $1,272,456 (M); expenditures, $232,119, including $220,300 for 2 grants (high: $200,300; low: $20,000).
Purpose and activities: Support traditionally for Jewish welfare funds and higher education.
Limitations: Giving primarily in New York, NY.
Application information: Contributes only to pre-selected organizations. Applications not accepted.
Officers: Ira D. Wallach,* Pres.; Armand P. Bartos,* V.P.; Joy G. Ungerleider-Mayerson,* V.P.; Edgar Wachenheim III, V.P.; James G. Wallach, V.P.; Peter C. Siegfried, Secy.; Benjamin Glowatz, Treas.
Directors:* Celeste G. Bartos, Philip Mayerson, Miriam G. Wallach.
Employer Identification Number: 136101701

4476
Adolph and Esther Gottlieb Foundation, Inc. ¤
380 West Broadway
New York 10012 (212) 226-0581

Established in 1976 in NY.
Donor(s): Adolph Gottlieb,† Esther Gottlieb.†
Foundation type: Independent
Financial data (yr. ended 6/30/88): Assets, $2,751,521 (M); expenditures, $263,493, including $133,400 for 21 grants to individuals (high: $10,000; low: $1,700; average: $1,700-$10,000).
Purpose and activities: Two separate grant programs: 1) Individual support program for painters, sculptors, and printmakers who have at least 20 years in a mature phase of their art, and are in current financial need; and 2) Emergency assistance program for painters, sculptors, and printmakers who have at least 10 years in a mature phase of their art and are in current financial need in excess of and unrelated to their normal economic situation, and which is the result of a recent emergency occurence such as a fire, flood or medical emergency.
Types of support: Grants to individuals.
Limitations: No support for support organizations, educational institutions, projects, or those working in crafts.

Publications: Informational brochure, application guidelines.
Application information: Emergency grant applications may be submitted and reviewed year round. Application form required.
Initial approach: Letter
Copies of proposal: 1
Deadline(s): Dec. 15 for individual support program
Board meeting date(s): Quarterly
Final notification: Early Mar.
Officers and Directors: Dick Netzer, Pres.; Lawrence Alloway, V.P.; Sanford Hirsch, Secy.-Treas.; Charlotte Kotik, Robert Mangold.
Number of staff: 2 full-time professional; 1 part-time support.
Employer Identification Number: 132853957

4477
The Florence Gould Foundation ▼
(Formerly Florence J. Gould Foundation, Inc.)
c/o Cahill Gordon and Reindel
80 Pine St.
New York 10005 (212) 701-3400

Incorporated in 1957 in NY.
Donor(s): Florence J. Gould.†
Foundation type: Independent
Financial data (yr. ended 12/31/88): Assets, $57,894,637 (M); gifts received, $3,865,249; expenditures, $4,954,654, including $4,119,878 for 59 grants (high: $750,000; low: $1,500; average: $1,500-$750,000) and $300,000 for in-kind gifts.
Purpose and activities: Established "to promote French-American amity and understanding" and for general charitable giving; support for museums, higher education, and the arts in the U.S. and France, and for a hospital in Paris.
Limitations: No grants to individuals.
Application information: Application form not required.
Deadline(s): None
Board meeting date(s): As necessary
Final notification: Varies
Write: John R. Young, Pres.
Officers and Directors: John R. Young, Pres.; William E. Hegarty, V.P. and Secy.; Daniel Davison, V.P. and Treas.; Daniel Wildenstein, V.P.; Walter C. Cliff.
Number of staff: None.
Employer Identification Number: 136176855

4478
Edwin Gould Foundation for Children ▼
23 Gramercy Park South
New York 10003 (212) 982-5200

Incorporated in 1923 in NY.
Donor(s): Edwin Gould.†
Foundation type: Independent
Financial data (yr. ended 12/31/88): Assets, $27,989,150 (M); expenditures, $1,986,072, including $1,031,165 for 170 grants (high: $150,000; low: $250; average: $500-$5,000).
Purpose and activities: "To promote the welfare of children...and to improve social and living conditions"; support primarily to children's services, with priority to agencies formerly affiliated with the foundation; some scholarship support to institutions for young people who have passed through foundation-affiliated institutions and programs developed by the foundation.
Types of support: Operating budgets, continuing support, seed money, special projects, conferences and seminars, scholarship funds, exchange programs, general purposes, internships, program-related investments, technical assistance, emergency funds.
Limitations: Giving primarily in New York, NY, and for special projects elsewhere in the U.S. No grants to individuals, or for building or endowment funds, or matching gifts; no loans.
Publications: Multi-year report, informational brochure, program policy statement.
Application information: Applications generally not encouraged; most grants support foundation's own programs. Application form not required.
Initial approach: Letter or proposal
Copies of proposal: 1
Deadline(s): None
Board meeting date(s): Monthly except July and Aug.
Final notification: Less than 1 month
Write: Michael W. Osheowitz, Pres.
Officers and Trustees:* Michael W. Osheowitz,* Pres.; Martha M. Innes,* V.P.; Herschel E. Sparks, Jr.,* Secy.; Brandt R. Allen, Malcolm J. Edgerton, Jr., Frances K. Field, Patricia Trudell Gordan, Daniel W. Joy, Newton P.S. Merrill, Aileen (Chuca) Meyer, Schuyler M. Meyer, Jr., Elsie V. Newburg, George C. Seward, Richard H. Valentine.
Advisory Trustees: Byron T. Hipple, John W. McDermott, Lelan F. Sillin, Jr.
Number of staff: 10 full-time professional; 1 part-time professional; 2 full-time support; 1 part-time support.
Employer Identification Number: 135675642

4479
Grace Foundation, Inc. ▼
1114 Ave. of the Americas
New York 10036-7794 (212) 819-6640

Incorporated in 1961 in NY.
Donor(s): W.R. Grace & Co.
Foundation type: Company-sponsored
Financial data (yr. ended 12/31/89): Assets, $18,056,936 (M); gifts received, $19,485,863; expenditures, $2,241,547, including $2,005,656 for 296 grants (high: $145,000; low: $100; average: $1,000-$20,000) and $223,144 for 399 employee matching gifts.
Purpose and activities: Grants primarily to organizations in communities in which the corporation does business, for education (including employee matching gifts and scholarships to children of domestic employees of W.R. Grace & Co.), urban and minority affairs, cultural programs, including performing arts, community funds, and health and hospitals.
Types of support: Operating budgets, continuing support, annual campaigns, building funds, equipment, matching funds, employee matching gifts, scholarship funds, employee-related scholarships, fellowships.
Limitations: No grants to individuals (except for employee-related scholarships), or for endowment funds, seed money, emergency funds, deficit financing, land acquisition, publications, demonstration projects, conferences, or specific research projects.
Application information: Application form not required.
Initial approach: Letter
Copies of proposal: 1
Deadline(s): None
Board meeting date(s): As required
Final notification: 2 to 3 months
Write: Paul D. Paganucci, Chair.
Officers and Directors:* Paul D. Paganucci,* Chair.; Brian J. Smith,* Pres.; Francis J. Brennan,* V.P. and Treas.; Thomas M. Doyle,* V.P.; Robert B. Lamm,* Secy.; J.P. Bolduc, James W. Frick, George P. Jenkins, Eben W. Pyne, Harold A. Stevens, John R. Young.
Number of staff: None.
Employer Identification Number: 136153305

4480
The Gramercy Park Foundation, Inc. ⌑
c/o Zemlock, Levy, Bick & Karnbad
225 Broadway
New York 10007 (212) 964-4140

Incorporated in 1952 in NY.
Donor(s): Benjamin Sonnenberg, Helen Sonnenberg Tucker.
Foundation type: Independent
Financial data (yr. ended 12/31/88): Assets, $1,546,571 (M); expenditures, $104,695, including $77,985 for 60 grants (high: $25,000; low: $50).
Purpose and activities: Grants for arts and cultural programs, with emphasis on libraries and the performing arts; support also for higher education, including music education.
Limitations: Giving primarily in the New York City metropolitan area. No grants to individuals.
Application information:
Write: Norman Motechin
Officers: Helen Sonnenberg Tucker, Pres. and Treas.; Steven Tucker, Secy.; William Spears.
Number of staff: 1 part-time support.
Employer Identification Number: 132507282

4481
Grand Street Foundation, Inc. ⌑ ☆
50 Riverside Dr.
New York 10024-6504

Established in 1985 in NY.
Foundation type: Independent
Financial data (yr. ended 3/31/89): Assets, $690,109 (M); expenditures, $189,510, including $175,950 for 6 grants (high: $171,000; low: $250).
Purpose and activities: "Primarily to advance the study and appreciation of literature and literary criticism."
Application information:
Deadline(s): None
Write: Benjamin Sonnenberg, Pres.
Officers and Directors: Benjamin Sonnenberg, Pres. and Treas.; Dorothy Gallagher, Secy.; Howard Sobel.
Employer Identification Number: 133247663

4482
Charles L. Grannon Foundation ¤
c/o Goldman Sachs & Co.
85 Broad St.
New York 10004

Established in 1977 in NY.
Donor(s): Charles L. Grannon.
Foundation type: Independent
Financial data (yr. ended 2/28/88): Assets, $192,929 (M); gifts received, $75,000; expenditures, $186,469, including $186,005 for 46 grants (high: $100,000; low: $50).
Purpose and activities: Grants primarily for higher education; some support also for hospitals, youth organizations and Protestant churches.
Trustees: Alice Fay Grannon, Charles L. Grannon, Craig C. Grannon, Michael L. Grannon.
Employer Identification Number: 132921501

4483
Charles M. & Mary D. Grant Foundation ¤
c/o Morgan Guaranty Trust Co. of New York
23 Wall St.
New York 10015 (212) 483-2097

Trust established in 1967 in NY.
Donor(s): Mary D. Grant.†
Foundation type: Independent
Financial data (yr. ended 12/31/88): Assets, $5,047,365 (M); expenditures, $238,057, including $200,000 for 9 grants (high: $50,000; low: $15,000).
Purpose and activities: Emphasis on higher education and hospitals.
Types of support: Operating budgets, continuing support, seed money, building funds, equipment, land acquisition, publications, special projects, general purposes.
Limitations: Giving primarily in the southern U.S. No grants to individuals, or for research, endowment funds, or matching gifts; generally no scholarships or fellowships; no loans.
Application information:
Initial approach: Letter
Copies of proposal: 1
Deadline(s): None
Board meeting date(s): May and Aug.
Write: Robert F. Longley, Sr. V.P., Morgan Guaranty Trust Co. of New York
Trustee: Morgan Guaranty Trust Co. of New York.
Number of staff: 5
Employer Identification Number: 136264329

4484
William T. Grant Foundation ▼
515 Madison Ave., 6th Fl.
New York 10022-5403 (212) 752-0071

Incorporated in 1936 in DE.
Donor(s): William T. Grant.†
Foundation type: Independent
Financial data (yr. ended 12/31/89): Assets, $154,300,000 (M); expenditures, $8,201,000, including $6,655,431 for 90 grants (high: $400,000; low: $1,500; average: $190,000).
Purpose and activities: Supports research in any medical or social-behavioral scientific discipline on the development of school-age children, adolescents and youth. The foundation is especially interested in interdisciplinary research employing multiple methods to investigate several problems simultaneously. Support is available in four forms, all of which are investigator-initiated: 1) research grants; 2) evaluations of innovative community-based interventions aimed at reducing problem behaviors; 3) Faculty Scholars Program; and 4) a limited number of small one-time grants for child-related community service projects in the New York metropolitan area.
Limitations: No grants to individuals (except Faculty Scholars Program), or for annual fundraising campaigns, equipment and materials, land acquisition, building or renovation projects, operating budgets, endowments, or scholarships; no loans.
Publications: Annual report, informational brochure (including application guidelines), newsletter.
Application information: Application to Faculty Scholars Program by nomination only. All applicants will be notified as to required copies of proposals. Application form not required.
Initial approach: Letter
Deadline(s): July 1 for Faculty Scholars Program nominations; no set deadline for grants
Board meeting date(s): Feb., May, Sept., and Dec.
Final notification: Immediately following board meeting; Mar. for Faculty Scholars Program
Write: Robert Johns Haggerty, M.D., Pres.
Officers: Robert P. Patterson, Jr.,* Chair.; Robert Johns Haggerty, M.D.,* Pres.; Lonnie Sherrod, V.P. for Prog.; Mary Goodley-Thomas, V.P. for Finance and Admin.; William H. Chisholm,* Treas.; Eileen Dorann, Controller.
Trustees:* William Bevan, Ellis T. Gravette, Jr., Beatrix A. Hamburg, M.D., Martha L. Minow, Henry W. Riecken, Kenneth S. Rolland, Rivington R. Winant.
Number of staff: 5 full-time professional; 10 full-time support.
Employer Identification Number: 131624021

4485
Eleanor and Wilson Greatbatch Foundation ☆
P.O. Box 135
Clarence 14031 (716) 759-8620

Established in 1986 in NY.
Foundation type: Independent
Financial data (yr. ended 9/30/89): Assets, $1,247,544 (M); qualifying distributions, $288,873, including $13,710 for 6 grants (high: $4,500; low: $755), $15,000 for 1 grant to an individual and $254,198 for 1 loan.
Purpose and activities: Giving for the performing arts and museums, historic preservation, a community playground, and social services, including programs benefitting children and the handicapped.
Types of support: Equipment, program-related investments, seed money, special projects.
Limitations: Giving limited to Clarence and Newstead, NY. No grants to individuals.
Publications: Occasional report, informational brochure (including application guidelines).
Application information: Application form required.
Initial approach: Letter or telephone
Copies of proposal: 1
Deadline(s): None
Board meeting date(s): Quarterly
Write: Peter Greatbatch, Pres.
Officer and Directors: Peter Greatbatch, Pres.; Warren Greatbatch, John E. Siegel.
Employer Identification Number: 222844999

4486
Green Foundation, Inc. ¤
570 Elmont Rd.
Elmont 11003-3532 (516) 328-9000

Donor(s): Investors Collateral Corp.
Foundation type: Independent
Financial data (yr. ended 10/31/89): Assets, $671,236 (M); gifts received, $30,000; expenditures, $171,365, including $169,799 for 32 grants (high: $43,800; low: $49).
Purpose and activities: Giving primarily to Jewish organizations, educational institutions, and health associations.
Limitations: Giving primarily in NY. No grants to individuals.
Application information:
Initial approach: Letter
Deadline(s): None
Write: Allan Green, Pres.
Officers: Allan Green, Pres.; Vincent Errante, V.P.; Hana Green, V.P.; Steven Tarloff, Secy.-Treas.
Employer Identification Number: 116014459

4487
The Green Fund, Inc. ▼
501 Fifth Ave., Suite 1814
New York 10017 (212) 697-9531

Incorporated in 1947 in NY.
Donor(s): Evelyn Green Davis,† Louis A. Green.†
Foundation type: Independent
Financial data (yr. ended 01/31/89): Assets, $25,907,457 (M); gifts received, $437,600; expenditures, $1,494,742, including $1,292,547 for 218 grants (high: $340,000; low: $25; average: $250-$15,000).
Purpose and activities: Giving primarily for Jewish welfare funds, hospitals within the Jewish Federation network, services to the aged and mentally handicapped, higher and secondary education, the performing arts, social services, and youth agencies.
Limitations: Giving primarily in the New York, NY, metropolitan area. No grants to individuals.
Application information: Grants initiated by the fund's members. Applications not accepted.
Board meeting date(s): Varies
Write: Cynthia Green Colin, Pres.
Officers and Directors: Cynthia Green Colin, Pres.; S. William Green, Treas.; Patricia F. Green.
Number of staff: 1 part-time support.
Employer Identification Number: 136160950

4488
Greenacre Foundation ☆
30 Rockefeller Plaza, Rm. 5600
New York 10112-0001 (212) 649-5674

Established in 1968 in NY.
Donor(s): Abby M. O'Neill, Abby R. Mauze.†
Foundation type: Operating
Financial data (yr. ended 12/31/88): Assets, $15,957,307 (M); gifts received, $29,795; expenditures, $425,164, including $20,000 for 2 grants (high: $15,000; low: $5,000) and $401,232 for 6 foundation-administered programs.
Purpose and activities: A private operating foundation; support for a local civic association and conservation group.
Limitations: Giving primarily in Manhattan, NY. No grants to individuals.
Application information: Contributes only to pre-selected organizations. Applications not accepted.
Write: Mrs. Jean M. Branscombe
Officers and Trustees:* Abby M. O'Neill,* Pres.; Donal C. O'Brien,* V.P.; James Sligar,* Secy.; George Pipino,* Treas.; and 9 additional trustees.
Number of staff: 1
Employer Identification Number: 132621502

4489
The Alan C. Greenberg Foundation, Inc. ▼ ⌑
c/o Bear Stearns & Co.
245 Park Ave.
New York 10167 (212) 272-2000

Established in 1964.
Donor(s): Alan C. Greenberg.
Foundation type: Independent
Financial data (yr. ended 12/31/88): Assets, $1,510,882 (M); gifts received, $1,225,000; expenditures, $607,645, including $596,688 for 109 grants (high: $250,350; low: $78; average: $500-$20,000).
Purpose and activities: Emphasis on Jewish organizations, higher education, medical research, and cultural programs.
Limitations: Giving primarily in NY and Israel.
Application information: Contributes only to pre-selected organizations. Applications not accepted.
Board meeting date(s): As necessary
Write: Alan C. Greenberg, Pres.
Officers and Directors: Alan C. Greenberg, Pres. and Treas.; Maynard Greenberg, V.P. and Secy.
Number of staff: None.
Employer Identification Number: 136271740

4490
The David J. Greene Foundation, Inc. ⌑
c/o Ms. Florence B. Weingart
30 Wall St.
New York 10005 (212) 344-5180

Incorporated in 1966 in NY.
Donor(s): David J. Greene,† and members of the Greene family.
Foundation type: Independent
Financial data (yr. ended 12/31/88): Assets, $5,918,096 (M); gifts received, $10,000; expenditures, $400,105, including $366,487 for 259 grants.
Purpose and activities: Grants largely for hospitals, higher and secondary education, social service and youth agencies, and Jewish welfare funds.
Types of support: General purposes.
Limitations: Giving primarily in the New York, NY, metropolitan area. No grants to individuals.
Application information:
Initial approach: Letter
Board meeting date(s): Mar., June, Sept., and Dec.
Officers and Directors: Alan I. Greene, Pres.; Robert J. Ravitz, V.P.; Florence B. Weingart, Secy.; James R. Greene, Treas.; Michael Greene.
Number of staff: None.
Employer Identification Number: 136209280

4491
The Jerome L. Greene Foundation, Inc. ⌑
450 Park Ave.
New York 10022

Established in 1978.
Donor(s): Jerome L. Greene.
Foundation type: Independent
Financial data (yr. ended 11/30/89): Assets, $7,852,798 (M); gifts received, $1,011,860; expenditures, $1,331,220, including $1,296,217 for 45 grants (high: $500,060; low: $25).
Purpose and activities: Grants primarily for cultural programs and Jewish welfare funds.
Limitations: Giving primarily in NY.
Application information:
Deadline(s): None
Officer and Directors:* Jerome L. Greene,* Pres.; Dawn Greene.
Employer Identification Number: 132960852

4492
Robert Z. Greene Foundation ▼ ⌑
1211 Ave. of the Americas
New York 10036

Established in 1947.
Donor(s): Robert Z. Greene.†
Foundation type: Independent
Financial data (yr. ended 12/31/88): Assets, $2,896,294 (L); gifts received, $2,512,378; expenditures, $828,885, including $797,420 for 47 grants (high: $150,000; low: $50; average: $5,000-$100,000).
Purpose and activities: Giving primarily for higher education, hospitals, and health agencies.
Limitations: Giving primarily in FL and NY.
Application information: Contributes only to pre-selected organizations. Applications not accepted.
Board meeting date(s): Monthly
Write: Seymour Levine, Trustee
Trustees: Monroe Chapin, Seymour Levine.
Number of staff: None.
Employer Identification Number: 136121751

4493
Greentree Foundation
110 West 51st St., Rm. 4600
New York 10020 (212) 582-2300

Established in 1982 in NY.
Donor(s): Betsey C. Whitney.
Foundation type: Independent
Financial data (yr. ended 12/31/89): Assets, $7,254,455 (M); expenditures, $325,169, including $285,500 for 34 grants (high: $25,000; low: $1,500).
Purpose and activities: Giving to reduce educational, social, and cultural deficiencies in urban areas, preferably through programs initiated by local community groups.
Types of support: Special projects.
Limitations: Giving primarily in the New York, NY, metropolitan area. No grants to individuals.
Application information: Application form not required.
Initial approach: Letter
Write: Kathryn Ritchie, Asst. Secy.
Officers: Betsey C. Whitney, Pres.; Kate R. Whitney, V.P. and Secy.; Sara R. Wilford, V.P. and Treas.
Number of staff: 2 part-time professional.
Employer Identification Number: 133132117

4494
The Greenwall Foundation ▼
370 Lexington Ave., Rm. 310
New York 10017 (212) 661-0831

Incorporated in 1949 in NY.
Donor(s): Anna A. Greenwall,† Frank K. Greenwall.†
Foundation type: Independent
Financial data (yr. ended 12/31/89): Assets, $51,188,548 (M); gifts received, $112,489; expenditures, $2,945,579, including $2,091,565 for 92 grants (high: $210,375; average: $2,500-$100,000).
Purpose and activities: Giving primarily for medical research, especially in bone cancer, diabetes, immunology, molecular biology, and dementia; education, especially scholarships through institutions; and the arts and humanities. The foundation expects to expand its efforts in arts and education.
Types of support: Continuing support, seed money, emergency funds, equipment, scholarship funds, professorships, fellowships, research, special projects.
Limitations: Giving primarily in New York, NY for arts and humanities; giving nationally for medical research and education. No support for state or religious schools, or private foundations. No grants to individuals, or for building or endowment funds, operating budgets, annual campaigns, deficit financing, publications, or conferences; no loans.
Publications: Annual report (including application guidelines).
Application information: Application form not required.
Initial approach: Letter
Copies of proposal: 1
Deadline(s): Submit proposal preferably in Jan. or July; deadlines Feb. 1 and Aug. 1
Board meeting date(s): May and Nov.
Final notification: After next board meeting
Write: William Charles Stubing, Pres.
Officers: Oscar M. Ruebhausen,* Chair.; Donald J. Donahue,* Vice-Chair.; William Charles Stubing, Pres.; Richard L. Salzer,* V.P.; William S. Vaun, M.D.,* V.P.; Edith Levett, Corp. Secy.; C. Richard MacGrath,* Treas.
Directors:* Chester Billings, Jr., George Bugliarello, George F. Cahill, Jr., M.D., Beatrix A. Hamburg, M.D., Edward M. Kresky, Andrew

A. MacGrath, Francis F. MacGrath, Susan A. MacGrath, Carl B. Menges, Richard L. Salzer, Jr., M.D.
Number of staff: 2 full-time professional; 1 part-time professional; 1 full-time support.
Employer Identification Number: 136082277

4495
The Greer Family Foundation ☆
c/o Weiss, Peck & Greer
One New York Plaza, 30th Fl.
New York 10004 (212) 908-9500

Established in 1985 in NY.
Donor(s): Philip Greer.
Foundation type: Independent
Financial data (yr. ended 12/31/89): Assets, $1,600,000 (M); gifts received, $274,949; qualifying distributions, $147,914, including $147,914 for 58 grants (high: $57,500; low: $100).
Purpose and activities: Giving primarily for higher and secondary education; support also for the handicapped.
Types of support: Operating budgets, capital campaigns.
Limitations: No grants to individuals.
Application information: Applications not accepted.
Write: Philip Greer, Pres.
Officers and Directors:* Philip Greer,* Pres. and Treas.; Norman M. Gold,* V.P. and Secy.; Arthur W. Brown, Jr.,* V.P.; Stephen B. Weiss,* V.P.; Karen Greer.
Number of staff: None.
Employer Identification Number: 133321858

4496
The William and Mary Greve Foundation, Inc. ⌑
630 Fifth Ave., No. 1750
New York 10111 (212) 758-8032

Incorporated in 1964 in NY.
Donor(s): Mary P. Greve.†
Foundation type: Independent
Financial data (yr. ended 12/31/88): Assets, $17,365,985 (M); expenditures, $939,102, including $581,065 for 49 grants (high: $75,000; low: $750; average: $1,000-$5,000).
Purpose and activities: Grants largely for education and related fields, including U.S.-Eastern Bloc relations and the performing arts.
Types of support: Seed money, endowment funds, matching funds, general purposes, continuing support.
Limitations: No grants to individuals, or for scholarships or fellowships; no loans.
Publications: Program policy statement, application guidelines.
Application information: Application form not required.
Initial approach: Letter
Copies of proposal: 1
Deadline(s): None
Board meeting date(s): Variable
Final notification: 2 months
Write: Anthony C.M. Kiser, Pres.
Officers and Directors: John W. Kiser III, Chair.; Anthony C.M. Kiser, Pres.; John A. Buckbee, Exec. V.P. and Treas.; John J. Tommaney, Secy.; James W. Sykes, Jr.
Number of staff: 1 full-time support; 2 part-time support.
Employer Identification Number: 136020724

4497
Grigg-Lewis Trust ⌑
c/o Earl, DeLange, May & Jones
P.O. Box 450
Lockport 14094

Established in 1968 in NY.
Donor(s): Henrietta G. Lewis, Grigg Share Corp.
Foundation type: Independent
Financial data (yr. ended 12/31/87): Assets, $2,043,246 (M); gifts received, $293,469; expenditures, $91,897, including $68,500 for 4 grants (high: $30,000; low: $3,500).
Purpose and activities: Support for general charitable purposes.
Limitations: Giving limited to western NY. No grants to individuals.
Application information: Contributes only to pre-selected organizations. Applications not accepted.
Trustees: Raymond C. Clair, Henrietta G. Lewis, William B. May, Norman Sinclair.
Employer Identification Number: 237013826

4498
Jennie Grossinger Foundation, Inc. ⌑ ☆
271 Madison Ave., 22nd Fl.
New York 10016

Established in 1970.
Donor(s): Joseph Alpert, Charles Alpert.
Foundation type: Independent
Financial data (yr. ended 06/30/89): Assets, $48,915 (M); gifts received, $85,000; expenditures, $249,173, including $248,182 for 138 grants (high: $39,385; low: $18).
Purpose and activities: Support for Jewish welfare and concerns.
Limitations: Giving primarily in NY.
Officers: Joseph Alpert, Secy.; Charles Alpert, Treas.
Employer Identification Number: 132726085

4499
Lila Gruber Research Foundation ⌑
19 Laurel Dr.
Great Neck 11021 (516) 442-1171

Established in 1962.
Donor(s): Barry Gruber, Daryl Gruber, Murray P. Gruber.
Foundation type: Independent
Financial data (yr. ended 12/31/88): Assets, $2,208,406 (M); gifts received, $8,000; expenditures, $55,007, including $53,327 for 75 grants (high: $15,000; low: $15).
Purpose and activities: Giving for Jewish religious and educational institutions and medical research; support also for social services, including a Jewish welfare fund.
Types of support: Research.
Limitations: Giving primarily in NY.
Application information: Application form not required.
Deadline(s): None
Write: Murray P. Gruber, Trustee
Trustee: Murray P. Gruber.
Employer Identification Number: 116035223

4500
Stanley and Kathleen Grumbacher Foundation, Inc. ⌑
900 Fifth Ave.
New York 10021

Incorporated in 1951 in NY.
Donor(s): Stanley Grumbacher.†
Foundation type: Independent
Financial data (yr. ended 4/30/87): Assets, $1,145,789 (M); expenditures, $77,822, including $72,928 for 29 grants (high: $30,000; low: $18).
Purpose and activities: Grants largely for hospitals and Jewish welfare funds.
Limitations: Giving primarily in the New York, NY, metropolitan area. No grants to individuals.
Application information: Contributes only to pre-selected organizations. Applications not accepted.
Officers and Directors: Kathleen Grumbacher Silberstein, Pres. and Treas.; Alex Silberstein, V.P.; Jack J. Roland, Secy.
Employer Identification Number: 136161277

4501
The Herbert Grunfeld Trust of 2/1/66 ⌑
c/o Hartman and Craven
460 Park Ave.
New York 10022

Established in 1966 in NY.
Donor(s): Herbert Grunfeld.†
Foundation type: Independent
Financial data (yr. ended 12/31/88): Assets, $87,714 (M); expenditures, $9,346,886, including $9,346,306 for 2 grants (high: $9,344,306; low: $2,000).
Purpose and activities: Grants primarily for higher education.
Types of support: General purposes.
Application information: Applications not accepted.
Trustees: Chester Inwald, Steven N. Rappaport.
Employer Identification Number: 136214777

4502
Oscar and Regina Gruss Charitable and Educational Foundation, Inc. ⌑
c/o Spicer & Oppenheim
Seven World Trade Ctr.
New York 10048

Incorporated in 1952 in NY.
Donor(s): Emanuel Gruss, Oscar Gruss,† Regina Gruss.
Foundation type: Independent
Financial data (yr. ended 3/31/88): Assets, $7,040,760 (M); expenditures, $378,448, including $370,301 for 8 grants (high: $238,476; low: $75).
Purpose and activities: Grants largely for education, Jewish welfare funds, and temple support.
Limitations: Giving primarily in New York, NY. No grants to individuals.
Application information: Contributes only to pre-selected organizations. Applications not accepted.
Officers: Regina Gruss, Pres.; Elizabeth Goldberg, V.P.; Emanuel Gruss, Secy.; Riane Gruss, Treas.
Employer Identification Number: 136061333

4503
Emanuel & Riane Gruss Charitable Foundation, Inc. ¤
c/o Spicer & Oppenheim
Seven World Trade Ctr.
New York 10048

Established in 1978 in NY.
Donor(s): Emanuel Gruss, Riane Gruss.
Foundation type: Independent
Financial data (yr. ended 3/31/89): Assets, $6,492,521 (M); expenditures, $305,330, including $294,556 for 52 grants (high: $78,000; low: $10).
Purpose and activities: Support for hospitals, Jewish giving, and education.
Limitations: Giving primarily in New York, NY. No grants to individuals.
Application information: Contributes only to pre-selected organizations. Applications not accepted.
Officers and Directors: Riane Gruss, Pres. and Treas.; Emanuel Gruss, V.P. and Secy.; Brenda Gruss, Leslie Gruss.
Employer Identification Number: 132969811

4504
Joseph & Caroline Gruss Charitable Foundation, Inc. ¤
900 Third Ave.
New York 10022 (212) 688-1500

Incorporated in 1952 in NY.
Donor(s): Joseph S. Gruss Charitable Trust, Joseph S. Gruss, and others.
Foundation type: Independent
Financial data (yr. ended 8/31/87): Assets, $178,184 (M); gifts received, $252,540; expenditures, $454,493, including $449,694 for 50 grants (high: $50,000; low: $150).
Purpose and activities: Grants to Jewish educational institutions, temples, and welfare funds.
Application information:
Write: Joseph S. Gruss, Pres.
Officers and Directors: Joseph S. Gruss, Pres.; Martin D. Gruss, Secy.-Treas.; Harvey Brecher, Abraham Israelite, Evelyn Gruss Lipper, Solomon Litt, Leon Meyers, Rabbi Joseph B. Soloveitchik.
Employer Identification Number: 136128429

4505
The Martin D. Gruss Foundation ¤
(Formerly The Martin and Agneta Gruss Foundation)
900 Third Ave.
New York 10022 (212) 688-1500

Established in 1982 in NY.
Donor(s): Gruss Petroleum Corp.
Foundation type: Independent
Financial data (yr. ended 8/31/87): Assets, $546,725 (M); expenditures, $275,052, including $264,000 for 23 grants (high: $100,000; low: $100).
Purpose and activities: Giving primarily for secondary education, museums, and Jewish organizations, including welfare funds; some support also for hospitals.
Limitations: Giving primarily in the New York, NY, metropolitan area.
Application information:
Write: Martin D. Gruss, Trustee
Trustee: Martin D. Gruss.
Employer Identification Number: 133132987

4506
The Daniel and Florence Guggenheim Foundation
950 Third Ave., 30th Fl.
New York 10022 (212) 755-3199

Incorporated in 1924 in NY.
Donor(s): Daniel Guggenheim,† Florence Guggenheim.†
Foundation type: Independent
Financial data (yr. ended 12/31/89): Assets, $6,462,598 (M); expenditures, $542,636, including $378,024 for 10 grants (high: $161,500; low: $3,000).
Purpose and activities: The main thrust is criminal justice; some seed money to possible breakthrough medical research; support also for UJA/Federation of Jewish Philanthropies annual campaign.
Types of support: Seed money, matching funds, research.
Limitations: No grants to individuals, or for scholarships or fellowships.
Publications: Annual report.
Application information: Application form not required.
Initial approach: Letter
Copies of proposal: 1
Deadline(s): Feb.; by mid-Mar. at latest
Board meeting date(s): May
Write: Oscar S. Straus II, Pres.
Officers: Oscar S. Straus II,* Pres.; Oscar S. Straus III,* V.P.; Joan G. Van de Maele,* V.P.; Rowley Bialla, Secy.; John T. Barnes, Treas.
Directors:* Powell M. Cabot, Michael B. Davies, Dana Draper, Daniel Guggenheim, Robert Guggenheim, Jr., Mrs. Max A. Hart, Pamela H. Metcalf, Alfred Ogden, Henry Patton, Oscar Schafer, Kenneth Taylor, Albert C. Van de Maele.
Number of staff: 2
Employer Identification Number: 135562232

4507
The Harry Frank Guggenheim Foundation ▼
527 Madison Ave., 15th Fl.
New York 10022-4301 (212) 644-4907

Incorporated in 1929 in NY.
Donor(s): Harry Frank Guggenheim.†
Foundation type: Independent
Financial data (yr. ended 06/30/89): Assets, $49,528,883 (M); expenditures, $2,544,263, including $1,165,769 for grants (average: $15-$40,000), $325,305 for grants to individuals and $167,760 for foundation-administered programs.
Purpose and activities: Grants for research projects at the post-doctoral level (though not necessarily requiring a Ph.D.) directed toward providing a better understanding of violence, aggression, and dominance; Dissertation Fellowship program to support individuals only during the writing of their Ph.D. thesis; research grants can be applied for directly; support also for higher education.
Types of support: Research, seed money, general purposes, grants to individuals.
Limitations: No grants for capital or endowment funds, or for matching gifts; no loans. No funds for overhead costs of institutions, travel to professional meetings, publications, conferences (except for those organized by the foundation), subsidiaries, self-education, elaborate fixed equipment, or pre-doctoral support (apart from that indirectly involved in research assistantships).
Publications: Multi-year report, newsletter, informational brochure (including application guidelines), application guidelines.
Application information: Career Development Awards program has been discontinued. New program: Dissertation Fellowship. Application form required.
Initial approach: Letter
Copies of proposal: 6
Deadline(s): Feb. 1 for Ph.D. support; Aug. 1 and Feb. 1 for research grants
Board meeting date(s): June and Dec.
Final notification: Within 3 days of meeting
Write: Karen Colvard, Prog. Officer
Officers: Peter O. Lawson-Johnston,* Chair.; James M. Hester,* Pres.; Mary-Alice Yates, Secy.; Joseph A. Koenigsberger, Treas.; Karen Colvard, Prog. Officer.
Directors:* William O. Baker, Josiah Bunting III, Peyton Cochran, James B. Edwards, George J. Fountaine, Donald R. Griffin, Peter Lawson-Johnston II, Theodore D. Lockwood, Alan Pifer, Floyd Ratliff, Rudy L. Ruggles, Jr., Roger W. Straus, Jr., Joan G. Van de Maele, William C. Westmoreland.
Number of staff: 3 full-time professional; 1 part-time professional.
Employer Identification Number: 136043471

4508
John Simon Guggenheim Memorial Foundation ▼
90 Park Ave.
New York 10016 (212) 687-4470

Incorporated in 1925 in NY.
Donor(s): Simon Guggenheim,† Mrs. Simon Guggenheim.†
Foundation type: Independent
Financial data (yr. ended 12/31/89): Assets, $134,596,683 (M); gifts received, $150,000; expenditures, $8,295,815, including $6,040,850 for grants to individuals (high: $30,000; low: $12,000; average: $26,500).
Purpose and activities: Fellowships offered to further the development of scholars and artists by assisting them to engage in research in any field of knowledge and creation in any of the arts, under the freest possible conditions and irrespective of race, color, or creed. Fellowships are awarded by the trustees upon nomination by a Committee of Selection. Awards are made to citizens and permanent residents of the U.S. and Canada, and Latin America and the Caribbean. Guggenheim fellowships may not be held concurrently with other fellowships.
Types of support: Fellowships.
Limitations: No grants for building or endowment funds, operating budgets, or special projects.

Publications: Annual report, informational brochure (including application guidelines).
Application information: Grants are awarded to individuals rather than institutions. Application form required.
Initial approach: Letter
Deadline(s): Oct. 1 for U.S. and Canada; Dec. 1 for Latin America and the Caribbean
Board meeting date(s): Apr. and June and as required
Final notification: Approximately 6 months
Write: Joel Conarroe, Pres.
Officers and Trustees:* W. Clarke Wescoe,* Chair.; Joel Conarroe,* Pres.; G. Thomas Tanselle, V.P. and Secy.; Coleen P. Higgins-Jacob, Treas.; Richard W. Couper, Edward E. David, Jr., Helene L. Kaplan, Robert V. Lindsay, Joseph A. Rice, Charles Andrew Ryskamp, Malcolm B. Smith, Jean Strouse.
Number of staff: 10 full-time professional; 15 full-time support.
Employer Identification Number: 135673173

4509
Guilden Foundation, Inc.
c/o Richard A. Eisner & Co.
575 Madison Ave.
New York 10022

Established in 1984 in NY.
Donor(s): Ira Guilden.†
Foundation type: Independent
Financial data (yr. ended 05/31/88): Assets, $997,485 (M); expenditures, $157,036, including $149,606 for 29 grants (high: $45,000; low: $150).
Purpose and activities: Support for higher education, civic affairs, Jewish concerns, and the performing arts.
Types of support: Continuing support.
Limitations: Giving primarily in New York, NY. No grants to individuals.
Application information: Contributes only to pre-selected organizations. Applications not accepted.
Write: Paul Guilden, Pres.
Officer and Trustees:* Paul Guilden, Pres. and Secy.; Tamara Guilden.
Number of staff: None.
Employer Identification Number: 133185270

4510
The Guinzburg Fund ⌑
Three West 29th St.
New York 10001

Incorporated in 1955 in NY.
Donor(s): Harold K. Guinzburg.†
Foundation type: Independent
Financial data (yr. ended 12/31/88): Assets, $1,550,169 (M); expenditures, $226,977, including $169,016 for grants (average: $1,000).
Purpose and activities: Giving for hospitals, higher education, cultural activities, and community development.
Types of support: Annual campaigns, research, special projects.
Limitations: Giving primarily in NY. No grants to individuals.
Application information: Contributes only to pre-selected organizations. Applications not accepted.
Officer and Director: Thomas H. Guinzburg, Pres. and Treas.
Number of staff: 1 part-time support.
Employer Identification Number: 136108425

4511
J. Gurwin Foundation, Inc. ⌑
P.O. Box 798
Great Neck 11022 (516) 466-3800

Incorporated in 1959 in NY.
Donor(s): Joseph Gurwin, Kings Point Industries, Inc.
Foundation type: Independent
Financial data (yr. ended 07/31/89): Assets, $9,029,028 (M); expenditures, $519,742, including $515,725 for 54 grants (high: $270,500; low: $40).
Purpose and activities: Giving for Jewish welfare funds; grants also for temple support and hospitals.
Limitations: Giving primarily in NY. No grants to individuals.
Application information: Contributes only to pre-selected organizations. Applications not accepted.
Write: Joseph Gurwin, Pres.
Officers: Joseph Gurwin, Pres.; Rosalind Gurwin, Secy.-Treas.
Directors: Laura Gurwin Flug, Eric Gurwin.
Employer Identification Number: 136059258

4512
The Gutfreund Foundation, Inc.
c/o John Gutfreund, Salomon Brothers Inc.
One New York Plaza
New York 10004 (212) 627-7710
Application address: c/o Joint Foundation Support, Inc., 40 West 20th St., 10th Fl., New York, NY 10011

Incorporated in 1967 in NY.
Donor(s): John H. Gutfreund.
Foundation type: Independent
Financial data (yr. ended 4/30/89): Assets, $1,162,889 (M); expenditures, $190,934, including $158,000 for 16 grants (high: $25,000; low: $5,000; average: $7,500-$15,000).
Purpose and activities: Small grants (averaging $10,000) to support projects designed to ensure civil rights and civil liberties, encourage self-help, and promote equality of opportunity for the urban and rural poor; giving also to promote appreciation for the arts; grants to groups organizing for change at the community level, as well as to organizations seeking new ways to deliver services. Grants sometimes made outside the New York City area to organizations that do not have access to larger sources of funding. Occasional larger grants to projects or institutions of personal interest to the trustees.
Types of support: Operating budgets, seed money, general purposes, matching funds, special projects.
Limitations: Giving primarily in New York, NY. No grants to individuals, or for building or endowment funds, scholarships, or fellowships; no loans.
Publications: Annual report, application guidelines.
Application information: Contributes only to pre-selected organizations. Applications not accepted.
Board meeting date(s): Spring and fall
Write: Nanette Falkenberg, Pres., Joint Foundation Support
Officers and Trustees: John H. Gutfreund, Pres.; Lawrence B. Buttenwieser, Secy.-Treas.
Number of staff: 3 full-time professional; 3 full-time support.
Employer Identification Number: 136227515

4513
Edna and Monroe C. Gutman Foundation, Inc. ⌑
c/o Hertz, Herson & Co.
Two Park Ave.
New York 10016

Incorporated in 1947 in NY.
Donor(s): Edna C. Gutman,† Monroe C. Gutman.†
Foundation type: Independent
Financial data (yr. ended 06/30/89): Assets, $3,021,281 (M); expenditures, $243,767, including $204,500 for 9 grants (high: $160,000; low: $1,000).
Purpose and activities: Grants largely for a hospital and secondary and higher education.
Application information: Contributes only to pre-selected organizations. Applications not accepted.
Officers: Margaret S. Nathan, Pres.; Cyrus Nathan, V.P. and Secy.; Philip Kimmel, V.P.
Employer Identification Number: 136094013

4514
Irwin & Marjorie Guttag Foundation, Inc. ⌑
575 Park Ave.
New York 10021

Established in 1956 in NY.
Donor(s): Irwin Guttag, Marjorie Guttag.
Foundation type: Independent
Financial data (yr. ended 12/31/88): Assets, $2,054,857 (M); expenditures, $90,712, including $79,809 for 31 grants (high: $40,000; low: $25).
Purpose and activities: Support primarily for Jewish concerns.
Limitations: Giving primarily in New York, NY. No grants to individuals.
Application information: Contributes only to pre-selected organizations. Applications not accepted.
Officers: Irwin Guttag, Pres. and Secy.; Marjorie Guttag, V.P. and Treas.
Employer Identification Number: 136061339

4515
Stella and Charles Guttman Foundation, Inc. ▼
595 Madison Ave., Suite 1604
New York 10022 (212) 371-7082

Incorporated in 1959 in NY.
Donor(s): Charles Guttman,† Stella Guttman.†
Foundation type: Independent
Financial data (yr. ended 12/31/88): Assets, $20,704,369 (M); expenditures, $1,359,795, including $1,110,000 for 109 grants (high:

$300,000; low: $500; average: $1,000-$10,000).
Purpose and activities: Support for organizations providing social, physical, medical, mental health, cultural and educational services. The foundation has also supported ongoing programs, such as its college scholarship program which provides annual grants to 20 liberal arts colleges. Support also for a limited number of charities that conduct activities in the state of Israel.
Types of support: Capital campaigns, general purposes, operating budgets, special projects.
Limitations: Giving primarily in the New York, NY, metropolitan area. No support for religious organizations for religious purposes, public interest litigation, or anti-vivisectionist causes. No grants to individuals, or for foreign travel or foreign study.
Publications: Program policy statement, grants list, informational brochure (including application guidelines).
Application information: Application form not required.
Initial approach: Letter
Copies of proposal: 1
Deadline(s): None
Board meeting date(s): As required
Write: Elizabeth Olofson, Exec. Dir.
Officers and Directors:* Abraham Rosenberg,* Pres.; Edgar H. Brenner,* V.P.; Sonia Rosenberg,* Secy.; Robert S. Gassman,* Treas.; Elizabeth Olofson,* Exec. Dir.; Charles S. Brenner, Peter A. Herbert, Ernest Rubenstein.
Number of staff: 2 part-time professional.
Employer Identification Number: 136103039

4516
H & M Charitable Fund, Inc. ⌑
1567 East Ninth St.
Brooklyn 11230 (718) 998-1951

Established in 1984 in NY.
Foundation type: Independent
Financial data (yr. ended 10/31/88): Assets, $68,937 (M); gifts received, $500,072; expenditures, $600,054, including $600,000 for 4 grants (high: $250,000; low: $100,000).
Purpose and activities: Support for religious schools of the Jewish faith.
Limitations: Giving primarily in NY.
Application information: Application form not required.
Deadline(s): None
Write: Harry Muller, Trustee
Trustees: Harry Muller, Hyman Muller.
Employer Identification Number: 112720493

4517
Charlotte Cuneen Hackett Charitable Trust
c/o Marine Midland Bank, N.A.
250 Park Ave.
New York 10177 (212) 503-2779

Established in 1971.
Donor(s): Charlotte Cuneen Hackett.†
Foundation type: Independent
Financial data (yr. ended 12/31/89): Assets, $1,684,886 (M); expenditures, $141,778, including $119,277 for 15 grants (high: $25,000; low: $300).
Purpose and activities: Giving for a cultural center and youth agencies, with emphasis on a youth center building.
Types of support: Continuing support, lectureships, renovation projects.
Limitations: Giving limited to Dutchess County, NY.
Publications: Multi-year report, 990-PF.
Application information: Contributes only to pre-selected organizations. Applications not accepted.
Write: Peter B. Miller, V.P., Marine Midland Bank, N.A.
Co-Trustees: John J. Gartland, Jr., Marine Midland Bank, N.A.
Number of staff: None.
Employer Identification Number: 237215233

4518
Hagedorn Fund ▼
c/o Manufacturers Hanover Trust Co.
270 Park Ave.
New York 10017 (212) 270-9107

Trust established in 1953 in NY.
Donor(s): William Hagedorn.†
Foundation type: Independent
Financial data (yr. ended 12/31/89): Assets, $20,487,405 (M); expenditures, $1,558,640, including $1,110,000 for 114 grants (high: $85,000; low: $1,000; average: $5,000-$10,000).
Purpose and activities: Support for higher and secondary education, and church support; grants also for hospitals and health agencies, AIDS programs and medical research, the aged, youth agencies, social welfare, community funds, and cultural organizations.
Types of support: Operating budgets, annual campaigns, building funds, capital campaigns, general purposes.
Limitations: Giving limited to the New York, NY, metropolitan area, including NJ and CT. No grants to individuals, or for continuing support, seed money, emergency funds, deficit financing, endowment funds, matching gifts, scholarships, fellowships, research, special projects, publications, or conferences; no loans.
Application information: Application form not required.
Initial approach: Proposal
Copies of proposal: 1
Deadline(s): Submit proposal preferably in Nov.; deadline Nov. 15
Board meeting date(s): Dec.
Final notification: 1 month
Write: Robert Rosenthal, V.P., Manufacturers Hanover Trust Co.
Trustees: William J. Fischer, Jr., Charles B. Lauren, Manufacturers Hanover Trust Co.
Number of staff: 5
Employer Identification Number: 136048718

4519
Margaret Voorhies Haggin Trust in Memory of Her Late Husband, James Ben Ali Haggin ⌑ ☆
c/o The Bank of New York
48 Wall St.
New York 10015

Trust established in 1938 in NY.
Donor(s): Margaret Voorhies Haggin.†
Foundation type: Independent
Financial data (yr. ended 12/31/88): Assets, $13,816,253 (M); expenditures, $681,406, including $620,612 for 13 grants (high: $334,295; low: $2,600).
Purpose and activities: Giving primarily for higher education and a hospital.
Limitations: Giving limited to KY.
Trustees: Laura C. Christianson, The Bank of New York.
Employer Identification Number: 136078494

4520
Hahn Family Foundation ⌑
1800 M & T Plaza
Buffalo 14203 (716) 885-4931

Established in 1965.
Donor(s): Charles Hahn.†
Foundation type: Independent
Financial data (yr. ended 12/31/87): Assets, $1,806,228 (M); gifts received, $24,650; expenditures, $92,627, including $86,600 for 76 grants (high: $8,500; low: $100; average: $2,500).
Purpose and activities: Emphasis on ecology, particularly in the areas of renewable energy sources, organic farming, preservation of farmland, and waste management; support also for local organizations of various types.
Types of support: General purposes, matching funds, publications, seed money, special projects.
Limitations: Giving primarily in Buffalo and Erie County, NY. No support for organizations eligible for membership in, but not belonging to, the United Way. No grants to individuals.
Publications: Application guidelines.
Application information: Application form not required.
Initial approach: Letter or proposal
Copies of proposal: 1
Write: Anne D. Hahn, Trustee
Trustees: Anne D. Hahn, Anne H. Hahn, Charles D. Hahn, Charles J. Hahn, Eric S. Hahn.
Number of staff: 1 part-time support.
Employer Identification Number: 166128499

4521
Mary P. Dolciani Halloran Foundation ⌑ ☆
c/o Wormser, Kiely, Alessandroni et al
100 Park Ave.
New York 10017-5516

Established in 1982.
Donor(s): Mary P. Dolciani Halloran.†
Foundation type: Independent
Financial data (yr. ended 12/31/88): Assets, $1,762,062 (M); gifts received, $250,415; expenditures, $426,558, including $375,500 for 11 grants (high: $302,000; low: $500).
Purpose and activities: Giving primarily for higher education; support also for cancer care and religious schools.
Types of support: Matching funds.
Limitations: Giving primarily in Greenwich, CT, and NY. No grants to individuals.
Application information: Contributes only to pre-selected organizations. Applications not accepted.

Officers: James J. Halloran, Pres.; Eugene J. Callahan, V.P.; Concepcion G. Halloran, V.P.; Denise Halloran Thomas, V.P.
Employer Identification Number: 133147449

4522
D. A. Hamel Family Charitable Trust ⌑ ☆
Morgan Guaranty Trust Co. of NY
616 Madison Ave.
New York 10153-0001

Established in 1986 in NY.
Foundation type: Independent
Financial data (yr. ended 11/30/88): Assets, $3,563,658 (M); expenditures, $208,592, including $109,500 for 29 grants (high: $25,000; low: $500).
Purpose and activities: Support for an environmental conservation trust, a community fund, higher and other education, and social services.
Trustees: Dana A. Hamel, Kathryn P. Hamel, Morgan Guaranty Trust Co. of New York.
Employer Identification Number: 136873334

4523
Handy & Harman Foundation ⌑
850 Third Ave.
New York 10022

Foundation type: Company-sponsored
Financial data (yr. ended 12/31/87): Assets, $13,145 (M); gifts received, $149,000; expenditures, $146,790, including $146,720 for 181 grants (high: $36,300; low: $100).
Purpose and activities: Giving primarily to the United Way, for education, particularly higher education, civic affairs, and health.
Application information:
Initial approach: Letter
Deadline(s): None
Write: R.N. Daniel, Pres.
Officers and Directors:* R.N. Daniel,* Pres.; S.B. Mudd,* V.P.; G.P. Ekern, Secy.
Employer Identification Number: 237408431

4524
Irving A. Hansen Memorial Foundation ⌑ ☆
c/o Chemical Bank
30 Rockefeller Plaza
New York 10112-0002 (212) 621-2148

Established in 1983 in NY.
Donor(s): Irving A. Hansen.†
Foundation type: Independent
Financial data (yr. ended 7/31/87): Assets, $2,151,611 (M); gifts received, $243,904; expenditures, $109,171, including $52,000 for 6 grants (high: $12,000; low: $5,000).
Purpose and activities: Giving for medical education and research including cancer research.
Limitations: No grants to individuals.
Application information:
Initial approach: Letter
Deadline(s): None
Write: Ms. Diane McGuire
Trustees: Elizabeth H. Cutting, Louis B. Frost, Elizabeth Hansen, William F. Hibberd, Chemical Bank.
Employer Identification Number: 133177338

4525
Harbor Lights Foundation ⌑ ☆
85 Broad St.
New York 10004-2408

Established in 1980.
Donor(s): J. Fred Weintz, Jr.
Foundation type: Independent
Financial data (yr. ended 4/30/89): Assets, $1,275,897 (M); gifts received, $100,000; expenditures, $66,682, including $58,600 for 68 grants (high: $10,000; low: $75).
Purpose and activities: Support for higher education, health associations, Protestant churches, and conservation.
Limitations: Giving primarily in NY and CT. No grants to individuals.
Application information: Applications not accepted.
Trustee: H. Frederick Krimendahl II, Elisabeth B. Weintz, J. Fred Weintz, Jr.
Employer Identification Number: 133052490

4526
The Harding Educational and Charitable Foundation ⌑
c/o The Chase Manhattan Bank, N.A.
1211 Sixth Ave., 34th Fl.
New York 10036 (212) 730-3244

Trust established in 1945 in NY.
Donor(s): Henry J. Harding, Robert L. Harding.
Foundation type: Independent
Financial data (yr. ended 12/31/88): Assets, $3,399,899 (M); expenditures, $213,399, including $177,000 for 19 grants (high: $35,000; low: $1,000).
Purpose and activities: Giving primarily for Protestant churches, higher education, and conservation.
Limitations: Giving primarily in NY.
Application information:
Initial approach: Letter
Deadline(s): None
Write: Joyce Schwartz
Trustees: Arthur R. Douglass, The Chase Manhattan Bank, N.A.
Employer Identification Number: 136083440

4527
Harkness Ballet Foundation, Inc. ⌑ ☆
145 East 48th St., Suite 26C
New York 10017-0025

Established in 1986 in NY.
Donor(s): Rebekah Harkness.
Foundation type: Independent
Financial data (yr. ended 12/31/88): Assets, $9,079,137 (M); gifts received, $2,633,186; expenditures, $498,385, including $238,490 for 67 grants (high: $40,000; low: $150).
Purpose and activities: Giving for the performing arts, especially dance companies.
Limitations: No grants to individuals.
Application information:
Initial approach: Letter
Deadline(s): None
Write: Theodore S. Bartwink, Secy.-Treas.
Officers and Directors: Barrett G. Kreisberg, Pres.; Theodore S. Bartwink, Secy.-Treas.; Bernard E. Brandes, William A. Perlmuth.
Employer Identification Number: 131926551

4528
William Hale Harkness Foundation, Inc.
145 East 48th St., Suite 26C
New York 10017 (212) 755-5540

Established in 1936 in NY.
Foundation type: Independent
Financial data (yr. ended 12/31/88): Assets, $8,200,000 (M); expenditures, $500,000, including $432,000 for 80 grants.
Purpose and activities: Emphasis on the the performing arts.
Types of support: General purposes, lectureships, operating budgets, scholarship funds, special projects.
Limitations: No grants to individuals.
Application information: Application form not required.
Initial approach: In writing; no telephone calls
Copies of proposal: 1
Deadline(s): None
Board meeting date(s): Quarterly
Final notification: After meetings
Write: Theodore S. Bartwink, Exec. Dir.
Officers and Directors: Barnett G. Kriesberg, Pres.; William A. Perlmuth, V.P.; Theodore S. Bartwink, Exec. Dir.; Bernard Brandes.
Number of staff: 2 full-time professional.
Employer Identification Number: 131790755

4529
Gladys and Roland Harriman Foundation ▼
63 Wall St., 23rd Fl.
New York 10005 (212) 493-8182

Established in 1966 in NY.
Donor(s): Roland Harriman,† Gladys Harriman.†
Foundation type: Independent
Financial data (yr. ended 12/31/88): Assets, $69,094,898 (M); gifts received, $2,466,050; expenditures, $4,717,076, including $4,077,504 for 65 grants (high: $750,000; low: $1,000; average: $3,000-$50,000).
Purpose and activities: Giving primarily for education; support also for youth and social service agencies, and health agencies and hospitals.
Limitations: No grants to individuals.
Application information:
Initial approach: Letter
Copies of proposal: 1
Deadline(s): None
Board meeting date(s): Apr. and Oct.
Write: William F. Hibberd, Secy.
Officers and Directors:* Elbridge T. Gerry, Sr.,* Pres.; William Rich III, V.P.; William F. Hibberd, Secy.; William J. Corcoran, Treas.; Thomas F. Dixon, Terrence M. Farley, Elbridge T. Gerry, Jr., Edward H. Northrup.
Number of staff: 3
Employer Identification Number: 510193915

4530
Mary W. Harriman Foundation
63 Wall St., 23rd Fl.
New York 10005 (212) 493-8182

Trust established in 1925 in NY; incorporated in 1973.
Donor(s): Mary W. Harriman.†
Foundation type: Independent

Financial data (yr. ended 12/31/88): Assets, $16,041,620 (M); expenditures, $946,696, including $817,452 for 91 grants (high: $70,000; low: $1,000; average: $1,000-$10,000).
Purpose and activities: Emphasis on higher and secondary education, hospitals and health agencies, cultural programs, public policy, civic affairs, and social service and youth agencies.
Types of support: Annual campaigns, capital campaigns, general purposes, operating budgets.
Limitations: Giving primarily in the New York, NY, metropolitan area. No grants to individuals.
Publications: 990-PF.
Application information:
Initial approach: Proposal
Copies of proposal: 1
Deadline(s): Sept. 15
Board meeting date(s): Dec.
Final notification: 1 month
Write: William F. Hibberd, Secy.
Officers and Directors:* Kathleen L.H. Mortimer,* Pres.; William Rich III, V.P.; William F. Hibberd, Secy.; William J. Corcoran, Treas.; Mary A. Fisk, Elbridge T. Gerry, Sr., Pamela C. Harriman, Edward H. Northrop.
Number of staff: 2 full-time professional; 2 full-time support.
Employer Identification Number: 237356000

4531
W. Averell and Pamela C. Harriman Foundation ⌑
63 Wall St., 23rd Fl.
New York 10005

Established in 1969 in NY.
Donor(s): W. Averell Harriman.†
Foundation type: Independent
Financial data (yr. ended 12/31/87): Assets, $1,838,369 (M); gifts received, $379,300; expenditures, $177,172, including $107,500 for 24 grants (high: $20,000; low: $500).
Purpose and activities: Giving for general charitable purposes, including to cultural orgainzations and for international affairs.
Application information:
Initial approach: Proposal
Deadline(s): None
Write: William F. Hibberd, Secy.
Officers: Pamela C. Harriman,* Pres.; William Rich III, V.P.; William F. Hibberd, Secy.; William J. Corcoran, Treas.
Directors:* Kathleen L.H. Mortimer, Mary A. Fisk, Elbridge T. Gerry, John B. Madden.
Employer Identification Number: 510193921

4532
The John A. Hartford Foundation, Inc. ▼
55 East 59th St.
New York 10022 (212) 832-7788

Established in 1929; incorporated in 1942 in NY.
Donor(s): John A. Hartford,† George L. Hartford.†
Foundation type: Independent
Financial data (yr. ended 12/31/89): Assets, $259,328,174 (M); expenditures, $10,594,026, including $7,335,587 for 75 grants (high: $600,000; low: $5,000; average: $50,000-$200,000) and $288,148 for 216 employee matching gifts.
Purpose and activities: The foundation provides support through (1) the Aging and Health Program, to address the unique health needs of the elderly, including long-term care, the use of medication in chronic health problems, increasing the nation's geriatric research and training capability, and improving hospital outcomes for frail elderly inpatients; and (2) the Health Care Cost and Quality Program concerned with balancing the quality and cost of medical procedures, particularly by developing systems for assessing their appropriateness, quality, and value. The Health Care Financing Program and the John A. and George L. Hartford Fellowship Program were both terminated in 1985; the Hartford Geriatric Faculty Development Award Program was terminated in 1987.
Types of support: Operating budgets, continuing support, program-related investments, special projects, research, publications, conferences and seminars, loans.
Limitations: No grants to individuals, or for annual campaigns, seed money, emergency, capital, or endowment funds, or deficit financing.
Publications: Program policy statement, application guidelines.
Application information: No new grants to individuals will be awarded. Application form not required.
Initial approach: Letter or proposal
Copies of proposal: 1
Deadline(s): No set deadline, but initial inquiry should be made at least 6 months before funding is required
Board meeting date(s): Mar., May, Sept., and Dec.
Final notification: 6 weeks
Write: Richard S. Sharpe, Prog. Dir.
Officers: James D. Farley,* Chair.; William Corbus,* Vice-Chair.; Charles E. Murphy, Jr.,* Vice-Chair.; Robert H. Mulreany,* Secy.; Stephen C. Eyre, Exec. Dir. and Treas.; Samuel R. Gische, Finance Dir. and Controller; Richard S. Sharpe, Prog. Dir.
Trustees:* Richard Cramer, Michael D. Dingman, Alexander Laughlin, Charles Moeller, Jr., Nuala Pell, Norman Volk, Matthew E. Welsh.
Number of staff: 6 full-time professional; 6 full-time support.
Employer Identification Number: 131667057

4533
Alexander & Sima Hartman Family Foundation ⌑ ☆
3356 Perry Ave.
Bronx 10467-3204 (212) 655-1700

Donor(s): Alexander Hartman.
Foundation type: Independent
Financial data (yr. ended 10/31/88): Assets, $1,040,171 (M); gifts received, $277,000; expenditures, $122,140, including $121,588 for grants (high: $23,000).
Purpose and activities: Giving primarily for Jewish organizations, including temples and yeshivas.
Limitations: Giving primarily in NY.
Application information:
Initial approach: Letter
Deadline(s): None
Write: Alexander Hartman, Mgr.
Officer: Alexander Hartman, Mgr.
Employer Identification Number: 136277775

4534
Jesse and Dorothy Hartman Foundation ⌑
c/o Proskauer, Rose, Goetz and Mendelsohn
300 Park Ave.
New York 10022

Established in 1954 in NY.
Donor(s): Jesse Hartman.†
Foundation type: Independent
Financial data (yr. ended 12/31/88): Assets, $2,340,154 (M); expenditures, $138,744, including $123,500 for 6 grants (high: $53,000; low: $2,500).
Purpose and activities: Support primarily for the media arts and higher education.
Limitations: No grants to individuals.
Application information: Contributes only to pre-selected organizations. Applications not accepted.
Officers and Trustees: Margot Hartman Tenney, Pres.; Charles Looker, V.P.; Milton Mann, Secy.; Delbert Tenney.
Employer Identification Number: 066044501

4535
Hasbro Children's Foundation ▼
32 West 23rd St.
New York 10010 (212) 645-2400

Established in 1985 in RI.
Donor(s): Hasbro, Inc.
Foundation type: Company-sponsored
Financial data (yr. ended 12/30/88): Assets, $5,519,589 (M); gifts received, $1,750,000; expenditures, $1,880,382, including $1,719,843 for 54 grants (high: $150,000; low: $500; average: $5,000-$150,000).
Purpose and activities: Giving to improve the quality of life of children; emphasis on health, including pediatric AIDS, and special education, with focus on handicapped, abused, and neglected children, literacy, the impact of homelessness on children, minority education, and hunger. The Foundation contributes to direct service programs on a national basis, for children under the age of twelve.
Types of support: Seed money, special projects.
Limitations: No grants to individuals, or for operating expenses, or capital improvements.
Publications: Informational brochure (including application guidelines).
Application information: Application form not required.
Initial approach: Letter and proposal
Copies of proposal: 3
Deadline(s): Two months prior to meeting
Board meeting date(s): Feb., June, and Oct.
Final notification: 1 week following meeting
Write: Eve Weiss, Exec. Dir.
Officers and Trustees: Ellen Block, Chair.; Barry J. Alperin, Secy.; Eve Weiss, Exec. Dir.; Carole Lewis Anderson, William Birenbaum, Roger Hart, Alan G. Hassenfeld, Samuel Katz,

Jerome Lowenstein, Alvin Poussaint, Lee Salk, B.J. Seabury, William Whaley.
Number of staff: 1 full-time professional; 1 full-time support.
Employer Identification Number: 222570516

4536
Merrill G. and Emita E. Hastings Foundation ⌑
c/o Conceptual Planning, Inc.
245 Fifth Ave.
New York 10016 (212) 779-1300

Trust established in 1966 in NY.
Donor(s): Emita E. Hastings.†
Foundation type: Independent
Financial data (yr. ended 2/28/88): Assets, \$2,579,809 (M); expenditures, \$124,214, including \$58,900 for 36 grants (high: \$15,000; low: \$100; average: \$2,000).
Purpose and activities: Giving for cultural programs, including museums, and for education and conservation.
Limitations: Giving primarily in the New York, NY, area. No grants to individuals, or for endowment funds.
Publications: 990-PF.
Application information:
Initial approach: Letter
Copies of proposal: 1
Deadline(s): None
Board meeting date(s): As required
Write: Lee R. Robins, Accountant
Trustees: Elizabeth H. Peterfreund, Janis Peterfreund, Joshua Peterfreund, Liza Peterfreund.
Employer Identification Number: 136203465

4537
Margaret Milliken Hatch Charitable Trust ⌑
c/o The Bank of New York, Tax Dept.
48 Wall St.
New York 10015

Trust established in 1970 in NY.
Donor(s): Margaret Milliken Hatch.†
Foundation type: Independent
Financial data (yr. ended 10/31/89): Assets, \$9,563,785 (M); expenditures, \$2,117,210, including \$2,055,000 for 39 grants (high: \$300,000; low: \$4,000).
Purpose and activities: Emphasis on higher education, international welfare and understanding, and hospitals; support also for the aged, social service agencies, and Protestant churches. Grants almost entirely limited to institutions originally favored by creators of the trust.
Limitations: Giving primarily in NY and CT. No grants to individuals, or for building funds.
Application information:
Initial approach: Letter
Copies of proposal: 1
Deadline(s): Submit proposal in Jan. or June
Board meeting date(s): Apr. and Sept.
Write: Donna Daniels, V.P., The Bank of New York
Trustees: Rakia I. Hatch, Richard L. Hatch, The Bank of New York.
Employer Identification Number: 136330533

4538
Hausman Belding Foundation, Inc.
1430 Broadway
New York 10018 (212) 944-6040

Established in 1953.
Donor(s): Belding Heminway Co., Inc.
Foundation type: Company-sponsored
Financial data (yr. ended 12/31/88): Assets, \$866 (M); gifts received, \$401,861; expenditures, \$408,488, including \$408,448 for 175 grants (high: \$20,000; low: \$10; average: \$500-\$1,000).
Purpose and activities: Grants primarily for Jewish welfare funds; support also for hospitals, health agencies, cancer research, education, and child development and welfare.
Limitations: Giving primarily in NY.
Application information: Applications not accepted.
Write: Cynthia Grushack
Administrator: Jack Hausman.
Employer Identification Number: 136119189

4539
The Havens Relief Fund Society
105 East 22nd St., Suite 805
New York 10010 (212) 475-1990

Incorporated in 1870 in NY.
Donor(s): Charles G. Havens.†
Foundation type: Operating
Financial data (yr. ended 12/31/88): Assets, \$10,366,616 (M); expenditures, \$609,061, including \$406,429 for grants to individuals.
Purpose and activities: A private operating foundation established for "the relief of poverty and distress, and especially the affording of temporary relief to unobtrusive suffering endured by industrious or worthy persons." Income distributed by almoners, appointed by the Society, who are responsible for distribution of their respective grants among individual beneficiaries of their own selection in greater New York City.
Types of support: Grants to individuals.
Limitations: Giving limited to New York, NY. No support for institutions.
Application information: Individuals are not referred to almoners. Applications not accepted.
Board meeting date(s): Feb. and Nov.
Write: Mrs. Marilyn Lamarr, Exec. Dir.
Officers: Arthur V. Savage, Pres.; William S. Ellis, V.P.; Michael Loening, Secy.; Paul J. Brignola, Treas.
Number of staff: 2 full-time professional.
Employer Identification Number: 135562382

4540
Hawley Foundation for Children ⌑
Eight Medical Arts Ln.
Saratoga Springs 12866-1097
Application address: Chamber of Commerce Bldg., 494 Broadway, Saratoga Springs, NY 12866; Tel.: (518) 584-3255

Foundation type: Independent
Financial data (yr. ended 10/31/88): Assets, \$1,336,619 (M); expenditures, \$80,108, including \$18,693 for 13 grants (high: \$6,000; low: \$500; average: \$500-\$6,000) and \$56,650 for 80 grants to individuals (high: \$3,000; low: \$300).
Purpose and activities: Support for higher education and child welfare.
Types of support: Student aid, general purposes.
Limitations: Giving limited to Saratoga County, NY.
Application information: Application form required.
Initial approach: Telephone or written request
Write: Linda Toohey
Officers: Paul Rouillard, Pres.; Harry Snyder, V.P.; Walker Stroup, Secy.; Leo Roohan, Treas.
Trustee: Adirondack Trust Co.
Number of staff: None.
Employer Identification Number: 141340069

4541
Charles Hayden Foundation ▼
One Bankers Trust Plaza
130 Liberty St.
New York 10006 (212) 938-0790

Incorporated in 1937 in NY.
Donor(s): Charles Hayden.†
Foundation type: Independent
Financial data (yr. ended 09/30/89): Assets, \$155,023,000 (M); expenditures, \$7,668,000, including \$6,370,078 for 166 grants (high: \$250,000; low: \$2,250; average: \$5,000-\$100,000).
Purpose and activities: To assist young people; emphasis on helping to provide physical facilities and equipment for organizations primarily concerned with the mental, moral, and physical development of youth; some limited program support available for experimental projects with well-defined goals and the potential for replication by others.
Types of support: Building funds, equipment, land acquisition, matching funds, renovation projects, special projects, seed money, technical assistance.
Limitations: Giving limited to the New York, NY (including northern NJ), and Boston, MA, metropolitan areas. No support for fraternal groups, religious organizations for other than community youth-related projects, or hospitals, hospices, and projects essentially medical in nature. No grants to individuals, or for endowment funds, operating budgets, general support, continuing support, fellowships, annual campaigns, emergency funds, deficit financing, publications, or conferences; no loans.
Publications: Annual report (including application guidelines), application guidelines.
Application information: Application form not required.
Initial approach: Proposal
Copies of proposal: 1
Deadline(s): None
Board meeting date(s): Monthly
Final notification: 4 to 6 weeks
Write: William T. Wachenfeld, Pres.
Officers and Trustees:* William T. Wachenfeld,* Pres.; David B. Stone,* V.P.; Gilda G. Wray, V.P., Program; Howard F. Cerny,* Secy.; John L. Kidde,* Treas.; Andrew Ardito.
Number of staff: 3 full-time professional; 6 part-time professional; 1 full-time support.
Employer Identification Number: 135562237

4542
Fred Hazan Foundation, Inc. ⌘
224 West 35th St.
New York 10001 (212) 736-8350

Established in 1955 in NY.
Donor(s): Isaac M. Hazan, Victor Hazan, Aaron Hazan, Lawrence Hazan, Lloyd Sportswear, Inc.
Foundation type: Independent
Financial data (yr. ended 1/31/89): Assets, $369,695 (M); gifts received, $70,000; expenditures, $151,225, including $150,685 for grants.
Purpose and activities: Support for Jewish giving, medical research, hospitals, and the Sephardic Temple.
Limitations: No grants to individuals.
Application information:
Initial approach: Letter
Deadline(s): None
Write: Isaac M. Hazan, Trustee
Trustees: Aaron Hazan, Isaac M. Hazan, Lawrence Hazan, Victor Hazan.
Employer Identification Number: 136159194

4543
The Edward W. Hazen Foundation, Inc.
505 Eighth Ave., 23rd. Fl.
New York 10018 (212) 967-5920

Incorporated in 1925 in CT.
Donor(s): Edward Warriner Hazen,† Helen Russell Hazen,† Lucy Abigail Hazen,† Mary Hazen Arnold.†
Foundation type: Independent
Financial data (yr. ended 12/31/89): Assets, $10,000,000 (M); expenditures, $706,000, including $387,000 for 48 grants (high: $25,000; low: $250; average: $15,000).
Purpose and activities: "Support focused on advocacy, community and parent organizing, and community-based initiatives designed to foster effective schools for all students and to promote full partnerships for parents and communities in education reform and restructuring initiatives."
Types of support: Seed money, matching funds, special projects.
Limitations: No support for programs or projects in medicine or health sciences, engineering, law, or public and business administration. No grants to individuals, or for annual campaigns, deficit financing, capital or endowment funds, scholarships, or fellowships; no loans.
Publications: Biennial report, informational brochure (including application guidelines), grants list.
Application information: Request guidelines for detailed program and support limitations. Application form required.
Initial approach: Letter
Copies of proposal: 2
Deadline(s): Jan. 15 and July 15
Board meeting date(s): Apr. and Oct.
Final notification: 10 days
Write: Sharon B. King, Pres.
Officers and Trustees:* Mary L. Bundy,* Chair.; Sharon B. King,* Pres.; Edward M. Harris, Jr.,* V.P.; Vilma S. Martinez,* V.P.; Carol Anastasio,* Secy.; Harry Wugalter,* Treas.; Adrienne Y. Bailey, Jose A. Cardenas, Lewis Feldstein, Claire Guadiani, Barbara K. Hatton, Richard Schall.
Number of staff: 1 full-time professional; 1 full-time support; 1 part-time support.
Employer Identification Number: 060646671

4544
Joseph H. Hazen Foundation ⌘
645 Madison Ave.
New York 10022

Incorporated in 1957 in NY.
Donor(s): Joseph H. Hazen.
Foundation type: Independent
Financial data (yr. ended 12/31/88): Assets, $1,675,413 (M); expenditures, $257,785, including $243,490 for 22 grants (high: $50,000; low: $250).
Purpose and activities: Emphasis on Jewish welfare funds, museums and other cultural organizations, and educational institutions; support also for hospitals.
Limitations: Giving primarily in New York, NY, and Israel. No grants to individuals.
Application information:
Initial approach: Letter
Officers and Directors: Joseph H. Hazen, Pres.; Cynthia H. Polsky, V.P.; Robert Anthoine, Secy.; Lita A. Hazen.
Employer Identification Number: 136161536

4545
The Hearst Foundation, Inc. ▼
888 Seventh Ave.
New York 10106-0057 (212) 586-5404
Address for applicants from west of the Mississippi River: Thomas Eastham, V.P. and Western Dir., 90 New Montgomery St., Suite 1212, San Francisco, CA 94105; Tel.: (415) 543-0400

Incorporated in 1945 in NY.
Donor(s): William Randolph Hearst.†
Foundation type: Independent
Financial data (yr. ended 12/31/89): Assets, $136,000,000 (M); expenditures, $6,100,000, including $5,571,000 for 271 grants (high: $250,000; low: $5,000; average: $15,000-$35,000).
Purpose and activities: Giving for programs to aid poverty-level and minority groups, educational programs with emphasis on private secondary and higher education, health-delivery systems, and cultural programs with records of public support. Organizations serving larger geographic areas generally favored over those of a narrow community nature.
Types of support: Special projects, scholarship funds, research, endowment funds, general purposes, matching funds, operating budgets.
Limitations: Giving limited to the U.S. and its territories. No support for political purposes. No grants to individuals or for the purchase of tickets, tables, or advertising for fundraising events.
Publications: Program policy statement, application guidelines.
Application information: Application form not required.
Initial approach: Letter or proposal
Copies of proposal: 1
Deadline(s): None
Board meeting date(s): Mar., June, Sept., and Dec.
Final notification: 4 to 6 weeks
Write: Robert M. Frehse, Jr., Exec. Dir. (east of the Mississippi River); Thomas Eastham, V.P. and Western Dir. (west of the Mississippi River)
Officers and Directors:* George R. Hearst, Jr.,* Pres.; Thomas Eastham, V.P. and Western Dir.; Robert M. Frehse, Jr., V.P. and Exec. Dir.; Harvey L. Lipton,* V.P. and Secy.; Frank A. Bennack, Jr.,* V.P.; Millicent H. Boudjakdji,* V.P.; Richard E. Deems,* V.P.; John R. Hearst, Jr.,* V.P.; Randolph A. Hearst, V.P.; William R. Hearst, Jr.,* V.P.; J. Kingsbury-Smith,* V.P.; Frank Massi,* V.P.; Gilbert C. Maurer,* V.P.; Raymond J. Petersen,* V.P.; Franklin C. Snyder,* V.P.; Ralph J. Cuomo, Treas.
Number of staff: 10 full-time professional; 4 full-time support; 1 part-time support.
Employer Identification Number: 136161746

4546
William Randolph Hearst Foundation ▼
888 Seventh Ave., 27th Fl.
New York 10106-0057 (212) 586-5404
Address for applicants from west of the Mississippi River: Thomas Eastham, V.P. and Western Dir., 90 New Montgomery St., Suite 1212, San Francisco, CA 94105; Tel.: (415) 543-0400

Incorporated in 1948 in CA.
Donor(s): William Randolph Hearst.†
Foundation type: Independent
Financial data (yr. ended 12/31/89): Assets, $297,000,000 (M); expenditures, $11,600,000, including $8,387,500 for 271 grants (high: $1,000,000; low: $5,000; average: $15,000-$35,000).
Purpose and activities: Programs to aid poverty-level and minority groups, educational programs with emphasis on private secondary and higher education, health delivery systems, and cultural programs with records of public support. Organizations serving larger geographic areas are generally favored over those of a narrow community nature. Support also through two independent scholarship programs: Journalism Awards Program and United States Senate Youth Program.
Types of support: Endowment funds, research, scholarship funds, matching funds, general purposes, special projects, operating budgets.
Limitations: Giving limited to the U.S. and its territories. No support for political purposes. No grants to individuals, or for the purchase of tickets, tables, or advertising for fundraising events.
Publications: Program policy statement, application guidelines.
Application information: Application form not required.
Initial approach: Letter or proposal
Copies of proposal: 1
Deadline(s): None
Board meeting date(s): Mar., June, Sept., and Dec.
Final notification: 4 to 6 weeks
Write: Robert M. Frehse, Jr., Exec. Dir. (east of the Mississippi River); Thomas Eastham,

V.P. and Western Dir. (west of the Mississippi River)
Officers and Directors:* Randolph A. Hearst,* Pres.; Thomas Eastham, V.P. and Western Dir.; Robert M. Frehse, Jr., V.P. and Exec. Dir.; Harvey L. Lipton,* V.P. and Secy.; Frank A. Bennack, Jr.,* V.P.; Millicent H. Boudjakdji,* V.P.; Richard E. Deems,* V.P.; George R. Hearst, Jr.,* V.P.; John R. Hearst, Jr.,* V.P.; William R. Hearst, Jr.,* V.P.; J. Kingsbury-Smith,* V.P.; Frank Massi,* V.P.; Gilbert C. Maurer,* V.P.; Raymond J. Petersen,* V.P.; Franklin C. Snyder,* V.P.; Ralph J. Cuomo, Treas.
Number of staff: 10 full-time professional; 4 full-time support; 1 part-time support.
Employer Identification Number: 136019226

4547
Heathcote Art Foundation, Inc. ☆
3 South Eastway
Bronxville 10166

Incorporated in 1981 in NY.
Foundation type: Operating
Financial data (yr. ended 10/31/88): Assets, $1,795,670 (M); expenditures, $56,196, including $5,000 for 1 grant.
Purpose and activities: "To promote and encourage the arts and interest in the arts in all matters."
Application information:
Initial approach: Letter
Deadline(s): None
Write: Mercy Bona Pavelic, Pres.
Officers: Mercy Bona Pavelic, Pres.; Lorraine Miles, V.P.; Josephine Newsom, Secy.
Employer Identification Number: 136213535

4548
Hebrew Technical Institute ⌑
c/o Murphy, Hauser, O'Connor & Quinn
469 Seventh Ave.
New York 10018
Application address: Anita Goodberg, Lawrence Properties, 855 Ave. of the Americas, New York, NY, 10021

Established in 1884.
Foundation type: Independent
Financial data (yr. ended 12/31/86): Assets, $2,943,922 (M); gifts received, $18,062; expenditures, $173,405, including $158,114 for grants.
Purpose and activities: Giving primarily to organizations in the field of vocational education.
Limitations: Giving primarily in NY.
Application information:
Deadline(s): None
Officer and Directors: Robert Korn, Secy.; Lawrence A. Benenson, Seth Dubin, Myron S. Falk, Jr., Irving Lipkowitz, John R. Menke, Herbert A. Raisler, Hyman B. Ritchin, Mrs. Frederick Rose, Robert Rosenthal.
Employer Identification Number: 135562240

4549
The Heckscher Foundation for Children ▼
17 East 47th St.
New York 10017 (212) 371-7775

Incorporated in 1921 in NY.
Donor(s): August Heckscher.†
Foundation type: Independent
Financial data (yr. ended 12/31/88): Assets, $32,347,906 (M); expenditures, $1,542,773, including $1,447,703 for 116 grants (high: $100,000; low: $1,000; average: $100-$25,000).
Purpose and activities: To promote the welfare of children; grants particularly for child welfare and family service agencies, education, recreation, music and the performing arts, health and hospitals, summer youth programs and camps, and aid to the handicapped.
Types of support: Seed money, emergency funds, building funds, equipment, land acquisition, renovation projects, special projects, scholarship funds.
Limitations: Giving primarily in the greater New York, NY, area. No grants to individuals, or for operating budgets, annual campaigns, deficit financing, fellowships, or endowment funds; no loans.
Publications: Application guidelines.
Application information: Application form not required.
Initial approach: Letter or proposal
Copies of proposal: 1
Deadline(s): None
Board meeting date(s): Monthly except July and Aug.
Final notification: 1 month
Write: Virginia Sloane, Pres.
Officers and Trustees:* Louis Smadbeck,* Chair.; Virginia Sloane,* Pres.; Howard G. Sloane,* V.P. and Treas.; William D. Hart, Jr.,* Secy.; Mrs. J. Clarence Davis, Jr., Richard N. Kerst, John D. MacNeary, Gail Meyers, John M. O'Mara, Howard Grant Sloane, Arthur J. Smadbeck, Mina Smadbeck, Paul Smadbeck, Florence Wallach.
Number of staff: 1 full-time professional; 1 part-time professional; 1 part-time support.
Employer Identification Number: 131820170

4550
Heineman Foundation for Research, Educational, Charitable and Scientific Purposes, Inc. ⌑
c/o Brown Brothers Harriman & Co.
59 Wall St.
New York 10005

Incorporated in 1947 in DE.
Donor(s): Dannie N. Heineman.†
Foundation type: Independent
Financial data (yr. ended 12/31/88): Assets, $6,965,365 (M); expenditures, $327,655, including $295,000 for grants.
Purpose and activities: Support for research programs in mathematical sciences and medicine; grants for higher education, Jewish giving, specialized libraries (including the Heineman Library of Rare Books and Manuscripts given to The Pierpont Morgan Library, New York), music schools and two annual physics awards.
Application information: Contributes only to pre-selected organizations. Applications not accepted.
Board meeting date(s): Sept.-Oct.
Officers: David Rose, Pres.; Agnes Gautier, Esq., V.P.; Ann R. Podlipny, Secy.; Simon M.D. Rose, Treas.
Directors: Sibylle Evelt, Robert O. Fehr, James H. Heineman, Marian Rose, Hans Tauber, M.D.
Employer Identification Number: 136082899

4551
Heller Brothers Foundation, Inc. ☆
600 Madison Ave.
New York 10022-1615

Foundation type: Independent
Financial data (yr. ended 8/31/89): Assets, $1,011,743 (M); expenditures, $93,939, including $92,308 for 30 grants (high: $30,000; low: $100).
Purpose and activities: Giving primarily to Jewish welfare and religious organizations; support also for hospitals, health associations, and the performing arts.
Limitations: Giving primarily in FL and New York, NY.
Application information: Applications not accepted.
Write: James Heller, Secy.
Officers: Seymour Heller, Pres.; James Heller, Secy.
Number of staff: None.
Employer Identification Number: 136108261

4552
Hellman Family Foundation ⌑
c/o Barry M. Strauss Assoc.
245 Fifth Ave., Suite 1102
New York 10016-8775

Established in 1983 in CA.
Foundation type: Independent
Financial data (yr. ended 11/30/87): Assets, $219 (L); gifts received, $434,500; expenditures, $433,412, including $431,750 for 29 grants (high: $80,000; low: $1,750).
Purpose and activities: Support for higher education and cultural programs, social services and Jewish organizations.
Application information:
Deadline(s): None
Write: F. Warren Hellman
Officers and Directors*: Patricia C. Hellman,* Pres.; Marco Hellman, V.P.; Maureen Cantor, Secy.-Treas.; Patricia Hellman Gibbs, Richard Dwight Gibbs, F. Warren Hellman, Frances Hellman, Judith Hellman, Sabrina Hellman.
Employer Identification Number: 942880118

4553
The Harry B. Helmsley Foundation, Inc. ▼ ⌑
60 East 42nd St.
New York 10165

Incorporated in 1954 in NY.
Donor(s): Harry B. Helmsley.
Foundation type: Independent
Financial data (yr. ended 5/31/87): Assets, $31,496,487 (M); gifts received, $15,000,000; expenditures, $1,082,473, including

$1,044,200 for 19 grants (high: $875,000; low: $50; average: $100-$50,000).
Purpose and activities: Grants largely for hospitals, higher education, medical research, and religious organizations.
Application information:
Deadline(s): None
Officers and Directors: Harry B. Helmsley, Pres.; Leona M. Helmsley, V.P. and Treas.
Employer Identification Number: 136123336

4554
The Victor Herbert Foundation ⌑
c/o Burns, Summit, Rovins & Feldesman
445 Park Ave.
New York 10022

Established in 1969 in NY.
Foundation type: Independent
Financial data (yr. ended 04/30/89): Assets, $1,476,495 (M); gifts received, $5,000; expenditures, $135,059, including $102,850 for 46 grants (high: $20,000; low: $100).
Purpose and activities: Emphasis on promoting musical performances and cultural programs and higher education in music and the arts.
Limitations: Giving primarily in New York, NY. No grants to individuals.
Application information:
Deadline(s): None
Write: Herbert P. Jacoby, Pres.
Officers and Directors:* Herbert P. Jacoby,* Pres.; Arthur H. Schwartz,* V.P.; Carolyn B. Jacoby,* Secy.; Lois C. Schwartz.
Employer Identification Number: 237044623

4555
Harry Herskowitz Foundation, Inc.
c/o Dr. Ruth Skydell
975 Park Ave.
New York 10028

Established in 1958 in NY.
Foundation type: Independent
Financial data (yr. ended 11/30/88): Assets, $876,700 (M); expenditures, $135,742, including $126,849 for grants.
Purpose and activities: Support for education, Jewish welfare, hospitals, Israel, libraries, museums, and social services.
Types of support: Continuing support.
Application information: Applications not accepted.
Officers: Ruth H. Skydell, Pres. and Treas.; Adrian Skydell, V.P.; Harry Skydell, V.P.; Laurie S. Goldberg, Secy.
Employer Identification Number: 136115242

4556
Emy & Emil Herzfeld Foundation, Inc. ⌑
420 Lexington Ave., Suite 1745
New York 10170 (212) 682-2280

Established in 1952 in NY.
Foundation type: Independent
Financial data (yr. ended 12/31/88): Assets, $1,304,253 (M); expenditures, $91,459, including $71,700 for 66 grants (high: $4,000; low: $200; average: $500-$2,000).
Purpose and activities: Support for indigent young and indigent aged.
Limitations: Giving primarily in metropolitan NY area. No grants to individuals.
Application information:
Initial approach: Proposal
Deadline(s): None
Write: William Holm, Secy.
Officer and Directors: William Holm, Secy.; Emilie De Rohan Chandor, Jane H. Rowen, Joseph R. Rowen, Gary B. Schriener, Alice E. Schwartz.
Employer Identification Number: 136161598

4557
Hess Foundation, Inc. ▼ ⌑
1185 Ave. of the Americas
New York 10036 (212) 997-8500

Incorporated in 1954 in DE.
Donor(s): Leon Hess.
Foundation type: Independent
Financial data (yr. ended 11/30/88): Assets, $66,450,587 (M); gifts received, $2,111,240; expenditures, $3,743,059, including $3,725,944 for 61 grants (high: $296,250; low: $1,000; average: $1,000-$100,000).
Purpose and activities: Emphasis on higher education, a disaster relief fund, and hospitals; grants also for a football foundation, performing arts organizations, synagogues, and social welfare agencies.
Limitations: No grants to individuals.
Application information: Contributes only to pre-selected organizations. Applications not accepted.
Board meeting date(s): As required
Final notification: Varies
Write: Leon Hess, Pres.
Officers and Directors: Leon Hess, Pres.; Steven Gutman, V.P. and Secy.; Norma Hess, V.P. and Treas.; John B. Hess, V.P.
Number of staff: 1 full-time professional.
Employer Identification Number: 221713046

4558
Hettinger Foundation ⌑
c/o William R. Hettinger, Jr.
R.R. One, Box 50
Pawling 12564

Trust established in 1961 in NY.
Donor(s): Albert J. Hettinger, Jr.†
Foundation type: Independent
Financial data (yr. ended 12/31/88): Assets, $10,626,384 (M); gifts received, $50,000; expenditures, $553,722, including $470,471 for 21 grants (high: $260,000; low: $700).
Purpose and activities: Grants largely for higher and secondary education at certain schools with which there is a long-standing relationship, including scholarship funds; some support for welfare agencies.
Types of support: General purposes, scholarship funds.
Limitations: No grants to individuals.
Application information: Contributes only to pre-selected organizations. Applications not accepted.
Trustees: Betty Hettinger, James F. Hettinger, John Hettinger, William R. Hettinger.
Employer Identification Number: 136097726

4559
The DuBose and Dorothy Heyward Memorial Fund ⌑ ☆
c/o The Bank of New York, Tax Dept.
48 Wall St.
New York 10015 (212) 495-1177

Donor(s): Jenifer Heyward.†
Foundation type: Independent
Financial data (yr. ended 12/31/88): Assets, $2,434,577 (M); gifts received, $1,372,220; expenditures, $952,858, including $730,575 for 17 grants (high: $150,000; low: $35).
Purpose and activities: Grants to arts organizations and cancer research and treatment.
Types of support: General purposes.
Application information:
Initial approach: Letter
Deadline(s): None
Write: Kathleen Shoemaker
Trustees: Albert Cardinal Thacher, The Bank of New York.
Employer Identification Number: 136840999

4560
Hickrill Foundation, Inc. ⌑
147 East 48th St.
New York 10022

Incorporated in 1946 in NY.
Donor(s): The Norman Foundation, Frank A. Weil.
Foundation type: Independent
Financial data (yr. ended 12/31/88): Assets, $1,691,815 (M); expenditures, $156,836, including $134,678 for 31 grants (high: $50,000; low: $25).
Purpose and activities: Grants primarily for higher education, with emphasis on a school for government studies.
Application information:
Initial approach: Letter
Deadline(s): None
Write: Denie S. Weil, V.P.
Officers: Frank A. Weil, Pres.; Denie S. Weil, V.P.; Deborah W. Harrington, Secy.
Employer Identification Number: 136002949

4561
Jacob Hidary Foundation, Inc. ⌑
Ten West 33rd St.
New York 10001

Donor(s): M. Hidary Co., Inc., and members of the Hidary family.
Foundation type: Independent
Financial data (yr. ended 12/31/88): Assets, $981,331 (M); gifts received, $943,358; expenditures, $874,228, including $866,506 for 571 grants (high: $25,000; low: $18).
Purpose and activities: Support primarily for Jewish welfare and Jewish giving.
Limitations: Giving primarily in NY.
Application information:
Initial approach: Letter
Deadline(s): None
Write: Moses Hidary, V.P., or Abraham Hidary, Treas.
Officers: Moses Hidary, V.P.; Isaac Hidary, Secy.; Abraham Hidary, Treas.
Employer Identification Number: 136125420

4562
The Alex Hillman Family Foundation ☒
630 Fifth Ave.
New York 10111 (212) 265-3115

Incorporated in 1966 in NY.
Donor(s): Alex L. Hillman,† Rita K. Hillman.
Foundation type: Independent
Financial data (yr. ended 12/31/88): Assets, $16,996,301 (M); expenditures, $67,965, including $61,750 for 26 grants (high: $23,200; low: $100) and $4,070 for foundation-administered programs.
Purpose and activities: A private operating foundation; emphasis on the encouragement of the arts, including the fine and performing arts; support also for higher education.
Types of support: Operating budgets.
Limitations: Giving primarily in the New York, NY, metropolitan area. No grants to individuals, or for continuing support.
Publications: Annual report.
Application information: Application form not required.
Initial approach: Letter
Copies of proposal: 1
Deadline(s): None
Board meeting date(s): Semiannually
Final notification: 2 months
Write: Mrs. Rita K. Hillman, Pres.
Officers: Rita K. Hillman, Pres.; William M. Griffin, V.P.; Harold L. Schiff, Secy.-Treas.
Number of staff: None.
Employer Identification Number: 132560546

4563
Hilson Fund, Inc. ☒
c/o Wertheim Schroder Holdings, Inc.
787 Seventh Ave., 6th Fl.
New York 10019 (212) 492-6910

Established in 1947 in NY.
Donor(s): John S. Hilson, Mildred S. Hilson.
Foundation type: Independent
Financial data (yr. ended 11/30/88): Assets, $1,649,366 (M); expenditures, $135,367, including $121,563 for 37 grants (high: $60,333; low: $50).
Purpose and activities: Emphasis on the arts and hospitals, including medical research.
Limitations: Giving primarily in New York City, NY.
Application information:
Initial approach: Letter
Deadline(s): None
Write: John S. Hilson, V.P.
Officers: Mildred S. Hilson, Pres.; John S. Hilson, V.P.; Peter J. Repetti, Secy.; Howard D. Taylor, Treas.
Employer Identification Number: 136028783

4564
Grove W. & Agnes M. Hinman Charitable Foundation ☒
30 Broad St.
Hamilton 13346
Application address: P.O. Box 209, Hamilton, NY 13346; Tel.: (315) 824-1550

Established in 1970 in NY.
Foundation type: Independent
Financial data (yr. ended 4/30/88): Assets, $1,072,320 (M); expenditures, $79,088, including $18,636 for 5 grants (high: $9,000; low: $1,000) and $41,500 for 42 grants to individuals (high: $2,000; low: $500).
Purpose and activities: Support primarily for scholarships and health services.
Types of support: Student aid.
Limitations: Giving primarily in Morrisville, Hamilton, and Madison, NY.
Application information: Application form required.
Deadline(s): May 1
Write: Susan Schapiro, Trustee
Trustees: Robert Kallett, Raymond T. Ryan, Susan Schapiro, Frank O. White.
Employer Identification Number: 237194828

4565
The Richard L. Hirsch Foundation, Inc. ☆
c/o Welbilt Corp.
3333 New Hyde Park Rd.
New Hyde Park 11042-1205 (516) 365-5040

Incorporated in 1986 in NY.
Donor(s): Richard L. Hirsch.
Foundation type: Independent
Financial data (yr. ended 12/31/88): Assets, $1,525,242 (M); expenditures, $168,649, including $164,143 for 46 grants (high: $29,000; low: $50).
Purpose and activities: Giving primarily for Jewish religious, educational, and welfare organizations; support also for higher and other education.
Application information: Contributes only to pre-selected organizations. Applications not accepted.
Write: Richard Hirsch
Officers: Richard L. Hirsch, Pres.; David A. Hirsch, V.P. and Treas.; Joyce Hirsch, V.P.; Lawrence R. Gross, Secy.
Employer Identification Number: 133343606

4566
Irma T. Hirschl Trust for Charitable Purposes ▼ ☒
c/o Manufacturers Hanover Trust Co.
600 Fifth Ave.
New York 10020 (212) 957-1654

Trust established in 1973 in NY.
Donor(s): Irma T. Hirschl.†
Foundation type: Independent
Financial data (yr. ended 10/31/88): Assets, $30,634,369 (M); gifts received, $12,292; expenditures, $1,810,541, including $1,543,000 for 61 grants (high: $105,000; low: $4,000; average: $4,000-$110,000).
Purpose and activities: Grants primarily to eight medical schools for partial funding of selected medical research projects; annual medical scholarships to six designated medical schools; support also for 14 designated social service and health agencies.
Types of support: Research, scholarship funds.
Limitations: Giving primarily in New York, NY. No support for private foundations. No grants to individuals.
Application information: All applications submitted by designated medical schools. Application form required.
Deadline(s): Oct. 15
Final notification: After Dec. 10
Write: Uwe Linder, V.P., Manufacturers Hanover Trust Co.
Trustees: Manufacturers Hanover Trust Co.
Employer Identification Number: 136356381

4567
HKH Foundation ▼
33 Irving Place, 10th Fl.
New York 10003 (518) 352-7391

Foundation established in 1980 in NY.
Foundation type: Independent
Financial data (yr. ended 12/31/89): Assets, $31,468,554 (M); expenditures, $1,507,983, including $1,230,000 for 28 grants (high: $800,000; low: $5,000; average: $5,000-$25,000).
Purpose and activities: Major portion of funding earmarked for the Adirondack Historical Association; suggestions for funding priorities accepted in the following three additional areas only: 1) disarmament and the prevention of war; 2) civil liberties and human rights; and 3) environmental protection.
Types of support: Continuing support, general purposes, special projects.
Limitations: No grants to individuals.
Application information: The foundation does not solicit proposals. Applications not accepted.
Deadline(s): None
Board meeting date(s): Spring and fall
Final notification: Following board meeting
Write: Harriet Barlow
Staff: Harriet Barlow.
Number of staff: 1 part-time professional; 1 part-time support.
Employer Identification Number: 136784950

4568
The John H. Hobbs Charitable Trust ☒
466 Lexington Ave.
New York 10017-3140 (212) 421-1000

Established in 1984 in NY.
Donor(s): John H. Hobbs.
Foundation type: Independent
Financial data (yr. ended 12/31/88): Assets, $2,096,443 (M); gifts received, $33,643; expenditures, $64,044, including $60,000 for 3 grants (high: $40,000; low: $5,000).
Purpose and activities: Support primarily for higher education.
Limitations: No grants to individuals.
Application information: Contributes only to pre-selected organizations. Applications not accepted.
Trustee: John H. Hobbs.
Number of staff: None.
Employer Identification Number: 136847765

4569
A. W. Hoernle Foundation
c/o F.W. Lessing
Cross County Office Bldg., Rm. 603
Yonkers 10704

Established in 1978 in NY.
Donor(s): Adolph W. Hoernle.
Foundation type: Independent
Financial data (yr. ended 05/31/89): Assets, $6,126,283 (M); expenditures, $288,254, including $258,405 for 26 grants (high: $154,500; low: $80).

Purpose and activities: Support primarily for hospitals and health agencies, cultural programs, education, and social service agencies.
Limitations: Giving limited to NY and FL. No grants to individuals.
Application information: Application form not required.
Board meeting date(s): Annually
Write: Fred W. Lessing, Secy.-Treas.
Officers: Adolph W. Hoernle, Pres.; Fred W. Lessing, Secy.-Treas.
Number of staff: None.
Employer Identification Number: 132945331

4570
Marion O. & Maximilian Hoffman Foundation ⌘
Six Village Sq., Bldg. A
Glen Cove 11542

Established in 1984 in NY.
Foundation type: Independent
Financial data (yr. ended 06/30/88): Assets, $9,868,147 (M); expenditures, $790,475, including $555,000 for 5 grants (high: $250,000; low: $5,000).
Purpose and activities: Giving primarily to an animal medical center; support also for the arts, public television, and social services.
Limitations: Giving primarily in New York, NY. No grants to individuals.
Application information: Contributes only to pre-selected organizations. Applications not accepted.
Write: Ursula Niarakis, Pres.
Officer: Ursula C. Niarakis, Pres.
Employer Identification Number: 112697957

4571
Libby Holman Foundation, Inc. ☆
121 East 61st St.
New York 10021-8146 (212) 751-1583

Established in 1962.
Foundation type: Independent
Financial data (yr. ended 2/28/89): Assets, $1,183,058 (M); expenditures, $75,979, including $59,825 for 13 grants (high: $10,000; low: $2,500; average: $1,000-$10,000).
Purpose and activities: Giving primarily to organizations benefiting the aged and the handicapped; support also for secondary education and the arts.
Limitations: Giving primarily in New York, NY.
Application information: Application form not required.
Initial approach: Letter
Copies of proposal: 4
Deadline(s): 30 days prior to board meeting
Board meeting date(s): Jan.
Write: Jack Clareman, Pres.
Officers and Directors: Jack Clareman, Pres.; Anthony Reynolds, V.P.; Timothy H. Reynolds, V.P.; Lloyd S. Clareman, Secy.
Number of staff: 1 part-time professional.
Employer Identification Number: 116037769

4572
Jacob L. and Lillian Holtzmann Foundation ⌘
c/o Holtzmann, Wise & Shepard
745 Fifth Ave.
New York 10151

Trust established in 1958 in NY.
Donor(s): Jacob L. Holtzmann,† Lillian Holtzmann,† Howard M. Holtzmann.
Foundation type: Independent
Financial data (yr. ended 12/31/88): Assets, $4,039,528 (M); gifts received, $66,000; expenditures, $136,917, including $90,550 for 30 grants (high: $35,000; low: $100).
Purpose and activities: Grants largely for Jewish welfare funds and higher education, including a theological seminary.
Limitations: Giving primarily in NY. No grants to individuals.
Application information: Contributes only to pre-selected organizations. Applications not accepted.
Trustees: Howard M. Holtzmann, Benjamin C. O'Sullivan, Susan H. Richardson.
Employer Identification Number: 136174349

4573
Homeland Foundation, Inc. ⌘ ☆
c/o Kelley, Drye & Warren
101 Park Ave.
New York 10178 (212) 808-7800

Incorporated in 1938 in NY.
Donor(s): Chauncey Stillman,† and others.
Foundation type: Independent
Financial data (yr. ended 04/30/89): Assets, $487,805 (M); gifts received, $310,000; expenditures, $358,199, including $353,086 for 28 grants (high: $274,886; low: $500).
Purpose and activities: Giving predominantly for Roman Catholic church support, including welfare organizations in the U.S. and abroad and educational institutions.
Types of support: General purposes, building funds, operating budgets, lectureships, scholarship funds.
Limitations: No grants to individuals.
Application information: Application form not required.
Initial approach: Letter
Deadline(s): None
Officers and Trustees:* E. Lisk Wyckoff, Jr., Chair. and Treas.; Theodora Stillman Budnik, V.P.; Msgr. Eugene V. Clark, Secy.; Fr. Ralph F. Caamano, John J. Costello, Charles B. Grimes, Louis E. Lehrman, Carl Schmitt, Charles Scribner III.
Employer Identification Number: 136113816

4574
Josephine Lawrence Hopkins Foundation ⌘
61 Broadway, Suite 2912
New York 10006

Incorporated in 1968 in NY.
Donor(s): Josephine H. Graeber.†
Foundation type: Independent
Financial data (yr. ended 12/31/88): Assets, $3,499,394 (M); expenditures, $276,244, including $189,000 for 36 grants (high: $25,000; low: $1,000).
Purpose and activities: Emphasis on hospitals and medical research, Roman Catholic church support, animal welfare, youth agencies, and cultural programs including the performing arts.
Limitations: Giving primarily in NY. No grants to individuals; no loans.
Application information: Contributes only to pre-selected organizations. Applications not accepted.
Board meeting date(s): Once a year, usually in Oct.
Officers and Directors: Ivan Obolensky, Pres. and Treas.; Vera L. Colage, V.P.; Meredith N. Stiles, Jr., V.P.; Susan H. Whitmore, V.P.
Employer Identification Number: 136277593

4575
Horncrest Foundation, Inc.
Six Sleator Dr.
Ossining 10502 (914) 941-5533

Established in 1960 in NY.
Foundation type: Independent
Financial data (yr. ended 9/30/89): Assets, $2,255,296 (M); gifts received, $5,095; expenditures, $201,963, including $184,095 for 9 grants (high: $105,000; low: $1,000).
Purpose and activities: Grants for education, with emphasis on a university loan program; support also for social services and the disadvantaged, cultural programs, medical education, and organizations that develop interest in governmental issues, including arms control, housing, and civic affairs.
Types of support: General purposes, matching funds, scholarship funds.
Publications: Annual report.
Application information: Application form not required.
Initial approach: Proposal
Deadline(s): None
Write: Lawrence Blau, Pres.
Officers and Directors: Lawrence Blau, Pres.; Olivia Blau, V.P. and Secy.
Employer Identification Number: 136021261

4576
Gedale B. and Barbara S. Horowitz Foundation ⌘
c/o Solomon Brothers, Inc.
One New York Plaza
New York 10004

Established in 1970 in NY.
Donor(s): Gedale B. Horowitz, Gedale B. Horowitz Charitable Lead Trust.
Foundation type: Independent
Financial data (yr. ended 06/30/89): Assets, $2,521,222 (M); gifts received, $187,050; expenditures, $568,355, including $567,650 for 29 grants (high: $220,000; low: $50).
Purpose and activities: Grants primarly for Jewish giving, including welfare and temple support; support also for higher and legal education, a medical center, and culture.
Types of support: General purposes.
Limitations: Giving primarily in New York, NY, and Nassau County. No grants to individuals.
Application information: Contributes only to pre-selected organizations. Applications not accepted.
Officers and Directors:* Gedale B. Horowitz,* Pres.; David Horowitz,* V.P.;

William Donovan,* Secy.; Barbara S. Horowitz,* Treas.; Ruth Horowitz, Seth Horowitz.
Employer Identification Number: 237101730

4577
The Houghton Foundation, Inc. ⌑
80 East Market St.
Corning 14830 (607) 962-6876

Incorporated in 1955 in NY.
Donor(s): Arthur A. Houghton, Jr.,† Amory Houghton.†
Foundation type: Independent
Financial data (yr. ended 11/30/88): Assets, $1,318,479 (M); expenditures, $179,214, including $169,000 for 15 grants (high: $50,000; low: $1,000).
Purpose and activities: Support for human services, hospitals, education, and Protestant churches.
Limitations: Giving primarily in Corning, NY.
Application information: Applications not accepted.
Officers and Trustees: Amory Houghton, Jr.,* Pres.; Alanson B. Houghton II,* V.P.; James R. Houghton,* V.P.; Rowland Stebbins III,* Secy.-Treas.; Laura R. Houghton.
Employer Identification Number: 166028719

4578
Stewart W. & Willma C. Hoyt Foundation
300 Security Mutual Bldg.
80 Exchange St.
Binghamton 13901 (607) 722-6706

Established in 1970 in NY.
Donor(s): Willma C. Hoyt.†
Foundation type: Independent
Financial data (yr. ended 12/31/89): Assets, $12,060,014 (M); expenditures, $611,711, including $480,887 for 37 grants (high: $85,000; low: $210; average: $1,500-$30,000).
Purpose and activities: Giving for the arts and humanities, education, health, and social and human services, with preference for capital campaigns, special projects, seed money, and operating expenses.
Types of support: General purposes, building funds, matching funds, seed money, special projects, operating budgets, continuing support, emergency funds, equipment, technical assistance, consulting services, scholarship funds, conferences and seminars, capital campaigns.
Limitations: Giving limited to Broome County, NY. No support for religious purposes. No grants to individuals, or for annual campaigns, deficit financing, land acquisition, general endowments, research, or publications; no loans.
Publications: Annual report, informational brochure (including application guidelines).
Application information: No grants considered at Jan. meeting. Application form required.
Initial approach: Telephone or letter
Copies of proposal: 1
Deadline(s): The 1st of months prior to board meetings
Board meeting date(s): Bimonthly, beginning in Jan.; no grants awarded in Jan.
Final notification: 1 to 3 days following board meetings
Write: Judith C. Peckham, Exec. Dir.
Officers and Directors:* John F. Russell,* Chair.; Jane M. Park,* Vice-Chair.; William Rincker,* Secy.-Treas.; Denise M. Balkas, Silvia Fenton, John M. Keeler, Albert Mamary.
Trustee: Chase Lincoln First Bank, N.A.
Number of staff: 1 full-time professional; 1 part-time support.
Employer Identification Number: 237072539

4579
The Charles Evans Hughes Memorial Foundation, Inc. ⌑
175 Water St., 10th Fl.
New York 10038-4924 (212) 269-2500

Incorporated in 1962 in NY.
Donor(s): Mrs. Chauncey L. Waddell,† Chauncey L. Waddell.†
Foundation type: Independent
Financial data (yr. ended 7/31/88): Assets, $8,000,000 (M); expenditures, $475,000, including $375,000 for 18 grants.
Purpose and activities: Support for organizations engaged in education, legal aid, and organizations combatting prejudice based on race, color, or religious belief.
Types of support: Continuing support, general purposes, research, scholarship funds, seed money.
Limitations: No grants to individuals.
Application information: Application form not required.
Copies of proposal: 6
Deadline(s): June 1
Board meeting date(s): Oct.
Write: Mitchel J. Valicenti, Pres.
Officers: Mitchel J. Valicenti,* Pres. and Treas.; William T. Gossett,* V.P.; Suzanne T. Reardon, Secy.
Directors:* H. Stuart Hughes, Marjory Hughes Johnson, Betty J. Stebman, Theodore H. Waddell.
Number of staff: None.
Employer Identification Number: 136159445

4580
Hugoton Foundation ▼
900 Park Ave.
New York 10021 (212) 734-5447

Established in 1981 in DE.
Donor(s): Wallace Gilroy.†
Foundation type: Independent
Financial data (yr. ended 12/31/88): Assets, $24,494,312 (M); gifts received, $1,079,265; expenditures, $1,239,728, including $1,100,500 for 24 grants (high: $502,000; low: $1,500; average: $5,000-$25,000).
Purpose and activities: Giving primarily for hospitals, medical research, and equipment needs; some support for higher education.
Types of support: Equipment, special projects, research.
Limitations: Giving primarily in New York, NY, and Miami, FL.
Application information:
Initial approach: Proposal
Deadline(s): None
Board meeting date(s): As necessary
Final notification: 2 months
Write: Joan K. Stout, Pres.
Officers and Directors:* Joan K. Stout, Pres.; Arthur Jansen, V.P.; Joan M. Stout, Secy.; Jean C. Stout, Treas.; Frank S. Fejes.
Number of staff: None.
Employer Identification Number: 341351062

4581
Huguenot Society of America ☆
122 East 58th St.
New York 10022 (212) 755-0592

Established in 1883 in NY.
Foundation type: Independent
Financial data (yr. ended 2/28/89): Assets, $1,414,428 (M); gifts received, $7,975; expenditures, $98,302, including $30,000 for 25 grants to individuals of $1,200 each.
Purpose and activities: Giving limited to scholarships for higher education at listed colleges to descendants of Huguenots.
Types of support: Student aid.
Application information: Applications are made to universities. Application form required.
Initial approach: Letter
Deadline(s): None
Write: Mrs. N.P. Christy
Officers: Clifford V. Brokaw III, Pres.; Elizabeth M. Waite, Secy.; John H.G. Stuurman III, Treas.
Number of staff: 1 part-time support.
Employer Identification Number: 136117102

4582
Hultquist Foundation, Inc. ⌑
c/o Price, Miller, Evans & Flowers
Fenton Bldg.
Jamestown 14701 (716) 664-7414

Established in 1965 in NY.
Foundation type: Independent
Financial data (yr. ended 06/30/89): Assets, $6,860,874 (M); expenditures, $458,113, including $424,643 for 16 grants (high: $100,000; low: $1,000).
Purpose and activities: Giving primarily for a hospital, social services, and higher education.
Limitations: Giving primarily in Chautauqua County, NY.
Application information:
Initial approach: Letter
Deadline(s): June 1 and Dec. 1
Write: Thomas I. Flowers, Pres.
Officers and Directors:* Thomas I. Flowers,* Pres.; Robert E. Halsted,* V.P.; Charles H. Price,* V.P.; William L. Wright,* V.P.; Robert F. Rohm, Jr.,* Secy.-Treas.
Employer Identification Number: 160907729

4583
The Hunt Alternatives Fund
1255 Fifth Ave.
New York 10029 (212) 722-7606
Denver application address: 500 East 8th Ave., Suite 100, Denver, CO 80203; Tel.: (303) 839-1933

Established in 1981 in NY.
Donor(s): Helen Hunt, Swanee Hunt.
Foundation type: Independent
Financial data (yr. ended 11/30/89): Assets, $5,485,622 (L); expenditures, $1,262,744, including $1,051,272 for 99 grants (high: $20,000; low: $2,000) and $100,000 for loans.

Purpose and activities: Support for human services, particularly programs that offer opportunities to individuals who struggle against disenfranchisement, discrimination, violence, or poverty and are disadvantaged by mental, emotional, or contextual disabilities; recent emphasis has been on children and youth, empowerment of women, and the East Harlem community.
Types of support: Technical assistance, equipment, special projects, operating budgets, scholarship funds, seed money.
Limitations: Giving limited to the Denver, CO, Dallas, TX, and New York, NY, metropolitan areas. No support for federal, state, or municipal agencies, or cultural, educational, or religious projects except those concerned with the disabilities stated in the fund's purpose. No grants to individuals, or for institutional or general program needs.
Publications: Annual report, informational brochure (including application guidelines).
Application information: Application form not required.
Initial approach: Proposal
Copies of proposal: 1
Board meeting date(s): Apr., June, and Nov.
Final notification: Following board meeting
Write: Alice Radosh, Exec. Dir. for New York and Dallas applicants, at the NY address; Lauren Casteel for Denver applicants
Officers and Directors:* Alice Radosh,* Exec. Dir. (New York); Lauren Casteel,* Exec. Dir. (Denver); Helen Hunt, Swanee Hunt.
Number of staff: 2 part-time professional; 2 full-time support.
Employer Identification Number: 751763787

4584
Virginia Hunt Trust for Episcopal Charitable Institutions ☆
c/o Manufacturers Hanover Trust Co.
270 Park Ave.
New York 10017

Foundation type: Independent
Financial data (yr. ended 03/31/89): Assets, $2,429,563 (M); expenditures, $237,701, including $203,500 for 7 grants (high: $48,500; low: $5,000).
Purpose and activities: Giving limited to Episcopal charitable institutions, including a diocese, churches, a convent, and a hospital.
Limitations: Giving primarily in NY and VT. No grants to individuals.
Application information: Application form not required.
Initial approach: Letter
Deadline(s): None
Write: J.J. Kindred, III, V.P.
Trustees: Parker C. Risley, Manufacturers Hanover Trust Co.
Employer Identification Number: 237426415

4585
Graham Hunter Foundation, Inc. ⌘
c/o McGladrey & Pullen
1133 Sixth Ave., 26th Fl.
New York 10036
Application address: One East 42nd St., New York, NY 10017

Established in 1946 in NY.
Donor(s): Graham Hunter.†
Foundation type: Independent
Financial data (yr. ended 12/31/88): Assets, $1,399,458 (M); expenditures, $55,769, including $31,410 for 8 grants (high: $26,060; low: $150).
Purpose and activities: Grants primarily for higher education, including medical education; support also for cultural programs.
Limitations: No grants to individuals.
Application information: Application form not required.
Deadline(s): None
Write: Thomas G. Burke, V.P.
Officers: Carol Hunter Kelley, Pres.; William McClarene, V.P. and Secy.; Thomas G. Burke, V.P. and Treas.
Trustee: Thomas W. Burke.
Employer Identification Number: 136161726

4586
The Hurford Foundation ☆
c/o Townley & Updike
405 Lexington Ave.
New York 10174

Donor(s): John B. Hurford, Bea Associates.
Foundation type: Independent
Financial data (yr. ended 12/31/89): Assets, $808,741 (M); gifts received, $687,046; expenditures, $113,066, including $109,000 for 9 grants (high: $37,500; low: $1,000).
Purpose and activities: Giving primarily for higher education, youth, and cultural programs.
Types of support: General purposes.
Limitations: Giving primarily in New York, NY.
Application information: Contributes only to pre-selected organizations. Applications not accepted.
Officers and Directors:* John B. Hurford,* Pres.; Jayne M. Kurzman,* V.P.; Robert C. Miller,* Secy.
Employer Identification Number: 133394688

4587
Mary J. Hutchins Foundation, Inc. ⌘
110 William St.
New York 10038 (212) 602-8529

Incorporated in 1935 in NY.
Donor(s): Mary J. Hutchins,† Caspar J. Voorhis.†
Foundation type: Independent
Financial data (yr. ended 12/31/88): Assets, $19,003,127 (M); gifts received, $4,600; expenditures, $1,060,594, including $906,000 for 47 grants (high: $60,000; low: $3,000) and $43,795 for 14 grants to individuals (high: $4,980; low: $250).
Purpose and activities: To assist the poor and needy; grants also largely to hospitals, community funds, and religious welfare funds.
Types of support: Grants to individuals.
Limitations: Giving primarily in the New York, NY, area. No support for educational purposes or national health funds. No grants for seed money, scholarships, or annual campaigns.
Application information: Application form not required.
Initial approach: Proposal
Write: Richard J. Mirabella, V.P.
Officers and Directors:* Waldo Hutchins III,* Pres.; Richard J. Mirabella,* V.P. and Treas.; Robert A. Fromel,* V.P.; Julia L. Zeller, Secy.; Waldo Hutchins, Jr., John N. Huwer.
Employer Identification Number: 136083578

4588
The Hycliff Foundation, Inc.
c/o Bernhard Associates Ltd.
Six East 43rd St., 28th Fl.
New York 10017 (212) 986-7500

Incorporated in 1977 in DE as partial successor to The Bernhard Foundation, Inc.
Donor(s): The Bernhard Foundation, Inc.
Foundation type: Independent
Financial data (yr. ended 02/28/89): Assets, $1,099,607 (M); expenditures, $70,792, including $62,500 for 6 grants (high: $25,000; low: $2,500).
Purpose and activities: Emphasis on small experimental projects, including civil rights and civil liberties. Report on foundation included in annual report of Joint Foundation Support which administers the foundation.
Types of support: Operating budgets, continuing support, seed money.
Limitations: Giving primarily in New York, NY. No grants to individuals, or for building or endowment funds, scholarships, fellowships, or matching gifts; no loans.
Application information: Funds currently committed. Applications not accepted.
Board meeting date(s): Spring, fall, and winter
Write: Robert A. Bernhard, Pres.
Officers and Directors:* Robert A. Bernhard,* Pres.; Michael R. Bernhard,* V.P. and Treas.; Joan M. Bernhard,* V.P.; Adele Bernhard,* Secy.; Steven G. Bernhard, Susan Bernhard Collins.
Number of staff: None.
Employer Identification Number: 132893039

4589
Fannie C. Hyde Testamentary Trust ⌘
c/o Owego National Bank
203 Main St.
Owego 13827

Established in 1963 in NY.
Donor(s): Fannie C. Hyde.†
Foundation type: Independent
Financial data (yr. ended 4/30/88): Assets, $1,199,152 (M); expenditures, $125,371, including $108,770 for 37 grants (high: $32,458; low: $226).
Purpose and activities: Support for youth programs and community funds; some support for hospitals, education and social services.
Types of support: Equipment, general purposes, scholarship funds, special projects.
Limitations: Giving primarily in Tioga County, NY.
Trustee: Owego National Bank.
Employer Identification Number: 156020596

4590
I Have a Dream Foundation - New York ☆
330 Seventh Ave., 20th Fl.
New York 10001

Established in 1986 in NY.

Foundation type: Operating
Financial data (yr. ended 8/31/88): Assets, $4,454,499 (M); gifts received, $1,065,355; expenditures, $1,137,607, including $964,554 for 22 grants (high: $212,002; low: $1,960).
Purpose and activities: Projects include programs to motivate disadvantaged grade school students to attend college by offering scholarships, reading materials, support groups, and counseling services.
Types of support: Scholarship funds.
Limitations: No grants to individuals.
Application information: Giving only for pre-determined educational projects organized by the foundation's sponsors. Applications not accepted.
Officers and Directors:* George Friedman, Chair.; Eugene M. Lang, Pres.; Peter M. Flanigan,* V.P.; Joseph H. Flom,* Secy.; Augustus K. Oliver, Treas.
Number of staff: 2 full-time professional; 2 full-time support.
Employer Identification Number: 133370648

4591
I. & L. Association, Inc. ⌑ ☆
c/o Leonard H. Goldenson
77 West 66th St., 6th Fl.
New York 10023

Established in 1946.
Foundation type: Independent
Financial data (yr. ended 12/31/88): Assets, $4,073,018 (M); expenditures, $326,850, including $294,437 for 41 grants (high: $115,500; low: $100).
Purpose and activities: Giving primarily for medical research, health associations, with emphasis on the handicapped; support also for Jewish organizations and higher education.
Limitations: No grants to individuals.
Application information: Contributes only to pre-selected organizations. Applications not accepted.
Officers: Leonard H. Goldenson,* Pres. and Treas.; Isabelle W. Goldenson,* V.P.; Jerome B. Golden, Secy.
Directors:* Frederick S. Pierce, Martin J. Raynes.
Employer Identification Number: 136115597

4592
The Iacocca Foundation ⌑
75 Rockefeller Plaza, 6th Fl.
New York 10019 (212) 484-7460

Established in 1964 in MI; became active in 1985.
Donor(s): Lido A. Iacocca.
Foundation type: Independent
Financial data (yr. ended 12/31/87): Assets, $8,524,000 (M); gifts received, $2,703,000; expenditures, $395,000, including $324,000 for 9 grants (high: $200,000; low: $2,000; average: $50-$100,000).
Purpose and activities: Support limited to fellowships and endowed research positions in diabetes research; also awards scholarships for higher education for children of Chrysler employees through the Citizen's Scholarship Foundation of America.
Types of support: Capital campaigns, endowment funds, fellowships, professorships, research, employee-related scholarships.
Limitations: No grants for building funds or operating budgets.
Publications: 990-PF, informational brochure.
Application information:
Initial approach: Letter
Board meeting date(s): Quarterly
Write: Kathryn I. Hentz, Pres.
Officers and Trustees: Kathryn I. Hentz, Pres.; Lido A. Iacocca, V.P.; Joseph A. Califano, Jr., Secy.-Treas.; Jay J. Dugan, William R. Winn.
Number of staff: 2 full-time professional.
Employer Identification Number: 386071154

4593
IBM South Africa Projects Fund ☆
c/o IBM Corp.
Old Orchard Rd., Rm. 3C-45
Armonk 10504-1709 (914) 765-5040

Established in 1985 in NY.
Donor(s): IBM Corp.
Foundation type: Company-sponsored
Financial data (yr. ended 12/31/88): Assets, $1,952,731 (M); gifts received, $2,005,850; expenditures, $2,508,352, including $2,174,798 for 10 grants (high: $1,131,594; low: $5,500; average: $50,000-$75,000).
Purpose and activities: Support for education, legal reform, and the fostering of black enterprise in South Africa.
Application information: Application form required.
Initial approach: Proposal
Deadline(s): None
Final notification: 1 month
Write: Prog. Mgr.
Officers: James G. Parker,* Pres.; J.M. Sabater, V.P.; Robert S. Stone, V.P.; Chuck Taylor, V.P.; Amy Fliegelman, Secy.; John H. Stewart, Treas.; Michael H. Van Vranken, Controller.
Directors:* Edward T. Buhl, David A. Finley.
Number of staff: 1 full-time professional.
Employer Identification Number: 133267906

4594
Carl C. Icahn Foundation ▼ ⌑
100 South Bedford Rd.
Mt. Kisco 10549 (914) 242-4010

Established in 1980 in NY and DE.
Donor(s): Carl C. Icahn.
Foundation type: Independent
Financial data (yr. ended 11/30/86): Assets, $11,415,755 (M); gifts received, $596,351; expenditures, $1,815,265, including $796,800 for 50 grants (high: $500,000; low: $100; average: $750-$20,000).
Purpose and activities: Giving for cultural programs, hospitals, and for child welfare, including a child abuse prevention clinic.
Limitations: Giving primarily in New York, NY. No grants to individuals.
Application information:
Initial approach: Letter
Deadline(s): None
Board meeting date(s): As necessary
Write: Gail Golden
Officers: Carl C. Icahn, Pres.; Leba Icahn, Secy.-Treas.
Number of staff: 1
Employer Identification Number: 133091588

4595
The IFF Foundation, Inc. ⌑
521 West 57th St.
New York 10019 (212) 765-5500

Incorporated in 1963 in NY.
Donor(s): International Flavors & Fragrances, Inc.
Foundation type: Company-sponsored
Financial data (yr. ended 12/31/88): Assets, $753,252 (M); gifts received, $325,000; expenditures, $247,161, including $246,040 for 89 grants (high: $40,000; low: $100).
Purpose and activities: Grants primarily for higher education, including medical education and matching gifts; support also for research in chemistry and international affairs, for hospitals and mental health services, civic affairs agencies, and cultural activities.
Types of support: Research, employee matching gifts.
Application information:
Write: John P. Winandy, Treas.
Officers: Eugene P. Grisanti, Pres.; W. Dempsey, Secy.; John P. Winandy, Treas.
Employer Identification Number: 136159094

4596
The Indian Point Foundation, Inc.
1095 Park Ave., Rm. 11A
New York 10128 (212) 722-5752

Established in 1986 in CT.
Donor(s): Clement C. Moore.
Foundation type: Independent
Financial data (yr. ended 06/30/89): Assets, $1,258,660 (M); expenditures, $66,535, including $66,535 for 32 grants (high: $10,000; low: $100; average: $2,500-$5,000).
Purpose and activities: Broad purposes with emphasis on providing seed money for new projects. Areas of interest include wildlife preservation and land conservation, performing arts and museums and other cultural organizations, women's health agencies, and leadership development.
Types of support: Annual campaigns, capital campaigns, general purposes, endowment funds, publications, seed money, special projects.
Limitations: Giving primarily in NY and the New England region, with emphasis on CT. No grants to individuals.
Publications: Application guidelines.
Application information: Application form required.
Initial approach: Letter
Copies of proposal: 2
Deadline(s): None
Board meeting date(s): Jan., Apr., and Oct.
Final notification: 60 days
Write: Elizabeth Moore
Officers and Directors:* C.C. Moore,* Pres.; E.W.Y. Moore,* V.P. and Secy.; S.G. Yinkey.
Number of staff: 1 part-time professional; 1 part-time support.
Employer Identification Number: 222795753

4597
Indonesian Cultural Foundation, Inc.
60 East 42nd St.
New York 10165-0001 (212) 687-0517

Established in 1970 in NY.
Foundation type: Independent
Financial data (yr. ended 12/31/89): Assets, $1,918,968 (M); expenditures, $163,446, including $2,250 for 1 grant and $106,452 for 26 grants to individuals (high: $14,074; low: $600).
Purpose and activities: Support primarily for scholarships to Indonesian citizens engaged in graduate study in the U.S.
Types of support: Student aid.
Publications: Annual report.
Application information: Application form required.
Initial approach: Letter
Copies of proposal: 1
Deadline(s): None
Board meeting date(s): Mar., June, Sept., and Dec.
Write: James W. Clauson, V.P.
Officers and Directors: Ruth Sheldon Knowles, Pres.; James W. Clauson, V.P. and Treas.; George C. Benson, V.P.; David Fisher, V.P.; Carl J. Morelli, Secy.; R. Hasmoro, Janus J. Pitoy, Abdul Rachman Ramly, Ben Samsu.
Number of staff: 1 full-time professional.
Employer Identification Number: 237055841

4598
Inisfad Foundation, Inc. ⌘ ☆
c/o Teitler & Teitler
230 Park Ave.
New York 10169

Established in 1925.
Foundation type: Independent
Financial data (yr. ended 12/31/87): Assets, $1,114,062 (M); expenditures, $61,864, including $48,840 for 55 grants (high: $10,300; low: $100).
Purpose and activities: Support primarily for Catholic churches, community funds and social services, and higher education; support also for cultural programs and health.
Limitations: No grants to individuals.
Application information: Contributes only to pre-selected organizations. Applications not accepted.
Officers: Lawrence D. Cavanagh, Sr., Pres.; Mona Cavanagh, V.P.; Monica Cavanagh Cegrian, Secy.; Lawrence D. Cavanagh, Jr., Treas.
Employer Identification Number: 136157475

4599
Initial Teaching Alphabet Foundation, Inc.
32 Thornwood Ln.
Roslyn Heights 11577 (516) 621-6772

Incorporated in 1965 in NY.
Donor(s): Eugene Kelly.†
Foundation type: Operating
Financial data (yr. ended 12/31/89): Assets, $263,403 (M); expenditures, $637,537, including $336,512 for 35 grants (high: $45,000; low: $1,500; average: $1,500-$45,000) and $262,054 for foundation-administered programs.
Purpose and activities: A private operating foundation; giving to promote, maintain, and advance education, in all its fields, and in particular, but without limiting the generality of the foregoing, by the development, standardization, propagation, dissemination, teaching, and use of the Initial Teaching Alphabet, with the aim of improving reading and writing skills. Grants presently limited to support of projects and programs in support of the Initial Teaching Alphabet.
Types of support: Special projects, research, publications, consulting services, technical assistance, conferences and seminars.
Limitations: No grants to individuals, or for building or endowment funds, general support, scholarships, fellowships, or matching gifts; no loans.
Publications: 990-PF, informational brochure, program policy statement, occasional report, application guidelines.
Application information: Application form required.
Initial approach: Letter
Copies of proposal: 7
Deadline(s): Submit letters of intent by Mar. 15; proposal deadline Apr. 15
Board meeting date(s): May or June
Final notification: 1 month
Write: Betty E. Thompson, Exec. Dir.
Officers and Directors:* Frank G. Jennings,* Pres.; Gerald L. Knieter,* V.P.; Maurice S. Spanbock,* Secy.-Treas.; Betty E. Thompson,* Exec. Dir.; Max Bogart, Rebecca W. Stewart.
Number of staff: 1 full-time professional; 1 part-time professional.
Employer Identification Number: 112074243

4600
The Institute for Aegean Prehistory ⌘
c/o The Millburn Corp.
1270 Ave. of the Americas
New York 10020

Established in 1983 in NY.
Donor(s): Malcolm H. Wiener.
Foundation type: Operating
Financial data (yr. ended 6/30/89): Assets, $4,544,610 (M); gifts received, $36,000; expenditures, $475,179, including $169,703 for 19 grants (high: $25,000; low: $1,000) and $275,396 for 38 grants to individuals (high: $21,673; low: $185).
Purpose and activities: A private operating foundation; opportunities to participate in the organization's activities are given only for the purpose of allowing and encouraging persons to study Aegean prehistory with expectation of research publication under the direct supervision of the institute.
Types of support: Grants to individuals.
Application information:
Initial approach: Letter
Deadline(s): None
Write: Malcolm H. Wiener, Pres.
Officers and Trustees: Malcolm H. Wiener, Pres. and Treas.; Harvey Beker, V.P.; George E. Crapple, V.P.; Martin J. Whitman.
Employer Identification Number: 133137391

4601
International Fund for Health and Family Planning ⌘ ☆
c/o Alan Dolinsky
Nine Spruce Place
Great Neck 11021-1903

Donor(s): Philip D. Harvey.
Foundation type: Independent
Financial data (yr. ended 12/31/88): Assets, $2,864,513 (M); gifts received, $125,000; expenditures, $351,024, including $225,000 for 4 grants (high: $85,000; low: $10,000).
Purpose and activities: Giving to organizations for international family planning in underdeveloped countries.
Limitations: No grants to individuals.
Application information: Contributes only to pre-selected organizations. Applications not accepted.
Officers and Directors: Robert Ciszewski, Pres.; Steven Delibert, V.P. and Secy.; Philip D. Harvey, V.P.; Alan Dolinsky, Treas.; Tim Black, Richard Frank.
Employer Identification Number: 133000463

4602
International Paper Company Foundation ▼
Two Manhattanville Rd.
Purchase 10577 (914) 397-1581

Incorporated in 1952 in NY.
Donor(s): International Paper Co.
Foundation type: Company-sponsored
Financial data (yr. ended 12/31/87): Assets, $21,265,985 (M); gifts received, $4,000,000; expenditures, $1,535,000, including $1,119,186 for 170 grants (high: $116,500; low: $1,000; average: $2,500-$5,000) and $225,594 for 349 employee matching gifts.
Purpose and activities: Grants primarily for model projects in company communities and selected programs with potental national impact, with focus on pre-college levels of economic and career education, programs for minorities and women in engineering, health and welfare, and community and cultural affairs. Operates own program EDCORE (Education and Community Resource Program) in selected International Paper communities for public schools.
Types of support: Seed money, special projects, annual campaigns, research, publications, matching funds, employee matching gifts, continuing support, fellowships, operating budgets, capital campaigns, program-related investments.
Limitations: Giving primarily in communities where there are company plants and mills in AL, AR, LA, ME, MS, NY, OR, SC, TN, and TX. No support for athletic organizations or religious groups. No grants to individuals, or for endowment funds, capital expenses (except in company communities), or general operating expenses of health and welfare agencies or higher educational institutions; no loans.
Publications: Occasional report, informational brochure (including application guidelines).
Application information: Address requests from organizations in company communities to the local company mill or plant manager; no applications accepted for EDCORE (Education

and Community Resource Program) or for fellowships. Application form not required.
Initial approach: Letter, telephone, or proposal
Copies of proposal: 1
Deadline(s): Previous summer for next calendar year
Board meeting date(s): Jan.
Final notification: 6 to 8 weeks
Write: Sandra Wilson, V.P.
Officers: Arthur Wallace, Pres.; Sandra Wilson, V.P.; Tracy Doolittle, Secy.; Myra Drucker, Treas.
Directors: John A. Georges, W. Craig McClelland, James P. Melican, Jr., David W. Oskin.
Trustee: State Street Bank & Trust Co.
Number of staff: 1 full-time professional; 1 full-time support; 1 part-time support.
Employer Identification Number: 136155080

4603
Hope Goddard Iselin Foundation ⌑
c/o U.S. Trust Co. of New York, Tax Dept.
114 West 47th St.
New York 10036-1532
Application address: 65 Parker Hill Rd. Extension, Killington, CT 06417

Foundation type: Independent
Financial data (yr. ended 3/31/88): Assets, $1,299,418 (M); expenditures, $61,250, including $45,000 for 2 grants (high: $30,000; low: $15,000).
Purpose and activities: Support primarily for environmental organizations that promote outdoor activity.
Application information:
Initial approach: Letter
Deadline(s): None
Write: Robert T.H. Davidson, Trustee
Trustees: Robert T.H. Davidson, U.S. Trust Co. of New York.
Employer Identification Number: 136583545

4604
O'Donnell Iselin Foundation, Inc. ⌑
40 Wall St., Suite 2102
New York 10005 (212) 425-0105
IRS filing state: DE

Donor(s): Peter Iselin, Emilie I. Wiggin.
Foundation type: Independent
Financial data (yr. ended 12/31/88): Assets, $1,584,091 (M); gifts received, $100,000; expenditures, $134,977, including $114,750 for 38 grants (high: $20,000; low: $250).
Purpose and activities: Support for secondary education, cultural programs, and health associations.
Limitations: Giving primarily in NY. No grants to individuals.
Application information: Application form not required.
Deadline(s): None
Write: Peter Iselin, Pres.
Officers: Peter Iselin, Pres. and Treas.; Emilie I. Wiggin, V.P.; John F. Walsh, Secy.
Employer Identification Number: 516016471

4605
Ittleson Foundation, Inc. ▼
645 Madison Ave., 16th Fl.
New York 10022 (212) 838-5010

Trust established in 1932 in NY.
Donor(s): Henry Ittleson,† Blanche F. Ittleson,† Henry Ittleson, Jr.,† Lee F. Ittleson,† Nancy S. Ittleson.†
Foundation type: Independent
Financial data (yr. ended 12/31/89): Assets, $17,772,970 (M); gifts received, $564,838; expenditures, $1,388,877, including $834,338 for grants (high: $100,000).
Purpose and activities: For the promotion of the well-being of mankind throughout the world, including research, publication, and the establishment, maintenance, and aid of charitable activities and institutions. Current areas of particular interest are: mental health, including the consequences of AIDS on the mental health of people; the environment; the elderly and other underserved populations, such as the poor and minority communities; and crime and justice, including the prevention of crime and assisting youthful offenders to outgrow criminality.
Types of support: Seed money, matching funds, professorships, special projects, research, publications, technical assistance.
Limitations: No support for the humanities or cultural projects, general education, or to social service agencies offering direct service to people in local communities. No grants to individuals, or for continuing support, scholarships, fellowships, internships, annual or capital campaigns, travel, emergency, or endowment funds, or deficit financing; no loans.
Publications: Annual report.
Application information: Application form not required.
Initial approach: Letter
Copies of proposal: 1
Deadline(s): None
Board meeting date(s): May and Dec.
Final notification: 3 weeks to 3 months
Write: David M. Nee, Exec. Dir.
Officers and Directors:* H. Anthony Ittleson,* Chair. and Pres.; Pamela Lee Syrmis,* V.P.; David M. Nee,* Secy. and Exec. Dir.; Bernard W. Schwartz,* Treas.; Marianne S. Ittleson, Lionel I. Pincus, Victor Syrmis, M.D.
Number of staff: 1 part-time professional; 1 part-time support.
Employer Identification Number: 510172757

4606
Ittleson-Beaumont Fund ⌑ ☆
c/o The C.I.T. Group Holdings, Inc.
135 West 50th St.
New York 10020 (212) 408-6000
Application address: c/o The C.I.T. Group, Inc., 650 C.I.T. Dr., Livingston, NJ 07039

Established in 1932 in NY.
Foundation type: Independent
Financial data (yr. ended 12/31/88): Assets, $1,744,689 (M); expenditures, $204,936, including $128,800 for 13 grants (high: $100,000; low: $500) and $58,946 for 20 grants to individuals (high: $18,000; low: $261).
Purpose and activities: Giving primarily as relief assistance to needy current and former employees, and their families, of C.I.T. Financial Corp. and its affiliates; support also for a community fund.
Types of support: Grants to individuals.
Application information:
Initial approach: Letter
Deadline(s): None
Write: Clare Carmichael, AVP-OD Admin.
Trustees: William Baronoff, Joseph H. Carroll, Albert R. Gamper, Jr., H. Anthony Ittleson, William M. O'Grady, Thomas J. O'Rourke, Joseph A. Pollicino.
Employer Identification Number: 136083909

4607
J.J.J. Foundation, Inc. ⌑ ☆
445 Hamilton Ave., Suite 1200
White Plains 10601-1804

Established in 1985 in NY.
Donor(s): John R. Butler.
Foundation type: Independent
Financial data (yr. ended 9/30/88): Assets, $1,848,683 (M); expenditures, $87,425, including $62,679 for 30 grants (high: $25,000; low: $24).
Purpose and activities: Giving primarily for social services, with emphasis on associations and programs concerned with mental retardation; support also for higher and other education.
Limitations: Giving primarily in NY and Washington, DC. No grants to individuals.
Application information: Contributes only to pre-selected organizations. Applications not accepted.
Officers and Directors: John R. Butler, Pres. and Treas.; Charles Kingsley, V.P. and Secy.; Myron Arlen, Stuart Lemle, Richard Weill.
Employer Identification Number: 133379770

4608
The J.M. Foundation ▼
60 East 42nd St., Rm. 1651
New York 10165 (212) 687-7735

Incorporated in 1924 in NY.
Donor(s): Jeremiah Milbank,† Katharine S. Milbank.†
Foundation type: Independent
Financial data (yr. ended 12/31/89): Assets, $26,067,056 (M); expenditures, $3,427,877, including $2,290,208 for 100 grants (high: $250,000; low: $1,000; average: $15,000-$35,000), $72,285 for 44 employee matching gifts and $180,000 for 2 foundation-administered programs.
Purpose and activities: Giving primarily for rehabilitation of the physically handicapped; prevention and wellness, with an emphasis on individual responsibility for health; education, prevention, and early intervention in alcohol and other drug abuse; expansion of effective extramural care; health-related public policy research; and selected projects in biomedical research and medical education. The foundation also has a strong interest in educational activities which strengthen America's pluralistic system of free markets, individualism, entrepreneurship, voluntarism, and private enterprise. It also supports organizations that enhance the quality of family life, and provide today's youth with meaningful life experiences, productive employment

opportunities, healthy lifestyles, and positive character development. Support also for two in-house operating projects: the Medical Student Scholarship Program in Alcohol and Other Drug Dependencies and National Awards for Excellence in Vocational Programs. The foundation also sponsors a matching gift program for its board members and full-time staff.
Types of support: Research, special projects, publications, internships, scholarship funds, matching funds, conferences and seminars, technical assistance, seed money, employee matching gifts.
Limitations: No support for the arts. No grants to individuals, or for operating expenses, international activities, annual fundraising campaigns, capital campaigns, or endowment funds; no loans.
Publications: Annual report (including application guidelines), application guidelines.
Application information: Application form not required.
Initial approach: Summary letter accompanied by proposal
Copies of proposal: 1
Deadline(s): Submit proposal preferably in Feb., July, or Oct.; deadline 45 days prior to meetings
Board meeting date(s): Jan., May, and Oct.
Final notification: Preliminary response within 20 working days
Write: Chris K. Olander, Exec. Dir.
Officers and Directors:* Jeremiah Milbank, Jr.,* Pres.; Mrs. H. Lawrence Bogert,* V.P.; Daniel G. Tenney, Jr.,* Secy.; William Lee Hanley, Jr.,* Treas.; Chris K. Olander, Exec. Dir.; Jack Brauntuch, Special Counselor; Mary E. Caslin, Peter C. Morse, Michael Sanger.
Members: Jeremiah M. Bogert, Jeremiah Milbank III.
Number of staff: 2 full-time professional; 1 part-time professional; 3 full-time support; 1 part-time support.
Employer Identification Number: 136068340

4609
Jackson Hole Preserve, Inc.
30 Rockefeller Plaza, Rm. 5402
New York 10112 (212) 649-5600

Incorporated in 1940 in NY.
Donor(s): John D. Rockefeller, Jr.,† Laurance S. Rockefeller, Rockefeller Brothers Fund.
Foundation type: Independent
Financial data (yr. ended 12/31/89): Assets, $38,789,201 (M); expenditures, $3,146,500, including $2,294,000 for 14 grants (high: $2,000,000; low: $5,000).
Purpose and activities: Grants to restore, protect, and preserve for the benefit of the public the primitive grandeur and natural beauties of the landscape in areas notable for picturesque scenery; and to promote, encourage, and conduct other activities germane to these purposes.
Types of support: Land acquisition, matching funds, publications, consulting services, general purposes, special projects.
Limitations: Giving primarily in Jackson Hole, WY, the Eastern Caribbean, and Hudson River Valley, NY. No grants to individuals, or for building or endowment funds, scholarships, or fellowships; no loans.
Application information: Application form not required.
Initial approach: Letter or proposal
Copies of proposal: 1
Deadline(s): Preferably mid-late spring
Board meeting date(s): Sept. or Oct.; executive committee meets frequently
Write: George R. Lamb, Pres.
Officers: George R. Lamb,* Pres.; Gene W. Setzer,* V.P.; Franklin E. Parker,* Secy.; Ruth C. Haupert, Treas.
Trustees:* Nash Castro, Henry L. Diamond, William M. Dietel, Clayton W. Frye, Jr., Mrs. Lyndon B. Johnson, Howard Phipps, Jr., Laurance Rockefeller, Laurance S. Rockefeller, Fred Smith, Conrad L. Wirth.
Number of staff: 3 part-time professional; 1 part-time support.
Employer Identification Number: 131813818

4610
The Benjamin Jacobson and Sons Foundation ⌑
61 Broadway
New York 10006

Established in 1968 in NY and DE.
Donor(s): Benjamin Jacobson & Sons.
Foundation type: Company-sponsored
Financial data (yr. ended 06/30/89): Assets, $132,360 (M); gifts received, $140,000; expenditures, $314,097, including $310,278 for 373 grants (high: $40,000; low: $10).
Purpose and activities: Grants primarily for health services and medical research, religious support, with emphasis on Jewish giving, education, youth programs, and social services.
Limitations: Giving primarily in the New York, NY, metropolitan area. No grants to individuals.
Application information: Contributes only to pre-selected organizations. Applications not accepted.
Officers and Directors:* Robert J. Jacobson, Sr.,* Pres.; Benjamin J. Jacobson, Jr.,* V.P.; Robert J. Jacobson, Jr., Secy.; Arthur L. Jacobson,* Treas.; James A. Jacobson.
Employer Identification Number: 132630862

4611
Sid Jacobson Foundation, Inc. ⌑
151 Sunnyside Blvd.
Plainview 11803-1589

Established in 1955 in NY.
Donor(s): Sid Tool Co., Inc.
Foundation type: Independent
Financial data (yr. ended 08/31/89): Assets, $1,495 (M); gifts received, $211,000; expenditures, $225,924, including $225,900 for 88 grants (high: $125,000; low: $10).
Purpose and activities: Support primarily for Jewish concerns; also support for health services, hospitals, and medical research.
Application information: Application form not required.
Deadline(s): None
Write: Sid Jacobson, Trustee
Trustees: Bernice Jacobson, Mitchell Jacobson, Sid Jacobson.
Employer Identification Number: 116038028

4612
JBT Cultural Exchange Corp. ☆
787 Seventh Ave., 11th Fl.
New York 10019 (212) 698-4956

Established in 1988 in NY.
Foundation type: Independent
Financial data (yr. ended 03/31/90): Assets, $2,500,000 (M); gifts received, $1,000,000; qualifying distributions, $79,625, including $79,625 for 29 grants to individuals (high: $2,995; low: $1,790).
Purpose and activities: Grants to U.S. citizens to promote understanding of Japanese life through cultural exchange programs between the U.S. and Japan.
Types of support: Grants to individuals.
Application information:
Deadline(s): None
Write: Masako Osada, Assistant to the Dir.
Directors: Takato Ayabe, Mitsuo Manai, Shunichi Oyama, Akira Yasada.
Employer Identification Number: 133456886

4613
JCT Foundation
145 Central Park West, Apt. 25C
New York 10023

Established in 1984 in NY.
Donor(s): Jeff C. Tarr.
Foundation type: Independent
Financial data (yr. ended 12/31/88): Assets, $12,469,298 (M); gifts received, $4,627,360; expenditures, $400,780, including $385,031 for grants.
Purpose and activities: Support primarily for cultural programs, including the performing arts; some support for higher education.
Limitations: Giving primarily in the New York, NY, area. No grants to individuals.
Application information: Contributes only to pre-selected organizations. Applications not accepted.
Directors: Jeff C. Tarr, Patricia C. Tarr.
Employer Identification Number: 133237111

4614
The JDR 3rd Fund, Inc.
30 Rockefeller Plaza, Rm. 5600
New York 10112 (212) 649-5600

Incorporated in 1963 in NY.
Donor(s): John D. Rockefeller, 3rd.†
Foundation type: Independent
Financial data (yr. ended 8/31/89): Assets, $336,079 (M); expenditures, $303,188, including $283,096 for 9 grants (high: $100,000; low: $2,497).
Purpose and activities: Support primarily for cultural programs, including Asian cultural institutions and performing arts; support also for family planning.
Types of support: Exchange programs, endowment funds, operating budgets.
Limitations: No grants to individuals.
Application information: Contributes only to pre-selected organizations. Applications not accepted.
Officers: Mrs. John D. Rockefeller, 3rd,* Pres. and Chair.; Elizabeth J. McCormack,* V.P.; Paulette Walther, Secy.; George J. Pipino, Treas.

Trustees:* Hope Aldrich, Alida Rockefeller Dayton, Richard Lanier, Donal C. O'Brien, Jr.
Number of staff: 3 full-time professional.
Employer Identification Number: 131988876

4615
Richard Hampton Jenrette Foundation, Inc. ⌑
c/o Wood, Struthers & Winthrop
P.O. Box 18
New York 10005

Established in 1967 in NY.
Donor(s): Richard H. Jenrette.
Foundation type: Independent
Financial data (yr. ended 11/30/88): Assets, $900,206 (M); expenditures, $196,559, including $183,998 for 35 grants (high: $62,000; low: $100).
Purpose and activities: Emphasis on giving for the arts, historical preservation, and higher education; contributes also to an educational foundation.
Types of support: General purposes.
Limitations: Giving primarily in SC.
Application information: Contributes only to pre-selected oganizations. Applications not accepted.
Officers and Directors: Richard H. Jenrette, Pres.; Joseph M. Jenrette III, V.P.; Thomas E. Siegler, Secy.-Treas.; Charles H.P. Duell, John W. Smith, William L. Thompson.
Employer Identification Number: 136271770

4616
Jephson Educational Trust No. 1 ⌑
c/o The Chase Manhattan Bank, N.A.
1211 Ave. of the Americas, 36th Fl.
New York 10036 (212) 730-3415

Trust established in 1946 in NY.
Donor(s): Lucretia Davis Jephson.†
Foundation type: Independent
Financial data (yr. ended 12/31/88): Assets, $3,459,113 (M); expenditures, $207,102, including $132,000 for 16 grants (high: $50,000; low: $100).
Purpose and activities: To support four-year educational institutions through scholarship aid for youth throughout the U.S.
Types of support: Scholarship funds.
Limitations: No grants to individuals, or for matching gifts; no loans.
Application information:
Write: Jean P. Crawford, Trust Officer, The Chase Manhattan Bank, N.A.
Trustees: Dermod Ives, J. Stanley Parkin, The Chase Manhattan Bank, N.A.
Employer Identification Number: 136023169

4617
Jephson Educational Trust No. 2 ⌑
c/o The Chase Manhattan Bank, N.A.
1211 Ave. of the Americas
New York 10036 (212) 730-3795

Trust established in 1979 in NY.
Donor(s): Lucretia Davis Jephson.†
Foundation type: Independent
Financial data (yr. ended 9/30/88): Assets, $6,023,573 (M); gifts received, $8,619; expenditures, $246,794, including $129,211 for 27 grants (high: $10,000; low: $2,000).
Purpose and activities: Grants for higher and secondary education, including scholarship aid for worthy and needy students.
Types of support: Scholarship funds.
Limitations: No grants to individuals, or for matching gifts; no loans.
Application information: Application form not required.
Initial approach: Proposal
Copies of proposal: 1
Deadline(s): Submit proposal preferably in Mar. or Apr.; deadline Apr. 30
Board meeting date(s): June and Oct.
Final notification: 6 months
Write: Jean P. Crawford, Personal Trust Officer, The Chase Manhattan Bank, N.A.
Trustees: Dermod Ives, David S. Plume, The Chase Manhattan Bank, N.A.
Number of staff: 1
Employer Identification Number: 136777236

4618
Jesselson Foundation ▼ ⌑
1221 Ave. of the Americas
New York 10020 (212) 790-5722

Incorporated in 1955 in NY.
Donor(s): Ludwig Jesselson.
Foundation type: Independent
Financial data (yr. ended 4/30/88): Assets, $20,608,606 (M); expenditures, $1,489,487, including $1,444,065 for 294 grants (high: $250,000; low: $30; average: $100-$10,000).
Purpose and activities: Grants largely for higher and Jewish education, welfare funds, health agencies, and synagogues; some support for cultural programs.
Application information:
Initial approach: Letter
Deadline(s): None
Write: Ludwig Jesselson, Pres.
Officers: Ludwig Jesselson, Pres. and Treas.; Erica Jesselson, V.P. and Secy.; Michael Jesselson, 2nd V.P.
Employer Identification Number: 136075098

4619
Jewish Foundation for Education of Women
330 West 58th St., 5J
New York 10019 (212) 265-2565

Incorporated in 1884 in NY.
Foundation type: Independent
Financial data (yr. ended 06/30/89): Assets, $19,025,900 (M); gifts received, $24,366; expenditures, $994,517, including $739,185 for 485 grants to individuals (high: $4,000; low: $250) and $6,500 for 3 loans to individuals.
Purpose and activities: To provide scholarship assistance to women in the form of grants and loans for undergraduate, graduate, and professional studies. No support for law studies.
Types of support: Student aid, student loans.
Limitations: Giving limited to legal residents of the greater New York, NY, metropolitan area. No grants for general support, operating budgets, capital or endowment funds, matching gifts, research, special projects, publications, or conferences.
Publications: Application guidelines.
Application information: Application form required.
Initial approach: Letter
Copies of proposal: 1
Deadline(s): Submit proposal preferably between Oct. and Jan.; deadline Jan. 31
Board meeting date(s): Oct., Jan., June, and as required
Final notification: 6 weeks to 4 months
Write: Florence Wallach, Exec. Dir.
Officers and Directors:* Charles J. Tanenbaum,* Chair.; Ellen B. Kallman,* Pres.; Susan J. Schatz,* 1st V.P.; Alan D. Cohn,* V.P.; Suzanne H. Keusch,* V.P.; Jean G. Bronstein,* Secy.; Alan R. Kahn,* Treas.; Jack R. Ackerman, Sylvia Biederman, Mrs. F.H. Block, Martin Blumenthal, Lasalle Felheim, Linda Gabriel, Enid Goldberg, Mrs. Warren R. Goldsmith, Mrs. Carl Goldmark, Jr., Susan R. Knafel, Essie Lee, Brenda L. Lehman, Nadine Liebhardt, Marjorie Madonick, Reva Mager, Ruth Messinger, David Rosenberg, Mrs. Jack M. Schatz, Marion H. Spanbock, Ann Freda Thomas.
Number of staff: 1 full-time professional; 2 full-time support; 2 part-time support.
Employer Identification Number: 131860415

4620
The JMC Foundation ⌑ ☆
c/o Bear Stearns Companies, Inc.
245 Park Ave.
New York 10167

Established in 1985 in NY.
Donor(s): The Monterey Fund, Inc.
Foundation type: Independent
Financial data (yr. ended 9/30/88): Assets, $58,833 (M); gifts received, $11,400; expenditures, $156,419, including $156,419 for 7 grants (high: $54,000; low: $5,000).
Purpose and activities: Giving primarily for higher and other education, and the welfare of youth.
Types of support: Scholarship funds.
Limitations: Giving primarily in New York, NY. No grants to individuals.
Application information: Contributes only to pre-selected organizations. Applications not accepted.
Officers and Directors: Jeremiah Callaghan, Pres.; Karen Callaghan, V.P. and Secy.; Eugene Callaghan, Treas.; Joseph Gottlieb, Michael Shapiro.
Employer Identification Number: 133320959

4621
Jockey Club Foundation ⌑
380 Madison Ave.
New York 10017 (212) 599-1919

Incorporated in 1943 in NY.
Donor(s): New York Racing Assn., Clark Foundation.
Foundation type: Independent
Financial data (yr. ended 12/31/87): Assets, $4,755,177 (M); gifts received, $104,360; expenditures, $338,925, including $43,247 for 19 grants and $240,550 for 46 grants to individuals (high: $10,496; low: $18).
Purpose and activities: To support indigent employees of turf and racing clubs.
Types of support: Grants to individuals.

Limitations: Giving primarily in NY and FL.
Application information:
Deadline(s): None
Write: Nancy Colletti, Secy. to the Trustees
Officers: James B. Moseley,* Managing Trustee; Nancy Colletti, Secy.; Alan Marzelli, Treas.
Trustees:* Stephen C. Clark, Jr., James P. Ryan.
Employer Identification Number: 136124094

4622
The Keith Wold Johnson Charitable Trust ⌑ ☆
c/o The Johnson Co., Inc.
630 Fifth Ave., Suite 918
New York 10111

Established in 1986 in NY.
Donor(s): Betty Wold Johnson.
Foundation type: Independent
Financial data (yr. ended 12/31/88): Assets, $1,971,964 (M); gifts received, $500,000; expenditures, $67,325, including $50,000 for 1 grant.
Purpose and activities: Support for juvenile diabetes research.
Limitations: No grants to individuals.
Application information: Application form not required.
Deadline(s): None
Write: Robert W. Johnson, Trustee
Trustees: Christopher W. Johnson, Elizabeth Ross Johnson, Robert W. Johnson IV.
Employer Identification Number: 112845826

4623
Christian A. Johnson Endeavor Foundation ▼
1060 Park Ave.
New York 10128 (212) 534-6620

Incorporated in 1952 in NY.
Donor(s): Christian A. Johnson.†
Foundation type: Independent
Financial data (yr. ended 09/30/89): Assets, $62,767,653 (M); expenditures, $2,553,456, including $1,637,600 for 25 grants (high: $725,000; low: $500; average: $10,000-$25,000) and $528,138 for 1 foundation-administered program.
Purpose and activities: Giving concentrated on private institutions of higher learning at the baccalaureate level and on educational outreach programs of visual and performing arts organizations; occasional support for perceived needs in other areas of education and the arts.
Types of support: Operating budgets, seed money, building funds, equipment, matching funds, professorships, scholarship funds, renovation projects.
Limitations: Giving limited to the eastern U.S. No support for government agencies, or for community or neighborhood projects, religious institutions, or for health care. No grants to individuals, or for continuing support, annual campaigns, emergency funds, deficit financing, land acquisitions, medical research, demonstration projects, publications, or conferences; no loans.
Publications: Annual report (including application guidelines), financial statement, program policy statement, application guidelines.
Application information: Proposals by invitation only. Application form not required.
Initial approach: Letter of inquiry
Deadline(s): Submit proposal upon foundation's request between Oct. 1 and Mar. 30
Board meeting date(s): Fall, winter, spring, and early summer
Final notification: June
Write: Mrs. Wilmot H. Kidd, Pres.
Officers and Trustees:* Mrs. Christian A. Johnson,* Chair. and Treas.; Julie Kidd,* Pres.; Charles H. Harff, Donald Kersting.
Number of staff: 2 full-time professional; 1 part-time professional; 3 full-time support.
Employer Identification Number: 136147952

4624
Willard T. C. Johnson Foundation, Inc. ⌑
c/o The Johnson Co., Inc.
630 Fifth Ave., Suite 918
New York 10111

Incorporated in 1979 in NY.
Donor(s): Willard T.C. Johnson.†
Foundation type: Independent
Financial data (yr. ended 12/31/88): Assets, $25,565,953 (M); expenditures, $1,324,110, including $1,090,000 for 5 grants (high: $575,000; low: $20,000).
Purpose and activities: Emphasis on culture, including museums and opera, social services, conservation, and higher education.
Limitations: No grants to individuals.
Application information: Application form not required.
Deadline(s): None
Write: Robert W. Johnson IV, Pres.
Officers and Directors:* Betty W. Johnson,* Chair.; Robert W. Johnson IV,* Pres.; Robert J. Mortimer,* V.P. and Secy.-Treas.
Employer Identification Number: 132993310

4625
Daisy Marquis Jones Foundation ▼
620 Granite Bldg.
130 East Main St.
Rochester 14604-1620 (716) 263-3331

Established in 1968 in NY.
Donor(s): Daisy Marquis Jones.†
Foundation type: Independent
Financial data (yr. ended 12/31/89): Assets, $21,324,391 (M); expenditures, $1,683,484, including $1,410,705 for 106 grants (high: $150,000; low: $250; average: $250-$150,000) and $30,000 for 1 loan.
Purpose and activities: Grants primarily to improve the quality of health care for local residents; support also for services for senior citizens, women and youth, with special emphasis on the disadvantaged; support also toward improving the administration of justice. Special attention to preventive programs.
Types of support: Operating budgets, seed money, emergency funds, building funds, equipment, land acquisition, matching funds, technical assistance, special projects, publications, renovation projects, conferences and seminars, lectureships.
Limitations: Giving limited to Monroe and Yates counties, NY. No support for the arts or for religious purposes. No grants to individuals, or for endowment funds, research, continuing support, scholarships, fellowships, annual campaigns, or deficit financing; no loans.
Publications: Annual report (including application guidelines), application guidelines.
Application information: Application form required.
Initial approach: Letter
Copies of proposal: 1
Deadline(s): None
Board meeting date(s): Monthly (except summer)
Final notification: 2 to 3 months
Write: Pearl W. Rubin, Pres.
Officers and Trustees:* Leo M. Lyons,* Chair.; Helen G. Whitney,* Vice-Chair.; Pearl W. Rubin,* Pres.; Sydney R. Rubin,* Gen. Counsel; Marine Midland Bank, N.A.
Number of staff: 1 full-time professional; 1 part-time professional; 1 part-time support.
Employer Identification Number: 237000227

4626
Janet Stone Jones Foundation ⌑ ☆
c/o Investors' Records Corp.
One Penn Plaza, Suite 3331, 250 West 34th St.
New York 10119

Established in 1978 in NY.
Donor(s): Janet Stone Jones Charitable Lead Trust.
Foundation type: Independent
Financial data (yr. ended 12/31/88): Assets, $30,130 (M); gifts received, $75,000; expenditures, $129,504, including $127,660 for 57 grants (high: $20,175; low: $50).
Purpose and activities: Giving to educational institutions, health associations, and general charitable organizations.
Types of support: General purposes.
Limitations: Giving primarily in the northeastern U.S. No grants to individuals.
Application information:
Initial approach: Letter
Deadline(s): None
Write: Benjamin Brewster, Treas.
Officers and Directors:* William J. Kramer,* Secy.; Benjamin Brewster,* Treas.; Whitney Brewster Armstrong, Diana Brewster Clark, Janet Brewster York.
Employer Identification Number: 132988287

4627
Joselow Foundation ⌑
c/o Summit Rovins & Feldesman
445 Park Ave., 3rd Fl.
New York 10022 (212) 702-2200

Established in 1967 in NY.
Donor(s): Irving Joselow,† Florence Joselow.†
Foundation type: Independent
Financial data (yr. ended 12/31/87): Assets, $3,372,675 (M); expenditures, $357,410, including $290,100 for 43 grants (high: $36,500; low: $1,000; average: $1,000-$10,000).
Purpose and activities: Support for Jewish welfare and educational funds; support also for international activities, higher education and women's organizations.

Types of support: Continuing support, emergency funds, general purposes, special projects.
Limitations: No grants to individuals.
Publications: Annual report, 990-PF.
Application information: Application form not required.
Initial approach: Letter
Copies of proposal: 2
Deadline(s): None
Board meeting date(s): No set dates
Write: Mildred Robbins Leet and Jacquin D. Bierman, Trustees
Trustees: Jacquin D. Bierman, Mildred Robbins Leet.
Number of staff: None.
Employer Identification Number: 237028908

4628
Joukowsky Family Foundation ⌑
70 Pine St., 22nd Fl.
New York 10270 (212) 770-5125
Mailing address: 250 West 24th St., Suite 4EE, New York, NY 10011

Established in 1981 in NY.
Foundation type: Independent
Financial data (yr. ended 10/31/88): Assets, $16,887,277 (M); expenditures, $1,082,548, including $881,600 for 26 grants (high: $200,000; low: $50) and $42,250 for 2 grants to individuals (high: $31,750; low: $10,500).
Purpose and activities: Giving primarily for higher and secondary education.
Types of support: Annual campaigns, building funds, capital campaigns, endowment funds, fellowships, general purposes, matching funds, professorships, scholarship funds, seed money.
Application information:
Write: Randall G. Drain, Dir.
Directors: Randall G. Drain, Artemis A.W. Joukowsky, Martha Content Joukowsky.
Employer Identification Number: 133242753

4629
The John M. and Mary A. Joyce Foundation
Seven Forest Circle
New Rochelle 10804

Incorporated in 1956 in IL.
Donor(s): John M. Joyce,† Mary McCann Joyce,† Seven-Up Bottling Co.
Foundation type: Independent
Financial data (yr. ended 07/31/88): Assets, $4,586,679 (M); expenditures, $248,576, including $222,000 for 31 grants (high: $50,000; low: $1,000).
Purpose and activities: Emphasis on church support, schools and universities, hospitals, and social services.
Types of support: Matching funds, continuing support, emergency funds, building funds.
Limitations: Giving primarily in NY. No grants to individuals, or for endowment funds, scholarships, or fellowships.
Application information: Contributes only to pre-selected organizations. Applications not accepted.
Board meeting date(s): Mar., June, Sept., and Dec.
Officers and Trustees:* Catherine P. Joyce,* Pres. and Treas.; Timothy J. Joyce,* V.P. and Secy.; George J. Gillespie.
Number of staff: None.
Employer Identification Number: 366054112

4630
Julia R. and Estelle L. Foundation, Inc. ▼ ⌑
817 Washington St.
Buffalo 14203 (716) 857-3325

Incorporated in 1941 in NY.
Donor(s): Peter C. Cornell Trust, R. John Oishei.†
Foundation type: Independent
Financial data (yr. ended 12/31/88): Assets, $20,748,360 (M); gifts received, $1,332,611; expenditures, $1,856,873, including $1,820,000 for 129 grants (high: $94,500; low: $200; average: $2,000-$28,000).
Purpose and activities: Emphasis on hospitals and medical research, higher and secondary education, and social services, including programs for the aged and youth; some support for health agencies and cultural programs.
Types of support: General purposes, research, building funds.
Limitations: Giving primarily in Buffalo, NY. No grants to individuals.
Application information: Application form not required.
Deadline(s): None
Write: Richard L. Wolf
Officers and Directors:* R. John Oishei,* Pres.; Rupert Warren,* V.P. and Secy.-Treas.; Carl E. Larson,* V.P.
Members: Patricia O. Colby, Julian R. Oishei.
Number of staff: None.
Employer Identification Number: 160874319

4631
Jurodin Fund, Inc. ⌑
630 Fifth Ave., Rm. 1418
New York 10111

Incorporated in 1960 in DE.
Donor(s): Julius Silver.
Foundation type: Independent
Financial data (yr. ended 12/31/88): Assets, $9,627,490 (M); expenditures, $501,129, including $445,425 for grants (high: $100,500).
Purpose and activities: Grants largely for hospitals, higher education, and Jewish welfare funds.
Limitations: Giving primarily in NY.
Application information: Application form not required.
Deadline(s): None
Write: Julius Silver, Pres.
Officers: Julius Silver, Pres.; Roslyn Silver, V.P.; Enid Winslow, V.P.
Employer Identification Number: 136169166

4632
Alfred Jurzykowski Foundation, Inc. ▼
21 East 40th St.
New York 10016 (212) 689-2460
Address for award nominations by scholarly and cultural institutions: Cultural Advisory Comm., 15 East 65th St., New York, NY 10021

Incorporated in 1960 in NY.
Donor(s): Alfred Jurzykowski.†
Foundation type: Independent
Financial data (yr. ended 12/31/88): Assets, $17,099,790 (M); expenditures, $1,114,674, including $913,576 for 75 grants (high: $100,000; low: $500; average: $5,000-$15,000) and $56,000 for 16 grants to individuals (high: $5,000; low: $1,000; average: $1,000-$5,000).
Purpose and activities: Grants primarily for projects in the fields of culture and education. Annual awards, by nomination only, for achievement in science, the arts, medicine, and literary translations by scholars, writers, and artists of Polish ethnic background regardless of their residence or citizenship.
Types of support: Operating budgets, annual campaigns, special projects, general purposes, exchange programs, matching funds, continuing support.
Limitations: Giving primarily in the New York, NY, metropolitan area. No grants to individuals (except for awards made by nomination only), or for endowment funds; no loans.
Publications: Application guidelines.
Application information: Application form not required.
Initial approach: Proposal
Copies of proposal: 1
Deadline(s): 1 month before board meetings
Board meeting date(s): Jan., May, and Sept.
Final notification: 2 weeks after board meeting
Write: Mrs. Bluma D. Cohen, V.P.
Officers and Trustees:* Yolande L. Jurzykowski,* Exec. V.P.; Bluma D. Cohen,* V.P. and Exec. Dir.; M. Christine Jurzykowski,* Secy.-Treas.; Karin Falencki, William Pyka, M.D.
Number of staff: None.
Employer Identification Number: 136192256

4633
Max Kade Foundation, Inc. ▼
100 Church St., Rm. 1604
New York 10007 (212) 964-7980

Incorporated in 1944 in NY.
Donor(s): Max Kade.†
Foundation type: Independent
Financial data (yr. ended 12/31/89): Assets, $48,023,120 (M); expenditures, $2,396,936, including $1,986,325 for 111 grants (high: $75,000; low: $1,000; average: $1,000-$30,000).
Purpose and activities: Grants primarily to higher educational institutions, with present emphasis on postdoctoral research exchange programs between the U.S. and Europe in medicine or in the natural and physical sciences. Foreign scholars and scientists are selected by the sponsoring universities upon nomination by the respective Academy of Sciences. Grants also for visiting faculty exchange programs, the training of language teachers, and the development of language centers at qualified colleges and universities.
Types of support: Exchange programs.
Limitations: No grants to individuals, or for operating budgets, capital funds, development campaigns, or endowment funds; no loans.
Application information:
Initial approach: Letter or proposal

Deadline(s): None
Board meeting date(s): As required
Write: Erich H. Markel, Pres.
Officers and Directors:* Erich H. Markel,* Pres.; Edgar Schwaibold,* V.P.; Reimer Koch-Weser,* Secy.; Hans G. Hachmann,* Treas.; Berteline Dale-Baier, Fritz Kade, Fritz Kade, Jr., M.D.
Number of staff: 4 full-time professional.
Employer Identification Number: 135658082

4634
Irving B. Kahn Foundation ¤ ☆
375 Park Ave.
New York 10152-0001

Donor(s): Irving B. Kahn.
Foundation type: Independent
Financial data (yr. ended 11/30/89): Assets, $18,662 (M); gifts received, $40,000; expenditures, $143,701, including $142,900 for grants (high: $105,000).
Purpose and activities: Support for Jewish welfare funds, higher education, and hospitals.
Limitations: Giving primarily in NY.
Directors: Milton H. Hendler, Irving B. Kahn, David Rosenzweig.
Employer Identification Number: 133150036

4635
Peter S. Kalikow Foundation, Inc.
101 Park Ave.
New York 10178-0002

Estalbished in 1983 in NY.
Donor(s): Peter S. Kalikow.
Foundation type: Independent
Financial data (yr. ended 06/30/89): Assets, $39,747 (M); gifts received, $1,697,994; expenditures, $1,995,423, including $1,987,850 for 85 grants (high: $1,000,000; low: $175).
Purpose and activities: Support primarily for Jewish organizations, hospitals and medical research, a Christian church, cultural programs, child welfare, and higher and other education.
Types of support: Building funds.
Limitations: Giving primarily in NY.
Application information: Application form not required.
Deadline(s): None
Officers: Peter S. Kalikow, Pres.; Mary Kalikow, Exec. V.P.; Gerald Shrager, V.P.; Florence Fletcher, Secy.; Daniel F. Cremins, Treas.
Employer Identification Number: 133182633

4636
Kalkin Family Foundation, Inc. ¤ ☆
c/o Saul L. Klaw & Co., PC
275 Madison Ave.
New York 10016

Established in 1983.
Foundation type: Independent
Financial data (yr. ended 12/31/88): Assets, $1,621,065 (M); expenditures, $148,604, including $147,389 for 39 grants (high: $107,289; low: $10).
Purpose and activities: Support primarily for a university and other higher education institutions, cultural programs, and Jewish organizations, including welfare funds.
Trustees: Adam Kalkin, Eugene W. Kalkin, Joan Kalkin, Nancy Kalkin, Saul L. Klaw, Stanley Lesser.
Employer Identification Number: 133185333

4637
Kane Lodge Foundation, Inc. ¤
P.O. Box 12446, Church St. Station
New York 10249
Application address: One Wall St., Suite 3600, New York, NY 10015; Tel.: (212) 344-3488

Established in 1960 in NY.
Foundation type: Independent
Financial data (yr. ended 09/30/88): Assets, $1,136,038 (M); expenditures, $61,622, including $39,500 for 13 grants (high: $5,000; low: $1,000).
Purpose and activities: Support primarily for museums, education, and social services.
Limitations: Giving primarily in New York, NY.
Application information:
Initial approach: Letter
Deadline(s): None
Write: John Stitcher, Pres.
Officers: John Stitcher, Pres.; Herman E. Muller, Jr., V.P.; John R. Ahlgren, Secy.; John Campbell Henry, Treas.
Directors: Albert C. Valentine, Rodney I. Woods.
Employer Identification Number: 136105390

4638
Lazare and Charlotte Kaplan Foundation, Inc.
P.O. Box 216
Livingston Manor 12758 (914) 439-4544

Established in 1965 in NY.
Donor(s): Lazare Kaplan,† George Kaplan.
Foundation type: Independent
Financial data (yr. ended 12/31/89): Assets, $1,484,000 (M); expenditures, $124,000, including $20,000 for 7 grants (high: $3,500; low: $1,500; average: $2,000) and $92,000 for 110 grants to individuals (high: $2,000; low: $400; average: $800-$1,000).
Purpose and activities: Giving primarily for scholarships for higher education with priority to students or former graduates from Livingston Manor, Rosene, Liberty, and Jeffersonville, NY.
Types of support: Student aid, fellowships.
Limitations: Giving limited to Sullivan County, NY, particularly Livingston Manor.
Application information: Payments are made directly to colleges on behalf of individuals. Application form required.
Initial approach: Contact high school guidance counselor
Deadline(s): May 1
Board meeting date(s): Quarterly and as required
Final notification: June 30
Write: Irving Avery, Treas.
Officers and Directors:* Russell Ludlum, V.P.; Mary Fried, Secy.; Irving Avery, Treas.; George Kaplan, Paul Alan Kaplan, Leon Siegel.
Selection Committee Members: Irving Avery, Chair.; Mary Fried, Otto Hoos, Russell Ludlum.
Number of staff: None.
Employer Identification Number: 136193153

4639
Rita J. and Stanley H. Kaplan Foundation, Inc.
866 United Nations Plaza
New York 10017 (212) 688-1047

Incorporated in 1984 in NY.
Donor(s): Stanley H. Kaplan, Rita J. Kaplan.
Foundation type: Independent
Financial data (yr. ended 12/31/88): Assets, $11,580,690 (M); gifts received, $3,100,676; expenditures, $601,272, including $527,166 for 192 grants (high: $125,000; low: $10).
Purpose and activities: Emphasis on Jewish welfare organizations; support also for cutural programs, including music, arts, theater, dance, performing arts, and museums; medical research and education, including AIDS and cancer programs; higher and other education; and social and family services.
Types of support: Annual campaigns, capital campaigns, building funds, continuing support, general purposes, research.
Limitations: Giving primarily in NY.
Application information: Contributes only to pre-selected organizations. Applications not accepted.
Officers and Directors:* Stanley H. Kaplan,* Pres.; Rita J. Kaplan,* Secy.; Nancy Kaplan Belsky, Paul Alan Kaplan, Susan Beth Kaplan.
Number of staff: 1 part-time professional; 1 part-time support.
Employer Identification Number: 133221298

4640
The J. M. Kaplan Fund, Inc. ▼
30 Rockefeller Plaza, Suite 4250
New York 10112 (212) 767-0630

Incorporated in 1948 in NY as Faigel Leah Foundation, Inc.; The J.M. Kaplan Fund, Inc., a DE corporation, merged with it in 1975 and was renamed The J.M. Kaplan Fund, Inc.
Donor(s): Members of the J.M. Kaplan family.
Foundation type: Independent
Financial data (yr. ended 11/30/89): Assets, $85,050,185 (M); qualifying distributions, $10,891,366, including $6,908,000 for grants (average: $5,000-$50,000) and $3,983,366 for 2 loans.
Purpose and activities: Giving in four areas: 1) New York Environment--conservation, architecture, historic preservation, and strong neighborhoods; rational planning by government; and enhancement of natural resources, public gardens, and parks; 2) Rural New York--protection of farmlands and open space; 3) Arts--libraries, writers' organizations, special publications, exhibitions, catalogues, and music groups of a high order; and 4) Civil Liberties and Human Needs--to end prejudice and ensure First Amendment rights and other legal protections, basic public services, and worldwide human rights.
Types of support: Continuing support, seed money, special projects, publications, technical assistance, general purposes, operating budgets, land acquisition.
Limitations: Giving primarily in NY, with emphasis on New York City; and for rural open space and farmland preservation programs in NY State, with emphasis on the Hudson River Valley. No support for medicine, science, theater, or dance. No grants to individuals;

films or video; building, operating, or endowment funds; annual campaigns; deficit financing; equipment and materials; renovation projects; or scholarships, fellowships, conferences, research, prizes, study, or travel.
Publications: Annual report (including application guidelines).
Application information: Application form required.
Initial approach: Telephone or letter
Copies of proposal: 1
Deadline(s): Submit proposal only from Mar. 1 to Oct. 15; Music proposals in Sept. only
Board meeting date(s): As required
Final notification: 2 months
Write: Joan K. Davidson, Pres.
Officers: Joan K. Davidson,* Pres.; Elizabeth K. Fonseca,* V.P.; Mary E. Kaplan,* V.P.; Richard D. Kaplan,* V.P.; John Matthew Davidson,* Secy.; Henry Ng, Chief Admin. Officer; Anthony C. Wood,* Prog. Officer; Suzanne Davis, Exec. Dir.
Trustees:* Maurice Austin, Betsy Davidson, Bradford Davidson, Peter Davidson, Bruno Fonseca, Caio Fonseca, Isabel Fonseca, Quina Fonseca, Maurice C. Kaplan.
Number of staff: 4 full-time professional; 4 full-time support.
Employer Identification Number: 136090286

4641
Morris J. and Betty Kaplun Foundation ⌑
c/o Zvi Levavy, Wertheim & Co.
225 West 34th St., No. 1910
New York 10001 (212) 953-1800

Incorporated in 1955 in NY.
Donor(s): Morris J. Kaplun.†
Foundation type: Independent
Financial data (yr. ended 8/31/88): Assets, $2,863,996 (M); expenditures, $147,974, including $87,530 for 35 grants (high: $17,500; low: $180).
Purpose and activities: Grants largely for Jewish-sponsored education, especially higher education, and welfare funds.
Limitations: Giving primarily in New York, NY.
Application information: Application form not required.
Deadline(s): None
Officers: Zvi Levavy, Pres.; Gloria Isakower, V.P.; Lawrence Marin, V.P.; Herbert Rothman, V.P.; Aaron Seligson, V.P.; Moshe Sheinbaum, V.P.
Employer Identification Number: 136096009

4642
The Howard Karagheusian Commemorative Corporation
386 Park Ave. South, Suite 1601
New York 10016 (212) 725-0973

Incorporated in 1921 in NY.
Donor(s): Miran Karagheusian,† Zabelle Karagheusian,† Leila Karagheusian, Vartan H. Jinishian,† and others.
Foundation type: Operating
Financial data (yr. ended 12/31/89): Assets, $19,081,825 (M); expenditures, $851,755, including $75,500 for 19 grants (high: $25,000; low: $200) and $665,408 for foundation-administered programs.
Purpose and activities: A private operating foundation established to promote child welfare, public health services, and relief programs in Armenian refugee communities of Greece, Lebanon, and Syria and, on a smaller scale, in native Moslem Arab groups in the same communities.
Limitations: Giving primarily in the Middle East. No grants to individuals; no loans.
Publications: Annual report.
Application information: Applications for scholarships and research projects not accepted. Applications not accepted.
Write: Walter C. Bandazian, Exec. Dir.
Officers: Leila Karagheusian,* Pres.; Pergrouhi Svajian,* V.P.; Walter J. Corno,* Secy.-Treas.; Walter C. Bandazian, Exec. Dir.
Directors:* Harry A. Dorian, Michael Haratunian, Edward Janjigian, Vasken L. Parsegian, Alan G. Philibosian, Irma Der Stepanian, Richard J. Varadian.
Number of staff: 2 full-time professional; 3 part-time professional.
Employer Identification Number: 136149578

4643
The Harvey L. Karp Foundation, Inc. ⌑
P.O. Box 30
East Hampton 11937

Established in 1968 in NY.
Foundation type: Independent
Financial data (yr. ended 06/30/89): Assets, $1,347,195 (M); expenditures, $51,263, including $38,630 for 41 grants (high: $3,400; low: $20).
Purpose and activities: Emphasis on the arts, higher education, medical research, and Jewish giving.
Limitations: Giving primarily in New York, NY.
Application information: Contributes only to pre-selected organizations. Applications not accepted.
Officers: Harvey L. Karp, Pres. and Treas.; Robert B. Hodes, Secy.
Employer Identification Number: 132621240

4644
Suzanne T. and Irving D. Karpas Jr. Foundation, Inc.
(Formerly Karpas Family Foundation, Inc.)
c/o Polakoff & Michaelson
90 West St.
New York 10006 (212) 227-0634

Incorporated in 1947 in DE.
Foundation type: Independent
Financial data (yr. ended 12/31/89): Assets, $1,572,027 (M); expenditures, $127,747, including $118,593 for 26 grants (high: $62,340; low: $25).
Purpose and activities: Giving primarily for hospitals and Jewish welfare organizations.
Limitations: Giving primarily in NY. No grants to individuals.
Application information: Contributes only to pre-selected organizations. Applications not accepted.
Officers: Irving D. Karpas, Jr., Pres.; Bruce T. Karpas, V.P.; Matthew P. Karpas, V.P.; Patricia E. Karpas, V.P.; Suzanne T. Karpas, V.P.; Arnold R. Beiles, Secy.; Theodore R. Shiffman, Treas.
Number of staff: None.
Employer Identification Number: 136116217

4645
Otsar Kassin Foundation, Inc. ⌑
313 Fifth Ave.
New York 10016 (212) 889-7602

Established in 1974.
Donor(s): Members of the Kassin family, Transworld Textile.
Foundation type: Independent
Financial data (yr. ended 11/30/88): Assets, $12,538 (M); gifts received, $141,002; expenditures, $133,932, including $133,839 for grants (high: $17,200).
Purpose and activities: Grants primarily for Jewish educational institutions.
Limitations: No grants to individuals.
Application information:
Initial approach: Letter
Deadline(s): None
Write: Saul Kassin, Pres.
Officer: Saul Kassin, Pres.
Employer Identification Number: 510168548

4646
Howard & Holly Katz Foundation ⌑
Goldman, Sachs & Co.
85 Broad St., Tax Dept.
New York 10004-2408

Established in 1983 in NY.
Donor(s): Howard C. Katz.
Foundation type: Independent
Financial data (yr. ended 8/31/88): Assets, $201,526 (M); gifts received, $125,000; expenditures, $202,964, including $202,607 for 46 grants (high: $50,000; low: $100).
Purpose and activities: Support for Jewish welfare, health services, cultural organizations and educational institutions.
Limitations: Giving primarily in New York, NY. No grants to individuals; or for scholarships; no loans.
Application information: Contributes only to pre-selected organizations. Applications not accepted.
Trustees: Holly M. Katz, Howard C. Katz, Ronald S. Tauber.
Employer Identification Number: 133199938

4647
M. D. Katz Foundation, Inc. ⌑ ☆
1399 Carroll St.
Brooklyn 11213-4449

Established in 1960.
Donor(s): Mordecai D. Katz, Monique C. Katz.
Foundation type: Independent
Financial data (yr. ended 7/31/88): Assets, $1,104,494 (M); gifts received, $100,000; expenditures, $58,390, including $46,667 for 66 grants (high: $20,000; low: $10).
Purpose and activities: Support for higher education, including medical education; support also for Jewish organizations, including welfare funds, religious associations, and yeshivas.
Limitations: Giving primarily in NY and NJ. No grants to individuals.
Application information: Contributes only to pre-selected organizations. Applications not accepted.

Officers: Mordecai D. Katz, Pres. and Treas.; Frieda Katz, V.P. and Secy.; Monique C. Katz, V.P.
Employer Identification Number: 116035541

4648
The Katzenberger Foundation, Inc. ⌑
c/o Golieb & Golieb
Six East 43rd St.
New York 10017 (212) 687-3340

Incorporated in 1952 in NY.
Donor(s): Walter B. Katzenberger,† Helen Katherine Katzenberger,† The Advertising Checking Bureau, Inc.
Foundation type: Independent
Financial data (yr. ended 11/30/88): Assets, $9,834,082 (M); expenditures, $682,694, including $600,000 for 46 grants (high: $150,000; low: $1,000).
Purpose and activities: Grants for church support, welfare, higher and secondary education, the performing arts, and youth agencies.
Limitations: No grants to individuals; or for scholarships.
Application information:
Initial approach: Letter
Copies of proposal: 2
Deadline(s): Submit proposal preferably between July and Oct.; deadline Oct. 31
Board meeting date(s): Nov. and May
Write: Abner J. Golieb, Pres.
Officers and Directors:* Abner J. Golieb,* Pres.; Edward Davis,* Secy.; Richard Eason, Warren Grieb, Jon McIntyre, Earl Swanson.
Employer Identification Number: 136094434

4649
Eric & Ruth Katzenstein Foundation, Inc. ⌑ ☆
100 Overlook Terrace
New York 10040-3852

Established in 1960.
Donor(s): Eric S. Katzenstein.
Foundation type: Independent
Financial data (yr. ended 12/31/87): Assets, $277,142 (M); gifts received, $110,250; expenditures, $116,893, including $116,275 for 131 grants (high: $10,000; low: $36).
Purpose and activities: Giving for Jewish welfare and Jewish giving, including yeshivas and temple support.
Application information:
Deadline(s): None
Write: Eric S. Katzenstein, Pres.
Officers: Eric S. Katzenstein, Pres. and Treas.; Ruth B. Katzenstein, V.P. and Secy.
Directors: Theodore D. Katzenstein, Morris B. Klugman.
Employer Identification Number: 136089435

4650
Henry & Elaine Kaufman Foundation, Inc. ⌑
767 Fifth Ave.
New York 10153

Established in 1969.
Donor(s): Elaine Kaufman, Henry Kaufman, Henry Kaufman Charitable Lead Trust.
Foundation type: Independent
Financial data (yr. ended 12/31/87): Assets, $5,925,581 (M); gifts received, $353,459; expenditures, $381,844, including $258,055 for 50 grants (high: $50,000; low: $25).
Purpose and activities: Grants primarily for higher education and Jewish welfare funds and temple support.
Application information:
Initial approach: Letter
Deadline(s): None
Write: Dr. Henry Kaufman, Pres. or Elaine Kaufman, V.P.
Officers and Directors: Henry Kaufman, Pres. and Treas.; Elaine Kaufman, V.P.; George DeSipio, Secy.; Glen Kaufman.
Employer Identification Number: 237045903

4651
Henry Kaufmann Foundation ▼
300 Park Ave.
New York 10022 (212) 909-5951

Incorporated in 1928 in NY.
Donor(s): Henry Kaufmann.†
Foundation type: Independent
Financial data (yr. ended 12/31/89): Assets, $7,286,484 (M); expenditures, $1,234,154, including $1,168,868 for 23 grants (high: $275,000; low: $2,500; average: $15,000-$100,000).
Purpose and activities: Capital grants principally for geriatric care facilities, arts and educational institutions, Jewish giving and welfare funds, and camping and community centers.
Types of support: Building funds, equipment, general purposes, capital campaigns, land acquisition, professorships, renovation projects.
Limitations: Giving primarily in the New York, NY, and Pittsburgh, PA, metropolitan areas. No grants to individuals, or for endowment funds, operating budgets, scholarships, fellowships, or matching gifts; no loans.
Publications: 990-PF, annual report.
Application information: Application form not required.
Initial approach: Written proposal
Copies of proposal: 2
Deadline(s): Submit written proposal preferably 1 or 2 months before board meeting dates; no set deadline
Board meeting date(s): May and Nov.
Final notification: After board meetings (positive replies only)
Write: Jeffrey A. Horwitz, Asst. Secy.
Officers: Walter Mendelsohn,* Chair. and Pres.; Maurice B. Hexter,* V.P. and Treas.; Daniel D. Mielnicki, Secy.
Directors:* Leonard N. Block, William T. Golden, Charles Looker, Frederick P. Rose, John M. Wolf, Sr.
Number of staff: None.
Employer Identification Number: 136034179

4652
Marion Esser Kaufmann Foundation ⌑ ☆
c/o Weber & Cardillo
2525 Palmer Ave.
New Rochelle 10801
Application address: 11 Westway, Bronxville, NY 10708; Tel.: (914) 337-3332

Established in 1986 in NY.
Donor(s): Marion Esser Kaufmann.†
Foundation type: Independent
Financial data (yr. ended 12/31/88): Assets, $5,193,382 (M); gifts received, $40,000; expenditures, $240,896, including $150,000 for 3 grants (high: $100,000; low: $20,000).
Purpose and activities: Giving for higher education and research on Alzheimer's disease.
Types of support: Research, scholarship funds.
Limitations: Giving primarily in NY. No grants to individuals.
Application information:
Deadline(s): None
Final notification: Within 3 months
Write: Frederick L. Bissinger, Trustee
Trustees: Frederick L. Bissinger, Richard Esser.
Employer Identification Number: 133339941

4653
Kautz Family Foundation ⌑ ☆
c/o Goldman Sachs & Co., Tax Dept.
85 Broad St.
New York 10004-2106

Established in 1981 in NY.
Donor(s): James C. Kautz.
Foundation type: Independent
Financial data (yr. ended 2/28/89): Assets, $2,836,140 (M); gifts received, $420,938; expenditures, $98,358, including $95,025 for 47 grants (high: $20,000; low: $100).
Purpose and activities: Giving primarily for higher education; support also for human services, including child welfare and youth groups.
Limitations: Giving primarily in NY. No grants to individuals.
Application information: Applications not accepted.
Trustees: Caroline M. Kautz, Daniel P. Kautz, James C. Kautz, Leslie B. Kautz, Roy J. Zuckerberg.
Employer Identification Number: 133103149

4654
Kaye Foundation ⌑
c/o Fred N. Fishman
425 Park Ave.
New York 10022

Donor(s): Kaye, Scholer, Fierman, Hays & Handler.
Foundation type: Company-sponsored
Financial data (yr. ended 11/30/88): Assets, $8,378 (M); gifts received, $110,000; expenditures, $178,000, including $178,000 for 5 grants (high: $110,000; low: $2,500).
Purpose and activities: Support for community funds and organizations that promote progressive and public law.
Limitations: Giving primarily in NY.
Application information: Application form not required.
Initial approach: Letter
Deadline(s): None
Write: Alan Capilupi, Controller
Trustees: Peter M. Fishbein, Fred N. Fishman, David Klingsberg, Sheldon Oliensis, Stanley D. Robinson, Sidney Silberman.
Employer Identification Number: 237161546

4655
Ezra Jack Keats Foundation, Inc. ⌑ ☆
c/o Moses & Schreiber
3000 Marcus Ave., Suite 1625
Lake Success 11042
Application address: 1005 East Fourth St., Brooklyn, NY 11230; Tel.: (718) 252-4047

Foundation type: Independent
Financial data (yr. ended 12/31/88): Assets, $182,991 (M); expenditures, $122,100, including $105,450 for 43 grants (high: $23,000; low: $30).
Purpose and activities: Support for higher education, the arts, and organizations concerned with Israel.
Application information: Application form not required.
Deadline(s): None
Write: Martin Pope, Pres.
Officers: Martin Pope, Pres.; Melvin Schreiber, Secy.
Employer Identification Number: 237072750

4656
Anna Maria & Stephen Kellen Foundation, Inc. ⌑ ☆
45 Broadway, 29th Fl.
New York 10006-3007

Donor(s): Stephen M. Kellen, Anna Maria Kellen.
Foundation type: Independent
Financial data (yr. ended 4/30/89): Assets, $1,388,728 (M); gifts received, $647,228; expenditures, $128,484, including $125,975 for grants.
Purpose and activities: Giving primarily to cultural programs, including museums and performing arts groups; support also for higher and secondary education and a cancer research institute.
Limitations: Giving primarily in NY.
Application information: Contributes only to pre-selected organizations. Applications not accepted.
Officers and Directors: Anna Maria Kellen, Pres.; Michael Kellen, V.P. and Secy.; Stephen M. Kellen, Treas.; Anna Maria Kellen.
Employer Identification Number: 133173593

4657
J. C. Kellogg Foundation ⌑
c/o Spear, Leeds & Kellogg
115 Broadway
New York 10006

Established in 1954 in NY.
Donor(s): Morris W. Kellogg, James C. Kellogg IV, Elizabeth I. Kellogg.
Foundation type: Independent
Financial data (yr. ended 8/31/88): Assets, $2,635,225 (M); gifts received, $248,244; expenditures, $127,628, including $73,700 for 19 grants (high: $25,000; low: $50).
Purpose and activities: Support for hospitals, schools, and youth programs.
Application information: Contributes only to pre-selected organizations. Applications not accepted.
Write: Frank E. Witt
Officers and Trustees: Elizabeth I. Kellogg, Pres.; James C. Kellogg IV, Secy.; Nancy K. Gifford, Morris W. Kellogg, Peter R. Kellogg, Richard I. Kellogg.
Employer Identification Number: 136092448

4658
Kellogg Free Library
Main St.
Cincinnatus 13040

Established in 1930 in NY.
Foundation type: Independent
Financial data (yr. ended 12/31/88): Assets, $1,556,598 (M); gifts received, $2,977; expenditures, $78,123, including $3,805 for 3 grants (high: $1,805; low: $1,000).
Purpose and activities: Grants primarily for community services and libraries.
Types of support: Equipment.
Limitations: Giving limited to Cortland County, NY, for libraries and the Cincinnatus, NY, School District for community development.
Application information: Applications not accepted.
Write: Robert Burt, Pres.
Officers: Robert Burt, Pres.; Franklin Ufford, V.P.; Carol Harrington, Secy.; Marion Curry, Treas.
Number of staff: 3 part-time support.
Employer Identification Number: 150594533

4659
The Kempner Foundation, Inc. ⌑
c/o Peat Marwick Main & Co.
345 Park Ave., 29th Fl.
New York 10154

Incorporated in 1955 in NY.
Donor(s): Alan H. Kempner, Margaret L. Kempner, Thomas L. Kempner, and others.
Foundation type: Independent
Financial data (yr. ended 11/30/86): Assets, $104,585 (M); gifts received, $76,762; expenditures, $137,158, including $133,272 for 143 grants (high: $15,000; low: $25).
Purpose and activities: Giving largely for higher education, hospitals, and Jewish welfare funds; support also for youth agencies.
Application information: Contributes only to pre-selected organizations. Applications not accepted.
Officers: Margaret L. Kempner, Pres.; Charles H. Guggenheimer, Secy.
Employer Identification Number: 136085600

4660
Ethel Kennedy Foundation ⌑ ☆
Box 82
Cold Spring Harbor 11724

Established in 1986.
Foundation type: Independent
Financial data (yr. ended 12/31/88): Assets, $3,981,282 (M); expenditures, $176,089, including $172,000 for 64 grants (high: $25,000; low: $500).
Purpose and activities: Giving for higher and secondary education, social services and child welfare organizations, health associations, hospitals, and community funds.
Limitations: No grants to individuals.
Application information:
Initial approach: Letter
Deadline(s): None
Write: Ethel K. Marran
Officers: Ethel K. Marran, Pres. and Treas.; Elizabeth Marran, V.P.; Laura Marran, Secy.
Employer Identification Number: 112768682

4661
Karen A. & Kevin W. Kennedy Foundation ⌑ ☆
85 Broad St., Tax Dept.
New York 10004

Donor(s): Kevin W. Kennedy.
Foundation type: Independent
Financial data (yr. ended 04/30/89): Assets, $140,036 (M); gifts received, $106,703; expenditures, $142,675, including $141,700 for 33 grants (high: $100,000; low: $100).
Purpose and activities: Support for community funds and health services.
Limitations: Giving primarily in NY and NJ. No grants to individuals.
Application information: Contributes only to pre-selected organizations. Applications not accepted.
Trustees: Alfred C. Eckert III, Karen A. Kennedy, Kevin W. Kennedy.
Employer Identification Number: 133318161

4662
Marion E. Kenworthy - Sarah H. Swift Foundation, Inc.
300 East 34th St., 19C
New York 10016 (212) 685-4918

Established about 1963 in NY.
Foundation type: Independent
Financial data (yr. ended 12/31/88): Assets, $5,789,157 (M); expenditures, $372,492, including $350,745 for 25 grants (high: $53,000; low: $3,000; average: $1,000-$40,000).
Purpose and activities: Giving primarily for mental health programs; social services, including programs for youth and child welfare and development, education programs for minorities, family services, delinquency and drug abuse, welfare, and legal services; the advancement of psychiatry; and the performing arts.
Types of support: Continuing support, deficit financing, research, seed money, general purposes, publications, special projects.
Limitations: Giving primarily in Washington, DC, CT, and NY. No grants to individuals, or for building funds.
Application information: Application form not required.
Initial approach: Telephone conversation with president for new applicants
Copies of proposal: 6
Deadline(s): Apr. 1 and Nov. 1
Board meeting date(s): May and Dec.
Final notification: 2 months after board meeting
Write: Dr. Maurice V. Russell, Pres.
Officers: Maurice V. Russell, Chair. and Pres.; M. John Rockmore, V.P.; Stephen Wise Tulin, Secy.-Treas.
Number of staff: 1 part-time support.
Employer Identification Number: 136140940

4663
Keren Alta Fiega Teitelbaum Fund, Inc. ⌑ ☆
P.O. Box 566
Monroe 10950

Established in 1984 in NY.
Foundation type: Independent
Financial data (yr. ended 5/31/87): Assets, $54,233 (M); gifts received, $158,039; expenditures, $168,614, including $168,600 for 1 grant.
Purpose and activities: Initial year of grantmaking activity, fiscal 1987; support for a Jewish congregation.
Types of support: Deficit financing.
Trustees: Joseph Ashkenazy, Abraham Lefkowitz, Joseph Wassner.
Employer Identification Number: 222675996

4664
Hagop Kevorkian Fund ▼ ⌑
1411 Third Ave.
New York 10028

Trust established in 1950; incorporated in 1951 in NY.
Donor(s): Hagop Kevorkian.†
Foundation type: Independent
Financial data (yr. ended 12/31/88): Assets, $7,976,773 (M); expenditures, $961,626, including $765,680 for 11 grants (high: $489,186; low: $1,000; average: $6,700-$79,000).
Purpose and activities: To promote interest in Near and Middle Eastern art through exhibitions and through fellowships administered by the recipient institutions for research and study in this field.
Types of support: Fellowships, research.
Limitations: No grants to individuals.
Application information: Contributes only to pre-selected organizations. Applications not accepted.
Write: Ralph D. Minasian, Secy.-Treas.
Officers and Trustees: Stephen Chan, Chair. and Exec. V.P.; Marjorie Kevorkian, Pres. and Curator; Ralph D. Minasian, Secy.-Treas.; Miriam Chan, Martin D. Polevoy.
Employer Identification Number: 131839686

4665
Key Food Stores Foundation, Inc. ⌑ ☆
8925 Ave. D
Brooklyn 11236-1679 (718) 451-1000

Donor(s): Camillo Durso, Camillo Supermarkets.
Foundation type: Company-sponsored
Financial data (yr. ended 08/31/89): Assets, $113,789 (M); gifts received, $100,203; expenditures, $110,610, including $110,585 for 29 grants (high: $69,000; low: $25).
Purpose and activities: Emphasis on Jewish giving, health, hospitals, and health clinics.
Application information: Application form not required.
Deadline(s): None
Write: Allen Newman, Trustee
Trustees: Sheldon Geller, Lawrence Mandel, Allen Newman.
Employer Identification Number: 116035538

4666
The Kidder Peabody Foundation ▼ ⌑
c/o Kidder, Peabody & Co., Inc.
20 Exchange Pl.
New York 10005 (212) 510-5502

Incorporated in 1959 in NY.
Donor(s): Kidder, Peabody & Co., Inc.
Foundation type: Company-sponsored
Financial data (yr. ended 12/31/87): Assets, $3,299,233 (M); expenditures, $372,898, including $355,050 for 73 grants.
Purpose and activities: Emphasis on higher and secondary education; support also for arts, culture, and hospitals.
Limitations: Giving primarily in NY and areas where company maintains offices. No support for religious organizations. No grants to individuals; no loans.
Application information: Application form not required.
Initial approach: Letter
Deadline(s): None
Board meeting date(s): Annually
Write: Helen B. Platt, V.P.
Officers and Directors: Silas S. Cathcart, Chair.; Max C. Chapman, Jr., Pres.; Helen B. Platt, V.P.; John Liftin, Secy.; Joseph Martorella, Treas.
Number of staff: None.
Employer Identification Number: 136085918

4667
Walter H. D. Killough Trust
c/o Marine Midland Bank, N.A.
250 Park Ave., 2nd Fl.
New York 10177 (212) 503-2774

Trust established in 1929 in NY.
Donor(s): Walter H.D. Killough.†
Foundation type: Independent
Financial data (yr. ended 07/31/89): Assets, $2,325,953 (M); expenditures, $157,969, including $104,189 for grants (high: $29,136; low: $938).
Purpose and activities: Specific grants to designated educational and humane organizations; discretionary grants restricted primarily to hospitals and homes for the aged; scholarships limited to graduates of Erasmus High School, Brooklyn, New York.
Types of support: Equipment, general purposes, operating budgets, research, special projects, building funds.
Limitations: Giving primarily in NJ, NY, and PA. No grants to individuals.
Application information: Application form not required.
Initial approach: Submit proposal and most recent audited financial report
Copies of proposal: 1
Deadline(s): Oct. 15
Board meeting date(s): Nov. 30
Final notification: Jan. 15
Write: W. Gary Ogburn, V.P.
Officer: W. Gary Ogburn, V.P.
Trustees: Norman S. Fink, Rt. Rev. Robert C. Witcher, Marine Midland Bank, N.A.
Employer Identification Number: 136063894

4668
Helen & Milton Kimmelman Foundation ⌑
745 Fifth Ave., Suite 2204
New York 10151-0001

Established in 1982 in NY.
Donor(s): Milton Kimmelman.†
Foundation type: Independent
Financial data (yr. ended 11/30/88): Assets, $10,834,316 (M); gifts received, $2,369,316; expenditures, $3,826,152, including $3,775,727 for 95 grants (high: $950,000).
Purpose and activities: Giving primarily for Jewish welfare funds and other Jewish organizations, and the visual and performing arts, including museums; support also for medical research and education, and the environment.
Types of support: General purposes, matching funds, program-related investments, building funds.
Application information: Contributes only to pre-selected organizations. Applications not accepted.
Trustee: Helen Kimmelman.
Employer Identification Number: 133110688

4669
Don King Foundation, Inc.
c/o Don King Productions, Inc.
32 East 69th St.
New York 10021 (212) 794-2900

Established in 1969 in NY.
Donor(s): Donald King, Don King Productions, Inc.
Foundation type: Independent
Financial data (yr. ended 11/30/88): Assets, $1,241 (M); gifts received, $110,600; expenditures, $112,700, including $112,700 for 12 grants (high: $550,000; low: $200).
Purpose and activities: Support primarily for minority advocacy organizations; giving also to churches, higher education, youth groups, and a Jewish organization.
Application information: Individuals should submit resume of academic qualifications; organizations should submit proposal. Application form not required.
Copies of proposal: 3
Deadline(s): None
Board meeting date(s): June
Write: Henrietta King, V.P.
Officers: Donald King, Pres.; Henrietta King, V.P. and Secy.
Number of staff: None.
Employer Identification Number: 237047401

4670
Kings Point Richmond Foundation, Inc. ⌑
11 West 19th St.
New York 10011-4298 (212) 627-4646

Established in 1965 in NY.
Donor(s): Howard S. Richmond.
Foundation type: Independent
Financial data (yr. ended 12/31/88): Assets, $1,859,791 (M); gifts received, $313,281; expenditures, $120,459, including $114,883 for 120 grants (high: $20,000; low: $25).
Purpose and activities: Support for general charitable giving and education.

Application information: Application form not required.
Deadline(s): None
Write: Howard S. Richmond, Pres.
Officers: Howard S. Richmond, Pres., Treas., and Mgr.; Anita B. Richmond, V.P.; Bernard Gartlir, Secy.
Directors: Elizabeth Richmond, Frank Richmond, Larry Richmond, Phillip Richmond, Robert Richmond.
Employer Identification Number: 136180873

4671
KKR Charitable Trust ⌑
c/o Kohlberg, Kravis, Roberts & Co.
Nine West 57th St.
New York 10019

Established in 1985 in NY.
Donor(s): Jerome Kohlberg, Henry Kravis, George R. Roberts.
Foundation type: Independent
Financial data (yr. ended 6/30/88): Assets, $81,208 (M); gifts received, $50,000; expenditures, $478,099, including $464,620 for 3 grants (high: $339,620; low: $25,000).
Purpose and activities: Giving for higher education and health care.
Limitations: No grants to individuals.
Application information: Contributes only to pre-selected organizations. Applications not accepted.
Trustees: Thomas W. Hudson, Jr., John P. McLoughlin.
Employer Identification Number: 136857396

4672
The David and Sadie Klau Foundation
c/o Rochlin, Lipsky, Goodkin, Stoler & Company, P.C.
510 Fifth Ave.
New York 10036 (212) 840-6444
Application address: 993 Fifth Ave., New York, NY 10028

Incorporated in 1942 in NY.
Donor(s): David W. Klau.†
Foundation type: Independent
Financial data (yr. ended 12/31/87): Assets, $18,438,012 (M); expenditures, $723,818, including $649,249 for 164 grants (high: $200,000; low: $10).
Purpose and activities: Emphasis on health and hospitals, AIDS programs, higher and other education, Jewish welfare funds and temple support, child development and welfare, human services, and culture, including music and museums.
Types of support: General purposes, annual campaigns, building funds, capital campaigns.
Limitations: Giving primarily in New York, NY.
Application information:
Initial approach: Written request
Deadline(s): None
Board meeting date(s): As required
Write: Sadie K. Klau, Pres.
Officers and Directors:* Sadie K. Klau,* Pres.; Paula K. Oppenheim,* V.P., Secy., and Treas.; Lucille K. Carothers, James D. Klau, Felice K. Shea.
Number of staff: None.
Employer Identification Number: 136161378

4673
Klaus Family Foundation, Inc. ⌑
16 East 34th St.
New York 10016

Established in 1979 in NY.
Foundation type: Independent
Financial data (yr. ended 11/30/88): Assets, $2,913,202 (M); gifts received, $120,000; expenditures, $168,462, including $121,050 for 46 grants (high: $50,000; low: $100).
Purpose and activities: Emphasis on Jewish giving, education, and hospitals.
Limitations: Giving primarily in NY.
Application information: Contributes only to pre-selected organizations. Applications not accepted.
Trustees: Arthur Klaus, Lester Klaus, Mortimer Klaus.
Employer Identification Number: 133053197

4674
The Conrad and Virginia Klee Foundation, Inc. ⌑
700 Security Mutual Bldg.
80 Exchange St.
Binghamton 13901 (607) 723-5341

Incorporated in 1957 in NY.
Donor(s): Conrad C. Klee,† Virginia Klee.†
Foundation type: Independent
Financial data (yr. ended 12/31/88): Assets, $6,196,205 (M); gifts received, $899,765; expenditures, $362,641, including $362,641 for 35 grants (high: $77,000; low: $1,500).
Purpose and activities: Giving for community funds, Protestant church support, and higher education.
Limitations: Giving primarily in NY, especially Broome County and Guilford. No grants to individuals.
Application information: Application form not required.
Initial approach: Letter
Copies of proposal: 1
Deadline(s): None
Board meeting date(s): Apr. and Nov.
Write: Clayton M. Axtell, Jr., Pres.
Officers and Directors:* Clayton M. Axtell, Jr.,* Pres.; Richard R. Millar,* V.P. and Treas.; David K. Patterson,* Secy.
Employer Identification Number: 156019821

4675
The Calvin Klein Foundation ⌑
c/o Nathan Berkman & Co.
29 Broadway, Rm. 2800
New York 10006

Established in 1981 in NY.
Donor(s): Calvin Klein Industries, Inc.
Foundation type: Independent
Financial data (yr. ended 6/30/89): Assets, $38,342 (M); gifts received, $215,000; expenditures, $187,460, including $187,202 for grants (high: $25,000).
Purpose and activities: Giving primarily for medical research and health associations, including AIDS research; support also for Jewish organizations.
Limitations: Giving primarily in NY.
Application information: Application form not required.
Deadline(s): None
Trustees: Robert DiPaola, John Kabay.
Employer Identification Number: 133094765

4676
David L. Klein, Jr. Memorial Foundation, Inc. ⌑
c/o L.J. Podell
2181 Ralph Ave.
Brooklyn 11234

Incorporated in 1959 in NY.
Donor(s): David L. Klein,† Miriam Klein, Endo Laboratories, Inc.
Foundation type: Independent
Financial data (yr. ended 2/28/89): Assets, $2,273,276 (M); expenditures, $136,189, including $105,212 for 92 grants (high: $25,000; low: $10).
Purpose and activities: Emphasis on hospitals, medical research, Jewish welfare funds, temple support, higher education, and cultural activities.
Limitations: Giving primarily in NY. No grants to individuals.
Application information: Contributes only to pre-selected organizations. Applications not accepted.
Officer and Trustees: Miriam Klein, Pres.; Saretta Barnet, Marjorie Traub.
Employer Identification Number: 136085432

4677
Jack Kleinoder Foundation, Inc. ⌑ ☆
P.O. Box 310
Roslyn Heights 11577-0310

Donor(s): Jack Kleinodor.
Foundation type: Independent
Financial data (yr. ended 12/31/87): Assets, $159,553 (M); expenditures, $174,982, including $174,450 for 14 grants (high: $98,800; low: $200).
Purpose and activities: Giving primarily for the YMCA; giving also for higher education, Protestant churches, and hospitals.
Limitations: Giving primarily in New York, NY. No grants to individuals.
Application information: Contributes only to pre-selected organizations. Applications not accepted.
Officer and Directors: Jack Kleinoder, Pres.; Richard Wolfeld, Norman Zapolsky.
Employer Identification Number: 136191490

4678
The Esther A. and Joseph Klingenstein Fund, Inc. ▼
787 Seventh Ave.
New York 10019-6016 (212) 492-6181

Incorporated in 1945 in NY.
Donor(s): Esther A. Klingenstein,† Joseph Klingenstein.†
Foundation type: Independent
Financial data (yr. ended 09/30/89): Assets, $69,977,411 (M); gifts received, $62,000; expenditures, $3,947,885, including $3,429,643 for 107 grants (high: $333,333; low: $4,000; average: $5,000-$50,000).
Purpose and activities: Primary interests in neuroscientific research bearing on epilepsy

and independent secondary education. Some support also for health and health policy, church and state separation, public and social policy, communications and journalism, population and family planning, environment, and minority affairs.
Types of support: Research, special projects, publications, conferences and seminars, fellowships, operating budgets, seed money, general purposes, continuing support.
Limitations: No grants to individuals (except in fund's own programs in neuroscience and independent secondary education), or for building or endowment funds.
Publications: Informational brochure.
Application information: Application form not required.
Initial approach: Letter or proposal
Copies of proposal: 1
Deadline(s): None
Board meeting date(s): Generally 5 or 6 times a year
Write: John Klingenstein, Pres.
Officers and Directors:* John Klingenstein,* Pres. and Treas.; Frederick A. Klingenstein,* V.P. and Secy.; Claire List, V.P.; Patricia D. Klingenstein, Sharon L. Klingenstein.
Number of staff: 2 full-time professional; 1 part-time professional; 1 full-time support.
Employer Identification Number: 136028788

4679
Klock Company Trust ⌑
(also known as Jay E. and Lucia DeL. Klock Kingston Foundation)
c/o Key Trust Co.
253 Wall St.
Kingston 12401 (914) 339-6750

Established in 1966 in NY.
Foundation type: Independent
Financial data (yr. ended 12/31/88): Assets, $3,149,490 (M); expenditures, $247,035, including $221,965 for 28 grants (high: $25,000; low: $1,000).
Purpose and activities: Grants for hospitals and health services, youth organizations, social services, religious support, cultural programs, and education.
Limitations: Giving limited to Kingston and Ulster counties, NY.
Application information:
Initial approach: Letter
Deadline(s): Before quarters ending: Mar., June, Sept., and Dec. 31
Write: Earle H. Foster
Trustee: Key Trust Co.
Employer Identification Number: 146038479

4680
Louis & Rose Klosk Fund ⌑
c/o Chemical Bank
30 Rockefeller Plaza, 60th Fl.
New York 10112 (212) 621-2148

Trust established in 1970 in NY.
Donor(s): Louis Klosk.†
Foundation type: Independent
Financial data (yr. ended 12/31/87): Assets, $3,108,659 (M); expenditures, $125,438, including $94,500 for 34 grants (high: $12,500; low: $500).
Purpose and activities: Giving for Jewish welfare funds, hospitals, care for the aged, arts, and higher education.
Limitations: Giving primarily in NY.
Application information: Application form not required.
Deadline(s): None
Write: Barbara Strohmeier, V.P., Chemical Bank
Trustees: Barry Cooper, Nathan Cooper, Chemical Bank.
Employer Identification Number: 136328994

4681
The Knapp Fund ⌑
c/o James C. Edwards & Co., Inc.
805 Third Ave., 8th Fl.
New York 10022 (212) 319-8488

Incorporated in 1917 in NY.
Donor(s): George O. Knapp.†
Foundation type: Independent
Financial data (yr. ended 8/31/88): Assets, $1,978,440 (M); expenditures, $156,954, including $112,000 for grants (high: $25,000).
Purpose and activities: Activities largely confined to support for higher and secondary educational institutions.
Types of support: General purposes, continuing support, annual campaigns, building funds, research, scholarship funds, special projects.
Limitations: No grants to individuals, or for matching gifts; no loans.
Application information: Funds committed. Applications not accepted.
Board meeting date(s): Sept.
Write: George O. Knapp III, Pres.
Officers: George O. Knapp III,* Pres.; Frank A. Sprole,* V.P.; James T. Twomey, Secy.-Treas.
Directors:* James C. Edwards, Frank Jared Sprole, Sarah Knapp Sprole.
Number of staff: None.
Employer Identification Number: 136068384

4682
Knox Family Foundation
P.O. Box 387
Johnstown 12095

Incorporated in 1961 in NY.
Donor(s): Eleanor E. Knox,† Knox Gelatine, Inc.
Foundation type: Independent
Financial data (yr. ended 12/31/88): Assets, $4,370,304 (M); expenditures, $220,628, including $197,350 for 143 grants (high: $13,550; low: $50).
Purpose and activities: Emphasis on higher and secondary education, hospitals, Protestant church support, and social services.
Limitations: No grants to individuals.
Application information: Contributes only to pre-selected organizations. Applications not accepted.
Officers and Directors:* Eleanor G. Nalle,* Pres. and Treas.; John K. Graham,* V.P. and Secy.; Paul Armstrong,* V.P.; Rose Ann Armstrong,* V.P.; Roseann K. Beaudoin,* V.P.; Rosemary Birchard,* V.P.; Charles K. Brumley,* V.P.; Richard W. Hallock,* V.P.
Employer Identification Number: 146017797

4683
The Seymour H. Knox Foundation, Inc. ⌑
3750 Marine Midland Ctr.
Buffalo 14203 (716) 854-6811

Incorporated in 1945 in NY.
Donor(s): Seymour H. Knox, Marjorie K.C. Klopp,† Dorothy K.G. Rogers.†
Foundation type: Independent
Financial data (yr. ended 12/31/88): Assets, $18,498,699 (M); expenditures, $983,175, including $805,784 for 66 grants (high: $300,000; low: $100).
Purpose and activities: Giving for the arts, higher and secondary education, hospitals, civic organizations, and community funds.
Types of support: General purposes.
Limitations: Giving primarily in the Buffalo, NY, area. No grants to individuals.
Application information:
Initial approach: Letter
Deadline(s): None
Board meeting date(s): May and Dec.
Write: Seymour H. Knox, Pres.
Officers: Seymour H. Knox, Pres.; Northrup R. Knox, V.P. and Treas.; Hazard K. Campbell, V.P.; Seymour H. Knox III, V.P.; Samuel D. Magavern, Secy.
Director: Henry Z. Urban.
Employer Identification Number: 160839066

4684
The Kohlberg Foundation ⌑
c/o Kohlberg & Co.
116 Radio Circle
Mt. Kisco 10549 (914) 241-8598

Established in 1962 in New York.
Donor(s): Jerome Kohlberg.
Foundation type: Independent
Financial data (yr. ended 11/30/88): Assets, $13,836,281 (M); gifts received, $2,064,800; expenditures, $736,016, including $643,615 for 90 grants (high: $126,000; low: $100).
Purpose and activities: Emphasis on higher education, Jewish giving, and social services; support also for museums, hospitals, the arts and for a children's center.
Types of support: Continuing support.
Application information: Application form not required.
Write: Morton I. Cohen
Trustees: Karen K. Davis, Jerome Kohlberg, Jr., Nancy S. Kohlberg, Pamela K. Vinal.
Employer Identification Number: 136116079

4685
Robert Lee Kohns Foundation, Inc. ⌑ ☆
c/o Jeffrey A. Lowin, Shereff, Friedman et al
919 Third Ave.
New York 10022-9998

Established in 1956.
Foundation type: Independent
Financial data (yr. ended 12/31/88): Assets, $1,280,768 (M); expenditures, $1,335,404, including $1,321,850 for 8 grants (high: $400,000; low: $15,000).
Purpose and activities: Support primarily for Jewish organizations, international affairs and studies, and a university.
Limitations: Giving primarily in NY. No grants to individuals.

Application information: Contributes only to pre-selected organizations. Applications not accepted.
Officers: Jeffrey Lowin, Pres.; Joyce Arnoff Cohen, V.P.; S. Andrew Schaffer, V.P.; Sidney Greenman, Secy.; Stephen J. Epstein, Treas.
Employer Identification Number: 136126246

4686
William & Sheila Konar Foundation ⌑
110 Commerce Dr.
Rochester 14623-3504 (716) 334-4110

Donor(s): Sheila Konar, William B. Konar.
Foundation type: Independent
Financial data (yr. ended 12/31/87): Assets, $1,040,406 (M); gifts received, $212,730; expenditures, $166,772, including $165,862 for grants (high: $132,500).
Purpose and activities: Support primarily for Jewish giving and higher education.
Limitations: Giving primarily in NY.
Application information:
Initial approach: Proposal
Deadline(s): None
Write: William B. Konar, Trustee
Trustees: Rachel K. Guttenberg, Howard E. Konar, Sheila Konar, William B. Konar.
Employer Identification Number: 222434846

4687
Koochner Foundation ⌑ ☆
c/o Laventhal and Horwath
1776 Broadway
New York 10019

Donor(s): Raul Julia, Merel Julia.
Foundation type: Operating
Financial data (yr. ended 12/31/88): Assets, $1,992 (M); gifts received, $157,000; expenditures, $156,385, including $156,333 for 7 grants (high: $152,250; low: $200).
Purpose and activities: Giving primarily for the relief of hunger; support also for the theater.
Limitations: Giving primarily in NY. No grants to individuals.
Application information: Contributes only to pre-selected organizations. Applications not accepted.
Trustees: Merel Julia, Raul Julia, Martin Leaf.
Employer Identification Number: 133402062

4688
Kopf Foundation, Inc. ⌑
c/o Kelley, Drye & Warren
101 Park Ave.
New York 10178

Incorporated in 1967 in NY.
Foundation type: Independent
Financial data (yr. ended 12/31/88): Assets, $3,413,083 (M); expenditures, $256,242, including $215,000 for 2 grants (high: $200,000; low: $15,000).
Purpose and activities: Grants primarily for health, church support, and higher education.
Application information: Contributes only to pre-selected organizations. Applications not accepted.
Officers: Patricia Ann Colagiuri, Pres.; Nancy Sue Mueller, V.P.; Michael S. Insel, Secy.; Brenda Christy Helies, Treas.
Employer Identification Number: 136228036

4689
Elizabeth Christy Kopf Foundation ⌑ ☆
134 East 40th St.
New York 10016

Established in 1982 in NY.
Donor(s): R.C. Kopf.
Foundation type: Independent
Financial data (yr. ended 12/31/88): Assets, $2,587,850 (M); expenditures, $106,467, including $81,000 for 7 grants (high: $30,000; low: $1,000).
Purpose and activities: Support primarily for social services, hospitals and emergency care, and higher education.
Limitations: Giving primarily in NY and MA. No grants to individuals.
Application information: Contributes only to pre-selected organizations. Applications not accepted.
Officers: Patricia Ann Colagiuri, Pres.; Nancy Sue Mueller, V.P.; Michael S. Insel, Secy.; Brenda Christy Helies, Treas.
Employer Identification Number: 133127936

4690
Korean Association of New York, Inc. ⌑ ☆
149 West 24th St., No. 3
New York 10011-1917

Foundation type: Independent
Financial data (yr. ended 4/30/87): Assets, $1,089,946 (M); gifts received, $352,015; expenditures, $449,727, including $71,544 for grants (high: $13,458).
Purpose and activities: Grants limited to Korean-Americans and Korean organizations.
Types of support: Grants to individuals.
Limitations: Giving primarily in NY.
Officers and Directors: Byung Chang Cho, Pres.; Kyu Tak Chae, V.P.; O Young Juan, V.P.; Hyung Hoon Kim, V.P.; Tae Sik Park, V.P.; Hakjong Riew, V.P.; and 70 other directors.
Employer Identification Number: 237329822

4691
Richard & Peggy Korn Foundation, Inc. ⌑ ☆
c/o Osborne & McLellan
155 Sixth Ave.
New York 10013

Donor(s): Peggy Korn.
Foundation type: Independent
Financial data (yr. ended 12/31/88): Assets, $190,134 (M); gifts received, $40,938; expenditures, $126,175, including $123,075 for 51 grants (high: $92,000; low: $25).
Purpose and activities: Support for health organizations and general charitable activities.
Limitations: Giving primarily in New York, NY.
Officers: Peggy Korn, Pres.; William J. Kridel, V.P.; Gloria Neuwirth, Secy.
Employer Identification Number: 136114557

4692
Matthew R. & Susanne L. Kornreich Foundation ⌑ ☆
919 Third Ave.
New York 10022 (212) 688-7700

Donor(s): Matthew R. Kornreich.
Foundation type: Independent
Financial data (yr. ended 12/31/88): Assets, $126,583 (M); gifts received, $50,000; expenditures, $116,500, including $116,500 for 14 grants (high: $39,700; low: $100).
Purpose and activities: Support primarily for health, higher education, and Jewish organizations.
Types of support: General purposes.
Application information: Application form not required.
Deadline(s): None
Write: Sanford H. Hersch, Mgr.
Officers and Directors:* Matthew R. Kornreich,* Pres.; Susanne L. Kornreich,* Secy.; Catherine Kornreich, William D. Kornreich.
Employer Identification Number: 133283806

4693
Morton A. and Jo Anne Kornreich Foundation, Inc. ⌑ ☆
919 Third Ave.
New York 10022-3904 (212) 688-9700

Established in 1985 in NY.
Donor(s): Morton A. Kornreich.
Foundation type: Independent
Financial data (yr. ended 12/31/88): Assets, $185,900 (M); gifts received, $175,000; expenditures, $199,300, including $199,300 for 13 grants (high: $100,000; low: $800).
Purpose and activities: Support primarily for Jewish organizations, including Jewish welfare; support also for higher education.
Limitations: No grants to individuals.
Application information: Application form not required.
Deadline(s): None
Write: Morton A. Kornreich, Pres.
Officers and Directors: Morton A. Kornreich, Pres.; James Kornreich, V.P.; Jo Anne Kornreich, Secy.
Employer Identification Number: 133327179

4694
Kosciuszko Foundation, Inc.
15 East 65th St.
New York 10021-6595 (212) 734-2130

Incorporated in 1925 in NY.
Foundation type: Operating
Financial data (yr. ended 06/30/89): Assets, $10,520,370 (M); gifts received, $589,059; expenditures, $1,103,039, including $5,000 for 1 grant and $500,000 for 192 grants to individuals (high: $10,930; low: $4,480).
Purpose and activities: A private operating foundation which promotes Polish cultural and educational actvities in the U.S. and Poland. Scholarship grants for Polish scholars and academics desiring to study in the U.S., and for American scholars desiring to study in Poland, or for graduate and postgraduate Polish coursework in the U.S. The foundation also organizes summer courses at Polish universities for American students and has a bookstore for Polish-related publications.
Types of support: Student aid, fellowships, exchange programs, publications, grants to individuals, research.
Limitations: Giving primarily in Poland and the U.S.

Publications: Newsletter, informational brochure (including application guidelines).
Application information: Application form required.
Initial approach: Letter
Copies of proposal: 1
Deadline(s): Nov. 15 for foreign exchange students, Mar. 15 for summer session, and Jan. 15 for domestic program
Board meeting date(s): Apr. and Nov.
Final notification: May for domestic program; varies for foreign exchange program
Write: Maryla Janiak, Grants Officer
Officers: Joseph E. Gore, Pres. and Exec. Dir.; Leslie M. Burgess, Chair.; Andrew Lawn, Sr., Vice-Chair.; Witold Sulimirski, Vice-Chair.; Michael Wrotniak, Vice-Chair.; Gregory T. Lawn, Treas.
Number of staff: 10 full-time professional; 3 full-time support.
Employer Identification Number: 131628179

4695
Koussevitzky Music Foundation, Inc.
200 Park Ave.
New York 10166 (212) 351-3092

Established in 1942 in NY.
Donor(s): Olga Koussevitzky,† Serge Koussevitsky.†
Foundation type: Independent
Financial data (yr. ended 3/31/88): Assets, $1,410,494 (M); expenditures, $48,906, including $9,000 for 2 grants and $10,000 for 1 grant to an individual.
Purpose and activities: The foundation has suspended giving pending development of a new program.
Types of support: Grants to individuals.
Application information: Application form not required.
Deadline(s): Dec. 1 through Jan. 15
Write: Ellis J. Freedman, Esq., Secy.
Officers: Jacob Druckman, Pres.; Ellis J. Freedman, Secy.; John Grozier, Treas.
Directors: Leonard Bernstein, Elliott Carter, Mario Davidovsky, Andrew Imbrie, Fred Lerdahl, Gunther Schuller, Michael Tilson Thomas.
Employer Identification Number: 046128361

4696
E. A. Kraft Charitable Trust ¤
c/o Chemical Bank
30 Rockefeller Plaza, 60th Fl.
New York 10112 (212) 621-2143

Established in 1978.
Foundation type: Independent
Financial data (yr. ended 7/31/87): Assets, $37,153 (M); expenditures, $138,408, including $136,000 for 31 grants (high: $10,000; low: $1,000).
Purpose and activities: Giving for secondary and higher education, hospitals and health, social services, cultural programs, and Episcopal religious organizations.
Limitations: Giving primarily in New York, NY.
Application information: Application form not required.
Deadline(s): None
Write: Mrs. Barbara Strohmeier
Trustees: Alfred Ferguson, Logan Fulrath, Jr., Chemical Bank.
Employer Identification Number: 136761770

4697
Kramer Foundation ¤
c/o Wald & Wald
500 Fifth Ave., Rm. 1802
New York 10110

Established about 1951 in NY.
Donor(s): Saul Kramer.
Foundation type: Independent
Financial data (yr. ended 12/31/88): Assets, $2,480,474 (M); expenditures, $145,738, including $130,263 for 123 grants (high: $23,078; low: $10).
Purpose and activities: Emphasis on Jewish welfare, religious, and social service organizations; higher education, including medical education; and health services.
Limitations: Giving primarily in NY.
Application information:
Initial approach: Letter
Deadline(s): None
Write: Saul Kramer, Mgr.
Officers: Saul Kramer, Mgr.; Bernard Wald, Mgr.
Employer Identification Number: 221713053

4698
C. L. C. Kramer Foundation ¤
c/o Zabelle, Shechter & Marks
250 West 57th St.
New York 10107 (212) 277-0991

Established in 1966.
Donor(s): Catherine Kramer.†
Foundation type: Independent
Financial data (yr. ended 09/30/89): Assets, $5,593,675 (M); expenditures, $443,544, including $408,500 for 19 grants (high: $80,000; low: $1,000).
Purpose and activities: Giving primarily for hospitals and health agencies.
Limitations: Giving primarily in New York, NY.
Application information: Contributes only to pre-selected organizations. Applications not accepted.
Write: Robert Zabelle, Pres., or David Marks, Treas.
Officers: Robert Zabelle, Pres.; Charles Looker, Secy.; David Marks, Treas.
Employer Identification Number: 136226513

4699
Henry R. Kravis Foundation, Inc. ▼
c/o Kohlberg Kravis Roberts & Co.
Nine West 57th St.
New York 10019

Established in 1985 in NY.
Donor(s): Henry R. Kravis.
Foundation type: Independent
Financial data (yr. ended 11/30/88): Assets, $9,643,225 (M); gifts received, $5,000,000; expenditures, $4,997.
Purpose and activities: Support primarily for the arts and culture, including a museum, and for Jewish welfare.
Types of support: General purposes.
Limitations: No grants to individuals.
Application information: Contributes only to pre-selected organizations. Applications not accepted.
Officers and Directors:* Henry R. Kravis,* Chair. and Pres.; Thomas Hudson, Secy.; Richard I. Beattie, Jerome Kohlberg, Jr.
Number of staff: None.
Employer Identification Number: 133341521

4700
Samuel H. Kress Foundation ▼
174 East 80th St.
New York 10021 (212) 861-4993

Incorporated in 1929 in NY.
Donor(s): Samuel H. Kress,† Claude W. Kress,† Rush H. Kress.†
Foundation type: Independent
Financial data (yr. ended 08/31/89): Assets, $59,874,015 (M); expenditures, $2,912,826, including $1,661,950 for 93 grants (high: $200,000; low: $100; average: $50,000), $380,780 for 72 grants to individuals (high: $12,000; low: $1,000) and $14,050 for 15 employee matching gifts.
Purpose and activities: Giving through six main programs: 1) fellowships for pre-doctoral research in art history; 2) advanced training and research in conservation of works of art; 3) development of scholarly resources in the fields of art history and conservation; 4) conservation and restoration of monuments in western Europe; 5) archaeological fieldwork emphasizing art history; 6) occasional related projects.
Types of support: Professorships, internships, fellowships, research, publications, conferences and seminars.
Limitations: No support for art history programs below the pre-doctoral level, or the purchase of works of art. No grants for living artists, or for operating budgets, continuing support, annual campaigns, endowments, deficit financing, capital funds, or films; no loans.
Publications: Annual report (including application guidelines).
Application information: Application forms required for fellowships in art history and art conservation.
Initial approach: Proposal
Copies of proposal: 1
Deadline(s): Nov. 30 for research fellowships in art history; Feb. 28 for fellowships in art conservation; Mar. 30 for art history dissertation fellowships
Board meeting date(s): Usually in Oct. and May
Final notification: 3 months
Write: Dr. Marilyn Perry, Pres.
Officers and Trustees:* Franklin D. Murphy,* Chair.; W. Clarke Wescoe,* Vice-Chair. and Treas.; Marilyn Perry,* Pres.; John C. Fontaine,* V.P.; William Bader,* Secy.; Lyman Field, Immaculada de Habsburgo.
Number of staff: 2 full-time professional; 1 part-time professional; 3 full-time support; 1 part-time support.
Employer Identification Number: 131624176

4701
Krieger Charitable Trust ☆
120 West 45th St., Suite 412
New York 10036 (212) 642-3406

Foundation type: Independent
Financial data (yr. ended 11/30/89): Assets, $2,331,632 (M); expenditures, $116,133, including $111,042 for 73 grants (high: $81,524; low: $10).
Purpose and activities: Support primarily for higher education and Jewish organizations, including welfare funds and temples.
Application information:
Deadline(s): None
Write: Jacqueline Klein, Trustee
Trustee: Jacqueline Klein.
Employer Identification Number: 226374448

4702
The Mathilde and Arthur B. Krim Foundation, Inc.
c/o Orion Pictures
711 Fifth Ave.
New York 10022 (212) 758-5100

Donor(s): Arthur B. Krim.
Foundation type: Independent
Financial data (yr. ended 12/31/88): Assets, $253,069 (M); gifts received, $122,125; expenditures, $226,013, including $219,514 for 110 grants (high: $30,000; low: $30; average: $3,000).
Purpose and activities: Emphasis on higher education, medical research, cultural programs, health agencies, public policy, social services, civil rights, Jewish organizations, and an institute of sociology.
Types of support: Continuing support, research.
Limitations: Giving primarily in NY.
Publications: 990-PF.
Application information: Applications not accepted.
Write: Arthur B. Krim, Chair.
Director: Arthur B. Krim, Chair.
Number of staff: None.
Employer Identification Number: 136219851

4703
The H. Frederick Krimendahl II Foundation ⌘
c/o Goldman, Sachs & Co., Tax Dept.
85 Broad St., 30th Fl.
New York 10004-2106

Established in 1968 in NY.
Donor(s): H. Frederick Krimendahl II.
Foundation type: Independent
Financial data (yr. ended 5/31/88): Assets, $2,908,129 (M); gifts received, $274,000; expenditures, $79,325, including $68,928 for 67 grants (high: $5,000; low: $50).
Purpose and activities: Support primarily for youth; support also for education, arts, and culture.
Limitations: No grants to individuals.
Application information: Contributes only to pre-selected organizations. Applications not accepted.
Trustees: Constance M. Krimendahl, H. Frederick Krimendahl II, Nancy C. Krimendahl, James S. Marcus, Elizabeth K. Wolf.
Employer Identification Number: 237000391

4704
Charles and Bertha Kriser Foundation, Inc. ⌘
211 East 43rd St.
New York 10017

Established in NY.
Donor(s): Sidney P. Kriser, Richard Feldstein, Judy Feldstein, R.C. Mahon & Co., and others.
Foundation type: Independent
Financial data (yr. ended 5/31/89): Assets, $1,191,204 (M); gifts received, $200,000; expenditures, $242,044, including $241,103 for 32 grants (high: $50,000; low: $23).
Purpose and activities: Emphasis on Jewish welfare organizations; support also for health and hospitals, cultural programs, and higher education.
Limitations: Giving primarily in NY. No grants to individuals.
Application information: Contributes only to pre-selected organizations. Applications not accepted.
Officers: David Kriser, Pres.; Sidney Kriser, Secy.
Employer Identification Number: 136188243

4705
Michael J. Kugler Foundation, Inc. ⌘ ☆
c/o Spicer & Oppenheim
Seven World Trade Ctr.
New York 10048

Established in 1986 in NY.
Donor(s): Michael J. Kugler.
Foundation type: Independent
Financial data (yr. ended 9/30/88): Assets, $255,721 (M); gifts received, $80,068; expenditures, $202,642, including $189,680 for 51 grants (high: $50,000; low: $25).
Purpose and activities: Giving primarily for Jewish welfare and educational institutions, hospitals, and the performing arts; support also for museums, land conservation, health associations, and youth.
Limitations: Giving primarily in the greater New York, NY, metropolitan area. No grants to individuals.
Application information: Contributes only to pre-selected organizations. Applications not accepted.
Officers and Directors: Michael J. Kugler, Pres. and Treas.; David Warmflash, V.P. and Secy.; Allen S. Sexter.
Employer Identification Number: 133423317

4706
The Albert Kunstadter Family Foundation ⌘
1035 Fifth Ave.
New York 10028 (212) 249-1733

Incorporated in 1952 in IL.
Donor(s): Members of the Kunstadter family.
Foundation type: Independent
Financial data (yr. ended 12/31/88): Assets, $2,636,738 (M); expenditures, $233,237, including $192,737 for 67 grants (high: $10,000; low: $1,000; average: $2,000-$5,000).
Purpose and activities: Local, national, and, where possible, international giving, including support for education and the arts.
Types of support: Special projects, general purposes, operating budgets.
Limitations: Giving primarily in East Coast states between Boston, MA, and Washington, DC. No support for religious purposes. No grants to individuals, or for deficit financing, building funds, land acquisition, scholarships and fellowships, or matching gifts; no loans.
Publications: Biennial report (including application guidelines).
Application information: Application form not required.
Initial approach: Letter
Copies of proposal: 1
Deadline(s): Submit short proposal preferably before Nov.
Board meeting date(s): June and as required
Final notification: 3 weeks for negative responses, 1 to 3 months for positive ones
Write: John W. Kunstadter, Pres., or Geraldine S. Kunstadter, Chair.
Officers and Directors: Geraldine S. Kunstadter, Chair.; John W. Kunstadter, Pres. and Treas.; Christopher Kunstadter, V.P.; Peter Kunstadter, V.P.; Lisa Kunstadter, Secy.; Elizabeth Kunstadter, Sally Lennington Kunstadter.
Number of staff: None.
Employer Identification Number: 366047975

4707
Kupferberg Foundation ⌘ ☆
131-38 Sanford Ave.
Flushing 11352 (718) 461-7000

Established in 1961.
Donor(s): Kepco, Inc.
Foundation type: Company-sponsored
Financial data (yr. ended 11/30/88): Assets, $1,017,393 (M); expenditures, $53,575, including $51,100 for 26 grants (high: $5,000; low: $100).
Purpose and activities: Emphasis on Jewish giving and community services, including ambulance corps.
Limitations: Giving primarily in Queens, NY. No grants to individuals.
Application information: Contributes only to pre-selected organizations. Applications not accepted.
Officers: Jack Kupferberg, Pres.; Jesse Kupferberg, V.P.; Kenneth Kupferberg, V.P.; Max Kupferberg, Secy.-Treas.
Employer Identification Number: 116008915

4708
L and L Foundation ⌘
c/o Mildred C. Brinn
570 Park Ave., Suite 1A
New York 10021

Incorporated in 1963 in NY.
Donor(s): Lawrence E. Brinn.
Foundation type: Independent
Financial data (yr. ended 12/31/88): Assets, $5,635,196 (M); gifts received, $1,000; expenditures, $285,846, including $248,375 for 37 grants (high: $104,000; low: $75).
Purpose and activities: Emphasis on hospitals, higher education, cultural programs, including the performing arts, and youth and child welfare agencies.

Limitations: Giving primarily in NY. No grants to individuals.
Application information: Contributes only to pre-selected organizations. Applications not accepted.
Officers and Directors: Lawrence E. Brinn, Pres. and Treas.; Mildred F. Cunningham, V.P.; Peter F. De Gaetano, Secy.
Employer Identification Number: 136155758

4709
Asmund S. Laerdal Foundation, Inc. ¤
One Labriola Court
Armonk 10504

Established in 1977 in NY.
Donor(s): Laerdal Medical Corp.
Foundation type: Independent
Financial data (yr. ended 12/31/88): Assets, $3,330,355 (M); expenditures, $264,704, including $230,292 for 6 grants (high: $150,000; low: $5,000) and $1,332 for 1 grant to an individual.
Purpose and activities: Giving primarily for medicine, emergency medical services, and medical research.
Types of support: Research.
Application information: Contributes only to pre-selected organizations. Applications not accepted.
Officer: Hans H. Dahll, Pres.
Employer Identification Number: 132885659

4710
The Lagemann Foundation ¤
c/o John H. Olding
28 West 44th St., Suite 304
New York 10036-6603

Established in 1944 in NY.
Foundation type: Independent
Financial data (yr. ended 12/31/88): Assets, $1,628,554 (M); expenditures, $146,416, including $132,000 for 12 grants (high: $35,000; low: $2,000).
Purpose and activities: Support for Christian religious activities and youth centers.
Limitations: Giving primarily in the East Coast, especially NY.
Application information:
Deadline(s): None
Officers: Peter J. Lagemann, Pres.; John H. Olding, Secy.; Franklin E. Parker, Treas.
Employer Identification Number: 136115306

4711
Gerard B. Lambert Memorial Foundation, Inc. ▼
713 Park Ave.
New York 10021 (212) 472-2702

Established in 1976 in NY.
Donor(s): Rachel L. Mellon.
Foundation type: Independent
Financial data (yr. ended 03/31/89): Assets, $13,591 (M); gifts received, $372,000; expenditures, $377,235, including $321,483 for 1 grant (high: $441,377; low: $175,500).
Purpose and activities: Support primarily to the government of Antigua for a hospital laboratory and a clinic; also support for general charitable purposes.
Types of support: General purposes.
Limitations: Giving primarily in MA, VA, and Antigua, West Indies. No grants to individuals.
Application information: Applications not accepted.
Board meeting date(s): As necessary
Write: Anita Engel Malon, Secy.
Officers and Directors:* Rachel L. Mellon,* Pres.; Charles Ryskamp,* V.P.; Kenneth I. Starr,* V.P.; Anita Engel Malon, Secy.; Alexander D. Forger,* Treas.; Rev. Richard T.C. Peard.
Number of staff: None.
Employer Identification Number: 132831262

4712
Eugene M. Lang Foundation ▼ ¤
100 East 42nd St., 3rd Fl.
New York 10017 (212) 687-4741

Established in 1968 in NY.
Donor(s): Eugene M. Lang.
Foundation type: Independent
Financial data (yr. ended 12/31/88): Assets, $22,695,000 (M); expenditures, $1,928,000, including $1,749,749 for 85 grants (high: $1,257,000; low: $25; average: $100-$20,000).
Purpose and activities: Support for higher education, cultural programs, and hospitals.
Types of support: Operating budgets, continuing support, annual campaigns, seed money, emergency funds, scholarship funds, professorships, internships, fellowships, special projects, conferences and seminars, land acquisition.
Limitations: Giving primarily in NY and neighboring area, including PA. No grants to individuals, or for building funds, equipment and materials, capital or endowment funds, deficit financing, publications, or matching gifts; no loans.
Application information: Application form not required.
Initial approach: Letter
Deadline(s): None
Board meeting date(s): Apr. and Nov.
Write: Eugene M. Lang, Trustee
Trustees: David A. Lang, Eugene M. Lang, Stephen Lang, Theresa Lang.
Number of staff: 1 part-time professional; 1 full-time support.
Employer Identification Number: 136153412

4713
The Jacob and Valeria Langeloth Foundation ▼
One East 42nd St.
New York 10017 (212) 687-3760

Incorporated in 1915 in NY as the Valeria Home; renamed in 1975.
Donor(s): Jacob Langeloth.†
Foundation type: Independent
Financial data (yr. ended 11/30/89): Assets, $34,912,359 (M); expenditures, $1,918,165, including $1,451,000 for 25 grants (high: $100,000; low: $15,000; average: $25,000-$100,000).
Purpose and activities: Grants to nonprofit hospitals and health-care facilities, primarily to defray costs incurred by in-patients who are "people of education," or are involved in the arts, who normally would not ask for or be justified in accepting charity, but who nevertheless have difficulty in meeting their obligations.
Types of support: Continuing support.
Limitations: Giving primarily in NY, with emphasis on New York City and Westchester County. No grants to individuals.
Application information: Applications for grants are not invited except from previous recipients. Application form not required.
Initial approach: Letter
Copies of proposal: 1
Deadline(s): Sept. 1
Board meeting date(s): Feb. and Sept.
Final notification: Varies
Write: William R. Cross, Jr., Pres.
Officers and Directors:* John L. Loeb,* Chair.; William R. Cross, Jr.,* Pres. and Exec. Dir.; George Labalme, Jr.,* V.P.; Julian B. Beaty, Jr.,* Secy.; Henry A. Loeb,* Treas.; Mrs. Claude Boillot, Adam Hochschild, John L. Loeb, Jr., Peter K. Loeb, Richard G. Poole.
Number of staff: 1 part-time professional; 2 full-time support.
Employer Identification Number: 131773646

4714
Larsen Fund, Inc.
Time & Life Bldg.
New York 10020
Application address: c/o Mrs. Patricia S. Palmer, Grants Admin., 2960 Post Rd., Suite 100, Southport, CT 06490; Tel.: (203) 255-5318

Incorporated in 1941 in NY.
Donor(s): Roy E. Larsen.†
Foundation type: Independent
Financial data (yr. ended 12/31/88): Assets, $6,662,738 (M); expenditures, $437,823, including $338,531 for 43 grants (high: $26,000; low: $500).
Purpose and activities: Grants largely for higher and other education, conservation and wildlife, the arts, research, and social and health services.
Types of support: General purposes, fellowships, professorships, research, annual campaigns, building funds, capital campaigns, conferences and seminars, consulting services, endowment funds, internships, land acquisition, lectureships, scholarship funds, seed money, special projects.
Limitations: Giving primarily in the New York, NY, area, Minneapolis, MN, area, and CT. No grants to individuals.
Publications: Annual report (including application guidelines).
Application information: Application form not required.
Initial approach: Letter
Copies of proposal: 1
Deadline(s): Submit proposal at least 60 days prior to meeting dates
Board meeting date(s): Beginning of June and Dec.
Write: Mrs. Marcelle Coudrai, Asst. Treas.
Officers and Directors:* Robert R. Larsen,* Pres. and Treas.; Christopher Larsen,* V.P.; Ann Larsen Simonson,* V.P.; Jonathan Z. Larsen,* Secy.; Marcelle Coudrai.
Number of staff: 2 full-time support.
Employer Identification Number: 136104430

4715
Lasdon Foundation, Inc. ⌑
Ten Rockefeller Plaza, Suite 1111
New York 10020-1903 (212) 977-8420

Incorporated in 1946 in DE.
Donor(s): W.S. Lasdon,† Stanley S. Lasdon, J.S. Lasdon,† M.S. Lasdon.†
Foundation type: Independent
Financial data (yr. ended 11/30/88): Assets, $2,678,677 (M); expenditures, $239,013, including $162,625 for 70 grants (high: $25,000; low: $25).
Purpose and activities: To further research in the medical sciences through grants to universities and medical institutions; support also for the performing arts and general civic projects.
Types of support: Research, matching funds, continuing support, annual campaigns.
Limitations: No grants to individuals, or for building or endowment funds, operating budgets, or program support.
Application information: Application form not required.
Initial approach: Letter
Copies of proposal: 1
Deadline(s): Submit proposal preferably in Mar. or Sept.; no set deadline
Board meeting date(s): Annually
Final notification: Application for grants not necessarily acknowledged
Write: Stanley S. Lasdon, Pres.
Officers and Directors: Stanley S. Lasdon, Pres. and Treas.; Gene S. Lasdon, V.P.; Mildred D. Lasdon, V.P.
Number of staff: 1 full-time support.
Employer Identification Number: 131739997

4716
William and Mildred Lasdon Foundation ⌑
Ten Rockefeller Plaza, Suite 1111
New York 10020-1903

Established in 1947 in DE.
Donor(s): Jacob S. Lasdon, William S. Lasdon.
Foundation type: Independent
Financial data (yr. ended 12/31/87): Assets, $1,818,443 (M); gifts received, $1,065,000; expenditures, $58,190, including $53,008 for 73 grants (high: $5,000; low: $75).
Purpose and activities: Giving primarily for hospitals, museums, and other arts organizations.
Limitations: Giving primarily in NY.
Officers: Mildred D. Lasdon, Pres.; Nanette L. Laitman, Secy.-Treas.
Employer Identification Number: 237380362

4717
Albert and Mary Lasker Foundation, Inc. ⌑
865 First Ave., Apt. 15E
New York 10017 (212) 421-9010

Incorporated in 1942 in NY.
Donor(s): Albert D. Lasker,† Mary W. Lasker.
Foundation type: Operating
Financial data (yr. ended 12/31/87): Assets, $3,567,409 (M); gifts received, $41,250; expenditures, $721,832, including $290,082 for grants (high: $24,999), $8,934 for 1 grant to an individual and $127,683 for foundation-administered programs.
Purpose and activities: Primarily concerned with medical research; annual Lasker awards given to honor and encourage outstanding medical research; support also for a beautification program, health programs, and the arts.
Application information: Application form not required.
Deadline(s): None
Write: Mary W. Lasker, Pres.
Officers and Directors: Mary W. Lasker, Pres.; Alice Fordyce, Exec. V.P.; Catherine G. Blair, V.P.; William McC. Blair, V.P.; James W. Fordyce, Secy.-Treas.; Christopher Brody, Anne B. Fordyce, Dr. Jordan Gutterman, David Morse, Edwin C. Whitehead.
Employer Identification Number: 131680062

4718
B. J. Lasker Foundation, Inc. ⌑
20 Broad St.
New York 10005

Established in 1957 in NY.
Donor(s): Bernard J. Lasker.
Foundation type: Independent
Financial data (yr. ended 11/30/88): Assets, $1,588,857 (M); gifts received, $27,000; expenditures, $5,200.
Purpose and activities: General charitable giving.
Application information: Contributes only to pre-selected organizations. Applications not accepted.
Officer: Bernard J. Lasker, Pres. and Treas.
Director: James J. Fuld.
Employer Identification Number: 136051635

4719
Lassalle Fund, Inc. ⌑ ☆
c/o Abacus & Assoc.
147 East 48th St.
New York 10017

Established in 1966.
Foundation type: Independent
Financial data (yr. ended 12/31/88): Assets, $1,200,320 (M); expenditures, $89,064, including $64,628 for 10 grants (high: $40,500; low: $300).
Purpose and activities: Giving primarily for ballet companies and schools.
Limitations: Giving primarily in New York, NY. No grants to individuals.
Application information:
Initial approach: Letter
Deadline(s): None
Write: Nancy Lassalle, Pres.
Officers: Nancy N. Lassalle, Pres. and Secy.-Treas.; Andrew E. Norman, V.P.
Employer Identification Number: 136213551

4720
Abe and Frances Lastfogel Foundation ⌑
c/o Wallin, Simon, Black and Co.
1350 Ave. of the Americas
New York 10019 (212) 586-5100

Established in 1972 in CA.
Donor(s): Abe Lastfogel,† Frances Lastfogel.†
Foundation type: Independent
Financial data (yr. ended 12/31/87): Assets, $4,578,683 (M); gifts received, $1,110,068; expenditures, $490,760.
Purpose and activities: Grants for Jewish welfare funds, education, cultural programs, health and social service agencies, including those affiliated with the motion picture industry.
Types of support: Annual campaigns, endowment funds, program-related investments, special projects.
Limitations: Giving primarily in the Los Angeles, CA, area and NY.
Publications: 990-PF.
Application information:
Write: Lawrence Lewis, V.P.
Officers and Directors:* Walter Zifkin,* Pres.; Lawrence Lewis,* V.P.; Lee Stevens,* V.P.; Roger Davis, Secy.-Treas.
Employer Identification Number: 237146829

4721
The Lauder Foundation, Inc. ▼
767 Fifth Ave., 37th Floor
New York 10153 (212) 572-4426

Incorporated in 1962 in NY.
Donor(s): Estee Lauder, Joseph H. Lauder,† Leonard A. Lauder, Ronald S. Lauder.
Foundation type: Independent
Financial data (yr. ended 11/30/89): Assets, $8,050,155 (M); expenditures, $1,269,227, including $1,257,511 for grants.
Purpose and activities: Emphasis on museums, education, medical research, Jewish organizations, social service agencies, cultural programs, and conservation; some support for public affairs organizations and hospitals.
Limitations: Giving primarily in the New York, NY, metropolitan area. No grants to individuals.
Application information: Application form not required.
Initial approach: Proposal
Copies of proposal: 1
Deadline(s): None
Board meeting date(s): As needed
Final notification: 4 to 8 weeks
Write: Sharon Yeramian
Officers and Directors:* Estee Lauder,* Pres.; Leonard A. Lauder,* Secy.-Treas.
Number of staff: None.
Employer Identification Number: 136153743

4722
Fred L. Lavanburg Foundation
950 Third Ave., 30th Fl.
New York 10022 (212) 371-5060

Incorporated in 1927 in NY.
Donor(s): Fred L. Lavanburg.†
Foundation type: Independent
Financial data (yr. ended 12/31/89): Assets, $1,860,614 (M); gifts received, $1,984; expenditures, $113,652, including $47,000 for 5 grants (high: $20,000; low: $2,000; average: $18,000).
Purpose and activities: Major objectives related to the improvement of low- and middle-income housing and design, the development of neighborhood, city, and regional planning, and the movement to resolve problems associated with family and community living.

Types of support: Seed money, matching funds.
Limitations: Giving primarily in NY. No grants to individuals, or for endowment funds, scholarships, fellowships, or operating budgets.
Publications: Multi-year report.
Application information: Application form not required.
Initial approach: Brief proposal
Copies of proposal: 1
Deadline(s): Submit proposal preferably in Feb.
Board meeting date(s): Apr.
Write: Oscar S. Straus II, Pres.
Officers and Trustees: Oscar S. Straus II, Pres.; Rowley Bialla, Secy.; John T. Barnes, Treas.; Pauline Falk, Leonard A. Hockstader II, James A. Kingsland, Anne Lindgren, Alfred Ogden, Peter D. Salins, Oscar S. Schafer, Jr., Roger Schafer, Oscar S. Straus III, Harold S. Williams.
Number of staff: None.
Employer Identification Number: 131850830

4723
The Lavanburg-Corner House, Inc.
130 East 59th St., Rm. 545
New York 10022 (212) 836-1358

Incorporated in 1928 in NY.
Donor(s): Fred L. Lavanburg,† Sara Lavanburg Strauss.
Foundation type: Independent
Financial data (yr. ended 12/31/88): Assets, $2,475,961 (M); expenditures, $585,128, including $505,818 for 45 grants (high: $30,000; low: $800; average: $6,000).
Purpose and activities: Grants to community agencies and schools for demonstration, innovative pilot projects dealing with welfare and health services to seriously disadvantaged children and youth through high school.
Types of support: Seed money, matching funds, scholarship funds, special projects.
Limitations: Giving limited to the New York, NY, metropolitan area. No grants to individuals, or for operating budgets, continuing support, annual campaigns, emergency funds, deficit financing, capital or endowment funds, research, publications, or conferences; no loans.
Publications: Application guidelines.
Application information: Application form required.
Initial approach: Letter or proposal
Copies of proposal: 1
Deadline(s): 2 months prior to board meetings
Board meeting date(s): June and Jan.
Final notification: 1 week after board meetings
Write: Lauren Katzowitz, Staff Consultant
Officers and Trustees: Robert L. Popper, Pres.; Ira H. Lustgarten, V.P.; Herbert Millman, Secy.; Mrs. Leonard H. Bernheim, Louise Greilsheimer, Henry Kohn, Jack A. Krauskopf, Mark D. Litt, Mrs. Henry A. Loeb, John H. Loeb, Millard L. Midonick, Ann Sand, Sanford Solender, Estelle Tanner.
Number of staff: 1 part-time professional.
Employer Identification Number: 131960060

4724
Lawrence Foundation ⌑
c/o Lawrence Aviation Industries, Inc.
Sheep Pasture Rd.
Port Jefferson Station 11776 (516) 473-1800

Established in 1943 in MA and NY.
Donor(s): Lawrence Aviation Industries, Inc.
Foundation type: Independent
Financial data (yr. ended 12/31/88): Assets, $2,246,943 (M); expenditures, $141,744, including $124,350 for 86 grants (high: $10,000; low: $25).
Purpose and activities: Giving primarily for higher education, hospitals and health associations; support also for social services and cultural affairs.
Limitations: Giving primarily in New York, NY, with emphasis on Long Island.
Application information: Application form not required.
Deadline(s): None
Write: Gerald Cohen, Trustee
Trustee: Gerald Cohen.
Employer Identification Number: 116035412

4725
Alice Lawrence Foundation, Inc. ⌑
c/o Graubard, Mollen, Dunnett Horowitz & Pomeranz
600 Third Ave.
New York 10016-1903

Incorporated in 1985 in NY.
Donor(s): Alice Lawrence.
Foundation type: Independent
Financial data (yr. ended 12/31/88): Assets, $2,826,184 (M); expenditures, $47,073, including $45,500 for 6 grants (high: $30,000; low: $1,000).
Purpose and activities: Support for Jewish organizations.
Limitations: No grants to individuals.
Application information: Contributes only to pre-selected organizations. Applications not accepted.
Officers and Directors:* Alice Lawrence,* Pres.; E. Reich,* Secy.; C. Daniel Chill.
Employer Identification Number: 133317659

4726
John S. and Florence G. Lawrence Foundation, Inc.
Eight Freer St., Suite 160
Lynbrook 11563 (516) 887-9485

Established in 1955 in NY.
Donor(s): John S. Lawrence.
Foundation type: Independent
Financial data (yr. ended 04/30/89): Assets, $1,832,652 (M); expenditures, $89,611, including $78,492 for 99 grants (high: $27,950; low: $50).
Purpose and activities: Giving primarily for Jewish welfare organizations and religious activities; support also for education, hospitals, and the arts.
Types of support: Operating budgets, continuing support, annual campaigns, emergency funds, fellowships, general purposes, research, scholarship funds.
Limitations: No grants to individuals, or for seed money, deficit financing, capital funds, endowment funds, matching gifts, non-grant support, research, demonstration projects, program support, publications, conferences or seminars; no loans.
Application information: Application form not required.
Initial approach: Letter
Deadline(s): None
Board meeting date(s): Mar.
Write: John S. Lawrence, Pres.
Officers and Directors:* John S. Lawrence,* Pres. and Treas.; Florence G. Lawrence,* V.P. and Secy.; James G. Lawrence,* V.P.; Betsy P. Schiff,* V.P.; George J. Hutt, David M. Levitan.
Number of staff: 1 part-time support.
Employer Identification Number: 136099026

4727
The Lazar Foundation
c/o Helen Lazar, Pres.
680 Madison Ave.
New York 10021

Incorporated in 1957 in DE.
Donor(s): Jack Lazar, Helen Lazar, and others.
Foundation type: Independent
Financial data (yr. ended 12/31/88): Assets, $5,973,172 (L); gifts received, $18,825; expenditures, $324,504, including $288,025 for 44 grants (high: $75,000; low: $100).
Purpose and activities: Support for Jewish welfare funds, higher education, including medical education, the environment, and hospitals.
Types of support: Special projects.
Limitations: Giving primarily in NY. No grants to individuals.
Publications: 990-PF.
Application information: Contributes only to pre-selected organizations. Applications not accepted.
Officers and Trustees:* Helen B. Lazar,* Pres.; William Lazar,* V.P.; Jeanne Morency,* Secy.
Number of staff: 1 part-time professional.
Employer Identification Number: 136088182

4728
LCP Charitable Foundation
730 Fifth Ave., Rm. 2101
New York 10019 (212) 247-1300

Incorporated in 1983 in DE.
Donor(s): Anthony M. Pilaro, and members of the Pilaro family.
Foundation type: Independent
Financial data (yr. ended 12/31/88): Assets, $1,250,000 (M); gifts received, $500,000; expenditures, $500,000, including $500,000 for grants.
Purpose and activities: Emphasis on higher and other education, including teacher development and training, children's welfare, and social services; support also for museums, hospitals, and community funds.
Limitations: Giving primarily in the New York, NY, area.
Application information: Contributes only to pre-selected organizations. Applications not accepted.
Board meeting date(s): May and as required
Officers and Trustees:* Linda C. Pilaro,* Pres.; Susan Ader,* V.P.; Craigh Leonard,* Secy.; Anthony M. Pilaro.
Employer Identification Number: 133185378

4729
The Lebensfeld Foundation ⌑
600 Fifth Ave.
New York 10020 (212) 581-7660

Incorporated in 1959 in NY.
Donor(s): Harry Lebensfeld.
Foundation type: Independent
Financial data (yr. ended 8/31/88): Assets, $1,595,690 (M); expenditures, $79,699, including $71,500 for 32 grants (high: $10,000; low: $150).
Purpose and activities: Grants primarily for higher and secondary education, hospitals, and Jewish welfare funds.
Limitations: Giving primarily in NY.
Application information: Application form not required.
Deadline(s): None
Write: Harry Lebensfeld, Pres.
Officers: Harry Lebensfeld, Pres.; Edward Brodsky, V.P. and Secy.; Joseph F. Arrigo, V.P. and Treas.; Lynne Pasculano, V.P.
Director: Andrew G. Petrini.
Employer Identification Number: 136086169

4730
The LeBrun Foundation ⌑
2100 Main Place Tower
Buffalo 14202 (716) 853-1521

Established in 1974.
Donor(s): Jennifer L. Jacobs.
Foundation type: Independent
Financial data (yr. ended 6/30/88): Assets, $2,794,646 (M); expenditures, $189,820.
Purpose and activities: Grants primarily for international welfare, refugee aid, and justice organizations, including those under Roman Catholic and Jewish auspices, and an amnesty organization.
Types of support: Research.
Trustees: Thomas R. Beecher, Jr., Jennifer L. Jacobs.
Employer Identification Number: 237408547

4731
James T. Lee Foundation, Inc.
P.O. Box 1856
New York 10185

Incorporated in 1958 in NY.
Donor(s): James T. Lee.†
Foundation type: Independent
Financial data (yr. ended 11/30/88): Assets, $4,169,880 (M); expenditures, $269,150, including $230,000 for 18 grants (high: $25,000; low: $5,000).
Purpose and activities: Emphasis on higher education, including medical education, hospitals, religious associations, and child welfare.
Types of support: Continuing support, annual campaigns, emergency funds, deficit financing, scholarship funds, special projects, research.
Limitations: Giving primarily in NY. No grants to individuals, or for operating budgets, seed money, capital or endowment funds, publications, or conferences; no loans.
Application information: Contributes only to pre-selected organizations. Applications not accepted.
Board meeting date(s): Feb., May, Aug., and Nov.
Final notification: 3 months
Write: Raymond T. O'Keefe, Pres.
Officers and Directors:* Raymond T. O'Keefe,* Pres.; Robert Rivel, V.P. and Treas.; John J. Duffy,* Secy.; Thomas Appleby, Verne S. Atwater, James Bloor, Robert Graber, Delcour Potter, Wesley Rivel.
Number of staff: None.
Employer Identification Number: 131878496

4732
The Marvin & Annette Lee Foundation, Inc. ⌑
878 Highland Rd.
Ithaca 14850-1444

Established in 1959 in NY.
Donor(s): Marvin Lee, Annette Lee.
Foundation type: Independent
Financial data (yr. ended 12/31/88): Assets, $1,238,965 (M); expenditures, $62,223, including $55,345 for 43 grants (high: $15,000; low: $50).
Purpose and activities: Support for higher education, health and hospitals, and cultural programs.
Limitations: Giving primarily in NY. No grants to individuals or for scholarships; no loans.
Application information: Contributes only to pre-selected organizations. Applications not accepted.
Officers: Marvin Lee, Pres.; Annette Lee, Secy.; David M. Lee, Treas.
Employer Identification Number: 066034414

4733
The Leeds Foundation, Inc. ⌑ ☆
300 Hawkins Ave.
Lake Ronkonkoma 11779-4238

Established in 1964 in NY.
Donor(s): Kenneth Leeds.†
Foundation type: Independent
Financial data (yr. ended 2/28/89): Assets, $10,124 (M); gifts received, $350,000; expenditures, $407,273, including $406,000 for 6 grants (high: $135,000; low: $1,000).
Purpose and activities: Giving for higher education, mental health, a Catholic church, and an AIDS organization.
Limitations: Giving primarily in Long Island and New York, NY. No grants to individuals.
Application information: Contributes only to pre-selected organizations. Applications not accepted.
Officers: Helen DiBiase, Pres.; Edwin S. Brown, V.P.; Ivan Mann, Secy.-Treas.
Employer Identification Number: 116042627

4734
Leff Foundation, Inc. ⌑
c/o National Spinning Co., Inc.
183 Madison Ave.
New York 10016

Incorporated in 1942 in NY.
Donor(s): Carl Leff, Phillip Leff, National Spinning Co., Inc.
Foundation type: Independent
Financial data (yr. ended 12/31/87): Assets, $1,195,644 (M); gifts received, $163,100; expenditures, $216,985.
Purpose and activities: Support primarily for Jewish welfare funds and educational and religious organizations, including institutions in Israel.
Application information: Contributes only to pre-selected organizations. Applications not accepted.
Officers: Carl Leff, Pres.; Eleanor Leff, V.P.; Lilian Leff, V.P.; Joseph Leff, Secy.-Treas.
Employer Identification Number: 116007845

4735
Samuel J. & Ethel Lefrak Foundation, Inc. ⌑
97-77 Queens Blvd.
Rego Park 11374 (718) 495-9021

Established in 1963.
Donor(s): Samuel J. Lefrak, L.S.S. Leasing Corp.
Foundation type: Independent
Financial data (yr. ended 12/31/88): Assets, $329,131 (M); gifts received, $77,220; expenditures, $118,899, including $118,590 for 115 grants (high: $11,000; low: $10).
Purpose and activities: Giving primarily for education, hospitals and health agencies, and cultural institutions; some support for Jewish giving and general charitable giving.
Limitations: Giving primarily in New York, NY.
Application information:
Initial approach: Letter
Deadline(s): None
Write: Maxwell Goldpin, Admin. Asst.
Officer: Samuel J. Lefrak, Pres.
Employer Identification Number: 116043788

4736
Lefteria Foundation, Inc. ⌑ ☆
c/o 61 Associates
350 Fifth Ave., Suite 3410
New York 10118-0001

Established in 1984 in NY.
Donor(s): Eli S. Garber, Helen S. Cohen, Thomas Cohen.
Foundation type: Independent
Financial data (yr. ended 11/30/88): Assets, $766,539 (M); gifts received, $137,163; expenditures, $127,654, including $114,500 for 5 grants (high: $100,000; low: $500).
Purpose and activities: Giving primarily for a political science organization; minor support for higher education.
Limitations: Giving primarily in NY and MA. No grants to individuals.
Application information: Contributes only to pre-selected organizations. Applications not accepted.
Officers and Directors: Eli S. Garber, Pres. and Secy.; Mayer Miller, V.P.; Steven Ungerleider, Treas.
Employer Identification Number: 133337436

4737
Edith and Herbert Lehman Foundation, Inc.
c/o Cleary, Gottlieb, Steen & Hamilton
One State St. Plaza, 27th Fl.
New York 10004

Incorporated in 1952 in NY.
Donor(s): Edith A. Lehman,† Herbert Lehman.†
Foundation type: Independent

Financial data (yr. ended 09/30/89): Assets, $3,486,227 (M); expenditures, $130,694, including $114,673 for 30 grants (high: $50,000; low: $250).
Purpose and activities: Grants largely for welfare, education, health services, and the arts.
Types of support: General purposes.
Limitations: Giving primarily in NY. No grants to individuals.
Publications: Annual report.
Application information: Contributes only to pre-selected organizations. Applications not accepted.
Officers and Directors:* John R. Lehman,* Pres.; Arthur G. Altschul,* V.P.; Wendy Lash,* V.P.; Camilla M. Rosenfeld,* V.P.; Stephanie Wise,* V.P.; George DeSipio,* Secy.-Treas.; Steven M. Loeb.
Employer Identification Number: 136094015

4738
Robert Lehman Foundation, Inc. ▼
c/o Hertz, Herson, & Co.
Two Park Ave.
New York 10016 (212) 808-7946

Incorporated in 1943 in NY.
Donor(s): Robert Lehman.†
Foundation type: Independent
Financial data (yr. ended 9/30/88): Assets, $39,595,329 (M); expenditures, $1,823,398, including $1,360,453 for 20 grants (high: $634,138; low: $5,000; average: $5,000-$60,000).
Purpose and activities: Support for the maintenance, conservation, and preservation of the Robert Lehman collection at the Metropolitan Museum of Art; some support also for higher education and cultural programs, with emphasis on visual arts and related teaching activities and publications.
Limitations: Giving primarily in the northeastern U.S., with emphasis on New York, NY.
Application information: Unsolicited applications generally not accepted.
Deadline(s): None
Board meeting date(s): As required
Write: Paul C. Guth, Exec. Secy.
Officers and Directors: Philip H. Isles, Pres.; Edwin L. Weisl, Jr., V.P.; Paul C. Guth, Exec. Secy.; Robert A. Bernhard, Treas.; James M. Hester.
Number of staff: None.
Employer Identification Number: 136094018

4739
Lemberg Foundation, Inc. ⌑
60 East 42nd St., Rm. 1814
New York 10165 (212) 682-9595

Incorporated in 1945 in NY.
Donor(s): Samuel Lemberg.†
Foundation type: Independent
Financial data (yr. ended 12/31/88): Assets, $7,923,716 (M); expenditures, $373,701, including $340,131 for 109 grants (high: $50,000; low: $20).
Purpose and activities: Support for Jewish welfare funds, higher education, temple support, and the performing arts.
Types of support: Building funds, endowment funds, special projects, research, scholarship funds, fellowships.
Limitations: No grants for matching gifts.
Application information:
Initial approach: Letter, proposal, or telephone
Copies of proposal: 1
Board meeting date(s): As required
Write: John Usdan, Treas.
Officers: Suzanne Usdan, Pres.; Adam Usdan, Secy.; John Usdan, Treas.
Number of staff: 2 part-time support.
Employer Identification Number: 136082064

4740
The Dorothea L. Leonhardt Foundation, Inc. ☆
One Chase Manhattan Plaza, 47th Fl.
New York 10005 (212) 530-5016

Incorporated in 1988 in NY.
Donor(s): Frederick H. Leonhardt.†
Foundation type: Independent
Financial data (yr. ended 07/31/89): Assets, $7,797,015 (M); gifts received, $7,240,560; expenditures, $292,661, including $230,200 for 16 grants (high: $63,200; low: $120).
Purpose and activities: First year of grantmaking activities fiscal, 1989; grants primarily for the arts, music, and medical research.
Types of support: General purposes, research.
Limitations: Giving primarily in NY and CT. No grants to individuals.
Application information: Contributes only to pre-selected organizations. Applications not accepted.
Write: Guilford W. Gaylord, Asst. Secy.
Officers and Directors: Joanne L. Cassullo, Pres.; Richard A. Stark, Secy.-Treas.; Alexander D. Forger.
Number of staff: 1
Employer Identification Number: 133420520

4741
Florence and Edgar Leslie Charitable Trust ⌑
230 Park Ave.
New York 10169

Established in 1977 in NY.
Foundation type: Independent
Financial data (yr. ended 12/31/88): Assets, $1,220,651 (M); expenditures, $91,180, including $61,500 for 8 grants (high: $25,000; low: $1,500).
Purpose and activities: Giving for research and advancements in medical science.
Limitations: Giving primarily in NY.
Application information: Application form not required.
Initial approach: Letter
Deadline(s): None
Write: Edward G. Brucker, Esq., Trustee
Trustees: Andrew G. Brucker, Edward G. Brucker, Arthur M. Tunick.
Employer Identification Number: 136720542

4742
Edgar M. Leventritt Foundation, Inc. ⌑
Jay Cox Rd.
Cold Spring 10516

Established in 1939 in NY.
Foundation type: Independent
Financial data (yr. ended 12/31/88): Assets, $1,525,208 (M); expenditures, $83,289, including $73,950 for 28 grants (high: $25,000; low: $100).
Purpose and activities: Support for higher education and cultural programs, including music.
Limitations: No grants to individuals, or for scholarships; no loans.
Application information: Contributes only to pre-selected organizations. Applications not accepted.
Officers: Edgar R. Berner, Pres.; T. Roland Berner, V.P. and Treas.; Thomas R. Berner, V.P.; Olga Formissano, Secy.
Employer Identification Number: 136111037

4743
Levien Foundation ⌑
745 Fifth Ave., Suite 312
New York 10151-0016

Established in 1960 in NY.
Foundation type: Independent
Financial data (yr. ended 12/31/88): Assets, $1,253,526 (M); expenditures, $51,527, including $50,483 for 30 grants (high: $10,000; low: $25).
Purpose and activities: Giving primarily for Jewish organizations and health; support also for social services.
Types of support: Research, general purposes.
Limitations: Giving primarily in NY. No grants to individuals.
Application information: Contributes only to pre-selected organizations. Applications not accepted.
Officer: Francis Levien, Mgr.
Employer Identification Number: 136077798

4744
Louis Levin Foundation ⌑ ☆
c/o A. Zell
299 Broadway, Suite 1520
New York 10007

Established in 1967.
Foundation type: Independent
Financial data (yr. ended 12/31/88): Assets, $1,021,561 (M); expenditures, $62,953, including $47,600 for grants.
Purpose and activities: Support for synagogues, the aged, orphanages, medical research, and medical colleges.
Limitations: No grants to individuals.
Application information: Application form not required.
Initial approach: Proposal
Deadline(s): None
Write: Murray Rose, Trustee
Trustees: Max Leon, Murray Rose, Saul Rose.
Employer Identification Number: 226076671

4745
Morris L. Levinson Foundation, Inc. ⌑
c/o Becker Ross Stone DeStefano and Klein
41 East 42nd St.
New York 10012

Incorporated in 1952 in NY.
Donor(s): Morris L. Levinson, Associated Products, Inc.
Foundation type: Independent
Financial data (yr. ended 6/30/88): Assets, $3,246,059 (M); expenditures, $266,634, including $252,153 for 81 grants (high: $25,000; low: $2).
Purpose and activities: Emphasis on Jewish welfare funds, temple support, and higher education in Israel.
Limitations: Giving primarily in NY and Israel. No grants to individuals.
Application information: Contributes only to pre-selected organizations. Applications not accepted.
Officers and Directors: Morris L. Levinson, Pres.; Barbara S. Levinson, V.P.; Daniel G. Ross, Secy.
Employer Identification Number: 136132727

4746
Leviton Foundation, Inc. - New York ⌑
59-25 Little Neck Pkwy.
Little Neck 11362

Incorporated in 1952 in NY.
Donor(s): Leviton Manufacturing Co., American Insulated Wire Corp.
Foundation type: Company-sponsored
Financial data (yr. ended 12/31/88): Assets, $1,355,920 (M); gifts received, $7,500; expenditures, $376,785, including $374,483 for 27 grants (high: $100,000; low: $100).
Purpose and activities: Emphasis on Jewish welfare funds; some support for education and community funds.
Limitations: Giving primarily in NY and RI. No grants to individuals.
Application information: Contributes only to pre-selected organizations. Applications not accepted.
Officers: Harold Leviton, Pres.; Jack Amsterdam, Secy.-Treas.; Shirley Leviton, Treas.
Employer Identification Number: 116006368

4747
Mortimer Levitt Foundation, Inc. ⌑
c/o E. Rubenstein
215 East 68th St.
New York 10021-5718
Application address: 18 East 50th St., New York, NY 10022; Tel.: (212) 223-3600

Established in 1966 in NY.
Donor(s): Mortimer Levitt, The Custom Shops.
Foundation type: Independent
Financial data (yr. ended 2/28/89): Assets, $1,467,786 (M); gifts received, $94,600; expenditures, $57,462, including $57,296 for 73 grants (high: $5,850; low: $40).
Purpose and activities: Support for museums and other arts groups and youth.
Limitations: Giving primarily in New York, NY.
Application information:
Initial approach: Letter
Deadline(s): None
Write: Mortimer Levitt, Pres.
Officers: Mortimer Levitt, Pres.; A. Levitt, V.P. and Secy.; E. Rubenstein, Treas.
Employer Identification Number: 136204678

4748
The Betty & Norman F. Levy Foundation, Inc. ⌑
522 Fifth Ave.
New York 10036-7601

Established in 1965 in NY.
Donor(s): Norman F. Levy.
Foundation type: Independent
Financial data (yr. ended 9/30/89): Assets, $3,990,678 (M); gifts received, $1,476,346; expenditures, $220,130, including $219,100 for 17 grants (high: $100,000; low: $300).
Purpose and activities: Giving primarily for Jewish organizations, including a welfare fund and a yeshiva; support also for health.
Limitations: Giving primarily in NY.
Officers and Directors: Norman F. Levy, Pres.; Francis N. Levy, V.P.; Albert L. Maltz, Secy.
Employer Identification Number: 132553674

4749
The Jerome Levy Foundation ⌑
c/o Warshaw, Burstein, Cohen, Schlesinger & Kuh
555 Fifth Ave.
New York 10017
Application address: P.O. Box 26, Chappaqua, NY 10514; Tel.: (914) 238-3267

Trust established in 1955 in NY.
Donor(s): Leon Levy, S. Jay Levy.
Foundation type: Independent
Financial data (yr. ended 10/31/88): Assets, $173,078 (M); expenditures, $468,647, including $464,085 for 29 grants (high: $325,000; low: $35).
Purpose and activities: Grants largely for Jewish welfare funds, the fine arts, and higher education; support also for organizations interested in freedom of expression.
Limitations: No grants to individuals.
Application information: Primarily contributes to pre-selected organizations. Applications not accepted.
Write: S. Jay Levy, Trustee
Trustees: Leon Levy, S. Jay Levy.
Employer Identification Number: 136159573

4750
The Lewis Foundation, Inc. ⌑
c/o Sullivan & Cromwell
250 Park Ave.
New York 10177

Incorporated in 1952 in NY.
Donor(s): Salim B. Lewis,† Diana B. Lewis, Barbara Lewis.
Foundation type: Independent
Financial data (yr. ended 8/31/89): Assets, $1,288,071 (M); expenditures, $147,254, including $130,218 for 24 grants (high: $30,000; low: $39).
Purpose and activities: Emphasis on higher and secondary education, Jewish welfare funds, and child development.
Limitations: Giving primarily in NY.
Application information: Contributes only to pre-selected organizations. Applications not accepted.
Officers: Salim B. Lewis, Pres.; Barbara Lewis, V.P.; Henry Christensen III, Secy.-Treas.
Employer Identification Number: 136062713

4751
Wadsworth Lewis Trust ⌑
c/o Citibank, N.A., PB & I Tax Dept.
20 Exchange Place, Sort No. 4850
New York 10043
Application address: Joe Valentine, c/o Citibank, N.A. 641 Lexington Ave., 4th Fl., New York, NY 10043

Foundation type: Independent
Financial data (yr. ended 12/31/88): Assets, $1,239,502 (M); expenditures, $30,321, including $3,506 for 1 grant.
Purpose and activities: Giving to a community fund in NYC.
Limitations: Giving primarily in NY.
Application information:
Initial approach: Letter
Deadline(s): Dec. 31
Trustees: Joseph W. Drake, Jr., Citibank, N.A.
Employer Identification Number: 136053996

4752
The Li Foundation, Inc. ⌑
66 Herbhill Rd.
Glen Cove 11542
Application address: State Education Commission, Beijing, People's Republic of China

Established in 1944.
Foundation type: Independent
Financial data (yr. ended 12/31/86): Assets, $6,000,202 (M); expenditures, $372,685, including $3,282 for 2 grants and $266,076 for 37 grants to individuals (high: $13,931; low: $1,250).
Purpose and activities: Giving entirely for scholarships to Chinese students.
Types of support: Student aid.
Limitations: Giving primarily in China.
Publications: Annual report.
Application information: Application form required.
Deadline(s): None
Board meeting date(s): May
Write: E. Leong Way, Pres.
Officers: E. Leong Way,* Pres.; Marie Chun,* V.P.; Madeline L. Way, Treas.
Directors:* Mildred L. Distin, K.C. Li, Jr.
Number of staff: 3
Employer Identification Number: 136098783

4753
Bertha & Isaac Liberman Foundation ⌑
c/o Richard Mark, Peat Marwick Main & Co.
599 Lexington Ave.
New York 10022
Application address: 45 East 89th St., New York, NY 10028

Established in 1947 in NY.
Donor(s): Isaac Liberman.†
Foundation type: Independent
Financial data (yr. ended 06/30/89): Assets, $4,106,961 (M); expenditures, $220,433,

including $200,015 for 15 grants (high: $60,000; low: $350).
Purpose and activities: Support primarily for a Young Men's Hebrew Association, higher education, and a Jewish welfare organization.
Types of support: General purposes.
Limitations: No grants to individuals.
Application information: Application form not required.
Deadline(s): None
Write: Jeffrey Klein, Pres.
Officer: Jeffrey Klein, Pres.
Employer Identification Number: 136119056

4754
David L. Lieb Foundation, Inc. ⌑ ☆
270 Madison Ave.
New York 10016-0601 (212) 683-7110

Donor(s): David L. Lieb.
Foundation type: Independent
Financial data (yr. ended 9/30/88): Assets, $1,034,596 (M); gifts received, $482,400; expenditures, $265,245, including $250,909 for 29 grants (high: $106,880; low: $100).
Purpose and activities: Giving primarily for a Jewish welfare fund and other Jewish organizations; support also for higher education and hospitals.
Limitations: Giving primarily in NY. No grants to individuals.
Application information: Contributes only to pre-selected organizations. Applications not accepted.
Officers: David L. Lieb, Pres.; Charles H. Lieb, Secy.
Employer Identification Number: 136077728

4755
J. S. Liebowitz Foundation, Inc. ⌑
75 Rockefeller Plaza, Suite 1105
New York 10019-6908

Incorporated in 1945 in NY.
Donor(s): J.S. Liebowitz.
Foundation type: Independent
Financial data (yr. ended 11/30/88): Assets, $402,298 (M); expenditures, $194,571, including $192,685 for 31 grants (high: $50,800; low: $15).
Purpose and activities: Grants primarily for Jewish welfare funds, higher education, and health agencies.
Limitations: No grants to individuals.
Application information:
Initial approach: Letter
Deadline(s): None
Write: J.S. Liebowitz, Pres.
Officers and Directors: J.S. Liebowitz, Pres. and Treas.; Shirley W. Liebowitz, V.P.; Bernard Kashdan, Secy.
Employer Identification Number: 136100091

4756
Lighting Research Institute, Inc. ⌑ ☆
345 East 47th St.
New York 10017

Established in 1983.
Donor(s): National Electric Manufacturers Assn., General Electric Co.
Foundation type: Operating
Financial data (yr. ended 12/31/88): Assets, $347,701 (M); gifts received, $350,380; expenditures, $472,262, including $314,762 for 12 grants (high: $50,000; low: $8,000).
Purpose and activities: A private operating foundation; support for higher education and medical research.
Types of support: Research.
Limitations: No grants to individuals.
Application information: Contributes only to pre-selected organizations. Applications not accepted.
Officer and Director: Richard Vincent, Secy.
Employer Identification Number: 133147071

4757
The Lincoln Fund ⌑
292 Madison Ave., 24th Fl.
New York 10017 (212) 889-4109

Incorporated in 1898 in NY.
Foundation type: Independent
Financial data (yr. ended 6/30/88): Assets, $4,927,425 (M); expenditures, $325,965, including $285,000 for 19 grants (high: $25,000; low: $5,000; average: $11,667).
Purpose and activities: Giving for aid to the elderly, education, nursing, and medical programs; grants limited to pilot projects, demonstrations, and expansion of programs.
Types of support: Continuing support, seed money, matching funds, scholarship funds, special projects.
Limitations: Giving limited to New York, NY. No grants to individuals, or for building or endowment funds, operating budgets, or general corporate purposes.
Application information: Application form not required.
Initial approach: Letter
Copies of proposal: 1
Deadline(s): None
Board meeting date(s): Sept., Dec., Mar., and June
Final notification: 3 to 4 months
Write: Mrs. James C. Sargent, Pres.
Officers and Directors: Mrs. James C. Sargent, Pres.; Mrs. Duer McLanahan, V.P.; Mrs. William Brown, Secy.; Lawrence L. Lanier, Treas.; Mrs. Paule R. Alexander, Jeanne M. Greene, E. Eldred Hill.
Number of staff: 1 part-time support.
Employer Identification Number: 131740466

4758
Lindau Foundation, Inc. ⌑
Box 329, R.D. 2
Pine City 14871

Established in 1973 in NY.
Foundation type: Independent
Financial data (yr. ended 4/30/88): Assets, $1,045,947 (M); expenditures, $101,034, including $93,250 for 29 grants (high: $25,000; low: $500).
Purpose and activities: Emphasis on community funds, cultural programs, hospitals, and education.
Types of support: General purposes.
Limitations: Giving primarily in Elmira, NY.
Application information: Contributes primarily to pre-selected organizations. Applications not accepted.
Officers: Whitney S. Powers, Jr., Pres.; Patricia L. Powers, V.P.; Bela C. Tifft, Secy.
Employer Identification Number: 161020706

4759
The Lindemann Foundation, Inc. ⌑
c/o Mahoney Cohen Paul & Co., P.C.
111 West 40th St., 12th Fl.
New York 10018

Incorporated in 1943 in NY.
Donor(s): Joseph S. Lindemann.†
Foundation type: Independent
Financial data (yr. ended 12/31/88): Assets, $2,945,949 (M); expenditures, $102,575, including $83,312 for 83 grants (high: $16,667; low: $25).
Purpose and activities: Support for higher education in Israel and the U.S., and Jewish welfare funds.
Officers: Lilyan S. Lindemann, V.P.; George L. Lindemann, Secy.-Treas.
Directors: Carol L. Abend, Barbara L. Schlei.
Employer Identification Number: 136140249

4760
Albert A. & Bertram N. Linder Foundation, Inc.
305 East 40th St., PH C
New York 10016 (212) 986-7983

Incorporated in 1947 in NY.
Donor(s): Bertram N. Linder.
Foundation type: Independent
Financial data (yr. ended 5/31/89): Assets, $1,415,444 (M); expenditures, $107,061, including $78,515 for grants (high: $16,000; low: $10).
Purpose and activities: Emphasis on Jewish welfare funds, community funds, higher education, hospitals, and church and temple support.
Types of support: Annual campaigns, building funds, capital campaigns, endowment funds, research, scholarship funds, seed money, continuing support.
Limitations: Giving primarily in NY and Scranton, PA. No grants to individuals, or for scholarships, fellowships, or matching gifts; no loans.
Application information:
Initial approach: Letter
Copies of proposal: 1
Deadline(s): Submit application preferably in Apr. or early May; deadline May 15
Board meeting date(s): June and Dec.
Write: Bertram N. Linder, Pres.
Officers and Trustees: Bertram N. Linder, Pres. and Treas.; Mary Ellen Linder, V.P. and Secy.; Robert Allen Linder, V.P.
Employer Identification Number: 136100590

4761
Fay J. Lindner Foundation ⌑
1161 Meadowbrook Rd.
North Merrick 11566

Established in 1966.
Donor(s): Fay J. Lindner.
Foundation type: Independent

Financial data (yr. ended 8/31/88): Assets, $2,679,547 (M); gifts received, $300,000; expenditures, $387,808, including $378,668 for 45 grants (high: $150,000; low: $250).
Purpose and activities: Giving primarily for hospitals and health agencies; grants also to a university and Jewish organizations, including a Jewish welfare fund.
Limitations: Giving primarily in Long Island, NY.
Application information: Contributes only to pre-selected organizations. Applications not accepted.
Director: Diane Lindner Goldberg.
Employer Identification Number: 116043320

4762
Trustees of Lingnan University ⌑
1290 Ave. of the Americas, Rm. 3450
New York 10104 (212) 373-4200

Established in 1893 in NY.
Foundation type: Independent
Financial data (yr. ended 6/30/88): Assets, $8,652,345 (M); gifts received, $6,388; expenditures, $310,099, including $252,500 for 12 grants.
Purpose and activities: Grants only for support of higher education of Chinese students.
Types of support: Operating budgets, continuing support, seed money, professorships, internships, exchange programs, research, publications, conferences and seminars.
Limitations: Giving primarily in Hong Kong and People's Republic of China. No grants to individuals, or for annual campaigns or emergency, capital, or endowment funds; no loans.
Publications: Program policy statement.
Application information: Application form not required.
Initial approach: Proposal or letter
Copies of proposal: 1
Deadline(s): None
Board meeting date(s): May and Nov.
Final notification: 2 months after meetings
Write: Russell A. Phillips, Jr., Pres.
Officers and Trustees: Russell A. Phillips, Jr., Pres.; Robert Chin, V.P.; Ralph E. Lerner, Secy.; Stuyvesant Wainwright III, Treas.; and 21 additional trustees.
Number of staff: 1 part-time professional; 1 part-time support.
Employer Identification Number: 136400470

4763
George Link, Jr. Foundation, Inc. ▼ ⌑
c/o Emmet, Marvin and Martin
48 Wall St.
New York 10005 (212) 422-2974

Incorporated in 1980 in NY.
Donor(s): George Link, Jr.†
Foundation type: Independent
Financial data (yr. ended 12/31/88): Assets, $19,978,335 (M); expenditures, $1,663,110, including $1,489,400 for 106 grants (high: $210,000; low: $5,000).
Purpose and activities: Giving primarily for hospitals and medical research, higher and secondary education, welfare, and Christian religious giving.
Types of support: Building funds, scholarship funds, fellowships, endowment funds.
Limitations: Giving primarily in NY, MA, and NJ. No grants to individuals, or for general support, operating budgets, continuing support, annual campaigns, seed money, emergency funds, deficit financing, equipment, land acquisition, renovation projects, or matching gifts; no loans.
Application information: Application form not required.
Initial approach: Proposal
Copies of proposal: 5
Deadline(s): None
Board meeting date(s): Monthly except July and Aug.
Final notification: 6 weeks
Write: Michael J. Catanzaro, V.P.
Officers and Directors: Eleanor Irene Link, Chair.; Robert Emmet Link, Vice-Chair.; Bernard F. Joyce, V.P. and Secy.; Michael J. Catanzaro, V.P. and Treas.; Coleman Clougherty, V.P.
Number of staff: None.
Employer Identification Number: 133041396

4764
Jacques and Yulla Lipchitz Foundation, Inc. ⌑
Six East 43rd St.
New York 10017

Established in 1962.
Donor(s): Yulla Lipchitz.
Foundation type: Independent
Financial data (yr. ended 02/28/89): Assets, $2,488,368 (M); expenditures, $24,776, including $24,500 for 4 grants (high: $9,500; low: $5,000).
Purpose and activities: Gifts of works of art by Jacques Lipchitz to various museums.
Application information: Contributes only to pre-selected organizations. Applications not accepted.
Initial approach: Letter
Write: Hanno D. Mott, V.P.
Officers: Yulla Lipchitz, Pres.; Hanno D. Mott, V.P.
Employer Identification Number: 136151503

4765
Howard and Jean Lipman Foundation, Inc.
522 Fifth Ave.
New York 10036

Established in 1959 in NY.
Donor(s): Howard W. Lipman, Jean Lipman.
Foundation type: Independent
Financial data (yr. ended 06/30/89): Assets, $1,113,525 (L); expenditures, $65,888, including $61,150 for 16 grants (high: $20,000; low: $250; average: $2,921).
Purpose and activities: Giving primarily for art museums; support also for hospitals.
Types of support: Endowment funds.
Publications: 990-PF.
Application information: Contributes only to pre-selected organizations. Applications not accepted.
Officers: Howard W. Lipman, Pres.; Peter W. Lipman, V.P.; Charles H. Leavitt, Secy.; Jean Lipman, Treas.
Employer Identification Number: 136066963

4766
Lippman Rose Schnurmacher Fund, Inc. ⌑
1114 First Ave.
New York 10021 (212) 838-7766

Incorporated in 1945 in NY.
Donor(s): Rose Schnurmacher.†
Foundation type: Independent
Financial data (yr. ended 12/31/88): Assets, $1,762,610 (M); expenditures, $84,510, including $80,580 for 14 grants (high: $35,000; low: $50).
Purpose and activities: Emphasis on Jewish welfare funds and hospitals; grants also for an optometric center.
Limitations: Giving primarily in NY.
Application information:
Write: Adolph Schnurmacher, Mgr.
Officers: Adolph Schnurmacher, Mgr.; Irwin Schnurmacher, Mgr.
Employer Identification Number: 136126002

4767
Meno Lissauer Foundation, Inc. ⌑
530 Park Ave.
New York 10021

Incorporated in 1951 in NY.
Donor(s): Associated Metals and Minerals Corp.
Foundation type: Independent
Financial data (yr. ended 12/31/88): Assets, $1,056,998 (M); expenditures, $71,267, including $54,380 for 39 grants (high: $10,000; low: $50).
Purpose and activities: Grants largely for Jewish welfare funds.
Limitations: Giving primarily in NY.
Application information: Contributes only to pre-selected organizations. Applications not accepted.
Officer: Peter Eliel, Mgr.
Employer Identification Number: 136161478

4768
Albert A. List Foundation, Inc. ▼ ⌑
998 Fifth Ave.
New York 10028

Incorporated in 1953 in CT.
Donor(s): Albert A. List,† Vera G. List.
Foundation type: Independent
Financial data (yr. ended 6/30/89): Assets, $13,559,113 (M); expenditures, $938,505, including $834,166 for 11 grants (high: $250,000; low: $5,000; average: $2,000-$60,000).
Purpose and activities: Grants largely for Jewish welfare funds, hospitals, and higher education; giving also for the aged and cultural programs.
Limitations: Giving primarily in NY and CT. No grants to individuals.
Application information:
Initial approach: Letter
Deadline(s): None
Board meeting date(s): Oct. and Apr.
Final notification: Varies
Write: Olga List Mack, Pres.
Officers: Olga List Mack, Pres.; Viki List, Secy.; JoAnn List Levinson,* Treas.
Directors:* Vera G. List, Carol List Schwartz.
Number of staff: None.
Employer Identification Number: 510188408

4769
The Lucius N. Littauer Foundation, Inc. ▼
60 East 42nd St., Suite 2910
New York 10165 (212) 697-2677

Incorporated in 1929 in NY.
Donor(s): Lucius N. Littauer.†
Foundation type: Independent
Financial data (yr. ended 12/31/88): Assets, $19,000,499 (M); gifts received, $2,000; expenditures, $1,508,117, including $1,227,800 for 148 grants (high: $125,000; low: $250; average: $1,000-$25,000).
Purpose and activities: Grants primarily for the social sciences and the humanities; support for higher education with emphasis on Jewish and Middle Eastern studies, and for refugee aid, including resettlement and rehabilitation; other interests include history and biography, language and literature, philosophy, political science, environmental projects, medical ethics, and religion.
Types of support: Research, publications, conferences and seminars, endowment funds, matching funds, fellowships, lectureships, professorships, scholarship funds, special projects.
Limitations: Giving primarily in NY for medical ethics and environmental projects. No grants to individuals, or for capital projects or operating funds.
Application information: Application form not required.
Initial approach: Proposal
Copies of proposal: 1
Deadline(s): None
Board meeting date(s): Semiannually and as required
Final notification: 3 months
Write: William Lee Frost, Pres.; or Pamela Ween Brumberg, Prog. Officer
Officers and Directors: Harry Starr, Chair.; William Lee Frost, Pres. and Treas.; Issai Hosiosky, V.P. and Secy.; Charles Berlin, Berthold Bilski, George Harris, Henry A. Lowett, Peter J. Solomon.
Number of staff: 2 full-time professional.
Employer Identification Number: 131688027

4770
Mollie Parnis Livingston Foundation, Inc. ⌑ ☆
135 Madison Ave.
New York 10016
Journalism award application address: C.R. Eisendrath, Exec. Dir., 2098 Frieze Bldg., Univ. of Michigan, Ann Arbor, MI 48109; Tel.: (313) 764-0420

Established in 1967 in NY.
Donor(s): Mollie Parnis Livingston, Robert L. Livingston.†
Foundation type: Independent
Financial data (yr. ended 12/31/87): Assets, $468,800 (M); expenditures, $180,905, including $174,643 for grants.
Purpose and activities: Giving primarily for urban affairs; support also for a journalism awards program for journalists under 35 who are not students and are working for a U.S.-owned publication or broadcast organization.
Types of support: Grants to individuals.
Limitations: Giving primarily in New York, NY, for organizations.
Application information: Application form required for journalism awards.
Deadline(s): Feb. 1
Officers: Mollie Parnis Livingston, Pres.; Alan U. Schwartz, Secy.-Treas.
Directors: Charlotte Curtis, Richard M. Clurman, Carole Hochman, Neil Hochman, Mike Wallace.
Employer Identification Number: 136265280

4771
Frances and John L. Loeb Foundation ⌑
c/o Peat Marwick Main Co.
599 Lexington Ave., 16th Fl.
New York 10022 (212) 909-5000

Incorporated in 1937 in NY.
Donor(s): John L. Loeb, Frances L. Loeb.
Foundation type: Independent
Financial data (yr. ended 10/31/88): Assets, $3,932,970 (M); expenditures, $755,864, including $731,764 for 158 grants (high: $252,512; low: $100; average: $100-$10,000).
Purpose and activities: Giving for higher education, hospitals and health services, and cultural programs, including museums and the performing arts; some support also for social services and international activities.
Application information: Contributes only to pre-selected organizations. Applications not accepted.
Officers and Trustees: Frances L. Loeb, Pres. and Treas.; John L. Loeb, V.P.; Deborah L. Brice, Ann L. Bronfman, Judith L. Chiara, Arthur L. Loeb, John L. Loeb, Jr.
Number of staff: None.
Employer Identification Number: 136085598

4772
Loewenberg Foundation, Inc. ⌑ ☆
450 Park Ave.
New York 10022 (212) 753-4100

Established in 1959 in NY.
Donor(s): Ralph E. Loewenberg, Kurt Loewenberg.†
Foundation type: Independent
Financial data (yr. ended 10/31/88): Assets, $2,379,833 (M); expenditures, $128,408, including $109,500 for 8 grants (high: $100,000; low: $1,000).
Purpose and activities: Support primarily for Jewish welfare; giving also for the arts and secondary education.
Limitations: No grants to individuals.
Application information:
Initial approach: Letter
Deadline(s): None
Write: Ralph E. Loewenberg, Pres.
Officers and Directors: Ralph E. Loewenberg, Pres.; Jeffrey N. Grabel, Secy.; Frederick Lubeker.
Employer Identification Number: 136075586

4773
Loews Foundation ▼
One Park Ave., 15th Fl.
New York 10016 (212) 545-2643

Trust established in 1957 in NY.
Donor(s): Loews Corp., and subsidiaries.
Foundation type: Company-sponsored
Financial data (yr. ended 12/31/88): Assets, $1,753 (M); gifts received, $1,187,000; expenditures, $1,563,677, including $1,551,032 for 53 grants (high: $1,050,000; low: $100; average: $1,000-$25,000) and $12,565 for employee matching gifts.
Purpose and activities: Grants primarily for Jewish welfare funds, higher education, including employee matching gifts and employee-related scholarships through the National Merit Scholarship Corp., and cultural organizations.
Types of support: Employee matching gifts, employee-related scholarships.
Limitations: No grants to individuals.
Application information: Applications for employee-related scholarship program available from foundation.
Deadline(s): None
Board meeting date(s): As required
Write: Daria Mychajluk
Trustees: Roy Posner, C.G. Sposato, Jr., Laurence A. Tisch, Preston R. Tisch.
Employer Identification Number: 136082817

4774
Loewy Family Foundation, Inc. ⌑
19 Rector St., Rm. 2805
New York 10006

Established in 1966 in NY.
Donor(s): Alfred Loewy,† Edna Loewy Butler.†
Foundation type: Independent
Financial data (yr. ended 6/30/88): Assets, $4,741,764 (M); gifts received, $4,370,656; expenditures, $24,834, including $6,000 for 1 grant.
Purpose and activities: Support for engineering, science, and technology.
Limitations: Giving primarily in New York, NY.
Application information:
Initial approach: Proposal
Deadline(s): None
Write: John P. Reiner, Secy.-Treas.
Officers and Directors: Andrew Linz, Pres.; Michael Green, V.P.; William W. Reiner, V.P.; John P. Reiner, Secy.-Treas.
Employer Identification Number: 136225288

4775
The Lorber Foundation ⌑ ☆
c/o Jerome Z. Lorber
40 Cuttermill Rd., Suite 410
Great Neck 11021

Established in 1986 in NY.
Donor(s): Jerome Z. Lorber.
Foundation type: Independent
Financial data (yr. ended 6/30/89): Assets, $200,146 (M); gifts received, $414,313; expenditures, $242,398, including $239,355 for 15 grants (high: $100,500; low: $205).
Purpose and activities: Support primarily for Jewish welfare, hospitals, and higher education.
Limitations: Giving primarily in New York, NY. No grants to individuals.
Application information: Contributes only to pre-selected organizations. Applications not accepted.
Officers: Jerome Z. Lorber, Pres. and Treas.; Harvey Brecher, V.P. and Secy.
Director: Eli S. Garber.
Employer Identification Number: 133387946

4776
Lucille Lortel Foundation, Inc. ¤
c/o Hecht & Co.
1500 Broadway
New York 10036

Established in 1980 in NY.
Donor(s): Lucille Lortel.
Foundation type: Independent
Financial data (yr. ended 6/30/88): Assets, $503,686 (M); expenditures, $173,380, including $159,875 for 40 grants (high: $100,000; low: $75).
Purpose and activities: Support for cultural organizations, including theaters, and libraries.
Limitations: Giving primarily in New York, NY.
Application information: Contributes only to pre-selected organizations. Applications not accepted.
Officers: Lucille Lortel, Pres.; Michael Hecht, Secy.-Treas.
Employer Identification Number: 133036521

4777
Richard Lounsbery Foundation, Inc. ▼
159A East 61st St.
New York 10021 (212) 319-7033

Incorporated in 1959 in NY.
Donor(s): Richard Lounsbery Foundation Trust, Inc.
Foundation type: Independent
Financial data (yr. ended 12/31/89): Assets, $16,591,229 (M); gifts received, $1,206,635; qualifying distributions, $2,038,741, including $2,038,741 for 149 grants (high: $50,000; low: $72; average: $1,000-$25,000).
Purpose and activities: Support primarily for biomedical research, the improvement of the teaching and learning of science and mathematics at the secondary and elementary levels, and human rights.
Types of support: Seed money, emergency funds, matching funds, fellowships, research.
Limitations: No grants to individuals, or for capital or building funds, conferences or seminars, or endowment funds; no loans.
Publications: Application guidelines.
Application information: Funds mainly committed to projects developed by the directors; other projects sometimes considered, but applications not encouraged. Application form not required.
Initial approach: Letter
Copies of proposal: 1
Deadline(s): 6 weeks prior to board meetings
Board meeting date(s): Last Wednesday of Jan., Apr., July, and Oct.
Final notification: 2 weeks
Write: Alan F. McHenry, Pres.
Officers and Directors:* Alan F. McHenry,* Pres. and Treas.; Benjamin J. Borden,* V.P. and Secy.; William J. McGill, M.D., Frederick Seitz, M.D., Lewis Thomas, M.D.
Number of staff: 1 full-time professional; 1 full-time support.
Employer Identification Number: 136081860

4778
Low Foundation, Inc. ☆
700 Park Ave.
New York 10021-4930

Established in 1952.
Donor(s): Barbara L. Karatz.
Foundation type: Independent
Financial data (yr. ended 8/31/88): Assets, $1,125,184 (M); expenditures, $103,329, including $88,007 for 61 grants (high: $24,100; low: $18).
Purpose and activities: Giving primarily for hospitals; support also for higher education, a library, cultural programs, and family planning services.
Limitations: Giving primarily in NY. No grants to individuals.
Application information: Contributes only to pre-selected organizations. Applications not accepted.
Officers and Directors: Barbara L. Karatz, Pres.; William W. Karatz, V.P.; Lawrence Buttenwieser, Treas.
Employer Identification Number: 136062712

4779
Leon Lowenstein Foundation, Inc. ▼
126 East 56th St., 28th Fl.
New York 10022 (212) 319-0670
FAX: (212) 688-0134

Incorporated in 1941 in NY.
Donor(s): Leon Lowenstein.†
Foundation type: Independent
Financial data (yr. ended 12/31/89): Assets, $66,800,000 (M); expenditures, $3,300,000, including $2,700,000 for 107 grants (high: $500,000; low: $250; average: $1,000-$25,000).
Purpose and activities: Support primarily for medical research, New York City public schools, and youth programs.
Types of support: General purposes, research, seed money, special projects.
Limitations: Giving primarily in the New York, NY, metropolitan area.
Application information: Application form not required.
Initial approach: Letter
Copies of proposal: 1
Deadline(s): None
Board meeting date(s): As necessary
Final notification: 3 months
Write: John F. Van Gorder, Exec. Dir.
Officers: Robert Bendheim, Pres.; John M. Bendheim, V.P.; Bernard R. Rapoport, Secy.-Treas.; John F. Van Gorder, Exec. Dir.
Number of staff: 2 full-time professional.
Employer Identification Number: 136015951

4780
Theodore Luce Charitable Trust ¤ ☆
c/o Chemical Bank, Admin. Services Dept.
30 Rockefeller Plaza
New York 10112 (212) 621-2148

Foundation type: Independent
Financial data (yr. ended 7/31/89): Assets, $6,697,049 (M); expenditures, $333,406, including $294,000 for 44 grants (high: $11,000; low: $6,000; average: $6,000).
Purpose and activities: Giving for hospitals and health associations, animal welfare, social services, and youth and child welfare organizations.
Limitations: Giving primarily in New York, NY. No grants to individuals, or for conferences or research papers.
Application information: Application form not required.
Deadline(s): None
Write: Mrs. M. Peterson
Trustee: Chemical Bank.
Employer Identification Number: 136029703

4781
The Henry Luce Foundation, Inc. ▼
111 West 50th St., Rm. 3710
New York 10020 (212) 489-7700

Incorporated in 1936 in NY.
Donor(s): Henry R. Luce,† Clare Booth Luce.†
Foundation type: Independent
Financial data (yr. ended 12/31/89): Assets, $419,279,061 (M); gifts received, $286,595; expenditures, $21,396,368, including $19,264,772 for 312 grants (high: $1,000,000; low: $1,600; average: $25,000-$300,000) and $324,573 for 18 grants to individuals (average: $14,000-$17,000).
Purpose and activities: Grants for specific projects in the broad areas of Asian affairs, higher education and scholarship, theology, the arts, and public affairs. The Luce Scholars Program gives a select group of young Americans, not Asian specialists, a year's work/study experience in the East and Southeast Asia. The Henry R. Luce Professorship Program provides five- or eight-year support for a limited number of integrative academic programs in the humanities and social sciences at private colleges and universities. Funding in the arts focuses on research and scholarship in American art; direct support for specific projects at major museums throughout the country; dissertation support to selected university departments of art history. The Luce Fund for Southeast Asian Studies offers support to an invited group of ten American universities on a competitive basis to improve the quality of Southeast Asian Studies. The United States-China Cooperative Research Program is a competitive grant program to encourage thematic research projects jointly directed by American and Chinese Scholars.
Types of support: Seed money, special projects, research, professorships, internships, scholarship funds.
Limitations: Giving for international activities limited to East and Southeast Asia. No support for journalism or media projects. No grants to individuals (except for the Luce Scholars Program), or for endowment or domestic building funds, general operating support, scholarships, or fellowships, annual fund drives; no loans.
Publications: Annual report (including application guidelines), informational brochure.
Application information: Nominees for scholars programs accepted from institutions only; individual applications cannot be considered; Luce Fund for Southeast Asian Studies by invitation only; American Art proposals by invitation only; Clare Booth Luce Fund by invitation only. Application form not required.

Initial approach: Letter
Copies of proposal: 1
Deadline(s): Apr. 1, Henry R. Luce Professorship; June 15, American Art; 1st Monday in Dec., Luce Scholar nominations; Oct. 3, Luce Fund for Southeast Asian Studies; Jan. 15, U.S.-China Cooperative Research; none, program grants
Board meeting date(s): June, Sept., and Dec.
Final notification: 1 month to 1 year; program grants awarded in late fall and end of year
Write: Robert E. Armstrong, Exec. Dir.
Officers and Directors:* Henry Luce III,* Pres.; Robert E. Armstrong,* V.P. and Exec. Dir.; John C. Evans,* V.P. and Secy.-Treas.; Mrs. Maurice T. Moore,* V.P.; Margaret Boles Fitzgerald, Thomas L. Pulling, David V. Ragone, Charles C. Tillinghast, Jr.
Number of staff: 6 full-time professional; 5 full-time support.
Employer Identification Number: 136001282

4782
Georges Lurcy Charitable and Educational Trust ⌑
520 Madison Ave.
New York 10022

Donor(s): Georges Lurcy.†
Foundation type: Independent
Financial data (yr. ended 6/30/87): Assets, $15,110,480 (M); expenditures, $873,141, including $637,873 for 37 grants (high: $85,526; low: $1,000).
Purpose and activities: Support primarily for fellowships for students of American colleges or universities to study in France and students of French colleges or universities to study in the U.S.
Types of support: Fellowships.
Application information: Fellowship applicants from America must be recommended by their universities; applicants from France must apply to the Franco-American Commission for Educational Exchange. Applicants cannot apply directly to the foundation.
Write: Seth E. Frank, Trustee
Trustees: Alan S. Bernstein, Daniel L. Bernstein, George Lurcy Bernstein, Seth E. Frank, Sidney O. Friedman.
Employer Identification Number: 136372044

4783
MacAndrews and Forbes Foundation ▼ ⌑
36 East 63rd St.
New York 10021

Established in 1982 in NY.
Donor(s): MacAndrews & Forbes Co., MacAndrews & Forbes Group, Technicolor, Inc., Wilbur Chocolate Co.
Foundation type: Company-sponsored
Financial data (yr. ended 12/31/88): Assets, $86,241 (M); gifts received, $725,000; expenditures, $723,797, including $723,602 for 32 grants (high: $226,000; low: $100; average: $500-$50,000).
Purpose and activities: Support for Jewish giving, health services, culture, and higher education.
Limitations: Giving primarily in New York, NY. No grants to individuals.
Application information: Contributes only to pre-selected organizations. Applications not accepted.
Write: Richard E. Halperin, Pres.
Officers: Richard E. Halperin,* Pres.; Fred L. Tepperman,* V.P. and Treas.; Frederick W. McNabb, Jr., Secy.
Directors:* Ronald O. Perelman, Bruce Slovin.
Employer Identification Number: 133116648

4784
James A. Macdonald Foundation ⌑
One North Broadway
White Plains 10601 (914) 428-9305

Incorporated in 1966 in NY.
Donor(s): Flora Macdonald Bonney.†
Foundation type: Independent
Financial data (yr. ended 12/31/88): Assets, $4,943,138 (M); expenditures, $368,547, including $324,170 for 252 grants (high: $25,000; low: $100; average: $200-$600).
Purpose and activities: Emphasis on Protestant church support, secondary education, community funds, hospitals, youth agencies, and historic preservation.
Types of support: Operating budgets, continuing support, annual campaigns, seed money, emergency funds, building funds, equipment, land acquisition, endowment funds, scholarship funds, special projects, research, fellowships, renovation projects.
Limitations: Giving primarily in NY. No grants to individuals or for matching gifts; no loans.
Application information: Application form not required.
Initial approach: Letter
Copies of proposal: 1
Deadline(s): None
Board meeting date(s): Irregularly, but at least quarterly
Write: Walter J. Handelman, Secy.
Officers: Blanche B. Handelman,* Pres.; Walter J. Handelman,* Secy.; Alan L. Model, Treas.
Directors:* Alice H. Model.
Number of staff: None.
Employer Identification Number: 136199690

4785
Marquis George MacDonald Foundation, Inc.
c/o The Chase Manhattan Bank, N.A.
1211 Ave. of the Americas, 37th Fl.
New York 10036 (212) 730-5379

Incorporated in 1951 in NY.
Donor(s): Marquis George MacDonald.†
Foundation type: Independent
Financial data (yr. ended 12/31/89): Assets, $5,144,027 (M); expenditures, $264,106, including $199,000 for 138 grants (high: $7,500; low: $300).
Purpose and activities: Giving for the arts, environment, higher and secondary education, church support, religious associations, hospitals, health, cancer and AIDS research, welfare funds, and organizations providing benefit to the community and serving the public interest.
Types of support: Special projects.
Limitations: No grants to individuals, or for matching gifts; no loans.
Application information:
Initial approach: Proposal
Deadline(s): None
Write: Jeannine Merrien, Admin.
Officers and Directors:* Gerald MacDonald,* Pres.; Catherine MacDonald,* V.P.; John L. McDonald, Jr.,* V.P.; Helen McDonald, Joseph MacDonald, Kevin McDonald.
Employer Identification Number: 131957181

4786
The Paul MacKall & Evanina Evans Bell MacKall Trust ⌑
c/o Morgan Guaranty Trust Co. of New York
Nine West 57th St.
New York 10019
Application address: The Presbyterian Univ. of Pennsylvania Medical Center, 51 North 39th St., Philadelphia, PA 19104; Tel.: (215) 662-8100

Established in 1982.
Foundation type: Independent
Financial data (yr. ended 8/31/88): Assets, $7,304,672 (M); expenditures, $415,640, including $358,149 for 2 grants (high: $250,000; low: $108,149).
Purpose and activities: Giving limited to medical facilities, with emphasis on opthalmological research.
Application information:
Initial approach: Letter
Deadline(s): None
Write: Dr. Harold G. Schie, Trustee
Trustees: Harold G. Schie, Morgan Guaranty Trust Co. of New York.
Employer Identification Number: 136794686

4787
Mary W. MacKinnon Fund ⌑ ☆
c/o Wilber National Bank, Trust Dept.
245 Main St.
Oneonta 13820 (607) 432-1700

Established in 1968.
Donor(s): Mary W. MacKinnon.†
Foundation type: Independent
Financial data (yr. ended 12/31/88): Assets, $1,109,328 (M); expenditures, $55,110, including $48,453 for grants to individuals.
Purpose and activities: To provide medical, hospital, rehabilitation, and nursing home care for the aged and the indigent.
Types of support: Grants to individuals.
Limitations: Giving limited to Sidney, NY, residents.
Application information:
Initial approach: Application must be submitted through doctor or hospital
Deadline(s): None
Trustees: Rev. Irving Ballert, Jr., Roma Hoag, John MacDonald.
Employer Identification Number: 237234921

4788
Robert L. and Kathrina H. Maclellan Foundation ⌘
c/o U.S. Trust Co. of New York
114 West 47th St.
New York 10036-1532 (212) 852-1000

Established in 1972 in TN.
Donor(s): Kathrina H. Maclellan.
Foundation type: Independent
Financial data (yr. ended 12/31/87): Assets, $3,104,631 (M); gifts received, $236,697; expenditures, $98,659, including $81,000 for 6 grants (high: $25,000; low: $1,000).
Purpose and activities: Giving primarily to evangelistic Christian educational programs.
Types of support: General purposes.
Application information: Application form not required.
Initial approach: Letter
Deadline(s): May
Board meeting date(s): May
Write: Debra A. Hausser
Officers and Directors: Kathrina H. Maclellan, Pres. and Treas.; Joseph F. Decosimo, Secy.; Lee S. Anderson, Richard L. Heffner, Robert H. Maclellan.
Number of staff: None.
Employer Identification Number: 237159802

4789
The Macmillan Foundation ⌘
866 Third Ave.
New York 10022 (212) 702-2000

Incorporated in 1967 in DE.
Donor(s): Macmillan, Inc.
Foundation type: Company-sponsored
Financial data (yr. ended 12/31/88): Assets, $3,499,516 (M); expenditures, $208,318, including $183,559 for 66 grants (high: $15,000; low: $250).
Purpose and activities: Emphasis on cultural organizations, including the performing arts, libraries, and higher education.
Types of support: General purposes, operating budgets, annual campaigns, endowment funds.
Limitations: Giving primarily in NY, particularly in the New York City metropolitan area. No grants to individuals, or for building funds, scholarships, fellowships, or matching gifts; no loans.
Application information: Application form not required.
Initial approach: Proposal
Copies of proposal: 1
Deadline(s): None
Board meeting date(s): As required
Final notification: 2 months
Write: Philip E. Hoversten, V.P.
Officers and Directors:* Robert Maxwell,* Chair.; Kevin Maxwell,* Vice-Chair.; William F. Reilly,* Pres.; Ellis J. Freedman,* Secy.-Treas.
Number of staff: None.
Employer Identification Number: 136260248

4790
Josiah Macy, Jr. Foundation ▼
44 East 64th St.
New York 10021 (212) 486-2424

Incorporated in 1930 in NY.
Donor(s): Kate Macy Ladd.†
Foundation type: Independent
Financial data (yr. ended 06/30/89): Assets, $94,465,198 (M); expenditures, $5,432,247, including $3,048,555 for 49 grants (high: $275,000; low: $1,500; average: $20,000-$200,000), $57,874 for 46 employee matching gifts and $743,525 for 3 foundation-administered programs.
Purpose and activities: Major interest in medicine and health. Major grant programs are Minorities in Medicine, Medical Education, with emphasis on improving its effectiveness, and training of physicians and other health care professionals; support also for Macy Conferences, usually on issues relevant to current program areas.
Types of support: Special projects.
Limitations: No grants to individuals, or for travel, capital or endowment funds, operating budgets, annual fund appeals, seed money, emergency funds, deficit financing, research, publications, conferences not run by the foundation, scholarships, or fellowships; no loans.
Publications: Annual report.
Application information: The Pathobiology Program has been discontinued. Receipt of proposal acknowledged; no interviews. Application form not required.
Initial approach: Letter
Copies of proposal: 1
Deadline(s): None
Board meeting date(s): Jan., May, and Sept.
Final notification: Within 1 month
Write: Thomas H. Meikle, Jr., M.D., Pres.
Officers and Directors:* Clarence F. Michalis,* Chair.; Thomas H. Meikle, Jr.,* Pres.; Maxine E. Bleich, V.P.; Rina Forlini, Secy.-Treas.; Lawrence K. Altman, M.D., Harold Amos, Louis Auchincloss, Alexander G. Bearn, E. Virgil Conway, Charles B. Finch, S. Parker Gilbert, Patricia Albjerg Graham, Bernard W. Harleston, Lawrence S. Huntington, John Jay Iselin, David L. Luke III, Mary Patterson McPherson, Walter N. Rothschild, Jr.
Number of staff: 3 full-time professional; 5 full-time support.
Employer Identification Number: 135596895

4791
Mad River Foundation ⌘
c/o Barrett and Associates
521 Fifth Ave.
New York 10175

Incorporated in 1961 in DE.
Donor(s): Godfrey S. Rockefeller.†
Foundation type: Independent
Financial data (yr. ended 12/31/87): Assets, $1,568,135 (M); expenditures, $142,594, including $121,250 for 63 grants (high: $10,000; low: $200).
Purpose and activities: Support primarily for higher and secondary education, including a medical school, welfare programs, and social service agencies; support also for conservation and wildlife preservation.
Application information:
Write: Peter H. Blair, Secy.-Treas.
Officers: Richard G. Stone,* Pres.; Peter H. Blair, Secy.-Treas.
Directors:* Audrey R. Blair, Godfrey A. Rockefeller, Marion R. Stone.
Employer Identification Number: 136097034

4792
The Russell Maguire Foundation, Inc. ⌘
c/o Berman and Hecht
Ten East 40th St., Rm. 710
New York 10016
Application address: 74 Harbor Dr., Greenwich, CT 06830

Incorporated in 1941 in NY.
Donor(s): Russell Maguire,† and others.
Foundation type: Independent
Financial data (yr. ended 12/31/88): Assets, $2,792,115 (M); expenditures, $214,225, including $108,915 for 57 grants (high: $15,000; low: $30).
Purpose and activities: Emphasis on arts and cultural programs; support also for a community fund, education, health associations, and social service agencies.
Limitations: Giving primarily in NY and CT.
Application information:
Write: Elizabeth Gale, Dir.
Directors: F. Richards Ford III, Natasha B. Ford, Elizabeth S. Gale, Suzanne S. Maguire.
Employer Identification Number: 136162698

4793
A. L. Mailman Family Foundation, Inc.
707 Westchester Ave.
White Plains 10604 (914) 681-4448

Foundation established in 1976 in FL as The Dr. Marilyn M. Segal Foundation, Inc.
Donor(s): Abraham L. Mailman,† The Mailman Foundation, Inc.
Foundation type: Independent
Financial data (yr. ended 12/31/88): Assets, $13,875,944 (M); gifts received, $36,125; expenditures, $916,208, including $727,075 for 81 grants (high: $50,000; low: $100).
Purpose and activities: Support primarily for programs committed to the preservation and strengthening of the family, with a special interest in children and youth who are disadvantaged by socio-economic status, race, and emotional or physical disabilities; giving also for educational efforts to stimulate moral and intellectual growth and the development of social responsibility; and for research in and refinement of developmental, individualized education.
Types of support: Seed money, matching funds, special projects, research, publications, technical assistance.
Limitations: No grants to individuals, or for operating budgets, capital or endowment funds, continuing support, annual campaigns, emergency funds, or deficit financing.
Publications: Annual report (including application guidelines).
Application information: Application form not required.
Initial approach: Letter
Copies of proposal: 1
Deadline(s): Submit proposal preferably in Sept. and Feb.; deadline Mar. 1 and Oct. 1
Board meeting date(s): Jan. and June
Final notification: 5 months
Write: Luba H. Lynch, Secy.
Officers: Marilyn M. Segal,* Chair.; Richard D. Segal,* Pres.; Luba H. Lynch, Secy.; Kurt Lichten, Treas.

Trustees:* Betty S. Bardige, Jonathan R. Gordon, Jay B. Langner, Patricia S. Lieberman, Wendy S. Masi.
Number of staff: 2 full-time professional; 1 part-time support.
Employer Identification Number: 510203866

4794
The Mailman Foundation, Inc.
477 Madison Ave., 17th Fl.
New York 10022 (212) 751-7171
FAX: (212) 752-1437

Incorporated in 1943 in DE.
Donor(s): Joseph L. Mailman,† Abraham L. Mailman.†
Foundation type: Independent
Financial data (yr. ended 12/31/89): Assets, $4,307,501 (M); expenditures, $230,653, including $230,302 for 65 grants (high: $50,000; low: $30).
Purpose and activities: Support for Jewish welfare funds, hospitals, higher education, temple support, and the arts.
Limitations: No grants to individuals.
Publications: Annual report.
Application information: Contributes only to pre-selected organizations. Applications not accepted.
Write: Vito G. DiCristina, Secy.-Treas.
Officers and Trustees: Joshua L. Mailman, V.P.; Phyllis Mailman, V.P.; Joan M. Wolfe, V.P.; Vito G. DiCristina, Secy.-Treas.
Employer Identification Number: 136161556

4795
Maleh-Shalom Foundation, Inc. ⌑ ☆
c/o Cradle Togs, Inc.
112 West 34th St.
New York 10001

Established in 1967.
Donor(s): Cradle Togs, Inc.
Foundation type: Independent
Financial data (yr. ended 12/31/88): Assets, $122,824 (M); gifts received, $120,150; expenditures, $133,172, including $132,913 for 69 grants (high: $60,000; low: $36).
Purpose and activities: Support for Jewish religious and educational institutions.
Limitations: Giving primarily in NJ and NY. No grants to individuals.
Application information:
Initial approach: Proposal
Deadline(s): None
Write: Murray Maleh, Mgr.
Officer: Murray Maleh, Mgr.
Employer Identification Number: 136265282

4796
The Mandeville Foundation, Inc. ⌑
230 Park Ave.
New York 10169 (212) 697-4785

Incorporated in 1963 in CT.
Donor(s): Ernest W. Mandeville.
Foundation type: Independent
Financial data (yr. ended 12/31/88): Assets, $6,201,023 (M); gifts received, $200,000; expenditures, $902,648, including $661,523 for 82 grants (high: $229,315; low: $150; average: $1,000-$15,000).
Purpose and activities: Giving primarily for higher and secondary education, cultural programs, and social service agencies.
Limitations: Giving primarily in NY and CT.
Application information: Application form not required.
Deadline(s): None
Final notification: 90 days
Write: Hubert T. Mandeville, Pres.
Officers and Directors:* Hubert T. Mandeville,* Pres.; P. Kempton Mandeville,* V.P.; Maurice C. Greenbaum,* Secy.; Meredith H. Hollis, Deborah S. Mandeville, Matthew T. Mandeville.
Number of staff: 2
Employer Identification Number: 066043343

4797
Manealoff Foundation, Inc. ⌑
One North Lexington Ave.
White Plains 10601

Incorporated in 1956 in NY.
Donor(s): Dorothy Manealoff,† William Manealoff, Adams Fabricated Steel Corp., J.B. Kendall Co., and others.
Foundation type: Independent
Financial data (yr. ended 4/30/89): Assets, $684,155 (M); expenditures, $539,517, including $533,900 for grants (high: $500,000).
Purpose and activities: Grants primarily for higher education, Jewish welfare and educational funds, and hospitals.
Limitations: No grants to individuals.
Application information: Contributes only to pre-selected organizations. Applications not accepted.
Officer: Molly Manealoff, Pres.
Employer Identification Number: 136067649

4798
Meyer & Min Manischewitz Foundation, Inc. ⌑
c/o Robert A. Mann
785 Fifth Ave.
New York 10022-1051

Established in 1965 in NY.
Foundation type: Independent
Financial data (yr. ended 12/31/87): Assets, $1,509,409 (M); expenditures, $61,166, including $57,675 for 69 grants (high: $6,000; low: $100).
Purpose and activities: Support primarily for arts and culture, social services, and Jewish organizations.
Limitations: Giving primarily in NY and CA. No grants to individuals.
Application information: Contributes only to pre-selected organizations. Applications not accepted.
Officers and Directors: Robert A. Mann, Pres.; Gerald Barrett, Secy.; Alan Bralower.
Employer Identification Number: 136185013

4799
The James Hilton Manning and Emma Austin Manning Foundation ⌑
45 Fifth Ave.
New York 10003

Incorporated in 1958 in NY.
Donor(s): Beatrice Austin Manning.†
Foundation type: Independent
Financial data (yr. ended 07/31/89): Assets, $4,356,278 (M); gifts received, $16,667; expenditures, $325,440, including $264,167 for 17 grants (high: $50,000; low: $5,000).
Purpose and activities: Support only for "medical research in human physiology and the diseases thereof."
Types of support: Research.
Limitations: No grants to individuals, or for student aid, general support, capital or endowment funds, scholarships, fellowships, or matching gifts; no loans.
Publications: Annual report.
Application information: Contributes only to pre-selected organizations. Applications not accepted.
Board meeting date(s): Semiannually
Write: Jean Scully, Dir.
Officers and Directors:* Ella A. Severin,* V.P. and Secy.; Leonard T. Scully,* V.P. and Treas.; Jean Scully.
Number of staff: 1 part-time professional.
Employer Identification Number: 136123540

4800
Manufacturers Hanover Foundation ▼
270 Park Ave.
New York 10017 (212) 286-7124

Trust established in 1956 in NY.
Donor(s): Manufacturers Hanover Trust Co.
Foundation type: Company-sponsored
Financial data (yr. ended 12/31/88): Assets, $15,401,317 (M); expenditures, $1,252,955, including $754,500 for 54 grants (high: $341,500; low: $1,000; average: $10,000-$50,000) and $450,007 for employee matching gifts.
Purpose and activities: Interests include a community fund, higher and secondary education, hospitals, cultural programs, youth agencies, public policy and community development organizations, and health agencies.
Types of support: Employee matching gifts, annual campaigns, building funds, endowment funds, general purposes, continuing support.
Limitations: Giving primarily in areas in which the company operates, primarily the New York, NY, metropolitan area. No support for private foundations. No grants to individuals, or for scholarships, fellowships, or special projects; no loans.
Publications: Annual report.
Application information: Application form not required.
Initial approach: Letter
Copies of proposal: 1
Deadline(s): Submit proposal preferably between Sept. and Dec.; deadline Mar. 31
Board meeting date(s): May
Final notification: June 1
Write: Matthew Trachtenberg, Agent
Advisory Committee: John F. McGillicuddy, Chair.
Trustee: Manufacturers Hanover Trust Co.
Employer Identification Number: 136143284

4801
Marble Fund, Inc. ⌑
200 Park Ave., Rm. 4406
New York 10166-0001 (212) 687-0466

Established in 1952 in NY.
Donor(s): M. William Levy, Marion H. Levy, Caryn L. Magid.
Foundation type: Independent
Financial data (yr. ended 12/31/88): Assets, $543,915 (M); expenditures, $120,058, including $115,862 for 127 grants (high: $25,000; low: $25).
Purpose and activities: Giving for education, health and medical research, community and rural development, the performing arts, and the environment and wildlife conservation.
Types of support: Annual campaigns, building funds, capital campaigns, general purposes, research, seed money, technical assistance.
Limitations: Giving primarily in NY.
Application information:
Initial approach: Letter
Deadline(s): None
Write: Marion H. Levy, Pres.
Officers and Director:* Marion H. Levy,* Pres.; William G. Levy, V.P.; Caryn L. Magid, V.P.
Number of staff: 2 part-time support.
Employer Identification Number: 136084387

4802
The Marcelle Foundation ⌑
R.D. 2
South Bethlehem 12161

Foundation type: Independent
Financial data (yr. ended 12/31/88): Assets, $1,269,196 (M); expenditures, $30,623, including $25,000 for 1 grant.
Purpose and activities: Primarily giving to a college and a medical center.
Types of support: Capital campaigns, general purposes.
Application information: Contributes only to pre-selected organizations. Applications not accepted.
Officers: Ann W. Marcelle, Pres.; Ruthann Marcelle, V.P.; Michael Sonnewick, Secy.-Treas.
Employer Identification Number: 112647245

4803
James S. Marcus Foundation ⌑
c/o Goldman, Sachs & Co.
85 Broad St., Tax Dept.
New York 10004

Established in 1969.
Donor(s): James S. Marcus.
Foundation type: Independent
Financial data (yr. ended 05/31/89): Assets, $1,577,322 (M); expenditures, $70,403, including $68,620 for 68 grants (high: $16,000; low: $25).
Purpose and activities: Giving for the arts and cultural programs, particularly opera; some support for health agencies, social services, and higher education.
Limitations: Giving primarily in NY. No grants to individuals.
Application information: Contributes only to pre-selected organizations. Applications not accepted.
Trustees: H. Frederick Krimendahl II, Ellen F. Marcus, James S. Marcus.
Employer Identification Number: 237044611

4804
Mariposa Foundation, Inc. ⌑ ☆
1251 Ave. of the Americas
New York 10020 (212) 703-8099

Donor(s): Lewis W. Bernard.
Foundation type: Independent
Financial data (yr. ended 11/30/88): Assets, $1,989,267 (M); gifts received, $886,938; expenditures, $56,959, including $49,735 for 31 grants (high: $12,000; low: $10).
Purpose and activities: Giving primarily for social services and cultural programs; support also for education.
Application information:
Initial approach: Letter
Deadline(s): None
Write: Lewis Bernard, Pres.
Officers: Lewis W. Bernard, Pres. and Treas.; Jill Bernard, V.P. and Secy.
Employer Identification Number: 510170409

4805
Mark IV Industries Foundation, Inc. ☆
P.O. Box 450
Williamsville 14231 (716) 689-4972

Established in 1976 in NY.
Donor(s): Mark IV Industries, Inc.
Foundation type: Company-sponsored
Financial data (yr. ended 04/30/89): Assets, $2,131,798 (M); gifts received, $21,265; qualifying distributions, $16,473, including $11,473 for 63 grants (high: $2,400; low: $25; average: $1,000-$1,500) and $5,000 for loans.
Purpose and activities: Giving for higher education, youth and child welfare, the performing arts and other cultural programs, community development, and Jewish organizations.
Types of support: Continuing support, employee matching gifts.
Limitations: Giving primarily in Buffalo, NY.
Publications: Annual report.
Application information: Application form not required.
Initial approach: Letter
Copies of proposal: 1
Deadline(s): None
Board meeting date(s): Apr.
Write: Jeri J. Herrington-Serrianne
Officers: Sal Alfiero, Chair.; Clement R. Arrison, Pres.; Gerald S. Lippes, Secy.
Number of staff: 1
Employer Identification Number: 161082605

4806
Pauline Yuells Markel Charitable Trust ⌑ ☆
114 Perth Ave.
New Rochelle 10804-3528 (914) 235-0318
Additional application address: c/o Mrs. Lucille Greenblatt, 430 East 56th St., New York, NY 10022

Established in 1958.
Foundation type: Independent
Financial data (yr. ended 11/30/88): Assets, $1,223,350 (M); expenditures, $108,725, including $102,000 for 100 grants (high: $25,000; low: $100).
Purpose and activities: Giving primarily for Jewish organizations, especially welfare funds; minor support also for health, higher education, and social services.
Limitations: Giving primarily in NY. No grants to individuals.
Application information: Application form not required.
Initial approach: Letter; telephone solicitations not accepted
Deadline(s): Sept. 1
Write: Mrs. Barbara S. Italie, Trustee
Trustees: Lucille Greenblatt, Barbara S. Italie.
Employer Identification Number: 136110485

4807
The John and Mary R. Markle Foundation ▼
75 Rockefeller Plaza, Suite 1800
New York 10019-6908 (212) 489-6655

Incorporated in 1927 in NY.
Donor(s): John Markle.†
Foundation type: Independent
Financial data (yr. ended 06/30/89): Assets, $99,068,908 (M); gifts received, $16,228,277; expenditures, $5,195,125, including $2,779,948 for 37 grants (high: $462,740; low: $3,000; average: $3,000-$462,740), $3,240 for 1 grant to an individual and $958,018 for 11 foundation-administered programs.
Purpose and activities: Giving primarily for the improvement of mass communications, including services growing out of new technologies for the processing and transfer of information, with current emphasis on the following areas: the potential of communications and information technologies to enhance political participation; the benefits of communications and information technologies for an aging population; developments in electronic publishing; the educational and entertainment use and value of computer software in the home; and analysis of issues of public policy and public interest in the communications field.
Types of support: Research, special projects.
Limitations: No grants to individuals (except for pensions to specified beneficiaries); generally no grants for general support, operating budgets, continuing support, annual campaigns, seed money, emergency funds, equipment, land acquisition, renovations, capital or endowment funds, matching gifts, scholarships, or fellowships; no loans. No grants generally for publications, conferences, or film, radio, or video production.
Publications: Annual report (including application guidelines), informational brochure.
Application information: Application form not required.
Initial approach: Letter
Copies of proposal: 1
Deadline(s): 6 weeks prior to board meetings
Board meeting date(s): Mar., June, and Nov.
Final notification: 2 weeks to 2 months
Write: Lloyd N. Morrisett, Pres.

Officers: Lloyd N. Morrisett,* Pres.; Dolores E. Miller, Secy.; Fanny L. Stiller, Financial Officer.
Directors:* Joel L. Fleishman, Chair.; Michael L. Ainslie, David O. Beim, Michael Collins, Lawrence A. Cremin, D. Ronald Daniel, Stephen W. Fillo, John G. Heimann, Alice S. Ilchman, Gertrude G. Michelson, Donald M. Stewart, George B. Weiksner.
Number of staff: 4 full-time professional; 6 full-time support; 1 part-time support.
Employer Identification Number: 131770307

4808
Marks Family Foundation ⌑ ☆
c/o Carl Marks & Co.
77 Water St.
New York 10005

Established in 1986.
Donor(s): Edwin S. Marks, Nancy A. Marks.
Foundation type: Independent
Financial data (yr. ended 6/30/88): Assets, $480,294 (M); expenditures, $205,060, including $201,218 for 37 grants (high: $50,000; low: $60).
Purpose and activities: Support primarily for fine and performing arts groups, social services, and a hospital.
Limitations: Giving primarily in NY.
Application information: Contributes only to pre-selected organizations. Applications not accepted.
Officers: Edwin S. Marks, Pres. and Treas.; Nancy A. Marks, V.P. and Secy.
Employer Identification Number: 133385770

4809
The James Harper Marshall Foundation ⌑ ☆
100 East 42nd St., Suite 1800
New York 10017

Established in 1982 in NY.
Donor(s): James Harper Marshall, John H. Peace.
Foundation type: Independent
Financial data (yr. ended 12/31/88): Assets, $1,022,017 (M); gifts received, $55,000; expenditures, $28,505, including $27,750 for 8 grants (high: $25,000; low: $100).
Purpose and activities: Giving primarily for higher education.
Limitations: No grants to individuals.
Application information: Contributes only to pre-selected organizations. Applications not accepted.
Officers and Directors: James Harper Marshall, Pres.; Edward G. Beimfohr, Secy.-Treas.
Employer Identification Number: 133157280

4810
Glenn L. Martin Foundation ⌑
c/o Fiduciary Trust Co. of New York
Two World Trade Ctr.
New York 10048 (212) 466-4100

Established in 1941 in NY.
Donor(s): Glenn L. Martin.†
Foundation type: Independent
Financial data (yr. ended 12/31/87): Assets, $1,467,002 (M); expenditures, $77,481, including $16,820 for 17 grants (high: $2,145; low: $500) and $47,750 for 45 grants to individuals (high: $2,500; low: $250).
Purpose and activities: Emphasis on the handicapped, civic organizations, social services, and grants to retired employees of Martin Marietta Corp. suffering hardship.
Types of support: Grants to individuals.
Limitations: Giving primarily in Baltimore, MD.
Application information:
Initial approach: Letter
Deadline(s): None
Write: Edmund Murphy
Officer: Elizabeth H. Restivo, Secy.
Trustee: Fiduciary Trust Co. of New York.
Committee Members: B.F. Leonard, Richard F. Weber.
Employer Identification Number: 136086736

4811
The Sylvia Martin Foundation, Inc. ⌑
645 Madison Ave.
New York 10022-1010 (212) 836-4430

Incorporated in 1962 in NY.
Donor(s): The Martin Foundation, Inc., Sylvia Martin.†
Foundation type: Independent
Financial data (yr. ended 12/31/88): Assets, $520,909 (M); expenditures, $326,842, including $264,350 for 126 grants (high: $20,000; low: $100).
Purpose and activities: Giving primarily for medical research, higher education, including matching funds, hospitals, and Jewish welfare funds.
Types of support: Matching funds.
Limitations: No grants to individuals, or for endowment funds, scholarships, or fellowships; no loans.
Application information:
Deadline(s): Submit proposal preferably in Jan.
Board meeting date(s): June and Dec.
Write: Alana Martin Frumkes, 1st V.P., or R. Allan Martin, V.P.
Officers: Theodore Mann, Pres.; Alana Martin Frumkes, 1st V.P.; R. Allan Martin, V.P.; Louis Frumkes, Secy.-Treas.
Trustees: M.R. Feinberg, Philip J. Hirsch.
Number of staff: 1 full-time support.
Employer Identification Number: 132690799

4812
Joseph Martinson Memorial Fund ⌑
c/o Citibank, N.A., Fiduciary Tax Dept.
20 Exchange Place, Suite 4850
New York 10043

Trust established in 1950 in NY.
Donor(s): Joseph B. Martinson.†
Foundation type: Independent
Financial data (yr. ended 12/31/88): Assets, $1,626,103 (M); expenditures, $153,472, including $122,200 for 26 grants (high: $22,000; low: $600).
Purpose and activities: Support largely for the performing arts and museums.
Limitations: Giving primarily in NY, VT, AZ, and CT. No grants to individuals.
Application information:
Initial approach: Letter
Deadline(s): Dec. 31
Write: Lee Gaguardo
Trustees: Howard Graff, Paul Martinson, F. Martinson, Citibank, N.A.
Employer Identification Number: 136161532

4813
Virginia & Leonard Marx Foundation ⌑ ☆
18 Heathcote Rd.
Scarsdale 10583-4418

Established in 1959 in NY.
Donor(s): Leonard Marx, Virginia Marx.
Foundation type: Independent
Financial data (yr. ended 12/31/87): Assets, $669,463 (M); gifts received, $494,278; expenditures, $725,329, including $724,975 for 82 grants (high: $420,000; low: $50).
Purpose and activities: Giving primarily for a fine arts museum and other cultural programs, Jewish welfare services, and higher education.
Limitations: Giving primarily in New York, NY.
Application information: Application form not required.
Deadline(s): None
Trustees: Leonard Marx, Virginia Marx.
Employer Identification Number: 136162557

4814
The William Marx Foundation ⌑
16 Court St.
Brooklyn 11241-0103

Donor(s): Helen Schulman Marx.
Foundation type: Independent
Financial data (yr. ended 10/31/88): Assets, $5,215 (M); gifts received, $159,000; expenditures, $159,036, including $159,000 for 6 grants (high: $50,000; low: $5,000).
Purpose and activities: Giving primarily for Jewish welfare and medical research.
Application information: Contributes only to pre-selected organizations. Applications not accepted.
Officers: Helen Schulman Marx, Pres.; Harry Marx, Secy.-Treas.
Employer Identification Number: 116020448

4815
The Charles A. Mastronardi Charitable Foundation ⌑
c/o Morgan Guaranty Trust Co. of New York
Nine West 57th St.
New York 10019
Application address: 14 Vanderenter Ave., Port Washington, NY 10050; Tel.: (516) 883-4600

Established in 1964 in NY.
Donor(s): Charles A. Mastronardi.†
Foundation type: Independent
Financial data (yr. ended 12/31/88): Assets, $8,130,964 (M); expenditures, $450,750, including $379,930 for 93 grants (high: $60,000; low: $100).
Purpose and activities: Giving largely for higher education, child welfare, hospitals, and Roman Catholic church support.
Limitations: Giving primarily in NY and FL. No grants to individuals.
Application information:
Initial approach: Letter or proposal
Deadline(s): None
Write: Alfred C. Turino, Exec. V.P.

Officers: Carrie Mastronardi, Pres.; Alfred C. Turino, Exec. V.P.; Edward F. Bennett, V.P.; Nicholas D. Mastronardi, V.P.; Olga De Felippo, Secy.; Joseph Mastronardi, Treas.
Employer Identification Number: 136167916

4816
The Richard Mather Fund
c/o Key Trust Co.
201 South Warren St.
Syracuse 13202 (315) 470-5222
Additional address: c/o W.L. Broad, Box 4967, Syracuse, NY 13221

Trust established in 1955 in NY.
Donor(s): Flora Mather Hosmer,† R.C. Hosmer, Jr.,† Hosmer Descendants Trust.
Foundation type: Independent
Financial data (yr. ended 12/31/88): Assets, $2,328,000 (M); gifts received, $22,180; expenditures, $161,552, including $141,792 for 14 grants (high: $50,000; low: $100; average: $1,000-$5,000).
Purpose and activities: Emphasis on cultural organizations, including museums, music, theater, and other performing arts.
Types of support: Capital campaigns, endowment funds, general purposes, matching funds, publications, special projects.
Limitations: Giving primarily in central NY, with emphasis on Syracuse. No grants to individuals; no loans.
Publications: Informational brochure (including application guidelines).
Application information: Funds substantially committed. Application form not required.
Initial approach: Letter; mass mail solicitations not considered
Copies of proposal: 1
Board meeting date(s): As required
Write: John S. Hancock, Trustee
Trustees: William L. Broad, John S. Hancock, S. Sterling McMillan III, Elizabeth H. Schaefer.
Number of staff: None.
Employer Identification Number: 156018423

4817
G. Harold & Leila Y. Mathers Charitable Foundation ▼ ⌑
707 Westchester Ave.
White Plains 10604 (914) 681-0852

Established in 1975 in NY.
Foundation type: Independent
Financial data (yr. ended 12/31/87): Assets, $109,886,855 (M); expenditures, $7,002,010, including $5,745,207 for 63 grants (high: $1,000,000; low: $2,500; average: $10,000-$35,000).
Purpose and activities: Giving primarily for basic medical research.
Types of support: Research, general purposes.
Limitations: No grants to individuals.
Application information:
Initial approach: Letter, with 1 copy of research proposal
Deadline(s): None
Board meeting date(s): 3 or 4 times a year
Final notification: Varies
Write: James H. Handelman, Exec. Dir.
Officers and Directors: Donald E. Handelman, Pres.; William R. Handelman, V.P.; John Hay, V.P.; Don Fizer, Secy.; Joseph W. Handelman, Treas.; John R. Young.
Number of staff: 1 full-time professional; 1 full-time support; 1 part-time support.
Employer Identification Number: 237441901

4818
Mathis-Pfohl Foundation ⌑
5-46 46th Ave.
Long Island City 11101 (718) 784-4800

Incorporated in 1947 in IA.
Donor(s): Members of the Pfohl family and associated companies.
Foundation type: Independent
Financial data (yr. ended 11/30/88): Assets, $3,173,090 (M); gifts received, $28,988; expenditures, $121,924, including $111,725 for 69 grants (high: $12,000; low: $100; average: $200-$2,000).
Purpose and activities: Grants for higher and secondary education, hospitals and health organizations, religious institutions, social service and youth agencies, and cultural programs.
Application information:
Initial approach: Letter
Deadline(s): None
Board meeting date(s): As required
Write: James M. Pfohl, Pres.
Officers: James M. Pfohl, Pres.; Ann Pfohl Kirby, V.P. and Secy.; Lynn P. Quigley, V.P. and Treas.
Employer Identification Number: 116013764

4819
Hale Matthews Foundation ⌑
100 Park Ave., 33rd Fl.
New York 10017

Established in 1963.
Donor(s): Hale Matthews.†
Foundation type: Independent
Financial data (yr. ended 12/31/88): Assets, $1,686,749 (M); expenditures, $124,552, including $110,500 for 10 grants (high: $25,000; low: $2,500; average: $7,500).
Purpose and activities: Giving for the theatre and the performing arts, health, and conservation.
Types of support: Matching funds, fellowships, general purposes.
Limitations: Giving primarily in NY. No grants to individuals.
Application information:
Initial approach: Proposal
Officers and Directors:* William N. Ashbey,* Pres.; Frances G. Scaife,* V.P.; Helen Brann,* Secy.; Richard G. Hewitt,* Treas.
Employer Identification Number: 136157267

4820
Reuben & Rose Mattus Foundation, Inc. ⌑
c/o Janover Rubincort & Co.
450 Seventh Ave., Rm. 3400
New York 10123

Established in 1983 in NY.
Donor(s): Reuben Mattus, Rose Mattus, Doris Mattus Hurley.
Foundation type: Independent
Financial data (yr. ended 6/30/88): Assets, $2,825,322 (M); gifts received, $200,000; expenditures, $222,796, including $215,625 for 36 grants (high: $50,000; low: $200).
Purpose and activities: Support primarily for Jewish organizations.
Limitations: Giving primarily in NY and NJ. No grants to individuals.
Officers: Reuben Mattus, Pres.; Doris Mattus Hurley, V.P.; Rose Mattus, Treas.
Employer Identification Number: 133183976

4821
Edelman Division Matz Foundation ⌑
253 Broadway
New York 10007

Trust established in 1970 in NY as one of two successor trusts to the Matz Foundation.
Donor(s): Israel Matz.†
Foundation type: Independent
Financial data (yr. ended 6/30/88): Assets, $2,424,169 (M); expenditures, $155,007, including $132,000 for 36 grants (high: $26,000; low: $400).
Purpose and activities: Emphasis on Jewish welfare funds and cultural institutions, higher and other education, and health services.
Limitations: Giving primarily in NY.
Application information:
Write: The Trustees
Trustees: Richard M. Edelman, Louise E. Sagalyn.
Employer Identification Number: 237082997

4822
Israel Matz Foundation ⌑
14 East Fourth St., Rm. 403
New York 10012 (212) 673-8142

Trust established in 1925 in NY.
Donor(s): Israel Matz.†
Foundation type: Independent
Financial data (yr. ended 12/31/88): Assets, $1,498,785 (M); expenditures, $139,390, including $44,678 for 16 grants (high: $19,500; low: $250) and $40,790 for 28 grants to individuals (high: $3,900; low: $600).
Purpose and activities: To extend financial grants-in-aid to indigent Hebrew scholars, writers, and public workers and their dependents, primarily in Israel; also to publish Hebrew classics and to advance Hebrew literature and culture.
Types of support: Grants to individuals, publications.
Limitations: Giving primarily in Israel and New York, NY.
Application information:
Initial approach: Letter
Deadline(s): 6 months before needed
Write: Dr. Milton Arfa, Chair.
Officers and Trustees: Milton Arfa, Chair.; Rachel Arfa, Abraham S. Halkin, Shlomo Sharan.
Employer Identification Number: 136121533

4823
Helen Mayer Charitable Trust ⌑
c/o Norstar Trust Co.
One East Ave.
Rochester 14638

Established in 1959 in NY.
Donor(s): Helen Shumway Mayer.
Foundation type: Independent
Financial data (yr. ended 11/30/88): Assets, $945,603 (M); gifts received, $200,000; expenditures, $171,879, including $167,500 for 36 grants (high: $25,000; low: $500).
Purpose and activities: Grants for religious support, historic preservation, and culture.
Application information: Contributes only to pre-selected organizations. Applications not accepted.
Trustees: Helen Shumway Mayer, Norstar Trust Co.
Employer Identification Number: 166022958

4824
Chaim Mayer Foundation, Inc. ⌑ ☆
c/o Stockel and Press
39 Broadway
New York 10006 (212) 269-4444

Established in 1981 in NY.
Donor(s): Joseph Neumann.
Foundation type: Independent
Financial data (yr. ended 4/30/88): Assets, $25,605 (M); gifts received, $1,586,624; expenditures, $1,888,226, including $1,712,499 for 260 grants (high: $278,800; low: $55) and $174,525 for 170 grants to individuals (high: $25,000; low: $50).
Purpose and activities: Giving limited to Jewish concerns, including yeshivas, synagogues, and grants to individuals for research and study of the Bible, the Talmud, and similar theological works.
Types of support: Grants to individuals, student aid.
Application information:
Initial approach: Letter
Deadline(s): None
Write: Donald Press, V.P.
Officers: Joseph Neumann, Pres.; Rachel Neumann, V.P.; Donald Press, V.P.; Rabbi Joseph A. Luria, Controller; Hirsch Wulliger, Controller.
Employer Identification Number: 133119407

4825
The Louis B. Mayer Foundation ▼
165 East 72nd St., Suite 1B
New York 10021 (212) 737-1011

Trust established in 1947 in CA.
Donor(s): Louis B. Mayer.†
Foundation type: Independent
Financial data (yr. ended 12/31/89): Assets, $8,357,285 (M); expenditures, $1,345,558, including $1,180,000 for 5 grants (high: $1,000,000; low: $25,000; average: $25,000-$1,000,000).
Purpose and activities: Support for basic innovation, research, and development in areas of education, the arts, letters, and medicine.
Types of support: Building funds, continuing support, endowment funds, equipment, operating budgets, professorships, renovation projects, research, seed money, special projects.
Limitations: No grants to individuals; no loans.
Application information: Contributes only to pre-selected organizations. Applications not accepted.
Board meeting date(s): Quarterly
Write: Ann Brownell Sloane
Officers and Trustees: Jeffrey Selznick, Pres.; Robert A. Gottlieb, Secy.; Carol Farkas, Treas.; Irene Mayer Selznick.
Number of staff: 1 full-time professional; 1 full-time support; 2 part-time support.
Employer Identification Number: 952232340

4826
Joseph & Ceil Mazer Foundation, Inc. ▼ ⌑
c/o Becker, Ross, Stone, et al.
41 East 42nd St.
New York 10017 (212) 697-2310

Established in 1941.
Donor(s): Joseph M. Mazer.†
Foundation type: Independent
Financial data (yr. ended 12/31/88): Assets, $3,723,653 (M); expenditures, $933,970, including $902,783 for 44 grants (high: $213,000; low: $50; average: $1,000-$70,000).
Purpose and activities: Grants primarily for Jewish welfare and educational funds in the U.S. and Israel.
Types of support: Endowment funds, building funds, general purposes, seed money, scholarship funds.
Limitations: No grants to individuals.
Application information:
Initial approach: Written request
Deadline(s): None
Board meeting date(s): As required
Final notification: Within 4 months
Write: Foundation Directors
Officers and Directors:* William Mazer,* Pres.; Daniel G. Ross,* V.P.; Jesse Margolin, Secy.-Treas.; Grace J. Ross.
Number of staff: None.
Employer Identification Number: 136111730

4827
William and Helen Mazer Foundation, Inc. ⌑
c/o Cohen and Randall
1100 Franklin Ave.
Garden City 11530 (516) 877-2720

Incorporated in 1979 in NY.
Donor(s): Abraham Mazer Family Fund, Inc., William Mazer.
Foundation type: Independent
Financial data (yr. ended 09/30/88): Assets, $1,141,150 (M); gifts received, $2,000; expenditures, $123,653, including $111,239 for 93 grants (high: $25,000; low: $18).
Purpose and activities: Emphasis on higher education, including medical education, and hospitals; support also for the performing arts, Jewish welfare organizations, and a peace fund.
Application information:
Initial approach: Proposal
Deadline(s): None
Write: William Mazer, Pres.
Officers and Directors:* William Mazer,* Pres. and Treas.; Norman H. Cohen.
Employer Identification Number: 133029517

4828
The McCaddin-McQuirk Foundation, Inc. ⌑
1002 Madison Ave.
New York 10021 (212) 772-9090

Incorporated in 1902 in NY.
Donor(s): Rt. Rev. John McQuirk,† Ann Eliza McCaddin Walsh.†
Foundation type: Independent
Financial data (yr. ended 12/31/88): Assets, $1,649,599 (M); expenditures, $87,784, including $79,200 for 59 grants (high: $6,000; low: $600).
Purpose and activities: To foster educational opportunities for poorer students to be priests or lay teachers of the Roman Catholic Church throughout the world.
Types of support: Scholarship funds.
Application information: Applications must be made through a bishop, rector, or head of a seminary.
Initial approach: Letter
Deadline(s): Dec. 1
Write: Robert W. Dumser, Pres.
Officers: Robert W. Dumser, Pres.; William A. White, V.P.; Henry J. Humphreys, Secy.; Richard A. Mumma, Treas.
Trustees: Most Rev. John W. Comber, Leo A. Egan, Frederic J. Fuller, Francis M. Hartman, Carol A. Muccia, Jr., Rev. Norbert Rans, John G. Scott, Thomas A. Turley, Douglas Wyatt.
Employer Identification Number: 136134444

4829
Penny McCall Foundation ☆
c/o McCaffrey & McCall
575 Lexington Ave.
New York 10022 (212) 350-1777

Established in 1987 in NY.
Donor(s): Mrs. James Mills.
Foundation type: Independent
Financial data (yr. ended 12/31/88): Assets, $1,068,827 (M); gifts received, $71,251; expenditures, $111,836, including $101,000 for 16 grants to individuals (high: $15,000; low: $1,000).
Purpose and activities: Awards grants to individuals "to promote artistic development."
Types of support: Grants to individuals.
Limitations: Giving limited to U.S. citizens, with emphasis on New York, NY, area residents. No grants for students.
Application information: Applications not accepted.
Write: Joan McCall, Pres. or Anne Joyce, Secy.
Officers: Joan McCall, Pres.; David McCall, V.P. and Treas.; Claudia Demonte, V.P.; William McGowin, V.P.; Jerome Traum, V.P.; Anne Joyce, Secy.
Number of staff: 1
Employer Identification Number: 133376289

4830
James J. McCann Charitable Trust and McCann Foundation, Inc.
(also known as McCann Foundation)
35 Market St.
Poughkeepsie 12601 (914) 452-3085

McCann Foundation, Inc. established in NY in 1967; trust established in 1969 in NY;

foundations function as single unit and financial data is combined.
Donor(s): James J. McCann.†
Foundation type: Independent
Financial data (yr. ended 12/31/89): Assets, $24,829,821 (M); expenditures, $2,168,206, including $1,999,539 for 35 grants (high: $855,000; low: $100; average: $100-$1,000,000) and $50,000 for 1 loan.
Purpose and activities: Giving primarily for secondary and higher education (including scholarship funds), recreation, civic projects, social services, cultural programs, church support and religious associations, and hospitals.
Types of support: Continuing support, annual campaigns, seed money, building funds, equipment, land acquisition, scholarship funds, fellowships, publications, conferences and seminars.
Limitations: Giving limited to Poughkeepsie and Dutchess County, NY. No grants to individuals, or for operating budgets, emergency or endowment funds, deficit financing, or matching gifts; no loans.
Publications: Annual report.
Application information: Application form not required.
Initial approach: Letter or proposal
Copies of proposal: 1
Deadline(s): Submit proposal preferably in Feb. or Aug.; no deadline
Board meeting date(s): Jan. and July
Final notification: 60 days
Write: John J. Gartland, Jr., Pres.
Officers and Trustees:* John J. Gartland, Jr.,* Pres.; William L. Gardner, Jr.,* V.P.; Richard V. Corbally, Secy.
Number of staff: 1 part-time professional; 1 full-time support.
Employer Identification Number: 146050628

4831
The McCarthy Charities, Inc. ⌑
P.O. Box 576
Troy 12181

Incorporated in 1917 in NY.
Donor(s): Robert H. McCarthy, Lucy A. McCarthy.†
Foundation type: Independent
Financial data (yr. ended 12/31/88): Assets, $5,104,499 (M); expenditures, $237,065, including $227,375 for 78 grants (high: $25,000; low: $100).
Purpose and activities: Giving for Roman Catholic church support and church-related education and welfare agencies; support also for community funds, social service agencies, and hospitals.
Limitations: Giving primarily in the Albany Capital District, NY, area.
Application information: Contributes only to pre-selected organizations. Applications not accepted.
Write: Peter F. McCarthy, Pres.
Officers: Peter F. McCarthy, Pres. and Treas.; James A. McCarthy, V.P.; Marion P. McCarthy, Secy.
Employer Identification Number: 146019064

4832
Mary A. and John M. McCarthy Foundation ☆
c/o Lord Abbett & Co.
767 Fifth Ave.
New York 10153 (212) 848-1800
Additional address: 69 First St., Garden City, NY 11530

Established in 1985.
Donor(s): Mary A. McCarthy, John M. McCarthy.
Foundation type: Independent
Financial data (yr. ended 11/30/88): Assets, $1,308,776 (M); gifts received, $303,738; expenditures, $67,238, including $60,000 for 6 grants (high: $20,000; low: $5,000).
Purpose and activities: Giving primarily for education, health and hospitals, animal welfare, the arts, and Catholic organizations.
Types of support: Scholarship funds, capital campaigns.
Limitations: No grants to individuals.
Application information: Contributes only to pre-selected organizations. Applications not accepted.
Write: John M. McCarthy, Trustee
Trustees: John M. McCarthy, Mary A. McCarthy, Stephen J. McCarthy.
Number of staff: None.
Employer Identification Number: 136863980

4833
The Michael W. McCarthy Foundation ⌑
World Financial Ctr., South Tower
New York 10080

Trust established in 1958 in NY.
Donor(s): Michael W. McCarthy, Margaret E. McCarthy.
Foundation type: Independent
Financial data (yr. ended 12/31/87): Assets, $2,269,802 (M); expenditures, $166,520, including $143,491 for 17 grants (high: $98,366; low: $225).
Purpose and activities: Support largely for higher education and for Roman Catholic church support and religious associations.
Application information: Contributes only to pre-selected organizations. Applications not accepted.
Trustee: Michael W. McCarthy.
Employer Identification Number: 136150919

4834
Neil A. McConnell Foundation, Inc.
113 East 55th St.
New York 10022 (212) 980-9090
Application address: P.O. Box 1990, Church St. Station, New York, NY 10008

Incorporated in 1960 in NY.
Donor(s): Neil A. McConnell.
Foundation type: Independent
Financial data (yr. ended 03/31/90): Assets, $3,500,000 (M); expenditures, $300,000, including $230,000 for 11 grants (high: $35,000; low: $5,000; average: $5,000-$35,000).
Purpose and activities: Giving for special educational projects identified or developed by the foundation; interests include the arts, medical sciences, child development, and the aged.
Types of support: Special projects, annual campaigns, conferences and seminars, general purposes, research.
Limitations: Giving limited to the northeastern U.S. and the New York, NY, metropolitan area. No grants to individuals.
Application information: Application form not required.
Initial approach: Letter
Copies of proposal: 1
Deadline(s): None
Board meeting date(s): Annually and as required
Write: Concetta Matranga, Exec. Dir.
Officers and Trustees:* Neil A. McConnell,* Pres.; James G. Niven,* V.P. and Treas.; B. Scott McConnell,* V.P.; Douglas F. Williamson, Jr., Secy.; Concetta Matranga, Exec. Dir.
Number of staff: 1 full-time professional.
Employer Identification Number: 136114121

4835
J. M. McDonald Foundation, Inc.
2057 East River Rd.
Cortland 13045-9752 (607) 756-9283

Incorporated in 1952 in NE.
Donor(s): James M. McDonald, Sr.†
Foundation type: Independent
Financial data (yr. ended 12/31/88): Assets, $9,757,305 (M); expenditures, $500,674, including $405,000 for 26 grants (high: $30,000; low: $2,500; average: $10,000-$30,000).
Purpose and activities: Grants for the aged, orphans, and children who are sick, infirm, blind, or crippled; youth and child care in an effort to combat juvenile delinquency and to aid underprivileged, mentally or physically handicapped children; other interests include health and hospitals and education, especially higher education.
Types of support: Annual campaigns, building funds, equipment, research, general purposes, continuing support, renovation projects.
Limitations: Giving primarily in the Northeast. No grants to individuals, or for seminars, workshops, endowment funds, scholarships, fellowships, travel, exhibits, or conferences; no loans.
Publications: Application guidelines.
Application information: Application form not required.
Initial approach: Letter, proposal, or telephone
Copies of proposal: 1
Deadline(s): Apr. 15 and Sept. 15
Board meeting date(s): May and Oct.
Final notification: May 30 or Oct. 30 for positive responses
Write: Reed L. McJunkin, Secy.
Officers and Trustees:* Eleanor F. McJunkin,* Pres.; Donald R. McJunkin,* V.P.; Reed L. McJunkin,* Secy.; Donald C. Berry, Jr.,* Treas.
Number of staff: 1 part-time support.
Employer Identification Number: 471431059

4836
Frederick McDonald Trust ⌘
c/o Norstar Trust Co.
69 State St.
Albany 12201 (518) 447-4189

Established in 1950.
Donor(s): Frederick McDonald.
Foundation type: Independent
Financial data (yr. ended 12/31/88): Assets, $1,000,860 (M); expenditures, $131,878, including $129,500 for 33 grants (high: $20,000; low: $1,000; average: $2,000-$4,000).
Purpose and activities: Giving primarily for hospitals and health agencies; support also for youth agencies and a community fund.
Types of support: Annual campaigns, equipment, operating budgets.
Limitations: Giving limited to Albany, NY. No grants to individuals.
Application information: Application form required.
Deadline(s): Oct. 1
Write: R.F. Galvin, Sr. Trust Officer
Trustee: Norstar Trust Co.
Number of staff: None.
Employer Identification Number: 146014233

4837
John McEnroe Foundation ⌘ ☆
c/o Paul Weiss Rifkind et al
1285 Ave. of the Americas
New York 10019

Established in 1986 in NY.
Donor(s): John McEnroe.
Foundation type: Independent
Financial data (yr. ended 12/31/88): Assets, $1,566,850 (M); expenditures, $92,840, including $89,320 for 20 grants (high: $12,000; low: $200).
Purpose and activities: Support primarily for higher education, social services, and health associations.
Limitations: Giving primarily in NY. No grants to individuals.
Application information: Contributes only to pre-selected organizations. Applications not accepted.
Officers: John McEnroe, Pres. and Treas.; John P. McEnroe, Sr. V.P.; Mark T. McEnroe, V.P. and Secy.; Patrick McEnroe, V.P.
Employer Identification Number: 133389114

4838
Dextra Baldwin McGonagle Foundation, Inc.
445 Park Ave.
New York 10022 (212) 758-8970
Additional address: 40 Crossing at Blind Brook, Purchase, NY 10577-2210

Incorporated in 1967 in NY.
Donor(s): Mrs. Dextra Baldwin McGonagle.†
Foundation type: Independent
Financial data (yr. ended 12/31/89): Assets, $8,165,006 (M); expenditures, $461,833, including $401,150 for 93 grants (high: $110,000; low: $25; average: $4,300).
Purpose and activities: Support for hospitals, health services, medical research, and higher and medical education; grants also for social service agencies, religious organizations, and cultural programs.
Types of support: Annual campaigns, seed money, building funds, equipment, research, endowment funds.
Limitations: Giving primarily in NY and CA. No grants to individuals, or for matching gifts.
Application information: Application form not required.
Initial approach: Letter
Board meeting date(s): As required
Write: David B. Spanier, Pres.
Officers and Directors:* Maury L. Spanier,* Chair.; David B. Spanier,* Pres.; Helen G. Spanier,* V.P. and Secy.-Treas.
Number of staff: 3 part-time support.
Employer Identification Number: 136219236

4839
The Donald C. McGraw Foundation, Inc. ⌘
46 Summit Ave.
Bronxville 10708 (914) 779-1682

Incorporated in 1963 in NY.
Donor(s): Donald C. McGraw.†
Foundation type: Independent
Financial data (yr. ended 1/31/88): Assets, $4,828,818 (L); gifts received, $145,369; expenditures, $312,039, including $308,000 for 33 grants (high: $50,000; low: $1,000).
Purpose and activities: Grants largely for hospitals and medical research, education, church support, cultural programs, and social service agencies.
Limitations: Giving primarily in NY and NJ.
Application information:
Initial approach: Letter
Deadline(s): None
Write: John L. Cady, V.P.
Officers and Directors: Donald C. McGraw, Jr., Pres.; John L. Cady, V.P. and Secy.; John L. McGraw, V.P. and Treas.
Employer Identification Number: 136165603

4840
The McGraw-Hill Foundation, Inc. ▼
1221 Ave. of the Americas, Rm. 3517
New York 10020 (212) 512-6113

Incorporated in 1978 in NY.
Donor(s): McGraw-Hill, Inc.
Foundation type: Company-sponsored
Financial data (yr. ended 12/31/89): Assets, $18,923 (M); gifts received, $1,900,000; expenditures, $1,973,751, including $1,022,456 for 184 grants (high: $160,000; low: $100; average: $1,000-$5,000) and $951,295 for 3,122 employee matching gifts.
Purpose and activities: Program emphasis is on education; significant support also given in the areas of health and welfare, arts and cultural organizations, and civic activities.
Types of support: General purposes, operating budgets, continuing support, annual campaigns, seed money, special projects, research, scholarship funds, employee-related scholarships, matching funds, employee matching gifts.
Limitations: Giving limited to areas of company operations, or to national organizations. No support for religious or political organizations or United Way member agencies. No grants to individuals, or for capital, building, or endowment funds, conferences, travel, courtesy advertising, films, or publications; no loans.
Publications: Application guidelines.
Application information: Application form not required.
Initial approach: Proposal
Copies of proposal: 1
Deadline(s): None
Board meeting date(s): Quarterly
Final notification: 4-6 weeks
Write: Susan A. Wallman, Admin.
Officers and Directors:* Mary A. Cooper,* Pres.; Frank D. Penglase, V.P. and Treas.; Susan A. Wallman, Admin. and Secy.; Frank J. Kaufman, Robert N. Landes, Donald S. Rubin, Ralph R. Schulz, Thomas J. Sullivan.
Number of staff: 2 full-time professional; 2 full-time support.
Employer Identification Number: 132955464

4841
Meadows Charitable Trust ⌘ ☆
c/o Market St. Trust Co.
Two East Market St.
Corning 14830-2666

Foundation type: Independent
Financial data (yr. ended 10/31/88): Assets, $1,136,318 (M); expenditures, $81,224, including $76,000 for 10 grants (high: $29,000; low: $1,000).
Purpose and activities: Giving primarily for religious welfare organizations.
Limitations: Giving primarily in NY. No grants to individuals.
Application information: Application form not required.
Deadline(s): None
Trustees: Adelaide C. Griswold, Alanson B. Houghton II, Amory Houghton, Jr.
Employer Identification Number: 166093057

4842
William M. & Miriam F. Meehan Foundation, Inc. ⌘ ☆
39 Broadway
New York 10006

Established in 1951.
Donor(s): Terence S. Meehan, Miriam F. Meehan, Maureen M. Sennott.
Foundation type: Independent
Financial data (yr. ended 9/30/88): Assets, $1,945,081 (M); gifts received, $524,313; expenditures, $147,263, including $144,333 for 172 grants (high: $25,000; low: $16).
Purpose and activities: Support primarily for Catholic and Protestant churches and human services, including youth and a mental health institute; grants also for cultural programs and higher education.
Limitations: Giving primarily in New York, NY. No grants to individuals.
Application information: Contributes only to pre-selected organizations. Applications not accepted.
Officers and Directors: Miriam F. Meehan, Pres.; Maureen M. Sennott, V.P.; Barbara A. Byrnes, Secy.; Terence S. Meehan, Treas.; Joanne M. Berghold.
Employer Identification Number: 136062834

4843
Mellam Family Foundation ⌑ ☆
c/o U.S. Trust Co. of New York
45 Wall St.
New York 10005

Established in 1987 in NY.
Foundation type: Independent
Financial data (yr. ended 12/31/88): Assets, $3,077,310; expenditures, $107,877, including $65,000 for 4 grants (high: $50,000; low: $5,000).
Purpose and activities: Support primarily for medical research and hospitals.
Limitations: Giving primarily in NY. No grants to individuals.
Application information: Contributes only to pre-selected organizations. Applications not accepted.
Trustee: U.S. Trust Co. of New York.
Employer Identification Number: 136894208

4844
The Andrew W. Mellon Foundation ▼
140 East 62nd St.
New York 10021 (212) 838-8400

Trust established in 1940 in DE as Avalon Foundation; incorporated in 1954 in NY; merged with Old Dominion Foundation and renamed The Andrew W. Mellon Foundation in 1969.
Donor(s): Ailsa Mellon Bruce,† Paul Mellon.
Foundation type: Independent
Financial data (yr. ended 12/31/89): Assets, $1,832,347,000 (M); gifts received, $49,212; expenditures, $75,501,129, including $75,501,129 for 302 grants (high: $5,000,000; low: $5,000; average: $25,000-$800,000).
Purpose and activities: Grants on selective basis in higher education, cultural affairs, including historic preservation, the humanities, museums, performing arts, population, and in certain environmental and public affairs areas. Graduate fellowship program in the humanities administered by the Woodrow Wilson National Fellowship Foundation, which makes all awards.
Types of support: Continuing support, endowment funds, research, internships, fellowships, matching funds, special projects.
Limitations: No support for primarily local organizations. No grants to individuals (including scholarships and fellowships); no loans.
Publications: Annual report (including application guidelines).
Application information: Application form not required.
Initial approach: Descriptive letter or proposal
Copies of proposal: 1
Deadline(s): None
Board meeting date(s): Mar., June, Oct., and Dec.
Final notification: After board meetings
Write: Neil L. Rudenstine, Exec. V.P.
Officers: William G. Bowen,* Pres.; Neil L. Rudenstine, Exec. V.P.; James M. Morris, Secy.; Kenneth J. Herr, Treas.
Trustees:* William O. Baker, Chair.; William G. Bowen, Charles E. Exley, Jr., Hanna Holborn Gray, Timothy Mellon, Arjay Miller, Frank H.T. Rhodes, Charles A. Ryskamp, John R. Stevenson, John C. Whitehead.
Number of staff: 13 full-time professional; 20 full-time support.
Employer Identification Number: 131879954

4845
L. Thomas Melly Foundation ⌑
c/o Goldman Sachs & Co., Tax Dept.
85 Broad St.
New York 10004-2408

Established in 1969 in NY.
Donor(s): L. Thomas Melly.
Foundation type: Independent
Financial data (yr. ended 5/31/88): Assets, $1,185,546 (M); gifts received, $49,874; expenditures, $58,254, including $53,215 for 31 grants (high: $12,200; low: $25).
Purpose and activities: Support primarily for higher education, youth organizations, social services, and health services and associations.
Limitations: Giving primarily in CT, MA, and NY.
Application information: Applications not accepted.
Trustees: Alice P. Melly, L. Thomas Melly, Laura A. Melly, Thomas L. Melly.
Employer Identification Number: 237059703

4846
Joseph and Martha Melohn Chesed Fund ⌑ ☆
c/o Altman & Dick
1350 Sixth Ave.
New York 10019-4703

Established in 1986 in NY.
Donor(s): Johny Melohn.
Foundation type: Independent
Financial data (yr. ended 11/30/87): Assets, $21,781 (M); gifts received, $152,000; expenditures, $134,168, including $134,168 for 31 grants (high: $50,000; low: $25).
Purpose and activities: Support for Jewish organizations, including synagogues and yeshivas.
Limitations: No grants to individuals.
Application information: Contributes only to pre-selected organizations. Applications not accepted.
Officer: Johny Melohn, Pres.
Employer Identification Number: 133395217

4847
The Melohn Foundation, Inc. ⌑
1995 Broadway, 14th Fl.
New York 10023-5882

Established in 1965.
Donor(s): Members of the Melohn family.
Foundation type: Independent
Financial data (yr. ended 7/31/88): Assets, $3,150,479 (M); gifts received, $321,000; expenditures, $401,311, including $115,358 for 12 grants (high: $75,000; low: $1,000).
Purpose and activities: Giving for Jewish schools and temple support.
Limitations: Giving primarily in NY.
Application information:
Initial approach: Letter
Deadline(s): None
Officers: Martha Melohn, Pres.; Alfons Melohn, Secy.; Leon Melohn, Treas.
Employer Identification Number: 136197827

4848
The Memton Fund, Inc.
60 East 42nd St., Suite 1651
New York 10165 (212) 972-0398

Incorporated in 1936 in NY.
Donor(s): Albert G. Milbank,† Charles M. Cauldwell.†
Foundation type: Independent
Financial data (yr. ended 12/31/89): Assets, $6,450,149 (M); expenditures, $366,928, including $259,850 for 108 grants (high: $15,000; low: $500; average: $1,000-$5,000).
Purpose and activities: Emphasis on higher education, health, human services, and culture.
Types of support: General purposes, annual campaigns, endowment funds, scholarship funds, capital campaigns.
Limitations: No grants to individuals.
Application information: Applications not accepted.
Board meeting date(s): Mar. and Oct.
Write: Lillian Daniels, Secy.-Treas.
Officers and Directors:* Daphne M. White,* Pres.; Elenita M. Drumwright,* V.P.; Lillian I. Daniels, Secy.-Treas.; Marjorie M. Farrar, David M. Milbank, Samuel L. Milbank, Francis H. Musselman, Deborah Piccone, Samuel S. Polk, Barrie M. White, Pamela White.
Number of staff: 1 full-time professional.
Employer Identification Number: 136096608

4849
The Robert and Joyce Menschel Foundation
c/o Goldman Sachs & Co.
85 Broad St.
New York 10004

Established in 1958 in NY.
Donor(s): Robert B. Menschel.
Foundation type: Independent
Financial data (yr. ended 10/31/89): Assets, $4,520,006 (M); expenditures, $206,050, including $205,925 for 130 grants (high: $25,000; low: $100).
Purpose and activities: Giving for social welfare, the arts, hospitals, and higher education.
Application information: All grants initiated by the foundation. Applications not accepted.
Officers: Robert B. Menschel, Pres. and Treas.; Joyce F. Menschel, V.P. and Secy.
Number of staff: None.
Employer Identification Number: 136098443

4850
The Sue and Eugene Mercy, Jr. Foundation ⌑
c/o Goldman, Sachs & Co., Tax Dept.
85 Broad St.
New York 10004

Established in 1967 in NY.
Donor(s): Eugene Mercy, Jr.
Foundation type: Independent
Financial data (yr. ended 12/31/88): Assets, $3,106,050 (M); gifts received, $200,001;

expenditures, $560,123, including $555,775 for 137 grants (high: $255,000; low: $50).
Purpose and activities: Emphasis on Jewish giving, including welfare funds, secondary education, and hospitals; support also for higher education and culture, particularly music.
Limitations: Giving primarily in New York, NY. No grants to individuals.
Application information: Applications not accepted.
Officers and Directors:* Eugene Mercy, Jr.,* Pres. and Treas.; Sue Mercy,* V.P.; Robert E. Mnuchin,* Secy.
Employer Identification Number: 136217050

4851
Merlin Foundation ¤
c/o Schulte, Roth & Zabel
900 Third Ave.
New York 10022 (212) 758-0404

Established in 1978 in NY.
Donor(s): Audrey Sheldon Poon.†
Foundation type: Independent
Financial data (yr. ended 9/30/88): Assets, $1,203,353 (M); expenditures, $70,684, including $54,050 for 19 grants (high: $7,500; low: $500).
Purpose and activities: Emphasis on cultural programs and higher education in music and the arts; some support also for welfare funds.
Application information:
Initial approach: Letter
Deadline(s): None
Write: William D. Zabel, Pres.
Officers: William D. Zabel, Pres. and Treas.; Roger S. Altman, V.P.; Thomas H. Baer, V.P.; John J. McLaughlin, Secy.
Employer Identification Number: 237418853

4852
The Ingram Merrill Foundation ¤
104 East 40th St., Suite 302
New York 10016
Application address: P.O. Box 202, Village Station, New York, NY 10014

Trust established in 1956 in NY.
Donor(s): James I. Merrill.
Foundation type: Independent
Financial data (yr. ended 12/31/87): Assets, $132,214 (M); gifts received, $10,000; expenditures, $213,010, including $189,300 for 22 grants to individuals (high: $15,000; low: $3,000).
Purpose and activities: Concerned primarily with the advancement of the cultural and fine arts through aid to individual writers, poets, and artists.
Types of support: Grants to individuals.
Limitations: No grants for the performing arts.
Application information: Application form required.
Board meeting date(s): May
Write: Milton Maurer, Trustee
Selection Committee: Harry Ford, Chair.; Patrick Marla, Secy.; John Hollander, David M. Kalstone, Joseph D. McClatchy, Jr.
Trustees: Huyler C. Held, Robert A. Magowan, Jr., Milton Maurer.
Employer Identification Number: 136042498

4853
Merrill Lynch & Company Foundation, Inc. ▼
World Headquarters, South Tower
World Financial Ctr.
New York 10080-6106 (212) 236-4319

Incorporated in 1950 in DE.
Donor(s): Merrill Lynch, Pierce, Fenner & Smith, Inc.
Foundation type: Company-sponsored
Financial data (yr. ended 12/31/89): Assets, $19,600,000 (M); gifts received, $3,000,000; expenditures, $3,342,642, including $3,257,096 for 387 grants (high: $250,000; low: $1,000).
Purpose and activities: Emphasis on education, especially higher education; support also for the arts, cultural programs, health, civic affairs, and community services.
Types of support: General purposes, operating budgets, special projects, research, capital campaigns, continuing support, endowment funds, publications, renovation projects, scholarship funds.
Limitations: No support for religious purposes or social, fraternal, or athletic organizations. No grants to individuals, or for deficit financing, matching gifts, or conferences; no loans.
Publications: Corporate giving report, 990-PF, application guidelines.
Application information: Application form not required.
Initial approach: Letter
Copies of proposal: 1
Deadline(s): None
Board meeting date(s): Mar., June, Sept., and Dec.
Final notification: 3 months
Write: Westina L. Matthews, Secy.
Officers and Trustees:* John A. Fitzgerald,* Pres.; William A. Schreyer,* V.P.; Daniel P. Tully,* V.P.; Westina L. Matthews, Secy.; Thomas Lombardi, Treas.; Matthew W. McKenna.
Number of staff: 3 full-time professional; 1 part-time professional; 3 full-time support; 2 part-time support.
Employer Identification Number: 136139556

4854
Martha Mertz Foundation, Inc. ¤
295 Madison Ave., Rm. 1228
New York 10017

Incorporated in 1939 in NY.
Donor(s): DeWitt W. Mertz.†
Foundation type: Independent
Financial data (yr. ended 12/31/88): Assets, $3,466,867 (M); expenditures, $235,656, including $161,000 for 10 grants (high: $51,000; low: $1,500).
Purpose and activities: To administer to, provide for, and rehabilitate unmarried girls who have become mothers or prostitutes, or who, from such causes, shall be homeless or in fear of becoming homeless or social outcasts.
Limitations: Giving primarily in NY. No grants to individuals.
Application information: Contributes only to pre-selected organizations. Applications not accepted.
Write: Jonathan Reilly, Pres.
Officers and Directors:* Jonathan Reilly,* Pres.; Charlotte F. Andress,* V.P. and Secy.; Robert A.N. Cudd,* Treas.; Barbara Lee Cudd, Nancy H. Cudd.
Employer Identification Number: 136129085

4855
Joyce Mertz-Gilmore Foundation ▼
218 East 18th St.
New York 10003 (212) 475-1137

Incorporated in 1959 in NY.
Donor(s): Joyce Mertz Gilmore.†
Foundation type: Independent
Financial data (yr. ended 12/31/89): Assets, $39,861,523 (M); gifts received, $3,315,000; expenditures, $5,550,183, including $4,917,085 for 349 grants (high: $400,000; low: $700; average: $5,000-$25,000).
Purpose and activities: Current concerns include human rights and democratic values, the protection and enhancement of the environment, alternative defense and common security issues, and New York City cultural, social, and civic concerns.
Types of support: Operating budgets, general purposes, special projects, technical assistance.
Limitations: No grants to individuals, or for capital or endowment funds, conferences, scholarships, fellowships, or matching gifts; no loans.
Publications: Annual report (including application guidelines), financial statement.
Application information: Submit proposal upon request of foundation only. Application form required.
Initial approach: Letter
Copies of proposal: 1
Deadline(s): Jan. 31 and July 31
Board meeting date(s): Apr. and Nov. for grant decisions
Final notification: Within 2 weeks of meeting
Write: Robert Crane, V.P., Program
Officers and Directors:* LuEsther T. Mertz,* Chair.; Larry E. Condon,* Pres.; Elizabeth Burke Gilmore,* Secy.; Charles Bloomstein,* Treas.; Harlan Cleveland, C. Virgil Martin, Richard J. Mertz, Patricia Ramsay, Franklin W. Wallin.
Number of staff: 4 full-time professional; 2 full-time support; 1 part-time support.
Employer Identification Number: 132872722

4856
Stanley W. Metcalf Foundation, Inc. ¤
120 Genesee St., Rm. 503
Auburn 13021 (315) 253-9321

Established in 1962.
Donor(s): Stanley W. Metcalf.†
Foundation type: Independent
Financial data (yr. ended 12/31/88): Assets, $472,683 (M); expenditures, $347,806, including $297,000 for 52 grants (high: $40,000; low: $500).
Purpose and activities: Emphasis on youth organizations and church support; grants also for hospitals, welfare, and education.
Types of support: Annual campaigns, building funds, capital campaigns, continuing support, emergency funds, endowment funds, general purposes, matching funds, operating budgets, scholarship funds.

Limitations: Giving primarily in Cayuga County, NY.
Application information: Application form not required.
Deadline(s): None
Write: J. Douglas Pedley, Pres.
Officer and Directors:* J. Douglas Pedley, Pres.; Herbert T. Anderson, James P. Costello, Marjorie S. Pedley, Madeline M. Schneider, Ronald D. West.
Number of staff: 1
Employer Identification Number: 156017859

4857
Metropolitan Life Foundation ▼
One Madison Ave.
New York 10010-3690 (212) 578-6272

Incorporated in 1976 in NY.
Donor(s): Metropolitan Life Insurance Co.
Foundation type: Company-sponsored
Financial data (yr. ended 12/31/89): Assets, $100,257,489 (M); qualifying distributions, $17,627,632, including $7,832,696 for 800 grants (high: $196,770; low: $100; average: $1,000-$25,000), $70,000 for 2 grants to individuals, $499,893 for 600 employee matching gifts and $9,225,043 for loans.
Purpose and activities: To make donations for elementary, secondary, and higher education, health, including medical research and substance abuse programs, civic purposes, and United Way chapters; grants also for cultural programs, including public broadcasting, music, dance, and theater, and urban development, including housing and public policy; also makes program-related investments.
Types of support: Operating budgets, continuing support, employee matching gifts, research, program-related investments, general purposes, publications, special projects, capital campaigns, equipment, matching funds, scholarship funds, employee-related scholarships, seed money.
Limitations: No support for private foundations, religious, fraternal, athletic, political, social, or veterans' organizations; organizations already receiving support through United Way campaigns; local chapters of national organizations; disease-specific organizations; labor groups; organizations with international programs; organizations primarily engaged in patient care or direct treatment, drug treatment centers and community health clinics; hospital capital fund campaigns; or elementary or secondary schools. No grants to individuals (except for 1 medical research award), or for endowment funds, courtesy advertising, or festival participation.
Publications: Corporate giving report, application guidelines, program policy statement, financial statement, informational brochure (including application guidelines).
Application information: Application form required for special programs where requests for proposals are issued.
Initial approach: Letter
Copies of proposal: 1
Deadline(s): Varies for competitive awards programs; none for grants
Board meeting date(s): About 6 times a year
Final notification: 4 to 6 weeks
Write: Sibyl C. Jacobson, Pres. and C.E.O.
Officers and Directors:* John J. Creedon,* Chair.; Sibyl C. Jacobson,* Pres. and C.E.O.; Paul S. Entmacher, M.D.,* V.P.; William J. Howard, Counsel and Secy.; Arthur G. Typermass,* Treas.; Kenneth W. Malcolm, Controller; Richard W. Keough, Donald A. Odell, William G. Takacs.
Number of staff: None.
Employer Identification Number: 132878224

4858
Metzger-Price Fund, Inc. ¤
230 Park Ave.
New York 10169 (212) 867-9500

Trust established in 1970 in NY.
Donor(s): Estelle Metzger,† Leonard Metzger.†
Foundation type: Independent
Financial data (yr. ended 06/30/89): Assets, $649,567 (M); gifts received, $168,769; expenditures, $215,645, including $201,000 for 114 grants (high: $5,000; low: $500; average: $1,000-$2,500).
Purpose and activities: Giving for aid to the handicapped and health services; support also for child welfare and social service agencies, recreation, and the elderly.
Limitations: Giving primarily in New York, NY. No grants to individuals.
Publications: Financial statement.
Application information: Application form not required.
Initial approach: Letter
Copies of proposal: 1
Deadline(s): Submit proposal preferably 1 month before board meetings
Board meeting date(s): Jan., Apr., July, and Oct.
Final notification: Only if decision is affirmative
Write: Marie Mallot, Secy.-Treas.
Officers: Rabbi Ronald B. Sobel, Pres.; Robert Johnson, V.P.; Marie Mallot, Secy.-Treas.
Number of staff: None.
Employer Identification Number: 237072764

4859
Mex-Am Cultural Foundation, Inc. ¤
c/o Grant, Herrmann, Schwartz & Klinger
One Wall St.
New York 10005 (212) 943-8126

Established in 1985 in NY.
Donor(s): The Wolfgang Schoenborn Trust.
Foundation type: Independent
Financial data (yr. ended 9/30/88): Assets, $2,401,155 (M); expenditures, $147,979, including $105,000 for 8 grants (high: $50,000; low: $5,000).
Purpose and activities: Support for Mexico through cultural organizations that promote programs related to Mexican arts and its culture and welfare assistance, including hurricane disaster relief and child welfare.
Limitations: Giving primarily in New York, NY.
Application information:
Initial approach: Letter
Deadline(s): None
Write: Andrew M. Klinger, Trustee
Trustees: William J. Brown, Andrew M. Klinger, Evelyn Rather, Milton Schwartz.
Employer Identification Number: 133328723

4860
The Meyer Foundation ☆
c/o Lazard Freres & Co.
One Rockefeller Plaza
New York 10020

Established in 1985 in NY.
Foundation type: Independent
Financial data (yr. ended 12/31/87): Assets, $6,753,410 (M); expenditures, $315,962, including $253,000 for 4 grants (high: $90,000; low: $35,000).
Purpose and activities: Support for medical research, the arts, and higher education.
Types of support: General purposes, research.
Limitations: No grants to individuals.
Application information: Applications not accepted.
Write: George J. Ames, Secy.-Treas.
Officers and Directors:* Dr. Phillipe Meyer,* Pres.; Vincent Meyer,* V.P.; George J. Ames,* Secy.-Treas.
Number of staff: None.
Employer Identification Number: 133317912

4861
Roger and Barbara Michaels Family Fund, Inc. ¤
c/o David Tarlow & Co.
60 East 42nd St.
New York 10165

Foundation type: Independent
Financial data (yr. ended 12/31/88): Assets, $1,244,008 (M); expenditures, $65,986, including $54,050 for 123 grants (high: $26,000; low: $10).
Purpose and activities: Giving primarily to a community trust.
Limitations: Giving primarily in NY.
Application information:
Initial approach: Letter
Deadline(s): None
Write: Foundation Mgr.
Directors: Alice M. Ginandes, Barbara R. Michaels, Roger A. Michaels.
Employer Identification Number: 133022845

4862
Barbara and Clifford Michel Foundation, Inc. ¤
80 Pine St.
New York 10005 (212) 701-3200
Additional tel.: (212) 344-3090

Incorporated in 1951 in NY.
Donor(s): Barbara R. Michel,† Clifford W. Michel.†
Foundation type: Independent
Financial data (yr. ended 12/31/87): Assets, $596,888 (M); gifts received, $120,000; expenditures, $123,621, including $114,500 for 14 grants (high: $35,000; low: $1,000).
Purpose and activities: Support for higher and secondary education, hospitals, cultural programs, and projects concerned with law and justice.
Types of support: Operating budgets, continuing support, annual campaigns, building funds, equipment, endowment funds, capital campaigns.
Limitations: No grants to individuals, or for seed money, emergency funds, deficit financing, land acquisition, demonstration

projects, publications, conferences, research, scholarships, or fellowships; no loans.
Publications: 990-PF.
Application information: Application form not required.
Deadline(s): None
Board meeting date(s): June and Dec.
Final notification: 2 to 3 weeks
Write: Clifford L. Michel, Pres.
Officers: Clifford L. Michel, Pres.; Clifford F. Michel, V.P.; Denise Riccardelli, Secy.; Lynn R. Falcone, Treas.
Number of staff: None.
Employer Identification Number: 136082879

4863
The Dunlevy Milbank Foundation, Inc. ▼
c/o Sullivan & Cromwell
125 Broad St.
New York 10004 (212) 558-3724

Incorporated in 1941 in NY.
Donor(s): Dunlevy Milbank.†
Foundation type: Independent
Financial data (yr. ended 12/31/89): Assets, $2,224,079 (M); expenditures, $1,168,940, including $1,126,250 for 29 grants (high: $740,000; low: $250; average: $250-$740,000).
Purpose and activities: Emphasis on hospitals, a zoological society, a medical center, and local community organizations.
Types of support: Renovation projects, scholarship funds, building funds, general purposes, capital campaigns, emergency funds, endowment funds, seed money, special projects.
Limitations: Giving primarily in New York, NY, and FL. No grants to individuals.
Application information: Application form not required.
Initial approach: Letter
Copies of proposal: 1
Deadline(s): Oct.
Board meeting date(s): Nov. or Dec. and as required
Final notification: 1 to 2 months
Write: Donald R. Osborn, Secy.-Treas.
Officers and Directors:* William Ward Foshay,* Pres.; Barbara Foshay Duke,* V.P.; Donald R. Osborn,* Secy.-Treas.
Number of staff: None.
Employer Identification Number: 136096738

4864
Milbank Memorial Fund
One East 75th St.
New York 10021 (212) 570-4800

Incorporated in 1905 in NY.
Donor(s): Elizabeth Milbank Anderson.†
Foundation type: Operating
Financial data (yr. ended 12/31/89): Assets, $40,328,918 (M); gifts received, $18,000; expenditures, $1,763,955, including $251,414 for 16 grants (high: $40,000; low: $1,000; average: $1,000-$40,000) and $574,131 for foundation-administered programs.
Purpose and activities: A private operating foundation currently supporting projects which promote improvement in occupational health, with initial emphasis upon the health and welfare of migrant workers. In addition to grantmaking, the foundation has published the Milbank Quarterly, a scholarly journal in the health field since 1923.
Types of support: Research.
Limitations: No grants for annual campaigns, building or endowment funds, deficit financing, operating budgets, general purposes, matching gifts, or scholarships; no loans.
Publications: Annual report, informational brochure (including application guidelines).
Application information: Application form not required.
Initial approach: Letter
Board meeting date(s): Mar., May, Oct., and Dec.
Write: Daniel M. Fox, Ph.D., Pres.
Officers: Daniel M. Fox, Pres.; David P. Willis, V.P.; Sara C. Romano, Secy.-Treas.
Directors:* Samuel L. Milbank,* Chair.; Francis H. Musselman,* Vice-Chair.; Leroy E. Burney, M.D., Robert H. Ebert, Peter M. Gottsegen, Thomas Harvey, Jeremiah Milbank, Jr., Rosemary A. Stevens, Alan T. Wenzell.
Number of staff: 11
Employer Identification Number: 135562282

4865
Millbrook Tribute Garden, Inc. ▼ ⌑
c/o George T. Whalen, Inc.
P.O. Box AC
Millbrook 12545 (914) 677-3434

Incorporated in 1943 in NY.
Foundation type: Independent
Financial data (yr. ended 9/30/88): Assets, $22,846,108 (M); expenditures, $1,176,026, including $1,067,025 for 42 grants (high: $318,700; low: $25; average: $1,000-$30,000).
Purpose and activities: Emphasis on secondary education, church support, child welfare, hospitals, and civic projects; operates and maintains a playground and memorial park in honor of war veterans.
Types of support: General purposes, capital campaigns, equipment.
Limitations: Giving limited to Millbrook, NY. No grants to individuals.
Application information:
Initial approach: Proposal
Deadline(s): None
Write: George T. Whalen, Jr., Trustee
Officers: Oakleigh B. Thorne, Pres.; Daryl Parshall, V.P.
Trustees: Felicitas S. Thorne, Vincent N. Turletes, George T. Whalen, Jr., Robert W. Whalen.
Employer Identification Number: 141340079

4866
Kathryn & Gilbert Miller Fund, Inc. ⌑
c/o Proskauer, Rose, Goetz & Mendelsohn
300 Park Ave.
New York 10022

Incorporated in 1952 in NY.
Donor(s): Kathryn B. Miller.†
Foundation type: Independent
Financial data (yr. ended 3/31/89): Assets, $2,331,189 (M); expenditures, $1,030,684, including $1,005,233 for 28 grants (high: $498,732; low: $500).
Purpose and activities: Grants primarily for cultural programs, hospitals and medical research, and higher and secondary education.
Limitations: Giving primarily in NY. No grants to individuals.
Application information: Contributes only to pre-selected organizations. Applications not accepted.
Officers and Directors: Charles Looker, Pres.; Philip J. Hirsch, V.P. and Treas.; Jerold Zieselman, Secy.
Employer Identification Number: 136121254

4867
Milliken Foundation ▼ ⌑
1045 Ave. of the Americas
New York 10018

Trust established in 1945 in NY.
Donor(s): Milliken & Co., and others.
Foundation type: Company-sponsored
Financial data (yr. ended 12/31/88): Assets, $6,245,230 (M); gifts received, $2,211,690; expenditures, $1,409,866, including $1,176,203 for 114 grants (high: $231,690; low: $100; average: $500-$20,000).
Purpose and activities: Emphasis on higher and secondary education, community funds, public affairs, and youth agencies.
Application information: Contributes only to pre-selected organizations. Applications not accepted.
Advisory Committee: Lawrence Heagney, Thomas J. Malone, Gerrish H. Milliken, Minot K. Milliken, Roger Milliken.
Trustee: Citibank, N.A.
Number of staff: None.
Employer Identification Number: 136055062

4868
Milstein Family Foundation, Inc. ▼ ⌑
1271 Ave. of the Americas, Suite 4200
New York 10020 (212) 708-0800

Established in 1975 in NY.
Donor(s): Builtland Partners, Seymour Milstein, Paul Milstein, Gloria M. Flanzer.
Foundation type: Independent
Financial data (yr. ended 09/30/89): Assets, $3,277,990 (M); gifts received, $6,200,000; expenditures, $5,859,258, including $5,837,638 for 47 grants (high: $5,033,600; low: $500; average: $500-$25,000).
Purpose and activities: For at least the next five years, the foundation will give primarily for medicine, including medical research.
Types of support: Research.
Limitations: Giving primarily in NY.
Application information:
Initial approach: Letter
Write: Seymour Milstein, Chair.
Officers: Seymour Milstein, Chair.; Paul Milstein, Pres.; David V. Habif, V.P.; Philip L. Milstein, Secy.-Treas.
Employer Identification Number: 510190133

4869
Mitrani Family Foundation, Inc. ▼
c/o Rashba & Pokart
469 Seventh Ave.
New York 10018 (212) 736-3340

Incorporated in 1959 in NY.

Donor(s): Members of the Mitrani family, Milco Industries, Inc., and others.
Foundation type: Independent
Financial data (yr. ended 12/31/88): Assets, $1,239,893 (M); gifts received, $1,640,884; expenditures, $819,880, including $812,621 for 86 grants (high: $500,000; low: $50; average: $200-$10,000).
Purpose and activities: Grants largely for Jewish-sponsored higher and secondary education and for vocational and technological training schools in Israel and the U.S.; support also for Jewish welfare funds, non-secular colleges and universities, and social service and health agencies.
Application information: Application form not required.
Deadline(s): None
Write: Norman Nadel, Secy.
Officers and Directors: Norman Belmonte, V.P.; Leonard Comerchero, V.P.; Ira Hecht, V.P.; Selma Mitrani, V.P.; Norman Nadel, Secy.
Employer Identification Number: 246018102

4870
The Mnuchin Foundation ¤
c/o Goldman, Sachs & Co.
85 Broad St., Tax Dept., 30th Fl.
New York 10004

Established in 1980 in NY.
Donor(s): Robert E. Mnuchin.
Foundation type: Independent
Financial data (yr. ended 04/30/89): Assets, $3,563,331 (M); gifts received, $700,000; expenditures, $443,725, including $439,254 for 81 grants (high: $100,000; low: $25).
Purpose and activities: Emphasis on Jewish welfare, health, the arts, dance, and education.
Limitations: Giving primarily in NY.
Application information:
Deadline(s): None
Trustees: Eugene Mercy, Jr., Adrian Mnuchin, Robert E. Mnuchin.
Employer Identification Number: 133050751

4871
The Dom Mocquereau Foundation, Inc. ¤
c/o Davis Polk & Wardwell
499 Park Ave.
New York 10022 (212) 759-3076

Incorporated about 1926 in NY.
Donor(s): Justine B. Ward.†
Foundation type: Independent
Financial data (yr. ended 9/30/88): Assets, $900,200 (M); expenditures, $179,072, including $110,500 for 8 grants (high: $24,000; low: $1,000).
Purpose and activities: Support only for teaching of Gregorian chant by gifts to charitable organizations in the U.S., France, Switzerland, Holland, Italy, and Portugal, and by direct payment of salary of teachers of Gregorian chant.
Types of support: Grants to individuals, professorships.
Limitations: No grants for scholarships; no loans.
Application information:
Initial approach: Letter
Deadline(s): None
Write: James F. Dolan, Pres.
Officers: James F. Dolan,* Pres.; Theodore Marier, Exec. V.P.; Bernard F. Curry,* 2nd V.P. and Treas.; Maureen S. Bateman,* Secy.
Trustees:* Jean C. Lallemand, Thomas Mastroianni, Martin F. Shea.
Employer Identification Number: 237118643

4872
Leo Model Foundation, Inc. ¤
c/o Schneidman & Assoc.
405 Park Ave.
New York 10022

Established in 1970 in NY.
Donor(s): Model Charitable Lead Trust, Jane and Leo Model Foundation.
Foundation type: Independent
Financial data (yr. ended 12/31/87): Assets, $6,457,595 (M); gifts received, $1,312,077; expenditures, $865,699, including $817,520 for 117 grants (high: $175,000; low: $500).
Purpose and activities: Support for museums and the arts, secondary and higher education, and public interest organizations.
Application information: Contributes only to pre-selected organizations. Applications not accepted.
Officers: Allen Model, Pres.; Peter H. Model, V.P.; John A. Nevins, Secy.-Treas.
Employer Identification Number: 237084119

4873
Mohawk-Hudson Community Foundation, Inc.
901A Madison Ave.
Albany 12208 (518) 438-1673

Incorporated in 1968 in NY.
Foundation type: Community
Financial data (yr. ended 12/31/89): Assets, $2,196,588 (M); gifts received, $1,313,243; expenditures, $491,039, including $310,203 for 434 grants (high: $4,000; low: $19; average: $500-$1,000) and $1,500 for 1 loan.
Purpose and activities: Some funds restricted by donor designation; for others, emphasis on giving to otherwise unfinanced projects in the public interest.
Types of support: Special projects, equipment, scholarship funds, seed money.
Limitations: Giving primarily in Albany, Renssalaer and Saratoga counties, NY. No support for sectarian religious purposes. No grants to individuals, or for endowment or building funds, operating budgets, deficit financing, consulting services, continuing support, emergency funds, land acquisition, annual campaigns, scholarships, or fellowships; no loans.
Publications: Annual report, application guidelines, newsletter, informational brochure.
Application information: Application form required.
Initial approach: Proposal
Copies of proposal: 2
Deadline(s): Apr. 1 and Oct. 1
Board meeting date(s): Apr. and Dec.
Write: Judith Lyons, Exec. Dir.
Officers and Directors:* Marvin A. Freedman,* Pres.; Charles C. Freihofer III,* 1st V.P.; Ned Pattison,* 2nd V.P.; Ellen K. Lang,* Secy.; Susan S. Clarke,* Treas.; Judith Lyons,* Exec. Dir.; and 32 additional directors.
Number of staff: 2 full-time professional; 1 part-time professional; 1 full-time support; 1 part-time support.
Employer Identification Number: 141505623

4874
The Ambrose Monell Foundation ▼ ¤
c/o Fulton, Duncombe & Rowe
30 Rockefeller Plaza, Rm. 3217
New York 10112 (212) 586-0700

Incorporated in 1952 in NY.
Donor(s): Maude Monell Vetlesen.†
Foundation type: Independent
Financial data (yr. ended 12/31/88): Assets, $120,686,432 (M); expenditures, $6,294,872, including $5,693,500 for 95 grants (high: $500,000; low: $1,000; average: $5,000-$100,000).
Purpose and activities: For the "improvement of the physical, mental, and moral condition of humanity throughout the world"; giving largely for hospitals and health services, medical and chemical research, museums, performing arts, and other cultural activities, and higher and secondary education; support also for social services, research in political science, mental health, aid to the handicapped, and geophysical research.
Types of support: General purposes, research, building funds, endowment funds, operating budgets.
Limitations: No grants to individuals.
Application information: Application form not required.
Initial approach: Proposal
Copies of proposal: 1
Deadline(s): None
Board meeting date(s): Dec.
Write: Harmon Duncombe, Pres.
Officers and Directors:* Harmon Duncombe,* Pres. and Treas.; George Rowe, Jr.,* V.P. and Secy.; Eugene P. Grisanti, Henry G. Walter, Jr.
Number of staff: None.
Employer Identification Number: 131982683

4875
Monterey Fund, Inc. ▼ ¤
c/o Bear, Stearns & Co.
245 Park Ave.
New York 10167 (212) 272-4384

Incorporated in 1967 in NY.
Donor(s): Bear Stearns & Co., employees of Bear, Stearns & Co.
Foundation type: Independent
Financial data (yr. ended 4/30/88): Assets, $7,913,161 (M); gifts received, $8,634,978; expenditures, $8,490,734, including $8,268,654 for 2,962 grants (high: $500,000; low: $10; average: $200-$10,000).
Purpose and activities: Grants primarily for Jewish welfare funds and other Jewish organizations; support also for hospitals, health services, community funds, higher and other education, social services, and youth and child welfare.
Limitations: No grants to individuals.
Application information:
Deadline(s): None

Board meeting date(s): As required
Final notification: Varies
Write: William J. Montgoris, Treas.
Officers and Directors: Jeremiah Callaghan, Pres.; Denis Coleman, Jr., Secy.; William J. Montgoris, Treas.
Employer Identification Number: 136255661

4876
MONY Financial Services Foundation
1740 Broadway, MD 9-5
New York 10019

Established in 1987 in NY; direct corporate giving since the early 1940's.
Donor(s): The Mutual Life Insurance Co. of New York.
Foundation type: Company-sponsored
Financial data (yr. ended 12/31/88): Assets, $484,683 (M); gifts received, $2,189,135; expenditures, $2,133,145, including $2,112,527 for grants.
Purpose and activities: The foundation has identified "The Changing American Family" as its principal focus for funding. As always, change creates new needs and problems. The MONY Financial Services address the changes of society in transition by directing resources to organizations and programs that demonstrate an ability to effectively combat the social problems arising from these changes. MONY will consider grants that address such areas as, but not limited to: affordable and accessible child care alternatives for single parents; improved educational and training opportunities for women and minorities; and increased community-based services that allow the elderly to remain at home and prevent institutionalization with emphasis on innovative and well-managed programs that will enhance the quality of life of the individuals and families who comprise our diverse communities. Types of support include employee volunteer programs, employee matching gifts, challenge matches, and in-kind donations.
Types of support: Employee matching gifts, special projects, employee-related scholarships, matching funds, in-kind gifts.
Limitations: Giving primarily in communities where MONY maintains offices, including Teaneck, NJ; Purchase, Syracuse, and New York, NY. No support for private foundations, fully participating members of the United Way, or religious, fraternal, athletic, social, or veterans' organizations. No grants for capital fund drives, endowments, or deficit financing.
Publications: Application guidelines.
Application information: Application form not required.
Initial approach: Letter of inquiry
Copies of proposal: 1
Deadline(s): May 1
Board meeting date(s): Sept. 15
Final notification: Oct. 1
Write: Lynn Stekas, Pres.
Officers: Lynn Stekas, Pres.; Thomas G. Napurano, C.F.O.; Robert F. Colby, Secy.; Frederick P. Winters, Treas.
Directors: Thomas Conklin, Gordon E. Perry, Albert J. Schiff, Floyd L. Smith.
Number of staff: 3 full-time professional.
Employer Identification Number: 133398852

4877
Edward S. Moore Foundation, Inc. ▼
c/o Walter, Conston, Alexander and Green
90 Park Ave.
New York 10016 (212) 210-9400
Application address: 55 Old Field Point Rd., Greenwich, CT 06830; Tel.: (203) 629-4591

Established in 1957 in NY.
Donor(s): Edward S. Moore, Jr.,† Evelyn N. Moore,† Carolyn N. Moore, and others.
Foundation type: Independent
Financial data (yr. ended 12/31/89): Assets, $26,927,626 (M); expenditures, $1,246,636, including $1,073,868 for 82 grants (high: $50,000; low: $1,500; average: $2,500-$30,000).
Purpose and activities: Support for youth agencies, hospitals, education, and cultural programs, including museums, and churches.
Types of support: Operating budgets, continuing support, annual campaigns, seed money, emergency funds, building funds, equipment, land acquisition, endowment funds, matching funds, internships, scholarship funds, special projects, research.
Limitations: Giving primarily in NY and CT. No grants to individuals, or for deficit financing, publications, or conferences; no loans.
Publications: Annual report, 990-PF.
Application information: Application form not required.
Initial approach: Letter
Deadline(s): None
Board meeting date(s): Jan., Apr., July, and Oct.
Final notification: 3 to 6 months
Write: John W. Cross III, Pres.
Officers and Directors:* John W. Cross III,* Pres.; Marion Moore Gilbert,* V.P.; Donald Vail,* Secy.; Alexander Jackson,* Treas.; Jeffrey Gilbert, Lois Cross Willis.
Number of staff: 1 full-time professional.
Employer Identification Number: 136127365

4878
Morania Foundation, Inc. ¤
c/o Morgan Guaranty Trust Co.
Nine West 57th St.
New York 10019 (212) 826-7190

Incorporated in 1960 in NY.
Foundation type: Independent
Financial data (yr. ended 10/31/89): Assets, $6,630,137 (M); expenditures, $330,663, including $309,000 for 19 grants (high: $150,000; low: $1,000).
Purpose and activities: Grants largely for Roman Catholic church-related institutions, foreign missions, and welfare funds.
Application information: Application form not required.
Initial approach: Proposal
Deadline(s): None
Write: William J. McCormack, Pres.
Officers and Directors:* William J. McCormack,* Pres. and Treas.; William M. Waterman,* Secy.; Julie M. Greenough.
Employer Identification Number: 136141577

4879
Morgan Guaranty Trust Company of New York Charitable Trust ▼
60 Wall St.
New York 10260 (212) 648-9673

Trust established in 1961 in NY.
Donor(s): Morgan Guaranty Trust Co. of New York.
Foundation type: Company-sponsored
Financial data (yr. ended 12/31/89): Assets, $4,775,595 (M); gifts received, $5,000,000; expenditures, $8,310,746, including $6,597,039 for 349 grants (high: $400,000; low: $500; average: $2,000-$25,000) and $1,713,707 for 8,494 employee matching gifts.
Purpose and activities: Emphasis is on helping to find solutions to social problems and needs through support of competent agencies in fields of health, social services, culture, education, the environment, and international affairs. Special attention to job training, youth programs, international relief, housing, economic development, and advocacy and citizen involvement programs in New York City. Matches employee gifts to educational programs, cultural institutions, hospitals and health care agencies, human services and local development organizations, environmental and international organizations.
Types of support: Employee matching gifts, operating budgets, annual campaigns, seed money, building funds, equipment, special projects, matching funds, technical assistance, general purposes, capital campaigns, endowment funds, renovation projects.
Limitations: Giving limited to New York, NY, except for selected institutions of higher education, and international affairs. No support for organizations working with specific disabilities or diseases. No grants to individuals, or for scholarships, fellowships, or conferences; no loans.
Publications: Corporate giving report, application guidelines, program policy statement.
Application information: Application form required.
Initial approach: Proposal
Copies of proposal: 1
Deadline(s): Sept. 15
Board meeting date(s): Monthly
Final notification: 3 months
Write: Roberta Ruocco, V.P., Morgan Guaranty Trust Co. of New York
Advisory Committee: Lewis T. Preston, John F. Ruffle, Dennis Weatherstone.
Trustee: Morgan Guaranty Trust Co. of New York.
Number of staff: 4 full-time professional; 4 full-time support.
Employer Identification Number: 136037931

4880
Morgan Stanley Foundation ▼
1251 Ave. of the Americas, 31st Fl.
New York 10020 (212) 703-6610

Trust established in 1961 in NY.
Donor(s): Morgan Stanley & Co., Inc.
Foundation type: Company-sponsored
Financial data (yr. ended 12/31/89): Assets, $8,000,000 (M); gifts received, $2,500,000; expenditures, $1,370,000, including

$1,140,000 for grants (high: $20,000; low: $1,000; average: $3,500-$10,000) and $230,000 for employee matching gifts.
Purpose and activities: Giving primarily for programs in social welfare, including programs for housing and the homeless, employment, and child welfare; grants also for business schools, cultural programs and the performing arts, and hospitals.
Types of support: Operating budgets, continuing support, employee matching gifts, general purposes.
Limitations: Giving primarily in the New York, NY, metropolitan area. No support for United Way member agencies. No grants to individuals, or for emergency, endowment or building funds, deficit financing, equipment, land acquisition, scholarships, fellowships, special projects, research, publications, or conferences; no loans.
Publications: Program policy statement.
Application information: Application form not required.
Initial approach: Letter
Copies of proposal: 1
Deadline(s): None
Board meeting date(s): Quarterly and as required
Final notification: 3-6 months
Write: Patricia Schaefer
Trustees: Anson Beard, Jr., Kenneth DeRegt, Edward Dunn, John Wilson.
Number of staff: 2 full-time professional.
Employer Identification Number: 136155650

4881
Morris Morgenstern Foundation ▼
100 Merrick Rd., Rm. 506E
Rockville Centre 11570 (516) 536-3030

Trust established in 1949 in NY.
Donor(s): Morris Morgenstern.†
Foundation type: Independent
Financial data (yr. ended 12/31/88): Assets, $10,412,670 (M); gifts received, $3,487; expenditures, $1,503,131, including $1,330,416 for 129 grants (high: $320,000; low: $10; average: $50-$10,000).
Purpose and activities: Support for Jewish welfare funds; religious institutions, particularly synagogues; religious and secular education, health and hospitals, and youth agencies.
Types of support: General purposes.
Limitations: Giving primarily in the New York, NY, metropolitan area.
Application information:
Initial approach: Letter
Deadline(s): None
Final notification: Within 1 month after board meeting
Write: Hannah Klein, Exec. Dir.
Officer: Hannah Klein, Exec. Dir.
Trustee: Frank N. Morgenstern.
Employer Identification Number: 131635719

4882
Norman M. Morris Foundation, Inc. ¤
Six Corporate Park Dr.
White Plains 10604 (914) 694-1380

Incorporated in 1947 in NY.
Donor(s): Norman M. Morris.
Foundation type: Independent
Financial data (yr. ended 12/31/88): Assets, $5,540,483 (M); expenditures, $262,513, including $253,025 for 210 grants (high: $100,000; low: $20).
Purpose and activities: Emphasis on Jewish welfare funds, higher education, and hospitals.
Limitations: Giving primarily in NY.
Application information: Application form not required.
Initial approach: Letter
Deadline(s): None
Write: Norman M. Morris, Pres.
Officers and Trustees:* Norman M. Morris,* Pres.; Marvin Lubin,* V.P.; Robert E. Morris,* Secy.-Treas.; Arline J. Lubin, Kenneth A. Lubin, Leland M. Morris.
Employer Identification Number: 136119134

4883
The William T. Morris Foundation, Inc. ▼ ¤
230 Park Ave., Suite 622
New York 10169 (212) 986-8036
Scholarship application address: c/o Robert Ripa, Wyoming Area High School, Exeter, PA 18643

Trust established in 1937; incorporated in 1941 in DE.
Donor(s): William T. Morris.†
Foundation type: Independent
Financial data (yr. ended 6/30/89): Assets, $39,243,085 (M); expenditures, $2,025,289, including $1,531,000 for 60 grants (high: $50,000; low: $5,000; average: $5,000-$20,000) and $12,000 for 4 grants to individuals.
Purpose and activities: Giving primarily to religious, charitable, scientific, and/or educational institutions; support also for student aid.
Types of support: Student aid.
Limitations: Giving primarily in the northeastern states, especially NY and CT; scholarships limited to residents of West Pittston, PA.
Application information: Completion of application form required for student aid.
Initial approach: Letter and proposal
Copies of proposal: 1
Deadline(s): July 31 for scholarships; no set dealine for grants
Board meeting date(s): As required
Final notification: 6 to 8 weeks
Write: Edward A. Antonelli, Pres.
Officers and Directors: Edward A. Antonelli, Pres.; W.F. Wheeler, Jr., V.P.; P.W. Krehbiel, Secy.; A.C. Laske, Jr., Treas.; Arthur C. Laske.
Number of staff: 3 full-time professional.
Employer Identification Number: 131600908

4884
Carl A. Morse Foundation ¤
c/o Fleischman & Co.
307 Fifth Ave.
New York 10016

Established about 1966 in NY.
Donor(s): Carl A. Morse, Morse-Diesel, Inc.
Foundation type: Independent
Financial data (yr. ended 10/31/88): Assets, $22,981 (M); gifts received, $50,000; expenditures, $123,030, including $122,975 for 17 grants (high: $32,500; low: $25).
Purpose and activities: Emphasis on higher education, including engineering, and Jewish giving, including Israel; some support also for secondary education.
Limitations: No grants to individuals.
Application information:
Initial approach: Proposal
Deadline(s): None
Write: Carl A. Morse, Mgr.
Officer: Carl A. Morse, Mgr.
Employer Identification Number: 136208704

4885
Enid & Lester S. Morse, Jr. Foundation, Inc. ¤
60 East 42nd St.
New York 10165-0015

Established in 1967 in NY.
Donor(s): Lester S. Morse, Jr.
Foundation type: Independent
Financial data (yr. ended 3/31/89): Assets, $2,590,737 (M); gifts received, $2,639,262; expenditures, $131,576, including $129,151 for 113 grants (high: $13,333; low: $25).
Purpose and activities: Support primarily for higher education and cultural programs, including fine and performing arts groups.
Limitations: Giving primarily in New York, NY. No grants to individuals.
Application information: Contributes only to pre-selected organizations. Applications not accepted.
Officers: Lester S. Morse, Jr., Pres.; Enid Morse, V.P.; Richard Morse, Treas.
Director: Lawrence A. Wien.
Employer Identification Number: 136220174

4886
Morton Foundation, Inc. ¤
c/o B. Suss, Goldstein, Golub, Kessler & Co.
1185 Ave. of the Americas, 5th Fl.
New York 10036-2602

Established in 1961.
Donor(s): J. Morton Davis.
Foundation type: Independent
Financial data (yr. ended 12/31/88): Assets, $2,141,252 (M); gifts received, $237,714; expenditures, $127,747, including $125,273 for 36 grants (high: $23,000; low: $80).
Purpose and activities: Emphasis on Jewish education and temple support; support also for higher education.
Limitations: Giving primarily in NY. No grants to individuals, or for scholarships.
Application information: Contributes only to pre-selected organizations. Applications not accepted.
Officer and Directors:* Rosalind Davidowitz,* Pres. and Treas.; Ruki Renov, Esther Staller.
Employer Identification Number: 136107817

4887
Mosbacher Foundation, Inc. ¤
375 Park Ave. 8th Fl.
New York 10152

Incorporated in 1948 in NY.

Donor(s): Emil Mosbacher, Gertrude Mosbacher, Emil Mosbacher, Jr., Barbara Mosbacher, Robert Mosbacher.
Foundation type: Independent
Financial data (yr. ended 12/31/88): Assets, $30,253 (M); expenditures, $407,734, including $407,441 for 169 grants (high: $30,000; low: $25).
Purpose and activities: Grants primarily for higher education, museums and other cultural programs, and international studies.
Application information: Contributes only to pre-selected organizations. Applications not accepted.
Officers: Robert Mosbacher, Pres.; Barbara Mosbacher, Secy.-Treas.
Employer Identification Number: 136155392

4888
Henry and Lucy Moses Fund, Inc. ▼
c/o Moses and Singer
1271 Ave. of the Americas
New York 10020 (212) 246-3700

Incorporated in 1942 in NY.
Donor(s): Henry L. Moses,† Lucy G. Moses.†
Foundation type: Independent
Financial data (yr. ended 12/31/88): Assets, $7,484,021 (M); gifts received, $1,219,800; expenditures, $4,170,228, including $4,136,121 for 189 grants (high: $750,000; low: $250; average: $1,000-$50,000).
Purpose and activities: Support for hospitals, including building funds, and rehabilitation and medical schools; Jewish and other welfare funds; higher and legal education and educational programs for minorities; social service agencies, including those for youth, child welfare, minorities, the aged, and the handicapped; the arts and cultural programs, including dance; environmental concerns, including Central Park in New York City; and AIDS programs.
Types of support: Building funds, endowment funds, research, scholarship funds, fellowships, general purposes, matching funds, professorships, continuing support, annual campaigns, capital campaigns, operating budgets.
Limitations: Giving primarily in the New York, NY, metropolitan area. No grants to individuals; no loans.
Application information: Support generally limited to previous grant recipients. Applications not accepted.
Board meeting date(s): Usually in Feb., May, Aug., and Oct.
Write: Henry Schneider, Treas.
Officers and Directors:* Alfred W. Bressler,* V.P.; Felix A. Fischman,* V.P.; Arthur M. Fishberg, M.D.,* V.P.; Lillian E. Rachlin,* Secy.; Henry Schneider,* Treas.
Number of staff: None.
Employer Identification Number: 136092967

4889
Edwin H. Mosler, Jr. Foundation ⌘
307 Fifth Ave., 12th Fl.
New York 10016

Trust established in 1962 in NY.
Donor(s): Edwin H. Mosler, Jr.†
Foundation type: Independent
Financial data (yr. ended 11/30/88): Assets, $1,029,835 (M); gifts received, $269,079; expenditures, $379,364, including $350,000 for 10 grants (high: $90,000; low: $17,500).
Purpose and activities: Emphasis on support for the U.S. Olympic Committee, sports and recreation activities, youth agencies, and Jewish welfare agencies.
Application information:
Initial approach: Letter
Deadline(s): None
Write: Joan Johnson and Edmund W. Badgley, Trustees
Trustees: Edmund W. Badgley, Joan Johnson.
Employer Identification Number: 136108682

4890
J. Malcolm Mossman Charitable Trust ⌘
c/o Chemical Bank
30 Rockefeller Plaza
New York 10112 (212) 621-2148

Established in 1971.
Foundation type: Independent
Financial data (yr. ended 12/31/88): Assets, $404,966 (M); expenditures, $145,410, including $139,800 for 74 grants (high: $10,000; low: $300).
Purpose and activities: Giving primarily for social service and youth agencies, higher and secondary education, cultural programs, health, and church support, with some emphasis on Roman Catholic organizations.
Limitations: Giving primarily in NY. No grants to individuals.
Application information: Application form not required.
Initial approach: Letter
Deadline(s): None
Write: Mrs. Barbara Strohmeier
Trustees: Irving Goodstein, Chemical Bank.
Employer Identification Number: 136354042

4891
The Mostazafan Foundation of New York ▼
500 Fifth Ave., 34th Fl.
New York 10110-0397 (212) 944-8333

Incorporated in 1973 in NY.
Donor(s): Bank Melli of Iran.
Foundation type: Independent
Financial data (yr. ended 03/31/89): Assets, $85,840,014 (M); gifts received, $28,671; expenditures, $14,946,446, including $1,805,115 for 62 grants (high: $384,825; low: $50; average: $100-$50,000), $531,279 for 81 grants to individuals (high: $23,928; low: $156; average: $10,000-$15,000) and $3,301,628 for 3 foundation-administered programs.
Purpose and activities: To provide scholarships to Iranian students studying in the U.S., counsel students, and conduct research in the areas of Islamic religion and economic development; also distributes educational and religious books, and administers an educational center and a Sunday school for teaching Islamic religion and culture.
Types of support: Student aid, continuing support, endowment funds, lectureships, publications, special projects.
Publications: Program policy statement, application guidelines.
Application information: Application form required.
Copies of proposal: 1
Deadline(s): None
Board meeting date(s): Annually
Final notification: 1 to 3 months for scholarships and fellowships
Write: Mrs. N. Rouzati for student aid and Mr. N. Mardi for organizations
Officers and Directors:* Mohammad Badr-Taleh,* Pres.; Habib Zobeidi,* V.P. and Treas.; Hoshang Ahmadi,* V.P.; Mojtaba Hesami,* Secy.; Mohamad Pirayandeh.
Number of staff: 10 full-time professional; 10 full-time support.
Employer Identification Number: 237345978

4892
Mostyn Foundation, Inc. ⌘
c/o James C. Edwards & Co.
805 Third Ave., 8th Fl.
New York 10022

Trust established in 1949 in NY; incorporated in 1965.
Donor(s): Harvey D. Gibson,† Mrs. Harvey D. Gibson,† Mrs. Whitney Bourne Atwood.
Foundation type: Independent
Financial data (yr. ended 12/31/88): Assets, $2,574,224 (M); expenditures, $192,833, including $150,000 for 26 grants (high: $25,000; low: $1,000).
Purpose and activities: Grants largely for Protestant church support and religious associations, social service agencies, higher education, health agencies, hospitals, and youth agencies.
Limitations: No grants to individuals.
Application information: Contributes only to pre-selected organizations. Applications not accepted.
Write: Arthur B. Choate, Pres.
Officers: Arthur B. Choate, Pres.; Mrs. Whitney Bourne Atwood, V.P.; Charles C. Newbery, V.P.; Peter Megaree Brown, Secy.-Treas.
Employer Identification Number: 136171217

4893
Stewart R. Mott Charitable Trust/Spectemur Agendo
(Formerly Stewart R. Mott Charitable Trust)
515 Madison Ave.
New York 10022
Application address: 1133 Fifth Ave., New York, NY 10128; Tel.: (212) 289-0006

Trust established in 1968 in NY; reorganized in 1989 in NY.
Donor(s): Stewart R. Mott, Ruth R. Mott.
Foundation type: Independent
Financial data (yr. ended 12/31/89): Assets, $6,397,000 (M); expenditures, $283,000, including $241,900 for 65 grants (high: $65,000; low: $400; average: $500-$3,000).
Purpose and activities: Support primarily for arms control and international family planning.
Limitations: No support for local or state organizations. No grants to individuals, or for media or direct services.

Application information: Application form not required.
Initial approach: Proposal
Copies of proposal: 1
Deadline(s): None
Write: Stewart R. Mott, Trustee
Trustees: John P. Hodgkin, Stewart R. Mott, Kappy J. Wells.
Number of staff: 3 part-time professional; 1 full-time support.
Employer Identification Number: 237002554

4894
Mary S. Mulligan Charitable Trust ⌑
c/o Norstar Trust Co.
One East Ave.
Rochester 14604 (716) 546-9104

Established in 1967 in NY.
Donor(s): Mary S. Mulligan.†
Foundation type: Independent
Financial data (yr. ended 05/31/89): Assets, $2,306,169 (M); gifts received, $1,680; expenditures, $192,575, including $177,100 for 21 grants (high: $25,000; low: $400).
Purpose and activities: Giving primarily for higher and secondary education, including a medical scholarship fund, and hospitals.
Types of support: Building funds, continuing support, endowment funds, research, scholarship funds.
Limitations: No grants to individuals.
Application information: Contributes only to pre-selected organizations. Applications not accepted.
Trustee: Norstar Trust Co.
Employer Identification Number: 166076169

4895
Charles & Constance Murcott Charitable Trust ⌑ ☆
Ten Matinecock Farms Rd.
Glen Cove 11542

Established in 1986 in NY.
Foundation type: Independent
Financial data (yr. ended 8/31/88): Assets, $1,809,824 (M); expenditures, $142,648, including $111,200 for 24 grants (high: $50,000; low: $100).
Purpose and activities: Giving primarily for a conservation association and a hospital; some support for health associations and services.
Limitations: Giving primarily in NY. No grants to individuals.
Application information: Contributes only to pre-selected organizations. Applications not accepted.
Trustees: Charles Murcott, Constance Murcott.
Employer Identification Number: 112826619

4896
Musicians Foundation, Inc. ⌑
200 West 55th St., No. 41
New York 10019-5218 (212) 247-5332

Established in 1914 in NY.
Donor(s): Noel Murphy,† and others.
Foundation type: Independent
Financial data (yr. ended 4/30/89): Assets, $1,230,663 (M); gifts received, $51,800; expenditures, $133,347, including $91,095 for 39 grants to individuals (high: $5,950; low: $250).
Purpose and activities: Provides financial assistance to needy professional musicians and their families.
Types of support: Grants to individuals.
Publications: Informational brochure, application guidelines.
Application information: Application form not required.
Deadline(s): None
Write: Brent Williams, Secy.-Treas.
Officer: Brent Williams, Secy.-Treas.
Number of staff: None.
Employer Identification Number: 131790739

4897
H. Herbert Myers Memorial Foundation ⌑
c/o Lapatin, Lewis, Green, Kitzler & Blattels
989 Ave. of the Americas
New York 10017
Additional address: c/o Philip Berman, Trustee, 8 Fernwood Rd., Florham Park, NJ; Tel.: (201) 822-1000

Established in 1964 in NY.
Donor(s): Various donors.
Foundation type: Independent
Financial data (yr. ended 12/31/88): Assets, $1,633,582 (M); expenditures, $78,747, including $71,200 for 6 grants (high: $63,000; low: $100).
Purpose and activities: Emphasis on Jewish welfare funds, including those benefiting Israel.
Limitations: No grants to individuals.
Application information: Contributes only to pre-selected organizations. Applications not accepted.
Trustees: Philip Berman, Martin Myers.
Employer Identification Number: 116044697

4898
N've Shalom Foundation, Inc. ⌑
411 Fifth Ave.
New York 10016

Incorporated about 1938 in NY.
Donor(s): Joseph Attie.
Foundation type: Independent
Financial data (yr. ended 12/31/88): Assets, $2,065,382 (M); gifts received, $5,000; expenditures, $189,881, including $185,570 for 43 grants (high: $40,000; low: $50).
Purpose and activities: Giving for Jewish educational institutions and welfare funds.
Limitations: Giving primarily in NY. No grants to individuals.
Application information: Contributes only to pre-selected organizations. Applications not accepted.
Officers: Joseph Shalom, Pres.; Henry Shalom, V.P. and Secy.; Stephen Shalom, Treas.
Employer Identification Number: 136168301

4899
The Napier Foundation ⌑
c/o Chemical Bank
30 Rockefeller Plaza, 60th Fl.
New York 10112 (212) 621-2148
Application address: Michael Cunsolini, Napier Co., Napier Park, Meriden, CT 06450

Donor(s): Napier Co.
Foundation type: Independent
Financial data (yr. ended 7/31/87): Assets, $2,451,813 (M); expenditures, $133,035, including $118,984 for 71 grants (high: $11,400; low: $100).
Purpose and activities: Emphasis on higher and secondary education, youth and social agencies, hospitals, and cultural programs.
Limitations: Giving primarily in the Meriden, CT, area.
Application information: Application form not required.
Deadline(s): None
Write: Barbara Strohmeier, V.P., Chemical Bank
Trustees: John E. Benison, Eugene E. Bertolli, Michael G. Consolini, Eleanor S. Cooney, Ronald J. Meoni, Robert M. Meyers, Howard C. Schaefer, John A. Shulga, Carter H. White, Chemical Bank.
Employer Identification Number: 136029883

4900
The Nash Family Foundation, Inc. ⌑
c/o Spicer & Oppenheim
Seven World Trade Center
New York 10048

Established in 1964 in NY.
Donor(s): Jack Nash, Leo Levy, Helen Nash.
Foundation type: Independent
Financial data (yr. ended 6/30/88): Assets, $2,757,996 (M); expenditures, $49,487, including $41,387 for 42 grants (high: $15,000; low: $10).
Purpose and activities: Emphasis on Jewish giving, education, the arts, and museums.
Limitations: Giving primarily in New York, NY.
Application information: Contributes only to pre-selected organizations. Applications not accepted.
Officers and Directors: Jack Nash, Pres.; Arthur Aeder, V.P.; Ludwig Braumann, V.P.; Helen Nash, Treas.; Joshua Nash, Pamela Rohr.
Employer Identification Number: 136168559

4901
Nathanson-Abrams Family Foundation ⌑
c/o Roberta Abrams
1230 Ave. of the Americas, Suite 2010
New York 10020

Established in 1980.
Foundation type: Independent
Financial data (yr. ended 2/28/87): Assets, $1,102,930 (M); expenditures, $120,385, including $112,295 for grants.
Purpose and activities: Support for museums, universities, and public charities.
Types of support: Annual campaigns, building funds, capital campaigns, conferences and seminars, operating budgets.
Officer: Roberta Abrams, Treas.
Employer Identification Number: 133030314

4902
National Center for Automated Information Retrieval
165 East 72nd St., Suite 1B
New York 10021 (212) 249-0760

Established in 1966 in NY.
Foundation type: Independent
Financial data (yr. ended 12/31/89): Assets, $2,777,809 (M); expenditures, $174,644, including $39,000 for 1 grant and $45,000 for 3 grants to individuals (average: $15,000).
Purpose and activities: Grants to further the development of computer assisted methods of research or information retrieval for use by the legal and accounting professions.
Types of support: Grants to individuals, research.
Application information: Application form required.
Initial approach: Letter explaining relation of proposed project to automatic data retrieval
Write: A.B. Sloane
Officers: Timothy C. Leixner, Chair.; William C. Bruschi, Vice-Chair.; Winslow Christian, Pres.
Number of staff: None.
Employer Identification Number: 146037296

4903
The National City Foundation ⌑
c/o Corp. Tax Dept.
399 Park Ave.
New York 10043
Application address: National City Fdn. Scholarship Program, c/o CSS Educational Testing Service, CN 6730, Princeton, NJ 08541

Foundation type: Independent
Financial data (yr. ended 12/31/88): Assets, $2,599,407 (M); gifts received, $4,767; expenditures, $126,889, including $30,600 for 33 grants (high: $1,800; low: $250).
Purpose and activities: Support only for scholarships to children of Citibank/Citicorp employees.
Types of support: Employee-related scholarships.
Publications: Annual report.
Application information: Scholarship recipients chosen by committee selected by College Scholarship Service. Application form required.
Deadline(s): Nov. 28
Officers: Pamela P. Flaherty, Chair.; Paul H. Kolterjahn, Pres.; Mary Jane Henry, V.P.; Vivian Longo, V.P.; Rose Anne Gifford, Secy.
Directors: Helen Tomm, Mgr.; Michael T. Corcoran, Olga Girod, James H. Maher, Nicholas Onorato, Gerald N. Rhodes.
Employer Identification Number: 136097628

4904
M. & H. Neiman Foundation, Inc. ⌑
1616 49th St.
Brooklyn 11204-1133 (718) 851-9000

Established in 1972 in NY.
Donor(s): Marvin Neiman.
Foundation type: Independent
Financial data (yr. ended 10/31/87): Assets, $246,333 (M); gifts received, $217,632; expenditures, $221,665, including $220,525 for grants.
Purpose and activities: Support primarily for education.
Application information:
Initial approach: Letter
Deadline(s): None
Write: Marvin Neiman, Pres.
Officers: Marvin Neiman, Pres.; Louis Neiman, V.P.; Helen Neiman, Secy.
Employer Identification Number: 237042788

4905
Nelco Foundation, Inc. ⌑
164 West 25th St.
New York 10001 (212) 924-7604

Incorporated in 1953 in NY.
Donor(s): Leon Jolson, Nelco Sewing Machine Sales Corp.
Foundation type: Company-sponsored
Financial data (yr. ended 5/31/88): Assets, $1,488,186 (M); gifts received, $310,000; expenditures, $123,557, including $122,022 for 64 grants (high: $20,000; low: $10).
Purpose and activities: Support primarily for Jewish giving, Jewish welfare, and for educational associations.
Limitations: Giving primarily in NY.
Application information:
Initial approach: Letter
Deadline(s): None
Write: Leon Jolson, Pres.
Officers: Leon Jolson, Pres.; Barbara J. Blumenthal, Secy.
Employer Identification Number: 136089850

4906
Alice & Fred Netter Foundation, Inc.
c/o K. Fred Netter
411 Theodore Fremd Ave.
Rye 10580-0908

Established in 1965 in NY.
Donor(s): K. Fred Netter.
Foundation type: Independent
Financial data (yr. ended 12/31/89): Assets, $1,512,000 (M); expenditures, $65,387, including $62,207 for 178 grants (high: $8,000; low: $25; average: $50-$5,000).
Purpose and activities: Support for music, education, including education for minorities, Jewish welfare, medical research, sociology, and general charitable giving.
Types of support: Annual campaigns, building funds, capital campaigns, research.
Limitations: Giving primarily in NY. No grants to individuals.
Application information: Contributes only to pre-selected organizations. Applications not accepted.
Officers and Trustees: K. Fred Netter, Pres. and Treas.; Alfred E. Netter, V.P.; Ronald A. Netter, V.P.; Kenneth J. Bialkin, Secy.; Alice Netter.
Number of staff: None.
Employer Identification Number: 136176542

4907
Hugo and Doris Neu Foundation, Inc. ⌑
c/o Hugo Neu & Sons
1185 Ave. of the Americas, Suite 310
New York 10036

Incorporated in 1955 in NY.
Donor(s): Hugo Neu, Union Minerals & Alloys Corp., Hugo Neu & Sons, Inc.
Foundation type: Independent
Financial data (yr. ended 12/31/88): Assets, $4,410,042 (M); gifts received, $1,300,000; expenditures, $390,881, including $389,350 for 69 grants (high: $67,500; low: $250).
Purpose and activities: Emphasis on Jewish welfare funds; support also for hospitals and higher and secondary education.
Types of support: General purposes.
Limitations: Giving primarily in NY. No grants to individuals.
Application information: Contributes only to pre-selected organizations. Applications not accepted.
Officers and Directors:* Doris Neu,* Pres. and Treas.; John L. Neu,* V.P. and Secy.; Richard W. Neu,* V.P.; Herman Caro, Donald Schapiro.
Employer Identification Number: 136107504

4908
Roy R. and Marie S. Neuberger Foundation, Inc.
522 Fifth Ave.
New York 10036 (212) 790-9676

Incorporated in 1954 in NY.
Donor(s): Roy R. Neuberger, Marie S. Neuberger.
Foundation type: Independent
Financial data (yr. ended 12/31/89): Assets, $10,545,120 (M); gifts received, $946,250; expenditures, $705,380, including $667,600 for 148 grants (high: $200,000; low: $50; average: $1,808).
Purpose and activities: Grants primarily for cultural programs, including the fine arts, and higher education.
Limitations: Giving primarily in NY. No grants to individuals.
Application information: Application form not required.
Initial approach: Letter
Board meeting date(s): Apr.
Write: Mary Piatoff, Dir.
Officers and Directors:* Roy R. Neuberger,* Pres. and Treas.; Ann N. Aceves,* V.P.; James A. Neuberger,* V.P.; Marie S. Neuberger,* V.P.; Roy S. Neuberger,* V.P.; Charles H. Levitt,* Secy.; Mary Piatoff.
Number of staff: None.
Employer Identification Number: 136066102

4909
New Cycle Foundation ⌑ ☆
515 Madison Ave., Rm. 4100
New York 10022

Established in 1985 in NY.
Donor(s): Michael Currier.
Foundation type: Independent
Financial data (yr. ended 12/31/88): Assets, $9,354,012 (M); expenditures, $522,505, including $357,353 for 14 grants (high: $100,000; low: $660).
Purpose and activities: Giving primarily for an organization promoting scientific, educational, and cultural development in Tibet and a health institute; support also for higher and other education and child and youth development.

Limitations: Giving primarily in New York, NY. No grants to individuals.
Application information: Contributes only to pre-selected organizations. Applications not accepted.
Officer: Saville Ryan, Exec. Dir.
Trustee: Michael Currier.
Employer Identification Number: 133260471

4910
New Hope Foundation, Inc. ☆
c/o Howard Bindelglass
445 Park Ave., Suite 1700
New York 10022-2638 (212) 702-2421
Application address for Lenore Marshall Poetry Prize Book Award: c/o The Nation, 72 Fifth Ave., New York, NY 10011; Tel.: (212) 242-8400

Established in 1949 in NY.
Donor(s): Lenore Marshall.†
Foundation type: Independent
Financial data (yr. ended 12/31/89): Assets, $1,096,387 (M); expenditures, $104,178, including $83,024 for 4 grants (high: $40,000; low: $3,584).
Purpose and activities: Support for an environmental organization, anti-nuclear and civil liberties groups; awards the annual L.G. Marshall Poetry Prize Book Award.
Types of support: Conferences and seminars, general purposes, seed money, special projects.
Limitations: Giving primarily in New York, NY.
Application information: Application form not required.
Initial approach: Applicants must be recommended to the foundation
Copies of proposal: 10
Deadline(s): 2 weeks prior to meeting
Board meeting date(s): Spring (Apr. or May) and autumn (Oct.)
Write: Sarah Katz, Asst. Secy.
Officers: Jonathan Marshall, Chair.; Linda Scholle, Vice-Chair.; Arthur L. Kimmelfield, Secy.; Howard Bindelglass, Treas.
Directors: David Finn, Lawrence K. Grossman, Robert L. Marshall, Lawrence Pitkethly, Ellen Scholle, Harold Taylor.
Number of staff: 1 part-time support.
Employer Identification Number: 136088891

4911
The New World Foundation ▼
100 East 85th St.
New York 10028 (212) 249-1023

Incorporated in 1954 in IL.
Donor(s): Anita McCormick Blaine.†
Foundation type: Independent
Financial data (yr. ended 09/30/89): Assets, $32,813,334 (M); expenditures, $2,673,033, including $1,617,000 for 132 grants (high: $35,000; low: $500; average: $1,000-$25,000).
Purpose and activities: Program places emphasis on (a) equal rights and opportunity, with emphasis on minorities' rights; (b) public education, especially the roles of parents and the community working together; (c) public health, particularly helping the disadvantaged, raising occupational health and safety standards, and reducing environmental hazards to health; (d) community initiative for rural and urban communities; and (e) avoidance of war, especially nuclear war, and seeking peace; some support also for youth advocacy and child welfare agencies.
Types of support: Special projects, conferences and seminars, program-related investments, technical assistance, seed money, loans.
Limitations: No support for community fund drives, schools, hospitals, or cultural, arts, or media programs, organizations which discriminate against women or members of ethnic minority groups, or that do not have an affirmative action policy and practice. No grants to individuals, or for general operating budgets, deficit financing, continuing support, capital, building, or endowment funds, research that is not action- or policy-oriented with regard to current issues and is not of limited scope or duration, scholarships, fellowships, or matching gifts; emergency loans to current grantees only.
Publications: Biennial report (including application guidelines).
Application information: Application form not required.
Initial approach: Letter
Copies of proposal: 1
Deadline(s): None
Board meeting date(s): 3 times a year
Final notification: 3 months
Write: Colin Greer, Pres.
Officers: Hillary Rodham Clinton,* Chair.; Maria Echaveste,* Vice-Chair.; Colin Greer, Pres. and Exec. Dir.; Byllye Y. Avery,* Secy.; David B. Harrison,* Treas.
Directors:* James P. Breeden, Adrian W. De Wind, Harold C. Fleming, John W. Hatch, Charles Heymaestre, Joyce Kramer, Karl Mathiasen III, Linda A. Randolph, Phyllis Ross Schloss.
Number of staff: 3 full-time professional; 3 full-time support.
Employer Identification Number: 131919791

4912
The New York Community Trust ▼
Two Park Ave.
New York 10016 (212) 686-0010

Established in 1923 in NY by resolution and declaration of trust.
Foundation type: Community
Financial data (yr. ended 12/31/89): Assets, $829,783,809 (M); gifts received, $36,291,336; expenditures, $54,061,422, including $46,284,030 for 6,694 grants (high: $571,243; low: $100; average: $5,000-$35,000), $138,532 for 262 employee matching gifts, $806,346 for 1 foundation-administered program and $50,000 for 1 loan.
Purpose and activities: A composite of many charitable funds. The grant program of each fund is handled separately, designed to meet objectives suggested by founder. Priority given to applications for special support for projects having particular significance for the New York City area. Loan guarantee program improves access to commercial lending.
Types of support: Seed money, matching funds, consulting services, technical assistance, special projects, research, publications, conferences and seminars, loans, scholarship funds, employee matching gifts.
Limitations: Giving limited to the metropolitan New York, NY, area. No support for religious purposes, or for transportation, or manpower development by non-advised grant program. No grants to individuals, or for deficit financing, emergency funds, building campaigns, endowment funds, or general operating support.
Publications: Informational brochure, annual report, application guidelines, newsletter, occasional report.
Application information: Application form not required.
Initial approach: Proposal with cover letter
Copies of proposal: 1
Deadline(s): None
Board meeting date(s): Feb., Apr., June, July, Oct., and Dec.
Final notification: 10 to 12 weeks
Write: Lorie A. Slutsky, Dir.
Officers: Lorie A. Slutsky,* Pres. and Dir.; Karen Metcalf, V.P., Finance and Admin.; Joyce M. Bove, V.P., Program and Projects; Sidney S. Whelan, Jr., V.P., Donor Relations; Kieran J. Lawlor, Controller.
Distribution Committee:* Barbara S. Preiskel, Chair.; Arthur G. Altschul, Aida Alvarez, William H. Donaldson, William M. Evarts, Jr., Barry H. Garfinkel, Judah Gribetz, Robert M. Kaufman, William Parsons, Bernard J. Pisani, M.D., Mrs. Laurance S. Rockefeller.
Trustees: The Bank of New York, Bankers Trust Co., Barclays Bank of New York, N.A., Bessemer Trust Co., N.A., Brown Brothers Harriman Trust Co., The Chase Manhattan Bank, N.A., Chemical Bank, Citibank, N.A., Fiduciary Trust Co. International, Manufacturers Hanover Trust Co., Marine Midland Bank, N.A., Morgan Guaranty Trust Co. of New York, Republic National Bank of New York, Rockefeller Trust Co., IBJ Schroder Bank & Trust Co., J. & W. Seligman Trust Co., U.S. Trust Co. of New York.
Number of staff: 16 full-time professional; 4 part-time professional; 18 full-time support; 1 part-time support.
Employer Identification Number: 133062214

4913
New York Foundation ▼
350 Fifth Ave., No. 2901
New York 10118 (212) 549-8009

Incorporated in 1909 in NY.
Donor(s): Louis A. Heinsheimer,† Alfred M. Heinsheimer,† Lionel J. Salomon.†
Foundation type: Independent
Financial data (yr. ended 12/31/89): Assets, $50,264,000 (M); expenditures, $3,239,000, including $2,318,000 for 88 grants (high: $50,000; low: $10,000; average: $20,000-$35,000).
Purpose and activities: Support for projects designed to improve the quality of life for disadvantaged, handicapped, and minority populations, with extra emphasis on youth and the elderly, especially projects with a strong community base. Some support for advocacy and coalition work and health services, including AIDS programs.
Types of support: Operating budgets, continuing support, seed money, matching funds, technical assistance, general purposes, special projects.

Limitations: Giving primarily in the New York, NY, metropolitan area. No support for the arts, medical research, or films. No grants to individuals, or for annual campaigns, renovations, emergency funds, deficit financing, building or endowment funds, equipment, scholarships, fellowships, land acquisition, research, conferences, publications, or demonstration projects; no loans.
Publications: Annual report (including application guidelines).
Application information: Application form not required.
Initial approach: Letter
Copies of proposal: 1
Deadline(s): Nov. 1, Mar. 1, and July 1
Board meeting date(s): Feb., June, and Oct.
Final notification: 3 to 6 months
Write: Madeline Lee, Exec. Dir.
Officers and Trustees:* Rebecca S. Straus,* Chair.; Stephen D. Heyman,* Vice-Chair.; Joan Leiman,* Secy.; William M. Kelly,* Treas.; Michael Diaz, R. Harcourt Dodds, Myron S. Falk, Jr., Barbara D. Finberg, Marilyn Gittell, Theodora Jackson, Michael M. Kellen, Mack Lipkin, Jr., Josephine Morales, Archibald R. Murray, Stephanie K. Newman, Robert Pollack, Alice Radosh, Helen Rehr, M.D. Taracido, Edward Wachenheim III.
Number of staff: 4 full-time professional; 3 full-time support.
Employer Identification Number: 135626345

4914
New York Friends Group, Inc. ¤
218 East 18th St.
New York 10003

Established in 1956 in NY as an operating foundation; changed to private foundation status in 1985.
Foundation type: Independent
Financial data (yr. ended 6/30/89): Assets, $866,638 (M); expenditures, $330,797, including $253,254 for 23 grants (high: $35,000; low: $1,115).
Purpose and activities: Giving primarily in the following areas: 1) International peace, including programs seeking alternatives to national security, promotion and dissemination of peace issues, and exploration of the theory of nonviolence; 2) Human rights in the U.S. and abroad in South Africa, Haiti, Central America, and the Philippines; 3) Education and youth, with emphasis on programs for secondary school age youth; and 4) Environment policy issues on both national and local levels.
Limitations: Giving primarily in the New York, NY, metropolitan area for projects which are local in nature, as distinct from national or international programs. No grants to individuals.
Officers and Directors: George Rubin, Chair.; Charles Bloomstein, Vice-Chair.; Doris Shamleffer, Pres.; Edward G. Doty, Secy.-Treas.; William A. Delano, Harry Fleischman, Elizabeth Burke Gilmore, Daniel A. Seeger.
Employer Identification Number: 135680254

4915
New York Life Foundation ▼ ¤
51 Madison Ave.
New York 10010 (212) 576-7341

Established in 1979 in NY.
Donor(s): New York Life Insurance Co.
Foundation type: Company-sponsored
Financial data (yr. ended 12/31/88): Assets, $34,729,453 (M); gifts received, $8,211,888; expenditures, $2,282,280, including $2,227,077 for 593 grants (high: $360,000; low: $25; average: $500-$10,000).
Purpose and activities: Grants to national and local organizations. Priority areas are AIDS and literacy; support also for higher education, including insurance education, in both direct grants and employee matching gifts; community funds; community development and urban affairs; hospitals; cultural programs; and youth and social service agencies.
Types of support: General purposes, scholarship funds, operating budgets, building funds, special projects, employee matching gifts.
Limitations: No support for public educational institutions; fraternal, social, professional, veterans', or athletic organizations; religious or sectarian organizations or activities whose services are limited to members of any one religious group; grant-making foundations; preschool, primary, or secondary educational institutions; or United Way-member organizations already receiving foundation support. No grants to individuals, or for seminars, conferences, trips, memorials, endowments, capital campaigns, research-related programs, or matching gifts; no loans.
Publications: Application guidelines.
Application information: Application form not required.
Initial approach: Letter
Copies of proposal: 1
Deadline(s): None
Board meeting date(s): No formal schedule
Final notification: Varies
Write: Carol J. Reuter, Exec. Dir.
Officers: Donald K. Ross,* Chair.; Edmund R. Harnedy,* Secy.; William E. Keiter,* Treas.; Carol J. Reuter, Exec. Dir.
Directors:* George A.W. Bundschuh, John T. DeBardeleben, Harry G. Hohn, Malcolm MacKay, Walter Shur.
Number of staff: 3 full-time professional; 1 full-time support.
Employer Identification Number: 132989476

4916
New York Society for the Relief of Widows & Orphans of Medical Men
c/o Davies & Davies
50 East 42nd St.
New York 10017

Established in 1939 in NY.
Foundation type: Independent
Financial data (yr. ended 03/31/88): Assets, $1,924,940 (M); expenditures, $110,894, including $96,727 for grants to individuals.
Purpose and activities: Financial support for widows and orphans of physicians.
Types of support: Grants to individuals.
Application information:
Deadline(s): Nov. 15
Write: Walter Wichern, Secy.
Officers: Charles Schetlin, Pres.; Walter Wichern, Jr., Secy.; Chen B. Yeoh, Treas.
Employer Identification Number: 237156733

4917
New York Stock Exchange Foundation, Inc. ¤
11 Wall St.
New York 10005 (212) 656-2060

Incorporated in 1983 in NY.
Donor(s): New York Stock Exchange.
Foundation type: Company-sponsored
Financial data (yr. ended 12/31/88): Assets, $6,296,451 (M); gifts received, $500,000; expenditures, $853,074, including $793,774 for 49 grants (high: $500,000; low: $500) and $46,561 for employee matching gifts.
Purpose and activities: Support for higher education, community development, social services, and arts and cultural institutions.
Types of support: Employee matching gifts.
Limitations: Giving primarily in New York, NY.
Application information:
Initial approach: Letter
Deadline(s): None
Write: James E. Buck, Secy.
Officers: Richard R. Shinn,* Chair.; James E. Buck, Secy.; John P. Johnson, Treas.
Directors:* James C. Bradford, Jr., John A. Georges, William A. Schreyer, Donald Stone.
Employer Identification Number: 133203195

4918
The New York Times Company Foundation, Inc. ▼
229 West 43rd St.
New York 10036 (212) 556-1091

Incorporated in 1955 in NY.
Donor(s): The New York Times Co.
Foundation type: Company-sponsored
Financial data (yr. ended 12/31/88): Assets, $2,289,526 (M); gifts received, $5,000,000; expenditures, $5,091,791, including $4,302,090 for 595 grants (high: $250,000; low: $500; average: $1,000-$10,000) and $542,008 for 608 employee matching gifts.
Purpose and activities: Grants primarily for higher and secondary education, including employee-related scholarships through the National Merit Scholarship Corp., support for minority education, and a matching gifts program; support also for urban affairs, cultural programs, journalism, and environmental concerns.
Types of support: Annual campaigns, conferences and seminars, continuing support, emergency funds, employee matching gifts, endowment funds, fellowships, general purposes, internships, operating budgets, research, scholarship funds, seed money, employee-related scholarships.
Limitations: Giving primarily in the New York, NY, metropolitan area and in localities served by affiliates of the company. No support for sectarian religious institutions or for health-related purposes; grants for urban affairs seldom made on the neighborhood level. No grants to individuals, or for capital and building funds; no loans.

Publications: Annual report (including application guidelines).
Application information: Application form not required.
Initial approach: Letter
Copies of proposal: 1
Deadline(s): Submit proposal in the early part of the year; no set deadline
Board meeting date(s): Mar. and Sept.
Final notification: Varies
Write: Arthur Gelb, Sr. V.P.
Officers and Directors:* Arthur Ochs Sulzberger,* Chair.; Fred M. Hechinger,* Pres.; Arthur Gelb, Exec. V.P.; Walter E. Mattson,* Exec. V.P.; David L. Gorham, Sr. V.P.; Michael E. Ryan, Sr. V.P.; Solomon B. Watson IV, V.P.; Laura Corwin, Secy.; John F. Akers, William R. Cross, Jr., Richard L. Gelb, Louis V. Gerstner, Jr., Marian S. Heiskell, Ruth S. Holmberg, George B. Munroe, George L. Shinn, Donald M. Stewart, Judith P. Sulzberger, M.D., Cyrus R. Vance, Esq.
Number of staff: 2 full-time professional; 2 full-time support.
Employer Identification Number: 136066955

4919
The New-Land Foundation, Inc. ▼
1345 Ave. of the Americas, 45th Fl.
New York 10105 (212) 841-6000

Incorporated in 1941 in NY.
Donor(s): Muriel M. Buttinger.†
Foundation type: Independent
Financial data (yr. ended 12/31/88): Assets, $15,822,407 (M); gifts received, $161,036; expenditures, $1,787,803, including $1,575,343 for 139 grants.
Purpose and activities: Grants for civil rights, mental health, environmental preservation, public interest, arms control and disarmament, cultural programs, minority and medical education, and social service and youth agencies.
Types of support: General purposes, annual campaigns, seed money, research, continuing support, internships, matching funds, operating budgets, special projects.
Limitations: No grants to individuals; no loans.
Publications: Application guidelines.
Application information: Application form not required.
Initial approach: Letter requesting guidelines
Copies of proposal: 1
Deadline(s): Feb. 1 and Aug. 1
Board meeting date(s): Spring and fall
Final notification: For positive responses only
Write: Robert Wolf, Pres.
Officers and Directors:* Robert Wolf,* Pres.; Constance Harvey,* V.P.; Hal Harvey,* V.P.; Renee G. Schwartz,* Secy.-Treas.; Joan Harvey, Anna Frank Loeb, Albert Solnit.
Number of staff: None.
Employer Identification Number: 136086562

4920
Newbrook Charitable Foundation, Inc. ⌑
(Formerly Gerald David Neuman Foundation, Inc.)
1102 53rd St.
Brooklyn 11219

Established in 1981 in NY.
Foundation type: Independent
Financial data (yr. ended 12/31/88): Assets, $1,401,022 (M); expenditures, $1,045,713, including $1,025,100 for 7 grants (high: $350,000; low: $100).
Purpose and activities: Emphasis on Jewish giving; support also for a hospital.
Application information: Contributes only to pre-selected organizations. Applications not accepted.
Officer: Gerald David Newman, Mgr.
Employer Identification Number: 112554328

4921
Samuel I. Newhouse Foundation, Inc. ▼ ⌑
c/o Paul Scherer & Co.
330 Madison Ave.
New York 10017

Incorporated in 1945 in NY.
Donor(s): Samuel I. Newhouse,† Mitzi E. Newhouse.†
Foundation type: Independent
Financial data (yr. ended 10/31/88): Assets, $60,479,612 (M); gifts received, $4,000; expenditures, $4,304,769, including $4,118,260 for 419 grants (high: $250,000; low: $100; average: $500-$1,000).
Purpose and activities: Establishment of Newhouse Communications Center at Syracuse University for education and research in mass communications; giving for community funds, hospitals, Jewish welfare funds, higher and secondary education, music and the arts, and youth agencies; support also for journalism associations.
Limitations: No grants to individuals.
Application information: Contributes only to pre-selected organizations. Applications not accepted.
Officers and Directors: Donald E. Newhouse, V.P.; Samuel I. Newhouse, Jr., V.P.; Norman N. Newhouse, Secy.; Theodore Newhouse, Treas.; Richard E. Diamond.
Number of staff: None.
Employer Identification Number: 116006296

4922
Jerome A. and Estelle R. Newman Assistance Fund, Inc. ▼
c/o Howard A. Newman
925 Westchester Ave., Suite 308
White Plains 10604-3507 (914) 993-0777

Incorporated in 1954 in NY.
Donor(s): Howard A. Newman, Jerome A. Newman.†
Foundation type: Independent
Financial data (yr. ended 06/30/88): Assets, $7,846,036 (M); expenditures, $1,012,248, including $982,440 for grants (average: $250-$15,000).
Purpose and activities: Support for higher education, hospitals, aid to the handicapped, Jewish welfare funds, and the performing arts.
Limitations: Giving primarily in NY. No grants to individuals or loans to individuals.
Application information:
Initial approach: Letter
Deadline(s): None
Board meeting date(s): Sept.
Final notification: Varies
Officers: Howard A. Newman,* Chair.; William C. Newman,* Pres.; Patricia Nanon,* V.P.; Elizabeth L. Newman,* V.P.; Robert H. Haines,* Secy.; Michael Greenberg, Treas.
Directors:* Andrew H. Levy, William C. Scott.
Number of staff: None.
Employer Identification Number: 136096241

4923
Henry Nias Foundation, Inc.
639 Seney Ave.
Mamaroneck 10543 (914) 698-5036

Incorporated in 1955 in NY.
Donor(s): Henry Nias.†
Foundation type: Independent
Financial data (yr. ended 11/30/89): Assets, $12,300,000 (M); expenditures, $676,600, including $612,500 for 59 grants (high: $37,500; low: $2,500; average: $5,000-$15,000).
Purpose and activities: Emphasis on hospitals, aid to the handicapped, medical school student loan funds, education, cultural programs, child welfare and youth, the aged, and Jewish organizations, including welfare funds.
Types of support: Continuing support.
Limitations: Giving limited to the New York, NY, metropolitan area.
Application information: Applications by invitation only.
Deadline(s): Aug. 31
Board meeting date(s): Sept. and Oct.
Final notification: Grants paid in Nov.
Write: Henry L. Fleischman, Pres.
Officers and Directors:* Henry L. Fleischman,* Pres. and Treas.; Albert J. Rosenberg,* V.P. and Secy.; Stanley Edelman, M.D.,* V.P.; Richard J. Edelman, Charles D. Fleischman, William F. Rosenberg.
Number of staff: None.
Employer Identification Number: 136075785

4924
Nichols Foundation, Inc.
630 Fifth Ave., Rm. 1964
New York 10111 (212) 581-1160

Incorporated in 1923 in NY.
Donor(s): Members of the Nichols family.
Foundation type: Independent
Financial data (yr. ended 01/31/89): Assets, $6,650,843 (M); qualifying distributions, $386,525, including $386,525 for 43 grants (high: $85,000; low: $75).
Purpose and activities: Emphasis on higher and secondary education, research in cancer, chemistry, biology, and the medical sciences, environmental conservation, hospitals, and social services agencies, including child welfare and youth groups.
Types of support: Research, matching funds, continuing support, annual campaigns, building funds, equipment, endowment funds, scholarship funds, fellowships.
Limitations: Giving primarily in the New York, NY, metropolitan area. No grants to individuals; no loans.
Application information: Application form not required.
Initial approach: Letter
Copies of proposal: 1

Deadline(s): Submit proposal preferably in Apr. or Oct.; deadlines Apr. 30 and Oct. 31
Board meeting date(s): June and Jan.
Final notification: 4 months to 1 year
Write: Peter C. Coxhead, Pres.
Officers and Directors:* Peter C. Coxhead,* Pres.; David H. Nichols,* V.P.; Mary H. Vinton, Secy.; C. Walter Nichols III,* Treas.
Number of staff: 1 full-time professional.
Employer Identification Number: 136400615

4925
Ethel & Alexander Nichoson Foundation ⌑ ☆
18 West Carver St.
Huntington 11743 (516) 421-9051

Established in 1970.
Foundation type: Independent
Financial data (yr. ended 5/31/89): Assets, $1,468,692 (M); expenditures, $73,963, including $62,485 for 42 grants (high: $10,000; low: $25).
Purpose and activities: Support primarily for Jewish organizations, including welfare funds.
Limitations: No grants to individuals.
Application information: Contributes only to pre-selected organizations. Applications not accepted.
Write: Arthur Goldstein, Trustee
Trustee: Arthur Goldstein.
Employer Identification Number: 116101005

4926
John H. and Ethel G. Noble Charitable Trust
c/o Bankers Trust Co.
One North Lexington Ave.
White Plains 10601

Trust established in 1969 in CT.
Donor(s): Ethel G. Noble,† John H. Noble.†
Foundation type: Independent
Financial data (yr. ended 05/31/89): Assets, $10,738,443 (M); expenditures, $562,543, including $499,500 for 11 grants (high: $100,000; low: $13,500).
Purpose and activities: Grants for organizations that provide shelter or support to the aged and places for the care and treatment of handicapped children.
Limitations: Giving primarily in CT, NY, and FL.
Application information: Application form not required.
Initial approach: Proposal
Copies of proposal: 1
Write: Paul J. Bisset, V.P., Bankers Trust Co.
Trustee: Bankers Trust Co.
Employer Identification Number: 136307313

4927
Edward John Noble Foundation, Inc. ▼
32 East 57th St.
New York 10022 (212) 759-4212
Business office address: P.O. Box 162, Washington Depot, CT 06794

Trust established in 1940 in CT; incorporated in 1982.
Donor(s): Edward John Noble.†
Foundation type: Independent
Financial data (yr. ended 12/31/89): Assets, $95,332,162 (M); expenditures, $3,841,109, including $2,728,419 for 64 grants (high: $500,000; low: $250; average: $5,000-$50,000).
Purpose and activities: Grants to major cultural organizations in New York City, especially for their educational programs. Selected projects concerned with conservation and ecology primarily related to activities on an island off the coast of GA. Supports private college and university environmental studies programs in the Northeast and programs to improve educational opportunity for gifted and talented disadvantaged children in New York City. Programs in health education efforts related to family planning and the problems of overpopulation.
Types of support: Continuing support, scholarship funds, matching funds, general purposes, endowment funds, special projects.
Limitations: Giving primarily in the metropolitan New York, NY, area for arts organizations and their educational programs; St. Catherine's Island, GA, and the eastern states for conservation projects and population control; and the Northeast for private colleges and universities. No support for television, films, or performances. No grants to individuals, or for publications, building funds, or equipment; no loans.
Publications: Biennial report (including application guidelines).
Application information: Application form not required.
Initial approach: Letter or proposal
Copies of proposal: 1
Deadline(s): 6 weeks before board meeting dates
Board meeting date(s): June and Dec.
Final notification: 3 months
Write: June Noble Larkin, Chair.
Officers and Directors:* June Noble Larkin,* Chair. and Pres.; Nancy K. Breslin,* Secy.; Frank Y. Larkin,* Treas.; E.J. Noble Smith,* Exec. Dir.; Mimi Coleman, Robert G. Goelet, Howard Phipps, Jr., Frank P. Piskor, Jeremy T. Smith, Carroll L. Wainwright, Jr., Alan N. Weeden.
Number of staff: 3 full-time professional; 3 full-time support.
Employer Identification Number: 061055586

4928
Robert J. Nolan Foundation, Inc. ⌑ ☆
Two Potter St.
Glens Falls 12801 (518) 792-8841

Established in 1986 in NY.
Donor(s): Robert J. Nolan.
Foundation type: Independent
Financial data (yr. ended 9/30/89): Assets, $1,100,927 (M); expenditures, $52,287, including $47,465 for 10 grants to individuals (high: $7,500; low: $2,500).
Purpose and activities: Awards scholarships for higher education to local area secondary school students.
Types of support: Student aid.
Limitations: Giving limited to residents of the greater Glens Falls, NY, area.
Application information: Application form required.
Deadline(s): June 1
Officers: Robert J. Nolan, Pres.; Suzanne Farnett Nolan, 1st V.P. and Treas.; Paul Keihak, 2nd V.P.; Jane Barton, Secy.
Employer Identification Number: 222826285

4929
Norcross Wildlife Foundation, Inc. ⌑
1322 Empire State Bldg.
New York 10118 (212) 947-0220

Established in 1964 in NY.
Foundation type: Independent
Financial data (yr. ended 12/31/88): Assets, $28,453,625 (M); expenditures, $1,173,827, including $496,650 for 36 grants (high: $50,000; low: $50).
Purpose and activities: Support for social services, environmental and wildlife organizations, and civic affairs.
Limitations: Giving primarily in NY.
Application information: Application form not required.
Deadline(s): None
Write: Anthony Schoendorf, Pres.
Officers and Directors:* Anthony Schoendorf,* Pres. and Treas.; Ethel Stella,* Exec. V.P.; Fred C. Anderson,* Secy.; Arthur Douglas, Edward Gallagher, Arthur D. Norcross, Jr., Richard Reagan.
Employer Identification Number: 132041622

4930
Norman Foundation, Inc. ⌑
c/o Abacus and Associates
147 East 48th St.
New York 10017 (212) 230-9830

Incorporated in 1935 in NY.
Donor(s): Aaron E. Norman,† and directors of the foundation.
Foundation type: Independent
Financial data (yr. ended 12/31/88): Assets, $21,023,238 (M); gifts received, $5,000; expenditures, $1,054,132, including $849,675 for 86 grants (high: $30,000; low: $50).
Purpose and activities: Major interests include the protection of civil rights and civil liberties and, in general, broadening and improving the quality of citizen participation in the political, economic, and social processes of American communities. A major portion of grants are currently being made to projects which address the economic plight of the working and non-working poor and which enable them to have more voice in the institutions which allocate jobs and resources in their communities.
Types of support: General purposes, matching funds, seed money, special projects, operating budgets.
Limitations: No support for programs having broad public support or dealing only with local issues, or for media or art projects, direct social service agencies, community fund drives, schools, or hospitals. No grants to individuals, or for building or endowment funds, publications, continuing support, conferences, research, scholarships, or fellowships; generally no loans.
Publications: Application guidelines, program policy statement, multi-year report.
Application information: Application form not required.

Initial approach: Letter or proposal
Copies of proposal: 1
Deadline(s): None
Board meeting date(s): Quarterly
Final notification: 1 to 5 months
Write: Phyllis Ekhaus, Prog. Dir.
Officers: Frank A. Weil,* Pres.; Lucinda W. Bunnen,* V.P.; Nancy N. Lassalle,* Secy.; Jody Weisbrod, Treas.; Phyllis Ekhaus, Prog. Dir.
Directors:* Andrew E. Norman, Chair.; Belinda Bunnen, Melissa Bunnen, Robert L. Bunnen, Jr., Alice Franklin, Andrew D. Franklin, Deborah Weil Harrington, Diana Lassalle, Honor Lassalle, Philip E. Lassalle, Abigail Norman, Margaret Norman, Sarah Norman, Amanda Weil, Sandison E. Weil.
Number of staff: 1 part-time professional; 1 full-time support.
Employer Identification Number: 131862694

4931
Normandie Foundation, Inc.
c/o Abacus and Associates
147 East 48th St.
New York 10017 (212) 230-9800

Incorporated in 1966 in NY.
Donor(s): Andrew E. Norman, The Aaron E. Norman Fund, Inc.
Foundation type: Independent
Financial data (yr. ended 12/31/89): Assets, $2,100,000 (M); expenditures, $136,700, including $117,500 for 25 grants (high: $20,000; low: $50).
Purpose and activities: Grants primarily for civil liberties, minority and civil rights both in the U.S. and elsewhere; support also for local civic, charitable, educational, and cultural insitutions.
Types of support: General purposes.
Limitations: Giving primarily in Rockland County and New York, NY, and Barnstable County, MA. No grants to individuals, or for building or endowment funds, scholarships, fellowships, or matching gifts; generally no loans.
Application information: Generally, grants are only to organizations with which the officers are personally familiar. Application form not required.
Initial approach: Letter
Copies of proposal: 1
Deadline(s): None
Board meeting date(s): June and Dec.
Final notification: 6 months
Write: Andrew E. Norman, Pres.
Officers: Andrew E. Norman, Pres. and Treas.; Nancy N. LaSalle, V.P. and Secy.; Helen D. Norman, V.P.
Number of staff: 1
Employer Identification Number: 136213564

4932
Norstar Bank of Upstate NY Foundation ⌑
c/o Norstar Bank of Upstate New York, Trust Dept.
69 State St.
Albany 12201 (518) 447-4162

Trust established in 1962 in NY.
Donor(s): Norstar Bank of Upstate New York.
Foundation type: Company-sponsored
Financial data (yr. ended 9/30/89): Assets, $6,087,815 (M); gifts received, $288,199; expenditures, $692,731, including $686,740 for 138 grants (high: $125,000; low: $25).
Purpose and activities: Emphasis on community funds, higher education, hospitals and health associations, and youth agencies; support also for civic affairs and the arts.
Types of support: Building funds, equipment, land acquisition, research, capital campaigns.
Limitations: Giving primarily in the Albany, Utica, and Newburgh, NY, areas. No grants to individuals, or for endowment funds, scholarships, fellowships, or matching gifts; no loans.
Application information: Application form required.
Initial approach: Proposal
Copies of proposal: 2
Deadline(s): None
Board meeting date(s): Distribution committee meets 3 or 4 times a year as required
Final notification: Shortly after meeting
Write: Robert F. MacFarland, Chair.
Trustee: Norstar Bank of Upstate New York.
Number of staff: None.
Employer Identification Number: 146014607

4933
North American Philips Foundation ⌑
100 East 42nd St.
New York 10017

Established in 1979 in NY.
Donor(s): North American Philips Corp.
Foundation type: Company-sponsored
Financial data (yr. ended 12/31/88): Assets, $8,927 (M); gifts received, $231,400; expenditures, $234,864, including $234,800 for 225 grants to individuals (high: $3,000; low: $250).
Purpose and activities: Awards scholarships for employees' dependents.
Types of support: Employee-related scholarships.
Application information: Application form required.
Initial approach: Letter requesting application
Deadline(s): Mar. 1
Officers: D. Hamilton, Pres.; J. Kanter, V.P.; S. Cundey, Treas.
Director: B. Bengtson.
Employer Identification Number: 132961300

4934
Northeastern New York Community Trust
c/o Key Trust Co.
60 State St.
Albany 12207

Established in 1955 in NY.
Foundation type: Community
Financial data (yr. ended 12/31/87): Assets, $1,374,310 (M); expenditures, $82,148, including $69,650 for 10 grants (high: $14,000; low: $1,650).
Purpose and activities: Support for higher education through awards to scholarship programs.
Types of support: Scholarship funds.
Limitations: Giving primarily in northeastern NY.
Application information: Application form not required.
Initial approach: Letter
Deadline(s): Nov. 1
Board meeting date(s): Varies
Trustee: Key Trust Co.
Employer Identification Number: 146030063

4935
Northern New York Community Foundation, Inc.
(Formerly Watertown Foundation, Inc.)
P.O. Box 6106
Watertown 13601 (315) 782-7110

Incorporated in 1929 in NY.
Foundation type: Community
Financial data (yr. ended 12/31/88): Assets, $3,109,621 (M); gifts received, $141,014; expenditures, $739,666, including $395,023 for 46 grants (high: $80,000; low: $333) and $200,834 for 199 grants to individuals (high: $2,500; low: $250).
Purpose and activities: To promote charitable, educational, cultural, recreational, and health programs through grants to community organizations and agencies and a student scholarship program.
Types of support: Annual campaigns, seed money, building funds, equipment, land acquisition, matching funds, student aid, special projects, research, publications, conferences and seminars, renovation projects, capital campaigns.
Limitations: Giving limited to Jefferson County, NY. No grants for endowment funds or deficit financing.
Publications: Annual report.
Application information: Application form not required.
Initial approach: Letter or telephone
Copies of proposal: 1
Deadline(s): Feb. 1, May 1, Aug. 1, and Nov. 1
Board meeting date(s): Mar., June, Sept., and Dec.
Final notification: 1 to 2 months
Write: James W. Higgins, Exec. Dir.
Officers: Robert G. Horr, Jr.,* Pres.; Everett G. Foster,* V.P.; Anderson Wise,* Secy.-Treas.; James W. Higgins, Exec. Dir.
Directors:* Norman R. Ahlheim, Frances P. Carter, Floyd J. Chandler, John Doldo, Jr., Richard O. Flechtner, Barbara D. Hanrahan, Lee T. Hirschey, P. Owen Willaman.
Number of staff: 1 full-time professional; 1 part-time professional; 2 full-time support.
Employer Identification Number: 156020989

4936
Norwood Foundation, Inc.
c/o Bessemer Trust Co.
630 Fifth Ave.
New York 10111
Mailing address: P.O. Box 238, East Norwich, NY 11732, Tel.: (516) 626-0288

Incorporated in 1952 in NY.
Donor(s): Thomas M. Bancroft,† Edith W. Bancroft.†
Foundation type: Independent

Financial data (yr. ended 12/31/89): Assets, $1,993,364 (M); expenditures, $86,247, including $66,000 for 14 grants (high: $15,000; low: $1,000).
Purpose and activities: Grants primarily for secondary education, hospitals, health services, and museums.
Types of support: Operating budgets, continuing support, annual campaigns, seed money, building funds, equipment, endowment funds, scholarship funds, deficit financing, capital campaigns.
Limitations: Giving primarily in NY. No grants to individuals, or for emergency funds, exchange programs, land acquisition, matching gifts, fellowships, professorships, internships, special projects, research, publications, or conferences; no loans.
Application information: Application form not required.
Initial approach: Letter
Deadline(s): None
Officer: Thomas M. Bancroft, Jr., Pres. and Treas.
Number of staff: None.
Employer Identification Number: 136111530

4937
Jessie Smith Noyes Foundation, Inc. ▼
16 East 34th St.
New York 10016 (212) 684-6577

Incorporated in 1947 in NY.
Donor(s): Charles F. Noyes.†
Foundation type: Independent
Financial data (yr. ended 12/31/89): Assets, $61,180,601 (M); expenditures, $5,095,763, including $4,540,264 for grants.
Purpose and activities: Basic goal is to prevent irreversible damage to the natural systems upon which all life depends through grants in the following areas: 1) tropical ecology, with special interest in preventing the destruction of tropical ecosystems, in particular, tropical forests in Latin America; 2) sustainable agriculture promoting long-term sustainability in North America and Latin America; 3) water resources, especially the protection of groundwater in the U.S.; 4) and reproductive rights in North America and Latin America. Grants, which are to institutions only, emphasize the strengthening of individuals and institutions committed to sustaining natural systems and a sustainable society.
Types of support: Continuing support, special projects, seed money.
Limitations: Giving primarily in North America, Central America and South America. No grants to individuals, or for endowment funds, capital construction funds, land acquisition, or general fundraising drives; generally no support for conferences, research, or media; no loans.
Publications: Annual report (including application guidelines), program policy statement, application guidelines.
Application information: Applications not accepted for discretionary or founder-designated funds. Application form required.
Initial approach: 1- or 2-page letter of inquiry, including budget estimate; if project is of interest, full proposal will be requested
Copies of proposal: 2
Deadline(s): Letters of inquiry will be received at any time during the year; proposals will usually be due 1 month after being requested
Board meeting date(s): Jan., June, and Nov.
Final notification: Within 6 weeks of receipt of letters; within 2 weeks of board meetings for final proposals
Write: Stephen Viederman, Pres.
Officers and Directors:* Ann F. Wiener,* Chair.; Pamela W. McCann,* Vice-Chair.; Dorothy E. Muma,* Vice-Chair.; Stephen Viederman,* Pres.; Nicholas Jacangelo,* Secy.-Treas.; Catherine Bedell, Barbara B. Dow, Very Rev. James P. Morton, Edith N. Muma, David Orr, Emily Smith, Greg Watson.
Number of staff: 3 full-time professional; 2 full-time support; 1 part-time support.
Employer Identification Number: 135600408

4938
NYNEX Foundation ▼
1113 Westchester Ave., 1st Fl.
White Plains 10604-3510 (914) 644-7226

Established in 1985 in NY.
Donor(s): NYNEX Corp.
Foundation type: Company-sponsored
Financial data (yr. ended 12/31/88): Assets, $27,720,000 (M); gifts received, $3,000,000; expenditures, $2,070,000, including $2,000,000 for 46 grants (average: $10,000-$50,000).
Purpose and activities: Giving in three areas: for organizations of all educational levels, economic and community development, including support for cultural institutions, and innovative solutions to the problems of the less advantaged, such as the elderly and unemployed.
Types of support: Special projects.
Limitations: Giving primarily in areas of company operations concentrated in New England and NY. No support for organizations which duplicate work of federal, state, or local public agencies, or religious organizations. No grants to individuals, or for advertising, or operating expenses of organizations supported by the United Way.
Publications: Annual report (including application guidelines), informational brochure (including application guidelines).
Application information:
Initial approach: Proposal with letter
Deadline(s): None
Board meeting date(s): Contributions Committee meets 4 times a year
Final notification: 4 to 6 months
Write: Barbara W. Bates, Prog. Dir.
Officers: W.G. Burns,* Pres.; R.F. Burke,* V.P. and Secy.; G. J. Fippinger, V.P. and Treas.; D.K. Emmons, Exec. Dir.; M. Goldstein, Comptroller.
Directors:* D. C. Staley.
Number of staff: 5 part-time professional; 2 part-time support.
Employer Identification Number: 133319048

4939
O.C.F. Foundation, Inc. ⌘
122 East 42nd St.
New York 10168

Incorporated in 1940 in NY.
Donor(s): International Minerals and Metals Corp.
Foundation type: Company-sponsored
Financial data (yr. ended 12/31/89): Assets, $1,611,466 (M); expenditures, $138,609, including $118,380 for 45 grants (high: $60,000; low: $75).
Purpose and activities: Support for Jewish welfare funds and cultural activities; some support for social services.
Limitations: Giving primarily in NY.
Application information: Contributes only to pre-selected organizations. Applications not accepted.
Officers: H. Fred Baerwald, Pres.; Anne Halpern, V.P.; Philip J. Maron, Secy.; Gregor Leinsdorf, Treas.
Employer Identification Number: 136007727

4940
A. Lindsay and Olive B. O'Connor Foundation ▼
P.O. Box D
Hobart 13788 (607) 538-9248

Trust established in 1965 in NY.
Donor(s): Olive B. O'Connor.†
Foundation type: Independent
Financial data (yr. ended 12/31/88): Assets, $35,758,754 (M); expenditures, $1,704,714, including $1,405,326 for 119 grants (high: $250,000; low: $142; average: $1,000-$20,000).
Purpose and activities: Emphasis on "quality of life," including hospitals, libraries, community centers, higher education, nursing and other vocational education, child development and youth agencies, religious organizations, museums, and historic restoration; support also for civic affairs and town, village, and environmental conservation and improvement.
Types of support: General purposes, continuing support, annual campaigns, seed money, emergency funds, building funds, equipment, land acquisition, endowment funds, special projects, research, publications, conferences and seminars, scholarship funds, matching funds, loans, technical assistance, program-related investments, renovation projects.
Limitations: Giving primarily in Delaware County, NY, and contiguous rural counties in upstate NY. No grants to individuals, or for operating budgets or deficit financing.
Publications: Program policy statement.
Application information: Limited funding available until 1992. Application form required.
Initial approach: Letter
Copies of proposal: 1
Deadline(s): Apr. 1 and Sept. 1
Board meeting date(s): May or June and Sept. or Oct.; committee meets monthly to consider grants under $5,000
Final notification: 1 week to 10 days after semiannual meeting
Write: Donald F. Bishop II, Exec. Dir.
Officer: Donald F. Bishop II, Exec. Dir.

Advisory Committee: Olive B. Price, Chair.; Robert L. Bishop II, Vice-Chair.; Robert L. Bishop, Exec. Secy.; Donald F. Bishop, Charlotte Bishop Hill, William J. Murphy, Eugene E. Peckham.
Trustee: Chase Lincoln First Bank, N.A.
Number of staff: 2 full-time professional.
Employer Identification Number: 166063485

4941
Jonathan & Shirley O'Herron Foundation ⌑
c/o Lazard Freres & Co.
One Rockefeller Plaza
New York 10020-1902

Established in 1984 in NY.
Donor(s): Jonathan O'Herron, Shirley O'Herron.
Foundation type: Independent
Financial data (yr. ended 06/30/89): Assets, $378,245 (M); gifts received, $115,000; expenditures, $168,692, including $167,000 for 50 grants (high: $16,500; low: $500).
Purpose and activities: Giving primarily for Catholic churches, secondary and higher education; support also for hospitals and social services.
Limitations: Giving primarily in in MA, CT, VT, and NY. No grants to individuals.
Application information: Application form not required.
Initial approach: Letter
Deadline(s): None
Write: Jonathan O'Herron, Pres.
Officers: Jonathan O'Herron, Pres.; Shirley O'Herron, V.P.; Thomas F.X. Mullarkey, Secy.-Treas.
Employer Identification Number: 133244207

4942
Cyril F. and Marie E. O'Neil Foundation ⌑
c/o Richards, O'Neil & Allegaert
885 Third Ave.
New York 10022 (212) 207-1200

Incorporated in 1957 in OH.
Donor(s): Members of the O'Neil family.
Foundation type: Independent
Financial data (yr. ended 12/31/89): Assets, $4,057,187 (M); expenditures, $419,522, including $377,900 for 29 grants (high: $250,000; low: $200).
Purpose and activities: Grants largely for higher and secondary education, and Catholic church support.
Limitations: Giving primarily in NY and OH.
Application information:
Initial approach: Letter
Deadline(s): None
Write: Ralph O'Neil, Pres.
Officers: Ralph M. O'Neil, Pres.; Cyril F. O'Neil, V.P.
Employer Identification Number: 346523819

4943
The O'Sullivan Children Foundation, Inc. ⌑ ☆
355 Post Ave.
Westbury 11590 (516) 334-3209

Established in 1981.
Donor(s): Kevin P. O'Sullivan, Carole O'Sullivan.
Foundation type: Independent
Financial data (yr. ended 9/30/88): Assets, $5,580,288 (M); gifts received, $5,102,031; expenditures, $163,254, including $148,687 for grants (high: $54,380).
Purpose and activities: Giving primarily for Catholic organizations, including churches and a school; support also for hospitals and health associations.
Types of support: Capital campaigns, endowment funds.
Limitations: No grants to individuals.
Application information:
Initial approach: Proposal
Write: Kevin P. O'Sullivan, Pres.
Officers and Directors: Kevin P. O'Sullivan, Pres.; Carole O'Sullivan, V.P. and Treas.; Neil M. Delman, Secy.
Number of staff: 1 full-time professional.
Employer Identification Number: 133126389

4944
The Oaklawn Foundation ⌑
420 Lexington Ave.
New York 10170 (212) 986-8660

Incorporated in 1948 in NY.
Donor(s): Mabel B. Kies,† W.S. Kies,† Margaret K. Gibb, and others.
Foundation type: Independent
Financial data (yr. ended 12/31/88): Assets, $9,098,707 (M); gifts received, $218,282; expenditures, $655,819, including $492,760 for 76 grants (high: $75,000; low: $500; average: $2,500-$10,000).
Purpose and activities: Assistance primarily to higher and secondary education; support also for the performing arts and social services.
Types of support: Endowment funds, scholarship funds.
Limitations: Giving primarily in the Northeast. No grants to individuals, or for operating budgets, deficit financing, emergency funds, capital funds, research, special projects, publications, or conferences; no loans.
Application information: Application form not required.
Initial approach: Proposal
Deadline(s): None
Board meeting date(s): May and Oct.
Final notification: 2 to 3 months
Write: Walter B. Levering, Pres.
Officers and Directors: Walter B. Levering, Pres.; John L. Montgomery, Jr., V.P.; Standish F. Medina, Secy.; A.S. Paight, Treas.; A.K. Arnold, W.A. Arnold IV, William S. Kies III, M. Leslie, A.S. Paight, L. Romanucci.
Number of staff: None.
Employer Identification Number: 136127896

4945
The Odysseus Foundation ⌑
c/o RHO Management, Co.
767 Fifth Ave., 43rd Fl.
New York 10153

Established in 1986 in NJ.
Donor(s): Bernd Diethelm Hoener.
Foundation type: Independent
Financial data (yr. ended 12/31/88): Assets, $380,816 (M); gifts received, $225,000; expenditures, $500,793, including $497,773 for 8 grants (high: $300,000; low: $5,000).
Purpose and activities: Support primarily for community funds and social services; support also for civic organizations in a city in France.
Limitations: Giving primarily in New York, NY and Cannes, France. No grants to individuals.
Application information: Contributes only to pre-selected organizations. Application form not required.
Officers: Bernd Diethelm Hoener, Pres.; Henry Christensen III, V.P. and Secy.; William F. Indoe, V.P.; Irene March, Treas.
Employer Identification Number: 133391991

4946
Odyssey Partners Foundation, Inc. ⌑ ☆
437 Madison Ave., 29th Fl.
New York 10022

Donor(s): Odyssey Partners.
Foundation type: Company-sponsored
Financial data (yr. ended 1/31/89): Assets, $160,624 (M); gifts received, $150,000; expenditures, $103,300, including $103,275 for 70 grants (high: $19,500; low: $25).
Purpose and activities: Support for higher education, Jewish organizations, and general charitable giving.
Types of support: General purposes.
Limitations: Giving primarily in New York, NY. No grants to individuals.
Application information: Contributes only to pre-selected organizations. Applications not accepted.
Officers: Jack Nash, Pres.; Ludwig Braumann, V.P.; Lawrence Levitt, Secy.-Treas.
Employer Identification Number: 136186566

4947
Sylvan and Ann Oestreicher Foundation, Inc. ⌑
645 Madison Ave.
New York 10022 (212) 759-8500

Incorporated in 1948 in NY.
Donor(s): Sylvan Oestreicher.†
Foundation type: Independent
Financial data (yr. ended 4/30/88): Assets, $3,091,374 (M); expenditures, $147,307, including $135,639 for 134 grants (high: $21,000; low: $75).
Purpose and activities: Grants primarily for religious welfare funds, hospitals, and higher education; support also for the handicapped, youth agencies, religious associations, and cultural programs.
Application information: Application form not required.
Deadline(s): None
Write: Robert F. Welch, Secy.
Officers and Directors: Ann Oestreicher, Pres.; Merwin Lewis, V.P.; Robert F. Welch, Secy.
Employer Identification Number: 136085974

4948
Ralph E. Ogden Foundation, Inc. ⌑
Pleasant Hill Rd.
Mountainville 10953

Incorporated in 1947 in DE.

Donor(s): Ralph E. Ogden,† H. Peter Stern, Margaret H. Ogden.†
Foundation type: Independent
Financial data (yr. ended 12/31/89): Assets, $19,212,887 (M); expenditures, $955,888, including $836,155 for 22 grants (high: $739,655; low: $1,000).
Purpose and activities: Support primarily for the arts, especially a local art center; minor support for international relief and affairs, higher education, and community welfare.
Limitations: Giving primarily in Mountainville and New York, NY.
Application information: Contributes only to pre-selected organizations. Applications not accepted.
Officers and Trustees:* H. Peter Stern, Pres.; Leslie A. Jacobson, V.P.; Spencer L. Koslan, Secy.; Eugene L. Cohan, Treas.; Frederick Lubcher, David Sachs, Beatrice Stern, Elisabeth Ellen Stern, John Peter Stern.
Employer Identification Number: 141455902

4949
The Ogilvy Foundation ⌑ ☆
Two East 48th St.
New York 10017-1002

Established in 1984 in NY.
Donor(s): The Ogilvy Group, Inc.
Foundation type: Independent
Financial data (yr. ended 6/30/88): Assets, $1,161,388 (M); gifts received, $96,000; expenditures, $80,761, including $76,500 for 4 grants (high: $25,000; low: $1,500).
Purpose and activities: Giving primarily for wildlife conservation; support also for an outdoor educational program.
Limitations: No grants to individuals.
Application information:
Initial approach: letter
Deadline(s): None
Officers and Directors:* William E. Phillips,* Pres.; John Elliott, Jr.,* V.P.; Graham Phillips,* V.P.; Nancy Nolan, Secy.; John P. Gill,* Treas.; David Ogilvy.
Employer Identification Number: 133230406

4950
Nathan M. Ohrbach Foundation, Inc. ⌑
c/o Mitchell Rabbino
51 East 42nd St., 17th Fl.
New York 10017-5497 (212) 682-8383

Established in 1943 in NY.
Foundation type: Independent
Financial data (yr. ended 04/30/89): Assets, $1,137,136 (M); expenditures, $82,285, including $68,000 for 17 grants (high: $15,000; low: $1,000).
Purpose and activities: Support primarily for higher education, community development, medical research, cultural organizations, youth, and wilderness conservation and the environment.
Limitations: Giving primarily in NY and CA. No grants to individuals.
Application information:
Initial approach: Proposal
Deadline(s): None
Write: Caryl E. Ohrbach, Pres.
Officers and Directors:* Caryl E. Ohrbach,* Pres.; Lisa K. Ohrbach,* V.P.; Thomas Silk, Secy.-Treas.; Barbara Kennedy Martin, Suzan N. Ohrbach, Mitchell W. Rabbino.
Employer Identification Number: 136111585

4951
F. W. Olin Foundation, Inc. ▼
780 Third Ave.
New York 10017 (212) 832-0508
Minnesota address: William B. Horn, V.P., 2700 Foshay Tower, Minneapolis, MN 55402; Tel.: (612) 341-2581

Incorporated in 1938 in NY.
Donor(s): Franklin W. Olin.†
Foundation type: Independent
Financial data (yr. ended 12/31/89): Assets, $263,959,853 (M); expenditures, $10,997,175, including $9,290,658 for 13 grants (high: $5,500,000; low: $5,000; average: $3,000,000-$6,300,000).
Purpose and activities: Primarily for constructing and equipping new academic buildings and libraries at private four-year, accredited, degree-granting colleges and universities, with a preference for funding undergraduate buildings. Awards limited to institutions with enrollment of more than 500 full-time students.
Types of support: Building funds, equipment.
Limitations: No support for colleges and universities with enrollments of less than 500 full-time undergraduate students. No grants to individuals, or for operating budgets, research, scholarships, fellowships, matching gifts, special projects, general support, or non-academic buildings and facilities funds; no loans.
Publications: Program policy statement (including application guidelines).
Application information: Submit original application to New York office and 1 copy to Minneapolis office; geographic location is given negative weight for proposals in areas of previous foundation support, especially during the last 2 years. Application form not required.
Initial approach: Letter (no more than 5 pages)
Copies of proposal: 2
Deadline(s): Submit applications from Jan. 1 to Oct. 31
Board meeting date(s): As required
Final notification: Mar. of following year
Write: Lawrence W. Milas, Pres.
Officers and Directors:* Lawrence W. Milas,* Pres.; William B. Horn,* V.P.; William B. Norden,* Secy. and Counsel; William J. Schmidt,* Treas.
Number of staff: 4 full-time professional; 2 part-time professional; 2 full-time support.
Employer Identification Number: 131820176

4952
John M. Olin Foundation, Inc. ▼
100 Park Ave., Suite 2701
New York 10017 (212) 661-2670

Incorporated in 1953 in DE.
Donor(s): John M. Olin.†
Foundation type: Independent
Financial data (yr. ended 12/31/89): Assets, $90,000,000 (M); gifts received, $4,900,000; expenditures, $16,000,000, including $14,840,000 for grants (high: $2,441,000; low: $1,000; average: $10,000-$200,000).
Purpose and activities: Support for public policy research, strategic and international studies, studies of American political institutions, and law and the legal system, with emphasis on the application of fundamental American principles of freedom and justice.
Types of support: Seed money, research, special projects, publications, conferences and seminars, general purposes, professorships, fellowships, continuing support, lectureships.
Limitations: No support for programs without significant importance for national affairs. No grants to individuals, or for annual campaigns, operating budgets, or building or endowment funds; no loans.
Publications: Annual report (including application guidelines), application guidelines.
Application information: Application form not required.
Initial approach: Proposal
Copies of proposal: 1
Deadline(s): None
Board meeting date(s): 4 times a year
Final notification: Usually within 90 days
Write: James Piereson, Exec. Dir.
Officers and Trustees:* William E. Simon,* Pres.; George J. Gillespie III,* Secy.-Treas.; James Piereson,* Exec. Dir.; Richard M. Furlaud, Charles F. Knight, Walter F. O'Connell, Eugene F. Williams, Jr.
Number of staff: 4 full-time professional; 1 part-time professional; 1 full-time support; 1 part-time support.
Employer Identification Number: 376031033

4953
Olive Bridge Fund, Inc. ⌑
40 Wall St., Rm. 4201
New York 10005

Incorporated in 1952 in NY.
Donor(s): Harold F. Linder.†
Foundation type: Independent
Financial data (yr. ended 12/31/88): Assets, $8,764,509 (M); gifts received, $65,000; expenditures, $268,914, including $171,950 for 97 grants (high: $20,000; low: $25).
Purpose and activities: Grants primarily for higher education and Jewish welfare funds.
Application information: Contributes only to pre-selected organizations. Applications not accepted.
Officers and Directors:* Daniel L. Steiner,* Pres.; William T. Golden,* V.P. and Treas.; Susan E. Linder,* V.P.; Prudence L. Steiner,* V.P.; May L. Linder,* Secy.; Anna Lou Dehavenon.
Employer Identification Number: 136161669

4954
William & Miriam Olsten Foundation, Inc. ⌑ ☆
c/o Milton J. Kain
25 Willets Rd., Box 326
Old Westbury 11568-1522

Donor(s): Miriam Olsten, William Olsten.
Foundation type: Independent
Financial data (yr. ended 12/31/88): Assets, $115,276 (M); gifts received, $100,000;

expenditures, $111,419, including $111,019 for 22 grants (high: $50,000; low: $50).
Purpose and activities: Support for general charitable organizations.
Limitations: No grants to individuals.
Application information: Contributes only to pre-selected organizations. Applications not accepted.
Trustees: Andrew N. Heine, Miriam Olsten, William Olsten.
Employer Identification Number: 133206285

4955
The Oncologic Foundation of Buffalo, Inc. ⌑
225 Oak St.
Buffalo 14203 (716) 855-0183

Established in 1981 in New York.
Donor(s): Photomedica, Inc., Thomas J. Dougherty.
Foundation type: Independent
Financial data (yr. ended 4/30/88): Assets, $5,079,501 (M); gifts received, $560,000; expenditures, $615,000, including $45,000 for 3 grants (average: $10-$15,000) and $16,000 for 1 grant to an individual.
Purpose and activities: Support limited to research in photodynamic therapy.
Types of support: Research, endowment funds.
Application information: Applicant must be researcher employed by research institute or university. Applications not accepted.
Initial approach: Proposal
Write: Kenneth R. Weishaupt, Exec. Dir.
Officers: Thomas J. Dougherty, Pres.; Rev. John Buerk, V.P.; Raymond Riechert, Secy.; Kenneth R. Weishaupt, Treas. and Exec. Dir.
Number of staff: 4 full-time professional; 5 full-time support.
Employer Identification Number: 161183425

4956
Ontario Children's Home ⌑
P.O. Box 82
Canandaigua 14424-0383
Additional address: 3467 West Lake Rd., Canandaigua, NY 14424

Established in 1863 in NY.
Foundation type: Independent
Financial data (yr. ended 9/30/88): Assets, $1,082,009 (M); expenditures, $68,951, including $20,516 for 8 grants (high: $6,756; low: $960), $9,075 for 37 grants to individuals (high: $536; low: $55) and $29,921 for 31 loans to individuals.
Purpose and activities: Giving primarily for child welfare and recreation; support also for student loans.
Types of support: Loans, grants to individuals, student loans.
Limitations: Giving limited to children in Ontario County, NY.
Application information: Application form not required.
Deadline(s): None
Write: Mrs. Arthur Hamlin, Trustee
Officer and Managers: Mrs. James Anlt, Pres.; and 23 other managers.
Employer Identification Number: 166028318

4957
Open Society Fund, Inc. ▼
888 Seventh Ave., 33rd Fl.
New York 10106 (212) 262-6300

Established about 1981 in NY.
Donor(s): George Soros, Tivadar Charitable Lead Trust.
Foundation type: Independent
Financial data (yr. ended 12/31/87): Assets, $2,315,182 (M); gifts received, $530,656; expenditures, $1,551,517, including $1,356,246 for grants (high: $112,000; low: $1,000).
Purpose and activities: Grants for higher education, international studies and affairs, human rights, and the medical sciences. Scholarships to students who are financially or culturally deprived or who are members of racial, religious, or ethnic minorities for studies in the U.S., Europe, Africa, and Asia. Fellowships for scholarly research or analysis, creation of educational materials, or other projects consistent with the charitable purposes of the fund, such as improving or enhancing a literary, artistic, musical, scientific, or other skill or talent. Applicants must be affiliated with an institution.
Types of support: Student aid, fellowships.
Limitations: No grants for No loans to individuals.
Application information:
Write: Sheila Other
Officers: George Soros,* Pres.; Susan Weber,* Exec. V.P., Treas., and Prog. Dir.; Gary Gladstein, V.P. and Secy.
Directors:* Aryeh Neier.
Employer Identification Number: 133095822

4958
Leo Oppenheimer and Flora Oppenheimer Haas Trust ⌑
c/o The Chase Manhattan Bank, N.A., Tax Srvc. Div.
1211 Ave. of the Americas, 36th Fl.
New York 10036

Trust established in 1950 in NY.
Donor(s): Flora Oppenheimer Haas.†
Foundation type: Independent
Financial data (yr. ended 12/31/87): Assets, $7,432,771 (M); expenditures, $544,058, including $486,350 for grants.
Purpose and activities: Grants, out of income only, for the care, aid, and comfort of needy children of the Hebrew faith through grants to established agencies.
Limitations: Giving primarily in the New York, NY, metropolitan area.
Trustees: Maurice Josephberg, Jacob M. Robbins, The Chase Manhattan Bank, N.A.
Employer Identification Number: 136013101

4959
Edward B. Osborn Charitable Trust ⌑
c/o U.S. Trust Co. of New York
114 West 47th St.
New York 10036-1532 (212) 852-1000

Trust established in 1961 in NY.
Donor(s): Edward B. Osborn.
Foundation type: Independent
Financial data (yr. ended 10/31/88): Assets, $3,936,247 (M); expenditures, $345,049, including $302,373 for 55 grants (high: $25,000; low: $500).
Purpose and activities: Giving for hospitals and medical research, with some support for cultural programs, secondary schools, parks, and youth agencies.
Limitations: Giving primarily in NY and FL.
Application information: Application form not required.
Deadline(s): None
Officer and Trustees: James W. Anderson, V.P.; Mrs. Edward B. Osborn, U.S. Trust Co. of New York.
Employer Identification Number: 136071296

4960
Osceola Foundation, Inc. ⌑
51 East 42nd St., Suite 1601
New York 10017

Incorporated in 1963 in NY.
Donor(s): Katherine Sperry Beinecke Trust.
Foundation type: Independent
Financial data (yr. ended 12/31/88): Assets, $3,233,235 (M); expenditures, $474,079, including $277,802 for 77 grants (high: $77,870; low: $15) and $44,627 for 4 grants to individuals (high: $24,740; low: $1,000).
Purpose and activities: Giving primarily for higher education, including scholarships to individuals, and historic preservation, including a rare book library; some support for performing arts organizations.
Types of support: Student aid.
Application information:
Initial approach: Letter
Deadline(s): Prior to end of year; scholarship applications should be made well in advance of tuition due dates
Write: Walter Beinecke, Jr., Pres.
Officers and Directors: Walter Beinecke, Jr., Pres. and Treas.; Perry Ashley, Secy.; Deborah Kinsella Beale, Walter Beinecke III, Barbara Collar, Ann Oliver.
Employer Identification Number: 136094234

4961
OSG Foundation ⌑
1114 Ave. of the Americas, 12th Fl.
New York 10036

Donor(s): Overseas Shipholding Group, Inc.
Foundation type: Company-sponsored
Financial data (yr. ended 12/31/87): Assets, $812,511 (M); gifts received, $348,400; expenditures, $654,269, including $652,781 for 112 grants (high: $150,000; low: $50).
Purpose and activities: Giving for Jewish welfare funds, hospitals, education, and the arts.
Application information: Applications not accepted.
Officers and Directors: Raphael Recanati, Pres.; Michael A. Recanati, V.P. and Secy.-Treas.; Morton P. Hyman, V.P.; Morris Feder.
Employer Identification Number: 133099337

4962
Nicholas B. Ottaway Foundation, Inc. ⌑
P.O. Box 401
Campbell Hall 10916 (914) 294-8181

Established in 1967 in NY.
Donor(s): Members of the Ottway family.

Foundation type: Independent
Financial data (yr. ended 10/31/88): Assets, $339,774 (M); gifts received, $174,332; expenditures, $172,183, including $161,237 for 68 grants (high: $15,000; low: $250).
Purpose and activities: Giving for education, social services, and youth.
Types of support: Scholarship funds.
Application information: Application form not required.
Initial approach: Letter
Deadline(s): Dec. 30
Write: Laura K. Crozier, Secy.
Officers and Trustees: David B. Ottaway, Pres.; Marina S. Ottaway, V.P.; Laura K. Crozier, Secy.; James H. Ottaway, Sr., Treas.; Alexandra H. Ottaway, Christopher H. Ottaway, Eric B. Ottaway, James H. Ottaway, Jr., James W. Ottaway, Ruth B. Ottaway, Frank Alexie Sherer.
Employer Identification Number: 141505939

4963
The Overbrook Foundation ▼ ⌑
521 Fifth Ave., Rm. 1821
New York 10175 (212) 661-8710

Incorporated in 1948 in NY.
Donor(s): Frank Altschul,† Helen G. Altschul,† Arthur G. Altschul, Margaret A. Lang.
Foundation type: Independent
Financial data (yr. ended 12/31/89): Assets, $51,929,293 (M); gifts received, $290,730; expenditures, $2,244,499, including $1,773,232 for 181 grants (high: $330,000; low: $250; average: $1,000-$10,000).
Purpose and activities: Grants for arts and cultural programs, child welfare, civil rights, community funds, environment and conservation, elementary, secondary, and higher education, hospitals, international affairs, medical research, museums, and social services.
Types of support: General purposes.
Limitations: Giving primarily in NY and CT. No grants to individuals.
Application information: Application form not required.
Initial approach: Letter
Deadline(s): None
Board meeting date(s): Usually in Apr. and Nov.
Final notification: Within 3 months
Write: M. Sheila McGoldrick
Officers and Directors:* Arthur G. Altschul,* Pres. and Treas.; Edith A. Graham,* V.P.; Margaret A. Lang,* V.P.; Diana L. Altschul,* Secy.; Stephen F. Altschul, Robert C. Graham, Jr., Frances L. Labaree, Bethuel M. Wester.
Number of staff: 2 part-time professional; 4 part-time support.
Employer Identification Number: 136088860

4964
Overlock Family Foundation ⌑ ☆
c/o Goldman Sachs & Co.
85 Broad St., Tax Dept., 30th Fl.
New York 10004-2408 (212) 902-6897

Established in 1984 in NY.
Donor(s): Willard J. Overlock, Jr.
Foundation type: Independent
Financial data (yr. ended 2/28/89): Assets, $231,272 (M); gifts received, $150,000; expenditures, $176,823, including $176,606 for 81 grants (high: $30,000; low: $100).
Purpose and activities: Giving primarily for elementary education and drug abuse prevention, counseling, and rehabilitation; support also for health and hospitals.
Limitations: Giving primarily in New York, NY. No grants to individuals.
Application information: Contributes only to pre-selected organizations. Applications not accepted.
Trustees: Geoffrey T. Boisi, Katherine S. Overlock, Willard J. Overlock, Jr.
Employer Identification Number: 133247601

4965
PaineWebber Foundation ⌑
1285 Ave. of the Americas
New York 10019 (212) 713-4545

Established in 1983 in NY.
Donor(s): Paine Webber.
Foundation type: Company-sponsored
Financial data (yr. ended 12/31/87): Assets, $2,952,326 (M); expenditures, $155,330, including $110,000 for 8 grants (high: $30,000; low: $5,000).
Purpose and activities: Support for research on economics.
Types of support: Research.
Application information:
Initial approach: Letter
Deadline(s): Dec. 1
Write: Monika Dillon, Trustee
Trustees: Monika Dillon, Paul Guenther, Donald B. Marron.
Employer Identification Number: 046032804

4966
William S. Paley Foundation, Inc.
51 West 52nd St., Rm. 3490
New York 10019 (212) 765-3333

Incorporated in 1936 in NY.
Donor(s): William S. Paley.
Foundation type: Independent
Financial data (yr. ended 12/31/89): Assets, $19,599,451 (M); gifts received, $755,150; expenditures, $1,311,029, including $755,150 for 49 grants (high: $275,000; low: $150).
Purpose and activities: Emphasis on a museum of broadcasting, education, cultural programs, and health services and hospitals.
Types of support: General purposes, annual campaigns, continuing support.
Limitations: Giving primarily in NY. No grants to individuals.
Application information: Application form not required.
Initial approach: Proposal
Copies of proposal: 1
Deadline(s): None
Board meeting date(s): 3rd Wednesday in Oct.
Write: Patrick S. Gallagher, Asst. Secy.
Officers and Directors:* William S. Paley,* Pres.; Sidney W. Harl,* V.P.; John S. Minary,* Secy.; Patrick S. Gallagher,* Treas.; George J. Gillespie III, Kate C. Paley, William C. Paley, Phillip A. Raspe, Jr.
Number of staff: None.
Employer Identification Number: 136085929

4967
The Palisades Educational Foundation, Inc.
c/o Gibney, Anthony & Flaherty
665 Fifth Ave., Suite 200
New York 10022 (201) 461-0170
Application address: 2050 Center Ave., Suite 200, Fort Lee, NJ 07024

Incorporated in 1949 in DE.
Donor(s): Prentice-Hall, Inc.
Foundation type: Independent
Financial data (yr. ended 12/31/88): Assets, $4,638,000 (M); expenditures, $338,017, including $305,200 for 25 grants (high: $75,000; low: $1,000).
Purpose and activities: Giving for hospitals, medical research, and higher and other education.
Types of support: Continuing support, operating budgets, scholarship funds.
Limitations: Giving primarily in areas of company operations, with emphasis on northern NJ, NY, and southern CT. No grants to individuals, or for fellowships; no loans.
Application information:
Initial approach: Letter
Deadline(s): None
Board meeting date(s): Nov. or Dec.
Write: Frank J. Dunnigan, Pres.
Officers: Frank J. Dunnigan,* Pres.; Ralph F. Anthony,* V.P. and Treas.; Frederick W. Anthony, Secy.
Trustees:* Colin Gunn.
Number of staff: None.
Employer Identification Number: 516015053

4968
Palisades Geophysical Institute, Inc. ⌑
180 Route 59
P.O. Box 251
West Nyack 10994 (914) 358-6500

Established in 1970 in NY.
Foundation type: Operating
Financial data (yr. ended 12/31/87): Assets, $1,743,377 (M); expenditures, $2,112,909, including $400,000 for 2 grants (high: $250,000; low: $150,000).
Purpose and activities: A private operating foundation maintaining a research institute. Some support for higher education.
Application information:
Initial approach: Letter
Deadline(s): 1 month before board meeting
Board meeting date(s): Mar.
Write: Catherine M. Acevedo, Secy.
Officers: John Lamar Werzel,* Chair. and Pres.; Dean P. Seifried,* V.P.; Catherine M. Acevedo, Secy.; Frank Mongelli,* Treas.
Directors:* Edwin P. Bledsoe, Robert H. Ewing, W. Arnold Finck, Carl Hartdegen III, Hollis D. Hedberg, Gary V. Latham, Arthur E. Maxwell.
Employer Identification Number: 237069955

4969
The Vincent and Harriet Palisano Foundation ⌑
135 Huntley Rd.
Buffalo 14215

Established in 1962 in NY.

Donor(s): Vincent H. Palisano,† Harriet A. Palisano.†
Foundation type: Independent
Financial data (yr. ended 5/31/88): Assets, $3,579,567 (M); expenditures, $262,938, including $187,976 for 22 grants (high: $50,000; low: $1,500).
Purpose and activities: Emphasis on higher and secondary education, including scholarship aid for selected colleges and high schools in Erie County administered through The Buffalo Foundation; support also for Roman Catholic associations.
Types of support: Scholarship funds.
Limitations: Giving primarily in the Buffalo, NY, area.
Application information: Application form not required.
Write: V.M. DiAngelo
Trustees: James G. Hurley, Charles J. Palisano, Joseph S. Palisano.
Employer Identification Number: 166052186

4970
The Francis Asbury Palmer Fund ⌑ ☆
c/o U.S. Trust Co. of New York
45 Wall St.
New York 10005

Incorporated in 1897 in NY.
Donor(s): Francis Asbury Palmer.†
Foundation type: Independent
Financial data (yr. ended 4/30/88): Assets, $2,466,679 (M); expenditures, $158,792, including $150,000 for 13 grants (high: $12,000; low: $9,000).
Purpose and activities: Support for home missions and educational institutions and Christian ministers and workers; support also for needy persons desiring to become Christian ministers, teachers, or workers and for placing Bible teachers and lecturers in colleges and schools.
Limitations: No grants to individuals.
Application information: Applications not accepted.
Board meeting date(s): May and Nov.
Directors: William A. Chisolm, E. Gayle McGuigan, Jr., Robert P. Patterson, Jr., William H. Sword.
Employer Identification Number: 136400635

4971
Paramount Communications Foundation, Inc. ▼
(Formerly Gulf + Western Foundation, Inc.)
15 Columbus Circle
New York 10023 (212) 373-8508

Incorporated in 1954 in NY.
Donor(s): Paramount Communications, Inc.
Foundation type: Company-sponsored
Financial data (yr. ended 10/31/89): Assets, $153,000 (M); gifts received, $1,900,000; expenditures, $1,916,000, including $1,595,495 for 225 grants (high: $175,000; low: $10; average: $1,000-$5,000) and $320,505 for 763 employee matching gifts.
Purpose and activities: Administers philanthropic giving of operating units on behalf of the corporation. Purposes relate to employee needs or interests and/or business interests of the corporation. Administers an employee matching gifts program.
Types of support: Operating budgets, continuing support, employee matching gifts, employee-related scholarships.
Limitations: Giving primarily in areas of company operations, and to national organizations. No grants to individuals, or for annual campaigns, seed money, emergency funds, deficit financing, equipment, land acquisition, renovation, endowment funds, research, demonstration projects, publications, or conferences; no loans.
Application information: Applications not accepted.
Write: Edward T. Weaver, Pres.
Officers: Samuel J. Silberman,* Chair.; Edward T. Weaver,* Pres.; Elsa M. Rivlin, Secy.; Raymond M. Nowak, Treas.
Trustees:* Donald Oresman.
Number of staff: 1 full-time professional; 1 full-time support.
Employer Identification Number: 136089816

4972
Parapsychology Foundation, Inc.
228 East 71st St.
New York 10021 (212) 628-1550

Incorporated in 1951 in DE.
Foundation type: Operating
Financial data (yr. ended 12/31/89): Assets, $1,720,445 (M); gifts received, $5,638; expenditures, $377,950, including $3,500 for 2 grants (high: $2,000; low: $1,000) and $14,750 for 9 grants to individuals (high: $3,000; low: $500).
Purpose and activities: A private operating foundation; to conduct and further research in parapsychology through an operating program of its own and grants to educational institutions throughout the world.
Types of support: Research, grants to individuals.
Limitations: No grants for building or endowment funds, or operating budgets.
Publications: Annual report, informational brochure, application guidelines.
Application information: Application form required.
Initial approach: Letter
Copies of proposal: 2
Deadline(s): Submit proposal preferably between Jan. and Mar.; no set deadline
Board meeting date(s): Quarterly
Final notification: 4 to 6 weeks
Write: Mrs. Eileen Coly, Pres.
Officers and Trustees:* Eileen Coly,* Pres.; Lisette Coly,* V.P.; Robert R. Coly,* Secy.-Treas.; William Martin, Sandra R. Miller, Stephen E. Powers.
Number of staff: 6 full-time professional.
Employer Identification Number: 131677742

4973
The Park Foundation ⌑
100 East 42nd St., Suite 1850
New York 10017

Incorporated in 1949 in DC.
Donor(s): John P. Kennedy, Jr. Foundation.
Foundation type: Independent
Financial data (yr. ended 12/31/88): Assets, $11,283 (M); gifts received, $183,300; expenditures, $184,677, including $184,395 for grants (high: $19,750).
Purpose and activities: Assistance to "the indigent, sick, and infirm"; emphasis on higher and secondary education and child welfare; support also for rehabilitation of the handicapped, Roman Catholic welfare agencies, and cultural programs.
Types of support: General purposes.
Limitations: Giving primarily in NY, MA, and DC.
Application information: Application form not required.
Deadline(s): None
Write: Richard S. Waite, Asst. Treas.
Officers: Jean K. Smith,* V.P.; Joseph E. Hakim, Treas.
Trustees:* Stephen E. Smith.
Employer Identification Number: 136163065

4974
E. & H. Parnes Foundation, Inc. ⌑
1606 49th St.
Brooklyn 11204-1133

Established in 1971 in NY.
Donor(s): Emanuel Parnes, Herschel Parnes.
Foundation type: Independent
Financial data (yr. ended 06/30/89): Assets, $4,960,741 (M); gifts received, $172,196; expenditures, $125,118, including $117,230 for 28 grants (high: $20,000; low: $50).
Purpose and activities: Support primarily for Jewish giving.
Application information:
Write: Herschel Parnes, Mgr.
Managers: Emanuel Parnes, Herschel Parnes.
Employer Identification Number: 237237932

4975
Moses L. Parshelsky Foundation
26 Court St., Rm. 904
Brooklyn 11242 (718) 875-8883

Trust established in 1949 in NY.
Donor(s): Moses L. Parshelsky.
Foundation type: Independent
Financial data (yr. ended 12/31/89): Assets, $5,576,010 (M); expenditures, $327,938, including $293,850 for 61 grants (high: $30,000; low: $100; average: $100-$30,000).
Purpose and activities: Emphasis on hospitals, higher and secondary education, and temple support and religious activities; grants also for care of the aged, the handicapped, youth agencies, mental health, and Jewish welfare funds.
Limitations: Giving primarily in Brooklyn and Queens, NY. No grants to individuals, or for building or endowment funds, or operating budgets.
Application information: Application form not required.
Initial approach: Letter
Copies of proposal: 1
Deadline(s): May 31
Board meeting date(s): Monthly
Write: Tony B. Berk, Trustee
Trustees: Tony B. Berk, Josephine B. Krinsky, Robert D. Krinsky.
Number of staff: 1 part-time professional.
Employer Identification Number: 111848260

4976
Betty Parsons Foundation ☆
c/o Brauner, Baron, et al
61 Broadway, 18th Fl.
New York 10006-2802 (212) 797-9100

Established in 1983 in NY.
Donor(s): Betty Parsons.†
Foundation type: Independent
Financial data (yr. ended 08/31/88): Assets, $2,699,561 (M); expenditures, $48,095, including $25,500 for 5 grants (high: $10,000; low: $150).
Purpose and activities: Giving for "1) programs for the development of modern art, and 2) programs for the protection or conservation of the seas." Support also for youth.
Types of support: General purposes, in-kind gifts.
Limitations: Giving primarily in NY.
Publications: Annual report, application guidelines, 990-PF.
Application information:
Initial approach: Letter or proposal
Deadline(s): None
Write: Christopher C. Schwabacher, V.P.
Officers: William P. Rayner, Pres. and Treas.; Christopher C. Schwabacher, V.P. and Secy.
Director: Chasbrough H. Rayner.
Number of staff: 1 part-time professional.
Employer Identification Number: 133193737

4977
Martin Paskus Foundation, Inc. ⌑
230 Park Ave.
New York 10017

Established in 1950 in NY.
Donor(s): Elsie Paskus.†
Foundation type: Independent
Financial data (yr. ended 12/31/87): Assets, $303,757 (M); expenditures, $128,047, including $126,000 for 3 grants (high: $100,000; low: $1,000).
Purpose and activities: Support for education.
Application information: Contributes only to pre-selected organizations. Applications not accepted.
Officers: Richard P. Danziger, Pres.; Frederick M. Danziger, Treas.
Employer Identification Number: 510166266

4978
Josephine Bay Paul and C. Michael Paul Foundation, Inc.
c/o Martin L. Schneider Associates
12 Monroe Pl.
Brooklyn 11201-2630 (718) 875-5100

Incorporated in 1962 in NY.
Donor(s): Josephine Bay Paul.†
Foundation type: Independent
Financial data (yr. ended 1/31/88): Assets, $2,821,533 (M); expenditures, $449,921, including $220,060 for 41 grants (high: $65,000; low: $1,000).
Purpose and activities: Grants for professional chamber music ensembles, selected festivals or presenters, and conservatories to promote chamber music and career development opportunities for performers.
Types of support: Continuing support, operating budgets, general purposes, matching funds, seed money, special projects, technical assistance.
Publications: Program policy statement, 990-PF.
Application information: Application form not required.
Initial approach: Letter
Copies of proposal: 1
Deadline(s): Preferably Jan. and Aug.
Board meeting date(s): Apr. and Oct.
Write: Frederick Bay, Pres. and Exec. Dir.
Officers and Directors: Synnova B. Hayes, Chair.; Frederick Bay, Pres. and Exec. Dir.; Daniel A. Demarest, Secy.; Hans A. Ege, Treas.
Number of staff: 1 part-time professional; 1 part-time support.
Employer Identification Number: 131991717

4979
Henry M. Paulson, Jr. & Wendy J. Paulson Foundation ⌑ ☆
c/o Goldman, Sachs & Co., Tax Dept.
85 Broad St.
New York 10004

Established in 1985 in NY.
Donor(s): Henry M. Paulson, Jr.
Foundation type: Independent
Financial data (yr. ended 3/31/89): Assets, $351,544 (M); gifts received, $43,142; expenditures, $109,165, including $107,095 for 49 grants (high: $20,000; low: $45).
Purpose and activities: Support primarily for Christian Science churches, environmental conservation and wildlife preservation, and higher education; minor support for the arts.
Types of support: General purposes.
Limitations: Giving primarily in Barrington and Chicago, IL. No grants to individuals; no loans.
Application information: Contributes only to pre-selected organizations. Applications not accepted.
Trustees: Henry M. Paulson, Jr., Marianna G. Paulson, Wendy J. Paulson.
Employer Identification Number: 942988627

4980
PBP Foundation of New York, Inc. ⌑
c/o Willkie, Farr and Gallagher
153 East 53rd St.
New York 10022 (212) 935-8000

Incorporated in 1978 in NY.
Donor(s): Fiona F. Beck.
Foundation type: Independent
Financial data (yr. ended 12/31/88): Assets, $34,618 (M); gifts received, $210,425; expenditures, $199,595, including $172,500 for 8 grants (high: $120,000; low: $1,000).
Purpose and activities: Emphasis on public policy, equal rights, and political science; support also for media and for higher education.
Types of support: General purposes, annual campaigns, building funds, operating budgets, special projects, fellowships.
Application information:
Initial approach: Letter
Deadline(s): None
Write: Arthur D. Kowaloff, Treas.
Officers and Directors:* Stuart J. Beck,* Pres.; Fiona Field,* V.P.; Arthur D. Kowaloff,* Treas.
Employer Identification Number: 132939192

4981
Henry and Rose Pearlman Foundation, Inc. ⌑
c/o Gettry Marcus Stern & Lehrer
220 Fifth Ave.
New York 10001 (212) 684-3399

Incorporated in 1953 in NY.
Donor(s): Henry Pearlman,† Rose Pearlman, Eastern Cold Storage Insulation Co., Inc.
Foundation type: Operating
Financial data (yr. ended 11/30/88): Assets, $20,775,561 (M); gifts received, $20,000; expenditures, $19,985, including $19,900 for 31 grants (high: $5,500; low: $25).
Purpose and activities: A private operating foundation; grants locally for museums, arts organizations, social service agencies, and Jewish welfare organizations.
Limitations: Giving primarily in NY.
Application information: Application form not required.
Deadline(s): None
Write: Rose Pearlman, Pres.
Officers and Directors: Rose Pearlman, Pres.; Alex W. Pearlman, V.P.; Marge Scheuer, Secy.; Dorothy Edelman, Treas.
Employer Identification Number: 136159092

4982
The Peierls Foundation, Inc. ⌑
c/o Bankers Trust Co.
P.O. Box 829, Church St. Station
New York 10008

Incorporated in 1956 in NY.
Donor(s): Edgar S. Peierls.†
Foundation type: Independent
Financial data (yr. ended 10/31/88): Assets, $4,288,052 (M); expenditures, $238,576, including $204,393 for 31 grants (high: $36,793; low: $2,500).
Purpose and activities: Grants primarily for youth and social service agencies, aid to the handicapped, minority rights and opportunities programs, higher education, medical research, and population control.
Limitations: No grants to individuals.
Application information: Application form not required.
Deadline(s): None
Write: Walter Johnson, V.P., Bankers Trust Co.
Officers: E.J. Peierls, Pres.; Brian Eliot Peierls, V.P. and Treas.; Ethel Peierls, Secy.
Employer Identification Number: 136082503

4983
James C. Penney Foundation, Inc.
1633 Broadway, 39th Fl.
New York 10019 (212) 830-7490

Incorporated in 1954 in NY.
Donor(s): James C. Penney,† Caroline A. Penney.
Foundation type: Independent
Financial data (yr. ended 12/31/89): Assets, $5,714,894 (M); expenditures, $623,858, including $460,513 for 50 grants (high: $10,000; low: $3,500; average: $7,000-$7,500).
Purpose and activities: The Foundation's primary mission is to empower and benefit people who are economically and politically

disenfranchised. Giving primarily for special projects, with emphasis on community-based organizations operating in the areas of environment, especially toxic waste clean-up, low income/homeless housing, domestic violence, teenage pregnancy prevention, economic development, employment, homelessness, social and economic justice.
Types of support: Special projects, general purposes, operating budgets, program-related investments, seed money, technical assistance.
Limitations: Giving limited to the Northeast and Appalachia, including CT, NY, MA, ME, PA, VT, NH, MD, KY, WV, TN, NJ, NC, and DC. No support for medical, educational, or cultural institutions. No grants to individuals, or for capital improvements, endowments, scholarships, media, research, conferences, or for film or media presentations.
Publications: Multi-year report, grants list, application guidelines.
Application information: New requests for support not presently being accepted; will accept new requests beginning in 1991. Application form required.
Initial approach: Letter
Copies of proposal: 1
Deadline(s): None
Board meeting date(s): 3 times per year
Final notification: 1 to 6 months
Write: Anne L. Romasco, Managing Dir.
Administrator: Anne L. Romasco, Managing Dir.
Officers and Directors: Carol P. Guyer, Pres.; Mary Frances Wagley, V.P. and Treas.; Andrew W. Bisset, Secy.; Mary Wagley Copp, Anne W. Gow, Shelly D. Guyer, Alissa C. Keny-Guyer, Caroline A. Penney, James F. Wagley.
Number of staff: 1 full-time professional; 1 full-time support.
Employer Identification Number: 136114301

4984
Penzance Foundation ▼
237 Park Ave., 21st Fl.
New York 10017 (212) 551-3559

Established in 1981 in DE.
Donor(s): Edna McConnell Clark.†
Foundation type: Independent
Financial data (yr. ended 04/30/89): Assets, $45,240,527 (M); expenditures, $2,112,645, including $1,935,150 for 12 grants (high: $500,000; low: $5,000).
Purpose and activities: During its early years of operation, the foundation's grantmaking will reflect personal preferences of donor.
Types of support: General purposes.
Limitations: No grants to individuals.
Application information: Applications not accepted.
Write: John M. Emery, V.P.
Officers and Trustees:* Hays Clark,* Pres.; John M. Emery,* V.P. and Secy.; James McConnell Clark,* V.P. and Treas.
Number of staff: 1
Employer Identification Number: 133081557

4985
PepsiCo Foundation, Inc. ▼ ⌑
700 Anderson Hill Rd.
Purchase 10577 (914) 253-3153

Incorporated in 1962 in NY.
Donor(s): PepsiCo, Inc., Frito-Lay, Inc.
Foundation type: Company-sponsored
Financial data (yr. ended 12/31/87): Assets, $15,053,941 (M); gifts received, $20,341,635; expenditures, $5,641,086, including $5,639,251 for 1,956 grants (high: $484,383; low: $20).
Purpose and activities: Support for education and other non-profit organizations where employees are involved as volunteers.
Types of support: Employee matching gifts.
Limitations: Giving primarily in areas of company operations in NY; and to national and regional organizations. No grants to individuals.
Publications: Informational brochure, program policy statement, application guidelines.
Application information:
Initial approach: Proposal
Deadline(s): None
Board meeting date(s): At least annually
Final notification: Within 3 months
Write: Jacqueline R. Millan, V.P., Contribs.
Officers: Donald M. Kendall,* Chair.; Joseph F. McCann,* Pres.; Jacqueline R. Millan, V.P., Contribs.; Douglas Cram, Secy.; Claudia Morf, Treas.
Directors:* D. Wayne Calloway, Robert G. Dettmer, Roger A. Enrico, Michael H. Jordan, Harvey C. Russell.
Number of staff: 2 full-time professional; 2 full-time support.
Employer Identification Number: 136163174

4986
The George W. Perkins Memorial Foundation ⌑
660 Madison Ave.
New York 10021

Incorporated in 1961 in NY.
Donor(s): Mrs. George W. Perkins.
Foundation type: Independent
Financial data (yr. ended 12/31/88): Assets, $8,266,848 (M); expenditures, $452,265, including $397,000 for 51 grants (high: $35,000; low: $1,000).
Purpose and activities: Grants largely for higher and secondary education, hospitals, and conservation.
Application information: Contributes only to pre-selected organizations. Applications not accepted.
Officers: Linn M. Perkins, Pres.; George W. Perkins, Jr., V.P.; Penelope P. Wilson, V.P.; Anne P. Cabot, Secy.
Trustees: Antoinette Burns, Arthur V. Savage.
Employer Identification Number: 136085859

4987
Fred & Gertrude Perlberg Foundation, Inc. ⌑ ☆
c/o William F. Sullivan
100 Merrick Rd., No. 510E
Rockville Centre 11570-3813

Established in 1956.
Donor(s): Perlberg Holding Corp.
Foundation type: Independent
Financial data (yr. ended 7/31/88): Assets, $1,006,146 (M); gifts received, $45,000; expenditures, $48,853, including $42,610 for 57 grants (high: $10,000; low: $25).
Purpose and activities: Giving primarily for Jewish organizations, especially a welfare fund; support also for the fine and performing arts, hospitals, and higher and other education.
Limitations: Giving primarily in NY and FL.
Application information:
Deadline(s): None
Write: Fred Perlberg, Pres.
Officers: Fred Perlberg, Pres.; Gertrude Perlberg, Secy.; Edward Perlberg, Treas.
Employer Identification Number: 136100032

4988
Victor E. Perley Fund
One Irving Place Park, No. 28C
New York 10003

Established in 1967 in NY.
Foundation type: Independent
Financial data (yr. ended 12/31/89): Assets, $2,900,000 (M); expenditures, $210,000, including $140,000 for 9 grants (high: $30,000; low: $3,000).
Purpose and activities: Giving primarily for underprivileged children.
Limitations: Giving primarily in New York, NY.
Application information:
Initial approach: Letter
Deadline(s): None
Write: Joseph J. Famularo, Trustee
Trustees: Rabbi Irving Block, H. Daniel Carpenter, Joseph J. Famularo, Barry McCarthy, Rev. Albert Neibacher.
Number of staff: None.
Employer Identification Number: 136219298

4989
The Perrin Foundation ⌑ ☆
72 Reade St.
New York 10007
Application address: 926 Coolidge St., Westfield, NJ 07090; Tel.: (201) 295-5944

Established in 1928.
Donor(s): Mary Ricks.
Foundation type: Independent
Financial data (yr. ended 12/31/88): Assets, $668,472 (M); gifts received, $50,000; expenditures, $106,872, including $105,000 for 6 grants (high: $81,600; low: $300).
Purpose and activities: Giving limited to Christian organizations, including churches, missionary programs, and schools.
Limitations: No grants to individuals.
Application information: Application form not required.
Deadline(s): None
Write: John G. Jeffers, Pres.
Officers: John G. Jeffers, Pres. and Treas.; Curtis B. Myers, V.P.; George C. Sharp, Secy.
Directors: Robert Q. Bennett, Francis B. Macmillan, Mary Ricks.
Employer Identification Number: 226049335

4990
The Pfizer Foundation, Inc. ▼
235 East 42nd St.
New York 10017 (212) 573-3351

Incorporated in 1953 in NY.
Donor(s): Pfizer Inc.
Foundation type: Company-sponsored
Financial data (yr. ended 12/31/89): Assets, $2,986,631 (M); expenditures, $1,198,234, including $1,198,000 for 142 grants (high: $100,000; low: $1,000; average: $1,000-$5,000).
Purpose and activities: Grants primarily for higher and other education, health, hospitals, and medicine, civic and community welfare, arts and culture, international affairs, and social services for the disabled, youth, the aged, and women.
Types of support: Operating budgets, continuing support, annual campaigns, seed money, emergency funds, building funds, equipment, matching funds, professorships, internships, scholarship funds, fellowships, special projects, research, publications, conferences and seminars, capital campaigns, endowment funds, exchange programs, technical assistance.
Limitations: Giving primarily in areas of company operations, with emphasis on local New York City or national organizations. No support for religious organizations for religious purposes, veterans', fraternal or labor organizations, non tax-exempt foundations, or anti-business organizations. No grants to individuals, or for deficit financing, employee matching gifts, goodwill advertising, or land acquisition; no loans.
Publications: Corporate giving report (including application guidelines).
Application information: Application form not required.
Initial approach: Proposal
Copies of proposal: 1
Deadline(s): None
Board meeting date(s): As required
Final notification: 3 months
Write: Wyndham Anderson, Exec. V.P.
Officers and Directors:* Robert A. Wilson,* Pres.; Wyndham Anderson,* Exec. V.P.; James R. Gardner,* V.P.; Terence J. Gallagher,* Secy.; Kevin S. Keating,* Treas.
Number of staff: None.
Employer Identification Number: 136083839

4991
The Carl and Lily Pforzheimer Foundation, Inc. ▼
650 Madison Ave., 23rd Fl.
New York 10022 (212) 223-6500

Incorporated in 1942 in NY.
Donor(s): Members of the Pforzheimer family and others.
Foundation type: Independent
Financial data (yr. ended 12/31/87): Assets, $26,351,311 (M); expenditures, $885,880, including $454,062 for 18 grants (high: $80,000; low: $2,000).
Purpose and activities: Maintains publishing and research activities in connection with the Carl H. Pforzheimer Library collection at the New York Public Library in the general field of American and English literature; giving primarily for higher and secondary education; support also for cultural programs, a national municipal organization, and health care.
Types of support: Seed money, professorships, internships, scholarship funds, endowment funds, fellowships, matching funds, program-related investments, publications, special projects.
Limitations: No grants to individuals, or for building funds; no loans.
Application information:
Initial approach: Letter or proposal
Copies of proposal: 1
Deadline(s): None
Board meeting date(s): Apr., June, Oct., and Dec.
Final notification: Immediately following board meeting, generally
Write: Carl H. Pforzheimer, Jr., Pres.
Officers and Directors:* Carl H. Pforzheimer, Jr.,* Pres.; Carl H. Pforzheimer III,* V.P. and Treas.; Martin F. Richman, Secy.; Nancy P. Aronson, Richard W. Couper, George Frelinghuysen, Carol K. Pforzheimer.
Number of staff: 3 full-time professional; 2 full-time support.
Employer Identification Number: 135624374

4992
Philippe Foundation, Inc.
122 East 42nd St.
New York 10168 (212) 687-3290

Incorporated in 1953 in NY.
Donor(s): Pierre Philippe.
Foundation type: Independent
Financial data (yr. ended 12/31/88): Assets, $2,690,852 (M); gifts received, $99,137; expenditures, $158,985, including $143,430 for 61 grants to individuals (high: $12,760; low: $522; average: $1,000-$6,000).
Purpose and activities: Grants to individuals for advanced study and scientific research; exchange of doctors between the U.S. and France.
Types of support: Internships, exchange programs, research, conferences and seminars, grants to individuals, fellowships.
Publications: Application guidelines.
Application information: Application form not required.
Initial approach: Letter
Deadline(s): 1st day of board meeting months
Board meeting date(s): Mar., June, Sept., and Dec.
Final notification: 3 months
Write: Merton Holman, V.P.
Officers and Directors:* Beatrice Philippe,* Pres.; Merton Holman,* V.P. and Secy.-Treas.; Anne Marie Philippe,* V.P.; Helene P. Grenier, Marie-Josette Larrieu, Irving London, Alain Philippe, Anne Philippe.
Number of staff: None.
Employer Identification Number: 136087157

4993
Charlotte Palmer Phillips Foundation, Inc.
c/o Walter, Conston, Alexander & Green
90 Park Ave.
New York 10016 (212) 210-9400

Incorporated in 1958 in NY.
Donor(s): Charlotte Palmer Phillips.†
Foundation type: Independent
Financial data (yr. ended 12/31/88): Assets, $1,696,548 (M); expenditures, $93,201, including $59,000 for 34 grants (high: $6,500; low: $100).
Purpose and activities: Grants primarily for higher and secondary education, church support, and hospitals and medical research.
Types of support: Operating budgets, continuing support, building funds, equipment, endowment funds, scholarship funds.
Limitations: No loans.
Application information: Contributes only to pre-selected organizations. Applications not accepted.
Board meeting date(s): May
Write: Robert L. Strong, Pres.
Officers and Trustees: Robert L. Strong, Pres. and Treas.; James R. Cogan, Secy.; Rev. George T. Cook, Charles E. Rogers.
Number of staff: 1 part-time professional.
Employer Identification Number: 136100994

4994
Phillips-Van Heusen Foundation, Inc. ⌑
1290 Ave. of the Americas
New York 10104 (212) 541-5200

Incorporated in NY in 1969.
Donor(s): Phillips-Van Heusen Corp., and others.
Foundation type: Company-sponsored
Financial data (yr. ended 12/31/87): Assets, $1,962,281 (M); gifts received, $1,169,525; expenditures, $447,227, including $443,850 for 97 grants (high: $100,000; low: $100).
Purpose and activities: Emphasis on Jewish organizations, including those in Israel, community funds, health and hospitals, and higher education; support also for child welfare, youth and social service agencies, and international affairs; the corporation runs a clothing bank and donates clothes and shoes to the homeless.
Types of support: Operating budgets, continuing support, annual campaigns, emergency funds, special projects, research.
Limitations: No grants to individuals.
Application information:
Initial approach: Letter
Board meeting date(s): Sept.
Write: Lawrence S. Phillips, Chair.
Officers: Lawrence S. Phillips, Chair.; Irwin W. Winter, V.P. and Treas.; Bruce J. Klatsky, V.P.; Pamela Hootkin, Secy.
Number of staff: None.
Employer Identification Number: 237104639

4995
Tatiana Piankova Foundation ⌑
570 Park Ave., Suite 1A
New York 10021

Established about 1983 in NY.
Donor(s): Susan Polachek.
Foundation type: Independent
Financial data (yr. ended 7/31/89): Assets, $2,509,166 (M); expenditures, $115,817, including $99,915 for 22 grants (high: $30,500; low: $65).

Purpose and activities: Giving primarily for the arts, cultural institutions, and social service organizations.
Limitations: No grants to individuals.
Application information: Contributes only to pre-selected organizations. Applications not accepted.
Write: Mildred C. Brinn, V.P.
Officers and Directors: Mildred C. Brinn, V.P. and Treas.; Peter F. De Gaetano, Secy.
Employer Identification Number: 133142090

4996
Picotte Family Foundation Trust ⌑ ☆
120 Washington Ave.
P.O. Box 219
Albany 12210-0219

Established in 1987 in NY.
Donor(s): Picotte Charitable Lead Trusts, Kathleen M. Picotte.
Foundation type: Independent
Financial data (yr. ended 07/31/89): Assets, $127,600 (M); gifts received, $226,250; expenditures, $159,048, including $152,000 for 23 grants (high: $30,000; low: $500).
Purpose and activities: Support primarily for higher and other education and hospitals.
Limitations: Giving primarily in the Albany, NY, area. No grants to individuals.
Application information: Contributes only to pre-selected organizations. Applications not accepted.
Trustees: Rhea P. Clark, Marcia P. Floyd, John D. Picotte, Kathleen M. Picotte, Michael B. Picotte.
Employer Identification Number: 141699412

4997
The Lionel I. Pincus Foundation, Inc. ⌑
466 Lexington Ave.
New York 10017

Established in 1961 in NY.
Donor(s): Lionel I. Pincus.
Foundation type: Independent
Financial data (yr. ended 12/31/88): Assets, $3,490,577 (M); gifts received, $500,000; expenditures, $517,606, including $511,000 for 20 grants (high: $110,000; low: $1,000).
Purpose and activities: Grants for higher education, health services, and Jewish giving.
Limitations: Giving primarily in NY. No grants to individuals.
Application information: Contributes only to pre-selected organizations. Applications not accepted.
Officers: Lionel I. Pincus, Pres.; Suzanne Pincus, V.P.; Kenneth T. Bialkin, Secy.
Employer Identification Number: 136089184

4998
Pine Level Foundation, Inc. ⌑
c/o Ernst & Whinney
787 Seventh Ave.
New York 10019

Incorporated in 1968 in CT as a successor to the Stetson Foundation, a trust established in 1936 in CT.
Donor(s): Iola Wise Stetson.
Foundation type: Independent
Financial data (yr. ended 12/31/87): Assets, $1,108,172 (M); expenditures, $94,083, including $74,264 for 72 grants (high: $6,000; low: $250).
Purpose and activities: Giving for cultural programs, conservation, education, and health agencies.
Limitations: Giving primarily in CT and NY.
Application information: Application form not required.
Initial approach: Letter
Deadline(s): None
Write: Iola Haverstick, Pres.
Officers and Directors: Iola Haverstick, Pres.; Elizabeth Kratovil, V.P.; S. Alexander Haverstick, Secy.
Employer Identification Number: 237008912

4999
Pine Street Foundation ⌑ ☆
1251 Ave. of the Americas
New York 10020-1104

Donor(s): R.W. Ash,† T.A. Donahoe,† T.L. Raleigh.†
Foundation type: Independent
Financial data (yr. ended 10/31/88): Assets, $286,154 (M); gifts received, $20,000; expenditures, $113,929, including $109,180 for grants.
Purpose and activities: Support for higher education, community funds, family planning, and cultural programs.
Limitations: No grants to individuals.
Application information: Contributes only to pre-selected organizations. Applications not accepted.
Officers: Harold Haddock, Jr., Pres.; James E. Daley, V.P.; Dominic A. Tarantino, V.P.; Charles E. Hoagland, Secy.-Treas.
Employer Identification Number: 136119394

5000
The Pines Bridge Foundation ⌑ ☆
1114 Ave. of the Americas, Suite 3400
New York 10036

Established in 1986 in NY.
Foundation type: Independent
Financial data (yr. ended 11/30/88): Assets, $877,616 (M); expenditures, $190,793, including $187,450 for 42 grants (high: $50,000; low: $100).
Purpose and activities: Support for higher education and cultural programs, including performing arts groups and museums.
Limitations: Giving primarily in New York, NY. No grants to individuals.
Application information: Contributes only to pre-selected organizations. Applications not accepted.
Write: Alan G. Weiler, Trustee
Trustees: Alan G. Weiler, Elaine Weiler.
Employer Identification Number: 136872045

5001
Pinewood Foundation ▼ ⌑
100 Park Ave.
New York 10017

Incorporated in 1956 in NY as Celeste and Armand Bartos Foundation.
Donor(s): Celeste G. Bartos, D.S. and R.H. Gottesman Foundation.
Foundation type: Independent
Financial data (yr. ended 10/31/88): Assets, $10,096,334 (M); expenditures, $1,561,432, including $1,428,450 for 58 grants (high: $200,300; low: $38).
Purpose and activities: Giving for higher education and cultural programs, with emphasis on the arts.
Limitations: Giving primarily in New York, NY.
Application information: Contributes only to pre-selected organizations. Applications not accepted.
Officers: Celeste G. Bartos,* Pres.; Armand P. Bartos,* V.P.; Edgar Wachenheim III, V.P.; Peter C. Siegfried, Secy.; Benjamin Glowatz, Treas.
Directors:* Adam Bartos.
Employer Identification Number: 136101581

5002
Ann Pinkerton Charitable Trust ⌑
c/o Morgan Guaranty Trust Co. of New York
616 Madison Ave.
New York 10153
Application address: c/o Morgan Guaranty Trust Co., 725 Park Ave., New York, NY 10021

Established in 1977 in NY.
Foundation type: Independent
Financial data (yr. ended 12/31/88): Assets, $1,908,165 (M); expenditures, $100,917, including $83,000 for 13 grants (high: $25,000; low: $2,000).
Purpose and activities: Giving primarily for civic organizations; support also for a school, an orchestra, and social service agencies.
Types of support: General purposes.
Limitations: Giving primarily in NY, including the East End of Long Island.
Application information:
Initial approach: Letter
Deadline(s): None
Write: Joan Colello, Advisory Committee
Advisory Committee: Joan Colello, George J. Gillespie.
Trustee: Morgan Guaranty Trust Co. of New York.
Employer Identification Number: 136747629

5003
The Pinkerton Foundation ⌑
725 Park Ave.
New York 10021 (212) 772-6110

Incorporated in 1966 in DE.
Donor(s): Robert A. Pinkerton.†
Foundation type: Independent
Financial data (yr. ended 12/31/87): Assets, $10,861,790 (M); expenditures, $560,484, including $485,946 for 25 grants (high: $100,000; low: $500).
Purpose and activities: Giving for the prevention of crime and juvenile delinquency; emphasis on youth training and employment programs and special education.
Limitations: Giving primarily in NY. No grants to individuals.
Publications: 990-PF.
Application information:
Initial approach: Letter
Copies of proposal: 1

Deadline(s): Submit proposal preferably in Apr. or Oct.
Board meeting date(s): June and Dec.
Write: Ms. Joan Colello, Secy.
Officers and Trustees: Edward J. Bednarz, Chair.; George J. Gillespie III, Pres.; Joan Colello, Secy. and Exec. Dir.; Eugene C. Fey, Treas.; Michael S. Joyce, John C. Overhiser, Thomas J. Sweeney.
Employer Identification Number: 136206624

5004
The Pioneer Fund, Inc.
299 Park Ave.
New York 10171 (212) 207-1808

Incorporated in 1937 in NY.
Foundation type: Independent
Financial data (yr. ended 12/31/89): Assets, $6,057,000 (M); expenditures, $888,000, including $797,000 for 17 grants (high: $105,000; low: $3,000).
Purpose and activities: Education and research in heredity and eugenics and psychology; support also for immigration reform.
Types of support: Research.
Limitations: No grants to individuals.
Application information: Application form not required.
Deadline(s): None
Board meeting date(s): Annually
Write: Harry F. Weyher, Pres.
Officers and Directors: Harry F. Weyher, Pres.; John B. Trevor, Jr., Treas.; William D. Miller, Marion A. Parrott, Randolph L. Speight.
Number of staff: None.
Employer Identification Number: 510242968

5005
Henry B. Plant Memorial Fund, Inc. ⌑
c/o U.S. Trust Co. of New York
114 West 47th St.
New York 10036-1532

Incorporated in 1947 in NY.
Donor(s): Amy P. Statter.
Foundation type: Independent
Financial data (yr. ended 12/31/88): Assets, $5,463,547 (M); expenditures, $278,702, including $241,000 for 81 grants (high: $30,000; low: $500).
Purpose and activities: Emphasis on hospitals, population control, cultural programs, the environment, and health agencies.
Limitations: Giving primarily in NY.
Application information:
Initial approach: Letter
Deadline(s): None
Officers: Mrs. J. Phillip Lee, Pres.; Phyllis S. Oxman, V.P.
Advisor: U.S. Trust Co. of New York.
Employer Identification Number: 136077327

5006
Pluta Family Foundation, Inc. ⌑
3385 Brighton Henriette Town Line Rd.
Rochester 14623

Incorporated in 1966 in NY.
Donor(s): James Pluta, Helen Pluta, Peter Pluta, Mrs. Peter Pluta, General Circuits, Inc., Pluta Manufacturing Corp.
Foundation type: Independent
Financial data (yr. ended 12/31/87): Assets, $3,574,193 (M); expenditures, $305,434, including $270,000 for 5 grants (high: $150,000; low: $5,000) and $22,172 for 37 grants to individuals of $600 each.
Purpose and activities: Support for hospitals and higher education, including scholarship funds and student aid for General Circuits employees and their families.
Types of support: Scholarship funds, employee-related scholarships.
Limitations: Giving limited to Monroe County, NY.
Application information:
Initial approach: Letter
Board meeting date(s): Semiannually
Officer and Directors: Peter Pluta, Pres.; Andrew Pluta, John Pluta.
Employer Identification Number: 510176213

5007
Plymouth Foundation, Inc. ⌑
c/o I.N. Burnham, II
60 Broad St., 11th Fl.
New York 10004

Established in 1957 in NY.
Donor(s): Members of the Burnham family.
Foundation type: Independent
Financial data (yr. ended 12/31/86): Assets, $79,539 (M); gifts received, $124,092; expenditures, $143,938, including $142,479 for 86 grants (high: $12,000; low: $20).
Purpose and activities: Giving for Jewish welfare, social services, and civic affairs.
Application information: Contributes only to pre-selected organizations. Applications not accepted.
Officer: I.N. Burnham II, Pres.
Director: Jon Burnham.
Employer Identification Number: 136163070

5008
The Pollock-Krasner Foundation, Inc. ⌑
725 Park Ave.
New York 10021 (212) 517-5400
Application address: P.O. Box 4957, New York, NY 10185; FAX No.: (212) 288-2836

Established in 1984 in DE.
Donor(s): Lee Krasner.†
Foundation type: Independent
Financial data (yr. ended 6/30/88): Assets, $24,101,514 (M); expenditures, $1,588,728, including $833,175 for 94 grants to individuals (high: $25,000; low: $1,000).
Purpose and activities: Giving exclusively to needy and worthy individual working artists (painters, sculptors, and graphic and mixed-media artists) who have embarked on professional careers; grants may be used for professional or personal requirements.
Types of support: Grants to individuals.
Limitations: No support for organizations or institutions; no individual grants to students, photographers, commercial or performance artists, or craftsmen. No grants for no tuition payments.
Publications: Informational brochure (including application guidelines), annual report, application guidelines.
Application information: Application form required.
Initial approach: Letter
Deadline(s): None
Board meeting date(s): Regularly throughout the year
Final notification: As soon as possible
Write: Charles C. Bergman, Exec. V.P.
Officers and Directors:* Gerald Dickler,* Chair.; Eugene Victor Thaw,* Pres.; Charles C. Bergman, Exec. V.P.
Number of staff: 6 full-time professional; 1 part-time professional; 2 full-time support.
Employer Identification Number: 133255693

5009
The Pope Foundation ▼ ⌑
211 West 56th St., Suite 5-E
New York 10019

Incorporated in 1947 in NY.
Donor(s): Generoso Pope.†
Foundation type: Independent
Financial data (yr. ended 12/31/86): Assets, $22,376,153 (M); expenditures, $1,463,953, including $1,177,500 for 65 grants (high: $201,490; low: $250; average: $1,000-$50,000).
Purpose and activities: Emphasis on Roman Catholic church support, religious associations and welfare funds, higher and secondary education, and hospitals.
Limitations: Giving primarily in the New York, NY, metropolitan area, including Westchester County.
Application information:
Write: Fortune Pope, V.P.
Officers and Directors: Catherine Pope, Pres.; Anthony Pope, V.P. and Secy.; Fortune Pope, V.P. and Treas.
Employer Identification Number: 136096193

5010
Port Royal Foundation, Inc. ⌑ ☆
350 Fifth Ave., Suite 4606
New York 10118 (212) 736-2030

Incorporated in 1983 in NY.
Foundation type: Independent
Financial data (yr. ended 10/31/87): Assets, $1,075,766 (M); expenditures, $244,277, including $234,565 for 33 grants (high: $60,000; low: $100).
Purpose and activities: Support primarily for higher education, historical preservation, and cultural programs; minor support for medical research.
Limitations: Giving primarily in NY and HI. No grants to individuals.
Application information:
Initial approach: Letter
Deadline(s): None
Write: Mrs. Sally Sample Aall, Pres.
Officers: Sally Sample Aall, Pres.; Hiram Johnson Cuthrell, V.P. and Secy.; Maureen Anderson, Treas.
Employer Identification Number: 133162050

5011
Mrs. Cheever Porter Foundation ⌑
c/o Adams & Becker
Seven High St.
Huntington 11743
Application address: c/o Kelley, Drye & Warren, 101 Park Ave., New York, NY 10178

Established in 1962 in NY.
Foundation type: Independent
Financial data (yr. ended 06/30/89): Assets, $2,761,789 (M); expenditures, $237,208, including $208,750 for 37 grants (high: $45,000; low: $500).
Purpose and activities: Giving primarily for higher education, the arts, and animal welfare.
Application information:
Initial approach: Letter
Deadline(s): None
Write: Alton E. Peters, Dir.
Directors: Alton E. Peters, Edgar Scott, Jr., Clifford E. Starkins.
Employer Identification Number: 136093181

5012
Ralph B. Post Trust ⌑ ☆
c/o Marine Midland Bank
P.O. Box 4203, 17th Fl.
Buffalo 14240

Established in 1985 in NY.
Foundation type: Independent
Financial data (yr. ended 9/30/88): Assets, $1,682,460 (M); gifts received, $26,853; expenditures, $46,471, including $30,284 for 9 grants to individuals.
Purpose and activities: Award scholarships for higher education.
Application information: Contributes only to pre-selected individuals. Applications not accepted.
Trustee: Marine Midland Bank, N.A.
Employer Identification Number: 146052967

5013
The Potts Memorial Foundation
P.O. Box 1015
Hudson 12534 (518) 828-3366

Incorporated in 1922 in NY.
Foundation type: Independent
Financial data (yr. ended 12/31/88): Assets, $2,423,919 (M); expenditures, $70,462, including $51,284 for 6 grants (high: $25,757; low: $1,000).
Purpose and activities: A private foundation established to provide for the care, treatment, and rehabilitation of persons afflicted with tuberculosis; support for tuberculosis eradication, including fellowship programs for physicians.
Types of support: Seed money, building funds, equipment, research, special projects, publications, conferences and seminars, internships, scholarship funds, fellowships.
Limitations: No grants to individuals, or for endowment funds or matching gifts; no loans.
Application information:
Initial approach: Proposal
Copies of proposal: 8
Deadline(s): One month prior to board meeting
Board meeting date(s): May and Oct.
Write: Charles E. Inman, Secy.
Officers and Trustees:* Carl G. Whitbeck, M.D.,* Pres.; James M. Blake, M.D.,* V.P.; Charles E. Inman,* Secy.; J. Warren Van Deusen,* Treas.; Stanley Bardwell, M.D., Gerald D. Dorman, M.D., Frank C. Maxon, Jr., M.D.
Employer Identification Number: 141347714

5014
Elaine E. & Frank T. Powers, Jr. Foundation, Inc. ⌑ ☆
c/o Seaman & Ashley
51 East 42nd St.
New York 10017-5404

Established in 1987 in NY.
Foundation type: Independent
Financial data (yr. ended 2/28/89): Assets, $146,729 (M); gifts received, $357,600; expenditures, $393,361, including $358,360 for 148 grants (high: $47,000; low: $100; average: $1,000-$5,000).
Purpose and activities: Giving primarily for elementary and secondary education; support also for health and hospitals, Protestant churches, and youth.
Limitations: Giving primarily in NY. No grants to individuals.
Application information:
Initial approach: Letter
Deadline(s): None
Write: David Seaman, Esq.
Officers and Directors: Althea Powers, Pres.; Marjorie Ade, V.P.; F. Thomas Powers.
Employer Identification Number: 133388970

5015
The Pratt-Northam Foundation ⌑
c/o Hunt & Hunt
5564 Woodlawn Ave.
Lowville 13367
Application address: P.O. Box 104, Lowville, NY 13367

Incorporated in 1962 in NY.
Donor(s): Hazel Northam.†
Foundation type: Independent
Financial data (yr. ended 12/31/87): Assets, $1,897,869 (M); expenditures, $219,797, including $174,945 for 42 grants (high: $35,000; low: $1,125).
Purpose and activities: Grants and workerships provided for educational, cultural or charitable objectives.
Limitations: Giving limited to the Black River Valley region of NY.
Application information: Application form required.
Deadline(s): None
Write: Donald Exford
Directors: John A. Beach, Richard C. Cummings, Lee Hirschey, Lyle W. Hornbeck, Donald M. Hunt, Livingston Lansing, Edward Sieber.
Number of staff: None.
Employer Identification Number: 166088207

5016
The Louis and Harold Price Foundation, Inc. ▼
654 Madison Ave., Suite 2005
New York 10021 (212) 753-0240
Additional tel.: (212) 752-9335

Incorporated in 1951 in NY.
Donor(s): Louis Price,† Harold Price.
Foundation type: Independent
Financial data (yr. ended 12/31/88): Assets, $30,215,310 (M); expenditures, $1,448,829, including $1,250,160 for 269 grants (high: $724,500; low: $25; average: $100-$5,000).
Purpose and activities: Support for a business institute, Jewish welfare funds, hospitals, community funds, and higher education, including scholarship funds; grants also for youth agencies, camps for children, temple support, medical research, the arts, and services for the handicapped, including the blind.
Types of support: Endowment funds, operating budgets, scholarship funds, special projects, continuing support, research, annual campaigns.
Limitations: Giving primarily in metropolitan New York, NY, and Los Angeles, CA. No grants to individuals, or for building funds.
Publications: 990-PF.
Application information: Application form not required.
Initial approach: Letter or proposal
Copies of proposal: 1
Deadline(s): None
Board meeting date(s): Feb., May, and as required
Final notification: 1 to 3 months
Write: Harold Price, Pres.
Officers and Trustees: Harold Price, Pres.; Pauline Price, V.P. and Secy.; Rosemary L. Guidone, Exec. Dir.; Gloria Appel, George Asch, David Gerstein, Milton Slotkin, Linda Vitti.
Number of staff: 1 full-time professional.
Employer Identification Number: 136121358

5017
Price Institute for Entrepreneurial Studies, Inc.
654 Madison Ave.
New York 10021 (212) 752-9335

Established in 1979 in NY.
Donor(s): The Louis & Harold Price Foundation, Inc.
Foundation type: Operating
Financial data (yr. ended 12/31/88): Assets, $2,305,937 (M); gifts received, $724,500; expenditures, $683,092, including $413,962 for grants.
Purpose and activities: Giving primarily to a center for entrepreneurial studies and institutions of higher education; support also for research and education related to entrepreneurial work.
Limitations: Giving primarily in NY and CA.
Application information:
Initial approach: Letter
Deadline(s): For higher education - Dec. 1 for a grant in the subsequent year; no deadline for other applicants
Write: Gloria Appel, Pres.
Officers: Harold Price, Chair.; Gloria W. Appel, Pres.
Employer Identification Number: 133008173

5018
Price Waterhouse Foundation ▼
1251 Ave. of the Americas
New York 10020 (212) 489-8900

Incorporated in 1956 in NY.
Donor(s): Active and retired partners, and employees of Price Waterhouse.
Foundation type: Company-sponsored
Financial data (yr. ended 12/31/87): Assets, $252,180 (M); gifts received, $422,570; expenditures, $188,817, including $188,770 for 10 grants (high: $30,000; low: $1,000; average: $1,000-$20,000).
Purpose and activities: The advancement of higher education in the field of accountancy; grants to four-year and postgraduate degree-granting colleges and universities for aid to teachers, scholarships, fellowships, and student loans; support for an employee matching gift program and for research programs, libraries, and other facilities.
Types of support: Professorships, fellowships, scholarship funds, research, employee matching gifts, annual campaigns, building funds, capital campaigns, endowment funds, general purposes, matching funds, conferences and seminars.
Limitations: Giving limited to the U.S. No support for athletic funds. No grants to individuals; no loans.
Publications: Program policy statement, informational brochure (including application guidelines).
Application information: Applications should be made through local offices of Price Waterhouse. Application form not required.
Initial approach: Letter and summary of proposal
Copies of proposal: 1
Deadline(s): Submit letter of inquiry and summary of proposal preferably before July; no set deadline
Board meeting date(s): 3 to 4 times a year
Write: Larry P. Scott, Exec. Dir.
Officers: R.G. Nichols,* Pres.; Francis N. Bonsignore,* V.P. and Secy.; H. Haddock, Jr., Treas.
Directors:* R.A. Mulshine, W.D. Pugh, A.H. Siegel, N.R. Walker.
Number of staff: 1 part-time professional.
Employer Identification Number: 136119208

5019
Primerica Foundation ▼ ¤
65 East 55th St.
New York 10022 (212) 891-8884

Incorporated in 1960 in NY.
Donor(s): Primerica Corp.
Foundation type: Company-sponsored
Financial data (yr. ended 12/31/88): Assets, $2,512,456 (M); gifts received, $2,300,000; expenditures, $2,334,436, including $1,938,980 for 243 grants (high: $135,000; low: $200; average: $1,000-$50,000), $146,850 for 132 grants to individuals (high: $3,400; low: $250) and $146,318 for 281 employee matching gifts.
Purpose and activities: The foundation is undergoing a review of its grantmaking activities.
Types of support: Operating budgets, seed money, emergency funds, employee matching gifts, scholarship funds, employee-related scholarships, fellowships, special projects, continuing support, program-related investments.
Limitations: Giving primarily to national organizations, with some emphasis on areas of company operations. No support for strictly recreational, sectarian, or denominational organizations. Usually no grants to veterans' or fraternal organizations for their own benefit. No grants for for building or endowment funds, continuing support, courtesy advertising, annual campaigns, deficit financing, land acquisition, or special events; no loans. Generally, no grants for capital drives.
Publications: Annual report, program policy statement, application guidelines.
Application information: Application form not required.
Initial approach: Letter or proposal
Copies of proposal: 1
Deadline(s): None
Board meeting date(s): Every 8 to 10 weeks
Final notification: 2 months
Officers and Directors:* Dee Topol,* Chair.; Kenneth A. Yarnell, Jr.,* V.P. and Treas.; Gerald Tsai, Jr.,* V.P.; John T. Andrews, Jr.,* Secy.; Robert B. Bogart, David A. Frank, JoAnn H. Heisen, John G. Polk, Walter A. Scott.
Number of staff: 4 full-time professional; 2 full-time support.
Employer Identification Number: 136161154

5020
William E. and Maude S. Pritschard Charitable Trust ¤
c/o Chase Manhattan Bank, N.A., Tax Serv. Div.
1211 Ave. of the Americas
New York 10036 (212) 730-5883

Established in 1983 in NY.
Foundation type: Independent
Financial data (yr. ended 12/31/88): Assets, $8,240,032 (M); gifts received, $131,086; expenditures, $725,937, including $600,000 for 27 grants (high: $125,000; low: $1,000).
Purpose and activities: Support for education, hospitals, social services, and religion.
Types of support: General purposes.
Application information:
Initial approach: Summary of academic qualifications
Deadline(s): None
Write: Howard P. Serrell
Trustees: Edward J. Cunnigle, Herbert C. Wellington, The Chase Manhattan Bank, N.A.
Employer Identification Number: 136824965

5021
Morris and Anna Propp Sons Fund, Inc. ¤
405 Park Ave., Suite 1103
New York 10022

Incorporated in 1944 in NY.
Donor(s): Members of the Propp family.
Foundation type: Independent
Financial data (yr. ended 12/31/88): Assets, $3,867,635 (M); gifts received, $26,891; expenditures, $149,889, including $140,512 for 101 grants (high: $22,500; low: $18).
Purpose and activities: Giving primarily for Jewish welfare funds, temple support, and religious education; some support for higher education.
Limitations: No grants to individuals.
Application information: Contributes only to pre-selected organizations. Applications not accepted.
Directors: Ephraim Propp, M.J. Propp, Seymour Propp.
Employer Identification Number: 136099110

5022
The Prospect Hill Foundation, Inc. ▼
420 Lexington Ave., Suite 3020
New York 10170 (212) 370-1144

Incorporated in 1960 in NY; absorbed The Frederick W. Beinecke Fund in 1983.
Donor(s): William S. Beinecke.
Foundation type: Independent
Financial data (yr. ended 12/31/89): Assets, $38,102,128 (M); expenditures, $2,236,416, including $1,398,540 for 76 grants (high: $75,000; low: $2,500; average: $5,000-$25,000) and $97,770 for 78 employee matching gifts.
Purpose and activities: The Prospect Hill Foundation has a broad range of philanthropic interests. Prospective applicants are requested to obtain guidelines prior to submitting an inquiry.
Types of support: Matching funds, operating budgets, general purposes.
Limitations: Giving primarily in the northeastern U.S., including NY, NJ, and RI; support for youth and social agencies primarily in NY. No support for religious activities. No grants to individuals, or for research.
Publications: Grants list, informational brochure (including application guidelines).
Application information: Application form not required.
Initial approach: Letter
Deadline(s): None
Board meeting date(s): 4 times annually
Final notification: 4 weeks
Write: Constance Eiseman, Exec. Dir.
Officers and Directors:* William S. Beinecke,* Pres.; Elizabeth G. Beinecke,* V.P.; John B. Beinecke,* V.P.; Constance Eiseman, Secy. and Exec. Dir.; Michael A. Yesko, Treas.; Frederick W. Beinecke, Frances Beinecke Elston, Sarah Beinecke Richardson.
Number of staff: 1 full-time professional; 1 full-time support; 6 part-time support.
Employer Identification Number: 136075567

5023
Prudential-Bache Foundation ¤
100 Gold St.
New York 10292 (212) 214-7507

Incorporated in 1965 in NY.
Donor(s): Bache Halsey Stuart Shields, Inc.
Foundation type: Company-sponsored
Financial data (yr. ended 1/31/88): Assets, $22,020 (M); gifts received, $435,000; expenditures, $435,580, including $435,535 for 150 grants (high: $25,000; low: $100).
Purpose and activities: Emphasis on social services, higher education, hospitals, cultural

programs, and Jewish and Roman Catholic welfare funds.
Application information: Application form not required.
Deadline(s): None
Write: Bruno G. Bissetta, Treas.
Officers: H. Virgil Sherrill, Pres.; Charles Christofilis, V.P. and Secy.; Bruno G. Bissetta, Treas.
Directors:* George McGough, Leland Paton.
Employer Identification Number: 136193023

5024
The Pumpkin Foundation ⌑
c/o Joseph H. Reich & Co.
900 Third Ave.
New York 10022 (212) 753-5150

Donor(s): Joseph H. Reich.
Foundation type: Independent
Financial data (yr. ended 6/30/88): Assets, $1,263,827 (M); expenditures, $17,916, including $13,835 for 26 grants (high: $3,400; low: $40).
Purpose and activities: Support primarily for education, the arts and museums.
Application information:
Write: Joseph H. Reich
Trustees: Carol F. Reich, Janet H. Reich, Joseph H. Reich.
Employer Identification Number: 136279814

5025
The R. and D. Fund, Inc. ⌑
1700 Broadway, Rm. 1702
New York 10019

Incorporated in 1952 in NY.
Donor(s): Members of the Straus family.
Foundation type: Independent
Financial data (yr. ended 12/31/87): Assets, $72,721 (M); gifts received, $141,213; expenditures, $154,358, including $152,211 for 75 grants (high: $35,700; low: $10).
Purpose and activities: Grants only to charities of personal interest to the donors, with emphasis on fine arts and cultural programs, international affairs, higher education, and hospitals.
Application information: Contributes only to pre-selected organizations. Applications not accepted.
Officers: Ralph I. Straus, Pres.; Donald B. Straus, V.P.; Tricia McKenna, Secy.-Treas.
Employer Identification Number: 136118829

5026
The Harold K. Raisler Foundation, Inc. ⌑
599 Lexington Ave.
New York 10022 (212) 319-2660

Incorporated in 1957 in NY.
Foundation type: Independent
Financial data (yr. ended 12/31/88): Assets, $1,690,972 (M); expenditures, $84,915, including $77,090 for grants (high: $20,000).
Purpose and activities: Grants for higher education, hospitals, cultural programs, temple support, and Jewish welfare funds.
Limitations: Giving primarily in New York, NY. No grants to individuals.
Application information: Contributes only to pre-selected organizations. Applications not accepted.
Board meeting date(s): May
Write: Harold K. Raisler, Pres.
Officer and Directors: Harold K. Raisler, Pres. and Treas.; Robert K. Raisler, V.P. and Secy.
Employer Identification Number: 136094406

5027
The Robert K. Raisler Foundation, Inc. ⌑
599 Lexington Ave.
New York 10022 (212) 319-2660

Incorporated in 1958 in NY.
Foundation type: Independent
Financial data (yr. ended 12/31/88): Assets, $1,708,245 (M); expenditures, $91,053, including $83,095 for grants (high: $18,000).
Purpose and activities: Emphasis on higher education, Jewish welfare funds, cultural programs, temple support, and health agencies.
Limitations: No grants to individuals.
Application information: Contributes only to pre-selected organizations. Applications not accepted.
Officers and Directors: Robert K. Raisler, Pres. and Treas.; Harold K. Raisler, V.P. and Secy.
Employer Identification Number: 136094433

5028
Charles S. Raizen Foundation, Inc. ⌑
31 Meadow Rd.
Scarsdale 10585

Established in 1945 in NY.
Donor(s): Charles S. Raizen,† Patricia T. Raizen,† Transogram Co., Inc., Transogram Midwest, Playwood Plastics, Anchor Toy Corp.
Foundation type: Independent
Financial data (yr. ended 12/31/88): Assets, $1,918,695 (M); expenditures, $137,326, including $122,785 for 94 grants (high: $45,000; low: $50).
Purpose and activities: Giving for Jewish welfare, medical research, and social services.
Limitations: No grants to individuals.
Application information: Contributes only to pre-selected organizations. Applications not accepted.
Officers: Roy Raizen, Pres.; Edna Mae Fadem, V.P.; Nancy Raizen, Secy.; Leroy Fadem, Treas.
Employer Identification Number: 136122579

5029
Ramapo Trust ▼
126 East 56th St.
New York 10022 (212) 308-7355

Trust established in 1973 in NY.
Donor(s): Henry L. Schwartz,† Montebello Trust.
Foundation type: Independent
Financial data (yr. ended 06/30/89): Assets, $36,203,832 (M); qualifying distributions, $5,677,001, including $5,677,001 for 52 grants (high: $1,200,000; average: $1,000-$1,200,000).
Purpose and activities: Giving for gerontological and geriatric research and innovative services; support also for health, higher education, and youth.
Types of support: Seed money, matching funds, professorships, scholarship funds, fellowships, special projects, research, publications, conferences and seminars, emergency funds, equipment, internships.
Limitations: Giving primarily in the metropolitan New York, NY, and NJ areas. No grants to individuals, or for capital or building campaigns, operating budgets, continuing support, annual campaigns, or deficit financing; no loans.
Publications: Newsletter, application guidelines.
Application information: Application form not required.
Initial approach: Letter
Deadline(s): None
Board meeting date(s): Monthly
Write: Danyelle Rudin by telephone, or Steven L. Schwartz by mail
Trustees: Arthur Norman Field, Karen Schwartz Hart, Harold Resnik, Andrew M. Schreier, William Schreier, Rebecca Schwartz, Stephen L. Schwartz, Mary Ann Van Clief.
Number of staff: 1 full-time professional; 1 part-time professional; 2 part-time support.
Employer Identification Number: 136594279

5030
William Rankin and Elizabeth Forbes Rankin Trust ⌑
c/o The Chase Manhattan Bank, N.A., Tax Serv. Div.
1211 Ave. of the Americas, 36th Fl.
New York 10036

Established in 1971 in NY.
Foundation type: Independent
Financial data (yr. ended 12/31/87): Assets, $4,692,000 (M); expenditures, $250,420, including $180,069 for 5 grants (high: $36,014; low: $36,013).
Purpose and activities: Support primarily for health associations and social service organizations.
Trustees: Estate of John A. Murray, Jr., The Chase Manhattan Bank, N.A.
Employer Identification Number: 136584984

5031
Hirsch and Braine Raskin Foundation, Inc. ⌑
270 Madison Ave., Rm. 1201
New York 10016

Incorporated in 1957 in NY.
Donor(s): Hirsch Raskin,† Braine Raskin.†
Foundation type: Independent
Financial data (yr. ended 2/29/88): Assets, $2,105,872 (M); expenditures, $107,298, including $96,000 for 5 grants (high: $35,000; low: $11,000).
Purpose and activities: Grants for Israeli higher educational and scientific institutions and for Jewish welfare funds.
Limitations: Giving primarily in New York, NY.
Application information: Application form not required.
Deadline(s): None
Write: William Prager, Jr., V.P.

Officers and Directors: Rose Raskin, Pres.; William W. Prager, Jr., V.P.; William W. Prager, Sr., Secy.
Employer Identification Number: 136085867

5032
Rauch Foundation, Inc. ⌑
118 Huntington Rd.
Port Washington 11050 (516) 944-5244

Incorporated in 1960 in NY.
Donor(s): Philip J. Rauch, Louis Rauch.
Foundation type: Independent
Financial data (yr. ended 11/30/88): Assets, $11,935,536 (M); gifts received, $6,699,275; expenditures, $754,820, including $659,358 for 51 grants (high: $503,000; low: $34).
Purpose and activities: Support for innovative programs in the area of early childhood and daycare. Funds for local ongoing support of educational, cultural, health, and social service organizations currently fully committed.
Types of support: Seed money, special projects, research, publications, conferences and seminars, matching funds.
Limitations: Giving primarily in east coast states between Boston, MA, and Washington, DC. No support for religious purposes. No grants to individuals, or for deficit financing, building funds, land acquisition, scholarships, or fellowships; no loans.
Application information: Contributes only to pre-selected organizations. Applications not accepted.
Board meeting date(s): Jan., July, and Oct.
Officers and Directors: Louis Rauch, Pres.; Philip J. Rauch, V.P. and Secy.-Treas.; Nancy R. Douzinas, V.P.; Gerald I. Lustig, V.P.; Philip J. Rauch, V.P.
Number of staff: 1 part-time support.
Employer Identification Number: 112001717

5033
Richard Ravitch Foundation, Inc. ⌑ ☆
c/o Richard Ravitch
1021 Park Ave.
New York 10028

Foundation type: Independent
Financial data (yr. ended 11/30/89): Assets, $621,696 (M); gifts received, $184,764; expenditures, $213,474, including $207,675 for 37 grants (high: $198,075; low: $100).
Purpose and activities: Support for Jewish organizations and general charitable giving.
Limitations: Giving primarily in NY. No grants to individuals.
Application information: Contributes only to pre-selected organizations. Applications not accepted.
Officers: Richard Ravitch,* Pres. and Principal Mgr.; Junn Lipkowitz,* Secy.; Joseph Ravitch,* Treas.
Directors:* Judah Gribetz, Michael Ravitch.
Employer Identification Number: 136093139

5034
Raymond Foundation
c/o Raymond Corp.
45 Lewis St.
Binghamton 13901 (607) 656-2311

Trust established in 1964 in NY.
Donor(s): George G. Raymond.†
Foundation type: Company-sponsored
Financial data (yr. ended 12/31/88): Assets, $2,561,104 (M); gifts received, $41,000; expenditures, $60,430, including $54,503 for 52 grants (high: $5,000; low: $100; average: $200-$1,000).
Purpose and activities: Grants for community funds, higher education, and youth agencies.
Types of support: Annual campaigns, building funds, capital campaigns, matching funds, renovation projects, special projects.
Limitations: Giving limited to areas of company operations in NY and CA. No grants to individuals, or for endowment funds, or operating budgets; no loans.
Publications: 990-PF, application guidelines, program policy statement, annual report.
Application information: Applications not accepted.
Deadline(s): None
Board meeting date(s): Mar., June, Sept., and Dec.
Write: Terri Brant, Asst. Exec. Secy.
Officers: George G. Raymond III,* Exec. Secy.; Patrick J. McManus, Treas.
Trustees:* James F. Barton, Chair.; Stephen S. Raymond, Vice-Chair.; Terri Brant, Robert C. Eldred, George G. Raymond, Jr., Jean C. Raymond, John Riley, David E. Sonn, Jeanette L. Williamson, Lee J. Wolf, Madeleine R. Young.
Employer Identification Number: 166047847

5035
Robert Raymond Foundation, Inc. ⌑ ☆
61 Broadway
New York 10006

Established in 1961.
Donor(s): Robert Raymond.
Foundation type: Independent
Financial data (yr. ended 12/31/88): Assets, $1,190,506 (M); gifts received, $136,250; expenditures, $48,332, including $45,975 for 52 grants (high: $5,000; low: $100).
Purpose and activities: Support for health associations, hospitals, Jewish organizations, and higher education.
Limitations: Giving primarily in NY and NJ. No grants to individuals, or for scholarships, fellowships, or prizes; no loans.
Application information: Contributes only to pre-selected organizations. Applications not accepted.
Officer: Robert Raymond, Pres.
Employer Identification Number: 136105866

5036
Walter Reade Foundation, Inc. ⌑
c/o Simpson, Thacher, and Bartlett
One Battery Park Plaza
New York 10004 (212) 908-2713

Donor(s): Walter Reade Organization, Inc.
Foundation type: Independent
Financial data (yr. ended 12/31/88): Assets, $1,751,666 (M); expenditures, $370,506, including $366,200 for 5 grants (high: $350,000; low: $200).
Purpose and activities: Grants primarily for a theater institute and a film society; support also for education and a political science institute.
Limitations: No grants to individuals.
Application information: Contributes only to pre-selected organizations. Applications not accepted.
Write: Stephen P. Duggan, Treas.
Officers: Gertrude B. Reade, Pres.; Dolly Reade Borgia, V.P.; Stephen P. Duggan, Treas.
Employer Identification Number: 216014506

5037
Reader's Digest Foundation ▼
Pleasantville 10570 (914) 241-5370

Incorporated in 1938 in NY.
Donor(s): The Reader's Digest Association, Inc., DeWitt Wallace,† Lila Acheson Wallace.†
Foundation type: Company-sponsored
Financial data (yr. ended 12/31/89): Assets, $21,275,691 (M); expenditures, $3,647,478, including $2,563,414 for 86 grants (high: $100,000; low: $1,000; average: $10,000-$60,000) and $1,084,064 for 3,551 employee matching gifts.
Purpose and activities: Particular interest in journalism education and in programs that offer pre-college youth a variety of character-building experiences, including programs that assist young people in acquiring those basic skills critical to building a solid educational base.
Types of support: Employee matching gifts, general purposes, scholarship funds, program-related investments, employee-related scholarships.
Limitations: No support for religious organizations or endeavors; legislative or lobbying efforts; veterans', political, or fraternal organizations; charitable dinners or fundraising events; private foundations; cultural organizations; environmental groups; television, film or video productions; local chapters of national organizations; or medical research or health-related activities. No grants to individuals, or for capital, building or endowment funds, operating budgets, annual campaigns, seed money, emergency funds, deficit financing, special projects, publications, workshops, or conferences or seminars; no loans.
Publications: Annual report (including application guidelines).
Application information: Application form not required.
Initial approach: Letter
Copies of proposal: 1
Deadline(s): Jan. 15, April 15, and Sept. 15
Board meeting date(s): Feb., June, and Oct.
Final notification: 90 days
Write: J. Edward Hall, Pres.
Officers and Directors:* George V. Grune,* Chair.; J. Edward Hall,* Pres.; Richard F. McLoughlin,* V.P.; Mary Graniero, Secy.; Ross Jones, Treas.; Kenneth O. Gilmore, Barbara J. Morgan, John A. Pope, Jr., Francis G. Ronnenberg.
Number of staff: 2 part-time professional; 1 full-time support; 1 part-time support.
Employer Identification Number: 136120380

5038
Realty Foundation of New York
551 Fifth Ave.
New York 10017

Scholarship application address: Scholarship Aid Committee, 531 Fifth Ave., Suite 1105, New York, NY 10017

Established in 1956 in NY.
Foundation type: Independent
Financial data (yr. ended 6/30/87): Assets, $1,204,997 (M); gifts received, $67,691; expenditures, $303,829, including $92,500 for 4 grants (high: $50,000; low: $7,500) and $80,712 for 46 grants to individuals (high: $10,000; low: $500).
Purpose and activities: Support for higher education, including scholarships limited to employees of the real estate industry and their children.
Types of support: Employee-related scholarships.
Limitations: Giving limited to the five boroughs of New York City.
Application information: Application form required.
Deadline(s): None
Officers: Harry B. Helmsley, Chair.; Jack D. Weiler, Pres.; Mary Lilly, Exec. V.P.; David M. Baldwin, V.P.; Charles B. Benenson, V.P.; Seymour B. Durst, V.P.; Aaron Gural, V.P.; Edwin A. Malloy, V.P.; S. Dudley Nostrand, V.P.; Vincent James Peters, V.P.; Irving Schneider, V.P.; Alvin Schwartz, V.P.; Larry A. Silverstein, V.P.; Conrad D. Stephenson, V.P.; Charles J. Urstadt, V.P.; John R. White, V.P.; Daniel Rose, Secy.; Eugene M. Grant, Treas.
Directors: Lawrence D. Ackman, and 48 additional directors.
Employer Identification Number: 136016622

5039
Rebny Foundation, Inc. ⌑ ☆
c/o The Real Estate Board of NY, Inc.
12 East 41st St.
New York 10017-6221 (212) 532-3100

Incorporated in 1985 in NY.
Donor(s): The Real Estate Board of New York, Inc., New York City House, Inc.
Foundation type: Independent
Financial data (yr. ended 6/30/88): Assets, $86,257 (M); gifts received, $310,376; expenditures, $268,792, including $108,065 for 42 grants (high: $50,000; low: $50).
Purpose and activities: Giving for "projects concerning housing and the homeless"; support also for the physically disabled.
Limitations: Giving limited to New York, NY. No grants to individuals.
Application information:
Initial approach: Letter
Deadline(s): None
Write: Marolyn Davenport
Officers and Directors: Jerry I. Speyer, Pres.; George M. Brooker, V.P.; Aaron Gural, V.P.; Alton G. Marshall, V.P.; Burton P. Resnick, V.P.; Larry A. Silverstein, V.P.; Conrad D. Stephenson, V.P.; Fred Wilpon, Secy.; Bertram F. French, Treas.; Dan J. Gronich, Edward A. Riguardi.
Employer Identification Number: 133317104

5040
Recanati Foundation ⌑
511 Fifth Ave.
New York 10017 (212) 578-1845

Incorporated in 1956 in NY.
Donor(s): Israel Discount Bank Limited, and others.
Foundation type: Independent
Financial data (yr. ended 06/30/89): Assets, $2,438,331 (M); gifts received, $177,964; expenditures, $94,276, including $64,195 for 65 grants (high: $5,000; low: $20).
Purpose and activities: Grants for welfare funds, cultural relations, and educational, scientific, and Jewish religious support.
Limitations: Giving primarily in NY. No grants to individuals, or for building funds.
Application information: Applications not accepted.
Write: Marvin Alexander
Member-Directors: Eliahu Cohen, Ran Hettena, Morton P. Hyman, Frank J. Klein, Diane Recanati, Michael Recanati, Raphael Recanati, Gertrud Stark.
Employer Identification Number: 136113080

5041
Morton & Beverley Rechler Foundation, Inc. ⌑ ☆
131 Jericho Tpke.
Jericho 11753
Application address: 17 Blue Sea Ln., Kings Point, NY 11024

Established in 1986.
Donor(s): Morton Rechler, Beverley Rechler.
Foundation type: Independent
Financial data (yr. ended 12/31/88): Assets, $205,477 (M); gifts received, $10,000; expenditures, $125,825, including $120,000 for 4 grants (high: $50,000; low: $20,000).
Purpose and activities: Giving primarily for a Jewish welfare fund and a temple; support also for a medical college.
Application information:
Initial approach: Letter
Write: Morton Rechler, Pres.
Officers: Morton Rechler, Pres.; Beverley Rechler, Secy.; Bennett Rechler, Treas.
Employer Identification Number: 592828631

5042
The Reed Foundation, Inc. ▼
444 Madison Ave.
New York 10022 (212) 223-1330

Incorporated in 1949 in NY.
Donor(s): Samuel Rubin.†
Foundation type: Independent
Financial data (yr. ended 12/31/89): Assets, $11,516,023 (M); expenditures, $1,301,708, including $1,190,482 for 93 grants (high: $56,250; low: $1,000; average: $1,000-$10,000).
Purpose and activities: Emphasis on higher, minority, and other education, the performing and fine arts and other cultural affairs, the environment, youth agencies, and civil and human rights; provides support for "projects of newly-formed organizations or innovative or timely programs of existing institutions for which other funding may be difficult to obtain."
Types of support: Endowment funds, research, conferences and seminars, scholarship funds, fellowships, exchange programs, matching funds, general purposes, building funds, capital campaigns, continuing support, operating budgets, program-related investments, publications, renovation projects, seed money, special projects.
Limitations: Giving primarily in the New York, NY, metropolitan area; some giving in New York State, CT, DC, IL, and VT. No grants to individuals.
Publications: Program policy statement.
Application information: Application form not required.
Initial approach: Letter
Copies of proposal: 1
Deadline(s): None
Board meeting date(s): Bimonthly
Final notification: Immediately following board meetings
Write: J. Sinclair Armstrong, Secy.
Officers and Directors:* Reed Rubin,* Pres.; J. Sinclair Armstrong,* Secy.; Jane Gregory Rubin,* Treas.
Number of staff: 1 part-time professional; 1 part-time support.
Employer Identification Number: 131990017

5043
Philip D. Reed Foundation, Inc.
570 Lexington Ave., Rm. 923
New York 10022

Incorporated in 1955 in NY.
Donor(s): Philip D. Reed.†
Foundation type: Independent
Financial data (yr. ended 06/30/89): Assets, $3,421,711 (M); expenditures, $1,338,926, including $1,317,950 for 35 grants (average: $1,000-$50,000).
Purpose and activities: Grants mainly for hospitals, higher education, international studies, public policy organizations, and community funds.
Limitations: No grants to individuals.
Application information:
Deadline(s): None
Write: Patricia Anderson, Secy.
Officers and Trustees:* Philip D. Reed, Jr.,* Chair. and Pres.; Harold A. Segall,* V.P. and Treas.; Patricia Anderson,* Secy.
Employer Identification Number: 136098916

5044
The Reich Fund ⌑ ☆
c/o Seymour Reich
640 Park Ave.
New York 10021-6126

Foundation type: Independent
Financial data (yr. ended 10/31/89): Assets, $1,132,031 (M); expenditures, $39,825, including $38,430 for 33 grants (high: $7,925; low: $50).
Purpose and activities: Giving primarily to Jewish organizations; support also for higher education, libraries, and hospitals and medical research.
Limitations: No grants to individuals.

Application information: Contributes only to pre-selected organizations. Applications not accepted.
Trustees: Lilian Reich, Seymour Reich.
Employer Identification Number: 510166322

5045
Anne & Harry J. Reicher Foundation ⌑
1173-A Second Ave.
Box 363
New York 10021

Established in 1961 in PA.
Foundation type: Independent
Financial data (yr. ended 12/31/88): Assets, $4,850,884 (M); expenditures, $779,626, including $718,250 for 96 grants (high: $250,000; low: $25).
Purpose and activities: Giving primarily to hospitals and health organizations, particularly a hospital for joint diseases, and to Jewish welfare funds.
Limitations: Giving primarily in the greater New York, NY, metropolitan area. No grants to individuals.
Application information:
Initial approach: Proposal
Write: Hermia Gould, Secy.-Treas.
Officers: Harold Lamberg, Pres.; Rabbi Bulfour Buckner, V.P.; Leonard Zalkin, V.P.; Hermia Gould, Secy.-Treas.
Employer Identification Number: 136115086

5046
The Reichmann Family Foundation ⌑ ☆
15 Harbor Park Dr.
Port Washington 11050

Established in 1986 in NY.
Donor(s): Andre Reichmann.
Foundation type: Independent
Financial data (yr. ended 12/31/88): Assets, $1,031,930 (M); gifts received, $545,000; expenditures, $231,861, including $231,653 for 105 grants (high: $18,000; low: $100).
Purpose and activities: Support for Jewish organizations, including synagogues and yeshivas.
Limitations: Giving primarily in NY. No grants to individuals.
Application information: Contributes only to pre-selected organizations. Applications not accepted.
Officers: Charles Reichmann, Pres.; Andre Reichmann, V.P.; Louis Reichmann, V.P.; Marianne Reichmann, V.P.
Employer Identification Number: 112813890

5047
Floyd J. Reinhart Memorial Scholarship Foundation ⌑ ☆
P.O. Box 29
Amsterdam 12010

Foundation type: Independent
Financial data (yr. ended 6/30/89): Assets, $1,757,077 (M); expenditures, $93,558, including $66,750 for grants.
Purpose and activities: Support for education.
Application information:
Write: Frances Allen, Trustee
Trustee: Frances Allen.
Employer Identification Number: 141605307

5048
Mahir A. & Helene Reiss Foundation, Inc. ⌑
445 Park Ave., 16th Fl.
New York 10022

Established in 1981 in NY.
Donor(s): Mahir A. Reis.
Foundation type: Independent
Financial data (yr. ended 12/31/87): Assets, $1,979 (M); gifts received, $380,100; expenditures, $387,267, including $386,131 for 116 grants (high: $23,680; low: $100).
Purpose and activities: Support for Jewish educational and religious organizations.
Application information:
Write: Mahir A. Reis, Pres.
Officer: Mahir A. Reis, Pres.
Employer Identification Number: 133050322

5049
Szerena & Albert Reitman Foundation, Inc. ⌑
350 Broadway
New York 10013

Established in 1955 in NY.
Foundation type: Independent
Financial data (yr. ended 12/31/87): Assets, $1,793,967 (M); expenditures, $142,494, including $112,068 for grants.
Purpose and activities: Giving primarily for medical education and research; support also for Jewish giving.
Application information:
Write: Richard Tannenbaum, Pres.
Officers: Richard Tannenbaum, Pres.; Hyman Tannenbaum, Secy.; Philip Berkowitz, Treas.
Trustee: Walter Berkowitz.
Employer Identification Number: 136202503

5050
Revlon Foundation, Inc. ⌑
c/o Macandrews & Forbes Group, Inc.
36 East 63rd St.
New York 10021

Incorporated in 1955 in NY.
Donor(s): Revlon, Inc., and its subsidiaries.
Foundation type: Company-sponsored
Financial data (yr. ended 12/31/88): Assets, $498,647 (M); gifts received, $4,430,000; expenditures, $4,084,630, including $4,047,592 for 34 grants (high: $1,000,000; low: $100) and $36,855 for 139 employee matching gifts (high: $1,375; low: $25).
Purpose and activities: Emphasis on women's interest groups, minorities, and health care which are national in scope or where company has subsidiaries, and cultural organizations which focus on main areas of interest listed above; support also for higher education, including an employee matching gift program, Jewish giving and welfare funds, conservation, and community funds.
Types of support: Employee matching gifts.
Limitations: No grants to individuals; employee matching gifts awarded to educational institutions only.
Application information: Applications not accepted.
Write: Roger Shelley, Pres.
Officers: Richard E. Halperin,* Pres.; Nancy T. Gardiner, Exec. V.P.; Wade H. Nichols III, V.P. and Secy.; John Bulzacchelli, V.P. and Treas.
Directors:* Howard Gittis, Ronald O. Perelman.
Employer Identification Number: 136126130

5051
Charles H. Revson Foundation, Inc. ▼ ⌑
444 Madison Ave., 30th Fl.
New York 10022 (212) 935-3340

Incorporated in 1956 in NY.
Donor(s): Charles H. Revson.†
Foundation type: Independent
Financial data (yr. ended 12/31/87): Assets, $87,101,932 (M); gifts received, $230,973; expenditures, $7,697,188, including $6,035,034 for 89 grants (high: $350,000; low: $2,000; average: $5,000-$125,000).
Purpose and activities: Grants for urban affairs and public policy, with a special emphasis on New York City problems as well as national policy issues; education, including higher education; biomedical research policy; and Jewish philanthropy and education. Particular emphasis within these program areas on the future of New York City, accountability of government, the changing role of women (especially leadership development for public life), minority groups, and the role of modern communications in education and other aspects of society.
Types of support: Research, fellowships, internships, special projects.
Limitations: Giving primarily in New York, NY. No support for local health appeals. No grants to individuals, or for building or endowment funds, general support, or matching gifts; no loans.
Publications: Biennial report, application guidelines.
Application information: Application form not required.
Initial approach: Letter or full proposal
Copies of proposal: 1
Deadline(s): None
Board meeting date(s): Apr., June, Oct., and Dec.
Final notification: 6 months
Write: Eli N. Evans, Pres.
Officers: Eli N. Evans,* Pres.; Lisa E. Goldberg, V.P.; Harry Meresman,* Secy.-Treas.
Directors:* Adrian W. DeWind, Chair.; Victor J. Barnett, Benjamin J. Buttenwieser, Alice Chandler, Robert Curvin, Matina S. Horner, Joshua Lederberg, Paul A. Marks, Robert B. McKay, Charles H. Revson, Jr., John C. Revson, Simon H. Rifkind.
Number of staff: 4 full-time professional; 1 part-time professional; 4 full-time support; 1 part-time support.
Employer Identification Number: 136126105

5052
Rexford Fund, Inc. ⌑
c/o Marcus Schloss Co., Inc.
One Whitehall St.
New York 10004

Established in 1967 in NY.
Donor(s): Marcus Schloss & Co.

Foundation type: Company-sponsored
Financial data (yr. ended 12/31/88): Assets, $1,198,243 (M); gifts received, $208,014; expenditures, $144,738, including $139,310 for 161 grants (high: $15,000; low: $25).
Purpose and activities: Giving for Jewish welfare, education, and social services.
Limitations: No grants to individuals.
Application information: Contributes only to pre-selected organizations. Applications not accepted.
Officers and Directors:* Alan S. Sexter,* Pres.; Irwin Schloss,* Secy.; Paul J. Zuckerberg,* Treas.; Bryant M. Yunker.
Employer Identification Number: 136222049

5053
Edith Grace Reynolds Estate Residuary Trust
c/o Key Trust Co.
60 State St.
Albany 12207

Established in 1971 in NY.
Donor(s): Edith Grace Reynolds.†
Foundation type: Independent
Financial data (yr. ended 03/31/89): Assets, $1,128,639 (M); expenditures, $77,841, including $17,000 for 16 grants (high: $5,000; low: $100) and $51,825 for 172 grants to individuals (high: $750; low: $250; average: $200-$375).
Purpose and activities: Giving primarily for scholarships for higher education; some support also for local community development.
Types of support: Student aid.
Limitations: Giving limited to School District 1, in Rensselaer County, NY.
Application information:
Initial approach: Application and high school transcript for scholarships
Deadline(s): Feb. 15 for scholarship applications
Write: Stanley Lepkowski, Trust Officer, Key Trust Co.
Trustee: Key Trust Co.
Employer Identification Number: 237170056

5054
The Christopher Reynolds Foundation, Inc.
121 East 61st St.
New York 10021 (212) 838-2920

Incorporated in 1952 in NY.
Donor(s): Libby Holman Reynolds.†
Foundation type: Independent
Financial data (yr. ended 1/31/89): Assets, $21,383,615 (M); expenditures, $2,006,528, including $1,718,720 for 50 grants (high: $164,250; low: $1,000; average: $5,000-$100,000).
Purpose and activities: Grants primarily in the field of international relations, with current focus on Indochina.
Types of support: Continuing support, conferences and seminars, research, technical assistance, exchange programs.
Limitations: Giving primarily in the U.S. for organizations providing humanitarian aid to Indochina (Vietnam, Laos, and Cambodia) and promoting reconciliation with these countries. No grants to individuals, or for capital or endowment funds, operating budgets, annual campaigns, seed money, emergency funds, deficit financing, special projects, publications, scholarships, fellowships, or matching gifts; no loans.
Publications: Multi-year report (including application guidelines), 990-PF, financial statement, grants list.
Application information: Application form not required.
Initial approach: Letter
Copies of proposal: 6
Deadline(s): Submit proposal preferably 30 days prior to board meeting
Board meeting date(s): Mar., June, Sept., and Dec.
Final notification: 1 week
Write: Jack Clareman, Exec. Dir.
Officers and Directors:* Michael Kahn,* Pres.; Margaret Randol,* Sr. V.P.; John R. Boettiger,* V.P.; Jack Clareman,* Secy.-Treas. and Exec. Dir.; Andrea Panaritis,* Assoc. Exec. Dir.; Suzanne Derrer.
Number of staff: 3 full-time professional.
Employer Identification Number: 136129401

5055
Rhodebeck Charitable Trust ☆
575 Lexington Ave.
New York 10022-6102

Established in 1987 in AZ.
Donor(s): Mildred T. Rhodebeck.†
Foundation type: Independent
Financial data (yr. ended 04/30/89): Assets, $14,730,637 (M); expenditures, $721,172, including $598,016 for 20 grants (high: $100,000; low: $4,555).
Purpose and activities: "To alleviate the plight of disadvantaged people including homeless, hungry, elderly, children, and sick by making grants to publicly supported tax-exempt organizations concerned with one or more of these objectives."
Types of support: General purposes, special projects.
Limitations: Giving limited to AZ and New York, NY. No grants to individuals.
Application information: Unsolicited applications are discouraged.
Trustee: Huyler C. Held.
Number of staff: 1 part-time support.
Employer Identification Number: 133413293

5056
Rich Foundation, Inc. ⌑
1145 Niagara St.
P.O. Box 245
Buffalo 14213 (716) 878-8305

Established in 1961.
Foundation type: Company-sponsored
Financial data (yr. ended 12/31/88): Assets, $771,554 (M); gifts received, $280,000; expenditures, $288,977, including $275,968 for 143 grants (high: $90,000; low: $18).
Purpose and activities: Emphasis on community funds, the arts, hospitals, church support, youth programs, and education, especially higher education.
Limitations: Giving primarily in NY.
Application information:
Initial approach: Letter
Deadline(s): None
Officer: David A. Rich, Exec. Dir.
Employer Identification Number: 166026199

5057
The Richard Foundation ⌑
Three Crosswood Ln.
Glen Head 11545
Application address: 181 Oleander Way, Vero Beach, FL, 32963

Established in 1948 in NY.
Foundation type: Independent
Financial data (yr. ended 12/31/88): Assets, $1,364,055 (M); expenditures, $102,392, including $98,910 for 282 grants (high: $10,000; low: $10).
Purpose and activities: Giving primarily for education and medicine; support also for youth.
Limitations: Giving primarily in NY.
Application information: Application form not required.
Deadline(s): None
Write: Harold Van B. Richard, V.P.
Officers: Vera R. Wood, Pres.; Harold Van B. Richard, V.P.; Trumbull Richard, V.P.; Merrell Clark, Jr., Secy.
Employer Identification Number: 136083721

5058
Anne S. Richardson Charitable Trust ⌑
c/o Chemical Bank
30 Rockefeller Plaza
New York 10112 (212) 621-2143

Trust established in 1965 in CT.
Donor(s): Anne S. Richardson.†
Foundation type: Independent
Financial data (yr. ended 7/31/88): Assets, $8,000,301 (M); expenditures, $486,113, including $396,400 for 25 grants (high: $10,000; low: $700).
Purpose and activities: Interests include conservation, education, and cultural programs.
Limitations: Giving primarily in CT and NY. No grants to individuals, or for endowment funds, scholarships, or fellowships; no loans.
Application information: Application form not required.
Initial approach: Letter or proposal
Copies of proposal: 2
Deadline(s): Submit proposal preferably in Jan., Mar., June, or Oct.; no set deadline
Board meeting date(s): Feb., Apr., July, and Nov.
Write: Patricia Kelly
Trustees: Chemical Bank.
Employer Identification Number: 136192516

5059
Frank E. and Nancy M. Richardson Foundation ⌑ ☆
c/o Wesray Capital Corp.
375 Park Ave.
New York 10152-0103 (212) 752-1900

Established in 1987 in NY.
Donor(s): Frank E. Richardson III.
Foundation type: Independent
Financial data (yr. ended 3/31/88): Assets, $1,453,271 (M); gifts received, $1,511,866;

expenditures, $95,532, including $83,800 for 17 grants (high: $30,000; low: $300).
Purpose and activities: Giving primarily for international affairs and elementary education; support also for the performing and visual arts.
Limitations: Giving primarily in NY.
Application information: Application form not required.
Initial approach: Letter
Deadline(s): None
Write: Frank E. Richardson III, Trustee
Trustees: Frank E. Richardson III, Nancy M. Richardson.
Employer Identification Number: 133440317

5060
Smith Richardson Foundation, Inc. ▼
210 East 86th St., 6th Fl.
New York 10028 (212) 861-8181
Application address for Early Intervention, Education and Indigenous Self-Help projects: c/o Peter L. Richardson, V.P., 266 Post Rd. East, Westport, CT 06880

Incorporated in 1935 in NC.
Donor(s): H.S. Richardson, Sr.,† Grace Jones Richardson.†
Foundation type: Independent
Financial data (yr. ended 12/31/88): Assets, $248,907,833 (M); expenditures, $17,672,946, including $15,311,787 for 136 grants (high: $5,177,162; low: $5,000).
Purpose and activities: The grants-in-aid program has two main thrusts: 1) a public affairs program, aimed at supporting and promoting a vigorous economy and free society, mainly through support of public policy research projects and educational programs focusing on business and the economy; 2) to aid in developing the qualities of leadership that will make society fully responsive to the great demands being placed upon it in today's world, through support of the Center for Creative Leadership in Greensboro, NC. Two new grants programs were established in 1986: Early Intervention/Education projects for at-risk children, and Indigenous Self-Help/Mutual Aid projects which would include community oriented efforts that focus on child development and family support issues in economically disadvantaged areas.
Types of support: Research, publications, conferences and seminars, seed money, matching funds, special projects.
Limitations: No support for programs in the arts, historic restoration, or regional or community programs concerning employment, recreation, or regional or community health and welfare. No grants to individuals, or for deficit financing, building or endowment funds, scholarships, fellowships, operating budgets, or research in the physical sciences; no loans.
Publications: Annual report (including application guidelines).
Application information: Most projects funded are initiated by the foundation. Application form not required.
Initial approach: Proposal
Copies of proposal: 1
Deadline(s): None
Board meeting date(s): Usually in Mar., June, Sept., and Dec.
Final notification: 30 to 60 days
Write: Mrs. Devon Gaffney Cross, Dir. of Research
Officers: H. Smith Richardson, Jr.,* Chair.; R. Randolph Richardson,* Vice-Chair. and Pres.; Peter L. Richardson,* V.P. and Secy.; R. Larry Coble, Treas.
Trustees:* C.W. Cheek, Robert H. Mulreany, Heather S. Richardson, Stuart S. Richardson.
Number of staff: 5 full-time professional; 2 full-time support.
Employer Identification Number: 560611550

5061
Richenthal Foundation ⌑ ☆
122 East 42nd St.
New York 10168-0001 (212) 687-8360

Established in 1964.
Foundation type: Independent
Financial data (yr. ended 12/31/88): Assets, $1,570,602 (M); expenditures, $51,004, including $40,865 for 23 grants (high: $10,000; low: $100).
Purpose and activities: Support for Jewish organizations, including welfare funds; grants also for the performing arts, health associations, and hospitals.
Limitations: Giving primarily in NY. No grants to individuals.
Application information:
Initial approach: Proposal
Deadline(s): None
Write: Arthur Richenthal or Vivian Richenthal, Directors
Directors: Arthur Richenthal, Donald Richenthal, Vivian Richenthal.
Employer Identification Number: 136113616

5062
The Frederick W. Richmond Foundation, Inc. ⌑
P.O. Box 33
Wantagh 11793 (516) 579-3373

Incorporated in 1962 in NY.
Donor(s): Frederick W. Richmond.
Foundation type: Independent
Financial data (yr. ended 4/30/89): Assets, $3,349,162 (M); gifts received, $177,250; expenditures, $279,821, including $229,400 for 65 grants (high: $12,500; low: $350; average: $2,000).
Purpose and activities: Major interest in pilot projects in education and the arts; support also for AIDS research.
Types of support: Special projects, seed money, fellowships.
Limitations: No grants to individuals.
Publications: 990-PF, program policy statement.
Application information: Application form not required.
Initial approach: Letter
Copies of proposal: 1
Deadline(s): None
Board meeting date(s): Biannually
Final notification: 3 months
Write: Pauline Nunen, Exec. Dir.
Officers: Timothy E. Wyman,* Pres.; William J. Butler,* Secy.; Barbara Brown, Treas.; Beatrice Hinch, Treas.; Gerald K. Warner, Treas.; Pauline Nunen, Exec. Dir.
Directors:* Barbara Bode, Helen Fioratti, Steven N. Kaufmann, Frederick W. Richmond.
Number of staff: 1 full-time professional; 1 part-time professional; 1 part-time support.
Employer Identification Number: 136124582

5063
The Ridgefield Foundation ⌑
641 Lexington Ave., 26th Fl.
New York 10022 (212) 750-9330

Incorporated in 1956 in NY.
Donor(s): Henry J. Leir, Erna D. Leir, Continental Ore Corp., International Ore and Fertilizer Corp.
Foundation type: Independent
Financial data (yr. ended 02/28/89): Assets, $4,655,934 (M); expenditures, $392,884, including $303,450 for 70 grants (high: $25,000; low: $100; average: $100-$500).
Purpose and activities: Support for education in the U.S. and Israel, Jewish welfare funds, social service agencies, and cultural programs; most support is for past donees or for organizations recommended by board members.
Limitations: Giving primarily in NY for local services; giving in the U.S. and Israel for education. No grants to individuals, or for scholarships, fellowships, or matching gifts; no loans.
Application information: Contributes only to pre-selected organizations. Applications not accepted.
Board meeting date(s): Oct.
Write: Marguerite M. Riposanu, Secy.
Officers: Henry J. Leir,* Pres.; Louis J. Lipton,* V.P.; Marguerite M. Riposanu, Secy.; Samuel Sitkoff,* Treas.
Directors:* Alan K. Docter, Arthur S. Hoffman, Marcelo Leipziger, Jean Mayer, Jerome Shelby.
Number of staff: 1 part-time professional.
Employer Identification Number: 136093563

5064
Jessie Ridley Foundation, Inc. ⌑
250 West 57th St.
New York 10019

Incorporated in 1973 in NY.
Foundation type: Independent
Financial data (yr. ended 12/31/86): Assets, $1,275,260 (M); expenditures, $76,192, including $56,400 for 9 grants (high: $10,500; low: $2,000).
Purpose and activities: Grants to higher educational institutions, primarily for scholarships for physically handicapped students selected by the institutions.
Types of support: Scholarship funds.
Limitations: No grants to individuals.
Officers and Trustees: Murry Kalik, Pres.; P. Douglass Martin, V.P.; Mark Kalik, Secy.; Edward Ridley Finch, Jr., Treas.; Elizabeth Lathrop Finch, Lawrence Kalik, Richard W. Martin.
Employer Identification Number: 237379436

5065
Simon H. Rifkind Foundation ⌑
c/o Paul, Weiss, Rifkind, Wharton, & Garrison
1285 Ave. of the Americas
New York 10019-6064

Established in 1957 in NY.
Donor(s): Members of the Rifkind Family.
Foundation type: Independent
Financial data (yr. ended 1/31/89): Assets, $1,075,714 (M); gifts received, $35,000; expenditures, $113,601, including $112,650 for 27 grants (high: $35,500; low: $25).
Purpose and activities: Support for Jewish giving, including welfare funds; higher education, including medical education; and hospitals.
Limitations: Giving primarily in NY. No grants to individuals.
Application information: Contributes only to pre-selected organizations. Applications not accepted.
Trustees: Richard A. Rifkind, Robert S. Rifkind, Simon H. Rifkind.
Employer Identification Number: 136110890

5066
The Riklis Family Foundation, Inc. ⌑
888 Seventh Ave., 43rd Fl.
New York 10106 (212) 621-4500

Incorporated in 1960 in NY.
Donor(s): McCrory Corp.
Foundation type: Company-sponsored
Financial data (yr. ended 6/30/87): Assets, $5,122,863 (M); gifts received, $780,000; expenditures, $427,822, including $421,660 for 53 grants (high: $90,000; low: $360).
Purpose and activities: Emphasis on Jewish welfare funds, children, and education.
Application information: Application form not required.
Initial approach: Letter
Deadline(s): None
Write: Simona Ackerman, Pres.
Officers: Simona Ackerman, Pres.; Meshulam Riklis, V.P.; Avigdor Shwartzstein, Secy.-Treas.
Employer Identification Number: 136163061

5067
The Ring Foundation, Inc. ⌑
20 West 47th St.
New York 10036-3303

Established in 1979 in NY.
Donor(s): Frank Ring, Leo Ring, Michael Ring.
Foundation type: Independent
Financial data (yr. ended 5/31/87): Assets, $1,301,564 (M); gifts received, $515,000; expenditures, $55,717, including $55,646 for 13 grants (high: $30,000; low: $36).
Purpose and activities: Support primarily for Jewish giving; support also for higher and secondary education.
Types of support: Building funds.
Application information: Contributes only to pre-selected organizations. Applications not accepted.
Officers: Leo Ring, Pres.; Michael Ring, V.P.; Frank Ring, Secy.
Employer Identification Number: 133015418

5068
The Ritter Foundation, Inc.
1776 Broadway
New York 10019 (212) 757-4646

Incorporated in 1947 in NY.
Donor(s): Gladys Ritter Livingston, Irene Ritter,† Lena Ritter,† Louis Ritter,† Sidney Ritter.†
Foundation type: Independent
Financial data (yr. ended 11/30/89): Assets, $4,811,489 (M); expenditures, $264,518, including $248,050 for 107 grants (high: $42,138; low: $25).
Purpose and activities: Grants for higher education, including medical education, Israel, mental health, and local Jewish welfare funds.
Limitations: No grants to individuals.
Application information: Funds committed through 1995. Applications not accepted.
Board meeting date(s): May and Nov.
Write: Toby G. Ritter, V.P.
Officers and Trustees:* Gladys Ritter Livingston,* Pres.; Toby G. Ritter,* V.P. and Secy.; David Ritter,* V.P.; Alan I. Ritter,* Treas.; Frances R. Weisman.
Number of staff: 1 part-time support.
Employer Identification Number: 136082276

5069
May Ellen and Gerald Ritter Foundation ⌑
9411 Shore Rd.
Brooklyn 11209

Foundation established in 1980 in NY.
Donor(s): Gerald Ritter,† May Ellen Ritter.†
Foundation type: Independent
Financial data (yr. ended 12/31/88): Assets, $6,928,292 (M); expenditures, $226,981, including $183,735 for 27 grants (high: $111,000; low: $50).
Purpose and activities: Giving primarily for health agencies and Roman Catholic welfare funds.
Limitations: No grants to individuals.
Application information: Application form not required.
Initial approach: Letter and proposal
Deadline(s): None
Board meeting date(s): Quarterly
Write: Emma A. Daniels, Pres.
Officers: Emma A. Daniels, Pres.; John Parker, V.P.; Helen Rohan, Secy.; Sophie Distanovich, Treas.
Number of staff: None.
Employer Identification Number: 136114269

5070
The Gerald & May Ellen Ritter Memorial Fund ⌑
c/o Proskauer Rose Goetz & Mendelsohn
300 Park Ave.
New York 10022 (212) 909-7708

Fund established in 1980 in NY.
Donor(s): May Ellen Ritter,† Gerald Ritter.†
Foundation type: Independent
Financial data (yr. ended 4/30/89): Assets, $1,263,747 (M); expenditures, $278,729, including $265,500 for grants (average: $500-$50,000).
Purpose and activities: Support for higher education; cultural organizations, including music and other performing arts; social service and youth agencies; and Jewish organizations, including temples and welfare funds.
Types of support: Building funds, equipment, land acquisition, endowment funds, matching funds, scholarship funds, fellowships, research, loans, publications, conferences and seminars, continuing support, operating budgets, annual campaigns, seed money, emergency funds, deficit financing, special projects.
Limitations: Giving primarily in New York, NY. No grants to individuals.
Application information: Application form not required.
Initial approach: Letter or proposal
Deadline(s): None
Board meeting date(s): Quarterly
Final notification: Varies
Write: Gerald Silbert, Pres.
Officers and Directors: Gerald Silbert, Chair. and Pres.; Lawrence Lachman, Sr. V.P.; Ramie J. Silbert, V.P.; Terry F. Silbert, V.P.; Rita Rothman, Secy.; Herbert T. Weinstein, Treas.
Number of staff: None.
Employer Identification Number: 133037300

5071
Robbins Foundation, Inc. ⌑ ☆
515 Madison Dr.
New York 10022

Established in 1945.
Foundation type: Independent
Financial data (yr. ended 2/28/89): Assets, $1,138,214 (M); expenditures, $53,623, including $39,500 for 32 grants (high: $5,000; low: $100).
Purpose and activities: Support primarily for higher and secondary education and Jewish welfare.
Limitations: Giving primarily in NY. No grants to individuals.
Application information: Contributes only to pre-selected organizations. Applications not accepted.
Officers: Mary Robbins, Pres.; Allan J. Robbins, V.P. and Secy.; Edgar B. Robbins, Treas.
Employer Identification Number: 136116442

5072
Edward R. & Rosalind S. Roberts Foundation ☆
85 Broad St., 30th Fl.
New York 10004-2408

Established in 1981.
Donor(s): Edward R. Roberts.
Foundation type: Independent
Financial data (yr. ended 11/30/88): Assets, $881,171 (M); gifts received, $46,467; expenditures, $140,126, including $132,160 for 41 grants (high: $23,285; low: $50).
Purpose and activities: Giving primarily for the performing arts and higher education; support also for hospitals, health, and museums and other cultural programs.
Limitations: Giving primarily in New York, NY. No grants to individuals.

Application information: Contributes only to pre-selected organizations. Applications not accepted.
Trustees: Alfred Olono II, Edward R. Roberts, Marc Roberts, Nancy C. Roberts.
Employer Identification Number: 133087877

5073
James E. Robinson Foundation ☆
20 Haarlem Ave.
White Plains 10603 (914) 428-5350

Established in 1960 in NY.
Donor(s): James E. Robinson.
Foundation type: Independent
Financial data (yr. ended 11/30/89): Assets, $1,084,591 (M); expenditures, $66,227, including $64,000 for grants (average: $1,000-$10,000).
Purpose and activities: Giving primarily for higher and other education; support also for performing arts groups.
Types of support: Annual campaigns.
Limitations: No grants to individuals.
Application information: Application form not required.
Initial approach: Letter
Copies of proposal: 1
Deadline(s): None
Board meeting date(s): Winter
Write: James E. Robinson, Pres.
Officers: James E. Robinson, Pres.; Christine Beshar, V.P.; Jeanie McAlpin, Secy.
Employer Identification Number: 136075171

5074
Maurice R. Robinson Fund, Inc. ¤
c/o Scholastic, Inc.
730 Broadway
New York 10003 (212) 505-3449

Established in 1960 in NY.
Donor(s): Maurice R. Robinson.
Foundation type: Independent
Financial data (yr. ended 3/31/89): Assets, $2,155,970 (M); gifts received, $10,000; expenditures, $112,895, including $89,760 for 43 grants (high: $20,000; low: $200).
Purpose and activities: Preference given to educational institutions from early childhood through higher education, especially colleges offering majors in communications, including print and broadcast journalism.
Types of support: Internships.
Application information: Application form not required.
Initial approach: Letter or proposal
Deadline(s): Preferably before Mar. 1
Board meeting date(s): Mid-Mar.
Write: Jack K. Lippert, Pres.
Officers: Jack K. Lippert,* Pres.; Sidney P. Marland, Jr.,* V.P.; Anne Devanie, Secy.; Raymond A. Occhipinti, Treas.; Claudia Cohl.
Trustees:* Sturges F. Cary, Jeanne Krier.
Number of staff: 2 part-time professional.
Employer Identification Number: 136161094

5075
The Ellis H. and Doris B. Robison Foundation ¤
161 River St., P.O. Box 809
Troy 12181 (518) 274-6000

Trust established in 1980 in NY.
Donor(s): Ellis Robison.†
Foundation type: Independent
Financial data (yr. ended 12/31/87): Assets, $2,684,833 (M); expenditures, $120,605, including $111,175 for grants.
Purpose and activities: Grants for educational, religious, social services, and medical purposes initiated solely by the president.
Types of support: Continuing support, building funds, general purposes.
Limitations: Giving limited to Rensselaer County, NY. No grants to individuals, or for endowment funds, scholarships, fellowships, or matching gifts; no loans.
Application information: Contributes only to pre-selected organizations. Applications not accepted.
Officers: James A. Robison, Pres.; Richard G. Robison, V.P.; Elissa R. Prout, Secy.
Employer Identification Number: 222470695

5076
Edward & Ellen Roche Relief Foundation
c/o U.S. Trust Co. of New York
114 West 47th St.
New York 10036-1532 (212) 852-3683

Established in 1930 in NY.
Donor(s): Edward Roche.†
Foundation type: Independent
Financial data (yr. ended 12/31/89): Assets, $4,000,000 (M); expenditures, $205,000, including $167,000 for 44 grants (high: $13,000; low: $1,000; average: $1,000-$5,000).
Purpose and activities: Emphasis on aid to destitute women and children, grants largely for child welfare, youth organizations, and social service agencies.
Types of support: Seed money, special projects, general purposes.
Limitations: Giving primarily in NY, CT, and NJ. No grants to individuals, or for building or endowment funds, research, fellowships, or matching gifts; no loans.
Publications: Program policy statement.
Application information: Letter or proposal. Application form not required.
Initial approach: Telephone for guidelines
Copies of proposal: 1
Deadline(s): Apr. 15 and Oct. 1
Board meeting date(s): May and Nov.
Final notification: Positive replies only
Write: Anne Smith-Ganey, Asst. V.P., U.S. Trust Co. of New York
Trustee: U.S. Trust Co. of New York.
Number of staff: None.
Employer Identification Number: 135622067

5077
Rochester Area Foundation
335 Main St. East, Suite 402
Rochester 14604 (716) 325-4353

Incorporated in 1972 in NY.
Foundation type: Community
Financial data (yr. ended 02/28/90): Assets, $21,355,974 (M); gifts received, $6,388,332; expenditures, $2,315,472, including $1,831,842 for 593 grants (high: $80,000; low: $100; average: $5,000-$10,000) and $85,616 for 193 grants to individuals (high: $4,000; low: $100; average: $250-$750).
Purpose and activities: Giving for broad purposes related to community betterment, including education, the environment, cultural programs, health services, commmunity development, and social services, including family and legal services, minorities, women, and youth; scholarship recipients chosen by institutions.
Types of support: Seed money, equipment, fellowships, renovation projects, technical assistance, consulting services, scholarship funds, publications, student aid, special projects, building funds, conferences and seminars.
Limitations: Giving limited to Monroe, Livingston, Ontario, Orleans, Genesee, and Wayne counties, NY. No support for religious projects. No grants to individuals (except from restricted funds), or for operating budgets, continuing support, annual campaigns, deficit financing, land acquisition, endowment or emergency funds, matching or challenge grants, or research.
Publications: Annual report, program policy statement, application guidelines.
Application information: Scholarship recipients chosen by institutions. Application form required.
Initial approach: Letter
Copies of proposal: 3
Board meeting date(s): Jan., Mar., May, July, Sept., and Nov.
Write: Linda S. Weinstein, Pres.
Officers and Directors:* Pete C. Merrill,* Chair.; Charles Pickhardt,* Vice-Chair., Endowment; Jon Schumacher,* Vice-Chair., Administration; Ruth Scott,* Vice-Chair., Grantmaking; Linda S. Weinstein, Pres.; Mary-Francis Winters,* Secy.; Richard Gray,* Treas.; and 26 other directors.
Number of staff: 2 full-time professional; 4 part-time professional; 4 full-time support; 1 part-time support.
Employer Identification Number: 237250641

5078
Rochester Female Charitable Society ¤
c/o Chase Lincoln First Bank, N.A.
P.O. Box 1412
Rochester 14603
Application address: 87 Grosvenor Rd., Rochester, NY 14610; Tel.: (716) 244-2979

Established in 1822.
Foundation type: Independent
Financial data (yr. ended 03/31/89): Assets, $1,399,386 (M); expenditures, $73,940, including $49,255 for 30 grants (high: $5,000; low: $200) and $16,276 for 170 grants to individuals (high: $700; low: $10).
Purpose and activities: Emphasis on recreation programs and facilities for youth, child welfare, hospitals, and social service agencies; also award grants to local area public welfare agencies on behalf of individuals.

Limitations: Giving limited to the greater Rochester, NY, area.
Application information:
Initial approach: Letter
Deadline(s): None
Write: Mrs. Bruce B. Bates, Allocations Chair.
Officers and Directors:* Jane Gorsline,* Pres.; Mimi Whitbeck,* V.P.; Gina Strasenburgh,* Recording Secy.; Nora Ward,* Corresponding Secy.; Carol Rees,* Treas.; and 18 additional directors.
Trustee: Chase Lincoln First Bank, N.A.
Employer Identification Number: 237166180

5079
Rockefeller Brothers Fund ▼
1290 Ave. of the Americas
New York 10104 (212) 373-4200

Incorporated in 1940 in NY.
Donor(s): John D. Rockefeller, Jr.,† Martha Baird Rockefeller,† Abby Rockefeller Mauze,† David Rockefeller, John D. Rockefeller, 3rd,† Laurance S. Rockefeller, Nelson A. Rockefeller,† Winthrop Rockefeller.†
Foundation type: Independent
Financial data (yr. ended 12/31/88): Assets, $242,120,725 (M); gifts received, $188,267; expenditures, $12,032,313, including $7,999,659 for 146 grants (high: $225,000; low: $3,000; average: $10,000-$75,000).
Purpose and activities: "Support of efforts in the U.S. and abroad that contribute ideas, develop leaders, and encourage institutions in the transition to global interdependence and that counter world trends of resource depletion, militarization, protectionism, and isolation which now threaten to move humankind everywhere further away from cooperation, trade and economic growth, arms restraint, and conservation." There are four major giving categories: 1) One World, with two major components: sustainable resource use and world security, including issues related to arms control, international relations, development, trade, and finance; 2) New York City; 3) Nonprofit Sector; and 4) Special Concerns. Two new concerns include focusing effective action on public health and related issues involved with the AIDS crisis in New York City, and dealing with the current crisis in South Africa.
Types of support: General purposes, seed money, special projects, conferences and seminars, internships, exchange programs, matching funds, consulting services, continuing support, research, technical assistance, endowment funds.
Limitations: No support for churches, hospitals, or community centers. No grants to individuals (including research, graduate study, or the writing of books), or for endowment or building funds; no loans.
Publications: Annual report (including application guidelines).
Application information: Application form not required.
Initial approach: Letter
Copies of proposal: 1
Deadline(s): None
Board meeting date(s): June and Nov.
Final notification: 3 months
Write: Benjamin R. Shute, Jr., Secy.
Officers: Colin G. Campbell,* Pres.; Russell A. Phillips, Jr., Exec. V.P.; Benjamin R. Shute, Jr., Secy.; David G. Fernald, Treas.
Trustees:* David Rockefeller, Jr., Chair.; Abby M. O'Neill, Vice-Chair.; Laura R. Chasin, Peggy Dulany, Neva R. Goodwin, Richard D. Parsons, George Putnam, Laurance Rockefeller, Rodman C. Rockefeller, Sharon P. Rockefeller, Steven C. Rockefeller, S. Frederick Starr, Russell E. Train.
Number of staff: 6 full-time professional; 1 part-time professional; 13 full-time support; 1 part-time support.
Employer Identification Number: 131760106

5080
Rockefeller Family Fund, Inc. ▼
1290 Ave. of the Americas, Rm. 3450
New York 10104 (212) 373-4252

Incorporated in 1967 in NY.
Donor(s): Members of the Rockefeller family.
Foundation type: Independent
Financial data (yr. ended 12/31/88): Assets, $30,530,537 (M); gifts received, $550,384; expenditures, $2,747,150, including $2,037,414 for 105 grants (high: $40,000; low: $1,000).
Purpose and activities: "In 1990, the fund will make grants to support advocacy programs that are action-oriented and likely to yield tangible results in five program areas: Citizen Education and Participation; Economic Justice for Women; Education; Environment; and Institutional Responsiveness: 1) Citizen Education and Participation: supports nonpartisan organizations that help citizens comprehend and exercise their right to vote and work for the removal of institutional barriers to voting; 2) Economic Justice for Women: supports projects that seek to provide women with equitable employment opportunities and the improvement of their work lives; 3) Education: support for advocacy projects designed to improve the quality of American public education, primarily in the preschool and the elementary school years; emphasis given to projects designed to assist economically and socially disadvantaged children and families. Supports proposals to advance public policy, strengthen educational institutions, and enhance the ability of children to learn; 4) Environment: emphasizes conservation of natural resources, protection of health as affected by the environment, the cessation of pollution caused by the Department of Energy and military services, and domestic efforts to broaden the definition of national security and global stability to include environmental security; and 5) Institutional Responsiveness: traditionally the most open-ended of the fund's program areas, its purpose is to provide individuals and organizations with the means to influence the policies and actions of public and private institutions."
Types of support: Operating budgets, continuing support, seed money, special projects.
Limitations: No support for international programs. No grants to individuals, or for building funds, renovation projects, deficit financing, research, endowment funds, matching gifts, scholarships, or fellowships; no loans.
Publications: Annual report (including application guidelines).
Application information: Application form not required.
Initial approach: Letter or proposal
Copies of proposal: 1
Deadline(s): None
Board meeting date(s): June and Dec.; executive committee usually meets 3 additional times a year
Final notification: 1 to 3 months
Write: Donald K. Ross, Dir.
Officers and Trustees:* Richard M. Chasin,* Pres.; Nancy Anderson,* V.P.; Anne Bartley,* V.P.; Clare Buden,* V.P.; Diana N. Rockefeller,* V.P.; Wendy Rockefeller,* V.P.; Donald K. Ross, Dir. and Secy.; Hope Aldrich, Dana Chasin, Laura R. Chasin, Bruce Mazlish, Alida R. Messinger, Catharine O'Neill, Mary Louise Pierson, Richard G. Rockefeller, Steven C. Rockefeller, Abby R. Simpson.
Number of staff: 2 full-time professional; 1 full-time support; 1 part-time support.
Employer Identification Number: 136257658

5081
The Rockefeller Foundation ▼
1133 Ave. of the Americas
New York 10036 (212) 869-8500

Incorporated in 1913 in NY.
Donor(s): John D. Rockefeller, Sr.†
Foundation type: Independent
Financial data (yr. ended 12/31/89): Assets, $2,140,244,924 (M); gifts received, $67,932; expenditures, $90,702,898, including $59,996,580 for 910 grants (high: $975,000; low: $1,000; average: $10,000-$150,000), $5,693,062 for 320 grants to individuals (high: $70,000; low: $500; average: $5,000-$20,000), $28,021 for 153 employee matching gifts, $5,777,335 for 5 foundation-administered programs and $5,000,000 for 1 loan.
Purpose and activities: "To promote the well-being of mankind throughout the world." Concentrates its activities on science-based, international development in agriculture, health, and population sciences; arts and humanities; and equal opportunity. A "Special Interests and Explorations" category permits the foundation to maintain flexibility in grantmaking. Programs are carried out through the awarding of grants and fellowships, and the dissemination of information through publications and close association with the media. In addition, the foundation operates a Study and Conference Center in Bellagio, Italy, which is available for international conferences and brief residencies.
Types of support: Fellowships, research, publications, conferences and seminars, special projects, grants to individuals, program-related investments, employee matching gifts.
Limitations: No support for appraising or subsidizing cures or inventions; the establishment of local hospitals, churches, schools, libraries, or welfare agencies or their building or operating funds; financing altruistic movements involving private profit; or propaganda or attempts to influence legislation. No grants for personal aid to

individuals, or for capital or endowment funds, general support, or scholarships; no loans, except program-related investments.
Publications: Annual report, program policy statement, informational brochure (including application guidelines), application guidelines.
Application information: Informational brochures available for fellowship programs. Application form not required.
Initial approach: Letter or proposal
Copies of proposal: 1
Deadline(s): Specified in individual brochures
Board meeting date(s): Usually in Mar., June, Sept., and Dec.
Write: Lynda Mullen, Secy.
Officers: Peter C. Goldmark, Jr.,* Pres.; Kenneth Prewitt, Sr. V.P.; Hugh B. Price, V.P.; Frank Karel, V.P. for Communications; Lynda Mullen, Secy.; Jack R. Meyer, Treas.; Sally Ferris, Dir. for Administration.
Trustees:* John R. Evans, Chair.; Alan Alda, John Brademas, Harold Brown, Henry G. Cisneros, Peggy Dulany, Frances FitzGerald, Daniel P. Garcia, Ronald E. Goldsberry, W. David Hopper, Karen N. Horn, Alice Stone Ilchman, Richard H. Jenrette, Tom Johnson, Arthur Levitt, Jr., Robert C. Maynard, Eleanor Holmes Norton, Harry Woolf.
Number of staff: 108 full-time professional; 1 part-time professional; 43 full-time support; 3 part-time support.
Employer Identification Number: 131659629

5082
Richard & Dorothy Rodgers Foundation ⌑
c/o Mrs. Dorothy Rodgers
598 Madison Ave.
New York 10022

Established in 1952 in NY.
Donor(s): Richard Rodgers,† Dorothy F. Rodgers.
Foundation type: Independent
Financial data (yr. ended 12/31/88): Assets, $1,907,368 (M); gifts received, $699,994; expenditures, $1,319,069, including $1,297,200 for 104 grants (high: $510,000; low: $50).
Purpose and activities: Support for hospitals, culture, including museums, Jewish organizations, and general charitable giving.
Limitations: Giving primarily in New York, NY. No grants to individuals.
Application information: Contributes only to pre-selected organizations. Applications not accepted.
Officers: Dorothy F. Rodgers, Pres. and Treas.; Lawrence B. Buttenwieser, Secy.
Employer Identification Number: 136062852

5083
The Felix and Elizabeth Rohatyn Foundation, Inc.
(Formerly Felix G. Rohatyn Foundation)
c/o Lazard Freres & Co.
One Rockefeller Plaza
New York 10020

Established in 1968.
Donor(s): Felix G. Rohatyn.
Foundation type: Independent
Financial data (yr. ended 12/31/89): Assets, $4,357,588 (M); gifts received, $400,000; expenditures, $518,925, including $515,891 for 125 grants (high: $50,000; low: $100).
Purpose and activities: Support for education, particularly elementary and secondary education.
Types of support: General purposes, equipment.
Limitations: Giving primarily in the New York, NY, area. No grants to individuals.
Application information: Application form not required.
Initial approach: Letter
Deadline(s): None
Write: Felix G. Rohatyn, Pres.
Officers: Felix G. Rohatyn, Pres.; Elizabeth Rohatyn, V.P.; Melvin L. Heineman, Secy.-Treas.
Director: Vivien Stiles Duffy.
Number of staff: 1 part-time professional.
Employer Identification Number: 237015644

5084
Martin Romerovski Foundation, Inc. ⌑
812 Fifth Ave.
New York 10021 (212) 758-1638

Established in 1965.
Donor(s): Martin Romerovski, Romerovski Brothers, Inc.
Foundation type: Independent
Financial data (yr. ended 12/31/88): Assets, $150,370 (M); gifts received, $190,000; expenditures, $161,653, including $161,598 for 72 grants (high: $40,000; low: $10).
Purpose and activities: Giving primarily for Jewish welfare funds and educational institutions, both in the U.S. and Israel.
Limitations: No grants to individuals.
Application information: Contributes only to pre-selected organizations. Applications not accepted.
Write: Martin Romerovski, Pres.
Officers: Martin Romerovski, Pres.; Rose Romerovski, V.P. and Secy.; Philip J. Maron, Treas.
Employer Identification Number: 136172511

5085
Romill Foundation ▼
1045 Sixth Ave.
New York 10018
Additional address: c/o Wilmington Trust Company, 10th and Market Sts., Wilmington, DE 19890

Trust established in 1960 in SC.
Donor(s): Roger Milliken.
Foundation type: Independent
Financial data (yr. ended 12/31/88): Assets, $2,001,166 (M); gifts received, $363,999; expenditures, $1,531,037, including $1,521,015 for 24 grants (high: $1,000,000; low: $600; average: $2,500-$65,000).
Purpose and activities: Grants primarily for educational associations and higher education; some support for public interest and cultural organizations.
Types of support: General purposes.
Limitations: Giving primarily in Spartanburg County, SC.
Application information: Application form not required.
Initial approach: Letter
Deadline(s): None
Board meeting date(s): As required
Write: Lawrence Heagney, Treas.
Officer: Lawrence Heagney, Treas.
Trustees: Gerrish H. Milliken, Justine V.R. Milliken, Minot K. Milliken.
Number of staff: None.
Employer Identification Number: 136102069

5086
The Theodore Roosevelt Association ☆
P.O. Box 720
Oyster Bay 11771

Chartered by Act of Congress in 1920.
Foundation type: Independent
Financial data (yr. ended 09/30/89): Assets, $1,153,729 (M); gifts received, $110,676; expenditures, $127,166, including $5,000 for 5 grants (high: $1,500; low: $600).
Purpose and activities: Support for libraries and historic preservation programs and sites related to Theodore Roosevelt.
Limitations: No grants to individuals.
Application information: Contributes only to pre-selected organizations. Applications not accepted.
Officers: Theodore R. Kupferman, Pres.; R.D. Dalziel, V.P.; Stephen Jeffries, Secy.; John Gable, Exec. Dir.
Number of staff: 1 full-time professional; 1 part-time professional.
Employer Identification Number: 135593999

5087
The Roothbert Fund, Inc.
475 Riverside Dr., Rm. 252
New York 10115 (212) 870-3116

Incorporated in 1958 in NY.
Donor(s): Albert Roothbert,† Toni Roothbert.†
Foundation type: Independent
Financial data (yr. ended 12/31/88): Assets, $1,897,443 (M); expenditures, $126,386, including $84,700 for 76 grants to individuals (high: $2,000; low: $500; average: $1,000).
Purpose and activities: To assist college or university students who are primarily motivated by spiritual values, with preference to those considering teaching as a vocation.
Types of support: Student aid.
Limitations: No grants for capital or endowment funds, operating budgets, general support, special projects, or matching gifts; no loans.
Publications: Annual report, application guidelines.
Application information: Interview with Scholarship Committee is a requirement in the application process; interviews take place in Mar. in New York City and currently in Washington, Philadelphia, and Providence. Application form required.
Initial approach: Letter
Copies of proposal: 1
Deadline(s): Submit Fund form in Jan. or Feb.; deadline Mar. 1
Board meeting date(s): Apr. and Oct.; awards grants annually in Apr.
Final notification: 1 month

Write: Jacob van Rossum, Admin. Secy.
Officers and Directors:* Carl Solberg,* Pres. and Secy.; Blake T. Newton III,* V.P. and Treas.; Sylvia A. Boone,* V.P.; Susan S. Purdy,* V.P.; James P. Carse, Jane F. Century, Adriaan T. Halfhide, Toby M. Horn, Donna M. Johnson, John W. Johnson, Lowell W. Livezey, Michael Mooney, Grace A. Troisi, Charles Van Horne.
Number of staff: None.
Employer Identification Number: 136162570

5088
Billy Rose Foundation, Inc. ▼ ⌑
One Dag Hammarskjold Plaza, 47th Fl.
New York 10163 (212) 349-4141

Incorporated in 1958 in NY.
Donor(s): Billy Rose.†
Foundation type: Independent
Financial data (yr. ended 12/31/88): Assets, $9,081,987 (M); expenditures, $1,262,671, including $1,237,000 for 88 grants (high: $325,000; low: $2,500; average: $2,500-$25,000).
Purpose and activities: Support for museums, particularly a museum in Israel, the performing and fine arts, higher education, and medical research.
Types of support: Research, special projects.
Limitations: Giving primarily in New York, NY. No grants to individuals.
Application information: Application form not required.
Initial approach: Letter
Deadline(s): None
Board meeting date(s): Usually in June
Final notification: Varies
Write: Terri C. Mangino, Exec. Dir.
Officers and Directors:* Arthur Cantor,* Chair.; Morris Shilensky,* Pres.; James R. Cherry,* V.P. and Secy.-Treas.; Charles Wohlstetter, V.P.; Terri C. Mangino, Exec. Dir.
Number of staff: 1 full-time professional.
Employer Identification Number: 136165466

5089
Frederick P. & Sandra P. Rose Foundation ⌑
380 Madison Ave., 4th Fl.
New York 10017

Established in 1982 in DE.
Donor(s): Frederick P. Rose.
Foundation type: Independent
Financial data (yr. ended 11/30/88): Assets, $1,581,977 (M); gifts received, $965,000; expenditures, $132,250, including $131,385 for 53 grants (high: $25,100; low: $100).
Purpose and activities: Giving primarily for higher education; support also for cultural organizations.
Limitations: No grants to individuals.
Application information: Contributes only to pre-selected organizations. Applications not accepted.
Officers and Directors:* Frederick P. Rose,* Pres.; Sandra P. Rose,* V.P.; Jonathan F.P. Rose,* Secy.-Treas.; Deborah Rose, Elihu Rose.
Employer Identification Number: 133136740

5090
The Rose Fund, Inc. ⌑
380 Madison Ave.
New York 10017-2513

Donor(s): David Rose.
Foundation type: Independent
Financial data (yr. ended 9/30/88): Assets, $108,655 (M); gifts received, $65,000; expenditures, $126,879, including $126,400 for 16 grants (high: $25,000; low: $200).
Purpose and activities: Support primarily for higher education, medical research, the arts, and for Jewish giving.
Limitations: Giving primarily in NY.
Application information: Contributes only to pre-selected organizations. Applications not accepted.
Officers: Frederick P. Rose, Pres.; Daniel Rose, V.P. and Treas.; Elihu Rose, Secy.
Employer Identification Number: 136161403

5091
Joseph Rosen Foundation, Inc. ⌑
P.O. Box 334, Lenox Hill Station
New York 10021 (212) 249-1550

Incorporated in 1948 in NY.
Foundation type: Independent
Financial data (yr. ended 6/30/87): Assets, $9,012,532 (M); gifts received, $434,050; expenditures, $364,718, including $342,169 for 235 grants (high: $24,000; low: $50).
Purpose and activities: Grants largely for Jewish welfare funds, and temple support, child welfare, higher education, health services, and cultural organizations, especially the performing arts.
Application information: Contributes only to pre-selected organizations. Applications not accepted.
Officers and Directors: Abraham A. Rosen, Pres.; Jonathan P. Rosen, V.P. and Secy.; Miriam Rosen, Treas.
Employer Identification Number: 136158412

5092
Jacob & Belle Rosenbaum Foundation ⌑
15 Highview Rd.
Monsey 10952-2943

Established in 1982 in NY.
Foundation type: Independent
Financial data (yr. ended 12/31/88): Assets, $263,165 (M); gifts received, $207,658; expenditures, $203,810, including $197,418 for grants (high: $82,000; low: $10).
Purpose and activities: Contributing primarily for Jewish giving and Jewish welfare organizations.
Application information:
Write: Jack Rosenbaum
Trustees: Belle Rosenbaum, Jacob Rosenbaum.
Employer Identification Number: 133100072

5093
Abraham & Lillian Rosenberg Foundation, Inc. ⌑
80 White St.
New York 10013

Established in 1964 in NY.
Foundation type: Independent
Financial data (yr. ended 04/30/89): Assets, $1,306,893 (M); gifts received, $75,000; expenditures, $62,565, including $58,149 for 32 grants (high: $12,500; low: $10).
Purpose and activities: Emphasis on Jewish giving.
Types of support: General purposes.
Application information: Applications not accepted.
Officer: Dorothy Weinstein, Pres.
Employer Identification Number: 136167434

5094
Sunny and Abe Rosenberg Foundation, Inc. ⌑
c/o Gassman, Rebuhn & Co.
350 Fifth Ave.
New York 10118
Application address: c/o Star Industries, Inc., 345 Underhill Blvd., Syosset, NY 11791; Tel.: (718) 895-8950

Incorporated in 1966 in NY.
Donor(s): Abraham Rosenberg.
Foundation type: Independent
Financial data (yr. ended 12/31/88): Assets, $8,094,898 (M); gifts received, $500,000; expenditures, $283,349, including $233,620 for 83 grants (high: $81,500; low: $50).
Purpose and activities: Grants largely for Jewish welfare funds, higher education, and hospitals.
Application information:
Initial approach: Letter
Deadline(s): None
Write: Sonia Rosenberg, V.P.
Officers: Abraham Rosenberg, Pres. and Treas.; Sonia Rosenberg, V.P. and Secy.
Employer Identification Number: 136210591

5095
Rosenblatt Family Foundation, Inc. ⌑
155 Riverside Dr.
New York 10024

Incorporated in 1956 in NY.
Donor(s): Marcus Retter, Betty Retter, C. Rosenblatt.
Foundation type: Independent
Financial data (yr. ended 11/30/88): Assets, $490,665 (M); gifts received, $50,000; expenditures, $178,678, including $176,692 for grants (high: $100,000).
Purpose and activities: Support primarily for Jewish concerns.
Application information: Application form not required.
Deadline(s): None
Officer and Directors:* Marcus Retter,* Pres.; Betty Retter, Mary Schreiber.
Employer Identification Number: 136145385

5096
The Max Rosenfeld Foundation, Inc. ⌑
c/o David Berdon & Co.
415 Madison Ave.
New York 10017

Established in 1945 in DE.
Foundation type: Independent
Financial data (yr. ended 11/30/88): Assets, $1,717,718 (M); expenditures, $105,258,

including $87,433 for 14 grants (high: $31,000; low: $100).
Purpose and activities: Giving primarily for education and Jewish organizations; support also for cultural programs.
Application information: Contributes only to pre-selected organizations. Applications not accepted.
Directors: Suzanne Lehmann, Michael Rosenfeld, Maxine Sekir.
Employer Identification Number: 136137869

5097
The Rosenstiel Foundation
c/o Goldstein, Golub, Kessler & Co.
1185 Ave. of the Americas
New York 10036-2602

Incorporated in 1950 in OH.
Donor(s): Lewis S. Rosenstiel.†
Foundation type: Independent
Financial data (yr. ended 12/31/88): Assets, $11,937,644 (M); expenditures, $744,747, including $590,075 for 84 grants (high: $103,125; low: $500).
Purpose and activities: Grants largely for Polish cultural programs, the performing arts, health organizations, hospitals, and higher education.
Limitations: Giving primarily in NY and FL.
Application information: Contributes only to pre-selected organizations. Applications not accepted.
Officers: Blanka A. Rosenstiel, Pres.; Elizabeth R. Kabler, V.P.; Maurice C. Greenbaum, Secy.
Employer Identification Number: 066034536

5098
The Ida and William Rosenthal Foundation, Inc.
90 Park Ave.
New York 10016 (212) 953-1418

Incorporated in 1953 in NY.
Donor(s): Ida Rosenthal,† William Rosenthal.†
Foundation type: Independent
Financial data (yr. ended 08/31/89): Assets, $4,435,996 (M); expenditures, $364,853, including $356,090 for 44 grants (high: $100,000; low: $250).
Purpose and activities: Grants primarily for scholarships at selected secondary, undergraduate, and graduate institutions; support also for community and minority organizations in the NY metropolitan area and Hudson County, NJ; support for educational projects in the Dominican Republic.
Types of support: Seed money, scholarship funds, special projects.
Limitations: Giving primarily in NY and Hudson County, NJ; some support also in GA, FL, and WV; support for projects in the Dominican Republic through national organizations. No grants to individuals, or for matching gifts; no loans.
Application information: Application form not required.
Initial approach: Letter
Copies of proposal: 1
Deadline(s): None
Board meeting date(s): Quarterly
Write: Catherine C. Brawer, Pres.
Officers and Directors:* Catherine Coleman Brawer,* Pres.; David C. Masket,* V.P. and Treas.; Robert A. Brawer,* V.P.; Elizabeth J. Coleman,* V.P.; Abraham P. Kanner, V.P.; Steven N. Masket, Secy.; Robert N. Stroup.
Number of staff: 1 full-time professional; 1 part-time professional; 1 full-time support; 1 part-time support.
Employer Identification Number: 136141274

5099
Richard and Lois Rosenthal Foundation ⌑
Spicer and Oppenheim
Seven World Trade Ctr.
New York 10048

Established in 1969 in NY.
Donor(s): Richard Rosenthal.†
Foundation type: Independent
Financial data (yr. ended 12/31/87): Assets, $739,320 (M); expenditures, $358,464, including $350,231 for 3 grants (high: $230,000; low: $50,000).
Purpose and activities: Support primarily for hospitals, Jewish welfare, and Jewish giving.
Limitations: Giving primarily in New York, NY. No grants to individuals.
Application information: Contributes only to pre-selected organizations. Applications not accepted.
Officers and Directors: Richard Rosenthal, Pres. and Treas.; Lois Rosenthal, V.P.
Employer Identification Number: 237048452

5100
The William Rosenwald Family Fund, Inc. ⌑
122 East 42nd St., 24th Fl.
New York 10168 (212) 697-2420

Incorporated in 1938 in CT.
Donor(s): William Rosenwald, and family.
Foundation type: Independent
Financial data (yr. ended 12/31/88): Assets, $15,158,989 (M); expenditures, $986,859, including $938,953 for 57 grants (high: $530,000; low: $100).
Purpose and activities: Emphasis on Jewish welfare funds; some support for higher education, including medical education, cultural activities, and hospitals.
Types of support: General purposes.
Limitations: Giving primarily in NY.
Application information: Application form not required.
Initial approach: Proposal
Deadline(s): None
Write: David P. Steinmann, Secy.
Officers: William Rosenwald,* Pres. and Treas.; Nina Rosenwald,* V.P.; Alice R. Sigelman,* V.P.; Elizabeth R. Varet,* V.P.; David P. Steinmann, Secy.
Directors:* Hulbert S. Aldrich, Bernard E. Brandes, Henry Z. Steinway, Frank D. Williams.
Employer Identification Number: 131635289

5101
Ross Foundation, Inc. ⌑ ☆
15 East 40th St., Rm. 906
New York 10016-0401 (212) 686-8006

Established in 1950.
Foundation type: Independent
Financial data (yr. ended 12/31/88): Assets, $1,457,857 (M); expenditures, $67,992, including $61,350 for 46 grants (high: $2,000; low: $50).
Purpose and activities: Giving primarily for higher education; minor support for Episcopal churches and a community fund.
Limitations: No grants to individuals.
Application information:
Initial approach: Letter
Deadline(s): None
Write: Catherine R. Loveland, Pres.
Officers and Trustees: William E. Ross, Chair.; Catherine R. Loveland, Pres.; William L. Loveland, V.P.; Samuel Bly, Secy.; Louise A. Ross, Treas.; A.G. MacLean, Jr.
Employer Identification Number: 136106681

5102
Arthur Ross Foundation, Inc.
20 East 74th St., 4-C
New York 10021 (212) 737-7311

Incorporated in 1955 in NY.
Donor(s): Arthur Ross.
Foundation type: Independent
Financial data (yr. ended 12/31/89): Assets, $6,569,532 (M); gifts received, $658,706; expenditures, $1,213,187, including $1,179,487 for 108 grants (high: $234,000; low: $21).
Purpose and activities: Giving for higher education and cultural institutions, especially museums and parks; support also for environmental organizations and historic preservation.
Limitations: Giving primarily in NY.
Publications: Annual report.
Application information: Contributes only to pre-selected organizations. Applications not accepted.
Write: Arthur Ross, Pres.
Officers and Directors:* Arthur Ross,* Pres. and Treas.; Clifford A. Ross,* Exec. V.P.; Janet C. Ross,* V.P.; George J. Gillespie III,* Secy.; Tom Bernstein, John H. Dobkin, William T. Golden, William J. Vanden Heuval, Ralph M. Sussman, Paul E. Taylor, Jr., Edgar Wachenheim III.
Employer Identification Number: 136121436

5103
The Dorothea Haus Ross Foundation
1036 Monroe Ave.
Rochester 14620 (716) 473-6006

Established in 1979 in NY.
Donor(s): Dorothea Haus Ross.
Foundation type: Independent
Financial data (yr. ended 5/31/89): Assets, $1,747,387 (M); gifts received, $150,000; expenditures, $167,286, including $126,286 for 34 grants (high: $5,396; low: $50; average: $2,723).
Purpose and activities: To advance the moral, mental, and physical well-being of children of all races and creeds in all parts of the world; to

aid and assist in providing for the basic needs of food, shelter, and education of such children by whatever means and methods necessary or advisable; to prevent by medical research or otherwise the mental and physical handicaps of children.
Types of support: Seed money, equipment, matching funds, special projects, research, publications, emergency funds, endowment funds, technical assistance, renovation projects.
Limitations: No grants to individuals, or for operating budgets, continuing support, annual campaigns, deficit financing, land acquisition, conferences, scholarships, or fellowships; no emergency funds outside Monroe County, NY; no loans.
Publications: Application guidelines.
Application information: 1 copy only of appendix material. Application form not required.
Initial approach: Telephone, letter, or proposal
Copies of proposal: 4
Deadline(s): None
Board meeting date(s): Quarterly
Final notification: 2 months
Write: Wayne S. Cook or Patricia Hans, Directors
Trustees: Kathleen Borkhuis, Philetus M. Chamberlain, Marine Midland Bank, N.A.
Directors: Wayne S. Cook, Patricia Hans.
Number of staff: 2 part-time professional.
Employer Identification Number: 161080458

5104
Lyn & George M. Ross Foundation ¤ ☆
c/o Goldman Sachs & Co.
85 Broad St., Tax Dept.
New York 10004-2106

Established in 1977.
Donor(s): George M. Ross.
Foundation type: Independent
Financial data (yr. ended 2/28/89): Assets, $3,361,588 (M); gifts received, $611,545; expenditures, $115,267, including $104,000 for 9 grants (high: $50,000; low: $500).
Purpose and activities: Giving primarily for Jewish welfare and higher education; some support for the arts.
Limitations: Giving primarily in Philadelphia, PA. No grants to individuals.
Application information: Applications not accepted.
Trustees: George M. Ross, Lyn M. Ross.
Employer Identification Number: 232049592

5105
Stanley & Elsie Roth Foundation, Inc.
c/o Stanley Roth, Jr.
10 East 70th St., Apt. 14C
New York 10021-4947

Incorporated in 1974 in NJ.
Donor(s): Stanley Roth, Sr.†
Foundation type: Independent
Financial data (yr. ended 12/31/88): Assets, $1,441,756 (M); expenditures, $262,757, including $240,000 for 30 grants (high: $100,000; low: $500).
Purpose and activities: Giving largely for universities, museums, care for the aged, and hospitals.
Limitations: No grants to individuals.
Publications: 990-PF.
Application information: Application form not required.
Initial approach: Letter
Deadline(s): Sept. 30
Final notification: Dec. 31
Write: Richard S. Borisoff, V.P.
Officers and Directors:* Stanley Roth, Jr.,* Pres.; Richard S. Borisoff,* V.P.; Robert Roth,* V.P.; Joseph S. Iseman,* Secy.-Treas.
Number of staff: None.
Employer Identification Number: 237400784

5106
Robert and Maurine Rothschild Fund, Inc.
c/o Perelson Johnson & Rones
560 Lexington Ave.
New York 10022

Incorporated in 1948 in NY.
Donor(s): Herbert M. Rothschild,† Nannette F. Rothschild,† and others.
Foundation type: Independent
Financial data (yr. ended 12/31/89): Assets, $1,770,884 (M); expenditures, $171,232, including $156,019 for 83 grants (high: $101,650; low: $15).
Purpose and activities: Emphasis on the arts, including museums, community development, and higher and elementary education.
Limitations: Giving primarily in ME.
Application information:
Initial approach: Letter
Deadline(s): None
Write: The Directors
Directors: Katherine Jackson, Maurine Rothschild, Peter Rothschild, Robert F. Rothschild.
Number of staff: None.
Employer Identification Number: 136059064

5107
Royce Family Fund, Inc. ¤ ☆
1414 Ave. of the Americas
New York 10019-2514

Established in 1985 in NY.
Donor(s): Charles M. Royce.
Foundation type: Independent
Financial data (yr. ended 12/31/87): Assets, $883,939 (M); gifts received, $565,563; expenditures, $255,111, including $254,860 for grants.
Purpose and activities: General charitable giving.
Limitations: No grants to individuals.
Application information: Contributes only to pre-selected organizations. Applications not accepted.
Officers: Charles M. Royce, Pres.; Noreen McKee, Secy.-Treas.
Director: Karen P. Free.
Employer Identification Number: 133318620

5108
Frank Rubenstein Foundation, Inc. ¤ ☆
c/o Albert Rubenstein
781 Fifth Ave., Suite 1911
New York 10022 (212) 355-5281

Incorporated in 1951 in NY.
Donor(s): Mrs. Frank Rubenstein,† Albert Rubenstein, Denia Levin, and others.
Foundation type: Independent
Financial data (yr. ended 12/31/88): Assets, $584,016 (M); expenditures, $167,413, including $157,636 for grants.
Purpose and activities: Emphasis on Jewish welfare funds, temple support, hospitals, and education.
Application information:
Initial approach: Letter or telephone
Deadline(s): None
Officer: Albert Rubenstein, Pres.
Employer Identification Number: 136103808

5109
Robert E. & Judith O. Rubin Foundation ¤
c/o Goldman, Sachs & Co. - Tax Dept.
85 Broad St., 30th Fl.
New York 10004

Established in 1980 in NY.
Donor(s): Robert E. Rubin.
Foundation type: Independent
Financial data (yr. ended 8/31/88): Assets, $1,529,114 (M); gifts received, $1,000,000; expenditures, $748,546, including $745,545 for 59 grants (high: $250,000; low: $200).
Purpose and activities: Giving primarily for higher education, hospitals, and Jewish welfare; support also for cultural programs.
Limitations: Giving primarily in New York, NY. No grants to individuals.
Application information: Applications not accepted.
Trustees: Judith O. Rubin, Robert E. Rubin, Roy J. Zuckerberg.
Employer Identification Number: 133050749

5110
Samuel Rubin Foundation, Inc. ▼ ¤
777 United Nations Plaza
New York 10017 (212) 697-8945

Established in 1958 in NY.
Donor(s): Samuel Rubin Foundation, Inc.
Foundation type: Independent
Financial data (yr. ended 6/30/88): Assets, $11,656,801 (M); expenditures, $993,973, including $779,800 for 74 grants (high: $200,000; low: $800; average: $2,000-$15,000).
Purpose and activities: Grants for the pursuit of peace and justice; for an equitable reallocation of the world's resources; and to promote social, economic, political, civil, and cultural rights.
Types of support: General purposes, seed money.
Limitations: No grants to individuals, or for endowments or building funds.
Publications: Program policy statement, 990-PF.
Application information:
Initial approach: Proposal
Deadline(s): None
Board meeting date(s): Quarterly
Final notification: 2 weeks following board meetings
Write: Cora Weiss, Pres.
Officers and Directors: Cora Weiss, Pres.; Judy Weiss, V.P.; Charles L. Mandelstam,

Secy.; Peter Weiss, Treas.; Ralph Shikes, Daniel Weiss, Tamara Weiss.
Number of staff: 1 full-time professional; 1 part-time professional; 1 full-time support.
Employer Identification Number: 136164671

5111
Helena Rubinstein Foundation, Inc. ▼
405 Lexington Ave.
New York 10174 (212) 986-0806

Incorporated in 1953 in NY.
Donor(s): Helena Rubinstein Gourielli.†
Foundation type: Independent
Financial data (yr. ended 05/31/89): Assets, $37,580,774 (M); expenditures, $5,425,052, including $5,035,518 for grants (high: $300,000; low: $1,500; average: $5,000-$25,000).
Purpose and activities: Focus on projects that benefit women and children. Funding primarily for higher and other education, community and social services, health care and medical research, and the arts.
Types of support: Operating budgets, seed money, internships, scholarship funds, fellowships, research, continuing support, general purposes.
Limitations: Giving primarily in New York, NY. No grants to individuals, or for emergency funds, or film or video projects; no loans.
Publications: Annual report (including application guidelines), application guidelines.
Application information: Application form not required.
Initial approach: Letter
Copies of proposal: 1
Deadline(s): None
Board meeting date(s): Nov. and May
Final notification: 1 to 3 months
Write: Diane Moss, Exec. Dir.
Officers and Directors:* Oscar Kolin,* Pres.; Diane Moss,* V.P. and Exec. Dir.; Robert S. Friedman,* Secy.-Treas.; Gertrude G. Michelson, Martin E. Segal, Louis E. Slesin, Suzanne Slesin.
Number of staff: 4 full-time professional; 1 full-time support; 1 part-time support.
Employer Identification Number: 136102666

5112
The Rudin Foundation, Inc.
345 Park Ave.
New York 10154 (212) 644-8500

Incorporated in 1960 in NY.
Donor(s): Jack Rudin, Lewis Rudin.
Foundation type: Independent
Financial data (yr. ended 12/31/88): Assets, $881,721 (M); gifts received, $469,900; expenditures, $570,069, including $550,347 for 140 grants (high: $200,000; low: $100; average: $500-$2,000).
Purpose and activities: Grants for Jewish wefare funds, higher education, community development, and cultural organizations.
Limitations: Giving primarily in New York, NY. No grants to individuals.
Application information:
Initial approach: Letter
Deadline(s): None
Write: Susan H. Rapaport, Admin.
Officers and Directors:* Jack Rudin,* Pres.; Lewis Rudin,* V.P.; Morton Witzling,* Secy.; David B. Levy,* Treas.; Milton N. Hoffman, May Rudin, Lewis Steinman, Adelaide Rudin Zisson.
Employer Identification Number: 136113064

5113
The Louis and Rachel Rudin Foundation, Inc.
345 Park Ave.
New York 10154 (212) 644-8500

Incorporated in 1968 in NY.
Foundation type: Independent
Financial data (yr. ended 07/31/88): Assets, $27,252,612 (M); expenditures, $1,327,781, including $1,197,000 for 29 grants (high: $95,000; low: $5,000).
Purpose and activities: Grants to medical and nursing schools only for educational training programs.
Types of support: Scholarship funds.
Limitations: Giving primarily in New York, NY. No grants to individuals, or for building funds.
Application information:
Initial approach: Letter
Write: Susan H. Rapaport, Admin.
Officers and Directors:* Jack Rudin,* Pres.; Lydia Heimlich,* V.P.; Lewis Rudin,* Secy.; Natalie Lewin,* Treas.; Lewis Steinman.
Employer Identification Number: 237039549

5114
Samuel and May Rudin Foundation, Inc. ▼
345 Park Ave.
New York 10154 (212) 644-8500

Incorporated in 1976 in NY.
Donor(s): Samuel Rudin.†
Foundation type: Independent
Financial data (yr. ended 6/30/89): Assets, $2,197,910 (M); gifts received, $5,989,540; expenditures, $6,327,666, including $6,101,200 for 219 grants (high: $800,000; low: $1,000; average: $10,000-$50,000).
Purpose and activities: Support primarily for higher education, social service and religious welfare agencies, hospitals and health associations, and museums, performing arts groups, and other cultural programs.
Limitations: Giving primarily in New York, NY.
Application information:
Initial approach: Letter
Deadline(s): None
Write: Susan H. Rapaport, Admin.
Officers and Directors:* May Rudin,* Chair.; Jack Rudin,* Pres.; Lewis Rudin,* Exec V.P. and Secy.-Treas.; Beth Rudin DeWoody,* V.P.; Eric C. Rudin,* V.P.; Madeleine Rudin Johnson, Katherine L. Rudin, William Rudin.
Employer Identification Number: 132906946

5115
Peter B. & Adeline W. Ruffin Foundation, Inc. ⌑
150 East 42nd St.
New York 10017-5612

Established in 1964 in NY.
Foundation type: Independent
Financial data (yr. ended 11/30/88): Assets, $11,358,138 (M); gifts received, $2,077,320; expenditures, $669,113, including $607,500 for 12 grants (high: $200,000; low: $2,500).
Purpose and activities: Support primarily for higher and secondary education.
Types of support: Endowment funds, professorships.
Application information: Funds largely committed; unsolicited applications not recommended.
Deadline(s): None
Write: Edward G. McAnaney, Pres.
Officers and Trustees:* Edward G. McAnaney,* Pres. and Treas.; Francis A. McAnaney,* V.P.; Marion Simmons, Secy.; Brian T. McAnaney, Kevin G. McAnaney.
Employer Identification Number: 136170484

5116
The Russ Togs Foundation ⌑
c/o Eli L. Rousso, Trustee
1411 Broadway
New York 10018

Established in 1960 in NY.
Donor(s): Russ Togs, Inc.
Foundation type: Company-sponsored
Financial data (yr. ended 12/31/88): Assets, $4,605 (M); gifts received, $146,000; expenditures, $148,100, including $148,060 for 49 grants (high: $64,100; low: $50).
Purpose and activities: Giving for Jewish welfare funds, hospitals, and the aged; support also for higher education and youth.
Application information: Contributes only to pre-selected organizations. Applications not accepted.
Trustees: Eli L. Rousso, Irving L. Rousso, Herman Saporta.
Employer Identification Number: 136086149

5117
The Nina M. Ryan Foundation, Inc. ⌑
Jaycox Rd.
Cold Spring 10516

Incorporated in 1947 in NY.
Foundation type: Independent
Financial data (yr. ended 12/31/88): Assets, $2,422,710 (M); gifts received, $4,082; expenditures, $56,256, including $50,080 for 51 grants (high: $6,300; low: $50).
Purpose and activities: Grants primarily for cultural programs, with emphasis on music and music education, and for higher education; support also for community funds.
Limitations: No grants to individuals, or for scholarships; no loans.
Application information: Contributes only to pre-selected organizations. Applications not accepted.
Officers: Winifred B. Parker, Pres.; T. Roland Berner, V.P. and Treas.; R.F. Bell, V.P.; Richard O. Berner, V.P.; Olga Formissano, Secy.
Employer Identification Number: 136111038

5118
Sacharuna Foundation ⌘
c/o Palisades Management Corp.
515 Madison Ave., Rm. 4100
New York 10022

Established in 1985 in NY.
Donor(s): Lavinia Currier, Jack Robinson.
Foundation type: Independent
Financial data (yr. ended 12/31/88): Assets, $10,472,331 (M); gifts received, $4,000; expenditures, $288,591, including $209,498 for 16 grants (high: $70,000; low: $90).
Purpose and activities: Giving primarily for conservation, environmental, and wildlife organizations. Some support for historic preservation and cultural programs.
Application information: Contributes only to pre-selected organizations. Applications not accepted.
Trustee: Lavinia Currier.
Employer Identification Number: 133264132

5119
Arthur M. Sackler Foundation ☆
461 East 57th St.
New York 10022 (212) 980-5400

Established in 1965 in NY.
Donor(s): Arthur M. Sackler, and family.
Foundation type: Operating
Financial data (yr. ended 12/31/88): Assets, $9,997,288 (M); gifts received, $597,164; expenditures, $696,748, including $380,911 for 3 grants (high: $313,500; low: $18,800).
Purpose and activities: A private operating foundation; support for educational and charitable purposes, including the arts and medical research.
Limitations: No grants to individuals.
Application information: Contributes only to pre-selected organizations. Applications not accepted.
Officers: Elizabeth Sackler-Berner, Pres.; Else Sackler, V.P.
Directors: Carol Master, Arthur F. Sackler.
Employer Identification Number: 521074954

5120
Raymond and Beverly Sackler Foundation, Inc.
15 East 62nd St.
New York 10021-7204

Established in 1967 in NY.
Donor(s): Raymond R. Sackler, R.S. Sackler, J.D. Sackler.
Foundation type: Operating
Financial data (yr. ended 12/31/89): Assets, $9,767,953 (M); expenditures, $684,499, including $45,000 for 2 grants (high: $25,000; low: $20,000; average: $20,000-$25,000) and $601,519 for 3 foundation-administered programs.
Purpose and activities: Giving primarily for medical research in biological and physical sciences, hospitals, education, and cultural institutions.
Application information: Applications not accepted.
Officers: Raymond R. Sackler, Pres.; J.D. Sackler, V.P.; R.S. Sackler, V.P.; B. Sackler, Secy.-Treas.
Number of staff: 9 full-time professional; 3 part-time professional.
Employer Identification Number: 237022467

5121
Russell Sage Foundation
112 East 64th St.
New York 10021 (212) 750-6000

Incorporated in 1907 in NY.
Donor(s): Mrs. Russell Sage.†
Foundation type: Operating
Financial data (yr. ended 08/31/89): Assets, $108,939,032 (M); expenditures, $5,167,092, including $1,536,231 for 58 grants (high: $230,092; low: $4,000; average: $10,000-$75,000) and $4,004,290 for foundation-administered programs.
Purpose and activities: A private operating foundation created for "the improvement of social and living conditions in the United States." Primary attention is on basic research in the social and behavioral sciences, on strengthening methodology in the social sciences, and on social research with public policy implications. The foundation conducts a Visiting Scholar program in which scholars working in areas of interest to the foundation are invited, usually as part of a collaborative group, to pursue research and writing in residence for periods of up to a year. The foundation also makes grants to scholars at other institutions in support of research that advances the foundation's programmatic goals. Special seminars and non-residential working groups are also supported. The foundation participates in the planning and operation of each study or program it supports and usually reserves the right to publish any resulting manuscripts. This assures widespread dissemination of the research it sponsors through publication of books and monographs.
Types of support: Seed money, special projects, research, publications, conferences and seminars.
Limitations: No grants for capital or endowment funds, independent ongoing activities of other institutions, scholarships, annual campaigns, emergency funds, deficit financing, operating budgets, or continuing support; no loans.
Publications: Biennial report, informational brochure, program policy statement, application guidelines, newsletter.
Application information: Application form not required.
Initial approach: Letter
Copies of proposal: 1
Deadline(s): None
Board meeting date(s): Nov., Mar., and June
Final notification: 3 months
Write: Eric Wanner, Pres.
Officers: Eric Wanner,* Pres.; Peter de Janosi, V.P.; Madeline Spitaleri, Secy.; Loren Ross, Treas.
Trustees:* Gary E. MacDougal, Chair.; Patricia King, Vice-Chair.; Robert McCormick Adams, Anne P. Carter, Joel E. Cohen, Philip E. Converse, Peggy C. Davis, Gardner Lindzey, James G. March, Howard Raiffa, Madelon Talley, Harold Tanner, William Julius Wilson.
Number of staff: 21 full-time professional; 14 full-time support; 5 part-time support.
Employer Identification Number: 131635303

5122
The William R. and Virginia F. Salomon Family Foundation, Inc. ⌘
c/o Salomon Brothers
One State St. Plaza, 42nd Fl.
New York 10004 (212) 747-7000

Incorporated in 1954 in NY.
Donor(s): William R. Salomon.
Foundation type: Independent
Financial data (yr. ended 12/31/88): Assets, $1,657,546 (M); expenditures, $194,111, including $174,425 for 75 grants (high: $26,000; low: $15).
Purpose and activities: Emphasis on Jewish welfare funds, higher education, and hospitals.
Types of support: Annual campaigns, building funds, general purposes, research.
Limitations: Giving primarily in NY. No grants to individuals.
Application information: Contributes only to pre-selected organizations. Applications not accepted.
Board meeting date(s): Annually
Write: William R. Salomon, Pres.
Officers and Directors:* William R. Salomon,* Pres. and Treas.; Virginia F. Salomon,* V.P.; Susan S. Havens, Peter F. Salomon.
Number of staff: None.
Employer Identification Number: 136088823

5123
Richard & Edna Salomon Foundation, Inc. ⌘
45 Rockefeller Plaza
New York 10111 (212) 903-1216

Established in 1964 in NY.
Donor(s): Richard B. Salomon.
Foundation type: Independent
Financial data (yr. ended 12/31/87): Assets, $2,894,655 (M); expenditures, $584,140, including $578,250 for 47 grants (high: $201,000; low: $250).
Purpose and activities: Giving for the arts, education, and social services.
Types of support: General purposes.
Limitations: No grants to individuals.
Application information:
Initial approach: Letter
Deadline(s): None
Write: R.M. Schleicher, V.P.
Officers: Richard B. Salomon,* Pres.; Raymond M. Schleicher,* V.P. and Treas.; Merwin Lewis, Secy.
Directors:* Edna Salomon, Richard E. Salomon.
Employer Identification Number: 136163521

5124
The Salomon Foundation Inc ▼
One New York Plaza
New York 10004 (212) 747-2400

Established in 1985 in NY.
Donor(s): Salomon Inc.
Foundation type: Company-sponsored

Financial data (yr. ended 12/31/89): Assets, $5,400,000 (M); expenditures, $2,125,307, including $1,230,905 for grants (high: $100,000; low: $1,000; average: $1,000-$5,000) and $891,812 for employee matching gifts.
Purpose and activities: Support for higher, elementary and secondary education; arts and culture; community activities; libraries; and medical research and health. The foundation also sponsors an employee matching gift program for education.
Types of support: Employee matching gifts.
Limitations: Giving primarily in the New York, NY, area and other geographic locations where branch offices are situated, notably Los Angeles and San Francisco, CA; Dallas, TX; Chicago, IL; Atlanta, GA; and Boston, MA. No grants to individuals.
Application information: Application form not required.
Initial approach: Letter (3 pages)
Copies of proposal: 1
Deadline(s): None
Write: Jane Heffner, V.P. and Secy.
Officers and Directors:* John H. Gutfreund,* Pres.; Jane E. Heffner, V.P. and Secy.; Donald M. Feuerstein, Treas.; Warren E. Buffett, Gedale B. Horowitz, James L. Massey, William F. May.
Number of staff: 1 full-time professional; 1 full-time support.
Employer Identification Number: 133388259

5125
The Gary Saltz Foundation, Inc. ⌑
600 Madison Ave., 20th Fl.
New York 10022 (212) 980-0910

Incorporated in 1985 in NY.
Donor(s): Jack Saltz, Anita Saltz.
Foundation type: Independent
Financial data (yr. ended 04/30/89): Assets, $3,322,538 (M); gifts received, $500,000; expenditures, $75,775, including $52,000 for 2 grants (high: $35,000; low: $17,000).
Purpose and activities: Grants primarily for medical research with emphasis on juvenile diabetes and cancer in children.
Types of support: Research.
Application information: Contributes only to pre-selected organizations. Applications not accepted.
Write: Anita Saltz, Pres.
Officers: Anita Saltz, Pres.; Ronald Saltz, V.P.; Susan Saltz, Secy.; Leonard Saltz, Treas.
Employer Identification Number: 133267114

5126
Saltzman Foundation, Inc. ⌑
350 Fifth Ave.
New York 10118-0001

Established in 1950 in NY.
Foundation type: Independent
Financial data (yr. ended 3/31/88): Assets, $1,160,367 (M); gifts received, $25,000; expenditures, $55,908, including $52,100 for 19 grants (high: $30,000; low: $50).
Purpose and activities: Support primarily for higher education, museums, health, hospitals, libraries, and child development.
Limitations: Giving primarily in NY.
Application information:
Write: Arnold A. Saltzman, Pres.
Officers and Directors: Arnold A. Saltzman, Pres. and Treas.; Joan Saltzman, Secy.; Roth Tuishoff.
Employer Identification Number: 136142471

5127
The Fan Fox and Leslie R. Samuels Foundation, Inc. ▼
30 Rockefeller Plaza, Suite 1933
New York 10112 (212) 315-2940

Incorporated in 1959 in UT; reincorporated in 1981 in NY.
Donor(s): Leslie R. Samuels,† Fan Fox Samuels.†
Foundation type: Independent
Financial data (yr. ended 07/31/89): Assets, $98,303,982 (M); gifts received, $300,000; expenditures, $4,307,211, including $3,984,512 for 102 grants (high: $300,000; low: $250; average: $5,000-$400,000).
Purpose and activities: Grants largely for the performing arts and other cultural programs; hospitals and health care, including AIDS and cancer research; social services, especially programs for the young and the elderly; and education.
Types of support: Continuing support, seed money, building funds, equipment, research, matching funds, special projects.
Limitations: Giving primarily in the New York, NY, metropolitan area. No grants to individuals, or for scholarships or fellowships; no loans.
Publications: Biennial report (including application guidelines).
Application information: Application form not required.
Initial approach: Letter
Copies of proposal: 1
Deadline(s): None
Board meeting date(s): Oct., Jan., Apr., July, and as necessary
Final notification: 1 month
Write: Marvin A. Kaufman, Pres.
Officers and Directors:* Morton J. Bernstein,* Chair.; Marvin A. Kaufman,* Pres.; Joseph C. Mitchell,* V.P. and Treas.; Carlos D. Moseley,* V.P.; Muriel Nasser,* Secy.
Number of staff: 3 full-time professional; 1 full-time support.
Employer Identification Number: 133124818

5128
Sandoz Foundation of America ⌑
608 Fifth Ave.
New York 10020 (201) 386-0880

Incorporated in 1965 in DE.
Donor(s): Sandoz Corp.
Foundation type: Company-sponsored
Financial data (yr. ended 12/31/88): Assets, $5,261,201 (M); expenditures, $84,673, including $40,919 for 5 grants (high: $33,264; low: $650).
Purpose and activities: Grants primarily to educational and charitable institutions engaged in medical and scientific research.
Limitations: No grants to individuals, or for building or endowment funds or operating budgets.
Publications: Application guidelines.
Application information:
Initial approach: Letter
Copies of proposal: 1
Deadline(s): None
Board meeting date(s): As required
Write: Craig D. Burrell, M.D., V.P.
Officers: Daniel Wagniere, Pres.; Kenneth L. Brewton, Jr., V.P.; Craig D. Burrell, M.D., V.P.; Herbert J. Brennan, Secy.
Trustees: Marc Moret, Chair.; Ulrich H. Oppikofer, M.D.
Employer Identification Number: 136193034

5129
Santa Maria Foundation, Inc. ⌑
c/o Patrick P. Grace, Secy.
43 West 42nd St.
New York 10036

Established in 1978.
Donor(s): J. Peter Grace, Margaret F. Grace.
Foundation type: Independent
Financial data (yr. ended 12/31/88): Assets, $2,317,577 (M); expenditures, $146,930, including $106,275 for 25 grants (high: $25,000; low: $25).
Purpose and activities: Support largely for higher education and Roman Catholic religious organizations.
Types of support: General purposes, operating budgets.
Limitations: Giving primarily in NY.
Application information: Contributes only to pre-selected organizations. Applications not accepted.
Officers and Directors:* J. Peter Grace,* Pres.; J.P. Bolduc, V.P. and Treas.; Patrick P. Grace,* Secy.; Margaret F. Grace, Theresa G. Sears.
Employer Identification Number: 132938749

5130
Peg Santvoord Foundation, Inc. ☆
c/o M. Handelman Co.
2500 Westchester Ave.
Purchase 10577-2515
Application address: 200 Waverly Place, New York, NY 10014; Tel.: (212) 242-5249

Incorporated in 1966 in NY.
Foundation type: Independent
Financial data (yr. ended 06/30/89): Assets, $1,225,644 (M); expenditures, $74,146, including $61,000 for 10 grants (high: $10,000; low: $3,000).
Purpose and activities: Support limited to experimental theater groups.
Types of support: Special projects.
Limitations: Giving limited to the Manhattan area in New York, NY. No grants to individuals.
Application information: Application form not required.
Initial approach: Letter
Deadline(s): None
Write: Donn Russell, Dir.
Officers: Nancy M.S. Stover, Pres.; William R. Handelman, V.P.; Russell J. Handelman, Secy.; Donald E. Handelman, Treas.
Director: Donn Russell.
Employer Identification Number: 136183822

5131
Sasco Foundation
c/o Manufacturers Hanover Trust Co.
600 Fifth Ave., 5th Fl.
New York 10020

Trust established in 1951 in NY.
Donor(s): Leila E. Riegel,† Katherine R. Emory.
Foundation type: Independent
Financial data (yr. ended 12/31/88): Assets, $4,157,181 (M); expenditures, $279,561, including $239,000 for 93 grants (high: $25,000; low: $500; average: $500-$2,000).
Purpose and activities: Grants for hospitals, higher and secondary education, youth agencies, cultural programs, and conservation.
Limitations: Giving primarily in NY, CT, and ME. No grants to individuals.
Application information: Application form not required.
Initial approach: Proposal
Deadline(s): Nov. 30
Write: Mr. Uwe Lindner
Trustee: Manufacturers Hanover Trust Co.
Employer Identification Number: 136046567

5132
Denise & Andrew Saul Foundation ▼ ⌑
c/o Eisner & Lubin
250 Park Ave.
New York 10177

Established in 1984 in NY.
Donor(s): Andrew M. Saul.
Foundation type: Independent
Financial data (yr. ended 09/30/87): Assets, $1,095,165 (M); expenditures, $839,974, including $836,627 for 14 grants (high: $250,000; low: $866; average: $10,000-$100,000).
Purpose and activities: Giving primarily for cultural programs; support also for education and hospitals.
Application information: Contributes only to pre-selected organizations. Applications not accepted.
Officers and Trustees: Andrew M. Saul, Pres. and Treas.; Denise M. Saul, V.P. and Secy.; Lynn T. Fischer, Sidney J. Silberman.
Number of staff: None.
Employer Identification Number: 133254182

5133
Joseph E. & Norma G. Saul Foundation, Inc. ⌑
c/o Saul Partners
630 Fifth Ave., Suite 2518
New York 10111

Established in 1984 in NY.
Donor(s): Joseph E. Saul.
Foundation type: Independent
Financial data (yr. ended 9/30/88): Assets, $3,237,978 (M); expenditures, $306,677, including $299,500 for 1 grant.
Purpose and activities: Support primarily for the United Jewish Appeal.
Application information: Contributes only to pre-selected organizations. Applications not accepted.
Officers and Trustees: Joseph E. Saul, Pres. and Treas.; Andrew M. Saul, V.P.; Norma G. Saul, Secy.; Lynn T. Fischer, Sidney J. Silberman.
Employer Identification Number: 133254180

5134
Elias Sayour Foundation, Inc. ⌑
185 Madison Ave.
New York 10016
Application address: 17 Harbor Ln., Brooklyn, NY 11209; Tel.: (718) 680-8378

Incorporated in 1951 in NY.
Donor(s): Elias Sayour,† George Sayour, and associates.
Foundation type: Independent
Financial data (yr. ended 10/31/88): Assets, $1,141,577 (M); expenditures, $86,539, including $69,070 for 66 grants (high: $7,500; low: $50).
Purpose and activities: Grants primarily for Roman Catholic church support, welfare funds, and religious organizations; support also for hospitals.
Application information:
Initial approach: Letter
Deadline(s): None
Write: Jeanette Sayour, Pres.
Officers: Jeanette Sayour, Pres.; Mary Jane Gosen, V.P.; John Sayour, Secy.; Paul T. Sayour, Treas.
Employer Identification Number: 136109953

5135
H. Schaffer Foundation, Inc. ⌑
670 Franklin St.
Schenectady 12305

Established in 1980 in NY.
Donor(s): Harry M. Schaffer,† Schaffer Stores Co., Inc.
Foundation type: Independent
Financial data (yr. ended 10/31/88): Assets, $6,673,396 (M); expenditures, $3,460,971, including $3,346,500 for 15 grants (high: $2,500,000; low: $10,000).
Purpose and activities: Giving for higher education, medicine, social services, and performing arts groups.
Application information: Application form not required.
Initial approach: Letter
Deadline(s): None
Write: Herman Stall, Pres.
Officers: Herman Stall, Pres.; Lawrence A. Wien, V.P.; Richard R. Bieber, Secy.-Treas.
Employer Identification Number: 222325485

5136
Michael & Helen Schaffer Foundation, Inc. ⌑
295 Madison Ave.
New York 10017

Established about 1963 in NY.
Donor(s): Michael I. Schaffer.
Foundation type: Independent
Financial data (yr. ended 7/31/88): Assets, $4,759,358 (M); expenditures, $312,289, including $251,780 for 25 grants (high: $60,000; low: $100).
Purpose and activities: Emphasis on Jewish giving, particularly welfare funds, and hospitals.
Officer: Michael I. Schaffer, Mgr.
Employer Identification Number: 136159235

5137
Robert Schalkenbach Foundation, Inc.
41 East 72nd St.
New York 10021 (212) 988-1680

Incorporated in 1925 in NY.
Donor(s): Robert Schalkenbach.†
Foundation type: Operating
Financial data (yr. ended 06/30/89): Assets, $8,155,556 (M); gifts received, $217,596; expenditures, $440,387, including $223,000 for 14 grants (high: $64,000; low: $750) and $59,400 for 2 foundation-administered programs.
Purpose and activities: A private operating foundation established to teach the social and economic philosophy of Henry George, especially his views concerning the single tax on land values and international free trade, primarily through publication of books and other forms of educational work, including research.
Types of support: Continuing support, matching funds, research, publications, conferences and seminars.
Limitations: No grants to individuals, or for capital funds, operating budgets, annual campaigns, demonstration projects, start-up or emergency funds, or deficit financing; no loans.
Publications: Annual report.
Application information: Application form not required.
Initial approach: Letter or proposal
Copies of proposal: 1
Deadline(s): None
Board meeting date(s): Bimonthly, beginning in Feb.
Final notification: 2 months
Write: Oscar B. Johannsen, Secy.
Officers and Directors:* C. Lowell Harriss,* Pres.; Will Lissner,* V.P.; Oscar Johannsen,* Secy. and Exec. Dir.; Thomas A. Larkin,* Treas.; Charles Abramovitz, Robert V. Andelson, T.H. Bonaparte, John Burger, Steven B. Cord, William P. Davidson, Roy A. Foulke, Jr., Mason Gaffney, Frank C. Genovese, Lancaster M. Greene, J. Ted Gwartney, Albert S. Hartheimer, Richard Noyes, Lawrence S. Ritter, Frances Soriero, Nicolaus Tideman.
Number of staff: 2 full-time professional; 1 full-time support; 1 part-time support.
Employer Identification Number: 131656331

5138
Harold & Bette Wolfson Schapiro Foundation ⌑
c/o Pepper & Altman
1350 Ave. of the Americas
New York 10019

Established about 1957 in NY.
Donor(s): Members of the Schapiro family.
Foundation type: Independent
Financial data (yr. ended 2/28/87): Assets, $451,888 (M); expenditures, $146,053, including $139,960 for 147 grants (high: $13,100; low: $12).
Purpose and activities: Emphasis on Jewish giving, including welfare funds, and higher education.
Trustees: Bette W. Schapiro, Gerald E. Schapiro, Stuart Schapiro.
Employer Identification Number: 136157602

5139
M. A. Schapiro Fund ⌑
One Chase Manhattan Plaza
New York 10005

Established in 1955 in NY.
Donor(s): Morris A. Schapiro.
Foundation type: Independent
Financial data (yr. ended 12/31/88): Assets, $2,969,364 (M); expenditures, $130,688, including $121,500 for 25 grants (high: $25,000; low: $150).
Purpose and activities: Support primarily for civil rights legal funds and Jewish welfare; giving also for welfare agencies, institutions for the handicapped, and an association for voluntary sterilization.
Limitations: Giving primarily in New York, NY. No grants to individuals.
Application information: Contributes only to pre-selected organizations. Applications not accepted.
Officers and Directors:* Morris A. Schapiro,* Pres.; Thomas J. Mirante, V.P.; Nathaniel Whitehorn, Treas.
Employer Identification Number: 136089254

5140
The Schenectady Foundation ⌑
P.O. Box 1020
Schenectady 12301 (518) 372-4761

Established in 1963 in NY.
Donor(s): Eleanor F. Green,† Mabel Birdsall,† General Electric Foundation.
Foundation type: Community
Financial data (yr. ended 12/31/89): Assets, $2,826,000 (M); expenditures, $207,786, including $193,159 for 13 grants and $10,800 for 1 foundation-administered program.
Purpose and activities: Support for general charitable purposes; awards scholarships for persons entering the teaching profession.
Types of support: Student aid, seed money, building funds, equipment, land acquisition, renovation projects, matching funds, fellowships, program-related investments, research.
Limitations: Giving limited to Schenectady County, NY. No grants for operating budgets, continuing support, annual campaigns, emergency or deficit financing, general or special endowments, demonstration projects, publications, or conferences or seminars; no loans.
Publications: Annual report.
Application information: Application form required.
Write: William D. Gustin, Secy.
Officers: Charles W. Carl, Chair.; William D. Gustin, Secy.; W.H. Milton III, Treas.
Number of staff: None.
Employer Identification Number: 146019650

5141
Leopold Schepp Foundation
15 East 26th St., Suite 1900
New York 10010 (212) 889-9737

Incorporated in 1925 in NY.
Donor(s): Leopold Schepp,† Florence L. Schepp.†
Foundation type: Independent
Financial data (yr. ended 2/28/89): Assets, $10,377,488 (M); expenditures, $593,900, including $593,900 for grants to individuals.
Purpose and activities: Primarily to assist young men and women of character and ability who have insufficient means to complete their vocational or professional education. Undergraduate scholarships to individuals under 30 years of age; graduate scholarships to individuals under 40 years of age; a small number of postdoctoral fellowships for independent study and research awarded annually to individuals in the arts and literature, medicine, and oceanography.
Types of support: Fellowships, student aid.
Publications: Program policy statement, application guidelines.
Application information: Application form required.
Initial approach: Letter
Copies of proposal: 1
Deadline(s): Submit application request between June and Dec.; deadline Dec. 31
Board meeting date(s): May and Oct.
Final notification: 1st week in May
Write: Mrs. Edythe Bobrow, Exec. Dir.
Officers: Barbara Tweed Estill,* Pres.; William L.D. Barrett,* V.P.; Elizabeth N. Gaillard,* V.P.; Charles E. Hodges,* V.P.; Samuel Thorne, Jr.,* Treas.; Edythe Bobrow, Exec. Dir.
Trustees:* William L.D. Barrett, Carvel H. Cartmell, Kathryn Batchelber Cashman, Sue Ann Dawson, Clementine Z. Estes, Henry E. Gaillard, C. Edwin Linville, Linda B. McKean, Barbara McLendon, Thomas W. McNealy, Priscilla C. Perkins, Benjamin Phillips, Elizabeth Jones Thorne, George R. Walker, Eugenia B. Willard.
Number of staff: 1 full-time professional; 1 full-time support; 2 part-time support.
Employer Identification Number: 135562353

5142
The Scherman Foundation, Inc. ▼
315 West 57th St., Suite 2D
New York 10019 (212) 489-7143

Incorporated in 1941 in NY.
Donor(s): Members of the Scherman family.
Foundation type: Independent
Financial data (yr. ended 12/31/89): Assets, $60,750,712 (M); expenditures, $4,068,841, including $3,519,900 for 148 grants (high: $900,000; low: $4,900; average: $10,000-$25,000) and $51,000 for 1 loan.
Purpose and activities: Grants largely for conservation, disarmament and peace, family planning, human rights and liberties, the arts, and social welfare.
Types of support: Operating budgets, continuing support, seed money, emergency funds, matching funds, program-related investments, special projects, general purposes, technical assistance.
Limitations: Giving primarily in New York, NY, for arts and social welfare. No support for colleges, universities, or other higher educational institutions. No grants to individuals, or for building or endowment funds, scholarships, or fellowships.
Publications: Annual report (including application guidelines), application guidelines.
Application information: Application form not required.
Initial approach: Letter
Copies of proposal: 1
Deadline(s): None
Board meeting date(s): Quarterly
Final notification: 3 months
Write: David F. Freeman, Exec. Dir.
Officers and Directors:* Axel G. Rosin,* Pres.; Katharine S. Rosin,* Secy.; David F. Freeman, Treas. and Exec. Dir.; Helen Edey, M.D., Archibald R. Murray, Susanna Sahatdjian, Anthony M. Schulte, Sandra Silverman, Karen R. Sollins, Marcia Thompson.
Number of staff: 1 full-time professional; 1 part-time professional; 1 full-time support.
Employer Identification Number: 136098464

5143
S. H. and Helen R. Scheuer Family Foundation, Inc. ▼ ⌑
104 East 40th St.
New York 10016-1801 (212) 573-8350

Incorporated in 1943 in NY.
Donor(s): Members of the Scheuer family.
Foundation type: Independent
Financial data (yr. ended 11/30/89): Assets, $38,916,391 (M); gifts received, $4,443,494; expenditures, $8,025,672, including $7,050,545 for 258 grants (high: $1,121,096; low: $100; average: $5,000-$50,000).
Purpose and activities: Emphasis on local Jewish welfare funds, higher education, and cultural programs.
Limitations: Giving primarily in New York, NY.
Application information: Applications not accepted.
Board meeting date(s): As necessary
Write: Wilbur Daniels, Exec. Dir.
Officers: Amy Scheuer Cohen, Pres.; Richard J. Scheuer, V.P.; Harvey Brecher, Secy.; Harold Cohen, Treas.
Number of staff: 1 full-time professional.
Employer Identification Number: 136062661

5144
Sarah I. Schieffelin Residuary Trust
c/o The Bank of New York
48 Wall St.
New York 10015

Established in 1976.
Donor(s): Sarah I. Schieffelin.†
Foundation type: Independent
Financial data (yr. ended 03/31/89): Assets, $5,690,504 (M); expenditures, $308,521, including $243,290 for 27 grants (high: $24,329; low: $1,000).
Purpose and activities: Giving for conservation, wildlife preservation, cultural programs, health, social services, and church support.
Types of support: Continuing support.
Limitations: Giving primarily in New York, NY. No grants to individuals.
Application information: Contributes only to pre-selected organizations. Applications not accepted.
Write: A. Bostley
Trustees: Thomas B. Fenlon, The Bank of New York.
Employer Identification Number: 136724459

5145
The Schiff Foundation ▼
485 Madison Ave., 20th Fl.
New York 10022 (212) 751-3180

Incorporated in 1946 in NY.
Donor(s): John M. Schiff,† Edith B. Schiff,† David T. Schiff, Peter G. Schiff.
Foundation type: Independent
Financial data (yr. ended 12/31/89): Assets, $10,616,000 (M); gifts received, $40,800; expenditures, $1,010,000, including $1,004,000 for 125 grants (high: $400,000; low: $100; average: $500-$25,000).
Purpose and activities: Giving for special medical programs, certain youth and social service agencies, museums, animal welfare, and education; funds substantially committed to organizations of interest to the donors.
Types of support: Annual campaigns, capital campaigns, general purposes, professorships, research, special projects.
Limitations: Giving primarily in NY. No grants to individuals.
Application information: Contributes only to pre-selected organizations. Applications not accepted.
Write: David T. Schiff, Pres.
Officers and Directors:* David T. Schiff,* Pres.; Peter G. Schiff,* V.P.; Sandra Frey Davies, Secy.; Andrew N. Schiff, Treas.
Employer Identification Number: 136088221

5146
The Dorothy Schiff Foundation
(Formerly The Pisces Foundation)
53 East 66th St.
New York 10021 (212) 619-6255

Incorporated in 1951 in NY.
Donor(s): Dorothy Schiff,† New York Post Corp.
Foundation type: Independent
Financial data (yr. ended 12/31/87): Assets, $6,625,248 (M); gifts received, $102,031; expenditures, $447,830, including $339,460 for 113 grants (high: $50,000; low: $50).
Purpose and activities: Emphasis on education, hospitals, public television, juvenile delinquency, AIDS research, family planning, and environmental organizations.
Limitations: Giving primarily in NY. No grants to individuals, or for endowment or capital funds, or matching gifts; no loans.
Application information:
Initial approach: Letter
Deadline(s): None
Board meeting date(s): Monthly except Aug.
Write: Adele Hall Sweet, Pres.
Officers: Adele Hall Sweet, Pres.; Sarah-Ann Kramarsky, Secy.; Mortimer W. Hall, Treas.
Number of staff: None.
Employer Identification Number: 136018311

5147
Frederick and Amelia Schimper Foundation ⌑
805 Third Ave., 20th Fl.
New York 10022 (212) 702-5700

Incorporated in 1943 in NY.
Donor(s): Amelia S. Ehrmann.†
Foundation type: Independent
Financial data (yr. ended 12/31/88): Assets, $1,635,997 (M); expenditures, $110,582, including $79,952 for 3 grants (high: $29,952; low: $2,500).
Purpose and activities: Giving primarily for seed money for significant research designed to benefit indigent, aged persons.
Types of support: Continuing support, seed money, research, publications.
Limitations: No grants to individuals, or for building or endowment funds, annual campaigns, emergency funds, deficit financing, equipment, land acquisition, matching gifts, special projects, conferences, scholarships, fellowships, or operating budgets; no loans.
Publications: Application guidelines.
Application information: Contributes only to pre-selected organizations. Applications not accepted.
Board meeting date(s): June and Dec.
Officers and Directors: William E. Friedman, Pres. and Treas.; Myles A. Cane, V.P. and Secy.; Stanley S. Weithorn.
Number of staff: None.
Employer Identification Number: 136108507

5148
Schlumberger Foundation, Inc. ▼
277 Park Ave.
New York 10172 (212) 350-9455

Schlumberger Foundation established as a trust in 1954 in TX; terminated in 1982 and assets transferred to Schlumberger Horizons, Inc., a DE foundation; in 1982 name changed from Schlumberger Horizons, Inc. to Schlumberger Foundation, Inc.
Donor(s): Schlumberger, Ltd.
Foundation type: Company-sponsored
Financial data (yr. ended 12/31/89): Assets, $15,161,408 (M); expenditures, $655,000, including $604,848 for 71 grants (high: $60,000; low: $1,000; average: $3,000-$20,000).
Purpose and activities: Grants limited to selected colleges and universities for scholarships and fellowships in engineering and other natural sciences; small number of grants awarded in the educational, medical, and humanitarian areas.
Types of support: Scholarship funds, fellowships, general purposes, research, special projects, program-related investments.
Limitations: Giving limited to the North American continent. No grants to individuals, or for building funds or operating budgets.
Application information: Application form not required.
Initial approach: Letter
Deadline(s): None
Board meeting date(s): Feb. or Mar.
Final notification: Within 3 weeks
Write: Arthur W. Alexander, Exec. Secy.
Officer and Directors:* Arthur W. Alexander,* Exec. Secy.; John D. Ingram, George H. Jewell, Pierre M. Schlumberger, Roy Shourd.
Trustee Banks: The Northern Trust Co., Texas Commerce Bank.
Number of staff: None.
Employer Identification Number: 237033142

5149
Priscilla & Richard Schmeelk Foundation, Inc. ⌑ ☆
c/o Noble, Speer, & Fulvio
60 East 42nd St.
New York 10165

Established in 1983 in NY.
Donor(s): Richard J. Schmeelk.
Foundation type: Independent
Financial data (yr. ended 12/31/88): Assets, $1,267,269 (M); gifts received, $470,000; expenditures, $339,725, including $332,125 for 69 grants (high: $50,000; low: $10).
Purpose and activities: Giving for social services, hospitals, youth, Jewish organizations, and support for the United Nations.
Limitations: Giving primarily in New York, NY. No grants to individuals.
Application information: Contributes only to pre-selected organizations. Applications not accepted.
Officers and Directors: Richard J. Schmeelk, Pres. and Treas.; Priscilla M. Schmeelk, V.P. and Secy.; George De Sipio.
Employer Identification Number: 133126387

5150
Adolph & Ruth Schnurmacher Foundation, Inc. ⌑ ☆
1114 First Ave.
New York 10021-8325 (212) 838-7766

Donor(s): Hippman Rose Scholarship Fund, Inc.
Foundation type: Independent
Financial data (yr. ended 11/30/88): Assets, $697,001 (M); gifts received, $75,000; expenditures, $148,189, including $146,657 for 54 grants (high: $75,000; low: $100).
Purpose and activities: Support for hospitals and general charitable organizations.
Limitations: Giving primarily in NY.
Application information:
Initial approach: Telephone
Write: Adolph Schnurmacher, Pres.
Officers: Adolph Schnurmacher, Pres.; Ruth Schnurmacher, Secy.-Treas.
Employer Identification Number: 132938935

5151
Charles & Mildred Schnurmacher Foundation, Inc. ⌑
1114 First Ave.
New York 10021

Established in 1977 in NY.
Donor(s): Charles M. Schnurmacher.†
Foundation type: Independent
Financial data (yr. ended 11/30/87): Assets, $2,071,592 (M); gifts received, $892,258; expenditures, $246,055, including $237,967 for 29 grants (high: $207,100; low: $15).
Purpose and activities: Emphasis on medical research and hospitals.
Application information: Contributes only to pre-selected organizations. Applications not accepted.
Officers: Mildred Schnurmacher, Pres.; Adolph Schnurmacher, Secy.; Fred Plotkin, Treas.
Trustee: Ira J. Weinstein.
Employer Identification Number: 132937218

5152
The Marvin & Edie Schur Charitable Foundation, Inc. ⌑
126 East 56th St., Suite 2300
New York 10022-3613

Established in 1985 in NY.
Donor(s): Marvin H. Schur.
Foundation type: Independent
Financial data (yr. ended 10/01/88): Assets, $10,623 (M); gifts received, $123,000; expenditures, $389,005, including $387,750 for 9 grants (high: $250,000; low: $500).
Purpose and activities: Support primarily for hospitals, Jewish welfare funds, and higher education.
Limitations: Giving primarily in NY. No grants to individuals.
Application information: Contributes only to pre-selected organizations. Applications not accepted.
Officer and Trustees:* Marvin H. Schur,* Pres.; Kathleen Greene, Edith A. Schur, Ronald J. Stein.
Employer Identification Number: 133251453

5153
Alvin & Dorothy Schwartz Foundation ⌑
33 Beverly Rd.
Great Neck 11021-1329 (212) 687-6400

Established in 1966 in NY.
Donor(s): Alvin Schwartz.
Foundation type: Independent
Financial data (yr. ended 12/31/88): Assets, $1,727,608 (M); gifts received, $200,000; expenditures, $53,540, including $52,600 for 5 grants (high: $50,000; low: $100).
Purpose and activities: Giving primarily for Jewish giving; support also for hospitals and medical schools.
Limitations: No support for private foundations. No grants to individuals.
Application information:
Initial approach: Letter
Deadline(s): None
Write: Alvin Schwartz, Mgr.
Officers: Alvin Schwartz, Mgr.; Dorothy Schwartz, Mgr.
Employer Identification Number: 116112410

5154
Bernard & Irene Schwartz Foundation, Inc. ⌑ ☆
c/o Loral Corp.
600 Third Ave.
New York 10016-1903

Established in 1981 in NY.
Donor(s): Bernard L. Schwartz.
Foundation type: Independent
Financial data (yr. ended 11/30/88): Assets, $809,402 (M); expenditures, $151,367, including $145,452 for 18 grants (high: $53,000; low: $18).
Purpose and activities: Giving primarily for a social welfare fund for providing aid to Israel and a Jewish organization; support also for museums and other cultural programs, higher education, and a business association.
Limitations: Giving primarily in New York, NY. No grants to individuals.
Application information: Contributes only to pre-selected organizations. Applications not accepted.
Officers and Directors: Bernard L. Schwartz, Pres.; Judy Linksman, Treas.; Robert Hodes, Irene Schwartz.
Employer Identification Number: 133099518

5155
David Schwartz Foundation, Inc. ▼ ⌑
720 Fifth Ave.
New York 10019 (212) 682-6640

Incorporated in 1945 in NY.
Donor(s): Jonathan Logan, Inc., David Schwartz, and others.
Foundation type: Independent
Financial data (yr. ended 5/31/87): Assets, $18,791,449 (M); expenditures, $1,672,051, including $1,458,896 for 90 grants (high: $231,500; low: $10).
Purpose and activities: Emphasis on higher education, cultural programs, and social welfare; support also for hospitals, health agencies, and Jewish organizations.
Types of support: General purposes.
Limitations: Giving primarily in NY, with emphasis on New York City. No grants to individuals.
Application information: Funds currently committed. Applications not accepted.
Board meeting date(s): At least once a year, usually in May or June
Write: Richard J. Schwartz, Pres.
Officers and Directors: Richard J. Schwartz, Pres.; Lois R. Zenkel, V.P.; Stephen D. Gardner, Irene Schwartz, Bruce Zenkel.
Number of staff: None.
Employer Identification Number: 226075974

5156
Samuel & Bertha Schwartz Foundation, Inc. ⌑ ☆
501 National Bank Bldg.
Auburn 13021 (315) 253-6205

Established in 1951.
Donor(s): Herman H. Schwartz.
Foundation type: Independent
Financial data (yr. ended 12/31/88): Assets, $1,299,730 (M); expenditures, $158,388, including $143,493 for 35 grants (high: $52,300; low: $50).
Purpose and activities: Giving primarily for Jewish welfare and temple support, higher education, and hospitals; support also for social and human services, including programs for youth and the aged.
Types of support: Building funds, annual campaigns, scholarship funds, equipment.
Limitations: Giving primarily in Auburn, Rochester and New York, NY, and Palm Beach and Miami, FL. No grants to individuals.
Application information:
Initial approach: Letter
Deadline(s): None
Write: Herman H. Schwartz, Pres.
Officers and Trustees: Herman H. Schwartz, Pres. and Treas.; Vincent M. Klein, Secy.; Lois Ellenoff, Bradley W. Schwartz, Margaret A. Schwartz.
Employer Identification Number: 156017667

5157
Arnold and Marie Schwartz Fund for Education and Health Research ⌑
465 Park Ave.
New York 10022

Incorporated in 1971 in DE.
Donor(s): Arnold Schwartz Charitable Trust.
Foundation type: Independent
Financial data (yr. ended 3/31/88): Assets, $5,561,943 (M); expenditures, $513,722, including $422,090 for 69 grants (high: $103,810; low: $20; average: $500-$10,000).
Purpose and activities: Grants largely for higher education, hospitals, medical research, music, and religious organizations.
Limitations: Giving primarily in the New York City, NY, area.
Application information:
Deadline(s): None
Officers: Marie D. Schwartz, Pres.; Ruth Kerstein,* Secy.
Directors:* Sylvia Kassel.
Employer Identification Number: 237115019

5158
Edith M. Schweckendieck Trusts ⌑
Citibank Private Banking Div.
641 Lexington Ave., 4th Fl.
New York 10043 (212) 715-0100

Trust established in 1922 in NY; second trust established in 1936 in NY.
Donor(s): Edith M. Schweckendieck.†
Foundation type: Independent
Financial data (yr. ended 12/31/86): Assets, $2,200,000 (M); expenditures, $140,000, including $117,000 for 17 grants (high: $15,000; low: $5,000).
Purpose and activities: Grants to charitable institutions to provide assistance for care and maintenance of the aged and feeble; care, maintenance, and education of crippled children; and prevention and relief of cancer.
Types of support: General purposes, building funds, endowment funds.
Limitations: Giving limited to NY. No grants to individuals.
Application information:
Initial approach: Letter
Deadline(s): Submit proposal preferably in July; deadline Aug. 31
Board meeting date(s): Oct.
Write: Joseph P. Valentine, V.P., Citibank, N.A.
Trustee: Citibank, N.A.
Employer Identification Number: 136055135

5159
Louis Schweitzer Charitable Trust ⌑
c/o Hecht & Co., P.C.
1500 Broadway
New York 10036

Trust established in 1972 in NY.
Donor(s): Louis Schweitzer.†
Foundation type: Independent
Financial data (yr. ended 4/30/88): Assets, $1,578,323 (M); expenditures, $131,842, including $120,000 for 4 grants (high: $95,000; low: $5,000).
Purpose and activities: Grants largely for a theatre foundation, and for hospitals.

Application information: Contributes only to pre-selected organizations. Applications not accepted.
Trustees: Daniel G. Ross, Lucille Schweitzer, M. Peter Schweitzer.
Employer Identification Number: 136517711

5160
Scovill Foundation, Inc. ¤
499 Park Ave.
New York 10022 (212) 750-0200

Incorporated in 1961 in CT.
Donor(s): Scovill Manufacturing Co.
Foundation type: Company-sponsored
Financial data (yr. ended 12/31/86): Assets, $1,034,611 (M); expenditures, $259,015, including $255,620 for 122 grants (high: $38,000; low: $25).
Purpose and activities: Emphasis on community funds, hospitals, youth agencies, cultural organizations, and educational institutions.
Types of support: Operating budgets, continuing support, seed money, building funds, employee matching gifts.
Limitations: Giving primarily in areas of company operations. No grants to individuals.
Application information: Application form not required.
Initial approach: Proposal
Copies of proposal: 1
Deadline(s): None
Board meeting date(s): Mar.
Final notification: 3 months
Write: Laura B. Resnikoff, Trustee
Trustees: John W. Moore, Jr., Laura B. Resnikoff.
Employer Identification Number: 066022942

5161
The Scudder Association, Inc. ¤ ☆
525 East 68th St., Rm. 2024
New York 10021 (212) 535-8499

Foundation type: Independent
Financial data (yr. ended 12/31/88): Assets, $1,063,306 (M); gifts received, $12,773; expenditures, $90,959, including $27,200 for grants and $25,500 for 18 grants to individuals (high: $2,000; low: $500).
Purpose and activities: Awards scholarship grants to individuals for higher education; support also for a hospital and medical education.
Types of support: Student aid.
Application information:
Deadline(s): None
Write: Paul A. Scudder, M.D.
Officers: Cynthia Sherman, Secy.; Scudder Stevens, Treas.; Richard Scudder.
Employer Identification Number: 135647705

5162
Sea Coast Foundation ¤ ☆
c/o Gelfand, Rennert & Feldman
Six East 43rd St.
New York 10017
Application address: P.O. Box 870, Cooper Station, New York, NY 10276

Foundation type: Operating
Financial data (yr. ended 12/31/88): Assets, $18,721 (M); expenditures, $123,649, including $123,500 for 7 grants (high: $50,000; low: $500).
Purpose and activities: A private operating foundation; support for Jewish and Christian organizations.
Application information: Application form not required.
Initial approach: Letter
Deadline(s): None
Write: Naomi Saltzman, Trustee
Trustees: David Braun, Bob Dylan, Sara Dylan, Marshall Gelfand, Naomi Saltzman.
Employer Identification Number: 237034949

5163
Seevak Family Foundation ¤
c/o Goldman, Sachs & Co., Tax Dept.
85 Broad St., 30th Fl.
New York 10004

Established in 1981 in NY.
Donor(s): Sheldon Seevak, Elinor A. Seevak.
Foundation type: Independent
Financial data (yr. ended 3/31/89): Assets, $2,036,191 (M); gifts received, $135,250; expenditures, $115,053, including $114,740 for 43 grants (high: $50,000; low: $50).
Purpose and activities: Support for Jewish welfare funds, higher education, and hospitals.
Limitations: No grants to individuals.
Application information: Applications not accepted.
Trustee: Elinor A. Seevak, Sheldon Seevak.
Employer Identification Number: 133102898

5164
The Seidman Foundation ¤ ☆
c/o BDO Seidman
15 Columbus Circle
New York 10023-7788
Application address: 2190 Commerce Tower, Memphis, TN 38150

Established in 1947.
Donor(s): J.S. Seidman.†
Foundation type: Independent
Financial data (yr. ended 12/31/88): Assets, $1,065,711 (M); gifts received, $62,496; expenditures, $92,216, including $85,000 for 5 grants (high: $50,000; low: $2,500).
Purpose and activities: Giving primarily for higher education, including support to an affiliated trust for a lecture series and scholarship awards; support also for culture and health.
Types of support: Lectureships, scholarship funds.
Application information:
Initial approach: Letter or proposal
Deadline(s): None
Write: P.K. Seidman, Trustee
Trustees: H.R. Seidman, L.J. Seidman, P.K. Seidman.
Employer Identification Number: 136022257

5165
Seligson Foundation ¤
Valley Rd.
Locust Valley 11560

Established in 1982 in NY.
Donor(s): Alan Seligson.
Foundation type: Independent
Financial data (yr. ended 11/30/89): Assets, $823,742 (M); expenditures, $186,000, including $182,948 for 6 grants (high: $73,723; low: $11,470).
Purpose and activities: Giving primarily for medical research.
Application information:
Initial approach: Letter
Deadline(s): None
Write: Alan Seligson, Pres.
Officers: Alan Seligson, Pres.; Kate Seligson, V.P.; Nancy Seligson, V.P.; Edith Seligson, Secy.
Employer Identification Number: 112625463

5166
Sequa Foundation of Delaware ¤
(Formerly Sun Chemical Foundation)
200 Park Ave.
New York 10166

Established in 1967.
Donor(s): Sun Chemical Corp., Sequa Corp.
Foundation type: Company-sponsored
Financial data (yr. ended 12/31/88): Assets, $443,054 (M); gifts received, $276,029; expenditures, $344,680, including $344,640 for 38 grants (high: $250,000; low: $40).
Purpose and activities: Giving to Jewish welfare funds and higher education.
Limitations: Giving primarily in NY. No grants to individuals.
Application information:
Initial approach: Proposal
Deadline(s): None
Write: Monroe Adlman, Asst. Secy.
Officers and Trustees:* Norman E. Alexander,* Pres.; S.Z. Krinsly,* Secy.; D.J. O'Brien, Treas.
Employer Identification Number: 237000821

5167
The Sexauer Foundation ¤
531 Central Park Ave.
Scarsdale 10583

Incorporated in 1961 in DE.
Donor(s): John A. Sexauer.†
Foundation type: Independent
Financial data (yr. ended 8/31/88): Assets, $1,761,748 (M); expenditures, $132,370.
Purpose and activities: Emphasis on hospitals and higher education; support also for churches.
Application information: Contributes only to pre-selected organizations. Applications not accepted.
Officers and Trustee: James M. Sexauer, Pres. and Treas.; Nancy S. Walsh, V.P.; Donald Byrne, Secy.; Thomas J. Abbamont.
Employer Identification Number: 136156256

5168
Sharp Foundation ⌘ ☆
1370 Ave. of the Americas, 20th Fl.
New York 10019-4602

Established in 1984 in NY.
Donor(s): Peter J. Sharp.
Foundation type: Independent
Financial data (yr. ended 6/30/89): Assets, $2,462,391 (M); gifts received, $1,039,375; expenditures, $651,511, including $641,430 for 15 grants (high: $283,750; low: $1,500).
Purpose and activities: Support primarily for museums and the performing arts, with emphasis on music.
Types of support: Scholarship funds.
Limitations: Giving primarily in New York, NY. No grants to individuals.
Application information: Contributes only to pre-selected organizations. Applications not accepted.
Officers: Peter J. Sharp, Pres.; Joy Weber, Secy.; Charles Herrick, Treas.
Employer Identification Number: 133253731

5169
The Evelyn Sharp Foundation ⌘
1370 Ave. of the Americas
New York 10019 (212) 603-1333

Incorporated in 1952 in NY.
Donor(s): Evelyn Sharp, and others.
Foundation type: Independent
Financial data (yr. ended 06/30/89): Assets, $4,612,778 (M); expenditures, $105,133, including $97,000 for 19 grants (high: $15,000; low: $1,000).
Purpose and activities: Emphasis on the performing arts and museums, education, population control, and medical research and hospitals.
Limitations: Giving primarily in NY.
Application information:
Initial approach: Letter
Deadline(s): None
Write: Mrs. Evelyn Sharp, Pres.
Officers and Trustees:* Evelyn Sharp, Pres.; Mrs. Philip Bastedo,* V.P.; Mary Cronson,* V.P.; Emerson Foote,* V.P.; Albert Francke III,* V.P.; Jeremiah Milbank, Jr.,* V.P.; Peter J. Sharp,* V.P.
Employer Identification Number: 136119532

5170
Sharpe Family Foundation ⌘ ☆
c/o Fiduciary Trust Co. of New York
Two World Trade Ctr.
New York 10048-0001 (212) 466-4100

Established in 1966.
Donor(s): Mary Elizabeth Sharpe.
Foundation type: Independent
Financial data (yr. ended 12/31/87): Assets, $1,169,039 (M); gifts received, $133,004; expenditures, $56,078, including $49,024 for grants.
Purpose and activities: Support for landscape design and improvement grants to educational and other organizations.
Limitations: Giving primarily in RI. No grants to individuals.
Application information:
Initial approach: Letter
Deadline(s): None
Write: Henry D. Sharpe, Jr., Trustee
Trustees: Henry D. Sharpe, Jr., Peggy B. Sharpe, Fiduciary Trust Co. of New York.
Employer Identification Number: 136208422

5171
J. D. Shatford Memorial Trust ⌘
c/o Chemical Bank
30 Rockefeller Plaza
New York 10112 (212) 621-2148

Trust established in 1955 in NY.
Foundation type: Independent
Financial data (yr. ended 12/31/88): Assets, $3,208,972 (M); gifts received, $26,623; expenditures, $188,914, including $5,598 for grants and $154,202 for 70 grants to individuals (high: $24,172; low: $331).
Purpose and activities: Emphasis on scholarship aid, secondary and higher education, and charities in Hubbards, Nova Scotia.
Types of support: Student aid, grants to individuals.
Limitations: Giving limited to Nova Scotia, Canada.
Application information: Application form available for scholarship grants.
Deadline(s): None
Write: Mrs. Barbara Strohmeier
Trustees: Willard R. Brown, Chemical Bank.
Employer Identification Number: 136029993

5172
Shaykin Family Foundation ☆
c/o Adler & Skaykin
375 Park Ave.
New York 10151

Established in 1986 in NY.
Donor(s): Leonard Shaykin.
Foundation type: Independent
Financial data (yr. ended 11/30/89): Assets, $881,811 (M); gifts received, $664,815; qualifying distributions, $643,715, including $493,715 for 76 grants (high: $215,813; low: $25) and $150,000 for loans.
Purpose and activities: Giving primarily for an institution of Torah studies in Israel; support also for Jewish organizations.
Application information: Applications not accepted.
Write: Leonard Shaykin, Pres.
Officers: Leonard Shaykin, Pres.; Norah Shaykin, V.P.
Director: Richard Lang.
Number of staff: None.
Employer Identification Number: 363486772

5173
Emma A. Sheafer Charitable Trust
c/o Morgan Guaranty Trust Co. of New York
Nine West 57th St.
New York 10019
Application address: c/o Morgan Guaranty Trust Co. of NY, 60 Wall St., New York, NY 10260; Tel.: (212) 648-9667

Trust established in 1975 in NY.
Donor(s): Emma A. Sheafer.†
Foundation type: Independent
Financial data (yr. ended 12/31/88): Assets, $3,692,127 (M); expenditures, $168,526, including $138,200 for 10 grants (high: $15,000; low: $1,150).
Purpose and activities: Giving limited to performing arts groups.
Types of support: General purposes, continuing support, seed money, deficit financing, building funds, land acquisition, endowment funds, capital campaigns, operating budgets, renovation projects, special projects.
Limitations: Giving limited to NY, with emphasis on New York City. No grants to individuals, or for research, scholarships, fellowships, or matching gifts; no loans.
Application information: Application form not required.
Initial approach: Letter
Copies of proposal: 1
Deadline(s): Mid-Apr. and mid-Oct.
Board meeting date(s): June and Dec.
Final notification: 2 months
Write: Ms. Hildy Simmons, V.P., Morgan Guaranty Trust Co. of New York
Trustees: John C. Russell, Morgan Guaranty Trust Co. of New York.
Number of staff: None.
Employer Identification Number: 510186114

5174
Eric P. Sheinberg Foundation ⌘
c/o Goldman, Sachs & Co., Tax Dept.
85 Broad St., 30th Fl.
New York 10004

Donor(s): Eric P. Sheinberg.
Foundation type: Independent
Financial data (yr. ended 06/30/89): Assets, $2,870,930 (M); gifts received, $68,122; expenditures, $98,155, including $89,360 for 46 grants (high: $20,000; low: $25).
Purpose and activities: Support for health and welfare organizations, arts and cultural programs, and higher education.
Types of support: General purposes.
Limitations: Giving primarily in New York, NY. No grants to individuals.
Application information: Applications not accepted.
Trustees: Eric P. Sheinberg, Michael Steinhardt.
Employer Identification Number: 137004291

5175
Ralph C. Sheldon Foundation, Inc. ⌘
710 Hotel Jamestown Bldg.
Jamestown 14701 (716) 664-9850

Incorporated in 1948 in NY.
Donor(s): Julia S. Livengood, Isabell M. Sheldon.
Foundation type: Independent
Financial data (yr. ended 5/31/87): Assets, $4,372,536 (M); gifts received, $1,149,192; expenditures, $1,194,838, including $797,593 for 37 grants (high: $194,100; low: $800; average: $35,000).
Purpose and activities: Giving primarily for youth and social service agencies, and cultural programs.
Types of support: General purposes, building funds, equipment, annual campaigns, capital campaigns, emergency funds.
Limitations: Giving primarily in southern Chautauqua County, NY. No support for religious organizations. No grants to individuals.

Application information: Application form required.
Copies of proposal: 1
Deadline(s): None
Final notification: Immediately after determination
Write: Paul B. Sullivan, Exec. Dir.
Officers and Directors: Elizabeth Y. Sheldon, Pres.; Walter L. Miller, V.P.; Robert G. Wright, V.P.; Paul B. Sullivan, Secy. and Exec. Dir.; Miles L. Lasser, Treas.; Barclay O. Wellman.
Number of staff: 1 part-time professional; 1 full-time support; 1 part-time support.
Employer Identification Number: 166030502

5176
Shendell Foundation ⌑
122 East 42nd St., Suite 2500
New York 10168-0002

Established in 1962 in NY.
Donor(s): Isaac Shendell.
Foundation type: Independent
Financial data (yr. ended 10/31/88): Assets, $716,252 (M); expenditures, $169,529, including $162,000 for 6 grants (high: $60,000; low: $10,000).
Purpose and activities: Giving primarily for recreation, music and for higher education, including medical education.
Application information:
Initial approach: Proposal
Deadline(s): None
Write: Gordon S. Oppenheimer, Trustee
Trustees: Gordon S. Oppenheimer, Andrew Segal, Charles Segal.
Employer Identification Number: 136097659

5177
C. D. Shiah Charitable Foundation ⌑
75 Rockefeller Plaza, Suite 1501
New York 10019 (212) 484-8780

Established in 1981 in NY.
Foundation type: Independent
Financial data (yr. ended 06/30/89): Assets, $1,591,997 (M); expenditures, $76,589, including $73,600 for 5 grants (high: $30,000; low: $3,600).
Purpose and activities: Emphasis on secondary and higher education and the performing arts.
Limitations: Giving primarily in New York, NY. No grants to individuals.
Application information: Contributes only to pre-selected organizations. Applications not accepted.
Write: Oded Aboodi, Trustee
Trustee: Oded Aboodi.
Employer Identification Number: 133076929

5178
The Shimkin Foundation ⌑ ☆
c/o S. J. Levitan, Esq.
445 Park Ave.
New York 10022

Established in 1985 in NY.
Foundation type: Independent
Financial data (yr. ended 12/31/88): Assets, $1,011,751 (M); gifts received, $1,000,000; expenditures, $4,125, including $4,000 for 2 grants (high: $2,500; low: $1,500).
Purpose and activities: Support for a temple and an environmental group.
Limitations: Giving primarily in NY. No grants to individuals.
Application information: Contributes only to pre-selected organizations. Applications not accepted.
Officers and Directors: Rebecca Shimkin, V.P.; Selig J. Levitan, Secy.; Michael Shimkin, Treas.; Emily S. Gindin.
Employer Identification Number: 136022234

5179
The Shubert Foundation, Inc. ▼
234 West 44th St.
New York 10036 (212) 944-3777

Incorporated in 1945 in DE.
Donor(s): Lee Shubert,† J.J. Shubert.†
Foundation type: Independent
Financial data (yr. ended 05/31/89): Assets, $113,168,506 (M); gifts received, $181,407; expenditures, $4,297,181, including $2,758,200 for 132 grants (high: $250,000; low: $2,500; average: $10,000-$20,000) and $173,988 for 1 foundation-administered program.
Purpose and activities: To build and perpetuate the live performing arts, particularly the professional theater, in the U.S. Support both of theatrical institutions and of those other elements of the performing arts and related institutions necessary to maintain and support the theater. The foundation also operates a theatrical archive. Grants almost always made exclusively for general operating funds.
Types of support: Operating budgets.
Limitations: No grants to individuals, or for capital or endowment funds, research, conduit organizations, audience development, direct subsidies to reduce admission prices, productions for specialized audiences, scholarships, fellowships, or matching gifts; no loans.
Publications: Annual report (including application guidelines).
Application information: Application form required.
Initial approach: Letter or telephone
Copies of proposal: 2
Deadline(s): Submit proposal preferably in Oct. or Nov.; deadline Dec. 1
Board meeting date(s): Monthly
Final notification: May
Write: Lynn L. Seidler, Exec. Dir.
Officers and Directors:* Gerald Schoenfeld,* Chair.; Bernard B. Jacobs,* Pres.; John W. Kluge,* V.P.; Michael I. Sovern,* V.P.; Irving M. Wall,* Secy.; Lee J. Seidler,* Treas.; Lynn L. Seidler, Exec. Dir.
Number of staff: 2 full-time professional; 1 full-time support.
Employer Identification Number: 136106961

5180
The Franz W. Sichel Foundation ⌑
c/o Galef & Jacobs
711 Third Ave.
New York 10017

Incorporated in 1961 in NY.
Donor(s): Employees of Fromm & Sichel, Inc.
Foundation type: Independent
Financial data (yr. ended 05/31/89): Assets, $906,283 (M); expenditures, $172,353, including $163,378 for 63 grants (high: $107,559; low: $69).
Purpose and activities: Giving primarily for a museum of fine arts and other cultural programs and health organizations.
Types of support: General purposes.
Limitations: Giving primarily in New York, NY.
Application information: Contributes only to pre-selected organizations. Applications not accepted.
Officers: Peter M.F. Sichel, Pres.; Victor Jacobs, Secy.-Treas.
Trustees: Alfred Fromm, Noel Rubinton, Margaret Sichel, Sylvia Sichel.
Employer Identification Number: 136115904

5181
The Lois and Samuel Silberman Fund, Inc. ⌑
133 East 79th St.
New York 10021 (212) 737-8500

Incorporated in 1951 in NY.
Donor(s): Samuel J. Silberman.
Foundation type: Independent
Financial data (yr. ended 7/31/88): Assets, $8,936,723 (M); expenditures, $1,211,960, including $1,157,392 for 4 grants (high: $1,134,501; low: $2,149) and $10,044 for 2 grants to individuals (high: $9,028; low: $1,016).
Purpose and activities: From 1986 to 1989, the primary focus will be on programs for the benefit of the Hunter College School of Social Work; support also for programs that encourage study of emerging social problems.
Types of support: Grants to individuals.
Limitations: No grants for building or endowment funds, general purposes, operating budgets, scholarships, fellowships, or matching gifts.
Publications: Multi-year report, informational brochure.
Application information: Field Education Awards are by nomination only. Application form required.
Initial approach: Letter
Copies of proposal: 10
Deadline(s): Sept. 30 for Senior Faculty Awards, Nov. 15 for Junior Faculty Awards, and Dec. 31 for Field Education Awards nominations
Board meeting date(s): Varies
Final notification: Jan. for Senior Faculty Awards, Mar. for Junior Faculty Awards, and June for Field Education Awards
Write: Lois V. Silberman, V.P.
Officers and Trustees: Samuel J. Silberman, Pres.; Lois V. Silberman, V.P.; Allen H. Russell, Secy.; J. Robert Baylis, Treas.; Herbert L. Abrons, Kevin R. Brine, Thomas R. Horton, Seymour Milstein, Jayne M. Silberman, Edward T. Weaver.
Number of staff: None.
Employer Identification Number: 136097931

5182
David and Lyn Silfen Foundation ⌑
c/o Goldman, Sachs & Co., Tax Dept.
85 Broad St., 30th Fl.
New York 10004-2106

Established in 1981 in NY.
Donor(s): David M. Silfen.
Foundation type: Independent
Financial data (yr. ended 3/31/88): Assets, $1,171,371 (M); gifts received, $536,000; expenditures, $152,208, including $149,150 for 76 grants (high: $50,000; low: $25).
Purpose and activities: Support primarily for Jewish welfare organizations; giving also for the handicapped, higher education and medical research.
Limitations: Giving primarily in NY. No grants to individuals.
Application information: Presently contributes only to pre-selected organizations. Applications not accepted.
Trustees: Robert M. Freeman, Patricia Gordon, David M. Silfen, Lyn Silfen.
Employer Identification Number: 133103011

5183
Louis & Martha Silver Foundation, Inc. ⌑
c/o Gassman Rebhun & Co., P.C.
350 Fifth Ave.
New York 10118
Application address: 345 Underhill Blvd., Syosset, NY 11791; Tel.: (718) 895-8950

Established in 1964 in NY.
Donor(s): Louis Silver, Martha Silver.
Foundation type: Independent
Financial data (yr. ended 12/31/88): Assets, $2,566,513 (M); gifts received, $150,000; expenditures, $115,186, including $106,716 for 123 grants (high: $20,000; low: $10).
Purpose and activities: Emphasis on Jewish giving, including temple support, welfare funds, hospitals, and higher education.
Application information:
Initial approach: Letter
Deadline(s): None
Write: Louis Silver, Pres.
Officers: Louis Silver, Pres.; Stanley Silver, V.P.; Martha Silver, Secy.-Treas.
Employer Identification Number: 136165326

5184
Simon Foundation, Inc. ⌑
c/o Charles Simon
One New York Plaza
New York 10004 (212) 747-6013

Incorporated in 1954 in NY.
Donor(s): Charles Simon.
Foundation type: Independent
Financial data (yr. ended 12/31/88): Assets, $362,692 (M); expenditures, $249,923, including $241,375 for 61 grants (high: $39,000; low: $100).
Purpose and activities: Emphasis on cultural programs and museums, higher education, hospitals, and youth agencies.
Types of support: General purposes, scholarship funds.
Limitations: Giving primarily in NY. No grants to individuals.
Application information: Contributes only to pre-selected organizations. Applications not accepted.
Officers and Directors: Charles Simon, Pres. and Treas.; George DeSipio, V.P. and Secy.; Daniel M. Kelly.
Employer Identification Number: 136088838

5185
Sidney, Milton and Leoma Simon Foundation ⌑
23 Crestview Dr.
Pleasantville 10570

Established in 1964.
Donor(s): Milton Simon.†
Foundation type: Independent
Financial data (yr. ended 05/31/89): Assets, $10,264,135 (M); expenditures, $606,999, including $412,500 for 62 grants (high: $12,000; low: $2,500).
Purpose and activities: Grants primarily for the handicapped, performing arts, medical research, Jewish welfare funds, and hospitals.
Types of support: Research.
Application information:
Initial approach: Letter or proposal
Deadline(s): None
Write: Joseph C. Warner, Trustee
Trustees: Joseph C. Warner, Meryl Warner, Alan Wechsler.
Employer Identification Number: 136175218

5186
The Harry & Anna Singer Foundation ⌑
c/o Saul Singer
Two Osceola Ave.
Dobbs Ferry 10522

Established in 1969 in NY.
Foundation type: Independent
Financial data (yr. ended 06/30/89): Assets, $30,002 (M); expenditures, $1,190,504, including $1,189,140 for 18 grants (high: $1,075,000; low: $100).
Purpose and activities: Support primarily for Jewish giving and higher education.
Limitations: Giving primarily in NY.
Application information:
Initial approach: Letter
Deadline(s): None
Officer: Saul Singer, Mgr.
Employer Identification Number: 237078853

5187
Herbert & Nell Singer Foundation, Inc. ⌑ ☆
745 Fifth Ave.
New York 10151

Donor(s): Herbert N. Singer, The Peter Singer Trust, The Steven Singer Trust.
Foundation type: Independent
Financial data (yr. ended 12/31/88): Assets, $424,538 (M); gifts received, $300,000; expenditures, $165,724, including $165,500 for 29 grants (high: $70,000; low: $250).
Purpose and activities: Support for Jewish organizations, higher education, film programs, and general charitable organizations.
Limitations: Giving primarily in New York, NY. No grants to individuals.
Application information: Contributes only to pre-selected organizations. Applications not accepted.
Trustees: Richard Netter, Herbert N. Singer, Nell Singer.
Employer Identification Number: 133151548

5188
Louis P. Singer Fund, Inc. ⌑ ☆
211 Broadway
Lynbrook 11563

Established in 1961.
Donor(s): Berkshire Hathaway Corp.
Foundation type: Independent
Financial data (yr. ended 8/31/88): Assets, $1,471,165 (M); gifts received, $8,561; expenditures, $88,639, including $73,282 for 70 grants (high: $32,000; low: $35).
Purpose and activities: Support primarily for Jewish welfare, including support for Israel; giving also for public television and radio and other cultural programs, hospitals, health associations, medical research, and education.
Application information: Applications not accepted.
Officers: Louis P. Singer, Pres.; Paula Singer, V.P.; John Viener, Secy.-Treas.
Employer Identification Number: 136077788

5189
The Alexandrine and Alexander L. Sinsheimer Fund ⌑
c/o Manufacturers Hanover Trust Co.
600 Fifth Ave.
New York 10020 (212) 957-1603

Trust established in 1959 in NY.
Donor(s): Alexander L. Sinsheimer,† Alexandrine Sinsheimer.†
Foundation type: Independent
Financial data (yr. ended 04/30/89): Assets, $7,516,858 (M); expenditures, $393,881, including $351,312 for 7 grants (high: $57,104; low: $20,000).
Purpose and activities: To support scientific research relating to prevention and cure of human disease.
Limitations: Giving limited to the New York, NY, metropolitan area.
Application information: Application form required.
Deadline(s): Feb. 15
Write: T.E. Roepe, V.P., Manufacturers Hanover Trust Co.
Trustee: Manufacturers Hanover Trust Co.
Employer Identification Number: 136047421

5190
Morris & Eddie Sitt Family Foundation ⌑ ☆
10 West 33rd St., Rm. 626
New York 10001 (212) 947-4111

Established in 1977.
Donor(s): Morris Sitt, and members of the Sitt family.
Foundation type: Independent
Financial data (yr. ended 6/30/89): Assets, $58,521 (M); gifts received, $147,000; expenditures, $109,553, including $109,506 for 136 grants (high: $18,000; low: $10).

Purpose and activities: Giving primarily for Jewish organizations, including congregations, yeshivas, and a welfare fund.
Application information:
Initial approach: Letter
Deadline(s): None
Directors: Eddie Sitt, Jeffrey Sitt, Morris Sitt.
Employer Identification Number: 132886778

5191
The Jack Sitt 1986 Charitable Trust, Inc. ⌑ ☆
c/o Baby Togs
450 West 33rd St.
New York 10001

Established in 1986 in NY.
Donor(s): Jack Sitt.
Foundation type: Independent
Financial data (yr. ended 12/31/88): Assets, $820 (M); gifts received, $349,000; expenditures, $471,887, including $471,603 for 53 grants (high: $248,611; low: $10).
Purpose and activities: Giving primarily for Jewish organizations; support also for hospitals and health.
Trustees: Jack Sitt, Joseph J. Sitt.
Employer Identification Number: 133441744

5192
Skiers Injuries Charities Trust ⌑ ☆
488 Madison Ave., 4th Fl.
New York 10021

Established in 1983.
Donor(s): Martin J. Raynes, Beatrice Raynes.
Foundation type: Independent
Financial data (yr. ended 4/30/89): Assets, $372 (M); gifts received, $176,000; expenditures, $175,879, including $172,900 for 2 grants (high: $157,900; low: $15,000).
Purpose and activities: Giving primarily for a shelter for injured skiers; some support for a medical center.
Limitations: Giving primarily in Aspen, CO. No grants to individuals.
Application information: Contributes only to pre-selected organizations. Applications not accepted.
Trustees: Frederic Heller, Martin J. Raynes, Robert Stong.
Employer Identification Number: 133183448

5193
Skirball Foundation ▼ ⌑
c/o Bergreen & Bergreen
660 Madison Ave.
New York 10021 (212) 832-8500

Established in 1950 in OH.
Donor(s): Members of the Skirball family, Skirball Investment Co.
Foundation type: Independent
Financial data (yr. ended 12/31/87): Assets, $28,830,944 (M); gifts received, $24,752,376; expenditures, $2,187,176, including $2,106,360 for 31 grants (high: $1,000,000; low: $100; average: $500-$10,000).
Purpose and activities: Giving primarily for Jewish welfare and temple support; support also for education, the arts, and medicine.
Limitations: Giving primarily in CA. No grants to individuals.
Application information:
Write: Morris H. Bergreen, Pres.
Officers and Trustees: Morris H. Bergreen, Pres.; Martin Blackman, Secy.; Robert D. Goldfarb, V.P.; A. Skirball-Kenis, V.P.; George H. Heyman, Jr., Treas.; Robert M. Tanenbaum.
Employer Identification Number: 346517957

5194
Dr. Louis Sklarow Memorial Fund ⌑ ☆
c/o The Bank of New York, Tax Dept.
48 Wall St.
New York 10015
Application address: c/o Key Trust Co., 284 Main St., Buffalo, NY 14202; Tel.: (716) 847-2227

Established in 1975.
Foundation type: Independent
Financial data (yr. ended 5/31/89): Assets, $1,172,312 (M); expenditures, $98,695, including $90,164 for 2 grants (high: $58,495; low: $31,669).
Purpose and activities: "To support biomedical research into the causes and cures of disabling or fatal diseases for which there has been no known solution to date." Emphasis on heart diseases, cancer, stroke, and neuromuscular disorders.
Types of support: Research.
Application information:
Initial approach: Proposal
Copies of proposal: 1
Deadline(s): Sept. 30
Final notification: Nov. 30
Write: Irene R. Hypnarowski, Trust Officer, Key Trust Co.
Trustees: Joseph Hoffman, The Bank of New York.
Employer Identification Number: 166201243

5195
The Slade Foundation, Inc. ⌑
c/o Bear Stearns Companies, Inc.
245 Park Ave.
New York 10167

Incorporated in 1952 in NY.
Donor(s): John H. Slade.
Foundation type: Independent
Financial data (yr. ended 7/31/88): Assets, $541,173 (M); gifts received, $255,000; expenditures, $158,612, including $156,443 for 16 grants (high: $150,000; low: $20).
Purpose and activities: Giving for Jewish welfare funds and organizations, and for cultural programs and social services; support also for organizations in Israel.
Limitations: Giving primarily in New York, NY, and Israel.
Application information: Contributes only to pre-selected organizations. Applications not accepted.
Officers and Directors:* John H. Slade,* Pres.; Milton B. Evlau,* V.P.; George Maxwell, Secy.-Treas.
Employer Identification Number: 136065039

5196
C. F. Roe Slade Foundation ⌑
c/o J.T. Jackson
P.O. Box 1944
New York 10116-1944

Established in 1969 in NY.
Donor(s): Marie-Antoinette Slade.†
Foundation type: Independent
Financial data (yr. ended 6/30/88): Assets, $572,574 (M); gifts received, $79,000; expenditures, $128,151, including $120,750 for 9 grants (high: $30,000; low: $5,000).
Purpose and activities: Support for education, culture, health services, and conservation.
Types of support: Research, building funds, general purposes.
Limitations: Giving primarily in NY.
Application information: Contributes only to pre-selected organizations. Applications not accepted.
Trustees: Kathleen McLaughlin Jeffords, Jean T.J. Scully, Leonard T. Scully, Donald Vail.
Employer Identification Number: 136205873

5197
The Slaner Foundation, Inc. ⌑
645 Fifth Ave.
New York 10022

Established in 1960 in NY.
Donor(s): Alfred P. Slaner, Felix Zandman.
Foundation type: Independent
Financial data (yr. ended 11/30/88): Assets, $2,369,767 (M); expenditures, $113,746, including $103,000 for 12 grants (high: $50,000; low: $250).
Purpose and activities: Support primarily for Jewish welfare organizations, health and medical associations, and for public policy organizations.
Limitations: Giving primarily in NY and Washington, DC.
Application information:
Initial approach: Letter
Deadline(s): None
Write: Alfred P. Slaner, Pres.
Officers and Directors: Alfred P. Slaner, Pres. and Treas.; Luella Slaner, V.P. and Secy.; Millie Bluth Allinson, Eugenia Ames, Milton N. Scofield.
Employer Identification Number: 136143119

5198
The Slant/Fin Foundation, Inc. ⌑
100 Forest Dr.
Greenvale 11548

Established in 1985 in NY.
Donor(s): Slant/Fin Corp.
Foundation type: Company-sponsored
Financial data (yr. ended 06/30/89): Assets, $1,359,147 (M); gifts received, $400,000; expenditures, $313,346, including $312,182 for grants (high: $116,700).
Purpose and activities: Giving primarily for Jewish organizations.
Application information: Contributes only to pre-selected organizations. Applications not accepted.
Officers and Directors:* Melvin Dubin,* Pres.; Delcy Brooks,* Secy.; Donald Brown,* Treas.
Employer Identification Number: 112752009

5199
The Charles Slaughter Foundation
c/o Milgrim, Thomajan & Lee
53 Wall St.
New York 10005-2815 (212) 858-5342

Established in 1980 in NY.
Foundation type: Independent
Financial data (yr. ended 10/31/89): Assets, $2,399,095 (M); expenditures, $165,116, including $105,000 for 2 grants (high: $65,000; low: $40,000).
Purpose and activities: Grants to hospitals for medical research activities.
Types of support: Research.
Limitations: Giving primarily in New York, NY. No grants to individuals.
Publications: Financial statement.
Application information: Contributes only to pre-selected organizations. Applications not accepted.
Write: Myles A. Cane, Pres.
Officers: Myles A. Cane, Pres.; William E. Friedman, Secy.-Treas.
Director: Kenneth T. Donaldson.
Number of staff: 1 part-time professional; 1 part-time support.
Employer Identification Number: 133055995

5200
Alan B. Slifka Foundation, Inc. ⌑
11 Hanover Sq.
New York 10005

Established in 1963 in NY.
Donor(s): Alan B. Slifka.
Foundation type: Independent
Financial data (yr. ended 11/30/88): Assets, $1,402,516 (M); gifts received, $435,400; expenditures, $463,533, including $459,554 for 275 grants (high: $50,000; low: $10).
Purpose and activities: Support primarily for Jewish welfare organizations and cultural activities; some support also for education and child welfare.
Limitations: Giving primarily in NY.
Application information: Application form not required.
Deadline(s): None
Officer: Alan B. Slifka, Pres.
Employer Identification Number: 136192257

5201
Joseph & Sylvia Slifka Foundation ⌑
477 Madison Ave.
New York 10022

Established in 1944.
Foundation type: Independent
Financial data (yr. ended 10/31/88): Assets, $2,264,122 (M); gifts received, $100,000; expenditures, $151,079, including $131,960 for 34 grants (high: $50,000; low: $100).
Purpose and activities: Support primarily for Jewish welfare, hospitals, higher education, culture, and the arts.
Application information:
Initial approach: Letter
Deadline(s): None
Write: Joseph Slifka, Pres.
Officer: Joseph Slifka, Pres.
Employer Identification Number: 136106433

5202
Alfred P. Sloan Foundation ▼
630 Fifth Ave., 25th Fl.
New York 10111-0242 (212) 649-1649

Incorporated in 1934 in DE.
Donor(s): Alfred P. Sloan, Jr.,† Irene Jackson Sloan,† New Castle Corp.
Foundation type: Independent
Financial data (yr. ended 12/31/89): Assets, $622,070,457 (M); expenditures, $21,217,968, including $14,049,581 for grants (high: $2,395,000; average: $10,000-$300,000) and $3,200,000 for grants to individuals.
Purpose and activities: Interests in science and technology, education, economics and management, and related problems of society; Sloan fellowships for basic research in the sciences are administered entirely through institutions.
Types of support: General purposes, seed money, research, fellowships, conferences and seminars, special projects.
Limitations: No support for the creative or performing arts, humanities (except through the New Liberal Arts Program), medical research, religion, or primary or secondary education. No grants to individuals directly, or for endowment or building funds, or equipment not related directly to foundation-supported projects; no loans.
Publications: Annual report, informational brochure, program policy statement, application guidelines.
Application information: Nomination forms available for fellowship candidates; direct applications not accepted. Application form not required.
Initial approach: Letter
Copies of proposal: 1
Deadline(s): Sept. 15 for fellowship program; no deadline for others
Board meeting date(s): Throughout the year (grants of $30,000 or less); 5 times a year (grants over $30,000)
Final notification: Early in year for research fellowships; within 3 months for others
Write: Ralph E. Gomory, Pres.
Officers: Ralph E. Gomory,* Pres.; Stewart F. Campbell, Financial V.P. and Secy.; Arthur L. Singer, Jr., V.P.
Trustees:* Howard W. Johnson, Chair.; Lucy Wilson Benson, Stephen L. Brown, Lloyd C. Elam, S. Parker Gilbert, Marvin L. Goldberger, Ralph E. Gomory, Howard H. Kehrl, Donald N. Langengerg, Cathleen Synge Morawetz, Frank Press, Lewis T. Preston, James D. Robinson III, Harold T. Shapiro, Roger B. Smith.
Number of staff: 8 full-time professional; 9 full-time support.
Employer Identification Number: 131623877

5203
John Sloan Memorial Foundation, Inc. ⌑
220 East 42nd St., 16th Fl.
New York 10017 (212) 682-3060

Established in 1979 in NY.
Foundation type: Independent
Financial data (yr. ended 12/31/88): Assets, $1,422,555 (M); expenditures, $146,160, including $133,900 for 18 grants (high: $51,400; low: $2,000).
Purpose and activities: Giving limited to organizations and activities concerning American art, preferably for the period from 1880 to 1950.
Application information: Application form not required.
Initial approach: Letter
Deadline(s): None
Write: Harry B. Clark, Treas.
Officers: Helen F. Sloan, Pres.; Donald E. McNicol, V.P.; Harry B. Clark, Treas.
Employer Identification Number: 132988798

5204
Mary Jean & Frank P. Smeal Foundation ⌑ ☆
85 Broad St.
New York 10004-2454

Established in 1985 in NY.
Donor(s): Frank P. Smeal.
Foundation type: Independent
Financial data (yr. ended 2/28/89): Assets, $2,325,973 (M); expenditures, $496,523, including $471,752 for 41 grants (high: $150,000; low: $50).
Purpose and activities: Support for higher education, youth, and social services.
Limitations: Giving primarily in NY, NJ, PA, MA, and Washington, DC. No grants to individuals; no loans.
Application information: Applications not accepted.
Trustees: Frank P. Smeal, Mary Jean Smeal.
Employer Identification Number: 133318167

5205
George Graham and Elizabeth Galloway Smith Foundation, Inc. ⌑ ☆
84 South Davis St.
Orchard Park 14127-2683 (716) 662-9749

Donor(s): Elizabeth G. Smith, Beatrice Erlin.†
Foundation type: Independent
Financial data (yr. ended 5/31/89): Assets, $1,811,226 (M); gifts received, $908,031; expenditures, $43,156, including $36,250 for grants (high: $7,550).
Purpose and activities: Support for higher education and the arts, including museums.
Limitations: Giving primarily in western NY.
Application information:
Initial approach: Letter
Deadline(s): June 15 for requests above $1,000
Write: Graham Wood Smith, Pres.
Officers: Elizabeth G. Smith, Chair.; Graham Wood Smith, Pres.; Geo G. Smith III, V.P.
Employer Identification Number: 166031530

5206
Roy & Marianne Smith Foundation ⌑ ☆
c/o Goldman Sachs & Co.
85 Broad St.
New York 10004-2408

Established in 1980.
Donor(s): Roy C. Smith, Marianne F. Smith.
Foundation type: Independent
Financial data (yr. ended 3/31/89): Assets, $969,236 (M); gifts received, $300,000; expenditures, $187,995, including $182,718 for 22 grants (high: $100,000; low: $1,000).

Purpose and activities: Giving primarily for higher and other education, including a U.S. naval academy; support also for the fine and performing arts, and child welfare.
Limitations: Giving primarily in NY, NJ, MA, MD, and CT. No grants to individuals; no loans.
Application information: Applications not accepted.
Trustees: Michael H. Coles, Marianne F. Smith, Roy C. Smith.
Employer Identification Number: 133050754

5207
George D. Smith Fund, Inc. ▼ ⌑
c/o Lawrence W. Milas, V.P.
805 Third Ave., 20th Fl.
New York 10022

Incorporated in 1956 in DE.
Donor(s): George D. Smith, Sr.†
Foundation type: Independent
Financial data (yr. ended 12/31/88): Assets, $24,920,219 (M); expenditures, $1,132,680, including $1,106,286 for 10 grants (high: $324,186; low: $100; average: $20,000-$130,000).
Purpose and activities: Primarily supports basic research in molecular and cellular physiology and in cardiovascular diagnostic methods at two university medical centers; support also for higher education and public television.
Types of support: Research.
Limitations: Giving primarily in CA and UT.
Application information: Applications not accepted.
Officers and Trustees:* George D. Smith, Jr.,* Pres. and Secy.-Treas.; H.D. Burgess, V.P.; Lawrence W. Milas, V.P.; C.M. Smith,* V.P.
Employer Identification Number: 136138728

5208
The Christopher D. Smithers Foundation, Inc.
P.O. Box 67, Oyster Bay Rd.
Mill Neck 11765 (516) 676-0067

Incorporated in 1952 in NY.
Donor(s): Christopher D. Smithers,† Mrs. Mabel B. Smithers,† R. Brinkley Smithers.
Foundation type: Independent
Financial data (yr. ended 12/31/89): Assets, $6,576,010 (M); gifts received, $32,366; expenditures, $1,229,399, including $1,150,975 for 30 grants (high: $852,663; low: $50) and $35,106 for 1 foundation-administered program.
Purpose and activities: Supports organizations performing prevention, educational service, treatment, and research in the field of alcoholism; initiates its own projects in this field primarily by writing and publishing specialized booklets for industry, educational organizations, and the general public.
Types of support: Operating budgets, special projects, research, conferences and seminars.
Limitations: No grants to individuals, or for building or endowment funds, or matching gifts; no loans.
Publications: Annual report.
Application information: Application form not required.
Initial approach: Proposal
Copies of proposal: 2
Deadline(s): Submit proposal between Sept. and Dec.; no set deadline
Board meeting date(s): May
Write: Adele C. Smithers, Pres.
Officers and Directors:* R. Brinkley Smithers,* Chair.; Adele C. Smithers,* Pres.; M. Elizabeth Brothers,* V.P.; Henry S. Ziegler,* Secy.; Charles F. Smithers, Jr.,* Treas.; Shirley B. Klusener, Christopher B. Smithers.
Number of staff: 1 part-time professional.
Employer Identification Number: 131861928

5209
The John Ben Snow Foundation, Inc.
P.O. Box 376
Pulaski 13142 (315) 298-6401
New Jersey office: 202 Mountain Ave., Westfield, NJ 07090

Incorporated in 1948 in NY.
Donor(s): John Ben Snow.†
Foundation type: Independent
Financial data (yr. ended 03/31/89): Assets, $4,015,631 (M); expenditures, $224,866, including $162,095 for 20 grants (high: $20,000; low: $350; average: $5,000-$10,000).
Purpose and activities: Giving for higher, secondary, elementary, early childhood, and minority educational institutions; child development and youth agencies; hospitals and sevices for the disabled; and community betterment projects.
Types of support: Building funds, matching funds, scholarship funds, special projects, fellowships, equipment.
Limitations: Giving limited to central NY, with focus on Oswego County. No grants to individuals, or for operating budgets, endowment funds, or contingency financing.
Publications: Annual report (including application guidelines).
Application information: Application form required.
Initial approach: Letter
Copies of proposal: 1
Deadline(s): Submit proposal between Sept. and Apr.; deadline Mar. 15
Board meeting date(s): June
Write: Vernon F. Snow, Pres.
Officers and Directors:* Vernon F. Snow,* Pres.; Allen R. Malcolm,* Exec. V.P. and Secy.-Treas.; Bruce Malcolm, Rollan Melton, Royle Melton, Joseph Mitchell, David H. Snow.
Number of staff: 2 part-time support.
Employer Identification Number: 136112704

5210
John Ben Snow Memorial Trust ▼
P.O. Box 378
Pulaski 13142 (315) 298-6401

Trust established in 1974 in NY.
Donor(s): John Ben Snow.†
Foundation type: Independent
Financial data (yr. ended 12/31/88): Assets, $16,940,550 (M); expenditures, $1,161,570, including $836,840 for 36 grants (high: $75,000; low: $2,000; average: $5,000-$25,000).
Purpose and activities: Giving primarily for education, especially scholarship funds and for research; cultural institutions, especially libraries; medical and health organizations; environmental groups; and community development.
Types of support: Seed money, equipment, research, publications, scholarship funds, fellowships, matching funds, renovation projects, conferences and seminars, internships.
Limitations: Giving primarily in central NY, and New York City. No support for government agencies or unspecified projects. No grants to individuals or for operating budgets or endowment funds; no loans.
Publications: Annual report (including application guidelines).
Application information: Application form required.
Initial approach: Letter
Copies of proposal: 1
Deadline(s): Submit proposal preferably from July through Mar.; deadline Mar. 15
Board meeting date(s): June
Final notification: 3 months
Write: Vernon F. Snow, Trustee
Trustees: Allen R. Malcolm, Rollan D. Melton, Vernon F. Snow, The Bank of New York.
Number of staff: 2 part-time support.
Employer Identification Number: 136633814

5211
The Valentine Perry Snyder Fund ⌑
c/o Morgan Guaranty Trust Co. of New York
Nine West 57th St.
New York 10019 (212) 483-2248
Application address: c/o Morgan Guaranty Trust Co. of New York, 23 Wall St., New York, NY 10005

Trust established in 1942 in NY.
Donor(s): Mrs. Sheda T. Snyder.†
Foundation type: Independent
Financial data (yr. ended 12/31/86): Assets, $4,849,763 (M); expenditures, $280,658, including $249,850 for 16 grants (high: $25,000; low: $50,000).
Purpose and activities: Giving for social services, including religious welfare organizations, child welfare, health, community development, and church support.
Types of support: General purposes, operating budgets, continuing support, seed money, emergency funds, building funds, equipment, land acquisition, endowment funds, special projects.
Limitations: Giving primarily in the New York, NY, metropolitan area. No grants to individuals, or for research-related programs, scholarships, fellowships, or matching gifts; no loans.
Application information:
Initial approach: Letter
Copies of proposal: 1
Deadline(s): None
Board meeting date(s): May and Nov.
Write: Robert F. Longley, Sr. V.P., Morgan Guaranty Trust Co. of New York
Trustee: Morgan Guaranty Trust Co. of New York.
Number of staff: 1
Employer Identification Number: 136036765

5212
Society for the Relief of Women & Children ☆
575 Lexington Ave.
New York 10022-6102

Established in 1802 in NY.
Foundation type: Independent
Financial data (yr. ended 10/31/89): Assets, $1,523,478 (M); expenditures, $80,281, including $43,900 for 14 grants (high: $7,000; low: $900) and $25,159 for 12 grants to individuals (high: $6,180; low: $105).
Purpose and activities: "Awards grants to individuals who after leading productive lives are unable because of circumstances beyond their control to adequately support themselves"; support also for organizations with programs to aid same class of persons.
Types of support: Grants to individuals.
Limitations: Giving primarily in New York, NY.
Application information: Unsolicited applications discouraged. Application form not required.
Deadline(s): None
Officers and Directors:* Mrs. Charles J. Irwin,* Pres.; Mrs. J. Michael Loening,* Secy.; Mrs. William H. Savage,* Treas.; and 15 additional directors.
Number of staff: None.
Employer Identification Number: 136161272

5213
Sofaer Foundation ⌑ ☆
c/o 61 Associates
350 Fifth Ave., Suite 3410
New York 10118

Established in 1985 in NY.
Donor(s): Marian B. Scheuer-Sofaer.
Foundation type: Independent
Financial data (yr. ended 11/30/88): Assets, $11,746 (M); gifts received, $111,631; expenditures, $196,684, including $193,945 for 85 grants (high: $50,000; low: $50).
Purpose and activities: Giving primarily for Jewish organizations and higher and religious education; support also for museums.
Application information: Contributes only to pre-selected organizations. Applications not accepted.
Officers and Directors: Marian B. Scheuer-Sofaer, Pres. and Treas.; Abraham D. Sofaer, V.P. and Secy.; Richard J. Scheuer.
Employer Identification Number: 133336722

5214
Sofia American Schools, Inc.
850 Third Ave.
New York 10022 (212) 319-2453

Established in 1926 in MA.
Foundation type: Independent
Financial data (yr. ended 6/30/89): Assets, $2,003,956 (M); expenditures, $164,411, including $115,550 for 4 grants (high: $48,000; low: $14,500).
Purpose and activities: All contributions are to aid American-sponsored educational institutions in the Near and Middle East. In 1990, the foundation hopes to initiate Bulgarian-American student exchanges.
Types of support: Scholarship funds, general purposes.
Limitations: Giving primarily in Greece and Turkey.
Application information:
Initial approach: Letter
Deadline(s): Feb.
Board meeting date(s): Mar.
Write: Board of Trustees
Officers: Irwin T. Sanders, Pres.; Robert C. Hubbard, V.P.; Walter Prosser, Secy.; Donald B. Murphy, Treas.; John H. Clymer, Clerk.
Trustees: Corrine M. Black, Carl S. Dorn, Stephen Grant, Alfred H. Howell, Elizabeth Michaels, Richard C. Robarts, Joel Studebaker, Roger Whitaker.
Number of staff: None.
Employer Identification Number: 136400773

5215
Sokoloff Foundation, Inc. ⌑
200 East 78th St.
New York 10021 (212) 744-5337

Foundation type: Independent
Financial data (yr. ended 12/31/88): Assets, $1,934,391 (M); expenditures, $82,106, including $74,550 for 55 grants (high: $15,000; low: $50).
Purpose and activities: Giving for Jewish welfare funds, social services, and the arts.
Application information: Application form not required.
Deadline(s): None
Write: Stephen Sokoloff, Pres.
Officers: Stephen Sokoloff, Pres.; H. Sol Tunick, Secy.
Employer Identification Number: 136155196

5216
The Soling Family Foundation ⌑
c/o Solico Penthouse
205 East 42nd St.
New York 10017

Established in 1985 in NY.
Donor(s): Chester Soling.
Foundation type: Independent
Financial data (yr. ended 5/31/88): Assets, $2,147,048 (M); expenditures, $351,661, including $277,035 for grants (high: $191,335).
Purpose and activities: Support primarily for a child care organization; giving also for museums, theaters and higher education.
Limitations: Giving primarily in MA and NY. No grants to individuals.
Application information: Contributes only to pre-selected organizations. Applications not accepted.
Officers: Chester Soling, Pres.; Carole Soling, Secy.; Caytha Jentis.
Employer Identification Number: 133288798

5217
Peter J. & Linda N. Solomon Foundation ⌑ ☆
c/o Barry M. Strauss Associates, Ltd.
245 Fifth Ave., Suite 1102
New York 10016-8775

Established in 1986 in NY.
Donor(s): Peter J. Solomon.
Foundation type: Independent
Financial data (yr. ended 3/31/88): Assets, $945,278 (M); gifts received, $565,375; expenditures, $122,160, including $116,817 for 45 grants (high: $30,000; low: $25).
Purpose and activities: Giving primarily for education, including elementary schools and universities; support also for Jewish organizations, museums, and conservation.
Application information:
Initial approach: Letter
Deadline(s): None
Write: Peter J. Solomon, Trustee
Trustees: Linda N. Solomon, Peter J. Solomon.
Employer Identification Number: 133384028

5218
Solow Foundation ▼ ⌑
Nine West 57th St.
New York 10019-2601 (212) 751-1100

Established in 1978 in DE.
Donor(s): Sheldon H. Solow.
Foundation type: Independent
Financial data (yr. ended 10/31/88): Assets, $7,201,167 (M); expenditures, $2,126,865, including $2,104,750 for 33 grants (high: $650,000; low: $250).
Purpose and activities: Support for higher education, cultural programs, a park conservancy, and Jewish organizations, including a holocaust memorial committee.
Types of support: General purposes.
Application information: Application form not required.
Deadline(s): None
Write: Sheldon H. Solow, Pres.
Officers: Sheldon H. Solow, Pres.; Rosalie S. Wolff, V.P.; Leonard Lazarus, Secy.; Steven Cherniak, Treas.
Employer Identification Number: 132950685

5219
Sheldon H. Solow Foundation, Inc. ⌑ ☆
Nine West 57th St.
New York 10019-2601 (212) 751-1100

Incorporated in 1986 in NY.
Donor(s): Sheldon H. Solow.
Foundation type: Independent
Financial data (yr. ended 11/30/87): Assets, $6,338,779 (M); gifts received, $6,000,000; expenditures, $10.
Purpose and activities: Initial year of operation, fiscal 1987; no grants awarded.
Application information: Application form not required.
Initial approach: Letter
Deadline(s): None
Write: Sheldon H. Solow, Pres.
Officers: Sheldon H. Solow, Pres. and Treas.; Rosalie S. Wolff, V.P.; Leonard Lazarus, Secy.
Employer Identification Number: 133386646

5220
The Abraham & Beverly Sommer Foundation ⌑
810 Seventh Ave.
New York 10019-5818

Established in 1977 in NY.
Donor(s): Beverly Sommer.
Foundation type: Independent
Financial data (yr. ended 12/31/88): Assets, $952,572 (M); gifts received, $250,000;

expenditures, $108,447, including $107,800 for 21 grants (high: $50,000; low: $30).
Purpose and activities: Giving primarily for Jewish organizations; support also for higher education, environmental preservation, and culture, including an opera company.
Limitations: Giving primarily in NY. No grants to individuals.
Application information: Contributes only to pre-selected organizations. Applications not accepted.
Officers: Beverly Sommer, Pres.; Amy Sommer, V.P.; Herman Abbott, Secy.-Treas.
Employer Identification Number: 132960992

5221
Sonnenblick Foundation, Inc. ⌑ ☆
445 Park Ave., 2nd Fl.
New York 10022 (212) 980-7600

Established in 1954.
Donor(s): Arthur I. Sonnenblick, Jack E. Sonnenblick.
Foundation type: Independent
Financial data (yr. ended 3/31/89): Assets, $169,366 (M); gifts received, $125,000; expenditures, $154,631, including $153,220 for 66 grants (high: $109,000; low: $10).
Purpose and activities: Giving primarily for a Jewish welfare fund and synagogues; support also for higher education, including medical education.
Limitations: Giving primarily in NY. No grants to individuals.
Application information:
Initial approach: Letter
Deadline(s): None
Write: Arthur I. Sonnenblick, Treas.
Officers and Directors: Jack E. Sonnenblick, Pres.; Arthur I. Sonnenblick, Treas.
Employer Identification Number: 136122775

5222
Sony Corporation of America Foundation, Inc. ⌑
Nine West 57th St.
New York 10019 (212) 418-9404

Established in 1972 in NY.
Donor(s): Sony Corp. of America.
Foundation type: Company-sponsored
Financial data (yr. ended 12/31/86): Assets, $1,763,503 (M); gifts received, $342,500; expenditures, $498,603, including $476,286 for grants and $22,317 for employee matching gifts.
Purpose and activities: Grants largely for hospitals, higher education, including scholarships for children of company employees, community funds, the performing arts, and Japanese and other cultural programs.
Types of support: General purposes, operating budgets, continuing support, annual campaigns, seed money, emergency funds, deficit financing, building funds, equipment, land acquisition, endowment funds, employee matching gifts, internships, employee-related scholarships.
Limitations: No grants to individuals (except for scholarships for children of company employees), or for special projects, research, publications, or conferences; no loans.
Application information: Application form not required.
Initial approach: Letter
Copies of proposal: 1
Deadline(s): None
Board meeting date(s): Quarterly
Final notification: 1 week
Write: Kenneth L. Nees, V.P.
Officers and Directors: Akio Morita, Chair.; Kenji Tamiya, Pres.; Kenneth L. Nees, V.P. and Secy.; Robert D. Dillon, Jr., V.P.; Norio Ohga, V.P.; Harvey L. Schein, V.P.
Number of staff: None.
Employer Identification Number: 237181637

5223
The Soros Foundation-Hungary, Inc. ⌑ ☆
888 Seventh Ave., Suite 3301
New York 10106

Established in 1983 in NY.
Donor(s): George Soros, George Soros Charitable Lead Trust, Tivadar Charitable Lead Trust.
Foundation type: Independent
Financial data (yr. ended 12/31/88): Assets, $3,548,599 (M); gifts received, $4,577,604; expenditures, $4,411,789, including $3,624,967 for 70 grants (high: $522,395; low: $715) and $272,332 for 56 grants to individuals (high: $63,528; low: $58).
Purpose and activities: Supports Hungarian organizations and projects, including the fields of language, culture, and education; also awards grants and scholarships to individuals for higher education and medical research.
Types of support: Grants to individuals, student aid, research.
Application information:
Write: Elizabeth Agocs, Secy.-Treas.
Officers and Directors:* George Soros,* Pres.; Philip Kaiser,* V.P.; William D. Zabel,* V.P.; Elizabeth Agocs, Secy.-Treas.
Employer Identification Number: 133210361

5224
Spektor Family Foundation, Inc. ⌑ ☆
261 Fifth Ave.
New York 10016 (212) 679-6868

Established in 1968.
Donor(s): Eryk Spektor.
Foundation type: Independent
Financial data (yr. ended 6/30/89): Assets, $921,359 (M); gifts received, $290,000; expenditures, $130,239, including $129,400 for 35 grants (high: $30,000; low: $200).
Purpose and activities: Support primarily for Jewish organizations, including welfare funds; grants also for higher education and hospitals.
Types of support: Scholarship funds.
Limitations: No grants to individuals.
Application information:
Initial approach: Letter
Deadline(s): None
Write: Eryk Spektor, Pres.
Officers: Eryk Spektor, Pres.; Mira Spektor, V.P. and Secy.
Employer Identification Number: 136277982

5225
The Sperry Fund
(Formerly The S & H Foundation, Inc.)
420 Lexington Ave., Suite 3020
New York 10170 (212) 370-1144
Application address: Coleman Associates, P.O. Box 1283, New Canaan, CT 06840; Tel.: (203) 966-7517

Established in 1962 in NY.
Foundation type: Independent
Financial data (yr. ended 12/31/88): Assets, $8,354,418 (M); expenditures, $240,100, including $12,500 for 1 grant and $129,950 for 79 grants to individuals (average: $500-$6,000).
Purpose and activities: Giving primarily to college juniors for support during two years of graduate education.
Types of support: Special projects, student aid.
Publications: Informational brochure (including application guidelines).
Application information: College or university must be invited to nominate juniors for scholarship program; individual applications not accepted. Application form required. Applications not accepted.
Write: Henry S. Coleman
Officers and Directors:* Frederick W. Beinecke,* Pres.; William S. Beinecke,* V.P.; Thane Benedict III,* Secy.; Michael A. Yesko, Treas.; R. Scott Greathead, Melvyn L. Shaffir.
Number of staff: 1 part-time support.
Employer Identification Number: 136114308

5226
Jerry and Emily Spiegel Family Foundation, Inc. ⌑
(Formerly Jerry Spiegel Foundation, Inc.)
375 North Broadway
Jericho 11753

Established in 1958 in NY.
Donor(s): Jerry Spiegel.
Foundation type: Independent
Financial data (yr. ended 3/31/89): Assets, $2,526,693 (M); gifts received, $1,082,200; expenditures, $370,137, including $364,640 for 78 grants (high: $175,000; low: $25).
Purpose and activities: Giving primarily for Jewish welfare organizations and temples; support also for health associations and hospitals, a tennis association, and education, particularly higher education.
Limitations: Giving primarily in NY. No grants to individuals.
Application information: Contributes only to pre-selected organizations. Applications not accepted.
Officer: Jerry Spiegel, Pres.
Employer Identification Number: 116006020

5227
Nate B. and Frances Spingold Foundation, Inc. ▼ ⌑
c/o Lankenau & Bickford
1740 Broadway
New York 10019

Incorporated in 1955 in NY.
Donor(s): Frances Spingold,† Nathan Breither Spingold.†
Foundation type: Independent
Financial data (yr. ended 11/30/89): Assets, $9,762,999 (M); gifts received, $10,000;

expenditures, $808,332, including $222,400 for 6 grants (high: $75,000; low: $12,400; average: $10,000-$50,000).
Purpose and activities: To improve the human condition through health and human services, with emphasis on meeting pediatric, geriatric and gerontological needs; expand opportunities for research and higher education, particularly in the medical sciences; and foster the development of the visual, performing and communication arts by providing opportunities for talented young artists, and by making arts available to more people.
Types of support: Conferences and seminars, fellowships, internships, matching funds, professorships, research, scholarship funds, special projects.
Limitations: Giving primarily in the New York, NY, metropolitan area and in Israel. No support for international activities. No grants to individuals, or for building or endowment funds, annual campaigns, or general operating purposes; no loans.
Publications: Annual report (including application guidelines).
Application information: Application form not required.
Initial approach: Proposal
Copies of proposal: 1
Deadline(s): None
Board meeting date(s): Monthly
Final notification: 90 days
Write: Daniel L. Kurtz, Pres.
Officers: Daniel L. Kurtz, Pres. and C.E.O.; Sherry Klein Heitler, V.P. and Secy.; Lorance Hockert, V.P. and Treas.
Directors: James R. Halperin, Melvyn C. Levitan.
Number of staff: None.
Employer Identification Number: 136107659

5228
Spirit Foundation, Inc.
c/o Kimmelman, Sexter, Warmflash & Leitner
61 Broadway, 24th Fl.
New York 10006 (212) 422-8300

Established in 1978 in NY.
Donor(s): John Lennon,† Yoko Ono Lennon.
Foundation type: Independent
Financial data (yr. ended 11/30/88): Assets, $98,527 (M); gifts received, $12,370; expenditures, $107,000, including $107,000 for 13 grants (high: $20,000; low: $1,000).
Purpose and activities: Support for underprivileged children and for the aged.
Publications: 990-PF.
Application information: Contributes only to pre-selected organizations. Applications not accepted.
Write: David Warmflash, Secy.-Treas.
Officers and Directors:* Yoko Ono Lennon,* Pres.; David Warmflash,* Secy.-Treas.; Allen S. Sexter.
Number of staff: None.
Employer Identification Number: 132971714

5229
The Spiritus Gladius Foundation
(Formerly D.C. Foundation, Inc.)
c/o Meyer Handelman Co.
2500 Westchester Ave.
Purchase 10577-2515

Established in 1959 in NY.
Donor(s): Nedenia H. Hartley.
Foundation type: Independent
Financial data (yr. ended 8/31/89): Assets, $2,574,668 (M); gifts received, $46,662; expenditures, $140,903, including $136,650 for 29 grants (high: $25,000; low: $250).
Purpose and activities: Support for youth and child welfare, higher education, medical research, and the arts.
Limitations: Giving primarily in NY, CT, and MA. No grants to individuals.
Application information: Contributes only to pre-selected organizations. Applications not accepted.
Officers: Nedenia H. Hartley, Pres.; Donald E. Handelman, V.P. and Secy.-Treas.
Trustees: Nedenia R. Craig, Joseph W. Handelman, Heather M. Robertson, Stanley H. Rumbough.
Employer Identification Number: 136113272

5230
The Bernard & Anne Spitzer Foundation, Inc. ¤
800 Fifth Ave.
New York 10021-7299

Donor(s): Bernard Spitzer.
Foundation type: Independent
Financial data (yr. ended 12/31/88): Assets, $1,642,571 (M); gifts received, $1,000,000; expenditures, $14,830, including $10,825 for grants (high: $5,000).
Purpose and activities: Support primarily for culture and Jewish welfare.
Limitations: Giving primarily in NY. No grants to individuals.
Application information: Contributes only to pre-selected organizations. Applications not accepted.
Officer and Directors:* Bernard Spitzer,* Pres.; Anne Spitzer.
Employer Identification Number: 133098005

5231
The Seth Sprague Educational and Charitable Foundation ▼
c/o U.S. Trust Co. of New York
114 West 47th St.
New York 10036-1532 (212) 852-3683

Trust established in 1939 in NY.
Donor(s): Seth Sprague.†
Foundation type: Independent
Financial data (yr. ended 12/31/89): Assets, $35,900,000 (M); expenditures, $2,100,000, including $1,560,000 for 386 grants (high: $25,000; low: $1,000; average: $1,000-$5,000).
Purpose and activities: Emphasis on health and human services, education, culture and the arts, and civic affairs and community development.
Types of support: Operating budgets, seed money, general purposes, matching funds, special projects.
Limitations: Giving primarily in NY and MA. No grants to individuals, or for building funds; no loans.
Publications: Application guidelines.
Application information: Application form not required.
Initial approach: Proposal or letter
Copies of proposal: 1
Deadline(s): Apr. 15 and Oct. 1
Board meeting date(s): Mar., June, Sept., and Nov. (grants awarded at June and Nov. meetings)
Final notification: No notice unless grant is made
Write: Maureen Auguściak, Sr. V.P., or Anne L. Smith Ganey, Asst. V.P., U.S. Trust Co. of New York
Trustees: Walter G. Dunnington, Jr., Arline Ripley Greenleaf, Jacqueline DeN. Simpkins, U.S. Trust Co. of New York.
Number of staff: None.
Employer Identification Number: 136071886

5232
The Spunk Fund, Inc.
675 Third Ave., Suite 1510
New York 10017 (212) 972-8330

Incorporated in 1981 in NY.
Donor(s): Marianne Gerschel.
Foundation type: Independent
Financial data (yr. ended 06/30/89): Assets, $10,731,123 (M); gifts received, $600,000; expenditures, $1,116,890, including $725,086 for 47 grants (high: $52,495; low: $1,000).
Purpose and activities: Support initiatives that contribute to the enrichment and well-being of children, including medical research, education, cultural programs, and programs for the prevention and treatment of child abuse and neglect.
Types of support: General purposes, research.
Limitations: Giving primarily in NY. No grants for capital programs.
Publications: Informational brochure (including application guidelines).
Application information: Proposals must be requested by the fund to receive consideration. Application form not required.
Initial approach: Letter of inquiry
Copies of proposal: 1
Deadline(s): Letters of inquiry accepted year round; requested proposals due Apr. 1
Board meeting date(s): June
Final notification: July 1
Write: Anna Matheny-Cartier, Exec.-Dir.
Officers: Marianne Gerschel, Pres. and Treas.; Joseph Erdman, Secy.; Anna Metheny-Cartier,* Exec. Dir.
Number of staff: 3 full-time professional; 2 full-time support.
Employer Identification Number: 133116094

5233
St. Faith's House Foundation
16 Crest Dr.
Tarrytown 10591 (914) 631-6065
Additional address: P.O. Box 7189, Ardsley-on-Hudson, NY 10503

Incorporated in 1901 in NY as St. Faith's House; reorganized in 1973.
Foundation type: Independent

Financial data (yr. ended 06/30/89): Assets, $5,954,215 (M); expenditures, $303,180, including $190,000 for 24 grants (high: $20,000; low: $1,500; average: $5,000-$10,000).
Purpose and activities: To make grants for services to and for children and young people.
Types of support: Continuing support, seed money, emergency funds, equipment, matching funds, special projects.
Limitations: Giving limited to Westchester County, NY. No support for public or private educational institutions. No grants to individuals, or for building or endowment funds, or operating budgets.
Publications: Application guidelines, 990-PF.
Application information: Application form required.
Initial approach: Letter
Copies of proposal: 11
Deadline(s): Submit proposal preferably in Aug., Nov., or Jan.; deadlines Sept. 1, Dec. 1, and Mar. 1
Board meeting date(s): Oct., Jan., and Apr.
Final notification: Nov., Mar., and June
Write: Ann D. Phillips, Chair., Grants Comm.
Officers and Directors:* Mrs. Maarten van Hengel,* Pres.; Mrs. William Shore,* V.P.; Horace J. McAfee,* Secy.; Daniel H. Childs,* Treas.; Mrs. Robert L. Huston, Mrs. John C. Keenan, Mrs. Robert W. Lyman, Mrs. Arthur O. Mojo, Robert C. Myers, Ann D. Phillips, Mrs. Joseph E. Rogers, Mrs. J.B. Stewart, Harvey J. Struthers, Jr.
Number of staff: None.
Employer Identification Number: 131740123

5234
St. George's Society of New York ⌑
71 West 23rd St.
New York 10010 (212) 924-1434

Established in 1770 in NY.
Foundation type: Operating
Financial data (yr. ended 12/31/88): Assets, $2,164,628 (M); gifts received, $15,979; expenditures, $203,949, including $101,003 for grants to individuals.
Purpose and activities: A private operating foundation; stipends to augment income of elderly, with assistance limited to former members of the British Commonwealth and their offspring.
Types of support: Grants to individuals.
Limitations: Giving primarily in the New York, NY, metropolitan area.
Application information:
Initial approach: Personal interviews and visits from the Society's social worker
Deadline(s): None
Board meeting date(s): 2nd Wed. of month, except July and Aug.
Write: David Loovis
Officers and Members: Colton P. Wagner, Pres.; Michael J.G. Chapman, 1st V.P.; E.A.G. Manton, 2nd V.P.; Peter J. Prill, Secy.; James S.G. Pigott, Treas.; and 17 additional members.
Employer Identification Number: 237426425

5235
St. Giles Foundation ⌑
(Formerly The House of St. Giles the Cripple)
One Hanson Place
Brooklyn 11243 (718) 638-1996

Donor(s): James Tisdale Trust, Louis W. Arnold,† Marvin Leavens,† Jesse Ridley,† and others.
Foundation type: Independent
Financial data (yr. ended 3/31/88): Assets, $11,303,467 (M); gifts received, $71,850; expenditures, $525,582, including $405,500 for 7 grants (high: $150,000; low: $36,500).
Purpose and activities: Grants for hospitals and organizations to help the handicapped; special interest in childrens' orthopedics.
Types of support: Equipment, research, general purposes.
Application information:
Initial approach: Proposal
Deadline(s): None
Write: Richard Croker
Officers: Richard T. Arkwright, Pres.; John H. Livingston, V.P.; John J. Bennett, Jr., Secy.; Samuel H. Owens, Treas.
Employer Identification Number: 111630806

5236
St. Vincent De Paul Foundation, Inc. ⌑
1045 Park St., Suite C
Peekskill 10566-3891 (914) 737-0030

Established about 1980 in NY.
Foundation type: Independent
Financial data (yr. ended 12/31/88): Assets, $1,284,798 (M); expenditures, $73,824, including $48,000 for 14 grants (high: $15,000; low: $1,000).
Purpose and activities: "To aid and advance the welfare, development, and education of indigent, distressed, or underprivileged children"; grants to homes and agencies with some emphasis on Catholic welfare organizations.
Limitations: Giving primarily in NY and NJ. No grants to individuals.
Application information: Application form not required.
Initial approach: Proposal
Deadline(s): None
Write: Thomas R. Langan, Secy.
Officers and Directors:* Thomas J. Langan, Jr.,* Pres. and Chair.; James J. Marett,* V.P.; Thomas R. Langan,* Secy.; M. Eileen Dolphin, John Duffy, Jr., Lucia Marett, Daniel M. McKeon, William E. Nielson, Robert V. Tiburzi, Sr., Robert V. Tiburzi, Jr.
Employer Identification Number: 135596824

5237
Thomas F. Staley Foundation
Four Chatsworth Ave., No. 3
Larchmont 10538-2932 (914) 834-2669

Trust established in 1943 in MI.
Donor(s): Thomas F. Staley,† Shirley H. Hunter.
Foundation type: Independent
Financial data (yr. ended 12/31/88): Assets, $4,751,124 (M); expenditures, $313,672, including $209,795 for 138 grants (high: $3,200; low: $192).
Purpose and activities: Support only for Christian scholar lectureship programs on college campuses.
Types of support: Lectureships.
Publications: Program policy statement, informational brochure (including application guidelines).
Application information: Funding restricted to those institutions scheduled to participate in the Staley Distinguished Christian Scholar Lecture Program for the coming years.
Initial approach: Letter
Copies of proposal: 1
Deadline(s): Submit proposal preferably in July or Aug.
Board meeting date(s): June
Write: Mrs. Elizabeth D. Halliday
Officers: Thomas F. Staley, Pres.; Robert G. Howard, Treas.
Trustees: Rev. Joseph P. Bishop, Shirley H. Hunter, Rev. Peter C. Moore, Alfred Sunderwirth.
Number of staff: 1 full-time professional.
Employer Identification Number: 136071888

5238
The Joan Stanton Irrevocable Charitable Trust ⌑ ☆
c/o Starr & Co.
350 Park Ave.
New York 10022

Established in 1988 in NY.
Foundation type: Independent
Financial data (yr. ended 12/31/88): Assets, $143,590 (M); gifts received, $520,068; expenditures, $392,607, including $392,495 for 71 grants (high: $50,000; low: $25).
Purpose and activities: Giving primarily for the arts, including music and the performing arts; support also for health organizations, higher and other education, and public affairs.
Limitations: Giving primarily in NY. No grants to individuals.
Application information: Contributes only to pre-selected organizations. Applications not accepted.
Officer: Joan Stanton, Pres.
Employer Identification Number: 133442844

5239
The Starr Foundation ▼
70 Pine St.
New York 10270 (212) 770-6882

Incorporated in 1955 in NY.
Donor(s): Cornelius V. Starr,† and others.
Foundation type: Independent
Financial data (yr. ended 12/31/88): Assets, $464,860,690 (M); expenditures, $21,633,497, including $20,305,018 for 327 grants (high: $2,000,000; low: $1,000) and $842,004 for 359 grants to individuals (high: $6,000; low: $100).
Purpose and activities: Grants largely for education with emphasis on higher education, including scholarships under specific programs; support also for culture, health, welfare, and social sciences.
Types of support: Continuing support, building funds, endowment funds, professorships, student aid, scholarship funds, fellowships, research, general purposes.

Limitations: No grants to individuals (except through foundation's scholarship programs), or for matching gifts; no loans.
Publications: 990-PF.
Application information: Application form not required.
Initial approach: Letter
Copies of proposal: 1
Deadline(s): None
Board meeting date(s): Feb. and Sept.
Final notification: Varies
Write: Mr. Ta Chun Hsu, Pres.
Officers: Ta Chun Hsu,* Pres.; Marion I. Breen,* V.P.; Ida E. Galler, Secy.; Frank R. Tengi, Treas.
Directors:* Maurice R. Greenberg, Chair.; Houghton Freeman, Edwin A.G. Manton, John J. Roberts, Ernest E. Stempel.
Number of staff: 1 full-time professional; 3 full-time support.
Employer Identification Number: 136151545

5240
Anne & Jacob Starr Foundation ☆
2109 Broadway, No. 14-41
New York 10023

Incorporated in 1964 in NY.
Donor(s): Jacob Starr.
Foundation type: Independent
Financial data (yr. ended 11/30/88): Assets, $1,069,674 (M); expenditures, $59,157, including $53,899 for 21 grants (high: $16,000; low: $25).
Purpose and activities: Giving primarily for Jewish welfare, educational, and religious organizations, including support for Israel; support also for mental health, higher and other education, and the performing arts.
Application information: Foundation initiates application process. Applications not accepted.
Write: Jean M. Starr, Pres.
Officers: Jean M. Starr, Pres.; Tama Starr, V.P.; Jonathan Starr, Secy.
Employer Identification Number: 136193022

5241
The Statler Foundation
Statler Tower, Suite 508
Buffalo 14202 (716) 852-1104

Trust established in 1934 in NY.
Donor(s): Ellsworth Milton Statler.†
Foundation type: Independent
Financial data (yr. ended 12/31/88): Assets, $22,861,385 (M); expenditures, $1,228,920, including $797,004 for 19 grants (high: $156,600; low: $4,081; average: $10,000).
Purpose and activities: Education and research for the benefit of the hotel industry in the U.S. Income used for endowments, scholarship funds, and awards to colleges and schools teaching hotel techniques and for grants to schools and others for research projects and for programs to train and increase the proficiency of hotel workers. The foundation also provides funds to local social service agencies to support food services to the needy.
Types of support: Endowment funds, scholarship funds, research, building funds, professorships, program-related investments, equipment.
Limitations: Giving primarily in upstate NY.
Application information: Application form required for scholarships in the hospitality field.
Initial approach: Letter
Deadline(s): Apr. 15 for scholarships
Board meeting date(s): Monthly
Final notification: Dec. 1
Write: Peter J. Crotty, Chair.
Officer and Trustees:* Peter J. Crotty,* Chair.; M. Robert Koren, Arthur F. Musarra.
Number of staff: 1 full-time professional.
Employer Identification Number: 131889077

5242
Amy Plant Statter Foundation ⌑
598 Madison Ave., 9th Fl.
New York 10022

Established in 1958 in NY.
Donor(s): Amy Plant Statter Clark.
Foundation type: Independent
Financial data (yr. ended 12/31/87): Assets, $2,176,698 (M); expenditures, $163,213, including $138,000 for 43 grants (high: $5,000; low: $1,000).
Purpose and activities: Support primarily for hospitals and health agencies, and social services.
Application information:
Initial approach: Letter
Deadline(s): None
Write: John H. Reilly, Jr., Trustee
Trustees: Amy Plant Statter Clark, John H. Reilly, Jr.
Employer Identification Number: 136152801

5243
Janet Upjohn Stearns Charitable Trust ⌑
c/o Morgan Guaranty Trust Co. of New York
616 Madison Ave.
New York 10153

Established in 1961 in NY.
Foundation type: Independent
Financial data (yr. ended 12/31/88): Assets, $1,380,801 (M); expenditures, $63,446, including $50,500 for 28 grants (high: $20,000; low: $500).
Purpose and activities: Funds for secondary education, culture, and social services.
Application information:
Deadline(s): None
Trustee: Morgan Guaranty Trust Co. of New York.
Advisory Committee: Robin Munn Aldie, Janet T. Beck, G.E. Eisenhardt, Janet W. Ley.
Employer Identification Number: 136035045

5244
The Stebbins Fund, Inc. ⌑ ☆
R.D. Box 1792, Route 106
Syosset 11791 (516) 921-5028

Incorporated in 1947 in NY.
Donor(s): Members of the Stebbins family.
Foundation type: Independent
Financial data (yr. ended 12/31/88): Assets, $1,796,037 (M); expenditures, $130,357, including $70,500 for 39 grants (high: $12,500; low: $250).
Purpose and activities: Giving primarily for higher, art, and other education and museums; support also for historic preservation.
Limitations: Giving primarily in the northeastern U.S. No grants to individuals, or for endowment funds; no loans.
Application information: Contributes only to pre-selected organizations. Applications not accepted.
Board meeting date(s): June
Write: James F. Stebbins, Pres.
Officers: James F. Stebbins,* Pres.; Jane S. Sykes,* V.P. and Treas.; Theodore E. Stebbins,* V.P.; Meredith M. Brown, Secy.
Directors:* Greenleaf Victoria Stebbins, J. Wright Rumbough, Jr., Edwin E.F. Stebbins, Michael Morgan Stebbins.
Employer Identification Number: 116021709

5245
Philip H. & Lois R. Steckler Foundation, Inc. ⌑
c/o Philip H. Steckler, Jr.
522 Fifth Ave.
New York 10036

Established in 1969 in NY.
Donor(s): Philip H. Steckler, Jr.
Foundation type: Independent
Financial data (yr. ended 7/31/87): Assets, $1,719,006 (M); gifts received, $368,667; expenditures, $209,597, including $182,616 for 164 grants (high: $50,000; low: $10).
Purpose and activities: Giving primarily for hospitals and health services; some support for education, churches, youth services, and cultural activities.
Limitations: Giving primarily in New York, NY.
Application information: Contributes only to pre-selected organizations. Applications not accepted.
Officers and Directors: Philip H. Steckler, Jr., Pres. and Treas.; Philip H. Steckler, V.P.; Lois R. Steckler, Secy.; Donald R. Kurtz, Charles H. Levitt, Philip H. Steckler III, Philip A. Straus.
Employer Identification Number: 132621420

5246
The Steele-Reese Foundation ▼
c/o Messrs. Davidson, Dawson & Clark
330 Madison Ave.
New York 10017 (212) 557-7700
Application addresses: John R. Bryden, 760 Malabu Dr., Lexington, KY 40502; Christine Brady, P.O. Box 7263, Boise, ID 83707

Trust established in 1955 in NY.
Donor(s): Eleanor Steele Reese,† Emmet P. Reese.†
Foundation type: Independent
Financial data (yr. ended 08/31/89): Assets, $20,287,131 (M); expenditures, $1,215,246, including $1,056,250 for 45 grants (high: $125,000; low: $500).
Purpose and activities: Principally to aid organized charities in southern Appalachia and ID and adjacent states. Support for education, including scholarships, health and hospices, welfare, including programs for drug abuse and youth, conservation, and the humanities, with a strong preference for rural projects; student aid paid through institutions.

Types of support: General purposes, operating budgets, equipment, endowment funds, matching funds, professorships, scholarship funds.
Limitations: Giving primarily in southern Appalachia, particularly KY, and in the northwest, with emphasis on ID; scholarship program limited to students from Lemhi and Custer counties, ID. No grants to individuals, or for continuing support, annual campaigns, seed money, emergency or building funds, deficit financing, research, or land acquisition; no loans; grants to individuals confined to scholarships and paid through institutions.
Publications: Annual report (including application guidelines).
Application information: High school seniors should apply for scholarships through their schools. Application form not required.
Initial approach: Letter
Copies of proposal: 3
Deadline(s): None; payments are generally made in Feb. and Aug.
Board meeting date(s): Monthly
Final notification: 3 to 6 months
Write: William T. Buice, III, in NY for general matters; Dr. John R. Bryden for southern applicants; and Mrs. Christine Brady for northwestern applicants
Trustees: William T. Buice III, Robert T.H. Davidson, Morgan Guaranty Trust Co. of New York.
Number of staff: 3 part-time support.
Employer Identification Number: 136034763

5247
Joseph F. Stein Foundation, Inc.
28 Aspen Rd.
Scarsdale 10583 (914) 725-1770

Incorporated in 1954 in NY.
Donor(s): Joseph F. Stein,† Allen A. Stein, Esq.,† and others.
Foundation type: Independent
Financial data (yr. ended 12/31/88): Assets, $8,100,507 (M); gifts received, $342,843; expenditures, $733,293, including $696,241 for 221 grants (high: $211,218; low: $20).
Purpose and activities: Grants largely for local Jewish welfare and social activities; some support for higher and secondary education, including religious education, and medical research.
Types of support: General purposes, scholarship funds, equipment, research.
Limitations: Giving primarily in NY and FL. No grants to individuals (including scholarships), or for matching gifts; no loans.
Application information:
Initial approach: Letter
Copies of proposal: 1
Board meeting date(s): Monthly
Write: Melvin M. Stein, Pres.
Officers and Directors:* Melvin M. Stein,* Pres.; Melvin M. Stein,* V.P.; Stuart M. Stein,* Secy.
Number of staff: None.
Employer Identification Number: 136097095

5248
Ruth and Milton Steinbach Fund, Inc.
c/o Klingstein, Fields & Co., L.P.
787 Seventh Ave.
New York 10019-6016 (212) 492-6190

Incorporated in 1950 in NY.
Donor(s): Milton Steinbach.†
Foundation type: Independent
Financial data (yr. ended 10/31/89): Assets, $7,627,000 (M); expenditures, $410,217, including $364,000 for 21 grants (high: $50,000; low: $2,000).
Purpose and activities: Grants for Jewish welfare funds, secondary and higher education, hospitals and a social science research institute.
Limitations: Giving primarily in NY.
Application information:
Initial approach: Letter
Deadline(s): None
Write: John Klingenstein, V.P.
Officers and Directors:* Ruth A. Steinbach,* Pres.; John S. Hilson,* V.P.; John Klingenstein,* V.P.; Frederick A. Klingenstein,* Treas.
Employer Identification Number: 136028785

5249
The Steinberg Family Fund, Inc. ⌑
c/o Bear Stearns & Co., Inc.
245 Park Ave.
New York 10167

Established in 1984 in NY.
Donor(s): Robert Steinberg.
Foundation type: Independent
Financial data (yr. ended 11/30/89): Assets, $1,184,082 (M); expenditures, $32,495.
Purpose and activities: Support primarily for Jewish giving.
Limitations: Giving primarily in NY. No grants to individuals.
Application information: Contributes only to pre-selected organizations. Applications not accepted.
Officers: Robert Steinberg, Pres. and Treas.; Suzanne Steinberg, Pres. and Treas.
Employer Identification Number: 133254493

5250
Meyer Steinberg Foundation, Inc. ⌑
11 East 44th St.
New York 10017 (212) 867-6899

Established in 1965 in NY.
Donor(s): Meyer Steinberg.
Foundation type: Independent
Financial data (yr. ended 12/31/88): Assets, $3,813,900 (M); gifts received, $800,000; expenditures, $464,661, including $462,234 for 108 grants (high: $278,840; low: $50).
Purpose and activities: Giving primarily to a Jewish welfare fund and other Jewish organizations.
Application information:
Initial approach: Letter
Deadline(s): None
Write: Meyer Steinberg, Pres.
Officers: Meyer Steinberg, Pres. and Treas.; Jean Steinberg, V.P. and Secy.
Employer Identification Number: 136199973

5251
The Miriam & Harold Steinberg Foundation, Inc. ▼ ⌑
527 West 34th St.
New York 10001

Established in 1960 in NY.
Donor(s): Harold Steinberg, Grammercy Holding Corp., Harmir Realty Co.
Foundation type: Independent
Financial data (yr. ended 6/30/88): Assets, $1,835,479 (M); expenditures, $445,903, including $441,575 for 23 grants (high: $401,000; low: $50; average: $100-$10,000).
Purpose and activities: Support primarily for Jewish welfare and cultural programs.
Limitations: Giving primarily in NY. No grants to individuals.
Application information: Contributes only to pre-selected organizations. Applications not accepted.
Officers: Harold Steinberg, Pres. and Treas.; Morris Steinberg, Secy.
Employer Identification Number: 136126000

5252
Albert & Marie Steinert Foundation ☆
c/o Moses & Singer
1271 Ave. of the Americas
New York 10020-1302

Established in 1969 in NY.
Donor(s): Marie A.P. Steinert.†
Foundation type: Independent
Financial data (yr. ended 12/31/88): Assets, $507,715 (M); expenditures, $124,256, including $119,750 for 41 grants (high: $50,000; low: $250).
Purpose and activities: Support primarily for the arts and cultural organizations, cancer research, Jewish giving, hospitals, social services, and a university and a college.
Types of support: Continuing support, scholarship funds.
Limitations: Giving primarily in New York, NY.
Application information: Contributes only to pre-selected organizations. Applications not accepted.
Officers and Directors:* Henry Schneider,* Pres.; Felix Fishman,* Secy.-Treas.; Steven Glaser.
Number of staff: None.
Employer Identification Number: 237027970

5253
Jane Stern Family Foundation, Inc. ☆
778 Park Ave.
New York 10021

Established in 1986 in NY.
Donor(s): Jane Stern.
Foundation type: Independent
Financial data (yr. ended 02/28/89): Assets, $1,516,284 (M); expenditures, $88,611, including $68,727 for 52 grants (high: $11,500; low: $10).
Purpose and activities: Support for education, including universities, yeshivas, and schools; culture and the arts; medical organizations; and a synagogue.
Limitations: Giving primarily in New York, NY. No grants to individuals.

Application information: Contributes only to pre-selected organizations. Applications not accepted.
Officers and Directors:* Jane Stern,* Pres. and Treas.; Geoffrey Stern,* Secy.; Ronald Stern.
Employer Identification Number: 133389567

5254
Jerome L. Stern Family Foundation, Inc.
(Formerly Jerome L. and Jane Stern Foundation, Inc.)
342 Madison Ave., Rm. 1912
New York 10173 (212) 972-8165

Incorporated in 1944 in NY.
Donor(s): Members of the Stern family.
Foundation type: Independent
Financial data (yr. ended 2/28/89): Assets, $1,458,882 (M); expenditures, $139,832, including $128,795 for 45 grants (high: $58,250; low: $50).
Purpose and activities: Emphasis on Jewish religious education, temple support, and Jewish welfare funds; some support also for museums.
Limitations: Giving primarily in NY.
Application information: Applications not accepted.
Write: Jerome L. Stern, Pres.
Officers and Directors: Jerome L. Stern, Chair., Pres., and Secy.; Geoffrey S. Stern, V.P.; Henriette J. Stern, Treas.; Lynda Stern, Michael Stern, Ronald A. Stern.
Number of staff: None.
Employer Identification Number: 136127063

5255
Bernice and Milton Stern Foundation ⌑
335 Madison Ave.
New York 10017 (212) 503-1701

Established in 1982 in DE.
Foundation type: Independent
Financial data (yr. ended 4/30/87): Assets, $5,856,578 (M); gifts received, $5,000,000; expenditures, $254,994, including $239,167 for 28 grants (high: $20,000; low: $100).
Purpose and activities: Grants for Jewish welfare, social services, and health services.
Application information: Application form required.
Write: Bernice Stern, V.P.
Officers: Milton Stern, Pres.; Bernice Stern, V.P.; Michael Stern, Secy.-Treas.
Employer Identification Number: 510264122

5256
Gustav Stern Foundation, Inc. ⌑ ☆
c/o Weitzner, Levine & Louis
230 Park Ave.
New York 10023

Donor(s): James O. Herland, Ray Stern.
Foundation type: Independent
Financial data (yr. ended 3/31/88): Assets, $411,667 (M); gifts received, $6,947; expenditures, $395,212, including $377,946 for 17 grants (high: $350,000; low: $86).
Purpose and activities: Giving primarily for Jewish organizations, including synagogues and education; support also for elementary schools.
Application information:
Initial approach: Letter
Deadline(s): None
Officers: Irene Stern, Pres.; Steven Stern, V.P.; Joyce Herland, Secy.-Treas.
Director: Ralph Suskind.
Employer Identification Number: 136121155

5257
Isidore Stern Foundation ⌑
60 East 42nd St., Rm. 1148
New York 10165-0033

Established in 1943 in NY.
Foundation type: Independent
Financial data (yr. ended 12/31/88): Assets, $1,353,443 (M); gifts received, $5,141; expenditures, $74,902, including $69,000 for 11 grants (high: $45,000; low: $500).
Purpose and activities: Grants for social services and youth programs, support also for a Jewish welfare organization.
Limitations: No grants to individuals.
Application information: Contributes only to pre-selected organizations. Applications not accepted.
Trustees: James A. Stern, Richard M. Stern, Theodore L. Stern.
Employer Identification Number: 136113256

5258
Leonard N. Stern Foundation ▼
667 Madison Ave.
New York 10001 (212) 308-3336

Established in 1963 in NY.
Donor(s): Leonard N. Stern.
Foundation type: Independent
Financial data (yr. ended 12/31/89): Assets, $230,908 (M); gifts received, $1,957,500; expenditures, $1,810,702, including $1,806,430 for 46 grants (high: $354,455; low: $100; average: $5,000-$70,000).
Purpose and activities: Grants for Jewish organizations, higher education, and social services for homeless families.
Types of support: Continuing support, equipment, general purposes, matching funds, operating budgets, renovation projects, seed money, special projects.
Limitations: Giving primarily in the New York, NY, metropolitan area.
Application information: Contributes only to pre-selected organizations. Applications not accepted.
Write: Carol Kellermann, Exec. Dir.
Officers and Directors:* Leonard N. Stern,* Pres.; Armand Lindenbaum, V.P.; Curtis Schwartz,* Secy.-Treas.; Carol Kellermann, Exec. Dir.
Number of staff: 1 full-time professional; 1 full-time support.
Employer Identification Number: 136149990

5259
Marjorie & Michael Stern Foundation ⌑ ☆
c/o Yohalem Gillman & Co.
477 Madison Ave.
New York 10022

Established in 1987 in DE.
Donor(s): Marjorie Stern, Michael Stern.
Foundation type: Independent
Financial data (yr. ended 12/31/88): Assets, $1,443,558 (M); gifts received, $650,500; expenditures, $435,560, including $433,312 for 14 grants (high: $397,662; low: $100).
Purpose and activities: Support primarily for education, especially an organization that works to motivate disadvantaged grade school students to attend college.
Limitations: No grants to individuals.
Application information: Contributes only to pre-selected organizations. Applications not accepted.
Officers: Michael Stern, Pres. and Treas.; Marjorie Stern, Secy.
Directors: Erica Stern, Mark Stern.
Employer Identification Number: 133440362

5260
The Stevens Kingsley Foundation, Inc. ⌑
125 Broad St.
New York 10004-2425
Application address: North George St., Rome, NY 13440

Established in 1960 in NY.
Foundation type: Independent
Financial data (yr. ended 12/31/88): Assets, $1,118,668 (M); gifts received, $78,824; expenditures, $68,400, including $68,400 for 13 grants (high: $18,000; low: $500).
Purpose and activities: Support primarily for libraries, community development, historic preservation, and education.
Types of support: Building funds, equipment, seed money, renovation projects.
Limitations: Giving limited to Rome, NY, area. No grants to individuals, or for operating expenses.
Application information:
Initial approach: Letter
Deadline(s): None
Board meeting date(s): Fall
Write: George B. Waters, Dir.
Officers and Directors:* Donald R. Osborn,* Pres.; Henry Christensen III,* Secy.-Treas.; George B. Grow, Mark F. Hinman, William Curtis Pierce, George B. Waters.
Employer Identification Number: 136150722

5261
Stanley Steyer Family Foundation, Inc. ⌑ ☆
c/o Harold Orlin
1440 Broadway
New York 10018

Donor(s): Thomas M. Steyer, Helen Steyer.
Foundation type: Independent
Financial data (yr. ended 05/31/89): Assets, $208,229 (M); gifts received, $110,000; expenditures, $171,335, including $170,440 for 3 grants (high: $159,940; low: $500).
Purpose and activities: Support for medical research.
Limitations: No grants to individuals.
Application Information: Contributes only to pre-selected organizations. Applications not accepted.
Officers: Stanley Steyer, Pres.; Thomas M. Steyer, V.P.; Helen Steyer, Secy.-Treas.
Employer Identification Number: 133207413

5262
The Stone Foundation, Inc. ⌘ ☆
20 Broad St., Rm. 1123
New York 10005

Incorporated in 1985 in NY.
Donor(s): Donald Stone.
Foundation type: Independent
Financial data (yr. ended 11/30/88): Assets, $1,061,235 (M); gifts received, $100,000; expenditures, $105,562, including $104,481 for 8 grants (high: $49,981; low: $1,000).
Purpose and activities: Support primarily for higher education and Jewish organizations, including welfare funds.
Types of support: Scholarship funds.
Limitations: No grants to individuals.
Application information: Contributes only to pre-selected organizations. Applications not accepted.
Officers: Robert L. Stone, Pres.; Donald Stone, Secy.-Treas.
Employer Identification Number: 136066290

5263
Stony Wold-Herbert Fund, Inc.
136 East 57th St., Rm. 1705
New York 10022 (212) 753-6565

Incorporated in 1974 in NY.
Foundation type: Independent
Financial data (yr. ended 12/31/87): Assets, $3,840,961 (M); gifts received, $3,582; expenditures, $290,359, including $137,525 for 13 grants (high: $20,765; low: $1,550; average: $2,000-$10,000) and $47,390 for grants to individuals.
Purpose and activities: Support for four programs: research grants to doctors within the greater New York area involved in studying respiratory diseases; pulmonary fellowships to doctors in the greater New York area training in the respiratory field; grants for community service projects in the pulmonary field; and supplementary scholarships for college or vocational school students, 16 years or older, living in the greater New York area only, with respiratory illnesses.
Types of support: Continuing support, deficit financing, fellowships, special projects, research, conferences and seminars, student aid.
Limitations: Giving primarily in NY. No grants for capital or endowment funds, operating budgets, annual campaigns, seed money, emergency funds, or matching gifts; no loans.
Publications: Application guidelines.
Application information: Application form required.
Initial approach: Letter or telephone
Copies of proposal: 6
Deadline(s): Oct. 15 for research and fellowship grants; Mar. 1 for community service proposals
Board meeting date(s): Nov., Mar., and June
Final notification: 2 to 3 weeks
Write: Cheryl S. Friedman, Exec. Dir.
Officers: Sheila C. Davidson, Pres.; Cheryl S. Friedman, Exec. Dir.
Number of staff: 2 part-time professional.
Employer Identification Number: 132784124

5264
Robert L. Stott Foundation, Inc. ⌘
c/o Wagner, Stott & Co.
20 Broad St.
New York 10005

Incorporated in 1957 in NY.
Donor(s): Robert L. Stott.†
Foundation type: Independent
Financial data (yr. ended 12/31/88): Assets, $2,644,411 (M); expenditures, $161,230, including $144,500 for 34 grants (high: $25,000; low: $250).
Purpose and activities: Grants largely for hospitals and secondary education.
Limitations: Giving primarily in NY and in Palm Beach, FL. No grants to individuals.
Application information: Contributes only to pre-selected organizations. Applications not accepted.
Officers and Directors: Robert L. Stott, Jr., Pres.; Leonard Wagner, V.P.; Donald B. Stott, Secy.-Treas.; Donald F. Young.
Employer Identification Number: 136061943

5265
Martha Washington Straus & Harry H. Straus Foundation, Inc. ⌘
Sky Meadow Farm
Lincoln Ave.
Port Chester 10573

Incorporated in 1949 in NC.
Donor(s): Harry H. Straus, Sr.†
Foundation type: Independent
Financial data (yr. ended 12/31/88): Assets, $3,136,262 (M); gifts received, $27,263; expenditures, $123,826, including $116,900 for 102 grants (high: $12,500; low: $100).
Purpose and activities: Grants for medical research, higher education (including medical education), hospitals, and health and welfare funds.
Limitations: No grants to individuals.
Application information: Contributes only to pre-selected organizations. Applications not accepted.
Board meeting date(s): As required
Write: Roger J. King, Secy.
Officers and Trustees: Louise Straus King, Pres.; Betty B. Straus, V.P.; Roger J. King, Secy.-Treas.; Harry H. Straus III.
Employer Identification Number: 560645526

5266
The Philip A. and Lynn Straus Foundation, Inc. ⌘
1037 Constable Dr. South
Mamaroneck 10543

Incorporated about 1957 in NY.
Donor(s): Philip A. Straus.
Foundation type: Independent
Financial data (yr. ended 3/31/89): Assets, $12,518,481 (M); expenditures, $675,180, including $670,900 for 99 grants (high: $313,000; low: $100).
Purpose and activities: Giving for higher education, Jewish welfare funds, international cooperation, child welfare, civil rights organizations, and museums and cultural programs.
Limitations: Giving primarily in NY. No grants to individuals.
Application information: Contributes only to pre-selected organizations. Applications not accepted.
Write: Philip A. Straus, Pres.
Officers and Trustees: Philip A. Straus, Pres.; Lynn G. Straus, V.P. and Treas.; John W. Hertz, Secy.
Employer Identification Number: 136161223

5267
Alan & Katherine Stroock Fund ⌘
c/o Stroock & Stroock & Lavan
Seven Hanover Sq.
New York 10004-2594 (212) 806-6068

Established in 1958 in NY.
Donor(s): Alan M. Stroock,† Katherine W. Stroock.
Foundation type: Independent
Financial data (yr. ended 12/31/87): Assets, $49,484 (M); gifts received, $313,249; expenditures, $359,925, including $357,470 for 30 grants (high: $200,000; low: $25).
Purpose and activities: Support primarily for higher education, cultural programs, and Jewish concerns.
Limitations: No grants to individuals.
Application information: Contributes only to pre-selected organizations. Applications not accepted.
Officers and Directors: Ronald J. Stein, Pres.; Henry A. Loeb, V.P.; Judith Jahnke, Secy.; Morton L. Deitch, Treas.; Barbara Lamar.
Employer Identification Number: 136086102

5268
Structured Employment/Economic Development Corporation ⌘ ☆
130 West 42nd St., Suite 801
New York 10036 (212) 302-0540

Established in 1983.
Donor(s): The Ford Foundation, Charles Stewart Mott Foundation, UPS Foundation, Primerica Foundation, Lilly Endowment, Carnegie Corp. of New York.
Foundation type: Operating
Financial data (yr. ended 9/30/87): Assets, $2,515,395 (M); gifts received, $1,497,140; expenditures, $718,201, including $245,813 for 8 grants (high: $47,500; low: $10,000).
Purpose and activities: A private operating foundation, support for community development activities in low-income neighborhoods through the Urban Institutions Program.
Types of support: Technical assistance, program-related investments.
Limitations: No grants to individuals.
Application information:
Initial approach: Letter
Deadline(s): None
Write: Mark Weinheimer, Prog. Mgr.
Officers: James Pickman, Pres.; Ronald Monroe, Secy.; Thomas Seessel, Treas.
Directors: Lawrence Sills, Chair.; Ronald Gault, Vice-Chair.; Graham Finney, Clifford Goldman, William Grinker, Nan Miller, Juan Patlan, Hugh Price, Phyllis Quan, Herman Wilson.
Employer Identification Number: 132875743

5269
The Stuart Foundation, Inc.
126 East 56th St.
New York 10022 (212) 753-0800

Incorporated in 1951 in NY.
Donor(s): Members of the Stuart family.
Foundation type: Independent
Financial data (yr. ended 12/31/89): Assets, $2,550,000 (M); expenditures, $141,500, including $101,500 for 76 grants (high: $30,000; low: $15; average: $15-$30,000).
Purpose and activities: Giving primarily for higher and secondary education, and for Jewish organizations.
Limitations: Giving primarily in NY and New England.
Application information:
Write: James M. Stuart, Treas.
Officers and Directors:* Alan L. Stuart,* V.P. and Secy.; James M. Stuart,* V.P., Treas., and Mgr.
Employer Identification Number: 136066191

5270
William Matheus Sullivan Musical Foundation, Inc.
251 West 89th St., Suite 10-B
New York 10024 (212) 874-2373

Incorporated in 1956 in NY.
Donor(s): William Matheus Sullivan,† Arcie Lubetkin.†
Foundation type: Independent
Financial data (yr. ended 12/31/88): Assets, $3,015,404 (M); gifts received, $3,600; expenditures, $167,647, including $92,917 for 15 grants (high: $55,000; low: $225) and $7,066 for 21 grants to individuals (high: $1,261; low: $105).
Purpose and activities: To advance the careers of gifted young singers who have completed their formal music training, either directly or by finding engagements for them via assistance given to orchestras, operatic societies, or other musical groups; grants based on financial need of applicant. Awards to individuals range from $250 to a maximum of $1,000.
Types of support: Grants to individuals, continuing support, special projects.
Limitations: No support for general fields of music education and vocal or instrument training. No grants for building or endowment funds, or for operating budgets.
Publications: Application guidelines.
Application information: Requests for New York auditions should be accompanied by resume and copy of contract for at least one engagement with full orchestra after Nov.; San Francisco and Chicago auditions in early Nov., New York auditions in mid-Nov. Application form required.
Initial approach: Letter or proposal, detailing educational and musical experience
Copies of proposal: 1
Deadline(s): Oct. 15th for the following fall
Board meeting date(s): 5 or 6 times a year as required
Write: David Lloyd, Exec. Dir.
Officers and Trustees: Barbara B. Last, Pres.; Jose T. Moscoso, Secy.; Peter J. Merrill, Treas.; David Lloyd, Exec. Dir.; Rose Bampton, George L. Boveroux, Jr., Spencer Byard, Bruce Donnell, Edward O. Downes, Gail M.L. Lavielle, Stanley Reese, Lee Schaenen.
Number of staff: 1 full-time professional.
Employer Identification Number: 136069096

5271
The Sulzberger Foundation, Inc. ⌑
229 West 43rd St.
New York 10036 (212) 556-1750

Incorporated in 1956 in NY.
Donor(s): Arthur Hays Sulzberger,† Iphigene Ochs Sulzberger.†
Foundation type: Independent
Financial data (yr. ended 12/31/88): Assets, $14,633,263 (M); gifts received, $1,547,490; expenditures, $785,326, including $675,331 for 180 grants (high: $40,125; low: $100).
Purpose and activities: Grants largely for education, cultural programs, hospitals, community funds, and welfare funds.
Types of support: Annual campaigns, building funds, capital campaigns, conferences and seminars, consulting services, continuing support, emergency funds, endowment funds, equipment, exchange programs, fellowships, general purposes, internships, lectureships, operating budgets, professorships, program-related investments, renovation projects, scholarship funds, seed money, special projects, technical assistance.
Limitations: Giving primarily in NY and Chattanooga, TN. No grants to individuals, or for matching gifts; no loans.
Publications: 990-PF.
Application information:
Initial approach: Telephone
Deadline(s): None
Board meeting date(s): Jan. and as required
Write: Marian S. Heiskell, Pres.
Officers and Directors: Marian S. Heiskell, Pres.; Arthur Ochs Sulzberger, V.P. and Secy.-Treas.; Ruth S. Holmberg, V.P.; Judith P. Sulzberger, V.P.
Number of staff: 3 part-time support.
Employer Identification Number: 136083166

5272
Benjamin & Hedwig Sulzle Foundation, Inc. ⌑ ☆
616 Rugby Rd.
Syracuse 13203 (315) 454-3221

Established in 1966 in NY.
Donor(s): H.G. Sulzle.
Foundation type: Independent
Financial data (yr. ended 09/30/89): Assets, $1,044,431 (M); gifts received, $150,000; expenditures, $5,839, including $3,000 for 1 grant.
Purpose and activities: Support for hospitals and higher education; giving also for cultural activities and volunteerism.
Application information:
Initial approach: Proposal
Deadline(s): None
Write: H.G. Sulzle, Mgr.
Officer: H.G. Sulzle, Mgr.
Trustees: A.J. Flanagan, L.S. Flanagan.
Employer Identification Number: 166075456

5273
Solon E. Summerfield Foundation, Inc. ▼ ⌑
270 Madison Ave.
New York 10016 (212) 685-5529

Incorporated in 1939 in NY.
Donor(s): Solon E. Summerfield.†
Foundation type: Independent
Financial data (yr. ended 12/31/88): Assets, $31,170,330 (M); expenditures, $1,575,151, including $1,243,255 for 108 grants (high: $467,995; low: $250; average: $500-$10,000).
Purpose and activities: Three-fourths of funds paid to designated recipients; remaining one-fourth distributed largely for higher education; some support for social services, and hospitals and health.
Types of support: Endowment funds, scholarship funds.
Application information: Funds largely committed. Applications not accepted.
Write: William W. Prager, Pres.
Officers and Trustees:* William W. Prager,* Pres.; Clarence R. Treeger,* V.P.; Joseph A. Tiano,* Secy.-Treas.
Number of staff: None.
Employer Identification Number: 131797260

5274
Sunflower Foundation
305 Madison Ave., Suite 1166
New York 10165 (212) 682-0889

Established in 1969 in CA.
Donor(s): Katherine W. Tremaine.
Foundation type: Independent
Financial data (yr. ended 12/31/89): Assets, $1,209,715 (M); expenditures, $618,413, including $530,610 for grants (average: $5,000).
Purpose and activities: Giving primarily for research and advocacy organizations concerned with public policy, environmental issues, civil and human rights, labor, poverty, and minorities.
Types of support: General purposes.
Limitations: No grants to individuals, or for films or books.
Application information: Application form not required.
Initial approach: Proposal
Copies of proposal: 1
Deadline(s): 1 month prior to board meetings
Board meeting date(s): Feb., June, and Oct.
Write: Katherine W. Tremaine, Pres.
Officers and Directors:* Katherine W. Tremaine,* Pres.; Richard Parker,* Exec. Dir.; Katherine Peake, David L. Peri.
Number of staff: 1 full-time professional; 1 part-time support.
Employer Identification Number: 952644098

5275
The David J. Supino Foundation ⌑ ☆
c/o Lazard Freres and Co.
One Rockefeller Plaza
New York 10020

Established in 1986 in NY.
Donor(s): David J. Supino.
Foundation type: Independent
Financial data (yr. ended 9/30/88): Assets, $89,057 (M); gifts received, $100,000;

expenditures, $121,633, including $121,400 for 5 grants (high: $100,000; low: $150).
Purpose and activities: Giving for land conservation and museums.
Limitations: Giving primarily in NY and CT. No grants to individuals.
Application information:
Initial approach: Letter
Deadline(s): None
Write: David J. Supino, Pres.
Officers and Directors: David J. Supino, Pres.; Melvin Heineman, V.P.; Howard Sontag, Secy.-Treas.
Employer Identification Number: 133371585

5276
Surdna Foundation, Inc. ▼
1155 Ave. of the Americas, 16th Fl.
New York 10036 (212) 730-0030
FAX: (212) 391-4384

Incorporated in 1917 in NY.
Donor(s): John E. Andrus.†
Foundation type: Independent
Financial data (yr. ended 06/30/89): Assets, $312,534,326 (M); gifts received, $1,524,072; expenditures, $20,702,563, including $9,585,839 for 160 grants (high: $300,000; low: $9,720) and $8,620,000 for 2 foundation-administered programs.
Purpose and activities: "The foundation's guidelines focus on two areas: 1) the environment, specifically transportation and energy, urban and suburban issues, and biological and cultural diversity; and 2) community revitalization, which takes a comprehensive and holistic approach to restoring communities in America. The foundation is particularly interested in fostering catalytic, entreprenurial programs that offer solutions to difficult systemic problems."
Types of support: Seed money, special projects, technical assistance, continuing support, general purposes.
Limitations: No grants to individuals, or for annual campaigns, building funds, endowments, or land acquisition.
Publications: Annual report, informational brochure (including application guidelines).
Application information: Application form not required.
Initial approach: Letter and preliminary outline
Copies of proposal: 1
Deadline(s): None
Board meeting date(s): Sept., Nov., Feb., and May
Final notification: 2 weeks
Write: Edward Skloot, Exec. Dir.
Officers and Directors:* John E. Andrus III,* Chair.; Peter B. Benedict,* Vice-Chair.; Samuel S. Thorpe III, Pres.; John J. Lynagh,* V.P. and Secy.; Lawrence S.C. Griffith, V.P.; Frederick F. Moon III,* Treas.; Julia Moon Aubry, Christopher F. Davenport, Sandra T. Kaupe, Elizabeth Andrus Kelly.
Number of staff: 4 full-time professional; 3 full-time support; 1 part-time support.
Employer Identification Number: 136108163

5277
Edna Bailey Sussman Fund ☆
c/o Boyce, Hughes, & Farrell
1025 Northern Blvd.
Roslyn 11576
Application address: 75 Cos Cob Ave., No. 10, Cos Cob, CT 06807

Established in 1984 in NY.
Donor(s): Arthur H. Dean,† Edward S. Miller.
Foundation type: Independent
Financial data (yr. ended 04/30/89): Assets, $3,472,335 (M); expenditures, $184,338, including $161,962 for 15 grants to individuals (high: $30,000; low: $3,000).
Purpose and activities: To further the preservation of wildlife, the control of pollution, and the preservation of natural land and resources by funding internships for individuals in a field of study at an institution of higher learning in an area that significantly impacts upon the environment.
Types of support: Internships.
Application information: Stipends disbursed to institution on behalf of intern selected by fund trustees. Application form required.
Initial approach: Application process must conform with host institution's general procedures
Deadline(s): None
Write: Dorothy Bertine, Admin.
Trustees: Robert H. Frey, Edward S. Miller.
Employer Identification Number: 133187064

5278
Otto Sussman Trust
P.O. Box 1374
Trainsmeadow Station
Flushing 11370-9998

Trust established in 1947 in NY.
Donor(s): Otto Sussman.†
Foundation type: Independent
Financial data (yr. ended 12/31/88): Assets, $2,820,666 (M); expenditures, $118,168, including $80,323 for 36 grants to individuals (high: $6,049; low: $329).
Purpose and activities: Assistance to persons in need due to death or illness in their immediate families or some other unusual or unfortunate circumstance.
Types of support: Grants to individuals, student aid.
Limitations: Giving limited to residents of NY, NJ, OK, and PA.
Application information: Applicants must be recommended by agencies known to the trustees. Application form required. Applications not accepted.
Deadline(s): None
Write: Edward S. Miller, Trustee
Trustees: Edward S. Miller, Alice M. Ullmann, Erwin A. Weil.
Employer Identification Number: 136075849

5279
Abraham, David & Solomon Sutton Family Foundation ⌑ ☆
One East 33rd St.
New York 10016-5011

Established in 1979.
Donor(s): Bag Bazaar, Inc.
Foundation type: Independent
Financial data (yr. ended 12/31/88): Assets, $221,412 (M); gifts received, $355,000; expenditures, $345,051, including $344,986 for 306 grants (high: $31,928; low: $10).
Purpose and activities: Giving for Jewish organizations, especially yeshivas.
Limitations: Giving primarily in NY. No grants to individuals.
Application information: Contributes only to pre-selected organizations. Applications not accepted.
Trustees: David Sutton, Solomon Sutton.
Employer Identification Number: 132984908

5280
Stephen C. Swid and Nan G. Swid Foundation ⌑ ☆
c/o SCS Communications
1290 Ave. of the Americas
New York 10104

Established in 1985 in NY.
Donor(s): Stephen C. Swid, Charles Koppleman, Martin Bandier.
Foundation type: Independent
Financial data (yr. ended 9/30/89): Assets, $565,944 (M); gifts received, $350,000; expenditures, $167,938, including $167,600 for 18 grants (high: $50,000; low: $100).
Purpose and activities: Giving primarily for an international studies institute; support also for Jewish organizations, including institutes of higher education, a museum, and a hospital.
Limitations: Giving primarily in New York, NY. No grants to individuals.
Application information: Contributes only to pre-selected organizations. Applications not accepted.
Officers: Stephen C. Swid, Pres.; Nan G. Swid, Secy.
Employer Identification Number: 133369493

5281
Switzer Foundation
350 Hudson St., 4th Fl.
New York 10014 (212) 989-9393

Incorporated in 1909 in NY.
Donor(s): Margaret Switzer,† Sarah Switzer.†
Foundation type: Independent
Financial data (yr. ended 12/31/89): Assets, $3,885,151 (M); expenditures, $225,775, including $179,600 for 41 grants (high: $9,000; low: $1,000).
Purpose and activities: To provide scholarships for girls and women, particularly nursing students, through grants directly to schools.
Types of support: Scholarship funds.
Limitations: Giving primarily in the New York, NY, metropolitan area. No grants to individuals, or for building or endowment funds, operating budgets, or special projects.
Publications: Informational brochure.
Application information: Application form not required.
Initial approach: Letter
Copies of proposal: 1
Deadline(s): Submit proposal preferably between Jan. and June; deadline June 30
Board meeting date(s): Apr. and Oct.
Final notification: 3 months
Write: Mrs. Mary D. Butler, Secy.-Treas.

Officers: John A. Pilski, Pres.; John D. Bamonte, V.P.; Mary D. Butler, Secy.-Treas.
Number of staff: 1 full-time professional.
Employer Identification Number: 135596831

5282
Taconic Foundation, Inc. ▼
745 Fifth Ave., Suite 1608
New York 10151 (212) 758-8673

Incorporated in 1958 in DE.
Donor(s): Stephen R. Currier,† Mrs. Stephen R. Currier.†
Foundation type: Independent
Financial data (yr. ended 12/31/88): Assets, $16,330,964 (M); gifts received, $112,699; expenditures, $1,332,384, including $945,391 for 35 grants (high: $182,000; low: $1,800; average: $5,000-$20,000).
Purpose and activities: Grants primarily for programs furthering equal opportunity; current emphasis on housing and youth employment.
Types of support: General purposes, continuing support.
Limitations: Giving primarily in the New York, NY, area. No support for higher education, arts and cultural programs, mass media, crime and justice, health, medicine, mental health, ecology and the environment, individual economic development projects, or local community programs outside New York City. No grants to individuals, or for building or endowment funds, scholarships, or fellowships; grants rarely made for research; no loans.
Publications: Program policy statement, application guidelines.
Application information: Application form not required.
Initial approach: Letter or proposal
Copies of proposal: 1
Deadline(s): None
Board meeting date(s): 4 to 6 times a year
Final notification: 2 to 3 months
Write: Mrs. Jane Lee J. Eddy, Exec. Dir.
Officers and Directors:* John G. Simon,* Pres. and Treas.; Lloyd K. Garrison,* V.P.; Jane Lee J. Eddy,* Secy. and Exec. Dir.; Sheila M. Bautz, Susan P. Curnan, L.F. Boker Doyle, Alan J. Dworsky, Harold C. Fleming, Dorothy Hirshon, Vernon E. Jordan, Jr., Melvin A. Mister.
Number of staff: 1 full-time professional; 1 part-time professional; 2 full-time support; 1 part-time support.
Employer Identification Number: 131873668

5283
J. T. Tai & Company Foundation, Inc. ⌑
18 East 67th St.
New York 10021

Incorporated in 1983 in DE.
Donor(s): Jun Tsei Tai, J.T. Tai & Co.
Foundation type: Independent
Financial data (yr. ended 12/31/88): Assets, $10,249,397 (M); gifts received, $419,306; expenditures, $297,041, including $177,012 for 25 grants (high: $30,000; low: $1,000) and $108,680 for grants to individuals.
Purpose and activities: Giving for an international education organization and for medical education expenses.
Types of support: Student aid.
Application information: Application form not required.
Initial approach: Letter
Deadline(s): None
Write: Jun Tsei Tai, Pres.
Officers and Directors:* Jun Tsei Tai,* Pres. and Managing Dir.; Richard Chu, Ping Y. Tai.
Employer Identification Number: 133157279

5284
Tamiment Institute, Inc. ⌑
1501 Broadway
New York 10036 (212) 354-8330

Established in 1920 in NY.
Foundation type: Independent
Financial data (yr. ended 12/31/86): Assets, $1,695,430 (M); expenditures, $202,752, including $180,250 for 2 grants (high: $180,000; low: $250).
Purpose and activities: Support for labor-related activities and Jewish welfare.
Officers and Directors: Shelley Appleton, Pres.; Mitchell Levitas, V.P.; Myron Kolatch, Secy.; Jack Soska, Treas.; Norman Jacobs, Robert Lekachman, Richard Margulis, Harvey Shapiro, Bruce Vladek.
Employer Identification Number: 134981835

5285
Martin Tananbaum Foundation, Inc. ⌑
450 Seventh Ave., Suite 1509
New York 10123 (212) 687-3440

Incorporated in 1958 in NY.
Donor(s): Martin Tananbaum.†
Foundation type: Independent
Financial data (yr. ended 12/31/88): Assets, $1,383,739 (M); expenditures, $244,716, including $177,746 for 74 grants (high: $25,550; low: $36).
Purpose and activities: Grants largely for Jewish welfare funds, temple support, theological education, and health agencies.
Limitations: No grants to individuals, or for building or endowment funds.
Application information:
Initial approach: Letter
Copies of proposal: 7
Deadline(s): Submit proposal between Oct. and Apr.
Board meeting date(s): Monthly
Write: Arnold Alperstein, Pres.
Officers and Directors: Arnold Alperstein, Pres.; Elbert Brodsky, V.P.; Barbara Tananbaum DeGeorge, V.P.; Florence Levine, Secy.; Minnie Lee Tananbaum, Treas.
Members: Eileen Alperstein, Amy Coplon, Janet Weiner Dewild, Dorothy T. Kelly.
Employer Identification Number: 136162900

5286
The Tang Fund ⌑ ☆
c/o Morris & McVeigh
767 Third Ave.
New York 10017
Application address: c/o Reich & Tang, Inc., 100 Park Ave., New York, NY 10017; Tel.: (212) 370-1110

Established in 1984 in NY.
Donor(s): Oscar L. Tang, Reich & Tang, and members of the Tang family.
Foundation type: Independent
Financial data (yr. ended 11/30/87): Assets, $5,874,859 (M); gifts received, $550,756; expenditures, $90,567, including $82,650 for 22 grants (high: $45,000; low: $75).
Purpose and activities: Giving primarily for higher and secondary education; support also for cultural programs, community development, and a cancer research fund.
Application information:
Initial approach: Letter
Deadline(s): None
Write: Oscar L. Tang, Pres.
Officers: Oscar L. Tang, Pres.; Lorraine Husler, Secy.
Employer Identification Number: 133256296

5287
Michael & Lynne Tarnopol Foundation, Inc. ☆
c/o Bear Stearns Companies, Inc.
245 Park Ave.
New York 10167

Established in 1969 in NY.
Donor(s): Michael Tarnopol, Lynne Tarnopol.
Foundation type: Independent
Financial data (yr. ended 12/31/88): Assets, $1,287,866 (M); gifts received, $376,875; expenditures, $211,070, including $210,970 for 85 grants (high: $75,000; low: $25).
Purpose and activities: Giving primarily for higher education and Jewish organizations; support also for social services.
Limitations: Giving primarily in New York, NY, and PA. No grants to individuals.
Application information: Contributes only to pre-selected organizations. Applications not accepted.
Officers and Directors:* Michael L. Tarnopol,* Pres. and Treas.; Lynne Tarnopol,* V.P.; Joel Chrenkesnz,* Secy.
Number of staff: None.
Employer Identification Number: 132626280

5288
Fred and Harriett Taylor Foundation ⌑
c/o Chase Lincoln First Bank, N.A.
P.O. Box 1412
Rochester 14603

Trust established in NY.
Donor(s): Fred C. Taylor.†
Foundation type: Independent
Financial data (yr. ended 12/31/88): Assets, $5,897,313 (M); expenditures, $503,166, including $468,584 for 39 grants (high: $80,000; low: $55).
Purpose and activities: Emphasis on education, hospitals, Protestant church support and religious associations, youth agencies, community development, and health associations.
Limitations: Giving limited to the Hammondsport, NY, area.
Application information: Contributes only to pre-selected organizations. Applications not accepted.
Trustee: Chase Lincoln First Bank, N.A.
Employer Identification Number: 166205365

5289
The Teagle Foundation, Inc. ▼
30 Rockefeller Plaza, Rm. 2835
New York 10112 (212) 247-1946

Incorporated in 1944 in CT.
Donor(s): Walter C. Teagle,† Rowena Lee Teagle,† Walter C. Teagle, Jr.†
Foundation type: Independent
Financial data (yr. ended 05/31/89): Assets, $86,138,301 (M); expenditures, $3,785,523, including $2,288,932 for 264 grants (high: $50,000; low: $500; average: $15,000-$30,000), $44,397 for 8 grants to individuals (high: $13,840; low: $390) and $73,382 for 77 employee matching gifts.
Purpose and activities: General and project grants in support of higher education. Scholarships for children of employees of Exxon Corporation and its affiliates (program administered by College Scholarship Service, Princeton, N.J.). Limited support for New York City community organizations with youth activities. Direct assistance grants to needy employees, annuitants, and widows of deceased employees of Exxon Corporation. In 1990, the foundation will discontinue its program of scholarship grants to institutions and begin an invitation-only grants program to small, private colleges in the eastern U.S. The foundation's funding of traditional nursing scholarships will be replaced with a program designed to encourage nursing schools to help nursing students attain their BSN through alternatives to the 4-year format. The foundation has discontinued funding scholarships and fellowships for medicine and science at the graduate level.
Types of support: Scholarship funds, employee-related scholarships, continuing support, matching funds, special projects, employee matching gifts, general purposes, seed money.
Limitations: Giving limited to the U.S. and (for Exxon Scholarship Program only) Canada. No grants to community organizations outside New York City. No grants to U.S. organizations for foreign programmatic activities. No grants to individuals not connected with Exxon Corp.; no loans.
Publications: Annual report.
Application information: Application form not required.
Initial approach: Letter
Copies of proposal: 1
Deadline(s): Applications for Exxon Scholarship Program due Nov. 1 at College Scholarship Service; no deadline for other grants
Board meeting date(s): Feb., May, and Nov.
Final notification: Promptly after decision
Write: Richard W. Kimball, Exec. V.P.
Officers: Donald M. Cox,* Pres.; Richard W. Kimball, Exec. V.P. and C.E.O.; Margaret B. Sullivan, Secy.; James C. Anderson, Treas.
Directors:* Mary R. Williams, Chair.; George Bugliarello, Elliot R. Cattarulla, John S. Chalsty, Robert G. Engel, Richard L. Morrill, Vincent J. Motto, Walter C. Teagle III, Albert J. Wetzel.
Number of staff: 2 full-time professional; 1 part-time professional; 2 full-time support.
Employer Identification Number: 131773645

5290
Texaco Foundation ▼
(Formerly Texaco Philanthropic Foundation Inc.)
2000 Westchester Ave.
White Plains 10650 (914) 253-4150

Incorporated in 1979 in DE.
Donor(s): Texaco, Inc.
Foundation type: Company-sponsored
Financial data (yr. ended 12/31/88): Assets, $14,163,644 (M); expenditures, $6,710,926, including $5,649,255 for 440 grants (high: $850,000; low: $300; average: $1,000-$10,000) and $998,265 for 2,451 employee matching gifts.
Purpose and activities: To enhance the quality of life by providing support for cultural programs, higher education, social welfare, public and civic organizations, hospitals and health agencies, and environmental protection.
Types of support: Employee matching gifts, fellowships, research, employee-related scholarships, special projects, scholarship funds.
Limitations: Giving primarily in areas of company operations to local organizations; support also for national organizations that serve a large segment of the population. No support for religious organizations, private foundations, fraternal, social, or veterans' organizations, social functions, commemorative journals, or meetings, or political activities. No grants to individuals(except for employee-related scholarships), or for general operating support, capital funds (except for selected private non-profit hospitals), or endowments; no loans.
Publications: Annual report (including application guidelines).
Application information: Application form not required.
Initial approach: Proposal
Copies of proposal: 1
Deadline(s): None
Board meeting date(s): Quarterly
Final notification: 2 months
Write: Maria Mike-Mayer, Secy.
Officers and Directors:* Lorene L. Rogers,* Chair.; Maria Mike-Mayer, Secy.; Carl B. Davidson, Pres.; David C. Crikelair, Treas.; John D. Ambler, William S. Barrack, Jr., Paul B. Hicks, Jr., George Parker, Jr., L. Stanton Williams.
Number of staff: 5
Employer Identification Number: 133007516

5291
Texaco, Inc. Foundation ⌑
c/o Texaco, Inc.
2000 Westchester Ave.
White Plains 10650 (914) 253-4150

Incorporated in 1969 in OK; renamed as Texaco, Inc. Foundation in 1984 following Getty Oil Co.'s merger with Texaco, Inc.
Donor(s): Texaco, Inc.
Foundation type: Company-sponsored
Financial data (yr. ended 12/31/88): Assets, $727,761 (M); expenditures, $525,355, including $525,300 for 7 grants (high: $400,000; low: $8,800; average: $10,000-$50,000).
Purpose and activities: To enhance the quality of life by providing support for cultural programs, higher education, social welfare, public affairs and civic organizations, hospitals and health agencies, and environmental protection.
Types of support: Research, special projects.
Limitations: No support for religious organizations or private foundations. No grants to individuals, or for capital funds or endowments.
Application information: Application form not required.
Initial approach: Proposal or letter
Copies of proposal: 1
Deadline(s): None
Board meeting date(s): As required
Final notification: 2 months
Write: Maria Mike-Mayer, Secy.
Officers: William C. Weitzel, Jr.,* Pres.; Maria Mike-Mayer, Secy.; David C. Crikelair, Treas.
Directors:* Lorene L. Rogers, Chair.; William S. Barrack, Jr., Paul B. Hicks, Jr., George Parker, Jr.
Employer Identification Number: 237063751

5292
Thanksgiving Foundation ⌑
c/o Fiduciary Trust Co.
Two World Trade Ctr.
New York 10048

Established in 1985 in NJ.
Donor(s): Thomas M. Peters, Marion Post Peters.
Foundation type: Independent
Financial data (yr. ended 07/31/89): Assets, $5,268,073 (M); expenditures, $266,128, including $217,500 for 52 grants (high: $21,000; low: $500).
Purpose and activities: Support for social service and child welfare agencies, higher and elementary education, family planning, and religion.
Limitations: Giving primarily in NY and NJ. No grants to individuals.
Application information: Contributes only to pre-selected organizations. Applications not accepted.
Trustees: Thomas Henry Stone, Mark C. Winmill, Fiduciary Trust Co.
Employer Identification Number: 136861874

5293
Eugene V. & Clare E. Thaw Charitable Trust
726 Park Ave.
New York 10021

Established in 1981 in NY.
Donor(s): Eugene V. Thaw.
Foundation type: Operating
Financial data (yr. ended 05/31/89): Assets, $51,469,381 (M); gifts received, $47,900,000; expenditures, $619,272, including $585,996 for 15 grants (high: $273,787; low: $1,000).
Purpose and activities: A private operating foundation; giving for arts and culture; limited support for social services.
Application information: Contributes only to pre-selected organizations. Applications not accepted.
Trustees: Clare E. Thaw, Eugene V. Thaw.
Employer Identification Number: 133081491

5294
J. Walter Thompson Company Fund, Inc.
466 Lexington Ave.
New York 10017 (212) 210-7000

Incorporated in 1953 in NY.
Donor(s): J. Walter Thompson Co.
Foundation type: Company-sponsored
Financial data (yr. ended 11/30/89): Assets, $1,088,004 (M); gifts received, $100,000; expenditures, $145,596, including $113,650 for 14 grants (high: $40,000; low: $1,000; average: $1,500-$5,000) and $26,593 for 100 employee matching gifts.
Purpose and activities: Giving to the arts and educational organizations, including an employee matching gift program for education. Grants generally restricted to organizations which have received longstanding support from the fund.
Types of support: Employee matching gifts, employee-related scholarships, scholarship funds.
Limitations: No grants to individuals.
Application information:
Initial approach: Letter
Copies of proposal: 1
Deadline(s): Feb.
Board meeting date(s): Mar.-Apr.
Write: Nancy Fitzpatrick, Secy.
Officers and Directors:* Edward A. Haymes,* Chair.; Burt Manning,* Pres.; Susan Mirsky,* V.P.; Nancy Fitzpatrick,* Secy.; Donna Matteo, Treas.
Number of staff: None.
Employer Identification Number: 136020644

5295
The Thorne Foundation ¤
435 East 52nd St.
New York 10022 (212) 758-2425

Incorporated in 1930 in NY.
Donor(s): Landon K. Thorne,† Julia L. Thorne.†
Foundation type: Independent
Financial data (yr. ended 12/31/88): Assets, $2,456,984 (M); expenditures, $236,176, including $213,130 for 34 grants (high: $25,000; low: $25).
Purpose and activities: Emphasis on higher education, museums, and cultural programs; support also for medical organizations.
Limitations: Giving primarily in NY.
Application information:
Initial approach: Proposal
Deadline(s): None
Write: Miriam A. Thorne, Pres.
Officers: Miriam A. Thorne, Pres.; David H. Thorne, V.P.; John B. Jessup, Secy.-Treas.
Employer Identification Number: 136109955

5296
The Oakleigh L. Thorne Foundation
1633 Broadway, 30th Fl.
New York 10019 (212) 246-5070

Incorporated in 1959 in NY.
Donor(s): Commerce Clearing House, Inc.
Foundation type: Company-sponsored
Financial data (yr. ended 12/31/88): Assets, $190,843 (M); gifts received, $330,000; expenditures, $331,530, including $331,100 for 119 grants (high: $80,000; low: $100).
Purpose and activities: Emphasis on community funds, hospitals, health agencies, higher and secondary education, youth agencies, conservation programs, and cultural programs.
Types of support: General purposes, operating budgets, continuing support, annual campaigns, seed money, emergency funds, deficit financing, building funds, equipment, land acquisition, endowment funds, special projects, research, publications, capital campaigns, renovation projects.
Limitations: No grants to individuals, or for scholarships, fellowships, or matching gifts; no loans.
Application information: Application form not required.
Initial approach: Letter
Copies of proposal: 1
Deadline(s): None
Board meeting date(s): Quarterly
Final notification: 6 months
Write: Oakleigh B. Thorne, Pres.
Officers and Directors:* Oakleigh B. Thorne,* Chair., Pres., and Treas.; Oakleigh Thorne,* V.P. and Secy.; Theresa A. Milone,* V.P.
Number of staff: None.
Employer Identification Number: 510243758

5297
Louis Comfort Tiffany Foundation ¤
P.O. Box 480
Canal St. Station
New York 10013 (212) 431-9880

Association established in 1918 in NY.
Donor(s): Louis Comfort Tiffany.†
Foundation type: Independent
Financial data (yr. ended 12/31/87): Assets, $4,210,046 (M); expenditures, $391,765, including $300,000 for 20 grants to individuals.
Purpose and activities: To encourage talented and advanced artists of the fine arts (painting, sculpture, and the graphic arts) and the industrial crafts (ceramics, textile design, glass design, metal work) by awarding a limited number of grants biannually.
Types of support: Grants to individuals.
Limitations: No grants for general support, or capital or endowment funds.
Application information: Awards are by nomination only. Applications not accepted.
Write: Angela Westwater, Pres.
Officers and Trustees: Angela Westwater, Pres.; Gerard E. Jones, Secy.; Robert Meltzer, Treas.; William Bailey, Robert Blackburn, Thomas S. Buechner, Amanda Burden, Stephen Greene, Lewis Iselin, Bill N. Lacy, Roy Lichtenstein, David Pease, Martin Puryear, David A. Ross, Paul J. Smith, Diane Waldman.
Number of staff: None.
Employer Identification Number: 131689389

5298
Time Inc. Foundation ¤
Time & Life Bldg., Rm. 4173
Rockefeller Ctr.
New York 10020 (212) 841-8030

Established in 1983 in NY.
Donor(s): Time-Warner, Inc.
Foundation type: Company-sponsored
Financial data (yr. ended 12/31/88): Assets, $167,227 (M); gifts received, $125,236; expenditures, $415,619, including $415,500 for 32 grants (high: $54,000; low: $500).
Purpose and activities: Giving mainly for cultural programs, urban affairs, and youth agencies.
Types of support: Operating budgets.
Application information: Contributes only to pre-selected organizations. Applications not accepted.
Officers: Emelda M. Cathcart, Pres.; Sara Wentworth, Secy.; Kevin D. Senie, Treas.
Directors: Philip R. Bochner, Jr., Glenn A. Britt, Gerald M. Levin, Louis J. Slovinsky.
Employer Identification Number: 133131902

5299
The Tinker Foundation, Inc. ▼
55 East 59th St.
New York 10022 (212) 421-6858

Trust established in 1959 in NY; incorporated in 1975 in NY.
Donor(s): Edward Larocque Tinker.†
Foundation type: Independent
Financial data (yr. ended 12/31/89): Assets, $53,037,776 (M); expenditures, $2,303,200, including $2,295,200 for grants and $8,000 for 4 grants to individuals.
Purpose and activities: To promote better understanding among the peoples of the U.S., Latin America, Portugal, and Spain. Grants in aid of projects in the social sciences, international relations, marine sciences, natural resource development and some assistance for projects focused on Antarctica. Support also offered for conferences, meetings, seminars, and public affairs programs, and occasionally for programs furthering the education of the Spanish- and Portuguese-speaking peoples in the U.S.
Types of support: Special projects, research, conferences and seminars, exchange programs, matching funds, lectureships, seed money.
Limitations: Giving limited to projects related to Latin America, Spain, Portugal, and Antarctica. No support for projects concerned with health or medical issues or the arts and humanities. No grants to individuals, or for building or endowment funds, annual campaigns, operating budgets, or production costs for film, television, and radio projects.
Publications: Annual report, grants list, application guidelines.
Application information: The foundation has terminated its Postdoctoral Fellowship Program. Application form required.
Initial approach: Letter
Copies of proposal: 2
Deadline(s): Institutional grants: Mar. 1 for summer meeting and Oct. 1 for winter meeting; Field Research Grants: Oct. 1
Board meeting date(s): Institutional grants: June and Dec.; Field Research Grants: Dec.
Final notification: Institutional and Field Research grants: 2 weeks after board meetings
Write: Martha T. Muse, Chair.
Officers and Directors:* Martha T. Muse,* Chair., Pres., and C.E.O.; Grayson Kirk,* V.P.; Raymond L. Brittenham,* Secy.; Gordon T. Wallis,* Treas.; Renate Rennie,* Exec. Dir.;

James H. Billington, John N. Irwin II, Charles McC. Mathias, W. Clarke Wescoe.
Number of staff: 5 full-time professional; 3 full-time support.
Employer Identification Number: 510175449

5300
Tisch Foundation, Inc. ▼ ⌑
667 Madison Ave.
New York 10021-8087 (212) 545-2000

Incorporated in 1957 in FL.
Donor(s): Hotel Americana, Tisch Hotels, Inc., members of the Tisch family, and closely held corporations.
Foundation type: Independent
Financial data (yr. ended 12/31/88): Assets, $84,496,505 (M); expenditures, $2,523,418, including $2,238,580 for 114 grants (high: $777,000; low: $100; average: $1,000-$56,000).
Purpose and activities: Emphasis on higher education, including institutions in Israel, and research related programs; support also for Jewish organizations and welfare funds, museums, and secondary education.
Types of support: Continuing support, building funds, equipment, research.
Limitations: No grants to individuals, or for endowment funds, scholarships, fellowships, or matching gifts; no loans.
Application information: Contributes only to pre-selected organizations. Applications not accepted.
Board meeting date(s): Mar., June, Sept., Dec., and as required
Write: Laurence A. Tisch, Sr. V.P.
Officers and Directors:* Preston R. Tisch, Pres.; Laurence A. Tisch, Sr. V.P.; E. Jack Beatus,* Secy.-Treas.; Joan H. Tisch, Wilma S. Tisch.
Number of staff: None.
Employer Identification Number: 591002844

5301
Rose & John Tishman Fund, Inc. ⌑
175 East 79th St.
New York 10021-0432

Established in 1957 in NY.
Donor(s): Rose F. Tishman.
Foundation type: Independent
Financial data (yr. ended 12/31/88): Assets, $878,232 (M); gifts received, $230,000; expenditures, $266,585, including $230,495 for 87 grants (high: $100,000; low: $20) and $22,500 for 1 grant to an individual.
Purpose and activities: Giving primarily for Jewish organizations, higher education, scientific research, and health; grants also to indigent individuals to help defray medical costs.
Types of support: Grants to individuals.
Limitations: Giving primarily in NY.
Application information:
Initial approach: Letter
Deadline(s): None
Write: Mrs. Rose F. Tishman, V.P.
Officers: John Tishman, Pres.; Daniel R. Tishman, V.P. and Treas.; Katherine Blacklock, V.P.; Rose F. Tishman, V.P.; Kathleen E. Kotown, Secy.
Employer Identification Number: 136151766

5302
The Titan Industrial Foundation, Inc. ⌑
c/o Titan Industrial Co.
555 Madison Ave., 10th Fl.
New York 10022

Incorporated in 1951 in NY.
Donor(s): Titan Industrial Corp., Dominion Steel Export Co., Ltd.
Foundation type: Company-sponsored
Financial data (yr. ended 11/30/89): Assets, $849,563 (M); gifts received, $200,000; expenditures, $115,694, including $113,477 for 79 grants (high: $17,000; low: $25).
Purpose and activities: Support primarily for Jewish organizations, including welfare funds, higher education, cultural organizations, and programs for the disabled.
Limitations: Giving primarily in NY. No grants to individuals.
Application information: Contributes only to pre-selected organizations. Applications not accepted.
Officer and Director:* Jerome A. Siegel,* Pres. and Treas.
Employer Identification Number: 136066216

5303
William S. & Frances B. Todman Foundation
c/o Reid & Priest
40 West 57th St.
New York 10019

Established in 1980 in NY.
Donor(s): Frances B. Todman.
Foundation type: Independent
Financial data (yr. ended 11/30/88): Assets, $3,490 (M); gifts received, $213,723; expenditures, $214,010, including $214,000 for 12 grants (high: $150,000; low: $1,000).
Purpose and activities: Support primarily for medical research, Jewish giving, and the arts.
Limitations: Giving primarily in NY and FL. No grants to individuals.
Application information: Contributes only to pre-selected organizations. Applications not accepted.
Trustees: Lisa Todman Plough, Frances B. Todman, William S. Todman, Jr.
Number of staff: None.
Employer Identification Number: 133064427

5304
Topstone Fund ⌑
c/o H.G. Wellington & Co., Inc.
14 Wall St., Suite 1702
New York 10005 (212) 732-6800

Established in 1968 in NY.
Foundation type: Independent
Financial data (yr. ended 12/31/87): Assets, $1,487,013 (M); expenditures, $90,189, including $80,000 for 16 grants (high: $11,000; low: $2,000).
Purpose and activities: Giving primarily for social service agencies, churches and other religious associations, and higher education, including theological education.
Types of support: General purposes.
Limitations: Giving primarily in NJ and NY.
Application information:
Initial approach: Letter or proposal
Deadline(s): None
Write: John Baumann, Trustee
Trustees: John Baumann, John B. Jessup.
Employer Identification Number: 136274973

5305
Tortuga Foundation
c/o Siegel, Sacks & Co.
630 Third Ave., 22nd Fl.
New York 10017

Established in 1979 in NY.
Donor(s): William C. Breed III, J.L. Tweedy.
Foundation type: Independent
Financial data (yr. ended 09/30/89): Assets, $4,481,140 (M); gifts received, $600,025; expenditures, $488,791, including $450,000 for 22 grants (high: $50,000; low: $5,000).
Purpose and activities: Support primarily for land preservation, the environment, and women's and family planning groups; support also for health organizations and education.
Limitations: No grants to individuals.
Application information: Contributes only to pre-selected organizations. Applications not accepted.
Officers and Trustees:* George H.P. Dwight,* Pres.; Hugh J. Freund,* V.P. and Secy.-Treas.; Patricia P. Livingston,* V.P.; Robert C. Livingston, Millie L. Siceloff.
Number of staff: 2
Employer Identification Number: 510245279

5306
Ross E. Traphagen, Jr. Fund ⌑ ☆
c/o Goldman Sachs & Co., Tax Dept.
85 Broad St., 30th Fl.
New York 10004-2106

Established in 1976.
Donor(s): Ross E. Traphagen, Jr.
Foundation type: Independent
Financial data (yr. ended 3/31/88): Assets, $1,066,039 (M); expenditures, $106,389, including $103,360 for 155 grants (high: $25,000; low: $15).
Purpose and activities: Giving to churches, higher education, social services, and cultural organizations.
Limitations: Giving primarily in NY, FL, and NJ. No grants to individuals.
Application information: Applications not accepted.
Trustee: Ross E. Traphagen, Jr.
Employer Identification Number: 132894831

5307
Triangle Foundation ⌑
900 Third Ave., 31st Fl.
New York 10022 (212) 230-3000
Additional application address: Nelson Peltz, Trustee, 777 South Flagler Dr., West Palm Beach, FL

Established in 1964 in NY.
Foundation type: Company-sponsored
Financial data (yr. ended 12/31/88): Assets, $132,662 (M); gifts received, $2,320,000; expenditures, $2,463,597, including $242,919 for 279 grants (high: $150,000; low: $50).
Purpose and activities: Support primarily for Jewish welfare and temples; support also for

higher education, hospitals, health organizations, and educational broadcasting.
Limitations: No grants to individuals.
Application information:
Initial approach: Letter
Deadline(s): None
Write: Peter W. May, Trustee
Trustees: Peter W. May, Nelson Peltz.
Employer Identification Number: 226064018

5308
Robert Mize & Isa White Trimble Family Foundation ⌑
c/o Gerard L. Finneran
50 East 77th St., Apt 12D
New York 10021

Established in 1978 in New York.
Donor(s): Mary Ray Finneran.†
Foundation type: Independent
Financial data (yr. ended 6/30/88): Assets, $2,231,036 (M); expenditures, $86,184, including $78,000 for 16 grants (high: $10,000; low: $500).
Purpose and activities: Giving primarily for hospitals, children's homes, and Catholic religious organizations.
Limitations: Giving primarily in NY and for a few organizations in KY. No grants to individuals, or for scholarships or fellowships; no loans.
Application information: Contributes only to pre-selected organizations. Applications not accepted.
Officers and Directors: Gerard L. Finneran, Pres.; Daniel J. Ashley, V.P.; Rita H. Rowan, Secy.; Gerard B. Finneran.
Employer Identification Number: 132972532

5309
Tripp Foundation, Inc. ⌑ ☆
c/o S. Roberts Rose
One West Church St.
Elmira 14901

Foundation type: Independent
Financial data (yr. ended 04/30/89): Assets, $1,234,631 (M); expenditures, $135,222, including $129,350 for 21 grants (high: $50,000; low: $750).
Purpose and activities: Support primarily for arts organizations, including museums and the performing arts.
Types of support: General purposes, building funds.
Limitations: Giving primarily in NY. No grants to individuals.
Officers and Trustees:* Nancy T. Rose,* Pres.; Bela C. Tifft,* Secy.; S. Roberts Rose,* Treas.; Nancy M. Kimball, Edward T. Marks, Mary T. Marks, Frank T. Rose, Mary Elizabeth Smith.
Employer Identification Number: 160986346

5310
Jean L. & Raymond S. Troubh Fund ⌑ ☆
c/o Peat Marwick Main
599 Lexington Ave.
New York 10022

Donor(s): Jean L. Troubh.
Foundation type: Independent
Financial data (yr. ended 5/31/89): Assets, $202,325 (M); expenditures, $154,835, including $154,060 for 76 grants (high: $25,000; low: $20).
Purpose and activities: Giving primarily for higher and secondary education; support also for hospitals and medical centers.
Limitations: Giving primarily in NY. No grants to individuals.
Application information: Contributes only to pre-selected organizations. Applications not accepted.
Officers and Trustees: Jean L. Troubh, Pres.; Raymond S. Troubh, V.P.; Henry A. Loeb, Treas.
Employer Identification Number: 136178229

5311
Mildred Faulkner Truman Foundation ⌑
c/o Chase Lincoln First Bank, N.A.
P.O. Box 1412
Rochester 14603
Application address: 212 Front St., P.O. Box 236, Owego, NY 13827; Tel.: (607) 687-1350 or (607) 785-2355

Established in 1985 in NY.
Donor(s): Mildred Faulkner Truman.†
Foundation type: Independent
Financial data (yr. ended 8/31/88): Assets, $4,564,405 (M); gifts received, $1,159,812; expenditures, $216,263, including $161,402 for 36 grants (high: $25,287; low: $208).
Purpose and activities: Giving for youth and child welfare, education, social services, and cultural programs.
Limitations: Giving primarily in Tioga County, NY, with emphasis on the Owego, NY, area.
Publications: Application guidelines, informational brochure.
Application information: Application form not required.
Initial approach: Proposal
Deadline(s): 3 weeks before board meeting
Board meeting date(s): Quarterly
Write: Irene C. Graven, Exec. Dir.
Officers: Carl Saddlemire, Chair.; Edwin B. Bartow, Vice-Chair.; Robert Williams, Secy.; Dorothy Goodrich, Treas.; Irene C. Graver, Exec. Dir.
Directors: John J. Donnelly, James V. Guido, Fred R. McFadden, John R. Murphy.
Corporate Trustee: Chase Lincoln First Bank, N.A.
Employer Identification Number: 166293320

5312
The Fred C. Trump Foundation ⌑
c/o Irwin Durben
200 Garden City Plaza
Garden City 11530

Incorporated in 1952 in NY.
Donor(s): Beach Haven Apartments, Inc., Green Park Essex, Inc., Shore Haven Apartments, Inc., Trump Village Construction Corp., and others.
Foundation type: Independent
Financial data (yr. ended 12/31/88): Assets, $16,085 (M); gifts received, $100,000; expenditures, $116,422, including $116,338 for 53 grants (high: $25,000; low: $50).
Purpose and activities: Grants primarily for hospitals, higher education, Jewish welfare funds, and youth and health agencies.
Limitations: Giving primarily in NY.
Application information: Application form not required.
Deadline(s): None
Write: Fred C. Trump, Dir.
Directors: Irwin Durben, Donald J. Trump, Fred C. Trump.
Employer Identification Number: 116015006

5313
The Trust for Mutual Understanding ⌑
30 Rockefeller Plaza, Rm. 5600
New York 10112

Established in 1984 in NY.
Foundation type: Independent
Financial data (yr. ended 04/30/89): Assets, $17,754,569 (M); expenditures, $1,042,622, including $743,952 for 25 grants (high: $75,000; low: $5,000).
Purpose and activities: Support for an academy of the sciences, an opera company, theater and other cultural programs.
Application information: Contributes only to pre-selected organizations. Applications not accepted.
Trustees: Richard Lanier, Elizabeth J. McCormack, Donal C. O'Brien, Jr.
Employer Identification Number: 133212724

5314
Michael Tuch Foundation, Inc.
122 East 42nd St., No. 2905
New York 10168 (212) 986-9082

Incorporated in 1946 in NY.
Donor(s): Michael Tuch.†
Foundation type: Independent
Financial data (yr. ended 12/31/88): Assets, $4,893,969 (M); gifts received, $62,677; expenditures, $327,629, including $263,082 for 99 grants (high: $6,100; low: $500; average: $1,000).
Purpose and activities: Emphasis on higher and other education, cultural programs, including the performing arts, and the disadvantaged, including Jewish welfare funds and child welfare.
Types of support: Scholarship funds, fellowships, internships, special projects.
Limitations: Giving primarily in New York, NY. No support for religion or health. No grants to individuals, or for study, or new general support.
Application information: Application form not required.
Initial approach: Proposal
Copies of proposal: 1
Deadline(s): None
Board meeting date(s): May
Write: Eugene Tuck, Pres.
Officers: Eugene Tuck, Pres. and Exec. Dir.; Elizabeth Tuck, 1st V.P.; Martha Rozett, 2nd V.P.; Jacques J. Stone, Secy.-Treas.
Trustee: Jonathon S. Tuck.
Number of staff: 3 part-time professional; 2 part-time support.
Employer Identification Number: 136002848

5315
Tudor Foundation, Inc.
420 Lexington Ave., 15th Fl.
New York 10170 (212) 682-8490

Incorporated in 1945 in NY.
Donor(s): Aaron Rabinowitz,† Clara G. Rabinowitz.
Foundation type: Independent
Financial data (yr. ended 3/31/89): Assets, $5,763,508 (M); gifts received, $100,922; expenditures, $448,309, including $376,500 for 31 grants (high: $75,000; low: $1,000; average: $5,000-$10,000).
Purpose and activities: Grants primarily to educational institutions of higher learning and research libraries.
Types of support: General purposes, continuing support, endowment funds, special projects.
Limitations: Giving primarily in the Northeast, especially NY, NJ, PA, CT, and MA. No grants to individuals.
Application information: Application form not required.
Initial approach: Letter
Copies of proposal: 1
Deadline(s): Submit proposal in Feb. or Mar.; deadline Apr. 15
Board meeting date(s): May
Final notification: Aug.
Write: Edwin A. Malloy, Pres.
Officers and Directors: Edwin A. Malloy, Pres.; Susan R. Malloy, V.P.; Joseph A. Weinberger, Secy.; Timon J. Malloy, Treas.; David G. Fulton, Jennifer Malloy, Simon H. Rifkind, Ralph Sheffer, Ann Sheffer Stolpen.
Employer Identification Number: 136119193

5316
Ruth Turner Fund, Inc. ☆
c/o William J. Kridel
360 Lexington Ave.
New York 10017-6502

Established in 1973.
Donor(s): Ruth Turner.†
Foundation type: Independent
Financial data (yr. ended 12/31/90): Assets, $4,000,000 (M); expenditures, $210,000, including $172,000 for 13 grants (high: $25,000; low: $3,000).
Purpose and activities: Support for medical research, including AIDS research, and programs for the visually impaired; grants also for youth and social services and primary and secondary education.
Types of support: Research, scholarship funds.
Limitations: Giving primarily in New York, NY. No grants to individuals.
Officers: William J. Kridel, Pres.; Daniel L. Hartman, V.P.; Gloria S. Neuwirth, Secy.
Number of staff: None.
Employer Identification Number: 237240889

5317
Twentieth Century Fund, Inc. ⌑
41 East 70th St.
New York 10021 (212) 535-4441

Incorporated in 1919 in MA.
Donor(s): Edward A. Filene.†
Foundation type: Operating
Financial data (yr. ended 6/30/88): Assets, $42,189,198 (M); expenditures, $3,371,393, including $29,583 for 2 grants (high: $25,000; low: $4,583) and $3,237,730 for 61 foundation-administered programs.
Purpose and activities: A private operating foundation engaged in research and public education on significant contemporary issues, with an emphasis on communications, economic and social questions, and international affairs.
Limitations: Generally no grants to individuals or institutions.
Publications: Annual report, program policy statement, application guidelines, newsletter.
Application information: Generally, no grants to institutions or individuals, but foundation will review independent project proposals within program guidelines as well as soliciting its own. Application form not required.
Initial approach: Letter
Copies of proposal: 1
Deadline(s): Submit proposal preferably in Dec., Mar., or Sept.
Board meeting date(s): Jan., May, and Nov.
Write: M.J. Rossant, Dir.
Officers: Charles V. Hamilton,* Secy.; Richard Ravitch,* Treas.; Matina S. Horner,* Clerk; M.J. Rossant, Dir.
Trustees:* Brewster C. Denny,* Chair.; James A. Leach, Vice-Chair.; Morris B. Abram, H. Brandt Ayers, Peter A.A. Berle, Jose A. Cabranes, Alexander Morgan Capron, Edward E. David, Jr., P. Michael Pitfield, Albert Shanker, Harvey I. Sloane, M.D., Theodore C. Sorensen, James Tobin, Shirley Williams.
Number of staff: 11 full-time professional; 1 part-time professional; 10 full-time support; 3 part-time support.
Employer Identification Number: 131624235

5318
Underhill Foundation ☆
18 East 74th St.
New York 10021 (212) 628-9077

Donor(s): Gladys R. Underhill.
Foundation type: Operating
Financial data (yr. ended 11/30/89): Assets, $4,987,830 (M); gifts received, $705,000; expenditures, $300,043, including $29,000 for 9 grants (high: $7,500; low: $200) and $186,061 for 19 foundation-administered programs.
Purpose and activities: A private operating foundation; giving for conservation of the environment and wildlife. Support also for minority education programs, employment, and public policy.
Types of support: Conferences and seminars, general purposes, grants to individuals, land acquisition, scholarship funds.
Publications: Annual report, financial statement.
Application information: Applications not accepted.
Officer: John Echeverria, Prog. Dir.
Trustees: Christopher Elliman, David Elliman.
Number of staff: 2 part-time professional; 1 part-time support.
Employer Identification Number: 133096073

5319
S. J. Ungar Foundation ⌑
299 Broadway
New York 10007 (212) 233-2662

Incorporated in 1958 in NY.
Donor(s): Sidney J. Ungar.
Foundation type: Independent
Financial data (yr. ended 6/30/88): Assets, $3,398,256 (M); expenditures, $196,852, including $164,365 for grants (high: $60,000).
Purpose and activities: Emphasis on Jewish welfare funds, health agencies and hospitals, youth agencies, and higher education.
Limitations: Giving primarily in NY.
Application information:
Initial approach: Proposal
Deadline(s): None
Write: John Ungar, Dir.
Directors: Joan Shapiro, John Ungar.
Employer Identification Number: 136188247

5320
Unilever United States Foundation
(Formerly Lever Brothers Company Foundation)
390 Park Ave.
New York 10022 (212) 906-4685

Incorporated in 1952 in NY.
Donor(s): Lever Brothers Co.
Foundation type: Company-sponsored
Financial data (yr. ended 12/31/89): Assets, $599,133 (M); expenditures, $585,255, including $550,375 for 202 grants (high: $25,000; low: $500) and $34,880 for 16 grants to individuals.
Purpose and activities: Grants largely for health and human services, education, civil rights, community development, and civic affairs.
Types of support: Operating budgets, employee-related scholarships, employee matching gifts.
Limitations: Giving primarily in areas of company operations in NY, CA, GA, IN, MD, and MO. No support for religious or international organizations. No grants to individuals (except for employee-related scholarships), or for building funds or endowment funds; no loans.
Publications: Application guidelines.
Application information: Application form not required.
Initial approach: Letter or proposal
Copies of proposal: 1
Deadline(s): Dec. 31
Board meeting date(s): Feb.
Final notification: 1 month after meeting
Write: Rachel R. Greenstein, Community Affairs Mgr., Unilever United States, Inc.
Officers: Ned W. Bandler,* Pres.; John T. Gould, Jr., V.P.; T.J. Hoolihan, Secy.; C.L. Roberts, Jr., Treas.
Directors:* T.C. Mullins, W.M. Volpi.
Number of staff: 2 part-time professional; 1 part-time support.
Employer Identification Number: 136122117

5321
United Armenian Charities, Inc.
c/o Sal Sica
168 Canal St., Suite 207
New York 10013

Established in 1951 in NY.
Donor(s): Dadour Dadourian.
Foundation type: Independent
Financial data (yr. ended 12/31/88): Assets, $1,678,750 (M); expenditures, $86,544, including $81,984 for 11 grants (high: $32,000; low: $90).
Purpose and activities: Grants primarily for Armenian religious support; grants also for Armenian education and social services.
Types of support: General purposes.
Limitations: Giving primarily in NY.
Officers: Dadour Dadourian, Pres.; Alex Dadourian, V.P. and Treas.; Haig Dadourian, Secy.
Number of staff: None.
Employer Identification Number: 136125023

5322
United Merchants Foundation, Inc. ⌘
1407 Broadway, 6th Fl.
New York 10018-5103 (212) 930-3999

Incorporated in 1944 in NY.
Foundation type: Company-sponsored
Financial data (yr. ended 6/30/88): Assets, $1,152,850 (M); expenditures, $117,241, including $116,533 for 23 grants (high: $50,000; low: $250).
Purpose and activities: Emphasis on Jewish welfare funds, community funds, higher education, youth programs, and hospitals.
Limitations: Giving primarily in NY. No grants to individuals.
Application information: Application form required.
Initial approach: Letter
Copies of proposal: 1
Deadline(s): None
Board meeting date(s): Dec.
Write: Lawrence Marx, Jr., Pres.
Officers and Trustees: Lawrence Marx, Jr., Pres.; Martin J. Schwab, V.P.; Oliver G. Seidman, Secy.-Treas.
Employer Identification Number: 136077135

5323
United States Trust Company of New York Foundation
c/o U.S. Trust Co. of New York
114 West 47th St.
New York 10036 (212) 852-1000

Trust established in 1955 in NY.
Donor(s): U.S. Trust Co. of New York.
Foundation type: Company-sponsored
Financial data (yr. ended 12/31/88): Assets, $32,716 (L); gifts received, $382,965; expenditures, $402,906, including $292,945 for 46 grants (high: $50,000; low: $1,000; average: $3,000-$5,000) and $109,820 for 298 employee matching gifts (high: $15,000; low: $10).
Purpose and activities: Support for the performing arts and other cultural programs; health; adult, minority, and other education; and civic and urban affairs and development organizations, including programs for employment, housing, and the disadvantaged that assist in building or maintaining an improved quality of life. Preference given to innovative, broad-based, privately supported, and efficient organizations in which company employees are active.
Types of support: Operating budgets, annual campaigns, seed money, equipment, endowment funds, matching funds, employee matching gifts, special projects, research, capital campaigns, general purposes, publications, program-related investments, renovation projects.
Limitations: Giving primarily in the New York metropolitan area and other primary market areas of the company. No support for religious or political organizations or member agencies of the United Way. No grants to individuals, or for emergency funds, deficit financing, scholarships, or fellowships; no loans.
Publications: Informational brochure (including application guidelines).
Application information: Education, cultural, and arts proposals reviewed in the spring; health, human services, civic and community proposals reviewed in the fall. Application form not required.
Initial approach: Letter or proposal
Copies of proposal: 1
Deadline(s): Apr. 1
Board meeting date(s): Mar., May, and Oct.
Final notification: 2 to 6 months, depending on date proposal submitted
Write: Carol A. Strickland, V.P.
Corporate Contributions Committee: Carol A. Strickland, V.P. and Corp. Secy.
Number of staff: 2 part-time professional; 1 part-time support.
Employer Identification Number: 136072081

5324
United States-Japan Foundation ▼
145 East 32nd St., 12th Fl.
New York 10016 (212) 481-8753
Tokyo, Japan, office address: Nihon Shobo Kaikan, 9th Fl., 2-9-16 Toranomon, Minato-ku, Tokyo 105, Japan; Tel.: 03-591-4002

Foundation incorporated in 1980 in NY.
Donor(s): The Japan Shipbuilding Industry Foundation.
Foundation type: Independent
Financial data (yr. ended 12/31/88): Assets, $84,747,547 (M); expenditures, $4,994,535, including $3,229,880 for 47 grants (high: $230,206; low: $965; average: $10,000-$25,000).
Purpose and activities: To strengthen cooperation and understanding between the people of the U.S. and Japan through grants in: 1) Exchange of persons and ideas, involving American and Japanese leaders drawn from local communities, the professions, state and local governments, and other groups; 2) Education, with emphasis on pre-college education; and 3) Nongovernmental dialogue in such fields as energy, technology, international finance, and defense.
Types of support: Exchange programs, special projects, internships, fellowships, matching funds, conferences and seminars, research, seed money.
Limitations: No support for projects in the arts involving performances, exhibitions, or productions, or for sports exchanges, student exchanges, scholarly research, or scholarly conferences. No grants to individuals, or for building or endowment funds; no loans.
Publications: Annual report, newsletter.
Application information: Application form not required.
Initial approach: Letter
Copies of proposal: 1
Deadline(s): Mar. and Sept.
Board meeting date(s): May and Nov.
Final notification: 6 months to 1 year
Write: Stephen W. Bosworth, Pres.
Officers: Stephen W. Bosworth,* Pres.; Ronald Aqua, V.P.; Maximilian Kempner, Secy.; Stephen W. Montanye, Controller.
Trustees:* William D. Eberle, Chair.; Kiichi Saeki, Vice-Chair.; Thomas A. Bartlett, Robin Chandler Duke, Orville L. Freeman, Tadao Ishikawa, Hiroyuki Itami, Jonathan Mason, Robert S. McNamara, Isao Nakauchi, Shizuo Saito, Robert W. Sarnoff, Yohei Sasakawa, Ryuzo Sejima, Ayako Sono, Phillips Talbot, Yoshio Terasawa, Joseph D. Tydings, Henry G. Walter, Jr., John S. Wadsworth, Jr.
Number of staff: 6 full-time professional; 4 full-time support; 2 part-time support.
Employer Identification Number: 133054425

5325
Bella & Israel Unterberg Foundation, Inc. ⌘
c/o Leipziger & Breskin
230 Park Ave.
New York 10169

Incorporated in 1948 in NY.
Donor(s): Members of the Unterberg family.
Foundation type: Independent
Financial data (yr. ended 12/31/88): Assets, $949,085 (M); gifts received, $192,801; expenditures, $180,984, including $169,975 for 64 grants (high: $25,000; low: $50).
Purpose and activities: Giving primarily for Jewish welfare funds, higher education, hospitals, and community development.
Limitations: No grants to individuals.
Application information: Contributes only to pre-selected organizations. Applications not accepted.
Officers: Edgar J. Nathan, 3rd., Pres.; Selma S. Unterberg, 1st V.P.; Carol R. Meyer, 2nd V.P.; Thomas I. Unterberg, 3rd V.P.; James H. Powell, 4th V.P.; Frank E. Joseph, Jr., 5th V.P.; Lilian V. Desecktor, Secy.
Employer Identification Number: 136099080

5326
Uris Brothers Foundation, Inc. ▼
300 Park Ave.
New York 10022 (212) 355-7107

Incorporated in 1956 in NY.
Donor(s): Percy Uris,† Harold D. Uris,† and related business interests.
Foundation type: Independent
Financial data (yr. ended 10/31/89): Assets, $21,741,527 (M); qualifying distributions, $1,920,464, including $1,620,464 for 91 grants (high: $100,000; low: $500) and $300,000 for 2 loans.

Purpose and activities: Since 1984, the foundation's primary focus has been on low-income housing and homeless issues relating to families. Support also for education and the New York City public school system.
Types of support: Building funds, special projects, capital campaigns, technical assistance, general purposes, loans, program-related investments, renovation projects.
Limitations: Giving primarily in New York, NY. No grants to individuals, or for endowment funds, video or film production, or research.
Application information: Application form not required.
Initial approach: Letter or brief proposal
Copies of proposal: 1
Deadline(s): None
Board meeting date(s): Quarterly
Write: Ms. Alice Paul, Exec. Dir.
Officers: Susan Halpern,* Pres.; Jane Bayard,* V.P.; Linda Sanger,* V.P.; Alice Paul,* Secy. and Exec. Dir.; Benjamin Gessula, Treas.
Directors:* Ruth Uris, Chair.; Robert H. Abrams, Robert L. Bachner.
Number of staff: 1 part-time professional.
Employer Identification Number: 136115748

5327
Ushkow Foundation, Inc. ⌘
c/o Sedco Industries, Inc.
98 Cutter Mill Rd., Suite 475
Great Neck 11021

Incorporated in 1956 in NY.
Donor(s): Joseph Ushkow.
Foundation type: Independent
Financial data (yr. ended 10/31/87): Assets, $5,195,940 (M); expenditures, $174,428, including $172,225 for 37 grants (high: $100,000; low: $15).
Purpose and activities: Grants primarily for hospitals, higher education, and Jewish welfare funds.
Limitations: Giving primarily in NY. No grants to individuals.
Application information: Contributes only to pre-selected organizations. Applications not accepted.
Write: Maurice A. Deane, Secy., or Jerome Serchuck, V.P.
Officer: Joan Serchuck, Pres.; Barbara Deane, V.P.; Jerome Serchuck, V.P.; Maurice A. Deane, Secy.-Treas.
Employer Identification Number: 116006274

5328
Utica Foundation, Inc.
270 Genesee St.
Utica 13502 (315) 735-8212

Incorporated in 1952 in NY.
Foundation type: Community
Financial data (yr. ended 12/31/88): Assets, $8,956,512 (L); gifts received, $5,748,124; expenditures, $351,710, including $316,577 for 44 grants (high: $72,500; low: $700).
Purpose and activities: Support for social and health services, scholarship programs of institutions for aid to local students, and cultural programs.
Types of support: General purposes, seed money, building funds, equipment, conferences and seminars, professorships, matching funds, scholarship funds, capital campaigns.
Limitations: Giving limited to Utica, Oneida, and Herkimer counties, NY. No support for religious purposes. No grants to individuals, or for endowment funds, deficit financing, or operating budgets; no loans.
Publications: Annual report, application guidelines.
Application information: Application form required.
Initial approach: Letter
Copies of proposal: 7
Board meeting date(s): 3 to 4 times a year, in May and as required
Final notification: 2 to 3 months
Write: Addison M. White, Pres.
Officers and Directors: Addison M. White, Pres.; Mrs. Thomas G. Hineline, V.P.; Arthur H. Turner, V.P.; William L. Schrauth, Secy.; James S. Kernan, Jr., Treas.; Rev. P. Arthur Brindisi, Vincent R. Corrou, Jr., Irving Cramer, M.D., Victor T. Ehre, John L. Knower, Harold J. Moore, Burrel Samuels, Msgr. Charles Sewall, Dwight E. Vicks, Jr., William B. Westcott, Jr.
Trustee Banks: Marine Midland Bank, N.A., Norstar Bank of Upstate New York.
Number of staff: 1 full-time professional; 1 full-time support.
Employer Identification Number: 156016932

5329
van Ameringen Foundation, Inc. ▼
509 Madison Ave.
New York 10022 (212) 758-6221

Incorporated in 1950 in NY.
Donor(s): Arnold Louis van Ameringen.†
Foundation type: Independent
Financial data (yr. ended 12/31/89): Assets, $32,674,316 (M); expenditures, $2,233,233, including $1,960,935 for 52 grants (high: $80,000; low: $2,500; average: $20,000-$50,000).
Purpose and activities: Grants chiefly to promote mental health and social welfare through preventive measures, treatment, and rehabilitation; support also for child development, medical education, and health, including the fields of psychology and psychiatry.
Types of support: Operating budgets, continuing support, seed money, matching funds, special projects, research, publications, endowment funds.
Limitations: Giving primarily in the urban Northeast from Boston, MA, to Washington, DC, including NY and PA. No support for international activities and institutions in other countries, or for mental retardation, the physically handicapped, drug abuse, or alcoholism. No grants to individuals, or for annual campaigns, deficit financing, emergency funds, capital campaigns, scholarships, or fellowships; no loans.
Publications: Annual report, informational brochure (including application guidelines).
Application information: Application form not required.
Initial approach: Proposal
Copies of proposal: 1
Deadline(s): 2 months before board meetings
Board meeting date(s): Mar., June, and Nov.
Final notification: Within 60 days
Write: Patricia Kind, Pres.
Officers and Directors:* Patricia Kind,* Pres., Treas., and C.E.O.; Lily vA. Auchincloss,* V.P.; Harmon Duncombe,* Secy.; Mrs. Arnold Louis van Ameringen,* Honorary Chair.; Henry P. van Ameringen, Henry G. Walter, Jr.
Number of staff: 1 full-time professional; 1 full-time support.
Employer Identification Number: 136125699

5330
H. van Ameringen Foundation ⌘
509 Madison Ave.
New York 10022

Established in 1950.
Donor(s): Henry P. van Ameringen, Mrs. Arnold Louis van Ameringen.
Foundation type: Independent
Financial data (yr. ended 12/31/88): Assets, $471,589 (M); gifts received, $300,000; expenditures, $166,695, including $165,985 for 40 grants (high: $25,000; low: $500).
Purpose and activities: Giving for cultural programs, conservation, mental health, education, and social services.
Limitations: Giving primarily in NY.
Application information: Unsolicited applications not accepted. Applications not accepted.
Trustee: Henry P. van Ameringen.
Employer Identification Number: 136215329

5331
The Ann & Erlo Van Waveren Foundation, Inc. ☆
210 East 86th St., Suite 204
New York 10128 (212) 517-0060

Incorporated in 1986 in NY.
Donor(s): Ann Van Waveren.†
Foundation type: Independent
Financial data (yr. ended 3/31/89): Assets, $1,544,719 (M); expenditures, $179,277, including $22,500 for 4 grants (high: $12,500; low: $2,000), $29,000 for 7 grants to individuals (high: $6,000; low: $2,500) and $42,441 for foundation-administered programs.
Purpose and activities: Grants awarded "to promote and advance study and research in the field of Jungian psychology."
Types of support: Research, grants to individuals, publications, seed money.
Application information: Application form not required.
Initial approach: Letter
Deadline(s): Dec. 31
Write: Olivier Bernier, Pres.
Officers: Olivier Bernier, Pres.; Diana Swayer, Secy.; Theodore Young, Treas.
Employer Identification Number: 133343738

5332
The Vanneck-Bailey Foundation ⌘
100 Park Ave.
New York 10017 (212) 725-2850

Established in 1971 in NY through the consolidation of The Vanneck Foundation, incorporated in 1949 in NY, and The Frank and Marie Bailey Foundation.

Donor(s): John Vanneck,† Barbara Bailey Vanneck.
Foundation type: Independent
Financial data (yr. ended 12/31/87): Assets, $4,924,001 (M); expenditures, $208,226, including $190,775 for 77 grants (high: $50,000; low: $60).
Purpose and activities: Emphasis on higher and secondary education, hospitals, and youth agencies.
Types of support: Continuing support, research.
Limitations: No grants to individuals.
Application information: Unsolicited applications not accepted; grantees are organizations of personal interest to family members.
Write: John B. Vanneck, V.P.
Officers: Barbara Bailey Vanneck, Pres.; John B. Vanneck, V.P.; Jeanne M. Wiedenman, Secy.; William P. Vanneck, Treas.
Employer Identification Number: 237165285

5333
Miles Hodsdon Vernon Fund, Inc. ⌑
49 Beekman Ave.
North Tarrytown 10591 (914) 631-4226

Incorporated in 1953 in NY.
Donor(s): Miles Hodsdon Vernon,† Martha Hodsdon Kinney,† Louise Hodsdon.†
Foundation type: Independent
Financial data (yr. ended 12/31/88): Assets, $3,996,455 (M); expenditures, $229,287, including $198,750 for 46 grants (high: $30,000; low: $250).
Purpose and activities: Grants for medical research, especially on encephalitis and other brain disorders; support also for youth agencies, aid for the aged, and education.
Types of support: Scholarship funds.
Application information:
Initial approach: Proposal
Deadline(s): None
Write: Robert C. Thomson, Jr., Pres.
Officers and Directors:* Robert C. Thomson, Jr.,* Pres. and Treas.; Dennis M. Fitzgerald,* V.P. and Secy.; Eleanor C. Thomson, Gertrude Whalen.
Employer Identification Number: 136076836

5334
G. Unger Vetlesen Foundation ▼ ⌑
c/o Fulton, Duncombe, and Rowe
30 Rockefeller Plaza
New York 10112 (212) 586-0700

Incorporated in 1955 in NY.
Donor(s): George Unger Vetlesen.†
Foundation type: Independent
Financial data (yr. ended 12/31/88): Assets, $35,415,270 (M); expenditures, $2,029,649, including $1,900,000 for 20 grants (high: $650,000; low: $5,000; average: $5,000-$50,000).
Purpose and activities: Established a biennial international science award for discoveries in the earth sciences; grants for biological, geophysical, and environmental research, including scholarships, and cultural organizations, including those emphasizing Norwegian-American relations and maritime interests. Support also for public policy research and libraries.
Types of support: General purposes, special projects.
Limitations: No grants to individuals.
Application information: Application form not required.
Initial approach: Proposal
Copies of proposal: 1
Deadline(s): Nov. 1
Board meeting date(s): Dec.
Final notification: Positive determination, by Dec. 31; negative determination, no response
Write: George Rowe, Jr., Pres.
Officers: George Rowe, Jr., Pres.; Harmon Duncombe, V.P. and Treas.; Joseph T.C. Hart, Secy.
Directors: Eugene P. Grisanti, Henry G. Walter, Jr.
Number of staff: None.
Employer Identification Number: 131982695

5335
The Vidda Foundation ▼
c/o Carter, Carter, & Rupp
10 East 40th St., Suite 2103
New York 10016 (212) 696-4052

Established in 1979 in NY.
Donor(s): Ursula Corning.
Foundation type: Independent
Financial data (yr. ended 5/31/89): Assets, $1,002,292 (M); gifts received, $810,075; expenditures, $875,655, including $728,134 for 22 grants (high: $200,000; low: $750).
Purpose and activities: Giving primarily to educational projects, cultural programs, including an educational film-making company, church music funds, conservation, hospitals, and social services.
Types of support: General purposes, building funds, special projects, endowment funds, research, operating budgets.
Limitations: Giving primarily in NY. No grants to individuals.
Application information: Application form not required.
Initial approach: Letter or proposal
Copies of proposal: 3
Deadline(s): None
Board meeting date(s): Nov. and May
Final notification: Approximately 2 months
Write: Gerald E. Rupp, Mgr.
Trustees: Gerald E. Rupp, Mgr.; Ann Fraser Brewer, Ursula Corning, Thomas T. Fraser, Christophe Velay.
Number of staff: 2 part-time professional; 1 part-time support.
Employer Identification Number: 132981105

5336
Doris Warner Vidor Foundation, Inc. ⌑
317 East 64th St.
New York 10021

Established in 1972.
Foundation type: Independent
Financial data (yr. ended 11/30/88): Assets, $1,500,210 (M); gifts received, $10,000; expenditures, $195,394, including $187,055 for 80 grants (high: $20,350; low: $50).
Purpose and activities: Emphasis on cultural programs; support also for higher and secondary education, health, and hospitals.
Limitations: Giving primarily in the greater New York City, NY, metropolitan area.
Application information: Contributes only to pre-selected organizations. Applications not accepted.
Officers: Warner Leroy, Pres.; Quentin Vidor, V.P.; Lewis Brian Vidor, Secy.; Linda Janklow, Treas.
Employer Identification Number: 237252504

5337
Vinmont Foundation, Inc.
888 East 19th St.
Brooklyn 11230 (718) 377-0178

Incorporated in 1947 in NY.
Donor(s): Lily H. Weinberg,† Robert C. Weinberg,† Ruth Weinberg.†
Foundation type: Independent
Financial data (yr. ended 12/31/89): Assets, $1,429,299 (M); expenditures, $120,371, including $114,000 for 60 grants (high: $6,000; low: $500; average: $500-$6,000).
Purpose and activities: Giving primarily for black and Native American development nationally; and for social service agencies, urban planning, and restoration in metropolitan New York City.
Types of support: Operating budgets, continuing support, annual campaigns, seed money, emergency funds.
Limitations: Giving primarily in the New York, NY, metropolitan area; national support for minorities. No grants to individuals, or for capital or endowment funds, research, special projects, publications, conferences, scholarships, fellowships, or matching gifts; no loans.
Publications: Program policy statement.
Application information: Rarely funds unsolicited proposals. Application form not required.
Initial approach: Letter or proposal
Copies of proposal: 1
Deadline(s): None
Board meeting date(s): Feb., Apr., Sept., and Nov.
Final notification: 6 months
Write: William R. Nye, Pres.
Officers: William R. Nye, Pres.; Carolyn S. Whittle, V.P.; Paul S. Byard, Secy.; Ellen Edwards, Treas.
Directors: Bruce Bozeman, L. Franklyn Lowenstein.
Number of staff: None.
Employer Identification Number: 131577203

5338
The Laura B. Vogler Foundation, Inc.
P.O. Box 94
Bayside 11361 (718) 423-3000

Incorporated in 1959 in NY.
Donor(s): Laura B. Vogler,† John J. Vogler.†
Foundation type: Independent
Financial data (yr. ended 10/31/89): Assets, $3,583,873 (M); expenditures, $190,096, including $139,200 for 49 grants (high: $5,000; low: $1,000; average: $1,000-$5,000).

Purpose and activities: Giving for education, health care, services for minorities, and conservation.
Types of support: Seed money, emergency funds, special projects, research, scholarship funds.
Limitations: Giving limited to the New York, NY, metropolitan area, including Long Island. No grants to individuals, or for building or endowment funds, annual fundraising campaigns, or matching gifts; no loans.
Publications: Annual report (including application guidelines).
Application information: Application form required.
Initial approach: Letter
Copies of proposal: 1
Deadline(s): Jan. 1, Apr. 1, July 1, and Oct. 1
Board meeting date(s): Jan., Apr., July, and Oct.
Final notification: 2 to 3 months
Write: D. Donald D'Amato, Pres.
Officers and Trustees:* D. Donald D'Amato,* Pres. and C.E.O.; Lawrence L. D'Amato,* Secy.-Treas.; Max L. Kupferberg, I. Jerry Lasurdo, Stanley C. Pearson, Robert T. Waldbauer, Karen M. Yost.
Number of staff: 2 part-time professional.
Employer Identification Number: 116022241

5339
The Sunny von Bulow Coma and Head Trauma Research Foundation ☆
555 Madison Ave., Suite 2001
New York 10022-3303 (212) 753-5003

Established in 1986 in NY.
Donor(s): Annie-Laurie Atkin Trust.
Foundation type: Independent
Financial data (yr. ended 12/31/89): Assets, $662,991 (M); gifts received, $520,000; expenditures, $148,750, including $148,750 for 6 grants (high: $60,000; low: $2,500).
Purpose and activities: Support primarily for medical research.
Limitations: No grants to individuals.
Publications: Informational brochure (including application guidelines), 990-PF, financial statement.
Application information: Application form required.
Initial approach: 1-2 page letter of intent
Copies of proposal: 8
Deadline(s): June 30 and Dec. 31
Board meeting date(s): Fall
Final notification: One month after board meeting
Write: Dominic Introcaso
Officers and Directors:* Annie-Laurie Isham,* Pres.; George Morris Gurley,* V.P.; Alexander von Auersperg,* Secy.; Ralph Isham,* Treas.
Number of staff: 1 full-time professional; 1 full-time support.
Employer Identification Number: 133349779

5340
Mary Jane & William J. Voute Foundation, Inc. ⌑
c/o Salomon Brothers, Inc.
One New York Plaza
New York 10004

Established in 1977 in New York.
Donor(s): Mary Jane Voute, William J. Voute.
Foundation type: Independent
Financial data (yr. ended 6/30/88): Assets, $4,961 (M); gifts received, $185,000; expenditures, $377,780, including $377,255 for 82 grants (high: $30,000; low: $10).
Purpose and activities: Grants primarily for Catholic church support and higher education; giving also for health and social services.
Types of support: Scholarship funds.
Limitations: Giving primarily in the New York, NY, metropolitan area, including Westchester County.
Application information: Contributes only to pre-selected organizations. Applications not accepted.
Officers: William J. Voute, Pres. and Treas.; Mary Jane Voute, V.P. and Secy.
Directors: Stanley L. Cohen, Salvatore Traini, Michael Walsh.
Employer Identification Number: 510249510

5341
Sue and Edgar Wachenheim Foundation ⌑
100 Park Ave.
New York 10017-5516

Donor(s): Sue W. Wachenheim, Edgar Wachenheim III.
Foundation type: Independent
Financial data (yr. ended 10/31/89): Assets, $1,692,696 (M); gifts received, $80,250; expenditures, $44,746, including $43,925 for 14 grants (high: $25,000; low: $25).
Purpose and activities: Support primarily for higher education.
Limitations: Giving primarily in NY. No grants to individuals.
Application information: Contributes only to pre-selected organizations. Applications not accepted.
Officers: Edgar Wachenheim III, Pres.; Sue W. Wachenheim, Exec. V.P.; Benjamin Glowatz, V.P. and Treas.; James G. Wallach, V.P.; Kenneth L. Wallach, Secy.
Director: Ira D. Wallach.
Employer Identification Number: 237011002

5342
The Wachtell, Lipton, Rosen & Katz Foundation ▼ ⌑
299 Park Ave.
New York 10171

Established in 1981 in New York.
Donor(s): Wachtell, Lipton, Rosen & Katz.
Foundation type: Company-sponsored
Financial data (yr. ended 9/30/88): Assets, $6,026,737 (M); gifts received, $4,000,000; expenditures, $2,492,446, including $2,478,907 for 129 grants (high: $925,000; low: $15; average: $1,000-$50,000).
Purpose and activities: Emphasis on Jewish organizations and higher education.
Application information: Contributes only to preselected organizations. Applications not accepted.
Board meeting date(s): As necessary
Officers: Martin Lipton, Pres.; Leonard M. Rosen, V.P. and Secy.; George A. Katz, V.P. and Treas.; Herbert M. Wachtell, V.P.
Number of staff: None.
Employer Identification Number: 133099901

5343
Wahrsager Foundation ⌑
c/o Spicer & Oppenheim
Seven World Trade Center
New York 10048 (212) 422-1000

Established in 1961 in NY.
Donor(s): Members of the Wahrsager family.
Foundation type: Independent
Financial data (yr. ended 9/30/88): Assets, $1,237,701 (M); expenditures, $71,358, including $49,557 for 32 grants (high: $20,000; low: $25).
Purpose and activities: Giving primarily for higher education.
Limitations: Giving primarily in New York, NY. No grants to individuals.
Application information: Contributes only to pre-selected organizations. Applications not accepted.
Officer and Directors: Karel Wahrsager, Pres. and Treas.; Eve Wahrsager.
Employer Identification Number: 136034241

5344
George P. Wakefield Residuary Trust ⌑
c/o The Bank of New York, Tax Dept.
48 Wall St.
New York 10015

Foundation type: Independent
Financial data (yr. ended 6/30/88): Assets, $1,911,593 (M); expenditures, $123,314, including $89,000 for 22 grants (high: $8,200; low: $1,500).
Purpose and activities: Support primarily for Jewish welfare agencies; giving also to child welfare organizations and hospitals; support also for medical research.
Limitations: Giving primarily in NY.
Trustees: Samuel Weinberg, The Bank of New York.
Employer Identification Number: 136079388

5345
Wallace Genetic Foundation, Inc. ▼ ⌑
Farvue Farm
South Salem 10590
Grant application address: Polly Lawrence, Research Secy., 4801 Massachusetts Ave., Suite 400, Washington, DC 20016; Tel.: (202) 966-2932

Incorporated in 1959 in NY.
Donor(s): Henry A. Wallace.†
Foundation type: Independent
Financial data (yr. ended 12/31/88): Assets, $46,974,737 (M); gifts received, $190,000; expenditures, $2,691,102, including $2,517,231 for 74 grants (high: $500,000; low: $1,000; average: $1,000-$50,000).
Purpose and activities: Support for agricultural research and preservation of farmland, higher education, nutritional research, conservation, and environmental activities.
Types of support: Research.
Limitations: No grants to individuals, or for scholarships or overhead expenses; no loans.
Application information: Application form required.
Initial approach: Letter and proposal
Copies of proposal: 1
Board meeting date(s): As required
Final notification: Sept. 1

Directors: Jean W. Douglas, Henry B. Wallace, Robert B. Wallace.
Number of staff: 3
Employer Identification Number: 136162575

5346
DeWitt Wallace-Reader's Digest Fund, Inc. ▼
(Formerly DeWitt Wallace Fund, Inc.)
261 Madison Ave., 24th Fl.
New York 10016 (212) 953-1201
FAX: (212) 953-1279

Incorporated in 1965 in NY.
Donor(s): DeWitt Wallace.†
Foundation type: Independent
Financial data (yr. ended 12/31/89): Assets, $697,122,307 (M); expenditures, $19,277,844, including $17,754,259 for grants.
Purpose and activities: The fund is primarily interested in the improvement of public education (K through 12), including programs for teacher development and training, minorities, and libraries; giving also for youth leadership development, using employment training and the exploration of career options and programs which provide opportunities for community service.
Types of support: Operating budgets, continuing support, internships, scholarship funds, special projects.
Limitations: No support for public television, film, or media projects; colleges and universities; local chapters of national organizations; religious, fraternal, or veterans' organizations; government and public policy organizations; or private foundations. No grants to individuals, or for annual campaigns, endowments, emergency or capital funds, deficit financing, or scholarly research; no loans.
Publications: Annual report (including application guidelines), application guidelines.
Application information: A significant number of projects are initiated by the fund. Application form not required.
Initial approach: Letter (no more than 3 pages)
Copies of proposal: 1
Deadline(s): None
Board meeting date(s): 3 to 4 times per year
Final notification: 12 weeks
Write: Donna V. Dunlop, Prog. Dir.
Officers and Directors:* George V. Grune,* Chair.; M. Christine DeVita, Pres.; Donald C. Platten,* Secy.; Rob D. Nagel, Treas.; William G. Bowen, Theodore F. Brophy, Kenneth O. Gilmore, J. Edward Hall, Melvin R. Laird, Laurance S. Rockefeller.
Number of staff: 10 full-time professional; 5 full-time support.
Employer Identification Number: 136183757

5347
Lila Wallace-Reader's Digest Fund, Inc. ▼
(Formerly L.A.W. Fund, Inc.)
261 Madison Ave., 24th Fl.
New York 10016 (212) 953-1200
FAX: (212) 953-1279

Incorporated in 1956 in NY.
Donor(s): Lila Acheson Wallace.†
Foundation type: Independent
Financial data (yr. ended 12/31/89): Assets, $527,739,800 (M); expenditures, $12,474,984, including $11,086,288 for grants (average: $20,000-$60,000).
Purpose and activities: The fund promotes the arts through projects of national or regional impact in the performing, visual, and literary arts that target the following goals: audience development, outreach, or education; creation or presentation of new work; revival and reinterpretation of masterworks; and professional development of talented emerging artists.
Types of support: Operating budgets, continuing support, special projects, general purposes.
Limitations: Giving primarily in New York, NY, and the Northeast; some support for national programs. No support for health and medical services or research; child or social welfare programs or projects serving special populations; conservation or environmental programs; historic preservation; colleges and universities; religious, fraternal, or veterans' organizations; government and public policy organizations; or private foundations. No grants to individuals, or for annual campaigns, building or endowment funds, capital purposes, or scholarly research.
Publications: Annual report (including application guidelines), application guidelines.
Application information: Funds largely committed; most new projects initiated by the fund; proposals considered for funding from only 1 Wallace Fund per year. Application form not required.
Initial approach: Letter (no more than 3 pages)
Copies of proposal: 1
Deadline(s): None
Board meeting date(s): 3 to 4 times a year
Final notification: 12 weeks
Write: Jessica Chao, Prog. Officer, Arts and Culture
Officers and Directors:* George V. Grune,* Chair.; M. Christine DeVita, Pres.; Donald C. Platten,* Secy.; Rob D. Nagel, Treas.; William G. Bowen, Theodore F. Brophy, Kenneth O. Gilmore, J. Edward Hall, Melvin R. Laird, Laurance S. Rockefeller.
Number of staff: 9 full-time professional; 5 full-time support.
Employer Identification Number: 136086859

5348
Miriam G. and Ira D. Wallach Foundation ⌑
100 Park Ave.
New York 10017

Incorporated in 1956 in NY.
Foundation type: Independent
Financial data (yr. ended 10/31/88): Assets, $13,244,061 (M); expenditures, $1,495,173, including $1,278,939 for 91 grants (high: $200,300; low: $100).
Purpose and activities: Support primarily for higher education, and international relations, including peace; support also for social services, Jewish organizations, and cultural programs.
Limitations: Giving primarily in NY.
Application information: Contributes only to pre-selected organizations. Applications not accepted.
Officers: Ira D. Wallach,* Pres.; Edgar Wachenheim III,* V.P.; James G. Wallach,* V.P.; Kenneth L. Wallach,* V.P.; Miriam G. Wallach,* V.P.; Peter C. Siegfried, Secy.; Benjamin Glowatz, Treas.
Directors:* Sue W. Wachenheim, Kate B. Wallach, Mary K. Wallach, Susan S. Wallach.
Employer Identification Number: 136101702

5349
The Marcus Wallenberg Foundation ⌑
c/o Sullivan & Cromwell
250 Park Ave.
New York 10177

Established in 1983 in NY.
Donor(s): National Union Electric Corp., The Tappan Co.
Foundation type: Independent
Financial data (yr. ended 3/31/87): Assets, $2,045,760 (M); gifts received, $205,000; expenditures, $142,477, including $119,500 for 11 grants to individuals (high: $15,000; low: $2,500).
Purpose and activities: Support for the enhancement of education in the fields of international enterprise and commerce.
Types of support: Student aid.
Application information:
Deadline(s): None
Officers: Peter Wallenberg,* Pres.; Henry Christensen III, V.P.; Johan Stalhand, Secy.; P. Henry Mueller, Treas.
Directors:* Russell E. Palmer, Nils Svenson.
Employer Identification Number: 133176307

5350
The Walters Family Foundation, Inc. ⌑ ☆
548 Manhasset Woods Rd.
Manhasset 11030

Established in 1960.
Foundation type: Independent
Financial data (yr. ended 12/31/88): Assets, $1,625,488 (M); expenditures, $111,140, including $106,500 for 5 grants (high: $80,000; low: $2,000).
Purpose and activities: Giving primarily for cancer research and treatment.
Types of support: Research.
Application information:
Deadline(s): None
Write: Bernard F. Walters, Pres.
Officers: Bernard F. Walters, Pres. and Treas.; Norma C. Walters, V.P.
Employer Identification Number: 136107423

5351
The Andy Warhol Foundation for the Visual Arts
22 East 33rd St.
New York 10016 (212) 683-6496

Established in 1987 in NY.
Donor(s): Andy Warhol.†
Foundation type: Independent
Financial data (yr. ended 04/30/88): Assets, $1,134,649 (M); gifts received, $1,135,650; expenditures, $50,912.

Purpose and activities: Giving for the arts and cultural activities, including music, theater, and dance; support also for education and conservation.
Types of support: Building funds, conferences and seminars, equipment, fellowships, general purposes, internships, matching funds, publications, renovation projects, research, special projects, technical assistance.
Publications: Grants list, informational brochure (including application guidelines).
Application information: Repeat-year funding is discouraged. Application form not required.
Initial approach: 1-2 page letter
Deadline(s): Jan. 15 and Aug. 15
Final notification: Apr. 30 and Oct. 31
Write: Emily Todd, Prog. Dir.
Officers: Frederick Hughes, Chair.; Archibald L. Gilles, Pres.; John Warhola, V.P.; Vincent Fremont, Secy.-Treas.
Number of staff: 4 full-time professional.
Employer Identification Number: 133410749

5352
Albert and Bessie Warner Fund ¤
c/o Joint Foundation Support
40 W. 20th St., 10th Fl.
New York 10011 (212) 661-4080

Trust established in 1955 in NY.
Foundation type: Independent
Financial data (yr. ended 12/31/88): Assets, $3,685,144 (M); expenditures, $192,695, including $145,358 for 40 grants (high: $12,000; low: $100).
Purpose and activities: Primary areas of giving include advancing civil rights and civil liberties; strengthening the movement toward peace and disarmament; empowering young people; and preserving the environment.
Limitations: Giving primarily in New York City and Suffolk County, NY. No grants to individuals, or for building or endowment funds.
Application information: Application form not required.
Initial approach: Letter
Deadline(s): None
Board meeting date(s): Feb., May, Aug., and Nov.
Write: Nanette Falkenberg
Trustees: Arthur J. Steel, Lewis M. Steel, Ruth M. Steel.
Number of staff: 1 part-time support.
Employer Identification Number: 136095213

5353
Riley J. and Lillian N. Warren and Beatrice W. Blanding Foundation ¤
Six Ford Ave.
Oneonta 13820 (607) 432-6720

Trust established in 1972 in NY.
Donor(s): Beatrice W. Blanding.
Foundation type: Independent
Financial data (yr. ended 12/31/87): Assets, $4,354,779 (L); expenditures, $230,902, including $179,750 for 24 grants (high: $75,000; low: $500).
Purpose and activities: Emphasis on higher and secondary education; support also for churches and civic affairs programs.
Limitations: Giving primarily in NY.
Application information:
Initial approach: Letter
Deadline(s): Nov. 1
Write: Henry L. Hulbert, Mgr.
Officer and Trustees: Henry L. Hulbert, Mgr.; Beatrice W. Blanding, Robert A. Harlem.
Employer Identification Number: 237203341

5354
Washington Square Fund
P.O. Box 7938, F.D.R. Station
New York 10150

Foundation type: Independent
Financial data (yr. ended 09/30/88): Assets, $2,168,458 (M); expenditures, $131,186, including $95,180 for 7 grants (high: $30,000; low: $4,680).
Purpose and activities: Grants for child welfare, youth agencies, and families, including welfare and social programs, education about health, teenage pregnancy prevention, guidance of troubled teenagers, and family planning and counseling; preference is for pilot and special projects, usually of two-to-three years duration.
Types of support: Seed money, special projects.
Limitations: Giving limited to New York, NY. No grants to individuals, or for operating funds.
Application information:
Initial approach: Letter or proposal
Deadline(s): None
Write: L. Kirk Payne, Pres.
Officers: L. Kirk Payne, Pres.; Theresa R. Schaff, V.P.; Louise Chinn, Secy.; Susan J. Baisley, Treas.
Directors: James D. Johnson, Mrs. James D. Johnson, Margo Lynden, William Taggart, Theresa Thompson, Jeff Wallis.
Employer Identification Number: 131624213

5355
The Wasily Family Foundation, Inc. ¤ ☆
c/o Chemical Bank
30 Rockefeller Plaza, 60th Fl.
New York 10112

Established in 1988 in NY.
Donor(s): Anne Wasily, H. Vira Kolisch.
Foundation type: Independent
Financial data (yr. ended 06/30/89): Assets, $1,156,582 (M); expenditures, $2,839.
Purpose and activities: Initial year of operation, fiscal 1989; no grants awarded.
Application information:
Initial approach: Letter
Deadline(s): None
Write: Patrick N. Moloney, Secy.-Treas.
Officers: Anne Wasily, Pres.; H. Vira Kolisch, V.P.; Patrick N. Moloney, Secy.-Treas.
Employer Identification Number: 133503227

5356
The David Wasserman Foundation, Inc. ¤
107 Division St.
Amsterdam 12010 (518) 843-2800

Incorporated in 1953 in NY.
Donor(s): David Wasserman.†
Foundation type: Independent
Financial data (yr. ended 2/29/88): Assets, $1,323,238 (M); expenditures, $113,991, including $85,750 for 3 grants (high: $65,000; low: $750).
Purpose and activities: Grants for scientific, educational, and charitable purposes, including a scholarship fund.
Types of support: Building funds, equipment, general purposes, special projects.
Limitations: Giving limited to Montgomery County, NY. No grants for operating budgets.
Publications: 990-PF.
Application information: Application form not required.
Initial approach: Letter
Copies of proposal: 1
Deadline(s): Submit proposal preferably in Jan.
Board meeting date(s): Monthly
Write: Norbert J. Sherbunt, Pres.
Officers and Directors: Norbert J. Sherbunt, Pres. and Treas.; Judith M. Sherbunt, V.P. and Secy.; Peter W. Hosner.
Number of staff: 1 part-time professional; 1 part-time support.
Employer Identification Number: 237183522

5357
Lucius P. Wasserman Foundation, Inc. ¤
c/o Greenberg & Kamras
855 Ave. of the Americas
New York 10001

Incorporated in 1951 in NY.
Donor(s): L.P. Wasserman,† and others.
Foundation type: Independent
Financial data (yr. ended 12/31/86): Assets, $2,169,797 (M); expenditures, $121,716, including $110,280 for 62 grants (high: $20,050; low: $100).
Purpose and activities: Emphasis on higher and secondary education, Jewish welfare funds, hospitals, and social agencies.
Limitations: Giving primarily in NY. No grants to individuals, or for building or endowment funds, operating budgets, or special projects.
Application information:
Initial approach: Letter
Board meeting date(s): As required
Officers and Trustees:* Peter Wasserman,* Pres.; Judith Soley,* V.P.; Robert Soley, V.P.; Judith Wasserman, V.P.; Bernard A. Green,* Secy.; J.S. Chinitz, Treas.
Employer Identification Number: 136098895

5358
Abraham Wassner & Sons Foundation, Inc. ¤
c/o Berlack, Israels & Liberman
1155 Ave. of the Americas
New York 10036

Established in 1981 in NY.
Foundation type: Independent
Financial data (yr. ended 12/31/88): Assets, $716,278 (M); expenditures, $104,907, including $103,350 for 32 grants (high: $24,000; low: $260).
Purpose and activities: Support primarily for Jewish giving.

Application information: Contributes only to pre-selected organizations. Applications not accepted.
Officers and Directors:* I. Robert Wassner,* Pres.; Diane Wassner,* Secy.
Employer Identification Number: 136219360

5359
Waterfowl Research Foundation, Inc. ⌘
c/o Wood, Struthers & Winthrop
P.O. Box 18
New York 10005

Established in 1955 in NY.
Donor(s): M.E. Davis.†
Foundation type: Independent
Financial data (yr. ended 12/31/87): Assets, $5,783,384 (M); gifts received, $5,000; expenditures, $339,230, including $300,000 for 1 grant.
Purpose and activities: To preserve waterfowl; support primarily for a wetland preservation program.
Application information: Contributes only to pre-selected organizations. Applications not accepted.
Officers and Directors: Henry E. Coe III, Chair.; Edison I. Gaylord, Pres.; Carroll L. Wainwright, Jr., V.P. and Secy.; Robert Winthrop, Treas.; and 10 other directors.
Employer Identification Number: 136122167

5360
Jacques Weber Foundation, Inc. ☆
1460 Broadway
New York 10036 (717) 784-7701
Application address: P.O. Box 420, Bloomsburg, PA 17815

Established in 1948.
Foundation type: Independent
Financial data (yr. ended 09/30/89): Assets, $1,295,707 (M); gifts received, $4,212; expenditures, $59,154, including $50,702 for 18 grants to individuals (high: $5,735; low: $1,848).
Purpose and activities: Primarily awards scholarships for textile studies; minor support for higher education, civic affairs, and a community fund.
Types of support: Student aid.
Limitations: Giving primarily in Abbeville, SC, and within a 70-mile radius of Bloomsburg, PA.
Application information: Completion of application form required for scholarships.
Deadline(s): Scholarship applications accepted from Aug. to Nov. 30
Write: Martin A. Satz, Chair., Scholarship Committee
Officers and Trustees:* Boyd F. Buckingham,* Pres.; John D. Griffith,* V.P.; James P. Marion, Jr.,* Secy.-Treas.; Gordon C. Boop, Lester Jones, Martin A. Satz, Ph.D.
Employer Identification Number: 136101161

5361
Frank Weeden Foundation
11 Broadway
New York 10004 (212) 344-8470

Established about 1963 in CA.
Donor(s): Frank Weeden,† Alan N. Weeden, Donald E. Weeden, John D. Weeden, William F. Weeden, M.D.
Foundation type: Independent
Financial data (yr. ended 06/30/89): Assets, $21,633,085 (M); expenditures, $950,117, including $810,000 for 42 grants (high: $100,000; low: $500; average: $10,000-$20,000).
Purpose and activities: Giving primarily to environmental organizations working to insure species diversity, and organizations working to keep population within the limits of the world's resources to sustain them.
Types of support: General purposes, land acquisition.
Limitations: No grants to individuals.
Publications: Annual report.
Application information: Application form not required.
Initial approach: Letter
Copies of proposal: 1
Deadline(s): None
Board meeting date(s): Mar., June, Sept., and Dec.
Write: Alan N. Weeden, Pres.
Officers and Directors: Alan N. Weeden, Pres.; William F. Weeden, V.P.; John D. Weeden, Secy.-Treas.; Donald E. Weeden.
Number of staff: 1 part-time support.
Employer Identification Number: 946109313

5362
The Weezie Foundation ⌘
c/o Morgan Guaranty Trust Co. of New York
616 Madison Ave.
New York 10153 (212) 826-7717

Trust established in 1961 in NY.
Donor(s): Adelaide T. Corbett.†
Foundation type: Independent
Financial data (yr. ended 12/31/87): Assets, $12,309,317 (M); expenditures, $478,342, including $349,500 for 19 grants (high: $50,000; low: $5,000).
Purpose and activities: Support for education, hospitals, the handicapped and youth agencies.
Limitations: Giving primarily in MA and New York, NY.
Application information:
Initial approach: Letter
Deadline(s): None
Write: Robert Schwecherl, Secy.
Officer and Trustees: Robert Schwecherl, Secy.-Treas.; Morgan Guaranty Trust Co. of New York.
Advisory Committee: D. Nelson Adams, Adelrick Benziger, Jr., James F. Dolan, Mrs. George F. Fiske, Jr., Mrs. William H. Hays III, Charles H. Thieriot.
Employer Identification Number: 136090903

5363
The Louis A. Wehle Foundation
445 St. Paul St.
Rochester 14605

Established in 1952 in NY.
Donor(s): Genesee Brewing Co., Inc.
Foundation type: Independent
Financial data (yr. ended 04/30/89): Assets, $695,465 (M); gifts received, $50,000; expenditures, $119,331, including $114,216 for 21 grants (high: $58,433; low: $50).
Purpose and activities: Grants primarily for social services, a community fund, culture, and higher and other education.
Types of support: General purposes, building funds, annual campaigns, capital campaigns, continuing support, equipment, operating budgets.
Limitations: Giving primarily in the greater Rochester, NY, area. No grants to individuals.
Application information: Application form not required.
Initial approach: Proposal
Copies of proposal: 1
Deadline(s): None
Board meeting date(s): As required
Final notification: Following board meeting
Write: John L. Wehle, Jr., Trustee
Trustees: John L. Wehle, Sr., John L. Wehle, Jr., Marjorie S. Wehle, Robert G. Wehle.
Number of staff: None.
Employer Identification Number: 166027209

5364
The Weight Watchers Foundation, Inc. ⌘
Jericho Atrium
500 North Broadway
Jericho 11753 (516) 939-0400

Incorporated in 1968 in NY.
Donor(s): Weight Watchers International, Inc.
Foundation type: Company-sponsored
Financial data (yr. ended 12/31/88): Assets, $42,463 (M); gifts received, $137,259; expenditures, $116,743, including $116,731 for 22 grants (high: $15,000; low: $4,375).
Purpose and activities: For research into the causes and control of obesity; grants to higher educational institutions and hospitals for medical research and conferences on obesity.
Types of support: Conferences and seminars, research.
Limitations: No grants to individuals, or for general support, building or endowment funds, scholarships, fellowships, matching gifts, overhead, or travel funds; no loans.
Publications: Annual report, application guidelines.
Application information:
Write: W. Henry Sebrell, Exec. Dir.
Officer: W. Henry Sebrell, Exec. Dir.
Directors: Albert Lippert, Chair.; Charles M. Berger, Robert Birnhak, Lester Fein, Barbara Ecker Gordon, Robert Machiz, Les G. Parducci, Richard Patton.
Employer Identification Number: 112165046

5365
Weil Gotshal & Manges Foundation, Inc. ▼ ⌘
767 Fifth Ave.
New York 10153 (212) 310-8000

Established in 1983 in New York.
Donor(s): Robert Todd Lang, Ira M. Millstein, Harvey R. Miller.
Foundation type: Independent
Financial data (yr. ended 12/31/88): Assets, $2,346,938 (M); gifts received, $1,500,000; expenditures, $1,070,727, including

$1,067,655 for 75 grants (high: $432,200; low: $50; average: $200-$10,000).
Purpose and activities: Giving primarily for Jewish welfare organizations; support also for public interest organizations and community funds.
Limitations: Giving primarily in NY.
Application information:
Deadline(s): Nov. 1
Write: Jesse D. Wolff, Treas.
Officers and Directors:* Robert Todd Lang,* Chair.; Ira M. Millstein,* Pres.; Harvey R. Miller,* Secy.; Jesse D. Wolff,* Treas.
Employer Identification Number: 133158325

5366
F. Weiler Charity Fund ¤
1114 Ave. of the Americas, Suite 3400
New York 10036

Trust established in 1946 in NY.
Donor(s): Weiler family and associates.
Foundation type: Independent
Financial data (yr. ended 12/31/88): Assets, $1,647,848 (M); expenditures, $255,948, including $230,700 for 109 grants (high: $30,000; low: $50).
Purpose and activities: Support primarily for Jewish welfare and for Jewish giving.
Limitations: Giving primarily in NY. No grants to individuals.
Application information: Contributes only to pre-selected organizations. Applications not accepted.
Write: Jack D. Weiler, Trustee
Trustees: Robert H. Arnow, Alan G. Weiler, Jack D. Weiler.
Employer Identification Number: 136161247

5367
Theodore & Renee Weiler Foundation, Inc. ¤
24 Rock St.
Brooklyn 11206

Established in 1965 in NY.
Donor(s): Theodore R. Weiler.
Foundation type: Independent
Financial data (yr. ended 12/31/88): Assets, $3,922,765 (M); gifts received, $2,087,099; expenditures, $156,659, including $144,810 for 83 grants (high: $24,150; low: $60).
Purpose and activities: Grants for Jewish giving, culture, education, and health and social services.
Limitations: Giving primarily in New York, NY, and Palm Beach, FL. No grants to individuals.
Application information: Contributes only to pre-selected organizations. Applications not accepted.
Officers: Alan Safir, Pres.; Richard Kandel, Secy.-Treas.
Employer Identification Number: 136181441

5368
Sanford I. Weill Charitable Foundation, Inc. ¤
65 East 55th St.
New York 10022 (212) 891-8878

Donor(s): Sanford I. Weill.
Foundation type: Independent
Financial data (yr. ended 12/31/88): Assets, $1,105,823 (M); expenditures, $27,851, including $23,950 for 12 grants (high: $15,000; low: $100).
Purpose and activities: Support for culture, education, social services, and the aged.
Limitations: Giving primarily in NY.
Application information: Application form required.
Initial approach: Proposal
Deadline(s): None
Write: Sanford I. Weill, Pres.
Officers: Sanford I. Weill, Pres.; Kenneth J. Bailkin, Mgr.; Joan H. Weill, Mgr.
Employer Identification Number: 136223609

5369
Kurt Weill Foundation for Music, Inc. ¤
Seven East 20th St.
New York 10003 (212) 505-5240
Application address: 142 West End Ave., Suite 1R, New York, NY 10023

Established in 1962.
Donor(s): Lotte Lenya.†
Foundation type: Operating
Financial data (yr. ended 12/31/88): Assets, $2,210,773 (M); expenditures, $405,913, including $18,165 for 9 grants (high: $6,500; low: $450) and $109,111 for foundation-administered programs.
Purpose and activities: A private operating foundation; programs include maintenance of archives and research center and production consultation. Awards grants to organizations and individuals for projects "intended to promote greater understanding of the artistic legacies of Kurt Weill or Lotte Lenya."
Types of support: Research, publications, fellowships, grants to individuals, special projects.
Publications: Informational brochure (including application guidelines), newsletter.
Application information: Application form required.
Initial approach: Proposal
Copies of proposal: 1
Deadline(s): Nov. 15
Final notification: Feb. 1
Write: David Farneth, Dir., Prog.
Officers and Trustees:* Kim Kowalke,* Pres.; Henry Marx,* V.P.; Lys Symonette,* V.P.; Guy Stern,* Secy.; Milton Coleman,* Treas.; Harold Prince, Julius Rudel.
Number of staff: 4 full-time professional; 2 full-time support; 1 part-time support.
Employer Identification Number: 136139518

5370
Monique Weill-Caulier Trust ¤
c/o Weil, Gotshal & Manges
767 Fifth Ave.
New York 10153

Established in 1981 in NY.
Foundation type: Independent
Financial data (yr. ended 10/31/88): Assets, $1,773,962 (M); expenditures, $142,700, including $120,000 for 5 grants (high: $40,000; low: $6,667).
Purpose and activities: Grants to medical schools, a university, and a hospital.
Limitations: Giving primarily in NY. No grants to individuals.
Application information: Contributes only to pre-selected organizations. Applications not accepted.
Trustees: Robert Todd Lang, John M. Lewis.
Employer Identification Number: 133020092

5371
Harold M. & Anna M. Weinberg Family Foundation, Inc.
25 Robert Pitt Dr.
Monsey 10952

Established in 1956 in NY.
Donor(s): Edward Weinberg, James Weinberg.
Foundation type: Independent
Financial data (yr. ended 12/31/87): Assets, $85,246 (M); gifts received, $68,000; expenditures, $120,625, including $119,355 for 91 grants (high: $72,500; low: $10).
Purpose and activities: Support primarily for Jewish welfare; some support for cultural programs and health.
Limitations: No grants to individuals.
Application information: Contributes only to pre-selected charitable organizations. Applications not accepted.
Officers: James Weinberg, Pres.; Edward Weinberg, Treas.
Employer Identification Number: 136160074

5372
The John L. Weinberg Foundation
c/o Goldman, Sachs & Co.
85 Broad St., 22nd Fl.
New York 10004

Trust established in 1959 in NY.
Donor(s): John L. Weinberg.
Foundation type: Independent
Financial data (yr. ended 4/30/89): Assets, $13,896,706 (M); gifts received, $1,150,001; expenditures, $587,059, including $561,251 for 111 grants (high: $200,000; low: $15).
Purpose and activities: Emphasis on hospitals, medical research, secondary and higher education, and Jewish welfare funds.
Types of support: Annual campaigns, operating budgets, professorships, program-related investments, renovation projects, research.
Limitations: Giving primarily in New York, NY, and Greenwich, CT. No grants to individuals.
Application information: Applications not accepted.
Trustees: Arthur G. Altschul, Jean H. Weinberg, John L. Weinberg, John S. Weinberg, Sue Ann Weinberg.
Employer Identification Number: 136028813

5373
Louis Weinberg Foundation, Inc. ¤ ☆
c/o Marine Midland Bank, N.A.
P.O. Box 4203, 17th Fl.
Buffalo 14240

Established in 1964.
Foundation type: Independent
Financial data (yr. ended 12/31/88): Assets, $1,030,478 (M); expenditures, $48,625, including $44,500 for 51 grants (high: $10,000; low: $10).

Purpose and activities: Giving for Jewish welfare and religious organizations and social services.
Limitations: No grants to individuals.
Application information: Contributes only to pre-selected organizations. Applications not accepted.
Officers and Trustees: Cecelia Weinberg, Pres.; Henry Dolgin, V.P.; William M. Connors, Secy.-Treas.; Marine Midland Bank, N.A.
Employer Identification Number: 146030952

5374
Sidney J. Weinberg, Jr. Foundation
c/o Goldman, Sachs & Co.
85 Broad St., Tax Dept., 30th Fl.
New York 10004

Established in 1979 in NY.
Donor(s): Sidney J. Weinberg, Jr.
Foundation type: Independent
Financial data (yr. ended 05/31/89): Assets, $9,977,343 (M); gifts received, $2,106,720; expenditures, $685,676, including $685,553 for 77 grants (high: $250,000; low: $50).
Purpose and activities: Grants primarily for hospitals and higher education.
Types of support: General purposes.
Limitations: Giving primarily in the eastern U.S., especially New York, NY. No grants to individuals.
Application information: Contributes only to pre-selected organizations. Applications not accepted.
Trustees: Elizabeth W. Smith, Peter A. Weinberg, Sidney J. Weinberg, Jr., Sydney H. Weinberg.
Number of staff: None.
Employer Identification Number: 132998603

5375
The Richard and Gertrude Weininger Foundation, Inc. ⌘ ☆
c/o Stroock & Stroock & Lavan
Seven Hanover Sq.
New York 10004

Established in 1982.
Donor(s): Gertrude Weininger.†
Foundation type: Independent
Financial data (yr. ended 11/30/88): Assets, $2,575,684 (M); gifts received, $182,246; expenditures, $115,545, including $67,600 for 5 grants (high: $30,000; low: $5,000).
Purpose and activities: Support primarily for Jewish giving and welfare.
Application information:
Initial approach: Letter
Deadline(s): None
Write: Peter Simon, Pres.
Officers: Peter Simon, Pres.; William A. Perlmuth, V.P. and Secy.; T.J. Stevenson, Jr., V.P. and Treas.
Employer Identification Number: 132362019

5376
The Alex J. Weinstein Foundation, Inc. ⌘
c/o Herbert Feinberg
60 Cutter Mill Rd., No. 504
Great Neck 11021

Established in 1953.
Foundation type: Independent
Financial data (yr. ended 11/30/88): Assets, $2,028,841 (M); expenditures, $93,925, including $84,650 for 23 grants (high: $25,000; low: $150).
Purpose and activities: Support largely for hospitals, higher education, Jewish giving, and museums and the performing arts.
Limitations: No grants to individuals.
Application information: Contributes only to pre-selected organizations. Applications not accepted.
Trustees and Directors: Herbert D. Feinberg, Barrie W. Selesko.
Employer Identification Number: 136160964

5377
J. Weinstein Foundation, Inc. ⌘
Rockridge Farm, Route 52
Carmel 10512

Incorporated in 1948 in NY.
Donor(s): Joe Weinstein,† J.W. Mays, Inc., and others.
Foundation type: Independent
Financial data (yr. ended 12/31/88): Assets, $3,365,489 (M); gifts received, $35,000; expenditures, $176,586, including $160,084 for 62 grants (high: $52,500; low: $15).
Purpose and activities: Support for higher education in the U.S. and Israel, temple support, hospitals, and Jewish welfare funds.
Types of support: Continuing support, endowment funds, general purposes.
Limitations: Giving primarily in NY.
Application information: Contributes only to pre-selected organizations. Applications not accepted.
Officers and Directors:* Max L. Shulman,* Pres.; Lloyd J. Shulman,* V.P.; Sylvia W. Shulman,* V.P.; Melvin M. Kazdin,* Secy.
Employer Identification Number: 116003595

5378
The Stephen and Suzanne Weiss Foundation ⌘ ☆
One New York Plaza
New York 10004

Established in 1986 in NY.
Donor(s): Stephen Weiss.
Foundation type: Independent
Financial data (yr. ended 12/31/88): Assets, $2,504,686 (M); gifts received, $370,000; expenditures, $180,788, including $163,995 for 65 grants (high: $25,000; low: $25).
Purpose and activities: Giving for secondary education; support also for hospitals, health associations, medical research, culture, and Jewish organizations.
Limitations: Giving primarily in New York, NY. No grants to individuals.
Application information: Contributes only to pre-selected organizations. Applications not accepted.
Officers: Stephen Weiss, Pres.; Suzanne Weiss, V.P.; Roger J. Weiss, Secy.-Treas.
Employer Identification Number: 133384021

5379
Paul M. Weissman Family Foundation, Inc. ⌘
c/o Oppenheim, Appel, Dixon & Co.
Two Oxford Rd.
White Plains 10605

Established in 1969 in NY.
Donor(s): Paul M. Weissman.
Foundation type: Independent
Financial data (yr. ended 2/28/88): Assets, $1,598,383 (M); expenditures, $72,355, including $67,459 for 75 grants (high: $25,000; low: $20).
Purpose and activities: Support primarily for Jewish organizations; giving also to private schools and universities, health and social services, and child welfare associations.
Limitations: Giving primarily in NY. No grants to individuals.
Application information: Contributes only to pre-selected organizations. Applications not accepted.
Officers and Directors: Paul M. Weissman, Pres. and Treas.; Harriet L. Weissman, V.P.; Robert M. Dubrow, Secy.; Richard M. Sanuier.
Employer Identification Number: 237049744

5380
Wellington Foundation, Inc. ⌘
14 Wall St., Suite 1702
New York 10005

Incorporated in 1955 in NY.
Donor(s): Herbert G. Wellington,† Herbert G. Wellington, Jr., Elizabeth D. Wellington.†
Foundation type: Independent
Financial data (yr. ended 12/31/88): Assets, $1,617,386 (M); expenditures, $300,800, including $297,000 for 22 grants (high: $100,000; low: $1,000).
Purpose and activities: To support recognized medical, educational, and cultural programs.
Limitations: Giving primarily in the greater New York, NY, metropolitan area. No grants to individuals.
Application information: Contributes only to pre-selected organizations. Applications not accepted.
Officers and Directors: Herbert G. Wellington, Jr., Pres. and Treas.; Patricia B. Wellington, V.P.; Thomas D. Wellington, Secy.
Employer Identification Number: 136110175

5381
The Margaret L. Wendt Foundation ⌘
1325 Liberty Bldg.
Buffalo 14202 (716) 855-2146

Trust established in 1956 in NY.
Donor(s): Margaret L. Wendt.†
Foundation type: Independent
Financial data (yr. ended 1/31/87): Assets, $41,280,939 (M); expenditures, $1,474,839, including $970,031 for 71 grants (high: $80,000; low: $200; average: $5,000-$15,000).
Purpose and activities: Emphasis on education, the arts, and social services; support also for churches and religious organizations, health associations, public interest organizations, and youth agencies.
Limitations: Giving primarily in Buffalo and western NY. No grants to individuals, or for scholarships.

Application information: Application form not required.
Initial approach: Letter
Copies of proposal: 4
Deadline(s): 1 month prior to board meeting
Board meeting date(s): Quarterly; no fixed dates
Final notification: Usually 4 to 6 months
Write: Robert J. Kresse, Secy.
Officers and Trustees: Ralph W. Loew, Chair.; Robert J. Kresse, Secy.; Thomas D. Lunt.
Number of staff: 1 part-time support.
Employer Identification Number: 166030037

5382
Wenner-Gren Foundation for Anthropological Research, Inc.
220 Fifth Ave., 16th Fl.
New York 10003 (212) 683-5000

Incorporated in 1941 in DE.
Donor(s): Axel L. Wenner-Gren.†
Foundation type: Operating
Financial data (yr. ended 12/31/89): Assets, $58,240,414 (M); expenditures, $3,235,910, including $899,459 for 149 grants to individuals and $1,475,756 for 4 foundation-administered programs.
Purpose and activities: A private operating foundation; international support of research in all branches of anthropology including cultural/social anthropology, ethnology, biological/physical anthropology, archeology, and anthropological linguistics, and in closely related disciplines so far as they pertain to human origins, development, and variation; grants-in-aid for programs of research; subsidizes conferences for anthropologists to promote reporting on results of research; publishes a journal and provides clearinghouse services for anthropological information.
Types of support: Research, conferences and seminars, seed money, publications, fellowships, grants to individuals.
Limitations: No support for intermediary funding agencies, non-project personnel, or institutional overhead or support. No grants for salaries or fringe benefits, tuition or travel to meetings; low priority given to dissertation writeup or revision, publication subvention, or filmmaking.
Publications: Annual report, program policy statement, application guidelines.
Application information: Contact foundation for most recent information.
Initial approach: Request application form for Small Grants Program; letter for all other programs
Copies of proposal: 5
Deadline(s): May 1 and Nov. 1 for Small Grants Program; no set deadline for other programs
Board meeting date(s): Oct. and Apr.
Final notification: Approximately 6 months after deadline
Write: Dr. Sydel Silverman, Pres.
Officers: Harold C. Martin,* Chair.; Richard Scheuch,* Vice-Chair.; Dr. Sydel Silverman, Pres.; Hiram F. Moody, Jr.,* Treas.
Trustees:* Nancy Bekavac, David L. Brigham, George Brockway, Marilyn Goldstein Fedak, Robert Garrett, Dr. Frank Wadsworth.
Number of staff: 3 full-time professional; 9 full-time support; 2 part-time support.
Employer Identification Number: 131813827

5383
Nina W. Werblow Charitable Trust ⌑
c/o Ehrenkranz, Ehrenkranz and Schultz
375 Park Ave.
New York 10152 (212) 751-5959

Trust established in NY.
Donor(s): Nina W. Werblow.†
Foundation type: Independent
Financial data (yr. ended 2/28/89): Assets, $4,758,674 (M); expenditures, $289,694, including $215,000 for 52 grants (high: $25,000; low: $1,000).
Purpose and activities: Giving for hospitals, Jewish welfare organizations, higher education, social service agencies, and cultural programs.
Limitations: Giving limited to New York, NY.
Application information:
Initial approach: Letter
Deadline(s): Sept. 30
Write: Roger A. Goldman, Esq., Trustee
Trustees: Lillian Ahrens Carver, Joel S. Ehrenkranz, Roger A. Goldman.
Employer Identification Number: 136742999

5384
Westchester Health Fund
3010 Westchester Ave.
Purchase 10577-2524 (914) 939-3879

Established in 1969 in NY New York.
Foundation type: Independent
Financial data (yr. ended 12/31/89): Assets, $2,074,186 (M); expenditures, $121,569, including $75,373 for grants.
Purpose and activities: To support efforts to provide better health care for lower cost.
Types of support: Consulting services, special projects, program-related investments.
Limitations: Giving limited to Westchester County, NY. No grants for research projects, endowment funds, or building programs; no annual support.
Application information:
Initial approach: Telephone or letter
Deadline(s): None
Write: Harry L. Staley, Exec. Dir.
Officers: Ross Weale,* Chair.; Richard Finucane, M.D.,* Pres.; Harry L. Staley, Secy. and Exec. Dir.
Directors:* Sandra Brown, Steven Galef, S.J. Schulman, Ivan G. Seidenberg.
Number of staff: 1 part-time support.
Employer Identification Number: 237071929

5385
The Western New York Foundation
Main Seneca Bldg., Suite 1402
237 Main St.
Buffalo 14203 (716) 847-6440

Incorporated in 1951 in NY as The Wildroot Foundation; present name adopted in 1958.
Donor(s): Welles V. Moot.†
Foundation type: Independent
Financial data (yr. ended 07/31/89): Assets, $4,696,329 (M); expenditures, $260,455, including $195,731 for 17 grants (high: $50,000; low: $320; average: $10-$15,000).
Purpose and activities: Grants to nonprofit institutions, with emphasis on capital needs, seed funds for new projects, or expanding services. Support primarily for the performing arts, youth agencies, the natural sciences, and social service agencies.
Types of support: Seed money, building funds, equipment, land acquisition, endowment funds, special projects, publications, conferences and seminars, matching funds, loans, capital campaigns, renovation projects, technical assistance, emergency funds.
Limitations: Giving limited to the 8th Judicial District of NY (Erie, Niagara, Genesee, Wyoming, Allegany, Cattaraugus, and Chautauqua counties). No support for hospitals or religious organizations. No grants to individuals, or for scholarships, fellowships, or generally for operating budgets or deficit financing.
Publications: Annual report.
Application information: Application form required.
Initial approach: Letter (not more than 1 and 1/2 pages) from officer of applicant organization, not staff member
Copies of proposal: 2
Deadline(s): None
Board meeting date(s): 3 or 4 times a year
Final notification: 6 to 8 weeks
Write: Welles V. Moot, Jr., Pres.
Officers and Trustees:* Welles V. Moot, Jr.,* Pres.; Cecily M. Johnson,* V.P.; Robert S. Scheu,* V.P.; John R. Moot,* Secy.; Richard Moot,* Treas.; Karr Parker, Jr., John N. Walsh III.
Number of staff: 1 full-time professional.
Employer Identification Number: 160845962

5386
Westvaco Foundation Trust ▼
c/o Westvaco Corp.
299 Park Ave.
New York 10171 (212) 688-5000

Trust established in 1951 in NY.
Donor(s): Westvaco Corp.
Foundation type: Company-sponsored
Financial data (yr. ended 9/30/88): Assets, $262,955 (M); gifts received, $1,010,000; expenditures, $1,183,776, including $1,033,805 for 153 grants (high: $65,000; low: $473; average: $1,000-$25,000) and $148,146 for 747 employee matching gifts.
Purpose and activities: Support primarily for community funds, higher education, hospitals, and a cancer center; also matches employee gifts to educational institutions.
Types of support: Employee matching gifts.
Limitations: Giving primarily in areas of plant operations. No grants to individuals, or in-kind gifts.
Publications: Multi-year report.
Application information: Contributions initiated primarily by plant managers; unsolicited requests usually not granted.
Initial approach: Letter
Deadline(s): None
Write: Roger Holmes

Trustees: William S. Beaum, George E. Cruser, Irving Trust Co.
Number of staff: 1 part-time professional; 1 part-time support.
Employer Identification Number: 136021319

5387
Harry R. & Rita White Foundation, Inc. ⌑ ☆
c/o Samuel Rothstein & Co.
31 William Park Center
Farmingdale 11735

Established in 1976.
Foundation type: Operating
Financial data (yr. ended 11/30/88): Assets, $2,274,827 (M); expenditures, $48,404, including $10,000 for 1 grant and $10,938 for 2 grants to individuals (high: $7,000; low: $3,938).
Purpose and activities: A private operating foundation; giving for a cancer fund and grants to individuals for education.
Types of support: Student aid.
Officers and Directors: Harry R. White, Jr., Pres.; Rita White, Jr., V.P.; Karl White, Secy.; Kris White, Treas.; Samuel Rothstein, Joseph White.
Employer Identification Number: 132874801

5388
The Whitehead Foundation
65 East 55th St.
New York 10022 (212) 755-3131

Established in 1982 in NY.
Donor(s): John C. Whitehead Foundation.
Foundation type: Independent
Financial data (yr. ended 06/30/89): Assets, $17,320,926 (M); expenditures, $1,708,103, including $1,707,810 for 114 grants (high: $300,000; low: $25).
Purpose and activities: General categories of interest: international affairs, economic and public policy, the arts, and higher education.
Limitations: Giving primarily in NY.
Application information: Unsolicited proposals are rarely approved. Applications not accepted.
Write: Marcia Townley, Exec. Dir.
Trustees: Arthur G. Altschul, Anne W. Crawford, John L. Weinberg, John C. Whitehead, Gregory Whitehead, Nancy D. Whitehead.
Employer Identification Number: 133119344

5389
Mrs. Giles Whiting Foundation ▼
30 Rockefeller Plaza
New York 10112 (212) 698-2500

Incorporated in 1963 in NY.
Donor(s): Mrs. Giles Whiting.†
Foundation type: Independent
Financial data (yr. ended 11/30/89): Assets, $22,209,026 (M); expenditures, $1,453,770, including $814,600 for 10 grants (high: $315,000; low: $1,600; average: $25,000-$150,000) and $255,000 for 21 grants to individuals (high: $25,000; low: $5,000).
Purpose and activities: Grants only to seven graduate schools conducting programs of Whiting Fellowships in the Humanities. Support also for emerging writers through Whiting Writers' Awards.
Types of support: Fellowships, grants to individuals.
Limitations: No grants to individuals (except for Whiting Writers' Award program for which applications are not invited), or for general support, capital funds, matching gifts, research, special projects, publications, or conferences; no loans.
Publications: Multi-year report.
Application information: Funds fully committed. Applications not accepted.
Board meeting date(s): May and Nov.
Write: Robert H.M. Ferguson, Secy.
Officers: Robert M. Pennoyer,* Pres.; Mary St. John Douglas,* V.P.; Harry W. Havemeyer,* V.P.; Robert H.M. Ferguson, Secy.-Treas.
Trustees:* Robert L. Belknap.
Number of staff: 1 full-time professional; 2 part-time professional.
Employer Identification Number: 136154484

5390
The Helen Hay Whitney Foundation ▼ ⌑
450 East 63rd St.
New York 10021-7999 (212) 751-8228

Trust established in 1947; incorporated in 1951 in NY.
Donor(s): Mrs. Charles S. Payson.†
Foundation type: Independent
Financial data (yr. ended 6/30/88): Assets, $24,267,763 (M); gifts received, $25,000; expenditures, $1,382,623, including $1,071,616 for 65 grants to individuals (high: $21,584; low: $4,750).
Purpose and activities: To support beginning postdoctoral training in basic biomedical research through research fellowships for residents of the U.S., Canada, or Mexico who are under 35 years of age. Fellowships are awarded to individuals but funds are administered largely by research institutions. American citizenship is not required, but applications are not accepted from individuals or organizations outside North America.
Types of support: Fellowships.
Limitations: Giving limited to North America. No grants to individuals over 35 years of age.
Publications: Annual report, informational brochure (including application guidelines).
Application information: Application form required.
Initial approach: Letter or telephone
Copies of proposal: 7
Deadline(s): Submit proposal in Aug.; deadline Aug. 15
Board meeting date(s): Jan. and June
Final notification: 5 months
Write: Barbara M. Hugonnet, Admin. Dir.
Officers and Trustees: Mrs. Henry B. Middleton, Pres.; Maclyn McCarty, M.D., V.P. and Chair., Scientific Advisory Comm.; Thomas A. Melfe, Secy.; Sandra deRoulet, M.D., Treas.; Alexander G. Bearn, M.D., Charles L. Christian, M.D., Jerome Gross, M.D., Lisa A. Steiner, M.D., W. Perry Welch.
Number of staff: 1 full-time professional; 6 part-time professional; 1 part-time support.
Employer Identification Number: 131677403

5391
Julia A. Whitney Foundation
c/o Thomas P. Whitney, Dir.
46 Circular St.
Saratoga Springs 12866

Established in 1965 in NY.
Foundation type: Independent
Financial data (yr. ended 12/31/88): Assets, $1,733,324 (M); expenditures, $71,175, including $64,400 for 6 grants (high: $30,000; low: $1,000).
Purpose and activities: Grants primarily to foster appreciation and preservation of Russian language, literature, and art, including support for a library of Russian literature; support also for higher education.
Limitations: No grants to individuals.
Application information: Contributes only to pre-selected organizations. Applications not accepted.
Trustees: Harrison E. Salisbury, Marguerite C. Whitney, Thomas P. Whitney.
Employer Identification Number: 136192314

5392
Wallace S. Whittaker Foundation ⌑
c/o Buchbinder Stein Tunick & Platkin
One Penn Plaza
New York 10119

Established in 1957 in NY.
Donor(s): Wallace S. Whittaker.†
Foundation type: Independent
Financial data (yr. ended 12/31/86): Assets, $0 (M); gifts received, $5,713; expenditures, $387,361, including $373,984 for grants.
Purpose and activities: Support primarily for education.
Officers: John Howley, Pres.; V. Schackelford, V.P.; Howard Herzog, Secy.; Irwin Schumer, Treas.
Employer Identification Number: 136130941

5393
Lawrence A. Wien Foundation, Inc. ⌑
c/o Wien, Malkin & Bettex
60 East 42nd St.
New York 10165

Incorporated in 1953 in NY.
Donor(s): Lawrence A. Wien, Mae L. Wien, and others.
Foundation type: Independent
Financial data (yr. ended 6/30/87): Assets, $5,052,133 (M); expenditures, $1,529,988, including $1,516,020 for 275 grants (low: $100).
Purpose and activities: Grants primarily for higher education, Jewish religious and social organizations and welfare funds, cultural programs, and social services; support also for hospitals and health services.
Limitations: Giving primarily in New York, NY.
Application information:
Write: Lawrence A. Wien, Pres.
Officers and Directors: Lawrence A. Wien, Pres. and Treas.; Peter L. Malkin, Secy.; Isabel W. Malkin, Enid W. Morse, Lester S. Morse, Jr.
Employer Identification Number: 136095927

5394
Malcolm Hewitt Wiener Foundation, Inc. ⌑ ☆
1270 Ave. of the Americas, 11th Fl.
New York 10020

Incorporated in 1984 in NY.
Donor(s): Malcolm H. Wiener.
Foundation type: Independent
Financial data (yr. ended 12/31/88): Assets, $20,496,222 (M); gifts received, $139,294; expenditures, $1,239,923, including $1,110,493 for 41 grants (high: $260,000; low: $100).
Purpose and activities: Giving primarily for foreign relations and world peace; support also for museums, higher and other education, economic policy, archaeology, and child welfare.
Limitations: No grants to individuals.
Application information: Contributes only to pre-selected organizations. Applications not accepted.
Officers and Directors: Malcolm H. Wiener, Pres. and Treas.; Harvey Beker, V.P.; George Crapple, V.P.; Thomas R. Moore, Secy.; Martin J. Whitman.
Employer Identification Number: 133250321

5395
Barrie A. & Deedee Wigmore Foundation ⌑
c/o Goldman, Sachs & Co., 30th Fl.
85 Broad St.
New York 10004

Established in 1978 in New York.
Donor(s): Barrie A. Wigmore.
Foundation type: Independent
Financial data (yr. ended 3/31/89): Assets, $745,152 (M); expenditures, $197,598, including $195,725 for 72 grants (high: $50,000; low: $100).
Purpose and activities: Support for higher education, the performing arts, and museums and other cultural programs.
Limitations: Giving primarily in New York, NY. No grants to individuals.
Application information: Applications not accepted.
Trustees: Donald Lenz, Barrie A. Wigmore, Deedee Wigmore.
Employer Identification Number: 132967487

5396
The Wikstrom Foundation ⌑
c/o Norstar Trust Co.
One East Ave.
Rochester 14638 (315)4247-707

Established in 1960 in NY.
Donor(s): A.S. Wikstrom.†
Foundation type: Independent
Financial data (yr. ended 12/31/88): Assets, $1,703,304 (M); expenditures, $208,979, including $181,580 for grants (high: $50,000; average: $1,000-$20,000).
Purpose and activities: Grants primarily for cultural programs and higher education; support also for programs for the elderly and Roman Catholic organizations, including church support.
Types of support: Operating budgets, annual campaigns, building funds, equipment, endowment funds, matching funds, capital campaigns, conferences and seminars, continuing support, general purposes, publications, renovation projects, research, seed money, special projects.
Limitations: Giving limited to NY and FL. No grants to individuals; no loans.
Application information: Contributes only to pre-selected organizations. Applications not accepted.
Trustees: Robert J. Hughes, Jr., Norstar Trust Co.
Number of staff: None.
Employer Identification Number: 146014286

5397
Ralph Wilkins Foundation ⌑
222 Groton Ave.
Cortland 13045 (607) 756-7548
Mailing address: P.O. Box 628, Cortland, NY 13045-0628

Established in 1981 in NY.
Foundation type: Independent
Financial data (yr. ended 9/30/88): Assets, $1,603,091 (M); expenditures, $103,848, including $89,350 for 34 grants (high: $12,000; low: $100).
Purpose and activities: Support primarily for community funds, social services, recreational activities, and medical research.
Types of support: Building funds, scholarship funds, research, general purposes.
Limitations: Giving primarily in Cortland County, NY.
Application information:
Deadline(s): None
Write: John Kimmich, Pres.
Officers and Directors: John Kimmich, Pres.; Patricia K. Porter, V.P.; Harley M. Albro, Secy.-Treas.; Lawrence J. Dippold, Grant Van Sant.
Employer Identification Number: 161188525

5398
The Williams Family Philanthropic Foundation ⌑ ☆
1200 Shames Dr.
Westbury 11590

Established in 1986 in NY.
Donor(s): Jerry Williams.
Foundation type: Independent
Financial data (yr. ended 11/30/88): Assets, $662,313 (M); expenditures, $231,527, including $230,559 for 259 grants (high: $12,500; low: $10).
Purpose and activities: Support for Jewish organizations, including religious associations, schools, and welfare funds.
Application information: Contributes only to pre-selected organizations. Applications not accepted.
Officer: Jerry Williams, Pres.
Employer Identification Number: 112849607

5399
Dave H. & Reba W. Williams Foundation ⌑ ☆
1345 Ave. of the Americas, 38th Fl.
New York 10105 (212) 969-1026

Established in 1986 in NY.
Donor(s): Dave H. Williams, Reba W. Williams.
Foundation type: Independent
Financial data (yr. ended 6/30/89): Assets, $12,545 (M); gifts received, $115,000; expenditures, $112,801, including $110,699 for 40 grants (high: $40,475; low: $100).
Purpose and activities: Support primarily for museums and the arts.
Limitations: Giving primarily in New York, NY. No grants to individuals.
Application information:
Initial approach: Proposal
Deadline(s): None
Write: Dave H. Williams, Trustee
Trustees: Dave H. Williams, Reba W. Williams.
Employer Identification Number: 133381821

5400
Fred & Floy Willmott Foundation ⌑ ☆
c/o Marine Midland Bank
P.O. Box 4203
Buffalo 14240

Established in 1984 in NY.
Foundation type: Independent
Financial data (yr. ended 12/31/88): Assets, $4,417,882 (M); expenditures, $294,476, including $206,744 for 37 grants (high: $25,000; low: $50).
Purpose and activities: Giving primarily for Protestant churches and other religious organizations; support also for higher and other education and social services.
Limitations: Giving primarily in NY. No grants to individuals.
Application information: Contributes only to pre-selected organizations. Applications not accepted.
Trustees: George Cook, Rev. John D. Cooke, Marine Midland Bank, N.A.
Employer Identification Number: 222587484

5401
Elaine P. and Richard U. Wilson Foundation ⌑
c/o Chase Lincoln First Bank, N.A.
P.O. Box 1412
Rochester 14603

Established in 1963 in NY.
Donor(s): Katherine M. Wilson.†
Foundation type: Independent
Financial data (yr. ended 12/31/88): Assets, $5,305,459 (M); expenditures, $396,174, including $375,941 for 19 grants (high: $150,000; low: $500).
Purpose and activities: Emphasis on higher and secondary education, Protestant church support, cultural programs, and museums.
Limitations: Giving primarily in NY.
Application information: Contributes only to pre-selected organizations. Applications not accepted.
Trustee: Chase Lincoln First Bank, N.A.
Employer Identification Number: 166042023

5402
The H. W. Wilson Foundation, Inc. ⌑
950 University Ave.
Bronx 10452 (212) 588-8400

Incorporated in 1952 in NY.
Donor(s): H.W. Wilson,† Mrs. H.W. Wilson,† The H.W. Wilson Co., Inc.

Foundation type: Independent
Financial data (yr. ended 11/30/88): Assets, $5,792,743 (M); expenditures, $314,375, including $258,525 for 42 grants (high: $25,000; low: $2,000).
Purpose and activities: Grants largely to accredited library schools for scholarships; support also for cultural programs, including historical societies, and library associations.
Types of support: Research, scholarship funds.
Limitations: No grants for building or endowment funds or operating budgets.
Application information:
Initial approach: Letter
Copies of proposal: 1
Deadline(s): None
Board meeting date(s): Jan., Mar., May, July, and Oct.
Final notification: 3 months
Write: Leo M. Weins, Pres. or James Humphrey III, V.P.
Officers and Directors: Howard Haycraft, Chair.; Leo M. Weins, Pres. and Treas.; James Humphrey III, V.P.; William A. Ziegler, Secy.; Florence A. Arnold, Rutherford D. Rogers.
Employer Identification Number: 237418062

5403
Marie C. and Joseph C. Wilson Foundation
160 Allens Creek Rd.
Rochester 14618 (716) 461-4699

Trust established in 1963 in NY.
Donor(s): Katherine M. Wilson,† Joseph C. Wilson.†
Foundation type: Independent
Financial data (yr. ended 12/31/89): Assets, $11,138,459 (M); expenditures, $565,793, including $565,793 for 48 grants (high: $97,000; low: $100; average: $1,000-$25,000).
Purpose and activities: Giving primarily for social services, health and medical research, education, housing, and youth agencies; some support for the arts.
Types of support: Operating budgets, continuing support, annual campaigns, seed money, emergency funds, building funds, endowment funds, matching funds, internships, scholarship funds, fellowships, special projects, research, conferences and seminars.
Limitations: Giving primarily in Rochester, NY. No support for political organizations. No grants to individuals.
Publications: Annual report (including application guidelines).
Application information: Application form not required.
Initial approach: 1-page letter; submit full proposal only at request of foundation
Copies of proposal: 12
Deadline(s): 6 weeks before board meetings
Board meeting date(s): Feb., May, and Sept.; grants considered in Feb. and Sept. only
Final notification: 3 months
Write: Ruth H. Fleischmann, Exec. Dir.
Officer: Ruth H. Fleischmann, Exec. Dir.
Board of Managers: Katherine W. Roby, Chair.; Janet C. Wilson, Pres.; Joan W. Dalbey, R. Thomas Dalbey, Jr., Katherine Dalbey Ensign, Deirdre Wilson Garton, Breckenridge Kling, Judith W. Martin, Joseph R. Wilson.
Trustee: Chase Lincoln First Bank, N.A.
Number of staff: 1 part-time professional; 1 part-time support.
Employer Identification Number: 166042022

5404
Robert Wilson Foundation ⌑
990 Sixth Ave., No. 19G
New York 10018

Trust established in 1964 in NY.
Donor(s): Robert W. Wilson, Marillyn B. Wilson.
Foundation type: Independent
Financial data (yr. ended 12/31/87): Assets, $212,842 (L); expenditures, $318,053, including $299,045 for 70 grants (high: $30,000; low: $100; average: $500-$25,000).
Purpose and activities: Emphasis on music, especially opera, social services, historic preservation, population control, the arts, and conservation.
Types of support: Building funds, equipment, land acquisition, matching funds, loans.
Limitations: Giving primarily in New York City, NY. No grants to individuals, or for endowment funds, research, scholarships, or fellowships.
Publications: Annual report.
Application information: Application form not required.
Initial approach: Telephone or proposal
Copies of proposal: 1
Deadline(s): Submit proposal preferably in Jan. or Feb.; no set deadline
Board meeting date(s): As required
Write: Robert W. Wilson, Trustee
Trustees: Marillyn B. Wilson, Robert W. Wilson.
Number of staff: None.
Employer Identification Number: 116037280

5405
The Winfield Foundation ⌑
c/o D. Troxell
342 Madison Ave., No. 1818
New York 10173 (212) 245-7580

Incorporated in 1941 in NY.
Donor(s): Frasier W. McCann,† Helena M. Charlton.†
Foundation type: Independent
Financial data (yr. ended 12/31/88): Assets, $1,410,188 (M); gifts received, $100,000; expenditures, $147,010, including $117,250 for 25 grants (high: $53,750; low: $500; average: $1,000-$5,000).
Purpose and activities: Emphasis on historic preservation, music, and hospitals.
Limitations: Giving primarily in NY. No grants to individuals, or for research-related programs, scholarships, fellowships, or matching gifts; no loans.
Application information: Application form not required.
Initial approach: Letter
Copies of proposal: 1
Board meeting date(s): Semiannually
Write: Franklin W. McCann, Pres.
Officers and Directors:* Franklin W. McCann,* Pres.; Jonathan W. McCann,* V.P.; D. Chase Troxell, V.P. and Secy.; Helen Hooke, Secy.; Gordon S. Gavan.
Employer Identification Number: 136158017

5406
The Norman and Rosita Winston Foundation, Inc. ▼ ⌑
c/o Summit Rovins and Feldesman
445 Park Ave.
New York 10022 (212) 702-2200

Incorporated in 1954 in NY.
Donor(s): Norman K. Winston,† The N.K. Winston Foundation, Inc.
Foundation type: Independent
Financial data (yr. ended 12/31/88): Assets, $43,498,832 (M); expenditures, $2,675,811, including $2,034,300 for 83 grants (high: $300,000; low: $1,000; average: $5,000-$50,000).
Purpose and activities: Emphasis on higher education, including medical and theological education, hospitals, and cultural programs.
Types of support: General purposes.
Limitations: Giving primarily in NY. No grants to individuals.
Application information: Application form not required.
Initial approach: Proposal
Copies of proposal: 1
Deadline(s): None
Board meeting date(s): 2 to 4 times a year
Final notification: By the end of Dec.
Write: Joel M. Rudell, Secy.
Officers: Julian S. Perlman,* Pres.; Arthur Levitt, Jr.,* V.P. and Treas.; Joel M. Rudell, Secy.
Trustee: Simon H. Rifkind.
Number of staff: None.
Employer Identification Number: 136161672

5407
Harry Winston Research Foundation, Inc. ⌑
718 Fifth Ave.
New York 10019 (212) 245-2000

Incorporated in 1964 in NY.
Donor(s): Harry Winston,† Ronald Winston.
Foundation type: Independent
Financial data (yr. ended 12/31/88): Assets, $9,431,766 (M); expenditures, $777,986, including $593,793 for 18 grants (high: $264,950; low: $100).
Purpose and activities: Giving for programs of scientific research in the field of genetics and related medical research; includes support for hospitals and higher education.
Types of support: Research.
Limitations: Giving primarily in NY.
Application information: Application form not required.
Initial approach: Letter
Deadline(s): None
Write: Ronald Winston, Pres.
Officers: Ronald Winston, Pres.; Robert Holtzman, V.P.; Richard Copaken, Secy.
Employer Identification Number: 136168266

5408
Robert Winthrop Charitable Trust ⌑
c/o Wood Struthers & Winthrop
P.O. Box 18
New York 10005

Donor(s): Robert Winthrop.
Foundation type: Independent

Financial data (yr. ended 11/30/88): Assets, $1,570,414 (M); gifts received, $238,928; expenditures, $293,471, including $267,246 for 88 grants (high: $50,000; low: $100).
Purpose and activities: Support primarily for wildlife preservation; support also for higher education, historic preservation, medical research, and museums.
Application information: Contributes only to pre-selected organizations. Applications not accepted.
Trustees: Cornelia Bonnie, Robert Winthrop.
Employer Identification Number: 237441147

5409
Robert I. Wishnick Foundation ⌑
(Formerly The Witco Foundation)
520 Madison Ave.
New York 10022 (212) 605-3843

Incorporated in 1951 in IL.
Donor(s): Witco Chemical Corp.
Foundation type: Company-sponsored
Financial data (yr. ended 12/31/88): Assets, $7,634,784 (M); gifts received, $18,106; expenditures, $549,773, including $531,453 for 160 grants (high: $125,000; low: $75).
Purpose and activities: Grants largely for hospitals, higher education, community funds, and Jewish welfare funds; employee-related scholarships awarded through National Merit Scholarship Corp.
Types of support: Annual campaigns, endowment funds, research, conferences and seminars, scholarship funds, fellowships, employee-related scholarships, general purposes.
Limitations: No grants to individuals (except for employee-related scholarships), or for matching gifts; no loans.
Application information: Requests from outside New York City must be forwarded through local offices of the corporation. Application form not required.
Initial approach: Proposal
Copies of proposal: 1
Deadline(s): None
Board meeting date(s): Monthly
Final notification: 6 to 8 weeks
Write: Joseph Russo, Secy., for national and NY organizations; local company offices for local organizations
Officers: William Wishnick,* Pres.; Thomas J. Bickett,* V.P. and Treas.; William R. Toller, V.P.; Joseph Russo,* Secy.
Directors:* Robert L. Bachner, Simeon Brinberg.
Employer Identification Number: 136068668

5410
Esther & Morton Wohlgemuth Foundation, Inc. ⌑
1457 Broadway, Rm. 718
New York 10036

Incorporated in 1956 in NY.
Donor(s): Morton Wohlgemuth,† Esther Wohlgemuth, Alexander Wohlgemuth, Robert Wohlgemuth.
Foundation type: Independent
Financial data (yr. ended 12/31/88): Assets, $1,975,558 (M); expenditures, $117,335, including $103,025 for 69 grants (high: $15,000; low: $25).
Purpose and activities: Giving for Jewish welfare funds, higher education, health agencies, hospitals, and social service and youth agencies.
Limitations: Giving primarily in NY.
Application information: Contributes only to pre-selected organizations. Applications not accepted.
Officers: Esther Wohlgemuth, Pres.; Alexander Wohlgemuth, V.P.; Robert Wohlgemuth, V.P.; Samuel Zinman, Secy.-Treas.
Employer Identification Number: 136086849

5411
Wolowitz Family Foundation, Inc. ⌑ ☆
c/o Bernard Segal
122 East 42nd St., Suite 1911
New York 10168

Established in 1986.
Donor(s): Herbert Wolowitz.
Foundation type: Independent
Financial data (yr. ended 12/31/88): Assets, $201,185 (M); gifts received, $690,905; expenditures, $617,556, including $615,940 for 279 grants (high: $50,000; low: $18).
Purpose and activities: Support primarily for Jewish organizations, including welfare funds, schools, and congregations.
Limitations: No grants to individuals.
Application information: Contributes only to pre-selected organizations. Applications not accepted.
Officers and Managers: Herbert Wolowitz, Pres.; Marilyn Wolowitz, Secy.
Employer Identification Number: 133384435

5412
Women's Aid Society of 1844, Inc. ⌑
150 East 45th St.
New York 10017

Established in 1844 in NY; incorporated in 1860 as the German Ladies Society; current name adopted in 1972.
Foundation type: Independent
Financial data (yr. ended 12/31/88): Assets, $1,312,358 (M); gifts received, $1,651; expenditures, $93,723, including $66,750 for grants to individuals.
Purpose and activities: To provide regular and special relief assistance to the poor, indigent, aged, and sick, including destitute widows, children, and families; no longer provides educational aid.
Types of support: Grants to individuals.
Limitations: Giving limited to New York, NY. No grants for student aid or corporations and institutions.
Publications: Informational brochure.
Application information: Application form not required.
Initial approach: Letter
Deadline(s): None
Officers: Mrs. Curt Buhler, Pres.; Jacqueline Dwyer, V.P. and Secy.; Mrs. de Giers Armstrong, Treas.
Number of staff: 2 part-time professional.
Employer Identification Number: 136006486

5413
Charles R. Wood Foundation ⌑ ☆
P.O Box 511
Lake George 12845-0511

Established in 1978.
Donor(s): Charles R. Wood.
Foundation type: Independent
Financial data (yr. ended 12/31/87): Assets, $49,614 (M); expenditures, $131,890, including $131,798 for 42 grants (high: $100,000; low: $40).
Purpose and activities: Giving primarily to a medical center; minor support for arts and culture, higher education, and youth.
Limitations: Giving primarily in NY. No grants to individuals.
Application information: Contributes only to pre-selected organizations. Applications not accepted.
Trustees: Shirley Myott, Barbara Wages, Charles R. Wood.
Employer Identification Number: 222237193

5414
Woodland Foundation, Inc.
c/o Bankers Trust Co.
280 Park Ave.
New York 10017

Incorporated in 1950 in DE.
Donor(s): William Durant Campbell.
Foundation type: Independent
Financial data (yr. ended 12/31/89): Assets, $3,823,353 (M); gifts received, $350,000; expenditures, $269,356, including $219,250 for 40 grants (high: $45,000; low: $500).
Purpose and activities: Giving for higher and secondary education; grants also for youth agencies, Protestant church support, and hospitals.
Types of support: Annual campaigns, building funds, capital campaigns, endowment funds.
Limitations: No grants to individuals.
Application information: Applications not accepted.
Write: Harvey G. Burney, Treas.
Officers and Trustees:* Margot C. Bogert,* Pres.; Jeremiah M. Bogert,* V.P.; Winthrop Rutherford, Jr.,* Secy.; Harvey G. Burney,* Treas.; William Durant Campbell, George W. Knight, Frank J. Nulty.
Number of staff: None.
Employer Identification Number: 136018244

5415
The Ian Woodner Family Collection, Inc. ⌑ ☆
660 Madison Ave.
New York 10021 (212) 644-0630

Incorporated in 1986 in NY.
Donor(s): Ian Woodner, Shipley Corp.
Foundation type: Independent
Financial data (yr. ended 6/30/89): Assets, $37,494,674 (M); gifts received, $7,717,000; expenditures, $1,522,994, including $262,339 for 19 grants (high: $110,000; low: $300).
Purpose and activities: Lends works of art to museums and other institutions for public display and supports research related to the compilation and production of art works and art publications.
Types of support: Research, publications.

Limitations: No grants to individuals.
Application information:
Initial approach: Letter
Deadline(s): None
Write: Ian Woodner
Officers: Ian Woodner, Pres.; Paula A. Virl, V.P.; Andrea Woodner, V.P.; Dian Woodner, V.P.; Leo Wind, Secy.-Treas.
Employer Identification Number: 133317928

5416
Ann Eden Woodward Foundation ⌑ ☆
989 Sixth Ave.
New York 10009-7044

Established in 1963.
Donor(s): Ann Eden Woodward.†
Foundation type: Independent
Financial data (yr. ended 5/31/89): Assets, $323,457 (M); gifts received, $100,000; expenditures, $136,424, including $129,750 for 23 grants (high: $25,000; low: $750).
Purpose and activities: Giving for the performing arts and museums, hospitals, environmental and wildlife preservation, social services, and a public library.
Limitations: Giving primarily in New York, NY. No grants to individuals.
Application information: Applications not accepted.
Write: Joseph A. Lapatin, Mgr.
Managers: Joseph A. Lapatin, James A. Woods.
Employer Identification Number: 136126021

5417
The Woodward Fund
c/o Norstar Trust Co.
One East Ave.
Rochester 14638 (716) 546-9093

Established in 1965 in NY.
Donor(s): Florence S. Woodward.
Foundation type: Independent
Financial data (yr. ended 11/30/88): Assets, $2,063,140 (M); expenditures, $119,059, including $110,000 for 35 grants (high: $10,000; low: $1,000).
Purpose and activities: Giving for wildlife preservation and land conservation, Native Americans, rehabilitation of the handicapped, and community funds.
Limitations: Giving primarily in AZ and ME. No grants to individuals.
Application information: Contributes only to pre-selected organizations. Applications not accepted.
Write: Samuel A. Curtis, Jr.
Officers: Barbara W. Piel, Mgr.; Reid T. Woodward, Mgr.; Stephen S. Woodward, Mgr.; William S. Woodward, Mgr.
Trustee: Norstar Trust Co.
Employer Identification Number: 166064221

5418
Abraham Woursell Foundation ⌑
c/o CitiBank, N.A., Tax Dept.
20 Exchange Place
New York 10043

Foundation type: Independent
Financial data (yr. ended 12/31/87): Assets, $1,204,661 (M); expenditures, $59,310, including $37,336 for 2 grants to individuals of $18,668 each.
Purpose and activities: Support for general charitable giving.
Types of support: Grants to individuals.
Application information: Contributes only to pre-selected individuals. Applications not accepted.
Trustees: Frank Hayes, Citibank, N.A.
Employer Identification Number: 136140514

5419
Wrightson-Ramsing Foundation, Inc.
c/o Trident Oil Corp.
375 Park Ave., Suite 3408
New York 10152 (212) 758-2835

Incorporated in 1952 in NY.
Donor(s): Martha Wrightson Ramsing.
Foundation type: Independent
Financial data (yr. ended 12/31/89): Assets, $1,203,897 (M); expenditures, $119,690, including $98,095 for grants (high: $50,000).
Purpose and activities: Grants primarily for higher education and cultural programs, including dance and museums.
Types of support: General purposes.
Limitations: No grants to individuals.
Application information: Funds committed through 1991, but applications will be kept on file. Application form not required.
Initial approach: Letter
Deadline(s): None
Write: Thor H. Ramsing, Pres.
Officers and Directors:* Thor H. Ramsing,* Pres. and Treas.; Martha Wrightson Ramsing,* V.P.; Anthony A. Bliss, Byron L. Ramsing, Martha R. Zoubek.
Employer Identification Number: 131967462

5420
Wunsch Foundation, Inc. ⌑
841 63rd St.
Brooklyn 11220 (718) 238-2525

Incorporated in 1943 in NY.
Donor(s): Joseph W. Wunsch, Eric M. Wunsch, Samuel Wunsch, WEA Enterprises Co., Inc.
Foundation type: Independent
Financial data (yr. ended 12/31/88): Assets, $4,174,850 (M); gifts received, $40,000; expenditures, $153,778, including $149,500 for grants.
Purpose and activities: Giving primarily for higher education, fine arts, museums, and Israel.
Limitations: No grants to individuals.
Application information:
Initial approach: Letter
Deadline(s): None
Write: Eric M. Wunsch, Pres.
Officers: Eric M. Wunsch, Pres.; Ethel Wunsch, Secy.
Employer Identification Number: 116006013

5421
Harold L. Wyman Foundation, Inc. ⌑
33 Puritan Dr.
Port Chester 10573-2503

Established in 1965 in New York.
Foundation type: Independent
Financial data (yr. ended 9/30/88): Assets, $1,577,875 (M); expenditures, $102,365, including $88,600 for 44 grants (high: $7,500; low: $500).
Purpose and activities: Support for cultural activities, health associations, social services, and youth organizations.
Limitations: Giving primarily in NY. No grants to individuals.
Application information: Contributes only to pre-selected organizations. Applications not accepted.
Initial approach: Letter
Write: Walter G. Korntheuer, Secy.
Officers: Otto Korntheuer,* Pres.; Walter C. Korntheuer, Secy.-Treas.
Trustees:* George C. Barron.
Employer Identification Number: 136201289

5422
Wyman-Potter Foundation ☆
c/o Marine Midland Bank, N.A.
One Marine Midland Plaza, 7th Fl.
Rochester 14639 (716) 238-7721

Established in 1965.
Foundation type: Independent
Financial data (yr. ended 01/31/89): Assets, $1,123,623 (M); qualifying distributions, $80,644, including $79,704 for 6 grants (high: $62,964; low: $40).
Purpose and activities: Giving primarily for hospitals and health associations, and medical research and education.
Limitations: Giving primarily in Rochester, NY. No grants to individuals.
Application information: Application form not required.Applications not accepted.
Initial approach: Proposal
Board meeting date(s): As required
Write: Lawrence J. Oberlies
Trustee: Marine Midland Bank, N.A.
Employer Identification Number: 166060015

5423
William & Vina B. Yerdon Foundation ⌑
c/o First American Bank of New York
50 State St.
Albany 12207

Established in 1975 in NY.
Foundation type: Independent
Financial data (yr. ended 04/30/89): Assets, $1,228,887 (M); expenditures, $62,940, including $52,000 for 10 grants (high: $15,000; low: $1,000).
Purpose and activities: Support for community development, civic affairs, social services and cultural organizations.
Application information: Contributes only to pre-selected organizations. Applications not accepted.
Officer and Trustee:* Guy Trono,* Pres.
Employer Identification Number: 237366678

5424
The Young & Rubicam Foundation ⌑
c/o R. John Cooper, Pres.
285 Madison Ave.
New York 10017 (212) 210-3000

Incorporated in 1955 in NY.

Donor(s): Young & Rubicam, Inc.
Foundation type: Company-sponsored
Financial data (yr. ended 12/31/88): Assets, $445,895 (M); gifts received, $370,348; expenditures, $470,244, including $363,923 for 120 grants (high: $10,000; low: $100) and $106,225 for 254 employee matching gifts.
Purpose and activities: Grants primarily for a matching gifts program; foundation directors initiate contributions for selected community funds, cultural programs, including the performing arts, community development, and youth agencies.
Types of support: Employee matching gifts.
Limitations: No grants to individuals, or for capital or endowment funds, scholarships, fellowships, operating budgets, continuing support, annual campaigns, seed money, emergency funds, deficit financing, special projects, research, publications, or conferences; no loans.
Application information: Applications not accepted.
Board meeting date(s): June and Nov.
Officers and Directors: R. John Cooper, Pres.; Joan L. Hafey, V.P.; Mark Stroock, V.P.; Robert Tallman, Jr., Secy.; Dave Greene, Treas.
Number of staff: 5 part-time support.
Employer Identification Number: 136156199

5425
Youth Foundation, Inc. ⌑
36 West 44th St.
New York 10036

Incorporated in 1940 in NY.
Donor(s): Alexander M. Hadden,† Mrs. Alexander M. Hadden,† and others.
Foundation type: Independent
Financial data (yr. ended 12/31/87): Assets, $3,965,596 (M); gifts received, $4,618; expenditures, $218,262, including $101,667 for 48 grants to individuals (high: $2,000; low: $1,000).
Purpose and activities: Emphasis on assisting young people to a richer experience in living; scholarships awarded annually to undergraduate students who have demonstrated need as well as ability.
Types of support: Student aid.
Limitations: No support for post-graduate studies.
Publications: Application guidelines, program policy statement.
Application information: All entries must include self-addressed stamped envelope. Application form required.
Initial approach: Letter with recommendation
Copies of proposal: 1
Deadline(s): Apr. 15
Final notification: June
Write: Edward F.L. Bruen, V.P.
Officers and Directors: Mrs. Guy Norman Robinson, Pres.; Edward F.L. Bruen, V.P.; Henry S. Middendorf, Jr., Secy.; Jack L. Rubin, Treas.; Mrs. C. Kenneth Clinton, John L. Fenton, James W. Gerard, Jean S. Gerard, John Campbell Henry, Mrs. Donald M. Liddell, Jr., Asa E. Phillips, Jr., Harry Roberts, Horace B.B. Robinson, A. David Russell.
Employer Identification Number: 136093036

5426
Youths' Friends Association, Inc. ⌑
c/o Seidman & Seidman
15 Columbus Circle
New York 10023
Application address: P.O. Box 5387, Hilton Head, SC 29938; Tel.: (803) 671-5060

Incorporated in 1950 in NY.
Donor(s): Johan J. Smit,† Mrs. Johan J. Smit.†
Foundation type: Independent
Financial data (yr. ended 12/31/88): Assets, $5,461,593 (M); expenditures, $260,166, including $203,000 for 82 grants (high: $15,000; low: $1,000).
Purpose and activities: Grants largely for character-building, with emphasis on higher and secondary education, health agencies, hospitals, youth agencies, child welfare, and music; some support also for churches and religious associations.
Limitations: No grants to individuals.
Application information: Application form not required.
Initial approach: Letter
Copies of proposal: 1
Deadline(s): None
Board meeting date(s): Semiannually
Write: Walter J. Graver, Secy.
Officers and Directors:* Herman J. Meinert,* Pres.; Sheila Smit,* V.P.; Walter J. Graver,* Secy.-Treas.; Marion Meinert, Stephen C. Smit.
Employer Identification Number: 136097828

5427
Isaac Herman Zacharia Foundation, Inc. ⌑
c/o Weinick, Sanders and Co.
1515 Broadway
New York 10036
Application address: R.D. No. 31, KM24 12MG, Rico Blanco, Sun Cos, Puerto Rico

Incorporated in 1953 in NY.
Donor(s): Isaac Herman Zacharia, and others.
Foundation type: Independent
Financial data (yr. ended 12/31/87): Assets, $2,667,216 (M); expenditures, $152,215, including $139,732 for 38 grants (high: $25,000; low: $10).
Purpose and activities: Giving for education, including religious education; grants also for aid to the handicapped, temple support, Jewish welfare funds, and recreation.
Limitations: Giving primarily in NY.
Application information:
Initial approach: Letter
Deadline(s): None
Write: Isaac Herman Zacharia, Pres.
Officers: Isaac Herman Zacharia, Pres.
Employer Identification Number: 510108212

5428
Charles Zarkin Memorial Foundation, Inc. ⌑
c/o Wachtell, Lipton, Rosen & Katz
299 Park Ave.
New York 10171

Incorporated in 1969 in NY.
Donor(s): Fay Zarkin.†
Foundation type: Independent
Financial data (yr. ended 12/31/87): Assets, $3,778,819 (M); expenditures, $202,908, including $143,000 for 12 grants (high: $60,000; low: $3,000).
Purpose and activities: Emphasis on Jewish welfare funds, youth agencies, hospitals, higher education, and cultural programs.
Limitations: Giving primarily in New York, NY. No grants to individuals.
Application information: Contributes only to pre-selected organizations. Applications not accepted.
Board meeting date(s): Dec.
Officers: Martin Lipton,* Pres. and Treas.; Leonard Rosen,* V.P.; Estelle Oleck,* V.P.; Constance Monte, Secy.
Trustees:* Robert B. McKay, Lester Pollack.
Number of staff: None.
Employer Identification Number: 237149277

5429
Zenkel Foundation ☆
15 West 53rd St.
New York 10019-5410 (212) 333-5730

Established in 1987 in NY.
Foundation type: Independent
Financial data (yr. ended 12/31/88): Assets, $3,664,334 (M); expenditures, $180,561, including $144,457 for 79 grants (high: $30,000; low: $35).
Purpose and activities: Giving primarily for Jewish welfare, the arts, and museums; support also for health associations, AIDS and other medical research, race relations and human rights, the environment, and higher education.
Types of support: Annual campaigns, building funds, general purposes, scholarship funds.
Limitations: No grants to individuals.
Application information: Contributes only to pre-selected organizations. Applications not accepted.
Write: Lois Zenkel, Pres.
Officers and Directors:* Lois S. Zenkel,* Pres.; Daniel R. Zenkel,* Secy.; Bruce L. Zenkel,* Treas.; Gary B. Zenkel, Lisa R. Zenkel.
Number of staff: None.
Employer Identification Number: 133380631

5430
Aaron Ziegelman Foundation ⌑ ☆
c/o Chanales & Kuhun
200 West 57th St.
New York 10019

Established in 1986 in NY.
Foundation type: Independent
Financial data (yr. ended 12/31/88): Assets, $301,041 (M); expenditures, $613,592, including $595,271 for 53 grants (high: $131,689; low: $25).
Purpose and activities: Giving primarily for Jewish organizations, especially theological, higher, and other education; minor support for arts and culture.
Limitations: Giving limited to the New York, NY, metropolitan area. No grants to individuals.
Application information:
Initial approach: Letter
Deadline(s): None
Trustees: Irwin J. Chanales, William Diament, Leon Mandel.
Employer Identification Number: 133323659

5431
The Zilkha Foundation, Inc.
30 Rockefeller Plaza
New York 10112-0153 (212) 765-8661

Incorporated in 1948 in NY.
Donor(s): Ezra K. Zilkha, Zilkha & Sons, Inc.
Foundation type: Company-sponsored
Financial data (yr. ended 8/31/89): Assets, $170,190 (M); gifts received, $320,000; expenditures, $326,351, including $317,578 for 54 grants (high: $68,035; low: $60).
Purpose and activities: A small family foundation of which a large part of funds are designated for specific charities; grants primarily for higher education, Jewish welfare and educational funds, the performing arts, and intercultural organizations; support also for a hospital.
Limitations: No grants to individuals.
Application information: Grants awarded largely at the initiative of the officers.
Initial approach: Letter
Deadline(s): Aug. 31
Board meeting date(s): Dec.
Write: Ezra K. Zilkha, Pres.
Officers: Ezra K. Zilkha, Pres. and Treas.; Cecile E. Zilkha, V.P. and Secy.
Number of staff: None.
Employer Identification Number: 136090739

5432
Marie and John Zimmermann Fund, Inc.
c/o U.S. Trust Co. of New York
114 West 47th St.
New York 10036-1532 (212) 852-1000

Incorporated in 1942 in NY.
Donor(s): Marie Zimmermann,† Frank A. Zunio, Jr.
Foundation type: Independent
Financial data (yr. ended 12/31/89): Assets, $5,321,367 (M); expenditures, $220,799, including $190,000 for grants (high: $110,700).
Purpose and activities: Grants for higher education, particularly medical education.
Limitations: No grants to individuals.
Application information: Contributes only to pre-selected organizations. Applications not accepted.
Write: Anne L. Smith-Ganey, Asst. V.P., U.S. Trust Co. of New York
Officers and Directors:* John C. Zimmermann III,* Pres.; Anne L. Smith-Ganey,* Treas.; J. Robert Buchanan, M.D., Henry W. Grady, Jr., Anne C. Heller, A. Parks McCombs, Thomas H. Meikle, Jr., Robert Perret, Jr.
Employer Identification Number: 136158767

5433
Arthur Zimtbaum Foundation, Inc.
c/o Elihu H. Modlin
EAB Plaza
Uniondale 11556-0132 (516) 294-2660

Incorporated in 1955 in NY.
Donor(s): Arthur Zimtbaum,† Rose B. LeVantine.
Foundation type: Independent
Financial data (yr. ended 12/31/88): Assets, $1,291,926 (M); expenditures, $182,794, including $136,000 for 16 grants (high: $20,000; low: $2,000).
Purpose and activities: Giving for medical research, cultural programs, and higher education.
Limitations: Giving primarily in NY.
Application information:
Initial approach: Written proposal
Deadline(s): None
Write: Elihu H. Modlin, V.P.
Officers: Rose B. LeVantine, Pres.; Elihu H. Modlin, V.P. and Secy.; Herbert Merin, Treas.
Directors: William J. Burke, Paulette L. LeVantine, Andrew Merin, Charles Modlin.
Employer Identification Number: 116016391

5434
Sergei S. Zlinkoff Fund for Medical Research and Education, Inc. ¤
c/o Carter, Ledyard & Milburn
Two Wall St.
New York 10005

Incorporated in 1956 in NY.
Donor(s): Sergei S. Zlinkoff.†
Foundation type: Independent
Financial data (yr. ended 10/31/88): Assets, $2,421,095 (M); expenditures, $496,851, including $442,500 for 13 grants (high: $240,000; low: $1,000).
Purpose and activities: Grants primarily for higher education, including medical education, and research; some support for social services and a library.
Limitations: No grants to individuals.
Application information: Contributes only to pre-selected organizations. Applications not accepted.
Write: Jerome J. Cohen, Dir.
Officers: Mack Lipkin, Pres.; Milton Hamolsky, V.P.
Directors: Victor Brudney, Jerome J. Cohen, Ralph E. Hansmann, John O. Lipkin, Mack Lipkin, Jr.
Employer Identification Number: 136094651

5435
Zock Endowment Trust ¤ ☆
c/o Morgan Bank
616 Madison Ave.
New York 10153
Application address: 506 Crescent Pkwy., Sea Girt, NJ 08750

Foundation type: Independent
Financial data (yr. ended 9/30/88): Assets, $3,910,415 (M); expenditures, $159,259, including $122,001 for 31 grants (high: $100,000; low: $10).
Purpose and activities: Giving for an international relief association, Lutheran organizations, and health associations.
Limitations: Giving primarily in NJ, MD, and PA. No grants to individuals.
Application information: Application form not required.
Deadline(s): None
Write: Sara M. Zock, Trustee
Trustees: Robert A. Zock, Sara M. Zock.
Employer Identification Number: 226093288

5436
Roy J. Zuckerberg Foundation ¤
c/o Goldman, Sachs & Co.
85 Broad St., Tax Dept., 30th Fl.
New York 10004-2408

Established in 1980 in NY.
Donor(s): Roy J. Zuckerberg.
Foundation type: Independent
Financial data (yr. ended 09/30/89): Assets, $1,413,000 (M); gifts received, $456,281; expenditures, $377,391, including $376,580 for 118 grants (high: $65,000; low: $100).
Purpose and activities: Giving primarily for Jewish welfare and for health associations.
Limitations: Giving primarily in NY. No grants to individuals.
Application information: Applications not accepted.
Trustees: James C. Kautz, Barbara Zuckerberg, Roy J. Zuckerberg.
Employer Identification Number: 133052489

NORTH CAROLINA

5437
ABC Foundation ¤
c/o NCNB National Bank of North Carolina, T11-5
Charlotte 28255
Application address: c/o Cone Mills Corp., 1201 Maple St., Greensboro, NC 27405; Tel.: (919) 379-6220

Trust established in 1944 in NC.
Donor(s): Cone Mills Corp.
Foundation type: Company-sponsored
Financial data (yr. ended 10/31/89): Assets, $4,066,394 (M); expenditures, $412,511, including $344,304 for 60 grants (high: $50,000; low: $100) and $39,300 for 40 grants to individuals (high: $2,500; low: $500).
Purpose and activities: Grants for higher education, community funds, culture, and child welfare; support also for employee-related scholarships.
Types of support: Employee-related scholarships.
Limitations: Giving limited to areas of company operations in NC. No grants to individuals.
Application information:
Initial approach: Letter
Copies of proposal: 1
Deadline(s): None
Board meeting date(s): Annually and as required
Write: Lacy G. Baynes, Dir.
Directors: Lacy G. Baynes, W.O. Leonard, Dewey L. Trogdon.
Agent: NCNB National Bank of North Carolina.
Employer Identification Number: 581504894

5438
Maye Morrison Abernethy Testamentary Charitable Trust ⌑
c/o Claude S. Abernethy
P.O. Box 700
Newton 28658

Established in 1985 in NC.
Donor(s): Maye M. Abernethy.†
Foundation type: Independent
Financial data (yr. ended 2/28/89): Assets, $2,351,089 (M); expenditures, $158,472, including $150,000 for 2 grants of $75,000 each.
Purpose and activities: Support for education.
Limitations: Giving primarily in NC.
Application information: Contributes only to pre-selected organizations. Applications not accepted.
Trustees: Claude S. Abernethy, Jr., J.W. Abernethy, Jr.
Employer Identification Number: 566257481

5439
Akers Foundation, Inc.
P.O. Box 2726
Gastonia 28053 (704) 867-6846

Incorporated in 1955 in NC.
Foundation type: Independent
Financial data (yr. ended 12/31/88): Assets, $1,753,094 (M); expenditures, $131,652, including $111,735 for 62 grants (high: $16,000; low: $85).
Purpose and activities: Giving primarily for Protestant church support, education, and social services; support also for cultural programs.
Limitations: Giving primarily in NC.
Application information: Application form not required.
Initial approach: Letter
Deadline(s): None
Write: John M. Akers, Pres.
Officers: John M. Akers, Pres. and Treas.; C. Scott Akers, V.P.; Charles W. Akers, Secy.
Number of staff: None.
Employer Identification Number: 566044428

5440
American Otological Society, Inc. ⌑ ☆
c/o Dr. Robert Kohut
300 South Hawthorne Rd.
Winston-Salem 27103-2732
Application address: c/o Dr. Arnold Duvall III, Box 396, Univ. of Minnesota Hospitals, 420 Delware St., S.E., Minneapolis, MN 55455; Tel.: (612) 373-8607

Foundation type: Independent
Financial data (yr. ended 6/30/88): Assets, $4,075,824 (M); expenditures, $341,628, including $2,115 for 3 grants (high: $1,000; low: $515) and $241,782 for 10 grants to individuals (high: $25,000; low: $21,395).
Purpose and activities: Awards grants to individuals for research in the field of otosclerosis.
Types of support: Research.
Limitations: Giving limited to U.S. and Canadian citizens.
Application information:
Initial approach: Proposal
Deadline(s): Jan. 31
Officers: D. Thane Cody, M.D., Pres.; H.A. Ted Bailey, Jr., M.D., V.P.; Robert I. Kohut, M.D., Secy.-Treas.
Employer Identification Number: 136131376

5441
American Scholafhurst Foundation, Inc. ⌑ ☆
P.O. Box 240828
Charlotte 28224 (704) 554-0800

Established in 1987 in NC.
Foundation type: Independent
Financial data (yr. ended 12/31/88): Assets, $1,036,520 (M); gifts received, $2,129; expenditures, $5,625.
Purpose and activities: General charitable purposes.
Application information:
Deadline(s): None
Write: John C. Martin, Pres.
Officers: John C. Martin,* Pres.; Joel H. Myers, Secy.
Directors:* Frank Paetzold, Charles B. Park III, Jan Reiners.
Employer Identification Number: 561590110

5442
Robert C. and Sadie G. Anderson Foundation ⌑
c/o NCNB National Bank Trust Group
One NCNB Plaza T09-1
Charlotte 28255 (704) 374-5731

Trust established in 1952 in NC.
Donor(s): Robert C. Anderson,† Sadie Gaithêr Anderson.†
Foundation type: Independent
Financial data (yr. ended 12/31/88): Assets, $2,159,421 (M); expenditures, $157,507, including $140,000 for 16 grants (high: $64,000; low: $1,500).
Purpose and activities: Support only for Presbyterian causes or institutions.
Limitations: Giving primarily in NC and VA, with preference for NC. No grants to individuals, or for operating budgets, building or endowment funds, or matching gifts; no loans.
Publications: Program policy statement.
Application information: Contributes only to pre-selected organizations. Applications not accepted.
Board meeting date(s): Apr.
Write: Mgr., Institutional Services
Directors: William M.M. Barnhardt, Katherine McKay Belk, William Maynard Fountain, Jr., Voit Gilmore, Carl Horn, Jr., P. Greer Johnson, Ralph S. Robinson, Jr.
Trustee: NCNB National Bank Trust Group.
Employer Identification Number: 566065233

5443
Awards Committee for Education, Inc. ⌑
20 Battery Park Ave., Suite 310
Asheville 28801
Application address: 138 North Hawthorne Rd., Winston-Salem, NC 27104; Tel.: (704) 251-0144

Established in 1981 in NC.
Donor(s): Ann Forsythe.
Foundation type: Independent
Financial data (yr. ended 8/31/89): Assets, $93,487 (M); gifts received, $238,309; expenditures, $225,949, including $123,124 for grants (high: $16,080) and $13,130 for 2 grants to individuals.
Purpose and activities: Support primarily for higher education, including scholarships to individuals.
Types of support: Scholarship funds, student aid.
Limitations: Giving primarily in NC.
Application information: Application must include official transcript and SAT scores. Application form required.
Deadline(s): None
Write: Lillian D. Meredith, Treas.
Officers: Ann Forsyth, Chair.; John Ehle, Pres.; Lillian D. Meredith, Treas.
Employer Identification Number: 561308884

5444
Mary Reynolds Babcock Foundation, Inc. ▼
102 Reynolda Village
Winston-Salem 27106-5123 (919) 748-9222

Incorporated in 1953 in NC.
Donor(s): Mary Reynolds Babcock,† Charles H. Babcock.†
Foundation type: Independent
Financial data (yr. ended 08/31/89): Assets, $53,818,531 (M); expenditures, $3,414,149, including $3,007,828 for 115 grants (high: $100,000; low: $1,000) and $100,000 for 1 loan.
Purpose and activities: Supports active participation by citizens in the protection of the environment, the development of public policy, the well-being of children and adolescents, education, grassroots organizing, opportunity for women, rural issues, and the arts.
Types of support: Operating budgets, seed money, emergency funds, special projects, program-related investments, matching funds.
Limitations: Giving primarily in NC and the southeastern U.S., and to national organizations. No support for medical or health programs, research, film or video production, international activities, local or community programs (except where the program is a model for the region or nation), or for tax-supported educational institutions outside NC. No grants to individuals, or for endowment funds, building funds, renovation projects, scholarships, or fellowships; no student loans.
Publications: Annual report (including application guidelines), program policy statement.
Application information: Application form required.
Initial approach: Proposal
Copies of proposal: 1
Deadline(s): Mar. 1 and Sept. 1
Board meeting date(s): May and Nov.
Final notification: 1st week of months following board meetings
Write: William L. Bondurant, Exec. Dir.
Officers and Directors:* L. Richardson Preyer,* Pres.; Barbara B. Millhouse,* V.P.; Kenneth F. Mountcastle, Jr.,* Secy.; Zachary T. Smith,* Treas.; William L. Bondurant, Exec.

Dir.; Betsy M. Babcock, Bruce M. Babcock, Reynolds Lassiter, Katharine B. Mountcastle, Katharine R. Mountcastle, Laura Mountcastle, William R. Rogers, Isabel Stewart, Paul N. Ylvisaker.
Number of staff: 3 full-time professional; 2 full-time support.
Employer Identification Number: 560690140

5445
Pearl Dixon Balthis Foundation
c/o First Union National Bank
Capital Management Group, CMG-10-1159
Charlotte 28288 (704) 374-3464

Established in 1957 in NC.
Donor(s): W.L. Balthis.†
Foundation type: Independent
Financial data (yr. ended 06/30/89): Assets, $1,199,489 (M); expenditures, $77,816, including $66,250 for 17 grants (high: $10,250; low: $250).
Purpose and activities: Giving primarily to youth organizations and child development; support also for higher, secondary, and elementary education, religious organizations and schools, the handicapped and rehabilitation, mental health, recreation, cancer research, and social services, including family planning and services.
Types of support: Capital campaigns, endowment funds, fellowships, general purposes, scholarship funds.
Limitations: Giving primarily in Gaston and MceKlenburg counties, NC.
Application information: Application form not required.
Initial approach: Letter
Copies of proposal: 1
Deadline(s): May 1 and Dec. 1
Board meeting date(s): May 15 and Dec. 15
Final notification: One week after board meeting
Write: Miles V. Smith
Trustee: First Union National Bank.
Number of staff: 1
Employer Identification Number: 566041570

5446
BarclaysAmerican/Foundation, Inc.
201 South Tryon St.
P.O. Box 31488
Charlotte 28231 (704) 339-5000

Incorporated in 1959 in NC.
Donor(s): BarclaysAmerican Corp., and subsidiaries.
Foundation type: Company-sponsored
Financial data (yr. ended 12/31/89): Assets, $780,653 (M); expenditures, $324,258, including $302,910 for 287 grants (high: $50,000; low: $100) and $21,348 for 134 employee matching gifts.
Purpose and activities: Grants largely for education and community funds; support also for the arts and medical institutions.
Types of support: Continuing support, annual campaigns, building funds, employee matching gifts.
Limitations: Giving limited to areas of company operations. No grants to individuals, or for endowment funds, scholarships, fellowships, or research; no loans.
Application information: Application form not required.
Initial approach: Letter
Copies of proposal: 2
Deadline(s): None
Board meeting date(s): Quarterly
Final notification: 6 months
Write: Robert V. Knight, Jr., Secy.-Treas.
Officers and Directors: Edward F. Hill, Pres. and Chair.; Robert V. Knight, Jr., Secy.-Treas.; Douglas W. Booth, Terrance G. Vane, Jr.
Employer Identification Number: 566060973

5447
The Belk Foundation ¤
c/o I.N. Howard, Trustee
2801 West Tyvola Rd.
Charlotte 28217-4500

Trust established in 1928 in NC.
Donor(s): The Belk Mercantile Corps.
Foundation type: Company-sponsored
Financial data (yr. ended 5/31/88): Assets, $18,434,408 (M); gifts received, $587,794; expenditures, $817,621, including $710,200 for 40 grants (high: $100,000; low: $500).
Purpose and activities: Grants largely for community funds and higher education; support also for youth agencies and cultural programs.
Limitations: Giving primarily in NC and SC.
Application information:
Deadline(s): None
Trustees: I.N. Howard, First Union National Bank.
Advisors: Thomas M. Belk, Chair.; Claudia Belk, Irwin Belk, John M. Belk, Katherine Belk, B. Frank Matthews, Leroy Robinson.
Employer Identification Number: 566046450

5448
Thomas Milburn Belk Foundation ¤
c/o I.N. Howard, Trustee
2801 West Tyvola Rd.
Charlotte 28217-4500

Established in 1953 in NC.
Foundation type: Independent
Financial data (yr. ended 12/31/88): Assets, $1,226,744 (M); expenditures, $59,172, including $57,800 for 19 grants (high: $23,000; low: $200).
Purpose and activities: Giving primarily for higher and other education; support also for a Presbyterian church.
Types of support: Operating budgets.
Application information: Contributes only to pre-selected organizations. Applications not accepted.
Advisory Board: Irwin Belk, John M. Belk, Katherine McKay Belk, Sarah Belk Gambrell.
Trustee: I.N. Howard.
Employer Identification Number: 566046452

5449
The Mary Duke Biddle Foundation
1044 West Forest Hills Blvd.
Durham 27707 (919) 493-5591

Trust established in 1956 in NY.
Donor(s): Mary Duke Biddle.†
Foundation type: Independent
Financial data (yr. ended 12/31/89): Assets, $16,163,861 (M); expenditures, $869,719, including $650,972 for grants (high: $20,000; low: $500; average: $2,000-$5,000).
Purpose and activities: Support for private higher and secondary education, specified churches, cultural programs, particularly music and projects in the arts, and aid to the community and to the handicapped; half of the income is committed to Duke University.
Types of support: Seed money, research, conferences and seminars, scholarship funds, fellowships, professorships, general purposes, matching funds, special projects.
Limitations: Giving limited to New York, NY, and NC. No support for public education. No grants to individuals, or for building or endowment funds or operating budgets; no loans.
Publications: Annual report.
Application information: Application form not required.
Initial approach: Letter
Copies of proposal: 1
Deadline(s): None
Board meeting date(s): Mar., June, Sept., and Nov.
Final notification: Approximately 90 days for negative responses
Write: James H. Semans, Chair., or Douglas C. Zinn, Asst. to the Chair.
Officers and Trustees: James H. Semans, M.D., Chair.; Mary D.B.T. Semans, Vice-Chair.; Thomas S. Kenan III, Secy.-Treas.; Archie K. Davis, Mary T. Jones.
Number of staff: 2 part-time professional; 2 part-time support.
Employer Identification Number: 136068883

5450
Blue Bell Foundation ¤
c/o Wrangler Co.
335 Church Court
Greensboro 27401 (919) 373-3580

Trust established in 1944 in NC.
Donor(s): Blue Bell, Inc.
Foundation type: Company-sponsored
Financial data (yr. ended 12/31/88): Assets, $3,809,991 (M); expenditures, $46,680, including $41,257 for 15 grants (high: $10,000; low: $50).
Purpose and activities: Grants for higher and secondary education, including matching gifts, community funds, hospitals, and cultural programs.
Types of support: Employee matching gifts.
Limitations: Giving primarily in areas where corporation has plants.
Application information:
Initial approach: Letter
Deadline(s): None
Write: Mickey Conklin
Advisory Committee: D.P. Laws, H.V. Moore, T.L. Weatherford.
Trustee: Wachovia Bank & Trust Co., N.A.
Employer Identification Number: 566041057

5451
The Blumenthal Foundation ▼ ⌑
P.O. Box 34689
Charlotte 28234 (704) 377-6555

Trust established in 1953 in NC.
Donor(s): I.D. Blumenthal,† Herman Blumenthal, Radiator Specialty Co.
Foundation type: Independent
Financial data (yr. ended 4/30/88): Assets, $19,067,751 (M); gifts received, $63,927; expenditures, $975,287, including $922,904 for 178 grants (high: $300,500; low: $8; average: $100-$23,000).
Purpose and activities: Giving for higher education, Jewish welfare organizations, and programs in the arts and humanities; also supports Wildacres, a conference center in North Carolina, which invites groups in a variety of disciplines to use its facilities.
Types of support: Building funds, equipment, operating budgets, emergency funds, research, general purposes, publications, matching funds, annual campaigns, conferences and seminars, seed money, special projects.
Limitations: Giving primarily in NC, with emphasis on Charlotte. No grants to individuals, or for scholarships or fellowships; no loans.
Application information: Application form not required.
Initial approach: Letter or proposal
Copies of proposal: 1
Deadline(s): 15 days before board meetings
Board meeting date(s): Mar., June, Sept., and Dec.
Final notification: 1 to 3 months
Write: Herman Blumenthal, Trustee
Trustees: Herman Blumenthal, Chair.; Alan Blumenthal, Anita Blumenthal, Philip Blumenthal, Samuel Blumenthal, M.D.
Number of staff: 3
Employer Identification Number: 560793667

5452
The Bolick Foundation ⌑
P.O. Box 307
Conover 28613

Established in 1967 in NC.
Donor(s): Southern Furniture Co. of Conover, Inc.
Foundation type: Company-sponsored
Financial data (yr. ended 6/30/88): Assets, $2,350,717 (M); expenditures, $109,472, including $104,150 for 33 grants (high: $23,750; low: $50).
Purpose and activities: Giving primarily to a Lutheran high school and for Protestant church activities.
Limitations: Giving primarily in NC.
Trustees: Jerome W. Bolick, O.W. Bolick.
Employer Identification Number: 566086348

5453
W. H. Brady Foundation, Inc.
P.O. Box 610
Maggie Valley 28751

Incorporated in 1956 in WI.
Foundation type: Independent
Financial data (yr. ended 07/31/89): Assets, $5,740,537 (M); gifts received, $60,000; expenditures, $338,500, including $257,300 for 41 grants (high: $30,000; low: $500; average: $2,500).
Purpose and activities: About one-third of giving in WI; giving to national organizations with emphasis on public policy research and education, public affairs, and international affairs.
Types of support: Conferences and seminars, continuing support, publications, research, special projects.
Limitations: No support for elementary or secondary education, sectarian programs, or "umbrella" organizations. No grants to individuals.
Publications: Informational brochure (including application guidelines).
Application information: All mailings should be sent to the foundation's NC office. Funding to tax-supported institutions extremely limited. Application form not required.
Initial approach: 1-page summary of prospective proposal required; request application guidelines
Copies of proposal: 1
Deadline(s): Apr. 15, Aug. 15, and Dec. 15
Board meeting date(s): Jan., May, and Sept.
Final notification: 3-4 weeks following board meeting
Officers and Directors:* Elizabeth B. Lurie,* Pres. and Treas.; Michael S. Joyce,* V.P.; Beverly J. Riemer,* Secy.; William H. Brady III, Dinesh D'Souza, Sherry K. Hoel, Michael S. Joyce, Peter J. Lettenberger, Phillip M. McGoohan.
Number of staff: 1 part-time support.
Employer Identification Number: 396064733

5454
Brenner Foundation, Inc. ⌑ ☆
P.O. Box 76
Winston-Salem 27102

Incorporated in 1960 in NC.
Donor(s): Abe Brenner, Morris Brenner, Sanco Corp., Brenner Cos., Inc.
Foundation type: Independent
Financial data (yr. ended 4/30/88): Assets, $1,502,701 (M); gifts received, $176,500; expenditures, $156,684, including $151,300 for grants.
Purpose and activities: Giving primarily for Jewish welfare funds and higher education.
Limitations: Giving primarily in NC.
Officers: Abe Brenner, Pres.; Herb Brenner, V.P.; Gertrude Brenner, Secy.-Treas.; Robert G. Stockton, Dir.
Employer Identification Number: 566058174

5455
Broyhill Family Foundation, Inc. ▼
P.O. Box 500, Golfview Park
Lenoir 28645 (704) 758-6120

Incorporated in 1945 in NC.
Donor(s): Broyhill Furniture Industries, Inc., James E. Broyhill, and family.
Foundation type: Independent
Financial data (yr. ended 12/31/87): Assets, $23,903,141 (M); expenditures, $1,487,112, including $1,246,146 for 291 grants (high: $100,000; low: $50; average: $250-$5,000).
Purpose and activities: Support for scholarship loans through the College Foundation, Inc.; support also for health, child development and welfare, civic and community services, and the free enterprise system.
Types of support: Scholarship funds, special projects.
Limitations: Giving primarily in NC. No grants to individuals.
Application information:
Initial approach: Letter
Deadline(s): June 15 and Dec. 15
Board meeting date(s): Quarterly
Final notification: Within calendar year
Write: Paul H. Broyhill, Pres., or Mrs. Lee E. Pritchard, Asst. Secy.-Treas.
Officers and Directors:* Paul H. Broyhill,* Pres.; E.D. Beach,* Secy.-Treas.; Clarence E. Beach, Faye A. Broyhill, M. Hunt Broyhill, Mrs. Lee E. Pritchard.
Number of staff: 2 full-time professional.
Employer Identification Number: 566054119

5456
Kathleen Price and Joseph M. Bryan Family Foundation ▼
One North Pointe, Suite 170
3101 North Elm St.
Greensboro 27408 (919) 288-5455

Incorporated in 1955 in NC.
Donor(s): Kathleen Price Bryan,† Joseph M. Bryan, Sr., Kathleen Bryan Edwards, Nancy Bryan Faircloth, Joseph M. Bryan, Jr.
Foundation type: Independent
Financial data (yr. ended 12/31/89): Assets, $34,632,239 (M); expenditures, $1,808,751, including $1,418,425 for 63 grants (high: $125,000; low: $2,000; average: $5,000-$100,000).
Purpose and activities: Grants principally in the fields of higher, minority, and early childhood education; the fine and performing arts and other arts and cultural programs; health and human services, including AIDS programs; public interest; and youth.
Types of support: Continuing support, seed money, equipment, general purposes, operating budgets, scholarship funds, technical assistance, special projects, endowment funds, building funds, renovation projects, internships.
Limitations: Giving primarily in the southeast, with emphasis on NC. No support for private foundations. No grants to individuals, or generally for annual fund drives or research; no loans.
Publications: Program policy statement, application guidelines, grants list.
Application information: Telephone or personal interviews with Exec. Dir. are encouraged prior to deadlines; site visits are made when possible. Application form required.
Initial approach: Letter
Copies of proposal: 1
Deadline(s): Mar. 1 and Sept. 1
Board meeting date(s): May and Nov.
Final notification: 2 weeks after board meetings
Write: Robert K. Hampton, Exec. Dir.
Officers and Trustees:* Kathleen Bryan Edwards,* Pres.; Joseph M. Bryan, Jr.,* V.P. and Treas.; Robert K. Hampton,* Secy. and

Exec. Dir.; William C. Friday, R. Howard Taylor III.
Number of staff: 1 full-time professional; 1 full-time support.
Employer Identification Number: 566046952

5457
James E. and Mary Z. Bryan Foundation, Inc.
First Citizens Bank and Trust Co.
P.O. Box 151
Raleigh 27602 (919) 755-7101

Incorporated in 1954 in NC.
Donor(s): James E. Bryan,† Mary Z. Bryan.†
Foundation type: Independent
Financial data (yr. ended 06/30/89): Assets, $3,604,526 (M); qualifying distributions, $280,825, including $148,500 for 12 grants (high: $40,000; low: $1,000), $32,325 for 22 grants to individuals (average: $1,500) and $100,000 for loans.
Purpose and activities: To aid needy and worthy students who are residents of NC through grants to trade schools, colleges, or universities in or outside the state; support also to secondary schools.
Types of support: Scholarship funds, student aid.
Limitations: Giving limited to NC. No grants for general support.
Publications: 990-PF.
Application information: Application form not required.
Initial approach: Proposal
Copies of proposal: 3
Deadline(s): Submit proposal preferably in Nov. or Dec.
Board meeting date(s): Jan. or Feb.
Write: Byron E. Bryan, Pres.
Officers and Directors:* Byron E. Bryan,* Pres.; James M. Zealy,* V.P.; Lewis R. Holding,* Secy.-Treas.
Number of staff: 2 part-time support.
Employer Identification Number: 566034567

5458
Burlington Industries Foundation ▼
P.O. Box 21207
3330 West Friendly Ave.
Greensboro 27420 (919) 379-2515

Trust established in 1943 in NC.
Donor(s): Burlington Industries, Inc., and subsidiary companies.
Foundation type: Company-sponsored
Financial data (yr. ended 09/30/89): Assets, $7,302,684 (M); expenditures, $954,291, including $646,742 for 163 grants (high: $50,000; low: $100; average: $500-$5,000), $29,250 for 54 grants to individuals (high: $1,000; low: $250; average: $250-$1,000) and $278,299 for 765 employee matching gifts.
Purpose and activities: To support educational, charitable, cultural, and similar causes. Grants to colleges and universities generally in the geographical area of plants, where the company recruits annually for employees. Grants to various community and civic causes based upon recommendation of the company's local management; includes support for youth agencies, hospitals, and some health associations. Grants to individuals are only to help employees cope with hardship caused by disasters.
Types of support: Matching funds, annual campaigns, building funds, professorships, scholarship funds, fellowships, employee matching gifts.
Limitations: Giving primarily in areas of company operations in NC, SC, and VA. Generally no grants for sectarian or denominational religious organizations, national organizations, private secondary schools, or historic preservation projects. No grants to individuals (except for company employees and their families in distress), or for conferences, seminars, workshops, outdoor dramas, films, documentaries, endowment funds, or medical research operating expenses; no loans.
Publications: Program policy statement, application guidelines.
Application information: Application form not required.
Initial approach: Telephone, letter, or proposal
Copies of proposal: 1
Deadline(s): None
Board meeting date(s): Quarterly
Write: Park R. Davidson, Exec. Dir.
Officer and Trustees:* Park R. Davidson,* Exec. Dir.; J.C. Cowan, Jr., Donald R. Hughes, J. Kenneth Lesley, Charles A. McLendon, Jr.
Number of staff: None.
Employer Identification Number: 566043142

5459
The Burroughs Wellcome Fund ▼
3030 Cornwallis Rd.
Research Triangle Park 27709 (919) 248-4136

Incorporated in 1955 in NY.
Donor(s): Burroughs Wellcome Co.
Foundation type: Company-sponsored
Financial data (yr. ended 04/30/89): Assets, $19,316,711 (M); gifts received, $550,000; expenditures, $5,804,162, including $5,701,438 for 177 grants (high: $300,000; low: $500; average: $1,000-$50,000).
Purpose and activities: Primarily to give financial aid for the advancement of research in the basic medical sciences within the U.S.: (1) support for clinical pharmacology through a competitive annual award, now $300,000 paid over five years, and an annual series of Creasy Visiting Professorships of Clinical Pharmacology; (2) an annual competitive Toxicology Scholar Award of $300,000, paid over five years; (3) an annual competitive Molecular Parasitology Award of $300,000 paid over five years; (4) Wellcome Visiting Professorships in the Basic Medical Sciences administered by the Federation of American Societies for Experimental Biology; (5) Wellcome Visiting Professorships in Microbiological Sciences administered by the American Society of Microbiology; (6) Wellcome Research Travel Grants to Britain/Ireland; (7) competitive awards for postdoctoral research fellowships administered by national medical, pharmacy, and life sciences organizations; (8) Pharmacoepidemiology Scholar Award of $300,000 payable over five years; (9) an annual competitive award of $300,000 for Immunopharmacology of Allergic Diseases; (10) Young Investigator Award in virology of $90,000; occasional, modest grants made on a short-term basis to "institutions for specially talented investigators and innovative research projects in the basic medical sciences."
Types of support: Scholarship funds, special projects, research, professorships, fellowships, lectureships.
Limitations: No grants to individuals, or for building or endowment funds, operating budgets, continuing support, annual campaigns, deficit financing, publications, conferences, or matching gifts; no loans.
Publications: Annual report, application guidelines, newsletter, informational brochure (including application guidelines), 990-PF.
Application information: Application form required only for Wellcome Research Travel Grants Program.
Initial approach: Letter
Deadline(s): varies
Board meeting date(s): Bimonthly, beginning in Feb.
Final notification: 6 weeks
Write: Martha G. Peck, Exec. Dir.
Officers: George H. Hitchings,* Pres.; Martha G. Peck, Secy. and Exec. Dir.
Directors:* David Barry, M.D., Stephen Corman, Thomas Krenitsky, Howard J. Schaeffer, A.J. Shepperd, C.E. Gordon Smith, M.D., Philip Tracy.
Number of staff: 3 full-time professional; 2 full-time support.
Employer Identification Number: 237225395

5460
The Cannon Foundation, Inc. ▼
P.O. Box 548
Concord 28026-0548 (704) 786-8216

Incorporated in 1943 in NC.
Donor(s): Charles A. Cannon,† Cannon Mills Co.
Foundation type: Independent
Financial data (yr. ended 09/30/89): Assets, $97,652,868 (M); qualifying distributions, $3,969,832, including $3,969,832 for 74 grants (high: $800,000; low: $125; average: $125-$800,000).
Purpose and activities: Support for hospitals, higher and secondary education, and cultural programs; grants also for Protestant church support, and social service and youth agencies.
Types of support: Annual campaigns, building funds, equipment, matching funds, renovation projects.
Limitations: Giving primarily in NC, especially in the Cabarrus County area. No grants to individuals, or for operating budgets, seed money, emergency funds, deficit financing, land acquisition, endowment funds, demonstration projects, research, publications, conferences, seminars, scholarships, or fellowships; no loans.
Publications: Application guidelines.
Application information: Application form required.
Initial approach: Letter
Copies of proposal: 1
Deadline(s): Submit proposal in Jan., Apr., July, and Oct.; deadline Jan. 15, Apr. 15, July 15, and Oct. 15

Board meeting date(s): Mar., June, Sept., and Dec.
Final notification: Within 2 weeks of board action
Write: Dan L. Gray, Exec. Dir.
Officers and Directors:* Mariam C. Hayes,* Pres.; W.S. Fisher,* V.P.; T.C. Haywood,* Secy.-Treas.; Dan L. Gray,* Exec. Dir.; G.A. Batte, Jr., R.C. Hayes, Elizabeth L. Quick, T.L. Ross.
Number of staff: 1 full-time professional; 2 full-time support.
Employer Identification Number: 566042532

5461
Wilbur Lee Carter Charitable Trust ⌑
1012 Country Club Dr.
Greensboro 27408-6316

Foundation type: Independent
Financial data (yr. ended 12/31/87): Assets, $2,159,587 (M); expenditures, $135,792, including $97,110 for 5 grants (high: $29,133; low: $9,711).
Purpose and activities: Giving primarily to a Baptist children's home, a seminary, a church and a hospital.
Application information: Contributes only to pre-selected organizations. Applications not accepted.
Trustees: Marie E.C. Carter, Wilbur L. Carter, Jr., Charles T. Hagan, Jr., NCNB National Bank of North Carolina.
Employer Identification Number: 237420174

5462
James McKeen Cattell Fund ⌑
Dept. of Psychology
Duke University
Durham 27706 (919) 684-3902

Trust established in 1942 in NY.
Donor(s): James McKeen Cattell.†
Foundation type: Independent
Financial data (yr. ended 12/31/87): Assets, $1,999,796 (M); expenditures, $181,495, including $145,560 for 14 grants to individuals (high: $15,502; low: $1,550).
Purpose and activities: Grants for postdoctoral training to supplement sabbatical allowances of psychologists in universities.
Types of support: Fellowships.
Limitations: Giving limited to the U.S. and Canada. No grants for building or endowment funds, operating budgets, or special projects.
Publications: Annual report, application guidelines.
Application information: Application form required.
Initial approach: Letter
Copies of proposal: 5
Deadline(s): Dec. 1
Board meeting date(s): Jan. or Feb.
Final notification: Feb. or Mar.
Write: Dr. Gregory A. Kimble, Secy.-Treas.
Officers and Trustees: Gregory A. Kimble, Secy.-Treas.; Lyle V. Jones, Managing Trustee; Edward Jones, Janet Spence, Elliot Valenstein.
Number of staff: 1 part-time professional.
Employer Identification Number: 136129600

5463
CCB Foundation, Inc. ⌑
111 Corcoran St.
Durham 27701
Application address: P.O. Box 931, Durham, NC 27707

Established in 1985 in NC.
Donor(s): CCB Financial Corp.
Foundation type: Company-sponsored
Financial data (yr. ended 12/31/86): Assets, $144,558 (M); gifts received, $129,120; expenditures, $165,041, including $151,146 for 56 grants (high: $28,500; low: $100) and $12,138 for 93 employee matching gifts.
Purpose and activities: Grants primarily for higher education, including through an employee matching gift program.
Types of support: Employee matching gifts.
Application information:
Initial approach: Letter
Deadline(s): None
Write: John J. Zenner III, Pres.
Officers: John J. Zenner III, Pres.; James L. Nicholson, Jr., V.P.; Norwood A. Thomas, Jr., Secy.-Treas.
Employer Identification Number: 581611223

5464
The Cemala Foundation, Inc. ⌑ ☆
P.O. Box 997
Greensboro 27402-0997 (919) 274-3541

Established in 1986 in NC.
Donor(s): Martha A. Cone, Ceasar Cone II.†
Foundation type: Independent
Financial data (yr. ended 12/31/88): Assets, $51,551 (M); gifts received, $165,000; expenditures, $123,356, including $104,500 for 18 grants (high: $50,000; low: $200).
Purpose and activities: Giving primarily to an Episcopal diocese and a youth organization; support also for Jewish giving and higher education.
Types of support: Building funds, operating budgets.
Limitations: Giving primarily in Greensboro, NC. No grants to individuals.
Application information: Application form not required.
Initial approach: Proposal
Deadline(s): None
Final notification: Within 3 to 6 months
Write: Robert B. White, Secy.-Treas.
Officers: Martha A. Cone,* Pres.; Ceasar Cone III,* V.P.; Robert B. White, Secy.-Treas.
Directors:* Lawrence M. Cone, Martha C. Richmond.
Employer Identification Number: 561528982

5465
Chapin Foundation of Myrtle Beach, South Carolina ⌑
c/o NCNB National Bank Trust Group
One NCNB Plaza T09-1
Charlotte 28255
Application address: P.O. Box 2568, Myrtle Beach, SC 29577

Trust established in 1943 in SC.
Donor(s): S.B. Chapin.
Foundation type: Independent
Financial data (yr. ended 07/31/89): Assets, $7,934,227 (M); expenditures, $769,041, including $739,692 for 52 grants (high: $100,000; low: $570).
Purpose and activities: Support for local Protestant churches and libraries.
Limitations: Giving limited to the Myrtle Beach, SC, area.
Application information: Application form not required.
Initial approach: Letter or proposal
Copies of proposal: 1
Deadline(s): None
Board meeting date(s): Twice a year
Write: Harold D. Clardy, Chair.
Officers and Directors:* Harold D. Clardy,* Chair.; Claude M. Epps, Jr.,* Secy.; Ruth T. Gore, Harold Hartshorne, Jr.
Trustee: NCNB National Bank.
Employer Identification Number: 566039453

5466
Chatham Foundation, Inc. ⌑
c/o Chatham Manufacturing Co.
3100 Glen Ave.
Elkin 28621 (919) 723-7802

Incorporated in 1943 in NC.
Donor(s): Members of the Chatham and Hanes families, and corporations.
Foundation type: Company-sponsored
Financial data (yr. ended 12/31/87): Assets, $1,748,959 (M); gifts received, $75,000; expenditures, $106,419, including $54,100 for 15 grants (high: $10,000; low: $400) and $12,750 for 9 grants to individuals (high: $1,500; low: $750).
Purpose and activities: Emphasis on higher and secondary education, including scholarships to children of Chatham Manufacturing Co. employees, Protestant church support, youth agencies, and alcoholism programs.
Types of support: Operating budgets, continuing support, annual campaigns, building funds, employee-related scholarships.
Limitations: Giving primarily in Elkin, NC, and vicinity. No grants to individuals (except for employee-related scholarships), or for endowment funds, research, or matching gifts; no loans.
Application information:
Initial approach: Letter
Copies of proposal: 1
Deadline(s): None
Board meeting date(s): As required
Final notification: 30 days
Write: David H. Cline, Secy.
Officers and Directors: Lucy Chatham Everett, Pres.; Barbara F. Chatham, V.P.; David H. Cline, III, Secy.-Treas.; Alex Chatham, Jr., Mary M. Chatham, Thomas L. Chatham.
Number of staff: None.
Employer Identification Number: 560771852

5467
Christian Training Foundation ⌑
2004 Valencia Terr.
Charlotte 28226

Established in 1972 in MN.
Donor(s): C. Wilbur Peters, Bessie Peters.
Foundation type: Independent
Financial data (yr. ended 01/31/89): Assets, $12,132,850 (M); gifts received, $124,121;

qualifying distributions, $670,812, including $415,773 for 31 grants (high: $73,893; low: $38) and $228,860 for 1 loan.
Purpose and activities: Support primarily for Protestant organizations, with emphasis on religious studies.
Limitations: No grants to individuals.
Application information: Contributes only to pre-selected organizations. Applications not accepted.
Officer: C. Wilbur Peters, Pres.
Employer Identification Number: 237167181

5468
Coffey Foundation, Inc. ⌑
P.O. Box 1170
Lenoir 28645
Application address: 406 Norwood St. S.W., Lenoir, NC 28645; Tel.: (704) 754-6594

Established about 1979 in NC.
Donor(s): The Annie N. Coffey Trust, Harold F. Coffey Trust.
Foundation type: Independent
Financial data (yr. ended 11/30/88): Assets, $2,815,045 (M); gifts received, $50,584; expenditures, $231,252, including $88,083 for 27 grants (high: $11,000; low: $500) and $112,000 for grants to individuals.
Purpose and activities: Giving for higher education, youth, and social services; support also for student loans and individual scholarships.
Types of support: Student loans, student aid.
Limitations: Giving primarily in Caldwell County, NC; scholarships limited to residents of Caldwell County.
Application information: Application forms for student grants available at high schools in Caldwell County.
Deadline(s): Apr. 15
Write: Mrs. Hope Huffstetler
Trustees: Faith T. Austin, Gary W. Bradford, W. Ray Cunningham, Percy F. Deverick, Charles E. Dobbin, W.H. Maynard, Wayne J. Miller, Jr.
Employer Identification Number: 566047501

5469
Cole Foundation ⌑
c/o NCNB National Bank of North Carolina
One NCNB Plaza
Charlotte 28255

Donor(s): Elizabeth S. Cole,† Robert Cole.†
Foundation type: Independent
Financial data (yr. ended 07/31/89): Assets, $15,050,752 (M); gifts received, $1,860,873; expenditures, $428,505, including $291,194 for 12 grants (high: $50,000; low: $4,900).
Purpose and activities: Support primarily for new projects that address identified community needs.
Limitations: Giving primarily in Richmond County, NC.
Application information: Contributes only to pre-selected organizations. Applications not accepted.
Write: William L. Spencer
Directors: Elizabeth S. Cole, Robert Cole.
Trustee: NCNB National Bank of North Carolina.
Employer Identification Number: 566067376

5470
Harold M. Cole Scholarship Trust ⌑ ☆
115 East Massachusetts Ave.
Southern Pines 28387
Application address: Scholarship Committee, South National Bank of North Carolina, Southern Pines, NC 28387

Established in 1987 in NC.
Foundation type: Independent
Financial data (yr. ended 3/31/88): Assets, $1,278,909 (M); gifts received, $1,251,958; expenditures, $19,017, including $11,261 for 4 grants to individuals (high: $4,900; low: $1,000).
Purpose and activities: Support limited to student aid to local residents attending NC institutions pursuing accounting degrees.
Types of support: Student aid.
Limitations: Giving limited to Moore County, NC, residents.
Application information: Application form required.
Initial approach: Letter
Deadline(s): June 30
Trustee: Southern National Bank of North Carolina.
Committee: Scott A. Brewer, Frankie Page, Jr.
Employer Identification Number: 586212292

5471
Connemara Fund
P.O. Box 20124
Greensboro 27420

Established in 1968 in NC.
Donor(s): Mary R. Jackson.†
Foundation type: Independent
Financial data (yr. ended 06/30/89): Assets, $6,929,858 (M); expenditures, $262,406, including $245,250 for 75 grants (high: $40,000; low: $100; average: $3,000).
Purpose and activities: Grants primarily for church support and religious welfare associations; support also for child welfare, social services, and cultural programs.
Types of support: Continuing support, general purposes.
Limitations: Giving primarily in the New England area. No grants to individuals.
Application information: Application form not required.
Initial approach: Proposal or letter
Copies of proposal: 1
Board meeting date(s): As required
Final notification: 2 months
Write: Herrick Jackson, Trustee
Trustees: Herrick Jackson, Robert W. Jackson, Alison Jackson Van Dyk.
Number of staff: 1
Employer Identification Number: 566096063

5472
The Marion Stedman Covington Foundation ☆
P.O. Box 1108
Greensboro 27402 (919) 272-5100

Established in 1986 in NC.
Foundation type: Independent
Financial data (yr. ended 12/31/88): Assets, $3,074,718 (M); expenditures, $170,841, including $141,500 for 10 grants (high: $22,000; low: $2,500).
Purpose and activities: Giving for higher education, social services, and the arts and cultural organizations, with an emphasis on historic preservation.
Types of support: Annual campaigns, capital campaigns, continuing support, scholarship funds.
Limitations: Giving primarily in NC. No grants to individuals.
Application information: Application form required.
Initial approach: Letter or telephone
Copies of proposal: 1
Deadline(s): 3 weeks prior to board meeting dates
Board meeting date(s): Usually end of Apr. and Oct.
Final notification: Following board meeting
Write: Sarah Fish, Trust Officer, North Carolina Trust Co.
Trustees: Marion S. Covington, Kathleen Crockett, Jane C. Hildebrand, J. Myrick Howard, North Carolina Trust Co.
Employer Identification Number: 566286555

5473
Cumberland Community Foundation, Inc.
P.O. Box 2171
Fayetteville 28302 (919) 483-4449

Established in 1980 in NC.
Foundation type: Community
Financial data (yr. ended 06/30/89): Assets, $2,327,418 (M); gifts received, $18,182; expenditures, $51,417.
Purpose and activities: Support primarily for community funds and services.
Types of support: Building funds, conferences and seminars, consulting services, emergency funds, employee matching gifts, equipment, exchange programs, internships, matching funds, program-related investments, publications, renovation projects, seed money, technical assistance.
Limitations: Giving primarily in Cumberland County, NC.
Publications: Annual report.
Application information: Application form not required.
Initial approach: Letter
Deadline(s): Oct.
Write: Robert O. McCoy
Officers and Directors:* Robert O. McCoy, Jr.,* Pres.; Henry G. Hutaff,* V.P.; Mary Lynn McGree Bryan,* Secy.; Charles vonRosenberg,* Treas.; Reginald Barton, Jr., John Randolph Griffin, Jr., James S. Harper, Charles B.C. Holt, Tom McLean, Walter C. Moorman, Ruby S. Murchison, John E. Raper, Joel Schur, Iris Thornton, Terri S. Union.
Employer Identification Number: 581406831

5474
Harry L. Dalton Foundation, Inc. ⌑
736 Wachovia Ctr.
Charlotte 28285 (704) 332-5380

Established about 1979 in NC.
Foundation type: Independent
Financial data (yr. ended 07/31/89): Assets, $2,283,694 (M); expenditures, $85,490,

including $80,200 for 31 grants (high: $21,300; low: $20).
Purpose and activities: Giving primarily for education, including higher education and libraries; support also for cultural programs, youth, family planning, drug abuse programs, mental health, and historic preservation.
Application information: Application form not required.
Deadline(s): None
Write: Harry L. Dalton, Pres.
Officers and Directors:* Harry L. Dalton,* Pres. and Treas.; Mary E. Dalton,* V.P.; Elizabeth D. Brand, Secy.
Number of staff: 1 part-time support.
Employer Identification Number: 566061267

5475
The Josephus Daniels Charitable Foundation
215 South McDowell St.
Raleigh 27601-1331 (919) 829-4694

Established in 1964 in NC.
Donor(s): The News and Observer Publishing Co.
Foundation type: Company-sponsored
Financial data (yr. ended 12/31/88): Assets, $2,992,259 (M); gifts received, $617,368; expenditures, $544,611, including $516,763 for 107 grants (high: $55,000; low: $50).
Purpose and activities: Support for higher and other education, and community funds and development; support also for the fine and performing arts and other cultural programs, and social services, including AIDS programs, the disadvantaged, women, and youth.
Types of support: Annual campaigns, building funds, capital campaigns, continuing support, emergency funds, endowment funds, equipment, publications, renovation projects, scholarship funds, seed money, special projects, in-kind gifts, land acquisition.
Limitations: Giving primarily in NC. No support for religious or political organizations. No grants to individuals, or for conferences or seminars.
Publications: Informational brochure (including application guidelines).
Application information: Application form not required.
Initial approach: Letter
Deadline(s): None
Board meeting date(s): Quarterly
Write: Witt Clarke, Secy.-Treas.
Officers: Frank A. Daniels, Jr., Pres.; Melvin L. Finch, V.P.; Witt Clarke, Secy.-Treas.
Employer Identification Number: 566065260

5476
Champion McDowell Davis Charitable Foundation ⌑
2405 Oleander Dr.
Wilmington 28403

Established in 1963 in NC.
Donor(s): Champion McDowell Davis.†
Foundation type: Independent
Financial data (yr. ended 12/31/88): Assets, $8,662,416 (M); expenditures, $281,828, including $146,870 for 6 grants (high: $130,000; low: $1,000).
Purpose and activities: Giving for health services and care for the elderly; support also for conservation.
Limitations: Giving primarily in Wilmington, NC.
Application information:
Write: Michael C. Brown, Pres.
Officers and Trustees:* Michael C. Brown,* Pres.; John Codington, Cyrus D. Hogue, Jr., Emsley A. Laney, John Murchison II, Peter B. Ruffin, Robey T. Sinclair, Jr., M.D.
Employer Identification Number: 566055716

5477
Davis Hospital, Inc. ⌑ ☆
Rte. 1, Box 353
Sugar Grove 28679

Established in 1983 in NC.
Foundation type: Independent
Financial data (yr. ended 9/30/88): Assets, $4,614,538 (M); expenditures, $258,851, including $180,676 for 2 grants (high: $164,580; low: $16,095) and $29,708 for 1 grant to an individual.
Purpose and activities: Giving primarily for nursing education; support also for health care for individuals.
Types of support: Grants to individuals.
Application information: Contributes only to pre-selected organizations. Applications not accepted.
Officer and Trustees: John L. West, Mgr.; Ralph Bentley, John N. Gilbert, Jr., William R. Hill, Mildred Husking, Fred Lovette, William H. McElwee, Lillie Norket, J. Stewart, Hoyle L. Whiteside, Margaret Wilhide.
Employer Identification Number: 581528127

5478
Deichman-Lerner Foundation ☆
2600 Charlotte Plaza
201 South College St.
Charlotte 28244

Foundation type: Independent
Financial data (yr. ended 1/28/89): Assets, $1,589 (M); gifts received, $261,895; expenditures, $281,230, including $280,955 for 7 grants (high: $152,825; low: $1,500).
Purpose and activities: Giving primarily for an organization providing relief in India; support also for medical and higher education.
Limitations: No grants to individuals.
Application information: Contributes only to pre-selected organizations. Applications not accepted.
Officer: Dane Reynolds, Mgr.
Employer Identification Number: 581615694

5479
The Dickson Foundation, Inc. ⌑
2000 Two First Union Ctr.
Charlotte 28282 (704) 372-5404

Incorporated in 1944 in NC.
Donor(s): American and Efird Mills, Inc.
Foundation type: Independent
Financial data (yr. ended 12/31/88): Assets, $19,951,223 (M); expenditures, $856,164, including $789,699 for 233 grants (high: $50,000; low: $100).
Purpose and activities: Support for secondary and higher education, including scholarship funds, community funds, youth agencies, and hospitals.
Types of support: Scholarship funds, general purposes.
Limitations: Giving primarily in NC. No grants to individuals, or for building or endowment funds.
Application information:
Initial approach: Letter
Deadline(s): None
Board meeting date(s): Annually and as required
Officers and Directors:* R. Stuart Dickson,* Chair.; Alan T. Dickson,* Pres.; Rush S. Dickson III,* V.P.; Thomas W. Dickson,* V.P.; Colleen S. Colbert, Secy.-Treas.
Employer Identification Number: 566022339

5480
The Dillard Fund, Inc. ⌑
3900 Spring Garden St.
Greensboro 27407

Established in 1964 in NC.
Donor(s): Dillard Paper Co.
Foundation type: Company-sponsored
Financial data (yr. ended 12/31/88): Assets, $1,247,467 (M); gifts received, $100,000; expenditures, $126,885, including $121,725 for 72 grants (high: $50,000; low: $25).
Purpose and activities: Support for higher and other education, youth, the United Way, health, and social services.
Limitations: Giving primarily in NC.
Officers and Trustees: Geoffrey A. Clark, Chair.; G. Henry Jobe, Jr., Pres.; John H. Dillard, Sr. V.P.; Frank A. Sharpe, Jr., V.P. and Secy.; George R. Brumback, V.P. and Treas.; Thomas Ruffin, Jr., V.P.
Employer Identification Number: 566065838

5481
The Dover Foundation, Inc.
P.O. Box 208
Shelby 28150 (704) 847-2000

Incorporated in 1944 in NC.
Foundation type: Independent
Financial data (yr. ended 08/31/89): Assets, $13,000,000 (M); expenditures, $565,000, including $545,000 for 135 grants (high: $250,000; low: $100; average: $100-$250,000) and $20,000 for 12 grants to individuals (high: $6,000; low: $1,000; average: $1,000-$6,000).
Purpose and activities: Emphasis on higher and secondary education, museums, church support, health services, and social service agencies.
Types of support: Annual campaigns, building funds, capital campaigns, operating budgets, renovation projects, scholarship funds.
Limitations: Giving primarily in NC.
Application information: Application form not required.
Initial approach: Letter
Deadline(s): July
Board meeting date(s): Jan., Mar., July, and Sept.
Write: Hoyt Q. Bailey, Pres.

Officers: Hoyt Q. Bailey, Pres.; Harvey B. Hamrick, Secy.; W.W. Gainey, Jr., Treas.
Number of staff: 1 part-time support.
Employer Identification Number: 560769897

5482
Dowd Foundation, Inc. ⌑
P.O. Box 35430
Charlotte 28235

Donor(s): Charlotte Pipe & Foundry Co.
Foundation type: Independent
Financial data (yr. ended 10/31/88): Assets, $2,352,108 (M); gifts received, $650,000; expenditures, $287,171, including $278,901 for 54 grants (high: $50,000; low: $100).
Purpose and activities: Giving to youth and social services, education, and Protestant religious activities.
Application information:
Initial approach: Letter
Deadline(s): None
Officers: Roddey Dowd, Pres.; Frank Dowd, Jr., V.P.; E.H. Hardison, Secy.-Treas.
Employer Identification Number: 566061389

5483
The Duke Endowment ▼
200 South Tryon St., Suite 1100
Charlotte 28202 (704) 376-0291
Additional office: 3329 Chapel Hill Blvd., P.O. Box 51307, Durham, NC 27717-1307

Trust established in 1924 in NJ.
Donor(s): James Buchanan Duke.†
Foundation type: Independent
Financial data (yr. ended 12/31/89): Assets, $990,835,850 (M); expenditures, $52,378,941, including $45,940,739 for 853 grants.
Purpose and activities: "To make provision in some measure for the needs of mankind along physical, mental, and spiritual lines." Grants to nonprofit hospitals and child care institutions; rural United Methodist churches and retired ministers in NC and their dependents; and Duke, Furman, and Johnson C. Smith universities, and Davidson College.
Types of support: Operating budgets, seed money, emergency funds, matching funds, professorships, internships, scholarship funds, fellowships, endowment funds, research, special projects, publications, conferences and seminars, consulting services, technical assistance, continuing support, annual campaigns, building funds, capital campaigns, equipment, general purposes, renovation projects, grants to individuals.
Limitations: Giving primarily in NC and SC. No grants to individuals (except for retired ministers and their dependents), or for deficit financing; no loans.
Publications: Annual report, newsletter, informational brochure (including application guidelines).
Application information: Application form not required.
Initial approach: Letter
Deadline(s): None
Board meeting date(s): Monthly
Final notification: 2 to 8 months
Write: Billy G. McCall, Exec. Dir., or Jere W. Witherspoon, Deputy Exec. Dir.
Officers: Billy G. McCall, Exec. Dir.; Jere W. Witherspoon, Deputy Exec. Dir.; Myrna C. Fourcher, Secy.; Janice C. Walker, Treas.
Trustees: Mary D.B.T. Semans, Chair.; Hugh M. Chapman, Vice-Chair.; Louis C. Stephens, Jr., Vice-Chair.; Archie K. Davis, Doris Duke, W. Kenneth Goodson, Mary D.T. Jones, Juanita M. Kreps, Charles F. Myers, Jr., Marshall I. Pickens, Richard W. Riley, Russell M. Robinson II, James C. Self, Charles B. Wade, Jr.
Number of staff: 16 full-time professional; 19 full-time support.
Employer Identification Number: 560529965

5484
Duke Power Company Foundation ⌑
422 South Church St.
Charlotte 28242 (704) 373-3224
Scholarship application address: Scholastic Excellence Awards Program, P.O. Box 33189, Charlotte, NC 28242

Established in 1984 in NC.
Donor(s): Duke Power Co.
Foundation type: Company-sponsored
Financial data (yr. ended 12/31/88): Assets, $2,143,673 (M); gifts received, $573,120; expenditures, $5,022,843, including $4,967,474 for 1,768 grants (high: $100,000; low: $10; average: $500-$10,000) and $43,650 for 89 grants to individuals.
Purpose and activities: Supports those organizations, institutions, and programs that are able to demonstrate a broad base of support among the business and civic community. Support is directed to: health and human services, education, civic programs, the homeless, environment, engineering, and culture and art. Awards competitive scholarships to students whose parents live in company areas and to employees' or retirees' children.
Types of support: Employee-related scholarships, student aid, capital campaigns, employee matching gifts, general purposes, matching funds.
Limitations: Giving primarily in the company's headquarters and service areas in NC and SC. No support for single sectarian or denominational religious, veterans', or fraternal organizations; organizations where the foundation would be the only donor; hospitals supported by the Duke Endowment; or to organizations primarily supported by tax dollars (education excepted).
Application information: Application form required for scholarships only; students must be nominated by school official.
Initial approach: Proposal
Copies of proposal: 1
Deadline(s): Scholarships: Oct. 15; all others anytime
Write: Robert C. Allen, V.P.
Officers: William S. Lee,* Chair.; Douglas W. Booth,* Pres.; Robert C. Allen, V.P. and Exec. Dir.; John P. O'Keefe, Secy.; David L. Hauser, Treas.
Trustees:* Steve C. Griffith, Jr., William H. Grigg, Warren H. Owen.
Employer Identification Number: 581586283

5485
Elizabeth City Foundation ⌑
P.O. Box 574
Elizabeth City 27907-0574 (919) 335-7850

Community trust.
Foundation type: Community
Financial data (yr. ended 7/31/88): Assets, $1,847,688 (M); gifts received, $575; expenditures, $143,653, including $83,000 for 7 grants (high: $44,500; low: $2,000) and $28,633 for grants to individuals.
Purpose and activities: Giving for education and civic improvement; support also for scholarships for local students.
Types of support: Student aid, continuing support.
Limitations: Giving limited to the Albemarle area of northeastern NC for general grants, and Camden County, NC, for scholarships.
Application information: Scholarship application forms available at Wachovia Bank and Trust Co. and Camden High School. Application form required.
Deadline(s): Apr. 1 for scholarships; May 15 and Dec. 15 for other grants
Board meeting date(s): Jan. and June
Write: Ray S. Jones, Jr., Exec. Dir.
Officer: Ray S. Jones, Jr., Exec. Dir.
Trustees: First Citizens Bank & Trust Co., First Union National Bank, Peoples Bank and Trust, Wachovia Bank & Trust Co., N.A.
Employer Identification Number: 237076018

5486
Percy B. Ferebee Endowment ⌑
c/o Wachovia Bank & Trust Co., N.A.
P.O. Box 3099
Winston-Salem 27150 (919) 770-5991

Established in 1973 in NC.
Donor(s): Percy Ferebee.†
Foundation type: Independent
Financial data (yr. ended 12/31/88): Assets, $1,996,668 (M); gifts received, $1,302; expenditures, $128,706, including $61,000 for 6 grants (high: $16,424; low: $3,901; average: $5,000) and $47,100 for 77 grants to individuals (high: $1,200; low: $500; average: $600).
Purpose and activities: Emphasis on scholarships to individuals, and educational, cultural, and civic development.
Types of support: Student aid, annual campaigns, seed money, emergency funds, building funds, equipment, land acquisition.
Limitations: Giving primarily in Cherokee, Clay, Graham, Jackson, Macon, and Swain counties, NC, and the Cherokee Indian Reservation. No grants to individuals (except for scholarships), or for operating budgets.
Publications: Informational brochure (including application guidelines).
Application information: Application form required.
Initial approach: Proposal
Copies of proposal: 1
Deadline(s): Submit proposal preferably in Sept.; deadline for scholarships, Feb. 15; for grants, Oct. 1
Board meeting date(s): May and Nov.
Final notification: 10 days
Write: J. Wade Stinnette

Awards Advisory Committee: John Parris, Chair.; Mrs. Frela Owl Beck, Ty W. Burnette, James Conley, Maggie Alice Sandlin Crisp, J. Smith Howell, John Waldroup, Bill Walker.
Trustee: Wachovia Bank & Trust Co., N.A.
Number of staff: None.
Employer Identification Number: 566118992

5487
Ferree Educational & Welfare Fund ⌑
101 Sunset Ave.
P.O. Box 1328
Asheboro 27203 (919) 629-2960

Established in 1953 in NC.
Donor(s): Mabel P. Ferree.†
Foundation type: Independent
Financial data (yr. ended 12/31/88): Assets, $1,454,392 (M); qualifying distributions, $75,116, including $20,000 for 20 grants to individuals of $1,000 each and $48,000 for 91 loans to individuals.
Purpose and activities: Awards students loans and grants for higher education to residents of Randolph County, NC.
Types of support: Student loans, student aid.
Limitations: Giving limited to Randolph County, NC, residents.
Application information: Application form required.
Deadline(s): June 15, loan applicants must complete interview with foundation by June 1
Write: Claire C. Sprouse, Admin. Dir.
Officers: Claire C. Sprouse, Exec. Secy.; James M. Culberson, Jr.,* Treas.
Trustees:* George Fleetwood, Chair.; Darrell Frye, Bob W. Gordon, Thomas N. Moose, J.M. Ramsay III, Marion S. Smith, W. Joe Trogdon.
Number of staff: 1 part-time professional.
Employer Identification Number: 566062560

5488
Fieldcrest Foundation ⌑
326 East Stadium Dr.
Eden 27288
Application address: c/o Fieldcrest Cannon, Inc., General Office, Eden, NC 27288; Tel.: (919) 627-3046

Incorporated in 1959 in NC.
Donor(s): Fieldcrest Mills, Inc.
Foundation type: Company-sponsored
Financial data (yr. ended 12/31/88): Assets, $2,147,175 (M); gifts received, $922,978; expenditures, $707,477, including $705,626 for grants (high: $17,000).
Purpose and activities: Scholarships for children of company employees; grants primarily to community funds, youth agencies, and higher education, including building funds.
Types of support: Employee-related scholarships, building funds.
Limitations: Giving primarily in plant communities in NC, VA, GA, SC, and AL.
Application information: Application form required.
Deadline(s): For scholarships, May 1; for grants, July 1
Write: C.C. Barnhardt, Jr., Secy.
Officers: Charles G. Horn,* Pres.; C.C. Barnhardt, Jr., Secy.; K.W. Fraser, Jr.,* Treas.
Directors:* B.W. Binford, M.K. Doss, O.L. Raines, Jr., W.O. Stone, Jr.
Employer Identification Number: 566046659

5489
The Doak Finch Foundation
c/o NCNB National Bank Trust Group
One NCNB Plaza T09-1
Charlotte 28255 (704) 374-7581
Application address: 10 Welloskie Dr., Thomasville, NC 27360

Trust established in 1961 in NC.
Donor(s): Doak Finch.†
Foundation type: Independent
Financial data (yr. ended 10/31/89): Assets, $2,981,675 (M); expenditures, $210,826, including $190,300 for 23 grants (high: $50,000; low: $1,000; average: $3,000-$5,000).
Purpose and activities: Giving to schools, social service agencies, and cultural organizations.
Limitations: Giving limited to the Thomasville, NC, area.
Application information: Application form not required.
Initial approach: Letter or proposal
Copies of proposal: 1
Deadline(s): Feb.
Board meeting date(s): No established dates
Write: Manager of Institutional Services
Directors: J.C. Dorety, Helen Finch, Richard J. Finch, Jane F. Turner, David R. Williams.
Trustee Bank: NCNB National Bank.
Employer Identification Number: 566042823

5490
Thomas Austin Finch Foundation ⌑
c/o Wachovia Bank & Trust Co., N.A.
P.O. Box 3099
Winston-Salem 27150 (919) 770-6222

Trust established in 1944 in NC.
Donor(s): Ernestine L. Finch Mobley,† Thomas Austin Finch, Jr.†
Foundation type: Independent
Financial data (yr. ended 12/31/88): Assets, $5,673,259 (M); expenditures, $299,318, including $251,035 for 17 grants (high: $55,500; low: $1,000).
Purpose and activities: Interests include higher and secondary education, Protestant church support and church-related schools, and community funds.
Types of support: Operating budgets, continuing support, annual campaigns, building funds, equipment, scholarship funds, special projects.
Limitations: Giving limited to Thomasville, NC. No grants to individuals, or for emergency funds, deficit financing, endowment funds, or fellowships; no loans.
Publications: Informational brochure (including application guidelines).
Application information: Application form required for all grants over $5,000.
Initial approach: Letter
Copies of proposal: 1
Deadline(s): Feb. 15 and Oct. 15
Board meeting date(s): Mar. and Nov.
Final notification: 2 weeks
Write: Wade Stinnette
Foundation Committee: David Finch, Chair.; John Finch, Sumner Finch, Meredith Slane Person.
Trustee: Wachovia Bank & Trust Co., N.A.
Number of staff: None.
Employer Identification Number: 566037907

5491
A. E. Finley Foundation, Inc.
P.O. Box 27785
Raleigh 27611 (919) 782-0565

Incorporated in 1957 in NC.
Donor(s): A.E. Finley.†
Foundation type: Independent
Financial data (yr. ended 11/30/88): Assets, $16,972,446 (M); gifts received, $1,944,254; expenditures, $972,186, including $760,630 for 92 grants (high: $153,750; low: $20).
Purpose and activities: Giving for higher education and youth agencies.
Types of support: Fellowships, operating budgets, research.
Limitations: Giving primarily in NC.
Publications: Informational brochure.
Application information: Application form not required.
Initial approach: Letter
Copies of proposal: 1
Write: Bobby Brown
Officer and Directors:* R.C. Brown,* Pres.; A. Earle Finley II,* Secy.; W.C. Calton, A.E. Howard, C.D. Nottingham II, G.W. Wilson.
Number of staff: 1 full-time professional; 1 part-time professional; 1 full-time support.
Employer Identification Number: 566057379

5492
First Gaston Foundation, Inc.
(Formerly Myers-Ti-Caro Foundation, Inc.)
P.O. Box 2696
Gastonia 28053 (704) 865-6111

Incorporated in 1950 in NC.
Donor(s): Textiles, Inc., Threads, Inc.
Foundation type: Independent
Financial data (yr. ended 10/01/88): Assets, $6,741,895 (M); expenditures, $909,153, including $716,306 for 71 grants (high: $317,000; low: $500) and $96,000 for 57 grants to individuals (high: $12,000; low: $322).
Purpose and activities: Grants for higher and secondary education, including scholarships to students in Gaston County; also social services and youth, religious welfare, health and hospitals, and arts and culture.
Types of support: Student aid.
Limitations: Giving limited to communities in NC, with emphasis on Gaston County.
Application information: Application forms required for scholarships. Application form not required.
Deadline(s): None
Board meeting date(s): Spring and Dec.
Write: Albert G. Myers, Jr., Chair. or Nina Greene, Secy.
Officers and Trustees:* Albert G. Myers, Jr.,* Chair.; B. Frank Matthews II,* Vice-Chair.; J. Mack Holland, Jr.,* Secy.; Robert P. Caldwell, Jr.,* Treas.; A. Lionel Brunnemer, Tom D. Effird, J.C. Fry, Albert G. Myers III.
Number of staff: 1 full-time support.

Employer Identification Number: 560770083

5493
The First Union Foundation
First Union Plaza, 0143
Charlotte 28288 (704) 374-6649
Addresses of contributions coordinators: First Union Natl. Bank, Marketing Div. T-2, Box 1329, Greenville, SC 29602; First Union Corp., GA, P.O. Box 56566, Atlanta, GA 30343; First Union Natl. Bank, P.O. Box 2080, Jacksonville, FL 32231

Established in 1987 in NC.
Donor(s): First Union Corp.
Foundation type: Company-sponsored
Financial data (yr. ended 12/31/89): Assets, $3,268,030 (M); gifts received, $4,499,500; expenditures, $3,757,543, including $3,576,680 for grants and $178,183 for 724 employee matching gifts.
Purpose and activities: Support for higher education, special programs for public elementary and secondary schools, and other educational programs; arts funds or councils, public broadcasting, visual and performing arts, and historic preservation and libraries; community improvement and leadership development; family and social services, minorities, the handicapped, and the homeless; health, including drug abuse and mental health programs, cancer research, and rehabilitation; and environmental protection. Special consideration for children and youth and the disadvantaged to help them become productive and self-sufficient. Types of support include capital grants, made only when there is a community-wide fundraising campaign that includes the entire business community. A grant is made for one year only and does not imply that a grant will be made the following year unless a multi-year pledge is made.
Types of support: Building funds, capital campaigns, endowment funds, operating budgets, renovation projects, special projects, employee matching gifts, scholarship funds, seed money.
Limitations: Giving primarily in FL, GA, NC, and SC. No support for religious, veterans', or fraternal organizations, retirement homes, pre-college level schools except through employee matching gifts or for a special project for a public school, or organizations supported through the United Way, except for approved capital campaigns.
Publications: Application guidelines.
Application information: Application form not required.
Initial approach: Proposal to the nearest First Union Bank
Copies of proposal: 1
Deadline(s): Sept. 1 for consideration in next year's budget
Board meeting date(s): Mar., June, Sept., and Dec.
Write: Ann D. Thomas, V.P., Corp. Contribs.
Directors: Ann D. Thomas, Dir., Corp. Contribs.; Marion A. Cowell, Jr., Edward E. Crutchfield, Jr., John R. Georgius, J. Robert Lee, B.J. Walker.
Trustee: First Union National Bank of North Carolina.
Employer Identification Number: 566288589

5494
Foundation For The Carolinas ▼
301 South Brevard St.
Charlotte 28202 (704) 376-9541

Incorporated in 1958 in NC.
Foundation type: Community
Financial data (yr. ended 12/31/89): Assets, $52,085,210 (M); gifts received, $22,670,561; expenditures, $10,469,370, including $9,841,961 for 1,800 grants (high: $3,150,000; low: $100; average: $1,000-$20,000).
Purpose and activities: Support primarily for education, human services, religion, the arts, health and medical research, youth programs, the aged, the environment, historic preservation, and public interest and civic programs.
Types of support: Seed money, matching funds, scholarship funds.
Limitations: Giving primarily to organizations serving the citizens of NC and SC, with emphasis on the Central Piedmont region. No grants to individuals, or for deficit financing, capital campaigns, operating budgets, publications, conferences, or endowment funds.
Publications: Annual report (including application guidelines), newsletter, program policy statement.
Application information: Application form required.
Initial approach: Letter
Copies of proposal: 15
Deadline(s): Feb. 1, June 1, and Oct. 1
Board meeting date(s): Quarterly, with annual meeting in Mar.; distribution committee meets monthly
Final notification: 2 months
Write: William L. Spencer, Pres.
Officers: Larry J. Dagenhart,* Chair.; Robin L. Hinson,* 1st Vice-Chair.; A.F. Sloan,* Vice-Chair.; William L. Spencer, Pres.; Marilyn Bradbury,* V.P.; James Thompson,* Secy.; Crandall Close Bowles,* Treas.
Directors:* John V. Andrews, and 39 additional directors.
Number of staff: 6 full-time professional; 2 part-time professional; 6 full-time support; 1 part-time support.
Employer Identification Number: 566047886

5495
Community Foundation of Gaston County, Inc.
(Formerly Garrison Community Foundation of Gaston County, Inc.)
P.O. Box 123
Gastonia 28053 (704) 864-0927

Incorporated in 1978 in NC.
Foundation type: Community
Financial data (yr. ended 12/31/89): Assets, $3,870,388 (M); gifts received, $619,617; expenditures, $498,556, including $484,656 for grants.
Purpose and activities: Support for the arts, education, health services, museums and youth organizations; support also for medical grants to children 18 or under.
Types of support: Seed money, building funds, equipment, special projects, renovation projects, general purposes.
Limitations: Giving limited to Gaston County, NC. No grants for exchange programs, fellowships, program-related investments, annual campaigns, deficit financing, continuing support, technical assistance, professorships, scholarships, or internships; no loans.
Publications: Annual report, occasional report, informational brochure.
Application information: Application form is required for Children's Medical Aid Fund only.
Initial approach: Letter
Copies of proposal: 1
Deadline(s): Feb. 15 and Aug. 15
Board meeting date(s): Feb. and Sept.
Write: Rebecca B. Carter, Exec. Dir.
Officers: George C. Winecoff, Pres.; Rebecca B. Carter, Exec. Dir.
Employer Identification Number: 581340834

5496
The Edward C. Giles Foundation
736 Hempstead Place
Charlotte 28207 (704) 376-1293
Scholarship application address: P.O. Box 33056, Charlotte, NC 28233

Established in 1981 in NC.
Donor(s): Lucille P. Giles.
Foundation type: Independent
Financial data (yr. ended 12/31/88): Assets, $8,280,084 (M); expenditures, $690,007, including $511,500 for 26 grants (high: $50,000; low: $5,000) and $98,361 for 33 grants to individuals of $4,000 each.
Purpose and activities: Scholarships to descendants of employees of Caraustar Industries, Inc. and subsidiaries.
Types of support: Student aid, employee-related scholarships.
Limitations: Giving primarily in NC.
Publications: Informational brochure (including application guidelines).
Application information: Application form required.
Deadline(s): Feb. 15
Board meeting date(s): Spring and late fall
Write: Mrs. Lucille P. Giles, Pres.
Officers: Lucille P. Giles, Pres. and Treas.; Joseph W. Grier, Jr., V.P.; James Y. Preston, Secy.
Number of staff: None.
Employer Identification Number: 581450874

5497
Gilmer-Smith Foundation ⌑ ☆
P.O. Box 251
Mount Airy 27030

Foundation type: Independent
Financial data (yr. ended 11/30/89): Assets, $2,133,525 (M); expenditures, $202,670, including $95,119 for 13 grants (high: $39,396; low: $300).
Purpose and activities: Giving primarily for a park and a historical preservation society; support also for health.
Limitations: Giving primarily in Mount Airy, NC.
Officers: Edward N. Swanson, Pres.; P.M. Sharpe, Secy.
Trustees: David Beal, George T. Fawcett, Jr., Rachel B. Smith.
Employer Identification Number: 581463411

5498
Karl and Anna Ginter Foundation
c/o NCNB National Bank Trust Group
One NCNB Plaza T09-1
Charlotte 28255 (704) 374-7581

Established in 1968 in NC.
Donor(s): Karl Ginter.†
Foundation type: Independent
Financial data (yr. ended 12/31/89): Assets, $1,802,404 (M); expenditures, $111,422, including $100,138 for 15 grants (high: $20,000; low: $2,000; average: $5,000-$6,000).
Purpose and activities: Emphasis on higher education; support also for museums and other cultural programs, adult education, child development, religious missionaries, community development, and social services, including programs for the homeless and fighting hunger.
Types of support: Annual campaigns, building funds, capital campaigns, fellowships, general purposes, program-related investments, research, scholarship funds, seed money, special projects.
Limitations: Giving primarily in Mecklenburg County, NC.
Application information: Funds are mostly committed. Application form not required.
Initial approach: Proposal or letter
Copies of proposal: 1
Deadline(s): Sept. 30
Board meeting date(s): Nov.
Final notification: Dec. 31
Write: Mgr., Institutional Services
Directors: Stamford R. Brookshire, Joseph W. Grier, Jr., Thomas R. Payne.
Trustee: NCNB National Bank.
Employer Identification Number: 566094355

5499
The Glaxo Foundation
Five Moore Dr.
Research Triangle Park 27709 (919) 248-2140

Established in 1986 in NC.
Donor(s): Glaxo, Inc.
Foundation type: Company-sponsored
Financial data (yr. ended 6/30/88): Assets, $3,897,371 (M); gifts received, $1,438,572; expenditures, $127,977, including $124,950 for 3 grants (high: $68,400; low: $16,000).
Purpose and activities: Initial year of grantmaking activities, fiscal 1988; support for early childhood and elementary education, child development and child welfare, health, and programs for the disadvantaged.
Types of support: Operating budgets.
Limitations: Giving primarily in NC. No support for religious or fraternal organizations. No grants to individuals, or for general operating expenses.
Publications: Annual report, informational brochure (including application guidelines).
Application information: Application form not required.
Copies of proposal: 1
Deadline(s): Apr. 1 and Oct. 1
Board meeting date(s): June and Dec.
Final notification: June 30 and Dec. 30
Write: Kathryn H. Wallace, Contribs. Admin.
Officers and Directors: Joseph J. Ruvane, Jr., Pres.; Thomas R. Haber, V.P. and Treas.; Thomas W. D'Alonzo, Secy.; Stephen R. Conafay, Ernest Mario.
Number of staff: 1 full-time professional.
Employer Identification Number: 581698610

5500
Carrie E. & Lena V. Glenn Foundation ⌑
P.O. Box 308
Gastonia 28053-0308

Established in 1971 in NC.
Foundation type: Independent
Financial data (yr. ended 9/30/88): Assets, $3,824,476 (M); expenditures, $219,087, including $164,000 for 21 grants (high: $25,000; low: $1,000).
Purpose and activities: Support primarily for education, health organizations and medical education, libraries, drug abuse programs, community development, and religious welfare.
Types of support: General purposes.
Limitations: Giving primarily in Gaston County, NC.
Application information: Application form not required.
Deadline(s): None
Directors: Hugh F. Bryant, W.W. Dickson, Craig Fielding, Judith M. Miller, Elizabeth T. Stewart, James G. Stuart.
Trustee: Branch Banking & Trust Co.
Employer Identification Number: 237140170

5501
Goody's Manufacturing Corporation Foundation ⌑ ☆
P.O. Box 10518
Winston-Salem 27108-0518

Donor(s): Goody's Manufacturing Corp.
Foundation type: Company-sponsored
Financial data (yr. ended 12/31/88): Assets, $18,345 (M); gifts received, $74,000; expenditures, $106,578, including $106,301 for 75 grants (high: $15,000; low: $25).
Purpose and activities: Giving primarily for hospitals and health associations, and higher education; support also for Protestant welfare.
Limitations: Giving primarily in NC, with emphasis on Winston-Salem. No grants to individuals.
Application information: Contributes only to pre-selected organizations. Applications not accepted.
Trustees: T.A. Carter, T.H. Chambers, Jr., A.L. Spencer.
Employer Identification Number: 566075615

5502
The Foundation of Greater Greensboro, Inc.
First Citizens Bank, Suite 307
P.O. Box 207
Greensboro 27402 (919) 379-9100

Established in 1983.
Foundation type: Community
Financial data (yr. ended 06/30/89): Assets, $4,971,346 (M); gifts received, $2,242,439; expenditures, $423,844, including $303,194 for grants.
Purpose and activities: Grants primarily for cultural affairs and the arts, civic affairs and community development, education, and health and social services.
Types of support: Emergency funds, equipment, general purposes, renovation projects, seed money, special projects.
Limitations: Giving limited to the Greater Greensboro, NC, area.
Publications: Annual report, application guidelines, program policy statement, newsletter.
Application information: Application form required.
Initial approach: Proposal (3 pages or less)
Copies of proposal: 1
Deadline(s): 30 days prior to monthly meeting
Write: Wentworth L. Durgin, Exec. Dir.
Officers and Directors:* John Ellison, Jr.,* Pres.; Carolyn W. Fee,* Treas.; and 27 additional directors.
Number of staff: 1 full-time professional; 1 full-time support.
Employer Identification Number: 561380249

5503
The John W. and Anna H. Hanes Foundation
c/o Wachovia Bank & Trust Co., N.A.
P.O. Box 3099, MC 31022
Winston-Salem 27150 (919) 770-5274

Trust established in 1947 in NC.
Foundation type: Independent
Financial data (yr. ended 12/31/89): Assets, $14,412,034 (M); expenditures, $585,336, including $527,833 for 38 grants (high: $57,000; low: $1,000; average: $1,000-$25,000).
Purpose and activities: Support for cultural programs, historic preservation, conservation, health, education, child welfare, social services, and community programs.
Types of support: Annual campaigns, seed money, emergency funds, building funds, equipment, land acquisition, endowment funds, matching funds, special projects, research, publications, capital campaigns.
Limitations: Giving limited to NC, particularly Forsyth County. No grants to individuals, or for operating expenses.
Publications: Program policy statement, application guidelines.
Application information: Application form required.
Initial approach: Telephone or letter
Copies of proposal: 1
Deadline(s): 15th day of month preceding board meeting
Board meeting date(s): Jan., Apr., July, and Oct.
Final notification: 10 days
Write: Joyce T. Adger, V.P., Wachovia Bank & Trust Co., N.A.
Trustees: Frank Borden Hanes, Sr., Frank Borden Hanes, Jr., Gordon Hanes, R. Philip Hanes, Jr., Wachovia Bank & Trust Co., N.A.
Number of staff: None.
Employer Identification Number: 566037589

5504
James G. Hanes Memorial Fund/Foundation ⌑
c/o Wachovia Bank & Trust Co., N.A.
P.O. Box 3099, MC 31022
Winston-Salem 27150 (919) 770-5274

Trusts established in 1957 and 1972 in NC.
Foundation type: Independent
Financial data (yr. ended 10/31/88): Assets, $9,511,107 (M); gifts received, $437,112; expenditures, $11,602,307, including $1,033,830 for 39 grants (high: $380,000; low: $1,000; average: $1,000-$25,000).
Purpose and activities: Support for health and education projects, cultural programs, conservation, and community programs.
Types of support: Annual campaigns, seed money, emergency funds, building funds, equipment, land acquisition, matching funds, special projects, research, publications, endowment funds.
Limitations: Giving primarily in NC and the Southeast. No grants to individuals, or for general operational or maintenance purposes.
Publications: Informational brochure (including application guidelines).
Application information: Application form required.
Initial approach: Proposal
Copies of proposal: 1
Deadline(s): Mar. 15, June 15, Sept. 15, and Dec. 15
Board meeting date(s): Jan., Apr., July, and Oct.
Final notification: 10 days
Write: Joyce T. Adger, V.P., Wachovia Bank & Trust Co., N.A.
Distribution Committee: Eldridge C. Hanes, Chair.; Edward K. Crawford, James G. Hanes III, Douglas R. Lewis, Drewry Hanes Nostitz, Frank F. Willingham.
Trustee: Wachovia Bank & Trust Co., N.A.
Number of staff: None.
Employer Identification Number: 566036987

5505
James J. and Angelia M. Harris Foundation
c/o Wachovia Bank and Trust Co., N.A.
P.O. Box 3099
Winston-Salem 27150 (704) 364-6046
Application address: P.O Box 220427, Charlotte, NC 28222

Established as a trust in 1984 in NC.
Donor(s): James J. Harris,† and others.
Foundation type: Independent
Financial data (yr. ended 11/30/89): Assets, $12,478,206 (M); expenditures, $867,195, including $755,062 for 52 grants (high: $50,000; low: $1,000).
Purpose and activities: Support primarily for higher and other education; grants also to youth and social service agencies, Presbyterian churches, health services, and hospitals.
Types of support: Scholarship funds.
Limitations: Giving primarily in Clarke County, GA, and Mechlenburg County, NC.
Application information: Application form not required.
Initial approach: Letter (no more than 3 pages)
Copies of proposal: 1
Deadline(s): None
Board meeting date(s): May and Nov.
Write: Lillian Seaman
Officer and Managers:* William S. Lee III,* Chair.; Sara Harris Bissell, Cameron M. Harris, John W. Harris, James E.S. Hynes.
Number of staff: None.
Employer Identification Number: 561465696

5506
Felix Harvey Foundation, Inc. ¤
901 Dewey St.
Kinston 28501-3630

Donor(s): Felix Harvey, Margaret B. Harvey.
Foundation type: Independent
Financial data (yr. ended 08/31/89): Assets, $1,692,570 (M); gifts received, $122,967; expenditures, $129,396, including $121,771 for 33 grants (high: $26,225; low: $25).
Purpose and activities: Support for social services, educational institutions, and religious organizations.
Limitations: No grants to individuals.
Application information: Contributes only to pre-selected organizations. Applications not accepted.
Officers: Felix Harvey, Pres.; John McNairy, V.P.; Leigh McNairy, V.P.; Ruth Heath, Secy.; Margaret B. Harvey, Treas.
Employer Identification Number: 237038942

5507
Haworth Foundation, Inc. ¤
300 North Green St.
Morganton 28655 (704) 433-0087

Established in 1984 in NC.
Foundation type: Independent
Financial data (yr. ended 12/31/88): Assets, $792,210 (M); expenditures, $186,505, including $174,915 for 82 grants (high: $46,356; low: $135).
Purpose and activities: Support primarily for secondary and higher education, social services and general charitable giving.
Types of support: General purposes.
Limitations: Giving primarily in NC.
Application information:
Deadline(s): None
Write: Howard H. Haworth, Pres.
Officers: Howard H. Haworth, Pres. and Treas.; Patricia G. Haworth, V.P. and Secy.
Directors: E. Ellen Haworth Boardman, Lucy B. Haworth.
Employer Identification Number: 581574743

5508
Alex Hemby Foundation ¤
4419 Sharon Rd.
Charlotte 28211

Established in 1950 in NC.
Donor(s): Hemby Investment Co.
Foundation type: Independent
Financial data (yr. ended 12/31/87): Assets, $5,364,136 (M); expenditures, $353,411, including $306,700 for 37 grants (high: $75,000; low: $50).
Purpose and activities: Giving for higher and other education, health associations and hospitals, and cultural programs.
Application information:
Initial approach: Letter
Deadline(s): None
Write: T.E. Hemby, Jr., Trustee
Trustees: Mrs. B.W. Leahy, Mrs. Hilda W. Hemby, T.E. Hemby, Jr.
Employer Identification Number: 566046767

5509
Hillsdale Fund, Inc. ¤
P.O. Box 20124
Greensboro 27420 (919) 274-5471

Incorporated in 1963 in NC.
Donor(s): The L. Richardson family.
Foundation type: Independent
Financial data (yr. ended 12/31/88): Assets, $18,235,663 (M); expenditures, $761,528, including $588,700 for 48 grants (high: $50,000; low: $5,000).
Purpose and activities: Interests include the general fields of education, conservation, and the arts and humanities.
Limitations: Giving primarily in NC and the southeastern states. No grants to individuals, or for operating budgets.
Application information: Submit 13 copies of brochures and printed material. Application form not required.
Initial approach: Proposal
Copies of proposal: 1
Deadline(s): Approximately one month prior to biannual board meetings
Board meeting date(s): Usually in Apr. and Nov.
Write: Sion A. Boney, Admin. V.P.
Officers and Trustees: Lunsford Richardson, Jr., Pres.; Sion A. Boney, Admin. V.P. and Secy.-Treas.; Sion A. Boney III, J. Peter Gallagher, Margaret W. Gallagher, Laurinda V. Lowenstein, Louise Boney McCoy, Beatrix P. Richardson, Beatrix W. Richardson, Eudora L. Richardson, Molly R. Smith, Richard G. Smith III, Margaret R. White.
Number of staff: 1 part-time support.
Employer Identification Number: 566057433

5510
The Robert P. Holding Foundation, Inc. ¤
P.O. Box 1377
Smithfield 27577

Incorporated in 1955 in NC.
Donor(s): Robert Holding,† Maggie B. Holding.
Foundation type: Independent
Financial data (yr. ended 12/31/88): Assets, $8,066,243 (M); expenditures, $41,886, including $34,949 for 11 grants (high: $14,150; low: $100).
Purpose and activities: Grants for higher and secondary education.
Officers and Directors:* Frank B. Holding,* Pres.; Lewis R. Holding,* Pres.; Virginia Hopkins, Treas.; T.E. Williams.
Employer Identification Number: 566044205

5511
Huffman Cornwell Foundation ¤
c/o Wachovia Bank & Trust Co., N.A.
P.O. Box 3099
Winston-Salem 27150
Application address: P.O. Box 1113, Morgantown, NC 28653; Tel.: (704) 437-5872

Established in 1960 in NC.

Foundation type: Independent
Financial data (yr. ended 12/31/88): Assets, $1,344,687 (M); expenditures, $81,968, including $56,005 for 27 grants (high: $7,000; low: $500) and $10,000 for 14 grants to individuals (high: $1,250; low: $250).
Purpose and activities: Giving for higher education, social services, and youth; support also for a scholarship program.
Types of support: Student aid.
Limitations: Giving primarily in NC; scholarships limited to students of Burke County high schools.
Application information: Application form required.
Initial approach: Letter
Deadline(s): None
Write: Mary Louise McCombs, Secy.
Officers: Ann C. Patton, Chair.; Barbara C. Norvell, Vice-Chair.; Mary Louise McCombs, Secy.
Members: Graham S. DeVane, J.H. McCombs, Jr., J.T. Norvell, Jr., Lou Norvell, Frank C. Patton, Jr., Mary Lou Rogers.
Trustee Bank: Wachovia Bank & Trust Co., N.A.
Employer Identification Number: 566065286

5512
J. F. Hurley Foundation ⌑
P.O. Box 4354
Salisbury 28144

Established in 1982 in NC.
Donor(s): Gordon P. Hurley, J.F. Hurley, Jr., Gordon P. Hurley.
Foundation type: Independent
Financial data (yr. ended 12/31/88): Assets, $2,769,800 (M); gifts received, $35,772; expenditures, $404,684, including $392,123 for 29 grants (high: $270,000; low: $250).
Purpose and activities: Giving primarily for general and higher education institutions, health, and medical associations; support also for child welfare organizations and children's homes.
Limitations: Giving primarily in NC.
Application information:
Deadline(s): None
Write: Gordon P. Hurley, Pres.
Officers and Directors:* J.F. Hurley III,* Chair. and Secy.-Treas.; Gordon P. Hurley,* Pres.; Haden Hurley,* V.P.; Clyde Kiziah, V.P.
Employer Identification Number: 561318937

5513
Jewish Community Council of Winston-Salem ⌑
107 Briar Klage Circle
Winston-Salem 27104

Foundation type: Independent
Financial data (yr. ended 12/31/87): Assets, $104,751 (M); gifts received, $126,087; expenditures, $163,400, including $154,900 for 7 grants (high: $129,000; low: $1,500).
Purpose and activities: Giving primarily for Jewish welfare and education.
Officers: Alan Davis, Chair.; Arnold Sidman, Pres.; Ronald Goldman, Treas.
Employer Identification Number: 581410327

5514
The Kaplan Family Foundation ☆
Seven Monmouth Court
Greensboro 27410-6047

Established in 1982.
Donor(s): Leonard J. Kaplan.
Foundation type: Independent
Financial data (yr. ended 12/31/88): Assets, $1,410,456 (M); gifts received, $6,000; expenditures, $152,984, including $142,250 for 5 grants (high: $50,000; low: $1,000).
Purpose and activities: Giving for Jewish welfare services and synagogues.
Limitations: No grants to individuals.
Application information: Contributes only to pre-selected organizations. Applications not accepted.
Officers: Leonard J. Kaplan, Pres. and Treas.; Tobee W. Kaplan, V.P. and Secy.
Number of staff: None.
Employer Identification Number: 581496345

5515
May Gordon Latham Kellenberger Historical Foundation
c/o NCNB National Bank Trust Group
One NCNB Plaza T09-1
Charlotte 28255 (704) 374-7581
Application address: P.O. Box 908, New Bern, NC 28560

Established in 1979.
Donor(s): May Gordon Latham Kellenberger.†
Foundation type: Independent
Financial data (yr. ended 11/30/89): Assets, $5,822,645 (M); expenditures, $240,455, including $206,971 for 32 grants (high: $25,000; low: $100; average: $5,000-$10,000).
Purpose and activities: "To aid and support projects related to Tryon Palace and Historical New Bern," with emphasis on building, restoration, and preservation.
Types of support: Building funds, special projects, publications, renovation projects, research.
Limitations: Giving limited to New Bern, NC.
Application information: Application form not required.
Initial approach: Letter or proposal
Copies of proposal: 1
Deadline(s): June 1 and Dec. 1
Write: Mgr., Institutional Services
Officers and Directors:* Robert D. Douglas, Jr.,* Chair.; Gertrude S. Carraway,* Vice-Chair.; George A. Ives, Jr.,* Secy.-Treas.; Ella Bengel, Patrick Dorsey, Arthur Edmondson, Charles Potter, W.S. Price, Jr., John C. Thomas, Joshua W. Willey, Jr.
Trustee Bank: NCNB National Bank.
Employer Identification Number: 581360279

5516
Kenan Family Foundation
P.O. Box 2729
Chapel Hill 27515-2729

Established in 1984 in NC.
Donor(s): Frank H. Kenan.
Foundation type: Independent
Financial data (yr. ended 12/31/89): Assets, $2,681,293 (M); expenditures, $98,952, including $79,000 for 3 grants (high: $50,000; low: $5,000; average: $5,000-$50,000) and $4 for grants to individuals.
Purpose and activities: Support for education, economics, and humanities.
Limitations: Giving primarily in NC. No grants to individuals.
Application information: Contributes only to pre-selected organizations. Applications not accepted.
Officers and Directors:* Frank H. Kenan,* Pres.; Thomas S. Kenan III,* V.P. and Treas.; Braxton Schell,* Secy.; Owen Gwyn, Jr., Annice Hawkins Kenan, Elizabeth Price Kenan, Owen G. Kenan.
Number of staff: None.
Employer Identification Number: 581587972

5517
William R. Kenan, Jr. Charitable Trust ▼
Kenan Ctr.
P.O. Box 3858, Bowles Dr.
Chapel Hill 27515-3858 (919) 962-8150

Trust established in 1965 in NY.
Donor(s): William R. Kenan, Jr.†
Foundation type: Independent
Financial data (yr. ended 12/31/89): Assets, $234,367,668 (M); qualifying distributions, $8,630,000, including $8,630,000 for 25 grants (high: $3,000,000; low: $5,000; average: $500,000).
Purpose and activities: To support education, primarily teaching excellence, at private universities and colleges of recognized high quality; also challenge grant support to independent secondary schools which meet trustees' requirements and are located in states selected by trustees.
Types of support: Endowment funds, matching funds.
Limitations: Giving for secondary schools limited to eastern seaboard states. No support for medical, public health, or social welfare; or for designated educational programs, or independent day schools. No grants to individuals, or for building funds, operating budgets, scholarships, fellowships, research, or special programs.
Publications: Annual report, application guidelines.
Application information: Application by invitation only. Applications not accepted.
Board meeting date(s): As required
Write: William C. Friday, Exec. Dir.
Officer: William C. Friday, Exec. Dir.
Trustees: Frank H. Kenan, Thomas S. Kenan III, Morgan Guaranty Trust Co. of New York.
Number of staff: 1 part-time professional; 2 part-time support.
Employer Identification Number: 136192029

5518
The William Kenan, Jr. Fund
P.O. Box 3808, Bowles Dr.
Chapel Hill 27515-3808 (919) 962-8150

Established in 1983 in NC.
Donor(s): Frank H. Kenan, William R. Kenan, Jr. Charitable Trust, Thomas S. Kenan III.
Foundation type: Independent
Financial data (yr. ended 06/30/89): Assets, $26,713,448 (M); gifts received, $4,845,034;

expenditures, $1,180,747, including $746,570 for 4 grants (high: $636,570; low: $10,000).
Purpose and activities: Charitable purposes; grants awarded to an institute for the study of private enterprise and to the University of North Carolina for the support of the Kenan Center.
Types of support: Seed money.
Limitations: No grants to individuals.
Application information: Contributes only to pre-selected organizations. Applications not accepted.
Write: William Friday, Pres.
Officers and Directors:* Frank H. Kenan,* Chair.; William C. Friday,* Pres.; Thomas S. Kenan III,* V.P.; Braxton Schell,* Secy.-Treas.; Harry Barbee, Elizabeth Price Kenan, Owen G. Kenan, Thomas J. Sweeney.
Number of staff: 1 part-time professional; 2 part-time support.
Employer Identification Number: 570757568

5519
Senah C. and C. A. Kent Foundation ⌑
c/o Wachovia Bank & Trust Co., N.A.
P.O. Box 3099
Winston-Salem 27150

Established in 1971 in NC.
Foundation type: Independent
Financial data (yr. ended 12/31/88): Assets, $1,309,082 (M); expenditures, $83,962, including $52,287 for 13 grants (high: $5,147; low: $1,554) and $17,150 for grants to individuals.
Purpose and activities: Giving only to five specified institutions; support for a scholarship program at three specific schools.
Types of support: Student aid.
Limitations: Giving limited to NC.
Application information: Scholarships are limited to Wake Forest University, North Carolina School of the Arts, and Salem College; contact individual schools for application information. Application form required.
Deadline(s): July 1
Trustee: Wachovia Bank & Trust Co., N.A.
Employer Identification Number: 566037248

5520
Kirkland S. and Rena B. Lamb Foundation, Inc. ⌑
c/o Parks N. Austin
901 Greentree Dr.
Charlotte 28211
Application address for organizations: Lillian L. Williams, V.P., 1312 Eckles Dr., Tampa, FL 33612
Scholarship application address: Martha L. Johnston, Secy., 3213 Milton, Dallas, TX 75205

Incorporated in 1961 in NC.
Donor(s): Rena B. Lamb,† Kirkland S. Lamb.†
Foundation type: Independent
Financial data (yr. ended 12/31/87): Assets, $8,937,159 (M); expenditures, $493,340, including $479,935 for 24 grants (high: $215,506; low: $1,260).
Purpose and activities: Grants largely for Protestant church support, theological studies, and evangelical activities; applicants must subscribe to doctrinal position of the foundation.
Types of support: Student aid.
Application information:
Initial approach: Letter
Deadline(s): Sept.
Board meeting date(s): Nov.
Officers: Wendell G. Johnston, Pres.; Lillian L. Williams, V.P.; Martha L. Johnston, Secy.; Richard A. Williams, Treas.
Employer Identification Number: 566062394

5521
Lance Foundation ⌑
c/o NCNB National Bank of North Carolina
One NCNB Plaza T09-1
Charlotte 28255
Application address: c/o Lance, Inc., P.O. Box 32368, Charlotte, NC 28232

Trust established in 1956 in NC.
Donor(s): Lance, Inc., and members of the Van Every family.
Foundation type: Company-sponsored
Financial data (yr. ended 06/30/89): Assets, $4,669,044 (M); gifts received, $130,525; expenditures, $462,683, including $436,416 for 55 grants (high: $50,000; low: $500; average: $2,000-$5,000).
Purpose and activities: Emphasis on higher education, medical research, and community services, particularly in an area where donor is engaged in business.
Types of support: General purposes, operating budgets.
Limitations: Giving primarily in NC, SC, and southeastern states. No grants to individuals, or for scholarships or fellowships; no loans.
Application information: Application form not required.
Initial approach: Proposal or letter
Copies of proposal: 1
Deadline(s): None
Board meeting date(s): As required
Final notification: 2 to 3 months
Write: Zean Jamison, Dir.
Directors: J.W. Disher, Price Gwynn III, Thom B. Horack, Zean Jamison, J.S. Moore, Albert F. Sloan.
Trustee: NCNB National Bank of North Carolina.
Number of staff: 1
Employer Identification Number: 566039487

5522
Liberty Hosiery Mills Foundation ⌑
c/o Branch Banking & Trust Co.
223 West Nash St.
Wilson 27893

Established in 1952 in NC.
Foundation type: Company-sponsored
Financial data (yr. ended 06/30/89): Assets, $1,125,620 (M); gifts received, $51,000; expenditures, $16,481, including $2,500 for 2 grants (high: $1,500; low: $1,000).
Purpose and activities: Support primarily for religion; giving also to education and health.
Trustee: Branch Banking & Trust Co.
Employer Identification Number: 566040787

5523
Effie Allen Little Foundation ⌑
P.O. Box 340
Wadesboro 28170 (704) 694-3114

Established in 1954 in NC.
Donor(s): Charles L. Little, Sr.
Foundation type: Independent
Financial data (yr. ended 12/31/88): Assets, $1,383,304 (M); expenditures, $85,613, including $46,403 for 22 grants (high: $15,000; low: $100; average: $100-$5,000).
Purpose and activities: Giving primarily for higher and other education; support also for social service and youth organizations.
Types of support: Annual campaigns, scholarship funds, continuing support, operating budgets, special projects.
Limitations: Giving primarily in Anson County, NC.
Publications: 990-PF.
Application information: Applications not accepted.
Board meeting date(s): As needed
Write: Dora Anne Little, Pres.
Officers and Directors: Charles L. Little, Sr., Chair.; Dora Anne Little, Pres.; Henry W. Little III, Secy.-Treas.; Mrs. Charles L. Little, Mrs. Hal W. Little.
Number of staff: None.
Employer Identification Number: 566048449

5524
Solon E. & Espie Watts Little Scholarship Loan Fund, Inc. ⌑
c/o Wachovia Bank Bldg.
P.O. Box 26
Taylorsville 28681 (704) 632-2096

Incorporated in 1982 in NC.
Foundation type: Independent
Financial data (yr. ended 12/31/87): Assets, $2,302,976 (M); expenditures, $253,073, including $179,602 for 107 loans (high: $3,200; low: $300).
Purpose and activities: Support for educational loans to graduates of Alexander County High School who reside in Alexander County.
Types of support: Loans.
Limitations: Giving primarily in Alexander County, NC.
Application information: Must have resided in Alexander County for at least one year.
Deadline(s): Feb. 15
Officers: F. Paul Wiles, Pres.; Webster S. Medlin, Secy.-Treas.
Employer Identification Number: 581491453

5525
The Betty J. and J. Stanley Livingstone Charitable Foundation, Inc. ☆
1754 Sterling Rd.
Charlotte 28209

Established in 1986 in NC.
Donor(s): Betty J. Livingstone.†
Foundation type: Independent
Financial data (yr. ended 05/31/89): Assets, $1,692,964 (M); expenditures, $382,892, including $375,000 for 2 grants (high: $250,000; low: $125,000).
Purpose and activities: Giving primarily for higher education.

Limitations: Giving limited to Charlotte, NC.
Application information: Applications not accepted.
Officers and Directors:* Margaret D. Callen,* Pres.; David M. Bishop,* Secy.; Doris B. Smith,* Treas.
Number of staff: None.
Employer Identification Number: 566233211

5526
Martha and Spencer Love Foundation ¤
c/o NCNB National Bank
One NCNB Plaza T09-1
Charlotte 28255

Trust established in 1947 in NC.
Donor(s): J. Spencer Love,† Martha E. Love Ayers.
Foundation type: Independent
Financial data (yr. ended 12/31/88): Assets, $1,883,941 (M); expenditures, $205,313, including $185,000 for 3 grants (high: $175,000; low: $5,000).
Purpose and activities: Emphasis on higher education, the arts, Protestant church support, and social welfare programs.
Limitations: Giving primarily in NC.
Application information: Application form not required.
Initial approach: Proposal or letter
Copies of proposal: 1
Board meeting date(s): As required
Write: Mgr., Institutional Services
Trustee: NCNB National Bank.
Directors: Howard Holderness, Charles E. Love, Cornelia S. Love, Julian Love, Martin E. Love, Lela Porter Love, E.R. Zane.
Employer Identification Number: 566040789

5527
Lowe's Charitable and Educational Foundation ¤
c/o Lowe's Companies, Inc.
P.O. Box 1111
North Wilkesboro 28656 (919) 651-4200

Donor(s): Lowe's Companies, Inc.
Foundation type: Company-sponsored
Financial data (yr. ended 10/31/89): Assets, $808,265 (M); gifts received, $294,325; expenditures, $169,076, including $168,200 for 140 grants (high: $25,000; low: $25).
Purpose and activities: Giving primarily for education, medical, and community activities.
Limitations: Giving primarily in NC. No grants to individuals.
Application information: Application form not required.
Initial approach: Letter
Deadline(s): None
Write: Petro Kulynych, Pres.
Officers: Petro Kulynych, Pres. and Chair.; Leonard G. Herring, V.P.; Robert L. Strickland, V.P.; William F. Reins, Secy.-Treas.
Trustees: Wendell Emerine, Dwight E. Pardue, Harry Underwood.
Employer Identification Number: 566061689

5528
Lundy Foundation, Inc. ¤
P.O. Box 49
Clinton 28328

Established in 1966 in NC.
Foundation type: Independent
Financial data (yr. ended 11/30/89): Assets, $1,634,340 (M); expenditures, $55,139, including $45,722 for 32 grants (high: $15,000; low: $25).
Purpose and activities: Giving primarily for education and social services.
Limitations: No grants to individuals.
Application information: Contributes only to pre-selected organizations. Applications not accepted.
Officers: Annabelle L. Fetterman, Pres.; Lewis M. Fetterman, Jr., V.P.; Mabel F. Held, Secy.-Treas.
Employer Identification Number: 566093241

5529
Magee Christian Education Foundation
P.O. Box 754
Lake Junaluska 28745 (704) 452-5427

Established in 1938 in KY.
Donor(s): Ella G. Magee,† Magee Carpet Co.
Foundation type: Independent
Financial data (yr. ended 12/31/89): Assets, $2,024,328 (M); gifts received, $434,086; expenditures, $122,858, including $110,500 for 28 grants (high: $25,000; low: $1,000; average: $3,000-$4,000).
Purpose and activities: Giving only for scholarship programs for students studying for a full-time church-related vocation.
Types of support: Scholarship funds.
Limitations: Giving primarily in KY, PA, OH, IL, SC, NC, TX, NJ, VA, GA, and Washington, DC. No grants to individuals.
Application information: Application form required.
Initial approach: Letter requesting application
Deadline(s): Sept. 1
Board meeting date(s): Nov. 1
Write: Edward L. Tullis, Secy.-Treas.
Officers and Directors:* James Magee,* Pres.; Otis W. Erisman,* V.P.; Edward L. Tullis,* Secy.-Treas.; Glen S. Bagby, David Hilton, William R. Jennings, Mrs. Myles Katerman, Roy H. Short.
Number of staff: 1 part-time professional.
Employer Identification Number: 616034760

5530
Martin Marietta Philanthropic Trust
c/o First Union National Bank of NC
P.O. Box 3008
Raleigh 27602
Application address: c/o John F. Long, Jr., Dir. Govt. Affairs, Martin Marietta Aggregates, P.O. Box 30013, Raleigh, NC 27622; Tel.: (919) 781-4550

Trust established in 1952 in NC.
Donor(s): Superior Stone Co.
Foundation type: Company-sponsored
Financial data (yr. ended 12/31/88): Assets, $1,500,519 (M); expenditures, $156,701, including $145,075 for 143 grants (high: $8,000; low: $100; average: $100-$500).
Purpose and activities: Grants for community funds, social services, youth and child welfare agencies, rural and civic affairs, community development, higher and other education, health services and associations, the environment and animal welfare, and cultural programs, including museums and the performing arts. Support for building funds for education and hospitals.
Types of support: Annual campaigns, building funds, capital campaigns, continuing support, emergency funds, endowment funds, fellowships, general purposes, in-kind gifts, operating budgets, scholarship funds, special projects.
Limitations: Giving primarily in the Southeast and the Midwest, especially in areas of company operations. No grants to individuals, or for courtesy advertising, tickets for fundraising, or memberships in local Chambers of Commerce or other civic groups.
Application information: Application form not required.
Initial approach: Letter
Copies of proposal: 1
Deadline(s): None
Board meeting date(s): None
Advisory Committee: William B. Harwood, Chair.; Robert A. Bischoff, John F. Long, Jr.
Trustee: First Union National Bank of North Carolina.
Number of staff: 1 part-time professional.
Employer Identification Number: 566035971

5531
The McAdenville Foundation, Inc. ¤
The Main Mill Office
McAdenville 28101 (704) 824-3551

Incorporated in 1944 in NC.
Donor(s): Local textile mills.
Foundation type: Operating
Financial data (yr. ended 12/31/87): Assets, $1,619,049 (M); gifts received, $101,050; expenditures, $456,248, including $83,900 for 13 grants (high: $25,000; low: $100) and $347,520 for foundation-administered programs.
Purpose and activities: A private operating foundation which operates community social and recreational facilities; some giving to churches and church-affiliated colleges.
Types of support: Annual campaigns, building funds, capital campaigns, continuing support, general purposes, renovation projects, special projects.
Limitations: Giving limited to McAdenville, NC. No grants to individuals, or for endowment funds, research, scholarships, fellowships, or matching gifts.
Application information: Applications not accepted.
Board meeting date(s): May and Dec.
Officers and Trustees: Daniel J. Stowe, V.P. and Secy.; J.M. Carstarphen, V.P.
Employer Identification Number: 560623961

5532
Alexander Worth McAlister Foundation, Inc.

c/o Wachovia Bank & Trust Co., N.A.
P.O. Box 3099
Winston-Salem 27150 (919) 770-4819

Established in 1968 in NC.
Donor(s): Sarah L. McAlister.
Foundation type: Independent
Financial data (yr. ended 12/31/89): Assets, $1,537,862 (M); expenditures, $95,345, including $80,000 for 21 grants (high: $7,000; low: $1,000; average: $2,000-$5,000).
Purpose and activities: Support for social service and youth organizations, hospitals and health services, and education.
Limitations: Giving primarily in NC, particularly Greensboro and Charlotte.
Publications: Informational brochure.
Application information: Application form required.
Deadline(s): Feb. 15 and Aug. 15
Write: Martha B. Carlisle
Officers and Trustees:* John W. McAlister, Jr.,* Pres. and Secy.-Treas.; R. Vaughn McAlister,* V.P.; Mary M. Flora, Elizabeth M. Groves, R. Vaughn McAlister, Jr., Sarah L. McAlister, John Sealy, Margaret M. Sealy.
Employer Identification Number: 566095754

5533
James G. K. McClure Educational and Development Fund, Inc.

Hickory Nut Gap Farm
Rte. 1, Box 105
Fairview 28730 (704) 628-3105

Incorporated in 1944 in NC.
Foundation type: Independent
Financial data (yr. ended 06/30/89): Assets, $1,935,666 (L); qualifying distributions, $84,125, including $30,283 for 23 grants (high: $5,000; low: $30; average: $1,000-$5,000) and $53,842 for 101 grants to individuals (high: $2,400; low: $300).
Purpose and activities: Support primarily for scholarship funds and educational projects, a nurse recruitment program in the mountain counties of NC, and other activities for the welfare of the people of western NC, including community development, religion, and youth programs.
Types of support: Scholarship funds, building funds, student aid, exchange programs.
Limitations: Giving primarily in western NC. No grants to individuals (except for scholarships), or for endowment funds; no loans.
Publications: Annual report, application guidelines, informational brochure.
Application information: Application form required.
Initial approach: Letter
Copies of proposal: 1
Deadline(s): Apr. 1 and Sept. 1
Board meeting date(s): Apr. and Sept.
Write: John Curtis Ager, Exec. Dir.
Officers and Trustees:* Harold L. Bacon, M.D.,* Pres.; Richard G. Jennings, Jr.,* V.P.; James McClure Clarke,* Secy.; Martha Guy,* Treas.; John Curtis Ager,* Exec. Dir.; Mrs. John C. Ager, Jr., Mrs. Burnham S. Colburn, Reuben A. Holden.
Number of staff: 1 full-time professional.
Employer Identification Number: 560690982

5534
The McNair Foundation, Inc. ¤

127 Fairly St.
Laurinburg 28352 (919) 276-0861
Application address: Box 399, Laurinburg, NC 28352

Incorporated in 1943 in NC.
Donor(s): Local businesses.
Foundation type: Independent
Financial data (yr. ended 08/31/89): Assets, $285,833 (M); gifts received, $73,925; expenditures, $116,955, including $116,168 for 37 grants (high: $44,650; low: $10).
Purpose and activities: Emphasis on higher education and Protestant church support. Grants also to community development programs and youth agencies.
Limitations: Giving limited to NC, with an emphasis on Scotland County.
Application information:
Initial approach: Letter
Deadline(s): None
Write: John C. Edens, Secy.
Officers and Directors:* R.F. McCoy,* Pres.; David Burns,* V.P.; McNair Evans,* V.P.; S. Hewitt Fulton III,* V.P.; John C. Edens, Secy.-Treas.; James H. Pou Bailey, Jr., E. Hervey Evans, Jr., Halbert M. Jones, Jr., Leroy Marks.
Employer Identification Number: 560772091

5535
The John Motley Morehead Foundation ▼

P.O. Box 690
Chapel Hill 27514 (919) 962-1201

Trust established in 1945 in NY.
Donor(s): John Motley Morehead III.†
Foundation type: Independent
Financial data (yr. ended 6/30/88): Assets, $61,204,575 (M); expenditures, $4,184,093, including $367,470 for grants and $2,462,307 for grants to individuals.
Purpose and activities: The advancement of education, learning and/or research for public benefit, in the U.S. Currently makes awards for undergraduate study only at the University of North Carolina at Chapel Hill to graduates of NC high schools and preparatory schools, of selected preparatory schools outside the state and in Canada, and of thirty selected public schools in England; candidates for undergraduate scholarships must be nominated by their secondary schools.
Types of support: Internships, special projects, equipment, student aid.
Limitations: Giving primarily in the South.
Publications: Annual report.
Application information: Nomination form required.
Initial approach: By nomination only; no one may apply directly for Morehead Award
Deadline(s): Nov. 1 for nominations
Board meeting date(s): Feb., Apr., Aug., and Nov.
Final notification: March 1
Write: Charles E. Lovelace, Jr., Exec. Dir.
Officers: Charles E. Lovelace, Jr., Exec. Dir.; Forrest H. Page, Assoc. Dir.; Patricia L. Mercier, Treas.
Trustees: Alan Thomas Dickson, Chair.; Frank Borden Hanes, Vice-Chair.; Robert Cluett, Lucy Chatham Everett, Jean M. Larkin.
Number of staff: 4 full-time professional; 4 full-time support; 2 part-time support.
Employer Identification Number: 560599225

5536
The Morgan Trust for Charity, Religion, and Education

Old Wire Rd.
Laurel Hill 28351 (919) 462-2016

Trust established in 1949 in NC.
Donor(s): Edwin Morgan,† Elise McK. Morgan, Morgan Mills, Inc.
Foundation type: Independent
Financial data (yr. ended 4/30/89): Assets, $7,162,348 (M); gifts received, $46,701; expenditures, $412,222, including $374,770 for 37 grants (high: $175,000; low: $50; average: $500).
Purpose and activities: Support for higher education, a theological seminary, and Protestant church support.
Types of support: Continuing support, annual campaigns, seed money, building funds, matching funds, endowment funds.
Limitations: Giving primarily in NC. No grants to individuals, or for scholarships or fellowships; no loans. Generally no grants for operating budgets.
Application information: Application form not required.
Initial approach: Letter
Copies of proposal: 1
Deadline(s): None
Board meeting date(s): As required
Write: James L. Morgan, Chair.
Officers and Trustees:* James L. Morgan,* Chair.; William R. Dulin,* Secy.-Treas.; Elizabeth E. Morgan, M. Morrison Morgan.
Number of staff: None.
Employer Identification Number: 566056812

5537
E. A. Morris Charitable Foundation ▼ ¤

c/o Duke Univ. Medical Ctr.
110 Swift St.
Durham 27705 (919) 684-5332

Established in 1980.
Donor(s): E.A. Morris, Mrs. E.A. Morris.
Foundation type: Independent
Financial data (yr. ended 12/31/88): Assets, $5,335,557 (M); gifts received, $3,483,794; expenditures, $955,890, including $923,525 for 134 grants (high: $50,000; low: $50; average: $5,000-$20,000).
Purpose and activities: Giving mainly for Christian missionary organizations, education, and churches; some support also for national public policy research organizations concerned with free enterprise and government.
Types of support: General purposes.
Application information:
Initial approach: Letter
Deadline(s): None
Write: John S. Thomas, V.P.

Officers and Directors: E.A. Morris, Pres.; John S. Thomas, V.P. and Exec. Dir.; Mrs. E.A. Morris, V.P.; Mary Lou Morris, Secy.; Joseph E. Morris, Treas.
Employer Identification Number: 581413060

5538
Musicians Club of America ⌑ ☆
457 Rose Creek Rd.
Franklin 28734

Donor(s): Fletcher Foundation, Homer Gray.
Foundation type: Operating
Financial data (yr. ended 12/31/88): Assets, $1,206,921 (M); gifts received, $12,365; expenditures, $320,121, including $1,200 for 1 grant to an individual and $299,110 for 1 foundation-administered program.
Purpose and activities: A private operating foundation; activities restricted to music education, in grants and through the Franklin Center for the Performing Arts in NC; support also for an indigent musician.
Types of support: General purposes, grants to individuals.
Officers: Homer Gray, Pres.; John C. Dick, V.P.; Jon Koch, V.P.; Elaine Koch, Secy.; Robert D. Young, Treas.
Directors: Ellen Alexander, Mrs. Charles B. Kells, Barbara Lavietes, Ed Lowe, William Woodruff.
Employer Identification Number: 590531291

5539
Charles and Irene Nanney Foundation ⌑ ☆
P.O. Box 935
Gastonia 28053

Established in 1961.
Donor(s): C.P. Nanney,† Irene B. Nanney.†
Foundation type: Independent
Financial data (yr. ended 12/31/88): Assets, $2,878,867 (M); gifts received, $2,489,480; expenditures, $10,681, including $5,755 for 7 grants (high: $1,255; low: $500).
Purpose and activities: Giving primarily for higher education.
Limitations: Giving primarily in NC. No grants to individuals.
Application information: Contributes only to pre-selected organizations. Applications not accepted.
Trustee: Branch Banking & Trust Co.
Employer Identification Number: 566046763

5540
Neisler Foundation, Inc. ⌑
P.O. Box 99
Kings Mountain 28086

Established in 1952 in NC.
Foundation type: Independent
Financial data (yr. ended 12/31/88): Assets, $1,100,111 (M); expenditures, $71,547, including $58,494 for 45 grants (high: $4,000; low: $250).
Purpose and activities: Support primarily for education, community funds, local fire departments, historical societies, libraries, and religious giving.
Trustee: First Union National Bank of North Carolina.
Employer Identification Number: 566042484

5541
Nucor Foundation, Inc. ⌑
4425 Randolph Rd.
Charlotte 28211 (704) 366-7000

Established in 1973 in NC.
Donor(s): Nucor Corp.
Foundation type: Company-sponsored
Financial data (yr. ended 12/31/87): Assets, $231,461 (M); gifts received, $150,000; expenditures, $174,582, including $173,014 for 180 grants to individuals (high: $2,838; low: $15).
Purpose and activities: Giving only for a scholarship program for children of employees.
Types of support: Employee-related scholarships.
Application information: Application form required.
Deadline(s): Mar. 1
Write: James M. Coblin
Directors: F. Kenneth Iverson, Samuel Siegel.
Employer Identification Number: 237318064

5542
P & B Foundation ⌑
2004 Valencia Terr.
Charlotte 28226-3311

Established in 1970.
Donor(s): C. Wilbur Peters.
Foundation type: Independent
Financial data (yr. ended 8/31/88): Assets, $1,307,474 (M); expenditures, $83,535, including $75,563 for 6 grants (high: $72,917; low: $200).
Purpose and activities: Grants primarily for Baptist church-related educational and religious institutions.
Limitations: Giving primarily in MN and NC.
Application information: Applications not accepted.
Officer and Directors: C. Wilbur Peters, Pres.; Bessie Peters.
Employer Identification Number: 237083912

5543
The Palin Foundation ⌑
3600 Glenwood Ave.
Raleigh 27612 (919) 781-7800

Established in 1985 in NC.
Donor(s): Clifton L. Benson, Jr.
Foundation type: Independent
Financial data (yr. ended 12/31/87): Assets, $7,548,506 (M); expenditures, $726,364, including $622,390 for 44 grants (high: $200,000; low: $400).
Purpose and activities: Giving primarily to a university and a church.
Types of support: General purposes, building funds.
Application information:
Initial approach: Proposal
Deadline(s): None
Write: Dr. John F. Philips, V.P.
Officers: Clifton L. Benson, Jr., Pres.; John F. Philips, V.P.; Margaret P. Benson, Secy.; Clifton L. Benson III, Treas.
Employer Identification Number: 561490228

5544
Peoples Bank Foundation ⌑
c/o Peoples Bank & Trust Co.
Box 872
Rocky Mount 27802 (919) 977-4001

Established in 1954 in NC.
Foundation type: Company-sponsored
Financial data (yr. ended 12/31/88): Assets, $2,688 (M); gifts received, $180,600; expenditures, $183,059, including $178,590 for 158 grants (high: $15,000; low: $15).
Purpose and activities: Grants primarily for higher education; support also for youth, social services, culture, and community funds.
Limitations: Giving primarily in NC. No grants to individuals.
Application information: Contributes only to pre-selected organizations. Applications not accepted.
Write: Robert R. Mauldin
Trustee: Peoples Bank & Trust Co.
Employer Identification Number: 566050776

5545
The Perry-Griffin Foundation ⌑ ☆
P.O. Box 53
Oriental 28571
Application address: P.O. Box 82, Oriental, NC 28571; Tel.: (919) 249-0227

Foundation type: Independent
Financial data (yr. ended 8/31/88): Assets, $1,500,617 (M); expenditures, $54,628, including $500 for 1 grant.
Purpose and activities: Giving primarily to churches; support also for student loans for undergraduate study to local residents.
Limitations: Giving limited to Pamlico and Jones counties, NC.
Application information: Application form required.
Deadline(s): None
Write: Edward D. Lupton, Mgr.
Officers: Edward D. Lupton, Mgr.; Julia Whitty,* Secy.
Directors:* Ned Delamar II, Ned Delamar III, Lurley Hines.
Employer Identification Number: 560860864

5546
Peterson Family Foundation, Inc. ⌑ ☆
505 Old Haw Creek Rd.
Asheville 28805

Established in 1988 in NC.
Donor(s): M.C. Peterson.
Foundation type: Independent
Financial data (yr. ended 12/31/88): Assets, $1,065,149 (M); gifts received, $1,154,176; expenditures, $75,152, including $75,000 for 1 grant.
Purpose and activities: Initial year of operation, 1988; support for a community foundation.
Limitations: Giving primarily in NC.
Application information: Contributes only to pre-selected organizations. Applications not accepted.
Officers and Directors: M.C. Peterson, Pres.; Robert P. Peterson, V.P.; Sara P. Duyck, Secy.-Treas.
Employer Identification Number: 561624394

5547
Piedmont Aviation Foundation ¤
P.O. Box 2720
Winston-Salem 27102

Established in 1964 in NC.
Foundation type: Company-sponsored
Financial data (yr. ended 12/31/88): Assets, $1,690,499 (M); gifts received, $900,000; expenditures, $502,923, including $415,075 for 125 grants (high: $119,375; low: $100) and $74,794 for employee matching gifts.
Purpose and activities: Giving for education, social services, community funds, and an employee matching gift program for colleges and universities.
Types of support: Employee matching gifts.
Trustees: Edwin I. Colodny, T.H. Davis, Edward A. Horrigan, Jr., John G. Medlin, Jr., Thomas E. Schick.
Employer Identification Number: 566065806

5548
Polk County Community Foundation, Inc. ☆
One Depot St.
Tryon 28782 (704) 859-5314

Incorporated in 1975 in NC.
Foundation type: Community
Financial data (yr. ended 12/31/89): Assets, $2,735,390 (M); gifts received, $178,793; expenditures, $145,814, including $126,451 for grants.
Purpose and activities: Support for charitable organizations, health and hospices, and education, including medical education.
Types of support: Scholarship funds, matching funds.
Limitations: Giving limited to the Polk County, NC, area.
Publications: Annual report, application guidelines.
Application information: Application form required.
Copies of proposal: 5
Deadline(s): 3 weeks prior to end of each quarter
Board meeting date(s): 2nd Thursday in Apr., June, Oct., and Dec.
Final notification: Immediately following board meetings
Write: Paul E. Culberson, Exec. Dir.
Officers and Directors:* Henry W. Welch,* Chair.; Harry L. Evans,* Vice-Chair.; George A. Stinson, Pres.; Mrs. Hugh E. Replogle,* Secy.; Mrs. Joseph W. Stayman, Jr., Treas.; Paul E. Culberson, Exec. Dir.; Mrs. Joseph A. Wagner, Admin. Dir.; and 12 additional directors.
Number of staff: None.
Employer Identification Number: 510168751

5549
Mary Norris Preyer Fund
P.O. Box 20124
Greensboro 27420 (919) 274-5471

Established in 1965 in NC.
Donor(s): Members of the Preyer Family.
Foundation type: Independent
Financial data (yr. ended 06/30/89): Assets, $3,227,196 (M); expenditures, $182,639, including $180,994 for 35 grants (high: $10,000; low: $450; average: $3,000-$5,000).
Purpose and activities: Support for higher education and social services.
Types of support: General purposes, seed money.
Limitations: Giving primarily in NC.
Application information: Application form not required.
Initial approach: Proposal
Copies of proposal: 1
Deadline(s): 1 month before meeting
Board meeting date(s): Varies spring to fall, once annually
Write: Fred L. Preyer, Trustee
Trustees: Ellen P. Davis, Mary Norris Preyer Oglesby, Fred L. Preyer, Jill Preyer, Kelly Anne Preyer, L. Richardson Preyer, Norris W. Preyer, Norris Preyer, Jr., Robert O. Preyer, William Y. Preyer, Jr.
Number of staff: None.
Employer Identification Number: 566068167

5550
Lynn R. and Karl E. Prickett Fund
P.O. Box 20124
Greensboro 27420 (919) 274-5471

Established in 1964 in NC.
Donor(s): Lynn R. Prickett.†
Foundation type: Independent
Financial data (yr. ended 6/30/89): Assets, $14,408,897 (M); gifts received, $291,170; expenditures, $249,065, including $212,000 for 20 grants (high: $50,000; low: $1,000).
Purpose and activities: Giving for general charitable purposes, including support for a church and a community fund.
Types of support: General purposes.
Application information: Application form not required.
Initial approach: Proposal
Deadline(s): None
Board meeting date(s): None
Write: C.W. Cheek, Trustee
Trustees: Charles S. Chapin, Chester F. Chapin, Samuel C. Chapin, C.W. Cheek, Lynn C. Gunzenhauser, Lisa B. Prochnow.
Employer Identification Number: 566064788

5551
Proctor Foundation
c/o Wachovia Bank & Trust Co.
P.O. Box 3099
Winston-Salem 27150 (919) 770-4819
Application address: P.O. Box 829, Salisbury, NC 28145-0829

Established in 1974 in NC.
Donor(s): Lucille S. Proctor.†
Foundation type: Independent
Financial data (yr. ended 12/31/88): Assets, $1,338,340 (M); expenditures, $70,052, including $55,346 for 18 grants (high: $25,000; low: $200; average: $500-$3,000).
Purpose and activities: Emphasis on higher education and youth; some support also for the handicapped and cultural organizations.
Types of support: Continuing support, annual campaigns, seed money, emergency funds, general purposes, building funds, equipment, land acquisition, renovation projects, matching funds.
Limitations: Giving primarily in Rowan County, NC. No grants to individuals, or for deficit financing or endowments; no loans.
Application information:
Initial approach: Letter
Deadline(s): None
Board meeting date(s): Jan. and Sept.
Final notification: 10 days after board meetings
Write: Martha B. Carlisle
Officers and Directors: Lucille P. Norvell, Pres.; Patricia P. Rendleman, V.P.; James L. Woodson, Secy.; Richard J. Rendleman, Treas.; Henrietta S. Anthony, Edwin O. Norvell.
Employer Identification Number: 237398904

5552
Trent Ragland, Jr. Trust ¤ ☆
c/o First Union National Bank, Trust Tax Dept. CMG-12-1161
Charlotte 28288
Application address: P.O. Box 31343, Raleigh, NC 27622; Tel.: (919) 781-4550

Established in 1959.
Donor(s): W. Trent Ragland, Jr.
Foundation type: Independent
Financial data (yr. ended 12/31/88): Assets, $1,023,952 (M); gifts received, $90,625; expenditures, $62,353, including $49,140 for grants.
Purpose and activities: Support primarily for higher education and human services, including a women's center and community funds; support also for health and cultural programs, including historic preservation.
Limitations: Giving primarily in NC, FL, and VA.
Application information:
Initial approach: Letter
Deadline(s): None
Write: W.T. Ragland, Jr., Advisory Committee Member
Advisory Committee: Walton Joyner, Anna Ragland, W. Trent Ragland, Jr.
Trustee: First Union National Bank.
Employer Identification Number: 566035980

5553
Rexham Corporation Foundation
7315 Pineville Matthews Rd.
Charlotte 28226 (704) 541-2905

Established in 1958 in DE and NY.
Donor(s): Rexham Corp.
Foundation type: Company-sponsored
Financial data (yr. ended 12/31/88): Assets, $10,398 (M); gifts received, $123,000; expenditures, $127,836, including $114,766 for 65 grants (high: $20,842; low: $25) and $13,070 for 8 grants to individuals (high: $2,000; low: $500).
Purpose and activities: Support for health and welfare, community funds, youth, employee matching gifts for higher education, and employee-related scholarships to individuals.
Types of support: Capital campaigns, employee-related scholarships, scholarship funds, employee matching gifts, general purposes.
Limitations: Giving primarily in the Southeast, with emphasis on NC and SC.

Application information: Applications not accepted.
Deadline(s): None
Write: Rubina I. Grosso, Secy.
Officers: K.F. Kennedy,* Pres.; T.L. McVerry,* V.P.; Rubina I. Grosso, Secy.; Joseph Keniry, Treas.
Directors:* S.C. Lea.
Number of staff: None.
Employer Identification Number: 136165669

5554
Kate B. Reynolds Charitable Trust ▼
BB & T Building
Eight West Third St., Suite M3
Winston-Salem 27101 (919) 723-1456

Trust established in 1947 in NC.
Donor(s): Kate B. Reynolds.†
Foundation type: Independent
Financial data (yr. ended 08/31/89): Assets, $262,596,647 (M); expenditures, $12,986,367, including $12,628,574 for 97 grants (high: $4,500,000; low: $5,000; average: $10,000-$100,000).
Purpose and activities: Seventy-five percent of net income to be distributed for the health care of those in need statewide; twenty-five percent for the benefit of poor and needy residents of Winston-Salem and Forsyth County.
Types of support: Operating budgets, continuing support, annual campaigns, seed money, emergency funds, matching funds, building funds, capital campaigns, equipment, general purposes, renovation projects, research, special projects.
Limitations: Giving limited to NC; social welfare grants limited to Winston-Salem and Forsyth County; health care giving, statewide. No grants to individuals, or for endowment funds; grants on a highly selective basis for construction of facilities or purchase of equipment.
Publications: Annual report (including application guidelines), program policy statement, informational brochure, application guidelines.
Application information: Applicant should contact the executive secretary prior to submitting a written application. Application form required.
Initial approach: Proposal
Copies of proposal: 1
Deadline(s): Jan. 15, May. 15, and Aug. 15 for Poor and Needy Trust; Apr. 1 and Oct. 1 for Health Care Trust
Board meeting date(s): Advisory committee for Poor and Needy Trust meets in Feb., June, and Sept.; for Health Care grants in May and Nov.
Final notification: 1 week after committee meeting
Write: W. Vance Frye, Exec. Secy.
Trustee: Wachovia Bank & Trust Co., N.A.
Number of staff: 1 full-time professional; 1 full-time support.
Employer Identification Number: 566036515

5555
Z. Smith Reynolds Foundation, Inc. ▼
101 Reynolda Village
Winston-Salem 27106-5199 (919) 725-7541

Incorporated in 1936 in NC.
Donor(s): Nancy S. Reynolds,† Mary Reynolds Babcock,† Richard J. Reynolds, Jr.,† William N. Reynolds.†
Foundation type: Independent
Financial data (yr. ended 12/31/89): Assets, $220,214,158 (M); gifts received, $12,675,824; expenditures, $7,994,999, including $7,377,004 for 232 grants (high: $750,000; low: $2,000; average: $15,000-$35,000) and $15,000 for 3 grants to individuals of $5,000 each.
Purpose and activities: Giving primarily for primary and secondary education, community and economic development, social services, child welfare and development, citizenship and leadership development, public policy and affairs, conservation of the environment, improvement of the criminal justice system, and minority and women's issues.
Types of support: Operating budgets, continuing support, annual campaigns, seed money, matching funds, special projects, conferences and seminars, general purposes, technical assistance.
Limitations: Giving limited to NC. No grants to individuals (except for Nancy Susan Reynolds Awards for community leadership), or for research or program-related investments; no loans.
Publications: Annual report (including application guidelines).
Application information: Application form required.
Initial approach: Letter or telephone
Copies of proposal: 1
Deadline(s): Feb. 1 and Aug. 1
Board meeting date(s): 2nd Friday in May and Nov.
Final notification: 4 months after deadline
Write: Thomas W. Lambeth, Exec. Dir.
Officers: Zachary T. Smith,* Pres.; Smith W. Bagley,* V.P.; Thomas W. Lambeth, Secy. and Exec. Dir.; Joseph G. Gordon,* Treas.
Trustees:* Josephine D. Clement, Daniel G. Clodfelter, Hubert Humphrey, Katharine B. Mountcastle, Mary Mountcastle, Stephen L. Neal, Jane S. Patterson, Sherwood H. Smith, Jr.
Number of staff: 3 full-time professional; 3 full-time support.
Employer Identification Number: 586038145

5556
H. Smith Richardson Charitable Trust ▼
c/o Piedmont Financial Co.
P.O. Box 20124
Greensboro 27420

Trust established in 1976 in NC.
Donor(s): H. Smith Richardson.†
Foundation type: Independent
Financial data (yr. ended 6/30/88): Assets, $35,750,643 (M); expenditures, $1,792,805, including $1,530,122 for 46 grants (high: $150,000; low: $500; average: $10,000-$40,000).
Purpose and activities: Support primarily for higher education, educational organizations, and public policy research.
Types of support: General purposes, publications, special projects.
Limitations: No grants to individuals.
Application information:
Initial approach: Proposal
Write: H. Smith Richardson, Jr., Trustee
Trustees: C.W. Cheek, H. Smith Richardson, Jr., Peter L. Richardson, R.R. Richardson, Stuart S. Richardson.
Number of staff: 1 part-time professional.
Employer Identification Number: 237245123

5557
Grace Richardson Fund ⌘
c/o Piedmont Financial Co., Inc.
P.O. Box 20124
Greensboro 27420-0124 (919) 274-5471

Established in 1965 in NC.
Foundation type: Independent
Financial data (yr. ended 06/30/89): Assets, $1,891,798 (M); expenditures, $87,762, including $77,712 for 3 grants (high: $50,712; low: $5,000).
Purpose and activities: Support for health associations, universities, and hospitals to assist in research and treatment of cystic fibrosis; support also for community funds, education, and conservation.
Application information:
Initial approach: Letter or proposal
Deadline(s): None
Write: H.S. Richardson, Jr., Trustee
Trustees: H.S. Richardson, Jr., R.R. Richardson, Grace R. Stetson.
Employer Identification Number: 566067849

5558
The Mary Lynn Richardson Fund
P.O. Box 20124
Greensboro 27420 (919) 274-5471

Trust established in 1940 in NC.
Donor(s): Mary Lynn Richardson.†
Foundation type: Independent
Financial data (yr. ended 12/31/89): Assets, $4,760,144 (M); expenditures, $266,322, including $230,086 for 46 grants (high: $15,000; low: $750; average: $3,000) and $12,540 for 5 grants to individuals (high: $4,440; low: $900).
Purpose and activities: Grants to organizations which aid the needy and to foreign Presbyterian causes.
Types of support: General purposes, seed money.
Limitations: Giving limited to NC for domestic programs, and internationally. No grants to individuals, or for building funds, research programs, or matching gifts; no loans.
Application information: No new grants to individuals will be awarded. Application form not required.
Initial approach: Proposal
Copies of proposal: 1
Deadline(s): Submit proposal preferably between Jan. and Mar.; deadline Apr. 1 and Oct. 1
Board meeting date(s): In late spring and fall
Write: Adele Richardson Ray, Trustee

Officer: James F. Connolly, Mgr.
Trustees: Eric R. Calhoun, Betsy Boney Mead, William Y. Preyer, Jr., Lisa B. Prochnow, Adele Richardson Ray.
Employer Identification Number: 066025946

5559
Grace Jones Richardson Trust
P.O. Box 20124
Greensboro 27420

Trust established in 1962 in CT.
Donor(s): Grace Jones Richardson.†
Foundation type: Independent
Financial data (yr. ended 12/31/88): Assets, $25,589,551 (M); expenditures, $397,821, including $264,200 for 156 grants (high: $22,000; low: $100).
Purpose and activities: Emphasis on community funds, social services, religious giving, health services, conservation, higher education, and cultural programs.
Limitations: No grants to individuals.
Application information: Applications not accepted.
Board meeting date(s): As required
Trustees: Peter L. Richardson, Robert R. Richardson, Stuart S. Richardson.
Number of staff: 1 part-time support.
Employer Identification Number: 066023003

5560
J. P. Riddle Charitable Foundation ⌑ ☆
P.O. Box 53646
Fayetteville 28305-3646

Established in 1976 in NC.
Donor(s): Joseph P. Riddle, Jr.
Foundation type: Independent
Financial data (yr. ended 12/31/88): Assets, $1,167,610 (M); gifts received, $20,000; expenditures, $73,423, including $56,100 for 5 grants (high: $36,000; low: $100).
Purpose and activities: Giving primarily for a medical foundation and a methodist church.
Limitations: Giving primarily in NC.
Trustee: Joseph P. Riddle, Jr.
Employer Identification Number: 561152362

5561
Oscar C. Rixson Foundation, Inc.
P.O. Box 963
Hendersonville 28793 (704) 891-5490

Incorporated in 1925 in NY.
Foundation type: Independent
Financial data (yr. ended 12/31/87): Assets, $1,746,300 (M); expenditures, $214,731, including $95,500 for 78 grants (high: $2,800; low: $200; average: $400) and $31,400 for 157 grants to individuals of $200 each.
Purpose and activities: To assist evangelical churches, mission boards, and organizations in the support of missionaries, schools and activities "dedicated to the furtherance of the gospel of our Lord and Savior Jesus Christ."
Types of support: Grants to individuals.
Application information: Grant requests are neither solicited nor desired and will not receive favorable action. Applications not accepted.
Write: Thomas Elliott, Pres.
Officers and Directors:* Thomas Elliot,* Pres.; Nathan Dunkerton,* V.P. and Secy.; Alan Mojonnier,* Treas.; Donald Dunkerton, William R. Kusche, Jr.
Number of staff: 1 part-time support.
Employer Identification Number: 136129767

5562
The Florence Rogers Charitable Trust
P.O. Box 36006
Fayetteville 28303 (919) 484-2033

Trust established in 1961 in NC.
Donor(s): Florence L. Rogers.†
Foundation type: Independent
Financial data (yr. ended 03/31/90): Assets, $4,085,222 (M); expenditures, $232,034, including $205,878 for 78 grants (high: $50,000; low: $150; average: $2,975).
Purpose and activities: Support for music and the arts, education, recreation, hunger programs, child welfare, nursing and hospices, wildlife, and the general quality of life in the area. Preference is given to seed money for new ideas.
Types of support: Conferences and seminars, emergency funds, matching funds, operating budgets, publications, renovation projects, research, seed money, special projects.
Limitations: Giving primarily in Fayetteville, Cumberland County, and southeastern NC. No grants to individuals, or for building or endowment funds, scholarships, or fellowships; no loans.
Publications: Informational brochure (including application guidelines).
Application information: Application form not required.
Initial approach: Letter or telephone
Copies of proposal: 1
Deadline(s): Feb. 28, Apr. 30, July 31, Oct. 31, and Dec. 31
Board meeting date(s): Monthly
Final notification: By the end of the following month
Write: JoAnn Barnette Stancil, Admin.
Officer: JoAnn Barnette Stancil, Admin.
Trustees: Nolan P. Clark, John C. Tally.
Number of staff: 1 full-time professional; 1 part-time professional; 2 part-time support.
Employer Identification Number: 566074515

5563
The RosaMary Foundation ▼
c/o Wachovia Bank & Trust Co, N.A.
P.O. Box 3099
Winston-Salem 27150
Application address: P.O. Box 51299, New Orleans, LA 70151

Trust established in 1939 in LA.
Donor(s): Members of the A.B. Freeman family.
Foundation type: Independent
Financial data (yr. ended 12/31/88): Assets, $24,406,940 (M); expenditures, $1,453,720, including $1,247,430 for 35 grants (high: $200,000; low: $180; average: $5,000-$50,000).
Purpose and activities: Emphasis on a community fund, higher and secondary education, including church-related schools, social service agencies, civic affairs, and cultural programs.
Types of support: Annual campaigns, building funds, capital campaigns, continuing support, endowment funds, research, seed money, special projects.
Limitations: Giving primarily in the greater New Orleans, LA, area. No grants to individuals.
Application information:
Initial approach: Proposal in letter form
Copies of proposal: 1
Deadline(s): None
Board meeting date(s): Approximately 2 times a year beginning in spring
Write: Louis M. Freeman, Chair.
Trustees: Louis M. Freeman, Chair.; Adelaide W. Benjamin, Richard W. Freeman, Jr., Charles Keller, Jr., Rosa F. Keller, Mary Elizabeth Wisdom.
Number of staff: None.
Employer Identification Number: 726024696

5564
Salisbury Community Foundation, Inc. ⌑ ☆
P.O. Box 1327
Salisbury 28144 (704) 636-5211

Incorporated in 1944 in NC.
Foundation type: Community
Financial data (yr. ended 12/31/88): Assets, $4,488,279 (M); gifts received, $111,312; expenditures, $2,710,929, including $2,645,783 for 752 grants (high: $434,100; low: $15; average: $3,518).
Purpose and activities: Grants primarily for capital projects in Rowan County; some seed-money grants for special projects.
Types of support: Building funds, special projects, seed money.
Limitations: Giving primarily in NC. No grants to individuals, or for endowment funds or operating budgets.
Application information:
Initial approach: Proposal
Copies of proposal: 1
Deadline(s): 2 weeks before board meetings
Board meeting date(s): Feb., May, Aug., and Nov.
Write: Thomas M. Caddell, Trustee
Officers and Trustees:* James G. Whitton,* Pres.; W.A. Sherrill,* Secy.; Thomas M. Caddell, Irvin Oestreicher, Patsy Rendelman, Fred J. Stanback, Jr., W.C. Stanback.
Employer Identification Number: 560772117

5565
The Shelton Foundation ⌑ ☆
101 South Stratford Rd., Suite 450
Winston-Salem 27104

Established in 1985 in NC.
Donor(s): Shelco, Inc.
Foundation type: Independent
Financial data (yr. ended 12/31/88): Assets, $923,337 (M); gifts received, $342,833; expenditures, $221,777, including $212,725 for 34 grants (high: $50,000; low: $200).
Purpose and activities: Support primarily for higher and other education, including medical schools; grants also for a Baptist church.
Limitations: Giving primarily in NC. No grants to individuals.

Application information: Contributes only to pre-selected organizations. Applications not accepted.
Officers: Charles M. Shelton, Pres.; Edwin Shelton, V.P.
Director: Richard B. Howington.
Employer Identification Number: 581596729

5566
George Shinn Foundation, Inc. ⌑ ☆
Two First Union Plaza, Suite 2600
Charlotte 28282

Donor(s): George Shinn, George Shinn & Assocs., Inc.
Foundation type: Independent
Financial data (yr. ended 12/31/88): Assets, $204,436 (M); gifts received, $150,000; expenditures, $108,254, including $108,124 for 38 grants (high: $10,100; low: $100).
Purpose and activities: All grants are to underwrite program of recipient or for scholarships. Areas of interest include community funds and community development, youth, education, Christian organizations, and general charitable giving.
Types of support: Scholarship funds, general purposes.
Limitations: Giving primarily in NC.
Application information:
Initial approach: Letter
Deadline(s): None
Write: Spencer Stolpen, V.P.
Officer: Spencer Stolpen, V.P.
Employer Identification Number: 561083525

5567
The General William A. Smith Trust, Item XXII ⌑
United Carolina Bank
212 South Tryon St.
Charlotte 28200
Application address: c/o James A. Hardison, Jr., Trustee, Wadesboro, NC 28170; Tel.: (704) 694-3094

Trust established in 1940 in NC.
Donor(s): General William A. Smith.
Foundation type: Independent
Financial data (yr. ended 12/31/88): Assets, $3,246,505 (M); expenditures, $213,256, including $191,100 for 18 grants (high: $60,883; low: $575).
Purpose and activities: Support for education, health services, government, and religion.
Types of support: Annual campaigns, building funds, capital campaigns, continuing support, emergency funds, endowment funds, equipment, general purposes, professorships, renovation projects, scholarship funds, special projects.
Limitations: Giving primarily in Anson County, NC. No grants to individuals.
Application information: Application form not required.
Deadline(s): Dec. 31
Administrative Trustees: Bennett M. Edwards, Jr., Joe Gaddy, Mary Nelme Griffen, James A. Hardison, Jr.
Trustee Bank: United Carolina Bank.
Employer Identification Number: 566042630

5568
Spalding Health Care Trust ⌑ ☆
c/o First Union National Bank
First Union Plaza
Charlotte 28288

Established in 1986 in GA.
Foundation type: Independent
Financial data (yr. ended 12/31/88): Assets, $7,520,064 (M); gifts received, $17,235; expenditures, $1,969,834, including $1,917,248 for 1 grant.
Purpose and activities: Giving to a hospital providing care to the indigent.
Limitations: Giving primarily in GA.
Trustee: First Union National Bank.
Employer Identification Number: 581657005

5569
Sigmund Sternberger Foundation, Inc. ⌑
P.O. Box 3111
Greensboro 27402 (919) 373-1500

Incorporated in 1957 in NC.
Donor(s): Sigmund Sternberger,† Rosa Sternberger Williams.†
Foundation type: Independent
Financial data (yr. ended 3/31/87): Assets, $9,223,412 (M); gifts received, $499,000; expenditures, $489,229, including $404,950 for 38 grants (high: $75,000; low: $500) and $16,450 for 18 grants to individuals (high: $1,400; low: $500).
Purpose and activities: Support for higher education, including scholarship funds, and individual scholarships for children of members of the Revolution Masonic Lodge and to residents of Guilford County pursuing undergraduate studies in NC; grants also for the arts and human service agencies. Emphasis on special one-time projects, seed money and emergency needs.
Types of support: Seed money, emergency funds, special projects, scholarship funds, student aid, capital campaigns, operating budgets.
Limitations: Giving primarily in Guilford County, NC. No loans.
Publications: Application guidelines.
Application information: Application form required.
Initial approach: Letter
Copies of proposal: 1
Deadline(s): None
Board meeting date(s): Usually in Mar., June, Dec., and as required
Final notification: 3 months
Write: Robert O. Klepfer, Jr., Exec. Dir.
Officers: Mrs. A.J. Tannenbaum,* Pres.; Sidney J. Stern, Jr.,* Secy.-Treas.; Robert O. Klepfer, Jr., Exec. Dir.
Directors:* Howard E. Carr, Charles M. Reid, Jeanne Tannenbaum, Sigmund I. Tannenbaum, M.D., Rabbi Arnold S. Task.
Number of staff: 1 part-time professional.
Employer Identification Number: 566045483

5570
The Stewards Fund ☆
P.O. Box 17845
Raleigh 27619 (919) 782-8410

Established in 1986 in NC.
Donor(s): Nancy B. Faircloth, Anne B. Faircloth.
Foundation type: Independent
Financial data (yr. ended 12/31/89): Assets, $2,908,392 (M); gifts received, $194,350; expenditures, $90,153, including $86,500 for 12 grants (high: $33,000; low: $2,000).
Purpose and activities: Support for social services, with emphasis on meeting the needs of the disadvantaged.
Types of support: Continuing support, general purposes, matching funds, operating budgets, seed money, special projects.
Limitations: Giving primarily in Raleigh, NC. No support for political programs. No grants to individuals.
Application information:
Initial approach: Letter
Deadline(s): None
Write: Alton E. Howard, Secy.-Treas.
Officers: Nancy B. Faircloth, Pres.; Albert G. Edwards, V.P.; Anne B. Faircloth, V.P.; Alton E. Howard, Secy.-Treas.
Number of staff: None.
Employer Identification Number: 561482138

5571
Stonecutter Foundation, Inc. ⌑
300 Dallas St.
Spindale 28160 (704) 286-2341

Incorporated in 1944 in NC.
Donor(s): Stonecutter Mills Corp.
Foundation type: Company-sponsored
Financial data (yr. ended 8/31/88): Assets, $4,714,421 (M); gifts received, $17,320; expenditures, $323,791, including $217,420 for 29 grants (high: $98,000; low: $1,000) and $32,970 for 31 loans to individuals.
Purpose and activities: Giving for secondary and higher education (including student loans), youth agencies, and church support.
Types of support: Student loans.
Limitations: Giving primarily in NC; student loans restricted to Rutherford and Polk County, NC, areas.
Application information: Application forms provided for student loans.
Deadline(s): None
Write: V.H. Lonan, Treas.
Officers: Z.E. Dobbins,* Pres.; James R. Cowan,* V.P.; Adin H. Rucker,* V.P.; T.P. Walker, Secy.; V.H. Lonan, Treas.
Directors:* H.W. Crenshaw, Mark L. Summey, K.S. Tanner, Jr.
Employer Identification Number: 566044820

5572
Robert Lee Stowe, Jr. Foundation, Inc. ⌑
100 North Main St.
P.O. Box 351
Belmont 28012 (704) 825-5314

Incorporated in 1945 in NC.
Donor(s): Robert Lee Stowe, Jr.,† Robert Lee Stowe III, R.L. Stowe Mills, Inc.
Foundation type: Independent

Financial data (yr. ended 12/31/87): Assets, $2,391,392 (M); gifts received, $100,000; expenditures, $204,290, including $176,644 for 82 grants (high: $30,000; low: $100).
Purpose and activities: Emphasis on church support, child welfare, and higher education.
Limitations: Giving primarily in NC.
Application information:
Initial approach: Letter
Deadline(s): None
Write: Daniel Harding Stowe, Pres.
Officers: Daniel Harding Stowe, Pres.; David M. McConnell, V.P.; Richmond H. Stowe, V.P.; Robert Lee Stowe III, V.P.; Jean H. Gibson, Secy.-Treas.
Employer Identification Number: 566034773

5573
Adele M. Thomas Trust ☆
327 Burlage Circle
Chapel Hill 27514-2705 (919) 942-8198

Established in 1961 in IN.
Donor(s): Claude A. Thomas,† Adele M. Thomas.
Foundation type: Independent
Financial data (yr. ended 12/31/88): Assets, $1,393,781 (M); expenditures, $62,006, including $59,893 for 39 grants (high: $11,140; low: $25; average: $25-$11,140).
Purpose and activities: Giving for social services, including child welfare and family planning; support also for cultural programs, Christian religious organizations, and citizenship.
Limitations: Giving primarily in Orange County, NC; Marion County, IN; and Washington, DC.
Application information: Application form not required.
Deadline(s): None
Write: Adele M. Thomas, Trustee
Trustees: Adele M. Thomas, John V. Thomas.
Number of staff: None.
Employer Identification Number: 356042836

5574
Thomasville Furniture Industries Foundation ⌘
c/o Wachovia Bank & Trust Co., N.A.
P.O. Box 3099
Winston-Salem 27150 (919) 770-6222
Application address: c/o Carlyle A. Nance, Jr., Thomasville Furniture Industries Inc., P.O. Box 339, Thomasville, NC 27360; Tel.: (919) 475-1361

Trust established in 1960 in NC.
Donor(s): Thomasville Furniture Industries, Inc.
Foundation type: Company-sponsored
Financial data (yr. ended 12/31/87): Assets, $2,924,796 (M); gifts received, $100,000; expenditures, $251,464, including $220,812 for 96 grants (high: $25,000; low: $50; average: $1,500-$2,000).
Purpose and activities: Grants largely for higher and secondary education, including scholarships for children of employees of Thomasville Furniture Industries, and for hospitals, mainly in areas of company operations.
Types of support: Employee-related scholarships, annual campaigns.
Limitations: Giving primarily in NC.
Application information:
Initial approach: Letter
Deadline(s): None
Write: Susan Wiles
Administrative Committee: Frederick B. Starr, Chair.; Frank W. Burr, Carlyle A. Nance, Jr., Charles G. O'Brien.
Trustee: Wachovia Bank & Trust Co., N.A.
Employer Identification Number: 566047870

5575
Greater Triangle Community Foundation
P.O. Box 12834
Research Triangle Park 27709 (919) 549-9840

Incorporated in 1983 in NC.
Foundation type: Community
Financial data (yr. ended 06/30/89): Assets, $6,487,410 (M); gifts received, $1,724,221; expenditures, $606,663, including $454,391 for grants.
Purpose and activities: Support primarily for education, the arts, health, conservation, and the social sciences.
Types of support: Scholarship funds, seed money, special projects.
Limitations: Giving primarily in the Durham, Orange, and Wake County, NC, area. No grants for annual campaigns, continuing support, or operating budgets.
Publications: Annual report, newsletter, application guidelines.
Application information: Application form required.
Initial approach: Letter
Copies of proposal: 15
Deadline(s): Feb. 15 and Oct. 31
Board meeting date(s): Apr. and Dec.
Final notification: May 1 and Jan. 1
Write: Shannon St. John, Exec. Dir.
Officers and Directors:* K.v.R. Dey, Jr.,* Pres.; Frank A. Daniels, Jr.,* V.P.; Theodore E. Haigler, Jr.,* Secy.; Joseph J. Ruvane, Jr.,* Secy.; Edward G. Lilly, Jr.,* Finance Chair.; Mary L. Hill,* Distrib. Chair.; Shannon St. John,* Exec. Dir.; and 22 additional directors.
Number of staff: 2 full-time professional; 1 part-time professional; 1 full-time support.
Employer Identification Number: 561380796

5576
Philip L. Van Every Foundation ▼ ⌘
c/o NCNB National Bank of NC Trust Group
One NCNB Plaza, T09-1
Charlotte 28255
Application address: c/o Lance, Inc., P.O. Box 32368, Charlotte, NC 28232; Tel.: (704) 554-1421

Established in 1961 in NC.
Donor(s): Philip Van Every.
Foundation type: Independent
Financial data (yr. ended 12/31/88): Assets, $21,108,940 (M); gifts received, $13,413; expenditures, $1,363,708, including $1,304,120 for 109 grants (high: $100,000; low: $500; average: $5,000-$10,000).
Purpose and activities: Giving for social services, health and medical research, and education, especially higher education.
Limitations: Giving primarily in NC and SC.
Application information: Application form not required.
Initial approach: Letter or proposal
Deadline(s): None
Final notification: Immediately after board meeting
Write: Mgr., Institutional Services
Officer and Administrators: Zean Jamison, Exec. Dir.; J.W. Disher, Price Gwynn, T.B. Horack, J.S. Moore, Albert F. Sloan.
Trustee: NCNB National Bank of North Carolina.
Number of staff: 1
Employer Identification Number: 566039337

5577
The Wachovia Foundation Inc. ▼
c/o Wachovia Bank & Trust Co., N.A.
P.O. Box 3099
Winston-Salem 27150

Incorporated in 1982 in NC.
Donor(s): Wachovia Bank & Trust Co., N.A.
Foundation type: Company-sponsored
Financial data (yr. ended 12/31/89): Assets, $5,710,021 (M); gifts received, $2,309,803; expenditures, $2,022,126, including $2,018,150 for 140 grants (high: $708,310; low: $275; average: $2,000-$20,000).
Purpose and activities: Emphasis on higher education and community projects, including community funds.
Types of support: Building funds, capital campaigns, special projects, endowment funds, research, operating budgets, annual campaigns, renovation projects, grants to individuals.
Limitations: Giving primarily in NC. No grants to individuals.
Application information:
Initial approach: Contact local bank office
Deadline(s): None
Board meeting date(s): Monthly
Write: L.M. Baker, Jr., Pres. and C.E.O., Wachovia Bank & Trust Co., N.A.
Officers: John G. Medlin, Jr., Pres.; L.M. Baker, Jr., V.P.; Thomas A. Bennett, V.P.; Kenneth W. McAllister, Secy.; Graham P. Dozier, Treas.
Number of staff: None.
Employer Identification Number: 581485946

5578
Weaver Foundation, Inc. ☆
324 West Wendover, Suite 300
Greensboro 27408 (919) 275-9600
Application address: P.O. Box 26040, Greensboro, NC 27420-6040

Incorporated in 1967 in NC.
Donor(s): W.H. Weaver,† E.H. Weaver.
Foundation type: Independent
Financial data (yr. ended 12/31/89): Assets, $11,293,808 (M); gifts received, $198,339; expenditures, $206,221, including $170,382 for 59 grants (high: $25,000; low: $25).
Purpose and activities: Giving primarily for arts and culture and higher education; support also for social services, low-income housing, Protestant ministries, and health.
Limitations: Giving primarily in NC. No grants to individuals.
Application information: Application form not required.
Initial approach: Proposal

Copies of proposal: 1
Deadline(s): None
Write: Robert G. Kelley, V.P.
Officers and Trustees:* H.M. Weaver,* Pres. and Chair.; Robert G. Kelley, V.P. and Secy.-Treas.; Ashley E. Weaver, Edith H. Weaver, Michele D. Weaver.
Number of staff: None.
Employer Identification Number: 566093527

5579
Wellons Foundation, Inc. ⌑
P.O. Box 1254
Dunn 28334 (919) 892-3123

Established in 1958 in NC.
Foundation type: Independent
Financial data (yr. ended 12/31/88): Assets, $1,887,889 (M); gifts received, $27,800; expenditures, $190,200, including $12,122 for grants (high: $5,000) and $25,274 for loans to individuals.
Purpose and activities: Emphasis on higher education, including student loans, and Protestant giving.
Types of support: Student loans.
Application information: Application form required.
Deadline(s): None
Write: John H. Wellons, Sr., Pres.
Officers and Directors: John H. Wellons, Sr., Pres.; John H. Wellons, Jr., V.P.; Donald McCoy, Secy.; Sylvia W. Craft, Gene T. Jernigan, Llewellyn Jernigan.
Employer Identification Number: 566061476

5580
The Community Foundation of Western North Carolina, Inc.
13 Biltmore Ave.
Asheville 28802 (704) 254-4960
Mailing address: P.O. Box 1888, Asheville, NC 28802

Incorporated as the Community Foundation of Greater Asheville, Inc. in 1978 in NC.
Foundation type: Community
Financial data (yr. ended 06/30/89): Assets, $3,350,652 (M); gifts received, $744,612; expenditures, $753,315, including $670,093 for 230 grants (high: $55,500; low: $50).
Purpose and activities: Emphasis on higher and other education, social services, including youth agencies, religion, health, and the arts.
Types of support: Matching funds, renovation projects, seed money.
Limitations: Giving limited to western NC. No grants to individuals.
Publications: Annual report.
Application information: Application form required.
Copies of proposal: 1
Deadline(s): Sept. 1-Nov. 30
Board meeting date(s): Last Wednesday in Apr.
Final notification: May 31
Write: John Q. Schell, Exec. Dir.
Officers and Directors:* Charles T. McCullough, Jr.,* Chair.; Thomas C. Arnold,* Vice-Chair.; Brian F.D. Lavelle,* Secy.; Robert B. Armstrong,* Treas.; John Q. Schell, Exec. Dir.; and 23 additional directors.
Number of staff: 1 full-time professional; 2 part-time professional.
Employer Identification Number: 561223384

5581
Whitener Foundation ⌑
1941 English Rd., Box E
High Point 27260

Foundation type: Independent
Financial data (yr. ended 12/31/88): Assets, $2,747,815 (M); expenditures, $145,014, including $134,920 for 58 grants (high: $20,000; low: $20; average: $500-$1,000).
Purpose and activities: Giving for higher education, social service and youth agencies, particularly orphanages; and Protestant church support.
Limitations: Giving primarily in NC.
Officers and Directors: Orin Whitener, Pres.; Marshall Pittman, V.P.; Loraine Ward, Secy.-Treas.
Employer Identification Number: 521467548

5582
Thomas Henry Wilson & Family Foundation ⌑ ☆
P.O. Box 2276
High Point 27261

Established in 1967.
Donor(s): Thomas Henry Wilson, Jr., and members of the Wilson family.
Foundation type: Independent
Financial data (yr. ended 12/31/88): Assets, $1,057,840 (M); gifts received, $66,005; expenditures, $32,515, including $30,505 for 28 grants (high: $10,000; low: $25).
Purpose and activities: Giving for higher and secondary education and Protestant church support.
Limitations: No grants to individuals.
Application information: Contributes only to pre-selected organizations. Applications not accepted.
Trustee: High Point Bank & Trust Co.
Employer Identification Number: 566125766

5583
Wilson Foundation ⌑ ☆
c/o William W. Wilson
P.O. Box 1147
Statesville 28677 (704) 872-2411

Foundation type: Independent
Financial data (yr. ended 12/31/88): Assets, $1,164,516 (M); gifts received, $126,000; expenditures, $109,506, including $104,000 for 43 grants (high: $50,000; low: $100).
Purpose and activities: Support primarily for general charitable organizations.
Limitations: Giving primarily in NC.
Application information:
Initial approach: Letter
Deadline(s): None
Write: Thomas L. Wilson, Pres.
Officers: Thomas L. Wilson, Pres.; William W. Wilson, Secy.
Employer Identification Number: 561262432

5584
The Winston-Salem Foundation ▼
229 First Union National Bank Bldg.
Winston-Salem 27101 (919) 725-2382

Established in 1919 in NC by declaration of trust.
Foundation type: Community
Financial data (yr. ended 12/31/89): Assets, $57,917,827 (M); gifts received, $7,547,233; expenditures, $6,497,397, including $5,874,977 for grants (average: $15,000), $160,437 for 67 grants to individuals (high: $3,000; low: $500) and $321,400 for 136 loans to individuals.
Purpose and activities: Student aid primarily to bona fide residents of Forsyth County, NC; support also for nonprofit organizations of all types, especially educational, social service and health programs, the arts, and civic affairs.
Types of support: Seed money, emergency funds, student aid, special projects, matching funds, general purposes, student loans, fellowships, research, continuing support.
Limitations: Giving primarily in the greater Forsyth County, NC, area; some support for northwest NC. No grants for annual campaigns, land acquisition, publications, or conferences.
Publications: Annual report, application guidelines, newsletter, grants list.
Application information: Application form required for student aid or student loans and includes $20 application fee. Application form not required.
Initial approach: Telephone
Copies of proposal: 1
Deadline(s): Jan. 1, Apr. 1, July 1, and Oct. 1
Board meeting date(s): Jan., Mar., June, Sept., and Nov. (applications not considered at Jan. meeting)
Final notification: 1 month
Write: Henry M. Carter, Jr., Exec. Dir.
Officer: Henry M. Carter, Jr., Exec. Dir.
Foundation Committee: John F. McNair III, Chair.; F. Hudnall Christopher, Jr., Vice-Chair.; Herbert Brenner, Victor I. Flow, Jr., Roberta W. Irwin, Barbara K. Phillips, C. Edward Pleasants, Jr., Charles Shelton, A. Tab Williams III.
Trustees: Branch Banking & Trust Co., First Citizens Bank & Trust Co., First Union National Bank, NCNB National Bank, Southern National Bank, Wachovia Bank & Trust Co., N.A.
Number of staff: 4 full-time professional; 1 part-time professional; 4 full-time support.
Employer Identification Number: 566037615

5585
Margaret C. Woodson Foundation, Inc. ⌑
P.O. Box 829
Salisbury 28144 (704) 633-5000

Incorporated in 1954 in NC.
Donor(s): Margaret C. Woodson.†
Foundation type: Independent
Financial data (yr. ended 12/31/88): Assets, $7,166,119 (M); gifts received, $373,798; expenditures, $358,983, including $330,500 for 25 grants (high: $54,000; low: $300).
Purpose and activities: Giving for higher education, cultural programs, child welfare, and hospitals.

Limitations: Giving primarily in Davie and Rowan counties, NC. No grants for research.
Application information: Application form not required.
Deadline(s): Jan. 31
Write: James L. Woodson, Pres.
Officers: James L. Woodson,* Pres.; Esther C. Shay,* V.P.; Roy C. Hoffner, Secy.; Charles Cunningham,* Treas.
Directors:* Paul L. Bernhardt, Beulah Hillard, Mary Holt W. Woodson, Paul B. Woodson.
Trustee: U.S. Trust Co. of New York.
Employer Identification Number: 566064938

NORTH DAKOTA

5586
Gabriel J. Brown Trust
112 Ave. E West
Bismarck 58501 (701) 223-5916

Established in 1969 in ND.
Donor(s): Gabriel J. Brown.†
Foundation type: Independent
Financial data (yr. ended 03/31/89): Assets, $1,071,899 (M); expenditures, $127,636, including $102,000 for 91 loans to individuals (average: $1,000-$2,000).
Purpose and activities: Support for education through student loans.
Types of support: Student loans.
Limitations: Giving limited to residents of ND.
Application information: Application form required.
Initial approach: Letter or telephone
Copies of proposal: 1
Deadline(s): June 15
Board meeting date(s): About July 1
Final notification: July
Write: Robert Lundberg or Susan Lundberg, Trustees
Trustees: Robert Lundberg, Susan Lundberg.
Number of staff: 1 part-time professional.
Employer Identification Number: 237086880

5587
Fargo-Moorhead Area Foundation
15 Broadway, Suite 601
Fargo 58102 (701) 234-0756

Established in 1960 in ND.
Foundation type: Community
Financial data (yr. ended 12/31/88): Assets, $4,257,460 (M); gifts received, $1,255,857; expenditures, $335,520, including $242,520 for 78 grants (high: $15,000; low: $10; average: $1,000-$10,000).
Purpose and activities: Support primarily for the arts, civic improvement, education, health, and social services.
Types of support: Seed money, emergency funds, equipment, scholarship funds, renovation projects, capital campaigns, conferences and seminars, consulting services, exchange programs, general purposes, operating budgets, publications, special projects, technical assistance.
Limitations: Giving primarily in the city of Fargo and Cass County, ND, and the city of Moorhead and Clay County, MN. No grants to individuals, or for deficit financing, land acquisition, or medical research; no loans.
Publications: Program policy statement, application guidelines, informational brochure, annual report.
Application information: Application form required.
Initial approach: Letter or telephone
Copies of proposal: 8
Deadline(s): Dec. 31
Board meeting date(s): Quarterly
Final notification: May 30
Write: Susan M. Hunke, Exec. Dir.
Officer: Roger L. Sullivan, Secy.
Distribution Committee: Esther Allen, Richard B. Crockett, Mary Davies, Edward Ellenson, Robert Feder, Edward R. Stern, James M. Swedback.
Trustee Banks: American Bank & Trust Co., Dakota First Trust Co., First Interstate Bank and Trust, First Trust Co. of North Dakota, Norwest Capital Bank ND, N.A.
Number of staff: 1 full-time professional; 1 part-time support.
Employer Identification Number: 456010377

5588
Tom & Frances Leach Foundation, Inc.
P.O. Box 1136
Bismarck 58502 (701) 255-0479

Established in 1955 in ND.
Donor(s): Thomas W. Leach,† Frances V. Leach.†
Foundation type: Independent
Financial data (yr. ended 12/31/88): Assets, $4,819,653 (M); expenditures, $437,154, including $254,500 for 41 grants (high: $50,000; low: $500; average: $1,000-$10,000).
Purpose and activities: Giving for higher education, social service and youth agencies, hospitals and health services, and cultural programs.
Types of support: Scholarship funds, capital campaigns, continuing support, endowment funds, general purposes, operating budgets, special projects.
Limitations: Giving primarily in ND, particularly in Bismarck and Mandan, and in Tulsa, OK.
Publications: Annual report.
Application information: Application form required.
Initial approach: Letter
Copies of proposal: 1
Deadline(s): Oct. 1
Board meeting date(s): Nov.
Final notification: Dec.
Write: Clement C. Weber, Exec. Dir.
Officers: Ernest R. Fleck,* Pres.; James P. Wachter,* V.P.; Russell R. Mather,* Secy.-Treas.; Clement C. Weber, Exec. Dir.
Directors:* Frank J. Bavendick, Robert P. Hendrickson, Gilbert N. Olson, Paul D. Schliesman.
Number of staff: 1 full-time professional; 1 full-time support.
Employer Identification Number: 456012703

5589
MDU Resources Foundation
400 North Fourth St.
Bismarck 58501 (701) 222-7828

Established in 1983 in ND.
Donor(s): MDU Resources Group, Inc., Williston Basin Interstate Pipeline Co., Knife River, Coal Mining Co.
Foundation type: Company-sponsored
Financial data (yr. ended 12/31/89): Assets, $231,601 (M); expenditures, $193,820, including $183,820 for 163 grants (high: $17,000; low: $20) and $10,000 for 10 grants to individuals of $1,000 each.
Purpose and activities: Grants for education, including employee-related scholarships; support also for community development, hospitals and health services, and cultural programs.
Types of support: General purposes, scholarship funds, building funds, employee-related scholarships.
Limitations: Giving primarily in areas of company operations of MDU Resources Group and its divisions and subsidiaries in ND, MT, SD, and WY.
Application information: Application form required.
Deadline(s): None
Write: Robert E. Wood, Pres.
Officers and Directors:* Robert E. Wood,* Pres.; Alvin J. Wittmaier,* V.P.; H.J. Mellen, Jr.,* Secy.-Treas.; Douglas C. Kane, Joseph R. Maichel.
Employer Identification Number: 450378937

5590
Myra Foundation ⌑
P.O. Box 1536
Grand Forks 58206-1536 (701) 775-9420

Incorporated in 1941 in ND.
Donor(s): John E. Myra.†
Foundation type: Independent
Financial data (yr. ended 12/31/87): Assets, $2,489,194 (M); expenditures, $263,987, including $169,986 for 23 grants (high: $44,500; low: $500; average: $7,390).
Purpose and activities: Emphasis on civic projects, health, cultural organizations, higher and secondary education, social services, the aged, and youth development.
Limitations: Giving limited to Grand Forks County, ND. No grants to individuals, or for endowment funds, research, or matching gifts; no loans.
Publications: Informational brochure (including application guidelines).
Application information: Application form required.
Initial approach: Letter
Copies of proposal: 1
Deadline(s): None
Board meeting date(s): Quarterly

Write: Edward C. Gillig, Pres.
Officers: Edward C. Gillig, Pres.; Hilda Johnson, V.P.; Robert F. Hansen, Secy.-Treas.
Employer Identification Number: 450215088

5591
North Dakota Community Foundation
1025 North Third St.
Bismarck 58501 (701) 222-8349

Established in 1977 in ND.
Foundation type: Community
Financial data (yr. ended 12/31/89): Assets, $2,936,928 (M); gifts received, $582,052; expenditures, $300,319, including $104,294 for 82 grants (high: $10,000; low: $60; average: $1,000) and $17,625 for 49 grants to individuals (high: $1,200; low: $50).
Purpose and activities: Unrestricted funds largely for aid to the elderly and disadvantaged; support also for health services, including mental health, youth agencies, parks and recreation, and arts and cultural programs.
Types of support: Operating budgets, continuing support, annual campaigns, seed money, building funds, equipment, matching funds, scholarship funds, special projects, research, publications, conferences and seminars, student aid.
Limitations: Giving primarily in ND. No support for lobbying or sectarian purposes; low priority given to national or out-of-state organizations, hospitals, organizations with substantial and professional fundraising programs, or organizations that raise money through gambling activities. No grants to individuals (except for scholarships), or for emergency or endowment funds, deficit financing, or land acquisition; no loans.
Publications: Annual report, newsletter, informational brochure.
Application information: Application by foundation invitation only for unrestricted grants. Application form required.
Initial approach: Letter
Copies of proposal: 1
Deadline(s): Aug. 31
Board meeting date(s): Annually in 2nd quarter of year
Write: Richard H. Timmins, Pres.
Officers and Directors:* Vernon E. Wagner,* Chair.; Mark Butz,* Vice-Chair.; Richard H. Timmins,* Pres.; Donald L. Schmid,* Secy.-Treas.; Jan Berg, David Gipp, Sarah Andrews Herman, Ray Hoffman, J. Gerald Niles, John Pierson.
Number of staff: 2 full-time professional; 1 full-time support.
Employer Identification Number: 450336015

5592
Alex Stern Family Foundation
Bill Stern Bldg., Suite 202
609-1/2 First Ave., North
Fargo 58102 (701) 237-0170

Established in 1964 in ND.
Donor(s): William Stern,† Sam Stern,† Edward A. Stern.†
Foundation type: Independent
Financial data (yr. ended 12/31/89): Assets, $7,217,635 (M); expenditures, $417,419, including $343,323 for 49 grants (high: $30,000; low: $1,000; average: $7,007).
Purpose and activities: Giving primarily for arts and culture, including museums and the performing arts; child welfare and youth organizations; family and social services, including legal services, alcohol abuse programs, and welfare for the homeless, aged, and disabled; community organizaitons; higher, business, minority, and other education; and hospices and cancer research.
Types of support: Special projects, continuing support, annual campaigns, emergency funds, building funds, equipment, research, conferences and seminars, professorships, matching funds, lectureships, operating budgets, publications, scholarship funds.
Limitations: Giving limited to the Fargo, ND, and Moorhead, MN, areas. No grants to individuals, or for endowment funds; no loans.
Publications: Application guidelines.
Application information: Application form required.
Initial approach: Letter, telephone, or proposal
Copies of proposal: 3
Deadline(s): Submit application preferably between Apr. and Dec.; no set deadline
Final notification: Within a few months
Write: A.M. Eriksmoen, Exec. Dir.
Officer and Trustees:* A.M. Eriksmoen,* Exec. Dir.; W.R. Amundson, J.L. McCormick.
Number of staff: 1 full-time professional; 1 part-time professional.
Employer Identification Number: 456013981

OHIO

5593
Abington Foundation ☆
2000 Huntington Bldg.
Cleveland 44115 (216) 696-4700

Established in 1983 in OH.
Foundation type: Independent
Financial data (yr. ended 12/31/89): Assets, $1,535,364 (M); gifts received, $140,000; expenditures, $72,384, including $50,150 for 7 grants (high: $20,000; low: $150).
Purpose and activities: Giving primarily to educational institutions; support also for a community development organization.
Limitations: Giving primarily in Cleveland, OH. No grants to individuals.
Application information: Contributes only to pre-selected organizations. Applications not accepted.
Write: John J. Whitney, Secy.
Officers and Trustees:* David K. Ford,* Chair.; Amasa B. Ford, M.D.,* Pres.; Allen H. Ford,* V.P. and Treas.; David Kingsley Ford,* V.P.; Oliver M. Ford,* V.P.; John J. Whitney,* Secy.; Elizabeth B. Ford.
Employer Identification Number: 341404854

5594
Akron Community Foundation
900 Society Bldg.
159 South Main St.
Akron 44308 (216) 376-8522

Incorporated in 1955 in OH.
Foundation type: Community
Financial data (yr. ended 03/31/90): Assets, $16,795,333 (M); expenditures, $950,904, including $837,155 for 141 grants (high: $48,000; low: $50).
Purpose and activities: To promote charitable, benevolent, educational, recreational, health, esthetic, cultural, and public welfare activities; to support a program of research leading to the improvement of the health, education, and general well-being of all citizens of the Akron area; to give toward the support of experimental and demonstration programs, through established or new agencies; to test the validity of research findings in various fields of community planning directed toward the efficient and adequate coordination of public and private services organized to meet human needs.
Types of support: Operating budgets, building funds, matching funds, research, special projects.
Limitations: Giving primarily in Summit County, OH. No grants to individuals, or for endowment funds, scholarships, or fellowships; no loans.
Publications: Annual report, application guidelines, newsletter.
Application information: No more than 1 grant to an organization in a 12-month period. Application form not required.
Initial approach: Proposal, letter, or telephone
Copies of proposal: 1
Deadline(s): Mar. 15, July 15, and Dec. 1
Board meeting date(s): Generally May, Sept., and Jan.
Final notification: 6 weeks
Write: Gordon E. Heffern, Pres. and C.E.O.
Officers: George T. Parry,* Pres.; Gale R. Urda,* V.P.; Allan Johnson, Secy.; Ernest J. Novack, Jr.,* Treas.; John L. Feudner, Jr., Exec. Dir.
Trustees:* Randolph Baxter, Ann Amer Brennan, Robert W. Briggs, Don Fair, Howard L. Flood, J. Harvey Graves, Karl S. Hay, Judith Isroff, David A. Lieberth, Tom Merryweather, Bruce Rothmann, Sandra Smith, Gale R. Urda, Charles F. Zodrow.
Trustee Banks: Bank One Akron, N.A., First National Bank of Ohio, National City Bank, Society National Bank.
Number of staff: 1 part-time professional; 1 full-time support.
Employer Identification Number: 237029875

5595
The William H. Albers Foundation, Inc. ⌑
P.O. Box 38360
Cincinnati 45238-0360

Incorporated in 1982 in OH.
Foundation type: Independent
Financial data (yr. ended 4/30/88): Assets, $1,444,397 (M); expenditures, $114,858,

including $95,000 for 30 grants (high: $10,000; low: $200).
Purpose and activities: Emphasis on secondary and higher education, cultural programs, youth agencies, and hospitals.
Types of support: General purposes, building funds, operating budgets.
Limitations: Giving primarily in Cincinnati, OH.
Application information:
Write: Irene A. Dornheggen, Pres.
Officer and Trustees: Irene A. Dornheggen, Pres.; Ann M. Kallaher, James L. Leonard, Luke J. Leonard.
Employer Identification Number: 316023881

5596
The Allyn Foundation ⌑
2211 South Dixie Ave., Suite 302
Dayton 45409 (513) 299-2295

Incorporated in 1955 in OH.
Donor(s): S.C. Allyn.†
Foundation type: Independent
Financial data (yr. ended 12/31/88): Assets, $1,651,694 (M); expenditures, $93,257, including $71,350 for 51 grants (high: $6,000; low: $100).
Purpose and activities: Emphasis on higher and secondary education; support also for hospitals, social services, aid to the handicapped, and a community fund.
Types of support: Capital campaigns, continuing support, general purposes, scholarship funds.
Limitations: Giving primarily in southern OH, with the exception of certain schools and universities. No grants to individuals, or for endowment funds.
Publications: 990-PF, annual report (including application guidelines).
Application information:
Initial approach: Letter
Copies of proposal: 1
Board meeting date(s): Nov. 20; executive board meeting in June
Write: Charles S. Allyn, Jr., Pres.
Officers and Trustees: Charles S. Allyn, Jr., Pres.; Mary Louise Sunderland, V.P.; Compton Allyn, Secy.-Treas.; Sara A. Bahlman, Anne Reed Sunderland, Louise Allyn Sunderland, Mary Compton Sunderland.
Employer Identification Number: 316030791

5597
Eleanora C. U. Alms Trust
c/o Fifth Third Bank, Dept. 00864 Trust Div.
38 Fountain Sq. Plaza
Cincinnati 45263 (513) 579-6034

Trust established in 1939 in OH.
Donor(s): Eleanora C.U. Alms.†
Foundation type: Independent
Financial data (yr. ended 09/30/89): Assets, $3,310,259 (M); expenditures, $157,666, including $137,441 for 10 grants (high: $56,700; low: $2,246; average: $10,000).
Purpose and activities: Support primarily for performing and fine arts, including music, museums, and historic preservation; support also for education, a community fund, conservation, family services, leadership development, and a church.
Types of support: Building funds, annual campaigns, capital campaigns, equipment, renovation projects, seed money.
Limitations: Giving limited to Cincinnati, OH. No support for political or religious purposes, or to other foundations. No grants to individuals, or for operating budgets; no loans.
Publications: Annual report, application guidelines.
Application information: Application form not required.
Initial approach: Letter
Copies of proposal: 1
Deadline(s): Feb. 1, May 1, Aug. 1, and Nov. 1
Board meeting date(s): Mar., June, Sept., and Dec.
Final notification: Immediately following meeting
Write: Carolyn F. McCoy, Mgr.
Trustee: Fifth Third Bank.
Number of staff: 1 full-time professional; 1 full-time support.
Employer Identification Number: 316019723

5598
Amcast Industrial Foundation
3931 South Dixie Ave.
Kettering 45439 (513) 298-5251
Mailing address: P.O. Box 98, Dayton, OH 45401

Incorporated in 1952 in OH.
Donor(s): Amcast Industrial Corp. (formerly Dayton Malleable, Inc.).
Foundation type: Company-sponsored
Financial data (yr. ended 08/31/89): Assets, $539,013 (M); gifts received, $119,350; expenditures, $145,471, including $118,945 for 75 grants (high: $12,000; low: $100), $15,050 for grants to individuals and $5,402 for 29 employee matching gifts.
Purpose and activities: Grants mainly for community funds, arts and cultural programs, social services, health, and higher education; includes matching gifts for education.
Types of support: Continuing support, annual campaigns, emergency funds, building funds, employee matching gifts, special projects, research, employee-related scholarships.
Limitations: Giving primarily in areas of company operations. No grants to individuals (except employee-related scholarships), or for operating budgets, seed money, deficit financing, equipment, land acquisition, endowment funds, scholarships, fellowships, publications, or conferences; no loans.
Publications: Informational brochure.
Application information: Letters to the foundation are routed to the different divisions which then make grant recommendations to the foundations. Applicants may write to the division in their area directly. Application form not required.
Copies of proposal: 1
Deadline(s): Prior to board dates
Board meeting date(s): Feb., May, Aug., and Nov.
Write: Thomas G. Amato, Secy.
Officers and Trustees:* Leo W. Ladehoff,* Pres.; Thomas G. Amato,* Secy.
Number of staff: None.
Employer Identification Number: 316016458

5599
The American Financial Corporation Foundation ▼
One East Fourth St.
Cincinnati 45202 (513) 579-2400

Established in 1971 in OH.
Donor(s): American Financial Corp.
Foundation type: Company-sponsored
Financial data (yr. ended 12/31/88): Assets, $155,890 (M); gifts received, $2,500,000; expenditures, $2,476,428, including $2,472,572 for 100 grants (high: $250,000; low: $20; average: $500-$20,000).
Purpose and activities: Foundation is primarily a conduit for corporate contributions to local charities. Giving primarily for organizations promoting social change, economic study, and social welfare, including hospitals, and public interest organizations; grants also for education and the arts.
Types of support: Building funds, endowment funds, operating budgets, special projects.
Limitations: Giving primarily in the Cincinnati, OH, area. No grants to individuals.
Application information:
Initial approach: Letter
Copies of proposal: 1
Deadline(s): None
Board meeting date(s): As required
Final notification: 60 days
Write: Sandra W. Heimann, Secy.
Officers and Directors:* Carl H. Lindner,* Pres.; Robert D. Lindner,* V.P.; Sandra W. Heimann, Secy.
Number of staff: None.
Employer Identification Number: 237153009

5600
The American Foundation Corporation ▼ ⌑
720 National City Bank Bldg.
Cleveland 44114 (216) 241-6664

Incorporated in 1974 as successor to trust established in 1944 in OH.
Donor(s): Corning, Murfey and Norweb families and others.
Foundation type: Independent
Financial data (yr. ended 12/31/87): Assets, $16,946,361 (M); gifts received, $22,675; expenditures, $1,064,220, including $1,064,220 for 186 grants (high: $197,124; low: $8; average: $200-$36,000).
Purpose and activities: Emphasis on an arboretum, the arts, higher and secondary education, child welfare, and community funds.
Types of support: Annual campaigns, general purposes, continuing support.
Limitations: Giving primarily in the Cleveland, OH, area, and CA. No grants to individuals, or for capital or endowment funds, special projects, research, scholarships, fellowships, or matching gifts; no loans.
Application information: Funds presently committed. Applications not accepted.
Board meeting date(s): As necessary
Write: Maria G. Muth, Treas.
Officers: Malvin E. Bank, Secy.; Maria G. Muth, Treas.
Trustees: Henry H. Corning, Nathan E. Corning, T. Dixon Long, Spencer L. Murfey, Jr., William W. Murfey.
Number of staff: None.
Employer Identification Number: 237348126

5601
American Society of Ephesus, Inc. ⌑
(also known as George B. Quatman Foundation)
327 North Elizabeth St.
Lima 45801 (419) 225-2261

Incorporated in 1958.
Foundation type: Independent
Financial data (yr. ended 12/31/89): Assets, $3,980,049 (M); gifts received, $16,011; expenditures, $161,490, including $111,918 for 16 grants (high: $70,000; low: $1,000; average: $1,000-$5,000).
Purpose and activities: Formed primarily for the purpose of the restoration and preservation of the Christian shrines contained in the ruins of the ancient city of Ephesus that lies on the western coast of Turkey facing the Aegean Sea. Once the annual budget for this program is completed, it normally consumes all available income. Should any monies be remaining, consideration is primarily given to a donation to a Christian shrine that would have the common focal point and usage by the public in general.
Types of support: Renovation projects.
Limitations: Giving primarily in Ephesus, Turkey; some local giving in the Lima, OH, area. No grants for research, scholarships, or church maintenance or reconstruction.
Publications: 990-PF, occasional report, informational brochure.
Application information:
Deadline(s): None
Write: Joseph B. Quatman, V.P.
Officers: George W. Quatman, Jr.,* Pres.; Joseph B. Quatman,* V.P.; Anne Lehmann, Secy.-Treas.
Trustees:* Anthony J. Bowers, John D. Quatman, Joseph E. Quatman, Jr.
Number of staff: 1 part-time professional; 1 part-time support.
Employer Identification Number: 346560998

5602
Anderson Foundation ⌑
P.O. Box 119
Maumee 43537 (419) 891-6404

Trust established in 1949 in OH.
Donor(s): Partners in The Andersons.
Foundation type: Company-sponsored
Financial data (yr. ended 12/31/88): Assets, $4,536,469 (M); gifts received, $50,670; expenditures, $672,482, including $634,641 for 170 grants (high: $246,866; low: $50).
Purpose and activities: Grants for higher and secondary education, social service and youth agencies, community funds, civic and community efforts, cultural programs, religious organizations, and educational and research associations.
Types of support: Capital campaigns, conferences and seminars, employee matching gifts, employee-related scholarships, annual campaigns, building funds, emergency funds, general purposes, matching funds, publications, research, scholarship funds, seed money, special projects.
Limitations: Giving primarily in the greater Toledo, OH, area, including Maumee, Columbus, and Findlay. Grants also to organizations located within 50 miles of The Andersons plants in the following cities: Delphi, Frankfort, and Dunkirk, IN; Champaign, IL; and Albion, Potterville, Webberville, and White Pigeon, MI. No support for private foundations. No grants to individuals, or for endowment funds, travel, building or operating funds for churches or elementary schools.
Publications: Application guidelines.
Application information: Application form not required.
Initial approach: Letter or telephone
Copies of proposal: 1
Deadline(s): Three weeks before board meetings
Board meeting date(s): 4th Monday of Feb., Apr., June, Aug., Oct., and Dec.
Final notification: Generally 2 months; depends on completeness of proposal
Write: Mrs. Beverly J. Lange, Secy. to the Chair.
Trustees: Thomas H. Anderson, Chair.; Andrew T. Anderson, Christopher J. Anderson, Michael J. Anderson, Robert G. Bristow, Beverly J. McBride, Ruth M. Miller.
Number of staff: 1 full-time professional.
Employer Identification Number: 346528868

5603
William P. Anderson Foundation
c/o Central Trust Co.
Fifth and Main Sts.
Cincinnati 45202 (513) 651-8439

Incorporated in 1941 in OH.
Foundation type: Independent
Financial data (yr. ended 10/31/88): Assets, $3,875,116 (M); expenditures, $208,695, including $127,855 for 30 grants (high: $17,500; low: $500) and $40,521 for 4 grants to individuals (high: $34,667; low: $780).
Purpose and activities: Emphasis on hospitals, community funds, educational institutions, child welfare and youth agencies, including problems of juvenile delinquency, health agencies, conservation, and the arts.
Types of support: Annual campaigns, building funds, capital campaigns.
Limitations: Giving primarily in Cincinnati, OH, and Boston, MA. No grants to individuals.
Application information: The foundation no longer awards scholarships to individual students; existing commitments will be paid out. Application form not required.
Initial approach: Letter
Deadline(s): None
Board meeting date(s): Oct. and Nov.
Write: Paul D. Myers, Secy.
Officers and Trustees: William G. Anderson, Pres. and Treas.; Vachael Anderson Coombe, V.P.; Harry W. Whittaker, V.P.; Paul D. Myers, Secy.; Grenville Anderson, William P. Anderson V, Eva Jane Coombe, Michael A. Coombe, Margot A. Pattison, C. Lawson Reed, Dorothy W. Reed, Katharine W. Taft.
Employer Identification Number: 316034059

5604
The Andrews Foundation
1127 Euclid Ave., Suite 210
Cleveland 44115 (216) 621-3215

Incorporated in 1951 in OH.
Donor(s): Mrs. Matthew Andrews.†
Foundation type: Independent
Financial data (yr. ended 12/31/89): Assets, $5,613,336 (M); expenditures, $333,593, including $293,600 for 37 grants (high: $50,000; low: $500).
Purpose and activities: Giving for higher and secondary education, the performing arts, a child development center, and associations concerned with alcoholism and the handicapped.
Types of support: Annual campaigns, building funds, capital campaigns, endowment funds, general purposes.
Limitations: Giving limited to northeastern OH. No grants to individuals.
Application information: Application form not required.
Initial approach: Letter
Copies of proposal: 1
Deadline(s): None
Board meeting date(s): Usually in Nov.
Write: Richard S. Tomer, Pres.
Officers and Trustees:* Richard S. Tomer,* Pres. and Treas.; Barbara J. Baxter,* V.P.; James H. Dempsey, Jr.,* Secy.; Laura S. Baxter.
Number of staff: None.
Employer Identification Number: 346515110

5605
The Mildred Andrews Fund ⌑
1220 Huntington Bldg.
Cleveland 44115

Trust established in 1972 in OH.
Donor(s): Peter Putnam,† and others.
Foundation type: Operating
Financial data (yr. ended 12/31/87): Assets, $32,045,394 (M); gifts received, $18,506,069; expenditures, $1,008,304, including $363,934 for 33 grants (high: $100,112; low: $50).
Purpose and activities: A private operating foundation; giving for the arts and higher education.
Limitations: Giving primarily in the Cleveland, OH, area.
Application information:
Write: Robert C. Bouhall, Trustee
Trustee: Robert C. Bouhall.
Employer Identification Number: 237158695

5606
The Evenor Armington Fund ⌑
c/o Huntington Trust Co., N.A.
P.O. Box 1558
Columbus 43260
Application address: The Huntington National Bank, Trust Dept., 41 South High St., Columbus, OH 43216; Tel.: (614) 463-3707

Established in 1954 in OH.
Donor(s): Everett Armington, and members of the Armington family.
Foundation type: Independent
Financial data (yr. ended 6/30/88): Assets, $4,789,988 (M); expenditures, $48,392, including $18,000 for 3 grants (high: $8,000; low: $4,000).
Purpose and activities: Grants primarily for special projects, usually short-term, in education, child welfare, medical research, health, the arts, the environment, and public policy organizations, including human rights, peace and justice, and the struggle against poverty.

Types of support: Operating budgets, continuing support, annual campaigns, emergency funds, research, publications, special projects.
Limitations: No grants for deficit financing, or for general purposes.
Application information: Most grants are initiated by the advisors. Application form not required. Applications not accepted.
Deadline(s): Nov. 15
Board meeting date(s): Summer
Advisors: Catherine Armington, David E. Armington, Paul S. Armington, Peter Armington, Rosemary Armington.
Trustee: Huntington National Bank.
Number of staff: None.
Employer Identification Number: 346525508

5607
The Ashtabula Foundation, Inc. ⌑
c/o Society Bank of Eastern Ohio, N.A.
4717 Main Ave.
Ashtabula 44004 (216) 992-6818

Incorporated in 1922 in OH.
Foundation type: Community
Financial data (yr. ended 12/31/88): Assets, $8,122,829 (M); gifts received, $76,109; expenditures, $384,670, including $286,676 for grants (high: $79,164).
Purpose and activities: To administer charitable trusts; support for health, welfare, and cultural programs, with emphasis on a community fund and church support.
Types of support: Building funds, land acquisition, renovation projects, equipment.
Limitations: Giving limited to the Ashtabula, OH, area.
Publications: Application guidelines.
Application information: Application guidelines for scholarship funds available. Application form required.
Initial approach: Proposal
Copies of proposal: 4
Deadline(s): Feb. 1, May 1, Aug. 1, and Nov. 1
Board meeting date(s): Mar., June, Sept., and Dec.
Officers and Trustees: Frank Koski, Pres.; Wilbur Anderson, V.P.; Tom Anderson, Secy.-Treas.; Douglas Hedberg, Eleanor Jammal, Maynard Walker, Glen Warner, John Zaback, William C. Zweier.
Trustee Bank: Society Bank of Eastern Ohio, N.A.
Employer Identification Number: 346538130

5608
Associated Charities of Findlay, Ohio ⌑
233 South Main St.
Findlay 45840-3395 (419) 423-2021

Established in 1918 in OH.
Foundation type: Independent
Financial data (yr. ended 12/31/88): Assets, $1,292,995 (M); expenditures, $72,495, including $61,109 for grants.
Purpose and activities: Giving primarily to needy families and individuals, and to organizations that give similarly.
Limitations: Giving primarily in the Findlay, OH, area.
Application information:
Initial approach: Personal interview or telephone
Write: Mary Jane Roberts
Officers and Trustees: Marge Kennedy, Pres.; Charles Bishop, V.P.; Susan Smith, Secy.; Harry Cross, Treas.; and 18 additional trustees.
Employer Identification Number: 346400067

5609
The Austin Memorial Foundation ⌑
Aurora Commons Office Bldg., Suite 230
Aurora 44202 (216) 562-5515

Incorporated in 1961 in OH.
Donor(s): Members of the Austin family.
Foundation type: Independent
Financial data (yr. ended 12/31/88): Assets, $5,397,124 (M); gifts received, $40,367; expenditures, $439,000, including $352,623 for 39 grants (high: $47,540; low: $200).
Purpose and activities: Emphasis on higher and secondary education, hospitals, social services, and Protestant church support.
Limitations: Giving limited to the U.S. and its possessions. No grants to individuals.
Application information: Contributes only to pre-selected organizations. Applications not accepted.
Board meeting date(s): Semiannually
Officers: Donald G. Austin, Jr.,* Pres.; Donald G. Austin,* V.P.; Winifred N. Austin,* V.P.; Margaret A. Grumhaus,* V.P.; Colette Mylott, Secy.; David A. Rodgers,* Treas.
Trustees:* James W. Austin, Richard C. Austin, Stewart G. Austin, Thomas G. Austin, Sarah R. Cole, Ann R. Loeffler.
Number of staff: 1 part-time professional.
Employer Identification Number: 346528879

5610
Baird Brothers Company Foundation ⌑
c/o The Huntington Trust Co., N.A.
P.O. Box 1558
Columbus 43260
Application address: c/o The Huntington Trust Co., N.A., 41 South High St., Columbus, OH 43215; Tel.: (614) 463-3707

Established in OH.
Foundation type: Independent
Financial data (yr. ended 06/30/89): Assets, $3,293,680 (M); expenditures, $164,326, including $136,924 for 7 grants (high: $45,991; low: $300).
Purpose and activities: Grants primarily for a museum, civic affairs, a hearing center, and church support.
Limitations: Giving limited to Nelsonville, OH.
Application information: Application form not required.
Deadline(s): None
Write: Arlene B. Powell, Dir.
Directors: David S. Fraedrich, Arlene B. Powell, Wilbert W. Warren.
Trustee: Huntington Trust Co., N.A.
Employer Identification Number: 316194844

5611
Jessie Foos Baker Charitable Foundation ⌑
c/o Huntington National Bank
Box 1558
Columbus 43260
Application address: Huntington National Bank, Trust Dept., 41 South High St., Columbus, OH 43216; Tel.: (614) 463-3707

Established in 1952 in OH.
Foundation type: Independent
Financial data (yr. ended 12/31/88): Assets, $2,353,240 (M); expenditures, $163,702, including $92,834 for 1 grant.
Purpose and activities: Support for a memorial home association.
Application information:
Deadline(s): Nov. 15
Trustee: Huntington National Bank.
Employer Identification Number: 346547859

5612
C. Glenn Barber Foundation ⌑
c/o National City Bank
P.O. Box 5756
Cleveland 44101

Established in 1978 in Ohio.
Foundation type: Independent
Financial data (yr. ended 12/31/88): Assets, $1,596,354 (M); expenditures, $105,744, including $91,926 for 2 grants (high: $77,703; low: $14,223).
Purpose and activities: Giving limited to higher education.
Limitations: Giving primarily in OH.
Application information: Contributes only to pre-selected organizations. Applications not accepted.
Trustee: National City Bank.
Employer Identification Number: 346765153

5613
Bardes Fund ⌑
4730 Madison Rd.
Cincinnati 45227-1426 (513) 871-4000

Established in 1955 in OH.
Foundation type: Company-sponsored
Financial data (yr. ended 12/31/88): Assets, $1,694,316 (M); expenditures, $84,989, including $74,737 for 110 grants (high: $5,600; low: $20).
Purpose and activities: Giving primarily for general charitable organizations with an emphasis on welfare and higher and private secondary education.
Application information:
Initial approach: Letter
Deadline(s): None
Write: Marilyn Stoeckle, Secy.
Officers: Olivia Kiebach, Pres.; Marilyn Stoeckle, Secy.
Employer Identification Number: 316036206

5614
The Bares Foundation ☆
530 Washington St.
Chagrin Falls 44022 (216) 247-4600

Established in 1977 in OH.
Donor(s): Milbar Corp.
Foundation type: Independent
Financial data (yr. ended 06/30/89): Assets, $1,002,849 (M); expenditures, $95,034, including $90,100 for 15 grants (high: $45,000; low: $75).
Purpose and activities: Giving primarily to universities for research in artificial intelligence,

with particular interest in the Quayle phenomenon; support also for the performing arts.
Types of support: Research.
Application information:
Initial approach: Letter or proposal
Deadline(s): None
Write: Jack A. Bares, Pres.
Officers and Trustees:* Jack A. Bares,* Pres. and Secy.; Alice W. Bares,* V.P.; Brian K. Gothot, Treas.
Employer Identification Number: 341211995

5615
Barnitz Fund ⌘ ☆
c/o Bank One, Dayton, N.A.
Kettering Tower
Dayton 45401
Application address: c/o Bank One, Middletown, Two South Main St., Middletown, OH 45042; Tel.: (513) 425-8400

Established in 1951.
Foundation type: Independent
Financial data (yr. ended 12/31/88): Assets, $1,097,891 (M); expenditures, $59,517, including $38,208 for 24 grants (high: $10,500; low: $25) and $11,513 for 8 grants to individuals (high: $3,333; low: $280).
Purpose and activities: Awards scholarships to graduates of local area high schools who plan to go into Christian work; grants also for a YMCA and other human services.
Types of support: Student aid.
Limitations: Giving primarily in Middletown, OH.
Application information:
Deadline(s): None
Trustee: Bank One, Dayton, N.A.
Employer Identification Number: 316020687

5616
Edward M. Barr Charitable Trust
c/o Mahoning National Bank of Youngstown, Trust Dept.
23 Federal Plaza, P.O. Box 479
Youngstown 44501 (216) 742-7000

Established in 1973 in OH.
Foundation type: Independent
Financial data (yr. ended 12/31/89): Assets, $1,516,910 (M); expenditures, $89,403, including $77,600 for 6 grants (high: $50,000; low: $6,650).
Purpose and activities: Giving primarily for social services, especially the Salvation Army; support also for cultural programs and denominational giving.
Types of support: Building funds, capital campaigns, equipment, renovation projects.
Limitations: Giving primarily in Youngstown, OH.
Application information:
Initial approach: Letter
Deadline(s): None
Write: Patrick A. Sebastiano, Sr. V.P. and Sr. Trust Officer, Mahoning National Bank of Youngstown
Trustee: Mahoning National Bank of Youngstown.
Members: John C. Litty, Jr., Gregory L. Ridler, Patrick A. Sebastiano.
Number of staff: None.
Employer Identification Number: 346687006

5617
Barry Foundation
P.O. Box 129
Columbus 43216 (614) 864-6400

Incorporated in 1963 in OH.
Donor(s): Florence Melton, R.G. Barry Corp.
Foundation type: Independent
Financial data (yr. ended 12/31/88): Assets, $11,404 (M); gifts received, $182,381; expenditures, $182,237, including $180,933 for 65 grants (high: $65,000; low: $25).
Purpose and activities: Emphasis on Jewish welfare funds, community funds, theological and higher education in Israel; support also for educational associations and research and elementary and adult education, the fine and performing arts, international studies, medical research and health services, religious welfare organizations, and family and social services, including family planning, child welfare agencies, and programs for the disabled, homeless, and hungry.
Types of support: Annual campaigns, research, scholarship funds.
Limitations: Giving primarily in OH. No grants to individuals.
Publications: Financial statement.
Application information: Application form not required.
Initial approach: Letter
Copies of proposal: 1
Deadline(s): None
Board meeting date(s): Dec.
Write: Gordon Zacks, Pres.
Officers and Trustees:* Florence Melton,* Chair.; Gordon Zacks,* Pres.; William W. Ellis, Jr.,* Secy.; Richard L. Burrell,* Treas.; Harvey M. Kreuger.
Employer Identification Number: 316051086

5618
The Georgine E. Bates Memorial Fund, Inc. ⌘
1221 Lippincott Rd.
P.O. Box 351
Urbana 43078 (513) 653-7186

Established in 1979.
Foundation type: Independent
Financial data (yr. ended 10/31/88): Assets, $1,317,572 (M); expenditures, $84,310, including $65,960 for 19 grants (high: $7,240; low: $640).
Purpose and activities: Giving for higher and secondary education, youth agencies, health, Protestant church support, and a center for senior citizens.
Limitations: Giving limited to Champaign County, OH.
Application information:
Write: Henry W. Houston, Treas.
Officers: Marvin V. Humphrey, Pres.; James R. Wilson, Secy.; Henry W. Houston, Treas.
Employer Identification Number: 341296531

5619
Elsie and Harry Baumker Charitable Foundation, Inc. ⌘
2828 Barrington Dr.
Toledo 43606

Incorporated in 1982 in OH.
Donor(s): Elsie Baumker.†
Foundation type: Independent
Financial data (yr. ended 12/31/88): Assets, $1,597,237 (M); expenditures, $90,031, including $78,450 for 30 grants (high: $7,500; low: $500).
Purpose and activities: Giving primarily for health services and social service and youth agencies; support also for higher education and cultural programs.
Types of support: Endowment funds, scholarship funds, special projects.
Limitations: Giving primarily in OH, with emphasis on Toledo.
Application information: Application form required.
Deadline(s): None
Final notification: 3 months
Trustees: Gladys M. Preis, Mgr.; Howard L. Ness, Nancy Preis.
Employer Identification Number: 341300465

5620
The Ruth H. Beecher Charitable Trust ☆
c/o The Dollar Savings & Trust Co.
P.O. Box 450
Youngstown 44501

Established in 1986 in OH.
Foundation type: Independent
Financial data (yr. ended 09/30/89): Assets, $1,316,773 (M); expenditures, $77,748, including $69,600 for 11 grants (high: $25,000; low: $1,000; average: $1,000-$5,000).
Purpose and activities: Giving primarily for a symphony society; support also for civic affairs and a historical society.
Types of support: Renovation projects, land acquisition, equipment, capital campaigns, special projects.
Limitations: Giving primarily in Youngstown, OH.
Application information: Application form not required.
Copies of proposal: 3
Deadline(s): None
Write: Herbert H. Pridham, Sr. V.P. and Sr. Trust Off., The Dollar Savings & Trust Co.
Trustees: John Weed Powers, The Dollar Savings & Trust Co.
Employer Identification Number: 346861417

5621
Florence Simon Beecher Foundation
c/o Mahoning National Bank of Youngstown, Trust Dept.
P.O. Box 479
Youngstown 44501 (216) 742-7000

Established in 1969 in OH.
Donor(s): Florence Simon Beecher.
Foundation type: Independent
Financial data (yr. ended 12/31/89): Assets, $3,885,117 (M); expenditures, $209,124, including $185,000 for 15 grants (high: $115,000; low: $1,500).
Purpose and activities: Giving for youth agencies and community development.
Types of support: General purposes, equipment, building funds, capital campaigns, equipment, renovation projects.
Limitations: Giving limited to Youngstown, OH.
Application information:
Initial approach: Letter or proposal

Copies of proposal: 1
Deadline(s): Submit proposal Jan. through Mar.
Board meeting date(s): As required
Write: Patrick A. Sebastiano, Sr. V.P. and Sr. Trust Officer, Mahoning National Bank of Youngstown
Directors: Eleanor Beecher Flad, Erle L. Flad, Ward Beecher Flad, Arthur G. Young.
Trustee: Mahoning National Bank of Youngstown.
Number of staff: None.
Employer Identification Number: 346613413

5622
Ward Beecher Foundation
c/o Mahoning National Bank of Youngstown, Trust Dept.
P.O. Box 479
Youngstown 44501 (216) 742-7000

Established in 1958 in OH.
Donor(s): Ward Beecher.†
Foundation type: Independent
Financial data (yr. ended 12/31/89): Assets, $2,477,084 (M); expenditures, $90,902, including $76,000 for 5 grants (high: $35,000; low: $5,000).
Purpose and activities: Support for capital building drives for hospitals, community funds, and youth agencies.
Types of support: Building funds, annual campaigns, capital campaigns, equipment, renovation projects.
Limitations: Giving limited to the Youngstown, OH, area. No grants to individuals, or for scholarships, fellowships, matching gifts, endowment funds, or research; no loans.
Application information: Application form not required.
Initial approach: Letter or proposal
Copies of proposal: 1
Deadline(s): Submit proposal in the 1st quarter of the calendar year
Board meeting date(s): As required
Write: Patrick A. Sebastiano, Sr. V.P. and Sr. Trust Officer, Mahoning National Bank of Youngstown
Directors: Florence Simon Beecher, Eleanor Beecher Flad, Erle L. Flad, Ward Beecher Flad.
Trustee: Mahoning National Bank of Youngstown.
Number of staff: None.
Employer Identification Number: 346516441

5623
The Leon A. Beeghly Fund ⌑
c/o Bank One, Youngstown N.A.
Six Federal Plaza West
Youngstown 44503 (216) 743-3151
Mailing address: 808 Stambaugh Bldg., Youngstown, OH 44503

Trust established in 1940 in OH.
Donor(s): Leon A. Beeghly,† Mabel L. Beeghly.†
Foundation type: Independent
Financial data (yr. ended 12/31/88): Assets, $3,733,732 (M); expenditures, $853,433, including $808,182 for 67 grants (high: $80,000; low: $200; average: $5,000-$10,000).
Purpose and activities: Emphasis on Protestant church support and religious associations, higher education, cultural programs, community development, hospitals, community funds, and aid to the handicapped; support also for family services and programs that benefit women, youth, and the disadvantaged and the aged.
Types of support: General purposes, building funds, equipment, endowment funds, professorships, scholarship funds, capital campaigns, annual campaigns, continuing support, emergency funds, operating budgets, renovation projects, special projects.
Limitations: Giving primarily in the Youngstown, OH, metropolitan area; limited giving in western PA. No grants to individuals, or for research, special projects, publications, or conferences; no loans.
Publications: Program policy statement, application guidelines.
Application information: Application form not required.
Initial approach: Proposal
Copies of proposal: 1
Deadline(s): None
Board meeting date(s): Quarterly
Final notification: 1 to 6 months
Write: James L. Beeghly, Exec. Secy.
Appointing Committee: James L. Beeghly, Exec. Secy.; John D. Beeghly, R.T. Beeghly.
Trustee: Bank One, Youngstown, N.A.
Number of staff: 1 part-time support.
Employer Identification Number: 346514043

5624
The Beerman Foundation, Inc. ⌑
11 West Monument Bldg., 8th Fl.
Dayton 45402

Incorporated in 1945 in OH.
Donor(s): Arthur Beerman,† Jessie Beerman, and others.
Foundation type: Independent
Financial data (yr. ended 12/31/88): Assets, $7,114,283 (M); expenditures, $731,710, including $616,172 for 51 grants (high: $293,993; low: $35).
Purpose and activities: Support for a medical center, higher education, Jewish welfare funds, social services, and the arts.
Limitations: Giving primarily in Dayton, OH.
Publications: Annual report.
Application information:
Initial approach: Letter
Deadline(s): None
Write: William S. Weprin, V.P.
Officers: Barbara Beerman Weprin, Pres.; William S. Weprin, V.P. and Secy.; Val P. Hattemer, Treas.
Employer Identification Number: 316024369

5625
Anderton Bentley Fund ⌑ ☆
c/o First National Bank of Toledo
606 Madison Ave.
Toledo 43604-1108

Foundation type: Independent
Financial data (yr. ended 10/31/88): Assets, $369,522 (M); expenditures, $140,317, including $135,500 for 12 grants (high: $109,250; low: $1,000).
Purpose and activities: Giving for community funds, education, and cultural programs.
Limitations: Giving primarily in Toledo, OH.
Trustee: First National Bank of Toledo.
Employer Identification Number: 346509881

5626
The Bentz Foundation ⌑
P.O. Box 18191
Columbus 43218-0191
Application address: 580 South High St., Columbus, OH 43215; Tel.: (614) 221-5287

Incorporated in 1948 in OH.
Donor(s): George B. Bentz, Agnes C. McConnell, Mary E. Bentz, and others.
Foundation type: Independent
Financial data (yr. ended 10/31/88): Assets, $2,696,286 (M); expenditures, $94,404, including $57,000 for 3 grants (high: $50,000; low: $2,000).
Purpose and activities: Grants and loans primarily for Roman Catholic church support and missionary programs.
Limitations: No grants to individuals.
Application information: Application form not required.
Deadline(s): None
Board meeting date(s): As required
Write: Robert T. Cull, Pres.
Officers and Trustees: Robert T. Cull, Pres.; Hon. R. Patrick West, V.P.; Edmund D. Doyle, Secy.; William H. Boodro, Treas.
Employer Identification Number: 316036015

5627
The Benua Foundation, Inc. ⌑
17 South High St., Rm. 724
Columbus 43215

Incorporated in 1952 in DE.
Donor(s): A.R. Benua, Ebco Manufacturing Co.
Foundation type: Independent
Financial data (yr. ended 12/31/88): Assets, $11,530,591 (M); expenditures, $408,595, including $394,000 for 136 grants (high: $30,000; low: $500).
Purpose and activities: Giving for conservation, higher education, youth and health agencies, and cultural programs.
Limitations: Giving primarily in Columbus, OH.
Application information: Contributes only to pre-selected organizations. Applications not accepted.
Trustees: John M. Bowsher, Eleanor L. Craig, Mac Lee Henny.
Employer Identification Number: 316026443

5628
The Louis and Sandra Berkman Foundation ⌑
330 North Seventh St.
Steubenville 43952 (614) 283-3722
Application address: P.O. Box 576, Steubenville, OH 43952

Incorporated in 1952 in OH.
Donor(s): Louis Berkman, Sr.,† Mrs. Louis Berkman, The Louis Berkman Co., Follansbee Steel Corp., and others.
Foundation type: Independent
Financial data (yr. ended 12/31/88): Assets, $2,453,843 (M); expenditures, $74,816,

including $74,700 for 23 grants (high: $25,000; low: $50).
Purpose and activities: Grants primarily for Jewish welfare funds and higher education; support also for medical research and hospitals.
Limitations: Giving primarily in OH, PA, and MA.
Application information:
Initial approach: Proposal
Deadline(s): July 1 of year prior to year of grant
Write: Chester M. Anderson, Trustee
Officers and Trustees: Francis D. O'Leary, Louis Berkman, Pres. and Treas.; Marshall L. Berkman, V.P.; Robert A. Paul, V.P.; Chester M. Anderson, Secy.
Employer Identification Number: 346526694

5629
Loren M. Berry Foundation ⌑
3055 Kettering Blvd., Suite 418
Dayton 45439 (513) 293-0398

Incorporated in 1960 in OH.
Donor(s): Loren M. Berry.†
Foundation type: Independent
Financial data (yr. ended 12/31/88): Assets, $9,486,768 (M); gifts received, $219,656; expenditures, $615,099, including $519,925 for 113 grants (high: $30,000; low: $100).
Purpose and activities: Emphasis on higher education, hospitals, youth agencies, medical research, cultural programs, church support, and patriotic organizations.
Limitations: Giving primarily in OH. No grants to individuals, or for operating budgets.
Application information:
Initial approach: Letter
Deadline(s): None
Board meeting date(s): Mar., June, Sept., and Dec.
Write: William T. Lincoln, Treas.
Officers and Trustees: John W. Berry, Sr., Pres.; John W. Berry, Jr., V.P.; William T. Lincoln, Treas.; Charles D. Berry, David L. Berry, George W. Berry, Martha B. Fraim, William L. Fraim, Elizabeth B. Gray, Leland W. Henry, James O. Payne.
Employer Identification Number: 316026144

5630
Beta Theta Pi Fraternity Founders Fund ⌑
P.O. Box 111
208 East High St.
Oxford 45056 (513) 523-7591

Established in 1920 in OH.
Foundation type: Independent
Financial data (yr. ended 6/30/88): Assets, $1,462,302 (M); gifts received, $75,705; expenditures, $336,039, including $58,000 for 49 grants to individuals (high: $10,000; low: $750).
Purpose and activities: Scholarship assistance to members of Beta Theta Pi.
Types of support: Student aid.
Application information: Application form required.
Initial approach: Letter or telephone
Deadline(s): Apr. 15
Write: Thomas A. Beyer, Admin. Secy.
Trustees: Thomas L. Brennan, William G. Colby, Jr., Edward B. Vallone II, Robert A. Williams, Jr.
Employer Identification Number: 316050515

5631
Bicknell Fund
c/o Advisory Services, Inc.
1422 Euclid Ave., Rm. 1010
Cleveland 44115-2078 (216) 363-6482

Incorporated in 1949 in OH.
Donor(s): Kate H. Bicknell, Warren Bicknell, Jr.,† Warren Bicknell III, Kate B. Kirkham.
Foundation type: Independent
Financial data (yr. ended 12/31/89): Assets, $4,923,253 (M); expenditures, $260,345, including $237,900 for 53 grants (high: $30,000; low: $1,000; average: $1,000-$5,000).
Purpose and activities: Giving for a community fund, health and social services, and higher and secondary educational institutions.
Limitations: Giving primarily in OH. No grants to individuals; no loans.
Publications: Application guidelines.
Application information: Application form not required.
Initial approach: Proposal
Copies of proposal: 1
Deadline(s): Submit proposal prior to May or Nov.
Board meeting date(s): June and Dec.
Write: Robert G. Acklin, Secy.-Treas.
Officers: Kate B. Kirkham,* Pres.; Warren Bicknell III,* V.P.; Robert G. Acklin, Secy.-Treas.
Trustees:* Guthrie Bicknell, Wendy H. Bicknell, George D. Kirkham, Alexander S. Taylor, Lyman H. Treadway III.
Employer Identification Number: 346513799

5632
The William Bingham Foundation
1250 Leader Bldg.
Cleveland 44114 (216) 781-3275

Incorporated in 1955 in OH.
Donor(s): Elizabeth B. Blossom.†
Foundation type: Independent
Financial data (yr. ended 12/31/89): Assets, $25,779,000 (M); gifts received, $2,500; expenditures, $1,315,178, including $1,202,860 for 50 grants (high: $200,000; low: $1,000; average: $1,000-$25,000).
Purpose and activities: Support for the arts, education, including higher education, conservation, health, and welfare.
Types of support: General purposes, special projects, seed money, building funds, equipment, endowment funds, research, publications, conferences and seminars, scholarship funds, matching funds, program-related investments, operating budgets, capital campaigns, land acquisition, professorships, renovation projects.
Limitations: Giving primarily in the eastern U.S., with some emphasis on the Cleveland, OH, area. No grants to individuals; no loans.
Publications: Annual report (including application guidelines), application guidelines.
Application information: Full proposals accepted only on request of foundation in response to applicant's initial letter. Application form not required.
Initial approach: Letter of 2 pages or less
Copies of proposal: 1
Deadline(s): Submit letter preferably in Feb. or July; deadline for solicited proposal, 2 months prior to board meeting dates
Board meeting date(s): Usually May and Oct.
Final notification: 3 to 6 months
Write: Laura C. Hitchcox, Dir.
Officers: Dudley S. Blossom,* Pres.; Elizabeth B. Heffernan,* V.P.; Thomas F. Allen, Secy.; C. Bingham Blossom,* Treas.
Director: Laura C. Hitchcox.
Trustees: Laurel Blossom, Benjamin Gale, Mary E. Gale, Thomas H. Gale.
Number of staff: 1 full-time professional.
Employer Identification Number: 346513791

5633
Blade Foundation ⌑
c/o The Toledo Blade, Personnel Office
541 Superior St.
Toledo 43604 (419) 245-6290

Established in 1969 in OH.
Donor(s): Blade Communications, Inc.
Foundation type: Company-sponsored
Financial data (yr. ended 9/30/88): Assets, $447,511 (M); gifts received, $150,000; expenditures, $192,518, including $183,650 for 48 grants (high: $40,000; low: $200) and $8,000 for 9 grants to individuals (high: $1,000; low: $500).
Purpose and activities: Support for cultural and educational institutions and social service organizations; scholarships limited to children or legal dependents of full-time employees of the Toledo Blade with at least 3 years employment; officers' and directors' children are not eligible.
Types of support: Student aid.
Limitations: Giving primarily in OH.
Application information:
Deadline(s): Mar. 1 for scholarships
Officers and Trustees: William Block, Jr., Pres.; Allan Block, V.P.; John R. Block, V.P.; William Block, Jr., V.P.; Newell Kest, V.P.; Harold O. Davis, Secy.; John W. Harms, Treas.
Employer Identification Number: 346559843

5634
Peter J. Blosser Scholarship Trust ⌑
P.O. Box 6160
Chillicothe 45601-6160 (614) 773-2709

Established in 1977 in OH.
Foundation type: Independent
Financial data (yr. ended 12/31/88): Assets, $1,176,047 (M); expenditures, $63,071, including $50,300 for 35 loans to individuals (high: $1,500; low: $500; average: $1,500).
Purpose and activities: Support for loans to individuals for higher education.
Types of support: Student loans.
Limitations: Giving limited to residents of Ross County, OH.
Application information: Application form required.
Deadline(s): None
Write: Marie Rosebrook
Trustees: Raymond E. Pack, Robert Sigler, Maurice Smith, Lorene C. Washington.
Employer Identification Number: 310629687

5635
Borden Foundation, Inc. ▼
180 East Broad St., 34th Floor
Columbus 43215 (614) 225-4340

Incorporated in 1944 in NY.
Donor(s): Borden, Inc.
Foundation type: Company-sponsored
Financial data (yr. ended 12/31/88): Assets, $4,053,124 (M); gifts received, $1,415,000; qualifying distributions, $2,861,637, including $2,149,425 for 684 grants (high: $120,000; low: $25; average: $1,000-$5,000), $94,763 for 246 employee matching gifts and $617,449 for in-kind gifts.
Purpose and activities: Emphasis on higher education, civic affairs and community funds, child welfare and youth, and welfare agencies, including programs for the handicapped, minorities, and the homeless.
Types of support: Operating budgets, continuing support, annual campaigns, emergency funds, equipment, matching funds, employee matching gifts, technical assistance, consulting services.
Limitations: Giving primarily in areas of company operations. No support for organizations receiving major government funding, or political lobbying organizations. No grants to individuals, or for deficit financing, building funds, land acquisition, renovation projects, endowment funds, scholarships, fellowships, advertisements, membership drives, research, special projects, publications, or conferences; no loans.
Publications: Application guidelines.
Application information: Application form not required.
Initial approach: Letter
Copies of proposal: 1
Deadline(s): Mar. 1, July 1, and Oct. 1
Board meeting date(s): Apr., Aug., and Dec.
Final notification: 10 days following director's meeting
Write: Judy Barker, Pres.
Officers: James T. McCrory, Chair.; Judy Barker, Pres.; R.H. Byrd, Treas.
Directors: H. Cort Doughty, R.J. Ventres.
Number of staff: 2 full-time professional; 1 full-time support; 1 part-time support.
Employer Identification Number: 136089941

5636
The Bremer Foundation ⌑
709 Bank One Bldg.
Youngstown 44503

Incorporated in 1953 in OH.
Donor(s): Richard P. Bremer.†
Foundation type: Independent
Financial data (yr. ended 12/31/88): Assets, $1,824,252 (M); expenditures, $260,029, including $250,600 for 25 grants (high: $114,460; low: $500).
Purpose and activities: Giving for higher education and social welfare.
Limitations: Giving primarily in OH.
Application information:
Write: James E. Mitchell, Secy.
Officers and Trustees: Jonas S. Bremer, Pres.; W. Brooks Reed, V.P.; James E. Mitchell, Secy.; Morris S. Rosenblum, M.D., Treas.; Henry G. Cranblett, M.D., Joan L. McCoy.
Employer Identification Number: 346514168

5637
Brenlin Foundation ☆
Society Bldg., 6th Fl.
Akron 44308 (216) 762-2411

Established in 1983 in OH.
Donor(s): Gulf States Steel, Inc., Spartanburg Steel Products, Inc., Forged Products, Inc.
Foundation type: Company-sponsored
Financial data (yr. ended 12/31/88): Assets, $1,939,095 (M); gifts received, $1,274,000; expenditures, $57,701, including $56,875 for 20 grants (high: $15,000; low: $100).
Purpose and activities: Emphasis on education.
Types of support: General purposes.
Limitations: Giving primarily in OH, MI, and SC. No grants to individuals.
Application information: Proposals outside the field of education unlikely to receive consideration for funding.
Initial approach: Letter
Deadline(s): None
Write: David L. Brennan, Trustee
Trustees: David L. Brennan, Richard M. Hamlin, James P. McCready.
Number of staff: None.
Employer Identification Number: 346821141

5638
Bridgestone/Firestone Trust Fund ▼
(Formerly The Firestone Trust Fund)
1200 Firestone Pkwy.
Akron 44317 (216) 379-6590

Trust established in 1952 in OH.
Donor(s): Bridgestone/Firestone, Inc.
Foundation type: Company-sponsored
Financial data (yr. ended 10/31/88): Assets, $12,000,000 (M); expenditures, $6,125,616, including $6,125,616 for 530 grants (high: $3,000,000; low: $50; average: $1,000-$35,000).
Purpose and activities: Support for higher and other education, including employee matching gifts; community funds, health, and welfare; also supports civic and community affairs, and culture, including the fine and performing arts.
Types of support: Continuing support, annual campaigns, seed money, emergency funds, building funds, endowment funds, matching funds, employee matching gifts, research, special projects, capital campaigns, employee-related scholarships.
Limitations: Giving primarily in areas of company operations in AR, IL, IA, IN, LA, NC, OH, OK, TX, and VA. No grants to individuals, or for operating budgets, deficit financing, equipment, land acquisition, fellowships, publications, or conferences; no loans.
Publications: Application guidelines.
Application information: Application form not required.
Initial approach: Letter
Copies of proposal: 1
Deadline(s): Submit proposal preferably by July; no set deadline
Board meeting date(s): As required
Final notification: 3 to 4 weeks
Write: Bob Troyer, Secy.
Firestone Trust Fund Committee: J. Robert Anderson, Chair.; Bob Troyer, Secy.
Trustee: Ameritrust Co., N.A.
Directors: Michael J. Connor, Donald L. Groninger.
Number of staff: 1 full-time support.
Employer Identification Number: 346505181

5639
Britton Fund
1010 Hanna Bldg.
1422 Euclid Ave.
Cleveland 44115-2078 (216) 363-6487

Incorporated in 1952 in OH.
Donor(s): Gertrude H. Britton, Charles S. Britton, Brigham Britton.†
Foundation type: Independent
Financial data (yr. ended 12/31/89): Assets, $5,941,850 (M); gifts received, $70,000; expenditures, $352,757, including $333,000 for 43 grants (high: $61,000; low: $1,000; average: $2,000-$5,000).
Purpose and activities: Giving to community funds and social service agencies, higher and secondary education, hospitals and health services, youth agencies, and organizations aiding the handicapped.
Types of support: General purposes, operating budgets, emergency funds, annual campaigns, continuing support, endowment funds, scholarship funds.
Limitations: Giving primarily in OH. No grants to individuals.
Publications: Annual report.
Application information: Funds substantially committed.
Initial approach: Letter
Copies of proposal: 1
Deadline(s): Prior to board meetings
Board meeting date(s): May and Nov.
Write: Elizabeth C. Reed, Secy.
Officers: Charles S. Britton II,* Pres.; Gertrude H. Britton,* V.P.; Elizabeth C. Reed, Secy.; Donald C. Cook, Treas.
Trustees:* Lynda R. Britton.
Number of staff: 1 full-time professional.
Employer Identification Number: 346513616

5640
Louise Brown Foundation ⌑
2000 Huntington Bldg.
Cleveland 44115 (216) 696-4700

Established in 1971 in OH.
Donor(s): Louise I. Brown.
Foundation type: Independent
Financial data (yr. ended 11/30/88): Assets, $34,622 (M); gifts received, $267,826; expenditures, $214,240, including $210,015 for 46 grants (high: $50,115; low: $50).
Purpose and activities: Support for cultural organizations, higher and other education, and health services.
Limitations: Giving primarily in Cleveland, OH. No grants to individuals.
Application information:
Write: Richard T. Watson, Trustee
Trustees: Louise I. Brown, Willard W. Brown, Richard T. Watson.
Employer Identification Number: 237194549

5641
John N. Browning Family Fund, Inc. ⌑
c/o First National Bank of Cincinnati
P.O. Box 1118
Cincinnati 45201

Incorporated in 1969 in KY.
Donor(s): John N. Browning.†
Foundation type: Independent
Financial data (yr. ended 4/30/87): Assets, $2,428,528 (M); expenditures, $94,812, including $84,300 for 28 grants (high: $10,000; low: $200).
Purpose and activities: Grants primarily for higher and secondary education; some support for youth agencies.
Application information: Contributes only to pre-selected organizations. Applications not accepted.
Officers and Directors: Laura B. Van Meter, Pres.; Carlisle B. Van Meter, Secy.; George M. Van Meter, Jr., Treas.; Isaac C. Van Meter, Jr.
Employer Identification Number: 237009543

5642
Eva L. and Joseph M. Bruening Foundation ☆
c/o Ameritrust Co., N.A., Trust Tax
P.O. Box 5937
Cleveland 44101-9990 (216) 621-2632

Established in 1988 in OH.
Donor(s): Joseph M. Bruening,† Eva L. Bruening.†
Foundation type: Independent
Financial data (yr. ended 12/31/88): Assets, $15,897,614 (M); gifts received, $6,073,914; expenditures, $1,094,212, including $1,084,121 for 28 grants (high: $200,000; low: $3,000).
Purpose and activities: Initial year of operation, 1988; giving primarily for higher and other education; social services, including youth and child welfare, the elderly, the handicapped, and the disadvantaged; health and hospitals; and community development, including parks.
Types of support: Capital campaigns, building funds, equipment, renovation projects, seed money.
Limitations: Giving limited to the greater Cleveland, OH, area. No grants to individuals, or for endowment funds, general operating budgets, research, publications, or symposiums and seminars.
Publications: Informational brochure.
Application information: The foundation does not respond to mass mailings or annual campaign appeals. Application form not required.
Initial approach: Proposal
Copies of proposal: 6
Deadline(s): Mar. 1, July 1, and Nov. 1
Board meeting date(s): Apr., Aug, and Dec.
Final notification: Within several weeks of board meeting
Write: Janet E. Narten, Exec. Secy.
Distribution Committee: John R. Cunin, Chair.; Robert T. Blaine, E. Lorrie Robertson.
Trustee: Ameritrust Co., N.A.
Employer Identification Number: 341584378

5643
The Brush Foundation
c/o Ameritrust Co., N.A., Trust Tax Section
P.O. Box 5937
Cleveland 44101-0937 (216) 881-5121
Application address: 2027 Cornell Rd., Cleveland, OH 44106

Trust established in 1928 in OH.
Donor(s): Charles F. Brush,† Maurice Perkins.
Foundation type: Independent
Financial data (yr. ended 12/31/89): Assets, $3,374,020 (M); expenditures, $177,208, including $155,000 for 7 grants (high: $50,000; low: $1,600).
Purpose and activities: Grants for the regulation of population growth and betterment of the human race, including research in eugenics. The current major interests of the foundation are adolescent sexuality and the control of adolescent pregnancy, preservation of the freedom of choice of women to have abortions, and how laws and regulations may control population growth.
Types of support: General purposes, operating budgets, continuing support, annual campaigns, seed money, emergency funds, special projects, research, publications, conferences and seminars, matching funds.
Limitations: No grants to individuals, or for capital endowment funds, scholarships, or fellowships; no loans.
Application information: Application form not required.
Initial approach: Letter
Copies of proposal: 11
Deadline(s): None
Board meeting date(s): Apr., Sept., and Dec.
Final notification: 1 week after board meeting
Write: Doris B. Dingle, Pres.
Officers and Managers:* Doris B. Dingle,* Pres.; Meacham Hitchcock,* V.P.; Richard M. Donaldson,* Treas.; John J. Beeston, M.D., Charles F. Brush, Sally F. Burton, Virginia P. Carter, Jane Perkins Moffett, Edward A. Mortimer, Jr., M.D., William C. Weir, M.D.
Trustee Bank: Ameritrust Co., N.A.
Number of staff: None.
Employer Identification Number: 346000445

5644
Kenneth Calhoun Charitable Trust ⌑
c/o Society National Bank
800 Superior Ave.
Cleveland 44101
Application address: c/o Society National Bank, 157 South Main St., Akron, OH 44308; Tel.: (216) 379-1647

Established in 1982 in OH.
Donor(s): Kenneth Calhoun.†
Foundation type: Independent
Financial data (yr. ended 07/31/89): Assets, $3,771,049 (M); expenditures, $263,161, including $241,736 for 67 grants (high: $45,500; low: $100; average: $500-$10,000).
Purpose and activities: Giving for hospitals, cultural programs, education, youth agencies, and social services.
Limitations: Giving limited to the greater Akron, OH, area with an emphasis on Summit County. No grants to individuals.
Application information: Application form not required.
Initial approach: Letter
Copies of proposal: 1
Deadline(s): June 30
Write: Karen Krino, Sr. Trust Officer, Society National Bank
Trustee: Society National Bank.
Employer Identification Number: 341370330

5645
M. E. & F. J. Callahan Foundation ⌑
29500 Solon Rd.
Solon 44139-3474

Established in 1975 in OH.
Donor(s): F.J. Callahan.
Foundation type: Independent
Financial data (yr. ended 12/31/88): Assets, $1,387,864 (M); gifts received, $1,187,500; expenditures, $135,550, including $133,906 for 32 grants (high: $37,200; low: $25).
Purpose and activities: Giving to performing arts, especially music.
Limitations: Giving primarily in OH, with emphasis on Cleveland. No grants to individuals.
Application information: Contributes only to pre-selected organizations. Applications not accepted.
Officers: F.J. Callahan, Pres.; Mary E. Callahan, V.P.; John F. Fant, Jr., Secy.
Employer Identification Number: 510164320

5646
The Camden Foundation
c/o Fifth Third Bank
Dept. 00861
Cincinnati 45263 (513) 579-4327

Established in 1952 in OH.
Foundation type: Independent
Financial data (yr. ended 09/30/89): Assets, $1,440,600 (M); expenditures, $53,772, including $47,000 for 15 grants (high: $15,000; low: $1,000).
Purpose and activities: Giving primarily for museums, the arts, education, the environment, and general charitable projects.
Application information: Application form required.
Initial approach: Letter or telephone
Deadline(s): None
Write: Eileen McCaulay
Trustee: Fifth Third Bank.
Employer Identification Number: 316024141

5647
The Robert Campeau Family Foundation (U.S.) ▼
(Formerly Federated Department Stores Foundation)
Seven West Seventh St.
Cincinnati 45202 (513) 579-7166

Originally incorporated in 1952 in OH and later dissolved; reestablished in 1980 in OH.
Donor(s): Federated Department Stores, Inc.
Foundation type: Company-sponsored
Financial data (yr. ended 01/31/89): Assets, $15,966,757 (M); expenditures, $7,250,512, including $6,137,570 for 557 grants (high: $305,500; low: $500; average: $1,000-$15,000) and $1,005,003 for 136 employee matching gifts.

Purpose and activities: Emphasis on higher education, and cultural, civic, and health and welfare programs; matching employee gifts to educational and cultural organizations and contributions of $1,000 or more to local organizations at the request of the divisions of the company.
Types of support: Employee matching gifts, general purposes, building funds, matching funds, special projects.
Limitations: Giving primarily in communities of company operations: Miami, FL; Atlanta, GA; Boston and Somerville, MA; Brooklyn and New York, NY; Cincinnati and Columbus, OH; Memphis, TN; Seattle, WA; and Paramus, NJ. No support for religious organizations for religious purposes. No grants to individuals.
Publications: Annual report.
Application information: Local organizations should apply directly to local division of Federated Dept. Stores. Application form not required.
Initial approach: Proposal
Copies of proposal: 1
Deadline(s): None
Board meeting date(s): Approximately the 15th of each month
Final notification: 6 to 8 weeks
Write: Patricia Ikeda, Exec. Dir.
Officers: Ilse Campeau,* Chair. and Pres.; Robert Campeau,* Vice-Chair.; Ronald W. Tysoe,* Sr. V.P.; Roland Villemaire, V.P. and Treas.; Thomas G. Cody, Secy.
Trustees:* Cardinal G. Emmett Carter, J. Roy Weir, James M. Zimmerman.
Number of staff: 1 part-time professional; 2 part-time support.
Employer Identification Number: 310996760

5648
The Don M. Casto Foundation ⌑
209 East State St.
Columbus 43215

Incorporated in 1962 in OH.
Donor(s): Members of the Casto family and family-related businesses.
Foundation type: Independent
Financial data (yr. ended 05/31/89): Assets, $1,095,542 (M); gifts received, $50,000; expenditures, $152,078, including $142,625 for 40 grants (high: $20,000; low: $25).
Purpose and activities: Giving primarily for cultural programs, community funds, hospitals, and higher and secondary education.
Limitations: Giving primarily in OH.
Application information: Generally does not accept unsolicited applications.
Trustees: Frank S. Benson, Jr., Frank S. Benson III, Don M. Casto III.
Employer Identification Number: 316049506

5649
Cayuga Foundation ⌑
c/o Trustcorp Bank, Ohio
Three Seagate
Toledo 43603 (419) 259-8288
Application address: c/o Trustcorp Bank, Ohio, P.O. Box 10099, Toledo, OH 43699-0099

Established in 1960 in OH.
Foundation type: Independent
Financial data (yr. ended 12/31/88): Assets, $1,501,998 (M); expenditures, $124,722, including $105,600 for 57 grants (high: $20,000; low: $200).
Purpose and activities: Grants primarily for health and education, especially higher education; support also for cultural programs and denominational giving.
Types of support: General purposes, scholarship funds, building funds.
Limitations: Giving primarily in Toledo, OH, and NY.
Application information:
Initial approach: Proposal
Write: Gerald Miller
Corporate Trustee: Trustcorp Bank, Ohio.
Advisors: Donald J. Keume, Elizabeth M. Pfenzinger.
Employer Identification Number: 346504822

5650
Centerior Energy Foundation ▼
(Formerly The Cleveland Electric Illuminating Foundation)
P.O. Box 5000
Cleveland 44101 (216) 622-9800
Application address: 55 Public Sq., Cleveland, OH 44113; Tel.: (216) 479-4214

Incorporated in 1961 in OH.
Donor(s): The Cleveland Electric Illuminating Co.
Foundation type: Company-sponsored
Financial data (yr. ended 12/31/88): Assets, $13,525,093 (M); expenditures, $1,317,171, including $1,166,125 for 123 grants (high: $100,000; low: $100; average: $200-$10,000) and $151,046 for 1,005 employee matching gifts.
Purpose and activities: Emphasis on qualifying nonprofit organizations in health, welfare, civic, cultural, or educational endeavors; support also for community funds.
Types of support: Annual campaigns, building funds, equipment, operating budgets, employee matching gifts, continuing support.
Limitations: Giving limited to northeastern and northwestern OH, with emphasis on Cleveland and Toledo. No support for political organizations. Generally, no grants to individuals, or for endowment funds, deficit financing, research, scholarships, or fellowships; no loans.
Publications: Informational brochure (including application guidelines), program policy statement.
Application information: Application form not required.
Initial approach: Cover letter with proposal
Copies of proposal: 1
Deadline(s): None
Board meeting date(s): Contributions Committee usually meets monthly
Final notification: 8 weeks
Write: Jackie Hauserman, Chair., Contribs. Comm.
Officers: Richard A. Miller, Chair.; Robert J. Farling, Vice-Chair.; Lyman C. Phillips, Pres.; Victor F. Greenslade, V.P.; E. Lyle Pepin, Secy.; Gary Hawkinson, Treas.
Trustees: Richard P. Anderson, Leigh Carter, Thomas A. Commes, Robert M. Ginn, Roy H. Holdt, George H. Kaull, Frank E. Mosier, Sister Mary Martha Reinhard, S.N.D., Paul M. Smart, William J. Williams.
Number of staff: 2 part-time professional; 1 part-time support.
Employer Identification Number: 346514181

5651
Charities Foundation ▼
One Sea Gate, 22nd Fl.
Toledo 43666 (419) 247-1888

Trust established in 1937 in OH.
Donor(s): Owens-Illinois, Inc., William E. Levis,† Harold Boeschenstein,† and others.
Foundation type: Independent
Financial data (yr. ended 12/31/89): Assets, $5,184,477 (M); gifts received, $123,234; expenditures, $612,777, including $585,550 for 57 grants (high: $300,000; low: $100; average: $750-$20,000).
Purpose and activities: Contributions from the foundation are initiated internally, with emphasis on higher and other education, community funds, hospitals, cultural programs, including museums and performing arts, conservation, youth and social service agencies, and civic and public affairs organizations.
Types of support: General purposes, employee matching gifts.
Limitations: Giving primarily in OH, with emphasis on Toledo. No grants to individuals, or for scholarships.
Publications: Annual report, 990-PF.
Application information: All funds presently committed. Applications not accepted.
Write: Grayce A. Neimy, Secy.
Officer: David Van Hooser, Mgr.
Trustees: Jerome A. Bohland, Henry A. Page, Jr., Carter Smith.
Number of staff: 1 part-time support.
Employer Identification Number: 346554560

5652
Christ Foundation ⌑
88 Industry Rd.
Atwater 44201 (216) 947-2027

Established in 1971 in OH.
Donor(s): Jerry Moore.
Foundation type: Independent
Financial data (yr. ended 12/31/88): Assets, $1,397,369 (M); gifts received, $100,000; expenditures, $48,148, including $45,400 for 8 grants (high: $30,600; low: $100).
Purpose and activities: Giving limited to persons, projects, programs, and institutions affiliated with the Church of Christ.
Application information:
Initial approach: Letter
Deadline(s): None
Write: Patricia Moore, Secy.-Treas.
Officers and Trustees: Jerry Moore, Pres.; Patricia Moore, Secy.-Treas.; Daniel J. Moore, Randall V. Moore, Robert D. Moore.
Employer Identification Number: 237121546

5653
Christopher Foundation ⌑ ☆
100 Center St.
Chardon 44024 (216) 285-2242

Established in 1952.
Foundation type: Independent
Financial data (yr. ended 12/31/88): Assets, $718,164 (M); gifts received, $3,936; expenditures, $107,501, including $100,000 for 26 grants (high: $31,100; low: $100).
Purpose and activities: Support for Catholic organizations and churches and higher and other education.
Limitations: Giving primarily in OH. No grants to individuals.
Application information: Application form not required.
Initial approach: Proposal
Deadline(s): None
Write: Paul J. Dolan, Secy.
Officer: Paul J. Dolan, Secy.
Trustees: Lou Alexander, Helen Dolan, Sr., Helen Dolan, Jr.
Custodian: Bank One.
Employer Identification Number: 340961579

5654
Cincinnati Bell Foundation, Inc. ⌑
201 East Fourth St.
Cincinnati 45202 (513) 397-1250

Established in 1984 in OH.
Donor(s): Cincinnati Bell, Inc.
Foundation type: Company-sponsored
Financial data (yr. ended 12/31/88): Assets, $773,404 (M); gifts received, $1,000,000; expenditures, $616,192, including $614,283 for grants.
Purpose and activities: Support for the arts; education, including higher education; health and hospitals; welfare and youth; and media and communications. Priority to programs that are broadly supported by other organizations.
Types of support: Annual campaigns, capital campaigns, employee matching gifts.
Limitations: Giving primarily in the greater Cincinnati, OH area, and in northern KY, and any other city in which company has a significant corporate presence.
Publications: Informational brochure (including application guidelines).
Application information: Application form not required.
Initial approach: Letter
Copies of proposal: 1
Deadline(s): None
Write: C.W. Wright, Exec. Dir.
Officers: Dwight H. Hibbard, Pres.; Betty S. Kromer, Secy.-Treas.; C.W. Wright, Exec. Dir.
Trustees: Scott Aiken, John T. LaMacchia, Dennis J. Sullivan, Jr.
Number of staff: 1
Employer Identification Number: 311125542

5655
The Greater Cincinnati Foundation ▼
802 Carew Tower
441 Vine St.
Cincinnati 45202-2817 (513) 241-2880

Established in 1963 in OH by bank resolution and declaration of trust.
Foundation type: Community
Financial data (yr. ended 12/31/89): Assets, $82,517,098 (M); gifts received, $12,273,360; expenditures, $8,157,838, including $7,830,187 for grants.
Purpose and activities: Grants for a broad range of both new and existing activities in general categories of arts and culture and humanities, civic affairs, economic development, education, health, and social and human services, including youth agencies.
Types of support: Seed money, capital campaigns, building funds, equipment, program-related investments, special projects, matching funds, loans, technical assistance, renovation projects.
Limitations: Giving limited to the greater Cincinnati, OH, area. No support for sectarian religious purposes. No grants to individuals, or for operating budgets, annual campaigns, deficit financing, scholarships, fellowships, internships, exchange programs, or scholarly research.
Publications: Annual report (including application guidelines), newsletter, application guidelines, informational brochure.
Application information: Application form required.
Initial approach: Letter or telephone, followed by interview with foundation staff
Copies of proposal: 22
Deadline(s): 90 days prior to board meetings
Board meeting date(s): Feb., May, Aug., and Nov.
Final notification: Immediately following board meetings
Write: Ruth A. Cronenberg, Prog. Officer
Officers: William O. Coleman, Dir.; William T. Bahlman, Jr., Assoc. Dir.; Herbert R. Brown, Assoc. Dir.; Charles W. Goering, Assoc. Dir.; Daniel LeBlond, Assoc. Dir.; Walter L. Lingle, Jr., Assoc. Dir.; Nelson Schwab, Jr., Assoc. Dir.; Robert Westheimer, Assoc. Dir.
Governing Board: Kay Pettengill, Chair.; Charles S. Mechem, Jr., Vice-Chair.; William D. Atteberry, Cynthia Booth, William A. Friedlander, Louise A. Head, Sidney Peerless, M.D., Robert G. Stachler, John L. Strubbe.
Trustee Banks: Ameritrust Co., N.A., BancOne Ohio Corp., The Central Trust Co. of Northern Ohio, N.A., Fifth Third Bank, Huntington National Bank, Kentucky National Bank, The Lebanon-Citizens National Bank, The Northside Bank & Trust Co., Peoples Liberty Bank of Northern Kentucky, Provident Bank, Society Bank, N.A., Star Bank, N.A., Cincinnati.
Number of staff: 2 full-time professional; 3 full-time support.
Employer Identification Number: 310669700

5656
The Cincinnati Foundation for the Aged ⌑
2012 Central Trust Tower
Cincinnati 45202 (513) 381-6859

Established in 1891 in OH.
Donor(s): Oscar Cohrs,† Otto Luedeking,† and others.
Foundation type: Independent
Financial data (yr. ended 3/31/89): Assets, $5,084,579 (M); gifts received, $76,827; expenditures, $265,728, including $246,796 for 9 grants (high: $120,508; low: $1,050).
Purpose and activities: To financially assist worthy, aged, and indigent men and women to enter as residents into homes established for aged and retired persons.
Limitations: Giving primarily in the greater Cincinnati, OH, area.
Application information: Application form required.
Deadline(s): None
Officers: William Dock Meyer, Pres.; Robert Porter, Jr., 1st V.P.; Virginia Light, Secy.; Donald Hathaway, Treas.
Employer Identification Number: 310536971

5657
Cincinnati Milacron Foundation ▼ ⌑
4701 Marburg Ave.
Cincinnati 45209 (513) 841-8526

Incorporated in 1951 in OH.
Donor(s): Cincinnati Milacron, Inc.
Foundation type: Company-sponsored
Financial data (yr. ended 12/31/88): Assets, $138,144 (M); gifts received, $639,292; expenditures, $647,302, including $647,073 for 57 grants (high: $310,000; low: $500; average: $500-$30,000).
Purpose and activities: Emphasis on community funds and higher education; support also for youth and human service agencies.
Types of support: Annual campaigns, seed money, building funds, scholarship funds, research, continuing support, capital campaigns, special projects.
Limitations: Giving primarily in OH. No grants to individuals, or for endowment funds.
Application information:
Initial approach: Proposal
Copies of proposal: 1
Deadline(s): None
Board meeting date(s): Quarterly
Write: George G. Price, Asst. Secy.
Officers and Trustees: James A.D. Geier, Pres. and Treas.; Daniel J. Meyer, V.P. and Secy.; Lyle Everingham, Donald N. Frey, Gilbert G. McCurdy.
Number of staff: None.
Employer Identification Number: 316030682

5658
The Cleveland Foundation ▼
1400 Hanna Bldg.
Cleveland 44115 (216) 861-3810

Established in 1914 in OH by bank resolution and declaration of trust.
Foundation type: Community
Financial data (yr. ended 12/31/89): Assets, $579,897,967 (M); gifts received, $11,668,054; expenditures, $32,493,017, including $24,510,926 for 673 grants (high: $657,390; low: $43; average: $1,000-$800,000) and $3,050,000 for loans.
Purpose and activities: The pioneer community foundation which has served as a model for most community foundations in the U.S.; grants are made to private tax-exempt and governmental agencies and programs serving the greater Cleveland area in the fields of civic and cultural affairs, education and economic development, and health and social services. Current priorities are in economic

development, neighborhood development, downtown revitalization, lakefront enhancement, programs dealing with the young, the aged and special constituencies, health care for the medically indigent and for underserved populations, and the professional performing and visual arts. Grants mainly as seed money for innovative projects or to developing institutions or services addressing unmet needs in the community. Very limited support for capital purposes for highly selective construction or equipment projects which serve the program priorities listed above.
Types of support: Seed money, special projects, matching funds, consulting services, technical assistance, program-related investments, renovation projects.
Limitations: Giving limited to the greater Cleveland area, with primary emphasis on Cleveland, Cuyahoga, Lake, and Geauga Counties, OH, unless specified by donor. No support for sectarian or religious activities, community services such as fire and police protection, and library and welfare services. No grants to individuals, or for endowment funds, operating costs, debt reduction, fundraising campaigns, publications, films and audiovisual materials (unless they are an integral part of a program already being supported), memberships, travel for bands, sports teams, classes and similar groups; capital support for planning, construction, renovation, or purchase of buildings, equipment and materials, land acquisition, or renovation of public space unless there is strong evidence that the program is of priority to the foundation.
Publications: Annual report (including application guidelines), newsletter, occasional report, application guidelines, informational brochure.
Application information: Application form not required.
Initial approach: Letter, proposal, or telephone
Copies of proposal: 2
Deadline(s): Mar. 31, June 30, Sept. 15, and Dec. 31
Board meeting date(s): Distribution committee meets in Mar., June, Sept., and Dec.
Final notification: 1 month
Write: Steven A. Minter, Dir.
Officers: Steven A. Minter, Dir.; Michael J. Hoffmann, Secy.; Philip T. Tobin, Admin. Officer and Treas.
Distribution Committee: John J. Dwyer, Chair.; Henry J. Goodman, Vice-Chair.; Rev. Elmo A. Bean, James M. Delaney, Annie Lewis Ganda, Russell R. Gifford, Jerry V. Jarrett, Adrienne L. Jones, Lindsay J. Morgenthaler, Harvey G. Oppmann, Alfred M. Rankin, Jr.
Trustees: Ameritrust Co., N.A., Bank One, Cleveland, N.A., First National Bank of Ohio, Huntington National Bank, National City Bank, Society National Bank.
Number of staff: 15 full-time professional; 5 part-time professional; 17 full-time support.
Employer Identification Number: 340714588

5659
The Cleveland-Cliffs Foundation
1100 Superior Ave.
Cleveland 44114-2589 (216) 694-5700

Established in 1960 in OH.
Donor(s): The Cleveland-Cliffs Iron Co., Tilden Mining Co., Empire Iron Mining Partnership, Hibbing Taconite Co.
Foundation type: Company-sponsored
Financial data (yr. ended 12/31/89): Assets, $133,523 (M); gifts received, $450,000; expenditures, $383,180, including $313,675 for 102 grants (high: $100,000; low: $100) and $69,340 for 290 employee matching gifts.
Purpose and activities: Support for higher education, including an employee matching gift program, community funds, hospitals, and social services, including youth agencies. Priority given to innovative educational projects.
Types of support: General purposes, building funds, research, professorships, scholarship funds, employee matching gifts, annual campaigns, capital campaigns.
Limitations: Giving primarily in areas of company operations, with emphasis on Cleveland, OH, MI, and MN. No grants to individuals, or for endowment funds; no loans.
Publications: Application guidelines.
Application information: Application form not required.
Initial approach: Proposal
Copies of proposal: 1
Deadline(s): None
Board meeting date(s): July, disbursement committee meets monthly
Final notification: 3 months
Write: David L. Gardner, Secy.
Officers and Trustees:* M.T. Moore,* Chair. and C.E.O.; J.L. Kelly,* V.P., Public Affairs; D.L. Gardner, Secy.-Treas.; Harry J. Bolwell, E. Mandell de Windt, R.J. Flynn, James D. Ireland III, E. Bradley Jones, R. McInnes, Donald C. Platten, David V. Ragone, Samuel K. Scovil, Richard S. Sheetz, Jeptha H. Wade, Alton W. Whitehouse, Jr.
Number of staff: None.
Employer Identification Number: 346525124

5660
The George W. Codrington Charitable Foundation
c/o Ameritrust Co., N.A. Trust Tax
P.O. Box 5937
Cleveland 44101

Trust established in 1955 in OH.
Donor(s): George W. Codrington.†
Foundation type: Independent
Financial data (yr. ended 12/31/88): Assets, $8,742,928 (M); expenditures, $478,536, including $403,119 for 82 grants (high: $53,000; low: $64).
Purpose and activities: Giving primarily for higher education and hospitals; support also for community funds, museums, youth and health agencies, and music.
Limitations: Giving limited to Cuyahoga County, OH, and the surrounding area. No grants to individuals, or for endowment funds; no loans.
Publications: Annual report (including application guidelines).
Application information:
Initial approach: Full proposal
Copies of proposal: 5
Deadline(s): Submit proposal preferably the month before board meetings
Board meeting date(s): Mar., June, Sept., and Dec.
Write: Raymond T. Sawyer, Chair.
Officer: Raymond T. Sawyer, Chair.
Supervisory Board: W. Paul Cooper, Vice-Chair.; John J. Dwyer, William E. McDonald, Curtis E. Moll.
Trustee: Ameritrust Co., N.A.
Number of staff: None.
Employer Identification Number: 346507457

5661
Cole National Foundation ⌑ ☆
5915 Landerbrook Dr., Suite 300
Mayfield Heights 44124-4041 (216) 449-4100

Established in 1981 in OH.
Donor(s): Cole National Corp.
Foundation type: Company-sponsored
Financial data (yr. ended 12/31/88): Assets, $970,604 (M); gifts received, $218,000; expenditures, $210,636, including $208,000 for 8 grants (high: $120,000; low: $1,000).
Purpose and activities: Support primarily for Jewish community organizations, medical research and care facilities, higher education, and a community fund.
Limitations: Giving primarily in Cleveland, OH, area. No grants to individuals.
Application information: Application form not required.
Deadline(s): None
Write: Jeffrey A. Cole, Treas.
Officers and Trustees:* Joseph E. Cole,* Chair.; John F. Downie, Secy.; Jeffrey A. Cole,* Treas.
Employer Identification Number: 341341165

5662
The Columbus Foundation ▼
1234 East Broad St.
Columbus 43205 (614) 251-4000

Established in 1943 in OH by resolution and declaration of trust.
Foundation type: Community
Financial data (yr. ended 12/31/89): Assets, $156,000,000 (M); gifts received, $15,109,000; expenditures, $14,049,000, including $12,882,000 for 3,000 grants (high: $400,000; low: $100; average: $5,000-$25,000).
Purpose and activities: A public charitable foundation for receiving funds for distribution to charitable organizations mainly in the central OH region. Grants made to strengthen existing agencies or to initiate new programs in the following categories: arts and humanities, civic affairs, conservation and environmental protection, education, health, mental health and retardation, and social service agencies.
Types of support: Seed money, matching funds, capital campaigns, land acquisition, publications, renovation projects, special projects, technical assistance, continuing support.
Limitations: Giving limited to central OH from unrestricted funds. No support for religious purposes, or for projects normally the

responsibility of a public agency. No grants to individuals, or generally for budget deficits, conferences, scholarly research, or endowment funds.
Publications: Annual report, application guidelines, newsletter, informational brochure.
Application information: Grant requests to the Columbus Youth Foundation must be submitted by the 1st Fridays in Feb. and Oct. for consideration at meetings held in Apr. and Dec.; requests to the Ingram-White Castle Foundation must be submitted by the 1st Fridays in Feb. and Sept. for consideration in Apr. and Nov. Application form required.
Initial approach: Meeting with staff
Copies of proposal: 4
Deadline(s): 1st Friday in Dec., Mar., May, and Aug.
Board meeting date(s): Feb., May, July, and Oct.
Final notification: After quarterly meeting
Write: James I. Luck, Pres.
Officers: James I. Luck, Pres.; Raymond J Biddiscombe, V.P.; Tullia Brown Hamilton, V.P.; Dorothy M. Reynolds, V.P.
Governing Committee: Eldon W. Ward, Chair.; Leslie H. Wexner, Vice-Chair.; J.W. Wolfe, Vice-Chair.; Don M. Casto III, John B. Gerlach, Charlotte P. Kessler, Shirle N. Westwater.
Trustee Banks and Trustee Committee: BancOhio National Bank, Bank One Trust Co., N.A., Huntington Trust Co., N.A.
Number of staff: 8 full-time professional; 10 full-time support.
Employer Identification Number: 316044264

5663
Columbus Youth Foundation ☆
c/o The Columbus Foundation
1234 East Broad St.
Columbus 43205 (614) 251-4000

Trust established in 1955 in OH; supporting organization of Columbus Foundation.
Foundation type: Community
Financial data (yr. ended 12/31/88): Assets, $1,150,087 (M); expenditures, $158,865, including $149,232 for 10 grants.
Purpose and activities: "To find projects serving sick, underprivileged, and disabled inner-city youth, with particular interest in recreation and education projects."
Types of support: Building funds, equipment, land acquisition, matching funds, publications, renovation projects, seed money.
Limitations: Giving limited to Columbus and Franklin county, OH. No grants to individuals; or for annual campaigns, conferences and seminars, deficit financing, endowments, continuing support, emergency funds, or operating budgets.
Application information: Application form required.
Write: James I. Luck, Pres.
Officer: James I. Luck, Pres.
Number of staff: 1 part-time professional; 2 part-time support.
Employer Identification Number: 316034435

5664
Commercial Intertech Foundation
(Formerly Commercial Shearing Foundation)
1775 Logan Ave.
Youngstown 44501 (216) 746-8011

Trust established in 1953 in OH.
Donor(s): Commercial Intertech Corp., Inc.
Foundation type: Company-sponsored
Financial data (yr. ended 10/31/89): Assets, $257,000 (M); expenditures, $180,664, including $179,345 for 63 grants (high: $85,500; low: $25) and $1,100 for 1 employee matching gift.
Purpose and activities: Giving for hospitals, higher education, youth agencies, and community funds; support also for economic education.
Types of support: General purposes, annual campaigns, building funds.
Limitations: Giving limited to areas of company operations. No grants to individuals, or for operating budgets, endowment funds, scholarships, fellowships, or matching gifts; no loans.
Application information: Application form not required.
Copies of proposal: 1
Deadline(s): Submit proposal preferably 60 days before meeting dates
Board meeting date(s): Jan., Apr., July, and Oct.
Write: Gilbert M. Manchester, Secy.
Officers and Trustees:* Don E. Tucker,* Pres.; Gilbert M. Manchester,* Secy.; Kenneth W. Marcum,* Treas.; William W. Bresnahan, Charles B. Cushwa III, W.W. Cushwa, Neil D. Humphrey, Kipton C. Kumler, Jennings R. Lambeth, John Nelson, John F. Peyton, Paul J. Powers, Thomas J. Travers, Philip N. Winkelstern.
Number of staff: None.
Employer Identification Number: 346517437

5665
Cooper Tire and Rubber Foundation ⌑
Lima & Western Aves.
Findlay 45840 (419) 423-1321

Established in 1953 in OH.
Donor(s): Cooper Tire & Rubber Co.
Foundation type: Company-sponsored
Financial data (yr. ended 12/31/88): Assets, $967,691 (M); gifts received, $250,000; expenditures, $233,041, including $233,041 for grants.
Purpose and activities: Giving primarily for community funds, social services, and higher education.
Types of support: Employee matching gifts.
Application information:
Deadline(s): None
Trustees: J.A. Faisant, W.C. Hattendorf, J.A. Reinhardt.
Employer Identification Number: 237025013

5666
The Corbett Foundation ⌑
800 Broadway, Suite 1007
Cincinnati 45202-1333 (513) 241-3320

Incorporated in 1958 in OH.
Donor(s): J. Ralph Corbett, Patricia A. Corbett.
Foundation type: Independent
Financial data (yr. ended 4/30/88): Assets, $6,727,921 (M); gifts received, $190,000; expenditures, $1,106,466, including $810,813 for 13 grants (high: $500,000; low: $1,000).
Purpose and activities: Support primarily for culture and the arts, including music, education, and community projects.
Limitations: Giving primarily in OH, with emphasis on Cincinnati. No grants to individuals.
Application information:
Initial approach: Proposal
Deadline(s): None
Final notification: Within 2 months
Write: Jean S. Reis, V.P.
Officers and Trustees: Patricia A. Corbett, Pres. and Treas.; Jean S. Reis, V.P. and Secy.; William J. Baechtold, J. Ralph Corbett, Thomas R. Corbett, Alan J. Lehn, Jack M. Watson, Perry B. Wydman.
Employer Identification Number: 316050360

5667
Coshocton Foundation
P.O. Box 15
Coshocton 43812 (614) 622-2532

Established in 1966 in OH.
Donor(s): Adolph Golden,† Edward E. Montgomery.
Foundation type: Community
Financial data (yr. ended 09/30/89): Assets, $2,528,718 (M); gifts received, $552,475; expenditures, $324,817, including $283,311 for grants (high: $15,125; low: $1,000; average: $3,000) and $17,900 for 10 grants to individuals (high: $4,000; low: $600; average: $600-$4,000).
Purpose and activities: Support largely for the improvement of a park and the downtown area; giving also for a museum, health services, and higher education.
Types of support: Capital campaigns, continuing support, equipment, renovation projects, special projects, student aid, matching funds, employee matching gifts.
Limitations: Giving limited to Coshocton County, OH.
Publications: Annual report.
Application information: Application form not required.
Initial approach: Letter
Deadline(s): None
Board meeting date(s): Quarterly
Write: Orville Fuller, Treas.
Officers and Trustees:* Robert M. Thomas, Pres.; Paul Bryant, V.P.; Randall H. Peddicord, Secy.; Orville Fuller,* Treas.; Willard S. Breon, Samuel C. Clow, Seward D. Schooler.
Distribution Committee: R. Leo Prindle, Chair.; Robert B. Henderson, Fred E. Johnston, Bruce Wallace, Harry Zink.
Number of staff: None.
Employer Identification Number: 316064567

5668
James M. Cox, Jr. Foundation, Inc. ⌑
Fourth and Ludlow Sts.
Dayton 45402
Application address: c/o Cox Enterprises, Inc., P.O. Box 105720, Atlanta, GA 30348

Established in 1969 in GA.

Foundation type: Independent
Financial data (yr. ended 12/31/88): Assets, $6,510,778 (M); expenditures, $346,243, including $325,000 for 1 grant.
Purpose and activities: Support for a performing arts group, environmental conservation, and mental health; some support for museums and education.
Types of support: General purposes.
Limitations: Giving primarily in OH and GA.
Application information:
Write: Carl R. Gross, Treas.
Officers and Trustees:* James Cox Kennedy,* Pres.; Barbara Cox Anthony,* V.P.; James A. Hatcher, Secy.; Carl R. Gross,* Treas.
Employer Identification Number: 237256190

5669
J. Ford Crandall Memorial Foundation ⌑
1108 Mahoning Bank Bldg.
Youngstown 44503 (216) 744-2125

Trust established in 1975 in OH.
Donor(s): J. Ford Crandall.†
Foundation type: Independent
Financial data (yr. ended 12/31/88): Assets, $3,652,650 (M); expenditures, $242,049, including $181,138 for 18 grants (high: $31,427; low: $1,000).
Purpose and activities: Support for hospitals and social service agencies.
Types of support: Building funds, equipment, endowment funds, scholarship funds.
Limitations: Giving limited to Mahoning County, OH. No grants to individuals, or for operating budgets or research; no loans.
Application information: Application form not required.
Initial approach: Letter
Copies of proposal: 3
Deadline(s): Dec. 1
Board meeting date(s): Monthly
Write: R.M. Hammond, Secy. and Counsel
Officers and Trustees: Horace G. Tetlow, Chair.; Arthur G. Young, Vice-Chair.; Amy H. Gambrel, 2nd Vice-Chair.; R.M. Hammond, Secy.
Number of staff: None.
Employer Identification Number: 346513634

5670
Dana Corporation Foundation ▼ ⌑
P.O. Box 1000
Toledo 43697 (419) 535-4500

Incorporated in 1956 in OH.
Donor(s): Dana Corp.
Foundation type: Company-sponsored
Financial data (yr. ended 12/31/87): Assets, $8,535,794 (M); gifts received, $2,000,000; expenditures, $1,736,297, including $1,529,526 for 232 grants (high: $161,342; low: $100; average: $500-$20,000) and $179,589 for employee matching gifts.
Purpose and activities: Emphasis on community funds, higher education including an employee matching gifts program, social services, health services, civic affairs, youth agencies, and cultural programs.
Types of support: Employee matching gifts, annual campaigns, building funds, continuing support, emergency funds, equipment, land acquisition, operating budgets, seed money, capital campaigns.
Limitations: Giving primarily in areas of company operations. No grants to individuals, or for scholarships or fellowships; no loans.
Application information: Application form not required.
Initial approach: Proposal
Copies of proposal: 1
Deadline(s): None
Board meeting date(s): Apr., Aug., and Dec. or May, Sept., and Jan.
Final notification: 60 to 90 days
Write: Pauline Marzollini, Asst. Secy.
Officers and Directors: C.H. Hirsch, Pres.; T.J. Fairhurst, V.P.; R.M. Leonardi, Secy.; R.A. Habel, Treas.; B.N. Cole, Robert A. Cowie, J.R. Gregory, R.J. Lipford, N.L. Revenaugh.
Number of staff: 1 part-time professional.
Employer Identification Number: 346544909

5671
Danis Foundation, Inc.
P.O. Box 1510
Dayton 45401 (513) 228-1225

Established in 1957 in OH.
Donor(s): Danis Industries Corp.
Foundation type: Company-sponsored
Financial data (yr. ended 12/31/89): Assets, $876,421 (M); gifts received, $200,000; expenditures, $250,000, including $241,074 for 125 grants (high: $100,000; low: $25) and $5,200 for 8 grants to individuals of $650 each.
Purpose and activities: Support primarily for higher and other education, health, community and religious organizations, and social services; support also for employee-related scholarships.
Types of support: Building funds, capital campaigns, equipment, employee-related scholarships.
Limitations: Giving primarily in the Dayton, OH, area.
Application information: Application form required for scholarships.
Copies of proposal: 1
Deadline(s): None for grants; Mar. 31 for scholarships
Board meeting date(s): Monthly
Final notification: Usually within 30 days
Write: Richard R. Danis, Trustee
Trustees: Benjamin G. Danis, Jr., Charles W. Danis, Richard R. Danis.
Number of staff: None.
Employer Identification Number: 316041012

5672
Charles H. Dater Foundation, Inc.
508 Atlas Bank Bldg.
Cincinnati 45202 (513) 241-1234

Established in 1985 in OH.
Foundation type: Independent
Financial data (yr. ended 08/31/89): Assets, $5,123,606 (M); gifts received, $270,450; expenditures, $303,188, including $151,014 for 31 grants (high: $20,000; low: $600).
Purpose and activities: Support primarily for social services, with emphasis on services for children; support also for hospitals, education, including libraries, and the fine arts, including museums.
Types of support: Annual campaigns, building funds, consulting services, continuing support, equipment, general purposes, program-related investments, scholarship funds, seed money, special projects.
Limitations: Giving primarily in the greater Cincinnati, OH, area.
Publications: 990-PF.
Application information: Application form required.
Initial approach: Letter requesting application form
Copies of proposal: 4
Deadline(s): None
Board meeting date(s): Monthly
Final notification: Within 2 months
Write: Bruce A. Krone, Secy.
Officers and Trustees:* Paul W. Krone,* Pres.; Bruce A. Krone,* Secy.; Stanley J. Frank, Jr., David L. Olberding, John D. Silvati.
Employer Identification Number: 311150951

5673
William Dauch Foundation ⌑
(Formerly Believers Foundation)
1570 Dutch Hollow Rd.
Elida 45807-1803 (419) 339-4441

Established in 1986 in OH.
Donor(s): Gladys Dauch.
Foundation type: Independent
Financial data (yr. ended 12/31/89): Assets, $4,607,347 (M); expenditures, $291,298, including $252,670 for 22 grants (high: $104,470; low: $100) and $35,100 for 3 grants to individuals (high: $30,100; low: $1,000).
Purpose and activities: Support primarily to organizations and individuals that promote Christian knowledge and dissemination of the Gospel.
Types of support: Grants to individuals.
Application information:
Initial approach: Letter
Deadline(s): None
Write: Thomas E. Brown, Pres.
Officer and Trustees:* Thomas E. Brown, Pres.; Gladys Dauch, Debra Ann Grant, Tamara Brown LeRoux.
Employer Identification Number: 341516486

5674
Davis Foundation ⌑
c/o Huntington National Bank, Trust Dept.
41 South High St.
Columbus 43260 (614) 463-3707

Established in 1951 in OH.
Foundation type: Operating
Financial data (yr. ended 12/31/87): Assets, $1,873,260 (M); expenditures, $267,634, including $25,391 for 19 grants (high: $2,494; low: $840).
Purpose and activities: Support primarily for a college and a medical center, support also for a campus ministry and for crippled children.
Limitations: Giving primarily in OH.
Application information: Application form not required.
Deadline(s): None
Trustee: Huntington National Bank.
Employer Identification Number: 316023094

5675
The Dayton Foundation ▼
2100 Kettering Tower
Dayton 45423-1395 (513) 222-0410

Established in 1921 in OH by resolution and declaration of trust.
Foundation type: Community
Financial data (yr. ended 12/31/88): Assets, $24,517,381 (M); gifts received, $4,816,281; expenditures, $3,078,092, including $2,232,013 for 361 grants (high: $506,501; low: $25; average: $1,000-$10,000) and $66,065 for 126 grants to individuals.
Purpose and activities: To assist public charitable, benevolent and educational purposes which benefit local citizens and respond to a wide variety of community needs, including cultural programs, community development, health and social services, and youth; "to help launch new projects which represent a unique and unduplicated opportunity for the community," and to generate matching funds.
Types of support: Seed money, building funds, equipment, matching funds, technical assistance, special projects, capital campaigns, conferences and seminars, consulting services, emergency funds, endowment funds, renovation projects, internships, land acquisition, publications, research, scholarship funds.
Limitations: Giving limited to the greater Dayton, OH, area. No support for religious organizations for religious purposes. No grants to individuals (except for awards to teachers and municipal employees), or for operating budgets, exchange programs, professorships, continuing support, annual campaigns, or deficit financing; no loans or program-related investments.
Publications: Annual report (including application guidelines), newsletter, program policy statement, application guidelines, informational brochure.
Application information: Application form not required.
Initial approach: Proposal, telephone, or letter
Copies of proposal: 1
Deadline(s): Mar., July, Sept., and Nov.
Board meeting date(s): Bimonthly beginning in Jan.
Final notification: 4 to 6 weeks
Write: Marilyn Kaplan, Admin. Officer
Officer: Frederick Bartenstein III, Dir.
Governing Board: Frederick C. Smith, Chair.; John E. Moore, Vice-Chair.; Richard F. Glennon, Anne S. Greene, Lloyd E. Lewis, Jr., Jesse Philips, Burnell R. Roberts.
Trustees and Bank Trustees: Avery Allen, Michael J. Alley, William A. Harrell, Donald H. Kasle, Jerry L. Kirby, Frederick W. Schantz, Trace B. Swisher, Bank One, Dayton, N.A., The Central Trust Co. of Northern Ohio, N.A., Citizens Federal Savings and Loan Assn., Fifth Third Bank, First National Bank, Huntington National Bank, Society Bank, N.A.
Number of staff: 5 full-time professional; 5 part-time professional; 3 full-time support; 2 part-time support.
Employer Identification Number: 316027287

5676
Dayton Foundation Depository
2100 Kettering Tower
Dayton 45423 (513) 222-0410

Established in 1982 in OH.
Foundation type: Independent
Financial data (yr. ended 12/31/89): Assets, $4,778,000 (M); gifts received, $2,465,000; expenditures, $1,563,000, including $1,458,000 for 2,353 grants (high: $100,000; low: $10).
Purpose and activities: A "donor-directed pool", distributing funds to recipients designated by donors.
Limitations: No grants to individuals.
Publications: Annual report, newsletter, informational brochure (including application guidelines).
Application information: Contributes only to pre-selected organizations. Applications not accepted.
Write: Mary Jo Leet
Officers: John E. Moore,* Pres.; Anne S. Greene,* V.P.; Frederick Bartenstein III, Secy.
Trustees:* Charles Abromowitz, Thomas Danis, Richard F. Glennon, Sr., Lloyd E. Lewis, Jr., Jesse Philips, Burnell R. Roberts, Betsy Whitney.
Number of staff: 1 part-time professional; 1 part-time support.
Employer Identification Number: 311044298

5677
The Dayton Power & Light Company Foundation
Courthouse Plaza, S.W.
P.O. Box 1247
Dayton 45402 (513) 259-7225

Established in 1984 in OH.
Donor(s): Dayton Power & Light Co.
Foundation type: Company-sponsored
Financial data (yr. ended 12/31/88): Assets, $10,716,415 (M); expenditures, $884,315, including $812,027 for grants (high: $250,000; average: $25-$250,000).
Purpose and activities: Support for civic affairs and race relations, community development, energy and engineering, health and welfare, museums and other arts and cultural programs, the environment, and education; includes in-kind giving.
Types of support: Capital campaigns, operating budgets, employee-related scholarships, scholarship funds, in-kind gifts.
Limitations: Giving primarily in southwestern OH.
Application information:
Copies of proposal: 1
Deadline(s): None
Board meeting date(s): Apr. and Dec.
Write: Kathleen G. Zehenny
Officers and Trustees:* Stephen F. Kozair,* Pres.; Judy W. Lansaw,* Secy.; Thomas M. Jenkins,* Treas.
Number of staff: 1 full-time professional; 1 part-time support.
Employer Identification Number: 311138883

5678
Marie P. DeBartolo Foundation ⌑ ☆
c/o G.M. Walsh
7620 Market St.
Youngstown 44512-6052

Established in 1987 in OH.
Donor(s): Edward J. DeBartolo, Jr., Marie Denise DeBartolo York.
Foundation type: Independent
Financial data (yr. ended 12/31/87): Assets, $1,499,737 (M); gifts received, $1,524,881; expenditures, $42,500, including $42,500 for grants.
Purpose and activities: Initial year of operation, 1987; general charitable giving.
Trustees: Edward J. DeBartolo, Jr., Anthony W. Liberati, J. Ronald Mastriana, Marie Denise DeBartolo York.
Employer Identification Number: 341562415

5679
George H. Deuble Foundation
c/o Ameritrust Co., N.A.
Box 5937
Cleveland 44101
Mailing address: c/o DCC Corp., P.O. Box 2288, North Canton, OH 44720; Tel.: (216) 494-0494

Trust established in 1947 in OH.
Donor(s): George H. Deuble.†
Foundation type: Independent
Financial data (yr. ended 12/31/88): Assets, $13,638,048 (M); expenditures, $710,108, including $655,962 for 83 grants (high: $52,075; low: $20).
Purpose and activities: Grants for youth agencies, higher education, hospitals, cultural programs, and a community fund.
Types of support: Continuing support, annual campaigns, emergency funds, building funds, equipment, endowment funds, matching funds, scholarship funds, loans, conferences and seminars.
Limitations: Giving primarily in the Stark County, OH, area. No grants to individuals, or for operating budgets, seed money, deficit financing, general endowments, land acquisition, research, or publications.
Application information: Application form not required.
Initial approach: Letter
Copies of proposal: 1
Deadline(s): None
Board meeting date(s): Monthly
Final notification: 1 month
Write: Andrew H. Deuble, Trustee
Officer and Trustees:* Walter C. Deuble,* Pres.; Andrew H. Deuble, Stephen G. Deuble, Charles A. Morgan, Ameritrust Co., N.A.
Number of staff: None.
Employer Identification Number: 346500426

5680
Dicke Family Foundation ⌑ ☆
c/o Touche Ross & Co.
1700 Courthouse Plaza, N.E.
Dayton 45402

Established in 1984 in OH.
Donor(s): Members of the Dicke family.
Foundation type: Independent

Financial data (yr. ended 11/30/87): Assets, $321,041 (M); gifts received, $615,000; expenditures, $343,765, including $337,751 for 10 grants (high: $188,250; low: $500).
Purpose and activities: Giving primarily for an educational foundation; support also for a YMCA and a university.
Types of support: Building funds, general purposes.
Limitations: No grants to individuals.
Application information: Contributes only to pre-selected organizations. Applications not accepted.
Trustees: Dane Dicke, Eileen W. Dicke, James F. Dicke, Sr., James F. Dicke II.
Employer Identification Number: 341446513

5681
Geo. S. Dively Foundation
55 Public Sq.
Cleveland 44113
Application address: 1230 Seminary St., Key West, FL 33040; Tel.: (305) 296-4055

Incorporated in 1956 in OH.
Donor(s): George S. Dively.†
Foundation type: Independent
Financial data (yr. ended 12/31/88): Assets, $1,777,953 (M); expenditures, $161,691, including $144,682 for 21 grants (high: $40,000; low: $100).
Purpose and activities: Grants primarily for higher education, and awards for corporate leadership in civic and social areas.
Limitations: No grants to individuals.
Application information: Almost all grants initiated by the foundation and applications are generally not acknowledged. Application form not required. Applications not accepted.
Initial approach: Letter
Write: Michael Dively
Officers and Trustees:* Michael A. Dively,* Pres.; Juliette G. Dively,* V.P.; Thomas F. Allen,* Treas. and Secy.; James C. Hardie, Richard B. Tullis.
Number of staff: None.
Employer Identification Number: 346526304

5682
Donum Fund ☆
982 Mentor Ave.
Painesville 44077-2550 (216) 354-3362

Established in 1962.
Foundation type: Independent
Financial data (yr. ended 12/31/88): Assets, $1,033,569 (M); gifts received, $18,823; expenditures, $53,782, including $50,600 for 57 grants (high: $5,000; low: $100).
Purpose and activities: Contributions for education and social services, including youth groups; some support for culture and health services, including hospices.
Types of support: Operating budgets, special projects.
Limitations: Giving primarily in OH.
Application information: Application form not required.
Deadline(s): None
Board meeting date(s): 2-3 times per year
Write: Arthur S. Holden, Jr., Treas.
Officers: Constance Keen, Pres.; Sarah McLaren, V.P.; Jane Q. Outcalt, Secy.; Arthur S. Holden, Jr., Treas.
Number of staff: None.
Employer Identification Number: 346529430

5683
The Elizabeth G. & John D. Drinko Charitable Foundation ¤
(Formerly Cleveland Institute of Electronics Charitable Foundation)
3200 National City Ctr.
Cleveland 44114

Established in 1982 in OH.
Donor(s): John D. Drinko, Elizabeth G. Drinko.
Foundation type: Independent
Financial data (yr. ended 11/30/89): Assets, $1,985,325 (M); expenditures, $365,002, including $353,481 for 29 grants (high: $50,000; low: $600).
Purpose and activities: Giving primarily for higher education.
Limitations: Giving primarily in OH. No grants to individuals.
Application information: Contributes only to pre-selected organizations. Applications not accepted.
Officers and Trustees:* John D. Drinko,* Pres.; Elizabeth G. Drinko,* V.P.; James E. Chapman,* Secy.; J. Randall Drinko,* Treas.; and 5 additional trustees.
Employer Identification Number: 341391069

5684
Duriron Foundation ¤
P.O. Box 1145
Dayton 45401 (513) 226-4242

Established in 1983 in OH.
Foundation type: Company-sponsored
Financial data (yr. ended 12/31/88): Assets, $150,039 (M); gifts received, $275,000; expenditures, $126,105, including $126,000 for 54 grants (high: $30,250; low: $100).
Purpose and activities: Support for community funds, higher education, and operating funds for civic and charitable groups which do not receive United Way support and have a high priority of need.
Types of support: Capital campaigns, special projects, operating budgets.
Limitations: Giving primarily in areas of company operation, especially Dayton, OH and Cookeville, TN. No support for political activities, for theological functions of religious organizations, or organizations already receiving major support from United Way. No grants to individuals, or for medical research or social events.
Application information: Division presidents recommend grants within the established budget limit for the local community in which they are located.
Initial approach: Letter
Deadline(s): None
Board meeting date(s): Quarterly
Write: Gail Hamer
Officers and Trustees:* John S. Haddick,* Pres.; R.D. Gillaugh,* Secy.; Gregory L. Smith, Treas.
Employer Identification Number: 311080064

5685
The Eagle-Picher Foundation ¤
580 Walnut St.
P.O. Box 779
Cincinnati 45201 (513) 721-7010

Incorporated in 1953 in MI; merged with The Union Steel Foundation in 1969.
Donor(s): Eagle-Picher Industries, Inc.
Foundation type: Company-sponsored
Financial data (yr. ended 10/31/88): Assets, $42,535 (M); gifts received, $54,540; expenditures, $218,951, including $218,435 for 92 grants (high: $19,000; low: $100).
Purpose and activities: Grants largely for community funds, cultural programs, youth agencies, hospitals, social services, and higher education.
Limitations: Giving primarily in areas of company operations. No grants to individuals, or for endowment funds or matching gifts; no loans.
Application information:
Initial approach: Letter
Copies of proposal: 1
Deadline(s): None
Board meeting date(s): As required
Write: J. Rodman Nall, Pres.
Officers and Directors: J. Rodman Nall, Pres.; David N. Hall, V.P. and Treas.; Corinne M. Faris, Secy.; James A. Ralston.
Employer Identification Number: 316029997

5686
The Eaton Charitable Fund ▼ ¤
Eaton Ctr.
Cleveland 44114 (216) 523-4822

Trust established in 1953 in OH.
Donor(s): Eaton Corp.
Foundation type: Company-sponsored
Financial data (yr. ended 12/31/88): Assets, $9,457,466 (M); expenditures, $3,720,378, including $3,670,904 for grants (average: $1,000-$10,000).
Purpose and activities: High priority to local organizations which serve the needs of company's employees and offer them opportunity to provide leadership, voluntary service, and personal financial support, including vigorous support for United Way concept. General operating support and capital grants to health, human services, medical research, civic and cultural organizations, and independent college funds. Support for educational institutions preferably for engineering, scientific, technological, and business-related projects; capital campaigns limited to educational institutions with programs of direct interest to Eaton. Capital grants to health care facilities limited to geographic areas where there is a shortage of beds, facilities which serve needs of employees, and have reduced their ratio of beds to general public and shortened average stay, and projects that will increase productivity and lower cost of health care.
Types of support: Operating budgets, building funds, employee matching gifts, annual campaigns, special projects, in-kind gifts.
Limitations: Giving primarily in areas of company operations. No support for religious denominations, fraternal organizations, and organizations which could be members of a

United Fund or federated community fund but who choose not to participate. No grants to individuals, or for endowment funds, or fundraising events outside of specific company interests; no loans.
Publications: Corporate giving report, annual report, application guidelines.
Application information: Contribution requests should be made through a local Eaton manager wherever possible. Application form not required.
Initial approach: Letter or proposal
Copies of proposal: 1
Deadline(s): None
Board meeting date(s): Quarterly
Final notification: 60 to 90 days
Write: Frederick B. Unger, Dir., Community Affairs
Officer: Frederick B. Unger, Dir. of Community Affairs.
Corporate Contributions Committee: Marshall Wright, Chair.; William E. Butler, John D. Evans, Floyd M. Wilkerson.
Trustee: Society National Bank.
Number of staff: 2 part-time professional; 1 part-time support.
Employer Identification Number: 346501856

5687
The Cyrus Eaton Foundation
3552 Fairmount Blvd.
Shaker Heights 44118 (216) 932-9550

Established in 1955 in DE.
Foundation type: Independent
Financial data (yr. ended 12/31/88): Assets, $1,859,666 (M); expenditures, $108,153, including $95,250 for 29 grants (high: $26,250; low: $500).
Purpose and activities: Giving primarily for Cleveland-based, little-known or supported cultural programs, public affairs, social services, and international peace studies (through support of the Pugwash Conferences of Scientists); limited support also for ecological and environmental programs.
Types of support: Endowment funds, general purposes, seed money, special projects.
Limitations: Giving primarily in OH, with emphasis on Cleveland, and in CA, DC, FL, and IL. No grants to individuals.
Application information: Applications accepted only at the request of board members. Application form not required.
Copies of proposal: 5
Deadline(s): Sept. 30
Board meeting date(s): Oct.
Final notification: Following board meeting
Write: Henry W. Gulick, Pres.
Officers and Trustees:* Henry W. Gulick,* Pres.; Raymond Szabo,* V.P. and Secy.; Alice J. Gulick,* V.P. and Treas.; Mary Stephens Eaton,* V.P.; Barring Coughlin.
Number of staff: 1 part-time support.
Employer Identification Number: 237440277

5688
The Edwards Foundation, Inc. ⌑ ☆
1241 McKinley Ave.
Columbus 43222-1198
Mailing address: c/o Edwards Industries, Inc., 941 Chatham Ln., Columbus, OH 43221

Established in 1964.
Donor(s): Edwards Industries, Inc.
Foundation type: Company-sponsored
Financial data (yr. ended 6/30/88): Assets, $225,151 (M); gifts received, $117,161; expenditures, $111,102, including $109,310 for 31 grants (high: $40,000; low: $25).
Purpose and activities: Giving primarily for higher education, health associations and hospitals, and social service agencies.
Limitations: Giving primarily in OH, with emphasis on Columbus.
Application information: Contributes only to pre-selected organizations. Applications not accepted.
Trustees: D.A. Edwards, J.T. Edwards, Jr.
Employer Identification Number: 237447588

5689
El-An Foundation ⌑
1800 Moler Rd.
Columbus 43207

Incorporated in 1957 in OH.
Donor(s): Schottenstein Trustees, Value City Furniture, Inc., W.M. Whitney & Co., Elyria City, Inc., and others.
Foundation type: Independent
Financial data (yr. ended 12/31/87): Assets, $709,506 (M); gifts received, $700,000; expenditures, $307,822, including $307,228 for grants (high: $152,500; average: $500-$10,000).
Purpose and activities: Giving for Jewish welfare funds and religious education.
Limitations: Giving primarily in OH.
Directors: Jerome Schottenstein, Chair.; Saul Schottenstein, Secy.; Jay Schottenstein, Treas.
Employer Identification Number: 316050597

5690
The Thomas J. Emery Memorial
c/o Frost and Jacobs
2500 Central Trust Ctr.
Cincinnati 45202 (513) 621-3124

Incorporated in 1925 in OH.
Donor(s): Mary Muhlenberg Emery.†
Foundation type: Independent
Financial data (yr. ended 12/31/88): Assets, $15,779,416 (M); expenditures, $802,901, including $668,000 for 45 grants (high: $78,500; low: $1,000).
Purpose and activities: Emphasis on higher and secondary education, a community fund, cultural activities, social service and youth agencies, and hospitals.
Limitations: Giving primarily in Cincinnati, OH.
Application information: Application form not required.
Initial approach: Letter
Deadline(s): None
Board meeting date(s): 4 times a year
Final notification: 30 days to 3 months
Write: Henry W. Hobson, Jr., Pres.
Officers and Trustees:* Henry W. Hobson, Jr.,* Pres.; Frank T. Hamilton,* Secy.; Walter L. Lingle, Jr.,* Treas.; Charles M. Barrett, M.D., Lee A. Carter, John T. Lawrence, Jr.
Number of staff: 2 part-time support.
Employer Identification Number: 310536711

5691
Engineering and Science Foundation of Dayton
140 East Monument Ave.
Dayton 45402
Application address: c/o Thompson, Hine and Flory, P.O. Box 8801, 2000 Courthouse Plaza N.E., Dayton, OH 45401-8801; Tel.: (513) 443-6536

Established in 1966 in OH.
Foundation type: Independent
Financial data (yr. ended 06/30/89): Assets, $1,991,634 (M); expenditures, $176,827, including $159,459 for 19 grants (high: $34,400; low: $570).
Purpose and activities: Grants for the support and enhancement of engineering and science.
Types of support: Seed money.
Limitations: Giving limited to Montgomery County, OH, and adjacent counties. No grants for salaries.
Application information: Application form required.
Initial approach: 4 to 8 page proposal
Copies of proposal: 21
Deadline(s): None
Board meeting date(s): 4th Monday of each month except holidays
Final notification: One month after application has been filed
Write: Howard N. Thiele, Jr., Secy.
Officers: Gordon A. Sargent, Chair.; Richard R. Wolf, Vice-Chair.; Howard N. Thiele, Jr., Secy.; Charles Hoschouer, Treas.
Number of staff: None.
Employer Identification Number: 316063229

5692
Walter and Marian English Foundation
c/o Walter English Co.
1227 Bryden Rd.
Columbus 43205 (614) 253-7458
Application address: Station E, Box 6869, Columbus, OH 43205

Established about 1978 in Ohio.
Donor(s): Walter English.
Foundation type: Independent
Financial data (yr. ended 12/31/88): Assets, $1,738,046 (M); gifts received, $217,616; expenditures, $70,002, including $60,420 for 28 grants (high: $16,500; low: $70).
Purpose and activities: Giving primarily for civic affairs, cultural programs, education, health, and social services.
Limitations: Giving limited to Franklin County, OH. No grants to individuals.
Application information: Applications not accepted.
Write: Ellen E. Wiseman, Mgr.
Trustee: Walter English.
Officer: Ellen E. Wiseman, Mgr.
Employer Identification Number: 310921799

5693
The Ernst & Whinney Foundation ▼ ⌑
2000 National City Ctr.
Cleveland 44114 (216) 861-5000

Incorporated in 1937 in OH.
Donor(s): Ernst & Whinney Partnership.
Foundation type: Company-sponsored

Financial data (yr. ended 12/31/87): Assets, $7,469,922 (M); gifts received, $821,888; expenditures, $2,091,601, including $450,884 for 33 grants (high: $50,000; low: $200; average: $1,000-$25,000), $72,275 for 13 grants to individuals and $1,042,761 for 512 employee matching gifts.
Purpose and activities: Grants for higher educational institutions in the field of accounting, including employee matching gifts, and to doctoral candidates in accounting.
Types of support: Employee matching gifts, fellowships, professorships.
Limitations: No support for programs unrelated to business education. No grants for capital or endowment funds, special projects, continuing support, or general purposes; no loans.
Publications: Application guidelines.
Application information: Application form required for doctoral dissertation candidates.
Deadline(s): June 1
Board meeting date(s): Annually
Final notification: Aug. 1
Write: B.J. Mantia, Chair.
Officers and Trustees: B.J. Mantia, Chair.; P.C. Berry, Treas.
Number of staff: None.
Employer Identification Number: 346524211

5694
John F. and Doris E. Ernsthausen Charitable Foundation ⌑
c/o Society National Bank, Trust Tax Dept.
P.O. Box 6179
Cleveland 44101
Application address: Citizens Bank Bldg., Norwalk, OH 44857

Trust established in 1956 in OH.
Donor(s): John F. Ernsthausen, Doris E. Ernsthausen.
Foundation type: Independent
Financial data (yr. ended 6/30/88): Assets, $7,125,645 (M); expenditures, $301,382.
Purpose and activities: Giving for the Methodist church, care of the aged, higher and secondary education, a community fund, and cultural programs.
Limitations: Giving primarily in OH.
Application information: Application form not required.
Deadline(s): None
Write: Cornelius J. Ruffing, Mgr.
Officers: Paul L. Carpenter, Mgr.; Loyal L. Chaney, Mgr.; John F. Ernsthausen, Mgr.; Earle H. Lowe, Mgr.; Cornelius J. Ruffing, Mgr.
Trustee: Society National Bank.
Employer Identification Number: 346501908

5695
Hubert A. & Gladys C. Estabrook Charitable Trust ⌑ ☆
145 Manor Ln.
Dayton 45429

Established in 1977.
Donor(s): Gladys C. Estabrook Charitable Remainder Unitrust.
Foundation type: Independent
Financial data (yr. ended 3/31/89): Assets, $1,480,354 (M); gifts received, $867,008; expenditures, $42,260, including $30,425 for 3 grants (high: $24,000; low: $1,425).
Purpose and activities: "To benefit law schools and/or the study of law."
Types of support: Building funds, scholarship funds, renovation projects.
Limitations: Giving limited to OH. No grants to individuals.
Application information: Contributes only to pre-selected organizations. Applications not accepted.
Trustee: John O. Henry.
Employer Identification Number: 310909737

5696
The Thomas J. Evans Foundation
36 North Second St.
P.O. Box 919
Newark 43055-0764 (614) 345-3431

Established in 1965 in OH.
Donor(s): Thomas J. Evans.†
Foundation type: Independent
Financial data (yr. ended 10/31/89): Assets, $12,804,075 (M); expenditures, $379,442, including $315,841 for 11 grants (high: $124,021; low: $1,000).
Purpose and activities: Grants in the areas of public health, education, recreation, social services, church support, and protection of the environment; also land and buildings held for use by charitable organizations.
Types of support: Seed money, building funds, general purposes, scholarship funds, operating budgets.
Limitations: Giving primarily in Licking County, OH. No grants to individuals.
Application information:
Initial approach: Letter
Deadline(s): None
Board meeting date(s): Quarterly
Write: J. Gilbert Reese, Pres.
Officers and Trustees: John W. Alford, Chair. and Treas.; J. Gilbert Reese, Pres.; Sarah R. Wallace, Secy.
Employer Identification Number: 316055767

5697
Jesse Eyman Trust
c/o John S. Bath
132 1/2 Court St.
Washington Court House 43160

Trust established in 1924 in OH.
Donor(s): Jesse Eyman.†
Foundation type: Independent
Financial data (yr. ended 12/31/88): Assets, $2,547,428 (M); expenditures, $103,647, including $83,009 for 28 grants (high: $18,000; low: $29).
Purpose and activities: Emphasis on payments to support organizations for medical and dental care on behalf of needy persons; some support for social service and health agencies.
Limitations: Giving limited to Washington Court House and Fayette County, OH. No grants to individuals except through intermediary businesses providing services to the indigent; no loans.
Application information: Funds are disbursed only to support organizations. Applications not accepted.
Trustees: John S. Bath, Jesse Persinger.
Employer Identification Number: 316040007

5698
Ferro Foundation
1000 Lakeside Ave.
Cleveland 44114-1183 (216) 641-8580

Incorporated in 1959 in OH.
Donor(s): Ferro Corp.
Foundation type: Company-sponsored
Financial data (yr. ended 04/30/89): Assets, $163,982 (M); expenditures, $217,104, including $216,860 for 48 grants (high: $69,000; low: $500).
Purpose and activities: Emphasis on a community fund, higher education, cultural programs, and hospitals.
Types of support: Operating budgets, building funds.
Limitations: Giving primarily in OH.
Application information: Application form not required.
Write: Adolph Posnick, Pres.
Officers and Trustees:* Adolph Posnick,* Pres.; A.C. Bersticker,* V.P.; J.W. Adams, Secy.; H.R. Ortino,* Treas.
Employer Identification Number: 346554832

5699
The 1525 Foundation ▼
1525 National City Bank Bldg.
Cleveland 44114 (216) 696-4200

Incorporated in 1971 in OH.
Donor(s): Kent H. Smith.†
Foundation type: Independent
Financial data (yr. ended 12/31/89): Assets, $13,830,444 (M); expenditures, $2,645,167, including $2,474,695 for 40 grants (high: $2,000,000; low: $3,000; average: $5,000-$90,000).
Purpose and activities: Emphasis on higher and other education, environmental quality and conservation of natural resources, and social service agencies; charities of interest to the founder during his lifetime are favored.
Types of support: Operating budgets, building funds, capital campaigns, continuing support, general purposes, matching funds, professorships, seed money, endowment funds, equipment.
Limitations: Giving primarily in OH, with emphasis on Cuyahoga County.
Publications: 990-PF.
Application information: Application form not required.
Initial approach: Proposal
Copies of proposal: 1
Deadline(s): None
Board meeting date(s): As required - at least monthly
Final notification: Within 1 month of receipt
Write: Bernadette Walsh, Asst. Secy.
Officers: Hubert H. Schneider, Pres.; Thelma G. Smith, V.P.; Phillip A. Ranney, Secy.-Treas.
Employer Identification Number: 341089206

5700
The Fifth Third Foundation
c/o Fifth Third Bank
Dept. 00864, Fifth Third Ctr.
Cincinnati 45263 (513) 579-6034

Trust established in 1948 in OH.
Donor(s): Fifth Third Bank.
Foundation type: Company-sponsored

Financial data (yr. ended 09/30/89): Assets, $86,379,701 (M); gifts received, $905,500; expenditures, $807,600, including $752,236 for grants (high: $102,000; low: $100) and $13,030 for 111 employee matching gifts.
Purpose and activities: Emphasis on higher education, hospitals, health agencies, youth, social services, cultural programs, and community development.
Types of support: Continuing support, annual campaigns, seed money, building funds, equipment, special projects, publications, capital campaigns, renovation projects, scholarship funds, employee matching gifts.
Limitations: Giving primarily in the Cincinnati, OH, area, and other operating areas of the corporation. No grants to individuals, or for endowment funds, or fellowships; no loans.
Publications: Application guidelines, informational brochure, program policy statement.
Application information: Application form not required.
Initial approach: Proposal
Copies of proposal: 1
Deadline(s): None
Board meeting date(s): Monthly
Write: Carolyn F. McCoy, Foundation Officer
Trustee: Fifth Third Bank.
Number of staff: 1 full-time professional; 1 full-time support.
Employer Identification Number: 316024135

5701
Margaret H. Findeiss Trust B ¤
c/o The Central Trust Co.
434 Main St.
Zanesville 43701

Established in 1959 in OH.
Foundation type: Independent
Financial data (yr. ended 12/31/88): Assets, $1,249,873 (M); expenditures, $74,747, including $65,001 for 7 grants of $9,286 each.
Purpose and activities: Support primarily for a Methodist church, mission and seminary; support also for community funds and for social services.
Application information: Contributes only to pre-selected organizations. Applications not accepted.
Trustee: The Central Trust Co., N.A.
Number of staff: None.
Employer Identification Number: 316113258

5702
John D. Finnegan Foundation
c/o Mahoning National Bank of Youngstown, Trust Dept.
P.O. Box 479
Youngstown 44501 (216) 742-7000

Trust established in 1957 in OH.
Donor(s): John D. Finnegan.†
Foundation type: Independent
Financial data (yr. ended 12/31/89): Assets, $3,453,097 (M); expenditures, $238,991, including $219,000 for 18 grants (high: $50,000; low: $1,000).
Purpose and activities: Giving for care of the aged; support for Roman Catholic religious and welfare associations and for higher education.
Types of support: Building funds, capital campaigns, equipment, renovation projects.
Limitations: Giving primarily in Youngstown, OH. No grants to individuals, or for operating budgets, scholarships, fellowships, or matching gifts; no loans.
Application information:
Initial approach: Letter or proposal
Copies of proposal: 1
Deadline(s): Submit proposal preferably from Jan. through Mar.
Board meeting date(s): May, Sept., and Nov.
Final notification: Mar.
Write: Patrick A. Sebastiano, Sr. V.P. and Sr. Trust Officer, Mahoning National Bank of Youngstown
Directors: John M. Newman, Chair.; W.W. Bresnahan, Vice-Chair.; William J. Mullen, Gregory L. Ridler, Arthur G. Young.
Trustee: Mahoning National Bank of Youngstown.
Number of staff: None.
Employer Identification Number: 346516439

5703
Firan Foundation ¤
1115 South Main St.
Akron 44301

Established in 1983 in OH as a successor to Firestone Foundation.
Foundation type: Independent
Financial data (yr. ended 12/31/88): Assets, $3,277,004 (M); expenditures, $250,198, including $192,500 for 6 grants (high: $75,000; low: $2,500).
Purpose and activities: Grants primarily for hospitals and medical research; support also for education and recreation.
Types of support: General purposes, research, land acquisition.
Limitations: Giving primarily in U.S. and Canada. No grants to individuals.
Application information: Contributes only to pre-selected organizations. Applications not accepted.
Trustees: Herbert T. McDevitt, Exec. Dir.; D. Morgan Firestone, Mrs. D. Morgan Firestone.
Employer Identification Number: 341388250

5704
J. B. Firestone Charitable Trust ☆
c/o Elyria Savings & Trust National Bank
105 Court St.
Elyria 44035-5525 (216) 329-3000

Established in 1966.
Foundation type: Independent
Financial data (yr. ended 12/31/88): Assets, $1,006,586 (M); qualifying distributions, $145,357, including $49,854 for 20 grants (high: $15,732; low: $200) and $90,649 for 23 loans to individuals.
Purpose and activities: Awards loans for higher education to students or alumni of Black River High School in the Spencer, OH, area. Grants also for Protestant churches, education, and social services.
Types of support: Student loans.
Limitations: Giving limited to the Spencer, OH, area.
Application information: Application form required for student loans.
Deadline(s): None
Write: Georgia L. Bour, V.P., Elyria Savings & Trust National Bank
Trustee: Elyria Savings & Trust National Bank.
Employer Identification Number: 346577308

5705
Harvey S. Firestone No. 1 Fund A ¤
c/o Bank One Akron, N.A.
50 South Main St.
Akron 44308

Established in 1917 in Ohio.
Foundation type: Independent
Financial data (yr. ended 12/31/87): Assets, $1,361,836 (M); expenditures, $94,041, including $83,750 for 14 grants (high: $28,000; low: $250).
Purpose and activities: Primarily Christian religious giving.
Trustee Bank: Bank One Akron, N.A.
Employer Identification Number: 346505756

5706
Elizabeth Firestone-Graham Foundation
c/o Bank One Akron, N.A.
50 South Main St.
Akron 44308

Established in 1983 in Ohio.
Foundation type: Independent
Financial data (yr. ended 11/30/88): Assets, $1,954,313 (M); expenditures, $88,024, including $60,000 for 6 grants (high: $15,000; low: $5,000).
Purpose and activities: Giving primarily for the arts, including film, the fine arts, and museums.
Types of support: Lectureships, publications, special projects.
Application information: Application form not required.
Initial approach: Proposal
Copies of proposal: 1
Deadline(s): May 1 and Oct. 1
Write: C.J. Goldthorpe
Officer and Trustees:* Ray A. Graham III,* Pres.; Barbara F. Graham.
Employer Identification Number: 341388252

5707
Harvey Firestone, Jr. Foundation ¤
c/o Bank One, Akron
50 South Main St.
Akron 44308

Established in 1983 in Ohio.
Foundation type: Independent
Financial data (yr. ended 12/31/88): Assets, $8,338,100 (M); expenditures, $199,417, including $108,250 for 32 grants (high: $30,000; low: $250).
Purpose and activities: Emphasis on hospitals and education; support also for cultural programs, social services, and denominational giving.
Types of support: General purposes.
Limitations: Giving primarily in the eastern U.S.
Application information:
Initial approach: Proposal
Deadline(s): Submit application from July 1 through Sept. 30

Write: C.J. Goldthorpe
Trustees: Anne F. Ball, Martha F. Ford, Elizabeth F. Willis.
Employer Identification Number: 341388254

5708
Firman Fund ⌘
1010 Hanna Bldg.
1422 Euclid Ave.
Cleveland 44115-2078 (216) 363-6480

Incorporated in 1951 in OH.
Donor(s): Pamela H. Firman.
Foundation type: Independent
Financial data (yr. ended 12/31/88): Assets, $5,826,780 (M); expenditures, $358,899, including $309,710 for 100 grants (high: $26,000; low: $50; average: $100-$50,000).
Purpose and activities: Grants largely for hospitals, higher and secondary education, cultural programs, youth agencies, and community funds.
Types of support: Annual campaigns, general purposes, building funds.
Limitations: Giving primarily in OH. No grants to individuals, or for research; no loans.
Application information:
Initial approach: Proposal or letter
Copies of proposal: 1
Deadline(s): 6 weeks prior to meetings
Board meeting date(s): Apr. and Nov.
Write: Pamela H. Firman, Pres. or Carol L. Colangelo, Secy.
Officers: Pamela H. Firman, Pres.; Cynthia F. Webster, V.P.; Carol L. Colangelo, Secy.-Treas.
Trustee: Royal Firman III.
Employer Identification Number: 346513655

5709
The Fleischmann Foundation ⌘
4001 Carew Tower
Cincinnati 45202

Incorporated in 1931 in OH.
Donor(s): Julius Fleischmann.†
Foundation type: Independent
Financial data (yr. ended 12/31/88): Assets, $3,261,250 (M); expenditures, $138,477, including $125,195 for 41 grants (high: $66,824; low: $50).
Purpose and activities: Emphasis on arts and the humanities, including support for museums, especially for a museum of natural history.
Limitations: Giving primarily in OH.
Application information: Application form not required.
Deadline(s): None
Write: Charles Fleischmann III, Pres.
Officers: Charles Fleischmann III, Pres. and Treas.; Eric P. Yeiser, V.P.; Burd Blair S. Fleischmann, Secy.
Trustees: Burd S. Schlessinger, Leonard A. Weakly.
Employer Identification Number: 316025516

5710
The Flickinger Memorial Trust, Inc. ⌘
115 West North St.
P.O. Box 1255
Lima 45802-1255 (419) 227-6506

Trust established in 1965 in OH.
Donor(s): William J. Flickinger.†
Foundation type: Independent
Financial data (yr. ended 12/31/88): Assets, $1,853,506 (M); gifts received, $6,650; expenditures, $192,088, including $18,800 for 21 grants (high: $2,500; low: $50) and $97,633 for 68 loans to individuals.
Purpose and activities: Emphasis on higher education, including scholarship loans; support also for youth agencies.
Types of support: Student loans.
Limitations: Giving primarily in OH.
Application information:
Initial approach: Letter
Deadline(s): None
Write: F. Miles Flickinger, M.D., Chair.
Officers and Trustees: F. Miles Flickinger, M.D., Chair.; Marhl P. Flickinger, Treas.; Miriam Bandy, Irma L. Flickinger, Samuel O. Jeffrey.
Employer Identification Number: 346527156

5711
Albert W. and Edith V. Flowers Charitable Trust ⌘
c/o Society Bank of Eastern Ohio, N.A.
P.O. Box 9950
Canton 44701 (216) 489-5422

Trust established in 1968 in OH.
Donor(s): Albert W. Flowers,† Edith V. Flowers.†
Foundation type: Independent
Financial data (yr. ended 12/31/88): Assets, $1,528,550 (M); expenditures, $101,819, including $88,575 for 32 grants (high: $9,000; low: $200).
Purpose and activities: Emphasis on Protestant church support, a home for the aged, youth agencies, higher and secondary education, and cultural programs.
Limitations: Giving primarily in Stark County, OH. No grants to individuals.
Application information:
Initial approach: Letter
Deadline(s): Nov. 15
Write: Stephen C. Donatini
Distribution Committee: Ronald B. Tynan, Chair.; F.E. McCullough, Albert C. Printz.
Trustee: Society Bank of Eastern Ohio, N.A.
Employer Identification Number: 346608643

5712
H. Fort Flowers Foundation, Inc.
P.O. Box 238
Findlay 45839

Incorporated in 1951 in DE.
Donor(s): Flowers Trust.
Foundation type: Independent
Financial data (yr. ended 12/31/88): Assets, $1,149,306 (M); gifts received, $187,058; expenditures, $439,534, including $438,190 for 18 grants (high: $250,000; low: $190).
Purpose and activities: Grants mainly to schools of engineering.
Types of support: Professorships, endowment funds.
Limitations: No grants to individuals.
Application information: Application form not required.
Deadline(s): None
Write: Richard W. Flowers, Secy.
Officers: D.F. Flowers,* Pres.; S.N.F. Georges,* V.P.; K.L. Smith, V.P.; W.L. Woellert, V.P.; Richard W. Flowers,* Secy.
Trustees:* D.F. Flowers, Jr., J.R. Murray, Sr., J.R. Murray, Jr.
Employer Identification Number: 346513672

5713
The S. N. Ford and Ada Ford Fund
c/o Trustcorp Bank, OH
P.O. Box 10099
Toledo 43699-0099 (419) 526-3493
Application address: 42 North Main, Mansfield, OH 44902

Trust established in 1947 in OH.
Donor(s): Ada Ford, M.D.†
Foundation type: Independent
Financial data (yr. ended 12/31/88): Assets, $6,087,885 (M); expenditures, $401,970, including $36,100 for 10 grants (high: $7,500; low: $1,000) and $298,348 for 392 grants to individuals (high: $11,472; low: $16).
Purpose and activities: Assistance to the aged and the sick, and scholarships for the youth of Richland County.
Types of support: Building funds, student aid, grants to individuals.
Limitations: Giving primarily in Richland County, OH. No grants for endowment funds, or for operating budgets, special projects, general support, research, or matching gifts; no loans.
Publications: Annual report.
Application information: Application form required.
Initial approach: Telephone
Deadline(s): None
Board meeting date(s): Monthly
Final notification: 2 months
Write: Nick Gesouras, Trust Officer, Trustcorp Bank, OH
Distribution Committee: Ralph H. LeMunyon, Pres.; Burton Preston, V.P.; David L. Upham, Secy.; Stephen B. Bogner, Walter J. Kinkel.
Trustee: Trustcorp Bank.
Employer Identification Number: 340842282

5714
Forest City Enterprises Charitable Foundation, Inc. ⌘
10800 Brookpark Rd.
Cleveland 44130

Trust established in 1976 in OH.
Donor(s): Forest City Enterprises, Inc.
Foundation type: Company-sponsored
Financial data (yr. ended 1/31/89): Assets, $79,308 (M); gifts received, $525,000; expenditures, $507,760, including $507,632 for 316 grants (high: $82,000; low: $15).
Purpose and activities: Support for Jewish welfare funds, a community fund, and several other fields, including crime and law enforcement, leadership development, drug abuse programs, the homeless, and hunger. Additional support for education, including adult and elementary education, and cultural programs.
Types of support: Annual campaigns, employee-related scholarships.
Limitations: Giving primarily in OH.
Application information:

Copies of proposal: 1
Deadline(s): None
Write: Nathan Shafran
Officers and Trustees:* Max Ratner,* Pres.; Sam Miller,* V.P.; Helen F. Morgan, Secy.; Albert Ratner, Charles Ratner.
Number of staff: 3
Employer Identification Number: 341218895

5715
Donald J. Foss Memorial Employees Trust ¤
604 Madison Ave.
Wooster 44691-4764

Foundation type: Independent
Financial data (yr. ended 4/30/89): Assets, $1,546,174 (M); expenditures, $68,031, including $31,500 for 2 grants (high: $16,500; low: $15,000) and $36,431 for 60 grants to individuals (high: $1,125; low: $22).
Purpose and activities: Grants to individual employees of the Wooster Brush Co. in time of sickness, death or unfortunate circumstance; support also for a community fund.
Types of support: Grants to individuals.
Limitations: Giving primarily in Wooster, OH.
Application information: Application form required.
Deadline(s): None
Write: Woodrow J. Zook, Trustee
Trustees: Robert L. Weiss, Thomas W. Zook, Woodrow J. Zook.
Employer Identification Number: 346517801

5716
Clyde T. & Lyla C. Foster Foundation ¤ ☆
c/o National City Bank
P.O. Box 5756
Cleveland 44101 (216) 575-2748

Established in 1955 in OH.
Foundation type: Independent
Financial data (yr. ended 12/31/88): Assets, $1,226,187 (M); expenditures, $117,074, including $111,700 for 23 grants (high: $50,000; low: $250).
Purpose and activities: Giving primarily for Catholic welfare, community projects, and social services.
Application information: Application form not required.
Initial approach: Letter
Deadline(s): None
Write: Marianne Hobe
Trustee: National City Bank.
Employer Identification Number: 346511940

5717
The Harry K. & Emma R. Fox Charitable Foundation
c/o National City Bank
P.O. Box 5756
Cleveland 44101 (216) 621-8400
Application address: 900 Bond Court Bldg., Cleveland, OH 44114

Trust established in 1959 in OH.
Donor(s): Emma R. Fox.†
Foundation type: Independent
Financial data (yr. ended 12/31/88): Assets, $4,180,446 (M); expenditures, $296,695, including $253,600 for 63 grants (high: $17,000; low: $500; average: $1,000-$10,000).
Purpose and activities: Giving to hospitals, education, cultural programs, youth agencies, and human services.
Limitations: Giving primarily in northeastern OH. No grants to individuals, or for endowment funds or matching gifts; no loans.
Publications: Application guidelines.
Application information: Application form not required.
Initial approach: Full proposal
Copies of proposal: 4
Deadline(s): May 15 and Nov. 15
Board meeting date(s): June and Dec.
Final notification: 6 months
Write: Harold E. Friedman, Secy.
Officer: Harold E. Friedman, Secy.
Trustees: Marjorie S. Schweid, Chair.; George Rosenfeld, Vice-Chair.; National City Bank.
Number of staff: 1 part-time professional.
Employer Identification Number: 346511198

5718
France Stone Foundation
1000 National Bank Bldg.
Toledo 43603 (419) 241-2201

Established in 1952 in OH.
Donor(s): George A. France,† The France Stone Co., and subsidiaries.
Foundation type: Independent
Financial data (yr. ended 12/31/88): Assets, $7,324,876 (M); expenditures, $369,600, including $313,200 for 33 grants (high: $89,500; low: $250).
Purpose and activities: Giving primarily to hospitals, religious organizations, youth agencies, and higher and secondary education.
Types of support: Continuing support, annual campaigns, building funds, research, scholarship funds.
Limitations: Giving primarily in OH, MI, and IN. No grants to individuals, or for operating budgets or special projects.
Application information: Application form not required.
Initial approach: Proposal
Copies of proposal: 1
Deadline(s): Oct. 1
Board meeting date(s): June
Final notification: 6 months
Write: Joseph S. Heyman, Pres.
Officers and Trustees:* Joseph S. Heyman,* Pres.; Ollie J. Risner,* V.P.; Andrew E. Anderson,* Secy.-Treas.
Number of staff: 1 part-time support.
Employer Identification Number: 346523033

5719
Franklin Foundation, Inc. ¤ ☆
760 Northlawn Dr.
Columbus 43214

Established in 1986 in OH.
Donor(s): Sally L. Havens, Suzanne E. Havens-Nick, Ellen H. Hardymon, Thomas F. Havens, John C. Havens.
Foundation type: Operating
Financial data (yr. ended 11/30/88): Assets, $1,645,921 (M); expenditures, $144,210, including $136,750 for 1 grant.
Purpose and activities: A private operating foundation; support for a housing project for low-income senior citizens.
Trustees: Ellen H. Hardymon, John C. Havens, Thomas F. Havens, Philipp D. Nick.
Employer Identification Number: 311191673

5720
Laura B. Frick Trust ¤ ☆
c/o Wayne County National Bank
P.O. Box 550
Wooster 44691 (216) 264-1222

Foundation type: Independent
Financial data (yr. ended 12/31/88): Assets, $1,671,345 (M); expenditures, $62,431, including $46,141 for 26 grants (high: $7,500; low: $309).
Purpose and activities: Support primarily for elementary and secondary education.
Limitations: Giving primarily in the Wooster, OH, area.
Application information: Application form not required.
Initial approach: Letter
Deadline(s): None
Write: Stephen Kitchen, Sr. Trust Officer, Wayne County National Bank
Trustee: Wayne County National Bank.
Employer Identification Number: 346513247

5721
The Sidney Frohman Foundation ¤
c/o Muehlauser & Moore
P.O. Box 790
Sandusky 44870

Trust established in 1952 in OH.
Donor(s): Sidney Frohman,† Blanche P. Frohman.†
Foundation type: Independent
Financial data (yr. ended 12/31/88): Assets, $6,433,370 (M); expenditures, $326,845, including $302,500 for 39 grants (high: $60,000; low: $500).
Purpose and activities: To promote the well-being of mankind; assistance to the sick, aged, and needy; guidance of youth; aid to higher and secondary education; support of public health and recreation; and the furtherance of research.
Limitations: Giving primarily in OH, with emphasis on Erie County. No grants to individuals.
Application information: Contributes only to pre-selected organizations. Applications not accepted.
Trustees: Daniel C. Frohman, George T. Henderson, L.G. Parker, Max E. Stierwalt.
Employer Identification Number: 346517809

5722
Paul & Maxine Frohring Foundation, Inc. ¤
3200 National City Ctr.
Cleveland 44114

Established in 1958 in OH.
Foundation type: Independent
Financial data (yr. ended 12/31/88): Assets, $2,829,711 (M); expenditures, $122,279, including $111,500 for 24 grants (high: $25,000; low: $1,000).

Purpose and activities: Support primarily for higher education; support also for health agencies.
Limitations: Giving primarily in OH. No grants to individuals.
Application information: Application form not required.
Deadline(s): None
Write: William W. Falsgraf, Secy.
Officers and Trustees: Paul R. Frohring, Pres.; Maxine A. Frohring, V.P. and Treas.; William W. Falsgraf, Secy.; Elmer Jagow, Paula Frohring Kuslan.
Employer Identification Number: 346513729

5723
The William O. and Gertrude Lewis Frohring Foundation, Inc. ¤
3200 National City Ctr.
Cleveland 44114 (216) 621-0200

Trust established in 1958 in OH; incorporated in 1963.
Donor(s): William O. Frohring,† Gertrude L. Frohring.†
Foundation type: Independent
Financial data (yr. ended 12/31/87): Assets, $3,318,030 (M); expenditures, $281,141, including $248,250 for 47 grants (high: $50,000; low: $450; average: $3,864).
Purpose and activities: Giving mainly for health, education, and the arts.
Types of support: Operating budgets, continuing support, annual campaigns, seed money, emergency funds, building funds, equipment, land acquisition.
Limitations: Giving primarily in Geauga, Lake, and Cuyahoga counties, OH. No grants to individuals, or for deficit financing, endowment funds, matching gifts, scholarships, or fellowships; no loans.
Application information: Application form not required.
Initial approach: Letter
Copies of proposal: 1
Deadline(s): Submit proposal preferably in Mar. and Aug.; deadline 1 week before board meetings
Board meeting date(s): May and Oct.
Final notification: 3 weeks after board meetings
Write: William W. Falsgraf, Asst. Secy.
Officers and Trustees: Glenn H. Frohring, Chair.; Lloyd W. Frohring, Treas.; William W. Falsgraf, Elaine A. Szilagyi.
Employer Identification Number: 346516526

5724
Meshech Frost Testamentary Trust ¤
c/o BancOhio National Bank
155 East Broad St.
Columbus 43251
Application address: 109 South Washington St., Tiffin, OH 44883

Trust established in 1922 in OH.
Donor(s): Meshech Frost.†
Foundation type: Independent
Financial data (yr. ended 12/31/88): Assets, $2,528,417 (M); gifts received, $4,493; expenditures, $165,441, including $137,430 for 14 grants (high: $30,000; low: $150) and $1,822 for 5 grants to individuals (high: $690; low: $169).
Purpose and activities: One-half for civic improvement or beautification and one-half for the needy poor, including support for a local college and hospital.
Types of support: Grants to individuals.
Limitations: Giving limited to Tiffin, OH.
Application information:
Initial approach: Letter
Deadline(s): None
Write: Kenneth H. Myers, Secy.-Treas.
Officer and Advisory Committee:* Kenneth H. Myers,* Secy.-Treas.; Charles Hering, Wayne Marker, Robert McDonald.
Trustee: BancOhio National Bank.
Employer Identification Number: 316019431

5725
The Lewis P. Gallagher Family Foundation
c/o Society National Bank, Trust Dept.
800 Superior Ave.
Cleveland 44114
Application address: c/o Gilbert V. Kelling, Jr., Secy., 2817 2nd Ave. North, Billings, MT 59101

Established in 1980.
Donor(s): Lewis P. Gallagher Family Charitable Income Trust.
Foundation type: Independent
Financial data (yr. ended 12/31/87): Assets, $3,722,085 (M); gifts received, $823,299; expenditures, $482,372, including $422,055 for 13 grants (high: $100,000; low: $2,500).
Purpose and activities: Giving for higher and secondary education, hospitals, and Protestant welfare organizations.
Types of support: Matching funds, scholarship funds, building funds, operating budgets, general purposes.
Limitations: Giving primarily in OH. No grants to individuals.
Application information:
Initial approach: Letter
Deadline(s): Sept. 1
Write: Gilbert V. Kelling, Jr., Secy.
Officers: Howard H. Fraser, Pres.; Gilbert V. Kelling, Jr., Secy.; Monford D. Custer III, M.D., Treas.
Employer Identification Number: 341325313

5726
The GAR Foundation ▼
50 South Main St.
P.O. Box 1500
Akron 44309 (216) 376-5300

Trust established in 1967 in OH.
Donor(s): Ruth C. Roush,† Galen Roush.†
Foundation type: Independent
Financial data (yr. ended 12/31/89): Assets, $101,463,835 (M); expenditures, $5,843,677, including $5,515,739 for 159 grants (high: $800,000; low: $1,000; average: $10,000-$75,000).
Purpose and activities: Grants to higher and secondary educational institutions for programs promoting the private enterprise economic system, and for the arts, hospitals, and civic and social service agencies, including youth activities.
Types of support: Equipment, general purposes, endowment funds, matching funds, research, scholarship funds.
Limitations: Giving primarily in northeastern OH, with emphasis on Akron. No support for medical research. No grants to individuals, or for fundraising campaigns or general operating expenses of the donee not directly related to its exempt purpose.
Publications: Application guidelines.
Application information: Application form required.
Initial approach: Proposal
Copies of proposal: 1
Deadline(s): 1st of month prior to board meeting date
Board meeting date(s): Feb., May, Aug., and Nov.
Final notification: Jan. 1, Apr. 1, July 1 and Oct. 1
Write: Lisle M. Buckingham, Trustee
Distribution Committee: Lisle M. Buckingham,* Joseph Clapp, John L. Tormey, S.R. Werner, Charles F. Zodrow.
Trustees:* National City Bank, Akron.
Number of staff: 1 full-time professional; 4 part-time professional.
Employer Identification Number: 346577710

5727
The Gardner Foundation ¤
P.O. Box 126
Middletown 45042 (513) 423-1795

Incorporated in 1952 in OH.
Foundation type: Independent
Financial data (yr. ended 5/31/89): Assets, $2,863,082 (M); gifts received, $1,000; expenditures, $189,086, including $12,000 for 2 grants (high: $10,000; low: $2,000) and $136,500 for grants to individuals.
Purpose and activities: Support primarily for higher education, with emphasis on private colleges and universities and a scholarship program for graduating seniors from schools in Middletown and Hamilton County, OH.
Types of support: Student aid, annual campaigns.
Limitations: Giving primarily in OH, with emphasis on Middletown and Hamilton County.
Publications: Program policy statement, application guidelines.
Application information: Application form required.
Deadline(s): Apr. 1 (for scholarships)
Write: Robert Q. Millan, Pres.
Officers and Trustees: Robert Q. Millan, Pres.; E.T. Gardner, Jr., V.P., Finance; Ames Gardner, Jr., V.P.; Calvin F. Lloyd, Secy.-Treas.; Ames Gardner, Colin Gardner III, Colin Gardner IV, E. T. Gardner III, Mary G. Neill.
Number of staff: None.
Employer Identification Number: 316050604

5728
Virginia Gay Fund ¤ ☆
c/o Marjorie L. Ater
751 Grandon Ave.
Columbus 43209

Established in 1914.
Foundation type: Independent

Financial data (yr. ended 12/31/88): Assets, $1,025,386 (M); expenditures, $52,830, including $41,347 for 22 grants to individuals (high: $3,840; low: $500).
Purpose and activities: Provides relief assistance to retired, elderly female school teachers.
Types of support: Grants to individuals.
Limitations: Giving limited to OH residents.
Application information: Application form required.
Deadline(s): None
Write: Trustees
Officers and Trustees: L.D. Shuter, Pres.; Loren N. Hinton, V.P.; Marjorie Ater, Secy.-Treas.; C. Lucille Carroll, Maryellen Meredith, Orin E. Morris, George D. Norris.
Employer Identification Number: 314379588

5729
GenCorp Foundation, Inc. ▼
175 Ghent Rd.
Fairlawn 44313-3300 (216) 869-4292

Incorporated in 1961 in OH as successor to The General Tire Foundation, a trust established in 1950 in OH.
Donor(s): GenCorp, Inc.
Foundation type: Company-sponsored
Financial data (yr. ended 11/30/89): Assets, $30,354,561 (M); expenditures, $1,196,234, including $930,231 for 157 grants (high: $80,000; low: $300) and $195,178 for 648 employee matching gifts.
Purpose and activities: Emphasis on higher education, community funds, and youth agencies; support also for social services and cultural programs.
Types of support: Employee matching gifts, annual campaigns, employee-related scholarships, general purposes, continuing support.
Limitations: Giving primarily in areas of company operations, including AZ, AR, CA, IN, MS, NH, NY, OH, PA, and TN. No grants to individuals, or for endowment funds, or research; no loans.
Application information: Application form not required.
Initial approach: Letter
Copies of proposal: 1
Deadline(s): None
Board meeting date(s): As required
Final notification: 2 months
Write: Charles R. Tilden, Pres.
Officers and Trustees:* Charles R. Tilden,* Pres. and Secy.; Celeste Michalski,* Treas.; Russell A. Livigni, Robert L. Malcolm.
Number of staff: None.
Employer Identification Number: 346514223

5730
The Generation Trust ⌑ ☆
c/o Trustcorp Bank Ohio
P.O. Box 10099
Toledo 43699-0099

Established in 1986 in OH.
Donor(s): John D. Beckett, and other members of the Beckett family.
Foundation type: Independent
Financial data (yr. ended 12/31/88): Assets, $4,646,124 (M); gifts received, $2,001,393; expenditures, $148,728, including $140,000 for 12 grants (high: $40,000; low: $2,500).
Purpose and activities: Support limited "to organizations with a Christian purpose," including churches and ministries.
Limitations: No grants to individuals.
Application information:
Initial approach: Letter
Deadline(s): None
Write: J. Philip Ruyle, Trust Officer, Trustcorp Bank Ohio
Advisory Committee: John D. Beckett, Wendy Beckett, Robert S. Cook.
Trustee: Trustcorp Bank, Ohio.
Employer Identification Number: 346850815

5731
The George Foundation
P.O. Box 21609
Columbus 43221

Established in 1982 in OH.
Donor(s): Kaplan Trucking Co.
Foundation type: Independent
Financial data (yr. ended 12/31/88): Assets, $1,968,471 (M); expenditures, $135,753, including $127,585 for 160 grants (high: $100,000; low: $25).
Purpose and activities: Emphasis on higher education.
Limitations: Giving primarily in OH.
Application information:
Initial approach: Letter
Deadline(s): None
Write: Jack M. George, Secy.-Treas.
Officers and Trustees: Noel F. George, Pres.; James George, V.P.; Jack M. George, Secy-Treas.; Mildred George.
Employer Identification Number: 311030194

5732
Gerlach Foundation, Inc. ⌑
37 West Broad St., 5th Fl.
Columbus 43215

Incorporated in 1953 in OH.
Donor(s): Pauline Gerlach,† John J. Gerlach, John B. Gerlach.
Foundation type: Independent
Financial data (yr. ended 11/30/88): Assets, $6,127,311 (M); gifts received, $1,000; expenditures, $467,278, including $207,220 for 40 grants (high: $51,375; low: $100).
Purpose and activities: Emphasis on higher education and social services; support also for cultural programs.
Types of support: General purposes.
Limitations: Giving primarily in OH. No grants to individuals.
Application information: Contributes only to pre-selected organizations. Applications not accepted.
Officers: John J. Gerlach, Pres.; David P. Gerlach, V.P.; John B. Gerlach, Secy.; John B. Gerlach, Jr., Treas.
Employer Identification Number: 316023912

5733
Benjamin S. Gerson Family Foundation
2425 North Park Blvd., Apt. 2
Cleveland 44106 (216) 231-2928

Trust established in 1958 in OH; foundation established in 1973.
Donor(s): Benjamin S. Gerson,† Members of the Gerson family.
Foundation type: Independent
Financial data (yr. ended 12/31/88): Assets, $2,445,276 (M); expenditures, $138,616, including $129,400 for 23 grants (high: $30,000; low: $500; average: $2,000-$5,000).
Purpose and activities: Support for community organizations, programs emphasizing access to education, alternative and innovative education, civil liberties, and children and family concerns; some support for national issue advocacy organizations.
Types of support: Operating budgets, continuing support, seed money, emergency funds, matching funds, special projects, general purposes.
Limitations: Giving limited to the greater Cleveland, OH, community for operating programs. No grants to individuals, or for conferences.
Publications: Application guidelines, grants list.
Application information: Application form not required.
Initial approach: Telephone or letter requesting guidelines
Copies of proposal: 2
Deadline(s): Submit proposal preferably in Aug. or Sept.; deadline Sept. 15
Board meeting date(s): Jan.
Final notification: Suitable requests notified after board meets
Write: Eleanor R. Gerson, Chair.
Trustees: Eleanor R. Gerson, Chair.; Thomas E. Gerson, Richard Margolis, Rae Weil.
Number of staff: None.
Employer Identification Number: 346611446

5734
Charles H. and Fannie M. Giles Memorial Foundation ⌑
1100 Huntington Bldg.
Cleveland 44115 (216) 696-1100

Established in 1959 in OH.
Foundation type: Independent
Financial data (yr. ended 12/31/88): Assets, $1,574,879 (M); expenditures, $77,171, including $59,800 for 28 grants (high: $10,776; low: $250).
Purpose and activities: Giving primarily for social services and civic affairs.
Types of support: Scholarship funds, operating budgets.
Limitations: Giving limited to OH, with emphasis on Chagrin Falls and the Cleveland area.
Application information: Contributes only to pre-selected organizations. Applications not accepted.
Write: George M. Roudebush, Pres.
Officer and Trustees: George M. Roudebush, Pres.; Richard H. Brown, Laverne Yushik.
Employer Identification Number: 346554844

5735
Goerlich Family Foundation, Inc. ⌑
1200 National Bank Bldg.
Toledo 43604

Incorporated in 1965 in OH.
Foundation type: Independent
Financial data (yr. ended 12/31/88): Assets, $2,826,423 (M); expenditures, $156,698, including $138,093 for 74 grants (high: $24,800; low: $25).
Purpose and activities: Emphasis on child welfare, mental health, and community funds; grants also for church support and religious associations, the aged, handicapped, and youth agencies.
Limitations: Giving primarily in Toledo, OH.
Application information: Contributes only to pre-selected organizations. Applications not accepted.
Officers: John Goerlich,* Chair.; William F. Bates, Pres. and Secy.-Treas.; Paul Putnam,* V.P.
Directors:* Edward H. Alexander, Sandrea Sue Goerlich Alexander, Selma E. Goerlich, Robert R. Hessler, William S. Miller.
Employer Identification Number: 340970919

5736
Goodyear Tire & Rubber Company Fund ⌑
1144 East Market St.
Akron 44316-0001 (216) 796-2916

Incorporated in 1945 in DE.
Donor(s): The Goodyear Tire & Rubber Co.
Foundation type: Company-sponsored
Financial data (yr. ended 12/31/88): Assets, $7,506 (M); gifts received, $170,000; expenditures, $175,078, including $175,058 for 6 grants (high: $77,733; low: $2,000).
Purpose and activities: Aid to colleges and universities.
Types of support: Annual campaigns, building funds, continuing support, fellowships, operating budgets, research, scholarship funds, employee-related scholarships, special projects, general purposes.
Limitations: Giving primarily in areas where company plants and subsidiaries are located. No grants to individuals, or for endowment funds or matching gifts; no loans.
Application information: Application form not required.
Initial approach: Letter
Copies of proposal: 1
Deadline(s): Submit proposal preferably from July through Dec.; no set deadline
Board meeting date(s): May and as required
Final notification: 3 to 4 months
Write: Mrs. Patricia A. Kemph, Asst. Secy.
Officers: Robert E. Mercer,* Chair.; Tom H. Barrett,* Pres.; Oren G. Shaffer, Treas.
Trustees:* Thomas H. Cruikshank, Edwin D. Dodd, Gertrude G. Michelson, Steven A. Minter, Charles W. Parry, Robert H. Platt, F. Vincent Prus, Agnar Pytte, Jacques R. Sardas, Lloyd B. Smith, William C. Turner.
Number of staff: 2
Employer Identification Number: 346522959

5737
Gould Inc. Foundation
35129 Curtis Blvd.
Eastlake 44094 (216) 953-5000

Incorporated in 1951 in OH.
Donor(s): Gould, Inc.
Foundation type: Company-sponsored
Financial data (yr. ended 12/31/88): Assets, $1,810,280 (M); expenditures, $297,547, including $91,973 for 28 grants (high: $18,000; low: $250; average: $2,000-$5,000), $68,198 for grants to individuals and $81,384 for employee matching gifts.
Purpose and activities: To strengthen the socio-economic environment in areas of corporate operations and of selected educational and scientific institutions; grants largely for scholarships for children of employees, hospitals, cultural activities, and youth agencies; support also for national organizations recognized as beneficial to the broader national community.
Types of support: Employee-related scholarships, annual campaigns, research, employee matching gifts.
Limitations: Giving primarily in areas of corporate operations: Chandler, AZ; Pocatello, ID; Glen Burnie, MD; Newburyport, MA; and Cleveland, Eastlake, and McConnelsville, OH. No support for groups that discriminate against minorities; disease-related organizations, other than special projects undertaken within Gould Inc.; or religious and fraternal groups which do not benefit entire commmunities. No grants to individuals (except employee-related scholarships); no loans.
Publications: Application guidelines.
Application information: Write to principal manager of local Gould facility. Application form not required.
Initial approach: Letter or proposal
Copies of proposal: 1
Deadline(s): Jan. 31 for scholarships; Mar. 31 for general requests
Board meeting date(s): Apr. and as required
Write: Joseph Huss, V.P., Human Resources, Gould, Inc.
Officers and Directors:* C.D. Ferguson,* Pres.; M.C. Veysey,* V.P. and Secy.; Jerry W. Gaskin,* V.P.; L.J. Huss,* V.P.
Number of staff: None.
Employer Identification Number: 346525555

5738
The Gradison & Company Foundation ☆
c/o Donald E. Weston
580 Building
Cincinnati 45202 (513) 579-5000

Established in 1981.
Donor(s): Gradison & Co., Inc.
Foundation type: Company-sponsored
Financial data (yr. ended 12/31/88): Assets, $18,528 (M); gifts received, $20,000; expenditures, $101,777, including $101,650 for 86 grants (high: $17,500; low: $25).
Purpose and activities: Support for United Appeal, culture, youth, higher education, schools for the handicapped, civic affairs, health, and social services.
Limitations: Giving primarily in Cincinnati, OH. No grants to individuals.
Application information: Contributes only to pre-selected organizations. Applications not accepted.
Trustees: David W. Ellis, Robert B. Shott, Paul G. Sittenfeld, Donald E. Weston.
Employer Identification Number: 311018948

5739
Lucile and Robert H. Gries Charity Fund ⌑
1500 Statler Office Tower
Cleveland 44115 (216) 861-1146

Trust established in 1968 in OH.
Donor(s): Lucile D. Gries.
Foundation type: Independent
Financial data (yr. ended 12/31/88): Assets, $2,309,983 (M); expenditures, $174,604, including $127,225 for 14 grants (high: $25,000; low: $175; average: $500-$15,000).
Purpose and activities: Support for general charitable purposes, including performing arts groups and Jewish organizations.
Types of support: Operating budgets, continuing support, annual campaigns, emergency funds, equipment, endowment funds, matching funds, internships, scholarship funds, research, grants to individuals, seed money, building funds, land acquisition, publications, conferences and seminars.
Limitations: Giving primarily in the greater Cleveland, OH, area.
Publications: 990-PF.
Application information: Application form not required.
Initial approach: Proposal or letter
Copies of proposal: 1
Board meeting date(s): Usually in Mar., June, Sept., and Dec., and as required
Write: Robert D. Gries, Member, Distribution Committee
Distribution Committee: Ellen G. Cole, Robert D. Gries.
Trustee: Ameritrust Co., N.A.
Number of staff: None.
Employer Identification Number: 346507593

5740
Gries Family Foundation ☆
1500 Statler Office Bldg.
1127 Euclid Ave., Suite 1500
Cleveland 44115 (216) 861-1146

Established in 1986.
Donor(s): Robert D. Gries, Ellen D. Cole.
Foundation type: Independent
Financial data (yr. ended 12/31/89): Assets, $3,263,489 (M); gifts received, $5,000; expenditures, $200,000, including $162,555 for 40 grants (high: $25,000; low: $500).
Purpose and activities: Giving primarily for higher and other education; support also for hospitals and cultural programs, including performing arts groups.
Limitations: Giving limited to the greater Cleveland, OH, area. No grants to individuals.
Application information: Application form not required.
Initial approach: Proposal
Deadline(s): None
Board meeting date(s): 4 to 6 times annually
Write: Robert D. Gries, Pres.

Officers and Trustees:* Robert D. Gries,* Pres.; Ellen G. Cole,* V.P.; Sally P. Gries,* Secy.-Treas.
Employer Identification Number: 341536795

5741
The Grimes Foundation ⌑
200 South Main St.
Urbana 43078
Application address: 166 Tanglewood Dr., Urbana, OH 43078; Tel.: (513) 653-4865

Incorporated about 1951 in OH.
Donor(s): Warren G. Grimes.
Foundation type: Independent
Financial data (yr. ended 12/31/88): Assets, $2,310,565 (M); expenditures, $192,377, including $163,150 for 32 grants (high: $50,000; low: $300).
Purpose and activities: Emphasis on higher, secondary, and primary education and hospitals.
Types of support: General purposes, scholarship funds, building funds.
Limitations: Giving primarily in OH and FL. No grants to individuals, or for endowment funds, research, or matching gifts; no loans.
Application information: Application form not required.
Initial approach: Letter or telephone
Copies of proposal: 1
Deadline(s): None
Board meeting date(s): Mar. and Aug.
Write: Lewis B. Moore, Chair.
Officers and Trustees: Lewis B. Moore, Chair. and Pres.; James S. Mihori, Secy.-Treas.; C.J. Brown, Jr., Frank J. Lausche, Robert S. Oelman.
Number of staff: None.
Employer Identification Number: 346528288

5742
Walter L. and Nell R. Gross Charitable Trust
105 East Fourth St., Rm. 710
Cincinnati 45202 (513) 721-5086

Established in 1955 in OH.
Donor(s): Members of the Gross family.
Foundation type: Independent
Financial data (yr. ended 12/31/89): Assets, $3,712,498 (M); expenditures, $69,394, including $52,600 for 23 grants (high: $6,000; low: $750).
Purpose and activities: Support for higher and secondary education, youth agencies, cultural programs, hospitals and health agencies, and Protestant church support.
Limitations: Giving primarily in OH. No grants to individuals.
Application information: Applications not accepted.
Write: Walter L. Gross, Jr., or Thomas R. Gross, Trustees
Advisory Board: Thomas R. Gross, Walter L. Gross, Jr., Patricia G. Linnemann.
Employer Identification Number: 316033247

5743
The George Gund Foundation ▼
One Erieview Plaza
Cleveland 44114-1773 (216) 241-3114

Incorporated in 1952 in OH.
Donor(s): George Gund.†
Foundation type: Independent
Financial data (yr. ended 12/31/88): Assets, $257,234,830 (M); expenditures, $11,433,673, including $10,277,060 for 536 grants (high: $424,031; low: $1,000; average: $25,000-$35,000).
Purpose and activities: Priority to education projects, with emphasis on new concepts and methods of teaching and learning, and on increasing educational opportunities for the disadvantaged; programs advancing economic revitalization and job creation; projects promoting neighborhood development; projects for improving human services, employment opportunities, housing for minority and low-income groups, and meeting the special needs of women; support also for ecology, civic affairs, and the arts.
Types of support: Operating budgets, continuing support, seed money, emergency funds, land acquisition, matching funds, internships, scholarship funds, special projects, publications, conferences and seminars, program-related investments, exchange programs, renovation projects, research.
Limitations: Giving primarily in northeastern OH. Generally no grants to individuals, or for building or endowment funds, equipment, or renovation projects.
Publications: Annual report (including application guidelines).
Application information: Application form not required.
Initial approach: Proposal
Copies of proposal: 1
Deadline(s): Jan. 15, Mar. 30, June 30, and Sept. 30
Board meeting date(s): Mar., June, Oct., and Dec.
Final notification: 8 weeks
Write: David Bergholz, Exec. Dir.
Officers and Trustees: Frederick K. Cox, Pres. and Treas.; Geoffrey Gund, V.P.; David Bergholz, Exec. Dir.; Kathleen L. Barber, Ann L. Gund, George Gund III, Llura A. Gund.
Number of staff: 3 full-time professional; 3 full-time support.
Employer Identification Number: 346519769

5744
H.C.S. Foundation ▼ ⌑
c/o Ohio Savings Bank
1801 East 9th St., Suite 1235
Cleveland 44114 (216) 781-3502

Trust established in 1959 in OH.
Donor(s): Harold C. Schott.†
Foundation type: Independent
Financial data (yr. ended 12/31/88): Assets, $30,545,185 (M); gifts received, $5,000,282; expenditures, $1,191,296, including $1,042,333 for 14 grants (high: $250,000; low: $1,000; average: $1,000-$50,000).
Purpose and activities: Grants primarily for a hospital, health organizations, and education.
Types of support: Operating budgets, scholarship funds, endowment funds, building funds.
Limitations: Giving limited to OH. No grants to individuals.
Application information: Application form not required.
Initial approach: Letter
Copies of proposal: 1
Deadline(s): None
Write: Trustees
Trustees: Francie S. Hiltz, L. Thomas Hiltz, Betty Jane Mulcahy, William Dunne Saal, Milton B. Schott, Jr.
Number of staff: 1 full-time professional.
Employer Identification Number: 346514235

5745
The Hamilton Community Foundation, Inc.
319 North Third St.
Hamilton 45011 (513) 863-1389

Incorporated in 1951 in OH.
Foundation type: Community
Financial data (yr. ended 12/31/88): Assets, $9,198,587 (M); gifts received, $863,131; expenditures, $971,100, including $915,471 for 200 grants (high: $25,000; low: $10; average: $1,000-$20,000) and $6,665 for foundation-administered programs.
Purpose and activities: Grants for local institutions, with emphasis on youth and child welfare agencies and scholarships. Grants also for health agencies and cultural programs.
Types of support: Seed money, emergency funds, scholarship funds, conferences and seminars.
Limitations: Giving limited to Butler County, OH. No grants to individuals, or for operating budgets, continuing support, annual campaigns, deficit financing, capital or endowment funds, matching gifts, program support, research, demonstration projects, or publications; no loans.
Publications: Annual report, application guidelines.
Application information: Application form not required.
Initial approach: Proposal
Copies of proposal: 10
Deadline(s): Submit proposal 30 days prior to 1st Monday of months in which board meets
Board meeting date(s): Feb., Apr., June, Oct., and Dec.
Final notification: 2 months
Write: Cynthia V. Parrish, Exec. Dir.
Officers: Anne B. Carr, Pres.; Cynthia V. Parrish, Exec. Dir.
Trustees: David Belew, Don W. Fitton, Jr., Richard J. Fitton, William Hartford, Lamont Jacobs, William Keck, Joseph L. Marcum, Lee H. Parrish, Joel H. Schmidt, John A. Whalen.
Trustee Banks: First National Bank and Trust Co., Star Bank, N.A., Cincinnati.
Number of staff: 1 part-time professional; 1 full-time support.
Employer Identification Number: 316038277

5746
Grace and John T. Harrington Foundation
c/o Bank One, Youngstown, N.A.
P.O. Box 359
Youngstown 44501 (216) 742-6740
Application address: c/o Bank One, Youngstown, N.A., Trust Dept., Six Federal Plaza West, Youngstown, OH 44503

Established in 1954 in OH.

Foundation type: Independent
Financial data (yr. ended 12/31/88): Assets, $1,445,348 (M); expenditures, $109,335, including $90,667 for 3 grants (high: $66,667; low: $4,000; average: $200-$10,000).
Purpose and activities: Giving primarily for arts and culture, education, and social services.
Types of support: General purposes.
Publications: 990-PF.
Application information: Application form not required.
Deadline(s): None
Trustees: John T. Thornton, Peter Thornton, William W. Thornton, Bank One, Youngstown, N.A.
Employer Identification Number: 346514087

5747
Hartzell-Norris Charitable Trust ¤
c/o Fifth Third Bank of Miami Valley, N.A.
326 North Main St., Trust Dept.
Piqua 45356

Trust established in 1943 in OH.
Donor(s): Hartzell Industries, Inc.
Foundation type: Company-sponsored
Financial data (yr. ended 10/31/88): Assets, $3,924,986 (M); expenditures, $333,035, including $280,698 for 432 grants (high: $50,000; low: $15).
Purpose and activities: Giving for youth agencies, social services, including the Salvation Army, health and hospitals, community funds, Protestant church support and religious associations, and higher education.
Limitations: Giving primarily in OH.
Distribution Committee: G.W. Hartzell, Chair.; Roy H. DePriest, Miriam H. Hartzell.
Trustee: Fifth Third Bank of Miami Valley, N.A.
Employer Identification Number: 316024521

5748
Haskell Fund
1010 Hanna Bldg.
Cleveland 44115 (216) 696-5528

Incorporated in 1955 in OH.
Donor(s): Melville H. Haskell,† Coburn Haskell, Melville H. Haskell, Jr., Mark Haskell.
Foundation type: Independent
Financial data (yr. ended 12/31/89): Assets, $2,625,767 (M); expenditures, $135,226, including $118,700 for 51 grants (high: $16,000; low: $500; average: $1,000-$5,000).
Purpose and activities: Giving locally for community services and nationally for higher and secondary education, hospitals, health agencies, family planning, and the environment.
Types of support: Annual campaigns, building funds, continuing support, endowment funds, general purposes, operating budgets, scholarship funds, special projects.
Limitations: Giving primarily in the Cleveland, OH, area for community service grants; other grants awarded nationally. No grants to individuals.
Publications: Annual report.
Application information: Application form not required.
Initial approach: Proposal
Copies of proposal: 1
Deadline(s): May 31
Board meeting date(s): Within the first 2 weeks of June
Write: Donald C. Cook, Treas.
Officers: Coburn Haskell,* Pres.; Schuyler A. Haskell,* V.P.; Elizabeth C. Reed, Secy.; Donald C. Cook, Treas.
Trustees:* Melville H. Haskell, Jr., Mary H. Haywood.
Number of staff: None.
Employer Identification Number: 346513797

5749
The Hauss-Helms Foundation, Inc. ¤
Peoples National Bank Bldg.
P.O. Box 25
Wapakoneta 45895 (419) 738-4911

Incorporated in 1965 in OH.
Donor(s): Besse Hauss Helms,† W.B. Helms.†
Foundation type: Independent
Financial data (yr. ended 12/31/88): Assets, $6,355,161 (M); expenditures, $440,574, including $365,785 for 302 grants to individuals (high: $6,000; low: $35).
Purpose and activities: Scholarships for graduating high school students who are residents of Auglaize and Allen counties, OH.
Types of support: Student aid.
Limitations: Giving limited to residents of Auglaize and Allen counties, OH.
Publications: Program policy statement, application guidelines.
Application information: Application form required.
Initial approach: Letter
Copies of proposal: 1
Deadline(s): Jan. 15
Board meeting date(s): Jan., Mar., Apr., May, June, Dec., and as required
Write: James E. Weger, Pres.
Officers: James E. Weger, Pres.; Vincent G. Hudson, V.P.; Robert C. Lietz, Secy.-Treas.
Trustee: N. Thomas Cornell, Thomas R. Haehn.
Employer Identification Number: 340975903

5750
Hayfields Foundation ¤ ☆
4001 Carew Tower
Cincinnati 45202-2803

Established in 1946.
Donor(s): Louise F. Tate,† Charles F. Yeiser.
Foundation type: Independent
Financial data (yr. ended 12/31/88): Assets, $3,394,981 (M); gifts received, $633,300; expenditures, $1,862,915, including $1,815,960 for grants (high: $1,699,077).
Purpose and activities: Giving primarily for the benefit of a local village in the form of land for community development; support also for family planning, fine arts, education, welfare, and health associations.
Types of support: Land acquisition.
Limitations: Giving primarily in OH, particularly Indian Hill.
Officers: Eric B. Yeiser, Pres.; Charles F. Yeiser, V.P.; Robert E. Rich, Secy.-Treas.
Employer Identification Number: 316025518

5751
Hazelbaker Foundation ¤
1810 MacKenzie Dr.
Columbus 43220 (614) 457-7353

Established in 1985 in OH.
Donor(s): Ralph E. Hazelbaker.
Foundation type: Independent
Financial data (yr. ended 2/28/89): Assets, $1,102,161 (M); expenditures, $49,727, including $45,415 for 30 grants (high: $20,000; low: $50; average: $1,000-$20,000).
Purpose and activities: General charitable giving.
Types of support: Annual campaigns, fellowships, internships, matching funds, operating budgets, student aid.
Limitations: Giving primarily in OH.
Application information: Contributes only to pre-selected organizations. Applications not accepted.
Board meeting date(s): Quarterly
Write: Ralph E. Hazelbaker, Pres.
Officers: Ralph E. Hazelbaker, Pres.; Billie E. Hazelbaker, Secy.; R. Brian Hazelbaker, Treas.
Employer Identification Number: 311131197

5752
The Helping Hand Quilting Craft Foundation ¤
P.O. Box 295
Berlin 44610

Established in 1968.
Foundation type: Independent
Financial data (yr. ended 12/31/88): Assets, $1,625,245 (M); gifts received, $15,000; expenditures, $240,280, including $42,720 for 12 grants (high: $50,000; low: $200) and $18,914 for 1 foundation-administered program.
Purpose and activities: Giving for Mennonite church programs and community development, especially improvement of a park.
Limitations: Giving primarily in OH.
Application information:
Initial approach: Letter
Deadline(s): None
Write: The Trustees
Officers and Trustees: Alma Mullet, Pres.; Emanuel E. Mullet, V.P.; Ruby E. Hostetler, Secy.; Joe Yoder.
Employer Identification Number: 340996981

5753
The Hershey Foundation
Two Bratenahl Place
Bratenahl 44108

Established in 1986 in OH.
Donor(s): Jo Hershey Selden.
Foundation type: Independent
Financial data (yr. ended 12/31/89): Assets, $2,209,884 (M); gifts received, $1,010,000; expenditures, $56,781, including $54,365 for 14 grants (high: $30,000; low: $500).
Purpose and activities: Giving for "educational and charitable purposes with emphasis on innovative educational and cultural programs providing opportunities for children."
Types of support: Building funds, general purposes.
Limitations: Giving primarily in northeastern OH.

Application information: Application form required.
Copies of proposal: 2
Write: Jo Hershey Selden, Pres.
Officers and Trustees:* Jo Hershey Selden,* Pres.; Carole H. Walters,* V.P.; Debra S. Guren,* Secy.; Georgia A. Froelich, Loren Hershey.
Employer Identification Number: 341525626

5754
Heymann Foundation ⌑
c/o Ohio Citizens Bank
P.O. Box 1688
Toledo 43603-1688

Established in 1955 in OH.
Donor(s): Ohio Plate Glass.
Foundation type: Independent
Financial data (yr. ended 12/31/88): Assets, $1,198,895 (M); gifts received, $7,338; expenditures, $87,647, including $76,300 for 85 grants (high: $3,000; low: $100).
Purpose and activities: Giving primarily for higher and secondary educational institutions; support also for youth and child welfare organizations, social services, and Lutheran welfare and church organizations.
Limitations: Giving primarily in Toledo, OH. No grants to individuals.
Application information: Contributes only to pre-selected organizations. Applications not accepted.
Trustee: Ohio Citizens Bank.
Advisors: Paul F. Heymann, R.C. Heymann, Jr., James J. Murtagh.
Employer Identification Number: 346518714

5755
Charles F. High Foundation ⌑
1520 Melody Ln.
Bucyrus 44820 (419) 562-2074

Established in 1939 in Ohio.
Donor(s): Charles F. High.†
Foundation type: Independent
Financial data (yr. ended 12/31/88): Assets, $2,270,375 (M); expenditures, $209,133, including $190,853 for 104 grants to individuals (high: $2,479; low: $701).
Purpose and activities: Scholarships awarded only to male students of the State of OH to attend Ohio State University.
Types of support: Student aid.
Limitations: Giving limited to OH.
Application information: Application form required.
Initial approach: Letter
Deadline(s): June 1
Write: John R. Clime, Secy.-Treas.
Officers: J.H. Blicke, Pres.; John R. Clime, Secy.-Treas.
Trustees: F.J. Farmer, L.R. Likens, D.L. Wingate.
Employer Identification Number: 346527860

5756
Robert E. Hillier Family Charitable Trust
1365 Sharon-Copley Rd.
P.O. Box 70
Sharon Center 44274 (216) 239-2711

Established in 1974 in OH.
Donor(s): Pleadis Hillier,† Colon C. Hillier,† Ruth E. Hillier.†
Foundation type: Independent
Financial data (yr. ended 11/30/88): Assets, $4,355,550 (M); gifts received, $1,362,554; expenditures, $329,869, including $212,682 for 19 grants (high: $37,500; low: $90).
Purpose and activities: Support for youth, the aged, social service agencies, education, and churches.
Types of support: General purposes, scholarship funds.
Limitations: Giving primarily in Medina and Summit counties, OH.
Application information:
Initial approach: Letter
Deadline(s): Early in year
Write: Robert C. Bolon, Exec. Dir.
Officer: Robert C. Bolon,* Exec. Dir.
Trustees:* Henry S. Belden, Henry L. Metzger, John C. Swartz.
Employer Identification Number: 237425779

5757
C. C. Hobart Foundation ⌑
Hobart Sq.
Troy 45373

Established in 1942 in Ohio.
Donor(s): Hobart Brothers Co.
Foundation type: Independent
Financial data (yr. ended 12/31/88): Assets, $1,292,405 (M); gifts received, $50,000; expenditures, $151,267, including $140,750 for 53 grants (high: $40,000; low: $50).
Purpose and activities: Giving primarily for a hospital, social services, and education.
Limitations: Giving primarily in OH.
Officers and Directors: Ralph G. Ehlers, Pres. and Treas.; William H. Hobart, Secy.; Lucia H. Bravo, Peter C. Hobart, William B. Howell.
Employer Identification Number: 316030834

5758
Homan Foundation
6529 Willowhollow Ln.
Cincinnati 45243 (606) 341-6450
Application address: P.O. Box 17350, Edgewood, KY 41017

Foundation type: Independent
Financial data (yr. ended 12/31/88): Assets, $1,338,228 (M); expenditures, $95,475, including $92,950 for 66 grants (high: $15,000; low: $50).
Purpose and activities: Giving primarily for Roman Catholic schools and churches, other private schools, social services, and hospitals.
Limitations: Giving primarily in the Cincinnati, OH, area. No grants to individuals.
Application information: Application form not required.
Initial approach: Proposal
Deadline(s): Nov. 15
Write: John T. Collopy, Trustee
Trustees: John T. Collopy, Frank X. Homan, Margo S. Homan.
Employer Identification Number: 237038734

5759
Honda of America Foundation
Honda Pkwy.
Marysville 43040 (513) 642-5000

Established in 1981 in OH.
Donor(s): Honda of America Manufacturing, Inc.
Foundation type: Company-sponsored
Financial data (yr. ended 12/31/89): Assets, $2,000,000 (M); expenditures, $86,486, including $82,927 for 9 grants (high: $36,000; low: $978; average: $978-$36,000).
Purpose and activities: Support for educational institutions, cultural exchange, including an educators to Japan program, and medical research at a children's hospital.
Types of support: Scholarship funds.
Limitations: Giving primarily in areas where Honda of America facilities are located and associates reside in OH.
Application information: Application form not required.
Initial approach: Letter with proposal
Copies of proposal: 1
Write: Joan Burns, Staff Asst.
Officers and Trustees:* Hiroyuki Yoshino,* Pres.; Toshi Amino,* Exec. V.P.; Susan Insley,* Dir.; Tetsuo Chino.
Number of staff: None.
Employer Identification Number: 311006130

5760
The Hoover Foundation ▼
101 East Maple St.
North Canton 44720 (216) 499-9200

Trust established in 1945 in OH.
Donor(s): Members of the Hoover family.
Foundation type: Independent
Financial data (yr. ended 12/31/87): Assets, $37,128,847 (M); expenditures, $1,376,603, including $1,283,303 for 53 grants (high: $200,000; low: $100; average: $500-$50,000).
Purpose and activities: Grants for youth agencies, hospital building funds, community funds, and higher, secondary, and elementary education.
Types of support: Building funds, operating budgets, annual campaigns, scholarship funds, general purposes.
Limitations: Giving primarily in Stark County, OH. No grants to individuals, or for endowment funds.
Application information: Application form not required.
Initial approach: Letter
Deadline(s): None
Board meeting date(s): As required
Final notification: 1 week to 1 month
Write: Joseph S. Hoover, Chair.
Trust Committee: Joseph S. Hoover, Chair.; Ronald K. Bennington, Secy.; Herbert W. Hoover, Jr., Lawrence R. Hoover, W. Henry Hoover.
Trustee: Society Bank of Eastern Ohio, N.A.
Number of staff: None.
Employer Identification Number: 346510994

5761
W. Henry Hoover Fund-Trust ⌑
c/o Society Bank of Eastern Ohio, N.A.
126 Central Plaza North
Canton 44702
Application address: Society Bank of Eastern Ohio, N.A., P.O. Box 9950, Canton, OH 44711; Tel.: (216) 489-5419

Established in 1945 in OH.
Donor(s): W. Henry Hoover.†
Foundation type: Independent
Financial data (yr. ended 12/31/88): Assets, $2,836,404 (M); gifts received, $50,000; expenditures, $157,438, including $131,075 for 29 grants (high: $40,000; low: $50).
Purpose and activities: Giving primarily for a church, education, social services, and civic affairs.
Limitations: Giving primarily in OH.
Application information:
Initial approach: Proposal
Deadline(s): None
Write: Stephen C. Donatini
Trustee: Society Bank of Eastern Ohio, N.A.
Employer Identification Number: 346573738

5762
Dr. R. S. Hosler Memorial Educational Fund ⌑
50 Bortz St.
P.O. Box 5
Ashville 43103
Application address: 154 East Main St., Ashville, OH 43103

Foundation type: Independent
Financial data (yr. ended 12/31/88): Assets, $3,235,234 (M); expenditures, $208,024, including $118,876 for 1 grant and $49,452 for 5 grants to individuals (high: $24,179; low: $3,381).
Purpose and activities: Giving for scholarships and the Teays Valley and Amanda Clearcreek school districts.
Types of support: Student aid.
Limitations: Giving limited to graduates of Teays Valley and Amanda Clearcreek, OH, high schools.
Application information: Application form required.
Deadline(s): Mar. 1
Write: Leo J. Hall, Trustee
Trustee: Leo J. Hall.
Employer Identification Number: 311073939

5763
The Hostetler Foundation ⌑
3200 National City Ctr.
Cleveland 44114

Established in 1985 in OH.
Foundation type: Independent
Financial data (yr. ended 12/31/88): Assets, $1,047,037 (M); expenditures, $99,430, including $86,000 for 8 grants (high: $50,000; low: $1,000).
Purpose and activities: Giving primarily for higher education, especially legal education; support also for the United Way and a family planning organization.
Types of support: General purposes.
Limitations: Giving primarily in Cleveland, OH.
Application information: Application form not required.
Initial approach: Proposal
Deadline(s): None
Write: John D. Drinko, Treas.
Officers and Trustees:* John D. Drinko,* Chair. and Treas.; Daniel C. Prior,* Pres.; Jean T. Prior,* V.P.; James E. Chapman, Secy.; Elizabeth D. Drinko, J. Richard Hamilton.
Employer Identification Number: 341476061

5764
Letha E. House Foundation ⌑
698 East Washington St., Suite 1-B
Medina 44256 (216) 723-6404

Established in 1967 in OH.
Foundation type: Independent
Financial data (yr. ended 06/30/89): Assets, $1,340,497 (M); expenditures, $88,349, including $66,322 for 4 grants (high: $24,322; low: $4,000).
Purpose and activities: Support primarily for historical restoration projects.
Types of support: Renovation projects, operating budgets.
Limitations: Giving primarily in the Medina County, OH, area.
Application information:
Initial approach: Letter
Deadline(s): None
Write: Charles Clark Griesinger, Trustee
Trustees: Charles Clark Griesinger, Paul M. Jones, Old Phoenix National Bank of Medina.
Employer Identification Number: 237025122

5765
The Howland Memorial Fund ☆
2080 Stockbridge Rd.
Akron 44313 (216) 867-3020

Established in 1974 in OH.
Donor(s): Mame E. Howland.†
Foundation type: Independent
Financial data (yr. ended 12/31/88): Assets, $1,325,349 (M); expenditures, $96,273, including $75,520 for 17 grants (high: $30,320; low: $500).
Purpose and activities: Giving primarily for higher education, social services, the arts, and Episcopal churches.
Types of support: Building funds, capital campaigns, endowment funds, scholarship funds.
Limitations: Giving primarily in Akron, OH. No grants to individuals, or for conferences or workshops, operating budgets, or continuing support.
Application information: Majority of funding initiated by trustees. Application form not required.
Initial approach: Letter (not exceeding 3 pages)
Copies of proposal: 1
Deadline(s): Grant decisions generally made between Dec. 15 and Jan. 15
Write: John V. Frank, Trustee
Trustees: John V. Frank, Paul A. Frank.
Number of staff: None.
Employer Identification Number: 346709057

5766
The Huffy Foundation, Inc.
P.O. Box 1204
Dayton 45401 (513) 866-6251

Incorporated in OH in 1959 as Huffman Foundation; name changed in 1978.
Donor(s): Huffy Corp.
Foundation type: Company-sponsored
Financial data (yr. ended 06/30/89): Assets, $266,902 (M); expenditures, $247,278, including $236,120 for 83 grants (high: $45,000; low: $100; average: $1,000) and $9,235 for 34 employee matching gifts.
Purpose and activities: Support for higher education, cultural programs, youth agencies, community funds, civic affairs, and health.
Types of support: Operating budgets, continuing support, annual campaigns, seed money, emergency funds, matching funds, scholarship funds, special projects, publications, employee matching gifts, conferences and seminars, building funds, capital campaigns, consulting services, general purposes.
Limitations: Giving primarily in areas of company operations in OH, CO, CA, and WI. Generally no operational grant support for agencies covered by the United Way. No grants to individuals, or for deficit financing, endowment funds, research, or fellowships; no loans.
Publications: Informational brochure (including application guidelines).
Application information: Application form not required.
Initial approach: Letter or proposal
Copies of proposal: 1
Deadline(s): None
Board meeting date(s): Apr., Aug., and Dec.
Final notification: Approximately 2 weeks after board meetings
Write: R.R. Wieland, Secy.
Officers: Harry A. Shaw,* Pres.; R.R. Wieland, Secy.
Trustees:* F.C. Smith, Chair.; S.J. Northrop.
Number of staff: None.
Employer Identification Number: 316023716

5767
Gilbert W. & Louise Ireland Humphrey Foundation ⌑
1010 Hanna Bldg.
Cleveland 44115 (216) 363-6486

Incorporated in 1951 in OH.
Donor(s): Gilbert W. Humphrey,† Louise Ireland Humphrey.
Foundation type: Independent
Financial data (yr. ended 12/31/88): Assets, $1,467,504 (M); gifts received, $43,022; expenditures, $181,248, including $171,500 for 25 grants (high: $46,000; low: $500; average: $1,000-$5,000).
Purpose and activities: Emphasis on educational institutions, music, cultural programs, a community fund, hospitals, and social service agencies.
Limitations: Giving primarily in OH. No grants to individuals.
Publications: 990-PF.
Application information: Funds committed to the same charities each year; foundation rarely

considers new appeals. Application form not required.
Initial approach: Letter
Copies of proposal: 1
Deadline(s): Submit proposal preferably in 1st quarter of year; deadline Sept. 1
Board meeting date(s): 1st Tuesday of Nov.
Write: Louise Ireland Humphrey, Pres.
Officers and Trustees:* Louise Ireland Humphrey,* Pres.; Margaret H. Bindhardt,* V.P.; M.G. Mikolaj,* Secy.; George M. Humphrey II, Treas.
Employer Identification Number: 346525832

5768
George M. and Pamela S. Humphrey Fund ¤
c/o Advisory Services, Inc.
1010 Hanna Bldg., 1422 Euclid Ave.
Cleveland 44115-2078 (216) 363-6483

Incorporated in 1951 in OH.
Donor(s): George M. Humphrey,† Pamela S. Humphrey.†
Foundation type: Independent
Financial data (yr. ended 12/31/88): Assets, $6,653,572 (M); expenditures, $455,331, including $420,225 for 61 grants (high: $50,000; low: $500).
Purpose and activities: Support for hospitals, higher and secondary education, and community funds; support also for cultural programs and health agencies.
Types of support: Operating budgets, continuing support, annual campaigns, emergency funds, building funds, equipment, endowment funds, matching funds, professorships, internships, research, technical assistance.
Limitations: Giving primarily in OH. No grants to individuals; no loans.
Publications: Annual report.
Application information: Application form not required.
Initial approach: Letter or proposal
Copies of proposal: 1
Deadline(s): Prior to board meetings
Board meeting date(s): Apr., Nov., and Dec.
Final notification: 1 month
Write: Jackie A. Horning, Secy.-Treas.
Officers: Carol H. Butler,* Pres.; John G. Butler,* V.P.; Jackie A. Horning, Secy.-Treas.
Trustees:* Pamela B. Rutter.
Employer Identification Number: 346513798

5769
Hunter Fund ¤
c/o Advisory Services, Inc.
1010 Hanna Bldg., 1422 Euclid Ave.
Cleveland 44115-2078 (216) 363-6483

Established in 1956 in OH.
Foundation type: Independent
Financial data (yr. ended 12/31/88): Assets, $1,233,761 (M); expenditures, $118,318, including $105,700 for 19 grants (high: $20,000; low: $1,000).
Purpose and activities: Giving for hospitals and medical purposes, social services, higher education, and an environmental museum.
Limitations: Giving primarily in AZ and KY. No grants to individuals.
Application information:
Initial approach: Proposal
Deadline(s): Aug. 31
Board meeting date(s): 1st 2 weeks in Sept.
Write: Jackie A. Horning, Treas.
Officers and Trustees: Barbara Hunter,* Pres.; J. Rukin Jelks, Jr., V.P.; R.S. St. John, Secy.; Jackie A. Horning, Treas.; Carolyn G. Jelks.
Employer Identification Number: 346513679

5770
The John Huntington Fund for Education
822 National City Bank Bldg.
Cleveland 44114 (216) 861-0777

Incorporated in 1954 in OH.
Donor(s): John Huntington.†
Foundation type: Independent
Financial data (yr. ended 12/31/88): Assets, $22,923,945 (M); qualifying distributions, $1,000,000, including $1,000,000 for 10 grants (high: $420,700; low: $13,000).
Purpose and activities: A limited number of tuition grants and grants-in-aid varying in amount are available to residents of Cuyahoga County, OH, for study there in scientific and technological fields on full- or part-time, day or evening schedules. Grants are made to and administered by the educational institutions.
Types of support: Scholarship funds.
Limitations: Giving limited to Cuyahoga County, OH. No grants to individuals.
Application information:
Initial approach: Letter
Copies of proposal: 1
Deadline(s): Apr. 30
Board meeting date(s): Usually in June
Write: Morris Everett, Treas.
Officers: Peter W. Adams,* Pres.; Earla Mae Inks, Exec. Secy.; Oakley Andrews,* Secy.; Morris Everett,* Treas.
Trustees:* Albert J. Abramovitz, Robert M. Ginn, Karen Horn, Susan Murray, R. Henry Norweb, Jr., Leigh H. Perkins.
Number of staff: 1
Employer Identification Number: 340714434

5771
John F. and Loretta A. Hynes Foundation
c/o Mahoning National Bank of Youngstown
Box 479
Youngstown 44501 (216) 742-7000

Established in 1957 in OH.
Foundation type: Independent
Financial data (yr. ended 12/31/89): Assets, $1,421,897 (M); expenditures, $88,396, including $79,300 for 13 grants (high: $12,500; low: $1,000).
Purpose and activities: Giving primarily for arts organizations, hospitals, education, and youth programs.
Types of support: Equipment, capital campaigns, special projects, renovation projects.
Limitations: Giving primarily in the Youngstown, OH, area. No grants to individuals.
Application information: Application form not required.
Initial approach: Proposal
Deadline(s): None
Write: Patrick A. Sebastiano, Sr. V.P. and Sr. Trust Officer, Mahoning National Bank of Youngstown
Officers: John M. Newman, Chair.; W.W. Bresnahan, Vice-Chair.
Members: William J. Mullen, Gregory L. Ridler, Arthur G. Young.
Trustee Bank: Mahoning National Bank of Youngstown.
Number of staff: None.
Employer Identification Number: 346516440

5772
Iddings Foundation ¤
Kettering Tower, Suite 1620
Dayton 45423 (513) 224-1773

Trust established in 1973 in OH.
Donor(s): Roscoe C. Iddings,† Andrew S. Iddings.†
Foundation type: Independent
Financial data (yr. ended 12/31/88): Assets, $7,662,903 (M); expenditures, $521,897, including $454,806 for 67 grants (high: $30,000; low: $100; average: $5-$10,000).
Purpose and activities: Grants for pre-college and higher education, health care, mental health, care of the aged and handicapped, youth agencies, cultural programs, the environment, community welfare, and population control.
Types of support: Operating budgets, continuing support, annual campaigns, seed money, emergency funds, building funds, equipment, land acquisition, scholarship funds, special projects, publications, consulting services, capital campaigns, conferences and seminars, general purposes, matching funds, renovation projects.
Limitations: Giving limited to OH, with emphasis on the Dayton metropolitan area. No grants to individuals, or for endowment funds or deficit financing; no loans.
Publications: Informational brochure (including application guidelines), multi-year report.
Application information: Application form not required.
Initial approach: Letter or telephone
Copies of proposal: 8
Deadline(s): Mar. 1, June 1, Sept. 1, or Nov. 1
Board meeting date(s): Apr., July, Oct., and Dec.
Final notification: 1 week following meeting of distribution committee
Write: Maribeth A. Eiken, Admin.
Trustee: Bank One, Dayton, N.A.
Number of staff: 1 part-time professional.
Employer Identification Number: 316135058

5773
The Louise H. and David S. Ingalls Foundation, Inc. ¤
301 Tower East
20600 Chagrin Blvd.
Shaker Heights 44122 (216) 921-6000

Incorporated in 1953 in OH.
Donor(s): Louise H. Ingalls,† Edith Ingalls Vignos, Louise Ingalls Brown, David S. Ingalls,† David S. Ingalls, Jr., Jane I. Davison, Anne I. Lawrence.
Foundation type: Independent

Financial data (yr. ended 12/31/88): Assets, $11,110,658 (M); expenditures, $600,364, including $573,500 for 18 grants (high: $205,500; low: $2,500).
Purpose and activities: "The improvement of the physical, educational, mental, and moral condition of humanity throughout the world"; grants largely for higher and secondary education; support also for community funds, health, and cultural programs. Support mainly to organizations known to the trustees.
Types of support: Special projects, building funds, capital campaigns, research, endowment funds, equipment.
Limitations: Giving primarily in Cleveland, OH. No grants to individuals.
Application information: Application form not required.
Initial approach: Proposal
Copies of proposal: 5
Deadline(s): None
Board meeting date(s): As required
Write: David S. Ingalls, Jr., Pres.
Officers: David S. Ingalls, Jr.,* Pres. and Treas.; Louise Ingalls Brown,* V.P.; Edith Ingalls Vignos,* V.P.; James H. Dempsey, Jr., Secy.
Trustees:* Jane I. Davison, Anne I. Lawrence.
Number of staff: 2 part-time support.
Employer Identification Number: 346516550

5774
Ingram-White Castle Foundation
(Formerly Edgar W. Ingram Foundation)
1234 East Broad St.
Columbus 43205 (614) 251-4000

Incorporated in 1949 in OH.
Donor(s): Edgar W. Ingram,† White Castle System, Inc.
Foundation type: Independent
Financial data (yr. ended 12/31/89): Assets, $8,758,245 (M); expenditures, $714,309, including $680,865 for 52 grants (high: $100,000; low: $400; average: $5,000-$25,000).
Purpose and activities: A supporting organization of the Columbus Foundation, with support primarily for elementary, secondary, and higher education.
Types of support: General purposes, scholarship funds, capital campaigns, matching funds, publications, renovation projects, scholarship funds, seed money, special projects.
Limitations: Giving primarily in the central OH, area.
Publications: Informational brochure (including application guidelines).
Application information: Application form required.
Initial approach: Meeting with staff prior to submission of application
Copies of proposal: 4
Deadline(s): 1st Friday in Sept. and Feb.
Board meeting date(s): Apr., Sept., and Nov.
Write: Ann Bryson
Officers: Edgar W. Ingram III, Pres.; Mrs. Robert H. Jeffrey II, V.P.; Robert D. Hays, Secy.
Trustees: John S. Kobacker, Thekla R. Shackelford.
Number of staff: 18
Employer Identification Number: 316051433

5775
The Ireland Foundation ⌑
1010 Hanna Bldg., 1422 Euclid Ave.
Cleveland 44115 (216) 363-6486

Incorporated in 1951 in OH.
Donor(s): Margaret Allen Ireland,† R. Livingston Ireland,† Kate Ireland, and members of the Ireland family.
Foundation type: Independent
Financial data (yr. ended 12/31/88): Assets, $7,326,496 (M); expenditures, $462,396, including $390,000 for 73 grants (high: $100,000; low: $100; average: $1,000-$5,000).
Purpose and activities: Grants largely for educational and charitable programs, with emphasis on nursing, higher and secondary education, and hospitals; grants also for music.
Types of support: General purposes.
Limitations: Giving primarily in Cleveland, OH. No grants to individuals.
Application information: Funds committed to the same charities each year; foundation rarely considers new appeals. Applications not accepted.
Initial approach: Letter and brief proposal
Board meeting date(s): 1st Tuesday of Nov.
Officers: Louise Ireland Humphrey,* Pres. and Treas.; Kate Ireland,* V.P.; M.G. Mikolaj, Secy.
Trustees:* R.L. Ireland III.
Employer Identification Number: 346525817

5776
Irwin J. Jaeger Foundation
c/o Barbara S. Bromberg
1700 Central Trust Tower
Cincinnati 45202

Established in 1971 in OH.
Donor(s): Irwin J. Jaeger.
Foundation type: Independent
Financial data (yr. ended 11/30/89): Assets, $1,525,927 (M); qualifying distributions, $91,151, including $91,151 for 10 grants (high: $62,214; low: $150).
Purpose and activities: Giving primarily to Jewish organizations, underprivileged children, and the advancement of the arts.
Types of support: Continuing support, equipment, operating budgets.
Limitations: Giving primarily in southern CA.
Application information: Application form not required.
Copies of proposal: 1
Officer: Irwin J. Jaeger, Pres. and Treas.
Trustees: Patricia Jaeger, Richard Jaeger.
Employer Identification Number: 237154491

5777
Isaac & Esther Jarson - Stanley & Mickey Kaplan Foundation
(Formerly Isaac N. and Esther M. Jarson Charitable Trust)
105 East Fourth St., Suite 710
Cincinnati 45202 (513) 721-5086

Trust established in 1955 in OH.
Foundation type: Independent
Financial data (yr. ended 12/31/89): Assets, $3,243,975 (M); expenditures, $172,598, including $158,784 for 73 grants (high: $40,000; low: $25).
Purpose and activities: Giving for civic affairs, education, and cultural programs.
Limitations: Giving primarily in Cincinnati, OH.
Application information:
Write: Stanley M. Kaplan or Myran J. Kaplan, Mgrs.
Officers: Myran J. Kaplan, Mgr.; Stanley M. Kaplan, Mgr.
Employer Identification Number: 316033453

5778
Jasam Foundation, Inc. ⌑
3518 Rue de Fleur
Columbus 43221

Established in 1953 in OH.
Foundation type: Independent
Financial data (yr. ended 12/31/88): Assets, $6,833,806 (M); expenditures, $39,075, including $35,850 for 14 grants (high: $25,000; low: $250).
Purpose and activities: Giving for charitable purposes, including an academy.
Types of support: Seed money, special projects.
Limitations: Giving primarily in Franklin County, OH.
Application information: Contributes only to pre-selected organizations. Applications not accepted.
Officers: Jeanette A. Davis, Pres.; Jane Ferger, Secy.
Trustees: Samuel B. Davis, Joan Guylas.
Number of staff: None.
Employer Identification Number: 316036574

5779
The Martha Holden Jennings Foundation ▼
710 Halle Bldg.
1228 Euclid Ave.
Cleveland 44115 (216) 589-5700
Business office: 20620 North Park Blvd., No. 215, Shaker Heights, OH 44118; Tel.: (216) 932-7337

Incorporated in 1959 in OH.
Donor(s): Martha Holden Jennings.†
Foundation type: Independent
Financial data (yr. ended 12/31/88): Assets, $45,039,560 (M); gifts received, $9,287; expenditures, $2,703,642, including $1,354,912 for 114 grants (high: $57,000; low: $500; average: $1,000-$30,000) and $770,234 for 16 foundation-administered programs.
Purpose and activities: Giving to foster development of the capabilities of young people through improving the quality of teaching in secular elementary and secondary schools; program includes awards in recognition of outstanding teaching; special educational programs for teachers in the fields of the humanities, the arts, and the sciences; awards to deserving students in furtherance of their recognized abilities; curriculum development projects; school evaluation studies; and educational television programs.
Types of support: Continuing support, seed money, matching funds, special projects, conferences and seminars.
Limitations: Giving limited to OH. No grants to individuals (except awards by nomination), or for operating budgets, annual campaigns, travel, emergency funds, deficit financing,

capital or endowment funds, research, or publications; no loans.
Publications: Annual report, newsletter, program policy statement, application guidelines.
Application information: Application form required for Grants to Teachers Program. Application form not required.
Initial approach: 1-page project summary, cover letter, budget, and proposal
Copies of proposal: 9
Deadline(s): 20th of each month preceding month in which application is to be considered
Board meeting date(s): Advisory and Distribution Committee meets monthly, except July and Dec.
Final notification: 6 to 8 weeks
Write: Dr. Richard A. Boyd, Exec. Dir.
Officers and Trustees:* Arthur S. Holden, Jr.,* Chair.; George B. Chapman, Jr.,* Pres.; William F. Hauserman,* V.P.; John H. Gherlein,* Secy.; Allen H. Ford,* Treas.; Richard A. Boyd,* Exec. Dir.; Robert M. Ginn.
Number of staff: 3 full-time professional; 1 full-time support; 2 part-time support.
Employer Identification Number: 340934478

5780
The Andrew Jergens Foundation ⌑
c/o The Central Trust Co., N.A.
P.O. Box 1198
Cincinnati 45201 (513) 651-8377

Incorporated in 1962 in OH.
Donor(s): Andrew N. Jergens.†
Foundation type: Independent
Financial data (yr. ended 8/31/88): Assets, $5,258,598 (M); gifts received, $17,254; expenditures, $656,712, including $587,005 for 51 grants (high: $50,000; low: $300; average: $3,000-$8,000).
Purpose and activities: To promote the health, education, social welfare, and cultural experiences of children from pre-school through high school age.
Types of support: Seed money, special projects, building funds, capital campaigns, equipment, land acquisition, renovation projects.
Limitations: Giving limited to the greater Cincinnati, OH, area. No grants to individuals, or for continuing support, annual campaigns, endowment funds, deficit financing, scholarships, fellowships, or research; no loans.
Publications: Application guidelines, program policy statement.
Application information: Application form not required.
Initial approach: Letter or telephone
Copies of proposal: 9
Deadline(s): Submit proposal preferably in months when board does not meet; deadlines Oct. 1, Jan. 1, Apr. 1, or July 1
Board meeting date(s): Nov., Feb., May, and Aug.
Final notification: 1 month after meetings
Write: Nancy C. Gurney, Admin.
Officers and Trustees: Rev. Andrew N. Jergens, Jr., Pres.; Mary Ann Hays, V.P.; Leonard S. Meranus, Secy.-Treas.; John W. Beatty, Thomas C. Hays, Linda Busken Jergens, Lavatus V. Powell, Jr.
Number of staff: 1
Employer Identification Number: 316038702

5781
The Jochum-Moll Foundation ⌑
5389 West 130th St., P.O. Box 2741
Cleveland 44111

Incorporated in 1961 in OH.
Donor(s): MTD Products, Inc., and its subsidiaries.
Foundation type: Company-sponsored
Financial data (yr. ended 7/31/88): Assets, $11,214,781 (M); gifts received, $257,450; expenditures, $584,848, including $529,700 for 40 grants (high: $66,000; low: $200).
Purpose and activities: Emphasis on higher and secondary education and hospitals; grants also for a community fund, welfare, and Protestant church support.
Limitations: Giving primarily in OH.
Officers and Trustees: Theo Moll, Pres.; Emil Jochum, V.P.; David J. Hessler, Secy.; Curtis E. Moll, Treas.; Emma Gerhard, Darrell Moll.
Employer Identification Number: 346538304

5782
The Juilfs Foundation ⌑
8485 Broadwell Rd.
Cincinnati 45244

Established in 1962 in OH.
Foundation type: Independent
Financial data (yr. ended 12/31/88): Assets, $2,227,991 (M); expenditures, $117,589, including $113,400 for 43 grants (high: $47,000; low: $100).
Purpose and activities: Emphasis on higher education, hospitals, the arts, youth agencies, and a community fund.
Limitations: Giving primarily in the greater Cincinnati, OH, area.
Application information:
Initial approach: Letter
Deadline(s): None
Write: George C. Juilfs, Trustee
Trustees: George C. Juilfs, Howard W. Juilfs, Faye Kuluris.
Employer Identification Number: 316027571

5783
The Robert E., Harry A., and M. Sylvia Kangesser Foundation ⌑
1801 East Ninth St., No. 1220
Cleveland 44114 (216) 621-5747

Incorporated in 1947 in OH.
Donor(s): Robert E. Kangesser,† Harry A. Kangesser,† M. Sylvia Kangesser.†
Foundation type: Independent
Financial data (yr. ended 12/31/88): Assets, $3,500,000 (M); expenditures, $340,000, including $320,000 for 23 grants (high: $150,000; low: $200).
Purpose and activities: Support largely for Jewish educational organizations; support also for non-denominational health and medical services and civic affairs.
Types of support: General purposes, building funds, annual campaigns, continuing support, operating budgets, capital campaigns.
Limitations: Giving primarily in the greater Cleveland, OH, area.
Application information: Application form not required.
Initial approach: Proposal
Deadline(s): Aug. 31
Board meeting date(s): Usually in Sept. or Oct.
Write: David G. Kangesser, Pres.
Officers and Trustees: David G. Kangesser, Pres.; Helen Kangesser, V.P.; Hedy Kangesser, Treas.
Employer Identification Number: 346529478

5784
G. Martin Kenney Trust ⌑
100 East Broad St.
Columbus 43271-0191
Application address: American State Bank, Ligonier, IN 46767; Tel.: (219) 894-4141

Established in 1967 in OH.
Foundation type: Independent
Financial data (yr. ended 12/31/87): Assets, $607,647 (M); expenditures, $134,713, including $125,000 for 1 grant.
Purpose and activities: Giving primarily for community projects and religious institutions.
Limitations: Giving limited to Ligonier, IN.
Application information: Application form required.
Deadline(s): None
Write: Frederick Lamble
Trustees: American State Bank of Ligonier, Bank One, Columbus, N.A.
Employer Identification Number: 316068232

5785
The Kettering Family Foundation
1440 Kettering Tower
Dayton 45423 (513) 228-1021

Incorporated in 1955 in IL; reincorporated in 1966 in OH.
Donor(s): E.W. Kettering,† Virginia W. Kettering, J.K. Lombard, S.K. Williamson, P.D. Williamson, M.D., Richard D. Lombard, B. Weiffenbach,† Charles F. Kettering III.
Foundation type: Independent
Financial data (yr. ended 12/31/89): Assets, $7,715,412 (M); expenditures, $424,974, including $357,400 for 24 grants (high: $100,000; low: $400; average: $5,000-$25,000).
Purpose and activities: Support largely for higher and secondary education, cultural programs, conservation, and specialized medical research.
Types of support: Operating budgets, annual campaigns, seed money, deficit financing, building funds, equipment, land acquisition, endowment funds, special projects, research, publications, capital campaigns, continuing support, general purposes, matching funds.
Limitations: No support for foreign purposes or religious organizations. No grants to individuals, or for scholarships or fellowships; no loans.
Publications: Annual report.
Application information: Application form not required.
Initial approach: Letter stating amount requested
Copies of proposal: 1
Deadline(s): Mar. 1 and Sept. 1

Board meeting date(s): Mid-May and mid-Nov.
Final notification: 1 month after board meetings
Write: Jack L. Fischer, Secy.
Officers: Charles F. Kettering III,* Pres.; Susan K. Beck,* V.P.; Debra L. Williamson,* V.P.; Jane K. Lombard,* Secy.-Treas.; Jack L. Fischer, Secy.; Jonathan G. Verity, Treas.
Trustees:* Matthew B. Beck, Kyle W. Cox, Mark A. Cox, Douglas J. Cushnie, Karen W. Cushnie, Linda K. Danneberg, William H. Danneberg, Lisa S. Kettering, Virginia W. Kettering, Richard J. Lombard, Douglas E. Williamson, Leslie G. Williamson, P.D. Williamson, M.D., Susan K. Williamson.
Number of staff: None.
Employer Identification Number: 310727384

5786
Charles F. Kettering Foundation
200 Commons Rd.
Dayton 45459-2799 (513) 434-7300
Additional tel.: (800) 221-3657; in OH, (800) 523-0078

Incorporated in 1927 in OH.
Donor(s): Charles F. Kettering.†
Foundation type: Operating
Financial data (yr. ended 12/31/89): Assets, $144,308,137 (M); gifts received, $524,176; expenditures, $7,358,295, including $375,000 for 15 grants (high: $150,000; low: $4,500) and $2,948,032 for foundation-administered programs.
Purpose and activities: A private operating foundation concentrating in the areas of governing, educating, and science, particularly in how they interrelate on an international basis. Applies available funds to research efforts generally designed by foundation staff, but welcomes partnerships with other institutions and individuals who are actively working on similar problems.
Types of support: Research.
Limitations: No grants to individuals.
Publications: Newsletter.
Application information: Except for research partnerships, the foundation does not make grants. Applications not accepted.
Board meeting date(s): May and Nov.
Write: James P. Schwartzhoff, V.P. and Treas.
Officers: David Mathews,* Pres. and C.E.O.; James P. Schwartzhoff, V.P. and Treas.
Trustees:* Madeline H. McWhinney, Chair.; Lisle C. Carter, Jr., Nathaniel S. Colley, Sr., Lawrence A. Cremin, Katharine W. Fanning, Robert W. Lundeen, James R. Thomas, William F. Winter, Daniel Yankelovich.
Number of staff: 20 full-time professional; 22 full-time support; 13 part-time support.
Employer Identification Number: 310549056

5787
The Kettering Fund ▼
1440 Kettering Tower
Dayton 45423 (513) 228-1021

Established in 1958 in OH.
Donor(s): Charles F. Kettering.†
Foundation type: Independent
Financial data (yr. ended 06/30/89): Assets, $60,108,259 (M); expenditures, $3,680,111, including $3,641,925 for 36 grants (high: $2,000,000; low: $1,000; average: $5,000-$50,000).
Purpose and activities: Grants for scientific, medical, social, and educational studies and research; support also for community development and cultural programs, including the performing arts.
Limitations: Giving primarily in OH. No support for religious purposes. No grants to individuals, or for fellowships or scholarships; no loans.
Application information: Application form not required.
Initial approach: Brief outline of proposal in letter form
Copies of proposal: 1
Deadline(s): Apr. 1 and Oct. 1
Board meeting date(s): Usually in mid-May and mid-Nov.
Final notification: 10 days to 2 weeks after meeting date
Write: Jack L. Fischer
Distribution Committee and Trustee:* Susan K. Beck, Member; Virginia W. Kettering,* Member; Jane K. Lombard, Member; Susan K. Williamson, Member.
Trustee Bank: Bank One, Dayton, N.A.
Number of staff: None.
Employer Identification Number: 316027115

5788
Kibble Foundation ⌑
P.O. Box 723
Pomeroy 45769

Established in 1976.
Foundation type: Independent
Financial data (yr. ended 12/31/88): Assets, $2,714,753 (M); expenditures, $237,368, including $178,537 for grants to individuals.
Purpose and activities: Giving for scholarships only to local area full-time students pursuing four-year degrees or lesser technical degrees.
Types of support: Student aid.
Limitations: Giving limited to graduates of Meigs County, OH, high schools.
Trustee: Bernard V. Fultz.
Employer Identification Number: 316175971

5789
Charles Kilburger Scholarship Fund ⌑
Equitable Bldg.
Lancaster 43130 (614) 653-0461

Established in 1968 in OH.
Donor(s): Charles Kilburger.†
Foundation type: Independent
Financial data (yr. ended 5/31/89): Assets, $3,076,935 (M); expenditures, $237,036, including $176,020 for 80 grants to individuals (high: $5,000; low: $400).
Purpose and activities: Scholarship grants to local area students for higher education.
Types of support: Student aid.
Limitations: Giving limited to residents of Fairfield County, OH.
Application information: Students are recommended by guidance counselors at high schools and colleges. Applications not accepted.
Write: Mr. and Mrs. Kermit Sitterly
Trustee: Kermit Sitterley.
Employer Identification Number: 316086870

5790
William H. Kilcawley Fund ☆
c/o The Dollar Savings & Trust Co.
P.O. Box 450
Youngstown 44501-0450

Established in 1946.
Foundation type: Independent
Financial data (yr. ended 12/31/89): Assets, $1,830,276 (M); expenditures, $383,808, including $373,700 for 19 grants (high: $110,000; low: $500; average: $500-$25,000).
Purpose and activities: Giving primarily for higher and other education, Christian churches, community funds, performing and other arts, including museums, and health and social services, including youth and child development, programs for the aged and the homeless, and alcohol abuse programs.
Types of support: Annual campaigns, building funds, capital campaigns, equipment, general purposes.
Limitations: Giving primarily in OH. No grants to individuals.
Application information:
Initial approach: Letter or proposal
Copies of proposal: 1
Deadline(s): None
Appointing Committee: Anne K. Christman.
Trustee: The Dollar Savings & Trust Co.
Employer Identification Number: 346515643

5791
The Klein Foundation
1771 East 30th St.
Cleveland 44114-4469 (216) 623-0370

Established in 1979 in OH.
Foundation type: Independent
Financial data (yr. ended 9/30/89): Assets, $21,457 (M); gifts received, $101,512; expenditures, $113,363, including $109,513 for 68 grants (high: $13,000; low: $50).
Purpose and activities: Support primarily for the arts and museums; support also for higher education, churches, and environmental conservation.
Limitations: Giving primarily in Cleveland, OH.
Application information: Application form not required.
Deadline(s): None
Officers: G. Robert Klein, Chair.; George R. Klein, Pres.; Marilyn E. Brown, Secy.
Employer Identification Number: 341288590

5792
Knight Foundation ▼
One Cascade Plaza
Akron 44308 (216) 253-9301
FAX: (216) 253-8092

Incorporated in 1950 in OH.
Donor(s): John S. Knight,† James L. Knight, and their families and associates.
Foundation type: Independent
Financial data (yr. ended 12/31/89): Assets, $581,138,052 (M); gifts received, $9,090,417; expenditures, $20,562,205, including $16,665,311 for 337 grants (high: $1,000,000; low: $1,000; average: $5,000-$100,000).
Purpose and activities: Grants primarily for education, culture, health, and social service programs initiated by organizations in cities where Knight-Ridder newspapers are located;

giving on a national scale for print journalism, higher education, and arts and culture.
Types of support: Special projects, building funds, capital campaigns, endowment funds, fellowships, general purposes, matching funds, scholarship funds, seed money, renovation projects.
Limitations: Giving limited to areas where Knight-Ridder newspapers are published: CA, CO, FL, GA, IN, KS, KY, MI, MN, MS, NC, ND, OH, PA, SC, and SD for Cities Program; Journalism and Arts and Culture programs are national in scope. No support for organizations with grantmaking activities other than community foundations; organizations whose mission is to prevent, eradicate and/or alleviate the effects of a specific disease; religious purposes; or political campaigns. No grants to individuals, or for annual fundraising campaigns or dinners; general operating support; operating deficits; trips or uniforms for bands; films, videos, or television programs; honoraria; scholarly research leading to a book; group travel; memorials; or medical research.
Publications: Annual report (including application guidelines), application guidelines, informational brochure (including application guidelines).
Application information: Considers only 1 request from an organization during a 12-month period; all proposals must have endorsement of president of organization or institution requesting grant. Application form not required.
Initial approach: Letter
Copies of proposal: 2
Deadline(s): Jan. 1, Apr. 1, July 1, and Oct. 1
Board meeting date(s): Mar., June, Sept., and Dec.
Final notification: 2 weeks after meeting dates
Write: Creed C. Black, Pres.
Officers and Trustees:* James L. Knight,* Chair.; Lee Hills,* Vice-Chair.; Creed C. Black,* Pres.; James D. Spaniolo,* V.P. and Secy.; David J. Catrow,* Treas.; W. Gerald Austen, James K. Batten, Alvah H. Chapman, Jr., Charles E. Clark, C.C. Gibson, Gordon E. Heffern, Rolfe Neill, Beverly Knight Olson, Henry King Stanford, Barbara Knight Toomey.
Number of staff: 4 full-time professional; 3 full-time support; 1 part-time support.
Employer Identification Number: 346519827

5793
William & Elsie Knight Foundation ☆
c/o Society Bank & Trust
P.O. Box 10099
Toledo 43699-0099 (419) 259-8058

Established in 1957.
Foundation type: Independent
Financial data (yr. ended 12/31/88): Assets, $1,084,801 (M); expenditures, $116,788, including $105,200 for 40 grants (high: $25,000; low: $100).
Purpose and activities: Support for community funds, higher and other education, hospitals and health associations, social services, and cultural programs.
Limitations: Giving primarily in Toledo, OH.
Application information: Applications not accepted.
Write: Michael Judge
Trustee: Society Bank & Trust.
Advisors: Diana K. Foster, Elsie S. Knight, John L. Knight, Robert A. Stranahan, Jr.
Number of staff: None.
Employer Identification Number: 346504813

5794
Louise Kramer Foundation
c/o Society Bank Trust Dept.
34 North Main St.
Dayton 45402 (513) 226-6076

Established in 1965 in OH.
Donor(s): Louise Kramer.†
Foundation type: Independent
Financial data (yr. ended 12/31/87): Assets, $2,944,552 (M); expenditures, $258,420, including $233,000 for 38 grants (high: $50,000; low: $1,000).
Purpose and activities: Emphasis on higher and other education, health agencies, the handicapped, church support, community funds, youth agencies and child welfare, and the arts.
Types of support: Building funds, capital campaigns, operating budgets.
Limitations: Giving primarily in Dayton, OH.
Application information: Application form not required.
Copies of proposal: 1
Deadline(s): Mar. 31
Board meeting date(s): Varies
Final notification: Varies
Write: P.G. Gillespie, V.P. and Trust Officer, Society Bank Trust Dept.
Officers: Joseph F. Connelly,* Pres.; Hugh Wall III,* Secy.; P.G. Gillespie, Treas.
Trustees:* W.T. Lincoln.
Number of staff: None.
Employer Identification Number: 316055729

5795
The Kroger Company Foundation ⌑ ☆
1014 Vine St.
Cincinnati 45201 (513) 762-1304

Established in 1987 in OH.
Donor(s): The Kroger Co.
Foundation type: Company-sponsored
Financial data (yr. ended 12/31/88): Assets, $14,923,821 (M); expenditures, $2,637,271, including $2,533,211 for 717 grants (high: $76,782; low: $100).
Purpose and activities: To improve the quality of life in communities of company operations through support for united campaigns in communities which provide assistance and services to Kroger employees and customers, human services and substance abuse programs, cultural programs, educational institutions, and civic groups.
Types of support: Operating budgets, capital campaigns, seed money.
Limitations: Giving primarily in areas of company operations; certain national and regional groups will also be supported, but only to the extent to which they provide services to areas of company operations. No grants to individuals, or for endowment campaigns (but exceptions will be considered on a case-by-case basis where an endowment is an important part of a broader campaign that meets the foundation's objectives).
Application information:
Initial approach: Proposal
Deadline(s): None
Final notification: Within 6 to 8 weeks
Write: Paul Bernish, V.P.
Officers and Trustees: Jack W. Partridge, Pres.; Paul Bernish, V.P. and Secy.; Lawrence M. Turner, Treas.; William Boehm, Donald F. Dufek, Thomas E. Murphy, Norma S. Skoog, Richard Tillman.
Employer Identification Number: 312292929

5796
Kulas Foundation ▼ ⌑
1662 Hanna Bldg.
Cleveland 44115 (216) 861-3139

Incorporated in 1937 in OH.
Donor(s): Fynette H. Kulas,† E.J. Kulas.†
Foundation type: Independent
Financial data (yr. ended 12/31/88): Assets, $18,703,397 (M); gifts received, $296,871; expenditures, $1,221,158, including $1,053,729 for 67 grants (high: $119,779; low: $500; average: $2,000-$30,000).
Purpose and activities: Grants largely to music institutions and for higher education; some support also for local performing arts and social services.
Types of support: Building funds, continuing support, equipment, professorships, renovation projects, special projects.
Limitations: Giving limited to the greater Cleveland, OH, area. No grants to individuals, or for endowment funds.
Application information: Application form required.
Initial approach: Letter
Copies of proposal: 5
Deadline(s): Submit proposal preferably six weeks before a meeting; no set deadline
Board meeting date(s): Feb., May, Aug., and Nov.
Final notification: After board meetings
Write: Allen C. Holmes, Pres.
Officers: Allen C. Holmes,* Pres.; Richard W. Pogue,* V.P.; Sarah E. Werder, Secy.
Trustees:* Herbert E. Strawbridge.
Number of staff: 1 full-time support.
Employer Identification Number: 340770687

5797
The Kuntz Foundation ⌑
120 West Second St.
Dayton 45402 (513) 461-3870

Incorporated in 1946 in OH.
Donor(s): The Peter Kuntz Sr. family, The Peter Kuntz Co., and affiliated companies.
Foundation type: Independent
Financial data (yr. ended 12/31/88): Assets, $2,572,306 (M); expenditures, $235,307, including $221,280 for 122 grants (high: $25,000; low: $100).
Purpose and activities: Giving for higher education, hospitals, Catholic church support, community funds, youth agencies, and an art museum.
Limitations: Giving primarily in OH. No grants to individuals.

Officers and Trustees: Peter H. Kuntz, Pres.; Martin Kuntz, Secy.; Richard P. Kuntz, Treas.; Dorothy Hobstetter, Edward Kuntz.
Employer Identification Number: 316016465

5798
Lancaster Lens, Inc. ☒ ☆
37 West Broad St., Suite 500
Columbus 43215

Established in 1953.
Foundation type: Independent
Financial data (yr. ended 07/31/89): Assets, $1,440,329 (M); expenditures, $194,738, including $49,070 for 21 grants (high: $24,000; low: $50).
Purpose and activities: Giving for higher education and community services.
Limitations: Giving primarily in OH. No grants to individuals.
Application information: Contributes only to pre-selected organizations.
Write: Clarence Clapham, Secy.
Officers: Bruce L. Rosa, Pres.; Clarence Clapham, Secy.; Joseph E. Schmidhammer, Treas.
Employer Identification Number: 316023927

5799
The Laub Foundation
19583 Coffinberry Blvd.
Fairview Park 44126 (216) 331-4028
Application address: Five Ocean Ave., South Harwich, MA 02661

Incorporated in 1958 in OH.
Donor(s): Herbert J. Laub,† Elsie K. Laub.†
Foundation type: Independent
Financial data (yr. ended 10/31/89): Assets, $2,963,958 (M); expenditures, $191,439, including $151,225 for 40 grants (high: $6,000; low: $600).
Purpose and activities: Grants primarily for scholarship programs of colleges and private schools, cultural programs, and youth agencies.
Types of support: Scholarship funds, operating budgets, continuing support, annual campaigns, seed money, emergency funds, building funds, equipment, matching funds, fellowships, publications, conferences and seminars.
Limitations: Giving primarily in Cuyahoga County, OH, and adjacent counties. No grants to individuals, or for deficit financing or endowment funds; no loans.
Publications: Annual report.
Application information: Final distribution of grants made at Aug. meeting. Application form not required.
Initial approach: Letter followed by proposal
Copies of proposal: 2
Deadline(s): None
Board meeting date(s): Feb., May, Aug., and Nov.
Final notification: After Aug. meeting
Write: Malcolm D. Campbell, Jr., Pres.
Officers and Trustees:* Malcolm D. Campbell, Jr.,* Pres. and Treas.; Amie M. Campbell,* V.P.; Robert B. Nelson,* Secy.; Laurence A. Bartell, Katherine C. Berry, Thomas C. Westropp.
Number of staff: 1 part-time professional.
Employer Identification Number: 346526087

5800
LeBlond Foundation ☒ ☆
c/o LeBlond Makino Machine Tool Co.
2690 Madison Rd.
Cincinnati 45208-1386

Established in 1952 in OH.
Foundation type: Independent
Financial data (yr. ended 12/31/88): Assets, $1,029,630 (M); expenditures, $109,103, including $97,260 for 31 grants (high: $25,000; low: $50).
Purpose and activities: Giving primarily for a community fund and youth; support also for higher and other education, community development, and fine arts.
Types of support: Operating budgets.
Limitations: Giving primarily in OH.
Application information:
Initial approach: Letter
Deadline(s): None
Write: Ms. Barbara S. Cummins, Secy.
Officers: Richard E. LeBlond, Pres.; Daniel W. LeBlond, V.P.; Barbara S. Cummins, Secy.; Charles J. LeBlond, Treas.
Employer Identification Number: 316036274

5801
Fred A. Lennon Foundation ▼ ☒
29500 Solon Rd.
Solon 44139 (216) 248-4600

Established in 1965 in OH.
Foundation type: Independent
Financial data (yr. ended 11/30/87): Assets, $8,951,087 (M); gifts received, $800,000; expenditures, $1,710,596, including $1,689,310 for 158 grants (high: $401,800; low: $100; average: $100-$100,000).
Purpose and activities: Giving for higher education and Roman Catholic church support; grants also for public policy, hospitals, cultural programs, social services, and community funds.
Limitations: Giving primarily in OH.
Application information:
Initial approach: Proposal
Deadline(s): None
Write: John F. Fant, Jr., Asst. Secy.
Officers: Fred A. Lennon, Pres.; A.P. Lennon, V.P.; F.J. Callahan, Secy.
Employer Identification Number: 346572287

5802
The Lincoln Electric Foundation ☒
c/o Society National Bank
22801 St. Clair Ave.
Cleveland 44117 (216) 481-8100

Trust established in 1952 in OH.
Donor(s): Lincoln Electric Co.
Foundation type: Company-sponsored
Financial data (yr. ended 12/31/88): Assets, $1,123,353 (M); gifts received, $650,000; expenditures, $481,089, including $477,750 for 40 grants (high: $115,000; low: $250; average: $500-$20,000).
Purpose and activities: Emphasis on higher education and a community fund; grants also for hospitals and medical services, social service agencies, cultural programs, and civic institutions.
Limitations: Giving primarily in OH, with emphasis on Cleveland.
Application information: Application form not required.
Initial approach: Letter
Deadline(s): Sept. 20
Board meeting date(s): Nov.
Write: Ellis F. Smolik, Secy.-Treas.
Officer: Ellis F. Smolik, Secy.-Treas.
Trustee: Society National Bank.
Number of staff: 1
Employer Identification Number: 346518355

5803
Emil M. Linderme Foundation ☒
c/o National City Bank
P.O. Box 5756
Cleveland 44101 (216) 575-2706

Established in 1958 in OH.
Foundation type: Independent
Financial data (yr. ended 12/31/88): Assets, $1,733,883 (M); expenditures, $81,375, including $69,019 for 6 grants (high: $37,010; low: $6,402).
Purpose and activities: Giving primarily for Christian churches, food programs, and social services, especially for the disadvantaged.
Application information: Application form not required.
Initial approach: Letter
Deadline(s): None
Write: David S. Brown, V.P., National City Bank
Trustee: National City Bank.
Employer Identification Number: 346515216

5804
Jerome Lippman Family Foundation ☒ ☆
P.O. Box 991
Akron 44309-0991

Established in 1966.
Donor(s): Margaret Lippman, Jerome Lippman, Joseph Kanfer.
Foundation type: Independent
Financial data (yr. ended 12/31/88): Assets, $647,993 (M); gifts received, $750,000; expenditures, $321,318, including $321,060 for 31 grants (high: $253,000; low: $60).
Purpose and activities: Giving primarily to Jewish organizations, including welfare funds, temples, yeshivas, and social services.
Limitations: Giving primarily in OH.
Application information: Contributes only to pre-selected organizations. Applications not accepted.
Officers: Jerome Lippman, Pres.; Joseph Kanfer, Secy.-Treas.
Directors: Stan Bober, Paul Sobel.
Trustee: Margaret Lippman.
Employer Identification Number: 340974875

5805
The Community Foundation of Greater Lorain County
1865 North Ridge Rd., East, Suite A
Lorain 44055 (216) 277-0142
Additional tel.: (216) 323-4445

Incorporated in 1980 in OH.
Foundation type: Community
Financial data (yr. ended 12/31/89): Assets, $12,993,392 (M); gifts received, $2,058,882;

expenditures, $759,310, including $343,745 for 35 grants (high: $70,476; low: $250; average: $1,500-$10,000) and $37,067 for 36 grants to individuals (high: $2,500; low: $300; average: $300-$2,500).
Purpose and activities: Giving for social services, education, health, civic affairs, and cultural programs.
Types of support: Student aid, special projects, general purposes, matching funds, technical assistance, scholarship funds, seed money.
Limitations: Giving limited to Lorain County, OH, and its immediate vicinity. No grants to individuals (except for scholarships), or for annual campaigns, deficit financing, or capital campaigns.
Publications: Annual report, informational brochure (including application guidelines), application guidelines, newsletter.
Application information: Application form not required.
Initial approach: Proposal, letter, or telephone
Copies of proposal: 1
Deadline(s): Feb. and Aug. 15 for general grants; May 1 for scholarships
Board meeting date(s): Apr. and Oct. for general grants; June for scholarships
Write: Carol G. Simonetti, Exec. Dir.
Officers and Trustees: Scribner L. Fauver, Pres.; John S. Corogin, V.P.; Gerda Klein, Secy.; Billy S. Rowland, Treas.; Robert S. Cook, Frank Jacinto, Larry D. Jones, Sr., James W. McGlamery, Fannie Moore-Hopkins, Robert C. Singleton, Donald W. Stevenson, Kenneth S. Stumphauzer, Elizabeth W. Thomas, Rickie Weiss, J. Milton Yinger, Molly Young.
Number of staff: 3 full-time professional; 2 full-time support.
Employer Identification Number: 341322781

5806
The Lubrizol Foundation
29400 Lakeland Blvd.
Wickliffe 44092 (216) 943-4200
Application address: 29425 Chagrin Blvd., Suite 303, Pepper Pike, OH 44122; Tel.: (216) 591-1404

Incorporated in 1952 in OH.
Donor(s): The Lubrizol Corp.
Foundation type: Company-sponsored
Financial data (yr. ended 12/31/89): Assets, $1,249,447 (M); gifts received, $1,000,075; expenditures, $1,027,933, including $863,225 for grants and $143,805 for employee matching gifts.
Purpose and activities: Emphasis on higher education, social services, civic and cultural programs, youth agencies, and hospitals; the foundation also conducts an employee matching gift program.
Types of support: Operating budgets, continuing support, annual campaigns, emergency funds, building funds, equipment, matching funds, professorships, internships, scholarship funds, fellowships, research, employee matching gifts, capital campaigns, general purposes.
Limitations: Giving primarily in areas of major company operations, particularly the greater Cleveland, OH, and Houston, TX, areas. No grants to individuals, or for seed money, deficit financing, endowment funds, demonstration projects, publications, or conferences; no loans.
Publications: Annual report.
Application information: Application form not required.
Initial approach: Proposal
Copies of proposal: 1
Deadline(s): None
Board meeting date(s): As required, usually 4 times a year
Final notification: 2 weeks after meeting
Write: Douglas W. Richardson, Pres.
Officers and Trustees:* L.E. Coleman,* Chair. and C.E.O.; Douglas W. Richardson,* Pres. and C.O.O.; Martha L. Berens, Secy.; Jeffrey P. Hollis, Treas.; W.T. Beargie, J. Cody Davis, David K. Ford, George R. Hill, J.F. Klemens, W.M. LeSuer.
Number of staff: 1 full-time support; 1 part-time support.
Employer Identification Number: 346500595

5807
M/B Foundation ⌑ ☆
Fiberglas Tower
One Levy Sq.
Toledo 43659

Established in 1986.
Donor(s): William W. Boeschenstein.
Foundation type: Independent
Financial data (yr. ended 12/31/88): Assets, $255,563 (M); expenditures, $185,054, including $184,750 for 29 grants (high: $50,000; low: $500).
Purpose and activities: Giving primarily for health, including a medical center and substance addiction services; support also for historic preservation and other cultural programs.
Application information: Contributes only to pre-selected organizations. Applications not accepted.
Trustees: Josephine M. Boeschenstein, William W. Boeschenstein.
Employer Identification Number: 311195114

5808
Jack N. and Lilyan Mandel Foundation ⌑
4500 Euclid Ave.
Cleveland 44103 (216) 391-8300

Established in 1963 in OH.
Donor(s): Jack N. Mandel, Lilyan Mandel.
Foundation type: Independent
Financial data (yr. ended 12/31/86): Assets, $3,486,233 (M); gifts received, $48,000; expenditures, $49,312, including $35,371 for 26 grants (high: $21,166; low: $25).
Purpose and activities: Emphasis on Jewish welfare funds and religious organizations.
Limitations: Giving primarily in OH.
Application information: Application form not required.
Initial approach: Proposal
Deadline(s): None
Write: Jack N. Mandel, Pres.
Officers and Trustees: Jack N. Mandel, Pres.; Lilyan Mandel, V.P.; Morton L. Mandel, Secy.-Treas.
Employer Identification Number: 346546418

5809
Joseph and Florence Mandel Foundation ⌑
4500 Euclid Ave.
Cleveland 44103 (216) 391-8300

Established in 1963 in OH.
Donor(s): Florence Mandel, Joseph C. Mandel.
Foundation type: Independent
Financial data (yr. ended 12/31/86): Assets, $3,499,854 (M); gifts received, $48,000; expenditures, $186,642, including $177,672 for 23 grants (high: $143,000; low: $25).
Purpose and activities: Emphasis on Jewish welfare funds and religious organizations.
Limitations: Giving primarily in OH.
Application information: Application form not required.
Initial approach: Proposal
Deadline(s): None
Write: Joseph C. Mandel, Trustee
Officers: Joseph C. Mandel,* Pres.; Florence Mandel,* V.P.; Philip S. Sims, Secy.-Treas.
Trustees:* Michele Beyer, Penni Weinberg.
Employer Identification Number: 346546419

5810
Morton and Barbara Mandel Foundation ⌑
4500 Euclid Ave.
Cleveland 44103 (216) 391-8300

Established in 1963 in OH.
Donor(s): Morton L. Mandel, Barbara A. Mandel.
Foundation type: Independent
Financial data (yr. ended 12/31/88): Assets, $5,363,921 (M); gifts received, $73,903; expenditures, $229,445, including $224,806 for 39 grants (high: $186,483; low: $30).
Purpose and activities: Support primarily for Jewish welfare funds.
Application information: Application form not required.
Initial approach: Proposal
Deadline(s): None
Write: Morton L. Mandel, Pres.
Officers and Trustees:* Morton L. Mandel,* Pres.; Barbara A. Mandel,* V.P.; Henry L. Zucker,* Secy.-Treas.
Employer Identification Number: 346546420

5811
Marian Foundation ⌑
260 Reeb Ave.
Columbus 43207-1988

Established in 1954 in OH.
Foundation type: Independent
Financial data (yr. ended 4/30/88): Assets, $1,002,414 (M); expenditures, $62,478, including $59,425 for 28 grants (high: $5,000; low: $600).
Purpose and activities: Support primarily for Catholic welfare and youth organizations.
Limitations: Giving primarily in Columbus, OH.
Application information:
Initial approach: Proposal
Deadline(s): Mar. 1
Final notification: Apr. 30
Write: William Huber, Pres.
Officers: William Huber, Pres.; Norm Hausfeld, V.P.; Patrick Foley, Secy.; John Morrison, Treas.
Employer Identification Number: 316050535

5812
The John C. Markey Charitable Fund ⌑
P.O. Box 191
Bryan 43506

Established in 1966 in OH.
Donor(s): John C. Markey.†
Foundation type: Independent
Financial data (yr. ended 6/30/87): Assets, $3,321,404 (M); expenditures, $285,765, including $206,520 for 78 grants (high: $91,500; low: $100).
Purpose and activities: Grants for a local chapter of the YWCA, higher and other education, Protestant church support, hospitals, and libraries and other cultural organizations.
Application information:
Write: John R. Markey, Pres.
Officers and Trustees: John R. Markey, Pres. and Treas.; Catherine M. Anderson, V.P.; Arthur S. Newcomer, Secy.; L.W. Lisle.
Employer Identification Number: 346572724

5813
Roy & Eva Markus Foundation, Inc. ⌑
c/o Board of Education, Rm. 152
1380 East Sixth St.
Cleveland 44114

Trust established in 1954 in OH; incorporated in 1967.
Donor(s): Roy C. Markus,† Eva Markus, Eli C. Markus,† Seymour H. Levy,† Robert C. Coplan.
Foundation type: Independent
Financial data (yr. ended 7/31/87): Assets, $1,583,946 (M); gifts received, $100,000; expenditures, $241,887, including $212,900 for 34 grants (high: $70,000; low: $100).
Purpose and activities: Giving largely for higher education, mainly through local scholarship funds; support also for health, cultural programs, and Jewish welfare funds.
Types of support: Scholarship funds, research.
Limitations: Giving primarily in OH and CA. No grants to individuals.
Publications: Annual report.
Application information: Funds committed for the foreseeable future.
Officers and Trustees:* Eva Markus,* Pres.; Robert C. Coplan,* Exec. V.P. and Secy.; Mark A. Levy,* V.P.; Shirley H. Levy,* V.P.; E.M. Glickman, Treas.
Employer Identification Number: 341018827

5814
David Meade Massie Trust ⌑
65 East Second St.
P.O. Box 41
Chillicothe 45601 (614) 772-5070

Foundation type: Independent
Financial data (yr. ended 12/31/88): Assets, $3,551,804 (M); expenditures, $295,608, including $235,671 for 55 grants (high: $5,000; low: $750).
Purpose and activities: Emphasis on community development, especially volunteer fire departments, and on youth, health, and social service agencies; support also for education and cultural programs.
Limitations: Giving limited to Chillicothe and Ross County, OH.
Publications: Program policy statement, application guidelines.
Application information: Application form required.
Deadline(s): Mar. 15, June 15, Sept. 15, and Dec. 15
Write: Marilyn Carnes
Trustees: Louis A. Ginther, Joseph G. Kear, Joseph P. Sulzer.
Employer Identification Number: 316022292

5815
The S. Livingston Mather Charitable Trust
803 Tower East
20600 Chagrin Blvd.
Shaker Heights 44122 (216) 942-6484

Trust established in 1953 in OH.
Donor(s): S. Livingston Mather.†
Foundation type: Independent
Financial data (yr. ended 12/31/89): Assets, $3,413,445 (M); expenditures, $248,862, including $225,950 for 68 grants (high: $29,000; low: $100; average: $1,000-$10,000).
Purpose and activities: Support for education, child welfare, youth programs, mental health, social services, cultural programs, and the environment and natural resources. Support for both general operations and specific projects.
Types of support: Operating budgets, continuing support, seed money, emergency funds, building funds, equipment, special projects, annual campaigns, renovation projects, scholarship funds, capital campaigns.
Limitations: Giving primarily in northeastern OH. No support for science and medical research programs, or in areas "appropriately supported by the government and/or the United Way. No grants to individuals, or for deficit financing or mass mailing solicitation; no loans.
Publications: Biennial report (including application guidelines).
Application information: Mass mail solicitations not considered. Application form not required.
Initial approach: Letter or telephone
Copies of proposal: 1
Deadline(s): None
Board meeting date(s): Quarterly, and as required
Final notification: 2 months
Write: S. Sterling McMillan, Secy.
Distribution Committee: S. Sterling McMillan,* Secy.; Elizabeth M. McMillan, Madeleine M. Offutt.
Trustees:* Ameritrust Co., N.A.
Number of staff: 1 part-time support.
Employer Identification Number: 346505619

5816
Elizabeth Ring Mather and William Gwinn Mather Fund
650 Citizens Bldg.
850 Euclid Ave.
Cleveland 44114 (216) 861-5341

Incorporated in 1954 in OH.
Donor(s): Elizabeth Ring Mather.†
Foundation type: Independent
Financial data (yr. ended 12/31/89): Assets, $6,553,592 (M); gifts received, $443,384; expenditures, $1,031,209, including $952,132 for 51 grants (high: $575,941; low: $100).
Purpose and activities: Giving generally for specific civic purposes, including the arts, hospitals and health agencies, higher and secondary education, conservation, and social welfare.
Types of support: Annual campaigns, building funds, equipment, general purposes, publications, endowment funds.
Limitations: Giving primarily in OH, with emphasis on the greater Cleveland area. No grants to individuals, or for scholarships, fellowships, or matching gifts; no loans.
Application information:
Initial approach: Letter
Deadline(s): None
Board meeting date(s): June and Dec.
Write: James D. Ireland, Pres.
Officers and Trustees:* James D. Ireland,* Pres. and Treas.; Theodore R. Colborn,* Secy.; Cornelia I. Hallinan, Cornelia W. Ireland, George R. Ireland, James D. Ireland III, Lucy E. Ireland, R. Henry Norweb, Jr.
Number of staff: 1 part-time professional.
Employer Identification Number: 346519863

5817
The Matterhorn Foundation, Inc. ⌑ ☆
1800 Star Bank Ctr.
Cincinnati 45202

Donor(s): Priscilla Reed Gamble.
Foundation type: Independent
Financial data (yr. ended 12/31/88): Assets, $381,264 (M); gifts received, $187,992; expenditures, $158,058, including $75,000 for 1 grant and $80,000 for 1 grant to an individual of $80,000 each.
Purpose and activities: Support limited to medical research.
Limitations: Giving limited to the Cincinnati, OH, area.
Application information: Application form required.
Write: Donald C. Hess, Secy.
Officers: Priscilla Reed Gamble, Pres. and Treas.; Rosamund Reed Wulsin, V.P.; Donald C. Hess, Secy.
Employer Identification Number: 311167684

5818
John A. McAlonan Trust ⌑
c/o National City Bank
P.O. Box 2130
Akron 44309-2130 (216) 375-8398

Trust established in 1958 in OH.
Donor(s): John A. McAlonan.†
Foundation type: Independent
Financial data (yr. ended 12/31/88): Assets, $3,938,976 (M); expenditures, $206,929, including $176,200 for 49 grants (high: $10,000; low: $833).
Purpose and activities: Giving for cultural programs and facilities, youth agencies, hospitals, the handicapped, and education.
Limitations: Giving limited to the Akron, OH, area. No grants to individuals.
Application information:
Initial approach: Letter or proposal
Copies of proposal: 6
Board meeting date(s): May and Nov.

Write: Mary H. Hembree, Trust Officer, National City Bank
Trustee: National City Bank.
Employer Identification Number: 346513095

5819
The McCormack Foundation ⌑ ☆
c/o International Management Group, Inc.
One Erieview Plaza, Suite 1300
Cleveland 44114

Established in 1986 in OH.
Donor(s): Mark H. McCormack.
Foundation type: Independent
Financial data (yr. ended 12/31/87): Assets, $99,899 (M); expenditures, $111,430, including $111,300 for 15 grants (high: $50,000; low: $100).
Purpose and activities: Giving primarily for a national golf association and education, with emphasis on higher education.
Limitations: No grants to individuals.
Application information: Contributes only to pre-selected organizations. Applications not accepted.
Officer and Trustees: William H. Carpenter, Secy.; Mark H. McCormack, Mary Leslie McCormack, Scott B. McCormack, Todd H. McCormack.
Employer Identification Number: 341536692

5820
McDonald & Company Securities Foundation ⌑ ☆
2100 Society Bldg.
Cleveland 44114 (216) 443-2300

Donor(s): McDonald & Co. Securities, Inc.
Foundation type: Company-sponsored
Financial data (yr. ended 3/31/89): Assets, $597,258 (M); gifts received, $34,500; expenditures, $144,097, including $140,103 for 105 grants (high: $21,000; low: $100).
Purpose and activities: Support for community funds, education, cultural programs, and general charitable giving.
Types of support: General purposes.
Limitations: Giving primarily in northeastern OH, especially Cleveland. No support for secondary schools, sports, or sports-related events.
Application information: Support for higher education only through contributions to the Ohio Foundation for Independent Colleges and Cleveland area colleges not affiliated with the OFIC; religious and welfare support is restricted to local arms of United Way, United Jewish Welfare Fund, and Catholic Charities. Application form not required.
Initial approach: Letter
Deadline(s): None
Write: E. Robert Hawken Jr., Secy.
Officers: Thomas M. O'Donnell, Chair. and Pres.; Willard E. Carmel,* V.P.; E. Robert Hawken, Jr., Secy.; Gordon A. Price, Treas.
Trustees:* Dean G. Lauritzen, Edward L. Tabol.
Number of staff: None.
Employer Identification Number: 341386528

5821
Lois Sisler McFawn Trust No. 2
c/o Ameritrust Co., N.A.
P.O. Box 5937
Cleveland 44101-0937 (216) 737-5632

Trust established in 1956 in OH.
Donor(s): Lois Sisler McFawn.
Foundation type: Independent
Financial data (yr. ended 12/31/89): Assets, $10,514,419 (M); expenditures, $637,832, including $620,474 for 79 grants (high: $20,000; low: $500).
Purpose and activities: Emphasis on education, hospitals, minority group programs, cultural activities, and youth agencies.
Types of support: General purposes, building funds, equipment, research, internships.
Limitations: Giving primarily in the Akron, OH, area. No grants to individuals, or for matching gifts, continuing support, seed money, emergency funds, deficit financing, land acquisition, publications, or conferences; no loans.
Publications: Application guidelines.
Application information: Application form not required.
Initial approach: Proposal
Copies of proposal: 1
Deadline(s): None
Board meeting date(s): Usually in June and Dec.
Write: Donald F. Barney, V.P., Ameritrust Co., N.A.
Distribution Committee: Michael Connor, H. Flood, Patricia Kempk, John Ong, Justin T. Rogers.
Trustee: Ameritrust Co., N.A.
Number of staff: None.
Employer Identification Number: 346508111

5822
John McIntire Educational Fund ⌑
c/o First National Bank, Trust Dept.
P.O. Box 2668, 422 Main St.
Zanesville 43701 (614) 432-8444

Foundation type: Independent
Financial data (yr. ended 6/30/88): Assets, $3,996,653 (M); gifts received, $100; expenditures, $197,300.
Purpose and activities: Awards college scholarships to residents of Zanesville, OH, who are single and under twenty-one years of age.
Types of support: Student aid.
Limitations: Giving limited to Zanesville, OH.
Application information: Application form required.
Deadline(s): May 1
Officers: Milman H. Linn, Pres.; E.M. McHenry, V.P.; Nelson McCoy, Secy.; Charles A. Gorsuch, Treas.
Directors: Willis Bailey, Bill Brown, Fred Grant, Milman H. Linn III, John Mast.
Employer Identification Number: 316021239

5823
The Mead Corporation Foundation ▼
Courthouse Plaza N.E.
Dayton 45463 (513) 459-6323

Trust established in 1957 in OH.
Donor(s): The Mead Corp.
Foundation type: Company-sponsored
Financial data (yr. ended 12/31/89): Assets, $24,036,953 (M); expenditures, $3,498,017, including $3,016,158 for 510 grants (high: $500,000; low: $100; average: $200-$30,000) and $202,377 for 854 employee matching gifts.
Purpose and activities: Emphasis on community funds, elementary, secondary, higher, and minority education, critical human services needs, and arts.
Types of support: Building funds, emergency funds, employee matching gifts, equipment, matching funds, seed money, special projects, employee-related scholarships.
Limitations: Giving primarily in areas of company operations. No support for national, fraternal, labor, or veterans' organizations, political organizations, or religious organizations for religious purposes. Grants rarely to tax-supported institutions except for public colleges and universities. No grants to individuals, or for endowment funds, advertising, dinners, or tickets; no loans; normally no operating support for organizations already receiving substantial support through United Way.
Publications: Annual report, informational brochure (including application guidelines).
Application information: Applicants for grants in Mead operating communities should contact or apply to the local Mead unit manager. Application form not required.
Initial approach: Proposal
Copies of proposal: 1
Deadline(s): None
Board meeting date(s): Apr., Aug, and Nov.
Final notification: 2 months
Write: Ronald F. Budzik, Exec. Dir.
Officers: Ronald F. Budzik, Exec. Dir.; K.A. Strawn, Admin. Officer and Secy.; William D. Bloebaum, Jr., Treas.
Trustee: Bank One, Dayton, N.A.
Distribution Committee: James Van Vleck, Chair.; Charles W. Joiner, Elias M. Karter, Raymond W. Lane, Charles Mazza, Frederick J. Robbins.
Number of staff: None.
Employer Identification Number: 316040645

5824
Nelson Mead Fund ⌑
c/o Rend & Co.
2060 Kettering Tower
Dayton 45423

Established in 1965 in OH.
Donor(s): Ioka Fund.
Foundation type: Independent
Financial data (yr. ended 11/30/89): Assets, $4,879,978 (M); expenditures, $175,043, including $131,446 for 88 grants (high: $20,000; low: $25).
Purpose and activities: Support primarily for conservation and wildlife preservation; giving also for Episcopal churches, civic and cultural groups, health associations, and educational institutions.
Limitations: No grants to individuals.
Application information: Contributes only to pre-selected organizations. Applications not accepted.
Trustees: Nelson S. Mead, Ruth C. Mead.
Employer Identification Number: 316064591

5825
Meftah Scholarship Foundation
2777 McCoy Rd.
Columbus 43220 (614) 451-5859

Established in 1985 in OH.
Foundation type: Independent
Financial data (yr. ended 12/31/88): Assets, $1,073,196 (M); expenditures, $35,084, including $19,002 for grants to individuals.
Purpose and activities: Undergraduate and graduate scholarship support for recent immigrant and refugee youths who are or will be students at OH colleges.
Types of support: Student aid.
Limitations: Giving limited to OH.
Publications: Application guidelines, informational brochure.
Application information: Interviews required. Application form required.
Deadline(s): None
Board meeting date(s): Quarterly
Write: Michael Meftah, Trustee
Trustees: Bruce V. Heine, Michael Meftah, Patricia Meftah, Joseph J. Merrelli.
Number of staff: None.
Employer Identification Number: 316271327

5826
The Mellen Foundation ▼ ⌑
3200 National City Ctr.
Cleveland 44114
Address for nursing fellowship applications: c/o Lillie R. Marquis, 9519 Arban Dr., St. Louis, MO 63216

Established in 1963 in OH.
Donor(s): Edward J. Mellen.
Foundation type: Independent
Financial data (yr. ended 12/31/88): Assets, $13,049,130 (M); expenditures, $1,438,956, including $1,088,994 for 26 grants (high: $200,000; low: $1,000; average: $500-$400,000) and $99,571 for 16 grants to individuals (high: $10,000; low: $810).
Purpose and activities: Grants primarily for higher education, including graduate fellowships for critical care nursing education; some support also for churches and medical organizations.
Types of support: Fellowships.
Application information: Application form required for fellowships; applicants must have a current legal residence or be employed in a state east of the Mississippi River.
Deadline(s): Jan. 15 for requesting fellowship application form
Write: Stephanie Keane, Treas.
Officers and Trustees:* John D. Drinko,* Pres.; Elizabeth G. Drinko,* V.P.; John J. Dwyer,* V.P.; James E. Chapman,* Secy.; Stephanie Keane, Treas.; J. Raymond Barry, John H. Burlingame, Diana Lynn Drinko, J. Richard Hamilton, Lloyd F. Loux.
Employer Identification Number: 346560874

5827
Samuel Mendel Melton Foundation ⌑
17 South High St., Suite 1018
Columbus 43215 (614) 224-5239

Established in 1951 in OH.
Donor(s): Samuel Mendel Melton.
Foundation type: Independent
Financial data (yr. ended 09/30/89): Assets, $842,303 (M); gifts received, $272,811; expenditures, $1,102,217, including $1,096,625 for 86 grants (high: $400,000; low: $25).
Purpose and activities: Giving primarily for higher education and Jewish religious educational organizations.
Limitations: No grants to individuals.
Application information: Application form not required.
Deadline(s): None
Write: Samuel M. Melton, Trustee
Trustees: Donald Katz, Florence Melton, Mina Bess Melton, Samuel Mendel Melton.
Employer Identification Number: 316031944

5828
Lewis N. Miller Charitable Trust
Elyria Savings and Trust National Bank
105 Court St.
Elyria 44035

Established in 1985 in OH.
Foundation type: Independent
Financial data (yr. ended 12/31/88): Assets, $2,041,396 (M); expenditures, $150,351, including $136,119 for 9 grants (high: $15,125; low: $15,124).
Purpose and activities: Support for animal welfare, higher education, social services, cultural programs, health associations, and a church.
Limitations: No grants to individuals.
Application information: Contributes only to pre-selected organizations. Applications not accepted.
Trustee: Elyria Savings and Trust National Bank.
Employer Identification Number: 346834475

5829
George Lee Miller Memorial Trust ⌑
c/o Society Bank of Eastern Ohio, N.A.
P.O. Box 500
Canton 44702

Established about 1982 in OH.
Foundation type: Independent
Financial data (yr. ended 12/31/87): Assets, $2,002,807 (M); expenditures, $102,345, including $85,443 for 19 grants (high: $7,103; low: $3,284).
Purpose and activities: Grants for hospitals, youth agencies, and Protestant church support; grants also for a university and a historical society.
Limitations: Giving primarily in the Canton, OH, area.
Application information:
Initial approach: Letter
Deadline(s): None
Write: Stephen C. Donatini
Trustee: Society Bank of Eastern Ohio, N.A.
Employer Identification Number: 346748261

5830
Clement O. Miniger Memorial Foundation
Hillcrest Hotel, Rm. 229
Madison Ave. at 16th St.
Toledo 43612
Mailing address: P.O. Box 333, Toledo, OH 43691

Incorporated in 1952 in OH.
Donor(s): George M. Jones, Jr.,† Eleanor Miniger Jones.
Foundation type: Independent
Financial data (yr. ended 12/31/88): Assets, $5,378,711 (M); expenditures, $293,348, including $275,450 for 36 grants (high: $40,000; low: $500).
Purpose and activities: Giving for higher education, youth agencies, social services, and cultural programs.
Limitations: Giving primarily in OH. No grants to individuals.
Application information: Contributes only to pre-selected organizations. Applications not accepted.
Officers and Trustees:* George M. Jones III,* Pres.; Richard Day,* V.P.; Thomas DeVilbiss,* Exec. Secy and Treas.; Severn Joyce, John A. Morse.
Employer Identification Number: 346523024

5831
MLM Charitable Foundation ⌑
410 United Savings Bldg.
Toledo 43604 (419) 255-0500

Established in 1967 in OH.
Donor(s): Mary L. McKenny, Charles A. McKenny.
Foundation type: Independent
Financial data (yr. ended 12/31/89): Assets, $1,047,600 (M); gifts received, $100,000; expenditures, $128,334, including $126,300 for 44 grants (high: $30,000; low: $100).
Purpose and activities: Grants primarily for higher education and Protestant church support.
Types of support: Operating budgets.
Limitations: Giving primarily in OH and NY. No grants to individuals.
Application information: Contributes only to pre-selected organizations. Applications not accepted.
Write: Charles A. McKenny, Treas.
Officers: Mary L. McKenny, Pres. and Secy.; Anne E. McKenny, V.P.; Charles A. McKenny, Treas.
Employer Identification Number: 341018519

5832
Charles Moerlein Foundation ☆
c/o The Fifth Third Bank, Trust Div.
Dept. 00858, 38 Fountain Sq. Plaza
Cincinnati 45263 (513) 579-6034

Established in 1966 in OH.
Donor(s): Charles Moerlein.†
Foundation type: Independent
Financial data (yr. ended 09/30/89): Assets, $1,758,741 (M); expenditures, $106,119, including $94,255 for 13 grants (high: $30,000; low: $1,105).
Purpose and activities: Giving primarily for social services, cultural programs, and education; support also for community development and health.
Types of support: Seed money, renovation projects, building funds, equipment.
Limitations: Giving limited to the greater Cincinnati, OH, area. No support for religious or political organizations. No grants to individuals.

Publications: Annual report, application guidelines.
Application information: Application form required.
Initial approach: Letter
Copies of proposal: 1
Deadline(s): Feb. 1, May 1, Aug. 1, and Nov. 1
Board meeting date(s): Mar., June, Sept., and Dec.
Write: Carolyn F. McCoy, Mgr.
Trustee: Fifth Third Bank.
Number of staff: 1 full-time professional; 1 full-time support.
Employer Identification Number: 316020341

5833
Molyneaux Foundation ⌑ ☆
First National Bank of Southwestern OH
Third & High Sts., P.O. Box 476
Hamilton 45012

Donor(s): Kendle Molyneaux, Mrs. Kendle Molyneaux.
Foundation type: Independent
Financial data (yr. ended 6/30/89): Assets, $1,157,859 (M); gifts received, $26,799; expenditures, $60,548, including $49,000 for 5 grants (high: $39,000; low: $1,000).
Purpose and activities: Giving for human services, including a hospital, a hospice, health associations, and social services; grants also for higher education.
Types of support: Renovation projects, operating budgets, capital campaigns.
Limitations: Giving primarily in Oxford and Hamilton, OH. No grants to individuals.
Application information:
Initial approach: Proposal
Write: Dennis G. Walsh, Trust Officer, First National Bank of Southwestern Ohio
Trustee: First National Bank of Southwestern Ohio.
Employer Identification Number: 510154432

5834
Monarch Machine Tool Company Foundation ⌑
615 North Oak St.
Sidney 45365

Trust established in 1952 in OH.
Donor(s): Monarch Machine Tool Co.
Foundation type: Company-sponsored
Financial data (yr. ended 12/31/88): Assets, $2,017,761 (M); expenditures, $107,781, including $92,560 for 34 grants (high: $15,000; low: $100).
Purpose and activities: Giving for higher education, youth agencies, community funds, hospitals, community development, and the aged.
Limitations: Giving primarily in OH.
Application information: Application form not required.
Deadline(s): Dec.
Write: Robert M. Peters, Secy.-Treas.
Officers: Kermit T. Kuck, Pres.; Robert M. Peters, Secy.-Treas.
Trustee: N.V. Gushing.
Employer Identification Number: 346556088

5835
Montgomery Foundation ▼ ⌑
Roscoe Village
Coshocton 43812 (614) 622-2696

Established in 1972 in OH.
Donor(s): Edward E. Montgomery, Frances B. Montgomery.
Foundation type: Independent
Financial data (yr. ended 6/30/88): Assets, $8,945,469 (M); expenditures, $943,691, including $825,298 for 24 grants (high: $756,600; low: $100; average: $200-$15,000).
Purpose and activities: Grants for an historic restoration project; limited support also for local charities.
Types of support: Annual campaigns, matching funds, renovation projects, seed money.
Limitations: Giving primarily in Coshocton, OH.
Application information:
Initial approach: Letter or proposal
Deadline(s): None
Board meeting date(s): Feb., May, Aug., and Nov.; executive committee meets monthly to review requests
Final notification: 90 days
Write: Robert M. Thomas, Pres.
Officers and Trustees: Edward E. Montgomery, Chair., Exec. Comm.; Robert M. Thomas, Pres.; Robert W. Dunmire, V.P.; Floyd E. Friedli, Secy.; Richard E. Corbett, Treas.; Suzanne Bowen, Helen Breon, R.E. Hopkins, Jr., Michael Manning, Frances B. Montgomery, Joseph Montgomery, Scott Montgomery, R.L. Prindle, Seward D. Schooler.
Number of staff: 2 part-time professional; 1 part-time support.
Employer Identification Number: 237165768

5836
Harry W. and Margaret Moore Foundation, Inc. ⌑
c/o Society Bank
34 North Main St.
Dayton 45402
Application address: 5051 Litridge Rd., Dayton, OH 45402; Tel.: (513) 233-0233

Incorporated in 1959 in OH.
Donor(s): Harry W. Moore.†
Foundation type: Independent
Financial data (yr. ended 08/31/89): Assets, $1,794,584 (M); expenditures, $84,075, including $52,201 for 10 grants (high: $13,353; low: $948) and $11,490 for 3 loans to individuals.
Purpose and activities: Support primarily for health associations and religious organizations; also awards low-interest loans to Dayton, OH, students planning to attend local universities.
Types of support: Student loans.
Limitations: Giving primarily in southwestern OH. No support for graduate students. No grants for operating budgets, scholarships, fellowships, deficit financing, or endowment funds.
Application information:
Initial approach: Proposal
Copies of proposal: 1
Deadline(s): Submit proposal in Apr. through Sept.; no set deadline
Board meeting date(s): Dec.
Write: Arthur C. Reiger, Jr., Pres.
Officers: J. Milan Biddison,* Chair.; A.C. Reiger, Pres.; Edward H. O'Neil, V.P.; Mary Ann Price, Secy.-Treas.
Trustees:* Glen E. Bucholtz, John M. Cloud, James Doyle, David R. Setz, W. Patrick Winton.
Employer Identification Number: 316040186

5837
The Harry C. Moores Foundation
3010 Hayden Rd.
Columbus 43235 (614) 764-8999

Trust established in 1961 in OH.
Donor(s): Harry C. Moores.†
Foundation type: Independent
Financial data (yr. ended 09/30/89): Assets, $18,159,045 (M); expenditures, $905,967, including $879,000 for 71 grants (high: $200,000; low: $1,000; average: $1,000-$20,000).
Purpose and activities: Grants largely for rehabilitation of the handicapped, Protestant church support, hospitals, higher education, cultural programs, and social service agencies concerned with the aged, child welfare, and the retarded.
Types of support: Seed money, scholarship funds, general purposes, capital campaigns, annual campaigns.
Limitations: Giving primarily in the Columbus, OH, area. No support for private foundations. No grants to individuals, or for endowment funds, or matching gifts; no loans.
Application information: Application form not required.
Initial approach: Proposal in letter form
Copies of proposal: 1
Deadline(s): Submit proposal between Oct. and July; deadline Aug. 1
Board meeting date(s): Apr. or May and Aug. or Sept.
Final notification: By Oct. 15 (if affirmative)
Write: David L. Fenner, Secy.
Officers and Trustees:* Francis E. Caldwell,* Chair.; David L. Fenner, Secy.; William H. Leighner,* Treas.; Ronald D. Bardon, William C. Jones.
Number of staff: None.
Employer Identification Number: 316035344

5838
Burton D. Morgan Foundation, Inc.
P.O. Box 1500
Akron 44309-1500 (216) 258-6512
Additional tel.: (216) 376-5300

Established in 1967 in OH.
Donor(s): Burton D. Morgan.
Foundation type: Independent
Financial data (yr. ended 12/31/88): Assets, $5,195,721 (M); gifts received, $351,500; expenditures, $173,006, including $160,400 for 34 grants (high: $34,500; low: $400; average: $3,000).
Purpose and activities: Emphasis on research development and higher education.
Types of support: General purposes, building funds, special projects, research, endowment funds, operating budgets.
Limitations: Giving primarily in Summit County, OH. No grants to individuals.
Publications: Application guidelines, 990-PF.

Application information: Application form not required.
Initial approach: Letter
Copies of proposal: 1
Board meeting date(s): 3 times a year
Write: John V. Frank, Pres.
Officers and Trustees:* John V. Frank,* Pres.; Weldon W. Case,* V.P.; Richard A. Chenoweth,* Secy.-Treas.
Number of staff: 1 part-time professional.
Employer Identification Number: 346598971

5839
The Mount Vernon Community Trust ⌑
c/o First-Knox National Bank
One South Main St., P.O. Box 871
Mount Vernon 43050 (614) 397-6344

Established in 1944 in OH by declaration of trust.
Foundation type: Community
Financial data (yr. ended 12/31/86): Assets, $6,714,262 (M); gifts received, $755,387; expenditures, $525,013, including $490,213 for 142 grants (high: $50,000; low: $33; average: $300-$400).
Purpose and activities: "To assist public, educational, charitable or benevolent enterprises." Grants, in accordance with the donors' wishes, for student loan and scholarship funds, Protestant church support, community funds, higher education, and youth agencies.
Types of support: Scholarship funds, building funds, capital campaigns, continuing support, equipment, matching funds, seed money.
Limitations: Giving primarily in Knox County, OH. No grants to individuals, or for endowment funds or research; no loans.
Publications: Annual report.
Application information: Application form required.
Initial approach: Letter
Copies of proposal: 7
Board meeting date(s): Monthly
Write: Frederick N. Lorey, Chair.
Distribution Committee: Frederick N. Lorey, Chair.; James J. Cullers, Secy.; Maureen Buchwald, Winslow Curry, J. Robert Purdy, Helen M. Zelkowitz.
Trustee: The First-Knox National Bank.
Number of staff: 1 part-time professional.
Employer Identification Number: 316024796

5840
The Murch Foundation
830 Hanna Bldg.
Cleveland 44115

Incorporated in 1956 in OH.
Donor(s): Maynard H. Murch.†
Foundation type: Independent
Financial data (yr. ended 12/31/88): Assets, $8,471,014 (M); expenditures, $613,229, including $600,000 for 29 grants (high: $307,500; low: $1,000; average: $1,000-$90,000).
Purpose and activities: Emphasis on museums and cultural programs, higher and secondary education, hospitals and health agencies, and community recreation.
Types of support: Annual campaigns, capital campaigns, endowment funds, general purposes, renovation projects, scholarship funds.
Limitations: Giving primarily in OH. No grants to individuals.
Application information: Contributes only to pre-selected organizations. Applications not accepted.
Write: Maynard H. Murch IV, Pres.
Officers and Trustees: Maynard H. Murch IV, Pres. and Treas.; Creighton B. Murch, V.P. and Secy.; Robert B. Murch, V.P.
Number of staff: 1 part-time support.
Employer Identification Number: 346520188

5841
Thomas G. & Joy P. Murdough Foundation ⌑ ☆
P.O. Box 1500
Akron 44309-1500

Established in 1984.
Donor(s): Thomas G. Murdough.
Foundation type: Independent
Financial data (yr. ended 12/31/88): Assets, $473,524 (M); gifts received, $371,086; expenditures, $127,861, including $123,500 for 13 grants (high: $30,000; low: $2,000).
Purpose and activities: Giving primarily for hospitals, medical research, and higher and secondary education; support also for museums and a musical arts association.
Limitations: Giving primarily in OH.
Application information: Contributes only to pre-selected organizations. Applications not accepted.
Officers and Trustees: Thomas G. Murdough, Pres.; Joy P. Murdough, Secy.; William M. Oldham.
Employer Identification Number: 341454379

5842
The Murphy Family Foundation ⌑ ☆
25800 Science Park Dr.
Beachwood 44122-5525 (216) 831-0404

Established in 1986 in OH.
Donor(s): The Murphy-Phoenix Co.
Foundation type: Company-sponsored
Financial data (yr. ended 12/31/88): Assets, $52,333 (M); gifts received, $100,000; expenditures, $105,130, including $83,815 for 58 grants (high: $10,000; low: $500) and $21,125 for employee matching gifts.
Purpose and activities: Giving primarily for welfare, including food and housing; support also for higher and other education and Protestant and Catholic churches and welfare organizations.
Limitations: Giving primarily in OH. No grants to individuals.
Application information: Application form not required.
Deadline(s): None
Write: Rita M. Carfagna, Secy.-Treas.
Officers and Trustees: Murlan J. Murphy, Sr., Pres.; Murlan J. Murphy, Jr., V.P.; Rita Murphy Carfagna, Secy.-Treas.; Brian F. Murphy, Paul J. Murphy, Raymond M. Murphy.
Employer Identification Number: 341526161

5843
John P. Murphy Foundation ▼
Tower City Ctr.
610 Terminal Tower
Cleveland 44113-2204 (216) 623-4770

Incorporated in 1960 in OH.
Donor(s): John P. Murphy.†
Foundation type: Independent
Financial data (yr. ended 12/31/89): Assets, $34,099,470 (M); expenditures, $2,429,263, including $2,151,482 for 114 grants (high: $100,000; low: $500; average: $5,000-$50,000).
Purpose and activities: Giving for higher and secondary (restricted) education; support also for the arts, community and civic affairs, social service and youth agencies, and hospitals.
Types of support: Operating budgets, building funds, equipment, general purposes, capital campaigns, continuing support, annual campaigns, exchange programs, matching funds, publications, renovation projects, research, special projects.
Limitations: Giving primarily in the greater Cleveland, OH, area. No grants to individuals, or for endowment funds; no loans.
Publications: Annual report, informational brochure.
Application information: Application form not required.
Initial approach: Letter
Copies of proposal: 1
Deadline(s): None; all applications on hand considered at monthly meetings
Board meeting date(s): Monthly
Final notification: Within 2 weeks of meeting
Write: Herbert E. Strawbridge, Pres. and Secy.
Officers and Trustees: Herbert E. Strawbridge, Pres. and Secy.; Claude M. Blair, V.P.; Robert R. Broadbent, V.P.; Robert G. Wright, V.P.; Paul L. Volk, Treas.
Number of staff: 1 part-time support.
Employer Identification Number: 346528308

5844
R. C. and Katharine M. Musson Charitable Foundation ⌑
(Formerly R. C. and Katherine M. Musson Charitable Trust)
c/o Brouse & McDowell
500 First National Tower
Akron 44308 (216) 535-5711

Established in 1984 in OH as R. C. and Katherine M. Musson Charitable Trust; successor foundation established in 1988.
Donor(s): R.C. Musson.†
Foundation type: Independent
Financial data (yr. ended 06/30/89): Assets, $3,805,747 (M); expenditures, $331,084, including $304,712 for 46 grants (high: $25,000; low: $500; average: $1,000-$10,000).
Purpose and activities: Support primarily for social services and Protestant churches.
Types of support: General purposes.
Limitations: Giving primarily in Summit County, OH.
Application information:
Initial approach: Proposal
Deadline(s): None

Trustees: Irvin J. Musson, Jr., Robert B. Palmer, Ben Segers.
Number of staff: 1 part-time support.
Employer Identification Number: 341549070

5845
Louis S. and Mary Myers Foundation ¤
1293 South Main St.
Akron 44301

Established in 1956 in OH.
Foundation type: Independent
Financial data (yr. ended 12/31/88): Assets, $1,402,764 (M); gifts received, $155,000; expenditures, $99,952, including $98,900 for 21 grants (high: $37,500; low: $250).
Purpose and activities: Giving primarily to Jewish organizations, including welfare funds; support also for the arts.
Limitations: Giving primarily in OH. No grants to individuals.
Application information:
Write: Ms. Pat Hill
Officer: Louis S. Myers, Pres.
Trustees: Mary Myers, Stephen E. Myers.
Employer Identification Number: 346555862

5846
National Machinery Foundation, Inc. ¤
Greenfield St.
P.O. Box 747
Tiffin 44883 (419) 447-5211

Incorporated in 1948 in OH.
Donor(s): National Machinery Co.
Foundation type: Company-sponsored
Financial data (yr. ended 12/31/87): Assets, $7,314,651 (M); expenditures, $511,428, including $331,089 for 81 grants (high: $100,000; low: $61) and $108,287 for 300 grants to individuals (high: $6,000; low: $50).
Purpose and activities: Grants to charitable, religious, and youth organizations, higher education, including scholarships, and aid to needy individuals, including former company employees.
Types of support: Scholarship funds, grants to individuals, annual campaigns.
Limitations: Giving primarily in Seneca County and Tiffin, OH.
Application information: Application form required.
Initial approach: Letter
Copies of proposal: 1
Board meeting date(s): Monthly
Write: D.B. Bero, Admin.
Officers and Trustees: Paul N. Aley, Pres.; P.A. Stevens, V.P.; Larry F. Baker, Secy.-Treas.; R.L. Callaghan, J.T. Cassell, L.D. Cook, C.F. Kalnow, D.E. King, Paul R. Martin, Jr.
Number of staff: 1 part-time professional; 1 part-time support.
Employer Identification Number: 346520191

5847
Nationwide Foundation ▼
One Nationwide Plaza
Columbus 43216 (614) 249-4310

Incorporated in 1959 in OH.
Donor(s): Nationwide Mutual Insurance Co., and affiliates.
Foundation type: Company-sponsored
Financial data (yr. ended 12/31/88): Assets, $18,577,456 (M); expenditures, $2,968,749, including $2,667,449 for 142 grants (high: $1,133,994; low: $52; average: $1,000-$15,000) and $242,689 for 333 employee matching gifts.
Purpose and activities: Giving primarily for human services agencies; support also for cultural programs, community funds, and higher education, including employee matching gifts.
Types of support: Operating budgets, continuing support, annual campaigns, seed money, emergency funds, special projects, research, scholarship funds, employee matching gifts, capital campaigns.
Limitations: Giving primarily in OH, particularly Columbus, and other communities where the company maintains offices. No support for public elementary and secondary schools, or fraternal or veterans' organizations. No grants to individuals, or for building funds; no loans.
Publications: Informational brochure (including application guidelines).
Application information: The foundation has a specific format for requests for funding, which is listed in the Guidelines for Grant Consideration brochure. Application form not required.
Initial approach: Letter
Copies of proposal: 1
Deadline(s): Sept. 1
Board meeting date(s): Feb., May, Aug., and Nov.
Final notification: Feb.
Write: Stephen A. Rish, V.P., Public Relations
Officers and Trustees:* John E. Fisher,* Chair.; John L. Marakas,* Pres.; Thomas E. Kryshak,* Exec. V.P., Finance; Peter F. Frenzer, Exec. V.P., Investments; Gordon E. McCutchan, Sr. V.P. and General Counsel; Gerald W. Woodard, V.P. and Treas.; Stephen A. Rish, V.P., Public Relations; W.E. Fitzpatrick, Secy.; Paul A. Donald, Charles L. Fuellgraf, Jr., Dwight W. Oberschlake, Leonard E. Schnell, Frank B. Sollars.
Number of staff: 1 part-time professional; 1 part-time support.
Employer Identification Number: 316022301

5848
The NCR Foundation ▼ ¤
1700 South Patterson Blvd.
Dayton 45479 (513) 445-2577

Incorporated in 1953 in OH.
Donor(s): NCR Corp.
Foundation type: Company-sponsored
Financial data (yr. ended 12/31/88): Assets, $7,579,069 (M); expenditures, $3,964,327, including $2,173,328 for 62 grants (high: $863,639; low: $500; average: $1,000-$50,000).
Purpose and activities: Emphasis on cultural programs, higher education, including an employee matching gift program, and community funds.
Types of support: Operating budgets, annual campaigns, seed money, emergency funds, building funds, equipment, research, scholarship funds, employee-related scholarships, employee matching gifts, continuing support.
Limitations: Giving primarily in areas of company operations, with emphasis on Dayton, OH. No grants to individuals; no loans.
Application information: Application form not required.
Initial approach: Letter or proposal
Copies of proposal: 1
Deadline(s): None
Board meeting date(s): Mar., June, Sept., and Dec.
Final notification: 3 to 6 months
Write: R.F. Beach, V.P.
Officers: W.S. Anderson, Chair.; G. Biassini, Pres.; R.F. Beach, V.P.; C.P. Russ III, Secy.; P.T. Amstuz III, Treas.
Trustees: C.H. Hardesty, Jr., Harry Holiday, Jr., Cathleen Synge Morawetz, Gilbert P. Williamson.
Number of staff: 2
Employer Identification Number: 316030860

5849
New Orphan Asylum Scholarship Foundation ¤
2340 Victory Pkwy., Suite 1
Cincinnati 45206 (513) 961-6626

Donor(s): Various trusts and estates.
Foundation type: Independent
Financial data (yr. ended 12/31/88): Assets, $1,543,429 (L); gifts received, $64,744; expenditures, $109,815, including $200 for 1 grant and $68,930 for grants to individuals.
Purpose and activities: Awards scholarship grants primarily for college education.
Types of support: Student aid.
Limitations: Giving limited to residents of the greater Cincinnati, OH, area.
Application information: Postgraduate applications not accepted; payments are made directly to the institutions. Application form required.
Deadline(s): July 31 for new applicants
Write: Norma L. Lane
Officers: Matthew L. Fairfax, Pres.; Moss White, Jr., Secy.; Cornelius Wilson, Treas.
Directors: Willie Carden, Jr., Perry Davis, Blanche Kalfus, Melody Sparks.
Employer Identification Number: 310536683

5850
The L. and L. Nippert Charitable Foundation ¤
c/o The Central Trust Co. of Northern Ohio, N.A.
P.O. Box 1198
Cincinnati 45201 (513) 651-8421

Established in 1981.
Donor(s): Louis Nippert, Louise D. Nippert.
Foundation type: Independent
Financial data (yr. ended 12/31/88): Assets, $3,294,393 (M); expenditures, $739,456, including $722,050 for 56 grants (high: $500,000; low: $100).
Purpose and activities: Support for education, conservation, music, and social services.
Types of support: Annual campaigns, building funds, capital campaigns, endowment funds, equipment, land acquisition, operating budgets,

publications, renovation projects, scholarship funds, seed money, special projects.
Limitations: Giving primarily in OH.
Publications: Application guidelines.
Application information:
Initial approach: Proposal
Copies of proposal: 4
Deadline(s): First of Mar., July, and Nov.
Board meeting date(s): Apr., Aug., and Dec.
Final notification: 1 month after meetings
Write: Betty C. Scheid, Trust Officer, The Central Trust Co., of Northern Ohio, N.A.
Trustees: Louis Nippert, Louise D. Nippert, The Central Trust Co. of Northern Ohio, N.A.
Number of staff: 1
Employer Identification Number: 316219757

5851
The Nord Family Foundation
(Formerly Nordson Foundation)
347 Midway Blvd.
Elyria 44035 (216) 324-2822
Additional tel.: (216) 233-8401

Trust established in 1952 in OH; reorganized in 1988 under current name.
Donor(s): Walter G. Nord,† Mrs. Walter G. Nord,† Nordson Corp., Evan W. Nord.
Foundation type: Independent
Financial data (yr. ended 10/31/89): Assets, $56,129,427 (M); gifts received, $5,000; expenditures, $2,548,651, including $2,014,184 for 120 grants (high: $200,000; low: $200; average: $3,000-$5,000), $180,500 for 2 loans and $7,251 for 1 in-kind gift.
Purpose and activities: Emphasis on projects to assist the disadvantaged and minorities, including giving for early childhood, secondary, and higher education, social services, health, cultural affairs, and civic activities. New initiatives in 1988 were creation of Public Service Institute, Child Care Resource Center, and a day care center for low- to moderate-income families.
Types of support: Operating budgets, continuing support, seed money, emergency funds, equipment, matching funds, consulting services, technical assistance, loans, special projects, publications, employee matching gifts, general purposes, program-related investments.
Limitations: Giving primarily in the Lorain and Cuyahoga county areas, OH. No grants to individuals, or for deficit financing, research, scholarships, fellowships, or conferences.
Publications: Annual report (including application guidelines).
Application information: Application form not required.
Initial approach: Proposal, letter, or telephone
Copies of proposal: 1
Deadline(s): Submit proposal at least 6 weeks before meetings
Board meeting date(s): Feb., June, and Oct.
Final notification: 1 to 3 months
Write: Henry C. Doll, Exec. Dir.
Officers and Trustees:* Evan W. Nord,* Pres.; Eric T. Nord,* V.P.; William D. Ginn,* Secy.; Henry C. Doll, Exec. Dir.
Number of staff: 3 full-time professional; 1 part-time professional; 1 full-time support.
Employer Identification Number: 341595929

5852
Edwin D. Northrup II Fund Trust ¤ ☆
c/o National City Bank
P.O. Box 5756
Cleveland 44101 (216) 575-2740

Established in 1984.
Foundation type: Independent
Financial data (yr. ended 12/31/88): Assets, $1,157,618 (M); expenditures, $68,502, including $56,513 for 6 grants (high: $14,128; low: $6,782).
Purpose and activities: Support for a masonic home, a law school, an Episcopal church, and a library.
Limitations: Giving primarily in OH.
Application information:
Initial approach: Letter
Deadline(s): None
Write: Christopher A. Gray
Trustee: National City Bank.
Employer Identification Number: 346829894

5853
Charles G. O'Bleness Foundation No. 3 ¤
c/o Huntington National Bank, Trust Dept.
41 South High St.
Columbus 43216 (614) 463-3707

Established in 1963 in OH.
Donor(s): Charles O'Bleness,† Charles O'Bleness Foundation No. 1.
Foundation type: Independent
Financial data (yr. ended 12/31/88): Assets, $2,409,163 (M); gifts received, $5,000; expenditures, $181,905, including $144,464 for 13 grants (high: $35,714; low: $250).
Purpose and activities: Giving primarily for education; support also for a historical society.
Limitations: Giving limited to Athens County, OH.
Application information: Application form not required.
Deadline(s): Oct. 15
Advisors: John M. Jones, Theodore Vogt.
Trustee: Huntington National Bank.
Employer Identification Number: 316042978

5854
The M. G. O'Neil Foundation ¤
c/o Gencorp.
175 Ghent Rd.
Akron 44313 (216) 869-4412

Incorporated in 1953 in OH.
Donor(s): M.G. O'Neil.
Foundation type: Independent
Financial data (yr. ended 6/30/88): Assets, $4,648,889 (M); expenditures, $137,208, including $132,375 for 62 grants (high: $11,000; low: $100).
Purpose and activities: Giving primarily for Roman Catholic organizations; some support also for a community fund and social service agencies.
Types of support: General purposes.
Limitations: Giving primarily in OH. No grants for conferences, seminars, or special projects.
Application information: Application form not required.
Initial approach: Letter
Copies of proposal: 1
Deadline(s): None
Write: M.G. O'Neil, Pres.
Officers and Trustees: M.G. O'Neil, Pres. and Treas.; T.M. Haidnick, V.P.; E.R. Dye, Secy.
Number of staff: None.
Employer Identification Number: 346516968

5855
The O'Neill Brothers Foundation
3550 Lander Rd.
Cleveland 44122 (216) 464-2121

Incorporated in 1953 in MI.
Donor(s): William J. O'Neill,† P.J. O'Neill,† H.M. O'Neill,† Francis J. O'Neill.†
Foundation type: Independent
Financial data (yr. ended 12/31/88): Assets, $635,476 (M); gifts received, $16,725; expenditures, $164,031, including $153,916 for 84 grants (high: $10,750; low: $25).
Purpose and activities: Emphasis on Roman Catholic religious organizations and church support, health organizations, and higher and secondary education.
Types of support: General purposes.
Limitations: Giving primarily in Cleveland, OH.
Application information:
Deadline(s): None
Board meeting date(s): 4 times a year
Write: Robert K. Healey, Pres.
Officers and Trustees:* Robert K. Healey,* Pres.; William J. O'Neill, Jr.,* Secy.; P.F. Lang, F.J. O'Neill, Jr., Rev. A.M. Pilla, C.J. Rutt, Fr. J.J. Wright.
Employer Identification Number: 346545084

5856
The F. J. O'Neill Charitable Corporation ¤
3550 Lander Rd.
Cleveland 44124

Established in 1979 in OH.
Donor(s): Francis J. O'Neill.†
Foundation type: Independent
Financial data (yr. ended 8/31/88): Assets, $77,895,376 (M); expenditures, $4,147,670, including $3,483,859 for 58 grants (high: $1,000,000; low: $500).
Purpose and activities: Giving for higher and secondary education, and medical research, and to Roman Catholic organizations.
Types of support: General purposes.
Limitations: Giving primarily in greater Cleveland, OH. No grants for scholarships, fellowships, prizes, or similar benefits.
Application information: Applications not accepted.
Officers: Hugh O'Neill, Pres.; Nancy M. O'Neill, V.P.; Rev. E.P. Joyce, Secy.-Treas.
Employer Identification Number: 341286022

5857
H. M. O'Neill Charitable Trust ☆
3550 Lander Rd.
Cleveland 44124 (216) 464-2121

Established in 1973.
Foundation type: Independent
Financial data (yr. ended 05/31/89): Assets, $375,274 (M); expenditures, $833,820, including $806,890 for 27 grants (high: $300,000; low: $500).

Purpose and activities: Support primarily for Catholic organizations and secondary education; giving also for youth and social services, a museum, and health.
Types of support: Endowment funds.
Limitations: Giving primarily in Cleveland, OH. No grants to individuals.
Application information: Contributes only to pre-selected organizations. Applications not accepted.
Write: R.K. Healey, Trustee
Trustees: Robert K. Healey, Hugh O'Neill, Alice O'Neill Powers.
Employer Identification Number: 346695119

5858
The William J. and Dorothy K. O'Neill Foundation, Inc. ☆
30195 Chagrin Blvd., Suite 123
Cleveland 44124 (216) 831-9667

Established in 1987 in OH.
Donor(s): Dorothy K. O'Neill, Cleveland Research Institute.
Foundation type: Independent
Financial data (yr. ended 12/31/89): Assets, $1,562,832 (M); gifts received, $612,309; expenditures, $563,598, including $555,700 for 48 grants (high: $103,000; low: $1,000).
Purpose and activities: Giving primarily for Catholic organizations and higher and other education; support also for health.
Types of support: Endowment funds, general purposes, annual campaigns.
Limitations: Giving primarily in OH.
Application information:
Write: William J. O'Neill, Jr., Pres.
Officers and Trustees: William J. O'Neill, Jr., Pres. and Treas.; Sheldon M. Sager, Secy.; Dorothy K. O'Neill.
Employer Identification Number: 341560893

5859
Ohio Bell Foundation
45 Erieview Plaza, Rm. 870
Cleveland 44114 (216) 822-2423

Established in 1987 in OH.
Donor(s): Ohio Bell.
Foundation type: Company-sponsored
Financial data (yr. ended 12/31/89): Assets, $22,537,892 (M); gifts received, $1,750,000; expenditures, $2,382,947, including $2,121,051 for 400 grants (high: $500,000; low: $100; average: $100-$500,000) and $260,633 for 2,016 employee matching gifts.
Purpose and activities: Support for civic affairs, community development, science and technology, art and culture, higher, secondary, and elementary education, and health; support also for programs for literacy, and the aged.
Types of support: Continuing support, employee matching gifts, general purposes, special projects, capital campaigns.
Limitations: Giving limited to the Ohio Bell serving area, except for employee matching gifts for education. No support for religious organizations for religious purposes, lobbying, direct patient care, or sports or athletic events. No grants to individuals, or for special event advertising.
Publications: Annual report.
Application information: Application form not required.
Initial approach: Proposal
Copies of proposal: 1
Deadline(s): None
Board meeting date(s): Periodic
Final notification: Varies
Write: William W. Boag, Jr., Exec. Dir.
Officers: Thomas L. Elliott,* Pres.; Donald W. Morrison,* Secy.; Robert E. Cogan, Treas.; William W. Boag, Jr., Exec. Dir.
Trustees:* Douglas E. Fairbanks, Robert J. Hudzik, Donald W. Morrison, Leo R. Reichard.
Number of staff: 1 full-time professional; 2 full-time support.
Employer Identification Number: 341536258

5860
The Ohio Citizens Trust Company Foundation ⌑
405 Madison Ave.
P.O. Box 1688
Toledo 43603 (419) 259-7065

Trust established in 1953 in OH.
Donor(s): Ohio Citizens Bank.
Foundation type: Company-sponsored
Financial data (yr. ended 12/31/88): Assets, $7,109 (M); gifts received, $145,680; expenditures, $155,855, including $155,745 for 45 grants (high: $95,000; low: $25).
Purpose and activities: Emphasis on community funds, higher education, youth agencies, and hospitals.
Types of support: Operating budgets, continuing support, annual campaigns, building funds, capital campaigns, employee matching gifts, renovation projects.
Limitations: Giving primarily in the northwest OH area. No grants to individuals, or for endowment funds, scholarships, or fellowships; no loans.
Application information:
Initial approach: Proposal
Copies of proposal: 1
Deadline(s): Submit proposal preferably in month prior to board meetings; deadlines Mar. 1, June 1, Sept. 1, and Dec. 1
Board meeting date(s): Mar., June, Sept., and Dec.
Final notification: 1 month
Write: Jennifer J. Plummer, Asst. V.P., Ohio Citizens Bank
Trustees: Jennifer J. Plummer, Robert A. Robinson, Robert G. Siefers.
Employer Identification Number: 346519189

5861
The Ohio National Foundation ☆
237 William Howard Taft Rd.
Cincinnati 45219 (513) 559-6221

Established in 1987 in OH.
Donor(s): The Ohio National Life Insurance Co.
Foundation type: Company-sponsored
Financial data (yr. ended 12/31/89): Assets, $1,410,613 (M); expenditures, $162,403, including $141,825 for 60 grants (high: $57,500; low: $100) and $15,892 for 92 employee matching gifts.
Purpose and activities: Giving primarily to a community fund; support also for health, hospitals, and medical research, including AIDS, cancer, and heart disease; social services and youth; arts and culture, including museums; and education, including an employee matching gift program for higher education.
Types of support: Employee matching gifts, annual campaigns, building funds, capital campaigns, research, scholarship funds.
Limitations: Giving primarily in Cincinnati, OH. No grants to individuals.
Application information:
Initial approach: Letter
Deadline(s): None
Write: Howard C. Becker, Secy.
Officers and Trustees:* Bradley L. Warnemunde,* Pres.; Wendell C. True,* V.P.; Howard C. Becker,* Secy.; Joseph P. Brom,* Treas.; Stuart G. Summers, Bradley D. Warnemunde, Donald J. Zimmerman.
Employer Identification Number: 311230164

5862
The Ohio Valley Foundation
c/o The Fifth Third Bank
Dept. 00864
Cincinnati 45263 (513) 579-6034

Incorporated in 1946 in OH.
Donor(s): John J. Rowe,† Wm. L. McGrath, John W. Warrington.
Foundation type: Independent
Financial data (yr. ended 09/30/89): Assets, $3,356,813 (M); expenditures, $153,294, including $138,307 for 15 grants (high: $25,000; low: $4,000).
Purpose and activities: Giving primarily for education, youth agencies, cultural programs, and a children's hospital.
Types of support: Building funds, capital campaigns, renovation projects.
Limitations: Giving primarily in the greater Cincinnati, OH, area. No grants to individuals, or for endowment funds or operating budgets.
Publications: Annual report.
Application information: Application form not required.
Initial approach: Proposal
Copies of proposal: 1
Deadline(s): Aug. 1
Board meeting date(s): Sept.
Final notification: Immediately after meeting
Write: Carolyn F. McCoy, Fdn. Officer
Trustees: Clement Buenger, Philip C. Long, David Sharrock, N. Beverly Tucker, John W. Warrington.
Number of staff: 1 full-time professional; 1 full-time support.
Employer Identification Number: 316008508

5863
The Parker-Hannifin Foundation ▼ ⌑
17325 Euclid Ave.
Cleveland 44112 (216) 531-3000

Incorporated in 1953 in OH.
Donor(s): Parker-Hannifin Corp.
Foundation type: Company-sponsored
Financial data (yr. ended 6/30/88): Assets, $1,268,957 (M); gifts received, $2,406,328; expenditures, $1,771,656, including $1,645,345 for grants.

Purpose and activities: Grants largely for higher education, community funds, hospitals, and youth and health agencies.
Types of support: Employee matching gifts.
Limitations: No support for fraternal or labor organizations.
Application information: Application form not required.
Copies of proposal: 1
Board meeting date(s): Jan. and July
Write: Joseph D. Whiteman, V.P.
Officers and Trustees:* Patrick S. Parker,* Chair.; Paul G. Schloemer,* Pres. and C.E.O.; Joseph D. Whiteman, V.P., Secy., and General Counsel.
Number of staff: None.
Employer Identification Number: 346555686

5864
Paulstan, Inc. ⌑
P.O. Box 921
Cuyahoga Falls 44223

Established in 1984 in OH.
Donor(s): Stanley Myers, Pauline Myers.
Foundation type: Independent
Financial data (yr. ended 12/31/88): Assets, $649,167 (M); gifts received, $35,800; expenditures, $550,940, including $540,957 for 20 grants (high: $485,007; low: $250).
Purpose and activities: Support primarily for religious organizations, missionary programs, and a community foundation.
Limitations: No grants to individuals.
Application information: Contributes only to pre-selected organizations. Applications not accepted.
Officers: Stanley D. Myers, Pres.; S. Myers, V.P.; P.W. Myers, Secy.; D. Myers, Treas.
Employer Identification Number: 341462129

5865
The Payne Fund ⌑
1770 Huntington Bldg.
Cleveland 44115 (216) 696-1621

Incorporated in 1929 in OH.
Donor(s): Frances P. Bolton.†
Foundation type: Independent
Financial data (yr. ended 12/31/88): Assets, $2,387,965 (M); gifts received, $341,786; expenditures, $516,718, including $428,033 for 28 grants (high: $50,000; low: $3,000).
Purpose and activities: To initiate, assist, or conduct research and experiments in education and other activities in behalf of the welfare of mankind; support also for higher education and cultural programs.
Application information: Contributes only to pre-selected organizations. Applications not accepted.
Officers and Directors: Charles P. Bolton, Pres.; Kenyon C. Bolton III, V.P.; Philip P. Bolton, V.P.; Thomas C. Bolton, V.P.; William B. Bolton, Secy.-Treas.; John B. Bolton, Barbara Bolton Gratry, Mary Bolton Hooper, Frederick B. Taylor.
Employer Identification Number: 135563006

5866
Pearce Foundation ☆
c/o Mahoning National Bank
23 Federal Plaza, P.O. Box 479
Youngstown 44501-0479 (216) 742-7000

Established in 1966.
Foundation type: Independent
Financial data (yr. ended 12/31/89): Assets, $1,425,579 (M); expenditures, $71,470, including $50,000 for 15 grants (high: $8,000; low: $1,000) and $10,921 for 6 grants to individuals (high: $3,500; low: $1,000).
Purpose and activities: Support primarily for churches, historical societies, social services, and scholarships for higher education.
Types of support: Student aid.
Limitations: Giving primarily in OH, with emphasis on Salem.
Application information:
Initial approach: Letter or proposal
Deadline(s): None
Write: Carol Chamberlain, Asst. Trust Officer, Mahoning National Bank
Directors: Marjorie Barnes, Mildred Courtney, John Oesch.
Trustee: Mahoning National Bank of Youngstown.
Employer Identification Number: 346572300

5867
The Peerless Foundation ⌑ ☆
1821 Summit Rd., Suite 101
Cincinnati 45237
Application address: 3180 East Galbraith Rd., Cincinnati, OH 45236; Tel.: (513) 793-4558

Donor(s): Sidney A. Peerless.
Foundation type: Independent
Financial data (yr. ended 12/31/88): Assets, $134,175 (M); gifts received, $116,000; expenditures, $284,044, including $206,730 for 8 grants (high: $73,000; low: $2,000).
Purpose and activities: Giving primarily for medical research at universities and hospitals.
Types of support: Equipment, research.
Application information:
Deadline(s): None
Write: Sidney A. Peerless, Chair.
Officers: Sidney A. Peerless, Chair.; Louis Peerless, Pres.; Howard Schwartz, Secy.; Charles Froikin, Treas.
Employer Identification Number: 310741546

5868
The Perkins Charitable Foundation ⌑
401 Euclid Ave., Rm. 480
Cleveland 44114

Trust established in 1950 in OH.
Donor(s): Members of the Perkins family.
Foundation type: Independent
Financial data (yr. ended 12/31/88): Assets, $7,501,586 (M); expenditures, $422,843, including $394,000 for 46 grants (high: $50,000; low: $200).
Purpose and activities: Giving for higher and secondary education, museums, hospitals, community funds, and conservation.
Limitations: Giving primarily in OH. No grants to individuals.
Application information: Contributes only to pre-selected organizations. Applications not accepted.
Officer: Marilyn Best, Secy.-Treas.
Trustees: George Oliva III, Jacob B. Perkins, Leigh H. Perkins, Sallie P. Sullivan.
Employer Identification Number: 346549753

5869
Peterloon Foundation
1900 Carew Tower
Cincinnati 45202

Established in 1958.
Donor(s): John J. Emery.†
Foundation type: Independent
Financial data (yr. ended 11/30/89): Assets, $2,986,620 (M); expenditures, $225,533, including $50,750 for 14 grants (high: $10,000; low: $1,000).
Purpose and activities: Giving for arts and cultural programs, education, and social service agencies.
Limitations: Giving primarily in the metropolitan Cincinnati, OH, area. No grants for general operating funds.
Application information: Application form not required.
Copies of proposal: 4
Deadline(s): None
Board meeting date(s): As required
Officers: Lela Emery Steele, Pres. and Treas.; Melissa Emery Lanier, V.P.; Henry H. Chatfield, Secy.
Trustees: Ethan Emery, Irene E. Goodale, Paul George Sittenfeld.
Number of staff: None.
Employer Identification Number: 316037801

5870
The Thomas F. Peterson Foundation ⌑
3200 National City Ctr.
Cleveland 44114 (216) 621-0200

Established in 1953.
Foundation type: Independent
Financial data (yr. ended 10/31/88): Assets, $1,528,358 (M); gifts received, $20,000; expenditures, $68,117, including $53,000 for 13 grants (high: $7,500; low: $500).
Purpose and activities: Giving for higher education, cultural programs, and youth agencies.
Types of support: General purposes, scholarship funds.
Limitations: Giving primarily in OH. No grants to individuals.
Application information: Application form not required.
Deadline(s): None
Write: James E. Chapman, Secy.
Officers and Trustees: Ethel B. Peterson, Chair.; Barbara P. Ruhlman, Pres.; John D. Drinko, V.P.; James E. Chapman, Secy.; J. Richard Hamilton, Treas.
Employer Identification Number: 346524958

5871
Jesse Philips Foundation ▼ ⌑
4801 Springfield St.
Dayton 45401
Scholarship application address: c/o Ruth Richardson, Dayton Board of Education, Dayton Public Schools, 348 West First St., Dayton, OH 45402

Incorporated in 1960 in OH.
Donor(s): Jesse Philips, Philips Industries, Inc., and subsidiaries.
Foundation type: Company-sponsored
Financial data (yr. ended 2/28/89): Assets, $14,705,556 (M); gifts received, $1,688,185; expenditures, $2,560,999, including $2,419,319 for 117 grants (high: $452,500; low: $16; average: $500-$25,000).
Purpose and activities: Giving for Jewish welfare funds, hospitals, higher education, cultural programs, social services, and community development. Scholarships or study loans limited to high school students in Montgomery County, OH, or to Jesse Philips Scholars and paid through institutions.
Types of support: Scholarship funds.
Limitations: Giving primarily in Dayton, OH.
Application information: Application forms required for scholarship program.
Deadline(s): May I for scholarships
Write: Jesse Philips, Pres.
Officers and Trustees:* Jesse Philips,* Pres.; Caryl Philips,* V.P.; Milton Roisman,* V.P.; E.L. Ryan, Jr.,* Secy.; Thomas C. Haas,* Treas.
Employer Identification Number: 316023380

5872
Philips Industries Foundation ⌑ ☆
4801 Springfield St.
P.O. Box 943
Dayton 45401

Established in 1986 in OH.
Donor(s): Philips Industries, Inc.
Foundation type: Company-sponsored
Financial data (yr. ended 12/31/88): Assets, $2,035,523 (M); gifts received, $1,000,000; expenditures, $61,568, including $50,000 for 1 grant.
Purpose and activities: Support for a museum of natural history.
Limitations: Giving primarily in OH. No grants to individuals.
Application information: Contributes only to pre-selected organizations. Applications not accepted.
Officers: Jesse Philips, Pres.; Robert H. Brethen, V.P.; Leonard Reardon, V.P., Finance; E.L. Ryan, Sr., Secy.; T. Haas, Treas.
Employer Identification Number: 311207183

5873
The William B. Pollock Company Foundation
c/o Bank One, Youngstown, N.A.
Six Federal Plaza West
Youngstown 44503 (216) 742-6721

Established in 1952 in OH.
Foundation type: Independent
Financial data (yr. ended 12/31/89): Assets, $1,674,657 (M); qualifying distributions, $73,500, including $73,500 for 33 grants (high: $16,000; low: $100; average: $100-$4,000).
Purpose and activities: Emphasis on health and social services; some support for education, youth agencies, the handicapped, and the arts.
Types of support: General purposes.
Limitations: Giving primarily in the Youngstown, OH, area.
Publications: 990-PF.
Application information: Application form not required.
Initial approach: Letter
Copies of proposal: 1
Deadline(s): None
Trustee: Bank One, Youngstown, N.A.
Number of staff: None.
Employer Identification Number: 346514078

5874
The William B. Pollock II and Kathryn Challiss Pollock Foundation
c/o Bank One, Youngstown, N.A.
Six Federal Plaza West
Youngstown 44503

Trust established in 1952 in OH.
Donor(s): William B. Pollock II, Kathryn Challiss Pollock.
Foundation type: Independent
Financial data (yr. ended 12/31/89): Assets, $1,349,826 (M); qualifying distributions, $91,050, including $91,050 for 54 grants (high: $16,000; low: $50; average: $50-$7,000).
Purpose and activities: Support for hospitals, community funds, Protestant church support, cultural activities, education, youth and health agencies, and population control.
Types of support: Operating budgets, continuing support, annual campaigns, seed money, emergency funds, deficit financing, building funds, equipment, land acquisition, endowment funds, research, special projects, publications, conferences and seminars.
Limitations: Giving limited to the Youngstown, OH, area. No grants to individuals, or for matching gifts, or scholarships and fellowships; no loans.
Publications: 990-PF.
Trustees: Franklin S. Bennett, Jr., Bank One, Youngstown, N.A.
Number of staff: None.
Employer Identification Number: 346514079

5875
Porthouse Foundation ⌑ ☆
313 West North St.
Akron 44303-2397
Application address: 128 Ridge Crest Dr., Chesterfield, MO 63017

Donor(s): C.R. Porthouse.
Foundation type: Independent
Financial data (yr. ended 12/31/88): Assets, $1,040,983 (M); gifts received, $13,246; expenditures, $67,691, including $57,240 for 30 grants (high: $11,000; low: $40).
Purpose and activities: Giving primarily for higher education; support also for fishing and game organizations and community funds.
Application information:
Initial approach: Letter
Deadline(s): Oct. 1
Write: J. David Porthouse, Pres.
Officers: J. David Porthouse, Pres.; D.L. Gindlesberger, Secy.-Treas.
Director: C.R. Porthouse.
Employer Identification Number: 346525861

5876
Premier Industrial Foundation ⌑
4500 Euclid Ave.
Cleveland 44103 (216) 391-8300

Trust established in 1953 in OH.
Donor(s): Jack N. Mandel, Joseph C. Mandel, Morton L. Mandel, Premier Industrial Corp., and others.
Foundation type: Company-sponsored
Financial data (yr. ended 12/31/87): Assets, $4,477,795 (M); expenditures, $510,598, including $351,337 for 71 grants (high: $200,000; low: $100).
Purpose and activities: To support charitable organizations operating in the fields of education, welfare, and civic affairs; grants largely for Jewish welfare funds, the United Way, neighborhood development, and higher education, including scholarships to relatives of Premier Industrial Corporation employees. The Premier Industrial Philanthropic Fund is a fund of the Jewish Community Federation. The Federation makes recommendations to the company as to which organizations to fund.
Types of support: Employee-related scholarships, building funds.
Application information: Application form not required.
Initial approach: Proposal
Deadline(s): None
Board meeting date(s): Bimonthly
Write: Morton L. Mandel, Trustee
Trustees: Jack N. Mandel, Joseph C. Mandel, Morton L. Mandel, Philip S. Sims.
Number of staff: 2 full-time professional; 1 part-time support.
Employer Identification Number: 346522448

5877
The Elisabeth Severance Prentiss Foundation ▼
c/o National City Bank
P.O. Box 5756
Cleveland 44101 (216) 575-2760

Trust established in 1944 in OH.
Donor(s): Elisabeth Severance Prentiss,† Luther L. Miller, Kate W. Miller.
Foundation type: Independent
Financial data (yr. ended 12/31/88): Assets, $43,327,045 (M); gifts received, $5,182; expenditures, $2,909,666, including $2,647,241 for 19 grants (high: $1,228,740; low: $5,000; average: $5,000-$100,000).
Purpose and activities: To promote medical and surgical research and to assist in the acquisition, advancement and dissemination of knowledge of medicine and surgery, and of means of maintaining health; to promote public health; to aid hospitals and health institutions in Cuyahoga County, OH, that are organized and operated exclusively for public charitable purposes by contributions for capital improvements or equipment, purchase of rare and expensive drugs, and expenses of operation or maintenance; to improve methods of hospital management and administration; to support programs to make hospital and medical care available to all, especially those of low income.
Types of support: Research, operating budgets, continuing support, seed money, general purposes, building funds, equipment,

endowment funds, special projects, renovation projects.
Limitations: Giving primarily in the greater Cleveland, OH, area. No support for national fundraising organizations and foundations. No grants to individuals, or for scholarships, fellowships, or matching gifts; no loans.
Publications: Annual report (including application guidelines).
Application information: Application form not required.
Initial approach: Proposal
Copies of proposal: 1
Deadline(s): Submit proposal prior to May 15 and Nov. 15
Board meeting date(s): June and Dec.
Final notification: 1 week to 10 days following board meetings
Write: Frank Dinda
Officers: Quentin Alexander,* Pres.; Richard A. Beeman, Secy.
Managers:* Harry J. Bolwell, William J. DeLancey, J. Robert Killpack, William A. Mattie.
Trustee: National City Bank.
Number of staff: None.
Employer Identification Number: 346512433

5878
Price Brothers Foundation ⌑
367 West Second St., P.O. Box 825
Dayton 45402-1721 (513) 226-8849

Foundation type: Independent
Financial data (yr. ended 12/31/87): Assets, $335,611 (M); gifts received, $60,000; expenditures, $116,548, including $115,445 for 54 grants (high: $42,500; low: $24).
Purpose and activities: Support primarily for community funds.
Types of support: Matching funds.
Application information: Application form not required.
Initial approach: Letter
Deadline(s): None
Write: John B. Henry
Trustees: Donald N. Lorenz, Gayle B. Price, Jr., Harry S. Price, Jr.
Employer Identification Number: 316049364

5879
The Procter & Gamble Fund ▼
P.O. Box 599
Cincinnati 45201 (513) 983-3913

Incorporated in 1952 in OH.
Donor(s): The Procter & Gamble Cos.
Foundation type: Company-sponsored
Financial data (yr. ended 06/30/89): Assets, $24,259,320 (M); expenditures, $14,695,779, including $14,622,593 for 1,083 grants (high: $1,830,000; low: $50).
Purpose and activities: Grants nationally for private higher education and economic and public policy research organizations; support also for community funds, hospitals, youth agencies, urban affairs, and aid to the handicapped; generally limited to areas of domestic company operations.
Types of support: Annual campaigns, building funds, continuing support, emergency funds, equipment, land acquisition, matching funds, employee-related scholarships, employee matching gifts.
Limitations: Giving primarily in areas in the U.S. and where the company and its subsidiaries have large concentrations of employees; national giving for higher education and economic and public affairs. No grants to individuals.
Publications: Informational brochure.
Application information: Grant requests from colleges and universities are discouraged, as most grants are initiated by the trustees within specified programs. Application form not required.
Initial approach: Proposal
Copies of proposal: 1
Deadline(s): None
Board meeting date(s): Jan., Apr., July, and Oct.
Final notification: 1 month
Write: R.R. Fitzpatrick, V.P.
Officers and Trustees:* G.S. Gendell,* Pres.; R.R. Fitzpatrick,* V.P. and Secy.; S.J. Fitch,* V.P.; P.F. Wieting,* V.P.; George M. Gibson, Treas.; J.W. Nethercott.
Number of staff: 5 full-time professional; 2 full-time support.
Employer Identification Number: 316019594

5880
The Provident Foundation ⌑
One East Fourth St.
Cincinnati 45201
Application address: P.O. Box 2176, Cincinnati, OH 45201; Tel.: (513) 579-2067

Established in 1980 in OH.
Foundation type: Independent
Financial data (yr. ended 12/31/87): Assets, $8,656 (M); gifts received, $160,000; expenditures, $185,005, including $184,524 for 50 grants (high: $90,000; low: $100).
Purpose and activities: Support primarily for community funds, hospitals and health services, and education, especially higher education.
Limitations: Giving primarily in Hamilton County, OH.
Application information:
Initial approach: Letter
Deadline(s): None
Write: Eugenia Kelly
Officers and Trustees: Allen L. Davis, Pres.; Phillip R. Myers, V.P.; Leslie C. Nomelond, Secy.; James Berry, Treas.
Number of staff: None.
Employer Identification Number: 310999986

5881
Ada & Helen Rank Charitable Trust ⌑ ☆
P.O. Box 9950
Canton 44701-0950

Established in 1950.
Foundation type: Independent
Financial data (yr. ended 9/30/88): Assets, $1,493,988 (M); expenditures, $84,705, including $71,611 for 32 grants (high: $21,680; low: $431).
Purpose and activities: Support primarily for youth and social services.
Trustee: Society Bank of Eastern Ohio, N.A.
Employer Identification Number: 346576279

5882
P. K. Ranney Foundation
1525 National City Bank Bldg.
Cleveland 44114 (216) 696-4200

Incorporated in 1973 in OH.
Foundation type: Independent
Financial data (yr. ended 12/31/89): Assets, $5,354,914 (M); expenditures, $262,247, including $250,000 for 10 grants (high: $150,000; low: $5,000; average: $5,000-$10,000).
Purpose and activities: Support primarily for a local community foundation, health services, and marine sciences.
Types of support: Continuing support, endowment funds, general purposes, research.
Limitations: Giving primarily in OH.
Publications: 990-PF.
Application information:
Initial approach: Proposal
Deadline(s): None
Board meeting date(s): As required
Write: Phillip A. Ranney, Secy.
Officers: Peter K. Ranney, Pres. and Treas.; Robert K. Bissell, V.P.; Phillip A. Ranney, Secy.
Number of staff: 1 part-time professional.
Employer Identification Number: 237343201

5883
The Ratner, Miller, Shafran Foundation
10800 Brookpark Rd.
Cleveland 44130 (216) 267-1200

Incorporated in 1952 in OH.
Foundation type: Independent
Financial data (yr. ended 11/30/89): Assets, $458,613 (M); gifts received, $53,000; expenditures, $202,908, including $170,652 for 30 grants (high: $33,588; low: $100) and $31,556 for 92 grants to individuals (high: $6,032; low: $175).
Purpose and activities: Emphasis on Jewish giving, including education in the U.S. and Israel. Scholarships for residents of Cuyahoga County, OH.
Types of support: Student aid.
Application information: Application form required for scholarships. Application form required.
Deadline(s): May 1 for scholarships
Write: Nathan Shafran
Officers: Max Ratner, Pres.; Sam Miller, V.P. and Treas.; Albert Ratner, Secy.
Employer Identification Number: 346521216

5884
George J. Record School Foundation
P.O. Box 581
Conneaut 44030 (216) 599-8283

Incorporated in 1958 in OH.
Donor(s): George J. Record.†
Foundation type: Independent
Financial data (yr. ended 12/31/89): Assets, $2,753,166 (M); expenditures, $247,736, including $194,096 for 82 grants to individuals (high: $2,700; low: $500).
Purpose and activities: Scholarships to qualified residents of Ashtabula County, OH; applicants must attend an approved private college and complete six semesters or nine quarters of religious study.
Types of support: Student aid.

Limitations: Giving limited to residents of Ashtabula County, OH.
Application information: Formal interview at foundation is required. Application form required.
Deadline(s): May 20 for freshmen, June 20 for upperclassmen
Write: Charles N. Lafferty, Pres.
Officers and Trustees:* Charles N. Lafferty,* Pres. and Exec. Dir.; Harold M. Ladner,* V.P.; Howard T. Glover,* Secy.-Treas.; William H. Gerdes, William N. Runion.
Employer Identification Number: 340830818

5885
Reeves Foundation
232-4 West Third St.
P.O. Box 441
Dover 44622 (216) 364-4660

Trust established in 1966 in OH.
Donor(s): Margaret J. Reeves,† Helen F. Reeves,† Samuel J. Reeves.†
Foundation type: Independent
Financial data (yr. ended 12/31/89): Assets, $13,862,615 (M); expenditures, $572,664, including $461,186 for grants.
Purpose and activities: Emphasis on historical societies and health agencies; grants also for cultural activities, youth agencies, higher and other education, and public administration. Priority given to capital improvement projects.
Types of support: Operating budgets, continuing support, building funds, equipment, matching funds, research, scholarship funds, special projects.
Limitations: Giving primarily in OH, with emphasis on the Dover area. No grants to individuals, or for annual campaigns, seed money, emergency funds, deficit financing, land acquisition, renovation projects, endowment funds, fellowships, special projects, publications, or conferences; no loans.
Application information: Application form not required.
Initial approach: Proposal
Copies of proposal: 2
Deadline(s): 10 days prior to those months when board meets
Board meeting date(s): Bimonthly starting in Feb.
Final notification: 1 month
Write: Don A. Ulrich, Exec. Dir.
Officers and Trustees:* Margaret H. Reeves,* Pres.; Thomas R. Scheffer,* V.P.; W.E. Lieser,* Treas.; Don A. Ulrich, Exec. Dir.; Thomas J. Patton, Ronald L. Pissocra, Jeffry Wagner.
Number of staff: 1 part-time professional; 1 part-time support.
Employer Identification Number: 346575477

5886
The Reinberger Foundation ▼
27600 Chagrin Blvd.
Cleveland 44122 (216) 292-2790

Established in 1968 in OH.
Donor(s): Clarence T. Reinberger,† Louise F. Reinberger.†
Foundation type: Independent
Financial data (yr. ended 12/31/89): Assets, $49,595,473 (M); qualifying distributions, $1,872,921, including $1,872,921 for 51 grants (high: $200,000; low: $500; average: $20,000-$50,000).
Purpose and activities: Support for the arts, social welfare, Protestant churches, higher education, and medical research.
Types of support: Operating budgets, continuing support, annual campaigns, building funds, equipment, endowment funds, matching funds, scholarship funds, research, publications, special projects, deficit financing, capital campaigns.
Limitations: Giving primarily in the Cleveland and Columbus, OH, areas. No grants to individuals, or for seed money, emergency funds, land acquisition, demonstration projects, or conferences; no loans.
Publications: 990-PF.
Application information: Application form not required.
Initial approach: Proposal
Copies of proposal: 1
Deadline(s): None
Board meeting date(s): Mar., June, Sept., and Dec.
Final notification: 6 months
Write: Robert N. Reinberger, Co-Dir.
Officer: Richard H. Oman, Secy.
Directors: Robert N. Reinberger, William C. Reinberger.
Trustee: Ameritrust Co., N.A.
Number of staff: 2 full-time professional.
Employer Identification Number: 346574879

5887
Reliance Electric Company Charitable, Scientific and Educational Trust
6065 Parkland Blvd.
Cleveland 44124 (216) 266-1923

Trust established in 1952 in OH.
Donor(s): Reliance Electric Co.
Foundation type: Company-sponsored
Financial data (yr. ended 12/31/89): Assets, $155,000 (M); gifts received, $650,000; expenditures, $705,000, including $550,000 for 112 grants (high: $20,000; low: $200; average: $500-$5,000) and $155,000 for employee matching gifts.
Purpose and activities: Emphasis on community funds, higher education, hospitals, cultural programs, and social services; also funds an employee matching gifts program.
Types of support: Employee matching gifts, capital campaigns, continuing support.
Limitations: Giving primarily in areas of major company facilities. No support for national health organizations. No grants to individuals, or for dinners or special events.
Application information: Application form not required.
Initial approach: Proposal
Copies of proposal: 1
Deadline(s): None
Board meeting date(s): Quarterly
Write: William C. Gallagher, Secy.
Officer: William C. Gallagher, Secy.
Trustee: Ameritrust Co., N.A.
Number of staff: None.
Employer Identification Number: 346505329

5888
Renner Foundation ⌑
6151 Wilson Mills Rd., No. 215
Highland Heights 44143 (216) 473-0119

Incorporated in 1947 in OH as Renner Clinic Foundation.
Donor(s): R. Richard Renner, M.D.†
Foundation type: Independent
Financial data (yr. ended 5/31/88): Assets, $2,371,787 (M); expenditures, $174,501, including $123,140 for 4 grants (high: $100,000; low: $5,500).
Purpose and activities: Grants for a college, a hospital, and a Christian religious organization.
Limitations: No grants to individuals.
Application information:
Initial approach: Letter
Deadline(s): Submit proposal preferably in Jan. or Feb.; deadline Mar.
Board meeting date(s): Apr.
Write: Robert R. Renner, Pres.
Officers: Robert R. Renner,* Pres.; John W. Renner,* V.P.; Lillian M. Kozan, Secy.; Richard R. Renner,* Treas.; Gary L. Slapnicker, Exec. Dir.
Trustees:* David F. Percy, Frank E. Percy, Ruth A. Percy, Daniel S. Renner, Jane Renner, Jennie S. Renner, Carlton B. Schnell.
Employer Identification Number: 340684303

5889
Resler Foundation ⌑ ☆
P.O. Box 9715
Columbus 43209-9715

Established in 1946.
Foundation type: Independent
Financial data (yr. ended 12/31/88): Assets, $1,298,355 (M); expenditures, $61,750, including $59,000 for 5 grants (high: $15,000; low: $6,000).
Purpose and activities: Support primarily for social services.
Limitations: Giving primarily in Columbus, OH. No grants to individuals.
Application information: Contributes only to pre-selected organizations. Applications not accepted.
Officers: Eleanor S. Resler, Pres. and Secy.; John B. Resler, V.P. and Treas.
Employer Identification Number: 316042069

5890
The Reynolds and Reynolds Company Foundation
P.O. Box 2608
Dayton 45401 (513) 449-4490

Established in 1986 in OH.
Donor(s): The Reynolds and Reynolds Co.
Foundation type: Company-sponsored
Financial data (yr. ended 09/30/89): Assets, $11,281 (M); gifts received, $215,000; expenditures, $226,204, including $220,677 for grants and $5,000 for 2 grants to individuals.
Purpose and activities: "The foundation focuses attention on a program of giving to promote a healthy environment for neighbors, employees and their families, and the business community." Support for health, education, arts, and community activities; organizations not falling precisely into these categories may also be considered for grants. Programs will be

judged on their impact in the local community and how they fit into the total contributions program. Support is given to traditional, established organizations and to organizations which propose worthy, innovative programs. At times, when the foundation sees a need for a specific program for which it has not received an application, it may solicit a grant that addresses the perceived need. The United Way is also strongly supported.
Types of support: Annual campaigns, capital campaigns, operating budgets, program-related investments, special projects.
Limitations: Giving primarily in areas of company operations, with emphasis on Dayton, OH. No support for sectarian organizations with an exclusively religious purpose, fraternal or veterans' organizations, primary or secondary schools (except for occasional special projects), or tax-supported universities and colleges (except for occasional special projects); organizations receiving funds from the United Way generally not considered. No grants to individuals, or for courtesy advertising.
Publications: Application guidelines.
Application information: Outside of Dayton area, write to local facility manager. Application form not required.
Initial approach: Proposal
Copies of proposal: 1
Board meeting date(s): Bimonthly
Final notification: 3 months
Write: Mary Green, Admin.
Officer and Trustee:* Jack R. Martin,* Chair.
Employer Identification Number: 311168299

5891
The Helen Steiner Rice Foundation
221 East Fourth St., Suite 2100, Atrium 2
Cincinnati 45202 (513) 451-4939

Established in 1980 in OH.
Donor(s): Helen Steiner Rice.†
Foundation type: Independent
Financial data (yr. ended 06/30/89): Assets, $3,678,436 (M); expenditures, $216,370, including $149,500 for 27 grants (high: $15,000; low: $1,000; average: $5,000-$10,000).
Purpose and activities: Grants for the elderly and needy, family and health services, youth and child welfare, women, and adult, early childhood, and elementary education; preference for meeting immediate needs.
Types of support: Consulting services, continuing support, emergency funds, general purposes, seed money, special projects, operating budgets.
Limitations: Giving limited to the greater Cincinnati area and Lorain, OH. No grants to individuals, or for capital campaigns or building funds.
Publications: Annual report (including application guidelines), application guidelines, informational brochure, program policy statement.
Application information: Application form required.
Initial approach: Letter
Copies of proposal: 5
Deadline(s): July 1
Board meeting date(s): As required
Final notification: Nov.
Write: Virginia J. Ruehlmann, Admin.
Trustees: Willis D. Gradison, Jr., Eugene P. Ruehlmann, Donald E. Weston.
Number of staff: 1 full-time professional; 1 part-time support.
Employer Identification Number: 310978383

5892
The Richland County Foundation of Mansfield, Ohio ⌑
34-1/2 South Park St., Rm. 202
Mansfield 44902 (419) 525-3020

Incorporated in 1945 in OH.
Foundation type: Community
Financial data (yr. ended 12/31/88): Assets, $16,847,115 (M); gifts received, $1,387,918; expenditures, $1,201,770, including $865,278 for 43 grants (high: $187,240; low: $38), $154,783 for 230 grants to individuals and $44,573 for employee matching gifts.
Purpose and activities: To promote activities "of a charitable, educational, cultural, recreational and inspirational nature for the people of Richland County"; grants for local scholarships (paid directly to colleges), programs for the indigent aged, youth programs, hospital additions and health services, the handicapped, and the local community fund.
Types of support: Seed money, building funds, equipment, scholarship funds, operating budgets, emergency funds, student aid.
Limitations: Giving primarily in Richland County, OH. No support for sectarian religious purposes. No grants to individuals (except for undergraduate scholarships), or for endowment funds, annual campaigns, fellowships, highly technical or specialized research, operating or maintenance funds, or travel; no loans.
Publications: Annual report (including application guidelines).
Application information: Application form required for scholarships; available after Jan. 1.
Initial approach: Proposal
Copies of proposal: 1
Deadline(s): None
Board meeting date(s): Feb., May, Aug., and Nov.
Final notification: At least 6 weeks
Write: Betty J. Crawford, Exec. Dir.
Officers: Miles Christian,* Pres.; W.R. Cress, V.P.; James C. Gorman, V.P.; Pamela Siegenthaler,* V.P.; Betty J. Crawford, Secy. and Exec. Dir.; Rex E. Collins,* Treas.
Trustees:* F. Loyal Bemiller, Margaret Black, David L. Carto, Otis M. Cummins III, James D. Curry, M.D., Robert H. Enskat, John C. Fernyak, John Frecka, Miriam T. Gilbert, Jeff Gorman, James Kehoe, Darrell Kelley, K. Robert May, Robert B. Meese, John Robinson, John S. Roby, Tom Ross, Allen Sanford, Jean U. Sauter, John H. Siegenthaler, Richard G. Taylor, F.J. Wiecher.
Trustee Banks: Bank One of Mansfield, First Buckeye Bank, Richland Bank.
Number of staff: 1
Employer Identification Number: 340872883

5893
Richman Brothers Foundation ⌑
P.O. Box 657
Chagrin Falls 44022 (216) 247-5426

Incorporated in 1932 in OH.
Donor(s): Nathan G. Richman, Charles L. Richman, Henry C. Richman.
Foundation type: Independent
Financial data (yr. ended 12/31/89): Assets, $1,673,325 (M); expenditures, $109,778, including $45,097 for 25 grants (high: $10,000; low: $500) and $45,745 for 192 grants to individuals (high: $1,995; low: $100).
Purpose and activities: Giving principally for health care and to agencies providing support to children and aged; also provides relief assistance to pensioners or their widows of Richman Brothers Co.
Types of support: Grants to individuals.
Limitations: Giving primarily in OH, particularly Cleveland.
Application information: Application form required.
Initial approach: Proposal
Deadline(s): Nov. 15
Officers and Trustees:* Richard R. Moore,* Pres.; Ernest J. Marvar,* V.P.; John F. Miller,* V.P.; Raymond J. Novack.
Employer Identification Number: 346504927

5894
The Charles E. and Mabel M. Ritchie Memorial Foundation ⌑
c/o First National Bank of Ohio
106 South Main St.
Akron 44308 (216) 384-7313

Trust established in 1954 in OH.
Donor(s): Mabel M. Ritchie.†
Foundation type: Independent
Financial data (yr. ended 12/31/88): Assets, $4,393,573 (M); expenditures, $229,170, including $190,810 for 49 grants (high: $10,000; low: $900).
Purpose and activities: Grants to hospitals, youth agencies, and for higher education.
Types of support: Capital campaigns.
Limitations: Giving limited to Summit County, OH. No grants to individuals.
Application information:
Initial approach: Proposal
Copies of proposal: 4
Deadline(s): Jan. 1, Apr. 1, July 1, and Oct.1
Board meeting date(s): Distribution Committee meets first week of Feb., May, Aug., and Nov.
Write: Ronald B. Tynan, V.P., First National Bank of Ohio
Advisory Committee: Edward F. Carter, Kathryn M. Hunter, John D. Ong.
Trustee: First National Bank of Ohio.
Employer Identification Number: 346500802

5895
George W. & Mary F. Ritter Charitable Trust ⌑ ☆
c/o Trustcorp Bank, Ohio
P.O. Box 10099
Toledo 43699-0099

Established in 1982 in OH.
Foundation type: Independent

Financial data (yr. ended 11/30/88): Assets, $3,864,475 (M); expenditures, $209,080, including $185,715 for 25 grants (high: $27,857; low: $10) and $10,661 for 2 grants to individuals (high: $6,933; low: $3,728).
Purpose and activities: Giving primarily for hospitals and higher education; support also for Christian organizations, a library, and a museum.
Types of support: Operating budgets, student aid.
Limitations: Giving primarily in the Toledo, OH, area.
Application information: Completion of application form required for scholarships.
Deadline(s): None
Write: James E. Lupe, V.P., Trustcorp Bank, Ohio
Trustee: Trustcorp Bank, Ohio.
Scholarship Selection Committee: Larry Fierstien, Edgar A. Gibson, James D. Harvey, James Lupe.
Employer Identification Number: 346781636

5896
Roscoe Village Foundation ⌑
381 Hill St.
Coshocton 43812 (614) 622-5235

Trust established in 1952 in OH.
Donor(s): The Montgomery family.
Foundation type: Operating
Financial data (yr. ended 12/31/88): Assets, $10,033,345 (M); gifts received, $895,466; expenditures, $2,208,652.
Purpose and activities: A private operating foundation; all funds currently committed to the restoration of an historic canal town.
Limitations: Giving limited to the Roscoe Village, OH.
Publications: Newsletter, informational brochure.
Application information: Funds currently committed. Applications not accepted.
Write: Joel L. Hampton, Pres.
Officers and Trustees:* Fred E. Johnston,* Chair.; Samuel C. Clow,* Vice-Chair.; Joel L. Hampton, Pres.; Andrew L. Carter, V.P.; Dalvin Donovan, Treas.; and 11 additional trustees.
Number of staff: 15 full-time professional; 5 part-time professional; 65 full-time support; 90 part-time support.
Employer Identification Number: 316022295

5897
The Samuel Rosenthal Foundation
Halle Bldg., Suite 810
1228 Euclid Ave.
Cleveland 44115-8125 (216) 523-8125

Trust established in 1959 in OH.
Donor(s): Work Wear Corp., Inc., and subsidiaries.
Foundation type: Independent
Financial data (yr. ended 03/31/89): Assets, $9,633,828 (M); expenditures, $642,029, including $601,530 for 39 grants (high: $414,500; low: $50).
Purpose and activities: Grants for general, secular, vocational, Hebrew, and Jewish education; support also for the arts, health and welfare funds, medical research, and the aged.
Types of support: General purposes.
Limitations: Giving primarily in Cleveland, OH. No grants to individuals.
Publications: Application guidelines.
Application information: Application form not required.
Initial approach: Proposal
Copies of proposal: 1
Deadline(s): None
Board meeting date(s): 4 times a year
Final notification: After meeting
Write: Charlotte R. Kramer, Trustee
Trustees: Cynthia R. Boardman, Jane R. Horvitz, Charlotte R. Kramer, Mark R. Kramer, Leighton A. Rosenthal.
Number of staff: 2 part-time support.
Employer Identification Number: 346558832

5898
Helen L. & Marie F. Rotterman Trust ⌑
1000 Courthouse Plaza, S.W.
Dayton 45402 (513) 228-1111

Established in 1982 in OH.
Foundation type: Independent
Financial data (yr. ended 7/31/88): Assets, $2,456,720 (M); expenditures, $129,792, including $108,000 for 5 grants (high: $72,000; low: $6,000) and $7,750 for 4 grants to individuals (high: $4,000; low: $750).
Purpose and activities: Grants to Catholic colleges and missionary organizations; awards scholarships mainly to young women enrolled in Trinity College or who are in high school and plan to enroll there.
Application information:
Initial approach: Individual applicants should include Trinity College application and a copy of high school record and certification of Catholic church affiliation where applicable
Deadline(s): 4 to 6 months prior to beginning of school year for scholarships
Write: Louis T. Shulman, Trustee
Trustees: Charles F. Collins, John O. Hubler, Louis T. Shulman.
Employer Identification Number: 316236156

5899
The Rubbermaid Foundation ⌑
1147 Akron Rd.
Wooster 44691-0800 (216) 264-6464

Established in 1986 in OH.
Donor(s): Rubbermaid, Inc.
Foundation type: Company-sponsored
Financial data (yr. ended 12/31/88): Assets, $3,950,370 (M); gifts received, $1,400,000; expenditures, $534,856, including $525,571 for 60 grants (high: $252,206; low: $100).
Purpose and activities: Support for the arts, higher and secondary education, economics, and health.
Types of support: Annual campaigns.
Limitations: Giving primarily in OH, with emphasis on Wooster. No grants to individuals.
Application information:
Initial approach: Letter
Deadline(s): None
Write: Richard Gates, Pres.
Officers: Richard D. Gates,* Pres.; James A. Morgan,* Secy.; Jean W. Dean III, Treas.
Trustees:* Stanley C. Gault, Richard W. Hider, Joseph G. Meehan, Walter W. Williams.
Employer Identification Number: 341533729

5900
Fran and Warren Rupp Foundation ⌑
40 Sturges Ave.
Mansfield 44902-1912 (419) 522-2345

Established in 1977.
Donor(s): Fran Rupp, Warren Rupp.
Foundation type: Independent
Financial data (yr. ended 12/31/88): Assets, $2,635,005 (M); gifts received, $851,675; expenditures, $91,516, including $71,552 for 11 grants (high: $25,000; low: $1,000).
Purpose and activities: Emphasis on the arts and social service agencies.
Types of support: General purposes.
Limitations: Giving primarily in Mansfield, OH. No grants to individuals.
Application information: Application form not required.
Initial approach: Letter
Deadline(s): None
Write: Donald Smith, Secy.-Treas.
Officers and Trustees: Fran Rupp, Pres.; Donald Smith, Secy.-Treas.
Employer Identification Number: 341230690

5901
Josephine S. Russell Charitable Trust ⌑
c/o The Central Trust Co., N.A.
P.O. Box 1198
Cincinnati 45201 (513) 651-8377

Trust established in 1976 in OH.
Donor(s): Josephine Schell Russell.†
Foundation type: Independent
Financial data (yr. ended 06/30/89): Assets, $5,350,947 (M); expenditures, $221,634, including $197,030 for 27 grants (high: $30,000; low: $2,500; average: $5,000-$10,000).
Purpose and activities: Emphasis on education and aid to the handicapped; support also for social service agencies, cultural programs, health, and scientific and literary purposes.
Types of support: Seed money, equipment, land acquisition, special projects, publications, building funds, capital campaigns, renovation projects.
Limitations: Giving limited to the greater Cincinnati, OH, area. No grants to individuals, or for endowment funds, operating budgets, continuing support, annual campaigns, deficit financing, scholarships, or conferences; no loans.
Publications: Informational brochure (including application guidelines).
Application information: Application form not required.
Initial approach: Letter, telephone, or proposal
Copies of proposal: 8
Deadline(s): 1 month prior to board meetings
Board meeting date(s): 3rd Friday in Jan. and July
Final notification: 3 months
Write: Mrs. Nancy C. Gurney, Exec. Asst.
Trustee: The Central Trust Co., N.A.
Number of staff: 1 part-time professional.
Employer Identification Number: 316195446

5902
RWK Foundation ⌑ ☆
P.O. Box 1081
Findlay 45839-0551 (419) 423-4343

Donor(s): members of the Kirk Family.
Foundation type: Independent
Financial data (yr. ended 12/31/88): Assets, $63,416 (M); gifts received, $17,000; expenditures, $290,601, including $286,175 for 15 grants (high: $157,069; low: $260).
Purpose and activities: Giving primarily for religious welfare and education; support also for hazardous waste programs and child welfare.
Limitations: Giving primarily in OH.
Application information: Application form required.
Deadline(s): None
Write: Robert W. Kirk, Pres.
Officers: Robert W. Kirk, Pres.; James L. Kirk, V.P.; Joseph R. Kirk, V.P; Richard C. Kirk, V.P; William T. Kirk, Secy.; Catherine M. Smith, Treas.
Employer Identification Number: 341250065

5903
Salem Lutheran Foundation ⌑ ☆
c/o Michael Lerch
750 Northlawn Dr.
Columbus 43214
Application address: c/o Prince of People Church, 6470 Centennial Dr., Reynoldsburg, OH 43062; Tel.: (614) 863-3124

Established in 1968.
Donor(s): George A. Skestos, Homewood Corp.
Foundation type: Company-sponsored
Financial data (yr. ended 12/31/88): Assets, $1,704,390 (M); gifts received, $35,000; expenditures, $92,826, including $86,000 for 189 grants to individuals (high: $1,000; low: $200).
Purpose and activities: Awards scholarships to men entering the pastoral ministry of the Wisconsin Evangelical Lutheran Synod.
Types of support: Student aid.
Application information: Application form required.
Deadline(s): July 1
Write: Rev. Marc Schroeder, Trustee
Officers and Trustees: William Goldman, Pres.; Michael Saad, Secy.; Michael Lerch, Treas.; Rev. Marc Schroeder, Roger Zehms.
Employer Identification Number: 316084166

5904
Ruth G. & Sam H. Sampliner Foundation ⌑
27500 Cedar Rd., Apt. 305
Beachwood 44122-1150 (216) 464-6046

Donor(s): Sam H. Sampliner.
Foundation type: Independent
Financial data (yr. ended 12/31/88): Assets, $1,128,378 (M); expenditures, $78,380, including $69,484 for 21 grants (high: $25,000; low: $50).
Purpose and activities: Support primarily for culture, hospitals, and Jewish organizations.
Application information:
Initial approach: Letter
Deadline(s): None
Write: Sam H. Sampliner, Trustee
Trustee: Sam H. Sampliner.
Employer Identification Number: 346520228

5905
The Sapirstein-Stone-Weiss Foundation ⌑
(Formerly The Jacob Sapirstein Foundation of Cleveland)
10500 American Rd.
Cleveland 44144 (216) 252-7300

Incorporated in 1952 in OH.
Donor(s): Jacob Sapirstein.†
Foundation type: Independent
Financial data (yr. ended 5/31/88): Assets, $17,070,939 (M); expenditures, $1,755,947, including $1,620,938 for 62 grants (high: $498,613; low: $100).
Purpose and activities: Giving locally, nationally, and internationally for Jewish welfare funds and secondary and higher religious education.
Types of support: General purposes.
Limitations: No grants to individuals, or for scholarships or fellowships; no loans.
Application information:
Initial approach: Letter
Copies of proposal: 1
Deadline(s): Submit proposal in Apr.
Board meeting date(s): Quarterly
Write: Irving I. Stone, Pres.
Officers and Trustees: Irving I. Stone, Pres.; Morry Weiss, V.P. and Treas.; Gary Weiss, Jeffrey Weiss.
Employer Identification Number: 346548007

5906
The Schey Foundation ⌑
2167 Savannah Pkwy.
Westlake 44145

Established in 1985 in OH.
Donor(s): Ralph E. Schey, Walter A. Rajki.
Foundation type: Independent
Financial data (yr. ended 6/30/89): Assets, $2,744,511 (M); expenditures, $125,666, including $119,920 for 35 grants (high: $35,000; low: $50).
Purpose and activities: Giving primarily to a school of business building fund, a business education foundation, and an opera association; support also for performing arts groups.
Types of support: Building funds.
Limitations: Giving primarily in OH.
Application information: Contributes only to pre-selected organizations. Applications not accepted.
Officer and Trustees: Ralph E. Schey, Pres.; David E. Cook, Lucille L. Schey.
Employer Identification Number: 341502219

5907
John J. and Mary R. Schiff Foundation ⌑
P.O. Box 145496
Cincinnati 45214

Established in 1983 in OH.
Donor(s): John J. Schiff, Mary R. Schiff.
Foundation type: Independent
Financial data (yr. ended 06/30/89): Assets, $8,572,852 (M); expenditures, $280,998, including $274,413 for 12 grants (high: $61,413; low: $500).
Purpose and activities: Support primarily for a museum; giving also for cultural programs, secondary and other education, and Protestant churches.
Limitations: Giving primarily in OH.
Officer and Trustees:* John J. Schiff, Jr.,* Chair.; Susan S. Rheingold, Thomas R. Schiff.
Employer Identification Number: 311077222

5908
Albert G. and Olive H. Schlink Foundation ⌑
401 Citizens National Bank Bldg.
Norwalk 44857

Established in 1966 in OH.
Foundation type: Independent
Financial data (yr. ended 12/31/88): Assets, $6,087,327 (M); expenditures, $330,080, including $275,000 for 15 grants (high: $77,500; low: $2,500).
Purpose and activities: Grants to organizations providing aid to the indigent, including health agencies and hospitals; support also for the blind.
Limitations: Giving primarily in OH. No grants to individuals.
Application information:
Deadline(s): None
Write: Robert A. Wiedemann, Pres.
Officers and Trustees: Robert A. Wiedemann, Pres. and Secy.; Dorothy E. Wiedemann, V.P.; John D. Allton, Treas.; Lawrence P. Furlong, Charles Koppleman.
Employer Identification Number: 346574722

5909
Charlotte R. Schmidlapp Fund
c/o Fifth Third Bank
Dept. 00864, Fifth Third Ctr.
Cincinnati 45263 (513) 579-6034
Application address: Fifth Third Ctr., 31st Fl., Cincinnati, OH 45202

Trust established in 1907 in OH.
Donor(s): Jacob G. Schmidlapp.†
Foundation type: Independent
Financial data (yr. ended 09/30/89): Assets, $16,244,421 (M); gifts received, $109,326; expenditures, $639,984, including $562,065 for grants and $124,863 for loans to individuals.
Purpose and activities: "To aid young girls in the preparation for womanhood, by bringing their minds and hearts under the influence of education, relieving their bodies from disease, suffering or constraint and assisting them to establish themselves in life." Student loan program recently discontinued, however, prior commitments are still being honored; the foundation will make direct grants, primarily to colleges, universities, and nursing schools.
Types of support: Seed money, special projects.
Limitations: Giving primarily in Cincinnati, OH. No grants for building or endowment funds, or operating budgets.
Publications: Application guidelines.
Application information:
Initial approach: Letter

Copies of proposal: 1
Deadline(s): Mar. 1
Board meeting date(s): Mar. and Oct.
Write: Carolyn M. McCoy, Fdn. Officer, Fifth Third Bank
Trustee: Fifth Third Bank.
Number of staff: 1 full-time professional; 1 full-time support.
Employer Identification Number: 310532641

5910
Jacob G. Schmidlapp Trust No. 1 ▼
c/o Fifth Third Bank
Dept. 00864, Foundation Office
Cincinnati 45263 (513) 579-6034

Trust established in 1927 in OH.
Donor(s): Jacob G. Schmidlapp.†
Foundation type: Independent
Financial data (yr. ended 09/30/89): Assets, $32,443,966 (M); expenditures, $1,677,055, including $1,548,705 for 51 grants (high: $250,000; low: $500; average: $5,000-$100,000).
Purpose and activities: Grants for the relief of sickness, suffering, and distress, and for care of young children or the helpless and afflicted; support also for education related to the care of young children, including child care training.
Types of support: Seed money, building funds, equipment, land acquisition, capital campaigns.
Limitations: Giving primarily in the greater Cincinnati, OH, area. No support for religious or political purposes. No grants to individuals, or for annual campaigns, emergency funds, deficit financing, general support, scholarships, fellowships, operating budgets, or continuing support; no loans.
Publications: Annual report (including application guidelines).
Application information: Application form not required.
Initial approach: Letter, telephone, or proposal
Copies of proposal: 1
Deadline(s): Feb. 1, May 1, Aug. 1, and Nov. 1
Board meeting date(s): Mar., June, Sept., and Dec.
Final notification: Middle of months in which board meets
Write: Carolyn McCoy
Trustee: Fifth Third Bank.
Number of staff: 1 full-time professional; 1 full-time support.
Employer Identification Number: 316019680

5911
Jacob G. Schmidlapp Trust No. 2
c/o Fifth Third Bank
Dept. 00864, Trust Div.
Cincinnati 45263 (513) 579-6034

Trust established in 1916 in OH.
Donor(s): Jacob G. Schmidlapp.†
Foundation type: Independent
Financial data (yr. ended 09/30/89): Assets, $2,617,861 (M); expenditures, $117,489, including $89,442 for 6 grants (high: $30,000; low: $2,882; average: $5,000).
Purpose and activities: Grants for education, with emphasis on capital programs for higher educational institutions and cultural programs, primarily in the greater Cincinnati area.
Types of support: Equipment, building funds, capital campaigns, land acquisition, seed money, renovation projects.
Limitations: Giving primarily in the greater Cincinnati, OH, area; support also in KY and IN. No support for religious or political purposes. No grants to individuals, or for endowment funds, operating budgets, scholarships, or fellowships; no loans.
Publications: Annual report (including application guidelines), application guidelines.
Application information:
Initial approach: Letter or telephone
Copies of proposal: 1
Deadline(s): Feb. 1, May 1, Aug. 1, and Nov. 1
Board meeting date(s): Mar., June, Sept., and Dec.
Final notification: Middle of months in which board meets
Write: Carolyn F. McCoy, Fdn. Officer, Fifth Third Bank
Trustee: Fifth Third Bank.
Number of staff: 1 full-time professional; 1 full-time support.
Employer Identification Number: 316020109

5912
The Schooler Family Foundation ⌑ ☆
36 North Second St.
P.O. Box 919
Newark 43055

Established in 1987 in OH.
Donor(s): Seward D. Schooler.
Foundation type: Independent
Financial data (yr. ended 12/31/88): Assets, $70,561 (M); expenditures, $276,567, including $270,000 for 5 grants (high: $175,000; low: $15,000).
Purpose and activities: Support primarily for higher education; minor support for a Methodist church, a local park district, and a hospital.
Limitations: Giving primarily in OH. No grants to individuals.
Application information: Contributes only to pre-selected organizations. Applications not accepted.
Officers and Trustees: Seward Schooler, Pres. and Treas.; Edith I. Schooler, V.P.; J. Gilbert Reese, Secy.; Willard S. Broen, David R. Schooler, Seward Dean Schooler, Jr.
Employer Identification Number: 311157433

5913
Jerome & Saul Schottenstein Foundation ⌑ ☆
1800 Moler Rd.
Columbus 43207-1698

Established in 1982.
Donor(s): Saul Schottenstein, Jerome Schottenstein.
Foundation type: Independent
Financial data (yr. ended 12/31/88): Assets, $1,359,964 (M); gifts received, $500,000; expenditures, $491,458, including $491,000 for 6 grants (high: $267,000; low: $2,000).
Purpose and activities: Giving primarily for Jewish organizations and historical preservation; support also for medical research.
Types of support: Renovation projects, research, building funds.
Limitations: Giving primarily in Columbus, OH.
Application information: Contributes only to pre-selected organizations. Applications not accepted.
Officers: Saul Schottenstein, Pres.; Jerome Schottenstein, V.P.; Jay L. Schottenstein, Treas.
Employer Identification Number: 311038192

5914
The Scioto County Area Foundation
BancOhio Bldg., Suite 801
Portsmouth 45662 (614) 354-4612

Established in 1974 in OH.
Foundation type: Community
Financial data (yr. ended 09/30/89): Assets, $5,141,351 (M); gifts received, $264,248; expenditures, $388,753, including $318,170 for 41 grants (high: $21,330; low: $200).
Purpose and activities: Giving for charitable purposes to benefit the citizens of Scioto County.
Types of support: Seed money, equipment, matching funds, scholarship funds, special projects, publications, conferences and seminars, research.
Limitations: Giving limited to Scioto County, OH. No grants to individuals, or for operating budgets, continuing support, annual campaigns, emergency funds, deficit financing, building funds, land acquisition, endowments, consulting services, technical assistance, foundation-managed projects, professorships, internships, exchange programs, fellowships, or program support; no loans.
Publications: Application guidelines, annual report, informational brochure.
Application information: Application form required.
Initial approach: Telephone or letter
Deadline(s): Last Monday of each month
Board meeting date(s): 2nd Tuesday of each month
Write: Daniel Ruggiero, Chair.
Officer: Daniel Ruggiero, Chair.
Number of staff: 1 full-time professional.
Employer Identification Number: 510157026

5915
Scripps Howard Foundation
P.O. Box 5380
Cincinnati 45201 (513) 977-3035

Incorporated in 1962 in OH.
Donor(s): Scripps Howard, Inc., and Scripps Howard executives, employees and friends.
Foundation type: Company-sponsored
Financial data (yr. ended 12/31/89): Assets, $13,338,440 (M); gifts received, $1,181,692; expenditures, $1,691,058, including $1,015,470 for 68 grants (high: $250,000; low: $333; average: $3,000-$5,000) and $352,150 for 301 grants to individuals (high: $3,000; low: $500; average: $500-$3,000).
Purpose and activities: The improvement and advancement of journalism through education and research, and to support the First Amendment; support also for journalism

scholarship grants to both graduate and undergraduate students pursuing a career in communications as it pertains to print or broadcast media. Also grants for special journalism educational projects and National Journalism Awards.
Types of support: Scholarship funds, student aid, special projects.
Limitations: Giving primarily in areas of company operations for scholarship grants, and nationally for special grants and awards; national giving only for journalism and communications endeavors. No support for private foundations; generally no special grants to public causes, public radio and television, campus newspapers, governmental studies, or international projects. No grants for seminars, operating funds, or capital or annual campaigns.
Publications: Annual report, informational brochure (including application guidelines).
Application information: Information on journalism award contests available from foundation. Application form required for scholarships. Application form not required.
Initial approach: Proposal for any special grants
Copies of proposal: 1
Deadline(s): Submit proposal Mar. 31 for special grants; deadline Dec. 20 for scholarship applicants to request application, to be completed and returned by Feb. 25
Board meeting date(s): Semiannually
Final notification: May 15 for scholarships; July or Aug. for all other grants
Write: Albert J. Schottelkotte, Pres. or Mary Lou Marusin, Exec. Dir.
Officers: Jacques A. Caldwell,* Chair.; Albert J. Schottelkotte,* Pres.; Naoma Lowensohn,* V.P.; David Stolberg,* V.P.; M. Denise Kuprionis, Secy.; D.J. Castellini, Treas.
Trustees:* Michael Callaghan, Ron Klayman, Paul Knue, Sue Porter, Marilyn Scripps, Paul K. Scripps, Robert P. Scripps, Dan Thomasson, M.C. Watters, Joseph R. Williams, Jerome Wright.
Number of staff: 1 full-time professional; 1 full-time support.
Employer Identification Number: 316025114

5916
The Sears Family Foundation ⌑
907 Park Bldg.
Cleveland 44114 (216) 241-6434

Trust established in 1949 in OH.
Donor(s): Anna L. Sears,† Lester M. Sears,† Ruth P. Sears,† Mary Ann Swetland.†
Foundation type: Independent
Financial data (yr. ended 12/31/88): Assets, $2,104,675 (M); gifts received, $29,655; expenditures, $181,073, including $167,300 for 55 grants (high: $50,000; low: $100).
Purpose and activities: Giving for health, education, welfare, and environmental projects.
Types of support: General purposes, operating budgets, continuing support, annual campaigns, seed money, emergency funds, deficit financing, building funds, equipment, land acquisition, matching funds, research, capital campaigns.
Limitations: Giving limited to the Cleveland, OH, area. No grants to individuals, or for scholarships or fellowships; no loans.
Publications: 990-PF.
Application information: Application form not required.
Initial approach: Letter
Copies of proposal: 1
Deadline(s): Submit proposal preferably before Dec.
Board meeting date(s): As needed
Final notification: 60 days
Write: David W. Swetland, Trustee
Officer and Trustees: Polly M. Swetland, Secy.; Ruth Swetland Eppig, David Sears Swetland, David W. Swetland.
Number of staff: 2 part-time support.
Employer Identification Number: 346522143

5917
Murray and Agnes Seasongood Good Government Foundation ☆
1006 Mercantile Library Bldg.
Cincinnati 45202 (513) 721-2181
Application address: 414 Walnut St., Suite 1006, Cincinnati, OH 45202

Established in 1987 in OH.
Foundation type: Independent
Financial data (yr. ended 12/31/88): Assets, $2,618,218 (M); expenditures, $200,463, including $131,487 for 15 grants (high: $60,020; low: $326).
Purpose and activities: Giving for the legal profession, legal education, and government internships.
Types of support: Internships.
Limitations: Giving primarily in Cincinnati, OH.
Publications: Informational brochure.
Application information: Application form required.
Initial approach: Request for application
Copies of proposal: 15
Deadline(s): 15th of even-numbered months
Board meeting date(s): Odd-numbered months
Write: D. David Altman, Exec. Secy.
Officers: Bruce I. Petrie, Sr., Pres.; Henry R. Winkler, 1st V.P.; David D. Black, 2nd V.P.; D. David Altman, Exec. Secy.; William Baughin, Secy.; William T. Bahlman, Jr., Treas.
Trustees: William R. Burleigh, Robert W. Hilton, Jr., Mrs. Herbert Hoffheimer, Jon Hoffheimer, Gail Levin, Nancy Minson, Edward Padgett.
Number of staff: 1 part-time professional.
Employer Identification Number: 311220827

5918
Second Foundation ▼
1525 National City Bank Bldg.
Cleveland 44114 (216) 696-4200

Established in 1984 in OH.
Donor(s): 1525 Foundation.
Foundation type: Independent
Financial data (yr. ended 12/31/89): Assets, $25,335,198 (M); expenditures, $2,026,850, including $1,959,770 for 16 grants (high: $1,409,346; low: $1,000; average: $5,000-$100,000).
Purpose and activities: Support primarily for culture, education, social sciences, and environmental protection and conservation.
Types of support: Continuing support, endowment funds, general purposes, matching funds, research, equipment, professorships, building funds, capital campaigns, operating budgets, seed money.
Limitations: Giving primarily in OH, especially the Cleveland area.
Publications: 990-PF.
Application information: Application form not required.
Initial approach: Proposal
Copies of proposal: 1
Deadline(s): None
Board meeting date(s): As required; at least monthly
Final notification: Within 1 month of receipt
Write: Bernadette Walsh, Asst. Secy.
Officers and Directors:* Hubert H. Schneider,* Pres.; Thelma G. Smith,* V.P.; Phillip A. Ranney,* Secy.-Treas.
Number of staff: 2
Employer Identification Number: 341436198

5919
The Della Selsor Trust ⌑
P.O. Box 1488
Springfield 45501 (513) 324-5541

Established in 1966 in OH.
Donor(s): Della Selsor.†
Foundation type: Independent
Financial data (yr. ended 12/31/88): Assets, $2,250,681 (M); expenditures, $114,115, including $83,400 for 40 grants (high: $15,000; low: $200).
Purpose and activities: Grants to youth, cultural organizations, hospitals, and education; support also for a church.
Types of support: Annual campaigns, building funds, capital campaigns.
Limitations: Giving primarily in Clark and Madison counties, OH.
Application information:
Initial approach: Letter or telephone call
Deadline(s): None
Write: Trustees
Trustees: Glenn W. Collier, Oscar T. Martin.
Employer Identification Number: 510163338

5920
The Louise Taft Semple Foundation ▼
1800 Star Bank Ctr.
Cincinnati 45202 (513) 381-2838
Application address: 1808 Cincinnati Commerce Ctr., 600 Vine St., Cincinnati, OH 45202; Tel.: (513) 241-8880

Incorporated in 1941 in OH.
Donor(s): Louise Taft Semple.†
Foundation type: Independent
Financial data (yr. ended 12/31/89): Assets, $13,295,144 (M); expenditures, $619,218, including $533,450 for 26 grants (high: $75,000; low: $2,000; average: $2,000-$75,000).
Purpose and activities: Support for the fine arts, social services and a community fund, higher and secondary education, hospitals, and health organizations.

Types of support: Building funds, endowment funds, scholarship funds, matching funds.
Limitations: Giving primarily in the Cincinnati or Hamilton County, OH, area. No grants to individuals, or for general purposes or research; no loans.
Application information: Application form not required.
Initial approach: Letter
Deadline(s): None
Board meeting date(s): 1st Monday in Apr., July, Oct., and Dec.
Final notification: 3 months
Write: Dudley S. Taft, Pres. and Trustee
Officers: Dudley S. Taft,* Pres.; James R. Bridgeland, Jr.,* Secy.; Norma F. Gentzler, Treas.
Trustees:* Mrs. John T. Lawrence, Jr., Walter L. Lingle, Jr., Nellie L. Taft, Robert A. Taft, Jr., Mrs. Robert A. Taft II.
Number of staff: None.
Employer Identification Number: 310653526

5921
The Richard H. and Ann Shafer Foundation ⌑
Eight East Long St., Rm. 400
Columbus 43215 (614) 224-8111

Donor(s): Richard A. Shafer,† Ohio Road Paving Co.
Foundation type: Independent
Financial data (yr. ended 12/31/88): Assets, $1,689,520 (M); gifts received, $5,000; expenditures, $130,045, including $101,900 for 30 grants (high: $30,000; low: $400).
Purpose and activities: Emphasis on hospitals and health agencies, higher education, cultural programs, and social service agencies.
Limitations: Giving limited to OH.
Application information: Application form not required.
Initial approach: Proposal
Deadline(s): Dec. 10
Write: Fannie L. Shafer, Mgr.
Officer and Trustees: Fannie L. Shafer, Mgr.; Homer W. Lee, John Reese.
Employer Identification Number: 316029095

5922
Share Foundation, Inc. ⌑
10925 Reed Hartman Hwy., Suite 200
Cincinnati 45242

Established in 1966 in OH.
Donor(s): Robert M. Blatt.
Foundation type: Independent
Financial data (yr. ended 12/31/88): Assets, $637,115 (M); gifts received, $150,000; expenditures, $197,398, including $196,775 for 16 grants (high: $159,600; low: $50).
Purpose and activities: Funds primarily for Jewish giving.
Application information: Contributes only to pre-selected organizations. Applications not accepted.
Officer: Robert M. Blatt, Mgr.
Trustees: Berdye Blatt, David Blatt.
Employer Identification Number: 316067758

5923
Jasper H. Sheadle Trust ⌑
c/o Ameritrust Co., N.A.
900 Euclid Ave.
Cleveland 44101

Trust established in 1917 in OH.
Donor(s): Jasper H. Sheadle.†
Foundation type: Independent
Financial data (yr. ended 12/31/88): Assets, $2,371,697 (M); expenditures, $135,596, including $104,781 for 357 grants to individuals (high: $681; low: $50).
Purpose and activities: To provide pensions for aged couples or aged women (60 and over) only, who are residing in Cuyahoga or Mahoning counties, OH.
Types of support: Grants to individuals.
Limitations: Giving limited to Cuyahoga and Mahoning counties, OH.
Application information: Applicants usually nominated by outside organizations.
Officers: Frank I. Harding III, Mgr.; Rt. Rev. James R. Moodey, Mgr.; Francis J. Talty, Mgr.
Trustee: Ameritrust Co., N.A.
Employer Identification Number: 346506457

5924
Sheller-Globe Foundation ⌑
c/o Ohio Citizens Bank
P.O. Box 1688
Toledo 43603 (419) 255-8840
Application address: Sheller-Globe Corp., 1505 Jefferson Ave., Toledo, OH 43697

Trust established in 1956 in OH.
Donor(s): Sheller-Globe Corp.
Foundation type: Company-sponsored
Financial data (yr. ended 12/31/88): Assets, $181,147 (M); expenditures, $139,652, including $136,266 for 26 grants (high: $22,000; low: $250).
Purpose and activities: Emphasis on community funds, youth agencies, hospitals, the arts, and higher education.
Limitations: Giving primarily in OH. No grants to individuals.
Application information:
Initial approach: Letter
Copies of proposal: 1
Deadline(s): None
Board meeting date(s): As required
Write: William H. Patterson, Mgr.
Advisory Committee: George A. Berry, Chester Devenow, Alfred Grava, Ralph Hill, Lawrence King.
Trustee: Ohio Citizens Bank.
Employer Identification Number: 346518486

5925
The Sherman-Standard Register Foundation ⌑
626 Albany St.
Dayton 45408

Incorporated in 1955 in OH.
Donor(s): Standard Register Co.
Foundation type: Company-sponsored
Financial data (yr. ended 11/30/88): Assets, $616,647 (M); gifts received, $200,000; expenditures, $190,528, including $190,033 for 66 grants (high: $47,000; low: $120).
Purpose and activities: Giving for community funds, higher education, youth agencies, health, civic affairs, and culture.
Limitations: Giving primarily in OH.
Application information: Applications not accepted.
Officers: William P. Sherman, Pres.; J.L. Sherman, V.P.; Otto F. Stock, Secy.; Craig J. Brown, Treas.
Employer Identification Number: 316026027

5926
The Sherwick Fund ⌑
c/o The Cleveland Foundation
1400 Hanna Bldg.
Cleveland 44115 (216) 861-3810

Incorporated in 1953 in OH.
Donor(s): John Sherwin, Frances Wick Sherwin.
Foundation type: Independent
Financial data (yr. ended 12/31/87): Assets, $9,660,556 (M); expenditures, $583,212, including $512,933 for grants.
Purpose and activities: A supporting fund of The Cleveland Foundation; emphasis on youth agencies, health, education, social services, cultural programs, and community funds.
Types of support: Seed money.
Limitations: Giving limited to the greater Cleveland, OH, area and Lake County. No grants to individuals, or for endowment funds, general operating budgets, or deficit financing; no loans.
Publications: Annual report, application guidelines, program policy statement.
Application information: Application form not required.
Initial approach: Full proposal or letter of inquiry
Copies of proposal: 2
Deadline(s): Apr. 1 and Oct. 1
Board meeting date(s): Usually in June and Dec.
Final notification: 1 month after board meets
Write: Mary Louise Hahn, Secy.-Treas.
Officers: John Sherwin,* Chair.; John Sherwin, Jr.,* Pres.; Homer C. Wadsworth,* V.P.; Mary Louise Hahn, Secy.-Treas.
Trustees:* John J. Dwyer, Harvey G. Oppmann.
Number of staff: 1 full-time professional; 1 part-time support.
Employer Identification Number: 346526395

5927
The Sherwin-Williams Foundation
101 Prospect Ave., N.W., 12th Fl.
Cleveland 44115 (216) 566-2511

Incorporated in 1964 in OH.
Donor(s): The Sherwin-Williams Co.
Foundation type: Company-sponsored
Financial data (yr. ended 12/31/88): Assets, $4,497,451 (M); gifts received, $2,765,414; expenditures, $524,136, including $457,116 for 144 grants (high: $140,000; low: $250; average: $1,000-$2,000) and $64,187 for 305 employee matching gifts.
Purpose and activities: Supports health and human services agencies, higher education, civic affairs, and cultural programs.
Types of support: Operating budgets, building funds, equipment, employee matching gifts.

Limitations: Giving primarily in areas of company headquarters and plants; most grants are in Cleveland, OH. No support for sectarian, labor, veterans' or fraternal organizations, or organizations assisted by taxes; no operating support for organizations assisted by United Way. No grants to individuals, or for endowment funds, annual campaigns, seed money, emergency funds, deficit financing, land acquisition, special projects, research, scholarships, fellowships, publications, advertising, or conferences; no loans.
Application information: Application form not required.
Initial approach: Letter
Copies of proposal: 1
Deadline(s): Submit proposal preferably in Jan., Apr., July, or Oct.
Board meeting date(s): Mar., June, Sept., and Dec.
Final notification: 1 month
Write: Barbara Gadosik, Dir., Corp. Contribs.
Trustees: John G. Breen, Chair.; Thomas A. Commes, T. Kroeger, Thomas R. Miklich.
Number of staff: 1 full-time professional; 1 full-time support.
Employer Identification Number: 346555476

5928
William M. Shinnick Educational Fund ⌑
534 Market St.
Zanesville 43701 (614) 452-2273

Established in 1923 in OH.
Donor(s): William M. Shinnick, Eunice Hale Buckingham.
Foundation type: Independent
Financial data (yr. ended 6/30/87): Assets, $2,384,005 (M); gifts received, $75,311; expenditures, $2,238,343, including $528 for grants to individuals and $141,305 for 109 loans to individuals.
Purpose and activities: Loans and scholarships to students for educational purposes and grants for higher education.
Types of support: Student aid, student loans.
Limitations: Giving limited to Muskingum, OH.
Application information: Application form not required.
Deadline(s): June 30
Officers: Hazel L. Butterfield,* Pres.; Annabelle Kinney, Secy.
Trustees:* William S. Barry, Harold Gottlieb, J. Linsalm Knapp, Norma Littick.
Employer Identification Number: 314394168

5929
John Q. Shunk Association ⌑
P.O. Box 625
Bucyrus 44820
Scholarship application address: 1201 Timber Ln., Marion, OH 43302

Established in 1938 in OH.
Foundation type: Independent
Financial data (yr. ended 12/31/88): Assets, $1,287,697 (M); expenditures, $104,282, including $1,496 for 1 grant and $81,750 for grants to individuals.
Purpose and activities: Giving primarily for undergraduate scholarships.
Types of support: Student aid.
Limitations: Giving primarily in Bucyrus and Crawford counties, OH; scholarships limited to graduates of four high schools in Crawford County.
Application information: Application form required for scholarships is available from foundation or high school guidance offices.
Initial approach: Letter
Deadline(s): Feb. 15 for scholarships, none for other grants
Write: Jane C. Peppard, Secy.-Treas.
Officers: Fred Christman, Pres. and Mgr.; Jane C. Peppard, Secy.-Treas. and Mgr.; Jim Gillenwater, Mgr.; John Kennedy, Mgr.; Paul Kennedy, Mgr.
Employer Identification Number: 340896477

5930
The Simmons Charitable Trust ⌑
c/o Miners and Mechanics Savings & Trust Co.
124 North 4th St.
Steubenville 43952-2132

Established in 1977 in OH.
Foundation type: Independent
Financial data (yr. ended 5/31/88): Assets, $1,846,855 (M); expenditures, $81,961, including $68,725 for 29 grants (high: $10,000; low: $225) and $7,329 for 1 grant to an individual.
Purpose and activities: Grants for health and social services agencies, youth organizations, education, and religious giving; awards music scholarships to students of Steubenville High School.
Types of support: Student aid.
Limitations: Giving primarily in Jefferson County, OH, with emphasis on Steubenville.
Application information: Application form not required.
Initial approach: Letter
Trustee: Miners and Mechanics Savings & Trust.
Employer Identification Number: 346743541

5931
The Simmons Charitable Trust ⌑ ☆
c/o Miners and Mechanics Savings & Trust
124 North 4th St.
Steubenville 43952-2132

Established in 1977 in OH.
Foundation type: Independent
Financial data (yr. ended 5/31/88): Assets, $1,846,855 (M); expenditures, $81,961, including $68,725 for 29 grants (high: $10,000; low: $225) and $7,329 for 1 grant to an individual.
Purpose and activities: Giving primarily for human and social services, civic affairs, higher education, and historic preservation; also awards scholarships to individuals for higher education.
Types of support: Student aid.
Limitations: Giving primarily in Jefferson County, OH.
Application information:
Initial approach: Letter
Deadline(s): None
Trustee: Miners and Mechanics Savings & Trust.
Employer Identification Number: 341313062

5932
The Slemp Foundation ⌑
c/o Star Bank, N.A., Cincinnati
P.O. Box 1118
Cincinnati 45201 (513) 632-4585

Trust established in 1943 in VA.
Donor(s): C. Bascom Slemp.†
Foundation type: Independent
Financial data (yr. ended 6/30/87): Assets, $7,618,752 (M); gifts received, $1,300; expenditures, $449,037, including $177,750 for 26 grants (high: $54,000; low: $50) and $205,600 for 257 grants to individuals of $800 each.
Purpose and activities: Giving for the maintenance of three named institutions; charitable and educational purposes and for the improvement of health of residents of Lee and Wise counties, VA, or their descendants, wherever located; also giving for scholarships, a museum, libraries, and hospitals.
Types of support: Student aid, building funds, emergency funds, endowment funds, equipment, lectureships, renovation projects, scholarship funds, seed money.
Limitations: Giving limited to Lee and Wise counties, VA.
Publications: 990-PF.
Application information: Application forms provided for scholarship applicants.
Initial approach: Letter
Copies of proposal: 1
Deadline(s): Oct. 1 for scholarships
Board meeting date(s): Apr., July, and Nov.
Trustees: Campbell S. Edmonds, Mary Virginia Edmonds, John A. Reid, Nancy E. Smith.
Employer Identification Number: 316025080

5933
The Eleanor Armstrong Smith Charitable Fund
1100 National City Bank Bldg.
Cleveland 44114 (216) 566-5500

Established in 1974 in OH.
Donor(s): Kelvin Smith.†
Foundation type: Independent
Financial data (yr. ended 12/31/89): Assets, $3,558,166 (M); expenditures, $128,450, including $128,335 for 26 grants (high: $50,000; low: $35).
Purpose and activities: Support primarily for the environment, including nature and horticulture, health care, non-sectarian education, performing and visual arts, and health.
Types of support: General purposes.
Limitations: Giving primarily in the Cleveland, OH, area. No grants to individuals; no loans.
Application information: Telephone inquiries discouraged. Application form not required.
Initial approach: Letter
Copies of proposal: 1
Deadline(s): None
Write: Andrew L. Fabens, III
Trustee: Eleanor A. Smith.
Number of staff: None.
Employer Identification Number: 237374137

5934
The Smith Family Foundation ☒
19701 North Park Blvd.
Shaker Heights 44122

Incorporated in 1986 in OH.
Foundation type: Independent
Financial data (yr. ended 10/31/88): Assets, $129,722 (M); expenditures, $159,306, including $158,990 for 56 grants (high: $75,000; low: $25).
Purpose and activities: Support primarily for higher education, community funds, and the performing arts.
Types of support: General purposes.
Limitations: Giving primarily in Cleveland, OH. No grants to individuals.
Application information: Contributes only to pre-selected organizations. Applications not accepted.
Trustees: Gretchen P. Smith, Ward Smith.
Employer Identification Number: 346874008

5935
The Kelvin and Eleanor Smith Foundation ☒
1100 National City Bank Bldg.
Cleveland 44114
Application address: 29425 Chagrin Blvd., Suite 303, Pepper Pike, OH 44122

Incorporated in 1955 in OH.
Donor(s): Kelvin Smith.†
Foundation type: Independent
Financial data (yr. ended 10/31/88): Assets, $29,857,125 (M); gifts received, $651,727; expenditures, $1,225,997, including $952,833 for 41 grants (high: $133,333; low: $1,500).
Purpose and activities: Giving for education, cultural affairs, hospitals, and conservation.
Types of support: Operating budgets, continuing support, annual campaigns, seed money, building funds, equipment.
Limitations: Giving primarily in the greater Cleveland, OH, area. No grants to individuals, or for endowment funds, scholarships, fellowships, or matching gifts; no loans.
Publications: Application guidelines.
Application information: Application form not required.
Initial approach: Letter
Copies of proposal: 2
Deadline(s): None
Board meeting date(s): May and Oct.
Final notification: 2 to 3 months
Write: Douglas W. Richardson, Trustee
Officers and Trustees: John L. Dampeer, Pres. and Treas.; Lucia S. Nash, V.P.; Cara S. Stirn, V.P.; Ellen Mavec, Secy.; Douglas W. Richardson, Ralph S. Tyler, Jr.
Number of staff: None.
Employer Identification Number: 346555349

5936
Kelvin Smith 1980 Charitable Trust ☆
1100 National City Bank Bldg.
Cleveland 44114 (216) 566-5500

Established in 1980 in OH.
Donor(s): Kelvin Smith.†
Foundation type: Independent
Financial data (yr. ended 05/31/89): Assets, $2,884,364 (M); expenditures, $150,114, including $150,000 for 1 grant.
Purpose and activities: Support primarily in the field of aquarium and other marine activities.
Types of support: Operating budgets, special projects.
Limitations: Giving primarily in Cleveland, OH. No support for private foundations. No grants to individuals, or for scholarships or fellowships; generally no grants for endowments; no loans.
Application information: Telephone inquiries not encouraged. Application form not required.
Initial approach: Proposal
Copies of proposal: 1
Deadline(s): None
Write: John L. Dampeer, Trustee
Trustees: John L. Dampeer, Howard F. Stirn.
Number of staff: None.
Employer Identification Number: 346789395

5937
Jack J. Smith, Jr. Charitable Trust ☒
c/o The Central Trust Co., N.A.
P.O. Box 1198
Cincinnati 45201 (513) 651-8377

Established in 1972 in OH.
Donor(s): Jack J. Smith, Jr.†
Foundation type: Independent
Financial data (yr. ended 9/30/88): Assets, $3,411,950 (M); gifts received, $10,985; expenditures, $199,150, including $173,100 for 31 grants (high: $15,000; low: $250; average: $5,000-$10,000).
Purpose and activities: Giving primarily for social services, with emphasis on programs for needy or handicapped children.
Types of support: Seed money, equipment, land acquisition, special projects, publications, building funds, capital campaigns, renovation projects.
Limitations: Giving limited to the greater Cincinnati, OH, area. No grants to individuals, or for operating budgets, continuing support, annual campaigns, emergency funds, deficit financing, endowment funds, scholarships, research, or conferences; no loans.
Publications: Informational brochure (including application guidelines).
Application information: Application form not required.
Initial approach: Letter, telephone, or proposal
Copies of proposal: 7
Deadline(s): 1 month before meetings
Board meeting date(s): Bimonthly on the 3rd Friday of the month
Final notification: 3 months
Write: Nancy C. Gurney, Exec. Asst.
Trustees: Thomas J. Reis, The Central Trust Co., N.A.
Number of staff: 1 part-time professional.
Employer Identification Number: 310912146

5938
Willard E. Smucker Foundation ☒
2026 Wayne St., Rte. 2
Orrville 44667

Established in 1968 in OH.
Donor(s): J.M. Smucker Co., and members of the Smucker family.
Foundation type: Company-sponsored
Financial data (yr. ended 12/31/88): Assets, $3,213,134 (M); gifts received, $87,000; expenditures, $130,287, including $128,260 for 26 grants (high: $30,000; low: $1,000).
Purpose and activities: Support primarily for education and youth activities.
Limitations: Giving primarily in OH.
Application information: Contributes only to pre-selected organizations. Applications not accepted.
Officers and Trustees:* Paul H. Smucker,* Pres. and Treas.; Marcella S. Clark,* Exec V.P.; H. Ray Clark,* V.P.; Lorraine E. Smucker,* V.P.; Steven J. Ellcessor, Secy.; Richard K. Smucker, Timothy P. Smucker.
Employer Identification Number: 346610889

5939
The South Waite Foundation
Ameritrust Co., N.A.
900 Euclid Ave.
Cleveland 44101

Incorporated in 1953 in OH.
Donor(s): Francis M. Sherwin,† Margaret H. Sherwin.
Foundation type: Independent
Financial data (yr. ended 12/31/88): Assets, $2,020,512 (M); expenditures, $147,527, including $134,334 for 28 grants (high: $15,000; low: $1,000).
Purpose and activities: Grants usually to those local organizations with which the foundation is familiar; emphasis on community funds, the arts, secondary education, health and medical research, and youth organizations.
Types of support: Operating budgets, capital campaigns, annual campaigns.
Limitations: Giving limited to the Cleveland, OH, area. No grants to individuals, or for scholarships.
Application information: Application form not required.
Initial approach: Letter
Deadline(s): None
Write: Thomas P. Demeter
Officers and Trustees:* Brian Sherwin,* Pres.; Margaret H. Sherwin,* V.P.; Donald W. Gruetner,* Secy.-Treas.; Sherman Dye, Member.
Members: Dennis Sherwin, Peter Sherwin.
Agent: Ameritrust Co., N.A.
Employer Identification Number: 346526411

5940
The Springfield Foundation ☆
c/o Robertson Can Co.
14 North Lowry Ave.
Springfield 45504 (513) 323-3747

Incorporated in 1948 in OH.
Foundation type: Community
Financial data (yr. ended 3/31/89): Assets, $3,215,101 (M); gifts received, $280,700; qualifying distributions, $177,684, including $177,684 for 99 grants (high: $17,500; low: $250).
Purpose and activities: Support for education, social services, the fine arts and music, recreation, health services, and the handicapped.

Types of support: General purposes, program-related investments, special projects, student loans.
Limitations: Giving limited to Springfield and Clark counties, OH. No grants to individuals.
Publications: Informational brochure, application guidelines.
Application information: Application form not required.
Initial approach: Letter
Copies of proposal: 1
Deadline(s): Mar. 31
Board meeting date(s): Feb., June, and Oct.
Write: Reed Robertson, Secy.
Officers: Daniel R. Shouvlin, Jr., Pres.; Reed Robertson, Secy.
Number of staff: None.
Employer Identification Number: 316030764

5941
Standard Products Charitable Foundation ⌑ ☆
2130 West 110th St.
Cleveland 44102-3590 (216) 281-8300

Established in 1984.
Donor(s): Standard Products Co.
Foundation type: Company-sponsored
Financial data (yr. ended 6/30/88): Assets, $1,016,546 (M); gifts received, $330,000; expenditures, $32,337, including $29,850 for 8 grants (high: $20,000; low: $500).
Purpose and activities: Support for higher education and youth clubs and organizations.
Types of support: Scholarship funds.
Limitations: Giving primarily in OH.
Application information: Application form not required.
Initial approach: Letter
Deadline(s): None
Write: Robert C. Jacob, V.P.
Officers and Trustees: James S. Reid, Jr., Pres.; Robert C. Jacob, V.P. and Secy.; Joseph A. Robinson, Treas.
Employer Identification Number: 341440117

5942
The Standard Products Foundation ⌑
2130 West 110th St.
Cleveland 44102 (216) 281-8300

Incorporated in 1953 in OH.
Donor(s): Standard Products Co.
Foundation type: Company-sponsored
Financial data (yr. ended 06/30/89): Assets, $6,685,162 (M); gifts received, $423,000; expenditures, $590,310, including $585,624 for 90 grants (high: $323,187; low: $125).
Purpose and activities: Emphasis on community funds, higher education, hospitals, cultural programs, and social service and youth agencies.
Limitations: Giving primarily in Cleveland, OH.
Application information:
Initial approach: Letter
Deadline(s): None
Write: Robert C. Jacob, V.P.
Officers and Trustees:* James S. Reid, Jr.,* Pres.; Robert C. Jacob,* V.P.; James E. Chapman,* Secy.; Joseph A. Robinson,* Treas.; E.B. Brandon.
Employer Identification Number: 346525047

5943
Star Bank, N.A., Cincinnati Foundation ⌑
(Formerly The First National Bank of Cincinnati Foundation)
c/o The First National Bank of Cincinnati
425 Walnut St.
Cincinnati 45202 (513) 632-4524

Trust established in 1967 in OH.
Foundation type: Company-sponsored
Financial data (yr. ended 12/31/87): Assets, $1,155,860 (M); gifts received, $220,000; expenditures, $503,350, including $500,804 for 49 grants (high: $87,500; low: $200).
Purpose and activities: Grants for community funds, hospitals, cultural programs, and higher education.
Types of support: General purposes, building funds, equipment, land acquisition, operating budgets.
Limitations: Giving limited to the greater Cincinnati, OH, area. No grants to individuals, or for endowment funds, research, scholarships, fellowships, or matching gifts; no loans.
Application information: Application form not required.
Initial approach: Letter
Deadline(s): None
Board meeting date(s): Monthly
Write: David L. Dowen
Officers and Trustees: Oliver W. Waddell, Chair.; Samuel M. Cassidy, Pres.; Herman J. Guckenberger, Jr., Secy.; James R. Bridgeland, Jr., J.P. Hayden, Jr., Mark T. Johnson, Thomas J. Klinedinst, William N. Liggett, Philip M. Meyers, Jr., Thomas E. Petry, William W. Wommack.
Number of staff: None.
Employer Identification Number: 316079013

5944
The Stark County Foundation
United Bank Bldg., Suite 350
220 Market Ave., South
Canton 44702 (216) 454-3426

Established in 1964 in OH by resolution and declaration of trust.
Foundation type: Community
Financial data (yr. ended 12/31/89): Assets, $31,462,000 (L); gifts received, $5,464,000; expenditures, $1,697,344, including $1,082,000 for 76 grants (high: $150,000; low: $250; average: $2,500-$20,000), $24,000 for 32 grants to individuals (high: $1,200; low: $250; average: $250-$1,200) and $107,000 for 82 loans to individuals.
Purpose and activities: To maintain the sound health and general welfare of the citizens through support for civic improvement programs, including the Newmarket Project for redevelopment of downtown Canton, hospitals, and educational institutions.
Types of support: Seed money, emergency funds, building funds, equipment, land acquisition, matching funds, scholarship funds, special projects, research, conferences and seminars, consulting services, technical assistance, capital campaigns, general purposes, student loans, student aid, loans.
Limitations: Giving limited to Stark County, OH. No grants for endowment funds, operating budgets, continuing support, annual campaigns, publications, or deficit financing; no grants or loans to individuals (except to college students who are residents of Stark County).
Publications: Multi-year report, program policy statement, application guidelines, financial statement, grants list.
Application information: Application form not required.
Initial approach: Letter or proposal
Copies of proposal: 8
Deadline(s): Mar. 1 for student aid; none for other grants
Board meeting date(s): Monthly
Final notification: 60 to 90 days
Write: James A. Bower, Exec. Dir.
Officers: William F. Schumacher, Financial Secy.; James A. Bower, Exec. Dir.
Distribution Committee: William H. Belden, Jr., Donald A. Hart, Dr. Thomas H. Hoover, William L. Luntz, Randolph L. Snow.
Trustee Banks: Ameritrust Co. of Stark County, Bank One of Alliance, The Central Trust Co. of Northern Ohio, N.A., First National Bank in Massillon, Society National Bank, United National Bank.
Number of staff: 1 full-time professional; 1 part-time professional; 1 full-time support.
Employer Identification Number: 340943665

5945
Justine Sterkel Trust ⌑
c/o Bank One, Mansfield
28 Park Ave. West
Mansfield 44902

Trust established in 1966 in OH.
Donor(s): Justine Sterkel.†
Foundation type: Independent
Financial data (yr. ended 12/31/87): Assets, $2,803,588 (M); expenditures, $161,803, including $137,000 for 7 grants (high: $40,000; low: $2,500).
Purpose and activities: Support largely for health and social service agencies.
Limitations: Giving primarily in OH.
Trustees: H. Eugene Ryan, Bank One, Mansfield.
Employer Identification Number: 346576810

5946
Burton E. Stevenson Endowment for Children ⌑
Box 572
Chillicothe 45601 (614) 772-5070

Established in 1963 in OH.
Foundation type: Independent
Financial data (yr. ended 12/31/88): Assets, $1,556,472 (M); gifts received, $4,542; expenditures, $100,948, including $51,206 for 12 grants (high: $10,800; low: $40) and $31,886 for 18 grants to individuals.
Purpose and activities: Grants given for the education, health, and welfare of underprivileged children including university scholarships.
Types of support: Student aid.
Limitations: Giving limited to Ross County, OH.
Application information:
Initial approach: Letter with financial information
Deadline(s): None

Write: Marilyn Carnes, Exec. Secy.
Officer: Marylyn Carnes, Exec. Secy.
Trustee: Huntington Trust Co., N.A.
Employer Identification Number: 136107576

5947
The Stocker Foundation

3535 East Erie Ave.
Lorain 44054 (216) 288-4581
Additional address: P.O. Box 2118, Lorain, OH 44054

Incorporated in 1979 in OH.
Donor(s): Beth K. Stocker.
Foundation type: Independent
Financial data (yr. ended 09/30/89): Assets, $8,542,375 (M); gifts received, $125,000; expenditures, $670,031, including $602,625 for 64 grants (high: $25,000; low: $500; average: $2,000-$1,500).
Purpose and activities: Emphasis on short-term youth development programs; social service agencies offering solutions to specific problems, such as literacy, hunger, and homelessness; education (including higher education); aid to the handicapped; self-help programs; and cultural programs.
Types of support: Operating budgets, continuing support, seed money, emergency funds, building funds, equipment, endowment funds, matching funds, scholarship funds, publications, renovation projects, research, special projects.
Limitations: Giving primarily in Lorain County, OH, and southern AZ. No support for religious organizations for religious purposes, governmental services, or public school services required by law. No grants to individuals, or for annual campaigns or deficit financing; no loans.
Publications: Application guidelines, informational brochure (including application guidelines).
Application information: Application form not required.
Initial approach: Telephone, letter, or proposal
Copies of proposal: 5
Deadline(s): Feb. 1, May 15, and Oct. 1
Board meeting date(s): Mid-winter, summer, and fall
Final notification: 1 month after board meetings
Write: Sara Jane Norton, Secy.-Treas.
Officers and Trustees:* Beth K. Stocker,* Pres.; Sara Jane Norton,* Secy.-Treas. and Dir.; Mary Ann Dobras, Anne Woodling, Nancy Elizabeth Woodling.
Corporate Trustee: Ameritrust Co., N.A.
Number of staff: 1 part-time professional; 1 part-time support.
Employer Identification Number: 341293603

5948
The Stouffer Corporation Fund ⌑

29800 Bainbridge Rd.
Solon 44139 (216) 248-3600

Incorporated in 1952 in OH.
Donor(s): The Stouffer Corp.
Foundation type: Company-sponsored
Financial data (yr. ended 6/30/88): Assets, $1,629,020 (M); gifts received, $500,000; expenditures, $407,808, including $402,550 for 277 grants (high: $77,500; low: $100; average: $250-$1,000).
Purpose and activities: Grants primarily for community funds, higher education, cultural programs, and health.
Types of support: Operating budgets, continuing support, annual campaigns, seed money, emergency funds, building funds, equipment, endowment funds, scholarship funds, special projects, capital campaigns, renovation projects.
Limitations: Giving primarily in OH. No grants to individuals, or for matching gifts, research, publications, or conferences; no loans.
Application information: Application form not required.
Initial approach: Letter
Copies of proposal: 1
Deadline(s): Submit proposal preferably in Aug. through Oct.
Board meeting date(s): Sept., Nov., Feb., and May
Write: Robert W. Loehr, Secy.-Treas.
Officers: Thomas Stauffer, Pres.; Powell Woods, V.P.; Robert W. Loehr, Secy.-Treas.
Trustees: Richard Atkinson, James M. Biggar, Ed Frantz, William Hulett, David Jennings, Anthony Martino, Wayne Partin, John Quagliata.
Number of staff: None.
Employer Identification Number: 346525245

5949
Stranahan Foundation ▼

900 Upton Ave.
Toledo 43607 (419) 535-2567

Trust established in 1944 in OH.
Donor(s): Robert A. Stranahan,† Frank D. Stranahan,† and others.
Foundation type: Independent
Financial data (yr. ended 12/31/87): Assets, $37,247,746 (M); expenditures, $1,643,788, including $1,414,616 for 44 grants (high: $275,000; low: $500; average: $500-$40,000).
Purpose and activities: Giving largely for higher education; support also for a community fund, youth, and social service and health agencies.
Types of support: Annual campaigns, building funds, equipment, land acquisition, endowment funds, general purposes, renovation projects, continuing support.
Limitations: Giving primarily in Toledo, OH. No grants to individuals.
Application information: Application form not required.
Initial approach: Letter
Copies of proposal: 1
Deadline(s): Oct. 1
Board meeting date(s): As required
Final notification: 4 months
Write: R.A. Stranahan, Jr., Trustee
Trustees: Francis G. Pletz, Duane Stranahan, Sr., Duane Stranahan, Jr., Robert A. Stranahan, Jr., Charles G. Yeager.
Number of staff: None.
Employer Identification Number: 346514375

5950
Switzer Foundation ⌑

2000 Huntington Bldg.
Cleveland 44115
CA application address: Oakland Scottish Rite Scholarship Foundation, 1547 Lakeside Dr., Oakland, CA 94612; Tel.: (415) 451-1906; New England application address: New Hampshire Charitable Fund, P.O. Box 1335, Concord, NH 03301

Established in 1985 in CA.
Donor(s): Members of the Switzer family.
Foundation type: Independent
Financial data (yr. ended 6/30/88): Assets, $6,974,835 (M); expenditures, $368,594, including $278,471 for 4 grants (high: $100,000; low: $38,000).
Purpose and activities: Scholarships and research grants for the reduction of air, water, or land pollution. Scholarships awarded only to students in CA through the Oakland Scottish Rite Scholarship Foundation and in northern New England through the New Hampshire Charitable Fund.
Types of support: Research, scholarship funds.
Limitations: Giving limited to CA and northern New England. No grants to individuals.
Publications: Application guidelines.
Application information: Application form required.
Initial approach: Letter
Deadline(s): Mar. 31
Board meeting date(s): Mar., May, Sept., and Nov.
Write: Ann Swander, Trustee
Trustees: Lincoln Reavis, Ann P. Swander, Fred E. Switzer, Marge Switzer, Patricia D. Switzer, Paul E. Switzer, Robert Switzer.
Employer Identification Number: 341504501

5951
The Frank M. Tait Foundation

Courthouse Plaza, S.W., 10th Fl.
Dayton 45402 (513) 222-2401

Incorporated in 1955 in OH.
Donor(s): Frank M. Tait,† Mrs. Frank M. Tait.†
Foundation type: Independent
Financial data (yr. ended 12/31/88): Assets, $4,446,744 (M); expenditures, $268,545, including $215,785 for 40 grants (high: $22,130; low: $50; average: $1,000-$5,000).
Purpose and activities: Support for youth agencies and cultural programs.
Types of support: Annual campaigns, seed money, building funds, equipment, special projects, capital campaigns, matching funds.
Limitations: Giving limited to Montgomery County, OH. No grants to individuals, or for endowment funds, operating budgets, continuing support, emergency funds, deficit financing, research, publications, conferences, scholarships, or fellowships; no loans.
Publications: Annual report (including application guidelines).
Application information: Application form not required.
Initial approach: Letter
Copies of proposal: 1
Deadline(s): Mar. 15, June 15, Sept. 15, and Dec. 15
Board meeting date(s): Apr., July, Oct., and Jan.

Final notification: 2 months
Write: Susan T. Rankin, Exec. Dir.
Officers: Richard F. Beach,* Pres.; Frederick W. Schantz, V.P.; Susan T. Rankin, Secy.-Treas. and Exec. Dir.
Trustees:* Irvin G. Bieser, Peter H. Forster, Alexander J. Williams.
Number of staff: 1 part-time professional.
Employer Identification Number: 316037499

5952
Nelson Talbott Foundation
911 East Ohio Bldg.
Cleveland 44114

Established in 1947 in OH.
Donor(s): Nelson S. Talbott.
Foundation type: Independent
Financial data (yr. ended 09/30/89): Assets, $1,419,356 (M); expenditures, $59,422, including $40,121 for 68 grants (high: $9,000; low: $25).
Purpose and activities: Support primarily for cultural institutions, wilderness societies, environmental concerns, and social services.
Limitations: Giving primarily in Cleveland, OH.
Trustees: Josephine L. Talbott, Nelson S. Talbott.
Employer Identification Number: 316039441

5953
Tamarkin Foundation ⌑
20 Federal Plaza West
Youngstown 44503 (216) 743-1786

Established in 1968.
Donor(s): Tamarkin Co., Project Four, Inc., S&H Co., members of the Tamarkin family.
Foundation type: Company-sponsored
Financial data (yr. ended 12/31/88): Assets, $399,382 (M); gifts received, $200,000; expenditures, $200,528, including $198,400 for 27 grants (high: $160,000; low: $100).
Purpose and activities: Primarily giving for Jewish welfare agencies and temple support; also support for hospitals and cultural institutions.
Types of support: Operating budgets, special projects, building funds.
Limitations: Giving primarily in OH.
Application information: Application form not required.
Deadline(s): None
Write: Bertram Tamarkin, Pres., or Nathan H. Monus, Secy.
Officers and Trustees: Bertram Tamarkin, Pres.; Jerry P. Tamarkin, V.P.; Nathan H. Monus, Secy.; Jack P. Tamarkin, Treas.; Arthur N.K. Friedman, Michael I. Monus.
Employer Identification Number: 341023645

5954
Lydia M. Taylor Trust ⌑ ☆
c/o First National Bank
P.O. Box 2668
Zanesville 43702-2668

Established in 1986.
Foundation type: Independent
Financial data (yr. ended 12/31/87): Assets, $3,502,502 (M); expenditures, $209,325, including $157,359 for 2 grants (high: $152,359; low: $5,000).
Purpose and activities: Support for a historical society and a hospital.
Application information:
Deadline(s): None
Trustee: First National Bank.
Employer Identification Number: 316307982

5955
Richard M. & Lydia McHenry Taylor Trust ⌑
c/o First National Bank, Trust Dept.
P.O. Box 2668
Zanesville 43702-2688 (614) 455-7060

Established in 1964 in OH.
Foundation type: Independent
Financial data (yr. ended 12/31/88): Assets, $1,250,390 (M); expenditures, $57,920, including $51,500 for 10 grants (high: $8,000; low: $2,000).
Purpose and activities: Support for community development and services.
Limitations: Giving limited to Muskingum County, OH.
Application information:
Initial approach: Letter
Deadline(s): None
Trustee: First National Bank.
Employer Identification Number: 316063772

5956
Paul P. Tell Foundation
1105 TransOhio Bldg.
156 South Main St.
Akron 44308 (216) 434-8355

Incorporated in 1952 in OH.
Donor(s): Tell family members, and their business interests.
Foundation type: Independent
Financial data (yr. ended 12/31/89): Assets, $3,072,601 (M); gifts received, $334,068; expenditures, $225,684, including $212,300 for 116 grants (high: $34,500; low: $100; average: $1,000).
Purpose and activities: For the furtherance of Evangelical Christianity; grants primarily for foreign missions and church-related educational institutions.
Types of support: Operating budgets, continuing support, seed money.
Limitations: No grants to individuals, or for building or endowment funds, scholarships, fellowships, or matching gifts; no loans.
Application information: Applications not accepted.
Board meeting date(s): June
Write: David J. Schipper, Exec. Dir.
Officers: Paul P. Tell, Jr.,* Pres.; Peter Keslar, V.P.; Jean Anne Schipper, Secy.-Treas.; David J. Schipper, Exec. Dir.
Trustees:* David Fair, Anne Tell, Michael Tell, Paul P. Tell, Sr.
Number of staff: None.
Employer Identification Number: 346537201

5957
The Thendara Foundation, Inc. ⌑ ☆
1800 Star Bank Ctr.
Cincinnati 45202

Established in 1984.
Donor(s): C. Lawson Reed, Dorothy W. Reed.
Foundation type: Independent
Financial data (yr. ended 12/31/88): Assets, $1,533,585 (M); gifts received, $500,100; expenditures, $24,950, including $24,167 for 4 grants (high: $12,000; low: $500).
Purpose and activities: Support primarily for the fine arts and performing arts.
Limitations: Giving primarily in Cincinnati, OH. No grants to individuals.
Application information: Contributes only to pre-selected organizations. Applications not accepted.
Trustees: James M. Anderson, Janet Reed Goss, Dorothy Reed Hagist, C.L. Reed III, C. Lawson Reed, Dorothy W. Reed, Foster A. Reed, Peter S. Reed.
Employer Identification Number: 311126072

5958
R. David Thomas Foundation ⌑
5131 Post Rd., Suite 302
Dublin 43017

Established in 1985 in OH.
Donor(s): R. David Thomas.
Foundation type: Independent
Financial data (yr. ended 12/31/88): Assets, $492,532 (M); expenditures, $474,738, including $449,268 for 5 grants (high: $289,058; low: $1,000).
Purpose and activities: Support for higher education, a recreation program, and a children's home society.
Limitations: Giving primarily in OH. No grants to individuals.
Application information: Contributes only to pre-selected organizations. Applications not accepted.
Officers and Trustees: R.L. Richards, Pres. and Treas.; Duke W. Thomas, Secy.; W.L. Thomas, Mgr.; Molly J. Postewaite, Lori D. Thomas.
Employer Identification Number: 311143830

5959
Joseph H. Thompson Fund ⌑
c/o C.E. Bartter, C.P.A.
503 Lyme Circle
Berea 44017
Application address: 1649 35th St. N.W., Washington, DC 20007; Tel.: (202) 342-7595

Incorporated in 1957 in OH.
Donor(s): Joseph H. Thompson.
Foundation type: Independent
Financial data (yr. ended 12/31/88): Assets, $1,446,692 (M); expenditures, $93,057, including $81,500 for 30 grants (high: $9,000; low: $500).
Purpose and activities: Support primarily for hospitals, higher and secondary education, conservation, and family planning.
Application information:
Initial approach: Letter
Deadline(s): None
Write: Lacey Neuhaus Dorn, Pres.
Officers: Lacey Neuhaus Dorn, Pres.; William J. Clark, Jr., V.P. and Treas.; Robert A. Toepfer, Secy.
Employer Identification Number: 346520252

5960
The Timken Company Charitable Trust ⌑
1835 Dueber Ave., S.W.
Canton 44706 (216) 438-4005

Trust established in 1947 in OH.
Donor(s): The Timken Co.
Foundation type: Company-sponsored
Financial data (yr. ended 12/31/87): Assets, $1,004,902 (M); expenditures, $226,182, including $214,675 for 30 grants (high: $33,250; low: $350; average: $1,000-$15,000).
Purpose and activities: Support primarily for higher education and community funds; some support for cultural programs.
Types of support: Operating budgets.
Limitations: Giving primarily in OH. No grants to individuals.
Application information: Application form not required.
Deadline(s): None
Final notification: Varies
Write: Ward J. Timken, Advisor
Advisor: Ward J. Timken.
Trustee: The Central Trust Co. of Northern Ohio, N.A.
Number of staff: 3 full-time professional; 3 full-time support.
Employer Identification Number: 346534265

5961
The Timken Company Educational Fund, Inc. ⌑
1835 Dueber Ave., S.W.
Canton 44706 (216) 438-3944

Established in 1957.
Donor(s): Timken Co. Charitable Trust.
Foundation type: Company-sponsored
Financial data (yr. ended 12/31/86): Assets, $259,408 (M); expenditures, $344,392, including $36,000 for 14 grants (high: $6,000; low: $2,000) and $307,800 for 31 grants to individuals.
Purpose and activities: Grants for higher education, including individual scholarships for children of company employees.
Types of support: Employee-related scholarships.
Application information: Application form required.
Deadline(s): Announced annually
Write: Thomas E. Grove, Supervisor - Education Programs
Officers and Trustees: Ward J. Timken, Pres.; R.W. Lang, V.P.; J.K. Ramsey, Secy.-Treas.; P.J. Ashton, C.P. Weigel, C.H. West.
Employer Identification Number: 346520257

5962
Timken Foundation of Canton ▼
236 Third St., S.W.
Canton 44702 (216) 455-5281

Incorporated in 1934 in OH.
Donor(s): Members of the Timken family.
Foundation type: Independent
Financial data (yr. ended 09/30/89): Assets, $138,713,451 (M); expenditures, $6,856,837, including $6,545,306 for 57 grants (high: $2,000,000; low: $750; average: $10,000-$300,000).
Purpose and activities: To promote broad civic betterment by capital fund grants; grants largely for colleges, schools, hospitals, cultural centers, conservation and recreation, and other charitable institutions.
Types of support: Building funds, equipment, capital campaigns.
Limitations: Giving primarily in areas of Timken Co. domestic operations in Canton, Columbus, Ashland, Bucyrus, and Wooster, OH; Gaffney, SC; Lincolnton, NC; and Latrobe, PA. No grants to individuals, or for operating budgets.
Application information: Proposal. Application form not required.
Deadline(s): None
Board meeting date(s): As required
Final notification: As soon as possible
Write: Don D. Dickes, Secy.-Treas.
Officers and Trustees* Ward J. Timken,* Pres.; W.R. Timken,* V.P.; W.R. Timken, Jr.,* V.P.; Don D. Dickes,* Secy.-Treas.
Number of staff: 1 full-time professional; 1 part-time support.
Employer Identification Number: 346520254

5963
Tipp City Foundation ⌑ ☆
c/o Star Bank
910 West Main St.
Troy 45373

Foundation type: Independent
Financial data (yr. ended 12/31/88): Assets, $1,084,406 (M); expenditures, $84,845, including $77,335 for grants.
Purpose and activities: Support for education, the elderly, historic preservation, and recreation.
Limitations: Giving limited to Tipp City, OH.
Application information:
Deadline(s): None
Trustee: Star Bank, N.A., Cincinnati.
Employer Identification Number: 316018697

5964
Toledo Community Foundation, Inc. ▼
1540 National Bank Bldg.
Toledo 43604-1108 (419) 241-5049

Established in 1924 in OH by trust agreement; reactivated in 1973.
Foundation type: Community
Financial data (yr. ended 12/31/88): Assets, $14,359,657 (M); gifts received, $1,418,061; expenditures, $1,971,240, including $1,710,823 for 417 grants.
Purpose and activities: Support for projects which promise to affect a broad segment of the citizens of northwestern OH or which tend to help those living in an area not being adequately served by local community resources. Areas of interest include social services and youth programs, arts and culture, hospitals and health associations, education, conservation, religion, government and urban affairs, and united funds.
Types of support: Seed money, matching funds, conferences and seminars, equipment, renovation projects, special projects.
Limitations: Giving primarily in northwestern OH, with emphasis on the greater Toledo area. No grants to individuals, or for annual campaigns, operating budgets, or endowment funds.
Publications: Annual report, informational brochure, application guidelines.
Application information: Application form required.
Copies of proposal: 1
Deadline(s): Submit proposal preferably in months when board meets; deadlines Mar. 1, June 1, Sept. 1, and Dec. 1
Board meeting date(s): Jan., Apr., July, and Oct.
Final notification: 2 months
Write: Pam Howell-Beach, Dir.
Officers and Trustees:* Steven Timonere,* Pres.; Duane Stranahan, Jr.,* V.P.; Thomas H. Anderson,* Secy.; Lawrence T. Foster,* Treas.; Robert V. Franklin, Jr., Robert J. Kirk, Marvin S. Kobacker, Joel Levine, Helen McMaster, Julie Taylor, H. Lawrence Thompson, Jr., Mrs. Frederic D. Wolfe.
Number of staff: 2 full-time professional; 2 part-time professional; 1 full-time support; 2 part-time support.
Employer Identification Number: 237284004

5965
Tranzonic Foundation
c/o The Tranzonic Companies
30195 Chagrin Blvd., Suite 224E
Pepper Pike 44124 (216) 831-5757

Established in 1976 in OH.
Donor(s): The Tranzonic Cos.
Foundation type: Company-sponsored
Financial data (yr. ended 06/30/89): Assets, $1,164 (M); gifts received, $230,575; expenditures, $230,300, including $230,300 for 30 grants (high: $21,000; low: $100).
Purpose and activities: Support primarily for Jewish welfare, community funds, health, and social services and community development.
Limitations: Giving primarily in northern OH. No grants to individuals.
Application information: Application form required.
Initial approach: Letter
Deadline(s): None
Final notification: Late Feb. or early Mar.
Write: Robert S. Reitman, V.P.
Officers: James H. Berick, Pres.; Robert S. Reitman, V.P.; Sam Pearlman, Secy.-Treas.
Number of staff: None.
Employer Identification Number: 341193613

5966
Tremco Foundation ⌑
10701 Shaker Blvd.
Cleveland 44104

Trust established in 1950 in OH.
Donor(s): Tremco Manufacturing Co.
Foundation type: Company-sponsored
Financial data (yr. ended 12/31/88): Assets, $1,584,380 (M); gifts received, $250,000; expenditures, $232,035, including $220,968 for 140 grants (high: $15,000; low: $10; average: $300).
Purpose and activities: Emphasis on community funds, higher education, and cultural programs.
Types of support: Building funds, capital campaigns, continuing support, employee

matching gifts, fellowships, general purposes, employee-related scholarships, scholarship funds.
Limitations: Giving primarily in Cleveland, OH. No grants to individuals, or for annual campaigns, conferences and seminars, consulting services, deficit financing, endowment funds, equipment, exchange programs, internships, land acquisition, matching funds, operating budgets, professorships, publications, renovation projects, research, seed money, special projects, or technical assistance; no loans.
Application information: Contributes only to pre-selected organizations. Applications not accepted.
Trustees: Leigh Carter, Gordon D. Harnett, Mark A. Steinbock.
Employer Identification Number: 346527566

5967
The Treu-Mart Fund ⌑
c/o The Cleveland Foundation
1400 Hanna Bldg.
Cleveland 44115 (216) 861-3810
Additional address: c/o R. Michael Cole, The Jewish Community Federation of Cleveland, 1750 Euclid Ave., Cleveland, OH 44115; Tel.: (216) 566-9200

Established in 1980 in OH.
Donor(s): Elizabeth M. Treuhaft, William C. Treuhaft.†
Foundation type: Independent
Financial data (yr. ended 12/31/87): Assets, $1,802,539 (M); gifts received, $1,000; expenditures, $103,531, including $93,800 for grants (high: $20,000; low: $1,000).
Purpose and activities: Supporting organization of The Cleveland Foundation and The Jewish Community Federation of Cleveland; organization grants primarily for projects benefitting residents of the greater Cleveland area, especially those incorporating demonstration or research elements. Support largely for community development, cultural programs, health planning, and social service activities, including Jewish welfare agencies.
Types of support: Research, special projects.
Limitations: Giving primarily in Cleveland, OH. No grants to individuals, or for operating budgets or annual campaigns.
Publications: Annual report, program policy statement, application guidelines.
Application information: Application form not required.
Initial approach: Proposal
Copies of proposal: 2
Deadline(s): Feb. 1 and Sept. 1
Board meeting date(s): Usually in Mar. and Oct.
Final notification: 3 months
Write: Mary Louise Hahn, Treas.
Officers: Elizabeth M. Treuhaft,* Chair.; Arthur W. Treuhaft,* Pres.; Homer C. Wadsworth,* V.P.; Henry L. Zucker,* V.P.; Howard R. Berger, Secy.; Mary Louise Hahn, Treas.
Trustees:* Frances M. King, Albert B. Ratner, Lloyd S. Schwenger.
Number of staff: 1 full-time professional; 1 full-time support.
Employer Identification Number: 341323364

5968
The Treuhaft Foundation ▼ ⌑
10701 Shaker Blvd.
Cleveland 44104 (216) 229-0166

Trust established in 1955 in OH.
Donor(s): Mrs. William C. Treuhaft, William C. Treuhaft.†
Foundation type: Independent
Financial data (yr. ended 12/31/87): Assets, $12,595,919 (M); expenditures, $1,188,963, including $1,101,049 for 78 grants (high: $240,000; low: $125; average: $200-$50,000).
Purpose and activities: Support for higher education, Jewish welfare funds, music and cultural programs, and health and welfare programs.
Types of support: Operating budgets, annual campaigns, seed money, emergency funds, building funds, endowment funds, professorships, special projects, research, publications, conferences and seminars.
Limitations: Giving primarily in the Cleveland, OH, area. No grants to individuals, or for capital grants, deficit financing, or hardware or software equipment; general support only to specific organizations of interest to the Treuhaft family; no loans.
Application information:
Initial approach: Letter
Deadline(s): None
Board meeting date(s): As required
Final notification: After board meeting
Write: Mrs. William C. Treuhaft, Chair.
Trustees: Mrs. William C. Treuhaft, Chair.; Irwin M. Feldman, Arthur W. Treuhaft.
Number of staff: None.
Employer Identification Number: 341206010

5969
The Troy Foundation
c/o Star Bank, N.A., Troy
910 West Main St.
Troy 45373 (513) 335-8351

Established in 1924 in OH by bank resolution and declaration of trust.
Donor(s): Nannie Kendall,† A.G. Stouder,† J.M. Spencer.†
Foundation type: Community
Financial data (yr. ended 12/31/89): Assets, $11,364,456 (M); gifts received, $1,058,837; expenditures, $594,313, including $553,226 for 44 grants (high: $151,083; low: $153).
Purpose and activities: To assist, encourage, and promote the well-being of mankind.
Types of support: Renovation projects, seed money, building funds, equipment, general purposes, annual campaigns, emergency funds, matching funds, program-related investments.
Limitations: Giving primarily in the Troy City, OH, School District and its vicinity. No support for religious organizations. No grants to individuals, or for endowment funds, operating budgets, continuing support, annual campaigns, emergency funds, deficit financing, land acquisition, research, demonstration projects, publications, conferences, scholarships, or fellowships; no loans.
Publications: Annual report, 990-PF, informational brochure, application guidelines.
Application information: Application form not required.
Initial approach: Proposal
Copies of proposal: 5
Deadline(s): None
Board meeting date(s): As required
Final notification: 1 to 2 months
Write: Richard J. Fraas, Secy.
Officers and Trustees: David L. Ault, Chair.; Richard J. Fraas, Secy.; Vernon T. Bowling, Robert J.M. Fisher, Thomas B. Hamler, William Hobart, Jr., Robert Koverman, Stewart I. Lipp, Robert B. Meeker, Max Myers, Jerrold R. Stammen.
Distribution Committee: Harold F. Willis, Chair.; Helen Meeker, Vice-Chair.; Doris Blackmore, R. Murray Dalton, G. Joseph Reardon.
Number of staff: None.
Employer Identification Number: 316018730

5970
Henry A. True Trust ⌑ ☆
c/o John K. Bartram
146 East Center St.
Marion 43302 (614) 387-6000

Established in 1964.
Foundation type: Independent
Financial data (yr. ended 12/31/88): Assets, $3,224,201 (M); expenditures, $216,543, including $106,000 for 27 grants (high: $15,000; low: $1,000).
Purpose and activities: Grants for Protestant church support, youth, and the arts, including museums.
Limitations: Giving limited to the Marion County, OH, area.
Application information:
Initial approach: Letter
Deadline(s): None
Write: John Kline Bartram, Trustee
Trustees: John C. Bartram, John Kline Bartram, Joe D. Donithen.
Employer Identification Number: 310679235

5971
Trustcorp Inc. Foundation
(Formerly The Toledo Trust Foundation)
c/o Society Bank & Trust
Three Seagate
Toledo 43603 (419) 259-8217

Trust established in 1953 in OH.
Donor(s): The Toledo Trust Co.
Foundation type: Company-sponsored
Financial data (yr. ended 12/31/88): Assets, $3,896 (M); gifts received, $620,025; expenditures, $619,453, including $604,911 for 85 grants (high: $100,000; low: $150; average: $1,000-$10,000) and $10,635 for 27 employee matching gifts.
Purpose and activities: Support for community funds and higher and secondary education; grants also for cultural activities and youth agencies.
Types of support: Operating budgets, continuing support, annual campaigns, emergency funds, building funds, equipment, land acquisition, consulting services, technical assistance, program-related investments, employee matching gifts, matching funds.
Limitations: Giving primarily in OH. No grants to individuals, or for start-up funds, deficit financing, or matching gifts; no loans.

Application information: Application form not required.
Initial approach: Letter
Deadline(s): None
Board meeting date(s): Monthly
Final notification: 2 months
Write: Thomas Cox, V.P., Society Bank & Trust
Number of staff: None.
Employer Identification Number: 346504808

5972
TRW Foundation ▼
1900 Richmond Rd.
Cleveland 44124 (216) 291-7166

Incorporated in 1953 in OH as the Thompson Products Foundation; became the Thompson Ramo Wooldridge Foundation in 1958, and adopted its present name in 1965.
Donor(s): TRW, Inc.
Foundation type: Company-sponsored
Financial data (yr. ended 12/31/88): Assets, $18,000,000 (M); gifts received, $14,000,000; expenditures, $7,117,708, including $5,610,212 for 367 grants (high: $375,000; low: $500; average: $2,500-$50,000), $7,000 for 5 grants to individuals (high: $1,500; low: $1,000) and $1,448,643 for 3,470 employee matching gifts.
Purpose and activities: Grants largely for higher education, particularly for engineering, technical, science, and/or business administration programs, and community funds; limited support for hospitals, welfare agencies, youth agencies, and civic and cultural organizations.
Types of support: Employee matching gifts, scholarship funds, professorships, fellowships, research, operating budgets, equipment, general purposes, matching funds, special projects.
Limitations: Giving primarily in TRW plant communities, with some emphasis on Cleveland, OH. No support for religious purposes, fraternal or labor organizations, or private elementary or secondary schools. No grants to individuals, or for endowment funds.
Publications: Annual report, program policy statement, application guidelines, grants list.
Application information: The employee-related scholarship program was discontinued in 1986; past obligations continue to be paid. Application form not required.
Initial approach: Proposal
Copies of proposal: 1
Deadline(s): Submit proposals preferably in Aug. or Sept.; deadline Sept. 1 for organizations already receiving support from the foundation
Board meeting date(s): Dec.
Final notification: 60 to 90 days
Write: Laura L. Johnson, Mgr.
Officers and Trustees:* Howard V. Knicely, Pres.; Robert M. Hamse, V.P.; Alan F. Senger, V.P.; James M. Roosevelt, Secy.; Robert G. Gornall, Treas.; Peter S. Hellman, Controller; Martin A. Coyle, Joseph T. Gorman.
Number of staff: 3 full-time professional; 1 full-time support; 1 part-time support.
Employer Identification Number: 346556217

5973
V and V Foundation ⌑
c/o Tinkham Veale II
Epping Rd.
Gates Mills 44040

Donor(s): Tinkham Veale II.
Foundation type: Independent
Financial data (yr. ended 12/31/88): Assets, $2,415,305 (M); gifts received, $152,000; expenditures, $84,212, including $79,975 for 36 grants (high: $19,875; low: $100).
Purpose and activities: Emphasis on higher and secondary education, Protestant giving, and for cardiovascular research.
Trustees: Helen V. Gelbach, Harriet V. Leedy, Harriet E. Veale, Tinkham Veale II, Tinkham Veale III.
Employer Identification Number: 346565830

5974
Van Dorn Foundation
2700 East 79th St.
Cleveland 44104 (216) 361-5234

Established in 1985 in OH.
Donor(s): Van Dorn Co.
Foundation type: Company-sponsored
Financial data (yr. ended 12/31/89): Assets, $8,323 (M); gifts received, $200,000; expenditures, $210,291, including $162,109 for 127 grants (high: $90,000; low: $50) and $48,182 for 42 employee matching gifts.
Purpose and activities: Interests include higher and secondary education, the performing arts and other cultural organizations, community funds and development, the disadvantaged, Catholic, Protestant, and Jewish giving, wildlife preservation, and health, including hospitals, nursing, and cancer research.
Types of support: Annual campaigns, capital campaigns, employee matching gifts.
Limitations: Giving primarily in the greater Cleveland, OH, area.
Application information: Application form not required.
Initial approach: Letter, outlining usage of monies requested
Copies of proposal: 1
Deadline(s): None
Board meeting date(s): Quarterly
Final notification: By end of calendar year
Write: Herman R. Ceccardi, Treas.
Officers and Trustees:* Lawrence C. Jones,* Chair.; Robert N. Jones,* Pres.; Campbell W. Elliott,* V.P., Public Affairs; Dennis A. Buss,* V.P.; Wolfgang Liebertz,* V.P.; Richard A. Plociak,* V.P.; William G. Pryor,* V.P.; George M. Smart,* V.P.; John L. Dampeer,* Secy.; Herman R. Ceccardi,* Treas.; James R. Heckman,* Controller.
Number of staff: None.
Employer Identification Number: 341464280

5975
The I. J. Van Huffel Foundation ⌑
c/o Bank One, Youngstown, N.A.
106 East Market St.
Warren 44481 (216) 841-7824
Application address: P.O. Box 231, Warren, OH 44482

Trust established in 1951 in OH.
Donor(s): Van Huffel Tube Corp.
Foundation type: Independent
Financial data (yr. ended 12/31/88): Assets, $1,618,595 (M); expenditures, $121,450, including $103,300 for 47 grants (high: $25,000; low: $250).
Purpose and activities: Emphasis on higher education, Roman Catholic and Protestant church support, hospitals, and social service agencies.
Limitations: Giving primarily in OH.
Application information:
Initial approach: Proposal
Deadline(s): None
Write: William Hanshaw, V.P., Bank One, Youngstown, N.A.
Directors: Joseph F. Dray, Dianne Knappenberger, Evelyn M. Reese, Edgar A. Van Huffel, Harold E. Van Huffel, Sr.
Trustee: Bank One, Youngstown, N.A.
Employer Identification Number: 346516726

5976
The Van Wert County Foundation ⌑
101-1/2 East Main St.
Van Wert 45891 (419) 238-1743

Incorporated in 1925 in OH.
Donor(s): Charles F. Wassenberg,† Gaylord Saltzgaber,† John D. Ault,† Kernan Wright,† Richard L. Klein,† Hazel Gleason,† Constance Eirich.†
Foundation type: Independent
Financial data (yr. ended 12/31/89): Assets, $7,124,457 (M); gifts received, $9,455; expenditures, $355,344, including $238,529 for grants (average: $500) and $58,762 for 100 grants to individuals (average: $200-$1,500).
Purpose and activities: Emphasis on scholarships in art, music, agriculture, and home economics; support also for elementary and secondary education, youth agencies, an art center, recreational facilities, and programs dealing with alcoholism and drug abuse.
Types of support: General purposes, equipment, student aid.
Limitations: Giving limited to Van Wert County, OH. No grants for endowment funds or matching gifts; no loans.
Publications: 990-PF, application guidelines.
Application information: Application forms and guidelines issued for scholarship program. Application form not required.
Initial approach: Letter or proposal
Copies of proposal: 1
Deadline(s): Submit proposal in May or Nov.; deadlines May 15 and Nov. 15
Board meeting date(s): Semiannually
Final notification: 1 week
Write: Robert W. Games, Exec. Secy.
Officers: A.C. Diller, Pres.; Larry L. Wendel, V.P.; D.L. Brumback, Jr., Secy.
Trustees: William S. Derry, Kenneth Koch, Gaylord E. Leslie, Watson Ley, Paul W. Purmort, Jr., Charles F. Ross, C. Allan Runser, Donald C. Sutton, Roger K. Thompson, Sumner J. Walters, G. Dale Wilson, Michael R. Zedaker.
Number of staff: 1 full-time professional; 1 full-time support.
Employer Identification Number: 340907558

5977
The Waddell Ladies Home Association ☆
P.O. Box 358
Marion 43301-0358 (614) 389-3677

Established in 1901 in OH.
Donor(s): Benjamin Waddell.†
Foundation type: Independent
Financial data (yr. ended 5/31/89): Assets, $1,257,710 (M); expenditures, $49,102, including $42,615 for 2 grants (high: $32,605; low: $10,010).
Purpose and activities: Giving primarily for social services, with emphasis on programs for senior citizens, including transportation and meals.
Limitations: Giving primarily in Marion County, OH.
Application information: Application form not required.
Initial approach: Letter
Copies of proposal: 2
Deadline(s): 1 week prior to board meetings
Board meeting date(s): 3rd Tuesday of Feb., May, Aug., and Nov.
Final notification: 2 weeks after board meetings
Write: James P. Waddell, Pres., or William E. Payette, Secy.-Treas.
Officers: James P. Waddell, Pres.; William Dunn, V.P.; William E. Payette, Secy.-Treas.
Trustees: Lewis Conkle, Betty Dendinger.
Number of staff: None.
Employer Identification Number: 314386851

5978
The Wagnalls Memorial
150 East Columbus St.
Lithopolis 43136 (614) 837-4765

Incorporated in 1924 in OH.
Donor(s): Mabel Wagnalls-Jones.†
Foundation type: Independent
Financial data (yr. ended 08/31/89): Assets, $16,874,285 (M); expenditures, $887,092, including $33,115 for grants, $217,069 for grants to individuals and $599,446 for foundation-administered programs.
Purpose and activities: Giving primarily for scholarships and fellowships; support also for community development, youth, libraries, and the arts.
Types of support: Student aid, fellowships, matching funds.
Limitations: Giving limited to the Bloom Township in Fairfield County, OH, area.
Publications: Annual report, newsletter, biennial report, application guidelines, informational brochure.
Application information: Application forms required for scholarships.
Initial approach: Letter or telephone
Deadline(s): June 15
Board meeting date(s): 1st Monday of each month
Write: Jerry W. Neff, Exec. Dir.
Officer: Jerry W. Neff, Exec. Dir.
Trustees: George W. Boving, W.W. Haynes, Benjamin C. Humphrey, Robert Rager, Dwayne R. Spence, John Watkins, Edwin Wisher.
Number of staff: 4 full-time professional; 2 part-time professional; 5 full-time support; 16 part-time support.
Employer Identification Number: 314379589

5979
Waite-Brand Foundation ⌑
c/o Schumaker, Loop & Kendrick
1000 Jackson Blvd.
Toledo 43624 (419) 241-4201

Established in 1965 in OH.
Foundation type: Independent
Financial data (yr. ended 2/28/88): Assets, $1,381,357 (M); expenditures, $88,065, including $63,750 for 7 grants (high: $29,750; low: $3,000).
Purpose and activities: Emphasis on Protestant giving, including ministries, and youth organizations.
Limitations: Giving primarily in Toledo, OH.
Application information:
Write: Gregory G. Alexander, Trustee
Trustees: Gregory G. Alexander, George M. Todd, The Toledo Trust Co.
Employer Identification Number: 346563471

5980
Evelyn E. Walter Foundation ⌑ ☆
116 South Main St.
Marion 43302

Established in 1987 in OH.
Foundation type: Independent
Financial data (yr. ended 12/31/88): Assets, $1,255,841 (M); expenditures, $57,531, including $50,000 for 10 grants (high: $13,000; low: $2,000).
Purpose and activities: Giving primarily for higher education and social services, including child welfare; support also for arts and culture.
Types of support: Scholarship funds, building funds, equipment.
Limitations: Giving primarily in Marion, OH. No grants to individuals.
Application information:
Initial approach: Letter
Deadline(s): None
Write: Ronald Cramer, Trustee
Trustees: Ronald Cramer, George Kennedy, William Rogers.
Employer Identification Number: 311171927

5981
The Grace High Washburn Trust ⌑
c/o John R. Clime
1520 Melody Ln.
Bucyrus 44820-3146
Application address: P.O. Box 389, Bucyrus, OH 44820

Established in 1949 in OH.
Foundation type: Independent
Financial data (yr. ended 12/31/88): Assets, $105,460,404 (M); expenditures, $69,304, including $54,472 for 90 grants to individuals (high: $2,000; low: $500).
Purpose and activities: Provides scholarships for Protestant female students to study at Ohio State University.
Types of support: Student aid.
Limitations: Giving limited to Bucyrus, OH, area.
Application information: Application form required.
Deadline(s): May 31
Officers: W.R. Mackling, Pres.; R. Miller, Secy.; M.R. Clime, Treas.
Employer Identification Number: 346521078

5982
Walter E. and Caroline H. Watson Foundation
P.O. Box 450
Youngstown 44501 (216) 744-9000

Trust established in 1964 in OH.
Donor(s): Walter E. Watson.†
Foundation type: Independent
Financial data (yr. ended 12/31/89): Assets, $4,683,426 (M); expenditures, $259,422, including $239,319 for 47 grants (high: $46,419; low: $500; average: $500-$5,000).
Purpose and activities: To support public institutions of learning in OH and public and charitable institutions in the Mahoning Valley, OH; emphasis on hospitals, child development and youth agencies, community development, health and family services, and arts and cultural programs.
Types of support: Annual campaigns, equipment, general purposes, renovation projects, special projects.
Limitations: Giving primarily in OH. No grants to individuals, or for endowment funds or operating budgets.
Application information: Application form not required.
Copies of proposal: 3
Board meeting date(s): Semiannually
Write: Herbert H. Pridham
Trustee: The Dollar Savings & Trust Co.
Employer Identification Number: 346547726

5983
The Raymond John Wean Foundation ▼ ⌑
c/o Second National Bank of Warren, Trust Dept.
108 Main St.
Warren 44481 (216) 394-5600

Trust established in 1949 in OH.
Donor(s): Raymond J. Wean.†
Foundation type: Independent
Financial data (yr. ended 12/31/86): Assets, $31,291,968 (M); gifts received, $6,597,590; expenditures, $1,083,775, including $933,834 for 608 grants (high: $75,000; low: $50; average: $100-$20,000).
Purpose and activities: Grants for higher and secondary education, hospitals, health agencies, youth agencies, Protestant church support, cultural programs, and social services.
Types of support: Continuing support.
Limitations: Giving primarily in OH, Palm Beach, FL, and PA, especially Pittsburgh.
Application information: Contributes only to pre-selected organizations. Applications not accepted.
Board meeting date(s): As required
Write: Raymond J. Wean, Jr., Chair.
Administrators: Raymond J. Wean, Jr., Chair.; Raymond J. Wean III, Vice-Chair.; Clara G. Petrosky, Secy.; Gordon B. Wean.
Trustee: Second National Bank of Warren.
Number of staff: None.
Employer Identification Number: 346505038

5984
The Weatherhead Foundation ⌑
c/o Thomas F. Allen
1800 Huntington Bldg.
Cleveland 44115 (216) 687-8664

Incorporated in 1953 in OH; foundation is income beneficiary of a perpetual trust; assets reflect assets of both feeder trust and foundation.
Donor(s): Albert J. Weatherhead, Jr.†
Foundation type: Independent
Financial data (yr. ended 12/31/88): Assets, $2,850,314 (M); gifts received, $1,083,238; expenditures, $1,401,232, including $1,255,000 for 7 grants (high: $600,000; low: $10,000).
Purpose and activities: Grants for endowments or programs, principally to universities and research organizations.
Types of support: Endowment funds, special projects, research, operating budgets.
Limitations: No support for religious purposes or for general support of church or denominational institutions. No grants to individuals.
Publications: Annual report, application guidelines, informational brochure.
Application information:
Initial approach: Letter
Deadline(s): None
Board meeting date(s): Spring, fall, and as required
Officers and Trustees:* Albert J. Weatherhead III,* Pres.; Dwight S. Weatherhead,* V.P. and Secy.; Don K. Price,* V.P.; Henry Rosovsky,* V.P.; Stanley Salmen,* V.P.; Celia Weatherhead,* V.P.; John P. Weatherhead,* V.P.; Michael H. Weatherhead,* V.P.; Thomas F. Allen, Treas.
Number of staff: 1 full-time professional.
Employer Identification Number: 132711998

5985
Maxwell C. Weaver Foundation ⌑
c/o Star Bank of Cincinnati
P.O. Box 1118
Cincinnati 45201 (513) 632-4579

Established in 1985 in OH.
Foundation type: Independent
Financial data (yr. ended 12/31/88): Assets, $1,066,362 (M); expenditures, $61,092, including $53,209 for 13 grants (high: $8,000; low: $1,000).
Purpose and activities: Giving primarily for the arts and health programs for youth; support also for secondary education.
Limitations: No grants to individuals.
Application information: Application form not required.
Deadline(s): None
Write: Terry Crilley
Trustee: Star Bank, N.A., Cincinnati.
Employer Identification Number: 316275346

5986
The Clara Weiss Fund ⌑
2225 Marks Rd.
Valley City 44280 (216) 225-8514

Trust established in 1955 in OH.
Donor(s): L.C. Weiss, Mrs. L.C. Weiss.
Foundation type: Independent
Financial data (yr. ended 12/31/88): Assets, $1,737,894 (M); expenditures, $120,314, including $89,700 for 112 grants (high: $5,000; low: $50).
Purpose and activities: Grants largely for higher and secondary education, health agencies, and welfare institutions, including child welfare.
Limitations: Giving primarily in the Cleveland, OH, area. No grants to individuals.
Application information: Application form not required.
Initial approach: Letter
Deadline(s): None
Write: David C. Weiss, Mgr.
Officer and Trustees:* David C. Weiss,* Mgr.; Arthur D. Weiss, Robert L. Weiss.
Employer Identification Number: 346556158

5987
The S. K. Wellman Foundation ⌑
1800 Huntington Bldg.
Cleveland 44115
Application address: 548 Leader Bldg., Cleveland, OH 44114; Tel.: (216) 696-4640

Incorporated in 1951 in OH.
Donor(s): S.K. Wellman.†
Foundation type: Independent
Financial data (yr. ended 12/31/88): Assets, $7,594,297 (M); expenditures, $390,301, including $341,000 for 66 grants (high: $20,000; low: $500).
Purpose and activities: Grants for education, cultural activities, health agencies, and social services.
Limitations: Giving primarily in OH. No grants to individuals.
Publications: Application guidelines.
Application information: Application form not required.
Initial approach: Letter
Deadline(s): Dec. 31
Write: R. Dugald Pearson, Exec. Secy.
Officers: John M. Wilson, Jr.,* Pres.; R. Dugald Pearson, Exec. Secy.
Trustees:* Franklin B. Floyd, Suzanne O'Gara, Mrs. John M. Wilson, Jr.
Employer Identification Number: 346520032

5988
Wexner Foundation ▼ ⌑
41 South High St., Suite 3390
Columbus 43215-6190 (614) 461-8112

Established in 1973.
Donor(s): Leslie Wexner, Bella Wexner.
Foundation type: Independent
Financial data (yr. ended 12/31/88): Assets, $67,905,615 (M); expenditures, $3,767,255, including $2,632,869 for 19 grants (high: $500,000; low: $610; average: $1,000-$500,000) and $423,100 for 2 foundation-administered programs.
Purpose and activities: General charitable giving locally, nationally, and internationally, including fellowship and institutional grants programs.
Types of support: Fellowships, special projects.
Limitations: Giving primarily in OH.
Publications: Informational brochure, program policy statement.
Application information: Contributes only to pre-selected organizations; applications accepted for fellowship programs.
Deadline(s): For fellowships, mid-Jan.
Write: Rabbi Maurice S. Corson, Pres.
Officers and Trustees:* Leslie H. Wexner,* Chair.; Bella Wexner,* Co-Chair.; Rabbi Maurice S. Corson, Pres.; Stanley Schwartz, Jr., Secy.; Harold L. Levin,* Treas.
Number of staff: 3 full-time professional; 2 full-time support.
Employer Identification Number: 237320631

5989
Wexner Institutional Grants Program, Inc. ⌑ ☆
41 South High St., Suite 3390
Columbus 43215-6103 (614) 461-8112

Established in 1986 in OH.
Foundation type: Independent
Financial data (yr. ended 12/31/88): Assets, $8,745 (M); gifts received, $423,100; expenditures, $401,227, including $287,600 for 6 grants (high: $72,750; low: $25,000).
Purpose and activities: "To stimulate improvement in the core curricula of graduate institutions which train congregational rabbis, Jewish educational leaders and Jewish communal professionals, or to assist graduate schools seeking to extend their training curricula to include those professions.
Limitations: No grants to individuals, or for capital campaigns or the purchase or maintenance of library, audio visual, computer equipment or supplies.
Application information:
Initial approach: Letter
Deadline(s): June 15 and Dec. 15
Final notification: Sept. 15 and Feb. 15
Write: Larry Moses, Dir.
Officers: Leslie H. Wexner, Chair.; Maurice Carson, Pres.; Harold L. Levin, V.P. and Treas.; Stanley Schwartz, Jr., Secy.
Employer Identification Number: 222854430

5990
White Consolidated Industries Foundation, Inc. ⌑
c/o White Consolidated Industries, Inc.
11770 Berea Rd.
Cleveland 44111 (216) 252-8385

Established in 1951 in OH.
Donor(s): White Consolidated Industries, Inc., The Tappan, Co.
Foundation type: Company-sponsored
Financial data (yr. ended 12/31/88): Assets, $1,137,600 (M); gifts received, $151,727; expenditures, $435,298, including $432,352 for 91 grants (high: $55,000; low: $75).
Purpose and activities: Emphasis on community funds, higher education, hospitals, and cultural organizations.
Types of support: General purposes, building funds, equipment, research, continuing support, operating budgets, employee matching gifts.
Limitations: Giving primarily in Cleveland and Columbus, OH.
Application information: Application form required.
Initial approach: Proposal
Copies of proposal: 1

Deadline(s): None
Board meeting date(s): As required
Write: Daniel R. Elliott, Jr., Chair.
Officers and Trustees: Daniel R. Elliott, Jr., Chair.; Lawrence W. Kenney, V.P. and Treas.; Donald C. Blasius, V.P.; W.G. Bleakley, V.P.
Employer Identification Number: 046032840

5991
The Thomas H. White Foundation
(Formerly Thomas H. White Charitable Trust)
c/o Ameritrust Co., N.A.
P.O. Box 5937
Cleveland 44101 (216) 737-5671

Trust established in 1913 in OH.
Donor(s): Thomas H. White.†
Foundation type: Independent
Financial data (yr. ended 12/31/89): Assets, $11,731,411 (M); expenditures, $670,993, including $617,642 for 71 grants (high: $50,000; low: $250; average: $9,170).
Purpose and activities: Subject to numerous life estates, the trust first became active in 1939 when surplus income became available; giving to support education and charitable purposes in Cleveland, to provide scholarships, to promote scientific research, to provide for care of the sick, aged, or helpless, and to improve living conditions or provide recreation for all classes.
Types of support: Seed money, emergency funds, building funds, equipment, matching funds, scholarship funds, special projects, capital campaigns, renovation projects, endowment funds.
Limitations: Giving limited to Cleveland, OH. No grants to individuals, or for annual campaigns, deficit financing, or land acquisition; no loans.
Publications: Annual report (including application guidelines).
Application information: Mass mailings not accepted. Application form not required.
Initial approach: Letter
Copies of proposal: 6
Deadline(s): Dec. 1, Mar. 1, June 1, and Sept. 1
Board meeting date(s): Distribution Committee meets in Jan., Apr., July, and Oct.
Final notification: 2 months
Write: Donald F. Barney, V.P., Ameritrust Co., N.A.
Distribution Committee: Donald Barney, Edward F. Bell, Frank Harding III, James Rode, Charles A. Thigpen.
Trustee: Ameritrust Co., N.A.
Number of staff: 1 part-time professional.
Employer Identification Number: 346505722

5992
The E. F. Wildermuth Foundation ⌑
4770 Indianola Ave., Suite 240
Columbus 43214 (614) 846-5838

Established in 1962.
Foundation type: Independent
Financial data (yr. ended 12/31/88): Assets, $2,967,159 (M); gifts received, $50,000; expenditures, $224,994, including $170,000 for 24 grants (high: $50,000; low: $500).
Purpose and activities: Grants primarily for higher education, particularly optometric schools and research; support also for the arts and a church.
Limitations: Giving primarily in OH.
Application information: Application form not required.
Initial approach: Letter
Deadline(s): Aug. 1
Write: Homer W. Lee, Treas.
Officers and Trustees: H. Wald Ewalt, Pres.; Faurest Borton, V.P.; Bettie A. Kalb, Secy.; Homer W. Lee, Treas.; Karl Borton, J. Patrick Campbell, Genevieve Connable, W. Daniel Driscoll, David T. Patterson, Phillip N. Phillipson.
Employer Identification Number: 316050202

5993
The Marguerite M. Wilson Foundation ⌑
29525 Chagrin Blvd., No. 305
Pepper Pike 44122 (216) 292-5730

Established in 1953 in Ohio.
Foundation type: Independent
Financial data (yr. ended 12/31/88): Assets, $1,745,545 (M); expenditures, $67,222, including $60,500 for 7 grants (high: $30,000; low: $1,000).
Purpose and activities: Emphasis on hospitals, private schools, cultural organizations, and social services.
Limitations: Giving primarily in OH. No grants to individuals.
Application information: Application form not required.
Deadline(s): None
Final notification: Response only to those applications which the trustees wish to pursue
Officers and Trustees: Pauline W. Horner, Pres. and Treas.; James H. Dempsey, Jr., Secy.; Holly Munger Book, Carol Horner Donaldson, Douglas M. Horner, James M. Horner, Jr., Myron W. Munger.
Employer Identification Number: 346521259

5994
Wodecroft Foundation ⌑
2100 DuBois Tower
Cincinnati 45202 (513) 621-6747

Trust established in 1958 in OH.
Donor(s): Roger Drackett.
Foundation type: Independent
Financial data (yr. ended 12/31/88): Assets, $5,797,414 (M); expenditures, $309,739, including $300,000 for 42 grants (high: $63,000; low: $500).
Purpose and activities: Emphasis on cultural programs, health and hospitals, social services, and conservation.
Limitations: Giving primarily in OH. No grants to individuals.
Application information:
Initial approach: Letter
Board meeting date(s): As required
Write: H. Truxtun Emerson, Jr., Secy.
Officers and Trustees: Richard W. Barrett, Chair.; H. Truxton Emerson, Jr., Secy.; Jeanne H. Drackett.
Employer Identification Number: 316047601

5995
Wolfe Associates, Inc. ▼ ⌑
34 South Third St.
Columbus 43216 (614) 461-5220

Incorporated in 1973 in OH.
Donor(s): The Dispatch Printing Co., The Ohio Co., WBNS TV, Inc., RadiOhio, Inc., Video Indiana, Inc.
Foundation type: Company-sponsored
Financial data (yr. ended 6/30/88): Assets, $5,765,431 (M); gifts received, $1,840,333; expenditures, $669,416, including $620,858 for 59 grants (high: $232,500; low: $500; average: $1,000-$10,000) and $38,750 for 26 employee matching gifts.
Purpose and activities: Giving for a community fund, higher and secondary education, hospitals and medical research, cultural activities, and youth and social service agencies.
Types of support: Operating budgets, continuing support, annual campaigns, emergency funds, building funds, equipment, matching funds, professorships, employee matching gifts, scholarship funds.
Limitations: Giving primarily in central OH. No grants to individuals, or for research, demonstration projects, publications, or conferences.
Publications: Program policy statement, application guidelines.
Application information: Application form not required.
Initial approach: Letter
Deadline(s): None
Board meeting date(s): Mar., June, Sept., and Dec.
Final notification: After board meeting
Write: A. Kenneth Pierce, Jr., V.P.
Officers: John W. Wolfe, Pres.; A. Kenneth Pierce, Jr., V.P. and Secy.-Treas.; Nancy Wolfe Lane, V.P.; William C. Wolfe, Jr., V.P.
Number of staff: None.
Employer Identification Number: 237303111

5996
Women's Project Foundation ☆
c/o Ameritrust Co., N.A.
P.O. Box 5937
Cleveland 44101-0937 (216) 737-5283

Established in 1986.
Foundation type: Independent
Financial data (yr. ended 11/30/89): Assets, $6,230,419 (M); expenditures, $376,967, including $316,000 for 4 grants (high: $116,000; low: $30,000).
Purpose and activities: Support for projects for women's and children's issues, including women filmmakers and domestic violence.
Application information: Application form not required.
Initial approach: Letter
Copies of proposal: 1
Deadline(s): None
Write: Joyce K. Alexander
Trustees: Louise L. Gund, Maximilian Kempner, Ameritrust Co., N.A.
Employer Identification Number: 133417304

5997
World Training Ministries ⌑ ☆
4664 West Tuscarawas St.
Canton 44708

Donor(s): Stark Truss Co., Inc.
Foundation type: Independent
Financial data (yr. ended 12/31/87): Assets, $8,275 (M); gifts received, $55,090; expenditures, $104,247, including $99,191 for 21 grants (high: $21,988; low: $100) and $4,600 for 3 grants to individuals (high: $2,500; low: $800).
Purpose and activities: Support primarily for evangelical ministries, missions, schools and churches.
Types of support: General purposes, grants to individuals.
Limitations: Giving primarily in OH, OK, WA, and TX; support also for missionary organizations in India.
Application information: Application form not required.
Deadline(s): None
Write: Esther Yoder, Secy.-Treas.
Officers: Abner Yoder, Pres.; John Schrock, V.P.; Esther Yoder, Secy.-Treas.
Employer Identification Number: 341454477

5998
Wright Foundation ⌑
1900 Richmond Rd.
Cleveland 44124

Incorporated in 1953 in OH.
Donor(s): J.D. Wright.
Foundation type: Independent
Financial data (yr. ended 12/31/88): Assets, $1,535,450 (M); gifts received, $6,551; expenditures, $133,368, including $113,265 for 44 grants (high: $75,250; low: $50).
Purpose and activities: Giving for hospitals and higher education.
Limitations: Giving primarily in OH.
Application information:
Write: J.D. Wright, Pres.
Officers and Trustees: J.D. Wright, Pres.; Bernadine G. Wright, V.P.; John D. Wright, Jr., V.P.; Doris M. Toth, Secy.-Treas.
Employer Identification Number: 346520282

5999
The Wuliger Foundation, Inc. ▼
Halle Bldg.
1228 Euclid Ave., 10th Fl.
Cleveland 44115 (216) 522-1310

Incorporated in 1956 in OH.
Donor(s): Ernest M. Wuliger, Allan M. Unger, Ohio-Sealy Mattress Manufacturing Co.
Foundation type: Company-sponsored
Financial data (yr. ended 12/31/88): Assets, $3,792,825 (M); gifts received, $1,265,072; expenditures, $1,301,528, including $1,300,777 for 127 grants (high: $375,000; low: $20; average: $500-$30,000).
Purpose and activities: Giving for Jewish welfare funds; support also for higher education, hospitals, and the arts.
Limitations: Giving primarily in OH. No grants to individuals.
Application information:
Initial approach: Proposal
Deadline(s): None
Board meeting date(s): As necessary
Final notification: Within 2 weeks if possible
Write: Ernest M. Wuliger, Pres.
Officers: Ernest M. Wuliger, Pres. and Treas.; Timothy F. Wuliger, Secy.
Number of staff: None.
Employer Identification Number: 346527281

6000
The Leo Yassenoff Foundation ▼
37 North High St., Suite 304
Columbus 43215 (614) 221-4315

Incorporated in 1947 in DE.
Donor(s): Leo Yassenoff.†
Foundation type: Independent
Financial data (yr. ended 12/31/88): Assets, $8,339,352 (M); expenditures, $1,836,280, including $1,208,717 for 104 grants (high: $300,000; low: $200; average: $1,000-$20,000).
Purpose and activities: Support primarily for social services, including programs for minorities and the disadvantaged, education, health and hospitals, youth agencies, religion, civic affairs, and arts and cultural programs.
Types of support: Seed money, emergency funds, equipment, matching funds, special projects, renovation projects.
Limitations: Giving limited to Franklin County, OH. No support for religious purposes, except to donor-designated recipients. No grants to individuals, or for operating support, annual campaigns, endowments, deficit financing, or debt reduction; no loans.
Publications: Annual report, application guidelines.
Application information: Application must follow foundation guidelines. Application form not required.
Initial approach: Telephone, letter, or proposal
Copies of proposal: 1
Board meeting date(s): Quarterly
Final notification: 3 months
Write: Cynthia A. Cecil Lazarus, Exec. Dir.
Officers and Trustees:* Melvin L. Schottenstein,* Chair.; Frederick E. Dauterman, Jr.,* Vice-Chair.; Mary J. Hoover,* Secy.-Treas.; Cynthia A. Cecil Lazarus, Exec. Dir.
Number of staff: 1 full-time professional; 1 part-time professional; 1 full-time support; 1 part-time support.
Employer Identification Number: 310829426

6001
Hugo H. and Mabel B. Young Foundation
416 North Wood St.
Loudonville 44842 (419) 994-4501

Incorporated in 1963 in OH.
Foundation type: Independent
Financial data (yr. ended 04/30/89): Assets, $3,704,710 (M); expenditures, $300,816, including $265,488 for 11 grants (high: $123,884; low: $2,500).
Purpose and activities: Giving primarily to civic, educational, and health organizations.
Types of support: Building funds, equipment, scholarship funds.
Limitations: Giving primarily in Ashland County, OH. No grants to individuals, or for general purposes or matching gifts; no loans.
Application information: Application form not required.
Initial approach: Letter
Copies of proposal: 6
Deadline(s): Submit proposal preferably in Mar.
Board meeting date(s): May
Write: R.D. Mayer, Secy.-Treas.
Officers and Trustees:* Phillip Ranney,* Chair.; James Dudte,* Pres.; Avery Hand,* V.P.; R.D. Mayer,* Secy.-Treas.; Robert Dubler, John Kirkpatrick.
Number of staff: None.
Employer Identification Number: 346560664

6002
The Youngstown Foundation ▼
c/o The Dollar Savings & Trust Co.
P.O. Box 450
Youngstown 44501 (216) 744-9000

Established in 1918 in OH by bank resolution.
Foundation type: Community
Financial data (yr. ended 12/31/88): Assets, $25,033,083 (M); gifts received, $817,157; expenditures, $2,362,938, including $2,160,438 for grants.
Purpose and activities: To support local charitable and educational agencies for the betterment of the community; grants for capital purposes, with emphasis on aid to crippled children, community funds, youth agencies, music and cultural programs, and hospitals.
Types of support: Building funds, equipment, annual campaigns, student loans, general purposes, renovation projects, special projects, conferences and seminars, continuing support, research.
Limitations: Giving limited to the Mahoning County, OH, with emphasis on Youngstown. No grants to individuals (except for limited student loans), or for endowment funds, operating budgets, seed money, emergency funds, deficit financing, land acquisition, demonstration projects, publications, scholarships, fellowships, or matching gifts.
Publications: Informational brochure, annual report.
Application information: Application form not required.
Initial approach: Proposal
Copies of proposal: 1
Deadline(s): None
Board meeting date(s): Jan., Mar., May, July, Sept., Nov., and Dec.
Write: Herbert H. Pridham, Secy.
Officer: Herbert H. Pridham, Secy.; Aileen Gottschling.
Distribution Committee: D.W. McGowan, Chair.; William M. Cafaro, Vice-Chair.; C. Gilbert James, William R. Powell, Bernard J. Yozwiak.
Trustee: The Dollar Savings & Trust Co.
Number of staff: None.
Employer Identification Number: 346515788

OKLAHOMA

6003
K. S. Adams Foundation ⌑
c/o WestStar Bank, N.A.
P.O. Box 2248
Bartlesville 74005-2248 (918) 337-3291

Established in 1953 in OK.
Foundation type: Independent
Financial data (yr. ended 12/31/88): Assets, $1,201,854 (M); expenditures, $72,972, including $68,750 for 29 grants (high: $5,000; low: $500).
Purpose and activities: Support for organizations that promote child development and education; giving also for medical research.
Limitations: Giving primarily in Bartlesville, OK.
Application information: Application form not required.
Initial approach: Letter
Deadline(s): None
Trustees: Dorothy Glynn Adams, WestStar Bank, N.A.
Employer Identification Number: 736091602

6004
Mary K. Ashbrook Foundation for El Reno, Oklahoma ⌑
P.O. Box 627
El Reno 73036 (405) 262-4684

Established in 1978 in OK.
Donor(s): Mary K. Ashbrook.†
Foundation type: Independent
Financial data (yr. ended 6/30/88): Assets, $1,512,870 (M); expenditures, $126,447, including $107,929 for 16 grants (high: $50,000; low: $335).
Purpose and activities: Grants for education, cultural programs, civic affairs, community development, and welfare; support also for a hospital.
Types of support: Continuing support, seed money, emergency funds, building funds, equipment, land acquisition, matching funds, scholarship funds, special projects.
Limitations: Giving limited to El Reno, OK. No grants to individuals, or for deficit financing, endowment funds, research, fellowships, demonstration projects, publications, or conferences; no loans.
Publications: Application guidelines.
Application information: Application form required.
Initial approach: Letter or telephone
Deadline(s): Submit proposal by first of each month
Board meeting date(s): Monthly
Final notification: 1 month
Write: The Board of Trustees
Trustees: Betty Dittmer, Virginia Sue Douglas, Alleen Poole.
Number of staff: None.
Employer Identification Number: 731049531

6005
Hu & Eva Maud Bartlett Foundation ⌑
P.O. Box 1368
Sapulpa 74067

Established in 1950 in OK.
Foundation type: Independent
Financial data (yr. ended 12/31/88): Assets, $1,092,071 (M); expenditures, $61,197, including $57,806 for 5 grants (high: $55,056; low: $500).
Purpose and activities: Support primarily for a medical center; giving also for historical preservation and general charitable purposes.
Limitations: Giving primarily in Sapulpa, OK.
Application information:
Initial approach: Letter
Deadline(s): None
Trustees: Barbara Benedict, Charley Sherwood, Sherry Sherwood.
Employer Identification Number: 736092249

6006
Cordelia Lunceford Beatty Trust ⌑
Security Bank Bldg., 2nd Fl.
101 North Main
Blackwell 74631 (405) 363-3684

Established in 1943 in OK.
Foundation type: Independent
Financial data (yr. ended 12/31/88): Assets, $1,514,925 (M); expenditures, $83,159, including $42,628 for 21 grants (high: $8,828; low: $17) and $17,806 for 75 grants to individuals (high: $1,000; low: $10).
Purpose and activities: Giving primarily for a scholarship program for local high school residents who are under 19 years of age; support also for youth and child welfare service organizations.
Types of support: Student aid.
Limitations: Giving limited to Blackwell, OK.
Application information: Application form required for scholarships.
Initial approach: Letter requesting application
Deadline(s): Prior to start of school year
Write: James R. Rodgers, Trustee
Trustees: James R. Rodgers, William W. Rodgers.
Employer Identification Number: 736094952

6007
Grace & Franklin Bernsen Foundation
2600 Fourth National Bank Bldg.
Tulsa 74119

Established in 1985 in OK.
Donor(s): Grace Bernsen,† Franklin Bernsen.†
Foundation type: Independent
Financial data (yr. ended 9/30/89): Assets, $20,756,407 (M); expenditures, $1,653,926, including $1,343,195 for 25 grants (high: $300,000; low: $1,000).
Purpose and activities: Support primarily for Christian religious organizations, the arts, medical sciences, and youth organizations.
Types of support: General purposes.
Limitations: Giving primarily in in the Tulsa, OK, area.
Application information: Application form not required.
Copies of proposal: 1
Write: Howard H. Maher, Trustee
Trustees: Howard M. Maher, Donald F. Marlar, Donald E. Pray, John D. Strong.
Number of staff: 2 full-time professional.
Employer Identification Number: 237009414

6008
Blair Foundation ⌑ ☆
2800 South Boston Ave.
Tulsa 74114-2434

Established in 1968 in OK.
Foundation type: Independent
Financial data (yr. ended 12/31/87): Assets, $1,180,115 (M); expenditures, $55,495, including $51,050 for 21 grants (high: $5,250; low: $100).
Purpose and activities: Giving primarily for health associations and hospitals, the performing arts, Christian organizations, and education; support also for a community fund and the Salvation Army.
Limitations: Giving primarily in Tulsa, OK. No grants to individuals.
Application information: Contributes only to pre-selected organizations. Applications not accepted.
Trustees: John Blair, Penelope Blair.
Employer Identification Number: 237003485

6009
The Mervin Bovaird Foundation ▼
800 Oneok Plaza
100 West Fifth St.
Tulsa 74103 (918) 583-1777

Established about 1956.
Donor(s): Mabel W. Bovaird.†
Foundation type: Independent
Financial data (yr. ended 12/31/88): Assets, $24,783,672 (M); expenditures, $1,421,500, including $1,219,420 for 55 grants (high: $434,000; low: $500; average: $500-$35,000).
Purpose and activities: Supports scholarship funds at the University of Tulsa and Oklahoma Baptist University; support also for community development, social services, education, and health.
Types of support: Scholarship funds.
Limitations: Giving primarily in Tulsa, OK.
Application information: Scholarship recipients are chosen by the universities and subsequently approved by the foundation.
Deadline(s): Dec. 1
Board meeting date(s): Irregularly
Final notification: Dec. 20
Write: Fenelon Boesche, Pres.
Officers and Trustees:* Fenelon Boesche,* Pres.; Tilford Eskridge,* V.P.; Thomas H. Trower,* V.P.; Franklin D. Hettinger,* Secy.-Treas.
Number of staff: 2
Employer Identification Number: 736102163

6010
C. Harold & Constance Brand Foundation ⌑ ☆
825 N.W. 58th St.
Oklahoma City 73118

Established in 1985 in OK.
Donor(s): Constance M. Brand.
Foundation type: Independent

Financial data (yr. ended 12/31/88): Assets, $1,184,359 (M); expenditures, $458,340, including $430,000 for 5 grants (high: $300,000; low: $10,000).
Purpose and activities: Giving primarily for secondary and higher education and health.
Limitations: Giving primarily in Shawnee and Oklahoma City, OK. No grants to individuals.
Application information: Contributes only to pre-selected organizations. Applications not accepted.
Officers: Constance M. Brand, Pres. and Treas.; Robert C. Fuegner, V.P.; Clara R. Stevens, Secy.
Director: Gerald L. Gamble.
Employer Identification Number: 726095799

6011
Broadhurst Foundation ⌑
401 South Boston, Suite 100
Tulsa 74103 (918) 584-0661

Trust established in 1951 in OK.
Donor(s): William Broadhurst.†
Foundation type: Independent
Financial data (yr. ended 12/31/87): Assets, $5,362,885 (M); expenditures, $388,888, including $241,927 for 82 grants (high: $40,000; low: $20; average: $4,000) and $40,000 for 1 loan.
Purpose and activities: Support for scholarship funds at institutions selected by the foundation, for students training for the Christian ministry; grants also to educational and religious institutions, and to medical research institutions, especially related to pediatric diseases; loans to churches for building projects.
Types of support: Continuing support, seed money, building funds, equipment, scholarship funds, fellowships, loans, renovation projects.
Limitations: Giving primarily in the Midwest, particularly OK. No grants to individuals or for scholarship funds, except at 31 schools the foundation currently supports.
Publications: Financial statement, annual report.
Application information: Application form not required.
Initial approach: Letter or proposal
Copies of proposal: 1
Deadline(s): None
Board meeting date(s): Quarterly
Final notification: 1 month
Write: Ann Shannon Cassidy, Chair.
Trustees: Ann Shannon Cassidy, Chair.; John Cassidy, Jr., Clint V. Cox, Ernestine Broadhurst Howard, Wishard Lemons.
Number of staff: 2 full-time professional; 1 part-time support.
Employer Identification Number: 736061115

6012
Brown Foundation ⌑ ☆
1707 Elmhurst
Oklahoma City 73120

Donor(s): William C. Brown.
Foundation type: Independent
Financial data (yr. ended 12/31/88): Assets, $43,641 (M); gifts received, $28,370; expenditures, $146,416, including $146,325 for 28 grants (high: $21,000; low: $1,000).
Purpose and activities: Support for Catholic organizations, health associations, and groups fighting hunger.
Application information: Contributes only to pre-selected organizations. Applications not accepted.
Trustees: Carolyn M. Brown, William C. Brown.
Employer Identification Number: 736230335

6013
Burbridge Foundation, Inc. ⌑
P.O. Box 82976
Oklahoma City 73148

Established in 1959 in OK.
Foundation type: Independent
Financial data (yr. ended 07/31/86): Assets, $1,490,061 (M); gifts received, $1,800; expenditures, $25,664, including $9,132 for 23 grants (high: $1,400; low: $100).
Purpose and activities: Giving for Christian religious organizations and missionary efforts.
Application information: Application form required.
Initial approach: Letter
Deadline(s): None
Write: Veyda P. Sarkey Burbridge, Pres.
Officers: Veyda P. Sarkey Burbridge, Pres. and Treas.; Bobbie Lane, Secy.
Employer Identification Number: 756028012

6014
Max and Tookah Campbell Foundation ⌑
P.O. Box 701051
Tulsa 74170

Trust established in 1964 in OK.
Donor(s): Max W. Campbell.†
Foundation type: Independent
Financial data (yr. ended 12/31/88): Assets, $5,370,478 (M); expenditures, $420,238, including $254,405 for 61 grants (high: $16,667; low: $100).
Purpose and activities: Emphasis on Protestant church support and higher education; grants also for hospitals and health agencies, cultural programs, and youth agencies.
Limitations: Giving primarily in OK. No grants to individuals.
Application information: Contributes only to pre-selected organizations. Applications not accepted.
Trustees: Pauline Holderman, Joan Lepley Hunt, Robert G. Hunt.
Employer Identification Number: 736111626

6015
H. A. and Mary K. Chapman Charitable Trust ▼
One Warren Place, Suite 1816
6100 South Yale
Tulsa 74136 (918) 496-7882

Trust established in 1976 in OK.
Donor(s): H.A. Chapman.†
Foundation type: Independent
Financial data (yr. ended 12/31/89): Assets, $40,000,000 (M); expenditures, $1,994,133, including $1,724,000 for 39 grants (high: $350,000; low: $500; average: $10,000-$50,000).
Purpose and activities: Grants largely for education, particularly higher education, health, social services, and cultural programs.
Limitations: Giving primarily in Tulsa, OK.
Application information: Application form required.
Deadline(s): None
Board meeting date(s): Quarterly and as needed
Write: Donne Pitman, Trustee
Trustees: Ralph L. Abercrombie, Donne W. Pitman.
Number of staff: None.
Employer Identification Number: 736177739

6016
Christian Life Foundation ⌑
Ten East Third St., Suite 700
Tulsa 74103

Established in 1985 in OK.
Donor(s): Gail R. Runnels.
Foundation type: Independent
Financial data (yr. ended 11/30/89): Assets, $379,463 (M); gifts received, $100,000; expenditures, $129,185, including $128,100 for 16 grants (high: $117,500; low: $100).
Purpose and activities: Giving primarily for Christian institutions and missionary efforts.
Types of support: General purposes.
Limitations: Giving primarily in Tulsa, OK.
Application information: Contributes only to pre-selected organizations. Applications not accepted.
Trustees: Gail R. Runnels, Virginia Runnels.
Employer Identification Number: 731263661

6017
The George and Jennie Collins Foundation ⌑
c/o Collins & Weese
2627 East 21st St., Suite 126
Tulsa 74114-1710 (918) 742-5456

Trust established in 1943 in OK.
Donor(s): George F. Collins, Jr.,† Liberty Glass Co., and others.
Foundation type: Independent
Financial data (yr. ended 12/31/88): Assets, $3,192,106 (M); expenditures, $241,281, including $230,800 for 8 grants (high: $80,500; low: $1,000).
Purpose and activities: Giving for higher and secondary education, and youth and social service agencies.
Types of support: Scholarship funds, building funds.
Limitations: Giving primarily in OK.
Application information:
Initial approach: Letter
Deadline(s): None
Write: Loreine C. Dietrich, Chair.
Officers and Trustees: Loreine C. Dietrich, Chair.; Frank P. Collins, Secy.; Helen Jayne Henley, Treas.
Employer Identification Number: 736093053

6018
George Fulton Collins, Jr. Foundation ⌘
2251 East Skelly Dr., Suite 105-A
Tulsa 74105 (918) 742-5456

Established in 1968 in OK.
Foundation type: Independent
Financial data (yr. ended 12/31/88): Assets, $3,167,497 (M); expenditures, $251,240, including $242,466 for 8 grants (high: $80,500; low: $2,500).
Purpose and activities: Emphasis on higher education, health agencies, and Protestant church support.
Limitations: Giving primarily in OK.
Application information:
Initial approach: Proposal
Deadline(s): None
Write: Fulton Collins, Chair.
Officers and Trustees: Fulton Collins, Chair.; Frank M. Engle, Secy.; Loreine C. Dietrich, Treas.
Employer Identification Number: 237008179

6019
Community Resource Development Foundation, Inc. ☆
525 N.W. 13th
Oklahoma City 73103 (405) 236-8109

Established in 1981 in OK.
Donor(s): Ray Potts, Pat Potts.
Foundation type: Operating
Financial data (yr. ended 12/31/88): Assets, $105,680 (M); gifts received, $194,800; expenditures, $126,652, including $5,715 for 6 grants (high: $1,500; low: $600; average: $500-$5,000) and $103,150 for 1 foundation-administered program.
Purpose and activities: A private operating foundation; support for prevention and resolution of family problems and improvement of nonprofit management, support also for vocational and other education and family planning.
Types of support: Annual campaigns, building funds, capital campaigns, conferences and seminars, consulting services, continuing support, general purposes, seed money, special projects.
Limitations: Giving primarily in Oklahoma City, OK.
Publications: Application guidelines.
Application information: Application form required.
Initial approach: Letter or proposal
Copies of proposal: 1
Deadline(s): June 15 and Dec. 15
Board meeting date(s): July 15 and Jan. 1
Write: Denis Greene, Mgr.
Officers: Mark Potts, Pres.; Pat Potts, V.P.; Geri Price, Treas.; Denis Greene, Mgr.
Number of staff: 1 part-time professional.
Employer Identification Number: 731119767

6020
The Cuesta Foundation, Inc.
One Williams Ctr., Suite 4400
Tulsa 74172

Incorporated in 1962 in OK.
Donor(s): Charles W. Oliphant, Allene O. Mayo, Allen G. Oliphant, Jr., Gertrude O. Sundgren, Eric B. Oliphant, Nancy B. Deane.
Foundation type: Independent
Financial data (yr. ended 04/30/88): Assets, $2,480,788 (M); gifts received, $6,000; expenditures, $160,271, including $145,750 for grants (average: $2,000).
Purpose and activities: Emphasis on higher education; support also for the performing arts, social service agencies, and a population control organization.
Types of support: Building funds, continuing support, endowment funds.
Limitations: Giving primarily in OK. No grants to individuals.
Publications: Financial statement, informational brochure.
Application information: Application form not required.
Initial approach: Letter or proposal
Copies of proposal: 1
Deadline(s): Sept. 1
Write: Donald P. Carpenter, Treas.
Officers and Directors:* Charles W. Oliphant,* Chair.; Eric B. Oliphant,* Pres.; Richard E. Wright III,* Secy.; Donald P. Carpenter,* Treas.; Allene O. Mayo, Arline B. Oliphant, Gertrude O. Oliphant.
Employer Identification Number: 736091550

6021
Educational Fund for Children of Phillips Petroleum Company Employees ⌘
180 Plaza Office Bldg.
Bartlesville 74004 (918) 661-5630

Established in 1939 in OK.
Donor(s): Phillips Petroleum Co.
Foundation type: Company-sponsored
Financial data (yr. ended 8/31/88): Assets, $481,418 (M); gifts received, $264,000; expenditures, $266,243, including $258,419 for 340 grants to individuals (high: $1,500; low: $500).
Purpose and activities: Scholarships for high school seniors who are the children of present or deceased full-time Phillips Petroleum Co. employees; awards limited to $1000 per year for a period not to exceed 4 years.
Types of support: Employee-related scholarships.
Application information: Application form required.
Write: Bill Dausses, Dir., Educational Funds
Administrator: W.F. Dausses.
Selection Committee: J.R. Morris, S.R. Parr, R.W. Poole.
Employer Identification Number: 736095141

6022
8:32, Inc. ⌘
4401 S.W. 23rd St.
Oklahoma City 73108

Established in 1984 in Oklahoma.
Donor(s): Members of the Humphreys family.
Foundation type: Independent
Financial data (yr. ended 12/31/88): Assets, $322,905 (M); gifts received, $97,462; expenditures, $137,152, including $135,797 for 34 grants (high: $31,125; low: $150).
Purpose and activities: Giving primarily for religious activities, especially Baptist church support and youth ministries.
Limitations: Giving primarily in OK. No grants to individuals.
Application information: Contributes only to pre-selected organizations. Applications not accepted.
Officers: Craig A. Humphreys, Pres.; Kent J. Humphreys, V.P.; Kirk D. Humphreys, Secy.-Treas.
Employer Identification Number: 731214621

6023
Howard E. Felt Foundation
700 Holarud Bldg.
10 East Third St.
Tulsa 74103

Established in 1945 in OK.
Foundation type: Independent
Financial data (yr. ended 12/31/88): Assets, $1,528,614 (M); expenditures, $85,521, including $80,898 for 25 grants (high: $25,750; low: $50).
Purpose and activities: Support for higher and other education, social service agencies, a Methodist church, and cultural programs.
Types of support: General purposes.
Limitations: Giving primarily in Tulsa, OK.
Application information: Contributes only to pre-selected organizations. Applications not accepted.
Officers and Trustees:* Joe M. Holliman,* Pres.; George W. Deck,* V.P.; Frank M. Engle,* V.P.; Jean F. Holliman,* Secy.-Treas.
Number of staff: None.
Employer Identification Number: 736092860

6024
Laura Fields Trust
P.O. Box 2394
Lawton 73502 (405) 355-3733

Trust established in 1950 in OK.
Donor(s): Laura Fields.†
Foundation type: Independent
Financial data (yr. ended 6/30/89): Assets, $1,652,199 (M); gifts received, $87,895; expenditures, $120,119, including $35,311 for 12 grants (high: $82,505; low: $711; average: $2,000) and $65,618 for 38 loans to individuals.
Purpose and activities: Emphasis on student loans; grants also for higher education and youth agencies.
Types of support: Lectureships, student loans.
Limitations: Giving limited to Comanche County, OK, residents.
Application information: Application form required.
Initial approach: Letter or telephone
Copies of proposal: 1
Deadline(s): None
Board meeting date(s): 2nd Tuesday of each month
Write: Jay Dee Fountain, Exec. Secy.
Officers: T.D. Nicklas, Chair.; Jay Dee Fountain, Exec. Secy.
Trustees: George Bridges, Jack Brock, David Dennis, Russell Money, Lee Woods.
Number of staff: 2 part-time professional.
Employer Identification Number: 736095854

6025
Charles W. & Pauline Flint Foundation ⌑
P.O. Box 490
Tulsa 74101

Established in 1961 in OK.
Donor(s): Charles W. Flint, Jr., Susan Seay.
Foundation type: Independent
Financial data (yr. ended 12/31/87): Assets, $1,083,486 (M); expenditures, $29,351, including $21,400 for 10 grants (high: $5,000; low: $500).
Purpose and activities: Grants primarily for education.
Limitations: Giving primarily in OK.
Application information: Contributes only to pre-selected organizations. Applications not accepted.
Trustees: George M. Davis, Charles W. Flint III, Charles C. Killin.
Employer Identification Number: 736093759

6026
The Glass-Glen Burnie Foundation
116 East Delaware
Nowata 74048

Established in 1986 in OK.
Donor(s): Julian W. Glass, Jr.
Foundation type: Operating
Financial data (yr. ended 12/31/88): Assets, $1,510,280 (M); gifts received, $123,085; expenditures, $70,472, including $10,000 for 1 grant.
Purpose and activities: A private operating foundation in the process of establishing a museum; support for historic preservation and general charitable purposes.
Limitations: Giving primarily in Winchester, VA. No grants to individuals.
Publications: 990-PF.
Application information: Contributes only to pre-selected organizations. Applications not accepted.
Officer: R. Lee Taylor, Exec. Dir.
Trustees: David D. Denham, Julian W. Glass, Jr., Patrick C. Hayes, Irene S. Wischer.
Number of staff: 1 part-time support.
Employer Identification Number: 731267576

6027
The Charles B. Goddard Foundation ⌑
1000 Energy Ctr., Suite 102
P.O. Box 1485
Ardmore 73402 (405) 226-6040

Trust established in 1958 in OK.
Donor(s): Charles B. Goddard.†
Foundation type: Independent
Financial data (yr. ended 6/30/89): Assets, $4,881,564 (M); expenditures, $238,114, including $231,068 for 54 grants (high: $25,000; low: $18).
Purpose and activities: Support for community funds, youth agencies, hospitals and health associations, and secondary and elementary education.
Types of support: Operating budgets, continuing support, annual campaigns, seed money, emergency funds, building funds, equipment, land acquisition, research.
Limitations: Giving limited to southern OK and northern TX, or to programs of nationwide impact. No grants to individuals, or for endowment funds; no loans.
Application information: Application form not required.
Initial approach: Letter
Copies of proposal: 1
Deadline(s): Submit proposal preferably in Mar. through Sept.
Board meeting date(s): Apr. and Oct.
Write: William R. Goddard, Jr., Chair.
Officers and Trustees: William R. Goddard, Jr., Chair.; William M. Johns, Secy.-Treas.; Elizabeth E. Cashman, Ann G. Corrigan, William R. Goddard.
Number of staff: None.
Employer Identification Number: 756005868

6028
Herbert and Roseline Gussman Foundation ⌑
3200 First National Tower
Tulsa 74103

Established in 1951 in OK.
Donor(s): Herbert Gussman, Roseline Gussman, Barbara Gussman, Ellen Jane Adelson.
Foundation type: Independent
Financial data (yr. ended 12/31/88): Assets, $2,205,953 (M); expenditures, $318,659, including $312,789 for 56 grants (high: $220,201; low: $25).
Purpose and activities: Emphasis on Jewish giving, cultural programs, health services, and educational institutions, including higher education.
Limitations: Giving primarily in OK. No grants to individuals.
Application information: Contributes only to pre-selected organizations. Applications not accepted.
Trustees: Herbert Gussman, Roseline Gussman.
Employer Identification Number: 736090063

6029
Pearl M. and Julia J. Harmon Foundation
P.O. Box 52568
Tulsa 74152 (918) 743-6191

Trust established in 1962 in OK.
Donor(s): Claude C. Harmon,† Julia J. Harmon.†
Foundation type: Independent
Financial data (yr. ended 05/31/89): Assets, $16,205,387 (M); qualifying distributions, $1,228,176, including $382,849 for grants (average: $80-$12,000), $2,949 for 4 grants to individuals (high: $1,250; low: $758) and $842,378 for loans.
Purpose and activities: Loans and program-related investments to charitable organizations.
Types of support: Loans, program-related investments.
Limitations: Giving limited to OK, AR, KS, NM, and TX, with preference given to northeastern OK. No support for research. No grants to individuals.
Publications: Application guidelines.
Application information: Application form required.
Initial approach: Letter or telephone
Copies of proposal: 1
Deadline(s): None
Board meeting date(s): Monthly
Write: George L. Hangs, Jr., Secy.-Treas.
Officer and Trustees:* George L. Hangs, Jr.,* Secy.-Treas.; Hugh Conine, George L. Hangs, Sr., Jean M. Kuntz, First National Bank.
Employer Identification Number: 736095893

6030
Harris Foundation, Inc.
6403 N.W. Grand Blvd., Suite 200
Oklahoma City 73116 (405) 848-3371

Incorporated in 1938 in OK.
Donor(s): Vernon V. Harris.†
Foundation type: Independent
Financial data (yr. ended 12/31/88): Assets, $1,571,153 (M); expenditures, $288,940, including $273,650 for 41 grants (high: $50,000; low: $150).
Purpose and activities: Support for higher education, youth and health agencies, Protestant church support, social services, and cultural programs.
Types of support: Building funds, equipment, fellowships, operating budgets, renovation projects.
Limitations: Giving primarily in OK, with emphasis on Oklahoma City, Lawton, and Enid.
Publications: Financial statement.
Application information: Application form not required.
Deadline(s): None
Write: William V. Harris, Pres., or Ann B. Patterson, Asst. Secy.
Officers and Directors:* William V. Harris,* Pres.; Pat J. Patterson,* V.P. and Secy.-Treas.; Judith Harris Garrett,* V.P.; William J. Harris,* V.P.; Robert F. Long,* V.P.
Employer Identification Number: 736093072

6031
The Helmerich Foundation ⌑
1579 East 21st St.
Tulsa 74114 (918) 742-5531

Established in 1965 in OK.
Donor(s): W.H. Helmerich.†
Foundation type: Independent
Financial data (yr. ended 9/30/88): Assets, $13,876,453 (M); gifts received, $1,143,381; expenditures, $1,094,481, including $1,000,000 for 5 grants (high: $250,000; low: $50,000).
Purpose and activities: Giving of large capital gifts, with emphasis on Protestant church support and religious organizations, cultural programs, youth and health agencies, and a community development project.
Types of support: Building funds, equipment, capital campaigns, operating budgets.
Limitations: Giving limited to the Tulsa, OK, area. No grants to individuals, or for general support, continuing support, annual campaigns, seed money, emergency funds, deficit financing, land acquisition, endowment funds, matching gifts, scholarships, fellowships, program support, research, demonstration projects, publications, or conferences; no loans.
Publications: Application guidelines, program policy statement.
Application information: Application form not required.
Initial approach: Letter

Copies of proposal: 1
Deadline(s): None
Board meeting date(s): As required
Final notification: 4 weeks
Write: W.H. Helmerich III, Trustee
Trustee: W.H. Helmerich III.
Number of staff: None.
Employer Identification Number: 736105607

6032
Historical Preservation, Inc. ⌑
429 N.W. 16th St.
Oklahoma City 73103 (405) 272-4363

Established in 1971 in OK.
Donor(s): Carolyn Skelly Burford, Mrs. Hugh M. Johnson.†
Foundation type: Independent
Financial data (yr. ended 12/31/88): Assets, $1,788,354 (L); expenditures, $109,489, including $6,525 for 4 grants (high: $5,000; low: $25; average: $25-$5,000).
Purpose and activities: Giving is primarily concerned with the preservation, restoration and maintenance of historic sites, located within and around the Heritage Hills Historical Preservation District; the perpetuation of the historical and cultural heritage of the area; and assisting in the development of projects for zoning and land use to eliminate blighting influences and foster planning, development, beautification, and improvement within the parameters of historical preservation.
Types of support: Equipment, building funds, renovation projects, special projects, publications.
Limitations: Giving limited to the Heritage Hills Historical Preservation District in Oklahoma City, OK, and surrounding urban areas. No grants to individuals.
Application information:
Write: G.P. Johnson Hightower, Treas.
Officers: Chuck Wiggin, Pres.; Bill Carey, 1st V.P.; John Hefner, 2nd V.P.; John Yoeckel, Community Liaison Representative; Gary Bloom, Secy.; G.P. Johnson Hightower, Treas.
Employer Identification Number: 237023817

6033
Dexter G. Johnson Educational and Benevolent Trust ⌑
900 First City Place
Oklahoma City 73102 (405) 232-3340

Trust established in 1971 in OK.
Foundation type: Independent
Financial data (yr. ended 12/31/88): Assets, $5,236,369 (M); expenditures, $396,641, including $185,684 for 59 grants to individuals (high: $30,083; low: $300) and $77,864 for 11 loans to individuals.
Purpose and activities: Giving for student loans to physically handicapped students and students who by misfortune or calamity cannot otherwise complete their education in OK high schools, Oklahoma A and M College, Oklahoma City University, the University of Oklahoma; grants or loans to handicapped individuals for audiological evaluations, corrective surgery, vocational training, speech therapy, and medical equipment.
Types of support: Student aid, equipment, grants to individuals, student loans.
Limitations: Giving limited to OK.
Application information: Application form required.
Deadline(s): None
Write: Phil C. Daugherty, Trustee
Trustee: Phil C. Daugherty.
Employer Identification Number: 237389204

6034
Willard Johnston Foundation, Inc. ⌑
6100 North Western
Oklahoma City 73118-1098 (405) 840-5585

Established in 1951 in OK.
Foundation type: Independent
Financial data (yr. ended 12/31/87): Assets, $1,170,060 (M); expenditures, $90,079, including $59,745 for grants.
Purpose and activities: Support for higher education, health and social services, and the arts.
Types of support: General purposes, scholarship funds.
Limitations: Giving primarily in Oklahoma City, OK.
Application information:
Initial approach: Letter
Deadline(s): None
Write: George J. Records, Mgr.
Officer: George J. Records, Mgr.
Employer Identification Number: 736093829

6035
Montfort Jones and Allie Brown Jones Foundation ⌑
P.O. Box 1234
Bristow 74010

Trust established in 1960 in OK.
Donor(s): Allie B. Jones.†
Foundation type: Independent
Financial data (yr. ended 8/31/88): Assets, $2,478,913 (M); expenditures, $161,923, including $105,775 for 11 grants (high: $60,000; low: $500).
Purpose and activities: Support for educational, civic, and charitable institutions.
Limitations: Giving limited to organizations that specifically benefit Bristow, OK. No grants for scholarships (except funds at Southern Methodist University and University of Mississippi).
Application information: Application form required.
Deadline(s): Nov. 1
Write: Hazel S. Earnhardt, Secy.
Officers and Trustees: David H. Loeffler, Chair.; Hazel S. Earnhardt, Secy.; Roger Collins, Velma J. Collins, Stan Earnhardt.
Employer Identification Number: 730721557

6036
Kerr Center for Sustainable Agriculture
P.O. Box 588
Poteau 74953 (918) 647-9123

Established in 1985 in OK.
Foundation type: Operating
Financial data (yr. ended 12/31/87): Assets, $17,165,467 (M); gifts received, $25,490; expenditures, $1,941,215, including $6,250 for 1 grant.
Purpose and activities: A private operating foundation; support primarily for a center for agricultural research.
Publications: Newsletter, informational brochure.
Application information: Applications not accepted.
Board meeting date(s): 1st. Saturday in Dec.
Write: Barbara Chester, Secy.
Officers: Kay Adair, Pres.; Jim Horne, V.P.; Robert Adair, Sr., Secy.-Treas.; Barbara Chester, Secy.
Trustees: Robert Adair, Jr., Lloyd Faulkner, Shrikrishna Kashyap.
Number of staff: 10 full-time professional; 1 part-time professional; 19 full-time support; 5 part-time support.
Employer Identification Number: 731256120

6037
The Kerr Foundation, Inc. ▼
6301 North Western, Suite 120
Oklahoma City 73118 (405) 842-1510

Incorporated in 1963 in OK, and reincorporated in 1985.
Donor(s): Grayce B. Kerr Flynn.†
Foundation type: Independent
Financial data (yr. ended 12/31/89): Assets, $22,042,600 (M); qualifying distributions, $784,844, including $769,844 for 56 grants (high: $115,000; low: $300; average: $10,000-$50,000) and $15,000 for loans.
Purpose and activities: Giving primarily for education, the fine arts and other cultural activities, and health. Generally all grants are challenge grants.
Types of support: Matching funds.
Limitations: Giving primarily in TX, AR, KS, CO, MO, NM, and OK. No grants to individuals, or generally for continuing support.
Publications: Application guidelines.
Application information: Application form required.
Initial approach: Letter
Copies of proposal: 4
Deadline(s): None
Board meeting date(s): Quarterly
Write: Anne Holzberlein, Admin. Asst.
Officers and Trustees:* Robert S. Kerr, Jr.,* Chair. and Pres.; Lou C. Kerr,* V.P. and Secy.; Gerald R. Marshall,* Treas.; Royce Hammons, Sharon Kerr, Steven Kerr, Elmer B. Staats.
Number of staff: 2 part-time professional; 1 full-time support.
Employer Identification Number: 731256122

6038
The Robert S. and Grayce B. Kerr Foundation, Inc.
6301 North Western, Suite 220
Oklahoma City 73118 (405) 848-0975
FAX: (405) 848-0978

Chartered in 1986 in OK.
Donor(s): Grayce B. Kerr Flynn.†
Foundation type: Independent
Financial data (yr. ended 01/31/88): Assets, $18,400,000 (M); gifts received, $9,850; expenditures, $1,159,838, including $889,037 for 45 grants (high: $200,000; low: $250).
Purpose and activities: "Grantmaking concentrated in the areas of cultural activities,

education, the environment, and human services.
Types of support: Emergency funds, equipment, fellowships, general purposes, matching funds, operating budgets, renovation projects, scholarship funds, seed money, special projects, technical assistance, building funds, conferences and seminars, internships.
Limitations: Giving limited to OK. No support for lobbying efforts, memberships, or political campaigns. No grants to individuals, or for endowments, annual campaigns, memberships, or medical or scientific research.
Publications: Annual report (including application guidelines), program policy statement.
Application information: Application form required.
Initial approach: Letter
Copies of proposal: 7
Deadline(s): Mar. 1 and Oct. 1
Board meeting date(s): June and Dec.
Final notification: 1 week after board meeting
Write: Anne Hodges Morgan, Pres.
Officers and Trustees:* Joffa Kerr,* Chair.; Anne Hodges Morgan,* Pres.; N. Martin Stringer,* Secy.; William G. Kerr,* Treas.
Number of staff: 1 full-time professional; 1 full-time support.
Employer Identification Number: 731256123

6039
Grayce B. Kerr Fund, Inc.
6305 Waterford Blvd., Suite 340
Oklahoma City 73118 (405) 843-3653

Chartered in 1986 in OK.
Donor(s): Grayce B. Kerr Flynn,† Breene M. Kerr.
Foundation type: Independent
Financial data (yr. ended 12/31/89): Assets, $21,699,000 (M); qualifying distributions, $1,171,292, including $1,171,292 for 50 grants (average: $100-$500,000).
Purpose and activities: Major area of interest is education, including higher education; support also for the arts.
Types of support: Capital campaigns, consulting services, endowment funds, equipment, general purposes, matching funds, professorships, renovation projects, scholarship funds, seed money, special projects.
Limitations: Giving primarily in OK. No grants to individuals, or for continuing support.
Publications: Application guidelines, annual report.
Application information: Application form required.
Initial approach: Letter or proposal
Copies of proposal: 1
Deadline(s): None
Final notification: 3 months after final proposal is submitted
Write: Phillis Stone, Exec. Dir.
Officers: Breene M. Kerr,* Chair., Pres., and Treas.; Sheryl V. Kerr,* V.P. and Secy.; Phillis Stone, Exec. Dir.
Trustees:* Bill W. Cameron, Collin W. Scarborough, Carol C. Wilkinson.
Number of staff: 1 full-time professional; 1 full-time support.
Employer Identification Number: 731256124

6040
Kirkpatrick Foundation, Inc.
1300 North Broadway Dr.
Oklahoma City 73103 (405) 235-5621

Incorporated in 1955 in OK.
Donor(s): Eleanor B. Kirkpatrick, John E. Kirkpatrick, Kirkpatrick Oil Co., Joan E. Kirkpatrick, Kathryn T. Blake.†
Foundation type: Independent
Financial data (yr. ended 12/31/89): Assets, $18,999,286 (M); expenditures, $1,028,591, including $932,175 for 130 grants (high: $388,900; low: $25; average: $100-$25,000) and $2,394 for 1 in-kind gift.
Purpose and activities: Support for community programs, education, cultural programs, including fine and performing arts groups and historic preservation, and social service projects.
Types of support: Operating budgets, continuing support, annual campaigns, emergency funds, endowment funds, seed money, special projects.
Limitations: Giving primarily in Oklahoma City, OK. No support for hospitals, religious organizations, or mental health agencies. No grants to individuals; no loans.
Publications: Informational brochure.
Application information: Application form required.
Copies of proposal: 1
Deadline(s): 2 weeks before board meets
Board meeting date(s): Mar., June, Sept., and Dec.
Write: Marilyn B. Myers, Dir. and Asst. Secy.
Officers and Directors: John E. Kirkpatrick, Chair.; Joan E. Kirkpatrick, Pres.; Christian K. Keesee, V.P.; Eleanor J. Maurer, Secy.; Eleanor B. Kirkpatrick, Treas.; Jack Abernathy, John L. Belt, Douglas Cummings, Dan Hogan, Marilyn B. Myers, Charles E. Nelson, Morrison G. Tucker.
Number of staff: 2 part-time professional; 1 part-time support.
Employer Identification Number: 730701736

6041
E. P. & Roberta L. Kirschner Foundation ☆
409 Commercial Bank Bldg.
Muskogee 74401 (918) 682-3151

Established in 1979 in OK.
Donor(s): E. Phil Kirschner,† Roberta L. Kirschner.†
Foundation type: Independent
Financial data (yr. ended 05/31/89): Assets, $1,237,229 (M); expenditures, $47,406, including $42,836 for 38 grants (high: $4,330; low: $25).
Purpose and activities: Support for general charitable, religious, scientific, literary, and educational organizations; special consideration given to institutions supported by the donors during their lifetime.
Limitations: Giving primarily in OK, especially northeastern OK. No support for public educational institutions. No grants to individuals, or for computer equipment.
Publications: Annual report.
Application information: Application form not required.
Initial approach: Proposal
Copies of proposal: 1
Deadline(s): Sept. 1
Board meeting date(s): Between Sept. 1 and Oct. 31
Final notification: By Dec. 1
Write: Miriam Freedman
Officer and Trustees:* Miriam Freedman,* Chair.; Sandra K. Gross, Susan Kirschner.
Number of staff: 3
Employer Identification Number: 736191753

6042
Liberty Foundation, Inc. ☆
c/o Rodney L. Lee
100 North Broadway
Oklahoma City 73102

Established in 1982.
Donor(s): Liberty National Bank.
Foundation type: Company-sponsored
Financial data (yr. ended 12/31/88): Assets, $214,897 (M); gifts received, $351,203; expenditures, $146,449, including $146,439 for 88 grants (high: $30,000; low: $25).
Purpose and activities: Giving primarily for community funds, medical research and health organizations, higher education, and cultural programs.
Limitations: Giving primarily in Oklahoma City, OK. No grants to individuals.
Application information: Contributes only to pre-selected organizations. Applications not accepted.
Officers: William M. Bell, Chair.; Mischa Gorkuscha, V.P. and Secy.; Rodney L. Lee, V.P. and Controller; Kenneth Brown, V.P.; Charles E. Nelson, V.P.
Employer Identification Number: 731171302

6043
E. H. Lyon and Melody Lyon Foundation, Inc. ⌑
P.O. Box 546
Bartlesville 74005
Application address: 416 East Fifth St., Bartlesville, OK 74003; Tel.: (918)336-0066

Established about 1975 in OK.
Donor(s): E.H. Lyon, Melody Lyon.†
Foundation type: Independent
Financial data (yr. ended 12/31/88): Assets, $12,171,430 (M); gifts received, $122,065; expenditures, $799,804, including $653,318 for 25 grants (high: $126,000; low: $250).
Purpose and activities: Emphasis on civic projects, particularly parks and recreation, and on education and a medical foundation.
Limitations: Giving primarily in Bartlesville, OK.
Application information: Application form not required.
Initial approach: Letter
Deadline(s): None
Write: Don Donaldson, Pres.
Officers and Directors: Don Donaldson, Pres.; Walter W. Allison, V.P.; Charles W. Selby, V.P.; James W. Conner, Secy.; John F. Kane, Treas.
Employer Identification Number: 237299980

6044
The J. E. and L. E. Mabee Foundation, Inc. ▼
3000 Mid-Continent Tower
401 South Boston
Tulsa 74103 (918) 584-4286

Incorporated in 1948 in DE.
Donor(s): J.E. Mabee,† L.E. Mabee.†
Foundation type: Independent
Financial data (yr. ended 08/31/89): Assets, $494,281,654 (M); expenditures, $20,443,168, including $18,664,903 for 79 grants (high: $1,250,000; low: $600; average: $100,000-$500,000).
Purpose and activities: To aid Christian religious organizations, charitable organizations, and institutions of higher learning; and to support hospitals and other agencies and institutions engaged in the discovery, treatment, and care of diseases.
Types of support: Building funds, matching funds, capital campaigns, land acquisition, renovation projects.
Limitations: Giving limited to OK, TX, KS, AR, MO, and NM. No support for secondary or elementary education, or tax-supported institutions. No grants to individuals, or for research, endowment funds, scholarships, fellowships, or operating expenses; no loans.
Publications: Program policy statement, application guidelines.
Application information: Application form not required.
Initial approach: Proposal
Copies of proposal: 1
Deadline(s): Mar. 1, June 1, Sept. 1, and Dec. 1
Board meeting date(s): Jan., Apr., July, and Oct.
Final notification: After board meetings
Write: John H. Conway, Jr., Vice-Chair.
Officers and Trustees:* Guy R. Mabee,* Chair.; John H. Conway, Jr.,* Vice-Chair. and Secy.-Treas.; John W. Cox,* Vice-Chair.; Joe Mabee,* Vice-Chair.; Donald P. Moyers,* Vice-Chair.
Number of staff: 1 full-time professional; 4 part-time professional; 7 full-time support.
Employer Identification Number: 736090162

6045
McCasland Foundation ▼ ⌑
P.O. Box 400
McCasland Bldg.
Duncan 73534 (405) 252-5580

Trust established in 1952 in OK.
Donor(s): Members of the McCasland family, Mack Oil Co., Jath Oil Co., and others.
Foundation type: Independent
Financial data (yr. ended 12/31/88): Assets, $23,205,541 (M); gifts received, $367,550; expenditures, $1,134,770, including $1,095,604 for 125 grants (high: $95,000; low: $300; average: $1,000-$50,000).
Purpose and activities: Emphasis on higher education, hospitals, community welfare, and cultural programs.
Types of support: Scholarship funds, general purposes, building funds.
Limitations: Giving primarily in OK and the Southwest, including TX and KS.
Application information:
Initial approach: Letter
Deadline(s): None
Board meeting date(s): Variable; usually quarterly
Final notification: After board meetings
Write: W.H. Phelps, Trustee
Trustees: Mary Frances Maurer, T.H. McCasland, Jr., W.H. Phelps.
Number of staff: None.
Employer Identification Number: 736096032

6046
The McGee Foundation, Inc.
P.O. Box 18127
Oklahoma City 73154 (405) 842-6266

Incorporated in 1963 in OK.
Donor(s): Dean A. McGee.†
Foundation type: Independent
Financial data (yr. ended 06/30/89): Assets, $3,399,615 (M); gifts received, $40,000; expenditures, $115,877, including $112,600 for grants.
Purpose and activities: Giving for higher education and medical research.
Limitations: Giving primarily in OK and CA. No grants to individuals, or for endowment funds.
Application information:
Write: Miss Elizabeth Zoernig, Secy.-Treas.
Officers and Directors:* Dorothea S. McGee,* V.P.; Elizabeth Zoernig,* Secy.-Treas.; Marcia Ann Bieber, Patricia McGee Maino.
Employer Identification Number: 736099203

6047
The McMahon Foundation ▼
714-716 C Ave.
P.O. Box 2156
Lawton 73502 (405) 355-4622

Incorporated in 1940 in OK.
Donor(s): Eugene D. McMahon,† Louise D. McMahon.†
Foundation type: Independent
Financial data (yr. ended 03/31/89): Assets, $27,421,321 (M); expenditures, $1,514,429, including $1,081,813 for 24 grants (high: $435,000; low: $400) and $154,918 for 1 foundation-administered program.
Purpose and activities: Support for education, social welfare and youth agencies, the arts, and community development projects.
Types of support: Annual campaigns, building funds, capital campaigns, emergency funds, equipment, general purposes, land acquisition, matching funds, renovation projects, scholarship funds.
Limitations: Giving limited to OK. No grants to individuals.
Application information: Application form not required.
Initial approach: Letter
Copies of proposal: 1
Deadline(s): 1 week prior to board meeting
Board meeting date(s): Monthly
Final notification: 2-3 days after board meeting
Write: James F. Wood, Dir.
Officers: Gale Sadler,* Secy.-Treas.; James F. Wood, Dir.
Trustees:* Charles S. Graybill, M.D., Chair.; Manville Redman, Vice-Chair.; Kenneth Bridges, Ronald E. Cagle, M.D., Orville Smith, Frank C. Sneed.
Number of staff: 2 full-time professional; 2 full-time support; 1 part-time support.
Employer Identification Number: 730664314

6048
The Merrick Foundation
P.O. Box 998
Ardmore 73402 (405) 226-7000

Trust established in 1947 in OK; incorporated in 1968.
Donor(s): Mrs. Frank W. Merrick,† and others.
Foundation type: Independent
Financial data (yr. ended 12/31/88): Assets, $5,331,986 (M); expenditures, $256,056, including $186,970 for 46 grants (high: $11,000; low: $100).
Purpose and activities: Giving for higher education and hospitals; grants also for medical research, youth agencies, and a community fund.
Types of support: Seed money, building funds.
Limitations: Giving primarily in OK, with emphasis on southern OK. No grants to individuals, or for endowment or operating funds.
Application information:
Initial approach: Letter
Copies of proposal: 1
Deadline(s): Submit proposal in Sept.
Board meeting date(s): Nov.
Write: Ward S. Merrick, Jr., V.P.
Officers and Trustees: Elizabeth Merrick Coe, Pres.; Ward S. Merrick, Jr., V.P.; Valda M. Buchanan, Secy.; Michael A. Cawley, Charles R. Coe, Jr., Ward I. Coe, Bill Goddard, Linda P. Mitchell, Frank W. Merrick, Jack D. Wilkes.
Number of staff: 2 full-time professional.
Employer Identification Number: 736111622

6049
Ruth Kaiser Nelson Family Foundation
P.O. Box 21468
Tulsa 741211468 (918) 491-4518

Established in 1983 in OK.
Foundation type: Independent
Financial data (yr. ended 12/31/88): Assets, $630,577 (M); gifts received, $60,845; expenditures, $106,128, including $105,786 for 32 grants (high: $22,153; low: $100).
Purpose and activities: Support for higher education and to welfare organizations.
Types of support: Scholarship funds.
Limitations: Giving primarily in Tulsa, OK.
Application information: Application form not required.
Deadline(s): None
Trustees: George B. Kaiser, Ruth Kaiser Nelson.
Employer Identification Number: 731210115

6050
The Samuel Roberts Noble Foundation, Inc. ▼
P.O. Box 2180
Ardmore 73402 (405) 223-5810

Trust established in 1945 in OK; incorporated in 1952.
Donor(s): Lloyd Noble.†
Foundation type: Independent

Financial data (yr. ended 10/31/89): Assets, $345,256,786 (M); expenditures, $17,613,107, including $4,945,771 for 100 grants (high: $463,316; low: $1,500; average: $5,000-$150,000), $69,000 for 48 grants to individuals (high: $2,000; low: $1,000; average: $1,000-$2,000), $26,365 for 46 employee matching gifts and $11,807,821 for 3 foundation-administered programs.
Purpose and activities: Supports its own three operating programs: 1) basic biomedical research pertaining to cancer and degenerative diseases; 2) plant research, with the objective of genetic engineering of plants; and 3) agricultural research, consultation, and demonstration, along with wildlife management, for the benefit of rural and urban people. Primarily, grants are for higher education, for health research pertaining to cancer and degenerative diseases, and for health delivery systems. Matching gift program for Noble Co. employees.
Types of support: Research, employee-related scholarships, seed money, building funds, equipment, endowment funds, matching funds, employee matching gifts.
Limitations: Giving primarily in the Southwest, with emphasis on OK. No grants to individuals (except through the scholarship program for children of employees of Noble organizations); no loans.
Publications: Annual report.
Application information: Application form required.
Initial approach: Letter
Copies of proposal: 1
Deadline(s): 6 weeks prior to board meeting dates
Board meeting date(s): Usually in Jan., Apr., July, and Oct.
Final notification: 2 weeks after board meetings
Write: John F. Snodgrass, Pres.
Officers: John F. Snodgrass,* Pres.; Larry Pulliam, V.P. and Treas.; M.K. Patterson, Jr., V.P.; Jackie N. Skidmore, Secy.
Trustees:* Ann Noble Brown, David R. Brown, Michael A. Cawley, Vivian N. Dubose, William R. Goddard, John R. March, Edward E. Noble, Mary Jane Noble, Sam Noble.
Number of staff: 73 full-time professional; 67 full-time support; 12 part-time support.
Employer Identification Number: 730606209

6051
The Vivian Bilby Noble Foundation, Inc.
P.O. Box 817
Ardmore 73402 (405) 223-5810

Trust established in 1936 in OK; incorporated in 1959.
Donor(s): Lloyd Noble.†
Foundation type: Independent
Financial data (yr. ended 12/31/89): Assets, $2,833,624 (M); expenditures, $105,395, including $92,300 for 17 grants (high: $25,000; low: $300; average: $5,000-$10,000).
Purpose and activities: Emphasis on education, church support, and youth agencies; some support also for cultural programs and community social service organizations.
Types of support: Operating budgets, continuing support, annual campaigns, building funds, equipment, land acquisition, endowment funds, capital campaigns, general purposes, renovation projects, special projects.
Limitations: Giving primarily in the southwestern U.S. No grants to individuals, or for seed money, emergency funds, deficit financing, matching gifts, scholarships, fellowships, research, publications, or conferences; no loans.
Publications: Application guidelines.
Application information: Application form required.
Initial approach: Letter
Copies of proposal: 1
Deadline(s): Submit proposal preferably in June through Aug.; deadline Aug. 31
Board meeting date(s): Oct. and as needed
Final notification: 2 months
Write: Donna Windel
Officers and Trustees:* Edward E. Noble,* Pres.; Sam Noble,* V.P.; Ann Noble Brown,* Secy.-Treas.
Number of staff: None.
Employer Identification Number: 736090116

6052
Occidental Oil and Gas Charitable Foundation
(Formerly Cities Service Foundation)
110 West Seventh St.
P.O. Box 300
Tulsa 74102 (918) 561-4745

Incorporated in 1954 in DE.
Donor(s): Occidental Oil and Gas Co.
Foundation type: Company-sponsored
Financial data (yr. ended 12/31/88): Assets, $8,685,213 (M); expenditures, $716,941, including $524,380 for 119 grants (high: $88,000; low: $350; average: $5,000) and $141,987 for employee matching gifts.
Purpose and activities: Giving primarily for higher education (including and employee matching gift program), cultural programs and the arts, health and welfare organizations, civic organizations, and community funds.
Types of support: Annual campaigns, employee matching gifts, operating budgets, renovation projects, employee-related scholarships.
Limitations: Giving limited to areas of company operations: Tulsa and Oklahoma City, OK, and Houston and Midland, TX. No support for political organizations. No grants to individuals.
Application information: Application form not required.
Initial approach: Letter
Copies of proposal: 1
Deadline(s): Sept. 1
Write: Joanne G. Sellers, Contribs. Coord.
Officers: David A. Hentschel,* Pres.; R.W. Archibald, V.P.; D.A. Kelsey, V.P.; R.G. Peters, Exec. Secy.; G.D. Luthey, Secy.; C.P. Marlowe,* Treas.
Trustees:* Paul C. Hebner, J.R. Niehaus, R.G. Peters, J.G. Sellers.
Number of staff: 2 part-time professional.
Employer Identification Number: 136081799

6053
Oklahoma City Community Foundation, Inc.
115 Park Ave.
Oklahoma City 73103 (405) 235-5603
Additional address: P.O. Box 1146, Oklahoma City, OK 73101

Incorporated in 1968 in OK.
Foundation type: Community
Financial data (yr. ended 06/30/88): Assets, $34,342,591 (M); gifts received, $3,838,758; expenditures, $1,598,289, including $1,358,826 for 284 grants (high: $335,289; low: $25; average: $3,000-$10,000) and $45,000 for 2 foundation-administered programs.
Purpose and activities: Giving to charitable, educational, health, and cultural organizations.
Types of support: Scholarship funds, fellowships, matching funds, operating budgets, continuing support, annual campaigns, seed money, emergency funds, building funds, equipment, research, special projects.
Limitations: Giving primarily in greater Oklahoma City, OK. No grants to individuals, or for endowment funds or deficit financing; no loans.
Publications: Annual report, newsletter.
Application information:
Initial approach: Telephone
Copies of proposal: 6
Deadline(s): July 31 and Jan. 31
Board meeting date(s): Jan., Apr., July, and Oct.
Write: Nancy B. Anthony, Exec. Dir.
Officers: James R. Tolbert III,* Pres.; Nancy Payne,* V.P.; John L. Belt, Secy.; Eleanor J. Maurer, Treas.; Nancy B. Anthony, Exec. Dir.
Trustees:* Ray Anthony, Edward Barth, John Kirkpatick, Frank McPherson, George Record, James Tolbert, Richard Van Horn.
Trustee Banks: Bank Oklahoma, First Interstate Bank and Trust, Liberty National Bank & Trust Co. of Oklahoma City, Trust Co. of Oklahoma.
Number of staff: 2 full-time professional; 1 full-time support; 1 part-time support.
Employer Identification Number: 237024262

6054
Oklahoma Gas and Electric Company Foundation, Inc.
321 North Harvey
P.O. Box 321
Oklahoma City 73101 (405) 272-3196

Incorporated in 1957 in OK.
Donor(s): Oklahoma Gas and Electric Co.
Foundation type: Company-sponsored
Financial data (yr. ended 12/31/89): Assets, $1,000,000 (M); qualifying distributions, $640,700, including $611,800 for 57 grants (high: $125,000; low: $200; average: $3,000-$10,000) and $28,900 for 131 employee matching gifts.
Purpose and activities: Support for higher educational institutions, hospitals, and youth agencies.
Types of support: Operating budgets, continuing support, annual campaigns, building funds, equipment, employee matching gifts, professorships, scholarship funds.

Limitations: Giving limited to OK, in areas of company operations. No grants to individuals; no loans.
Application information: Application form not required.
Initial approach: Letter or proposal
Copies of proposal: 1
Deadline(s): None
Board meeting date(s): As required
Final notification: 1 month
Write: James G. Harlow, Jr., Pres.
Officers and Directors:* James G. Harlow, Jr.,* Pres.; Patrick J. Ryan,* V.P.; Al M. Strecker,* V.P.; Irma B. Elliott,* Secy.-Treas.
Number of staff: None.
Employer Identification Number: 736093572

6055
Lucile Page Testamentary Trust ⌑
P.O. Box 308
Sand Springs 74063

Foundation type: Independent
Financial data (yr. ended 12/31/88): Assets, $1,396,144 (M); expenditures, $97,755, including $42,649 for 9 grants (high: $23,654; low: $145).
Purpose and activities: Giving primarily to fund dental care for the needy and general community welfare.
Limitations: Giving limited to the Sand Springs, OK, area. No grants to individuals.
Application information:
Initial approach: Proposal
Deadline(s): None
Write: The Trustees
Trustees: George E.M. Campbell, Dr. Charles Halm, Lawrence Hinson.
Employer Identification Number: 736188163

6056
The Robert L. Parker Foundation ⌑
Eight East Third St.
Tulsa 74103

Established in 1973.
Donor(s): Robert L. Parker.
Foundation type: Independent
Financial data (yr. ended 11/30/88): Assets, $198,482 (M); expenditures, $112,207, including $111,250 for 33 grants (high: $50,000; low: $100).
Purpose and activities: Giving primarily for a Methodist church and other Christian organizations; support also for youth and social service organizations.
Types of support: Operating budgets, building funds.
Application information: Contributes only to pre-selected organizations. Applications not accepted.
Trustees: Robert L. Parker, Jr., Jack E. Short.
Employer Identification Number: 510153008

6057
Frank Parkes Foundation, Inc. ⌑
P.O. Box 245
Hooker 73945

Established in 1977 in OK.
Foundation type: Independent
Financial data (yr. ended 3/31/87): Assets, $1,309,160 (M); expenditures, $276,676, including $109,080 for grants.
Purpose and activities: Giving for general charitable purposes.
Application information:
Initial approach: Letter
Deadline(s): None
Write: James P. Flanagan, Trustee
Trustees: James P. Flanagan, Ralph Flesher, Vernon Taylor, Henry Wacher.
Employer Identification Number: 731019708

6058
Robert A. Parman Foundation ⌑
c/o Liberty National Bank & Trust
100 Broadway
Oklahoma City 73102
Application address: 1414 West Reno, Oklahoma City, OK 73106

Trust established in 1962 in OK.
Donor(s): Robert A. Parman.†
Foundation type: Independent
Financial data (yr. ended 8/31/88): Assets, $4,548,227 (M); expenditures, $462,298, including $365,650 for 11 grants (high: $50,000; low: $650).
Purpose and activities: Support for higher education, social services and a hospital.
Limitations: Giving primarily in OK. No grants to individuals.
Application information:
Initial approach: Letter
Deadline(s): None
Write: John L. Hessel, Trustee
Trustees: Donald W. Burleson, John L. Hessel, Rev. J. Clyde Wheeler, Liberty National Bank & Trust Co. of Indiana.
Employer Identification Number: 736098053

6059
The Frank Phillips Foundation, Inc.
P.O. Box 1647
Bartlesville 74005 (918) 336-0307

Incorporated in 1937 in DE.
Donor(s): Frank Phillips,† Mrs. Frank Phillips.†
Foundation type: Operating
Financial data (yr. ended 12/31/88): Assets, $24,153,831 (M); gifts received, $39,569; qualifying distributions, $1,534,736, including $36,388 for 18 grants (high: $10,000; low: $190; average: $200-$5,000) and $1,496,529 for 1 foundation-administered program.
Purpose and activities: A private operating foundation; established primarily to maintain and operate Woolaroc, a 3,500-acre wildlife preserve, Western-Indian museum, historic lodge, and the national Y-Indian guide center and its connecting nature trails, owned and operated by the foundation. Some grants to local eligible charitable agencies as funds are available, with emphasis on youth programs.
Limitations: Giving limited to OK. No grants to individuals, or for building or endowment funds, research programs, scholarships, or fellowships; no loans.
Publications: Application guidelines, newsletter, informational brochure.
Application information: Application form not required.
Initial approach: Letter
Copies of proposal: 1
Deadline(s): None
Board meeting date(s): Bimonthly
Write: William R. Blakemore, General Mgr.
Officer: William R. Blakemore, General Mgr. and Secy.-Treas.
Trustees: V.M. Lockard, Chair.; Donald Doty, Vice-Chair.; William G. Creel, John Hughes, Leo H. Johnstone, Richard Kane, Robert Kane, Lee Phillips III, Robert B. Phillips, C.J. Silas.
Number of staff: 31 full-time professional; 8 part-time professional.
Employer Identification Number: 730636562

6060
Phillips Petroleum Foundation, Inc. ▼ ⌑
Phillips Bldg., 16th Fl.
Bartlesville 74004 (918) 661-6248

Incorporated in 1973 in OK.
Donor(s): Phillips Petroleum Co.
Foundation type: Company-sponsored
Financial data (yr. ended 12/31/88): Assets, $10,250 (M); gifts received, $3,485,855; expenditures, $3,217,770, including $2,126,364 for 436 grants (high: $87,920; low: $50; average: $1,000-$25,000) and $1,091,346 for employee matching gifts.
Purpose and activities: Support for education, civic and youth organizations, cultural programs, and social service and health agencies.
Types of support: Employee matching gifts, operating budgets, annual campaigns, seed money, building funds, equipment, land acquisition, renovation projects, research, conferences and seminars, scholarship funds, fellowships, professorships, internships, exchange programs, matching funds, continuing support, general purposes, capital campaigns.
Limitations: Giving primarily in areas of company operations, particularly OK, TX, CO, and other states in the South and Southwest. Generally no grants to religious organizations or specialized health agencies. No grants to individuals, or for trips or fundraising dinners; no loans.
Publications: Application guidelines.
Application information: Application form not required.
Initial approach: Proposal, letter, or telephone
Copies of proposal: 1
Deadline(s): None
Board meeting date(s): Mar. and as required
Final notification: 8 to 12 weeks
Write: John C. West, Exec. Mgr.
Officers and Directors:* R.W. Peters, Jr.,* Pres.; R.H. Schultz,* V.P.; J.B. Whitworth,* V.P.; G.C. Meese, Secy.; Betsy L. Swan, Treas.; John C. West, Exec. Mgr.; D.J. Billam, D.L. Cone, L.M. Francis, J.W. Middleton, Stanley R. Mueller, J.W. O'Toole, J.G. Wilson.
Number of staff: 1 part-time professional; 1 part-time support.
Employer Identification Number: 237326611

6061
Puterbaugh Foundation
215 East Choctaw, First National Ctr., Suite 117
P.O. Box 729
McAlester 74502 (918) 426-1591

Trust established in 1949 in OK.
Donor(s): Jay Garfield Puterbaugh,† Leela Oliver Puterbaugh.†
Foundation type: Independent
Financial data (yr. ended 12/31/89): Assets, $6,543,356 (L); expenditures, $353,709, including $249,856 for 32 grants (high: $42,456; low: $25) and $35,043 for 1 foundation-administered program.
Purpose and activities: Giving for education, medical research, child welfare and youth agencies, government, and social services.
Types of support: Annual campaigns, building funds, endowment funds, equipment, exchange programs, matching funds, professorships, scholarship funds, special projects.
Limitations: Giving primarily in OK. No grants to individuals.
Publications: Financial statement.
Application information: Budgets are set 1 year in advance of year of payment. Application form not required.
Initial approach: Letter
Deadline(s): Jan. 15 for payment in Dec.
Write: Don C. Phelps, Managing Trustee
Trustees: Don C. Phelps, Managing Trustee; Frank G. Edwards, Norris J. Welker.
Number of staff: 2 part-time support.
Employer Identification Number: 736092193

6062
Robert Glenn Rapp Foundation ⌑
2301 N.W. 39th Expressway, Suite 300
Oklahoma City 73112 (405) 525-8331

Trust established about 1953 in OK.
Donor(s): Florence B. Clark.†
Foundation type: Independent
Financial data (yr. ended 12/31/88): Assets, $5,549,709 (M); expenditures, $108,333, including $1,750 for 1 grant.
Purpose and activities: Emphasis on higher education; support also for medical research, hospitals, secondary education, and cultural programs.
Limitations: Giving primarily in OK, with emphasis on Oklahoma City. No grants to individuals.
Application information:
Initial approach: Letter
Deadline(s): Oct. 1
Board meeting date(s): Annually, usually in the latter part of the year
Write: Trustees
Trustees: Stanley B. Catlett, James H. Milligan, Lois Darlene Milligan.
Number of staff: None.
Employer Identification Number: 730616840

6063
Mike & Sharon Robinowitz Family Foundation ⌑
7130 South Lewis, Suite 910
Tulsa 74136

Established in 1966 in OK.
Foundation type: Independent
Financial data (yr. ended 12/31/88): Assets, $1,151,105 (M); expenditures, $49,514, including $48,276 for 20 grants (high: $31,200; low: $50).
Purpose and activities: Support primarily for Jewish welfare.
Limitations: Giving primarily in Tulsa, OK. No grants to individuals.
Application information: Contributes only to pre-selected organizations. Applications not accepted.
Officer and Trustee: Mike Robinowitz, Mgr.
Employer Identification Number: 736108970

6064
Sarkeys Foundation ▼
116 South Peters, Rm. 219
Norman 73069 (405) 364-3703

Established in 1962 in OK.
Donor(s): S.J. Sarkeys.†
Foundation type: Independent
Financial data (yr. ended 11/30/89): Assets, $50,874,253 (M); expenditures, $2,363,289, including $2,007,255 for 27 grants (high: $500,000; low: $1,500; average: $10,000-$125,000).
Purpose and activities: Emphasis on higher education; grants also for community services, health and welfare, and general charitable support. Preference given to project-oriented grants over general budgetary support.
Types of support: Endowment funds, capital campaigns, professorships, research, scholarship funds, special projects.
Limitations: Giving primarily in OK. No support for elementary or secondary education, or generally for local programs appropriately financed within the community, or direct mail solicitations. No grants to individuals.
Publications: Informational brochure (including application guidelines).
Application information: Application form not required.
Initial approach: Proposal or letter
Copies of proposal: 9
Deadline(s): Mar. 15 and Sept. 15
Board meeting date(s): Jan., Apr., July, and Oct.; grants considered at Apr. and Oct. meeting
Final notification: Shortly after Apr. and Oct. board meetings
Write: R. Boyd Gunning, Managing Trustee, or Cheri D. Cartwright, Project Mgr.
Officers and Trustees:* Richard Bell,* Pres.; Duane Draper,* V.P.; Philip C. Kidd,* Secy.-Treas.; R. Boyd Gunning,* Managing Trustee; Cheri D. Cartwright,* Project Mgr.; Robert Rennie, Robert S. Rizley.
Number of staff: 2 full-time professional.
Employer Identification Number: 730736496

6065
Charles Morton Share Trust ⌑
c/o Liberty National Bank & Trust Co.
P.O. Box 25848, Trust Dept.
Oklahoma City 73125 (405) 231-6815

Trust established in 1959 in OK.
Donor(s): Charles Morton Share.†
Foundation type: Independent
Financial data (yr. ended 6/30/87): Assets, $7,314,609 (M); expenditures, $889,857, including $632,560 for 11 grants (high: $495,000; low: $2,500; average: $15,000-$25,000).
Purpose and activities: Emphasis on higher education and hospitals; support also for community projects and a museum.
Types of support: Scholarship funds.
Limitations: Giving primarily in OK. No grants to individuals, or for operating budgets, continuing support, annual campaigns, seed money, emergency, building, or endowment funds; deficit financing, equipment, land acquisition, renovations, matching gifts, special projects, research, publications, or conferences; no loans.
Application information: Application form not required.
Initial approach: Proposal
Copies of proposal: 5
Deadline(s): None
Board meeting date(s): Quarterly and as required
Final notification: 6 weeks
Trustees: J.R. Holder, C.E. Johnson, Gertrude Myers, B.H. Thornton, Liberty National Bank & Trust Co. of Oklahoma City.
Number of staff: None.
Employer Identification Number: 736090984

6066
Shin'en Kan, Inc. ⌑
P.O. Box 1111
Bartlesville 74005

Established in 1980 in OK.
Foundation type: Operating
Financial data (yr. ended 12/31/88): Assets, $6,225,738 (M); gifts received, $140,000; expenditures, $57,489, including $16,000 for 3 grants (high: $10,000; low: $1,000).
Purpose and activities: Support primarily for the development and construction of a museum devoted to Japanese art and the furtherance of the understanding and appreciation of the architecture of Bruce Goff.
Types of support: Building funds, general purposes.
Application information: Contributes only to pre-selected organizations. Applications not accepted.
Write: Joe D. Price, Pres.
Officers: Joe D. Price,* Pres.; Etsuko Y. Price,* V.P.; W.E. Yount, Secy.-Treas.
Directors:* Ralph E. Lerner.
Employer Identification Number: 731106645

6067
Harold C. & Joan S. Stuart Foundation ⌑
Box 1349
Tulsa 74101 (918) 743-7814

Established in 1969 in OK.
Foundation type: Independent
Financial data (yr. ended 12/31/88): Assets, $1,006,785 (M); expenditures, $46,835, including $45,525 for 47 grants (high: $10,000; low: $25; average: $100-$500).
Purpose and activities: Giving primarily for social services and youth, including a community fund; support also for cultural programs and health associations.
Types of support: General purposes.

Limitations: Giving primarily in the Tulsa, OK, area.
Application information: Application form not required.
Deadline(s): None
Write: Harold C. Stuart, Trustee
Trustees: Harold C. Stuart, Joan S. Stuart.
Employer Identification Number: 237052178

6068
Herman P. and Sophia Taubman Foundation ⌑
1701 First National Bldg.
Tulsa 74103 (918) 585-9151

Trust established in 1955 in OK.
Donor(s): Herman P. Taubman,† Sophia Taubman.†
Foundation type: Independent
Financial data (yr. ended 12/31/88): Assets, $3,607,000 (M); expenditures, $233,041, including $200,034 for 36 grants (high: $30,700; low: $50).
Purpose and activities: Grants largely for Jewish welfare funds, hospitals, youth agencies and higher education.
Types of support: Research, building funds, general purposes.
Limitations: Giving primarily in OK. No grants to individuals.
Application information:
Initial approach: Letter
Copies of proposal: 3
Deadline(s): None
Board meeting date(s): As required
Write: Morris B. Taubman, Trustee
Trustees: David Fist, Louis Taubman, Morris B. Taubman.
Number of staff: None.
Employer Identification Number: 736092820

6069
C. W. Titus Foundation ⌑
1801 Philtower Bldg.
Tulsa 74103 (918) 582-8095

Established in 1968 in OK.
Foundation type: Independent
Financial data (yr. ended 12/31/88): Assets, $8,207,624 (M); expenditures, $293,546, including $250,269 for 43 grants (high: $50,000; low: $1,000; average: $1,000-$10,000).
Purpose and activities: Giving for hospitals and health services, cultural programs, the handicapped, and social service agencies.
Limitations: Giving primarily in OK and MO.
Application information: Application form not required.
Deadline(s): None
Trustees: Rosemary T. Reynolds, Timothy T. Reynolds.
Employer Identification Number: 237016981

6070
Tulsa Foundation ⌑ ☆
c/o First National Bank of Tulsa
P.O. Box One
Tulsa 74193 (918) 586-5594

Established in 1919 in OK.
Foundation type: Community
Financial data (yr. ended 12/31/88): Assets, $10,867,088 (M); gifts received, $252,149; expenditures, $956,885, including $886,804 for 22 grants.
Purpose and activities: Support to organizations "that provide services that enhance the quality of life for the citizens of Tulsa."
Limitations: Giving limited to Tulsa, OK, area. No grants to individuals.
Application information:
Write: J. Michael Bartel, Asst. V.P., First National Bank of Tulsa
Number of staff: None.
Employer Identification Number: 736090617

6071
Tulsa Royalties Company
3229-A South Harvard Ave.
Tulsa 74135 (918) 747-5638

Incorporated in 1951 in OK.
Donor(s): William S. Bailey, Jr.
Foundation type: Independent
Financial data (yr. ended 12/31/88): Assets, $3,966,951 (M); expenditures, $279,991, including $200,016 for 69 grants (high: $30,000; low: $25).
Purpose and activities: Emphasis on higher education, hospitals, social service agencies, and Protestant church support.
Types of support: Building funds, capital campaigns, endowment funds, equipment.
Limitations: Giving primarily in OK. No grants to individuals, or for matching gifts; no loans.
Application information: Funds largely committed.
Board meeting date(s): Mar.
Officers and Trustees:* William S. Bailey, Jr.,* Chair.; Lawrence A. Peitz,* Pres.; Albert J. Geiger,* V.P.; Donald E. Pray,* V.P.; R. Paul Henry,* Secy.-Treas.; Eleanor M. Jones.
Number of staff: 2 full-time professional.
Employer Identification Number: 736101744

6072
28:19, Inc. ⌑
7300 North Comanche
Oklahoma City 73132 (405) 721-2797

Foundation type: Independent
Financial data (yr. ended 11/30/88): Assets, $4,658,461 (M); gifts received, $261,214; expenditures, $367,082, including $287,096 for grants.
Purpose and activities: Grants for Protestant religious organizations.
Officers and Directors:* Max Barnett,* Pres.; John R. Repass,* V.P. and Secy.-Treas.
Employer Identification Number: 736091732

6073
Warren Charite ⌑
P.O. Box 470372
Tulsa 74147-0372

Established in 1968 in OK.
Donor(s): William K. Warren.
Foundation type: Independent
Financial data (yr. ended 11/30/88): Assets, $5,456,518 (M); expenditures, $304,979, including $283,665 for 62 grants (high: $50,000; low: $150).
Purpose and activities: Grants for a cancer research center and a hospital; some support for health associations and religion.
Types of support: General purposes.
Limitations: Giving primarily in OK.
Application information:
Initial approach: Letter
Officers and Trustees: William K. Warren, Pres.; Eleanor L. Corp, V.P.; W.R. Lissau, Secy.
Employer Identification Number: 730776064

6074
The William K. Warren Foundation ▼ ⌑
P.O. Box 470372
Tulsa 74147-0372 (918) 492-8100

Incorporated in 1945 in OK.
Donor(s): William K. Warren, Mrs. William K. Warren.
Foundation type: Independent
Financial data (yr. ended 12/31/88): Assets, $269,743,325 (M); gifts received, $605,537; expenditures, $16,788,323, including $15,389,470 for 32 grants (high: $5,700,000; low: $200; average: $5,000-$50,000).
Purpose and activities: Grants for local Catholic health care facilities, education, and social services; substantial support for a medical research program.
Types of support: Building funds, endowment funds, operating budgets, special projects.
Limitations: Giving primarily in OK. No grants to individuals.
Application information: Application form not required.
Initial approach: Letter
Deadline(s): None
Board meeting date(s): Semiannually
Write: W.R. Lissau, Pres.
Officers: W.R. Lissau,* Pres.; John A. Naughton, V.P. and Treas.; Dorothy Warren King,* Secy.
Directors:* Robert J. Stanton, Chair.; Natalie O. Warren, Vice-Chair.; W.K. Warren, Jr., Vice-Chair; John A. Gaberino, Jr., John J. King, Jr., Patricia Warren Swindle.
Number of staff: 10
Employer Identification Number: 730609599

6075
The Herman and Mary Wegener Foundation, Inc. ⌑
1711 First National Bldg.
Oklahoma City 73102 (405) 235-7200

Incorporated in 1954 in OK.
Donor(s): Herman H. Wegener.†
Foundation type: Independent
Financial data (yr. ended 12/31/88): Assets, $2,830,267 (M); gifts received, $100,000; expenditures, $306,917, including $249,700 for 32 grants (high: $15,000; low: $200).
Purpose and activities: Emphasis on hospitals and education; grants also for cultural programs, youth agencies, and social service agencies.
Types of support: Building funds, operating budgets, special projects.
Limitations: Giving primarily in Oklahoma City, OK. No grants to individuals, or for endowment funds.
Application information:

Initial approach: Letter
Deadline(s): Nov. 1
Board meeting date(s): Quarterly
Write: The Trustees
Officers and Trustees: Willis B. Sherin, Pres.; Lee Holmes, V.P.; May Fry, Secy.; Clenard Wegener, Treas.; Rosemary Fields, Kenneth Wegener, Raymond Lee Wegener, Willis B. Wegener.
Employer Identification Number: 736095407

6076
The Williams Companies Foundation, Inc. ▼
P.O. Box 2400
Tulsa 74102 (918) 588-2106

Incorporated in 1974 in OK.
Donor(s): The Williams Companies, Inc.
Foundation type: Company-sponsored
Financial data (yr. ended 12/31/89): Assets, $8,085,000 (M); expenditures, $1,360,124, including $911,368 for grants (high: $387,245; low: $50; average: $1,000-$30,000) and $435,756 for employee matching gifts.
Purpose and activities: Support primarily for education, especially higher education, health and human services, arts and cultural programs, and civic projects; employee matching gifts for United Way campaign.
Types of support: General purposes, building funds, equipment, seed money, emergency funds, matching funds.
Limitations: Giving primarily in locations where the Williams Companies has a strong business presence, with emphasis on Tulsa, OK. Generally, no support for national organizations. No grants to individuals, or for scholarships or fellowships; no loans.
Application information: Application form not required.
Initial approach: Proposal
Copies of proposal: 1
Deadline(s): None
Board meeting date(s): Varies
Final notification: Approximately 1 month
Write: Hannah D. Robson, Mgr.
Officers: Joseph H. Williams,* Chair.; Vernon T. Jones, Pres.; Keith E. Bailey,* V.P.; David M. Higbee, Secy.-Treas.; Hannah D. Robson, Mgr.
Directors:* John C. Bumgarner, Jr., J. Furman Lewis.
Number of staff: 1 part-time professional.
Employer Identification Number: 237413843

6077
The W. P. Wood Charitable Trust ⌘
P.O. Box 127
Shawnee 74801 (405) 273-2880

Established in 1973.
Foundation type: Independent
Financial data (yr. ended 12/31/88): Assets, $2,095,082 (M); expenditures, $331,591, including $263,000 for 17 grants (high: $50,000; low: $500).
Purpose and activities: Giving primarily for higher education, programs to aid the handicapped, and social services; support also for a museum.
Types of support: Operating budgets, building funds, scholarship funds, research.
Limitations: Giving primarily in OK. No grants to individuals.
Application information:
Initial approach: Proposal
Deadline(s): None
Write: Steve Garner, Mgr.
Officer and Trustees: Steve Garner, Mgr.; Gerald D. McGehee, Lindsay Peters.
Employer Identification Number: 736152038

6078
World Evangelism Services, Inc. ⌘ ☆
3417 Goodger Dr.
Oklahoma City 73112-1439 (405) 842-4503

Donor(s): Gene Thomas, Betty Lynn Thomas.
Foundation type: Independent
Financial data (yr. ended 6/30/89): Assets, $1,188,475 (M); gifts received, $91,383; expenditures, $247,400, including $9,548 for 88 grants (high: $500; low: $10) and $181,259 for 2 foundation-administered programs.
Purpose and activities: Support for evangelistic churches and organizations, especially ministries to the poor and needy.
Limitations: Giving primarily in Oklahoma City, OK.
Application information: Application form not required.
Deadline(s): None
Write: Betty Lynn Thomas, Secy.-Treas.
Officers: Gene Thomas, Pres.; David Lynn Thomas, V.P.; Steve Thomas, V.P.; Betty Lynn Thomas, Secy.-Treas.
Employer Identification Number: 730976027

6079
Logan Wright Foundation, Inc. ⌘
2701 60th Ave., N.W.
Norman 73072 (405) 329-4822

Incorporated about 1975 in OK.
Donor(s): Logan Wright, Brooks Wright.
Foundation type: Independent
Financial data (yr. ended 11/30/88): Assets, $2,326,950 (M); gifts received, $37,262; expenditures, $106,242, including $7,986 for grants (high: $4,206).
Purpose and activities: Giving primarily for higher education; some scholarship aid for needy students.
Types of support: Student aid.
Limitations: Giving primarily in OK.
Application information:
Initial approach: Letter
Deadline(s): None
Write: Logan Wright, Pres.
Officer: Logan Wright, Pres. and Mgr.
Directors: Jaye May, Rosine Miller, Brooks Wright.
Employer Identification Number: 730979754

6080
The R. A. Young Foundation ⌘
6401 North Pennsylvania Ave., Suite 209
Oklahoma City 73116 (405) 840-4444

Incorporated in 1953 in OK.
Donor(s): Raymond A. Young, Verna N. Young.
Foundation type: Independent
Financial data (yr. ended 11/30/89): Assets, $3,717,810 (M); expenditures, $201,944, including $196,640 for 31 grants (high: $50,000; low: $100).
Purpose and activities: Giving for Protestant church support and religious service associations, higher education, and arts and culture.
Limitations: Giving primarily in OK. No grants to individuals.
Application information: Application form not required.
Initial approach: Letter
Deadline(s): None
Write: Raymond A. Young, Pres.
Officers and Trustees:* Raymond A. Young,* Pres.; Carolyn Young Hodnett,* V.P.; Verna N. Young,* Secy.-Treas.
Employer Identification Number: 736092654

6081
The Anne and Henry Zarrow Foundation ⌘
P.O. Box 1530
Tulsa 74101 (918) 587-3391

Established in 1986 in OK.
Donor(s): Henry Zarrow.
Foundation type: Independent
Financial data (yr. ended 12/31/88): Assets, $4,076,946 (M); expenditures, $326,137, including $305,500 for 38 grants (high: $38,500; low: $2,000).
Purpose and activities: Support primarily for education, the handicapped, health, medical research, mental health, and programs and services for the disadvantaged and homeless.
Types of support: Annual campaigns, emergency funds.
Limitations: Giving primarily in Tulsa, OK, area.
Application information: Application form not required.
Initial approach: Letter
Copies of proposal: 1
Deadline(s): None
Board meeting date(s): Fall and spring
Write: Judith Z. Kishner
Officers and Directors: Henry Zarrow, Pres.; Anne Zarrow, V.P.; Robert H. Elliott, Secy.; Robert A. Mulholland, Treas.; Judith Z. Kishner, Stuart A. Zarrow.
Employer Identification Number: 731286874

6082
John Steele Zink Foundation ⌘
1259 East 26th St.
Tulsa 74114 (918) 749-8249

Established in 1972.
Donor(s): John Steele Zink,† Jacqueline A. Zink.
Foundation type: Independent
Financial data (yr. ended 10/31/88): Assets, $34,977,166 (M); expenditures, $1,066,308, including $998,973 for 54 grants (high: $414,000; low: $150).
Purpose and activities: Support for higher education and cultural programs.
Limitations: Giving primarily in Tulsa, OK.
Application information: Application form not required.
Initial approach: Letter or telephone
Deadline(s): None
Write: Jacqueline A. Zink, Trustee
Trustees: Horace Balling, Swannie Zink Tarbel, Jacqueline A. Zink, John Smith Zink.
Employer Identification Number: 237246964

OREGON

6083
The Autzen Foundation
P.O. Box 3709
Portland 97208 (503) 226-6051

Incorporated in 1951 in OR.
Donor(s): Thomas J. Autzen.†
Foundation type: Independent
Financial data (yr. ended 12/31/89): Assets, $8,799,705 (M); expenditures, $429,424, including $378,600 for 76 grants (high: $65,000; low: $50; average: $200-$10,000).
Purpose and activities: Support for higher education, conservation, the arts, including the performing arts, and youth agencies.
Types of support: Continuing support, seed money, building funds, matching funds, special projects.
Limitations: Giving primarily in OR. No grants to individuals, or for scholarships or fellowships; no loans.
Application information: Application form not required.
Initial approach: Letter
Copies of proposal: 1
Deadline(s): Apr. 30, July 31, and Oct. 31
Board meeting date(s): May, Aug., and Dec.
Final notification: 3 to 4 months
Write: Vivienne B. Snow, Admin.
Officers and Directors:* Thomas E. Autzen,* Pres.; Duane Autzen,* V.P.; Henry C. Houser,* Secy.; Vivienne B. Snow,* Admin.
Number of staff: 1 part-time professional.
Employer Identification Number: 936021333

6084
B. J. & S. M. Beattie Charitable Trust ⌑ ☆
c/o U.S. National Bank of Oregon
P.O. Box 3168
Portland 97208-3168

Established in 1982.
Foundation type: Independent
Financial data (yr. ended 6/30/89): Assets, $1,317,383 (M); expenditures, $82,524, including $68,676 for grants.
Purpose and activities: Giving primarily for a children's hospital and medical education.
Limitations: Giving primarily in Portland, OR. No grants to individuals.
Application information: Contributes only to pre-selected organizations. Applications not accepted.
Trustee: U.S. National Bank of Oregon.
Employer Identification Number: 936151155

6085
Bend Foundation
416 N.E. Greenwood
Bend 97701 (503) 382-1662

Trust established in 1947 in IL.
Donor(s): Brooks-Scanlon, Inc., Brooks Resources Corp.
Foundation type: Company-sponsored
Financial data (yr. ended 12/31/89): Assets, $2,134,053 (M); qualifying distributions, $131,241, including $131,241 for 18 grants (high: $25,000; low: $500).
Purpose and activities: Grants for higher education, cultural programs, and a community fund.
Types of support: Annual campaigns, seed money, building funds, equipment, land acquisition, matching funds, student aid.
Limitations: Giving limited to central OR, with preference for the city of Bend and Deschutes County. No grants for operating budgets, deficit financing, endowment funds, special projects, research, publications, or conferences; no loans.
Application information: Application form not required.
Initial approach: Letter or proposal
Copies of proposal: 1
Deadline(s): Submit proposal preferably in Dec.
Board meeting date(s): Feb. or Mar.
Final notification: A few months
Write: Michael P. Hollern, Trustee
Trustees: Conley Brooks, Conley Brooks, Jr., Michael P. Hollern, William L. Smith.
Number of staff: None.
Employer Identification Number: 416019901

6086
Bowerman Foundation ⌑ ☆
825 East Park St.
Eugene 97401

Established in 1982 in OR.
Donor(s): William Jay Bowerman, Jr., William J. Bowerman.
Foundation type: Independent
Financial data (yr. ended 6/30/89): Assets, $1,042,913 (M); gifts received, $160,689; expenditures, $25,520, including $16,300 for 10 grants (high: $5,000; low: $500) and $3,940 for 7 grants to individuals (high: $1,273; low: $167).
Purpose and activities: Support for medical research and health and the arts, including performing arts groups; also awards grants to individuals for scholarships and research.
Types of support: Student aid, grants to individuals.
Limitations: Giving primarily in Eugene, OR.
Application information:
Initial approach: Letter
Deadline(s): None
Write: Donald A. Gallagher, Jr., Secy.
Officers and Trustees: Orlando J. Hollis, Chair.; Donald A. Gallagher, Jr., Secy.; C. Wade Bell, Treas.; William J. Bowerman, William Jay Bowerman, Jr.
Employer Identification Number: 930813012

6087
The Robert Brady Trust ⌑
c/o U.S. National Bank of Oregon
P.O. Box 3168
Portland 97208-3168 (503) 275-4855

Incorporated in 1960 in OR.
Donor(s): Robert Brady.†
Foundation type: Independent
Financial data (yr. ended 06/30/89): Assets, $1,496,213 (M); expenditures, $112,778, including $99,189 for 25 grants (high: $19,244; low: $500).
Purpose and activities: Grants for child welfare, with emphasis on providing books and clothing for needy school children.
Limitations: Giving primarily in OR. No grants to individuals.
Application information:
Initial approach: Letter
Deadline(s): None
Board meeting date(s): Annually in Aug.
Write: Janis Tucker
Trustee: U.S. National Bank of Oregon.
Employer Identification Number: 936019516

6088
Archie C. & Gertrude C. Cammack Trust ⌑ ☆
P.O. Box 3168
Portland 97208
Application address: c/o The Medical Research Foundation of Oregon, P.O. Box 458, Portland, OR 97207; Tel.: (503) 297-1348

Foundation type: Independent
Financial data (yr. ended 6/30/89): Assets, $1,215,345 (M); expenditures, $71,709, including $59,198 for 1 grant.
Purpose and activities: "Funds dedicated to pure medical research as differentiated from clinical or applied medical research."
Limitations: Giving primarily in OR. No grants to individuals.
Application information: Completion of standard medical protocol required.
Copies of proposal: 4
Trustee: U.S. National Bank of Oregon.
Employer Identification Number: 936053590

6089
The Carpenter Foundation
711 East Main St., Suite 18
P.O. Box 816
Medford 97501 (503) 772-5851

Incorporated in 1957 in OR.
Donor(s): Helen Bundy Carpenter,† Alfred S.V. Carpenter,† Harlow Carpenter.
Foundation type: Independent
Financial data (yr. ended 06/30/89): Assets, $9,262,068 (M); expenditures, $483,454, including $382,547 for 60 grants (high: $22,500; low: $500; average: $2,000-$10,000).
Purpose and activities: Grants for higher and secondary education, including scholarship funds through local high schools, human services, art and architecture, and the performing arts.
Types of support: Operating budgets, seed money, equipment, matching funds, technical assistance, scholarship funds, research.
Limitations: Giving primarily in Jackson and Josephine counties, OR. No grants to

individuals, or for deficit financing, endowment funds, or demonstration projects.
Publications: Application guidelines, annual report.
Application information: Application form not required.
Initial approach: Proposal or letter
Copies of proposal: 1
Deadline(s): Submit proposal 4 weeks before board meeting
Board meeting date(s): Usually in Mar., June, Sept., and Dec.
Final notification: 1 to 2 weeks
Write: Dunbar Carpenter, Treas.
Officers and Trustees:* Jane H. Carpenter,* Pres.; Dunbar Carpenter,* Treas.; Karen C. Allan, Emily C. Mostue, Mrs. Robert Ogle.
Associate Trustees: Jerilyn Holt, Sheila Kimball, Bill Moffat, William Thorndike, Jr.
Number of staff: 1 part-time support.
Employer Identification Number: 930491360

6090
Chiles Foundation ▼ ⌑
111 S.W. Fifth Ave., Suite 4050
Portland 97204-3643 (503) 222-2143

Incorporated in 1949 in OR.
Donor(s): Eva Chiles Meyer,† Earle A. Chiles,† Virginia H. Chiles.
Foundation type: Independent
Financial data (yr. ended 12/31/88): Assets, $24,301,647 (M); expenditures, $3,847,328, including $3,265,684 for 83 grants (high: $550,000; low: $500; average: $1,000-$50,000).
Purpose and activities: Grants traditionally to institutions of higher education for business schools and medical research.
Types of support: Building funds, equipment.
Limitations: Giving primarily in OR, with emphasis on Portland, and the Pacific Northwest. No grants to individuals, or for deficit financing, mortgage retirement, projects involving litigation, or projects and conferences already completed; no loans.
Application information:
Initial approach: Telephone
Deadline(s): Submit proposal between Jan. 1 and Feb. 15
Board meeting date(s): As required
Final notification: By Dec. 31
Officer and Trustees:* Earle M. Chiles,* Pres.; Virginia H. Chiles, Frank E. Nash, Melvin E. Smith.
Number of staff: 4 full-time professional.
Employer Identification Number: 936031125

6091
Clark Foundation
255 S.W. Harrison St., GA 2
Portland 97201 (503) 223-5290

Established in 1968 in OR.
Donor(s): Maurie D. Clark.
Foundation type: Independent
Financial data (yr. ended 12/31/87): Assets, $66,691 (M); gifts received, $551,750; expenditures, $533,935, including $492,982 for grants.
Purpose and activities: Emphasis on building funds for higher education and for churches and religious associations; grants also for cultural programs, youth agencies, secondary education, the environment, and medical care.
Types of support: Building funds.
Limitations: Giving primarily in the Portland, OR, area. No grants to individuals, or for endowment funds, research, or matching gifts; no loans.
Application information:
Initial approach: Letter
Copies of proposal: 1
Deadline(s): None
Board meeting date(s): Bimonthly
Write: Jean Ameele
Officers: Maurie D. Clark, Pres. and Treas.; David A. Kekel, V.P.; Patrick E. Becker, Secy.
Number of staff: 1 part-time professional.
Employer Identification Number: 237423789

6092
Louis G. & Elizabeth L. Clarke Endowment Fund ⌑ ☆
c/o Scottish Rite Temple
709 S.W. Fifteenth Ave.
Portland 97205

Established in 1960 in OR.
Foundation type: Independent
Financial data (yr. ended 6/30/89): Assets, $1,104,359 (M); expenditures, $62,383, including $34,381 for grants to individuals.
Purpose and activities: Giving limited "to provide financial assistance to needy Masons or their immediate family members requiring hospitalization."
Types of support: Grants to individuals.
Limitations: Giving limited to the Portland, OR, metropolitan area, including Multnomah, Clackamas, and Washington counties.
Application information:
Write: Walter L. Peters, Exec. Secy., Scottish Rite Temple
Trustee: U.S. National Bank of Oregon.
Employer Identification Number: 936020655

6093
The Elizabeth Church Clarke Testamentary Trust/Fund Foundation ⌑
c/o Scottish Rite Temple
709 S.W. Fifteenth Ave.
Portland 97205

Established in 1961 in OR; incorporated in 1964.
Donor(s): Elizabeth Church Clark.†
Foundation type: Independent
Financial data (yr. ended 12/31/87): Assets, $1,229,861 (M); expenditures, $76,738, including $52,274 for grants.
Purpose and activities: Supports medical treatments for OR residents only.
Limitations: Giving limited to OR.
Application information:
Initial approach: Letter
Deadline(s): None
Write: Walter L. Peters, Exec. Secy., Scottish Rite Temple
Trustee: U.S. National Bank of Oregon.
Employer Identification Number: 936024205

6094
The Clemens Foundation ⌑
P.O. Box 427
Philomath 97370 (503) 929-3541

Incorporated in 1959 in OR.
Donor(s): Rex Clemens, Ethel M. Clemens, Rex Veneer Co.
Foundation type: Independent
Financial data (yr. ended 12/31/88): Assets, $17,710,535 (M); gifts received, $9,512,440; expenditures, $482,106, including $1,000 for 1 grant and $459,577 for 385 grants to individuals (high: $2,436; low: $30).
Purpose and activities: Tuition grants for local high school graduates to attend college or accredited vocational school on a full-time basis.
Types of support: Student aid.
Limitations: Giving limited to Philomath, Eddyville, Crane, and Alsea, OR.
Application information: Application form required.
Initial approach: Letter or telephone
Deadline(s): Application should be submitted before the school term begins; no set deadline
Write: Leon Stratton
Officers and Trustees: Ethel M. Clemens, Pres. and Treas.; Bernard C. Davis, Secy.; Elwood Berklund, Ron Edwards, Robert Hall, Wayne L. Howard, Frank Kochis, David Lowther, Fred Lowther, Steven Lowther, Thad Springer.
Employer Identification Number: 936023941

6095
The Collins Foundation ▼
1618 S.W. First Ave., Suite 305
Portland 97201 (503) 227-7171

Incorporated in 1947 in OR.
Donor(s): Members of the Collins family.
Foundation type: Independent
Financial data (yr. ended 12/31/89): Assets, $94,363,918 (M); expenditures, $2,930,415, including $2,571,871 for 159 grants (high: $500,000; low: $700; average: $3,000-$25,000).
Purpose and activities: Emphasis on higher education, youth, hospices, and health agencies, social welfare, and the arts and cultural programs.
Types of support: Building funds, equipment, research, matching funds, program-related investments, special projects.
Limitations: Giving limited to OR, with emphasis on Portland. No support for legislative lobbying or delayed projects. No grants to individuals, or for deficit financing, endowment funds, general purposes, scholarships, fellowships, operating budgets, or annual campaigns.
Publications: Annual report (including application guidelines), informational brochure.
Application information: Application form not required.
Initial approach: Letter
Copies of proposal: 1
Deadline(s): None
Board meeting date(s): Approximately 6 times a year
Final notification: 4 to 8 weeks
Write: William C. Pine, Exec. V.P.

Officers: Maribeth W. Collins,* Pres.; William C. Pine, Exec. V.P.; Grace Collins Goudy,* V.P.; Thomas B. Stoel, Secy.; Timothy R. Bishop, Treas.
Trustees:* Ralph Bolliger.
Number of staff: 1 part-time professional; 1 part-time support.
Employer Identification Number: 936021893

6096
Collins Medical Trust
1618 S.W. First Ave., Suite 300
Portland 97201 (503) 227-1219

Established in 1956 in OR.
Foundation type: Independent
Financial data (yr. ended 09/30/89): Assets, $3,393,075 (M); expenditures, $159,666, including $147,385 for 12 grants (high: $25,000; low: $1,000).
Purpose and activities: Grants for medical research and health services.
Types of support: Equipment, research, scholarship funds.
Limitations: Giving primarily in OR.
Application information:
Initial approach: Letter
Deadline(s): None
Write: Joseph A. Connolly, Administrator
Trustees: Maribeth W. Collins, Truman W. Collins, Jr., Joseph F. Paquet, M.D.
Employer Identification Number: 936021895

6097
Collins-McDonald Trust Fund ⌑
620 North First St.
Lakeview 97630 (503) 947-2196

Incorporated in 1940 in OR.
Foundation type: Independent
Financial data (yr. ended 12/31/88): Assets, $2,680,703 (M); expenditures, $170,161, including $99,950 for 10 grants (high: $60,000; low: $250) and $66,622 for 40 grants to individuals (high: $3,430; low: $700).
Purpose and activities: Awards scholarships for higher education to graduates of local high schools only; grants also for social services and a hospital.
Types of support: Equipment, student aid, renovation projects.
Limitations: Giving limited to Lake County, OR.
Application information: Completion of application form required for scholarships.
Initial approach: Proposal
Deadline(s): May 1 for scholarships
Write: James C. Lynch, Trustee
Trustees: Robert Evans, James C. Lynch, Eugene E. Sharp.
Employer Identification Number: 936021894

6098
Bernard Daly Educational Fund ⌑
P.O. Box 309
Lakeview 97630 (503) 947-2196
Application address: P.O. Box 351, Lakeview, OR 97630

Established in 1922 in OR.
Donor(s): Bernard Daly.†
Foundation type: Independent
Financial data (yr. ended 5/31/89): Assets, $1,832,860 (M); gifts received, $2,200; expenditures, $126,637, including $110,950 for 54 grants to individuals (high: $2,100; low: $700).
Purpose and activities: Financial aid for study at OR technical schools and colleges.
Types of support: Student aid.
Limitations: Giving limited to Lake County, OR, residents.
Publications: Application guidelines.
Application information: Application form required.
Initial approach: Telephone
Copies of proposal: 2
Deadline(s): May 1
Board meeting date(s): June
Write: James C. Lynch, Secy.-Treas.
Officers and Trustees: Dorothy Howard, Chair.; Mildred Harvey, Vice-Chair.; James C. Lynch, Secy.-Treas.; Carter E. Fetsch, Jack Pendleton.
Employer Identification Number: 936025466

6099
Leslie G. Ehmann Trust ⌑
c/o U.S. National Bank of Oregon, Trust Group
P.O. Box 3168
Portland 97208

Established in 1985 in OR.
Donor(s): Leslie G. Ehmann.†
Foundation type: Independent
Financial data (yr. ended 6/30/87): Assets, $1,436,933 (M); expenditures, $138,323, including $109,995 for 6 grants (high: $30,030; low: $12,455; average: $14,000-$18,000).
Purpose and activities: Grants primarily for animal welfare agencies.
Types of support: Special projects.
Application information: Application form required.
Initial approach: Letter
Write: Gordon Childs, Trustee
Trustees: Gordon Childs, U.S. National Bank of Oregon.
Employer Identification Number: 936176402

6100
Henry Failing Fund ⌑
c/o First Interstate Bank of Oregon, N.A.
P.O. Box 2971
Portland 97208

Established in 1947 in OR.
Foundation type: Independent
Financial data (yr. ended 12/31/88): Assets, $2,193,872 (M); gifts received, $2,922; expenditures, $23,661.
Purpose and activities: Support primarily for education and hospitals; giving also for an art association.
Limitations: Giving primarily in Portland, OR. No grants to individuals.
Application information: Contributes only to pre-selected organizations. Applications not accepted.
Trustee: First Interstate Bank of Oregon, N.A.
Employer Identification Number: 936021362

6101
First Interstate Bank of Oregon, N.A. Charitable Foundation ▼ ⌑
P.O. Box 3131
Portland 97208
Application address: 1300 S.W. Fifth Ave., Portland, OR 97201

Incorporated in 1983 in OR.
Donor(s): First Interstate Bank of Oregon, N.A.
Foundation type: Company-sponsored
Financial data (yr. ended 12/31/88): Assets, $1,880,154 (M); gifts received, $3,616,637; expenditures, $999,169, including $998,253 for 231 grants (high: $310,500; low: $20; average: $100-$5,000).
Purpose and activities: Support for community funds, education, with emphasis on higher education, cultural programs, and child and animal welfare.
Limitations: Giving limited to OR. No support for political or religious organizations. No grants to individuals, or for seminars or conferences.
Application information: Submit information on specific project budget material.
Initial approach: Letter or proposal
Deadline(s): None
Board meeting date(s): As necessary
Final notification: 2 to 4 months
Write: Harleen Katke, Trustee
Trustees: Robert Ames, David S. Belles, Floyd Bennett, Robert J. Derby, Harleen Katke, Robert G. Murray.
Agent: First Interstate Bank of Oregon, N.A.
Number of staff: None.
Employer Identification Number: 930836170

6102
Fohs Foundation ⌑
P.O. Box 1001
Roseburg 97470 (503) 673-0141

Trust established in 1937 in NY.
Donor(s): F. Julius Fohs,† Cora B. Fohs.†
Foundation type: Independent
Financial data (yr. ended 12/31/88): Assets, $764,207 (M); expenditures, $522,134, including $455,200 for 16 grants (high: $155,000; low: $700).
Purpose and activities: To promote science, art, education, health, healthful recreation and good citizenship of children and adults; research in general, charitable, humanitarian, sociological and educational problems; support for Ella Fohs children's and senior citizens' camps in CT; grants for Jewish-sponsored educational institutions, particularly in Israel.
Types of support: Scholarship funds, endowment funds.
Application information: Application form not required.
Initial approach: Letter
Copies of proposal: 1
Deadline(s): None
Board meeting date(s): Apr. or May
Write: Charlotte Richards, Secy.-Treas.
Officers: Frances F. Sohn, Chair.; Fred Sohn, Vice-Chair.; Charlotte Richards, Secy.-Treas.
Number of staff: 1 part-time support.
Employer Identification Number: 746003165

6103
Kenneth W. Ford Foundation ⌑
c/o Roseburg Forest Products Co.
P.O. Box 1088
Roseburg 97470

Incorporated in 1957 in OR.
Donor(s): Kenneth W. Ford, Hallie E. Ford, Roseburg Forest Products Co.
Foundation type: Independent
Financial data (yr. ended 4/30/89): Assets, $3,377,062 (M); gifts received, $151,000; expenditures, $148,396, including $147,500 for 32 grants (high: $25,500; low: $500).
Purpose and activities: Emphasis on community funds, youth agencies, and higher education.
Limitations: Giving primarily in OR.
Officers and Directors: Kenneth W. Ford, Pres.; Hallie E. Ford, V.P.; Frank H. Spears, Secy.
Employer Identification Number: 936026156

6104
Foreign Mission Foundation ⌑ ☆
4550 S.W. Lombard
Beaverton 97005

Foundation type: Independent
Financial data (yr. ended 2/28/89): Assets, $2,977,638 (M); expenditures, $152,721, including $22,916 for 10 grants (high: $8,000; low: $85).
Purpose and activities: Support for churches, ministries, missions and Christian education.
Officers and Directors: Eugene Davis, Pres.; Vivian Davis, Secy.; George Hughes.
Employer Identification Number: 930763215

6105
A. J. Frank Family Foundation ⌑
P.O. Drawer 79
Mill City 97360 (503) 897-2371

Incorporated in 1959 in OR.
Donor(s): A.J. Frank, L.D. Frank, Frank Lumber Co., Inc., Frank Timber Products, Inc., and members of the Frank family.
Foundation type: Independent
Financial data (yr. ended 9/30/88): Assets, $3,244,878 (M); gifts received, $856,400; expenditures, $103,287, including $98,900 for 27 grants (high: $10,000; low: $500).
Purpose and activities: Giving largely for Roman Catholic church support and welfare funds, and for secondary education.
Limitations: Giving primarily in OR. No grants to individuals.
Application information: Application form not required.
Initial approach: Letter
Deadline(s): Aug. 15 and Dec. 15
Final notification: Prior to Sept. 15 or Jan. 15
Write: Douglas Highberger
Officers: A.J. Frank, Pres.; J.T. Frank, V.P.; D.D. Frank, Secy.; L.D. Frank, Treas.
Employer Identification Number: 930523395

6106
The Friendly-Rosenthal Foundation, Inc.
1295 Gans St.
P.O. Box 562
Lake Oswego 97034 (503) 636-3110

Incorporated in 1946 in OR.
Donor(s): Jacob Rosenthal,† Seymour C. Friendly,† Julius C. Friendly.†
Foundation type: Independent
Financial data (yr. ended 12/31/88): Assets, $1,775,648 (M); expenditures, $157,901, including $125,000 for 30 grants (high: $30,000; low: $500; average: $500-$30,000).
Purpose and activities: Grants only to existing local institutions concerned with social welfare programs, including Jewish welfare funds, and assistance to the aged, women, minorities, youth, the homeless, the handicapped, and new immigrants.
Types of support: Continuing support, seed money, emergency funds.
Limitations: Giving primarily in Multnomah, Clackamas and Washington counties, OR, and organizations in Salem, OR, that serve these areas. No grants to individuals, or for building, capital, or endowment funds, scholarships, fellowships, or matching gifts; no loans.
Publications: 990-PF, application guidelines.
Application information: Application form not required.
Initial approach: Letter, proposal, or telephone
Copies of proposal: 1
Deadline(s): Submit proposal preferably from Sept. through Nov.; deadline Nov. 15
Board meeting date(s): Jan.
Write: Mrs. Evelyn J. Harriman, Secy. and Trustee
Officers and Trustees:* Milton Carl,* Pres. and Chair.; Stuart Durkheimer,* V.P.; Evelyn J. Harriman,* Secy.; Paul T. Akre,* Treas.; Henry Blauer, Melvyn C. Friendly, James A. Meyer, Grant Stebner, Elaine Weil, Merritt S. Yoelin, U.S. National Bank of Oregon.
Number of staff: 1 part-time professional.
Employer Identification Number: 930395711

6107
Helen Paulson Gunderson Trust ⌑
c/o The Oregon Bank
P.O. Box 2808
Portland 97208

Established about 1979 in OR.
Donor(s): Helen Gunderson.†
Foundation type: Independent
Financial data (yr. ended 11/30/87): Assets, $1,551,684 (M); expenditures, $119,213, including $101,849 for 4 grants.
Purpose and activities: Grants primarily for health and education services for the handicapped.
Limitations: Giving primarily in Portland, OR.
Trustee: The Oregon Bank.
Employer Identification Number: 936138283

6108
Lorene Sails Higgins Charitable Trust ⌑
c/o The Bank of California, N.A.
P.O. Box 3121
Portland 97208 (503) 225-2924

Trust established in 1968 in OR.
Donor(s): Lorene Sails Higgins.
Foundation type: Independent
Financial data (yr. ended 12/31/88): Assets, $3,833,140 (M); expenditures, $284,630, including $210,500 for 20 grants (high: $45,000; low: $1,000).
Purpose and activities: Emphasis on cultural programs, the performing arts, higher education, and religious institutions with emphasis on Christian Science projects.
Types of support: Building funds, equipment, matching funds.
Limitations: Giving primarily in the Portland, OR, metropolitan area. No grants to individuals, or for endowment funds, general support, scholarships, or fellowships; no loans.
Publications: Program policy statement, application guidelines.
Application information: Contributes only to pre-selected organizations. Applications not accepted.
Write: Marc Grignon, Trust Officer, The Bank of California, N.A.
Trustees: The Bank of California, N.A., Wood, Tatum, Mosser, Brooke, & Holder.
Number of staff: None.
Employer Identification Number: 936050051

6109
C. Giles Hunt Charitable Trust
c/o First Interstate Bank of Oregon, N.A.
P.O. Box 10566
Eugene 97440

Trust established in 1974 in OR.
Donor(s): C. Giles Hunt.†
Foundation type: Independent
Financial data (yr. ended 12/31/88): Assets, $3,725,657 (M); gifts received, $4,803; expenditures, $246,511, including $209,702 for 48 grants (high: $17,000; low: $500).
Purpose and activities: Giving for social services, youth agencies, and secondary education.
Types of support: Building funds, capital campaigns, equipment, general purposes, renovation projects.
Limitations: Giving primarily in Douglas County, OR. No grants to individuals.
Publications: Application guidelines.
Application information: Application form required.
Initial approach: Letter or proposal
Copies of proposal: 7
Deadline(s): Submit proposal in Jan. or Feb.; deadline Feb. 28
Board meeting date(s): Mar. or Apr.
Write: C.Q. Dukehart, Trust Officer, First Interstate Bank of Oregon, N.A.
Trustee: First Interstate Bank of Oregon, N.A.
Employer Identification Number: 237428278

6110
The Jackson Foundation ⌑
c/o U.S. National Bank of Oregon
P.O. Box 3168
Portland 97208 (503) 275-5718

Trust established in 1960 in OR; Philip Ludwell Jackson Charitable and Residual Trusts were merged into The Jackson Foundation in 1981.
Donor(s): Maria C. Jackson.†
Foundation type: Independent

Financial data (yr. ended 6/30/87): Assets, $8,836,487 (M); expenditures, $602,000, including $508,998 for 123 grants (high: $66,570; low: $500; average: $1,000-$5,000).
Purpose and activities: Support largely to aid needy persons through social service agencies; grants for higher and secondary education, cultural programs, hospitals, community and civic organizations, and youth agencies.
Types of support: Seed money, emergency funds, building funds, equipment, special projects, technical assistance, renovation projects, consulting services.
Limitations: Giving limited to OR. No support for churches or temples. No grants to individuals, or for endowment funds, matching gifts, scholarships, fellowships, or building or equipment funds for religious organizations; no loans to individuals.
Application information: Application form required.
Initial approach: Request for application form
Copies of proposal: 4
Deadline(s): Aug. 25, Nov. 25, and Mar. 25
Board meeting date(s): Sept., Dec., Apr., and as required
Final notification: 3 or 4 weeks
Write: Frank E. Staich, Asst. V.P., U.S. National Bank of Oregon
Trustees: Milo Ormseth, Gordon M. Tretheway, U.S. National Bank of Oregon.
Number of staff: 3
Employer Identification Number: 936020752

6111
The Jeld-Wen Foundation ¤
(Formerly Jeld-Wen, Wenco Foundation)
3303 Lakeport Blvd.
P.O. Box 1329
Klamath Falls 97601 (503) 882-3451

Established in 1969.
Donor(s): Jeld-Wen Fiber Products, Inc. of Iowa, Jeld-Wen Co. of Arizona, Wenco, Inc. of North Carolina, Wenco, Inc. of Ohio, and other Jeld-Wen, Wenco companies.
Foundation type: Company-sponsored
Financial data (yr. ended 12/31/88): Assets, $10,795,216 (M); gifts received, $2,726,929; expenditures, $1,022,012, including $881,102 for 92 grants (high: $100,000; low: $700).
Purpose and activities: The foundation prioritizes requests on the basis of demonstrated impact toward making our communities better places to live. An assessment is also made as to how many company employees will use the services. Projects that improve the existing service or provide new ones, usually involving capital or seed money, and annual support for existing organizations through the United Way are major categories for giving.
Types of support: General purposes, seed money, building funds, equipment, land acquisition, special projects, scholarship funds, matching funds.
Limitations: Giving primarily in areas of company operations; in AZ, FL, IA, KY, NC, OH, OR, SD, and WA projects should serve communities in which company plants exist; projects in adjacent communities may be accepted if sufficient members of employees reside in the area and would benefit. No support for activities that are specifically religious or that duplicate services provided by other government or private agencies. No grants to individuals; no loans.
Publications: Program policy statement, application guidelines.
Application information: Application form required.
Initial approach: Proposal or letter; prefer not to receive telephone calls
Copies of proposal: 1
Deadline(s): Submit proposal preferably in Mar.; no set deadline
Board meeting date(s): Mar., June, Sept., and Dec.
Final notification: 2 weeks after meetings
Write: R.C. Wendt, Secy.
Officer and Trustees: R.C. Wendt, Secy.; W.B. Early, T.H. Schnormeier, Richard L. Wendt, L.V. Wetter.
Number of staff: None.
Employer Identification Number: 936054272

6112
Jenkins Student Loan Fund ¤
c/o U.S. National Bank of Oregon, Trust Group
321 S.W. Sixth Ave., P.O. Box 3168
Portland 97208 (503) 275-4456

Established in 1960 in OR.
Donor(s): Hopkin Jenkins.†
Foundation type: Independent
Financial data (yr. ended 6/30/88): Assets, $1,314,177 (M); expenditures, $158,589, including $106,739 for 53 loans to individuals.
Purpose and activities: Loans to students for college education costs.
Types of support: Student loans.
Limitations: Giving limited to residents of OR.
Publications: Program policy statement, application guidelines.
Application information: Application form required.
Initial approach: Letter
Copies of proposal: 1
Deadline(s): Submit applications from June 1 to June 15 for the ensuing academic year
Board meeting date(s): Usually in Sept., Dec., Mar., and June
Final notification: By July 15
Write: Roberta G. Kinohi
Trustee: U.S. National Bank of Oregon.
Number of staff: 2
Employer Identification Number: 936020672

6113
The Samuel S. Johnson Foundation
(Formerly The S.S. Johnson Foundation)
P.O. Box 356
Redmond 97756 (503) 548-8104

Incorporated in 1948 in CA.
Donor(s): Samuel S. Johnson,† Elizabeth Hill Johnson.
Foundation type: Independent
Financial data (yr. ended 05/31/89): Assets, $3,431,347 (M); expenditures, $180,273, including $160,879 for 158 grants (high: $10,000; low: $100; average: $500-$1,000), $6,185 for 13 grants to individuals (high: $500; low: $185; average: $500-$1,000) and $4,000 for 5 loans to individuals.
Purpose and activities: Giving for higher and other education, including research associations and libraries; social services, including community funds, family services, and programs for the aged, women, and youth and child development; science and technology; health and hospitals, including nursing, cancer and other medical research, and the medical sciences; the environment and animal welfare; the fine and performing arts and other cutural programs; and religious organizations. Support primarily for limited emergency operational funds and limited non-recurring emergency grants or loans to students through educational institutions.
Types of support: Operating budgets, seed money, emergency funds, matching funds, scholarship funds, student aid, conferences and seminars, student loans, equipment, special projects, continuing support, lectureships, professorships, publications, research.
Limitations: Giving primarily in the Pacific Northwest, primarily OR and northern CA. No support for foreign organizations. No grants for annual campaigns, deficit financing, construction, sole underwriting of major proposals or projects, or endowments.
Publications: 990-PF, program policy statement, application guidelines.
Application information: Application form required for scholarships and loans.
Initial approach: Letter
Copies of proposal: 1
Deadline(s): June 1 for July meeting and Nov. 15 for Jan. meeting
Board meeting date(s): July and Jan.
Final notification: 2 to 3 weeks after board meeting
Write: Elizabeth Hill Johnson, Pres.
Officers: Elizabeth Hill Johnson,* Pres.; Shirley K. Comini, Secy.-Treas.
Directors:* Robert W. Hill, Elizabeth K. Johnson, Patricia Johnson Nelson, Ralf H. Stinson, M.D.
Number of staff: 1 part-time support.
Employer Identification Number: 946062478

6114
Louisiana-Pacific Foundation
111 S.W. Fifth Ave.
Portland 97204 (503) 221-0800

Established in 1973 in OR.
Donor(s): Louisiana-Pacific Corp.
Foundation type: Company-sponsored
Financial data (yr. ended 12/31/89): Assets, $19,160 (L); gifts received, $775,000; expenditures, $780,169, including $780,169 for 228 grants (high: $100,000; low: $100; average: $500-$5,000).
Purpose and activities: Giving for higher education, including employee-related scholarships, and community funds; some support for health, youth agencies, and the arts.
Types of support: Annual campaigns, capital campaigns, continuing support, general purposes, employee-related scholarships, emergency funds.
Limitations: Giving primarily in areas of plant locations.
Application information: Application form required for scholarships.
Initial approach: Letter

Copies of proposal: 1
Board meeting date(s): Quarterly
Write: Robert E. Erickson, Trustee
Officers and Trustees:* Harry A. Merlo,* Chair. and Pres.; Donald R. Holman, Secy.; John C. Hart, Treas.; Robert E. Erickson, Gary R. Maffei.
Number of staff: None.
Employer Identification Number: 237268660

6115
Maybelle Clark Macdonald Fund ⌑
405 N.W. 18th Ave.
Portland 97209
Application address: 5270-7 S.W. Landing Sq. Dr., Portland, OR 97201

Established about 1970.
Donor(s): Maybelle Clark Macdonald.
Foundation type: Independent
Financial data (yr. ended 6/30/88): Assets, $287,550 (M); gifts received, $102,212; expenditures, $108,671, including $105,481 for 43 grants (high: $20,000; low: $25).
Purpose and activities: Giving largely for local cultural programs and Roman Catholic church support.
Limitations: Giving primarily in OR.
Application information:
Initial approach: Letter
Deadline(s): None
Write: Maybelle Clark Macdonald, Pres.
Officers: Maybelle Clark Macdonald, Pres.; Fred C. Macdonald, Secy.; Daniel A. Callahan, Treas.
Employer Identification Number: 237108002

6116
Sophia Byers McComas Foundation ⌑ ☆
c/o U.S. National Bank of Oregon
P.O. Box 3168
Portland 97208 (503) 275-6564

Established in 1953.
Foundation type: Independent
Financial data (yr. ended 6/30/89): Assets, $1,303,511 (M); gifts received, $15,869; expenditures, $81,000, including $72,223 for grants to individuals.
Purpose and activities: "Provides limited financial assistance to aged and indigent persons monthly who are residents of the state of Oregon and who are not on welfare assistance."
Types of support: Grants to individuals.
Limitations: Giving limited to OR.
Application information: Applicants recommended by church groups, social service agencies, or similar groups.
Initial approach: Telephone
Write: U.S. National Bank of Oregon, Trustee
Trustee: U.S. National Bank of Oregon.
Employer Identification Number: 936019602

6117
Mentor Graphics Foundation ⌑
8500 S.W. Creekside Place
Beaverton 97005-7191 (503) 626-7000

Established in 1985 in OR.
Donor(s): Mentor Graphics.
Foundation type: Company-sponsored
Financial data (yr. ended 12/31/88): Assets, $140,606 (M); gifts received, $23,250; expenditures, $166,819, including $166,003 for 81 grants (high: $18,663; low: $20).
Purpose and activities: Support for community funds, the fine and performing arts, youth, social services, and higher education.
Limitations: Giving primarily in areas where the company has major operations. No grants to individuals.
Application information:
Initial approach: Letter
Deadline(s): 3 weeks prior to meeting
Board meeting date(s): Bimonthly
Write: Marti Brown, Admin.
Officers and Directors: Frank S. Delia, V.P. and Secy.; John C. Carveth, V.P. and Treas.; Berkley T. Merchant, V.P.; Richard J. Anderson, Frank J. Costa, Brian Kiernan.
Employer Identification Number: 930870309

6118
Meyer Memorial Trust ▼
(Formerly Fred Meyer Charitable Trust)
1515 S.W. Fifth Ave., Suite 500
Portland 97201 (503) 228-5512

Trust established by will in 1978; obtained IRS status in OR in 1982.
Donor(s): Fred G. Meyer.†
Foundation type: Independent
Financial data (yr. ended 03/31/90): Assets, $276,842,089 (M); expenditures, $12,976,696, including $11,953,746 for 209 grants (high: $2,000,000; low: $500; average: $20,000-$200,000).
Purpose and activities: The trust provides two types of funding: 1) general purpose grants, primarily in OR for education, the arts and humanities, health, and social welfare; and 2) special program grants, primarily in AK, ID, MT, OR, and WA, in the areas of Aging and Independence, and Support for Children at Risk. Under general purpose, the trust operates the Small Grants Program, which provides awards of $500 to $8,000 for small projects in OR.
Types of support: Seed money, building funds, equipment, matching funds, technical assistance, program-related investments, special projects, research, general purposes, operating budgets, renovation projects.
Limitations: Giving primarily in OR, except for special programs which also include WA, ID, MT, and AK. No support for sectarian or religious organizations for religious purposes. No grants to individuals, or for operating budgets, endowment funds, annual campaigns, deficit financing, scholarships or fellowships, or indirect or overhead costs, except as specifically and essentially related to the grant project; occasional program-related loans only.
Publications: Annual report, informational brochure (including application guidelines), program policy statement.
Application information: Special guidelines for aging program, Children at Risk program, and Small Grants Program. Application form required.
Initial approach: Proposal
Copies of proposal: 1
Deadline(s): 1990: Apr. 1 and Oct. 1 for Children at Risk program; Jan. 15, Apr. 15, July 15, and Oct. 15 for Small Grants Program; no set deadline for other grants. No applications in 1990 for Aging & Independence
Board meeting date(s): Monthly
Final notification: 3 to 5 months for proposals that pass first screening; 1 to 2 months for those that don't
Write: Charles S. Rooks, Exec. Dir.
Officers: Charles S. Rooks, Secy. and Exec. Dir.; Wayne G. Pierson, Treas.
Trustees: Travis Cross, Pauline Lawrence, Warne Nunn, G. Gerald Pratt, Oran B. Robertson.
Number of staff: 5 full-time professional; 5 full-time support.
Employer Identification Number: 930806316

6119
OCRI Foundation
P.O. Box 1682
Lake Oswego 97035 (503) 635-8010

Established in 1971 in OR.
Donor(s): Members of the Lamb family.
Foundation type: Independent
Financial data (yr. ended 12/31/88): Assets, $3,663,455 (M); expenditures, $230,112, including $199,162 for 55 grants (high: $35,000; low: $75).
Purpose and activities: Supports Christian religious organizations, higher education, youth programs, environmental organizations, the humanities, and programs for the homeless.
Types of support: Emergency funds, general purposes, matching funds, seed money, special projects.
Limitations: Giving limited to OR. No grants to individuals, or for building or endowment funds.
Publications: Annual report.
Application information: Application form not required.
Initial approach: Letter
Copies of proposal: 1
Deadline(s): None
Board meeting date(s): Mar., July, Sept., and Dec.
Write: Anita Lamb Bailey, Chair.
Officers and Directors:* Anita Lamb Bailey,* Chair.; Dorothy Lamb,* Vice-Chair.; Helen Lamb,* Secy.; F. Gilbert Lamb,* Treas.; Edna Lamb, Frank G. Lamb, Maryann Lamb, Paula L. Lamb, Peter Lamb, Walter Minnick.
Number of staff: 1 part-time support.
Employer Identification Number: 237120564

6120
The Oregon Community Foundation ▼
1110 Yeon Bldg.
522 S.W. Fifth Ave.
Portland 97204 (503) 227-6846

Established in 1973 in OR.
Foundation type: Community
Financial data (yr. ended 06/30/89): Assets, $51,170,977 (M); gifts received, $9,046,980; expenditures, $5,454,739, including $4,459,661 for grants (average: $3,500-$10,000).
Purpose and activities: To "meet educational, cultural, medical, social and civic needs in all

areas and at all levels of society throughout the state."
Types of support: Operating budgets, seed money, building funds, equipment, land acquisition, technical assistance, scholarship funds, special projects, matching funds, renovation projects.
Limitations: Giving limited to OR. No support for films, or for religious organizations for religious purposes. No grants to individuals, or for emergency funding, endowments, annual campaigns, deficit financing, research, publications, or conferences, unless so designated by a donor; no loans.
Publications: Annual report, newsletter, program policy statement, application guidelines.
Application information: Application form required.
Initial approach: 1-page letter
Copies of proposal: 12
Deadline(s): Submit application preferably in Mar. or Aug.; deadlines Apr. 1 and Sept. 1
Board meeting date(s): Jan., June, Sept., and Nov.
Final notification: 3 months
Write: Gregory A. Chaille, Exec. Dir.
Officers: John D. Gray,* Pres.; Robert W. Chandler,* V.P.; Richard F. Hensley,* V.P.; Sally McCracken,* V.P.; Gwyneth Gamble Booth,* Secy.; William Swindells, Jr., Treas.; Gregory A. Chaille, Exec. Dir.
Directors:* Edwin M. Baker, Donald C. Frisbee, Alice Koehler, Walter C. Reynolds, M.D., David Rhoten, Jess Rogerson.
Participating Banks: The Bank of California, N.A., First Interstate Bank of Oregon, N.A., The Oregon Bank, U.S. National Bank of Oregon.
Number of staff: 3 full-time professional; 1 part-time professional; 2 full-time support; 1 part-time support.
Employer Identification Number: 237315673

6121
Portland Women's Union ⌑
P.O. Box 1032
Portland 97202 (503) 239-5457

Established in 1983 in OR.
Foundation type: Independent
Financial data (yr. ended 4/30/88): Assets, $1,899,799 (M); expenditures, $139,319, including $97,200 for 30 grants (high: $9,000; low: $1,000).
Purpose and activities: Giving primarily for low-cost residences for women with low income.
Limitations: Giving primarily in OR.
Application information:
Initial approach: Proposal
Deadline(s): Feb. 1
Write: Selections Chair.
Officers: Pat Gambee, Pres.; Sally Gram, 1st V.P.; Dorothy Boothe, 2nd V.P.; Joan Metz, Corres. Secy.; Nancy Tang, Treas.
Employer Identification Number: 930386905

6122
The Salem Foundation
c/o Pioneer Trust Bank, N.A.
109 Commercial St., N.E.
Salem 97301 (503) 363-3136
Application address: P.O. Box 2305, Salem, OR 97308

Established in 1930 in OR.
Foundation type: Community
Financial data (yr. ended 12/31/88): Assets, $1,250,489 (M); gifts received, $438,574; expenditures, $95,115, including $67,547 for grants (high: $34,093; low: $300; average: $500-$1,000) and $14,060 for 21 grants to individuals (high: $5,500; low: $30).
Purpose and activities: Giving for charitable purposes to benefit the citizens of Salem, OR.
Types of support: Operating budgets, continuing support, seed money, emergency funds, equipment, special projects, conferences and seminars, general purposes, consulting services, publications, technical assistance, matching funds.
Limitations: Giving limited to the Salem, OR, area. No grants for annual campaigns, deficit financing, endowments, or capital campaigns.
Publications: 990-PF.
Application information: Application form not required.
Copies of proposal: 1
Deadline(s): Dec. 31
Board meeting date(s): Distribution Committee meets in Jan.
Write: Michael S. Compton, Trust Officer, Pioneer Trust Bank
Trustee: Pioneer Trust Bank, N.A.
Number of staff: None.
Employer Identification Number: 936018523

6123
Steinbach Foundation ☆
c/o U.S. National Bank of Oregon
P.O. Box 3168
Portland 97208

Established in 1961 in OR.
Foundation type: Independent
Financial data (yr. ended 6/30/89): Assets, $1,187,075 (M); expenditures, $72,114, including $41,700 for grants to individuals.
Purpose and activities: Awards scholarships and loans for higher education.
Types of support: Student aid, student loans.
Limitations: Giving primarily in OR.
Application information: Application forms available from local area high schools, college financial aid office, or trustee bank. Application form required.
Deadline(s): Jan. 1-Apr. 1 for scholarships; June 1-15 for loans
Final notification: June 30 for scholarships; July 15 for loans
Trustee: U.S. National Bank of Oregon.
Employer Identification Number: 936020885

6124
Harley and Mertie Stevens Memorial Fund ⌑ ☆
c/o U.S. National Bank of Oregon
P.O. Box 3168
Portland 97208-3168

Foundation type: Independent
Financial data (yr. ended 6/30/89): Assets, $1,153,017 (M); expenditures, $73,296, including $2,050 for 3 grants (high: $1,000; low: $50) and $29,600 for grants to individuals.
Purpose and activities: Primarily awards scholarships and loans to individuals for higher education.
Types of support: Student aid, student loans.
Limitations: Giving primarily in Clackamas County, OR.
Application information: Application forms available from local area high schools, college financial aid office, or trustee bank. Application form required.
Deadline(s): Jan. 1 to Apr. 1 for scholarships; June 1-15 for loans
Final notification: June 30 for scholarships; July 15 for loans
Trustee Bank: U.S. National Bank of Oregon.
Employer Identification Number: 936053655

6125
Tektronix Foundation ▼
P.O. Box 500
Beaverton 97077 (503) 627-7084

Incorporated in 1952 in OR.
Donor(s): Tektronix, Inc.
Foundation type: Company-sponsored
Financial data (yr. ended 12/31/88): Assets, $2,604,827 (M); gifts received, $2,029,622; expenditures, $1,295,598, including $999,795 for 150 grants (high: $135,000; low: $25), $59,940 for 35 grants to individuals (average: $2,000) and $215,682 for employee matching gifts.
Purpose and activities: Giving for education, especially physical sciences and employee matching gifts, community funds and other social service programs, health agencies, and some limited arts grants; support also for scholarship programs for children of company employees.
Types of support: Operating budgets, continuing support, annual campaigns, seed money, building funds, equipment, land acquisition, employee matching gifts, fellowships, employee-related scholarships, renovation projects.
Limitations: Giving primarily in OR. No grants to individuals (except for employee-related scholarships), or for emergency or endowment funds, demonstration projects, matching or challenge gifts, deficit financing, research, publications, or conferences; no loans.
Application information: Application form not required.
Initial approach: Proposal
Copies of proposal: 1
Deadline(s): 1 month before board meeting
Board meeting date(s): Feb., May, Aug., and Nov.
Final notification: Following board meeting, for grant recipients only
Write: Dianna Smiley, Exec. Dir.
Officers and Trustees:* Jean Vollum,* Chair.; Charles H. Frost,* Vice-Chair.; Tom Long,* Secy.; Terry Clifford,* Treas.; Pat Kunkle, Steve Vollum, William D. Walker.
Number of staff: 1 part-time professional; 1 part-time support.
Employer Identification Number: 936021540

6126
The Herbert A. Templeton Foundation
1717 S.W. Park Ave.
Portland 97201 (503) 223-0036

Incorporated in 1955 in OR.
Donor(s): Herbert A. Templeton,† members of the Templeton family.
Foundation type: Independent
Financial data (yr. ended 12/31/89): Assets, $4,711,181 (M); expenditures, $333,664, including $298,350 for 107 grants (high: $20,000; low: $100; average: $500-$5,000).
Purpose and activities: Grants for educational, youth, cultural, and social service organizations operating in OR or having programs significantly affecting OR residents; present emphasis on program and direct services.
Types of support: Operating budgets, continuing support, seed money, emergency funds, scholarship funds, special projects, general purposes.
Limitations: Giving limited to OR. No support for medical services, scientific research or technology, the aged, or parochial education. No grants to individuals, or for program-related investments, fellowships, building or endowment funds, or matching gifts; no loans.
Publications: Program policy statement (including application guidelines).
Application information: Application form not required.
Initial approach: Letter or proposal
Copies of proposal: 1
Deadline(s): Submit proposal preferably from July through Sept.; deadline Sept. 30
Board meeting date(s): Jan., Apr., July, Oct., and Nov.; most grant requests processed at meetings in Oct. or Nov.
Final notification: Nov. or Dec.
Write: Mrs. Ruth B. Richmond, Pres.
Officers and Trustees:* Ruth B. Richmond,* Pres.; Jane T. Bryson,* V.P.; Terrence R. Pancoast, Secy.-Treas.; James E. Bryson, John R. Olsen, Hall Templeton, William B. Webber.
Number of staff: 1 part-time support.
Employer Identification Number: 930505586

6127
Rose E. Tucker Charitable Trust ⌑
900 S.W. Fifth Ave., 24th Fl.
Portland 97204 (503) 224-3380

Trust established about 1976 in OR.
Donor(s): Rose E. Tucker,† Max and Rose Tucker Foundation.
Foundation type: Independent
Financial data (yr. ended 6/30/88): Assets, $13,350,953 (M); expenditures, $717,830, including $587,605 for 157 grants (high: $25,000; low: $500; average: $2,500-$12,000).
Purpose and activities: Priority given to programs in fields of education, health and welfare, community development, social services, arts and culture, and care and education of the underprivileged and handicapped.
Types of support: Building funds, scholarship funds, general purposes, operating budgets, equipment, special projects, capital campaigns, land acquisition.
Limitations: Giving primarily in OR, with emphasis on the Portland metropolitan area. No support for religion, or private foundations. No grants to individuals, or for fellowships, operating budgets, or debt reduction; no loans.
Publications: Application guidelines, annual report (including application guidelines), grants list.
Application information: Application form not required.
Initial approach: Proposal
Copies of proposal: 1
Deadline(s): None
Board meeting date(s): Approximately every 2 months
Final notification: Within 10 days of board meetings
Write: Thomas B. Stoel or Milo Ormseth, Trustees
Trustees: Milo Ormseth, Thomas B. Stoel, U.S. National Bank of Oregon.
Number of staff: 1 part-time support.
Employer Identification Number: 936119091

6128
Andrew E. Vanstrom Trust B. ⌑ ☆
c/o First Interstate Bank of Oregon, N.A.
P.O. Box 2971
Portland 97208

Foundation type: Independent
Financial data (yr. ended 7/31/89): Assets, $1,506,812 (M); expenditures, $99,247, including $81,148 for 4 grants of $20,287 each.
Purpose and activities: Support for scouting organizations, a hospitals for crippled children, and a Baptist church.
Types of support: General purposes.
Limitations: Giving primarily in OR and FL. No grants to individuals.
Application information: Contributes only to pre-selected organizations. Applications not accepted.
Trustee: First Interstate Bank of Oregon, N.A.
Employer Identification Number: 936107339

6129
William S. Walton Charitable Trust ⌑
c/o U.S. National Bank of Oregon
P.O. Box 3168
Portland 97208

Trust established in 1958 in OR.
Donor(s): William S. Walton.†
Foundation type: Independent
Financial data (yr. ended 5/31/87): Assets, $728,892 (M); expenditures, $152,833, including $135,000 for 15 grants (high: $25,000; low: $2,000; average: $2,500-$15,000).
Purpose and activities: Giving primarily for youth agencies, higher education, cultural programs, and Protestant welfare funds. Support for capital improvements only, including building funds, equipment and materials and renovation projects.
Types of support: Building funds, equipment, renovation projects.
Limitations: Giving limited to the Salem, OR, area. No grants to individuals, or for endowment funds, general operating support, scholarships, fellowships, or matching gifts; no loans.
Application information: Application form not required.
Initial approach: Full proposal
Copies of proposal: 1
Deadline(s): Submit proposal preferably from June through Aug.; deadline Sept. 15
Board meeting date(s): Oct.
Final notification: Oct. 30
Write: Floyd K. Bowers, Trustee
Trustees: Floyd K. Bowers, U.S. National Bank of Oregon.
Number of staff: 2 part-time professional.
Employer Identification Number: 930432836

6130
Wessinger Foundation ⌑
1133 West Burnside
Portland 97209 (503) 222-4351

Established in 1979.
Foundation type: Independent
Financial data (yr. ended 9/30/88): Assets, $4,060,016 (M); expenditures, $257,594, including $199,750 for 25 grants (high: $50,000; low: $250).
Purpose and activities: Giving for higher education, cultural programs, youth agencies, social services, and historic preservation organizations.
Limitations: Giving limited to the Pacific Northwest, with emphasis on the Tri-County area.
Application information:
Initial approach: Letter
Deadline(s): None
Officers and Directors: W.W. Wessinger, Pres.; Fred G. Wessinger, V.P.; Thomas B. Steol, Secy.; Donald Frisbee, John C. Hampton.
Employer Identification Number: 930754224

6131
Wheeler Foundation
1211 S.W. Fifth Ave., Suite 2906
Portland 97204-1911 (503) 228-0261

Established in 1965 in OR.
Donor(s): Coleman H. Wheeler,† Cornelia T. Wheeler.
Foundation type: Independent
Financial data (yr. ended 12/31/88): Assets, $4,286,526 (M); gifts received, $20,000; expenditures, $251,820, including $240,125 for 63 grants (high: $20,000; low: $250; average: $1,000).
Purpose and activities: Emphasis on higher and secondary education, medical services and research, cultural programs, and youth agencies.
Types of support: General purposes.
Limitations: Giving primarily in OR. No grants to individuals, or for endowment funds.
Application information: Application form not required.
Initial approach: Letter
Copies of proposal: 1
Deadline(s): None
Board meeting date(s): Mar., June, Sept., and Dec.
Write: Samuel C. Wheeler, Pres.
Officers and Directors: Samuel C. Wheeler, Pres.; John C. Wheeler, V.P.; David A. Kekel, Secy.-Treas.; Lil M. Hendrickson.
Number of staff: 1 part-time professional.
Employer Identification Number: 930553801

6132
The Woodard Family Foundation
P.O. Box 97
Cottage Grove 97424

Incorporated in 1952 in OR.
Foundation type: Independent
Financial data (yr. ended 6/30/89): Assets, $2,391,985 (M); expenditures, $106,343, including $89,892 for 45 grants (high: $21,000; low: $25).
Purpose and activities: Support for business and other education, community development, animal welfare, social services, and culture.
Limitations: Giving primarily in OR.
Officers: Carlton Woodard, Pres.; Dutee Woodard, V.P.; Kim Woodard, Secy.-Treas.
Employer Identification Number: 936026550

PENNSYLVANIA

6133
Action Industries Charitable Foundation ⌘ ☆
460 Nixon Rd.
Cheswick 15024 (412) 782-4800

Established in 1976 in PA.
Donor(s): Action Industries, Inc.
Foundation type: Company-sponsored
Financial data (yr. ended 12/31/88): Assets, $347,196 (M); expenditures, $308,440, including $307,449 for 25 grants (high: $125,000; low: $80).
Purpose and activities: Support for culture and the arts, community funds, Jewish giving, and education, including higher education.
Types of support: In-kind gifts, general purposes.
Limitations: Giving primarily in Pittsburgh, PA.
Application information:
Initial approach: Proposal
Deadline(s): None
Write: Sholom D. Comay, Trustee
Trustees: Steven H. Berez, Sholom D. Comay, David Shapira.
Employer Identification Number: 251299973

6134
Adams Foundation, Inc.
202 West Fourth St.
Bethlehem 18015

Incorporated in 1955 in PA.
Donor(s): Rolland L. Adams,† South Jersey Publishing Co., The Bethlehems' Globe Publishing Co., Cleveland Coca-Cola Bottling Co., Quaker State Coca-Cola Bottling Co., and others.
Foundation type: Independent
Financial data (yr. ended 12/31/88): Assets, $906,988 (M); qualifying distributions, $235,912, including $235,816 for 33 grants (high: $50,000; low: $250).
Purpose and activities: The foundation is in the process of being reorganized.
Application information:
Write: Nancy A. Taylor, Pres.
Officer: Nancy A. Taylor,* Pres.
Employer Identification Number: 240866511

6135
The Air Products Foundation ▼
Route 222
Trexlertown 18087 (215) 481-8079
Additional address: c/o Mgr., Corp. Philanthropy, Air Products and Chemicals, Inc., 7201 Hamilton Blvd., Allentown, PA 18195-1501

Incorporated in 1979 in PA.
Donor(s): Air Products and Chemicals, Inc.
Foundation type: Company-sponsored
Financial data (yr. ended 09/30/89): Assets, $2,636,241 (M); gifts received, $1,400,000; expenditures, $1,134,376, including $863,561 for 217 grants (high: $150,000; low: $42; average: $500-$5,000).
Purpose and activities: Support for the areas of higher and other education, including programs for minorities, health associations, welfare, community investment, and culture and the arts, including the fine arts.
Types of support: Operating budgets, continuing support, annual campaigns, seed money, emergency funds, building funds, equipment, special projects, capital campaigns, renovation projects.
Limitations: Giving primarily in areas of company operations throughout the U.S. No support for sectarian religious purposes, political or veterans' organizations, labor groups, national capital campaigns of health organizations, hospital capital campaigns or operating expenses, elementary or secondary schools, or organizations receiving support from the United Way. No grants to individuals; no loans.
Publications: Informational brochure (including application guidelines).
Application information: Application form not required.
Initial approach: Proposal
Copies of proposal: 1
Deadline(s): None
Board meeting date(s): Monthly
Final notification: 3 months
Write: Charlotte Walker, Contribs. Officer
Officers: Leon C. Holt, Jr.,* Chair.; C.P. Powell, V.P.; Richard A. Gray, Jr., Secy.
Trustees:* Dexter F. Baker, P.L. Thibaut Brian, R.M. Davis, R.F. Dee, Walter F. Light, Jack B. St. Clair.
Number of staff: None.
Employer Identification Number: 232130928

6136
Alco Standard Foundation ⌘
P.O. Box 834
Valley Forge 19482-0834 (215) 296-8000

Established in 1974 in PA.
Donor(s): Alco Standard Corp.
Foundation type: Company-sponsored
Financial data (yr. ended 12/31/88): Assets, $3,422,232 (M); gifts received, $2,937,500; expenditures, $193,446, including $104,499 for 122 grants (high: $12,870; low: $25) and $84,610 for 485 employee matching gifts.
Purpose and activities: Emphasis on community funds, education, including an employee matching gift program, hospitals, health, youth, and cultural programs.
Types of support: Employee matching gifts, matching funds.
Limitations: Giving primarily in areas of company operations. No grants to individuals.
Application information: Contributes only to pre-selected organizations. Applications not accepted.
Officers and Directors:* Ray B. Mundt,* Pres.; William F. Drake, Jr.,* V.P.; O. Gordon Brewer, Jr., Treas.; Tinkham Veale III.
Employer Identification Number: 237378726

6137
Alcoa Foundation ▼
1501 Alcoa Bldg.
Pittsburgh 15219-1850 (412) 553-2348

Trust established in 1952 in PA; incorporated in 1964.
Donor(s): Aluminum Co. of America.
Foundation type: Company-sponsored
Financial data (yr. ended 12/31/89): Assets, $250,314,828 (M); expenditures, $13,407,117, including $9,696,413 for grants (average: $5,000-$25,000), $428,000 for 214 grants to individuals of $2,000 each, $1,279,548 for 2,898 employee matching gifts and $250,000 for loans.
Purpose and activities: Grants chiefly for education, especially higher education, arts and cultural programs, health and welfare organizations, hospitals, civic and community development, and youth organizations.
Types of support: Annual campaigns, building funds, conferences and seminars, continuing support, emergency funds, employee matching gifts, equipment, fellowships, matching funds, operating budgets, research, scholarship funds, seed money, employee-related scholarships, capital campaigns, general purposes, renovation projects, special projects.
Limitations: Giving primarily in areas of company operations, including: Davenport, IA; Knoxville, TN; Massena, NY; Pittsburgh, PA; Evansville, IN; Cleveland, OH; and Rockdale, TX. No support for sectarian or religious organizations, political purposes, or elementary or secondary schools. No grants to individuals (except for employee-related scholarships), or for endowment funds, tickets, souvenir programs, advertising, golf outings, trips, tours, or student exchange programs; no loans.
Publications: Annual report, informational brochure (including application guidelines).
Application information: Application form not required.
Initial approach: Proposal
Copies of proposal: 1
Deadline(s): None
Board meeting date(s): Monthly
Final notification: 1 to 4 months
Write: Earl L. Gadbery, Pres.
Officers: Earl L. Gadbery,* Pres.; F. Worth Hobbs,* V.P.; Kathleen R. Burgan, Secy.-Treas.

Directors:* Ernest J. Edwards, Richard L. Fischer, Vincent R. Scorsone, Robert F. Slagle, Donald R. Whitlow.
Corporate Trustee: Mellon Bank, N.A.
Number of staff: 3 full-time professional; 1 part-time professional; 3 full-time support.
Employer Identification Number: 251128857

6138
Allegheny Foundation
P.O. Box 268
Pittsburgh 15230 (412) 392-2900

Incorporated in 1953 in PA.
Donor(s): Richard M. Scaife.
Foundation type: Independent
Financial data (yr. ended 12/31/89): Assets, $24,249,348 (M); expenditures, $383,172, including $149,500 for 11 grants (high: $35,000; low: $2,500; average: $2,500-$35,000).
Purpose and activities: Emphasis on organizations concerned with historic preservation and higher education.
Types of support: General purposes, publications, seed money, operating budgets.
Limitations: Giving primarily in western PA, with emphasis on Pittsburgh. No grants to individuals, or for endowment funds, scholarships, or fellowships; no loans.
Publications: 990-PF.
Application information: Application form not required.
Initial approach: Letter
Copies of proposal: 1
Deadline(s): None
Board meeting date(s): Dec.
Final notification: Dec.
Write: Joanne B. Beyer, Pres.
Officers and Trustees: Richard M. Scaife,* Chair.; Joanne B. Beyer,* Pres.; Margaret R. Battle, Peter B. Bell, Ralph H. Goettler, Doris O'Donnell, Nathan J. Stark, George Weymouth, Arthur P. Ziegler, Jr.
Number of staff: 3
Employer Identification Number: 256012303

6139
Allegheny Ludlum Foundation ⌑
1000 Six PPG Place
Pittsburgh 15222-5479 (412) 394-2836

Established in 1981 in PA.
Donor(s): Allegheny Ludlum Corp.
Foundation type: Company-sponsored
Financial data (yr. ended 12/31/88): Assets, $1,748,044 (M); gifts received, $500,000; expenditures, $630,348, including $623,107 for 99 grants (high: $211,000; low: $250; average: $500-$5,000).
Purpose and activities: Support primarily for community funds, hospitals, and youth agencies; some support for education.
Types of support: Annual campaigns, building funds, capital campaigns, continuing support, emergency funds, publications, employee-related scholarships, scholarship funds.
Limitations: Giving primarily in PA, IN, CT, NY, and OK. No grants to individuals.
Application information: Application form not required.
Initial approach: Letter
Copies of proposal: 1
Deadline(s): None
Write: Jon D. Walton, Chair. Contribs. Comm.
Trustees: J.L. Murdy, R.P. Simmons, Jon D. Walton, Pittsburgh National Bank.
Number of staff: None.
Employer Identification Number: 256228755

6140
Harriett Ames Charitable Trust
c/o St. Davids Ctr.
150 Radnor Chester Rd., A-200
St. Davids 19087 (215) 341-9270

Trust established in 1952 in NY.
Donor(s): Harriett Ames.†
Foundation type: Independent
Financial data (yr. ended 12/31/89): Assets, $11,554,265 (M); expenditures, $1,381,734, including $1,315,000 for 44 grants (high: $200,000; low: $2,500; average: $2,500-$20,000).
Purpose and activities: Grants to educational and charitable organizations, with emphasis on medical research, education, health associations, and Jewish welfare.
Types of support: General purposes.
Limitations: Giving primarily in the New York, NY, metropolitan area. No grants to individuals.
Application information: Applications not accepted.
Write: A.C. Cory
Trustee: Walter H. Annenberg.
Employer Identification Number: 236286757

6141
AMETEK Foundation, Inc. ▼
Station Sq. Two
Paoli 19301 (215) 647-2121

Incorporated in 1960 in NY.
Donor(s): AMETEK, Inc.
Foundation type: Company-sponsored
Financial data (yr. ended 12/31/89): Assets, $4,208,000 (M); gifts received, $650,000; expenditures, $970,000, including $950,000 for 115 grants (high: $100,000; low: $1,000; average: $1,000-$25,000).
Purpose and activities: Emphasis on community funds; hospitals and medical research, including cancer research; higher, elementary, and minority education; and welfare funds.
Types of support: Annual campaigns, building funds, research, employee-related scholarships, scholarship funds, technical assistance, matching funds, general purposes, exchange programs, equipment, endowment funds.
Limitations: No grants to individuals, or for matching gifts; no loans.
Application information: Application form not required.
Initial approach: Letter
Copies of proposal: 1
Deadline(s): Submit proposal preferably in Feb. or Sept.; deadlines Feb. 28 and Sept. 30
Board meeting date(s): Apr. and Nov.
Final notification: 2 weeks after board meets
Write: Robert W. Yannarell, Asst. Secy.-Treas.
Officers and Directors:* John H. Lux,* Pres.; John P. Dandalides, V.P.; Bernard E. Brandes,* Secy.-Treas.; Wallace E. Cowan, Helmut N. Friedlaender, Anthony A. Sirna III.
Number of staff: None.
Employer Identification Number: 136095939

6142
AMP Foundation ⌑
c/o AMP, Inc.
Harrisburg 17108 (717) 564-0100

Established in 1977 in PA.
Donor(s): AMP, Inc.
Foundation type: Company-sponsored
Financial data (yr. ended 12/31/88): Assets, $10,608,303 (M); gifts received, $1,000,000; expenditures, $757,129, including $720,211 for 305 grants (high: $102,650; low: $25; average: $5,000-$15,000).
Purpose and activities: Emphasis on hospitals, higher education, community funds, youth agencies, and social service organizations.
Limitations: Giving primarily in PA, with some emphasis on the Harrisburg and Carlisle areas. No grants to individuals.
Application information:
Initial approach: Proposal
Deadline(s): Submit proposal preferably in Nov.; no set deadline
Board meeting date(s): Jan. and July
Final notification: 4-6 weeks after Jan. meeting
Write: Hugo A. Walfred, Principal Mgr.
Officer: Hugo A. Walfred, Principal Mgr.
Trustee: Dauphin Deposit Bank & Trust Co.
Number of staff: 2 part-time professional; 1 part-time support.
Employer Identification Number: 232022928

6143
The Annenberg Fund, Inc. ▼
St. Davids Ctr.
150 Radnor Chester Rd., Suite A-200
St. Davids 19087 (215) 341-9270

Incorporated in 1951 in DE.
Donor(s): Walter H. Annenberg.
Foundation type: Independent
Financial data (yr. ended 12/31/89): Assets, $22,586,194 (M); expenditures, $6,057,757, including $6,020,616 for 150 grants (high: $1,666,667; low: $100; average: $100-$100,000).
Purpose and activities: Emphasis on higher education, health and medical research, including medical education, cultural programs, and community services.
Types of support: Research, building funds, general purposes.
Limitations: Giving primarily in PA, CA, and NY. No grants to individuals.
Application information: Applications not accepted.
Board meeting date(s): Irregularly
Write: Alice C. Cory, Secy.-Treas.
Officers and Directors:* Walter H. Annenberg,* Pres.; Leonore Annenberg,* V.P.; William J. Henrich, Jr.,* V.P.; Alice C. Cory,* Secy.-Treas; Wallis Annenberg.
Number of staff: None.
Employer Identification Number: 236286756

6144
The Arcadia Foundation ▼
105 East Logan St.
Norristown 19401 (215) 275-8460

Incorporated in 1964 in PA.
Donor(s): Edith C. Steinbright, Marilyn Lee Steinbright.
Foundation type: Independent
Financial data (yr. ended 09/30/89): Assets, $12,878,911 (M); expenditures, $795,027, including $768,710 for 109 grants (average: $500-$20,000).
Purpose and activities: Emphasis on hospitals and health agencies, higher education, child welfare agencies, and care of the handicapped.
Types of support: Operating budgets, annual campaigns, continuing support, emergency funds, building funds, equipment, endowment funds, research, special projects.
Limitations: Giving limited to PA. Generally, no support for cultural programs. No grants to individuals, or for deficit financing, land acquisition, fellowships, demonstration projects, publications, or conferences; no loans.
Application information: Application form not required.
Initial approach: Telephone, letter, or proposal (not exceeding 2 pages)
Copies of proposal: 1
Deadline(s): Submit proposal preferably between July 1 and Aug. 15; deadline Aug. 15
Board meeting date(s): Sept. and Nov.
Final notification: 3 months
Write: Marilyn Lee Steinbright, Pres.
Officers and Directors:* Marilyn Lee Steinbright,* Pres.; Tanya Hashorva,* V.P.; David P. Sandler,* Secy.; Harvey S.S. Miller,* Treas.; Edward L. Jones, Jr., Kathleen Shellington.
Number of staff: None.
Employer Identification Number: 236399772

6145
Aristech Foundation ⌑ ☆
600 Grant St., Rm. 2114
Pittsburgh 15230-0250

Established in 1987 in PA.
Foundation type: Company-sponsored
Financial data (yr. ended 12/31/89): Assets, $1,727,603 (M); gifts received, $500,000; expenditures, $248,613, including $219,975 for 54 grants (high: $55,000; low: $350) and $17,755 for 34 employee matching gifts.
Purpose and activities: Support for higher education, the performing arts and other cultural programs, and community services and funds.
Types of support: Employee matching gifts.
Limitations: No grants to individuals, or for conferences and seminars, symposia, travel, book or magazine publications, or film or telvision productions.
Application information: Application form not required.
Initial approach: Letter (1 to 2 pages)
Write: J. Harry Varner, Exec. Dir.
Officer: J. Harry Varner, Exec. Dir.
Trustees: Craig R. Andersson, Thomas Marshall, Anthony F. Mastro.
Employer Identification Number: 256298142

6146
Armstrong Foundation
(Formerly Armstrong World Industries Charitable Foundation)
P.O. Box 3001
Lancaster 17604 (717) 396-3403

Established in 1985 in PA.
Donor(s): Armstrong World Industries, Inc.
Foundation type: Company-sponsored
Financial data (yr. ended 12/31/88): Assets, $6,249,450 (M); gifts received, $627,000; expenditures, $635,089, including $630,959 for grants (high: $198,000).
Purpose and activities: Support primarily for a community fund and higher education; some support for public interest and civic affairs organizations and health and social services.
Types of support: Employee matching gifts, annual campaigns, building funds, scholarship funds.
Application information: Contributes only to pre-selected organizations. Applications not accepted.
Write: M. William Jones, Asst. to the Pres.
Officers: William W. Adams, Pres.; John N. Jordin, V.P.; Warren Posey, Treas.
Employer Identification Number: 232387950

6147
The Arronson Foundation
1101 Market St.
Philadelphia 19107

Established in 1957 in DE.
Donor(s): Gertrude Arronson.†
Foundation type: Independent
Financial data (yr. ended 10/31/89): Assets, $6,629,366 (M); expenditures, $586,461, including $583,136 for 53 grants (high: $200,000; low: $100).
Purpose and activities: Emphasis on Jewish organizations and education, particularly higher education; support also for the performing arts and other cultural programs and hospitals and medical research, and women's issues.
Types of support: Annual campaigns, endowment funds, scholarship funds, seed money.
Limitations: Giving primarily in Philadelphia, PA.
Application information: Application form not required.
Initial approach: Letter
Copies of proposal: 1
Deadline(s): None
Write: Harold E. Kohn, Pres.
Officers: Harold E. Kohn, Pres.; Edith Kohn, V.P.; Joseph C. Kohn, V.P.; Stuart H. Savett, V.P.; Bayard M. Graf, Secy.-Treas.
Number of staff: None.
Employer Identification Number: 236259604

6148
Asplundh Foundation ⌑
Blair Mill Rd.
Willow Grove 19090 (215) 784-4200

Incorporated in 1953 in PA.
Donor(s): Carl Hj. Asplundh,† Lester Asplundh.
Foundation type: Independent
Financial data (yr. ended 12/31/88): Assets, $3,973,445 (M); gifts received, $200,300; expenditures, $194,661, including $188,700 for 40 grants (high: $110,000; low: $100).
Purpose and activities: Giving for Protestant church support.
Limitations: Giving primarily in PA. No grants to individuals.
Application information:
Initial approach: Letter
Deadline(s): None
Write: E. Boyd Asplundh, Secy.
Officers and Directors:* Edward K. Asplundh,* Pres.; E. Boyd Asplundh,* Secy.; Barr E. Asplundh, Robert H. Asplundh.
Employer Identification Number: 236297246

6149
Atochem North America Foundation ▼
(Formerly Pennwalt Foundation)
Pennwalt Bldg.
Three Benjamin Franklin Pkwy.
Philadelphia 19102 (215) 587-7653

Trust established in 1957 in PA.
Donor(s): Atochem North America.
Foundation type: Company-sponsored
Financial data (yr. ended 12/31/88): Assets, $2,006,660 (M); gifts received, $2,990,000; expenditures, $1,336,657, including $1,169,240 for 627 grants (high: $66,552; low: $25; average: $100-$3,000) and $165,512 for employee matching gifts.
Purpose and activities: Grants primarily for community funds; higher education, including employee-related scholarships and matching gifts; and cultural programs, including museums and public broadcasting; support also for civic affairs, and health and medicine.
Types of support: Operating budgets, general purposes, continuing support, annual campaigns, seed money, emergency funds, deficit financing, building funds, equipment, land acquisition, matching funds, employee matching gifts, employee-related scholarships, renovation projects.
Limitations: Giving primarily in areas of company operations, with some emphasis on the Philadelphia, PA, area. No support for public education; veterans', fraternal, or labor organizations; or sectarian religious organizations. No grants to individuals (except for employee-related scholarships), or for endowment funds, special projects, research, publications, conferences, courtesy advertising, or entertainment promotions; no loans.
Application information: Application form not required.
Initial approach: Proposal
Copies of proposal: 1
Deadline(s): None
Board meeting date(s): Mar., June, Sept., and Dec.
Final notification: 1 to 3 months
Write: George L. Hagar, Exec. Secy.
Trustees: Anthony P. Fortino, Seymour S. Preston III, George Reath, Jr.
Number of staff: 1 part-time professional; 1 full-time support.
Employer Identification Number: 236256818

6150
Babcock Charitable Trust ⌑
2220 Palmer St.
Pittsburgh 15218 (412) 351-3515

Established in 1957 in PA.
Donor(s): Fred C. Babcock.
Foundation type: Independent
Financial data (yr. ended 12/31/88): Assets, $1,490,050 (M); expenditures, $27,628, including $27,265 for 74 grants (high: $1,900; low: $25).
Purpose and activities: Support primarily for secondary and higher education, community funds, youth organizations and cultural programs.
Application information: Application form not required.
Initial approach: Letter
Deadline(s): None
Write: Fred C. Babcock, Trustee
Trustees: Fred C. Babcock, Jean B. Harbeck, Carl P. Stillitano.
Employer Identification Number: 256035161

6151
Baltimore Family Foundation, Inc. ⌑
34 South River St.
Wilkes-Barre 18702-2406

Established in 1984 in PA.
Donor(s): Members of the Baltimore family.
Foundation type: Independent
Financial data (yr. ended 11/30/89): Assets, $1,125,730 (M); gifts received, $10,000; expenditures, $140,985, including $134,340 for 30 grants (high: $60,000; low: $40).
Purpose and activities: Support primarily for Jewish welfare and for higher education.
Limitations: Giving primarily in Wilkes-Barre, PA. No grants to individuals.
Application information: Contributes only to pre-selected organizations. Applications not accepted.
Officers: David M. Baltimore, Pres.; Muriel Baltimore, Secy.
Directors: Charles Baltimore, Lynn Baltimore, Terry S. Baltimore.
Employer Identification Number: 232308091

6152
Robert Bard Foundation ⌑ ☆
c/o Mellon Bank (East), N.A.
P.O. Box 7236
Philadelphia 19101 (215) 553-3208

Established in 1989 in PA.
Donor(s): Agnes Cook Bard.†
Foundation type: Independent
Financial data (yr. ended 06/30/89): Assets, $2,424,404 (M); gifts received, $2,442,800; expenditures, $109,404, including $107,575 for grants.
Purpose and activities: Initial year of grantmaking 1989; support for general charitable activities.
Limitations: Giving primarily in the Royerford, PA, area. No grants to individuals.
Application information:
Initial approach: Proposal
Deadline(s): Apr. 1
Write: Pat Kling
Trustee: Mellon Bank (East), N.A.
Employer Identification Number: 236806099

6153
Barra Foundation, Inc. ▼
8200 Flourtown Ave., Suite 12
Wyndmoor 19118 (215) 233-5115

Incorporated in 1963 in DE.
Donor(s): Robert L. McNeil, Jr.
Foundation type: Independent
Financial data (yr. ended 12/31/88): Assets, $23,290,370 (M); expenditures, $1,511,901, including $1,255,285 for 211 grants (high: $250,000; low: $500; average: $500-$10,000).
Purpose and activities: Giving for the advancement and diffusion of knowledge and its effective application to human needs in certain fields, particularly in Eighteenth Century American art and material culture. Projects must be pilot studies or enterprises requiring foresight, not supported by other agencies or individuals; publication or studies required.
Types of support: Matching funds, special projects.
Limitations: Giving primarily in the Philadelphia, PA, area. No grants to individuals, or for annual or capital campaigns, building or endowment funds, operating budgets, deficit drives, scholarships, fellowships, or ongoing programs; no loans.
Publications: Program policy statement.
Application information: Application form required.
Initial approach: Letter
Copies of proposal: 3
Deadline(s): None
Board meeting date(s): Dec. and as appropriate
Final notification: 3 to 6 months
Write: Robert L. McNeil, Jr., Pres.
Officers and Directors:* Robert L. McNeil, Jr.,* Pres. and Treas.; William T. Tredennick,* V.P.; George M. Brodhead,* Secy.; Herman R. Hutchinson, E. Marshall Nuckols, Jr.
Number of staff: 1 part-time support.
Employer Identification Number: 236277885

6154
Bayer-Mobay Foundation ⌑
Mobay Rd.
Pittsburgh 15205-9741 (412) 394-5542

Established in 1985 in PA.
Donor(s): Mobay Corp.
Foundation type: Company-sponsored
Financial data (yr. ended 12/31/87): Assets, $7,099,946 (M); gifts received, $295,000; expenditures, $490,347, including $457,620 for 67 grants (high: $115,000; low: $125).
Purpose and activities: Support for a community fund, higher education, culture, and civic affairs.
Application information: Application form required.
Deadline(s): None
Write: W.C. Ostern, Pres.
Officers: W.C. Ostern, Pres.; R.W. Brown, V.P. and Secy.-Treas.; E.L. Reichard, V.P.
Employer Identification Number: 251508079

6155
Helen D. Groome Beatty Trust ⌑
c/o Mellon Bank (East), N.A.
P.O. Box 7899
Philadelphia 19101-7899 (215) 585-3208

Trust established in 1951 in PA.
Donor(s): Helen D. Groome Beatty.†
Foundation type: Independent
Financial data (yr. ended 9/30/87): Assets, $5,275,840 (M); expenditures, $317,162, including $274,197 for 94 grants (high: $11,575; low: $1,000).
Purpose and activities: To provide capital support for charitable and educational institutions, with emphasis on higher education, hospitals, and cultural programs.
Types of support: Building funds, renovation projects.
Limitations: Giving primarily in the Philadelphia, PA, metropolitan area. No grants to individuals, or for endowment funds or operating budgets.
Publications: Application guidelines.
Application information:
Initial approach: Proposal, telephone, or letter
Copies of proposal: 1
Deadline(s): Apr. 15 or Oct. 15
Board meeting date(s): May 15 and Nov. 15
Write: Patricia M. Kling, Trust Officer, Mellon Bank (East), N.A.
Trustee: Mellon Bank (East), N.A.
Employer Identification Number: 236224798

6156
Will R. Beitel Childrens Community Foundation ⌑
c/o Lovine Keller
P.O. Box 292
Nazareth 18064-0292 (215) 759-0332

Established in 1874 in PA.
Foundation type: Independent
Financial data (yr. ended 9/30/87): Assets, $1,392,745 (M); expenditures, $84,893, including $61,105 for 19 grants (high: $7,500; low: $1,000).
Purpose and activities: Giving primarily to youth and community organizations and social services.
Types of support: Operating budgets, renovation projects.
Limitations: Giving primarily in Northampton County, PA.
Application information:
Initial approach: Letter
Deadline(s): Apr. 1
Write: Lovine Keller, Asst. Secy.
Officers: Conrad C. Shimer, Pres.; John M. Dusinski, V.P.; Lester H. Miller, Secy.; Grant W. Welizer, Treas.
Directors: Elwood G. Buss, Robert C. Hoch, Ivan D. Stamper.
Employer Identification Number: 240800920

6157
Claude Worthington Benedum Foundation ▼
1400 Benedum-Trees Bldg.
Pittsburgh 15222 (412) 288-0360

Incorporated in 1944 in PA.

Donor(s): Michael Late Benedum,† Sarah N. Benedum.†
Foundation type: Independent
Financial data (yr. ended 12/31/88): Assets, $146,790,484 (M); expenditures, $7,920,551, including $7,056,551 for 107 grants (high: $1,000,000; low: $3,000; average: $10,000-$125,000).
Purpose and activities: Grants are made in areas of education, health and human services, community and economic development, and the arts. Funds are provided for projects that address regional problems and needs, that establish demonstration projects with strong potential for replication in WV, or that make outstanding contributions to the area. Local initiatives and voluntary support are encouraged by the foundation.
Types of support: Matching funds, consulting services, building funds, operating budgets, technical assistance, special projects, program-related investments, seed money.
Limitations: Giving limited to WV and to the greater Pittsburgh, PA, area. No support for national health and welfare campaigns, medical research, or religious activities. No grants to individuals.
Publications: Biennial report (including application guidelines).
Application information: Application form not required.
Initial approach: Letter or telephone
Copies of proposal: 1
Board meeting date(s): Mar., June, Sept., and Dec.
Final notification: Up to 6 months
Write: Paul R. Jenkins, Pres.
Officers and Trustees:* Henry A. Bergstrom,* Chair.; Paul R. Jenkins,* Pres.; David L. Wagner, V.P. and Treas.; Elizabeth Pusateri, Secy.; Paul G. Benedum, Harry C. Hamm, Jennings Randolph, Hulett C. Smith, George A. Stinson.
Number of staff: 5 full-time professional; 1 part-time professional; 3 full-time support.
Employer Identification Number: 251086799

6158
Beneficia Foundation
One Pitcairn Place
Jenkintown 19046-3593

Incorporated in 1953 in PA.
Donor(s): Members of the Theodore Pitcairn Family.
Foundation type: Independent
Financial data (yr. ended 4/30/89): Assets, $12,726,588 (M); expenditures, $731,867, including $653,000 for 41 grants (high: $155,000; low: $2,000).
Purpose and activities: Emphasis on conservation, music, the arts, education, and church support.
Limitations: Giving primarily in PA. No grants to individuals.
Application information: Application form not required.
Initial approach: Letter
Copies of proposal: 1
Deadline(s): Mar. 15
Board meeting date(s): Apr.
Write: Feodor U. Pitcairn, Exec. Secy.
Officers and Directors: Laren Pitcairn, Pres.; Miriam P. Mitchell, V.P.; Feodor U. Pitcairn, Exec. Secy.; Mark J. Pennink, Treas.; Heather D. Cooper, Diene P. Duncan, J. Daniel Mitchell, John D. Mitchell, Eshowe P. Pennink, Kirstin O. Pitcairn, Mary Eleanor Pitcairn.
Number of staff: None.
Employer Identification Number: 246015630

6159
David Berger Foundation ⌑
c/o Heffler and Co.
1515 Market St., Suite 800
Philadelphia 19102
Application address: 1622 Locust St., Philadelphia, PA 19103

Established in 1965 in PA.
Foundation type: Independent
Financial data (yr. ended 12/31/89): Assets, $536,562 (M); expenditures, $223,943, including $222,925 for 16 grants (high: $102,000; low: $50).
Purpose and activities: Support primarily for Jewish welfare; support also for social services and health associations.
Types of support: General purposes.
Limitations: Giving primarily in Philadelphia, PA, and Palm Beach, FL.
Application information:
Initial approach: Letter
Deadline(s): None
Write: David Berger, Pres.
Officer: David Berger, Pres.
Employer Identification Number: 236424659

6160
Bergstrom Foundation ⌑
1800 Benedum Trees Bldg.
Pittsburgh 15222 (412) 471-1751

Established in 1960 in PA.
Donor(s): Henry A. Bergstrom, Margaret A. Bergstrom.
Foundation type: Independent
Financial data (yr. ended 12/31/88): Assets, $1,453,098 (M); expenditures, $83,071, including $63,400 for 28 grants (high: $25,000; low: $100).
Purpose and activities: Giving primarily for education, particularly higher education, and cultural programs.
Types of support: General purposes, endowment funds.
Limitations: Giving primarily in the Pittsburgh, PA, area. No grants to individuals.
Application information: Application form not required.
Deadline(s): None
Write: Henry A. Bergstrom, Pres.
Officers and Trustees: Henry A. Bergstrom, Pres.; Henry A. Bergstrom, Jr., V.P.
Employer Identification Number: 251112093

6161
Allen H. & Selma W. Berkman Charitable Trust
5000 Fifth Ave., No. 207
Pittsburgh 15232 (412) 355-8640
Application address: 5000 Fifth Ave., Pittsburgh, PA 15232

Established in 1972 in PA.
Donor(s): Allen H. Berkman, Selma W. Berkman.
Foundation type: Independent
Financial data (yr. ended 10/31/88): Assets, $1,732,295 (M); gifts received, $103,710; expenditures, $154,821, including $149,000 for 37 grants (high: $50,000; low: $250; average: $1,500).
Purpose and activities: Giving primarily for higher and other educational institutions, and social services, including programs for the aged, child development, and the handicapped; support also for health and hospitals, the performing arts, historic preservation, and other cultural programs, and community and urban development.
Types of support: Special projects, annual campaigns, building funds, capital campaigns, continuing support, emergency funds, endowment funds, fellowships, general purposes, operating budgets, scholarship funds, technical assistance, research, program-related investments.
Limitations: Giving primarily in the Pittsburgh, PA, area.
Publications: Annual report, 990-PF.
Application information: Application form not required.
Initial approach: Letter
Copies of proposal: 1
Deadline(s): Sept. 1
Write: Allen H. Berkman, Trustee
Trustees: Barbara B. Ackerman, Allen H. Berkman, Richard L. Berkman, Selma W. Berkman, Susan B. Rahm.
Number of staff: None.
Employer Identification Number: 256144060

6162
Charles G. Berwind Foundation
3000 Centre Sq. West
1500 Market St.
Philadelphia 19102

Foundation type: Independent
Financial data (yr. ended 09/30/89): Assets, $1,200,851 (M); expenditures, $71,740, including $59,967 for 18 grants to individuals (high: $10,000; low: $250; average: $500-$7,700).
Purpose and activities: Awards scholarships to individuals who are the children of an active, retired, or deceased employee of Berwind Corp. and it subsidiaries.
Types of support: Student aid, employee-related scholarships.
Application information: Application form required.
Deadline(s): Nov. 30
Write: Betty A. Olund, Fdn. Admin.
Selection Committee: Walter G. Arader, Macy Patterson McPherson, Julia Painter.
Employer Identification Number: 237382896

6163
Bethlehem Area Foundation
430 East Broad St.
Bethlehem 18018 (215) 867-7588

Established in 1967 in PA.
Foundation type: Community
Financial data (yr. ended 06/30/89): Assets, $2,579,111 (M); gifts received, $70,792;

expenditures, $213,942, including $178,533 for 45 grants (high: $10,000; low: $945; average: $2,000-$6,000).
Purpose and activities: Giving primarily for health, education and training, social services, and welfare; support also for cultural programs and civic needs.
Types of support: Seed money, emergency funds, building funds, equipment, land acquisition, matching funds, special projects, capital campaigns, renovation projects, publications.
Limitations: Giving limited to the Bethlehem, PA, area. No support for sectarian religious purposes. No grants to individuals, or for operating budgets, continuing support, annual campaigns, deficit financing, endowments, scholarships, or research; no loans.
Publications: Annual report (including application guidelines), grants list, application guidelines, program policy statement.
Application information: Capital funding: must submit invoice copies when requesting release of funds. Program: brief progress report in June; program evaluation by Oct. Application form not required.
Initial approach: Letter
Copies of proposal: 5
Deadline(s): Submit proposal from June 1 to Aug. 1
Board meeting date(s): Oct.
Final notification: Oct.
Write: Eleanor A. Boylston, Exec. Dir.
Officers: Joseph F. Leeson, Jr.,* Chair.; Cidney B. Spillman,* Vice-Chair.; Eleanor A. Boylston, Secy. and Exec. Dir.
Board of Governors:* Curtis H. Barnette, Martha Cusimano, Msgr. John McPeak, John R. Mendenhall, Jose Perna, Nancy W. Swan, Edwin F. Van Billiard.
Trustee Banks: First Valley Bank, Lehigh Valley Bank, Meridian Bank.
Number of staff: 1 part-time professional.
Employer Identification Number: 231686634

6164
Betts Foundation ⌑
1800 Pennsylvania Ave.
Warren 16365
Application address: P.O. Box 88, Warren, PA 16365; Tel.: (814) 723-1250

Established in 1957 in PA.
Donor(s): Betts Industries, Inc.
Foundation type: Company-sponsored
Financial data (yr. ended 12/31/87): Assets, $1,125,883 (M); gifts received, $28,900; expenditures, $71,275, including $68,931 for 42 grants (high: $18,637; low: $40).
Purpose and activities: Grants primarily for higher education; support also for community development.
Limitations: Giving primarily in Warren County, PA.
Application information:
Initial approach: Letter or telephone
Deadline(s): None
Write: Richard T. Betts, Trustee
Trustees: R.E. Betts, Richard T. Betts, C.J. Kauffman, M. Marshall.
Employer Identification Number: 256035169

6165
Binswanger Foundation ⌑ ☆
c/o The Binswanger Co.
1635 Market St.
Philadelphia 19103 (215) 448-6000

Donor(s): Binswanger Corp.
Foundation type: Company-sponsored
Financial data (yr. ended 12/31/88): Assets, $1,054,048 (M); gifts received, $102,070; expenditures, $170,993, including $160,886 for 54 grants (high: $55,000; low: $50).
Purpose and activities: Support for Jewish welfare, the United Way, civic affairs, higher education, and cultural programs, including the fine and performing arts and music.
Limitations: Giving primarily in Philadelphia, PA. No grants to individuals.
Application information: Application form not required.
Initial approach: Letter
Deadline(s): None
Write: Frank G. Binswanger, Sr., Chair.
Officers: Frank G. Binswanger, Sr., Chair.; Frank G. Binswanger, Jr., Vice-Chair.; Samuel Levy, Secy.; John K. Binswanger, Treas.
Employer Identification Number: 236296506

6166
Vernon & Doris Bishop Foundation ⌑
1616 Fieldcrest Rd.
Lebanon 17042 (717) 273-1462

Established in 1957 in PA.
Foundation type: Independent
Financial data (yr. ended 12/31/88): Assets, $2,319,812 (M); expenditures, $85,018, including $82,300 for 26 grants (high: $50,000; low: $100).
Purpose and activities: Support for social service and youth agencies, educational institutions, particularly for higher education, and religious organizations.
Types of support: General purposes.
Limitations: Giving primarily in PA.
Application information:
Initial approach: Letter
Deadline(s): None
Write: Vernon Bishop, Trustee
Trustees: Doris Bishop, Vernon Bishop.
Employer Identification Number: 236255835

6167
H. M. Bitner Charitable Trust
One Mellon Bank Ctr., Rm. 3845
Pittsburgh 15258 (412) 234-4695

Established in PA in 1955.
Donor(s): H.M. Bitner,† Evelyn H. Bitner.
Foundation type: Independent
Financial data (yr. ended 12/31/88): Assets, $1,390,274 (M); expenditures, $92,965, including $61,750 for 47 grants (high: $5,000; low: $250; average: $1,000).
Purpose and activities: Giving for higher and other education, performing arts and other cultural programs, hospitals and medical research, and social service agencies.
Types of support: General purposes, operating budgets.
Limitations: Giving primarily in IL, IN, NY, and PA.
Application information: Application guidelines available from the foundation upon request.
Deadline(s): None
Write: Helen Collins
Trustees: Jessie N. Bitner, Evelyn Bitner Pearson, Cynthia Pearson Turich, Mellon Bank (East), N.A.
Employer Identification Number: 256018931

6168
Philo and Sarah Blaisdell Foundation
50 Boylston St.
Bradford 16701
Scholarship application address: Office of Financial Aid, Univ. of Pittsburgh at Bradford, Bradford, PA 16701; Tel.: (814) 362-3801

Trust established in 1950 in PA.
Donor(s): George G. Blaisdell, Zippo Manufacturing Co.
Foundation type: Independent
Financial data (yr. ended 12/31/88): Assets, $1,894,332 (M); expenditures, $174,663, including $155,071 for 7 grants (high: $50,000; low: $1,000) and $2,442 for 5 grants to individuals (high: $1,250; low: $200).
Purpose and activities: Emphasis on youth and child welfare agencies, including a school for retarded children; support also for a university scholarship fund.
Types of support: Scholarship funds.
Limitations: Giving primarily in McKean County, PA.
Application information:
Write: Robert H. Wick, Exec. Secy.
Officer: Robert H. Wick, Exec. Secy.
Trustees: Sarah B. Dorn, Richard McDowell, Harriet B. Wick.
Employer Identification Number: 256035748

6169
Bozzone Family Foundation ⌑ ☆
101 Bayberry Dr.
New Kensington 15068-6701

Established in 1986 in PA.
Donor(s): Robert P. Bozzone.
Foundation type: Independent
Financial data (yr. ended 12/31/88): Assets, $1,389,690 (M); gifts received, $25,000; expenditures, $39,032, including $31,392 for 31 grants (high: $10,000; low: $45).
Purpose and activities: Giving for Catholic organizations, including churches and welfare programs; support also for a community fund.
Limitations: Giving primarily in PA.
Application information: Contributes only to pre-selected organizations. Applications not accepted.
Trustee: Robert P. Bozzone.
Employer Identification Number: 256277066

6170
The Brighter Days Foundation ⌑ ☆
1082 Bower Hill Rd., Suite 1
Pittsburgh 15243

Established in PA in 1986.
Donor(s): Edward M. Ryan.
Foundation type: Independent
Financial data (yr. ended 5/31/88): Assets, $154,607 (M); gifts received, $155,000;

expenditures, $528,186, including $527,290 for 30 grants (high: $127,840; low: $500).
Purpose and activities: Support primarily for higher and other education, including Catholic education; giving also for an economic development society, health associations, and social services.
Limitations: Giving primarily in PA. No grants to individuals.
Application information: Contributes only to pre-selected organizations. Applications not accepted.
Officers: Edward M. Ryan, Pres.; Ann C. Ryan, Secy.-Treas.
Employer Identification Number: 251528676

6171
Bristol Fund, Inc.
P.O. Box 33A
Carversville 18913

Established in 1962 in PA.
Foundation type: Independent
Financial data (yr. ended 12/31/88): Assets, $389,783 (M); gifts received, $119,730; expenditures, $146,148, including $143,965 for 62 grants (high: $32,500; low: $33).
Purpose and activities: Giving primarily for higher and other education; support also for music.
Types of support: General purposes, matching funds, scholarship funds, special projects.
Application information: Contributes only to pre-selected organizations. Applications not accepted.
Officers: Madeleine B. Kuckel, Pres.; Michael W. Bristol, Treas.
Employer Identification Number: 237209712

6172
The Soloman and Sylvia Bronstein Foundation ⌑ ☆
1200 Four Penn Ctr. Plaza
Philadelphia 19103 (215) 569-5571

Established in 1985 in PA.
Donor(s): Solomon Bronstein.†
Foundation type: Independent
Financial data (yr. ended 6/30/89): Assets, $3,631,222 (M); gifts received, $425,000; expenditures, $21,663, including $19,500 for 5 grants (high: $6,000; low: $1,500).
Purpose and activities: Support primarily for Jewish organizations and a health care foundation.
Limitations: Giving primarily in NY and PA.
Application information: Application form not required.
Initial approach: Letter
Deadline(s): None
Write: Bernard Glassman, Esq.
Trustees: Gerald Broker, Marvin Comisky, Rabbi Gerald I. Wolpe.
Employer Identification Number: 222656339

6173
Michael A. Bruder Foundation ⌑
600 Reed Rd.
P.O. Box 600
Broomall 19008 (215) 353-5100

Trust established in 1956 in PA.
Donor(s): M.A. Bruder and Sons, Inc., and others.
Foundation type: Independent
Financial data (yr. ended 12/31/88): Assets, $831,425 (M); gifts received, $12,100; expenditures, $175,299, including $163,880 for 27 grants (high: $43,000; low: $200) and $10,880 for 7 grants to individuals (high: $1,800; low: $900).
Purpose and activities: Emphasis on higher education, including scholarships restricted to children of company employees; grants also for community and welfare funds, Catholic church support, and hospitals.
Types of support: Employee-related scholarships.
Limitations: Giving primarily in areas covered by M.A. Bruder and Sons, Inc.
Application information: Application form not required.
Deadline(s): None
Final notification: Within 2 months of receipt of application
Write: Joseph S. Mirante
Trustees: James I. Bruder, Thomas A. Bruder, Jr., Edward G. Kucker, Andrew B. Young.
Employer Identification Number: 236298481

6174
Caroline Alexander Buck Foundation ☆
1600 Market St., Suite 3600
Philadelphia 19103

Established in 1960.
Donor(s): Caroline A. Churchman.
Foundation type: Independent
Financial data (yr. ended 12/31/88): Assets, $659,851 (M); gifts received, $196,250; expenditures, $130,562, including $113,500 for 75 grants (high: $6,000; low: $1,000).
Purpose and activities: Giving primarily for social services, including programs aiding minorities, the aged, women, children, and the disabled; support also for higher and other education, youth, and hospitals and health associations, including research on cancer and heart disease.
Limitations: Giving primarily in PA, with emphasis on Philadelphia. No grants to individuals.
Application information: Application form required.
Initial approach: Letter
Deadline(s): May and Nov.
Write: J. Pennington Strauss, Trustee
Trustees: Caroline A. Churchman, W. Morgan Churchman, William Machold, Michael Peters, J. Pennington Strauss.
Number of staff: None.
Employer Identification Number: 236257115

6175
Buckingham Mountain Foundation ⌑
3400 Spruce St.
Philadelphia 19104-4283

Established in 1952 in PA.
Foundation type: Independent
Financial data (yr. ended 12/31/88): Assets, $1,076,357 (M); expenditures, $8,427, including $5,000 for 3 grants (high: $2,500; low: $500).
Purpose and activities: Support primarily for higher and secondary education; medical research and education; and libraries.
Application information: Unsolicited applications for funds not encouraged. Application form not required.
Initial approach: Letter
Copies of proposal: 1
Board meeting date(s): June and Dec.
Officers: Mary B. Johnson, Pres.; Jonathan E. Rhoads, Sr., Secy.-Treas.
Directors: George Rhoads, Jonathan Rhoads, Jr.
Number of staff: 1 part-time support.
Employer Identification Number: 236254714

6176
The Buhl Foundation ▼
Four Gateway Ctr., Rm. 1522
Pittsburgh 15222 (412) 566-2711

Trust established in 1927 in PA.
Donor(s): Henry Buhl, Jr.†
Foundation type: Independent
Financial data (yr. ended 06/30/89): Assets, $36,965,038 (M); expenditures, $2,245,946, including $1,859,139 for 50 grants (high: $900,000; low: $750; average: $5,000-$50,000).
Purpose and activities: Emphasis on "developmental or innovative" grants to regional institutions, with special interest in education at all levels and in regional concerns, particularly those related to problems of children and youth.
Types of support: Seed money, special projects, research, continuing support.
Limitations: Giving primarily in southwestern PA, particularly the Pittsburgh area. No support for religious activities or nationally funded organizations. No grants to individuals, or for building or endowment funds, operating budgets, scholarships, fellowships, equipment, land acquisition, annual campaigns, emergency funds, deficit financing, renovation projects, publications, or conferences or seminars (unless grant-related); no loans.
Publications: Annual report, informational brochure (including application guidelines).
Application information: Submit final proposal upon invitation only. Application form not required.
Initial approach: Letter
Copies of proposal: 1
Deadline(s): None
Board meeting date(s): Monthly
Final notification: Approximately 3 months normally
Write: Dr. Doreen E. Boyce, Exec. Dir.
Officers: John G. Frazer, Jr., Pres. and Mgr.; Francis B. Nimick, Jr., V.P. and Mgr.; William H. Rea, V.P. and Mgr.; Katherine E. Schumacher, Secy.; John M. Arthur, Treas. and Mgr.; Doreen E. Boyce, Exec. Dir.
Number of staff: 2 full-time professional; 2 full-time support.
Employer Identification Number: 250378910

6177
Buncher Family Foundation ⌘
5600 Forward Ave.
Pittsburgh 15217 (412) 422-9900

Established in 1974 in PA.
Donor(s): The Buncher Co., Jack G. Buncher.
Foundation type: Independent
Financial data (yr. ended 11/30/89): Assets, $26,459 (M); gifts received, $316,500; expenditures, $400,037, including $398,668 for 73 grants (high: $120,000; low: $16).
Purpose and activities: Grants primarily to Jewish organizations, including Jewish welfare funds.
Limitations: Giving primarily in PA, with emphasis on Pittsburgh. No grants to individuals.
Application information:
Initial approach: Letter
Deadline(s): None
Write: Bernita B. Balter, Secy.-Treas.
Officers: Joanne K. Buncher, Pres.; Bernita B. Balter, Secy.-Treas.
Employer Identification Number: 237366998

6178
Albert M. Burki Foundation ⌘
1901 Liberty Ave.
Pittsburgh 15222-4499

Established in 1981 in PA.
Foundation type: Independent
Financial data (yr. ended 12/31/87): Assets, $340,270 (M); expenditures, $178,083, including $160,500 for 12 grants (high: $53,000; low: $2,500).
Purpose and activities: Support for community development funds and youth organizations.
Types of support: Endowment funds.
Limitations: Giving primarily in PA. No grants to individuals.
Application information: Contributes only to pre-selected organizations. Applications not accepted.
Trustees: Donald E. Hook, Howard J. Hook, Lawrence B. Nieman.
Employer Identification Number: 251402862

6179
Alpin J. and Alpin W. Cameron Memorial Fund ⌘
c/o First Pennsylvania Bank, N.A.
16th and Market Sts.
Philadelphia 19101

Trust established in 1957 in PA.
Donor(s): Alpin W. Cameron,† Alpin J. Cameron.†
Foundation type: Independent
Financial data (yr. ended 09/30/89): Assets, $2,582,594 (M); gifts received, $89,291; expenditures, $178,937, including $159,250 for 77 grants (high: $10,000; low: $500).
Purpose and activities: Emphasis on higher education, cultural programs, and hospitals.
Limitations: Giving primarily in the Philadelphia, PA, area.
Application information:
Write: Gregory D'Angelo, Trust Admin., First Pennsylvania Bank, N.A.
Trustee: First Pennsylvania Bank, N.A.
Employer Identification Number: 236213225

6180
Charles Talbot Campbell Foundation ⌘
c/o Union National Bank of Pittsburgh
P.O. Box 837
Pittsburgh 15230

Trust established in 1975 in PA.
Donor(s): Charles Talbot Campbell.†
Foundation type: Independent
Financial data (yr. ended 12/31/88): Assets, $4,225,000 (M); expenditures, $288,000, including $280,000 for 13 grants (high: $75,000; low: $5,000; average: $20,000).
Purpose and activities: Emphasis on hospitals and ophthalmological research, agencies for the handicapped, and music.
Limitations: Giving primarily in PA. No support for community funds, including United Way. No grants to individuals; no loans.
Application information: Application form not required.
Copies of proposal: 1
Write: William M. Schmidt, V.P.
Trustee: Union National Bank of Pittsburgh.
Employer Identification Number: 251287221

6181
Julius H. Caplan Charity Foundation, Inc. ⌘
14th & Cumberland Sts.
P.O. Box 208
Lebanon 17042 (717) 272-4665

Incorporated in 1944 in NY.
Donor(s): Hyman S. Caplan,† Keystone Weaving Mills, Inc.
Foundation type: Independent
Financial data (yr. ended 12/31/88): Assets, $3,713,193 (M); expenditures, $129,353, including $124,003 for 25 grants (high: $90,000; low: $25).
Purpose and activities: Emphasis on Jewish welfare funds; support also for higher education and hospitals.
Limitations: Giving primarily in PA and NY.
Application information: Application form not required.
Deadline(s): None
Write: Eli Caplan, Dir.
Directors: Eli Caplan, Helen Caplan, Perry Caplan.
Employer Identification Number: 136067379

6182
Gunard Berry Carlson Memorial Foundation, Inc. ⌘
350 Marshallton Rd.
Thorndale 19372 (215) 384-2800

Established in 1957 in PA.
Foundation type: Independent
Financial data (yr. ended 12/31/88): Assets, $1,265,051 (M); expenditures, $59,535, including $44,195 for grants.
Purpose and activities: Support primarily for education, health associations, and social services.
Application information: Application form not required.
Deadline(s): None
Write: Barbara C. Travaglini, Secy.
Officers: Nancy C. Bacharach, Pres.; Frederick C. Travaglini, 1st V.P.; Benjamin Bacharach, 2nd V.P.; Barbara C. Travaglini, Secy.-Treas.
Directors: Rev. Vincent R. Negherbon, A.F. Travaglini.
Employer Identification Number: 236261693

6183
Carnegie Hero Fund Commission
2307 Oliver Bldg.
Pittsburgh 15222-2394 (412) 281-1302

Trust established in 1904 in PA.
Donor(s): Andrew Carnegie.†
Foundation type: Operating
Financial data (yr. ended 12/31/89): Assets, $17,261,029 (M); expenditures, $1,095,432, including $50,000 for 2 grants of $25,000 each and $539,706 for 235 grants to individuals (high: $4,000; low: $600; average: $600-$4,000).
Purpose and activities: A private operating foundation established to recognize, with the award of medals and sums of money, heroism voluntarily performed by civilians within the U.S. and Canada in saving or attempting to save the lives of others; and to grant monetary assistance, including scholarship aid, to persons disabled in these efforts and to the dependents of those who have lost their lives or who have been disabled in such heroic manner.
Types of support: Grants to individuals, student aid, continuing support.
Limitations: Giving limited to the U.S. and Canada.
Publications: Annual report, program policy statement, application guidelines, informational brochure.
Application information: Awards by nomination only. Application form required.
Initial approach: Letter
Copies of proposal: 1
Deadline(s): Within 2 years of the act for nominations
Board meeting date(s): Feb., Apr., June, Sept., Oct., and Dec.
Final notification: Following board meetings
Write: Robert W. Off, Pres.
Officers and Trustees: Robert W. Off, Pres.; Walter F. Rutkowski, V.P. and Secy.; James M. Walton, Treas.; Henry H. Armstrong, F.J. Torrance Baker, E. Bayley Buchanan, A.H. Burchfield III, George S. Ebbert, Jr., John G. Frazer, Jr., T. Herbert Hamilton, Lawrence Wm. Haywiser, Thomas J. Hilliard, Jr., Priscilla J. McCrady, David B. Oliver II, John C. Oliver III, Frank Brooks Robinson, J. Evans Rose, Jr., Arthur M. Scully, Jr., William P. Snyder III, George H. Taber, Walter F. Toerge, Alfred W. Wishart, Jr.
Number of staff: 6 full-time professional; 2 full-time support.
Employer Identification Number: 251062730

6184
E. Rhodes & Leona B. Carpenter Foundation
c/o Joseph A. O'Connor, Jr., Morgan, Lewis & Bockius
2000 One Logan Sq.
Philadelphia 19103
Application address: P.O. Box 58880, Philadelphia, PA 19102-8880

Established in 1975 in VA.
Donor(s): E. Rhodes Carpenter,† Leona B. Carpenter.†
Foundation type: Independent
Financial data (yr. ended 12/31/88): Assets, $80,616,944 (M); gifts received, $1,000,000; expenditures, $2,144,846, including $1,194,951 for 25 grants (high: $500,000; low: $2,000).
Purpose and activities: Main areas of interest include the arts, including the performing arts and museums; education, including graduate theological education; and health.
Limitations: Giving primarily in areas east of the Mississippi River. No support for local church congregations or parishes, private secondary education, or large public charities. No grants to individuals.
Application information:
Initial approach: Letter
Deadline(s): None
Officers: Ann Day, Pres.; Paul Day, Jr., V.P. and Secy.-Treas.
Director: M.H. Reinhart.
Employer Identification Number: 510155772

6185
Carpenter Technology Corporation Foundation ⌑
101 West Bern St.
Reading 19601 (215) 371-2214

Incorporated in 1953 in NJ; re-incorporated in 1981 in DE as the Carpenter Technology Corporation Foundation.
Donor(s): Carpenter Technology Corp.
Foundation type: Company-sponsored
Financial data (yr. ended 09/30/89): Assets, $638,193 (M); gifts received, $300,000; expenditures, $274,166, including $240,035 for 90 grants (high: $89,000; low: $100) and $33,650 for 211 employee matching gifts.
Purpose and activities: Support for community funds, health and welfare, culture and the arts, civic and public affairs, and higher education, including giving toward scholarship funds. Company also has an employee matching gifts program toward colleges and universities.
Types of support: Employee matching gifts, scholarship funds, building funds, general purposes, fellowships, research, special projects, employee-related scholarships.
Limitations: Giving primarily in areas of company operations, especially the Reading, PA, area. No grants to individuals.
Publications: Program policy statement, application guidelines.
Application information: Application form required for scholarships.
Initial approach: Letter
Deadline(s): Dec. of preceding academic year for scholarships
Board meeting date(s): Semiannually
Write: W.J. Pendleton, V.P.
Officers: Paul R. Roedel,* Pres.; H.O. Beaver, Jr.,* Chair.; J.M. McHale, V.P.; W.J. Pendleton, Secy.; John A. Schuler, Treas.
Directors:* T. Beaver, Jr., W.E.C. Dearden, C.R. Garr, A.E. Humphrey, J.L. Jones, E.W. Kay, Frederick C. Langenberg, A.J. Lena, H.R. Sharbaugh, S. James Spitz, Jr., H.W. Walker II.
Employer Identification Number: 232191214

6186
The Carthage Foundation ▼
P.O. Box 268
Pittsburgh 15230 (412) 392-2900

Incorporated in 1964 in PA.
Donor(s): Richard M. Scaife.
Foundation type: Independent
Financial data (yr. ended 12/31/89): Assets, $13,721,863 (M); gifts received, $4,830,689; expenditures, $1,768,436, including $1,411,000 for 22 grants (high: $300,000; low: $15,000; average: $15,000-$450,000).
Purpose and activities: Grants primarily for public policy research, particularly in the areas of government and international affairs.
Types of support: Conferences and seminars, general purposes.
Limitations: No grants to individuals.
Publications: 990-PF.
Application information: Application form not required.
Initial approach: Letter
Copies of proposal: 1
Deadline(s): None
Board meeting date(s): Spring and fall
Final notification: 1 to 3 weeks
Write: Richard M. Larry, Treas.
Officers and Trustees:* Richard M. Scaife,* Chair.; George R. McCullough,* Vice-Chair.; R. Daniel McMichael,* Secy.; Richard M. Larry,* Treas.
Number of staff: 2 part-time professional; 2 part-time support.
Employer Identification Number: 256067979

6187
Louis N. Cassett Foundation ⌑
Two Mellon Bank Ctr., Suite 1804
Philadelphia 19102-2468

Trust established in 1946 in PA.
Donor(s): Louis N. Cassett.†
Foundation type: Independent
Financial data (yr. ended 12/31/88): Assets, $5,523,177 (M); expenditures, $427,616, including $357,600 for 143 grants (high: $55,000; low: $100; average: $3,000).
Purpose and activities: Giving primarily for social service and youth agencies, higher education, hospitals, medical research, and health agencies, including aid to the handicapped; some support also for cultural programs.
Types of support: Annual campaigns, building funds.
Limitations: Giving primarily in the northeastern U.S. No grants to individuals, or for endowment funds.
Application information:
Initial approach: Proposal
Copies of proposal: 1
Deadline(s): None
Board meeting date(s): As required
Write: Joseph Oberndorf, Trustee
Trustees: Albert J. Elias, Carol Gerstley, Joseph Oberndorf.
Number of staff: None.
Employer Identification Number: 236274038

6188
Castelli Charitable Trust ⌑ ☆
c/o Pittsburgh National Bank Trust Dept.
One Oliver Plaza, 29th Fl.
Pittsburgh 15265
Application address: c/o John F. Dent, Exec. Dir., Law & Finance Bldg., Greensburg, PA 15601

Established in 1984 in PA.
Foundation type: Independent
Financial data (yr. ended 06/30/89): Assets, $1,229,403 (M); expenditures, $62,305, including $39,931 for 79 grants to individuals.
Purpose and activities: Awards scholarships for higher education.
Types of support: Student aid.
Limitations: Giving limited to Westmoreland County, PA, residents.
Application information: Application form available from high school guidance counselors. Application form required.
Deadline(s): May 1
Trustee: Pittsburgh National Bank.
Employer Identification Number: 256242226

6189
CertainTeed Corporation Foundation ⌑
P.O. Box 860
Valley Forge 19482 (215) 341-7000

Established in 1955 in PA.
Donor(s): CertainTeed Products Corp.
Foundation type: Company-sponsored
Financial data (yr. ended 12/31/88): Assets, $62,624 (M); gifts received, $300,470; expenditures, $262,685, including $262,625 for 304 grants (high: $50,000; low: $25).
Purpose and activities: Emphasis on higher education through an employee matching gift program, support also for community funds.
Types of support: Employee matching gifts.
Limitations: Giving primarily in Philadelphia, PA. No support for religious organizations, or organizations receiving more than 20% of their funding from the government or the United Way. No grants to individuals.
Application information:
Deadline(s): None
Write: J.A. Gallagher, Secy.
Officers and Directors:* Michel Besson,* Pres.; M. Simmons,* V.P.; J. Gallagher,* Secy.; M. Walsh, Treas.; M. LeComte.
Employer Identification Number: 236242991

6190
The Charitable Fund
19 Vine Ave.
Sharon 16146 (412) 981-5522

Trust established in 1903 in PA.
Donor(s): Frank H. Buhl.†
Foundation type: Independent
Financial data (yr. ended 09/30/89): Assets, $1,797,340 (M); expenditures, $168,326, including $160,230 for 4 grants (high: $158,700; low: $330).
Purpose and activities: Charitable giving for the benefit of local citizens.
Limitations: Giving primarily in Sharon, PA, and vicinity. No grants to individuals, or for building funds.
Publications: Annual report.

Application information: Funds presently committed. Applications not accepted.
Board meeting date(s): Jan., Apr., June, Sept., and Nov.
Write: H.H. Hanson, Treas.
Officers and Trustees:* Carlton E. Hutchison,* Pres.; Ray W. Rowney,* V.P.; George M. Lanier,* Secy.; H.H. Hanson,* Treas.; A.E. Acker, Louis R. Epstein, J.E. Feeney, Leslie E. Spaulding, Mrs. William F. Whitla, G. Leo Winger.
Number of staff: 2 part-time professional.
Employer Identification Number: 237366997

6191
Julius and Ray Charlestein Foundation, Inc.
1710 Romano Dr.
Norristown 19401 (215) 277-3800

Established in 1963.
Donor(s): Premier Dental Products Co., Premier Medical Co.
Foundation type: Company-sponsored
Financial data (yr. ended 06/30/89): Assets, $2,915,664 (M); gifts received, $310,000; expenditures, $194,169, including $187,292 for 89 grants (high: $75,000; low: $10).
Purpose and activities: Giving primarily to Jewish associations, including welfare funds; support also for education and health organizations.
Limitations: Giving primarily in the Philadelphia, PA, area.
Application information:
Write: Morton Charlestein, Pres.
Officers: Morton Charlestein, Pres.; Jerrold A. Frezel, V.P.; Gary Charlestein, Secy.-Treas.
Number of staff: None.
Employer Identification Number: 232310090

6192
CIGNA Foundation ▼
One Liberty Place
1650 Arch St., P.O. Box 7716
Philadelphia 19101-7716 (215) 523-5255
Organizations in the greater Hartford area, write to: James N. Mason, Dir., Civic Affairs, CIGNA Corp., W-A, 900 Cottage Grove Rd., Bloomfield, CT 06002

Incorporated in 1962 in PA; merged with Connecticut General Contributions and Civic Affairs Department in 1982.
Donor(s): CIGNA Corp.
Foundation type: Company-sponsored
Financial data (yr. ended 12/31/89): Assets, $2,172,282 (M); gifts received, $7,244,403; qualifying distributions, $7,932,582, including $6,575,431 for 441 grants (high: $725,850; low: $100; average: $2,000-$100,000), $1,207,151 for employee matching gifts and $150,000 for in-kind gifts.
Purpose and activities: Support for a broad range of programs in education, health and human services, civic affairs, and the arts, with priority placed on public secondary education, higher education for minority students, programs which favorably influence CIGNA's business environment, community economic development, and culture and the arts. Special emphasis on increasing literacy, career education, and minority higher education, programs which contribute to an improved understanding of societal issues significant to business and economic development in Philadelphia, PA, and Hartford, CT.
Types of support: Employee matching gifts, general purposes, annual campaigns, seed money, emergency funds, fellowships, matching funds, operating budgets, scholarship funds, employee-related scholarships, special projects, conferences and seminars.
Limitations: Giving primarily in Hartford, CT, and Philadelphia, PA; and to selected national organizations. No support for religious organizations for religious purposes, political organizations or campaigns, or disease-specific research or treatment organizations. No grants to individuals, or endowment drives, capital campaigns, organizations receiving major support through the United Way or other CIGNA-supported federated funding agencies, or hospital capital improvements and expansions.
Publications: Corporate giving report (including application guidelines), annual report.
Application information: In the greater Hartford area, direct requests to Bloomfield, CT office; other requests go to Philadelphia, PA office. Application form not required.
Initial approach: Letter of 1 or 2 pages
Copies of proposal: 1
Deadline(s): None
Board meeting date(s): Biennially
Final notification: 6 weeks
Write: Arnold W. Wright, Jr., Exec. Dir.
Officers: Barry F. Wiksten, Pres.; Arnold W. Wright, Jr., Exec. Dir.
Directors: James W. Walker, Jr., Chair.; Thomas H. Dooley, Caleb L. Fowler, Donald M. Levinson, G. Robert O'Brien, James G. Stewart, George R. Trumbull.
Number of staff: 6
Employer Identification Number: 236261726

6193
Claneil Foundation, Inc.
630 West Germantown Pike, Suite 400
Plymouth Meeting 19462-1059

Incorporated in 1968 in DE.
Donor(s): Henry S. McNeil,† Langhorne B. Smith.
Foundation type: Independent
Financial data (yr. ended 12/31/89): Assets, $6,853,769 (M); expenditures, $428,904, including $396,800 for 79 grants (high: $75,000; low: $500; average: $500-$75,000).
Purpose and activities: Support largely for arts education, higher and secondary education, cultural programs, conservation, historic preservation, health and social services, and family planning.
Limitations: Giving primarily in PA. No grants to individuals.
Application information: Application form not required.
Initial approach: Proposal
Copies of proposal: 1
Deadline(s): Sept. 30
Board meeting date(s): Oct.
Final notification: Nov.
Write: Dr. Henry A. Jordan, Exec. Dir.
Officers and Directors: Lois F. McNeil, Pres.; Barbara M. Jordan, V.P.; Warrin C. Meyers, V.P.; George M. Brodhead, Secy.; Langhorne B. Smith, Treas.; Henry A. Jordan, Exec. Dir.
Employer Identification Number: 236445450

6194
The Anne L. and George H. Clapp Charitable and Educational Trust ⌘
c/o Mellon Bank, N.A.
One Mellon Bank Ctr.
Pittsburgh 15230 (412) 234-5598

Donor(s): George H. Clapp.†
Foundation type: Independent
Financial data (yr. ended 9/30/88): Assets, $9,221,105 (M); expenditures, $547,476, including $453,500 for 37 grants (high: $30,500; low: $3,000).
Purpose and activities: Giving primarily for education, hospitals, health and social services, cultural programs, a community fund, and youth agencies.
Limitations: Giving primarily in the Pittsburgh, PA, area.
Application information:
Initial approach: Letter; application form provided after initial contact
Deadline(s): None
Write: William B. Outy, V.P., Mellon Bank, N.A.
Trustees: William E. Collins, Katherine Clapp Galbraith, Mellon Bank, N.A.
Employer Identification Number: 256018976

6195
Charles S. & Mary Coen Family Foundation ⌘
1100 West Chestnut St.
Washington 15301

Established in 1959 in PA.
Donor(s): C.S. Coen,† Mary Coen,† Charles R. Coen, C.S. Coen Land Co.
Foundation type: Independent
Financial data (yr. ended 2/28/87): Assets, $4,023,313 (M); gifts received, $360,000; expenditures, $206,038, including $194,675 for 53 grants (high: $55,000; low: $20).
Purpose and activities: Giving primarily for health associations, hospitals, and social service and youth agencies; some support also for higher education.
Limitations: Giving primarily in the Washington, PA, and the St. Mary's, WV, areas. No grants to individuals.
Trustees: Carlton B. Coen, Charles R. Coen, Earl Coen.
Employer Identification Number: 256033877

6196
Ethel D. Colket Foundation ⌘
c/o Provident National Bank
1632 Chestnut St.
Philadelphia 19103

Established in 1964 in PA.
Foundation type: Independent
Financial data (yr. ended 08/31/89): Assets, $1,790,448 (M); expenditures, $74,455, including $62,500 for 13 grants (high: $12,500; low: $1,000).

Purpose and activities: Support primarily for hospitals; giving also for opera, ballet, and other musical activities; contributions to churches and other religious, scientific, literary or educational activities.
Limitations: Giving primarily in the Delaware Valley, PA, area.
Application information:
Initial approach: Letter
Deadline(s): None
Trustees: Ruth Colket, Tristram Colket, Jr., Provident National Bank.
Employer Identification Number: 236292917

6197
Connelly Foundation ¤
9300 Ashton Rd.
Philadelphia 19136 (215) 698-5203

Incorporated in 1955 in PA.
Donor(s): John F. Connelly,† Josephine C. Connelly.
Foundation type: Independent
Financial data (yr. ended 12/31/88): Assets, $196,355,181 (M); expenditures, $8,659,045, including $8,500,089 for 298 grants (high: $1,151,250; low: $100; average: $100-$5,000).
Purpose and activities: Giving to higher education; Christian religious institutions, including churches, schools and colleges, and welfare programs; hospitals; and social services.
Limitations: Giving primarily in the Philadelphia, PA, area. No grants to individuals, or for endowment funds or research; no loans.
Publications: 990-PF.
Application information: Application form not required.
Initial approach: Letter
Copies of proposal: 1
Deadline(s): Submit proposal preferably early in the year
Board meeting date(s): Feb., June, Sept. or Oct., and Dec.
Final notification: 6 to 9 months after receiving proposal
Officers and Trustees:* Josephine C. Connelly,* Vice-Chair.; Chester C. Hilinski,* V.P.; Josephine C. Mandeville,* V.P.; Christine Connelly, Danielle Connelly, John F. Connelly, Jr., Thomas S. Connelly, Judith Delouvrier, Philippe Delouvrier, Owen A. Mandeville, Jr., Emily Riley.
Number of staff: 3
Employer Identification Number: 236296825

6198
Consolidated Natural Gas Company Foundation ▼
c/o CNG Tower
625 Liberty Ave.
Pittsburgh 15222-3199 (412) 227-1185

Established about 1984 in PA.
Donor(s): Consolidated Natural Gas Co.
Foundation type: Company-sponsored
Financial data (yr. ended 12/31/88): Assets, $4,421,140 (M); gifts received, $3,250,000; expenditures, $3,671,148, including $3,405,766 for 628 grants (high: $100,000) and $159,988 for employee matching gifts.
Purpose and activities: Support for human services, community funds and development, education, and culture and the arts.
Types of support: Employee matching gifts, operating budgets, matching funds, annual campaigns, building funds, capital campaigns, conferences and seminars, continuing support, equipment, general purposes, matching funds, operating budgets, renovation projects, special projects.
Limitations: Giving primarily in PA, OH, WV, NY, LA, OK, VA, and areas where the company has business interests. No support for fraternal, political, or labor organizations, or organizations for strictly sectarian purposes. No grants to individuals, or for operating funds of United Way-supported organizations, fundraising activities, or courtesy advertising.
Publications: Multi-year report, informational brochure (including application guidelines).
Application information: Application form not required.
Initial approach: Letter
Copies of proposal: 1
Deadline(s): Sept. 1 for support renewal requests
Board meeting date(s): Varies
Write: Ray N. Ivey, V.P. and Exec. Dir.
Officers and Directors:* D.E. Weatherwax,* Pres.; Ray N. Ivey,* V.P. and Exec. Dir.; S.M. Banda,* Secy. and Mgr.; R.J. Bean, Jr., W.F. Fritsche, Jr., J.B. Hoey, D.P. Hunt, R.R. Gifford, L.J. Timms, Jr.
Trustee: Mellon Bank, N.A.
Number of staff: 3 full-time professional.
Employer Identification Number: 136077762

6199
Conston Foundation ¤
3250 South 76th St.
Philadelphia 19153

Established in 1959.
Donor(s): Conston, Inc.
Foundation type: Company-sponsored
Financial data (yr. ended 12/31/88): Assets, $1,544,492 (M); qualifying distributions, $71,918, including $71,852 for 37 grants (high: $16,000; low: $100).
Purpose and activities: Grants largely for Jewish welfare funds, a community fund, and higher and other education.
Limitations: Giving primarily in Philadelphia, PA.
Officer: Charles Conston, Mgr.
Employer Identification Number: 236297587

6200
Harry Cook Foundation ¤
1210 Ricewynne Rd.
Wyncote 19095

Foundation type: Independent
Financial data (yr. ended 11/30/88): Assets, $1,120,195 (M); expenditures, $90,999, including $88,770 for 7 grants (high: $70,000; low: $1,000).
Purpose and activities: Giving primarily for health associations and Jewish welfare funds.
Types of support: General purposes.
Limitations: Giving primarily in PA.
Officers: Herbert Cook, Pres.; Rose Small, Secy.; Seymour Saslow, Treas.
Trustee: D.W. Niesenbaum.
Employer Identification Number: 236439332

6201
Copernicus Society of America ¤
1950 Pennsylvania Ave.
P.O. Box 385
Ft. Washington 19034 (215) 628-3632

Established in 1972 in PA.
Donor(s): Edward J. Piszek, Sr.
Foundation type: Independent
Financial data (yr. ended 6/30/87): Assets, $6,045,225 (M); gifts received, $5,000; expenditures, $466,150, including $361,151 for 16 grants.
Purpose and activities: Grants largely for cultural programs and historic preservation.
Types of support: Continuing support, endowment funds, publications, conferences and seminars.
Limitations: No grants to individuals, or for special projects, operating budgets, annual campaigns, seed money, emergency funds, deficit financing, building funds, equipment and materials, land acquisition, matching gifts, scholarships, fellowships, or research; no loans.
Publications: Program policy statement, application guidelines.
Application information: Application form not required.
Initial approach: Proposal
Copies of proposal: 1
Deadline(s): None
Board meeting date(s): Monthly
Final notification: 5 to 6 weeks
Write: P. Erik Nelson, Exec. Dir.
Officers: Edward J. Piszek, Sr.,* Chair. and Pres.; Helen P. Nelson,* V.P. and Secy.; Francis Keenan, V.P.; Edward J. Piszek, Jr.,* V.P.; George Piszek,* V.P.; William P. Piszek,* V.P.; Anne P. Reitenbaugh,* V.P.; Olga P. Piszek,* Treas.; P. Erik Nelson, Exec. Dir.
Directors:* James Draper, Bernard J. McLafferty, Harold B. Montgomery.
Number of staff: 1 full-time professional; 3 part-time support.
Employer Identification Number: 237184731

6202
Earle M. Craig and Margaret Peters Craig Trust ¤
c/o Mellon Bank, N.A.
P.O. Box 185
Pittsburgh 15230 (412) 234-5784

Trust established in 1953 in PA.
Donor(s): Earle M. Craig,† Margaret Peters Craig.†
Foundation type: Independent
Financial data (yr. ended 12/31/88): Assets, $1,279,723 (M); gifts received, $5,000; expenditures, $999,732, including $983,000 for 249 grants (high: $100,000; low: $1,000; average: $1,000-$20,000).
Purpose and activities: Giving largely for higher education, private secondary schools, hospitals, Protestant churches and religious organizations, the arts, public policy research, and social service agencies.

Types of support: Operating budgets, continuing support, annual campaigns, seed money, emergency funds, building funds, equipment, land acquisition, endowment funds, research, publications, conferences and seminars.
Limitations: Giving primarily in PA; support also in TX, NY, and New England, including ME. No grants to individuals, or for deficit financing, matching gifts, scholarships, fellowships, or demonstration projects; no loans.
Application information: Family directs distribution of funds. Applications not accepted.
Board meeting date(s): As required
Write: Barbara K. Robinson, Asst. V.P., Mellon Bank, N.A.
Trustee: Mellon Bank, N.A.
Number of staff: None.
Employer Identification Number: 256018660

6203
Craig-Dalsimer Fund ¤ ☆
Packard Bldg., 12th Fl.
Philadelphia 19102

Established in 1987 in PA.
Donor(s): Janet Craig Dalsimer.†
Foundation type: Independent
Financial data (yr. ended 2/28/89): Assets, $2,069,658 (M); gifts received, $2,110,597; expenditures, $95,554, including $92,000 for 1 grant.
Purpose and activities: Giving to a university for the study of adolescent medicine.
Limitations: Giving primarily in Philadelphia, PA.
Application information:
Deadline(s): None
Trustees: Anna-Marie Chirico, Lida Freeman, David J. Kaufman.
Employer Identification Number: 236875197

6204
E. R. Crawford Estate ¤
Trust Fund "A", P.O. Box 487
McKeesport 15134

Trust established in 1936 in PA.
Donor(s): E.R. Crawford.†
Foundation type: Independent
Financial data (yr. ended 12/31/88): Assets, $5,430,167 (M); expenditures, $483,107, including $405,626 for 110 grants (high: $40,000; low: $500) and $30,559 for 31 grants to individuals (high: $1,440; low: $264).
Purpose and activities: Giving for hospitals, a library, higher education, Protestant church support, youth agencies, and community funds; scholarship aid to McKeesport Area High School and Duquesne High School seniors to attend the University of Pittsburgh or Pennsylvania State University, McKeesport Campus; grants to indigent individuals are limited to former employees of McKeesport Tin Plate Co. who meet income requirements and are not awarded to others.
Types of support: Operating budgets, scholarship funds, grants to individuals.
Limitations: Giving primarily in PA, with emphasis on Allegheny County. No grants to individuals (except former employees of the McKeesport Tin Plate Co.).
Application information: Application form required for needy individuals.
Initial approach: Proposal
Deadline(s): None
Write: Francis E. Neish, Jr., Trustee
Trustees: William O. Hunter, Frank J. Kelly, Francis E. Neish, Jr., George F. Young, Jr.
Number of staff: 4
Employer Identification Number: 256031554

6205
The Crels Foundation
P.O. Box 275
New Holland 17557 (717) 354-7901

Trust established in 1953 in PA.
Donor(s): Edwin B. Nolt.
Foundation type: Independent
Financial data (yr. ended 12/31/89): Assets, $4,311,261 (M); gifts received, $5,000; expenditures, $212,015, including $202,000 for 47 grants (high: $37,500; low: $1,000; average: $1,000-$37,500).
Purpose and activities: Support for hospitals, nursing homes, Mennonite-related religious associations, and parochial elementary education.
Types of support: General purposes, building funds, equipment, operating budgets.
Limitations: Giving primarily in PA, particularly the Lancaster County area. No grants to individuals, or for endowment funds, research programs, scholarships, fellowships, continuing support, annual campaigns, seed money, emergency funds, land acquisition, renovation projects, publications, conferences, matching gifts, or special projects; no loans.
Application information: Applications not encouraged. Application form not required.
Initial approach: Letter
Copies of proposal: 1
Deadline(s): Submit proposal preferably in Sept.
Board meeting date(s): Oct. and as required
Write: George C. Delp, Chair.
Officers and Trustees:* George C. Delp,* Chair.; Clarence J. Nelson,* Secy.; Eugene N. Burkholder, Kenneth N. Burkholder, John H. Frey, Edwin B. Nolt, Katie B. Nolt.
Number of staff: None.
Employer Identification Number: 236243577

6206
The Crossroads Foundation ¤
1082 Bower Hill Rd., Suite 1
Pittsburgh 15243

Established in 1985 in PA.
Donor(s): The Brighter Days Foundation, Edward M. Ryan.
Foundation type: Independent
Financial data (yr. ended 11/30/88): Assets, $162,589 (M); gifts received, $272,000; expenditures, $142,595, including $142,175 for 14 grants (high: $75,000; low: $1,000).
Purpose and activities: Support primarily for Catholic churches and welfare organizations.
Limitations: Giving primarily in Pittsburgh, PA. No grants to individuals.
Application information: Contributes only to pre-selected organizations. Applications not accepted.
Officers: Edward M. Ryan, Pres.; Ann C. Ryan, Secy.-Treas.
Employer Identification Number: 251513510

6207
Cyclops Foundation
650 Washington Rd.
Pittsburgh 15228 (412) 343-4000

Trust established in 1953 in PA.
Donor(s): Cyclops Corp.
Foundation type: Company-sponsored
Financial data (yr. ended 12/31/89): Assets, $180,555 (M); gifts received, $300,000; expenditures, $282,824, including $262,636 for 56 grants (high: $50,000; low: $500) and $19,910 for employee matching gifts.
Purpose and activities: Grants primarily for community funds and development, higher education, health services and hospitals, youth and child welfare, the environment, and cultural organizations located in communities where the company is a significant employer.
Types of support: Annual campaigns, seed money, building funds, equipment, land acquisition, employee matching gifts, capital campaigns, scholarship funds.
Limitations: Giving primarily in areas of company operations in PA and OH. No grants to individuals, or for endowment funds, research, fellowships, challenge grants, special projects, deficit financing, operating budgets, continuing support, emergency funds, publications, or conferences; no loans.
Application information: Application form not required.
Initial approach: Letter
Copies of proposal: 1
Deadline(s): None
Final notification: 1 to 2 months
Write: Susan R. Knapp, Mgr.-Cash & Banking
Trustees: Joseph J. Nowak, James F. Will.
Number of staff: None.
Employer Identification Number: 256067354

6208
Debemac Foundation ¤
c/o Drinker Biddle & Reath
1345 Chestnut St.
Philadelphia 19107-3426

Established in 1958 in PA.
Donor(s): Lewis H. Van Dusen, Jr., Maria P.W. Van Dusen, Marian A. Boyer.
Foundation type: Independent
Financial data (yr. ended 9/30/87): Assets, $260,762 (M); gifts received, $191,497; expenditures, $868,918, including $864,045 for 27 grants (high: $425,000; low: $20).
Purpose and activities: Support primarily for a science museum and planetarium and a hospital.
Application information: Contributes only to pre-selected organizations. Applications not accepted.
Officers: John E. Littleton, Pres.; John N. Childs, Jr., V.P.; Henry S. Robinson, Secy.; Robert J. Harbison, Treas.
Trustees: John C. Garner, Daniel R. Ross, Lewis H. Van Dusen, Jr.
Employer Identification Number: 236222789

6209
DeFrees Family Foundation, Inc.
419 Third Ave.
P.O. Box 708
Warren 16365 (814) 723-8150

Established in 1978 in PA.
Donor(s): Joseph H. DeFrees,† members of the DeFrees family.
Foundation type: Independent
Financial data (yr. ended 12/31/89): Assets, $3,471,442 (M); expenditures, $130,217, including $120,900 for 20 grants (high: $35,000; low: $500).
Purpose and activities: Giving primarily for education, particularly higher education.
Types of support: Special projects, research, publications, scholarship funds.
Limitations: Giving primarily in the Warren, PA, area. No support for relief projects. No grants to individuals; no loans.
Publications: Application guidelines.
Application information: Application form not required.
Initial approach: Proposal
Deadline(s): Mar. 1, July 1, and Oct. 1
Board meeting date(s): Apr., Aug., and Nov.
Write: Harold A. Johnson, Pres.
Officers and Directors:* Harold A. Johnson,* Pres. and Treas.; Barbara B. DeFrees,* V.P.; Charles W.S. DeFrees,* Secy.
Number of staff: None.
Employer Identification Number: 251320042

6210
Arthur S. DeMoss Foundation ▼
St. Davids Ctr. A 300
St. Davids 19087 (215) 254-5500
Financial office where 990-PF is filed:
Chattanooga, TN

Incorporated in PA in 1955 as the National Liberty Foundation of Valley Forge, Inc.
Donor(s): Arthur S. DeMoss.†
Foundation type: Independent
Financial data (yr. ended 12/31/87): Assets, $323,687,337 (M); gifts received, $82,505; expenditures, $20,477,650, including $5,916,295 for 59 grants (high: $2,174,857; low: $1,000) and $9,964,387 for 6 foundation-administered programs.
Purpose and activities: Support primarily for operating programs initiated and managed by the foundation that are evangelistic and discipling in nature in the U.S. and other countries; some grants to support certain activities of organizations which have these same goals.
Limitations: No support for local churches, denominational agencies and/or schools. No grants to individuals.
Application information:
Initial approach: Brief proposal of not more than 2 pages
Deadline(s): Submit proposal between Jan. 1 and Mar. 31, or between July 1 and Sept. 30
Board meeting date(s): Monthly
Final notification: 90 to 120 days
Officers and Directors: Nancy DeMoss, Chair. and C.E.O.; Robert G. DeMoss, Pres.; Theodore G. DeMoss, Secy.-Treas.; Charlotte A. DeMoss, Deborah L. DeMoss, Nancy L. DeMoss, R. Mark DeMoss.
Number of staff: 11 full-time professional; 1 part-time professional; 6 full-time support; 10 part-time support.
Employer Identification Number: 236404136

6211
Dentsply International Foundation ⌑
570 West College Ave.
York 17405

Established in 1955 in PA.
Donor(s): Dentsply International, Inc.
Foundation type: Company-sponsored
Financial data (yr. ended 12/31/87): Assets, $476,701 (M); gifts received, $200,000; expenditures, $151,690, including $151,225 for 51 grants (high: $37,500; low: $200).
Purpose and activities: Support primarily for higher education, including dental education, health and social services, and community funds.
Types of support: Building funds, equipment, scholarship funds.
Application information: Application form not required.
Deadline(s): None
Write: Marcus K. Dixon, Trustee
Trustees: John A. Behrmann, Burton C. Borgelt, Marcus K. Dixon, Leslie A. Jones.
Employer Identification Number: 236297307

6212
Dietrich American Foundation
1811 Chestnut St., Suite 304
Philadelphia 19103 (215) 988-0050

Established in 1963 in DE.
Foundation type: Operating
Financial data (yr. ended 12/31/89): Assets, $14,395,409 (M); expenditures, $661,524, including $510,600 for 9 grants (high: $250,000; low: $100).
Purpose and activities: Support primarily for the arts, including historic preservation and museums.
Types of support: Operating budgets.
Application information: Application form not required.
Initial approach: Letter
Copies of proposal: 1
Deadline(s): None
Board meeting date(s): Jan.
Write: H. Richard Dietrich, Jr., Pres.
Officers: H. Richard Dietrich, Jr., Pres.; Lowell S. Thomas, Jr., Secy.; Frederic C. Barth, Treas.
Number of staff: 2 part-time professional.
Employer Identification Number: 516017453

6213
The Dietrich Foundation, Inc.
1811 Chestnut St., Suite 304
Philadelphia 19103 (215) 988-0050

Incorporated in 1953 in DE.
Donor(s): Members of the Dietrich family, Dietrich American Foundation.
Foundation type: Independent
Financial data (yr. ended 12/31/89): Assets, $4,915,495 (M); gifts received, $250,000; expenditures, $453,793, including $375,000 for 24 grants (high: $60,000; low: $500; average: $15,000).
Purpose and activities: Grants primarily for museums, conservation, music, and visual, performing, and community arts.
Types of support: Continuing support, operating budgets, special projects, publications.
Limitations: Giving primarily in PA. No grants to individuals.
Application information: Application form not required.
Initial approach: Letter
Copies of proposal: 1
Board meeting date(s): Usually in Jan.
Write: Daniel W. Dietrich II, Pres.
Officers and Directors:* Daniel W. Dietrich II,* Pres. and Treas.; Joseph G.J. Connolly,* Secy.
Number of staff: 1
Employer Identification Number: 236255134

6214
William B. Dietrich Foundation
(Formerly The Dietrich Foundation, Inc.)
1811 Chestnut St., Suite 304
Philadelphia 19103 (215) 988-0050

Incorporated in 1936 in DE.
Donor(s): Daniel W. Dietrich Foundation, Inc., Henry D. Dietrich,† Dietrich American Foundation.
Foundation type: Independent
Financial data (yr. ended 12/31/89): Assets, $7,092,481 (M); gifts received, $250,000; expenditures, $590,745, including $518,782 for 11 grants (high: $300,000; low: $500; average: $15,000).
Purpose and activities: Grants largely for conservation, higher, secondary, and other education, museums, local historic restoration programs, AIDS programs, and community funds.
Types of support: Research, operating budgets, special projects, building funds, capital campaigns, matching funds.
Limitations: Giving primarily in PA. No grants to individuals.
Application information: Application form not required.
Initial approach: Letter
Copies of proposal: 1
Board meeting date(s): Jan., Apr., July, and Oct.
Write: William B. Dietrich, Pres.
Officers and Directors:* William B. Dietrich,* Pres. and Treas.; Frank G. Cooper,* Secy.; Frederic C. Barth.
Number of staff: 1
Employer Identification Number: 231515616

6215
Dolfinger-McMahon Foundation
One Franklin Plaza, 15th Fl.
Philadelphia 19102 (215) 854-6318

Trust established in 1957 in PA, and originally comprised of four separate trusts: T/W of Henry Dolfinger as modified by will of Mary McMahon; 1935 D/T of Henry Dolfinger as modified by will of Caroline D. McMahon; Residuary T/W of Caroline D. McMahon; Dolfinger-McMahon Trust for Greater Philadelphia. In 1986 the 1935 D/T of H. Dolfinger was merged with the residuary T/W of C. McMahon.

Donor(s): Caroline D. McMahon,† Mary M. McMahon.†
Foundation type: Independent
Financial data (yr. ended 09/30/89): Assets, $10,718,607 (M); expenditures, $602,301, including $465,528 for 73 grants (high: $15,000; low: $1,000).
Purpose and activities: Emphasis on experimental, demonstration, or "seed money" projects in race relations, aid to the handicapped, higher and secondary education, social and urban programs, church programs, and health agencies. Beginning in 1981, the foundation has given increased consideration to true emergency situations. Grants limited to $20,000 in any one year to a single project or program.
Types of support: Operating budgets, seed money, emergency funds, matching funds, special projects, publications, conferences and seminars, deficit financing, scholarship funds, loans.
Limitations: Giving limited to the greater Philadelphia, PA, area. No support for medical or scientific research or for special interest advocacy through legislative lobbying or solicitation of government agencies. No grants to individuals; no support for medical or scientific research or for special interest advocacy through legislative lobbying or solicitation of government agencies, or for endowment funds, physical facilities, renovations or building repairs, building funds, scholarships, or fellowships.
Publications: Annual report (including application guidelines), application guidelines.
Application information: Application form not required.
Initial approach: Proposal
Copies of proposal: 2
Deadline(s): Submit proposal preferably in Mar. or Sept.; must actually be received on or before Apr. 1 or Oct. 1 (or the preceding Friday if the 1st falls on a weekend)
Board meeting date(s): Apr., Oct., and as required
Final notification: 1 week to 10 days following semiannual meeting
Write: Joyce E. Robbins, Exec. Secy.
Officer: Joyce E. Robbins, Exec. Secy.
Trustees: Martin A. Heckscher, Roland Morris.
Number of staff: None.

6216
Mary J. Donnelly Foundation
2510 Centre City Tower
Pittsburgh 15222 (412) 471-5828

Trust established in 1951 in PA.
Donor(s): Mary J. Donnelly.†
Foundation type: Independent
Financial data (yr. ended 6/30/89): Assets, $2,540,693 (M); expenditures, $268,702, including $242,500 for 26 grants (high: $100,000; low: $1,000; average: $10,170).
Purpose and activities: Support for secondary and higher education, the handicapped, and Roman Catholic associations and welfare funds.
Types of support: Annual campaigns, building funds, capital campaigns, general purposes, special projects.
Limitations: Giving primarily in PA. No grants to individuals, or for endowment funds or matching gifts; no loans.
Application information: Application form not required.
Initial approach: Letter
Copies of proposal: 3
Deadline(s): None
Board meeting date(s): Dec. and June
Write: Thomas J. Donnelly, Trustee
Trustees: Thomas J. Donnelly, Ruth D. Egler, C. Holmes Wolfe.
Number of staff: None.
Employer Identification Number: 256037469

6217
The Douty Foundation
(also known as The Alfred and Mary Douty Foundation)
P.O. Box 540
Plymouth Meeting 19462 (215) 828-8145

Established in 1968 in PA.
Donor(s): Alfred Douty,† Mary M. Douty.†
Foundation type: Independent
Financial data (yr. ended 12/31/89): Assets, $3,130,300 (M); expenditures, $150,000, including $116,795 for 57 grants (high: $4,000; low: $595; average: $1,000-$5,000).
Purpose and activities: Emphasis on projects in the fields of elementary and other education, youth, and community welfare, with special emphasis on services to disadvantaged people.
Types of support: Operating budgets, general purposes, special projects, seed money.
Limitations: Giving primarily in the greater Philadelphia, PA, area, with preference given to Montgomery and Philadelphia counties. No support for religious or political purposes. No grants to individuals, or for matching gifts or agency promotion, such as marketing, development, publication of annual reports or sponsorship of fundraising events; generally no support for capital projects or endowments; no loans.
Publications: Annual report (including application guidelines).
Application information: Submit one application per calendar year except under special circumstances; organizations with budgets greater than $2 million are discouraged from applying. Application form required.
Initial approach: Proposal
Copies of proposal: 2
Deadline(s): Feb. 15, Apr. 15, and Oct. 15
Board meeting date(s): Mar., May, and Nov.
Final notification: 2 months
Write: Judith L. Bardes, Exec. Dir.
Officers and Trustees:* Judith L. Bardes,* Exec. Dir.; Richard G. Alexander, Norma Elias, Thomas B. Harvey, Carrolle Perry.
Number of staff: 1
Employer Identification Number: 236463709

6218
The Downs Foundation ⌑
P.O. Box 475
Davisville Rd. and Turnpike Dr.
Willow Grove 19090 (215) 672-1100

Trust established in 1960 in PA.
Donor(s): George T. Downs.
Foundation type: Independent
Financial data (yr. ended 12/31/89): Assets, $1,385,469 (M); expenditures, $86,728, including $79,025 for 44 grants (high: $12,000; low: $100).
Purpose and activities: Support primarily for secondary and higher education, including scholarships for children of Downs Carpet Co. employees, hospitals and health associations, social services, and religious organizations.
Types of support: Research, building funds, capital campaigns, annual campaigns, general purposes, operating budgets, employee-related scholarships.
Limitations: Giving primarily in the Philadelphia, PA, area.
Application information: Application form not required.
Initial approach: Letter
Copies of proposal: 1
Deadline(s): Submit proposal preferably between July and Sept.
Board meeting date(s): Sept. and Dec.
Write: T. George Downs, Trustee
Trustees: Joan Downs Brehm, George T. Downs III, T. George Downs.
Employer Identification Number: 236257328

6219
The Eberly Foundation
P.O. Box 2023
Uniontown 15401-0526 (412) 437-7557

Established in 1963 in PA.
Foundation type: Independent
Financial data (yr. ended 12/31/89): Assets, $6,399,892 (M); gifts received, $3,033,563; expenditures, $471,473, including $380,363 for 11 grants (high: $238,038; low: $300).
Purpose and activities: Support primarily for community development, elementary education, health organizations, the performing arts, and historic preservation.
Limitations: Giving primarily in PA, WV, and OK.
Application information: Application form not required.
Initial approach: Letter
Deadline(s): None
Write: Robert E. Eberly, Pres.
Officers: Robert E. Eberly, Pres. and Treas.; Patricia Hillman Miller, Secy.
Trustees: Carolyn E. Blaney, Ruth Ann Carter, Jill Drost, Robert E. Eberly, Jr., Margaret E. George, Jacob D. Moore.
Employer Identification Number: 237070246

6220
Ralph M. and Ella M. Eccles Foundation ⌑
First Seneca Bank
248 Seneca St.
Oil City 16301 (814) 677-5085

Trust established in 1972 in PA.
Foundation type: Independent
Financial data (yr. ended 12/31/86): Assets, $2,173,371 (M); expenditures, $148,818, including $93,766 for 8 grants (high: $48,148; low: $205; average: $5,000-$10,000).
Purpose and activities: Giving for operating expenses of Eccles-Lesher Memorial Library and for other community programs and projects.

Types of support: General purposes, operating budgets, continuing support, annual campaigns, seed money, emergency funds, deficit financing, building funds, equipment, land acquisition.
Limitations: Giving limited to Union School District of Clarion County, PA. No grants to individuals, or for endowment funds, special projects, research, publications, conferences, scholarships, fellowships, or matching gifts; no loans.
Publications: Application guidelines, 990-PF.
Application information: Application form required.
Initial approach: Letter
Copies of proposal: 3
Deadline(s): Submit proposal preferably in Apr. or Nov.; no set deadline
Board meeting date(s): May and Dec.
Final notification: 2 months
Write: Stephen P. Kosak, Consultant
Trustee: First Seneca Bank.
Number of staff: 1 full-time professional; 1 part-time support.
Employer Identification Number: 237261807

6221
Eden Hall Foundation ▼ ⌑
Pittsburgh Office and Research Park
5500 Corporate Dr., Suite 210
Pittsburgh 15237

1984.
Donor(s): Eden Hall Farm.
Foundation type: Independent
Financial data (yr. ended 12/31/88): Assets, $78,297,656 (M); expenditures, $3,773,921, including $3,552,000 for 71 grants (high: $300,000; low: $2,000; average: $5,000-$100,000).
Purpose and activities: Support for higher education, the prevention and alleviation of sickness and disease, the improvement of conditions of the poor and needy, and the advancement of good morals.
Types of support: Capital campaigns, scholarship funds, endowment funds, research.
Limitations: Giving limited to western PA. No support for private foundations. No grants to individuals, or for operating budgets, deficit financing, or general fundraising campaigns.
Publications: Application guidelines.
Application information: Application form not required.
Initial approach: Letter
Board meeting date(s): Quarterly
Write: Arthur H. Andersen, Secy.
Officers: Richard F. Herr, Pres.; George R. Shifler, V.P. and Treas.; Arthur H. Andersen, Secy.; Ralph D. McCracken, Gen. Mgr.
Number of staff: 2
Employer Identification Number: 251384468

6222
Abraham & Rose Ellis Foundation ⌑
c/o The Glenmede Trust Co.
229 South 18th St.
Philadelphia 19103-4252

Established in 1952 in PA.
Foundation type: Independent
Financial data (yr. ended 12/31/87): Assets, $796,089 (M); gifts received, $100; expenditures, $120,892, including $12,050 for 13 grants (high: $100,000; low: $250).
Purpose and activities: Support primarily for a university; support also for Jewish welfare.
Limitations: Giving primarily in Philadelphia, PA.
Application information: Contributes only to pre-selected organizations. Application form not required.
Officers: Michael D. Ellis, M.D., Pres.; Sylvia M. Ellis, V.P.; Ann Lieberman, Secy.
Employer Identification Number: 237442471

6223
Charles E. Ellis Grant and Scholarship Fund ▼
c/o Educational Advisory Services International
1101 Market, Suite 2850
Philadelphia 19107 (215) 928-0900

Established in 1981 in PA.
Donor(s): Charles E. Ellis.†
Foundation type: Independent
Financial data (yr. ended 2/28/89): Assets, $19,693,849 (M); expenditures, $1,278,284, including $1,061,305 for grants to individuals.
Purpose and activities: Grants for high school scholarships given to functionally orphaned female high school students who are residents of Philadelphia County, PA.
Types of support: Student aid.
Limitations: Giving limited to Philadelphia County, PA.
Publications: Application guidelines, informational brochure, program policy statement.
Application information: Funds paid directly to the educational institution the individual attends. Application form required.
Initial approach: Letter
Deadline(s): Mar. 1, Apr. 1, June 1, and Oct. 1
Board meeting date(s): Apr., May, Aug., and Nov.
Final notification: Two weeks after each board meeting
Trustee: Provident National Bank.
Number of staff: None.
Employer Identification Number: 236725618

6224
The Emergency Aid of Pennsylvania Foundation, Inc. ☆
c/o The Baldwin School
Montgomery Ave. & Morris Rd., Rm. 215
Bryn Mawr 19010 (215) 527-1712

Established in 1984 in PA.
Foundation type: Independent
Financial data (yr. ended 06/30/89): Assets, $1,831,728 (M); gifts received, $51,864; expenditures, $142,479, including $88,610 for grants (average: $500-$2,000).
Purpose and activities: Giving primarily for welfare, including children and youth, the elderly, the handicapped, and emergency assistance; support also for recreation, higher education, women's causes, and historic preservation.
Types of support: Emergency funds, renovation projects, special projects.
Limitations: Giving primarily in Philadelphia, PA.
Publications: Annual report, newsletter, informational brochure.
Application information: Application form required.
Initial approach: Letter
Copies of proposal: 1
Deadline(s): None
Board meeting date(s): 3rd Monday in Jan., Mar., May, Sept., and Nov.
Officers and Directors:* Mrs. Thomas F. Quinn,* Chair.; Mrs. William Thomas,* Vice-Chair.; Mrs. Daniel J. Haley, Jr.,* Secy.; Mrs. Daniel P. McDevitt, Treas. and Member, Distribution Committee; and 12 other directors.
Distribution Committee: Mrs. Thomas Bevan, Co-Chair.; Mrs. Lee H. Heist, Jr., Co-Chair.; and 8 other members.
Trustee: Provident National Bank.
Number of staff: 1 full-time support; 1 part-time support.
Employer Identification Number: 232321913

6225
The Emporium Foundation, Inc. ⌑
c/o Bucktail Bank and Trust Co.
Fourth and Broad Sts.
Emporium 15834 (814) 486-3333

Incorporated in 1929 in PA.
Foundation type: Community
Financial data (yr. ended 12/31/87): Assets, $2,572,785 (M); expenditures, $185,947.
Purpose and activities: Established for the benefit of local residents for maintaining or assisting public schools, public libraries, recreation areas, community buildings, and similar facilities.
Types of support: Building funds, equipment.
Limitations: Giving limited to Cameron County, PA.
Application information: Application form not required.
Initial approach: Letter
Deadline(s): None
Write: L. William Smith, Treas.
Officers and Directors: George B. Erskine, Pres.; James B. Miller, V.P.; Edwin W. Tomkins II, Secy.; L. William Smith, Treas.; Edward B. Lundberg, John T. Rogers.
Employer Identification Number: 250995760

6226
Bright & Christella Erichson Charitable Trust ⌑
1500 Fidelity Bldg.
Philadelphia 19109 (215) 893-5042

Established in 1980 in PA.
Foundation type: Independent
Financial data (yr. ended 10/31/89): Assets, $1,091,041 (M); expenditures, $54,945, including $50,000 for 5 grants of $10,000 each.
Purpose and activities: Support primarily to organizations which benefit the needy and the elderly.
Limitations: Giving primarily in Philadelphia, PA. No grants to individuals.
Application information: Contributes only to pre-selected organizations. Applications not accepted.
Write: Harvey N. Shapiro, Trustee
Trustees: Rev. Gonzalo Correa Santa Cruz, Harvey N. Shapiro.
Employer Identification Number: 236697739

6227
The Erie Community Foundation ▼
502 G. Daniel Baldwin Bldg.
P.O. Box 1818
Erie 16507 (814) 454-0843

Established as Erie Endowment Foundation in 1935 in PA; renamed in 1970.
Foundation type: Community
Financial data (yr. ended 12/31/89): Assets, $15,684,537 (M); gifts received, $450,518; expenditures, $1,139,519, including $1,008,821 for 112 grants (high: $77,050; low: $332; average: $300-$25,000).
Purpose and activities: Giving for social service and youth agencies, education, the visual and performing arts, hospitals, health agencies, and religious organizations.
Types of support: Seed money, emergency funds, building funds, equipment, matching funds, research, annual campaigns, capital campaigns, conferences and seminars.
Limitations: Giving primarily in Erie County, PA. No grants to individuals (except for scholarships from restricted funds), or for operating budgets, continuing support, deficit financing, land acquisition, endowment funds, special projects, or publications; no loans.
Publications: Annual report.
Application information: Application form required.
Initial approach: Letter or telephone
Copies of proposal: 6
Deadline(s): Submit proposal preferably in Feb., May, Aug., or Nov.; deadlines 1st of the month of board meetings
Board meeting date(s): Mar., June, Sept., and Dec.
Final notification: 3 to 4 weeks
Write: Edward C. Doll, Chair.
Officers and Trustees:* Edward C. Doll,* Chair.; Charles H. Bracken,* Pres.; William F. Grant,* V.P.; Ray L. McGarvey,* Secy.-Treas.; David W. Doupe, M.D., Albert F. Duval, John R. Falcone, Ann V. Greene, F. William Hirt, Ernest L. Lake.
Trustee Banks: First National Bank of Pennsylvania, Marine Bank, Mellon Bank, N.A., PennBank Erie.
Number of staff: 1 part-time professional; 2 part-time support.
Employer Identification Number: 256032032

6228
Fair Oaks Foundation ⌑ ☆
(Formerly AMPCO-Pittsburgh Foundation II, Inc.)
600 Grant St., Suite 4600
Pittsburgh 15219 (412) 456-4418

Established in 1988 in PA.
Donor(s): Pittsburgh Forgings Foundation.
Foundation type: Company-sponsored
Financial data (yr. ended 12/31/89): Assets, $5,502,584 (M); gifts received, $2,319,615; expenditures, $237,840, including $221,285 for 74 grants (high: $40,000; low: $35) and $9,500 for 18 grants to individuals (high: $1,000; low: $500; average: $500).
Purpose and activities: Support primarily for the United Way; giving also for a university.
Application information: Application form not required.
Initial approach: Letter or proposal
Deadline(s): Nov. 1
Write: Rose Hoover, Secy.
Officers and Trustees:* Louis Berkman,* Chair.; Marshall L. Berkman,* Pres.; Robert A. Paul,* V.P. and Treas.; Rose Ann Hoover, Secy.
Employer Identification Number: 251576560

6229
Maurice Falk Medical Fund ⌑
3317 Grant Bldg.
Pittsburgh 15219 (412) 261-2485

Incorporated in 1960 in PA.
Donor(s): Maurice and Laura Falk Foundation.
Foundation type: Independent
Financial data (yr. ended 8/31/88): Assets, $7,922,854 (M); expenditures, $467,389, including $225,911 for 49 grants (high: $125,000; low: $300; average: $1,000).
Purpose and activities: Grants program is limited to long-term commitments and endowments in the mental health field, including racism and mental health, and public policy.
Types of support: Continuing support, seed money, consulting services, technical assistance, special projects, publications, conferences and seminars, program-related investments, endowment funds.
Limitations: No grants to individuals, or for operating budgets, annual campaigns, deficit financing, capital funds, scholarships, fellowships, or matching gifts; no loans.
Publications: Application guidelines, occasional report.
Application information: Application form not required.
Initial approach: Letter or telephone
Copies of proposal: 1
Deadline(s): None
Board meeting date(s): Quarterly
Final notification: 2 to 3 weeks
Write: Philip B. Hallen, Pres.
Officers and Trustees:* Philip Baskin, Chair.; Sigo Falk, C.E.O.; Philip B. Hallen, Pres.; Bertram S. Brown, M.D., Exec. V.P.; Julian Ruslander,* Secy.; George A. Stinson,* Treas.
Number of staff: 2 full-time professional; 1 full-time support.
Employer Identification Number: 251099658

6230
Farber Foundation ⌑
1401 Walnut St.
Philadelphia 19102

Foundation type: Company-sponsored
Financial data (yr. ended 12/31/88): Assets, $1,942,996 (M); gifts received, $175,000; expenditures, $94,354, including $93,995 for 56 grants (high: $30,000; low: $50; average: $50-$30,000).
Purpose and activities: Giving primarily for Jewish organizations, higher education and a broad range of general charitable programs.
Application information: Contributes only to pre-selected organizations. Applications not accepted.
Officers: Jack Farber, Pres.; Stephen V. Dubin, V.P. and Secy.; James G. Baxter, V.P. and Treas.
Employer Identification Number: 236254221

6231
Federation Foundation of Greater Philadelphia ▼
226 South 16th St.
Philadelphia 19102 (215) 893-5823

Established in 1971 in PA.
Foundation type: Independent
Financial data (yr. ended 11/30/89): Assets, $7,477,320 (M); gifts received, $154,149; expenditures, $1,255,566, including $1,255,566 for 381 grants (high: $105,000; low: $100; average: $2,000).
Purpose and activities: Primarily giving to Jewish welfare and educational organizations, higher education, and Israel; support also for social services.
Types of support: Annual campaigns, endowment funds, general purposes, scholarship funds.
Application information: Grantees are pre-selected by individual donors of the foundation. Applications not accepted.
Write: Robert S. Hass, Exec. Secy.
Officers and Directors:* Annabelle Fishman,* Pres.; Harry K. Madway,* V.P.; Frank Newburger, Jr.,* V.P.; Robert S. Hass, Exec. Secy.; Stanley Ferst, Secy.; Charles G. Sunstein,* Treas.; Michael R. Belman, Louise Brown, Louis Fryman, Benjamin B. Levin.
Number of staff: 1 part-time support.
Employer Identification Number: 237083735

6232
Myer and Rosaline Feinstein Foundation
1700 Market St., 7th Fl.
Philadelphia 19103

Trust established in 1945 in PA; incorporated in 1960 in DE.
Donor(s): Myer Feinstein,† Rosaline B. Feinstein, and others.
Foundation type: Independent
Financial data (yr. ended 12/31/89): Assets, $4,111,480 (M); expenditures, $482,989, including $473,284 for 18 grants (high: $385,000; low: $200).
Purpose and activities: Support primarily for Jewish welfare funds, culture and education; some support for social services.
Types of support: Annual campaigns, building funds, scholarship funds, special projects.
Limitations: Giving primarily in PA. No grants to individuals.
Application information: Applications not accepted.
Board meeting date(s): July and as required
Write: I. Jerome Stern, Exec. V.P.
Officers and Directors:* Peggy Freedman,* Pres.; I. Jerome Stern,* Exec. V.P.; Samuel Feinstein,* V.P.; Bernice S. Chalphin,* Secy.; Pauline Green.
Number of staff: 1 part-time professional; 1 part-time support.
Employer Identification Number: 236235232

6233
Samuel S. Fels Fund ▼
2214 Land Title Bldg.
100 South Broad St.
Philadelphia 19110 (215) 567-2808

Incorporated in 1935 in PA.
Donor(s): Samuel S. Fels.†

Foundation type: Independent
Financial data (yr. ended 12/31/89): Assets, $29,768,796 (M); expenditures, $1,990,270, including $1,256,996 for 144 grants (high: $250,000; low: $500; average: $3,000-$20,000).
Purpose and activities: Grants for continuing support of two major projects instituted by the fund itself: the Fels Research Institute, Temple University Medical School and the Fels Center of Government, University of Pennsylvania. Additional grants for short-term assistance to projects and organizations that help to demonstrate and evaluate ways to prevent, lessen, or resolve contemporary social problems, or that seek to provide permanent improvements in the provision of services for the improvement of daily life; to increase the stability of arts organizations and enrich the cultural life of the city of Philadelphia; limited aid to locally based university presses.
Types of support: Seed money, emergency funds, matching funds, technical assistance, special projects, research, conferences and seminars, continuing support, general purposes, internships, publications.
Limitations: Giving limited to the city of Philadelphia, PA. No support for national organizations. No grants to individuals, or for endowment or building funds, travel, scholarships, or fellowships.
Publications: Annual report, application guidelines.
Application information: Applicant must request guidelines before submitting proposals. Application form required.
Initial approach: Proposal
Copies of proposal: 1
Board meeting date(s): Monthly except Aug.
Write: Kathryn Smith Pyle, Exec. Dir.
Officers and Member-Directors:* Iso Briselli,* Pres.; Kathryn Smith Pyle,* Secy. and Exec. Dir.; David C. Melnicoff,* Treas.; Brother Daniel Burke, F.S.C., Raymond K. Denworth, Jr., Sandra Featherman, Wilbur E. Hobbs, David H. Wice.
Number of staff: 1 full-time professional; 1 part-time support.
Employer Identification Number: 231365325

6234
Female Association of Philadelphia
c/o Provident National Bank
1632 Chestnut St.
Philadelphia 19103
Application address: 2185 Paper Mill Rd., Huntingdon Valley, PA 19006

Established in 1881.
Foundation type: Independent
Financial data (yr. ended 9/30/87): Assets, $1,891,203 (M); gifts received, $1,121; expenditures, $91,748, including $75,894 for grants to individuals.
Purpose and activities: Modest, individual grants awarded only to women over 60 years of age, who reside in the Philadelphia area, and are living in "reduced circumstances."
Types of support: Grants to individuals.
Limitations: Giving limited to the Philadelphia, PA, area.
Application information:
Deadline(s): Mar. 31 and Sept. 30
Board meeting date(s): Apr. and Oct.
Write: Elizabeth Harbison, Treas.
Officers: Mrs. John N. Childs, Jr., Pres.; Mrs. C. Craig Smith, V.P.; Mrs. Henry S. Robinson, Secy.; Mrs. Robert J. Harbison, Treas.
Number of staff: None.
Employer Identification Number: 236214961

6235
J. B. Finley Charitable Trust
c/o Pittsburgh National Bank
Pittsburgh 15265 (412) 762-2586

Trust established in 1919 in PA.
Donor(s): J.B. Finley.†
Foundation type: Independent
Financial data (yr. ended 12/31/89): Assets, $2,914,068 (M); expenditures, $185,986, including $161,345 for 30 grants (high: $10,000; low: $700).
Purpose and activities: Emphasis on Protestant church support and religious organizations, higher and secondary education, and cultural programs; support also for a community fund and a hospital.
Types of support: Building funds, general purposes, equipment, matching funds, seed money, special projects.
Limitations: Giving primarily in PA.
Publications: Informational brochure, application guidelines.
Application information: Application form required.
Initial approach: Letter
Copies of proposal: 1
Deadline(s): Apr. 15 and Oct. 15
Board meeting date(s): End of May and Nov.
Final notification: Mid June and Dec.
Write: Secy., Charitable Trust Comm.
Trustee: Pittsburgh National Bank.
Employer Identification Number: 256024443

6236
Roger S. Firestone Foundation
Two South Bryn Mawr Ave., Suite 102
Bryn Mawr 19010

Established in 1983 in Ohio.
Foundation type: Independent
Financial data (yr. ended 12/31/88): Assets, $6,921,707 (M); expenditures, $321,229, including $231,100 for 10 grants (high: $111,000; low: $5,000).
Purpose and activities: Emphasis on art institutions, cultural programs, and education, particularly higher education; support also for social service agencies.
Types of support: General purposes.
Limitations: Giving primarily in AZ, Washington, DC, and NY.
Application information: Application form not required.
Initial approach: Proposal
Copies of proposal: 1
Deadline(s): None
Write: Herbert T. McDevitt, Exec. Admin.
Trustees: John D. Firestone, Herbert T. McDevitt, Susan F. Semegen, Gay F. Wray.
Number of staff: 1 part-time professional; 1 part-time support.
Employer Identification Number: 341388255

6237
Bernard & Annabelle Fishman Foundation ⌑ ☆
The Fairmont, Suite 409
Bala-Cynwyd 19004

Established in 1971.
Foundation type: Independent
Financial data (yr. ended 12/31/88): Assets, $102,614 (M); expenditures, $126,964, including $125,715 for 43 grants (high: $47,000; low: $100).
Purpose and activities: Support primarily for Jewish associations, including a Jewish welfare organization and a Jewish theological seminary.
Limitations: Giving limited to Philadelphia, PA. No grants to individuals.
Application information: Applications not accepted.
Manager: Bernard Fishman.
Employer Identification Number: 237113420

6238
Percival E. and Ethel Brown Foerderer Foundation
P.O. Box 7734
Philadelphia 19101-7734 (215) 828-8145

Trust established in 1962 in PA.
Donor(s): Ethel Brown Foerderer,† Percival E. Foerderer.†
Foundation type: Independent
Financial data (yr. ended 12/31/89): Assets, $6,273,666 (M); qualifying distributions, $370,758, including $370,758 for 19 grants (high: $263,900; low: $500).
Purpose and activities: Funds largely committed to the Foerderer Fellowship Program for students in the College of Graduate Studies of Thomas Jefferson University; remainder currently focused on a research project concerning achondroplasia, the failure of normal development of cartilage resulting in dwarfism.
Types of support: Fellowships, research.
Limitations: Giving primarily in the Philadelphia, PA, area.
Publications: Biennial report.
Application information: Fund presently commited; no new proposals are being considered at this time. Applications not accepted.
Deadline(s): Sept. 1 (for previous commitments)
Board meeting date(s): Apr., Sept., and Oct.
Write: Thomas L. Higginson, Secy.
Officers and Trustees:* Shirley Foerderer Higginson,* Chair.; N. Ramsay Pennypacker,* Secy.; Spencer D. Wright III,* Treas.; Ethel F. Davis, Mrs. John M.K. Davis, Mignon Foerderer Davis, Shelley A. Hartz, James W. Stratton.
Number of staff: 1
Employer Identification Number: 236296084

6239
Foster Charitable Trust ⌑
P.O. Box 67
Pittsburgh 15230 (412) 928-8900

Trust established in 1962 in PA.
Donor(s): Foster Industries, Inc.
Foundation type: Independent
Financial data (yr. ended 12/31/88): Assets, $3,144,233 (M); gifts received, $468,967;

expenditures, $539,421, including $526,933 for 87 grants (high: $200,000; low: $333).
Purpose and activities: Grants primarily to Jewish welfare funds, hospitals, higher education, and the arts.
Limitations: Giving primarily in PA. No grants to individuals, or for endowment funds or operating budgets.
Application information: Application form not required.
Initial approach: Letter
Copies of proposal: 1
Deadline(s): None
Board meeting date(s): As required
Write: Bernard S. Mars, Trustee
Trustees: J.R. Foster, Jay L. Foster, H. Roy Gordon, Bernard S. Mars, Milton Porter.
Number of staff: None.
Employer Identification Number: 256064791

6240
Founders' Memorial Fund of the American Sterilizer Co.
American Sterilizer Co.
2424 West 23rd St.
Erie 16506 (814) 870-8448

Established in 1938 in PA.
Foundation type: Independent
Financial data (yr. ended 12/31/87): Assets, $1,674,665 (M); expenditures, $134,409, including $118,865 for 16 grants to individuals.
Purpose and activities: Support for higher education; scholarship grants to dependents of employees of the American Sterilizer Co.
Types of support: Employee-related scholarships.
Application information:
Write: Gerri Leonard
Officers: Frank DeFazio, Mgr.; Henry E. Fish, Mgr.
Employer Identification Number: 256062068

6241
The Richard J. Fox Foundation ⌑
1325 Morris Dr., Suite 201
Wayne 19087-5506

Established in 1983 in PA.
Foundation type: Independent
Financial data (yr. ended 12/31/88): Assets, $5,675,025 (M); gifts received, $4,000,000; expenditures, $14,132, including $12,000 for 2 grants (high: $9,000; low: $3,000).
Purpose and activities: Giving primarily for international relations and Israel.
Limitations: No grants to individuals.
Application information: Contributes only to pre-selected organizations. Applications not accepted.
Officer: Richard J. Fox, Pres.
Trustee: Harry D. Fox.
Employer Identification Number: 232267786

6242
Freas Foundation, Inc. ⌑
2032 Wyntre Brooke South
York 17403
Application address: 11 Halstead Ln., Branford, CT 06405

Foundation type: Independent
Financial data (yr. ended 12/31/88): Assets, $3,480,421 (M); expenditures, $188,460, including $160,802 for 45 grants (high: $43,500; low: $250).
Purpose and activities: Giving primarily for health services and higher and other education.
Limitations: Giving primarily in PA.
Application information:
Initial approach: Letter
Deadline(s): None
Write: David M. Trout, Mgr.
Officers: Arthur K. Freas, Mgr.; Margery H. Freas, Mgr.; David M. Trout, Mgr.; Rebecca F. Trout, Mgr.
Employer Identification Number: 221714810

6243
The Fredricksen Foundation ☆
4718 Old Gettysburg Rd., Suite 405
Mechanicsburg 17055-4325 (717) 731-9405

Established in 1987 in PA.
Donor(s): L.B. Smith Medical Foundation, Inc., C.J. Fredricksen.
Foundation type: Independent
Financial data (yr. ended 12/31/89): Assets, $1,216,328 (M); gifts received, $200,000; expenditures, $56,884, including $52,000 for 10 grants (high: $15,000; low: $1,000; average: $1,000-$15,000).
Purpose and activities: Giving primarily for hospitals; support also for nursing education.
Types of support: Scholarship funds, capital campaigns, general purposes.
Limitations: Giving limited to the Harrisburg, PA, and Marco Island, FL, areas. No grants to individuals.
Application information: Application form not required.
Initial approach: Letter
Copies of proposal: 1
Deadline(s): None
Write: Miles J. Gibbons, Jr., Exec. Dir.
Officer: Miles J. Gibbons, Jr., Exec. Dir.
Trustees: Cleve J. Fredricksen, Dauphin Deposit Bank & Trust Co.
Number of staff: 2 part-time professional; 1 part-time support.
Employer Identification Number: 222852610

6244
Freeport Brick Company Charitable Trust ⌑
Drawer F
Freeport 16229

Established in 1964 in PA.
Foundation type: Company-sponsored
Financial data (yr. ended 12/31/87): Assets, $1,080,840 (M); expenditures, $56,011, including $53,291 for 14 grants (high: $30,000; low: $500).
Purpose and activities: Support primarily for a community park; support also for community, youth and health organizations.
Application information: Application form not required.
Initial approach: Letter
Write: F.H. Laube, Secy.-Treas.
Officers: R.A. Keasey, Chair.; J.C. Overholt, Vice-Chair.; F.H. Laube, Secy.-Treas.
Trustees: F.H. Laube III, H.R. Laube, D.J. Stefl.
Employer Identification Number: 256074334

6245
Henry C. Frick Educational Commission
Centre City Tower
650 Smithfield St.
Pittsburgh 15222 (412) 232-3335

Trust established in 1909 in PA.
Donor(s): Henry C. Frick.†
Foundation type: Independent
Financial data (yr. ended 12/31/89): Assets, $4,461,682 (M); expenditures, $121,690, including $121,690 for 35 grants (high: $10,800; low: $50; average: $1,000-$10,000).
Purpose and activities: To improve or enhance the quality of public elementary and secondary education. Invites and gives preference to proposals that provide for or encourage interaction among the various community elements that make up and contribute to public education.
Types of support: Seed money, matching funds, special projects, research, publications, conferences and seminars.
Limitations: Giving limited to the city of Pittsburgh, and Allegheny, Fayette, Greene, Washington, and Westmoreland counties in southwestern PA. No grants to individuals, or for annual campaigns, deficit financing, capital or endowment funds, scholarships, or fellowships; no loans.
Publications: Program policy statement, application guidelines, informational brochure, grants list.
Application information: Application form not required.
Initial approach: Letter or telephone
Copies of proposal: 1
Deadline(s): Oct. and Feb.
Board meeting date(s): Mar., June, and Dec.
Final notification: 2 weeks after board meetings
Write: Jane C. Burger, Exec. Dir.
Officers: Albert C. Van Dusen,* Pres.; Sandra J. McLaughlin,* V.P.; Joseph C. Swaim, Jr.,* Secy.-Treas.; Jane C. Burger, Exec. Dir.
Trustees:* David Bergholz, Doreen E. Boyce, William J. Copeland, Henry Clay Frick II, David Henderson, Lloyd Kaiser, George D. Lockhart.
Number of staff: 1 part-time professional; 2 part-time support.
Employer Identification Number: 250965374

6246
The Helen Clay Frick Foundation ▼
7200 Penn Ave.
Pittsburgh 15208 (412) 371-0600

Trust established in 1947 in PA.
Donor(s): Helen C. Frick.†
Foundation type: Independent
Financial data (yr. ended 12/31/89): Assets, $65,519,733 (M); gifts received, $46,851; expenditures, $3,489,133, including $1,905,450 for 38 grants (high: $1,325,000; low: $1,000; average: $1,000-$25,000).
Purpose and activities: Grants to an art reference library in New York City, a nature sanctuary in Westchester County, NY, a historical society in Westmoreland County, PA; support also for cultural organizations, groups concerned with conservation and horticulture, and educational institutions.

Types of support: Annual campaigns, publications, operating budgets, general purposes, continuing support, capital campaigns.
Limitations: Giving primarily in Pittsburgh, PA, and NY. No grants to individuals.
Application information: The foundation has suspended grantmaking for an indefinite length of time. No grant applications will be accepted until further notice.
Board meeting date(s): Apr., June, Sept., and Dec.
Write: DeCourcy E. McIntosh, Exec. Dir.
Officers and Trustees:* Henry Clay Frick II,* Chair.; I. Townsend Burden III,* Vice-Chair.; DeCourcy E. McIntosh, Secy. and Exec. Dir.; Peter P. Blanchard III, Walter F. Cooley, Jr., Mrs. Edward N. Dane, Henry Clay Frick III, Thomas J. Hilliard, J. Fife Symington III, Edward R. Weidlein, Jr., C. Holmes Wolfe, Jr., Mellon Bank, N.A.
Number of staff: 5 full-time professional; 16 full-time support; 9 part-time support.
Employer Identification Number: 256018983

6247
Edwin B. Garrigues Trust ⌑
c/o Duane Morris & Heckscher
1500 One Franklin Plaza
Philadelphia 19102 (215) 854-6379

Established in 1922 in PA.
Foundation type: Independent
Financial data (yr. ended 12/31/88): Assets, $2,013,000 (M); expenditures, $124,492, including $110,000 for 4 grants (high: $60,000; low: $15,000).
Purpose and activities: Grants to accredited schools of music for scholarship assistance.
Types of support: Scholarship funds.
Limitations: Giving primarily in the Philadelphia, PA, area. No grants to individuals.
Application information:
Initial approach: Letter
Deadline(s): None
Write: Seymour Wagner, Secy.
Officers: Robert Montgomery Scott, Chair.; Seymour Wagner, Secy.
Trustee: Fidelity Bank, N.A.
Employer Identification Number: 236220616

6248
Elsie Lee Garthwaite Memorial Foundation ⌑
c/o Quinlan and Co., Ltd.
510 Walnut St., 11th Fl.
Philadelphia 19106
Application address: 1100 Barberry Rd., Bryn Mawr, PA 19010

Donor(s): Albert A. Garthwaite, Jr.
Foundation type: Independent
Financial data (yr. ended 12/31/87): Assets, $1,179,881 (M); gifts received, $74,417; expenditures, $10,166.
Purpose and activities: Support primarily for health associations and educational and cultural institutions.
Application information: Application form not required.
Deadline(s): None
Write: Albert A. Garthwaite, Jr., Pres.
Officers: Albert A. Garthwaite, Jr., Pres.; John B. Webb, V.P.; Patricia J. Turney, Secy.; C. Robert Turney, Treas.
Trustees: John Acuff, and 8 other trustees.
Employer Identification Number: 236290877

6249
General Accident Insurance Charitable Trust ⌑ ☆
436 Walnut St.
Philadelphia 19106

Established in 1987 in PA.
Donor(s): General Accident Insurance Co. of America.
Foundation type: Company-sponsored
Financial data (yr. ended 12/31/88): Assets, $4,280,004 (M); gifts received, $263,250; expenditures, $335,192, including $226,775 for 73 grants (high: $158,249; low: $50) and $61,118 for 116 employee matching gifts.
Purpose and activities: Giving primarily for community funds; support also for community development and civic affairs, health associations, arts and culture, social services, including programs for youth, and higher education, including support through an employee matching gift program.
Types of support: Employee matching gifts.
Limitations: No grants to individuals.
Application information: Contributes only to pre-selected organizations. Applications not accepted.
Trustees: James C. Corcoran, Francis J. Coyne, George N. Morris, John J. Naughton.
Employer Identification Number: 232441567

6250
Joel Gershman Foundation ⌑
1027 Pheasant Rd.
Rydal 19046-1817

Donor(s): Joel Gershman.
Foundation type: Independent
Financial data (yr. ended 11/30/87): Assets, $2,410,344 (M); gifts received, $1,000,000; expenditures, $129,643, including $126,625 for 31 grants (high: $80,100; low: $50).
Purpose and activities: Support primarily for community funds and Jewish organizations.
Limitations: Giving primarily in Philadelphia, PA.
Application information: Application form not required.
Deadline(s): None
Write: Joel Gershman, Pres.
Officers: Joel Gershman, Pres.; Philip Sheikman, Secy.-Treas.
Employer Identification Number: 222529629

6251
Giant Eagle Foundation ⌑ ☆
101 Kappa Dr.
Pittsburgh 15238 (412) 963-6200

Donor(s): Giant Eagle, Inc.
Foundation type: Company-sponsored
Financial data (yr. ended 8/31/88): Assets, $2,868,847 (M); gifts received, $475,000; expenditures, $247,692, including $239,615 for 108 grants (high: $40,000; low: $25).
Purpose and activities: Giving primarily for Jewish organizations, higher education, and cultural programs.
Limitations: No grants to individuals.
Application information: Contributes only to pre-selected organizations. Applications not accepted.
Trustees: Milton Chat, Stanley Morovitz, Donald Plung, Irwin Porter, David Shapira, Norman Weinerbaum.
Employer Identification Number: 256033905

6252
Addison H. Gibson Foundation ▼ ⌑
Two PPG Place, Suite 310
Pittsburgh 15222 (412) 261-1611

Trust established in 1936 in PA.
Donor(s): Addison H. Gibson.†
Foundation type: Independent
Financial data (yr. ended 12/31/88): Assets, $15,341,404 (M); gifts received, $10,000; expenditures, $1,200,410, including $397,500 for 28 grants (high: $16,000; low: $12,500), $166,530 for 79 grants to individuals (high: $12,000; low: $60) and $403,930 for 89 loans to individuals.
Purpose and activities: To provide (1) medical and hospital care for local needy persons and (2) loans to male students residing in western PA for college or university expenses after at least one year's self-maintenance; grants also to hospitals and rehabilitation institutions.
Types of support: Grants to individuals, student loans.
Limitations: Giving limited to western PA. No grants for building funds, endowments, operating budgets, or special projects.
Publications: Informational brochure (including application guidelines).
Application information: Application form required.
Initial approach: For loans, letter or telephone to schedule personal interview; for medical assistance, letter or telephone from referring physician or agency prior to patient interview
Deadline(s): None
Board meeting date(s): About 10 times a year
Final notification: Varies
Write: Charlotte G. Kisseleff, Secy.
Officer: Charlotte G. Kisseleff, Secy.
Trustees: Frank J. Gaffney, Earl F. Reed, Jr., Union National Bank of Pittsburgh.
Number of staff: 1 full-time professional; 2 full-time support.
Employer Identification Number: 250965379

6253
Glencairn Foundation ▼ ⌑
One Pitcairn Place
Jenkintown 19046-3593 (215) 887-6700

Incorporated in 1950 in PA.
Donor(s): Raymond Pitcairn,† and members of the Pitcairn family.
Foundation type: Independent
Financial data (yr. ended 12/31/88): Assets, $11,662,453 (M); expenditures, $2,476,363, including $2,394,176 for 4 grants (high: $1,832,676; low: $100,000).
Purpose and activities: Giving for Protestant church support and a church-related school.

Limitations: Giving primarily in Bryn Athyn, PA.
Application information: Funds are committed until 1998. Application form not required.
Deadline(s): None
Board meeting date(s): As necessary
Write: Lachlan Pitcairn, Secy.
Officers and Directors:* Garthowen Pitcairn,* Pres.; Michael Pitcairn, V.P.; Lachlan Pitcairn,* Secy.; James F. Junge,* Treas.; Charles S. Cole, Jr., Kirk P. Pendleton.
Number of staff: None.
Employer Identification Number: 231429828

6254
Glendorn Foundation
78 Main St.
Bradford 16701 (814) 368-7171

Trust established in 1953 in TX.
Donor(s): Forest Oil Corp., Ruth H. Dorn.†
Foundation type: Company-sponsored
Financial data (yr. ended 12/31/88): Assets, $3,388,896 (M); gifts received, $219,538; expenditures, $211,332, including $205,000 for 1 grant.
Purpose and activities: Support for medical research.
Types of support: Research.
Publications: Financial statement.
Application information: Funds currently committed. Applications not accepted.
Write: William F. Higie, Fdn. Mgr.
Officer and Trustees:* William F. Higie,* Fdn. Mgr.; Clayton D. Chisum, David F. Dorn, John C. Dorn, Richard B. Dorn, Wendy M. Hitt, Jay Bird Lawson, Leslie D. Young.
Number of staff: None.
Employer Identification Number: 251024349

6255
David A. Glosser Foundation ⌑
72 Messenger St.
Johnstown 15902 (814) 535-7521

Incorporated in 1962 in PA.
Donor(s): David A. Glosser.†
Foundation type: Independent
Financial data (yr. ended 06/30/89): Assets, $2,209,699 (M); expenditures, $165,052, including $93,433 for 35 grants (high: $70,000; low: $50).
Purpose and activities: Emphasis on social services, including Jewish welfare funds, and educational organizations.
Limitations: Giving primarily in Johnstown, PA. No grants to individuals, or for endowment funds.
Application information:
Initial approach: Letter
Copies of proposal: 1
Deadline(s): None
Board meeting date(s): As required
Final notification: 2 months
Write: Lester Edelstein, Pres.
Officers: Lester Edelstein, Pres. and Secy.; Robert Krantzler, Treas.
Director: Lester Goldstein.
Employer Identification Number: 256066913

6256
William Goldman Foundation
1700 Walnut St., Suite 800
Philadelphia 19103 (215) 546-2779

Trust established in 1952 in PA.
Donor(s): William Goldman,† Helen L. Goldman.†
Foundation type: Independent
Financial data (yr. ended 12/31/88): Assets, $2,645,334 (M); expenditures, $134,010, including $28,000 for 36 grants (high: $7,500; low: $200; average: $250-$3,000) and $40,000 for 62 grants to individuals (high: $1,000; low: $250; average: $1,000).
Purpose and activities: Grants for graduate studies (including medical education and graduate school scholarships), hospitals, child welfare, community funds, and Jewish welfare funds.
Types of support: Operating budgets, annual campaigns, research, scholarship funds, continuing support, special projects, student aid.
Limitations: Giving primarily in the metropolitan Philadelphia, PA, area. No grants for endowment funds or matching gifts; generally no loans.
Publications: Application guidelines.
Application information: Application form required for scholarships.
Initial approach: Letter
Copies of proposal: 1
Deadline(s): Mar. 15 for scholarships; no deadline for other requests
Board meeting date(s): Quarterly
Write: Ms. Marilyn Klein, Exec. Dir.
Officers and Trustees:* William Goldman, Jr.,* Chair. and Treas.; Alice S. Goldman,* Vice-Chair.; William R. Goldman,* Secy.; Marilyn Klein, Exec. Dir.; Lowell H. Dubrow, Randolph Louis Goldman, Anne Goldman Kravitz, Barbara G. Susman, Ronald M. Wiener.
Number of staff: 1 part-time professional.
Employer Identification Number: 236266261

6257
Grable Foundation
309 Smithfield St., Suite 4000
Pittsburgh 15222 (412) 566-1818

Established in 1977 in PA.
Donor(s): Minnie K. Grable.
Foundation type: Independent
Financial data (yr. ended 12/31/88): Assets, $2,571,742 (M); gifts received, $360,000; expenditures, $193,228, including $163,500 for 20 grants (high: $30,000; low: $1,000).
Purpose and activities: Support primarily for health and social service agencies, youth organizations, and education.
Types of support: Annual campaigns, building funds, capital campaigns, continuing support, general purposes, operating budgets, program-related investments, special projects.
Limitations: Giving primarily in Pittsburgh, PA, Orlando, FL, and their vicinities.
Publications: 990-PF.
Application information: Application form not required.
Initial approach: Proposal
Copies of proposal: 1
Deadline(s): None
Board meeting date(s): Varies
Write: Charles R. Burke, Pres.
Officers and Trustees:* Charles R. Burke,* Pres. and Secy.; Patricia G. Burke,* V.P.; Marion G. Nicholson,* V.P.; William B. Nicholson,* Treas.; Minnie K. Grable.
Number of staff: None.
Employer Identification Number: 251309888

6258
Grandom Institution ⌑ ☆
4132 Presidential Dr.
Lafayette Hill 19444

Incorporated in 1841.
Donor(s): Hartt Grandom.†
Foundation type: Independent
Financial data (yr. ended 7/31/87): Assets, $1,288,545 (M); expenditures, $48,527, including $41,745 for 1 grant.
Purpose and activities: Giving limited to aid organizations in "furnishing winter fuels to the worthy poor."
Limitations: Giving primarily in Germantown, PA.
Officers and Managers: F. Preston Buckman, Pres.; Robert S. Jones, Secy.-Treas.; Robert C. Bodine, Francis H. Brown, John A. Childs, Thomas O. Ely, Francis J. Haines.
Employer Identification Number: 230640770

6259
Grass Family Foundation ⌑
4025 Crooked Hill Rd.
Harrisburg 17110

Established in 1972.
Donor(s): Alex Grass.
Foundation type: Independent
Financial data (yr. ended 11/30/88): Assets, $4,078,084 (M); gifts received, $150,000; expenditures, $212,250, including $186,500 for 10 grants (high: $100,000; low: $500).
Purpose and activities: Grants largely for Jewish welfare funds, including those in Israel; some support also for higher education.
Limitations: Giving primarily in New York, NY, and Harrisburg, PA. No grants to individuals.
Application information: Contributes only to pre-selected organizations. Applications not accepted.
Officers and Directors:* Alex Grass,* Chair.; Linda Grass Shapiro,* Secy.; Martin L. Grass, Roger L. Grass, Elizabeth Grass Weese.
Employer Identification Number: 237218002

6260
Lois F. Grass Foundation ⌑
P.O. Box 1003
Harrisburg 17108

Established in 1972 in PA.
Donor(s): Lois F. Grass.
Foundation type: Independent
Financial data (yr. ended 11/30/86): Assets, $1,595,707 (M); expenditures, $28,415, including $26,000 for 7 grants (high: $8,000; low: $2,000).
Purpose and activities: Giving for Jewish welfare funds and other social services.
Types of support: Annual campaigns, building funds, capital campaigns, continuing support, endowment funds, general purposes.
Limitations: Giving primarily in PA.
Officer: Lois F. Grass, Chair.
Employer Identification Number: 237218005

6261
The Albert M. Greenfield Foundation ⌑
2207 Oakwyn Rd.
Lafayette Hill 19444
Application address: One Beekman Pl., Apt. 2A, New York, NY 10022

Incorporated in 1953 in PA.
Donor(s): Albert M. Greenfield,† Etelka J. Greenfield.†
Foundation type: Independent
Financial data (yr. ended 8/31/88): Assets, $5,274,018 (M); expenditures, $256,144, including $231,000 for 21 grants (high: $50,000; low: $1,000).
Purpose and activities: Emphasis on the arts, music, and higher education.
Limitations: Giving primarily in the Philadelphia, PA, area. No grants for endowment funds; no loans.
Application information: Application form not required.
Initial approach: Letter
Copies of proposal: 1
Deadline(s): None
Board meeting date(s): As required
Write: Elizabeth M. Petrie, Chair.
Officers and Trustees: Elizabeth M. Petrie, Chair.; Gordon K. Greenfield, Pres.; Elizabeth G. Zeidman, Secy.; Gustave G. Amsterdam, Bruce H. Greenfield.
Employer Identification Number: 236050816

6262
M. S. Grumbacher Foundation ⌑
2801 East Market St., P.O. Box 2821
York 17405 (717) 757-7660

Established in 1958.
Donor(s): M.S. Grumbacher, Mailman Stores, Inc.
Foundation type: Independent
Financial data (yr. ended 8/31/88): Assets, $4,239,152 (M); expenditures, $217,226, including $97,256 for 16 grants (high: $56,699; low: $200).
Purpose and activities: Grants largely for Jewish welfare funds and education.
Types of support: Capital campaigns.
Limitations: Giving limited to PA, with emphasis on York.
Application information:
Initial approach: Letter
Deadline(s): Submit applications from Nov. 1 to Apr. 30
Write: M.S. Grumbacher, Chair.
Officer and Trustees: M.S. Grumbacher, Chair.; R. Grumbacher, David J. Kaufman, A.G. Lowengard.
Employer Identification Number: 236406993

6263
The Grundy Foundation ⌑
680 Radcliffe St.
P.O. Box 701
Bristol 19007 (215) 788-5460

Trust established in 1961 in PA.
Donor(s): Joseph R. Grundy.†
Foundation type: Independent
Financial data (yr. ended 12/31/87): Assets, $33,106,408 (M); expenditures, $1,262,650, including $205,100 for 27 grants (high: $50,000; low: $500; average: $1,000-$30,000).
Purpose and activities: Grants for civic affairs and community planning; social service and youth agencies, including a community fund; cultural programs, higher education, and health. Giving restricted to activities in which the donor was interested during his lifetime.
Types of support: Building funds, equipment, land acquisition, seed money, conferences and seminars, special projects, renovation projects, operating budgets.
Limitations: Giving limited to Bucks County, PA. No grants to individuals, or for endowment funds, research, scholarships, or fellowships; no loans.
Application information: Application form not required.
Initial approach: Letter
Copies of proposal: 1
Deadline(s): None
Board meeting date(s): Monthly except in Aug.
Final notification: 1 week
Write: Leonard N. Snyder, Exec. Dir.
Officer: Leonard N. Snyder, Exec. Dir.
Trustees: W. James MacIntosh, Chair.; James M. Gassaway, Stanton C. Kelton, Jr., William P. Wood, Fidelity Bank, N.A.
Number of staff: 2 full-time professional.
Employer Identification Number: 231609243

6264
Evelyn A. J. Hall Charitable Trust ▼
150 Radnor Chester Rd., Suite A200
St. Davids 19087 (215) 341-9270

Trust established in 1952 in NY.
Donor(s): Evelyn A. Hall.
Foundation type: Independent
Financial data (yr. ended 12/31/89): Assets, $11,073,263 (M); expenditures, $650,449, including $569,505 for 120 grants (high: $60,000; low: $100; average: $1,000-$25,000).
Purpose and activities: Giving for museums, hospitals, medical research, higher education, conservation, historic preservation, social services, and youth agencies.
Types of support: General purposes.
Limitations: Giving primarily in New York, NY, and FL. No grants to individuals.
Application information: Applications not accepted.
Write: Alice C. Cory
Trustee: Walter H. Annenberg.
Number of staff: 5
Employer Identification Number: 236286760

6265
The Hall Foundation ⌑
444 South Second St.
Harrisburg 17104 (717) 236-0384

Trust established in 1952 in PA.
Donor(s): John N. Hall, Hall's Motor Transit Co., and others.
Foundation type: Independent
Financial data (yr. ended 9/30/89): Assets, $6,184,751 (M); expenditures, $407,755, including $152,536 for 26 grants (high: $40,000; low: $100) and $192,363 for 194 grants to individuals (high: $1,070; low: $133).
Purpose and activities: Emphasis on scholarship grants for the children of Hall's Motor Transit Co. employees and customers; support also for higher education, youth agencies, and sports and recreation.
Types of support: Employee-related scholarships.
Limitations: Giving primarily in PA.
Application information: Application form provided for scholarship requests.
Deadline(s): 3 months before Fall semester for scholarships
Write: Gerald N. Hall, Pres.
Officers and Trustees: Gerald N. Hall, Pres.; Robert E. Hall, Secy.-Treas.; Shirley Hall Carr, Leroy S. Zimmerman.
Employer Identification Number: 236243044

6266
The Hallowell Foundation ⌑
980 Meetinghouse Rd.
Rydal 19046

Trust established in 1956 in PA.
Foundation type: Independent
Financial data (yr. ended 12/31/87): Assets, $3,716,406 (M); expenditures, $457,955, including $434,450 for 20 grants (high: $150,000; low: $100).
Purpose and activities: Giving primarily for hospitals and higher and secondary education.
Types of support: Building funds, operating budgets.
Limitations: Giving primarily in PA.
Application information: Contributes only to pre-selected organization. Applications not accepted.
Trustees: Dorothy W. Hallowell, H. Thomas Hallowell, Jr., Howard T. Hallowell III, Merritt W. Hallowell, Anne H. Miller.
Employer Identification Number: 236234545

6267
Halpern Foundation ⌑
810 Penn Ave.
Pittsburgh 15222 (412) 391-6130

Established in 1952 in PA.
Donor(s): Members of the Halpern family.
Foundation type: Independent
Financial data (yr. ended 12/31/88): Assets, $1,232,368 (M); gifts received, $3,764; expenditures, $94,049, including $82,503 for grants.
Purpose and activities: Grants primarily for Jewish organizations.
Application information:
Initial approach: Letter
Deadline(s): None
Trustees: Bernard M. Halpern, Irving J. Halpern, Richard F. Halpern, Steven F. Halpern.
Employer Identification Number: 256060720

6268
James T. Hambay Foundation ⌑
c/o Dauphin Deposit Bank & Trust Co.
P.O. Box 2961
Harrisburg 17105 (717) 255-2174

Trust established in 1941 in PA.
Donor(s): J.T. Hambay.†
Foundation type: Independent
Financial data (yr. ended 12/31/87): Assets, $1,826,970 (M); expenditures, $159,680, including $104,281 for 42 grants (high:

$41,289; low: $52) and $25,232 for 24 grants to individuals (high: $5,150; low: $35).
Purpose and activities: To aid blind, crippled, and indigent children; support includes grants to individuals for medical and dental expenses; payments are to the attending physician or hospital on behalf of the individual.
Types of support: Grants to individuals.
Limitations: Giving limited to Harrisburg, PA, and vicinity. No grants for building or endowment funds or operating budgets.
Application information:
Initial approach: Letter stating medical expenses and current income
Copies of proposal: 1
Board meeting date(s): Monthly
Write: Joseph A. Macri, Trust Officer, Dauphin Deposit Bank & Trust Co.
Trustees: Worthington C. Flowers, Dauphin Deposit Bank & Trust Co.
Employer Identification Number: 236243877

6269
Hamilton Bank Foundation ⌑
(Formerly The National Central Foundation)
c/o Hamilton Bank
P.O. Box 3959
Lancaster 17604 (717) 291-3512

Incorporated in 1965 in PA.
Donor(s): Hamilton Bank.
Foundation type: Company-sponsored
Financial data (yr. ended 12/31/87): Assets, $60,067 (M); gifts received, $358,588; expenditures, $441,723, including $441,629 for 283 grants (high: $25,000; low: $25).
Purpose and activities: Emphasis on community funds and higher education, including employee matching gifts; support also for hospitals, youth agencies, and arts organizations.
Types of support: Employee matching gifts.
Limitations: Giving limited to seven counties of south central PA.
Application information:
Write: Eloise C. Aurand, Dir., Pub. Rel.
Employer Identification Number: 236444555

6270
William Stucki Hansen Foundation ☆
2600 Neville Rd.
Pittsburgh 15225

Established in 1984 in PA.
Donor(s): Hansen, Inc.
Foundation type: Independent
Financial data (yr. ended 11/30/89): Assets, $950,327 (M); gifts received, $400,000; expenditures, $123,440, including $122,150 for 23 grants (high: $52,500; low: $100).
Purpose and activities: Support primarily for higher and secondary education, and Christian religious purposes.
Types of support: Endowment funds, equipment, operating budgets.
Limitations: Giving primarily in PA.
Application information: Application form not required.
Deadline(s): None
Write: William S. Hansen, Pres.
Officers and Directors:* William S. Hansen,* Pres.; Nancy K. Hansen,* V.P.; William Gregg Hansen,* Secy.-Treas.
Employer Identification Number: 251483674

6271
The Greater Harrisburg Foundation
P.O. Box 678
Harrisburg 17108-0678 (717) 236-5040

Established in 1920 in PA; assets first acquired in 1940; grants first made in the mid-1940's.
Foundation type: Community
Financial data (yr. ended 12/31/89): Assets, $3,383,095 (M); gifts received, $1,102,046; expenditures, $659,557, including $487,437 for 241 grants (high: $20,000; low: $10).
Purpose and activities: Giving for education, health, human services, community development, and arts and humanities; priority assigned to funding new projects and awarding seed money to organizations which may not be eligible for support elsewhere.
Types of support: Seed money, special projects, conferences and seminars, matching funds, publications, research, scholarship funds.
Limitations: Giving primarily in PA, with emphasis on Dauphin, Cumberland, Franklin, and Perry counties in central PA. No grants to individuals, or for operating or capital expenses.
Publications: Annual report (including application guidelines), informational brochure, application guidelines.
Application information: Contact foundation for application guidelines. Application form not required.
Initial approach: Proposal
Copies of proposal: 1
Deadline(s): Apr. 15 for spring round; Sept. 1 for fall round
Board meeting date(s): June and Nov. for grantmaking; Feb. for policy review
Final notification: 2 weeks following meeting date
Write: Diane Sandquist Swartzkopf, Pres.
Officers and Distribution Committee:* Lois Lehrman Grass,* Chair.; Gerald H. Hempt,* Vice-Chair.; John M. Aichele, William H. Alexander, Tita Eberly, Jacqueline M. Little, John M. Schrantz, John McD. Sharpe, Conrad M. Siegel, Elsie W. Swenson, Nathan H. Waters, Jr., Esq.
Staff: Diane Sanquist Swartzkopf, Pres.
Trustee Banks: CCNB Bank, N.A., Citizens National Bank & Trust Co., Citizens National Bank of Greencastle, Commonwealth National Bank, Dauphin Deposit Bank & Trust Co., Farmers and Merchants Trust Co., Farmers Trust Co. of Carlisle, First National Bank of Greencastle, The First Bank and Trust Co. of Mechanicsburg, First National Bank and Trust Co. of Waynesboro, Fulton Bank, GHF, Inc., Hamilton Bank, The Juniata Valley Bank, Pennsylvania National Bank and Trust Co., Valley Bank and Trust Co.
Number of staff: 1 full-time professional; 2 part-time professional; 1 full-time support.
Employer Identification Number: 236294219

6272
Harsco Corporation Fund ⌑
c/o Harsco Corp.
P.O. Box 8888
Camp Hill 17011-8888 (717) 763-7064

Trust established in 1956 in PA.
Donor(s): Harsco Corp.
Foundation type: Company-sponsored
Financial data (yr. ended 12/31/88): Assets, $7,773,002 (M); expenditures, $446,170, including $421,889 for 227 grants (high: $101,910; low: $50).
Purpose and activities: Grants largely to community funds and health agencies in areas of corporation operations; educational and performing arts grants primarily for matching gifts. Requests for contributions originate with local operating management and are approved or disapproved at the fund's central office. Scholarship program for children of employees administered through National Merit Scholarship Corp.
Types of support: General purposes, operating budgets, continuing support, employee-related scholarships, employee matching gifts.
Limitations: Giving primarily in areas of company operations. No grants to individuals, or for special projects, building or endowment funds, or research programs; no loans.
Publications: Program policy statement.
Application information: Application form required for employee-related scholarships.
Initial approach: Letter
Deadline(s): Jan. 12 for scholarships; no set deadline for grants
Board meeting date(s): Apr. and as required
Write: Richard Y. Eby, Secy. (Grants); Demaris K. Hetrick, Dir., Public Relations (Scholarship Prog.)
Officers and Trustees:*: Jeffrey J. Burdge,* Pres.; M.W. Gambill,* V.P.; Richard Y. Eby, Secy.; George F. Rezich, Treas.; Robert F. Nation.
Employer Identification Number: 236278376

6273
The Hassel Foundation ⌑
c/o Michael Krekstein
1760 Market St., 13th Fl.
Philadelphia 19103 (215) 561-6400

Trust established in 1961 in PA.
Donor(s): Morris Hassel,† Calvin Hassel.†
Foundation type: Independent
Financial data (yr. ended 12/31/88): Assets, $3,710,834 (M); expenditures, $228,856, including $183,500 for 20 grants (high: $35,000; low: $500) and $13,000 for 8 grants to individuals (high: $2,500; low: $1,000).
Purpose and activities: Support for hospitals, and higher and other education; two scholarships are awarded annually to graduating seniors of two specific high schools.
Types of support: General purposes, building funds, student aid.
Limitations: Giving primarily in PA. No grants to individuals (except for scholarships at specified high schools).
Application information: Scholarship applications are available from the high school principal's office; no application form for grants.
Initial approach: Letter
Deadline(s): None
Board meeting date(s): June and as required
Write: Herman H. Krekstein, Secy.
Officer and Trustees: Herman H. Krekstein, Secy.; Barbara Cohen, Sarle H. Cohen, Jay L. Goldberg, Marilyn Khoury, Theodore Kobrin, I.H. Krekstein, Michael H. Krekstein, Ephram Royfe, Morton M. Silton, Merle Wolfson.
Employer Identification Number: 236251862

6274
Lita Annenberg Hazen Charitable Trust
150 Radnor Chester Rd., Suite A200
St. Davids 19087 (215) 341-9270

Trust established in 1952 in NY.
Donor(s): Lita A. Hazen.
Foundation type: Independent
Financial data (yr. ended 12/31/89): Assets, $5,579,978 (M); expenditures, $2,361,324, including $2,356,234 for 61 grants (high: $1,000,000; low: $100).
Purpose and activities: Grants largely for medical research, hospitals, education, and cultural programs; some support for social services, especially Jewish welfare agencies.
Types of support: Annual campaigns, general purposes, scholarship funds.
Limitations: Giving primarily in New York, NY. No grants to individuals.
Application information: Contributes only to pre-selected organizations. Applications not accepted.
Write: A.C. Cory
Trustee: Walter H. Annenberg.
Number of staff: 5
Employer Identification Number: 236286759

6275
H. J. Heinz Company Foundation ▼
P.O. Box 57
Pittsburgh 15230 (412) 456-5772

Trust established in 1951 in PA.
Donor(s): H.J. Heinz Co.
Foundation type: Company-sponsored
Financial data (yr. ended 4/30/87): Assets, $8,336,715 (M); gifts received, $6,700,000; expenditures, $4,699,352, including $3,830,783 for grants and $840,333 for 2,037 employee matching gifts.
Purpose and activities: Support mainly for community funds; grants also for higher education, including employee matching gifts, hospitals, youth and social agencies, cultural programs, and research in nutrition.
Types of support: Annual campaigns, building funds, continuing support, employee matching gifts, operating budgets, seed money, technical assistance, emergency funds, equipment, internships, scholarship funds, fellowships, special projects, research, publications, conferences and seminars, professorships, endowment funds, capital campaigns.
Limitations: Giving primarily in areas of company operations. No grants to individuals, or for deficit financing, or land acquisition; no loans.
Publications: Program policy statement, application guidelines.
Application information: Application form not required.
Initial approach: Letter
Copies of proposal: 1
Deadline(s): None
Board meeting date(s): As necessary
Final notification: Varies
Write: Elizabeth Atkinson, Admin.
Officers and Trustees: Anthony F.J. O'Reilly, Chair.; Karyll A. Davis, Secy.; R. Derek Finlay, S.D. Wiley, Mellon Bank, N.A.
Number of staff: 1 full-time professional; 1 full-time support.
Employer Identification Number: 256018924

6276
Howard Heinz Endowment ▼ ⌑
30 CNG Tower
625 Liberty Ave.
Pittsburgh 15222-3199 (412) 391-5122

Trust established in 1941 in PA.
Donor(s): Howard Heinz,† Elizabeth Rust Heinz.†
Foundation type: Independent
Financial data (yr. ended 12/31/88): Assets, $433,860,577 (M); expenditures, $16,707,947, including $15,299,077 for 177 grants (high: $1,500,000; low: $300; average: $20,000-$250,000).
Purpose and activities: After gifts to certain agencies with which Mr. Heinz was associated during his life, the endowment supports music and the arts, education, health, social services, and urban and international affairs, usually with one-time, non-renewable grants for new programs, seed money, and capital projects.
Types of support: Seed money, building funds, annual campaigns, emergency funds, general purposes, equipment, endowment funds, research, scholarship funds, matching funds, program-related investments, operating budgets, renovation projects, capital campaigns.
Limitations: Giving limited to PA, with emphasis on Pittsburgh and the Allegheny County area; educational grants limited to Pittsburgh and Allegheny County. No grants to individuals; no loans.
Publications: Annual report (including application guidelines).
Application information: Application form required.
Initial approach: Letter, proposal, or telephone
Copies of proposal: 1
Deadline(s): 90 days before meeting date
Board meeting date(s): June and Dec.
Final notification: 3 to 4 months
Write: Alfred W. Wishart, Jr., Exec. Dir.
Officers: Jack E. Kime, Assoc. Dir., Chief Financial and Admin. Officer; Alfred W. Wishart, Jr., Exec. Dir.; Dixon R. Brown, Dir. of Finance.
Trustees: Henry John Heinz III, Chair.; Drue Heinz, Joseph W. Oliver, William H. Rea, William W. Scranton, Mellon Bank, N.A.
Number of staff: 7 full-time professional; 2 part-time professional; 9 full-time support.
Employer Identification Number: 251064784

6277
Vira I. Heinz Endowment ▼
The CNG Tower
625 Liberty Ave., 30th Fl.
Pittsburgh 15222-3199 (412) 391-5122

Trust established in 1983 in PA.
Donor(s): Vira I. Heinz.†
Foundation type: Independent
Financial data (yr. ended 12/31/88): Assets, $212,563,283 (M); expenditures, $7,699,916, including $6,913,371 for 125 grants (high: $1,000,000; low: $388; average: $5,000-$150,000).
Purpose and activities: Support for education, human services, arts and humanities, health and nutrition, religion and values, and economic development.
Types of support: Capital campaigns, general purposes, renovation projects, seed money, special projects, technical assistance, building funds.
Limitations: Giving limited to Pittsburgh and western PA, although in certain cases support may be considered on a national or international basis. No grants for general endowments.
Publications: Annual report, informational brochure.
Application information: Application form required.
Initial approach: Letter, proposal, or telephone
Deadline(s): 60 days prior to board meeting
Board meeting date(s): Mar. and Oct.
Final notification: 3 to 4 months
Write: Alfred W. Wishart, Jr., Exec. Dir.
Administrator: Alfred W. Wishart, Jr., Exec. Dir.
Trustees: James M. Walton, Chair.; William H. Rea, Helen P. Rush, John T. Ryan, S. Donald Wiley, Mellon Bank, N.A.
Number of staff: 8 full-time professional; 1 part-time professional; 8 full-time support.
Employer Identification Number: 256235878

6278
Heinz Family Foundation ⌑
4440 USX Tower, Suite 4440
600 Grant St.
Pittsburgh 15219

Established in 1984 in PA.
Foundation type: Independent
Financial data (yr. ended 12/31/88): Assets, $1,684,833 (M); expenditures, $159,728, including $155,000 for 4 grants (high: $67,500; low: $5,000).
Purpose and activities: Giving primarily for secondary and higher education; support also for a museum.
Application information: Contributes only to pre-selected organizations. Applications not accepted.
Trustees: Dixon R. Brown, Dolores Senanis.
Employer Identification Number: 251485640

6279
H. J. & Drue Heinz Foundation ▼
USX Tower, Suite 4440
600 Grant St.
Pittsburgh 15219 (412) 456-5731

Established in 1954 in PA.
Foundation type: Independent
Financial data (yr. ended 12/31/88): Assets, $2,228,079 (M); gifts received, $1,196,451; expenditures, $1,394,236, including $1,378,125 for 62 grants (high: $250,000; low: $250; average: $1,000-$25,000).
Purpose and activities: Emphasis on culture, conservation, and higher education.
Types of support: Special projects.
Limitations: Giving primarily in PA, NY, and Washington, DC.
Application information: Contributes only to pre-selected organizations. Applications not accepted.
Board meeting date(s): Nov.

Write: Dixon R. Brown, Trustee
Trustee: Dixon R. Brown.
Number of staff: 1 full-time professional.
Employer Identification Number: 256018930

6280
The Hershey Foods Corporation Fund ▼
14 East Chocolate Ave.
Hershey 17033-0814 (717) 534-7574

Trust established in 1960 in PA.
Donor(s): Hershey Foods Corp.
Foundation type: Company-sponsored
Financial data (yr. ended 12/31/89): Assets, $4,911,000 (M); expenditures, $2,177,000, including $1,478,000 for 203 grants (high: $395,000; low: $150; average: $500-$5,000) and $344,000 for 716 employee matching gifts.
Purpose and activities: Emphasis on higher education, including employee matching gifts, social services, civic affairs, and community funds; some support for health associations.
Types of support: Employee matching gifts, operating budgets, continuing support, annual campaigns, seed money, emergency funds, building funds, equipment, endowment funds, fellowships, research, publications, conferences and seminars, capital campaigns, general purposes, scholarship funds.
Limitations: Giving primarily in PA. No grants to individuals, or for endowment funds that are not part of the higher education capital funds campaign; no loans.
Application information: Application form not required.
Initial approach: Letter
Copies of proposal: 1
Deadline(s): None
Board meeting date(s): Monthly, with some exceptions
Final notification: 1 to 2 months
Write: L.W. Simmons, Corp. Contribs. Dir., Hershey Foods Corp.
Officer and Trustees:* Richard A. Zimmerman,* Chair.; J.P. Viviano, Kenneth L. Wolfe.
Number of staff: None.
Employer Identification Number: 236239132

6281
The High Foundation
P.O. Box 10008
Lancaster 17605-0008

Established in 1980 in PA.
Foundation type: Independent
Financial data (yr. ended 08/31/89): Assets, $1,948,253 (M); gifts received, $285,653; expenditures, $278,547, including $265,887 for 15 grants (high: $150,000; low: $250; average: $250-$150,000) and $6,000 for 6 grants to individuals of $1,000 each.
Purpose and activities: Giving for scholarships in higher education; support also for social services and religious organizations, including schools.
Types of support: Capital campaigns, general purposes.
Trustees: Calvin G. High, and 9 additional trustees.
Number of staff: None.
Employer Identification Number: 232149972

6282
Allen Hilles Fund
P.O. Box 8777
Philadelphia 19101-8777 (215) 828-8145

Trust established in 1983 in PA.
Donor(s): Edith Hilles Dewees.†
Foundation type: Independent
Financial data (yr. ended 12/31/89): Assets, $3,416,904 (M); expenditures, $196,633, including $153,200 for 62 grants (high: $5,000; low: $200; average: $3,000-$5,000).
Purpose and activities: "Support in the areas of education, health, counseling, and activities of the Religious Society of Friends."
Types of support: General purposes, operating budgets, seed money, special projects.
Limitations: Giving primarily in the greater Philadelphia, PA, and Wilmington, DE, areas. No grants to individuals, or for capital projects, endowments, conferences and seminars, or agency promotion, such as marketing, development, publication of annual reports, or sponsorship of fundraising events.
Publications: Annual report (including application guidelines).
Application information: Applicants limited to 1 request per calendar year. Application form required.
Initial approach: Proposal
Copies of proposal: 4
Deadline(s): Mar. 1, May 1, Sept.1, and Nov. 1
Board meeting date(s): Apr., June, Oct., and Dec.
Final notification: 2 months
Write: Judith L. Bardes, Mgr.
Officer: Judith L. Bardes, Mgr.
Trustees: Doris H. Darnell, Robert L. Dewees, Jr., Polly Dewees Moffett, Bryn Mawr Trust Co.
Number of staff: 1 part-time professional.
Employer Identification Number: 516154986

6283
The Hillman Foundation, Inc. ▼
2000 Grant Bldg.
Pittsburgh 15219 (412) 338-3466

Incorporated in 1951 in DE.
Donor(s): John Hartwell Hillman, Jr.,† J.H. Hillman & Sons Co., Hillman Land Co., and family-owned corporations.
Foundation type: Independent
Financial data (yr. ended 12/31/89): Assets, $44,268,934 (M); gifts received, $990,017; expenditures, $3,340,325, including $2,964,100 for 58 grants (high: $780,000; low: $2,000; average: $4,000-$200,000).
Purpose and activities: Program areas include cultural advancement and the arts, education, health and medicine, civic and community affairs, social services, youth, and religion.
Types of support: Continuing support, seed money, endowment funds, matching funds, professorships, special projects, building funds, equipment, land acquisition, capital campaigns, renovation projects.
Limitations: Giving primarily in Pittsburgh and southwestern PA. No grants to individuals, or for operating budgets, annual campaigns, deficit financing, travel, or conferences; no loans.
Publications: Annual report (including application guidelines).
Application information: Application form not required.
Initial approach: Letter
Copies of proposal: 1
Deadline(s): None
Board meeting date(s): Apr., June, Oct., and Dec., and at annual meeting in May
Final notification: 3 to 4 months
Write: Ronald W. Wertz, Pres.
Officers: Henry L. Hillman,* Chair.; Ronald W. Wertz, Pres.; C.G. Grefenstette,* V.P.; David H. Ross, Treas.
Directors:* H. Vaughan Blaxter III, Elise H. Hillman, Lawrence M. Wagner.
Number of staff: 3 full-time professional; 1 full-time support.
Employer Identification Number: 256011462

6284
The Henry L. Hillman Foundation
2000 Grant Bldg.
Pittsburgh 15219 (412) 338-3466

Established in 1964 in PA.
Donor(s): Henry L. Hillman.
Foundation type: Independent
Financial data (yr. ended 12/31/89): Assets, $14,330,556 (M); expenditures, $767,307, including $741,700 for 48 grants (high: $381,950; low: $250; average: $1,000-$5,000).
Purpose and activities: Support for the arts and cultural programs, youth, conservation, civic affairs, community development, church support, higher and secondary education, social services, and hospitals.
Types of support: Operating budgets, continuing support, annual campaigns, seed money, emergency funds, building funds, equipment, matching funds, special projects, renovation projects, capital campaigns.
Limitations: Giving primarily in Pittsburgh and southwestern PA. No grants to individuals, or for deficit financing, land acquisition, endowment funds, research, publications, or conferences; no loans.
Publications: Financial statement.
Application information: Application form not required.
Initial approach: Letter
Copies of proposal: 1
Deadline(s): None
Board meeting date(s): Mar. and Dec.
Final notification: 3 to 4 months
Write: Ronald W. Wertz, Exec. Dir. and Secy.
Officers: Henry L. Hillman,* Pres.; Ronald W. Wertz,* Exec. Dir. and Secy.; David H. Ross, Treas.
Directors:* H. Vaughan Blaxter III.
Number of staff: 1 part-time professional.
Employer Identification Number: 256065959

6285
The Margaret Mellon Hitchcock Foundation ⌑
c/o Mellon Bank, N.A.
P.O. Box 185
Pittsburgh 15258 (412) 234-5892

Trust established in 1961 in PA.
Donor(s): Margaret Mellon Hitchcock.
Foundation type: Independent
Financial data (yr. ended 12/31/86): Assets, $1,900,424 (M); expenditures, $168,238,

including $151,000 for 25 grants (high: $50,000; low: $1,000).
Purpose and activities: Grants largely for hospitals, music, aid to the handicapped, and secondary education.
Limitations: Giving primarily in the New York, NY, area. No grants to individuals, or for building or endowment funds, operating budgets, or special projects.
Application information: Application form required.
Board meeting date(s): Oct. or Nov.
Write: Leonard B. Richards III, V.P., Mellon Bank, N.A.
Officer: A.A. Vestal, Secy.
Trustees: Margaret Mellon Hitchcock, Thomas Hitchcock III, Alexander M. Laughlin, Mellon Bank, N.A.
Employer Identification Number: 256018992

6286
The Holstrom Family Foundation
P.O. Box 1310
Doylestown 18901

Established in 1984 in NY.
Donor(s): Carleton Holstrom, Bear Stearns & Co.
Foundation type: Independent
Financial data (yr. ended 11/30/88): Assets, $597,189 (M); expenditures, $116,900, including $109,875 for 33 grants (high: $25,000; low: $100).
Purpose and activities: Giving primarily for the arts and other cultural programs, education, Jewish welfare, hospitals, and social services.
Types of support: Annual campaigns, capital campaigns, endowment funds, research.
Limitations: Giving primarily in New York, NY, and NJ. No grants to individuals.
Application information: Contributes only to pre-selected organizations. Applications not accepted.
Officers: Carleton Holstrom, Pres.; Christina L. Holstrom, V.P.; Mary Beth Kineke, V.P.; Marcia O. Holstrom, Secy.; Cynthia J. Cawthorne, Treas.
Employer Identification Number: 222611162

6287
Esther Gowen Hood Trust ⌘ ☆
c/o Mellon Bank (East), N.A.
P.O. Box 7236
Philadelphia 19101 (215) 553-3208

Foundation type: Independent
Financial data (yr. ended 9/30/88): Assets, $1,076,107 (M); expenditures, $67,109, including $57,000 for 21 grants (high: $5,000; low: $1,000).
Purpose and activities: Support primarily to organizations helping the needy, including health services and programs for youth, the aged, and women.
Types of support: General purposes, operating budgets.
Limitations: Giving limited to Philadelphia, PA. No grants to individuals.
Application information:
Initial approach: Proposal
Deadline(s): Apr. 15
Write: Pat Kling, Mgr.
Officer: Pat Kling, Mgr.
Trustee: Mellon Bank (East), N.A.
Employer Identification Number: 236223619

6288
Janet A. Hooker Charitable Trust
150 Radnor Chester Rd., Suite A200
St. Davids 19087 (215) 341-9270

Trust established in 1952 in NY.
Donor(s): Janet A. Neff Hooker.
Foundation type: Independent
Financial data (yr. ended 12/31/89): Assets, $8,265,528 (M); expenditures, $621,420, including $567,800 for 59 grants (high: $45,000; low: $1,000).
Purpose and activities: Support largely for arts and culture, historic preservation, conservation, medical research and health services, and social service agencies; giving also for animal welfare, religion, and education.
Types of support: Annual campaigns, general purposes.
Limitations: Giving primarily in NY, FL, and Washington, DC. No grants to individuals.
Application information: Applications not accepted.
Write: A.C. Cory
Trustee: Walter H. Annenberg.
Number of staff: 5 full-time professional.
Employer Identification Number: 236286762

6289
Elizabeth S. Hooper Foundation
223 West Lancaster Ave., Suite 200
Devon 19333

Established in 1967.
Donor(s): Interstate Marine Transport Co., Interstate Towing Co., Interstate Ocean Transport Co., and members of the Hooper family.
Foundation type: Independent
Financial data (yr. ended 06/30/89): Assets, $1,513,733 (M); gifts received, $350,000; expenditures, $381,057, including $371,670 for 82 grants (high: $100,000; low: $250).
Purpose and activities: Giving largely for higher and secondary education; grants also for cultural programs, public policy organizations, health, and Protestant church support.
Types of support: Building funds, special projects, general purposes, emergency funds, research, scholarship funds, operating budgets.
Application information: Foundation is not considering any new grant requests. Applications not accepted.
Officers and Directors:* Adrian S. Hooper,* Pres.; Thomas Hooper,* V.P.; Bruce H. Hooper,* Secy.; Ralph W. Hooper,* Treas.; John P. Lally.
Employer Identification Number: 236434997

6290
John M. Hopwood Charitable Trust ⌘
c/o Pittsburgh National Bank
Trust Dept. - 965
Pittsburgh 15265

Trust established about 1948 in PA.
Donor(s): John M. Hopwood.†
Foundation type: Independent
Financial data (yr. ended 12/31/88): Assets, $10,270,927 (M); gifts received, $94,816; expenditures, $577,585, including $509,600 for 77 grants (high: $50,000; low: $250).
Purpose and activities: Giving for hospitals, higher education, youth and social service agencies, cultural programs, community funds, and church support.
Limitations: Giving primarily in PA and FL.
Application information:
Initial approach: Letter
Deadline(s): None
Write: James R. Smith, V.P., Pittsburgh National Bank
Trustees: William T. Hopwood, Pittsburgh National Bank.
Employer Identification Number: 256022634

6291
The Houghton-Carpenter Foundation ⌘
P.O. Box 930
Valley Forge 19482 (215) 666-4000

Established in 1951 in PA.
Donor(s): Aaron E. Carpenter,† Edythe A. Carpenter,† E.F. Houghton & Co.
Foundation type: Independent
Financial data (yr. ended 6/30/88): Assets, $1,676,940 (M); gifts received, $100,000; expenditures, $94,419, including $87,845 for 74 grants (high: $5,000; low: $150).
Purpose and activities: Giving for youth organizations, education, community affairs, and social services.
Types of support: General purposes, annual campaigns, equipment, emergency funds.
Limitations: Giving primarily in Philadelphia, PA. No grants to individuals.
Application information: Application form not required.
Initial approach: Letter
Deadline(s): None
Write: William F. MacDonald, Jr., Trustee
Trustees: William F. MacDonald, Jr., Robert Osborne, Bruce A. Schuck.
Employer Identification Number: 236230874

6292
The Hoyt Foundation ⌘
c/o First National Bank Bldg.
P.O. Box 1488
New Castle 16103 (412) 652-5511

Incorporated in 1962 in PA.
Donor(s): May Emma Hoyt,† Alex Crawford Hoyt.
Foundation type: Independent
Financial data (yr. ended 10/31/88): Assets, $8,390,487 (M); expenditures, $522,145, including $287,050 for 36 grants (high: $65,000; low: $200) and $147,859 for 208 grants to individuals (high: $4,000; low: $75).
Purpose and activities: Emphasis on higher education, including scholarships, and a hospital; some support also for cultural programs.
Types of support: Student aid, annual campaigns, building funds, capital campaigns, continuing support, seed money.
Limitations: Giving limited to residents of, or organizations located in Lawrence County, PA.
Application information: Application form required.

Initial approach: Proposal
Deadline(s): July 15 and Dec. 15 for scholarships
Board meeting date(s): Monthly
Write: Dorothy A. Patton
Officer and Directors: Thomas V. Mansell, Pres. and Secy.; A. Wayne Cole, Thomas J. O'Shane, Paul H. Reed, John W. Sant.
Number of staff: 1 part-time support.
Employer Identification Number: 256064468

6293
Hughes Foundation, Inc.
34 North Crystal St.
East Stroudsburg 18301

Established in 1959 in PA.
Donor(s): Russell C. Hughes Trust.
Foundation type: Independent
Financial data (yr. ended 04/30/89): Assets, $441,922 (M); gifts received, $76,000; expenditures, $121,847, including $118,000 for 15 grants (high: $30,000; low: $2,000; average: $2,000).
Purpose and activities: Grants primarily for education and youth organizations; support also for a community association, a public library, and a hospital.
Limitations: Giving primarily in the Stroudsburg, PA, area.
Application information: Contributes only to pre-selected organizations. Applications not accepted.
Directors: Ed V. Adamiak, Paul Dellaria, Alan S. Holliday, R. Clinton Hughes, R. Dale Hughes, Betty A. Rowe.
Employer Identification Number: 236298104

6294
Milton G. Hulme Charitable Foundation ⌑
720 Frick Bldg.
Pittsburgh 15219 (412) 281-2007

Established in 1960 in PA.
Donor(s): Glover & MacGregor, Inc.
Foundation type: Independent
Financial data (yr. ended 12/31/86): Assets, $3,107,113 (M); expenditures, $126,082, including $123,100 for 49 grants (high: $20,000; low: $250).
Purpose and activities: Giving primarily for hospitals, higher education, and music; some support for youth agencies.
Limitations: Giving primarily in PA. No grants to individuals.
Application information: Application form not required.
Initial approach: Letter, proposal, or telephone
Copies of proposal: 1
Deadline(s): Submit proposal preferably in early Dec.; deadline Dec. 15
Board meeting date(s): Dec.
Final notification: 2 weeks after application deadline
Write: Helen C. Hulme, Trustee
Trustees: Nathalie H. Curry, Helen C. Hulme, Jocelyn H. MacConnell, Helen H. Shoup.
Number of staff: 2 part-time support.
Employer Identification Number: 256062896

6295
The Hunt Foundation ⌑
One Bigelow Sq., Suite 630
Pittsburgh 15219 (412) 281-8734

Trust established in 1951 in PA.
Donor(s): Roy A. Hunt,† and members of the Hunt family.
Foundation type: Independent
Financial data (yr. ended 12/31/88): Assets, $9,980,622 (M); expenditures, $639,113, including $544,789 for 194 grants (high: $10,000; low: $500; average: $1,000).
Purpose and activities: Grants generally initiated by the trustees, with emphasis on higher education; smaller grants for secondary education, and cultural and conservation programs.
Types of support: Annual campaigns, building funds, capital campaigns, endowment funds, general purposes.
Limitations: Giving primarily in the Pittsburgh, PA, and Boston, MA, areas. No grants to individuals.
Application information:
Initial approach: Letter
Copies of proposal: 1
Deadline(s): May 1 and Oct. 1
Board meeting date(s): June and Nov.
Final notification: July and Dec.
Write: L.B. Richards
Trustees: Susan Hunt Hollingsworth, Andrew McQ. Hunt, Christopher M. Hunt, Daniel K. Hunt, Helen McM. Hunt, John B. Hunt, Marion McM. Hunt, Richard McM. Hunt, Roy A. Hunt III, Torrence M. Hunt, Jr., William E. Hunt, Rachel Hunt Knowles, Mellon Bank, N.A.
Number of staff: 2 part-time professional; 2 part-time support.
Employer Identification Number: 256018925

6296
The Roy A. Hunt Foundation ▼
One Bigelow Sq., Suite 630
Pittsburgh 15219 (412) 281-8734

Established in 1966 in PA.
Donor(s): Roy A. Hunt.†
Foundation type: Independent
Financial data (yr. ended 5/31/88): Assets, $19,514,824 (M); expenditures, $593,065, including $428,000 for 21 grants (high: $50,000; low: $5,000; average: $7,500-$50,000).
Purpose and activities: Grants initiated by the trustees, primarily to support the Hunt Institute for Botanical Documentation at Carnegie-Mellon University; smaller grants for higher and secondary education, Protestant church support, and cultural programs.
Types of support: Annual campaigns, building funds, endowment funds, general purposes.
Limitations: Giving primarily in the Pittsburgh, PA, area. No grants to individuals.
Application information: Applications not accepted.
Deadline(s): May 1 and Oct. 1 for solicited proposals only
Board meeting date(s): June and Nov.
Final notification: July and Dec.
Write: Torrence M. Hunt, Jr., Admin. Trustee
Officer: K. Sidney Neuman, Secy.
Trustees: Susan Hunt Hollingsworth, Andrew McQ. Hunt, Christopher M. Hunt, Daniel K. Hunt, Helen McM. Hunt, John B. Hunt, Marion McM. Hunt, Richard McM. Hunt, Roy A. Hunt III, Torrence M. Hunt, Torrence M. Hunt, Jr., Rachel Hunt Knowles.
Number of staff: 2 part-time professional; 2 part-time support.
Employer Identification Number: 256105162

6297
Hunt Manufacturing Company Foundation
230 South Broad St.
Philadelphia 19102 (215) 732-7700

Established in 1955 in NJ.
Donor(s): Hunt Manufacturing Co.
Foundation type: Company-sponsored
Financial data (yr. ended 11/28/89): Assets, $3,116 (M); gifts received, $616,167; expenditures, $621,686, including $589,484 for 140 grants (high: $58,500; low: $150; average: $1,000-$5,000), $30,762 for 18 grants to individuals (high: $2,000; low: $1,000; average: $1,000-$2,000) and $1,440 for 18 employee matching gifts.
Purpose and activities: Grants largely for cultural programs, inner-city revitalization, public policy research, civic groups, and higher education, including scholarships for the children of company employees; some support also for youth and health agencies and community funds.
Types of support: Operating budgets, continuing support, annual campaigns, seed money, building funds, equipment, scholarship funds, employee-related scholarships, employee matching gifts, special projects, technical assistance.
Limitations: Giving primarily in Philadelphia, PA; Fresno, CA; Florence, KY; Statesville, NC; and Florence, AL. No grants to individuals (except for employee-related scholarships), or for endowment funds or matching gifts; no loans.
Publications: Application guidelines, 990-PF.
Application information: Application form not required.
Initial approach: Proposal
Copies of proposal: 1
Deadline(s): 6 weeks prior to board meeting dates
Board meeting date(s): Jan., Apr., July, and Oct.
Final notification: 3 months
Write: William E. Parshall, Secy.
Officers: Ronald Naples,* Pres.; William E. Parshall, Secy.; Rudolph M. Peins, Jr.,* Treas.
Trustees:* John Carney, Thomas Duffy, Rudolph Peins, Phyllis Perry, Scott Venella.
Number of staff: 1 full-time professional; 1 full-time support.
Employer Identification Number: 226062897

6298
The Huston Foundation ⌑
P.O. Box 139
Gladwyne 19035 (215) 527-4371

Incorporated in 1957 in PA.
Donor(s): Charles Lukens Huston, Jr.,† Mrs. Charles Lukens Huston, Jr., Ruth Huston.†
Foundation type: Independent

Financial data (yr. ended 12/31/88): Assets, $20,452,974 (M); expenditures, $842,855, including $613,180 for 72 grants (high: $50,000; low: $500).
Purpose and activities: Giving for social services and Protestant missionary programs.
Types of support: Operating budgets, special projects, annual campaigns, building funds, capital campaigns, equipment, general purposes.
Limitations: Giving primarily in southeastern PA. No grants to individuals, or for research programs or fellowships; no loans.
Publications: Grants list, informational brochure, application guidelines.
Application information: Application form required.
Initial approach: Letter
Copies of proposal: 1
Deadline(s): Submit proposal preferably in Mar. through Apr. or Sept. through Oct.; deadlines Apr. 1 and Oct. 1
Board meeting date(s): May and Nov.
Write: Dorothy C. Hamilton
Officer: Dorothy C. Hamilton.
Directors: Loring Catlin, Mrs. William M. Galt III, Mrs. Richard L. Hansen, Charles L. Huston III, Elinor H. Lashley.
Number of staff: 1 part-time support.
Employer Identification Number: 236284125

6299
Hyman Family Foundation ⌑
6315 Forbes Ave.
Pittsburgh 15217

Trust established in 1957 in PA.
Donor(s): Samuel M. Hyman, and others.
Foundation type: Independent
Financial data (yr. ended 8/31/88): Assets, $1,423,163 (M); gifts received, $1,000; expenditures, $94,347, including $87,201 for 29 grants (high: $50,000; low: $36).
Purpose and activities: Giving for Jewish welfare funds, higher education, and temple support.
Limitations: Giving primarily in PA.
Application information: Contributes only to pre-selected organizations. Applications not accepted.
Officer: Yetta Elinoff, Mgr.
Members: Saul Elinoff, William Elinoff, Lois Rubin.
Employer Identification Number: 256065761

6300
Independence Foundation ▼
2500 Philadelphia National Bank Bldg.
Philadelphia 19107-3493 (215) 563-8105

Established in 1932 as International Cancer Research Foundation; incorporated as Donner Foundation in 1945 in DE; divided in 1961 into Independence Foundation and a newly formed William H. Donner Foundation.
Donor(s): William H. Donner.†
Foundation type: Independent
Financial data (yr. ended 12/31/89): Assets, $76,378,000 (M); expenditures, $3,825,847, including $3,354,065 for 36 grants (high: $250,000; low: $1,000; average: $10,000-$300,000).
Purpose and activities: Support for educational and cultural organizations; support also for student aid in nursing education.
Types of support: Endowment funds, professorships, general purposes, scholarship funds, fellowships.
Limitations: No grants to individuals, or for building and development funds, travel, research, publications, operating budgets, college scholarships, graduate fellowships, or matching gifts.
Publications: Program policy statement, application guidelines, annual report.
Application information: Exhibit material, if sent, should be in single form. Receipt of proposals is acknowledged. Should the original prove to be within the scope of the foundation's interests, interviews with the board will be arranged prior to final determination. Application form not required.
Initial approach: Letter
Copies of proposal: 5
Deadline(s): 3 weeks before meetings
Board meeting date(s): Mar., June, Sept., and Dec.
Final notification: 3 to 6 weeks
Write: Robert A. Maes, Pres.
Officers and Directors:* Robert A. Maes,* Pres.; Alexander F. Barbieri,* Secy.; Viola MacInnes,* Treas.; Frederick H. Donner, Robert M. Scott.
Number of staff: 3 full-time professional.
Employer Identification Number: 231352110

6301
Ingerman-Ginsburg Israeli Fellowship Foundation ⌑ ☆
c/o Ira Ingerman
1429 Walnut St., 8th Fl.
Philadelphia 19102

Established in 1983.
Donor(s): Ira Ingerman, Stanley Ginsberg.
Foundation type: Independent
Financial data (yr. ended 11/30/88): Assets, $2,600 (M); gifts received, $100,008; expenditures, $101,985, including $100,000 for grants.
Purpose and activities: Support for a university.
Limitations: No grants to individuals.
Application information: Contributes only to pre-selected organizations. Applications not accepted.
Officers: Stanley Ginsburg,* Chair.; Ira Ingerman, Pres. and Treas.
Directors:* Arlene Ginsburg, Eileen Ingerman.
Employer Identification Number: 232278199

6302
The J.D.B. Fund ⌑
404 Swedesford Rd.
P.O. Box 157
Gwynedd 19436 (215) 699-2233

Trust established in 1966 in PA.
Donor(s): John Drew Betz.
Foundation type: Independent
Financial data (yr. ended 12/31/87): Assets, $7,675,891 (M); expenditures, $1,820,201, including $1,767,611 for 43 grants (high: $725,000; low: $1,000).
Purpose and activities: All grants originate with the trustees. Grants to health associations, hospitals, conservation organizations, societies or agencies devoted to historic preservation, and civic affairs.
Types of support: Building funds, equipment, land acquisition, matching funds.
Limitations: Giving primarily in Philadelphia, PA, and the surrounding area. No support for arts and sciences or medical research. No grants to individuals, or for endowment funds; scholarships, fellowships, demonstration projects, publications, or conferences; no loans for general support of established universities, charities, foundations, or hospitals.
Application information: Contributes only to pre-selected organizations. Applications not accepted.
Board meeting date(s): Monthly
Write: Paul J. Corr, Mgr.
Officer: Paul J. Corr, Mgr.
Trustees: Claire S. Betz, John Drew Betz.
Number of staff: 2
Employer Identification Number: 236418867

6303
Henry Janssen Foundation, Inc. ⌑
2650 Westview Dr.
Wyomissing 19610

Incorporated in 1931 in DE.
Donor(s): Members of the Janssen family.
Foundation type: Independent
Financial data (yr. ended 12/31/88): Assets, $9,869,022 (M); expenditures, $633,883, including $553,000 for 41 grants (high: $50,000; low: $1,000).
Purpose and activities: Emphasis on hospitals, health, cultural programs, Protestant church support, higher education, and community funds.
Limitations: Giving primarily in PA, particularly Reading and Berks County.
Application information: Contributes only to pre-selected organizations. Applications not accepted.
Officers and Trustees: Elsa L. Bowman, Pres.; Helene L. Master, V.P.; John W. Bowman, Secy.; El Roy P. Master, Treas.; David F. Rick, F. Eugene Stapleton.
Employer Identification Number: 231476340

6304
The Mary Hillman Jennings Foundation ▼
2325 Pittsburgh National Bldg.
Pittsburgh 15222 (412) 566-2510

Incorporated in 1968 in PA.
Donor(s): Mary Hillman Jennings.†
Foundation type: Independent
Financial data (yr. ended 12/31/89): Assets, $29,373,000 (M); qualifying distributions, $1,430,000, including $1,430,000 for 148 grants (high: $100,000; low: $750; average: $1,000-$50,000).
Purpose and activities: Grants to schools, youth agencies, and hospitals and health associations.
Types of support: Annual campaigns, building funds, capital campaigns, endowment funds, equipment, general purposes, renovation projects, research, special projects.

Limitations: Giving primarily in the Pittsburgh, PA, area. No grants to individuals.
Application information: Application form not required.
Initial approach: Letter
Deadline(s): Submit proposal in Feb., May, or Aug.; deadline Sept. 15
Board meeting date(s): Mar., June, Sept., Dec., and as required
Final notification: 3 to 6 months
Write: Paul Euwer, Jr., Exec. Dir.
Officers and Directors:* Evan D. Jennings II,* Pres.; Andrew L. Weil,* Secy.; Irving A. Wechsler,* Treas.; Paul Euwer, Jr.,* Exec. Dir.; Christina Jennings.
Number of staff: 1 full-time professional; 1 part-time support.
Employer Identification Number: 237002091

6305
Donald P. Jones Foundation ⌑
P.O. Box 58910
Philadelphia 19102-3910

Established in 1953 in PA.
Foundation type: Independent
Financial data (yr. ended 12/31/88): Assets, $1,102,758 (M); qualifying distributions, $64,505, including $37,161 for 70 grants (high: $3,533; low: $50) and $27,344 for 41 in-kind gifts.
Purpose and activities: Support primarily for health, youth, the arts, education, and labor.
Limitations: Giving primarily in PA.
Application information: Application form not required.
Deadline(s): None
Write: Donald P. Jones, Trustee
Trustees: Arthur W. Jones, Donald P. Jones, Ethel G. Jones.
Employer Identification Number: 236259820

6306
The Robert Junge Trust ⌑ ☆
3400 Centre Sq., West
Philadelphia 19102

Established in 1969.
Foundation type: Independent
Financial data (yr. ended 12/31/87): Assets, $1,258,640 (M); expenditures, $87,247, including $64,500 for 6 grants (high: $27,500; low: $1,000).
Purpose and activities: Giving to Protestant churches and affiliated educational organizations connected with them.
Limitations: Giving primarily in PA and MD. No grants to individuals.
Application information: Contributes only to pre-selected organizations. Applications not accepted.
Trustees: Kent Junge, Robert S. Junge, Lawson M. Smith.
Employer Identification Number: 236482504

6307
Samuel Justus Charitable Trust
P.O. Box 374
Oil City 16301 (814) 677-5085

Trust established in 1967 in PA.
Donor(s): Samuel Justus.†
Foundation type: Independent
Financial data (yr. ended 12/31/86): Assets, $9,168,220 (M); expenditures, $572,864, including $497,679 for 25 grants (high: $49,789; low: $83; average: $5,000-$30,000).
Purpose and activities: Giving to benefit orphans, dependent, neglected, delinquent, disadvantaged, and disabled children and youth.
Types of support: General purposes, operating budgets, building funds, land acquisition, equipment, continuing support, annual campaigns, seed money, emergency funds, deficit financing, renovation projects.
Limitations: Giving limited to Venango County, PA. No grants to individuals, or for endowment funds, matching gifts, scholarships, fellowships, special projects, research, publications, or conferences; no loans.
Publications: Annual report, application guidelines.
Application information: Application form required.
Initial approach: Letter
Copies of proposal: 2
Deadline(s): Submit proposal preferably in Apr., Aug., or Nov.; no set deadline
Board meeting date(s): May, Sept., and Dec.
Final notification: 2 months
Write: Stephen P. Kosak, Consultant
Trustee: First Seneca Bank.
Officer and Directors: R. Grant Carner, Secy.; William E. Breene, Leonard M. Carroll, Thomas Golonski, Joseph S. Harvey, E.G. Heffelfinger, Jr., Carl Hitechew, William White, Wallace E. Witmer.
Number of staff: 1 full-time professional; 1 part-time support.
Employer Identification Number: 256031058

6308
Edith C. Justus Trust ⌑
P.O. Box 374
Oil City 16301 (814) 677-5085

Trust established in 1931 in PA.
Donor(s): Edith C. Justus.†
Foundation type: Independent
Financial data (yr. ended 12/31/86): Assets, $3,087,965 (M); expenditures, $197,088, including $173,284 for 17 grants (high: $36,398; low: $25; average: $5,000-$20,000).
Purpose and activities: Giving largely for community development and civic affairs, including a library and public parks, and for social service and health agencies.
Types of support: General purposes, operating budgets, building funds, equipment, land acquisition, continuing support, annual campaigns, seed money, emergency funds, deficit financing, matching funds, renovation projects.
Limitations: Giving primarily in Venango County, PA, with emphasis on Oil City. No grants to individuals, or for endowment funds, matching gifts, scholarships, fellowships, special projects, research, publications, or conferences; no loans.
Publications: Application guidelines, 990-PF, grants list.
Application information: Application form required.
Initial approach: Letter
Copies of proposal: 3
Deadline(s): Submit proposal in Apr., Aug., or Nov.; no set deadline
Board meeting date(s): May, Sept., and Dec.
Final notification: 2 months
Write: Stephen P. Kosak, Consultant
Trustee: First Seneca Bank.
Number of staff: 1 full-time professional; 1 part-time support.
Employer Identification Number: 256031057

6309
Samuel and Rebecca Kardon Foundation ⌑
c/o Landsburg Platt & Flax
117 South 17th St.
Philadelphia 19103 (215) 561-6633

Trust established in 1952 in PA.
Donor(s): Emanuel S. Kardon, American Bag & Paper Corp.
Foundation type: Independent
Financial data (yr. ended 12/31/88): Assets, $6,800,468 (M); gifts received, $3,000; expenditures, $149,628, including $132,380 for 32 grants (high: $60,000; low: $100; average: $500-$2,000).
Purpose and activities: Emphasis on Jewish welfare funds, higher, secondary, and music education; support also for hospitals and social service agencies.
Limitations: Giving primarily in PA.
Application information:
Initial approach: Letter
Deadline(s): None
Write: Emanuel S. Kardon, Pres.
Officer and Trustee:* Emanuel S. Kardon,* Pres.
Employer Identification Number: 236278123

6310
The Katz Foundation ⌑
Gateway Towers, Suite 22K
Pittsburgh 15222 (412) 362-8000

Trust established in 1960 in PA.
Donor(s): Members of the Katz family.
Foundation type: Independent
Financial data (yr. ended 12/31/88): Assets, $757,260 (M); expenditures, $410,143, including $406,684 for 64 grants (high: $100,000; low: $50).
Purpose and activities: Giving primarily for Jewish welfare funds, youth, and cultural programs.
Limitations: Giving primarily in PA. No grants to individuals, or for operating budgets.
Application information: Contributes only to pre-selected organizations. Applications not accepted.
Write: William Katz, Trustee
Trustees: Hyman I. Katz, Joseph M. Katz, Marshall P. Katz, William Katz.
Employer Identification Number: 256062917

6311
T. James Kavanagh Foundation
57 Northwood Rd.
Newtown Square 19073-4322 (215) 356-0743
Mailing address: P.O. Box 609, Broomall, PA 19008

Established in 1968 in PA.
Donor(s): T. James Kavanagh.†

Foundation type: Independent
Financial data (yr. ended 12/31/88): Assets, $5,613,043 (M); qualifying distributions, $216,642, including $216,642 for 130 grants (high: $10,000; low: $300; average: $1,000).
Purpose and activities: At least 55 percent of funding for Catholic church support, welfare, and religious associations; support also for education, including religious schools.
Types of support: Operating budgets, continuing support, annual campaigns, emergency funds, building funds, equipment, special projects, research, general purposes.
Limitations: Giving primarily in PA. No support for private foundations; no grants to organizations outside the U.S., including Catholic organizations with missions overseas. No grants to individuals, or for endowment funds, seed money, deficit financing, land acquisition, publications, conferences, scholarships, fellowships, or matching gifts; no loans.
Publications: Application guidelines.
Application information: Application guidelines available from the foundation. Application form not required.
Initial approach: Proposal
Copies of proposal: 1
Deadline(s): Submit proposal preferably by the end of Feb., July, or Oct.
Board meeting date(s): Mid Mar., Aug., and Nov.
Final notification: End of month preceding board meeting date
Write: Brenda S. Brooks, C.E.O.
Officer: Brenda S. Brooks, C.E.O.
Trustees: Frank J. Brooks, Louis J. Esposito, Thomas E. Kavanagh.
Number of staff: 1 full-time professional; 1 part-time professional.
Employer Identification Number: 236442981

6312
Kate M. Kelley Foundation ⌘
c/o Hosack, Specht, Muetzel & Wood
305 Mt. Lebanon Blvd.
Pittsburgh 15234
Application address: 341 West Penn Pl., Pittsburgh, PA 15224; Tel.: (412) 661-0134

Established in 1976 in PA.
Donor(s): Edward J. Kelley.†
Foundation type: Independent
Financial data (yr. ended 12/31/88): Assets, $4,434,826 (M); expenditures, $283,212, including $243,000 for 44 grants (high: $10,000; low: $1,000).
Purpose and activities: Giving largely for Roman Catholic church support and church-related education; some support also for other higher and secondary education, and health education.
Limitations: Giving primarily in Pittsburgh, PA.
Application information: Application form not required.
Initial approach: Letter
Deadline(s): None
Write: Edward C. Ifft, Trustee
Trustees: Rev. Roy G. Getty, Edward C. Ifft, Rev. Leo V. Vanyo.
Employer Identification Number: 256090985

6313
Kennametal Foundation
P.O. Box 231
Latrobe 15650 (412) 539-5203

Trust established in 1955 in PA.
Foundation type: Company-sponsored
Financial data (yr. ended 06/30/89): Assets, $904,362 (M); gifts received, $400,000; expenditures, $180,712, including $179,248 for 167 grants.
Purpose and activities: Emphasis on higher education, hospitals, museums, and social services, including community funds.
Types of support: Continuing support, building funds, equipment, endowment funds, program-related investments, matching funds.
Limitations: No grants to individuals, or for scholarships or fellowships; no loans.
Application information: Contributes only to pre-selected organizations. Applications not accepted.
Board meeting date(s): Monthly
Write: Alex G. McKenna, Trustee
Trustees: James R. Breisinger, Alex G. McKenna, Quentin C. McKenna, Richard J. Orwig.
Employer Identification Number: 256036009

6314
Killeshandra Foundation ⌘ ☆
c/o Keeley Management Co.
259 Radnor-Chester Rd.
Radnor 19087 (215) 293-2010

Established in 1982.
Donor(s): Bruce H. Hooper.
Foundation type: Independent
Financial data (yr. ended 12/31/88): Assets, $96,758 (M); gifts received, $100,000; expenditures, $106,451, including $105,700 for 15 grants (high: $30,000; low: $200).
Purpose and activities: Giving primarily to education, especially military academies and higher education; support also for international affairs and foreign policy research, social services, and cultural programs.
Types of support: Scholarship funds, operating budgets.
Limitations: Giving primarily in PA.
Application information:
Initial approach: Proposal
Deadline(s): None
Write: Bruce H. Hooper, Trustee
Trustees: Cynthia H. Bell, Bruce H. Hooper, Eileen Hooper.
Employer Identification Number: 232205924

6315
Charles and Figa Kline Foundation
626 North Main St.
Allentown 18104 (215) 437-4077

Incorporated in 1957 in PA.
Donor(s): Charles Kline,† Figa Cohen Kline.†
Foundation type: Independent
Financial data (yr. ended 10/31/88): Assets, $6,249,834 (M); expenditures, $480,476, including $452,170 for 27 grants (high: $175,000; low: $200).
Purpose and activities: Giving largely for Jewish welfare and community service agencies, temple support, a community fund, and education.
Limitations: Giving primarily in Allentown, PA. No grants to individuals.
Application information: Application form not required.
Deadline(s): Sept. 30
Write: Fabian I. Fraenkel, Dir.
Directors: Fabian I. Fraenkel, Lynn B. Hirshorn, Leonard Rapoport.
Employer Identification Number: 236262315

6316
Josiah W. and Bessie H. Kline Foundation, Inc. ▼
42 Kline Village
Harrisburg 17104 (717) 232-0266

Incorporated in 1952 in DE.
Donor(s): Josiah W. Kline,† Bessie H. Kline.†
Foundation type: Independent
Financial data (yr. ended 12/31/89): Assets, $18,066,941 (M); expenditures, $1,079,097, including $958,700 for 53 grants (high: $200,000; low: $250).
Purpose and activities: Support primarily for higher education, hospitals, and the handicapped; support also for scientific or medical research, educational associations and building funds, health associations, child welfare organizations, historic preservation, and legal education and projects for the improvement of the law.
Types of support: General purposes, continuing support, annual campaigns, emergency funds, building funds, equipment, scholarship funds, matching funds, renovation projects, capital campaigns, land acquisition, lectureships, research.
Limitations: Giving primarily in south central PA. No grants to individuals, or for endowment funds, operating budgets, special projects, publications, conferences, or fellowships; no loans.
Publications: 990-PF.
Application information: Application form not required.
Initial approach: Proposal
Copies of proposal: 2
Deadline(s): None
Board meeting date(s): Semiannually
Final notification: 6 months
Write: Harry R. Bughman, Secy.
Officers and Directors:* Robert F. Nation,* Pres.; Richard E. Jordan,* V.P.; Harry R. Bughman,* Secy.; William J. King,* Treas.; William D. Boswell, Jeffrey J. Burdge, Cleve J. Fredricksen, James A. Marley, William S. Masland, John C. Tuten.
Number of staff: 1 full-time professional.
Employer Identification Number: 236245783

6317
Earl Knudsen Charitable Foundation
P.O. Box 1791
Pittsburgh 15230

Established about 1975.
Donor(s): Earl Knudsen.†
Foundation type: Independent
Financial data (yr. ended 12/31/89): Assets, $3,500,000 (M); expenditures, $193,800, including $172,900 for 41 grants (high: $40,000; low: $500; average: $5,000).

Purpose and activities: Emphasis on higher education, hospitals, youth agencies, Protestant church support, and cultural programs.
Types of support: General purposes.
Limitations: Giving primarily in PA. No grants to individuals, or for endowment funds, scholarships, fellowships, or matching gifts; no loans.
Application information: Application form not required.
Initial approach: Proposal
Copies of proposal: 1
Deadline(s): None
Board meeting date(s): Quarterly and as required
Final notification: Affirmative replies only
Write: William M. Schmidt, Secy.
Trustees: Roy Thomas Clark, Edwin F. Rodenbaugh, Union National Bank of Pittsburgh.
Number of staff: None.
Employer Identification Number: 256062530

6318
Hyman Korman Family Foundation ¤
Two Neshaminy Interplex
P.O. Box 2000
Trevose 19047

Trust established in 1947 in PA.
Donor(s): Members of the Korman family, Hyman Korman, Inc., and others.
Foundation type: Independent
Financial data (yr. ended 12/31/88): Assets, $6,073,306 (M); gifts received, $10,000; expenditures, $248,556, including $185,150 for 11 grants (high: $100,000; low: $100).
Purpose and activities: Emphasis on Jewish welfare funds and religious organizations and a hospital.
Limitations: Giving primarily in Philadelphia, PA. No grants to individuals.
Publications: 990-PF.
Application information: Contributes only to pre-selected organizations. Applications not accepted.
Trustees: Berton E. Korman, Leonard I. Korman, Samuel J. Korman, Steven H. Korman, I. Barney Moss.
Employer Identification Number: 236297326

6319
John Crain Kunkel Foundation ¤
1400 Market St., Suite 203
Camp Hill 17011 (717) 763-1784

Established in 1965 in PA.
Foundation type: Independent
Financial data (yr. ended 12/31/88): Assets, $7,631,114 (M); expenditures, $594,309, including $481,800 for 40 grants (high: $100,000; low: $300).
Purpose and activities: Emphasis on a hospital, higher and secondary education, cultural programs, a municipality, and social service agencies.
Limitations: Giving primarily in PA.
Application information:
Initial approach: Letter
Deadline(s): None
Write: Hasbrouck S. Wright, Exec. Trustee
Trustees: Hasbrouck S. Wright, Exec. Trustee; W.M. Kunkel, K.R. Stark.
Employer Identification Number: 237026914

6320
Edna G. Kynett Memorial Foundation, Inc.
P.O. Box 8228
Philadelphia 19101-8228 (215) 828-8145

Incorporated in 1954 in DE.
Donor(s): Harold H. Kynett.†
Foundation type: Independent
Financial data (yr. ended 12/31/87): Assets, $3,173,055 (M); expenditures, $293,196, including $280,000 for 5 grants (high: $165,000; low: $5,000).
Purpose and activities: Grants to hospitals for medical education and research, to help educate primary care physicians in the field of cardiovascular disease.
Types of support: Conferences and seminars, fellowships, special projects.
Limitations: Giving primarily in the Philadelphia, PA, area. No grants for endowment purposes.
Application information: Application form not required.
Initial approach: Proposal
Copies of proposal: 12
Write: Judith L. Bardes, Mgr.
Officers and Trustees: Joseph B. VanderVeer, M.D., Pres.; F.W. Elliott Farr, V.P.; Barclay Hallowell, Secy.; Michael W. Walsh, Treas.; Dr. Elmer H. Funk, Jr., Davis W. Gregg, Norman B. Makous, M.D., James Shea, Edward J. Stemmler, Edward S. Weyl, D. Straton Woodruff, Jr., M.D.
Number of staff: 1 part-time professional.
Employer Identification Number: 236296592

6321
The Lancaster County Foundation
Horst Group Bldg.
29 East King St., Rm. 14
Lancaster 17602 (717) 397-1629

Established in 1924 in PA.
Donor(s): Martin M. Harnish.†
Foundation type: Community
Financial data (yr. ended 04/30/89): Assets, $7,312,614 (M); expenditures, $390,627, including $378,012 for 52 grants (high: $89,614; low: $92; average: $3,000-$10,000) and $4,741 for 3 grants to individuals.
Purpose and activities: Giving for welfare, social services, especially aid to the handicapped, health services, youth agencies, education, and cultural programs.
Types of support: Building funds, equipment, renovation projects, special projects, seed money, student aid, matching funds, emergency funds, program-related investments, publications, research.
Limitations: Giving limited to Lancaster County, PA. No support for governmental agencies. No grants to individuals (except for a limited number of scholarships from donor-designated funds), or for operating budgets, continuing support, annual campaigns, deficit financing, land acquisition, endowment funds, fellowships, consulting services, or conferences and seminars; no loans.
Publications: Annual report, application guidelines.
Application information: Application form required.
Copies of proposal: 2
Deadline(s): Oct. 15
Board meeting date(s): Varies
Final notification: Jan. 31
Write: Nancy L. Neff, Exec. Secy.
Trustees: Robert S. Luttrell, Chair.; and 11 trustee banks.
Governing Committee: Donald B. Hostetter, Chair.; R. Wesley Shope, Vice-Chair.; Nancy L. Neff, Exec. Secy.; John R. Baldwin, Rev. David L. Gockley, John I. Hartman, Jr., S. Dale High, C. Edwin Ireland, Dawn K. Johnston, Bruce P. Ryder.
Number of staff: 1 part-time professional.
Employer Identification Number: 236419120

6322
The R. K. Laros Foundation ¤
3529 Magnolia Dr.
Easton 18042

Trust established in 1952 in PA.
Donor(s): Russell K. Laros.†
Foundation type: Independent
Financial data (yr. ended 12/31/88): Assets, $2,396,338 (M); expenditures, $192,656, including $178,402 for 15 grants (high: $75,000; low: $1,000).
Purpose and activities: Emphasis on higher education, the arts, community programs, historic preservation, and a hospital.
Types of support: General purposes.
Limitations: Giving primarily in the Lehigh Valley area of eastern PA. No grants to individuals, or for endowment funds or operating budgets.
Application information:
Initial approach: Proposal
Copies of proposal: 6
Deadline(s): None
Board meeting date(s): Annually between May and Sept.
Write: Robert A. Spillman, Secy.
Officers: R.K. Laros, Jr., M.D., Pres.; Talbot Shelton, V.P.; Robert A. Spillman, Secy.; James G. Whildin, M.D., Treas.
Employer Identification Number: 236207353

6323
The Lasko Family Foundation ¤
101 Clarke St.
West Chester 19380

Established in 1984 in PA.
Foundation type: Independent
Financial data (yr. ended 6/30/88): Assets, $450,301 (M); expenditures, $115,018, including $114,500 for 6 grants (high: $50,000; low: $1,500).
Purpose and activities: Support primarily for Jewish giving and medical research.
Application information: Contributes only to pre-selected organizations. Applications not accepted.
Officers and Directors: Oscar Lasko, Pres.; William E. Lasko, Treas.; Bernard Eizen.
Employer Identification Number: 232307053

6324
Laurel Foundation ⌑
Three Gateway Ctr., 6 North
Pittsburgh 15222 (412) 765-2400

Incorporated in 1951 in PA.
Donor(s): Cordelia S. May.
Foundation type: Independent
Financial data (yr. ended 12/31/88): Assets, $17,001,950 (M); expenditures, $968,875, including $747,000 for 46 grants (high: $50,000; low: $500).
Purpose and activities: Grants largely to organizations operating in the fields of higher and secondary education, conservation, health, cultural programs, and population planning, with concentration on projects originating in the Pittsburgh area; support also for immigration reform.
Types of support: General purposes, building funds, special projects, conferences and seminars, equipment, land acquisition, operating budgets, publications, lectureships.
Limitations: Giving primarily in western PA. No grants to individuals.
Publications: Annual report, application guidelines.
Application information:
Initial approach: Letter
Copies of proposal: 1
Deadline(s): Submit proposal preferably between Jan. and Apr. or July and Oct.; deadlines are May 1 and Nov. 1
Board meeting date(s): June and Dec.
Write: Gregory D. Curtis, Pres.
Officers: Gregory D. Curtis, Pres. and Secy.; Roger F. Meyer, V.P. and Treas.; Mrs. John F. Kraft, Jr.,* V.P.
Trustees:* Cordelia S. May, Chair.; Curtis S. Scaife, Robert E. Willison.
Number of staff: 2 part-time professional; 2 part-time support.
Employer Identification Number: 256008073

6325
The Lebovitz Fund ⌑
3050 Tremont St.
Allentown 18104 (215) 820-5053

Established in 1944 in PA.
Foundation type: Independent
Financial data (yr. ended 07/31/89): Assets, $1,801,767 (M); gifts received, $1,000; expenditures, $65,104, including $50,459 for 92 grants (high: $10,000; low: $20).
Purpose and activities: Support for conservation, culture, and Jewish giving.
Limitations: Giving primarily in MI.
Application information: Application form not required.
Initial approach: Letter
Deadline(s): None
Write: Herbert C. Lebovitz, Treas.
Officers: Clara H. Lebovitz, Pres.; Beth Ann Segal, Secy.; Herbert C. Lebovitz, Treas.
Directors: Jonathan Jayitch, James Lebovitz.
Employer Identification Number: 236270079

6326
James E. & Kathleen E. Lee Charitable Trust ⌑
c/o Pittsburgh National Bank, Trust Dept. 970
One Oliver Plaza
Pittsburgh 15265

Established in 1984 in PA.
Foundation type: Independent
Financial data (yr. ended 12/31/87): Assets, $364,063 (M); expenditures, $235,604, including $230,000 for 2 grants (high: $20,000; low: $3,000).
Purpose and activities: Support for a theological seminary; giving also to a Presbyterian church.
Limitations: Giving primarily in PA.
Application information: Contributes only to pre-selected organizations. Applications not accepted.
Trustees: James E. Lee, Kathleen E. Lee, Pittsburgh National Bank.
Employer Identification Number: 256253314

6327
Lehigh Portland Cement Company Charitable Trust ⌑ ☆
c/o Lehigh Portland Cement Co.
718 Hamilton Mall
Allentown 18105 (215) 776-2689

Established in 1953 in PA.
Donor(s): Lehigh Portland Cement Co.
Foundation type: Company-sponsored
Financial data (yr. ended 12/31/88): Assets, $931,740 (M); gifts received, $299,900; expenditures, $117,537, including $98,056 for 200 grants (high: $16,790; low: $20) and $9,184 for 41 employee matching gifts.
Purpose and activities: Emphasis in giving for health associations, United Way, children, and higher and elementary education, including an employee matching gift program; minor support also for religious organizations.
Types of support: Employee matching gifts, general purposes.
Limitations: Giving primarily in areas of company operations.
Application information: Form required for employee matching gift program.
Initial approach: Letter
Deadline(s): None
Write: Edward W. Hyland, V.P.
Officers and Trustees: R. Memmer, Pres.; H. Leube, V.P., Admin.; Edward W. Hyland, V.P. and Secy.; F.R. Snyder II, V.P. and Treas.; J. Stofflet, Merchants Bank.
Employer Identification Number: 236291364

6328
Margaret and Irvin Lesher Foundation ⌑
P.O. Box 374
Oil City 16301 (814) 677-5085

Trust established in 1963 in PA.
Donor(s): Margaret W. Lesher.†
Foundation type: Independent
Financial data (yr. ended 12/31/86): Assets, $1,521,646 (M); expenditures, $92,296, including $79,272 for 51 grants to individuals (high: $2,150; low: $100; average: $100-$2,000).
Purpose and activities: Giving limited to scholarships for graduates of Union High School, Clarion County; support also for a rural medical center, and for research concerning the treatment of cancer and heart diseases.
Types of support: Student aid.
Limitations: Giving limited to Union School District of Clarion County, PA. No grants to individuals (except for scholarships), or for endowment funds; no loans.
Publications: 990-PF, application guidelines.
Application information: Application form required.
Initial approach: Letter
Copies of proposal: 2
Deadline(s): Submit proposal preferably in Apr., Aug., or Nov.
Board meeting date(s): May and Sept. and Dec. if needed
Final notification: 2 months after board meeting
Write: Stephen P. Kosak, Consultant
Trustee: First Seneca Bank.
Number of staff: 1 full-time professional; 1 part-time support.
Employer Identification Number: 256067843

6329
Polly Annenberg Levee Charitable Trust ⌑
100 Matsonford Rd.
P.O. Box 750
Radnor 19088 (215) 293-8902

Trust established in 1952 in NY.
Donor(s): Polly Annenberg Levee.†
Foundation type: Independent
Financial data (yr. ended 12/31/88): Assets, $9,950,331 (M); expenditures, $951,875, including $885,000 for 11 grants (high: $450,000; low: $10,000; average: $5,000-$25,000).
Purpose and activities: Grants for hospitals, medical research, social services, and higher education.
Types of support: General purposes.
Limitations: Giving primarily in the Philadelphia, PA, and New York, NY, metropolitan areas and in FL. No grants to individuals.
Application information: Contributes only to pre-selected organizations. Applications not accepted.
Board meeting date(s): Irregularly
Trustee: Walter H. Annenberg.
Number of staff: None.
Employer Identification Number: 236286761

6330
Lindback Foundation
(also known as Christian and Mary Lindback Foundation)
c/o Fidelity Bank, N.A.
Broad & Walnut Sts.
Philadelphia 19109
Application address: 1500 One Franklin Plaza, Philadelphia, PA 19102; Tel.: (215) 854-6329

Trust established in 1955, registered in NJ.
Donor(s): Mary F. Lindback.†
Foundation type: Independent
Financial data (yr. ended 12/31/89): Assets, $11,304,671 (M); expenditures, $668,358,

including $492,000 for 100 grants (high: $40,000; low: $1,000).
Purpose and activities: Support primarily for higher education, including medical education, and hospitals and medical research.
Types of support: Fellowships, scholarship funds, capital campaigns, endowment funds.
Limitations: Giving primarily in PA and NJ. No grants to individuals, or for building or endowment funds.
Application information: Applications not accepted.
Write: Maureen Evans, Admin.
Trustees: Martin A. Heckscher, David J. Jones, Roland Morris.
Employer Identification Number: 236290348

6331
Live Oak Foundation ¤
P.O. Box 7618
Philadelphia 19101
Application address: c/o William A. Powell, V.P., Philadelphia National Bank, Philadelphia, PA 19101; Tel.: (215) 973-3798

Established in 1966 in PA.
Donor(s): Charlotte C. Weber.
Foundation type: Independent
Financial data (yr. ended 8/31/88): Assets, $1,013,973 (M); gifts received, $269,562; expenditures, $2,031,029, including $1,955,000 for grants.
Purpose and activities: Support for hospitals and medical research projects; art museums and collections of paintings, sculptures, antiques, and other art objects; churches and other religious institutions; theater, opera, ballet, and other performing arts groups; and other educational activities, including animal welfare and wildlife preservation.
Application information: Application form not required.
Initial approach: Letter
Deadline(s): Feb. 28 for July awards
Trustees: Charlotte C. Weber, John C. Weber, Philadelphia National Bank.
Employer Identification Number: 236424637

6332
The Thomas Lord Charitable Trust ¤
c/o Pennbank, Trust Dept.
801 State St.
Erie 16538 (814) 871-1811

Trust established in 1955.
Donor(s): Thomas Lord.
Foundation type: Independent
Financial data (yr. ended 12/31/86): Assets, $1,987,582 (M); expenditures, $27,563, including $25,000 for 1 grant.
Purpose and activities: Grants primarily for a Christian religious organization, a hospital, and a university.
Application information: Application form not required.
Deadline(s): None
Officer: Douglas F. Ziegler, Mgr.
Trustees: Thomas Lord, Edward P. Selden, PennBank.
Employer Identification Number: 256028793

6333
George H. and Margaret McClintic Love Foundation ¤
c/o Helen M. Collins, Mellon Bank, N.A.
One Mellon Bank Ctr., Rm. 3845
Pittsburgh 15258-0001 (412) 234-4695

Trust established in 1952 in PA.
Donor(s): George H. Love.
Foundation type: Independent
Financial data (yr. ended 12/31/88): Assets, $1,736,154 (M); gifts received, $340,505; expenditures, $685,044, including $638,575 for 53 grants (high: $300,000; low: $100; average: $1,000).
Purpose and activities: Emphasis on hospitals, higher and secondary education, and youth and social service agencies.
Types of support: Annual campaigns, building funds, capital campaigns.
Application information:
Write: George H. Love, Dir. of Distrib.
Officers: George H. Love, Dir. of Distrib.; Lois R. O'Connor, Asst. Dir. of Distrib. and Secy.
Trustee: Mellon Bank, N.A.
Employer Identification Number: 256018655

6334
The Ludwick Institute
c/o Ballard, Spahr, Andrews & Ingersoll
30 South 17th St., 20th Fl.
Philadelphia 19103 (215) 636-4964

Foundation type: Independent
Financial data (yr. ended 4/30/89): Assets, $2,334,156 (M); expenditures, $113,633, including $98,500 for 16 grants (high: $32,000; low: $1,000).
Purpose and activities: Support for education, particularly of local area disadvantaged youths, and the study of the natural sciences.
Types of support: Scholarship funds, special projects.
Limitations: Giving limited to Philadelphia, PA.
Application information:
Initial approach: Proposal
Copies of proposal: 1
Deadline(s): Apr.
Board meeting date(s): May and Oct.
Write: Hugh A.A. Sargent, Pres.
Officers: Hugh A.A. Sargent, Pres.; F.W. Elliott Farr, V.P.; L. Wilbur Zimmerman, V.P.; Roger Moss, Secy.; William M. Davison IV, Treas.; and 9 managers.
Employer Identification Number: 236256408

6335
The Lukens Foundation ¤
50 South First Ave.
Coatesville 19320 (215) 383-2504

Trust established in 1966 in PA.
Donor(s): Lukens, Inc.
Foundation type: Company-sponsored
Financial data (yr. ended 12/31/87): Assets, $918,939 (L); expenditures, $177,388, including $163,968 for grants (high: $22,500; low: $100) and $8,154 for employee matching gifts.
Purpose and activities: Emphasis on community funds; conservation; cultural programs, including museums and performing arts; health and welfare efforts; human service projects; and education, including an employee matching gift program supporting institutions of secondary and higher education.
Types of support: Continuing support, annual campaigns, emergency funds, building funds, equipment, matching funds, employee matching gifts.
Limitations: Giving primarily in areas of domestic company operations. No grants to individuals, or for endowment funds or research; no loans.
Publications: Informational brochure.
Application information: Application form required.
Initial approach: Letter
Copies of proposal: 1
Deadline(s): Submit proposal preferably in Oct.; deadline Dec. 1
Board meeting date(s): Jan., Feb., Mar., and Apr.
Final notification: 4 months
Write: W. Evelyn Walker, Secy.
Officer: W. Evelyn Walker, Secy. and Admin.
Trustees: W.R. Wilson, Chair.; John R. Bartholdson, John van Roden, Robert Schaal.
Employer Identification Number: 236424112

6336
The J. S. Mack Foundation ¤
P.O. Box 34
Indiana 15701

Trust established in 1935 in PA.
Foundation type: Independent
Financial data (yr. ended 12/31/88): Assets, $6,005,705 (M); expenditures, $266,717, including $98,530 for 16 grants (high: $35,000; low: $300).
Purpose and activities: Emphasis on higher and secondary education; support also for youth agencies and welfare organizations.
Limitations: Giving primarily in IN. No grants to individuals, or for scholarships, fellowships, or prizes; no loans.
Application information: Application form not required.
Initial approach: Letter
Copies of proposal: 1
Deadline(s): None
Board meeting date(s): Jan. and as required
Officers and Trustees: L. Blaine Grube, Pres.; Pete Stewart, V.P.; Joseph N. Mack, Secy.-Treas.; L. Merle Rife.
Employer Identification Number: 256002036

6337
Magee Foundation ¤
480 West Fifth St.
Bloomsburg 17815-1598

Established in 1964 in PA.
Foundation type: Independent
Financial data (yr. ended 10/31/88): Assets, $1,456,080 (M); expenditures, $239,029, including $171,236 for 35 grants (high: $118,996; low: $30).
Purpose and activities: Support for higher education, health associations, youth and child welfare, and a Methodist church.
Limitations: Giving primarily in Bloomsburg, PA. No grants to individuals.

Application information: Contributes only to pre-selected organizations. Applications not accepted.
Trustees: Joanne M. Katerman, Myles W. Katerman, Audrey R. Magee, James A. Magee.
Employer Identification Number: 236398294

6338
Samuel P. Mandell Foundation
Two Mellon Bank Ctr., Suite 1104
Philadelphia 19102 (215) 569-3600

Trust established in 1955 in PA.
Donor(s): Samuel P. Mandell.†
Foundation type: Independent
Financial data (yr. ended 12/31/89): Assets, $9,667,311 (M); qualifying distributions, $875,000, including $875,000 for 233 grants (high: $273,000; low: $32).
Purpose and activities: Emphasis on Israel and Jewish organizations, including welfare funds; hospitals, AIDS and other medical research and health associations and services; higher and other education; the fine arts and other cultural programs; community affairs; and the environment.
Limitations: Giving primarily in PA. No support for private operating foundations. No grants to individuals.
Application information: Application form not required.
Initial approach: Letter
Deadline(s): None
Board meeting date(s): Quarterly
Write: John L. Ricketts, Exec. Secy.
Officer: John L. Ricketts, Exec. Secy.
Trustees: Judith Delfiner, Gerald Mandell, M.D., Morton Mandell, M.D., Ronald Mandell, Seymour Mandell.
Number of staff: 2 part-time support.
Employer Identification Number: 236274709

6339
The Martin Foundation ¤
c/o MME, Inc., Huntington Plaza
3993 Huntington Pike
Huntingdon Valley 19006-1927

Established in 1981 in PA.
Donor(s): Alfred S. Martin.
Foundation type: Independent
Financial data (yr. ended 3/31/88): Assets, $1,613,359 (M); expenditures, $91,775, including $72,200 for 27 grants (high: $10,000; low: $500).
Purpose and activities: Grants for culture, higher and secondary education, youth programs, and community funds.
Application information:
Initial approach: Letter
Deadline(s): None
Write: Jovina Armento
Officer and Trustees: Alfred S. Martin, Mgr.; William W. Allen III, George J. Hartnett, Mary M. Martin, W. James Quigley.
Employer Identification Number: 232182719

6340
Massey Charitable Trust
P.O. Box 1178
Coraopolis 15108 (412) 262-5992

Established in 1968.
Donor(s): H.B. Massey,† Doris J. Massey, Massey Rental.
Foundation type: Independent
Financial data (yr. ended 12/31/88): Assets, $24,776,928 (M); gifts received, $7,998,845; expenditures, $882,014, including $738,715 for 65 grants (high: $100,000; low: $100).
Purpose and activities: Giving primarily for the medical sciences, including medical research, hospitals, and health agencies; Protestant and Catholic church support; the arts; and literacy.
Limitations: Giving primarily in Pittsburgh, PA.
Application information: Application form not required.
Copies of proposal: 1
Deadline(s): None
Board meeting date(s): May and Oct.
Write: Walter J. Carroll, Exec. Dir. and Trustee
Officer and Trustees:* Walter J. Carroll,* Exec. Dir.; Daniel B. Carroll, Joe B. Massey.
Number of staff: 1 full-time professional; 1 full-time support.
Employer Identification Number: 237007897

6341
Anne McCormick Trust ¤
c/o Dauphin Deposit Bank & Trust Co.
P.O. Box 2961
Harrisburg 17105 (717) 255-2045

Trust established in PA.
Donor(s): Anne McCormick.†
Foundation type: Independent
Financial data (yr. ended 12/31/87): Assets, $4,051,636 (M); expenditures, $447,562, including $384,880 for 63 grants (high: $50,000; low: $100).
Purpose and activities: Emphasis on hospitals, youth agencies, and higher education.
Limitations: Giving limited to Dauphin, Cumberland, and Perry counties, PA.
Application information:
Initial approach: Proposal
Deadline(s): None
Write: Larry A. Hartman, V.P., Dauphin Deposit Bank & Trust Co.
Trustee: Dauphin Deposit Bank & Trust Co.
Employer Identification Number: 236471389

6342
John R. McCune Charitable Trust ▼
P.O. Box 1749
Pittsburgh 15230 (412) 644-7664

Established in 1972 in PA.
Foundation type: Independent
Financial data (yr. ended 11/30/88): Assets, $49,108,480 (M); expenditures, $2,270,867, including $1,993,900 for 63 grants (high: $142,500; low: $5,000; average: $10,000-$50,000).
Purpose and activities: Emphasis on secondary and higher education, health services, Presbyterian-related institutions, and social services.
Types of support: General purposes.
Limitations: Giving primarily in PA.
Application information:
Initial approach: Proposal
Deadline(s): May 1
Board meeting date(s): Annually
Write: James M. Edwards, Member, Dispensing Comm.
Dispensing Committee: Janet McCune Edwards Anti, Molly McCune Cathey, David L. Edwards, James M. Edwards, John H. Edwards, Michael M. Edwards, Carrie McCune Katigan, Laurie M. Lewis, Sara McCune Losinger, John R. McCune V, John R. McCune VI.
Trustee: Union National Bank of Pittsburgh.
Employer Identification Number: 256160722

6343
McCune Foundation ▼
1104 Commonwealth Bldg.
316 Fourth Ave.
Pittsburgh 15222 (412) 644-8779

Established in 1979 in PA.
Donor(s): Charles L. McCune.†
Foundation type: Independent
Financial data (yr. ended 09/30/89): Assets, $251,109,513 (M); expenditures, $14,465,283, including $13,364,994 for 37 grants (high: $1,500,000; low: $40,000; average: $100,000-$400,000).
Purpose and activities: Giving primarily for independent higher education, health, and social services; support includes challenge grants. Preference is given to the organizations supported by the donor.
Types of support: Equipment, endowment funds, building funds, matching funds, capital campaigns, renovation projects, scholarship funds, seed money, special projects, professorships.
Limitations: Giving primarily in southwestern PA, with emphasis on the Pittsburgh area. No grants to individuals, or for general operating purposes; no loans.
Publications: Annual report (including application guidelines), grants list, financial statement.
Application information: Applicants are encouraged to wait 3 years after receiving a grant before reapplying. Application form not required.
Initial approach: Letter
Copies of proposal: 1
Deadline(s): Nov. 1 and Mar. 15
Board meeting date(s): Jan. and June
Final notification: 4 months
Write: Earland I. Carlson, Exec. Dir.
Distribution Committee: Richard D. Edwards, John R. McCune, Robert F. Patton.
Trustee: Union National Bank of Pittsburgh.
Number of staff: 2 full-time professional; 2 full-time support.
Employer Identification Number: 256210269

6344
McFeely-Rogers Foundation
1110 Ligonier St., Suite 300
P.O. Box 300
Latrobe 15650 (412) 537-5588

Incorporated in 1953 in PA.
Donor(s): James H. Rogers,† Nancy K. McFeely,† Nancy M. Rogers.†

Foundation type: Independent
Financial data (yr. ended 12/31/89): Assets, $11,098,128 (M); expenditures, $604,531, including $397,245 for 57 grants (high: $40,000; low: $100; average: $500-$1,000).
Purpose and activities: Support mainly to local educational and charitable institutions, including civic affairs, community development, recreation programs, Protestant giving, hunger projects, aid for Native Americans, and cultural programs.
Types of support: Operating budgets, annual campaigns, seed money, emergency funds, deficit financing, building funds, equipment, matching funds, scholarship funds, general purposes, endowment funds, capital campaigns.
Limitations: Giving primarily in the Latrobe and Pittsburgh, PA, areas. No grants to individuals, or for land acquisition, special projects, research, publications, or conferences; no loans.
Publications: Program policy statement, application guidelines.
Application information: Application form not required.
Initial approach: Letter or telephone
Copies of proposal: 2
Deadline(s): Apr. 1 and Nov. 1
Board meeting date(s): End of Apr. and Nov.
Final notification: 2 weeks after board meeting
Write: James R. Okonak, Exec. Dir.
Officers and Trustees:* Fred M. Rogers,* Pres.; Nancy R. Crozier,* V.P.; James R. Okonak,* Secy. and Exec. Dir.; Grant F. Neely,* Treas.; William P. Barker, Douglas R. Nowicki, James B. Rogers.
Number of staff: 2 full-time professional; 1 part-time professional.
Employer Identification Number: 251120947

6345
Lalitta Nash McKaig Foundation
c/o Pittsburgh National Bank
Trust Dept. 970
Pittsburgh 15265
Cumberland office address: P.O. Box 1360, Cumberland, MD 21502; Tel.: (301) 777-1533

Established in 1973 in PA.
Foundation type: Independent
Financial data (yr. ended 9/30/89): Assets, $6,413,349 (M); expenditures, $345,410, including $317,718 for 274 grants to individuals (high: $1,500; low: $125).
Purpose and activities: Awards scholarships for higher education.
Types of support: Student aid.
Limitations: Giving limited to residents of Bedford and Somerset counties, PA; Mineral and Hampshire counties, WV; and Allegany and Garrett counties, MD.
Application information: Application forms can be obtained from high school guidance offices in the Cumberland, MD, area, the financial aid offices of Frostburg State College and Allegany Community College, the foundation's office in Cumberland, MD, or the Pittsburgh National Bank. Application form required.
Deadline(s): May 30
Write: Patricia M. Laird, Trust Officer, Pittsburgh National Bank
Trustee: Pittsburgh National Bank.
Employer Identification Number: 256071908

6346
Virginia A. McKee Poor Fund
c/o Pittsburgh National Bank
Trust Dept. 970
Pittsburgh 15265 (412) 762-3390

Trust established in 1929 in PA.
Donor(s): Virginia A. McKee.†
Foundation type: Independent
Financial data (yr. ended 09/30/89): Assets, $2,189,459 (M); expenditures, $114,877, including $105,000 for 4 grants (high: $58,000; low: $7,000).
Purpose and activities: Support "for such deserving poor persons in the City of Pittsburgh" through grants to local welfare organizations, particularly for emergency funds.
Types of support: Emergency funds.
Limitations: Giving limited to Pittsburgh, PA. No grants to individuals, or for building or endowment funds, research, scholarships, fellowships, or matching gifts; no loans.
Publications: Informational brochure, application guidelines.
Application information: Application form required.
Initial approach: Proposal
Copies of proposal: 1
Deadline(s): None
Board meeting date(s): May and Nov.
Final notification: One month
Write: John Culbertson, Trust Officer, Pittsburgh National Bank
Trustee: Pittsburgh National Bank.
Employer Identification Number: 256023292

6347
Katherine Mabis McKenna Foundation, Inc. ⌑
c/o Mellon Bank, N.A.
P.O. Box 185
Pittsburgh 15230
Application address: P.O. Box 186, LaTrobe, PA 15650; Tel.: (412) 537-6901

Incorporated in 1969 in PA.
Donor(s): Katherine M. McKenna.
Foundation type: Independent
Financial data (yr. ended 12/31/88): Assets, $14,744,850 (M); gifts received, $203,126; expenditures, $750,933, including $608,950 for 53 grants (high: $112,500; low: $200; average: $1,000-$10,000).
Purpose and activities: Giving for higher education, medical organizations, civic affairs, and cultural programs.
Types of support: General purposes, operating budgets, annual campaigns, seed money, building funds, equipment, endowment funds, special projects, scholarship funds, capital campaigns, internships, land acquisition.
Limitations: Giving primarily in western PA. No grants to individuals, or for matching gifts; no loans.
Application information: Application form not required.
Initial approach: Letter
Copies of proposal: 1
Deadline(s): Submit proposal preferably in Jan. through July; deadline Nov. 1
Board meeting date(s): Mar., June, Sept., and Dec.
Final notification: 3 to 6 months
Write: T. William Boxx, Secy.-Treas.
Officers and Directors:* Alex G. McKenna,* Chair.; Donald C. McKenna,* Vice-Chair.; T. William Boxx, Secy.-Treas.; Richard M. Larry, Norbert J. Pail.
Trustee: Mellon Bank, N.A., Linda McKenna Boxx.
Number of staff: 2
Employer Identification Number: 237042752

6348
Philip M. McKenna Foundation, Inc. ⌑
P.O. Box 186
Latrobe 15650 (412) 537-6901

Incorporated in 1967 in PA.
Donor(s): Philip M. McKenna.†
Foundation type: Independent
Financial data (yr. ended 12/31/87): Assets, $13,885,555 (M); expenditures, $1,413,630, including $1,198,059 for 88 grants (high: $300,000; low: $500; average: $10,000-$50,000).
Purpose and activities: Support for public policy research and economic education; grants for higher education generally to specified institutions of significance to the donor or in the foundation's local area; support locally for community and civic programs.
Types of support: Operating budgets, annual campaigns, seed money, building funds, equipment, research, scholarship funds.
Limitations: Giving primarily in southwestern PA for community and civic programs; grants to national organizations for public policy research and economic education. No grants to individuals, or for endowments or matching gifts; no loans; single-year grants only.
Application information: Application form not required.
Initial approach: Letter
Copies of proposal: 1
Deadline(s): Submit proposal preferably Jan. through July; deadline Nov. 1
Board meeting date(s): Apr. and Dec.; sometimes in the fall
Final notification: 3 to 6 months
Write: T. William Boxx, Secy.-Treas.
Officers and Directors: Alex G. McKenna, Chair.; Donald C. McKenna, Vice-Chair.; T. William Boxx, Secy.-Treas.; Norbert J. Pail.
Number of staff: 1 full-time professional; 1 part-time support.
Employer Identification Number: 236082635

6349
The McLean Contributionship
945 Haverford Rd.
Bryn Mawr 19010 (215) 527-6330

Trust established in 1951 in PA.
Donor(s): William L. McLean, Jr.,† Robert McLean, Bulletin Co.
Foundation type: Independent
Financial data (yr. ended 12/31/88): Assets, $16,395,978 (M); gifts received, $101,703; expenditures, $1,001,496, including $847,566

for 74 grants (high: $50,000; low: $500; average: $10,000-$15,000).
Purpose and activities: Giving primarily for education, hospitals, youth agencies, and conservation. Trustees prefer special projects rather than continuing programs.
Types of support: Special projects, building funds, capital campaigns, conferences and seminars, consulting services, endowment funds, equipment, land acquisition, publications, renovation projects, scholarship funds, seed money.
Limitations: Giving primarily in the greater Philadelphia, PA, metropolitan area.
Publications: Application guidelines.
Application information: Application form not required.
Initial approach: Proposal
Copies of proposal: 2
Board meeting date(s): Quarterly
Write: John H. Buhsmer, Pres.
Officers: John H. Buhsmer,* Pres.; Charles E. Catherwood, Treas.
Trustees:* William L. McLean III, Chair.; Jean Bodine, R. Jean Brownlee, Joseph K. Gordon.
Number of staff: None.
Employer Identification Number: 236396940

6350
William J. McMannis and A. Haskell McMannis Educational Fund
c/o Marine Bank Trust Div.
P.O. Box 8480
Erie 16553 (814) 871-9204

Established in 1974.
Donor(s): Haskell McMannis.†
Foundation type: Independent
Financial data (yr. ended 08/31/89): Assets, $3,288,201 (M); gifts received, $500,000; expenditures, $153,513, including $93,342 for 114 grants to individuals (high: $2,000; low: $500).
Purpose and activities: Giving for higher education scholarship funds only; grants paid directly to institutions for the benefit of students (U.S. citizens only) who "are enrolled and in good standing."
Types of support: Student aid.
Publications: Informational brochure (including application guidelines).
Application information: Application form required.
Initial approach: Letter
Copies of proposal: 4
Deadline(s): Apr. 1
Write: Sr. M. Lawreace Antoun, SSJ, Exec. Dir.
Officer: Sister M. Lawreace Antoun, Exec. Dir.
Trustees: Fred B. Sieber, Marine Bank.
Number of staff: 1 full-time support.
Employer Identification Number: 256191302

6351
John McShain Charities, Inc. ▼
540 North Seventeenth St.
Philadelphia 19130 (215) 564-2322

Incorporated in 1949 in PA.
Donor(s): John McShain, John McShain, Inc., and others.
Foundation type: Independent
Financial data (yr. ended 3/31/87): Assets, $47,775,889 (M); expenditures, $2,805,542, including $2,355,620 for 196 grants (high: $300,000; low: $10; average: $1,000-$50,000).
Purpose and activities: Support for higher and secondary education, Roman Catholic church support, and social welfare and cultural programs.
Limitations: Giving primarily in Philadelphia, PA. No grants to individuals.
Application information:
Initial approach: Letter
Deadline(s): None
Board meeting date(s): Mar.
Final notification: 3 months
Write: John McShain, Fdn. Dir.
Officers and Directors: John McShain, Fdn. Dir.; William L. Shinners, V.P.; Mary Tompkins, Secy.-Treas.; Henry B. Fitzpatrick, Sr. Pauline Mary McShain.
Number of staff: None.
Employer Identification Number: 236276091

6352
The Benjamin and Mary Siddons Measey Foundation
225 North Olive St.
P.O. Box 258
Media 19063 (215) 566-5800

Trust established in 1958 in PA.
Donor(s): William Maul Measey.†
Foundation type: Independent
Financial data (yr. ended 12/31/89): Assets, $21,600,000 (M); expenditures, $920,000, including $782,000 for 15 grants (high: $143,000; low: $7,000).
Purpose and activities: Grants to medical schools in Philadelphia for scholarships and fellowships.
Types of support: Scholarship funds, fellowships.
Limitations: Giving limited to Philadelphia, PA. No grants to individuals.
Application information: Applications should be made to the dean of the particular medical school. Application form not required.
Copies of proposal: 1
Deadline(s): 1 month prior to meeting
Board meeting date(s): Second Tuesday in Mar., June, Sept., and Dec.
Final notification: 1 month following meeting
Write: James C. Brennan, Mgr.
Officer: Matthew S. Donaldson, Jr., Secy.
Board of Managers: Jonathan E. Rhoads, M.D., Chair.; James C. Brennan, Brooke Roberts, M.D., Willis J. Winn, Francis C. Wood, M.D.
Number of staff: 1 part-time support.
Employer Identification Number: 236298781

6353
Mellon Bank (East) Foundation ⌑
c/o Mellon Bank (East), N.A.
P.O. Box 7236
Philadelphia 19102-7236 (215) 553-3032

Trust established in 1955 in PA.
Donor(s): Girard Trust Bank.
Foundation type: Company-sponsored
Financial data (yr. ended 11/30/88): Assets, $1,565,665 (M); expenditures, $127,500, including $115,250 for grants.
Purpose and activities: Emphasis on senior citizens, youth, cultural programs, community funds, civic affairs, and conservation.
Types of support: General purposes, operating budgets.
Limitations: Giving primarily in PA. No grants to individuals.
Application information:
Deadline(s): None
Trustee: Mellon Bank (East), N.A.
Employer Identification Number: 236227144

6354
Mellon Bank Foundation ▼
One Mellon Bank Ctr., Rm. 572
Pittsburgh 15258-0001 (412) 234-6266

Established in 1974 in PA.
Donor(s): Mellon Bank, N.A.
Foundation type: Company-sponsored
Financial data (yr. ended 12/31/87): Assets, $2,260,020 (M); gifts received, $1,202,500; expenditures, $1,290,245, including $1,275,954 for 83 grants (high: $125,000; low: $500; average: $1,500-$10,000).
Purpose and activities: Giving primarily to serve the overall vitality of local communities, with emphasis on economic development, including business development, employment and retraining initiatives, health and welfare, higher education, and cultural programs.
Types of support: Operating budgets, continuing support, annual campaigns, building funds, matching funds, technical assistance, special projects, capital campaigns, general purposes, seed money.
Limitations: Giving primarily in southwestern PA. No support for fraternal or religious organizations, specialized health campaigns or other highly specialized projects with little or no positive impact on local communities, or United Way agencies (unless authorized to solicit corporations). No grants to individuals, or for emergency funds, deficit financing, equipment, land acquisition, scholarships, fellowships, research, publications, or conferences; no loans.
Publications: Corporate giving report (including application guidelines), informational brochure.
Application information: Application form not required.
Initial approach: Proposal
Copies of proposal: 1
Deadline(s): None
Board meeting date(s): Monthly
Final notification: 2 months
Write: Sylvia Clark, V.P.
Officers: Sandra J. McLaughlin,* Chair. and Pres.; Sylvia Clark, V.P. and Secy.; Steven G. Elliott, Treas.
Trustees:* Joseph F. DiMario, George T. Farrell, Richard A. Gaugh, Martin G. McGuinn, W. Keith Smith.
Number of staff: None.
Employer Identification Number: 237423500

6355
R. K. Mellon Family Foundation ▼
525 William Penn Place
Pittsburgh 15219 (412) 392-2800
Mailing address: P.O. Box 1138, Pittsburgh, PA 15230

Incorporated in PA in 1978 through consolidation of Landfall, Loyalhanna, Rachelwood, and Cassandra Mellon Henderson Foundations.
Donor(s): Seward Prosser Mellon, Richard P. Mellon, Constance B. Mellon,† Cassandra M. Milbury.
Foundation type: Independent
Financial data (yr. ended 12/31/89): Assets, $27,405,148 (M); expenditures, $1,332,415, including $1,103,950 for 70 grants (high: $100,000; low: $1,000; average: $5,000-$50,000).
Purpose and activities: Grants largely for education, health care, social and human services, and conservation programs.
Types of support: Annual campaigns, seed money, building funds, equipment, research, special projects, capital campaigns, continuing support, general purposes, operating budgets, renovation projects.
Limitations: Giving primarily in western PA. No grants to individuals, or for endowment funds, scholarships, fellowships, or matching gifts; no loans.
Publications: Informational brochure (including application guidelines).
Application information: Application form not required.
Initial approach: Proposal
Copies of proposal: 1
Deadline(s): Submit proposal preferably Jan. through Mar. or July through Sept.; deadlines Apr. 1 and Oct. 1
Board meeting date(s): June and Nov.
Final notification: 1 to 6 months
Write: Robert B. Burr, Jr., Dir.
Officers: Robert B. Burr, Jr.,* Secy. and Dir.; Eileen Prince, Treas.
Trustees:* George H. Taber, Chair.; Andrew W. Mathieson, Seward Prosser Mellon, Mason Walsh, Jr.
Number of staff: 8
Employer Identification Number: 251356145

6356
Matthew T. Mellon Foundation ⌑
c/o Mellon Bank, N.A.
One Mellon Bank Ctr.
Pittsburgh 15258 (412) 234-5892

Established in 1946 in PA.
Foundation type: Independent
Financial data (yr. ended 12/31/87): Assets, $1,154,703 (M); gifts received, $500,000; expenditures, $194,290, including $189,000 for 4 grants (high: $84,000; low: $5,000).
Purpose and activities: Support primarily for a medical institute; support also for a Scottish-Irish trust and the arts.
Types of support: Building funds.
Application information:
Deadline(s): None
Write: Leonard B. Richards
Trustees: George D. Lockhart, James R. Mellon, A.A. Vestal, James M. Walton, Mellon Bank, N.A.
Employer Identification Number: 251286841

6357
Richard King Mellon Foundation ▼
525 William Penn Place
Pittsburgh 15219 (412) 392-2800

Trust established in 1947 in PA; incorporated in 1971 in PA.
Donor(s): Richard K. Mellon.†
Foundation type: Independent
Financial data (yr. ended 12/31/89): Assets, $878,877,690 (M); expenditures, $20,680,023, including $15,431,712 for 127 grants (high: $3,000,000; low: $1,000).
Purpose and activities: Local grant programs emphasize conservation, higher education, cultural and civic affairs, social services, medical research and health care; support also for conservation of natural areas and wildlife preservation elsewhere in the U.S.
Types of support: Seed money, building funds, equipment, land acquisition, research, matching funds, general purposes, continuing support, operating budgets, renovation projects.
Limitations: Giving primarily in Pittsburgh and western PA, except for nationwide conservation programs. No grants to individuals, or for fellowships or scholarships except through National Merit Scholarship Corp.
Publications: Annual report (including application guidelines), informational brochure.
Application information: Application form not required.
Initial approach: Proposal
Copies of proposal: 1
Deadline(s): Apr. 1 and Oct. 1; submit proposal between Jan. and Mar. or July and Sept.
Board meeting date(s): June and Dec.
Final notification: 1 to 6 months
Write: George H. Taber, V.P.
Officers and Trustees:* Richard P. Mellon,* Chair.; Seward Prosser Mellon,* Pres.; George H. Taber,* V.P. and Dir.; Robert B. Burr, Jr., Secy.; Andrew W. Mathieson,* Treas.; Arthur M. Scully, Jr., Mason Walsh, Jr.
Number of staff: 8 part-time professional; 1 full-time support; 10 part-time support.
Employer Identification Number: 251127705

6358
Glenn and Ruth Mengle Foundation ⌑
c/o Deposit Bank, Trust Dept.
P.O. Box 1046
Du Bois 15801

Trust established in 1956 in PA.
Donor(s): Glenn A. Mengle,† Ruth E. Mengle Blake.†
Foundation type: Independent
Financial data (yr. ended 12/31/88): Assets, $8,666,940 (M); expenditures, $546,032, including $455,050 for 40 grants (high: $75,000; low: $1,000).
Purpose and activities: Emphasis on youth agencies, hospitals, civic affairs, and community funds.
Limitations: Giving limited to the Brockway-Dubois and Erie, PA, areas.
Application information:
Initial approach: Proposal
Deadline(s): Sept. 1
Write: D. Edward Chaplin, V.P. and Sr. Trust Officer, Deposit Bank
Trustees: DeVere L. Sheesley, Deposit Bank.
Employer Identification Number: 256067616

6359
Merchants-Oliver Fund ⌑
c/o Peter Hemingway
107 Rutgers Ave., No. 4
Swarthmore 19081

Established prior to 1913.
Donor(s): Lewis Elkins Fund, Charles Fearon.†
Foundation type: Operating
Financial data (yr. ended 12/31/86): Assets, $3,623,871 (M); gifts received, $85,671; expenditures, $255,539, including $199,128 for 48 grants to individuals (high: $5,652; low: $900).
Purpose and activities: Giving "to provide relief to indigent merchants or their widows and families."
Types of support: Grants to individuals.
Limitations: Giving primarily in Philadelphia, PA.
Application information: Application form required.
Deadline(s): None
Officers and Directors: James D. Winsor III, Pres.; Henry Winsor, V.P.; Richard D. Wood, Sr., V.P.; Rev. Henry W. Kaufmann, Secy.-Treas.; G. Lester Blankin, Jr., Willis S. Delacour, Albert L. Doering, Richard N. Knight, Jr., David McMullen, J. Stephen Peake, Jr., John A. Philbrick III, William Schuster, G. Stephen Vorhees, Jr., Charles S. Webb II, H. St. John Webb III, Peter Wilminding.
Employer Identification Number: 231980213

6360
Meridian Foundation
c/o Meridian Bancorp, Inc.
1700 Arch St., Mezzanine
Philadelphia 19103 (215) 854-3114

Established in 1956 in PA as the American Bank Foundation.
Donor(s): Meridian Bancorp, Inc.
Foundation type: Company-sponsored
Financial data (yr. ended 12/31/88): Assets, $30,649 (M); gifts received, $119,250; expenditures, $128,280, including $127,958 for 32 grants (high: $35,700; low: $100).
Purpose and activities: Support for community funds, higher education, health and welfare, arts and culture, and civic affairs. Maximum grant for capital campaigns is 5 percent of goal; special emphasis on economic and community development.
Types of support: Annual campaigns, building funds, capital campaigns.
Limitations: Giving primarily in southeastern PA: Berks, Bucks, Chester, Dauphin, Delaware, Lancaster, Lebanon, Lehigh, Montgomery, Philadelphia, and Schuylkill counties. No grants to individuals, or for endowment funds, scholarships, or fellowships; no loans.
Publications: Application guidelines.
Application information: Requests for multi-year support, capital campaigns, or grants over $5,000 handled by foundation directly. Smaller, single-year gifts are decided on by the local foundation committee for each subsidiary.
Initial approach: Proposal
Copies of proposal: 1
Deadline(s): 1 month prior to board meetings
Board meeting date(s): Feb., May, Aug., and Nov.

Write: Nora Mead Brownell, Dir., Corp. Communications and Community Relations
Officer: Nora Mead Brownell, Dir., Corp. Communications and Community Relations.
Trustee: Meridian Bancorp, Inc.
Number of staff: None.
Employer Identification Number: 231976387

6361
The Merit Gasoline Foundation
551 West Lancaster Ave.
Haverford 19041 (215) 527-7900

Trust established in 1956 in PA.
Donor(s): Merit Oil Co., and affiliates.
Foundation type: Company-sponsored
Financial data (yr. ended 8/31/89): Assets, $641,847 (M); gifts received, $275,000; expenditures, $187,457, including $174,448 for 89 grants (high: $60,000; low: $15; average: $3,000-$7,000) and $13,009 for 98 employee matching gifts.
Purpose and activities: Support for scholarship aid to children (including step-children) of employees of donor companies, civic affairs, higher education, social service programs, health agencies, and Jewish welfare.
Types of support: Operating budgets, continuing support, seed money, employee-related scholarships, employee matching gifts.
Limitations: Giving primarily in the urban areas of the New England and mid-Atlantic states where Merit Oil Co. has gas stations. No grants to individuals (except college scholarships for children, including step-children, of company employees), or for building or endowment funds, research, or special projects; no loans.
Publications: Program policy statement, application guidelines.
Application information: Application form not required.
Initial approach: Proposal
Copies of proposal: 1
Deadline(s): Submit proposal preferably in Jan. and July; no set deadline
Board meeting date(s): Usually in Aug.
Write: Robert M. Harting, Exec. Dir.
Officer: Robert M. Harting, Exec. Dir.
Trustees: Carl A. Levinson, Chair.; Ivan H. Gabel, Leonard Gilmar, Robert M. Harting, Joseph M. Jerome, Lois B. Rice, Morton Sand.
Number of staff: None.
Employer Identification Number: 236282846

6362
Frank J. Michaels Scholarship Fund ☆
c/o Fidelity Bank, N.A.
Broad & Walnut Sts.
Philadelphia 19109 (215) 985-7320
Application address: c/o Fidelity Bank, N.A., Oxford Branch, Third & Locust Sts., Oxford, PA 19363; Tel.: (215) 734-5294

Established in 1977 in PA.
Donor(s): Frank J. Michaels.†
Foundation type: Independent
Financial data (yr. ended 01/31/89): Assets, $1,914,700 (M); expenditures, $127,915, including $115,142 for 124 grants to individuals (high: $3,000; low: $30).
Purpose and activities: Awards scholarships to local area residents for higher education.
Types of support: Student aid.
Limitations: Giving limited to the Oxford, PA, area.
Application information: Application form required.
Deadline(s): Apr. 15
Board meeting date(s): May
Final notification: June 15
Write: Maureen B. Evans, Co-Trustee
Trustees: Maureen B. Evans, Andrew B. Young, Fidelity Bank, N.A.
Number of staff: None.
Employer Identification Number: 236680399

6363
The Millstein Charitable Foundation
North Fourth St. & Gaskill Ave.
Jeannette 15644

Established in 1964.
Foundation type: Independent
Financial data (yr. ended 09/30/89): Assets, $2,737,720 (M); expenditures, $130,236, including $115,711 for 222 grants (high: $25,000; low: $15).
Purpose and activities: Grants primarily for Jewish welfare funds and temple support.
Types of support: Annual campaigns, building funds, capital campaigns, emergency funds, research, special projects.
Limitations: Giving primarily in western PA.
Application information: Requests are reviewed as they are received. Application form not required.
Initial approach: Letter
Copies of proposal: 1
Board meeting date(s): Annually, usually in Sept.
Officer and Trustee:* David J. Millstein,* Exec. Secy.
Number of staff: 1 part-time support.
Employer Identification Number: 256064981

6364
Mine Safety Appliances Company Charitable Trust ▼
c/o Mine Safety Appliances Co.
P.O. Box 426
Pittsburgh 15230

Trust established in 1951 in PA.
Donor(s): Mine Safety Appliances Co.
Foundation type: Company-sponsored
Financial data (yr. ended 12/31/89): Assets, $5,388,489 (M); expenditures, $690,747, including $607,818 for 132 grants (high: $125,000; low: $100; average: $500-$5,000).
Purpose and activities: Emphasis on community funds, higher education, hospitals, and health care; some support for the performing arts.
Types of support: General purposes.
Limitations: Giving primarily in PA. No grants to individuals, or for matching gifts; no loans.
Application information: Application form not required.
Initial approach: Letter
Copies of proposal: 1
Deadline(s): None
Board meeting date(s): Quarterly
Final notification: Varies
Write: James E. Herald, Secy.
Officer: James E. Herald, Secy.
Trustee: Pittsburgh National Bank.
Number of staff: None.
Employer Identification Number: 256023104

6365
P. M. Moore Foundation ⌑
382 Franklin Ave.
Aliquippa 15001 (412) 375-7701

Incorporated in 1958 in PA.
Donor(s): Paul M. Moore.†
Foundation type: Independent
Financial data (yr. ended 12/31/86): Assets, $1,931,219 (M); expenditures, $108,838, including $104,000 for 35 grants (high: $35,000; low: $100).
Purpose and activities: Emphasis on higher education, Protestant church support, libraries, and social services.
Limitations: Giving primarily in Beaver County, PA.
Application information: Application form not required.
Deadline(s): None
Write: James S. Ruffner, Pres.
Officers: James S. Ruffner, Pres.; Ruth Ann Duff, Secy.; Dana L. Duff, Treas.
Employer Identification Number: 256066268

6366
Mudge Foundation ⌑
c/o Pittsburgh National Bank
Trust Div.
Pittsburgh 15265 (412) 762-3866

Established in 1955 in PA.
Foundation type: Independent
Financial data (yr. ended 12/31/88): Assets, $1,747,970 (M); expenditures, $164,127, including $147,250 for grants.
Purpose and activities: Grants for natural resources and science projects, including medical research; support also for museums of natural history.
Types of support: General purposes, research.
Limitations: Giving primarily in TX, ME, and PA.
Application information: Application form not required.
Initial approach: Letter
Deadline(s): None
Write: Henry Flood, V.P., Pittsburgh National Bank
Trustee: Pittsburgh National Bank.
Employer Identification Number: 256023150

6367
C. John & Josephine Muller Foundation ⌑
2800 Grant Ave.
Philadelphia 19114

Established in 1984 in PA.
Donor(s): C. John Muller, Josephine Muller.
Foundation type: Independent
Financial data (yr. ended 12/31/88): Assets, $3,988,986 (M); gifts received, $1,050,000; expenditures, $364,642, including $364,637 for 13 grants (high: $250,000; low: $200).
Purpose and activities: Support for social services, churches, and education.

Types of support: Scholarship funds, building funds.
Limitations: Giving primarily in PA, especially the Philadelphia area. No grants to individuals.
Application information: Contributes only to pre-selected organizations. Applications not accepted.
Directors: Michael Goldman, C. John Muller, Emanuel C. Pachman.
Employer Identification Number: 232324413

6368
G. C. Murphy Company Foundation ⌑
531 Fifth Ave.
McKeesport 15135 (412) 751-6649

Incorporated in 1952 in PA.
Foundation type: Independent
Financial data (yr. ended 12/31/86): Assets, $2,716,439 (M); expenditures, $175,993, including $146,885 for 27 grants (high: $32,000; low: $200).
Purpose and activities: Emphasis on education, a community fund, youth, and social service agencies.
Limitations: Giving primarily in southwestern PA.
Application information: Application form not required.
Initial approach: Letter
Deadline(s): None
Write: Edwin W. Davis, Secy.
Officers: M.M. Lewis,* Pres.; T.F. Hudak,* V.P. and Treas.; R.T. Messner,* V.P.; Charles E. Palmer,* V.P.; Edwin W. Davis, Secy.
Directors:* C.H. Lytle, S.W. Robinson, W.L. Shaw, Jr.
Number of staff: 1 part-time professional.
Employer Identification Number: 256028651

6369
Emma G. Musselman Foundation ⌑
c/o Philadelphia National Bank, Personal Trust Tax Dept.
Broad and Chestnut Sts.
Philadelphia 19101
Application address: c/o Franklin R. Bigham, P.O. Box 338, Gettysburg, PA 17325; Tel.: (717) 334-2159

Trust established in 1955 in PA.
Donor(s): Emma G. Musselman.†
Foundation type: Independent
Financial data (yr. ended 6/30/88): Assets, $845,321 (M); expenditures, $363,170, including $326,750 for 11 grants (high: $225,000; low: $1,250).
Purpose and activities: Giving primarily for community development, higher education, social services, youth, and hospitals.
Limitations: Giving limited to Adams County, PA.
Application information:
Initial approach: Letter
Deadline(s): None
Trustee: Philadelphia National Bank.
Advisory Committee: Thomas E. Arnold, Franklin R. Bigham, Nancy A. Oas.
Employer Identification Number: 236233856

6370
Warren V. Musser Foundation ⌑ ☆
630 Park Ave.
King of Prussia 19406
Application address: 2000 One Logan Sq., Philadelphia, PA 19103; Tel.: (215) 963-5283

Established in 1980.
Donor(s): Claire V. Sams, Warren V. Musser.
Foundation type: Independent
Financial data (yr. ended 11/30/88): Assets, $1,025,075 (M); gifts received, $160,846; expenditures, $287,417, including $280,917 for 71 grants (high: $150,000; low: $20).
Purpose and activities: Support primarily for higher education, youth, and social services.
Limitations: Giving primarily in Philadelphia, PA.
Application information:
Initial approach: Letter
Deadline(s): None
Write: Alan L. Reed, V.P.
Officers: Warren V. Musser, Pres. and Treas.; Alan L. Reed, V.P. and Secy.; Vincent G. Bell, Jr., V.P.
Employer Identification Number: 232162497

6371
Grace S. & W. Linton Nelson Foundation ☆
West Valley Business KCtr.
940 West Valley Rd., Suite 1601
Wayne 19087 (215) 975-9169

Established in 1984 in PA.
Donor(s): W. Linton Nelson,† William P. Brady, Delaware Management Co.
Foundation type: Independent
Financial data (yr. ended 12/31/88): Assets, $1,004,409 (M); gifts received, $1,091,770; expenditures, $250,922, including $237,500 for 16 grants (high: $50,000; low: $1,000).
Purpose and activities: Giving primarily for a military academy and higher education, including medical education; support also for the disabled, child welfare and youth clubs and agencies, the elderly, arts and culture, and cancer research and hospitals.
Types of support: Capital campaigns, equipment, endowment funds, operating budgets.
Limitations: Giving primarily in PA, with emphasis on Philadelphia. No grants to individuals.
Application information: Application form not required.
Deadline(s): None
Write: Fred C. Aldridge, Jr., Esq., Pres.
Officers: Fred C. Aldridge, Jr., Pres. and Treas.; James P. Schellenger, V.P. and Secy.; William P. Brady, V.P.
Number of staff: 1 part-time professional.
Employer Identification Number: 222583922

6372
Mary Margaret Nestor Foundation ⌑ ☆
c/o Reiff & Nestor Co.
Reiff & West Sts.
Lykens 17048 (717) 453-7113

Established in 1953.
Donor(s): Reiff & Nestor Co.
Foundation type: Independent
Financial data (yr. ended 6/30/89): Assets, $242,310 (M); gifts received, $60,000; expenditures, $119,757, including $900 for 2 grants (high: $700; low: $200) and $116,807 for 155 grants to individuals (high: $1,600; low: $100; average: $400-$800).
Purpose and activities: Primarily awards scholarships to local area students; minor support for the needy.
Types of support: Student aid, grants to individuals.
Limitations: Giving limited to the Lykens, PA, area.
Application information:
Initial approach: Letter
Deadline(s): None
Write: Robert E. Nestor, V.P.
Officers: John P. Nestor, Pres.; Robert E. Nestor, V.P.
Employer Identification Number: 236277570

6373
Neuman-Publicker Trust ⌑ ☆
c/o Cogen Sklar Levier & Co.
Box 1000, Suite 100, 225 City Line Ave.
Bala Cynwyd 19004

Trust established in 1946 in PA.
Donor(s): Harry Publicker, Rose Publicker.
Foundation type: Independent
Financial data (yr. ended 12/31/88): Assets, $1,102,213 (M); expenditures, $51,189, including $48,750 for 11 grants (high: $17,000; low: $1,000).
Purpose and activities: Giving primarily for anmimal welfare, including wildlife; support also for higher and other education.
Limitations: Giving primarily in PA, NY, and NJ. No grants to individuals.
Application information:
Initial approach: Letter
Deadline(s): None
Write: Priscilla N. Cohn, Trustee
Trustees: Priscilla N. Cohn, A. Bruce Neuman.
Employer Identification Number: 236232559

6374
The 1957 Charity Trust
c/o Mellon Bank (East), N.A.
660 Sentry Pkwy.
Blue Bell 19422 (215) 941-4144

Trust established in 1957 in PA.
Donor(s): Elizabeth R. Moran.
Foundation type: Independent
Financial data (yr. ended 6/30/88): Assets, $9,613,041 (M); expenditures, $489,205, including $395,905 for 125 grants (high: $20,000; low: $500; average: $1,000-$10,000).
Purpose and activities: Emphasis on human services, education, hospitals, health associations, youth agencies, and community funds.
Types of support: Annual campaigns, building funds, capital campaigns, conferences and seminars, consulting services, continuing support, deficit financing, emergency funds, endowment funds, equipment, fellowships, general purposes, land acquisition, matching funds, operating budgets, publications, renovation projects, research, scholarship funds, seed money, special projects, technical assistance.

Limitations: Giving primarily in PA, with emphasis on the Delaware Valley. No grants to individuals; no loans.
Publications: Application guidelines.
Application information:
Initial approach: Proposal
Copies of proposal: 1
Deadline(s): Jan. 15, May 15, and Sept. 15
Board meeting date(s): Feb., June, and Oct.
Final notification: Within 3 weeks
Write: Roderic Zengerl, V.P.
Committee Members: Elizabeth R. Moran, James M. Moran, Jr., Roderic Zengerl.
Trustee: Mellon Bank (East), N.A.
Number of staff: 1 part-time professional.
Employer Identification Number: 236227603

6375
Gustav Oberlaender Foundation, Inc. ¤
P.O. Box 896
Reading 19603

Incorporated in 1934 in DE.
Donor(s): Gustav Oberlaender.†
Foundation type: Independent
Financial data (yr. ended 12/31/88): Assets, $1,911,967 (M); expenditures, $117,846, including $97,900 for 49 grants (high: $15,000; low: $300).
Purpose and activities: Emphasis on cultural programs, hospitals, community funds, social services, higher education, and youth agencies.
Limitations: Giving primarily in PA.
Application information:
Initial approach: Letter or proposal
Deadline(s): None
Write: Harold O. Leinbach, Pres.
Officers and Trustees:* Harold O. Leinbach,* Pres.; Richard O. Leinbach,* V.P.; John M. Ennis,* Secy.-Treas.; Paula Leinbach, Henry B. Sellers, Greta Smith, Jean L. Ziemer.
Employer Identification Number: 236282493

6376
Isadore & Anna Oritsky Foundation ¤
106 Grape St.
Reading 19602

Established in 1967 in PA.
Donor(s): H. Oritsky, Inc.
Foundation type: Independent
Financial data (yr. ended 6/30/88): Assets, $1,496,015 (M); expenditures, $134,705, including $125,015 for 4 grants (high: $65,000; low: $15).
Purpose and activities: Emphasis on Jewish giving.
Manager: Herbert Oritsky.
Employer Identification Number: 236419027

6377
Oxford Foundation, Inc. ¤
55 South Third St.
Oxford 19363

Incorporated in 1947 in DE.
Donor(s): John H. Ware III, Marian S. Ware.
Foundation type: Independent
Financial data (yr. ended 12/31/88): Assets, $24,040,955 (M); expenditures, $1,304,724, including $1,276,500 for 149 grants (high: $152,000; low: $500; average: $500-$1,000).
Purpose and activities: Emphasis on higher education and church support; support also for social welfare agencies, health and hospitals, and environmental conservation.
Limitations: Giving primarily in PA. No grants to individuals, or for scholarships; no loans.
Application information:
Initial approach: Letter
Deadline(s): None
Final notification: Only to applications approved by the trustees
Write: John H. Ware III, Pres.
Officers and Trustees: John H. Ware III, Pres.; Marian S. Ware, V.P.; John H. Ware IV, Treas.; Marilyn W. Lewis, Secy.; Carol W. Gates, Paul W. Ware.
Employer Identification Number: 236278067

6378
Horace B. Packer Foundation, Inc. ¤
P.O. Box 35
Wellsboro 16901

Incorporated in 1951 in PA.
Donor(s): Horace B. Packer.†
Foundation type: Independent
Financial data (yr. ended 12/31/88): Assets, $1,582,535 (M); expenditures, $113,557, including $80,750 for 20 grants (high: $15,000; low: $500) and $16,114 for 50 grants to individuals (high: $950; low: $14).
Purpose and activities: To provide relief assistance or to furnish services to benefit the youth of Tioga County; grants to educational institutions for scholarships for students residing in the county; awards to students attending medical institutions who intend to work in Tioga County.
Types of support: Scholarship funds, student aid.
Limitations: Giving limited to Tioga County, PA.
Application information:
Initial approach: Letter
Deadline(s): None
Board meeting date(s): Annually
Write: Hon. Charles G. Webb, Pres.
Officer: Charles G. Webb, Pres.; Don Gill, V.P.; Rev. George Lineker, Secy.
Trustees: Carl Carson, Harold Hershberger, Jr., John D. Lewis, William Nichols, Northern Central Bank and Trust Co.
Employer Identification Number: 236390932

6379
The Goldie Paley Foundation ¤
c/o Alex Satinsky
2000 Market St., 10th Fl.
Philadelphia 19103-3293

Established in 1964 in PA.
Donor(s): Goldie Paley.†
Foundation type: Independent
Financial data (yr. ended 10/31/89): Assets, $1,999,477 (M); expenditures, $27,239, including $25,000 for 1 grant.
Purpose and activities: Grants to universities.
Limitations: Giving limited to Philadelphia, PA. No grants to individuals.
Application information: Contributes only to pre-selected organizations. Applications not accepted.
Trustees: Patrick S. Gallagher, William S. Paley, Alex Satinsky.
Employer Identification Number: 236392054

6380
W. I. Patterson Charitable Fund
407 Oliver Bldg.
Pittsburgh 15222 (412) 281-5580

Trust established in 1955 in PA.
Donor(s): W.I. Patterson.†
Foundation type: Independent
Financial data (yr. ended 07/31/89): Assets, $2,770,587 (M); expenditures, $152,798, including $115,921 for 49 grants (high: $23,184; low: $500; average: $500-$6,000).
Purpose and activities: Support for higher and other education, a library, health associations and hospitals, and welfare funds.
Types of support: Operating budgets, continuing support, annual campaigns, seed money, emergency funds, deficit financing, building funds, equipment, land acquisition, research, publications, capital campaigns, general purposes.
Limitations: Giving primarily in Allegheny County, PA. No grants to individuals, or for endowment funds, special projects, scholarships, fellowships, or matching gifts; no loans.
Application information: Application form not required.
Initial approach: Proposal
Copies of proposal: 1
Deadline(s): Submit proposal preferably in May or June; deadline June 30
Board meeting date(s): At least 6 times a year, including Feb., May, July, Sept., and Nov.
Write: Robert B. Shust, Trustee
Trustees: Martin L. Moore, Jr., Robert B. Shust, Lester K. Wolf.
Number of staff: None.
Employer Identification Number: 256028639

6381
Patton M for Charities ¤
c/o Mellon Bank (East), N.A.
P.O. Box 185
Pittsburgh 15230
Additional address: Mellon Bank (East), N.A., One Mellon Bank Ctr., Pittsburgh 15258; Tel.: (412) 234-5784

Established in 1976 in PA.
Foundation type: Independent
Financial data (yr. ended 12/31/87): Assets, $1,428,178 (M); gifts received, $4,000; expenditures, $125,456, including $104,223 for 33 grants (high: $6,000; low: $500).
Purpose and activities: Grants primarily for education and health and social services.
Limitations: Giving primarily in Armstrong County, PA. No support for capital fund drives.
Application information: Application form required.
Deadline(s): None
Write: Barbara Robinson, Asst. V.P.
Trustees: John W. Rohrer III, Mellon Bank (East), N.A.
Employer Identification Number: 256170579

6382
The William Penn Foundation ▼

1630 Locust St.
Philadelphia 19103-6305 (215) 732-5114

Incorporated in 1945 in DE.
Donor(s): Otto Haas,† Phoebe W. Haas,† Otto Haas & Phoebe W. Haas Charitable Trusts.
Foundation type: Independent
Financial data (yr. ended 12/31/89): Assets, $470,442,587 (M); gifts received, $10,938,202; expenditures, $28,107,617, including $25,318,071 for 412 grants (high: $3,500,000; low: $500) and $99,857 for 262 employee matching gifts.
Purpose and activities: The foundation supports the following categories: (1) environment; (2) culture; (3) human development, including programs for children, adolescents, and the elderly; and (4) community fabric (institutions, services, and intergroup relations). Also sponsors a matching gift program for board members, former board members, and employees of the foundation.
Types of support: Seed money, equipment, matching funds, special projects, emergency funds, land acquisition, renovation projects, technical assistance, employee matching gifts.
Limitations: Giving limited to the Philadelphia, PA, area, and Camden County, NJ; environmental giving in southeastern PA and southern NJ. No support for sectarian religious activities, recreational programs, or programs focusing on a particular disease or treatment for addiction. No grants to individuals, or for operating budgets, continuing support, annual campaigns, deficit financing, hospital building funds, endowment funds, scholarships, fellowships, research, publications, travel, films, or conferences; no loans.
Publications: Annual report (including application guidelines), application guidelines.
Application information: Application form not required.
Initial approach: Proposal
Copies of proposal: 1
Deadline(s): None
Board meeting date(s): Jan., Mar., Apr., June, July, Sept., Oct., and Dec.
Final notification: 2 to 3 months
Write: Bernard C. Watson, Ph.D., Pres. and C.E.O.
Officers and Directors:* John C. Haas,* Chair.; John O. Haas,* Vice-Chair.; Bernard C. Watson,* Pres. and C.E.O.; Fran M. Coopersmith, V.P. for Finance and Treas.; Harry E. Cerino, V.P. for Progs.; Roland H. Johnson, Secy. and Sr. Prog. Officer; Frederick W. Anton III, Ernesta Drinker Ballard, Mary C. Carroll, Gloria Twine Chisum, Nelson A. Diaz, Richard G. Gilmore, Carole F. Haas, Chara C. Haas, David W. Haas, Frederick R. Haas, Janet F. Haas, Melinda A. Haas, Nancy Haas, Thomas W. Haas, Barbara H. Hanrahan, Philip C. Herr II, Robert Montgomery Scott, Edmund B. Spaeth, Paul M. Washington.
Number of staff: 10 full-time professional; 3 part-time professional; 9 full-time support.
Employer Identification Number: 231503488

6383
The Charles F. Peters Foundation ⌘

2008 Duquesne Ave.
McKeesport 15132

Trust established in 1965 in PA.
Donor(s): Charles F. Peters.†
Foundation type: Independent
Financial data (yr. ended 12/31/87): Assets, $2,003,483 (M); expenditures, $131,647, including $102,500 for 97 grants (high: $5,000; low: $250).
Purpose and activities: Giving for Protestant church support, youth agencies, and community services.
Limitations: Giving limited to the McKeesport, PA, area. No grants to individuals.
Application information:
Initial approach: Proposal or letter
Copies of proposal: 1
Deadline(s): None
Board meeting date(s): Monthly
Write: J. Charles Peterson, Admin.
Administrators: William H. Balter, J. Charles Peterson, Kathryn Peters Schoeller.
Trustee: Equibank.
Employer Identification Number: 256070765

6384
The Pew Charitable Trusts

Three Pkwy., Suite 501
Philadelphia 19102-1305 (215) 568-3330

Pew Memorial Trust, J.N. Pew, Jr. Charitable Trust, J. Howard Pew Freedom Trust, Mabel Pew Myrin Trust, Medical Trust, Knollbrook Trust, and Mary Anderson Trust, created in 1948, 1956, 1957, 1957, 1975, 1965, and 1957 respectively.
Donor(s): Mary Ethel Pew,† Mabel Pew Myrin,† J. Howard Pew,† Joseph N. Pew, Jr.†
Foundation type: Independent
Financial data (yr. ended 12/31/89): Assets, $3,321,890,529 (M); expenditures, $143,798,962, including $137,083,529 for grants.
Purpose and activities: Giving primarily in culture, education, health and human services, conservation and the environment, public policy, and religion. In culture, support is given in the Philadelphia area to foster cultural activities of the highest quality, promote an environment that encourages artistic and institutional advancement, and increase awareness and appreciation of Philadelphia's diverse cultural resources. Nationally, support is given to advance specific cultural areas or disciplines, address critical cultural needs, and support the dissemination of creative solutions to problems shared by broad national constituencies. In education, support is given to maintain academic excellence, strengthen the liberal arts and sciences, support institutional diversity, make higher education more accessible to disadvantaged populations, and encourage better understanding of major issues affecting the quality of education. In health and human services, support is given to programs that encourage community development in the Philadelphia area, promote greater self-sufficiency and meaningful, productive lifestyles among groups at risk, strengthen institutions in the health professions, advance the biomedical sciences, improve health care delivery systems, encourage the elderly and the physically and mentally handicapped to live to their fullest potential, build the capacities of individuals and communities, strengthen indigenous policies and programs in developing countries that promote improved health status and sustained economic and social development. In conservation and the environment, support is given to advance the field of conservation through research and training, strengthen the field's infrastructure, and encourage collaboration among the various disciplines involved with resource management and development. In public policy, support is given to improve understanding of the free enterprise system and American civic values and responsibilities, and to encourage research and debate on the implications of contemporary policy concerns on U.S. security, international relations, and the economy. In religion, support is given to promote the development and application of Judeo-Christian values and encourage better understanding of how those values shape our lives and civic responsibilities. Support is also given to strengthen religious scholarship, foster international understanding, and develop the ministry of congregations in their communities.
Types of support: Seed money, matching funds, continuing support, renovation projects, building funds, equipment, research, operating budgets, special projects, capital campaigns, general purposes, internships, technical assistance.
Limitations: No grants to individuals, or for endowment funds, deficit financing, scholarships, or fellowships except those identified or initiated by the trusts.
Publications: Annual report (including application guidelines), grants list, occasional report, informational brochure (including application guidelines).
Application information: Contact foundation for specific guidelines and limitations in each program area. Culture applicants must submit a letter of intent form, obtained from the Culture Program office, 6 weeks in advance of deadlines. Application form not required.
Initial approach: Letter, telephone, or proposal
Copies of proposal: 1
Deadline(s): Culture: Music-Dec. 1, Museums/visual arts-Mar. 1, Theater-June 1, and Dance-Sept. 1; Education (including component requests): Feb. 1 for review in June and Aug. 1 for review in Dec.; all others, no set deadline
Board meeting date(s): Mar., June, Sept., and Dec.
Final notification: Approximately 3 weeks after board meetings
Write: Rebecca W. Rimel, Exec. Dir.
Officers and Board:* Thomas W. Langfitt, M.D.,* Pres.; Rebecca W. Rimel, Exec. Dir.; Susan W. Catherwood, Robert G. Dunlop, Robert E. McDonald, J. Howard Pew II, J.N. Pew III, John G. Pew, Jr., Joseph N. Pew IV, M.D., R. Anderson Pew.
Trustee: The Glenmede Trust Co.
Number of staff: 20 full-time professional; 44 full-time support; 2 part-time support.

6385
The Philadelphia Foundation ▼
1400 South Penn Sq.
Two Mellon Bank Ctr., Suite 2017
Philadelphia 19102 (215) 563-6417

Established in 1918 in PA by bank resolution.
Donor(s): 140 different funds.
Foundation type: Community
Financial data (yr. ended 04/30/90): Assets, $63,646,921 (M); gifts received, $1,403,012; expenditures, $5,491,320, including $4,914,946 for 470 grants (high: $100,173; low: $150).
Purpose and activities: For the purpose of promoting charitable, educational, and civic activities; most of the funds have specific purposes or named beneficiary institutions, with emphasis on health and welfare, including hospitals and community activities; grants also for education and cultural programs.
Types of support: Operating budgets, continuing support, seed money, emergency funds, matching funds, special projects, consulting services, technical assistance.
Limitations: Giving limited to Philadelphia and to Bucks, Chester, Delaware, and Montgomery counties in southeastern PA, except for designated funds. No support for national organizations, government agencies, large budget agencies, private schools, religious organizations, or umbrella-funding organizations. No grants to individuals, or for annual or capital campaigns, building funds, land acquisition, endowment funds, scholarships, fellowships, research, publications, tours or trips, conferences, or deficit financing; no loans.
Publications: Annual report, application guidelines, informational brochure, newsletter.
Application information: Application form required.
Initial approach: Proposal, including cover sheet and statistical form
Copies of proposal: 1
Deadline(s): Submit proposal preferably during May and June or Nov. and Dec.; proposals not accepted Aug.-Oct. and Feb.-Apr.; deadlines July 31 and Jan. 15
Board meeting date(s): Apr. and Nov.
Final notification: 3 to 4 months
Managers: Don Jose Stovall, Chair.; Ernesta Drinker Ballard, David Brenner, Peter Hearn, Walter R. Livingston, Jr., Carmen Febo-San Miguel, M.D., Christian Murphy, Leon C. Sunstein, Jr., Peter Vaughn.
Trustees: Continental Bank, N.A., Fidelity Bank, N.A., First National Bank & Trust of Newtown, First Pennsylvania Bank, N.A., The Glenmede Trust Co., Mellon Bank, N.A., Meridian Trust Co., Philadelphia National Bank, Provident National Bank.
Number of staff: 5 full-time professional; 3 full-time support.
Employer Identification Number: 231581832

6386
Dr. & Mrs. Arthur William Phillips Charitable Trust ⌑
229 Elm St.
P.O. Box 316
Oil City 16301 (814) 676-2736

Trust established in 1978 in PA.
Donor(s): Arthur William Phillips.†
Foundation type: Independent
Financial data (yr. ended 9/30/88): Assets, $8,343,801 (M); expenditures, $542,122, including $449,740 for 25 grants (high: $75,000; low: $790).
Purpose and activities: Giving for health agencies; support also for Protestant churches and welfare funds, youth agencies, and higher and secondary education.
Types of support: Renovation projects, capital campaigns, equipment, matching funds, student aid, special projects.
Limitations: Giving primarily in northwestern PA.
Application information: Application form not required.
Initial approach: Proposal
Copies of proposal: 3
Deadline(s): None
Write: William J. McFate, Trustee
Trustees: Hugh R. Gilmore, Jr., William J. McFate.
Employer Identification Number: 256201015

6387
Pine Tree Foundation ⌑ ☆
c/o Zweig, Ramick & Associates
2320 Faunce St.
Philadelphia 19152
Application address: 120 Righters Mill Rd., Gladwyne, PA 19035

Established in 1986 in PA.
Donor(s): A. Morris Williams, Jr., Ruth W. Williams.
Foundation type: Independent
Financial data (yr. ended 7/31/88): Assets, $1,840,094 (M); gifts received, $923,460; expenditures, $48,926, including $47,000 for 2 grants (high: $35,000; low: $12,000).
Purpose and activities: Support for a school and a welfare organization.
Application information:
Initial approach: Letter
Deadline(s): None
Write: A. Morris Williams, Jr., Dir.
Officers and Directors: A. Morris Williams, Jr., Pres.; Ruth W. Williams, Secy.-Treas.
Employer Identification Number: 222751187

6388
Piper Foundation, Inc. ⌑ ☆
P.O. Box 227
Lock Haven 17745-1312

Donor(s): Piper Aircraft Corp.
Foundation type: Company-sponsored
Financial data (yr. ended 9/30/88): Assets, $1,220,972 (M); expenditures, $67,026, including $60,950 for 21 grants (high: $15,000; low: $300).
Purpose and activities: Support primarily for community funds, higher education, and a library.
Officers: W.T. Piper, Jr., Pres.; Thomas F. Piper, V.P.; Henry W. Ebeling, Secy.-Treas.
Employer Identification Number: 240863140

6389
Pitcairn-Crabbe Foundation ⌑
c/o The CNG Tower
625 Liberty Ave., 30th Fl.
Pittsburgh 15222-3199 (412) 391-5122

Incorporated in 1940 in PA.
Donor(s): Susan Lee Hunt.†
Foundation type: Independent
Financial data (yr. ended 12/31/86): Assets, $5,536,132 (M); expenditures, $313,756, including $261,305 for 18 grants (high: $28,000; low: $850; average: $5,000-$20,000).
Purpose and activities: Giving for Christian education, primary and higher education, Protestant religious and church work, youth agencies, community welfare, and relief.
Types of support: General purposes, seed money, emergency funds, building funds, equipment, endowment funds, matching funds.
Limitations: Giving primarily in western PA. No support for the arts, or the medical needs of hospitals and scientific causes. No grants to individuals, or for operating budgets, scholarships, fellowships, annual campaigns of national organizations, or research; no loans.
Publications: Multi-year report, program policy statement, application guidelines.
Application information: Application form required.
Initial approach: Letter, proposal, or telephone
Copies of proposal: 1
Deadline(s): None
Board meeting date(s): Jan., May, and Oct.
Final notification: 2 months
Write: Alfred W. Wishart, Jr., Exec. Secy.
Officers: G. Dickson Shrum, Jr.,* Pres.; Richard M. Johnston,* V.P.; W. Bruce McConnell,* Secy.-Treas.; Alfred W. Wishart, Jr., Exec. Secy.
Directors:* Richard D. Baker, Elizabeth B. Behrend, Nathalie H. Curry, William H. Genge, Charles R. Rhine, Robert G. Runnette, Jean M. Schaefer, Arthur M. Scully, Jr., G. Dixon Shrum, Jr., John C. Wain, Farley W. Whetzel.
Number of staff: 2 full-time professional; 1 full-time support.
Employer Identification Number: 250965459

6390
Pittsburgh Child Guidance Foundation
580 South Aiken Ave.
Pittsburgh 15232-1502 (412) 683-7243

Established in 1982 in PA.
Foundation type: Independent
Financial data (yr. ended 12/31/89): Assets, $3,118,805 (M); expenditures, $322,484, including $245,459 for 15 grants (high: $117,640; low: $500).
Purpose and activities: The foundation's focus is on children's mental health, including preventative and early intervention programs and those fostering healthy development.
Types of support: Matching funds, seed money, special projects, research.
Limitations: Giving limited to western PA, northern WV, and eastern OH. Generally support for children's mental health only. No grants to individuals, scholarships, annual or capital campaigns, or endowments.

Publications: Informational brochure (including application guidelines), application guidelines, informational brochure, grants list.
Application information: The foundation initiates application for a Program Grant by issuing a Request for Proposal. Discretionary Grants are initiated by the applicant. Applicants should contact the foundation prior to submitting a proposal. Application form not required.
Initial approach: Telephone
Copies of proposal: 1
Deadline(s): Mar. 1, June 1, and Nov. 1
Board meeting date(s): Apr., July, Oct., and Jan.
Write: Brigitte Alexander, Exec. Dir.
Officers and Trustees:* Munro J. Grant,* Pres.; John D. Houston II, Esq.,* V.P.; Judith M. Davenport,* Secy.; Alan A. Axelson,* Treas.; Rose M. Alvin, Mark B. Aronson, Irvin Chamovitz, M.D., Joseph T. Christy, David B. Hartmann, M.D., Janet F. Krieger, Ann P. Leibrick, Don A. Linzer, Evelyn L. Murrin, Marie Ford Reilly, Karen VanderVen.
Number of staff: 1 part-time professional; 1 part-time support.
Employer Identification Number: 250965465

6391
The Pittsburgh Foundation ▼ ⌑
30 CNG Tower
625 Liberty Ave., 30th Fl.
Pittsburgh 15222-3199 (412) 391-5122

Established in 1945 in PA by bank resolution and declaration of trust.
Foundation type: Community
Financial data (yr. ended 12/31/87): Assets, $108,690,270 (M); gifts received, $4,331,215; expenditures, $5,256,531, including $4,608,585 for 274 grants (high: $100,000; low: $500; average: $5,000-$50,000).
Purpose and activities: Organized for the permanent administration of funds placed in trust for public charitable and educational purposes; funds used for programs to support special projects of regularly established agencies, capital and equipment needs, research of a nontechnical nature, and demonstration projects. Grants primarily for human services, health, education, urban affairs, and the arts. Unless specified by the donor, grants are generally nonrecurring.
Types of support: Special projects, seed money, building funds, equipment, research, renovation projects, technical assistance.
Limitations: Giving limited to Pittsburgh and Allegheny County, PA. No support for churches, private schools, or hospitals. No grants to individuals, or for annual campaigns, endowment funds, travel, operating budgets, scholarships, fellowships, or research of a highly technical or specialized nature; no loans to individuals.
Publications: Annual report, application guidelines, newsletter.
Application information: Application form required.
Initial approach: Letter or proposal
Copies of proposal: 1
Deadline(s): 60 days prior to board meeting
Board meeting date(s): Mar., June, Sept., and Dec.
Final notification: 4 to 6 weeks
Write: Alfred W. Wishart, Jr., Exec. Dir.
Officers: Alfred W. Wishart, Jr., Exec. Dir.; Jack E. Kime, Assoc. Dir. and Chief Financial and Admin. Officer; Dana M. Phillips, Planning and Evaluation Officer.
Distribution Committee: Sholom D. Comay, Chair.; William J. Copeland, Vice-Chair.; Dorothy R. Williams, Treas.; Byrd R. Brown, Jeanne C. Caliguiri, Douglas D. Danforth, Robert Dickey III, Arthur J. Edmunds, Benjamin R. Fisher, Jr., Phyllis Moorman Goode, Sherin H. Knowles, John L. Propst, Frieda G. Shapira.
Trustee Banks: First Seneca Bank, Equibank, Mellon Bank, N.A., Pittsburgh National Bank, Union National Bank of Pittsburgh.
Number of staff: 8 full-time professional; 1 part-time professional; 12 full-time support.
Employer Identification Number: 250965466

6392
Pittsburgh National Bank Foundation ▼ ⌑
(Formerly Pittsburgh National Foundation)
c/o Pittsburgh National Bldg., 14th Fl.
Fifth Ave. and Wood St.
Pittsburgh 15222 (412) 762-4222

Established in 1970 in PA.
Donor(s): Pittsburgh National Bank.
Foundation type: Company-sponsored
Financial data (yr. ended 12/31/89): Assets, $5,103,014 (M); gifts received, $1,059,042; expenditures, $1,585,589, including $1,541,055 for 277 grants (high: $363,500; low: $25; average: $1,000-$35,000) and $40,134 for 88 employee matching gifts.
Purpose and activities: Giving for community funds, education, hospitals and health, cultural programs, youth agencies, public policy, community development, and social services.
Types of support: Operating budgets, continuing support, annual campaigns, seed money, emergency funds, deficit financing, general purposes, building funds, equipment, land acquisition, matching funds, employee matching gifts.
Limitations: Giving limited to southwestern PA. No support for religious purposes. No grants to individuals, or for endowment; no loans.
Application information: Application form not required.
Initial approach: Letter
Copies of proposal: 1
Deadline(s): None
Board meeting date(s): Monthly
Final notification: Approximately 6 weeks
Write: D. Paul Beard, Secy.
Officer: D. Paul Beard, Secy.
Trustee: Pittsburgh National Bank.
Number of staff: 2 part-time professional; 2 part-time support.
Employer Identification Number: 251202255

6393
Pittsburgh-Des Moines Steel Company Charitable Trust ⌑
3400 Grand Ave., Neville Island
Pittsburgh 15225 (412) 331-3000

Established in 1952 in PA.
Foundation type: Company-sponsored
Financial data (yr. ended 12/31/87): Assets, $1,037,704 (M); expenditures, $37,898, including $34,525 for 28 grants (high: $10,000; low: $100).
Purpose and activities: Support primarily for community organizations and higher education.
Application information:
Write: W.R. Jackson, Trustee
Trustees: R.A. Dyers, W.R. Jackson, W.R. Jackson, Jr.
Employer Identification Number: 256032139

6394
The Harry Plankenhorn Foundation, Inc. ⌑
c/o Abram M. Snyder
R.D. 2
Cogan Station 17728

Incorporated in 1959 in PA.
Donor(s): Harry Plankenhorn.†
Foundation type: Independent
Financial data (yr. ended 12/31/88): Assets, $3,186,694 (M); expenditures, $200,266, including $189,975 for 32 grants (high: $45,000; low: $300).
Purpose and activities: Giving for youth agencies and child welfare, including handicapped children; some support also for health and social service agencies.
Limitations: Giving primarily in Lycoming County, PA.
Application information:
Initial approach: Letter
Deadline(s): None
Officers and Directors:* A. William Gehron,* Pres.; Charles F. Greevy III,* V.P.; Carl H. Sump,* Secy.; Abram M. Snyder,* Treas.; John H. Archer, Grove W. Deming, Rev. Bruce Druckenmiller, Barbara Ertel, Fred A. Foulkrod, Dean F. Rabert, Lucinda A. Wagner, Eleanor W. Whiting.
Employer Identification Number: 246023579

6395
PMA Foundation ⌑
925 Chestnut St.
Philadelphia 19107

Established in 1981 in PA.
Donor(s): PMA Industries, Inc.
Foundation type: Company-sponsored
Financial data (yr. ended 12/31/87): Assets, $59,826 (M); gifts received, $150,000; expenditures, $117,878, including $117,731 for 86 grants (high: $25,000; low: $25).
Purpose and activities: Grants primarily for higher education through an employee matching gift program, culture, and community funds.
Types of support: Employee matching gifts.
Limitations: Giving primarily in PA.
Trustees: Frederick W. Anton III, David L. Johnson, Douglas M. Moe.
Employer Identification Number: 232159233

6396
The Polk Foundation, Inc.
2000 Grant Bldg.
Pittsburgh 15219 (412) 338-3466

Incorporated in 1957 in PA.
Donor(s): Patricia Hillman Miller.†

Foundation type: Independent
Financial data (yr. ended 12/31/89): Assets, $3,489,784 (M); expenditures, $164,383, including $133,000 for 2 grants (high: $128,000; low: $5,000; average: $5,000-$128,000).
Purpose and activities: Emphasis on a school for exceptional children, programs for mentally or physically handicapped youth, and medical research.
Types of support: Seed money, building funds, equipment, capital campaigns, renovation projects.
Limitations: Giving limited to Pittsburgh and southwestern PA. No grants to individuals, or for operating budgets, continuing support, annual campaigns, emergency funds, deficit financing, land acquisition, endowment funds, matching gifts, scholarships, fellowships, research, special projects, publications, or conferences; no loans.
Publications: Financial statement.
Application information: Application form not required.
Initial approach: Letter
Copies of proposal: 1
Deadline(s): None
Board meeting date(s): May and Dec.
Final notification: 4 to 6 months
Write: Ronald W. Wertz, Exec. Dir.
Officers: Henry L. Hillman,* Pres.; H. Vaughan Blaxter III,* Secy.; Lawrence M. Wagner, Treas.; Ronald W. Wertz, Exec. Dir.
Directors:* Patricia M. Duggan, C.G. Grefenstette.
Number of staff: 1 part-time professional.
Employer Identification Number: 251113733

6397
The Potamkin Foundation ⌘
c/o Robert Potamkin
Grant and Academy Rds.
Philadelphia 19114

Established in 1985 in PA.
Foundation type: Independent
Financial data (yr. ended 5/31/88): Assets, $732,895 (M); expenditures, $165,572, including $162,750 for 15 grants (high: $50,000; low: $250).
Purpose and activities: Support for higher and other education, hospitals, the aged, and performing arts groups.
Limitations: No grants to individuals.
Application information: Contributes only to pre-selected organizations. Applications not accepted.
Directors: Alan Potamkin, Robert Potamkin, Victor Potamkin.
Employer Identification Number: 236800690

6398
PPG Industries Foundation ▼
One PPG Place
Pittsburgh 15272 (412) 434-2962

Incorporated in 1951 in PA.
Donor(s): PPG Industries, Inc.
Foundation type: Company-sponsored
Financial data (yr. ended 12/31/88): Assets, $10,051,501 (M); gifts received, $186,533; expenditures, $4,731,165, including $3,864,451 for 1,011 grants (high: $363,000; average: $5,000-$20,000) and $572,335 for 3,502 employee matching gifts.
Purpose and activities: Giving primarily for social services, including community funds and youth organizations, higher education, health and safety organizations, cultural programs, and civic and community affairs.
Types of support: Annual campaigns, capital campaigns, operating budgets, emergency funds, research, scholarship funds, employee-related scholarships, employee matching gifts, continuing support, special projects.
Limitations: Giving primarily in areas of company operations, with emphasis on the Pittsburgh, PA, region. No support for religious groups for religious purposes. No grants to individuals, or for endowment funds, advertising, benefits, grants (other than matching gifts) of less than $100, or operating support of United Way member agencies; no loans.
Publications: Annual report (including application guidelines).
Application information: Grant decisions made by the Screening Committee and the Board of Directors. Application form not required.
Initial approach: Letter
Copies of proposal: 1
Deadline(s): Sept. 1
Board meeting date(s): Usually in June and Dec.
Final notification: Following board meetings
Write: Roslyn Rosenblatt, Exec. Dir.
Officers and Directors:* Vincent Sarni,* Chair.; Frank V. Breeze,* Vice-Chair.; E.J. Slack,* Pres.; Robert H. Mitchel,* V.P.; Guy Zoghby,* V.P.; Edward Mazeski, Jr., Secy.; Lawrence M. Call, Treas.; Roslyn Rosenblatt,* Exec. Dir.
Number of staff: 1 full-time professional; 1 full-time support; 1 part-time support.
Employer Identification Number: 256037790

6399
The Presser Foundation ⌘
Presser Place
Bryn Mawr 19010 (215) 525-4797

Founded in 1916; incorporated in 1939 in PA.
Donor(s): Theodore Presser.†
Foundation type: Independent
Financial data (yr. ended 06/30/89): Assets, $10,726,977 (M); gifts received, $1,171,008; expenditures, $1,443,121, including $925,205 for grants, $50,558 for grants to individuals and $326,613 for foundation-administered programs.
Purpose and activities: To provide scholarship aid grants to accredited colleges and universities for worthy undergraduate students of music; to increase music education in institutions of learning and to popularize the teaching of music as a profession; to administer emergency aid through small grants to worthy music teachers in need.
Types of support: Grants to individuals, scholarship funds, building funds, conferences and seminars, equipment, fellowships, matching funds, renovation projects, seed money, special projects.
Application information: Application forms available for financial aid to needy music teachers and for scholarships.
Deadline(s): None
Write: Henderson Supplee III, Pres.
Officers and Trustees:* Henderson Supplee III,* Pres.; Thomas M. Hyndman, Jr.,* V.P.; Bruce Montgomery,* Secy.; Charles F. Nagel,* Treas.; Boyd T. Barnard, Robert Capanna, William M. Davison IV, Morris Duane, Raymond S. Green, Edwin F. Heidakka, Helen Laird, Edith A. Reinhardt, Felix C. Robb, Michael Stairs, James D. Winsor III, Philip W. Young.
Number of staff: 1 full-time professional.
Employer Identification Number: 232164013

6400
The Progress Education Foundation ⌘ ☆
P.O. Box 810
Carlisle 17013-0810 (717) 243-0583

Established in 1978.
Foundation type: Independent
Financial data (yr. ended 12/31/87): Assets, $440,801 (M); expenditures, $104,065, including $10,160 for 18 grants (high: $25,000; low: $100).
Purpose and activities: Giving primarily for higher education and social services; support also for community funds and theological education.
Limitations: No grants to individuals.
Application information: Application form not required.
Initial approach: Letter
Deadline(s): None
Write: Grant Mgr.
Trustees: C. Marius Haayan, Benjamin James, D.E. Lutz, June B. Lutz.
Employer Identification Number: 232053536

6401
Progress Foundation ⌘ ☆
c/o Dauphin Deposit Bank & Trust Co.
Box 2961
Harrisburg 17105
Application address: 1076 Harrisburg Pike, Carlisle, PA 17013

Established in 1961.
Donor(s): Urie D. Lutz,† Robert Long.
Foundation type: Independent
Financial data (yr. ended 12/31/87): Assets, $1,035,428 (M); gifts received, $2,810; expenditures, $111,836, including $14,100 for 3 grants (high: $12,000; low: $600).
Purpose and activities: Giving primarily for welfare agencies, children and youth, and education, including libraries.
Limitations: Giving primarily in Carlisle and Harrisburg, PA. No grants to individuals.
Application information:
Initial approach: Letter
Deadline(s): None
Write: D.E. Lutz, Trustee
Trustees: D.E. Lutz, June B. Lutz, Dauphin Deposit Bank & Trust Co.
Employer Identification Number: 236265833

6402
The Provincial Foundation
2023 Pine St.
Philadelphia 19103 (215) 735-3862

Established in 1958 in PA.
Foundation type: Independent
Financial data (yr. ended 1/31/89): Assets, $1,123,539 (M); expenditures, $89,333, including $56,250 for 130 grants (high: $3,000; low: $100; average: $438).
Purpose and activities: Grants for the arts, culture, health and social services, Jewish organizations, and higher education.
Limitations: Giving primarily in Philadelphia, PA. No grants to individuals.
Publications: Annual report (including application guidelines).
Application information: Application form not required.
Initial approach: Letter
Copies of proposal: 1
Board meeting date(s): Jan., Apr., July, and Sept.
Officers: Arthur Klein, Pres.; Esther Klein, V.P.; Michael Temin, Secy.
Number of staff: 1 part-time professional.
Employer Identification Number: 231422090

6403
The Quaker Chemical Foundation
Elm and Lee Sts.
Conshohocken 19428 (215) 828-4250

Trust established in 1959 in PA.
Donor(s): Quaker Chemical Corp.
Foundation type: Company-sponsored
Financial data (yr. ended 6/30/89): Assets, $470,918 (M); gifts received, $186,000; expenditures, $329,233, including $151,152 for 142 grants (high: $25,000; low: $2,750; average: $2,500), $95,528 for 38 grants to individuals (high: $4,000; low: $1,000; average: $1,000-$4,000) and $82,552 for 383 employee matching gifts.
Purpose and activities: Grants largely for higher education, including scholarships and employee matching gifts, local community funds, health, hospitals, social services, and cultural programs.
Types of support: Scholarship funds, employee matching gifts, employee-related scholarships, matching funds.
Limitations: Giving primarily in CA, MI, and PA. No grants to individuals (except for employee-related scholarships), or for building or endowment funds; no loans.
Publications: Application guidelines.
Application information: Application form not required.
Initial approach: Proposal
Copies of proposal: 1
Deadline(s): Apr. 30
Board meeting date(s): Quarterly
Final notification: July
Write: Karl H. Spaeth, Chair.
Trustees: Karl H. Spaeth, Chair.; Katherine N. Coughenour, Edwin J. Delattre, Alan G. Keyser, J. Everett Wick, Jane Williams.
Number of staff: None.
Employer Identification Number: 236245803

6404
John Charles & Kathryn S. Redmond Foundation ⌑
1700 Market St.
Philadelphia 19103

Foundation type: Independent
Financial data (yr. ended 12/31/88): Assets, $1,183,897 (M); expenditures, $89,505, including $68,700 for 13 grants (high: $30,000; low: $750).
Purpose and activities: Giving primarily for higher and secondary education, and church support.
Application information: Contributes only to pre-selected organizations. Applications not accepted.
Officers: John C. Redmond, Jr., Pres.; John C. Redmond III, Secy.; Dorothy Roche, Treas.
Employer Identification Number: 236279089

6405
Herbert M. Rehmeyer Trust ⌑
c/o The York Bank & Trust Co.
21 East Market St.
York 17401
Application address: 35 South Duke St., York, PA 17401; Tel.: (717) 843-7841

Established in 1981.
Foundation type: Independent
Financial data (yr. ended 4/30/88): Assets, $1,251,097 (M); expenditures, $138,063, including $118,650 for 37 grants (high: $10,000; low: $400).
Purpose and activities: Grants largely for arts and cultural programs, including historical societies; support also for youth and social service agencies, higher education, and hospitals and health agencies.
Limitations: Giving primarily in York County, PA.
Application information: Application form required.
Deadline(s): Oct. 1
Write: Henry Leader, Trustee
Trustees: Henry Leader, Lester Naylor, The York Bank & Trust Co.
Employer Identification Number: 236708035

6406
Reidler Foundation
Hazleton National Bank Bldg.
Broad and Laurel Sts.
Hazleton 18201 (717) 459-4242

Incorporated in 1944 in PA.
Donor(s): John W. Reidler.
Foundation type: Independent
Financial data (yr. ended 10/31/88): Assets, $4,299,249 (M); gifts received, $24,558; expenditures, $219,310, including $175,000 for 71 grants (high: $20,000; low: $500).
Purpose and activities: Grants for Protestant church support, higher education, hospitals, and youth agencies.
Limitations: Giving primarily in the Ashland and Hazleton, PA, areas. No grants to individuals.
Application information:
Initial approach: Letter
Deadline(s): Submit proposal preferably between Oct. and Mar.
Board meeting date(s): Apr., June, and Oct.
Write: Elizabeth Corcoran, Secy.-Treas.
Officers: Paul G. Reidler, Pres.; Ann B. Fegan, V.P.; Robert K. Gicking, V.P.; Elizabeth Corcoran, Secy.-Treas.
Directors: Howard D. Fegan, Eugene C. Fish, Carl J. Reidler.
Employer Identification Number: 246022888

6407
W. H. and Althea F. Remmel Foundation
c/o Pittsburgh National Bank
C & I Trust Div.
Pittsburgh 15265 (412) 752-2586

Established in 1951 in PA.
Donor(s): William H. Remmel,† Althea F. Remmel.†
Foundation type: Independent
Financial data (yr. ended 12/31/89): Assets, $1,866,599 (M); expenditures, $95,193, including $82,000 for 23 grants (high: $30,000; low: $1,000).
Purpose and activities: Grants primarily for education, health, religion, and social services.
Types of support: General purposes.
Limitations: Giving primarily in Pittsburgh, PA. No grants to individuals, or for operating budgets or scholarships; no loans.
Publications: Informational brochure, application guidelines.
Application information: Application form required.
Initial approach: Letter
Deadline(s): Mid-Apr. and mid-Oct.
Board meeting date(s): May and Nov.
Final notification: One month
Write: Charitable Trust Committee
Trustee: Pittsburgh National Bank.
Employer Identification Number: 237009732

6408
George W. Rentschler Foundation ⌑
c/o Provident National Bank
1632 Chestnut St.
Philadelphia 19103
Application address: Packard Bldg., 14th Fl., Philadelphia, PA 19102

Established in 1975 in PA.
Foundation type: Independent
Financial data (yr. ended 1/31/87): Assets, $1,445,516 (M); expenditures, $95,317, including $79,000 for 17 grants (high: $35,000; low: $1,000).
Purpose and activities: Grants for health services, education, and social services, including child welfare.
Types of support: Equipment, operating budgets.
Limitations: Giving primarily in Philadelphia, PA. No grants to individuals.
Application information: Application form required.
Initial approach: Letter
Deadline(s): None; however, grants are made in the fall of each year
Write: Hugh Sutherland, Esq., Secy.-Treas.
Officers: William O'Neill, Pres.; Samuel Evans III, V.P.; Hugh Sutherland, Secy.-Treas.
Employer Identification Number: 236627872

6409
Richardson Foundation, Inc. ⌑
Washington Trust Bldg., Rm. 412
Washington 15301
Application address: P.O. Box 339, Vero Beach, FL 32961-0339

Established in 1963 in PA.
Donor(s): Danforth K. Richardson, Marjorie H. Richardson.
Foundation type: Independent
Financial data (yr. ended 12/31/88): Assets, $1,269,517 (M); expenditures, $364,457, including $52,521 for 104 grants (high: $5,000; low: $20) and $221,390 for 96 grants to individuals (high: $5,000; low: $100).
Purpose and activities: Giving primarily for education, including secondary and higher education, and scholarships to individuals and through funds; support also for Protestant churches.
Types of support: Scholarship funds, student aid.
Limitations: Giving primarily in Indian River, FL.
Application information: Application form required.
Initial approach: Letter
Deadline(s): None
Write: Gary Lindsey
Officers: Danforth K. Richardson, Pres.; Marjorie H. Richardson, V.P.; Sandra R. Kahle, Secy.; Nancy R. Luther, Treas.
Employer Identification Number: 591027379

6410
Rider-Pool Foundation
1050 Cedar Crest Blvd.
Allentown 18103 (215) 770-9386

Established in 1957 in PA.
Donor(s): Dorothy Rider-Pool.
Foundation type: Independent
Financial data (yr. ended 12/31/88): Assets, $4,956,211 (M); expenditures, $328,731, including $316,096 for 9 grants (high: $100,000; low: $5,000; average: $15,000).
Purpose and activities: Giving for the prevention of cruelty to children or animals; some support for cultural programs.
Types of support: General purposes, building funds, emergency funds, endowment funds, fellowships, renovation projects, research, special projects.
Limitations: Giving primarily in Allentown, PA.
Application information:
Initial approach: Letter or proposal
Deadline(s): None
Write: Edwin F. Meehan
Trustees: Edward L. Donnely, Leon C. Holt, Provident National Bank.
Employer Identification Number: 236207356

6411
Rittenhouse Foundation
225 South 15th St.
Philadelphia 19102 (215) 735-3863

Incorporated in 1952 in PA.
Donor(s): Philip Klein.†
Foundation type: Independent
Financial data (yr. ended 12/31/87): Assets, $1,815,000 (M); expenditures, $168,406, including $114,675 for 137 grants (high: $14,000; low: $100).
Purpose and activities: To assist charitable and educational institutions, with emphasis on higher education, music and the arts, and youth agencies.
Types of support: Continuing support, seed money, equipment, publications.
Limitations: Giving primarily in the Philadelphia, PA, area. No grants to individuals, or for endowment funds or operating budgets; no loans.
Publications: Annual report (including application guidelines).
Application information: Application form not required.
Initial approach: Letter
Copies of proposal: 1
Deadline(s): None
Board meeting date(s): Jan., Apr., July, and Sept.
Final notification: 30 days
Write: Arthur Klein, Pres.
Officers and Directors:* Arthur Klein,* Pres. and Treas.; Esther Klein,* Exec. V.P.; Michael Temin, Secy.
Number of staff: 1 part-time professional; 2 part-time support.
Employer Identification Number: 236005622

6412
Donald & Sylvia Robinson Family Foundation
6507 Wilkins Ave.
Pittsburgh 15217 (412) 661-1200

Foundation type: Independent
Financial data (yr. ended 10/31/88): Assets, $1,665,198 (M); expenditures, $76,522, including $69,458 for 74 grants (high: $22,500; low: $25).
Purpose and activities: Support for Jewish welfare funds, Israel, the performing arts, ecology and the environment, and hunger programs.
Types of support: Annual campaigns, emergency funds.
Limitations: No grants to individuals.
Application information:
Write: Donald Robinson, Trustee
Trustees: Donald Robinson, Sylvia Robinson.
Number of staff: None.
Employer Identification Number: 237062017

6413
The Robinson Foundation ⌑
c/o Provident National Bank, M.S. No. 100-01-01
P.O. Box 7648
Philadelphia 19101 (215) 585-8184
Additional tel.: (215) 585-8185

Trust established in 1952 in PA.
Donor(s): Members of the William M.M. Robinson family.
Foundation type: Independent
Financial data (yr. ended 12/31/88): Assets, $1,457,808 (M); expenditures, $221,653, including $209,000 for 13 grants (high: $20,000; low: $2,500).
Purpose and activities: Grants for Protestant church support and social service agencies, higher and secondary education, and family planning.
Types of support: Continuing support, general purposes, scholarship funds.
Publications: Application guidelines.
Application information:
Initial approach: Letter
Deadline(s): Sept. 1
Board meeting date(s): Oct. or Nov.
Write: Diane D. Bakley, Asst. V.P., Provident National Bank
Distribution Committee: Diane D. Bakley, Anne B. Nutt, Kelsey P. Robinson, Mary R. Talbot.
Trustee: Margaret R. Bailey, Samuel W. Robinson, Provident National Bank.
Number of staff: None.
Employer Identification Number: 236207354

6414
Milton and Shirley Rock Foundation
229 South 18th St.
Philadelphia 19103 (215) 790-7055

Established in 1985 in PA.
Foundation type: Independent
Financial data (yr. ended 08/31/89): Assets, $1,876,225 (M); expenditures, $140,038, including $134,165 for 5 grants (high: $108,165; low: $1,000; average: $1,000-$134,000).
Purpose and activities: Support primarily for cultural programs and a university.
Limitations: Giving primarily in Philadelphia, PA.
Application information: Contributes only to pre-selected organizations. Applications not accepted.
Write: Milton L. Rock, Pres.
Officers and Directors:* Milton L. Rock,* Pres.; Susan Rock Herzog,* V.P.; Robert H. Rock,* V.P.
Number of staff: None.
Employer Identification Number: 222670382

6415
The Rockwell Foundation
3212 USX Tower
600 Grant St.
Pittsburgh 15219 (412) 765-3990

Trust established in 1956 in PA.
Donor(s): Willard F. Rockwell,† and family.
Foundation type: Independent
Financial data (yr. ended 12/31/89): Assets, $9,303,238 (M); expenditures, $458,727, including $441,000 for 120 grants (high: $25,000; low: $500).
Purpose and activities: Giving for higher and secondary education; support also for the fine and performing arts, child welfare and family services, conservation, hospitals and health agencies, historic preservation, and religion.
Types of support: Annual campaigns, building funds, capital campaigns, continuing support, endowment funds, equipment, general purposes, operating budgets, scholarship funds, seed money.
Limitations: Giving primarily in PA. No grants to individuals, or for fellowships; no loans.
Application information: Application form not required.
Initial approach: Letter or telephone
Copies of proposal: 1
Board meeting date(s): As required

Write: H. Campbell Stuckeman, Secy.
Officer and Trustees:* H. Campbell Stuckeman,* Secy.; George Peter Rockwell, Russell A. Rockwell, Willard F. Rockwell, Jr.
Number of staff: None.
Employer Identification Number: 256035975

6416
Rockwell International Corporation Trust ▼ ⌑
600 Grant St.
Pittsburgh 15219 (412) 565-7436

Trust established in 1959 in PA.
Donor(s): Rockwell International Corp.
Foundation type: Company-sponsored
Financial data (yr. ended 9/30/88): Assets, $33,415,497 (M); gifts received, $20,000,000; expenditures, $10,300,555, including $9,602,606 for 1,289 grants (high: $500,000; low: $25; average: $1,000-$50,000) and $598,902 for 628 employee matching gifts.
Purpose and activities: Giving for higher education, primarily engineering education, and organizations which provide services in communities where donor has facilities; support also for cultural programs, health, and human services.
Types of support: Operating budgets, building funds, employee matching gifts, scholarship funds, fellowships, professorships.
Limitations: Giving primarily in areas of corporate operations, except for selected national organizations and universities which are sources of recruits. No grants to individuals, or for hospital building campaigns or general endowments; no loans.
Publications: Informational brochure.
Application information: Application form not required.
Initial approach: Proposal
Copies of proposal: 1
Deadline(s): None
Board meeting date(s): Monthly
Final notification: 60 to 90 days
Write: J.J. Christin, Secy., Trust Comm., or W.R. Fitz, Asst. Secy.
Trust Committee: J.J. Christin, Secy.
Trustee: Pittsburgh National Bank.
Number of staff: 4
Employer Identification Number: 251072431

6417
Sidney R. Rosenau Foundation ⌑ ☆
c/o Frank B. Johnson
1207-A Skipack Pike
Blue Bell 19422

Foundation type: Independent
Financial data (yr. ended 12/31/87): Assets, $849,294 (M); expenditures, $119,658, including $104,200 for 59 grants (high: $12,000; low: $500).
Purpose and activities: Giving primarily for Jewish organizations and arts and culture; support also for recreation, health, and education.
Trustees: Donald Bean, Gary Rosenau.
Employer Identification Number: 236259121

6418
Alexis Rosenberg Foundation ⌑
c/o Fidelity Bank, N.A.
Broad & Walnut Sts.
Philadelphia 19109

Established in 1983 in PA.
Donor(s): Alexis Rosenberg.†
Foundation type: Independent
Financial data (yr. ended 06/30/89): Assets, $2,057,982 (M); expenditures, $84,384, including $66,000 for 25 grants (high: $10,000; low: $200).
Purpose and activities: Giving only to organizations to aid "Youth of America," including grants for higher education, hospitals and rehabilitation, and cultural programs.
Limitations: Giving primarily in PA. No grants to individuals.
Application information:
Initial approach: Proposal
Deadline(s): None
Officers and Trustees:* Robert Greenfield,* Pres.; Charles Kahn,* Secy.-Treas.; Edward Daley.
Trustee Bank: Fidelity Bank, N.A.
Employer Identification Number: 232222722

6419
Roth Foundation ⌑
410 Vernon Rd.
Jenkintown 19046 (215) 576-1191

Established in 1953 in PA.
Donor(s): Edythe M. Roth, Abraham Roth.†
Foundation type: Independent
Financial data (yr. ended 10/31/88): Assets, $2,830,395 (M); gifts received, $126,763; expenditures, $177,563, including $160,100 for 10 grants (high: $120,000; low: $1,800).
Purpose and activities: Scholarships for nursing education; some support also for medical research.
Types of support: Student aid, research.
Limitations: Giving primarily in PA.
Application information: Applicants must have completed one year in a recognized school of nursing. Scholarship awards are made directly to nursing institution on recipient's behalf. Application form not required.
Initial approach: Letter
Deadline(s): None
Write: Linda Schwartz, Trustee
Trustees: Henry Boreen, Edythe M. Roth, Roland Roth, Linda Schwartz.
Employer Identification Number: 236271428

6420
George B. Rudy, Jr. Trust ⌑
c/o The York Bank & Trust Co.
21 East Market St.
York 17401

Established in 1985 in PA.
Foundation type: Independent
Financial data (yr. ended 9/30/88): Assets, $4,391,591 (M); expenditures, $291,666, including $256,223 for 5 grants (high: $51,245; low: $51,244).
Purpose and activities: Support for a YMCA and other social services, a Lutheran church, a health agency, and a college.
Types of support: Operating budgets.
Limitations: Giving primarily in York, PA. No grants to individuals.
Application information: Contributes only to pre-selected organizations. Applications not accepted.
Trustee: The York Bank & Trust Co.
Employer Identification Number: 236708045

6421
The Rust Foundation
1801 Commonwealth Bldg.
316 Fourth Ave.
Pittsburgh 15222-2002 (412) 566-2233

Trust established in 1950 in PA.
Donor(s): The Rust family.
Foundation type: Independent
Financial data (yr. ended 12/31/88): Assets, $377,565 (M); expenditures, $259,434, including $227,750 for 147 grants (high: $1,000; low: $300; average: $300-$25,000).
Purpose and activities: Giving limited to interests of individual trustees, including grants for health care, education, environmental conservancy, church support, and community funds.
Application information: Direct contact with a trustee is desirable. Application form not required.
Initial approach: Letter
Copies of proposal: 1
Deadline(s): None
Board meeting date(s): Late Dec.
Officer: D.A. Nimick, Secy.
Trustees: Barbara R. Gillies, Mary Rust Gillies, Nancy L. Gillies, William B. Gillies III, Molly Rust Montgomery, Helen Rust, James O. Rust, John M. Rust, S.M. Rust, Jr., S.M. Rust III, Alice Rust Scheetz, J. Paul Scheetz.
Number of staff: None.
Employer Identification Number: 256049037

6422
Lawrence Saunders Fund
c/o Fidelity Bank, N.A.
Broad & Walnut Sts.
Philadelphia 19109

Established in 1970 in PA.
Foundation type: Independent
Financial data (yr. ended 12/31/88): Assets, $1,156,406 (M); expenditures, $72,244, including $62,000 for 82 grants (high: $7,800; low: $100).
Purpose and activities: Support primarily for higher and other educational institutions and libraries, social services, women, religion and Protestant welfare, youth and child development organizations, and cultural programs, including the arts, music, and historic preservation.
Limitations: Giving primarily in Philadelphia and Chester and Montgomery counties, PA.
Application information: Application form required.
Initial approach: Letter
Copies of proposal: 1
Deadline(s): None
Trustees: Kenneth N. Gemmill, Fidelity Bank, N.A.
Number of staff: 1
Employer Identification Number: 236488524

6423
Scaife Family Foundation ▼
P.O. Box 268
Pittsburgh 15230 (412) 392-2900

Established about 1983 in PA.
Donor(s): Sarah Mellon Scaife.†
Foundation type: Independent
Financial data (yr. ended 12/31/89): Assets, $77,211,995 (M); gifts received, $8,938,325; expenditures, $4,587,386, including $4,081,550 for 80 grants (high: $1,000,000; low: $1,000; average: $25,000-$50,000).
Purpose and activities: Grants for programs that address issues relating to the family, education, alcoholism, drug abuse, and community development.
Types of support: General purposes, operating budgets, research, special projects.
Limitations: No grants to individuals; no loans.
Publications: 990-PF.
Application information: Application form not required.
Initial approach: Letter
Copies of proposal: 1
Deadline(s): Grant applications are normally considered in June and Dec.; no set deadline
Board meeting date(s): Quarterly
Final notification: Following board meetings
Write: Joanne B. Beyer, V.P.
Officers: Sanford B. Ferguson, Pres.; Joanne B. Beyer, V.P. and Secy.
Trustees: Donald A. Collins, Richard M. Larry, David N. Scaife, Jennie K. Scaife, James M. Walton.
Number of staff: 1 full-time professional; 1 part-time professional; 1 full-time support.
Employer Identification Number: 251427015

6424
Sarah Scaife Foundation, Inc. ▼
P.O. Box 268
Pittsburgh 15230 (412) 392-2900

Trust established in 1941; incorporated in 1959 in PA; present name adopted in 1974.
Donor(s): Sarah Mellon Scaife.†
Foundation type: Independent
Financial data (yr. ended 12/31/89): Assets, $203,133,504 (M); expenditures, $10,506,674, including $8,304,000 for 97 grants (high: $900,000; low: $1,000; average: $25,000-$100,000).
Purpose and activities: Grants primarily directed toward public policy programs that address major international and domestic issues; also supports local cultural, health, and recreational projects.
Types of support: Operating budgets, continuing support, seed money, equipment, matching funds, fellowships, research, special projects, publications, conferences and seminars, general purposes.
Limitations: No support for national organizations for general fundraising campaigns. No grants to individuals, or for deficit financing or scholarships; no loans.
Publications: Annual report (including application guidelines).
Application information: Application form not required.
Initial approach: Letter or proposal
Copies of proposal: 1
Deadline(s): None
Board meeting date(s): Feb., May, Sept., and Nov.
Final notification: 2 to 4 weeks
Write: Richard M. Larry, Pres.
Officers: Richard M. Scaife,* Chair.; Richard M. Larry,* Pres.; Donald C. Sipp, V.P., Investments and Treas.; Barbara L. Slaney, V.P.; R. Daniel McMichael, Secy.
Trustees:* Anthony J.A. Bryan, Peter Denby, Edwin J. Feulner, Jr., Allan H. Meltzer, James M. Walton.
Number of staff: 5
Employer Identification Number: 251113452

6425
The Walter L. Schautz Foundation ⌑
150 East Grove St.
Dunmore 18512

Incorporated in 1948 in PA.
Donor(s): Walter L. Schautz, Madalene L. Schautz, Grove Silk Co.
Foundation type: Independent
Financial data (yr. ended 1/31/87): Assets, $2,480,586 (M); expenditures, $98,968, including $52,755 for 38 grants (high: $4,000; low: $100) and $21,188 for 1 foundation-administered program.
Purpose and activities: Grants for welfare programs, youth agencies, church support, higher education, including theological seminaries, and a community fund. The foundation also operates a sports stadium.
Limitations: Giving primarily in PA.
Application information: Contributes only to pre-selected organizations.
Write: Madalene L. Schautz, Pres.
Officers: Madalene L. Schautz, Pres.; Walter L. Schautz, Jr., Treas.
Employer Identification Number: 246018362

6426
The Scholler Foundation
1100 One Penn Ctr. Plaza
Philadelphia 19103 (215) 568-7500

Trust established in 1939 in PA.
Donor(s): F.C. Scholler.†
Foundation type: Independent
Financial data (yr. ended 12/31/88): Assets, $9,179,071 (M); expenditures, $520,000, including $444,889 for 23 grants (high: $50,000; low: $5,600; average: $10,000-$25,000).
Purpose and activities: Giving for the alleviation of poverty and destitution, for the promotion of scientific research, including the branches of chemistry, and for other literary, educational, and public purposes; support largely for hospitals, with emphasis on grants for small community hospitals to purchase medical equipment.
Limitations: Giving limited to the Delaware Valley, PA. No grants to individuals, or for general support, endowment funds, scholarships, fellowships, or matching gifts; no loans.
Application information: Application form not required.
Initial approach: Proposal
Copies of proposal: 1
Deadline(s): Feb. 1, May 1, Aug. 1, and Nov. 1
Board meeting date(s): Feb., May, Aug., and Nov.
Write: Frederick L. Fuges, Secy.
Officer and Trustees:* Frederick L. Fuges,* Secy.; Edwin C. Dreby III, E. Brooks Keffer, Jr., Charles S. Strickler.
Number of staff: None.
Employer Identification Number: 236245158

6427
Lucy Kay Schoonmaker Foundation ⌑ ☆
c/o Mellon Bank, N.A.
One Mellon Bank Ctr., 3845
Pittsburgh 15258 (412) 234-4695

Trust established in 1957.
Donor(s): Lucy K. Schoonmaker.†
Foundation type: Independent
Financial data (yr. ended 12/31/87): Assets, $466,561 (M); expenditures, $120,973, including $113,000 for grants.
Purpose and activities: Emphasis on social services, hospitals, education, and church support; support also for community funds.
Types of support: Continuing support, annual campaigns, building funds, general purposes, matching funds.
Limitations: Giving primarily in PA. No grants to individuals, or for research, scholarships, or fellowships; no loans.
Application information:
Initial approach: Letter
Copies of proposal: 1
Deadline(s): Early fall
Board meeting date(s): Monthly
Write: Eileen M. Wilhem, Asst. V.P., Mellon Bank
Officer: G. Donald Gerlach, Dir. of Distribs.
Trustee: Mellon Bank, N.A.
Employer Identification Number: 256018687

6428
Schoonmaker J-Sewkly Val Hospital Trust ⌑ ☆
c/o Mellon Bank
P.O. Box 185
Pittsburgh 15230
Application address: One Mellon Bank Ctr., Pittsburgh, PA 15258; Tel.: (412) 234-4695

Foundation type: Independent
Financial data (yr. ended 9/30/88): Assets, $3,077,167 (M); expenditures, $181,441, including $159,441 for 7 grants (high: $39,860; low: $7,972).
Purpose and activities: Giving primarily for health and social services, including a community fund; support also for a university.
Limitations: Giving primarily in Pittsburgh, PA.
Application information: Application form required.
Initial approach: Letter
Deadline(s): None
Write: Helen M. Collins
Trustee: Mellon Bank, N.A.
Employer Identification Number: 256016020

6429
The Bernard Schwartz and Robert Schwartz Foundation, Inc. ⌑
c/o Jay Goldberg
12th Fl., Packard Bldg.
Philadelphia 19102 (609) 778-9200

Established in 1983 in PA.
Donor(s): Robert S. Schwartz.
Foundation type: Independent
Financial data (yr. ended 08/31/89): Assets, $10,546,406 (M); gifts received, $5,295,000; expenditures, $232,741, including $221,150 for 9 grants (high: $155,500; low: $500; average: $250-$40,250).
Purpose and activities: Support primarily for Jewish giving.
Limitations: Giving primarily in PA and NY. No grants to individuals.
Application information: Contributes only to pre-selected organizations. Applications not accepted.
Officers: Bernard Schwartz, Pres.; Robert S. Schwartz, Treas.
Employer Identification Number: 232267403

6430
Scott Paper Company Foundation ▼
One Scott Plaza
Philadelphia 19113 (215) 522-5398

Trust established in 1953 in PA.
Donor(s): Scott Paper Co.
Foundation type: Company-sponsored
Financial data (yr. ended 12/31/89): Gifts received, $3,899,778; expenditures, $3,899,778, including $3,899,778 for grants.
Purpose and activities: Primary focus is on helping children reach their full potential through grants in education, including employee-related scholarships through Citizens' Scholarship Corp. of America, health and human services, including AIDS research, and arts and culture; also has international relief interests.
Types of support: Seed money, employee-related scholarships, employee matching gifts, publications, consulting services, continuing support, emergency funds, equipment, matching funds, special projects, technical assistance.
Limitations: Giving primarily in areas of major company operations in Chester, PA; Dover, DE; Everett, WA; Fort Edward, NY; Hattiesburg, MS; Landisville, NJ; Marinette and Oconto Falls, WI; Mobile, AL; Muskegon, MI; Rogers, AR; Skowhegan, Westbrook and Winston, ME. No support for veterans', labor, or fraternal organizations, government agencies, political parties or candidates for public office, religious organizations for religious purposes, national health funds, or entertainment groups. No grants to individuals, or for endowment funds, deficit financing, land acquisition, good-will advertising, research, or generally, for capital campaigns; no loans.
Publications: Corporate giving report, newsletter, application guidelines, annual report.
Application information: Scholarship program for children of Scott Paper Co. employees administered through Citizens' Scholarship Corp. of America. Application form not required.
Initial approach: Letter requesting guidelines
Copies of proposal: 1
Deadline(s): None
Board meeting date(s): June and Dec.
Final notification: 3 months
Write: Cynthia D. Giroud, Mgr. of Corporate Social Investment
Trustees: J. Lawrence Shane, Chair.; Cynthia D. Giroud, Philip E. Lippincott, Paul N. Schregel, H.W. Sterritt.
Number of staff: 3 full-time professional; 1 part-time professional; 3 full-time support; 1 part-time support.
Employer Identification Number: 236231564

6431
The Scranton Area Foundation
204 Wyoming Ave.
Scranton 18503 (717) 347-6203

Established in 1954 in PA by resolution and declaration of trust.
Foundation type: Community
Financial data (yr. ended 12/31/89): Assets, $6,276,897 (M); gifts received, $159,018; expenditures, $348,366, including $212,670 for grants (high: $57,000; low: $2,500).
Purpose and activities: Encourages and helps to build community endowment through grants for new projects and services to address unmet needs; provides a variety of donor services.
Types of support: Seed money, general purposes, research, special projects, publications, conferences and seminars, matching funds, consulting services, renovation projects, scholarship funds.
Limitations: Giving limited to the Scranton, PA, area. No grants to individuals, or for building or endowment funds, operating budgets, annual campaigns, continuing support, deficit financing, or emergency funds; no loans.
Publications: Informational brochure (including application guidelines), annual report, newsletter.
Application information: Application form required.
Initial approach: Telephone
Copies of proposal: 11
Deadline(s): Submit proposal by first of month preceding board meeting
Board meeting date(s): Jan., Apr., July, and Oct.
Final notification: Jan., Apr., July, and Oct.
Write: Jeanne A. Bovard, Exec. Dir.
Officers: Jeanne A. Bovard, Exec. Dir.; William J. Calpin, Jr., Secy.
Governors: Marion M. Isaacs, Chair.; Francis E. Crowley, Vice-Chair.; Venald W. Bovard, Eugene Cosgrove, Donald J. Fendrick, Mary Graham, Judith Graziano, Eugene J. Kane, William Lynett.
Trustee: Northeastern Bank.
Number of staff: 1 full-time professional; 1 full-time support.
Employer Identification Number: 246022055

6432
Adam and Maria Sarah Seybert Institution for Poor Boys and Girls ⌑
(also known as Seybert Institution)
P.O. Box 8228
Philadelphia 19101-8228 (215) 828-8145

Incorporated in 1914 in PA.
Donor(s): Henry Seybert.†
Foundation type: Independent
Financial data (yr. ended 12/31/88): Assets, $4,002,346 (M); gifts received, $15,000; expenditures, $282,705, including $228,562 for 43 grants (high: $26,525; low: $1,000).
Purpose and activities: Assistance of needy children through support for educational programs, including a scholarship program providing financial assistance for poor Philadelphia youth with leadership and academic potential at participating schools; innovative teaching methods; and counseling services in the areas of child abuse, drugs, and parenting.
Types of support: Scholarship funds, seed money, emergency funds, research, matching funds.
Limitations: Giving limited to Philadelphia, PA. No grants to individuals, or for building or endowment funds.
Publications: Application guidelines, annual report.
Application information: Applicants limited to 1 request per calendar year. Application form not required.
Initial approach: Proposal
Copies of proposal: 10
Deadline(s): Jan. 2, Apr. 1, July 1, and Oct. 1
Board meeting date(s): Last Wednesday in Jan., Apr., July, and Oct.
Write: Judith L. Bardes, Mgr.
Officers and Trustees:* William C. Bullitt,* Pres.; Hon. Lois G. Forer,* V.P.; Steven R. Garfinkel,* Secy.-Treas.; Susan C. Day, M.D., Graham S. Finney, Rev. David I. Hagan, Lallie L. O'Brien, Carver A. Portlock.
Number of staff: 1
Employer Identification Number: 236260105

6433
The Samuel E., Howard T. and Jason H. Shapiro Charitable Trust ⌑
234 Forbes Ave.
Pittsburgh 15222-1806 (412) 355-0314

Established in 1986 in PA.
Donor(s): Samuel E. Howard, Jason H. Shapiro, Howard T. Shapiro.
Foundation type: Independent
Financial data (yr. ended 12/31/87): Assets, $23,070 (M); gifts received, $41,000; expenditures, $240,837, including $240,720 for 20 grants (high: $150,000; low: $100).
Purpose and activities: Support primarily for Jewish welfare and Jewish organizations.
Limitations: No grants to individuals.
Application information: Application form not required.
Deadline(s): None
Write: Jason H. Shapiro, Trustee
Trustees: Samuel E. Shapiro, Howard T. Shapiro, Jason H. Shapiro.
Employer Identification Number: 256252736

6434
Sharon Steel Foundation ⌑
P.O. Box 190
Farrell 16120 (412) 981-1375

Trust established in 1953 in PA.
Donor(s): Sharon Steel Corp.
Foundation type: Company-sponsored

Financial data (yr. ended 12/31/87): Assets, $3,390,406 (M); expenditures, $433,116, including $423,750 for 58 grants (high: $100,000; low: $100).
Purpose and activities: Support for higher education, music, community funds, hospitals, medical research, civic affairs, and youth activities.
Officers and Trustees: Victor Posner, Chair.; Steven Posner, Mgr.; Jack Coppersmith.
Employer Identification Number: 256063133

6435
Lawrence B. Sheppard Foundation, Inc. ⌑
c/o Hanover Shoe Farms, Inc.
P.O. Box 339
Hanover 17331 (717) 637-8931

Incorporated in 1946 in PA.
Donor(s): Lawrence B. Sheppard.
Foundation type: Independent
Financial data (yr. ended 11/30/87): Assets, $2,214,633 (M); gifts received, $100,400; expenditures, $88,935, including $81,000 for 22 grants (high: $12,500; low: $1,000).
Purpose and activities: Giving for secondary education, health agencies, Protestant church support, youth agencies, and community development.
Types of support: General purposes, building funds, land acquisition.
Limitations: Giving primarily in the Hanover, PA, area.
Application information:
Initial approach: Letter
Deadline(s): Oct. 31
Write: Paul E. Spears, Pres.
Officers: Paul E. Spears, Pres.; Charlotte S. Devan, V.P.; Horace E. Smith, Secy.; Betty J. Nolt, Treas.
Directors: Lawrence S. Devan, W. Todd Devan, Patricia S. Winder.
Employer Identification Number: 236251690

6436
The Thomas H. and Mary Williams Shoemaker Fund ⌑
c/o First Pennsylvania Bank, N.A.
P.O. Box 7558/TRTX CTSQ 9
Philadelphia 19101-7558 (215) 542-1340
Application address: c/o First Pennsylvania Bank, N.A., 16th and Market Sts., Philadelphia, PA 19102

Trust established in 1953 in PA.
Donor(s): Mary Williams Shoemaker,† Thomas H. Shoemaker,† Thomas H. and Mary Williams Shoemaker Trust.
Foundation type: Independent
Financial data (yr. ended 12/31/89): Assets, $5,605,906 (M); expenditures, $300,181, including $280,053 for 72 grants (high: $33,000; low: $97; average: $2,000-$5,000).
Purpose and activities: Emphasis on religious, charitable, and educational institutions of the Religious Society of Friends.
Types of support: General purposes, continuing support, seed money, building funds, endowment funds, scholarship funds, operating budgets, publications.
Limitations: Giving primarily in PA. No grants to individuals, or for matching gifts; no loans.
Publications: Application guidelines.
Application information: Application form not required.
Initial approach: Proposal
Copies of proposal: 6
Deadline(s): Apr. 15 and Oct. 15
Board meeting date(s): May and Nov.
Final notification: 3 weeks after meetings
Write: Gregory J. D'Angelo
Managers: Barbara Sprogell Jacobson, Secy.; William P. Camp, Alan Reeve Hunt, H. Mather Lippincott, Jr., Regina Hallowell Peasley.
Trustee: First Pennsylvania Bank, N.A.
Number of staff: 1 full-time support.
Employer Identification Number: 236209783

6437
Ray S. Shoemaker Trust for Shoemaker Scholarship Fund ⌑ ☆
c/o Commonwealth National Bank
P.O. Box 1010
Harrisburg 17108
Application address: c/o Dir. of Admissions, Harrisburg Community College, Cameron St., Harrisburg, PA 17108; Tel.: (717) 780-2400

Donor(s): Ray S. Shoemaker.
Foundation type: Independent
Financial data (yr. ended 9/30/88): Assets, $2,690,196 (M); gifts received, $250; expenditures, $130,598, including $86,738 for 60 grants to individuals (high: $4,000; low: $200).
Purpose and activities: Giving restricted to a scholarship program for graduates of greater Harrisburg, PA, area high schools.
Types of support: Student aid.
Application information: Application form required.
Initial approach: Letter
Deadline(s): Mar. 15
Trustee: Commonwealth National Bank.
Employer Identification Number: 236237250

6438
Sickles Charitable Trust ⌑
1625 Amity Rd.
Rydal 19046-1204

Established in 1972 in PA.
Foundation type: Independent
Financial data (yr. ended 11/30/88): Assets, $1,126,920 (M); expenditures, $85,028, including $79,250 for 29 grants (high: $25,000; low: $100).
Purpose and activities: Support primarily for Jewish welfare, education, and medical research.
Limitations: Giving primarily in PA.
Application information:
Initial approach: Letter
Deadline(s): None
Trustees: Ann Sickles, Edward Sickles.
Employer Identification Number: 237250391

6439
The SICO Foundation ⌑
15 Mount Joy St.
Mt. Joy 17552 (717) 653-1411

Incorporated in 1941 in DE.
Donor(s): Clarence Schock.†
Foundation type: Independent
Financial data (yr. ended 5/31/89): Assets, $10,762,510 (M); expenditures, $624,624, including $455,000 for 10 grants (high: $105,500; low: $7,500).
Purpose and activities: Support for public higher education and the education of elementary school teachers.
Types of support: Scholarship funds.
Limitations: Giving limited to DE and specified counties in PA and NJ.
Publications: Informational brochure, application guidelines.
Application information: Contributes only to pre-selected organizations. Applications not accepted.
Officers and Directors: Harry K. Gerlach, Pres.; William H. Duncan, V.P.; Fred S. Engle, Secy.; Franklin R. Eichler, Treas.; Anthony F. Ceddia, Harrison L. Diehl, Jr., Carl R. Hallgren, Joseph D. Moore, Forrest R. Schaeffer, John N. Weidman.
Number of staff: 5 part-time support.
Employer Identification Number: 236298332

6440
Alexander Silberman Foundation ⌑
1831 North Fifth St.
Philadelphia 19122

Established in 1950 in PA.
Donor(s): Alexander Silberman, Billy Penn Corp.
Foundation type: Independent
Financial data (yr. ended 4/30/87): Assets, $1,583,250 (M); gifts received, $35,783; expenditures, $37,899, including $37,363 for grants (high: $9,546).
Purpose and activities: Emphasis on Jewish giving, including education, temple support, and social services.
Types of support: General purposes.
Officers: Philip Pollack, Pres.; S. Alan Yulsman, Secy.; Alexander Silberman, Treas.
Employer Identification Number: 237072977

6441
Louis Silverstein No. 4 Charitable Trust ⌑
c/o Provident National Bank
1632 Chestnut St.
Philadelphia 19103

Established in 1976.
Donor(s): Louis J. Silverstein.†
Foundation type: Independent
Financial data (yr. ended 1/31/88): Assets, $1,047,290 (M); expenditures, $80,533.
Purpose and activities: Support primarily for a local university.
Limitations: Giving primarily in PA.
Application information:
Initial approach: Letter
Deadline(s): None
Trustee: Provident National Bank.
Employer Identification Number: 232030953

6442
R. P. Simmons Family Foundation ⌑ ☆
Witherow Rd., R.D. 3
Pittsburgh 15143

Established in 1987 in PA.
Donor(s): Richard P. Simmons.

Foundation type: Independent
Financial data (yr. ended 12/31/88): Assets, $2,757,337 (M); gifts received, $440,000; expenditures, $406,794, including $390,410 for 34 grants (high: $250,000; low: $100).
Purpose and activities: Giving primarily for higher education.
Types of support: Scholarship funds, professorships, endowment funds, general purposes.
Limitations: Giving primarily in PA. No grants to individuals.
Application information: Contributes only to pre-selected organizations. Applications not accepted.
Trustee: Richard P. Simmons.
Employer Identification Number: 256277068

6443
Esther Simon Charitable Trust
150 Radnor Chester Rd., A200
Radnor 19087 (215) 341-9270

Trust established in 1952 in NY.
Donor(s): Esther Simon.
Foundation type: Independent
Financial data (yr. ended 12/31/89): Assets, $9,128,897 (M); expenditures, $615,058, including $554,000 for 51 grants (high: $100,000; low: $50).
Purpose and activities: Grants to charitable, cultural, and educational institutions, including hospitals and social service organizations.
Types of support: Annual campaigns, general purposes.
Limitations: Giving primarily in New York, NY. No grants to individuals.
Application information: Applications not accepted.
Write: A.C. Cory
Trustee: Walter H. Annenberg.
Number of staff: 5
Employer Identification Number: 236286763

6444
Joseph T. & Helen M. Simpson Foundation ¤ ☆
c/o Dauphin Deposit Bank & Trust Co.
P.O. Box 2961
Harrisburg 17105-2961
Application address: 4031 Ridgeview Dr., Harrisburg, PA 17112

Established in 1954.
Foundation type: Independent
Financial data (yr. ended 12/31/88): Assets, $1,002,946 (M); expenditures, $73,619, including $61,050 for 83 grants (high: $2,700; low: $50).
Purpose and activities: Support for hospitals and health associations, higher education, and social services, including a community fund.
Limitations: Giving primarily in Washington, DC, and Harrisburg, PA. No grants to individuals.
Application information:
Initial approach: Letter
Deadline(s): None
Trustees: Helen M. Simpson, Jerry T. Simpson, Joseph T. Simpson, Dauphin Deposit Bank & Trust Co.
Employer Identification Number: 236242538

6445
W. W. Smith Charitable Trust ▼
101 Bryn Mawr Ave., Suite 200
Bryn Mawr 19010 (215) 525-9667

Trust established in 1977 in PA.
Donor(s): William Wikoff Smith.†
Foundation type: Independent
Financial data (yr. ended 06/30/89): Assets, $95,815,419 (M); expenditures, $5,422,760, including $4,916,799 for 227 grants (high: $100,000; low: $5,000; average: $5,000-$40,000).
Purpose and activities: Support for financial aid programs for qualified needy undergraduate students at accredited universities and colleges, hospital programs for the medical care of the poor and needy, basic scientific medical research programs dealing with cancer, AIDS, and heart disease, and programs of organizations providing shelter, food, and clothing for children and the aged.
Types of support: Scholarship funds, research, operating budgets, seed money, emergency funds, building funds, equipment, land acquisition, special projects, publications, matching funds, general purposes, continuing support, renovation projects.
Limitations: Giving primarily in the Delaware Valley, including Philadelphia and its 5 neighboring counties; grants to colleges and hospitals (for indigent care) by invitation only. No grants to individuals, or for deficit financing, existing endowment funds, or retroactive funding for non-emergencies; no loans; no grants over 3 years.
Publications: Biennial report (including application guidelines).
Application information: Free medical care and college financial aid programs by invitation only; applications for medical research grants must be submitted in quadruplicate; application forms required for medical research only.
Initial approach: Proposal or letter
Copies of proposal: 1
Deadline(s): For free medical care, Feb. 1; for social service programs, Feb. 1 and Aug. 1; for college scholarships, May 1; for cancer and AIDS research, June 15; and for heart research, Sept. 15
Board meeting date(s): For medical care, Mar.; social services, Mar. and Sept.; scholarships, June; cancer and AIDS research, Sept.; heart research, Dec.
Final notification: 1 month after trustees meet
Write: Bruce M. Brown, Trust Admin.
Trustees: Mary L. Smith, Philadelphia National Bank.
Number of staff: 7 part-time professional; 2 part-time support.
Employer Identification Number: 236648841

6446
Smith Foundation
210 Fairlamb Ave.
Havertown 19083 (215) 446-4651

Incorporated in 1920 in PA.
Donor(s): W. Hinckle Smith,† H. Harrison Smith.†
Foundation type: Independent
Financial data (yr. ended 12/31/88): Assets, $5,398,345 (M); expenditures, $431,706, including $383,700 for 67 grants (high: $25,000; low: $1,000).
Purpose and activities: To aid the sick, aged, and poor, as well as to aid in the education of needy boys and girls through local organizations engaged in such work; grants for hospitals, child welfare, the aged, and the handicapped.
Types of support: Building funds, operating budgets, special projects.
Limitations: Giving limited to southeastern PA. No grants to individuals, or for endowment funds.
Publications: Annual report.
Application information: Application form required.
Initial approach: Letter
Copies of proposal: 1
Deadline(s): Oct. 1
Board meeting date(s): Semiannually
Write: Joseph H. Barber, Secy.-Treas.
Officers and Directors:* Roger P. Hollingsworth,* Pres.; Robert L. Strayer,* V.P.; Joseph H. Barber,* Secy.-Treas.; Philip C. Burnham, Martin Evoy, William Buchanan Gold, Jr., Lewis R. Good, Francis Veale.
Trustee Bank: Philadelphia National Bank.
Employer Identification Number: 236238148

6447
Ethel Sergeant Clark Smith Memorial Fund
101 Bryn Mawr Ave., Suite 200
Bryn Mawr 19010 (215) 525-9667

Trust established in 1977 in PA.
Donor(s): Ethel Sergeant Clark Smith.†
Foundation type: Independent
Financial data (yr. ended 05/31/89): Assets, $10,337,664 (M); gifts received, $2,900; expenditures, $555,296, including $465,500 for 24 grants (high: $50,000; low: $1,000; average: $5,000-$25,000).
Purpose and activities: Giving for hospitals, higher and other education, child welfare and development, social service organizations, libraries, arts and culture, museums and historical buildings, recreation, music and drama facilities, and programs for women, the handicapped, and exceptional persons.
Types of support: Building funds, continuing support, emergency funds, equipment, general purposes, land acquisition, operating budgets, research, special projects, exchange programs, matching funds, renovation projects, scholarship funds, seed money.
Limitations: Giving limited to Delaware County, PA, or organizations benefitting county residents. No support for one-disease organizations, salaries, or consultants. No grants to individuals, or for deficit financing, scholarships, or fellowships; no gifts longer than 3 years; no loans.
Publications: Multi-year report (including application guidelines).
Application information: Personal visits prior to proposal submission discouraged. Application form not required.
Initial approach: Letter or proposal
Copies of proposal: 1
Deadline(s): Mar. 1 and Sept. 1 for completed proposals
Board meeting date(s): May and Nov.

Final notification: 1 month
Write: Bruce M. Brown, V.P. for Charitable Trusts, Philadelphia National Bank
Trustee: Philadelphia National Bank.
Number of staff: 7 part-time professional; 2 part-time support.
Employer Identification Number: 236648857

6448
SmithKline Beecham Foundation ▼
(Formerly SmithKline Beckman Foundation)
One Franklin Plaza
P.O. Box 7929
Philadelphia 19101 (215) 751-7096

Trust established in 1967 in DE.
Donor(s): SmithKline Beecham.
Foundation type: Company-sponsored
Financial data (yr. ended 12/31/88): Assets, $4,683,207 (M); expenditures, $4,624,737, including $3,821,936 for 141 grants (high: $570,508; low: $1,000), $66,083 for 21 grants to individuals (high: $5,647; low: $477) and $676,103 for 901 employee matching gifts.
Purpose and activities: Foundation maintains an employee matching gift program for qualifying educational institutions and hospitals; support also for community funds, the arts, health and medicine, and public policy.
Types of support: Employee matching gifts, general purposes, operating budgets, research, special projects.
Limitations: No grants to individuals.
Publications: Annual report.
Application information: The scholarship program has been terminated. Application form not required.
Board meeting date(s): May, and as required to review proposals
Write: Tod R. Hullin, Pres.
Officers and Directors: Thomas M.. Collins, Chair.; Tod R. Hullin, Pres. and C.E.O.; Richard V. Holmes, Secy.; Kenneth N. Kermes, Treas.; John F. Chappel, Thomas M. Landin.
Number of staff: 2
Employer Identification Number: 232120418

6449
Harry E. and Florence W. Snayberger Memorial Foundation ⌑
c/o Pennsylvania National Bank and Trust Co.
One South Centre St.
Pottsville 17901-3003 (717) 622-4200

Established in 1976 in PA.
Donor(s): Harry E. Snayberger.†
Foundation type: Independent
Financial data (yr. ended 3/31/88): Assets, $3,511,055 (M); expenditures, $294,806, including $39,107 for 84 grants (high: $2,500; low: $57) and $221,252 for 473 grants to individuals (high: $800; low: $300).
Purpose and activities: Emphasis on higher education, youth programs, church support, public libraries and community affairs.
Types of support: Student aid, operating budgets, special projects.
Limitations: Giving limited to Schuylkill County, PA.
Application information: Application form required.
Initial approach: Letter
Copies of proposal: 1
Deadline(s): Feb. 28
Board meeting date(s): Weekly as required
Final notification: Middle of Oct. for scholarships
Write: Paul J. Hanna II, Sr. V.P. and Trust Officer, Pennsylvania National Bank and Trust Co.
Trustee: Pennsylvania National Bank and Trust Co.
Employer Identification Number: 232056361

6450
Snee-Reinhardt Charitable Foundation ⌑ ☆
c/o Mellon Bank, N.A.
P.O. Box 185
Pittsburgh 15230

Established in 1987 in PA.
Foundation type: Independent
Financial data (yr. ended 12/31/87): Assets, $2,577,139 (M); gifts received, $1,578,031; expenditures, $4,195, including $3,000 for 1 grant.
Purpose and activities: Initial year of operation, 1987; support for a program benefitting cancer patients.
Limitations: No grants to individuals.
Application information: Contributes only to pre-selected organizations. Applications not accepted.
Officer and Directors: Paul A. Hemsley, Chair.; Virginia Davis, Karen L. Hemsley, Timothy Hemsley, Richard T. Vale.
Trustee: Mellon Bank, N.A.
Employer Identification Number: 256292908

6451
The Snider Foundation ⌑
1804 Rittenhouse Sq.
Philadelphia 19103

Established in 1977 in PA.
Donor(s): Edward M. Snider.
Foundation type: Independent
Financial data (yr. ended 4/30/88): Assets, $1,728,821 (M); gifts received, $519,950; expenditures, $349,311, including $346,731 for 83 grants (high: $150,000; low: $36).
Purpose and activities: Support primarily for museums and the arts, higher education, and Jewish welfare.
Limitations: Giving primarily in Philadelphia, PA. No grants to individuals.
Application information: Contributes only to pre-selected organizations. Applications not accepted.
Officers: Edward M. Snider, Pres.; Sanford Lipstein, Secy.-Treas.
Trustee: Fred A. Shabel.
Employer Identification Number: 232047668

6452
W. P. Snyder Charitable Fund ⌑
3720 One Oliver Plaza
Pittsburgh 15222 (412) 471-1331

Trust established in 1950 in PA.
Donor(s): W.P. Snyder, Jr.,† W.P. Snyder III, The Shenango Furnace Co.
Foundation type: Independent
Financial data (yr. ended 12/31/86): Assets, $8,845,363 (M); expenditures, $488,606, including $452,700 for 37 grants (high: $150,000; low: $500).
Purpose and activities: Emphasis on community funds, higher and secondary education, and hospitals; support also for cultural programs, including historic preservation, and social service agencies.
Types of support: General purposes.
Limitations: Giving primarily in PA.
Application information:
Deadline(s): None
Write: John K. Foster, Trustee
Trustees: John K. Foster, G. Whitney Snyder, W.P. Snyder III.
Employer Identification Number: 256034967

6453
Sordoni Foundation, Inc.
45 Owen St.
Forty Fort 18704 (717) 283-1211

Incorporated in 1946 in PA.
Donor(s): Andrew J. Sordoni, Sr.,† Andrew J. Sordoni, Jr.,† Andrew J. Sordoni III, Mrs. Andrew J. Sordoni, Sr.,† Mrs. Andrew J. Sordoni, Jr.,† Mrs. Andrew J. Sordoni III, and others.
Foundation type: Independent
Financial data (yr. ended 7/31/89): Assets, $8,289,539 (M); gifts received, $3,500; expenditures, $437,522, including $421,062 for 41 grants (high: $240,000; low: $100).
Purpose and activities: Giving for education; support also for cultural programs, health, social services, and civic affairs.
Types of support: Building funds, equipment, capital campaigns, continuing support, seed money, special projects, annual campaigns, endowment funds.
Limitations: Giving primarily in northeastern PA. No grants to individuals, or for scholarships.
Application information: The foundation has discontinued the scholarships to individuals program. No new grants will be awarded.
Initial approach: Letter
Deadline(s): None
Board meeting date(s): As required
Write: Benjamin Badman, Jr., Exec. V.P.
Officers and Directors: Andrew J. Sordoni III, Pres.; Benjamin Badman, Jr., Exec. V.P. and Secy.-Treas.; Helen Mary Sekera, V.P.; Jule Ayers, Roy E. Morgan, Stephen Sordoni, William J. Umphred.
Number of staff: 1 full-time professional; 1 part-time support.
Employer Identification Number: 246017505

6454
Alexander C. & Tillie S. Speyer Foundation ⌑
1202 Benedum Trees Bldg.
Pittsburgh 15222 (412) 281-7225

Established in 1962 in PA.
Donor(s): Members of the Speyer family.
Foundation type: Independent
Financial data (yr. ended 12/31/88): Assets, $3,250,410 (M); expenditures, $131,287, including $95,005 for 64 grants (high: $20,250; low: $25).
Purpose and activities: Giving primarily for education, culture, and Jewish organizations.

Application information: Application form not required.
Deadline(s): None
Write: A.C. Speyer, Jr., Mgr.
Trustees: A.C. Speyer, Jr., Darthea Speyer.
Employer Identification Number: 256051650

6455
SPS Foundation
c/o SPS Technologies
P.O. Box 1000
Newtown 18940 (215) 572-3000

Trust established in 1953 in PA.
Donor(s): SPS Technologies, Inc.
Foundation type: Company-sponsored
Financial data (yr. ended 12/31/88): Assets, $621,883 (M); gifts received, $232,191; expenditures, $229,970, including $225,280 for 205 grants (high: $55,000; low: $25; average: $100-$500).
Purpose and activities: Giving for community funds, higher education, health and hospitals, youth activities and child welfare, the arts and culture, law and justice, science, and welfare.
Types of support: Operating budgets, continuing support, annual campaigns, emergency funds, building funds, equipment, employee matching gifts, special projects, research, capital campaigns, matching funds.
Limitations: Giving primarily in PA; Cleveland, OH; Santa Ana, CA; Muskelon, MI; Marengo, IL; and Mayaguez, PR. No grants to individuals, or for seed money, land acquisition, matching funds, scholarships, fellowships, demonstration projects, publications, or conferences and seminars; no loans.
Application information: Application form not required.
Initial approach: Letter
Copies of proposal: 1
Deadline(s): None
Final notification: 1 month
Write: Rockwell M. Groves, Chair., Gifts Comm.
Manager: Rockwell M. Groves, Chair., Gifts Comm.
Trustees: A.B. Belden, John R. Selby, Jr., Harry J. Wilkinson.
Number of staff: None.
Employer Identification Number: 236294553

6456
St. Mary's Catholic Foundation
1935 State St.
St. Marys 15857 (814) 781-1591

Incorporated in 1960 in PA.
Donor(s): Benedict R. Reuscher,† Alfred A. Gleixner,† Richard J. Reuscher, R.B. Reuscher, E.H. Gleixner, William E. Reuscher, EB & Associates, Keystone Carbon Co.
Foundation type: Independent
Financial data (yr. ended 01/31/90): Assets, $3,585,790 (M); gifts received, $706,228; expenditures, $621,186, including $614,290 for 24 grants (high: $216,360; low: $400; average: $25,000).
Purpose and activities: Grants to local Roman Catholic-sponsored elementary and secondary schools and colleges to supplement teachers' salaries and for school equipment; support also for Roman Catholic religious associations and organizations of interest to the donor.
Types of support: Equipment, operating budgets, general purposes, continuing support, seed money, research, publications.
Limitations: Giving primarily in Erie Diocese, PA, with emphasis on the St. Mary's area. No grants to individuals, or for endowment funds, scholarships, or fellowships; no loans.
Application information: Contributes only to pre-selected organizations. Applications not accepted.
Board meeting date(s): Quarterly
Write: Richard J. Reuscher, Trustee
Officers and Trustees:* E.H. Gleixner,* Pres.; William E. Reuscher,* V.P.; Richard J. Reuscher,* Secy.-Treas.; C.J. Kogousek, R.B. Reuscher.
Number of staff: None.
Employer Identification Number: 256036961

6457
The Donald B. and Dorothy L. Stabler Foundation ⌑
c/o Dauphin Deposit Bank and Trust Co.
Box 2961
Harrisburg 17105 (717) 255-2044

Established in 1966 in PA.
Donor(s): Stabler Companies, Inc.
Foundation type: Independent
Financial data (yr. ended 12/31/87): Assets, $3,948,003 (L); gifts received, $815,808; expenditures, $242,266, including $223,970 for 66 grants (high: $100,000; low: $100; average: $1,400).
Purpose and activities: Giving for higher education, hospitals, and religious purposes.
Types of support: Operating budgets, continuing support, annual campaigns, building funds, equipment, endowment funds, matching funds, scholarship funds, professorships.
Limitations: Giving primarily in PA. No grants to individuals, or for seed money, research programs, land acquisition, special projects, publications, conferences, deficit financing, or emergency funds; no loans.
Application information: Application form not required.
Initial approach: Letter
Copies of proposal: 1
Deadline(s): 1 month prior to board meetings
Board meeting date(s): Usually in May, Sept., and Oct.
Final notification: 1 month after board meetings
Write: William King, Chair.
Officers and Trustees: William King, Chair.; Frank A. Sinon, Secy.; Richard E. Jordan, Harold S. Mohler, David Schaper, W. Stewart Taylor.
Number of staff: None.
Employer Identification Number: 236422944

6458
Stackpole-Hall Foundation
44 South St. Marys St.
St. Marys 15857 (814) 834-1845

Trust established in 1951 in PA.
Donor(s): Lyle G. Hall,† J. Hall Stackpole,† Harrison C. Stackpole.
Foundation type: Independent
Financial data (yr. ended 12/31/89): Assets, $17,955,903 (M); expenditures, $759,068, including $659,768 for 54 grants (high: $53,000; low: $800; average: $800-$53,000).
Purpose and activities: Support for higher and secondary education, and literacy and vocational projects; social services, including youth and child welfare agencies; the arts and cultural programs; health services, including mental health and drug abuse issues; and community development, including civic affairs and leadership development, conservation concerns, rural development, and volunteerism.
Types of support: Building funds, annual campaigns, seed money, equipment, matching funds, capital campaigns, renovation projects, special projects.
Limitations: Giving primarily in Elk County, PA. No grants to individuals, or for scholarships or fellowships; generally, no grants for operating budgets or endowment funds; no loans.
Publications: Annual report.
Application information: Application form not required.
Initial approach: Letter
Copies of proposal: 1
Deadline(s): None
Board meeting date(s): Feb., May, Aug., and Dec.
Final notification: 3 months
Write: William C. Conrad, Exec. Secy.
Officer: William C. Conrad, Exec. Secy.
Trustees: Harrison C. Stackpole, Chair.; Douglas R. Dobson, Helen Hall Drew, Lyle G. Hall, Jr., J.M. Hamlin Johnson, Alexander Sheble-Hall, R. Dauer Stackpole.
Number of staff: 1 full-time professional; 1 part-time support.
Employer Identification Number: 256006650

6459
Staunton Farm Foundation Trust ⌑
c/o Mellon Bank, N.A.
One Mellon Bank Ctr., 40th Fl.
Pittsburgh 15258
Application address: Philip B. Hallen, 3317 Grant Bldg., Pittsburgh, PA 15219; Tel.: (412) 261-2485

Incorporated in 1937 in PA.
Donor(s): Mathilda Craig Staunton.
Foundation type: Independent
Financial data (yr. ended 12/31/87): Assets, $21,088,464 (M); expenditures, $865,519, including $768,142 for 18 grants (high: $250,000; low: $10,000; average: $10,000-$50,000).
Purpose and activities: Grants limited to hospitals or local organizations concerned with mental health, the emotionally handicapped, and child welfare.
Types of support: Continuing support.
Limitations: Giving limited to Allegheny County, PA, and contiguous counties.
Publications: Informational brochure (including application guidelines).
Application information:
Initial approach: Letter
Deadline(s): None
Board meeting date(s): Quarterly
Final notification: Immediately following board meetings

Write: Philip B. Hallen
Officers and Directors: Albert B. Craig, Jr., Pres.; Barbara K. Robinson, Secy.-Treas.; Mrs. George L. Craig, Jr., John P. Davis, Jr., Joseph D. Dury, Jr., Joseph Craig Ferree, Elizabeth C. Griffiths, Kathleen C. Knight, George D. Lockhart, Mrs. David McCargo, Charles J. Ramsburg, Jr., William L. Standish.
Manager: Mellon Bank, N.A.
Number of staff: 1 part-time professional; 1 part-time support.
Employer Identification Number: 250965573

6460
Louis & Bessie Stein Foundation ▼ ⌑
1700 Walnut St., Suite 925
Philadelphia 19103 (215) 546-8100

Established in 1953 in NJ.
Donor(s): Louis Stein, Walter Liventhal, Stanley Merves, Stein, Stein & Engel, and others.
Foundation type: Independent
Financial data (yr. ended 12/31/88): Assets, $1,912,075 (M); gifts received, $279,192; expenditures, $648,604, including $639,623 for grants.
Purpose and activities: Giving primarily to Jewish welfare funds and universities; some support also to health agencies.
Application information:
Initial approach: Letter
Deadline(s): None
Write: Louis Stein, Trustee
Trustees: Marilyn Bellet, Louis Stein.
Employer Identification Number: 236395253

6461
Sidney J. Stein Foundation ☆
416 East Church Rd.
P.O. Box 1533
King of Prussia 19406-1533

Established in 1980 in PA.
Donor(s): Electro Science Laboratories Inc.
Foundation type: Independent
Financial data (yr. ended 3/31/89): Assets, $1,086,358 (M); gifts received, $71,000; expenditures, $59,314, including $58,550 for 39 grants (high: $15,000; low: $100).
Purpose and activities: Emphasis on Jewish giving, cultural institutions, education, and the United Way.
Limitations: No grants to individuals.
Application information: Contributes only to pre-selected organizations. Applications not accepted.
Trustees: Bertha Stein, Michael Alan Stein, Sidney J. Stein.
Employer Identification Number: 222315982

6462
James Hale Steinman Foundation
P.O. Box 128
Lancaster 17603
Scholarship application address: Eight West King St., Lancaster, PA 17603

Trust established in 1952 in PA.
Donor(s): James Hale Steinman,† Louise Steinman von Hess,† Lancaster Newspapers, Inc., and others.
Foundation type: Independent
Financial data (yr. ended 12/31/88): Assets, $6,654,864 (M); gifts received, $300,000; expenditures, $533,213, including $465,599 for 38 grants (high: $308,499; low: $250) and $38,000 for grants to individuals (average: $2,000).
Purpose and activities: Giving for the arts and historic preservation, higher and other education (including scholarships to newspaper carriers and children of employees of Steiman Enterprises), youth and social services, health, family planning, and a community fund.
Types of support: Employee-related scholarships, annual campaigns, capital campaigns.
Limitations: Giving primarily in Lancaster, PA.
Application information: Application form available for employee-related scholarships. Application form required.
Deadline(s): For scholarships, Feb. 28 of senior year of high school
Board meeting date(s): Dec.
Write: Dennis A. Getz, Secy.
Officers and Trustees:* Caroline S. Nunan,* Chair.; Beverly R. Steinman,* Vice-Chair.; Dennis A. Getz,* Secy.; Willis W. Shenk,* Treas.; John M. Buckwalter, Jack S. Gerhart, Caroline N. Hill, Hale S. Krasne.
Number of staff: None.
Employer Identification Number: 236266377

6463
John Frederick Steinman Foundation
Eight West King St.
Lancaster 17603
Additional address: P.O. Box 128, Lancaster, PA 17603

Trust established in 1952 in PA.
Donor(s): John Frederick Steinman,† Shirley W. Steinman,† Lancaster Newspapers, Inc., and others.
Foundation type: Independent
Financial data (yr. ended 12/31/89): Assets, $11,373,565 (M); gifts received, $300,000; expenditures, $542,081, including $489,300 for 86 grants (high: $75,000; low: $250) and $30,000 for grants to individuals (high: $1,750; low: $1,000).
Purpose and activities: Giving for higher and secondary education, community funds, social services, youth, hospitals, and the handicapped; also funds a fellowship program limited to graduate study in mental health or a related field.
Types of support: Fellowships, annual campaigns, capital campaigns.
Limitations: Giving primarily in PA, with emphasis on the Lancaster area.
Application information: Application for fellowship program available upon request.
Deadline(s): Feb. 1 for fellowships
Board meeting date(s): Dec.
Write: Dennis A. Getz, Secy., or Jay H. Wenrich, Fellowship Prog. Secy. for fellowships
Officers and Trustees:* Pamela M. Thye,* Chair.; Dennis A. Getz,* Secy.; Willis W. Shenk, Treas.; John M. Buckwalter, Jack S. Gerhart, Shirley N. Katzenbach, Henry Pildner, Jr.
Number of staff: None.
Employer Identification Number: 236266378

6464
Julius L. and Libbie B. Steinsapir Family Foundation ⌑
900 Lawyers Bldg.
Pittsburgh 15219 (412) 391-2920

Established in 1969 in PA.
Donor(s): I.H. Steinsapir,† Standard Emblem Jewelers.
Foundation type: Independent
Financial data (yr. ended 1/31/88): Assets, $1,759,780 (M); expenditures, $135,624, including $97,975 for 59 grants (high: $12,500; low: $15).
Purpose and activities: Emphasis on temple support, Jewish welfare funds, and secondary education; some support for Christian churches and religious orders.
Limitations: Giving primarily in PA. No grants to individuals.
Application information: Application form not required.
Deadline(s): None
Write: Samuel Horovitz, Trustee
Trustees: Samuel Horovitz, Melvin L. Mallit, Albert C. Shapira, Lewis Silverboard.
Employer Identification Number: 256104248

6465
The Harry Stern Family Foundation ⌑
c/o Mervin J. Hartman
Three Pkwy., 20th Fl.
Philadelphia 19102

Established in 1985 in PA.
Donor(s): Members of the Stern family.
Foundation type: Independent
Financial data (yr. ended 12/31/87): Assets, $5,692,128 (M); expenditures, $834,892, including $754,342 for 245 grants (high: $101,000; low: $18; average: $20-$100,000).
Purpose and activities: Support for education, health, and religion, with emphasis on Jewish giving.
Limitations: Giving primarily in the greater Philadelphia, PA, area.
Publications: 990-PF.
Application information: Applications not accepted.
Initial approach: Letter
Deadline(s): None
Write: Jerome Stern, Secy.
Officers: Harry Stern, Pres.; Jerome Stern,* Secy.
Directors:* Rebecca Stern Herschkopf, Sheva Stern Mann, Sareva Stern Naor, Amram Stern, Zelda Stern.
Number of staff: 1 full-time professional; 1 full-time support; 1 part-time support.
Employer Identification Number: 236806751

6466
Alexander Stewart Foundation ⌑ ☆
c/o Mellon Bank (East), N.A.
P.O. Box 7236
Philadelphia 19101 (215) 585-3690

Established in 1981 in PA.
Foundation type: Independent
Financial data (yr. ended 06/30/89): Assets, $3,451,095 (M); expenditures, $240,227, including $214,136 for grants.
Purpose and activities: Support for education.

Limitations: Giving primarily in Shippensburg, PA, and vicinity, including Cumberland, Franklin, Fulton, and Perry counties.
Application information:
Initial approach: Proposal
Deadline(s): Apr. 1
Write: Richard C. Thomas, Trust Officer, Mellon Bank (East), N.A.
Trustee: Mellon Bank (East), N.A.
Employer Identification Number: 236732616

6467
Stockton Rush Bartol Foundation ⌑
230 South Broad St., Suite 1300
Philadelphia 19102 (215) 875-5402

Established in 1984 in PA.
Donor(s): George E. Bartol III.
Foundation type: Independent
Financial data (yr. ended 11/30/89): Assets, $7,454,172 (M); gifts received, $1,465,695; expenditures, $266,753, including $216,250 for 57 grants (average: $1,000-$5,000).
Purpose and activities: Support for the arts and cultural organizations.
Types of support: General purposes, special projects, building funds, continuing support, operating budgets, publications, renovation projects, seed money, research.
Limitations: Giving limited to Bucks, Chester, Delaware, Montgomery, and Philadelphia counties, PA. No support for religious, social, or political organizations. No grants to individuals.
Publications: Annual report (including application guidelines), grants list, application guidelines.
Application information: Applicants must reapply annually. Application form required.
Initial approach: Letter requesting application
Deadline(s): May 1 and Nov. 1
Board meeting date(s): June and Dec.
Write: Mary L. Kuhn, Exec. Dir.
Officers: Mildred Blair Bartol MacInnes, Chair.; Cynthia W. Drayton, Pres.; Mary L. Kuhn, Secy.-Treas. and Exec. Dir.
Trustees: Mary Farr Bartol, Katherine Selma Bartol Lunt, Victoria Grier Bartol Valley, Mary Rush Bartol Wolszon.
Number of staff: 1 part-time professional.
Employer Identification Number: 232318470

6468
Lydia B. Stokes Foundation ⌑
3400 Centre Sq. West
1500 Market St.
Philadelphia 19102 (215) 981-2594

Trust established in 1959 in NJ.
Donor(s): Lydia B. Stokes.†
Foundation type: Independent
Financial data (yr. ended 6/30/89): Assets, $2,818,351 (M); expenditures, $178,346, including $155,000 for 5 grants (high: $50,000; low: $10,000).
Purpose and activities: Support for social services and educational institutions affiliated with the Religious Society of Friends, a hospital, and a community fund.
Types of support: Annual campaigns, building funds, capital campaigns, general purposes.
Limitations: Giving primarily in PA and southern NJ. No grants to individuals.
Application information: Application form not required.
Initial approach: Letter
Copies of proposal: 1
Deadline(s): None
Board meeting date(s): As required
Final notification: 1 month
Write: Kenneth W. Gemmill, Trustee
Trustees: Kenneth W. Gemmill, Lydia B. Stokes, Samuel Emlen Stokes, Jr., First Fidelity Bank, N.A., NJ.
Number of staff: None.
Employer Identification Number: 216016107

6469
The Louis L. Stott Foundation
2000 One Logan Sq.
Philadelphia 19103 (215) 963-5281
Mailing address: 1400 Waverly Rd., Blair 225, Gladwyne, PA 19035

Trust established in 1968 in PA.
Donor(s): Martha Stott Diener.
Foundation type: Independent
Financial data (yr. ended 9/30/89): Assets, $2,352,320 (M); expenditures, $139,304, including $116,250 for 36 grants (high: $20,000; low: $500; average: $1,000-$5,000).
Purpose and activities: Support for scientific and technological research, education, medical research, encouragement of art, and preservation of wildlife; giving also for elementary and secondary education, and population and environmental control.
Types of support: Operating budgets, continuing support, annual campaigns, seed money, emergency funds, building funds, equipment, land acquisition, special projects, research, publications, renovation projects.
Limitations: Giving primarily in Berks County, PA. No grants to individuals, or for endowment funds, scholarships, fellowships, conferences, or matching gifts; no loans.
Publications: Application guidelines, program policy statement.
Application information: Application form not required.
Initial approach: Proposal or letter
Copies of proposal: 1
Deadline(s): Submit proposal preferably between Jan. and Aug.; no set deadline
Board meeting date(s): July and Aug.
Final notification: 2 to 3 months
Write: William P. Wood, Esq., Secy.
Officers and Trustees: Martha Stott Diener, Chair.; William P. Wood, Secy.; Brady O. Bryson, Benjamin W. Stott, Edward Barrington Stott, Jonathan D. Stott.
Number of staff: 1 part-time professional; 1 part-time support.
Employer Identification Number: 237009027

6470
Strauss Foundation ⌑
c/o Fidelity Bank, N.A.
Broad & Walnut Sts.
Philadelphia 19109 (215) 985-6326

Trust established in 1951 in PA.
Donor(s): Maurice L. Strauss.
Foundation type: Independent
Financial data (yr. ended 12/31/88): Assets, $30,922,264 (M); expenditures, $1,832,366, including $1,681,344 for 327 grants (high: $447,656; low: $100).
Purpose and activities: Emphasis on Jewish welfare funds in the U.S. and Israel, child welfare and youth agencies, education, hospitals, and cultural programs.
Limitations: Giving primarily in PA and for organizations in Israel. No grants to individuals.
Application information: Unsolicited applications are not encouraged.
Initial approach: Letter
Deadline(s): None
Write: Mrs. Lisa Peters
Trustees: Henry A. Gladstone, Scott R. Isdaner, Sandra S. Krause, Benjamin Strauss, Robert Perry Strauss.
Corporate Trustee: Fidelity Bank, N.A.
Employer Identification Number: 236219939

6471
Margaret Dorrance Strawbridge Foundation of Pennsylvania I, Inc.
c/o Robert L. Freedman, Dechert Price & Rhoads
3400 Center Sq. West, 1500 Market St.
Philadelphia 19102
Mailing address: P.O. Box 135, Mendenhall, PA 19357

Established in 1985 in PA.
Donor(s): Margaret Dorrance Strawbridge Foundation.
Foundation type: Independent
Financial data (yr. ended 12/31/88): Assets, $3,812,987 (M); gifts received, $160,917; expenditures, $226,775, including $208,000 for 13 grants (high: $50,000; low: $1,000).
Purpose and activities: Grants for hospitals and medical research, and culture; some support for education.
Limitations: No grants to individuals, or for endowment funds.
Application information: Application form not required.
Initial approach: Proposal
Deadline(s): None
Board meeting date(s): Quarterly
Write: George Strawbridge, Jr., Pres.
Officers: George Strawbridge, Jr., Pres. and Treas.; Nina S. Strawbridge, V.P. and Secy.
Employer Identification Number: 232373081

6472
Margaret Dorrance Strawbridge Foundation of Pennsylvania II, Inc.
125 Strafford Ave.
Bldg. 3, Suite 108
Wayne 19087-3367 (215) 688-0743

Established in 1985 in PA.
Donor(s): Margaret Dorrance Strawbridge Foundation.
Foundation type: Independent
Financial data (yr. ended 12/31/87): Assets, $3,237,177 (M); gifts received, $113,287; expenditures, $333,192, including $205,310 for 66 grants (high: $25,000; low: $200; average: $1,000-$5,000).
Purpose and activities: Emphasis on higher and secondary education, hospitals and medical research, and community funds and programs. Nearly all grants are for operating expenses.

Types of support: Operating budgets, continuing support, research, annual campaigns.
Limitations: Giving primarily in the eastern U.S., especially PA and FL. No grants to individuals, or for capital or endowment funds, scholarships, or fellowships; no loans.
Application information: Application form not required.
Initial approach: Letter
Deadline(s): None
Officers and Directors: Diana S. Norris, Pres.; Charles S. Norris, Jr., V.P. and Secy.-Treas.
Number of staff: None.
Employer Identification Number: 232371943

6473
The Stroud Foundation ⌑
c/o Mellon Bank (East), N.A.
P.O. Box 7236
Philadelphia 19101
Application address: Landhope R.D. 2, West Grove, PA 19390

Trust established in 1961 in PA.
Donor(s): Joan M. Stroud.
Foundation type: Independent
Financial data (yr. ended 12/31/88): Assets, $2,662,414 (M); gifts received, $352,927; expenditures, $345,722, including $333,500 for 42 grants (high: $30,000; low: $100).
Purpose and activities: Grants largely for higher and secondary education and a natural science museum; some support also for cultural programs and environment.
Types of support: General purposes, continuing support, annual campaigns, seed money, emergency funds, building funds, equipment, land acquisition, endowment funds, research, scholarship funds.
Limitations: No grants to individuals, or for matching gifts; no loans.
Application information: Application form not required.
Initial approach: Letter
Copies of proposal: 1
Deadline(s): None
Board meeting date(s): Quarterly
Write: W.B. Dixon Stroud, Mgr.
Officers: Joan S. Blaine, Mgr.; T. Sam Means, Mgr.; Joan M. Stroud, Mgr.; Morris W. Stroud, Mgr.; W.B. Dixon Stroud, Mgr.; Truman Welling, Mgr.
Number of staff: None.
Employer Identification Number: 236255701

6474
Superior-Pacific Fund ⌑
Seven Wynnewood Rd.
Wynnewood 19096
Scholarship application address: Superior Tube Co. Scholarship Comm., P.O. Box 616, Devault, PA 19432; Tel.: (215) 647-2701

Trust established in 1952 in PA.
Donor(s): Superior Tube Co., Pacific Tube Co., Cawsl Enterprises, Inc.
Foundation type: Company-sponsored
Financial data (yr. ended 12/31/87): Assets, $9,296,941 (M); gifts received, $3,000,000; expenditures, $356,240, including $310,146 for 91 grants (high: $50,000; low: $25) and $12,250 for 15 grants to individuals (high: $1,500; low: $300).
Purpose and activities: Grants primarily for higher and secondary education, including scholarships for children of company employees, community funds, hospitals, health agencies, and music.
Types of support: Employee-related scholarships.
Application information: Application form required.
Deadline(s): Jan. 2 for Personal Data Form A; Jan. 9 for High School Certification Form B
Officer and Directors: Paul E. Kelly, Pres.; Richard H. Gabel, Paul E. Kelly, Jr., William G. Warden III.
Employer Identification Number: 236298237

6475
Susquehanna-Pfaltzgraff Foundation ⌑
P.O. Box 2026
York 17405
Application address: 140 East Market St., York, PA 17401; Tel.: (717) 848-5500

Established in 1966 in PA.
Donor(s): Susquehanna Radio Corp., The Pfaltzgraff Co., and affiliates.
Foundation type: Company-sponsored
Financial data (yr. ended 12/31/88): Assets, $369,470 (M); gifts received, $226,500; expenditures, $197,914, including $197,308 for 32 grants (high: $35,000; low: $100).
Purpose and activities: Primarily giving to youth and social service organizations, and cultural programs.
Application information:
Initial approach: Letter
Write: John L. Finlayson
Officers and Directors:* Louis J. Appell, Jr.,* Pres. and Treas.; George N. Appell,* V.P.; Helen P. Appell,* V.P.; William H. Simpson, Secy.
Employer Identification Number: 236420008

6476
James Sutton Home for Aged & Infirm Men Trust ⌑
c/o Robert W. Hall
39 Public Sq., Suite 300
Wilkes-Barre 18701

Established in 1917 in PA.
Foundation type: Independent
Financial data (yr. ended 6/30/88): Assets, $1,426,082 (M); expenditures, $89,194, including $62,120 for 4 grants of $15,530 each.
Purpose and activities: Support primarily for hospitals, churches, and social services.
Officers: Richard Hogoboom, George Johnson, Earl Phillips.
Employer Identification Number: 240795490

6477
Samuel Tabas Family Foundation ⌑
915 North Delaware Ave.
Philadelphia 19123

Trust established in 1951 in PA.
Donor(s): Members of the Tabas family.
Foundation type: Independent
Financial data (yr. ended 5/31/86): Assets, $1,650,409 (M); expenditures, $187,277, including $179,634 for 116 grants (high: $34,706; low: $18).
Purpose and activities: Emphasis on Jewish welfare funds, health services, higher education, and prevention of cruelty to animals and children.
Application information:
Write: Daniel M. Tabas, Trustee
Trustees: James McSwiggan, Daniel M. Tabas.
Employer Identification Number: 236254348

6478
Tasty Baking Foundation
2801 Hunting Park Ave.
Philadelphia 19129 (215) 221-8500

Established in 1955 in PA.
Donor(s): Tasty Baking Co.
Foundation type: Company-sponsored
Financial data (yr. ended 12/31/88): Assets, $232,580 (M); gifts received, $150,000; expenditures, $140,678, including $140,475 for 88 grants (high: $10,500; low: $100).
Purpose and activities: Giving for arts, education, health, the disadvantaged, general welfare, and low-income housing.
Types of support: General purposes.
Limitations: Giving limited to the greater Philadelphia, PA, area.
Application information: Application form required.
Initial approach: Letter
Copies of proposal: 1
Deadline(s): 2 weeks prior to monthly meeting of trustees
Write: K. Grim
Officers and Trustees:* Philip J. Baur, Jr.,* Chair.; John M. Pettine,* Secy.-Treas.; Elizabeth H. Gemmill, Nelson G. Harris.
Number of staff: 1 part-time professional.
Employer Identification Number: 236271018

6479
Teleflex Foundation ⌑
155 South Limerick Rd.
Limerick 19468-1699 (215) 948-5100

Established in 1980 in PA.
Donor(s): Teleflex, Inc.
Foundation type: Company-sponsored
Financial data (yr. ended 12/31/88): Assets, $430,000 (M); gifts received, $300,000; expenditures, $190,000, including $190,000 for 106 grants (high: $12,500; low: $100; average: $1,000-$5,000).
Purpose and activities: Support for higher and elementary education, hospitals and health, medical research, science and technology, community and social services, public affairs, culture, environmental issues, and urban affairs and welfare.
Types of support: General purposes, employee matching gifts, seed money.
Limitations: Giving primarily in areas of plant locations in CA, DE, MA, ME, MI, NJ, NY, OH, PA, and TX.
Application information: Application form not required.
Initial approach: Written request
Copies of proposal: 1
Deadline(s): None
Board meeting date(s): Fall and spring
Final notification: Within 60 days
Write: Robert Bertschy, Treas.

Officers: Lennox K. Black, Pres.; Bonnie Groff, Secy.; Robert Bertschy, Treas.
Directors: M.C. Chisholm, Diane Fukuda, William Haussmann, John H. Remer, Palmer Retzlaff.
Number of staff: 1 part-time professional; 1 part-time support.
Employer Identification Number: 232104782

6480
Thayer Corporation ⌑
346 Barren Rd.
Media 19063
Additional address: c/o Glenmede Trust Co., 229 South 18th St., Philadelphia, PA 19103; Tel.: (215) 875-3273

Established in 1951 in PA.
Foundation type: Independent
Financial data (yr. ended 12/31/86): Assets, $1,451,559 (M); expenditures, $83,234, including $74,600 for 72 grants (high: $5,000; low: $100).
Purpose and activities: Giving primarily for medical and other higher education; support also for social services.
Limitations: Giving primarily in PA. No grants to individuals.
Application information: Application form not required.
Initial approach: Proposal
Deadline(s): None
Write: Walter D. Macht, Pres.
Officers and Directors: Walter D. Macht, Pres.; Alice T. Macht, V.P.; Elmer L. Macht, V.P.; Albert L. Doering III, Secy.; Robert H.E. Lauer, Treas.; Paul E. Macht.
Employer Identification Number: 236266383

6481
The John Edgar Thomson Foundation
The Rittenhouse Claridge, Suite 318
Philadelphia 19103 (215) 545-6083

Endowment established in 1882 in PA.
Donor(s): John Edgar Thomson.†
Foundation type: Operating
Financial data (yr. ended 12/31/89): Assets, $5,894,970 (M); expenditures, $369,464, including $241,395 for 141 grants to individuals.
Purpose and activities: A private operating foundation; active in the education and maintenance of daughters of deceased railroad employees.
Types of support: Employee-related scholarships, grants to individuals.
Publications: Annual report, newsletter, informational brochure (including application guidelines).
Application information: Application form required.
Board meeting date(s): Monthly
Write: Gilda Verstein, Dir.
Officers: Gilda Verstein, Dir.; H. William Brady, Secy.; Wayne E. Bogardus, Treas.
Trustees: H. William Brady, John J. Maher, Carl L. Rugart, Jr.
Number of staff: 1 full-time professional; 1 full-time support.
Employer Identification Number: 231382746

6482
Frank Thomson Scholarship Trust ⌑
c/o Fidelity Bank, N.A.
135 South Broad St.
Philadelphia 19109

Foundation type: Independent
Financial data (yr. ended 12/31/87): Assets, $1,372,334 (M); expenditures, $67,646, including $56,425 for 70 grants to individuals (high: $1,000; low: $100).
Purpose and activities: Scholarships only to sons of employees of Conrail, Amtrak, and Penn Central prior to 1976.
Types of support: Employee-related scholarships.
Application information: Application form required.
Initial approach: Letter requesting application
Deadline(s): Mar. 31
Write: Frank Thomson, Chair.
Trustee: Fidelity Bank, N.A.
Employer Identification Number: 236217801

6483
Sylvan M. & Frances E. Tobin Foundation ⌑
101 Cheswold Ln., Unit 5D
Haverford 19041-1801

Established in 1966 in PA.
Foundation type: Independent
Financial data (yr. ended 12/31/88): Assets, $612,824 (M); expenditures, $110,220, including $109,000 for 14 grants (high: $50,000; low: $200).
Purpose and activities: Support primarily for medical research.
Limitations: Giving primarily in Philadelphia, PA. No grants to individuals.
Application information: Contributes only to pre-selected organizations. Applications not accepted.
Officers: Francis E. Tobin, Mgr.; Sylvan M. Tobin, Mgr.
Employer Identification Number: 236420013

6484
Harry C. Trexler Trust ▼
1227 Hamilton St.
Allentown 18102 (215) 434-9645

Trust established in 1934 in PA.
Donor(s): Harry C. Trexler,† Mary M. Trexler.†
Foundation type: Independent
Financial data (yr. ended 03/31/89): Assets, $54,566,777 (M); gifts received, $4,903; expenditures, $2,217,474, including $2,016,097 for 68 grants (high: $631,617; low: $500; average: $7,000-$40,000).
Purpose and activities: The will provides that one-fourth of the income shall be added to the corpus, one-fourth paid to the City of Allentown for park purposes, and the remainder distributed to such charitable organizations and objects as shall be "of the most benefit to humanity," but limited to Allentown and Lehigh County, particularly for hospitals, churches, institutions for the care of the crippled and orphans, youth agencies, social services, cultural programs, and support of ministerial students at two named PA institutions.
Types of support: Building funds, matching funds, general purposes, operating budgets, continuing support, land acquisition, capital campaigns, renovation projects.
Limitations: Giving limited to Allentown and Lehigh County, PA. No grants to individuals, or for endowment funds, research, scholarships, or fellowships; no loans.
Publications: Annual report, application guidelines.
Application information: Application form not required.
Initial approach: Letter
Copies of proposal: 3
Deadline(s): Jan. 31 for consideration at annual fund distribution
Board meeting date(s): Monthly; however, grant distribution takes place annually after Mar. 31
Final notification: June 1
Write: Thomas H. Christman, Secy. to the Trustees
Trustees: Kathryn Stephanoff, Chair.; Dexter F. Baker, Philip I. Berman, Carl J.W. Hessinger, Richard K. White, M.D.
Staff: Thomas H. Christman, Secy. to the Trustees.
Number of staff: 2
Employer Identification Number: 231162215

6485
Union Benevolent Association
c/o First Pennsylvania Bank, N.A.
16th and Market Sts.
Philadelphia 19101
Additional address: Joanne Denworth, Esq., Pennsylvania Environmental Ctr., 1211 Chestnut St., Philadelphia, PA 19107; Tel.: (215) 563-7860

Incorporated in 1830 in PA.
Foundation type: Independent
Financial data (yr. ended 12/31/88): Assets, $1,972,568 (M); gifts received, $1,239; expenditures, $107,697, including $88,473 for 39 grants (high: $8,250; low: $500).
Purpose and activities: Giving for the encouragement of industry, suppression of pauperism, and relief of suffering among the worthy poor; grants for community development, health and social service agencies, and youth programs.
Limitations: Giving limited to the greater Philadelphia, PA, area. No support for national organizations or government agencies. No grants to individuals, or for capital funds or deficit financing.
Publications: Program policy statement, application guidelines.
Application information:
Initial approach: Letter
Copies of proposal: 1
Deadline(s): Feb. 1, May 1, and Dec. 1
Board meeting date(s): Feb., May, and Dec.
Final notification: 3 months
Write: Floyd W. Alston, Pres.
Board of Managers: Floyd W. Alston, Pres.; William L. Elkins, M.D., V.P.; G. Malcolm Laws, Jr., Secy.; Lloyd M. Coates, Jr., Treas.; Martin A. Heckscher, Legal Counsel; Joanne R. Denworth, Graham Finney, William J. Lee, Theodore T. Newbold, Nettie Taylor, Roberta Griffin Torian.
Number of staff: None.

Employer Identification Number: 231360861

6486
Union Pacific Foundation ▼
Martin Tower
Eighth and Eaton Aves.
Bethlehem 18018 (215) 861-3225

Incorporated in 1955 in UT.
Donor(s): Union Pacific Corp.
Foundation type: Company-sponsored
Financial data (yr. ended 12/31/89): Assets, $852,020 (M); expenditures, $7,146,160, including $7,129,000 for 775 grants (high: $200,000; low: $200; average: $1,000-$10,000).
Purpose and activities: Grants primarily to non-tax-supported institutions of higher education, health (including hospitals and hospices), social services, and fine and performing arts groups and other cultural programs.
Types of support: Continuing support, building funds, equipment, matching funds, scholarship funds, renovation projects, capital campaigns, special projects, program-related investments.
Limitations: Giving primarily in areas of company operations, particularly in the midwestern and western U.S. in AR, CA, CO, ID, IL, KS, LA, MO, NE, NV, OK, OR, TX, UT, WA, and WY. No support for tax-supported institutions or affiliates (other than United Ways); specialized national health and welfare organizations; political, religious, or labor groups; social clubs, fraternal or veterans' organizations; support for United Way-affiliated organizations restricted to capital projects. No grants to individuals, or for sponsorship of dinners, benefits, seminars, or other special events.
Publications: Application guidelines, informational brochure.
Application information: The foundation does not sponsor an employee matching gift program. Application form required.
Initial approach: Letter
Copies of proposal: 1
Deadline(s): Aug. 15
Board meeting date(s): Late Jan. for consideration for the following year
Final notification: Feb. through May
Write: Mrs. Judy L. Swantak, Pres.
Officers: Judy L. Swantak,* Pres.; L.W. Matthews III, Sr. V.P., Finance; John R. Mendenhall, V.P., Taxes; G.M. Stuart, Treas.
Trustees:* Drew Lewis, Chair.; and 18 additional trustees.
Number of staff: 1 full-time professional; 1 full-time support.
Employer Identification Number: 136406825

6487
USX Foundation, Inc. ▼
(Formerly United States Steel Foundation, Inc.)
600 Grant St., Rm. 2640
Pittsburgh 15219-4776 (412) 433-5237

Incorporated in 1953 in DE.
Donor(s): USX Corp., and certain subsidiaries.
Foundation type: Company-sponsored
Financial data (yr. ended 11/30/89): Assets, $13,397,912 (M); gifts received, $2,590,000; expenditures, $5,691,871, including $5,295,000 for 168 grants and $83,807 for 130 employee matching gifts.
Purpose and activities: Support for higher education, primarily in the private sector, including college and university development grants, special purpose grants, project assistance, matching gifts, manpower development grants, and support to educational associations; scientific and research grants, including capital, operating, project, and research support; civic and cultural grants for capital and operating needs; medicine and health grants for research, capital, and operating purposes; and national and community social services support, including the United Way and other voluntary agencies.
Types of support: General purposes, operating budgets, continuing support, annual campaigns, seed money, emergency funds, building funds, equipment, land acquisition, endowment funds, special projects, research, employee matching gifts, capital campaigns, renovation projects.
Limitations: Giving primarily in areas of company operations, including: Bucks County and Pittsburgh, PA; Birmingham, AL; Gary, IN; and northeastern MN; support also to activities of a national nature. No support for religious organizations for religious purposes. No grants to individuals, or for conferences, seminars, travel, scholarships, fellowships, publications, or films; no loans.
Publications: Annual report (including application guidelines), application guidelines.
Application information: Application form not required.
Initial approach: 1- or 2-page proposal letter
Copies of proposal: 1
Deadline(s): Public, cultural, and scientific affairs, Jan. 15; aid to education, Apr. 15; medical, health, and national and community social services, July 15
Board meeting date(s): May, July, and Sept.
Final notification: Following board meetings
Write: William A. Gregory, Jr., Mgr.
Officers: Charles A. Corry,* Chair.; W. Bruce Thomas,* Vice-Chair.; Peter B. Mulloney,* Pres.; Rex D. Cooley,* V.P. and Comptroller; William E. Lewellen, V.P. and Treas.; Gary A. Glynn, V.P., Investments; Richard M. Hays, Secy.; William A. Gregory, Jr., Mgr.; Dominic B. King, General Counsel; John T. Mills, Tax Counsel.
Trustees:* Ramon G. Clements, Dan D. Sandman, Thomas J. Usher, Louis A. Valli, Richard E. White.
Number of staff: 2 full-time professional; 2 full-time support.
Employer Identification Number: 136093185

6488
Vesuvius Crucible Company Charitable Foundation
c/o Pittsburgh National Bank, Trust Div.
One Oliver Plaza, 27th Fl.
Pittsburgh 15265 (412) 762-3340

Established in 1966 in PA.
Foundation type: Company-sponsored
Financial data (yr. ended 12/31/89): Assets, $2,119,435 (M); expenditures, $120,173, including $106,625 for 30 grants (high: $25,000; low: $100).
Purpose and activities: Support primarily for higher education.
Types of support: General purposes.
Limitations: Giving primarily in Pittsburgh, PA.
Application information:
Initial approach: Letter
Copies of proposal: 1
Deadline(s): None
Write: John Culbertson
Trustee: Pittsburgh National Bank.
Employer Identification Number: 256076182

6489
Vicary Foundation, Inc.
5050 West 38th St.
Erie 16506-1307 (814) 833-5120
Application address: c/o Cheryl G. Vicary, P.O. Box 530, Waterford, PA 16441

Established in 1958 in PA.
Donor(s): Arthur C. Vicary,† Mary W. Vicary.†
Foundation type: Independent
Financial data (yr. ended 12/31/89): Assets, $1,126,740 (M); qualifying distributions, $58,050, including $58,050 for 27 grants (high: $5,000; low: $250; average: $1,500-$2,500).
Purpose and activities: Support primarily for community organizations and social services; support also for education and the arts.
Limitations: Giving primarily in Erie, PA.
Application information:
Deadline(s): None
Board meeting date(s): June 15 and Dec. 15
Write: Charles A. Curtze, Trustee
Officers and Trustees:* Charles C. Vicary,* Pres.; Thomas C. Vicary, V.P.; Cheryl W. Vicary, Secy.; Charles A. Curtze,* Treas.; Louise Curtze, Wilma Vicary.
Number of staff: None.
Employer Identification Number: 256035971

6490
Anna M. Vincent Trust ⌑
c/o Mellon Bank (East), N.A.
P.O. Box 7899
Philadelphia 19101-7899 (215) 553-3208

Trust established in 1967 in PA.
Donor(s): Anna M. Vincent.†
Foundation type: Independent
Financial data (yr. ended 6/30/87): Assets, $3,738,177 (M); expenditures, $132,525, including $101,400 for 90 grants to individuals (high: $2,500; low: $300).
Purpose and activities: Scholarships for graduate or undergraduate study at any recognized college, university, or other institution of higher learning.
Types of support: Student aid.
Limitations: Giving limited to the Delaware Valley, PA, area. No grants for building or endowment funds, operating budgets, or special projects.
Publications: Application guidelines.
Application information: Application forms available at high schools. Application form required.
Initial approach: Letter
Copies of proposal: 1
Deadline(s): Mar. 1
Board meeting date(s): Mar. and Apr.

Write: Patricia M. Kling, Trust Officer, Mellon Bank (East), N.A.
Trustees: Robert I. Whitelaw, Mellon Bank (East), N.A.
Employer Identification Number: 236422666

6491
The Waldorf Educational Foundation ▼ ⌑
c/o The Glenmede Trust Co.
229 South 18th St.
Philadelphia 19103 (215) 875-3200

Established in 1951 in PA.
Foundation type: Independent
Financial data (yr. ended 12/31/88): Assets, $7,336,641 (M); expenditures, $909,176, including $887,660 for 40 grants (high: $151,000; low: $890; average: $7,000-$25,000).
Purpose and activities: Grants primarily for education, with emphasis on faculty development.
Application information:
Write: A.E. Piscopo
Trustees: Samuel W. Morris, Karin Myrin, The Glenmede Trust Co.
Employer Identification Number: 236254206

6492
Alex C. Walker Educational and Charitable Foundation ⌑
c/o Pittsburgh National Bank, Trust Dept. 970
One Oliver Plaza, 28th Fl.
Pittsburgh 15265 (412) 762-3866

Trust established in 1967 in PA.
Donor(s): Alex C. Walker.†
Foundation type: Independent
Financial data (yr. ended 12/31/88): Assets, $3,933,323 (M); expenditures, $217,121, including $154,700 for 22 grants (high: $25,000; low: $500).
Purpose and activities: Grants for research in economics, including the effect of legislation, causes of depressions, recessions, and unemployment, the free enterprise system, and the monetary system of the U.S., including the advisability of a return to the gold standard.
Types of support: Research, general purposes.
Limitations: No grants to individuals, or for building or endowment funds.
Publications: Program policy statement.
Application information:
Initial approach: Proposal
Copies of proposal: 1
Deadline(s): None
Board meeting date(s): Quarterly
Write: Henry C. Flood, Jr.
Trustees: Barrett C. Walker, T. Urling Walker, Pittsburgh National Bank.
Employer Identification Number: 256109746

6493
Wardle Family Foundation ⌑ ☆
P.O. Box 2219
Lower Burrell 15068-0744

Established in 1987 in PA.
Donor(s): Robert V. Wardle.
Foundation type: Independent
Financial data (yr. ended 12/31/88): Assets, $2,099,954 (M); gifts received, $1,666,000; expenditures, $24,903, including $15,350 for 14 grants (high: $10,000; low: $100).
Purpose and activities: Giving primarily to a community fund; support also for social services.
Limitations: Giving primarily in Pittsburgh, PA. No grants to individuals.
Application information: Contributes only to pre-selected organizations. Applications not accepted.
Trustees: Corinne G. Wardle, Robert V. Wardle.
Employer Identification Number: 256290322

6494
The Warwick Foundation
108 West Court St.
Doylestown 18901 (215) 348-3199

Established in 1961 in PA.
Donor(s): Helen H. Gemmill, Kenneth Gemmill.
Foundation type: Independent
Financial data (yr. ended 12/31/88): Assets, $3,450,070 (M); expenditures, $152,717, including $139,700 for 46 grants (high: $10,000; low: $200).
Purpose and activities: Giving primarily for the United Way and higher education in the form of scholarship money to colleges and universities; support also for culture, civic affairs, and historic preservation.
Types of support: Scholarship funds, operating budgets.
Limitations: Giving primarily in the Bucks County and Philadelphia, PA, areas. No grants to individuals.
Application information: Application form not required.
Initial approach: Letter
Deadline(s): None
Final notification: No response to application unless affirmative
Write: Grace M. Huber, Secy.
Officer: Grace M. Huber, Secy. and Mgr.
Trustees: Catharine Cowen, Elizabeth Gemmill, Helen H. Gemmill, John Gemmill, William Gemmill.
Number of staff: None.
Employer Identification Number: 236230662

6495
Robert S. Waters Charitable Trust ⌑
c/o Mellon Bank (East), N.A.
One Mellon Bank Ctr.
Pittsburgh 15258 (412) 234-5784

Trust established in 1952 in PA.
Donor(s): Robert S. Waters.†
Foundation type: Independent
Financial data (yr. ended 12/31/86): Assets, $3,422,529 (M); gifts received, $111,804; expenditures, $179,705, including $141,800 for 36 grants (high: $23,000; low: $500).
Purpose and activities: Emphasis on cultural programs, conservation, secondary education, social services, and historic preservation.
Limitations: Giving primarily in PA. No grants to individuals, or scholarships, or fellowships; no loans.
Application information: Application form required.
Initial approach: Letter
Copies of proposal: 2
Deadline(s): None
Board meeting date(s): Sept.
Write: Barbara K. Robinson, V.P., Mellon Bank (East), N.A.
Trustees: John P. Davis, Jr., Mellon Bank (East), N.A.
Employer Identification Number: 256018986

6496
Robert and Mary Weisbrod Foundation
Trust Dept.
c/o Union National Bank of Pittsburgh
Pittsburgh 15278-2241

Established in 1968 in PA.
Donor(s): Mary E. Weisbrod.†
Foundation type: Independent
Financial data (yr. ended 12/31/88): Assets, $7,152,098 (M); expenditures, $458,268, including $410,308 for 23 grants (high: $100,000; low: $1,000).
Purpose and activities: Emphasis on hospitals and medical research, social service and child welfare agencies, music organizations, and historic preservation.
Types of support: Capital campaigns, equipment.
Limitations: Giving primarily in the Pittsburgh, PA, area.
Application information: Application form not required.
Initial approach: Proposal
Copies of proposal: 1
Deadline(s): None
Board meeting date(s): As required
Write: The Distribution Committee
Distribution Committee: John R. Echement, Donald L. McCaskey, Francis B. Nimick.
Trustee: Union National Bank of Pittsburgh.
Number of staff: None.
Employer Identification Number: 256105924

6497
Franklin H. & Ruth L. Wells Foundation
4718 Old Gettysburg Rd., Suite 405
Mechanicsburg 17055 (717) 763-1157

Established in 1983 in PA.
Donor(s): Ruth L. Wells Annuity Trust, Frank Wells Marital Trust.
Foundation type: Independent
Financial data (yr. ended 05/31/89): Assets, $4,749,980 (M); gifts received, $196,648; expenditures, $427,058, including $372,944 for 36 grants (high: $100,000; low: $500; average: $2,000-$15,000).
Purpose and activities: Support for social service agencies; health associations, hospices, and hospitals; cultural programs, including museums and historic preservation; and education, including elementary and secondary education, libraries, and literacy programs.
Types of support: Building funds, capital campaigns, emergency funds, equipment, land acquisition, renovation projects, seed money, special projects.
Limitations: Giving primarily in Dauphin, Cumberland, and Perry counties, PA. No support for religious activities. No grants for operating expenses, endowments, or debts.
Application information: Application form not required.
Initial approach: Letter

Copies of proposal: 1
Deadline(s): None
Write: Miles J. Gibbons, Exec. Dir
Committee: Miles J. Gibbons, Exec. Dir.; Clifford S. Charles, Gladys R. Charles, Ellen R. Cramer.
Trustee: Dauphin Deposit Bank & Trust Co.
Number of staff: 2 part-time professional; 1 part-time support.
Employer Identification Number: 222541749

6498
The H. O. West Foundation

(Formerly Herman O. West Foundation)
P.O. Box 808
Phoenixville 19460 (215) 935-4500

Established in 1972 in PA.
Donor(s): The West Co., and members of the West family.
Foundation type: Company-sponsored
Financial data (yr. ended 12/31/87): Assets, $427,740 (M); gifts received, $219,034; expenditures, $299,160, including $255,120 for 30 grants (high: $50,000; low: $500), $30,250 for 28 grants to individuals (high: $1,500; low: $307) and $10,345 for employee matching gifts.
Purpose and activities: Giving primarily for hospitals, pharmacy and health care, and social services; support also for higher education, including an employee-related scholarship program and an employee matching gift program.
Types of support: Employee matching gifts, building funds, research, employee-related scholarships, matching funds.
Limitations: Giving primarily in areas of company operations in FL, NJ, PA, and NE.
Application information: Contact company for scholarship application.
Initial approach: Proposal
Copies of proposal: 1
Deadline(s): Feb. 28
Board meeting date(s): Apr., Aug., and Nov.
Write: Mr. Geo Bennyhoff, Trustee
Trustees: Geo R. Bennyhoff, C.F. Sterling, J.A. West.
Number of staff: None.
Employer Identification Number: 237173901

6499
Western Association of Ladies for the Relief and Employment of the Poor

c/o Fidelity Bank, N.A.
Broad & Walnut Sts.
Philadelphia 19109 (215) 431-4679
Application address: 404 Baumont Circle, West Chester, PA 19380; Tel.: (215) 692-7962

Established in 1847 in PA.
Foundation type: Independent
Financial data (yr. ended 12/31/88): Assets, $1,408,494 (M); gifts received, $2,734; expenditures, $85,174, including $67,385 for grants to individuals.
Purpose and activities: Support for programs providing supplemental aid to the poor and homeless, including welfare for children and other individuals, family services, and programs for the disabled; support also for elementary, higher, and other education, dentistry, and citizenship.
Types of support: Emergency funds, equipment, general purposes, grants to individuals.
Limitations: Giving limited to Philadelphia County, PA.
Application information: Application must be submitted through a social service organization. Application form not required.
Initial approach: Letter
Deadline(s): None
Board meeting date(s): 2nd Tuesday of month: Sept.-June
Write: Marlane Bohon, Exec. Secy.
Officer: Marlane Bohon, Exec. Secy.
Number of staff: 1
Employer Identification Number: 231353393

6500
Westinghouse Foundation ▼

c/o Westinghouse Electric Corp.
11 Stanwix St.
Pittsburgh 15222 (412) 642-3017

Established in 1987 in PA as a result of the merger of Westinghouse Educational Foundation, Westinghouse International Educational Foundation and Westinghouse Electric Fund.
Donor(s): Westinghouse Electric Corp.
Foundation type: Company-sponsored
Financial data (yr. ended 12/31/88): Assets, $8,373,427 (M); gifts received, $8,150,000; expenditures, $10,709,847, including $9,361,655 for 630 grants (high: $907,500; low: $1,000) and $1,331,114 for employee matching gifts.
Purpose and activities: Grants primarily for United Way organizations where the company has a major presence. Support also for youth, the disadvantaged, minority education, educational associations, social service agencies, hospitals, and selected cultural grants in plant cities; expanded emphasis on civic and economic development; support also for grants to targeted colleges and universities for science and engineering.
Types of support: Employee matching gifts, special projects.
Limitations: Giving primarily in areas of company operations. No support for religious organizations or specialized health campaigns. No grants to individuals (except employee-related scholarships), or for operating budgets, annual campaigns, seed money, land acquisition, equipment, renovation projects, deficit financing, conferences, research, emergency or endowment funds, scholarships, or fellowships; no loans.
Publications: Annual report (including application guidelines), application guidelines.
Application information:
Initial approach: Telephone or proposal
Copies of proposal: 1
Deadline(s): None
Board meeting date(s): Feb., May, Sept., and Nov.
Final notification: 2 months
Write: G. Reynolds Clark, Pres., or C.L. Kubelick, Mgr., Contribs. & Comm. Affairs
Officers: G. Reynolds Clark, Pres.; C.L. Kubelick, Secy.
Trustees: R.F. Pugliese, Chair.; G.C. Dorman, W. Hollinshead, R.A. Linder, E.P. Massaro, H.F. Murray, W.A. Powe, M.C. Sardi, J.B. Yasinsky.
Number of staff: 3 full-time professional; 3 full-time support.
Employer Identification Number: 251357168

6501
Westmoreland Coal Company and Penn Virginia Corporation Foundation ⌑

700 The Bellvue
200 South Broad St.
Philadelphia 19102 (215) 545-2500

Trust established in 1974 in PA.
Donor(s): Westmoreland Coal Co., Penn Virginia Corp.
Foundation type: Company-sponsored
Financial data (yr. ended 12/31/88): Assets, $1,465,228 (M); gifts received, $3,624; expenditures, $168,942, including $5,000 for 1 grant and $117,985 for 176 grants to individuals (high: $2,600; low: $150).
Purpose and activities: Grants primarily for college scholarships for children of company employees or for residents in areas of company operations; some support for community development in areas of company operations.
Types of support: Employee-related scholarships.
Limitations: Giving primarily in areas of company operations in Lee, Scott, and Wise counties, VA; Boone, Fayette, Greenbrier, Logan, Nicholas, Raleigh, and Wyoming counties, WV; and Delta County, CO.
Application information: Application form required for scholarships.
Deadline(s): Dec. 1 for scholarships
Board meeting date(s): Annually
Write: Philip D. Weinstock, Mgr.
Officer: Philip D. Weinstock, Mgr.
Trustees: Charles E. Brinley, John P. Lamond, H. Kenneth Nelson.
Employer Identification Number: 237398163

6502
Whalley Charitable Trust ⌑

1205 Graham Ave.
Windber 15963
Application address: c/o G. Lesko, 1210 Graham Ave., Windber, PA 15963

Trust established in 1961 in PA.
Donor(s): John J. Whalley, John Whalley, Jr., Mary Whalley.
Foundation type: Independent
Financial data (yr. ended 12/31/86): Assets, $2,506,185 (M); expenditures, $133,449, including $113,988 for 60 grants (high: $20,000; low: $15).
Purpose and activities: Support for health, civic affairs, education, religious organizations, and cultural programs.
Limitations: Giving primarily in PA.
Trustees: David Klementik, G. Lesko.
Employer Identification Number: 237128436

6503
The Whitaker Foundation ▼
4718 Old Gettysburg Rd., Suite 405
Mechanicsburg 17055-4325 (717) 763-1391

Trust established in 1975 in NY.
Donor(s): U.A. Whitaker,† Helen F. Whitaker.†
Foundation type: Independent
Financial data (yr. ended 12/31/88): Assets, $287,225,775 (M); gifts received, $216,811; expenditures, $11,592,583, including $10,527,861 for 225 grants (high: $1,000,000; low: $250; average: $40,000-$60,000).
Purpose and activities: Support for projects which integrate engineering with biomedical research; grants also to local community service agencies, educational institutions, and cultural organizations.
Types of support: Seed money, building funds, equipment, land acquisition, research, special projects, renovation projects, capital campaigns.
Limitations: Giving primarily in the U.S. and Canada for Biomedical Engineering Research Program; and in the Harrisburg, PA, area for community service, educational, and cultural organizations. No support for sectarian religious purposes. No grants to individuals, or for operating budgets of established programs, deficit financing, annual campaigns, emergency funds, publications, conferences, seminars, or endowment funds; no loans.
Publications: Program policy statement, informational brochure (including application guidelines).
Application information: Application procedures are outlined in program policy statements for medical research grants and regional program. Application form not required.
Initial approach: Letter or telephone for regional program; preliminary application for medical research program
Copies of proposal: 1
Deadline(s): Jan. 2, May 1, and Sept. 1 for regional program proposals, and Feb. 15, June 15, and Oct. 15 for Biomedical Engineering Research Program
Board meeting date(s): Feb., June, and Oct. for governing committee
Final notification: 5 months
Write: Miles J. Gibbons, Jr., Exec. Dir.
Officer: Miles J. Gibbons, Jr., Exec. Dir.
Committee Members: C.J. Fredricksen, Chair.; Robert K. Campbell, Allen W. Cowley, M.D., Eckley B. Coxe IV, G. Burton Holmes, Ruth W. Holmes, Portia W. Shumaker.
Trustee: Chemical Bank.
Number of staff: 3 full-time professional; 2 full-time support.
Employer Identification Number: 222096948

6504
The Helen F. Whitaker Fund
4718 Old Gettysburg Rd., Suite 405
Mechanicsburg 17055 (717) 763-1600

Established in 1983 in NY.
Donor(s): Helen F. Whitaker.†
Foundation type: Independent
Financial data (yr. ended 07/31/89): Assets, $20,617,410 (M); gifts received, $6,006,194; expenditures, $902,445, including $844,472 for 8 grants (high: $232,472; low: $50,000).
Purpose and activities: Support primarily for educational institutions and charitable organizations supporting the development of the professional careers of young musicians and arts administrators, or the development of the business and professional careers of women.
Types of support: General purposes, seed money.
Application information: Application form not required.
Initial approach: Letter
Copies of proposal: 3
Deadline(s): None
Board meeting date(s): As needed
Write: Miles J. Gibbons, Jr., Comm. Member
Committee Members: Carmelita Biggie, Miles J. Gibbons, Jr., Ruth W. Holmes.
Trustee Bank: Chemical Bank.
Number of staff: 2 part-time professional; 1 part-time support.
Employer Identification Number: 222459399

6505
Widener Memorial Foundation in Aid of Handicapped Children
665 Thomas Rd.
P.O. Box 178
Lafayette Hill 19444 (215) 836-7500

Incorporated in 1912 in PA.
Donor(s): Peter A.B. Widener.†
Foundation type: Independent
Financial data (yr. ended 12/31/89): Assets, $4,257,117 (M); gifts received, $557,169; expenditures, $718,068, including $708,812 for 13 grants (high: $235,000; low: $3,200; average: $15,000-$100,000).
Purpose and activities: Support for research into the causes, treatment, and prevention of diseases and conditions which handicap children orthopedically; to aid and assist public and private charitable institutions and associations in the care, education, and rehabilitation of children so handicapped.
Types of support: Seed money, building funds, equipment, special projects, research, renovation projects.
Limitations: Giving limited to Delaware Valley, PA, for projects relating to orthopedically handicapped children. No grants to individuals, or for endowment funds, scholarships, fellowships, or matching gifts; no loans.
Application information: Application form not required.
Initial approach: Letter
Copies of proposal: 1
Deadline(s): Apr. 15 and Oct. 15
Board meeting date(s): May and Nov.
Final notification: Immediately after board meetings
Write: F. Eugene Dixon, Jr., Pres.
Officers and Trustees:* F. Eugene Dixon, Jr.,* Pres.; Peter M. Mattoon,* V.P.; George Widener Dixon,* Secy.-Treas.; Bruce L. Castor, Edith Robb Dixon.
Number of staff: None.
Employer Identification Number: 236267223

6506
Widgeon Foundation, Inc. ⌑
c/o George V. Strong, Jr.
1700 Two Mellon Bank Ctr.
Philadelphia 19102
Application address: P.O. Box 1084, Easton, MD 21601; Tel.: (301) 822-7707

Established in 1969 in PA.
Donor(s): Elizabeth H. Robinson.
Foundation type: Independent
Financial data (yr. ended 12/31/88): Assets, $1,767,839 (M); expenditures, $99,205, including $94,261 for 11 grants (high: $60,000; low: $161).
Purpose and activities: Giving primarily for youth, higher education, Christian religious groups, hospitals, and a YMCA.
Types of support: General purposes.
Limitations: Giving primarily in MD. No grants to individuals.
Application information: Application form not required.
Initial approach: Proposal
Deadline(s): None
Write: Elizabeth H. Robinson, Pres.
Officers and Directors: Elizabeth H. Robinson, Pres. and Treas.; Richard Robinson, V.P.; George V. Strong, Jr., Secy.
Employer Identification Number: 136113927

6507
Willary Foundation ⌑
c/o Northeastern Bank of Pennsylvania
P.O. Box 937
Scranton 18501-0937

Established in 1968 in PA.
Foundation type: Independent
Financial data (yr. ended 12/31/88): Assets, $1,066,968 (M); expenditures, $48,714, including $40,902 for 24 grants (high: $12,000; low: $30).
Purpose and activities: Support primarily for music, churches, and a community fund.
Limitations: Giving primarily in northeastern PA. No grants to individuals; no loans.
Trustees: Mary L. Scranton, William W. Scranton, Northeastern Bank of Pennsylvania.
Employer Identification Number: 237014785

6508
John C. Williams Charitable Trust
c/o Pittsburgh National Bank, Trust Division
One Oliver Plaza, 27th Fl.
Pittsburgh 15265 (412) 762-3796

Trust established in 1936 in PA.
Donor(s): John C. Williams.†
Foundation type: Independent
Financial data (yr. ended 12/31/89): Assets, $4,226,394 (M); expenditures, $202,908, including $175,909 for 7 grants (high: $35,000; low: $10,000).
Purpose and activities: Emphasis on higher education, hospitals, a community center, and youth agencies.
Types of support: General purposes, renovation projects, capital campaigns, equipment.
Limitations: Giving limited to Steubenville, OH, and Weirton, WV. No grants to individuals, or for fellowships or matching gifts; no loans.

Publications: Application guidelines.
Application information: Application form required.
Initial approach: Letter
Copies of proposal: 3
Deadline(s): None
Board meeting date(s): Mar. and Sept.
Write: Steve Bonnett
Trustee: Pittsburgh National Bank.
Employer Identification Number: 256024153

6509
The C. K. Williams Foundation ⌑
c/o Mellon Bank (East), N.A.
P.O. Box 7236
Philadelphia 19101-7236

Established in 1963 in PA.
Foundation type: Independent
Financial data (yr. ended 12/31/88): Assets, $3,846,264 (M); expenditures, $202,124, including $184,500 for 13 grants (high: $50,000; low: $1,000).
Purpose and activities: Giving primarily for higher education; support also for public television and housing.
Types of support: General purposes.
Limitations: Giving primarily in PA.
Application information: Contributes only to pre-selected organizations. Applications not accepted.
Officers and Directors: Joan W. Rhame, Pres. and Secy.; Charles K. Williams, Josephine C. Williams.
Employer Identification Number: 236292772

6510
Willock C. Jr.-Willock Memorial Fund ⌑ ☆
c/o Mellon Bank (East), N.A.
P.O. Box 185
Pittsburgh 15230
Application address: One Mellon Bank Ctr., Pittsburgh, PA 15258; Tel.: (412) 234-4695

Foundation type: Independent
Financial data (yr. ended 9/30/88): Assets, $1,853,313 (M); expenditures, $110,567, including $86,580 for 6 grants of $14,430 each.
Purpose and activities: Giving primarily for animal welfare; support also for a Presbyterian church.
Limitations: Giving primarily in PA.
Application information: Application form required.
Write: Helen Collins, Trustee
Trustee: Mellon Bank (East), N.A.
Employer Identification Number: 256170449

6511
Thomas A. Wilson Foundation
c/o Union National Bank of Pittsburgh
Pittsburgh 15278-2241 (412) 644-8359

Established in 1971 in PA.
Foundation type: Independent
Financial data (yr. ended 12/31/88): Assets, $4,186,069 (M); expenditures, $300,384, including $255,000 for 1 grant.
Purpose and activities: Emphasis on Christian education and health care.
Application information:
Initial approach: Proposal
Deadline(s): None
Write: Barbara L. Beech, Asst. V.P., Union National Bank of Pittsburgh
Trustee: Union National Bank of Pittsburgh.
Employer Identification Number: 237358862

6512
Wolf Foundation ⌑
P.O. Box 1267
York 17405 (218) 846-0250

Established in 1969 in PA.
Donor(s): Wolf Distributing Co., The Lumber Yard.
Foundation type: Company-sponsored
Financial data (yr. ended 12/31/88): Assets, $475,117 (M); gifts received, $243,167; expenditures, $222,350, including $220,885 for 60 grants (high: $30,000; low: $75).
Purpose and activities: Support for health organizations, and youth; some support for religion and arts.
Types of support: General purposes.
Application information:
Initial approach: Letter
Deadline(s): None
Write: William B. Zimmerman, Chair.
Officers: William B. Zimmerman, Chair.; Thomas W. Wolf, Pres.; George Hodged, Secy.-Treas.
Employer Identification Number: 237028494

6513
Benjamin & Fredora K. Wolf Foundation ⌑
Park Towne Place - North Bldg. 1205
Parkway at 22nd St.
Philadelphia 19130 (215) 787-6079

Incorporated in 1955 in PA.
Donor(s): Fredora K. Wolf.†
Foundation type: Independent
Financial data (yr. ended 5/31/88): Assets, $1,835,703 (M); expenditures, $100,829, including $92,375 for 203 grants to individuals (high: $4,975; low: $300).
Purpose and activities: Grants to needy individuals for college scholarships.
Types of support: Student aid.
Limitations: Giving limited to Philadelphia, PA, area residents. No grants for any purpose except student aid; no loans.
Application information: Application form required.
Initial approach: Letter
Copies of proposal: 1
Deadline(s): None
Board meeting date(s): June and Dec.
Write: Dr. David A. Horowitz, Admin.
Officers: Max Kohn, Pres.; Mrs. Howard Hurtig, V.P.; Mrs. Herbert Fogel, Secy.; Richard I. Abrahams, Treas.
Trustees: Mrs. John Briscoe, Mrs. J. Ronald Gray, John Tuton, Clarence Wolf, Mrs. Edwin Wolf, Provident National Bank.
Number of staff: 1 part-time support.
Employer Identification Number: 236207344

6514
Women's Aid of the Penn Central Transportation Company ⌑ ☆
c/o Conrail Trans. Co.
Six Penn Ctr., Rm. 1010
Philadelphia 19103

Foundation type: Company-sponsored
Financial data (yr. ended 12/31/88): Assets, $1,044,754 (M); expenditures, $55,762, including $45,383 for 136 grants to individuals (high: $750; low: $67).
Purpose and activities: Awards scholarships for higher education to dependents of employees and retirees of Conrail and its predecessor roads now employed by Amtrak or Penn Central Corp.
Types of support: Student aid.
Application information:
Initial approach: Letter
Deadline(s): Apr. 1
Director: J.P. Fox.
Associates: R.G. Kondan, D. Scott Morgan.
Employer Identification Number: 236232572

6515
Henrietta Tower Wurts Memorial ⌑
c/o Fidelity Bank, N.A.
135 South Broad St.
Philadelphia 19109 (215) 985-7320

Incorporated in 1934 in PA.
Donor(s): Henrietta Tower Wurts.†
Foundation type: Independent
Financial data (yr. ended 12/31/88): Assets, $2,542,655 (M); expenditures, $150,628, including $125,348 for 61 grants (high: $4,000; low: $1,500; average: $2,000).
Purpose and activities: To contribute to nonsectarian corporate institutions which are engaged in helping or caring for people in need, or alleviating the conditions under which they live; grants primarily for family and child welfare services, community development, and health services.
Types of support: General purposes, building funds, equipment, operating budgets, continuing support, annual campaigns, seed money, emergency funds.
Limitations: Giving limited to Philadelphia, PA. No grants to individuals, or for endowment funds, scholarships, fellowships, or matching gifts; no loans.
Publications: Application guidelines.
Application information: Application form required.
Initial approach: Letter
Copies of proposal: 1
Deadline(s): Submit proposal preferably before Jan. 1, May 1, or Sept. 1
Board meeting date(s): Feb., June, and Oct.
Final notification: 2 weeks after meeting
Officers and Directors:* S. Stoney Simons,* Pres.; Mrs. Henry T. Reath,* V.P.; Mrs. H. Carton Dittmann, Jr., Howard Kellogg, Pamela G. Model, Sidney N. Repplier, Richard Ferree Smith, Fidelity Bank, N.A.
Number of staff: None.
Employer Identification Number: 236297977

6516
Wyomissing Foundation, Inc.
1015 Penn Ave.
Wyomissing 19610 (215) 376-7496

Incorporated in 1929 in DE.
Donor(s): Ferdinand Thun,† and family.
Foundation type: Independent
Financial data (yr. ended 12/31/89): Assets, $12,874,534 (M); expenditures, $652,640, including $493,250 for 52 grants (high: $63,000; low: $1,000; average: $1,000-$20,000).
Purpose and activities: Giving primarily for hospitals and health services, higher education, civic affairs, youth and social service agencies, child welfare, family planning and services, and a community fund; support also for the environment and conservation and the arts, including performing arts and music.
Types of support: Operating budgets, continuing support, annual campaigns, seed money, emergency funds, building funds, equipment, matching funds, capital campaigns.
Limitations: Giving primarily in Berks County, PA, and contiguous counties; limited support also in the mid-Atlantic area. No grants to individuals, or for endowment funds, deficit financing, land acquisition, publications, conferences, scholarships, or fellowships; no loans.
Publications: Program policy statement, application guidelines, annual report, financial statement.
Application information: Application form not required.
Initial approach: Proposal not exceeding 2 pages (excluding supporting materials)
Copies of proposal: 1
Deadline(s): Submit proposal preferably in Feb., May, Aug., or Oct.; deadline 25th of month preceding board meeting
Board meeting date(s): Mar., June, Sept., and Nov.
Final notification: 3 months
Write: Lawrence A. Walsky, Secy.
Officers: Marlin Miller, Jr.,* Pres.; Peter Thun,* V.P.; Lawrence A. Walsky, Secy.; Alfred Hemmerich,* Treas.
Trustees:* Thomas A. Beaver, Victoria F. Guthrie, Sidney D. Kline, Jr., Nicholas Muhlenberg, Paul R. Roedel, David L. Thun.
Number of staff: 1 part-time professional; 1 part-time support.
Employer Identification Number: 231980570

6517
York Container Foundation
138 Mt. Zion Rd.
York 17402-8985 (717) 757-7611

Established in 1983 in PA.
Foundation type: Independent
Financial data (yr. ended 12/31/88): Assets, $248,436 (M); gifts received, $125,000; expenditures, $121,550, including $121,095 for 48 grants (high: $25,000; low: $45).
Purpose and activities: Support primarily for churches, youth and community organizations, and higher education.
Limitations: Giving primarily in PA, with emphasis on York. No grants to individuals.
Application information: Contributes only to pre-selected organizations. Applications not accepted.
Write: Dennis E. Willman, Secy.
Officers: Charles S. Wolf, Pres.; Dennis E. Willman, Secy.; Charles S. Wolf, Jr., Treas.
Director: Constance L. Wolf.
Employer Identification Number: 222473590

PUERTO RICO

6518
Harvey Foundation, Inc. ⌑
First Federal Bldg., Suite 507
1519 Ponce de Leon Ave.
Santurce 00909

Incorporated in 1963 in PR.
Foundation type: Independent
Financial data (yr. ended 12/31/86): Assets, $1,464,901 (M); expenditures, $128,594, including $60,200 for 6 grants (high: $50,000; low: $1,200) and $13,035 for 5 grants to individuals (high: $3,000; low: $2,000).
Purpose and activities: Emphasis on higher education, including scholarships.
Types of support: Scholarship funds, general purposes, student aid.
Limitations: Giving primarily in PR.
Officers: Arthur J. Harvey, Jr., Pres.; Emma C. Harvey, V.P.; Alfonso Miranda, Secy.; Charles M. Hitt, Treas.
Employer Identification Number: 660271454

6519
Puerto Rico Community Foundation ▼
Royal Bank Ctr. Bldg., Suite 1417
Hato Rey 00917 (809) 751-3822

Incorporated in 1984 in PR.
Foundation type: Community
Financial data (yr. ended 12/31/89): Assets, $8,008,570 (M); gifts received, $3,177,761; expenditures, $1,870,073, including $1,209,382 for 40 grants (high: $141,305; low: $400).
Purpose and activities: The foundation "seeks to contribute to the achievement of a healthier economy and enhance quality of life in Puerto Rico"; giving in areas such as economic development, education, community development, science and technological innovation, health, including AIDS programs, the arts, criminal justice, agriculture, animal welfare, and civic affairs.
Types of support: Conferences and seminars, continuing support, matching funds, operating budgets, professorships, publications, renovation projects, research, program-related investments.
Limitations: Giving primarily in PR. No support for religious organizations or commonly accepted community services. No grants to individuals, or for annual campaigns, technical assistance, consulting services, emergency funds, seed money, endowments, deficit financing, or scholarships; generally no grants for equipment or building funds.
Publications: Annual report, newsletter, informational brochure (including application guidelines), 990-PF, financial statement.
Application information:
Initial approach: Letter
Deadline(s): June 1, Sept. 1, Nov. 1, and Feb. 15
Board meeting date(s): June, Sept., Dec., and Mar.
Final notification: Within 2 weeks of board meetings
Write: Jose R. Crespo, Administrator
Officers: Ethel Rios de Betancourt, Pres.; Jose R. Crespo, Administrator.
Directors: Manuel H. Dubon, Chair.; Amalia Betanzos, and 18 additional directors.
Number of staff: 3 full-time professional; 2 part-time professional; 6 full-time support; 2 part-time support.
Employer Identification Number: 660413230

RHODE ISLAND

6520
Allendale Insurance Foundation ⌑
c/o The R.I. Hospital Trust National Bank
One Hospital Trust Plaza
Providence 02903 (401) 278-8889

Established in 1986 in RI.
Foundation type: Company-sponsored
Financial data (yr. ended 12/31/88): Assets, $4,660,069 (M); gifts received, $88,267; expenditures, $479,223, including $413,462 for 589 grants (high: $119,212; low: $25).
Purpose and activities: Grants primarily for community funds and educational institutions.
Application information:
Initial approach: Proposal and annual report
Deadline(s): None
Trustee: The Rhode Island Hospital Trust National Bank.
Director: George R. West.
Employer Identification Number: 222773230

6521
The Alperin Foundation ⌑
160 Taunton Ave.
East Providence 02914 (401) 751-2000

Established in 1956 in RI.
Donor(s): Members of the Alperin family.
Foundation type: Independent
Financial data (yr. ended 4/30/89): Assets, $3,946,294 (M); gifts received, $359,386; expenditures, $262,006, including $149,252 for 143 grants (high: $26,000; low: $10).

Purpose and activities: Giving primarily for Jewish organizations, including welfare funds, schools, and temple support; giving also for higher and secondary education.
Limitations: No grants to individuals.
Application information:
Initial approach: Letter
Deadline(s): None
Write: Max Alperin, Trustee
Trustees: Barry Alperin, Max Alperin, Melvin G. Alperin, Ruth Alperin, David Hirsch.
Employer Identification Number: 056008387

6522
Armbrust Foundation ⌑
735 Allens Ave.
Providence 02905

Trust established about 1951 in RI.
Donor(s): Armbrust Chain Co.
Foundation type: Company-sponsored
Financial data (yr. ended 12/31/88): Assets, $1,468,442 (M); gifts received, $40,581; expenditures, $87,893, including $82,876 for 52 grants (high: $14,000; low: $50).
Purpose and activities: Emphasis on a community fund, Protestant church support, and hospitals and health services; support also for education, and cultural and environmental programs.
Limitations: Giving primarily in RI. No grants to individuals.
Application information: Contributes only to pre-selected organizations. Applications not accepted.
Trustees: Adelaide P. Armbrust, Howard W. Armbrust.
Employer Identification Number: 056088332

6523
Paul O. & Mary Boghossian Memorial Trust ⌑ ☆
c/o The R.I. Hospital Trust National Bank
One Hospital Trust Plaza
Providence 02903

Established in 1974.
Foundation type: Independent
Financial data (yr. ended 4/30/89): Assets, $1,233,296 (M); expenditures, $84,023, including $42,250 for 33 grants (high: $10,000; low: $250; average: $500-$1,000) and $31,000 for 25 grants to individuals (high: $2,500; low: $500).
Purpose and activities: Giving primarily for higher education, especially through scholarships; support also for youth.
Types of support: Student aid.
Limitations: Giving primarily in RI.
Application information: Application form required for scholarships.
Initial approach: Proposal
Deadline(s): None
Trustees: David Boghossian, Paul O. Boghossian, The Rhode Island Hospital Trust National Bank.
Scholarship Committee Managers: John Boyce, Peter Koughassian, Ted Lowe.
Employer Identification Number: 056051815

6524
Bristol Home for Aged Women ⌑
20 Harborview Ave.
Bristol 02809-1710 (401) 253-9260

Established in 1873 in RI.
Foundation type: Independent
Financial data (yr. ended 6/30/89): Assets, $1,014,866 (M); gifts received, $1,768; expenditures, $46,533, including $27,300 for 9 grants (high: $10,500; low: $500) and $9,300 for 8 grants to individuals (high: $4,900; low: $100).
Purpose and activities: Support primarily for needy, elderly women in both direct support and through service organizations.
Types of support: General purposes, grants to individuals.
Limitations: Giving primarily in Bristol County, RI.
Application information:
Initial approach: Letter
Deadline(s): June 1
Write: Mrs. Alfred E. Newton, Treas.
Officers: Mrs. Ralph Peters, Pres.; Mrs. Walter J. St. Germain, V.P.; Mrs. John B. McGregor, Secy.; Mrs. Alfred E. Newton, Treas.
Employer Identification Number: 050262707

6525
Chace Fund, Inc. ⌑
731 Hospital Trust Bldg.
Providence 02903

Established in 1947 in RI.
Donor(s): Malcolm G. Chace III, Arnold B. Chace.
Foundation type: Independent
Financial data (yr. ended 12/31/88): Assets, $624,056 (M); gifts received, $170,030; expenditures, $195,054, including $183,290 for 73 grants (high: $15,000; low: $50).
Purpose and activities: Support primarily for community organizations; support also for education, social services, hospitals, and the arts.
Types of support: General purposes.
Limitations: Giving primarily in NY, RI, and MA. No grants to individuals.
Application information:
Initial approach: Letter
Deadline(s): None
Write: Malcolm G. Chace, III, Pres.
Officers: Malcolm G. Chace III, Pres.; Arnold B. Chace, Jr., V.P.; Robert A. Casale, Secy.-Treas.
Employer Identification Number: 056008849

6526
Mary Dexter Chafee Fund
c/o The R.I. Hospital Trust National Bank
One Hospital Trust Plaza, MS 450111
Providence 02903 (401) 278-7816

Established in 1933 in RI.
Foundation type: Independent
Financial data (yr. ended 06/30/87): Assets, $1,393,904 (M); expenditures, $119,010, including $94,500 for 20 grants (high: $20,000; low: $500).
Purpose and activities: Giving primarily for social services, education, cultural organizations, conservation, and historic preservation.
Limitations: Giving primarily in RI. No grants to individuals.
Application information: Application form not required.
Initial approach: Proposal
Deadline(s): None
Write: Kelly E. Cummings, Acct. Mgr., The Rhode Island Hospital Trust National Bank
Officers: Dorothy C. Scott, Pres.; Richard S. Chafee, Secy.; William G. Chafee, Treas.
Agent: The Rhode Island Hospital Trust National Bank.
Employer Identification Number: 056006295

6527
The Champlin Foundations ▼
P.O. Box 637
Providence 02901-0637 (401) 421-3719

Trusts established in 1932, 1947, and 1975 in DE.
Donor(s): George S. Champlin,† Florence C. Hamilton,† Hope C. Neaves.
Foundation type: Independent
Financial data (yr. ended 12/31/89): Assets, $243,569,771 (M); gifts received, $100,000; expenditures, $14,378,583, including $12,677,323 for 155 grants (high: $2,000,000; low: $720; average: $15-$50,000).
Purpose and activities: Support for conservation; higher, secondary, and other education, including libraries; health and hospitals; cultural activities, including historic preservation; scientific activities; and social and family sevices, including programs for youth and the elderly.
Types of support: Building funds, equipment, land acquisition, renovation projects, scholarship funds, capital campaigns.
Limitations: Giving primarily in RI. No grants to individuals, or for general support, program or operating budgets, matching gifts, special projects, research, publications, conferences, or continuing support; no loans.
Publications: Program policy statement, application guidelines, annual report, grants list.
Application information: Application form not required.
Initial approach: 1-page letter
Copies of proposal: 1
Deadline(s): Submit proposal preferably between Apr. 1 and Aug. 31; deadline Aug. 31
Board meeting date(s): Nov.
Final notification: After Nov. meeting; 1 month for rejections
Write: David A. King, Exec. Dir.
Distribution Committee: David A. King, Exec. Dir.; Francis C. Carter, John Gorham, Louis R. Hampton, Earl W. Harrington, Jr., Robert W. Kenyon, Norma B. LaFreniere, John W. Linnell.
Trustee: Bank of Delaware.
Number of staff: 1 full-time professional; 2 part-time professional; 1 full-time support.
Employer Identification Number: 516010168

6528
Citizens Charitable Foundation
c/o Citizens Bank
One Citizens Plaza
Providence 02903 (401) 456-7285

Established in 1967 in RI.

Donor(s): Citizens Savings Bank, Citizens Trust Co.
Foundation type: Company-sponsored
Financial data (yr. ended 12/31/88): Assets, $923,738 (M); gifts received, $325,000; expenditures, $390,944, including $380,200 for 53 grants (high: $160,000; low: $500; average: $2,500).
Purpose and activities: Giving primarily for the environment, community and urban development, and urban affairs.
Types of support: Building funds, equipment, land acquisition, special projects, technical assistance, employee-related scholarships.
Limitations: Giving limited to RI. No support for United Way member agencies except for capital funds. No grants to individuals, or for endowment funds, general support, research programs, or matching gifts; no loans.
Publications: Annual report (including application guidelines).
Application information: Application form not required.
Initial approach: Letter
Copies of proposal: 6
Deadline(s): Submit proposal preferably in June; no set deadline
Board meeting date(s): Mar., June, Sept., and Dec.
Final notification: 3 to 6 months
Write: D. Faye Sanders, Chair.
Trustees: D. Faye Sanders, Chair.; George Anter, Ann Langlois, George Oliveira.
Number of staff: None.
Employer Identification Number: 056022653

6529
John Clarke Trust ⌑ ☆
c/o The R.I. Hospital Trust National Bank
One Hospital Trust Plaza
Providence 02903
Application address: The R.I. Hospital Trust National Bank, P.O. Box 600, Newport, RI 02840; Tel.: (401) 847-2280

Foundation type: Independent
Financial data (yr. ended 12/31/88): Assets, $2,300,992 (M); expenditures, $155,989, including $98,391 for 29 grants (high: $7,500; low: $500) and $24,350 for 19 grants to individuals (high: $2,500; low: $500).
Purpose and activities: Support primarily for youth through welfare services, student aid, and scholarship funds for higher education.
Types of support: Scholarship funds, student aid.
Application information: Application form required.
Deadline(s): None
Trustees: William G. Corcoran, Wilbur Nelson, Jr., The Rhode Island Hospital Trust National Bank.
Employer Identification Number: 056006062

6530
The Cranston Foundation ⌑
c/o Leo G. Hutchings, Trustee
1381 Cranston St.
Cranston 02920 (401) 943-4800

Trust established in 1960 in RI.
Donor(s): Cranston Print Works Co.
Foundation type: Company-sponsored
Financial data (yr. ended 6/30/87): Assets, $826,466 (M); gifts received, $414,492; expenditures, $261,918, including $184,300 for 138 grants (high: $15,000; low: $50), $61,819 for 35 grants to individuals (high: $6,000; low: $35) and $13,375 for employee matching gifts.
Purpose and activities: Grants largely for higher education, including a scholarship program for children of Cranston Corporation employees. Support also for community funds, hospitals, and cultural programs.
Types of support: Employee-related scholarships, operating budgets, scholarship funds, employee matching gifts.
Limitations: Giving primarily in RI and MA.
Application information: Application form not required.
Initial approach: Proposal
Deadline(s): Apr. 15
Board meeting date(s): At least quarterly
Trustees: Leo G. Hutchings, Frederic L. Rockefeller, Richard Schein, George W. Shuster.
Employer Identification Number: 056015348

6531
Robert B. Cranston/Theophilus T. Pitman Fund ⌑ ☆
18 Market Sq.
Newport 02840 (401) 847-4260

Foundation type: Independent
Financial data (yr. ended 06/30/89): Assets, $1,210,648 (M); expenditures, $69,820, including $51,827 for grants and $6,856 for grants to individuals.
Purpose and activities: Support for the aged, the temporarily indigent, indigent individuals, and organizations which assist them.
Limitations: Giving limited to Newport County, RI.
Application information: Application form not required.
Initial approach: Personal appearance or reference from local welfare agencies
Deadline(s): None
Write: Rev. D.C. Hambly, Jr., Admin.
Trustees: Allen S. Harlow, Vernon A. Harvey, Wilbur Nelson.
Employer Identification Number: 056008897

6532
Norman & Rosalie Fain Fund Trust ⌑
505 Central Ave.
Pawtucket 02861 (401) 725-8028

Established in 1964 in RI.
Foundation type: Independent
Financial data (yr. ended 12/31/87): Assets, $1,184,594 (M); expenditures, $102,212, including $96,595 for 26 grants (high: $25,000; low: $100).
Purpose and activities: Support primarily for Planned Parenthood; support also for Jewish welfare and the arts.
Limitations: Giving primarily in RI.
Application information:
Initial approach: Letter
Deadline(s): None
Write: Norman M. Fain
Trustees: Norman M. Fain, Rosalie B. Fain.
Employer Identification Number: 056022655

6533
Fleet Charitable Trust ▼
c/o Fleet National Bank
111 Westminster St.
Providence 02903 (401) 278-6325

Trust established in 1955 in RI.
Donor(s): Fleet National Bank.
Foundation type: Company-sponsored
Financial data (yr. ended 12/31/89): Assets, $31,085,023 (M); expenditures, $1,834,851, including $1,595,138 for 114 grants (high: $525,000; low: $100; average: $2,100-$5,000), $14,000 for 14 grants to individuals of $1,000 each and $41,223 for employee matching gifts.
Purpose and activities: Giving primarily for capital purposes of major charities, including United Way, health, higher education, including an employee matching gift program, hospitals, arts, and museums. Support also for work/study scholarships paid to colleges on behalf of RI high school seniors from minority groups.
Types of support: Annual campaigns, emergency funds, building funds, equipment, employee matching gifts, capital campaigns, matching funds.
Limitations: Giving limited to RI-based nonprofit organizations. No grants for endowment or operating funds; no loans.
Publications: Application guidelines, program policy statement.
Application information: Scholarship candidates must be nominated by high school guidance counselor and submit a letter stating needs. Application form not required.
Initial approach: Proposal
Copies of proposal: 1
Deadline(s): None
Board meeting date(s): Quarterly
Final notification: 2 months after board meeting
Write: Ms. Sheila Devin McDonald, Secy.
Trustee: Fleet National Bank.
Number of staff: None.
Employer Identification Number: 056007619

6534
The Edward E. Ford Foundation ▼
297 Wickenden St.
Providence 02903 (401) 751-2966

Trust established in 1957 in NY.
Donor(s): Edward E. Ford.†
Foundation type: Independent
Financial data (yr. ended 09/30/89): Assets, $47,078,816 (M); qualifying distributions, $2,208,290, including $2,208,290 for 64 grants (high: $35,000; low: $20,000).
Purpose and activities: Primary interest in independent secondary education. Independent secondary schools must hold full and active membership in National Association of Independent Schools to be eligible for consideration.
Types of support: Annual campaigns, seed money, building funds, equipment, land acquisition, endowment funds, matching funds, scholarship funds, special projects, research, publications, renovation projects.
Limitations: Giving limited to the U.S. and its protectorates. No support for elementary or college-level schools, or to organizations that

have been applicants within the last three years. No grants to individuals, or for emergency funds or deficit financing.
Publications: Annual report (including application guidelines).
Application information: Application form required.
Initial approach: Letter or telephone
Copies of proposal: 12
Deadline(s): Submit proposal during months prior to stated deadlines: Feb. 1, Apr. 1, and Sept. 15
Board meeting date(s): Apr., June, and Nov.
Final notification: 6 weeks for formal reply; informal reply sooner
Write: Philip V. Havens, Exec. Dir.
Officer: Philip V. Havens, Exec. Dir.
Advisory Board: Lawrence L. Hlavacek, Chair.; H. Ward Reighley, Vice-Chair.; Gillian Attfield, Gillian R. Brooks, Frank H. Detweiler, Julia F. Menard, Lyman W. Menard.
Trustee: Manufacturers Hanover Trust Co.
Number of staff: 1 full-time professional; 1 full-time support.
Employer Identification Number: 136047243

6535
Ira S. and Anna Galkin Charitable Trust ☐
c/o Midwood, Northrup & Assoc.
27 Dryden Ln.
Providence 02904 (401) 331-6851

Trust established in 1947 in RI.
Donor(s): Ira S. Galkin.
Foundation type: Independent
Financial data (yr. ended 12/31/86): Assets, $2,801,036 (M); expenditures, $147,675, including $115,903 for 88 grants (high: $25,000; low: $10).
Purpose and activities: Emphasis on hospitals and health services, social service and youth agencies, Jewish welfare and community funds, temple support, and education, including medical education.
Limitations: Giving primarily in RI.
Application information:
Initial approach: Proposal
Deadline(s): None
Write: Arnold T. Galkin, Trustee
Trustees: Anna Galkin, Arnold T. Galkin.
Employer Identification Number: 056006231

6536
Genesis Foundation ☐
173 Waterman St.
Providence 02906 (401) 861-4323

Established in 1981 in RI.
Donor(s): Solon Foundation.
Foundation type: Independent
Financial data (yr. ended 12/31/88): Assets, $155,447 (L); gifts received, $1,016,732; expenditures, $1,700,243, including $1,519,375 for 75 grants (high: $100,000; low: $500; average: $10,000).
Purpose and activities: Emphasis on pre-school, primary, secondary, and adult basic educational needs in rural areas of southern Africa through financial assistance to schools and other educational resources; some support for adult basic educational needs of selected refugee populations in cases where government support is not available.
Types of support: Scholarship funds, special projects, seed money, equipment, matching funds, consulting services, technical assistance.
Limitations: Giving limited to rural areas of Botswana, Lesotho, South Africa, Swaziland, Zimbabwe, and for Southeast Asian refugees in RI. No support for non-educational programs, education in urban areas, or sectarian education. No grants to individuals, or for operating budgets, continuing support, annual campaigns, emergency funds, deficit financing, land acquisition, renovation projects, endowments, research, publications, workshops, or conferences and seminars; no loans.
Publications: Informational brochure (including application guidelines), grants list.
Application information: Application form not required.
Initial approach: Letter or telephone
Copies of proposal: 1
Deadline(s): None
Board meeting date(s): Annually
Final notification: 4 months
Write: John K. Harwood, Pres.
Officer and Directors: John K. Harwood, Pres. and Secy.-Treas.; Charlynn Wright Goins, John W. Mattern.
Number of staff: 1 full-time professional; 1 full-time support.
Employer Identification Number: 050391649

6537
The Thomas & William Gilbane Foundation ☐
Seven Jackson Walkway
Providence 02940

Established in 1954 in RI.
Foundation type: Independent
Financial data (yr. ended 11/30/88): Assets, $1,704,642 (M); expenditures, $98,339, including $85,146 for 3 grants (high: $83,896; low: $250).
Purpose and activities: Giving primarily to a university; support also for religious organizations.
Limitations: Giving primarily in RI.
Application information: Contributes only to pre-selected organizations. Applications not accepted.
Trustees: Jean A. Gilbane, William J. Gilbane.
Employer Identification Number: 056006170

6538
Haffenreffer Family Fund
400 Massasoit Ave., Suite 105
East Providence 02914

Trust established in 1943 in RI.
Donor(s): Members of the Haffenreffer family.
Foundation type: Independent
Financial data (yr. ended 12/31/88): Assets, $4,868,726 (M); expenditures, $269,033, including $227,250 for 92 grants (high: $40,000; low: $100).
Purpose and activities: Giving only to charities that are actively supported by members of the family.
Limitations: Giving primarily in RI.
Application information: Contributes only to pre-selected organizations. Applications not accepted.
Trustees: Melvin G. Alperin, Patricia H. Blackall, Paul J. Choquette, Jr., Robert H.I. Goddard, Carl W. Haffenreffer, David H. Haffenreffer, Rudolph F. Haffenreffer III, Rudolf F. Haffenreffer IV, William H. Heisler III.
Employer Identification Number: 056012787

6539
Hasbro Industries Charitable Trust, Inc.
c/o Hasbro, Inc.
1027 Newport Ave.
Pawtucket 02861 (401) 727-5429

Donor(s): Hasbro, Inc.
Foundation type: Company-sponsored
Financial data (yr. ended 12/28/88): Assets, $2,700,004 (M); gifts received, $1,250,000; expenditures, $515,156, including $513,145 for 68 grants (high: $118,000; low: $125; average: $500-$5,000).
Purpose and activities: Support for education, including early childhood education, health, and social services, including family services and youth organizations.
Types of support: Capital campaigns, program-related investments.
Limitations: Giving primarily in RI, and areas of major company operations. No grants for scholarships, endowments, or fundraising events.
Publications: Application guidelines.
Application information: Application form not required.
Initial approach: Letter
Copies of proposal: 1
Deadline(s): July 1
Board meeting date(s): Throughout spring and summer
Write: Mary Louise Fazzano
Officers: Alan G. Hassenfeld, Pres.; Alfred Verrecchia, C.F.O.
Number of staff: 1 full-time professional; 1 full-time support.
Employer Identification Number: 222538470

6540
The Hassenfeld Foundation ☐
1027 Newport Ave.
Pawtucket 02861 (401) 726-4100
Additional address: 32 West 23rd St., New York, NY 10010

Established in 1944 in RI.
Donor(s): Hasbro, Inc., and members of the Hassenfeld family.
Foundation type: Independent
Financial data (yr. ended 12/31/88): Assets, $2,207,715 (M); gifts received, $340,394; expenditures, $564,030, including $561,502 for 16 grants (high: $232,952; low: $50).
Purpose and activities: Giving primarily for Jewish welfare funds; grants also for higher education, including religious education.
Limitations: No grants to individuals.
Application information: Contributes only to pre-selected organizations. Applications not accepted.

Officers: Sylvia Hassenfeld,* Pres.; Alan G. Hassenfeld, V.P.
Directors:* Joan Engle, Leon S. Mann, Frank Supnick.
Employer Identification Number: 056015373

6541
Mary E. Hodges Fund
2115 Broad St.
Cranston 02905 (401) 467-2970

Foundation type: Independent
Financial data (yr. ended 10/31/89): Assets, $2,779,949 (M); expenditures, $159,873, including $107,461 for 31 grants (high: $15,000; low: $50) and $24,000 for grants to individuals (high: $600; low: $100).
Purpose and activities: Grants primarily for education, hospitals, and health and social services. Student aid for individuals who have a Masonic affiliation or who have been residents of RI for 5 years or more.
Types of support: Student aid.
Limitations: Giving limited to RI.
Application information:
Deadline(s): June 1
Write: Julio A. Paniccia, Secy.
Officers: Herbert H. McGuire, Pres.; Julio A. Paniccia, Secy.; Norman P. Jehan, Treas.
Employer Identification Number: 056049444

6542
The Jaffe Foundation ⌑
222 Richmond St., Suite 208
Providence 02903 (401) 421-2920

Established in 1962 in MA.
Donor(s): Meyer Jaffe,† Edwin A. Jaffe.
Foundation type: Independent
Financial data (yr. ended 06/30/89): Assets, $5,249,180 (M); expenditures, $379,060, including $345,718 for 82 grants (high: $40,000; low: $50; average: $2,000).
Purpose and activities: Giving primarily for Jewish organizations and higher education.
Limitations: Giving primarily in MA. No grants to individuals.
Application information: Contributes only to pre-selected organizations. Applications not accepted.
Board meeting date(s): Jan. and July
Write: Edwin A. Jaffe, Chair.
Officers and Trustees:* Edwin A. Jaffe,* Chair.; Lola Jaffe,* Vice-Chair.; David S. Greer, Donna Jaffe, Robert Jaffe.
Employer Identification Number: 046049261

6543
Phyllis Kimball Johnstone and H. Earle Kimball Foundation ⌑
c/o The R.I. Hospital Trust National Bank
One Hospital Trust Plaza
Providence 02903 (401) 278-8700

Established in 1957 in DE.
Donor(s): Phyllis Kimball Johnstone.†
Foundation type: Independent
Financial data (yr. ended 11/30/89): Assets, $2,900,905 (M); gifts received, $1,234; expenditures, $244,538, including $198,850 for 41 grants (high: $25,000; low: $500).
Purpose and activities: Emphasis on hospitals, social service and youth agencies, and a community fund.
Limitations: Giving primarily in RI.
Application information:
Initial approach: Proposal
Deadline(s): None
Trustees: John R. Fales, Jr., Gordon A. Feiner, Avery Seaman, Jr.
Employer Identification Number: 056015723

6544
Horace A. Kimball and S. Ella Kimball Foundation
c/o The R.I. Hospital Trust National Bank
One Hospital Trust Plaza
Providence 02903 (401) 364-3565
Additional address: P.O. Box 1068, Hope Valley, RI 02832

Incorporated in 1956 in DE.
Donor(s): H. Earle Kimball.†
Foundation type: Independent
Financial data (yr. ended 09/30/89): Assets, $3,866,425 (M); expenditures, $230,987, including $196,100 for 25 grants (high: $35,000; low: $500).
Purpose and activities: Emphasis on health services, secondary education, community funds, youth agencies, programs for the elderly, the disadvantaged, the homeless, and cultural programs; support also for volunteer fire and ambulance corps.
Types of support: Emergency funds, general purposes, matching funds, seed money.
Limitations: Giving limited to RI. No grants to individuals.
Publications: 990-PF.
Application information: Application form required.
Copies of proposal: 3
Deadline(s): None
Board meeting date(s): Varies
Write: Thomas F. Black III, Pres.
Officers and Trustees:* Thomas F. Black III,* Pres.; T. Dexter Clarke,* Secy.-Treas.; Norman D. Baker, Jr.
Number of staff: 1 part-time support.
Employer Identification Number: 056006130

6545
The Koffler Family Foundation ⌑
c/o The Koffler Corp.
170 Westminster St., Suite 300
Providence 02903

Established in 1978 in RI.
Donor(s): The Koffler Corp.
Foundation type: Independent
Financial data (yr. ended 7/31/88): Assets, $4,519,469 (M); expenditures, $248,553, including $214,434 for 127 grants (high: $65,009; low: $5).
Purpose and activities: Giving primarily to Jewish welfare funds and religious organizations, and higher education.
Limitations: Giving primarily in RI.
Application information: Contributes only to pre-selected organizations. Applications not accepted.
Trustees: Richard S. Bornstein, Leonard Granoff, Lillian Koffler, Sol Koffler.
Employer Identification Number: 050376269

6546
Little Family Foundation ▼
c/o The R.I. Hospital Trust National Bank
P.O. Box 1597
Providence 02901-1597 (401) 278-8752

Trust established in 1946 in RI.
Donor(s): Royal Little.†
Foundation type: Independent
Financial data (yr. ended 12/31/88): Assets, $12,746,724 (M); expenditures, $1,238,918, including $1,100,000 for 150 grants (high: $250,000; low: $1,000; average: $5,000).
Purpose and activities: Support for scholarship funds at designated business schools; Rhode Island Junior Achievement for programs in secondary schools; and various charities in New England, including youth agencies, cultural programs, and hospitals.
Types of support: Operating budgets, continuing support, annual campaigns, emergency funds, building funds, equipment, endowment funds, matching funds, scholarship funds.
Limitations: No grants to individuals, or for seed money, deficit financing, or land acquisition; no loans.
Publications: Application guidelines.
Application information: For scholarships, application is by letter to designated business school; deadline Sept. 1. Application form not required.
Initial approach: Letter
Copies of proposal: 1
Deadline(s): None
Board meeting date(s): Quarterly
Write: Shawn P. Buckless, Trust Off., The Rhode Island Hospital Trust National Bank
Trustees: Augusta Willoughby Little Bishop, E. Janice Leeming, Arthur D. Little, Cameron R. Little, The Rhode Island Hospital Trust National Bank.
Number of staff: None.
Employer Identification Number: 056016740

6547
Joseph W. Martin Trust ☆
781 Main St.
Warren 02885-4320 (401) 245-7480

Foundation type: Independent
Financial data (yr. ended 05/31/89): Assets, $1,627,583 (M); expenditures, $70,140, including $40,600 for 4 grants (high: $18,000; low: $4,000).
Purpose and activities: Support for health services, including a nursing association and a mental health center.
Limitations: Giving limited to Warren, RI.
Application information:
Initial approach: Proposal
Final notification: July
Write: S. George McVey, Trustee
Trustees: Douglas M. Domina, Judith A. Gomes, S. George McVey.
Employer Identification Number: 056011809

6548
Mustard Seed Foundation, Inc. ⌑ ☆
2700 Hospital Trust Tower
Providence 02903 (401) 274-9200

Established in 1984 in RI.
Donor(s): Russell Family Charitable Lead trust.

Foundation type: Independent
Financial data (yr. ended 11/30/88): Assets, $6,484 (M); gifts received, $147,834; expenditures, $151,456, including $134,791 for 18 grants (high: $20,000; low: $250) and $8,181 for 2 grants to individuals (high: $8,000; low: $181).
Purpose and activities: Giving for higher education, environmental concerns, and Episcopal churches.
Limitations: Giving primarily in RI and MA.
Application information:
Write: Philip Barr, Esq.
Officers: Rev. Thomas L. Crum,* Pres.; Philip B. Brock, Jr., Secy.; Benjamin G. Paster,* Treas.
Trustees:* Carol L. Russell, Robert J. Russell.
Employer Identification Number: 222714666

6549
Nortek Foundation ⌑
50 Kennedy Plaza
Providence 02903-2360

Established in 1974 in CA.
Donor(s): Nortek, Inc.
Foundation type: Company-sponsored
Financial data (yr. ended 12/31/87): Assets, $1,615,841 (M); gifts received, $86,097; expenditures, $95,495, including $59,065 for 56 grants (high: $7,500; low: $20).
Purpose and activities: Support primarily for higher education, arts and culture, health associations, and various civic organizations.
Limitations: Giving primarily in Providence, RI. No grants to individuals.
Application information: Contributes only to pre-selected organizations. Applications not accepted.
Officers and Directors: Ralph R. Papitto, Chair.; Richard L. Bready, Vice-Chair.; John R. Potter, Secy.; Richard J. Harris, Treas.
Employer Identification Number: 237376137

6550
Old Stone Bank Charitable Foundation
150 South Main St.
Providence 02903 (401) 278-2213

Established in 1969 in RI.
Donor(s): Old Stone Bank.
Foundation type: Company-sponsored
Financial data (yr. ended 12/31/89): Assets, $329,452 (M); gifts received, $300,000; expenditures, $392,260, including $378,883 for 39 grants (high: $185,000; low: $1,000) and $13,377 for 105 employee matching gifts.
Purpose and activities: Giving primarily for community funds, education, cultural activities, social services, health, and civic improvement.
Types of support: Seed money, building funds, land acquisition, program-related investments, employee matching gifts, special projects, capital campaigns, matching funds, renovation projects.
Limitations: Giving limited to RI. No support for member agencies of United Way or other united appeals, or religious or political organizations. No grants to individuals, or for endowment funds, scholarships, fellowships, publications, conferences, or general operating support; no loans.
Publications: Annual report (including application guidelines), financial statement, grants list, program policy statement, informational brochure (including application guidelines), application guidelines.
Application information: Application form not required.
Initial approach: Letter or telephone
Copies of proposal: 1
Deadline(s): 1st day of month when board meets
Board meeting date(s): Bimonthly beginning in Jan.
Final notification: 4 to 6 weeks
Write: Kay H. Low, Coord.
Distribution Committee: Robert A. Riesman, Chair.; Kay H. Low, Coord.; Theodore W. Barnes, Bernard V. Buonanno, Thomas P. Dimeo, Beverly Ledbetter, Winfield W. Major, Thomas F. Schutte, Richmond Viall, Jr.
Number of staff: 1 part-time professional.
Employer Identification Number: 237029175

6551
Providence Journal Charitable Foundation ⌑
75 Fountain St.
Providence 02902 (401) 277-7286

Trust established in 1956 in RI.
Donor(s): Providence Journal Co.
Foundation type: Company-sponsored
Financial data (yr. ended 12/31/88): Assets, $2,195,100 (M); gifts received, $6,890; expenditures, $590,487, including $584,734 for 64 grants (high: $162,500; low: $1,000).
Purpose and activities: Emphasis on higher education and a community fund; support also for youth agencies, cultural programs, and hospitals.
Types of support: Capital campaigns, operating budgets.
Limitations: Giving primarily in RI. No grants to individuals.
Application information:
Initial approach: Letter or proposal
Copies of proposal: 1
Deadline(s): None
Board meeting date(s): Monthly
Write: Harry Dyson, Trustee
Trustees: Benjamin L. Cook, Jr., Harry Dyson, Stephen Hamblett, Paul C. Nicholson, Jr., John C.A. Watkins.
Employer Identification Number: 056015372

6552
The Samuel Rapaporte, Jr. Foundation ⌑
c/o Rieka Rapaporte
395 Rochambeau Ave.
Providence 02906

Trust established in 1946 in RI.
Donor(s): Samuel Rapaporte, Jr.
Foundation type: Independent
Financial data (yr. ended 11/30/89): Assets, $2,063,220 (M); expenditures, $85,924, including $85,742 for 48 grants (high: $42,000; low: $25).
Purpose and activities: Giving for social services, higher and other education, and health, with emphasis on Jewish organizations.
Limitations: Giving primarily in RI.
Application information: Contributes only to pre-selected organizations. Applications not accepted.
Trustees: Renee Burrows, Rieka Rapaporte.
Employer Identification Number: 056006254

6553
Ress Family Foundation ⌑
c/o Joseph W. Ress, Trustee
P.O. Box 6485
Providence 02940-6485

Trust established in 1955 in RI.
Donor(s): Joseph W. Ress, Anne Ress.
Foundation type: Independent
Financial data (yr. ended 12/31/88): Assets, $1,538,090 (M); expenditures, $162,858, including $145,851 for 92 grants (high: $53,000; low: $15).
Purpose and activities: Giving for Jewish welfare funds and temple support, and higher education.
Limitations: Giving primarily in RI. No grants to individuals.
Application information: Contributes only to pre-selected organizations. Applications not accepted.
Officer: Joseph W. Ress, Mgr.
Trustees: Ellen Reeves, Joan Reeves.
Employer Identification Number: 056006308

6554
The Rhode Island Foundation/The Rhode Island Community Foundation
957 North Main St.
Providence 02904 (401) 274-4564

Incorporated in 1916 in RI (includes The Rhode Island Community Foundation).
Foundation type: Community
Financial data (yr. ended 12/31/89): Assets, $75,000,000 (M); gifts received, $3,543,618; expenditures, $3,755,872, including $3,389,921 for grants and $31,600 for 8 grants to individuals (high: $10,000; low: $2,000).
Purpose and activities: To promote educational and charitable activities which will tend to improve the living conditions and well-being of the inhabitants of RI; grants for capital and operating purposes principally to agencies working in the fields of education, health care, the arts and cultural affairs, youth, the aged, social services, urban affairs, historic preservation, and the environment. Some restricted grants for scholarships and medical research.
Types of support: Fellowships, operating budgets, seed money, emergency funds, building funds, equipment, land acquisition, matching funds, consulting services, technical assistance, special projects, scholarship funds, research, publications, conferences and seminars, renovation projects, capital campaigns, general purposes.
Limitations: Giving limited to RI. No support for sectarian purposes, or medical research (except as specified by donors). No grants to individuals, or for endowment funds, annual campaigns, or deficit financing; no loans.
Publications: Annual report, program policy statement, application guidelines, newsletter, informational brochure.

Application information: Priority given to first 25 applications received prior to each board meeting. Application form not required.
Initial approach: Telephone, meeting, or letter
Copies of proposal: 5
Deadline(s): None
Board meeting date(s): Jan., Mar., May, July, Sept., and Nov.
Final notification: 3 to 6 months
Write: Douglas M. Jansson, Exec. Dir.
Officer: Douglas M. Jansson, Secy. and Exec. Dir.
Distribution Committee and Board of Directors: Robert H.I. Goddard, Chair.; Melvin Alperin, Patricia H. Blackall, Paul J. Choquette, B. Jae Clanton, William H. Heisler, Edward Maggiacomo.
Trustees: Citizens Bank, Fleet National Bank, Old Stone Trust Co., The Rhode Island Hospital Trust National Bank, Van Liew Trust, The Washington Trust Co.
Number of staff: 2 full-time professional; 2 part-time professional; 2 full-time support; 1 part-time support.
Employer Identification Number: 050208270

6555
Fred M. Roddy Foundation, Inc. ⌑
c/o The R.I. Hospital Trust National Bank
One Hospital Trust Plaza
Providence 02903 (401) 278-8700

Trust established in 1969.
Donor(s): Fred M. Roddy.†
Foundation type: Independent
Financial data (yr. ended 12/31/86): Assets, $7,832,170 (M); expenditures, $497,923, including $440,000 for 20 grants (high: $130,000; low: $3,000; average: $5,000-$15,000).
Purpose and activities: Grants for higher education and medical research; support also for hospitals.
Limitations: Giving primarily in RI and MA.
Application information:
Initial approach: Letter
Deadline(s): None
Directors: Charles E. Gleadow, Jr., Lee Kintzel, John W. McIntyre.
Employer Identification Number: 056037528

6556
The Charles Salmanson Family Foundation ⌑ ☆
155 South Main St.
Providence 02903

Established in 1984 in RI.
Donor(s): Charles Salmanson.
Foundation type: Independent
Financial data (yr. ended 9/30/89): Assets, $1,239,978 (M); expenditures, $45,092, including $40,909 for 76 grants (high: $10,000; low: $20).
Purpose and activities: Giving primarily for Jewish welfare and temple support; limited giving for a community fund.
Application information: Applications not accepted.
Trustees: Charles Salmanson, Donald Salmanson.
Employer Identification Number: 222571909

6557
Donald Salmanson Foundation ⌑
155 South Main St.
Providence 02903-2963

Established in 1984 in RI.
Donor(s): Donald Salmanson.
Foundation type: Independent
Financial data (yr. ended 09/30/89): Assets, $1,258,691 (M); expenditures, $39,777, including $35,929 for 58 grants (high: $10,000; low: $10).
Purpose and activities: Support primarily for Jewish organizations, including welfare funds.
Limitations: Giving primarily in RI.
Application information: Applications not accepted.
Trustees: Charles Salmanson, Donald Salmanson.
Employer Identification Number: 222571911

6558
Edwin S. Soforenko Foundation ⌑ ☆
c/o Laventhol & Horworth
One Hospital Trust Plaza, 7th Fl.
Providence 02903

Established in 1967 in RI.
Donor(s): Edwin S. Soforenko.
Foundation type: Independent
Financial data (yr. ended 12/31/88): Assets, $1,324,702 (M); gifts received, $247,863; expenditures, $71,026, including $60,600 for 5 grants (high: $49,000; low: $500).
Purpose and activities: Support for Jewish organizations, including a welfare fund.
Limitations: No grants to individuals.
Application information:
Initial approach: Letter
Deadline(s): None
Final notification: 1 month
Write: Jerome L. Lafkowitz
Directors: Edwin S. Soforenko, Larry Soforenko.
Employer Identification Number: 056019803

6559
The Herbert E. & Daisy A. Stride Memorial Foundation
c/o Aquidneck Medical Assn.
Memorial Blvd.
Newport 02840-3699 (401) 847-2290

Established in 1959 in RI.
Foundation type: Independent
Financial data (yr. ended 12/31/89): Assets, $1,152,463 (M); qualifying distributions, $38,500, including $38,500 for 10 grants (high: $6,584; low: $500).
Purpose and activities: Giving primarily to education, with emphasis on health and higher education.
Types of support: Building funds, capital campaigns, conferences and seminars, equipment, lectureships, scholarship funds.
Limitations: Giving limited to RI. No grants to individuals.
Application information: Application form required.
Deadline(s): None
Board meeting date(s): Quarterly
Write: A.R.G. Wallace, M.D., Dir.
Directors: William D. Levin, C.P. Shoemaker, A.R.G. Wallace.
Number of staff: 1 part-time support.
Employer Identification Number: 237097640

6560
Frederick C. Tanner Memorial Fund, Inc. ⌑
c/o Citizens Trust Co.
870 Westminster St.
Providence 02907
Application address: c/o George Irvin Charles, Secy.-Treas., 340 Newman Ave., Rumford, RI 02916; Tel.: (401) 434-5118

Established in 1952 in RI.
Foundation type: Independent
Financial data (yr. ended 3/31/89): Assets, $1,207,530 (M); expenditures, $97,681, including $77,050 for 50 grants (high: $20,000; low: $50).
Purpose and activities: Emphasis on higher education; support also for hospitals and a community fund.
Limitations: Giving limited to RI.
Application information:
Initial approach: Letter
Deadline(s): None
Board meeting date(s): Quarterly
Officers and Directors: Frederick E. Bowerman, Pres.; Harold Melkonian, V.P.; William H. Metcalf, V.P.; George Irvin Charles, Secy.-Treas.; William H. Heisler III, DeWitte T. Kersh, Jr., H. Nord Kitchen, Johnathan R. Knowles, William F. Lunnie, Michael Shepard.
Employer Identification Number: 056011617

6561
The Textron Charitable Trust ▼
P.O. Box 878
Providence 02903 (401) 457-2430
Scholarship application addresses: Arthur Sussman, National Merit Scholarship Corp., One American Plaza, Evanston, IL 60201; Elaine Jacob, College Scholarship Service, P.O. Box CN6730, Princeton, NJ 08541

Trust established in 1953 in VT.
Donor(s): Textron, Inc.
Foundation type: Company-sponsored
Financial data (yr. ended 12/31/88): Assets, $14,232,841 (M); expenditures, $2,627,571, including $1,928,826 for 406 grants (high: $120,000; low: $100; average: $500-$50,000) and $672,969 for 910 employee matching gifts.
Purpose and activities: Giving primarily for community funds, higher education, including scholarship programs, and hospitals and health agencies; support also for youth clubs, urban programs, minorities, and cultural programs.
Types of support: Building funds, equipment, matching funds, employee matching gifts, technical assistance, employee-related scholarships, capital campaigns, general purposes, special projects.
Limitations: Giving primarily in areas of company operations nationwide. No grants to individuals, or for endowment funds, land acquisition, deficit financing, research, demonstration projects, or publications; no loans.
Publications: Application guidelines.
Application information: Application form not required.
Initial approach: Proposal
Copies of proposal: 1
Deadline(s): None
Board meeting date(s): Quarterly
Final notification: 8 weeks

Write: Elizabeth A. Wise, Contribs. Asst.
Contributions Committee: Raymond W. Caine, Jr., Chair.
Trustee: The Rhode Island Hospital Trust National Bank.
Number of staff: 1 full-time professional.
Employer Identification Number: 256115832

6562
Townsend Aid for the Aged ⌑
c/o Fleet National Bank
100 Westminster St.
Providence 02903

Established in 1882 in RI.
Foundation type: Independent
Financial data (yr. ended 4/30/89): Assets, $1,408,940 (M); expenditures, $89,479, including $74,700 for grants to individuals.
Purpose and activities: Provides aid to the needy elderly.
Types of support: Grants to individuals.
Application information: Foundation initiates application process. Applications not accepted.
Officers: Helen S. Tennant, Pres.; Carolyn Kaull, V.P.; Hilda N. Kaull, Secy.; Anna L. MacLaughlin, Treas.
Employer Identification Number: 056009549

6563
Richard Waterman Trust ⌑
One Old Stone Sq., Rm. 8DCW
Providence 02903
Application address: P.O. Box 55, Green, RI 02827; Tel.: (203) 376-2228

Established in 1847 in RI.
Foundation type: Independent
Financial data (yr. ended 12/31/88): Assets, $1,628,344 (M); expenditures, $81,773, including $38,300 for 2 grants (high: $21,300; low: $17,000) and $24,750 for 9 grants to individuals (high: $24,150; low: $75).
Purpose and activities: Support for Baptist churches, and also for individuals preaching the Calvinist Baptist doctrine within two miles of the late Richard Waterman's house in Greene, RI.
Types of support: Grants to individuals.
Limitations: Giving primarily in RI.
Application information: Application form not required.
Deadline(s): None
Write: Rev. Byron O. Waterman, Trustee
Officer and Trustees:* Wilma S. Waterman,* Principal Mgr.; Byron O. Waterman, Walter D. Waterman III.
Employer Identification Number: 056040728

6564
The Thomas J. Watson Foundation ▼
217 Angell St.
Providence 02906 (401) 274-1952

Trust established in 1961 in NY.
Donor(s): Jeannette K. Watson,† Arthur K. Watson,† Thomas J. Watson, Jr., Mrs. John N. Irwin II,† Helen W. Buckner.
Foundation type: Independent
Financial data (yr. ended 05/31/89): Assets, $47,770,561 (M); expenditures, $2,507,892, including $1,037,500 for 46 grants (high: $250,000; low: $1,000; average: $1,000-$250,000) and $1,000,328 for 75 grants to individuals (high: $18,000; low: $13,000; average: $13,000-$18,000).
Purpose and activities: Sponsors fellowship program for independent study and travel abroad through 55 colleges and universities; occasional other foundation-initiated grants.
Types of support: Fellowships, building funds, capital campaigns, continuing support, general purposes.
Publications: Informational brochure.
Application information: Applicant for fellowship must be nominated by our participating colleges and must be a graduating senior; other grants are initiated by the foundation. Application form required.
Deadline(s): 1st Tuesday in Nov.
Board meeting date(s): As required
Final notification: Approximately Mar. 17
Write: Steven V. Licata, Exec. Dir.
Officers: Steven V. Licata, Exec. Dir.; David McKinney,* Exec. Secy.
Advisory Committee:* Helen W. Buckner, Thomas J. Watson, Jr., Thomas J. Watson III.
Trustee: Morgan Guaranty Trust Co. of New York.
Number of staff: 2 full-time professional.
Employer Identification Number: 136038151

6565
The Winter Family Foundation ⌑ ☆
c/o Sansiveri, Ryan & Sullivan Co.
55 Dorrance St.
Providence 02903

Established in 1986.
Donor(s): V. Paul Winter.
Foundation type: Independent
Financial data (yr. ended 11/30/88): Assets, $1,279,528 (M); gifts received, $74,559; expenditures, $81,494, including $47,200 for grants.
Purpose and activities: General charitable activities.
Trustees: Edward Grogan, Lucy I. Sherman, Michael P. Winter, V. Paul Winter.
Employer Identification Number: 050426485

SOUTH CAROLINA

6566
The Abney Foundation ▼
P.O. Box 1138
Greenwood 29648-1138 (803) 229-5777

Trust established in 1957 in SC.
Donor(s): John S. Abney,† Susie M. Abney,† and others.
Foundation type: Independent
Financial data (yr. ended 12/31/89): Assets, $23,779,084 (M); expenditures, $1,165,708, including $1,061,230 for 28 grants (high: $400,000; low: $30; average: $5,000-$100,000).
Purpose and activities: Support primarily for higher education; some grants for social service and youth organizations.
Types of support: Annual campaigns, seed money, emergency funds, building funds, land acquisition, general purposes, endowment funds, research, scholarship funds, fellowships, professorships, internships, continuing support.
Limitations: Giving primarily in SC. No grants to individuals, or for matching gifts; no loans.
Application information: Application form not required.
Initial approach: Letter
Copies of proposal: 1
Deadline(s): Submit proposal preferably during the first half of the year; no set deadline
Board meeting date(s): Jan., Apr., July, and Oct.
Write: D. Wellsman Johnson, Vice-Chair.
Officers and Trustees:* J.R. Fulp, Jr.,* Chair.; D. Wellsman Johnson,* Vice-Chair.; William N. Bobo, John R. Fulp III, Labrena Spall Fulp, Carlette F. Holmes, Sally A. Rose.
Number of staff: 2
Employer Identification Number: 576019445

6567
The Aiken Foundation, Inc. ⌑
c/o Southern National Bank
P.O. Box 1351
Florence 29503

Incorporated in 1947 in SC.
Donor(s): Members of the Aiken family.
Foundation type: Independent
Financial data (yr. ended 12/31/88): Assets, $1,774,094 (M); expenditures, $129,353, including $111,000 for 9 grants (high: $50,000; low: $1,000).
Purpose and activities: Emphasis on higher education.
Limitations: Giving primarily in SC.
Officers: O.S. Aiken, Pres.; J.B. Aiken, Jr., V.P.; John D. Aiken, V.P.; P.S. Knox, Jr., V.P.; David H. McLeod, V.P.; O.S. Aiken, Jr., Secy.
Employer Identification Number: 576019769

6568
Saul Alexander Foundation ⌑ ☆
c/o C & National Bank of SC, Trust Dept.
P.O. Box 10608
Charleston 29402 (803) 745-8100

Established in 1957.
Foundation type: Independent
Financial data (yr. ended 12/31/87): Assets, $1,009,744 (M); expenditures, $88,159, including $72,650 for 27 grants (high: $19,000; low: $500).
Purpose and activities: Support primarily for Jewish organizations, including synagogues and social services; support also for cultural programs, including museums and the performing arts.
Limitations: Giving primarily in Charleston, SC.
Application information:
Initial approach: Proposal
Deadline(s): None
Write: Steven D. Bowen

Trustees: Gary C. Banks, Karl Keresh, Max Krawchek, Henry B. Smythe, Walter H. Solomon, Theodore S. Stern.
Employer Identification Number: 237420175

6569
The Arcadia Foundation ⌑
Mayfair Mills
Arcadia 29320

Foundation type: Independent
Financial data (yr. ended 12/31/87): Assets, $1,166,560 (M); gifts received, $47,000; expenditures, $74,248, including $50,947 for 32 grants (high: $8,333; low: $100).
Purpose and activities: Giving primarily for higher education.
Application information:
Initial approach: Letter
Deadline(s): July 31
Write: F.B. Dent, Pres.
Officers and Directors:* F.B. Dent,* Pres. and Treas.; L.O. Bragg, V.P. and Treas.; R.F. Bonsal,* V.P.; H.D. Towles, Secy.
Employer Identification Number: 570298275

6570
The Arkwright Foundation ⌑
P.O. Box 1086
Spartanburg 29301 (803) 585-9213

Incorporated in 1945 in SC.
Donor(s): Members of the M.L. Cates family, and members of the W.S. Montgomery family.
Foundation type: Independent
Financial data (yr. ended 12/31/88): Assets, $7,058,332 (M); expenditures, $308,423, including $268,518 for 100 grants (high: $45,000; low: $15).
Purpose and activities: Grants largely for a community fund, higher and secondary education, youth agencies, cultural programs, and Protestant church support.
Limitations: Giving primarily in SC.
Application information:
Initial approach: Letter, personal visit, or telephone
Deadline(s): None
Write: Joe W. Smith, Secy.-Treas.
Officers and Trustees:* MacFarlane L. Cates, Sr.,* Chair.; Walter S. Montgomery, Sr.,* Vice-Chair.; Joe W. Smith,* Secy.-Treas.; MacFarlane L. Cates, Jr., J.C. Kirkland, W.S. Montgomery, Jr.
Employer Identification Number: 576000066

6571
The Bailey Foundation
P.O. Box 1276
Clinton 29325 (803) 833-6830

Trust established in 1951 in SC.
Donor(s): M.S. Bailey & Son, Bankers, Clinton Investment Co., Clinton Mills.
Foundation type: Independent
Financial data (yr. ended 8/31/89): Assets, $4,053,300 (M); gifts received, $54,442; expenditures, $330,805, including $225,500 for 10 grants (high: $67,000; low: $1,000), $22,507 for 10 grants to individuals (high: $4,000; low: $1,000), $16,915 for 15 employee matching gifts and $48,735 for 25 loans to individuals.
Purpose and activities: Support primarily for higher education, including a student loan and scholarship program for children of employees of M.S. Bailey & Son, Bankers and others; support also for churches, community services, social services, libraries, museums, and child development.
Types of support: Employee-related scholarships, student loans, employee matching gifts, building funds, capital campaigns, endowment funds, matching funds, renovation projects.
Limitations: Giving primarily in Laurens County, SC, and in NC. No support for political organizations. No grants to individuals (except scholarships for students attending local high schools), or for operating expenses.
Application information: Applications for students available from guidance counselors at Clinton High School and Laurens High School.
Initial approach: For grants, write administrator
Deadline(s): For scholarships, Apr. 15 of applicant's senior year in high school
Board meeting date(s): Quarterly
Write: H. William Carter, Jr., Admin.
Trustee: M.S. Bailey & Son, Bankers.
Advisory Committee: Emily F. Bailey, George H. Cornelson, C. Bailey Dixon, Toccoa W. Switzer, Robert M. Vance, James Von Hollen.
Grants Advisory Committee: Joseph O. Nixon, Chair.; Clarice W. Johnson, W.E. Little, Virginia McMurray, Susan Polson, Donny Ross, Donny Wilder.
Number of staff: 1
Employer Identification Number: 576018387

6572
Baker & Baker Foundation, Inc. ☆
P.O. Box 12397
Columbia 29211-2397 (803) 254-8987

Foundation type: Company-sponsored
Financial data (yr. ended 12/31/89): Assets, $228,641 (M); gifts received, $75,000; expenditures, $101,174, including $101,125 for grants.
Purpose and activities: Giving for health associations, Jewish organizations, community development, government and law enforcement groups, and the fine arts; support for building funds of hospitals and educational institutions.
Types of support: Annual campaigns.
Publications: Annual report.
Application information: Contributes only to pre-selected organizations. Applications not accepted.
Officers: David Baker, Chair.; Lee Baker, V.P. and Secy.
Employer Identification Number: 570752311

6573
The Bannon Foundation ⌑ ☆
119 Manly St.
Greenville 29601
Application address: P.O. Box 91, Greenville, SC 29602

Foundation type: Independent
Financial data (yr. ended 12/31/88): Assets, $2,039,954 (M); gifts received, $1,965,363; expenditures, $34,877, including $23,000 for 9 grants (high: $11,000; low: $1,000).
Purpose and activities: Support for education, including higher education, and church support.
Limitations: Giving primarily in SC and TX.
Application information:
Initial approach: Letter
Deadline(s): None
Write: John M. Dillard, Trustee
Trustees: John M. Dillard, John R. Thomas.
Employer Identification Number: 570833931

6574
Belk-Simpson Foundation ⌑
P.O. Box 528
Greenville 29602

Trust established in 1944 in SC.
Donor(s): Belk-Simpson Co.
Foundation type: Company-sponsored
Financial data (yr. ended 12/31/87): Assets, $3,352,178 (M); gifts received, $42,282; expenditures, $146,431, including $123,900 for 91 grants (high: $7,500; low: $100).
Purpose and activities: Emphasis on Protestant church support; grants also to social service agencies.
Limitations: Giving primarily in SC. No grants to individuals.
Application information:
Initial approach: Letter
Copies of proposal: 1
Board meeting date(s): May and Nov.
Write: Willou R. Bichel, Trustee
Directors: Sarah Belk Gambrell, Lucy S. Kuhne, Nell M. Rice, Kate M. Simpson, Charles W. White.
Trustee: Willou R. Bichel.
Employer Identification Number: 576020261

6575
Lucy Hampton Bostick Charitable Trust ⌑
c/o H. Simmons Tate, Jr.
P.O. Box 11889
Columbia 29211

Established in 1968 in SC.
Foundation type: Independent
Financial data (yr. ended 7/31/88): Assets, $1,296,563 (M); expenditures, $99,284, including $79,800 for 7 grants (high: $25,000; low: $300).
Purpose and activities: Grants for cultural organizations and education.
Types of support: General purposes.
Limitations: Giving primarily in SC.
Application information: Contributes only to pre-selected organizations. Applications not accepted.
Trustees: A. Mason Gibbs, H. Simmons Tate, Jr., George R.P. Walker.
Employer Identification Number: 576042059

6576
W. W. Burgiss Charities, Inc. ⌑
P.O. Box 969
Greenville 29602 (803) 239-6841

Incorporated in 1952 in SC.
Donor(s): W.W. Burgiss.
Foundation type: Independent

Financial data (yr. ended 12/31/87): Assets, $1,491,198 (M); expenditures, $131,780, including $113,500 for 14 grants (high: $25,000; low: $1,229).
Purpose and activities: Support primarily for youth and social services, higher education, health concerns, and a science center.
Limitations: Giving primarily in SC, with emphasis on Greenville.
Application information:
Initial approach: Letter
Deadline(s): None
Trustee: South Carolina National Bank.
Employer Identification Number: 576020262

6577
James F. Byrnes Foundation ⌑
P.O. Box 9596
Columbia 29290 (803) 776-1211

Trust established in 1947 in SC.
Donor(s): James F. Byrnes,† and others.
Foundation type: Operating
Financial data (yr. ended 06/30/89): Assets, $1,914,760 (M); gifts received, $17,793; expenditures, $195,822, including $134,250 for 23 grants to individuals and $13,623 for 1 foundation-administered program.
Purpose and activities: A private operating foundation offering college scholarship assistance to orphans or part-orphans; also provides counseling and hosts a yearly retreat for grantees.
Types of support: Student aid.
Limitations: Giving limited to residents of SC.
Publications: Application guidelines.
Application information: Application form required.
Initial approach: Letter or telephone
Copies of proposal: 1
Deadline(s): Submit application preferably in Jan. or Feb.; deadline Mar. 15
Board meeting date(s): June and Dec.
Write: Margaret Courtney, Exec. Secy.
Officers and Directors:* Hal Norton,* Pres.; Robert R. Mallard,* V.P.; Lois H. Anderson, Secy.; William E. Rowe,* Treas.; Nancy N. Drews, Carol Ann Green, Deaver D. McGraw III.
Number of staff: 1 part-time professional.
Employer Identification Number: 576024756

6578
Citizens and Southern National Bank of South Carolina Foundation ⌑
1801 Main St.
Columbia 29222 (803) 765-8408

Trust established in 1960 in SC.
Donor(s): Citizens & Southern National Bank of South Carolina, C & S Systems.
Foundation type: Company-sponsored
Financial data (yr. ended 12/31/88): Assets, $755,737 (M); gifts received, $879,328; expenditures, $788,185, including $679,954 for 75 grants (high: $30,000; low: $500; average: $1,000-$10,000), $61,000 for 18 grants to individuals (high: $4,000; low: $1,000; average: $1,000-$4,000) and $15,531 for 133 employee matching gifts.
Purpose and activities: Grants for community funds and higher education, including employee-related scholarships; support also for hospitals and youth agencies.
Types of support: Continuing support, annual campaigns, building funds, matching funds, employee matching gifts, employee-related scholarships, capital campaigns, endowment funds.
Limitations: Giving primarily in SC. No grants to individuals (except employee-related scholarships), or for scholarship funds, fellowships, operating budgets, research, special projects, publications, or conferences; no loans.
Publications: Application guidelines, program policy statement.
Application information: Application form not required.
Initial approach: Letter or proposal
Copies of proposal: 1
Deadline(s): None
Board meeting date(s): Apr., July, Oct., and Dec.
Final notification: 3 months
Write: John C. Troutman, Trustee
Trustees: Gayle O. Avery, Chair.; MacFarlane L. Cates, Jr., Hugh M. Chapman, Joseph H. McGee, Robert V. Royall, Jr., John C. Troutman.
Number of staff: 1 part-time support.
Employer Identification Number: 576024906

6579
Close Foundation, Inc.
P.O. Drawer 460, 104 East Springs St.
Lancaster 29720 (803) 286-2196

Incorporated in 1968 in SC as Frances Ley Springs Foundation, Inc.; renamed Close Foundation in 1985.
Donor(s): Members of the Springs and Close families.
Foundation type: Independent
Financial data (yr. ended 12/31/88): Assets, $9,629,629 (M); gifts received, $10,150; expenditures, $490,091, including $391,340 for 25 grants (high: $60,000; low: $500) and $6,000 for 4 loans to individuals.
Purpose and activities: Support for recreation, higher education, including student loans, health care, and community services.
Types of support: General purposes, annual campaigns, seed money, building funds, land acquisition, renovation projects, endowment funds, conferences and seminars, professorships, matching funds, student loans.
Limitations: Giving primarily in Lancaster County, Chester Township of Chester County, and Fort Mill Township, SC and in NC.
Publications: Annual report.
Application information: Application form required for student loans.
Initial approach: Proposal
Copies of proposal: 1
Board meeting date(s): Apr., Sept., and Dec.
Write: Charles A. Bundy, Pres.
Officers and Directors: Anne Springs Close, Chair.; Charles A. Bundy, Pres.; R.C. Hubbard, V.P. and Secy.; Crandall Close Bowles, V.P. and Treas.; James Bradley, Derick S. Close, Elliott Springs Close, H.W. Close, Jr., Katherine Anne Close, Leroy Springs Close, Frances Close Hart, Pat Close Hastings.
Number of staff: 1 full-time professional; 1 full-time support; 1 part-time support.
Employer Identification Number: 237013986

6580
CSI Foundation ⌑ ☆
P.O. Box 830
Conway 29526-0830 (803) 347-4251

Donor(s): Canal Industries, Canal Wood, Inc., Pelican Companies, Inc., New South, Inc., Canal Investment Society.
Foundation type: Company-sponsored
Financial data (yr. ended 11/30/88): Assets, $48,943 (M); gifts received, $100,991; expenditures, $105,287, including $102,703 for 88 grants (high: $28,571; low: $25).
Purpose and activities: Support primarily for higher education and literacy programs.
Limitations: Giving primarily in SC.
Application information:
Initial approach: Proposal
Write: Fran B. Gilbert, Trustee
Trustees: Daniel M. Campbell III, M.C. Gibson, Fran B. Gilbert, C.W. Godfrey, R.A. Hard, J.M. Singleton.
Employer Identification Number: 570678822

6581
The Daniel Foundation of South Carolina
P.O. Box 9278
Greenville 29604-9278

Established in 1978 in SC as partial successor to The Daniel Foundation.
Donor(s): Daniel International Corp., Charles E. Daniel.†
Foundation type: Company-sponsored
Financial data (yr. ended 12/31/87): Assets, $9,287,484 (M); gifts received, $35,000; expenditures, $838,601, including $797,550 for grants (high: $200,000).
Purpose and activities: Grants largely for higher education.
Limitations: Giving primarily in SC and the Southeast. No grants to individuals.
Application information:
Write: Barbara C. Lewis, Secy.-Treas.
Officers and Trustees:* H.M. Daniel,* Chair.; Buck Mickel,* Pres.; James F. Daniel III,* V.P.; Barbara C. Lewis, Secy.-Treas.
Number of staff: 1
Employer Identification Number: 570673409

6582
Kittie M. Fairey Educational Fund
c/o South Carolina National Bank
101 Greystone Blvd., No. 9344
Columbia 29226 (803) 771-3740
Application address: South Carolina National Bank, Trust Dept., 1401 Main St., Columbia, SC 29226

Trust established in 1967 in SC.
Donor(s): Kittie Moss Fairey.†
Foundation type: Independent
Financial data (yr. ended 9/30/88): Assets, $1,808,794 (M); expenditures, $119,994, including $109,336 for grants to individuals.
Purpose and activities: To provide scholarships for South Carolinians attending a college or university within the state.
Types of support: Student aid.
Limitations: Giving limited to SC.
Application information: Applicants for scholarships must attend a four-year college or

university in the state of SC. Application form required.
Initial approach: Letter
Deadline(s): Mar. 15
Write: Joyce Sweeney
Trustee: South Carolina National Bank.
Employer Identification Number: 576037140

6583
C. G. Fuller Foundation
c/o NCNB National Bank of South Carolina
P.O. Box 2307
Columbia 29202 (803) 758-2317

Established in 1972 in SC.
Donor(s): Cornell G. Fuller.†
Foundation type: Independent
Financial data (yr. ended 12/31/87): Assets, $2,226,026 (M); gifts received, $600,766; expenditures, $199,643, including $174,900 for grants.
Purpose and activities: Scholarships only for residents of SC attending colleges or universities in the state; some support also for children's welfare organizations, medical research, and religious organizations.
Types of support: Annual campaigns, seed money, building funds, equipment, student aid.
Limitations: Giving limited to SC. No grants for endowment funds or matching gifts; no loans.
Publications: 990-PF.
Application information: Application form required.
Initial approach: Letter
Deadline(s): Feb. 15 for scholarships
Board meeting date(s): Quarterly
Final notification: 6 to 9 months
Write: R. Westmoreland Clarkson
Trustees: Victor B. John, Clinton Lemon, NCNB National Bank of South Carolina.
Number of staff: None.
Employer Identification Number: 576050492

6584
The Fullerton Foundation, Inc.
515 West Buford St.
Gaffney 29340 (803) 489-6678
Application address: P.O. Box 1146, Gaffney, SC 29342

Established in 1954 in NY.
Donor(s): Alma H. Fullerton.†
Foundation type: Independent
Financial data (yr. ended 11/30/88): Assets, $26,226,658 (M); expenditures, $1,539,868, including $1,203,000 for 34 grants (high: $132,900; low: $1,000).
Purpose and activities: Giving for hospitals, health care, and medical research; some support for higher education.
Types of support: Equipment, scholarship funds, special projects, matching funds, seed money.
Limitations: Giving primarily in NC and SC. No grants to individuals.
Application information:
Initial approach: Letter
Deadline(s): Apr. 1 and Aug. 1
Board meeting date(s): Twice yearly
Final notification: No set time
Write: Walter E. Cavell, Exec. Dir.
Officers and Directors:* John M. Hamrick,* Chair.; Wylie L. Hamrick,* Vice-Chair. and Treas.; Volina Cline Valentine,* Secy.; Walter E. Cavell, Exec. Dir.; Catherine Hamrick Beattie, Charles F. Hamrick.
Number of staff: 1 part-time professional; 1 part-time support.
Employer Identification Number: 570847444

6585
Community Foundation of Greater Greenville, Inc.
616 South Carolina National Bank Bldg.
Greenville 29601 (803) 233-5925

Established in 1956 in SC; incorporated in 1970.
Foundation type: Community
Financial data (yr. ended 12/31/89): Assets, $5,662,442 (M); gifts received, $750,002; expenditures, $442,151, including $157,000 for 31 grants (high: $80,000; low: $400).
Purpose and activities: "For such charitable purposes as...will make for the mental, moral, intellectual and physical improvement, assistance and relief of the people of Greenville County."
Types of support: Conferences and seminars, equipment, internships, matching funds, publications, renovation projects, scholarship funds, seed money.
Limitations: Giving limited to Greenville County, SC. No grants for capital campaigns or ongoing operational expenses of existing organizations.
Publications: Annual report, application guidelines, program policy statement, financial statement, grants list, newsletter, informational brochure.
Application information: Application form required.
Initial approach: Telephone or letter
Copies of proposal: 17
Deadline(s): Feb. 15, May 15, and Sept. 15
Board meeting date(s): Jan., Mar., May, Sept., and Nov.
Write: Jack Cromartie, Exec. Dir.
Officers and Directors:* E. Arthur Dreskin, M.D.,* Pres.; Vincent C. Brown,* V.P.; Jefferson V. Smith, Jr.,* Secy.; Irving T. Welling,* Treas.
Staff: Jack Cromartie, Exec. Dir.
Number of staff: 1 full-time professional; 1 full-time support.
Employer Identification Number: 576019318

6586
Gregg-Graniteville Foundation, Inc. ¤
P.O. Box 418
Graniteville 29829 (803) 663-7552

Incorporated in 1949 in SC.
Foundation type: Independent
Financial data (yr. ended 12/31/88): Assets, $12,828,686 (M); expenditures, $708,058, including $204,807 for 38 grants (high: $25,000; low: $100; average: $5,000), $49,540 for 34 grants to individuals (high: $2,625; low: $250) and $359,012 for 1 foundation-administered program.
Purpose and activities: Emphasis on education, recreation, religion, health, youth agencies, community funds, community development, and cultural programs; scholarships only for children of Graniteville Co. employees and residents of Graniteville, Vaucluse, and Warrenville, SC.
Types of support: Continuing support, annual campaigns, seed money, emergency funds, building funds, endowment funds, matching funds, employee-related scholarships, research, special projects, capital campaigns, equipment.
Limitations: Giving primarily in Aiken County, SC, and Richmond County, GA. No grants to individuals (except for scholarships for children of company employees and residents of specified areas), or for operating budgets, deficit financing, land acquisition, publications, or conferences; no loans.
Publications: Annual report.
Application information: Application form required.
Initial approach: Letter
Copies of proposal: 1
Deadline(s): None
Board meeting date(s): Bimonthly or as required
Final notification: 1 month
Write: Joan F. Phibbs, Secy.
Officers: Robert P. Timmerman,* Pres.; John W. Cunningham,* V.P.; Jerry R. Johnson,* V.P.; Joan F. Phibbs, Secy.-Treas.
Directors:* Robert M. Bell, Carl W. Littlejohn, Jr., William C. Lott, James A. Randall, Clyde F. Strom.
Number of staff: 1 full-time professional.
Employer Identification Number: 570314400

6587
Hartz Foundation ¤
10 Valencia Circle
Myrtle Beach 29572

Incorporated in 1956 in MN.
Foundation type: Independent
Financial data (yr. ended 7/31/88): Assets, $4,427,080 (M); expenditures, $262,185, including $227,029 for 99 grants (high: $25,000; low: $75).
Purpose and activities: Giving for Protestant church support, higher and secondary education, hospitals, community development, and public broadcasting.
Limitations: Giving primarily in MN. No grants to individuals, or for building or endowment funds; no loans.
Application information:
Initial approach: Proposal
Copies of proposal: 1
Deadline(s): None
Board meeting date(s): Sept.
Write: Onealee Hartz, Secy.-Treas.
Officers: Gene Beito, Pres.; Dwight Tanquist, V.P.; Onealee Hartz, Secy.-Treas.
Director: Orin Green.
Employer Identification Number: 416041638

6588
Hopewell Foundation, Inc. ¤
P.O. Box 470
Rock Hill 29731

Established in 1985 in SC.
Donor(s): Rock Hill Telephone Co.
Foundation type: Independent
Financial data (yr. ended 2/28/87): Assets, $1,500,715 (M); gifts received, $600,000;

expenditures, $199,447, including $198,775 for 2 grants (high: $198,490; low: $285).
Purpose and activities: Grants for Protestant church support.
Application information: Contributes only to pre-selected organizations. Applications not accepted.
Officers and Directors: Frank S. Barnes, Jr., Pres.; Edwin L. Barnes, Secy.-Treas.; John M. Barnes, Ladson A. Barnes, Jr.
Employer Identification Number: 570792719

6589
Dick Horne Foundation ⌘
P.O. Box 306
Orangeburg 29116
Application address: 360 Russell St., S.E., Orangeburg, SC 29115; Tel.: (803) 534-2096

Established in 1966 in SC.
Donor(s): Amelia S. Horne.†
Foundation type: Independent
Financial data (yr. ended 12/31/88): Assets, $2,640,106 (M); gifts received, $492,871; expenditures, $111,746, including $15,437 for 13 grants (high: $9,300; low: $195) and $67,096 for 125 grants to individuals (high: $1,350; low: $50).
Purpose and activities: Primarily awards scholarships for higher and vocational education; limited support for community affairs and social services.
Types of support: Student aid.
Limitations: Giving primarily in the Orangeburg, SC, area.
Application information: Application form required.
Initial approach: Letter
Deadline(s): None
Write: Helen Williams, Exec. Dir.
Officer and Trustees: Andrew Berry, Mgr.; Lenora R. Player, John F. Shuler.
Number of staff: 1 full-time professional.
Employer Identification Number: 237015996

6590
Inman-Riverdale Foundation ⌘
Inman Mills
Inman 29349 (803) 472-2121

Incorporated in 1946 in SC.
Donor(s): Inman Mills.
Foundation type: Company-sponsored
Financial data (yr. ended 11/30/88): Assets, $3,610,463 (M); gifts received, $333,141; expenditures, $478,382, including $273,039 for 55 grants (high: $100,000; low: $100) and $49,670 for grants to individuals.
Purpose and activities: Grants for higher education, including an employee-related scholarship fund, Protestant church support, youth agencies, community funds, recreation, and health activities.
Types of support: Employee-related scholarships.
Limitations: Giving primarily in Inman and Enoree, SC.
Application information: Contributes only to pre-selected organizations. Applications not accepted.
Write: W. Marshall Chapman, Chair.
Officers: W. Marshall Chapman,* Chair.; Robert H. Chapman, Jr.,* Vice-Chair.; Dorothy D. Maxwell, Secy.; John F. Renfro, Jr.,* Treas.
Trustees:* Robert H. Chapman III, Robert C. Martin, James C. Pace, Jr.
Employer Identification Number: 576019736

6591
Francis Nathaniel and Katheryn Padgett Kennedy Foundation
P.O. Box 1178
Greenwood 29649 (803) 942-1400

Established in 1973 in SC.
Donor(s): Katheryn Padgett Kennedy,† Francis Nathanial Kennedy.†
Foundation type: Independent
Financial data (yr. ended 06/30/87): Assets, $1,210,893 (M); expenditures, $123,000, including $77,500 for grants (high: $17,000; low: $300) and $25,000 for 48 grants to individuals.
Purpose and activities: Grants largely for higher education and missionary programs; scholarships to young men and women primarily in the Piedmont section of SC studying at an accredited college for the ministry in the Southern Baptist Church and for foreign mission work or Christian education in their local church; support also for youth agencies and a church.
Types of support: Student aid.
Limitations: Giving primarily in the Piedmont section of SC. No grants for capital needs; no loans.
Publications: Informational brochure (including application guidelines).
Application information: Application form required for scholarships for ministry students.
Deadline(s): May 15 for scholarships
Board meeting date(s): Oct., June, and as required
Final notification: Prior to July 10
Write: Dr. Sam M. Smith, Trustee
Trustees: J. Hewlette Wasson, Chair.; John P. Faris, E. Leon Patterson, G.D. Sherer, Sam M. Smith.
Number of staff: 1 part-time support.
Employer Identification Number: 237347655

6592
The Liberty Corporation Foundation ⌘
P.O. Box 789
Greenville 29602 (803) 292-4367

Established in 1965 in SC.
Donor(s): Liberty Corp.
Foundation type: Company-sponsored
Financial data (yr. ended 8/31/88): Assets, $198,094 (M); gifts received, $185,000; expenditures, $323,296, including $268,866 for 37 grants (high: $84,850; low: $1,500) and $53,975 for employee matching gifts.
Purpose and activities: Support primarily for higher education, including an employee matching gift program, and a community fund; some grants also to youth agencies and cultural institutions.
Types of support: Employee matching gifts.
Limitations: No grants to individuals.
Application information:
Initial approach: Proposal
Deadline(s): None
Write: Mary Anne Bunton, V.P.
Officers: W. Hayne Hipp,* Pres.; Mary Anne Bunton, V.P.; R.G. Hilliard,* V.P.; R.T. Coleman, Secy.; Barry L. Edwards, Treas.
Directors:* F.M. Hipp, Chair.; Macon G. Patton.
Employer Identification Number: 570468195

6593
Marlboro County General Hospital Charity Trust
c/o First Union National Bank of South Carolina
P.O. Box 728
Columbia 29202 (803) 251-4411

Established in 1983 in SC.
Foundation type: Operating
Financial data (yr. ended 12/31/88): Assets, $4,408,727 (M); expenditures, $374,915, including $352,375 for 1 grant.
Purpose and activities: A private operating foundation; support limited to hospitals for health care and aid to the indigent.
Types of support: General purposes.
Limitations: Giving limited to Marlboro County, SC.
Application information:
Write: S.S. Benson, Trust Officer, First Union National Bank of South Carolina
Trustees: William H. Bellinger, First Union National Bank of South Carolina.
Number of staff: None.
Employer Identification Number: 570737029

6594
Everett N. McDonnell Foundation
c/o Wallace Evans, Managing Agent
16 Starboard Tack
Salem 29676

Incorporated in 1946 in IL.
Donor(s): Everett N. McDonnell.†
Foundation type: Independent
Financial data (yr. ended 10/31/89): Assets, $2,948,648 (M); expenditures, $143,832, including $125,700 for 64 grants (high: $35,000; low: $100).
Purpose and activities: Giving for hospitals, health agencies, church support, cultural programs, and higher education.
Limitations: Giving primarily in IL and GA.
Application information: Applications not accepted.
Officers and Directors:* Florence L. McDonnell,* Pres. and Treas.; Gwyneth O. Moran, V.P.; John D. Marshall,* Secy.
Employer Identification Number: 366109359

6595
Merck Family Fund ⌘
15 Broad St.
Charleston 29401 (803) 722-3453

Incorporated in 1954 in NJ.
Donor(s): Members of the Merck family.
Foundation type: Independent
Financial data (yr. ended 11/30/88): Assets, $15,896,317 (M); expenditures, $879,482, including $792,500 for 33 grants (high: $75,000; low: $5,000).
Purpose and activities: Grants largely for conservation, education, and mental health;

support also for medical research, rehabilitation of the handicapped, and social service agencies.
Limitations: No grants to individuals; no loans.
Application information:
Initial approach: Letter
Deadline(s): Sept. 1
Write: Antony M. Merck, Pres.
Officers and Trustees:* Antony M. Merck,* Pres.; Anne Merck-Abeles,* V.P.; Francis W. Hatch III,* Secy.; Wilhelm M. Merck, Treas.; Judith M. Buechner, Josephine M. Coy.
Employer Identification Number: 226063382

6596
Alfred Moore Foundation ⌑
c/o C.L. Page Enterprises, Inc.
P.O. Box 18426
Spartanburg 29318 (803) 583-6844

Incorporated in 1949 in SC.
Donor(s): Jackson Mills.
Foundation type: Company-sponsored
Financial data (yr. ended 12/31/88): Assets, $2,178,296 (M); expenditures, $112,587, including $57,144 for 36 grants (high: $5,000; low: $250) and $33,500 for 34 grants to individuals (high: $2,000; low: $500).
Purpose and activities: Emphasis on higher education, including scholarships to individuals; support also for youth, health, and social services.
Types of support: Student aid.
Limitations: Giving limited to Anderson and Spartanburg counties, SC.
Application information:
Initial approach: Letter
Deadline(s): Scholarships, Mar. 29; loans, varies
Write: Cary L. Page, Jr., Chair.
Officers: Cary L. Page, Jr., Chair.; Bernelle Demo, Vice-Chair.
Employer Identification Number: 576018424

6597
Mount Vernon Mills Foundation ⌑ ☆
One Shelter Place
P.O. Box 3478
Greenville 29602 (803) 233-4151

Donor(s): Mount Vernon Mills, Inc.
Foundation type: Company-sponsored
Financial data (yr. ended 12/31/88): Assets, $56,477 (M); gifts received, $11,704; expenditures, $195,557, including $195,490 for 193 grants (high: $20,000; low: $50).
Purpose and activities: Support primarily for community funds, cultural programs, and social services.
Application information: Application form not required.
Deadline(s): None
Write: E.G. Cochrane II, Trustee
Trustees: E.G. Cochrane II, J.L. Jennings, Jr., R.B. Pamplin.
Employer Identification Number: 136111574

6598
Mary Barratt Park Foundation ⌑ ☆
P.O. Box 31
Greenwood 29648-0031

Donor(s): George W. Park Seed Co., Inc.
Foundation type: Independent
Financial data (yr. ended 12/31/88): Assets, $1,769 (M); gifts received, $114,499; expenditures, $114,258, including $113,950 for grants (high: $25,000).
Purpose and activities: Giving primarily for Protestant churches, welfare and missionary programs, and religious education; giving also for higher and other education, child welfare, a museum, and the performing arts.
Types of support: General purposes.
Limitations: Giving primarily in SC.
Officer: William John Park,* Mgr..
Directors:* Karen P. Jennings, George B. Park, Jr., J. Leonard Park.
Employer Identification Number: 237025200

6599
Piedmont Health City Foundation, Inc. ☆
P.O. Box 2585
Greenville 29602 (803) 242-5133

Established in 1985 in SC.
Foundation type: Independent
Financial data (yr. ended 12/31/88): Assets, $2,246,251 (M); expenditures, $163,418, including $111,836 for 6 grants (high: $66,000; low: $3,300).
Purpose and activities: Support for health, hospitals, and a science center.
Limitations: Giving limited to the Piedmont and Greenville, SC, areas.
Application information: Application form required.
Initial approach: Letter
Copies of proposal: 7
Deadline(s): Aug. 15
Board meeting date(s): Mar., June, Sept., and Dec.
Write: Schaefer Kendrick, Dean
Officers and Directors: Leonard Byrne, Chair.; Grady Wyatt, Vice-Chair.; David Evans, Secy.; Rob Hamby, Treas.; and 10 additional directors.
Number of staff: 1
Employer Identification Number: 570782523

6600
Post and Courier Foundation
134 Columbus St.
Charleston 29403-4800 (803) 577-7111

Incorporated in 1951 in SC.
Donor(s): Evening Post Publishing Co.
Foundation type: Company-sponsored
Financial data (yr. ended 12/31/89): Assets, $2,231,353 (M); gifts received, $702,225; expenditures, $475,216, including $472,364 for 98 grants (high: $76,707; low: $50).
Purpose and activities: Support for community development, conservation, crime and law enforcement, health services and associations, and cultural programs.
Types of support: Building funds, capital campaigns, continuing support, program-related investments.
Limitations: Giving primarily in Charleston, SC. No grants to individuals.
Application information: The foundation's employee-related scholarship program has been discontinued. Application form not required.
Initial approach: Proposal
Deadline(s): None
Write: J.F. Smoak, Fdn. Mgr.
Officers: Peter Manigault, Pres.; Ivan V. Anderson, Jr., Exec. V.P.; Joseph F. Smoak, V.P., Treas., and Fdn. Mgr.; Arthur M. Wilcox, Secy.
Employer Identification Number: 576020356

6601
The Roe Foundation
712 Crescent Ave.
Greenville 29601 (803) 235-8955

Incorporated in 1968 in SC.
Donor(s): Thomas A. Roe.
Foundation type: Independent
Financial data (yr. ended 12/31/89): Assets, $9,904,344 (M); expenditures, $636,058, including $533,480 for 65 grants (high: $100,000; low: $50; average: $50-$100,000).
Purpose and activities: Giving primarily for public policy organizations promoting free market and limited government.
Types of support: Operating budgets, continuing support, annual campaigns, seed money, emergency funds, building funds, equipment, land acquisition, fellowships.
Limitations: No grants to individuals, or for matching gifts; no loans.
Publications: Program policy statement.
Application information: Application form not required.
Initial approach: Letter
Copies of proposal: 1
Deadline(s): Apr. 15 and Nov. 15
Board meeting date(s): Semiannually
Final notification: 6 months
Write: Thomas A. Roe, Chair.
Officers and Trustees:* Thomas A. Roe,* Chair. and Treas.; Edwin Feulner, Jr.,* Vice-Chair.; Shirley W. Roe,* Secy.; Alfred F. Burgess, Roger E. Meiners, Paul M. Weyrich.
Number of staff: None.
Employer Identification Number: 237011541

6602
Sargent Foundation
P.O. Box 3714 Park Place
Greenville 29608 (803) 233-2769

Established in 1954.
Donor(s): Earle W. Sargent,† Eleanor G. Sargent.
Foundation type: Independent
Financial data (yr. ended 04/30/89): Assets, $1,710,267 (M); expenditures, $69,901, including $48,790 for 14 grants (high: $12,765; low: $1,000).
Purpose and activities: Giving for community funds and a hospital.
Types of support: Annual campaigns, capital campaigns, general purposes, scholarship funds.
Limitations: Giving primarily in SC.
Application information: Application form not required.
Initial approach: Proposal
Copies of proposal: 1
Deadline(s): Apr. 1
Board meeting date(s): Mid-Apr. and as required
Write: Ruth Nicholson, V.P.
Officers and Trustees:* Eleanor G. Sargent,* Pres.; Ruth Nicholson,* V.P. and Secy.; John R. McAdams,* Treas.; Richard Sargent, Robert A. Wilson.
Number of staff: None.

Employer Identification Number: 576019317

6603
Schafer Foundation
c/o Alan Schafer
P.O. Box 1328
Dillon 29536

Established in 1961 in SC.
Foundation type: Independent
Financial data (yr. ended 12/31/88): Assets, $1,256,353 (M); gifts received, $16,006; expenditures, $197,658, including $92,300 for 34 grants (high: $25,000; low: $100) and $3,250 for 4 grants to individuals (high: $2,000; low: $250).
Purpose and activities: Grants primarily for religion, education, and social services.
Application information: Contributes only to pre-selected organizations. Applications not accepted.
Officers: Patricia C. Schafer, Pres.; Ann U. Tyndall, V.P.; Lulu F. Holiday, Secy.
Employer Identification Number: 576033789

6604
D. L. Scurry Foundation ⌘
P.O. Box 10885, Federal Station
Greenville 29603 (803) 232-6880

Trust established in 1968 in SC.
Donor(s): D.L. Scurry.†
Foundation type: Independent
Financial data (yr. ended 6/30/87): Assets, $3,544,319 (M); expenditures, $156,700, including $126,000 for 52 grants (high: $5,000; low: $250).
Purpose and activities: Emphasis on higher education; support also for child welfare.
Types of support: Endowment funds, scholarship funds.
Limitations: Giving limited to SC. No grants to individuals, or for building funds or matching gifts; no loans.
Application information:
Initial approach: Proposal
Copies of proposal: 1
Deadline(s): None
Write: James F. Burgess, Trustee
Trustee: James F. Burgess.
Employer Identification Number: 576036622

6605
The Self Foundation ▼
P.O. Drawer 1017
Greenwood 29648 (803) 229-2571

Incorporated in 1942 in SC.
Donor(s): James C. Self.†
Foundation type: Independent
Financial data (yr. ended 12/31/89): Assets, $25,058,501 (M); expenditures, $1,293,666, including $1,032,817 for 28 grants (high: $125,000; low: $500; average: $15,000).
Purpose and activities: Primary interest in health care and higher education; support also for cultural programs, and activities for youth and the elderly; grants mainly for capital or special purposes.
Types of support: Seed money, emergency funds, building funds, equipment, matching funds, technical assistance, special projects, renovation projects.
Limitations: Giving limited to SC, with emphasis on Greenwood. No grants to individuals, or for endowment funds, land acquisition, operating budgets, continuing support, annual campaigns, deficit financing, publications, conferences, scholarships, fellowships, or research-related programs; no loans.
Publications: Annual report (including application guidelines).
Application information: Application form not required.
Initial approach: Proposal
Copies of proposal: 1
Deadline(s): Submit proposal preferably in the 2 months prior to board meetings; deadlines, 1st day of month in which board meets
Board meeting date(s): 3rd week in Mar., June, Sept., and Dec.
Final notification: 10 days after board meeting
Write: Frank J. Wideman, Jr., Exec. V.P.
Officers: James C. Self,* Pres.; Frank J. Wideman, Jr., Exec. V.P.; James C. Self, Jr.,* V.P.; W.M. Self,* Secy.; Kenneth E. Young, Treas.
Trustees:* Joan M. Anderson, Virginia S. Brennan, Emmett I. Davis, William B. Patrick, Jr., Sally E. Self, M.D., Paul E. Welder.
Number of staff: 1 full-time professional.
Employer Identification Number: 570400594

6606
The Simpson Foundation ⌘
P.O. Box 528
Greenville 29602 (803) 297-3451

Trust established in 1956 in SC.
Donor(s): W.H.B. Simpson, Mrs. W.H.B. Simpson.
Foundation type: Independent
Financial data (yr. ended 12/31/88): Assets, $3,245,806 (M); gifts received, $1,404; expenditures, $77,349, including $64,580 for 30 grants (high: $7,500; low: $100).
Purpose and activities: Giving for Protestant church support and religious organizations and social services.
Limitations: Giving primarily in NC and SC.
Application information:
Initial approach: Letter
Deadline(s): Before board meetings
Board meeting date(s): Nov. 1 and May 1
Write: W.H.B. Simpson
Directors: C.L. Efrid, Jr., Sarah Belk Gambrell, Nell M. Rice, Charles W. White.
Trustee: Willou R. Bichel.
Employer Identification Number: 576017451

6607
John I. Smith Charities, Inc. ⌘
c/o NCNB South Carolina, Trust Dept.
P.O. Box 608
Greenville 29602 (803) 271-5934

Established in 1985 in SC.
Donor(s): John Q. Smith.†
Foundation type: Independent
Financial data (yr. ended 07/31/89): Assets, $15,443,674 (M); gifts received, $1,058,159; expenditures, $987,842, including $905,047 for 27 grants (high: $250,000; low: $47).
Purpose and activities: Support for higher and other education, including medical and theological education, and literacy programs; museums and other fine and performing arts groups; religious associations; and community funds, child welfare, and programs for the handicapped.
Types of support: Capital campaigns, emergency funds, endowment funds, general purposes, scholarship funds.
Limitations: Giving primarily in SC.
Application information: Application form not required.
Initial approach: Letter
Board meeting date(s): Quarterly
Write: Wilbur Y. Bridgers, Pres.
Officers: Wilbur Y. Bridgers, Pres. and Secy.; W. Thomas Smith, V.P. and Treas.
Director: Jefferson V. Smith III.
Trustee: NCNB South Carolina.
Number of staff: None.
Employer Identification Number: 570806327

6608
Sonoco Foundation ⌘
North Second St.
Hartsville 29550 (803) 383-7000

Established in 1983 in SC.
Donor(s): Sonoco Products Co.
Foundation type: Company-sponsored
Financial data (yr. ended 12/31/87): Assets, $635,876 (M); gifts received, $825,000; expenditures, $748,504, including $748,504 for 162 grants (high: $217,000; low: $25).
Purpose and activities: Grants for higher education through an employee-matching gift program; support also for business associations, youth organizations, and social service agencies.
Types of support: Employee matching gifts.
Limitations: Giving primarily in areas of company operations.
Application information:
Initial approach: Letter; applications may also be submitted through any employee of Sonoco
Deadline(s): None
Write: Joyce Beasley
Trustees: Charles W. Coker, T.C. Coxe III, F. Treat Hill, Jr., R.C. King, Jr., F.B. Williams.
Employer Identification Number: 570752950

6609
The Spartanburg County Foundation
320 East Main St.
Spartanburg 29302-1943 (803) 582-0138

Incorporated in 1943 in SC.
Foundation type: Community
Financial data (yr. ended 12/31/89): Assets, $16,201,537 (M); gifts received, $1,339,192; expenditures, $1,097,914, including $829,898 for 162 grants (high: $50,000; low: $400; average: $5,000-$10,000).
Purpose and activities: To provide "for the mental, moral, intellectual and physical improvement, assistance and relief of the inhabitants of Spartanburg County." Support for local projects in education, arts, humanities, recreation, health, and welfare.
Types of support: Continuing support, seed money, emergency funds, building funds, equipment, matching funds, conferences and

seminars, consulting services, scholarship funds, renovation projects, lectureships.
Limitations: Giving limited to Spartanburg County, SC. No grants to individuals, or for operating budgets, annual campaigns, deficit financing, land acquisition, or endowment funds; no loans.
Publications: Annual report (including application guidelines), informational brochure.
Application information: Application form not required.
Initial approach: Telephone
Copies of proposal: 1
Deadline(s): Submit proposal preferably in 1st 6 months of year, and at least 40 days before board meetings. Grants are considered in Mar., June, Sept., and Dec.
Board meeting date(s): Monthly
Final notification: 1 month following board meeting
Write: James S. Barrett, Exec. Dir.
Officers: Elaine Freeman,* Secy.; John E. Keith,* Treas.; James S. Barrett, Exec. Dir.
Trustees:* Richard H. Pennell, Chair.; W. Marshall Chapman, Vice-Chair.; Joab M. Lesesne, Jr., Harry R. Phillips, Jr., Kurt Zimmerli.
Number of staff: 1 full-time professional; 1 part-time professional; 1 full-time support; 1 part-time support.
Employer Identification Number: 570351398

6610
Springs Foundation, Inc. ▼
104 East Springs St.
Lancaster 29720 (803) 286-2196
Mailing address: P.O. Drawer 460, Lancaster, SC 29720

Incorporated in 1942 in DE.
Donor(s): Elliott W. Springs,† Anne Springs Close, Frances Ley Springs.†
Foundation type: Independent
Financial data (yr. ended 12/31/89): Assets, $22,705,059 (M); expenditures, $1,833,814, including $1,401,548 for 32 grants (high: $1,151,000; low: $400; average: $5,000-$50,000) and $237,995 for loans.
Purpose and activities: Support largely for recreation, and education, including public schools and student loans; support for community services, churches, hospitals, and medical scholarships.
Types of support: Building funds, equipment, endowment funds, publications, professorships, matching funds, general purposes, special projects, student aid, student loans.
Limitations: Giving primarily in Lancaster County and/or the townships of Fort Mill and Chester, SC. No grants to individuals (except through the Springs Medical Scholarship Program).
Publications: Annual report (including application guidelines).
Application information: Application form required for student loans.
Initial approach: Telephone or brief letter
Copies of proposal: 1
Deadline(s): None
Board meeting date(s): Apr., Sept., and Dec.
Final notification: 3 months
Write: Charles A. Bundy, Pres.
Officers and Directors:* Anne Springs Close,* Chair.; Charles A. Bundy,* Pres.; Crandall Close Bowles,* V.P. and Treas.; James Bradley, Derick S. Close, Elliott Springs Close, H.W. Close, Jr., Katherine Anne Close, Leroy Springs Close, Frances Close Hart, Patricia Close, R.C. Hubbard.
Number of staff: 1 full-time professional; 2 full-time support.
Employer Identification Number: 570426344

6611
John T. Stevens Foundation ⌑
P.O. Box 158
Kershaw 29067

Established in 1948 in SC.
Donor(s): John T. Stevens.
Foundation type: Independent
Financial data (yr. ended 05/31/89): Assets, $3,699,360 (M); expenditures, $201,443, including $163,279 for 37 grants (high: $31,010; low: $500).
Purpose and activities: Giving for Protestant church support, medical and secondary education, and youth agencies.
Limitations: Giving primarily in SC.
Officers: John S. Davidson, Pres. and Secy.-Treas.; Steve L. Williams, V.P.
Employer Identification Number: 576005554

6612
The Stone Foundation ⌑
P.O. Box 3725
Greenville 29608

Established in 1944 in SC.
Foundation type: Independent
Financial data (yr. ended 12/31/88): Assets, $1,071,524 (M); expenditures, $89,493, including $73,030 for 159 grants (high: $5,000; low: $10).
Purpose and activities: Giving primarily to wildlife and environmental organizations.
Limitations: Giving primarily in SC and NC.
Officer: John J. Brausch, Admin. Dir.
Trustees: C. Rivers Stone, Eugene E. Stone III.
Employer Identification Number: 576025125

6613
F. W. Symmes Foundation
c/o South Carolina National Bank
P.O. Box 969
Greenville 29602 (803) 239-6843

Trust established in 1954 in SC.
Donor(s): F.W. Symmes.†
Foundation type: Independent
Financial data (yr. ended 03/31/89): Assets, $8,154,423 (M); expenditures, $526,805, including $446,000 for 9 grants (high: $125,000; low: $1,000; average: $36,000).
Purpose and activities: Emphasis on church support, child welfare, hospitals, youth agencies, music and the fine arts, recreation, and education, including libraries.
Limitations: Giving primarily in SC. No grants to individuals.
Publications: Application guidelines, informational brochure.
Application information: Application form not required.
Initial approach: Letter or telephone
Copies of proposal: 10
Deadline(s): 4 weeks before board meetings
Board meeting date(s): Semiannually
Final notification: 2 weeks following meeting
Write: Victoria G. Dotson, Trust Officer, South Carolina National Bank
Trustees: William H. Orders, Wilson C. Wearn, F. McKinnon Wilkinson, South Carolina National Bank.
Number of staff: None.
Employer Identification Number: 576017472

6614
Trident Community Foundation
11 Broad St.
Charleston 29401-3001 (803) 723-3635
Additional tel.: (803) 723-2124

Incorporated in l974 in SC.
Foundation type: Community
Financial data (yr. ended 6/30/88): Assets, $2,682,540 (M); gifts received, $1,376,616; expenditures, $286,259, including $116,030 for grants (high: $15,000; low: $100; average: $1,500-$5,000), $10,500 for grants to individuals (high: $1,000; low: $500; average: $500-$1,000), $33,000 for 2 foundation-administered programs and $13,475 for loans.
Purpose and activities: Giving for the arts and humanities, education, environment, and health and social services.
Types of support: Emergency funds, program-related investments, publications, renovation projects, scholarship funds, seed money, special projects, technical assistance, student aid, operating budgets.
Limitations: Giving primarily in Berkeley, Charleston, and Dorchester counties, SC. No grants for scholarships, annual campaigns, endowments, equipment, deficit financing, or generally for building funds; no loans.
Publications: Annual report (including application guidelines), newsletter.
Application information: Application form required.
Initial approach: Letter
Copies of proposal: 5
Board meeting date(s): 3rd Tuesday of every other month
Final notification: Within 3 months of each proposal deadline
Write: Ruth Heffron, Exec. Dir.
Officers and Directors: Henry Smythe, Jr., Pres.; George Bullwinkel, Jr., V.P.; Louise Maybank, Secy.; Conrad Zimmerman, Jr., Treas.; Ruth H. Heffron, Exec. Dir.; Richard Hendry, Dir. of Program Development; Ann Stein.
Number of staff: 2 full-time professional; 2 part-time professional; 2 part-time support.
Employer Identification Number: 237390313

6615
E. Craig Wall, Sr. Foundation ⌑ ☆
P.O. Box 830
Conway 29526-0830 (803) 347-4251

Established in 1970.
Donor(s): E.C. Wall, Sr.†
Foundation type: Independent
Financial data (yr. ended 11/30/88): Assets, $1,159,218 (M); gifts received, $1,068,883; expenditures, $319,308, including $316,431 for 28 grants (high: $200,000; low: $25).

Purpose and activities: Giving primarily for higher and secondary education; support also for churches.
Limitations: Giving primarily in SC.
Application information:
Initial approach: Letter
Deadline(s): None
Write: Fran B. Gilbert
Trustees: Harriet Wall Martin, Nell Wall Otto, E. Craig Wall, Jr., May Howard Wall.
Employer Identification Number: 237095547

SOUTH DAKOTA

6616
The Hatterscheidt Foundation, Inc. ⌑
c/o First Bank-Aberdeen
320 South First St.
Aberdeen 57401 (605) 225-9400

Incorporated in 1947 in DE.
Donor(s): Ruth K. Hatterscheidt, F.W. Hatterscheidt Trusts.
Foundation type: Independent
Financial data (yr. ended 12/31/88): Assets, $2,767,484 (M); gifts received, $11,283; expenditures, $210,119, including $57,750 for 36 grants (high: $7,000; low: $100) and $101,500 for grants to individuals.
Purpose and activities: Giving primarily to assist graduating high school seniors in the top quarter of their class in their first year of college; support also for local charitable organizations.
Types of support: Student aid.
Limitations: Giving primarily in SD and 100-mile radius of Jamestown, ND. No grants for endowment funds or matching gifts; no loans.
Application information: Application forms required for scholarships.
Initial approach: Letter
Copies of proposal: 1
Deadline(s): Submit proposal preferably in Feb.
Board meeting date(s): Mar. and Oct.
Write: Kenneth P. Johnson
Officers and Trustees: Margaret M. Meyers, Pres.; Arthur J. Eagleson, V.P.; Clarence L. Herges, Terence A. O'Keefe, Francis Rinke.
Employer Identification Number: 466012543

6617
Maas Foundation ⌑
P.O. Box 7
Watertown 57201

Established in 1986 in SD.
Donor(s): George E. Maas.
Foundation type: Independent
Financial data (yr. ended 12/31/87): Assets, $1,001,778 (M); gifts received, $80,000; expenditures, $7,278, including $4,000 for 2 grants.
Purpose and activities: Support for education.
Application information: Not currently accepting applications.
Trustees: Thomas K. Berg, George E. Maas, Patricia A. Maas.
Employer Identification Number: 460393558

6618
Sheldon F. Reese Foundation ⌑
P.O. Box 1107
Mitchell 57301

Established about 1980 in SD.
Donor(s): Sheldon F. Reese, Mayo Foundation, and other members of the Reese family.
Foundation type: Independent
Financial data (yr. ended 12/31/87): Assets, $2,049,185 (M); gifts received, $270,531; expenditures, $304,253, including $131,178 for grants.
Purpose and activities: Support for a doll museum and a medical research foundation; giving also for general charitable purposes.
Types of support: General purposes.
Officers: Oscar Austad, Pres.; Sheldon F. Reese, V.P.; Herbert Heidepriem, Secy.
Director: John Quello.
Employer Identification Number: 460358682

6619
South Dakota Community Foundation ☆
207 East Capitol
P.O. Box 296
Pierre 57501 (605) 224-1025

Incorporated in 1987 in SD.
Foundation type: Community
Financial data (yr. ended 12/31/88): Assets, $10,360,707 (M); gifts received, $5,613,574; expenditures, $207,372.
Purpose and activities: First year of operation, 1988; no grants awarded. Interest in the arts, citizenship, and education programs for minorities.
Types of support: Matching funds, publications.
Limitations: Giving limited to SD. No grants to individuals.
Publications: Annual report (including application guidelines).
Application information: Application form not required.
Copies of proposal: 7
Deadline(s): Feb. 1 and Sept. 1
Board meeting date(s): Apr. and Nov.
Write: Bernard W. Christenson, Exec. Dir.
Officer: Bernard W. Christenson, Exec. Dir.
Number of staff: 1 full-time professional; 1 full-time support.
Employer Identification Number: 460398115

TENNESSEE

6620
Arthur F. Adams Foundation, Inc. ⌑
4487 Talltrees Dr.
Memphis 38117

Foundation type: Independent
Financial data (yr. ended 12/31/87): Assets, $130,370 (M); expenditures, $133,634, including $132,000 for 3 grants (high: $80,000; low: $2,000).
Purpose and activities: Support primarily for a hospital and an opera company.
Limitations: Giving primarily in Miami, FL.
Application information: Application form not required.
Deadline(s): None
Write: Henry W. Clark, Pres.
Officers: Henry W. Clark, Pres.; William Warren, Exec. V.P.; H. Willis Day, V.P.; Richard Chadman, Secy.-Treas.
Employer Identification Number: 596151030

6621
Aladdin Industries Foundation, Inc. ⌑
703 Murfreesboro Rd.
Nashville 37210-4521 (615) 748-3360

Incorporated in 1964 in TN.
Donor(s): Aladdin Industries.
Foundation type: Company-sponsored
Financial data (yr. ended 12/31/88): Assets, $1,290,580 (M); expenditures, $48,255, including $41,000 for 12 grants (high: $10,000; low: $500).
Purpose and activities: Support primarily for youth; giving also for the elderly, music groups, business, education, and drug abuse programs.
Types of support: General purposes, employee-related scholarships, seed money.
Limitations: Giving primarily in TN. No grants to individuals.
Application information:
Initial approach: Letter
Deadline(s): Current calender year
Board meeting date(s): Quarterly
Write: L.B. Jenkins, Secy.-Treas.
Officer and Directors: L.B. Jenkins, Secy.-Treas.; V.S. Johnson III, F.R. Meyer.
Employer Identification Number: 620701769

6622
American Snuff Company Charitable Trust ⌑
Union Planters National Bank
P.O. Box 387
Memphis 38147
Application address: P.O. Box 217, Memphis, TN 38101

Established in 1952 in TN.
Donor(s): American Snuff Co.
Foundation type: Company-sponsored
Financial data (yr. ended 12/31/88): Assets, $2,297,724 (M); expenditures, $76,732, including $57,560 for 29 grants (high: $21,500; low: $35).
Purpose and activities: Giving primarily for the United Way and other social service agencies; support also for higher education and for the prevention of cruelty to children.
Limitations: Giving primarily in the Memphis, TN, area. No grants to individuals.
Application information:
Initial approach: Letter or proposal

Deadline(s): None
Write: David L. Simpson III, Trustee
Trustees: David L. Simpson III, Union Planters National Bank.
Employer Identification Number: 626036034

6623
Dantzler Bond Ansley Foundation ⌑
c/o Third National Bank, Trust Dept.
P.O. Box 305110
Nashville 37230-5110 (615) 748-5207

Incorporated in 1980 in TN.
Donor(s): Mildred B. Ansley.†
Foundation type: Independent
Financial data (yr. ended 4/30/88): Assets, $5,248,441 (M); expenditures, $283,587.
Purpose and activities: Support primarily for health and medical research, higher and secondary education, and cultural programs.
Types of support: Annual campaigns, capital campaigns.
Limitations: Giving primarily in middle TN and Nashville, TN.
Application information: Application form not required.
Copies of proposal: 3
Deadline(s): May 31
Write: Kim Williams, Trust Officer, Third National Bank
Trustees: Frank Drowota, Thomas F. Frist, Fred Russell.
Employer Identification Number: 592111990

6624
BBC Foundation ⌑
450 Machellan Bldg.
722 Chestnut St.
Chattanooga 37402
Application address: 428 McCallie Ave., Chattanooga, TN 37402; Tel.: (615) 756-5880

Foundation type: Independent
Financial data (yr. ended 12/31/88): Assets, $1,512,089 (M); expenditures, $116,915, including $110,750 for 34 grants (high: $45,000; low: $500).
Purpose and activities: Support primarily for elementary and secondary schools, cultural programs, and health services.
Types of support: General purposes.
Limitations: Giving primarily in Chattanooga, TN, and Atlanta, GA.
Application information:
Deadline(s): None
Write: Carl J. Arnold, Secy.-Treas.
Officers and Trustees: H. Clay Evans Johnson, Chair.; Betty J. Farmer, Vice-Chair.; Barbara J. Prickett, Vice-Chair.; Carl J. Arnold, Secy.-Treas.; H. Clay Evans Johnson, Jr.
Employer Identification Number: 581577719

6625
Belz Foundation ⌑
P.O. Box 171199
Memphis 38187-1199

Incorporated in 1952 in TN.
Donor(s): Jack A. Belz, Philip Belz, and others.
Foundation type: Independent
Financial data (yr. ended 12/31/86): Assets, $5,182,801 (M); gifts received, $1,170,874; expenditures, $394,574, including $391,130 for 352 grants (high: $223,955; low: $5).
Purpose and activities: Emphasis on Jewish welfare funds, temple support, education, and cultural organizations.
Limitations: Giving primarily in Memphis, TN. No grants to individuals.
Officers: Jack A. Belz, Mgr.; Martin S. Belz, Mgr.; Philip Belz, Mgr.; Raymond Shainberg, Mgr.; Jack Weil, Mgr.; Jimmie D. Williams, Mgr.
Employer Identification Number: 626046715

6626
Benwood Foundation, Inc. ▼ ⌑
1600 American National Bank Bldg.
Chattanooga 37402 (615) 267-4311

Incorporated in 1944 in DE, and 1945 in TN.
Donor(s): George Thomas Hunter.†
Foundation type: Independent
Financial data (yr. ended 12/31/88): Assets, $57,188,929 (M); expenditures, $4,176,176, including $3,779,822 for 105 grants (high: $625,000; low: $195; average: $1,000-$100,000).
Purpose and activities: Support for higher and secondary education, welfare, health agencies and hospitals, cultural programs, including the performing arts, beautification, and Christian organizations.
Types of support: Research, annual campaigns, seed money, emergency funds, deficit financing, building funds, equipment, land acquisition, conferences and seminars, endowment funds, professorships, scholarship funds, matching funds, general purposes, continuing support, renovation projects.
Limitations: Giving primarily in the Chattanooga, TN, area. No grants to individuals, or for building or operating funds of churches; no loans.
Publications: Application guidelines.
Application information: Application form required.
Initial approach: Letter
Copies of proposal: 6
Deadline(s): End of each month preceding board meetings
Board meeting date(s): Jan., Apr., July, and Oct.
Final notification: 3 days after board meeting
Write: William A. Walter, Exec. Dir.
Officers and Trustees: Walter R. Randolph, Jr., Chair.; Sebert Brewer, Jr., Pres.; Scott L. Probasco, Jr., V.P.; E.Y. Chapin III, Secy.-Treas.; William A. Walter, Exec. Dir.
Number of staff: 1 full-time professional; 2 full-time support.
Employer Identification Number: 620476283

6627
Bernal Foundation
c/o Werthan Industries, Inc.
P.O. Box 1310
Nashville 37202 (615) 259-9331

Established in 1953 in TN.
Donor(s): Albert Werthan, Members of the Werthan Family.
Foundation type: Independent
Financial data (yr. ended 12/31/89): Assets, $662,339 (M); gifts received, $152,886; expenditures, $288,340, including $278,215 for 257 grants (high: $25,000; low: $100).
Purpose and activities: Support primarily for higher and other education, Jewish temples, and Jewish welfare funds; giving also for a community fund.
Limitations: Giving primarily in TN. No grants to individuals.
Application information: Application form not required.
Initial approach: Letter
Deadline(s): None
Board meeting date(s): June
Write: Albert Werthan, Chair.
Officers and Trustees:* Albert Werthan,* Chair.; Bernard Werthan, Jr.,* Secy.; Morris Werthan II,* Treas.; Herbert M. Shayne, Leah Rose B. Werthan.
Employer Identification Number: 626037906

6628
J.C. Bradford & Co. Foundation ⌑ ☆
330 Commerce St.
Nashville 37201

Established in 1986 in TN.
Donor(s): J.C. Bradford & Co.
Foundation type: Company-sponsored
Financial data (yr. ended 12/30/88): Assets, $376,455 (M); gifts received, $33,706; expenditures, $135,079, including $134,559 for 33 grants (high: $31,000; low: $300).
Purpose and activities: Giving for a community fund, the performing arts, higher education, and a Jewish welfare fund.
Limitations: Giving primarily in Nashville, TN. No grants to individuals.
Application information: Contributes only to pre-selected organizations. Applications not accepted.
Officers: James C. Bradford, Jr., Pres.; W. Lucas Simons, V.P.; C. Taxin Malott, Secy.-Treas.
Employer Identification Number: 621303221

6629
T. W. Briggs Welcome Wagon Foundation, Inc. ⌑
2670 Union Ave. Extension, Suite 1122
Memphis 38112-4402 (901) 323-0213

Established in 1957.
Foundation type: Independent
Financial data (yr. ended 9/30/88): Assets, $4,445,067 (M); gifts received, $19,000; expenditures, $249,715, including $179,950 for 29 grants (high: $42,000; low: $500).
Purpose and activities: Emphasis on youth and education; support also for the arts, health, and social services, including a community fund.
Limitations: Giving primarily in AR, MS, TN, with emphasis in the Memphis, TN, area.
Application information:
Initial approach: Letter
Deadline(s): None
Officers and Directors: Hubert A. McBride, Chair.; S. Herbert Rhea, Pres. and Treas.; William T. Morris, V.P.; Eleanor Prest, Secy.; Margaret Hyde, Harry J. Phillips, Sr., Spence Wilson.
Employer Identification Number: 626039986

6630
The Brinkley Foundation ¤
c/o National Bank of Commerce, Trust Div.
One Commerce Sq.
Memphis 38103

Trust established in 1968 in TN.
Donor(s): Hugh M. Brinkley.†
Foundation type: Independent
Financial data (yr. ended 12/31/88): Assets, $1,932,393 (M); expenditures, $150,969, including $135,000 for 14 grants (high: $15,000; low: $4,000; average: $5,000-$10,000).
Purpose and activities: Giving primarily for hospitals, cultural programs, and secondary and higher education.
Limitations: Giving primarily in TN and AR.
Application information: Application form not required.
Deadline(s): None
Trustee: National Bank of Commerce.
Employer Identification Number: 626079631

6631
The Dora Maclellan Brown Charitable Trust
1001 McCallie Ave.
Chattanooga 37403 (615) 266-4574

Trust established in 1965 in TN; incorporated in 1976 in TN.
Donor(s): Dora Maclellan Brown.†
Foundation type: Independent
Financial data (yr. ended 12/31/89): Assets, $10,562,381 (M); expenditures, $951,225, including $793,825 for 134 grants (high: $36,000; low: $262).
Purpose and activities: To promote the work of the Christian church through scholarships to schools, colleges, and theological seminaries, and through grants to evangelical ministries.
Types of support: Scholarship funds, conferences and seminars, fellowships, lectureships, matching funds, special projects, continuing support, general purposes, student aid, operating budgets.
Limitations: Giving primarily in Chattanooga, TN. No support for secular education. No grants to individuals, or for seed money, emergency funds, deficit financing, capital funds, endowment funds, equipment and materials, land acquisition, renovation projects, research, or publications; no loans.
Publications: Informational brochure (including application guidelines).
Application information: Application form required for scholarships to seminaries only; interviews required for scholarship applicants; scholarships limited to residents of Chattanooga, TN. Application form required.
Initial approach: Letter
Copies of proposal: 8
Deadline(s): Submit proposal prior to 2nd week of any month
Board meeting date(s): Monthly
Final notification: Last week of each month
Write: Henry A. Henegar, Pres.
Officers: Henry A. Henegar,* Pres.; Llewellyn Boyd,* V.P.; Robert F. Huffaker,* V.P.; Raymond R. Murphy, Jr.,* Secy.; Harold J. Weekley, Treas.
Directors:* Thomas J. Patrick, Jr., John E. Steffner.
Custodian and Fiscal Agent: American National Bank & Trust Co.
Number of staff: 1 part-time professional; 1 part-time support.
Employer Identification Number: 510200174

6632
L. P. Brown Foundation ¤ ☆
119 Racine St.
P.O. Box 11514
Memphis 38111 (901) 323-0333

Established in 1956.
Donor(s): L.P. Brown III.
Foundation type: Independent
Financial data (yr. ended 5/31/89): Assets, $1,476,417 (M); expenditures, $68,088, including $66,870 for 31 grants (high: $25,000; low: $50).
Purpose and activities: Giving for health associations, hospitals, higher education, and churches; support also for the arts and a community foundation.
Limitations: Giving primarily in Memphis, TN.
Application information: Application form not required.
Deadline(s): None
Write: L.P. Brown III, Pres.
Officers: L.P. Brown III, Pres.; Bryan Morgan, V.P.; C.W. Butler, Jr., Secy.-Treas.
Directors: Hubert A. McBride, Axson Brown Morgan.
Employer Identification Number: 626036338

6633
John Dustin Buckman Charitable Trust ¤
165 Madison Ave.
P.O. Box 84
Memphis 38101
Application address: Advisory Panel, John D. Buckman Fdn., Burch Porter and Johnson, 130 North Court Ave., Memphis, TN 38103

Established in 1980.
Donor(s): John Dustin Buckman.†
Foundation type: Independent
Financial data (yr. ended 9/30/86): Assets, $5,536,366 (M); expenditures, $404,414, including $359,530 for 16 grants (high: $100,000; low: $500).
Purpose and activities: Emphasis on education, child health and welfare, and youth agencies.
Limitations: Giving primarily in Memphis, TN.
Application information:
Initial approach: Proposal
Deadline(s): None
Board meeting date(s): May and Oct.
Write: Joe Duncan, Secy.
Officer: Joe Duncan, Secy.
Trustee: First Tennessee Bank.
Employer Identification Number: 626155483

6634
Hardwick Caldwell Foundation, Inc. ☆
c/o American National Bank & Trust Co.
P.O. Box 1638
Chattanooga 37401-1638 (615) 757-3203

Donor(s): L. Hardwick Caldwell.†
Foundation type: Independent
Financial data (yr. ended 05/31/89): Assets, $5,590,672 (M); gifts received, $3,836,486; expenditures, $69,232, including $66,300 for 10 grants (high: $40,000; low: $500; average: $1,000-$3,000).
Purpose and activities: Support for education, a YMCA, community development, and Protestant churches and Christian organizations.
Types of support: Building funds, capital campaigns.
Limitations: Giving primarily in Chattanooga, TN. No grants to individuals.
Application information: Applications not accepted.
Write: Peter T. Cooper
Officers: Robert H. Caldwell,* Pres.; L.H. Caldwell, Jr., V.P. and Secy.-Treas.
Trustees:* Summer Bryan, L.H. Caldwell III, Robert H. Caldwell, Jr.
Number of staff: None.
Employer Identification Number: 626042101

6635
Camelot Foundation, Inc. ¤ ☆
108 West Price Ln.
Oak Ridge 37830 (615) 482-1492

Foundation type: Independent
Financial data (yr. ended 06/30/89): Assets, $1,047,886 (M); expenditures, $125,544, including $40,000 for 1 grant.
Purpose and activities: Giving limited to the care and treatment of disturbed children.
Limitations: No grants to individuals.
Application information:
Initial approach: Letter
Deadline(s): None
Write: John F. Terrell, Sr., Mgr.
Officers and Directors:* Charles B. Owen,* Pres.; Vincent Vivirito, V.P.; William Weiskopf, V.P.; Vivian N. Joyce,* Secy.; June Hardy,* Treas.; John F. Terrell, Sr., Mgr.; and 17 additional directors.
Employer Identification Number: 362935664

6636
Robert M. and Lenore W. Carrier Foundation ☆
c/o Union Planters National Bank
P.O. Box 387
Memphis 38147 (901) 523-6196

Established in 1952.
Foundation type: Independent
Financial data (yr. ended 12/31/88): Assets, $1,455,416 (M); expenditures, $100,663, including $86,000 for 25 grants to individuals (high: $4,000; low: $3,000).
Purpose and activities: Awards scholarships for higher education to MS residents attending the University of MS.
Types of support: Student aid.
Limitations: Giving limited to MS residents.
Application information: Application form available from Univ. of MS Financial Aid Office, University, MS 38677.
Deadline(s): Jan. 31, senior year of high school
Write: Ed Walton, Trust Officer, Union Planters National Bank
Trustees: Gordon Beasley, Leslie C. Daniel, Robert C. Khayat, Union Planters National Bank.
Employer Identification Number: 626035575

6637
Cartinhour Foundation, Inc.
c/o American National Bank & Trust Co.
736 Market St.
Chattanooga 37402 (615) 757-3203

Established in 1961 in DE.
Donor(s): W.C. Cartinhour.†
Foundation type: Independent
Financial data (yr. ended 6/30/89): Assets, $1,828,403 (M); expenditures, $90,908, including $81,000 for 20 grants (high: $16,000; low: $1,000; average: $1,000-$4,000).
Purpose and activities: Emphasis on higher education and religious giving, including religious schools.
Types of support: Operating budgets, scholarship funds.
Limitations: Giving primarily in Chattanooga, TN. No grants to individuals.
Application information: Applications not accepted.
Officers and Trustees: Kathleen G. Cartinhour, Pres.; Marie Cartinhour Woods, V.P.; Peter T. Cooper, Secy.-Treas.; William G. Brown, Margaret W. Denkler, Scott L. Pobasco, Jr., Ellen Woods Polansky, Kathleen Woods Van Devender, J. Ralston Wells, Caroline T. Woods.
Number of staff: None.
Employer Identification Number: 626036308

6638
The Community Foundation of Greater Chattanooga, Inc. ⌑
1600 American National Bank Bldg.
Chattanooga 37402 (615) 267-4311
Additional address: 736 Market St., Chattanooga, TN 37402

Incorporated in 1963 in TN.
Foundation type: Community
Financial data (yr. ended 12/31/88): Assets, $9,004,099 (M); gifts received, $865,459; expenditures, $1,917,924, including $543,528 for 91 grants.
Purpose and activities: "To promote and enhance the well-being of the inhabitants of the greater Chattanooga area."
Types of support: Student aid, continuing support, seed money, building funds, conferences and seminars, annual campaigns, matching funds, operating budgets, program-related investments, renovation projects.
Limitations: Giving limited to the greater Chattanooga, TN, area. No loans.
Publications: 990-PF, program policy statement, application guidelines.
Application information: Application form required.
Initial approach: Brief letter
Copies of proposal: 30
Deadline(s): End of month preceding Grants Committee meeting
Board meeting date(s): Annually; Grants Committee meets in Feb., May, Aug., and Nov.
Final notification: 3 weeks after meeting
Write: William A. Walter, Exec. Secy.
Officers: Llewellyn Boyd,* Pres.; Lynn Woodworth,* 1st V.P.; Robert J. Sudderth,* 2nd V.P.; J. Guy Beatty, Jr., Secy.; S.L. Probasco, Jr.,* Treas.
Directors:* Jerry V. Adams, Alton Chapman, Kay K. Chitty, Susan Davenport, R. Allan Edgar, John P. Franklin, Daniel K. Frierson, Jane W. Harbaugh, Barbara Haskew, Ruth Holmberg, N.C. Hughes, Jr., Carl D. Long, Spencer McCallie III, P. Robert Philip, David P. Phillips, James Robinson, Harold Ruck, Frances Smith, Yvonne Smith, William P. Sudderth.
Number of staff: 1 part-time professional; 2 part-time support.
Employer Identification Number: 626045999

6639
Christy-Houston Foundation, Inc. ☆
122 North Spring St.
Murfreesboro 37130 (615) 898-1140

Established in 1987 in TN.
Donor(s): Lady Houston Brown Trust.
Foundation type: Independent
Financial data (yr. ended 4/30/88): Assets, $45,307,547 (M); gifts received, $1,740,731; expenditures, $569,953, including $158,245 for 5 grants (high: $49,865; low: $16,000).
Purpose and activities: Giving primarily for hospitals and health-related projects.
Types of support: Building funds, equipment, matching funds.
Limitations: Giving limited to Rutherford County, TN. No support for religious or veterans' organizations or historical societies. No grants to individuals.
Publications: Grants list, application guidelines.
Application information: Application form not required.
Copies of proposal: 1
Deadline(s): Jan. 31
Board meeting date(s): Mar., June, Sept., and Dec.
Final notification: Apr. 1
Write: James R. Arnhart, Exec. Dir.
Directors: James R. Arnhart, Exec. Dir.; Granville S. R. Bouldin, Henry King Butler, Ed Delbridge, Ed Elam, Clyde Fite, Larry N. Haynes, John S. Holmes, Jr., William H. Huldleston, Louis C. Jennings, Roger C. Maples, Hubert McCullough, Edward E. Miller, Jr., Matt B. Murfree III, Myers B. Parsons.
Number of staff: 1 part-time support.
Employer Identification Number: 621280998

6640
The Robert H. and Monica M. Cole Foundation ⌑
c/o First American Trust Co., Trust Dept.
505 South Gay St.
Knoxville 37902

Established in 1976.
Foundation type: Independent
Financial data (yr. ended 9/30/88): Assets, $2,235,246 (M); expenditures, $172,894, including $137,172 for 41 grants (high: $50,000; low: $300; average: $1,000-$5,000).
Purpose and activities: Grants for medical research on Parkinson's disease, cultural programs, and civic affairs.
Types of support: Operating budgets, research.
Limitations: Giving limited to eastern TN, including Knoxville, and southeast KY.
Application information:
Write: Mark A. Goodson, Trust Officer, First American Trust Co.
Trustees: Monica M. Cole, William W. Davis, J. Robert Page, First American Trust Co.
Employer Identification Number: 626137973

6641
Brownlee Currey Foundation ⌑
c/o Sovran Bank/Central South, Trust Dept.
One Commerce Place
Nashville 37219 (615) 749-3336

Established in 1967.
Foundation type: Independent
Financial data (yr. ended 12/31/88): Assets, $2,292,113 (M); expenditures, $134,499, including $122,250 for 25 grants (high: $20,000; low: $250).
Purpose and activities: Giving primarily for cultural programs, education, health, and a community fund.
Types of support: Annual campaigns, research.
Application information:
Initial approach: Letter
Deadline(s): None
Write: M. Kirk Scobey, Sr. V.P. and Trust Officer, Sovran Bank/Central South
Officers: Margaret C. Henley, Pres.; Brownlee O. Currey, Jr., V.P.
Trustee: Sovran Bank/Central South.
Employer Identification Number: 626077710

6642
Daelansa Foundation ⌑
450 Maclellan Bldg.
Chattanooga 37402
Application address: 428 McCallie Ave., Chattanooga, TN 37402; Tel.: (615) 756-5880

Established about 1983 in TN.
Foundation type: Independent
Financial data (yr. ended 12/31/87): Assets, $1,579,757 (M); expenditures, $72,383, including $66,033 for 28 grants (high: $15,000; low: $500).
Purpose and activities: Support primarily for education; giving also to hospitals and a community fund.
Limitations: Giving primarily in TN, with emphasis on Chattanooga.
Application information:
Deadline(s): None
Write: Carl J. Arnold, Secy.-Treas.
Officers and Trustees: David F.S. Johnson, Chair.; Anita J. Hamilton, Vice-Chair.; Elise E. Johnson, Vice-Chair.; Sally J. Shy, Vice-Chair.; Carl J. Arnold, Secy.-Treas.
Employer Identification Number: 581577718

6643
Joe C. Davis Foundation
28 White Bridge Rd.
Nashville 37205
Application address: 72 Round Pond Rd., Greenville, SC 29607; Tel.: (803) 288-6417

Established in 1976 in TN.
Donor(s): Joe C. Davis.†
Foundation type: Independent
Financial data (yr. ended 9/30/89): Assets, $3,544,965 (M); gifts received, $210,021; expenditures, $275,362, including $245,200 for 34 grants (high: $125,000; low: $200).

Purpose and activities: Support for educational and health-related endeavors.
Types of support: Matching funds, research, seed money, special projects, student loans.
Limitations: Giving primarily in the Nashville, TN, area.
Application information: Application form not required.
Copies of proposal: 1
Deadline(s): Aug. 15
Board meeting date(s): Sept. 10
Final notification: Sept. 15
Write: Dr. or Mrs. William R. DeLoache
Trustees: Bond Davis DeLoache, William DeLoache, M.D., William R. DeLoache, Jr.
Number of staff: 1
Employer Identification Number: 626125481

6644
Dixie Yarns Foundation, Inc. ⌑
P.O. Box 751
Chattanooga 37401

Established in 1944 in DE.
Donor(s): Dixie Yarns, Inc.
Foundation type: Company-sponsored
Financial data (yr. ended 12/31/88): Assets, $671,978 (M); gifts received, $670,000; expenditures, $490,165, including $482,725 for 59 grants (high: $111,000; low: $250; average: $500-$10,000) and $4,350 for 21 grants to individuals (high: $400; low: $150).
Purpose and activities: Giving primarily for the United Way and other social services; support also for youth and education; also provides aid to indigent employees or former employees of Dixie Yarns, Inc.
Types of support: Grants to individuals.
Limitations: Giving generally confined to the Chattanooga, TN, area.
Application information: Giving generally confined to organizations in which Dixie Yarns, Inc. employees are directly involved.
Write: Thomas C. Robinson, Jr., Secy.-Treas.
Officers: J. Burton Frierson,* Pres.; Daniel K. Frierson,* V.P.; Thomas C. Robinson, Jr., Secy.-Treas.
Trustees:* Raymond B. Witt, Jr.
Number of staff: None.
Employer Identification Number: 620645090

6645
H. W. Durham Foundation ⌑
5050 Poplar Ave., Suite 1522
Memphis 38157 (901) 386-4531

Incorporated in 1955 in TN.
Foundation type: Operating
Financial data (yr. ended 09/30/88): Assets, $8,688,762 (M); gifts received, $57,734; expenditures, $564,427, including $19,849 for 3 grants (high: $10,000; low: $849).
Purpose and activities: A private operating foundation; support primarily for the elderly, including higher education and social services.
Limitations: Giving primarily in Memphis, TN.
Application information:
Deadline(s): None
Officers: Thomas H. Durham, Jr., Pres.; J.M. Scott, V.P.; Erich W. Merrill, Secy.; A. Earl Priest, Treas.
Directors: O.L. Cruzen, Ralph Lawrence, Bergen Merrill, Thomas Ratts, M.J. Scott.
Employer Identification Number: 620583854

6646
East Tennessee Foundation
360 Sovran Ctr.
550 West Main Ave.
Knoxville 37902 (615) 524-1223

Incorporated in 1958 in TN.
Foundation type: Community
Financial data (yr. ended 12/31/89): Assets, $6,646,316 (M); gifts received, $1,782,470; expenditures, $1,008,763, including $589,968 for grants and $5,000 for 2 grants to individuals of $2,500 each.
Purpose and activities: Support for the arts, education, community development, and youth services.
Types of support: Conferences and seminars, consulting services, equipment, matching funds, operating budgets, publications, renovation projects, research, technical assistance, fellowships, special projects.
Limitations: Giving limited to Knoxville, TN, and its 18 surrounding counties.
Publications: Biennial report (including application guidelines), newsletter, informational brochure.
Application information: Application form provided for application to the arts fund and the youth endowment. Application form not required.
Initial approach: Letter or phone
Copies of proposal: 1
Deadline(s): Unsolicited applications reviewed Apr. and Oct.; no set deadline
Write: Katharine Pearson, Exec. Dir.
Officers: Natalie L. Haslam, Chair.; John R. Cooper, Pres.; Katherine Pearson, Exec. Dir.
Number of staff: 4 full-time professional; 2 part-time support.
Employer Identification Number: 620807696

6647
The Evans Foundation, Inc. ⌑
450 Maclellan Bldg.
Chattanooga 37402 (615) 756-5880
Application address: P.O. Box 71, Lookout Mountain, TN 37350; Tel.: (615) 821-1368

Incorporated in 1952 in DE.
Donor(s): Nell Evans Johnson,† Joseph W. Johnson, Jr., M.D., H. Clay Evans Johnson, David F.S. Johnson.
Foundation type: Independent
Financial data (yr. ended 12/31/88): Assets, $1,225,386 (M); expenditures, $168,460, including $166,500 for 11 grants (high: $35,000; low: $3,000).
Purpose and activities: Emphasis on higher and secondary education, including awards to high school teachers and scholarship funds, youth agencies, and a community fund.
Types of support: Scholarship funds.
Limitations: Giving primarily in TN.
Publications: Application guidelines.
Application information:
Initial approach: Letter
Deadline(s): None
Write: Douglas A. Nelson, Pres.
Officers and Trustees: Douglas A. Nelson, Pres.; Margaret J. Curtis, Secy.-Treas.; Nell Evans Johnson, Anna K. Johnson-Chase, Mary J. Nelson.
Employer Identification Number: 626040820

6648
M. Stratton Foster Charitable Foundation ⌑ ☆
c/o First American Trust Co.
Nashville 37237-0402

Established in 1986 in TN.
Foundation type: Independent
Financial data (yr. ended 04/30/89): Assets, $2,953,193 (M); gifts received, $1,422; expenditures, $218,511, including $162,667 for 9 grants (high: $85,000; low: $1,000).
Purpose and activities: Support primarily for higher education, athletics and recreation, welfare, the performing arts, and a Presbyterian church.
Limitations: Giving primarily in Nashville, TN. No grants to individuals.
Application information:
Initial approach: Proposal
Deadline(s): Mar. 1 and Sept. 1
Write: Bob L. Andrews, Trust Officer, First American Trust Co.
Trustees: Reber Boult, Joe Thompson, Jr., First American Trust Co.
Employer Identification Number: 626195713

6649
Mary G. K. Fox Foundation ⌑ ☆
P.O. Box 1991
Knoxville 37901-1991

Established in 1981.
Foundation type: Independent
Financial data (yr. ended 1/31/88): Assets, $1,226,531 (M); expenditures, $87,721, including $79,523 for 9 grants (high: $58,023; low: $200).
Purpose and activities: Giving primarily to a YMCA; support also for community organizations.
Limitations: Giving primarily in Greeneville, TN.
Officers: C. Ray Adams, Mgr.; Helen L. Horner, Mgr.; Davis Stroud, Mgr.
Trustee: Valley Fidelity Bank & Trust Co.
Employer Identification Number: 626160483

6650
Gherkin Foundation, Inc. ☆
700 Krystal Bldg.
Chattanooga 37402 (615) 756-6585

Established in 1986 in TN.
Donor(s): Sharon Mills.
Foundation type: Independent
Financial data (yr. ended 12/31/87): Assets, $1,029,517 (M); expenditures, $37,500, including $37,500 for 1 grant.
Purpose and activities: Initial year of grantmaking activity, 1987; support in the areas of health, education, the humanities, religion, culture, and social welfare.
Types of support: Renovation projects.
Limitations: Giving primarily in the Chattanooga, TN, area.
Application information: Applications not accepted.
Write: W.E. Landis, Treas.
Officers: Sharon Mills, Pres.; W.E. Landis, V.P. and Treas.; Mrs. Felix G. Miller, Jr., Secy.
Employer Identification Number: 621289460

6651
Goldsmith Foundation, Inc. ¤
123 South Main St.
P.O. Box 449
Memphis 38143

Incorporated in 1944 in TN.
Donor(s): Members of the Goldsmith family.
Foundation type: Independent
Financial data (yr. ended 12/31/88): Assets, $3,854,994 (M); gifts received, $1,838; expenditures, $277,632, including $244,338 for 246 grants (high: $48,250; low: $20; average: $1,000-$10,000).
Purpose and activities: Emphasis on Jewish welfare funds, health, higher and other education, and social services.
Limitations: Giving primarily in TN.
Officers and Trustees: Robert T. Goldsmith, Pres.; Fred Goldsmith, Jr., V.P.; Fred Goldsmith III, V.P.; Edwin M. Marks, V.P.; Elias J. Goldsmith, Jr., Secy.-Treas.; Larry J. Goldsmith.
Employer Identification Number: 626039604

6652
Golightly Foundation, Inc. ¤
First Tennessee Bldg., Suite 2020
165 Madison Ave.
Memphis 38103

Established in 1955 in TN.
Foundation type: Independent
Financial data (yr. ended 12/31/88): Assets, $1,182,172 (M); expenditures, $56,563, including $52,200 for 2 grants (high: $37,200; low: $15,000).
Purpose and activities: General charitable giving in local area.
Limitations: Giving limited to TN.
Application information: Application form not required.
Deadline(s): None
Write: Ernest B. Williams III, Trustee
Officers: David Williams, V.P.; William F. Kirsch, Secy.-Treas.
Trustee: Ernest B. Williams III.
Employer Identification Number: 626047757

6653
Guzikowski Family Foundation ¤ ☆
c/o Sovran Bank-Central South
One Commerce Place
Nashville 37219 (615) 749-3336

Established in 1986 in TN.
Foundation type: Independent
Financial data (yr. ended 11/30/88): Assets, $42,182 (M); expenditures, $284,332, including $282,150 for 54 grants (high: $91,000; low: $250).
Purpose and activities: Giving primarily for Catholic churches and welfare organizations; support also for secondary and higher education.
Limitations: No grants to individuals.
Application information:
Initial approach: Letter
Deadline(s): None
Write: M. Kirk Scobey, Sr. V.P. and Trust Officer, Sovran Bank-Central South
Trustee: Sovran Bank/Central South.
Employer Identification Number: 626195892

6654
Hamico, Inc. ¤
1715 West 38th St.
Chattanooga 37409

Incorporated in 1956 in TN.
Donor(s): Chattem, Inc.
Foundation type: Independent
Financial data (yr. ended 12/31/88): Assets, $2,814,339 (M); gifts received, $57,406; expenditures, $77,702, including $76,100 for 27 grants (high: $10,000; low: $150).
Purpose and activities: Emphasis on higher, secondary, and elementary education, culture, and health programs.
Types of support: Continuing support, endowment funds.
Limitations: Giving primarily in Chattanooga, TN. No grants to individuals.
Application information: Contributes only to pre-selected organizations. Applications not accepted.
Officers and Trustees: Alex Guerry, Pres.; James E. Abshire, Jr., V.P.; Durwood C. Harvey, Secy.-Treas.; Ray W. Evans, Alexander Guerry III, James M. Holbert, Vernon L. Staggs.
Number of staff: None.
Employer Identification Number: 626040782

6655
Harris Foundation ☆
P.O. Box 2225
Johnson City 37605

Foundation type: Independent
Financial data (yr. ended 12/31/88): Assets, $1,446,068 (M); expenditures, $148,132, including $146,809 for grants.
Purpose and activities: Giving locally to educational and charitable organizations.
Limitations: Giving primarily in northeast TN.
Officers: Allen Harris III, Pres.; Allen Harris, Jr., V.P.; Sabe Hawkins, Secy.; W.L. Holmes, Treas.
Employer Identification Number: 626046613

6656
The HCA Foundation ▼
c/o Hospital Corp. of America
One Park Plaza, P.O. Box 550
Nashville 37202-0550 (615) 320-2165

Established in 1982 in TN.
Donor(s): Hospital Corp. of America.
Foundation type: Company-sponsored
Financial data (yr. ended 12/31/89): Assets, $54,789,897 (L); expenditures, $3,114,371, including $2,516,103 for 261 grants (high: $393,000; low: $200; average: $1,000-$20,000) and $217,933 for 903 employee matching gifts.
Purpose and activities: Giving primarily for health management and policy exploration; support also for education, especially higher education, the arts and cultural programs, social services, civic and community affairs, and the United Way.
Types of support: Matching funds, general purposes, land acquisition, special projects, building funds, professorships, publications, conferences and seminars, renovation projects, capital campaigns, equipment, continuing support, employee matching gifts, operating budgets, research, employee-related scholarships.
Limitations: Giving primarily in Nashville, TN, and to groups that are national in scope. No support for social, religious, fraternal, labor, athletic, or veterans' groups (except for specific programs of broad public benefit), political entities, schools below the college level, private foundations, or individual United Way agencies. No grants to individuals (except for employee-related scholarships), or for endowment funds, dinners, tables, or tickets to fund-raising events, promotional materials including goodwill advertising, publications, trips, or tours.
Publications: Biennial report (including application guidelines), informational brochure.
Application information: Information brochures available for HCA Teacher Awards Program, HCA Volunteer Service Awards, HCA Achievement Awards for Non-Profit Management, and employee-related scholarship program. Application form not required.
Initial approach: Telephone or letter
Copies of proposal: 1
Deadline(s): None
Board meeting date(s): Jan., Apr., July, and Oct.
Final notification: Within 4 months
Write: Ida F. Cooney, Exec. Dir.
Officers and Directors:* Donald S. MacNaughton,* Chair. and Pres.; Ida F. Cooney, V.P. and Exec. Dir.; Peter F. Bird, Secy.-Treas. and Sr. Prog. Officer; Robert C. Crosby, Frank F. Drowota III, Thomas F. First, Jr., Charles J. Kane, R. Clayton McWhorter, Roger E. Mick.
Number of staff: 3 full-time professional; 1 full-time support.
Employer Identification Number: 621134070

6657
Hohenberg Charity Trust ¤
266 South Front St.
Memphis 38101
Application address: P.O. Box 193, Memphis, TN 38101; Tel.: (901) 529-4200

Established in 1954 in TN.
Donor(s): Hohenberg Brothers Co.
Foundation type: Company-sponsored
Financial data (yr. ended 12/31/87): Assets, $1,203,028 (M); expenditures, $74,487, including $67,458 for 13 grants (high: $20,000; low: $500).
Purpose and activities: Giving primarily for a community fund and Jewish organizations; support also for education.
Limitations: Giving primarily in the Memphis, TN, area. No grants to individuals.
Application information: Application form not required.
Deadline(s): None
Write: Julien J. Hohenberg or Rudi E. Scheidt, Trustees
Trustees: Susan Scheidt Arney, Julien J. Hohenberg, Rudi E. Scheidt, Rudi E. Scheidt, Jr., Juliet Hohenberg Thompson.
Employer Identification Number: 626036168

6658
The Houghland Foundation ☒ ☆
c/o Davis Carr
P.O. Box 198062, 222 Third Ave., North
Nashville 37219

Established in 1986 in TN.
Donor(s): Calvin Houghland.
Foundation type: Independent
Financial data (yr. ended 6/30/88): Assets, $1,397,935 (M); gifts received, $1,098,091; expenditures, $13,549, including $1 for grants to individuals.
Purpose and activities: Giving to a youth club.
Application information: Contributes only to pre-selected organizations. Applications not accepted.
Officers and Trustees: James A. Webb, Jr., Pres.; George A. Ragsdale, V.P.; Davis H. Carr, Secy.-Treas.
Employer Identification Number: 626199041

6659
Orion L. & Emma B. Hurlbut Memorial Fund ☒
c/o First Tennessee Bank
701 Market St.
Chattanooga 37401
Application address: Jo Ann Clifford, c/o Chattanooga Tumor Clinic, 975 East Third St., Chattanooga, TN 37403; Tel.: (615) 266-3029

Established in 1937 in TN.
Foundation type: Independent
Financial data (yr. ended 4/30/87): Assets, $9,590,395 (M); expenditures, $439,649, including $247,941 for 1 grant and $80,171 for 29 grants to individuals (high: $10,352; low: $110).
Purpose and activities: Giving primarily for a tumor clinic; support also for treatment of cancer patients.
Types of support: Grants to individuals.
Limitations: Giving primarily in TN.
Application information:
Deadline(s): None
Administrators: C. Windon Kimsey, M.D., Harry Stone, M.D., First Tennessee Bank.
Employer Identification Number: 626034546

6660
Hazel Montague Hutcheson Foundation
c/o American National Bank & Trust Co.
736 Market St.
Chattanooga 37402 (615) 757-3203

Established in 1962 in TN.
Donor(s): Hazel G.M. Montague.†
Foundation type: Independent
Financial data (yr. ended 06/30/89): Assets, $2,891,516 (M); expenditures, $134,616, including $120,000 for 38 grants (high: $14,000; low: $200; average: $1,000-$3,000).
Purpose and activities: Support for private secondary schools, Protestant church support, health agencies, and cultural programs.
Types of support: Annual campaigns.
Limitations: Giving primarily in TN and FL. No grants for scholarships; no loans.
Application information: Applications not accepted.
Board meeting date(s): Varies
Write: Peter T. Cooper
Trustees: Betty R. Hutcheson, Theodore M. Hutcheson, W. Frank Hutcheson, Hazel Hutcheson Meadow.
Number of staff: None.
Employer Identification Number: 626045925

6661
J. R. Hyde Foundation, Inc. ☒
3030 Poplar Ave.
Memphis 38111 (901) 325-4245

Incorporated in 1961 in TN.
Donor(s): J.R. Hyde.†
Foundation type: Independent
Financial data (yr. ended 8/31/88): Assets, $14,688,291 (M); gifts received, $750,000; expenditures, $835,523, including $765,179 for 91 grants (high: $50,000; low: $600) and $17,500 for 7 grants to individuals of $2,500 each.
Purpose and activities: Grants for higher education, including scholarships for the children of Malone & Hyde employees, secondary education, cultural programs, community funds, social service and youth agencies, and Protestant church support.
Types of support: Scholarship funds, employee-related scholarships.
Limitations: Giving primarily in the mid-South. No grants to individuals (except for company-employee scholarships), or for general support, capital or endowment funds, research programs, or matching grants; no loans.
Application information: Application form not required.
Deadline(s): None
Board meeting date(s): Sept. and as required
Write: Ms. Margaret R. Hyde, Pres.
Officers: Margaret R. Hyde, Pres.; Joe R. Hyde III, V.P.; Jane Hyde Scott, Secy.-Treas.
Trustee: First Tennessee Bank.
Employer Identification Number: 620677725

6662
The Daniel Ashley and Irene Houston Jewell Memorial Foundation
c/o American National Bank & Trust Co.
P.O. Box 1638
Chattanooga 37401 (615) 757-3203

Trust established in 1951 in GA.
Donor(s): The Crystal Springs Textiles Corp.
Foundation type: Independent
Financial data (yr. ended 6/30/89): Assets, $2,653,699 (M); expenditures, $117,618, including $89,400 for 16 grants (high: $15,000; low: $300; average: $2,000) and $12,000 for 10 grants to individuals of $2,000 each.
Purpose and activities: Giving for a hospital, public schools and higher education, and local area scholarships.
Types of support: Student aid, annual campaigns, building funds, capital campaigns, equipment, operating budgets.
Limitations: Giving limited to Chickamauga, GA. Scholarships available only to high school seniors who are residents of Walker, Dade, and Catoosa counties, GA. No grants to individuals.
Application information: Applications not accepted, except for scholarships. Application form not required.
Board meeting date(s): Aug.
Write: Peter T. Cooper, Treas.
Officers and Trustees: William H. Jewell, Chair.; George M. McMillan, Vice-Chair.; E. Dunbar Jewell, Secy.; Peter T. Cooper, Treas.; Elizabeth J. Barry, Juanita Crowder, D.A. Jewell V.
Number of staff: None.
Employer Identification Number: 586034213

6663
Lichterman-Loewenberg Foundation ☒ ☆
P.O. Box 6
Memphis 38101

Established in 1945.
Donor(s): William A. Lowenberg, Martin J. Lichterman, Sr.
Foundation type: Independent
Financial data (yr. ended 11/30/89): Assets, $1,458,577 (M); gifts received, $209,693; expenditures, $198,507, including $194,160 for 65 grants (high: $110,250; low: $100).
Purpose and activities: Giving primarily for Jewish organizations and a Christian missionary program; support also for museums and higher education.
Types of support: Building funds, capital campaigns.
Limitations: Giving primarily in Memphis, TN. No grants to individuals.
Application information: Contributes only to pre-selected organizations. Applications not accepted.
Officers: William A. Loewenberg, Pres.; Hills H. Lichterman, V.P.; Martin J. Lichterman, Sr., V.P.; William Ira Lowenberg, Secy.
Employer Identification Number: 626048265

6664
Liff Family Foundation ☒
c/o Kraft Bros.
404 James Robertson Pkwy.
Nashville 37219-5025

Established in 1974 in TN.
Foundation type: Independent
Financial data (yr. ended 8/31/88): Assets, $1,200,886 (M); gifts received, $232,000; expenditures, $169,566, including $155,415 for 77 grants (high: $116,350; low: $10).
Purpose and activities: Giving primarily for Jewish welfare; support also for higher education.
Application information: Contributes only to pre-selected organizations. Applications not accepted.
Trustees: Adam Liff, Noah Liff.
Employer Identification Number: 237410352

6665
William P. and Marie R. Lowenstein Foundation ☒
100 North Main Bldg., Rm. 3020
Memphis 38103 (901) 525-5744

Incorporated about 1959 in TN.
Donor(s): Marie R. Lowenstein.†
Foundation type: Independent
Financial data (yr. ended 12/31/88): Assets, $2,752,233 (M); expenditures, $226,199, including $159,528 for 62 grants (high: $42,500; low: $100).

Purpose and activities: Giving primarily for Jewish welfare funds, higher education, hospitals, and health agencies.
Types of support: Operating budgets, seed money, equipment, scholarship funds, fellowships.
Limitations: Giving limited to TN and Israel. No grants to individuals, or for endowment funds or matching gifts; no loans.
Application information: Application form required.
Initial approach: Letter or proposal
Copies of proposal: 1
Deadline(s): None
Board meeting date(s): May and Dec.
Final notification: 10 months
Write: Alvin A. Gordon, Exec. Dir.
Officers and Directors: Alvin A. Gordon, Pres. and Exec. Dir.; Elaine K. Gordon, Marshall D. Gordon, Robert Gordon, Ed Marlowe, Ted M. Winestone.
Number of staff: 1 full-time professional; 1 full-time support.
Employer Identification Number: 626037976

6666
Lyndhurst Foundation ▼
Suite 701, Tallan Bldg.
100 West Martin Luther King Blvd.
Chattanooga 37402-2561 (615) 756-0767

Incorporated in 1938 in DE.
Donor(s): T. Cartter Lupton,† Central Shares Corp.
Foundation type: Independent
Financial data (yr. ended 12/31/89): Assets, $108,873,642 (M); expenditures, $7,090,377, including $4,938,200 for 53 grants (high: $1,250,000; low: $1,000; average: $4,000-$75,000) and $660,000 for 25 grants to individuals (high: $30,000; low: $20,000).
Purpose and activities: Support primarily for revitalization in Chattanooga, including grants for education, the arts, public participation, and community development. Limited number of grants are made to projects within the Southeast region. Lyndhurst Prizes, awarded to individuals whose work embodies values the foundation considers important, are given solely at the initiative of the foundation.
Types of support: General purposes, seed money, matching funds, operating budgets, program-related investments, special projects, grants to individuals.
Limitations: Giving limited to the southeastern U.S., especially Chattanooga, TN. No grants to individuals, or for scholarships, fellowships, building or endowment funds, equipment, deficit financing, medical or university-based research, publications, or conferences; no general support for hospitals, colleges, universities, or religious organizations; no loans.
Publications: Annual report, application guidelines.
Application information: Applications or nominations not accepted for Lyndhurst Prizes; application form required for Lyndhurst Teachers' Awards. Application form not required.
Initial approach: Letter
Copies of proposal: 1
Deadline(s): Feb. 15 for Lyndhurst Teachers' Awards; Jan. 25, Mar. 25, June 25, Aug. 25, and Oct. 25 for other grants
Board meeting date(s): Jan., Mar., May, Aug., Oct., and Dec.
Final notification: 3 months
Write: Jack E. Murrah, Pres.
Officers: Jack E. Murrah,* Pres.; Eleanor McCallie Cooper, V.P.; Allen McCallie, Secy.; Charles B. Chitty, Treas.
Trustees:* John T. Lupton,* Chair.; Robert Coles, Deaderick C. Montague.
Number of staff: 4 full-time professional; 3 full-time support; 1 part-time support.
Employer Identification Number: 626044177

6667
R. J. Maclellan Charitable Trust ▼
Provident Bldg., Suite 501
Chattanooga 37402 (615) 755-1291

Trust established in 1954 in TN.
Donor(s): Robert J. Maclellan.†
Foundation type: Independent
Financial data (yr. ended 12/31/89): Assets, $53,541,945 (M); expenditures, $3,826,016, including $3,752,654 for 59 grants (high: $290,000; low: $1,000).
Purpose and activities: Giving for higher and theological education, social service and youth agencies, Protestant religious associations, and cultural programs.
Types of support: Continuing support, annual campaigns, seed money, building funds, equipment, matching funds, scholarship funds, operating budgets.
Limitations: Giving primarily in the Chattanooga, TN, area. No grants to individuals, or for emergency funds, deficit financing, land acquisition, renovations, endowment funds, special projects, research, publications, or conferences; no loans.
Application information: Application form not required.
Initial approach: Letter
Copies of proposal: 1
Deadline(s): 3 weeks before board meetings
Board meeting date(s): Last Tues. of each month except Jan. and Nov.
Final notification: 1 week after meeting
Write: Hugh O. Maclellan, Sr., Trustee
Trustees: Hugh O. Maclellan, Sr., Dudley Porter, Jr., American National Bank & Trust Co. of Chattanooga.
Number of staff: 1 full-time professional; 1 full-time support.
Employer Identification Number: 626037023

6668
The Maclellan Foundation, Inc. ▼
Provident Bldg., Suite 501
Chattanooga 37402 (615) 755-1366

Incorporated in 1945 in DE.
Donor(s): Robert J. Maclellan,† and members of the Maclellan family.
Foundation type: Independent
Financial data (yr. ended 12/31/89): Assets, $129,235,513 (M); expenditures, $5,171,430, including $4,821,654 for 50 grants (high: $475,000; low: $330; average: $50,000-$150,000).
Purpose and activities: Grants largely for higher education, Protestant missions support and religious associations, youth agencies, and social services.
Types of support: Continuing support, annual campaigns, seed money, building funds, equipment, matching funds, operating budgets.
Limitations: Giving primarily in the Chattanooga, TN, area. No grants to individuals, or for emergency funds, deficit financing, land acquisition, renovations, endowment funds, research, demonstration projects, publications, or conferences; no loans.
Application information: Application form not required.
Initial approach: Letter
Copies of proposal: 1
Deadline(s): 3 weeks prior to board meetings
Board meeting date(s): Last Tues. of each month, except Jan. and Nov.
Final notification: 1 week after meeting
Write: Hugh O. Maclellan, Sr., Chair.
Officers: Hugh O. Maclellan, Sr.,* Chair.; Hugh O. Maclellan, Jr.,* Pres. and Treas.; Kathrina H. Maclellan, V.P.; Thomas H. McCallie III, Secy.
Trustees:* Frank A. Brock, G. Richard Hostetter, Pat MacMillan, Dudley Porter, Jr.
Number of staff: 1 full-time professional; 1 full-time support.
Employer Identification Number: 626041468

6669
Maddox Foundation ⌑
601 Broadway
Nashville 37203-3997

Foundation type: Independent
Financial data (yr. ended 12/31/87): Assets, $113,439 (M); expenditures, $103,628, including $101,925 for 53 grants (high: $22,500; low: $25).
Purpose and activities: Support primarily for higher and secondary education; support also for health associations, child and youth development, and welfare organizations.
Trustees: Dan W. Maddox, James N. Maddox, Margaret H. Maddox.
Employer Identification Number: 237017790

6670
Magdovitz Family Foundation
P.O. Box 650
Memphis 38101

Established in 1975 in TN.
Foundation type: Independent
Financial data (yr. ended 06/30/88): Assets, $1,029,324 (M); expenditures, $48,904, including $43,086 for grants.
Purpose and activities: Support primarily for Jewish organizations; support also for museums and other arts groups, religion, animal welfare, social service agencies, and health associations, including cancer programs.
Officers: Joseph A. Magdovitz, Pres. and Treas.; Earl J. Magdovitz, V.P. and Secy.
Employer Identification Number: 510164695

6671
Magic Chef Foundation, Inc. ⌑
740 King Edward Ave., S.E.
Cleveland 37311

Established in 1984 in TN.
Donor(s): Magic Chef Industries.
Foundation type: Company-sponsored
Financial data (yr. ended 06/30/89): Assets, $1,744,299 (M); expenditures, $301,569, including $298,120 for grants (high: $100,000).
Purpose and activities: Giving primarily for higher education, social services, with an emphasis of child welfare and youth organizations, and the arts.
Limitations: Giving primarily in TN. No grants to individuals.
Application information: Contributes only to pre-selected organizations. Applications not accepted.
Officers and Directors:* S.B. Rymer, Jr.,* Pres.; D.J. Krumm,* V.P.; Donald C. Byers, Secy.; Jerry Schiller,* Treas.
Employer Identification Number: 626047469

6672
Massengill-DeFriece Foundation, Inc.
Holston Plaza, Suite 208
516 Holston Ave.
Bristol 37620 (615) 764-3833

Incorporated in 1949 in TN.
Donor(s): Frank W. DeFriece,† Pauline M. DeFriece,† Frank W. DeFriece, Jr., Josephine D. Wilson.
Foundation type: Independent
Financial data (yr. ended 12/31/89): Assets, $3,671,913 (M); expenditures, $168,454, including $160,580 for 13 grants (high: $64,580; low: $500; average: $12,000).
Purpose and activities: Support for a historical association, private higher education, museums, health, youth, and religion.
Types of support: Continuing support, annual campaigns, emergency funds, equipment, matching funds, capital campaigns, endowment funds, operating budgets, professorships, special projects.
Limitations: Giving primarily in the Bristol, TN, and Bristol, VA, areas. No grants to individuals, or for research, publications, or conferences; no loans.
Application information: Application form not required.
Initial approach: Letter
Copies of proposal: 1
Board meeting date(s): Usually quarterly
Final notification: 2 to 4 months
Write: Frank W. DeFriece, Jr., V.P.
Officers: Albert S. Kelly, Jr., Pres.; Frank W. DeFriece, Jr., V.P.; Josephine D. Wilson, V.P.; John C. Paty, Jr., Secy.-Treas.
Directors: Mark W. DeFriece, Paul E. DeFriece, C. Richard Hagerstrom, Jr.
Number of staff: 1 part-time support.
Employer Identification Number: 626044873

6673
Jack C. Massey Foundation ⌑
310 25th Ave. North, Suite 109
Nashville 37203

Trust established in 1966 in TN.
Donor(s): Jack C. Massey.
Foundation type: Independent
Financial data (yr. ended 12/31/86): Assets, $6,063,882 (M); expenditures, $961,737, including $877,481 for 191 grants (high: $200,000; low: $50).
Purpose and activities: Emphasis on higher and secondary education and medical research; grants also for cultural programs.
Types of support: Research.
Limitations: Giving primarily in TN.
Application information: Contributes only to pre-selected organizations. Applications not accepted.
Write: Jack C. Massey, Trustee
Officers: Omega C. Sattler, Secy.; Clarence Edmonds,* Treas.
Trustees:* Barbara M. Clark, Jack C. Massey, J. Brad Reed.
Employer Identification Number: 626065672

6674
Meade Haven Charitable Trust ⌑
c/o Third National Bank
P.O. Box 76
Nashville 37244

Trust established in 1961 in TN.
Donor(s): Jesse E. Wills.
Foundation type: Independent
Financial data (yr. ended 12/31/87): Assets, $412,897 (M); expenditures, $497,808, including $481,000 for 54 grants (high: $55,000; low: $410).
Purpose and activities: Emphasis on higher and secondary education, Protestant church support, and a children's museum.
Limitations: Giving primarily in TN.
Trustees: Walter Robinson, Vernon Sharp, Robert W. Sturdivant, Ellen Buchner Wills, Jesse W. Wills, Matthew Buchner Wills, William Ridley Wills, Third National Bank.
Employer Identification Number: 626032780

6675
Melrose Foundation, Inc. ⌑
P.O. Box 18184
Knoxville 37928-2184

Incorporated in 1945 in TN.
Foundation type: Independent
Financial data (yr. ended 12/31/88): Assets, $1,280,821 (M); expenditures, $424,646, including $415,850 for 53 grants (high: $90,000; low: $500).
Purpose and activities: Giving for higher education, youth and social service agencies, health associations and hospitals, and a community fund.
Limitations: Giving primarily in TN, with emphasis on Knoxville. No grants to individuals.
Application information: Contributes only to pre-selected organizations. Applications not accepted.
Officers: J.E. Gettys,* Pres.; J.C. Kramer,* V.P.; J.B. Woolsey, Secy.-Treas.
Directors:* E.H. Rayson.
Employer Identification Number: 626037984

6676
Community Foundation of Greater Memphis ☆
1755 Lynnfield, Suite 285
Memphis 38119 (901) 761-3806

Established in 1969 in TN; combined operations with The Memphis-Plough Community Foundation in 1989.
Foundation type: Community
Financial data (yr. ended 4/30/89): Assets, $20,632,526 (M); gifts received, $3,111,727; expenditures, $3,036,626, including $2,640,882 for 397 grants (high: $200,000; low: $50; average: $100-$100,000).
Purpose and activities: Giving primarily for education, social services, and religion; support also for the arts and health associations.
Types of support: Seed money.
Limitations: Giving limited to Memphis and Shelby County, TN, western TN, and northern MS. No grants to individuals, or for budget deficits, endowments, capital or building funds, or annual campaigns.
Publications: Annual report, newsletter, informational brochure.
Application information: Application form required.
Initial approach: Letter or telephone
Copies of proposal: 4
Deadline(s): Apr. 16 and Nov. 1
Board meeting date(s): June and Dec.
Final notification: Following board meeting
Write: Gid H. Smith, Pres.
Officers: James D. Witherington, Jr., Chair.; Willis H. Willey III, Vice-Chair.; Gid H. Smith, Pres.; J. Martin Regan, Secy.; Robert S. Hester, Treas.
Number of staff: 5 full-time professional; 1 part-time professional; 2 full-time support.
Employer Identification Number: 581723645

6677
1939 Foundation ⌑
1600 Riverview Tower
900 South Gay St.
Knoxville 37902

Established in 1983 in TN.
Donor(s): F. Rodney Lawler.
Foundation type: Independent
Financial data (yr. ended 11/30/88): Assets, $3,072,494 (M); gifts received, $1,000,000; expenditures, $91,937, including $72,691 for 19 grants (high: $50,340; low: $100) and $9,590 for 2 grants to individuals (high: $8,190; low: $1,400).
Purpose and activities: Support for youth organizations and scholarships for higher education.
Types of support: Student aid.
Limitations: Giving primarily in TN.
Application information: Contributes only to pre-selected organizations and to individuals for scholarships.
Officers: F. Rodney Lawler,* Pres.; Phillip O. Lawson, Secy.
Directors:* Robin L. Gibson, Dell R. Lawler, Jon R. Lawler.
Employer Identification Number: 621183557

6678
North American Royalties Inc. Welfare Fund
200 East Eighth St.
Chattanooga 37402 (615) 265-3181

Established in 1966 in TN.
Donor(s): North American Royalties, Inc.
Foundation type: Company-sponsored
Financial data (yr. ended 12/31/89): Assets, $138,853 (M); gifts received, $293,385; expenditures, $320,733, including $286,810 for 24 grants (high: $38,300; low: $300) and $33,667 for 17 grants to individuals.
Purpose and activities: Giving primarily for social services, including community funds, and for education. Also supports a scholarship program for dependents of company employees.
Types of support: Building funds, general purposes, equipment, employee-related scholarships.
Limitations: Giving primarily in Chattanooga, TN. No grants to individuals (except for employee-related scholarships).
Application information: Application forms are provided for scholarships which are on behalf of the recipient. Scholarships are only for dependents of company employees.
Initial approach: Letter or telephone
Deadline(s): Mar. 1 for scholarships
Write: Gordon L. Smith, Jr., V.P., Planning, North American Royalties, Inc.
Trustees: Karl L. Landgrebe, Chair.; John P. Gaither, Gordon L. Smith, Jr., Gordon P. Street, Jr.
Employer Identification Number: 626052490

6679
Plough Foundation ▼
6077 Primacy Pkwy., Suite 230
Memphis 38119 (901) 761-9180

Trust established in 1972 in TN.
Donor(s): Abe Plough.†
Foundation type: Independent
Financial data (yr. ended 12/31/89): Assets, $74,684,084 (M); gifts received, $800,000; expenditures, $4,590,321, including $3,884,643 for 79 grants (high: $500,000; low: $100; average: $5,000-$100,000).
Purpose and activities: Grants to community projects, including a community fund, early childhood and elementary education, social service agencies, and civic affairs groups.
Types of support: Operating budgets, continuing support, annual campaigns, seed money, emergency funds, deficit financing, equipment, matching funds, general purposes, building funds, capital campaigns, endowment funds, professorships.
Limitations: Giving primarily in Memphis and Shelby counties, TN. No grants to individuals; no loans.
Application information: Application form not required.
Initial approach: Proposal
Copies of proposal: 1
Deadline(s): 15th of month prior to board meeting
Board meeting date(s): Feb., May, Aug., and Nov.
Final notification: 2 weeks
Write: Noris R. Haynes, Jr., Exec. Dir.
Officer and Trustees:* Noris R. Haynes, Jr.,* Exec. Dir.; Hallam Boyd, Jr., Patricia R. Burnham, Eugene J. Callahan, Sharon R. Eisenberg, Dianne R. Goldstein, Cecil C. Humphreys, Jocelyn P. Rudner, Steve Wishnia, Union Planters National Bank.
Number of staff: 1 full-time professional; 1 full-time support.
Employer Identification Number: 237175983

6680
The Justin and Valere Potter Foundation ▼
c/o Sovran Bank/Central South
One Commerce Place
Nashville 37219 (615) 749-3336

Trust established in 1951 in TN.
Donor(s): Justin Potter,† Valere Blair Potter.
Foundation type: Independent
Financial data (yr. ended 12/31/87): Assets, $17,559,527 (M); expenditures, $1,614,629, including $1,477,300 for 33 grants (high: $250,000; low: $5,000; average: $10,000-$75,000).
Purpose and activities: Giving primarily for higher education, including scholarship funds and medical education; support also for cultural programs, social services, and medical research.
Types of support: Scholarship funds, operating budgets, special projects, research.
Limitations: Giving primarily in Nashville, TN.
Application information:
Initial approach: Letter
Deadline(s): None
Board meeting date(s): As needed
Write: M. Kirk Scobey, Sr. V.P. & Trust Officer, Sovran Bank/Central South
Distribution Committee: Justin P. Wilson, Chair.; Albert L. Menefee, Jr., David K. Wilson.
Trustee: Sovran Bank/Central South.
Number of staff: None.
Employer Identification Number: 626033081

6681
James H. Prentiss Foundation ⌑ ☆
770 Estate Place
Memphis 38119-2770

Established in 1985 in TN.
Donor(s): James H. Prentiss.
Foundation type: Independent
Financial data (yr. ended 12/31/88): Assets, $1,206,324 (M); gifts received, $730,000; expenditures, $59,920, including $59,888 for 39 grants (high: $20,654; low: $25).
Purpose and activities: Giving primarily for a Presbyterian church and other Protestant organizations; support also for a community fund and higher education.
Officers and Directors: Raymond M. Shainberg, Pres.; Carol Wandling, Secy.-Treas.; Carol Prentiss, James H. Prentiss, James H. Prentiss, Jr.
Employer Identification Number: 621237684

6682
Reflection Riding, Inc. ⌑
c/o J. Nelson Irvine
1000 Tallan Bldg., Two Union Sq.
Chattanooga 37402

Established in 1956 in TN.
Foundation type: Independent
Financial data (yr. ended 12/31/88): Assets, $2,062,795 (M); gifts received, $68,898; expenditures, $173,460, including $169,060 for 1 foundation-administered program.
Purpose and activities: "Operate and maintain a modified arboretum open to the general public, to promote the conservation of resources, to educate the public as to and to demonstrate the need for conserving beauty, and to acquaint the public with the history of the area in which Reflection Riding is located."
Limitations: Giving primarily in TN.
Officers and Directors:* Mrs. John Woodworth,* Pres.; Mrs. John M. Martin,* V.P. and Secy.; H. Grant Law, Jr.,* V.P. and Treas.; and 11 additional directors.
Employer Identification Number: 620570240

6683
The Eleanor T. Reynolds Foundation ⌑ ☆
P.O. Box 156
Bristol 37621

Established in 1988.
Donor(s): Eleanor T. Reynolds.†
Foundation type: Independent
Financial data (yr. ended 12/31/88): Assets, $1,924,883 (M); gifts received, $1,831,803; expenditures, $90,948, including $62,199 for 4 grants (high: $29,400; low: $2,500).
Purpose and activities: Support for organizations with programs for the handicapped.
Trustees: Alethia P. Haynes, David Bruce Haynes, David S. Haynes.
Employer Identification Number: 621342279

6684
The Caudle Rymer Foundation, Inc. ⌑
1790 Ocoee St., N.E.
Cleveland 37311

Donor(s): S.B. Rymer, Jr.
Foundation type: Independent
Financial data (yr. ended 12/31/88): Assets, $1,476,078 (M); expenditures, $43,500, including $41,350 for 15 grants (high: $10,000; low: $100).
Purpose and activities: Support primarily to an athletic foundation, higher education (including bible colleges), and civic affairs organizations.
Limitations: Giving primarily in TN. No grants to individuals.
Application information: Contributes only to pre-selected organizations. Applications not accepted.
Officers: S.B. Rymer, Jr.,* Pres. and Treas.; Anne Caudle Rymer,* V.P. and Secy.
Directors:* S. Bradford Rymer III, Elise R. Turner.
Employer Identification Number: 581514882

6685
The Schadt Foundation, Inc. ⌑
One Commerce Sq., Rm. 1550
P.O. Box 241604
Memphis 38124-1604 (901) 526-8637

Incorporated in 1958 in TN.
Donor(s): Charles F. Schadt, Sr., Harry E. Schadt, Sr.,† Harry E. Schadt, Jr.

Foundation type: Independent
Financial data (yr. ended 12/31/88): Assets, $3,061,979 (M); expenditures, $164,460, including $151,000 for grants.
Purpose and activities: Emphasis on secondary education and youth agencies.
Limitations: Giving limited to Shelby County, TN. No grants to individuals.
Application information: Contributes only to pre-selected organizations. Applications not accepted.
Board meeting date(s): Annually
Write: Charles F. Schadt, Sr., Pres.
Officers and Directors: Stephen C. Schadt, Sr., Pres.; Lynn Schadt Thomas, Secy.; Charles F. Schadt, Jr., Charles F. Schadt, Sr., Harry E. Schadt, Jr., Reid Schadt.
Employer Identification Number: 626040050

6686
James A. Scheibler Jr. Trust ⌑ ☆
One Commerce Sq.
Memphis 38150

Foundation type: Operating
Financial data (yr. ended 11/30/88): Assets, $1,727,502 (M); gifts received, $1,275,596; expenditures, $191,479.
Purpose and activities: A private operating foundation; giving for general charitable activities.
Trustee: National Bank of Commerce.
Employer Identification Number: 626184539

6687
Schilling Foundation ⌑
P.O. Box 172079
Memphis 38187-2079

Established in 1983 in TN.
Donor(s): Steel City Wholesalers, Inc., Schilling Motors, Inc., Schilling Imports, Inc., Foxgate Lincoln-Mercury, Inc.
Foundation type: Company-sponsored
Financial data (yr. ended 12/31/87): Assets, $96,457 (M); gifts received, $285,000; expenditures, $243,525, including $243,502 for 77 grants (high: $100,000; low: $10).
Purpose and activities: Giving primarily for religious organizations, particularly Baptist and Presbyterian churches; support also for general charitable purposes.
Limitations: Giving primarily in TN.
Application information: Contributes only to pre-selected organizations. Applications not accepted.
Officers: Nettie W. Schilling,* Chair.; Harry L. Smith,* Pres.; Gary W. Curbo, Secy.-Treas.
Directors:* Mary E. Smith.
Employer Identification Number: 621185878

6688
Virginia & George Scholze, Jr. Foundation ⌑
Maclellan Bldg., Third Fl.
Chattanooga 37402

Established in 1984 in TN.
Donor(s): Maurine D. Scholze.†
Foundation type: Independent
Financial data (yr. ended 06/30/89): Assets, $1,390,408 (M); expenditures, $186,897, including $180,000 for 3 grants (high: $130,000; low: $20,000).
Purpose and activities: Support for organizations and programs whose function is the elimination of alcoholism and other drug addictions.
Limitations: Giving primarily in Chattanooga, TN.
Application information: Application form not required.
Deadline(s): None
Write: John C. Stophel, Pres.
Officers and Trustees:* John C. Stophel,* Pres.; G. William Oliphant,* V.P.; Glenn C. Stophel,* Secy.-Treas.; Carl B. Allen, Thomas A. Caldwell, Jr., E. Wayne Gilley.
Employer Identification Number: 581514413

6689
Sells Foundation, Inc. ⌑
410 South Roan St.
Box 410
Johnson City 37601 (615) 928-7591

Established in 1973 in TN.
Foundation type: Independent
Financial data (yr. ended 10/31/89): Assets, $1,155,040 (M); gifts received, $10,000; expenditures, $89,914, including $87,227 for 11 grants to individuals (high: $12,398; low: $2,879).
Purpose and activities: Support primarily for educational grants for needy theological students attending seminaries.
Types of support: Student aid.
Application information: Potential applicants are contacted by the foundation and furnished with forms to complete. Application form required.
Deadline(s): None
Write: Sam R. Sells, Pres.
Officers and Directors:* Sam R. Sells,* Pres. and Treas.; Ellen W. Sells,* V.P.; Ted F. Thomas,* Secy.; Francis Grimes, Harry H. Jones, Jr., Ben F. Lyle.
Employer Identification Number: 237322421

6690
The Shulman Family Foundation ⌑ ☆
P.O. Box 5585 EKS
Johnson City 37603 (615) 928-8438

Donor(s): Helen A. Shulman.
Foundation type: Independent
Financial data (yr. ended 12/31/88): Assets, $277,322 (M); gifts received, $52,484; expenditures, $103,045, including $52,433 for 42 grants and $48,650 for 47 grants to individuals (high: $7,452; low: $125).
Purpose and activities: Support for welfare agencies and the arts; also awards scholarships for higher education, primarily to former employees and their dependents and descendents, of the former Tri-State Container Corp. in Elizabethton, TN.
Types of support: Student aid, general purposes.
Limitations: Giving primarily in TN.
Application information: Application form available for scholarship requests.
Write: Barbara J. Silvers, Pres.
Officer and Trustees:* Barbara J. Silvers,* Pres.; Constance Ann Shulman, Diane Shulman, Helen A. Shulman, James David Shulman, Lori Shulman, William Shulman, H.R. Silvers.
Employer Identification Number: 626081798

6691
Speech Foundation of America
P.O. Box 11749
Memphis 38111-0749 (800) 992-9392
Application address: 5139 Klingle St., Washington, DC 20016; Tel.: (202) 363-3199

Established in 1947 in TN.
Donor(s): Members of the Fraser family.
Foundation type: Operating
Financial data (yr. ended 12/31/89): Assets, $6,800,000 (M); gifts received, $250,000; expenditures, $375,000, including $375,000 for foundation-administered programs.
Purpose and activities: A private operating foundation; support for foundation-initiated programs in therapy and prevention of stuttering.
Types of support: Conferences and seminars, publications.
Limitations: No grants to individuals, or for building or endowment funds, general purposes, scholarships, or fellowships.
Publications: Informational brochure.
Application information: Funds largely committed to support of operating programs; few grants awarded. Application form not required.
Initial approach: Letter
Board meeting date(s): Dec.
Write: Jane Fraser Fulcher, Pres.
Officers and Directors:* Jane Fraser Fulcher,* Pres.; Malcolm H. Fraser,* V.P.; Hubert A. McBride,* Secy.; Donald Edwards,* Treas.; Joseph Fulcher, James W. Garrison, Donald Lineback, Mary L. Ottensmeyer, William Parker, Joseph Walker, W.E. White.
Number of staff: 1 full-time professional; 2 full-time support.
Employer Identification Number: 626047678

6692
Steiner-Liff Foundation ⌑
c/o Steiner-Liff Iron and Metal Co.
710 South Second St.
Nashville 37213 (615) 252-2740
Additional address: P.O. Box 1182, Nashville, TN 37202

Established in 1965 in TN.
Foundation type: Independent
Financial data (yr. ended 07/31/89): Assets, $1,067,242 (M); gifts received, $410,010; expenditures, $380,689, including $378,521 for 69 grants (high: $250,000; low: $100; average: $100-$500).
Purpose and activities: Giving primarily for higher and other education, Jewish welfare funds, and Jewish temples; support also for general charitable purposes.
Types of support: Continuing support, general purposes, scholarship funds.
Limitations: Giving primarily in TN.
Publications: Annual report.
Application information:

Write: Trustees
Trustees: Noah Liff, Mitchell Magid.
Number of staff: None.
Employer Identification Number: 626050068

6693
Stephens Foundation Trust ⌑ ☆
Route 5, Pasquo Rd.
Nashville 37221

Established in 1987 in TN.
Donor(s): W.E. Stephens, Jr., Juanita Stephens, Stephens Foundation, Inc.
Foundation type: Independent
Financial data (yr. ended 7/31/89): Assets, $2,737,301 (M); gifts received, $145,495; expenditures, $170,306, including $115,900 for 18 grants (high: $100,000; low: $50).
Purpose and activities: Giving primarily to a university and Christian schools and churches.
Limitations: Giving primarily in TN.
Application information: Contributes only to pre-selected organizations. Applications not accepted.
Trustees: W.E. Stephens, Jr., Chair.; J. Greg Hardeman, Walter C. Leaver III, Juanita Stephens, James Vandiver.
Employer Identification Number: 626201842

6694
The William B. Stokely, Jr. Foundation ⌑
620 Campbell Station Rd.
Station West, Suite Y
Knoxville 37922 (615) 966-4878

Incorporated in 1951 in IN.
Donor(s): William B. Stokely, Jr.†
Foundation type: Independent
Financial data (yr. ended 12/31/88): Assets, $7,643,441 (M); expenditures, $444,158, including $415,060 for 96 grants (high: $50,000; low: $50).
Purpose and activities: Emphasis on higher education; some support also for hospitals, health agencies, and cultural programs.
Limitations: Giving primarily in eastern TN. No grants to individuals.
Application information: Application form not required.
Initial approach: Letter or proposal
Copies of proposal: 1
Deadline(s): Submit proposal preferably in the fall
Board meeting date(s): Feb., May, Aug., and Nov.
Write: William B. Stokely, III, Pres.
Officers: William B. Stokely III,* Pres.; Kay H. Stokely,* Exec. V.P.; Andrea A. White-Randall, V.P. and Secy.-Treas.
Directors:* Mrs. Horace Burnett, William B. Stokely IV.
Number of staff: 1 full-time professional.
Employer Identification Number: 356016402

6695
John Templeton Foundation ⌑ ☆
c/o Ann Cameron
Route One, Box 171
Sewanee 37375

Established in 1988 in TN.
Donor(s): John Marks Templeton.
Foundation type: Independent
Financial data (yr. ended 3/31/88): Assets, $2,079,425 (M); gifts received, $2,000,000; expenditures, $39,415, including $36,000 for 1 grant.
Purpose and activities: Initial year of operation, 1988; support for an association of Unity churches.
Application information:
Deadline(s): None
Officers: John Marks Templeton, Chair.; John Marks Templeton, Jr., Pres.; Harvey Maxwell Templeton III, Secy.; Ann Templeton Cameron, Treas.
Employer Identification Number: 621322826

6696
The Toms Foundation
Valley Fidelity Bank Bldg., Ninth Fl.
P.O. Box 2466
Knoxville 37901 (615) 544-3000

Trust established in 1954 in TN.
Donor(s): W.P. Toms.†
Foundation type: Independent
Financial data (yr. ended 06/30/89): Assets, $3,138,716 (M); expenditures, $100,732, including $11,969 for 10 grants (high: $4,000; low: $200; average: $650) and $83,525 for foundation-administered programs.
Purpose and activities: Emphasis on higher education and youth agencies; foundation also operates a museum and gardens.
Types of support: Seed money, emergency funds, building funds, equipment, land acquisition, professorships, research.
Limitations: Giving primarily in eastern TN. No grants to individuals, or for endowment funds, operating budgets, continuing support, annual campaigns, publications, demonstration projects, conferences, deficit financing, matching gifts, scholarships, or fellowships; no loans.
Publications: Annual report.
Application information: Application form not required.
Initial approach: Letter of inquiry followed by proposal
Copies of proposal: 1
Deadline(s): Submit proposal preferably in June; deadline June 30
Board meeting date(s): Aug. and as required
Final notification: 1 month after annual meeting
Write: William C. Wilson, Pres., or Ronald L. Grimm, Secy.-Treas.
Officers and Trustees:* William C. Wilson,* Chair. and Pres.; Eleanor C. Krug,* V.P.; Ronald L. Grimm,* Secy.-Treas.; Mary Mayne Perry, Dorothy B. Wilson.
Employer Identification Number: 626037668

6697
Tonya Memorial Foundation ▼
c/o American National Bank and Trust Co., Trust Dept.
736 Market St.
Chattanooga 37402

Incorporated in 1949 in DE.
Donor(s): Burkett Miller.†
Foundation type: Independent
Financial data (yr. ended 12/31/88): Assets, $13,769,255 (M); expenditures, $2,677,727, including $2,503,768 for 26 grants (high: $508,807; low: $500; average: $2,000-$200,000).
Purpose and activities: Grants to new donees limited to capital projects of a nonsectarian nature; emphasis on downtown rehabilitation, parks, hospitals, and community educational projects; continuing support for a few existing projects approved during the founder's lifetime.
Types of support: Building funds, land acquisition, equipment.
Limitations: Giving primarily in Chattanooga, TN, for new grant recipients. No grants to individuals, or for scholarships, endowment funds, or operating budgets; no loans.
Application information: Application form not required.
Initial approach: Letter
Copies of proposal: 4
Deadline(s): None
Board meeting date(s): Jan., Apr., July, and Oct.
Final notification: 6 months
Write: Maurice H. Martin, Pres. or H. James Hitching, Chair.
Officers and Trustees:* H. James Hitching,* Chair.; Maurice H. Martin,* Pres. and Treas.; James R. Hedges III,* V.P.; H. Whitney Durand,* Secy.
Number of staff: 1 part-time professional.
Employer Identification Number: 626042269

6698
Van Vleet Foundation ⌑
c/o National Bank of Commerce
One Commerce Sq.
Memphis 38150

Established in 1962 in TN.
Donor(s): Harriet Smith Van Vleet.†
Foundation type: Independent
Financial data (yr. ended 12/31/88): Assets, $6,299,462 (M); expenditures, $274,117, including $203,470 for 2 grants (high: $103,470; low: $100,000).
Purpose and activities: Grants to local area universities.
Types of support: Equipment, scholarship funds.
Limitations: Giving limited to Memphis, TN.
Application information: Contributes only to pre-selected organizations. Applications not accepted.
Write: Fletcher Haaga, 1st V.P. and Trust Officer, National Bank of Commerce
Trustees: National Bank of Commerce.
Employer Identification Number: 626034067

6699
Washington Foundation ⌑
(Formerly Church of Christ Foundation, Inc.)
3815 Cleghorn Ave.
P.O. Box 159057
Nashville 37215 (615) 244-0600

Incorporated in 1946 in TN.
Donor(s): G.L. Comer.
Foundation type: Independent
Financial data (yr. ended 12/31/88): Assets, $11,892,278 (M); expenditures, $758,669,

including $682,450 for 132 grants (high: $65,000; low: $200).
Purpose and activities: Support mainly for Church of Christ-related organizations, including churches, schools, and colleges; grants also for health and welfare.
Types of support: Operating budgets.
Limitations: Giving limited to U.S. for Church of Christ-related organizations; support primarily in the Nashville, TN, area for health and welfare. No grants to individuals.
Application information:
Deadline(s): Dec. 1
Board meeting date(s): Quarterly
Write: Paul A. Hargis, Pres.
Officers and Trustees: Paul A. Hargis, Pres.; E.M. Shepherd, V.P.; R. Hix Clark, Secy.; Paschall H. Young, Treas.; Howard R. Amacher, Andrew Benedict, Bill Berry, James M. Denton III, Neal L. Jennings, Robert C. Taylor.
Number of staff: 1
Employer Identification Number: 680649477

6700
Webster Foundation ¤ ☆
c/o Third National Bank
P.O. Box 305110
Nashville 37230

Established in 1958.
Foundation type: Independent
Financial data (yr. ended 12/31/88): Assets, $722,311 (M); expenditures, $351,775, including $338,750 for 28 grants (high: $230,000; low: $250).
Purpose and activities: Support primarily for Methodist churches and higher education.
Trustee: Third National Bank.
Employer Identification Number: 626032866

6701
Werthan Foundation
P.O. Box 1310
Nashville 37202 (615) 259-9331

Trust established in 1945 in TN.
Donor(s): Werthan Bag Corp., Bernard Werthan, Albert Werthan, Werthan Industries, Inc.
Foundation type: Independent
Financial data (yr. ended 11/30/89): Assets, $6,760,451 (M); gifts received, $329,439; expenditures, $641,511, including $571,290 for 87 grants (high: $135,000; low: $100; average: $200-$5,000).
Purpose and activities: Emphasis on Jewish welfare funds, higher education, and a community fund; support also for cultural programs.
Limitations: Giving primarily in TN. No grants to individuals.
Application information:
Initial approach: Letter
Deadline(s): None
Board meeting date(s): June
Write: Albert Werthan, Chair.
Officers and Trustees:* Albert Werthan,* Chair.; Bernard Werthan, Jr.,* Secy.; Herbert M. Shayne,* Treas.; Morris Werthan II.
Number of staff: None.
Employer Identification Number: 626036283

6702
Westend Foundation, Inc. ¤
c/o American National Bank and Trust Co.
736 Market St.
Chattanooga 37402 (615) 265-8881

Incorporated in 1956 in DE.
Donor(s): George West.†
Foundation type: Independent
Financial data (yr. ended 12/31/88): Assets, $2,479,370 (M); expenditures, $253,696, including $164,257 for 31 grants (high: $50,000; low: $1,000) and $63,000 for 40 grants to individuals (high: $3,000; low: $750).
Purpose and activities: Emphasis on scholarships, higher education, a university medical research laboratory in AZ, and Protestant church support.
Types of support: General purposes, student aid, scholarship funds.
Limitations: Giving primarily in the Chattanooga, TN, area.
Application information: Application form required.
Write: Raymond B. Witt, Jr., Secy.-Treas.
Officers and Trustees: L.W. Oehmig, Pres.; J. Burton Frierson, Jr., V.P.; Raymond B. Witt, Jr., Secy.-Treas.; Daniel W. Oehmig.
Employer Identification Number: 626041060

6703
Donald B. Wiener Fund ¤ ☆
c/o National Bank of Commerce, Trust Div.
One Commerce Sq.
Memphis 38150

Donor(s): Members of the Wiener Family.
Foundation type: Independent
Financial data (yr. ended 12/31/88): Assets, $110,148 (M); expenditures, $202,276, including $200,000 for 1 grant.
Purpose and activities: Giving for higher education, social services, youth organizations, and arts and culture.
Types of support: Operating budgets.
Limitations: Giving primarily in the Memphis, TN, area. No grants to individuals.
Trustee: National Bank of Commerce.
Employer Identification Number: 626033947

6704
Woods-Greer Foundation
c/o American National Bank and Trust Co., Trust Dept.
736 Market St., P.O. Box 1638
Chattanooga 37401 (615) 757-3203

Established in 1976.
Donor(s): C. Cecil Woods.†
Foundation type: Independent
Financial data (yr. ended 5/31/89): Assets, $1,822,609 (M); expenditures, $93,365, including $81,000 for 19 grants (high: $10,000; low: $500; average: $1,000-$5,000).
Purpose and activities: Giving mainly for higher education, Christian religious organizations, and the arts.
Types of support: Operating budgets, continuing support, annual campaigns, building funds, equipment, publications, scholarship funds, matching funds.
Limitations: Giving primarily in the southeastern U.S. No grants to individuals; no loans.
Application information: Application form not required.
Initial approach: Proposal
Copies of proposal: 1
Deadline(s): Submit proposal preferably in Apr. or May; no set deadline
Board meeting date(s): July
Write: Peter T. Cooper, Secy.-Treas.
Officers: The Very Rev. C. Cecil Woods, Jr., Chair.; Marie Cartinhour Woods, Vice-Chair.; Peter T. Cooper, Secy.-Treas.
Trustees: William G. Brown, Ellen Woods Polansky, Kathleen Woods Van Devender, Carolyn Taylor Woods, Margaret C. Woods-Denkler.
Number of staff: None.
Employer Identification Number: 626126272

6705
Raymond Zimmerman Family Foundation ¤
c/o Jack Byrd
3818 Cleghorn Ave., Suite 200
Nashville 37215

Established in 1982 in TN.
Donor(s): Raymond Zimmerman.
Foundation type: Independent
Financial data (yr. ended 5/31/87): Assets, $2,550,171 (M); gifts received, $1,638,500; expenditures, $17,252, including $15,000 for 2 grants (high: $10,000; low: $5,000).
Purpose and activities: Giving primarily to a hospital in Israel.
Application information: Contributes only to pre-selected organizations. Applications not accepted.
Trustees: Arlene G. Zimmerman, Fred E. Zimmerman, Raymond Zimmerman, Robyn Zimmerman.
Employer Identification Number: 626166380

6706
The Zimmerman Foundation ¤
c/o Byrd, Land & Proctor
3818 Cleghorn Ave., Suite 200
Nashville 37215-2514

Established in 1979.
Donor(s): Jack Byrd Trust.
Foundation type: Independent
Financial data (yr. ended 11/30/88): Assets, $540,189 (M); expenditures, $129,451, including $122,358 for 12 grants (high: $50,000; low: $250).
Purpose and activities: Giving for Jewish welfare funds, education, and hospitals.
Limitations: Giving primarily in TN.
Application information:
Write: Raymond Zimmerman, Pres.
Officers and Directors: Raymond Zimmerman, Pres.; Peggy Steine, Secy.; Rabbi Randall Falk, Sue Kresge, Doris Tenenbaum.
Employer Identification Number: 621058309

TEXAS

6707
Abell-Hanger Foundation ▼
303 West Wall, Rm. 615
Midland 79701 (915) 684-6655
Mailing address: P.O. Box 430, Midland, TX 79702

Incorporated in 1954 in TX.
Donor(s): George T. Abell,† Gladys H. Abell.†
Foundation type: Independent
Financial data (yr. ended 06/30/89): Assets, $92,381,151 (M); expenditures, $4,886,035, including $3,827,099 for 110 grants (high: $600,000; low: $1,000; average: $10,000-$50,000).
Purpose and activities: Support primarily for higher education, youth activities, cultural programs, health services, the handicapped, and social welfare agencies.
Types of support: General purposes, operating budgets, continuing support, annual campaigns, seed money, building funds, endowment funds, matching funds, scholarship funds, research, equipment, capital campaigns, special projects.
Limitations: Giving limited to TX, preferably within the Permian Basin. No grants to individuals, or for individual scholarships or fellowships; no loans.
Publications: 990-PF, annual report (including application guidelines).
Application information: Application form required.
Initial approach: Request and complete application forms
Copies of proposal: 1
Deadline(s): Sept. 30, Jan. 31, and May 31
Board meeting date(s): Oct. 15, Feb. 15, and June 15
Final notification: 1 month
Write: David L. Smith, Mgr.
Officers and Trustees:* John F. Younger,* Pres.; James I. Trott,* V.P.; Lester Van Pelt, Jr.,* Secy.-Treas.; David L. Smith, Mgr.; John P. Butler, Robert L. Leibrock.
Number of staff: 1 full-time professional; 2 part-time professional; 2 full-time support.
Employer Identification Number: 756020781

6708
The Abercrombie Foundation ⌑ ☆
5005 Riverway, Suite 500
Houston 77056 (713) 627-2500

Established in 1988 in TX as partial successor to The J.S. Abercrombie Foundation.
Donor(s): Josephine E. Abercrombie.
Foundation type: Independent
Financial data (yr. ended 12/31/88): Assets, $6,212,319 (M); expenditures, $904,219, including $781,000 for 12 grants (high: $105,000; low: $5,000).
Purpose and activities: Support primarily for higher and secondary education, including medical education; giving also for child welfare and hospitals.
Types of support: Building funds, operating budgets, research.
Limitations: Giving primarily in Houston, TX.
Application information:
Initial approach: Proposal
Copies of proposal: 1
Deadline(s): May 15 and Nov. 15
Write: Thomas M. Weaver, Mgr.
Officers: Josephine E. Abercrombie,* Pres.; John B. Howenstine,* Treas.; Thomas M. Weaver, Mgr.
Trustees:* Donald F. Wood.
Employer Identification Number: 760229183

6709
Community Foundation of Abilene
402 Cypress, Suite 708
P.O. Box 1001
Abilene 79604 (915) 676-3883

Incorporated in 1985 in TX.
Foundation type: Community
Financial data (yr. ended 06/30/89): Assets, $5,041,679 (M); gifts received, $2,579,841; expenditures, $1,290,040, including $1,125,223 for 107 grants (high: $150,000; low: $25; average: $2,000-$8,000) and $49,313 for foundation-administered programs.
Purpose and activities: Support for social services, health organizations, education, and civic affairs.
Types of support: Annual campaigns, building funds, conferences and seminars, consulting services, equipment, matching funds, operating budgets, publications, renovation projects, scholarship funds, seed money, technical assistance.
Limitations: Giving primarily in the Abilene, TX, area. No grants to individuals, or for continuing support, deficit financing, endowment funds, or program-related investments; no loans.
Publications: Annual report.
Application information: Application form not required.
Initial approach: Letter
Write: Nancy E. Dark, Exec. Dir.
Officers and Trustees:* Joe Canon,* Chair.; Tucker S. Bridwell,* Vice-Chair.; Lawrence E. Gill,* Secy.; John L. Shelton, Jr.,* Treas.; Nancy E. Dark, Exec. Dir.; Dr. Jesse C. Fletcher, and 10 additional trustees.
Number of staff: 1 full-time professional; 1 full-time support.
Employer Identification Number: 752045832

6710
The Akin Foundation ⌑
14515 Briarhills Pkwy., No. 1B
Houston 77077 (713) 524-7237

Incorporated in 1948 in TX.
Donor(s): J.W. Akin.
Foundation type: Independent
Financial data (yr. ended 12/31/88): Assets, $188,902 (M); expenditures, $231,697, including $205,200 for 35 grants (high: $23,000; low: $1,200).
Purpose and activities: Aid to various Churches of Christ.
Officers and Trustees: Harry J. Pickup, Jr., Pres.; James D. Yates, Secy.; Fred A. Hutson, Treas.
Employer Identification Number: 756036487

6711
Alcon Foundation
6201 South Freeway
Fort Worth 76134 (817) 551-8328

Established in 1962 in TX.
Donor(s): Alcon Laboratories, Inc.
Foundation type: Company-sponsored
Financial data (yr. ended 12/31/89): Assets, $4,081 (M); gifts received, $313,500; expenditures, $312,891, including $312,824 for 120 grants (high: $50,000; low: $37).
Purpose and activities: Contributions mostly limited to education and research within areas of specialization of Alcon Laboratories: ophthalmology, vision care, dermatology, etc.; grants also to community activities that benefit company employees.
Types of support: Annual campaigns, lectureships, research.
Limitations: No grants for building programs.
Application information:
Initial approach: Letter
Deadline(s): None
Board meeting date(s): Feb., Apr., June, Aug., Oct., and Dec.
Write: H.U. Fleck, Chair.
Trustees: H.U. Fleck, Co-Chair.; W.H. Rhue, Co-Chair.; C.H. Beasley, M.D., S.W. Clark, J. Hiddemen, P. Maley, R.H. Sisson.
Employer Identification Number: 756034736

6712
Robert D. & Catherine R. Alexander Foundation
Suite 617
4200 South Hulen
Fort Worth 76109 (817) 731-1317

Established in 1962 in TX.
Donor(s): R.D. Alexander Trust.
Foundation type: Independent
Financial data (yr. ended 12/31/88): Assets, $1,687,403 (M); gifts received, $50,000; expenditures, $97,031, including $71,875 for 21 grants (high: $42,750; low: $100).
Purpose and activities: Giving primarily for Christian churches, secondary education, and programs for visually impaired children.
Limitations: Giving primarily in Tarrant County, TX, with emphasis on Fort Worth. No grants to individuals.
Application information: Application form not required.
Initial approach: Letter
Copies of proposal: 1
Deadline(s): None
Write: R. Denny Alexander, Trustee
Trustees: Catherine R. Alexander, R. Denny Alexander, Lane Anne Kimzey, Anita Taylor.
Employer Identification Number: 756012124

6713
The Stanford & Joan Alexander Foundation ⌑
203 Timberwilde
Houston 77024

Established in 1986 in TX.
Donor(s): Stanford Alexander, Joan Alexander.
Foundation type: Independent
Financial data (yr. ended 12/31/88): Assets, $1,312,195 (M); gifts received, $504,621;

expenditures, $50,143, including $47,300 for 23 grants (high: $11,000; low: $50).
Purpose and activities: Support for Christian organizations, Jewish giving and health, including medical research.
Types of support: Operating budgets, research, general purposes.
Limitations: Giving primarily in Houston, TX.
Application information: Contributes only to pre-selected organizations. Applications not accepted.
Officers and Directors: Stanford Alexander, Pres. and Treas.; Joan Alexander, V.P. and Secy.; Andrew M. Alexander, Eric P. Alexander, Ilene S. Alexander, Melvin Dow.
Employer Identification Number: 760204170

6714
The Allbritton Foundation
5615 Kirby Dr., Suite 310
Houston 77005

Established in 1958 in TX.
Donor(s): Joe L. Allbritton, Perpetual Corp., and others.
Foundation type: Independent
Financial data (yr. ended 11/30/89): Assets, $6,206 (M); gifts received, $315,000; expenditures, $328,675, including $327,682 for 27 grants (high: $75,000; low: $250).
Purpose and activities: Grants mainly for Christian religious organizations, higher and secondary education, and cultural programs.
Types of support: Continuing support, endowment funds, fellowships, general purposes, scholarship funds.
Publications: Annual report.
Application information: Application form not required.
Deadline(s): None
Officers: Joe L. Allbritton,* Pres.; Barbara B. Allbritton,* V.P.; Virginia L. White, Secy.-Treas.
Trustees:* Lawrence I. Hebert, Stephen A. Massey, Thomas W. Wren.
Number of staff: 1 part-time support.
Employer Identification Number: 746051876

6715
Amarillo Area Foundation, Inc.
700 First National Place I
801 South Fillmore
Amarillo 79101 (806) 376-4521

Established as a trust in 1957 in TX.
Foundation type: Community
Financial data (yr. ended 12/31/88): Assets, $18,266,372 (M); gifts received, $1,538,578; expenditures, $2,368,319, including $2,076,639 for 63 grants (high: $744,500; low: $74; average: $10,000-$20,000).
Purpose and activities: Support for community development, including education, arts and cultural programs, and health organizations, especially a medical center.
Types of support: Seed money, emergency funds, building funds, equipment, land acquisition, matching funds, consulting services, technical assistance, scholarship funds, special projects, research, student aid.
Limitations: Giving limited to the 26 most northern counties of TX Panhandle. No grants to individuals (except for limited scholarships from designated funds), or for operating budgets, annual campaigns, deficit financing, endowment funds, publications, or conferences; no loans.
Publications: Annual report, application guidelines.
Application information: Specific application format required. Application form not required.
Initial approach: Letter or telephone
Copies of proposal: 1
Deadline(s): Quarterly
Board meeting date(s): Quarterly; executive committee meets bimonthly
Write: Jim Allison, Pres. and Exec. Dir.
Officers and Directors:* Betty Cooper,* Chair.; Tom Patterson,* 1st Vice-Chair.; Greg Mitchell,* 2nd Vice-Chair.; Becky Dodson,* Secy.; Jay O'Brien,* Treas.; and 19 additional directors.
Number of staff: 3 full-time professional.
Employer Identification Number: 750978220

6716
AMR/American Airlines Foundation ⌑ ☆
P.O. Box 619616
Dallas-Ft. Worth Airport 75261-9616 (817) 355-1575

Established in 1985 in TX.
Donor(s): AMR Corp.
Foundation type: Company-sponsored
Financial data (yr. ended 12/31/88): Assets, $3,213,635 (M); expenditures, $810,813, including $776,709 for 1,254 grants (high: $68,575; low: $20).
Purpose and activities: Giving primarily for higher education and community funds; support also for health associations, social services and youth, and the arts, including performing arts.
Limitations: No grants to individuals.
Application information:
Initial approach: Proposal
Deadline(s): None
Final notification: Within 2 months
Write: L.C. Duncan, Jr., Secy.
Officers and Director:* R.L. Crandall,* Pres.; R.A. Lempert, V.P.; L.C. Duncan, Jr., Secy. and Mgr.; D.J. Carty, Treas.
Employer Identification Number: 762086656

6717
Josephine Anderson Charitable Trust ⌑
P.O. Box 8
Amarillo 79105 (806) 376-7873

Trust established in TX.
Donor(s): Josephine Anderson.†
Foundation type: Independent
Financial data (yr. ended 2/28/89): Assets, $4,932,626 (M); expenditures, $500,744, including $330,478 for 10 grants (high: $296,476; low: $500).
Purpose and activities: Giving primarily for handicapped housing; support also for health associations, social services and youth agencies, cultural programs, churches, and education.
Types of support: Building funds.
Limitations: Giving primarily in Amarillo, TX. No grants to individuals.
Application information:
Initial approach: Letter
Deadline(s): None
Write: L.A. White, Managing Trustee, or Imadell Carter, Secy.
Officers and Trustees: L.A. White, Managing Trustee; Imadell Carter, Secy.
Employer Identification Number: 751469596

6718
M. D. Anderson Foundation ▼
1301 Fannin St., 21st Fl.
P.O. Box 809
Houston 77001 (713) 658-2316

Trust established in 1936 in TX.
Donor(s): M.D. Anderson.†
Foundation type: Independent
Financial data (yr. ended 12/31/87): Assets, $67,083,475 (M); gifts received, $10,000; expenditures, $4,777,812, including $3,893,825 for 77 grants (high: $500,000; low: $325; average: $5,000-$100,000).
Purpose and activities: "The improvement of working conditions among workers generally...; the establishment, support and maintenance of hospitals, homes, and institutions for the care of the sick, the young, the aged, the incompetent and the helpless among the people; the improvement of living conditions among people generally." Support for a large local medical center and for educational and related projects.
Types of support: Building funds, equipment, matching funds, research, seed money.
Limitations: Giving limited to TX, primarily the Houston area. No grants to individuals, or for endowment funds or operating budgets.
Publications: Multi-year report, application guidelines.
Application information: Application form not required.
Initial approach: Letter
Copies of proposal: 5
Deadline(s): None
Board meeting date(s): Monthly
Final notification: 1 month
Write: John W. Lowrie, Secy.-Treas.
Officers and Trustees: A.G. McNeese, Jr., Pres.; Uriel E. Dutton, V.P.; Gibson Gayle, Jr., V.P.; Charles W. Hall, V.P.; John W. Lowrie, Secy.-Treas.
Number of staff: None.
Employer Identification Number: 746035669

6719
The Andress Foundation ⌑
P.O. Box 5198
Abilene 79608 (915) 698-8800

Established in 1977.
Donor(s): Tony D. Andress, Sr.
Foundation type: Independent
Financial data (yr. ended 11/30/88): Assets, $1,186,000 (M); gifts received, $45,000; expenditures, $120,164, including $118,500 for 14 grants (high: $45,000; low: $500).
Purpose and activities: Giving for higher education, the Church of Christ, and social services, including a rehabilitation center.
Limitations: Giving primarily in Abilene, TX.
Application information:
Initial approach: Proposal
Deadline(s): None
Write: Tony D. Andress, Sr., Pres.

Officers and Directors: Tony D. Andress, Sr., Pres.; Tony D. Andress, Jr., Secy.-Treas.; Kellie Andress Alegre, Dawn Wylie.
Employer Identification Number: 751577382

6720
The Dene Anton Foundation ⌘
(Formerly The Judge Roy and Dene Hofheinz Trust)
c/o NCNB Texas National Bank, Trust Dept.
P.O. Box 2518
Houston 77001 (713) 652-6526

Established in 1984 in TX.
Donor(s): Roy M. Hofheinz Charitable Foundation.
Foundation type: Independent
Financial data (yr. ended 9/30/88): Assets, $1,603,748 (M); expenditures, $885,955, including $869,820 for 28 grants (high: $237,750; low: $100).
Purpose and activities: Support primarily for music organizations, medical research, and general charitable giving.
Types of support: Operating budgets, program-related investments.
Limitations: Giving primarily in CA. No grants to individuals.
Application information:
Initial approach: Letter
Deadline(s): None
Write: Mrs. Dene Hofheinz Anton, Trustee
Trustees: Dene Hofheinz Anton, NCNB Texas National Bank.
Employer Identification Number: 760093912

6721
The Armstrong Foundation ⌘
(Formerly The Texas Educational Association)
P.O. Box 470338
Fort Worth 76147-0338 (817) 737-7251
Application address: P.O. Drawer 2299, Matchez, MS 39120

Incorporated in 1949 in TX.
Donor(s): George W. Armstrong, Sr.†
Foundation type: Independent
Financial data (yr. ended 12/31/87): Assets, $9,155,664 (M); expenditures, $595,500, including $434,258 for 94 grants (high: $45,000; low: $100).
Purpose and activities: To support educational undertakings "through financial assistance to schools, colleges, universities and other educational mediums advocating the perpetuation of constitutional government." Grants only for educational programs on American ideals and traditional values; support also for youth agencies, cultural programs and religious activities.
Types of support: Conferences and seminars, internships, publications, research, general purposes.
Limitations: Giving primarily in TX. No grants to individuals, or for capital or endowment funds, or operating budgets; no loans.
Publications: Application guidelines.
Application information: Application form not required.
Initial approach: Proposal
Copies of proposal: 1
Deadline(s): None
Board meeting date(s): Mar., June, Sept., and Dec.
Final notification: 2 months
Write: Thomas K. Armstrong, Pres.
Officers: Thomas K. Armstrong, Pres.; John H. James, V.P. and Treas.; Thomas K. Armstrong, Jr., V.P.; J. Hatcher James III, V.P.; Laura J. Harrison, Secy.
Number of staff: 3 part-time professional; 1 full-time support; 1 part-time support.
Employer Identification Number: 756003209

6722
Morris & Ann Ashendorf Foundation, Inc. ⌘
8323 S.W. Freeway, Suite 300
Houston 77074

Incorporated in 1985 in TX.
Donor(s): Kalman & Ida Wolens Foundation, Inc.
Foundation type: Independent
Financial data (yr. ended 1/31/89): Assets, $1,084,231 (M); gifts received, $2,000; expenditures, $115,622, including $115,415 for 23 grants (high: $25,000; low: $25).
Purpose and activities: Support primarily for Jewish organizations.
Limitations: Giving primarily in Houston, TX.
Application information: Contributes only to pre-selected organizations. Applications not accepted.
Officers and Directors: H. Wesley Ashendorf, Pres.; Anne V. Ashendorf, V.P.; Carole S. Ashendorf, Secy.
Employer Identification Number: 760121343

6723
Austin Community Foundation
P.O. Box 5159
Austin 78763 (512) 472-4483

Established in 1977 in TX.
Foundation type: Community
Financial data (yr. ended 12/31/88): Assets, $4,940,970 (M); gifts received, $975,386; expenditures, $783,043, including $680,006 for 255 grants (high: $166,409).
Purpose and activities: Support for general charitable purposes, including education, community affairs and services, history, religious giving, medical research and rehabilitation, beautification, public health, child development, and recreation.
Types of support: Seed money, capital campaigns, general purposes, annual campaigns, building funds, conferences and seminars, consulting services, continuing support, equipment, land acquisition, matching funds, professorships, publications, renovation projects, research, technical assistance.
Limitations: Giving limited to Travis County, TX, for discretionary grants. No grants to individuals or for deficit financing, emergency funds, endowments, operating budgets, scholarships, or fellowships; no loans.
Publications: Newsletter, program policy statement, application guidelines.
Application information: Application form required.
Initial approach: Letter
Copies of proposal: 1
Deadline(s): Dec. 1
Board meeting date(s): Quarterly
Write: Richard G. Slaughter, Exec. Dir.
Board of Governors: George H. More III, Pres.; Sander Shapiro, V.P.; Mrs. Sam A. Wilson, Secy.; Malcolm L. Cooper, Treas.; Richard G. Slaughter, Exec. Dir.; and 14 additional governors.
Number of staff: 2 full-time professional; 1 part-time support.
Employer Identification Number: 741934031

6724
Fay T. Barnes Scholarship Trust ⌘
P.O. Box 550
Austin 78789-0001

Established in 1982 in TX.
Foundation type: Independent
Financial data (yr. ended 12/31/87): Assets, $2,146,907 (M); expenditures, $427,934, including $377,500 for grants to individuals.
Purpose and activities: Scholarship fund for high school seniors from Williamson and Travis counties to attend colleges and universities in TX.
Types of support: Student aid.
Limitations: Giving limited to Williamson and Travis counties, TX.
Publications: Informational brochure (including application guidelines).
Application information: Applications made through local high school counselors only in Travis and Williamson counties. Application form required.
Deadline(s): Jan. 15
Trustee: Texas Commerce Bank.
Employer Identification Number: 742256469

6725
Joe & Wilhelmina Barnhart Foundation ⌘
5620 Greenbriar
Houston 77005

Established in 1967 in TX.
Donor(s): Joseph M. Barnhart, Robert J. Barnhart, Wilhelmina B. Traylor.
Foundation type: Independent
Financial data (yr. ended 12/31/87): Assets, $1,001,152 (M); gifts received, $100,000; expenditures, $59,000, including $45,020 for 19 grants (high: $30,000; low: $25).
Purpose and activities: Support for an elementary school; giving also to community arts and cultural institutions, a college and a children's hospital.
Limitations: Giving primarily in Beeville and Houston, TX.
Application information: Contributes only to pre-selected organizations. Applications not accepted.
Trustees: Walter S. Baker, Jr., Joseph M. Barnhart, Robert J. Barnhart, Robert Leslie, Bland McReynolds, Margaret Price, Wilhelmina B. Traylor.
Employer Identification Number: 746088946

6726
Barrow Foundation ⌑
5000 Montrose, No. 7H
Houston 77006 (512) 346-3800

Established in 1952 in TX.
Donor(s): Nellie Dell Barrow.†
Foundation type: Independent
Financial data (yr. ended 11/30/87): Assets, $2,032,368 (M); gifts received, $516,345; expenditures, $125,952, including $91,615 for 8 grants (high: $50,000; low: $680).
Purpose and activities: Emphasis on secondary education.
Application information: Contributes only to pre-selected organizations. Applications not accepted.
Write: Sarah Barrow Seline, Pres.
Officers: Sarah Barrow Seline, Pres.; Carol Billups, Secy.-Treas.
Directors: Randall E. Kemper, Marvin H. Seline, Jay C. Tapp.
Employer Identification Number: 746041372

6727
Bass Foundation
309 Main St.
Fort Worth 76102 (817) 336-0494

Established in 1945 in TX.
Donor(s): Perry R. Bass, Lee Bass, Edward Bass, Sid Richardson Carbon and Gasoline Co., Perry R. Bass, Inc.
Foundation type: Independent
Financial data (yr. ended 12/31/89): Assets, $14,476,651 (M); gifts received, $300,000; expenditures, $930,763, including $840,000 for 9 grants (high: $430,000; low: $5,000; average: $5,000-$100,000).
Purpose and activities: Giving primarily for the arts and cultural institutions; some support for conservation.
Types of support: General purposes.
Limitations: Giving primarily in Fort Worth, TX.
Publications: 990-PF.
Application information: Contributes only to pre-selected organizations. Applications not accepted.
Write: Valleau Wilkie, Jr.
Officers and Directors:* Perry R. Bass,* Pres.; Nancy Lee Bass,* V.P.; Shaye Arnold,* Secy.-Treas.
Number of staff: 1 part-time professional.
Employer Identification Number: 756033983

6728
The Bass Foundation ⌑
1601 Elm St., Suite 4224
Dallas 75201
Application address: 4224 Thanksgiving Tower, Dallas, TX 75201; Tel.: (214) 754-7190

Trust established in 1945 in TX; in 1983, foundation split up into Bass Foundation and Harry Bass Foundation.
Donor(s): Harry W. Bass, Sr., Mrs. Harry W. Bass, Sr.
Foundation type: Independent
Financial data (yr. ended 12/31/88): Assets, $2,576,120 (M); expenditures, $204,348, including $195,180 for 66 grants (high: $25,000; low: $100; average: $200-$10,000).
Purpose and activities: Support for cultural programs, education, and hospitals.
Types of support: Building funds, general purposes.
Limitations: Giving primarily in the Dallas, TX, metropolitan area, and the Salt Lake City, UT, area.
Application information:
Initial approach: Proposal
Deadline(s): None
Board meeting date(s): As required
Write: Richard D. Bass, Trustee
Trustees: Richard D. Bass, Mary L. Stanley, Thurman R. Taylor, Harry W. Wittingdon.
Number of staff: None.
Employer Identification Number: 756013540

6729
Harry Bass Foundation
8333 Douglas Ave., Suite 1400
Dallas 75225 (214) 696-0557

Established in 1983 in TX.
Donor(s): Harry W. Bass, Jr.
Foundation type: Independent
Financial data (yr. ended 12/31/88): Assets, $5,153,174 (M); expenditures, $251,738, including $240,900 for 61 grants (high: $119,100; low: $100; average: $100-$10,000).
Purpose and activities: Support for numismatic organizations nationwide; support for museums, religious organizations, education, and health associations and hospitals in the Dallas, TX, area.
Types of support: General purposes, annual campaigns, continuing support, equipment, scholarship funds.
Limitations: Giving primarily in the Dallas, TX, area. No grants to individuals.
Publications: 990-PF.
Application information: Contributes only to pre-selected organizations. Applications not accepted.
Board meeting date(s): Dec.
Write: Harry W. Bass, Jr., Trustee
Trustees: Doris L. Bass, Harry W. Bass, Jr., Carol Ann McLean.
Number of staff: None.
Employer Identification Number: 751876307

6730
Baumberger Endowment ▼
P.O. Box 6067
San Antonio 78209 (512) 822-8915

Trust established in 1972 in TX.
Donor(s): Charles Baumberger, Jr.†
Foundation type: Independent
Financial data (yr. ended 12/31/87): Assets, $784,873 (M); gifts received, $1,603,510; expenditures, $1,626,349, including $1,426,398 for 366 grants to individuals.
Purpose and activities: Scholarships for Bexar County students attending TX colleges and universities.
Types of support: Student aid.
Limitations: Giving limited to Bexar County, TX.
Publications: Program policy statement, application guidelines.
Application information: Contact foundation office or high school counselor for guidelines and application forms. Application form required.
Deadline(s): Jan. 31 for financial aid forms; Feb. 15 for high school transcript and application form
Board meeting date(s): Mar., June, Sept., and Dec.
Final notification: May
Officers and Trustees:* S.H. Schmidt,* Chair. and Treas.; Travis M. Moursund,* Secy.; Cynthia Guyon,* Exec. Dir.; James F. Bartlett, Ronald Schmidt, Jerome Weynand.
Employer Identification Number: 237225925

6731
The Beal Foundation ⌑
c/o First National Bank of Midland, Trust Dept.
P.O. Box 270
Midland 79702-0270 (915) 682-3753

Incorporated in 1962 in TX.
Donor(s): Carlton Beal, W.R. Davis.
Foundation type: Independent
Financial data (yr. ended 12/31/87): Assets, $2,816,904 (M); expenditures, $474,760, including $454,500 for 48 grants (high: $110,000; low: $1,500).
Purpose and activities: Emphasis on education, social service and youth agencies, and health associations and hospitals.
Limitations: Giving primarily in the Midland, TX, area.
Application information: 1st-time applicants complete longer application form. Application form required.
Deadline(s): 1 month before meetings for 1st-time applicants; 2 weeks for repeat applicants
Board meeting date(s): Apr. 1 and Nov. 1
Write: Carlton Beal, Chair., or Herb Cartwright, Secy.-Treas.
Officers and Trustees: Carlton Beal, Chair.; Keleen Beal, Vice-Chair.; Herb Cartwright, Secy.-Treas.; Barry A. Beal, Carlton Beal, Jr., Spencer Beal, Mitchell A. Cappadonna, Robert J. Cowen, Karlene Garber, Jane B. Ramsland, Pomeroy Smith, Tom Welch.
Employer Identification Number: 756034480

6732
Theodore and Beulah Beasley Foundation, Inc. ▼ ⌑
3811 Turtle Creek Village, Suite 1370
Dallas 75219-4419 (214) 522-8790

Incorporated in 1957 in TX.
Donor(s): Theodore P. Beasley.
Foundation type: Independent
Financial data (yr. ended 12/31/88): Assets, $6,609,820 (M); expenditures, $647,712, including $476,500 for 18 grants (high: $200,000; low: $150; average: $1,000-$10,000).
Purpose and activities: Emphasis on higher education, youth agencies, hospitals, and Protestant church support.
Limitations: Giving primarily in the Dallas, TX, area. No grants to individuals.
Application information: Contributes only to pre-selected organizations. Applications not accepted.
Board meeting date(s): As required
Write: Mary Beasley, Pres.

Officers: Mary E. Beasley, Pres.; Samuel Dashefsky, V.P. and Treas.; Linda Tinney, Secy.
Number of staff: None.
Employer Identification Number: 756035806

6733
Behmann Brothers Foundation ⌑
5250 Weber, Suite C
Corpus Christi 78411
Application address: Route 3, Box 443, Corpus Christi, TX 78415-9715; Tel.: (512) 265-9396

Established in 1979.
Donor(s): Herman W. Behmann.†
Foundation type: Independent
Financial data (yr. ended 6/30/88): Assets, $5,292,753 (M); expenditures, $309,212, including $284,025 for 64 grants (high: $50,000; low: $25).
Purpose and activities: Giving for agricultural research programs; support also for Christian church support and youth agencies.
Limitations: Giving primarily in the southern TX area. No grants to individuals.
Application information:
Initial approach: Proposal
Deadline(s): May 1
Write: Charles L. Kosarek, Pres.
Officers and Directors: Charles L. Kosarek, Pres.; John Lloyd Bluntzer, V.P.; Ross Mitchon, Secy.; Willie J. Kosarek, Treas.; Ted M. Anderson.
Employer Identification Number: 742146739

6734
Bell Trust ⌑
10726 Plano Rd.
Dallas 75238 (214) 349-0060

Trust established in 1957 in TX.
Donor(s): R.S. Bell, Katherine Bell.
Foundation type: Independent
Financial data (yr. ended 12/31/87): Assets, $7,292,604 (M); expenditures, $315,131, including $262,665 for 93 grants (high: $6,800; low: $400).
Purpose and activities: Grants exclusively to the Church of Christ.
Limitations: No grants to individuals, or for building or endowment funds, scholarships, fellowships, or matching gifts; no loans.
Application information:
Initial approach: Proposal
Copies of proposal: 1
Deadline(s): None
Board meeting date(s): Mar., June, Sept., and Dec.
Write: H.L. Packer, Trustee
Trustees: Hulen L. Jackson, James N. Muns, H.L. Packer.
Number of staff: None.
Employer Identification Number: 756020180

6735
Bertha Foundation ⌑ ☆
P.O. Box 1110
Graham 76046 (817) 549-1400

Established in 1967 in TX.
Donor(s): E. Bruce Street, M. Boyd Street.
Foundation type: Independent
Financial data (yr. ended 4/30/88): Assets, $2,080,105 (M); gifts received, $257,944; expenditures, $166,705, including $138,109 for 18 grants (high: $87,252; low: $42).
Purpose and activities: Giving primarily for a library; support also for education and civic affairs.
Types of support: Operating budgets, scholarship funds.
Limitations: Giving primarily in TX, with emphasis on Graham. No grants to individuals.
Application information:
Initial approach: Letter
Deadline(s): None
Write: E. Bruce Street, Jr., V.P.
Officers: E. Bruce Street, Pres.; E. Bruce Street, Jr., V.P.; M. Boyd Street, V.P.; J. R. Montgomery, Secy.
Employer Identification Number: 756050023

6736
Biological Humanics Foundation ⌑
3808 Euclid Ave.
Dallas 75205 (214) 521-2924

Trust established in 1950 in TX.
Donor(s): Eugene McDermott.†
Foundation type: Independent
Financial data (yr. ended 12/31/88): Assets, $4,894,538 (M); expenditures, $336,646, including $297,300 for 4 grants (high: $198,000; low: $5,300).
Purpose and activities: To advance knowledge in the field of human growth and development with emphasis on medical aspects of symmetry and asymmetry.
Types of support: Research, scholarship funds.
Limitations: Giving primarily in Dallas, TX. No grants to individuals, or for endowment funds.
Application information: Application form not required.
Initial approach: Letter
Copies of proposal: 1
Deadline(s): None
Board meeting date(s): Semiannually
Write: Mrs. Mary M. Cook, Pres.
Officers and Trustees: Mary McDermott Cook, Pres.; Philip O'B. Montgomery, Jr., V.P.; Patricia Brown, Secy.; Kevin McBride, Treas.; Charles A. LeMaistre, Philip O'B. Montgomery III.
Number of staff: 1
Employer Identification Number: 756009766

6737
Mary E. Bivins Foundation ⌑
414 Polk St.
P.O. Box 708
Amarillo 79105
Application address: 6214 Elmhurst, Amarillo, TX 79106

Incorporated in 1949 in TX.
Donor(s): Mary E. Bivins Trust, and others.
Foundation type: Operating
Financial data (yr. ended 8/31/88): Assets, $51,484,818 (M); gifts received, $2,422,729; expenditures, $7,192,192, including $545,761 for 13 grants (high: $100,000; low: $1,000), $18,297 for 10 grants to individuals and $3,805,391 for 2 foundation-administered programs.
Purpose and activities: A private operating foundation; operates nursing homes for the aged; also giving for social service agencies and Christian colleges, including scholarships.
Types of support: Operating budgets, student aid.
Limitations: Giving primarily in TX.
Application information:
Initial approach: Letter
Deadline(s): Oct. 31
Write: Mr. Lindy Ward, Dir.
Officers and Directors: Tom Bivins, Pres.; Don McFarland, V.P.; Jim Moore, Secy.; Miles Childers, Glen B. Gibson, Forrest Skinner, Lindy L. Ward.
Employer Identification Number: 750842370

6738
Sarah Campbell Blaffer Foundation
12 Greenway Plaza, Suite 716
Houston 77046 (713) 623-8690

Incorporated in 1964 in TX.
Donor(s): Sarah C. Blaffer.†
Foundation type: Operating
Financial data (yr. ended 12/31/88): Assets, $32,792,895 (M); gifts received, $1,274,349; expenditures, $1,148,957, including $389,500 for 39 grants (high: $66,400; low: $100) and $475,223 for foundation-administered programs.
Purpose and activities: A private operating foundation; grants for cultural programs, medical research, church support, and secondary and higher education; also operates a program of art exhibits.
Limitations: Giving primarily in TX. No grants to individuals, or for endowment funds, scholarships, or fellowships; no loans.
Application information:
Initial approach: Letter
Copies of proposal: 1
Deadline(s): Submit proposal from Jan. through Aug.; deadline Aug. 31
Board meeting date(s): Mar. and Oct.
Final notification: Dec.
Write: Edward Joseph Hudson, Jr., Secy.
Officers and Trustees:* Charles W. Hall,* Pres.; Jane Blaffer Owen,* V.P. and Treas.; Cecil Blaffer von Furstenberg,* V.P.; Edward Joseph Hudson, Jr.,* Secy.; Gilbert M. Denman, Jr.
Number of staff: 2 full-time professional.
Employer Identification Number: 746065234

6739
J. B. & Margaret Blaugrund Foundation
918 First City National Bank
El Paso 79901 (915) 532-6196

Established in 1958 in TX.
Donor(s): Joseph B. Blaugrund,† Margaret A. Blaugrund.†
Foundation type: Independent
Financial data (yr. ended 07/31/89): Assets, $1,328,273 (M); expenditures, $50,708, including $46,750 for 31 grants (high: $10,000; low: $250).
Purpose and activities: Giving primarily for the United Jewish Appeal and other Jewish welfare organizations; support also for museums and the performing arts and other cultural programs, social service and youth agencies, women, health associations and

hospitals, and organizations promoting world peace.
Types of support: Endowment funds.
Limitations: No support for individuals.
Application information: Contributes only to pre-selected organizations. Applications not accepted.
Write: Ann B. Marks, Pres.
Officers: Ann B. Marks, Pres.; Maurice H. Blauguard, V.P.; J. Alan Marks, Secy.-Treas.
Number of staff: None.
Employer Identification Number: 746040400

6740
Bosque Foundation ▼ ⌑
2911 Turtle Creek Blvd., Suite 1080
Dallas 75219 (214) 559-0088

Established in 1983 in TX.
Donor(s): Louis A. Beecherl, Jr.
Foundation type: Independent
Financial data (yr. ended 12/31/88): Assets, $7,481,498 (M); expenditures, $1,320,481, including $1,304,000 for 32 grants (high: $500,000; low: $500; average: $1,000-$50,000).
Purpose and activities: Grants for health and hospitals, higher and secondary education, youth, and social services.
Types of support: Operating budgets, capital campaigns, building funds, research, equipment.
Limitations: Giving primarily in TX. No grants to individuals.
Application information:
Deadline(s): None
Board meeting date(s): As required
Final notification: Within 2 weeks
Write: Louis A. Beecherl, Jr., Trustee
Trustees: Julia T. Beecherl, Louis A. Beecherl, Jr., Julianna B. Davis, Mary B. Dillard.
Number of staff: None.
Employer Identification Number: 751865011

6741
Bowers Foundation ⌑ ☆
P.O. Box 56048
Houston 77256

Established in 1988 in TX.
Donor(s): Hugh R. Bowers, Ryn R. Bowers.
Foundation type: Independent
Financial data (yr. ended 12/31/88): Assets, $2,457,521 (M); gifts received, $2,500,000; expenditures, $74,681, including $72,200 for 4 grants (high: $45,000; low: $5,000).
Purpose and activities: Initial year of operation, 1988; giving primarily for ministry programs; support also for a school and a health association.
Limitations: No grants to individuals.
Application information: Contributes only to pre-selected organizations. Applications not accepted.
Officers: Hugh R. Bowers, Pres.; Ryn R. Bowers, V.P.; C.M. Barth, Treas.
Employer Identification Number: 760260739

6742
Ruth McLean Bowman Bowers Foundation ⌑
615 Belknap
P.O. Box 12199
San Antonio 78212-0199 (512) 733-0911

Established in 1956 in TX.
Donor(s): Ruth McLean Bowers.
Foundation type: Independent
Financial data (yr. ended 12/31/88): Assets, $1,165,210 (M); expenditures, $65,406, including $63,850 for 42 grants (high: $10,000; low: $250).
Purpose and activities: Contributions for medical and youth organizations; support also for the women's movement.
Limitations: Giving limited to TX. No grants to individuals.
Application information:
Initial approach: Letter
Deadline(s): None
Officers: Ruth McLean Bowers, Pres.; William O. Bowers III, V.P.; Sarah Weddington, Secy.
Employer Identification Number: 746062585

6743
George W. Brackenridge Foundation
535 Travis Park Plaza
711 Navarro St.
San Antonio 78205 (512) 224-1011

Trust established in 1920 in TX.
Donor(s): George W. Brackenridge.†
Foundation type: Independent
Financial data (yr. ended 12/31/89): Assets, $14,031,250 (M); expenditures, $753,788, including $637,787 for 30 grants (high: $100,000; low: $500; average: $3,000-$50,000).
Purpose and activities: Giving limited to support of accredited educational institutions.
Types of support: Endowment funds, research, special projects, scholarship funds.
Limitations: Giving limited to TX. No grants to individuals, or for general purposes, continuing support, seed money, emergency funds, land acquisition, renovation projects, building funds, operating budgets, annual campaigns, deficit financing, or matching gifts; no loans.
Publications: 990-PF.
Application information: All grants made on the foundation's own initiative. Applications not accepted.
Board meeting date(s): Mar., June, Sept., and Dec.
Write: Gilbert M. Denman, Jr., Trustee
Trustees: Gilbert M. Denman, Jr., Leroy G. Denman, Jr., Charles W. Harper, John B. McDaniel, Jr.
Number of staff: None.
Employer Identification Number: 746034977

6744
Louis and Allison Brandt Foundation ⌑
2001 Kirby, Suite 914
Houston 77019

Established about 1983 in TX.
Donor(s): Louis K. Brandt, Allison Brandt.
Foundation type: Independent
Financial data (yr. ended 11/30/86): Assets, $6,272 (M); gifts received, $157,500; expenditures, $155,170, including $153,975 for 30 grants (high: $52,800; low: $25).
Purpose and activities: Giving for social services, education, and a church.
Limitations: Giving primarily in TX.
Trustee: Louis K. Brandt.
Employer Identification Number: 760069463

6745
The Mr. & Mrs. Joe W. Bratcher, Jr. Foundation ⌑
c/o H. David Hughes
1400 One Congress Plaza, 111 Congress Ave.
Austin 78701

Established in 1985 in TX.
Donor(s): Joe W. Bratcher, Jr., Mrs. Joe W. Bratcher, Jr.
Foundation type: Independent
Financial data (yr. ended 12/31/88): Assets, $1,088,412 (M); expenditures, $146,653, including $142,999 for 11 grants (high: $35,000; low: $1,999).
Purpose and activities: Giving primarily for a capital raising fund for a hospital; support also for the performing arts and animal welfare.
Limitations: Giving primarily in Austin, TX. No grants to individuals.
Application information:
Initial approach: Letter
Deadline(s): Sept. 30
Write: Joe W. Bratcher, Jr., Pres.
Officers: Joe W. Bratcher, Jr., Pres.; Rhobie K. Bratcher, Secy.
Director: Joe W. Bratcher III.
Employer Identification Number: 742387803

6746
The J. S. Bridwell Foundation ▼ ⌑
500 City National Bldg.
Wichita Falls 76303 (817) 322-4436

Incorporated in 1949 in TX.
Donor(s): J.S. Bridwell,† Margaret B. Bowdle.
Foundation type: Independent
Financial data (yr. ended 12/31/88): Assets, $22,912,948 (M); expenditures, $3,372,959, including $3,263,750 for 48 grants (high: $3,000,000; low: $150; average: $200-$50,000).
Purpose and activities: Emphasis on higher and secondary education, social service and youth agencies, and civic affairs; some religious giving.
Types of support: Building funds, special projects, equipment, operating budgets.
Limitations: Giving limited to TX. No grants to individuals, or for endowment funds.
Application information: Contributes only to pre-selected organizations. Applications not accepted.
Officers: Herbert B. Story, Pres.; Clifford G. Tinsley, Secy.-Treas.
Directors: Ralph S. Bridwell, Garrett Oliver.
Employer Identification Number: 756032988

6747
Maureen Connolly Brinker Girls' Tennis Foundation, Inc. ⌑
5419 Wateka Dr.
Dallas 75209 (214) 357-1604

Donor(s): Phillip Morris.

Foundation type: Independent
Financial data (yr. ended 4/30/87): Assets, $1,792,767 (M); gifts received, $379,652; expenditures, $295,493, including $125,311 for 39 grants (high: $30,450; low: $25) and $9,197 for 7 grants to individuals (high: $3,871; low: $300).
Purpose and activities: Grants to individuals and organizations for the "furtherance of women's tennis."
Types of support: Grants to individuals.
Application information:
Initial approach: Letter
Deadline(s): None
Write: Mrs. Frank A. Jeffett, Pres.
Officer: Mrs. Frank A. Jeffett, Pres.
Trustees: Norman Brinker, Robert C. Taylor.
Employer Identification Number: 237040481

6748
Brochstein Foundation, Inc. ⌑
11530 South Main St.
Houston 77025

Established in 1975 in TX.
Donor(s): Brochsteins, Inc.
Foundation type: Company-sponsored
Financial data (yr. ended 10/31/88): Assets, $2,380,972 (M); gifts received, $305,205; expenditures, $68,924, including $66,000 for 7 grants (high: $30,000; low: $1,000).
Purpose and activities: Support primarily for higher education and a medical center foundation.
Limitations: Giving primarily in TX.
Application information: Contributes only to pre-selected organizations. Applications not accepted.
Trustees: Bertha Brochstein, I.S. Brochstein, Joel Brochstein, Mildred Brochstein, Raymond Brochstein, S.J. Brochstein, Jack Neal, Bernard Sampson, J. Richard Trellue, Gerald Trudeau.
Employer Identification Number: 746039346

6749
B. C. & Addie Brookshire Kleberg County Charitable Foundation ⌑
c/o Texas Commerce Bank-Corpus Christi, Trust Dept.
P.O. Drawer 749
Corpus Christi 78403 (512) 883-3621

Established in 1958.
Foundation type: Independent
Financial data (yr. ended 6/30/88): Assets, $1,143,409 (M); expenditures, $82,813, including $71,894 for 17 grants (high: $12,500; low: $500).
Purpose and activities: Giving for youth recreation agencies, community centers, education, and cultural programs.
Types of support: Building funds, equipment, renovation projects, scholarship funds, special projects.
Limitations: Giving primarily in Kleberg County, TX.
Application information:
Deadline(s): None
Write: Carly M. Ivy
Trustee: Texas Commerce Bank-Corpus Christi.
Employer Identification Number: 746108397

6750
T. J. Brown and C. A. Lupton Foundation, Inc. ⌑
Fort Worth Club Tower
777 Taylor St., Suite 800
Fort Worth 76102 (817) 332-1541

Incorporated in 1942 in TX.
Donor(s): T.J. Brown,† C.A. Lupton,† V.J. Earnhart, J.A. Gooch.
Foundation type: Independent
Financial data (yr. ended 12/31/87): Assets, $20,142,580 (M); expenditures, $975,538, including $795,000 for 16 grants (high: $604,000; low: $1,500).
Purpose and activities: Emphasis on higher education; some support for youth agencies, and medical research and hospitals.
Limitations: Giving primarily in Fort Worth, TX. No grants to individuals, or for scholarships, prizes, or similar benefits; no loans.
Application information:
Initial approach: Letter
Deadline(s): None
Board meeting date(s): Quarterly
Final notification: Within 3 months
Write: Sam P. Woodson, III, Pres.
Officer and Directors: Sam P. Woodson III, Pres. and Managing Dir.; Whitfield J. Collins, Bayard H. Friedman, Kit Tennison Moncrief, Gloria Lupton Tennison, William C. Tucker.
Number of staff: 1 full-time professional; 1 part-time professional.
Employer Identification Number: 750992690

6751
The Brown Foundation, Inc. ▼
2118 Welch Ave.
P.O. Box 130646
Houston 77219 (713) 523-6867

Incorporated in 1951 in TX.
Donor(s): Herman Brown,† Margarett Root Brown,† George R. Brown,† Alice Pratt Brown.†
Foundation type: Independent
Financial data (yr. ended 6/30/89): Assets, $413,019,005 (M); expenditures, $23,240,805, including $21,090,350 for 171 grants (high: $2,648,778; low: $1,500; average: $10,000-$100,000).
Purpose and activities: Support principally for the encouragement and assistance to education and the arts.
Types of support: Operating budgets, continuing support, annual campaigns, building funds, equipment, endowment funds, matching funds, professorships, fellowships, special projects, publications, capital campaigns, renovation projects.
Limitations: Giving primarily in TX, with emphasis on Houston. No support for religious organizations, private foundations, or political activities. No grants to individuals, or for advertising, testimonial dinners, deficit financing, or fundraising events; no loans.
Publications: Application guidelines, informational brochure (including application guidelines).
Application information: Will consider 1 grant proposal per 12 month period from an organization. No grant funds pledged beyond the current year. Application form not required.
Initial approach: Proposal
Copies of proposal: 1
Deadline(s): None
Board meeting date(s): Feb., May, Sept., and Nov.
Final notification: 3 months
Write: Katherine B. Dobelman, Exec. Dir.
Officers and Trustees:* Maconda Brown O'Connor,* Chair.; Isabel Brown Wilson,* Pres.; Louisa Stude Sarofim,* 1st V.P.; M.S. Stude,* V.P.; Nancy Brown Wellin,* V.P.; C.M. Hudspeth,* Secy.; Katherine B. Dobelman, Treas. and Exec. Dir.; Nancy O'Connor Abendshein, Thomas I. O'Connor, James R. Paden, Christopher B. Sarofim.
Number of staff: 1 full-time professional; 6 full-time support; 1 part-time support.
Employer Identification Number: 746036466

6752
M. K. Brown Foundation, Inc. ⌑
P.O. Box 662
Pampa 79066-0662 (806) 669-6851

Established in 1960 in TX.
Donor(s): M.K. Brown.†
Foundation type: Independent
Financial data (yr. ended 12/31/88): Assets, $3,503,974 (M); expenditures, $329,218, including $292,749 for 28 grants (high: $110,000; low: $1,000).
Purpose and activities: Emphasis on Christian church support, youth agencies, community projects, and social service agencies.
Limitations: Giving limited to the Panhandle area of TX, with emphasis on Pampa and Gray County. No grants to individuals.
Application information:
Initial approach: Proposal
Deadline(s): July 1 and Dec. 1
Write: Bill W. Waters, Chair.
Officers and Trustees: Bill W. Waters, Chair.; David E. Holt, Secy.; Alice T. Smith, Sandra Waters.
Employer Identification Number: 756034058

6753
William and Catherine Bryce Memorial Fund ⌑
c/o Team Bank, N.A.
P.O. Box 2050
Fort Worth 76113 (817) 884-4266

Trust established in 1944 in TX.
Foundation type: Independent
Financial data (yr. ended 09/30/89): Assets, $12,578,886 (M); expenditures, $532,693, including $451,100 for 44 grants (high: $60,000; low: $1,000).
Purpose and activities: Emphasis on child welfare, higher education, the aged, cultural programs, youth agencies, hospitals, and a community fund.
Limitations: Giving primarily in TX, particularly in the Fort Worth area. No grants to individuals.
Application information:
Initial approach: Letter
Copies of proposal: 1
Deadline(s): Sept. 30
Board meeting date(s): Nov.

Write: Kelly A. Bradshaw, Asst. V.P. and Trust Officer, Team Bank, N.A.
Trustee: Team Bank, N.A.
Employer Identification Number: 756013845

6754
The Burkitt Foundation ⌑
5847 San Felipe, Suite 4290
Houston 77057 (713) 780-7638

Incorporated in 1962 in TX.
Donor(s): Elizabeth B. Crane.†
Foundation type: Independent
Financial data (yr. ended 9/30/88): Assets, $8,854,492 (M); expenditures, $344,406, including $148,050 for 45 grants (high: $10,000; low: $600; average: $2,000-$5,000).
Purpose and activities: Giving for private higher and secondary education, churches and religious organizations, and social services, with emphasis on Roman Catholic church-sponsored programs.
Types of support: Operating budgets, continuing support, annual campaigns, seed money, endowment funds, matching funds, scholarship funds, fellowships, professorships, internships, exchange programs, special projects, research, publications, conferences and seminars, building funds, capital campaigns, general purposes.
Limitations: Giving primarily in the southwestern U.S., with emphasis on TX, NM, AZ, and LA. No grants to individuals, or for deficit financing; no loans.
Publications: Annual report, informational brochure (including application guidelines).
Application information: Application form not required.
Initial approach: Letter
Copies of proposal: 1
Deadline(s): Feb. 15 and Aug. 15
Board meeting date(s): Mar. and Sept.; screening committee meets monthly for initial review
Final notification: 30 days after board meetings
Write: Cornelius O. Ryan, Pres.
Officers and Trustees: Cornelius O. Ryan, Pres.; Joseph W. Ryan, V.P. and Secy.-Treas.; Carl E. Ryan, Rev. James F. Wilson.
Number of staff: None.
Employer Identification Number: 746053270

6755
Burlington Northern Foundation ▼ ⌑
3000 Continental Plaza
777 Main St.
Fort Worth 76102

Incorporated in 1953 in MN; renamed in 1970.
Donor(s): Burlington Northern, Inc.
Foundation type: Company-sponsored
Financial data (yr. ended 12/31/88): Assets, $18,405,341 (M); gifts received, $8,241,435; expenditures, $14,706,452, including $14,086,111 for 943 grants (high: $1,500,000; low: $80; average: $500-$50,000) and $504,666 for 259 employee matching gifts (high: $23,140; low: $50).
Purpose and activities: Grants primarily for higher education, cultural programs, community funds, social services, including American Red Cross, civic and recreation programs, and hospitals.
Types of support: Employee matching gifts, annual campaigns, building funds, equipment, general purposes.
Limitations: Giving primarily in areas of company operations, particularly Seattle, WA. No support for religious organizations for religious purposes, veterans' or fraternal organizations, national health organizations and programs, chambers of commerce, taxpayer associations, state railroad associations, and other bodies whose activities might benefit the company, or political organizations, campaigns, or candidates. No grants to individuals, or for operating budgets of hospitals, fundraising events, corporate memberships, endowment funds, scholarships, or fellowships; no loans.
Publications: Annual report, program policy statement, application guidelines.
Application information: Application form required.
Initial approach: Letter
Copies of proposal: 1
Deadline(s): None
Board meeting date(s): As required
Final notification: 4 to 5 months
Write: Don S. Snyder, V.P.
Officers and Directors:* Christopher T. Bayley,* Chair.; Donald K. North,* Pres.; Don S. Snyder, V.P., Secy. and Controller; Danell I. Tobey, Treas.; Ronald H. Reimann.
Trustees: Sanford C. Bernstein & Co., Inc., Ranier National Bank.
Number of staff: 1 full-time professional.
Employer Identification Number: 416022304

6756
The George and Anne Butler Foundation
2220 Allied Bank Plaza
1000 Louisiana
Houston 77002

Incorporated in 1956 in TX.
Donor(s): George A. Butler,† Anne G. Butler,† Houston Corp., McEvoy Co.
Foundation type: Independent
Financial data (yr. ended 12/31/88): Assets, $1,598,007 (M); expenditures, $353,876, including $340,750 for 23 grants (high: $145,000; low: $100).
Purpose and activities: Emphasis on higher and secondary education, arts and cultural programs, health, youth, and Protestant church support.
Types of support: Annual campaigns, emergency funds, lectureships.
Limitations: Giving primarily in TX.
Publications: Annual report.
Application information: Application form not required.
Deadline(s): None
Write: George V. Grainger, V.P.
Officers and Trustees:* Anne B. Leonard,* Pres.; Ida Jo B. Moran,* V.P.
Number of staff: None.
Employer Identification Number: 746063429

6757
H. E. Butt Foundation ⌑
P.O. Box 670
Kerrville 78029 (512) 896-2505

Incorporated in 1933 in TX.
Donor(s): Howard E. Butt, Sr., Howard E. Butt, Jr., H.E. Butt Grocery Co., and others.
Foundation type: Operating
Financial data (yr. ended 12/31/88): Assets, $8,930,342 (M); gifts received, $1,351,074; expenditures, $1,081,634, including $15,055 for 7 grants (high: $10,055; low: $500) and $1,046,505 for foundation-administered programs.
Purpose and activities: A private operating foundation supporting the operation of youth camps in TX used by qualifying groups and programs related to church renewal, lay theological education, and mental health.
Types of support: Operating budgets.
Limitations: Giving limited to TX. No grants to individuals, or for building or endowment funds.
Application information: Funds are reserved primarily for the foundation's operating programs. Application form not required.
Deadline(s): None
Board meeting date(s): Dec.
Write: Howard E. Butt, Jr., Pres.
Officers and Trustees: Howard E. Butt, Jr., Pres.; Barbara Dan Butt, Secy.-Treas.; Charles C. Butt, Howard E. Butt, Sr., Mary Butt.
Number of staff: 7 full-time professional; 9 full-time support.
Employer Identification Number: 741239819

6758
C.I.O.S. ▼
315 Washington Ave.
Waco 76701 (817) 752-5551

Incorporated about 1952 in TN; corporation liquidated into a charitable trust in 1987.
Donor(s): Paul P. Piper, Mrs. Paul P. Piper.
Foundation type: Independent
Financial data (yr. ended 6/30/89): Assets, $52,771,257 (M); gifts received, $89,000; qualifying distributions, $2,208,102, including $1,698,102 for 76 grants (high: $623,767; low: $25) and $510,000 for loans.
Purpose and activities: Grants for Protestant church support and religious programs, including Christian education, evangelism, welfare, and support for foreign missions.
Application information:
Initial approach: Letter or proposal
Deadline(s): June
Board meeting date(s): Monthly
Write: Paul P. Piper, Trustee
Trustees: Mary J. Piper, Paul P. Piper, Paul P. Piper, Jr., Ronald K. Piper.
Number of staff: None.
Employer Identification Number: 742472778

6759
The Effie and Wofford Cain Foundation ▼
6116 North Central Expressway, Suite 909-LB65
Dallas 75206 (214) 361-4201

Incorporated in 1952 in TX.
Donor(s): Effie Marie Cain, R. Wofford Cain.†
Foundation type: Independent

Financial data (yr. ended 10/31/89): Assets, $45,887,138 (M); expenditures, $1,976,397, including $1,615,230 for 56 grants (high: $500,000; low: $500; average: $2,000-$35,000).
Purpose and activities: Giving primarily for higher and secondary education, public service organizations, and cultural programs; grants also for religious organizations, aid to the handicapped, and medical services and research.
Types of support: Building funds, endowment funds, seed money, operating budgets, research, scholarship funds.
Limitations: Giving limited to TX. No grants to individuals.
Publications: Application guidelines.
Application information: Application form required.
Copies of proposal: 1
Deadline(s): Aug. 31 for Oct. meeting
Board meeting date(s): Oct. (annual); 4 to 6 interim meetings (dates vary)
Final notification: Varies
Write: Harvey L. Walker, Exec. Dir.
Officers and Directors:* Effie Marie Cain,* Pres.; Franklin W. Denius,* V.P.; R.J. Smith, Jr.,* Secy.-Treas.; Harvey L. Walker, Exec. Dir.; James B. Cain.
Number of staff: 2 full-time professional; 1 full-time support; 1 part-time support.
Employer Identification Number: 756030774

6760
The Gordon and Mary Cain Foundation ⌑ ☆
Eight Greenway Plaza, Suite 702
Houston 77046 (713) 960-9283

Established in 1988 in TX.
Donor(s): Gordon A. Cain, Mary H. Cain.
Foundation type: Independent
Financial data (yr. ended 12/31/88): Assets, $29,683,832 (M); gifts received, $29,186,000; expenditures, $363,003, including $281,050 for 37 grants (high: $50,000; low: $250).
Purpose and activities: Support for a leadership development association, higher and secondary education, social services, hospitals and health associations, and the arts.
Types of support: General purposes.
Limitations: Giving primarily in Houston, TX. No grants to individuals.
Application information:
Initial approach: Proposal
Deadline(s): None
Write: James D. Weaver, Pres.
Officers: Gordon A. Cain, Chair.; James D. Weaver, Pres. and C.O.O.; Mary H. Cain, V.P.; Margaret W. Oehmig, V.P.; Sharyn A. Weaver, V.P.; William C. Oehmig, Secy.-Treas. and C.F.O.
Employer Identification Number: 760251558

6761
Flora Cameron Foundation ⌑
4600 Broadway, Suite 106
San Antonio 78209 (512) 824-8301

Established in 1952 in TX.
Foundation type: Independent
Financial data (yr. ended 08/31/89): Assets, $1,544,803 (M); expenditures, $45,000, including $22,900 for 24 grants (high: $6,200; low: $35).
Purpose and activities: Giving for schools and cultural programs.
Types of support: General purposes.
Limitations: Giving primarily in the San Antonio, TX, area. No grants to individuals.
Application information:
Initial approach: Letter
Deadline(s): None
Write: Mrs. Flora C. Atherton, Pres.
Officers: Flora C. Atherton, Pres. and Treas.; Gloria Labatt, V.P.
Trustees: Robert Barclay, Everitt H. Jones.
Employer Identification Number: 746038681

6762
Harry S. and Isabel C. Cameron Foundation ⌑
P.O. Box 2555
Houston 77252-2555 (713) 652-6230

Established in 1966 in TX.
Donor(s): Isabel C. Cameron.†
Foundation type: Independent
Financial data (yr. ended 6/30/87): Assets, $14,443,733 (M); expenditures, $690,503, including $552,690 for 105 grants (high: $100,000; low: $500; average: $100-$10,000).
Purpose and activities: Emphasis on higher, elementary, and secondary education, Roman Catholic church support, health, and social service and youth agencies.
Types of support: Building funds, research, equipment, scholarship funds, general purposes.
Limitations: Giving primarily in TX, especially Houston. No grants to individuals, or for operating support, endowment funds, or matching gifts; no loans.
Application information: Application form not required.
Initial approach: Letter
Copies of proposal: 6
Deadline(s): Prior to board meetings
Board meeting date(s): Apr., Aug., and Dec.
Final notification: 2 weeks after board meetings, when action is favorable
Write: Carl W. Schumacher, Jr., or Sally Braddy
Directors: Charlotte Cameron, David W. Cameron, V.M. Cameron, Frances Cameron Miller, Estelle Cameron Mounger.
Trustee: InterFirst Bank Houston.
Number of staff: None.
Employer Identification Number: 746073312

6763
Amon G. Carter Foundation ▼
1212 NCNB Ctr.
P.O. Box 1036
Fort Worth 76101 (817) 332-2783

Incorporated in 1945 in TX.
Donor(s): Amon G. Carter,† N.B. Carter,† Star-Telegram Employees Fund, Carter Foundation Production Co.
Foundation type: Independent
Financial data (yr. ended 12/31/89): Assets, $184,753,824 (M); expenditures, $8,662,133, including $8,532,133 for 115 grants (high: $3,918,902; low: $500; average: $10,000-$175,000).
Purpose and activities: Grants primarily for the visual and performing arts, education, health care, social service and youth agencies, programs for the aged, and civic and community endeavors that enhance the quality of life. The foundation sponsors and largely supports an art museum.
Types of support: Continuing support, annual campaigns, seed money, emergency funds, building funds, equipment, land acquisition, matching funds, professorships, research, renovation projects, capital campaigns, general purposes, special projects.
Limitations: Giving largely restricted to Fort Worth and Tarrant County, TX. No grants to individuals, or for ongoing operating budgets, deficit financing, publications, or conferences; no loans.
Publications: Program policy statement.
Application information: Grants outside local geographic area usually initiated by board. Application form not required.
Initial approach: Letter
Copies of proposal: 1
Deadline(s): None
Board meeting date(s): Apr., Sept., and Dec.
Final notification: Within 10 days of board meeting
Write: Bob J. Crow, Exec. Dir.
Officers and Directors:* Ruth Carter Stevenson,* Pres.; Robert W. Brown, M.D.,* V.P.; Paul W. Mason,* Secy.-Treas.; Bob J. Crow, Exec. Dir.; J. Lee Johnson IV, Mark L. Johnson.
Number of staff: 3 full-time professional; 3 full-time support.
Employer Identification Number: 756000331

6764
Amon G. Carter Star Telegram Employees Fund
P.O. Box 17480
Fort Worth 76102 (817) 332-3535

Established in 1945 in TX.
Donor(s): Amon G. Carter,† Fort Worth Star Telegram, KXAS-TV, WBAP Radio.
Foundation type: Company-sponsored
Financial data (yr. ended 04/30/89): Assets, $12,815,130 (M); expenditures, $672,299, including $362,039 for 18 grants (high: $160,000; low: $2,000; average: $5,000-$50,000) and $292,517 for 92 grants to individuals (high: $7,964; low: $500; average: $1,000-$5,000).
Purpose and activities: Giving primarily for pension supplements and medical and hardship assistance for employees, and for scholarships for children of employees; support also for a few hospitals and local charities.
Types of support: Grants to individuals, employee-related scholarships.
Limitations: Giving limited to TX. No grants to individuals (except for employee-related scholarships and grants).
Application information: Assistance available only to employees and children of employees of the Fort Worth Star-Telegram, KXAS-TV, and WBAP Radio. Application form not required.
Initial approach: Letter and proposal
Copies of proposal: 1
Deadline(s): None
Board meeting date(s): Apr. and June

Write: Nenetta Tatum, Pres.
Officers: Nenetta Tatum, Pres.; John H. Robinson, Secy.-Treas.
Directors: George Carter, Mark L. Johnson.
Number of staff: 1 part-time professional; 1 part-time support.
Employer Identification Number: 756014850

6765
M. C. & Mattie Caston Foundation, Inc. ⌑
P.O. Box 837
Corsicana 75110
Application address: Navarro College, P.O. Box 1170, Corsicana, TX 75110; Tel.: (214) 874-6501, Ext. 287

Established in 1983 in TX.
Foundation type: Independent
Financial data (yr. ended 12/31/87): Assets, $5,669,586 (M); expenditures, $276,344, including $250 for 1 grant and $222,000 for grants to individuals.
Purpose and activities: Graduate and undergraduate scholarships for residents of Navarro and surrounding counties.
Types of support: Student aid.
Limitations: Giving limited to Navarro, TX, and surrounding counties.
Application information: Application information made available in high schools and on campuses in Jan.
Deadline(s): Mar. 1
Final notification: May 1
Write: Harold Nolte
Officers: Leighton B. Dawson, Pres.; Blake Gillen, V.P.; O.H. Moore, Secy.-Treas.
Employer Identification Number: 751844992

6766
Catto Foundation ⌑
110 East Crockett
San Antonio 78205 (512) 222-2161

Established in 1967 in TX.
Donor(s): Henry E. Catto, Jr., Jessica Hobby Catto, A & C Communications.
Foundation type: Independent
Financial data (yr. ended 12/31/88): Assets, $401,461 (M); gifts received, $250,000; expenditures, $254,623, including $246,866 for 43 grants (high: $66,666; low: $100).
Purpose and activities: Support primarily for higher education; grants also for cultural programs.
Types of support: General purposes.
Limitations: Giving primarily in Washington, DC, and San Antonio, TX. No grants to individuals.
Application information:
Initial approach: Letter
Deadline(s): None
Write: Jessica H. Catto, Pres.
Officers: Jessica Hobby Catto,* Pres.; Henry E. Catto, Jr.,* V.P.; Susan R. Farrimond, Secy.-Treas.
Directors:* William P. Hobby, Heather C. Kohout.
Employer Identification Number: 746089609

6767
John & Mildred Cauthorn Charitable Trust ⌑
P.O. Box 678
Sonora 76950-0678
Application address: 209 N.E. Main, Sonora, TX 76950; Tel.: (915) 387-3529

Established in 1985 in TX.
Foundation type: Independent
Financial data (yr. ended 12/31/88): Assets, $3,082,888 (M); expenditures, $113,467, including $88,387 for 5 grants (high: $45,910; low: $870).
Purpose and activities: Giving primarily to religious, youth, and community organizations.
Types of support: General purposes, operating budgets.
Limitations: Giving primarily in the Sonora, TX, area.
Application information: Application form required for scholarship program.
Deadline(s): None
Write: J.W. Elliott, Trustee
Trustees: J.W. Elliott, Michael V. Hale, Nelda Mayfield, Nelson Stubblefield, Bob Teaff.
Employer Identification Number: 751977779

6768
Central and South West Foundation ⌑
P.O. Box 660164
Dallas 75266 (214) 751-1000

Trust established in 1962 in IL.
Donor(s): Central and South West Corp., Central Power and Light Co., Public Service Co. of Oklahoma, Southwestern Electric Power Co., West Texas Utilities Co.
Foundation type: Company-sponsored
Financial data (yr. ended 10/31/88): Assets, $2,479,522 (M); gifts received, $636,710; expenditures, $331,564, including $300,963 for 121 grants (high: $26,560; low: $30).
Purpose and activities: Support for higher education, science and technology, studies in economics and agriculture, youth, and community funds; includes a matching gift program in which the foundation contributes 150 percent of the amount donated by an employee or director to an educational institution. The maximum annual donation qualifying for gift matching is $2,000 per gift, per employee; the total amount of donations not to exceed $3,000 per employee, per year.
Types of support: Employee matching gifts.
Limitations: Giving primarily in areas of company operations.
Application information:
Deadline(s): None
Trustee: First Republic Bank Dallas, N.A.
Advisors: Merle L. Borchelt, E.R. Brooks, Glen D. Churchill, Martin E. Fate, Jr., Philip McConnell.
Employer Identification Number: 366031631

6769
The Chilton Foundation Trust ▼
c/o NCNB Texas National Bank
P.O. Box 830241
Dallas 75283-0241 (214) 508-1687

Trust established in 1945 in TX.
Donor(s): Arthur L. Chilton,† Leonore Chilton.†
Foundation type: Independent
Financial data (yr. ended 12/31/87): Assets, $8,005,448 (M); expenditures, $920,913, including $854,182 for grants (average: $5,000-$25,000).
Purpose and activities: Giving primarily for youth, hospitals, health, education, and social service agencies.
Limitations: Giving primarily in TX. No grants to individuals.
Application information: Application form not required.
Deadline(s): None
Board meeting date(s): As necessary
Final notification: 2 months
Write: Alice J. Gayle, Trust Officer, NCNB Texas National Bank
Trustee: NCNB Texas National Bank.
Number of staff: None.
Employer Identification Number: 756006996

6770
Clampitt Foundation ⌑ ☆
9207 Ambassador Row
Dallas 75247-4695 (214) 638-3300

Donor(s): Maxwell A. Clampitt.
Foundation type: Independent
Financial data (yr. ended 12/31/88): Assets, $1,069,843 (M); gifts received, $150,000; expenditures, $59,818, including $58,730 for 68 grants (high: $7,000; low: $10).
Purpose and activities: Giving primarily for community development and medical research and hospitals; support also for Protestant churches and organizations.
Limitations: Giving primarily in TX. No grants to individuals.
Application information:
Initial approach: Letter
Deadline(s): None
Write: Maxwell A. Clampitt, Pres.
Officers and Director:* Maxwell A. Clampitt,* Pres.; Richard Clampitt, V.P.; Donald Gay, Secy.
Employer Identification Number: 756034280

6771
The Clark Foundation
6116 North Central Expressway, Suite 906
Dallas 75206 (214) 361-7498

Trust established in 1951 in TX.
Donor(s): Anson L. Clark, M.D.†
Foundation type: Independent
Financial data (yr. ended 12/31/89): Assets, $1,475,004 (M); expenditures, $124,620, including $100,000 for 9 grants (high: $15,000; low: $10,000).
Purpose and activities: Grants largely for higher and secondary education, including scholarships; support also for cultural programs and social services, including programs for the disadvantaged.
Types of support: Endowment funds, general purposes, scholarship funds.
Limitations: Giving limited to TX, with emphasis on the Dallas-Fort Worth metropolitan area. No grants to individuals, or for operating budgets, continuing support, annual campaigns, emergency or building funds, deficit financing, land acquisition, special projects, publications, or conferences; no loans.

Application information: Application form not required.
Initial approach: Letter
Copies of proposal: 1
Board meeting date(s): Varies
Final notification: 45 days
Write: Robert H. Middleton, Trustee
Trustees: Ray Bell, Robert H. Middleton, DeWitt T. Weaver.
Number of staff: 1 part-time professional.
Employer Identification Number: 756015614

6772
The John R. and Mary Margaret Clay Charitable Foundation
3221 Collinsworth
Fort Worth 76107 (817) 332-3709

Established in 1986 in TX.
Donor(s): John R. Clay.
Foundation type: Independent
Financial data (yr. ended 12/31/89): Assets, $1,423,891 (M); expenditures, $64,223, including $62,140 for 47 grants (high: $10,330; low: $100).
Purpose and activities: Support primarily for local area charitable organizations, including education, family services, and alcohol and drug abuse programs.
Types of support: Scholarship funds, annual campaigns, continuing support, operating budgets, seed money.
Limitations: Giving primarily in Tarrant County, TX. No grants to individuals.
Application information: Funding limited to programs of personal interest to trustees. Applications not accepted.
Initial approach: Personal contact (no telephone calls)
Write: John R. Clay, Pres.
Officers: John R. Clay, Pres. and Treas.; Mary Margaret Clay, Secy.
Number of staff: None.
Employer Identification Number: 752055174

6773
The Clayton Fund ▼ ⌑
Five Post Oak Park, Suite 1980
Houston 77027 (713) 623-0113

Trust established in 1952 in TX.
Donor(s): William L. Clayton,† Susan V. Clayton.†
Foundation type: Independent
Financial data (yr. ended 12/31/88): Assets, $22,823,209 (M); expenditures, $984,063, including $829,578 for 84 grants (high: $100,000; low: $300; average: $5,000-$25,000).
Purpose and activities: Support largely for higher education, including medical education and scholarships; grants also for hospitals, medical research, social services, population control, and cultural programs.
Types of support: Scholarship funds, continuing support, operating budgets, program-related investments, employee-related scholarships.
Limitations: Giving primarily in TX.
Application information: Request application guidelines for scholarship program. Application form not required.
Copies of proposal: 1
Write: S.M. McAshan, Jr., Trustee
Trustees: W.L. Garwood, Jr., S.M. McAshan, Jr., Burdine Venghiattis.
Number of staff: 1 full-time professional; 1 full-time support.
Employer Identification Number: 746042331

6774
Clements Foundation ⌑
1901 North Akard St.
Dallas 75201 (214) 720-0377

Established in 1968 in TX.
Foundation type: Independent
Financial data (yr. ended 12/31/88): Assets, $3,645,131 (M); expenditures, $153,631, including $144,400 for 18 grants (high: $90,000; low: $100).
Purpose and activities: Support primarily for youth groups, education, the arts, and medicine.
Types of support: General purposes.
Limitations: Giving primarily in the Dallas, TX, area.
Application information:
Deadline(s): None
Write: Janie Harris
Officers: William P. Clements, Jr., Pres.; Nancy Clements Seay, V.P. and Treas.; B. Gill Clements, V.P.
Employer Identification Number: 756065076

6775
Hubert E. Clift Foundation ☆
2710 West Alabama
Houston 77098-2199
Application address: 804 South Post Oak Ln., Houston, TX 77056; Tel.: (713) 621-9214

Donor(s): Jeannette E. Clift George.
Foundation type: Independent
Financial data (yr. ended 12/31/88): Assets, $894,408 (M); gifts received, $40,000; expenditures, $138,044, including $125,400 for 15 grants (high: $93,000; low: $500).
Purpose and activities: Giving primarily for Christian organizations, higher education, drug abuse programs, and the performing arts, including music and theater.
Limitations: Giving primarily in Houston, TX. No grants to individuals.
Application information: Application form not required.
Initial approach: Letter
Deadline(s): None
Write: T.E. Kennerly, Secy.-Treas.
Officers and Trustees:* Jeannette E. Clift George,* Pres.; T.E. Kennerly,* Secy.-Treas.; Robert W. Goodman, Jr.
Number of staff: None.
Employer Identification Number: 746072539

6776
Coastal Bend Community Foundation
860 First City Bank Tower - FCB 276
Corpus Christi 78477 (512) 882-9745

Established in 1980 in TX.
Foundation type: Community
Financial data (yr. ended 12/31/88): Assets, $2,852,499 (M); gifts received, $910,220; expenditures, $765,748, including $705,962 for 82 grants (high: $326,978; low: $125; average: $1,000-$2,000) and $4,101 for 10 grants to individuals (high: $800; low: $186; average: $200-$400).
Purpose and activities: Giving primarily for social services, including alcohol and drug abuse programs, youth and child welfare, literacy, the homeless and hungry, and welfare; higher and other education, including scholarship funds and libraries; culture, including museums and history; hospitals; community development; and animal welfare.
Types of support: Seed money, scholarship funds, equipment, general purposes, special projects, student aid, fellowships.
Limitations: Giving limited to Aransas, Bee, Jim Wells, Kleberg, Nueces, Refugio, and San Patricio counties, TX.
Publications: Grants list, newsletter, informational brochure (including application guidelines).
Application information: Application form not required.
Initial approach: Letter
Copies of proposal: 1
Deadline(s): Sept. 15
Board meeting date(s): Feb., May, Aug., and Nov.
Final notification: Nov.
Write: Dana Williams, Exec. V.P.
Officer: Dana Williams, Exec. V.P.
Number of staff: 1 full-time professional; 1 full-time support.
Employer Identification Number: 742190039

6777
Cockrell Foundation ▼
1600 Smith, Suite 4600
Houston 77002-7348 (713) 651-1271

Trust established in 1957 in TX; incorporated in 1966.
Donor(s): Mrs. Dula Cockrell,† Ernest Cockrell, Jr.,† Virginia H. Cockrell.†
Foundation type: Independent
Financial data (yr. ended 12/31/88): Assets, $51,657,179 (M); gifts received, $545,572; expenditures, $2,540,469, including $2,337,617 for 43 grants (high: $700,000; low: $500; average: $1,000-$50,000).
Purpose and activities: Giving for higher education; support also for cultural programs, social services, youth, religion, and hospitals.
Types of support: Annual campaigns, building funds, capital campaigns, endowment funds, fellowships, general purposes, matching funds, operating budgets, professorships, research, scholarship funds, special projects.
Limitations: Giving primarily in Houston, TX. No grants to individuals.
Publications: Annual report, 990-PF.
Application information: Application form not required.
Initial approach: Proposal
Copies of proposal: 1
Deadline(s): None
Board meeting date(s): Mar. and Oct.
Final notification: 6 weeks
Write: Mary McIntier, Exec. V.P.
Officers and Directors:* Alf Roark,* Pres.; Mary McIntier, Exec. V.P.; Ernest H. Cockrell,* V.P.; W.F. Wright, Jr., Secy.-Treas.; Janet S. Cockrell, Carol Cockrell Curran, Richard B. Curran.
Number of staff: None.
Employer Identification Number: 746076993

6778
Carr P. Collins Foundation, Inc. ▼ ⌑
P.O. Box 1330
Lewisville 75067 (214) 221-6202

Incorporated in 1962 in TX.
Donor(s): Carr P. Collins.
Foundation type: Independent
Financial data (yr. ended 12/31/88): Assets, $24,351,565 (M); expenditures, $1,206,824, including $995,625 for 34 grants (high: $750,000; low: $200; average: $10,000-$100,000).
Purpose and activities: Support for social services, cultural programs, and youth programs.
Limitations: Giving primarily in TX. No grants to individuals.
Application information: Contributes only to pre-selected organizations. Applications not accepted.
Board meeting date(s): Annually
Write: Connie G. Romans, Treas.
Officers: Ruth Collins Sharp,* Pres.; Michael J. Collins,* V.P.; R. Hubbard Hardy, Secy.; Connie G. Romans, Treas.
Directors:* J.C. Cantrell, Mrs. Calvert K. Collins, James M. Collins, Lynn Craft, W. Dewey Presley, Robert H. Stewart III.
Number of staff: 1 full-time professional.
Employer Identification Number: 756011615

6779
The James M. Collins Foundation
3131 Turtle Creek Blvd., Suite 810
Dallas 75219 (214) 522-0671

Established in 1964 in TX.
Donor(s): James M. Collins.†
Foundation type: Independent
Financial data (yr. ended 12/31/88): Assets, $5,530,133 (M); expenditures, $274,385, including $258,583 for 121 grants (high: $20,000; low: $50).
Purpose and activities: Emphasis on higher education, including business and medical education; church support and religious associations; and hospitals and medical research.
Limitations: Giving primarily in TX. No grants to individuals; no loans.
Application information: Applications not accepted.
Deadline(s): None
Write: Dorothy Collins, Pres.
Officers and Trustees:* Dorothy Dann Collins,* Pres.; Michael J. Collins,* V.P.; Kimberly K. Karalija,* Secy.; Hubbard Hardy, Treas.
Number of staff: None.
Employer Identification Number: 756040743

6780
Communities Foundation of Texas, Inc. ▼
4605 Live Oak St.
Dallas 75204 (214) 826-5231

Established in 1953 in TX; incorporated in 1960.
Foundation type: Community
Financial data (yr. ended 06/30/89): Assets, $152,028,702 (M); gifts received, $23,847,653; expenditures, $22,767,381, including $21,499,977 for 2,500 grants (average: $500-$25,000).
Purpose and activities: Grants from unrestricted funds are generally for education, health and hospitals, social services, youth, and cultural programs.
Types of support: Seed money, emergency funds, building funds, equipment, land acquisition, matching funds, technical assistance, special projects, research, capital campaigns.
Limitations: Giving primarily in the Dallas, TX, area. No support for religious purposes from general fund, media projects, publications, or organizations which redistribute funds to other organizations. No grants to individuals, or for continuing support, deficit financing, endowment funds, scholarships, or fellowships.
Publications: Program policy statement, application guidelines, financial statement, newsletter, annual report, 990-PF.
Application information: Application form not required.
Initial approach: Letter requesting guidelines
Copies of proposal: 1
Deadline(s): Feb., July 1, and Oct. 1
Board meeting date(s): Distribution Committee for unrestricted funds meets in Mar., Aug., and Nov.
Final notification: 1 week after Distribution Committee meeting
Write: Kimberly Floyd, Grant Administrator
Officers and Trustees:* John Stephens,* Chair. and C.E.O.; Edward M. Fjordbak,* Pres.; Margaret E. Shumake, Corp. Secy.; J. Michael Redfearn, Controller; Charlotte A. Nelson, Dir., Finance; Kimberly Floyd, Grant Administrator; Ebby Halliday Acers, Ruth Sharp Altshuler, Louis A. Beecherl, Jr., Durwood Chalker, Joe D. Denton, Jack B. Jackson, Thomas C. Unis.
Number of staff: 10 full-time professional; 1 part-time professional; 13 full-time support; 4 part-time support.
Employer Identification Number: 750964565

6781
Community Hospital Foundation, Inc. ⌑ ☆
P.O. Box 24185
Houston 77229

Incorporated in 1986 in TX.
Foundation type: Independent
Financial data (yr. ended 5/31/89): Assets, $4,241,053 (M); expenditures, $270,077, including $200,000 for 21 grants (high: $35,000; low: $500) and $20,000 for grants to individuals.
Purpose and activities: Giving primarily for higher education and Protestant churches; also provides scholarships to individuals for medical education.
Types of support: Student aid, capital campaigns, scholarship funds.
Limitations: Giving primarily in TX.
Application information:
Initial approach: Proposal
Deadline(s): None
Write: Dr. Loren Rohr, Pres.
Officers: Loren Rohr, Pres.; J.H. Kritzler, V.P.; Edythe Tompson, Secy.-Treas.
Directors: G. Cobb, J. Ward.
Employer Identification Number: 741470290

6782
The Constantin Foundation ▼
3811 Turtle Creek Blvd., Suite 900-LB 39
Dallas 75219 (214) 760-6950

Trust established in 1947 in TX.
Donor(s): E. Constantin, Jr.,† Mrs. E. Constantin, Jr.†
Foundation type: Independent
Financial data (yr. ended 12/31/88): Assets, $25,874,439 (M); expenditures, $1,687,619, including $1,524,395 for 17 grants (high: $1,000,000; low: $2,000).
Purpose and activities: Emphasis on higher and other education; some support for cultural programs, social service and youth agencies, and hospitals and health, including alcohol and drug abuse programs.
Types of support: Building funds, matching funds, general purposes, land acquisition, equipment, capital campaigns, continuing support, renovation projects.
Limitations: Giving limited to the Dallas, TX, metropolitan area. No support for state schools, theater, or churches. No grants to individuals, or for research; no loans.
Publications: Application guidelines.
Application information: Application form not required.
Initial approach: Proposal
Copies of proposal: 6
Deadline(s): Oct. 31; grants considered only at Dec. meeting
Board meeting date(s): Mar., June, Sept., and Dec.
Final notification: Jan.
Write: Betty S. Hillin, Exec. Dir.
Officer: Betty S. Hillin, Exec. Dir.
Trustees: Henry C. Beck, Jr., Gene H. Bishop, Walter L. Fleming, Jr., Paul A. Lockhart, Jr., Joel T. Williams, Jr.
Number of staff: 1 full-time professional; 1 full-time support.
Employer Identification Number: 756011289

6783
Kelly Gene Cook Charitable Foundation, Inc.
882 Hwy. 19
Huntsville 77340 (409) 291-3506

Incorporated in 1986 in TX.
Donor(s): Mrs. Kelly G. Cook, Kelly G. Cook.†
Foundation type: Independent
Financial data (yr. ended 12/31/88): Assets, $2,111,942 (M); expenditures, $123,351, including $115,378 for 5 grants (high: $37,398; low: $5,000).
Purpose and activities: Support primarily for scholarship funds at Millsap College, the University of Mississippi, and Mississippi State University.
Types of support: Scholarship funds.
Limitations: Giving primarily in MS.
Application information: Apply to the financial aid office at the above named institutions.
Deadline(s): Apr. 15
Write: Peggy J. Cook, Pres.
Officers: Peggy J. Cook, Pres.; Ray S. Mikell, V.P.; Deborah Rochelle, Secy.; J. Erik Hearon, Treas.
Employer Identification Number: 760201807

6784
Loring Cook Foundation ⌑
P.O. Box 1060
McAllen 78502
Scholarship application address: Counselor, McAllen Memorial High School, McAllen, TX 78502

Incorporated in 1953 in TX.
Foundation type: Independent
Financial data (yr. ended 3/31/87): Assets, $1,764,020 (M); expenditures, $70,384, including $54,145 for 34 grants (high: $21,320; low: $100) and $6,250 for grants to individuals.
Purpose and activities: Emphasis on Protestant church support, cancer and heart disease research, higher education, youth and social service agencies, and cultural programs; also awards scholarships to students graduating from a local high school.
Types of support: Student aid.
Limitations: Giving primarily in TX.
Application information: Application form required for scholarships.
Deadline(s): Mar. 1 for scholarships
Officers and Directors:* Vannie E. Cook, Jr.,* Pres.; Clarence Johnstone,* V.P.; Mrs. Vannie E. Cook, Jr., Secy.-Treas.
Employer Identification Number: 746050063

6785
The Denton A. Cooley Foundation ⌑
6655 Travis, Suite 900
Houston 77030 (713) 522-6655

Incorporated in 1960 in TX.
Donor(s): Denton A. Cooley, M.D., Louise T. Cooley.
Foundation type: Independent
Financial data (yr. ended 11/30/88): Assets, $804,811 (M); gifts received, $5,000; expenditures, $227,204, including $204,604 for 62 grants (high: $40,000; low: $35).
Purpose and activities: Emphasis on medical education and research, higher education, and health agencies.
Types of support: Operating budgets, building funds, endowment funds, special projects, research.
Limitations: Giving primarily in the Houston, TX, area. No grants to individuals, or for scholarships, fellowships, publications, or conferences; no loans.
Publications: 990-PF.
Application information: Application form not required.
Initial approach: Proposal
Copies of proposal: 1
Deadline(s): None
Board meeting date(s): Quarterly
Final notification: 4 to 6 months
Write: Gerald Maley, Secy.-Treas.
Officers and Trustees: Denton A. Cooley, M.D., Pres.; Louise T. Cooley, V.P.; Gerald A. Maley, Secy.-Treas.; Richard C. Hudson.
Number of staff: None.
Employer Identification Number: 746053213

6786
Cooper Industries Foundation ▼
First City Tower, Suite 4000
P.O. Box 4446
Houston 77210 (713) 739-5607

Incorporated in 1964; absorbed Crouse-Hinds Foundation in 1982; absorbed McGraw-Edison Foundation in 1985.
Donor(s): Cooper Industries, Inc.
Foundation type: Company-sponsored
Financial data (yr. ended 12/31/88): Assets, $2,385,651 (M); expenditures, $2,919,364, including $2,642,545 for 509 grants (high: $65,000; low: $250; average: $1,000-$5,000) and $276,819 for employee matching gifts.
Purpose and activities: Functions solely as a conduit through which Cooper Industries, Inc. and its operating units throughout the country make contributions to local charities, United Funds, education, civic and community affairs and limited health and welfare programs where company's operations are located; emergency funds are for local organizations only.
Types of support: Operating budgets, continuing support, annual campaigns, seed money, emergency funds, matching funds, employee matching gifts, employee-related scholarships, special projects, building funds, capital campaigns, general purposes.
Limitations: Giving primarily in Houston, TX, and other communities of company operations in AL, CA, CT, GA, IL, IN, ME, MI, MO, MS, NJ, NY, NC, OH, OK, PA, SC, TN, TX, and VA. No support for religious, fraternal, veterans', or lobbying organizations; national or state health and welfare organizations (except through the United Way and the company's matching gift program); or private elementary and secondary schools. No grants to individuals (except for scholarships to children of company employees), or for endowment funds, publications, conferences and seminars, or, generally, for hospital capital fund drives or their operating campaigns; no loans.
Publications: Application guidelines.
Application information: Requests that are local in nature will be referred to the nearest local operation for recommendation. Application form not required.
Initial approach: Letter
Copies of proposal: 1
Deadline(s): Fall for funding the following year
Board meeting date(s): Feb.; distribution committee meets quarterly
Final notification: Within 90 days
Write: Margie Joe, Secy.
Officers and Trustees:* Robert Cizik,* Chair.; Thomas W. Campbell,* Pres.; Alan E. Riedel,* V.P.; Margie Joe, Secy.; Dewain K. Cross,* Treas.
Number of staff: 2 part-time professional; 1 full-time support.
Employer Identification Number: 316060698

6787
Coral Reef Foundation ▼
1001 Fannin, Suite 4468
First City Tower
Houston 77002

Established in 1978 in TX.
Donor(s): Jayne L. Wrightsman, Charles B. Wrightsman.†
Foundation type: Independent
Financial data (yr. ended 12/31/88): Assets, $6,821,934 (M); expenditures, $3,644,881, including $3,630,000 for 7 grants (high: $2,200,000; low: $5,000; average: $10,000-$100,000).
Purpose and activities: Giving to cultural organizations, including museums and libraries.
Limitations: Giving primarily in New York, NY. No grants to individuals.
Application information: Contributes only to pre-selected organizations. Applications not accepted.
Board meeting date(s): Nov.
Write: Larry A. Lenz, Treas.
Officers: Jayne L. Wrightsman,* Pres.; James F. Dolan,* Secy.; Larry A. Lenz, Treas.
Directors:* Taggart Whipple.
Number of staff: None.
Employer Identification Number: 741969035

6788
Aubrey M. Costa Foundation ⌑
5580 LBJ Freeway, Suite 530
Dallas 75240

Established in 1968 in TX.
Donor(s): Aubrey M. Costa.†
Foundation type: Independent
Financial data (yr. ended 3/1/89): Assets, $1,326,933 (M); expenditures, $171,521, including $137,500 for 24 grants (high: $30,000; low: $300).
Purpose and activities: Emphasis on education; support also for health agencies, culture, community funds, Jewish welfare, and religious support.
Limitations: Giving primarily in TX. No grants to individuals.
Application information: Contributes only to pre-selected organizations. Applications not accepted.
Copies of proposal: 1
Board meeting date(s): As required
Final notification: 2 weeks
Trustees: Edward C. Greene, M.J. Greene.
Number of staff: None.
Employer Identification Number: 756085394

6789
Opal G. Cox Charitable Trust ⌑
c/o NCNB Texas National Bank
P.O. Box 908
Austin 78781
Application address for Baylor Univ. students: W.J. Dube III, c/o Baylor Univ., Box 7028, Waco, TX 76798-7028; Tel.: (817) 755-2611; Application address for seminary students: D.G. McQuitty, c/o Southwestern Baptist Theological Seminary, Box 22000, Fort Worth, TX 76122; Tel.: (817) 923-1921

Established in 1982 in TX.
Foundation type: Independent
Financial data (yr. ended 8/31/88): Assets, $1,766,490 (M); gifts received, $79,704; expenditures, $214,801, including $185,000 for 71 grants to individuals (high: $5,000; low: $1,500).
Purpose and activities: Support primarily for educational grants to individuals attending

Baylor University and Southwestern Theological Seminary.
Types of support: Student aid.
Limitations: Giving primarily in TX.
Application information: Application form required.
Deadline(s): For Southwestern Theological Seminary - Apr. 1; for Baylor University - Mar. 21
Trustee: NCNB Texas National Bank.
Employer Identification Number: 746307500

6790
Una Chapman Cox Foundation
P.O. Box 749
Corpus Christi 78403 (512) 883-3621
Application address: 1726 M St. N.W., Suite 800, Washington, DC 20016; Tel.: (202) 223-0887

Established in 1980 in TX.
Donor(s): Una Chapman Cox.†
Foundation type: Independent
Financial data (yr. ended 11/30/87): Assets, $10,102,798 (M); expenditures, $340,548, including $211,548 for 9 grants (high: $80,000; low: $3,000).
Purpose and activities: Support for the U.S. Foreign Service through grants to finance leaves of absence of State Dept. personnel.
Types of support: Conferences and seminars, special projects.
Publications: Informational brochure.
Application information: See information brochure. Application form not required.
Deadline(s): None
Write: Alfred L. Atherton, Jr., Exec. Dir.
Officers: Harvie Branscomb, Jr., Pres.; Alfred L. Atherton, Jr., Secy. and Exec. Dir.
Trustees: Jane C. Owen, George S. Vest.
Number of staff: 1 part-time professional.
Employer Identification Number: 742150104

6791
J. Paul Craig Foundation
c/o Amarillo National Bank, Trust Dept.
Box 1611
Amarillo 79181 (806) 378-8334

Donor(s): Gertrude Craig,† J. Paul Craig,† Norah Craig.†
Foundation type: Independent
Financial data (yr. ended 9/30/88): Assets, $2,220,064 (M); expenditures, $200,453, including $174,320 for 15 grants (high: $46,320; low: $3,000).
Purpose and activities: Giving for youth and child welfare, the aged, and education. Erection of permanent structures preferred.
Types of support: Building funds.
Limitations: Giving primarily in the Panhandle area of TX. No grants to individuals.
Application information:
Deadline(s): Sept. 1
Write: Trust Officer, Amarillo National Bank
Distribution Committee: J. Walter Browers, L.R. Hammer, Jr., William K. Irwin, Warren Jordan, Warren Kincaid.
Trustee: Amarillo National Bank.
Employer Identification Number: 756196164

6792
Joe and Jessie Crump Fund
c/o Texas American Bank, Fort Worth
P.O. Box 2050
Fort Worth 76113 (817) 884-4151

Trust established in 1965 in TX.
Foundation type: Independent
Financial data (yr. ended 09/30/88): Assets, $7,919,438 (M); gifts received, $59,810; expenditures, $983,205, including $655,291 for 10 grants (high: $170,291; low: $5,000) and $150,000 for loans.
Purpose and activities: Giving primarily for an Episcopal theological seminary; support also for cancer research, aid to handicapped children, and the Episcopal church.
Types of support: Research, scholarship funds, loans, lectureships.
Limitations: Giving limited to TX. No grants to individuals, or for building or endowment funds, matching gifts, or general purposes.
Application information: Application form not required.
Initial approach: Letter
Copies of proposal: 1
Deadline(s): None
Board meeting date(s): As required
Write: Robert M. Lansford, Sr. V.P., Texas American Bank
Trustees: Robert M. Lansford, Texas American Bank.
Number of staff: 1
Employer Identification Number: 756045044

6793
The Cullen Foundation ▼
601 Jefferson, 40th Fl.
Houston 77002 (713) 651-8835
Mailing address: P.O. Box 1600, Houston, TX 77251

Trust established in 1947 in TX.
Donor(s): Hugh Roy Cullen,† Lillie Cullen.†
Foundation type: Independent
Financial data (yr. ended 12/31/88): Assets, $137,566,307 (M); expenditures, $5,859,798, including $5,771,500 for grants (average: $50,000-$300,000).
Purpose and activities: Giving for charitable, educational, medical, and other eleemosynary purposes; grants for hospitals, medical, including eye, research, and higher education; support also for music, the performing arts, social services, drug abuse prevention, and community funds.
Types of support: Annual campaigns, deficit financing, building funds, equipment, land acquisition, general purposes, matching funds, professorships, research, renovation projects.
Limitations: Giving limited to TX, with emphasis on Houston. No grants to individuals; no loans.
Publications: 990-PF, application guidelines.
Application information: Application form not required.
Initial approach: Proposal, letter, or telephone
Copies of proposal: 1
Deadline(s): None
Board meeting date(s): Usually in Jan., Apr., July, Oct., and as required
Final notification: Varies
Write: Joseph C. Graf, Exec. Secy.
Officers: Wilhelmina Cullen Robertson,* Pres.; Roy Henry Cullen,* V.P.; Isaac Arnold, Jr.,* Secy.-Treas.; Joseph C. Graf, Exec. Secy.
Trustees:* Bert Campbell, Douglas B. Marshall, Jr.
Number of staff: 1 full-time professional; 1 full-time support.
Employer Identification Number: 746048769

6794
The Dallas Foundation
8333 Douglas Ave., Suite 1555
Dallas 75248 (214) 373-6080

Established in 1929 in TX.
Foundation type: Community
Financial data (yr. ended 12/31/88): Assets, $12,840,820 (M); gifts received, $490,416; expenditures, $1,124,782, including $899,459 for 22 grants (high: $250,000; low: $3,100; average: $20,000-$75,000).
Purpose and activities: Giving to promote charitable, educational, cultural, recreational, and health programs through grants to community organizations and agencies, principally for capital purposes.
Types of support: Building funds, capital campaigns, equipment, general purposes, special projects, matching funds, renovation projects.
Limitations: Giving limited to the City and County of Dallas, TX. No grants to individuals, or for endowment or emergency funds, operating budgets, annual campaigns, seed money, land acquisition, conferences and seminars, continuing support, publications, deficit financing, consulting services, technical assistance, research, scholarships, or fellowships; no loans.
Publications: Newsletter, program policy statement, application guidelines, informational brochure.
Application information: Application form not required.
Initial approach: 1-page proposal
Deadline(s): None
Board meeting date(s): Usually in Feb., May, Sept., and Nov.
Final notification: Following Nov. board meeting
Write: Mary M. Jalonick, Exec. Dir.
Officer: Mary M. Jalonick, Exec. Dir.
Governors: George Schrader, Chair.; Margaret J. Charlton, Robert W. Decherd, David G. Fox, Joseph R. Musolino, Joe Boyd Neuhoff, Caren H. Prothro, John Field Scovell, Joel T. Williams, Jr.
Trustee Bank: NCNB Texas National Bank.
Number of staff: 1 full-time professional; 1 full-time support.
Employer Identification Number: 756038529

6795
The Dallas Morning News - WFAA Foundation
c/o A.H. Belo Corp.
Communications Ctr., P.O. Box 655237
Dallas 75265 (214) 977-6661

Trust established in 1952 in TX.
Donor(s): A.H. Belo Corp.
Foundation type: Company-sponsored

Financial data (yr. ended 12/31/88): Assets, $3,643,180 (M); expenditures, $349,382, including $335,000 for 15 grants (high: $100,000; low: $5,000).
Purpose and activities: Giving for journalism education, civic improvement programs, cultural programs, and health and social service organizations.
Types of support: Building funds, endowment funds, capital campaigns.
Limitations: Giving primarily in Dallas, TX, and in cities where Belo has operating companies. No grants to individuals.
Application information: Application form required.
Initial approach: Letter or proposal; no visits
Copies of proposal: 1
Deadline(s): None
Board meeting date(s): Once a year
Write: Judith M. Garrett, Secy. and Admin.
Officer and Trustees: Robert W. Decherd, Chair. and Pres.; Joe M. Dealey, Ward L. Huey, James M. Moroney, Jr., James P. Sheehan.
Number of staff: 1 part-time professional.
Employer Identification Number: 756012569

6796
Dallas Rehabilitation Foundation ⌑
8828 Stemmons Freeway, Suite 106, LB-39
Dallas 75247 (214) 630-6181

Established in 1981 in TX; corpus derived from sale of Dallas Rehabilitation Institute to National Medical Enterprises, Inc.
Foundation type: Independent
Financial data (yr. ended 10/31/87): Assets, $6,455,484 (M); gifts received, $460,000; expenditures, $1,045,240, including $646,045 for 10 grants (high: $43,000; low: $15,000; average: $25,000-$40,000) and $399,195 for 4 foundation-administered programs.
Purpose and activities: Giving for projects that advance the science and art of rehabilitation of severely physically handicapped individuals, primarily through research activities; some support also for educational projects, such as educational conferences and film production.
Types of support: Equipment, special projects, research, seed money, matching funds, scholarship funds, professorships, internships, fellowships, publications, conferences and seminars.
Limitations: Giving primarily in TX. No grants to individuals, or for operating budgets, continuing support, annual campaigns, emergency funds, deficit financing, building funds, land acquisition, renovation projects, endowments, program-related investments, or exchange programs; no loans.
Publications: Program policy statement, application guidelines, newsletter, informational brochure.
Application information: Application form not required.
Initial approach: Proposal or letter
Copies of proposal: 1
Deadline(s): Sept. 15
Board meeting date(s): Feb., May, Aug., and Nov. or Dec.
Final notification: Dec.
Officers and Trustees: Jack W. Hawkins, V.P.; Mark Sinclair, Treas.; Linda Alesi-Miller, Manuel Avila, Robert O. Helberg, Hilton Hemphill, Randolph B. Marston, Mrs. Paul W. Phy, Francis W. Thayer, George W. Wharton, Robert J. Wright.
Number of staff: 2 full-time professional; 1 full-time support.
Employer Identification Number: 751783741

6797
Davidson Family Charitable Foundation
223 West Wall St., Suite 423
Midland 79701 (915) 687-0995

Trust established in 1961 in TX.
Donor(s): C.J. Davidson.†
Foundation type: Independent
Financial data (yr. ended 06/30/88): Assets, $17,672,895 (M); gifts received, $4,000; expenditures, $954,639, including $753,128 for 70 grants (high: $45,428; low: $1,000).
Purpose and activities: Emphasis on higher and other education, welfare, medical research, hospitals, health services, community services, and youth.
Types of support: Building funds, equipment, scholarship funds, endowment funds, general purposes.
Limitations: Giving limited to TX. No grants to individuals.
Application information: Apply at school financial office for scholarships. Application form required.
Initial approach: Letter
Copies of proposal: 6
Deadline(s): 30 days before semi-annual meetings
Board meeting date(s): June and Dec.
Final notification: 2 weeks after meetings
Write: H.W. Davidson, Chair.
Officers and Trustees:* H.W. Davidson, Chair.; Steve Davidson,* Vice-Chair.; Barry A. McClenahan, Hilton T. Ray, James H. Stewart, Jr., John J. Wilson.
Trustee Bank: Texas American Bank/Fort Worth.
Number of staff: 1 full-time professional.
Employer Identification Number: 237440630

6798
Theodore P. Davis Charitable Trust ⌑ ☆
c/o Texas Commerce Bank, Trust Dept.
700 Lavaca
Austin 78701

Established in 1987 in TX.
Foundation type: Independent
Financial data (yr. ended 12/31/87): Assets, $1,129,375 (M); expenditures, $61,943, including $45,000 for 9 grants (high: $10,000; low: $3,000).
Purpose and activities: Initial year of operation, 1987; giving primarily for social services, including child welfare and women's programs.
Types of support: Renovation projects, capital campaigns, special projects.
Limitations: Giving primarily in Austin, TX.
Trustees: Billy Ramsey, Texas Commerce Bank.
Employer Identification Number: 746254895

6799
Ken W. Davis Foundation ⌑
P.O. Box 3419
Fort Worth 76113 (817) 332-4081

Incorporated in 1954 in TX.
Donor(s): Ken W. Davis,† Ken W. Davis, Jr., T.C. Davis, W.S. Davis, Mid-Continent Supply Co.
Foundation type: Independent
Financial data (yr. ended 10/31/88): Assets, $2,778,581 (M); expenditures, $176,419, including $149,450 for 39 grants (high: $15,000; low: $100).
Purpose and activities: Support for health, the handicapped, hospitals, rehabilitation, community development, animal welfare and other civic affairs, the arts, and the homeless.
Types of support: Continuing support, general purposes, matching funds, program-related investments.
Limitations: Giving primarily in TX and OK. No support for religious organizations or drug or alcohol abuse programs. No grants to individuals.
Publications: Annual report.
Application information: Application form not required.
Initial approach: Proposal
Copies of proposal: 1
Deadline(s): None; however, fiscal year end is Oct. 31 for present year funding
Board meeting date(s): Quarterly
Officers and Directors: Ken W. Davis, Jr., Pres.; Kay Davis, V.P. and Secy.-Treas.; T.C. Davis, V.P.
Employer Identification Number: 756012722

6800
Del Norte Foundation ⌑ ☆
2000 MBank Plaza
El Paso 79901
Application address: P.O. Box 982, El Paso, TX 79960-0071

Established in 1987 in TX.
Donor(s): El Paso Electric Co.
Foundation type: Company-sponsored
Financial data (yr. ended 12/31/87): Assets, $128,336 (M); gifts received, $412,500; expenditures, $292,552, including $292,500 for grants.
Purpose and activities: Support primarily for community funds, social services, and youth organizations.
Limitations: Giving primarily in El Paso, TX. No grants to individuals.
Application information: Application form required.
Deadline(s): None
Write: Charles Mais, Chair.
Officer: Charles Mais, Chair.
Employer Identification Number: 742429543

6801
Daniel Deupree Foundation ⌑ ☆
Box 345
Bonham 75418
Application address: 119 North Ctr., Bonham, TX 75418; Tel.: (214) 583-5612

Established in 1981.
Foundation type: Independent

Financial data (yr. ended 12/31/88): Assets, $1,577,447 (M); expenditures, $106,659, including $95,964 for 301 grants to individuals (high: $1,500; low: $200).
Purpose and activities: Support for scholarship grants to individuals attending colleges and universities.
Types of support: Student aid.
Limitations: Giving limited to Fannin County, TX, residents.
Application information: Application form required.
Deadline(s): None
Write: M. Sorrells
Trustees: Bryan Caylor, Joe Duepree, Janie Eller, James Hicks, Mary Law.
Employer Identification Number: 759033769

6802
The Diamond M Foundation, Inc. ⌑
911 25th St.
P.O. Box 1149
Snyder 79549 (915) 573-6311

Trust established in 1950; incorporated in 1957 in TX.
Donor(s): C.T. McLaughlin.†
Foundation type: Operating
Financial data (yr. ended 12/31/87): Assets, $3,805,925 (M); gifts received, $5,000; expenditures, $121,017, including $101,169 for 1 foundation-administered program.
Purpose and activities: A private operating foundation; primary activity is to operate a museum; limited giving for charitable activities, including community funds, community services, and higher education.
Limitations: Giving primarily in TX.
Application information: Applications not accepted.
Write: Evelyn McLaughlin Davies, Dir.
Directors: Evelyn McLaughlin Davies, Jay Huckabee, John H. Jarrell, Jean McLaughlin Kahle, John Mark McLaughlin, Ruth McLaughlin Riddle, Max von Roeder.
Number of staff: 1 full-time professional; 1 full-time support; 1 part-time support.
Employer Identification Number: 756015426

6803
The Raymond Dickson Foundation ⌑
P.O. Box 406
Hallettsville 77964 (512) 798-2531

Trust established in 1958 in TX.
Donor(s): Raymond Dickson.†
Foundation type: Independent
Financial data (yr. ended 12/31/88): Assets, $1,189,345 (M); expenditures, $42,969, including $38,000 for 22 grants (high: $12,500; low: $500).
Purpose and activities: Emphasis on youth agencies, higher education, and medical research.
Types of support: Operating budgets.
Limitations: Giving limited to TX. No grants to individuals, or for building funds.
Publications: Program policy statement, application guidelines.
Application information: Application form not required.
Initial approach: Proposal
Copies of proposal: 1
Board meeting date(s): Nov. or Dec.
Write: Robert K. Jewett, Chair.
Officer and Trustees: Robert K. Jewett, Chair.; W.W. Allen, Wilbur H. Baber, Jr., G. Cameron Duncan, Vaughan B. Meyer.
Employer Identification Number: 746052983

6804
H. E. and Kate Dishman Charitable Foundation Trust ☆
c/o First City, Texas-Beaumont, N.A.
P.O. Box 3391
Beaumont 77704 (409) 838-9398

Established in 1985 in TX.
Donor(s): The Dishman Foundation, H.E. Dishman,† Kate Dishman.
Foundation type: Independent
Financial data (yr. ended 12/31/87): Assets, $2,078,974 (M); gifts received, $1,000,764; expenditures, $51,864, including $35,000 for 1 grant.
Purpose and activities: Support primarily for higher education, family services, the disadvantaged, and minorities, hospices, and the humanities.
Limitations: Giving primarily in Georgetown, TX.
Publications: Application guidelines.
Application information: Application form required.
Initial approach: Letter
Copies of proposal: 1
Deadline(s): Nov. 15
Final notification: Jan.
Write: Pam Parish, V.P. and Trust Officer, First City, Texas-Beaumont, N.A.
Trustee: First City, Texas-Beaumont, N.A.
Number of staff: None.
Employer Identification Number: 766024806

6805
Dodge Jones Foundation ▼
P.O. Box 176
Abilene 79604 (915) 673-6429

Incorporated in 1954 in TX.
Donor(s): Ruth Leggett Jones,† and others.
Foundation type: Independent
Financial data (yr. ended 12/31/88): Assets, $37,000,510 (M); expenditures, $2,926,318, including $2,465,387 for 94 grants (high: $500,000; low: $100; average: $1,000-$15,000).
Purpose and activities: Support for education, the arts, health, community funds, and youth programs.
Types of support: General purposes.
Limitations: Giving primarily in Abilene, TX. No grants to individuals.
Application information: Application form not required.
Initial approach: Letter
Copies of proposal: 1
Deadline(s): None
Board meeting date(s): Varies
Final notification: Varies; rejections are immediate
Write: Lawrence E. Gill, V.P., Grants Admin.
Officers: Julia Jones Matthews,* Pres.; Joseph E. Canon,* V.P. and Exec. Dir.; Lawrence E. Gill,* V.P., Grants Admin.; Melvin W. Holt,* V.P.; Eugene Allen, Secy.-Treas.
Directors:* Joe B. Matthews, John A. Matthews, Jr., Kade L. Matthews, Julia Matthews Wilkinson.
Number of staff: 2 full-time professional; 1 part-time support.
Employer Identification Number: 756006386

6806
Donsky Foundation ⌑ ☆
9633 Westheimer
Houston 77063

Established in 1968 in TX.
Donor(s): Abe H. Donsky.
Foundation type: Independent
Financial data (yr. ended 12/31/88): Assets, $417,532 (M); expenditures, $206,750, including $200,506 for 31 grants (high: $42,019; low: $25).
Purpose and activities: Support primarily for Jewish organizations, including welfare funds.
Limitations: Giving primarily in TX. No grants to individuals.
Publications: Annual report, 990-PF.
Application information: Contributes only to pre-selected organizations. Applications not accepted.
Officers: Abe H. Donsky, Pres.; Margaret Donsky, V.P.; Andrew Solomon, Secy.-Treas.
Employer Identification Number: 746104789

6807
The Dorset Foundation, Inc. ⌑
412 MBank Bldg.
Sherman 75090 (214) 893-6103

Incorporated about 1957 in TX.
Donor(s): W.S. Dorset.†
Foundation type: Independent
Financial data (yr. ended 12/31/88): Assets, $1,352,664 (M); expenditures, $63,280, including $52,884 for 5 grants (high: $25,000; low: $784).
Purpose and activities: Emphasis on community projects, social and health services, and youth programs.
Types of support: Operating budgets.
Limitations: Giving primarily in Grayson County, TX.
Application information:
Initial approach: Letter
Deadline(s): None
Write: Roy C. Sewell, Pres.
Officers: Roy C. Sewell, Pres. and Treas.; Ben G. Sewell, V.P.; Carolyn Nail Sewell, Secy.
Employer Identification Number: 756013384

6808
James & Dorothy Doss Foundation, Inc. ⌑
P.O. Box 388
Weatherford 76086-0388

Established in 1972 in TX.
Donor(s): James Doss.
Foundation type: Independent
Financial data (yr. ended 12/31/88): Assets, $1,363,632 (M); gifts received, $10,000; expenditures, $64,743, including $61,475 for 24 grants (high: $37,500; low: $25).
Purpose and activities: Support primarily for religious and educational institutions.

Types of support: Building funds, operating budgets.
Limitations: Giving primarily in Parker County, TX. No grants to individuals.
Application information:
Initial approach: Proposal
Deadline(s): None
Write: James Doss, Pres.
Officers: James Doss, Pres.; Dorothy Doss, V.P.; Nancy Knight, Secy.
Employer Identification Number: 756170120

6809
M. S. Doss Foundation, Inc. ⌑
P.O. Box 1677
Seminole 79360-1677 (915) 758-2770

Established in 1985 in TX.
Donor(s): M.S. Doss,† Meek Lane Doss.†
Foundation type: Independent
Financial data (yr. ended 12/31/88): Assets, $21,590,383 (M); expenditures, $1,455,098, including $612,213 for 13 grants (high: $352,867; low: $500; average: $15,000-$40,000) and $61,288 for 4 foundation-administered programs.
Purpose and activities: Support primarily for youth organizations.
Types of support: Building funds, program-related investments, renovation projects.
Limitations: Giving primarily in western TX.
Application information: Application form not required.
Initial approach: Letter
Copies of proposal: 1
Deadline(s): 30 days prior to the end of the calendar year
Board meeting date(s): Feb. and as required
Final notification: Following board meeting
Write: Joe K. McGill, Chair., or James W. Satterwhite, Exec. Dir.
Officers and Directors: Joe K. McGill, Chair.; James W. Satterwhite, Exec. Dir.; Rebecca Narvarte, Stuart Robertson, Fannie Smith, Richard Spraberry, Billie Thompson.
Number of staff: 1 full-time professional; 1 full-time support; 1 part-time support.
Employer Identification Number: 751945227

6810
The James R. Dougherty, Jr., Foundation
P.O. Box 640
Beeville 78104-0640 (512) 358-3560

Trust established in 1950 in TX.
Donor(s): James R. Dougherty,† Mrs. James R. Dougherty.†
Foundation type: Independent
Financial data (yr. ended 11/30/89): Assets, $8,009,748 (M); expenditures, $666,568, including $517,097 for 188 grants (high: $10,000; low: $310; average: $1,000-$5,000).
Purpose and activities: Support for Roman Catholic church-related institutions, including higher, secondary, and other education; cultural programs, including museums and the performing arts; health and hospitals; youth and social service agencies, particularly those benefitting the homeless, hunger, and women; and civil and human rights and international relief.
Types of support: Operating budgets, land acquisition, research, endowment funds, building funds, scholarship funds, equipment, annual campaigns, capital campaigns, conferences and seminars, general purposes, renovation projects.
Limitations: Giving primarily in TX. No grants to individuals; no loans.
Application information: Application form not required.
Initial approach: Proposal
Copies of proposal: 1
Deadline(s): 10 days prior to board meeting
Board meeting date(s): Semiannually
Final notification: 6 months or less
Write: Hugh Grove, Jr., Asst. Secy.
Officers and Trustees:* May Dougherty King,* Chair.; Mary Patricia Dougherty,* Secy.-Treas.; F. William Carr, Jr., James R. Dougherty III, Ben F. Vaughan III, Genevieve Vaughan.
Number of staff: 3
Employer Identification Number: 746039858

6811
Dresser Foundation, Inc. ▼
P.O. Box 718
Dallas 75221 (214) 740-6078
Harbison-Walker scholarship program application address: Scholarship Comm., One Gateway Ctr., Pittsburgh, PA 15222; Dresser Harbison Fdn. scholarship program application address: c/o Assoc. of Universities and Colleges of Canada, 151 Slater St., Ottawa, Canada KIP 5N1

Trust established in 1953 in TX.
Donor(s): Dresser Industries, Inc.
Foundation type: Company-sponsored
Financial data (yr. ended 10/31/89): Assets, $10,029,969 (M); expenditures, $1,481,701, including $1,232,071 for 245 grants (high: $108,347; low: $100; average: $1,000-$5,000), $55,697 for 73 grants to individuals (high: $1,350; low: $10; average: $300-$900) and $156,779 for 230 employee matching gifts.
Purpose and activities: Emphasis on community funds and higher education, including employee-related scholarships through National Merit Scholarship Corp. and through two foundation programs; support also for hospitals, youth agencies, and cultural programs; provides minor welfare assistance to retired employees.
Types of support: General purposes, employee matching gifts, building funds, employee-related scholarships.
Limitations: Giving primarily in areas of company operations, particularly Pittsburgh, PA, Waukesha, WI, Marion, OH, and Houston and Dallas, TX. No grants to individuals (except for employee-related scholarships and old age assistance payments), or for endowment funds; no loans.
Publications: Application guidelines.
Application information: Completion of application forms required for all employee-related scholarship programs but not for other programs.
Initial approach: Proposal
Copies of proposal: 1
Deadline(s): None for general grants; Feb. 14 for Harbison-Walker employee scholarships, and June 1 for Dresser Canada, Inc. employee scholarships
Board meeting date(s): As required
Final notification: 3 months
Write: Richard E. Hauslein, Chair. of Contrib. Comm.
Officers and Directors:* John J. Murphy,* Chair.; J.J. Corboy,* Pres.; R.E. Hauslein,* V.P.; Bill D. St. John,* V.P.; M.S. Nickson, Secy.; Paul W. Willey, Treas.
Trustees: NCNB Texas National Bank, Merrill Lynch Asset Management, Inc.
Number of staff: 1 full-time support.
Employer Identification Number: 237309548

6812
Cesle C. & Mamie Dues Charitable Foundation ⌑
c/0 Texas Commerce Bank-El Paso
Main and Mesa Sts.
El Paso 79901 (915) 546-6515

Established in 1974 in TX.
Foundation type: Independent
Financial data (yr. ended 12/31/87): Assets, $2,677,962 (M); expenditures, $212,926, including $69,029 for 20 grants (high: $10,000; low: $225) and $81,375 for 341 grants to individuals (high: $1,493; low: $9).
Purpose and activities: Support primarily to crippled and blind children under the age of twenty-one for medical care and equipment.
Types of support: Equipment.
Limitations: Giving primarily in TX.
Application information:
Deadline(s): None
Write: Terry Crenshaw, Char. Services Officer
Trustee: Texas Commerce Bank-El Paso.
Employer Identification Number: 746209610

6813
Dunagan Foundation, Inc.
1107 South Dwight
Monahans 79756

Established in 1976 in TX.
Donor(s): J. Conrad Dunagan, Kathlyn C. Dunagan, John C. Dunagan.
Foundation type: Independent
Financial data (yr. ended 12/31/88): Assets, $2,108,208 (M); gifts received, $43,100; expenditures, $120,317, including $108,910 for 17 grants (high: $27,058; low: $1,000; average: $1,000-$25,000).
Purpose and activities: Giving for charitable activities, including theatres, a youth organization, and a family planning agency.
Types of support: Continuing support, professorships, scholarship funds, special projects.
Limitations: Giving primarily in TX; limited support in IL, CT, and MO. No grants to individuals.
Application information: Usually contributes only to pre-selected organizations. Applications not accepted.
Write: J. Conrad Dunagan, Pres.
Officers: J. Conrad Dunagan, Pres.; Kathlyn C. Dunagan, V.P.; John C. Dunagan, Secy.-Treas.
Number of staff: None.
Employer Identification Number: 751561848

6814
The Lillian H. and C. W. Duncan Foundation ⌑
c/o Texas Commerce Bank, N.A.
P.O. Box 2558
Houston 77252-8037 (713) 236-4457

Established in 1964 in TX.
Donor(s): C.W. Duncan.†
Foundation type: Independent
Financial data (yr. ended 09/30/89): Assets, $4,345,196 (M); expenditures, $350,441, including $317,056 for 43 grants (high: $29,500; low: $500).
Purpose and activities: Emphasis on medical research; grants also for education, Protestant religious organizations, and youth agencies.
Limitations: Giving primarily in TX. No grants to individuals.
Application information:
Initial approach: Letter
Deadline(s): None
Board meeting date(s): Semiannually
Write: Inez Winston
Officers and Directors:* John H. Duncan,* Chair.; Charles W. Duncan, Jr.,* Pres.; Robert J. Faust, Secy.-Treas.; Anne S. Duncan, Brenda Duncan, C.W. Duncan III, Jeaneane Duncan, John H. Duncan, Jr., Mary Anne Duncan.
Employer Identification Number: 746064215

6815
John S. Dunn Research Foundation ☆
3355 West Alabama, Suite 720
Houston 77098-1718 (713) 626-0368

Established in 1985 in TX.
Donor(s): John S. Dunn, Sr.†
Foundation type: Independent
Financial data (yr. ended 12/31/89): Assets, $72,320,277 (M); gifts received, $126,924; expenditures, $3,501,218, including $2,950,472 for 20 grants (high: $1,000,000; low: $5,000; average: $5,000-$1,000,000).
Purpose and activities: Giving limited to health and medical-related organizations, especially hospitals; support also for cancer and other medical research.
Types of support: Endowment funds, matching funds.
Limitations: Giving limited to TX. No grants to individuals.
Publications: Application guidelines.
Application information: Application form not required.
Initial approach: Letter
Copies of proposal: 1
Deadline(s): None
Board meeting date(s): Third Wednesday of each month
Final notification: Written notice one week following meeting
Write: Robert D. Moreton, M.D., Exec. V.P. and Medical Advisor
Officers and Trustees:* Milby Dow Dunn,* Pres.; Robert D. Moreton, M.D.,* Exec. V.P. and Medical Advisor; Murry D. Kennedy,* V.P. and Secy.; John S. Dunn, Jr.,* V.P. and Treas.; Dagmar Dunn Pickens Gipe,* V.P.; Jerome L. Howard,* V.P.
Number of staff: 1 full-time professional; 2 full-time support.
Employer Identification Number: 741933660

6816
Early Foundation, Inc. ⌑
6319 Mimosa Lane
Dallas 75230 (214) 373-7114

Established in 1963 in TX.
Foundation type: Independent
Financial data (yr. ended 05/31/89): Assets, $2,048,421 (M); expenditures, $69,550, including $68,600 for 48 grants (high: $13,500; low: $250).
Purpose and activities: Emphasis on education, particularly higher education, and culture; some support also for the aged, and for Protestant giving.
Limitations: Giving primarily in Dallas, TX.
Application information: Application form not required.
Initial approach: Letter
Deadline(s): None
Write: Mrs. Jeannette B. Early, Pres.
Officer: Jeannette B. Early, Pres.
Employer Identification Number: 756011853

6817
J. E. S. Edwards Foundation
4413 Cumberland Rd. North
Fort Worth 76116 (817) 737-6924

Foundation established about 1975.
Donor(s): Jareen E. Schmidt.
Foundation type: Independent
Financial data (yr. ended 07/31/89): Assets, $1,808,761 (M); gifts received, $102,939; expenditures, $94,195, including $83,500 for 19 grants (high: $20,000; low: $1,000).
Purpose and activities: Grants largely for social services, including programs for women, hunger, the disadvantaged, and child welfare; support also for health and youth agencies and Protestant giving, including churches, schools, and missionary programs.
Types of support: Operating budgets.
Limitations: Giving primarily in TX and HI.
Application information: Application form not required.
Initial approach: Letter
Deadline(s): None
Write: Jareen E. Schmidt, Pres.
Officers: Jareen E. Schmidt, Pres.; Stacey Sewey, V.P.; Clifford Schmidt, Secy.; Sheryl Bowen, Treas.
Number of staff: None.
Employer Identification Number: 510173260

6818
El Paso Community Foundation
Texas Commerce Bank Bldg., Suite 1616
El Paso 79901 (915) 533-4020

Incorporated in 1977 in TX.
Foundation type: Community
Financial data (yr. ended 12/31/89): Assets, $23,251,391 (M); gifts received, $2,201,769; expenditures, $3,149,911, including $2,462,002 for grants (average: $25-$25,000).
Purpose and activities: Giving for education, social service agencies, health, arts and humanities, environment, and community development.
Types of support: Matching funds, special projects, continuing support, technical assistance, program-related investments.
Limitations: Giving limited to the El Paso, TX, area. No grants to individuals (except for scholarships), or for deficit financing or research.
Publications: Annual report, application guidelines, 990-PF.
Application information: Application form required.
Initial approach: Letter
Copies of proposal: 1
Deadline(s): Feb. 1
Board meeting date(s): May
Final notification: Following May meeting
Write: Janice W. Windle, Exec. Dir.
Officers: John Kelley,* Pres.; Frances Roderick Smith,* 1st V.P.; Guillermo Licon,* 2nd V.P.; Carl E. Ryan,* Secy.; Joe Kidd,* Treas.; Janice W. Windle, Exec. Dir.
Trustees:* H.M. Daugherty, Jr., Bernice Dittmer, Richard H. Feuille, Hugh K. Frederick, Jr., Morris Galatzan, Richard Hickson, Betty M. MacGuire, Charles Mais, Mary Lou Moreno, Guillermo Ochoa, Jim Phillips, Patricia Rogers, Mary Carmen Saucedo.
Number of staff: 3 full-time professional; 2 full-time support.
Employer Identification Number: 741839536

6819
J. A. and Isabel M. Elkins Foundation ⌑
3866 First City Tower
Houston 77002

Trust established in 1956 in TX.
Foundation type: Independent
Financial data (yr. ended 08/31/89): Assets, $2,836,151 (M); expenditures, $86,529, including $83,824 for 6 grants (high: $35,000; low: $3,324).
Purpose and activities: Grants primarily for child welfare and hospitals and health agencies; grants also for churches and religious associations.
Limitations: Giving primarily in Houston, TX.
Application information: Applications not accepted.
Trustees: J.A. Elkins, Jr., J.A. Elkins III.
Employer Identification Number: 746047894

6820
Margaret & James A. Elkins, Jr. Foundation ⌑
713 River Oaks Bank Tower
2001 Kirby Dr.
Houston 77019 (713) 526-6374

Established in 1956 in TX.
Foundation type: Independent
Financial data (yr. ended 10/31/88): Assets, $3,318,421 (M); expenditures, $177,257, including $158,600 for 7 grants (high: $60,000; low: $2,500).
Purpose and activities: Support primarily for education, social services, religion, cultural programs, and science.
Limitations: Giving primarily in Houston, TX.
Application information:
Initial approach: Letter
Deadline(s): None
Write: Howard Sides, Pres.
Officers: Howard Sides, Pres.; W.C. Menasco, V.P.; R.A. Seale, Jr., Secy.-Treas.
Employer Identification Number: 746051746

6821
The Ellwood Foundation ¤
P.O. Box 52482
Houston 77002 (713) 652-0613

Trust established in 1958 in TX.
Donor(s): D.C. Ellwood,† Irene L. Ellwood.†
Foundation type: Independent
Financial data (yr. ended 09/30/89): Assets, $15,281,459 (M); expenditures, $667,885, including $615,000 for 35 grants (high: $100,000; low: $1,000).
Purpose and activities: Emphasis on medical institutions, including medical education, research, health agencies, and hospitals; support for social welfare agencies and youth organizations.
Types of support: Renovation projects, operating budgets, scholarship funds, research.
Limitations: Giving primarily in the Houston, TX, area.
Application information: Application form not required.
Initial approach: Letter
Deadline(s): None
Write: H. Wayne Hightower, Trustee
Officers: H. Wayne Hightower, Pres.; Raybourne Thompson, Jr., V.P. and Secy.; Louis E. Scherck, V.P. and Treas.
Employer Identification Number: 746039237

6822
Enron Foundation ¤
(Formerly The Enron Foundation - Omaha)
1400 Smith
P.O. Box 1188
Houston 77251 (713) 853-5400

Established in 1979 in NE as InterNorth Foundation; in 1986 name changed to Enron Foundation - Omaha; in 1988 absorbed Enron Foundation - Houston (name changed from HNG Foundation) and name changed to Enron Foundation.
Donor(s): Enron Corp.
Foundation type: Company-sponsored
Financial data (yr. ended 12/31/87): Assets, $9,538,739 (M); gifts received, $2,455,527; expenditures, $4,479,438, including $3,958,268 for 424 grants (high: $200,000; low: $100; average: $5,000-$10,000) and $277,921 for 865 employee matching gifts.
Purpose and activities: Support primarily for higher education, arts and culture, community funds and civic organizations, and social service and youth agencies.
Types of support: General purposes, operating budgets, continuing support, annual campaigns, seed money, emergency funds, building funds, matching funds, employee matching gifts, capital campaigns, equipment, renovation projects, research.
Limitations: Giving limited to areas of company operations, with preference given to the Midwest and the Houston, TX, area; giving also in Omaha, NE, and Winter Park, FL. No support for non-educational religious organizations. No grants to individuals, or for fellowships; generally no grants for endowment funds or advertising for benefit purposes; no loans.
Publications: Annual report, informational brochure (including application guidelines).
Application information: Application form not required.
Initial approach: Letter
Copies of proposal: 1
Deadline(s): 30 days before board meeting
Board meeting date(s): May, Aug., Nov., and Feb.
Final notification: Generally, within 30 days; grants for over $10,000 are considered at quarterly board meetings and may require a longer response period
Write: Deborah Christie, Exec. Dir.
Officers and Directors: Kenneth L. Lay, Chair.; Rich Kinder, Vice-Chair.; Larry DeRoin, Sr. V.P.; Peggy Menchaca, V.P. and Secy.; Elizabeth Labanowski, V.P.; Edward Segner, V.P.; Ross Workman, V.P.; Deborah Christie, Exec. Dir.
Number of staff: 2 full-time professional; 1 full-time support; 1 part-time support.
Employer Identification Number: 470615943

6823
Fain Foundation ¤
500 City National Bldg.
Wichita Falls 76303

Established in 1942 in TX.
Donor(s): Minnie Rhea Wood.
Foundation type: Independent
Financial data (yr. ended 12/31/88): Assets, $1,357,050 (M); expenditures, $111,400, including $100,750 for 23 grants (high: $50,000; low: $250).
Purpose and activities: Giving for health and social services, youth agencies, and Protestant organizations.
Types of support: Operating budgets, special projects.
Limitations: Giving primarily in Wichita Falls, TX. No grants to individuals.
Application information: Contributes only to pre-selected organizations. Applications not accepted.
Officers and Directors: Minnie Rhea Wood, Pres. and Treas.; Martha Fain White, V.P.; Herbert B. Story, Secy.
Employer Identification Number: 756016679

6824
The R. W. Fair Foundation ▼ ¤
P.O. Box 689
Tyler 75710 (214) 592-3811

Trust established in 1936; incorporated in 1959 in TX.
Donor(s): R.W. Fair,† Mattie Allen Fair.†
Foundation type: Independent
Financial data (yr. ended 12/31/87): Assets, $15,192,264 (M); expenditures, $1,695,762, including $1,084,372 for 114 grants (high: $197,500; low: $200; average: $1,000-$20,000).
Purpose and activities: Grants largely for Protestant church support and church-related programs and secondary and higher education, including legal education; some support for hospitals, youth and social service agencies, libraries, and cultural activities.
Types of support: Seed money, building funds, equipment, general purposes, endowment funds, research, special projects, scholarship funds, matching funds.
Limitations: Giving primarily in the Southwest, with emphasis on TX. No grants to individuals, or for operating budgets.
Publications: Application guidelines.
Application information: Application form required.
Initial approach: Letter
Copies of proposal: 1
Deadline(s): Mar. 1, June 1, Sept. 1, and Dec. 1
Board meeting date(s): Mar., June, Sept., and Dec.
Final notification: 3 months
Write: Wilton H. Fair, Pres.
Officers and Directors: Wilton H. Fair, Pres.; James W. Fair, Sr. V.P.; Sam Bright, V.P.; Marvin N. Wilson, Secy.-Treas.; Calvin N. Clyde, Sr., Will Knight, B.B. Palmore, C.E. Peeples, Richard L. Ray.
Number of staff: 2 part-time professional.
Employer Identification Number: 756015270

6825
I.D. & Marguerite Fairchild Foundation
P.O. Box 150143
Lufkin 75915-0143

Established in 1977 in TX.
Donor(s): Marguerite Fairchild.†
Foundation type: Independent
Financial data (yr. ended 06/30/89): Assets, $1,610,299 (M); expenditures, $92,920, including $84,385 for 6 grants (high: $30,000; low: $2,400).
Purpose and activities: Support primarily for a higher education scholarship foundation; support also for a library, a museum, and a zoo.
Types of support: Building funds, capital campaigns, scholarship funds, special projects.
Limitations: Giving limited to Angelina County, TX.
Application information: Application form not required.
Initial approach: Letter
Copies of proposal: 9
Deadline(s): May 1
Board meeting date(s): June
Final notification: June 30
Write: Virginia R. Allen, Pres.
Officers: Virginia R. Allen, Pres.; Hilda Mitchell, V.P.; Mary Duncan, Secy.
Number of staff: None.
Employer Identification Number: 751572514

6826
The William Stamps Farish Fund ▼
1100 Louisiana, Suite 1200
Houston 77002 (713) 757-7313

Incorporated in 1951 in TX.
Donor(s): Libbie Rice Farish.
Foundation type: Independent
Financial data (yr. ended 6/30/88): Assets, $75,789,394 (M); expenditures, $3,915,736, including $3,615,000 for 110 grants (high: $200,000; low: $1,200; average: $10,000-$60,000).
Purpose and activities: Giving primarily for higher and secondary education, the humanities, hospitals and medical research, and social services.
Types of support: Research, general purposes.

Limitations: Giving primarily in TX. No grants to individuals, or for annual campaigns, deficit financing, operating budgets, exchange programs, or consulting services; no loans.
Publications: Application guidelines.
Application information: Application form not required.
Initial approach: Proposal
Copies of proposal: 1
Deadline(s): Mar. 30
Board meeting date(s): Semiannually
Write: W.S. Farish, Pres.
Officers: W.S. Farish,* Pres.; Martha Farish Gerry,* V.P.; J.O. Winston, Jr.,* V.P.; Caroline Rotan, Secy.; Terry W. Ward, Treas.
Trustees:* Myrtle M. Camp, Cornelia G. Corbett, Dan R. Japhet.
Number of staff: 1 full-time professional.
Employer Identification Number: 746043019

6827
The Fasken Foundation ▼
500 West Texas Ave., Suite 1160
Midland 79701 (915) 683-5401

Incorporated in 1955 in TX.
Donor(s): Andrew A. Fasken,† Helen Fasken House,† Vickie Mallison,† Howard Marshall Johnson,† Ruth Shelton.†
Foundation type: Independent
Financial data (yr. ended 12/31/88): Assets, $11,747,675 (M); gifts received, $321,888; expenditures, $1,254,537, including $1,028,066 for 72 grants (high: $105,000; low: $1,000; average: $1,500-$25,000).
Purpose and activities: Support for higher education, including scholarship funds to TX institutions for graduates of Midland County high schools and Midland Community College; support also for health and social services, including hospices and programs for alcoholism, drug abuse, mental health, and rehabilitation.
Types of support: Operating budgets.
Limitations: Giving limited to the Midland, TX, area; scholarship funds only for graduates of Midland high schools and junior college. No grants to individuals; no loans.
Publications: Application guidelines.
Application information: Application form required.
Initial approach: Letter
Copies of proposal: 1
Deadline(s): Submit proposal in Dec. or July; no set deadline
Board meeting date(s): Feb. and Sept.
Final notification: 6 months
Write: B.L. Jones, Exec. Dir.
Officers and Trustees:* Murray Fasken,* Pres.; Steven P. Fasken,* Secy.-Treas.; B.L. Jones,* Exec. Dir.; F. Andrew Fasken, William P. Franklin, Durward M. Goolsby.
Number of staff: 1 full-time professional; 1 part-time support.
Employer Identification Number: 756023680

6828
The Favrot Fund ⌑
909 Wirt Rd., No. 101
Houston 77024-3444 (713) 956-4009

Incorporated in 1952 in TX.
Donor(s): Laurence H. Favrot,† Johanna A. Favrot, George B. Strong.
Foundation type: Independent
Financial data (yr. ended 12/31/87): Assets, $6,738,467 (M); expenditures, $378,629, including $310,000 for 24 grants (high: $25,000; low: $2,000).
Purpose and activities: Emphasis on community-based programs directed toward health, support of the needy, and the arts, including the performing arts; grants also for education and social service agencies, including family planning and youth agencies.
Types of support: Operating budgets, building funds, equipment, general purposes.
Limitations: Giving primarily in TX, CA, NY, and Washington, DC.
Application information: Application form not required.
Initial approach: Letter
Copies of proposal: 1
Deadline(s): None
Board meeting date(s): Oct. or Nov.
Write: Mrs. Carol Parker
Officers and Trustees: Johanna A. Favrot, Pres.; Lenoir M. Josey, V.P. and Mgr.; Celestine Favrot Arndt, Laurence de Kanter Favrot, Leo Mortimer Favrot, Marcia Favrot-Anderson, Romelia Favrot, Jeanette Favrot Peterson.
Employer Identification Number: 746045648

6829
The Feldman Foundation
7800 Stemmons Freeway
P.O. Box 1046
Dallas 75221 (214) 689-4337

Trust established in 1946 in TX.
Donor(s): Commercial Metals Co. subsidiaries.
Foundation type: Company-sponsored
Financial data (yr. ended 12/31/88): Assets, $14,472,227 (M); gifts received, $1,431,040; expenditures, $1,226,386, including $801,900 for 22 grants (high: $250,000; low: $500; average: $1,000-$100,000).
Purpose and activities: Giving primarily for Jewish welfare funds; some support for cultural programs, medical research, hospitals, higher education, and social service agencies.
Types of support: Research, building funds, general purposes, scholarship funds, special projects.
Limitations: Giving primarily in TX and NY.
Application information: Application form not required.
Initial approach: Proposal
Copies of proposal: 1
Deadline(s): None
Board meeting date(s): As needed
Final notification: Upon receipt of proposal
Write: Jacob Feldman, Trustee
Trustees: Daniel E. Feldman, Jacob Feldman, Moses Feldman, Robert L. Feldman, M.B. Zale.
Number of staff: 1 full-time support.
Employer Identification Number: 756011578

6830
Kittie and Rugeley Ferguson Family Foundation ⌑
c/o Frost National Bank
P.O. Box 1600
San Antonio 78296

Established in 1984 in TX.
Donor(s): Kittie Ferguson, H. Rugeley Ferguson.
Foundation type: Independent
Financial data (yr. ended 11/30/88): Assets, $2,668,461 (M); expenditures, $147,576, including $125,000 for grants.
Purpose and activities: Support for a zoological society.
Application information: Contributes only to pre-selected organizations. Applications not accepted.
Trustee: Frost National Bank.
Employer Identification Number: 746320178

6831
Arch L. Ferguson Foundation, Inc. ⌑
601 East Abram St.
P.O. Box 1839
Arlington 76004-1839

Established in 1970.
Donor(s): Edwin V. Bonneau, Mrs. Edwin V. Bonneau.
Foundation type: Independent
Financial data (yr. ended 12/31/88): Assets, $3,529,818 (M); gifts received, $8,055; expenditures, $197,380, including $90,670 for 80 grants (high: $5,000; low: $300) and $13,209 for 19 grants to individuals (high: $1,500; low: $100).
Purpose and activities: Giving limited to church support, religious welfare funds, and missionary activities of the Church of Christ.
Types of support: Grants to individuals.
Application information: Contributes only to pre-selected organizations. Applications not accepted.
Officers and Directors: Wayne Hood, Pres.; Delos V. Johnson, Mgr.; Edwin V. Bonneau, Ralph Gage.
Employer Identification Number: 237103241

6832
Fifth Avenue Foundation ⌑
801 Cherry St., Suite 2100
Fort Worth 76102 (817) 877-2800

Established in 1979 in TX.
Donor(s): Pauline G. Evans.†
Foundation type: Independent
Financial data (yr. ended 12/31/89): Assets, $2,103,332 (M); expenditures, $120,629, including $108,000 for 68 grants (high: $6,000; low: $500; average: $1,000-$5,000).
Purpose and activities: Support primarily for cultural programs, hospitals and health associations, and social service agencies.
Types of support: Annual campaigns, capital campaigns, continuing support, emergency funds, renovation projects.
Limitations: Giving limited to local organizations in the Dallas-Ft. Worth, TX, area and national organizations. No grants for scholarships.
Application information: Application form not required.
Initial approach: Letter
Deadline(s): None
Write: Whitfield J. Collins, Pres.
Officers: Whitfield J. Collins, Pres.; Marie Harper, V.P.
Employer Identification Number: 751659424

6833
Leland Fikes Foundation, Inc. ▼
3050 Lincoln Plaza
500 North Akard
Dallas 75201 (214) 754-0144

Incorporated in 1952 in DE.
Donor(s): Leland Fikes,† Catherine W. Fikes.
Foundation type: Independent
Financial data (yr. ended 12/31/88): Assets, $55,148,902 (M); expenditures, $3,990,942, including $3,264,173 for 136 grants (high: $300,000; low: $25).
Purpose and activities: Giving primarily for medical research, health, youth, and social services, public interest groups, and education; grants also for population research and control, and cultural programs.
Types of support: Annual campaigns, seed money, emergency funds, building funds, equipment, land acquisition, endowment funds, research, scholarship funds, matching funds, continuing support, capital campaigns, general purposes, operating budgets, professorships, special projects.
Limitations: Giving primarily in the Dallas, TX, area. No grants to individuals; no loans.
Publications: Application guidelines.
Application information: Submit proposal upon request. Application form not required.
Initial approach: Letter
Copies of proposal: 1
Deadline(s): None
Board meeting date(s): Bimonthly
Write: Nancy Solana, Research and Grant Administration
Officers and Trustees:* Catherine W. Fikes,* Chair.; Lee Fikes,* Pres. and Treas.; Nancy Solana, Secy.; Amy L. Fikes.
Number of staff: 1 full-time professional; 3 part-time professional; 1 full-time support; 1 part-time support.
Employer Identification Number: 756035984

6834
FINA Foundation
(Formerly American Petrofina Foundation)
8350 North Central Expressway
Dallas 75206 (214) 750-2400
Application address: P.O. Box 2159, Dallas, TX 75221

Incorporated in 1974 in TX.
Donor(s): American Petrofina, Inc.
Foundation type: Company-sponsored
Financial data (yr. ended 06/30/89): Assets, $4,500,000 (M); expenditures, $335,808, including $327,512 for 139 grants (high: $64,659; low: $25).
Purpose and activities: Interests include health, especially hospitals and cancer and other medical research; community funds and civic affairs; the fine and performing arts, museums, and other cultural programs; higher and other education; family and social services; and the environment.
Types of support: Continuing support, annual campaigns, seed money, emergency funds, building funds, equipment, research, scholarship funds, employee matching gifts, matching funds.
Limitations: Giving primarily in TX. No grants to individuals.
Publications: Annual report (including application guidelines).
Application information: Application form required for employee matching gifts. Application form not required.
Initial approach: Proposal
Copies of proposal: 1
Deadline(s): None
Board meeting date(s): Approximately once per calendar quarter
Write: M. Leon Oliver, V.P.
Officers and Directors:* Ronald W. Haddock,* Pres.; M. Leon Oliver,* V.P. and Secy.; Brendan O'Connor,* V.P. and Treas.; Kenneth W. Perry,* V.P.; William W. Phelps,* V.P.; Glenn E. Selvidge,* V.P.
Employer Identification Number: 237391423

6835
First Interstate Foundation ⌑
(Formerly Allied Banks Foundation, Inc.)
815 Walker
P.O. Box 1515
Houston 77253-3326
Application address: 1000 Louisiana, Houston, TX 77002-5081; Tel.: (713) 226-1682

Incorporated in 1979 in TX.
Donor(s): Allied Bank of Texas, First Interstate Bank of Texas.
Foundation type: Company-sponsored
Financial data (yr. ended 12/31/88): Assets, $840,493 (M); expenditures, $354,830, including $352,662 for 87 grants (high: $70,700; low: $25).
Purpose and activities: Emphasis on cultural programs, including the performing arts, community funds, and social service agencies; support also for civic affairs, youth agencies, health, and education.
Limitations: Giving primarily in TX.
Application information:
Write: Bob Ward, Dir.
Officers and Directors: Gerald H. Smith, Pres.; Bob Grundy, Secy.; Jules C. Pollard, Treas.; Walter E. Johnson, Bob D. Ward.
Employer Identification Number: 742066478

6836
Ray C. Fish Foundation ⌑
2001 Kirby Dr., Suite 1005
Houston 77019 (713) 522-0741

Incorporated in 1957 in TX.
Donor(s): Raymond Clinton Fish,† Mirtha G. Fish.†
Foundation type: Independent
Financial data (yr. ended 06/30/89): Assets, $19,576,148 (M); gifts received, $79,335; expenditures, $1,118,950, including $827,000 for 110 grants (high: $100,000; low: $500).
Purpose and activities: Emphasis on educational institutions, hospitals, medical research, youth and social service agencies, and cultural organizations, including the performing arts.
Types of support: General purposes.
Limitations: Giving primarily in TX, with emphasis on Houston. No grants to individuals.
Application information: Contributes only to pre-selected organizations. Applications not accepted.
Officers: Barbara F. Daniel, Pres.; Robert J. Cruikshank, V.P.; James L. Daniel, Jr., V.P.; Maxine Costello, Secy.; Christopher J. Daniel, Treas.
Number of staff: 1
Employer Identification Number: 746043047

6837
The Fleming Foundation ▼
500 West 7th St., Suite 1007
Fort Worth 76102 (817) 335-3741

Incorporated in 1936 in TX.
Donor(s): William Fleming.†
Foundation type: Independent
Financial data (yr. ended 12/31/88): Assets, $12,858,902 (M); expenditures, $1,671,859, including $1,379,237 for 29 grants (high: $600,000; low: $200; average: $1,000-$10,000).
Purpose and activities: Emphasis on cultural programs and Protestant church support and church-related activities; support also for higher education and youth and social service agencies.
Types of support: Operating budgets, continuing support, annual campaigns, emergency funds, professorships, research, special projects.
Limitations: Giving primarily in TX, with emphasis on Fort Worth. No grants to individuals, or for deficit financing, building or endowment funds, land acquisition, matching or challenge grants, scholarships, fellowships, exchange programs, publications, or conferences; single-year grants only; no loans.
Application information: Application form not required.
Initial approach: Proposal
Copies of proposal: 1
Deadline(s): None
Board meeting date(s): Jan., Apr., July, and Sept.
Final notification: 2 months
Write: G. Malcolm Louden, Asst. Secy.
Officers and Directors: Mary D. Walsh, Pres.; F. Howard Walsh, V.P.; F. Howard Walsh, Jr., Secy.-Treas.; G. Malcolm Louden.
Number of staff: 2
Employer Identification Number: 756022736

6838
Rena Fleming Foundation for Boys, Inc. ⌑
P.O. Box 624
Corsicana 75110 (214) 874-7472

Established in 1970 in TX.
Foundation type: Independent
Financial data (yr. ended 10/31/89): Assets, $1,754,463 (M); expenditures, $57,017, including $37,950 for 9 grants (high: $12,000; low: $2,000).
Purpose and activities: Giving for youth organizations; also operates a camp for boys.
Types of support: Operating budgets.
Limitations: Giving primarily in Navarro County, TX.
Application information: Application must include a copy of IRS letter of exempt status. Application form not required.
Initial approach: Letter
Deadline(s): None

Write: Gary Brown, Secy.-Treas.
Officers: J.I. Walton, Pres.; S.L. Dublin, V.P.; Gary D. Brown, Secy.-Treas.
Employer Identification Number: 751045968

6839
The Florence Foundation
c/o NCNB Texas National Bank, Trust Dept.
P.O. Box 830241
Dallas 75283-0241 (214) 508-1931
Additional tel.: (214) 508-1932

Established in 1956.
Donor(s): The Fred F. Florence Trust.
Foundation type: Independent
Financial data (yr. ended 11/30/88): Assets, $1,850,000 (M); expenditures, $87,250, including $75,030 for 23 grants (high: $5,000; low: $500).
Purpose and activities: Giving for social services, hospitals, higher education, and cultural programs.
Types of support: General purposes, matching funds, equipment, building funds, special projects.
Limitations: Giving primarily in TX. No grants for scholarships; no loans.
Application information: Application form not required.
Initial approach: Letter
Copies of proposal: 1
Deadline(s): Feb. 1 and Aug. 1
Board meeting date(s): Spring and fall
Write: Dan M. White, Secy.
Trustee: NCNB Texas National Bank.
Members: Cecile Cook, Chair.; Dan M. White, Secy.; James Aston, David Florence, Paul Harris, John T. Stuart.
Employer Identification Number: 756008029

6840
The Fondren Foundation ▼ ⌑
7 TCT 37
P.O. Box 2558
Houston 77252-8037 (713) 236-4403

Trust established in 1948 in TX.
Donor(s): Mrs. W.W. Fondren, Sr.,† and others.
Foundation type: Independent
Financial data (yr. ended 10/31/89): Assets, $81,300,679 (M); gifts received, $58,508; expenditures, $3,402,049, including $3,201,750 for 63 grants (high: $500,000; low: $1,000; average: $5,000-$50,000).
Purpose and activities: Emphasis on higher and secondary education, social service and youth agencies, cultural organizations, and health.
Limitations: Giving primarily in TX, with emphasis on Houston, and in the Southwest. No grants to individuals, or for annual or operating fund drives.
Application information: Application form not required.
Initial approach: Letter
Copies of proposal: 1
Deadline(s): None
Board meeting date(s): Quarterly
Write: Melanie A. Boone, Asst. Secy.
Officers and Trustees:* Sue Trammell Whitfield,* Chair.; Linda Knapp Underwood,* Vice-Chair.; Walter W. Fondren III,* Secy.-Treas.; Doris Fondren Allday, R. Edwin Allday, Melanie A. Boone, Ann Gordon Trammell, David M. Underwood, William F. Whitfield, Sr.
Number of staff: None.
Employer Identification Number: 746042565

6841
Ershel Franklin Charitable Trust
P.O. Box 790
Post 79356 (806) 495-2051

Established in 1985 in TX.
Foundation type: Independent
Financial data (yr. ended 12/31/88): Assets, $1,815,194 (M); expenditures, $293,271, including $293,271 for 60 grants (high: $106,246; low: $200).
Purpose and activities: Support primarily for medical education and hospitals, higher education, religious organizations, and civic affairs.
Application information: Contributes only to pre-selected organizations. Applications not accepted.
Write: Giles C. McCrary, Trustee
Trustee: Giles C. McCrary.
Employer Identification Number: 756305761

6842
The Frees Foundation
5373 West Alabama, Suite 404
Houston 77056 (713) 623-0515

Established in 1983 in TX.
Donor(s): C. Norman Frees, Shirley B. Frees, Cumamex, S.A.
Foundation type: Independent
Financial data (yr. ended 12/31/89): Assets, $6,158,492 (M); expenditures, $311,937, including $153,571 for 13 grants (high: $100,000; low: $300; average: $1,000-$100,000).
Purpose and activities: "Focus on community organizations in TX and the Republic of Mexico," including support for hospitals and health services; organizations benefitting families, women, youth, the homeless and disadvantaged, and minorities; and intercultural relations and international relief.
Types of support: Building funds, continuing support, equipment, land acquisition, special projects.
Limitations: Giving primarily in TX and Mexico. No grants to individuals, or for endowment funds, deficit financing, or ongoing operating expenses.
Publications: Occasional report.
Application information: Application form not required.
Initial approach: Proposal
Copies of proposal: 1
Deadline(s): None
Board meeting date(s): Feb. 14
Write: Nancy Frees Rosser, Dir.
Directors: C. Norman Frees, C. Norman Frees, Jr., Shirley B. Frees, Nancy Frees Rosser, Carol Frees Watkins.
Employer Identification Number: 760053200

6843
The Fuller Foundation, Inc. ⌑
2020 Texas American Bank Bldg.
Fort Worth 76102 (817) 336-2020

Incorporated in 1951 in TX and in DE.
Foundation type: Independent
Financial data (yr. ended 12/31/88): Assets, $4,354,943 (M); expenditures, $246,583, including $217,430 for 27 grants (high: $75,000; low: $30).
Purpose and activities: Giving primarily for hospitals, secondary and higher education, and the arts and music; grants also for Protestant church support, youth agencies, and a botanical garden conservatory.
Application information:
Initial approach: Proposal
Deadline(s): None
Write: William M. Fuller, V.P.
Officers and Directors: Andrew P. Fuller, Pres.; William M. Fuller, V.P.; R.L. Bowen, Treas.
Employer Identification Number: 756015942

6844
Gailo Trust ⌑
1802 First City National Bank Bldg.
Houston 77002-6603

Established in 1963 in TX.
Foundation type: Independent
Financial data (yr. ended 12/31/88): Assets, $699,550 (M); expenditures, $692,283, including $690,705 for 4 grants (high: $673,205; low: $1,000).
Purpose and activities: Support for educational institutions.
Limitations: Giving primarily in Houston, TX. No grants to individuals.
Application information: Contributes only to pre-selected organizations. Applications not accepted.
Trustees: Gail F. Adler, Alice G. Spriggs, Lois F. Stark.
Employer Identification Number: 746054992

6845
Garvey Texas Foundation, Inc.
P.O. Box 9600
Fort Worth 76147-0600

Incorporated in 1962 in TX.
Donor(s): James S. Garvey, Shirley F. Garvey, Garvey Foundation.
Foundation type: Independent
Financial data (yr. ended 12/31/89): Assets, $5,186,873 (M); gifts received, $47,000; expenditures, $231,000, including $230,000 for 60 grants (high: $15,000; low: $50).
Purpose and activities: Support primarily for child welfare and youth agencies, higher, business, and other education, cultural activities, community funds, and hospitals and cancer research.
Types of support: Capital campaigns, program-related investments.
Limitations: Giving primarily in TX, OK, KS, NE, and CO. No grants to individuals.
Publications: 990-PF.
Application information: Application form required.
Initial approach: Letter
Copies of proposal: 1

Deadline(s): None
Write: Shirley F. Garvey, Pres.
Officers: Shirley F. Garvey,* Pres.; James S. Garvey,* V.P.; Jeffrey L. Ault, Secy.
Trustees:* Richard F. Garvey, Carol G. Sweat.
Employer Identification Number: 756031547

6846
The George Foundation ▼ ⌑
207 South Third St.
P.O. Drawer C
Richmond 77469 (713) 342-6109

Trust established in 1945 in TX.
Donor(s): A.P. George,† Mamie E. George.†
Foundation type: Independent
Financial data (yr. ended 12/31/88): Assets, $92,991,782 (M); gifts received, $150,000; expenditures, $3,944,389, including $2,151,272 for 47 grants (high: $500,000; low: $200; average: $2,500-$50,000).
Purpose and activities: Giving primarily for religious, charitable, scientific, literary, and/or educational purposes.
Types of support: Seed money, emergency funds, building funds, land acquisition, renovation projects, endowment funds, scholarship funds, matching funds, continuing support.
Limitations: Giving primarily in Fort Bend County, TX. No grants to individuals.
Publications: 990-PF.
Application information: Application form not required.
Initial approach: Letter
Copies of proposal: 1
Deadline(s): None
Board meeting date(s): 12 times a year
Final notification: Approximately 6 months
Write: Trustees
Trustees: J.A. Elkins, Jr., Hill Kemp, R. George Molina, Richard Trabulsi, Jr., Joe C. Wessendorff.
Number of staff: 2 part-time professional; 5 part-time support.
Employer Identification Number: 746043368

6847
Kenneth P. Gifford Foundation ⌑
c/o MTrust El Paso
P.O. Box 1072
El Paso 79901 (915) 592-9922

Established in 1977.
Foundation type: Independent
Financial data (yr. ended 12/31/88): Assets, $1,280,548 (M); expenditures, $68,819, including $57,000 for 10 grants (high: $25,000; low: $1,000).
Purpose and activities: Emphasis on organizations concerned with care for the aged and youth; supports scholarship program sponsored by El Paso Community Foundation for students of local high schools for undergraduate study at University of Texas-El Paso.
Types of support: Scholarship funds.
Limitations: Giving primarily in El Paso County, TX. No grants to individuals.
Application information: Application form not required.
Initial approach: Letter
Copies of proposal: 1
Deadline(s): Mar. 1
Board meeting date(s): Mar.
Write: Chris Rhoads
Board of Managers: Henry Ellis, W.A. Thurmond, Robert Young.
Employer Identification Number: 741977400

6848
Thomas Gilcrease Foundation
7540 Louis Pasteur, Suite 300
San Antonio 78229 (512) 692-3599

Incorporated in 1942 in OK.
Donor(s): Thomas Gilcrease.†
Foundation type: Independent
Financial data (yr. ended 9/30/89): Assets, $1,502,932 (M); expenditures, $69,356, including $44,000 for 12 grants (high: $10,000; low: $500).
Purpose and activities: Emphasis on social services and higher education.
Limitations: Giving primarily in TX.
Application information: Funds rarely made available to unsolicited applicants. Application form not required.
Initial approach: Letter
Copies of proposal: 1
Deadline(s): None
Write: Barta Gilcrease Busby, Pres.
Officers and Trustees: Barta Gilcrease Busby, Pres. and Mgr.; Peter D. Denney, V.P.; Eugene F. Gilcrease, V.P.; Jana Gilcrease, V.P.; Thomas G. Denney, Secy.
Number of staff: 1 part-time support.
Employer Identification Number: 736009934

6849
Pauline Gill Foundation ⌑ ☆
1901 North Akard
Dallas 75201-2330

Established in 1975 in TX.
Donor(s): Pauline G. Sullivan.
Foundation type: Independent
Financial data (yr. ended 12/31/88): Assets, $8,965,025 (M); expenditures, $401,976, including $400,850 for 23 grants (high: $200,000; low: $100).
Purpose and activities: Giving primarily for education, youth, and social services.
Application information: Contributes only to pre-selected organizations. Applications not accepted.
Officers and Trustees:* Pauline G. Sullivan, Pres. and Mgr.; B. Gill Clements,* V.P.; Nancy Clements Seay,* V.P.
Employer Identification Number: 237431528

6850
Sondra & Charles Gilman, Jr. Foundation, Inc. ⌑
P.O. Box 18925
Corpus Christi 78480 (512) 937-2520

Established in NY in 1981 as a successor to the Gilman Foundation.
Foundation type: Independent
Financial data (yr. ended 04/30/89): Assets, $10,297,558 (M); expenditures, $815,366, including $256,158 for 94 grants (high: $50,000; low: $15).
Purpose and activities: Support for health organizations, education, especially secondary education, museums, music, contemporary art and theater, and environmental organizations.
Application information:
Initial approach: Letter
Deadline(s): None
Write: Sondra Gilman, Pres.
Officers and Directors:* Sondra Gilman,* Chair.; Celso M. Gonzalez,* Pres.; John Mosler,* Secy.; Walter Baur,* Treas.; Jack Friedland, Charles Gilman III, Myrna Schatz.
Employer Identification Number: 133097485

6851
Robert and Ruth Glaze Foundation ⌑
2001 Bryan Tower, Suite 3131
Dallas 75201 (214) 969-5595

Established in 1986 in TX.
Donor(s): Robert E. Glaze, Ruth T. Glaze.
Foundation type: Independent
Financial data (yr. ended 12/31/88): Assets, $2,941,632 (M); expenditures, $245,470, including $214,724 for 21 grants (high: $108,000; low: $100).
Purpose and activities: Primarily for religious organizations, particularly a Baptist church and groups promoting Christian ministry. Some support also for a symphonic association.
Limitations: Giving primarily in Dallas, TX.
Application information:
Initial approach: Letter
Deadline(s): None
Write: Robert E. Glaze, Pres.
Officers and Directors: Robert E. Glaze, Pres. and Treas.; Ruth T. Glaze, V.P. and Secy.; Maryanne Romano.
Employer Identification Number: 752102493

6852
Meyer and Ida Gordon Foundation ⌑
2401 Fountain View, Suite 350
Houston 77057

Incorporated in 1950 in TX.
Donor(s): Members of the Gordon family, Gordon's Jewelry Co., and others.
Foundation type: Independent
Financial data (yr. ended 12/31/88): Assets, $3,705,825 (M); expenditures, $187,424, including $186,500 for 7 grants (high: $180,000; low: $100).
Purpose and activities: Grants largely for Jewish welfare funds.
Limitations: Giving primarily in Houston, TX.
Application information: Contributes only to pre-selected organizations. Applications not accepted.
Write: Harry B. Gordon, Pres.
Officers and Trustees: Harry B. Gordon, Pres.; Aron S. Gordon, V.P. and Treas.; James C. Gordon, V.P.; W.L. Barfield, Secy.
Employer Identification Number: 746046795

6853
The Green Foundation ⌑
3300 First City Ctr.
Dallas 75201 (214) 969-1700

Established in 1958 in TX.
Donor(s): Cecil H. Green, Ida M. Green.†
Foundation type: Independent
Financial data (yr. ended 12/31/88): Assets, $5,585,556 (M); gifts received, $150,711;

expenditures, $526,726, including $482,150 for 26 grants (high: $150,000; low: $250).
Purpose and activities: Emphasis on hospitals and medical services, cultural programs, historical preservation, higher education, a secondary school, and a community fund.
Types of support: Operating budgets.
Limitations: Giving primarily in the Dallas, TX, area.
Application information: Application form not required.
Deadline(s): None
Write: William E. Collins, Trustee
Trustees: William E. Collins, Cecil H. Green, Bryan Smith.
Employer Identification Number: 756015446

6854
Morris Greenspun Foundation
3717 Maplewood Ave.
Dallas 75205-2826 (214) 871-8619

Established in 1964 in TX.
Foundation type: Independent
Financial data (yr. ended 12/31/88): Assets, $1,141,771 (M); expenditures, $70,250, including $64,247 for 131 grants (high: $3,500; low: $10).
Purpose and activities: Giving primarily for cultural programs and museums, higher education, Jewish welfare funds, and medical research.
Limitations: Giving primarily in Los Angeles, CA; New York, NY; and Dallas, TX. No grants to individuals.
Application information: Applications not accepted.
Write: Theodore S. Hochstim, Dir.
Directors: Iva G. Hochstim, Theodore S. Hochstim, Raymond Marcus.
Number of staff: None.
Employer Identification Number: 756019227

6855
Rosa May Griffin Foundation
P.O. Box 1775
Kilgore 75662 (214) 983-2051

Incorporated in 1960 in TX.
Donor(s): Rosa May Griffin.†
Foundation type: Independent
Financial data (yr. ended 12/31/88): Assets, $3,422,562 (M); expenditures, $235,833, including $171,231 for 17 grants (high: $25,000; low: $100; average: $1,200).
Purpose and activities: Giving for Presbyterian church support, higher education, and hospitals.
Types of support: General purposes, operating budgets, continuing support, annual campaigns, emergency funds, building funds, equipment, matching funds.
Limitations: Giving limited to TX. No grants to individuals, or for endowment funds, scholarships, or fellowships; no loans.
Publications: Program policy statement.
Application information: Application form not required.
Initial approach: Letter or proposal
Copies of proposal: 1
Deadline(s): Submit proposal in Oct.
Board meeting date(s): Monthly
Final notification: 1 month
Write: Byron G. Bronstad, Secy.-Treas.
Officers and Trustees: O.N. Pederson, Pres.; E.B. Mobley, V.P.; Byron G. Bronstad, Secy.-Treas. and Mgr.
Number of staff: None.
Employer Identification Number: 756011866

6856
Leon and Beatrice Obenhaus Grodhaus Foundation ¤
P.O. Box 867
Columbus 78934 (409) 732-5706

Established in 1984 in TX.
Foundation type: Independent
Financial data (yr. ended 12/31/88): Assets, $1,351,864 (M); expenditures, $78,143, including $65,000 for 7 grants (high: $30,000; low: $1,000).
Purpose and activities: Giving primarily to welfare for needy families and the elderly and health organizations; support also for secondary education.
Types of support: Endowment funds, scholarship funds.
Limitations: Giving limited to Weimar, Colorado County, TX.
Application information: Application form not required.
Initial approach: Letter
Deadline(s): None
Write: James H. Whitcomb, Secy.-Treas.
Officer and Trustees: James H. Whitcomb, Secy.-Treas.; F.T. Barfield, Alfred Flournoy, Gus H. Miller, Jr., Harvey Vornsand.
Employer Identification Number: 746328959

6857
Paul and Mary Haas Foundation
P.O. Box 2928
Corpus Christi 78403 (512) 888-9301

Trust established in 1954 in TX.
Donor(s): Paul R. Haas, Mary F. Haas.
Foundation type: Independent
Financial data (yr. ended 12/31/89): Assets, $1,694,937 (M); gifts received, $1,000,000; expenditures, $415,700, including $243,397 for grants (high: $27,500; low: $50; average: $3,500) and $136,474 for grants to individuals (high: $750; low: $100; average: $750).
Purpose and activities: Grants for social service and youth agencies, including alcohol abuse programs, church support, higher, early childhood, and adult education, and the arts and cultural programs; scholarships only to undergraduates and vocational school students; limited medical support, including cancer and other medical research.
Types of support: Special projects, student aid, annual campaigns, building funds, capital campaigns, emergency funds, equipment, general purposes, renovation projects, seed money, operating budgets.
Limitations: Giving primarily in the Corpus Christi, TX, area. No grants to individuals (except for student aid); no support for graduate students.
Publications: Annual report (including application guidelines), application guidelines.
Application information: Application form provided for scholarship applicants.
Initial approach: Proposal
Copies of proposal: 1
Deadline(s): For scholarships preference is 3 months before the semester; none for other grants
Board meeting date(s): As needed
Final notification: Within a few weeks of receipt of proposal
Write: Paul R. Haas, Trustee
Trustees: Mary F. Haas, Paul R. Haas, Raymond P. Haas, Rene Haas, Rheta Haas Page.
Number of staff: 1 part-time professional; 1 part-time support.
Employer Identification Number: 746031614

6858
D. D. Hachar Charitable Trust Fund ¤
Laredo National Bank
P.O. Box 59
Laredo 78404 (512) 723-1151
Additional address: 700 San Bernardo, 6th Fl., LNB Plaza Towers, Laredo, TX 78404

Established in 1980 in TX.
Foundation type: Independent
Financial data (yr. ended 4/30/87): Assets, $7,164,959 (M); expenditures, $673,258, including $237,000 for 15 grants (high: $100,000; low: $3,000), $182,500 for 190 grants to individuals (high: $3,000; low: $250) and $56,500 for 31 loans to individuals.
Purpose and activities: Grants primarily for higher education, including scholarships and loans.
Types of support: Student aid, student loans, scholarship funds, general purposes.
Limitations: Giving limited to Laredo and Webb County, TX.
Publications: Annual report, informational brochure, program policy statement, application guidelines.
Application information: Application form required for scholarships.
Deadline(s): Last Friday in Apr. and Oct. for scholarships
Write: Margie H. Weatherford, Admin.
Trustee: Laredo National Bank.
Number of staff: 2 full-time professional.
Employer Identification Number: 742093680

6859
The Haggar Foundation ▼ ¤
6113 Lemmon Ave.
Dallas 75209
Scholarship application address: Haggar Scholarship Program, The University of North Texas, P.O. Box 13707, Denton, TX 76203-3707

Trust established in 1950 in TX.
Donor(s): Joseph M. Haggar, Rose M. Haggar, Haggar Co., and others.
Foundation type: Independent
Financial data (yr. ended 6/30/88): Assets, $19,354,689 (M); expenditures, $2,198,855, including $2,004,246 for 269 grants (high: $250,000; low: $100).
Purpose and activities: Emphasis on higher and secondary education, including a scholarship program for children of company employees, and hospitals; contributions also for youth agencies, cultural programs, and Catholic church support.

Types of support: Employee-related scholarships, building funds.
Limitations: Giving primarily in southern TX, and in OK, in areas of company operations.
Publications: Application guidelines.
Application information: Application guidelines available for employee-related scholarship program. Application form required.
Deadline(s): Submit scholarship application on or before Apr. 30; deadline Mar. 31
Write: Rosemary Haggar Vaughan, Exec. Dir.
Trustees: Edmond R. Haggar, Sr., Joseph M. Haggar, Jr., Joseph M. Haggar III, Robert C. Qualls, Rosemary Haggar Vaughan.
Employer Identification Number: 756019237

6860
Haggerty Foundation ⌑
5455 Northbrook Dr.
Dallas 75220

Established in 1950 in TX.
Donor(s): Patrick E. Haggerty.†
Foundation type: Independent
Financial data (yr. ended 12/31/88): Assets, $7,453,729 (M); expenditures, $530,565, including $480,000 for 13 grants (high: $300,000; low: $3,500).
Purpose and activities: Giving primarily for social services and higher education.
Types of support: General purposes.
Limitations: Giving primarily in TX.
Application information: Contributes only to pre-selected organizations. Applications not accepted.
Officers: Beatrice M. Haggerty, Pres.; Patrick E. Haggerty, Jr., V.P.; Michael G. Haggerty, Secy.-Treas.; Teresa Haggerty Parravano, Secy.-Treas.
Trustees: Kathleen Haggerty Strahan, Sheila Haggerty Turner.
Employer Identification Number: 752076387

6861
G. A. C. Halff Foundation ⌑
745 East Mulberry, Suite 400
San Antonio 78212 (512) 735-3300

Incorporated in 1951 in TX.
Donor(s): G.A.C. Halff.†
Foundation type: Independent
Financial data (yr. ended 2/29/88): Assets, $5,036,537 (M); expenditures, $356,363, including $214,000 for 34 grants (high: $25,000; low: $2,000).
Purpose and activities: Giving for social service agencies, aid to the handicapped, youth agencies, population control, and a community fund.
Limitations: Giving primarily in San Antonio, TX. No grants to individuals.
Application information: Application form not required.
Initial approach: Letter
Deadline(s): May 15
Write: Roland R. Arnold, V.P.
Officers and Trustees: Hugh Halff, Jr., Pres.; Roland R. Arnold, V.P. and Treas.; Catherine H. Edson, Secy.; Thomas H. Edson, Marie M. Halff, Catherine H. Luhn, George M. Luhn.
Employer Identification Number: 746042432

6862
F. V. Hall, Jr. & Marylou Hall Children's Crisis Foundation
c/o NCNB Texas National Bank
P.O. Box 830241
Dallas 75283-0241

Established in 1978 in TX.
Foundation type: Independent
Financial data (yr. ended 04/30/89): Assets, $1,234,816 (M); expenditures, $89,554, including $80,407 for grants to individuals.
Purpose and activities: Support for infants and children less than twelve years of age who are in a situation of crisis, critical need, or critical want.
Types of support: Grants to individuals.
Limitations: Giving limited to Tom Green County, TX.
Application information: Application form required.
Deadline(s): None
Write: Alice J. Gayle, Trust Officer, NCNB Texas National Bank
Officers: Robert Grant, Mgr.; Marvin Hunter, Mgr.; Linda Jacks, Mgr.; Susan Marshall, Mgr.; Craig Porter, Mgr.; Jerry Roach, Mgr.
Trustee: NCNB Texas National Bank.
Employer Identification Number: 756260350

6863
Halliburton Foundation, Inc. ▼
3600 Lincoln Plaza
500 North Akard St.
Dallas 75201-3391 (214) 978-2600

Incorporated in 1965 in TX.
Donor(s): Halliburton Co., Brown & Root, Inc., and other subsidiaries.
Foundation type: Company-sponsored
Financial data (yr. ended 12/31/88): Assets, $10,871,966 (M); expenditures, $1,369,489, including $1,021,000 for 86 grants (high: $100,000; low: $500; average: $1,000-$25,000) and $333,291 for 165 employee matching gifts.
Purpose and activities: Giving for higher education restricted to faculty support in engineering and technical schools, and a program that matches employee gifts to higher education; some limited support for select charitable organizations.
Types of support: Operating budgets, continuing support, annual campaigns, employee matching gifts, research, conferences and seminars, special projects.
Limitations: Giving primarily in the Southwest, with emphasis on TX. No grants to individuals, or for seed money, emergency funds, deficit financing, building funds, equipment and materials, land acquisition, renovation projects, endowment funds, scholarships, fellowships, demonstration projects, or publications; no loans.
Application information: Application form not required.
Initial approach: Proposal
Copies of proposal: 1
Deadline(s): None
Board meeting date(s): Feb. and Sept.
Final notification: Within 3 months
Write: Karen S. Stuart, V.P.
Officers: Thomas H. Cruikshank,* Pres.; Karen S. Stuart, V.P. and Secy.; C. Robert Fielder, V.P. and Treas.; Robert M. Kennedy, V.P.-Legal.
Trustees:* T. Louis Austin, Jr., Dale P. Jones.
Number of staff: None.
Employer Identification Number: 751212458

6864
The Ewing Halsell Foundation ▼
711 Navarro St.
San Antonio Bank and Trust Bldg., Suite 537
San Antonio 78205 (512) 223-2640

Trust established in 1957 in TX.
Donor(s): Ewing Halsell,† Mrs. Ewing Halsell,† Grace F. Rider.†
Foundation type: Independent
Financial data (yr. ended 6/30/88): Assets, $32,212,477 (M); expenditures, $1,789,579, including $1,381,847 for 51 grants (high: $1,000,000; low: $50; average: $1,000-$15,000).
Purpose and activities: Grants primarily for education, cultural programs, health organizations, and social service and youth agencies.
Types of support: Operating budgets, annual campaigns, building funds, equipment, land acquisition, research, publications, technical assistance, seed money.
Limitations: Giving limited to TX, with emphasis on southwestern TX, and particularly San Antonio. No grants to individuals, or for deficit financing, emergency funds, general endowments, matching gifts, scholarships, fellowships, demonstration projects, general purposes, or conferences; no loans.
Publications: Biennial report (including application guidelines), program policy statement.
Application information: Application form not required.
Initial approach: Letter or proposal
Copies of proposal: 1
Deadline(s): None
Board meeting date(s): Quarterly
Final notification: 3 months
Officers and Trustees: Gilbert M. Denman, Jr., Chair.; Helen Campbell, Secy.-Treas.; Leroy G. Denman, Jr., Hugh A. Fitzsimmons, Jr., Jean Holmes McDonald.
Number of staff: 1 full-time professional; 2 part-time support.
Employer Identification Number: 746063016

6865
George and Mary Josephine Hamman Foundation ▼
910 Travis St., No. 1438
Houston 77002-5816 (713) 658-8345

Incorporated in 1954 in TX.
Donor(s): Mary Josephine Hamman,† George Hamman.
Foundation type: Independent
Financial data (yr. ended 04/30/89): Assets, $23,391,000 (M); expenditures, $1,559,712, including $637,400 for grants (high: $65,000; low: $500; average: $1,000-$10,000) and $245,000 for 98 grants to individuals of $2,500 each.
Purpose and activities: Giving for construction and operation of hospitals, medical treatment,

and research organizations and programs; grants to churches and affiliated religious organizations (nondenominational); individual scholarship program for local high school students; grants to building programs or special educational projects at colleges and universities, mostly local; contributions also to cultural programs, social services, and youth agencies.
Types of support: Annual campaigns, emergency funds, building funds, equipment, research, professorships, scholarship funds, continuing support, matching funds, student aid.
Limitations: Giving limited to TX, primarily the Houston area. No support for post-graduate education. No grants to individuals (except for scholarships), or for deficit financing, maintenance of buildings, or endowment funds.
Publications: Application guidelines, financial statement, 990-PF.
Application information: Application form required for scholarships; none for other grants.
Initial approach: Letter
Copies of proposal: 1
Deadline(s): Feb. 28 for scholarships, none for other grants
Board meeting date(s): Monthly
Final notification: 60 days
Write: Stephen I. Gelsey, Admin.
Officers and Directors:* Charles D. Milby,* Pres.; Henry R. Hamman,* Secy.; Louise Milby Feagin.
Number of staff: 4 full-time professional.
Employer Identification Number: 746061447

6866
The Curtis & Doris K. Hankamer Foundation ⌑
9039 Katy Freeway, Suite 430
Houston 77024-1623

Established in 1981 in TX.
Donor(s): Doris K. Hankamer, Earl Curtis Hankamer, Jr.
Foundation type: Independent
Financial data (yr. ended 12/31/87): Assets, $4,507,494 (M); expenditures, $944,077, including $890,000 for 13 grants (high: $725,000; low: $5,000).
Purpose and activities: Giving primarily for medical research, higher education, and Christian ministry.
Application information: Applications not accepted.
Trustees: S. Terry Bracken, Doris K. Hankamer, Scott Hunsaker.
Employer Identification Number: 760022687

6867
The Harding Foundation
Harding Foundation Bldg.
Fifth and Hidalgo, P.O. Box 130
Raymondville 78580 (512) 689-2706

Incorporated in 1947 in TX.
Donor(s): W.A. Harding,† Laura V. Harding.†
Foundation type: Independent
Financial data (yr. ended 12/31/88): Assets, $1,554,112 (M); gifts received, $93,563; expenditures, $125,639, including $34,998 for 21 grants (high: $25,000; low: $54; average: $100-$1,500) and $23,150 for 11 grants to individuals (high: $4,500; low: $390).
Purpose and activities: For the furthering of Christian education in homes, schools, and churches; emphasis on Christian church support and religious associations, evangelical programs, and child welfare; scholarships to seminary students.
Types of support: Student aid, special projects.
Limitations: No grants for scholarships (except for theological students).
Application information: Application form required.
Initial approach: Letter
Deadline(s): None
Board meeting date(s): 2nd Tuesday in Feb.
Write: Mrs. Glenn W. Harding, Corresponding Secy.
Officers and Directors:* Glenn W. Harding,* Pres.; Martin Dale Harding,* V.P.; Dorothy J. Parr,* Secy.
Number of staff: 1 full-time professional.
Employer Identification Number: 746025883

6868
Harkins Foundation ⌑
P.O. Box 1940
Alice 78333 (512) 664-3427

Established in 1969 in TX.
Donor(s): H. Burton Harkins.
Foundation type: Independent
Financial data (yr. ended 10/31/88): Assets, $1,249,615 (M); expenditures, $43,529, including $42,695 for 8 grants (high: $25,000; low: $595).
Purpose and activities: Giving primarily for higher education and health.
Types of support: General purposes.
Limitations: Giving primarily in TX.
Publications: 990-PF.
Application information:
Initial approach: Proposal
Write: H. Burt Harkins, Trustee
Trustees: H. Burton Harkins, H. Burton Harkins, Jr., Deirdre Harkins Richards.
Employer Identification Number: 746124115

6869
The Don and Sybil Harrington Foundation ▼
700 First National Place I, Suite 700
801 South Fillmore
Amarillo 79101 (806) 373-8353

Trust established in 1951 in TX; incorporated in 1971.
Donor(s): Donald D. Harrington,† Mrs. Sybil B. Harrington.
Foundation type: Independent
Financial data (yr. ended 12/31/89): Assets, $71,368,132 (M); expenditures, $6,956,861, including $5,961,502 for 56 grants (high: $2,064,585; low: $1,500; average: $10,000-$100,000).
Purpose and activities: Interests include hospitals and health agencies, medical research, the arts and cultural programs, higher and other education, including scholarship funds, youth agencies, social services, and civic affairs.
Types of support: Scholarship funds, equipment, research, renovation projects.
Limitations: Giving limited to the 26 northernmost counties of the Texas Panhandle. No grants to individuals, or for operating budgets.
Application information: Application form not required.
Initial approach: Letter
Copies of proposal: 1
Deadline(s): At least 1 month prior to board meeting
Board meeting date(s): Quarterly
Final notification: 2 months
Write: Jim Allison, Pres. or Patricia M. Smith, Grants Coord.
Officers and Directors:* Gene Edwards,* Chair.; Don L. Patterson,* Vice-Chair.; Jim Allison, Pres. and Exec. Dir.; Patricia M. Smith, Secy.-Treas.
Number of staff: 2 full-time professional.
Employer Identification Number: 751336604

6870
Hawn Foundation, Inc. ▼ ⌑
1540 RepublicBank Bldg.
Dallas 75201 (214) 220-2828

Incorporated in 1962 in TX.
Donor(s): Mildred Hawn.†
Foundation type: Independent
Financial data (yr. ended 8/31/88): Assets, $19,128,523 (M); expenditures, $1,046,900, including $782,000 for 41 grants (high: $250,000; low: $500; average: $3,500-$30,000).
Purpose and activities: Emphasis on medical research, health agencies, hospitals, higher education, social services, and cultural programs.
Limitations: Giving primarily in TX, with emphasis on Dallas.
Application information:
Initial approach: Letter
Deadline(s): None
Board meeting date(s): Aug. and as necessary
Final notification: Between 30 and 90 days
Write: E.S. Blythe, Secy.-Treas.
Officers and Directors: William Russell Hawn, Pres.; E.S. Blythe, Secy.-Treas.; W.A. Hawn, Jr., William Russell Hawn, Jr., R.S. Strauss, I.N. Taylor.
Number of staff: None.
Employer Identification Number: 756036761

6871
Earl Hayes Foundation, Inc. ⌑
511 East John Carpenter Freeway, Suite 400
Irving 75039 (214) 869-2400

Incorporated in 1949 in DE.
Donor(s): Frue Alline Hayes, Robert T. Hayes, Bob Hayes Chevrolet, Inc.
Foundation type: Independent
Financial data (yr. ended 11/30/88): Assets, $227,589 (M); gifts received, $325,000; expenditures, $136,145, including $125,350 for 32 grants (high: $50,000; low: $100).
Purpose and activities: Emphasis on culture, particularly dance and music, and hospitals.
Limitations: Giving primarily in the Dallas, TX, area.
Application information:
Initial approach: Proposal
Deadline(s): None
Write: Frue Alline Hayes, Dir.

Officers: Susie McQuade, Pres.; Douglas Dunlap, V.P.
Directors: Frue Alline Hayes, Robert T. Hayes.
Employer Identification Number: 756011537

6872
Ed and Mary Heath Foundation ⌑
P.O. Box 338
Tyler 75710 (214) 597-7436

Established in 1954 in TX.
Donor(s): J.E. Heath,† Mary M. Heath.†
Foundation type: Independent
Financial data (yr. ended 12/31/88): Assets, $2,142,207 (M); expenditures, $238,496, including $94,250 for grants.
Purpose and activities: Giving for Protestant church support, youth agencies, recreation, and health services.
Limitations: Giving limited to TX, particularly Smith County. No grants to individuals, or for endowment funds.
Application information:
Initial approach: Letter
Copies of proposal: 1
Deadline(s): None
Board meeting date(s): Mar., June, Sept., and Dec.
Write: W.R. Smith, Chair.
Officers and Directors: W.R. Smith, Chair.; L.H. Reese, Secy.-Treas.; Russell Cooper, Gary Fenton, Jack Jackson, James Oliver, Wendell Pool.
Employer Identification Number: 756021506

6873
Simon and Louise Henderson Foundation ⌑
P.O. Box 1365
Lufkin 75902 (713) 634-3448

Established in 1958 in TX.
Donor(s): Louise Henderson.†
Foundation type: Independent
Financial data (yr. ended 12/31/88): Assets, $2,871,472 (M); expenditures, $171,836, including $150,181 for 35 grants (high: $20,000; low: $25).
Purpose and activities: Support for hospitals, education, and religious giving.
Limitations: Giving primarily in East TX.
Application information: Application form not required.
Deadline(s): None
Board meeting date(s): Dec. and as required
Write: Simon W. Henderson, Jr., Pres.
Officers: Simon W. Henderson, Jr., Pres.; Loucile J. Henderson, V.P.; Simon W. Henderson III, Secy.-Treas.
Employer Identification Number: 756022769

6874
The Patrick Henry Foundation ⌑ ☆
c/o NCNB Bank, Trust Div.
P.O. Box 908
Austin 78781 (512) 397-2574

Established in 1986 in TX.
Donor(s): Ellen Clayton Garwood.
Foundation type: Independent
Financial data (yr. ended 4/30/89): Assets, $2,734,697 (M); expenditures, $346,544, including $308,665 for 69 grants (high: $30,000; low: $500).
Purpose and activities: Giving primarily for international and domestic public policy and civil rights organizations, including international relief; support also for universities and other educational associations.
Limitations: No grants to individuals.
Application information: Application form required.
Deadline(s): None
Write: Ms. Anne Glanz
Officers and Trustees: Ellen Clayton Garwood, Pres. and Treas.; William L. Garwood, Jr., V.P.; Mary Garwood Yancy, Secy.; Susan Garwood Knapp.
Employer Identification Number: 742418070

6875
Hervey Foundation ⌑
909 North Mesa
El Paso 79901 (915) 532-2621

Trust established in 1957 in TX.
Foundation type: Independent
Financial data (yr. ended 1/31/87): Assets, $5,275,681 (M); expenditures, $324,481, including $276,900 for 28 grants (high: $75,000; low: $15).
Purpose and activities: Giving to community funds, youth agencies, and hospitals.
Types of support: Operating budgets, continuing support, annual campaigns, building funds, equipment, special projects, research, scholarship funds.
Limitations: Giving primarily in AZ and TX. No grants to individuals, or for endowment funds or matching gifts; no loans.
Application information: Application form not required.
Initial approach: Letter
Copies of proposal: 1
Deadline(s): None
Board meeting date(s): Monthly
Final notification: 2 months
Write: Fred Hervey, Trustee
Trustees: Bill J. Farmer, Fred Hervey, Robert E. Hutchinson, Millard Orick.
Number of staff: 1 part-time professional.
Employer Identification Number: 746068038

6876
Albert & Ethel Herzstein Charitable Foundation ⌑
6131 Westview
Houston 77055-5421 (713) 681-7868

Established in 1965 in TX.
Donor(s): Members of the Herzstein family.
Foundation type: Independent
Financial data (yr. ended 12/31/88): Assets, $25,166,454 (M); gifts received, $4,540,304; expenditures, $370,925, including $344,211 for 63 grants (high: $155,371; low: $25).
Purpose and activities: Support primarily for a food bank; some support for Jewish organizations.
Limitations: Giving primarily in TX.
Application information:
Initial approach: Letter or proposal
Deadline(s): None
Write: Albert H. Herzstein, Mgr.
Officer and Trustee: Albert H. Herzstein, Mgr.
Employer Identification Number: 746070484

6877
The Hevrdejs Foundation ☆
Eight Greenway Plaza, Suite 714
Houston 77046 (713) 961-5110

Established in 1988 in TX.
Donor(s): Frank J. Hevrdejs.
Foundation type: Independent
Financial data (yr. ended 12/31/89): Assets, $1,439,093 (M); expenditures, $94,513, including $58,935 for 2 grants (high: $35,000; low: $23,935).
Purpose and activities: Support for the development and encouragement of education, primarily to socially and economically disadvantaged youth, including projects to improve the quality of teaching and learning at all levels. Special consideration will be given to elementary and secondary educational programs which emphasize employment skills and/or enhance opportunities for further education. Priority given to such factors as innovation, the testing of new ideas, and the potential for replication.
Limitations: Giving primarily in TX. No support for medical research, health-related activities, or sectarian or denominational activities, except academic programs offered by religious institutions. No grants to individuals, or for capital improvement projects, building funds, fund raising drives, testimonial dinners, or advertising.
Publications: 990-PF, informational brochure (including application guidelines).
Application information: Application form not required.
Initial approach: Letter or preliminary proposal
Deadline(s): Nov. 30, Feb. 28, May 30, and Aug. 31
Board meeting date(s): Feb., May, Aug., and Nov.
Write: Pat Hevrdejs, Pres.
Officers and Trustees:* Frank J. Hevrdejs, Chair. and C.E.O.; Patricia A. Hevrdejs,* Pres. and C.F.O.; Sylvia J. Hurd,* V.P.; Bridget Tate Moore,* V.P.; Sylvia D. Hancock, Secy.
Number of staff: 1 part-time professional.
Employer Identification Number: 760267717

6878
Walter Hightower Foundation ⌑
c/o Texas Commerce Bank-El Paso
P.O. Drawer 140
El Paso 79980 (915) 546-6515

Established in 1980.
Donor(s): Walter Hightower.†
Foundation type: Independent
Financial data (yr. ended 12/31/88): Assets, $6,229,555 (M); expenditures, $303,795, including $250,000 for 1 grant and $25,162 for 159 grants to individuals (high: $3,617; low: $14).
Purpose and activities: Giving for health care for crippled children under the age of 21.
Types of support: General purposes, operating budgets, continuing support, annual campaigns, seed money, building funds, equipment, grants to individuals, capital campaigns, endowment funds, matching funds, publications.
Limitations: Giving limited to western TX and southern NM. No grants for scholarships or fellowships; no loans.

Publications: Program policy statement, application guidelines.
Application information: Application form required.
Initial approach: Letter
Copies of proposal: 2
Deadline(s): July 1
Board meeting date(s): Annually
Final notification: 2 months
Write: Terry Crenshaw, Charitable Services Officer, Texas Commerce Bank-El Paso
Trustee: Texas Commerce Bank-El Paso.
Number of staff: 1 full-time professional; 1 part-time professional.
Employer Identification Number: 746293379

6879
Hillcrest Foundation ▼
c/o NCNB Texas National Bank, Trust Div.
P.O. Box 830241
Dallas 75283-0241 (214) 508-1965

Trust established in 1959 in TX.
Donor(s): Mrs. W.W. Caruth, Sr.†
Foundation type: Independent
Financial data (yr. ended 05/31/89): Assets, $62,247,336 (M); expenditures, $3,299,008, including $3,144,339 for 119 grants (high: $150,000; low: $500; average: $1,000-$250,000).
Purpose and activities: To relieve poverty, advance education, and promote health; support for higher and other education, health and hospitals, social services, including programs for youth and child welfare, drug abuse, housing, and rehabilitation.
Types of support: Building funds, equipment, land acquisition, seed money, research, matching funds, continuing support, special projects, general purposes, renovation projects.
Limitations: Giving limited to TX, with emphasis on Dallas. No grants to individuals, or for endowment funds, operating budgets, scholarships, or fellowships; no loans.
Publications: Application guidelines.
Application information: Application form required.
Initial approach: Letter
Copies of proposal: 1
Deadline(s): None
Board meeting date(s): As required, usually 4 times annually
Write: Daniel Kelly, V.P., NCNB Texas National Bank
Trustees: D. Harold Byrd, Jr., W.W. Caruth, Jr., Donald Case, Harry A. Shuford, NCNB Texas National Bank.
Number of staff: 1 part-time professional.
Employer Identification Number: 756007565

6880
Hobby Foundation ⌘
3050 Post Oak Blvd., Suite 1330
Houston 77056 (713) 993-2580
Application address: P.O. Box 272389, Houston, TX 77277

Incorporated in 1945 in TX.
Donor(s): W.P. Hobby,† Oveta Culp Hobby, The Houston Post Co.
Foundation type: Independent
Financial data (yr. ended 12/31/88): Assets, $17,899,635 (M); gifts received, $250,000; expenditures, $960,812, including $846,514 for 149 grants (high: $496,679; low: $25).
Purpose and activities: Giving for higher and secondary education, museums, cultural programs, and hospitals.
Limitations: Giving primarily in TX.
Publications: Application guidelines.
Application information: Application form not required.
Deadline(s): None
Write: Oveta Culp Hobby, Pres.
Officers: Oveta Culp Hobby,* Pres.; William P. Hobby, Jr.,* V.P.; Audrey Horn, Secy.; Peggy C. Buchanan, Treas.
Trustees:* Jessica Hobby Catto, Diana P. Hobby.
Employer Identification Number: 746026606

6881
Hoblitzelle Foundation ▼
1410 Tower I
NCNB Ctr.
Dallas 75201 (214) 979-0321

Trust established in 1942 in TX; incorporated in 1953.
Donor(s): Karl St. John Hoblitzelle,† Esther T. Hoblitzelle.†
Foundation type: Independent
Financial data (yr. ended 04/30/89): Assets, $68,815,103 (M); expenditures, $4,031,205, including $3,289,518 for 59 grants (high: $300,000; low: $200; average: $60,000).
Purpose and activities: Grants for higher, secondary, vocational, and medical education, hospitals and health services, youth agencies, cultural programs, social services, and community development.
Types of support: Seed money, building funds, equipment, land acquisition, matching funds, general purposes, renovation projects, capital campaigns, special projects.
Limitations: Giving limited to TX, primarily Dallas. No support for religious organizations for sectarian purposes. No grants to individuals; only occasional board-initiated support for operating budgets, debt reduction, research, scholarships, or endowments; no loans.
Publications: Annual report, program policy statement, application guidelines, newsletter.
Application information: Application form not required.
Initial approach: Letter
Copies of proposal: 1
Deadline(s): Apr. 15, Aug. 15, and Dec. 15
Board meeting date(s): Latter part of May, Sept., and Jan.
Final notification: After next board meeting
Write: Paul W. Harris, Exec. V.P.
Officers: James W. Aston,* C.E.O. and Chair.; James W. Keay,* Pres.; Paul W. Harris, Exec. V.P.; Mary Stacy, Secy.; John M. Stemmons,* Treas.
Directors:* James D. Berry, Lillian M. Bradshaw, Dorothy R. Cullum, Gerald W. Fronterhouse, Robert Lynn Harris, Van Alen Hollomon, George L. MacGregor, Charles C. Sprague, M.D.
Number of staff: 1 full-time professional; 1 full-time support.
Employer Identification Number: 756003984

6882
Irene Cafcalas Hofheinz Foundation ⌘
c/o InterFirst Bank Houston
P.O. Box 2555
Houston 77001 (713) 652-6515

Established about 1984 in TX.
Donor(s): Roy M. Hofheinz Charitable Foundation.
Foundation type: Independent
Financial data (yr. ended 12/31/87): Assets, $2,658,115 (M); expenditures, $379,911, including $284,357 for 24 grants (high: $187,824; low: $100).
Purpose and activities: Giving primarily for higher education, the arts, with emphasis on museums and a music organization, and civic affairs and social service agencies.
Types of support: Loans, program-related investments.
Limitations: Giving primarily in Houston, TX. No grants to individuals.
Application information: Application form not required.
Initial approach: Letter
Deadline(s): None
Write: Fred Hofheinz, Trustee
Trustees: Fred Hofheinz, InterFirst Bank, N.A.
Employer Identification Number: 760083597

6883
The Hofheinz Fund ⌘
c/o NCNB Texas National Bank, Trust Dept.
P.O. Box 2518
Houston 77252-2518

Established in 1984 in TX.
Donor(s): Roy M. Hofheinz Charitable Foundation.
Foundation type: Independent
Financial data (yr. ended 9/30/88): Assets, $2,369,511 (M); expenditures, $237,553, including $142,052 for 11 grants (high: $113,696; low: $35).
Purpose and activities: Giving for community projects, higher education, and other charitable purposes.
Types of support: Operating budgets, program-related investments.
Limitations: No grants to individuals.
Application information:
Write: Roy Hofheinz, Jr., Trustee
Trustees: Roy Hofheinz, Jr., NCNB Texas National Bank.
Employer Identification Number: 760090167

6884
Bessie I. Hofstetter Trust ⌘
c/o InterFirst Bank Corsicana
P.O. Box 613
Corsicana 75110

Trust established in 1934 in TX.
Donor(s): Bessie I. Hofstetter.
Foundation type: Independent
Financial data (yr. ended 6/30/88): Assets, $2,404,438 (M); expenditures, $161,500, including $137,760 for 14 grants (high: $50,000; low: $500).
Purpose and activities: Grants largely for social service agencies, health agencies, and a Protestant church; support also for a community fund.

Limitations: Giving primarily in Navarro County, TX. No grants to individuals.
Application information:
Initial approach: Personal interview required
Deadline(s): None
Write: Gary Brown, Trust Officer, InterFirst Bank Corsicana
Trustee: InterFirst Bank Corsicana.
Employer Identification Number: 756006485

6885
Houston Endowment, Inc. ▼ ⌑
P.O. Box 52338
Houston 77052 (713) 223-4043

Incorporated in 1937 in TX.
Donor(s): Jesse H. Jones,† Mrs. Jesse H. Jones.†
Foundation type: Independent
Financial data (yr. ended 12/31/88): Assets, $614,658,550 (M); expenditures, $38,869,801, including $35,966,333 for 258 grants (high: $2,000,000; low: $1,000; average: $1,000-$1,000,000).
Purpose and activities: For "the support of any charitable, educational or religious undertaking." Grants largely for higher education and hospitals, and social service agencies.
Types of support: Building funds, equipment, scholarship funds, special projects, fellowships, professorships, continuing support.
Limitations: Giving primarily in TX; no grants outside the continental U.S. No grants to individuals, or for permanent endowment funds; no loans.
Publications: Biennial report (including application guidelines).
Application information: Application form not required.
Initial approach: Letter
Copies of proposal: 1
Deadline(s): None
Board meeting date(s): Monthly
Final notification: 1 to 2 months
Write: J.H. Creekmore, Pres.
Officers and Trustees:* J.H. Creekmore,* Pres. and Treas.; Jo Murphy,* V.P.; Alvin R. Thigpen,* Secy.; Audrey Jones Beck, H.J. Nelson III, Philip G. Warner, H.F. Warren.
Coordinator of Grants: Marshall F. Wells.
Number of staff: 3 full-time professional; 4 part-time professional.
Employer Identification Number: 746013920

6886
Houston Osteopathic Foundation, Inc. ☆
P.O. Box 19649
Houston 77224 (713) 464-6391
Application address: Grant Committee, 9225 Katy Freeway, Suite 201, Houston, TX 77024

Incorporated in 1975 in TX.
Foundation type: Independent
Financial data (yr. ended 12/31/88): Assets, $1,167,313 (M); expenditures, $141,735, including $24,000 for 1 grant and $75,000 for 35 grants to individuals (high: $5,000; low: $1,250; average: $1,250-$2,500).
Purpose and activities: Awards scholarships to students at Texas College of Osteopathic Medicine; support also for osteopathic organizations.
Types of support: Student aid.
Limitations: Giving limited to TX.
Application information: Application form required.
Initial approach: Letter
Deadline(s): None
Board meeting date(s): Quarterly
Final notification: Quarterly
Write: Robert L. Murphy, Dir.
Directors: William Badger, Bill Coltharp, Hunter Harang, Tom King, Joe Martin, Robert Murphy, Al Rosenthal, William Thomas, Lanny Vlasek.
Number of staff: None.
Employer Identification Number: 742426837

6887
Howard Foundation, Inc. ⌑
P.O. Box 5010
Texarkana 75501 (214) 793-4116

Incorporated in 1964 in TX.
Donor(s): V.E. Howard.
Foundation type: Independent
Financial data (yr. ended 12/31/86): Assets, $1,282,057 (M); gifts received, $21,970; expenditures, $56,245, including $51,620 for 4 grants (high: $34,800; low: $820).
Purpose and activities: Support for Protestant churches and evangelical radio stations and higher education, particularly Protestant-oriented colleges.
Application information:
Initial approach: Letter
Deadline(s): None
Write: V.E. Howard, Pres.
Officers and Directors: V.E. Howard, Pres.; Jasper Howard, Secy.-Treas.; Edgar Howard.
Employer Identification Number: 751216739

6888
The R. D. & Joan Dale Hubbard Foundation
(Formerly The R. Dee Hubbard Foundation)
301 Commerce, No. 3300
Fort Worth 76102 (817) 332-5006
Application address: 206 South Main, P.O. Box 387, Smith Center, KS 66967; Tel.: (913) 282-3378

Established in 1986 in CA.
Donor(s): R.D. Hubbard.
Foundation type: Independent
Financial data (yr. ended 12/31/88): Assets, $19,019,915 (M); gifts received, $16,187,500; expenditures, $68,500, including $66,500 for grants (high: $50,000).
Purpose and activities: Support primarily for elementary, secondary, and higher education; giving also for community funds, cancer research, museums and other cultural programs, and programs benefitting the disadvantaged, the handicapped, and Native Americans.
Types of support: Building funds, endowment funds, matching funds, professorships, scholarship funds.
Limitations: Giving primarily in TX, OK, KS, NM, and NE. No grants to individuals.
Publications: Program policy statement, annual report, application guidelines.
Application information: Application form not required.
Initial approach: Letter
Copies of proposal: 1
Deadline(s): None
Board meeting date(s): Varies
Write: Jim Stoddard
Officers: R.D. Hubbard, Pres.; Joan D. Hubbard, V.P.; Edward A. Burger, C.F.O.
Number of staff: 1 full-time professional.
Employer Identification Number: 330210158

6889
Leola W. and Charles H. Hugg Trust ⌑
c/o First City National Bank of Houston
P.O. Box 809
Houston 77001

Established in 1979.
Foundation type: Independent
Financial data (yr. ended 12/31/88): Assets, $2,172,719 (M); expenditures, $131,571, including $104,571 for 42 grants to individuals (high: $37,750; low: $500).
Purpose and activities: Grants for scholarships to students from Williamson County to attend colleges and universities in TX.
Types of support: Student aid.
Limitations: Giving limited to Williamson County, TX.
Publications: Application guidelines.
Application information: Application forms and guidelines available upon request from participating high schools, or from the Director of the Texas Baptist Children's Home in Round Rock, TX, or the Office of Student Financial Aid at Southwestern University, in Georgetown, TX. Application form required.
Deadline(s): May 1
Board meeting date(s): Annually
Final notification: May
Write: Glenda B. Tharp
Trustees: William Jones, William D. Swift, First City National Bank of Houston.
Employer Identification Number: 741907673

6890
The Humphreys Foundation ⌑
1915 Trinity St.
Box 550
Liberty 77575 (409) 336-3321

Incorporated in 1957 in TX.
Donor(s): Geraldine Davis Humphreys.†
Foundation type: Independent
Financial data (yr. ended 9/30/88): Assets, $5,331,535 (M); expenditures, $360,287, including $253,770 for 17 grants (high: $92,000; low: $1,000).
Purpose and activities: Giving largely for local theater and opera programs, and performing arts college scholarships.
Types of support: Scholarship funds, special projects.
Limitations: Giving limited to TX. No grants to individuals, or for building funds; no loans.
Publications: Application guidelines.
Application information: Application form required.
Initial approach: Letter or proposal
Copies of proposal: 4
Deadline(s): Submit proposal preferably in Aug.; deadline Aug. 25
Board meeting date(s): Sept. and as required
Write: L.Q. Van Deventer, Jr., Mgr.

Officers and Trustees: John S. Boles, Pres.; Claude C. Roberts, V.P. and Secy.; Mrs. J.G. Bertman, V.P. and Treas.
Number of staff: 1 part-time professional; 1 full-time support.
Employer Identification Number: 746061381

6891
Ed E. and Gladys Hurley Foundation ⌑

c/o NCNB Texas National Bank, Trust Div.
P.O. Box 831041
Dallas 75283-1041 (214) 508-1979

Established in 1957 in TX.
Donor(s): Ed E. Hurley.†
Foundation type: Independent
Financial data (yr. ended 08/31/89): Assets, $1,701,632 (M); expenditures, $174,954, including $8,300 for 2 grants (high: $7,500; low: $800) and $98,950 for grants to individuals.
Purpose and activities: Giving limited to scholarships for theological students in three states.
Types of support: Student aid.
Limitations: Giving limited to theological students in AR, LA, and TX.
Application information: Application form required.
Initial approach: Letter requesting application
Deadline(s): Apr. 15
Write: Alice Gayle, Trust Officer, NCNB Texas National Bank
Trustee Bank: NCNB Texas National Bank.
Employer Identification Number: 756006961

6892
Huthsteiner Fine Arts Trust ⌑

c/o Texas Commerce Bank-El Paso
P.O. Drawer 140
El Paso 79980 (915) 546-6515

Established in 1980.
Donor(s): Robert and Pauline Huthsteiner Trust.
Foundation type: Independent
Financial data (yr. ended 7/31/88): Assets, $1,530,907 (M); expenditures, $117,144, including $94,660 for 17 grants (high: $13,500; low: $500).
Purpose and activities: Support for the arts, especially music.
Types of support: Continuing support, emergency funds, endowment funds, equipment, general purposes, matching funds, operating budgets, publications.
Limitations: Giving primarily in West TX.
Application information: Application form not required.
Initial approach: Letter
Copies of proposal: 1
Deadline(s): None
Write: Terry Crenshaw, Charitable Services Officer, Texas Commerce Bank-El Paso
Trustee Bank: Texas Commerce Bank-El Paso.
Number of staff: 1 full-time professional; 1 part-time professional.
Employer Identification Number: 746308412

6893
Elton M. Hyder, Jr. Charitable & Educational Fund, Inc. ⌑

1918 Commerce Bldg.
Fort Worth 76102

Established in 1959 in TX.
Donor(s): Elton M. Hyder, Jr., Merle M. Rowan.
Foundation type: Independent
Financial data (yr. ended 10/31/89): Assets, $1,798,312 (M); expenditures, $8,222, including $4,150 for 14 grants (high: $600; low: $50).
Purpose and activities: Giving for higher education, including a law school, and social service agencies.
Types of support: Student aid.
Limitations: Giving primarily in Dallas and Fort Worth, TX.
Application information:
Initial approach: Letter
Deadline(s): None
Write: Elton M. Hyder, Jr., Pres.
Officers and Directors:* Elton M. Hyder, Jr.,* Pres.; Elton M. Hyder III,* V.P.; Martha R. Hyder,* V.P.; Nita Gothard,* Secy.-Treas.
Employer Identification Number: 756005547

6894
Hygeia Foundation ⌑ ☆

720 South F St.
Harlingen 78550 (512) 423-2050

Established in 1953.
Donor(s): Hygeia Dairy Co.
Foundation type: Independent
Financial data (yr. ended 3/31/88): Assets, $718,640 (M); gifts received, $47,800; expenditures, $112,033, including $88,285 for 95 grants (high: $10,000; low: $25) and $8,649 for 6 grants to individuals (high: $2,500; low: $599).
Purpose and activities: Giving for higher and secondary education, youth and child welfare organizations, social services, Protestant churches and welfare programs, health associations and hospitals, a zoo and an aquarium, and community funds; also awards educational grants and loans to individuals.
Types of support: Student aid, student loans.
Limitations: Giving primarily in TX.
Application information:
Initial approach: Letter
Deadline(s): None
Write: H. Lee Richards, Trustee
Trustee: H. Lee Richards.
Employer Identification Number: 746047054

6895
The Burdine Johnson Foundation

760 Southpark One Bldg.
1701 Directors Blvd.
Austin 78744-1066 (512) 441-1588

Trust established in 1960 in TX.
Donor(s): Burdine C. Johnson, J.M. Johnson.
Foundation type: Independent
Financial data (yr. ended 12/31/88): Assets, $12,100,035 (M); expenditures, $520,399, including $468,500 for 13 grants (high: $175,000; low: $1,000).
Purpose and activities: Giving for cultural programs, including a performing arts organization, education, social services, and religious organizations.
Limitations: Giving primarily in TX.
Application information: Application form not required.
Initial approach: Proposal
Deadline(s): None
Write: Robert C. Giberson, Trustee
Trustees: Robert C. Giberson, Burdine C. Johnson, William T. Johnson.
Employer Identification Number: 746036669

6896
M. G. and Lillie A. Johnson Foundation, Inc. ▼

P.O. Box 2269
Victoria 77902 (512) 575-7970

Incorporated in 1958 in TX.
Donor(s): M.G. Johnson,† Lillie A. Johnson.†
Foundation type: Independent
Financial data (yr. ended 11/30/89): Assets, $21,247,063 (M); gifts received, $910,075; expenditures, $1,247,089, including $1,086,710 for 21 grants (high: $100,000; low: $3,200; average: $10,000-$100,000).
Purpose and activities: Emphasis on building funds for hospitals, medical research centers, higher educational institutions, social services, civic affairs, and religious organizations.
Types of support: Building funds, equipment, land acquisition, matching funds, renovation projects.
Limitations: Giving primarily in TX, especially the Gulf Coast area located between San Patricio and Wharton counties. No grants to individuals, or for general support, operating budgets, endowment funds, scholarships, fellowships, research (except medical research), special projects, publications, or conferences; no loans.
Application information: Application form not required.
Initial approach: Proposal
Copies of proposal: 2
Deadline(s): Submit proposal 1 month before meetings; no set deadline
Board meeting date(s): Mar., July, and Oct.
Final notification: Varies
Write: Robert Halepeska, Exec. V.P.
Officers and Trustees:* Arnold Koop,* Pres.; Robert Halepeska, Exec. V.P.; Jack R. Morrison,* V.P.; Rev. M.H. Lehnhardt,* Secy.; Irving Moore, Jr.,* Treas.; M.H. Brock, Lloyd Rust.
Number of staff: 1 full-time professional; 1 part-time support.
Employer Identification Number: 746076961

6897
Ralph A. Johnston Foundation, Inc. ⌑

Nine Greenway Plaza, Suite 2112
Houston 77046 (713) 877-8954

Trust established in 1959 in TX; incorporated in 1963.
Donor(s): Ralph A. Johnston.
Foundation type: Independent
Financial data (yr. ended 5/31/89): Assets, $942,836 (M); expenditures, $126,057, including $119,868 for 20 grants (high: $35,000; low: $200).

Purpose and activities: Grants for hospitals and medical research, higher education, and social services, including child welfare.
Limitations: Giving primarily in TX.
Application information:
Initial approach: Letter
Deadline(s): None
Write: James J. Johnston, Pres.
Officers: James J. Johnston, Pres.; Jerry J. Andrew, V.P.; Lyle E. Carbaugh, V.P.; Gladys Watford, Secy.-Treas.
Employer Identification Number: 746051797

6898
Helen Jones Foundation, Inc. ⌑
P.O. Box 724
Lubbock 79408
Application address: 4603 92nd St., Lubbock, TX 79424; Tel.: (806) 794-8078

Established about 1984 in TX.
Donor(s): Helen DeVitt Jones.
Foundation type: Independent
Financial data (yr. ended 12/31/88): Assets, $10,389,094 (M); expenditures, $574,530, including $509,000 for 14 grants (high: $200,000; low: $500).
Purpose and activities: Support primarily for higher education.
Types of support: Operating budgets, equipment, scholarship funds.
Limitations: No grants to individuals.
Application information: Application form not required.
Initial approach: Letter
Deadline(s): None
Write: Louise Arnold, Secy.
Officers: Helen DeVitt Jones, Pres.; Louise Willson Arnold, V.P. and Secy.; L. Edwin Smith, Treas.
Employer Identification Number: 751977748

6899
The Jonsson Foundation
c/o NCNB Tower II, Suite 3300
325 North St. Paul
Dallas 75201-3803 (214) 969-5535

Incorporated in 1955 in TX.
Donor(s): J.E. Jonsson, Margaret E. Jonsson.†
Foundation type: Independent
Financial data (yr. ended 12/31/89): Assets, $4,005,115 (M); expenditures, $170,360, including $135,000 for 23 grants (high: $25,000; low: $500; average: $1,000-$10,000).
Purpose and activities: Giving in areas of health, education, culture, and general community interests.
Types of support: General purposes, building funds, equipment, matching funds, capital campaigns.
Limitations: Giving primarily in the Dallas, TX, area. No grants to individuals, or for endowment funds, scholarships, or fellowships; no loans.
Publications: Application guidelines.
Application information: Funds largely committed. Application form not required.
Initial approach: Letter
Copies of proposal: 1
Deadline(s): None
Board meeting date(s): Feb., May, and Sept.
Final notification: At next meeting
Write: Nelle C. Johnston, Secy.
Officers: Kenneth A. Jonsson,* Pres. and Treas.; Philip R. Jonsson,* V.P. and Treas.; Margaret J. Rogers,* V.P.; Nelle C. Johnston, Secy.
Trustees:* J.E. Jonsson.
Number of staff: 4
Employer Identification Number: 756012565

6900
Philip R. Jonsson Foundation ⌑
14951 Dallas Pkwy., Suite 1030
Dallas 75240 (214) 458-8400

Established in 1954 in TX.
Foundation type: Independent
Financial data (yr. ended 12/31/87): Assets, $1,092,522 (M); expenditures, $68,988, including $35,500 for 13 grants (high: $20,000; low: $500).
Purpose and activities: Support for the arts, education, environment, and social services; grants also for health agencies and for public policy organizations.
Types of support: Operating budgets, building funds.
Limitations: Giving primarily in the Dallas, TX, area. No grants to individuals.
Application information:
Initial approach: Proposal not exceeding 2 pages
Write: Janet W. Hill, Exec. Secy.
Officers and Directors: Philip R. Jonsson, Pres.; Eileen J. Lewis, 1st V.P.; Kenneth B. Jonsson, 2nd V.P.; Christina A. Jonsson, Secy.; Steven W. Jonsson, Treas.
Employer Identification Number: 751552642

6901
Katz Foundation ⌑ ☆
509 Lawrence St.
P.O. Box 1438
Corpus Christi 78403 (512) 882-4371

Established in 1956.
Donor(s): Abe M. Katz, Doris Katz.
Foundation type: Independent
Financial data (yr. ended 10/31/89): Assets, $1,202,750 (M); gifts received, $25,000; expenditures, $91,376, including $89,242 for 85 grants (high: $40,000; low: $10).
Purpose and activities: Giving primarily to Jewish organizations, including welfare funds, schools and religious associations.
Limitations: Giving primarily in TX. No grants to individuals.
Application information:
Initial approach: Letter
Deadline(s): None
Write: Abe M. Katz, Trustee
Trustees: Doris Katz, Abe M. Katz.
Employer Identification Number: 746054042

6902
The Kayser Foundation ⌑
Texas Commerce Bank Bldg.
712 Main St., Suite 1810
Houston 77002 (713) 222-7234

Incorporated in 1961 in TX.
Donor(s): Paul Kayser, Mrs. Paul Kayser.
Foundation type: Independent
Financial data (yr. ended 12/31/88): Assets, $3,117,783 (M); expenditures, $192,825, including $124,510 for 65 grants (high: $70,000; low: $50).
Purpose and activities: Emphasis on medical research, education, and social services.
Limitations: Giving primarily in TX. No grants to individuals.
Application information:
Initial approach: Letter
Deadline(s): None
Write: Henry O. Weaver, Pres.
Officer and Trustees: Henry O. Weaver, Pres.; Charles Sapp, V.P.; Juanita B. Stanley, Secy.-Treas.
Employer Identification Number: 746050591

6903
Ben E. Keith Foundation Trust
c/o Texas American Bank/Fort Worth
P.O. Box 2050
Fort Worth 76113 (817) 884-4161

Trust established in 1951 in TX.
Foundation type: Independent
Financial data (yr. ended 6/30/89): Assets, $9,420,162 (M); expenditures, $616,654, including $550,835 for 213 grants (high: $14,500; low: $500).
Purpose and activities: Giving for higher education and social service agencies; some support also for cultural programs and hospitals.
Types of support: General purposes, operating budgets, continuing support, annual campaigns, seed money, emergency funds, deficit financing, building funds, equipment, land acquisition, endowment funds, matching funds, capital campaigns.
Limitations: Giving limited to TX. No grants to individuals, or for scholarships or fellowships; no loans.
Publications: 990-PF.
Application information:
Initial approach: Letter
Board meeting date(s): Jan., Mar., June, and Oct.
Write: Richard L. Mitchell, Secy.
Officers and Directors: John Beauchamp, Chair.; Richard L. Mitchell, Secy.; Howard Hallam, Robert Hallam, Troy LaGrone, Ronnie Wallace, Hugh Watson.
Advisory Board: Texas American Bank/Fort Worth.
Number of staff: None.
Employer Identification Number: 756013955

6904
Harris and Eliza Kempner Fund
P.O. Box 119
Galveston 77553-0119 (409) 765-6671

Trust established in 1946 in TX.
Donor(s): Various interests and members of the Kempner family.
Foundation type: Independent
Financial data (yr. ended 12/31/89): Assets, $24,642,106 (M); gifts received, $69,394; expenditures, $1,179,796, including $877,083 for 119 grants (high: $125,000; low: $500; average: $1,000-$5,000), $55,845 for 107 employee matching gifts and $135,612 for 66 loans to individuals.

Purpose and activities: Emphasis on higher education, including medical education, programs for minorities, scholarship funds, student loans, and a matching gift program; community funds, welfare, population studies, and community projects; Jewish organizations, including welfare funds; and cultural programs, including historic preservation.
Types of support: General purposes, operating budgets, continuing support, seed money, emergency funds, building funds, equipment, scholarship funds, professorships, special projects, research, publications, conferences and seminars, student loans, capital campaigns, fellowships, lectureships, matching funds, renovation projects.
Limitations: Giving primarily in Galveston, TX. No grants to individuals.
Publications: 990-PF, annual report (including application guidelines).
Application information: Computerized solicitations not considered. Application form not required.
Initial approach: Letter requesting guidelines
Copies of proposal: 1
Deadline(s): For grant program: Mar. 1, Aug. 1 and Nov. 1
Board meeting date(s): Usually in Apr., Sept., Dec., and as required
Final notification: 2 weeks
Write: Elaine Perachio, Grants Admin.
Officers and Trustees:* Leonora K. Thompson,* Chair.; Harris K. Weston,* Vice-Chair.; Lyda Ann Q. Thomas,* Secy.-Treas.; Arthur M. Alpert, Jack T. Currie, Ann O. Hamilton, Hetta T. Kempner, Robert K. Lynch, Barbara Weston Sasser.
Number of staff: 1 part-time professional; 2 part-time support.
Employer Identification Number: 746042458

6905
The John G. and Marie Stella Kenedy Memorial Foundation ▼
1700 First City Tower II
Corpus Christi 78478 (512) 887-6565

Incorporated in 1960 in TX.
Donor(s): Sarita Kenedy East.†
Foundation type: Independent
Financial data (yr. ended 06/30/89): Assets, $130,532,639 (M); expenditures, $7,636,220, including $5,781,928 for 146 grants (high: $626,500; low: $131; average: $5,000-$60,000).
Purpose and activities: Ninety percent of grants issued are restricted to sectarian, primarily Roman Catholic activities; ten percent must be given to non-sectarian activities in TX. Support for education, arts and humanities, social services, youth, and health agencies.
Types of support: Building funds, equipment, land acquisition, matching funds, special projects.
Limitations: Giving limited to TX. No grants to individuals, or for operating budgets, annual fund drives, deficit financing, or scholarships; no support generally for endowments or requests in excess of $500,000.
Publications: Application guidelines, informational brochure, program policy statement.
Application information: Application form required.
Copies of proposal: 1
Deadline(s): Sectarian grants: Oct. 15, Jan. 15, Apr. 15, and July 15; non-sectarian grants: Mar. 5
Board meeting date(s): Monthly
Final notification: Sectarian grants awarded quarterly; non-sectarian grants awarded in May
Write: James R. McCown, General Mgr.
Officers and Directors: Rene H. Gracida, Pres.; Lee H. Lytton, Jr., V.P.; E.B. Groner, Secy.; Daniel Meaney, Treas.; Sister Bernard Marie Borgmeyer, Ronald W. Bradley.
Number of staff: 3 full-time professional; 5 full-time support.
Employer Identification Number: 746040701

6906
Winifred & B. A. Killson Educational Foundation ☆
c/o NCNB Texas National Bank
P.O. Box 2518
Houston 77252 (713) 751-6004

Established in 1971.
Foundation type: Independent
Financial data (yr. ended 01/31/89): Assets, $2,231,134 (M); expenditures, $161,387, including $140,000 for 4 grants of $35,000 each.
Purpose and activities: Giving limited to colleges and universities.
Limitations: Giving limited to TX. No grants to individuals.
Publications: 990-PF.
Application information: Application form not required.
Initial approach: Letter
Deadline(s): Dec. 1
Write: Elizabeth Calvert
Trustee Bank: NCNB Texas National Bank.
Employer Identification Number: 746147801

6907
William S. & Lora Jean Kilroy Foundation
1021 Main St., Suite 1900
Houston 77002-6662 (713) 651-0101

Established in 1985 in TX.
Donor(s): William S. Kilroy, Lora Jean Kilroy.
Foundation type: Independent
Financial data (yr. ended 12/31/89): Assets, $3,629,088 (M); expenditures, $85,890, including $76,125 for 23 grants (high: $15,570; low: $750).
Purpose and activities: Support primarily for higher education, museums, and community funds.
Types of support: Operating budgets, annual campaigns, capital campaigns.
Application information: Application form not required.
Initial approach: Letter
Deadline(s): None
Write: William S. Kilroy, Trustee
Trustee: William S. Kilroy.
Number of staff: None.
Employer Identification Number: 760169904

6908
Kimberly-Clark Foundation, Inc. ▼
P.O. Box 619100
Dallas 75261 (214) 830-1200

Incorporated in 1952 in WI.
Donor(s): Kimberly-Clark Corp.
Foundation type: Company-sponsored
Financial data (yr. ended 12/31/88): Assets, $2,639,637 (M); expenditures, $3,024,476, including $3,017,204 for 157 grants (high: $263,657; low: $100; average: $5,000-$45,000).
Purpose and activities: Emphasis on higher education, community funds, community development, social services, and cultural programs. The employee matching gift program was discontinued in 1986.
Types of support: Annual campaigns, building funds, continuing support, equipment, land acquisition, operating budgets, seed money, scholarship funds, general purposes, capital campaigns, program-related investments.
Limitations: Giving primarily in communities where the company has operations. No support for preschool, elementary, or secondary education, state-supported institutions, denominational religious organizations, or sports or athletics. No grants to individuals; no loans.
Publications: Annual report.
Application information: Application form not required.
Initial approach: Proposal
Copies of proposal: 1
Deadline(s): None
Board meeting date(s): Apr.
Final notification: By year end
Write: Colleen B. Berman, V.P.
Officers and Directors:* O. George Everbach,* Pres.; Colleen B. Berman, V.P.; Donald M. Crook, Secy.; W. Anthony Gamron,* Treas.; Brenda M. O'Neill, Darwin E. Smith.
Number of staff: 1 full-time professional; 1 full-time support.
Employer Identification Number: 396044304

6909
Carl B. and Florence E. King Foundation ⌑
5956 Sherry Ln., Suite 620
Dallas 75225

Incorporated in 1966 in TX.
Donor(s): Carl B. King,† Florence E. King,† Dorothy E. King.
Foundation type: Independent
Financial data (yr. ended 12/31/87): Assets, $26,472,034 (M); expenditures, $1,614,673, including $569,767 for 32 grants (high: $100,000; low: $250; average: $2,000-$15,000) and $210,000 for 141 grants to individuals (high: $4,000; low: $1,000).
Purpose and activities: Emphasis on higher and secondary education, youth and social service agencies, and cultural programs; scholarships and student loans limited to TX high school students; some support for hospitals and health agencies.
Types of support: Scholarship funds, special projects, student aid, student loans.
Limitations: Giving primarily in the Dallas, TX, area. No support for religious purposes.

Publications: Program policy statement, application guidelines.
Application information: Application forms required for scholarships only and available from the foundation and the Texas Interscholastic League; scholarships limited to TX high school students.
Initial approach: Letter
Copies of proposal: 1
Deadline(s): None for organizations; students should contact Texas Interscholastic League
Board meeting date(s): Quarterly
Final notification: 6 weeks
Write: Carl Yeckel, V.P.
Officers and Directors: Dorothy E. King, Pres.; Carl Yeckel, V.P.; Thomas W. Vett, Secy.-Treas.; M.E. Childs, Jack Phipps, Sam G. Winstead.
Number of staff: 4 full-time professional.
Employer Identification Number: 756052203

6910
King Ranch Family Trust ⌑
P.O. Drawer 911
Kingsville 78363
Application address: P.O. Box 17777, San Antonio, TX 78217; Tel.: (512) 822-2348

Trust established in 1946 in TX.
Donor(s): King Ranch, Inc.
Foundation type: Company-sponsored
Financial data (yr. ended 12/31/89): Assets, $6,059,606 (M); expenditures, $312,037, including $280,500 for 18 grants (high: $50,000; low: $1,000).
Purpose and activities: Emphasis on higher education; grants also for youth activities and religious organizations.
Types of support: Research, scholarship funds, matching funds.
Limitations: Giving primarily in TX, with emphasis on southern TX. No grants to individuals, or for endowment funds; no loans.
Publications: Application guidelines.
Application information: Application form not required.
Initial approach: Cover letter with proposal
Copies of proposal: 1
Deadline(s): None
Board meeting date(s): June and Dec.
Final notification: 30 days after board meeting
Write: Richard M. Kleberg III, Chair.
Gift Committee: Richard M. Kleberg III,* Chair.; Nelva Lou Shelton, Secy.; Ida L. Clement, Leslie C. Finger,* Helen K. Groves, Mary Lewis Kleberg, Michael Reynolds, Richard G. Sugden.
Trustees:* James H. Clement, Sr.
Number of staff: 1 part-time support.
Employer Identification Number: 746044809

6911
Robert J. Kleberg, Jr. and Helen C. Kleberg Foundation ▼
700 North St. Mary's St., Suite 1200
San Antonio 78205 (512) 271-3691

Incorporated in 1950 in TX.
Donor(s): Helen C. Kleberg,† Robert J. Kleberg, Jr.†
Foundation type: Independent
Financial data (yr. ended 12/31/88): Assets, $84,399,273 (M); expenditures, $4,153,446, including $3,271,366 for 45 grants (high: $500,000; low: $1,000; average: $5,000-$200,000).
Purpose and activities: Giving on a national basis for medical research, veterinary science, wildlife, and related activities; support also for local community organizations.
Types of support: Building funds, equipment, research, conferences and seminars, matching funds, renovation projects.
Limitations: No support for community organizations outside TX, for non-tax-exempt organizations, or for organizations limited by race or religion. No grants to individuals, or for general purposes, endowments, deficit financing, ongoing operating expenses, overhead or indirect costs, scholarships, or fellowships; no loans.
Publications: Annual report, application guidelines.
Application information: Application form not required.
Initial approach: Letter
Copies of proposal: 1
Deadline(s): None
Board meeting date(s): Usually in June and Dec.
Final notification: 6 months
Write: Robert L. Washington, Grants Coord.
Officers and Directors:* Helen K. Groves,* Pres.; John D. Alexander, Jr.,* V.P. and Secy.; Emory G. Alexander,* V.P. and Treas.; Helen C. Alexander,* V.P.; Caroline R. Alexander, Dorothy D. Alexander, Henrietta K. Alexander.
Number of staff: 1 full-time professional.
Employer Identification Number: 746044810

6912
Caesar Kleberg Foundation for Wildlife Conservation ⌑
711 Navarro St., Suite 535
San Antonio 78205 (512) 224-1011

Trust established about 1951 in TX.
Donor(s): Caesar Kleberg.†
Foundation type: Independent
Financial data (yr. ended 12/31/89): Assets, $14,760,432 (M); expenditures, $473,089, including $265,000 for 6 grants (high: $150,000; low: $5,000).
Purpose and activities: Giving to aid in the conservation of game and other wildlife.
Limitations: Giving primarily in southwest TX. No grants to individuals, or for building or endowment funds, scholarships, fellowships, or matching gifts; no loans.
Application information: Application form not required.
Initial approach: Letter
Copies of proposal: 3
Deadline(s): None
Board meeting date(s): Semiannually and as required
Final notification: 3 months
Write: Leroy G. Denman, Jr., Trustee
Trustees: Leroy G. Denman, Jr., Stephen J. Kleberg, Duane M. Leach.
Number of staff: None.
Employer Identification Number: 746038766

6913
Nathan J. Klein Fund ⌑
P.O. Box 20446
Houston 77225 (713) 790-0079

Trust established in 1953 in TX.
Donor(s): Nathan J. Klein, Almeda Harold Corp., and others.
Foundation type: Independent
Financial data (yr. ended 12/31/88): Assets, $8,656,605 (M); gifts received, $59,900; expenditures, $97,486, including $76,970 for 42 grants (high: $15,000; low: $10).
Purpose and activities: Grants largely for Jewish welfare funds and religious organizations, social and cultural organizations, and higher education, including a student loan fund and support for institutions in Israel.
Limitations: Giving primarily in TX. No grants to individuals.
Application information:
Initial approach: Letter or telephone
Deadline(s): None
Write: Nathan J. Klein, Mgr.
Officer and Trustees: Nathan J. Klein, Mgr.; Amelia Klein, Edward J. Klein, Martha K. Lottman, Shirley K. Markey.
Employer Identification Number: 746060543

6914
Knapp Foundation ⌑
118 East Tyler
Harlingen 78550

Donor(s): F.E. Knapp, J.A. Knapp.
Foundation type: Independent
Financial data (yr. ended 12/31/88): Assets, $1,268,485 (M); gifts received, $20,000; expenditures, $53,667, including $52,000 for 21 grants (high: $5,000; low: $1,000).
Purpose and activities: Giving for Protestant church support, religious organizations, and a hospital.
Limitations: Giving primarily in TX.
Officers and Directors: F. Gilson Knapp, Pres.; Adron Ming, Secy.-Treas.; A.S. Knapp, Sr., F.E. Knapp, Jr., Frederick Knapp, J.A. Knapp, Jr., Parker Knapp.
Employer Identification Number: 746060544

6915
Robert W. Knox, Sr. and Pearl Wallis Knox Charitable Foundation ⌑
NCNB Texas National Bank
P.O. Box 2518
Houston 77252-2518

Established in 1964 in TX.
Donor(s): Robert W. Knox, Jr.†
Foundation type: Independent
Financial data (yr. ended 8/31/88): Assets, $3,350,626 (M); expenditures, $170,224, including $139,301 for 28 grants (high: $16,666; low: $60).
Purpose and activities: Emphasis on cultural programs, social services, youth activities, parks and recreation, and religious organizations.
Limitations: Giving primarily in Houston, TX.
Application information:
Initial approach: Letter
Deadline(s): None
Write: Carl Schumacher, V.P., NCNB Texas National Bank
Trustee Bank: NCNB Texas National Bank.
Employer Identification Number: 746064974

6916
Marcia & Otto Koehler Foundation
P.O. Drawer 121
San Antonio 78291

Established in 1980 in TX.
Donor(s): Marcia Koehler.†
Foundation type: Independent
Financial data (yr. ended 07/31/89): Assets, $6,604,509 (M); expenditures, $344,757, including $309,100 for 41 grants (high: $25,000; low: $1,000).
Purpose and activities: Support for culture, higher education, youth, and social services.
Types of support: Operating budgets, renovation projects, building funds, research.
Limitations: Giving primarily in San Antonio, TX. No grants to individuals.
Application information: Application form required.
Copies of proposal: 1
Deadline(s): June 1
Write: Patricia M. Myers, Trust Officer, NBC Bank-San Antonio, N.A.
Trustee: NBC Bank-San Antonio, N.A.
Employer Identification Number: 742131195

6917
Mary Potishman Lard Trust ⌑
500 Throckmorton St., Suite 44225
Fort Worth 76102-3727 (817) 332-7559

Trust established in 1968 in TX.
Donor(s): Mary P. Lard.†
Foundation type: Independent
Financial data (yr. ended 12/31/88): Assets, $8,400,568 (M); expenditures, $835,028, including $688,100 for 63 grants (high: $175,000; low: $500).
Purpose and activities: Emphasis on education, including higher education; support also for social services, youth agencies, hospitals, medical research, and cultural organizations.
Limitations: Giving primarily in TX, with emphasis on Fort Worth. No grants to individuals.
Application information:
Initial approach: Letter
Deadline(s): None
Board meeting date(s): Generally in June or July, and Dec.
Final notification: Within 2 weeks of meeting
Write: Bayard H. Friedman, Trustee
Trustees: Bayard H. Friedman, Mayme Friedman, Walker C. Friedman.
Number of staff: 1 full-time professional.
Employer Identification Number: 756210697

6918
LBJ Family Foundation
13809 Research Blvd., Suite 700
Austin 78750

Trust established in 1957 in TX.
Donor(s): Lyndon B. Johnson,† Mrs. Lyndon B. Johnson, Texas Broadcasting Corp.
Foundation type: Independent
Financial data (yr. ended 12/31/89): Assets, $2,651,483 (M); qualifying distributions, $196,000, including $196,000 for 140 grants (high: $10,000; low: $100; average: $500).
Purpose and activities: Emphasis on conservation and recreation; some support for higher and secondary education, educational television, hospitals, and cultural programs, including support of presidential libraries.
Types of support: Continuing support, general purposes, scholarship funds, special projects.
Limitations: Giving primarily in Austin, TX. No grants to individuals, or for endowment funds; no loans.
Application information: Application form not required.
Initial approach: Letter
Copies of proposal: 1
Deadline(s): None
Board meeting date(s): June and Dec.
Write: John M. Barr, Mgr.
Officers: John M. Barr, Mgr.; Donald S. Thomas, Mgr.
Trustees: Claudia T. Johnson, Luci B. Johnson, Charles S. Robb, Lynda J. Robb.
Number of staff: None.
Employer Identification Number: 746045768

6919
Lennox Foundation ⌑
7920 Belt Line Rd.
Dallas 75240

Incorporated in 1951 in IA.
Donor(s): Lennox Industries, Inc.
Foundation type: Company-sponsored
Financial data (yr. ended 11/30/88): Assets, $7,531,544 (M); expenditures, $490,091, including $458,500 for 23 grants (high: $100,000; low: $5,000).
Purpose and activities: Grants primarily for private colleges and universities, and community development and nature conservancy.
Limitations: Giving limited to areas of company operations. No grants to individuals.
Application information: Contributes only to pre-selected organizations. Applications not accepted.
Board meeting date(s): Feb.
Write: Richard W. Booth, Chair.
Officers and Trustees: Richard W. Booth, Chair. and Treas.; David H. Anderson, Vice-Chair.; David V. Brown, Secy.
Employer Identification Number: 426053380

6920
J. A. Leppard Foundation Trust ⌑
1949 Donaldson Ave.
San Antonio 78228 (512) 433-4456

Trust established in 1980 in TX.
Donor(s): J.A. Leppard.†
Foundation type: Independent
Financial data (yr. ended 12/31/88): Assets, $1,677,421 (M); expenditures, $108,377, including $78,425 for 10 grants (high: $34,000; low: $250).
Purpose and activities: Grants exclusively for Christian churches, missions, and schools.
Limitations: Giving primarily in TX. No grants to individuals.
Application information: Application form not required.
Initial approach: Letter
Deadline(s): None
Write: Dorothy C. Mackey, Admin.
Officer and Trustees: Dorothy C. Mackey, Admin.; Harry James Fraser, Jr., J.A. Leppard, Jr., George Poppas, Jr.
Employer Identification Number: 742044159

6921
Harry and Devera Lerman Educational Trust ☆
300 Convent St., Suite 1500
San Antonio 78205-3732

Established in 1987 in TX.
Foundation type: Independent
Financial data (yr. ended 12/31/89): Assets, $1,106,107 (M); gifts received, $12,310; expenditures, $64,242, including $58,500 for 2 grants (high: $30,000; low: $28,500).
Purpose and activities: Support for higher education.
Types of support: Scholarship funds.
Limitations: Giving primarily in San Antonio, TX. No grants to individuals.
Application information: Contributes only to pre-selected organizations. Applications not accepted.
Trustees: Herman Cundiff, Cecil Schenker, Rabbi Samuel M. Stahl.
Employer Identification Number: 746335132

6922
The LeTourneau Foundation ⌑
P.O. Box 489
Rockwall 75087

Incorporated in 1935 in CA.
Donor(s): Robert G. LeTourneau,† Mrs. Robert G. LeTourneau.
Foundation type: Independent
Financial data (yr. ended 12/31/87): Assets, $5,466,440 (M); expenditures, $445,427, including $163,600 for 7 grants (high: $160,000; low: $100).
Purpose and activities: Grants limited to evangelical Christian activities in foreign missions, evangelism, and education.
Limitations: Giving primarily in TX.
Application information: All funds presently committed. Applications not accepted.
Board meeting date(s): Semiannually
Write: Roy S. LeTourneau, Pres.
Officers and Directors: Roy S. LeTourneau, Pres.; Brenda J. LeTourneau, Secy.-Treas.; Ken Gangel, M.D., Rev. Jeff Gonesky, Ben W. LeTourneau.
Number of staff: 2 full-time professional.
Employer Identification Number: 756001947

6923
Joe Levit Family Foundation ⌑
3131 East Holcombe Blvd.
Houston 77221
Application address: P.O. Box 14200, Houston, TX 77221; Tel.: (713) 747-5000

Established in 1968 in TX.
Donor(s): Max Levit, Milton Levit, Grocer's Supply Co., Inc.
Foundation type: Independent
Financial data (yr. ended 12/31/87): Assets, $3,213,481 (M); gifts received, $725,000; expenditures, $117,596, including $108,690 for 1 grant.

Purpose and activities: Support for Jewish welfare and general charitable purposes.
Limitations: Giving primarily in Houston, TX.
Application information: Application form not required.
Deadline(s): None
Write: Milton Levit, Dir.
Directors: Max Levit, Milton Levit.
Employer Identification Number: 746103403

6924
Lillian Kaiser Lewis Foundation ⌑
P.O. Box 809
Houston 77001 (713) 658-7237

Trust established in 1966 in TX.
Donor(s): Lillian Kaiser Lewis.†
Foundation type: Independent
Financial data (yr. ended 9/30/87): Assets, $1,701,965 (M); expenditures, $144,039, including $122,900 for 43 grants (high: $15,000; low: $500).
Purpose and activities: Support for programs relating to children, including grants to hospitals, health agencies, and educational activities.
Types of support: Operating budgets, continuing support, annual campaigns, emergency funds, deficit financing, building funds, equipment, endowment funds.
Limitations: Giving primarily in TX. No grants to individuals, or for scholarships, fellowships, or matching gifts; no loans.
Application information:
Initial approach: Proposal
Copies of proposal: 3
Board meeting date(s): Mar., June, Sept., and Dec.
Write: Carroll G. Sunseri, V.P., First City National Bank of Houston
Trustees: G. Sidney Buchanan, Hyman Judah Schachtel, First City National Bank of Houston.
Employer Identification Number: 746076511

6925
Lightner Sams Foundation, Inc.
11811 Preston Rd., Suite 200
Dallas 75230 (214) 458-8811

Established in 1981 in TX.
Foundation type: Independent
Financial data (yr. ended 12/31/88): Assets, $16,241,881 (M); expenditures, $1,054,928, including $822,912 for 75 grants (high: $100,000; low: $250; average: $5,000-$10,000).
Purpose and activities: Giving for the arts and cultural programs, including museums and the performing arts, and education; some support also for hospitals, health, youth organizations, Protestant religious organizations, community development, and social services; grants to a zoo and a playhouse.
Types of support: Annual campaigns, building funds, capital campaigns, equipment, operating budgets, renovation projects, research.
Limitations: Giving primarily in Dallas, TX, and WY. No grants to individuals.
Application information: Application form not required.
Initial approach: Letter
Copies of proposal: 1
Deadline(s): Submit proposal 2-3 weeks prior to board meetings
Board meeting date(s): 4 times annually; no specific dates
Final notification: As soon as possible after meetings
Write: Larry Lightner, Trustee
Trustees: Earl Sams Lightner, Larry Lightner, Robin Lightner, Sue B. Lightner.
Number of staff: 1 full-time professional.
Employer Identification Number: 742139849

6926
George B. and Irene Lindler Foundation ⌑ ☆
7811 Oak Vista Ln.
Houston 77087-5443

Established in 1980.
Donor(s): Irene B. Lindler.†
Foundation type: Independent
Financial data (yr. ended 12/31/88): Assets, $1,112,383 (M); gifts received, $277,950; expenditures, $74,513, including $40,655 for 80 grants (high: $9,000; low: $50).
Purpose and activities: Support primarily for hospitals and medical education, research, and services; minor support also for Protestant giving.
Types of support: Research.
Limitations: Giving primarily in Houston, TX. No grants to individuals.
Application information: Contributes only to pre-selected organizations. Applications not accepted.
Officers: George B. Lindler, Pres.; Bill Chenault, V.P.; Harry N. Holmes, V.P.; Joyce Lindler, V.P.; William S. Broughton, Secy.
Employer Identification Number: 742121178

6927
Franklin Lindsay Student Aid Fund ⌑
Texas Commerce Bank-Austin
P.O. Box 550
Austin 78789-0001 (512) 476-6611

Trust established in 1957 in TX.
Donor(s): Franklin Lindsay.†
Foundation type: Independent
Financial data (yr. ended 12/31/86): Assets, $9,289,658 (M); expenditures, $1,103,511, including $922,224 for 385 loans to individuals (high: $4,000; low: $500).
Purpose and activities: Student loans to students attending colleges or universities in TX.
Types of support: Student loans.
Limitations: Giving limited to students at institutions of higher learning in TX.
Publications: Program policy statement, application guidelines, informational brochure.
Application information: Address completed application to appropriate Loan Committee member (depending on area of TX where student resides). Application form required.
Copies of proposal: 1
Deadline(s): Varies according to each committee member
Board meeting date(s): July
Final notification: 1 month
Write: Rebecca Gassenmayer, Admin. Officer
Loan Committee: Charles Barnes, Alvin P. Bormann, Jr., M.H. Connelly, Lawrence L. Crum, Elwanda Griffith, John B. Hubbard, Mrs. Sherwood Inkley, James R. Kay, George C. Miller, B.G. Montgomery, H. Hart Nance, Mrs. Murray Nance, Robert F. Parker, V.P. Patterson; Mrs. Joseph M. Ray, James W. Stegall, John Stuart, Jim Valentine.
Trustee: Texas Commerce Bank-Austin.
Number of staff: 2
Employer Identification Number: 746031753

6928
Tom & Evelyn Linebery Foundation ⌑
P.O. Box 1536
Midland 79702

Established in 1976 in TX.
Donor(s): Tom Linebery, Evelyn Linebery.
Foundation type: Independent
Financial data (yr. ended 6/30/89): Assets, $1,201,241 (M); expenditures, $121,508, including $72,169 for 11 grants (high: $30,000; low: $1,000) and $26,649 for 7 grants to individuals (high: $15,000; low: $650).
Purpose and activities: Giving for higher and other education, including a seminar fund and scholarships to individuals; support also for hospitals.
Types of support: Student aid.
Limitations: Giving primarily in TX.
Application information:
Initial approach: Letter
Deadline(s): None
Write: Evelyn Linebery, Secy.-Treas.
Officers and Directors: Kelley Brown, Pres.; L.D. Crumley, Jr., V.P.; Evelyn Linebery, Secy.-Treas.; Taylor Henley, Tom Linebery, Charles C. Matthews, Jerry Stephens.
Employer Identification Number: 510187878

6929
The Link Foundation ⌑
c/o H. David Hughes
1400 One Congress Plaza, 111 Congress Ave.
Austin 78701

Established in 1985 in TX.
Donor(s): Joe W. Bratcher III.
Foundation type: Independent
Financial data (yr. ended 12/31/88): Assets, $1,238,122 (M); expenditures, $80,110, including $66,500 for 9 grants (high: $10,000; low: $1,500).
Purpose and activities: Support primarily for human services, including women and child welfare and international relief programs.
Limitations: Giving primarily in TX. No grants to individuals.
Application information:
Initial approach: Letter
Deadline(s): Sept. 30
Write: Joe W. Bratcher III, Pres.
Officers: Joe W. Bratcher III, Pres.; Brigid Anne Cockrum, Secy.
Director: Rhobie K. Bratcher.
Employer Identification Number: 742387802

6930
The Barbara Woodward Lips Foundation ⌑
305 Geneseo Rd.
San Antonio 78209

Established in 1986 in TX.
Donor(s): Barbara Woodward Lips.

Foundation type: Independent
Financial data (yr. ended 12/31/88): Assets, $3,806,454 (M); expenditures, $1,512,774, including $1,500,000 for 1 grant.
Purpose and activities: Support for a medical research and education foundation.
Application information: Contributes only to pre-selected organizations. Applications not accepted.
Trustee: Barbara Woodward Lips.
Employer Identification Number: 746143954

6931
Gillson Longenbaugh Foundation ⌑ ☆
6750 West Loop South, Suite 820
Bellaire 77401

Established in 1981.
Donor(s): Alta G. Longenbaugh.
Foundation type: Independent
Financial data (yr. ended 5/31/89): Assets, $1,086,784 (M); gifts received, $100,000; expenditures, $49,750, including $40,000 for 2 grants (high: $30,000; low: $10,000).
Purpose and activities: Giving for cancer research at a hospital and a rehabilitation institute.
Types of support: Research.
Limitations: Giving primarily in Houston, TX. No grants to individuals.
Application information: Contributes only to pre-selected organizations. Applications not accepted.
Officers: Alta G. Longenbaugh, Pres.; Lawrence I. Levy, V.P. and Secy.; Vernon V. Clinger, Treas.
Director: Adolph A. Pfeffer, Jr.
Employer Identification Number: 760001952

6932
The LTV Foundation ▼
c/o The LTV Corp.
P.O. Box 655003
Dallas 75265-5003 (214) 979-7726

Trust established in 1950 in OH.
Donor(s): Republic Steel Corp.
Foundation type: Company-sponsored
Financial data (yr. ended 12/31/89): Assets, $9,992,048 (M); expenditures, $1,268,389, including $1,161,809 for 443 grants (high: $50,000; low: $100; average: $1,000-$5,000).
Purpose and activities: Giving largely for community funds, hospitals, higher and other education, youth agencies, health agencies, urban renewal, and arts and cultural programs; employee-related scholarships through the National Merit Scholarship Corp.
Types of support: Operating budgets, annual campaigns, building funds, equipment, endowment funds, special projects, research, matching funds, capital campaigns, emergency funds, employee-related scholarships.
Limitations: Giving limited to areas of company operations, with emphasis on OH, TX, IL, IN, and NY. No support for religious or political purposes, fraternal or veterans' organizations, government agencies, or athletic teams. No grants to individuals, or for seed money, deficit financing, land acquisition, publications, conferences, or courtesy advertising; no loans.
Publications: Informational brochure (including application guidelines).
Application information: Application form not required.
Initial approach: Proposal
Copies of proposal: 1
Deadline(s): None
Board meeting date(s): Quarterly
Final notification: 2 to 4 months
Write: Brent Berryman, Exec. Dir.
Officer: Brent Berryman, Exec. Dir.
Trust Committee: Raymond A. Hay, David H. Hoag, James F. Powers.
Trustee Bank: Ameritrust Co., N.A.
Number of staff: 1 part-time professional; 1 part-time support.
Employer Identification Number: 346505330

6933
The Luling Foundation
523 South Mulberry Ave.
P.O. Drawer 31
Luling 78648 (512) 875-2438

Trust established in 1927 in TX.
Donor(s): Edgar B. Davis.†
Foundation type: Operating
Financial data (yr. ended 12/31/89): Assets, $5,574,749 (M); expenditures, $11,475, including $8,975 for 4 grants (high: $3,150; low: $75) and $2,500 for 3 grants to individuals (high: $1,000; low: $500; average: $500-$1,000).
Purpose and activities: A private operating foundation; giving to help the farmer through demonstrations of farming techniques and to help the 4-H and F.F.A. students for a period of two years with marketing show animals; principal activity is the operation of an agricultural demonstration farm; some support for scholarships to students working toward an agricultural degree.
Types of support: Special projects, student aid.
Limitations: Giving limited to Caldwell, Gonzales, and Guadalupe counties, TX. No grants for building or endowment funds, land acquisition, operating budgets, or matching gifts.
Publications: 990-PF, application guidelines, informational brochure, occasional report.
Application information: Application form required.
Initial approach: Letter
Copies of proposal: 1
Deadline(s): May 15
Board meeting date(s): Jan., Apr., July, and Oct., and as required
Write: Archie Abrameit, Mgr.
Officers: Debbie Miller, Secy.-Treas.; Archie Abrameit, Mgr.
Directors: Stan Reece, Chair.; Calvin Baker, Vice-Chair.; John Anderson, Tony Breitschopf, Lewis Freeman, Donald Lott, Tom Schoolcraft, Tom Wehe.
Number of staff: 2 full-time professional; 4 full-time support.
Employer Identification Number: 741143102

6934
W. P. & Bulah Luse Foundation ⌑ ☆
P.O. Box 231041
Dallas 75283-1041
Application address: P.O. Box 83041, Dallas, TX 75283-0241; Tel.: (214) 922-6521

Established in 1947 in TX.
Foundation type: Independent
Financial data (yr. ended 12/31/88): Assets, $3,354,258 (M); expenditures, $436,471, including $284,727 for 24 grants (high: $75,000; low: $1,000).
Purpose and activities: Giving limited to the "alleviation of poverty, education, and medical purposes."
Limitations: Giving limited to TX. No grants to individuals.
Application information: Application form not required.
Deadline(s): None
Board meeting date(s): Annually at the end of the year
Write: Bill Arrington
Trustees: Jack Burrell, Jack L. Burrell, Jr., Louise Delarios, NCNB Texas National Bank.
Employer Identification Number: 756007639

6935
Luttrell Trust ⌑ ☆
P.O. Box 1023
Arlington 76010-1929 (817) 860-9563

Established in 1959.
Donor(s): James Luttrell, George Ray Luttrell Trust, Will Ann Luttrell Trust.
Foundation type: Independent
Financial data (yr. ended 12/31/88): Assets, $1,854,085 (M); gifts received, $325,000; expenditures, $67,469, including $38,265 for 14 grants (high: $20,000; low: $25).
Purpose and activities: Support for hospitals, social services, and youth and child welfare organizations.
Limitations: Giving primarily in El Paso, Dallas, Arlington, and Fort Worth, TX.
Application information:
Deadline(s): None
Trustee: James Luttrell.
Employer Identification Number: 756036279

6936
Lyons Foundation ⌑
1266 First City National Bank Ctr.
Houston 77002

Established in 1961 in TX.
Donor(s): Richard T. Lyons.†
Foundation type: Independent
Financial data (yr. ended 12/31/89): Assets, $5,258,633 (M); expenditures, $357,181, including $251,200 for 24 grants (high: $50,000; low: $500).
Purpose and activities: Support for higher and secondary education and a hospital.
Types of support: Building funds, special projects.
Limitations: Giving primarily in TX.
Application information: Application form not required.
Initial approach: Letter
Copies of proposal: 1
Deadline(s): Nov. 1
Board meeting date(s): Dec. 10-15

Write: Mrs. Ruth Foster, Mgr.
Officers: R.A. Seale, Jr., Pres.; Frank Guthrie, Secy.-Treas.
Number of staff: 1
Employer Identification Number: 746038717

6937
The M.I.G. Foundation ⌑ ☆
P.O. Box 161235
Fort Worth 76161
Application address: 2000 Tom O'Shanter, Fort Worth, TX; Tel.: (817)429-6715

Foundation type: Independent
Financial data (yr. ended 06/30/88): Assets, $1,025,343 (M); expenditures, $128,630, including $12,000 for grants (high: $10,000; low: $2,000) and $79,932 for 7 grants to individuals (high: $19,700; low: $3,000).
Purpose and activities: Awards scholarships for undergraduate education.
Types of support: Student aid.
Limitations: Giving limited to TX residents.
Application information: Applications must be made prior to junior year of undergraduate studies. Application form required.
Deadline(s): Dec. 31
Write: Frank P. Turrella, Pres.
Officers: Frank P. Turrella, Pres.; Donald R. Ray, Secy.-Treas.
Directors: Chester W. Grudzinski, Jr., Frances G. Turrella.
Employer Identification Number: 752052592

6938
Sharon Lee MacDonald Charitable Trust ⌑
c/o Texas Commerce Bank
P.O. Box 2558
Houston 77252

Established in 1974 in TX.
Foundation type: Independent
Financial data (yr. ended 12/31/87): Assets, $1,273,412 (M); expenditures, $104,173, including $63,277 for 14 grants (high: $21,100; low: $1,000).
Purpose and activities: Support for social service and youth agencies and cultural programs.
Limitations: Giving primarily in Austin and Houston, TX.
Application information: Contributes only to pre-selected organizations. Applications not accepted.
Trustees: William S. Arendale, Texas Commerce Bank.
Employer Identification Number: 746203857

6939
Web Maddox Trust ⌑ ☆
c/o Texas American Bank
P.O. Box 2050
Fort Worth 76113 (817) 884-4153

Established in 1986 in TX.
Foundation type: Independent
Financial data (yr. ended 03/31/89): Assets, $12,436,211 (M); expenditures, $123,551, including $100,000 for 4 grants of $25,000 each.
Purpose and activities: Support for the fine and performing arts.
Limitations: Giving primarily in Tarrant County, TX. No support for organizations supported by the United Way.
Application information:
Initial approach: Letter
Deadline(s): None
Write: Suzanne Jennings
Trustee: Texas American Bank.
Employer Identification Number: 756347669

6940
Elizabeth Huth Maddux Foundation ⌑
P.O. Box 171717
San Antonio 78217

Established in 1968 in TX.
Donor(s): Elizabeth Huth Maddux.
Foundation type: Independent
Financial data (yr. ended 12/31/88): Assets, $2,394,558 (M); gifts received, $25,000; expenditures, $231,481, including $227,500 for 3 grants (high: $187,500; low: $20,000).
Purpose and activities: Giving for cultural programs; support also for general charitable purposes.
Limitations: Giving primarily in TX.
Application information: Contributes only to pre-selected organizations. Applications not accepted.
Trustees: Elizabeth Stieren Kelso, Elizabeth Huth Maddux, Arthur T. Stieren.
Employer Identification Number: 746107673

6941
David Malcolm Foundation ⌑ ☆
2929 Allen Pkwy., Suite 1700
Houston 77019-2120 (713) 520-1986

Established in 1960 in TX.
Donor(s): Zoe M. Vance.†
Foundation type: Independent
Financial data (yr. ended 11/30/89): Assets, $3,427,455 (M); expenditures, $555,751, including $468,000 for 7 grants (high: $428,000; low: $5,000).
Purpose and activities: Support for higher education.
Limitations: No grants to individuals.
Application information: Application form not required.
Deadline(s): None
Write: William Nathan Cabaniss, Treas.
Officers: Mary Katherine Leone, Pres.; William Nathan Cabaniss, Treas.
Trustees: Nicholas C. Leone, Diana MacDonald Moose, Erik G. Peterson, Philip M. Peterson.
Employer Identification Number: 746046681

6942
The Edward and Betty Marcus Foundation
One Preston Ctr.
8222 Douglas, Suite 360
Dallas 75225 (214) 361-4681

Established about 1984 in TX.
Donor(s): Betty B. Marcus.†
Foundation type: Independent
Financial data (yr. ended 12/31/89): Assets, $8,267,591 (M); gifts received, $357,437; expenditures, $303,981, including $206,127 for 2 grants (high: $171,127; low: $35,000).
Purpose and activities: Support primarily for visual arts institutions, organizations, and education.
Types of support: Exchange programs, program-related investments, publications, special projects.
Limitations: Giving primarily in TX. No grants to individuals, or for capital campaigns, operating support, or endowment funds.
Application information: Application form not required.
Initial approach: Letter
Copies of proposal: 1
Deadline(s): 60 days prior to board meeting
Board meeting date(s): First Tuesday in Feb., May, and Nov.
Write: Melba Davis Whatley, Chair.
Officers: Melba Davis Whatley, Chair.; Richard C. Marcus, Vice-Chair.; Mary O'Boyle English, Secy.; Carolyn Levy Clark, Treas.
Trustees: Peter J. Blum, Theodore S. Hochstim, Cary Shel Marcus.
Employer Identification Number: 751989529

6943
Mary Kay Foundation ⌑
8787 Stemmons Freeway
P.O. Box 47033
Dallas 75247 (214) 630-8787

Incorporated in 1969 in TX.
Donor(s): Mary Kay Ash.
Foundation type: Independent
Financial data (yr. ended 6/30/88): Assets, $1,982,113 (M); expenditures, $128,057, including $102,925 for 40 grants (high: $50,000; low: $100).
Purpose and activities: Giving for medical research, health agencies, social services, and public policy organizations.
Types of support: Research.
Limitations: Giving primarily in TX.
Application information: Application form not required.
Deadline(s): None
Trustees: Gerald M. Allen, Mary Kay Ash, Monty C. Barber, Michael Lunceford, Richard R. Rogers.
Employer Identification Number: 756081602

6944
Frank W. Mayborn Foundation ⌑
Ten South Third St.
Temple 76501-7619

Established in 1965 in TX.
Foundation type: Independent
Financial data (yr. ended 12/31/88): Assets, $2,269,875 (M); expenditures, $1,327,919, including $1,226,850 for 15 grants (high: $100,000; low: $100).
Purpose and activities: Support primarily for education, science, religion, and community organizations.
Types of support: General purposes.
Limitations: Giving primarily in the central TX, area. No grants to individuals.
Application information: Contributes only to pre-selected organizations. Applications not accepted.
Officers: Anyse Sue Mayborn,* Pres. and Treas.; Jerry Arnold, Secy.
Directors:* Jim B. Bowmer, Frank M. Burke, Jr.
Employer Identification Number: 746067859

6945
Oliver Dewey Mayor Foundation
c/o Ameritrust Texas, N.A.
P.O. Box 1088
Sherman 75091-1088 (214) 868-0819

Established in 1983 in TX.
Donor(s): Oliver Dewey Mayor.†
Foundation type: Independent
Financial data (yr. ended 06/30/89): Assets, $9,266,689 (M); expenditures, $444,332, including $278,581 for grants.
Purpose and activities: Support for education, community development, youth, and social and health services; support also for the construction of an outdoor theater.
Limitations: Giving limited to Grayson County, TX, and Mayes County, OK. No grants to individuals.
Publications: Application guidelines.
Application information: Application form not required.
Initial approach: Proposal
Deadline(s): None
Write: Philip McKinzie, Trust Officer, Ameritrust Texas, N.A.
Board of Governors: Samuel W. Graber, Tony J. Lyons, Philip McKinzie.
Number of staff: None.
Employer Identification Number: 751864630

6946
Mays Foundation ⌑
914 South Tyler St.
Amarillo 79101

Established in 1965.
Donor(s): W.A. Mays and Agnes Mays Trust.
Foundation type: Independent
Financial data (yr. ended 7/31/88): Assets, $1,607,862 (M); gifts received, $2,470; expenditures, $122,283, including $75,861 for 23 grants (high: $23,200; low: $25).
Purpose and activities: Emphasis on Baptist church organizations and higher education.
Limitations: Giving primarily in TX.
Application information: Contributes only to pre-selected organizations. Applications not accepted.
Trustees: Troy M. Mays, W.A. Mays.
Employer Identification Number: 751213346

6947
MBC Foundation ⌑
9826 Marek Rd.
Houston 77038 (713) 681-9213

Established in 1968 in TX.
Donor(s): Members of the Marek family.
Foundation type: Independent
Financial data (yr. ended 12/31/87): Assets, $1,743,508 (M); gifts received, $81,920; expenditures, $241,766, including $77,612 for 1 grant.
Purpose and activities: Giving for the welfare of the disadvantaged.
Limitations: Giving primarily in Houston, TX.
Application information: Application form not required.
Deadline(s): None
Write: Ralph S. Marek, Secy.
Officers: John L. Marek, Pres.; William A. Marek, V.P. and Treas.; Ralph S. Marek, Secy.
Directors: Bessie Marek, Frances Marek, Martha Marek.
Employer Identification Number: 746108373

6948
McAshan Educational and Charitable Trust ⌑
Five Post Oak Park, Suite 1980
Houston 77027

Trust established in 1952 in TX.
Donor(s): Susan C. McAshan, Susan Vaughn Clayton Trust No. 1.
Foundation type: Independent
Financial data (yr. ended 12/31/88): Assets, $37,163,719 (M); expenditures, $1,992,208, including $1,868,095 for 75 grants (high: $500,000; low: $250).
Purpose and activities: Emphasis on education, including the handicapped, population control, conservation, medical research, and the arts and music.
Limitations: Giving primarily in TX, with emphasis on Houston.
Application information:
Initial approach: Proposal
Trustees: Lucy Johnson Hadac, Susan C. McAshan, S.M. McAshan, Jr.
Director: W.W. Vann.
Employer Identification Number: 746042210

6949
McCombs Foundation, Inc. ⌑
9000 Tesoro, Suite 122
San Antonio 78217

Established in 1981 in TX.
Donor(s): Gary V. Woods, and members of the McCombs family.
Foundation type: Operating
Financial data (yr. ended 12/31/87): Assets, $233,412 (M); gifts received, $300,000; expenditures, $244,655, including $244,630 for 51 grants (high: $100,000; low: $100).
Purpose and activities: Giving for higher education, medical research, religious organizations, cultural and civic affairs, and social services.
Application information: Application form not required.
Initial approach: Letter
Deadline(s): None
Write: Billy J. McCombs, Pres.
Officers: Billy J. McCombs, Pres.; Charline McCombs, V.P.; Gary V. Woods, Secy.-Treas.
Employer Identification Number: 742204217

6950
Sollie & Lilla McCreless Foundation for Christian Evangelism, Christian Missions, and Christian Education
P.O. Box 2341
San Antonio 78298 (512) 736-6767

Established in 1958 in TX.
Donor(s): Sollie E. McCreless.†
Foundation type: Independent
Financial data (yr. ended 12/31/88): Assets, $2,322,215 (M); expenditures, $270,995, including $253,363 for 38 grants (high: $50,000; low: $65).
Purpose and activities: Support for Christian education, missions, and evangelical organizations.
Types of support: Special projects, general purposes.
Limitations: No grants to individuals.
Publications: Program policy statement.
Application information: Application form not required.
Initial approach: Letter
Deadline(s): None
Board meeting date(s): Annually
Write: G. Richard Ferdinandtsen, Secy.-Treas.
Officers: Frances Jean Sunderland,* Pres.; Robert B. Sunderland,* V.P.; G. Richardson Ferdinandtsen, Secy.-Treas.
Directors:* Dennis F. Kinlaw, William C. Reed.
Number of staff: None.
Employer Identification Number: 741485541

6951
The Eugene McDermott Foundation ▼
3808 Euclid
Dallas 75205 (214) 521-2924

Incorporated in 1972 in TX; The McDermott Foundation merged into above in 1977.
Donor(s): Eugene McDermott,† Mrs. Eugene McDermott.
Foundation type: Independent
Financial data (yr. ended 8/31/89): Assets, $41,442,971 (M); expenditures, $2,291,479, including $2,146,050 for 104 grants (high: $275,000; low: $1,000; average: $1,000-$25,000).
Purpose and activities: Support primarily for museums and other cultural programs, higher and secondary education, health, and general community interests.
Types of support: Building funds, equipment, operating budgets.
Limitations: Giving primarily in Dallas, TX. No grants to individuals.
Application information: Application form not required.
Initial approach: Letter
Copies of proposal: 1
Deadline(s): None
Board meeting date(s): Quarterly
Final notification: Prior to Aug. 31
Write: Mrs. Eugene McDermott, Pres.
Officers and Trustees:* Mrs. Eugene McDermott,* Pres.; Mary McDermott Cook,* Secy.-Treas.; Charles Cullom, C.J. Thomsen.
Number of staff: 1
Employer Identification Number: 237237919

6952
John P. McGovern Foundation ▼
6969 Brompton
Houston 77025 (713) 661-4808

Established in 1961 in TX.
Donor(s): John P. McGovern, M.D.
Foundation type: Independent
Financial data (yr. ended 08/31/90): Assets, $55,708,072 (M); gifts received, $1,303,463; expenditures, $2,148,940, including $2,056,052 for 4 grants (high: $2,000,000; low: $100).
Purpose and activities: "To provide assistance to organizations engaged in teaching, training, research, and treatment, particularly relating to

addiction (alcoholism, drug dependence, etc.), family dynamics, and the behavioral sciences; to provide scholarship funds to institutions for deserving students to study and train in these areas; also support for health agencies, higher education, and worthy charities."
Types of support: Research, scholarship funds, operating budgets, professorships, lectureships, endowment funds, building funds, conferences and seminars, continuing support, general purposes, matching funds, publications, emergency funds.
Limitations: Giving primarily in TX, with emphasis on Houston; giving also in the Southwest.
Application information: Grants primarily initiated by the foundation except for requests in the area of alcohol and/or drug addiction. Unsolicited grant requests are usually considered by the foundation. Application form not required.
Deadline(s): None
Board meeting date(s): Usually on or before Aug. 31
Write: Mrs. Sue Seymour
Officers: John P. McGovern, M.D., Pres.; Richard B. Davies, V.P.; Kathrine G. McGovern, Secy.-Treas.
Number of staff: 1 part-time professional; 6 part-time support.
Employer Identification Number: 746053075

6953
McGovern Fund for the Behavioral Sciences
(Formerly Texas Allergy Research Foundation)
6969 Brompton
Houston 77025 (713) 661-1444

Established in 1979 in TX.
Donor(s): John P. McGovern Foundation.
Foundation type: Independent
Financial data (yr. ended 11/30/89): Assets, $2,389,751 (M); gifts received, $1,972,500; expenditures, $1,644,578, including $1,630,817 for 197 grants (high: $250,000; low: $100; average: $1,000-$10,000).
Purpose and activities: "To provide assistance to organizations engaged in teaching, training, research, and treatment, particularly relating to addiction (alcoholism, drug dependence, etc.), family dynamics, and the behavioral sciences; to provide scholarship funds to institutions for deserving students to study and train in these areas; also support for health agencies, higher education, and worthy charities."
Types of support: Research, building funds, conferences and seminars, continuing support, emergency funds, endowment funds, general purposes, lectureships, matching funds, professorships, publications, scholarship funds.
Limitations: Giving primarily in TX, with emphasis on Houston; giving also in the Southwest.
Application information: Grants primarily initiated by the foundation except for requests in the area of alcohol and/or drug addiction. Unsolicited grant requests are usually considered by the foundation.
Deadline(s): None
Board meeting date(s): Usually on or before Nov. 30
Write: Mrs. Sue Seymour
Officers and Directors:* John P. McGovern,* Chair. and Pres.; Richard B. Davies,* V.P.; Kathrine G. McGovern,* Secy.
Number of staff: 1 part-time professional; 6 part-time support.
Employer Identification Number: 742086867

6954
Robert E. and Evelyn McKee Foundation
P.O. Box 220599
6006 North Mesa, Suite 906
El Paso 79913 (915) 581-4025

Incorporated in 1952 in TX.
Donor(s): Robert E. McKee,† Evelyn McKee,† Robert E. McKee, Inc., The Zia Co.
Foundation type: Independent
Financial data (yr. ended 12/31/88): Assets, $4,888,424 (M); expenditures, $366,088, including $313,100 for 95 grants (high: $50,000; low: $100).
Purpose and activities: Emphasis on local hospitals, community funds, and rehabilitation and the handicapped; grants also for higher and other education, youth agencies, child welfare, and medical research.
Types of support: Operating budgets, continuing support, annual campaigns, seed money, emergency funds, building funds, equipment, scholarship funds, research.
Limitations: Giving primarily in TX, with emphasis on El Paso. No support for organizations limited by race or ethnic origin; other private foundations, except for a local community foundation; or religious organizations, except local Episcopal churches. No grants to individuals, or for endowment funds or deficit financing; no loans.
Publications: Annual report, program policy statement, application guidelines.
Application information: Application form not required.
Initial approach: Proposal
Copies of proposal: 1
Deadline(s): Submit proposal preferably in Nov.; deadline Dec. 10
Board meeting date(s): May
Final notification: After Feb. 1
Write: Louis B. McKee, Pres.
Officers and Trustees:* Louis B. McKee,* Pres. and Treas.; Frances McKee Hays,* V.P.; Margaret McKee Lund,* V.P.; C. David McKee,* V.P.; John S. McKee,* V.P.; Philip S. McKee,* V.P.; Robert L. Hazelton,* Secy.; Charlotte McKee Cohen, Sharon Hays Herrera, C. Steven McKee, Louis B. McKee, Jr., Philip Russell McKee, Robert E. McKee III, Tad R. Smith, Helen Lund Yancey.
Number of staff: 1 part-time professional; 1 full-time support.
Employer Identification Number: 746036675

6955
Bruce McMillan, Jr. Foundation, Inc. ⌑
P.O. Box 9
Overton 75684 (214) 834-3148

Trust established in 1951 in TX.
Donor(s): V. Bruce McMillan, M.D.,† Mary Moore McMillan.†
Foundation type: Independent
Financial data (yr. ended 06/30/89): Assets, $13,599,562 (M); expenditures, $1,045,743, including $696,220 for 61 grants (high: $99,606; low: $500; average: $1,000-$40,000) and $69,690 for 100 grants to individuals (high: $1,250; low: $125).
Purpose and activities: Grants largely for higher education, including a scholarship program for graduates of 8 specific high schools in the immediate Overton, TX, area; support also for health agencies, church support, social service and youth agencies, agricultural conservation, and medical research.
Types of support: Student aid, general purposes, scholarship funds, special projects.
Limitations: Giving limited to eastern TX.
Publications: Application guidelines.
Application information: Application form required.
Initial approach: Letter
Deadline(s): May 31 for scholarship interviews; June 15 for scholarship applications; and May 15 for other requests
Board meeting date(s): June and Oct.
Final notification: July 1 (for scholarships)
Write: Ralph Ward, Pres.
Officers and Directors: Reginald H. Field, Chair.; Ralph Ward, Pres. and Treas.; Ralph B. Shank, V.P.; Ralph Ward, Jr., Secy.; John L. Pope.
Number of staff: 2 full-time professional; 4 full-time support.
Employer Identification Number: 750945924

6956
Amy Shelton McNutt Charitable Trust
1777 N.E. Loop 410, Suite 1512
San Antonio 78217

Established about 1983 in TX.
Foundation type: Independent
Financial data (yr. ended 09/30/89): Assets, $5,033,966 (M); expenditures, $261,791, including $237,078 for 47 grants (high: $25,000; low: $50).
Purpose and activities: Giving for higher education, the arts, research in the sciences, and a community fund.
Limitations: Giving primarily in TX, with emphasis on San Antonio.
Application information: Application form not required.
Initial approach: Proposal
Deadline(s): None
Write: Jack Guenther, Trustee
Trustees: R.B. Cutlip, Jack Guenther, Ruth Johnson, Edward D. Muir.
Employer Identification Number: 742298675

6957
Adeline and George McQueen Foundation of 1960 ⌑
c/o Texas American Bank
P.O. Box 2050
Fort Worth 76113 (817) 884-4266

Trust established in 1960 in TX.
Foundation type: Independent
Financial data (yr. ended 6/30/88): Assets, $8,005,832 (M); expenditures, $681,200, including $584,500 for 60 grants (high: $75,000; low: $500).
Purpose and activities: Emphasis on hospitals and youth agencies; support also for social

service agencies, medical research, and a Protestant theological seminary.
Limitations: Giving primarily in TX.
Application information:
Initial approach: Proposal
Copies of proposal: 1
Deadline(s): Sept. 30
Board meeting date(s): Nov.
Write: Kelly A. Bradshaw, Asst. V.P. and Trust Officer, Texas American Bank
Trustee: Texas American Bank.
Employer Identification Number: 756014459

6958
Meadows Foundation, Inc. ▼
Wilson Historic Block
2922 Swiss Ave.
Dallas 75204-5928 (214) 826-9431

Incorporated in 1948 in TX.
Donor(s): Algur Hurtle Meadows,† Mrs. Virginia Meadows.†
Foundation type: Independent
Financial data (yr. ended 12/31/89): Assets, $476,217,532 (M); gifts received, $103,897; expenditures, $24,236,740, including $18,608,011 for 255 grants (high: $2,450,000; low: $4,000; average: $25,000-$50,000).
Purpose and activities: Support for the arts, social services, health, education, and civic and cultural programs. Operates a historic preservation investment-related program using a cluster of Victorian homes as offices for nonprofit agencies.
Types of support: Operating budgets, continuing support, seed money, emergency funds, deficit financing, building funds, equipment, land acquisition, matching funds, scholarship funds, professorships, internships, fellowships, special projects, research, publications, conferences and seminars, program-related investments, technical assistance, consulting services, renovation projects.
Limitations: Giving limited to TX. No grants to individuals; no loans. In general, contributions are not made for annual fundraising appeals, media projects in initial planning stages, biomedical research projects, or for travel expenses for groups to perform or compete outside of TX.
Publications: Annual report (including application guidelines).
Application information: Application form not required.
Initial approach: Proposal
Copies of proposal: 1
Deadline(s): None
Board meeting date(s): Grants Review Committee meets monthly; full board meets 2 or 3 times a year to act on major grants
Final notification: 3 to 4 months
Write: Dr. Sally R. Lancaster, Exec. V.P.
Officers: Robert A. Meadows,* Chair. and V.P.; Curtis W. Meadows, Jr.,* Pres.; Sally R. Lancaster,* Exec. V.P.; G. Tomas Rhodus, V.P. and Secy.; Robert E. Wise, V.P. and Treas.; Judy B. Culbertson, V.P.; Linda S. Perryman,* V.P.; Eloise Meadows Rouse,* V.P.; Robert E. Weiss, V.P.
Directors:* Evelyn Meadows Acton, John W. Broadfoot, Vela Meadows Broadfoot, J.W. Bullion, Eudine Meadows Cheney, John A. Hammack, John H. Murrell, Charles H. Pistor, Evy Kay Ritzen, Dorothy C. Wilson.
Number of staff: 14 full-time professional; 2 part-time professional; 20 full-time support; 2 part-time support.
Employer Identification Number: 756015322

6959
Mechia Foundation ⌘
P.O. Box 1310
Beaumont 77704

Established in 1978.
Donor(s): Ben J. Rogers.
Foundation type: Independent
Financial data (yr. ended 12/31/88): Assets, $965,855 (M); expenditures, $289,941, including $286,928 for 94 grants (high: $152,400; low: $100).
Purpose and activities: Giving for cultural programs, higher education, health associations and hospitals, and Jewish welfare organizations and Jewish temples.
Limitations: Giving primarily in Beaumont and Houston, TX. No grants to individuals.
Application information: Contributes only to pre-selected organizations. Applications not accepted.
Officers: Ben J. Rogers, Pres.; Julie Rogers, V.P.; Regina Rogers, Secy.-Treas.
Employer Identification Number: 741948840

6960
Meredith Foundation ⌘
P.O. Box 117
Mineola 75773

Trust established in 1958 in TX.
Donor(s): Harry W. Meredith.†
Foundation type: Independent
Financial data (yr. ended 12/31/88): Assets, $8,389,589 (M); expenditures, $483,298, including $370,816 for 8 grants (high: $188,008; low: $2,000).
Purpose and activities: Emphasis on civic and cultural projects.
Limitations: Giving limited to Mineola, TX, and its environs.
Publications: Program policy statement.
Application information: Contributes only to pre-selected organizations. Applications not accepted.
Board meeting date(s): Monthly
Trustees: James Dear, Chair.; Sid Cox, Vice-Chair.; Ray Williams, Secy.-Treas.; Everett Smith, Coulter Templeton.
Employer Identification Number: 756024469

6961
Alice Kleberg Reynolds Meyer Foundation
P.O. Box 6985
San Antonio 78209 (512) 820-0552

Established in 1978 in TX.
Donor(s): Alice K. Meyer.
Foundation type: Independent
Financial data (yr. ended 12/31/89): Assets, $3,499,255 (M); gifts received, $214,450; expenditures, $151,954, including $141,566 for 29 grants (high: $70,000; low: $150; average: $150-$5,000).
Purpose and activities: Grants primarily for cultural organizations and medical research; support also for education.
Types of support: General purposes, building funds.
Limitations: Giving primarily in TX.
Application information: Application form not required.
Initial approach: Proposal
Copies of proposal: 1
Deadline(s): None
Write: Alice K. Meyer, Pres.
Officers: Alice K. Meyer, Pres. and Treas.; Vaughan B. Meyer, V.P. and Secy.
Number of staff: None.
Employer Identification Number: 742020227

6962
Nettie Millhollon Educational Trust Estate
304 North St. Peter
P.O. Box 643
Stanton 79782 (915) 756-2261

Trust established in 1963 in TX.
Donor(s): Nettie Millhollon.†
Foundation type: Independent
Financial data (yr. ended 06/30/89): Assets, $2,280,813 (M); qualifying distributions, $197,599, including $163,130 for loans to individuals.
Purpose and activities: Educational loans to needy deserving students.
Types of support: Student loans.
Limitations: Giving limited to residents of TX.
Officer and Trustees:* Rene Crosthwait,* Secy.-Treas.; Rodger Burch, Claude Ray Glaspie, F.E. Houston, Mary Belle Keaton, Kyle Kendall, W.E. Morrow, Dan Saunders.
Employer Identification Number: 756024639

6963
William A. and Elizabeth B. Moncrief Foundation
Ninth at Commerce
Fort Worth 76102 (817) 336-7232

Established in 1954.
Donor(s): W.A. Moncrief.†
Foundation type: Independent
Financial data (yr. ended 09/30/88): Assets, $8,295,652 (M); expenditures, $2,308,807, including $2,280,210 for 20 grants (high: $2,062,060; low: $250).
Purpose and activities: Giving for hospitals and higher education.
Types of support: General purposes, operating budgets.
Limitations: Giving primarily in TX.
Application information:
Initial approach: Letter
Deadline(s): None
Write: William A. Moncrief, Jr., Pres.
Officers and Directors:* William A. Moncrief, Jr.,* Pres.; R.W. Moncrief,* V.P.; C.B. Moncrief,* Secy.-Treas.
Employer Identification Number: 756036329

6964
The Moody Foundation ▼
704 Moody National Bank Bldg.
Galveston 77550 (409) 763-5333

Trust established in 1942 in TX.
Donor(s): William Lewis Moody, Jr.,† Libbie Shearn Moody.†
Foundation type: Independent
Financial data (yr. ended 12/31/88): Assets, $396,462,000 (M); expenditures, $17,419,064, including $15,460,064 for 79 grants (average: $10,000-$150,000).
Purpose and activities: Funds to be used for historic restoration projects, performing arts organizations, and cultural programs; promotion of health, science, and education; community and social services; and the field of religion.
Types of support: Seed money, emergency funds, building funds, equipment, consulting services, technical assistance, matching funds, professorships, special projects, research, publications, conferences and seminars, capital campaigns, land acquisition, renovation projects, student aid.
Limitations: Giving limited to TX. No grants to individuals (except for students covered by one scholarship program in Galveston County), or for operating budgets, except for start-up purposes, continuing support, annual campaigns, or deficit financing; no loans.
Publications: Annual report, application guidelines, 990-PF, financial statement.
Application information: Application format as outlined in guidelines required. Application form not required.
Initial approach: Letter or telephone
Copies of proposal: 1
Deadline(s): 6 weeks prior to board meetings
Board meeting date(s): Quarterly
Final notification: 2 weeks after board meetings
Write: Peter M. Moore, Grants Officer
Officer: Robert E. Baker, Exec. Admin. and Secy.
Trustees: Frances Moody Newman, Chair.; Robert L. Moody, Ross R. Moody.
Number of staff: 7 full-time professional; 6 full-time support.
Employer Identification Number: 741403105

6965
The Moores Foundation ⌑ ☆
One Sugar Creek Ctr. Blvd., Suite 500
Sugarland 77478

Established in 1988 in TX.
Donor(s): John J. Moores, Rebecca A. Moores.
Foundation type: Independent
Financial data (yr. ended 12/31/88): Assets, $3,315,100 (M); gifts received, $3,315,000; expenditures, $0.
Purpose and activities: Initial year of operation, 1988; no grants awarded.
Limitations: No grants to individuals.
Application information: Contributes only to pre-selected organizations. Applications not accepted.
Officers and Trustees: John J. Moores, Pres.; John J. Moores, Jr., V.P.; Jennifer A. Moores, Secy.; Rebecca A. Moores, Treas.
Employer Identification Number: 760266258

6966
The Morris Foundation ⌑
4850 Moss Hollow Court
Fort Worth 76109

Established in 1986 in TX.
Donor(s): Jack B. Morris, Linda C. Morris.
Foundation type: Independent
Financial data (yr. ended 12/31/88): Assets, $3,716,845 (M); expenditures, $137,631, including $134,900 for 16 grants (high: $50,000; low: $100).
Purpose and activities: Giving primarily for child development, including educational programs; support also for a Methodist church, health and social services, including family planning.
Limitations: Giving primarily in Fort Worth, TX. No grants to individuals.
Application information: Contributes only to pre-selected organizations. Applications not accepted.
Trustees: Jack B. Morris, Linda C. Morris.
Employer Identification Number: 752137184

6967
Ollege and Minnie Morrison Foundation ⌑ ☆
c/o Texas Commerce Bank
P.O. Box 2558
Houston 77252

Established in 1970.
Foundation type: Independent
Financial data (yr. ended 12/31/88): Assets, $1,000,052 (M); expenditures, $68,468, including $1,000 for 1 grant and $43,250 for 27 grants to individuals (high: $2,000; low: $750).
Purpose and activities: Awards for scholarships to individuals.
Types of support: Student aid.
Limitations: Giving primarily in Livingston, TX.
Application information: Contributes only to pre-selected organizations. Applications not accepted.
Trustees: Texas Commerce Bank.
Employer Identification Number: 237073336

6968
Louise L. Morrison Trust ☆
40 N.E. Loop 410, Suite 200
San Antonio 78216 (512) 342-8000

Foundation type: Independent
Financial data (yr. ended 09/30/89): Assets, $3,614,729 (M); expenditures, $243,989, including $195,355 for 7 grants (high: $104,189; low: $6,512).
Purpose and activities: Support primarily for higher education, services for the elderly, and an Episcopal Church.
Limitations: Giving primarily in San Antonio, TX.
Application information:
Initial approach: Proposal
Deadline(s): Sept. 30
Write: William T. Chumney, Jr., Mgr.
Officer: William T. Chumney, Jr., Mgr.
Trustees: Richard W. Calvert, W.W. Flannery, T.C. Frost, Jr.
Employer Identification Number: 741386236

6969
Harry S. Moss Foundation ⌑
970 San Jacinto Tower
2121 San Jacinto St.
Dallas 75210 (214) 754-2984

Incorporated in 1952 in TX.
Donor(s): Harry S. Moss, Florence M. Moss, Moss Petroleum Co.
Foundation type: Independent
Financial data (yr. ended 11/30/89): Assets, $3,152,176 (M); expenditures, $141,659, including $136,054 for 55 grants (high: $35,000; low: $475).
Purpose and activities: Emphasis on arts and cultural programs, youth agencies, and education.
Types of support: General purposes.
Limitations: Giving primarily in Dallas, TX.
Application information: Application form not required.
Deadline(s): None
Officers: Frank S. Ryburn, Pres.; John M. Little, Jr., V.P.; Frank M. Ryburn, Jr., V.P.; Mary Jane Ryburn, V.P.; F. Kenneth Travis, Treas.
Employer Identification Number: 756036333

6970
Harry S. Moss Heart Trust ▼ ⌑
c/o NCNB Texas National Bank
P.O. Box 830241
Dallas 75283-0241

Trust established in 1973 in TX.
Donor(s): Harry S. Moss, Florence M. Moss.
Foundation type: Independent
Financial data (yr. ended 9/30/86): Assets, $23,133,038 (M); gifts received, $1,018; expenditures, $1,237,579, including $1,030,000 for 4 grants (high: $750,000; low: $30,000; average: $30,000-$750,000).
Purpose and activities: Support for the prevention and cure of heart disease.
Types of support: Research.
Limitations: Giving limited to TX, with emphasis on Dallas County.
Application information: Application form not required.
Initial approach: Proposal
Copies of proposal: 1
Deadline(s): None
Board meeting date(s): As required
Final notification: 30 days
Write: Jimmy C. Green, Trust Officer, NCNB Texas National Bank
Trustees: Frank M. Ryburn, Jr., NCNB Texas National Bank.
Number of staff: None.
Employer Identification Number: 756147501

6971
William O. & Louise H. Mullins Foundation Trust ⌑ ☆
P.O. Box 1611
Amarillo 79181-0001

Established in 1987 in TX.
Foundation type: Independent
Financial data (yr. ended 12/31/88): Assets, $1,311,905 (M); expenditures, $180,219, including $160,717 for 20 grants (high: $25,000; low: $1,500) and $5,294 for 3 grants to individuals.

Purpose and activities: Giving priamrily for a hospice, a historical museum, youth organizations, and social services; also awards scholarships to individuals.
Types of support: Student aid.
Limitations: Giving primarily in Amarillo, TX.
Application information: Applications not accepted.
Trustee: Amarillo National Bank.
Employer Identification Number: 756353107

6972
W. B. Munson Foundation ⌑
c/o Texas American Bank-Denison
P.O. Box 341
Denison 75020 (214) 465-3030

Trust established in 1943 in TX.
Foundation type: Independent
Financial data (yr. ended 12/31/88): Assets, $5,171,833 (M); expenditures, $211,306, including $183,910 for 12 grants (high: $100,000; low: $200; average: $3,024) and $8,352 for 19 grants to individuals (high: $750; low: $175; average: $413).
Purpose and activities: Support for a hospital, an agricultural project, the arts, and scholarships for local high school graduates; applications not accepted for scholarships.
Types of support: Student aid, building funds, endowment funds, equipment, operating budgets, renovation projects.
Limitations: Giving limited to Grayson County, TX.
Application information: Applications not accepted for scholarships. Application form not required.
Initial approach: Letter
Deadline(s): None
Board meeting date(s): No set dates
Write: J. Brent Reed, Sr. V.P. & Trust Officer, Texas American Bank-Denison
Officer and Governors: Joseph W. Gay, Pres.; Roy L. McKinney III, W.B. Munson III.
Trustee: Texas American Bank/Denison.
Employer Identification Number: 756015068

6973
Kathryn Murfee Endowment ⌑
2200 Post Oak Blvd., Suite 320
Houston 77056 (713) 622-5855

Established in 1981 in TX.
Foundation type: Independent
Financial data (yr. ended 8/31/88): Assets, $4,109,160 (M); expenditures, $315,565, including $210,000 for 13 grants (high: $75,000; low: $5,000).
Purpose and activities: Support primarily for medical research, higher education, Protestant and other religious organizations, and the arts. When funding is available, also awards scholarships for higher education to students attending institutions in TX.
Types of support: General purposes, research.
Limitations: Giving primarily in the Houston, TX, area.
Application information: Application form required.
Deadline(s): 3 months prior to the commencement of the school term for which aid is requested
Write: June R. Nabb, Trustee
Trustees: Dan R. Japhet, June R. Nabb, James V. Walzel.
Employer Identification Number: 760007237

6974
Lynne Murray, Sr. Educational Foundation ⌑ ☆
1000 Louisiana, Suite 4600
Houston 77002 (713) 658-4444

Established in 1969.
Foundation type: Independent
Financial data (yr. ended 12/31/88): Assets, $1,235,189 (M); expenditures, $86,062, including $65,000 for 5 grants (high: $20,000; low: $5,000).
Purpose and activities: Support primarily for welfare, an opera company, and a family-affiliated educational trust.
Limitations: Giving limited to the Houston, TX, area.
Application information:
Initial approach: Letter
Deadline(s): None
Write: Robert J. Piro, Trustee
Trustees: Wilhelmine S. Murray, Robert J. Piro.
Employer Identification Number: 746137429

6975
Mike A. Myers Foundation
6310 Lemmon Ave., Suite 200
Dallas 75209 (214) 353-3777

Established in 1982 in TX.
Foundation type: Independent
Financial data (yr. ended 12/31/89): Assets, $1,486,812 (M); expenditures, $266,155, including $259,307 for 32 grants (high: $67,000; low: $100; average: $300-$10,000).
Purpose and activities: Support primarily to educational and arts institutions and organizations.
Limitations: Giving primarily in Dallas, TX. No grants to individuals.
Application information: Application form not required.
Initial approach: Letter
Copies of proposal: 1
Deadline(s): None
Board meeting date(s): Annually
Officers: Mike A. Myers,* Chair. and Pres.; Kathy Carver, Secy.; Joe Pipes, Treas.
Trustees:* Curtis W. Meadows, Jr., Alan D. Myers, Larry Temple, Carol M. Wilcox.
Number of staff: None.
Employer Identification Number: 751832130

6976
Nation Foundation
P.O. Box 180849
Dallas 75218-0849

Established in 1961 in TX.
Donor(s): First Co., Oslin Nation, James H. Nation, Patricia Walsh.
Foundation type: Operating
Financial data (yr. ended 01/31/90): Assets, $3,917,495 (M); gifts received, $253,515; expenditures, $213,327, including $176,825 for 16 grants (high: $35,000; low: $100; average: $10,000).
Purpose and activities: Support for Protestant churches, hospitals, and health services.
Limitations: Giving primarily in TX.
Trustees: Freida Ashworth, James H. Nation, Oslin Nation.
Employer Identification Number: 756036339

6977
The National Gypsum Company Foundation ⌑
4500 Lincoln Plaza
Dallas 75201

Trust established about 1952 in OH.
Donor(s): National Gypsum Co.
Foundation type: Company-sponsored
Financial data (yr. ended 12/31/87): Assets, $3,406,957 (M); gifts received, $46,202; expenditures, $167,826, including $160,622 for 79 grants (high: $21,772; low: $500).
Purpose and activities: Emphasis on community funds, higher education, and hospitals.
Application information:
Deadline(s): None
Write: David F. Byrne, Chair.
Officer and Trustees: David F. Byrne, Chair.; R. Beasley, A. Cecil, Paul T. Even.
Employer Identification Number: 346551614

6978
Navarro Community Foundation
512 Interfirst Bank Bldg.
P.O. Box 1035
Corsicana 75110 (214) 874-4301

Established in 1938 in TX.
Foundation type: Community
Financial data (yr. ended 12/31/88): Assets, $8,318,032 (M); expenditures, $127,220, including $57,970 for 9 grants (high: $24,300; low: $300).
Purpose and activities: Support largely for public schools, higher education, community development, and a community fund; grants also for Protestant church support, child welfare, youth agencies, a hospital, a library, and cultural programs.
Types of support: Annual campaigns, seed money, building funds, scholarship funds, matching funds, general purposes.
Limitations: Giving limited to Navarro County, TX. No grants to individuals, or for research, conferences, endowment funds, publications, or special projects; no loans.
Application information: Application form not required.
Initial approach: Proposal
Copies of proposal: 2
Deadline(s): Jan. 1, Apr. 1, July 1, or Oct. 1
Board meeting date(s): Jan., Apr., July, and Oct.
Write: David M. Brown, Exec. Secy.-Treas.
Officers and Trustees:* William Clarkson III,* Chair.; H.R. Stroube, Jr.,* 1st Vice-Chair.; David M. Brown,* Exec. Secy.-Treas.; O.L. Albritton, Jr., C. David Campbell, M.D., Tom Eady, Embry Ferguson, Mrs. Jack McFerran, C.E. Middleton.
Trustee Banks: Bank One, The Corsicana National Bank, NCNB Texas National Bank.
Number of staff: 1 full-time professional; 1 part-time professional.
Employer Identification Number: 750800663

6979
M. J. & Alice S. Neeley Foundation ⌑
c/o Team Bank, N.A.
P.O. Box 2050
Fort Worth 76113 (817) 884-4159

Established about 1983 in TX.
Donor(s): Alice S. Neeley, M.J. Neeley.
Foundation type: Independent
Financial data (yr. ended 09/30/89): Assets, $1,834,495 (M); gifts received, $2,446; expenditures, $130,515, including $112,200 for 10 grants (high: $50,000; low: $2,000).
Purpose and activities: Giving primarily for youth, education, and a hospital.
Types of support: General purposes, equipment.
Limitations: Giving primarily in TX.
Application information:
Initial approach: Letter
Deadline(s): Sept.
Write: Jim Wright
Trustees: James M. Moody, Marion Neeley Nettles, Kathleen Neeley Williams, Team Bank, N.A.
Employer Identification Number: 751911872

6980
Joseph O. Neuhoff Charitable Trust ⌑ ☆
4924 Greenville Ave., Suite 200
Dallas 75206-4099

Established in 1973.
Foundation type: Independent
Financial data (yr. ended 12/31/88): Assets, $1,151,181 (M); expenditures, $66,184, including $60,000 for 2 grants.
Purpose and activities: Support for a university and a Christian religious organization.
Application information: Contributes only to pre-selected organizations. Applications not accepted.
Trustees: Joseph O. Neuhoff, Sr., Rebecca Neuhoff.
Employer Identification Number: 756150214

6981
Mary Moody Northen, Inc.
2628 Broadway
Galveston 77553 (409) 765-9770

Established in 1964.
Donor(s): Mary Moody Northen.†
Foundation type: Independent
Financial data (yr. ended 06/30/89): Assets, $55,888,344 (M); gifts received, $26,866,594; expenditures, $4,209,797, including $79,940 for 9 grants (high: $10,000; low: $3,000).
Purpose and activities: Support for educational institutions, community development and civic affairs, and wildlife and the environment. The foundation is also in the process of restoring a museum of the W.L. Moody residence and conducts research of the history of that family.
Types of support: Continuing support, general purposes, professorships, research, special projects.
Limitations: Giving limited to TX and VA.
Application information: Application form not required.
Initial approach: Letter
Copies of proposal: 1
Deadline(s): None
Board meeting date(s): Monthly
Final notification: Grants are usually made in the 2nd quarter of each year
Write: R. Peter Mooz, Ph.D., Exec. Dir.
Officers: G.F. Orcutt, Pres. and Treas.; Edward L. Protz, V.P. and Secy.
Director: Robert L. Moody.
Number of staff: 2 full-time professional; 2 full-time support.
Employer Identification Number: 751171741

6982
The Kathryn O'Connor Foundation ⌑
One O'Connor Plaza, Suite 1100
Victoria 77901 (512) 578-6271

Incorporated in 1951 in TX.
Donor(s): Kathryn S. O'Connor,† Tom O'Connor, Jr., Dennis O'Connor.
Foundation type: Independent
Financial data (yr. ended 12/31/88): Assets, $5,342,437 (M); expenditures, $390,793, including $332,000 for 8 grants (high: $210,000; low: $1,000; average: $10,000-$50,000) and $45,684 for 1 foundation-administered program.
Purpose and activities: Support for institutions for the advancement of religion, education, and the relief of poverty; grants also for hospitals. The foundation also operates and maintains a church.
Types of support: Operating budgets, continuing support, annual campaigns, seed money, emergency funds, deficit financing, building funds, equipment, land acquisition, endowment funds, professorships, general purposes.
Limitations: Giving limited to southern TX, especially Victoria and Refugio counties and the surrounding area. No grants to individuals, or for matching gifts; no loans.
Application information: Application form not required.
Initial approach: Letter
Deadline(s): None
Board meeting date(s): As required
Write: Dennis O'Connor, Pres.
Officers: Dennis O'Connor, Pres.; Tom O'Connor, Jr., V.P.; Venable B. Proctor, Secy.; Mary O'Connor Braman, Treas.
Number of staff: None.
Employer Identification Number: 746039415

6983
O'Donnell Foundation ▼ ⌑
1401 Elm St., Suite 3388
Dallas 75202 (214) 698-9915

Incorporated in 1957 in TX.
Donor(s): Peter O'Donnell, Jr., Mrs. Peter O'Donnell, Jr.
Foundation type: Independent
Financial data (yr. ended 11/30/89): Assets, $86,879,224 (M); gifts received, $4,600,000; expenditures, $6,400,469, including $5,723,494 for 40 grants (high: $3,040,000; low: $1,000; average: $5,000-$250,000).
Purpose and activities: Giving primarily for science and engineering.
Limitations: Giving primarily in TX. No grants to individuals, or for scholarships.
Application information:
Initial approach: Letter with brief proposal
Deadline(s): None
Board meeting date(s): As required
Write: C.R. Bacon
Officers and Directors:* Peter O'Donnell, Jr.,* Pres.; Rita C. Clements,* V.P.; Edith Jones O'Donnell,* Secy.-Treas.; Duncan Boeckman, Philip O'B. Montgomery, Jr.
Number of staff: 1 full-time support.
Employer Identification Number: 756023326

6984
Oldham Little Church Foundation
5177 Richmond Ave., Suite 1068
Houston 77056-6701 (713) 621-4190

Trust established in 1949 in TX.
Donor(s): Morris Calvin Oldham.†
Foundation type: Independent
Financial data (yr. ended 12/31/89): Assets, $19,000,000 (M); expenditures, $1,319,000, including $1,156,000 for 339 grants (high: $5,000; low: $1,000; average: $2,000-$4,000).
Purpose and activities: To aid small Protestant churches and religious educational institutions.
Types of support: Special projects, equipment, renovation projects, special projects.
Limitations: No grants to individuals, or for operating budgets, endowments, or deficit financing.
Application information: Application form required.
Initial approach: Letter
Copies of proposal: 1
Deadline(s): None
Board meeting date(s): Monthly
Final notification: Usually within 60 days
Write: Louis E. "Ed" Finlay, Exec. Dir.
Officer and Trustees:* Louis E. "Ed" Finlay,* Exec. Dir.; Raymond E. Hankamer, Harry A. Kinney, John F. McIntyre, Carloss Morris, Jr., Stewart Morris, James S. Riley.
Number of staff: 1 part-time professional; 1 full-time support; 1 part-time support.
Employer Identification Number: 741240696

6985
Carrie S. Orleans Trust ⌑
c/o NCNB Texas National Bank
P.O. Box 831041
Dallas 75283-1041 (214) 922-5067

Foundation type: Independent
Financial data (yr. ended 6/30/88): Assets, $1,574,603 (M); expenditures, $96,637, including $81,500 for 17 grants (high: $12,500; low: $500).
Purpose and activities: To provide food and clothing for the poor and needy of Dallas County through public and private welfare agencies.
Limitations: Giving limited to Dallas County, TX. No grants to individuals.
Application information:
Initial approach: Letter
Deadline(s): None
Trustee: NCNB Texas National Bank.
Employer Identification Number: 756006730

6986
Oshman Foundation ⌑ ☆
P.O. Box 230234
Houston 77223-8234

Established in 1958.
Donor(s): Oshman Sporting Goods, Jeanette Oshman Efron.
Foundation type: Company-sponsored
Financial data (yr. ended 11/30/89): Assets, $2,220,304 (M); expenditures, $91,231, including $88,000 for 4 grants (high: $33,000; low: $5,000).
Purpose and activities: Support for the aged, cultural programs, Jewish organizations, and a college of medicine.
Limitations: Giving primarily in Houston, TX. No grants to individuals.
Application information: Contributes only to pre-selected organizations. Applications not accepted.
Officers and Directors:* Jeanette Oshman Efron,* Pres.; Marilyn O. Lubetkin,* V.P.; Judy O. Margolois,* V.P.; Marvin Aronowitz, Alvin Lubetkin.
Employer Identification Number: 746039864

6987
Overlake Foundation, Inc. ⌑
700 Preston Commons West
8117 Preston Rd.
Dallas 75225-6306 (214) 750-0722

Incorporated in 1981 in TX.
Donor(s): Mary Alice Fitzpatrick.
Foundation type: Independent
Financial data (yr. ended 11/30/88): Assets, $3,108,161 (M); gifts received, $200,000; expenditures, $234,428, including $203,000 for 26 grants (high: $100,000; low: $500; average: $1,000-$10,000).
Purpose and activities: Grants for social services, education, health associations, and cultural programs.
Limitations: Giving primarily in TX.
Application information:
Write: Donald J. Malouf, V.P.
Officers and Directors: Rayford L. Keller, Pres. and Treas.; Donald J. Malouf, V.P. and Secy.; Michael Scott Anderson, Steve Craig Anderson.
Employer Identification Number: 751793068

6988
B. B. Owen Trust ▼ ⌑
905 Custer Rd.
P.O. Box 68
Richardson 75080 (214) 783-7170

Trust established in 1974 in TX.
Donor(s): B.B. Owen.†
Foundation type: Independent
Financial data (yr. ended 9/30/88): Assets, $16,698,973 (M); expenditures, $1,486,041, including $1,059,220 for 16 grants (high: $660,000; low: $2,000; average: $1,000-$50,000).
Purpose and activities: Emphasis on hospitals, youth recreation agencies, civic affairs, and social service agencies.
Types of support: Building funds, equipment, special projects, capital campaigns.
Limitations: Giving primarily in Dallas, TX. No grants to individuals.
Application information: Application form not required.
Initial approach: Letter
Deadline(s): None
Board meeting date(s): As necessary
Final notification: 3-4 months
Write: Monty J. Jackson, Trustee
Officer: Mike Anderson, Mgr.
Trustees: Spencer Carver, Monty J. Jackson, Wendell W. Judd.
Number of staff: 1 full-time professional.
Employer Identification Number: 751385809

6989
Alvin and Lucy Owsley Foundation
3000 One Shell Plaza
Houston 77002 (713) 229-1271

Trust established in 1950 in TX.
Donor(s): Alvin M. Owsley,† Lucy B. Owsley.
Foundation type: Independent
Financial data (yr. ended 12/31/87): Assets, $4,852,989 (M); expenditures, $282,434, including $244,566 for grants (average: $1,000-$2,000).
Purpose and activities: Support for education, medicine, and social services.
Types of support: Operating budgets, continuing support, annual campaigns, seed money, emergency funds, building funds, matching funds, scholarship funds.
Limitations: Giving limited to TX. No grants to individuals, or for endowment funds; no loans.
Application information: Application form not required.
Initial approach: Letter
Copies of proposal: 1
Deadline(s): Submit proposal preferably in months when board meets; no set deadline
Board meeting date(s): Mar., June, Sept., and Dec.
Final notification: 2 months
Write: Alvin Owsley, General Mgr.
Officer and Trustees:* Alvin Owsley,* General Mgr.; Wendy Garrett, David T. Owsley, Lucy B. Owsley.
Number of staff: None.
Employer Identification Number: 756047221

6990
The Pangburn Foundation ⌑
c/o Texas American Bank, Fort Worth
500 Throckmorton St., P.O. Box 2050
Fort Worth 76113 (817) 884-4266

Established in 1962 in TX.
Foundation type: Independent
Financial data (yr. ended 3/31/88): Assets, $4,649,864 (M); expenditures, $304,313, including $259,805 for 18 grants (high: $55,000; low: $1,505).
Purpose and activities: Emphasis on cultural programs, especially music and the performing arts; grants also for education, social services, and youth agencies.
Limitations: Giving limited to the Fort Worth, TX, area. No grants to individuals.
Application information:
Initial approach: Letter
Copies of proposal: 1
Deadline(s): Sept. 30
Board meeting date(s): Oct. or Nov.
Write: Kelly Bradshaw
Trustee: Texas American Bank/Fort Worth.
Employer Identification Number: 756042630

6991
Pardee Cancer Treatment Association of Greater Brazosport ⌑
127-C Circle Way
Lake Jackson 77566

Donor(s): Elsa Pardee Foundation.
Foundation type: Operating
Financial data (yr. ended 12/31/88): Assets, $205,073 (M); gifts received, $126,088; expenditures, $106,303, including $100,647 for grants to individuals.
Purpose and activities: A private operating foundation; grants for expenses involved in the treatment of cancer, including the services of doctors, the use of hospitals and clinics, and the purchase of prescription drugs and medical equipment.
Limitations: Giving primarily in Southern Brazoria County, TX.
Application information: Application form required.
Deadline(s): None
Write: Shirley Funk
Officers and Directors: Everett Stovall, Chair.; Charles P. Quirk, Jr., Treas.; and 10 additional directors.
Number of staff: 1 part-time professional.
Employer Identification Number: 510169385

6992
The Parker Foundation ⌑
1111 Alamo Bldg.
San Antonio 78205 (512) 227-3128

Incorporated in 1957 in TX.
Donor(s): Members of the Parker family.
Foundation type: Independent
Financial data (yr. ended 3/31/88): Assets, $1,442,732 (M); expenditures, $34,371, including $23,500 for 21 grants (high: $4,620; low: $110).
Purpose and activities: Emphasis on secondary and higher education, social service agencies, cultural programs, hospitals, and Christian religious associations.
Limitations: Giving primarily in the San Antonio, TX, area.
Application information: Contributes only to pre-selected organizations. Applications not accepted.
Write: George Parker, Jr.
Officers and Directors: Mary H. Parker, Pres.; Camilla M. Parker, V.P.; Joseph B. Parker, V.P.; John M. Parker, Secy.-Treas.; Patricia H. Parker, William A. Parker.
Employer Identification Number: 746040454

6993
The Parten Foundation ⌑
1600 Smith, Suite 1650
Houston 77002

Incorporated in 1962 in TX.
Donor(s): John R. Parten, Grace P. Thomas.†
Foundation type: Independent
Financial data (yr. ended 3/31/87): Assets, $748,687 (M); gifts received, $168,556;

expenditures, $141,733, including $135,000 for 13 grants (high: $36,000; low: $1,000).
Purpose and activities: Emphasis on higher education, public affairs, and a medical research foundation.
Limitations: Giving primarily in TX.
Application information: Contributes only to pre-selected organizations. Applications not accepted.
Write: J.R. Parten, Pres.
Officers: John R. Parten, Pres.; John R. Parten, V.P. and Secy.; Robert F. Pratka, V.P. and Treas.
Employer Identification Number: 746043490

6994
J. C. Penney Company Fund, Inc. ¤
P.O Box 659000
Dallas 75265-9000 (214) 591-1341

Established in 1985 in TX.
Donor(s): J.C. Penney Co., Inc.
Foundation type: Company-sponsored
Financial data (yr. ended 03/31/89): Assets, $5,462,830 (M); gifts received, $3,000,000; expenditures, $151,250, including $151,250 for 3 grants (high: $100,000; low: $11,250).
Purpose and activities: Support primarily for community funds and development.
Limitations: No grants to individuals.
Application information:
Initial approach: Letter
Write: David Lenz, V.P.
Officers and Directors:* R.T. Erickson,* Chair.; M.C. Sears,* Pres.; David H. Lenz, V.P. and Exec. Dir.; R.S. Gorin, Secy.; R.O. Amick, Treas. and Controller; and 6 additional directors.
Employer Identification Number: 133274961

6995
The Joe and Lois Perkins Foundation ¤
1212 City National Bldg.
P.O. Box 360
Wichita Falls 76307 (817) 723-7163

Incorporated in 1941 in TX.
Donor(s): J.J. Perkins.†
Foundation type: Independent
Financial data (yr. ended 12/31/88): Assets, $9,854,902 (M); expenditures, $625,389, including $542,471 for 13 grants (high: $251,000; low: $500).
Purpose and activities: Giving for social services, education, hospitals, and church support.
Types of support: Operating budgets, building funds.
Limitations: Giving primarily in TX.
Application information: Contributes only to pre-selected organizations. Applications not accepted.
Officers: Elizabeth P. Prothro,* Pres.; Charles N. Prothro,* V.P.; Mark H. Prothro,* V.P.; Glynn D. Huff, Secy.-Treas.
Directors:* Charles V. Prothro, James E. Prothro, Joe N. Prothro, Herbert B. Story, Kathryn P. Yeager.
Employer Identification Number: 756012450

6996
Perkins-Prothro Foundation ¤
P.O. Box 360
Wichita Falls 76307

Established in 1967.
Donor(s): Lois Perkins,† Charles N. Prothro.
Foundation type: Independent
Financial data (yr. ended 6/30/89): Assets, $9,526,628 (M); expenditures, $289,846, including $255,102 for 12 grants (high: $175,000; low: $1,000).
Purpose and activities: Emphasis on higher education; support also for health and social services.
Limitations: Giving primarily in TX.
Application information: Unsolicited proposals rarely funded; most grantees are pre-selected.
Officers and Trustees:* Charles N. Prothro,* Pres.; Elizabeth P. Prothro,* V.P.; Joe N. Prothro,* V.P.; Kathryn Prothro Yeager,* V.P.; Glynn D. Huff, Secy.; Mark H. Prothro,* Treas.
Employer Identification Number: 751247407

6997
Perot Foundation ¤
12377 Merit Dr., Suite 1700
Dallas 75251 (214) 788-3000

Established in 1969 in TX.
Donor(s): H. Ross Perot.
Foundation type: Independent
Financial data (yr. ended 12/31/88): Assets, $58,965,938 (M); expenditures, $2,080,414, including $1,915,788 for 9 grants (high: $1,392,788; low: $1,000) and $686 for 1 grant to an individual.
Purpose and activities: Support primarily for higher education, a Salvation Army training school, and a Presbyterian church. The scholarship program for children of graduates of the class of 1953 of the United States Naval Academy is no longer active.
Limitations: Giving primarily in TX.
Application information:
Write: Bette Perot, V.P.
Officers: H. Ross Perot,* Pres.; Bette Perot, V.P.; Margaret B. Perot,* V.P.; Betty Taylor, Secy.
Directors:* Morton H. Meyerson, Nancy E. Mulford, H. Ross Perot, Jr., Margot Perot, Suzanne C. Perot, John T. Walker, Jr.
Employer Identification Number: 756093258

6998
The M. G. and Johnnye D. Perry Foundation
P.O. Box 466
Robstown 78380 (512) 387-2911

Trust established in 1946 in TX.
Donor(s): M.G. Perry,† Mrs. M.G. Perry.†
Foundation type: Operating
Financial data (yr. ended 12/31/88): Assets, $7,762,810 (M); expenditures, $767,901, including $5,529 for 11 grants (high: $2,500; low: $30) and $427,230 for 2 foundation-administered programs.
Purpose and activities: A private operating foundation; agricultural and economic research, including an experimental farm for benefit of farmers, stockmen, ranchers, and oil and gas producers; occasional educational loans, preferably for students planning a career in agriculture.
Types of support: Grants to individuals, matching funds, professorships, research, student loans.
Limitations: Giving limited to TX.
Publications: Application guidelines, annual report, 990-PF.
Application information: Application form not required.
Initial approach: Letter
Copies of proposal: 1
Deadline(s): None
Board meeting date(s): May
Write: Trustees
Trustees: James M. Perry, Richard H. Perry, Thomas E. Perry.
Number of staff: 3 full-time professional; 3 part-time professional; 4 full-time support; 1 part-time support.
Employer Identification Number: 741093218

6999
The Mary L. Peyton Foundation
Bassett Tower, Suite 908
303 Texas Ave.
El Paso 79901-1456 (915) 533-9698

Incorporated in 1937 in TX.
Donor(s): Joe C. Peyton.†
Foundation type: Operating
Financial data (yr. ended 05/31/89): Assets, $2,713,483 (M); expenditures, $242,055, including $173,551 for grants to individuals.
Purpose and activities: A private operating foundation; grants to provide health, welfare, and vocational educational benefits to those unable to obtain assistance elsewhere.
Types of support: Grants to individuals, student aid.
Limitations: Giving limited to legal residents of El Paso County, TX. No support for groups or organizations. No grants for building or endowment funds, scholarships, fellowships, or matching gifts; no loans.
Application information: Application form required.
Initial approach: Letter
Copies of proposal: 1
Deadline(s): None
Board meeting date(s): 3rd Thursday of each month
Write: James M. Day, Exec. Admin.
Officers and Trustees: Francis S. Ainsa, Chair.; Mrs. Alfred Blumenthal, Vice-Chair.; Mrs. R.F. Boverie, Freeman Harris, Mrs. William L. Massey, Ameritrust Texas, N.A.
Number of staff: 1 full-time professional; 1 full-time support; 1 part-time support.
Employer Identification Number: 741276102

7000
The Pine Foundation ¤
c/o H. David Hughes
1400 One Congress Plaza, 111 Congress Ave.
Austin 78701

Established in 1985 in TX.
Donor(s): Brigid Anne Cockrum.
Foundation type: Independent
Financial data (yr. ended 12/31/88): Assets, $1,084,553 (M); expenditures, $53,340,

including $40,500 for 11 grants (high: $10,000; low: $1,000).
Purpose and activities: Support primarily for health agencies and a hospital; giving also to a food bank and a Christmas fund.
Limitations: Giving primarily in the Austin, TX, area. No grants to individuals.
Application information: Application form not required.
Initial approach: Proposal
Deadline(s): Sept. 30
Write: Brigid Anne Cockrum, Pres.
Officers: Brigid Anne Cockrum, Pres.; James Bryant Cockrum, Secy.
Director: Wendy Albrecht.
Employer Identification Number: 742387801

7001
The Pineywoods Foundation
P.O. Box 1731
Lufkin 75901 (409) 634-7444

Established in 1984 in TX.
Donor(s): The Southland Foundation.
Foundation type: Independent
Financial data (yr. ended 12/31/88): Assets, $1,746,866 (M); expenditures, $174,453, including $65,005 for 21 grants (high: $10,000; low: $576; average: $1,000-$5,000).
Purpose and activities: Giving primarily for social and civic affairs.
Types of support: General purposes, equipment, building funds, matching funds, seed money, special projects.
Limitations: Giving limited to Angelina, Cherokee, Houston, Jasper, Nacogdoches, Panola, Polk, Sabine, San Augustine, San Jacinto, Shelby, Trinity, and Tyler counties, TX. No support for governmental agencies, state colleges, universities, churches, or other religious organizations. No grants to individuals, or for salaries or annual operating budgets.
Publications: Informational brochure, application guidelines.
Application information: Application form required.
Initial approach: Proposal
Copies of proposal: 7
Deadline(s): None
Board meeting date(s): Quarterly, at will
Final notification: Following board meetings
Write: Bob Bowman, Secy.
Officers and Trustees:* John F. Anderson,* Chair.; Bob Bowman,* Secy.; George Henderson,* Treas.; Jack McMullen, Jr., E.G. Pittman, Claude Smithhart.
Number of staff: 1 part-time professional.
Employer Identification Number: 751922533

7002
Minnie Stevens Piper Foundation ⌑
GPM South Tower, Suite 200
800 NW Loop 410
San Antonio 78216-5699 (512) 524-8494

Incorporated in 1950 in TX.
Donor(s): Randall G. Piper,† Minnie Stevens Piper.†
Foundation type: Independent
Financial data (yr. ended 12/31/88): Assets, $16,966,715 (M); expenditures, $1,056,423, including $30,000 for 20 grants (high: $2,500; low: $100; average: $1,000) and $254,080 for 2 foundation-administered programs.
Purpose and activities: Giving especially to contribute toward the education of worthy students and to support community funds and other organizations or activities dedicated to the furtherance of the general welfare; administers a student loan fund, annual Piper Professor awards to recognize teaching excellence at the college level, Piper Scholar awards of four-year college scholarships to outstanding high school graduates in TX, a Piper Fellows program for former Piper Scholars, a student aid library and information center, and a scholarship clearinghouse. Grants to individuals as educational loans, scholarships, and teaching awards are made only through the programs operated by the foundation.
Types of support: Scholarship funds, fellowships, student aid, student loans.
Limitations: Giving limited to TX. No grants for building or endowment funds.
Publications: Multi-year report, program policy statement, newsletter, application guidelines.
Application information: Recipients of scholarship and professorship award programs must be nominated; nomination not necessary for student loans.
Deadline(s): Feb. 1 and July 1 for grants
Board meeting date(s): Mar., June, Sept., and Dec.; student loan committee meets monthly
Write: Michael J. Balint, Exec. Dir.
Officer and Directors: Michael J. Balint, Exec. Dir.; Leatrice F. Cleveland, Martin R. Harris, Frank Slavik, J. Burleson Smith, Bruce Thomas, John H. Wilson II.
Number of staff: 5 full-time professional; 7 full-time support; 2 part-time support.
Employer Identification Number: 741292695

7003
The Polemanakos Foundation ⌑
c/o First City National Bank of Houston
P.O. Box 809
Houston 77001 (713) 668-7577

Established in 1964.
Foundation type: Independent
Financial data (yr. ended 12/31/88): Assets, $1,108,822 (M); expenditures, $47,383, including $29,726 for 19 grants (high: $11,226; low: $500).
Purpose and activities: Giving for higher education, social services, and a Greek Orthodox church.
Limitations: Giving primarily in TX.
Application information:
Initial approach: Proposal
Deadline(s): None
Officer: Tom Lykos, Mgr.
Trustee: First City National Bank of Houston.
Employer Identification Number: 746064811

7004
Pollock Foundation ⌑
2310 Cockrell Ave.
Dallas 75215
Application address: P.O. Box 66005, Dallas, TX 75266-0005; Tel.: (214) 428-7441

Established in 1955 in TX.
Donor(s): Lawrence S. Pollock, Sr.
Foundation type: Independent
Financial data (yr. ended 12/31/88): Assets, $812,287 (M); gifts received, $2,346; expenditures, $156,697, including $151,950 for 32 grants (high: $30,000; low: $250).
Purpose and activities: Giving primarily for culture and the arts, including a museum; support also for health services.
Limitations: Giving primarily in TX.
Application information: Application form required.
Deadline(s): None
Write: Lawrence S. Pollock, Jr., Trustee
Trustees: Lawrence S. Pollock, Jr., Robert G. Pollock.
Employer Identification Number: 756011985

7005
Potts and Sibley Foundation ⌑
P.O. Box 8907
Midland 79708
Application address: Ten Cambridge Court, Midland, TX 79705; Tel.: (915) 694-0694

Established in 1967.
Donor(s): Effie Potts Sibley Irrevocable Trust.
Foundation type: Independent
Financial data (yr. ended 7/31/87): Assets, $1,599,015 (M); expenditures, $176,718, including $100,800 for 29 grants (high: $13,300; low: $500).
Purpose and activities: Emphasis on higher education, cultural programs, and ecology programs.
Limitations: Giving primarily in TX.
Application information: Application form required.
Deadline(s): None
Write: Robert W. Bechtel, Trustee
Directors: Robert W. Bechtel, D.J. Sibley, Jr.
Trustees: M.R. Bullock, First RepublicBank.
Employer Identification Number: 756081070

7006
Powell Foundation ⌑ ☆
3900 Two Houston Ctr.
Houston 77010

Established in 1967.
Donor(s): Ben H. Powell, Jr.
Foundation type: Independent
Financial data (yr. ended 12/31/88): Assets, $1,074,671 (M); gifts received, $84,000; expenditures, $59,485, including $53,639 for 71 grants (high: $20,700; low: $100).
Purpose and activities: Support for higher and other education, including a military institute; support also for cultural programs, social and community services, and medical research.
Limitations: Giving primarily in Houston, TX, and VA.
Trustees: W.S. Gideon, Albert Maverick, Ben H. Powell, Jr.
Employer Identification Number: 746104592

7007
Prairie Foundation ⌑
303 West Wall, Suite 1901
Midland 79701-5116
Application address: 100 Larkspur Landing Circle, Suite 116, Larkspur, CA 94939; Tel.: (415) 461-2922

Established in 1957 in TX.
Donor(s): David Fasken Special Trust.
Foundation type: Independent
Financial data (yr. ended 12/31/88): Assets, $2,211,516 (M); expenditures, $121,505, including $115,815 for 17 grants (high: $25,000; low: $500).
Purpose and activities: Giving primarily for social service agencies; some support also for health organizations.
Limitations: Giving primarily in the San Francisco, CA, area.
Application information: Application form not required.
Deadline(s): None
Write: Barbara T. Fasken, Pres.
Officers and Directors:* Barbara T. Fasken,* Pres.; Richard S. Brooks,* V.P.; Louis A. Bartha, Secy.-Treas.
Employer Identification Number: 756012458

7008
Priddy Foundation
600 City National Bldg.
Wichita Falls 76301 (817) 723-2127

Established in 1963 in TX.
Donor(s): Ashley H. Priddy,† Robert T. Priddy, Swannanoa H. Priddy,† Walter M. Priddy.†
Foundation type: Independent
Financial data (yr. ended 11/30/89): Assets, $5,730,969 (M); gifts received, $735,738; expenditures, $299,732, including $250,083 for 26 grants (high: $118,500; low: $250).
Purpose and activities: Giving for social service agencies, particularly the YMCA, education, and the arts.
Types of support: Operating budgets, matching funds, special projects.
Limitations: Giving primarily in northern TX, with emphasis on Wichita Falls. No grants to individuals.
Publications: Program policy statement, application guidelines.
Application information: Application form required.
Initial approach: Proposal
Copies of proposal: 1
Deadline(s): Apr. 1 and Sept. 15
Board meeting date(s): May and Nov.
Write: Berneice Leath, Exec. Dir.
Officers and Directors:* Robert T. Priddy,* Pres.; Charles H. Priddy,* V.P.; Berneice Leath,* Secy.-Treas. and Exec. Dir.; John Raymond Clymer, Jr., Charles B. Kreutz, Leslie Priddy Moffett, Patricia M. Morgan, Hervey Amsler Priddy, Ruby N. Priddy.
Number of staff: None.
Employer Identification Number: 756029882

7009
Nelson Puett Foundation
P.O. Box 9038
Austin 78766 (512) 453-6611

Established in 1955 in TX.
Donor(s): Nelson Puett, Nelson Puett Mortgage Co.
Foundation type: Independent
Financial data (yr. ended 02/28/89): Assets, $3,686,993 (M); gifts received, $345,000; expenditures, $139,120, including $39,684 for 52 grants (high: $47,525; low: $25) and $91,525 for 2 loans to individuals.
Purpose and activities: Giving for education, religion, and social services; also provides homeowner loans.
Types of support: Scholarship funds, equipment, research, annual campaigns, fellowships, special projects, building funds.
Limitations: Giving primarily in TX. No grants to individuals.
Publications: Program policy statement, financial statement.
Application information: Information on scholarships available from individual high schools.
Write: Nelson Puett, Pres.
Officers: Nelson Puett, Pres.; Ruth B. Puett, V.P.; Robert C. Osborne, Secy.-Treas.
Number of staff: None.
Employer Identification Number: 746062365

7010
The Quanex Foundation ⌑
c/o Quanex Corp.
1900 West Loop South, Suite 1500
Houston 77027 (713) 961-4600

Incorporated in 1951 in IL.
Donor(s): La Salle Steel Co.
Foundation type: Company-sponsored
Financial data (yr. ended 12/31/88): Assets, $1,845,307 (M); expenditures, $120,259, including $102,153 for 118 grants (high: $13,772; low: $25).
Purpose and activities: Emphasis on community funds and community development.
Limitations: No support for organizations supporting dependent children. No grants to individuals.
Application information: Application form not required.
Initial approach: Letter or proposal
Copies of proposal: 1
Deadline(s): Oct. 31
Write: Paul Kraft, Mgr. Office Admin., Quanex Corp.
Officers and Directors: Robert C. Snyder, Pres.; J.K. Peery, V.P.; W.M. Rose, V.P.
Number of staff: None.
Employer Identification Number: 366065490

7011
Ed Rachal Foundation ⌑
204 Hopper Bldg.
Falfurrias 78355

Established in 1965 in TX.
Foundation type: Independent
Financial data (yr. ended 8/31/87): Assets, $12,472,902 (M); expenditures, $677,033, including $578,594 for 8 grants (high: $500,000; low: $100).
Purpose and activities: Giving for higher education, particularly Texas A&I University.
Types of support: General purposes.
Limitations: Giving primarily in TX.
Officers: Curtis D. Robert, Pres.; Curtis D. Robert, Jr., V.P. and Secy.; Adelfa B. Maldonado, Secy.
Employer Identification Number: 741116595

7012
Red River Valley Council for the Aid of Persons with Mental Problems, Inc. ⌑
c/o Dub Bassett
Box 1015
Paris 75460-1015 (214) 785-0351

Established in 1975 in TX.
Foundation type: Independent
Financial data (yr. ended 12/31/88): Assets, $1,054,902 (M); expenditures, $43,046, including $38,200 for 5 grants (high: $18,300; low: $300).
Purpose and activities: Support primarily for organizations which aid the intellectually or emotionally handicapped.
Types of support: Equipment.
Limitations: Giving primarily in northeastern TX and southeastern OK.
Application information: Application form not required.
Deadline(s): None
Officers: Clayton Forthman, Pres.; Mary Ayers, V.P.; Myrtice Broussard, Secy.; L.W. Bassett, Treas.
Employer Identification Number: 237455279

7013
Redman Foundation
7215 Skillman No. 310, Suite 287
Dallas 75231

Trust established in 1951 in MI.
Donor(s): Harold F. Redman,† Clara M. Redman.†
Foundation type: Independent
Financial data (yr. ended 12/31/88): Assets, $4,786,130 (M); gifts received, $60,000; expenditures, $241,003, including $200,480 for 31 grants (high: $12,480; low: $3,000).
Purpose and activities: Giving for higher education, Protestant church support, and social services.
Types of support: Capital campaigns, endowment funds, matching funds, operating budgets.
Limitations: Giving primarily in TX. No grants to individuals.
Publications: Application guidelines.
Application information: Application form not required.
Initial approach: Letter
Copies of proposal: 1
Deadline(s): 1 month prior to quarterly meetings
Board meeting date(s): 1st week of Mar., June, Sept., and Dec.
Write: Karen Baxter
Officer: Mary Redman, Mgr.
Trustees: James Redman, Chair.; William E. Collins, Mrs. James Redman, Ameritrust Co., N.A.
Number of staff: 1 part-time professional.
Employer Identification Number: 386045047

7014
N. D. & Mary Redmon Foundation, Inc. ⌑ ☆
Box 88
Tulia 79088-0088 (806) 995-3528
Additional tel.: (806) 9954325

Foundation type: Independent

Financial data (yr. ended 12/31/88): Assets, $1,016,831 (M); expenditures, $38,185, including $34,800 for 6 grants (high: $10,000; low: $1,000).
Purpose and activities: Giving for community development, youth organizations, the aged, and a halfway house.
Types of support: Operating budgets, capital campaigns.
Limitations: Giving primarily in Swisher County, TX, area. No grants to individuals.
Application information: Application form required.
Deadline(s): None
Board meeting date(s): Fall
Write: George Jennings, Jr., Dir.
Directors: Earl Bell Cosby, Kenneth B. Godwin, George J. Jennings, Jr.
Employer Identification Number: 751333002

7015
Elias & Hanna Regensburger Foundation ⌑ ☆
c/o Texas American Bank, Trust Dept.
231 West Main
Denison 75020 (214) 465-3030

Established in 1985 in TX.
Donor(s): Morris A. Regensburger Family Trust, William L. Regensburger Family Trust.
Foundation type: Independent
Financial data (yr. ended 12/31/88): Assets, $14,499,792 (M); gifts received, $774,020; expenditures, $65,616, including $58,825 for 13 grants (high: $22,500; low: $125).
Purpose and activities: Support for a Jewish congregation, social services, organizations benefitting youth, and higher education.
Types of support: Operating budgets.
Limitations: Giving primarily in Denison and Sherman, TX. No support for private foundations. No grants to individuals.
Application information:
Deadline(s): None
Trustee: Texas American Bank.
Employer Identification Number: 756322552

7016
RGK Foundation ▼
2815 San Gabriel
Austin 78705-3594 (512) 474-9298

Incorporated in 1966 in TX.
Donor(s): George Kozmetsky, Ronya Kozmetsky.
Foundation type: Independent
Financial data (yr. ended 12/31/89): Assets, $34,112,299 (M); gifts received, $1,274,347; expenditures, $1,349,020, including $721,685 for 80 grants (high: $85,000; low: $1,000; average: $1,000-$10,000) and $56,892 for foundation-administered programs.
Purpose and activities: Grants to higher educational institutions, with emphasis on medical and educational research; support also for business and economic associations.
Types of support: Matching funds, professorships, research, publications, conferences and seminars, special projects.
Limitations: No grants to individuals, or for deficit financing, building or endowment funds, operating budgets, or equipment; no loans.
Publications: Informational brochure (including application guidelines).
Application information: Proposals for medical research must follow NIH guidelines. Application form not required.
Initial approach: Letter or proposal
Copies of proposal: 1
Deadline(s): Submit proposal before Dec.; no set deadline
Board meeting date(s): Annually
Final notification: 2 to 3 months
Write: Ronya Kozmetsky, Pres.
Officers and Trustees:* George Kozmetsky,* Chair.; Ronya Kozmetsky,* Pres. and Treas.; Gregory Kozmetsky,* V.P. and Secy.; Daniel Fogel, Charles Hurwitz, Cynthia Kozmetsky, Nadya Kozmetsky Scott.
Number of staff: 3 full-time support; 1 part-time support.
Employer Identification Number: 746077587

7017
Sid W. Richardson Foundation ▼
309 Main St.
Fort Worth 76102 (817) 336-0494

Established in 1947 in TX.
Donor(s): Sid W. Richardson,† and associated companies.
Foundation type: Independent
Financial data (yr. ended 12/31/89): Assets, $249,876,981 (M); expenditures, $8,435,644, including $6,307,466 for 85 grants (high: $1,334,525; low: $2,000; average: $2,000-$350,000).
Purpose and activities: Giving primarily for education, health, the arts, and social service programs.
Types of support: Operating budgets, seed money, building funds, equipment, land acquisition, endowment funds, research, publications, conferences and seminars, matching funds, special projects, renovation projects, continuing support, general purposes.
Limitations: Giving limited to TX, with emphasis on Fort Worth for the arts and human services, and statewide for health and education. No support for religious organizations. No grants to individuals, or for scholarships or fellowships; no loans.
Publications: Annual report (including application guidelines).
Application information: Application form required.
Initial approach: Letter
Copies of proposal: 1
Deadline(s): Mar. 1, June 1, and Sept. 1
Board meeting date(s): Spring, summer, and fall
Final notification: Varies
Write: Valleau Wilkie, Jr., Exec. V.P.
Officers and Directors:* Perry R. Bass,* Pres.; Valleau Wilkie, Jr., Exec. V.P.; Lee M. Bass,* V.P.; Nancy Lee Bass,* V.P.; Sid R. Bass,* V.P.; Jo Helen Rosacker, Secy.; M.E. Chappell,* Treas.
Number of staff: 4 full-time professional; 2 full-time support; 4 part-time support.
Employer Identification Number: 756015828

7018
Sid Richardson Memorial Fund
309 Main St.
Fort Worth 76102 (817) 336-0494

Incorporated in 1965 in TX.
Donor(s): Sid W. Richardson.†
Foundation type: Independent
Financial data (yr. ended 12/31/89): Assets, $3,801,799 (M); expenditures, $261,836, including $174,000 for 57 grants to individuals (high: $12,000; low: $500; average: $2,600).
Purpose and activities: Giving limited to scholarships for spouses and direct descendants of donor's employees.
Types of support: Employee-related scholarships.
Limitations: No grants for capital or endowment funds, operating budgets, general purposes, special projects, research, or matching gifts; no loans.
Application information: Application form required.
Initial approach: Letter
Copies of proposal: 1
Deadline(s): Submit application between Jan. and Mar.; deadline Mar. 31
Board meeting date(s): July; selection committee meets annually in June
Final notification: 3 months
Write: JoHelen Rosacker, Admin.
Officers: C.T. Floyd,* Pres.; Valleau Wilkie, Jr.,* Exec. V.P.; Jo Helen Rosacker, Secy. and Admin.; Cynthia Kesey, Treas.
Directors:* William A. Landreth.
Number of staff: 2 part-time professional; 2 part-time support.
Employer Identification Number: 751220266

7019
Rienzi Foundation, Inc. ⌑
2001 Kirby Dr., Suite 714
Houston 77019

Established in 1958 in TX.
Foundation type: Independent
Financial data (yr. ended 12/31/88): Assets, $2,526,484 (M); expenditures, $139,917, including $130,525 for 127 grants (high: $15,000; low: $50).
Purpose and activities: Giving for cultural programs, social services, higher education, and hospitals.
Limitations: Giving primarily in Houston, TX. No grants to individuals.
Application information: Contributes only to pre-selected organizations. Applications not accepted.
Officer: Evangeline Thomas, Secy.-Treas.
Directors: Carroll S. Masterson, Harris Masterson, Isla C. Reckling, Randa R. Roach, Bert F. Winston, Lynn David Winston.
Employer Identification Number: 741484331

7020
Dora Roberts Foundation ⌑
c/o Texas American Bridge Bank/Fort Worth
P.O. Box 2050
Fort Worth 76113 (817) 884-4442

Trust established in 1948 in TX.
Donor(s): Dora Roberts.†
Foundation type: Independent

Financial data (yr. ended 12/31/89): Assets, $21,112,272 (M); gifts received, $7,834,344; expenditures, $1,118,730, including $874,294 for 20 grants (high: $230,000; low: $780).
Purpose and activities: Emphasis on higher education, social service and youth agencies, including a rehabilitation center, hospitals and health services, and Protestant church support.
Types of support: General purposes.
Limitations: Giving limited to TX, with emphasis on Big Spring.
Application information:
Initial approach: Proposal
Deadline(s): Sept. 30
Board meeting date(s): Annually in Oct. or Nov.
Final notification: End of Dec.
Write: Rick Piersall, V.P. and Trust Officer, Texas American Bridge Bank/Fort Worth
Advisory Board: Ralph W. Caton, Chair.; Roger Canter, Mrs. Horace Garrett, Sue Garrett Partee, J.P. Taylor, Ann Garrett Turner, R.H. Weaver.
Trustee: Texas American Bridge Bank/Fort Worth.
Number of staff: None.
Employer Identification Number: 756013899

7021
The Robinson Foundation ☆
5005 Riverway, Suite 200
Houston 77056-2123 (713) 627-2500
Application address: 5555 San Felipe, 17th Fl., Houston, TX 77056

Established in 1988 in TX as partial successor to The J. S. Abercrombie Foundation.
Donor(s): Jamie A. Robinson, George A. Robinson.
Foundation type: Independent
Financial data (yr. ended 12/31/88): Assets, $2,175,790 (M); expenditures, $197,951, including $125,000 for 4 grants (high: $45,000; low: $20,000).
Purpose and activities: Support primarily for medical education and child welfare; giving also for general charitable activities, including education, agriculture, and historic preservation.
Types of support: General purposes, operating budgets, research, technical assistance.
Limitations: Giving primarily in TX.
Application information: Application form not required.
Initial approach: Proposal
Copies of proposal: 1
Deadline(s): None
Board meeting date(s): Semiannually as determined
Final notification: Within 9 months of acceptance
Write: Gary A. Messersmith, Trustee
Trustees: Gary A. Messersmith, George A. Robinson, Jamie A. Robinson.
Number of staff: None.
Employer Identification Number: 760231150

7022
Rockwell Fund, Inc. ▼
910 Travis St., Suite 1921
Houston 77002 (713) 659-7204

Trust established in 1931; incorporated in 1949 in TX; absorbed Rockwell Brothers Endowment, Inc. in 1981.
Donor(s): Members of the James M. Rockwell family, Rockwell Bros. & Co., Rockwell Lumber Co.
Foundation type: Independent
Financial data (yr. ended 12/31/88): Assets, $49,223,111 (M); expenditures, $2,383,685, including $2,081,750 for grants (high: $60,000; low: $500; average: $5,000-$25,000).
Purpose and activities: Giving to causes of interest to the founders and donors, with emphasis on higher education, religious programs, hospitals, cultural programs, municipalities, and general welfare, and projects that fulfill the fund's philosophy of wanting to make its grants do as much good and touch the lives of as many people as possible.
Types of support: Annual campaigns, seed money, general purposes, building funds, equipment, land acquisition, scholarship funds, lectureships, operating budgets, professorships, renovation projects, research.
Limitations: Giving primarily in TX, with emphasis on Houston. No grants to individuals; no loans; grants awarded on a year-to-year basis only; no future commitments.
Publications: Application guidelines.
Application information: Application form required.
Initial approach: Letter
Copies of proposal: 1
Deadline(s): Nov. 1
Board meeting date(s): Quarterly
Final notification: Dec. 15
Write: Joe M. Green, Jr., Pres., or Mary Jo Loyd, Prog. Officer
Officers and Trustees:* Joe M. Green, Jr.,* Pres.; R. Terry Bell,* V.P.; Helen N. Sterling,* Secy.-Treas.
Number of staff: 2 full-time professional; 1 part-time professional; 2 full-time support.
Employer Identification Number: 746040258

7023
Rogers Brothers Foundation, Inc. ⌑ ☆
595 Orleans St.
P.O. Box 1310
Beaumont 77704 (409) 838-6681

Incorporated in 1961 in TX.
Donor(s): Members of the Rogers family.
Foundation type: Independent
Financial data (yr. ended 11/30/89): Assets, $344,240 (M); expenditures, $359,929, including $212,370 for 101 grants (high: $65,000; low: $100).
Purpose and activities: Giving primarily for Jewish welfare funds, arts and culture, education, health and hospitals, and social services.
Limitations: Giving primarily in TX. No grants to individuals.
Application information:
Board meeting date(s): As required
Write: Ben J. Rogers, Pres.
Officers: Ben J. Rogers, Pres.; Sol J. Rogers, V.P.; Victor J. Rogers, V.P.; Nate J. Rogers, Secy.-Treas.
Number of staff: None.
Employer Identification Number: 746063588

7024
The Victor J. Rogers Family Foundation ⌑
P.O. Box 1310
Beaumont 77704-8311

Established in 1980 in TX.
Donor(s): Roger Bros. Foundation, Inc.
Foundation type: Independent
Financial data (yr. ended 11/30/89): Assets, $1,093,711 (M); expenditures, $69,983, including $69,134 for 99 grants (high: $10,000; low: $10).
Purpose and activities: Support primarily for Jewish welfare, social services, higher education, and health.
Limitations: Giving primarily in Beaumont, TX. No grants to individuals.
Application information: Contributes only to pre-selected organizations. Applications not accepted.
Officer: Fred L. Brown, Mgr.
Trustees: J.W. Rogers, Victor J. Rogers.
Employer Identification Number: 742147665

7025
The Rogers Foundation ⌑
P.O. Box 130489
Tyler 75713 (214) 595-3701

Established in 1986 in TX.
Donor(s): Robert M. Rogers.
Foundation type: Independent
Financial data (yr. ended 12/31/88): Assets, $4,833,311 (M); expenditures, $258,096, including $249,716 for 19 grants (high: $200,000; low: $50).
Purpose and activities: To promote education by providing funds for schools and educational programs and for scholarships and scholarship funds.
Types of support: Building funds, general purposes.
Limitations: Giving primarily in Tyler, TX. No grants to individuals.
Application information:
Initial approach: Proposal
Deadline(s): None
Write: Robert M. Rogers, Dir.
Directors: Louise H. Rogers, Rebecca J. Rogers, Robert M. Rogers.
Employer Identification Number: 752143064

7026
Ralph B. Rogers Foundation
7610 Stemmons Freeway, Suite 600
Dallas 75247 (214) 647-6701

Trust established in 1953 in TX.
Donor(s): Ralph B. Rogers.
Foundation type: Independent
Financial data (yr. ended 12/31/88): Assets, $828,305 (M); gifts received, $57,850; expenditures, $316,305, including $288,950 for 25 grants (high: $250,000; low: $100; average: $1,000-$5,000).
Purpose and activities: Giving primarily for public broadcasting; support also for cultural programs, health education, medical research, and an independent school.
Types of support: Research, special projects.
Limitations: Giving primarily in TX.
Application information: Applications not accepted.

Board meeting date(s): Dec.
Write: Ralph B. Rogers, Trustee
Trustees: Robert Alpert, Ralph B. Rogers, Robert D. Rogers.
Number of staff: None.
Employer Identification Number: 136153567

7027
Earl C. Sams Foundation, Inc.
101 North Shoreline Dr., Suite 602
Corpus Christi 78401 (512) 888-6485

Incorporated in 1946 in NY; reincorporated in 1988 in TX.
Donor(s): Earl C. Sams.†
Foundation type: Independent
Financial data (yr. ended 12/31/88): Assets, $13,177,950 (M); expenditures, $1,015,649, including $733,622 for 11 grants (high: $375,000; low: $100).
Purpose and activities: Grants primarily for a zoological society, higher and secondary education, and medical purposes; support also for social service and youth agencies, and community funds.
Types of support: Annual campaigns, building funds, continuing support, endowment funds, equipment, special projects.
Limitations: Giving primarily in southern TX. No grants to individuals.
Application information:
Initial approach: Proposal
Copies of proposal: 5
Deadline(s): 3 weeks prior to board meeting
Board meeting date(s): Semiannually
Write: Dodie P. Tate, Pres.
Officers: Dodie P. Tate,* Pres.; Jack M. Roney,* V.P.; Susan Ohnmacht, Secy.
Directors:* Bruce Sams Hawn, Susan Hawn Thames.
Number of staff: 3 full-time professional.
Employer Identification Number: 741463151

7028
San Antonio Area Foundation ▼
808 Travis Bldg.
405 North St. Mary's St.
San Antonio 78205 (512) 225-2243

Established in 1964 in TX.
Foundation type: Community
Financial data (yr. ended 09/30/89): Assets, $16,169,311 (M); gifts received, $2,020,280; expenditures, $1,903,513, including $1,627,341 for 553 grants (average: $1,000-$10,000).
Purpose and activities: To provide an effective channel for private giving to meet educational, cultural, medical, research, social, religious, and civic needs at all levels of society.
Types of support: Operating budgets, continuing support, annual campaigns, seed money, emergency funds, building funds, equipment, land acquisition, endowment funds, matching funds, scholarship funds, special projects, research, publications, conferences and seminars, student aid, general purposes, lectureships, professorships, renovation projects.
Limitations: Giving limited to TX, with emphasis on the Bexar County and San Antonio areas, except when otherwise specified by donor. No support for political or lobbying programs. No grants to individuals (except for designated scholarship funds); or for deficit financing, endowment funds, or salaries (except as part of a project); no loans.
Publications: Annual report, 990-PF.
Application information: Application form required.
Initial approach: Letter or telephone
Copies of proposal: 15
Deadline(s): Feb. 15
Board meeting date(s): Annually and as required
Final notification: 8 weeks
Write: Katherine Netting Folbre, Exec. Dir.
Officer: Katherine Netting Folbre, Secy.-Treas. and Exec. Dir.
Distribution Committee: Gaines Voigt, Chair.; L. John Strieber, Jr., Vice-Chair.; John E. Banks, Sr., Clifton J. Bolner, Kenneth L. Farrimond, M.D., Richard E. Goldsmith, Pete R. Martinez, Edith McAllister, Al J. Notzon, Aaronetta Pierce, Jerome F. Weynand, Mary Beth Williamson, Mollie Zachry.
Trustee Banks: Broadway National Bank, First City Bank San Antonio, N.A., Frost National Bank, Groos Bank, Kelly Field National Bank, MTrust Corp., N.A., NBC of San Antonio, N.A., NCNB Texas National Bank.
Number of staff: 1 full-time professional; 1 part-time professional.
Employer Identification Number: 746065414

7029
San Marcos Civic Foundation ⌑
208 South Guadalupe
San Marcos 78666-5534 (512) 396-2411

Established in 1968 in TX.
Foundation type: Independent
Financial data (yr. ended 12/31/87): Assets, $1,106,108 (M); expenditures, $92,040, including $78,942 for 11 grants (high: $52,355; low: $120).
Purpose and activities: Support primarily for religious and educational institutions.
Limitations: Giving limited to Hays County, TX.
Application information: Oral presentation is required. Application form required.
Deadline(s): None
Write: Janis McBride, Trustee
Officer and Trustees: H.Y. Price, Jr., Mgr.; Janis McBride, James J. Pendergast, Jr.
Employer Identification Number: 746109230

7030
Sands Foundation ⌑
200 Crescent Court, Suite 300
Dallas 75201

Established in 1959 in TX.
Donor(s): Caroline Rose Hunt.
Foundation type: Independent
Financial data (yr. ended 12/31/87): Assets, $1,617,182 (M); gifts received, $1,200,000; expenditures, $33,309, including $31,600 for 8 grants (high: $16,000; low: $100).
Purpose and activities: Support for higher education, a church, a community fund, and social services.
Application information: Contributes only to pre-selected organizations. Applications not accepted.
Officers: Lloyd B. Sands, Pres.; Caroline Rose Hunt, V.P.; Stephen H. Sands, Secy.-Treas.
Employer Identification Number: 756010788

7031
Sarofim Foundation ⌑ ☆
Two Houston Ctr., Suite 2907
Houston 77010 (713) 654-4484

Established in 1968.
Donor(s): Fayez Sarofim, Louisa Stude Sarofim.
Foundation type: Independent
Financial data (yr. ended 6/30/89): Assets, $5,261,210 (M); expenditures, $265,029, including $258,850 for 4 grants (high: $185,000; low: $23,850).
Purpose and activities: Giving primarily for dance, including ballet; support also for education.
Limitations: Giving primarily in Houston, TX.
Application information: Application form not required.
Initial approach: Letter
Deadline(s): None
Write: Fayez Sarofim, Trustee
Trustees: E. Rudge Allen, Jr., Fayez Sarofim, Louisa Stude Sarofim.
Employer Identification Number: 237065248

7032
Scaler Foundation, Inc. ▼
2200 Post Oak Blvd., Suite 707
Houston 77056 (713) 627-2440

Incorporated in 1954 in TX.
Foundation type: Independent
Financial data (yr. ended 12/31/87): Assets, $7,502,026 (M); gifts received, $60,380; expenditures, $360,807, including $298,958 for 10 grants (high: $118,470; low: $1,000; average: $10,000-$30,000).
Purpose and activities: Grants for major national art museums to aid in acquiring objects of contemporary art from young talent.
Types of support: Operating budgets, seed money, special projects, general purposes, continuing support.
Limitations: Giving primarily in the U.S. and France. No grants to individuals, or for building and endowment funds, research, scholarships, fellowships, or matching gifts; no loans.
Application information: Contributes only to pre-selected organizations. Applications not accepted.
Officers and Directors: Eric Boissonnas, Pres.; Sylvie Boissonnas, V.P.; Elliott A. Johnson, Secy.-Treas.
Number of staff: None.
Employer Identification Number: 746036684

7033
Scarborough Foundation ⌑
P.O. Box 1536
Midland 79702 (915) 682-0357

Established in 1985 in TX.
Foundation type: Independent
Financial data (yr. ended 6/30/89): Assets, $864,760 (M); expenditures, $234,716, including $86,370 for 8 grants (high: $25,000; low: $1,200) and $127,276 for 66 grants to individuals (high: $11,337; low: $395).
Purpose and activities: Giving primarily for higher education.
Types of support: Student aid, scholarship funds.
Limitations: Giving primarily in TX.

Application information:
Initial approach: Letter
Deadline(s): None
Write: Mrs. Evelyn Linebery, Pres.
Officer and Trustee: Evelyn Linebery, Pres.
Employer Identification Number: 752056704

7034
William E. Scott Foundation
3200 Continental Plaza
Fort Worth 76102 (817) 336-0361

Incorporated in 1960 in TX.
Donor(s): William E. Scott.†
Foundation type: Independent
Financial data (yr. ended 5/31/89): Assets, $5,722,990 (M); expenditures, $407,686, including $321,750 for 23 grants (high: $107,750; low: $1,000; average: $5,000).
Purpose and activities: Giving primarily for programs in the arts; some grants for elementary and higher education, youth agencies, and community funds.
Types of support: Annual campaigns, capital campaigns, general purposes, special projects.
Limitations: Giving limited to TX, with emphasis on the Fort Worth-Tarrant County area, and in LA, OK, and NM. No grants to individuals.
Publications: Application guidelines.
Application information: Application form required.
Initial approach: Letter
Copies of proposal: 1
Deadline(s): None
Board meeting date(s): As required
Write: Robert W. Decker, Pres.
Officers and Directors:* Robert W. Decker,* Pres.; Raymond B. Kelly III,* V.P.
Number of staff: 1 part-time support.
Employer Identification Number: 756024661

7035
Scurlock Foundation
700 Louisiana, Suite 3920
Houston 77002 (713) 222-2041

Incorporated in 1954 in TX.
Donor(s): E.C. Scurlock,† Scurlock Oil Co., D.E. Farnsworth,† W.C. Scurlock,† J.S. Blanton, and other members of the Blanton family.
Foundation type: Independent
Financial data (yr. ended 12/31/88): Assets, $7,444,657 (M); gifts received, $42,085; expenditures, $773,676, including $741,936 for 129 grants (high: $95,133; low: $100).
Purpose and activities: Emphasis on hospitals and secondary and higher education; support also for health agencies, Protestant churches, social service and youth agencies, cultural programs, and public interest groups.
Types of support: Building funds, general purposes, annual campaigns, emergency funds, endowment funds, research, matching funds, continuing support.
Limitations: Giving primarily in TX. No grants to individuals, or for scholarships or fellowships; no loans.
Application information: Funds committed for approximately the next two years. Application form not required.
Initial approach: Letter
Copies of proposal: 1
Deadline(s): None
Board meeting date(s): Dec. and as required
Write: J.S. Blanton, Pres.
Officers and Directors: J.S. Blanton, Pres.; Ben Love, V.P.; Kenneth Fisher, Secy.-Treas.; Eddy S. Blanton, Jack S. Blanton, Jr., Laura Lee Blanton, Elizabeth B. Wareing.
Number of staff: None.
Employer Identification Number: 741488953

7036
Sarah M. & Charles E. Seay Charitable Trust ¤
300 Crescent Court, Suite 1370
Dallas 75201

Established in 1983 in TX.
Donor(s): Charles E. Seay, Sarah M. Seay.
Foundation type: Independent
Financial data (yr. ended 5/31/88): Assets, $1,860,065 (M); expenditures, $70,436, including $58,917 for 38 grants (high: $10,811; low: $50).
Purpose and activities: Giving for higher and other education, religious organizations, cultural programs, social service and youth agencies, and community affairs.
Limitations: Giving primarily in TX, with emphasis on Dallas. No grants to individuals.
Application information: Contributes only to pre-selected organizations. Applications not accepted.
Trustees: Charles E. Seay, Charles E. Seay, Jr., Sarah M. Seay, Stephen M. Seay.
Employer Identification Number: 751894505

7037
The Abe and Annie Seibel Foundation ¤
c/o The United States National Bank
P.O. Box 179
Galveston 77553 (409) 763-1151

Trust established in 1960 in TX.
Donor(s): Abe Seibel,† Annie Seibel.†
Foundation type: Independent
Financial data (yr. ended 7/31/88): Assets, $14,495,541 (M); qualifying distributions, $2,775,425, including $1,300,725 for 983 grants to individuals (high: $3,000; low: $1,000) and $1,474,700 for 560 loans to individuals.
Purpose and activities: Interest-free loans to needy and worthy students enrolled in four-year higher educational institutions.
Types of support: Student loans.
Limitations: Giving limited to graduates of TX high schools attending TX colleges and universities.
Application information: Application form required.
Initial approach: Telephone or letter
Deadline(s): Feb. 28
Write: Judith T. Whelton, V.P. and Trust Officer, The United States National Bank
Directors: Bernard Demoratsky, Rabbi Martin Levy, F.A. Odom.
Trustee: The United States National Bank.
Employer Identification Number: 746035556

7038
Semmes Foundation, Inc.
800 Navarro, Suite 210
San Antonio 78205 (512) 225-0887

Incorporated in 1952 in TX.
Donor(s): Douglas R. Semmes.†
Foundation type: Independent
Financial data (yr. ended 12/31/88): Assets, $7,569,142 (M); gifts received, $10,000; expenditures, $445,258, including $349,948 for 29 grants (high: $151,150; low: $100).
Purpose and activities: Giving for education, the arts, museums, and health services.
Types of support: Operating budgets, continuing support, annual campaigns, seed money, emergency funds, deficit financing, building funds, equipment, land acquisition, matching funds, professorships, special projects, research, publications, conferences and seminars, general purposes, capital campaigns.
Limitations: Giving primarily in the San Antonio, TX, area. No grants to individuals; no loans.
Application information: Application form not required.
Initial approach: Letter
Copies of proposal: 1
Deadline(s): None
Board meeting date(s): Feb. and as needed
Final notification: 6 months
Write: Thomas R. Semmes, Pres.
Officers and Directors:* Thomas R. Semmes,* Pres.; Carol Duffell, Secy.-Treas.; John R. Hannah, Lucian L. Morrison, Jr., D.R. Semmes, Jr., Julia Yates Semmes.
Number of staff: 1 part-time professional.
Employer Identification Number: 746062264

7039
James S. Seneker Trust for Religious Education ¤
c/o NCNB Texas National Bank
P.O. Box 83776
Dallas 75283
Application addresses: Bd. of Higher Education and Ministry, Box 871, Nashville, TN 37202-0871; Tel.: (615) 327-2700; Perkins School of Theology, Southern Methodist University, Dallas, TX 75275

Established in 1984 in TX.
Foundation type: Independent
Financial data (yr. ended 05/31/89): Assets, $1,549,520 (M); expenditures, $92,040, including $81,232 for grants to individuals.
Purpose and activities: Giving for two scholarship programs: John Q. Schisler Graduate Awards are for outstanding students studying in a professional graduate school who belong to the United Methodist Church and who have chosen a career as a professional Christian educator in the local church; Seneker Scholarship Awards are awarded to first-year students in the Master of Religious Education program at Perkins School of Theology.
Types of support: Student aid.
Application information: Application form required.

Deadline(s): John Q. Schisler Graduate Awards - Feb. 1; Seneker Scholarship Awards - Mar. 15
Final notification: Late Apr. for both awards
Trustee: NCNB Texas National Bank.
Employer Identification Number: 756318275

7040
W. L. & Louise E. Seymour Foundation ⌑
c/o MTrust El Paso, N.A.
P.O. Box 1072
El Paso 79958 (915) 546-4369

Established in 1983 in TX.
Donor(s): Louise E. Seymour.†
Foundation type: Independent
Financial data (yr. ended 3/31/87): Assets, $3,149,096 (M); expenditures, $101,687, including $83,000 for 4 grants (high: $50,000; low: $1,000; average: $20,000).
Purpose and activities: Grants primarily for handicapped and homeless children; some support for the aged.
Types of support: Endowment funds.
Limitations: Giving primarily in El Paso, TX. No grants to individuals.
Publications: 990-PF.
Application information:
Initial approach: Letter
Deadline(s): None
Write: Dorothy Hart, V.P. and Trust Officer, MTrust El Paso, N.A.
Trustee: MTrust El Paso, N.A.
Number of staff: None.
Employer Identification Number: 746315820

7041
The M. L. Shanor Foundation ⌑
P.O. Box 7522
Wichita Falls 76307 (817) 761-2401

Donor(s): N.T.P. Co.
Foundation type: Independent
Financial data (yr. ended 12/31/88): Assets, $1,932,541 (M); gifts received, $34,132; expenditures, $129,152, including $16,400 for 12 grants (high: $6,000; low: $100) and $92,175 for 70 loans to individuals.
Purpose and activities: Scholarship loans to individuals; grants also to local charitable organizations, including higher education.
Types of support: General purposes, student loans.
Limitations: Giving primarily in TX, with emphasis on Cherokee, Midland, Wichita, and Wilbarger counties.
Application information: Application form required for student loans.
Deadline(s): Aug. 1 for student loans
Write: J.B. Jarratt, Pres.
Officer and Directors: J.B. Jarratt, Pres.; Alvin Barnes, V.P.; J.C. Henderson, V.P.; Frank W. Jarratt, Secy.-Treas.; Ernestine Jarratt.
Employer Identification Number: 756012834

7042
Charles S. and Ruth C. Sharp Foundation, Inc. ⌑
c/o Security Bank Bldg., No. 504
2626 Cole Ave.
Dallas 75204

Incorporated in 1965 in TX.
Donor(s): Charles S. Sharp, Ruth Collins Sharp.
Foundation type: Independent
Financial data (yr. ended 12/31/86): Assets, $3,274,042 (M); gifts received, $56,393; expenditures, $316,396, including $279,000 for 21 grants (high: $65,000; low: $1,000).
Purpose and activities: Emphasis on Protestant church support, higher education, hospitals, and youth agencies.
Types of support: Operating budgets, general purposes.
Limitations: Giving primarily in Dallas, TX.
Application information:
Write: Ruth Collins Sharp, Pres.
Officers and Directors: Ruth Collins Sharp, Pres.; Margot Cryer, Secy.-Treas.; Sally S. Jacobson, Susan S. McAdam, Charles S. Sharp, Jr.
Employer Identification Number: 756045366

7043
Shell Oil Company Foundation ▼
(Formerly Shell Companies Foundation, Inc.)
Two Shell Plaza
P.O. Box 2099
Houston 77252 (713) 241-3616

Incorporated in 1953 in NY.
Donor(s): Shell Oil Co., and other participating companies.
Foundation type: Company-sponsored
Financial data (yr. ended 12/31/89): Assets, $14,067,360 (M); gifts received, $10,562,107; expenditures, $17,398,487, including $13,734,446 for 1,350 grants (high: $200,000; low: $500; average: $5,000-$150,000) and $1,498,956 for 700 employee matching gifts.
Purpose and activities: Preferred areas of giving are education and community funds. About 62 percent of the budget channeled through a number of planned programs that provide student aid, faculty development, basic research grants, and departmental grants to some 700 colleges and universities (three-quarters of these schools participate in Shell Matching Gifts Program only), and to a few national educational organizations. Main interests in education are engineering, science, and business. Approximately 18 percent of the budget directed to United Way organizations in cities or towns where Shell employees reside. The remaining funds paid to a number of national organizations concerned with a broad range of needs and to local organizations in communities where significant numbers of Shell employees reside.
Types of support: Continuing support, employee matching gifts, fellowships, general purposes, operating budgets, professorships, publications, research, scholarship funds, special projects, employee-related scholarships, renovation projects, capital campaigns.
Limitations: Giving primarily in areas of company operations. No support for special requests of colleges, universities, and college fundraising associations, or hospital operating expenses. No grants to individuals, or for endowment funds, capital campaigns of national organizations, or development funds; no loans.
Publications: Corporate giving report (including application guidelines).
Application information: Scholarship programs administered through National Merit Scholarship Corp. Application form not required.
Initial approach: Letter
Copies of proposal: 1
Deadline(s): Submit proposal Jan. through Aug.; deadline Aug. 31
Board meeting date(s): Dec. and Mar.
Final notification: 1 month
Write: Doris J. O'Connor, Sr. V.P., or R.L. Kuhns, Secy.
Officers and Directors:* Frank H. Richardson,* Pres. and Exec. Comm. Chair.; Doris J. O'Connor,* Sr. V.P. and Member, Exec. Comm.; L.E. Sloan,* V.P. and Member, Exec. Comm.; B.W. Levan,* V.P.; Ron L. Kuhns, Secy.; N.E. Gautier, Treas.; P.J. Carroll,* Member, Exec. Comm.; J.E. Little,* Member, Exec. Comm.; M.K. Seggerman,* Member, Exec. Comm.; R. Lopez, S.L. Miller, L.L. Smith, R.M. Sprague, J.R. Street, C.W. Wilson.
Number of staff: 5 full-time professional; 4 full-time support.
Employer Identification Number: 136066583

7044
M. C. Shook Trust ⌑ ☆
c/o Texas Commerce Bank, Trust Dept.
P.O. Box 5291
San Angelo 76902-5291

Established in 1955.
Donor(s): Melvin C. Shook.
Foundation type: Independent
Financial data (yr. ended 12/31/88): Assets, $1,165,576 (M); gifts received, $62,652; expenditures, $91,084, including $83,177 for 11 grants (high: $34,467; low: $25).
Purpose and activities: Giving primarily for a Christian church; support also for social service and youth agencies, a university, and health institutions.
Types of support: General purposes, scholarship funds.
Limitations: Giving primarily in San Angelo, TX.
Application information:
Initial approach: Letter
Deadline(s): None
Final notification: Within 1 month
Write: Spencer Kissell
Trustee: Texas Commerce Bank.
Employer Identification Number: 756022499

7045
Harold Simmons Foundation
Three Lincoln Ctr.
5430 LBJ Freeway, Suite 1700
Dallas 75240

Incorporated in 1988 in TX.
Donor(s): NL Industries, Inc., and subsidiaries, Contran Corp.
Foundation type: Company-sponsored
Financial data (yr. ended 12/31/89): Assets, $22,459 (M); gifts received, $1,000,000; qualifying distributions, $4,177,548, including $3,146,214 for 170 grants (high: $1,250,000; low: $100; average: $1,000-$5,000), $51,367 for 223 employee matching gifts and $979,967 for in-kind gifts.
Purpose and activities: Grants for community programs and projects, health and social

welfare agencies, culture and art, child development, youth, and education.
Types of support: Annual campaigns, building funds, continuing support, emergency funds, employee matching gifts, operating budgets, renovation projects, research, seed money, special projects.
Limitations: Giving limited to the Dallas, TX, area. No grants to individuals, or for endowment funds; no loans to individuals.
Publications: Application guidelines.
Application information: Application form not required.
Initial approach: Proposal
Copies of proposal: 1
Deadline(s): None
Board meeting date(s): As needed
Final notification: 3 months
Write: Lisa K. Simmons, Pres.
Officers and Directors:* Harold Simmons,* Chair.; Lisa K. Simmons,* Pres.; Steven L. Watson,* V.P. and Secy.; Gene Anderson, Treas.
Number of staff: 1 full-time professional; 1 full-time support.
Employer Identification Number: 752222091

7046
Clara Blackford Smith and W. Aubrey Smith Charitable Foundation ⌑
c/o NCNB Texas National Bank
300 West Main St.
Denison 75020 (214) 465-2131

Established in 1985 in TX.
Donor(s): Clara Blackford Smith.†
Foundation type: Independent
Financial data (yr. ended 6/30/88): Assets, $13,159,550 (M); expenditures, $827,425, including $737,248 for 15 grants (high: $400,000; low: $972).
Purpose and activities: Giving primarily for a medical center building fund, higher education, social services, and cultural organizations.
Types of support: Building funds.
Limitations: Giving primarily in Denison, TX.
Application information: Application form required.
Deadline(s): None
Officers: Charles H. Green, Chair.; Jane Ayres, Trust Officer.
Directors: Jack G. Berry, Wayne E. Delaney, Jerdy Gary, Roy L. McKinney III.
Trustee: NCNB Texas National Bank.
Employer Identification Number: 756314114

7047
Bob and Vivian Smith Foundation ⌑
2000 West Loop South, Suite 1900
Houston 77027 (713) 622-8611

Established about 1969.
Donor(s): R.E. Smith, Vivian L. Smith.
Foundation type: Independent
Financial data (yr. ended 12/31/88): Assets, $6,854,429 (M); expenditures, $356,504, including $350,000 for 11 grants (high: $75,000; low: $10,000).
Purpose and activities: Emphasis on medical research and secondary education.
Types of support: General purposes.
Limitations: Giving primarily in Houston, TX. No grants to individuals, or for program-related investments.
Application information: Application form not required.
Initial approach: Proposal
Deadline(s): None
Write: W.N. Finnegan III, Trustee
Officers: Vivian L. Smith,* Pres.; Suzanne R. Benson, Secy.
Trustees:* Bobby Smith Cohn, Sandra Smith Dompier, W.N. Finnegan III.
Employer Identification Number: 237029052

7048
Vivian L. Smith Foundation ⌑
2000 West Loop South, Suite 1900
Houston 77027 (713) 622-8611

Established in 1981 in TX.
Donor(s): Vivian L. Smith.
Foundation type: Independent
Financial data (yr. ended 12/31/87): Assets, $3,265,991 (M); expenditures, $163,956, including $162,318 for 20 grants (high: $71,000; low: $1,000).
Purpose and activities: Giving primarily for cultural programs; some support for education.
Types of support: General purposes.
Limitations: Giving primarily in Houston, TX. No grants to individuals.
Application information: Application form not required.
Initial approach: Letter or proposal
Deadline(s): None
Write: W.N. Finnegan
Officers and Trustees: Vivian L. Smith, Pres. and Treas.; R.A. Seale, Jr., V.P. and Secy.; Richard H. Skinner, Jack T. Trotter.
Employer Identification Number: 760101380

7049
Vivian L. Smith Foundation for Restorative Neurology ⌑
2000 West Loop South, Suite 1900
Houston 77027
Application address: 7000 Fannin, Suite 2140, Houston, TX 77030; Tel.: (713) 797-1388

Established in 1981 in TX.
Donor(s): Vivian L. Smith.
Foundation type: Operating
Financial data (yr. ended 12/31/87): Assets, $6,686,821 (M); gifts received, $5,475,399; expenditures, $1,627,242, including $95,947 for 10 grants to individuals (high: $30,000; low: $632).
Purpose and activities: A private operating foundation; primary purpose to promote the development of and provide support for research in restorative neurology.
Types of support: Research.
Application information:
Initial approach: Proposal
Deadline(s): None
Write: Dr. Milan Dimitrijevic, Research Dir.
Officers: Vivian L. Smith,* Pres.; R.A. Seale, Jr.,* V.P.; Ed McCraw, Secy.-Treas.
Trustees:* Delmer Q. Bowman, W.N. Finnegan, Dee S. Osborne.
Employer Identification Number: 742139770

7050
South Texas Charitable Foundation ⌑
P.O. Box 2549
Victoria 77902 (512) 573-4383

Established in 1981 in TX.
Donor(s): Maude O'Connor Williams.
Foundation type: Independent
Financial data (yr. ended 11/30/88): Assets, $7,157,270 (M); gifts received, $20,000; expenditures, $405,058, including $405,000 for 6 grants (high: $200,000; low: $6,000).
Purpose and activities: Support for cancer research and social services.
Limitations: Giving primarily in TX.
Application information: Application form not required.
Deadline(s): None
Write: Rayford L. Keller, Secy.-Treas.
Officers: Maude O'Connor Williams, Pres.; Roger P. Williams, V.P.; Rayford L. Keller, Secy.-Treas.
Employer Identification Number: 742148107

7051
Nelda C. and H. J. Lutcher Stark Foundation ⌑
602 West Main St.
P.O. Box 909
Orange 77631-0909 (409) 883-3513

Incorporated in 1961 in TX.
Donor(s): H.J. Lutcher Stark,† Nelda C. Stark.
Foundation type: Independent
Financial data (yr. ended 2/28/88): Assets, $73,655,532 (M); gifts received, $950,000; expenditures, $1,946,037, including $145,850 for 6 grants (high: $105,850; low: $3,000), $1,250 for 3 grants to individuals (high: $500; low: $250) and $1,386,149 for 2 foundation-administered programs.
Purpose and activities: Grants primarily for education, historical restoration, and the performing arts; operating programs include the construction, operation, and maintenance of a museum to house and exhibit an extensive art collection owned by the foundation and to underwrite performances of a theater for the performing arts.
Types of support: Student aid.
Limitations: Giving limited to TX and southwest LA. No grants to individuals (except limited scholarships), or for endowment funds or operating budgets.
Application information:
Initial approach: Brief letter
Deadline(s): None
Board meeting date(s): Monthly
Final notification: 1 month
Write: Clyde V. McKee, Jr., Secy.-Treas.
Officers and Trustees: Nelda C. Stark, Chair.; Eunice R. Benckenstein, Vice-Chair.; Clyde V. McKee, Jr., Secy.-Treas.; William J. Butler, Sidney H. Phillips, W.G. Riedel III, John C. Sargent, Homer B.H. Stark.
Number of staff: 6 full-time professional; 34 full-time support.
Employer Identification Number: 746047440

7052
Dorothy Richard Starling Foundation ⌑
P.O. Box 66527
Houston 77266 (713) 651-9102

Foundation established in 1969 in TX.
Donor(s): Frank M. Starling.†
Foundation type: Independent
Financial data (yr. ended 12/31/88): Assets, $11,943,120 (M); expenditures, $878,212, including $787,000 for 6 grants (high: $390,000; low: $15,000).
Purpose and activities: Support for classical violin performance, education, and programs.
Types of support: Endowment funds.
Application information:
Initial approach: Letter
Deadline(s): None
Final notification: Within 60 days
Write: Any of the trustees
Trustees: Robert K. Jewett, A.C. Speyer, Jr., H. Allen Weatherby.
Employer Identification Number: 746121656

7053
B. A. and Elinor Steinhagen Benevolent Trust
c/o First City, Texas-Beaumont, N.A.
P.O. Box 3391
Beaumont 77704

Trust established in 1939 in TX.
Donor(s): B.A. Steinhagen,† Elinor Steinhagen.†
Foundation type: Independent
Financial data (yr. ended 08/31/89): Assets, $3,393,149 (M); expenditures, $250,119, including $228,870 for 18 grants (high: $50,000; low: $1,500; average: $10,000-$20,000).
Purpose and activities: Giving for the housing and general assistance of the elderly and the helpless and afflicted of any age.
Types of support: Seed money, building funds, equipment, land acquisition, matching funds, research, publications, endowment funds.
Limitations: Giving limited to Jefferson County, TX. No grants to individuals, or for operating budgets, continuing support, annual campaigns, emergency funds, deficit financing, special projects, conferences, scholarships, or fellowships; no loans.
Publications: Application guidelines.
Application information: Application form required.
Initial approach: Letter
Copies of proposal: 1
Deadline(s): May 31
Board meeting date(s): Annually
Final notification: End of Aug.
Write: Pam Parish, Trust Officer
Trustee: First City, Texas-Beaumont, N.A.
Number of staff: None.
Employer Identification Number: 746039544

7054
Stemmons Foundation ⌑
1200 Tower East
2700 Stemmons Freeway
Dallas 75207 (214) 631-7910

Established in 1963 in TX.
Foundation type: Independent
Financial data (yr. ended 12/31/88): Assets, $3,460,519 (M); gifts received, $477,711; expenditures, $247,906, including $216,400 for 72 grants (high: $30,000; low: $100).
Purpose and activities: Giving for cultural programs, youth agencies, social services, health agencies, and education.
Types of support: Scholarship funds.
Limitations: Giving primarily in Dallas, TX.
Application information:
Initial approach: Proposal
Write: Ann M. Roberts, Secy.-Treas.
Officers: John M. Stemmons, Sr., Pres.; Allison S. Simon, V.P.; Heinz K. Simon, V.P.; Ruth T. Stemmons, V.P.; Ann M. Roberts, Secy.-Treas.; John M. Stemmons, Jr., Secy.-Treas.
Employer Identification Number: 756039966

7055
Arthur T. and Jane J. Stieren Foundation ⌑
D-101 Petroleum Ctr.
San Antonio 78209

Established in 1984 in TX.
Donor(s): Arthur T. Stieren, Jane J. Stieren.
Foundation type: Independent
Financial data (yr. ended 12/31/88): Assets, $2,110,438 (M); gifts received, $300,000; expenditures, $107,760, including $100,000 for 2 grants.
Purpose and activities: Giving for an opera company and a museum.
Limitations: Giving primarily in TX and NM. No grants to individuals.
Application information: Contributes only to pre-selected organizations personally known to the trustees. Applications not accepted.
Trustees: Arthur T. Stieren, Jane J. Stieren.
Employer Identification Number: 742346000

7056
Still Water Foundation, Inc.
c/o Arthur H. Coleman
P.O. Box 161957
Austin 78716

Established in 1982 in NM.
Donor(s): Julia Matthews Wilkinson.
Foundation type: Independent
Financial data (yr. ended 06/30/89): Assets, $115,228 (M); gifts received, $280,000; expenditures, $287,334, including $278,201 for 15 grants (high: $100,000; low: $1,691).
Purpose and activities: Emphasis on higher education.
Types of support: General purposes.
Limitations: No grants to individuals.
Application information: Application form not required.
Officers and Director:* Julia Matthews Wilkinson, Pres.; Arthur H. Coleman,* Secy.-Treas.
Number of staff: None.
Employer Identification Number: 850307646

7057
Ann Bradshaw Stokes Foundation ⌑
3204 Beverly Dr.
Dallas 75205 (214) 528-1924

Established in 1982 in TX.
Donor(s): Ann Bradshaw Stokes.†
Foundation type: Independent
Financial data (yr. ended 12/31/87): Assets, $1,804,693 (M); expenditures, $125,814, including $94,145 for 19 grants (high: $8,889; low: $1,408).
Purpose and activities: Grants limited to drama departments of TX colleges and universities for scholarship aid and department projects.
Types of support: Student aid, equipment, special projects.
Limitations: Giving limited to TX.
Publications: Informational brochure (including application guidelines).
Application information: Contact school's drama department. Application form required.
Copies of proposal: 1
Trustee: William N. Stokes, Jr.
Number of staff: None.
Employer Identification Number: 751866981

7058
Eusebia S. Stonestreet Trust ☆
c/o NCNB Texas National Bank
P.O. Box 1317
Fort Worth 76101

Foundation type: Independent
Financial data (yr. ended 10/31/88): Assets, $4,337,743 (M); expenditures, $420,987, including $365,272 for 2 grants of $182,636 each.
Purpose and activities: Support for social services for children and others.
Limitations: Giving primarily in Fort Worth, TX.
Trustee: NCNB Texas National Bank.
Employer Identification Number: 756009142

7059
Strake Foundation ▼
712 Main St., Suite 3300
Houston 77002-3210 (713) 546-2400

Trust established in 1952 in TX; incorporated in 1983.
Donor(s): George W. Strake, Sr.,† Susan K. Strake,† George W. Strake, Jr., Susan S. Dilworth,† Georganna S. Parsley.
Foundation type: Independent
Financial data (yr. ended 12/31/89): Assets, $23,230,017 (M); expenditures, $1,354,848, including $1,153,400 for 223 grants (high: $100,000; low: $500; average: $1,000-$15,000).
Purpose and activities: Giving primarily to Roman Catholic-affiliated associations, including hospitals and higher and secondary educational institutions; support also for the arts and social services, including programs for youth.
Types of support: Operating budgets, continuing support, annual campaigns, emergency funds, special projects, research, matching funds, general purposes.
Limitations: Giving primarily in TX, especially Houston; no grants outside the U.S. No support for elementary schools. No grants to individuals, or for deficit financing, consulting services, technical assistance, or publications; no loans.
Publications: Annual report (including application guidelines).
Application information: Application form not required.

Initial approach: Brief proposal
Copies of proposal: 1
Deadline(s): Submit proposal preferably in Mar. or Sept.; deadline 1 month prior to board meetings
Board meeting date(s): May or June and Nov. or Dec.
Final notification: 1 month after board meetings
Write: George W. Strake, Jr., Pres.
Officers and Trustees:* George W. Strake, Jr.,* Pres. and Treas.; Georganna S. Parsley,* V.P. and Secy.; Thomas B. Brennan, Robert W. Ligon, Burke M. O'Rourke, Brian S. Parsley, Stephen D. Strake, Colleen D. Stroup, Linda D. Walsh.
Number of staff: 1 part-time professional; 2 part-time support.
Employer Identification Number: 760041524

7060
Eugene Straus Charitable Trust
c/o NCNB Texas National Bank
P.O. Box 830241
Dallas 75283 (214) 508-1965

Trust established in 1975 in TX.
Donor(s): Eugene Straus.†
Foundation type: Independent
Financial data (yr. ended 08/31/89): Assets, $1,900,000 (M); expenditures, $115,000, including $95,000 for 8 grants (high: $24,550; low: $9,200; average: $15,000).
Purpose and activities: For building or maintenance of capital improvements for local charitable, health and social service, and educational organizations.
Types of support: Building funds, renovation projects.
Limitations: Giving limited to Dallas County, TX. No grants to individuals, or for operating budgets, continuing support, annual campaigns, seed money, emergency funds, deficit financing, equipment, land acquisition, special projects, publications, conferences, endowment funds, research, scholarships, fellowships, or matching gifts; no loans.
Publications: Application guidelines.
Application information: Application form not required.
Initial approach: Letter
Copies of proposal: 1
Deadline(s): Submit proposal preferably in Apr.; deadline June 30
Final notification: Aug. 31
Write: D.J. Kelly, V.P.-Trust, NCNB Texas National Bank
Trustee: NCNB Texas National Bank.
Number of staff: None.
Employer Identification Number: 756229249

7061
Hesta Stuart Christian Charitable Trust ⌑
c/o Texas American Bank/Fort Worth
P.O. Box 2050
Fort Worth 76113 (817) 884-4266

Established in 1973 in TX.
Foundation type: Independent
Financial data (yr. ended 6/30/88): Assets, $1,369,531 (M); expenditures, $72,825, including $51,500 for 8 grants (high: $12,500; low: $5,000).
Purpose and activities: Grants to Methodist organizations, including orphanages, hospitals, educational institutions, churches, homes for unwed mothers, and homes for the elderly; grants also for Methodist Church support.
Types of support: General purposes.
Limitations: No grants to individuals.
Application information:
Initial approach: Letter or proposal 2-3 pages long
Deadline(s): Sept. 30
Board meeting date(s): Nov.
Final notification: Prior to Dec. 31
Write: Kelly A. Bradshaw, Mgr.
Officer: Kelly A. Bradshaw, Mgr.
Trustee: Texas American Bank/Fort Worth.
Number of staff: None.
Employer Identification Number: 756177306

7062
Student Aid Foundation Enterprises ⌑
800 Commerce St.
Houston 77002

Established in 1956 in TX.
Donor(s): Frank T. Abraham, J.C. Brown.
Foundation type: Independent
Financial data (yr. ended 6/30/86): Assets, $2,233,094 (M); gifts received, $83,543; expenditures, $129,618, including $16,312 for 2 grants (high: $10,808; low: $5,504) and $5,441 for 4 grants to individuals (high: $1,973; low: $250).
Purpose and activities: Scholarship support for underprivileged youth; support also for higher education.
Types of support: Student aid.
Limitations: Giving primarily in Houston, TX.
Application information:
Initial approach: Letter
Deadline(s): None
Write: Frank T. Abraham, Pres.
Officers: Frank T. Abraham, Pres.; Robert E. Ballard, V.P.; Freeman Bullock, Secy.-Treas.
Directors: J.C. Brown, Chair.; James P. Wallare, Vice-Chair.; Tom Berry, Carl Mueller, Nick C. Nichols.
Employer Identification Number: 746060745

7063
H. E. Stumberg, Sr. Orphans, Crippled Children & Handicapped Persons Trust ☆
Tower Life Bldg., Suite 701
San Antonio 78205 (512) 225-0243

Established in 1960.
Foundation type: Independent
Financial data (yr. ended 12/31/88): Assets, $1,442,575 (M); expenditures, $52,307, including $49,000 for 21 grants (high: $8,500; low: $250).
Purpose and activities: Giving limited to organizations serving handicapped and crippled children or persons.
Limitations: Giving primarily in the Bexar County, TX, area. No grants to individuals.
Application information: Application form not required.
Initial approach: Letter
Copies of proposal: 1
Deadline(s): Oct. 31
Write: Louis H. Stumberg, Trustee
Trustees: Bond Davis, H.E. Stumberg, Jr., Louis H. Stumberg.
Number of staff: 1 part-time professional.
Employer Identification Number: 746063272

7064
Roy and Christine Sturgis Charitable and Educational Trust ▼ ⌑
c/o NCNB Texas National Bank, Trust Div.
P.O. Box 830241
Dallas 75283-0241

Established in 1981 in AR.
Foundation type: Independent
Financial data (yr. ended 9/30/88): Assets, $30,198,477 (M); gifts received, $317,755; expenditures, $2,109,216, including $1,695,500 for 28 grants (high: $300,000; low: $3,000; average: $10,000-$75,000).
Purpose and activities: Support primarily for religious, charitable, scientific, literary, and educational organizations.
Types of support: Building funds, capital campaigns, endowment funds, general purposes, matching funds, operating budgets, research, special projects.
Limitations: Giving primarily in AR and TX. No grants to individuals; no loans.
Publications: Application guidelines.
Application information: Requests are considered only once every two years. No personal interviews granted.
Initial approach: Letter or proposal
Copies of proposal: 2
Deadline(s): Mar. 1
Board meeting date(s): Apr.
Final notification: May
Trustee: NCNB Texas National Bank.
Number of staff: None.
Employer Identification Number: 756331832

7065
The Summerlee Foundation ⌑ ☆
One Preston Ctr.
8222 Douglas Ave., Suite 580
Dallas 75225

Established in 1988 in TX.
Donor(s): Annie Lee Roberts.
Foundation type: Independent
Financial data (yr. ended 06/30/89): Assets, $4,121,070 (M); gifts received, $4,014,356; expenditures, $70,901, including $13,500 for 2 grants (high: $11,000; low: $2,500).
Purpose and activities: Giving limited to: 1) the alleviation of pain and suffering and the prevention of cruelty to animals, and 2) for the study, promotion, preservation, and documentation of all facets of TX history.
Limitations: Giving primarily in TX and SD. No support for religious purposes. No grants to individuals; no loans.
Application information:
Initial approach: Letter
Deadline(s): Dec. 15, Mar. 15, June 15, and Sept. 15
Board meeting date(s): Jan., Apr., July, and Oct.
Write: David D. Jackson, V.P.

Officers: Annie Lee Roberts, Pres.; David D. Jackson, V.P., Secy.-Treas., and Mgr.; Mary Lavinia Griffith, V.P.
Employer Identification Number: 758314010

7066
Hatton W. Sumners Foundation ▼ ⌘
NCNB Center Tower III
325 North St. Paul, Suite 3333
Dallas 75201 (214) 220-2128

Trust established in 1949 in TX.
Foundation type: Independent
Financial data (yr. ended 12/31/88): Assets, $29,634,279 (M); gifts received, $6,000; expenditures, $1,553,432, including $1,306,500 for 27 grants (high: $323,000; low: $4,500; average: $20,000-$100,000).
Purpose and activities: Giving for youth organizations and higher education for the study and teaching of the science of self-government.
Types of support: Endowment funds.
Limitations: Giving primarily in TX and the southwestern states.
Application information:
Initial approach: Letter
Deadline(s): No set deadline for grants; scholarship program deadlines decided by university administering program
Board meeting date(s): Varies
Final notification: Usually in the fall
Write: Gordon R. Carpenter, Exec. Dir.
Officers and Trustees:* J. Cleo Thompson, Jr.,* Chair.; Charles E. Long, Jr.,* Vice-Chair.; William C. Pannell,* Secy.; Thomas S. Walker,* Treas.; Gordon R. Carpenter,* Exec. Dir.; Alfred P. Murrah, Jr.
Number of staff: 2
Employer Identification Number: 756003490

7067
Sunnyside, Inc. ⌘
8609 N.W. Plaza Dr., Suite 201
Dallas 75225 (214) 692-5686

Established in 1928 in TX.
Donor(s): I. Jalonick.†
Foundation type: Independent
Financial data (yr. ended 12/31/86): Assets, $1,303,662 (M); gifts received, $183,135; expenditures, $212,142, including $80,000 for 1 grant and $99,731 for 83 grants to individuals (high: $6,659; low: $150).
Purpose and activities: Grants to organizations and underprivileged children to provide for physical, moral, intellectual, and spiritual needs.
Types of support: Grants to individuals, student aid.
Application information: Application form required.
Deadline(s): None
Write: Mary Rothenflue, Exec. Dir.
Officers: Alex Bul,* Pres.; Fred Kull,* V.P.; Hugh E. Prather, Jr.,* V.P.-Finance; E.R. Slaughter, Jr.,* V.P.-Finance; Linda Slaughter,* Secy.; Alan Bashor,* Treas.; Mary Rothenflue, Exec. Dir.
Trustees:* Grace Lyon.
Employer Identification Number: 756037004

7068
Swalm Foundation ⌘
8707 Katy Freeway, Suite 300
Houston 77024

Established in 1980 in TX.
Donor(s): Dave C. Swalm, Ron Woliver, Texas Olefins Co.
Foundation type: Independent
Financial data (yr. ended 11/30/89): Assets, $12,813,020 (M); gifts received, $4,452,018; expenditures, $292,578, including $291,625 for 37 grants (high: $50,000; low: $1,000).
Purpose and activities: Support for social services and higher education.
Types of support: Scholarship funds, general purposes, endowment funds, building funds, renovation projects.
Limitations: Giving primarily in TX.
Application information:
Initial approach: Letter
Deadline(s): None
Write: Jo Beth Camp Swalm, Pres.
Officers and Trustees:* Jo Beth Camp Swalm,* Pres.; Dave C. Swalm,* V.P.; Mark C. Mendelovitz,* Secy.
Employer Identification Number: 742073420

7069
Anne Burnett and Charles D. Tandy Foundation ▼
801 Cherry St., Suite 1577
Fort Worth 76102 (817) 877-3344

Established in 1978 in TX.
Donor(s): Anne Burnett Tandy,† Charles D. Tandy,† Ben Bird.
Foundation type: Independent
Financial data (yr. ended 12/31/89): Assets, $186,291,319 (M); expenditures, $8,015,316, including $6,849,945 for 64 grants (high: $1,000,000; low: $5,000; average: $10,000-$100,000).
Purpose and activities: Support for health care and cultural organizations, including major museum projects; support also for social service and youth agencies, community affairs, and education.
Types of support: General purposes, capital campaigns, special projects, technical assistance, seed money.
Limitations: Giving primarily in the Fort Worth, TX, area. No grants to individuals, or for scholarships or fellowships.
Publications: Program policy statement, application guidelines, annual report (including application guidelines).
Application information: Application form required.
Initial approach: Letter
Copies of proposal: 1
Deadline(s): None
Board meeting date(s): Generally in Mar., June, and Nov.
Final notification: 90 days
Write: Thomas F. Beech, V.P.
Officers and Trustees:* Anne W. Marion,* Pres.; Edward R. Hudson, Jr.,* V.P. and Secy.; Benjamin J. Fortson, V.P. and Treas.; Perry R. Bass,* V.P.; Thomas F. Beech, V.P.; John L. Marion.
Number of staff: 1 full-time professional; 1 full-time support.
Employer Identification Number: 751638517

7070
David L. Tandy Foundation
8937 Random Rd.
Fort Worth 76179 (817) 236-7908

Established in 1968 in TX.
Foundation type: Independent
Financial data (yr. ended 05/31/88): Assets, $2,902,387 (M); expenditures, $143,872, including $126,000 for 30 grants (high: $20,000; low: $1,000).
Purpose and activities: Giving for educational and cultural programs and social services.
Limitations: Giving primarily in TX.
Application information: Applications not accepted.
Board meeting date(s): 2nd Monday in July
Write: William H. Michero, V.P. and Secy.
Officers and Directors:* Emmett Duemke,* Pres.; William H. Michero,* V.P. and Secy.; B.R. Roland,* V.P. and Treas.; A.R. Tandy, Jr., V.P.; Mrs. E.C. Whitney, V.P.
Number of staff: None.
Employer Identification Number: 756083140

7071
The Community Foundation of Metropolitan Tarrant County
(Formerly The Community Trust of Metropolitan Tarrant County)
Fort Worth Club Bldg.
306 West Seventh St., Suite 702
Fort Worth 76102 (817) 877-0702

Established in 1981 in TX as a program of the United Way; status changed to independent community foundation in 1989.
Foundation type: Community
Financial data (yr. ended 12/31/89): Assets, $18,980,205 (M); gifts received, $322,740; expenditures, $942,305, including $671,529 for 72 grants (high: $48,000; low: $253; average: $1,000-$5,000).
Purpose and activities: Support for community development, social services, education, youth, health, and arts and cultural programs; emphasis on one-time grants to new and innovative programs.
Types of support: General purposes, seed money, special projects, internships, renovation projects, scholarship funds.
Limitations: Giving primarily in Tarrant County, TX. No support for secular, religious, political, or fraternal organizations. No grants to individuals, or for annual or capital campaigns, deficit financing, endowment or emergency funds, matching grants, operating budgets, publications, research, continuing support, or conferences and seminars.
Publications: Application guidelines, annual report, informational brochure.
Application information: Application form not required.
Initial approach: Letter to request guidelines
Copies of proposal: 1
Deadline(s): Apr. 15 and Oct. 15
Board meeting date(s): June and Dec.
Final notification: June 30 and Dec. 31
Write: James R. Holcomb, Pres.
Officers and Directors:* Robert W. Decker,* Chair.; Leland Hodges, Vice-Chair.; James R. Holcomb, Pres. and Exec. Dir.; Lynda Roodhouse, Secy.; Lloyd J. Weaver, Treas.; Louise Appleman, Paul H. Brandt, Ronald

Clinkscale, Tom Cravens, Marcus Ginsburg, Marty Leonard, Jim Nichols, Robert S. Patterson, Bruce Petty, Earle A. Shields.
Number of staff: 1 full-time professional; 1 full-time support.
Employer Identification Number: 752267767

7072
Hope Pierce Tartt Scholarship Fund ⌑
P.O. Box 1964
Marshall 75671 (214) 938-6622

Trust established in 1978 in TX.
Donor(s): Hope Pierce Tartt.†
Foundation type: Independent
Financial data (yr. ended 05/31/89): Assets, $7,454,743 (M); expenditures, $542,003, including $491,000 for 28 grants (high: $100,250; low: $750).
Purpose and activities: To assist in providing education for East Texas students at private institutions.
Types of support: Scholarship funds.
Limitations: Giving primarily in Harrison, Gregg, Marion, Panola, and Upshur counties, TX.
Publications: Program policy statement, application guidelines.
Application information: Application form required.
Initial approach: Letter
Copies of proposal: 1
Deadline(s): None
Board meeting date(s): Feb. and as required
Write: Rev. Pat Day, Vice-Chair.
Officers: E.N. Smith, Jr., Chair.; Rev. R. Pat Day, Vice-Chair.; William L. Gaw, Vice-Chair.; James Heflin, Vice-Chair.; Robert L. Duvall, Secy.-Treas.
Employer Identification Number: 756263272

7073
The Taub Foundation ⌑
Texan Bldg.
333 West Loop North, 4th Fl.
Houston 77024 (713) 688-2426

Incorporated in 1953 in TX.
Donor(s): Henry J.N. Taub, Ben Taub.
Foundation type: Independent
Financial data (yr. ended 6/30/88): Assets, $3,116,728 (M); gifts received, $197,788; expenditures, $67,198, including $45,948 for 289 grants (high: $5,000; low: $25).
Purpose and activities: Support for education, social services, and health associations.
Limitations: Giving primarily in TX.
Application information: Contributes only to pre-selected organizations. Applications not accepted.
Trustees: Gail Hendryx, H. Ben Taub, Henry J.N. Taub, Henry J.N. Taub II, John B. Taub, Marcy E. Taub, I. Mark Westheimer.
Employer Identification Number: 746060216

7074
Taylor Family Foundation ⌑ ☆
4149 Ranier Court
Fort Worth 76109

Donor(s): Bob Benjamin Taylor, Linda R. Taylor, Sol Taylor, Thomas M. Taylor.
Foundation type: Independent
Financial data (yr. ended 12/31/88): Assets, $656,559 (M); gifts received, $200,300; expenditures, $124,378, including $123,592 for 19 grants (high: $55,750; low: $100).
Purpose and activities: Giving primarily for welfare, medical research, Jewish organizations, and wildlife preservation.
Types of support: Operating budgets, research, equipment.
Limitations: Giving primarily in Fort Worth, TX.
Application information: Contributes only to pre-selected organizations. Applications not accepted.
Trustees: Annette B. Taylor, Bob Benjamin Taylor, Linda R. Taylor, Sol Taylor, Thomas M. Taylor.
Employer Identification Number: 751665622

7075
T. L. L. Temple Foundation ▼
109 Temple Blvd.
Lufkin 75901 (409) 639-5197

Trust established in 1962 in TX.
Donor(s): Georgie T. Munz,† Katherine S. Temple.†
Foundation type: Independent
Financial data (yr. ended 11/30/89): Assets, $242,162,688 (M); gifts received, $100,000; expenditures, $10,290,979, including $10,009,877 for 178 grants (high: $1,250,000; low: $1,000; average: $1,000-$55,000).
Purpose and activities: Support for education, health, and community and social services; support also for civic affairs and cultural programs.
Types of support: Operating budgets, seed money, emergency funds, building funds, equipment, matching funds, scholarship funds, special projects, research, conferences and seminars.
Limitations: Giving primarily in counties in TX constituting the East Texas Pine Timber Belt. No support for private foundations, or religious organizations for religious purposes. No grants to individuals, or for continuing support, annual campaigns, deficit financing, or endowment funds; no loans.
Publications: Application guidelines, program policy statement.
Application information: Application form required.
Initial approach: Letter
Copies of proposal: 1
Deadline(s): None
Board meeting date(s): Monthly
Final notification: 2 months
Write: Ward R. Burke, Exec. Secy.
Officers and Trustees:* Arthur Temple,* Chair.; Ward R. Burke,* Exec. Secy.; M.F. Zeagler,* Controller; Phillip M. Leach, Arthur Temple III, W. Temple Webber, Jr.
Number of staff: 4 full-time professional; 2 full-time support.
Employer Identification Number: 756037406

7076
Temple-Inland Foundation
303 South Temple Dr.
P.O. Drawer 338
Diboll 75941 (409) 829-1313

Established in 1985 in TX.
Donor(s): Temple-Inland, Inc.
Foundation type: Company-sponsored
Financial data (yr. ended 06/30/89): Assets, $10,283,014 (M); gifts received, $5,000,000; expenditures, $1,088,413, including $544,404 for 50 grants (high: $100,000; low: $200), $335,200 for 293 grants to individuals (high: $3,000; low: $1,000) and $184,885 for 352 employee matching gifts.
Purpose and activities: Makes employee-matching contributions in various fields, including arts, culture, and higher and secondary education; and supports a scholarship program for children of employees of Temple-Inland.
Types of support: Employee matching gifts, general purposes, research, employee-related scholarships.
Limitations: No grants to individuals (except for employee-related scholarships).
Publications: 990-PF.
Application information: Contributes only to pre-selected organizations; application forms required for scholarships.
Initial approach: Letter
Copies of proposal: 1
Deadline(s): Mar. 15 for scholarships
Board meeting date(s): Varies
Final notification: June 1 for new scholarship applications; Aug. 15 for renewals
Write: M. Richard Warner, Pres.
Officers: M. Richard Warner, Pres.; Roger D. Ericson,* V.P.; James R. Wash, Secy.-Treas.
Directors:* Clifford J. Grum, W. Wayne McDonald.
Number of staff: None.
Employer Identification Number: 751977109

7077
The Terry Foundation ⌑ ☆
600 Jefferson, Suite 1600
Houston 77002

Established in 1986 in TX.
Donor(s): Howard L. Terry.
Foundation type: Independent
Financial data (yr. ended 12/31/89): Assets, $4,877,401 (M); gifts received, $1,582,071; expenditures, $368,406, including $356,250 for grants to individuals.
Purpose and activities: Scholarships for students attending local universities.
Types of support: Student aid.
Limitations: Giving limited to TX.
Application information: Contact the University of Texas at Austin and Texas A&M University for deadlines. Application form required.
Trustees: Rhett Campbell, Carter Overton, Darrell K. Royal, John W. Storms, Howard L. Terry.
Employer Identification Number: 760224312

7078
Texas Commerce Bank Foundation of Texas Commerce Bank - Houston, Inc. ▼
c/o Texas Commerce Bank-Houston
P.O. Box 2558
Houston 77252-8050 (713) 236-4004

Incorporated in 1952 in TX.
Donor(s): Texas Commerce Bank-Houston.

Foundation type: Company-sponsored
Financial data (yr. ended 12/31/88): Assets, $519,282 (M); gifts received, $840,000; expenditures, $648,952, including $618,553 for grants and $30,200 for employee matching gifts.
Purpose and activities: Giving for a community fund and community development, cultural programs, including museums and the performing arts, higher and other education, and health and medical research organizations; support also for social service agencies, including programs for minorities, child welfare, the homeless, and drug abuse.
Types of support: Annual campaigns, building funds, continuing support, employee matching gifts, research, capital campaigns, in-kind gifts.
Limitations: Giving limited to the Houston, TX, area. No grants to individuals, or for endowment funds; no loans.
Publications: Corporate giving report, application guidelines.
Application information: Application form not required.
Initial approach: Letter
Copies of proposal: 1
Deadline(s): 15th of each month
Board meeting date(s): Last Thursday of each month
Write: Carol Bohannon
Officers: Marc J. Shapiro, Chair.; Marshall Tyndall, Pres.; Shelby R. Rogers, Secy.; Beverly McCaskill, Treas.
Number of staff: 1 full-time professional.
Employer Identification Number: 746036696

7079
Texas Industries Foundation ⌑
8100 Carpenter Freeway
Dallas 75247 (214) 637-3100

Incorporated in 1965 in TX.
Donor(s): Texas Industries, Inc.
Foundation type: Company-sponsored
Financial data (yr. ended 12/31/88): Assets, $622 (M); gifts received, $150,063; expenditures, $150,063, including $133,491 for 47 grants (high: $22,400; low: $100; average: $2,000) and $16,572 for 5 grants to individuals.
Purpose and activities: Giving with emphasis on higher education, including scholarships for dependents of company employees, and community funds.
Types of support: Employee-related scholarships, building funds, research, scholarship funds, employee matching gifts.
Limitations: Giving primarily in TX, LA, and MS. No grants for operating funds.
Application information: Application form not required.
Deadline(s): Jan. 15 for scholarships
Write: James R. McCraw, Controller
Officers: Robert D. Rogers,* Pres.; R.W. Fowler, V.P. and Treas.; Robert C. Moore, Secy.
Directors:* Ralph B. Rogers, Chair.; Peter F. Carleton.
Number of staff: None.
Employer Identification Number: 756043179

7080
Texas Instruments Foundation ▼
13500 North Central Expressway
P.O. Box 655474, Mail Station 232
Dallas 75265 (214) 995-3172

Trust established in 1951 in TX; incorporated in 1964.
Donor(s): Texas Instruments, Inc., and wholly-owned subsidiaries.
Foundation type: Company-sponsored
Financial data (yr. ended 12/31/89): Assets, $13,024,146 (M); gifts received, $500,000; expenditures, $1,390,950, including $894,100 for 70 grants (high: $30,000; low: $1,000; average: $1,000-$10,000), $50,000 for 1 grant to an individual and $446,850 for employee matching gifts.
Purpose and activities: Giving largely for community funds; grants also for higher and secondary education, including employee matching gifts, hospitals, youth agencies, and cultural programs; Founders' Prize awarded for outstanding achievement in the physical, health, or management sciences, or mathematics.
Types of support: Employee matching gifts, building funds, scholarship funds, research, continuing support, capital campaigns, renovation projects.
Limitations: No grants to individuals (except for Founders' Prize award), or for company products or advertising; no loans.
Application information: Application for Founders' Prize by nomination only; application forms available from L.M. Rice, Jr., Pres. Application form not required.
Initial approach: Letter
Copies of proposal: 1
Deadline(s): Jan., Apr., July, and Nov.; Dec. 31 for Founders Prize
Board meeting date(s): Mar., June, Sept., and Dec.
Final notification: 3 weeks after board meetings
Write: Liston M. Rice, Jr., Pres.
Officers: Liston M. Rice, Jr.,* Pres.; William P. Weber,* V.P.; Joe Richardson, Secy.; William A. Aylesworth, Treas.
Directors:* Gerald W. Fronterhouse, S.T. Harris, Jerry R. Junkins, William B. Mitchell, Mark Shepherd, Jr., William P. Weber.
Number of staff: 2 full-time support.
Employer Identification Number: 756038519

7081
Mary Tabb & Clyde Berry Thompson Trust ⌑ ☆
c/o Texas American Bridge Bank/Fort Worth
P.O. Box 2050
Fort Worth 76113-2050 (817) 884-4266

Foundation type: Independent
Financial data (yr. ended 6/30/89): Assets, $1,255,874 (M); gifts received, $1,533; expenditures, $64,853, including $51,600 for 2 grants (high: $44,100; low: $7,500).
Purpose and activities: Giving to organizations for the blind.
Limitations: Giving primarily in Fort Worth, TX. No grants to individuals.
Application information:
Initial approach: Letter
Deadline(s): Sept.
Write: Kelly Bradshaw
Trustee: Texas American Bridge Bank/Fort Worth.
Employer Identification Number: 756186478

7082
The Tobin Foundation
P.O. Box 2101
San Antonio 78297 (512) 223-6203

Incorporated in 1951 in TX.
Donor(s): Edgar G. Tobin,† Margaret Batts Tobin.
Foundation type: Independent
Financial data (yr. ended 12/31/88): Assets, $2,277,642 (M); expenditures, $89,631, including $78,595 for 17 grants (high: $25,000; low: $120).
Purpose and activities: Giving to cultural programs, community funds, and education; support also for a church.
Limitations: Giving limited to TX. No grants to individuals.
Application information:
Initial approach: Letter
Deadline(s): None
Write: Arnold Swartz, Trustee
Officers: R.L.B. Tobin, Pres.; Harold Gasnell, Secy.
Trustees: James T. Hart, Arnold Swartz.
Employer Identification Number: 746035718

7083
The Trammell Foundation ⌑ ☆
c/o Texas Commerce Bank
P.O. Box 2558
Houston 77252-2558

Established in 1963.
Donor(s): W.B. Trammell, Ella F. Fondren 1982 Trust f/b/o Sue Trammell Whitfield.
Foundation type: Independent
Financial data (yr. ended 12/31/88): Assets, $1,360,588 (M); gifts received, $366,172; expenditures, $132,075, including $128,000 for 6 grants (high: $38,000; low: $5,000).
Purpose and activities: Giving primarily for the Methodist-affiliated universities and churches; support also for a hospital.
Types of support: Scholarship funds.
Limitations: Giving primarily in TX. No grants to individuals.
Application information:
Initial approach: Letter
Deadline(s): None
Write: Melanie Boone, Asst. Secy.-Treas.
Officers: Sue Trammell Whitfield,* Chair.; Walter W. Fondren III, Vice-Chair.; William F. Whitfield, Sr., Secy.-Treas.
Trustees:* Ernest C. Japhet, Harper Bryan Trammell, W. Trammell Whitfield.
Employer Identification Number: 746057690

7084
The Trull Foundation
404 Fourth St.
Palacios 77465 (512) 972-5241

Trust established in 1967 in TX.
Donor(s): R.B. Trull, Florence M. Trull,† Gladys T. Brooking, Jean T. Herlin, Laura Shiflett, and others.
Foundation type: Independent

Financial data (yr. ended 12/31/88): Assets, $14,003,918 (M); expenditures, $629,257, including $505,710 for 167 grants (high: $15,000; low: $50; average: $5,000).
Purpose and activities: Giving for Protestant church support and welfare programs, higher and secondary education, and welfare and youth agencies; support also for Hispanic concerns, community development and the environment, international relief activities, and population studies.
Types of support: Operating budgets, continuing support, annual campaigns, seed money, equipment, professorships, internships, scholarship funds, special projects, publications, conferences and seminars, fellowships, consulting services, general purposes, renovation projects, technical assistance.
Limitations: Giving primarily in southern TX. No grants to individuals, and rarely for building or endowment funds; no loans.
Publications: Biennial report (including application guidelines).
Application information: Application form not required.
Initial approach: Letter
Copies of proposal: 1
Deadline(s): None
Board meeting date(s): Usually 3 to 5 times a year; contributions committee meets monthly and as required
Final notification: 6 weeks
Write: Colleen Claybourn, Exec. Dir.
Officers and Trustees:* R.B. Trull,* Chair.; J. Fred Huitt,* Vice-Chair.; Colleen Claybourn,* Secy.-Treas. and Exec. Dir.; Jean T. Herlin, Rose C. Lancaster.
Number of staff: 1 full-time professional; 1 full-time support.
Employer Identification Number: 237423943

7085
Turner Charitable Foundation
811 Rusk, Suite 205
Houston 77002 (713) 237-1117

Incorporated in 1956 in TX.
Donor(s): Isla Carroll Turner,† P.E. Turner.†
Foundation type: Independent
Financial data (yr. ended 02/28/89): Assets, $14,008,092 (M); expenditures, $431,438, including $426,100 for 57 grants (high: $75,000; low: $500; average: $1,000-$5,000).
Purpose and activities: Giving for higher, secondary, and elementary education; social service and youth agencies; fine and performing arts groups and other cultural programs; Catholic, Jewish, and Protestant church support and religious programs; hospitals and health services; urban and community development; and conservation programs.
Types of support: Annual campaigns, building funds, capital campaigns, conferences and seminars, continuing support, emergency funds, endowment funds, equipment, fellowships, general purposes, land acquisition, lectureships, operating budgets, professorships, renovation projects, research.
Limitations: Giving limited to TX. No grants to individuals.
Application information: Application form not required.
Initial approach: Written request
Copies of proposal: 1
Deadline(s): Mar. 15
Board meeting date(s): Apr.
Final notification: None unless grant approved
Write: Eyvonne Moser, Asst. Secy.
Officers and Trustees: T.R. Reckling III, Pres.; Bert F. Winston, Jr., V.P.; Clyde J. Verheyden, Secy.; Isla S. Reckling, Treas.; Thomas E. Berry, Chaille W. Hawkins, Christiana R. McConn, T.R. "Cliffe" Reckling.
Number of staff: 1 full-time professional.
Employer Identification Number: 741460482

7086
The Tyler Foundation ⌑
3200 San Jacinto Tower
Dallas 75201 (214) 754-7800

Established in 1971 in TX.
Donor(s): Tyler Corp.
Foundation type: Company-sponsored
Financial data (yr. ended 12/31/88): Assets, $1,554,914 (M); expenditures, $185,548, including $182,865 for 64 grants (high: $20,000; low: $30; average: $500-$5,000).
Purpose and activities: Giving for welfare, the arts, youth agencies, and recreation.
Limitations: Giving primarily in TX. No grants to individuals, or for scholarships, fellowships, or matching gifts; no loans.
Application information: Application form not required.
Initial approach: Proposal
Copies of proposal: 1
Deadline(s): None
Board meeting date(s): As required
Final notification: 3 to 4 weeks
Write: Rick Margerison, Pres.
Officers: Rick Margerison,* Pres.; W. Michael Kipphut, Secy.; D.L. Smart,* Treas.
Trustees:* Joseph F. McKinney, Chair.
Number of staff: None.
Employer Identification Number: 237140526

7087
USAA Trust ⌑ ☆
USAA Bldg., Taxes, B-1-E
San Antonio 78288

Established in 1987 in TX.
Donor(s): United Services Automobile Assn., USAA Life Insurance Co.
Foundation type: Company-sponsored
Financial data (yr. ended 6/30/89): Assets, $3,020,954 (M); gifts received, $3,372,960; expenditures, $2,662,960, including $2,640,000 for 5 grants (high: $1,500,000; low: $40,000).
Purpose and activities: Giving to universities, especially U.S. Air Force, Naval, and other military academies.
Types of support: Endowment funds.
Limitations: No grants to individuals.
Application information: Contributes only to pre-selected organizations. Applications not accepted.
Trustee: Frost National Bank.
Employer Identification Number: 746363461

7088
USPA & IRA Educational Foundation ⌑
P.O. Box 2387
Fort Worth 76113

Established in 1983 in TX.
Foundation type: Independent
Financial data (yr. ended 12/31/88): Assets, $36,816 (M); gifts received, $135,500; expenditures, $117,349, including $116,393 for 122 grants to individuals (high: $1,000; low: $87).
Purpose and activities: Support for scholarships to undergraduates who are members of an active duty, retired or deceased military person's family.
Types of support: Student aid.
Application information: Applications are solicited by local military installations officer's wives clubs. Application form required.
Deadline(s): None
Officers and Directors: George C. Talley, Jr., Pres.; Freda J. Payne, V.P.; Lamar C. Smith, V.P.; G. Norman Coder, Secy.; William A. Dast, Treas.; Carroll H. Payne II.
Employer Identification Number: 860381200

7089
The Vale-Asche Foundation
910 River Oaks Bank Bldg.
2001 Kirby Dr., Suite 910
Houston 77019 (713) 520-7334

Incorporated in 1956 in DE.
Donor(s): Ruby Vale,† Fred B. Asche.†
Foundation type: Independent
Financial data (yr. ended 11/30/88): Assets, $4,467,063 (M); expenditures, $225,129, including $207,006 for 19 grants (high: $30,000; low: $1,000).
Purpose and activities: Grants for medical research, health care, child welfare, and aid to the aged and the handicapped; support also for secondary education and cultural programs, and projects that benefit the homeless.
Types of support: Equipment, research, special projects.
Limitations: Giving primarily in Houston, TX. No grants to individuals.
Application information: Request reviewed Sept.-Oct. Application form not required.
Initial approach: Letter
Deadline(s): None
Write: Mrs. Vale Asche Ackerman, Pres.
Officers and Trustees:* Mrs. Vale Asche Ackerman,* Pres.; Bettyann Asche Murray,* V.P.; Harry H. Hudson,* Secy.-Treas.; Asche Ackerman.
Employer Identification Number: 516015320

7090
Rachael & Ben Vaughan Foundation
P.O. Box 1579
Corpus Christi 78403 (512) 883-9266

Established in 1952 in TX.
Donor(s): Ben F. Vaughan, Jr.,† Rachael Vaughan.†
Foundation type: Independent
Financial data (yr. ended 11/30/89): Assets, $2,333,631 (M); expenditures, $111,802, including $108,500 for 33 grants (high: $15,000; low: $500).

Purpose and activities: Support for educational, cultural, environmental, community, and religious development of Central and South Texas; support for the needy and disadvantaged in this area.
Types of support: Annual campaigns, building funds, capital campaigns, conferences and seminars, consulting services, continuing support, emergency funds, employee matching gifts, endowment funds, equipment, exchange programs, fellowships, general purposes, internships, land acquisition, lectureships, matching funds, operating budgets, professorships, program-related investments, publications, renovation projects, research, seed money, special projects, technical assistance.
Limitations: Giving limited to south and central TX. No grants to individuals; no loans.
Publications: Application guidelines, 990-PF.
Application information: Application form not required.
Initial approach: Letter
Copies of proposal: 1
Deadline(s): Sept. 1
Board meeting date(s): Nov.
Final notification: End of first week in Dec.
Write: William R. Ward
Officers and Trustees:* Ben F. Vaughan III,* Pres.; Kleberg Eckhardt,* V.P.; Ben F. Vaughan IV,* V.P.; Genevieve Vaughan,* V.P.; Daphne duPont Vaughan,* Secy.-Treas.
Employer Identification Number: 746040479

7091
The Vaughn Foundation ⌑
P.O. Box 2266
Austin 78780 (214) 597-7652
Application address: 830 South Beckham, Tyler, TX 75701

Trust established in 1952 in TX.
Donor(s): Edgar H. Vaughn,† Lillie Mae Vaughn.†
Foundation type: Independent
Financial data (yr. ended 12/31/88): Assets, $4,835,198 (M); expenditures, $303,680, including $245,556 for 100 grants (high: $50,000; low: $10).
Purpose and activities: Interests include higher education, hospitals, health agencies, Protestant church support, and a related foundation.
Limitations: Giving primarily in the Southwest, with emphasis on Tyler, TX. No grants to individuals.
Application information:
Initial approach: Letter
Write: James M. Vaughn, Trustee
Trustees: James M. Vaughn, James M. Vaughn, Jr.
Employer Identification Number: 756008953

7092
James M. Vaughn, Jr. Foundation Fund ⌑
c/o MBank of Austin, Trust Dept.
P.O. Box 2266
Austin 78780

Established about 1971 in TX.
Foundation type: Independent
Financial data (yr. ended 12/31/86): Assets, $3,074,912 (M); expenditures, $552,130, including $298,777 for 26 grants (high: $33,818; low: $347) and $87,960 for 9 grants to individuals (high: $15,000; low: $1,250).
Purpose and activities: Support for cultural programs, including museums and a library, and for higher education; fellowships for mathematical research in format conjecture.
Types of support: Fellowships, research.
Application information: Application forms obtained through the American Mathematical Assn.; interviews required. Application form required.
Deadline(s): None
Officers: James M. Vaughn, Jr., Pres.; Bonna B. Vaughn, V.P.; Sally Vaughn, V.P.; Jan Werner, Secy.-Treas.
Employer Identification Number: 237166546

7093
Veritas Foundation, Inc.
221 West 6th St., Suite 1010
Austin 78701 (512) 472-1877

Established in 1983 in TX.
Donor(s): Joe Crow.†
Foundation type: Independent
Financial data (yr. ended 12/31/88): Assets, $1,668,462 (M); expenditures, $102,632, including $57,100 for 29 grants (high: $6,000; low: $100).
Purpose and activities: Giving primarily for social service and youth agencies, civic affairs groups, and schools.
Limitations: Giving primarily in Austin, TX. No grants to individuals.
Application information: Application form not required.
Initial approach: Proposal
Copies of proposal: 1
Deadline(s): None
Board meeting date(s): June and Dec.
Write: Diana Crow Leach, Pres., or Deborah Grote, Secy.
Officers: Diana Crow Leach, Pres. and Exec. Dir.; J.A. Crow, V.P.; Deborah A. Grote, Secy.; Chris Crow, Treas.
Employer Identification Number: 742254024

7094
The Waco Foundation ⌑
1801 Austin Ave.
Waco 76701 (817) 754-0315

Established in 1958 in TX.
Foundation type: Community
Financial data (yr. ended 3/31/87): Assets, $1,518,000 (L); gifts received, $18,374; expenditures, $66,387, including $30,319 for grants.
Purpose and activities: General giving in the community.
Types of support: Emergency funds, equipment, internships, matching funds, professorships, renovation projects, seed money.
Limitations: Giving primarily in Waco and McLennan counties, TX. No grants to individuals, or for continuing support, deficit financing, endowments, operating budgets, student loans, or technical assistance.
Publications: 990-PF.
Application information: Application form required.
Write: Jerome Cartwright, Exec. Dir.
Officer: Jerome Cartwright, Exec. Dir.
Employer Identification Number: 746054628

7095
Crystelle Waggoner Charitable Trust
c/o NCNB Texas National Bank
P.O. Box 1317
Fort Worth 76101 (817) 390-6114

Established in 1982 in TX.
Donor(s): Crystelle Waggoner.†
Foundation type: Independent
Financial data (yr. ended 06/30/89): Assets, $4,564,302 (M); expenditures, $359,164, including $286,224 for 55 grants (high: $37,000; low: $50; average: $2,000-$4,000).
Purpose and activities: Giving to charitable organizations in existence before Jan. 24, 1982, including health associations and services, the performing arts and other cultural programs, and social services, especially services for children and youth, the homeless, families, and women.
Types of support: General purposes, operating budgets, continuing support, annual campaigns, seed money, emergency funds, professorships, scholarship funds, building funds, capital campaigns, endowment funds, equipment, lectureships, publications, renovation projects, research, special projects.
Limitations: Giving limited to TX, especially Fort Worth and Decatur. No grants to individuals, or for challenge grants, consulting services, deficit financing, or conferences; no loans.
Publications: Annual report (including application guidelines).
Application information: Application form not required.
Initial approach: Letter
Copies of proposal: 1
Deadline(s): Mar. 31, June 30, Sept. 30, and Dec. 31
Board meeting date(s): Jan., Apr., July, and Oct.
Final notification: 6 months
Write: Darlene Mann, V.P., NCNB Texas National Bank
Trustee: NCNB Texas National Bank.
Number of staff: None.
Employer Identification Number: 751881219

7096
E. Paul and Helen Buck Waggoner Foundation, Inc. ⌑
P.O. Box 2130
Vernon 76384 (817) 552-2521

Incorporated in 1966 in TX.
Donor(s): E. Paul Waggoner,† Helen Buck Waggoner.†
Foundation type: Independent
Financial data (yr. ended 4/30/87): Assets, $6,323,661 (M); expenditures, $324,663, including $311,100 for 19 grants (high: $100,000; low: $100).
Purpose and activities: Giving for higher and secondary education, including agricultural research and scholarship funds; grants also for medical research and youth agencies.

Types of support: Building funds, scholarship funds, research.
Limitations: Giving primarily in TX.
Application information:
Initial approach: Proposal
Write: Gene W. Willingham, Dir.
Officers and Directors: Electra Waggoner Biggs, Pres.; Electra Biggs Winston, 1st V.P.; Helen Biggs Willingham, Secy.-Treas.; Gene W. Willingham, Charles F. Winston.
Employer Identification Number: 751243683

7097
Walsh Foundation ⌑
1007 NCNB Ctr.
Fort Worth 76102 (817) 335-3741

Established in 1956 in TX.
Donor(s): Mary D. Walsh, F. Howard Walsh, Sr.
Foundation type: Independent
Financial data (yr. ended 12/31/88): Assets, $1,392,224 (M); gifts received, $54,141; expenditures, $377,004, including $366,450 for 43 grants (high: $150,000; low: $100).
Purpose and activities: Emphasis on elementary and higher education, support also for cultural programs, including those for youth.
Types of support: Annual campaigns, continuing support, equipment, operating budgets, special projects.
Limitations: Giving primarily in Fort Worth, TX.
Application information:
Initial approach: Letter
Deadline(s): None
Write: F. Howard Walsh, Sr., Pres.
Officers: F. Howard Walsh, Sr., Pres.; Mary D. Walsh, V.P.; G. Malcolm Louden, Secy.-Treas.
Employer Identification Number: 756021726

7098
Marjorie T. Walthall Perpetual Charitable Trust ⌑
242 West Lynwood
San Antonio 78212 (512) 736-3712

Trust established in 1976 in TX.
Donor(s): Marjorie T. Walthall.
Foundation type: Independent
Financial data (yr. ended 12/31/88): Assets, $1,817,182 (M); expenditures, $117,919, including $94,945 for 22 grants (high: $10,000; low: $1,000).
Purpose and activities: Emphasis on health, medical and nursing education, scientific research and similar activities; support also for cultural programs.
Limitations: Giving primarily in San Antonio, TX. No grants to individuals.
Application information:
Initial approach: Letter
Deadline(s): Oct. 1
Write: Marjorie T. Walthall, Trustee
Trustees: Thomas W. Folbre, Marjorie T. Walthall, Paul T. Walthall.
Employer Identification Number: 510170313

7099
The Lillian Waltom Foundation ⌑ ☆
901 Oak St.
P.O. Box 517
Jourdanton 78026 (512) 769-2001

Established in 1988 in TX.
Donor(s): Lillian Waltom.†
Foundation type: Independent
Financial data (yr. ended 12/31/88): Assets, $2,902,247 (M); gifts received, $2,884,856; expenditures, $2,590.
Purpose and activities: Awards scholarships for higher education to local area students.
Types of support: Student aid.
Limitations: Giving limited to Atascosa County, TX, area residents.
Application information: Application form required.
Deadline(s): None
Write: W.F. Zuhlke, Jr., Trustee
Trustees: E.W. Norris, Leon F. Steinle, W.F. Zuhlke, Jr.
Employer Identification Number: 742509618

7100
Mamie McFaddin Ward Heritage Foundation
P.O. Box 3391
Beaumont 77704 (409) 838-9398

Established in 1976 in TX.
Donor(s): Mamie McFaddin Ward.†
Foundation type: Independent
Financial data (yr. ended 12/31/88): Assets, $19,783,513 (M); expenditures, $1,168,067, including $962,859 for 5 grants (high: $812,592; low: $1,500; average: $5,000-$7,500).
Purpose and activities: Support for the Mamie McFaddin Ward Heritage Museum and other cultural programs; some support for hospitals.
Limitations: Giving limited to Jefferson County, TX. No grants to individuals.
Application information: Application form required.
Initial approach: Letter
Copies of proposal: 5
Deadline(s): Sept. 15
Final notification: Nov.
Write: Pam Parish, V.P. and Trust Officer, First City, Texas-Beaumont, N.A.
Trustees: Eugene H.B. McFaddin, James L.C. McFaddin, Jr., Ida M. Pyle, Rosine M. Wilson, First City, Texas-Beaumont, N.A.
Number of staff: None.
Employer Identification Number: 746260525

7101
The Gil and Dody Weaver Foundation
500 West Seventh St., Suite 1714
Fort Worth 76102 (817) 877-1712

Established in 1980 in TX.
Donor(s): Galbraith McF. Weaver.
Foundation type: Independent
Financial data (yr. ended 09/30/88): Assets, $3,694,607 (M); expenditures, $222,599, including $190,000 for 55 grants (high: $13,000; low: $20).
Purpose and activities: Support largely for organizations helping needy or indigent people, including the aged, handicapped, and child development and welfare.
Types of support: Operating budgets, continuing support, equipment, special projects, research.
Limitations: Giving limited to TX, NM, OK, LA, KS, PA, and WV; mostly on a local basis. No grants to individuals, or for seed money, emergency funds, deficit financing, land acquisition, renovation projects, endowment funds, matching gifts, scholarships, fellowships, publications, or conferences; no loans.
Application information: Application form not required.
Initial approach: Letter or proposal
Copies of proposal: 1
Deadline(s): July 31
Board meeting date(s): Sept.
Write: Debbie Cain, Mgr.
Trustees: Eudora J. Weaver, Galbraith McF. Weaver, William R. Weaver, M.D.
Number of staff: 1
Employer Identification Number: 751729449

7102
Webber Foundation ⌑ ☆
1001 Fannin, Suite 4360
Houston 77002 (713) 951-9544

Foundation type: Independent
Financial data (yr. ended 12/31/88): Assets, $1,484,429 (M); expenditures, $465,479, including $458,050 for 55 grants (high: $250,000; low: $50).
Purpose and activities: Giving primarily for secondary education and a church; support also for museums.
Types of support: Operating budgets, building funds, capital campaigns.
Limitations: Giving primarily in Houston, TX.
Application information: Application form not required.
Initial approach: Letter
Deadline(s): None
Write: W. Temple Webber, Jr., Pres.
Officers: W. Temple Webber, Jr., Pres.; Barbara C. Webber, V.P.; W. Temple Webber III, Secy.-Treas.
Employer Identification Number: 756036145

7103
The Weiner Foundation, Inc. ⌑
P.O. Box 2612
Houston 77252

Incorporated in 1958 in TX.
Donor(s): Weiner's Stores, and others.
Foundation type: Independent
Financial data (yr. ended 12/31/87): Assets, $2,155,313 (M); gifts received, $87,341; expenditures, $477,827, including $469,709 for 65 grants (high: $295,240; low: $25).
Purpose and activities: Giving for Jewish welfare funds and temple support; some support for social services.
Limitations: Giving primarily in TX.
Officers and Directors: Sol B. Weiner, V.P.; Leon Weiner, Secy.-Treas.
Employer Identification Number: 746060381

7104
The Robert A. Welch Foundation ▼
4605 Post Oak Place, Suite 200
Houston 77027 (713) 961-9884

Trust established in 1954 in TX as a private operating foundation; status changed to private foundation in 1989.
Donor(s): Robert A. Welch.†
Foundation type: Independent
Financial data (yr. ended 08/31/89): Assets, $270,041,000 (M); expenditures, $16,039,867, including $12,472,645 for grants to individuals.
Purpose and activities: Grants for chemistry research, for which applicants must be full-time tenured or tenure-track faculty at educational institutions; for scholarships in chemistry; for the Welch Award in Chemistry; and for professorships in the field of chemistry research.
Types of support: Research, professorships, scholarship funds.
Limitations: Giving limited to TX. No support for any purpose other than basic chemistry research.
Publications: Annual report, application guidelines, newsletter.
Application information: Application form required.
Initial approach: Telephone or personal interview
Copies of proposal: 1
Deadline(s): Feb. 1 for regular research grant program and for Robert A. Welch Award in Chemistry
Board meeting date(s): Monthly
Final notification: Approximately 2 months
Write: Norbert Dittrich, Exec. Mgr.
Officers and Trustees:* Jack S. Josey,* Pres.; E.L. Wehner,* V.P.; Richard J.V. Johnson,* Secy.; Charles W. Duncan, Jr.,* Treas.; Norbert Dittrich, Exec. Mgr.; J. Evans Altman.
Number of staff: 2 full-time professional; 8 full-time support.
Employer Identification Number: 741216248

7105
Rob and Bessie Welder Wildlife Foundation
P.O. Box 1400
Sinton 78387 (512) 364-2643

Trust established in 1954 in TX.
Donor(s): R.H. Welder,† Mrs. R.H. Welder.†
Foundation type: Operating
Financial data (yr. ended 12/31/88): Assets, $14,222,662 (M); gifts received, $20,000; expenditures, $790,285, including $155,712 for 17 grants to individuals (high: $15,865; low: $1,075) and $257,867 for foundation-administered programs.
Purpose and activities: A private operating foundation established to further education in wildlife conservation, to support research into wildlife problems, and to develop scientific methods for increasing wildlife populations; operates a wildlife refuge.
Types of support: Fellowships, internships.
Limitations: No grants for building or endowment funds, or operating budgets.
Publications: Biennial report, informational brochure (including application guidelines).
Application information: Application form required.
Initial approach: Letter
Copies of proposal: 2
Deadline(s): Submit application preferably in fall; deadline Oct. 1
Board meeting date(s): Usually in Dec. and June
Write: James G. Teer, Dir.
Director: James G. Teer.
Trustees: M. Harvey Weil, John J. Welder, Patrick H. Welder.
Employer Identification Number: 741381321

7106
James L. and Eunice West Charitable Trust ▼ ⌑
c/o Shannon, Gracey, Ratliff, & Miller
2200 First City Bank Tower, 201 Main St.
Fort Worth 76102-3191

Established in 1980 in TX.
Donor(s): James L. West,† Eunice West.
Foundation type: Independent
Financial data (yr. ended 12/31/88): Assets, $14,419,744 (M); expenditures, $8,231,976, including $8,198,600 for 36 grants (high: $1,250,000; low: $1,000; average: $100-$500,000).
Purpose and activities: Giving primarily for youth and child welfare organizations, cultural programs, hospitals, higher education, social services, church support, and a community fund.
Types of support: General purposes, operating budgets, equipment, building funds, endowment funds.
Limitations: Giving primarily in Fort Worth, TX.
Application information:
Initial approach: Letter (including informational brochures, if any)
Deadline(s): None
Board meeting date(s): 3 or 4 times a year
Write: Loren Q. Hanson, Trustee
Trustees: Billy R. Roland, Managing Trustee; Loren Q. Hanson, Dean Lawrence, Eunice West, Herschel Winn.
Number of staff: None.
Employer Identification Number: 751724903

7107
West Foundation
P.O. Box 1675
Wichita Falls 76307

Established in 1973 in TX.
Donor(s): Gordon T. West,† Ellen B. West,† Gordon T. West, Jr.
Foundation type: Independent
Financial data (yr. ended 09/30/89): Assets, $10,030,071 (M); gifts received, $5,000; expenditures, $596,977, including $438,409 for 12 grants (high: $273,889; low: $5,000) and $50,000 for 20 grants to individuals of $2,500 each.
Purpose and activities: Support limited to education, through excellence in teaching awards to public school teachers and scholarship and other educational programs on the public school and university levels.
Types of support: Scholarship funds, grants to individuals.
Limitations: Giving limited to the Wichita Falls, TX, area.
Application information: Applications not accepted.
Write: Reece A. West, Pres.
Officers: Reece A. West, Pres.; Joe Sherrill, Jr., V.P.; Gordon T. West, Jr., V.P.; Lane T. West, V.P.
Number of staff: 1 full-time professional; 2 part-time support.
Employer Identification Number: 237332105

7108
The West Foundation ⌑
P.O. Box 491
Houston 77001

Trust established in 1938 in TX.
Donor(s): J.M. West,† Jessie Dudley West,† Wesley W. West, Leslie L. Appelt.
Foundation type: Independent
Financial data (yr. ended 12/31/87): Assets, $7,831,809 (M); expenditures, $444,038, including $371,000 for 10 grants (high: $100,000; low: $100).
Purpose and activities: Giving largely for education, medical research, health agencies, and religion.
Limitations: Giving primarily in TX.
Application information:
Initial approach: Letter
Deadline(s): None
Write: Coordinator of Grants
Trustees: William B. Blakemore II, Margene West Lloyd, William R. Lloyd, Jr., Robert H. Parsley, James A. Reichert.
Employer Identification Number: 746064039

7109
Neva and Wesley West Foundation
P.O. Box 7
Houston 77001 (713) 850-7911

Trust established in 1956 in TX.
Donor(s): Wesley West,† Mrs. Wesley West.
Foundation type: Independent
Financial data (yr. ended 12/31/88): Assets, $7,593,286 (M); expenditures, $667,952, including $625,000 for 12 grants (high: $250,000; low: $2,000).
Purpose and activities: Support for medical and educational purposes.
Types of support: General purposes, building funds, equipment, research, operating budgets.
Limitations: Giving primarily in TX. No grants to individuals, or for scholarships or fellowships; no loans.
Publications: Annual report.
Application information: Application form not required.
Initial approach: Letter
Copies of proposal: 1
Deadline(s): Submit proposal in Nov.; deadline Dec. 1
Board meeting date(s): Dec.
Write: Marylene Weir
Trustees: W.H. Hodges, Betty Ann West Stedman, Stuart West Stedman, Mrs. Wesley West.
Number of staff: None.
Employer Identification Number: 746039393

7110
J. M. West Texas Corporation ⌑
P.O. Box 491
Houston 77001

Incorporated in 1957 in TX.
Foundation type: Independent
Financial data (yr. ended 2/29/88): Assets, $5,092,698 (M); expenditures, $268,252, including $229,663 for 17 grants (high: $30,000; low: $1,000).
Purpose and activities: Emphasis on higher education and medical research; support also for youth agencies and cultural programs.
Limitations: Giving primarily in TX.
Application information:
Initial approach: Letter
Deadline(s): None
Write: Coord. of Grants
Officers: William R. Lloyd, Jr.,* Pres.; William B. Blakemore II,* V.P.; James A. Reichert, V.P.; Jack T. Trotter,* V.P.; Robert H. Parsley,* Secy.-Treas.
Trustees:* Margene West Lloyd.
Employer Identification Number: 746040389

7111
Erle and Emma White Foundation ⌑
P.O. Box 4669
Wichita Falls 76308

Established in 1981 in TX.
Foundation type: Independent
Financial data (yr. ended 12/31/88): Assets, $3,573,846 (M); expenditures, $341,617, including $319,000 for 42 grants (high: $30,000; low: $500).
Purpose and activities: Support for hospitals, health organizations, social services, and cultural programs.
Limitations: Giving primarily in the Wichita Falls, TX, area. No grants to individuals.
Application information: Contributes only to pre-selected organizations. Applications not accepted.
Officers: Emma White, Chair.; Marilyn Onstott, Secy.-Treas.
Trustee: Carolyn Brown.
Employer Identification Number: 751781596

7112
Tom C. White Foundation ⌑
900 Hamilton Bldg.
Wichita Falls 76301 (817) 723-1660

Established in 1959.
Donor(s): Tommie O. White.
Foundation type: Independent
Financial data (yr. ended 12/31/88): Assets, $1,321,950 (M); expenditures, $70,168, including $66,453 for 21 grants (high: $20,000; low: $80; average: $500-$10,000).
Purpose and activities: Emphasis on Protestant church support, social service and youth agencies, higher education, and health.
Types of support: General purposes, continuing support, annual campaigns, seed money, emergency funds, building funds, equipment, land acquisition, endowment funds, research, scholarship funds.
Limitations: Giving limited to TX. No grants to individuals, or for matching gifts; no loans.
Publications: 990-PF.
Application information: Application form not required.
Initial approach: Letter
Copies of proposal: 1
Deadline(s): Sept. 30
Board meeting date(s): Monthly
Final notification: 6 months
Write: David H. White, Trustee
Trustees: Evelyn C.W. Parkhurst, David H. White, Ora Belle White.
Number of staff: None.
Employer Identification Number: 756037052

7113
G. R. White Trust ⌑
c/o Texas American Bank, Fort Worth
P.O. Box 2050
Fort Worth 76113 (817) 884-4162

Trust established in TX.
Donor(s): G.R. White.†
Foundation type: Independent
Financial data (yr. ended 9/30/88): Assets, $7,570,862 (M); expenditures, $450,955, including $369,812 for 40 grants (high: $100,000; low: $1,000).
Purpose and activities: Emphasis on hospitals, youth agencies, higher education, and church support.
Types of support: General purposes, building funds, equipment, scholarship funds.
Limitations: Giving limited to TX. No grants to individuals.
Application information:
Initial approach: Letter
Deadline(s): Sept.
Board meeting date(s): Annually, usually in the spring
Final notification: Within 30 days
Write: Joe T. Lenamon
Trustee: Texas American Bank/Fort Worth.
Number of staff: None.
Employer Identification Number: 756094930

7114
Cecilia Young Willard Helping Fund ☆
c/o NBC Bank-San Antonio, N.A.
P.O. Box 121
San Antonio 78291-0125

Established in 1987 in TX.
Donor(s): Celia Young Willard Trust.
Foundation type: Independent
Financial data (yr. ended 5/31/88): Assets, $2,002,566 (M); gifts received, $2,004,571; expenditures, $37,036, including $31,593 for 4 grants (high: $11,283; low: $6,770).
Purpose and activities: Initial year of operation, fiscal 1988; support for a Presbyterian church, higher and other education, and a children's home.
Types of support: Operating budgets.
Limitations: Giving primarily in NC.
Application information: Funding limited to only those organizations that Dr. Willard contributed to during her lifetime. Grant requests are discouraged and will be declined. Applications not accepted.
Write: John Johnston, Trust Officer, NBC Bank-San Antonio, N.A.
Trustee: NBC Bank-San Antonio, N.A.
Employer Identification Number: 746350893

7115
The Wills Foundation ⌑
3436 Overbrook
Houston 77027 (713) 965-9043
Application address: P.O. Box 27534, Houston, TX 77227-7534

Established in 1966 in TX and AR.
Donor(s): Fletcher S. Pratt, Mrs. Fletcher S. Pratt, and others.
Foundation type: Independent
Financial data (yr. ended 7/31/89): Assets, $4,538,094 (M); gifts received, $443,662; expenditures, $150,316, including $115,000 for 5 grants (high: $25,000; low: $20,000).
Purpose and activities: Grants only for research regarding hereditary diseases, particularly Huntington's Chorea.
Types of support: Research, fellowships.
Application information:
Initial approach: Proposal
Write: Alice Evans Pratt, Pres.
Officers: Alice Evans Pratt, Pres. and Treas.; Peter E. Pratt, V.P. and Secy.
Directors: Charles Dillingham, Chair.; Charlotte B. Ferguson, Michael J. Murray, M.D., St. Clare Pratt Seifert.
Number of staff: 4 part-time professional; 1 part-time support.
Employer Identification Number: 746078200

7116
John & Nevils Wilson Foundation ⌑
P.O. Drawer S & P
Wichita Falls 76307-7511 (817) 322-3145
Application address: 1100 Hamilton Bldg., Wichita Falls, TX 76301

Established in 1968 in TX.
Donor(s): J.H. Wilson.†
Foundation type: Independent
Financial data (yr. ended 11/30/88): Assets, $2,575,758 (M); expenditures, $68,294, including $41,916 for 12 grants (high: $16,916; low: $200).
Purpose and activities: Grants primarily for churches and higher education.
Types of support: Building funds, equipment, general purposes.
Limitations: Giving primarily in Wichita County, TX. No grants to individuals or for scholarships or fellowships; no loans.
Application information: Application form not required.
Initial approach: Letter; no telephone calls
Copies of proposal: 5
Deadline(s): Submit proposal in Aug. through Oct.; deadline Oct. 30
Board meeting date(s): Feb. and Nov.
Final notification: Nov.
Write: Joseph N. Sherrill, Jr., V.P.
Officers and Trustees: Evelyn Wilson Egan, Pres.; Virginia Wilson Ewing, V.P.; Joseph N. Sherrill, Jr., V.P.; Earle W. Crawford, David A. Kimbell.
Number of staff: 1
Employer Identification Number: 756080151

7117
Ralph Wilson Public Trust ⌑
c/o Don Keen
600 South General Bruce Dr.
Temple 76501

Established in 1974.
Donor(s): Ralph Wilson.†
Foundation type: Independent
Financial data (yr. ended 12/31/87): Assets, $2,559,740 (M); expenditures, $181,957, including $180,000 for 5 grants (high: $125,000; low: $10,000).
Purpose and activities: Support mainly for the Ralph Wilson Youth Clubs; support also for cultural programs and child welfare.
Limitations: Giving primarily in TX.
Officers and Trustees: Jim Bowmer, Pres.; Ralph Wilson, Jr., V.P.; Betty Prescott, Secy.; Donald Keen, Treas.; and 9 additional trustees.
Employer Identification Number: 237351606

7118
The Wiseda Foundation ⌑
P.O. Box 122269
Fort Worth 76121-2269 (817) 737-6678

Established in 1976 in TX.
Donor(s): William S. Davis, Davoil, Inc.
Foundation type: Independent
Financial data (yr. ended 9/30/88): Assets, $1,139 (M); gifts received, $116,000; expenditures, $115,767, including $114,645 for 21 grants (high: $35,000; low: $100).
Purpose and activities: Emphasis on social service agencies, health, cultural programs, and historic preservation; substantial support for a local garden club.
Limitations: Giving primarily in TX. No grants for indivduals.
Application information:
Initial approach: Letter or proposal
Deadline(s): None
Write: William S. Davis, Trustee
Trustee: William S. Davis.
Employer Identification Number: 751533548

7119
Kalman & Ida Wolens Foundation
513 East Seventh Ave.
P.O. Box 2235
Corsicana 75151 (214) 874-2961

Established in 1972 in TX.
Donor(s): Louis Wolens.†
Foundation type: Independent
Financial data (yr. ended 7/31/89): Assets, $4,246,421 (M); gifts received, $3,000; expenditures, $146,853, including $113,500 for 13 grants (high: $50,000; low: $2,000; average: $5,000).
Purpose and activities: Giving primarily for Jewish welfare funds, education, and youth services.
Types of support: Endowment funds, research, scholarship funds, special projects.
Limitations: Giving primarily in TX and Israel. No grants to individuals.
Application information: Application form not required.
Initial approach: Letter
Copies of proposal: 1
Deadline(s): None
Board meeting date(s): Feb., Mar., Aug., and Nov.
Write: Dean Milkes, Pres.
Officers and Directors: Dean Milkes, Pres.; Bette Miller, V.P.; Marjorie Milkes, Secy.-Treas.; Cheryl Jerome.
Number of staff: None.
Employer Identification Number: 237222516

7120
Erving & Joyce Wolf Foundation ⌑ ☆
5353 West Alabama, Suite 303
Houston 77056

Established in 1972.
Donor(s): Erving Wolf, Joyce Wolf.
Foundation type: Independent
Financial data (yr. ended 2/28/89): Assets, $389,483 (M); expenditures, $434,742, including $426,801 for 17 grants (high: $225,000; low: $30).
Purpose and activities: Giving primarily to a fine arts museum; minor support for other cultural programs and higher education.
Limitations: No grants to individuals.
Application information: Contributes only to pre-selected organizations. Applications not accepted.
Officers and Directors: Erving Wolf, Pres.; Joyce Wolf, V.P. and Secy.; M. Daniel Wolf, Treas.; Diane R. Wolf, Mathew D. Wolf.
Employer Identification Number: 237275662

7121
Morris & Frieda Wolfe Foundation ⌑ ☆
500 Citicorp Ctr.
1200 Smith St.
Houston 77002-4307

Established in 1981 in TX.
Foundation type: Independent
Financial data (yr. ended 7/31/89): Assets, $204,489 (M); expenditures, $113,231, including $100,000 for 2 grants of $50,000 each.
Purpose and activities: Support for Jewish organizations, including welfare funds.
Limitations: Giving primarily in Houston, TX. No grants to individuals.
Application information: Contributes only to pre-selected organizations. Applications not accepted.
Trustees: Jay Bahme, John King, Frieda Wolfe, Henry Wolfe.
Employer Identification Number: 742137769

7122
The Pauline Sterne Wolff Memorial Foundation ⌑
c/o Texas Commerce Bank
P.O. Box 2558
Houston 77252 (713) 236-4407

Incorporated in 1922 in TX.
Foundation type: Independent
Financial data (yr. ended 12/31/87): Assets, $12,829,932 (M); expenditures, $811,264, including $585,207 for 15 grants (high: $239,722; low: $2,500).
Purpose and activities: Giving for medical education and research, and Jewish welfare organizations; support also for hospitals.
Limitations: Giving primarily in Harris County, TX.
Application information:
Initial approach: Letter
Deadline(s): Dec. 1
Write: Robert H. Richardson, Jr., Custodian, Texas Commerce Bank
Trustees: Jenard M. Gross, Marc J. Shapiro, Henry J.N. Taub, Henry J.N. Taub II.
Employer Identification Number: 741110698

7123
B. M. Woltman Foundation ⌑
2200 West Loop South, Suite 225
Houston 77027
Application address: c/o Frederick Boden, Exec. Dir., Lutheran Church-Synod, 7900 U.S. 290 East, Austin, TX 78724

Trust established in 1948 in TX.
Donor(s): B.M. Woltman,† Woltman Furniture Co., and others.
Foundation type: Independent
Financial data (yr. ended 12/31/86): Assets, $4,749,980 (M); gifts received, $3,200; expenditures, $221,152, including $102,500 for 11 grants (high: $33,000; low: $3,000) and $53,700 for 47 grants to individuals (high: $2,400; low: $500).
Purpose and activities: Giving only for Lutheran church support, local church-related secondary schools, hospitals, and higher education; scholarships for students preparing for the Lutheran ministry or for teaching in Lutheran schools.
Types of support: Student aid.
Limitations: Giving limited to TX.
Application information: Application forms provided for scholarships.
Deadline(s): Before school term begins for scholarships
Write: W.J. Woltman, Pres.
Officers and Trustees:* W.J. Woltman,* Pres.; W. Carloss Morris,* Secy.-Treas.; Robert H. McCanne, Mgr.; Richard D. Chandler, Jr., Rev. Hobart Meyer, Rev. Glenn O'Shoney.
Employer Identification Number: 741402184

7124
The Wortham Foundation ▼
2727 Allen Pkwy., Suite 2000
Houston 77019 (713) 526-8849

Trust established in 1958 in TX.
Donor(s): Gus S. Wortham,† Lyndall F. Wortham.†
Foundation type: Independent
Financial data (yr. ended 09/30/89): Assets, $132,466,811 (M); expenditures, $8,648,471, including $7,911,408 for 43 grants (high: $1,050,000; low: $1,000; average: $5,000-$100,000).
Purpose and activities: Support primarily for the arts, including the performing arts and museums, and community improvement, including civic beautification projects.
Types of support: Annual campaigns, seed money, emergency funds, deficit financing, general purposes, matching funds, continuing support.
Limitations: Giving limited to Houston and Harris County, TX. Generally no grants to

colleges, universities, or hospitals. No grants to individuals, or for building funds.
Publications: Informational brochure (including application guidelines).
Application information: Application form required.
Initial approach: Letter
Copies of proposal: 1
Deadline(s): Submit proposal preferably by the first week of Nov., Feb., May, or Aug.
Board meeting date(s): 3rd week of deadline months
Final notification: 1 month
Write: Allen H. Carruth, Pres.
Officer and Trustees:* Allen H. Carruth,* Pres.; H. Charles Boswell, Fred C. Burns, Brady F. Carruth, E.A. Stumpf III, R.W. Wortham III.
Number of staff: 2 full-time support.
Employer Identification Number: 741334356

7125
Worthing Scholarship Fund ¤
c/o NCNB Texas National Bank
P.O. Box 2518
Houston 77252-2518 (713) 652-6230
Application address: c/o F.D. Wesley, 119 East St., Houston, TX 77018

Established in 1951 in TX.
Foundation type: Independent
Financial data (yr. ended 09/30/89): Assets, $3,756,247 (M); expenditures, $186,570, including $173,000 for 122 grants to individuals (high: $3,000; low: $500).
Purpose and activities: Scholarship support for high school graduates in the Houston Independent School District who plan to attend a TX accredited college. Recipients are selected by the Worthing Scholarship Committee.
Types of support: Student aid.
Limitations: Giving limited to Houston, TX.
Application information: Application form required.
Deadline(s): May 1
Write: Carl W. Schumacher, Jr., Sr. V.P. & Trust Officer, NCNB Texas National Bank
Trustee: NCNB Texas National Bank.
Employer Identification Number: 741160916

7126
Mack Worthington Foundation, Inc. ¤
P.O. Box 2705
Houston 77252

Established in 1985 in TX.
Donor(s): Marshall H. Worthington.
Foundation type: Independent
Financial data (yr. ended 6/30/86): Assets, $6,674,000 (M); gifts received, $6,674,000; expenditures, $0.
Purpose and activities: First year of operation, 1985-86; no grants awarded. Giving resticted to Masonic organizations.
Application information: Contributes only to pre-selected organizations. Applications not accepted.
Officers and Directors:* J.D. Buddy Baccus,* Pres.; Gene S. Terry,* Secy.; G. Ronald Aldis, C.S. Inscho, Jr., Jess W. Pardue, Mack Worthington.
Employer Identification Number: 760180179

7127
Lola Wright Foundation, Inc.
P.O. Box 1138
Georgetown 78627-1138 (512) 255-3067

Incorporated in 1954 in TX.
Donor(s): Miss Johnie E. Wright.†
Foundation type: Independent
Financial data (yr. ended 12/31/87): Assets, $4,966,396 (M); expenditures, $779,221, including $564,884 for grants (average: $1,500-$25,000).
Purpose and activities: Emphasis on social services and the handicapped, health and hospitals, AIDS programs, cultural programs, the aged, youth and child development, higher and other education, community funds, and the environment.
Types of support: Matching funds, building funds, equipment, endowment funds, continuing support, renovation projects, research, special projects.
Limitations: Giving limited to TX, primarily the Austin area. No grants to individuals, or for operating budgets.
Publications: Application guidelines, annual report.
Application information: Application form not required.
Initial approach: Letter
Copies of proposal: 9
Deadline(s): Apr. 1 and Oct. 1
Board meeting date(s): Semiannually
Final notification: May 15 and Nov. 15
Write: Patrick H. O'Donnell, Pres.
Officers and Directors:* Patrick H. O'Donnell,* Pres.; William Hilgers,* V.P.; Vivian E. Todd,* Secy.-Treas; Martha Greenhill, James Meyers, Carole Rylander.
Number of staff: 1 part-time professional; 1 part-time support.
Employer Identification Number: 746054717

7128
The Zachry Foundation ¤
2500 Tower Life Bldg.
San Antonio 78205 (512) 554-4666

Incorporated in 1960 in TX.
Donor(s): H.B. Zachry Co. International, H.B. Zachry Co.
Foundation type: Independent
Financial data (yr. ended 12/31/88): Assets, $1,866,198 (M); gifts received, $1,090,000; expenditures, $689,154, including $660,240 for 25 grants (high: $125,000; low: $2,500).
Purpose and activities: Emphasis on higher education, music, and public television.
Types of support: Capital campaigns, annual campaigns, continuing support, endowment funds, internships, research, scholarship funds, special projects.
Limitations: Giving limited to TX, with emphasis on San Antonio. No grants to individuals.
Application information: Application form not required.
Initial approach: Telephone or letter
Copies of proposal: 1
Deadline(s): 1 month prior to board meetings
Board meeting date(s): Quarterly
Write: Dorothy G. Martin, Admin.
Officers and Trustees: H.B. Zachry, Jr., Pres.; Emma Leigh Carter, V.P.; Murray L. Johnston, Jr., Secy.; Charles Ebrom, Treas.; Dorothy G. Martin, Admin.; Mollie S. Zachry.
Number of staff: 1 part-time support.
Employer Identification Number: 741485544

7129
The Zale Foundation ▼ ¤
1445 Ross Ave., Suite 2600
Dallas 75202-2733 (214) 855-0627

Incorporated in 1951 in TX.
Donor(s): Members of the Zale and Lipshy families.
Foundation type: Independent
Financial data (yr. ended 12/31/88): Assets, $15,155,136 (M); gifts received, $12,900; expenditures, $903,490, including $694,686 for 17 grants (high: $629,286; low: $200).
Purpose and activities: Support primarily for a university medical center; support also for Jewish welfare agencies, higher education, hospitals, and social services.
Types of support: Operating budgets, seed money, building funds, professorships, consulting services, technical assistance, scholarship funds, capital campaigns.
Limitations: No grants to individuals, or for annual campaigns, emergency funds, deficit financing, renovation projects, endowment funds, conferences, study, films, publications, land acquisition, matching gifts, or continuing support; no loans. No grants for periods of more than 3 to 5 years.
Application information: Application form not required.
Initial approach: Letter and proposal of not more than 2 or 3 pages
Copies of proposal: 1
Deadline(s): None
Board meeting date(s): Semiannually
Final notification: 3 months
Write: Michael F. Romaine, Pres.
Officers: Michael F. Romaine,* Pres.; George Tobolowsky, Secy.-Treas.
Directors:* Donald Zale, Chair.; Leo Fields, Gloria Landsberg, Bruce A. Lipshy, Marvin Zale.
Number of staff: 1 full-time professional; 1 part-time support.
Employer Identification Number: 756037429

7130
William & Sylvia Zale Foundation ¤
P.O. Box 223566
Dallas 75222 (214) 987-4688
Application address: 5949 Sherry Ln., No. 1025, Dallas, TX 75225; Tel.: (214) 987-4688

Established in 1951 in TX.
Foundation type: Independent
Financial data (yr. ended 8/31/88): Assets, $3,935,339 (M); expenditures, $223,056, including $212,083 for 29 grants (high: $35,000; low: $350).
Purpose and activities: Support for Jewish welfare organizations and hospitals.
Limitations: No grants to individuals, or for scholarships, fellowships, or prizes; no loans.
Application information:
Initial approach: Letter
Deadline(s): None
Write: Lew D. Zale, Trustee
Trustees: Eugene Zale, Lew D. Zale, Sylvia Zale, Theodore Zale.
Employer Identification Number: 756037591

UTAH

7131
Ruth Eleanor Bamberger and John Ernest Bamberger Memorial Foundation ⌘
1201 Walker Bldg.
Salt Lake City 84111 (801) 364-2045

Incorporated in 1947 in UT.
Donor(s): Ernest Bamberger,† Eleanor F. Bamberger.†
Foundation type: Independent
Financial data (yr. ended 12/31/88): Assets, $7,683,414 (M); expenditures, $401,954, including $311,736 for 114 grants (high: $50,000; low: $100) and $54,428 for 63 grants to individuals (high: $2,412; low: $100).
Purpose and activities: Support for secondary and higher education, especially undergraduate scholarships for student nurses, and for schools, hospitals and health agencies, and youth and child welfare agencies; occasional loans for medical education.
Types of support: Operating budgets, continuing support, scholarship funds, equipment, student aid.
Limitations: Giving primarily in UT. No grants to individuals (except for scholarships to local students), or for endowment or building funds, research, or matching gifts.
Application information: Interview required for scholarship applicants. Application form not required.
Initial approach: Letter
Copies of proposal: 1
Deadline(s): None
Board meeting date(s): Bimonthly beginning in Feb.
Final notification: 2 months
Write: William H. Olwell, Secy.-Treas.
Officers and Members: Joseph E. Bernolfo, Jr., Chair.; William H. Olwell, Secy.-Treas.; Clifford L. Ashton, Clarence Bamberger, Jr., Roy W. Simmons.
Number of staff: 1 part-time support.
Employer Identification Number: 876116540

7132
Val A. Browning Charitable Foundation
P.O. Box 9936
Ogden 84409 (801) 626-9533
Application address: 1528 28th St., Ogden, UT 84401

Established in 1975 in UT.
Donor(s): Val A. Browning.
Foundation type: Independent
Financial data (yr. ended 12/31/88): Assets, $3,543,487 (M); gifts received, $820,000; expenditures, $522,845, including $506,000 for 12 grants (high: $382,000; low: $100).
Purpose and activities: Support primarily for a hospital and a secondary school; some support for health associations, social services, arts and culture, and higher and other education.
Types of support: Annual campaigns, building funds, capital campaigns, continuing support, endowment funds, special projects.
Limitations: Giving primarily in Ogden and Salt Lake City, UT.
Application information: Application form not required.
Initial approach: Letter
Copies of proposal: 1
Deadline(s): Preferably by Sept. 30
Write: Val A. Browning, Chair.
Directors: Val A. Browning, Chair.; Bruce Browning, John Val Browning, Carol Dumke, Judith B. Jones.
Trustee: First Security Bank of Utah, N.A.
Employer Identification Number: 876167851

7133
Robert Harold Burton Private Foundation ⌘ ☆
c/o First Security Bank of Utah, N.A.
P.O. Box 30007
Salt Lake City 84130-0007 (801) 350-5451

Established in 1985 in UT.
Donor(s): Robert H. Burton.†
Foundation type: Independent
Financial data (yr. ended 12/31/87): Assets, $10,708,441 (M); gifts received, $7,650,745; expenditures, $116,881.
Purpose and activities: Initial year of operation, 1985; no grants awarded in 1987.
Limitations: Giving primarily in Salt Lake County, UT.
Application information: Application form not required.
Deadline(s): None
Write: John Lamborn
Members: Richard Robert Burton, Chair.; Dan Harold Burton, Judith Covey Burton Moyle.
Trustee: First Security Bank of Utah, N.A.
Employer Identification Number: 746335785

7134
Marie Eccles Caine Charitable Foundation ⌘
P.O. Box 30007
Salt Lake City 84130
Application address: 324 North 500 East, Brigham City, UT 84302; Tel.: (801) 723-2770

Established in 1981 in UT.
Donor(s): Marie Eccles Caine.†
Foundation type: Independent
Financial data (yr. ended 05/31/89): Assets, $5,898,362 (M); expenditures, $253,898, including $230,643 for 44 grants (high: $22,000; low: $400).
Purpose and activities: Giving for the advancement of the fine arts, particularly at Utah State University, for other programs at that university which were of interest to the donor, and for other charitable purposes as determined by the committee from time to time.
Limitations: Giving primarily in Logan County, UT.
Application information:
Initial approach: Proposal
Copies of proposal: 4
Deadline(s): None
Write: Manon C. Russell or Dan C. Russell
Committee Members: Dan C. Russell, Manon C. Russell, George R. Wanlass, Kathryn C. Wanlass.
Trustee: First Security Bank of Utah, N.A.
Employer Identification Number: 942764258

7135
Louise E. Callister Foundation ⌘
2005 South 300 West
Salt Lake City 84115

Incorporated in 1958 in UT.
Donor(s): Paul Q. Callister, Mary B. Callister.
Foundation type: Independent
Financial data (yr. ended 6/30/88): Assets, $2,298,988 (M); expenditures, $117,823, including $100,000 for 13 grants (high: $74,000; low: $500).
Purpose and activities: Emphasis on the Mormon church and higher education.
Limitations: Giving primarily in UT. No grants to individuals.
Application information: Contributes only to pre-selected organizations. Applications not accepted.
Board meeting date(s): Quarterly and as required
Directors: Edward Callister, Jan E. Callister, Paul S. Callister, Marna C. Fryer, Jeanne Thorne.
Employer Identification Number: 876118299

7136
Castle Foundation ⌘
c/o Moore Trust Co.
200 South Main St.
Salt Lake City 84101 (801) 531-6075

Established in 1953.
Foundation type: Independent
Financial data (yr. ended 6/30/88): Assets, $1,963,897 (M); expenditures, $91,730, including $67,672 for 31 grants (high: $5,000; low: $1,000).
Purpose and activities: Giving for the arts, child welfare and social service agencies, higher and secondary education, and hospitals.
Types of support: Scholarship funds, special projects, equipment, operating budgets.
Limitations: Giving primarily in UT.
Application information: Application form required.
Initial approach: Letter
Deadline(s): None
Write: Gilbert M. Bean, Trust Officer, Moore Trust Co.
Trustee: Moore Trust Co.
Employer Identification Number: 876117177

7137
Annie Taylor Dee Foundation ⌘
c/o First Security Bank
P.O. Box 9936, Trust Dept.
Ogden 84409
Application address: c/o First Security Bank Bldg. No. 1212, 2404 Washington Blvd., Ogden, UT 84401

Trust established in 1961 in UT.
Donor(s): Maude Dee Porter.†
Foundation type: Independent

Financial data (yr. ended 12/31/88): Assets, $1,724,265 (M); expenditures, $31,949, including $22,500 for 7 grants (high: $7,500; low: $1,000).
Purpose and activities: Support primarily for the McKay-Dee Hospital; support also for higher and secondary education, cultural programs, religious purposes, and conservation.
Limitations: Giving primarily in UT. No grants to individuals; no loans.
Application information:
Initial approach: Letter
Copies of proposal: 1
Deadline(s): Submit proposal preferably by Sept. 30
Board meeting date(s): Apr. and Oct.
Write: Thomas D. Dee III, Vice-Chair.
Distribution Committee: Thomas D. Dee II, Chair.; David L. Dee, Vice-Chair.; Thomas D. Dee III, Vice-Chair.
Trustee: First Security Bank of Utah, N.A.
Employer Identification Number: 876116380

7138
Lawrence T. and Janet T. Dee Foundation
3905 Harrison Blvd., Suite W306
Ogden 84403 (801) 621-4863
Application address: c/o W. John Lamborn, First Security Bank of Utah, N.A., P.O. Box 30007, Salt Lake City, UT 84130

Established in 1971 in UT.
Donor(s): L.T. Dee,† Janet T. Dee.†
Foundation type: Independent
Financial data (yr. ended 12/31/89): Assets, $5,800,000 (M); expenditures, $335,000, including $200,000 for 24 grants (high: $100,000; low: $1,000).
Purpose and activities: Emphasis on health services, particularly the McKay-Dee Hospital; support also for higher education, cultural programs, including the fine and performing arts, and social service agencies.
Types of support: Annual campaigns, emergency funds, building funds, equipment, endowment funds, research, scholarship funds, matching funds.
Limitations: Giving primarily in UT. No grants to individuals; no loans.
Application information: Application form not required.
Initial approach: Letter
Copies of proposal: 3
Deadline(s): Submit proposal preferably by Sept. 30
Board meeting date(s): Mar., June, and Sept.
Write: Thomas D. Dee II, Chair.
Managers: Thomas D. Dee II, Chair.; Thomas D. Dee III, V.P.; David L. Dee, V.P.
Trustee: First Security Bank of Utah, N.A.
Employer Identification Number: 876150803

7139
Dialysis Research Foundation ⌑ ☆
c/o Bonneville Dialysis Assoc.
5575 South 500 East
Ogden 84405

Foundation type: Independent
Financial data (yr. ended 12/31/88): Assets, $317,122 (M); gifts received, $5,525; expenditures, $167,230, including $73,537 for 42 grants (high: $15,000; low: $18) and $53,609 for grants to individuals (high: $350; low: $10).
Purpose and activities: Giving limited to renal disease, including research on dialysis treatment and for grants to individuals undergoing dialysis.
Types of support: Grants to individuals, research.
Application information:
Initial approach: Proposal
Deadline(s): None
Officers and Trustees: Karen Stensrud, Chair.; H.J. Orme, Vice-Chair.; Mark Lindsay, Secy.-Treas.; Linda Clark, Charlie Davidson, Rev. Richard Reese, Becky Reis, Harry Senekjian, M.D., Judith Walser.
Employer Identification Number: 972819009

7140
Dr. Ezekiel R. and Edna Wattis Dumke Foundation ⌑
600 Crandall Bldg.
Ten West First South
Salt Lake City 84101 (801) 363-7863

Incorporated in 1959 in UT.
Foundation type: Independent
Financial data (yr. ended 12/31/88): Assets, $4,638,955 (M); expenditures, $310,524, including $262,113 for 27 grants (high: $40,000; low: $1,000).
Purpose and activities: Grants largely for higher education, cultural programs, medical and hospital services, and youth agencies.
Types of support: Building funds, technical assistance, research, general purposes, equipment.
Limitations: Giving primarily in UT and ID. No grants to individuals.
Application information: Application form required.
Deadline(s): Feb. 1 and July 1
Write: Max B. Lewis, Secy.
Officers and Directors: Ezekiel R. Dumke, Jr., Pres.; Martha Ann Dumke Healy, V.P.; Max B. Lewis, Secy. and Mgr.; Edmund E. Dumke, Treas.; Valerie Rork, Claire Dumke Ryberg, Nancy Healy Schwanfelder.
Employer Identification Number: 876119783

7141
Willard L. Eccles Charitable Foundation ▼
P.O. Box 45385
Salt Lake City 84145-0385 (801) 532-1500

Established in 1981 in UT.
Foundation type: Independent
Financial data (yr. ended 3/31/88): Assets, $20,151,116 (M); expenditures, $1,102,399, including $1,000,383 for 15 grants (high: $235,000; low: $2,000; average: $10,000-$150,000).
Purpose and activities: Support primarily for health care, medical research, and medical education.
Types of support: Equipment, research.
Limitations: Giving primarily in UT, with emphasis in the Ogden, UT, area. No grants to individuals, or for land acquisition, construction, building purposes, or to endow medical education positions.
Application information:
Initial approach: Letter
Deadline(s): Month preceeding meeting date
Board meeting date(s): Mar., June, and Oct.
Final notification: Following meeting
Write: Clark P. Giles, Secy.
Officers: Ruth P. Eccles, Chair.; Clark P. Giles, Secy.
Committee Members: Barbara E. Coit, William E. Coit, William H. Coit, Stephen E. Denkers, Stephen G. Denkers, Susan E. Denkers.
Trustee: First Security Bank of Utah, N.A.
Number of staff: None.
Employer Identification Number: 942759395

7142
The George S. and Dolores Dore Eccles Foundation ▼ ⌑
Deseret Bldg.
79 South Main St., 12th Fl.
Salt Lake City 84111 (801) 350-5336

Incorporated in 1958 in UT; absorbed Lillian Ethel Dufton Charitable Trust in 1981.
Donor(s): George S. Eccles.†
Foundation type: Independent
Financial data (yr. ended 12/31/88): Assets, $91,611,659 (M); gifts received, $800,000; expenditures, $4,667,611, including $4,260,464 for 85 grants (high: $700,000; low: $1,000; average: $2,500-$100,000).
Purpose and activities: Emphasis on higher education, hospitals and medical research, the performing and visual arts, and social services and youth agencies.
Types of support: Annual campaigns, building funds, capital campaigns, equipment, general purposes, matching funds, professorships, program-related investments, research, scholarship funds.
Limitations: Giving primarily in the Intermountain area, particularly UT. No grants to individuals, or for endowment funds; no loans.
Application information: Application form required.
Initial approach: Letter
Copies of proposal: 3
Deadline(s): None
Board meeting date(s): Quarterly
Final notification: Following meeting
Write: Karen Gardner, Exec. Asst.
Officers: David P. Gardner,* Chair.; Spencer F. Eccles,* Pres.; Alonzo W. Watson, Jr., Secy.; Robert Graham, Treas.
Directors:* Delores Dore Eccles.
Number of staff: 1
Employer Identification Number: 876118245

7143
Marriner S. Eccles Foundation ▼
701 Deseret Bldg.
79 South Main St.
Salt Lake City 84111 (801) 322-0116

Established in 1973.
Foundation type: Independent
Financial data (yr. ended 03/31/89): Assets, $16,824,307 (M); gifts received, $6,186; expenditures, $1,217,031, including $1,105,832 for 92 grants (high: $50,000; low: $250; average: $5,000-$25,000).

Purpose and activities: Giving primarily for higher education; health, hospitals, and medical research; arts and culture, including the performing arts, fine arts, and museums; and family and social services, including programs for rehabilitation, the aged, drug and alcohol abuse, welfare, youth, women, and the homeless.
Types of support: Equipment, seed money, operating budgets, general purposes, scholarship funds, research, matching funds.
Limitations: Giving limited to UT. No grants to individuals, or for capital expenditures for construction of buildings.
Application information: Application form not required.
Initial approach: Proposal
Copies of proposal: 7
Deadline(s): None
Board meeting date(s): Quarterly, usually beginning in July
Final notification: Within a week after meeting
Write: Erma E. Hogan, Mgr.
Officers and Committee Members:* Sara M. Eccles,* Chair.; Alonzo W. Watson, Jr.,* Secy.; John D. Eccles, Spencer F. Eccles, Harold J. Steele, Elmer D. Tucker.
Trustee: First Security Bank of Utah, N.A.
Number of staff: 1 full-time professional.
Employer Identification Number: 237185855

7144
Mrs. Fields Children's Health Foundation ☆
333 Main St.
P.O. Box 4000
Park City 84060

Established in 1986 in UT.
Donor(s): Randall K. Fields, Debra J. Fields, Mrs. Fields, Inc.
Foundation type: Independent
Financial data (yr. ended 12/31/88): Assets, $454,692 (M); gifts received, $99,797; expenditures, $301,038, including $300,919 for 12 grants (high: $181,683; low: $193).
Purpose and activities: Giving for the "advancement of medical research, care, and treatment of children, particularly in connection with cystic fibrosis and infant death syndrome."
Limitations: No grants to individuals.
Application information: Contributes only to pre-selected organizations. Applications not accepted.
Officers: Debra J. Fields, Chair. and V.P.; Randall K. Fields, Pres.; Robert K. Neilson, Mgr.
Employer Identification Number: 742450465

7145
Financial Foundation ⌑
185 South State St., Suite 202
Salt Lake City 84111

Established in 1979 in UT.
Donor(s): Various local banks.
Foundation type: Company-sponsored
Financial data (yr. ended 12/31/88): Assets, $95 (M); gifts received, $138,716; expenditures, $138,886, including $138,716 for 25 grants (high: $22,380; low: $100).
Purpose and activities: Emphasis on civic affairs, cultural programs including the performing arts, and social service and youth agencies.
Limitations: Giving primarily in UT. No grants to individuals.
Publications: 990-PF.
Application information:
Initial approach: Proposal
Copies of proposal: 8
Deadline(s): 2nd Wednesday of each month
Board meeting date(s): Monthly
Final notification: 2 months
Officer: Melanie R. Harris, Secy.-Treas.
Trustees: Bruce Baird, Marvin J. Hammond, Richard W. Kieffer, Gaylen C. Larsen, Brent Milne, Don Rocha.
Number of staff: 2
Employer Identification Number: 942662971

7146
Edith Dee Green Foundation ⌑
4245 Skyline Dr.
Ogden 84403 (801) 621-1485

Foundation type: Independent
Financial data (yr. ended 12/31/87): Assets, $1,418,885 (M); expenditures, $81,171, including $71,600 for 14 grants (high: $31,300; low: $350).
Purpose and activities: Emphasis on higher education and hospitals; grants also for social services and health agencies.
Limitations: Giving primarily in UT.
Application information:
Initial approach: Letter
Deadline(s): Preferably by Sept. 30; no set deadline
Write: Harold J. Mack
Trustees: Val A. Browning, Chair.; John Val Browning, Judith B. Jones, First Security Bank of Utah, N.A.
Employer Identification Number: 876149837

7147
The William H. and Mattie Wattis Harris Foundation ⌑
Crandall Bldg., Suite 600
10 West First South St.
Salt Lake City 84101 (801) 363-7863

Trust established in 1960 in UT.
Donor(s): Mattie Wattis Harris,† William H. Harris.
Foundation type: Independent
Financial data (yr. ended 12/31/87): Assets, $4,074,891 (M); expenditures, $384,945, including $278,300 for 66 grants (high: $24,500; low: $1,000).
Purpose and activities: Emphasis on arts, education, social service programs, conservation, and science.
Limitations: Giving primarily in the western U.S., with emphasis on UT. No support for religious or tax-supported organizations. No grants to individuals, or for scholarships; no loans.
Publications: Program policy statement, application guidelines.
Application information: Application form required.
Initial approach: Letter or proposal
Copies of proposal: 4
Deadline(s): Feb. 1 and Aug. 1
Board meeting date(s): Apr. and Oct.
Write: Max B. Lewis, Pres.
Officers and Trustees: Max B. Lewis, Pres. and Fdn. Mgr.; Marguerite Heydt, Exec. V.P.; James W. Hite, V.P.; Marilyn H. Hite, Secy.
Employer Identification Number: 870405724

7148
Preston G. Hughes Foundation, Inc.
195 West 200 North
Spanish Fork 84660-1714 (801) 798-9212

Established in 1963 in UT.
Foundation type: Independent
Financial data (yr. ended 12/31/88): Assets, $1,457,479 (M); expenditures, $53,979, including $53,180 for 3 grants (high: $52,455; low: $100).
Purpose and activities: Support primarily for a university; support also for missionary programs.
Types of support: Scholarship funds.
Limitations: Giving primarily in UT.
Application information: Applications not accepted.
Board meeting date(s): Dec.
Write: Preston G. Hughes, Pres.
Officers: Preston G. Hughes, Pres. and Treas.; Maurice M. Hughes, V.P.and Secy.; J. Preston Hughes, V.P.
Number of staff: None.
Employer Identification Number: 876122482

7149
Emma Eccles Jones Foundation ⌑
P.O. Box 30007
Salt Lake City 84130-0007
Application address: 300 Deseret Bldg., Salt Lake City, UT 84111; Tel.: (801) 350-5451

Established in 1972 in UT.
Foundation type: Independent
Financial data (yr. ended 8/31/88): Assets, $1,108,624 (M); expenditures, $68,679, including $60,000 for 1 grant.
Purpose and activities: Support primarily for higher education.
Types of support: Building funds.
Limitations: Giving primarily in UT.
Application information: Application form not required.
Deadline(s): None
Write: W. John Lamborn
Trustee: First Security Bank of Utah, N.A.
Employer Identification Number: 876155073

7150
Ben B. and Iris M. Margolis Charitable Foundation for Medical Research
c/o First Security Bank of Utah, N.A.
P.O. Box 30007
Salt Lake City 84130 (801) 350-5361

Established in 1979 in UT.
Donor(s): Iris M. Margolis, Ben B. Margolis.†
Foundation type: Independent
Financial data (yr. ended 03/31/88): Assets, $2,113,938 (M); expenditures, $131,477, including $110,000 for 9 grants (high: $22,500; low: $5,000).
Purpose and activities: Limited to the support of medical research.
Types of support: Research.

Limitations: No grants to individuals, or for scholarships, fellowships, or endowments; no loans.
Application information:
Initial approach: Proposal
Deadline(s): None
Board meeting date(s): Monthly
Trustee: First Security Bank of Utah, N.A.
Employer Identification Number: 876180864

7151
Masonic Foundation of Utah ⌑
650 East South Temple St.
Salt Lake City 84102 (801) 363-2936

Established in 1929.
Donor(s): Roy Craddock.†
Foundation type: Independent
Financial data (yr. ended 12/31/86): Assets, $2,735,882 (M); gifts received, $9,594; expenditures, $121,771, including $91,900 for 35 grants (high: $8,000; low: $150).
Purpose and activities: Giving for health, higher education, including student loan funds, and youth, and social service agencies.
Types of support: Research, equipment, general purposes.
Limitations: Giving primarily in UT.
Application information: Application form not required.
Deadline(s): None
Write: Robert D. Braman, Secy.-Treas.
Officers and Trustees: Francis W. Douglas, Chair.; Robert D. Braman, Secy.-Treas.; LeRoy S. Axland, Duane C. Carpenter, Tracy Smith.
Number of staff: 1 part-time professional; 1 part-time support.
Employer Identification Number: 870261722

7152
Herbert I. and Elsa B. Michael Foundation ⌑
200 South Main St.
Salt Lake City 84101
Application address: West One Trust Co., P.O. Box 3058, Salt Lake City, UT 84110

Established in 1950 in UT.
Donor(s): Elsa B. Michael.†
Foundation type: Independent
Financial data (yr. ended 9/30/88): Assets, $3,836,788 (M); expenditures, $285,266, including $233,600 for 38 grants (high: $100,000; low: $1,000).
Purpose and activities: Emphasis on cultural programs and higher and secondary education; support also for hospitals and social service agencies.
Limitations: Giving primarily in UT. No support for sectarian religious activities.
Application information:
Deadline(s): None
Write: Gilbert Bean
Trustees: William H. Adams, K. Jay Holdsworth, Continental Bank and Trust Co.
Advisory Committee: Francis W. Douglas, Gordon Hall, Chase N. Peterson.
Employer Identification Number: 876122556

7153
Samuel C. & Myra G. Powell Foundation
c/o First Security Bank of Utah, N.A.
P.O. Box 9936
Ogden 84409 (801) 393-5376
Application address: 714 Eccles Bldg., 385 24th St., Ogden, UT 84401

Established in 1974 in UT.
Foundation type: Independent
Financial data (yr. ended 12/31/88): Assets, $1,316,369 (M); gifts received, $10,600; expenditures, $39,123, including $27,775 for 11 grants (high: $10,000; low: $100).
Purpose and activities: Giving for higher and other education, the arts, historic preservation, religion, and health, including hospitals, a surgical society, and a burn center.
Limitations: Giving primarily in Ogden and Salt Lake City, UT.
Application information: Application form not required.
Initial approach: Letter
Deadline(s): Preferably by Sept. 30; no set deadline
Board meeting date(s): Dec.
Write: Samuel H. Barker, Chair.
Officers: Samuel H. Barker, Chair.; Charles Barker, Vice-Chair.; Jack Lampros, Secy.; Mary Barker, Rex Child.
Trustee: First Security Bank of Utah, N.A.
Number of staff: None.
Employer Identification Number: 876163275

7154
S. J. and Jessie E. Quinney Foundation ⌑
P.O. Box 45385
Salt Lake City 84145-0385 (801) 532-1500

Established about 1982 in UT.
Donor(s): S.J. Quinney.†
Foundation type: Independent
Financial data (yr. ended 12/31/86): Assets, $12,604,612 (M); gifts received, $3,815,625; expenditures, $292,627, including $248,965 for 40 grants (high: $10,900; low: $500).
Purpose and activities: Support for the arts, health associations, and higher education, a ballet, a museum, and a university.
Types of support: General purposes.
Limitations: Giving limited to UT.
Application information: Application form not required.
Deadline(s): June 30th of each year
Write: Herbert C. Livsey, Trustee
Trustees: Clark P. Giles, Janet Q. Lawson, Herbert C. Livsey, David E. Quinney, Jr.
Directors: James W. Freed, Frederick Q. Lawson, Peter Q. Lawson, Stephen B. Nobeker, JoAnne L. Shrontz, Alonzo W. Watson, Jr., Gene Q. Wilder.
Employer Identification Number: 870389312

7155
Charles Redd Foundation
La Sal 84530

Established in 1971 in UT.
Foundation type: Independent
Financial data (yr. ended 12/31/88): Assets, $1,576,360 (M); expenditures, $200,585, including $166,724 for 24 grants (high: $61,414; low: $50).
Purpose and activities: Support for agricultural, economic, and historical research at public and private universities in UT.
Types of support: Research, equipment, conferences and seminars, fellowships, land acquisition.
Limitations: Giving primarily in southeastern UT and southwestern CO.
Application information: Application form not required.
Copies of proposal: 8
Deadline(s): Nov. 30
Board meeting date(s): Jan.
Trustee: Charles Hardy Redd.
Number of staff: None.
Employer Identification Number: 876148176

7156
Junior E. & Blanche B. Rich Foundation ⌑
2826 Pierce Ave.
Ogden 84409

Established in 1975 in UT.
Foundation type: Independent
Financial data (yr. ended 12/31/87): Assets, $1,112,096 (M); expenditures, $65,903, including $53,950 for 8 grants (high: $6,000; low: $100).
Purpose and activities: Support primarily for higher education; support also for youth and arts organizations.
Types of support: Building funds, general purposes.
Limitations: Giving primarily in UT.
Application information: Application form not required.
Initial approach: Letter
Deadline(s): Sept. 30
Write: Sharon Rich Lewis, Chair.
Directors: Sharon Rich Lewis, Chair.; Blanche B. Rich, Edward B. Rich.
Trustee: First Security Bank of Utah, N.A.
Employer Identification Number: 876173654

7157
The Mary Elizabeth Dee Shaw Charitable Trust ☆
c/o First Security Bank of Utah, N.A.
P.O. Box 9936
Ogden 84409 (801) 626-9533

Trust established in 1959 in UT.
Donor(s): Mary Elizabeth Dee Shaw.†
Foundation type: Independent
Financial data (yr. ended 12/31/88): Assets, $2,316,680 (M); expenditures, $100,671, including $85,204 for 2 grants (high: $84,204; low: $1,000).
Purpose and activities: Primarily to assist Weber State College and McKay-Dee Hospital; some support for local charities.
Limitations: Giving limited to UT. No grants to individuals.
Application information: Funds largely committed for the next 10 years. Application form not required.
Initial approach: Letter
Copies of proposal: 1
Deadline(s): Submit proposal in Sept.
Board meeting date(s): Nov.

Write: Jack D. Lampros, Secy.
Distribution Committee: Elizabeth D.S. Stewart, Chair.; Donnell B. Stewart, Vice-Chair.; Dean W. Hurst, Venna Storey, C.W. Stromberg.
Trustee: First Security Bank of Utah, N.A.
Number of staff: None.
Employer Identification Number: 876116370

7158
Steiner Foundation, Inc. ⌑
505 East South Temple St.
Salt Lake City 84102-1061 (801) 328-8831
Application address: P.O. Box 2317, Salt Lake City, UT 84102

Established in 1959 in UT.
Donor(s): Steiner Corp.
Foundation type: Company-sponsored
Financial data (yr. ended 06/30/88): Assets, $1,906,379 (M); expenditures, $111,289, including $97,867 for 35 grants (high: $30,000; low: $500).
Purpose and activities: Support for culture and the arts, youth and community organizations, and social services.
Limitations: Giving primarily in UT.
Application information: Proposal.
Write: Kevin K. Steiner, Pres.
Officers: Kevin K. Steiner, Pres.; Timothy L. Weiler, Secy.
Employer Identification Number: 876119190

7159
Donnell B. and Elizabeth Dee Shaw Stewart Educational Foundation
c/o First Security Bank of Utah, N.A.
P.O. Box 9936
Ogden 84409 (801) 626-9533

Established in 1977 in UT.
Donor(s): Elizabeth D.S. Stewart.
Foundation type: Independent
Financial data (yr. ended 12/31/88): Assets, $2,124,437 (M); expenditures, $76,793, including $62,950 for 7 grants (high: $42,000; low: $150; average: $20,000).
Purpose and activities: Support primarily for Weber State College; minor giving also for other charitable activities.
Types of support: Building funds, capital campaigns, scholarship funds.
Limitations: Giving primarily in Ogden, UT.
Application information: Application form not required.
Initial approach: Letter
Copies of proposal: 1
Deadline(s): None, but submit request preferably by Sept. 30
Board meeting date(s): Nov.
Write: J.D. Lampros, Trust Officer, First Security Bank of Utah, N.A.
Officers: Elizabeth D.S. Stewart, Chair.; Donnell B. Stewart, Vice-Chair.
Member: Dean W. Hurst.
Trustee: First Security Bank of Utah, N.A.
Number of staff: None.
Employer Identification Number: 876179880

7160
Arthur L. Swim Foundation ⌑
1095 South 800 East, No. 4
Orem 84058

Established in 1942 in CA.
Foundation type: Independent
Financial data (yr. ended 12/31/88): Assets, $8,457,025 (M); expenditures, $144,933, including $65,000 for 3 grants (high: $50,000; low: $5,000).
Purpose and activities: Giving primarily for education, with emphasis on medical education; support also for legal organizations.
Limitations: No grants to individuals.
Application information: Contributes only to pre-selected organizations. Applications not accepted.
Trustees: Marilyn S. Lenahan, Gaylord K. Swim, Katherine M. Swim, Roger C. Swim.
Employer Identification Number: 826007432

7161
Tanner Charitable Trust ⌑
1930 South State St.
Salt Lake City 84115

Incorporated in 1965 in UT.
Donor(s): Obert C. Tanner.
Foundation type: Independent
Financial data (yr. ended 12/31/88): Assets, $382,013 (M); gifts received, $387,000; expenditures, $208,483, including $205,250 for 17 grants (high: $95,000; low: $100).
Purpose and activities: Grants for higher education and cultural programs, including music.
Types of support: Student aid.
Limitations: Giving primarily in UT.
Application information: Contributes only to pre-selected organizations. Applications not accepted.
Trustees: Carolyn T. Irish, Chair.; O. Don Ostler, Grace A. Tanner, Obert C. Tanner.
Employer Identification Number: 876125059

7162
Thrasher Research Fund ▼
50 East North Temple St., 7th Fl.
Salt Lake City 84150 (801) 240-3386
FAX: (801) 240-1417

Established in 1977 in UT.
Donor(s): E.W. "Al" Thrasher.
Foundation type: Independent
Financial data (yr. ended 12/31/89): Assets, $33,851,438 (M); expenditures, $1,630,806, including $1,290,348 for 23 grants.
Purpose and activities: To promote both national and international child health research. The fund currently emphasizes practical and applied interventions that have the potential to improve the health of children throughout the world.
Types of support: Research.
Limitations: No support for studies in the areas of abortions or reproductive physiology, including contraceptive technology; generally, no support for research in the area of sexually transmitted disease. No grants for conferences, workshops, or symposia. No support for general operations, construction or renovation of buildings or facilities, scholarships, or purchase of equipment; no loans.
Publications: Multi-year report (including application guidelines), informational brochure.
Application information: Application form required.
Initial approach: Consultation by telephone or letter, followed by a 3-page prospectus
Copies of proposal: 12
Deadline(s): None
Board meeting date(s): Apr. and Oct.
Final notification: 6 months
Write: Robert M. Briem, Assoc. Dir.
Executive Committee: Glenn L. Pace, Chair.; E.W. "Al" Thrasher, Vice-Chair.; Dan S. Bushnell, Isaac C. Ferguson, Addie Fuhriman, Harvey S. Glade, Alexander B. Morrison, Mary Ann Q. Wood, Donald Wright.
Number of staff: 2 full-time professional; 1 part-time professional; 1 full-time support; 2 part-time support.

VERMONT

7163
Copley Fund ⌑
P.O. Box 696
Morrisville 05661

Foundation type: Independent
Financial data (yr. ended 12/31/87): Assets, $1,579,602 (M); expenditures, $84,658, including $77,574 for 134 grants to individuals.
Purpose and activities: Housing assistance for the elderly.
Types of support: Grants to individuals.
Limitations: Giving limited to Lamoille County, VT.
Application information:
Initial approach: Letter
Deadline(s): Dec. 31
Write: Richard Sargent, Trustee
Trustees: Robert Parker, Richard Sargent.
Employer Identification Number: 036006013

7164
General Educational Fund, Inc. ⌑
c/o The Merchants Trust Co.
P.O. Box 1009, 123 Church St.
Burlington 05402

Incorporated in 1918 in VT.
Donor(s): Emma Eliza Curtis,† Lorenzo E. Woodhouse.†
Foundation type: Independent
Financial data (yr. ended 7/31/88): Assets, $16,183,562 (M); gifts received, $1,187; expenditures, $749,255, including $635,998 for grants to individuals.
Purpose and activities: Scholarships primarily for higher education; support also for secondary education and vocational training.
Types of support: Student aid.

Limitations: Giving primarily in VT. No grants for building or endowment funds, operating budgets, or special projects.
Application information: Application form required.
Initial approach: Letter
Copies of proposal: 1
Write: David W. Webster, Pres.
Officers and Trustees: David W. Webster, Pres. and Treas.; Fred G. Smith, V.P.; Frederick R. McGibney, Secy.
Employer Identification Number: 036009912

7165
Howfirma Foundation
14 Central St.
Woodstock 05091 (802) 457-1370
Application address: P.O. Box 417, Woodstock, VT 05091

Established about 1983 in VT.
Donor(s): Frank H. Teagle, Jr.
Foundation type: Operating
Financial data (yr. ended 12/31/88): Assets, $176,514 (M); gifts received, $308,541; expenditures, $168,723, including $156,683 for 355 grants (high: $25,000; low: $25).
Purpose and activities: A private operating foundation; support for youth and child welfare, social services, health associations, medical education, conservation, cultural organizations and historical preservation, and peace organizations.
Limitations: Giving primarily in the Woodstock, VT, area. No grants to individuals.
Application information: Application form required.
Deadline(s): None
Write: Gary R. Brown, Trustee
Trustees: Gary R. Brown, Frank H. Teagle, Jr., Ameritrust Co., N.A.
Employer Identification Number: 222495072

7166
Lintilhac Foundation
100 Harbor Rd.
Shelburne 05482 (802) 985-4106

Established in 1975.
Donor(s): Claire Malcolm Lintilhac.†
Foundation type: Independent
Financial data (yr. ended 12/31/88): Assets, $5,433,818 (M); gifts received, $688,596; expenditures, $562,524, including $502,187 for 29 grants (high: $166,667; low: $250).
Purpose and activities: Support for medical education programs at specified institutions in VT; support also for health services, community development, civic projects and educational institutions.
Types of support: Annual campaigns, building funds, capital campaigns, conferences and seminars, continuing support, equipment, general purposes, land acquisition, lectureships, matching funds, professorships, renovation projects, scholarship funds, seed money, special projects.
Limitations: Giving primarily in north central VT; including Chittenden, Lamoille, and Washington counties. No grants to individuals.
Publications: Annual report.
Application information:
Initial approach: Proposal
Deadline(s): None
Board meeting date(s): Quarterly
Write: Crea S. Lintilhac, V.P.
Officers and Directors:* Philip M. Lintilhac,* Pres.; Crea S. Lintilhac,* V.P. and Secy.; Raeman P. Sopher,* Treas.
Number of staff: 1 part-time support.
Employer Identification Number: 510176851

7167
Merchants Bank Foundation, Inc. ⌑ ☆
c/o The Merchants Bank
123 Church St.
Burlington 05401-8415

Donor(s): Merchants Bank.
Foundation type: Company-sponsored
Financial data (yr. ended 8/31/88): Assets, $654,492 (M); gifts received, $151,500; expenditures, $129,878, including $127,950 for 48 grants (high: $25,000; low: $100).
Purpose and activities: Support for secondary and higher education, hospitals, health associations, United Way, human services, the performing arts and museums.
Limitations: Giving primarily in VT. No grants to individuals.
Application information:
Initial approach: Letter
Deadline(s): None
Final notification: 2 months
Write: Fred G. Smith or Cheryl Mead, Trustees
Officers and Trustees: Dudley H. Davis, Pres.; Susan Struble, Secy.; Fred G. Smith, Treas.; Bruce B. Butterfield, Cheryl Mead.
Employer Identification Number: 036016628

7168
Mortimer R. Proctor Trust ⌑
c/o Proctor Bank
49 Main St.
Proctor 05765

Foundation type: Independent
Financial data (yr. ended 12/31/88): Assets, $2,367,215 (M); expenditures, $130,244, including $110,926 for 21 grants (high: $21,000; low: $310).
Purpose and activities: Giving for civic and community affairs.
Types of support: Emergency funds, exchange programs, operating budgets, special projects.
Limitations: Giving limited to Proctor, VT. No support for education, or charitable or religious organizations.
Publications: Annual report, 990-PF.
Application information:
Initial approach: Letter
Deadline(s): None
Trustee: Proctor Bank.
Employer Identification Number: 036020099

7169
Olin Scott Fund, Inc.
100 South St.
P.O. Box 1208
Bennington 05201 (802) 447-1096

Incorporated in 1920 in VT.
Donor(s): Olin Scott.†
Foundation type: Independent
Financial data (yr. ended 6/30/89): Assets, $2,378,588 (M); expenditures, $142,569, including $75,000 for 3 grants of $25,000 each and $64,700 for 33 loans to individuals.
Purpose and activities: Giving for higher education, including grants to colleges and universities in VT and student loans for young men in Bennington County.
Types of support: Student loans, scholarship funds.
Limitations: Giving limited to Bennington County, VT. No grants for building or endowment funds, operating budgets, or special projects.
Application information: Application form required.
Initial approach: Letter or telephone
Copies of proposal: 1
Deadline(s): None
Board meeting date(s): As required
Write: Melvin A. Dyson, Pres.
Officers and Trustees: Melvin A. Dyson, Pres. and Treas.; Kelton B. Miller, V.P.; Robert E. Cummings, Jr., Secy.
Number of staff: 2 full-time professional; 1 part-time support.
Employer Identification Number: 036005697

7170
The Windham Foundation, Inc.
P.O. Box 70
Grafton 05146 (802) 843-2211

Incorporated in 1963 in VT.
Donor(s): The Bunbury Co., Inc., Dean Mathey.†
Foundation type: Operating
Financial data (yr. ended 10/31/89): Assets, $34,741,897 (M); expenditures, $1,767,047, including $169,876 for 73 grants (high: $25,000; low: $76; average: $100-$5,000) and $162,333 for 409 grants to individuals (high: $1,000; low: $100).
Purpose and activities: A private operating foundation; eighty-five percent of adjusted net income applied to operating programs of foundation, including civic improvement and historic preservation; primary activity is preservation of properties in rural areas of VT to maintain their charm and historic, native, or unusual features, with emphasis on restoration of houses in Grafton; remaining fifteen percent of income for general charitable giving, primarily confined to the disadvantaged, youth activities, aid to students and to educational institutions, and organizations assisting the disabled.
Types of support: Operating budgets, seed money, building funds, matching funds, continuing support, student aid, special projects, equipment, general purposes.
Limitations: Giving limited to VT, with emphasis on Windham County. No grants to individuals (except for college scholarship program), or for endowment funds; no loans.
Publications: Annual report (including application guidelines), informational brochure, newsletter.
Application information: Application form required.
Initial approach: Letter
Copies of proposal: 5
Deadline(s): 1 month prior to board meeting

Board meeting date(s): Feb., May, July, and Oct.
Final notification: Following the board meeting
Write: Stephan A. Morse, Exec. Dir.
Officers: James R. Cogan,* Pres. and C.E.O.; William B. Wright,* V.P. and Treas.; Samuel W. Lambert III,* V.P.; Charles B. Atwater,* Secy. and Dir. of Scholarships; Stephan A. Morse, Exec. Dir.
Trustees:* Robert M. Olmsted, Edward J. Toohey, Charles C. Townsend, Edward R. Zuccaro.
Number of staff: 5 full-time professional; 1 full-time support.
Employer Identification Number: 136142024

VIRGINIA

7171
Aid Association for the Blind ⌑ ☆
c/o Jean K. Carry
6315 Evermay Dr.
McLean 22101

Foundation type: Independent
Financial data (yr. ended 06/30/89): Assets, $3,939,320 (M); expenditures, $230,300, including $202,500 for 10 grants (high: $75,000; low: $2,500).
Purpose and activities: Giving to hospitals, clinics, social service agencies, and public relations projects serving the blind.
Limitations: Giving primarily in Washington, DC, and MD. No grants to individuals.
Application information: Contributes only to pre-selected organizations. Applications not accepted.
Officers: Jean K. Carry, Pres. and Treas.; Sally B. Mann, V.P. and Secy.
Employer Identification Number: 530196564

7172
Scott B. and Annie P. Appleby Trust
c/o Crestar Bank, N.A.
P.O. Box 27385
Richmond 23261-7385
Application address: c/o Crestar Bank, N.A., 15th St. and New York Ave., N.W., Washington, DC 20005; Tel.: (202) 879-6341

Trust established in 1948 in DC.
Foundation type: Independent
Financial data (yr. ended 12/31/88): Assets, $2,772,009 (M); expenditures, $152,273, including $119,000 for 15 grants.
Purpose and activities: Emphasis on higher education for the handicapped, primarily in GA; some grants for cultural programs and child welfare in FL; support also for adult and other education, including religious schools.
Limitations: Giving primarily in GA, FL, and Washington, DC. No grants to individuals.
Application information: Application form not required.
Initial approach: Proposal
Copies of proposal: 1
Deadline(s): Submit proposal preferably in May; deadline June 1
Board meeting date(s): July or Aug.
Write: Virginia M. Herrin, V.P., Crestar Bank, N.A.
Trustees: F. Jordan Colby, Sarah P. Williams, Crestar Bank, N.A., Maryland National Bank.
Number of staff: 1 part-time support.
Employer Identification Number: 526334302

7173
George & Frances Armour Foundation, Inc. ⌑
c/o Stephen Wainger
7342 Ruthven Rd.
Norfolk 23505

Incorporated in 1957 in NY.
Donor(s): George L. Armour, Frances Armour.†
Foundation type: Independent
Financial data (yr. ended 3/31/89): Assets, $1,306,553 (M); expenditures, $95,989, including $61,950 for 31 grants (high: $10,000; low: $100).
Purpose and activities: Grants primarily for hospitals, health agencies, education, and Jewish welfare funds.
Limitations: No grants to individuals.
Application information: Applications not accepted.
Officers: Elizabeth Armour Wainger, Pres.; Stephen Wainger, V.P. and Secy.-Treas.; Anna Vanetsen, V.P.
Employer Identification Number: 136155619

7174
Beazley Foundation, Inc.
3720 Brighton St.
Portsmouth 23707-1788 (804) 393-1605

Incorporated in 1948 in VA.
Donor(s): Fred W. Beazley,† Marie C. Beazley,† Fred W. Beazley, Jr.†
Foundation type: Independent
Financial data (yr. ended 12/31/89): Assets, $20,229,424 (M); expenditures, $1,076,443, including $650,460 for 33 grants (high: $100,000; low: $50; average: $50-$100,000).
Purpose and activities: "To further the cause of charity, education, and religion." Grants for operation of community and senior citizens centers and a dental clinic for the indigent. Support also for secondary and medical education, community funds, the aged, youth agencies, and other endeavors.
Types of support: Capital campaigns, continuing support, scholarship funds.
Limitations: Giving primarily in the Hampton Roads area of VA. No grants to individuals.
Publications: Financial statement, application guidelines, program policy statement.
Application information: Application form not required.
Initial approach: Proposal
Copies of proposal: 1
Deadline(s): Month preceding board meetings
Board meeting date(s): Apr., July, Oct., and Jan.
Write: Lawrence W. I'Anson, Jr., Pres.
Officers and Trustees:* Lawrence W. I'Anson,* Chair.; Lawrence W. I'Anson, Jr.,* Pres.; Joseph J. Quadros, Jr.,* V.P. and Treas.; John T. Kavanaugh,* V.P.; Malcolm F. Beazley, Jr.,* Secy.; Jeanette C. Bridgeman,* Treas.; Jewel A. Bush, Mills E. Godwin, Jr.
Number of staff: 1 full-time professional; 6 full-time support; 2 part-time support.
Employer Identification Number: 540550100

7175
Bell Atlantic Charitable Foundation ☆
1310 North Courthouse Rd., 10th Fl.
Arlington 22201 (703) 974-5440

Established in 1987 in PA.
Donor(s): Bell Atlantic Corp.
Foundation type: Company-sponsored
Financial data (yr. ended 12/31/89): Assets, $5,152,566 (M); expenditures, $2,111,684, including $1,475,316 for 73 grants (high: $300,000; low: $1,000; average: $1,000-$300,000) and $631,734 for employee matching gifts.
Purpose and activities: Giving for national and regional organizations, with two main areas of support: 1) general grants, including health and human services, arts and culture, and social and economic development and 2) education, including science and technology and literacy. In 1989, the foundation pledged funds to finance the Bell Atlantic/ALA Family Literacy Project, in conjunction with the Association for Library Service to Children.
Limitations: Giving primarily in area of company operations.
Application information:
Initial approach: Letter or proposal; local organizations should contact the nearest Bell company
Deadline(s): None
Write: Ruth P. Caine, Dir.
Officers and Directors:* Christopher E. Clouser,* Pres.; A. Gray Collins, Jr.,* V.P.; Carolyn S. Burger,* Secy.-Treas.; James H. Brenneman, Tom Buens, Hank Butta, William S. Ford, Bruce S. Gordon, William Harval, Joe Hulihan, John M. Kelleher, Del Lewis, Hugh Stallard.
Employer Identification Number: 232502809

7176
Best Products Foundation ▼
P.O. Box 26303
Richmond 23260
Application address: 1616 P St. N.W., Suite 100, Washington, DC 20036; Tel.: (202) 328-5188

Established in 1967 in VA.
Donor(s): Best Products Co.
Foundation type: Company-sponsored
Financial data (yr. ended 01/31/90): Assets, $1,700,000 (M); expenditures, $1,000,000, including $810,000 for 500 grants (high: $100,000; low: $50,000; average: $100-$10,000).
Purpose and activities: Support primarily for higher, secondary, and elementary education, including educational programs for minorities and an employee matching gift program; museums and cultural programs; community and social welfare organizations, including

youth agencies; and projects concerning reproductive rights.
Types of support: Matching funds, special projects, employee matching gifts, seed money, emergency funds, scholarship funds.
Limitations: Giving primarily in areas of company operations. No support for religious institutions or government-supported organizations. No grants to individuals, or for publications, conferences, seminars, research, or building or endowment funds; no loans.
Publications: including application guidelines, 990-PF, informational brochure.
Application information: New proposals are not currently being accepted.
Initial approach: Letter
Copies of proposal: 1
Deadline(s): 2 months before board meetings
Board meeting date(s): Usually in Jan., Mar., June, Sept., and Nov.
Final notification: 45 days after completion of screening process
Write: Susan L. Butler, Exec. Dir.
Officers and Directors:* Frances A. Lewis,* Chair.; Sydney Lewis,* Pres.; Robert L. Burrus, Jr.,* Secy.; Susan L. Butler,* Treas. and Exec. Dir.
Number of staff: 1 full-time professional; 1 full-time support.
Employer Identification Number: 237139981

7177
The Elmer Bisbee Foundation
P.O. Box 7332
Arlington 22207-0332

Established in 1986 in VA.
Donor(s): Dorothy M. Bisbee.†
Foundation type: Independent
Financial data (yr. ended 12/31/88): Assets, $1,446,740 (M); expenditures, $75,606, including $72,800 for 24 grants (high: $5,000; low: $1,000).
Purpose and activities: Support primarily for evangelical Christian religious organizations, missionaries, and schools; support also for international studies and relief programs in Africa, Asia, Europe, and the United Kingdom; giving for child welfare, libraries, literacy, music, community development, theological education, and the needy.
Types of support: Emergency funds, lectureships, professorships, scholarship funds, special projects.
Application information: Contributes only to pre-selected organizations. Applications not accepted.
Officers: Helga B. Henry, Chair. and Pres.; Carl F. Henry, Secy.
Trustee: Edna F. Wyant.
Employer Identification Number: 541377732

7178
David S. Blount Educational Foundation ⌑
c/o Colonial American National Bank
P.O. Box 13888
Roanoke 24038 (703) 982-3201

Established in 1973 in VA.
Foundation type: Independent
Financial data (yr. ended 3/31/88): Assets, $1,770,169 (M); expenditures, $82,647, including $61,050 for 14 grants to individuals.
Purpose and activities: Awards scholarships to VA residents attending colleges and universities in VA.
Types of support: Student aid.
Limitations: Giving limited to VA residents.
Application information:
Initial approach: Apply for scholarships through college financial aid office
Deadline(s): None
Write: Harry L. Shinn Jr., Trust Officer, Colonial American National Bank
Trustee: Colonial American National Bank.
Employer Identification Number: 546111717

7179
John Stewart Bryan Memorial Foundation, Inc. ⌑
P.O. Box 1234
Richmond 23209-1234 (804) 643-8363

Established in 1946 in VA.
Foundation type: Independent
Financial data (yr. ended 12/31/87): Assets, $1,370,639 (M); gifts received, $17,000; expenditures, $96,915, including $89,345 for 39 grants (high: $17,600; low: $100).
Purpose and activities: Support primarily for community organizations; support also for higher education and Christian education.
Limitations: Giving primarily in VA.
Application information:
Write: D. Tennant Bryan, Pres.
Officers and Directors: D. Tennant Bryan, Pres.; C.M. Trible, V.P. and Secy.-Treas.; J. Stewart Bryan III, Mary Tennant Bryan, Florence Bryan Wishner.
Employer Identification Number: 237425357

7180
The Bryant Foundation ⌑
P.O. Box 275
Alexandria 22313 (703) 549-3500

Established about 1949.
Donor(s): J.C. Herbert Bryant.
Foundation type: Independent
Financial data (yr. ended 12/31/87): Assets, $3,239,316 (M); expenditures, $175,533, including $161,950 for 13 grants (high: $125,000; low: $50).
Purpose and activities: Giving primarily for education, with some support for social services and health.
Limitations: Giving primarily in VA. No grants to individuals.
Application information:
Initial approach: Letter or telephone
Deadline(s): None
Write: Arthur H. Bryant, II, Pres.
Officers: Arthur H. Bryant II, Pres. and Treas.; Howard W. Smith, Jr., Secy.
Employer Identification Number: 546032840

7181
N. R. Burroughs Educational Fund ⌑ ☆
c/o Piedmont Trust Bank
P.O. Box 4751
Martinsville 24115-4751 (703) 632-2971

Established in 1983 in VA.
Foundation type: Independent
Financial data (yr. ended 6/30/89): Assets, $3,136,666 (M); qualifying distributions, $130,000, including $130,000 for loans to individuals.
Purpose and activities: Provides educational support to qualified, deserving, and credit-worthy local area residents.
Types of support: Student loans.
Limitations: Giving limited to residents within 200-mile radius of Martinsville, VA.
Application information: Application form required.
Deadline(s): None
Write: Mabel Martin
Trustees: R.H. Dunn, Jr., I.M. Groves, Jr., Douglas T. Ramsey, Piedmont Trust Bank.
Employer Identification Number: 521303602

7182
The Robert G. Cabell III and Maude Morgan Cabell Foundation
P.O. Box 1377
Richmond 23211 (804) 780-2050

Incorporated in 1957 in VA.
Donor(s): Robert G. Cabell III,† Maude Morgan Cabell.†
Foundation type: Independent
Financial data (yr. ended 12/31/89): Assets, $22,619,737 (M); expenditures, $951,885, including $872,925 for 18 grants (high: $100,000; low: $15,000; average: $25,000-$100,000).
Purpose and activities: Grants primarily for higher education, health care, historic preservation, the arts and cultural projects, community development, and welfare.
Types of support: Building funds, capital campaigns, equipment, renovation projects, special projects.
Limitations: Giving primarily in VA. No support for political organizations or special interest groups. No grants to individuals, or for endowment funds, operating programs, or research projects.
Application information: Application form not required.
Initial approach: Letter
Copies of proposal: 1
Deadline(s): None
Board meeting date(s): Mar., May, and Nov.
Final notification: Before end of calendar year
Write: B. Walton Turnbull, Exec. Dir.
Officers: J. Read Branch,* Pres.; Robert G. Cabell, V.P.; Royal E. Cabell, Jr.,* Secy.; B. Walton Turnbull, Exec. Dir.
Directors:* Joseph L. Antrim III, J. Read Branch, Jr., Patteson Branch, Jr., Charles Cabell, Edmund A. Rennolds, Jr., John K.B. Rennolds.
Number of staff: 1 part-time professional; 2 part-time support.
Employer Identification Number: 546039157

7183
Camp Foundation
P.O. Box 813
Franklin 23851 (804) 562-3439

Incorporated in 1942 in VA.
Donor(s): James L. Camp, P.D. Camp, and their families.

Foundation type: Independent
Financial data (yr. ended 12/31/89): Assets, $12,360,600 (M); expenditures, $795,350, including $717,250 for 65 grants (high: $200,000; low: $1,000; average: $1,000-$20,000) and $66,000 for 29 grants to individuals (high: $4,000; low: $2,000; average: $2,000-$4,000).
Purpose and activities: "To provide or aid in providing in or near the town of Franklin, VA, ... parks, playgrounds, recreational facilities, libraries, hospitals, clinics, homes for the aged or needy, refuges for delinquent, dependent or neglected children, training schools, or other like institutions or activities." Grants also to select organizations statewide, with emphasis on youth agencies, hospitals, higher and secondary education, including scholarships filed through high school principals, recreation, historic preservation, and cultural programs.
Types of support: Annual campaigns, seed money, emergency funds, building funds, equipment, land acquisition, matching funds, scholarship funds, student aid, research.
Limitations: Giving primarily in Franklin, Southampton County, Isle of Wight County, and Tidewater, VA, and northeastern NC.
Publications: Informational brochure, 990-PF.
Application information: Application form not required.
Initial approach: Proposal
Copies of proposal: 7
Deadline(s): Submit proposal between June and Aug.; deadline Sept. 1; scholarship application deadlines Feb. 26 for filing with high school principals; Mar. 15 for principals to file with foundation
Board meeting date(s): May and Dec.
Final notification: 3 months
Write: Harold S. Atkinson, Exec. Dir.
Officers and Directors:* Robert C. Ray,* Chair.; Sol W. Rawls, Jr.,* Pres.; James L. Camp,* V.P.; John M. Camp, Jr.,* Treas.; Harold S. Atkinson,* Exec. Dir.; John M. Camp III, W.M. Camp, Jr., Clifford A. Cutchins III, William W. Cutchins, Mills E. Godwin, Jr., Paul Camp Marks, J. Edward Moyler, Jr., John D. Munford, S. Waite Rawls, Jr., J.E. Ray III, Richard E. Ray, Toy D. Savage, Jr., W.H. Story.
Number of staff: 1 full-time professional; 1 full-time support; 1 part-time support.
Employer Identification Number: 546052488

7184
Carrie S. Camp Foundation, Inc. ⌑
P.O. Box 557
Franklin 23851

Incorporated about 1949 in VA.
Donor(s): Edith Clay Camp.
Foundation type: Independent
Financial data (yr. ended 12/31/86): Assets, $1,512,421 (M); expenditures, $108,115, including $99,875 for 21 grants (high: $50,000; low: $175).
Purpose and activities: Support primarily for higher education and a student aid foundation; grants also for community services.
Limitations: Giving primarily in VA.
Application information:
Initial approach: Letter
Deadline(s): None
Write: William M. Camp, Jr., Pres.
Officers: William M. Camp, Jr., Pres.; Leon Clay Camp, V.P.; Mildred M. Branche, Secy.-Treas.
Employer Identification Number: 546052446

7185
J. L. Camp Foundation, Inc. ⌑
University Station
P.O. Box 3816
Charlottesville 22903 (804) 293-7004

Incorporated in 1946 in VA.
Donor(s): J.L. Camp, Jr.,† Mrs. J.L. Camp, Jr., James L. Camp III.
Foundation type: Independent
Financial data (yr. ended 12/31/88): Assets, $2,477,565 (M); expenditures, $146,047, including $133,733 for 20 grants (high: $45,760; low: $500).
Purpose and activities: Emphasis on higher and secondary education; support also for the arts and religion.
Types of support: Continuing support, scholarship funds.
Limitations: Giving primarily in VA. No support for private foundations. No grants to individuals.
Application information:
Initial approach: Proposal
Deadline(s): None
Write: James L. Camp III, Pres.
Officers and Directors: James L. Camp III, Pres.; Toy D. Savage, Jr., V.P.; Douglas B. Ellis, Secy.
Employer Identification Number: 540742940

7186
Ruth and Henry Campbell Foundation ⌑
c/o Sovran Bank, N.A., Trust Div.
P.O. Box 26903
Richmond 23261 (804) 788-2573

Established in 1957.
Foundation type: Independent
Financial data (yr. ended 12/31/87): Assets, $8,155,225 (M); expenditures, $545,308, including $473,650 for 46 grants (high: $42,250; low: $1,000).
Purpose and activities: Grants primarily for higher and secondary education and hospitals.
Limitations: Giving primarily in VA.
Application information:
Initial approach: Letter
Deadline(s): None
Write: Donnie Keence, 1st V.P., Sovran Bank, N.A.
Officer and Directors: Linda E. Beatty, Secy.; John M. Camp, Jr., Paul D. Camp III, Paul Camp Marks, H. Webster Walker III.
Trustee: Sovran Bank, N.A.
Employer Identification Number: 546031023

7187
The Beirne Carter Foundation
P.O. Box 26903
Richmond 23261 (804) 788-2964

Established in 1986 in VA.
Donor(s): Beirne B. Carter.†
Foundation type: Independent
Financial data (yr. ended 12/31/88): Assets, $3,131,172 (M); expenditures, $235,882, including $157,350 for 25 grants (high: $100,500; low: $50).
Purpose and activities: Giving primarily for a historical society, cultural programs, youth organizations, and health.
Limitations: Giving primarily in VA. No grants to individuals.
Application information: Contributes only to pre-selected organizations. Applications not accepted.
Write: J. Samuel Gillespie, Jr.
Officers: Mary Ross C. Hutcheson, Pres.; Mary T. Bryan, V.P.; Talfourd H. Kemper, Secy.-Treas.
Number of staff: 1 part-time professional; 1 part-time support.
Employer Identification Number: 541397827

7188
Cartledge Charitable Foundation, Inc. ⌑
P.O. Box 12528
Roanoke 24026-2528 (703) 343-1701

Established in 1960 in VA.
Foundation type: Independent
Financial data (yr. ended 8/31/88): Assets, $751,432 (M); gifts received, $151,059; expenditures, $234,380, including $233,734 for 117 grants (high: $30,000; low: $25).
Purpose and activities: Support primarily for private schools, colleges, social services, health services and associations, and youth organizations.
Application information:
Initial approach: Letter
Deadline(s): None
Officers: George B. Cartledge, Sr., Chair.; George B. Cartledge, Jr., Pres.; Henry Williamson, V.P.; Robert Bennett, Secy.
Employer Identification Number: 546044831

7189
Central Fidelity Banks, Inc. Foundation ⌑
c/o Central Fidelity Bank
P.O. Box 27602
Richmond 23261

Established in 1980.
Foundation type: Company-sponsored
Financial data (yr. ended 12/31/87): Assets, $41,453 (M); expenditures, $896,796, including $895,530 for 381 grants (high: $50,000; low: $25).
Purpose and activities: Giving for higher education, community funds, and cultural programs; support also for health and hospitals, youth agencies, and social services.
Limitations: Giving primarily in VA.
Application information:
Initial approach: Letter
Deadline(s): None
Write: Charles Tysinger, Mgr.
Officer and Directors: Charles Tysinger, Mgr.; Lewis N. Miller, Jr., Carroll L. Saine, William F. Shumadine, Jr.
Employer Identification Number: 546173939

7190
Chesapeake Corporation Foundation ⌑
1021 East Cary St.
P.O. Box 2350
Richmond 23218-2350 (804) 697-1000

Established in 1955 in VA.
Donor(s): Chesapeake Corp.
Foundation type: Company-sponsored
Financial data (yr. ended 12/31/88): Assets, $965,218 (M); gifts received, $510,000; expenditures, $419,744, including $403,322 for 87 grants (high: $50,421; low: $1,000) and $16,378 for 87 employee matching gifts.
Purpose and activities: Giving primarily for higher and other education, including an employee matching gift program for higher education, and scholarships for children of company employees; support also for community development, civic affairs, cultural programs, and health.
Types of support: Employee matching gifts, employee-related scholarships, matching funds, capital campaigns.
Limitations: Giving primarily in areas of company operations. No grants to individuals.
Application information:
Initial approach: Letter
Board meeting date(s): Feb., June, and Oct.
Write: Alvah H. Eubank, Jr., Secy.-Treas.
Officer: A.H. Eubank, Jr., Secy.-Treas.
Trustees: O.D. Dennis, T.G. Harris, G.P. Mueller, S.G. Olsson, W.T. Robinson.
Employer Identification Number: 540605823

7191
Circuit City Foundation ⌑
2040 Thalbro St.
Richmond 23230 (804) 257-4204

Established in 1962 in VA.
Donor(s): Wards Co., Inc., Circuit City Stores, Inc.
Foundation type: Company-sponsored
Financial data (yr. ended 2/28/89): Assets, $150,710 (M); gifts received, $950,000; expenditures, $896,029, including $766,686 for 355 grants (high: $99,999; low: $25) and $80,735 for 68 grants to individuals (high: $4,000; low: $150).
Purpose and activities: Giving for social services, education, and youth activities.
Types of support: Employee-related scholarships.
Limitations: Giving primarily in VA.
Application information: Application form not required.
Deadline(s): None
Write: Frances Rosi
Trustees: Alan L. Wurtzel, Chair.; Robert L. Burrus, Jr., Frances A. Lewis, Hyman Meyers, Elaine Rothenberg, Richard L. Sharp, Edward Villanueva.
Scholarship Committee: Adrienne Bank, Grace Harris, Barry Katz.
Employer Identification Number: 546048660

7192
The Clisby Charitable Trust ▼
(Formerly The Flager Foundation)
P.O. Box 1515
Richmond 23212-1515 (804) 648-5033

Incorporated in 1963 in VA.
Donor(s): Jessie Kenan Wise.†
Foundation type: Independent
Financial data (yr. ended 12/31/88): Assets, $18,610,174 (M); expenditures, $1,418,288, including $1,300,963 for 55 grants (high: $1,142,557; low: $500; average: $500-$5,000).
Purpose and activities: Support largely for higher and secondary education, historic restoration and preservation, and cultural programs.
Limitations: Giving primarily in VA, with emphasis on Richmond, and in FL, with emphasis on St. Augustine. No grants for capital programs or long-range projects.
Application information:
Initial approach: Proposal
Deadline(s): None
Board meeting date(s): Irregularly
Final notification: None
Write: Lawrence Lewis, Jr., Pres.
Officers and Directors: Lawrence Lewis, Jr., Pres. and Treas.; Mary L.F. Wiley, V.P.; Madeline B. McCarthy, Secy.; Janet P. Lewis.
Number of staff: 1
Employer Identification Number: 546051282

7193
Quincy Cole Trust ⌑
c/o Sovran Bank, N.A.
P.O. Box 26903
Richmond 23261
Grant application address: c/o Sovran Ctr., 12th & Main Sts., Richmond, VA 23261; Tel.: (804) 788-2143

Established in VA in 1969.
Donor(s): Quincy Cole.†
Foundation type: Independent
Financial data (yr. ended 06/30/89): Assets, $5,642,988 (M); expenditures, $309,524, including $264,982 for 15 grants (high: $41,982; low: $2,000).
Purpose and activities: Support for cultural programs, including the performing arts, museums, and historic preservation, and for higher education.
Limitations: Giving limited to the Richmond, VA, metropolitan area.
Application information:
Initial approach: Letter
Deadline(s): Apr. 20
Board meeting date(s): June
Write: Rita Smith
Trustee: Sovran Bank, N.A.
Employer Identification Number: 546086247

7194
Crestar Bank Charitable Trust ⌑
(Formerly United Virginia Charitable Trust)
c/o Crestar Bank, N.A.
P.O. Box 27385
Richmond 23261
Application address: 919 East Main St., Richmond, VA 23219; Tel.: (804) 782-7906

Established in 1964.
Donor(s): Crestar Bank, N.A.
Foundation type: Company-sponsored
Financial data (yr. ended 12/31/87): Assets, $978,995 (M); expenditures, $418,865, including $376,633 for 48 grants (high: $50,000; low: $100).
Purpose and activities: Giving for higher education, hospitals, and cultural programs.
Types of support: General purposes, continuing support, annual campaigns, building funds, equipment, land acquisition, endowment funds, matching funds.
Limitations: Giving primarily in VA. No support for government-supported organizations, or for religious or national health agencies. No grants to individuals, or for scholarships or fellowships; no loans.
Publications: Informational brochure, program policy statement, application guidelines.
Application information: Application form not required.
Initial approach: Proposal
Copies of proposal: 1
Deadline(s): Large grant requests should be made by Oct. for consideration for the following year
Board meeting date(s): Semiannually and as required
Final notification: 1 to 6 months
Write: J. Thomas Vaushan
Trustee: Crestar Bank, N.A.
Number of staff: 3
Employer Identification Number: 546054608

7195
Crestar Foundation
(Formerly UVB Foundation)
919 East Main St.
Richmond 23219 (804) 782-7907

Established in 1973 in VA.
Donor(s): Crestar Bank, N.A., and other affiliates of United Virginia Bankshares.
Foundation type: Company-sponsored
Financial data (yr. ended 12/31/89): Assets, $3,000,000 (M); gifts received, $1,300,000; expenditures, $2,015,000, including $1,900,000 for 750 grants (high: $150,000; low: $500) and $115,000 for 605 employee matching gifts.
Purpose and activities: Priority given to community funds and established educational and arts and cultural organizations in the communities served by bank affiliates; support also for capital campaigns of private colleges and universities in VA; grants also for business and health services.
Types of support: Building funds, employee matching gifts.
Limitations: Giving limited to VA and communities served by bank affiliates. No support for government-supported, religious, or national agencies. No grants to individuals, or for research, scholarships, or fellowships; no loans.
Publications: Informational brochure, program policy statement, application guidelines.
Application information: Application form not required.
Initial approach: Letter and proposal
Copies of proposal: 1
Deadline(s): Submit proposal before Oct.
Board meeting date(s): Semiannually as required
Write: J. Thomas Vaughan, Pres.
Officers: J. Thomas Vaughan, Pres.; Shirley Swarthout, Secy.-Treas.
Number of staff: 2 full-time professional.
Employer Identification Number: 237336418

7196
The Dalis Foundation ⌑
c/o Goodman & Co.
P.O. Box 3247
Norfolk 23514

Established in 1956.
Donor(s): M. Dan Dalis.†
Foundation type: Independent
Financial data (yr. ended 5/31/88): Assets, $3,952,879 (M); expenditures, $420,146, including $378,270 for 3 grants (high: $328,270; low: $25,000).
Purpose and activities: Emphasis on a Jewish welfare fund, hospitals, and a television station.
Limitations: Giving primarily in Norfolk, VA.
Application information:
Initial approach: Letter
Write: Joan D. Martone, Pres.
Officers: Joan Dalis Martone, Pres. and Treas.; Sandra W. Norment, V.P.
Number of staff: None.
Employer Identification Number: 546046229

7197
Dan River Foundation ⌑
P.O. Box 261
Danville 24541
Scholarship application address: Chair., Scholarship Comm., P.O. Box 2178, Danville, VA 24541; Tel.: (804) 799-7384

Incorporated in 1957 in VA.
Donor(s): Dan River, Inc.
Foundation type: Company-sponsored
Financial data (yr. ended 12/31/87): Assets, $1,934,916 (M); expenditures, $207,586, including $189,475 for 72 grants (high: $60,000; low: $100) and $3,945 for 3 grants to individuals (high: $2,250; low: $195).
Purpose and activities: Grants largely for community funds, higher education, including educational associations and scholarships to company employees and their children, and welfare organizations; some support for cultural programs, youth, health agencies, and hospitals.
Types of support: Employee-related scholarships.
Limitations: Giving primarily in areas of company operations, particularly Danville, VA, Greenville, SC, and New York, NY. No grants to individuals, except for employee-related scholarships.
Application information: Application form required.
Initial approach: Letter
Copies of proposal: 1
Deadline(s): Last day of Feb.
Board meeting date(s): Apr. and Dec.
Write: Grover S. Elliot, Pres.
Officers: Grover S. Elliot,* Pres. and Treas.; L.W. Van de Visser,* V.P.; H.H. Huntley, Secy.
Directors:* R.C. Crawford, Lester A. Hudson, Jr., David W. Johnston, Jr., W.J. Mika, R.S. Vigholo.
Employer Identification Number: 546036112

7198
Andrew H. & Anne O. Easley Trust ⌑
(also known as The Easley Foundation)
c/o Trust Dept., Central Fidelity Bank
P.O. Box 700
Lynchburg 24505

Established in 1968 in VA.
Donor(s): Andrew H. Easley.†
Foundation type: Independent
Financial data (yr. ended 6/30/88): Assets, $5,011,491 (M); expenditures, $239,725, including $195,399 for 11 grants (high: $50,000; low: $5,000).
Purpose and activities: Giving to youth organizations, education, health care, social services, and cultural programs, including historic preservation.
Limitations: Giving limited to the Lynchburg, VA, area. No support for religious organizations. No grants to individuals, or for research, deficit financing, seed money, annual campaigns, or conferences and seminars; no loans.
Publications: Application guidelines.
Application information: Application form not required.
Initial approach: Proposal not exceeding 2 pages
Copies of proposal: 6
Deadline(s): Apr. 1 and Oct. 1
Board meeting date(s): June and Dec.
Write: Secy., The Easley Foundation
Trustee: Central Fidelity Bank.
Number of staff: None.
Employer Identification Number: 546074720

7199
W. C. English Foundation ⌑
1522 Main St.
Altavista 24517 (804) 324-7241

Trust established in 1954 in VA.
Donor(s): Members of the English family.
Foundation type: Independent
Financial data (yr. ended 5/31/88): Assets, $7,205,417 (M); gifts received, $675,000; expenditures, $543,131, including $536,400 for 36 grants (high: $125,000; low: $200).
Purpose and activities: Giving for independent secondary schools and Protestant church activities, including missionary work.
Limitations: Giving primarily in VA.
Application information:
Initial approach: Letter
Deadline(s): None
Write: W.C. English, Chair.
Officers and Trustees: W.C. English, Chair.; Joan G. Allen, Louise T. English, Margaret Lester.
Employer Identification Number: 546061817

7200
The English Foundation-Trust ⌑
1522 Main St.
Altavista 24517 (804) 369-4771

Established in 1956 in VA.
Donor(s): E.R. English, W.C. English.
Foundation type: Independent
Financial data (yr. ended 12/31/88): Assets, $1,462,899 (M); expenditures, $104,774, including $54,880 for 38 grants (high: $26,000; low: $50) and $34,952 for grants to individuals.
Purpose and activities: Giving for civic affairs and community development, Protestant religious organizations and church support, and higher education, including scholarships.
Types of support: Student aid.
Limitations: Giving primarily in the Campbell County, VA, area.
Application information: Application form required for scholarships; request from manager.
Initial approach: Letter
Write: E.R. English, Sr., Trustee
Trustees: E.R. English, Sr., E.R. English, Jr., W.C. English, Sarah F. Simpson.
Number of staff: None.
Employer Identification Number: 546036409

7201
Estes Foundation ⌑
5600 Midlothian Tpke.
Richmond 23224

Established in 1969 in VA.
Donor(s): C.E. Estes.
Foundation type: Independent
Financial data (yr. ended 12/31/88): Assets, $1,616,415 (M); expenditures, $64,021, including $49,700 for 9 grants (high: $32,158; low: $200).
Purpose and activities: Giving primarily for religion, education, and social service and youth agencies.
Types of support: General purposes.
Limitations: Giving primarily in VA.
Application information: Contributes only to pre-selected organizations. Applications not accepted.
Officers: C.E. Estes, Pres. and Treas.; Carle E. Davis, Secy.
Directors: Dorothy Estes, Martha E. Grover.
Employer Identification Number: 237045252

7202
Fairchild Industries Foundation, Inc. ⌑
P.O. Box 10803
Chantilly 22021-9998

Incorporated in 1953 in MD.
Donor(s): Fairchild Industries, Inc.
Foundation type: Company-sponsored
Financial data (yr. ended 12/31/88): Assets, $460,000 (M); gifts received, $300,000; qualifying distributions, $238,180, including $193,000 for 78 grants (high: $10,000; low: $100), $26,000 for 23 grants to individuals (high: $2,500; low: $1,000; average: $500-$2,500) and $19,180 for 144 employee matching gifts.
Purpose and activities: Giving primarily for higher education, including employee matching gifts, community funds, and civic affairs; support also for scholarships to children of employees and aid to needy employees or retired employees.
Types of support: Operating budgets, continuing support, annual campaigns, emergency funds, general purposes, equipment, endowment funds, matching funds, scholarship funds, special projects, employee-related scholarships, research, fellowships, employee matching gifts.
Limitations: Giving primarily in areas of company operations. No grants to individuals (except to aid needy employees or retirees), or for deficit financing; no loans.
Application information: Application form not required.
Initial approach: Letter
Copies of proposal: 1

Deadline(s): None
Board meeting date(s): Jan. or as required
Write: John D. Jackson, Pres.
Officers: John D. Jackson,* Pres.; Hazel S. Chilcote, V.P. and Secy.; Karen L. Schneckenburger, Treas.
Trustees:* T.H. Moorer, R. James Woolsey.
Number of staff: 1 part-time professional.
Employer Identification Number: 526043638

7203
Fitz-Gibbon Charitable Trust
P.O. Box 1377
Richmond 23211 (804) 780-2012

Established about 1983 in VA.
Donor(s): T. David Fitz-Gibbon.†
Foundation type: Independent
Financial data (yr. ended 06/30/89): Assets, $2,461,590 (M); expenditures, $146,958, including $119,143 for 27 grants (high: $20,000; low: $100).
Purpose and activities: Support for higher and secondary education, hospitals, social services, and historic preservation.
Types of support: Endowment funds, professorships, scholarship funds.
Limitations: Giving primarily in VA. No grants to individuals.
Application information: Limited amount of funds available due to long-term commitments. Applications not accepted.
Write: Thomas Nelson Page Johnson, Jr., Chair.
Trustees: Thomas Nelson Page Johnson, Jr., Chair.; Thomas Nelson Page Johnson III, William M. Walsh, Jr.
Number of staff: None.
Employer Identification Number: 521272224

7204
Frederick Foundation, Inc.
3720 Brighton St.
Portsmouth 23707 (804) 393-1605

Established in 1986 in VA.
Donor(s): Fred W. Beazley,† Fred W. Beazley, Jr.,† Marie C. Beazley.†
Foundation type: Independent
Financial data (yr. ended 12/31/89): Assets, $25,066,500 (M); expenditures, $1,188,125, including $897,328 for 48 grants (high: $69,000; low: $50; average: $50-$69,000).
Purpose and activities: Support for education, health, religion, social services, community funds, recreation, and youth.
Types of support: Capital campaigns, continuing support, scholarship funds.
Limitations: Giving primarily in the Hampton Roads, VA, area. No grants to individuals.
Publications: Financial statement, application guidelines.
Application information: Application form not required.
Initial approach: Proposal
Copies of proposal: 1
Deadline(s): 15th of the month prior to board meetings
Board meeting date(s): Apr., July, Oct., Jan.
Write: Lawrence W. I'Anson, Jr., Pres.
Officers: Lawrence W. I'Anson, Jr., Pres.; Joseph J. Quadros, V.P.; Jeanette C. Bridgeman, Treas.
Trustees: Malcolm F. Beazley, Jr., Jewel A. Bush, Mills E. Godwin, Jr., John T. Kavanaugh, Eugene C. Lipscomb.
Number of staff: 1 full-time professional; 2 full-time support; 1 part-time support.
Employer Identification Number: 540604600

7205
Gannett Foundation ▼
1101 Wilson Blvd.
Arlington 22209

Incorporated in 1935 in NY.
Donor(s): Frank E. Gannett.†
Foundation type: Independent
Financial data (yr. ended 12/31/88): Assets, $547,540,276 (M); expenditures, $33,382,883, including $23,301,011 for 2,687 grants (high: $686,613; low: $20), $767,300 for 194 grants to individuals, $800,807 for 1,683 employee matching gifts and $2,939,036 for 2 foundation-administered programs.
Purpose and activities: Grants to nonprofit educational, charitable, civic, cultural, health, and social service institutions and organizations in areas served by daily newspapers, broadcast stations, outdoor advertising companies, and other properties of Gannett Co., Inc. in the U.S. and Canada. Primary national interests are support of journalism-related programs and the advancement of philanthropy, volunteerism, and the promotion of adult literacy. The foundation also operates the Gannett Center for Media Studies, the nation's first institute for the advanced study of mass communication and technological change, located at Columbia University in NY, and the Paul Miller Washington Reporting Fellowships in Washington, DC.
Types of support: Operating budgets, continuing support, seed money, emergency funds, deficit financing, building funds, equipment, land acquisition, scholarship funds, employee-related scholarships, special projects, publications, conferences and seminars, general purposes, capital campaigns, matching funds, renovation projects, technical assistance, fellowships, employee matching gifts.
Limitations: Giving primarily in areas of Gannett Co., Inc. operations in the U.S. and Canada. No support for national or regional organizations, medical or other research unrelated to journalism, literacy, philanthropy, or volunteerism; religious purposes; political groups; fraternal and similar organizations; or for primary or secondary school programs, except for those helping exceptional or disadvantaged children and youth. No grants to individuals (except for employee-related scholarships, fellowships and journalism-related research), or for annual campaigns (other than United Ways) or endowment funds; no loans.
Publications: Annual report, informational brochure (including application guidelines), newsletter.
Application information: Grant proposals from organizations in communities served by Gannett properties should be directed to the chief executive of the local property; executive committee of board approves grants monthly or as required. Journalism proposals should be directed to Gerald M. Sass, V.P./Education. Application form required.
Initial approach: Letter or proposal
Copies of proposal: 1
Deadline(s): None
Board meeting date(s): 3 to 4 times a year, and as required; annual meeting in Apr. or May
Final notification: 2 to 4 months for positive responses
Write: Charles L. Overby, Pres.; or local Gannett Co., Inc. chief executives or publishers, for requests originating in areas served by Gannett Co., Inc.
Officers: Charles L. Overby,* Pres. and C.E.O.; Gerald M. Sass, Sr. V.P.; Christy C. Bulkeley, V.P.; Harvey S. Cotter, V.P.; Everette E. Dennis, V.P.; Felix Gutierrez, V.P.; Calvin Mayne, V.P. - Grants Administration; Tracy A. Quinn, V.P. - Communications; Thomas L. Chapple, Secy.; Jimmy L. Thomas, Treas.
Trustees:* Allen H. Neuharth, Chair.; Martin F. Birmingham, Bernard B. Brody, M.D., Harry W. Brooks, Jr., John Curley, John E. Heselden, Madelyn P. Jennings, Bette Bao Lord, Douglas H. McCorkindale, Dillard Munford, John C. Quinn, Frank H.T. Rhodes, Carl Rowan, Carrie Rozelle, Josefina A. Salas-Porras.
Number of staff: 14 full-time professional; 2 part-time professional; 24 full-time support; 14 part-time support.
Employer Identification Number: 166027020

7206
Frank Gannett Newspapercarrier Scholarships, Inc.
1101 Wilson Blvd.
Arlington 22209 (703) 875-0921

Incorporated in 1952 in NY.
Donor(s): Gannett Foundation, Inc.
Foundation type: Independent
Financial data (yr. ended 12/31/88): Assets, $11,602 (M); gifts received, $588,709; expenditures, $580,839, including $504,363 for 424 grants to individuals (high: $2,000; low: $50).
Purpose and activities: College scholarships, awarded on a competitive basis, to current newspaper carriers of participating Gannett newspapers.
Types of support: Employee-related scholarships.
Limitations: No grants for general support, capital or endowment funds, matching gifts, program support, research, special projects, publications, or conferences; no loans.
Publications: 990-PF, program policy statement, application guidelines, annual report.
Application information: Application forms available in circulation departments of participating newspapers. Application form required.
Deadline(s): Jan. 1
Board meeting date(s): Apr., June, and either Oct., Nov., or Dec.
Final notification: May 1
Write: Nancy Katherine Higgins, Scholarships Admin.
Officers and Directors:* D. Robert Frisina,* Pres.; Alice H. Young,* V.P.; Gerald M. Sass,* Secy.-Treas.; Betty J. Altier, Harvey S. Cotter, William H. Dermody, M.D., Eugene C. Dorsey, Charles L. Overby.
Number of staff: None.
Employer Identification Number: 160766965

7207
C. W. Gooch, Jr. Charitable Trust ⌑
c/o United Virginia Bank
P.O. Box 26665
Richmond 23261
Application address: United Virginia Bank, Box 678, Lynchburg, VA 24505; Tel.: (804) 847-2236

Established in 1968 in VA.
Foundation type: Independent
Financial data (yr. ended 4/30/87): Assets, $2,513,539 (M); gifts received, $219,371; expenditures, $107,405, including $100,900 for 11 grants (high: $25,000; low: $100).
Purpose and activities: Support primarily for higher education and youth.
Types of support: Scholarship funds, equipment.
Limitations: Giving primarily in MD.
Application information:
Initial approach: Letter
Deadline(s): Apr. 1
Write: S.H. Williams, Jr.
Trustee: United Virginia Bank.
Employer Identification Number: 546074371

7208
Gottwald Foundation
c/o Floyd D. Gottwald, Jr.
P.O. Box 2189
Richmond 23217 (804) 788-5738

Established in 1957.
Donor(s): Floyd D. Gottwald, Sr.,† Floyd D. Gottwald, Jr.
Foundation type: Independent
Financial data (yr. ended 12/31/89): Assets, $10,955,897 (M); expenditures, $425,118, including $418,266 for 17 grants (high: $200,000; low: $100; average: $100-$200,000).
Purpose and activities: Emphasis on education, hospitals, the arts and cultural programs, and youth agencies; support also for a foundation benefiting a military institute.
Types of support: Operating budgets, capital campaigns, scholarship funds.
Limitations: Giving primarily in VA.
Application information: Contributes only to pre-selected organizations. Applications not accepted.
Write: Vernell B. Harris
Officers: Floyd D. Gottwald, Jr., Pres.; Anne C. Gottwald, V.P.; Bruce C. Gottwald, Secy.-Treas.
Number of staff: None.
Employer Identification Number: 546040560

7209
Graphic Arts Education and Research Foundation ⌑ ☆
1899 Preston White Dr.
Reston 22091 (703) 264-7200

Established in 1984 in VA.
Donor(s): Graphic Arts Show Co., Inc.
Foundation type: Independent
Financial data (yr. ended 12/31/88): Assets, $869,428 (M); gifts received, $300,000; expenditures, $523,400, including $486,773 for 5 grants (high: $145,600; low: $34,636).
Purpose and activities: Support for education and research pertaining to the graphic arts.
Types of support: Research, publications.
Application information:
Initial approach: Proposal
Deadline(s): Mar.
Officers: Regis J. Delmontagne, Pres.; Ray Roper, Secy.; Charles A. Alessandrini, Treas.
Directors: Nicholas P. Chiapelas, Gerald V. Harris, John C. Hedlund, Robert H. Houk, Edward Lemanski, Raymond J. Luca.
Employer Identification Number: 521321169

7210
Garland Gray Foundation ⌑
P.O. Box 397
Richmond 23203

Established in VA.
Donor(s): Garland Gray.†
Foundation type: Independent
Financial data (yr. ended 12/31/89): Assets, $13,652,318 (M); expenditures, $485,032, including $388,426 for 42 grants (high: $90,000; low: $1,000).
Purpose and activities: Emphasis on education and community development.
Types of support: Operating budgets, continuing support, annual campaigns, seed money, building funds, equipment, land acquisition, endowment funds, scholarship funds, matching funds, program-related investments.
Limitations: Giving limited to VA, with emphasis on Waverly. No grants to individuals, or for emergency funds, deficit financing, research, special projects, publications, or conferences; no loans.
Application information: Contributes only to pre-selected organizations. Applications not accepted.
Board meeting date(s): As required
Officers and Trustees:* Elmon T. Gray,* Pres. and Treas.; Charles F. Duff,* V.P.; Wallace Stettinius,* V.P.; Thomas H. Tullidge,* V.P.; W.Birch Douglass III,* Secy.; C. Taylor Everett, Thomas C. Gordon, Jr., Bruce B. Gray, Garland Gray II.
Number of staff: None.
Employer Identification Number: 546071867

7211
Richard and Caroline T. Gwathmey Memorial Trust
c/o Sovran Bank, N.A.
P.O. Box 26903
Richmond 23261 (804) 788-2964

Established in 1981 in VA.
Donor(s): Elizabeth G. Jeffress.†
Foundation type: Independent
Financial data (yr. ended 6/30/88): Assets, $7,542,327 (M); expenditures, $467,790, including $416,662 for 23 grants (high: $50,000; low: $3,000).
Purpose and activities: Support for a variety of charitable, cultural, and educational activities.
Types of support: General purposes.
Limitations: Giving primarily in VA. No grants to individuals.
Publications: Informational brochure (including application guidelines).
Application information: Application form not required.
Initial approach: Letter requesting guidelines
Deadline(s): Mar. 1 and Sept. 1
Final notification: Immediately following meeting at which proposal was considered
Write: Dr. J. Samuel Gillespie, Jr., Trust Advisor
Trustee: Sovran Bank, N.A.
Number of staff: 2
Employer Identification Number: 546191586

7212
Hands for Christ ⌑
P.O. Box 5426
Roanoke 24012 (703) 362-1214

Established in 1969 in VA.
Foundation type: Operating
Financial data (yr. ended 12/31/88): Assets, $91,771 (M); gifts received, $123,419; expenditures, $213,080, including $182,260 for grants.
Purpose and activities: A private operating foundation which supports evangelical Christian organizations; gives full gospel charismatic Christian cassette tape- and book-lending libraries to small churches, including churches in Third World countries, and to prisons.
Application information: Applications not accepted.
Write: R.W. Bowers, Pres.
Officers and Director:* R.W. Bowers,* Pres.; Joan C. Bowers, V.P.; Jean Self, Secy.
Employer Identification Number: 237074396

7213
Harrison & Conrad Memorial Trust ⌑
c/o Sovran Bank, N.A.
3401 Columbia Pike
Arlington 22204
Application address: c/o Loudoun Memorial Hospital, Office of the Administrator, 70 West Cornwall St., Leesburg, VA 22075; Tel.: (703) 777-3300

Established in 1982 in VA.
Donor(s): Mary J. Conrad.†
Foundation type: Independent
Financial data (yr. ended 1/31/88): Assets, $1,791,355 (M); expenditures, $104,189, including $77,693 for 1 grant.
Purpose and activities: To benefit children suffering from polio or muscular dystrophy or any other crippling disease whose families cannot afford treatment.
Types of support: Grants to individuals.
Limitations: Giving limited to Leesburg or Loudoun County, VA.
Application information: Individual applicants are interviewed.
Initial approach: Letter
Deadline(s): Apr. 1
Trustee: Sovran Bank, N.A.
Employer Identification Number: 521300410

7214
The Hastings Trust ⌑
544 Settlers Landing Rd.
Hampton 23669 (804) 722-2801

Established in 1964.
Donor(s): Charles E. Hastings,† Mary C. Hastings.†
Foundation type: Independent

Financial data (yr. ended 12/31/88): Assets, $2,083,966 (M); expenditures, $126,007, including $117,855 for 43 grants.
Purpose and activities: Grants primarily for a private school; support also for higher education, wildlife preservation, and environmental conservation.
Limitations: Giving primarily in VA. No grants to individuals.
Application information:
Deadline(s): None
Write: Robert C. Hastings, Trustee
Trustees: John A. Hastings, Robert C. Hastings, Carol H. Saunders.
Employer Identification Number: 546040247

7215
Hermitage Foundation ⌑
7637 North Shore Rd.
Norfolk 23505

Established in 1972.
Donor(s): Hermitage Foundation Trust.
Foundation type: Operating
Financial data (yr. ended 6/30/88): Assets, $3,701,429 (M); gifts received, $143,476; expenditures, $264,347, including $1,600 for 4 grants of $400 each.
Purpose and activities: A private operating foundation which owns and operates an art museum; some support for higher and other education.
Limitations: Giving primarily in VA.
Application information:
Initial approach: Letter
Deadline(s): None
Write: Phil Morrison
Officers and Trustees: William Marshall, Jr., Pres.; Lela Marshall Hine, V.P. and Secy.; John Ryan, V.P.; William S. Hull, Treas.; and 10 additional trustees.
Employer Identification Number: 540505909

7216
Herndon Foundation ⌑
c/o Floyd D. Gottwald, Jr.
300 Herndon Rd.
Richmond 23229

Established in 1965 in VA.
Donor(s): Floyd D. Gottwald, Jr.
Foundation type: Independent
Financial data (yr. ended 12/31/87): Assets, $3,501,454 (M); expenditures, $500,378, including $486,310 for 69 grants (high: $250,000; low: $20).
Purpose and activities: Emphasis on higher and other education.
Types of support: Operating budgets.
Limitations: Giving primarily in Richmond, VA.
Application information: Contributes only to pre-selected organizations. Applications not accepted.
Trustees: Elisabeth S. Gottwald, Floyd D. Gottwald, Jr.
Employer Identification Number: 546060809

7217
Eugene Holt Foundation
200 Massey Bldg.
Fourth & Main Sts.
Richmond 23219 (804) 649-9394

Foundation type: Independent
Financial data (yr. ended 8/31/88): Assets, $1,246,074 (M); expenditures, $69,911, including $63,750 for 16 grants (high: $29,000; low: $50).
Purpose and activities: Support primarily for a botanical garden and a museum of fine arts; support also for wildlife and ecological organizations, historical societies, and historical preservation associations.
Limitations: Giving primarily in Richmond, VA.
Application information: Application form not required.
Initial approach: Letter
Deadline(s): July 31
Write: Ivor Massey, Secy.-Treas.
Officers: Anne Holt Massey, Pres.; Ivor Massey, Jr., V.P.; Ivor Massey, Secy.-Treas.
Employer Identification Number: 540802044

7218
Hopeman Memorial Fund, Inc. ⌑
435 Essex Ave.
P.O. Box 1345
Waynesboro 22980 (703) 949-9200

Incorporated in 1980 in VA.
Donor(s): Hopeman Brothers, Inc., Royston Manufacturing Corp.
Foundation type: Independent
Financial data (yr. ended 12/31/88): Assets, $1,784,648 (M); expenditures, $155,237, including $155,100 for 9 grants (high: $80,000; low: $100).
Purpose and activities: Giving primarily to public policy institutes; support also for higher education.
Types of support: General purposes.
Limitations: Giving primarily in VA, PA, and IL.
Application information: Contributes only to pre-selected organizations. Applications not accepted.
Officers and Trustees: A.A. Hopeman, Jr., Pres.; Harriet M. Hopeman, V.P.; Henry W. Hopeman, Secy.-Treas.
Employer Identification Number: 541156930

7219
The John Jay Hopkins Foundation
1199 North Fairfax St.
P.O. Box 25047
Alexandria 22313

Trust established in 1954 in DC.
Donor(s): John J. Hopkins.†
Foundation type: Independent
Financial data (yr. ended 12/31/89): Assets, $2,108,233 (M); expenditures, $171,098, including $126,600 for 62 grants (high: $17,000; low: $100).
Purpose and activities: Giving for Protestant church support and church-related schools and higher education; support also for cultural programs, including historic preservation.
Types of support: Continuing support, annual campaigns, building funds, fellowships, general purposes.
Limitations: Giving primarily in VA and the Washington, DC, metropolitan area. No grants to individuals, or for endowment funds, operating budgets, seed money, emergency funds, deficit financing, land acquisition, matching gifts, special projects, research, publications, or conferences; no loans.
Publications: 990-PF.
Application information: Contributes only to pre-selected organizations. Applications not accepted.
Board meeting date(s): Nov. or Dec. and as required
Write: Lianne H. Conger, Pres., or Philip Tierney, Secy.
Officers and Trustees:* Lianne H. Conger,* Pres.; Philip Tierney,* Secy.; Clement E. Conger,* Treas.; Jay A. Conger, Harry Teeter.
Number of staff: None.
Employer Identification Number: 526036649

7220
Houff Foundation ⌑
P.O. Box 91
Weyers Cave 24486-0091 (703) 234-9233

Donor(s): Cletus E. Houff, Houff Transfer, Inc.
Foundation type: Independent
Financial data (yr. ended 12/31/88): Assets, $1,577,843 (M); gifts received, $292,500; expenditures, $107,776, including $99,500 for 9 grants (high: $50,000; low: $500).
Purpose and activities: Support primarily for higher education.
Limitations: Giving primarily in Shenandoah Valley, VA, area.
Application information: Application form not required.
Deadline(s): None
Write: Dwight E. Houff, Secy.
Officers: Cletus E. Houff, Pres. and Treas.; Dwight E. Houff, Secy.
Directors: Douglas Z. Houff, Roxie Houff White.
Employer Identification Number: 510236893

7221
HTW Foundation ⌑ ☆
22 Lower Tuckahoe Rd. West
Richmond 23233

Donor(s): Hays T. Watkins.
Foundation type: Independent
Financial data (yr. ended 12/31/87): Assets, $82,685 (M); gifts received, $69,000; expenditures, $128,164, including $128,063 for 1 grant.
Purpose and activities: Giving for a college.
Limitations: Giving primarily in VA. No grants to individuals.
Application information: Contributes only to pre-selected organizations. Applications not accepted.
Trustee: Hays T. Watkins.
Employer Identification Number: 541399048

7222
Ruth B. & George T. Huff Fund ☆
c/o Jefferson National Bank
P.O. Box 711
Charlottesville 22902-0711 (804) 972-1100

Established in 1966 in VA.

Donor(s): George T. Huff.†
Foundation type: Independent
Financial data (yr. ended 09/30/89): Assets, $1,188,232 (M); expenditures, $90,142, including $74,435 for 44 grants to individuals (high: $3,500; low: $235).
Purpose and activities: Awards scholarships for higher education to local area residents for first year costs.
Types of support: Student aid.
Limitations: Giving limited to Charlottesville and Floyd, Greene, and Patrick counties, VA.
Publications: Annual report.
Application information: Scholarships awarded to institution on behalf of named individual recipient. Application form required.
Initial approach: Contact superintendent or principal of schools in designated localities for application form
Deadline(s): Apr. 15
Final notification: May through June of scholarship year
Write: Hugh M. Leaveu
Trustee: Jefferson National Bank.
Number of staff: None.
Employer Identification Number: 546088063

7223
Emily S. and Coleman A. Hunter Trust
c/o Crestar Bank, N.A.
P.O. Box 26548
Richmond 23261 (804) 782-5248

Established in 1985 in VA.
Donor(s): Coleman A. Hunter,† Emily S. Hunter.†
Foundation type: Independent
Financial data (yr. ended 02/28/89): Assets, $3,214,698 (L); expenditures, $216,331, including $195,893 for grants.
Purpose and activities: Giving for hospitals and health associations, education, youth agencies, and a community fund.
Types of support: General purposes.
Limitations: Giving primarily in Richmond, VA. No grants to individuals.
Application information: Contributes only to pre-selected organizations. Applications not accepted.
Write: E.A. Flanagan
Trustee: Crestar Bank, N.A.
Employer Identification Number: 546219496

7224
Ivakota Association, Inc. ¤
901 North Pitt St.
Alexandria 22314

Established in 1919 in VA.
Donor(s): Dr. Kate Waller Barrett.†
Foundation type: Independent
Financial data (yr. ended 12/31/89): Assets, $2,684,601 (M); expenditures, $124,200, including $107,200 for grants.
Purpose and activities: Primary interest is support of needy women and children. Grants also for higher and other education.
Types of support: Continuing support, emergency funds, scholarship funds.
Limitations: Giving primarily in Alexandria, VA. No grants to individuals.
Application information: Application form not required.
Copies of proposal: 1
Deadline(s): Feb. 1
Board meeting date(s): Feb. 15
Final notification: Mar. 15
Write: Louis B. Rodenberg, Jr., Secy.
Officers: John T. Martyn, Jr., Pres.; David M. Burke, V.P.; Louis B. Rodenberg, Jr., Secy.-Treas.
Number of staff: None.
Employer Identification Number: 540505919

7225
Thomas F. and Kate Miller Jeffress Memorial Trust ¤
c/o Sovran Bank, N.A., Trust Div.
P.O. Box 26903
Richmond 23261 (804) 788-2964

Established in 1981 in VA.
Donor(s): Robert M. Jeffress.†
Foundation type: Independent
Financial data (yr. ended 6/30/88): Assets, $15,911,956 (M); gifts received, $11,671; expenditures, $742,948, including $606,769 for 11 grants (high: $224,378; low: $1,080; average: $7,750-$55,000).
Purpose and activities: Grants to colleges and universities for research activities.
Types of support: Research.
Limitations: Giving primarily in VA. No support for clinical research. No grants to individuals.
Publications: Informational brochure (including application guidelines).
Application information: Application form not required.
Copies of proposal: 6
Deadline(s): Mar. 1 and Sept. 1
Board meeting date(s): May and Nov.
Final notification: After meeting at which proposal has been considered
Write: Dr. J. Samuel Gillespie, Jr., Advisor
Trustee: Sovran Bank, N.A.
Advisor: J. Samuel Gillespie, Jr., M.D.
Allocations Committee: Robert V. Blanke, M.D., Richard L. Fields, M.D., William H. Groseclose, Julious P. Smith, Jr., John B. Werner.
Number of staff: 1 part-time professional; 1 part-time support.
Employer Identification Number: 546094925

7226
W. Alton Jones Foundation, Inc. ▼
232 East High St.
Charlottesville 22901 (804) 295-2134

Incorporated in 1944 in NY.
Donor(s): W. Alton Jones.†
Foundation type: Independent
Financial data (yr. ended 12/31/89): Assets, $193,450,890 (M); expenditures, $12,692,236, including $11,545,227 for grants (high: $1,875,000; average: $5,000-$100,000).
Purpose and activities: The foundation limits most of its grantmaking to two subject areas: environmental protection, with emphasis on conservation of biological diversity worldwide and protection of land, air, and water from pollution and toxic contamination; and prevention of nuclear war.
Types of support: General purposes, special projects, research, conferences and seminars, seed money, matching funds, exchange programs, loans, operating budgets, publications, program-related investments.
Limitations: No support for conduit organizations. No grants to individuals, or for building or endowment funds, deficit financing, scholarships, or fellowships.
Publications: Annual report, application guidelines.
Application information: Applicants must wait 1 year after a grant is approved or declined before submitting another application; applications accepted only for programs in environmental protection and arms control. Application form not required.
Initial approach: Proposal
Copies of proposal: 1
Deadline(s): None
Board meeting date(s): Quarterly
Final notification: 3 months
Write: John Peterson Myers, Dir.
Officers and Directors: Mrs. W. Alton Jones,* Chair.; Patricia Jones Edgerton,* Pres.; Bradford W. Edgerton,* V.P.; Diane Edgerton Miller,* Secy.; Bernard F. Curry,* Treas.
Trustees:* James S. Bennett, William A. Edgerton, Scott McVay.
Number of staff: 5 full-time professional; 4 full-time support.
Employer Identification Number: 136034219

7227
Lacy Foundation ¤
P.O. Box 3084
Martinsville 24115-3084

Established in 1980 in VA.
Foundation type: Independent
Financial data (yr. ended 08/31/89): Assets, $1,763,625 (M); expenditures, $175,868, including $157,500 for 18 grants (high: $25,000; low: $1,000).
Purpose and activities: Support for health services and Christian education.
Limitations: No grants to individuals.
Application information: Contributes only to pre-selected organizations. Applications not accepted.
Officers and Directors:* Frank M. Lacy, Jr.,* Pres.; Margaret A. James,* V.P.; Mary L. Cobbe,* Secy.
Employer Identification Number: 521205924

7228
Landmark Charitable Foundation ¤
150 West Brambleton Ave.
Norfolk 23510 (804) 446-2030

Incorporated in 1953 in VA.
Donor(s): The Virginian-Pilot and Ledger-Star, Greensboro Daily News and Greensboro Record, The Roanoke Times and The World-News, WTAR-AM and FM, WLTY-FM, KLAS-TV, KNTV-TV.
Foundation type: Company-sponsored
Financial data (yr. ended 10/31/88): Assets, $13,223,119 (M); gifts received, $1,354,000; qualifying distributions, $972,350, including $972,350 for 168 grants (high: $106,000; low: $500; average: $1,000-$10,000).
Purpose and activities: Grants largely for higher education, cultural organizations, and community funds in areas served by the donor

newspapers and TV stations; support also for journalism associations, literacy, secondary education, and business education.
Types of support: Annual campaigns, building funds, capital campaigns, endowment funds, scholarship funds, seed money, special projects.
Limitations: Giving primarily in communities served by a Landmark company participating in the foundation in the Hampton Roads and Roanoke, VA, areas; Greensboro, NC; San Jose, CA; and Las Vegas, NV. No support for non-tax exempt organizations or programs. No grants to individuals.
Application information:
Initial approach: Proposal or telephone
Copies of proposal: 1
Deadline(s): By Dec. of preceding year in which grant is expected
Board meeting date(s): As required
Write: Carolyn S. Wood, Exec. Dir.
Officers: Richard F. Barry III,* Pres.; J. William Diederich,* V.P.; Jane O. Pruitt, Secy.; James D. Wagner, Treas.
Directors:* Frank Batten, Chair.; Robert D. Benson, Conrad M. Hall, Carl W. Mangum, Walter Rugaber, Louis F. Ryan, John O. Wynne.
Number of staff: None.
Employer Identification Number: 546038902

7229
Minnie & Bernard Lane Foundation ⌑ ☆
c/o The Lane Co., Inc.
East Franklin Ave.
Altavista 24517

Donor(s): Bernard B. Lane, Minnie B. Lane.
Foundation type: Independent
Financial data (yr. ended 3/31/89): Assets, $3,163,626 (M); gifts received, $328,449; expenditures, $519,031, including $482,444 for 85 grants (high: $200,000; low: $10).
Purpose and activities: Giving primarily for national and international human services, especially a YMCA and a food distribution program; support also for Protestant churches, social services, and education.
Limitations: Giving primarily in VA. No grants to individuals.
Application information: Contributes only to pre-selected organizations. Applications not accepted.
Trustee: R.L. Short.
Employer Identification Number: 546052404

7230
Lind Lawrence Foundation ⌑
4132 Innslake Dr.
Glen Allen 23060-3307

Established in 1973 in VA.
Donor(s): Lind Lawrence.†
Foundation type: Independent
Financial data (yr. ended 9/30/88): Assets, $5,478,504 (M); gifts received, $5,274,818; expenditures, $482,041, including $446,580 for 12 grants (high: $188,000; low: $2,000).
Purpose and activities: Support primarily for neurosurgery research.
Limitations: Giving primarily in Richmond, VA, and Los Angeles, CA.
Application information:
Initial approach: Letter
Deadline(s): July 31
Write: Lee P. Martin, Jr., Trustee
Trustees: Fred J. Bernhardt, Jr., Lee P. Martin, Jr.
Employer Identification Number: 237310359

7231
Leggett Foundation ⌑
816 Monument St.
Danville 24543-1689 (804) 791-3600

Established in 1959 in VA.
Foundation type: Independent
Financial data (yr. ended 12/31/87): Assets, $202,922 (L); gifts received, $184,040; expenditures, $197,469, including $197,200 for 97 grants (high: $19,375; low: $100).
Purpose and activities: Support primarily for Christian churches and higher education.
Application information:
Initial approach: Letter
Deadline(s): None
Write: Alice C. Isom, Trustee
Officers: R.A. Leggett, Jr.,* Chair.; F.B. Leggett, Jr., Secy.-Treas.
Trustees:* Alice C. Isom, M.E. Mason, D.H. Stovall.
Employer Identification Number: 546037999

7232
Sydney & Frances Lewis Foundation ⌑
P.O. Box 26303
Richmond 23260

Established in 1966 in VA.
Donor(s): Sydney Lewis, Frances A. Lewis.
Foundation type: Operating
Financial data (yr. ended 6/30/88): Assets, $483,040 (M); gifts received, $333,682; expenditures, $549,899, including $547,840 for 165 grants (high: $107,000; low: $15).
Purpose and activities: A private operating foundation; support primarily for art museums and the arts; support also for Jewish organizations.
Application information: Contributes only to pre-selected organizations. Applications not accepted.
Officers and Directors: Sydney Lewis, Pres.; Susan L. Butler, V.P.; Frances A. Lewis, Secy.-Treas.; Robert L. Burrus, Jr., Robert E.P. Huntley, Andrew M. Lewis.
Employer Identification Number: 546061170

7233
The Lincoln-Lane Foundation
550 East Main St., Suite 1102
Norfolk 23510 (804) 622-2557

Incorporated in 1928 in VA.
Donor(s): John H. Rogers.†
Foundation type: Independent
Financial data (yr. ended 7/31/89): Assets, $6,249,701 (M); expenditures, $303,458, including $195,475 for 132 grants to individuals (high: $2,500; low: $350; average: $1,000-$1,500).
Purpose and activities: Giving limited to awards for college scholarships to individuals.
Types of support: Student aid.
Limitations: Giving limited to permanent residents of the Tidewater, VA, area. No grants for endowment or building programs, operating budgets, or special projects; no loans.
Publications: Application guidelines, program policy statement.
Application information: New applications available starting Oct. 1. Application form required.
Initial approach: Letter
Deadline(s): Oct. 31
Board meeting date(s): Apr., May, July, and Dec.
Final notification: Apr.
Write: Margaret B. Belvin, Admin. Asst.
Officers and Directors: M. Lee Payne, Pres.; Edward H. Burgess, V.P.; Arthur D. Liles, Secy.-Treas. and Exec. Dir.; Charles E. Jenkins II, Margery Loomis Krome.
Number of staff: 2 part-time professional; 1 part-time support.
Employer Identification Number: 540601700

7234
Little River Foundation ☆
Whitewood Farm
The Plains 22171 (703) 253-5540

Established in 1972.
Donor(s): Ohrstrom Foundation.
Foundation type: Independent
Financial data (yr. ended 11/30/89): Assets, $277,440 (M); gifts received, $282,500; expenditures, $292,640, including $289,500 for 48 grants (high: $30,000; low: $500).
Purpose and activities: Support primarily for hospitals and medical research, including AIDS and drug abuse programs; higher and other education, including a veterinary school and clinic, legal education, and international studies in Africa; environmental conservation and agriculture; legal services; religious organizations; and community funds.
Types of support: Building funds, conferences and seminars, endowment funds, operating budgets, research.
Publications: Annual report.
Application information: Application form not required.
Deadline(s): None
Board meeting date(s): Sept.-Oct.
Final notification: Nov.
Write: Dale D. Hogoboom, Asst. Treas.
Officers: George L. Ohrstrom, Pres.; G.A. Horkau, Jr., Secy.; Richard R. Ohrstorm, Treas.
Number of staff: 2 part-time support.
Employer Identification Number: 237218919

7235
Anthony Francis Lucas Foundation ⌑ ☆
c/o Crestar Bank, N.A.
P.O. Box 27385
Richmond 23261-7385
Application address: c/o Crestar Bank, N.A., 15th and New York Ave., N.W., Washington, DC 20005; Tel.: (202) 879-6274

Established in 1943.
Foundation type: Independent
Financial data (yr. ended 4/30/89): Assets, $1,079,645 (M); expenditures, $87,583, including $75,700 for grants.
Purpose and activities: Support for social services.
Application information:
Initial approach: Letter

Deadline(s): None
Write: Anne McBride
Trustee: Crestar Bank, N.A.
Employer Identification Number: 526034464

7236
The Mars Foundation ▼
6885 Elm St.
McLean 22101 (703) 821-4900

Incorporated in 1956 in IL.
Donor(s): Forrest E. Mars.
Foundation type: Independent
Financial data (yr. ended 12/31/88): Assets, $4,332,456 (M); gifts received, $600,334; expenditures, $1,154,817, including $1,104,000 for 117 grants (high: $100,000; low: $1,000; average: $2,000-$15,000).
Purpose and activities: Support for higher and secondary education; conservation, ecology, and wildlife preservation; fine arts groups; health agencies, AIDS and cancer programs and other medical research; youth organizations; hospices; and the homeless.
Types of support: Continuing support, annual campaigns, building funds, equipment, endowment funds, research, matching funds.
Limitations: No grants to individuals, or for scholarships; no loans.
Application information: Application form not required.
Initial approach: Proposal
Copies of proposal: 1
Deadline(s): 6 weeks prior to meeting
Board meeting date(s): June and Dec.
Final notification: 4 to 6 weeks after meeting
Write: Roger G. Best, Secy.
Officers: Forrest E. Mars, Jr., Pres.; John F. Mars, V.P.; Roger G. Best, Secy.; William C. Turnbull, Treas.
Directors: Adrienne B. Mars, Jacqueline M. Vogel.
Number of staff: 2
Employer Identification Number: 546037592

7237
Massey Foundation ▼ ⌑
P.O. Box 26765
Richmond 23261 (804) 788-1800

Established in 1958 in VA.
Donor(s): A.T. Massey Coal Co., Inc.
Foundation type: Company-sponsored
Financial data (yr. ended 11/30/89): Assets, $33,633,600 (M); expenditures, $1,533,789, including $1,367,250 for 76 grants (high: $210,000; low: $1,000; average: $1,000-$25,000).
Purpose and activities: Giving primarily for higher and secondary education; some support for hospitals and health services, cultural programs, and social services.
Limitations: Giving primarily in VA, particularly Richmond. No grants to individuals.
Application information:
Initial approach: Letter
Deadline(s): None
Board meeting date(s): Annually
Write: William E. Massey, Jr., Pres.
Officers and Directors:* William E. Massey, Jr.,* Pres.; William Blair Massey,* V.P. and Secy.; E. Morgan Massey,* Treas.; James B. Farinholt, Jr.
Number of staff: None.
Employer Identification Number: 546049049

7238
McCrea Foundation ⌑
P.O. Box 397
Richmond 23203

Established in 1960 in VA.
Donor(s): Mary Corling McCrea.†
Foundation type: Independent
Financial data (yr. ended 2/28/89): Assets, $3,049,726 (M); expenditures, $167,918, including $148,000 for 32 grants (high: $25,000; low: $500).
Purpose and activities: Grants for medical research, hospitals, and education.
Application information: Contributes only to pre-selected organizations. Applications not accepted.
Officers and Trustees: John L. Welsh, Jr., Pres.; George C. Baron, V.P.; Carle E. Davis, Secy.-Treas.; Edward C. Welsh, John L. Welsh III.
Employer Identification Number: 546052010

7239
Ruth Camp McDougall Charitable Trust ⌑
c/o Sovran Bank, N.A., Trust Tax Div.
P.O. Box 26903
Richmond 23261 (804) 788-2573

Trust established in 1976 in VA.
Donor(s): Ruth Camp McDougall.†
Foundation type: Independent
Financial data (yr. ended 12/31/87): Assets, $6,751,913 (M); expenditures, $436,802, including $398,800 for 76 grants (high: $75,000; low: $1,000).
Purpose and activities: Giving primarily for higher and secondary education; support also for youth agencies and cultural programs.
Limitations: Giving primarily in VA.
Application information:
Initial approach: Letter
Deadline(s): None
Write: Donnie E. Koonce, 1st V.P., Sovran Bank, N.A.
Directors: John M. Camp, Jr., Paul D. Camp III, Paul Camp Marks, Harry W. Walker.
Trustee: Sovran Bank, N.A.
Employer Identification Number: 546162697

7240
The Memorial Foundation for Children ⌑
c/o Capitoline Investment Services, Inc.
P.O. Box 436
Richmond 23203-0436
Application address: P.O. Box 8342, Richmond, VA 23226

Established about 1934 in VA.
Donor(s): Alexander S. George,† Elizabeth Strother Scott.†
Foundation type: Independent
Financial data (yr. ended 12/31/88): Assets, $6,976,355 (M); qualifying distributions, $317,042, including $317,042 for 36 grants (high: $20,250; low: $2,000).
Purpose and activities: Aid to nonprofit groups for the care and education of children.
Types of support: Operating budgets, continuing support, seed money, special projects.
Limitations: Giving limited to the Richmond, VA, area. No grants to individuals, or for capital or endowment funds, annual campaigns, emergency funds, deficit financing, matching gifts, publications, conferences, scholarships, or fellowships; no loans.
Publications: Program policy statement, application guidelines.
Application information: Application form required.
Initial approach: Letter or proposal
Copies of proposal: 1
Deadline(s): Sept. 1
Board meeting date(s): Mar., May, Oct., and Dec.
Final notification: By Dec.
Write: Mrs. Jack Spain, Jr., Chair., Grant Committee
Officers: Mrs. E. Armistead Talman, Pres.; Mrs. Daniel D. Talley III, V.P.; Mrs. William G. Ellyson, Rec. Secy.; Mrs. John P. Ackerly III, Treas.
Number of staff: None.
Employer Identification Number: 540536103

7241
Metropolitan Health Foundation, Inc.
700 West Grace St.
Richmond 23220 (804) 643-1958

Established in 1984 in VA.
Foundation type: Independent
Financial data (yr. ended 12/31/88): Assets, $14,814,335 (M); expenditures, $1,465,787, including $73,400 for 11 grants (high: $3,500; low: $500).
Purpose and activities: Support limited to health-related programs.
Types of support: General purposes.
Limitations: Giving primarily in the Richmond, VA, area.
Application information:
Initial approach: Letter
Deadline(s): None
Write: Charles P. Winkler, M.D., Pres.
Officers: William R. Hill, M.D., Chair.; Charles P. Winkler, M.D., Pres.; Charles P. Cardwell III, V.P.; Andres P. Franco, Jr., M.D., Secy.-Treas.
Directors: Renard A. Charity, M.D., K. Bruce Hobart, Raymond C. Hooker, Jr., M.D., Malcolm E. Ritsch, Jr., James Wood.
Employer Identification Number: 510186144

7242
Mobil Foundation, Inc. ▼
3225 Gallows Rd.
Fairfax 22037 (703) 846-3381

Incorporated in 1965 in NY.
Donor(s): Mobil Oil Corp.
Foundation type: Company-sponsored
Financial data (yr. ended 12/31/88): Assets, $13,253,485 (M); gifts received, $11,879,176; expenditures, $15,664,221, including $9,998,917 for 1,001 grants (high: $550,000; low: $100; average: $1,000-$10,000) and $3,867,994 for 2,104 employee matching gifts.
Purpose and activities: Support for arts and cultural programs, higher education, including grants in fields relating to the petroleum and

chemical industries, a scholarship program for children of employees, and an employee matching gift program; support also for community funds, civic affairs, social services, health agencies, and hospitals.
Types of support: Employee-related scholarships, employee matching gifts, research, exchange programs, general purposes.
Limitations: Giving primarily in areas of company operations in CA, CO, IL, LA, NJ, NY, TX, VA, and WA. No support for local and national organizations concerned with specific diseases or religious or fraternal organizations. No grants to individuals, or for building or endowment funds, operating budgets, charity benefits, athletic events, or advertising; no loans.
Publications: Financial statement, application guidelines, grants list.
Application information: Application form not required.
Initial approach: Letter or proposal
Copies of proposal: 1
Deadline(s): None
Board meeting date(s): Monthly
Final notification: 6 to 8 weeks
Write: Richard G. Mund, Secy.
Officers: Ellen Z. McCloy,* Pres.; Richard G. Mund, Secy. and Exec. Dir.; Anthony L. Cavaliere, Treas.
Directors:* Robert F. Amrhein, Donald J. Bolger, Douglas O. Fitzsimmons, John P. McCullough, Harold B. Olson, Jr., Michael A. Smith, Jerome F. Trautschold, Jr.
Number of staff: 3 full-time professional; 8 full-time support.
Employer Identification Number: 136177075

7243
Marietta McNeil Morgan & Samuel Tate Morgan, Jr. Foundation
c/o Sovran Bank, N.A., Trust Dept.
P.O. Box 26903
Richmond 23261 (804) 788-2963

Trust established in 1967 in VA.
Donor(s): Marietta McNeill Morgan,† Samuel T. Morgan, Jr.†
Foundation type: Independent
Financial data (yr. ended 06/30/88): Assets, $10,422,454 (M); gifts received, $13,000; expenditures, $787,696, including $690,900 for grants.
Purpose and activities: Grants of a capital nature only, with emphasis on promoting the cause of the church, fostering Christian education, and supporting agencies concerned with less fortunate local residents.
Types of support: Building funds, equipment, matching funds.
Limitations: Giving limited to VA. No support for private foundations. No grants to individuals, or for any purposes except capital expenses; no loans.
Publications: Informational brochure (including application guidelines).
Application information: Application form not required.
Initial approach: Letter
Copies of proposal: 1
Deadline(s): Submit proposal preferably in Feb., Mar., Sept. or Oct.; deadlines May 1 and Nov. 1
Board meeting date(s): June and Dec.
Final notification: 3 weeks after board meeting
Write: Elizabeth D. Seaman, Advisor, Sovran Bank, N.A., Trust Dept.
Trustee: Sovran Bank, N.A.
Number of staff: 2
Employer Identification Number: 546069447

7244
Mustard Seed Foundation, Inc. ☆
1001 North 19th St., Suite 1900
Arlington 22209 (703) 524-5620

Established in 1983 in PA.
Donor(s): Eileen Bakke, Dennis W. Bakke, and members of the Bakke and Harvey families.
Foundation type: Operating
Financial data (yr. ended 12/31/89): Assets, $857,500 (M); gifts received, $145,000; expenditures, $152,000, including $150,000 for grants.
Purpose and activities: "To advance the kingdom of God by awarding grants and loans to Christians engaged in or preparing for evangelism, ministry, education, and relieving human suffering."
Types of support: Loans, equipment, grants to individuals.
Limitations: No grants for general purposes.
Publications: Application guidelines, application guidelines.
Application information: Application must be recommended by a board member before being considered. Application form required.
Initial approach: Proposal
Copies of proposal: 1
Deadline(s): None
Board meeting date(s): Apr., July, and Dec.
Final notification: 60 days
Write: Craig E. Nauta, Exec. V.P.
Officers: Dennis W. Bakke,* Pres.; Craig E. Natua, Exec. V.P. and Secy.; Paul O. Pearson, Treas.
Directors:* Eileen Bakke, Chair.; K. Brian Bakke, Raymond J. Bakke, Tollef A. Bakke, Helen C. Harvey, W. Brantly Harvey, Margaret H. Thompson.
Number of staff: 1 part-time professional.
Employer Identification Number: 570748914

7245
Noland Company Foundation
2700 Warwick Blvd.
Newport News 23607

Established in 1962 in VA.
Donor(s): Noland Co.
Foundation type: Company-sponsored
Financial data (yr. ended 12/31/89): Assets, $553,350 (M); expenditures, $104,212, including $103,137 for 58 grants (high: $10,988; low: $150).
Purpose and activities: Giving for cultural programs, particularly museums and performing arts groups, social service and youth agencies, and higher education.
Limitations: Giving primarily in VA. No grants to individuals.
Application information: Contributes only to pre-selected organizations. Applications not accepted.
Officers: Lloyd U. Noland III, Pres.; Arthur P. Henderson, Jr., V.P.; J.E. Gullett, Secy.-Treas.
Employer Identification Number: 540754191

7246
Noland Memorial Foundation ⌑ ☆
P.O. Box 971
Newport News 23607

Established in 1955.
Donor(s): Members of the Noland family.
Foundation type: Independent
Financial data (yr. ended 12/31/88): Assets, $1,648,452 (M); gifts received, $86,500; expenditures, $81,128, including $51,840 for 40 grants (high: $9,500; low: $100).
Purpose and activities: Support for human services, including a community fund, higher and other education, and the environment.
Limitations: Giving primarily in VA, NY, and Washington, DC. No grants to individuals.
Application information: Contributes only to pre-selected organizations. Applications not accepted.
Officers: Lloyd U. Noland, Jr.,* Pres.; Susan C. Noland,* V.P.; M.D. Watt, Secy.-Treas.
Trustees:* Anne N. Edwards, Jane K. Noland, Lloyd U. Noland III.
Employer Identification Number: 546048597

7247
The Norfolk Foundation ▼
1410 Sovran Center
Norfolk 23510 (804) 622-7951

Established in 1950 in VA by resolution and declaration of trust.
Foundation type: Community
Financial data (yr. ended 12/31/89): Assets, $30,504,916 (M); gifts received, $791,859; expenditures, $1,651,311, including $1,239,734 for 36 grants (high: $226,350; low: $823; average: $25,000-$45,000) and $270,043 for 190 grants to individuals (high: $8,278; low: $125; average: $800-$2,000).
Purpose and activities: Support for hospitals, higher, medical, and other educational institutions, family and child welfare agencies, a community fund, programs for drug abuse, the aged, the homeless, and the handicapped, and cultural and civic programs; certain donor-designated scholarships restricted by residence in nearby localities and/or area colleges, and payable directly to the school.
Types of support: Seed money, building funds, equipment, land acquisition, research, special projects, capital campaigns, student aid.
Limitations: Giving primarily in Norfolk, VA, and a 50-mile area from its boundaries. No support for national or international organizations, or religious organizations for religious purposes. No grants to individuals (except for donor-designated scholarships), or for operating budgets, endowment funds, or deficit financing; no loans.
Publications: Annual report, application guidelines, program policy statement.
Application information: Application form not required.
Initial approach: Letter or telephone

Copies of proposal: 1
Deadline(s): For scholarships only, Dec. 1 to Mar. 1
Board meeting date(s): 4 times a year
Final notification: 3 to 4 months
Write: Lee C. Kitchin, Exec. Dir.
Officer: Lee C. Kitchin, Exec. Dir.
Distribution Committee: Charles F. Burroughs, Jr., Chair.; Toy D. Savage, Jr., Vice-Chair.; Jean C. Bruce, Joshua P. Darden, Jr., H.P. McNeal, H.B. Price III, Kurt M. Rosenbach.
Number of staff: 1 full-time professional; 2 part-time support.
Employer Identification Number: 540722169

7248
Norfolk Southern Foundation ▼
One Commercial Place
Norfolk 23510-2191 (804) 629-2650

Established in 1983 in VA.
Donor(s): Norfolk Southern Corp.
Foundation type: Company-sponsored
Financial data (yr. ended 12/31/87): Assets, $9,841,129 (M); gifts received, $4,918,467; expenditures, $2,749,692, including $2,076,630 for 209 grants (high: $95,000; low: $100; average: $750-$25,000) and $640,882 for employee matching gifts.
Purpose and activities: Giving primarily for cultural programs, including museums and performing arts groups, community funds, and higher education, including independent college funds. The foundation also sponsors an employee matching gift program to educational and cultural institutions.
Types of support: Employee matching gifts, operating budgets.
Limitations: Giving primarily in Atlanta, GA, and Hampton Roads and Roanoke, VA. No grants to individuals.
Application information:
Initial approach: Letter
Deadline(s): None
Board meeting date(s): As necessary
Final notification: 60 days
Write: Joseph R. Neikirk, V.P.
Officers: Arnold B. McKinnon, Chair., Pres., and C.E.O.; Joseph R. Neikirk, V.P. and Exec. Dir.; John S. Shannon, V.P.; John R. Turbyfill, V.P.; D.H. Watts, V.P.; Donald E. Middleton, Secy.; Thomas H. Kerwin, Treas.
Number of staff: None.
Employer Identification Number: 521328375

7249
North Shore Foundation ⌑
The Sovran Ctr.
Norfolk 23510 (804) 627-0611

Established in 1982 in VA.
Donor(s): Constance S. duPont Darden.
Foundation type: Independent
Financial data (yr. ended 4/30/86): Assets, $65,967 (M); gifts received, $668,055; expenditures, $606,471, including $605,950 for 25 grants (high: $100,000; low: $350).
Purpose and activities: Giving primarily for conservation and education.
Types of support: General purposes.
Limitations: No grants to individuals.
Application information: Application form not required.
Initial approach: Letter
Deadline(s): None
Write: Toy O. Savage, Jr., Secy.-Treas.
Officers and Directors: Joshua P. Darden, Jr., Pres.; Toy D. Savage, Jr., Secy.-Treas.; Constance S. DuPont Darden.
Employer Identification Number: 521296293

7250
The Tom and Claire O'Neil Foundation, Inc. ⌑
c/o Mark O'Neil
930 Graydon Ave.
Norfolk 23507

Incorporated in 1954 in CT.
Donor(s): Thomas F. O'Neil.
Foundation type: Independent
Financial data (yr. ended 12/31/88): Assets, $1,108,365 (M); expenditures, $71,286, including $58,975 for 12 grants (high: $25,000; low: $175).
Purpose and activities: Emphasis on Roman Catholic church support, church-related associations, and social service and youth agencies; support for educational institutions, hospitals, and cultural programs.
Limitations: Giving primarily in Norfolk, VA.
Application information: Contributes only to pre-selected organizations. Applications not accepted.
Officers and Directors: Thomas F. O'Neil, Pres.; Claire M. O'Neil, V.P.; Mark O'Neil, Secy. and Mgr.; William M. Regan, Treas.; Eileen O'Neil, Shane O'Neil.
Employer Identification Number: 066035099

7251
The Ohrstrom Foundation, Inc. ⌑
c/o Whitewood
The Plains 22171
Application address: 540 Madison Ave., 35th Fl., New York, NY 10022; Tel.: (212) 759-5380

Incorporated in 1953 in DE.
Donor(s): Members of the Ohrstrom family.
Foundation type: Independent
Financial data (yr. ended 05/31/89): Assets, $17,922,801 (M); expenditures, $877,312, including $830,000 for 139 grants (high: $282,500; low: $500; average: $1,000-$10,000).
Purpose and activities: Emphasis on elementary, secondary, and higher education; support also for civic affairs, conservation, hospitals and medical research, and museums.
Types of support: Operating budgets, continuing support, annual campaigns, seed money, emergency funds, building funds, equipment, land acquisition, endowment funds, matching funds.
Limitations: Giving primarily in VA and NY. No grants to individuals, or for deficit financing, scholarships, fellowships, research, special projects, publications, or conferences; no loans.
Application information: Application form not required.
Initial approach: Letter
Deadline(s): Mar. 31
Final notification: 3 to 6 months
Write: George L. Ohrstrom, Jr., V.P.
Officers: George L. Ohrstrom, Jr.,* V.P.; Ricard R. Ohrstrom, Jr.,* V.P.; Palma Cifu, Treas.
Trustees:* Magalen O. Bryant.
Number of staff: 1 part-time support.
Employer Identification Number: 546039966

7252
The George and Carol Olmsted Foundation
1515 North Courthouse Rd., Suite 305
Arlington 22201 (703) 527-9070

Incorporated in 1960 in VA.
Donor(s): George Olmsted.
Foundation type: Independent
Financial data (yr. ended 12/31/89): Assets, $8,600,000 (M); expenditures, $685,000, including $310,167 for 14 grants (high: $100,000; low: $1,500) and $125,469 for 48 grants to individuals (high: $5,500; low: $237).
Purpose and activities: Grants for higher education and charitable purposes. with emphasis on scholarships for nine career military officers per year, nominated by their branches of the Armed Forces only; scholarships not awarded to non-military students.
Types of support: Student aid.
Limitations: No grants to individuals (except for Olmsted Scholars).
Publications: Annual report, program policy statement, informational brochure (including application guidelines).
Application information: Applications handled through Military Services; funds largely committed. Applications not accepted.
Board meeting date(s): Jan., Apr., July, and Oct.
Write: Barbara S. Schimpff, Exec. V.P.
Officers: Howard Hussing,* Pres.; Barbara S. Schimpff, Exec. V.P.; Joseph McManus, Secy.-Treas.
Directors:* David S. Smith, Chair.; George L. Butler, Michael D. Fry, James L. Holloway III, Thomas E. Murphy, Carol S. Olmsted, George Olmsted.
Number of staff: 1 full-time professional; 1 part-time professional; 1 full-time support.
Employer Identification Number: 546049005

7253
Elis Olsson Memorial Foundation
c/o McGuire, Woods, Battle & Boothe
P.O. Box 397
Richmond 23203 (804) 644-4131

Established in 1966 in VA.
Donor(s): Inga Olsson Nylander,† Signe Maria Olsson.†
Foundation type: Independent
Financial data (yr. ended 12/31/88): Assets, $11,856,145 (M); gifts received, $520,287; expenditures, $584,865, including $516,175 for 76 grants (high: $125,000; low: $100).
Purpose and activities: Emphasis on higher, secondary, and other education, museums and the fine arts, medical and marine sciences, hospices, and Protestant church support.
Types of support: Fellowships, professorships.
Limitations: Giving primarily in VA. No grants to individuals.
Application information:

Initial approach: Letter
Deadline(s): None
Board meeting date(s): Oct. 1
Write: Carle E. Davis, Secy.
Officers and Trustees:* Sture G. Olsson,* Pres.; Shirley C. Olsson,* V.P. and Treas.; Carle E. Davis,* Secy.
Number of staff: 1 part-time professional.
Employer Identification Number: 546062436

7254
William G. Pannill Foundation ⌑
P.O. Box 5151
Martinsville 24115

Established in 1984 in VA.
Donor(s): William G. Pannill.
Foundation type: Independent
Financial data (yr. ended 12/31/88): Assets, $1,074,890 (M); gifts received, $60,000; expenditures, $337,243, including $334,500 for 12 grants (high: $125,000; low: $1,000).
Purpose and activities: Support for Christian religious purposes, higher education, and cultural activities.
Types of support: Operating budgets, research.
Limitations: Giving primarily in VA. No grants to individuals.
Application information: Contributes only to pre-selected organizations. Applications not accepted.
Officers and Directors: William G. Pannill, Pres. and Treas.; Catherine Stuart Pannill, V.P.; William L. Pannill, Secy.
Employer Identification Number: 541268236

7255
William Letcher Pannill Scholarship Foundation ⌑
P.O. Box 5151
Martinsville 24115

Established in 1985 in VA.
Foundation type: Independent
Financial data (yr. ended 2/28/88): Assets, $2,085,022 (M); gifts received, $66,667; expenditures, $150,446, including $140,556 for 40 grants to individuals (high: $5,000; low: $975).
Purpose and activities: Educational grants to children of Pannill employees.
Types of support: Student aid.
Limitations: Giving primarily in VA, NC, FL and AL.
Application information: Applicants must have worked for Pannill or its predecessor for three or more years.
Initial approach: Letter
Deadline(s): None
Officers: Frank M. Lacey, Jr., Pres.; James C. Smith, Jr., V.P.; Lucy C. Mattox, Secy.; William L. Pannill, Treas.
Employer Identification Number: 521375635

7256
Perry Foundation, Inc.
P.O. Box 558
Charlottesville 22902 (804) 977-8590

Incorporated in 1946 in VA.
Donor(s): Hunter Perry, Lillian Perry Edwards.
Foundation type: Independent
Financial data (yr. ended 12/31/88): Assets, $11,700,250 (M); expenditures, $566,664, including $495,716 for 15 grants (high: $100,000; low: $2,500).
Purpose and activities: Support for higher and secondary education; grants also for a community fund and aid to the handicapped.
Types of support: General purposes, building funds.
Limitations: Giving generally limited to Charlottesville and Albemarle, VA. No grants to individuals, or for operating budgets.
Application information: Application form not required.
Initial approach: Proposal
Copies of proposal: 6
Deadline(s): 1st day of Apr., July, Oct., and Dec.
Board meeting date(s): Quarterly
Write: Nancy Williams
Officers and Trustees:* George C. Palmer II,* Pres.; Francis H. Fife, V.P.; William A. Perkins, Secy.; Edward D. Taylor II, Treas.; Bernard J. Haggerty.
Employer Identification Number: 546036446

7257
Petersburg Methodist Home for Girls ⌑
c/o John G. Sayers
20 Franklin St., P.O. Box 270
Petersburg 23804
Application address: 910 Northampton Rd., Petersburg, VA 23805

Foundation type: Independent
Financial data (yr. ended 12/31/88): Assets, $1,885,287 (M); expenditures, $132,191, including $72,200 for 13 grants (high: $25,000; low: $1,000) and $37,300 for 33 grants to individuals (high: $2,500; low: $250).
Purpose and activities: Support for social services and scholarships for higher education.
Types of support: Student aid.
Limitations: Giving primarily in Southside, VA.
Application information: Application form required.
Deadline(s): July and Feb.
Write: Hilda T. Atkinson, Secy.
Officers: Howard D. Brown, Pres.; Robert E. Smith, V.P.; Hilda T. Atkinson, Secy.; John G. Sayers, Treas.
Directors: Mary E. Bailey, Carl D. Bedford, Henry Brigstock, James D. Fear, John Peyton Goodall.
Employer Identification Number: 540542500

7258
Portsmouth Community Trust
220 Swimming Point Walk
Portsmouth 23704 (804) 393-4192

Established in 1955 in VA.
Foundation type: Community
Financial data (yr. ended 12/31/89): Assets, $1,080,377 (M); gifts received, $222,815; expenditures, $290,851, including $274,076 for 42 grants (high: $153,000; low: $100; average: $100-$153,000).
Purpose and activities: Support for museums and other arts groups, public and civic affairs, community development and recreational programs, religious organizations, hospital building funds and medical education, libraries, and education, including higher and secondary institutions, adult education, and programs for minorities.
Types of support: Operating budgets, seed money, emergency funds, deficit financing, building funds, equipment, land acquisition, renovation projects, matching funds, scholarship funds, publications, conferences and seminars, capital campaigns.
Limitations: Giving limited to Portsmouth, VA, and the surrounding area. No grants to individuals.
Publications: Annual report, application guidelines, financial statement, grants list.
Application information: Application form required.
Initial approach: Letter requesting application form
Copies of proposal: 2
Deadline(s): Feb. 28, May 1, Aug. 1, and Nov. 1
Board meeting date(s): 1st Wed. in Mar., June, Sept., and Dec.
Write: Frank L. Kirby, Exec. Secy.
Officers: Herbert A. Haneman, Chair.; A. Lee Cherry III, Vice-Chair.; Frank L. Kirby, Exec. Secy.
Number of staff: 1 part-time professional.
Employer Identification Number: 546062589

7259
The Potomac Foundation ⌑ ☆
3211 Jermantown Rd., Suite 480
Fairfax 22030

Established in 1988 in VA.
Donor(s): BDM International Inc.
Foundation type: Independent
Financial data (yr. ended 12/31/88): Assets, $4,773,785 (M); gifts received, $5,000,000; qualifying distributions, $322,480, including $157,500 for 2 grants and $142,692 for foundation-administered programs.
Purpose and activities: Initial year of operation, 1988; support for organizations engaged in research in defense and international affairs.
Types of support: Conferences and seminars, research.
Limitations: Giving primarily in Washington, DC. No grants to individuals.
Application information: Contributes only to pre-selected organizations. Applications not accepted.
Officers and Directors: Stanley E. Harrison, Chair. and Pres.; F.N. Hofer, Secy.-Treas.; Joseph V. Braddock, Bernard J. Dunn, Daniel F. McDonald.
Employer Identification Number: 541468870

7260
Rangeley Educational Trust ⌑
c/o Crestar Bank, N.A.
P.O. Box 4911
Martinsville 24115 (703) 632-6301

Established about 1968 in VA.
Foundation type: Independent
Financial data (yr. ended 10/31/88): Assets, $1,545,918 (M); expenditures, $19,397, including $19,397 for loans to individuals.

Purpose and activities: Support limited to scholarship loans, based on scholastic ability, and family financial need.
Types of support: Student loans.
Limitations: Giving primarily in city of Martinsville and Henry County, VA.
Application information: Interviews usually required. Application form required.
Deadline(s): May 1
Write: Paul J. Turner, V.P., Personal Financial Services, Crestar Bank, N.A.
Trustee: Crestar Bank, N.A.
Employer Identification Number: 546077906

7261
Emerson G. & Dolores G. Reinsch Foundation ⌑
2040 Columbia Pike
Arlington 22204 (703) 920-3600

Established in 1964.
Foundation type: Independent
Financial data (yr. ended 12/31/86): Assets, $1,507,910 (M); expenditures, $52,158, including $45,690 for 44 grants (high: $6,890; low: $25).
Purpose and activities: Giving for health services, with emphasis on alcoholic rehabilitation; support also for education.
Types of support: Continuing support.
Limitations: Giving primarily in northern VA.
Application information:
Initial approach: Letter, except for continuing support
Deadline(s): None
Write: Dolores G. Reinsch
Trustees: Paul F. Neff, Lola C. Reinsch.
Employer Identification Number: 546055396

7262
Richard S. Reynolds Foundation ⌑
Reynolds Metals Bldg.
P.O. Box 27003
Richmond 23261
Application address: David P. Reynolds, 6601 West Broad St., Richmond, VA 23261; Tel.: (804) 281-4801

Incorporated in 1965 in VA.
Donor(s): Julia L. Reynolds.†
Foundation type: Independent
Financial data (yr. ended 6/30/87): Assets, $28,427,298 (M); gifts received, $15,158; expenditures, $801,010, including $701,000 for 22 grants (high: $500,000; low: $1,000).
Purpose and activities: Support for higher and secondary education, health, hospitals, and museums.
Limitations: Giving primarily in VA.
Application information:
Initial approach: Letter
Deadline(s): None
Officers and Directors: David P. Reynolds, Pres.; Mrs. Glenn R. Martin, V.P.; Richard S. Reynolds III, Secy.; William G. Reynolds, Jr., Treas.
Number of staff: None.
Employer Identification Number: 546037003

7263
Reynolds Metals Company Foundation ⌑
P.O. Box 27003
Richmond 23261-7003 (804) 281-2222

Foundation established around 1978.
Donor(s): Reynolds Metals Co.
Foundation type: Company-sponsored
Financial data (yr. ended 12/31/87): Assets, $1,750,847 (M); expenditures, $726,933, including $723,890 for 169 grants (high: $150,000; low: $100; average: $200-$75,000).
Purpose and activities: Emphasis on higher education, including an employee matching gift program, and community funds; support also for cultural programs, hospitals and health associations, youth agencies, and civic affairs.
Types of support: Employee matching gifts, building funds, scholarship funds, special projects.
Limitations: Giving primarily in areas of company operations, with emphasis on Richmond, VA.
Application information: Application form required.
Initial approach: Letter
Deadline(s): None
Write: Janice H. Bailey, Admin.
Officers: William O. Bourke,* Chair. and C.E.O.; John M. Noonan, Pres.; R. Bern Crowl,* Exec. V.P. and C.F.O.; John H. Galea,* Sr. V.P.; James E. Hertz,* V.P.; Donald T. Cowles, Secy.; Julian H. Taylor, Treas.
Directors:* Richard G. Holder.
Employer Identification Number: 541084698

7264
C. E. Richardson Benevolent Foundation ⌑
74 West Main St., Rm. 211
P.O. Box 1120
Pulaski 24301 (703) 980-6628
Additional tel.: (703) 980-1704

Established in 1979.
Foundation type: Independent
Financial data (yr. ended 5/31/88): Assets, $2,526,963 (M); expenditures, $163,142, including $139,400 for 37 grants (high: $40,000; low: $300).
Purpose and activities: Support for programs for needy children, aged people, and indigent or handicapped persons, and for private colleges and universities; support also for cultural programs.
Limitations: Giving limited to thirty miles north and south of Interstate 81 from Lexington to Abingdon, VA. No grants to individuals.
Publications: Program policy statement, application guidelines.
Application information: Application form required.
Initial approach: Letter or telephone
Copies of proposal: 1
Deadline(s): 1 month after the date of the published public notice; is stated in the notice, usually Sept. 15
Write: Betty S. King, Secy.
Officer: Betty S. King, Secy.
Trustees: James D. Miller, Annie S. Muire, James C. Turk.
Number of staff: 1 part-time support.
Employer Identification Number: 510227549

7265
Greater Richmond Community Foundation
4001 Fitzhugh Ave.
P.O. Box 11553
Richmond 23230 (804) 353-3406

Established in 1968 in VA.
Foundation type: Community
Financial data (yr. ended 12/31/88): Assets, $5,044,373 (M); gifts received, $678,582; expenditures, $864,326, including $688,760 for 45 grants (high: $448,500; low: $1,000; average: $1,000-$5,000) and $82,000 for 16 grants to individuals (high: $10,000; low: $1,000; average: $1,000-$10,000).
Purpose and activities: Giving for charitable purposes, including education, the arts, community development, youth organizations, and child welfare agencies.
Types of support: Technical assistance, renovation projects, emergency funds, equipment, general purposes, matching funds, seed money, special projects.
Limitations: Giving limited to metropolitan Richmond, VA. No grants for annual campaigns, deficit financing, land acquisition, or building funds.
Publications: Annual report, application guidelines, financial statement, newsletter, informational brochure.
Application information: Application form required.
Initial approach: Telephone or proposal
Copies of proposal: 1
Deadline(s): Jan. 15, Apr. 15, July 15 and Oct. 15
Board meeting date(s): Quarterly
Final notification: 60 days
Write: Darcy S. Oman, Exec. Dir.
Officers: Paul H. Riley, Chair.; Frank G. Louthan, Jr., Vice-Chair.; Wallace Stettinius, Vice-Chair.; Frances H. Rosi, Secy.; Robert L. Thalhimer, Treas.; Darcy S. Oman, Exec. Dir.; William L.S. Rowe, General Counsel.
Number of staff: 2 full-time professional.
Employer Identification Number: 237009135

7266
Robins Foundation ⌑
1516 Coggins Point Rd.
Hopewell 23860 (804) 458-2938

Estalished in 1957 in VA.
Foundation type: Independent
Financial data (yr. ended 12/31/87): Assets, $1,279,361 (M); expenditures, $41,470, including $39,500 for 6 grants (high: $35,000; low: $500).
Purpose and activities: Support for hospitals, youth organizations, education, cultural programs, and social services.
Application information:
Initial approach: Letter
Write: H.C. Townes, Secy.-Treas.
Officers and Directors: E.C. Robins, Pres.; E.B. Heilman, V.P.; H.C. Townes, Secy.-Treas.; A.B. Marchant, E.R. Porter, E.C. Robins, Jr., L.M. Robins.
Employer Identification Number: 540784484

7267
The William H., John G., and Emma Scott Foundation ⌑
c/o Davenport & Co.
801 East Main St.
Richmond 23219 (804) 780-2035

Incorporated in 1956 in VA.
Donor(s): John G. Scott,† Emma Scott Taylor.
Foundation type: Independent
Financial data (yr. ended 9/30/88): Assets, $5,304,341 (M); expenditures, $373,631, including $304,000 for 11 grants (high: $75,000; low: $2,000; average: $20,000) and $12,250 for 16 grants to individuals (high: $1,000; low: $750).
Purpose and activities: Emphasis on higher and secondary education; support also for a Christian diocese.
Types of support: Renovation projects, equipment, student aid.
Limitations: Giving primarily in VA. No grants for endowment funds, scholarships, or operating budgets.
Application information: Application form not required.
Initial approach: Letter
Copies of proposal: 2
Deadline(s): Mar. 1 for scholarships
Board meeting date(s): Nov., Dec., Jan., and June, and as required
Final notification: 1 year
Write: Clinton Webb, Treas.
Officers: Thomas W. Murrell, Jr., M.D.,* Pres.; T. Justin Moore, Jr.,* V.P.; R.E. Cabell, Jr.,* Secy.; Clinton Webb, Treas. and Asst. to Pres.
Trustees:* Rev. Don Raby Edwards, Charles M. Guthridge, Edwin P. Munson, Elizabeth Copeland Norfleet, C. Cotesworth Pinckney, E. Bryce Powell.
Number of staff: 1 full-time professional.
Employer Identification Number: 540648772

7268
George and Effie Seay Memorial Trust
c/o Sovran Bank, N.A., Trust Dept.
P.O. Box 26903
Richmond 23261 (804) 788-2963

Trust established in 1957 in VA.
Donor(s): George J. Seay,† Effie L. Seay.†
Foundation type: Independent
Financial data (yr. ended 06/30/89): Assets, $2,197,714 (M); expenditures, $125,829, including $111,300 for 21 grants (high: $15,000; low: $1,000; average: $5,000-$7,500).
Purpose and activities: Support for direct social service and youth programs and projects.
Types of support: General purposes, operating budgets, building funds, special projects, matching funds, renovation projects.
Limitations: Giving limited to VA. No support for private foundations. No grants to individuals, or for endowment funds or scholarships; no loans.
Publications: Informational brochure (including application guidelines).
Application information: Application form not required.
Initial approach: Letter
Copies of proposal: 1
Deadline(s): Submit proposal preferably in Feb. or Mar., and Sept. or Oct.; deadlines May 1 and Nov. 1
Board meeting date(s): June and Dec.
Final notification: 3 weeks after board meetings
Write: Elizabeth D. Seaman, Consultant
Trustee: Sovran Bank, N.A.
Number of staff: 1 part-time professional; 1 part-time support.
Employer Identification Number: 546030604

7269
Charles E. Smith Family Foundation ⌑ ☆
1735 Jefferson Davis Hwy.
Arlington 22202

Established in 1963 in VA.
Donor(s): Charles E. Smith, Robert H. Smith, Robert P. Kogod.
Foundation type: Independent
Financial data (yr. ended 2/29/88): Assets, $8,330 (M); gifts received, $515,000; expenditures, $528,128, including $526,150 for 18 grants (high: $500,000; low: $400).
Purpose and activities: Support primarily for a Jewish welfare fund and other Jewish organizations.
Limitations: Giving primarily in MD and Washington, DC. No grants to individuals.
Application information: Contributes only to pre-selected organizations. Applications not accepted.
Officers and Directors: Charles E. Smith, Pres.; Robert P. Kogod, V.P.; Robert H. Smith, Secy.-Treas.
Employer Identification Number: 520800784

7270
Sovran Foundation, Inc. ▼
c/o Trust Dept., Sovran Bank, N.A.
P.O. Box 26903
Richmond 23261 (804) 788-2963

Incorporated in 1966 in VA.
Donor(s): Sovran Bank, N.A.
Foundation type: Company-sponsored
Financial data (yr. ended 12/31/88): Assets, $70,313 (M); gifts received, $832,374; expenditures, $2,086,713, including $1,883,618 for 396 grants (high: $196,000; low: $100; average: $500-$25,000) and $116,940 for employee matching gifts.
Purpose and activities: Emphasis on higher education, economic education, health, the arts and culture, civic programs, and youth activities; social services supported through the United Way.
Types of support: Employee matching gifts, continuing support, annual campaigns, building funds, equipment, land acquisition, endowment funds, matching funds.
Limitations: Giving limited to communities in which Sovran Bank, N.A., has facilities, with emphasis on VA. No grants to individuals, or for scholarships or fellowships; no operating funds for United Way agencies; no loans.
Publications: Program policy statement, application guidelines.
Application information:
Initial approach: Letter
Copies of proposal: 1
Deadline(s): May 15 and Oct. 15
Board meeting date(s): July and Jan.
Write: Elizabeth D. Seaman, Secy.-Treas.
Officer: Elizabeth D. Seaman, Secy.-Treas.
Number of staff: 2
Employer Identification Number: 546066961

7271
The Taylor Foundation ⌑
6969 Tidewater Dr.
P.O. Box 2556
Norfolk 23501

Trust established in 1951 in VA.
Donor(s): West India Fruit and Steamship Co., Inc., members of the Taylor family, and others.
Foundation type: Independent
Financial data (yr. ended 12/31/86): Assets, $2,062,960 (M); expenditures, $68,566, including $53,450 for 34 grants (high: $9,000; low: $250; average: $1,000).
Purpose and activities: Giving for hospitals, higher education, Protestant church support, social service agencies, and a sailors' retirement home.
Types of support: Special projects.
Limitations: Giving primarily in NC, VA, and the Southeast. No grants to individuals.
Application information:
Initial approach: Letter
Deadline(s): Dec. 1
Write: Robert T. Taylor, Pres.
Officers and Trustees: Robert T. Taylor, Pres.; Leslie M. Taylor, V.P.; J. Lewis Rahls, Jr., Secy.; T.A. Bennett.
Employer Identification Number: 540555235

7272
Charles G. Thalhimer and Family Foundation ⌑
615 East Broad St.
Richmond 23219 (804) 643-4211

Established in 1976 in VA.
Donor(s): Members of the Thalhimer family.
Foundation type: Independent
Financial data (yr. ended 10/31/88): Assets, $2,065,551 (M); expenditures, $152,493, including $128,223 for 49 grants (high: $37,000; low: $25).
Purpose and activities: Giving primarily for cultural activities and higher education; support also for civic affairs.
Limitations: Giving primarily in VA. No grants to individuals.
Application information: Application form not required.
Initial approach: Letter
Deadline(s): None
Write: Charles Thalhimer, Pres.
Officers and Directors: Charles G. Thalhimer, Pres.; Charles G. Thalhimer, Jr., V.P.; Harry R. Thalhimer, V.P.; William B. Thalhimer, Jr., V.P.; Rhoda R. Thalhimer, Secy.-Treas.
Employer Identification Number: 546047108

7273
Thalhimer Brothers Foundation
615 East Broad St.
Richmond 23219 (804) 643-4211

Incorporated in 1950 in VA.
Donor(s): Thalhimer Brothers, Inc., Carter Hawley Hale Stores, Inc.

Foundation type: Company-sponsored
Financial data (yr. ended 11/30/89): Assets, $456 (M); gifts received, $244,000; expenditures, $244,721, including $241,925 for 72 grants (high: $70,000; low: $25).
Purpose and activities: Emphasis on community development, higher education, Jewish welfare funds, cultural programs, historic preservation, and youth.
Limitations: Giving primarily in VA and NC. No grants to individuals.
Application information: Applications not accepted.
Write: James E. Branson, Secy.-Treas.
Officers and Directors:* William B. Thalhimer, Jr.,* Pres.; Michael C. Weisberg,* V.P.; James E. Branson,* Secy.-Treas.; William B. Thalhimer III.
Number of staff: None.
Employer Identification Number: 546047107

7274
William B. Thalhimer, Jr. and Family Foundation
1513 Hearthglow Ln.
Richmond 23233 (804) 780-2992

Incorporated in 1953 in VA.
Donor(s): William B. Thalhimer, Jr., Barbara J. Thalhimer.
Foundation type: Independent
Financial data (yr. ended 10/31/89): Assets, $1,923,101 (M); gifts received, $5,284; expenditures, $97,840, including $92,098 for 80 grants (high: $30,000; low: $20).
Purpose and activities: Giving for Jewish welfare funds and temple support; grants also for cultural progams and higher education.
Limitations: Giving primarily in VA. No grants to individuals.
Application information:
Initial approach: Letter
Deadline(s): None
Write: Robert L. Thalhimer, V.P.
Officers and Directors:* William B. Thalhimer, Jr.,* Pres.; Robert L. Thalhimer,* V.P.; William B. Thalhimer III,* V.P.; Barbara J. Thalhimer,* Secy.-Treas.
Employer Identification Number: 546047110

7275
Theresa A. Thomas Memorial Foundation ⌑
c/o Sovran Ctr.
1111 East Main St., 21st Fl.
Richmond 23219
Application address: P.O. Box 1122, Richmond, VA 23208; Tel.: (804) 697-1200

Established in 1975.
Foundation type: Independent
Financial data (yr. ended 8/31/88): Assets, $8,938,355 (M); gifts received, $34,611; expenditures, $1,520,937, including $1,415,641 for 19 grants (high: $400,000; low: $2,500).
Purpose and activities: Giving for hospitals and health services, particularly for emergency rescue squads and medical training; support also for a college.
Types of support: Operating budgets.
Limitations: Giving primarily in VA.
Application information:
Initial approach: Letter
Deadline(s): None
Write: Charles L. Reed, Pres.
Officers and Directors: Charles L. Reed, Pres. and Treas.; James C. Roberts, V.P.; Thomas P. Carr, Secy.
Employer Identification Number: 510146629

7276
The Edgar A. Thurman Charitable Foundation for Children ⌑
P.O. Box 13888
Roanoke 24038 (703) 982-3201

Trust established in 1952 in VA.
Donor(s): Edgar A. Thurman.†
Foundation type: Independent
Financial data (yr. ended 6/30/87): Assets, $4,779,606 (M); expenditures, $261,017, including $189,300 for 36 grants (high: $12,000; low: $1,000).
Purpose and activities: To provide maintenance, care, and education for needy and necessitous children, support for orphanages, youth agencies, preschool education, and social service agencies.
Limitations: Giving limited to VA, with preference given to the Roanoke area. No grants to individuals, or for building or endowment funds, salaries, or deficit financing.
Publications: Program policy statement, application guidelines.
Application information: Application form required.
Initial approach: Letter
Copies of proposal: 2
Deadline(s): June 30
Board meeting date(s): Annually
Final notification: Aug. 30
Write: Harry L. Shinn, Jr., Fdn. Mgr.
Distribution Committee: G. Chapman Duffy, Kenneth L. Neathery, Jr., Charles W. Walker.
Trustee: Colonial American National Bank.
Employer Identification Number: 546113281

7277
The Bell and Horace Tilghman, Sr. Charitable Trust ⌑ ☆
c/o Rae H. Ely
P.O. Box 1550
Louisa 23093

Established in 1988 in VA.
Donor(s): Anne Tilghman Boyce.†
Foundation type: Independent
Financial data (yr. ended 12/31/88): Assets, $9,333,333 (M); gifts received, $9,333,333; expenditures, $0.
Purpose and activities: Initial year of operation, 1988; no grants awarded.
Limitations: No grants to individuals.
Application information: Contributes only to pre-selected organizations. Applications not accepted.
Trustees: Olivia Boyce-Abel, Rae H. Ely, Tyson B. van Auken.
Employer Identification Number: 222918521

7278
The Titmus Foundation, Inc.
P.O. Box 10
Sutherland 23885-0010 (804) 265-5834
Application address: Rte. 1, Box 358, Sutherland, VA 23885

Incorporated in 1945 in VA.
Donor(s): Edward Hutson Titmus, Sr.†
Foundation type: Independent
Financial data (yr. ended 01/31/90): Assets, $10,535,891 (M); expenditures, $473,589, including $453,779 for 146 grants (high: $140,200; low: $98; average: $98-$140,200).
Purpose and activities: Emphasis on Baptist church support and religious organizations, higher education, health, cancer research, and child welfare.
Limitations: Giving primarily in VA. No grants to individuals.
Application information: Application form not required.
Initial approach: Proposal
Deadline(s): None
Board meeting date(s): July
Write: Edward B. Titmus, Pres.
Officers: Edward B. Titmus, Pres.; George M. Modlin, V.P.; Margaret V. Beck, Secy.; John O. Muldowney, Treas.
Number of staff: 1 full-time support.
Employer Identification Number: 546051332

7279
The J. Edwin Treakle Foundation, Inc.
P.O. Box 1157
Gloucester 23061 (804) 693-3101

Incorporated in 1963 in VA.
Donor(s): J. Edwin Treakle.†
Foundation type: Independent
Financial data (yr. ended 04/30/89): Assets, $3,719,036 (M); expenditures, $235,750, including $147,000 for 40 grants (high: $20,000; low: $300).
Purpose and activities: Emphasis on Protestant church support, community development, youth agencies, higher education, hospitals, cancer research, and cultural organizations.
Types of support: Annual campaigns, building funds, capital campaigns, continuing support, equipment, general purposes, scholarship funds.
Limitations: Giving primarily in VA. No grants to individuals.
Application information: Application form required.
Copies of proposal: 1
Deadline(s): Submit proposal between Jan. 1 and Apr. 30
Board meeting date(s): Thursday after 2nd Monday in Feb., Apr., June, Aug., Oct., and Dec.
Write: John Warren Cooke, Treas.
Officers and Directors: James B. Martin, Pres.; Harry E. Dunn, V.P.; J. Kirkland Jarvis, Secy.; John W. Cooke, Treas.
Number of staff: 2 part-time professional; 2 part-time support.
Employer Identification Number: 546051620

7280
The Truland Foundation ⌑
1511 North 22nd St.
Arlington 22209

Trust established in 1954 in VA.
Donor(s): Truland of Florida, Inc., and members of the Truland family.
Foundation type: Independent
Financial data (yr. ended 3/31/89): Assets, $2,218,898 (M); expenditures, $107,322, including $101,304 for 62 grants (high: $70,000; low: $10).
Purpose and activities: Emphasis on conservation; some support also for community welfare, higher education, and the arts.
Limitations: Giving primarily in VA.
Application information: Applications not accepted.
Trustees: Alice O. Truland, Robert W. Truland, Walter R. Truland.
Employer Identification Number: 546037172

7281
Ukrop Foundation ⌑
600 Southlake Blvd.
Richmond 23236 (804) 794-2401

Established in 1983 in VA.
Donor(s): Ukrop's Super Markets, Inc.
Foundation type: Company-sponsored
Financial data (yr. ended 6/30/88): Assets, $263,308 (M); gifts received, $240,335; expenditures, $317,261, including $315,084 for 198 grants (high: $75,025; low: $25).
Purpose and activities: Giving for Christian church support, social services, and health associations; support also for an employee matching gift program.
Types of support: General purposes, building funds, special projects, employee matching gifts, land acquisition.
Limitations: Giving primarily in the greater Richmond, VA, area. No grants to individuals.
Application information: Application form not required.
Initial approach: Proposal
Deadline(s): None
Write: Gail Long
Officers and Directors: James E. Ukrop, Pres.; Robert S. Ukrop, V.P.; Jacqueline L. Ukrop, Secy.; J. Nelson Melton, Treas.; Joseph Ukrop.
Employer Identification Number: 541206389

7282
United Coal Company Charitable Foundation ⌑
P.O. Box 1280
Bristol 24203

Established in 1986 in VA.
Donor(s): Burton Fletcher, United Coal Co.
Foundation type: Operating
Financial data (yr. ended 12/31/89): Assets, $1,460,154 (M); expenditures, $133,411, including $131,770 for 1 grant.
Purpose and activities: Support primarily for a local YMCA.
Limitations: Giving primarily in VA.
Application information: Contributes only to pre-selected organizations. Applications not accepted.
Officers: Boyd Fowler, Vice-Chair.; James W. McGlothlin, Pres.; Wayne L. Bell, Secy.; Lois A. Clarke, Treas.
Employer Identification Number: 541390453

7283
Universal Leaf Foundation
Hamilton St. at Broad
P.O. Box 25099
Richmond 23260 (804) 359-9311

Established in 1975 in VA.
Donor(s): Universal Leaf Tobacco Co., Inc.
Foundation type: Company-sponsored
Financial data (yr. ended 6/30/89): Assets, $731,000 (M); expenditures, $433,581, including $354,176 for 175 grants (high: $31,000; low: $75; average: $500-$1,000) and $76,735 for 110 employee matching gifts.
Purpose and activities: Emphasis on higher education, community funds, museums, youth agencies, health, medical research, the environment and animal welfare, civic affairs, public policy, the homeless, and the arts.
Types of support: Annual campaigns, building funds, capital campaigns, emergency funds, employee matching gifts, operating budgets, renovation projects, research, technical assistance, internships, professorships, seed money.
Limitations: Giving primarily in VA.
Publications: Financial statement.
Application information: Application form not required.
Initial approach: Letter of inquiry
Deadline(s): None
Final notification: 3 to 4 weeks
Write: Nancy G. Powell, Mgr., Corp. Relations
Officers and Directors:* W.L. Chandler,* Vice-Chair.; T.R. Towers,* Vice-Chair.; Harry H. Harrell,* Pres. and C.E.O.; O. Kemp Dozier, V.P. and Treas.; J.M. White, V.P.; F.V. Lowden III, Secy.
Number of staff: 1 full-time professional; 1 full-time support.
Employer Identification Number: 510162337

7284
Virginia Environmental Endowment ▼
1051 East Cary St.
Richmond 23219 (804) 644-5000
Mailing address: P.O. Box 790, Richmond, VA 23206-0790

Incorporated in 1977 in VA.
Donor(s): Allied Chemical Corp., FMC Corp., Bethlehem Steel Corp.
Foundation type: Independent
Financial data (yr. ended 03/31/89): Assets, $15,902,010 (M); expenditures, $1,193,315, including $807,068 for 68 grants (high: $75,000; low: $1,000; average: $30,000).
Purpose and activities: Grants in VA are limited to support of activities to improve the quality of the environment. Grants in the Kanawha and Ohio River Valleys Program are limited to projects related to water quality in KY and WV.
Types of support: Operating budgets, continuing support, seed money, matching funds, scholarship funds, loans, special projects, research, conferences and seminars, publications.
Limitations: Giving limited to VA, and the Ohio River and Kanawha River valley regions, currently limited to KY and WV. No grants to individuals, or for indirect costs, construction, renovation, endowment funds, annual campaigns, lawsuits, or deficit financing.
Publications: Annual report (including application guidelines), informational brochure (including application guidelines).
Application information: Matching funds from applicant or other sources are generally required. Application form not required.
Initial approach: Proposal with copy of tax-exempt ruling
Copies of proposal: 4
Deadline(s): Jan. 15, May 15, and Sept. 15
Board meeting date(s): Usually in Mar., July, and Nov.
Final notification: 2.5 months
Write: Gerald P. McCarthy, Exec. Dir.
Officers: William B. Cummings,* Pres.; Virginia R. Holton,* Sr. V.P.; Ross P. Bullard,* V.P.; Gerald P. McCarthy, Secy. and Exec. Dir.; Dixon M. Butler,* Treas.
Directors:* Jeannie P. Baililes, Paul U. Elbling, Byron L. Yost.
Number of staff: 2 full-time professional; 1 full-time support.
Employer Identification Number: 541041973

7285
Washington Forrest Foundation
2300 Ninth St. South
Arlington 22204 (703) 920-3688

Incorporated in 1968 in VA.
Donor(s): Benjamin M. Smith.†
Foundation type: Independent
Financial data (yr. ended 06/30/89): Assets, $6,667,270 (M); expenditures, $1,099,323, including $626,751 for 87 grants (high: $250,000; low: $100; average: $500-$5,000).
Purpose and activities: Emphasis on the arts, education, youth programs, health, religion, and welfare.
Types of support: General purposes, operating budgets, continuing support, annual campaigns, seed money, emergency funds, building funds, equipment, matching funds, special projects, capital campaigns, renovation projects, scholarship funds.
Limitations: Giving primarily in northern VA. No support for public schools or colleges, national programs, or foreign programs. No grants to individuals, or for fellowships or multi-year pledges.
Publications: Program policy statement.
Application information: Application form required.
Initial approach: Letter or telephone
Copies of proposal: 1
Deadline(s): Contact foundation
Board meeting date(s): Contact foundation
Final notification: 2 weeks
Write: Lindsey Peete, Exec. Dir.
Officers: Margaret S. Peete, Pres.; Leslie Ariail, V.P.; Benjamin M. Smith, Jr., Secy.-Treas.; Lindsey Peete, Exec. Dir.
Members: Deborah Lucckese, James McKinney.
Number of staff: 1 part-time professional; 1 part-time support.
Employer Identification Number: 237002944

7286
Wheat Foundation
707 East Main St.
Richmond 23219 (804) 649-2311

Established in 1959.
Donor(s): Wheat First Securities, Inc.
Foundation type: Company-sponsored
Financial data (yr. ended 03/31/90): Assets, $1,100,000 (M); gifts received, $300,000; expenditures, $375,000, including $340,000 for 160 grants (high: $100,000; low: $500; average: $500-$100,000).
Purpose and activities: Support for higher and secondary education, hospitals, health services, and cultural institutions.
Types of support: Building funds, professorships, endowment funds, capital campaigns, renovation projects, scholarship funds.
Limitations: Giving primarily in VA, WV, NC, PA, GA, MD, DE, and Washington, DC. No grants to individuals, or for operating funds; no loans.
Application information: Application form not required.
Initial approach: Telephone
Copies of proposal: 1
Deadline(s): None
Board meeting date(s): Feb., May, Aug., and Nov.
Final notification: Within 30 days following board meeting
Write: William V. Daniel, Treas. and Trustee
Officers and Trustees:* James C. Wheat, Jr.,* Pres.; Howard T. Macrae, Jr.,* Secy.; William V. Daniel,* Treas.; Sharon L. Hobart, John L. McElroy, Jr., Marshall B. Wishnack.
Number of staff: None.
Employer Identification Number: 546047119

7287
Wildcat Foundation ⌑
c/o Arandel Communications
13873 Park Center Rd., Suite 301
Herndon 22071-3285

Established in 1981 in VA.
Donor(s): Marjorie S. Arundel Charitable Lead Trust.
Foundation type: Independent
Financial data (yr. ended 9/30/88): Assets, $13,885 (M); gifts received, $210,000; expenditures, $232,615, including $225,919 for 36 grants (high: $104,163; low: $200).
Purpose and activities: Support primarily for higher education and environmental and land conservation.
Limitations: No grants to individuals.
Application information: Contributes only to pre-selected organizations. Applications not accepted.
Officers: Jocelyn A. Alexander, Chair. and Pres.; Arthur W. Arundel, V.P. and Treas.; Annette J. Miller, Secy.
Director: Gerald W. Vesper.
Employer Identification Number: 521219474

7288
The Wilfred Fund ⌑
c/o Yount, Hyde & Barbour
P.O. Box 467
Middleburg 22117 (703) 687-6381

Incorporated in 1956 in NY.
Donor(s): Frederick M. Warburg,† Wilma S. Warburg.
Foundation type: Independent
Financial data (yr. ended 06/30/89): Assets, $502,543 (M); gifts received, $50,475; expenditures, $304,590, including $298,200 for 62 grants (high: $57,500; low: $50).
Purpose and activities: Emphasis on higher and secondary education, hospitals, and social service agencies.
Limitations: Giving primarily in New York, NY, and VA. No grants to individuals.
Application information:
Initial approach: Letter
Copies of proposal: 1
Deadline(s): None
Board meeting date(s): Monthly
Write: Mrs. Wilma S. Warburg, Pres.
Officers: Wilma S. Warburg, Pres.; Tom Slaughter, V.P.; Jerome A. Manning, Secy.; Marc Keller, Treas.
Employer Identification Number: 136088216

7289
Mark and Catherine Winkler Foundation ⌑
4900 Seminary Rd., No. 900
Alexandria 22311 (703) 998-0400

Established about 1964 in VA.
Donor(s): Catherine Winkler,† Mark Winkler.†
Foundation type: Independent
Financial data (yr. ended 1/31/88): Assets, $1,716,076 (M); expenditures, $559,656, including $521,689 for 45 grants (high: $100,600; low: $250).
Purpose and activities: Giving primarily for social services; support also for conservation and higher education, including a scholarship program.
Types of support: Student aid.
Limitations: Giving primarily in VA.
Application information: Application form provided for scholarship applicants.
Initial approach: Letter requesting application
Deadline(s): None
Write: Lynne S. Bromley, Asst. Secy.-Treas.
Officers and Directors: Catherine W. Herman, Chair.; Kathleen W. Wennesland, Pres.; Margaret W. Hecht, V.P.; Carolyn Winkler, Secy.
Employer Identification Number: 546054383

7290
Wrinkle in Time Foundation, Inc. ⌑
c/o Patterson & Assoc.
Route 626 & Stuart St., P.O. Box 306
The Plains 22171-0306 (703) 253-5266

Established in 1980 in NY.
Foundation type: Independent
Financial data (yr. ended 12/31/88): Assets, $2,023,958 (M); expenditures, $142,172, including $132,241 for 12 grants (high: $25,000; low: $150).
Purpose and activities: Support primarily for improving man's rural and urban environment; including wildlife and wilderness preservation; as well as to gather, preserve and disseminate information about the environment, make productive contributions to either the rural or urban surroundings; restore and maintain historic buildings, sites and antiquities; or encourage, promote and popularize art or design which enhances the rural or urban environment.
Types of support: Loans.
Limitations: Giving primarily in VA.
Application information: Application form not required.
Deadline(s): None
Write: Exec. Dir.
Officers: Andrea C. Patterson, Chair., Pres., and Treas.; Donald W. Patterson, V.P.
Employer Identification Number: 222351518

WASHINGTON

7291
Anderson Family Foundation
3500 First Interstate Ctr.
999 Third Ave.
Seattle 98104 (206) 223-4600

Established in 1974 in WA.
Donor(s): Barbara May Anderson, Charles L. Anderson.
Foundation type: Independent
Financial data (yr. ended 09/30/89): Assets, $1,377,075 (M); expenditures, $88,863, including $66,000 for 13 grants (high: $25,000; low: $1,000).
Purpose and activities: Grants to Christian organizations working in the areas of evangelism, education, and care of the needy.
Types of support: General purposes.
Publications: 990-PF.
Application information: Application form not required.
Initial approach: Letter
Deadline(s): None
Write: Christine Welch, Legal Asst.
Officers and Directors:* Charles L. Anderson,* Pres.; Barbara May Anderson,* V.P.; Richard B. Dodd,* Secy.; Rebecca L. Barton,* Treas.; Paul J. Anderson, Linda D. Aruffo.
Number of staff: None.
Employer Identification Number: 510147901

7292
Anderson Foundation ⌑
4755 First Ave. South
Seattle 98134 (206) 762-0600

Established in 1952.
Donor(s): Charles M. Anderson, Dorothy I. Anderson.
Foundation type: Independent

Financial data (yr. ended 6/30/88): Assets, $2,185,361 (M); gifts received, $49,000; expenditures, $121,928.
Purpose and activities: Giving for Protestant church support, higher education, and social services; support also for health agencies, hospitals and a medical research center.
Types of support: Building funds, equipment, land acquisition, program-related investments, research, scholarship funds, professorships.
Limitations: Giving primarily in the Pacific Northwest, particularly WA. No grants to individuals, or for endowment funds, or matching gifts; no loans.
Application information: Applications not accepted.
Copies of proposal: 1
Board meeting date(s): Semiannually
Officers: Charles M. Anderson, Pres.; Barbara J. Lawrence, V.P.; Dorothy I. Anderson, Secy.-Treas.
Employer Identification Number: 916031724

7293
Norman Archibald Charitable Foundation
c/o First Interstate Bank of Washington
P.O. Box 21927
Seattle 98111 (206) 292-3543

Established in 1976 in WA.
Donor(s): Norman Archibald.†
Foundation type: Independent
Financial data (yr. ended 09/30/89): Assets, $6,312,848 (M); expenditures, $329,008, including $279,860 for 80 grants (high: $12,500; low: $800).
Purpose and activities: Support for youth and child development programs; support also for medical research, education, the arts, the aged, the handicapped, housing programs, and conservation.
Types of support: General purposes, seed money, building funds, equipment, land acquisition, conferences and seminars, program-related investments, publications, renovation projects, research, special projects.
Limitations: Giving primarily in the Puget Sound region of WA. No support for government entities or private foundations. No grants to individuals, or for deficit financing, endowment funds, or scholarships or fellowships; no loans.
Publications: Annual report, application guidelines.
Application information: Application form not required.
Initial approach: Letter
Copies of proposal: 3
Deadline(s): None
Write: Lawrence E. Miller, V.P. and Trust Officer, First Interstate Bank of Washington
Advisors: Durwood Alkire, Lowell P. Mickelwait, Stuart H. Prestrud.
Trustee: First Interstate Bank of Washington.
Number of staff: None.
Employer Identification Number: 911098014

7294
The Arise Charitable Trust ⌑ ☆
P.O. Box 1014
Freeland 98249 (206) 321-5792

Established in 1986 in WA.
Donor(s): Judith P. Yeakel.
Foundation type: Independent
Financial data (yr. ended 09/30/89): Assets, $2,370,490 (M); expenditures, $151,688, including $20,401 for 8 grants (high: $4,600; low: $60) and $101,110 for 69 grants to individuals (high: $5,000; low: $10).
Purpose and activities: Giving limited to aid and programs for local area women in the form of scholarships to individuals and to social service agencies.
Types of support: Student aid.
Limitations: Giving limited to South Whidbey, WA.
Application information: Application form required.
Deadline(s): Apr. 15 and Oct. 15
Write: Charles W. Edwards, Trustee
Trustees: Charles W. Edwards, John Watson, Judith P. Yeakel.
Employer Identification Number: 911350780

7295
Clara & Art Bald Trust ⌑
P.O. Box 1757
Walla Walla 99362 (509) 527-3500

Established in 1985 in WA.
Foundation type: Independent
Financial data (yr. ended 3/31/88): Assets, $1,218,753 (M); expenditures, $48,418, including $15,950 for 10 grants (high: $4,000; low: $50).
Purpose and activities: Giving primarily for social services and agriculture and forestry education.
Limitations: Giving primarily in Walla Walla, WA. No grants to individuals.
Application information: Application form not required.
Deadline(s): None
Write: Robert L. Zagelow, Trustee
Trustee: Robert L. Zagelow.
Number of staff: None.
Employer Identification Number: 916275061

7296
Benaroya Foundation ⌑
1001 4th Ave. Plaza, Suite 4700
Seattle 98154

Established in 1984 in WA.
Donor(s): Jack A. Benaroya, Larry R. Benaroya.
Foundation type: Independent
Financial data (yr. ended 11/30/88): Assets, $1,343,222 (M); gifts received, $290,000; expenditures, $638,824, including $637,000 for 11 grants (high: $337,000; low: $2,500).
Purpose and activities: Support primarily for health, including medical research for diabetes and medical education; giving also for youth.
Types of support: Equipment.
Application information:
Initial approach: Proposal
Deadline(s): None
Write: Jack A. Benaroya, Pres.
Officers: Jack A. Benaroya, Pres.; Donna R. Benaroya, V.P.; Larry R. Benaroya, Secy.-Treas.
Directors: Alan G. Benaroya, Rebecca B. Benaroya, Sherry-Lee Benaroya.
Employer Identification Number: 911280516

7297
Bishop Foundation
c/o Security Pacific Bank Washington, N.A., Charitable Services Dept., T17-1
P.O. Box 3966
Seattle 98124 (206) 621-4445

Trust established in 1962 in WA.
Donor(s): E.K. Bishop,† Lillian F. Bishop.†
Foundation type: Independent
Financial data (yr. ended 07/31/87): Assets, $2,148,357 (M); expenditures, $82,241, including $59,267 for 2 grants (high: $57,267; low: $2,000).
Purpose and activities: Cure of diseases of the eye, the correction of faulty vision, the relief of needy sufferers from eye afflictions, and for use in related fields.
Types of support: Research.
Limitations: Giving primarily in WA. No grants to individuals.
Application information: Funds presently committed to the University of Washington School of Medicine. Applications not accepted.
Board meeting date(s): Semiannually
Directors: Charles H. Bagley, Winston D. Brown, John Hall, Carl D.F. Jensen, M.D., Walter Petersen, M.D.
Trustee: Security Pacific Bank Washington, N.A.
Employer Identification Number: 916027252

7298
E. K. and Lillian F. Bishop Foundation
c/o Security Pacific Bank Washington, N.A., Charitable Services Dept., T17-1
P.O. Box 3966
Seattle 98124 (206) 621-4445
Scholarship application address: Bishop Scholarship Committee, c/o Security Pacific Bank Washington, Grays Harbor Branch, P.O. Box 149, Aberdeen, WA 99520

Trust established in 1971 in WA.
Donor(s): E.K. Bishop,† Lillian F. Bishop.†
Foundation type: Independent
Financial data (yr. ended 04/30/89): Assets, $15,866,759 (M); expenditures, $800,691, including $562,349 for 65 grants (high: $100,000; low: $500; average: $5,000-$30,000) and $85,525 for 75 grants to individuals (high: $2,000; low: $500).
Purpose and activities: To promote the welfare of youths, ages 0 to 23, through scholarships and grants to educational, cultural, and welfare organizations.
Types of support: Seed money, building funds, equipment, matching funds, general purposes, student aid.
Limitations: Giving primarily in WA, with emphasis on Grays Harbor County; scholarship applicants must have resided in Grays Harbor County at least a year immediately before applying. No grants for endowment funds, research, or fellowships; no loans.
Publications: Program policy statement, application guidelines.

Application information: Application form provided for scholarships. Application form required.
Initial approach: Letter
Copies of proposal: 5
Deadline(s): Scholarship applications must be postmarked by June 1
Board meeting date(s): Jan., Apr., July, and Oct.
Final notification: 2 to 3 months
Write: Thomas J. Nevers
Directors: Isabelle Lamb, Gladys Phillips, Janet T. Skadon.
Trustee: Security Pacific Bank Washington, N.A.
Number of staff: None.
Employer Identification Number: 916116724

7299
Bishop-Fleet Foundation ⌑
1420 Fifth Ave., Suite 4400
Seattle 98101-2602 (206) 323-1345

Established in 1941 in WA.
Donor(s): E.K. Bishop, Reuben Fleet.
Foundation type: Independent
Financial data (yr. ended 12/31/88): Assets, $1,079,184 (M); expenditures, $54,023, including $41,228 for 60 grants (high: $6,465; low: $100).
Purpose and activities: Local giving primarily for education, including higher education, scholarships funds, and other educational organizations.
Types of support: Scholarship funds, general purposes.
Limitations: Giving limited to the Seattle, WA, area. No grants to individuals.
Application information: Application form not required.
Deadline(s): None
Write: William W. Brinkley, Pres.
Officers and Trustees:* William W. Brinkley,* Pres.; James R. Callaghan,* Secy.; Charles H. Badgley,* Treas.
Number of staff: None.
Employer Identification Number: 916031057

7300
The Bloedel Foundation, Inc. ⌑
7501 N.E. Dolphin Dr.
Bainbridge Island 98110

Incorporated in 1952 in DE.
Donor(s): Prentice Bloedel, J.H. Bloedel,† Eulalie Bloedel Schneider, Virginia Merrill Bloedel.
Foundation type: Independent
Financial data (yr. ended 6/30/87): Assets, $4,032,884 (M); expenditures, $170,977, including $140,080 for 61 grants (high: $29,916; low: $100).
Purpose and activities: Giving for museums, the performing arts, and Protestant church support; some support for secondary education, social service agencies, and conservation.
Limitations: Giving primarily in WA. No grants to individuals.
Application information:
Initial approach: Letter
Deadline(s): None
Write: Jack E. Gordon, Pres.
Officers and Trustees: Virginia Bloedel Wright, Chair.; John E. Gordon, Pres.; John F. Hall, Secy.; Prentice Bloedel, Virginia Merrill Bloedel, Maxwell Carlson, Solomon Katz, Eulalie Bloedel Schneider.
Employer Identification Number: 916035027

7301
Blue Mountain Area Foundation
11 South Second
P.O. Box 603
Walla Walla 99362 (509) 529-4371

Incorporated in 1984 in WA.
Foundation type: Community
Financial data (yr. ended 6/30/89): Assets, $1,641,795 (M); gifts received, $433,825; expenditures, $113,867, including $84,956 for grants (high: $7,031) and $7,609 for grants to individuals.
Purpose and activities: Giving primarily for higher education through scholarship funds; support also for organizations promoting welfare and education, social services, historical preservation, the arts, health, and animal welfare.
Types of support: Scholarship funds, equipment, program-related investments, renovation projects, seed money.
Limitations: Giving limited to Walla Walla, Columbia, Garfield, Benton and Franklin counties, WA, and Umatilla County, OR.
Publications: Annual report, application guidelines, newsletter.
Application information: Application form not required.
Initial approach: Letter
Deadline(s): Aug. 1
Board meeting date(s): Oct.
Write: Eleanor S. Kane, Admin.
Officers and Trustees: Arthur H. Griff, Pres.; W.W. Peery, V.P.; Richard D. Simon, M.D., Secy.-Treas.; Louis E. Keiler, Exec. Dir.; Tom Baker, Franklin B. Hanson, Barbara Hubbard, Eva M. Iverson, Vernon Marll, John M. Reese, Gary Sirmon, Mary Lou Tillay.
Number of staff: 1 part-time professional.
Employer Identification Number: 911250104

7302
Violet R. Bohnett Memorial Foundation
16149 Redmond Way, Suite 220
Redmond 93052

Established in 1969 in CA.
Donor(s): F. Newell Bohnett.
Foundation type: Independent
Financial data (yr. ended 12/31/89): Assets, $1,682,900 (M); gifts received, $6,100; expenditures, $151,531, including $34,402 for 50 grants (high: $4,000; low: $25; average: $100-$1,500) and $46,276 for 38 grants to individuals (high: $2,000; low: $100; average: $500-$1,500).
Purpose and activities: Grants largely for missionary programs and Protestant church support, youth agencies, and education, including scholarships.
Types of support: Student aid, grants to individuals, matching funds, program-related investments.
Limitations: Giving primarily in WA, OR, CA, AZ, and HI.
Application information:
Initial approach: Letter (no more than 1 page)
Board meeting date(s): Feb.
Final notification: June, Sept., Dec., and Feb.
Write: James N. Bohnett, Managing Trustee
Officers: F. Newell Bohnett, Mgr.; Owen G. Johnston, Mgr.; James A. Nelson, Mgr.
Trustees: James N. Bohnett, Joe Bohnett III, Thomas D. Bohnett, William C. Bohnett III.
Number of staff: 1 part-time professional.
Employer Identification Number: 956225968

7303
The Bullitt Foundation, Inc.
333 Dexter Ave. North
Seattle 98109 (206) 448-3992

Incorporated in 1952 in WA.
Donor(s): Members of the Bullitt family.
Foundation type: Independent
Financial data (yr. ended 02/28/90): Assets, $4,711,405 (M); gifts received, $3,804; expenditures, $282,814, including $246,733 for 24 grants (high: $75,000; low: $2,000; average: $5,000-$10,000).
Purpose and activities: Support for conservation and environmental programs, the health and education of children, and organizations to promote world peace.
Types of support: General purposes, operating budgets, special projects.
Limitations: Giving primarily in the Pacific Northwest. No grants to individuals.
Application information: Application form not required.
Initial approach: Letter
Copies of proposal: 1
Deadline(s): 5 weeks prior to board meetings
Board meeting date(s): Feb., June, and Oct.
Final notification: Mar., July, and Nov.
Write: Emory Bundy, Trustee
Officers and Trustees:* Priscilla Bullitt Collins,* Pres.; Katherine M. Bullitt,* V.P.; Stimson Bullitt,* Secy.-Treas.; Pam Brewster, Harriett Bullitt, Emory Bundy.
Number of staff: 1 part-time professional; 1 part-time support.
Employer Identification Number: 916027795

7304
Nellie Martin Carman Scholarship Trust ⌑
c/o Seattle Trust and Savings Bank
P.O. Box 12907
Seattle 98111 (206) 223-2220

Trust established in 1943 in WA.
Donor(s): Nellie M. Carman.†
Foundation type: Independent
Financial data (yr. ended 5/31/87): Assets, $1,775,863 (M); expenditures, $54,920, including $300 for 2 grants (high: $200; low: $100) and $40,000 for 81 grants to individuals (high: $500; low: $250).
Purpose and activities: To provide scholarships to graduating public high school students in King, Snohomish, and Pierce counties who attend WA colleges or universities; smaller grants paid annually to specified charitable organizations.
Types of support: Student aid.

Limitations: Giving primarily in WA, with emphasis on King, Snohomish, and Pierce counties.
Publications: Multi-year report.
Application information: Application form required for scholarships only.
Deadline(s): New applicants, Mar. 15; renewals, Apr. 2
Board meeting date(s): May and Dec.
Write: Mrs. Warren E. Kraft, Jr., Secy., Scholarship Comm.
Trustee: Seattle Trust and Savings Bank.
Scholarship Committee: Judge Francis E. Holman, Chair.; George Buck, Louis Roebke.
Number of staff: 1 full-time professional; 1 part-time support.
Employer Identification Number: 910668186

7305
Cawsey Trust, Inc. ⌑
700 Wall St. Bldg.
Everett 98201

Incorporated in 1960 in WA.
Donor(s): Mrs. Hugh R. Cawsey.†
Foundation type: Independent
Financial data (yr. ended 12/31/86): Assets, $1,636,822 (M); expenditures, $96,690, including $82,800 for 13 grants (high: $15,000; low: $300).
Purpose and activities: Giving for youth, social service agencies, and a hospital.
Limitations: Giving primarily in WA.
Officers and Trustees: W. Murray Campbell, Pres.; Dan Duryee, V.P.; J.P. Hunter, Secy.-Treas.; Elizabeth Campbell, Treas.; Harold Gunderson.
Employer Identification Number: 916053815

7306
Ben B. Cheney Foundation, Inc. ▼
First Interstate Plaza, Suite 1600
Tacoma 98402 (206) 572-2442

Incorporated in 1955 in WA.
Donor(s): Ben B. Cheney,† Marian Cheney Olrogg.†
Foundation type: Independent
Financial data (yr. ended 12/31/89): Assets, $56,940,666 (M); expenditures, $2,477,024, including $1,986,500 for 127 grants (high: $100,000; low: $1,500; average: $1,500-$20,000).
Purpose and activities: Giving primarily for education; health and social services, including programs for the elderly, the disabled, and youth; community development, including recreational facilities; and museums and other cultural programs.
Types of support: Seed money, building funds, equipment, general purposes, scholarship funds, special projects, emergency funds.
Limitations: Giving limited to WA and OR. No support for religious organizations for sectarian purposes. No grants to individuals, or for operating budgets, basic research, endowment funds, conferences or seminars, or book, film, or video production; no loans.
Publications: Annual report (including application guidelines), application guidelines, informational brochure.
Application information: Application form required.
Initial approach: Letter
Copies of proposal: 4
Deadline(s): 4 weeks prior to board meetings
Board meeting date(s): May, Oct., and Dec.
Final notification: Within 3 months
Write: Elgin E. Olrogg, Exec. Dir.
Officers and Trustees:* Francis I. Cheney,* Pres.; R. Gene Grant,* V.P.; John F. Hansler,* Secy.; Elgin E. Olrogg,* Treas. and Exec. Dir.
Number of staff: 2 full-time professional; 1 full-time support.
Employer Identification Number: 916053760

7307
Comstock Foundation ⌑
819 Washington Trust Financial Ctr.
Spokane 99204 (509) 747-1527

Trust established in 1950 in WA.
Donor(s): Josie Comstock Shadle.†
Foundation type: Independent
Financial data (yr. ended 12/31/88): Assets, $11,769,254 (M); expenditures, $1,001,478, including $937,546 for 68 grants (high: $100,000; low: $325; average: $300-$35,000).
Purpose and activities: Emphasis on capital grants to recreational facilities and other community development projects, social service agencies, aid to the handicapped, child welfare, and youth agencies. Giving also for arts, civic affairs, and higher education.
Types of support: Building funds, equipment, land acquisition, scholarship funds, research, general purposes, matching funds.
Limitations: Giving limited to Spokane County, WA. No grants to individuals, or for endowment funds or operating budgets; no loans. In general, no grants payable for reserve purposes, deficit financing, publications, films, emergency funds, conferences, or travel.
Publications: Informational brochure, program policy statement, application guidelines.
Application information: Application form required.
Initial approach: Proposal
Copies of proposal: 1
Deadline(s): None
Board meeting date(s): Weekly
Final notification: 10 days
Write: Horton Herman, Trustee
Trustees: Harold W. Coffin, Horton Herman, Luke G. Williams.
Number of staff: 1 part-time support.
Employer Identification Number: 916028504

7308
Louella Cook Foundation
c/o The Bank of California, N.A.
P.O. Box 3123
Seattle 98114 (206) 587-3623

Established in 1976 in WA.
Foundation type: Independent
Financial data (yr. ended 07/31/89): Assets, $2,241,243 (M); expenditures, $117,839, including $96,750 for 14 grants (high: $25,000; low: $250).
Purpose and activities: Provides food, clothing, and shelter for street people of Seattle, WA; also support for some specific educational institutions.
Types of support: Operating budgets.
Limitations: Giving limited to WA, with emphasis on Seattle.
Application information: Application form not required.
Initial approach: Letter
Copies of proposal: 1
Deadline(s): None
Board meeting date(s): Aug.
Write: J.W. Grubbs, Jr. or Michael G. Vranizan
Trustees: John Cook Jansing, The Bank of California, N.A.
Number of staff: None.
Employer Identification Number: 911098016

7309
Harriet Cheney Cowles Foundation, Inc. ⌑
West 999 Riverside Ave., Rm. 626
Spokane 99201

Incorporated in 1944 in WA.
Donor(s): Spokane Chronicle Co., Cowles Publishing Co., Inland Empire Paper Co.
Foundation type: Independent
Financial data (yr. ended 12/31/88): Assets, $6,313,839 (M); gifts received, $560,000; expenditures, $193,865, including $160,000 for 6 grants (high: $65,000; low: $10,000).
Purpose and activities: Support primarily for a historical society, the performing arts, YMCA, and a cathedral.
Types of support: Endowment funds, capital campaigns.
Limitations: Giving primarily in Spokane, WA. No grants to individuals.
Application information: Contributes only to pre-selected organizations. Applications not accepted.
Officers and Trustees: William H. Cowles III, Pres.; James P. Cowles, V.P.; M.K. Nielsen, Treas.
Employer Identification Number: 910689268

7310
William H. Cowles Foundation, Inc. ⌑
West 999 Riverside Ave., Rm. 626
Spokane 99201

Incorporated in 1952 in WA.
Foundation type: Independent
Financial data (yr. ended 12/31/88): Assets, $2,678,673 (M); expenditures, $165,364, including $150,000 for 3 grants.
Purpose and activities: Giving for higher education.
Types of support: Endowment funds.
Limitations: No grants to individuals.
Application information: Contributes only to pre-selected organizations. Applications not accepted.
Officers and Trustees: William H. Cowles III, Pres.; James P. Cowles, V.P.; M.K. Nielsen, Treas.
Employer Identification Number: 916020496

7311
Discuren Charitable Foundation
1201 Third Ave., 40th Fl.
Seattle 98101-3059

Established in 1983 in WA.
Foundation type: Independent

Financial data (yr. ended 10/31/89): Assets, $673,779 (M); gifts received, $179,092; expenditures, $327,366, including $297,912 for 7 grants (high: $96,787; low: $4,000).
Purpose and activities: Support primarily for science education and exhibits and higher education.
Types of support: Seed money, special projects.
Limitations: Giving primarily in WA. No support for church-affiliated missions.
Publications: including application guidelines, informational brochure.
Application information: Application form not required.
Initial approach: Letter or proposal
Copies of proposal: 4
Board meeting date(s): Quarterly
Final notification: 6 months
Write: Barbara D. Gage
Trustee: Security Pacific Bank Washington, N.A.
Employer Identification Number: 916249597

7312
Dupar Foundation
10604 N.E. 38th Place, Suite 223
Quad One North
Kirkland 98033 (206) 827-9997

Incorporated in 1954 in WA.
Donor(s): Frank A. Dupar, Ethel L. Dupar, Palmer Supply Co.
Foundation type: Independent
Financial data (yr. ended 01/31/89): Assets, $2,003,826 (M); expenditures, $153,586, including $128,316 for 65 grants (high: $12,500; low: $50; average: $1,730).
Purpose and activities: Emphasis on higher education, youth agencies, and community funds.
Types of support: Annual campaigns, building funds, capital campaigns, emergency funds, equipment, research, scholarship funds, special projects.
Limitations: Giving limited to WA.
Publications: Program policy statement, application guidelines, 990-PF.
Application information: Application form required.
Initial approach: Letter or telephone
Copies of proposal: 1
Deadline(s): May 1 and Nov. 1
Board meeting date(s): Jan. and June or July
Write: Frank A. Dupar, Jr., Pres.
Officers and Trustees:* Frank A. Dupar, Jr.,* Pres.; James W. Dupar, Jr.,* V.P.; Dorothy D. Lynch,* Secy.-Treas.; James W. Dupar, Robert W. Dupar, Thomas E. Dupar, Marilyn D. McIntosh.
Number of staff: 1 part-time professional.
Employer Identification Number: 916027389

7313
Fales Foundation Trust ⌑
c/o The Bank of California, N.A.
P.O. Box 3123
Seattle 98114

Established in 1986 in WA.
Foundation type: Independent
Financial data (yr. ended 1/31/88): Assets, $2,458,088 (M); expenditures, $172,630, including $134,714 for 22 grants (high: $13,800; low: $500).
Purpose and activities: Support primarily for community development, health and cultural programs, and the arts.
Types of support: Operating budgets.
Limitations: Giving limited to WA.
Trustees: Ward L. Sax, The Bank of California, N.A.
Employer Identification Number: 916087669

7314
First Interstate Bank of Washington Foundation
P.O. Box 160
Seattle 98111 (206) 292-3482

Established in 1983 in WA.
Donor(s): First Interstate Bank of Washington.
Foundation type: Company-sponsored
Financial data (yr. ended 12/31/88): Assets, $1,587,669 (M); gifts received, $730,000; expenditures, $526,848, including $502,148 for grants (high: $50,000; low: $1,000; average: $1,000-$5,000) and $23,700 for 143 employee matching gifts.
Purpose and activities: Giving primarily to the United Way, housing and community development, youth, social services, and higher and other education.
Types of support: Capital campaigns, employee matching gifts, special projects.
Limitations: Giving limited to WA.
Publications: Corporate giving report (including application guidelines), grants list, application guidelines, program policy statement, informational brochure (including application guidelines).
Application information: Application form required.
Deadline(s): Feb. 1, May 5, Aug. 4, and Nov. 1
Write: Susan Ingram, Registered Agent
Officers: Donn Spencer, Pres.; Dick Harding, Secy.; Mary Welk, Treas.
Trustees: Connie Best, John Deller, Tim Kirstein, Dave Wheelon, First Interstate Bank of Washington.
Registered Agent: Susan E. Ingram.
Employer Identification Number: 911199882

7315
Forest Foundation
820 A St., Suite 1276
Tacoma 98402 (206) 627-1634
Application address: 820 A St., Suite 545, Tacoma, WA 98402

Incorporated in 1962 in WA.
Donor(s): C. Davis Weyerhaeuser, William T. Weyerhaeuser.
Foundation type: Independent
Financial data (yr. ended 10/31/89): Assets, $20,064,437 (M); expenditures, $1,155,945, including $854,696 for 92 grants (high: $82,073; low: $500).
Purpose and activities: Giving primarily for social services, youth and child development and welfare, family services, the handicapped, Native Americans, health and medical research, the performing arts, and museums.
Types of support: Operating budgets, capital campaigns, special projects.
Limitations: Giving primarily in western WA, with emphasis on Pierce County, and southwest WA. No support for religious organizations for religious purposes. No grants to individuals, or for endowment funds, research, scholarships, or fellowships; no loans.
Publications: Program policy statement, application guidelines.
Application information: Application form required.
Initial approach: Letter or proposal
Copies of proposal: 5
Deadline(s): None
Board meeting date(s): At least 6 times per year
Final notification: 60 to 90 days
Write: Frank D. Underwood, Exec. Dir.
Officers: Gail T. Weyerhaeuser,* Pres. and Treas.; Annette B. Weyerhaeuser,* V.P.; Nicholas C. Spika, Secy.; Frank D. Underwood, Exec. Dir.
Directors:* C. Davis Weyerhaeuser, William T. Weyerhaeuser.
Number of staff: None.
Employer Identification Number: 916020514

7316
The Foster Foundation ⌑
1201 Third Ave., Suite 2101
Seattle 98101

Established in 1984 in WA.
Donor(s): Evelyn W. Foster.
Foundation type: Independent
Financial data (yr. ended 12/31/88): Assets, $4,973,018 (M); expenditures, $278,450, including $260,000 for 14 grants (high: $150,000; low: $3,000).
Purpose and activities: Support for cultural programs, education, social services, health, and the environment.
Types of support: Seed money, building funds, equipment, research, matching funds, special projects.
Limitations: Giving primarily in the Pacific Northwest and AK. No grants to individuals, or for fundraising, endowment funds, or unrestricted operating funds; no loans.
Application information:
Initial approach: Letter
Deadline(s): None
Final notification: 3 months
Write: Jill Goodsell, Admin.
Directors: Jill Goodsell Admin., Evelyn W. Foster, Michael G. Foster, Pamela Foster, Thomas B. Foster.
Employer Identification Number: 911265474

7317
Gottfried & Mary Fuchs Foundation ⌑
c/o The Bank of California, N.A.
P.O. Box 1917
Tacoma 98401 (206) 591-2549

Trust established in 1960 in WA.
Donor(s): Gottfried Fuchs,† Mary Fuchs.†
Foundation type: Independent
Financial data (yr. ended 12/31/87): Assets, $9,150,000 (M); expenditures, $555,215, including $438,243 for 64 grants (high: $22,000; low: $500).
Purpose and activities: Priority of support for charitable, educational, scientific, literary or

religious purposes not normally financed by tax funds; emphasis on child welfare and youth agencies, higher and secondary education, cultural programs, hospitals, and food programs. Prefers funding special capital or services projects rather than operating budgets.
Types of support: Continuing support, annual campaigns, emergency funds, building funds, equipment, scholarship funds, research, operating budgets, matching funds, special projects, capital campaigns.
Limitations: Giving primarily in Tacoma, Pierce County, and the lower Puget Sound area of WA. No grants to individuals.
Publications: Application guidelines.
Application information: Application form required.
Initial approach: Letter
Copies of proposal: 5
Deadline(s): 3 weeks prior to board meetings
Board meeting date(s): Apr., Aug., and Nov.
Write: Harlan Sachs, V.P. and Trust Officer, The Bank of California, N.A.
Trustee: The Bank of California, N.A.
Number of staff: 1 part-time professional.
Employer Identification Number: 916022284

7318
Geneva Foundation ⌑
1250 22nd Ave. East
Seattle 98112

Established in 1964 in WA.
Donor(s): Genevieve Albers.
Foundation type: Independent
Financial data (yr. ended 06/30/89): Assets, $1,891,606 (M); gifts received, $150,000; expenditures, $92,533, including $90,400 for 14 grants (high: $30,000; low: $32).
Purpose and activities: Support for Catholic churches and organizations, education, and social services.
Types of support: General purposes.
Trustee: Genevieve Albers.
Employer Identification Number: 916056767

7319
Glaser Foundation, Inc.
P.O. Box N
Edmonds 98020

Incorporated in 1952 in WA.
Donor(s): Paul F. Glaser.†
Foundation type: Independent
Financial data (yr. ended 11/30/89): Assets, $6,072,138 (M); expenditures, $258,722, including $236,772 for 62 grants (high: $10,245; low: $50; average: $1,000-$5,000).
Purpose and activities: Major focus on drug abuse; support also for direct-line service health agencies, and agencies serving children, youth, the handicapped, the aged, and the indigent; support also for some arts organizations.
Types of support: Matching funds, special projects, seed money, equipment.
Limitations: Giving primarily in the Puget Sound, WA, area. No grants to individuals, or for general purposes, building or endowment funds, scholarships, fellowships, publications, or conferences; no loans.
Publications: Application guidelines.
Application information: Application form required.
Initial approach: Letter
Copies of proposal: 2
Deadline(s): None
Board meeting date(s): Jan., Mar., May, July, Sept., and Nov.
Final notification: Last day in month of board meeting
Write: R.W. Carlstrom, Exec. Dir.
Officers and Directors:* Janet L. Politeo,* Pres.; P.F. Patrick,* V.P.; R. Thomas Olson,* Secy.; R.N. Brandenburg,* Treas.; R.W. Carlstrom,* Exec. Dir.
Number of staff: None.
Employer Identification Number: 916028694

7320
Joshua Green Foundation, Inc. ⌑
1414 Fourth Ave.
P.O. Box 720
Seattle 98111 (206) 344-2285

Trust established in 1956 in WA.
Donor(s): Joshua Green, Mrs. Joshua Green.
Foundation type: Independent
Financial data (yr. ended 12/31/87): Assets, $5,075,264 (M); gifts received, $14,800; expenditures, $272,121, including $269,423 for 60 grants (high: $80,000; low: $200; average: $1,000-$3,000).
Purpose and activities: Emphasis on higher and secondary education, community funds, cultural programs, health associations and services, and church support.
Limitations: Giving primarily in the Seattle, WA, area. No grants to individuals, or for scholarships or fellowships; no loans.
Application information:
Initial approach: Proposal
Copies of proposal: 1
Board meeting date(s): Mar., July, Sept., and Dec.
Officers and Trustees:* Joshua Green III,* Pres.; Charles P. Burnett III,* V.P.; Charles E. Riley,* V.P.; Wendy Cadman, Secy.; Steven E. Carlson, Treas.
Employer Identification Number: 916050748

7321
Frank J. & Adelaide Guse Endowment Trust ⌑ ☆
c/o Washington Trust Bank, Trust Dept.
P.O. Box 2127
Spokane 99210-2127

Established in 1988 in WA.
Foundation type: Independent
Financial data (yr. ended 12/31/88): Assets, $2,810,425 (M); expenditures, $121,332, including $113,870 for 1 grant.
Purpose and activities: Initial year of operation, 1988; support for a Catholic diocese.
Limitations: No grants to individuals.
Application information: Contributes only to pre-selected organizations. Applications not accepted.
Trustee: Washington Trust Bank.
Employer Identification Number: 916301489

7322
Saul and Dayee G. Haas Foundation, Inc.
5400 Columbia Seafirst Ctr.
701 Fifth Ave., Rm. 5376
Seattle 98104-7011 (206) 623-7580

Incorporated in 1971 in WA.
Donor(s): Saul Haas,† Dayee G. Haas.†
Foundation type: Independent
Financial data (yr. ended 06/30/89): Assets, $5,693,160 (M); gifts received, $18,505; expenditures, $478,474, including $395,359 for 456 grants (high: $43,920; low: $25).
Purpose and activities: Emphasis on a school-administered fund to aid indigent high school students to complete their education, and merit awards to university students in communications schools. Also sponsors a local university lecture series on broadcasting.
Types of support: Emergency funds.
Limitations: Giving primarily in WA. No grants to individuals, or for equipment, land acquisition, renovation projects, endowment funds, or matching gifts.
Publications: Informational brochure (including application guidelines).
Application information: Applications not encouraged.
Initial approach: Telephone
Board meeting date(s): Oct.
Write: Frank S. Hanawalt, Exec. Dir.
Officers and Directors:* Richard Roddis,* Chair. and Pres.; Jon Bowman,* 1st V.P.; Deesa Haas,* Secy.; Robert Nathane,* Treas.; Frank S. Hanawalt, Exec. Dir.; Emory Bundy, Ellen C. Dial, Bette B. Fletcher, Frederick T. Haley, Charles V. Johnson, Duff Kennedy, John McKenzie, Colleen S. Willoughby.
Number of staff: 2 part-time professional; 2 part-time support.
Employer Identification Number: 237189670

7323
Carl M. Hansen Foundation, Inc. ⌑ ☆
1420 One National Bldg.
Spokane 99201
Application address: 1600 Washington Bldg., Spokane, WA 99204; Tel.: (509) 455-9555

Established in 1965.
Donor(s): Carl M. Hansen.
Foundation type: Independent
Financial data (yr. ended 12/31/88): Assets, $1,051,518 (M); gifts received, $155,000; expenditures, $52,653, including $40,500 for 10 grants (high: $7,000; low: $500) and $6,000 for 6 grants to individuals of $1,000 each.
Purpose and activities: Awards scholarships and grants in "the fields of art, science, literature, and education, particularly as it applies to engineering."
Types of support: Student aid.
Limitations: Giving primarily in WA.
Application information:
Initial approach: Letter
Deadline(s): None
Write: Scott B. Lukins, Trustee
Trustees: Carl M. Hansen, Scott B. Lukins, Laurence D. Morse.
Employer Identification Number: 916063191

7324
Robert G. Hemingway Foundation ⌘ ☆
c/o Seattle First National Bank
P.O. Box 3586
Seattle 98124
Application address: 1354 Bellevue Way, N.E., Bellevue, WA 98004

Foundation type: Independent
Financial data (yr. ended 4/30/89): Assets, $3,726,786 (M); expenditures, $133,942, including $114,150 for 9 grants (high: $50,000; low: $1,000).
Purpose and activities: Giving for higher education, hospitals and medical research, social services, and Episcopal churches.
Types of support: Scholarship funds, research.
Limitations: Giving primarily in ID and WA. No grants to individuals.
Application information: Application form not required.
Initial approach: Letter
Deadline(s): Preferably before Mar. 1
Write: Susan H. Donahue, Admin.
Officer: Susan H. Donahue, Admin.
Trustee: Seattle-First National Bank.
Employer Identification Number: 876176774

7325
Mabel Horrigan Foundation ⌘
521 5th Ave. West, Suite 103
Seattle 98119

Established in 1952 in WA.
Foundation type: Independent
Financial data (yr. ended 12/31/88): Assets, $1,278,343 (M); expenditures, $76,986, including $58,000 for 42 grants (high: $4,500; low: $100).
Purpose and activities: Support for secondary education and Christian organizations.
Limitations: Giving primarily in Seattle, WA. No grants to individuals.
Application information:
Initial approach: Letter or proposal
Deadline(s): None
Write: Mary S. Horrigan, Trustee
Trustees: Mary S. Horrigan, U.S. Bank of Washington, N.A.
Employer Identification Number: 866022633

7326
Janson Foundation
c/o Seattle-First National Bank
P.O. Box 2729
Bellingham 98227 (206) 676-2831
Scholarship application address: Larry Lozier, 1515 East College Way, Mt. Vernon, WA 98273; Tel.: (206) 424-6181

Established in 1982 in WA.
Foundation type: Independent
Financial data (yr. ended 11/30/89): Assets, $1,168,292 (M); expenditures, $68,680, including $35,370 for 6 grants (high: $10,000; low: $1,613) and $27,770 for 50 grants to individuals (high: $750; low: $450).
Purpose and activities: Support primarily for higher education scholarships for local area students, recreation, youth, and social service organizations.
Types of support: Student aid.
Limitations: Giving limited to organizations and residents of Skagit County, WA.
Application information: Application form required.
Copies of proposal: 3
Deadline(s): Apr. 15 for scholarships; no deadline for grants
Write: James Weber
Trustee: Seattle-First National Bank.
Employer Identification Number: 916251624

7327
Johnston-Fix Foundation ☆
East 627 17th Ave.
Spokane 99203 (509) 838-2108

Established in 1948 as The Johnston Foundation; re-organized in 1988 under current name.
Donor(s): Eric Johnston.†
Foundation type: Independent
Financial data (yr. ended 12/31/89): Assets, $2,700,000 (M); expenditures, $133,640, including $111,763 for 34 grants (high: $17,250; low: $250).
Purpose and activities: Giving primarily for private higher and secondary education, youth agencies, and cultural programs.
Limitations: Giving limited to Spokane, WA, with the exception of independent education. No support for publicly supported educational institutions. No grants to individuals, or for scholarships or fellowships; no loans.
Application information: Application form not required.
Initial approach: Telephone or letter; suggest prior telephone call
Copies of proposal: 1
Deadline(s): None
Board meeting date(s): Usually in Apr., June, Sept., and Dec.
Final notification: 3 months
Write: Harriet J. Fix, Pres.
Officers and Trustees:* Harriet J. Fix,* Pres. and Treas.; William C. Fix,* V.P.; Allan C. Fix, Harold J. Fix, Katherine B. Fix, Ina H. Johnston, Scott B. Lukins, Maage E. LaCounte.
Number of staff: 1 part-time professional.
Employer Identification Number: 943076779

7328
Johnston-Hanson Foundation ☆
5118 South Perry St.
Spokane 99223 (509) 448-4708

Established in 1948 in WA as The Johnston Foundation; re-organized in 1988 under current name.
Donor(s): Eric Johnston.†
Foundation type: Independent
Financial data (yr. ended 01/01/90): Assets, $2,543,640 (M); expenditures, $147,115, including $123,294 for 28 grants.
Purpose and activities: Giving primarily for higher and other education; support also for the arts, including music and museums, and social services.
Types of support: Annual campaigns, building funds, continuing support, endowment funds, renovation projects, scholarship funds.
Limitations: Giving primarily in the Spokane, WA, area. No support for publicly supported institutions. No grants to individuals.
Publications: 990-PF.
Application information: Application form not required.
Initial approach: Letter
Copies of proposal: 1
Deadline(s): None
Board meeting date(s): Twice yearly; two conference calls yearly
Final notification: Following board meeting
Write: Mrs. Fred Hanson, Pres.
Officer and Trustees:* Mrs. Fred Hanson,* Pres. and Secy.-Treas.; Herbert Johnston Butler, Victoria Carney, Eric Hanson, Fred Hanson, Maage LaCounte, Scott Lukins.
Number of staff: None.
Employer Identification Number: 943077091

7329
Kawabe Memorial Fund ⌘
(also known as Harry S. Kawabe Trust)
c/o Seattle-First National Bank, Charitable Trust Administration
P.O. Box 3586
Seattle 98124 (206) 358-3388

Trust established in 1972 in WA.
Donor(s): Tomo Kawabe,† Harry Kawabe.†
Foundation type: Independent
Financial data (yr. ended 12/31/88): Assets, $1,718,198 (M); expenditures, $82,217, including $56,789 for 8 grants (high: $30,789; low: $500; average: $8,000) and $4,000 for 2 grants to individuals of $2,000 each.
Purpose and activities: Giving for Buddhist and Protestant church support, including training teachers and clergy and improving facilities; support also for colleges and universities, for scholarship funds and research, and for institutions devoted to the care of the indigent, children, and the aged. Preference given to AK citizens and institutions for scholarships and research.
Types of support: Operating budgets, continuing support, seed money, emergency funds, building funds, equipment, land acquisition, scholarship funds, research, publications, student aid.
Limitations: Giving primarily in the Seattle, WA, area and AK.
Publications: Application guidelines.
Application information: Scholarship applicants write for guidelines. Application form not required.
Initial approach: Proposal
Copies of proposal: 1
Deadline(s): None
Board meeting date(s): Approximately 4 times a year with no set schedule
Write: Rod. K. Kohnson, V.P., Seattle-First National Bank
Allocation Committee: Yasue Brevig, Tsuyoshi Horike, Harry H. Iwata, Jeanette Y. Otsuka, Rev. Sadmori Ouchi, Toru Sakahara, Terrance M. Toda, Chiyoko Yasutake, W.T. Yasutake.
Trustee: Seattle-First National Bank.
Number of staff: None.
Employer Identification Number: 916116549

7330
Bernice A. B. Keyes Trust ⌘
c/o Puget Sound National Bank
P.O. Box 11500, MS 8267
Tacoma 98411-5052

Application address: c/o Puget Sound National Bank, 1101 Pacific Ave., Tacoma, WA 98402; Tel.: (206) 593-3832

Established in 1978.
Foundation type: Independent
Financial data (yr. ended 12/31/88): Assets, $1,391,245 (M); expenditures, $103,463, including $30,750 for 2 grants (high: $24,000; low: $6,750) and $40,250 for 33 grants to individuals (high: $1,250; low: $250; average: $1,250).
Purpose and activities: Giving to high schools and to individuals for scholarships.
Types of support: Scholarship funds, student aid.
Limitations: Giving limited to the Tacoma, WA, area.
Application information: Scholarship application forms available through college counselors at local high schools; selections made by the high schools.
Write: John A. Cunningham, Trust Officer, Puget Sound National Bank
Trustees: Robert E. Ellis, Puget Sound National Bank, Skoog & Mullin.
Employer Identification Number: 916111944

7331
Florence B. Kilworth Charitable Foundation
c/o Puget Sound National Bank
P.O. Box 11500, MS 8262
Tacoma 98411-5052 (206) 593-3884

Established in 1977.
Foundation type: Independent
Financial data (yr. ended 12/31/89): Assets, $3,368,805 (M); qualifying distributions, $123,000, including $123,000 for 37 grants (high: $17,500; low: $1,000; average: $1,000-$17,500).
Purpose and activities: Giving for cultural programs, the arts, higher and medical education, hospitals, youth agencies, and Protestant church support.
Types of support: Annual campaigns, building funds, capital campaigns, operating budgets, research, scholarship funds, special projects.
Limitations: Giving primarily in the Tacoma and Pierce counties, WA, area. No grants to individuals.
Application information: Application form not required.
Initial approach: Letter
Copies of proposal: 1
Deadline(s): None
Board meeting date(s): Month following end of calendar quarter
Final notification: By letter
Write: John D. Baker, V.P., Puget Sound National Bank
Trustees: Florence Morris, Puget Sound National Bank.
Employer Identification Number: 916221495

7332
William Kilworth Charitable Trust
c/o Puget Sound National Bank
P.O. Box 11500, MS 8262
Tacoma 98411-5052

Trust established in 1968 in WA.
Foundation type: Independent
Financial data (yr. ended 12/31/89): Assets, $3,063,875 (M); qualifying distributions, $161,000, including $161,000 for 37 grants (high: $20,000; low: $1,500; average: $1,000-$20,000).
Purpose and activities: Emphasis on higher and other education, youth and child welfare agencies, and civic affairs.
Types of support: Scholarship funds, annual campaigns, building funds, capital campaigns, equipment, operating budgets, seed money.
Limitations: Giving limited to the Tacoma, WA, area. No grants to individuals.
Application information: Scholarship program administered by colleges; standard forms available from each school.
Initial approach: Letter
Copies of proposal: 1
Deadline(s): Nov. 15
Board meeting date(s): Dec.
Write: John D. Baker, V.P., Puget Sound National Bank
Trustee: Puget Sound National Bank.
Employer Identification Number: 916072527

7333
Kreielsheimer Foundation Trust
c/o Bogle & Gates
Two Union Sq., 601 Union St.
Seattle 98101-2322 (206) 682-5151
Additional application address: send 1 copy of proposal to Gary E. Grina, V.P., Seattle-First National Bank, P.O. Box 3586, Seattle, WA 98124

Established in 1979 in WA.
Donor(s): Leo T. Kreielsheimer,† Greye M. Kreielsheimer.†
Foundation type: Independent
Financial data (yr. ended 5/31/89): Assets, $31,953,696 (M); expenditures, $2,237,111, including $1,570,874 for 12 grants (high: $463,246; low: $5,000).
Purpose and activities: Giving for cultural programs and higher education; support also for a civic project.
Limitations: Giving limited to WA and AK. No support for religious or youth organizations. No grants to individuals.
Publications: Application guidelines.
Application information:
Initial approach: Proposal
Board meeting date(s): Semiannually
Final notification: Grants made within 30 days of the end of each calendar quarter
Write: Charles F. Osborn, Trustee
Trustees: Charles F. Osborn, Seattle-First National Bank.
Number of staff: None.
Employer Identification Number: 916233127

7334
Laird, Norton Foundation ⌑
801 Second Ave., Suite 1300
Seattle 98104 (206) 464-5292

Incorporated in 1940 in MN.
Donor(s): Founding family members and related businesses.
Foundation type: Independent
Financial data (yr. ended 12/31/87): Assets, $353,077 (M); gifts received, $405,662; expenditures, $638,725, including $614,718 for grants (average: $500-$1,500).
Purpose and activities: Funds devoted to distinctive programs of creative philanthropy that reflect the family's forest industry heritage and are directed generally to forestry, conservation, and economic education; grants also for continued support of designated recipients in other fields.
Types of support: Special projects, publications, internships, scholarship funds, matching funds, equipment, land acquisition, lectureships.
Limitations: No grants for capital campaigns, building funds, endowment funds, operating budgets, or general purposes; no loans.
Publications: 990-PF, program policy statement, application guidelines.
Application information: Application form required.
Initial approach: Letter
Copies of proposal: 1
Deadline(s): 1 month prior to board meetings
Board meeting date(s): Oct. and Feb.
Final notification: 2 weeks after board meeting
Write: Rebecca S. Richardson, Pres.
Officers: Rebecca S. Richardson,* Pres.; Tamsin O. Clapp,* Exec. V.P.; Patrick S. deFreitas, Secy.; Jeff Sullivan, Treas.
Directors:* Henry P. Brown, James Clapp, Elizabeth L. Helmholz, Gail Nettleton, Marie B. Pampush, Anne M. Storm, Christina B. Wilson.
Number of staff: 2 part-time support.
Employer Identification Number: 916048373

7335
The Irving A. Lassen Foundation
44 Silver Beach Dr.
Steilacoom 98388 (206) 584-8293

Established in 1973 in WA.
Donor(s): Irving A. Lassen.†
Foundation type: Independent
Financial data (yr. ended 12/31/87): Assets, $2,417,052 (M); expenditures, $195,977, including $110,800 for 34 grants (high: $10,000; low: $500).
Purpose and activities: Emphasis on social and health services, housing, children and youth, and secondary school scholarships; support also for two hospitals.
Types of support: Scholarship funds, building funds, continuing support, emergency funds.
Limitations: Giving limited to Thurston County, WA.
Publications: Annual report.
Application information: Application form not required.
Initial approach: Proposal
Copies of proposal: 1
Deadline(s): None
Write: Arleigh T. Jones, Trustee
Trustees: Arleigh T. Jones, Helen Lassen Mairs, Julia E. Weigman.
Number of staff: 1 part-time professional; 1 part-time support.
Employer Identification Number: 916215691

7336
Leuthold Foundation, Inc.
1006 Old National Bank Bldg.
Spokane 99201 (509) 624-3944

Incorporated in 1948 in WA.
Donor(s): Members of the Leuthold family.
Foundation type: Independent
Financial data (yr. ended 06/30/89): Assets, $6,979,248 (M); expenditures, $420,885, including $337,750 for 69 grants (high: $95,100; low: $75; average: $150-$10,000).
Purpose and activities: Giving primarily for youth agencies, hospitals, secondary and higher education, Protestant church support, community funds, and music.
Types of support: Operating budgets, continuing support, annual campaigns, building funds, matching funds, endowment funds, equipment, general purposes, scholarship funds.
Limitations: Giving limited to Spokane County, WA. No grants to individuals; no loans.
Publications: Application guidelines, program policy statement.
Application information: Application form required.
Initial approach: Letter
Copies of proposal: 1
Deadline(s): Submit proposal preferably in May or Nov.; deadlines May 15 and Nov. 15
Board meeting date(s): June and Dec.
Final notification: 1 week after board meets
Write: John H. Leuthold, Pres.
Officers and Trustees:* John H. Leuthold,* Pres.; Betty B. Leuthold,* V.P.; O.M. Kimmel, Jr.,* Secy.-Treas.; Caroline E. Leuthold, Allan H. Toole.
Number of staff: 1 part-time support.
Employer Identification Number: 916028589

7337
Byron W. and Alice L. Lockwood Foundation
8121 S.E. 44th St.
Mercer Island 98040 (206) 232-1881
Additional tel.: (206) 232-0131

Established in 1968 in WA.
Foundation type: Independent
Financial data (yr. ended 12/31/88): Assets, $9,177,646 (M); expenditures, $604,113, including $418,800 for 38 grants (high: $100,000; low: $500).
Purpose and activities: Support for health, culture, youth and social service organizations, and higher education.
Limitations: Giving primarily in Seattle, WA.
Application information:
Write: Sally Easterbrook
Officers and Trustees:* Paul R. Cressman,* Pres.; James R. Palmer,* Secy.-Treas.; Paul R. Cressman, Jr., Margaret Whiteman.
Employer Identification Number: 910833426

7338
Lozier Foundation ⌑
P.O. Box 98769
Des Moines 98198

Established in 1986 in WA.
Donor(s): Allan G. Lozier.
Foundation type: Independent
Financial data (yr. ended 12/31/87): Assets, $3,395,265 (M); gifts received, $590,754; expenditures, $277,183, including $270,710 for grants.
Purpose and activities: Support primarily to organizations providing social services, youth organizations, and cultural institutions.
Limitations: Giving primarily in Omaha, NE.
Application information: Contributes only to pre-selected organizations. Applications not accepted.
Trustees: Sheri L. Andrews, Allan G. Lozier, Lee E. Schultz.
Employer Identification Number: 943027928

7339
Elizabeth A. Lynn Foundation ⌑
P.O. Box 5024
Bellevue 98009 (206) 454-8329

Established in WA.
Donor(s): Elizabeth A. Lynn.†
Foundation type: Independent
Financial data (yr. ended 11/30/88): Assets, $1,300,038 (M); expenditures, $98,203, including $96,567 for 12 grants (high: $26,667; low: $900).
Purpose and activities: Support for secondary and higher education.
Types of support: General purposes, matching funds, seed money, special projects.
Limitations: Giving primarily in the Pacific Northwest. No grants to individuals.
Application information:
Initial approach: Letter
Deadline(s): None
Write: Laurie Jewett, Admin.
Trustees: Thomas J. Stephens, John M. Woodley.
Employer Identification Number: 911156982

7340
Matlock Foundation ▼ ⌑
1201 Third Ave., Suite 4900
Seattle 98101-3009 (206) 224-5000

Incorporated in 1954 in WA.
Donor(s): Simpson Timber Co., Simpson Paper Co., Pacific Western Extruded Plastics Co.
Foundation type: Company-sponsored
Financial data (yr. ended 12/31/88): Assets, $975,179; expenditures, $1,439,583, including $1,402,757 for 390 grants (high: $45,600; low: $50; average: $500-$15,000) and $36,826 for 87 employee matching gifts.
Purpose and activities: Allocates funds for giving by Simpson Fund and Simpson Reed Fund to community funds and for scholarships; giving also for arts and cultural programs, other education, social service and youth agencies, and health services and hospitals.
Types of support: Seed money, general purposes, emergency funds, building funds, equipment, land acquisition, employee matching gifts, annual campaigns, capital campaigns, operating budgets, special projects, renovation projects.
Limitations: Giving primarily in CA, MI, OH, OR, PA, TX, and WA. No grants to individuals, or for endowments; no loans.
Application information: Application form required.
Initial approach: Letter
Copies of proposal: 1
Deadline(s): Submit application preferably one month before fund committee meetings
Board meeting date(s): Apr., June, and Nov.
Final notification: 1 week following fund committee meeting
Write: Lin L. Smith
Officers: Joseph L. Leitzinger,* Pres.; Betty Y. Dykstra, Secy.; J. Thurston Roach, Treas.
Directors:* John J. Fannon, Robert B. Hutchinson, T.R. Ingham, Jr., Furman C. Moseley, Susan R. Moseley, Eleanor H. Reed, William G. Reed, Jr.
Number of staff: 4 part-time professional; 4 part-time support.
Employer Identification Number: 916029303

7341
D. V. & Ida J. McEachern Charitable Trust
(Formerly Ida J. McEachern Charitable Trust)
c/o The Bank of California, N.A.
P.O. Box 3123
Seattle 98114 (206) 587-3627

Trust established in 1966 in WA.
Donor(s): Ida J. McEachern,† D.V. McEachern.†
Foundation type: Independent
Financial data (yr. ended 08/31/89): Assets, $10,491,791 (M); expenditures, $564,528, including $473,509 for 36 grants (high: $65,000; low: $100).
Purpose and activities: Giving almost exclusively for capital funding of youth agencies serving children under the age of 18, where purpose is to give a better start in life to all children, both physically and mentally. Prefers organizations in existence at least 5 years and whose operational funding comes generally from a non-tax based source.
Types of support: Emergency funds, building funds, equipment, land acquisition, capital campaigns, renovation projects.
Limitations: Giving limited to the Puget Sound area of WA. No grants to individuals, or for endowment funds, scholarships, fellowships, operating budgets, continuing support, annual campaigns, seed money, deficit financing, publications, conferences, research programs, or matching gifts; no loans.
Publications: Application guidelines.
Application information: Application form not required.
Initial approach: Letter
Copies of proposal: 1
Deadline(s): None
Board meeting date(s): Usually in Feb., May, Aug., and Nov.
Final notification: 2 weeks after meeting
Write: Kim Cacace, Asst. V.P. and Trust Officer
Trustees: L.L. Allison, Robert B. McEachern, The Bank of California, N.A.
Number of staff: None.
Employer Identification Number: 916063710

7342
A. B. and Flavia McEachern Foundation ⌑
c/o The Bank of California, N.A.
P.O. Box 3123
Seattle 98114 (206) 587-3697

Established in 1958 in WA.
Foundation type: Independent
Financial data (yr. ended 12/31/88): Assets, $1,455,742 (M); expenditures, $96,447, including $72,625 for 63 grants (high: $13,000; low: $100).
Purpose and activities: Giving primarily for Christian religious organizations and cultural activities; support also for youth programs.
Types of support: Operating budgets.
Application information:
Initial approach: Letter
Deadline(s): None
Trustee: The Bank of California, N.A.
Employer Identification Number: 916113467

7344
Medina Foundation ▼ ⌑
1300 Norton Bldg.
801 Second Ave., 13th Fl.
Seattle 98104 (206) 464-5231

Incorporated in 1948 in WA.
Foundation type: Independent
Financial data (yr. ended 12/31/87): Assets, $28,731,281 (M); expenditures, $1,474,036, including $1,170,714 for 108 grants (high: $60,300; low: $300).
Purpose and activities: Giving for direct service delivery programs for emergency food and shelter, to aid the handicapped, and to improve the effectiveness of eleemosynary and/or governmental organizations; support also for cultural programs, youth and child welfare, community development, and education.
Types of support: Emergency funds, building funds, equipment, technical assistance, operating budgets, seed money.
Limitations: Giving limited to the greater Puget Sound, WA, area, with emphasis on Seattle. No support for public institutions. No grants to individuals, or for endowment funds, research, scholarships, or matching gifts; no loans.
Publications: Informational brochure, program policy statement, application guidelines.
Application information: Application form required.
Initial approach: Letter
Deadline(s): None
Board meeting date(s): Monthly
Final notification: 30 to 60 days
Write: Gregory P. Barlow, Exec. Dir.
Officers: Norton Clapp,* Pres.; Samuel H. Brown,* V.P.; Linda J. Henry,* V.P.; Margaret Ames, Secy.; Gary MacLeod,* Treas.; Gregory P. Barlow, Exec. Dir.
Trustees:* James N. Clapp II, K. Elizabeth Clapp, Kristina H. Clapp, Matthew N. Clapp, Jr., Marion Hand, Patricia M. Henry, Anne M. Simons.
Number of staff: 1 full-time professional; 1 full-time support.
Employer Identification Number: 910745225

7345
The R. D. Merrill Foundation ⌑
1411 Fourth Ave. Bldg., Suite 1415
Seattle 98101 (206) 682-3939

Incorporated in 1953 in WA.
Donor(s): R.D. Merrill, R.D. Merrill Co.
Foundation type: Independent
Financial data (yr. ended 6/30/88): Assets, $2,551,171 (M); expenditures, $165,229, including $129,333 for 58 grants (high: $20,000; low: $100).
Purpose and activities: Giving primarily to a community foundation, an art museum, health services, theaters and other cultural organizations, and the urban environment.
Limitations: Giving primarily in WA.
Application information: Application form not required.
Deadline(s): None
Write: Lois Hawkins, Asst. Secy.
Officers and Directors: Virginia Merrill Bloedel, Chair.; Corydon Wagner, Jr., Pres.; Virginia Bloedel Wright, V.P. and Treas.; Justin M. Martin, V.P.; Wendy Wagner Weyerhaeuser, V.P.; W.J. Wright, Secy.; Eulalie Merrill Wagner.
Employer Identification Number: 916029949

7346
Lila J. Miller Trust ⌑ ☆
c/o Security Pacific Bank Washington, N.A.
777 108th Ave., N.E., Suite 360
Bellevue 98004

Trust established in 1935 in WA.
Donor(s): Lila J. Miller.†
Foundation type: Independent
Financial data (yr. ended 12/31/88): Assets, $449,740 (M); expenditures, $163,838, including $155,800 for 4 grants (high: $100,000; low: $1,000).
Purpose and activities: Emphasis on cultural programs, youth and child welfare agencies, and education.
Types of support: Equipment.
Limitations: Giving primarily in Yakima, WA.
Trustee: Security Pacific Bank Washington, N.A.
Employer Identification Number: 916095701

7347
M. J. Murdock Charitable Trust ▼
703 Broadway, Suite 710
Vancouver 98660 (206) 694-8415
Mailing address: P.O. Box 1618, Vancouver, WA 98668

Trust established in 1975 in WA.
Donor(s): Melvin Jack Murdock.†
Foundation type: Independent
Financial data (yr. ended 12/31/89): Assets, $220,760,817 (M); expenditures, $13,218,002, including $11,940,078 for 109 grants (high: $1,250,000; low: $3,600; average: $20,000-$150,000).
Purpose and activities: Support primarily for special projects or programs of private, nonprofit charitable organizations aimed at the solution or prevention of significant problems with implications beyond the immediate geographical area and which are able to thrive after initial funding; support also for projects which address critical problems for the Portland, OR/Vancouver, WA, area. Desirable characteristics include self-help, free enterprise concepts leading to greater self-sufficiency and capability for organizations and the people they serve, a strategy for using up-front money including assistance from other supporters, and evidence that the problem-solving effort will make an important difference. Giving primarily for higher education; also provides seed money for selected medical and scientific research programs which have been identified as major priorities. Grants usually for a limited time, one or two years.
Types of support: Seed money, building funds, equipment, research, special projects.
Limitations: Giving primarily in the Pacific Northwest, (WA, OR, ID, MT, and AK); support for community projects only in the Portland, OR/Vancouver, WA, area. No support for government programs; projects common to many organizations without distinguishing merit; sectarian or religious organizations whose principal activities are for the benefit of their own members; agencies served by United Way of Columbia-Willamette, except for approved special projects; or institutes which unfairly discriminate by race, ethnic origin, sex, or creed. No grants to individuals, or for annual campaigns, general support, continuing support, deficit financing, endowment funds, operating budgets, emergency funds, scholarships, fellowships, or matching gifts; no loans.
Publications: Annual report, informational brochure (including application guidelines).
Application information: Submit original plus 3 copies of non-research proposal, original plus 9 copies of research or technical proposal. Application form not required.
Initial approach: Letter or telephone
Deadline(s): None
Board meeting date(s): Monthly
Final notification: 3 to 6 months
Write: Ford A. Anderson II, Exec. Dir.
Officer: Ford A. Anderson II, Exec. Dir.
Trustees: James B. Castles, Walter P. Dyke, Lynwood W. Swanson.
Number of staff: 4 full-time professional; 1 part-time professional; 5 full-time support; 1 part-time support.
Employer Identification Number: 237456468

7348
Murray Foundation
First Interstate Plaza, Suite 1750
Tacoma 98402 (206) 383-4911

Trust established in 1952 in WA.
Donor(s): L.T. Murray Trust.
Foundation type: Independent
Financial data (yr. ended 12/31/88): Assets, $3,200,971 (M); expenditures, $229,548, including $193,725 for 21 grants (high: $37,500; low: $25).
Purpose and activities: Giving for higher and secondary education, hospitals, cultural programs, and community funds. Priority given to capital programs in the Puget Sound area.
Types of support: Building funds, capital campaigns, endowment funds, matching funds, publications, scholarship funds, special projects.
Limitations: Giving primarily in Tacoma and Pierce County, WA. No grants to individuals,

or for endowment funds, research, scholarships, or fellowships; no loans.
Publications: 990-PF, informational brochure (including application guidelines).
Application information: Application form not required.
Initial approach: Letter
Copies of proposal: 1
Board meeting date(s): Dec. and as required (3 to 4 times a year)
Write: Lowell Anne Butson, Exec. Dir.
Officers and Directors:* Anne Murray Barbey,* Pres.; L.T. Murray, Jr.,* V.P.; Lowell Anne Butson,* Secy. and Exec. Dir.; Amy Lou Eckstrom,* Treas.; Steve Larson.
Number of staff: 1 part-time professional.
Employer Identification Number: 510163345

7349
Nesholm Family Foundation ☆
140 Lakeside Ave., Suite 230
Seattle 98122 (206) 324-3339

Established in 1987 in WA.
Donor(s): Elmer J. Nesholm.†
Foundation type: Independent
Financial data (yr. ended 12/31/89): Assets, $11,336,497 (M); expenditures, $407,666, including $316,842 for 21 grants (high: $50,000; low: $1,000).
Purpose and activities: Support primarily for education and health.
Types of support: Special projects.
Limitations: Giving limited to Seattle, WA. No grants to individuals.
Publications: Program policy statement, application guidelines.
Application information:
Initial approach: Proposal
Copies of proposal: 5
Deadline(s): None
Write: Dian Kallmer
Officers and Directors:* John F. Nesholm,* Pres.; Laurel Nesholm,* Exec. Dir.; Joseph M. Gaffney, Edgar K. Marcuse, M.D.
Number of staff: 1 part-time professional.
Employer Identification Number: 943055422

7350
New Horizon Foundation
820 A St., Suite 545
Tacoma 98402 (206) 627-1634

Established in 1983 in WA.
Donor(s): Sequoia Foundation.
Foundation type: Independent
Financial data (yr. ended 10/31/89): Assets, $84,925 (M); gifts received, $1,748,000; expenditures, $1,681,290, including $1,566,234 for 104 grants (high: $163,000; low: $250; average: $5,000-$25,000), $22,899 for 6 foundation-administered programs and $31,900 for 3 loans.
Purpose and activities: Giving primarily for social services, with an emphasis on food, shelter, and emergency aid programs; support also for arts and culture, education, the environment, community improvement, and mental health programs.
Types of support: Equipment, general purposes, operating budgets, renovation projects, special projects, matching funds.
Limitations: Giving primarily in western and southwestern WA, with primary emphasis on Pierce County. No support for private foundations or operating foundations, or political organizations. No grants to individuals, or for endowments, annual campaigns, debt reduction, film, publications, conferences, or travel.
Publications: Application guidelines.
Application information: Application form required.
Initial approach: Summary letter or proposal
Copies of proposal: 2
Deadline(s): None
Final notification: Between 30 and 60 days after submission of complete application
Write: Frank D. Underwood, Pres.
Officers and Directors:* Frank D. Underwood,* Pres. and Treas.; John F. Sherwood,* V.P.; Elvin J. Vandeburg.
Number of staff: None.
Employer Identification Number: 911228957

7351
The Norcliffe Fund
First Interstate Ctr.
999 Third Ave., Suite 1006
Seattle 98104 (206) 682-4820

Incorporated in 1952 in WA.
Donor(s): Theiline M. McCone.†
Foundation type: Independent
Financial data (yr. ended 11/30/89): Assets, $18,648,096 (M); gifts received, $360,225; expenditures, $1,121,666, including $1,083,331 for 318 grants (high: $125,000; low: $25; average: $1,000-$5,000).
Purpose and activities: Emphasis on cultural programs, Roman Catholic church support and religious associations, hospitals, higher and secondary education, and historic preservation; support also for medical research and health associations, conservation, and social services, including programs for the disabled, the homeless, child welfare, and the aged, and youth agencies.
Types of support: Operating budgets, continuing support, annual campaigns, seed money, emergency funds, building funds, equipment, land acquisition, research, special projects, capital campaigns, conferences and seminars, general purposes, lectureships, renovation projects, scholarship funds, endowment funds.
Limitations: Giving primarily in the Pacific Northwest, especially Seattle, WA; some grants in CA and nationally. No grants to individuals, or for deficit financing, matching gifts, scholarships, or fellowships; no loans.
Publications: Program policy statement, application guidelines.
Application information: Application form not required.
Initial approach: Letter
Copies of proposal: 1
Deadline(s): None
Board meeting date(s): As required
Final notification: 6 to 8 weeks
Write: Theiline P. Scheumann, Pres.
Officers and Trustees:* Theiline P. Scheumann,* Pres.; Carol R. Peterson, Secy. and Admin.; Mary Ellen Hughes,* Treas.; Virginia S. Helsell, Charles M. Pigott, James C. Pigott, Susan W. Pohl, Ann P. Wyckoff.
Number of staff: 1 part-time support.
Employer Identification Number: 916029352

7352
PACCAR Foundation ▼ ⌑
c/o PACCAR, Inc.
P.O. Box 1518
Bellevue 98009 (206) 455-7400

Incorporated in 1951 in WA.
Donor(s): PACCAR, Inc.
Foundation type: Company-sponsored
Financial data (yr. ended 11/30/87): Assets, $2,014,876 (M); gifts received, $750,000; expenditures, $1,430,881, including $1,402,398 for 85 grants (high: $264,850; low: $500).
Purpose and activities: Support for civic organizations, community funds, higher educational institutions, cultural programs, youth agencies, and hospitals.
Types of support: Employee matching gifts, annual campaigns, capital campaigns.
Limitations: Giving primarily in areas of company operations, particularly King County, WA. No grants to individuals, or for scholarships or fellowships.
Application information: Application form not required.
Initial approach: Proposal
Copies of proposal: 1
Deadline(s): None
Board meeting date(s): Quarterly; dates vary
Final notification: 2 to 3 months
Write: E.A. Carpenter, V.P.
Officers: Charles M. Pigott,* Pres.; E.A. Carpenter, V.P. and Treas.; G. Glen Morie, Secy.
Directors:* J.M. Dunn, J.M. Fluke, Jr., Harold J. Haynes, J.C. Pigott, John W. Pitts, James H. Wiborg, T.A. Wilson.
Number of staff: None.
Employer Identification Number: 916030638

7353
Palmer Charitable Foundation ⌑
c/o Cottle & Swanson
411 108th Ave., N.E., Suite 1050
Bellevue 98004

Established in 1959 in WA.
Foundation type: Independent
Financial data (yr. ended 12/31/87): Assets, $42,879 (M); gifts received, $3,231; expenditures, $118,002, including $117,250 for 29 grants (high: $50,000; low: $15).
Purpose and activities: Support primarily for Christian churches, publications, broadcasts, and missions; support also for higher education.
Officers: Dr. K. Robert Lang, Pres.; Zena Palmer, V.P.; Anita Lang, Secy.-Treas.
Employer Identification Number: 916055908

7354
Pemco Foundation ⌑
325 Eastlake Ave. East
Seattle 98109 (206) 628-7900

Established in 1965 in WA.
Donor(s): Pemco Corp., Washington School Employees Credit Union.
Foundation type: Company-sponsored

Financial data (yr. ended 06/30/89): Assets, $385,481 (M); gifts received, $377,355; expenditures, $400,526, including $335,504 for 127 grants (high: $23,020; low: $100) and $64,950 for 138 grants to individuals (high: $1,000; low: $100).
Purpose and activities: Grants for social services, youth activities, education, and hospitals and medical research; also awards scholarships.
Types of support: Research, student aid.
Limitations: Giving limited to WA residents for scholarships; organizational support mainly in Seattle.
Application information:
Initial approach: For scholarships, letter from school stating academic qualifications
Deadline(s): None
Final notification: 2 months for scholarships
Write: Stanley O. McNaughton, Secy.-Treas.
Officers: Sandra Kurack, Pres.; Stanley O. McNaughton, Secy.-Treas.
Employer Identification Number: 916072723

7355
Lorene M. Petrie Trust ¤
c/o Security Pacific Bank Washington, Tax Services Dept.
777 108th Ave., N.E., Suite 360
Bellevue 98004
Application address: c/o Security Pacific Bank Washington, P.O. Box 136, Yakima, WA 98907; Tel.: (509) 575-6720

Established in 1983 in WA.
Donor(s): Lorene Petrie.†
Foundation type: Independent
Financial data (yr. ended 07/31/89): Assets, $2,372,482 (M); expenditures, $144,071, including $120,000 for 1 grant.
Purpose and activities: Giving for charitable purposes.
Limitations: Giving limited to Yakima and Kittitas counties, WA.
Application information:
Write: Doug McIntyre, V.P. and Mgr., Security Pacific Bank Washington
Trustee: Security Pacific Bank Washington, N.A.
Employer Identification Number: 916256555

7356
Polack Foundation ¤ ☆
1024 South King St.
Seattle 98104-3097
Application address: P.O. Box 3065, Seattle, WA 98114; Tel.: (206) 323-8411

Established in 1969.
Donor(s): Morris Polack, Dean Polik, and members of the Polack family.
Foundation type: Independent
Financial data (yr. ended 12/31/88): Assets, $1,286,848 (M); gifts received, $70,000; expenditures, $160,734, including $156,380 for 28 grants (high: $55,000; low: $50).
Purpose and activities: Support primarily for Jewish welfare and other Jewish organizations.
Limitations: Giving primarily in WA. No grants to individuals.
Application information: Application form not required.
Deadline(s): None
Write: Morris Polack, Dir.
Directors: Jack Polack, James Polack, Morris Polack, Valerie Polack.
Employer Identification Number: 910850767

7357
Poncin Scholarship Fund ¤
c/o Seattle-First National Bank, Charitable Trust Administration
P.O. Box 3586
Seattle 98124 (206) 358-3388

Trust established in 1966 in WA.
Donor(s): Cora May Poncin.†
Foundation type: Independent
Financial data (yr. ended 12/31/88): Assets, $2,032,247 (M); expenditures, $63,267, including $34,200 for 14 grants to individuals (high: $3,600; low: $900; average: $1,000-$3,000).
Purpose and activities: Grants for medical research.
Types of support: Research, grants to individuals.
Limitations: Giving limited to the state of WA. No grants for operating budgets, continuing support, annual campaigns, seed money, emergency funds, deficit financing, building or endowment funds, scholarships, fellowships, matching gifts, special projects, publications, or conferences; no loans.
Application information: Application must be approved by head of applicant's institution. Application form not required.
Initial approach: Proposal
Deadline(s): None
Board meeting date(s): Trust officers committee meets weekly
Final notification: 2 weeks
Write: Rod Johnson, V.P., Seattle-First National Bank
Trustee: Seattle-First National Bank.
Number of staff: None.
Employer Identification Number: 916069573

7358
Quest for Truth Foundation ¤
221 First Ave. West, Suite 405
Seattle 98119-4224 (206) 284-4424

Established in 1982 in WA.
Foundation type: Independent
Financial data (yr. ended 9/30/88): Assets, $4,193,082 (M); expenditures, $108,505, including $100,000 for 1 grant.
Purpose and activities: Grants for research and publication of papers dealing with history, geography, politics, economics, sociology, and related subjects without restriction as to geographic areas or political jurisdiction, for the education of the reading public. Grants generally through organizations, grants to individuals will require advance approval of the IRS as required by the appropriate statute.
Types of support: Research, publications.
Application information: Application form required.
Deadline(s): None
Final notification: 2 months
Write: DeLancey B. Lewis, Secy.
Officers and Directors: Ellen S. Davies, Pres.; DeLancey B. Lewis, Secy.; Bradley F. Henke, V.P.; Paul K. Scripps, P.E. Swift.
Employer Identification Number: 911190760

7359
Ray Foundation
1111 Third Ave., Suite 2770
Seattle 98101 (206) 292-9101

Established in 1962 in MT.
Donor(s): James C. Ray, Joan L. Ray.†
Foundation type: Independent
Financial data (yr. ended 06/30/89): Assets, $10,188,096 (M); gifts received, $1,000,000; expenditures, $799,866, including $735,000 for 10 grants (high: $100,000; low: $10,000).
Purpose and activities: Giving primarily for higher education, scientific research, youth agencies, mental health, and drug abuse prevention for children and adolescents; support also for a museum.
Types of support: Operating budgets, continuing support, seed money, emergency funds, building funds, equipment, matching funds, special projects, research, publications, consulting services, technical assistance, general purposes.
Limitations: Giving primarily in AZ, OR, and WA. No grants to individuals, or for deficit financing; no loans.
Publications: Application guidelines.
Application information: Application form not required.
Initial approach: Letter or telephone
Copies of proposal: 1
Deadline(s): Deadlines Sept. 15 and Apr. 15
Board meeting date(s): Nov. and June
Final notification: Immediately following board meetings
Write: Shirley C. Brandenburg, Fdn. Admin.
Officer and Director:* James C. Ray,* Pres.
Number of staff: 1 full-time professional.
Employer Identification Number: 810288819

7360
Frank Rider Trust ¤
c/o Maurice Allert
P.O. Box 195
Rosalia 99170-0195 (509) 523-4693

Established in 1910 in WA.
Foundation type: Independent
Financial data (yr. ended 12/31/88): Assets, $1,038,094 (M); expenditures, $78,853, including $43,550 for 9 grants to individuals (high: $15,600; low: $800).
Purpose and activities: Grants primarily for indigent Masons.
Types of support: Grants to individuals.
Limitations: Giving limited to Whitman, Lincoln, Adams, Frank, and Grant counties, WA.
Application information: Application form required.
Deadline(s): None
Officers: William Kilpatrick, Chair.; Maurice Allert, Secy.-Treas.
Trustees: Lonny Ellis, Max Merritt.
Employer Identification Number: 910641308

7361
Robertson Charitable & Educational Trust ¤
c/o First Interstate Bank of Washington
P.O. Box 21927
Seattle 98111

Established in 1972 in WA.

Donor(s): W.H. Robertson,† Ruth Robertson,† Dorothy "Bill" Robertson.
Foundation type: Independent
Financial data (yr. ended 12/31/88): Assets, $858,500 (M); expenditures, $283,115, including $274,900 for 32 grants (high: $50,000; low: $1,000; average: $5,000).
Purpose and activities: Grants to youth agencies and cultural programs.
Types of support: Operating budgets, continuing support, annual campaigns, seed money, emergency funds, building funds, equipment, land acquisition, endowment funds, matching funds, internships, scholarship funds, exchange programs, fellowships, capital campaigns, general purposes, renovation projects, special projects.
Limitations: Giving limited to the Yakima, WA, area. No grants to individuals, or for deficit financing.
Application information: Contributes only to pre-selected organizations. Applications not accepted.
Board meeting date(s): As needed
Write: Shirley M. Nelson, Trust Officer, First Interstate Bank of Washington
Trustees: Dorothy "Bill" Robertson, First Interstate Bank of Washington.
Employer Identification Number: 916159252

7362
The Schoenfeld-Gardner Foundation ⌑
Columbia Ctr. 47th Fl.
Seattle 98104

Established in 1956 in WA.
Foundation type: Independent
Financial data (yr. ended 4/30/87): Assets, $1,220,115 (M); expenditures, $82,397, including $72,700 for 65 grants (high: $30,000; low: $200).
Purpose and activities: Giving largely for social services, including youth and child welfare agencies, and health agencies and hospitals.
Limitations: Giving primarily in WA.
Application information: Application form not required.
Deadline(s): None
Write: Trustees
Officers and Trustees: Ralph A. Schoenfeld, Pres.; Herbert Schoenfeld, Jr., V.P.; Judy B. Schoenfeld, Secy.; Nancy S. Burnett, Treas.; Sanford M. Bernbaum, Jr.
Employer Identification Number: 916055133

7363
Josephine Stedem Scripps Foundation ⌑
221 First Ave. West, Suite 405
Seattle 98119
Application address: P.O. Box 1861, San Diego, CA 92112

Established in 1958 in WA.
Donor(s): Members of the Scripps family.
Foundation type: Independent
Financial data (yr. ended 11/30/88): Assets, $1,072,452 (M); expenditures, $69,995, including $67,500 for 24 grants (high: $20,000; low: $250).
Purpose and activities: Support for hospitals, medical and scientific research, education, and agricultural and animal welfare organizations; some support for cultural programs.
Application information:
Deadline(s): None
Write: Ellen S. Davis, Treas.
Officers and Trustees:* Antonio Davis MacFarlane,* Pres.; Sally S. Weston,* V.P.; Roxanne D. Greene,* Secy.; Ellen S. Davis, Treas.
Employer Identification Number: 916053350

7364
Seafirst Foundation ▼ ⌑
P.O. Box 3586
Seattle 98124 (206) 358-3441

Established in 1979 in WA.
Donor(s): Seafirst Corp.
Foundation type: Company-sponsored
Financial data (yr. ended 12/31/88): Assets, $289,986 (M); gifts received, $1,386,000; expenditures, $1,313,240, including $1,308,055 for 107 grants (high: $100,000; low: $80; average: $3,000-$35,000).
Purpose and activities: Giving primarily for community development, including youth training and employment, higher and economic education, arts and culture, and to human service agencies through the United Way; multiple-year and capital grants sometimes considered but are limited in size and scope. All grants of more than one year are subject to review before funds are released for the subsequent year.
Types of support: Building funds, general purposes, seed money, special projects, capital campaigns, lectureships, operating budgets, renovation projects.
Limitations: Giving limited to WA. No support for fraternal organizations or religious organizations (unless the proposed project is non-denominational and does not promote religious advocacy), single disease organizations, or primary or secondary schools. No grants to individuals, or for research, endowment funds, travel expenses, operating deficits, fundraising events, scholarships (except for Seafirst scholarship programs), or film.
Publications: Informational brochure (including application guidelines).
Application information: Application form required.
Initial approach: Letter
Copies of proposal: 1
Deadline(s): None, but requests received after Oct. 1 will be carried forward to the following Jan.
Board meeting date(s): Quarterly
Final notification: 4 to 6 weeks
Write: Mary L. Bass, Community Relations Officer, Seafirst Bank
Officers and Trustees:* James Williams,* Pres.; Barbara Ells,* Treas.; Joan Enticknap, Jeffrey Farber, Jim Kirschbaum, Larry Ogg, Pat Prout, Tim Turnpaugh.
Number of staff: 2
Employer Identification Number: 911094720

7365
The Seattle Foundation
425 Pike St., Suite 510
Seattle 98101 (206) 622-2294

Incorporated in 1946 in WA.
Foundation type: Community
Financial data (yr. ended 06/30/88): Assets, $31,518,556 (M); gifts received, $3,249,000; expenditures, $4,522,000, including $4,522,000 for 300 grants (high: $75,000; low: $1,000; average: $5,000-$10,000).
Purpose and activities: To administer gifts and bequests for the benefit of charitable, cultural, educational, health, and welfare organizations.
Types of support: Building funds, equipment, renovation projects.
Limitations: Giving limited to the Seattle, WA, area. No grants to individuals, or for scholarships, fellowships, endowment funds, research, operating budgets, general purposes, matching gifts, conferences, exhibits, film production, or publications; no loans.
Publications: Annual report, informational brochure, program policy statement, application guidelines.
Application information: Application form not required.
Initial approach: Telephone, followed by proposal
Copies of proposal: 1
Deadline(s): Feb. 1, May 1, Aug. 1, and Nov. 1
Board meeting date(s): Mar., June, Sept., and Dec.
Final notification: 6 weeks to 2 months
Write: Anne V. Farrell, Pres.
Officers: Anne V. Farrell, Pres.; Susan Duffy, Secy.; James Ladd, Treas.
Trustees:* Christopher T. Bayley, Chair.; Elaine Monson, Vice-Chair.; and 22 additional trustees.
Trustee Banks: The Bank of California, N.A., First Interstate Bank, Old National Bank of Washington, Peoples National Bank of Washington, Rainier National Bank, Seattle-First National Bank, Seattle Trust and Savings Bank, Washington Mutual Savings Bank.
Number of staff: 2 full-time professional; 1 part-time professional; 1 full-time support; 1 part-time support.
Employer Identification Number: 916013536

7366
Sequoia Foundation ▼
820 A St., Suite 545
Tacoma 98402 (206) 627-1634

Established in 1982 in WA.
Donor(s): WBW Trust No. 1, W. John Driscoll, C. Davis Weyerhaeuser, F.T. Weyerhaeuser, William T. Weyerhaeuser.
Foundation type: Independent
Financial data (yr. ended 08/31/89): Assets, $17,732,712 (M); gifts received, $2,850,000; expenditures, $3,428,439, including $3,094,400 for 59 grants (high: $1,688,000; low: $1,000; average: $1,000-$75,000).
Purpose and activities: Giving primarily to serve the cultural and social needs of the world community. Grants are focused on the stimulation, encouragement, and support of established, voluntary, non-profit organizations set up to meet national and international need in the areas of cultural programs, education,

environment, hunger and emergency shelter, international peace, and world crisis relief. Current geographic and interest area priorities are Mexico, Central America, and the Himalayan Mountain region, but priorities may change annually.
Types of support: Special projects, general purposes.
Limitations: Giving primarily in Mexico, Central America, and the Himalayan Mountain region. No support for local organizations except for foundation-initiated grants. No grants to individuals, or for annual appeals, debt retirement, endowments, long-term commitments, lobbying or political propaganda, voter registration drives, travel, publications, or film projects.
Publications: Program policy statement, application guidelines.
Application information: Application form required.
Initial approach: Letter or proposal
Copies of proposal: 2
Deadline(s): None
Board meeting date(s): At least 6 times a year
Final notification: Between 60 and 90 days for complete applications
Write: Frank D. Underwood, Exec. Dir.
Officers and Directors:* William T. Weyerhaeuser,* Pres., Treas. and Member; Gail T. Weyerhaeuser,* V.P. and Member; Nicholas C. Spika, Secy.; Frank D. Underwood, Exec. Dir. and Member; Annette B. Weyerhaeuser,* Member.
Members: James R. Hanson.
Employer Identification Number: 911178052

7367
Tillie and Alfred Shemanski Testamentary Trust ⌑

c/o Seattle-First National Bank
P.O. Box 3586
Seattle 98124 (206) 358-3388

Trust established in 1974 in WA.
Donor(s): Alfred Shemanski, Tillie Shemanski.†
Foundation type: Independent
Financial data (yr. ended 12/31/88): Assets, $3,139,583 (M); expenditures, $204,884, including $167,042 for 29 grants (high: $22,766; low: $1,620; average: $5,100).
Purpose and activities: Giving for Jewish welfare funds, temple support, higher education, health associations and hospitals, and youth and child welfare agencies.
Limitations: Giving primarily in WA.
Application information:
Initial approach: Letter
Deadline(s): Nov. 30
Write: Rod Johnson, V.P., Seattle-First National Bank
Trustee: Seattle-First National Bank.
Employer Identification Number: 916196855

7368
Skinner Foundation ⌑

Skinner Bldg., Seventh Fl.
Seattle 98101 (206) 623-6480

Trust established in 1956 in WA.
Donor(s): Skinner Corp., Alpac Corp., NC Machinery.
Foundation type: Company-sponsored
Financial data (yr. ended 3/31/88): Assets, $2,869,461 (M); gifts received, $501,168; expenditures, $595,271, including $555,064 for 177 grants and $11,389 for employee matching gifts.
Purpose and activities: Grants for culture and the arts, health and human services, education, and civic and community affairs.
Types of support: Operating budgets, seed money, building funds, equipment, matching funds, technical assistance, professorships, fellowships, employee matching gifts, capital campaigns, endowment funds, renovation projects, general purposes, special projects.
Limitations: Giving primarily in areas of company operations in the Seattle, Tacoma, and Yakima areas of WA; and AK and HI. No support for religious organizations for religious purposes. No grants to individuals, or for continuing support, United Ways for operating funds, deficit financing, or conferences; no loans.
Publications: Annual report, informational brochure (including application guidelines).
Application information: Application form required.
Initial approach: Letter
Copies of proposal: 8
Deadline(s): Submit letter in May, Aug., Nov., or Feb.; deadline for application form 28 days before board meetings
Board meeting date(s): July, Oct., Jan., and Apr.
Final notification: 2 weeks
Write: Sandra Fry, Dir.
Trustees: Sally Skinner Behnke, Chair.; John S. Behnke, Robert J. Behnke, Shari D. Behnke, Arthur E. Nordhoff, Grace A. Nordhoff, Catherine E. Skinner.
Number of staff: 1 full-time professional.
Employer Identification Number: 916025144

7369
Frost and Margaret Snyder Foundation ⌑

c/o Puget Sound National Bank, Trust Dept.
P.O. Box 11500 MS 8262
Tacoma 98411-5052 (206) 593-3832

Trust established in 1957 in WA.
Donor(s): Frost Snyder,† Margaret Snyder.†
Foundation type: Independent
Financial data (yr. ended 12/31/88): Assets, $6,557,492 (M); expenditures, $355,963, including $281,897 for 16 grants (high: $50,000; low: $1,000).
Purpose and activities: Giving for the benefit of Roman Catholic educational and religious associations only.
Limitations: Giving primarily in WA. No grants to individuals.
Application information:
Initial approach: Letter
Deadline(s): Sept.
Write: John A. Cunningham, Trust Officer, Puget Sound National Bank
Trustees: Catherine S. Brockert, Margaret S. Cunningham, August Von Boecklin, Puget Sound National Bank.
Employer Identification Number: 916030549

7370
The Spitzer Foundation ⌑

P.O. Box 2008
Kirkland 98083-2008

Established in 1981 in WA.
Donor(s): Charlotte Spitzer, Jack J. Spitzer.
Foundation type: Independent
Financial data (yr. ended 12/31/87): Assets, $835,774 (M); expenditures, $151,938, including $106,114 for 61 grants (high: $12,700; low: $25).
Purpose and activities: Funds primarily for Jewish giving and Jewish welfare; support also for intercultural relations and international relief, law enforcement, and the United Way.
Types of support: Annual campaigns, building funds, capital campaigns, conferences and seminars.
Application information:
Write: Jack J. Spitzer, Pres.
Officer and Directors: Jack J. Spitzer, Pres.; Davis B. Fox, Jil Spitzer-Fox, Charlotte Spitzer, Kathleen Spitzer, Robert B. Spitzer.
Number of staff: None.
Employer Identification Number: 911160605

7371
Spokane Inland Northwest Community Foundation

400 Paulsen Ctr.
West 421 Riverside Ave.
Spokane 99201-0403 (509) 624-2606

Incorporated in 1974 in WA.
Foundation type: Community
Financial data (yr. ended 06/30/89): Assets, $6,577,787 (M); gifts received, $2,607,324; expenditures, $1,087,083, including $738,429 for 440 grants (average: $1,500) and $79,000 for 84 grants to individuals (average: $450).
Purpose and activities: Giving for charitable and philanthropic purposes in the fields of music, the arts, the elderly, education and youth, civic improvement, historical restoration, rehabilitation, and social and health services; four scholarship programs for students.
Types of support: Annual campaigns, land acquisition, endowment funds, special projects, publications, seed money, consulting services, technical assistance, student aid, general purposes, scholarship funds.
Limitations: Giving limited to the inland Northwest. No support for sectarian religious purposes. No grants to individuals (except for scholarships), or for deficit financing, building funds, emergency funds, research, or matching grants; no loans.
Publications: Annual report (including application guidelines), informational brochure (including application guidelines), newsletter, application guidelines.
Application information: Application form required.
Initial approach: Letter
Copies of proposal: 7
Deadline(s): Oct. 1 (Spokane, WA); Nov. 1 (Pullman and Dayton, WA); May 1 (northern ID); Apr. 15 and Oct. 15 (ISC Fund); Apr. 1 for scholarships
Board meeting date(s): Sept. through June
Final notification: 3 months
Write: Jeanne L. Ager, Exec. Dir.
Officer: Jeanne L. Ager, Exec. Dir.

Trustees: Harold B. Gilkey, Beverly N. Neraas, Allan H. Toole, and 26 additional trustees.
Number of staff: 3 full-time professional; 1 part-time support.
Employer Identification Number: 910941053

7372
The Stewardship Foundation ▼
Tacoma Financial Ctr., Suite 1500
1145 Broadway Plaza
Tacoma 98402 (206) 272-8336
Application address: P.O. Box 1278, Tacoma, WA 98401

Trust established in 1962 in WA.
Donor(s): C. Davis Weyerhaeuser Irrevocable Trust.
Foundation type: Independent
Financial data (yr. ended 12/31/89): Assets, $70,541,530 (M); gifts received, $300,000; expenditures, $4,760,975, including $3,991,408 for 223 grants (high: $390,000; low: $1,000; average: $5,000-$25,000) and $146,000 for 2 loans.
Purpose and activities: At least 85 percent of funds paid for evangelical religious organizations whose ministries reach beyond the local community; grants primarily for Christian colleges, universities, and seminaries, international development organizations, foreign missions, and youth ministries; some support also for local social service agencies.
Types of support: Annual campaigns, building funds, general purposes, continuing support, matching funds, operating budgets, publications, scholarship funds, special projects.
Limitations: Giving internationally, nationally and in the Pacific Northwest, including Tacoma and Pierce County, WA. No support for churches; religious support only to Christian parachurch organizations. No grants to individuals, or for endowment funds, deficit financing, research, or fellowships; no loans.
Publications: Biennial report, application guidelines.
Application information: Application form not required.
Initial approach: Letter
Copies of proposal: 2
Deadline(s): None
Board meeting date(s): Mar., June, Sept., and Dec.
Final notification: 90 days
Write: C. Davis Weyerhaeuser, Trustee; or George S. Kovats, Exec. Dir.
Trustees: Louis A. Flora, Annette B. Weyerhaeuser, C. Davis Weyerhaeuser, William T. Weyerhaeuser.
Number of staff: 1 full-time professional; 1 full-time support.
Employer Identification Number: 916020515

7373
Estate of Joseph L. Stubblefield ⌑
249 West Alder St.
P.O. Box 1757
Walla Walla 99362 (509) 527-3500

Trust established in 1902 in WA.
Donor(s): Joseph L. Stubblefield.†
Foundation type: Independent
Financial data (yr. ended 12/31/88): Assets, $2,666,161 (M); expenditures, $136,577, including $102,800 for 24 grants (high: $25,000; low: $100) and $14,974 for 37 grants to individuals (high: $2,000; low: $20).
Purpose and activities: Grants for indigent and elderly widows and orphans and organizations that assist such persons.
Types of support: Grants to individuals, scholarship funds.
Limitations: Giving limited to WA and OR.
Application information: Application form not required.
Initial approach: Letter
Deadline(s): None
Write: H.H. Hayner, Trustee
Trustees: H.H. Hayner, James K. Hayner, Robert O. Kenyon.
Employer Identification Number: 916031350

7374
Greater Tacoma Community Foundation
P.O. Box 1121
Tacoma 98401 (206) 383-5622

Incorporated in 1977 in WA.
Foundation type: Community
Financial data (yr. ended 05/31/89): Assets, $9,103,427 (M); gifts received, $2,184,327; expenditures, $875,311, including $516,854 for 170 grants (high: $211,085; low: $100; average: $100-$7,500), $4,800 for 48 grants to individuals of $100 each, $78,198 for 1 foundation-administered program and $50,000 for 4 loans.
Purpose and activities: Giving primarily for charitable, educational, cultural, health, social service, and civic purposes.
Types of support: Consulting services, technical assistance, emergency funds, seed money, building funds, equipment, matching funds, capital campaigns, loans, operating budgets, continuing support, scholarship funds, special projects.
Limitations: Giving limited to Pierce County, WA. No support for religious, political, or lobbying activities. No grants to individuals, or for annual campaigns, scholarships, fellowships, or publications, unless specified by donor.
Publications: Annual report, informational brochure (including application guidelines), newsletter.
Application information: Application form required.
Initial approach: Letter
Copies of proposal: 2
Deadline(s): Jan. 15, Mar. 15, and Sept. 15
Board meeting date(s): 5 times yearly
Final notification: Within 3 months
Write: Margy McGroarty, Exec. Dir.
Officers and Trustees:* Joe Gordon, Jr.,* Pres.; Ottie Ladd,* V.P.; John A. West,* Secy.; Sondra Purcell,* Treas.; Lowell Anne Butson, Elizabeth A. Gingrich, William L. Honeysett, Jerry McLaughlin, W. Howarth Meadowcroft, Carol Milgard, Dennis Seinfeld, Brewer B. Thompson, Constance Tice, Gail T. Weyerhaeuser, Howard H. Wong, M.D.
Number of staff: 2 full-time professional; 1 part-time professional.
Employer Identification Number: 911007459

7375
Teachers Foundation, Inc. ⌑
325 Eastlake Ave., East
Seattle 98109

Established in 1965 in WA.
Donor(s): The Handy Trust.
Foundation type: Independent
Financial data (yr. ended 12/31/87): Assets, $1,446,475 (M); gifts received, $30,000; expenditures, $301,229, including $301,013 for grants.
Purpose and activities: Support for child welfare, social services, aid for the handicapped, environmental and higher education, and some support for culture, including museums.
Limitations: Giving limited to WA, with emphasis on Seattle.
Officers: Lester R. Roblee, Pres.; Astrid I. Moen, V.P.; Stanley O. McNaughton, Secy.-Treas.
Employer Identification Number: 916068353

7376
Thurston Charitable Foundation ⌑
900 4th Ave., 38th Fl.
Seattle 98104 (206) 623-1031

Established in 1962 in WA.
Donor(s): Ellen E. Thurston.†
Foundation type: Independent
Financial data (yr. ended 06/30/89): Assets, $1,684,027 (M); gifts received, $137,850; expenditures, $51,136, including $40,200 for 12 grants (high: $10,000; low: $200).
Purpose and activities: Giving for hospitals and health services, local and national health and welfare organizations, civic and cultural affairs, and secondary and higher education; some support for religion.
Limitations: Giving primarily in WA. No grants to individuals.
Application information:
Initial approach: Letter
Deadline(s): None
Write: Harry Henke, Jr.
Officer: Harry Henke, Jr., Pres.
Employer Identification Number: 916055032

7377
Titcomb Foundation
P.O. Box 1278
Tacoma 98401-1278 (206) 272-8336

Established in 1960 in WA.
Foundation type: Independent
Financial data (yr. ended 12/31/89): Assets, $1,164,708 (M); gifts received, $89,500; expenditures, $213,350, including $204,350 for 53 grants (high: $10,000; low: $875).
Purpose and activities: Giving to help lessen immediate hardship and suffering, assist efforts that address long term societal problems, and support projects that demonstrate broad enhancements and improvement of the human condition.
Limitations: Giving primarily in WA. No grants to individuals.
Application information: Application form not required.
Initial approach: Letter
Copies of proposal: 1
Deadline(s): None

Final notification: Affirmative notifications by the end of the year
Write: Shirley Schmick
Officers: Stephen T. Titcomb,* Pres.; Peter C. Titcomb,* V.P.; James R. Hanson, Secy.-Treas.
Directors:* David R. Titcomb, John W. Titcomb, John W. Titcomb, Jr.
Number of staff: 2
Employer Identification Number: 916020513

7378
Univar/VWR Foundation ⌑
1600 Norton Bldg.
Seattle 98104

Established in 1967.
Donor(s): Univar Corp., VWR Corp.
Foundation type: Company-sponsored
Financial data (yr. ended 2/29/88): Assets, $247,878 (M); gifts received, $154,250; expenditures, $119,688, including $119,683 for 30 grants (high: $20,000; low: $400; average: $5,000).
Purpose and activities: Giving to community funds, cultural programs, higher education, and youth agencies.
Types of support: General purposes, building funds, operating budgets, research, publications.
Limitations: Giving primarily in the Seattle, WA, area.
Application information:
Write: Robert D. O'Brien, Pres.
Officers: Robert D. O'Brien,* Pres.; Susan Schmid, Secy.; N. Stewart Rogers,* Treas.
Trustees:* James W. Bernard, Richard E. Engebrecht, M.M. Harris, James H. Wiborg.
Number of staff: None.
Employer Identification Number: 910826180

7379
George Washington Foundation ⌑
3012 Tieton Dr.
Yakima 98902 (509) 457-4827

Established in 1921 in WA.
Foundation type: Independent
Financial data (yr. ended 06/30/89): Assets, $1,080,461 (M); expenditures, $97,459, including $85,582 for grants to individuals.
Purpose and activities: Higher education scholarships for deserving and needy students: grants are generally awarded for use at community colleges but exceptions are made.
Types of support: Student aid.
Limitations: Giving primarily in WA, but no formal restrictions apply. No grants for research projects.
Application information: Applications available through high school principal or counselor. Application form required.
Deadline(s): Apr. 1
Final notification: Mid Apr.
Write: Mr. Leslie Tripp, Secy.-Treas.
Officers: James B. Shrader, Pres.; Harry T. Sharpe, V.P.; Leslie Tripp, Secy.-Treas.
Employer Identification Number: 916024141

7380
Washington Mutual Savings Bank Foundation
c/o Washington Mutual Tower, P.O. Box 834
1201 Third Ave.
Seattle 98111 (206) 461-4663

Established in 1979 in WA.
Donor(s): Washington Mutual Savings Bank.
Foundation type: Company-sponsored
Financial data (yr. ended 12/31/89): Assets, $921,969 (M); gifts received, $750,000; expenditures, $602,363, including $593,113 for 176 grants (high: $40,000; low: $500; average: $500-$40,000) and $3,314 for 40 employee matching gifts.
Purpose and activities: "To provide assistance and encouragement to local communities through nonprofit organizations in the areas of health and welfare, cultural enhancement, education, and civic betterment;" in addition to making grants, the bank sponsors a variety of community and civic projects and activities.
Types of support: Operating budgets, scholarship funds, matching funds, special projects, employee matching gifts, building funds, capital campaigns, endowment funds, emergency funds, equipment, loans, renovation projects, seed money.
Limitations: Giving primarily in WA, especially Seattle, Tacoma, and Spokane. No support for religious organizations for religious purposes, or veterans' or labor organizations. No grants to individuals.
Publications: Annual report (including application guidelines).
Application information: Application form required.
Copies of proposal: 1
Deadline(s): Quarterly
Board meeting date(s): Quarterly
Write: Greg Tuke, Prog. Admin.
Officers and Directors: Sally Skinner Behnke, Pres.; Deloria Jones, Secy.; Ernest Jurdana, Treas.; Rev. Samuel B. McKinney, Lou H. Pepper, William G. Reed, Jr., Holt W. Webster.
Number of staff: 1 full-time professional; 1 part-time professional; 1 part-time support.
Employer Identification Number: 911070920

7381
Washington Trust Foundation
c/o Washington Trust Bank
P.O. Box 2127
Spokane 99210 (509) 353-3802

Established in 1981 in WA.
Donor(s): Washington Trust Bank.
Foundation type: Company-sponsored
Financial data (yr. ended 12/31/88): Assets, $35 (M); gifts received, $292,754; expenditures, $309,575, including $309,575 for 42 grants (high: $49,275; low: $1,000).
Purpose and activities: Support primarily for secondary and higher education, culture, and social services.
Types of support: General purposes.
Limitations: Giving primarily in Spokane, WA.
Application information: Application form not required.
Initial approach: Proposal
Copies of proposal: 1
Deadline(s): None
Board meeting date(s): As needed
Write: Thomas C. Garrett, Trustee
Trustees: Thomas C. Garrett, William K. Scammell, Jr., Peter F. Stanton, Philip H. Stanton.
Employer Identification Number: 911145506

7382
The Wasmer Foundation ☆
1100 Old National Bldg.
Spokane 99201-0390

Established in 1983.
Donor(s): Florence Wasmer.†
Foundation type: Independent
Financial data (yr. ended 12/31/88): Assets, $2,382,761 (M); gifts received, $2,362,237; expenditures, $94,882, including $82,000 for 17 grants (high: $34,000; low: $500).
Purpose and activities: Giving primarily for fine and performing arts groups; support also for social services and higher education.
Types of support: Endowment funds.
Limitations: Giving primarily in Spokane, WA. No grants to individuals.
Publications: Application guidelines.
Application information: Application form required.
Copies of proposal: 3
Deadline(s): Apr. 30 and Oct. 31
Board meeting date(s): May and Nov.
Final notification: June and Dec.
Write: Allan H. Toole, Trustee
Trustees: E.L. Rehn, T.H. Richardson, Allan H. Toole.
Employer Identification Number: 911205115

7383
George T. Welch Testamentary Trust ⌑
c/o Baker Boyer National Bank
P.O. Box 1796
Walla Walla 99362 (509) 525-2000

Established in 1938 in WA.
Foundation type: Independent
Financial data (yr. ended 09/30/89): Assets, $2,895,473 (M); expenditures, $167,759, including $43,480 for 11 grants (high: $18,500; low: $1,000) and $105,754 for 118 grants to individuals (high: $2,440; low: $39).
Purpose and activities: Grants to the needy, including medical assistance, and scholarships; some support also for youth agencies and cultural programs.
Types of support: Special projects, student aid, grants to individuals.
Limitations: Giving limited to Walla Walla County, WA. No grants for capital or endowment funds, general purposes, or matching gifts; no loans.
Publications: Program policy statement, application guidelines.
Application information: Application form required.
Initial approach: Proposal
Copies of proposal: 1
Deadline(s): May 1 for scholarships, July 1 for community projects, and Feb. 20, May 20, Aug. 20, and Nov. 20 for health and welfare for the needy
Board meeting date(s): Feb., May, Aug., and Nov.
Final notification: 30 days

Write: Bettie Loiacono, Asst. V.P., Baker Boyer National Bank
Trustee: Baker Boyer National Bank.
Number of staff: None.
Employer Identification Number: 916024318

7384
Carrie Welch Trust ⌘
P.O. Box 244
Walla Walla 99362

Trust established in 1946 in WA.
Donor(s): Carrie Welch.†
Foundation type: Independent
Financial data (yr. ended 10/31/88): Assets, $1,154,950 (M); expenditures, $96,945, including $50,407 for 11 grants (high: $10,000; low: $337) and $11,095 for 15 grants to individuals (high: $1,170; low: $35).
Purpose and activities: Giving for higher education, social services, and aid to needy individuals.
Types of support: Grants to individuals.
Limitations: Giving limited to WA state, with preference to the Walla Walla area.
Application information: Funds fully committed. Application form not required.
Deadline(s): None
Trustees: C.G. Conkey, Vera Conkey.
Employer Identification Number: 916030361

7385
A. Z. Wells Foundation ⌘
c/o Seattle-First National Bank
P.O. Box 3586
Seattle 98124

Trust established in 1950 in WA.
Donor(s): A.Z. Wells.
Foundation type: Independent
Financial data (yr. ended 12/31/88): Assets, $9,774,990 (M); expenditures, $866,061, including $580,620 for 16 grants (high: $61,060; low: $17,000; average: $30,000).
Purpose and activities: Giving for hospitals, youth, health associations, and a social service agency.
Limitations: Giving limited to north central WA, with emphasis on Wenatchee.
Application information: Contributes only to pre-selected organizations. Applications not accepted.
Trustee: Seattle-First National Bank.
Employer Identification Number: 916026580

7386
Weyerhaeuser Company Foundation ▼
CHIF 31
Tacoma 98477 (206) 924-3159

Incorporated in 1948 in WA.
Donor(s): Weyerhaeuser Co.
Foundation type: Company-sponsored
Financial data (yr. ended 12/31/89): Assets, $1,688,726 (M); gifts received, $6,908,080; expenditures, $5,686,775, including $5,318,850 for 662 grants (high: $532,000; low: $1,000; average: $1,000-$10,000) and $55,734 for 151 employee matching gifts.
Purpose and activities: Grants are awarded for two purposes: to improve the quality of life in areas where Weyerhaeuser Co. has a major presence; and to provide leadership that increases public understanding of the issues at the intersection of society's needs and the interests of the forest products industry. Support also for employee-related scholarships administered by the Citizens' Scholarship Foundation of America and National Merit Scholarship Corp.
Types of support: Seed money, emergency funds, building funds, equipment, land acquisition, employee-related scholarships, publications, conferences and seminars, fellowships, lectureships, renovation projects, operating budgets, research, special projects, technical assistance, employee matching gifts.
Limitations: Giving limited to areas of company operations, especially western WA (including Tacoma, Seattle, and Federal Way), western OR, northeastern OK, AL, AR, MS, and NC; giving to national organizations in fields related to the forest products industry. No support for religious organizations for religious purposes, or for political bodies. No grants to individuals, or for deficit financing, operating funds for United Way-supported organizations, indirect costs, conferences outside the forest products industry, endowments, or memorials.
Publications: Biennial report (including application guidelines).
Application information: Requests received in the fall will be considered for following year's budget. Application form not required.
Initial approach: Letter
Copies of proposal: 1
Deadline(s): None
Board meeting date(s): Jan. and mid-year
Final notification: 3 to 4 months
Write: Mary Stewart Hall, Pres.
Officers and Trustees:* Fred R. Fosmire,* Chair.; Mary Stewart Hall,* Pres.; Michael D. Munson, V.P.; Connie Bergeron, Secy.; William C. Stivers, Treas.; Charles W. Bingham, John W. Creighton, Jr., W. Howarth Meadowcroft, Gene C. Meyer, Robert L. Schuyler, George H. Weyerhaeuser, Robert B. Wilson.
Number of staff: None.
Employer Identification Number: 916024225

7387
The Wharton Foundation, Inc.
12168 S.E. 17th Place
Bellevue 98005 (206) 641-0589

Established in 1954 in MD.
Foundation type: Independent
Financial data (yr. ended 12/31/88): Assets, $3,166,314 (M); gifts received, $875,000; expenditures, $112,225, including $107,500 for 100 grants (high: $35,000; low: $35; average: $1,000-$5,000).
Purpose and activities: Giving primarily for higher, secondary, and theological education, social and family services, community development, health care, Protestant welfare and other giving, and youth agencies.
Types of support: Operating budgets, continuing support, annual campaigns, seed money, emergency funds, endowment funds, renovation projects, special projects, general purposes, research, scholarship funds.
Limitations: Giving primarily in AZ, IL, WA, CA, and FL. No grants to individuals; no multi-year commitments; no loans.
Publications: Application guidelines.
Application information: Unsolicited proposals not considered. Applications not accepted.
Board meeting date(s): Quarterly
Write: Martha Wharton, V.P.
Officers and Directors:* W.R. Wharton,* Pres.; M.W. Minnich,* V.P.; J.W. Pettitt,* V.P.; M.W. Wharton,* V.P.; Joseph B. Wharton III, Secy.-Treas.
Number of staff: None.
Employer Identification Number: 366130748

7388
Edgar E. Whitehead Foundation ⌘
P.O. Box 590
Prosser 99350

Established in 1985 in WA.
Foundation type: Independent
Financial data (yr. ended 12/31/88): Assets, $1,275,186 (M); expenditures, $85,713, including $20,877 for grants (high: $5,000).
Purpose and activities: Giving primarily for community affairs and education.
Limitations: Giving limited to the Prosser and Whitstran, WA, area.
Application information: Application form not required.
Deadline(s): None
Officers: Dwight Halstad, Pres.; Richard W. Gay, V.P.; Inez Thompson, Secy.; Jerry Ferguson, Treas.
Director: Max Berlitz, Sr.
Employer Identification Number: 911279093

7389
Wyman Youth Trust
304 Pioneer Bldg.
Seattle 98104

Trust established in 1951 in WA.
Donor(s): Members of the Wyman family.
Foundation type: Independent
Financial data (yr. ended 12/31/87): Assets, $2,713,502 (M); expenditures, $175,879, including $156,766 for 106 grants (high: $8,000; low: $50).
Purpose and activities: Support for "youth-oriented projects, civic and cultural development, and special community endeavors"; support also for schools and health services.
Limitations: Giving limited to King County, WA, and York County, NE. No grants to individuals, or for capital funds or aggregate donors.
Publications: Program policy statement, application guidelines.
Application information: Application form not required.
Initial approach: Proposal
Copies of proposal: 1
Deadline(s): Mar. 1, June 1, Sept. 1, and Dec. 1
Board meeting date(s): Mar., June, Sept., and Dec.
Final notification: 4 to 6 months
Trustees: Ann McCall Wyman, David C. Wyman, David E. Wyman, Deehan M. Wyman, Hal Wyman.
Number of staff: 1 part-time professional.
Employer Identification Number: 916031590

WEST VIRGINIA

7390
Beckley Area Foundation, Inc.
P.O. Box 1575
Beckley 25802-1575

Established in 1985 in WV.
Donor(s): Dr. Thomas Walker Memorial Health Foundation, and others.
Foundation type: Community
Financial data (yr. ended 3/31/89): Assets, $2,685,373 (M); gifts received, $15,189; expenditures, $132,994, including $102,302 for grants and $8,666 for grants to individuals.
Purpose and activities: Support primarily for education, social services, health, the arts, and recreation.
Types of support: Special projects.
Limitations: Giving primarily in the Beckley and Raleigh County, WV, area. No grants for operating budgets.
Publications: Annual report.
Application information: Application form not required.
Initial approach: Letter
Officers and Directors: Robert B. Sayre, Pres.; Paul Loflin, V.P.; Mrs. Albert M. Tieche, Secy.; Marion Massinople, Treas.; Charles K. Connor, Jr., Exec. Dir.; and 11 other directors.

7391
Ethel N. Bowen Foundation
c/o First National Bank of Bluefield
500 Federal St.
Bluefield 24701 (304) 325-8181

Established about 1968 in WV.
Donor(s): Ethel N. Bowen.†
Foundation type: Independent
Financial data (yr. ended 12/31/89): Assets, $6,324,762 (M); expenditures, $308,644, including $111,300 for 30 grants (high: $15,000; low: $100) and $167,935 for grants to individuals (high: $3,050; low: $500; average: $2,000).
Purpose and activities: Giving primarily for scholarships to further the education of students in southern WV and southwestern VA; support also for higher, secondary, and other education.
Types of support: Student aid, scholarship funds.
Limitations: Giving limited to southern WV and southwestern VA.
Application information:
Initial approach: Letter
Copies of proposal: 1
Deadline(s): For scholarships, Apr. 30
Board meeting date(s): Monthly
Write: R.W. Wilkinson, Secy.
Officers and Directors:* L.R. Coulling, Jr.,* Chair.; Virginia M. Bowen, Pres.; Richard W. Wilkinson, Secy.-Treas.; Henry Bowen, B.L. Jackson, B.K. Satterfield.
Trustee: First National Bank of Bluefield.
Number of staff: 2
Employer Identification Number: 237010740

7392
Carbon Fuel Foundation, Inc. ⌑
184 Summers St., Suite 201
Charleston 25301-2132
Application address: Morrison Bldg., 4th Fl., Charleston, WV 25301

Incorporated in 1953 in WV.
Donor(s): Carbon Fuel Co., Kentucky Carbon Corp.
Foundation type: Company-sponsored
Financial data (yr. ended 12/31/87): Assets, $1,018,045 (M); expenditures, $76,225, including $71,000 for 5 grants (high: $15,000; low: $3,000).
Purpose and activities: Giving to educational and charitable organizations, with emphasis on higher education, youth and child welfare agencies, and health agencies.
Types of support: Operating budgets, building funds, research, scholarship funds.
Limitations: Giving primarily in southern and central WV.
Application information:
Initial approach: Letter
Deadline(s): Nov. 15
Write: James R. Thomas II, Pres.
Officers and Trustees: James R. Thomas II, Pres.; David S. Long, V.P.; Sherman E. Witt, Jr., Secy.-Treas.; Robert F. Barroner, David M. Giltinan, Jr., L. Newton Thomas, Jr., John M. Wells, Sr.
Employer Identification Number: 556015917

7393
Carter Family Foundation ⌑
c/o Raleigh County National Bank
129 Main St.
Beckley 25801 (304) 256-7302

Established in 1981 in WV.
Donor(s): Bernard E. Carter,† Georgia Carter.†
Foundation type: Independent
Financial data (yr. ended 6/30/88): Assets, $2,733,575 (M); expenditures, $140,343, including $130,266 for 79 grants (high: $10,289; low: $500; average: $1,000-$2,000).
Purpose and activities: Emphasis on church support, social services, health, and education, including scholarship grants and loans to individuals to become teachers and teach for a period of time in WV.
Types of support: Student aid, scholarship funds, special projects.
Limitations: Giving limited to WV, with priority given to Raleigh County for scholarships.
Application information: Application form not required.
Initial approach: Letter and resume
Deadline(s): None
Write: Melvin Tolle, Trust Officer, Raleigh County National Bank
Trustee: Raleigh County National Bank.
Employer Identification Number: 550606479

7394
James B. Chambers Memorial ⌑
2207 National Rd.
Wheeling 26003 (304) 242-4000

Established in 1924 in WV.
Foundation type: Independent
Financial data (yr. ended 12/31/88): Assets, $3,960,650 (M); expenditures, $123,807, including $84,500 for grants.
Purpose and activities: Emphasis on education, including higher education, social services, youth agencies, and community development.
Limitations: Giving limited to the greater Wheeling, WV, area.
Application information:
Initial approach: Letter
Deadline(s): None
Write: Stephen Hanning, Exec. Dir.
Officers and Trustees:* Thomas L. Thomas,* Pres.; Philip L. Kirby,* V.P.; F. Lee Strasser,* Secy.; E. Lee Jones, Treas.; Stephen E. Hannig, Exec. Dir.
Employer Identification Number: 550360517

7395
Clay Foundation, Inc. ☆
1426 Kanawha Blvd. East
Charleston 25301 (304) 344-8656

Incorporated in 1986 in WV.
Donor(s): Charles M. Avampato, George Diab.
Foundation type: Independent
Financial data (yr. ended 10/31/88): Assets, $32,316,893 (M); gifts received, $16,866; expenditures, $1,557,967, including $905,965 for 17 grants (high: $300,000; low: $2,000).
Purpose and activities: Giving in the following areas: 1) Aging, 2) Health Care, including research and education, 3) Vocational Education, and 4) Disadvantaged Youth and their families.
Types of support: Renovation projects, research.
Limitations: Giving limited to WV, with emphasis on the greater Kanawha Valley area. No support for religious purposes or private functions. No grants to individuals, or for operating expenses, deficit financing, or annual campaigns.
Application information: Application form not required.
Initial approach: Letter (in triplicate)
Copies of proposal: 6
Deadline(s): No set deadline; 60 working days should be allowed for review of preliminary letter
Board meeting date(s): Jan., Apr., July, and Oct.
Final notification: 10 days after board meeting
Write: Charles M. Avampato, Pres.
Officers and Directors: Lyell B. Clay, Chair.; Charles M. Avampato, Pres.; Buckner W. Clay, V.P.; Whitney Clay Diller, Secy.; Hamilton G. Clay, Treas.
Number of staff: 1
Employer Identification Number: 550670193

7396
The Daywood Foundation, Inc. ⌘
1200 Charleston National Plaza
Charleston 25301 (304) 343-4841

Incorporated in 1958 in WV.
Donor(s): Ruth Woods Dayton.†
Foundation type: Independent
Financial data (yr. ended 12/31/88): Assets, $7,931,421 (M); expenditures, $746,024, including $695,890 for 45 grants (high: $320,090; low: $1,000).
Purpose and activities: Grants restricted to local organizations (except for a few out-of-state training institutions), with emphasis on higher education; some support for welfare agencies, youth agencies, and community funds.
Types of support: Annual campaigns, building funds, capital campaigns, emergency funds, equipment, general purposes, matching funds, renovation projects, seed money.
Limitations: Giving limited to Barbour, Charleston, Greenbrier, Kanawha, and Lewisburg counties, WV. No grants to individuals, or for endowment funds, research, scholarships, or fellowships; no loans.
Publications: Application guidelines.
Application information: Application form not required.
Initial approach: Letter
Copies of proposal: 1
Deadline(s): Submit proposal preferably in Jan. through May; deadline May 31
Board meeting date(s): July and Dec.
Final notification: Dec.
Write: William W. Booker, Secy.-Treas.
Officers and Directors: L. Newton Thomas, Pres.; Richard E. Ford, V.P.; William W. Booker, Secy.-Treas.
Number of staff: 1 part-time support.
Employer Identification Number: 556018107

7397
Sarita Kenedy East Foundation, Inc. ▼
c/o Frank Vest
Suite 1300, Charleston National Plaza, Box 3969
Charleston 25335

Established in 1962 in NY.
Donor(s): Sarita Kenedy East.†
Foundation type: Independent
Financial data (yr. ended 12/31/88): Assets, $14,776,988 (M); expenditures, $1,369,768, including $1,296,894 for 28 grants (high: $200,000; low: $100).
Purpose and activities: Giving to Roman Catholic organizations.
Types of support: General purposes, operating budgets.
Limitations: No grants to individuals.
Application information: Contributes only to pre-selected organizations. Applications not accepted.
Board meeting date(s): As necessary
Officers and Directors:* J. Peter Grace,* Pres.; Margaret F. Grace,* V.P.; Thomas M. Doyle,* Secy.; J.P. Bolduc, Treas.; Justine M. Carr, Patrick P. Grace, Theresa G. Sears.
Number of staff: None.
Employer Identification Number: 136116447

7398
Fenton Foundation, Inc.
310 Fourth St.
Williamstown 26187 (304) 375-7943

Established in 1955.
Foundation type: Independent
Financial data (yr. ended 12/31/88): Assets, $1,709,937 (M); expenditures, $108,780, including $106,309 for 79 grants (high: $10,000; low: $25).
Purpose and activities: Giving largely for higher education, church support, health associations, and community funds.
Limitations: Giving primarily in Wood County, WV, and Washington County, OH. No grants to individuals.
Application information:
Initial approach: Letter
Deadline(s): None
Write: Frank M. Fenton, Treas.
Officers and Directors: Wilmer C. Fenton, Pres.; Thomas K. Fenton, V.P.; Elinor P. Fenton, Secy.; Frank M. Fenton, Treas.
Employer Identification Number: 556017260

7399
Jamey Harless Foundation, Inc. ⌘
Drawer D
Gilbert 25621 (304) 664-3227

Established in 1967.
Donor(s): James H. Harless, Gilbert Imported Hardwoods, Hampden Coal Co., and others.
Foundation type: Independent
Financial data (yr. ended 12/31/88): Assets, $1,867,321 (M); gifts received, $110,000; expenditures, $99,952, including $86,129 for 24 grants (high: $50,000; low: $25; average: $100-$5,000), $4,722 for 24 grants to individuals (high: $817; low: $20; average: $20-$300) and $7,150 for loans to individuals.
Purpose and activities: Giving to higher and secondary education, and Protestant religious organizations; support also for scholarship loans to students and grants to distressed families.
Types of support: Grants to individuals, student aid, student loans.
Limitations: Giving primarily in WV.
Application information: Application form required.
Deadline(s): None
Write: Sharon Murphy, Secy.
Officers: James H. Harless, Pres.; Larry J. Harless, V.P.; Sharon Murphy, Secy.
Directors: Judy Burgess, J. Brooks Lawson, Jr.
Employer Identification Number: 237093387

7400
Herscher Foundation, Inc. ⌘ ☆
c/o United National Bank
P.O. Box 393
Charleston 25392

Established in 1959.
Foundation type: Independent
Financial data (yr. ended 12/31/88): Assets, $1,009,136 (M); expenditures, $56,144, including $48,000 for 24 grants (high: $12,000; low: $250).
Purpose and activities: Giving for higher education, the arts, health and social services, and civic affairs.
Limitations: Giving limited to WV, with emphasis on the Charleston area. No support for private foundations. No grants to individuals.
Application information:
Initial approach: Letter
Deadline(s): None
Write: Charles L. Jarrell, Pres.
Officers and Trustees: Charles L. Jarrell, Pres. and Treas.; Charles B. Stacy, V.P.; G. Thomas Battle, Secy.; George S. Herscher, Russell L. Isaacs, Stanley Loewenstein, Martha G. Wehrle.
Employer Identification Number: 556018744

7401
George D. Hott Memorial Foundation of Morgantown-Monongalia County, West Virginia ⌘ ☆
c/o First National Bank, Trust Dept.
201 High St.
Morgantown 26505-5414

Established in 1980.
Donor(s): George D. Hott.†
Foundation type: Operating
Financial data (yr. ended 12/31/88): Assets, $2,117,537 (M); gifts received, $1,885,471; expenditures, $114,656, including $109,500 for 22 grants (high: $15,000; low: $900).
Purpose and activities: Giving primarily for human services, including welfare agencies, youth, and a community fund; support also for Methodist churches and programs and hospitals.
Types of support: Scholarship funds.
Limitations: Giving primarily in Morgantown, WV.
Trustees: Jack Britton, Martin Piribek, Robert L. Shuman, First National Bank of Morgantown.
Employer Identification Number: 556085230

7402
The H. P. and Anne S. Hunnicutt Foundation, Inc. ☆
P.O. Box 309
Princeton 24740
Application address: c/o First Community Bank, Inc., P.O. Box 5939, Princeton, WV 24740

Established in 1987.
Donor(s): H.P. Hunnicutt.
Foundation type: Independent
Financial data (yr. ended 06/30/88): Assets, $1,299,019 (M); gifts received, $713,876; expenditures, $33,768, including $24,998 for 3 grants (high: $11,712; low: $5,000).
Purpose and activities: Giving primarily for civic affairs groups and a high school foundation.
Types of support: Equipment.
Limitations: Giving limited to the southern WV area.
Application information:
Initial approach: Letter
Deadline(s): None
Write: Robert L. Schumacher
Officers: H.P. Hunnicutt, Chair.; William P. Stafford, Pres.; James H. Salves, Secy.-Treas.
Trustee: First Community Bank, Inc.
Employer Identification Number: 550670462

7403
The Huntington Foundation, Inc. ⌑ ☆
P.O. Box 2548
Huntington 25726
Application address: 517 Ninth St., Suites 207 & 208, Huntington, WV 25701; Tel.: (304) 522-0611

Foundation type: Operating
Financial data (yr. ended 12/31/88): Assets, $6,704,594 (M); expenditures, $342,841, including $253,485 for 5 grants (high: $175,000; low: $3,200).
Purpose and activities: Giving primarily for higher education; support also for welfare and youth.
Limitations: Giving primarily in WV. No grants to individuals.
Application information: Application form required.
Deadline(s): None
Write: George S. Wallace, Jr., Exec. Dir.
Officers and Directors: C.H. McKown, Pres.; Cecil H. Underwood, V.P.; Kermit E. McGinnis, Secy.-Treas.; George S. Wallace, Jr., Exec. Dir.; Frank E. Hanshaw, Jr., Winfield C. John.
Employer Identification Number: 550370129

7404
Bernard H. and Blanche E. Jacobson Foundation ⌑
c/o One Valley Bank, N.A.
P.O. Box 1793
Charleston 25326
Application address: 1210 One Valley Sq., Charleston, WV 25301; Tel.: (304) 342-1141

Established in 1954 in WV.
Donor(s): Bernard H. Jacobson, Blanche E. Jacobson.
Foundation type: Independent
Financial data (yr. ended 12/31/88): Assets, $3,021,005 (M); gifts received, $30,900; expenditures, $139,845, including $121,100 for 38 grants (high: $21,000; low: $100).
Purpose and activities: Giving for education, social services (including local chapters of national associations), Jewish welfare funds, and a community fund.
Limitations: Giving primarily in WV, particularly Kanawha Valley and Charleston.
Application information: Application form not required.
Deadline(s): None
Write: John L. Ray, Trustee
Trustees: Charles W. Loeb, John L. Ray, L.N. Thomas, Jr., One Valley Bank, N.A.
Employer Identification Number: 556014902

7405
Kanawha Valley Bank Foundation, Inc. ⌑
c/o One Valley Bank, N.A.
P.O. Box 1793
Charleston 25326-1793 (304) 348-7000

Established in 1954 in WI.
Foundation type: Company-sponsored
Financial data (yr. ended 12/31/88): Assets, $893,853 (M); gifts received, $29,181; expenditures, $177,680, including $175,600 for 30 grants (high: $40,000; low: $100).
Purpose and activities: Support primarily for community organizations and higher education.
Types of support: General purposes.
Limitations: Giving primarily in Charleston, WV.
Application information: Applications not accepted.
Write: Michael W. Stajduhar
Trustees: Robert F. Baronner, Lloyd P. Calvert, Hugh A. Curry, J. Holmes Morrison, Virgil M. O'Dell, John L. Payne, A.S. Thomas, Jr., John M. Wells, Sr., Thomas D. Wilkerson.
Employer Identification Number: 556017269

7406
The Greater Kanawha Valley Foundation
1426 Kanawha Blvd., East
Charleston 25301 (304) 346-3620
Application address: P.O. Box 3041, Charleston, WV 25331

Established in 1962 in WV.
Foundation type: Community
Financial data (yr. ended 12/31/89): Assets, $30,519,135 (M); gifts received, $4,045,876; expenditures, $1,325,598, including $892,562 for 125 grants (high: $9,000; low: $500; average: $550-$5,000) and $433,036 for 275 grants to individuals (high: $100,000; low: $79; average: $100-$10,000).
Purpose and activities: Support for higher and other education; social services, including child welfare and family services, women, and housing; health and the medical sciences, including reseach on AIDS, heart disease, and cancer; the fine and performing arts; ecology and the environment; and recreation and community development programs.
Types of support: Operating budgets, continuing support, seed money, building funds, equipment, student aid, special projects, research, publications, conferences and seminars, technical assistance, annual campaigns, capital campaigns, general purposes, student loans.
Limitations: Giving limited to the Greater Kanawha Valley, WV, area, except scholarships which are limited to residents of WV; no loans. No grants for annual campaigns, deficit financing, or general endowments.
Publications: Annual report (including application guidelines), informational brochure, application guidelines, 990-PF.
Application information: Application form not required.
Initial approach: Proposal
Copies of proposal: 1
Deadline(s): Deadlines change yearly, write or call for information
Board meeting date(s): Quarterly, usually in Apr., July, Oct., and Dec.
Final notification: Immediately after board action
Write: Betsy B. VonBlond, Exec. Dir.
Officers and Trustees:* G. Thomas Battle,* Chair.; William O. McMillan, Jr., M.D.,* Vice-Chair.; Charles W. Loeb, Secy. and Advisory Committee member; Betsy B. VonBlond, Exec. Dir.; Deborah A. Faber, Brooks F. McCabe, Jr., Charles R. McElwee, Margaret C. Mills, William E. Mullett, K. Richard C. Sinclair, Louis S. Southworth II.
Advisory Committee: Frederick H. Belden, Jr., Bert A. Bradford, Jr., W.G. Caperton, Elizabeth E. Chilton, William M. Davis, Willard H. Erwin, Jr., J.W. Hubbard, Jr., Stanley Lowenstein, Thomas N. McJunkin, Harry Moore, James H. Nix, Mark H. Schaul, Dolly Sherwood, Charles B. Stacy, L. Newton Thomas, Jr.
Trustee Banks: United National Bank, One Valley Bank, N.A., Charleston National Bank, City National Bank of Charleston, National Bank of Commerce of Charleston.
Number of staff: 1 full-time professional; 2 full-time support.
Employer Identification Number: 556024430

7407
George A. Laughlin Trust ⌑ ☆
c/o Wheeling Dollar Bank, Trust Dept.
Bank Plaza
Wheeling 26003 (304) 234-9400

Established in 1936.
Foundation type: Independent
Financial data (yr. ended 12/31/88): Assets, $6,203,109 (M); expenditures, $457,949, including $378,194 for 82 loans to individuals.
Purpose and activities: Awards non-interest-bearing home loans to local area low-income individuals.
Types of support: Loans.
Limitations: Giving limited to Ohio County, WV, residents.
Application information: Application form required.
Deadline(s): May 1 through May 31
Write: Thomas Medovic
Trustee: Wheeling Dollar Bank.
Employer Identification Number: 556016889

7408
Sarah & Pauline Maier Foundation, Inc. ▼
P.O. Box 6190
Charleston 25362 (304) 343-2201

Established in 1958 in WV.
Donor(s): William J. Maier, Jr.,† Pauline Maier.
Foundation type: Independent
Financial data (yr. ended 10/31/89): Assets, $16,581,908 (M); expenditures, $1,787,714, including $1,242,883 for 18 grants (high: $350,000; low: $820; average: $10,000-$50,000).
Purpose and activities: Giving primarily for educational institutions; support also for a medical facility.
Types of support: Scholarship funds, annual campaigns, building funds, capital campaigns, endowment funds, equipment, matching funds, operating budgets, professorships, special projects.
Limitations: Giving limited to WV. No grants to individuals.
Application information: Grants limited to prior recipients, except in education. Application form required.
Initial approach: Letter
Copies of proposal: 9
Deadline(s): Oct. 1
Board meeting date(s): lst Friday in Dec.
Final notification: Dec. 31
Write: Ed Maier, Pres.
Officers: Pauline Maier, Chair.; Edward H. Maier, Pres.; W.J. Maier III, V.P.; Sara M. Rowe, Secy.-Treas.

Members: Thomas C. Burns, John T. Copenhaver, Elizabeth M. Culwell, Sidney P. Davis, Jr., Warren W. Point.
Number of staff: None.
Employer Identification Number: 556023833

7409
Bernard McDonough Foundation, Inc.
1000 Grand Central Mall
P.O. Box 1825
Parkersburg 26102 (304) 485-4494

Incorporated in 1961 in WV.
Donor(s): Bernard P. McDonough.†
Foundation type: Independent
Financial data (yr. ended 12/31/89): Assets, $2,593,030 (M); expenditures, $305,305, including $288,467 for 41 grants (high: $100,000; low: $100; average: $1,000-$15,000).
Purpose and activities: Priority given to programs with no other source of funding; support for higher education, civic affairs, health, and social service agencies, including programs for the handicapped.
Types of support: Annual campaigns, building funds, capital campaigns, continuing support, emergency funds, equipment, general purposes, operating budgets, renovation projects, special projects.
Limitations: Giving primarily in WV. No support for religious organizations, or national health or welfare campaigns. No grants to individuals, or for personnel, operating expenses, or publications.
Application information: Application form not required.
Initial approach: Letter
Copies of proposal: 1
Deadline(s): Submit proposal preferably in Oct.; no deadline
Board meeting date(s): Dec.
Final notification: 1 to 2 weeks
Write: James T. Wakley, Pres.
Officers: James T. Wakley,* Pres.; Alma G. McDonough,* V.P.; M. Norris, Secy.-Treas.
Directors:* Carl L. Broughton, Robert E. Evans, Mark C. Kury, F.C. McCusker.
Number of staff: 2 part-time professional.
Employer Identification Number: 556023693

7410
The Berkeley Minor and Susan Fontaine Minor Foundation ⌘
c/o John L. Ray
1210 One Valley Sq.
Charleston 25301

Trust established in 1957 in WV.
Donor(s): Berkeley Minor, Jr.†
Foundation type: Independent
Financial data (yr. ended 12/31/88): Assets, $1,663,901 (M); expenditures, $90,532, including $73,800 for 18 grants to individuals (high: $6,800; low: $1,000).
Purpose and activities: Scholarships for WV residents admitted to the Univ. of Charleston, the Univ. of Virginia, the Protestant Episcopal Theological Seminary of Virginia, or West Virginia Univ.
Types of support: Student aid.
Limitations: Giving limited to residents of WV attending specified colleges and universities in WV and VA.
Application information: Only students attending West Virginia Univ. should apply directly to the Foundation. Application form not required.
Initial approach: Letter
Deadline(s): Aug. 1
Board meeting date(s): Aug. and as required
Trustees: Charles W. Loeb, John L. Ray, William E. Thayer, Jr., One Valley Bank, N.A.
Employer Identification Number: 556014946

7411
Parkersburg Community Foundation ☆
1804 Market St.
P.O. Box 1762
Parkersburg 26102 (304) 428-4438
Additional tel.: (304) 428-2584

Established in 1963 in WV.
Donor(s): Albert Wolfe, and members of the Wolfe family, Keystone Foundation.
Foundation type: Community
Financial data (yr. ended 06/30/89): Assets, $1,060,387 (M); gifts received, $320,390; qualifying distributions, $105,161, including $80,459 for 53 grants (high: $13,811; low: $200), $7,202 for 32 grants to individuals (high: $1,000; low: $65) and $17,500 for 1 in-kind gift.
Purpose and activities: Support for programs leading toward the improvement or fulfillment of charitable, educational, cultural, health, or welfare activities, including direct human services and scholarships to individuals.
Types of support: Student aid, seed money, capital campaigns, deficit financing, scholarship funds.
Limitations: Giving limited to the Parkersburg, WV/Mid-Ohio Valley, area.
Publications: Annual report, program policy statement.
Application information: Application form required.
Copies of proposal: 1
Deadline(s): Apr. 1
Board meeting date(s): 3rd Friday in Jan., Mar., May, Sept., and Nov.
Final notification: May; grants paid in June but will consider emergency grants at other times
Write: Edwin L.D. Dils, Exec. Dir.
Officers and Governors: R. Bruce White, Chair.; Mrs. Charles F. Whitaker III, Vice-Chair.; Robert W. Burk, Jr., Secy.; Edwin L.D. Dils, Exec. Dir.; and 9 other members.
Trustee Banks: Commercial Banking & Trust Co., Mountain State Bank, United National Bank, Wood County Bank.
Number of staff: 1 part-time support.
Employer Identification Number: 556027764

7412
Herschel C. Price Educational Foundation
P.O. Box 179
Huntington 25706 (304) 529-3852

Trust established in 1975 in WV.
Donor(s): Herschel C. Price.†
Foundation type: Independent
Financial data (yr. ended 04/30/89): Assets, $2,789,784 (M); expenditures, $155,262, including $122,675 for 209 grants to individuals (high: $1,250; low: $150; average: $650).
Purpose and activities: Scholarships awarded directly to deserving students for attendance at accredited local educational institutions, with preference given to undergraduates residing in WV, or attending WV colleges and universities. Interviews generally required with selection based on financial need as well as scholastic standing.
Types of support: Student aid.
Limitations: Giving primarily in WV.
Application information: Application form required.
Initial approach: Letter
Copies of proposal: 1
Deadline(s): Submit application from Jan. to Mar. or Aug. to Sept.; deadlines Apr. 1 and Oct. 1
Board meeting date(s): May and Nov.
Final notification: Directly after board meeting dates
Write: E. JoAnn Price, Trustee
Officer: Jonna L. Hughes, Mgr.
Trustees: Chandos H. Peak, E. JoAnn Price, The First Huntington National Bank.
Number of staff: 2 full-time professional.
Employer Identification Number: 556076719

7413
Board of Trustees of the Prichard School ⌘
First Huntington National Bank, Trust Dept.
P.O. Box 179
Huntington 25706
Application address: Five Cavalier Dr., Huntington, WV 25701

Established in 1923.
Foundation type: Independent
Financial data (yr. ended 12/31/88): Assets, $4,032,834 (M); expenditures, $431,848, including $424,100 for 11 grants (high: $110,000; low: $10,000).
Purpose and activities: Giving for higher and secondary education, and youth organizations.
Limitations: Giving primarily in WV and VA. No grants to individuals.
Application information: Application form not required.
Deadline(s): None
Write: Phyllis R. White, Pres.
Officers: Phillis R. White, Pres.; Carter W. Wild, 1st V.P.; Robert M. Wild, 2nd V.P.; Paul W. McCreight, Secy.; William F. Agee, Treas.
Directors: Margaret B. Breece, Matilda Mynes, J. Seaton Taylor.
Employer Identification Number: 550435910

7414
Hugh I. Shott, Jr. Foundation
c/o First National Bank of Bluefield
500 Federal St.
Bluefield 24701 (304) 325-8181

Established in 1985 in WV.
Donor(s): Hugh J. Shott, Jr.†
Foundation type: Independent
Financial data (yr. ended 12/31/89): Assets, $20,135,426 (M); gifts received, $910,362;

expenditures, $482,984, including $404,500 for 9 grants (high: $300,000; low: $5,000).
Purpose and activities: Giving primarily for secondary and higher education, including business education; support also for historic preservation, the arts, community development, and health, including opthalmology.
Types of support: Annual campaigns, building funds, capital campaigns, matching funds.
Limitations: Giving limited to 9 counties within southwest VA and southern WV.
Application information: Application form not required.
Deadline(s): None
Write: Richard W. Wilkinson, Pres.
Officers: Richard W. Wilkinson, Pres.; Scott Shott, V.P.; John Shott, Secy.; B.K. Satterfield, Treas.
Director: L.R. Coulling, Jr.
Trustee: First National Bank of Bluefield.
Employer Identification Number: 550650833

7415
The James H. and Alice Teubert Charitable Trust ☆
P.O. Box 2131
Huntington 25701 (304) 525-6337

Established in 1987 in WV.
Foundation type: Independent
Financial data (yr. ended 09/30/89): Assets, $11,385,577 (M); expenditures, $509,542, including $409,100 for 9 grants (high: $314,811; low: $700).
Purpose and activities: Support for organizations which provide aid to the blind, including a public library and a youth baseball organization.
Limitations: Giving primarily in Cabell and Wayne Counties, WV.
Application information: Application form required.
Initial approach: Letter
Deadline(s): Oct. 1 and Mar. 1
Board meeting date(s): Nov. and Apr.
Write: Jimelle Bowen, Exec. Dir.
Officer: Jimelle Bowen, Exec. Dir.
Number of staff: 1 part-time professional.
Employer Identification Number: 556101813

7416
The Enrico Vecellio Family Foundation, Inc. ⌑
c/o Raleigh County National Bank
129 Main St.
Beckley 25801

Established in 1972.
Donor(s): Leo A. Vecellio, Sr.
Foundation type: Independent
Financial data (yr. ended 12/31/86): Assets, $1,833,716 (M); gifts received, $227,000; expenditures, $170,758, including $162,975 for 36 grants (high: $7,500; low: $500).
Purpose and activities: Grants for higher education, including employee-related scholarships, youth and social service agencies, health services, and church support.
Types of support: Employee-related scholarships.
Limitations: Giving primarily in WV.
Application information: Application form required.
Officers and Trustees:* Leo A. Vecellio, Sr.,* Pres.; Leo A. Vecellio, Jr.,* Exec. V.P.; Erma V. Grogan, V.P.; John L. Taylor, Secy.-Treas.
Employer Identification Number: 550538242

WISCONSIN

7417
Alexander Charitable Foundation, Inc. ⌑
100 Wisconsin River Dr.
Port Edwards 54469 (715) 887-5111

Incorporated in 1955 in WI.
Donor(s): John E. Alexander.†
Foundation type: Independent
Financial data (yr. ended 12/31/87): Assets, $8,385,150 (M); expenditures, $319,960, including $284,201 for 34 grants (high: $92,900; low: $500).
Purpose and activities: Emphasis on community centers, Protestant church support, and hospitals.
Limitations: Giving primarily in WI. No grants to individuals.
Application information: Contributes only to pre-selected charitable organizations. Applications not accepted.
Board meeting date(s): Quarterly
Write: Samuel A. Casey, Treas.
Officers and Directors:* Gerard E. Veneman,* Pres.; Charles R. Lester,* V.P.; Margaret Boyarski, Secy.; Samuel A. Casey,* Treas.
Employer Identification Number: 396045140

7418
Judd S. Alexander Foundation, Inc.
500 Third St., Suite 509
P.O. Box 2137
Wausau 54402-2137 (715) 845-4556

Incorporated in 1973 in WI.
Donor(s): Anne M. Alexander.†
Foundation type: Independent
Financial data (yr. ended 06/30/89): Assets, $20,534,277 (M); qualifying distributions, $753,697, including $445,278 for 56 grants (high: $60,000; low: $200; average: $3,000-$15,000) and $215,000 for 3 loans.
Purpose and activities: Support for civic affairs, youth agencies, higher education, cultural programs, and social service agencies.
Types of support: Seed money, emergency funds, building funds, equipment, land acquisition, matching funds, technical assistance, program-related investments, capital campaigns, scholarship funds.
Limitations: Giving primarily in WI, with emphasis on Marathon County. No grants to individuals, or for endowment funds, fellowships, special projects, research, publications, or conferences.
Application information: Application form not required.
Initial approach: Letter, proposal, or telephone
Copies of proposal: 1
Deadline(s): None
Board meeting date(s): Monthly
Final notification: 60 days
Write: Stanley F. Staples, Jr., Pres.
Officers and Directors:* Stanley F. Staples, Jr.,* Pres.; Harry Heinemann,* V.P.; John F. Michler,* Secy.; Richard D. Dudley,* Treas.
Number of staff: None.
Employer Identification Number: 237323721

7419
Walter Alexander Foundation, Inc.
500 Third St., Suite 509
P.O. Box 2137
Wausau 54402-2137 (715) 845-4556

Incorporated in 1952 in WI.
Donor(s): Ruth Alexander,† Anne M. Alexander.†
Foundation type: Independent
Financial data (yr. ended 11/30/88): Assets, $2,121,595 (M); expenditures, $106,053, including $85,522 for 14 grants (high: $15,860; low: $500; average: $1,500-$2,500).
Purpose and activities: Support for higher and secondary education, cultural programs, and social service agencies.
Types of support: Capital campaigns, seed money, emergency funds, building funds, equipment, land acquisition, matching funds, program-related investments, scholarship funds.
Limitations: Giving primarily in WI. No grants to individuals, or for endowment funds, fellowships, special projects, research, or conferences.
Application information: Application form not required.
Initial approach: Letter, proposal, or telephone
Copies of proposal: 1
Deadline(s): None, but preferably before June
Board meeting date(s): 3 times a year or as required
Final notification: 4 months
Write: Stanley F. Staples, Jr., Secy.
Officers and Directors:* Nancy Anne Cordaro,* Pres.; Jean A. Koskiner,* V.P.; Stanley F. Staples, Jr.,* Secy.; John F. Michler,* Treas.
Number of staff: None.
Employer Identification Number: 396044635

7420
Frank G. Andres Charitable Trust ⌑
1001 Superior Ave.
P.O. Box 753
Tomah 54660

Trust established in WI.
Foundation type: Independent
Financial data (yr. ended 06/30/89): Assets, $2,037,898 (M); expenditures, $131,724, including $109,460 for 11 grants (high: $23,475; low: $800).
Purpose and activities: Emphasis on civic affairs, a hospital, education, social agencies, and cultural programs.
Limitations: Giving primarily in Tomah, WI.

Application information: Application form required.
Deadline(s): May 15
Officer and Trustees:* Roxanne O'Conner,* Secy.-Treas.; A. Ahlstrom, Jay Charmichael, Donald Kortbein, David Meyer, R. Thomas Mockler, Raymond Paulis.
Employer Identification Number: 510172405

7421
Apollo Fund, Ltd.
c/o Foley & Lardner
777 East Wisconsin Ave.
Milwaukee 53202 (414) 289-3569

Established in 1948 in WI.
Foundation type: Independent
Financial data (yr. ended 07/31/89): Assets, $1,791,899 (M); expenditures, $135,000, including $130,000 for 50 grants (high: $10,000; low: $500).
Purpose and activities: Giving for higher and other education, youth agencies, recreation, cultural programs, health agencies, and hospitals.
Types of support: Annual campaigns, capital campaigns.
Limitations: Giving primarily in Milwaukee, WI.
Application information: Application form not required.
Initial approach: Letter
Deadline(s): None
Write: Orin Purintun, Secy.
Officers and Directors:* F.H. Roby,* Pres.; Orin Purintun,* Secy.; R.J. Maier,* Treas.; R.B. Bradley, James F. McKenna.
Number of staff: None.
Employer Identification Number: 396044029

7422
Badger Meter Foundation, Inc. ⌑
4545 West Brown Deer Rd.
Milwaukee 53223 (414) 355-0400

Incorporated in 1952 in WI.
Donor(s): Badger Meter, Inc.
Foundation type: Company-sponsored
Financial data (yr. ended 12/31/87): Assets, $2,525,270 (M); gifts received, $50,000; expenditures, $313,535, including $286,200 for 119 grants (high: $20,000; low: $25; average: $100-$10,000).
Purpose and activities: Grants largely for community funds, higher education, the arts, health care, and programs for the disabled.
Types of support: Operating budgets, continuing support, annual campaigns, seed money, emergency funds, deficit financing, building funds, equipment, land acquisition, endowment funds, research, special projects.
Limitations: Giving limited to WI, almost exclusively in the greater Milwaukee area. No grants to individuals, or for matching gifts, scholarships, fellowships, publications, or conferences; no loans.
Application information: Application form not required.
Initial approach: Letter
Copies of proposal: 1
Deadline(s): Aug. 31
Final notification: 3 to 4 months
Write: Mary George, Secy.
Officers: James O. Wright,* Pres.; R. Robert Howard,* V.P.; Mary George, Secy.; Rebecca Rush, Treas.
Directors:* Ronald H. Dix, Richard S. Gallagher, E.G. Smith, Barbara M. Wiley.
Number of staff: 1 part-time professional.
Employer Identification Number: 396043635

7423
Robert W. Baird and Company Foundation, Inc. ⌑
777 East Wisconsin Ave.
Milwaukee 53202

Established in 1967 in WI.
Donor(s): Robert W. Baird & Co., Inc.
Foundation type: Company-sponsored
Financial data (yr. ended 12/31/87): Assets, $1,630,171 (M); gifts received, $100,000; expenditures, $159,914, including $142,047 for 122 grants (high: $22,330; low: $50).
Purpose and activities: Giving primarily for higher education, community funds, cultural programs, civic affairs, and community development.
Limitations: Giving primarily in WI.
Application information: Contributes only to pre-selected organizations. Applications not accepted.
Trustees: G. Frederick Kasten, Jr., Arthur J. Laskin, Brenton H. Rupple.
Employer Identification Number: 396107937

7424
Banc One Wisconsin Foundation ⌑
(Formerly The Marine Foundation, Inc.)
111 East Wisconsin Ave.
P.O. Box 481
Milwaukee 53201 (414) 765-2624

Incorporated in 1958 in WI.
Donor(s): Marine Midland Bank, N.A., and other Marine banks in WI.
Foundation type: Company-sponsored
Financial data (yr. ended 12/31/87): Assets, $9,019 (L); gifts received, $360,905; expenditures, $356,170, including $311,725 for 50 grants (high: $115,500; low: $100; average: $6,235) and $44,417 for 559 employee matching gifts.
Purpose and activities: Emphasis on a community fund, cultural programs, higher education, and youth agencies.
Types of support: General purposes, operating budgets, continuing support, annual campaigns, seed money, emergency funds, deficit financing, building funds, equipment, employee matching gifts, special projects, research, conferences and seminars.
Limitations: Giving limited to WI; except for employee matching gifts to education. No grants to individuals, or for land acquisition, endowment funds, scholarships, fellowships, or publications; no loans.
Application information: Application form not required.
Initial approach: Proposal
Copies of proposal: 1
Deadline(s): 15 days before board meetings
Board meeting date(s): Jan., May, Aug., and Dec.
Final notification: 2 to 3 months
Write: Frances G. Smyth, Secy.
Officers and Directors:* George R. Slater,* Pres.; Ronald C. Baldwin,* V.P.; Frederick L. Cullen,* V.P.; Leila Fraser,* V.P.; Richard D. Headley,* V.P.; David J. Kunbert,* V.P.; James C. LaVelle,* V.P.; Jon R. Schumacher,* V.P.; Jon H. Stowe,* V.P.; Frances G. Smyth, Secy.; Clem F. Maslowski, Treas.
Number of staff: None.
Employer Identification Number: 396050680

7425
Banta Company Foundation, Inc. ⌑
P.O. Box 8003
100 Main St.
Menasha 54952-8003 (414) 722-7771

Incorporated in 1953 in WI.
Donor(s): George Banta Co., Inc.
Foundation type: Company-sponsored
Financial data (yr. ended 12/31/87): Assets, $271 (M); gifts received, $250,000; expenditures, $286,258, including $270,760 for 98 grants (high: $50,000; low: $100; average: $2,000-$3,000) and $15,465 for 40 employee matching gifts.
Purpose and activities: Emphasis on higher education and youth agencies; support also for cultural programs, including an historical society, and hospitals.
Types of support: Operating budgets, continuing support, annual campaigns, seed money, emergency funds, deficit financing, building funds, equipment, land acquisition, employee matching gifts, matching funds, special projects.
Limitations: Giving limited to areas of company operations including CA, IL, MN, MO, NC, NY, VA, and WI. No grants to individuals, or for scholarships, fellowships, or endowment funds; no loans.
Application information: Application form not required.
Initial approach: Letter
Copies of proposal: 1
Deadline(s): Nov. 1
Board meeting date(s): Apr., June, Sept., and Dec.
Write: Dean E. Bergstrom, V.P.
Officers: Harry W. Earle, Pres.; Dean E. Bergstrom, V.P. and Secy.-Treas.; Gerald A. Henseler, V.P.; Margaret Banta Humleker, V.P.; Donald S. Koskinen, V.P.
Number of staff: None.
Employer Identification Number: 396050779

7426
Norman Bassett Foundation - Wisconsin
7601 Ganser Way
Madison 53719
Application address: 201 Waubesa St., Madison, WI 53704

Established in 1954 in WI.
Foundation type: Independent
Financial data (yr. ended 3/31/89): Assets, $3,251,942 (M); expenditures, $342,579, including $309,352 for 37 grants (high: $50,000; low: $1,000).
Purpose and activities: Giving primarily for cultural programs, including performing arts groups, social service agencies, and education.
Types of support: Building funds, emergency funds, general purposes, professorships.

Limitations: Giving primarily in Madison and Dane County, WI.
Application information: Application form not required.
Initial approach: Letter
Copies of proposal: 1
Deadline(s): None
Write: J. Reed Coleman, Pres.
Officers: J. Reed Coleman, Pres.; F. Chandler Young, V.P.; Thomas R. Ragatz, Secy.; Robert W. Taplick, Treas.
Number of staff: None.
Employer Identification Number: 396043890

7427
Vina S. Beals Charitable Trust ⌘
c/o Bank One Wisconsin Trust Co., N.A.
111 East Wisconsin Ave.
Neenah 54956 (414) 725-4371

Established in 1957 in WI.
Foundation type: Independent
Financial data (yr. ended 12/31/88): Assets, $1,138,340 (M); expenditures, $76,632, including $65,000 for 12 grants (high: $37,600; low: $25).
Purpose and activities: Support primarily for a community foundation and for higher education.
Types of support: General purposes.
Limitations: Giving primarily in WI.
Application information: Application form not required.
Initial approach: Letter
Deadline(s): None
Write: Distributing Committee
Trustee: Bank One Wisconsin Trust Co., N.A.
Employer Identification Number: 396048856

7428
F. K. Bemis Family Foundation, Inc. ⌘
c/o Bemis Manufacturing Co.
300 Mill St.
Sheboygan 53085

Established about 1953 in WI.
Donor(s): Bemis Manufacturing Co.
Foundation type: Company-sponsored
Financial data (yr. ended 3/31/87): Assets, $63,722 (L); gifts received, $215,225; expenditures, $215,301, including $215,275 for 36 grants (high: $5,000; low: $50).
Purpose and activities: Giving primarily for education and youth.
Types of support: Operating budgets, building funds, scholarship funds.
Limitations: Giving primarily in Sheboygan County, WI.
Application information:
Initial approach: Letter
Deadline(s): None
Write: R.A. Bemis, Pres.
Officers: R.A. Bemis, Pres.; P.F. Bemis, V.P.; M.L. Parent, Secy.; P. Lukaszewicz, Treas.
Employer Identification Number: 396067930

7429
Alvin and Marion Birnschein Foundation, Inc. ⌘
740 North Plankinton Ave., Suite 510
Milwaukee 53203 (414) 276-3400

Established in 1968 in WI.
Foundation type: Independent
Financial data (yr. ended 12/31/87): Assets, $2,432,302 (M); expenditures, $236,914, including $179,538 for 26 grants (high: $20,000; low: $1,000).
Purpose and activities: Giving for social service and child welfare agencies, higher education, cultural programs, and hospitals.
Types of support: General purposes.
Limitations: Giving primarily in Milwaukee, WI.
Application information: Contributes only to pre-selected organizations. Applications not accepted.
Write: Peter C. Haensel, Pres.
Officers and Directors: Peter C. Haensel, Pres.; Loraine E. Schuffler, Secy.; Fred A. Erchul II.
Employer Identification Number: 396126798

7430
Blue Cross and Blue Shield United of Wisconsin Foundation, Inc. ⌘ ☆
401 West Michigan St.
Milwaukee 53203

Established in 1984 in WI.
Donor(s): Blue Cross & Blue Shield United of Wisconsin, Compcare Health Services Insurance Corp., United Wisconsin Insurance Co.
Foundation type: Independent
Financial data (yr. ended 12/31/88): Assets, $1,459 (M); gifts received, $100,000; expenditures, $138,997, including $138,947 for 39 grants (high: $45,350; low: $100).
Purpose and activities: Giving primarily for community funds; support also for community development, health associations, higher education, and youth.
Types of support: Research, scholarship funds, annual campaigns, operating budgets.
Limitations: Giving primarily in WI. No grants to individuals.
Application information: Contributes only to pre-selected organizations. Applications not accepted.
Officers: Thomas R. Hefty, Chair.; Thomas Gazzana, Pres.; Essie Whitelaw, V.P.; Mary Traver, Secy.-Treas.
Employer Identification Number: 391514703

7431
Eugenie Mayer Bolz Family Foundation ⌘
P.O. Box 8100
Madison 53708

Established in 1976 in WI and IL.
Donor(s): Eugenie M. Bolz.
Foundation type: Independent
Financial data (yr. ended 12/31/88): Assets, $3,911,481 (M); gifts received, $300,000; expenditures, $200,120, including $155,250 for 38 grants (high: $50,000; low: $500).
Purpose and activities: Giving primarily for social services, the arts, and a municipality.
Types of support: General purposes.
Limitations: Giving primarily in WI.
Application information: Application form not required.
Deadline(s): None
Write: Ronald Mattox, Dir.
Officers: Robert M. Bolz, Pres.; Marjorie B. Allen, V.P.; John A. Bolz, Secy.-Treas.
Director: Ronald Mattox.
Employer Identification Number: 237428561

7432
The Bradley Family Foundation, Inc. ⌘
c/o Arthur Andersen & Co.
P.O. Box 1215
Milwaukee 53201

Incorporated in 1967 in WI.
Donor(s): Margaret B. Bradley,† Jane Bradley Pettit.
Foundation type: Independent
Financial data (yr. ended 9/30/87): Assets, $2,698,318 (M); gifts received, $14,014; expenditures, $2,320,095, including $798,025 for grants.
Purpose and activities: Support primarily for a sculpture garden operated by the foundation; grants also for arts and cultural organizations, with emphasis on music.
Limitations: Giving primarily in WI and FL. No grants to individuals, or for building or endowment funds, or operating budgets.
Application information: Contributes only to pre-selected organizations. Applications not accepted.
Board meeting date(s): Annually
Officers and Directors: Jane Bradley Pettit, Pres.; Lloyd H. Pettit, V.P.; Lynde V. Uihlein, Secy.; David V. Uihlein, Jr., Treas.
Employer Identification Number: 396105450

7433
The Lynde and Harry Bradley Foundation, Inc. ▼
777 East Wisconsin Ave., Suite 2285
Milwaukee 53202 (414) 291-9915

Incorporated in 1942 in WI as the Allen-Bradley Foundation, Inc.; adopted present name in 1985.
Donor(s): Harry L. Bradley,† Caroline D. Bradley,† Margaret B. Bradley,† Margaret Loock Trust, Allen-Bradley Co.
Foundation type: Independent
Financial data (yr. ended 7/31/88): Assets, $339,775,000 (M); expenditures, $25,897,105, including $22,749,105 for 270 grants (high: $1,000,000; low: $2,080; average: $25,000-$200,000) and $291,188 for foundation-administered programs.
Purpose and activities: Support locally for cultural programs, education, social services, medical programs, health agencies, and public policy. National support for research and education in domestic, international, and strategic public policy; grants also for higher education; in particular, activities that investigate and nurture the moral, cultural, intellectual, and economic institutions which form a free society.
Types of support: Annual campaigns, capital campaigns, conferences and seminars, continuing support, equipment, fellowships, internships, lectureships, matching funds, operating budgets, professorships, publications, renovation projects, research, scholarship funds, special projects.

Limitations: No support for strictly denominational projects. No grants to individuals, or for endowment funds.
Publications: Multi-year report, informational brochure (including application guidelines).
Application information: Application form not required.
Initial approach: Letter of inquiry
Copies of proposal: 1
Deadline(s): Mar. 15, July 15, Sept. 15, and Dec. 15
Board meeting date(s): Feb., May, Sept., and Nov.
Final notification: 3 to 5 months
Write: Michael S. Joyce, Pres.
Officers: I. Andrew Rader,* Chair.; Michael S. Joyce,* Pres.; Hillel G. Fradkin, V.P. for Prog.; Richard H. Lillie, M.D.,* V.P.; Wayne J. Roper,* Secy.; James D. Ericson,* Treas.
Directors:* Sarah D. Barder, William J. Bennett, Urban T. Kuechle, J. Clayburn La Force, Francis J. Shakespeare, Allen M. Taylor, David V. Uihlein, Jr.
Number of staff: 4 full-time professional; 1 part-time professional; 5 full-time support; 1 part-time support.
Employer Identification Number: 396037928

7434
Victor F. Braun Foundation, Inc. ¤
7154 South 76th St.
Franklin 53132

Established in 1956 in WI.
Donor(s): Victor F. Braun.
Foundation type: Independent
Financial data (yr. ended 11/30/88): Assets, $2,429,203 (M); expenditures, $131,382, including $120,000 for 55 grants (high: $5,000; low: $1,000).
Purpose and activities: Emphasis on medical research and hospitals; higher, secondary, and vocational education; social service and youth agencies; and cultural programs.
Types of support: General purposes.
Limitations: Giving primarily in WI, with emphasis on Milwaukee; also in KY, MI, AR, and CT.
Application information: Contributes only to pre-selected organizations. Applications not accepted.
Officers and Directors: Victor F. Braun, Pres.; James V. Braun, V.P.; Roger Myers, Secy.; John H. Ladish, Treas.
Employer Identification Number: 396043684

7435
A. Keith Brewer Trust ¤ ☆
c/o Valley Trust Co.
P.O. Box 8915
Madison 53708-8915 (608) 252-3631

Foundation type: Independent
Financial data (yr. ended 12/31/88): Assets, $1,014,086 (M); expenditures, $107,383, including $92,144 for 2 grants (high: $67,144; low: $25,000).
Purpose and activities: Support for an affiliated private foundation and research in the physical sciences.
Types of support: Operating budgets.
Limitations: Giving primarily in WI. No grants to individuals.
Application information: Contributes only to pre-selected organizations. Applications not accepted.
Trustee: Valley Trust Co.
Employer Identification Number: 396432314

7436
Briggs & Stratton Corporation Foundation, Inc.
12301 West Wirth St.
Wauwatosa 53222 (414) 259-5333
Mailing address: P.O. Box 702, Milwaukee, WI 53201

Incorporated in 1954 in WI.
Donor(s): Briggs & Stratton Corp.
Foundation type: Company-sponsored
Financial data (yr. ended 11/30/89): Assets, $4,068,340 (M); expenditures, $452,481, including $433,250 for 38 grants (high: $198,000; low: $50; average: $500-$20,000) and $15,500 for 31 grants to individuals of $500 each.
Purpose and activities: Support primarily for higher and vocational education, health, rural issues, community funds, alcoholism programs, and cultural programs; scholarship program is open to the sons and daughters of company employees.
Types of support: Operating budgets, special projects, employee-related scholarships, capital campaigns.
Limitations: Giving limited to WI, with emphasis on Milwaukee. No support for religious organizations. No grants to individuals (except employee-related scholarships).
Publications: Annual report.
Application information: Application form not required.
Initial approach: Proposal
Copies of proposal: 1
Deadline(s): Jan. 31 for employee scholarship program; none for public charity grants
Board meeting date(s): June and Nov.
Final notification: Nov. 30
Write: Kasandra K. Preston, Secy.-Treas.
Officers and Directors:* Frederick P. Stratton, Jr.,* Pres.; John S. Shiely,* V.P.; Kasandra K. Preston,* Secy.-Treas.
Number of staff: None.
Employer Identification Number: 396040377

7437
Brookbank Foundation, Inc. ¤ ☆
P.O. Box 84
Grafton 53024-1955

Established in 1984.
Foundation type: Independent
Financial data (yr. ended 10/31/88): Assets, $291,370 (M); expenditures, $132,804, including $131,387 for 14 grants (high: $100,000; low: $1,000).
Purpose and activities: Support primarily for higher education.
Types of support: General purposes, capital campaigns, endowment funds, building funds.
Limitations: Giving primarily in WI.
Application information: Contributes only to pre-selected organizations. Applications not accepted.
Officers: Charles P. La Bahn, Pres.; Ridge A. Braunschweig, V.P. and Treas.; Pauline K. Morrison, Secy.
Director: Mary Ann La Bahn.
Employer Identification Number: 391516196

7438
Frank G. Brotz Family Foundation, Inc. ¤
3518 Lakeshore Rd.
P.O. Box 551
Sheboygan 53081 (414) 458-2121

Incorporated in 1953 in WI.
Donor(s): Plastics Engineering Co.
Foundation type: Independent
Financial data (yr. ended 9/30/88): Assets, $9,329,758 (M); gifts received, $700,000; expenditures, $412,973, including $398,175 for 66 grants (high: $50,000; low: $100).
Purpose and activities: Emphasis on hospitals, higher education, youth agencies, religious giving, and cultural programs.
Types of support: Building funds.
Limitations: Giving primarily in WI. No grants to individuals.
Application information:
Initial approach: Letter
Deadline(s): None
Board meeting date(s): Periodically
Write: Grants Comm.
Officers: Ralph T. Brotz,* Pres.; Stuart W. Brotz,* V.P. and Treas.; Ralph R. Brotz, Secy.
Trustees:* Roland M. Neumann.
Employer Identification Number: 396060552

7439
Bucyrus-Erie Foundation, Inc.
(Formerly Becor Western Foundation, Inc.)
1100 Milwaukee Ave.
South Milwaukee 53172 (414) 768-5005
Application address: P.O. Box 500, South Milwaukee, WI 53172

Incorporated in 1951 in WI.
Donor(s): Bucyrus-Erie Co.
Foundation type: Company-sponsored
Financial data (yr. ended 12/31/88): Assets, $10,153,753 (M); expenditures, $863,252, including $793,370 for 181 grants (high: $92,400; low: $25).
Purpose and activities: Grants for higher education, the arts, hospitals, and community funds; support also for social services and youth agencies.
Types of support: Operating budgets, continuing support, annual campaigns, building funds, equipment, endowment funds, employee matching gifts, employee-related scholarships, capital campaigns.
Limitations: Giving primarily in metropolitan Milwaukee, WI. No grants to individuals (except scholarships for children of employees), or for research, special projects, seed money, emergency funds, deficit financing, land acquisition, matching gifts, publications, or conferences; no loans.
Application information: Application form required for scholarships for children of employees.
Initial approach: Letter
Deadline(s): Dec. for scholarships
Board meeting date(s): Feb. and Oct.

Final notification: At the latest, after next board meeting
Write: D.L. Strawderman, Mgr. and Secy.
Officers and Directors:* W.B. Winter,* Pres.; N.J. Verville,* V.P. and Treas.; D.L. Strawderman,* Mgr. and Secy.; P.W. Cotter, D.E. Porter, B.H. Rupple.
Number of staff: 2 part-time support.
Employer Identification Number: 396075537

7440
Carrie Foundation ⌑
One East Milwaukee St.
Janesville 53545 (608) 756-4141

Established in 1984 in WI.
Foundation type: Independent
Financial data (yr. ended 11/30/88): Assets, $164,665 (M); expenditures, $153,744, including $152,000 for 24 grants (high: $60,000; low: $100).
Purpose and activities: Primarily supports higher education, Catholic institutions, and cultural programs.
Limitations: No grants to individuals.
Application information:
Initial approach: Letter
Deadline(s): None
Write: George K. Steil, Sr., Trustee
Trustees: James Fitzgerald, Marilyn Fitzgerald, George K. Steil, Sr.
Employer Identification Number: 391503227

7441
Chapman Foundation ⌑
777 East Wisconsin Ave., Suite 3090
Milwaukee 53202 (414) 276-6955

Established in 1944 in NY.
Donor(s): Laura Isabelle Miller,† and other donors.
Foundation type: Independent
Financial data (yr. ended 12/31/88): Assets, $1,108,060 (M); gifts received, $107,090; expenditures, $249,559, including $246,280 for 48 grants (high: $100,000; low: $100; average: $500).
Purpose and activities: Grants for education, health services, conservation, and culture; support also for the United Way.
Types of support: Capital campaigns, general purposes.
Limitations: Giving primarily in Milwaukee, WI. No grants to individuals.
Application information: Contributes only to pre-selected organizations. Applications not accepted.
Write: George M. Chester, Pres.
Officers and Directors:* George M. Chester,* Pres.; Marion C. Read, V.P.; Verne R. Read, V.P.; William M. Chester, Jr.,* Secy.-Treas.
Employer Identification Number: 396059569

7442
L. C. Christensen Charitable and Religious Foundation, Inc.
c/o Tompson & Coated, Ltd.
P.O. Box 516
Racine 53401 (414) 632-7541

Established in 1966 in WI.
Donor(s): Harold K. Christensen, Sr.†
Foundation type: Independent
Financial data (yr. ended 12/31/88): Assets, $1,929,226 (M); expenditures, $105,904, including $85,865 for 38 grants (high: $25,000; low: $150).
Purpose and activities: Grants for social services, youth agencies, and higher education, community development, and Christian church support.
Limitations: Giving primarily in Racine, WI. No grants for scholarships or fellowships; no loans.
Application information: Application form not required.
Initial approach: Letter
Deadline(s): None
Board meeting date(s): July and Dec.
Write: Stephen J. Smith, Secy.
Officers: Harold K. Christensen, Jr., Pres.; Russel L. Kortendick, Sr., V.P.; Stephen J. Smith, Secy.; John F. Thompson, Treas.
Directors: John E. Erskine, Jr., Dennis E. Schelling.
Employer Identification Number: 396096022

7443
Emory T. Clark Family Foundation
1033 North Mayfair Rd., Suite 200
Wauwatosa 53226

Established in 1982 in WI.
Donor(s): Emory T. Clark.†
Foundation type: Independent
Financial data (yr. ended 03/31/89): Assets, $5,416,505 (M); expenditures, $463,072, including $425,500 for 16 grants (high: $100,000; low: $3,000).
Purpose and activities: Support for higher education, hospitals, and charitable organizations.
Types of support: Capital campaigns.
Limitations: Giving primarily in WI.
Publications: Informational brochure.
Application information: Application form not required.
Initial approach: Proposal
Deadline(s): July
Board meeting date(s): Nov.
Write: William J. Labadie, Dir.
Trustee: First Wisconsin Trust Co.
Number of staff: None.
Employer Identification Number: 391410324

7444
Cleary Foundation, Inc. ⌑
First Bank Place, Suite 701
La Crosse 54601 (608) 782-7877

Established in 1982 in WI.
Donor(s): Russell G. Cleary, Gail K. Cleary.
Foundation type: Independent
Financial data (yr. ended 11/30/88): Assets, $2,186,984 (M); expenditures, $70,914, including $8,413 for 31 grants (high: $2,300; low: $10).
Purpose and activities: Giving to general charitable organizations, including education and health.
Types of support: Endowment funds.
Limitations: No grants to individuals.
Application information:
Initial approach: Letter
Deadline(s): None
Write: Russell G. Cleary, Pres.
Officers and Directors: Russell G. Cleary, Pres. and Treas.; Gail K. Cleary, V.P. and Secy.; Kristine H. Cleary, Sandra G. Cleary.
Employer Identification Number: 391426785

7445
Consolidated Papers Foundation, Inc. ▼
231 First Ave. North
P.O. Box 8050
Wisconsin Rapids 54495-8050 (715) 422-3368

Incorporated in 1951 in WI.
Donor(s): Consolidated Papers, Inc., Mead Inn.
Foundation type: Company-sponsored
Financial data (yr. ended 12/31/89): Assets, $21,360,667 (M); gifts received, $10,830,671; expenditures, $1,205,926, including $1,148,855 for grants (average: $5,000-$8,000) and $44,042 for 527 employee matching gifts.
Purpose and activities: Giving for local community funds, and youth and social service agencies in communities where Consolidated Papers, Inc. conducts operations; higher education grants generally limited to those in WI; support also for the fine and performing arts and other cultural programs.
Types of support: Operating budgets, continuing support, annual campaigns, seed money, emergency funds, building funds, equipment, endowment funds, employee matching gifts, scholarship funds, employee-related scholarships, capital campaigns, renovation projects, professorships.
Limitations: Giving primarily in WI, usually near areas of company operations. No grants to individuals (except scholarships), or for deficit financing, research, or conferences; no loans.
Application information: Application form not required.
Initial approach: Proposal
Copies of proposal: 1
Deadline(s): Mar. 31 and Sept. 30
Board meeting date(s): May or June, and Nov. or Dec.
Final notification: 3 months
Write: Daniel P. Meyer, Pres.
Officers and Directors:* Daniel P. Meyer,* Pres.; Mrs. Howard J. Bell,* V.P.; Carl R. Lemke, Secy.; J. Richard Matsch, Treas.; L.H. Boling, Lawrence H. Boling, I.F. Boyce, Patrick F. Brennan, Richard J. Kenney, George W. Mead, P.G. Meyers, D.L. Stein.
Number of staff: None.
Employer Identification Number: 396040071

7446
Cremer Foundation, Inc.
P.O. Box 1
Madison 53701 (608) 837-5166
Additional tel.: (608) 837-2124

Established in 1965 in WI.
Foundation type: Independent
Financial data (yr. ended 12/31/88): Assets, $1,909,875 (M); gifts received, $245,000; expenditures, $101,519, including $95,119 for 14 grants (high: $30,000; low: $115).
Purpose and activities: Giving primarily to social service agencies, especially those aiding

troubled youth, the homeless, the handicapped and senior citizens.
Types of support: General purposes, matching funds, scholarship funds, seed money.
Limitations: Giving limited to the Madison and Baraboo, WI, area. Generally, no support for religious-based programs. No grants to individuals, or generally for deficit financing and conferences and seminars.
Publications: Application guidelines.
Application information: Application form not required.
Initial approach: Letter or proposal
Deadline(s): None
Board meeting date(s): Twice a year; usually in Mar. and Aug.
Write: James A. Berkenstadt, Esq., Admin.
Officers and Directors:* J.T. Sykes,* Pres.; H.L. Cremer,* Secy.; P.T. Esser,* Treas.; James A. Berkenstadt,* Admin.; F.W. Haberman, H.B. Klotzbach, R.R. Stroud.
Employer Identification Number: 396086822

7447
William J. Cronin Foundation ⌑ ☆
c/o Management Operations, Inc.
P.O. Box 939
Janesville 53547 (608) 756-3151

Foundation type: Independent
Financial data (yr. ended 11/30/88): Assets, $1,594,801 (M); expenditures, $64,108, including $48,700 for 18 grants (high: $7,350; low: $500).
Purpose and activities: Giving for Catholic churches and schools, social service agencies, recreation programs, and a community fund.
Limitations: Giving limited to Janesville, WI.
Application information:
Initial approach: Letter
Deadline(s): Nov. 1
Write: James P. McGuire, Trustee
Trustees: James P. McGuire, Valley Trust Co.
Employer Identification Number: 930782568

7448
Patrick and Anna M. Cudahy Fund ▼
P.O. Box 11978
Milwaukee 53211 (414) 271-6020
Additional tel.: (708) 866-0760

Incorporated in 1949 in WI.
Donor(s): Michael F. Cudahy.†
Foundation type: Independent
Financial data (yr. ended 12/31/88): Assets, $17,558,175 (M); expenditures, $1,291,576, including $1,078,277 for 98 grants (high: $157,200; low: $300; average: $5,000-$10,000).
Purpose and activities: Support primarily for social services and the homeless, youth agencies, and education; support also for national programs concerned with environmental and public interest issues, and cultural and civic affairs programs.
Types of support: General purposes, operating budgets, continuing support, annual campaigns, seed money, emergency funds, deficit financing, building funds, equipment, land acquisition, matching funds, consulting services, technical assistance, scholarship funds, special projects, research, fellowships, renovation projects, capital campaigns.
Limitations: Giving primarily in Milwaukee, WI, and Chicago, IL, and for national programs. No grants to individuals, or for endowments; no loans.
Publications: Annual report, application guidelines.
Application information: Application form not required.
Initial approach: Letter
Copies of proposal: 1
Deadline(s): 6 weeks prior to board meetings
Board meeting date(s): Usually in Apr., June, Sept., and Dec.
Final notification: 2 weeks after meetings
Write: Sr. Judith Borchers, Exec. Dir.
Officers: Janet S. Cudahy,* Pres.; Louise A. McMenamin, Secy.; Sr. Judith Borchers, Exec. Dir.
Directors:* Richard D. Cudahy, Chair.; James Bailey, Tia Cudahy, Dudley J. Godfrey, Jr., Jean Holtz, Philip Lerman, Wesley Scott, Annette Stoddard-Freeman.
Number of staff: 1 part-time professional; 1 part-time support.
Employer Identification Number: 390991972

7449
CUNA Mutual Insurance Group Charitable Foundation, Inc. ⌑
5910 Mineral Point Rd.
Madison 53705 (608) 231-7314

Incorporated in 1967 in WI.
Foundation type: Company-sponsored
Financial data (yr. ended 12/31/87): Assets, $200,592 (M); gifts received, $498,573; expenditures, $439,419, including $439,010 for 174 grants (high: $135,000; low: $15; average: $500).
Purpose and activities: Giving for community funds, health promotion, higher and secondary education, cultural programs, and urban and civic affairs.
Types of support: Operating budgets, continuing support, annual campaigns, seed money, emergency funds, employee matching gifts, scholarship funds, fellowships, special projects, research, capital campaigns, matching funds.
Limitations: Giving primarily in WI. No grants to individuals, or for deficit financing, land acquisition, endowment funds, or publications; no loans.
Publications: Informational brochure (including application guidelines).
Application information: Application form required for requests of over $500.
Initial approach: Proposal, letter, or telephone
Copies of proposal: 1
Board meeting date(s): Feb., May, and Sept.
Final notification: 4 to 6 weeks
Write: Richard C. Radtke, Asst. Secy.-Treas.
Officers and Directors: James C. Barbe, Pres.; Rosemarie Shultz, V.P.; Robert L. Curry, Secy.-Treas. and Exec. Officer; Gerald J. Ping.
Number of staff: None.
Employer Identification Number: 396105418

7450
Gretchen & Andrew Dawes Endowment, Inc. ⌑
c/o Foley & Lardner
777 East Wisconsin Ave.
Milwaukee 53202-5373

Established in 1983 in WI.
Foundation type: Independent
Financial data (yr. ended 12/31/87): Assets, $9,809 (M); gifts received, $140,000; expenditures, $139,243, including $136,000 for 6 grants (high: $100,000; low: $1,000).
Purpose and activities: Support primarily for an exhibition and for the endowment of a staff position at a zoological society; support also for capital acquisitions for a public museum and a symphony orchestra.
Types of support: Endowment funds, capital campaigns.
Limitations: Giving primarily in Milwaukee, WI.
Application information: Application form not required.
Deadline(s): None
Write: Stephen M. Fisher, Secy.-Treas.
Officers and Directors: Gretchen N. Dawes, Pres.; Allen M. Taylor, V.P.; Stephen M. Fisher, Secy.-Treas.
Employer Identification Number: 391455825

7451
De Rance, Inc. ▼
7700 West Blue Mound Rd.
Milwaukee 53213 (414) 475-7700

Incorporated in 1946 in WI.
Donor(s): Harry G. John.
Foundation type: Independent
Financial data (yr. ended 12/31/88): Assets, $75,060,479 (M); expenditures, $9,020,074, including $912,117 for 204 grants (high: $62,000; low: $10; average: $1,000-$2,000), $30,839 for 2 foundation-administered programs and $3,062,400 for 3 in-kind gifts.
Purpose and activities: Emphasis on Roman Catholic church support, religious associations, missionary work, and welfare funds in the U.S. and abroad; support for higher education; support for educational and other programs for the Native American peoples, and for Latin American, African, and Asian educational and social development programs.
Types of support: Operating budgets, scholarship funds, general purposes, continuing support, building funds, conferences and seminars, equipment, in-kind gifts.
Limitations: No grants to individuals, or for endowment funds; no loans.
Publications: Program policy statement, application guidelines.
Application information: U.S. organizations must be listed in the Official Catholic Directory or submit a copy of their qualifying letter from I.R.S. determining their tax exempt status. Normally, all applications should be in English; applications from foreign countries should come from a diocese or religious order with the request from the bishop, archbishop, or the superior, as is appropriate. Application form not required.
Initial approach: Proposal
Copies of proposal: 1
Deadline(s): None
Board meeting date(s): Monthly

Final notification: 6 to 12 months
Write: Donald A. Gallagher, Ph.D., Exec. V.P.
Officers and Directors: Erica P. John, Pres.; Donald A. Gallagher, Exec. V.P.
Number of staff: 5 full-time professional; 6 full-time support; 1 part-time support.
Employer Identification Number: 391053272

7452
Edward U. Demmer Foundation ⌑
c/o Bank One Wisconsin Trust Co., N.A.
P.O. Box 1308
Milwaukee 53201 (414) 765-2800

Trust established in 1963 in WI.
Donor(s): Edward U. Demmer.†
Foundation type: Independent
Financial data (yr. ended 12/31/88): Assets, $1,984,527 (M); expenditures, $319,684, including $289,624 for 36 grants (high: $100,000; low: $1,000).
Purpose and activities: Giving restricted to Protestant or non-sectarian institutions, with emphasis on projects related to children; support also for cultural institutions, health agencies, and hospitals.
Limitations: Giving primarily in WI. No grants to individuals.
Application information:
Initial approach: Proposal
Copies of proposal: 4
Deadline(s): None
Board meeting date(s): Mar., June, Sept., and Dec.
Write: Robert L. Hanley, Sr. V.P., Bank One Wisconsin Trust Co., N.A.
Trustees: Lawrence Demmer, Harrold J. McComas, Carl N. Otjen, Bank One Wisconsin Trust Co., N.A.
Employer Identification Number: 396064898

7453
Ralph Evinrude Foundation, Inc.
c/o Quarles and Brady
411 East Wisconsin Ave.
Milwaukee 53202-4497 (414) 277-5000

Incorporated in 1959 in WI.
Donor(s): Ralph Evinrude.†
Foundation type: Independent
Financial data (yr. ended 07/31/89): Assets, $2,109,215 (M); expenditures, $148,712, including $131,750 for 53 grants (high: $25,000; low: $350; average: $1,000-$5,000).
Purpose and activities: Emphasis on education, hospitals, health agencies, including mental health, cultural programs, and social services, including programs for homelessness, hunger, the handicapped, and youth.
Types of support: Annual campaigns, building funds, capital campaigns, equipment, general purposes, operating budgets, renovation projects, research, scholarship funds.
Limitations: Giving primarily in Milwaukee, WI, and Stuart, FL. No grants to individuals; no loans.
Application information: Application form not required.
Initial approach: Proposal or letter
Copies of proposal: 1
Deadline(s): Submit proposal preferably in Jan., Apr., July, or Oct.
Board meeting date(s): Quarterly in Feb., May, Aug., and Nov.
Final notification: Within 2 weeks after meeting
Write: Patrick W. Cotter, V.P.
Officers and Directors:* Thomas J. Donnelly,* Pres.; Patrick W. Cotter,* V.P. and Treas.; Theodore F. Zimmer,* Secy.
Number of staff: 1 part-time professional.
Employer Identification Number: 396040256

7454
The Evjue Foundation, Inc.
1901 Fish Hatchery Rd.
P.O. Box 8060
Madison 53708 (608) 252-6401

Incorporated in 1958 in WI.
Donor(s): William T. Evjue.†
Foundation type: Independent
Financial data (yr. ended 02/28/89): Assets, $2,640,674 (M); gifts received, $921,531; expenditures, $680,980, including $621,520 for 107 grants (high: $100,000; low: $194; average: $1,000-$5,000).
Purpose and activities: Support for mental health, higher education, cultural programs, and youth and social service agencies.
Types of support: Continuing support, annual campaigns, seed money, emergency funds, special projects, scholarship funds, professorships, internships, publications, conferences and seminars, endowment funds.
Limitations: Giving primarily in Dane County, WI. No support for medical or scientific research. No grants to individuals, or for building funds, equipment, land acquisition, renovation projects, or operating expenses; no loans.
Publications: Program policy statement, application guidelines.
Application information: Application form not required.
Initial approach: Letter
Copies of proposal: 7
Deadline(s): Submit proposal preferably in Oct. or Nov.
Board meeting date(s): Jan., Mar., June, and Sept., and as required
Final notification: 3 months
Write: Marianne D. Pollard, Exec. Secy.
Officers and Directors:* John H. Lussier,* Pres.; Mrs. Frederick W. Miller,* V.P.; Frederick H. Gage,* Secy.; Frederick W. Miller,* Treas.; Nancy Brooke Gage, James D. Lussier, Gordon Sinykin.
Number of staff: 1 part-time support.
Employer Identification Number: 396073981

7455
First Wisconsin Foundation, Inc.
777 East Wisconsin Ave.
Milwaukee 53202 (414) 765-4292

Incorporated in 1954 in WI.
Donor(s): First Wisconsin National Bank of Milwaukee.
Foundation type: Company-sponsored
Financial data (yr. ended 12/31/89): Assets, $5,300,000 (M); expenditures, $946,000, including $938,000 for 136 grants (high: $256,000; low: $100; average: $1,000-$25,000).
Purpose and activities: Emphasis on a community fund, cultural programs, higher education, and youth and social service agencies.
Types of support: Annual campaigns, building funds, continuing support, equipment, general purposes.
Limitations: Giving primarily in the Milwaukee, WI, area. No grants to individuals, or for endowment funds, research, or matching gifts; no loans.
Publications: Annual report, program policy statement, application guidelines.
Application information: Application form not required.
Initial approach: Letter
Copies of proposal: 1
Deadline(s): None
Board meeting date(s): Monthly
Final notification: 60 days
Write: Ellen Hahn
Officers and Directors:* John H. Hendee, Jr.,* Chair.; Roger L. Fitzsimonds,* Vice-Chair.; John A. Becker,* Pres.; William H. Bergner, V.P.; William H. Risch, V.P.; Dennis R. Fredrickson, Secy.-Treas.; and 15 additional directors.
Employer Identification Number: 396042050

7456
A. Ward Ford Memorial Institute, Inc. ☆
813 Second St.
Wausau 54401-4799 (715) 845-9287

Incorporated in 1984 in WI.
Donor(s): Caroline S. Mark.
Foundation type: Independent
Financial data (yr. ended 06/30/89): Assets, $1,645,000 (M); gifts received, $1,700; expenditures, $136,484, including $62,630 for 5 grants (high: $20,820; low: $1,500).
Purpose and activities: Giving primarily for scientific health care projects, including cardiology research with the use of laser equipment.
Types of support: Research, consulting services.
Limitations: Giving primarily in WI and UT.
Application information: Application form not required.
Initial approach: Proposal
Deadline(s): Feb. 28
Board meeting date(s): Mar.
Write: Sandra S. Robarge, Administrator
Officers: Caroline S. Mark,* Chair.; Ellet H. Drake,* Pres.; Konrad Tuchscherer,* V.P.; Sandra Robarge, Secy.-Treas.
Trustees:* James Lundberg, Richard Morehead, William Owen.
Employer Identification Number: 370983948

7457
Fort Howard Foundation, Inc. ▼
(Formerly Fort Howard Paper Foundation, Inc.)
P.O. Box 11325
Green Bay 54307-1325 (414) 435-8821
Illinois office: 7575 South Kostner Ave., Chicago, IL 60652

Incorporated in 1953 in WI.
Donor(s): Fort Howard Paper Co.
Foundation type: Company-sponsored

Financial data (yr. ended 12/31/88): Assets, $13,900,023 (M); expenditures, $940,317, including $726,652 for 6 grants (high: $150,000; low: $13,732; average: $16,000-$125,000) and $12,050 for 8 grants to individuals (high: $2,500; low: $228).
Purpose and activities: Emphasis on education, cultural programs, and social service and youth agencies; support also for health-care facilities.
Types of support: Building funds, equipment, scholarship funds.
Limitations: Giving primarily in areas of company operations and limited surrounding areas; emphasis on Green Bay, WI, Muskogee, OK, and Effingham County, GA. No grants to individuals.
Application information: The foundation is honoring existing scholarship commitments to individuals, but is not making any new commitments.
Deadline(s): Mar. 1 and Aug. 1
Board meeting date(s): 3rd Saturdays of Mar. and Aug.
Final notification: Normally within 7-10 days following meeting
Write: Bruce W. Nagel, Exec. Dir.
Officers and Directors:* Paul J. Schierl,* Pres.; Kathleen J. Hempel,* V.P.; Robert E. Manger,* V.P.; Carol A. Schierl,* V.P.; Michael J. Schierl,* V.P.; James J. Schoshinski,* V.P.; Thomas L. Shaffer,* V.P.; Cheryl A. Thomson, Secy.; Susan M. Van Schyndle, Treas.; Bruce W. Nagel, Exec. Dir.; John W. Hickey.
Number of staff: None.
Employer Identification Number: 362761910

7458
Community Foundation for the Fox Valley Region, Inc.
222 West College Ave.
P.O. Box 563
Appleton 54912 (414) 730-3773

Organized in 1986 in WI.
Foundation type: Community
Financial data (yr. ended 06/30/89): Assets, $5,011,507 (M); gifts received, $65,200; expenditures, $199,879, including $69,634 for grants.
Purpose and activities: Support for social services, civic affairs, health, education, and cultural affairs, including the arts.
Limitations: Giving limited to the Fox Valley, WI, area. No support for sectarian or religious purposes, or specific research or medical projects. No grants for operating expenses, annual fund drives, deficit financing, endowment funds, capital projects, or travel expenses.
Publications: Biennial report, informational brochure.
Application information:
Initial approach: Letter or telephone
Deadline(s): Jan. 15, Apr. 15, July 15, and Sept. 30
Board meeting date(s): Feb., May, Aug., and Nov.
Write: Gordon Holten, Exec. Dir.
Officers: Roger A. Baird, Chair.; Paul H. Groth, Pres.; O.C. Boldt, V.P.; Mary Sensenbrenner, V.P.; Larry L. Kath, Secy.; Gail E. Janssen, Treas.; Gordon L. Holten, Exec. Dir.
Directors: F. John Barlow, and 44 other directors.
Number of staff: 3 full-time professional; 2 part-time support.
Employer Identification Number: 391548450

7459
John J. Frautschi Family Foundation, Inc. ⌑
c/o Webcrafters, Inc.
2211 Forden Ave., P.O. Box 7608
Madison 53707

Established in 1986 in WI.
Donor(s): members of the Frautschi family.
Foundation type: Independent
Financial data (yr. ended 12/31/87): Assets, $1,109,781 (M); gifts received, $263,875; expenditures, $99,430, including $88,500 for 15 grants (high: $50,000; low: $1,000).
Purpose and activities: First year of grantmaking, 1987; giving primarily to a cancer center; support also for education.
Limitations: Giving primarily in WI. No grants to individuals.
Application information: Contributes only to pre-selected organizations. Applications not accepted.
Officers and Directors: John J. Frautschi, Pres.; Mary W. Frautschi, V.P.; Peter W. Frautschi, Secy.; Christopher J. Frautschi, Treas.; Elizabeth J. Frautschi.
Employer Identification Number: 391561017

7460
Walter and Mabel Fromm Scholarship Trust ⌑
c/o First Wisconsin Trust Co.
P.O. Box 2054
Milwaukee 53201

Established in 1975.
Donor(s): Mabel Fromm,† Walter Fromm.†
Foundation type: Independent
Financial data (yr. ended 2/28/89): Assets, $1,835,475 (M); gifts received, $3,589; expenditures, $118,084, including $100,775 for 28 grants to individuals (high: $4,100; low: $1,150).
Purpose and activities: Support primarily for college and nursing school scholarships for graduates of the Maple Grove (elementary) School and/or Merrill Senior Public High School.
Types of support: Student aid.
Limitations: Giving limited to Hamburg and Merrill, WI.
Publications: Application guidelines.
Application information: Scholarship application guidelines available.
Write: G. Lindemann
Committee Members: Leonard Hamann, Richard Monka, Lanny Tibaldo, Gary Lee Woller.
Trustee: First Wisconsin Trust Co.
Employer Identification Number: 396250027

7461
The Gardner Foundation
111 East Wisconsin Ave., Suite 1359
Milwaukee 53202 (414) 272-0383

Incorporated in 1947 in NY.
Donor(s): Herman Gardner.†
Foundation type: Independent
Financial data (yr. ended 12/31/89): Assets, $1,334,779 (M); expenditures, $108,222, including $99,467 for 48 grants (high: $6,000; low: $100; average: $1,000-$5,000).
Purpose and activities: Grants for social services, education, community development, health services and hospices, and culture.
Types of support: Operating budgets, renovation projects, capital campaigns, emergency funds, scholarship funds.
Limitations: Giving primarily in the greater Milwaukee, WI, area.
Publications: Program policy statement, application guidelines.
Application information: Application form required.
Initial approach: Letter
Copies of proposal: 1
Deadline(s): Mar., Aug., and Nov.
Board meeting date(s): Apr., Sept., and Dec.
Final notification: Within one month of meeting
Write: Theodore Friedlander, Jr., Pres.
Officers and Directors:* Theodore Friedlander, Jr.,* Pres.; Gardner L. Friedlander,* V.P.; A. William Asmuth, Jr.,* Secy.; Gardner L.R. Friedlander, Jean W. Friedlander, Karen Friedlander, Louise Friedlander, Theodore Friedlander III, John C. Geilfuss, Norman Paulsen, Eleanor S. Poss.
Number of staff: None.
Employer Identification Number: 396076956

7462
The Gelatt Foundation, Inc.
P.O. Box 1087
La Crosse 54601 (608) 784-0110

Incorporated in 1954 in WI.
Donor(s): Charles D. Gelatt, Northern Engraving and Manufacturing Co.
Foundation type: Independent
Financial data (yr. ended 06/30/89): Assets, $1,694,521 (M); expenditures, $166,708, including $161,500 for 40 grants (low: $500; average: $4,000).
Purpose and activities: Emphasis on youth agencies, hospitals, community funds, and higher education.
Types of support: Operating budgets, continuing support, annual campaigns, building funds, matching funds.
Limitations: Giving primarily in WI. No grants to individuals, or for seed money, emergency or endowment funds, deficit financing, equipment, land acquisition, scholarships, fellowships, research, special projects, publications, or conferences; no loans.
Application information: Application form not required.
Initial approach: Letter
Copies of proposal: 1
Deadline(s): Submit proposal in Apr. or May; deadline June 1
Board meeting date(s): As required
Final notification: 1 month

Write: Donald B. Lee, Secy.-Treas.
Officers: Charles D. Gelatt, Pres.; Robert P. Smyth, V.P.; Donald B. Lee, Secy.-Treas.
Number of staff: None.
Employer Identification Number: 396044165

7463
Giddings and Lewis Foundation, Inc. ⌑
142 Doty St.
Fond du Lac 54935
Application address: P.O. Box 590, Fond du Lac, WI 54935; Tel.: (414) 921-9400

Incorporated in 1952 in WI.
Donor(s): Giddings and Lewis Machine Tool Co.
Foundation type: Company-sponsored
Financial data (yr. ended 12/31/87): Assets, $2,352,328 (M); expenditures, $221,001, including $211,080 for 38 grants (high: $25,000; low: $150) and $4,860 for 23 employee matching gifts (high: $900; low: $25).
Purpose and activities: Emphasis on education, community funds and community development, and local chapters of national social service organizations.
Types of support: Building funds, scholarship funds, matching funds, research, employee matching gifts, operating budgets.
Limitations: Giving primarily in WI. No grants to individuals.
Application information:
Initial approach: Letter
Deadline(s): May 1 and Dec. 1
Write: Richard C. Kleinfeldt, Pres.
Officers and Directors: Richard C. Kleinfeldt, Pres.; Joseph D. Carney, V.P.; William J. Fife, Jr., V.P.; Harry A. Hall, V.P.; Paul G. Holland, V.P.; Louis J. Lawrence, V.P.; Ronald F. Zweifel, Secy.-Treas.
Trustees: Peter G. Bolda, John K. Draeger, Orville W. Ehrhardt, John A. MacIntyre, John M. Rensink.
Employer Identification Number: 396061306

7464
Ray & Marie Goldbach Foundation, Ltd. ☆
c/o Marathon Cheese Corp.
304 East St.
Marathon 54448

Established in 1981 in WI.
Donor(s): Raymond A. Goldbach, Marie S. Goldbach, Marathon Cheese Corp.
Foundation type: Independent
Financial data (yr. ended 07/31/89): Assets, $2,273,339 (M); gifts received, $280,000; expenditures, $320,815, including $301,481 for grants.
Purpose and activities: Giving primarily for a swimming association; support also for Catholic relief and churches and secondary education.
Limitations: Giving primarily in WI. No grants to individuals.
Application information: Contributes only to pre-selected organizations. Applications not accepted.
Officers: Marie S. Goldbach, Pres. and Treas.; Raymond A. Goldbach, V.P. and Secy.
Directors: Mary Gallagher, Lisbeth J. Goldbach, Norbert Schumacher, John L. Skoug.
Number of staff: None.
Employer Identification Number: 391394328

7465
Grede Foundation, Inc. ☆
P.O. Box 26499
Milwaukee 53226 (414) 257-3600

Incorporated in 1954 in WI.
Donor(s): Grede Foundries, Inc.
Foundation type: Company-sponsored
Financial data (yr. ended 12/31/89): Assets, $256,369 (M); gifts received, $150,000; expenditures, $153,897, including $149,897 for 92 grants (low: $25; average: $25-$250,000).
Purpose and activities: Emphasis on youth agencies; support also for hospitals, higher and secondary education, community funds, community affairs, and public interest groups.
Types of support: Annual campaigns, building funds, capital campaigns.
Limitations: Giving primarily in WI. No grants to individuals.
Application information: Submit proposal preferably in Sept. Application form not required.
Initial approach: Telephone Loretta Tesch for information
Copies of proposal: 1
Deadline(s): None
Board meeting date(s): Quarterly
Write: James T. Williams, V.P. and Secy.-Treas.
Officers and Directors:* Burleigh E. Jacobs, Jr., Pres.; James T. Williams,* V.P. and Secy.-Treas.; Betty G. Davis.
Number of staff: 1 part-time support.
Employer Identification Number: 396042977

7466
H. J. Hagge Foundation, Inc. ☆
506 First American Ctr.
Wausau 54401 (715) 845-1818

Established in 1956.
Foundation type: Independent
Financial data (yr. ended 12/31/89): Assets, $1,181,620 (M); expenditures, $47,401, including $44,326 for 97 grants (high: $4,500; low: $50).
Purpose and activities: Support for health associations, social services, culture, and Protestant churches.
Types of support: General purposes.
Limitations: Giving primarily in WI. No grants to individuals.
Application information: Application form not required.
Initial approach: Letter
Copies of proposal: 1
Deadline(s): None
Board meeting date(s): Jan. and July
Write: Daniel L. Hagge, Pres.
Officers and Directors:* Daniel L. Hagge,* Pres. and Treas.; Robert S. Hagge, Jr.,* V.P.; Leigh Hagge Tuckey,* Secy.; Daniel L. Hagge, Jr., Kristin Single Hagge.
Number of staff: 1
Employer Identification Number: 396037112

7467
Harnischfeger Foundation, Inc.
120 Bishops Way, Suite 161
Brookfield 53005 (414) 784-4679

Incorporated in 1929 in WI.
Donor(s): Walter Harnischfeger,† Harnischfeger Corp.
Foundation type: Independent
Financial data (yr. ended 12/31/89): Assets, $2,230,000 (M); expenditures, $125,000, including $110,000 for 35 grants (high: $10,000; low: $100).
Purpose and activities: Emphasis on hospitals and health care, a community fund, higher education, cultural activities, and youth agencies.
Limitations: No grants to individuals, or for endowment funds, research, scholarships, fellowships, or matching gifts; no loans.
Application information: Application form not required.
Initial approach: Letter
Copies of proposal: 1
Board meeting date(s): May and Nov.
Write: Henry Harnischfeger, Pres.
Officers and Directors:* Henry Harnischfeger,* Pres.; Elizabeth Ogden,* V.P.; George B. Knight,* Secy.; Norman O. Rieboldt, Treas.
Number of staff: None.
Employer Identification Number: 396040450

7468
Hayssen Family Foundation, Inc. ⌑
1714 Cambridge
Sheboygan 53081-2640 (414) 457-5051

Established in 1944 in WI.
Foundation type: Independent
Financial data (yr. ended 12/31/88): Assets, $1,083,675 (M); expenditures, $27,145, including $16,950 for 18 grants (high: $3,000; low: $250).
Purpose and activities: Giving primarily for civic affairs, educational programs, and general charities.
Limitations: Giving primarily in WI.
Application information:
Initial approach: Letter
Deadline(s): None
Write: Daniel A. Merkel, Secy.
Officers and Directors: Marie Perry, V.P.; Daniel A. Merkel, Secy.
Employer Identification Number: 396044222

7469
Heileman Old Style Foundation, Inc. ⌑
100 Harborview Plaza
P.O. Box 459
La Crosse 54601 (608) 785-1000

Incorporated in 1966 in WI.
Donor(s): G. Heileman Brewing Co., Inc.
Foundation type: Company-sponsored
Financial data (yr. ended 12/31/88): Assets, $149,721 (M); gifts received, $47,945; expenditures, $251,380, including $179,626 for 120 grants (low: $30; average: $1,000-$2,000) and $71,057 for employee matching gifts.
Purpose and activities: Support for community funds; giving also for higher education and hospitals, cancer and other

medical research, museums and the theater, the environment, biological and other sciences, child development, minority education, and alcohol abuse programs.
Types of support: Building funds, capital campaigns, employee matching gifts, matching funds, scholarship funds.
Limitations: Giving primarily in areas of company operations: Perry, GA; Portland, OR; Baltimore, MD; Frankenmuth, MI; St. Paul, MN; Pittsburgh, PA; San Antonio, TX; Seattle, WA; and La Crosse, WI. No grants to individuals, or for endowment funds; no loans.
Publications: 990-PF.
Application information: Application form not required.
Initial approach: Telephone or proposal
Copies of proposal: 1
Deadline(s): Submit proposal preferably in month preceding board meeting
Board meeting date(s): Quarterly
Write: George E. Smith
Officer and Trustees: Murray Cutbush, Mgr.; Daniel J. Schmid, George E. Smith.
Number of staff: None.
Employer Identification Number: 396094334

7470
Evan and Marion Helfaer Foundation ¤
735 North Water St.
Milwaukee 53202 (414) 276-3600

Established in 1971 in WI.
Donor(s): Evan P. Helfaer.†
Foundation type: Independent
Financial data (yr. ended 7/31/88): Assets, $14,065,846 (M); expenditures, $1,048,268, including $867,250 for 140 grants (high: $50,000; low: $250).
Purpose and activities: Support for higher education, cultural programs, youth and social service agencies, and health.
Types of support: Lectureships, professorships, building funds, research.
Limitations: Giving limited to WI. No grants to individuals.
Application information: Application form available, but not required or preferred.
Initial approach: Letter
Deadline(s): None
Board meeting date(s): Periodically
Final notification: Within 90 days after end of fiscal year
Write: Thomas L. Smallwood, Trustee
Trustees: Thomas L. Smallwood, Admin.; Jack F. Kellner, Marshall & Ilsley Trust Co.
Number of staff: 1
Employer Identification Number: 396238856

7471
Heller Foundation, Inc. ¤
P.O. Box 886
Oshkosh 54902

Established in 1957 in WI.
Foundation type: Independent
Financial data (yr. ended 11/30/88): Assets, $1,707,765 (M); expenditures, $90,912, including $74,350 for 19 grants (high: $13,500; low: $350).
Purpose and activities: Support primarily for higher education and health services; grants also for the United Way.
Limitations: Giving primarily in Milwaukee, WI.
Application information:
Write: John E. Dempsey, Secy.
Officers and Trustees: William C. Heller, Jr., Pres. and Treas.; James K. Heller, V.P.; John E. Dempsey, Secy.
Employer Identification Number: 396045338

7472
Hobbs Foundation ¤
131 South Barstow St., Rm. 309
Eau Claire 54701 (715) 834-6645

Trust established in 1958 in WI.
Donor(s): Roswell H. Hobbs,† Jessie M. Hobbs.†
Foundation type: Independent
Financial data (yr. ended 12/31/88): Assets, $949,572 (M); expenditures, $184,234, including $151,382 for 30 grants (high: $73,755; low: $40) and $22,000 for 11 grants to individuals of $2,000 each.
Purpose and activities: Giving for youth and recreation programs, social services, and a library.
Types of support: Student aid.
Limitations: Giving primarily in Eau Claire, WI. No grants to individuals (except for limited special scholarships), or for endowment funds or operating budgets.
Application information: Scholarship program for special purposes only, and not open to any new applicants.
Initial approach: Letter
Copies of proposal: 3
Deadline(s): None
Board meeting date(s): Mar., June, Sept., and Dec.
Write: Francis J. Wilcox, Trustee
Trustees: Kempton L. German, Ray E. Wachs, Francis J. Wilcox.
Employer Identification Number: 396068746

7473
Margaret Banta Humleker Charitable Foundation, Inc. ¤
735 North Water St.
Milwaukee 53202

Established in 1982 in WI.
Donor(s): Margaret Banta Humleker.
Foundation type: Independent
Financial data (yr. ended 11/30/88): Assets, $6,058 (M); expenditures, $111,337, including $103,026 for 194 grants (high: $22,250; low: $15).
Purpose and activities: Support primarily for higher education and cultural organizations.
Limitations: Giving primarily in WI. No grants to individuals.
Application information: Contributes only to pre-selected organizations. Applications not accepted.
Trustees: John Hein, Ann Heinz, Bill Humleker, George Humleker, Margaret Banta Humleker, Peter D. Humleker III.
Employer Identification Number: 391427005

7474
Glenn & Gertrude Humphrey Foundation, Inc. ¤
1233 North Mayfair Rd., Suite 104
Wauwatosa 53226

Established in 1972 in WI.
Foundation type: Independent
Financial data (yr. ended 12/31/88): Assets, $4,844,965 (M); gifts received, $462,915; expenditures, $674,258, including $503,804 for 85 grants (high: $200,000; low: $25).
Purpose and activities: Giving primarily for higher education, medical research, and child development organizations.
Limitations: Giving primarily in Milwaukee, WI.
Application information: Application form required.
Initial approach: Letter
Write: Loraine Schuffler, Pres.
Officers and Directors: Gertrude Humphrey, Chair.; Loraine E. Schuffler, Pres.; Peter C. Haensel, Secy.; Roy Gruber, Joseph Tierney.
Employer Identification Number: 237207640

7475
Charles D. Jacobus Family Foundation ¤
c/o A. Peter McArthur
2323 North Mayfair Rd.
Wauwatosa 53226 (414) 475-6565

Established in 1986 in WI.
Donor(s): Jacobus Company.
Foundation type: Independent
Financial data (yr. ended 12/31/87): Assets, $1,025,518 (M); gifts received, $357,500; expenditures, $46,480, including $37,519 for 29 grants (high: $10,356; low: $100) and $2,250 for 6 grants to individuals of $375 each.
Purpose and activities: Support for higher education, social services, youth organizations, and community funds. Scholarships limited to children of employees of the Jacobus Co. or its subsidiaries.
Limitations: Giving primarily in WI.
Application information: Application form required.
Initial approach: Letter
Officers: Charles D. Jacobus, Pres. and Treas.; Eugenia T. Jacobus, V.P. and Secy.; Karim J. Campion, V.P.; Russell R. Campion, V.P.; Charles D. Jacobus, Jr., V.P.; Victoria B. Jacobus, V.P.
Employer Identification Number: 391559892

7476
Janesville Foundation, Inc.
121 North Parker Dr.
P.O. Box 1492
Janesville 53547 (608) 752-1032

Incorporated in 1944 in WI.
Donor(s): Merchants and Savings Bank, The Parker Pen Co., and others.
Foundation type: Independent
Financial data (yr. ended 12/31/89): Assets, $8,304,965 (M); gifts received, $1,025; expenditures, $619,636, including $437,430 for 43 grants (high: $80,000; low: $100; average: $5,000-$10,000) and $29,200 for 29 grants to individuals (high: $1,500; low: $50; average: $50-$1,500).

Purpose and activities: Support for the purpose of equipping individuals to help themselves and to aid the community; emphasis on higher and secondary education, scholarships for local high school graduates, youth and child welfare agencies, community funds, and historic restoration.
Types of support: Continuing support, seed money, building funds, equipment, land acquisition, matching funds, student aid, special projects, conferences and seminars.
Limitations: Giving limited to Janesville, WI; scholarships limited to Janesville, WI, high school students. No support for political projects. No grants to individuals (except for scholarships), or for operating budgets or endowment funds; no loans.
Publications: Informational brochure (including application guidelines).
Application information: Application form not required.
Initial approach: Letter with brief outline of proposal, or by telephone
Copies of proposal: 5
Deadline(s): 15th of month prior to each board meeting
Board meeting date(s): Feb., May, Aug., and Nov.
Final notification: As soon as possible after board meetings
Write: Alan W. Dunwiddie, Jr., Exec. Dir.
Officers: Alan W. Dunwiddie, Jr.,* Pres. and Exec. Dir.; Roger E. Axtell, V.P.; Alfred P. Diotte,* V.P.; Phyllis Saevre, Secy.-Treas.
Directors:* George S. Parker, Chair.; Rowland J. McClellan.
Number of staff: 1 full-time professional; 2 part-time support.
Employer Identification Number: 396034645

7477
Johnson Controls Foundation ▼
5757 North Green Bay Ave.
P.O. Box 591
Milwaukee 53201 (414) 228-2219

Trust established in 1952 in WI.
Donor(s): Johnson Controls, Inc.
Foundation type: Company-sponsored
Financial data (yr. ended 12/31/88): Assets, $17,026,046 (M); gifts received, $3,500,000; expenditures, $3,388,046, including $3,013,091 for 1,753 grants (low: $25), $84,500 for grants to individuals (average: $1,750) and $177,900 for 1,230 employee matching gifts.
Purpose and activities: Grants for higher education; health and hospitals; community funds; social services, including aid to the handicapped, care of children, and the aged; and civic, arts, and cultural organizations.
Types of support: Operating budgets, continuing support, annual campaigns, seed money, emergency funds, building funds, endowment funds, matching funds, employee-related scholarships, employee matching gifts.
Limitations: No support for political or religious purposes; public or private pre-schools; elementary or secondary schools; industrial groups or trade associations supported by industrial groups; foreign-based institutions; or fraternal, veterans', or labor groups. No grants to individuals (except employee-related scholarships), or for fundraising events, courtesy advertising, deficit financing, equipment, land acquisition, special projects, research, publications, conferences, or seminars; no loans.
Publications: Application guidelines.
Application information: Employee-related scholarship awards are paid directly to institutions and not to individuals. Application form not required.
Initial approach: Letter
Copies of proposal: 1
Deadline(s): None
Board meeting date(s): Usually Mar., June, and Sept.
Final notification: Up to 120 days
Write: Florence R. Klatt, Member, Advisory Board
Advisory Board: Fred L. Brengel, James H. Keyes, Florence R. Klatt, Philip R. Smith, R. Douglas Ziegler.
Trustee: First Wisconsin Trust Co.
Number of staff: 1 full-time professional; 1 part-time professional; 4 part-time support.
Employer Identification Number: 396036639

7478
The Johnson Foundation, Inc.
P.O. Box 547
Racine 53401-0547 (414) 681-3343

Incorporated in 1958 in NY.
Donor(s): S.C. Johnson & Son, Inc., and descendants of the late H.F. Johnson, H.F. Johnson.†
Foundation type: Operating
Financial data (yr. ended 06/30/89): Assets, $12,663,481 (M); gifts received, $1,820,267; expenditures, $2,465,077, including $9,338 for 5 grants (high: $5,331; low: $500) and $2,251,052 for foundation-administered programs.
Purpose and activities: A private operating foundation; supports four broad areas of activity: international understanding, educational excellence, intellectual and cultural growth, and improvement of the human environment; support also for family services, welfare, and the arts. The foundation's principal activity is planning and carrying out conferences at Wingspread, its educational conference center in Racine. Grants limited to activities directly related to Wingspread programs. Publications based on Wingspread conferences available on request.
Types of support: Conferences and seminars, publications.
Limitations: No grants to individuals.
Publications: Annual report (including application guidelines), informational brochure (including application guidelines).
Application information: Application form not required.
Initial approach: Letter
Copies of proposal: 1
Deadline(s): None
Board meeting date(s): June and Dec.
Final notification: Approximately 8 weeks
Write: Jo Ann Weibel, Program Secy.
Officers: Charles W. Bray,* Pres.; Catherine B. Cleary,* V.P. and Secy.; Harold F. Greiveldinger, Treas.
Trustees:* Samuel C. Johnson, Chair.; Robben W. Fleming, Patricia Albjerg Graham, Robert S. Ingersoll, Donald F. McHenry, Robert M. O'Neil, William J. Raspberry.
Number of staff: 6 full-time professional; 1 part-time professional; 10 full-time support.
Employer Identification Number: 390958255

7479
John A. Johnson Foundation ⌘
P.O. Box 8100
Madison 53708
Application address: 709 Lakewood Blvd., Madison, WI 53704; Tel.: (608) 249-2313

Incorporated in 1951 in WI.
Foundation type: Independent
Financial data (yr. ended 12/31/87): Assets, $1,636,423 (M); expenditures, $110,362, including $93,785 for 30 grants (high: $13,180; low: $205).
Purpose and activities: Giving primarily for a public park; support also for scholarships and higher education.
Types of support: Scholarship funds.
Limitations: Giving primarily in WI.
Application information: Application form not required.
Deadline(s): None
Write: John C. Weston, Pres.
Officers and Directors: John C. Weston, Pres. and Fund Mgr.; Toby F. Sherry, V.P.; Gordon G. Volz, Secy.-Treas.; John A. Bolz, Richmond Johnson, Stanley A. Johnson, John R. Pike, Thomas O. Zilavy.
Employer Identification Number: 396078592

7480
The Johnson Foundation Trust ⌘
1525 Howe St.
Racine 53403

Established in 1937.
Foundation type: Independent
Financial data (yr. ended 6/30/88): Assets, $1,373,295 (M); expenditures, $38,729, including $28,200 for 8 grants (high: $10,000; low: $1,000).
Purpose and activities: Giving primarily for higher education, cultural programs, conservation, and recreation programs.
Application information: Most grants are pre-selected by trustees. Application form not required.
Write: Robert C. Hart, Secy.
Officers: Samuel C. Johnson, Chair.; Robert C. Hart, Secy.
Trustees: John M. Schroeder, M & I Marshall & Ilsley Bank.
Employer Identification Number: 396052073

7481
The Johnson's Wax Fund, Inc. ▼ ⌘
1525 Howe St.
Racine 53403 (414) 631-2267

Incorporated in 1959 in WI.
Donor(s): S.C. Johnson & Son, Inc.
Foundation type: Company-sponsored
Financial data (yr. ended 6/30/88): Assets, $2,060,159 (M); gifts received, $2,622,142; expenditures, $2,117,623, including $1,247,898 for 112 grants (high: $195,350;

low: $500; average: $1,000-$40,000) and $771,522 for 3,209 employee matching gifts.
Purpose and activities: Scholarships for children of company employees through the Citizen's Scholarship Foundation of America and the National Merit Scholarship Corp.; scholarships and fellowships in specific areas of interest, i.e., chemistry, biology, marketing, and business; grants to local colleges; support for local welfare, cultural, and civic organizations; grants also for environmental protection, health, and education.
Types of support: Seed money, building funds, equipment, scholarship funds, exchange programs, fellowships, research, employee matching gifts, employee-related scholarships, capital campaigns.
Limitations: Giving primarily in WI and the Midwest in areas of company operations. No support for national health organizations or religious and social groups, organizations receiving support from the United Way, or veterans', labor, or fraternal organizations. No grants to individuals, or for operating budgets, emergency funds, deficit financing, demonstration projects, or conferences; no loans.
Publications: Informational brochure (including application guidelines), corporate giving report.
Application information: Application form not required.
Initial approach: Letter and proposal
Copies of proposal: 1
Deadline(s): None
Board meeting date(s): Mar., June, Sept., and Dec.
Final notification: 3 to 4 months
Write: Reva A. Holmes, V.P. and Secy.
Officers: Samuel C. Johnson,* Chair. and Pres.; David H. Cool,* Vice-Chair.; Reva A. Holmes, V.P. and Secy.; John M. Schroeder, Treas.
Trustees:* Richard A. Baradic, Wesley A. Coleman, Raymond F. Farley, Jane M. Hutterly, Serge E. Logan, Robert G. McCurdy.
Number of staff: 1 part-time professional; 1 part-time support.
Employer Identification Number: 396052089

7482
Kearney & Trecker Foundation, Inc.
11000 Theodore Trecker Way
West Allis 53214 (414) 476-8300

Incorporated in 1945 in WI.
Donor(s): Kearney and Trecker Corp.
Foundation type: Company-sponsored
Financial data (yr. ended 09/30/89): Assets, $1,106,000 (M); expenditures, $192,000, including $167,000 for 82 grants (high: $53,000; low: $250; average: $100-$2,000) and $22,000 for 60 employee matching gifts.
Purpose and activities: Support for 1) Education: any museum accredited by the American Association of Museums. Also any technical institution, graduate or professional school, two-year junior or community college, or four-year college or university which is listed in the Education Directory of the U.S. Department of Health, Education, and Welfare. Donations wholly or partially in lieu of tuition, or for tuition, will not be matched. Also support for any radio or television station affiliated with a technical institution, school, college or university. 2) Health and Welfare: any hospital accredited by the American Association, and any member of a United Way or equivalent community welfare fund, to which Kearney and Trecker Foundation made a contribution in its preceding fiscal year. 3) Arts: any United Performing Arts or equivalent community arts fund to which the foundation made a contribution in its preceding year.
Types of support: Employee matching gifts, capital campaigns, matching funds.
Limitations: Giving primarily in WI, with emphasis on the Milwaukee area. No support for government agencies. No grants to individuals, or for endowment funds; no loans.
Application information: Application form not required.
Initial approach: Proposal
Copies of proposal: 1
Board meeting date(s): Jan., May, and Sept.
Write: Donald P. Muench, V.P. and Treas.
Officers: W. Buck Cody,* Pres.; Donald P. Muench, V.P. and Treas.; Todd A. Dillman, Secy.
Directors:* Russell A. Hedden, Chair.; Patrick W. Cotter, Hebert W. Pohle, Donald E. Porter, Brenton H. Rupple, Robert R. Spitzer.
Number of staff: None.
Employer Identification Number: 396044253

7483
Herbert H. Kohl Charities, Inc. ☆
825 North Jefferson St., Suite 250
Milwaukee 53202

Established in 1977 in WI.
Donor(s): Herbert H. Kohl, Mary Kohl.
Foundation type: Independent
Financial data (yr. ended 06/30/89): Assets, $12,092,835 (M); gifts received, $150,000; expenditures, $190,745, including $125,517 for 2 grants (high: $125,000; low: $517).
Purpose and activities: Giving primarily for Jewish organizations; support also for health associations and medical research and education.
Limitations: Giving primarily in Milwaukee, WI. No grants to individuals.
Application information: Contributes only to pre-selected organizations. Applications not accepted.
Officers and Directors:* Herbert H. Kohl,* Pres.; Allen D. Kohl,* V.P.; Sidney A. Kohl,* Secy.; Delores K. Solovy,* Treas.
Employer Identification Number: 391300476

7484
Kohler Foundation, Inc.
104 Orchard Rd.
Kohler 53044 (414) 458-1972

Incorporated in 1940 in WI.
Donor(s): Herbert V. Kohler,† Marie C. Kohler,† Evangeline Kohler,† Lillie B. Kohler,† O.A. Kroos.†
Foundation type: Independent
Financial data (yr. ended 12/31/88): Assets, $30,278,849 (M); expenditures, $884,840, including $697,361 for 101 grants (high: $350,000; low: $150).
Purpose and activities: Supports education and the arts in WI. Annual program funds provide scholarships for students graduating from Sheboygen County high schools and to establish a Scholarship Endowment at private colleges in WI. All scholarship recipients are chosen by their schools.
Types of support: General purposes, seed money, building funds, equipment, land acquisition, endowment funds, publications, conferences and seminars, scholarship funds, fellowships, matching funds, special projects, program-related investments, capital campaigns.
Limitations: Giving limited to WI. No support for health care or medical programs. No grants to individuals, or for operating budgets or annual fundraising drives; no loans.
Publications: Application guidelines.
Application information: Application form not required.
Initial approach: Letter
Copies of proposal: 1
Deadline(s): Submit proposal preferably between Sept. and Nov. or Jan. and Apr.; deadlines Apr. 15 and Nov. 1
Board meeting date(s): May and Dec. and as required
Final notification: 1 week after contributions meetings
Write: Eleanor A. Jung, Exec. Dir.
Officers: Herbert V. Kohler, Jr.,* Chair.; Ruth DeYoung Kohler II, Pres.; Paul Tenpas,* Secy.; Eugene P. Seifert, Treas.; Eleanor A. Jung, Exec. Dir.
Directors:* Sam H. Davis, Frank C. Jacobson.
Number of staff: 2 part-time professional; 1 part-time support.
Employer Identification Number: 390810536

7485
Charles A. Krause Foundation
c/o Krause Consultants, Ltd.
330 East Kilbourne Ave., Two Plaza East 570
Milwaukee 53202 (414) 273-2733

Incorporated in 1952 in WI.
Foundation type: Independent
Financial data (yr. ended 12/31/89): Assets, $3,155,543 (M); expenditures, $197,418, including $192,091 for 64 grants (high: $25,000; low: $10).
Purpose and activities: Giving primarily for higher and secondary education, conservation, museums, and cultural programs.
Types of support: Capital campaigns, continuing support, general purposes.
Limitations: Giving primarily in WI. No grants to individuals.
Publications: 990-PF.
Application information: Employee-related scholarship program has been discontinued. Previous commitments honored; no new awards to individuals.
Copies of proposal: 1
Deadline(s): Nov. 1
Board meeting date(s): mid-Dec.
Write: Charles A. Krause III, Secy.-Treas.
Officers and Directors:* Carol Krause Wythes,* Pres.; E.A. Longenecker,* V.P.; Charles A. Krause III,* Secy.-Treas.; Eleanor T. Sullivan, Victoria K. Mayer.
Number of staff: None.
Employer Identification Number: 396044820

7486
The George Kress Foundation, Inc. ⌑
c/o Kellogg Trust
1700 North Webster Ave., P.O. Box 1107
Green Bay 54305

Incorporated in 1953 in WI.
Foundation type: Independent
Financial data (yr. ended 12/31/87): Assets, $1,721,077 (M); gifts received, $250,000; expenditures, $346,452, including $325,855 for 194 grants (high: $32,500; low: $50).
Purpose and activities: Emphasis on youth agencies, community funds, higher education, including scholarship funds, health agencies, the environment, community development, and church support.
Types of support: Scholarship funds.
Officers and Directors: George F. Kress, Pres.; James F. Kress, V.P.; S. Lawrence Mayer, Secy.-Treas.; Donald Kress, Max Sielaff, Marilyn Kress Swanson.
Employer Identification Number: 396050768

7487
Kurth Religious Trust ⌑
141 North Main, Suite 207
West Bend 53095

Trust established in 1946 in WI.
Donor(s): Kurth Malting Corp.
Foundation type: Company-sponsored
Financial data (yr. ended 12/31/88): Assets, $4,301,203 (M); expenditures, $242,350, including $211,525 for 59 grants (high: $35,000; low: $75).
Purpose and activities: Religious and charitable purposes; grants largely for Lutheran church support, religious associations and welfare funds; some support for higher education.
Limitations: No grants to individuals.
Application information: Application form not required.
Deadline(s): None
Write: Katherine Kurth, Trustee
Trustee: Katherine Kurth.
Employer Identification Number: 396048744

7488
La Crosse Community Foundation
(Formerly La Crosse Foundation)
P.O. Box 489
La Crosse 54602-0489 (608) 782-3223

Established in 1930 in WI.
Foundation type: Community
Financial data (yr. ended 12/31/89): Assets, $4,304,781 (M); gifts received, $926,894; expenditures, $297,230, including $248,054 for 107 grants (high: $37,000; low: $100).
Purpose and activities: Support for social programs, higher education, the arts, civic affairs, and youth.
Types of support: Operating budgets, continuing support, annual campaigns, seed money, emergency funds, building funds, equipment, matching funds, scholarship funds, research, conferences and seminars, grants to individuals, program-related investments, publications, employee matching gifts, capital campaigns, general purposes, renovation projects, special projects.
Limitations: Giving limited to La Crosse County, WI. No grants for deficit financing, land acquisition, consulting services, or technical assistance; grants to individuals for scholarships only, with payment made directly to the institution; no loans.
Publications: Annual report (including application guidelines), application guidelines.
Application information: Application form required.
Initial approach: Letter
Copies of proposal: 7
Deadline(s): Submit proposal by the 15th of Feb., May, Aug., and Nov.
Board meeting date(s): Mar., June, Sept., and Dec.
Final notification: Within 1 month of committee meetings
Write: Carol B. Popelka, Prog. Dir.
Officers and Directors: Jack H. Glendenning, Chair.; Signe G. Schroeder, Secy.; David D. Baptie, Ruth M. Dalton, M.D., Roberta Gelatt, Lindon Saline.
Trustee: La Crosse Trust Company.
Number of staff: 1 part-time professional.
Employer Identification Number: 396037996

7489
Ladish Company Foundation ⌑
5481 South Packard Ave.
Cudahy 53110

Trust established in 1952 in WI.
Donor(s): Ladish Co.
Foundation type: Company-sponsored
Financial data (yr. ended 11/30/88): Assets, $9,742,976 (M); expenditures, $491,903, including $466,685 for 111 grants (high: $45,000; low: $100; average: $2,000-$5,000).
Purpose and activities: Giving for community funds, youth agencies, hospitals and medical research, and higher education, including scholarship funds.
Types of support: General purposes, research, scholarship funds, endowment funds, annual campaigns.
Limitations: Giving primarily in WI. No grants to individuals.
Application information: Contributes only to pre-selected organizations. Applications not accepted.
Write: Walter D. Aumann, Trustee
Trustees: Walter D. Aumann, Victor F. Braun, John H. Ladish, L. Dean Welch.
Employer Identification Number: 396040489

7490
Herman W. Ladish Family Foundation, Inc. ⌑
c/o Ladish Malting Co.
790 North Jackson St., 2nd Fl.
Milwaukee 53202 (414) 271-4763
Additional address: P.O. Box 2044, Milwaukee, WI 53201

Incorporated in 1956 in WI.
Donor(s): Herman W. Ladish.†
Foundation type: Independent
Financial data (yr. ended 6/30/89): Assets, $17,322,767 (M); expenditures, $931,847, including $899,500 for 46 grants (high: $100,000; low: $2,000).
Purpose and activities: Emphasis on higher and secondary education, hospitals and health agencies, youth organizations, and cultural programs.
Limitations: Giving primarily in WI.
Application information: Application form not required.
Deadline(s): None
Board meeting date(s): Twice a year
Write: John H. Ladish, Pres.
Officers: John H. Ladish,* Pres.; Victor F. Braun,* V.P.; Robert T. Stollenwerk, Secy.-Treas.
Directors:* Elwin J. Zarwell.
Number of staff: None.
Employer Identification Number: 396063602

7491
Ladish Malting Company Foundation, Inc. ⌑
790 North Jackson St.
Milwaukee 53202 (414) 271-4763

Incorporated in 1957 in WI.
Donor(s): Ladish Malting Co.
Foundation type: Company-sponsored
Financial data (yr. ended 06/30/89): Assets, $2,718,896 (M); expenditures, $133,426, including $118,750 for 11 grants (high: $30,000; low: $250).
Purpose and activities: Giving primarily to hospitals; grants also for youth and social service agencies, including a community fund.
Types of support: General purposes.
Limitations: Giving primarily in WI and ND.
Application information: Application form not required.
Initial approach: Letter
Deadline(s): None
Write: John H. Ladish, Pres.
Officers and Directors:* John H. Ladish,* Pres. and Treas.; Victor F. Braun,* V.P.; Robert T. Stollenwerk,* Secy.
Employer Identification Number: 396045284

7492
The Elmer Leach Foundation, Inc. ⌑
c/o First Wisconsin National Bank of Oshkosh
P.O. Box 2448
Oshkosh 54903

Established in 1965 in WI.
Donor(s): Leach Co.
Foundation type: Independent
Financial data (yr. ended 12/31/87): Assets, $1,384,575 (M); gifts received, $54,000; expenditures, $76,983, including $58,710 for grants.
Purpose and activities: Support primarily for private secondary education, nursing education and aid for children with medical needs.
Limitations: Giving primarily in Oshkosh, WI.
Application information: Application form not required.
Initial approach: Letter
Deadline(s): Jan. 1 through Nov. 1
Write: David C. Leach, Pres.
Officers: David C. Leach, Pres.; Mary L. Smith, 1st V.P.; Frederick E. Leach, 2nd V.P.; Phyllis L. Leach, Secy.; Allen D. Beuth, Treas.
Employer Identification Number: 396093521

7493
Lindsay Foundation, Inc.
31982 West Treasure Isle Dr.
Hartland 53029

Established in 1963.
Donor(s): Walter Lindsay.†
Foundation type: Independent
Financial data (yr. ended 12/31/88): Assets, $1,753,259 (M); expenditures, $107,543, including $86,000 for 18 grants (high: $6,000; low: $2,000; average: $5,000).
Purpose and activities: Support for hospitals and health, including mental health, and family and social services.
Types of support: Continuing support.
Limitations: Giving primarily in WI. No support for arts or education. No grants to individuals.
Application information:
Write: Lorna L. Mayer, Pres.
Officer: Lorna L. Mayer, Pres.
Number of staff: None.
Employer Identification Number: 396086904

7494
Camille A. Lonstorf Trust ⌑
c/o Foley & Lardner
777 East Wisconsin Ave.
Milwaukee 53202 (414) 289-3528

Established in 1985 in WI.
Donor(s): Marge Long.†
Foundation type: Independent
Financial data (yr. ended 12/31/87): Assets, $1,248,082 (M); expenditures, $94,254, including $76,000 for 10 grants (high: $10,000; low: $1,000).
Purpose and activities: Support for higher education, social service agencies, cultural programs, and a community fund.
Limitations: Giving primarily in Milwaukee, WI.
Application information:
Initial approach: In writing
Deadline(s): None
Write: Harrold J. McComas, Trustee
Trustee: Harrold J. McComas.
Employer Identification Number: 391509343

7495
The Lubar Family Foundation, Inc. ⌑
777 East Wisconsin Ave., Suite 3380
Milwaukee 53202

Established in 1968 in WI.
Donor(s): Members of the Lubar family.
Foundation type: Independent
Financial data (yr. ended 12/31/88): Assets, $660,218 (M); expenditures, $289,907, including $289,006 for 70 grants (high: $150,000; low: $20).
Purpose and activities: Grants for higher education, Jewish organizations, and culture.
Types of support: Endowment funds, capital campaigns.
Limitations: Giving primarily in WI. No grants to individuals.
Application information: Contributes only to pre-selected organizations. Applications not accepted.
Officers and Directors: Marianne S. Lubar,* Pres.; Sheldon B. Lubar,* V.P. and Secy.; James C. Rowe, Treas.; Kristine L. Thompson.
Employer Identification Number: 391098690

7496
Madison Community Foundation
(Formerly United Madison Community Foundation)
615 East Washington Ave.
Madison 53703 (608) 255-0503
Application address: P.O. Box 71, Madison, WI 53701

Established as a trust in 1979 in WI.
Foundation type: Community
Financial data (yr. ended 04/30/89): Assets, $4,357,938 (M); gifts received, $516,516; expenditures, $512,850, including $356,826 for 48 grants.
Purpose and activities: To address emerging needs of the community in the areas of health and human services, youth, arts and culture, education, and economic development.
Types of support: Operating budgets, emergency funds, matching funds, continuing support, technical assistance, special projects, conferences and seminars, consulting services, equipment.
Limitations: Giving limited to Dane County, WI. No support for religious purposes. No grants to individuals, or for annual campaigns, building or endowment funds, deficit financing, renovation projects, seed money, scholarships, or fellowships.
Publications: Annual report, application guidelines, informational brochure.
Application information: Application form not required.
Initial approach: Letter followed by proposal
Copies of proposal: 6
Deadline(s): Feb. 1 for letter of intent, Mar. 15 for proposal
Board meeting date(s): Quarterly
Final notification: May 1
Write: Jane Taylor Coleman, Exec. Dir.
Board of Governors: W. Robert Koch, Chair.; and 14 other members.
Number of staff: 4 full-time professional.
Employer Identification Number: 396038248

7497
Madison Gas and Electric Foundation, Inc. ⌑
P.O. Box 1231
Madison 53701

Established in 1966 in WI.
Donor(s): Madison Gas & Electric.
Foundation type: Company-sponsored
Financial data (yr. ended 12/31/87): Assets, $1,377,365 (M); gifts received, $83,500; expenditures, $137,923, including $120,160 for 45 grants (high: $47,490; low: $25).
Purpose and activities: Support for children of company employees in the form of scholarship awards to attend the University of Wisconsin-Madison; support also for charitable institutions located in and serving areas served by Madison Gas and Electric.
Types of support: Employee-related scholarships.
Limitations: Giving primarily in WI.
Application information: Application forms for scholarships are published in the company newsletter in Apr. or May each year.
Write: Dale W. St. John, Treas.
Officers and Directors: Donald J. Helfrecht, Chair.; Frank C. Vendrasek, Pres.; Kent M. Barlow, V.P.; David C. Mebane, V.P.; Beverly R. Duncan, Secy.; Dale W. St. John, Treas.
Employer Identification Number: 396098118

7498
Marcus Corporation Foundation, Inc.
212 West Wisconsin Ave.
Milwaukee 53203 (414) 272-6020

Established in 1961 in WI.
Donor(s): Marcus Corp.
Foundation type: Company-sponsored
Financial data (yr. ended 12/31/88): Assets, $168,413 (M); gifts received, $282,665; expenditures, $356,612, including $356,325 for 87 grants (high: $100,000; low: $100).
Purpose and activities: Grants for cultural programs, medical research, higher and secondary education, and social services. The foundation's areas of interest vary from year to year.
Types of support: Building funds, research.
Limitations: Giving only in areas of company operations. No grants to individuals.
Application information: Applications not accepted.
Write: Ben Marcus, Pres., or Stephen Marcus, Treas.
Officers and Directors:* Ben Marcus,* Pres.; Robin Irwin,* Secy.; Stephen Marcus,* Treas.; C.E. Stevens.
Employer Identification Number: 396046268

7499
Marshall & Ilsley Foundation, Inc. ▼ ⌑
(Formerly Marshall & Ilsley Bank Foundation, Inc.)
770 North Water St.
Milwaukee 53202 (414) 765-7835

Incorporated in 1958 in WI.
Donor(s): Marshall & Ilsley Bank.
Foundation type: Company-sponsored
Financial data (yr. ended 12/31/88): Assets, $3,231,098 (M); gifts received, $738,147; expenditures, $926,836, including $903,225 for 90 grants (high: $123,250; low: $100; average: $1,000-$21,500) and $14,000 for grants to individuals.
Purpose and activities: Emphasis on higher education, including employee-related scholarships, social services, the arts, hospitals, and youth agencies.
Types of support: Student aid.
Limitations: Giving primarily in WI.
Application information: Scholarships only for children of permanent, full-time employees of the Marshall & Ilsley Corp.
Initial approach: Letter
Deadline(s): None
Board meeting date(s): As necessary
Final notification: Varies
Write: Diane Sebion, Secy.
Officers and Directors:* John A. Puelicher,* Pres.; James B. Wigdale,* V.P.; Diane L. Sebion, Secy.; Wendell F. Bueche, Burleigh E. Jacobs, Jack F. Kellner, James O. Wright.
Number of staff: None.
Employer Identification Number: 396043185

7500
Faye McBeath Foundation ▼
1020 North Broadway
Milwaukee 53202 (414) 272-2626

Trust established in 1964 in WI.
Donor(s): Faye McBeath.†
Foundation type: Independent
Financial data (yr. ended 12/31/89): Assets, $13,599,825 (M); expenditures, $1,555,416, including $1,414,337 for 53 grants (high: $75,000; low: $15,000; average: $10,000-$40,000).
Purpose and activities: To benefit the people of WI by providing homes and care for elderly persons; promoting education in medical science and public health; providing medical, nursing, and hospital care for the sick and disabled; promoting the welfare of children; and promoting research in civics and government directed towards improvement in the efficiency of local government.
Types of support: Seed money, building funds, equipment, special projects, matching funds, renovation projects, capital campaigns, continuing support, technical assistance.
Limitations: Giving limited to WI, with emphasis on the greater Milwaukee area. No support for specific medical or scientific research projects. No grants to individuals, or for annual campaigns, endowment funds, scholarships, or fellowships; grants rarely for emergency funds; no loans.
Publications: Annual report, program policy statement, application guidelines.
Application information: Application form not required.
Initial approach: Letter
Copies of proposal: 1
Deadline(s): 1 month prior to board meetings
Board meeting date(s): At least bimonthly, beginning in Jan.
Final notification: 2 weeks after meetings
Write: Sarah M. Dean, Exec. Dir.
Officers: Charles A. Krause,* Chair.; Bonnie R. Weigell,* Vice-Chair.; William L. Randall,* Secy.; Sarah M. Dean, Exec. Dir.
Trustees:* Joan Hardy, Thomas J. McCollow, First Wisconsin Trust Co.
Number of staff: 1 part-time professional; 1 part-time support.
Employer Identification Number: 396074450

7501
Menasha Corporation Foundation ⌑
P.O. Box 367
Neenah 54956 (414) 751-1326

Established in 1953 in WI.
Donor(s): Menasha Corp.
Foundation type: Company-sponsored
Financial data (yr. ended 12/31/88): Assets, $678,223 (M); gifts received, $345,005; expenditures, $438,980, including $360,642 for 158 grants (high: $100,000; low: $100), $51,850 for 59 grants to individuals (high: $1,050; low: $600; average: $600-$900) and $22,589 for 77 employee matching gifts.
Purpose and activities: Grants primarily for health, welfare, cultural, and higher educational organizations in areas of company operations; giving also for employee-related scholarships and an employee matching gift program.
Types of support: Employee matching gifts, employee-related scholarships.
Limitations: Giving primarily in areas of company operations.
Application information:
Initial approach: Proposal
Deadline(s): None
Write: Oliver C. Smith, Pres.
Officers: Oliver C. Smith, Pres.; D.C. Shepard, V.P.; Steven S. Kromholz, Secy.-Treas.
Employer Identification Number: 396047384

7502
Merkel Foundation, Inc. ⌑ ☆
1714 Cambridge Ave.
Sheboygan 53081

Established in 1986 in WI.
Donor(s): Daniel A. Merkel, Betty Merkel, American Orthodontics Corp.
Foundation type: Independent
Financial data (yr. ended 07/31/89): Assets, $160,260; gifts received, $151,500; expenditures, $131,424, including $131,300 for 30 grants (high: $67,300; low: $500).
Purpose and activities: Support primarily for Catholic services and organizations, social services and youth, and health associations.
Application information:
Initial approach: Letter
Deadline(s): None
Write: Daniel A. Merkel, Secy.
Officers and Directors: Betty Merkel, Pres.; Daniel A. Merkel, Secy.; Alvin R. Kloet.
Employer Identification Number: 391582624

7503
Midwest Charitable Trust Number 7 ⌑ ☆
404 West Ravine Baye Rd.
Bayside 53217

Established in 1988 in WI.
Donor(s): Peter A. Fischer.
Foundation type: Independent
Financial data (yr. ended 06/30/89): Assets, $109,670 (M); gifts received, $500,100; expenditures, $395,084, including $394,750 for 14 grants (high: $150,000; low: $750).
Purpose and activities: Giving primarily for Christian organizations, including athletic associations, youth groups, and churches; support also for secondary education and a theater.
Limitations: Giving primarily in WI. No grants to individuals.
Application information: Contributes only to pre-selected organizations. Applications not accepted.
Trustees: Doris L. Fischer, Peter A. Fischer.
Employer Identification Number: 391623861

7504
Mielke Family Foundation, Inc.
P.O. Box 2575
Appleton 54913 (414) 734-3416
Application address: Ten Sunnyslope Ct., Appleton, WI, 54911

Established in 1963 in WI.
Foundation type: Independent
Financial data (yr. ended 12/31/89): Assets, $4,787,000 (M); expenditures, $205,351, including $195,105 for 29 grants (high: $75,000; low: $65; average: $65-$3,000).
Purpose and activities: Support primarily for education, the arts, and health programs.
Limitations: Giving limited to the Appleton and Shawano, WI, areas.
Application information: Application form required.
Initial approach: Letter
Copies of proposal: 4
Deadline(s): Apr. 15 and Oct. 15
Board meeting date(s): May and Nov.
Final notification: Distributions normally made in Dec.
Write: Paul Groth, Dir.
Officers and Directors:* Jeffrey Riester,* Pres.; Philip Keller,* V.P.; Warren Parsons,* Secy.-Treas.; Harold C. Adams, Paul H. Groth, John E. Mielke, Marion Nemetz.
Number of staff: None.
Employer Identification Number: 396074258

7505
The Steve J. Miller Foundation ⌑
15 North Central Ave.
Marshfield 54449

Trust established about 1946 in WI.
Donor(s): Central Cheese Co., Inc., Steve J. Miller.†
Foundation type: Independent
Financial data (yr. ended 12/31/88): Assets, $3,002,837 (M); expenditures, $257,739, including $235,350 for 41 grants (high: $27,100; low: $200).
Purpose and activities: Grants largely for higher education, health agencies, community development, and cultural programs.
Limitations: Giving primarily in WI and Tucson, AZ.
Application information:
Initial approach: Letter
Deadline(s): None
Write: Harvey D. TeStrake, Secy.
Officers: Elizabeth Black Miller, Chair.; Norman C. Miller, Pres.; Isabell E. Black, V.P.; Harvey D. TeStrake, Secy. and Mgr.; William T. Gaus, Treas.
Employer Identification Number: 396051879

7506
Milwaukee Foundation ▼
1020 North Broadway
Milwaukee 53202 (414) 272-5805

Established in 1915 in WI by declaration of trust.
Foundation type: Community
Financial data (yr. ended 12/31/89): Assets, $83,018,628 (M); gifts received, $3,575,248; expenditures, $4,956,735, including $4,004,551 for 429 grants (high: $175,000; low: $100).
Purpose and activities: Present funds include many discretionary and some funds designated by the donors to benefit specific institutions or for special purposes, including educational institutions, the arts and cultural programs, social services, health care and hospitals; support also for community development, and conservation and historic preservation.

Types of support: Seed money, building funds, equipment, matching funds, scholarship funds, special projects, renovation projects.
Limitations: Giving primarily in the Milwaukee, WI, area. No support for the general use of churches or for sectarian religious purposes, or for specific medical or scientific projects except from components of the foundation established for such purposes. No grants to individuals (except for established awards), or for operating budgets, continuing support, annual campaigns, endowment funds, or deficit financing.
Publications: Annual report, informational brochure (including application guidelines), grants list, newsletter, program policy statement.
Application information: Capital requests such as construction and renovation for hospitals and health-related agencies are reviewed at June and Dec. board meetings. Application form required.
Initial approach: Proposal, telephone, or letter
Copies of proposal: 1
Deadline(s): Submit proposal preferably 10 weeks before board meetings; deadlines Jan. 2, Mar. 1, June 18, Sept. 17, and Dec. 17
Board meeting date(s): Mar., June, Sept., Dec., and as needed
Final notification: 2 weeks after board meetings
Write: David M.G. Huntington, Exec. Dir.
Officer: David M.G. Huntington, Secy. and Exec. Dir.
Foundation Board: Gwen T. Jackson, Chair.; Orren J. Bradley, Vice-Chair.; Doris H. Chortek, Harry F. Franke, Richard A. Gallun, Charles N. McNeer, Charles W. Parker, Jr., Dennis Purtell, Brenton H. Rupple, Polly H. Van Dyke.
Trustees: Bank One Wisconsin Trust Co., N.A., First Bank Milwaukee, First Wisconsin Trust Co., Marshall & Ilsley Trust Co.
Number of staff: 4 full-time professional; 1 part-time professional; 4 full-time support; 1 part-time support.
Employer Identification Number: 396036407

7507
Rose Monaghan Charitable Trust ⌑
c/o Walter Schmidt
2401 North Mayfair Rd.
Milwaukee 53226

Established in 1980 in WI.
Donor(s): Rose Monaghan.†
Foundation type: Independent
Financial data (yr. ended 6/30/89): Assets, $2,105,085 (M); expenditures, $117,350, including $97,000 for 17 grants (high: $25,000; low: $1,000).
Purpose and activities: Grants primarily for Catholic giving, including Catholic welfare and religious and secondary education.
Types of support: General purposes.
Limitations: Giving primarily in Milwaukee, WI. No grants to individuals.
Application information: Contributes only to pre-selected organizations. Applications not accepted.
Trustees: Joseph P. Callan, Walter F. Schmidt.
Employer Identification Number: 391363036

7508
National Institute of Biogerontology
4610 University Ave.
P.O. Box 55231
Madison 53705

Established in 1985 in WI.
Foundation type: Independent
Financial data (yr. ended 06/30/89): Assets, $611,457 (M); gifts received, $490,160; expenditures, $455,455, including $440,326 for grants.
Purpose and activities: Support limited to research on aging and disuse atrophy with emphasis on atrophy and osteoporosis.
Types of support: Grants to individuals, lectureships, research, seed money.
Limitations: Giving primarily in WI.
Application information:
Initial approach: Proposal
Deadline(s): None
Write: Dr. Everett L. Smith, Pres.
Officers and Directors:* Everett L. Smith,* Pres.; Robert O. Ray,* V.P.; Patricia Smith,* Secy.-Treas.; Vernon Dodson, William G. Reddan, Ronald T. Smith.
Number of staff: None.
Employer Identification Number: 391484704

7509
Neenah Foundry Foundation, Inc.
2121 Brooks Ave.
Neenah 54956 (414) 725-7000

Incorporated in 1953 in WI.
Donor(s): Neenah Foundry Co.
Foundation type: Company-sponsored
Financial data (yr. ended 12/31/89): Assets, $4,129,097 (M); expenditures, $227,649, including $219,275 for 54 grants (high: $31,200; low: $50).
Purpose and activities: Support for higher and secondary education, youth agencies, health agencies, and social services.
Types of support: Program-related investments.
Limitations: Giving primarily in WI. No grants to individuals.
Application information: Grants generally made only to pre-selected organizations. Applications not accepted.
Write: Thomas R. Franklin, Secy.-Treas.
Officers: E.W. Aylward, Sr., Pres.; E.W. Aylward, Jr., V.P.; T.R. Franklin, Secy.-Treas.
Employer Identification Number: 396042143

7510
Northwestern National Insurance Foundation ⌑
(Formerly ARMCO Insurance Group Foundation)
18650 West Corporate Dr.
Brookfield 53005

Established in 1967 in WI.
Donor(s): Armco Insurance Group, Inc.
Foundation type: Company-sponsored
Financial data (yr. ended 12/31/87): Assets, $1,694,545 (M); expenditures, $147,573, including $139,851 for 69 grants (high: $65,000; low: $50).
Purpose and activities: Emphasis on community funds, higher education, including employee matching gifts, cultural programs, and hospitals.
Types of support: Employee matching gifts.
Limitations: Giving primarily in areas of company operations.
Application information: Application form not required.
Deadline(s): None
Final notification: Within 6 months
Write: Robert C. Whitaker, V.P. and Secy.
Officers and Trustees: C. Robert Snyder, Chair.; Robert C. Whitaker, V.P. and Secy.; Howard Miller, Treas.
Number of staff: None.
Employer Identification Number: 396102416

7511
Oshkosh B'Gosh Foundation, Inc. ⌑
P.O. Box 300
Oshkosh 54902 (414) 231-8800

Established in 1985 in WI.
Donor(s): Oshkosh B'Gosh, Inc.
Foundation type: Company-sponsored
Financial data (yr. ended 12/31/88): Assets, $163,265 (M); expenditures, $290,520, including $209,950 for 48 grants (high: $39,000; low: $100) and $80,000 for 64 grants to individuals of $1,250 each.
Purpose and activities: Support for children and youth; scholarships for high school graduates in areas of company operations.
Types of support: Employee-related scholarships.
Limitations: Giving primarily in WI.
Application information: Application form required for scholarships.
Deadline(s): Schaolarship deadlines are established by each participating school; no set deadline for grants
Write: William P. Jacobsen, Treas.
Officers and Directors:* Thomas R. Wyman,* Pres.; Michael A. Wachtel,* Secy.; William P. Jacobsen,* Treas.
Employer Identification Number: 391525020

7512
Oshkosh Foundation ⌑
c/o First Wisconsin National Bank of Oshkosh
P.O. Box 2448
Oshkosh 54903 (414) 424-4283

Established in 1928 in WI by declaration of trust.
Donor(s): Combs Trust.
Foundation type: Community
Financial data (yr. ended 2/29/88): Assets, $5,732,860 (M); gifts received, $41,615; expenditures, $400,532, including $174,683 for 18 grants (high: $121,250; low: $43) and $141,608 for 224 grants to individuals (high: $4,809; low: $125).
Purpose and activities: Emphasis on scholarships, hospitals, medical care of the indigent, community funds, and cultural programs. Scholarships awarded for graduating Oshkosh high school seniors for a 4-year term only.
Types of support: Continuing support, annual campaigns, emergency funds, building funds, equipment, student aid, operating budgets, grants to individuals.
Limitations: Giving limited to Oshkosh, WI. No grants for endowments, matching gifts, seed

money, deficit financing, special projects, research, publications, or conferences; no loans.
Publications: Annual report, application guidelines.
Application information: Applications not accepted unless residency requirements are met. Application form not required.
Initial approach: Proposal
Copies of proposal: 1
Deadline(s): Submit proposal preferably in Apr.; no set deadline
Board meeting date(s): Usually in Apr. and as required
Final notification: 6 weeks
Write: Sandra A. Noe, Trust Officer
Officers and Foundation Committee: Marie Hoyer, Pres.; Edith Collins, V.P.; Virginia Nelson, Secy.; Hibbard H. Engler, Fred Leist, Edward Leyhe, Lewis C. Magnusen.
Trustee: First Wisconsin National Bank of Oshkosh.
Number of staff: 1 full-time professional; 1 full-time support.
Employer Identification Number: 396041638

7513
Oshkosh Truck Foundation, Inc. ⌑
2307 Oregon St.
P.O. Box 2566
Oshkosh 54903 (414) 235-9150

Incorporated in 1960 in WI.
Donor(s): Oshkosh Truck Corp.
Foundation type: Company-sponsored
Financial data (yr. ended 12/31/88): Assets, $417,635 (M); gifts received, $250,000; expenditures, $180,410, including $169,060 for 66 grants (high: $35,000; low: $10; average: $2,800) and $11,250 for 17 grants to individuals (high: $750; low: $60; average: $750).
Purpose and activities: Giving for youth agencies and higher and secondary education; support also for a hospital and a community fund. Scholarships to children of company employees who attend local high schools.
Types of support: Operating budgets, continuing support, annual campaigns, emergency funds, building funds, equipment, employee-related scholarships.
Limitations: Giving primarily in Winnebago County, WI. No grants for seed money, deficit financing, land acquisition, special projects, research, publications, conferences, general endowments, or matching gifts; no loans.
Publications: Application guidelines.
Application information: Application guidelines for scholarships for children of company employees only. Application form not required.
Initial approach: Letter
Deadline(s): Submit proposals in Feb.; no set deadline
Board meeting date(s): Mar., June, Sept., and Dec.
Final notification: 1 to 3 months
Write: J. Peter Mosling, Jr., Pres.
Officers: J. Peter Mosling, Jr., Pres.; T.M. Dempsey, V.P.; Barbara E. Boycks, Secy.; C.J. Hulsebosck, Treas.
Number of staff: None.
Employer Identification Number: 396062129

7514
Outagamie Charitable Foundation, Inc. ⌑ ☆
600 South Vulcan St.
Appleton 54912

Established in 1985.
Foundation type: Independent
Financial data (yr. ended 3/31/88): Assets, $1,841,890 (M); gifts received, $207,433; expenditures, $50,506, including $47,200 for 8 grants (high: $7,500; low: $3,000).
Purpose and activities: Giving primarily for arts and culture, including museums; support also for a library, youth, and cancer research.
Limitations: Giving primarily in NY, CT, and WI.
Application information: Applications not accepted.
Officers and Directors:* Joan Vitalis,* Pres.; Linda Jacob,* V.P.; Dwight Olver, Treas.; Barbara Aalfs, Charles Buchanan, Carolyn Fey, Josephine Lenfestey.
Employer Identification Number: 391526589

7515
Parker Foundation
c/o Valley Trust Co.
P.O. Box 5000
Janesville 53547 (608) 755-4249
Application address: 20 East Milwaukee, Suite 300, Janesville, WI 53545; Tel.: (608) 754-4700

Established in 1953 in WI.
Foundation type: Independent
Financial data (yr. ended 12/31/88): Assets, $1,517,940 (M); expenditures, $93,732, including $76,000 for 32 grants (high: $15,000; low: $500).
Purpose and activities: Giving primarily for higher education; support also for cultural programs and international affairs.
Types of support: General purposes, building funds.
Application information: Application form not required.
Initial approach: Letter
Deadline(s): None
Write: Robert E. Collins, V.P.
Officers and Directors:* Daniel Parker,* Pres.; Robert E. Collins,* V.P. and Secy.-Treas.; Peter C. Jacobs.
Number of staff: None.
Employer Identification Number: 396074582

7516
R. D. and Linda Peters Foundation, Inc. ⌑
c/o Bank One Wisconsin Trust Co., N.A.
P.O. Box 1308
Milwaukee 53201 (414) 765-2800

Established in 1965.
Donor(s): R.D. Peters.†
Foundation type: Independent
Financial data (yr. ended 12/31/88): Assets, $3,003,736 (M); expenditures, $538,044, including $481,000 for 15 grants (high: $200,000; low: $5,000).
Purpose and activities: Emphasis on higher and medical education, conservation, Protestant church support, metallurgical research, and youth activities.
Types of support: Equipment, research, general purposes.
Limitations: Giving primarily in the Brillion, WI, area.
Application information:
Initial approach: Proposal
Deadline(s): None
Board meeting date(s): Quarterly
Write: Edmond C. Young, Director
Directors: John S. Best, John P. Bosch, Harold Wolf.
Trustee: Bank One Wisconsin Trust Co., N.A.
Employer Identification Number: 396097994

7517
Fred J. Peterson Foundation, Inc.
101 Pennsylvania St.
Sturgeon Bay 54235 (414) 743-5574

Incorporated in 1962 in WI.
Donor(s): Peterson Builders, Inc., Fred J. Peterson, Irene Peterson,† Ellsworth L. Peterson.
Foundation type: Independent
Financial data (yr. ended 09/30/89): Assets, $2,912,637 (M); gifts received, $37,969; expenditures, $214,134, including $208,640 for 62 grants (high: $100,000; low: $50; average: $100-$5,000).
Purpose and activities: Giving to organizations working to improve the quality of life for WI citizens; grants for higher education, including scholarships through Rotary International, and various colleges, cultural programs, youth, and community development.
Types of support: Annual campaigns, building funds, capital campaigns, continuing support, equipment, general purposes, operating budgets, special projects.
Limitations: Giving primarily in Door County, WI. No grants to individuals.
Application information: All scholarship decisions made by Rotary International or individual colleges. Application form not required.
Initial approach: Letter only
Copies of proposal: 1
Deadline(s): Sept. 1
Board meeting date(s): As needed
Final notification: Sept. 10
Write: Marsha L. Kerley, Secy.-Treas.
Officers and Directors:* Ellsworth L. Peterson,* Pres.; Fred J. Peterson II,* V.P.; Marsha L. Kerley,* Secy.-Treas.; Fred J. Peterson.
Number of staff: 1
Employer Identification Number: 396075901

7518
Jane and Lloyd Pettit Foundation, Inc. ⌑ ☆
660 East Mason St.
Milwaukee 53202

Incorporated in 1986 in WI.
Donor(s): Jane Bradley Pettit, Lloyd H. Pettit.
Foundation type: Independent
Financial data (yr. ended 6/30/88): Assets, $1,505,041 (M); gifts received, $2,051,004; expenditures, $2,039,553, including $1,868,448 for 158 grants (high: $321,483; low: $40).
Purpose and activities: Giving for secondary and higher education, social services, including

a community fund, recreation, and health and hospitals.
Limitations: Giving primarily in Milwaukee, WI. No grants to individuals.
Application information: Contributes only to pre-selected organizations. Applications not accepted.
Officers and Directors:* Jane Bradley Pettit, Pres. and Treas.; Lloyd H. Pettit,* V.P.; Joseph E. Tierney, Jr.,* Secy.
Employer Identification Number: 391574123

7519
L. L. Phillips Charities, Inc. ⌑ ☆
P.O. Box 202
Eau Claire 54702-0202 (715) 832-3431

Established in 1956.
Foundation type: Independent
Financial data (yr. ended 7/31/89): Assets, $1,056,177 (M); expenditures, $109,431, including $82,726 for 14 grants (high: $27,500; low: $15).
Purpose and activities: Giving primarily for higher education; support also for hospitals and health associations and Jewish organizations.
Limitations: Giving primarily in WI. No grants to individuals.
Application information: Application form not required.
Deadline(s): None
Write: L. L. Phillips, Pres.
Officers and Directors: L.L. Phillips, Pres. and Mgr.; Arlene F. Phillips, V.P.; John F. Wilcox, Secy.; Jan Hasart, Treas.; Lisa Erickson, Mark Phillips.
Employer Identification Number: 396086011

7520
The L. E. Phillips Family Foundation, Inc. ▼
3925 North Hastings Way
Eau Claire 54703 (715) 839-2139
Additional address: P.O. Box 2105, Wilmington, DE 19899

Incorporated in 1943 in WI.
Donor(s): Members of the Phillips family and a family-related company.
Foundation type: Independent
Financial data (yr. ended 2/28/87): Assets, $34,024,682 (M); gifts received, $127,201; expenditures, $1,626,297, including $1,468,996 for 59 grants (high: $1,232,585; low: $10; average: $100-$10,000).
Purpose and activities: Support primarily for a Jewish welfare fund; giving also for higher education.
Types of support: Operating budgets, research, scholarship funds, building funds, endowment funds, special projects.
Limitations: Giving primarily in WI. No grants to individuals.
Application information: Application form not required.
Deadline(s): None; prefers to receive proposals before end of fiscal year
Board meeting date(s): As required
Final notification: 1 month
Write: Allan D. Hanson, Asst. Secy.
Officers and Directors: Melvin S. Cohen, Pres.; Maryjo R. Cohen, V.P.; Edith Phillips, V.P.; Arthur E. Petzold, Secy.-Treas.; Eileen Phillips Cohen.
Number of staff: 1 full-time professional; 2 part-time support.
Employer Identification Number: 396046126

7521
Melitta S. Pick Charitable Trust ⌑
c/o Foley and Lardner
777 East Wisconsin Ave., Suite 3800
Milwaukee 53202 (414) 289-3528

Trust established in 1972 in WI.
Donor(s): Melitta S. Pick.†
Foundation type: Independent
Financial data (yr. ended 1/31/87): Assets, $12,884,869 (M); expenditures, $596,168, including $518,000 for 49 grants (high: $80,000; low: $1,000).
Purpose and activities: Giving primarily to charities of interest to the trustees, with emphasis on the arts, youth agencies, and a community development fund.
Limitations: Giving primarily in southeastern WI. No grants to individuals.
Application information: The foundation's present plans preclude extensive consideration of unsolicited requests.
Initial approach: Letter
Deadline(s): None
Board meeting date(s): As required, usually quarterly
Write: Harrold J. McComas, Trustee
Trustees: Harrold J. McComas, Joan M. Pick.
Employer Identification Number: 237243490

7522
Pollybill Foundation, Inc. ⌑
735 North Water St., Suite 1328
Milwaukee 53202 (414) 273-4390

Incorporated in 1960 in WI.
Donor(s): William D. Van Dyke, Polly H. Van Dyke.
Foundation type: Independent
Financial data (yr. ended 12/31/87): Assets, $799,089 (M); gifts received, $421,300; expenditures, $417,963, including $400,000 for 30 grants (high: $100,000; low: $500).
Purpose and activities: Emphasis on private secondary education, higher education, the arts, conservation, health, and social services.
Limitations: Giving primarily in WI, especially Milwaukee.
Application information:
Deadline(s): None
Write: Paul F. Meissner, Dir.
Officers and Directors: Polly H. Van Dyke, Pres. and Treas.; William D. Van Dyke III, Secy.; Leonard G. Campbell, Jr., Paul F. Meissner.
Employer Identification Number: 396078550

7523
Racine County Area Foundation, Inc.
818 Sixth St.
Racine 53403 (414) 632-8474

Incorporated in 1975 in WI.
Foundation type: Community
Financial data (yr. ended 12/31/88): Assets, $2,141,656 (M); gifts received, $98,985; expenditures, $187,503, including $118,347 for 57 grants (high: $30,000; low: $50) and $6,456 for 18 grants to individuals (average: $500).
Purpose and activities: Giving primarily for health, community services and affairs, cultural activities, and education, including scholarships for individuals.
Types of support: Seed money, emergency funds, equipment, matching funds, student aid, conferences and seminars, operating budgets.
Limitations: Giving limited to Racine County, WI. No support for church or missionary groups unless for entire community benefit. No grants for capital expenditures, including building funds, endowment funds, research, travel, publications; no continuing support after three years.
Publications: Annual report, application guidelines.
Application information: Application form required.
Initial approach: Phone or letter
Copies of proposal: 10
Deadline(s): Jan. 15, Apr. 15, July 15, and Oct. 15
Board meeting date(s): Mar., June, Sept., and Dec.
Final notification: By letter after meeting in which proposal was discussed
Write: Marge Kozina, Exec. Secy.
Officers: Lloyd C. Meier, Pres.; Harry Mussie, V.P. and Treas.; Glenn R. Coates, V.P.; Deanna Parrish, V.P.; Roy J. Josten, Secy.
Number of staff: 1 part-time professional; 1 full-time support; 1 part-time support.
Employer Identification Number: 510188377

7524
Rahr Foundation
P.O. Box 130
Manitowoc 54221-0130 (414) 682-6571

Incorporated in 1942 in WI.
Donor(s): Rahr Malting Co.
Foundation type: Company-sponsored
Financial data (yr. ended 12/31/89): Assets, $2,686,841 (M); expenditures, $208,994, including $167,774 for 83 grants (high: $12,000; low: $40; average: $1,000) and $33,500 for 18 grants to individuals.
Purpose and activities: Support for charitable and educational institutions and public welfare, higher and secondary education, youth agencies, social services, cultural programs, and a scholarship program for children of company employees.
Types of support: Employee-related scholarships, annual campaigns, capital campaigns.
Limitations: Giving primarily in MN. No grants for endowment funds or research programs; no loans.
Application information: Application form not required.
Initial approach: Letter
Copies of proposal: 1
Deadline(s): None
Board meeting date(s): Annually
Write: JoAnn Weyenberg
Officers: Guido R. Rahr, Jr., Pres.; Frederick W. Rahr, V.P.; George D. Gackle, Secy.-Treas.

Directors: Jack D. Gage, Mary Gresham, Elizabeth B. Rahr.
Number of staff: None.
Employer Identification Number: 396046046

7525
The Oscar Rennebohm Foundation, Inc. ⌑
6333 Odana Rd.
P.O. Box 5187
Madison 53705 (608) 271-0297

Incorporated in 1949 in WI.
Donor(s): Oscar Rennebohm.†
Foundation type: Independent
Financial data (yr. ended 12/31/87): Assets, $19,614,943 (M); expenditures, $975,543, including $789,350 for 14 grants (high: $506,750; low: $1,000; average: $12,500-$120,000).
Purpose and activities: Emphasis on higher education; support also for social service agencies.
Limitations: Giving primarily in WI.
Application information: Application form not required.
Deadline(s): None
Write: John L. Sonderegger, Secy.
Officers and Directors: Steven Skolaski, Pres. and Treas.; Mary F. Rennebohm, V.P.; John L. Sonderegger, Secy.; Leona A. Sonderegger, William H. Young, Lenor Zeeh.
Employer Identification Number: 396039252

7526
Rexnord Foundation Inc. ▼
P.O. Box 2022
Milwaukee 53201-2022 (414) 384-3000

Incorporated in 1953 in WI.
Donor(s): Rexnord, Inc.
Foundation type: Company-sponsored
Financial data (yr. ended 10/31/89): Assets, $2,833,240 (M); expenditures, $511,355, including $427,000 for grants and $84,299 for employee matching gifts.
Purpose and activities: Grants primarily for community funds, higher education (including an employee matching gift program), hospitals, cultural programs, and youth agencies.
Types of support: Building funds, special projects, employee-related scholarships, employee matching gifts.
Limitations: Giving primarily in areas of company operations, with some emphasis on Milwaukee, WI. No support for political or religious organizations. No grants to individuals (except for employee-related scholarships), or for endowment funds.
Publications: Application guidelines.
Application information: Application form not required.
Initial approach: Letter or proposal
Copies of proposal: 1
Deadline(s): Submit grant proposals preferably in Feb.-Mar. or June-July; deadline mid-May for scholarship applications only
Board meeting date(s): 2 or 3 times a year
Final notification: 6 months
Write: Alice Lorenz, Foundation Admin.; Barb Alcorn for employee-related scholarships

Officers: Donald Taylor,* Pres.; John P. Calhoun,* V.P.; Charles R. Roy, Secy.; W.E. Schauer, Jr.,* Treas.
Directors:* F. Brengel, R.V. Krikorian, William C. Messinger, Gustave H. Moede, Jr., J. Swenson.
Number of staff: None.
Employer Identification Number: 396042029

7527
Hamilton Roddis Foundation, Inc. ⌑
c/o Augusta D. Roddis
1108 East Fourth St.
Marshfield 54449

Incorporated in 1953 in WI.
Donor(s): Hamilton Roddis,† Augusta D. Roddis, Catherine P. Roddis, Roddis Plywood Corp.
Foundation type: Independent
Financial data (yr. ended 12/31/87): Assets, $3,087,094 (M); expenditures, $166,864, including $143,100 for 47 grants (high: $17,500; low: $100).
Purpose and activities: Emphasis on Episcopal church support and religious education, social services, medical research, educational organizations, historic preservation, and local associations.
Limitations: No grants to individuals.
Application information: Grants only to pre-selected organizations. Applications not accepted.
Officers and Directors: William H. Roddis II, Pres.; Mrs. Gordon R. Connor, V.P.; Augusta D. Roddis, Secy.-Treas.
Employer Identification Number: 396077001

7528
Roehl Foundation, Inc. ⌑ ☆
P.O. Box 168
Oconomowoc 53066-0168 (414) 569-3000

Established in 1959.
Donor(s): Peter G. Roehl.
Foundation type: Independent
Financial data (yr. ended 6/30/89): Assets, $2,139,822 (M); gifts received, $9,452; expenditures, $112,647, including $100,376 for 43 grants (high: $8,000; low: $50).
Purpose and activities: Giving for Lutheran churches and welfare organizations; support also for higher and secondary education, hospitals, and medical research.
Limitations: Giving primarily in WI. No grants to individuals.
Application information:
Initial approach: Proposal
Deadline(s): None
Write: Peter Roehl, V.P.
Officers: Ora C. Roehl, Pres.; Peter G. Roehl, V.P. and Treas.; Nathalia E. Christian, Secy.
Director: Janet L. Roehl.
Employer Identification Number: 396048089

7529
Robert T. Rolfs Foundation, Inc. ⌑
735 South Main St.
West Bend 53095 (414) 338-6601

Established in 1981 in WI.
Foundation type: Independent
Financial data (yr. ended 9/30/88): Assets, $2,421,891 (M); gifts received, $475,000; expenditures, $98,441, including $80,900 for 16 grants (high: $20,000; low: $1,000) and $10,250 for 5 grants to individuals (high: $2,500; low: $1,250).
Purpose and activities: Support primarily for social services and education.
Types of support: Student aid.
Limitations: Giving primarily in IN and WI.
Application information: Application form not required.
Initial approach: Letter
Deadline(s): None
Write: Arthur P. Hoberg, V.P.
Officers: Robert T. Rolfs, Pres.; Arthur P. Hoberg, V.P.; John F. Rozek, Secy.-Treas.
Employer Identification Number: 391390015

7530
Thomas J. Rolfs Foundation, Inc. ⌑
735 South Main St.
West Bend 53095 (414) 338-6601

Established in 1959 in WI.
Donor(s): Amity Leather Products Co.
Foundation type: Independent
Financial data (yr. ended 9/30/88): Assets, $2,311,179 (M); gifts received, $475,000; expenditures, $93,411, including $75,000 for 23 grants (high: $15,000; low: $100) and $10,250 for 5 grants to individuals (high: $2,500; low: $1,250).
Purpose and activities: Support primarily for social services, education, and the performing arts.
Types of support: Student aid.
Limitations: Giving primarily in WI.
Application information:
Initial approach: Letter
Deadline(s): None
Write: Arthur P. Hoberg, V.P.
Officers: Thomas J. Rolfs, Pres.; Arthur P. Hoberg, V.P.; John F. Rozek, Secy.-Treas.
Employer Identification Number: 396043350

7531
Will Ross Memorial Foundation
c/o Bank One Wisconsin Trust Co., N.A.
P.O. Box 1308
Milwaukee 53201 (414) 765-2842

Foundation type: Independent
Financial data (yr. ended 12/31/89): Assets, $3,166,550 (M); gifts received, $589,908; expenditures, $420,069, including $388,200 for 38 grants (high: $75,000; low: $200).
Purpose and activities: Support primarily for the arts, social services, higher education, and health.
Limitations: Giving primarily in Milwaukee, WI.
Application information: Application form not required.
Initial approach: Letter
Deadline(s): None
Write: Mary Ann LaBahn, Treas.
Officers and Directors: Edmond C. Young, Pres.; John D. Bryson, Jr., V.P.; Richard R. Teschner, V.P.; David L. Kinnamon, Secy.; Mary Ann LaBahn, Treas.
Employer Identification Number: 396044673

7532
Philip Rubenstein Foundation, Inc. ⌑
160 South Second St.
Milwaukee 53204 (414) 272-2380

Established in 1978 in WI.
Donor(s): Philip Rubenstein.
Foundation type: Independent
Financial data (yr. ended 1/31/87): Assets, $2,625,574 (M); gifts received, $1,300,000; expenditures, $263,715, including $262,192 for 13 grants (high: $223,867; low: $25).
Purpose and activities: Support primarily for Jewish giving and Jewish welfare.
Application information: Application form not required.
Initial approach: Letter
Deadline(s): None
Write: Philip Rubenstein, Pres.
Officers and Directors Philip Rubenstein, Pres. and Treas.; Herbert Rubenstein, V.P.; Marvin E. Klitsner, Secy.
Employer Identification Number: 930757026

7533
Edward Rutledge Charity
404 North Bridge St.
Chippewa Falls 54729 (715) 723-6618
Mailing address: P.O. Box 758, Chippewa Falls, WI 54729

Incorporated in 1911 in WI.
Donor(s): Edward Rutledge.†
Foundation type: Independent
Financial data (yr. ended 5/31/89): Assets, $2,737,366 (M); expenditures, $139,136, including $19,415 for 23 grants (high: $6,000; low: $100; average: $100-$6,000) and $69,994 for 267 grants to individuals (high: $1,038; low: $10).
Purpose and activities: To furnish relief and charity for worthy poor and to aid charitable associations or institutions; grants for scholarships, youth agencies, the disadvantaged, a community fund, and a council on alcoholism.
Types of support: Grants to individuals, student aid, special projects, operating budgets, student loans.
Limitations: Giving limited to Chippewa County, WI. No grants for endowment funds.
Application information: Application form required for scholarships and other grants to individuals.
Initial approach: Telephone
Copies of proposal: 1
Deadline(s): Scholarship applications must be submitted by July 1; no deadline for other grants
Board meeting date(s): Twice a week
Final notification: July for scholarships
Write: John Frampton, Pres.
Officers and Directors:* John Frampton,* Pres.; Richard H. Stafford,* V.P.; Gerald Naiberg, Secy.-Treas.
Number of staff: 1 full-time professional; 1 full-time support.
Employer Identification Number: 390806178

7534
Schoenleber Foundation, Inc. ⌑
740 North Plankinton Ave., Suite 510
Milwaukee 53203-2403 (414) 276-3400

Established in 1965 in WI.
Donor(s): Marie Schoenleber,† Louise Schoenleber.†
Foundation type: Independent
Financial data (yr. ended 12/31/87): Assets, $3,734,529 (M); gifts received, $2,976,795; expenditures, $51,350, including $32,045 for 6 grants (high: $10,000; low: $1,000).
Purpose and activities: Support in the following areas: Education - including scholastic institutions, the library systems, and museums and historical societies; Social Welfare - with emphasis on the underpriviledged and handicapped; and the Arts - including music, theatre, and visual arts.
Limitations: Giving primarily in the greater Milwaukee, WI, area.
Application information: Application form required.
Initial approach: Letter
Copies of proposal: 1
Write: Peter C. Haensel, Pres.
Officers and Directors: Peter C. Haensel, Pres.; Frank W. Bastian, Secy.; Walter Schorrak.
Employer Identification Number: 391049364

7535
Walter Schroeder Foundation, Inc. ▼ ⌑
770 North Water St., Trust Dept.
Milwaukee 53202 (414) 287-7177

Incorporated in 1963 in WI.
Donor(s): Walter Schroeder Trust.
Foundation type: Independent
Financial data (yr. ended 6/30/88): Assets, $8,820,464 (M); expenditures, $1,569,258, including $1,490,911 for 102 grants (high: $150,000; low: $100; average: $1,000-$50,000).
Purpose and activities: Support for higher education, hospitals, community welfare, and youth agencies.
Types of support: Annual campaigns, building funds.
Limitations: Giving primarily in Milwaukee County, WI.
Application information: Application form not required.
Initial approach: Letter
Deadline(s): None
Board meeting date(s): Feb., May, Aug., and Nov.
Final notification: Varies
Write: William T. Gaus, Admin.
Officers and Directors: John A. Puelicher, Pres.; William T. Gaus, V.P., Treas., and Admin.; Marjorie A. Vallier, Secy.; Robert M. Hoffer, Ruthmarie M. Lawrenz.
Number of staff: None.
Employer Identification Number: 396065789

7536
Douglas Seaman Family Foundation, Inc. ⌑
5205 North Ironwood Rd., Suite 101
Milwaukee 53217 (414) 354-2310

Established in 1962 in WI.
Donor(s): Douglas Seaman, Douglas Securities Corp.
Foundation type: Independent
Financial data (yr. ended 6/30/89): Assets, $1,256,320 (M); gifts received, $25,000; expenditures, $110,432, including $99,525 for 56 grants (high: $45,200; low: $25).
Purpose and activities: Giving primarily for secondary and higher education, social services, and a hospital.
Limitations: Giving primarily in Milwaukee, WI. No grants to individuals.
Application information: Contributes only to pre-selected organizations. Applications not accepted.
Officers and Directors: Douglas Seaman, Pres.; Eleanor R. Seaman, V.P.; Gerald L. Hestekin, V.P. and Treas.; Joseph B. Tyson, Jr., Secy.
Employer Identification Number: 396073933

7537
Segel Family Foundation, Inc. ⌑
4700 North 132nd St.
Butler 53007
Application address: P.O. Box 1357, Milwaukee, WI 53201; Tel.: (414) 781-2400

Established in 1955 in WI.
Donor(s): Wis-Pac Foods, Inc.
Foundation type: Independent
Financial data (yr. ended 11/30/88): Assets, $1,284,882 (M); gifts received, $75,000; expenditures, $126,304, including $118,275 for 44 grants (high: $35,000; low: $25).
Purpose and activities: Giving primarily to Jewish welfare and other organizations; support also for higher education and cultural programs, including museums.
Types of support: Annual campaigns, general purposes.
Limitations: Giving primarily in Milwaukee, WI.
Application information:
Deadline(s): None
Write: Justin N. Segel, Pres.
Officers: Justin N. Segel, Pres. and Treas.; Floyd A. Segel, V.P. and Secy.
Employer Identification Number: 396040274

7538
Sentry Foundation, Inc. ⌑
c/o Sentry Insurance
1800 North Point Dr.
Stevens Point 54481 (715) 346-7232

Incorporated in 1963 in WI.
Donor(s): The Sentry Corp.
Foundation type: Company-sponsored
Financial data (yr. ended 12/31/87): Assets, $233,235 (M); gifts received, $75,000; expenditures, $251,550, including $250,875 for 48 grants (high: $69,500; low: $50).
Purpose and activities: Emphasis on higher education, corporate social responsibilities, and a community fund.
Types of support: Employee matching gifts.
Limitations: Giving primarily in WI. No support for political or religious organizations.
Publications: Annual report.
Application information: Application form not required.
Copies of proposal: 1
Deadline(s): Feb. 1

Board meeting date(s): Feb. and July
Write: Lillian Hanson, Exec. Dir.
Officers: Alfred C. Noel,* Pres.; Lillian P. Hanson,* V.P. and Exec. Dir.; Emil Fleischauer, Jr.,* Secy.; David L. Stephenson, Treas.
Directors:* Larry C. Ballard, Bernard C. Hlavac, Vernon H. Holmes, Philip R. Marshall, Jane R. Staples.
Number of staff: 1 part-time professional; 1 part-time support.
Employer Identification Number: 391037370

7539
Robert G. Sharp Trust ⌑
133 South Monroe Ave.
P.O. Box 1053
Green Bay 54305

Established in 1963 in WI.
Donor(s): Robert G. Sharp.†
Foundation type: Operating
Financial data (yr. ended 8/31/88): Assets, $1,105,482 (M); expenditures, $99,829, including $68,300 for 69 grants to individuals (high: $1,000; low: $500).
Purpose and activities: A private operating foundation; support for scholarships to graduates of local high schools who attend a college or university designated by the trust.
Types of support: Student aid.
Limitations: Giving limited to residents of Oconto and Brown counties, WI.
Publications: Application guidelines.
Application information: Application form required.
Deadline(s): Early May
Write: Robert Hugh Flatley, Trustee
Trustee: Robert Hugh Flatley.
Employer Identification Number: 396084979

7540
S.F. Shattuck Charitable Trust ⌑ ☆
c/o Bank One Wisconsin Trust Co., N.A.
P.O. Box 1308
Milwaukee 53201
Application address: c/o Bank One Wisconsin Trust Co., N.A., Neenah, WI; Tel.: (414) 727-3281

Established in 1951.
Foundation type: Independent
Financial data (yr. ended 10/31/88): Assets, $1,783,047 (M); expenditures, $86,463, including $71,000 for 12 grants (high: $28,000; low: $1,500).
Purpose and activities: Support primarily for higher and secondary education and hospitals.
Application information: Applications not accepted.
Write: Joe McGrane
Trustee: Bank One Wisconsin Trust Co., N.A.
Employer Identification Number: 396048820

7541
Siebert Lutheran Foundation, Inc. ▼
2600 North Mayfair Rd., Suite 390
Wauwatosa 53226 (414) 257-2656

Incorporated in 1952 in WI.
Donor(s): A.F. Siebert,† Reginald L. Siebert,† Milwaukee Electric Tool Corp.
Foundation type: Independent
Financial data (yr. ended 12/31/89): Assets, $53,108,719 (M); expenditures, $2,206,628, including $2,110,855 for 266 grants (high: $300,000; low: $100; average: $2,500-$10,000).
Purpose and activities: Support limited to Lutheran churches and other Lutheran institutions, including colleges, schools, programs for the aged, and other religious welfare agencies.
Types of support: Operating budgets, seed money, emergency funds, building funds, equipment, special projects, conferences and seminars, matching funds, consulting services, renovation projects.
Limitations: Giving primarily in WI. No grants to individuals, or for endowment funds, scholarships, or fellowships; no loans.
Publications: Program policy statement, application guidelines.
Application information: Grantees are required to sign Grant Agreement Form. Application form not required.
Initial approach: Letter or telephone
Copies of proposal: 1
Deadline(s): Mar. 15, June 15, Sept. 15, and Dec. 15
Board meeting date(s): Jan., Apr., July, and Oct.
Final notification: 1 week after board meeting
Write: Jack S. Harris, Pres.
Officers and Directors:* Raymond J. Perry,* Chair.; Glenn W. Buzzard,* Vice-Chair.; Jack S. Harris, Pres.; Armour F. Swanson,* Secy.; John E. Koenitzer,* Treas.; Richard C. Barkow, Edward A. Grede, Frederick H. Groth, Jack R. Jaeger, Neil A. Turnbull.
Number of staff: 1 full-time professional; 1 full-time support.
Employer Identification Number: 396050046

7542
Theda Clark Smith Family Foundation, Inc. ⌑
c/o Associated First Neenah Bank
100 West Wisconsin Ave.
Neenah 54956 (414) 722-3321

Established in 1968 in WI.
Foundation type: Independent
Financial data (yr. ended 12/31/88): Assets, $1,794,886 (M); expenditures, $93,585, including $76,300 for 22 grants (high: $10,000; low: $1,000).
Purpose and activities: Giving primarily for education, youth, and social services.
Limitations: Giving primarily in WI. No grants to individuals.
Application information:
Initial approach: Proposal
Board meeting date(s): May
Write: Michael Mahlik
Officers: Clark R. Smith, Pres.; Tablin C. Smith, V.P.; Robert Torgeson, Secy.
Trustee: Associated First Neenah Bank.
Employer Identification Number: 396125329

7543
A. O. Smith Foundation, Inc. ⌑
P.O. Box 23965
Milwaukee 53223-0965 (414) 359-4100
Application address: P.O. Box 23975, Milwaukee, WI 53223-0975

Incorporated in 1951 in WI.
Donor(s): A.O. Smith Corp.
Foundation type: Company-sponsored
Financial data (yr. ended 06/30/89): Assets, $14,766 (M); gifts received, $335,000; expenditures, $536,370, including $520,850 for 101 grants (high: $170,000; low: $200) and $15,276 for 54 employee matching gifts.
Purpose and activities: Support for community funds, civic and cultural affairs, social welfare, higher education, hospitals, and health services.
Types of support: Continuing support, annual campaigns, building funds, scholarship funds, employee matching gifts.
Limitations: Giving primarily in areas of company operations in CA, IL, KY, NC, OH, SC, TN, WA, and WI. No grants to individuals.
Publications: Annual report, application guidelines.
Application information: Application form not required.
Initial approach: Letter, telephone, or proposal
Copies of proposal: 1
Deadline(s): None
Board meeting date(s): June and as required
Final notification: 3 months
Write: Edward J. O'Connor, Secy.
Officers and Directors:* L.B. Smith,* Pres.; Thomas I. Dolan,* V.P.; A.O. Smith,* V.P.; E.J. O'Connor,* Secy.
Employer Identification Number: 396076924

7544
Stackner Family Foundation, Inc. ▼
411 East Wisconsin Ave.
Milwaukee 53202-4497 (414) 277-5000

Incorporated in 1966 in WI.
Donor(s): John S. Stackner,† Irene M. Stackner.†
Foundation type: Independent
Financial data (yr. ended 08/31/89): Assets, $11,945,678 (M); expenditures, $1,311,541, including $1,212,158 for 168 grants (high: $150,000; low: $500; average: $2,000-$20,000).
Purpose and activities: Grants largely for higher, secondary, and elementary education; social service and youth agencies, including family services, child welfare, employment, and minorities; medical research and health agencies, including those serving the mentally ill and the handicapped; environmental protection; drug and alcohol abuse programs; and the arts and cultural programs.
Types of support: Operating budgets, continuing support, annual campaigns, seed money, building funds, equipment, land acquisition, matching funds, special projects, research, publications, conferences and seminars, scholarship funds, capital campaigns.
Limitations: Giving limited to the greater Milwaukee, WI, area. No grants to individuals, or for deficit financing or fellowships; no loans.

Application information: Application form not required.
Initial approach: Proposal or letter
Copies of proposal: 1
Deadline(s): Mar. 31 and Aug. 31
Board meeting date(s): Apr. and Sept.
Final notification: 3 weeks after board meetings
Write: Patrick W. Cotter, Exec. Dir.
Officers and Directors:* Patricia S. Treiber,* Pres.; John A. Treiber,* V.P.; Phillip A. Treiber,* V.P.; Patrick W. Cotter, Secy. and Exec. Dir.; David L. MacGregor,* Treas.
Number of staff: 1 part-time professional.
Employer Identification Number: 396097597

7545
Arthur W. Strelow Trust ⌑
P.O. Box 830
Madison 53701 (608) 252-5952

Established in 1980 in WI.
Foundation type: Independent
Financial data (yr. ended 3/31/86): Assets, $1,278,554 (M); expenditures, $149,190, including $132,440 for 16 grants (high: $44,147; low: $500).
Purpose and activities: Giving primarily for hospitals, educational institutions, and Masonic charities.
Types of support: General purposes, equipment.
Application information: Application form not required.
Initial approach: Letter
Deadline(s): Oct. 1
Write: Oscar Seibel
Trustees: Floyd McBurney, Marshall & Ilsley Trust Services.
Employer Identification Number: 396335082

7546
E. C. Styberg Foundation, Inc. ⌑
P.O. Box 788
1600 Gould St.
Racine 53401-0788 (414) 637-9301

Established in 1981 in WI.
Foundation type: Independent
Financial data (yr. ended 6/30/88): Assets, $1,194,780 (M); expenditures, $42,892, including $41,519 for 48 grants (high: $12,000; low: $25).
Purpose and activities: Support primarily for a church, community development, and youth and health organizations.
Types of support: Capital campaigns, general purposes.
Limitations: Giving primarily in the southeastern, WI, area.
Application information:
Deadline(s): None
Final notification: Within 90 days
Write: E.C. Styberg, Jr., Pres.
Officers: E.C. Styberg, Jr., Pres.; Bernice M. Styberg, V.P. and Secy.; Paul L. Guenther, Treas.
Employer Identification Number: 391410323

7547
Surgical Science Foundation for Research & Development ⌑
c/o First Wisconsin National Bank
One South Pickney St.
Madison 53703

Established in 1983 in WI.
Foundation type: Independent
Financial data (yr. ended 12/31/87): Assets, $4,648,393 (M); gifts received, $840,000; expenditures, $84,963, including $35,143 for 1 grant.
Purpose and activities: Giving for medical education.
Trustees: Folkert Belzer, M.D., Herbert Berkoff, M.D., David Dibbell, M.D., Manucher J. Javid, M.D., Andrew A. McBeath, M.D., James R. Starling, M.D., David Vehling, M.D., Charles E. Yale, M.D.
Employer Identification Number: 930846339

7548
Time Insurance Foundation, Inc. ⌑
515 West Wells St.
Milwaukee 53203

Established in 1973 in WI.
Donor(s): Time Insurance Co.
Foundation type: Company-sponsored
Financial data (yr. ended 12/31/88): Assets, $753,301 (M); expenditures, $299,818, including $294,484 for 156 grants (high: $100,000; low: $50; average: $1,000), $500 for 1 grant to an individual and $4,800 for employee matching gifts.
Purpose and activities: Giving primarily for community services, including community funds, with emphasis on health care services, higher education, and the arts; priority given to projects which are operations as opposed to those which are capital in nature.
Types of support: Employee matching gifts, employee-related scholarships, consulting services, continuing support, endowment funds, general purposes, matching funds, operating budgets, renovation projects, research, special projects.
Limitations: Giving primarily in the greater Milwaukee, WI, area. No support for labor, political, or religious organizations, or hospitals.
Publications: Application guidelines.
Application information: Application form not required.
Initial approach: Letter requesting guidelines
Copies of proposal: 1
Board meeting date(s): Quarterly
Final notification: Ten days after board meeting
Write: John E. Krick, Pres.
Officers and Directors:* John E. Krick, Pres.; Arlene C. Ehret, V.P. and Secy.; Gerald L. Ganoni,* V.P.; Linda J. Hunn,* V.P.; Jacqueline V. Stone,* V.P.
Employer Identification Number: 237346436

7549
Trepte Family Fund
701 West Glendale Ave.
Milwaukee 53209-6509 (414) 962-3369

Established in 1953 in WI.
Donor(s): Gustave A. Trepte,† Florence L. Trepte,† Globe-Van Doorn Corp.
Foundation type: Independent
Financial data (yr. ended 09/30/88): Assets, $1,272,284 (M); expenditures, $77,986, including $76,200 for 48 grants (high: $5,000; low: $200).
Purpose and activities: Support primarily for health associations, social services, educational institutions, museums, religious organizations, hospitals, and youth organizations. Individual scholarship awards are made only to residents of Eastford, CT, who are attending post-secondary schools, colleges, or universities.
Types of support: Annual campaigns, building funds, capital campaigns, student aid.
Limitations: Giving limited to WI.
Application information: Application form not required.
Deadline(s): None
Board meeting date(s): Monthly
Write: Donald A. Trepte or Ralph N. Trepte, Trustees
Trustees: Donald A. Trepte, Ralph N. Trepte, Terry D. Trepte.
Number of staff: None.
Employer Identification Number: 396040308

7550
U.S. Oil/Schmidt Family Foundation, Inc. ☆
425 Washington St.
P.O. Box 25
Combined Locks 54113-1049

Established in 1984 in WI.
Donor(s): Raymond Schmidt, Arthur J. Schmidt, William Schmidt.
Foundation type: Independent
Financial data (yr. ended 07/31/89): Assets, $1,633,956 (M); gifts received, $36,165; expenditures, $199,996, including $196,810 for 144 grants (high: $50,000; low: $10).
Purpose and activities: Giving primarily for Catholic organizations and churches; support also for community funds, education, and hospitals.
Limitations: Giving primarily in WI. No grants to individuals.
Application information: Contributes only to pre-selected organizations. Applications not accepted.
Officers and Directors:* Arthur J. Schmidt,* Pres.; William Schmidt,* V.P.; Raymond Schmidt,* Secy.; Paul Bachman, Thomas Schmidt.
Employer Identification Number: 391540933

7551
Robert A. Uihlein Foundation ⌑ ☆
777 East Wisconsin Ave., Suite 2395
Milwaukee 53202-5385

Established in 1942.
Donor(s): Robert A. Uihlein III, James J. Uihlein.
Foundation type: Independent
Financial data (yr. ended 12/31/88): Assets, $1,142,107 (M); expenditures, $62,331, including $55,650 for 15 grants (high: $20,000; low: $100).
Purpose and activities: Support primarily for a leukemia association and other health organizations, youth, and the arts.
Limitations: Giving limited to Milwaukee, WI.
Application information:

Initial approach: Letter
Deadline(s): None
Write: R.T. Hoppe, Secy.-Treas.
Officers and Directors: Lorraine G. Uihlein, Pres.; Rudolph T. Hoppe, Secy.-Treas.; Thomas F. Lechner.
Employer Identification Number: 396033236

7552
Universal Foods Foundation, Inc. ⌑
433 East Michigan St.
Milwaukee 53202 (414) 271-6755

Incorporated in 1958 in WI.
Donor(s): Universal Foods Corp.
Foundation type: Company-sponsored
Financial data (yr. ended 9/30/88): Assets, $6,143,201 (M); gifts received, $100,000; expenditures, $503,884, including $452,778 for 128 grants (high: $55,000; low: $50) and $11,598 for 77 employee matching gifts.
Purpose and activities: Giving largely for community funds, social services and youth, arts and culture, hospitals, food-related research, higher education, and civic organizations.
Types of support: Employee matching gifts.
Limitations: No support for political organizations or sectarian religious organizations. No grants to individuals.
Application information: Contributes only to pre-selected organizations. Applications not accepted.
Write: John Heinrich, V.P., Admin.
Officers: John L. Murray, Pres.; Darrell E. Wilde, Sr. V.P.; John E. Heinrich, V.P.; Guy A. Osborn, V.P.; Dan E. McMullen, Secy.-Treas.
Number of staff: 1 part-time professional; 1 part-time support.
Employer Identification Number: 396044488

7553
Vilter Foundation, Inc. ⌑
2217 South First St.
Milwaukee 53207

Incorporated in 1961 in WI.
Donor(s): Vilter Manufacturing Co.
Foundation type: Company-sponsored
Financial data (yr. ended 7/31/88): Assets, $3,263,628 (M); expenditures, $170,554, including $137,332 for 103 grants (high: $20,000; low: $213).
Purpose and activities: Giving for community funds, hospitals, religious welfare funds and church support, and higher and secondary education.
Limitations: Giving primarily in WI.
Application information:
Write: A.A. Silverman, Pres.
Officers and Directors: A.A. Silverman, Pres.; E.J. Kocher, V.P.; C.D. Wegener, Secy.; W.I. Grant, Treas.
Employer Identification Number: 390678640

7554
Vollrath Company Foundation, Inc. ⌑
1236 North 18th St.
Sheboygan 53081 (414) 457-4851

Donor(s): Vollrath Co.
Foundation type: Company-sponsored
Financial data (yr. ended 9/30/88): Assets, $126,353 (M); gifts received, $183,856; expenditures, $180,486, including $178,165 for 63 grants (high: $29,487; low: $200) and $1,000 for 1 grant to an individual.
Purpose and activities: Support primarily for youth and social service organizations, higher education, and culture.
Limitations: Giving primarily in WI.
Application information:
Initial approach: Letter
Deadline(s): None
Write: Terry J. Kohler, Pres.
Officers and Directors:* Terry J. Kohler,* Pres.; Charlotte M. Kohler,* V.P.; Mary S. Kohler,* V.P.; Mary L. Ten Haken,* Secy.; Roland M. Neumann, Jr.,* Treas.
Trustee Bank: First Wisconsin National Bank of Sheboygan.
Employer Identification Number: 396046987

7555
R. H. Wagner Foundation, Ltd.
441 Milwaukee Ave.
Burlington 53105

Established in 1981 in WI.
Donor(s): Richard H. Wagner, Roberta Wagner.
Foundation type: Independent
Financial data (yr. ended 06/30/89): Assets, $4,090,314 (M); expenditures, $85,828, including $74,031 for 16 grants (high: $35,411; low: $10) and $1,700 for 4 grants to individuals (high: $800; low: $100).
Purpose and activities: Supports aviation-related programs, including a museum of aviation; support also for scholarships for aviation schooling.
Types of support: Equipment, scholarship funds.
Application information: Applications not accepted.
Write: Paul B. Edwards, Trustee
Officer: Roberta Wagner, Secy.-Treas.
Trustees: Paul B. Edwards, Richard H. Wagner.
Employer Identification Number: 391311452

7556
Byron L. Walter Family Trust
c/o Bank One Wisconsin Trust Co., N.A.
P.O. Box 19029
Green Bay 54307-9029 (414) 436-2610

Trust established in 1981 in WI.
Donor(s): Arlene B. Walter.†
Foundation type: Independent
Financial data (yr. ended 4/30/89): Assets, $6,904,571 (M); expenditures, $482,579, including $407,110 for 27 grants (high: $38,300; low: $750; average: $15,078).
Purpose and activities: Local giving for charitable purposes.
Types of support: Building funds, capital campaigns, equipment, special projects.
Limitations: Giving limited to Brown County, WI. No grants to individuals, or for matching gifts; no loans.
Publications: Application guidelines.
Application information: Application form not required.
Initial approach: Letter
Copies of proposal: 1
Deadline(s): Submit proposal preferably from Jan. through Mar.; no set deadline
Board meeting date(s): Jan., Apr., June, Sept., and Dec.
Final notification: 6 months
Write: Richard J. Blahnik
Trustees: Fred Will, Bank One Wisconsin Trust Co., N.A.
Number of staff: None.
Employer Identification Number: 396346563

7557
Wauwatosa Savings and Loan Foundation ⌑
7500 West State St.
Wauwatosa 53213 (414) 258-5880

Established in 1985 in WI.
Donor(s): Wauwatosa Savings and Loan Association.
Foundation type: Company-sponsored
Financial data (yr. ended 12/31/88): Assets, $1,828,668 (M); gifts received, $240,000; expenditures, $93,062, including $91,998 for 84 grants (high: $10,000; low: $20; average: $250-$1,500).
Purpose and activities: Support for historical societies and social services.
Types of support: Employee matching gifts, general purposes, matching funds, program-related investments, employee-related scholarships, scholarship funds, seed money, special projects.
Limitations: Giving primarily in areas of company facilities.
Application information:
Initial approach: Proposal
Deadline(s): None
Write: Raymond J. Perry, Trustee
Trustees: Charles A. Perry, Raymond A. Perry.
Number of staff: None.
Employer Identification Number: 391548588

7558
The Todd Wehr Foundation, Inc.
111 East Wisconsin Ave., Suite 2100
Milwaukee 53202 (414) 271-8210

Incorporated in 1953 in WI.
Donor(s): C. Frederic Wehr.†
Foundation type: Independent
Financial data (yr. ended 12/31/88): Assets, $9,023,495 (M); expenditures, $646,089, including $522,000 for 13 grants (high: $250,000; low: $2,000; average: $2,000-$750,000).
Purpose and activities: Support for higher education, including medical education, and community charitable institutions.
Types of support: Special projects.
Limitations: Giving limited to WI. No grants to individuals.
Application information: Application form not required.
Initial approach: Letter
Copies of proposal: 1
Deadline(s): None
Board meeting date(s): Quarterly
Write: Ralph G. Schulz, Pres.
Officers and Directors:* Ralph G. Schulz,* Pres.; William J. Hardy,* V.P. and Treas.; M. James Termondt,* Secy.; Robert P. Harland, Winfred W. Wuesthoff.
Number of staff: None.

Employer Identification Number: 396043962

7559
Frank L. Weyenberg Charitable Trust
c/o Quarles & Brady
411 East Wisconsin Ave.
Milwaukee 53202 (414) 277-5000

Established in 1983 in WI.
Foundation type: Independent
Financial data (yr. ended 07/31/89): Assets, $3,243,071 (M); expenditures, $230,661, including $198,400 for 17 grants (high: $50,000; low: $100).
Purpose and activities: Support primarily for cultural programs, education, and social services.
Application information: Contributes only to pre-selected organizations. Applications not accepted.
Write: Henry J. Loos, Trustee
Trustees: Henry J. Loos, First National Bank in Palm Beach.
Employer Identification Number: 391461670

7560
WICOR Foundation, Inc. ⌑
777 East Wisconsin Ave.
Milwaukee 53202 (414) 291-7026

Established in 1984 in WI.
Donor(s): WICOR, Inc.
Foundation type: Company-sponsored
Financial data (yr. ended 12/31/87): Assets, $133,807 (M); gifts received, $150,000; expenditures, $345,055, including $344,590 for 76 grants (high: $35,000; low: $100).
Purpose and activities: Emphasis on the arts, youth organizations, and health associations.
Limitations: Giving limited to areas of company operations; support primarily in Milwaukee, WI, area.
Application information:
Initial approach: In writing
Deadline(s): None
Write: B.W. Kostecke, Secy.-Treas.
Officers and Directors: R.M. Hoffer, Pres.; J.A. Brady, V.P.; W.W. Tisdale, V.P.; B.W. Kostecke, Secy.-Treas.
Employer Identification Number: 391522073

7561
Wildwood Foundation ⌑
141 North Main, Suite 207
West Bend 53095 (414) 338-6621

Established in 1970 in WI.
Donor(s): Red Arrow Products Co., North American Corp.
Foundation type: Independent
Financial data (yr. ended 12/31/88): Assets, $1,312,895 (M); gifts received, $4,480; expenditures, $74,989, including $64,700 for 31 grants (high: $15,300; low: $400).
Purpose and activities: Giving primarily for Christian religious organizations.
Limitations: Giving primarily in WI.
Application information: Application form not required.
Deadline(s): None
Write: Katherine Kurth, Dir.
Directors: Katherine Kurth, Thomas Kurth, Tineka Kurth, Elisabeth Wrean.
Employer Identification Number: 237096923

7562
Wisconsin Energy Corporation, Inc. ▼ ⌑
(Formerly Wisconsin Electric System Foundation, Inc.)
231 West Michigan St.
Milwaukee 53201 (414) 221-2105

Incorporated in 1982 in WI.
Donor(s): Wisconsin Electric Power Co., Wisconsin Natural Gas Co.
Foundation type: Company-sponsored
Financial data (yr. ended 12/31/88): Assets, $23,201,851 (M); gifts received, $10,000,000; expenditures, $2,356,820, including $2,322,810 for grants (average: $75-$10,000).
Purpose and activities: Giving primarily for community funds, higher education, youth and social service agencies, cultural programs, hospitals and health organizations, community development, and civic affairs.
Types of support: Employee matching gifts.
Limitations: Giving primarily in service territories in southeastern WI.
Application information: Application form not required.
Initial approach: Letter
Deadline(s): None
Board meeting date(s): As required
Final notification: Usually 2 weeks
Write: Jerry C. Remmel, Treas.
Officers: Charles S. McNeer, Pres.; Russell W. Britt, V.P.; John H. Goetsch, Secy.; Gerlad C. Remmel, Treas.
Number of staff: None.
Employer Identification Number: 391433726

7563
Wisconsin Power and Light Foundation, Inc.
222 West Washington Ave.
Madison 53703 (608) 252-3181
Additional address: P.O. Box 192, Madison, WI 53701

Established in 1984 in WI.
Donor(s): Wisconsin Power and Light Co.
Foundation type: Company-sponsored
Financial data (yr. ended 12/31/89): Assets, $5,194,139 (M); gifts received, $1,000,000; expenditures, $932,153, including $857,872 for grants and $26,433 for 128 employee matching gifts.
Purpose and activities: Support primarily for health, social services, education, cultural programs, and civic affairs. The foundation provides employee-related scholarships administered through Citizens' Scholarship Foundation of America.
Types of support: Annual campaigns, building funds, capital campaigns, continuing support, employee matching gifts, equipment, fellowships, operating budgets, scholarship funds, employee-related scholarships, seed money, renovation projects.
Limitations: Giving primarily in central and south-central WI, areas of company operations. No support for political or religious organizations. No grants to individuals.
Publications: Annual report, informational brochure (including application guidelines).
Application information: Application form not required.
Initial approach: Proposal
Copies of proposal: 1
Deadline(s): None
Board meeting date(s): Quarterly
Write: Donald R. Piepenburg, V.P.
Officers: A.J. (Nino) Amato,* Pres.; Donald R. Piepenburg, V.P.; Edward M. Gleason, Secy.-Treas.
Directors:* Willie Collins, Suzette M. Mullooly, Jules A. Nicolet, W. Keith Penniston, Michael J. Wish.
Number of staff: 1 part-time professional; 1 part-time support.
Employer Identification Number: 391444065

7564
Wisconsin Public Service Foundation, Inc. ⌑
700 North Adams St.
P.O. Box 19001
Green Bay 54307 (414) 433-1465
Scholarship application address: Wisconsin Public Service Foundation, Inc. Scholarship Program, College Scholarship Service, Sponsored Scholarships Program, CN 6730, Princeton, NJ 08541

Incorporated in 1964 in WI.
Donor(s): Wisconsin Public Service Corp.
Foundation type: Company-sponsored
Financial data (yr. ended 12/31/88): Assets, $7,184,839 (M); gifts received, $250,000; expenditures, $433,093, including $335,798 for 93 grants (high: $47,500; low: $25) and $77,800 for grants to individuals.
Purpose and activities: Grants largely for higher education and community services, with emphasis on health, arts and culture, and conservation.
Types of support: Operating budgets, building funds, equipment, student aid, employee-related scholarships.
Limitations: Giving limited to WI and upper MI. No grants for endowment funds.
Application information: Application form required for scholarships.
Initial approach: Letter
Copies of proposal: 1
Deadline(s): Dec. 15 for scholarships
Board meeting date(s): May and as required
Final notification: Feb.
Write: L.M. Stoll, Pres.
Officers: L.M. Stoll, Pres.; J.H. Liethen, V.P.; R.H. Knuth, Secy.; D.P. Bittner, Treas.
Employer Identification Number: 396075016

7565
Lester G. Wood Foundation, Inc. ⌑ ☆
3290 Vista Rd.
Green Bay 54301-2632 (414) 336-1222

Established in 1955.
Donor(s): members of the Baer and Lea families.
Foundation type: Independent
Financial data (yr. ended 12/31/88): Assets, $3,698,917 (M); gifts received, $3,000,000; expenditures, $157,760, including $154,965 for 37 grants (high: $50,000; low: $65).
Purpose and activities: Giving primarily for Methodist churches and social services; support also for higher and other education.
Limitations: Giving primarily in IL and WI. No grants to individuals.

Application information: Application form not required.
Deadline(s): None
Write: Patricia W. Baer, Secy.-Treas.
Officers and Directors: L. Bates Lea, Pres.; F.E. Baer, V.P.; Patricia W. Baer, Secy.-Treas.; Marcia W. Lea.
Employer Identification Number: 396055567

7566
The Aytchmonde Woodson Foundation, Inc. ⌘
P.O. Box 65
Wausau 54402-0065 (714) 845-9201

Incorporated in 1947 in WI.
Donor(s): Members of the Woodson family.
Foundation type: Independent
Financial data (yr. ended 06/30/89): Assets, $8,654,381 (M); expenditures, $320,221, including $243,526 for 11 grants (high: $80,000; low: $501).
Purpose and activities: Support almost exclusively for a museum.
Limitations: Giving primarily in Wausau, WI. No grants to individuals, or for endowment funds.
Application information:
Initial approach: Letter
Copies of proposal: 1
Board meeting date(s): Sept.
Write: San W. Orr, Jr., Treas.
Officers and Directors:* Nancy Woodson Spire,* Pres.; Alice Woodson Forester,* V.P.; John E. Forester,* Secy.; San W. Orr, Jr.,* Treas.; John M. Coates, Frederick W. Fisher, Lyman J. Spire.
Employer Identification Number: 391017853

7567
Irvin L. Young Foundation, Inc. ⌘
Snow Valley Ranch
Palmyra 53156 (414) 495-2568

Incorporated in 1949 in WI.
Donor(s): Irvin L. Young.†
Foundation type: Independent
Financial data (yr. ended 12/31/88): Assets, $8,035,749 (M); expenditures, $1,147,525, including $1,089,642 for 31 grants (high: $525,000; low: $500).
Purpose and activities: Grants largely for Protestant medical missionary programs in Africa, including the training of African medical workers.
Types of support: Building funds, equipment, general purposes, operating budgets, scholarship funds, matching funds.
Limitations: No grants to individuals.
Application information: Application form not required.
Initial approach: Letter
Copies of proposal: 1
Deadline(s): Submit proposal in Oct. or Nov.
Board meeting date(s): As required
Write: Fern D. Young, Pres.
Officers and Directors:* Fern D. Young,* Pres. and Treas.; Mary Longbrake,* V.P.; Robert W. Reninger,* Secy.; L. Arden Almquist, James H. Bird, David S. Fisher.
Number of staff: None.
Employer Identification Number: 396077858

7568
Youth Foundation, Inc. ⌘
P.O. Box 13735
Milwaukee 53213 (414) 327-6700

Incorporated about 1956 in WI.
Donor(s): Arthur L. Richards.†
Foundation type: Independent
Financial data (yr. ended 12/31/88): Assets, $1,082,828 (M); expenditures, $45,699, including $40,317 for 21 grants (low: $500).
Purpose and activities: To assist needy youth and support youth organizations.
Types of support: Seed money, emergency funds, matching funds, scholarship funds, special projects, research.
Limitations: Giving primarily in WI. No grants to individuals, or for operating budgets, continuing support, annual campaigns, building funds, equipment, publications, or conferences; no loans.
Application information: Application form required.
Initial approach: Letter
Deadline(s): None
Board meeting date(s): As required
Final notification: 2 months
Write: Jeraldine Marchant, Pres.
Officers: Jeraldine Marchant, Pres.; Rick Fricker, V.P.; James Zimanek,* Secy.; Nick Hoyer, Treas.
Directors:* Jackie Mickelson, John Ogden, Sr., Henry J. Wojcik.
Number of staff: None.
Employer Identification Number: 390945311

7569
The Ziegler Foundation, Inc.
215 North Main St.
West Bend 53095 (414) 334-5521

Incorporated in 1944 in WI.
Donor(s): Members of the Ziegler family.
Foundation type: Independent
Financial data (yr. ended 12/31/88): Assets, $4,800,000 (M); expenditures, $300,000, including $275,000 for 50 grants (high: $100,000; low: $200).
Purpose and activities: Support primarily for higher education, including a scholarship fund, church support, and youth agencies; support also for hospitals.
Limitations: Giving primarily in the West Bend, WI, area. No grants to individuals.
Application information: Present plans preclude extensive consideration of unsolicited requests. Application form not required.
Initial approach: Letter
Deadline(s): None
Board meeting date(s): May and Nov.
Write: Bernard C. Ziegler, Pres.
Officers and Directors:* Bernard C. Ziegler,* Pres.; R. Douglas Ziegler,* V.P. and Secy.-Treas.; Harrold J. McComas,* V.P.
Number of staff: None.
Employer Identification Number: 396044762

7570
Ziemann Foundation, Inc.
c/o First Wisconsin Trust
P.O. Box 2054
Milwaukee 53201 (414) 542-4996
Application address: P.O. Box 1408, Waukesha, WI 53187-1408

Established in 1963 in WI.
Donor(s): Lillian Ziemann,† H.J. Ziemann,† Mrs. H.J. Ziemann.†
Foundation type: Independent
Financial data (yr. ended 12/31/89): Assets, $1,818,000 (M); qualifying distributions, $61,750, including $61,750 for 16 grants (high: $30,000; low: $250; average: $1,000-$5,000).
Purpose and activities: Emphasis on social service agencies, community-based programs that enhance the quality of life of handicapped and developmentally disabled individuals in the southeastern WI community.
Types of support: Annual campaigns, continuing support, equipment, operating budgets, renovation projects, scholarship funds, special projects.
Limitations: Giving primarily in WI. No grants to individuals.
Publications: Program policy statement, application guidelines.
Application information: Applications sent between Sept. 30 and Dec. 31 will not be reviewed until the subsequent year. Application form not required.
Initial approach: Letter
Copies of proposal: 1
Deadline(s): Jan. 1 through Sept. 30
Board meeting date(s): Oct. or Nov.
Final notification: Dec.
Write: Cindy Linnan, V.P.
Officers and Directors:* Carolyn Wright,* Pres.; Cynthia Linnan,* V.P. and Treas.; Lila Pierce,* Secy.; Pam Praulins, Robert Veenendaal.
Number of staff: None.
Employer Identification Number: 396069677

WYOMING

7571
Dodd and Dorothy L. Bryan Foundation
P.O. Box 6287
Sheridan 82801 (307) 672-3535

Established in 1965 in WY.
Donor(s): Dorothy L. Bryan.†
Foundation type: Independent
Financial data (yr. ended 12/31/89): Assets, $3,920,792 (M); qualifying distributions, $224,300, including $10,000 for 1 grant and $214,300 for 131 loans to individuals.
Purpose and activities: Provides educational loans for local students.
Types of support: Student loans.
Limitations: Giving limited to Sheridan, Campbell, and Johnson counties, WY; and Powder River, Rosebud, and Big Horn counties, MT. No grants for general support, capital funds, endowment funds, matching gifts, scholarships, or fellowships.
Publications: Application guidelines.

Application information: Application form required.
Initial approach: Letter
Deadline(s): Submit application preferably in May or June; deadline July 15
Board meeting date(s): Monthly
Final notification: 2 months after board meeting
Write: J.E. Goar, Mgr.
Officers: W.D. Redle, Pres.; R.R. Loss, Treas.; J. Leonard Graham, V.P.; Jack E. Pellisier, Secy.; J.E. Goar, Mgr.
Director: Arthur G. Felker.
Number of staff: 1 full-time professional.
Employer Identification Number: 836006533

7572
The Goodstein Foundation ⌑
P.O. Box 1699
Casper 82602 (307) 237-0033

Incorporated in 1952 in CO.
Donor(s): J.M. Goodstein.
Foundation type: Independent
Financial data (yr. ended 06/30/89): Assets, $4,589,721 (M); expenditures, $1,463,731, including $1,451,513 for 43 grants (high: $1,143,513; low: $100).
Purpose and activities: Grants for higher education, Jewish temple support, and hospitals.
Limitations: Giving primarily in CO and WY.
Application information:
Initial approach: Letter
Deadline(s): None
Write: Charles L. Tangney, Pres.
Officers: Charles L. Tangney, Pres.; William H. Brown, V.P.
Employer Identification Number: 836003815

7573
Gertrude Kamps Memorial Foundation ⌑
c/o First Interstate Bank of Casper, N.A.
P.O. Box 40
Casper 82602
Application address: P.O. Box 2274, Casper, WY 82602

Established in 1976.
Donor(s): Gertrude Kamps.†
Foundation type: Independent
Financial data (yr. ended 07/31/89): Assets, $1,622,054 (M); expenditures, $153,371, including $144,472 for 23 grants (high: $29,662; low: $310).
Purpose and activities: Giving for youth, child welfare, and social service agencies.
Limitations: Giving limited to WY, with emphasis on Natrona County and the central region. No grants to individuals.
Application information: Application form not required.
Initial approach: Letter
Board meeting date(s): Annually in the 1st week of Sept.
Write: Brad Bochmann
Trustee: First Interstate Bank of Casper, N.A.
Employer Identification Number: 836024918

7574
The Nason Foundation ⌑
c/o First Wyoming Bank
P.O. Box 160
Laramie 82070-0160

Established in 1981 in WI.
Donor(s): Katherine H. Nason.
Foundation type: Independent
Financial data (yr. ended 11/30/87): Assets, $3,001,698 (M); gifts received, $683,400; expenditures, $222,572, including $168,500 for 14 grants (high: $100,000; low: $1,000).
Purpose and activities: Support primarily for higher education and hospitals.
Limitations: No grants to individuals.
Application information: Contributes only to pre-selected organizations. Applications not accepted.
Officers: John D. Merwin, Pres.; John Baird, V.P. and Secy.; Louis E. Scherck, V.P. and Treas.
Employer Identification Number: 742226170

7575
B. F. & Rose H. Perkins Foundation
P.O. Box 1064
Sheridan 82801 (307) 674-8871

Established in 1933 in WY.
Donor(s): Benjamin F. Perkins.
Foundation type: Independent
Financial data (yr. ended 12/31/88): Assets, $5,892,128 (M); qualifying distributions, $323,584, including $40,524 for 140 grants to individuals (high: $2,250; low: $10) and $264,788 for 143 loans to individuals.
Purpose and activities: Medical and educational assistance to individuals; recipients of educational grants and loans must be graduates of a Sheridan County High School.
Types of support: Student aid, grants to individuals, student loans.
Limitations: Giving primarily to residents of Sheridan County, WY.
Application information: Application form required.
Initial approach: Telephone
Copies of proposal: 1
Deadline(s): June 1 for fall registration; 1st of each month for other educational grants and for medical grants
Board meeting date(s): 2nd Monday of each month
Write: Margaret Sweem, Office Mgr.
Trustees: Paddy Bard, Donald R. Carrol, Victor Garber, Walter J. Pilch, William D. Redle.
Number of staff: 2 full-time professional; 5 full-time support.
Employer Identification Number: 830138740

7576
Newell B. Sargent Foundation ⌑ ☆
c/o Newell B. Sargent
821 Pulliam, P.O. Box 18
Worland 82401

Established in 1984.
Donor(s): Newell B. Sargent.
Foundation type: Independent
Financial data (yr. ended 10/31/89): Assets, $2,773,312 (M); gifts received, $800,000; expenditures, $129,153, including $119,831 for 17 grants (high: $99,335; low: $50).
Purpose and activities: Giving primarily for a municipality; support also for civic affairs groups. The foundation awards student aid to business students attending specified area colleges.
Types of support: Student aid, general purposes, land acquisition.
Limitations: Giving primarily in WY, with emphasis on Worland.
Trustees: Douglas W. Morrison, Newell B. Sargent, Charles W. Smith.
Employer Identification Number: 830271536

7577
Paul Stock Foundation
P.O. Box 2020
Cody 82414 (307) 587-5275
Scholarship application address: 1239 Rumsey Ave., Cody, WY 82414

Incorporated in 1958 in WY.
Donor(s): Paul Stock,† Eloise J. Stock.
Foundation type: Independent
Financial data (yr. ended 12/31/89): Assets, $8,143,346 (M); expenditures, $412,557, including $230,043 for 15 grants (high: $60,000; low: $500) and $137,599 for 77 grants to individuals (high: $3,000; low: $100).
Purpose and activities: Giving for higher education, including student aid to WY residents; grants also for the arts, hospitals, child welfare, youth agencies, a historical center, museums, medical research, and community development.
Types of support: Student aid, annual campaigns, building funds, research.
Limitations: Giving primarily in WY; student aid limited to those who have resided in WY for one year or more.
Application information: Application form and instructions for educational grants only.
Initial approach: Letter
Deadline(s): June 30 and Nov. 30 for educational grants
Board meeting date(s): July and Dec.
Write: Charles G. Kepler, Pres.
Officers: Charles G. Kepler, Pres.; Esther C. Brumage, V.P.; Donald M. Robirds, Secy.-Treas.
Number of staff: 1 part-time professional.
Employer Identification Number: 830185157

7578
Harry and Thelma Surrena Memorial Fund ⌑
P.O. Box 6286
Sheridan 82801 (307) 672-7491

Established in 1973 in WY.
Foundation type: Independent
Financial data (yr. ended 10/31/89): Assets, $3,348,439 (M); expenditures, $235,730, including $203,820 for 7 grants (high: $91,000; low: $1,000).
Purpose and activities: Giving for youth and social service agencies and a Methodist church.
Limitations: Giving primarily in WY.
Application information:
Initial approach: Letter
Deadline(s): None
Final notification: Usually in Oct.
Write: Henry A. Burgess, Trustee
Trustees: Henry A. Burgess, Ralph C. Robinson.
Employer Identification Number: 237435554

7579
Tom and Helen Tonkin Foundation
c/o Wyoming National Bank Casper
P.O. Box 2799
Casper 82602 (307) 266-1100

Trust established in 1956 in WY.
Donor(s): Helen B. Tonkin,† T.C. Tonkin.†
Foundation type: Independent
Financial data (yr. ended 07/31/89): Assets, $2,000,175 (M); expenditures, $116,035, including $86,008 for 20 grants (high: $15,336; low: $906; average: $1,000-$10,000).
Purpose and activities: To aid local youth, particularly those handicapped by illness, injury, or poverty, from ages 6-21.
Types of support: Operating budgets, seed money, emergency funds, deficit financing, matching funds, scholarship funds, publications, conferences and seminars.
Limitations: Giving limited to WY, with emphasis on the Casper area. No grants to individuals, or for continuing support, annual campaigns, building or endowment funds, land acquisition, special projects, or research; no loans.
Publications: 990-PF, application guidelines.
Application information: Application form not required.
Initial approach: Letter
Copies of proposal: 7
Deadline(s): None
Board meeting date(s): As required
Final notification: 60 days
Write: Elona Anderson
Members: A.F. Haskey, Chair.; James A. Barlow, Jr., Sheri Carlisle, Warren A. Morton, R.M. Robertson.
Trustee Bank: Wyoming National Bank Casper.
Number of staff: 1 part-time professional.
Employer Identification Number: 836002200

7580
True Foundation ⌑ ☆
P.O. Drawer 2360
Casper 82602 (307) 237-9301

Established in 1958.
Donor(s): True Oil Co.
Foundation type: Company-sponsored
Financial data (yr. ended 11/30/89): Assets, $615,879 (M); gifts received, $9,600; expenditures, $153,033, including $143,725 for 41 grants (high: $25,000; low: $25) and $9,300 for 11 grants to individuals (average: $600).
Purpose and activities: Support for education, including employee-related scholarships, community development, and social services.
Types of support: Employee-related scholarships.
Application information: Application form required for scholarships.
Deadline(s): Mar. 22 for scholarships
Trustee: H.A. True, Jr.
Employer Identification Number: 836004596

7581
William E. Weiss Foundation, Inc.
P.O. Box 1108
Jackson 83001 (307) 733-1680

Incorporated in 1955 in NY.
Donor(s): William E. Weiss, Jr.,† Helene K. Brown.†
Foundation type: Independent
Financial data (yr. ended 03/31/89): Assets, $4,086,157 (M); expenditures, $190,413, including $171,500 for 35 grants.
Purpose and activities: Grants largely for higher and secondary education, historic preservation, hospitals, and Protestant church support.
Types of support: Building funds, special projects, continuing support.
Limitations: Giving primarily in NY, WV, and WY. No grants to individuals.
Publications: Program policy statement, application guidelines.
Application information: Application form not required.
Initial approach: Proposal
Copies of proposal: 4
Deadline(s): Submit proposal preferably in Nov.
Board meeting date(s): Jan.
Final notification: Mar.
Write: Lulu Hughes, Secy.
Officers and Directors:* William D. Weiss,* Pres.; Daryl B. Uber,* V.P.; Lulu Hughes,* Secy.; P.W.T. Brown,* Treas.; Mary K. Weiss.
Number of staff: 1 part-time support.
Employer Identification Number: 556016633

7582
Whitney Benefits, Inc.
P.O. Box 691
Sheridan 82801 (307) 674-7303

Incorporated in 1927 in WY.
Donor(s): Edward A. Whitney.†
Foundation type: Independent
Financial data (yr. ended 12/31/89): Assets, $7,448,782 (M); qualifying distributions, $398,821, including $109,363 for 1 grant and $289,458 for 67 loans to individuals.
Purpose and activities: To provide interest-free student loans to graduates of Sheridan County, WY, high schools; loans for baccalaureate degrees only. Support also for a local youth agency.
Types of support: Student loans.
Limitations: Giving limited to Sheridan County, WY.
Publications: Annual report.
Application information: Applications accepted for loan program only. Foundation does not fund grants. Application form required.
Initial approach: Telephone, letter, or proposal
Copies of proposal: 1
Deadline(s): Submit application preferably between Mar. and June; deadline 5 days before 1st Monday of each month
Board meeting date(s): Monthly
Write: Jack R. Hufford, Secy.-Treas.
Officers and Trustees:* William E. Cook,* Pres.; Henry A. Burgess,* V.P.; Jack R. Hufford,* Secy.-Treas.; John P. Chase, George E. Ewan, George Gligorea, Ray V. Johnston, Dorothy King, C.B. Metz, Nels A. Nelson, Jr., R. David Parker, Jane S. Schroeder, Homer A. Scott, Sr., David Withrow.
Number of staff: 1 full-time professional; 1 full-time support.
Employer Identification Number: 830168511

APPENDIXES

APPENDIX A

The following foundations appeared in Edition 12 of *The Foundation Directory* but are not included in Edition 13 for the reasons stated. For those foundations which no longer qualify for inclusion on the basis of size, assets and grants figures are supplied for the year of record as well as the current address.

A-T Medical Research Foundation
344 Copa de Oro Rd., Los Angeles, CA 90077
Yr. ended 09/30/88: Assets, $7,052 (M); grants, $72,000

Abercrombie Foundation, J. S., The
Houston, TX
On May 31, 1988, the foundation distributed substantially all of its assets to the Abercrombie Foundation and the Robinson Foundation

Aliber Foundation
Des Moines, IA
The foundation has terminated

Allied Stores Foundation, Inc.
See Robert & Ilse Campeau Family Foundation, Inc.

Amis Foundation, Everett L.
P.O. Box 888, Spring Park, MN 55384
Yr. ended 11/30/88: Assets, $481,124 (M); grants, $11,500

Amont Foundation, Inc.
(Formerly Jeannette & Lafayette Montgomery Foundation, Inc.)
480 East Paces Ferry Rd., N.W., Suite 2, Atlanta, GA 30305
Yr. ended 12/31/88: Assets, $924,273 (M); grants, $57,970

AMPCO-Pittsburgh Foundation, Inc.
Pittsburgh, PA
The foundation merged with the Fair Oaks Foundation

Anderson Foundation, Ted and Peggy
Corpus Christi, TX
The foundation terminated in 1989

Annenberg Foundation, M. L., The
St. Davids, PA
The foundation terminated in 1989

Armstrong Rubber Co. Foundation, Inc.
See The Armtek Foundation, Inc.

Armtek Foundation, Inc., The
(Formerly Armstrong Rubber Co. Foundation, Inc.)
New Haven, CT
Due to the acquisition of Armtek Corp. by Mark IV Industries, the foundation has terminated

ARW Foundation, The
New York, NY
The foundation merged into The Pinkerton Foundation in 1988

Aslan Foundation
c/o Fiduciary Mgmt., Inc., 2400 Carew Tower, Cincinnati, OH 45202
Yr. ended 11/30/88: Assets, $17,726 (M); grants, $16,000

B Fund, The
c/o Edward H.R. Blitzer, 75 Central Park West, New York, NY 10023
Yr. ended 12/31/88: Assets, $837,916 (M); grants, $82,000

Bailey Trust, Frederick A.
c/o Boston Safe Deposit & Trust Co., One Boston Place, Boston, MA 02108
Yr. ended 08/31/88: Assets, $985,664 (M); grants, $42,500

Baird Foundation, Inc., David, Josephine, & Winfield
New York, NY
The foundation distributed its assets to the New York Community Trust in 1989

Barrett Foundation
Dallas, TX
The foundation has terminated

Bartels Foundation, Inc., Theodore R. and Grayce W.
70 Sunset Court, Mahwah, NJ 07430
Yr. ended 12/31/88: Assets, $6,077 (M); grants, $81,150

Barton-Malow Company Foundation
P.O. Box 5200, Oak Park, MI 48235
Yr. ended 03/31/89: Assets, $8,635 (M); grants, $65,700

Bates Foundation, Vernal W. & Florence H.
6503 29th Ave. West, Bradenton, FL 33529
Yr. ended 06/30/89: Assets, $925,180 (M); grants, $52,500

Baxter Foundation, Inc., George W.
6525 Morrison Blvd., Suite 501, Charlotte, NC 28211-3530
Yr. ended 6/30/88: Assets, $925,390 (M); grants, $47,475

Beech Foundation, Inc., The
138 Frogtown Rd., New Canaan, CT 06840
Yr. ended 10/31/89: Assets, $672,038 (M); grants, $89,700

Beefeater Foundation
See Kobrand Foundation

Belasco Foundation, Edna & Jack, The
139 East Main St., Moorestown, NJ 08057
Yr. ended 03/31/89: Assets, $558,568 (M); grants, $67,100

Belcher, Jr. Foundation, S. E.
c/o First Alabama Bank, 2222 Ninth St., Tuscaloosa, AL 35401
Yr. ended 12/31/88: Assets, $300,418 (M); grants, $49,889

Benson Foundation, Inc., Clifton L., The
2900 Yonkers Rd., Raleigh, NC 27604
Yr. ended 12/31/89: Assets, $8,101 (M); grants, $81,950

Beyer Charitable Foundation, Inc., Stanley & Lynn, The
132 South Rodeo Dr., Beverly Hills, CA 90212
Yr. ended 11/30/89: Assets, $46,385 (M); grants, $62,000

Biedenharn Foundation, The
P.O. Box 1114, Shreveport, LA 71163
Yr. ended 11/30/88: Assets, $100,387 (M); grants, $77,750

Block Foundation, Inc., James and Barbara
257 Cornelison Ave., Jersey City, NJ 07302
Yr. ended 06/30/89: Assets, $586,592 (M); grants, $1,671

Boeing Company Charitable Trust, The
Seattle, WA
Funds merged into corporate giving program

Bolton Foundation
Cleveland, OH
The foundation has terminated

Boone Foundation
11841 East Telegraph Rd., Santa Fe Springs, CA 90670
Yr. ended 9/30/88: Assets, $918,238 (M); grants, $0

Boren Foundation, Inc.
1909 South Main St., P.O. Box 218, Upland, IN 46989
Yr. ended 09/30/89: Assets, $612,766 (M); grants, $0

Boston Globe Foundation, Inc., The
Boston, MA
Status changed to public charity in 1987

Braden Trust, Clifford and Bonnie
P.O. Box 1757, Walla Walla, WA 99362
Yr. ended 03/31/89: Assets, $888,677 (M); grants, $25,200

Brandt Foundation, Elsie L. & Peter H.
350 Fifth Ave., New York, NY 10118
Yr. ended 12/31/88: Assets, $119,823 (M); grants, $79,627

Braver Foundation, Inc.
565 Park Ave., New York, NY 10021
Yr. ended 12/31/88: Assets, $230,357 (M); grants, $87,755

Brown Foundation, E. C., The
Portland, OR
Single-purpose endowment; generally does not make grants

California Tamarack Foundation
1100 Larkspur Landing Circle, Suite 294, Larkspur, CA 94939
Yr. ended 08/31/89: Assets, $53,122 (M); grants, $82,563

Calvert Trust
Chestnut Hill, MA
The trust terminated in 1989

Camp Carpenter, Trustees of
Auburn, NH
Single-purpose endowment

Campeau Family Foundation, Inc., Robert & Ilse
(Formerly Allied Stores Foundation, Inc.)
New York, NY
The foundation merged with the Federated Department Stores Foundation in Apr., 1989, to form the Robert Campeau Family Foundation (U.S.)

Candle Foundation, The
1999 Bundy Dr., Los Angeles, CA 90025
Yr. ended 12/31/88: Assets, $68,353 (M); grants, $65,468

Cantor Foundation, Joseph
Indianapolis, IN
The foundation will terminate in 1991

Capezio-Ballet Makers Dance Foundation, Inc.
One Campus Rd., Totowa, NJ 07512
Yr. ended 12/31/88: Assets, $61,921 (M); grants, $90,001

Carell, Jr. Foundation, Monroe, The
937 Church St., Nashville, TN 37203-3495
Yr. ended 12/31/88: Assets, $91,358 (M); grants, $34,226

Chicago Tribune Foundation
Chicago, IL
The foundation merged into the Chicago Tribune Charities, Inc., a public charity, in 1990

Christensen Family Foundation, A. Lee
1572 Orchard Dr., Salt Lake City, UT 84106
Yr. ended 12/31/88: Assets, $83,587 (M); grants, $15,000

Christian Foundation, The
Columbus, IN
Single-purpose endowment supporting a theological seminary

Clarke, Jr. Foundation, Henry D.
822 Beachland Blvd., Vero Beach, FL 32963
Yr. ended 11/30/88: Assets, $343,119 (M); grants, $79,650

Coler Foundation, The
c/o ATC Co., 441 Fifth Ave., New York, NY 10016
Yr. ended 12/31/88: Assets, $230,790 (M); grants, $0

Collins Foundation, Carol & James
P.O. Box 92092, Los Angeles, CA 90009
Yr. ended 11/30/88: Assets, $3,135 (M); grants, $1,000

Colt Industries Foundation, Inc.
New York, NY
The foundation terminated in 1988

Cook Charitable Trust, Peter C. and Emajean
Grand Rapids, MI
The trust terminated in 1987 and transferred its assets to the Peter C. and Emajean Cook Foundation

Copperweld Foundation
Four Gateway Ctr., 22nd Fl., Pittsburgh, PA 15222-1211
Yr. ended 06/30/89: Assets, $983,010 (M); grants, $86,830

Crary Home, The
304 Marine Bank Bldg., Warren, PA 16365
Yr. ended 12/31/88: Assets, $895,483 (M); grants, $5,000

Crivitz Youth, Inc.
Crivitz, WI
Non-grantmaking operating foundation

Cross and Trecker Foundation
505 North Woodward Ave., Suite 2000, Bloomfield Hills, MI 48013
Yr. ended 09/30/89: Assets, $110,457 (L); grants, $88,188

Crosset Charitable Trust, The
See Crosset Family Fund

Crosset Family Fund
(Formerly The Crosset Charitable Trust)
Cincinnati, OH
The trust terminated in 1987

Dauby Charity Fund, Nathan L.
Cleveland, OH
The foundation terminated in 1988 and transferred the bulk of its assets to the Gries Family Foundation

Davidhoff Foundation, Inc.
279 Graham Ave., Brooklyn, NY 11211
Yr. ended 06/30/89: Assets, $127,484 (M); grants, $85,792

Dayco Charitable Foundation, Inc.
1301 East 9th St., Suite 3600, Cleveland, OH 44114-1824
Yr. ended 12/31/88: Assets, $15,000 (M); grants, $750

de Santis Foundation
100 Drury Ln., Oak Brook Terrace, IL 60181
Yr. ended 12/31/88: Assets, $616,022 (M); grants, $78,171

Diller Charitable Foundation, William & Helen, The
297 97 St., Stone Harbor, NJ 08247
Yr. ended 09/30/89: Assets, $986,982 (M); grants, $78,959

Domino Foundation
343 East Jefferson Blvd., Los Angeles, CA 90011
Yr. ended 06/30/89: Assets, $112,308 (M); grants, $61,425

Dravo Corporation & Subsidiaries Charitable Trust
Pittsburgh, PA
The foundation terminated in 1990

Drexel Burnham Employees Scholarship Fund, Inc.
New York, NY
The fund terminated in 1990

Drexel Burnham Lambert Foundation, Inc., The
New York, NY
The foundation terminated in 1990

Duncan Foundation, A. J. and Jessie
1800 First City Bank Tower, 201 Main St., Fort Worth, TX 76102
Yr. ended 02/28/89: Assets, $650,483 (M); grants, $91,307

Duncan Foundation, Inc., Harry F.
4955 Linnean Ave., N.W., Washington, DC 20008
Yr. ended 12/31/89: Assets, $173,832 (M); grants, $36,664

Dyckman's Foundation, Inc.
73 West 47th St., New York, NY 10036
Yr. ended 08/31/89: Assets, $3,728 (M); grants, $41,078

E.D. Foundation
Ridgefield, NJ
The foundation is inactive

Elliott Foundation, Inc., Edward
c/o John B. Elliot, World Financial Ctr. & Oppenheimer Tower 35th Fl., New York, NY 10281
Yr. ended 6/30/89: Assets, $15,006 (M); grants, $5,750

Elser Foundation, Inc., Mathilde U. & Albert
777 East Wisconsin Ave., Suite 3800, Milwaukee, WI 53202-5366
Yr. ended 12/31/88: Assets, $115,244 (M); grants, $79,432

Enterprise Foundation, Inc.
Kendallville, IN
The foundation terminated in 1989

Eucalyptus Foundation, Inc.
New York, NY
Single-purpose endowment

Fairfield Foundation
4008 Shannon Ln., Dallas, TX 75205-1737
Yr. ended 12/31/88: Assets, $151,217 (M); grants, $5,000

Falk Family Trust, Leon
3315 Grant Bldg., Pittsburgh, PA 15219
Yr. ended 12/31/87: Assets, $314,386 (M); grants, $75,225

Favrot Family Fund, Clifford F.
1301 Napoleon Ave., New Orleans, LA 70115
Yr. ended 12/31/88: Assets, $898,287 (M); grants, $2,032

Federated Foundations, Inc.
c/o Theodore Present, 450 Seventh Ave., New York, NY 10123
Yr. ended 12/31/88: Assets, $286,160 (M); grants, $66,778

First Bank Foundation, Inc.
Milwaukee, WI
The foundation terminated in 1988

First National Foundation, Inc.
See Vose Foundation

Folsom Charitable Foundation, Inc.
16475 Dallas Pkwy., Suite 800, Dallas, TX 75248
Yr. ended 12/31/88: Assets, $239,460 (M); grants, $9,500

Fortunoff Foundation, Inc., Max & Clara
1300 Old Country Rd., Westbury, NY 11590-5102
Yr. ended 12/31/88: Assets, $17,628 (M); grants, $78,000

Foundation for Agronomic Research, Inc.
2801 Buford Hwy., N.E., Suite 401, Atlanta, GA 30329
Yr. ended 12/31/88: Assets, $556,672 (M); grants, $97,994

Francis Foundation, Parker B.
Kansas City, MO
The foundation has merged with the Parker B. Francis III Foundation to form the Francis Families Foundation

Francis III Foundation, Parker B.
Kansas City, MO
The foundation has merged with the Parker B. Francis Foundation to form the Francis Families Foundation

Freeman Foundation
3115 Netherland Ave., Bronx, NY 10463
Yr. ended 12/31/88: Assets, $436,830 (M); grants, $59,761

Freeze Trust, Macie Reagan
Statesville, NC
The trust is inactive

Garaventa Family Foundation, Silvio and Mary
4080 Mallard Dr., Concord, CA 94520
Yr. ended 03/31/89: Assets, $457,363 (M); grants, $81,300

Gateposts Foundation, Inc.
111 Great Neck Rd., Suite 402, Great Neck, NY 11021
Yr. ended 11/30/88: Assets, $223,353 (M); grants, $36,369

Gellerman Family Foundation, Herbert A.
7800 14th St., West, Rock Island, IL 61201-7402
Yr. ended 6/30/88: Assets, $18,741 (M); grants, $3,883

General Foods Fund, Inc., The
White Plains, NY
Due to the merger of General Foods and Kraft, the foundation terminated in 1989

Genshaft Family Foundation
5353 Laurel Dr., N.W., Canton, OH 44718
Yr. ended 12/31/88: Assets, $376,828 (M); grants, $97,200

Gill Trust, A. Smith
Fort Worth, TX
The trust has terminated

Gitt-Moul Historic Properties
Hanover, PA
Non-grantmaking operating foundation

God's Love, Inc.
533 North Main St., Helena, MT 59601
Yr. ended 09/30/88: Assets, $570,121 (M); grants, $49,409

Goulds Pumps Foundation
P.O. Box 330, 240 Fall St., Seneca Falls, NY 13148
Yr. ended 12/31/88: Assets, $2,257 (M); grants, $15,950

Green Bay Foundation
New York, NY
The foundation is under a 60-month termination

Greenberg Foundation, Inc., Leonard E. & Phyllis S.
5160 S.W. 15th Ave., Boyton Beach, FL 33437
Yr. ended 10/31/89: Assets, $6,221 (M); grants, $30,000

Griffin Foundation, Francis D. & Irene D.
c/o Dale Reis, 73453 Feather Trail, Palm Desert, CA 92260
Yr. ended 11/30/88: Assets, $895,992 (M); grants, $61,680

Griffith Foundation, Vernon S. & Rowena W.
Sheridan, WY
Support only for specified beneficiaries

Griswold Trust, Harry E.
Magna Trust Co., P.O. Box 1278, Decatur, IL 62525
Yr. ended 03/31/90: Assets, $935,288 (M); grants, $60,488

Gumpel-Lury Foundation
c/o Stroock & Stroock & Lavan, Seven Hanover Sq., New York, NY 10004
Yr. ended 10/31/89: Assets, $461,315 (M); grants, $93,534

Hall Family Foundation, The
P.O. Box 1479, Minden, NV 89423-1479
Yr. ended 12/31/88: Assets, $194,301 (M); grants, $82,670

Hammermill Foundation, The
Erie, PA
The foundation terminated in 1990

Harris Foundation, S. T. & Margaret D.
3428 St. John's Dr., Dallas, TX 75205
Yr. ended 10/31/89: Assets, $420,351 (M); grants, $42,500

Hasenfeld Foundation, Inc., A. & Z.
580 Fifth Ave., New York, NY 10036
Yr. ended 03/31/89: Assets, $5,842 (M); grants, $75,713

Hawthorne Foundation, Inc.
White Bear Lake, MN
The foundation was dissolved in 1988

Hayes Research Foundation, Inc., Stanley W.
Richmond, IN
Grantmaking suspended in 1990

Hayman Family Foundation, Fred
440 North Rodeo Dr., Penthouse, Beverly Hills, CA 90210
Yr. ended 12/31/88: Assets, $975,418 (M); grants, $89,500

Heitler Fund
1410 Grant St., Suite A101, Denver, CO 80203
Yr. ended 11/30/88: Assets, $291,586 (M); grants, $37,425

Heller Foundation, Dr. Bernard
New York, NY
Support only for specified beneficiaries

Hemingray Foundation, The
100 Alta St., No. 401, San Francisco, CA 94133-3532
Yr. ended 11/30/88: Assets, $44,868 (M); grants, $2,220

Higbee Foundation, The
Cleveland, OH
The foundation terminated in 1989

Honey Locust Foundation
Louisville, KY
The foundation is being dissolved

Hoover Charitable Trust 1916, Frank G.
c/o Society Bank of Eastern Ohio, N.A., 126 Central Plaza North, Canton, OH 44702
Yr. ended 12/31/88: Assets, $672,288 (M); grants, $0

Hope Charitable Foundation
Providence, RI
The foundation is a component fund of the Rhode Island Community Foundation

Horvitz Memorial Foundation, Inc., Samuel A.
Valley View, OH
The foundation terminated in 1987

Hubbell Foundation, James W. Hubbell, Jr. & Helen H.
c/o Bankers Trust Co., Trust Dept., P.O. Box 897, Des Moines, IA 50304-0897
Yr. ended 06/30/89: Assets, $1,037 (M); grants, $65,650

Ide Foundation, Dora Donner
c/o Chickering & Gregory, Two Embarcadero Ctr., Suite 740, San Francisco, CA 94111
Yr. ended 06/30/89: Assets, $651 (M); grants, $0

Interferon Foundation, The
Houston, TX
The foundation is no longer operational

Irving One Wall Street Foundation, Inc.
New York, NY
The foundation terminated in 1989 due to the takeover of Irving Bank by Bank of New York

J. & J. Foundation, Inc., The
Columbus, OH
The foundation merged into the George Foundation in 1988

Jacob Foundation, Inc., Thomas H.
P.O. Box 8010, Wausau, WI 54402-8010
Yr. ended 09/30/89: Assets, $607,066 (M); grants, $68,915

Jacobs Foundation, Charles B. & Irene B.
c/o Wormser, Kiely, Galef & Jacobs, 711 Third Ave., New York, NY 10017
Yr. ended 12/31/88: Assets, $98,860 (M); grants, $16,000

Jenkins Trust, Carolyn L.
Concord, NH
Non-grantmaking operating foundation

Jernigan Foundation
P.O. Box 848, Pelham, AL 35124-0848
Yr. ended 12/31/88: Assets, $2,630 (M); grants, $19,605

Johnston Foundation, The
Spokane, WA
The foundation was dissolved in 1988 and its assets distributed to the Johnston-Fix Foundation and the Johnston-Hanson Foundation

Kander Charitable Trust, Herbert
New York, NY
Support only for specified beneficiaries

Kapnek Charitable Trust
Philadelphia, PA
The trust is a foreign foundation

Keating-Crawford Foundation, Inc.
738 Schuyler Ave., Lyndhurst, NJ 07071
Yr. ended 12/31/88: Assets, $634,330 (M); grants, $96,550

Klafter Foundation, Herman & Gertrude
Chicago, IL
The foundation has terminated

Knapp Charitable Trust, Estelle
New York, NY
Specified beneficiaries

Kobrand Foundation
(Formerly Beefeater Foundation)
101 Park Ave., New York, NY 10178
Yr. ended 12/31/88: Assets, $918,921 (M); grants, $62,713

Kohl Charities, Inc., H. H.
Milwaukee, WI
The foundation merged with Herbert H. Kohl Charities, Inc. in 1989

Kresevich Foundation, Inc., The
184 West 237th St., Bronx, NY 10463
Yr. ended 11/30/88: Assets, $506,580 (M); grants, $91,510

Kritzer Charitable Trust
Chicago, IL
The foundation terminated in 1989. Its funds were distributed in full to the University of Illinois Foundation

Kroc Foundation, Joan B.
La Jolla, CA
The foundation is in the process of terminating; all remaining funds are committed

Kutak Foundation, Robert J.
1650 Farnam St., Omaha, NE 68102-2103
Yr. ended 12/31/88: Assets, $788,417 (M); grants, $73,076

LaFortune Foundation, J. A.
1801 Fourth National Bank Bldg., Tulsa, OK 74119
Yr. ended 12/31/88: Assets, $462,199 (M); grants, $26,400

Lambdyne Foundation
251 Merill St., Birmingham, MI 48011
Yr. ended 03/31/89: Assets, $229 (M); grants, $0

Landau Foundation, Inc., Fred & Anne
c/o Mann, Judd, Landau, 230 Park Ave., New York, NY 10169-0001
Yr. ended 12/31/88: Assets, $823,264 (M); grants, $61,788

Leeds & Northrup Foundation, The
Philadelphia, PA
The foundation is in the process of terminating

Leidesdorf Foundation, Inc.
203 South Lake Trail, Palm Beach, FL 33480
Yr. ended 12/31/88: Assets, $45,217 (M); grants, $7,725

Lineberger Foundation, Inc.
Belmont, NC
The foundation terminated in May, 1990

Lipper Foundation, Kenneth & Evelyn, The
c/o Lipper & Co., Inc., 101 Park Ave., 6th Fl., New York, NY 10178
Yr. ended 08/31/89: Assets, $748,008 (M); grants, $85,535

Lloyd Foundation, Ralph B., The
Los Angeles, CA
The foundation has terminated

London Memorial Hospital Foundation, George J.
c/o Shefsky, Saitlin & Froelich, Ltd., 444 North Michigan Ave., Chicago, IL 60611
Yr. ended 12/31/89: Assets, $864,816 (M); grants, $43,050

Loose Foundation, Jacob L. and Ella C.
c/o The Greater Kansas City Community Foundation, 127 West 10th St., Suite 406, Kansas City, MO 64105
Yr. ended 12/31/89: Assets, $0 (M); grants, $0

Lopin Foundation, Inc., Sam and Anna, The
936 Fifth Ave., New York, NY 10021
Yr. ended 06/30/88: Assets, $808,602 (M); grants, $87,313

LSI Foundation, The
Greenwich, CT
The foundation has terminated

Lucerna Fund
Port Washington, NY
Non-grantmaking operating foundation

MacDonald Trust, Mrs. Zoe Blunt
Houston, TX
Support only for a specified beneficiary

MacPherson Fund, Inc.
675 Mass Ave., Cambridge, MA 02139
Yr. ended 12/31/89: Assets, $272,910 (M); grants, $33,525

Madway Foundation
2200 Benjamin Franklin Pkwy., Apt. W-103, Philadelphia, PA 19130-3504
Yr. ended 12/31/88: Assets, $171,910 (M); grants, $10,820

Mank Foundation, Edward H., The
239 Lewis Wharf, Boston, MA 02109
Yr. ended 12/31/88: Assets, $71,512 (M); grants, $75,550

Mann Foundation for Scientific Research, Alfred E.
Sylmar, CA
Non-grantmaking operating foundation

Manpower Foundation, Inc.
5301 North Ironwood Rd., Milwaukee, WI 53201
Yr. ended 12/31/88: Assets, $646,416 (M); grants, $73,465

Marathon Oil Foundation, Inc.
Findlay, OH
The foundation merged into the USX Foundation in 1989

Markus Foundation Trust, Paula Anna
c/o Bank Of Boston, Po Box 1861, Boston, MA 02105
Yr. ended 12/31/88: Assets, $597,572 (M); grants, $35,957

Marlo Foundation, Ltd.
700 West Virginia St., Milwaukee, WI 53204-1580
Yr. ended 10/31/88: Assets, $340,844 (M); grants, $99,000

Marotta Family Foundation
30100 Chagrin Blvd., Suite 105, Pepper Pike, OH 44124
Yr. ended 12/31/88: Assets, $547 (M); grants, $59,000

Marquette Charitable Organization
Chicago, IL
The foundation terminated in 1989

Marx Residuary Trust, Robert S.
Cincinnati, OH
The foundation terminated in 1989

Massey Charitable Foundation
Nashville, TN
Single-purpose endowment

Mauze Charitable Trust, Jean
New York, NY
Support only for a college and a hospital

May Foundation, Morton J., The
St. Louis, MO
The foundation terminated in 1989

McBride Foundation
St. Louis, MO
The foundation terminated in Dec., 1990

McColl-Batts Foundation, The
Kalamazoo, MI
The foundation exists for the benefit of the Kalamazoo Nature Center and is no longer an active grantmaking organization

McCormick Foundation, Robert R.
Chicago, IL
All grants and loans are now made through the Robert R. McCormick Charitable Trust

McFarland Medical Trust
c/o Havana National Bank, 112 South Orange St., Havana, IL 62644
Yr. ended 12/31/88: Assets, $385,879 (M); grants, $93,675

McGregor Home, A. M., The
East Cleveland, OH
Grant program phased out May, 1990

McMillan-Avery Foundation
St. Louis, MO
The foundation merged into the St. Louis Community Foundation in 1989

McNally Charitable Trust, Rose
Saginaw, MI
The trust terminated in 1990

Mead Johnson & Company Foundation, Inc.
Evansville, IN
The foundation terminated in 1990

Memorial Fund for Curtis C. Spence and Jessie M. Spence
105 Court St., Elyria, OH 44035-5525
Yr. ended 12/31/88: Assets, $80,359 (M); grants, $93,595

Memphis-Plough Community Foundation, The
Memphis, TN
The foundation has merged into the Community Foundation of Greater Memphis

Menil Foundation, Inc.
Houston, TX
Operating foundation with specified beneficiaries

Mid-Nebraska Community Foundation, Inc.
117 North Dewey, P.O. Box 1321, North Platte, NE 69103
Yr. ended 5/31/89: Assets, $559,232 (M); grants, $16,630

Miller Charitable Fund, Stanley O.
P.O. Box 737, St. Joseph, MI 49085
Yr. ended 09/30/89: Assets, $781,544 (M); grants, $33,000

Montgomery Foundation, Inc., Jeannette & Lafayette
See Amont Foundation, Inc.

Moody Foundation, Inc., Robert
P.O. Box 1705, Santa Fe, NM 87504-1705
Yr. ended 12/31/88: Assets, $42,258 (M); grants, $11,584

Morgan Foundation, Roy T., The
Providence, RI
The foundation was succeeded by The Roy T. Morgan Foundation, Inc. in 1988

Morrison Foundation
Detroit, MI
The foundation is in the process of liquidation

Mueller Company Scholarship Foundation, C. F.
Jersey City, NJ
Due to the acquisition of C.F. Mueller Company by Best Foods, the foundation has terminated

Mugar Foundation, Inc., David G., The
One Bulfinch Place, Boston, MA 02114
Yr. ended 09/30/89: Assets, $191,784 (M); grants, $29,977

Mullarkey Foundation, Thomas & Theresa
c/o Lazard Freres & Co., One Rockefeller Plaza, New York, NY 10020-1902
Yr. ended 6/30/89: Assets, $41,945 (M); grants, $15,500

Murray Charitable Trust, Florence R. C.
Philadelphia, PA
The trust terminated in 1990

Muskiwinni Foundation, The
New York, NY
The foundation terminated in 1990

National Forge Foundation
c/o National Forge Company, Irvine, PA 16329
Yr. ended 12/31/89: Assets, $235,312 (M); grants, $76,375

Nelson Foundation, The
1125 18th St., West Des Moines, IA 50265-2320
Yr. ended 12/31/88: Assets, $377,431 (M); grants, $33,217

Newman Numismatic Education Society, Eric P.
St. Louis, MO
Non-grantmaking operating foundation

Nordman Charitable Trust, Amos
P.O. Box 479, Muskegon, MI 49443
Yr. ended 12/31/88: Assets, $940,789 (M); grants, $31,326

Norling Brothers Foundation
c/o American National Bank & Trust Co., Fifth & Minnesota Sts., St. Paul, MN 55101-4899
Yr. ended 12/31/88: Assets, $591,824 (M); grants, $70,900

Northwestern Bell Foundation
Omaha, NE
The foundation has merged with US WEST Foundation

O'Bleness Foundation No. 2, Charles G.
Columbus, OH
The foundation is in the process of terminating

Oak Hall Foundation, Inc.
840 Union St., Salem, VA 24153
Yr. ended 08/31/89: Assets, $4,781 (M); grants, $66,025

Oberlin Shansi Memorial Association
Oberlin, OH
Support only for specified beneficiaries

Osherow Foundation, The
c/o J. H. Cohn & Co., 75 Eisenhower Pkwy., Roseland, NJ 07068
Yr. ended 12/31/88: Assets, $539,440 (M); grants, $65,870

Ostrow Foundation, Seniel and Dorothy
c/o Cohen, Bender & Wall, 11999 San Vicente Blvd., Suite 300, Los Angeles, CA 90049-5042
Yr. ended 07/31/89: Assets, $954,484 (M); grants, $97,060

Parklands Foundation
1500 One Franklin Plaza, Philadelphia, PA 19102
Yr. ended 2/28/89: Assets, $308,359 (M); grants, $14,000

Patton Foundation, George Wm. Patton and Mary B.
Los Angeles, CA
Specified beneficiaries

Pearce Educational Foundation, Jack & Katherine
c/o United States National Bank, P.O. Box 179, Galveston, TX 77553-0179
Yr. ended 12/31/88: Assets, $776,637 (M); grants, $66,750

Pearson Memorial Fund, Patsy, The
Olympia Fields, IL
The foundation terminated in 1985

Philippian Foundation
c/o Townley & Updike, 405 Lexington Ave., New York, NY 10174
Yr. ended 10/31/89: Assets, $15,137 (M); grants, $38,500

Pittsburgh Forgings Foundation
Pittsburgh, PA
In 1988, the foundation terminated and transferred its assets to the AMPCO-Pittsburgh Foundation II, Inc.

Place Fund
6000 Parkland Blvd., Mayfield Heights, OH 44124
Yr. ended 12/31/88: Assets, $187,508 (M); grants, $18,000

Punia Foundation, The
16 Court St., Brooklyn, NY 11241-0103
Yr. ended 10/31/89: Assets, $128,001 (M); grants, $70,325

Quick Foundation, Inc., Edmund T. & Eleanor
1666 South University Blvd., Denver, CO 80210
Yr. ended 12/31/88: Assets, $392,085 (M); grants, $25,500

Rall Foundation, Inc., The
One Village Sq., Suite 121, Baltimore, MD 21210
Yr. ended 12/31/88: Assets, $100,391 (M); grants, $39,250

Reeves Brothers Foundation, Inc., The
Summit, NJ
The foundation transferred its funds to the Reeves Foundation in June, 1989

Reineke Foundation, Earl C.
505 Second Ave. North, Fargo, ND 58102
Yr. ended 12/31/88: Assets, $121,631 (M); grants, $0

Riesman Foundation, Joseph & Sadie
c/o Boston Safe Deposit & Trust Co., One Boston Place, Boston, MA 02108
Yr. ended 6/30/88: Assets, $346,761 (M); grants, $27,500

Roberts Foundation, The
520 Harbor Point Rd., Longboat Key, FL 33548
Yr. ended 9/30/88: Assets, $67,647 (M); grants, $84,104

Robertshaw Controls Company Charitable and Educational Foundation
c/o Robertshaw Controls Co., P.O. Box 26544, Richmond, VA 23261-6544
Yr. ended 03/31/90: Assets, $95,578 (M); grants, $95,107

Robin Hood Foundation, The
New York, NY
The foundation is a public charity

Roderick Foundation, Inc.
El Paso, TX
The foundation is now a component fund of the El Paso Community Foundation

Rogers Charitable Foundation, Kenny and Marianne
New York, NY
The foundation is currently inactive

Roosth Foundation, Sam
P.O. Box 2019, Tyler, TX 75701
Yr. ended 05/31/88: Assets, $960,785 (M); grants, $43,550

Roper Foundation
Kankakee, IL
The foundation has terminated

Rouback Family Foundation
Russell, KS
Support only for specified beneficiary organizations

Rowan Charitable & Educational Fund, Inc., C. L.
1918 Commerce Bldg., Fort Worth, TX 76102
Yr. ended 10/31/88: Assets, $818,871 (M); grants, $88,864

Sachs Foundation, Inc., The
Hingham, MA
The foundation is in the process of liquidation

Safdeye-Esses-Shalom Foundation, Inc.
20 West 33rd St., New York, NY 10001
Yr. ended 11/30/88: Assets, $3,434 (M); grants, $14,100

Salem Community Foundation, Inc.
Salem, OH
The foundation is inactive

Saltzman Foundation
7383 Orangewood Ln., Boca Raton, FL 33433
Yr. ended 12/31/88: Assets, $8,580 (M); grants, $25,565

Santa Fe Memorial Foundation
Temple, TX
The foundation makes grants to a specified beneficiary and is also in a 60-month termination

Sherman Fund, Saul & Devorah
208 South LaSalle St., Rm. 1840, Chicago, IL 60604
Yr. ended 09/30/89: Assets, $514,804 (M); grants, $79,660

Shuler Charitable Trust, John & Catherine
c/o Northern Trust Bank of Florida/Sarasota, 1515 Ringling Blvd., Sarasota, FL 33577
Yr. ended 12/31/88: Assets, $437,561 (M); grants, $22,000

Silberstein Foundation, Inc., William & Sylvia, The
93 Rye Rd., Rye, NY 10580
Yr. ended 11/30/88: Assets, $18,070 (M); grants, $86,304

Silverstein Family Foundation
1776 K St. N.W., Washington, DC 20006-2301
Yr. ended 11/30/88: Assets, $603,490 (M); grants, $76,925

Simon Foundation, Norton, The
Pasadena, CA
Non-grantmaking operating foundation

Simon Philanthropic Foundation - New York, Norton
Pasadena, CA
The foundation terminated in 1989

Smith Barney Foundation, The
New York, NY
The foundation has been merged into the Primerica Foundation

Smith Charitable Foundation, Caro Sewall Holmes
St. Louis, MO
Inactive foundation

Smith Charitable Trust, Emerson Sterling, The
101 East Main St., P.O. Box 167, Ravenna, OH 44266
Yr. ended 03/31/89: Assets, $413,514 (M); grants, $73,190

Sorensen Foundation, Harvey L. & Maud C.
San Francisco, CA
Specified beneficiaries, pursuant to the will of the donor

South Carolina National Charitable & Educational Foundation
Columbia, SC
The foundation has terminated

Stanadyne Foundation
Elyria, OH

Stark Foundation, The
c/o Rochelle Edwards, Burbank Studios, Columbia Plaza, West, Burbank, CA 91505
Yr. ended 11/30/88: Assets, $41,688 (M); grants, $5,000

Steinfeld Foundation
P.O. Box 3442, Chicago, IL 60654
Yr. ended 09/30/89: Assets, $6,985 (M); grants, $1,335

Stempler Foundation, Inc., Oscar & Lillian
4501 Connecticut Ave., N.W., Washington, DC 20008
Yr. ended 03/31/89: Assets, $574,368 (M); grants, $85,316

Stevens & Company, Inc. Foundation, J. P.
Greenville, SC
The foundation merged into West Point Pepperell Foundation in 1990

Stewards Foundation RGH Trust
Des Moines, WA
The trust terminated in 1989

Stockton Foundation, Inc., The
c/o First Union National Bank of Florida, P.O. Box 2080-0505, Jacksonville, FL 32231-0010
Yr. ended 11/30/88: Assets, $106,442 (M); grants, $16,400

Sukenik Foundation, The
118-75 Metropolitan Ave., Suite 1B, Kew Gardens, NY 11415
Yr. ended 11/30/88: Assets, $101,394 (M); grants, $64,406

Swanson Foundation, Inc., Carl and Caroline
Omaha, NE
Single-purpose endowment

Swartz Foundation, William & Mary
601 North Skokie Hwy., Lake Bluff, IL 60044
Yr. ended 11/30/88: Assets, $14,845 (M); grants, $65,000

Tallman Boys Fund Trust
c/o First of America Trust Co., 189 East Court St., Kankakee, IL 60901
Yr. ended 1/31/89: Assets, $965,270 (M); grants, $9,020

Taylor Foundation, The
2630 Exposition Blvd., Suite 103, Austin, TX 78703
Yr. ended 12/31/88: Assets, $102,472 (M); grants, $32,025

Teich Foundation, Curt
One First National Plaza, Suite 3148, Chicago, IL 60603-2279
Yr. ended 8/31/88: Assets, $432,929 (M); grants, $88,336

Templeton Foundation, Inc.
c/o Ann Cameron, Route 1, Box 171, Sewanee, TN 37375
Yr. ended 03/31/89: Assets, $67,270 (M); grants, $9,000

Terry Foundation, James W. and Norma Eliose
c/o Carl Lang, Rosenblum, Goldenhersh, Silverstein and Zaff, 7777 Bonhomme, 14th Fl., St. Louis, MO 63105
Yr. ended 12/31/88: Assets, $376,161 (M); grants, $64,710

Timken International Fund, The
Canton, OH
The fund merged with the Timken Foundation of Canton in 1988

Tosk Foundation
New York, NY
The foundation terminated in 1988

Traurig Foundation
21 Church St., P.O. Box 1285, Waterbury, CT 06702
Yr. ended 12/31/88: Assets, $289,627 (M); grants, $13,945

Treleaven Private Foundation, Richard W.
800 Hilltop Dr., Itasca, IL 60143
Yr. ended 06/30/89: Assets, $383,220 (M); grants, $67,172

Tuck Fund, Katherine
Detroit, MI
The foundation is in the process of terminating

Tull Foundation, J. M., The
Atlanta, GA
The foundation now reports as part of The Tull Charitable Foundation

Turner Construction Company Foundation
633 Third Ave., New York, NY 10017
Yr. ended 12/31/88: Assets, $1,111 (M); grants, $12,550

UCLA Foundation Charitable Fund
405 Hilgard Ave., Los Angeles, CA 90024
Yr. ended 06/30/89: Assets, $500,476 (M); grants, $32,058

Ullmann Foundation, Siegfried & Irma
c/o Weitzner, Levine, Hamburg et al., 230 Park Ave., New York, NY 10169
Yr. ended 12/31/88: Assets, $719,998 (M); grants, $38,108

Utopia Fund
New York, NY
The fund is inactive

Valentine Foundation
c/o Dechert Price & Rhoads, 3400 Centre Sq. West, Philadelphia, PA 19102
Yr. ended 11/30/89: Assets, $489,724 (M); grants, $52,621

Vernay Foundation, The
P.O. Box 184, Yellow Springs, OH 45387
Yr. ended 12/31/89: Assets, $131,386 (M); grants, $89,622

Vonderlieth Trust, Henry L.
Newark, NJ
Support only for a hospital facility in IL

Vose Foundation
(Formerly First National Foundation, Inc.)
9520 North May, Suite 320, Oklahoma City, OK 73120
Yr. ended 12/31/88: Assets, $505,134 (M); grants, $17,500

Wagner Fund
2221 North 30th, Tacoma, WA 98403
Yr. ended 06/30/89: Assets, $810,523 (M); grants, $75,100

Walter Foundation, Bill & Edith
c/o Schottenstein, Zox & Dunn, 41 South High St., Columbus, OH 43215
Yr. ended 12/31/88: Assets, $850,472 (M); grants, $37,267

Warner Communications Foundation, Inc.
New York, NY
The foundation is inactive due to merger of Warner Communications and Time, Inc.

Warner Electric Foundation
449 Gardner St., South Beloit, IL 61080
Yr. ended 12/31/88: Assets, $334,267 (M); grants, $99,895

Weller Investment Company
400 Westwood Dr., Denver, CO 80206-4132
Yr. ended 12/31/88: Assets, $749,638 (M); grants, $40,000

Williamsport Foundation
Williamsport, PA
The foundation is inactive

Wise Foundation, Jessie Kenan
Richmond, VA
The foundation has terminated

Wohl Family Foundation, Ignatz
See The Alfred Wohl Foundation, Inc.

Wohl Foundation, Inc., Alfred, The
(Formerly Ignatz Wohl Family Foundation)
c/o Paul Scherer & Co., 330 Madison Ave., New York, NY 10017
Yr. ended 03/31/89: Assets, $106,187 (M); grants, $28,930

Wolf, Sr. & Jr. Foundation, Harry H.
Wilmette, IL
The foundation terminated in 1986

Womack Foundation, Milton J.
c/o City National Bank, Trust Dept., P.O. Drawer 1231, Baton Rouge, LA 70821
Yr. ended 12/31/88: Assets, $770,069 (M); grants, $78,400

Woodner Foundation
660 Madison Ave., New York, NY 10021
Yr. ended 12/31/88: Assets, $0 (M); grants, $0

Woolley-Clifford Foundation
c/o Gerald A. Wolf, Two North Dean St., Englewood, NJ 07631
Yr. ended 12/31/88: Assets, $725,431 (M); grants, $42,150

Young Foundation, Inc., Stanton L.
P.O. Box 1466, Oklahoma City, OK 73101
Yr. ended 12/31/88: Assets, $522,928 (M); grants, $92,520

Younker Foundation Trust, Rachel
Des Moines, IA
Single-purpose endowment

Zuckerman Foundation, Paul
31731 Northwestern Hwy., Suite 107E, Farmington Hills, MI 48018-4566
Yr. ended 12/31/88: Assets, $983,052 (M); grants, $88,000

APPENDIX B

The following organizations are classified as private operating foundations under the IRS tax code. Their primary purpose is to conduct research, social welfare, or other programs determined by their individual governing bodies or establishment charters. Although they recently met the asset criteria set for *The Foundation Directory* (assets of $1 million or more), they are excluded from this volume because they do not maintain active grantmaking programs. E.I.N. refers to the Employer Identification Number assigned to the foundation by the IRS.

STATE	E.I.N.
Alabama	
Mobile Female Benevolent Society	630302149
Arizona	
Amerind Foundation, Inc., The	860122680
National Historical Fire Foundation	366111510
Tohono Chul Park, Inc.	860438592
Tucson Osteopathic Foundation	742449503
Arkansas	
Cooper Memorial Chapel, Mildred B.	581606828
HAR-BER Village Foundation, The	710541295
California	
Alta Vista Foundation	952576893
American Physical Fitness Research Institute, Inc.	952287919
Autry Western Heritage Museum, Gene	953947744
Beverly Foundation	953382956
Bleitz Wildlife Foundation, Inc.	956049593
Current Wisdom, Inc.	953893988
Djerassi Foundation, The	946115995
Doelger Animal & Wildlife Preserve Trust, Thelma	946582690
Foundation for American Christian Education	952393887
Fowler, Jr. Foundation, Francis E.	956092412
Hathaway Ranch Museum	954071530
Laboratory for the Advancement of Biomedical Research	953788451
Living Free	953628770
Loma Linda Faculty Medical Group, Inc.	330080787
Mama Foundation, The	954054650
Mechanics' Institute	941254644
Meditation Groups, Inc.	066054153
Monterey Bay Aquarium Foundation	942487469
Monterey Bay Aquarium Research Institute	771050580
Packard Humanities Institute, The	943038401
San Diego College of Retailing	330191784
Santa Catalina Island Conservancy	237228407
Schwab Foundation, Charles and Helen	943053861
Sea World Research Institute	952304740
Simon Art Foundation, Norton	956038921
Smith-Kettlewell Eye Research Foundation	946127237
Staley Educational Foundation, Richard Seth, The	953532336
Stanford Theater Foundation, The	770019543
Stuart Foundation, The	953353820
Walska Lotusland Foundation, Ganna	237082550

	E.I.N.
Western Foundation of Vertebrate Zoology	956096078
Whitman Institute, The	942984079
Wrigley Memorial Garden Foundation	952574307
Wunderman Museum, Severin, The	330082676
Colorado	
Canyon Colorado Equid Sanctuary	742140294
Gold Lake Foundation, Inc.	840949402
Harmsen Foundation, The	742299092
Museum of Outdoor Arts, The	742234944
Windstar Foundation	840740819
Connecticut	
Albers Foundation, Inc., Josef	237104223
Bacon Memorial Home	060662103
Burndy Library, Inc.	060709286
Card Home for the Aged, Inc.	060653041
Colony Foundation	060261454
Hascoe Foundation, The	222534970
Highstead Foundation, Inc.	061108612
Krieble Foundation, Inc., The	061011349
McLean Fund	066026241
Neustadt Museum of Tiffany Art, Egon & Hildegard	237361022
Newinton-Cropsey Foundation	060972155
Promisek, Inc.	060964701
Sterling Home of Bridgeport	060662169
Stone Trust Corporation, The	060552923
Stowe-Day Foundation	066042822
Wheeler School and Library	060728869
Wickham Park Trust Fund	066026059
Delaware	
Coxe Charitable Trust Foundation, Sophia G.	236001974
Delaware Museum of Natural History, Inc.	510083535
Longwood Gardens, Inc.	510110625
Palmer Home, Inc.	510066737
District of Columbia	
Cato Institute	237432162
Curry Foundation	436039016
Institute for Mental Health Initiatives	521273628
Lisner Home for Aged Women, Abraham and Laura	530228120
Montgomery Foundation, Inc., The	136153649
Phillips Collection, The	530204620
Remediation & Training Institute	521268332

	E.I.N.
Roosevelt Center for American Policy Studies, The	363163384
Shoemaker Home, Elizabeth R.	530211708
Tudor Place Foundation, Inc.	526070337

Florida

Azalea Trace, Inc.	591932549
Bok Tower Gardens Foundation, Inc.	231352009
Cooper Institute for Advanced Studies in Medicine and the Humanities	232012011
Cummer Museum Foundation Trust, DeEtte Holden	590870278
Dali Foundation, Inc., Salvador	346527073
Evans Foundation, Inc., J. E.	591146372
Historical Society of Martin County, Inc.	590913326
Kislak Foundation, Inc., Jay I.	592438331
Koger Foundation, Inc., Ira & Nancy, The	592440510
Margulies Foundation, Inc., Martin Z.	592130476
Mendez Foundation, Inc., C. E.	591086491
Morse Charitable Trust	341331872
Morse Foundation, Inc., Charles Hosmer	591659392
Neal Civic Center, Inc., W. T.	592140323
Regional Arts Foundation, Inc.	132914346
Selby Botanical Gardens, Inc., Marie, The	591848965
Society for the Prevention of Cruelty to Animals of Manatee County, Inc.	590826963
Weeks Air Museum, Inc.	592067321

Georgia

Broadway Towers, Inc.	581354973
Daughtry Foundation, Inc.	580673985
Garnett Senior Housing Foundation, Inc.	581395913
Hughston Sports Medicine Foundation	581354127
Kentucky Christian Senior Housing, Inc.	610937852
Lebanon Senior Housing, Inc.	581434676
Leitalift Foundation, Inc.	586058185
Lockerly Arboretum Foundation	581078686
St. Catherine's Island Foundation, Inc.	581449857
Walton County Foundation, Inc.	586034766

Hawaii

Lunalilo Home	990075244

Illinois

Amfund	362233542
Buehler Memorial, Christian	370661194
Cantigny First Division Foundation	362379641
Cantigny Trust	510203498
Chicago Access Corporation	363239826
Chicago Center Health Care System	363294834
Cook Foundation, David C.	366008100
Everly Home for the Aged Trust	376047799
Harding Museum, George F.	361190374
King-Bruwaert House	362167769
Logan County Park and Trails Foundation	237041808
Mark Home, Caroline	362284287
Page Foundation, Ruth, The	237069159
Proctor Endowment, John C.	370662595
Smith Home, Washington and Jane	362167948
Tatman Village, Inc.	371075972
Terra Museum of American Art	362999442
Wilderness Research Foundation	362355084

Indiana

Compton Oriental Arts Foundation, W. A.	510173635
Fourth Freedom Forum, Inc.	351546655
Golay Community Center, Inc.	351518699
Harris Homes for Widows & Orphans, Benjamin	351080834
Indianapolis Motor Speedway Foundation, Inc.	356013771
Minnetrista Cultural Foundation, Inc.	351628916
Olivet Foundation, Inc.	237026852
Sabin Home, Ruth C.	350886845
Solarbron Pointe, Inc.	351544098

Iowa

Cooks Home for the Friendless, Clarissa C.	420723017
Fisher Governor Foundation	426068730
Grout Trust, H. W.	237416881

	E.I.N.
Stanley Foundation, The	426071036
Warp Pioneer Village Foundation, Harold	363136921

Kansas

Logan Foundation, The	481061492

Kentucky

Home of the Innocents, The	610445834
Kentucky Derby Museum Corporation	311023459
Live Oak Gardens Foundation, Inc.	720857908
Maysville & Mason County Library Historical and Scientific Association	610444776
Moorman Home for Women, Charles P.	610444778
Oldham Civic Center & Game Preserve, Inc.	310908496

Louisiana

Brandon Hall Foundation	581691816
Brownell Foundation, The	726041231
Longue Vue Foundation	726029467
Milne Asylum for Destitute Orphan Girls	720261790
Noel Foundation, Inc.	237177629
Norton Art Foundation, R. W., The	720517182
Oak Alley Foundation	726032652
San Francisco Plantation	720789586
Six Foundation	726019187
Society for the Relief of Destitute Orphan Boys	720408986
Zigler Museum Foundation	726027971

Maine

Bangor Children's Home	010211481
Cape Elizabeth Home	010238086
Farmington Home for Aged People	010217212
Frye Home, Eunice	010211504
Good Samaritan Agency	010211507
Grand Banks Schooner Museum Trust	010359164
Kaler-Vaill Memorial Home	010261396
Lincoln House, Deborah	010226346
Malcolm Institute, Francis M.	942745577
McArthur Home for Aged People Association	010212437
Old Folks Home Association of Brunswick	010220389
Old Folks Home in Bath	010131950
Old York Historical Society	222474846
Owls Head Foundation Trust	237307367
Pine Tree Conservation Society, Inc.	237158781
Redington Memorial Home	010211547
Sawyer Foundation, Araxine Wilkins	010228468
Seal Cove Auto Museum	010277592
Vaill Trust, Addie Kaler	016007600

Maryland

B & O Railroad Museum, Inc.	521535426
Bethel Corporation	520888335
Chase Home, Inc.	520613676
Home for the Aged of Frederick City	520591486
Ladew Topiary Gardens, Inc., Trustees of the	132787826
Levi Foundation, Inc., Robert H. & Ryda H.	521217539
Logistics Management Institute	520741393
Maryland Anti-Vivisection Society	526001538
McManus Institute, Inc.	521304174
People for Better Housing, Inc.	521110633
Rothschild Art Foundation, Inc.	521301060

Massachusetts

Ames Free Library of Easton	237245953
Amherst Home for Aged Women	042127021
Anagnos Schools, Michael	046012768
Andover Historical Society	042312091
Art Complex, Inc., The	046155696
Berkeley Retirement Home, The	042104374
Berkshire Retirement Home, Inc.	042103875
Bertram Home for Aged Men	042103743
Biosciences Research Foundation, Inc.	222483849
Blanchard Fund, Inc., Henry Lawton	046054153
Boston Local Development Corporation	042681311
Cambridge Home, The	042103958
Carleton House, Elizabeth	042105924

	E.I.N.
Childs Park Foundation, Inc.	042143976
Clinton Home for Aged People	042131745
Colonial Society of Massachusetts	046110988
Colony Memorial	042633276
Concord's Home for the Aged	042103762
Cumberland Farms Conservation Trust	042616919
Dana Home of Lexington, Inc.	042111392
Deutsches Altenheim, Inc.	042104144
Fitch Home, Inc.	042111388
Fuller House of Stoneham	042121349
Fuller Trust, Inc.	042104243
Gardner Museum, Isabella Stewart	042104334
Griffin-White Home for Aged Men and Aged Couples, Inc.	042148009
Gund Art Foundation, The	042714713
Heritage Plantation of Sandwich, Inc.	042704457
Historic Boston, Inc.	046111819
Hitchcock Free Academy, Trustees of	042277210
Home for Aged Women in Salem	042104318
Hopedale Community House, Inc.	042133252
Insurance Library Association of Boston	042104331
Koch Foundation, Inc., William L., The	510179280
Lathrop Home	042104372
Leland Home, The	042104385
Loomis House, Inc.	042108366
Lynn Historical Society, Inc.	042269520
Lynn Home for Young Women, Inc.	042104409
Mann II Home for Aged & Infirm Women, Seth	042111410
Marblehead Female Humane Society	042104694
Montgomery Home for Aged People, Inc.	042131757
Mount Pleasant Home, The	042103822
National Health Research Foundation, Inc.	222521036
New England Home for the Deaf, The	042104760
Nichols House Museum, Inc.	046006789
North Andover Historical Society	042259628
Open Church Foundation	042108377
Orleans Conservation Trust	237418072
Park Trust, Francis William	046092035
Rowland Institute for Science, Inc., The	042704639
Roxbury Home for Aged Women	042104858
Seamen's Widow & Orphan Association	046014352
Springfield Home for the Elderly	042105936
Stanley Park of Westfield, Inc.	042131404
Wales Home for Aged Women	041940730
Whitehead Institute for Biochemical Research	061043412
Willard House and Clock Museum, Inc.	042671799
Winchester Mount Vernon House	042104317

Michigan

Ballenger Trust f/b/o Ballenger Park, W. S.	381408046
Detroit Neurosurgical Foundation	382127946
Ford House, Edsel & Eleanor	382218274
Gilmore Foundation, Genevieve and Donald	386154163
Kalamazoo Aviation History Museum, The	382144402
Lowell Area Housing	381945437
McFarlan Home	381390531
Walker Foundation, Carey, The	066071078

Minnesota

Bakken, The	510175508
Belwin Foundation	410967891
Burke Foundation, Mary & Jackson	237209330
Carpenter Foundation, Thomas and Edna	237275337
Charlson Research Foundation	411313302
Cook Waterfowl Foundation	363327050

Mississippi

Eastman Memorial Foundation	640308406

Missouri

Atkins Trust, Mary	436037928
Centre for International Understanding	430922802
Charless Home, The	430666753
Drumm Institute, Andrew	440569643
L-A-D Foundation, Inc.	436036974
Masonic Home of Missouri	430653370

	E.I.N.
Memorial Home, Inc.	430657946
Miniature Museum of Kansas City Foundation	431187852

Montana

Sweetgrass Lodge, Inc.	810383156
United States High Altitude Speed Skating Foundation	810428797

Nebraska

Swanson Center for Nutrition, Inc.	237175802

New Hampshire

Animal Rescue League of Manchester, New Hampshire	020222790
Blue Hills Foundation, Inc.	020366576
Chase Home for Children	022229190
Dover Children's Home	022233230
Eventide Home, Inc.	020228137
Foundation for Biblical Research, The	020243633
Franklin Home for the Aged Association	020202330
Gale Home, The	020223444
Harris Center for Conservation Education, Inc.	237085105
Home for Aged Women	020223603
Hunt Community	020369906
Manchester Historic Association	020223390
Milford Home for Aged Women	020223604
Nashua Historical Society	020246187
New Hampshire Centennial Home for the Aged	020224596
Norwell Home	020225753
Prospect Hill Home	020222146
Rolfe & Rumford Home of Concord, New Hampshire	020223340
Scott-Farrar Home, The	020241739
Shaker Village, Inc.	237035275
Sweeney Home, Mary A.	020312307
Webster Foundation, Rannie	020331198
Wentworth Home for Chronic Invalids, Mark H.	020222243
Wentworth Home for the Aged	020223354
Women's Aid Home	020222249
Woodward Home, Inc., The	020220400
Young Men's Christian Association of Portsmouth	020222251

New Jersey

Buehler Aviation Research, Inc.	221754787
Duke Gardens Foundation, Inc.	221630203
Elizabethtown Historical Foundation	226055641
Gund Collection of Western Art	346623289
Haines Home for Aged People, Job	220972180
Harbor Branch Oceangraphic Institution, Inc.	591542017
Indigent Widows and Single Women's Home Society of Trenton	210639869
Institute for Advanced Studies of World Religions	237085108
Liberty Hall Foundation	226109813
Mannheimer Primatological Foundation	221851590
Memorial Home of Upper Montclair for Aged People	221487239
Noyes Foundation, Mr. & Mrs. Fred Winslow	237247632
Polychronis Foundation, Constantinos C.	237172254
Ward Home, Marius L.	221574538

New Mexico

United World of the Universe Foundation	742173149

New York

Adirondack Historical Association	135635801
Advertising Educational Foundation, Inc.	133228986
Agricultural Development Council, Inc.	131771777
Albany Guardian Society	141363010
Andrus Memorial, Inc., John E.	135596795
Andrus Memorial, Inc., Julia Dyckman	132793295
Bismarck Foundation, Mona	133073031
Boscobel Restoration, Inc.	141458845
Branch-Wilbur Fund, Inc., The	166093008
Brewster House, Elizabeth	150533548
Brooklyn Section Community Senior Citizen Center	237389126
Canajoharie Library & Art Gallery	141398373
Chenango Valley Home for Aged People	150543650
Clark Manor House, The	160755755
Comunita Giovanile San Michele, Inc.	136102743
Corning Museum of Glass, The	160764349

	E.I.N.
Dia Art Foundation, Inc.	237397946
Dungkar Gompa Society, Inc.	132875931
Elizabethtown Social Center, Inc.	141338389
Fiscal Philatelic Foundation, Inc.	112506077
Fish Library, Alice and Hamilton	132933774
Frick Collection, The	131624012
Fuld Institute for Technology Nursing Education, Inc., The	133424850
Gardiner Foundation, Inc., Robert David Lion, The	133354308
Glens Falls Home	141340067
GreenPark Foundation, Inc.	136155738
Havemeyer Foundation, Inc., Dorothy Russell, The	133022482
Historic Hudson Valley	131692606
Home for the Aged	160766337
Hudson Home for the Aged	141436628
Human Potential Foundation	112670749
Huntington Free Library and Reading Room	135562384
Ingersoll Memorial for Aged Men, Inc.	141364550
Innisfree Foundation, Inc.	131972195
Jonas Foundation, Inc., Louis August	141387863
Koch Foundation, Frederick R.	133088563
Ladies Union Benevolent Society	150539106
Lehrman Institute, The	237218534
Lincoln Court Apartments Housing Development Fund Company, Inc.	222302282
Melville Memorial Foundation, Frank	116036411
Myrin Institute, Inc., The	111857581
Nantucket Ornithological Association	136176966
Neuroblastoma Foundation	363486770
Noguchi Foundation, Inc., Isamu	133059538
Orentreich Foundation for the Advancement of Science, Inc.	136154215
Osborn Memorial Home Association, Miriam	135562312
Pearson Art Foundation, Inc.	237087276
Performing Arts Foundation, Inc.	136149781
Public Art Fund, Inc.	132898805
Research Charitable Trust, The	222249971
Research Institute for the Study of Man	131874676
Rock Foundation	060944728
Rockwell Foundation, The	166052043
Rockwell Museum, The	222468604
Rojtman Foundation, Inc.	396050193
Rye Senior Citizens Apartment Housing Development Fund Corporation	133112042
Schweinfurth Memorial Art Center	161097876
Seabury Wilson Home, Inc., The	131740038
Sutton Place Foundation	980070731
That's the Spirit Productions, Inc.	133025846
Two Hundred Seventy-Two to Two Hundred Eighty Linwood Avenue, Inc.	237372052
Warner Home for the Aged	160743217
Welch Thanksgiving Home, Clara	150543655
Westmoreland Sanctuary, Inc.	131855977
Women's Christian Association of Fredonia, New York	160771085
Woodstock Foundation, Inc.	030221142
Young Morse Historic Site	141619998

North Carolina

College Foundation, Inc.	566046937
Reynolda House, Inc.	560810676
Walthour-Moss Foundation	237380583

Ohio

Abbot Home	341379421
Baker Family Museum, Inc., The	311131762
Blackburn Home for Aged People Association	340714543
Breiel Boulevard Care Center d/b/a Willow Knoll Nursing Center, Inc.	311059859
Bunker Hill Haven Trust	316040522
Dawes Arboretum, The	314379601
First 202 Housing Corporation	311070855
Kachelmacher Memorial, Inc.	310792046
King Trust No. 3, Charles Kelley	346506846
Masonic Toledo Trust	346560639
Palmer Home, Judson, The	344436480
Philada Home Fund	310677810
Rex Foundation	341320874
Sauder Museum, Inc.	237042835

Oklahoma

Goddard Youth Foundation	730749570
Sand Springs Home	730579278
Zink Foundation, John	736090267

Pennsylvania

Andalusia Foundation	232115358
Animal Care Fund	221837635
David Library of the American Revolution, Inc.	237289047
Easton Home for Aged Women	240801265
Garrett-Williamson Foundation	231433892
Gibbons Home	231381979
Glatfelter Memorial Field Trust	231640626
Hahn Home, The	231425032
Heinz House Association, Sarah	250965390
Henry Foundation for Botanical Research	231365145
Hershey Foundation, M. S.	236242734
Institute for Bio-Information Research	232528579
Jenkins Residuary Trust, H. Lawrence	236491966
Kirby Episcopal House, Inc., Fred M. and Jessie A.	240826175
Knox Home, Charles C.	231352347
Kuhn Day Camp, Henry J. & Willemina B.	231480672
Long Home, The	231352360
Lycoming House	231365326
Morris Animal Refuge	231352237
Newlin Foundation, Nicholas	231600703
Nursing Foundation of Pennsylvania	222479246
Open Land Conservancy of Chester County	237253755
Park Home, Inc.	240522575
Polk Foundation, Charles P. & Margaret E.	236296772
Roxborough Home for Indigent Women	231401566
Ryerss Infirmary for Dumb Animals Trust	236215037
Steinman Conestoga House Foundation, James Hale	232179646
Von Hess Foundation, Louise Steinman	237368611
Watson Memorial Home	250965602
Woods-Marchand Foundation	251014553
Yellow Springs Institute for Contemporary Studies & the Arts	231996473

Rhode Island

Brown Center for the Study of American Civilization, John Nicholas, The	222506553
Herreshoff Marine Museum	237102744
Lynette Home, Nina	050259061
Newport Restoration Foundation	050317816

South Carolina

Magill Foundation, Arthur and Holly	570713587
Muller, Jr. Trust, John D.	576107692
O'Neill, Jr. Education Fund, L. Arthur	237227009

South Dakota

Peterson-Bahde-Coleman Homes, Inc.	460343163

Tennessee

Caldsted Foundation	620696466
Memphis Sunshine Home for Aged Men	620202745

Texas

Anchorage Foundation of Texas	742071804
Bass Foundation, Anne T. & Robert M.	752001892
Breckenridge Library and Fine Arts Foundation	751891984
Brownson Home, Inc.	741237326
Center for Christian Growth, Inc.	751671920
Central Texas Museum Of Automotive History	742202758
Combat Jets Flying Museum	760197022
Davis Memorial Park, T. W.	746026891
Doss Youth Center, Inc., M. S.	751089342
Gihon Foundation	751612234
Guy Christian Music Ministry, Inc., Rita	770101026
Haley Memorial Library, Nita Stewart	237327454
Hall-Voyer Foundation	750868394
Heights Towers Services Company	237437989
Hendrick Home for Children	750818165

	E.I.N.
Hope Charities, Inc.	760202547
Kimbell Art Foundation	756036226
LDBrinkman Foundation	742374663
Majestic Foundation, Inc.	741908420
McDermott Fund, Eugene & Margaret	756008313
Menil Collection	760001544
Oldham Trust, Ida Mae	750993500
Pape Foundation, G. H.	746041756
PCCOA Housing Authority	751821147
Perry Gething Foundation	742359576
Pshigoda Foundation, Crist & Elizabeth	751783277
Rayburn Foundation, Sam	750984560
Read Youth Charities	237048642
Texas Energy Museum, Inc.	760225927
Thomsen Foundation	751833850
Tucker Foundation, The	746053182
Utah	
Stanley Research Foundation	870334696
Vermont	
Converse Home, Inc., The	030179406
Home for Aged Women of St. Johnsbury	030182054
Homestead, Inc.	030195636
Virginia	
Agecroft Association, The	540805729
American Foundation for the Study of Man	996001275
Ballentine Home for the Aged, Mary F.	540538201
Brookfield, Inc.	540638415
Chelonia Institute	521081407
Hunter Foundation	540801148
Jones Library Association, George M.	540505921
Kaufman Americana Foundation	510217081
Lafferty Foundation, The	541224308
McVitty Homes of Roanoke Valley, Inc.	510190114
Miller Home of Lynchburg, Virginia	540505999
Virginia Museum of Natural History Foundation	521356848
Williams Home, Inc., The	540524517
Winkler Botanical Preserve	510243204
Washington	
Casey Family Program, The	910793881
Frye Testamentary Trust f/b/o Charles & Emma Frye Free Public Art Museum, Inc., Charles H.	910659435
Jones Home, Franke Tobey, The	910575957
West Virginia	
Altenheim - The Home for the Aged	550371584
Foster Foundation, Inc.	550359756
Home for Aged Men	550359019
Wisconsin	
Fisher Philatelic Foundation, Inc., Margaret Woodson	237203064
Fox Cities Retirement Village, Inc.	391335177
Milwaukee Home for the Friendless	390837518
Paine Art Center and Arboretum	390785483
Phipps Center for the Arts, Inc.	391360778
Sand County Foundation	396089450
Uihlein Racing Museum Foundation, David	391284018
Woodson Art Museum, Inc., Leigh Yawkey	237281913
Wyoming	
Ucross Foundation	742188539
Whedon Cancer Detection Foundation, Earl & Bessie	830176313

APPENDIX C

The following organizations are classified as private nonoperating foundations under the IRS tax code. On the basis of statements from the organizations or an analysis of their most recent fiscal statements, it appears that these foundations contribute only to a few specified beneficiaries or to the support of a single organization or institution. Therefore, they are not included in this volume. Without further information, grantseekers are advised NOT to apply to these foundations for grant support. E.I.N. refers to the Employer Identification Number assigned to the foundation by the IRS.

STATE	E.I.N.
Alabama	
Bankhead Foundation	237047054
Brightwell School Trust, A. T.	636019162
Coastal Land Trust, Inc.	630849774
Edge Endowment Fund	630834443
Killgore Scholarship Trust Fund, J. A. & Ophelia	636055718
Marinos Trust, George	636018531
Warner Foundation Trust, David	630782745
Wheeler Memorial Foundation, Joe	630790958
Alaska	
Library Foundation	920072826
Arizona	
McCormick Trust, Ada P.	866097442
Metz Foundation, Arthur R.	366054389
Arkansas	
Rhew, Jr. Charitable Trust, J. C.	716132289
Richardson Foundation, Elizabeth Porter	581642867
Walthour Trust, J. D.	716082014
California	
Allensby Trust f/b/o Elks Lodge 1108 Charity Fund, Floyd D.	946572050
Anderson Foundation	952552375
Arboretum Fund	953310318
Bachrach Trust, Marguerite	946465724
Bacon Foundation, Inc., Francis, The	951921362
Beckman Laser Institute and Medical Center	953800459
Bothin Center, Henry E.	946118050
Bruml Trust, Simona	946461662
California Higher Education Loan Authority, Inc.	942618667
California Masonic Memorial Temple	941266937
Croft Trust, Gerald S. G.	956819409
DeHaven Trust, Madeline H.	946262074
Del Monte Forest Foundation, Inc.	946061665
Doelger Charitable Trust	946468716
Doheny Trust for St. Vincent de Paul Church, Carrie Estelle	956005702
Economic Development Foundation of Sacramento, Inc.	942674936
Free Scholarship Fund, William C. & Mazy Bell	956032103
Good Hope Medical Foundation	950782640
Hammer United World College Trust, Armand, The	954031114
Hansen Foundation, Fred J.	953247772
Houssels Trust, Hubert	956381605
Intra County Housing Corporation	953347447
Italian Welfare Agency Trust	946073585
Jewish Community Foundation Charitable Fund	953507310
Knapp Trust, Eloise M.	237338134
Knox Scholarship Trust, George & Mary	953751439
Kolb Foundation, Katherine	953582347
Lewis Charitable Trust, Cecile Woods	956550536
Link-Care Foundation	946121751
Lyons Trust, Austin E.	946412171
Morbio Trust, Adolph	946486955
Mudd Foundation, Mildred E. & Harvey S.	956021276
MW Anesthesia Pharmacology Research Foundation	942527684
Occidental College Charitable Fund	237327649
Palmuth Charitable Trust, Eugene & Edna	946478374
Perkins Trust, Nellie Thatcher	956652211
Peters Trust, John	946417522
Pfleger Foundation, George T.	952561117
Prescott Trust, Nellie	946054826
Robinson Trust, Harry W. & Virginia	956648391
Rohr Trust, Rosalie C.	946476435
Seaver Trust, Frank R.	956146676
Singleton Trust, Edward C.	946465282
Singleton Trust for Shriners Hospital for Crippled Children, Edward C.	946466283
Singleton Trust for the Salvation Army, Edward C.	946466282
Snelling Foundation, Gustavus J. & Helen Crowe	942924906
Southwest Hospital Foundation	952026888
Steiner Trust, Lionel	946445242
Stulsaft Testamentary Trust, Morris	946244806
Thompson Foundation, Porter E. & Helenmae	942831112
Van Nuys Trust, J. Benton	510193498
Veevers Charitable Trust, Eleanor	956795531
Walter Trust, Judith Scott	956007893
Weingart Center Association	956054617
Weingart Charitable Testamentary Trust, Ben	953646333
Weisbord Charitable Trust, Sam, The	956851741
Wiley Foundation, George R.	953923742
Williford Trust, Byron Lee	946399261
Wilson Fund, Jerry & Betty	956428914
Zabala Family Foundation	946079348
Zimmerman Memorial Fund, Robert & Adelaide May	956809322

	E.I.N.
Colorado	
Barnes Trust, Otis A. Barnes & Margaret T.	846023466
Koch Trust, Gwendolyn	846049291
Sachs Trust, Henry	846019399
Wann Foundation, Ralph J., The	846022561
Connecticut	
Belding Fund, Alvah N.	237425259
Bradley Home for the Aged, The	060646552
Burr Trust f/b/o Larabee Fund, Willie O.	061007619
Ferguson Trust, Andrew	066189534
Hunter Trust, Leila C.	066156777
Lloyd Trust f/b/o Metropolitan Museum of Art, Ruth	136844377
Miller Trust, Edward	060660911
Mitnick Fund, Louis	066291700
Pardee Estate Trust, Sarah N.	066029233
Riddle Trust f/b/o Hill-Stead Museum, Theodore Pope	136046213
Snider Charitable Trust, Dorothy & Samuel	066114143
Swebilius Trust, C. G.	066021035
Ward Trust, James E.	222589381
Delaware	
Bishop Trust B for the SPCA of Manatee County, Florida, Edward E.	237366312
Cohen Foundation, Inc., Harry, The	516015783
Kelly Trust dated July 30, 1969 f/b/o Initial Teaching Alphabet Foundation, Inc., Eugene V.	237277016
Miller Trust for Designated Charities, Ida J.	516012859
Pratt Trust for the Franke Tobey Jones Home for Aged People, Lillian T.	516012452
District of Columbia	
Plummer Trust, George P.	526181726
Scholz Foundation, Robert O.	521104075
Tarp Institute, Inc.	520955491
Wilson Scholarship Trust, J. Finley	526101438
Florida	
Bickel Charitable Trust, Karl A.	596515937
Buckner Foundation, Thad & Loca Lee	596171241
Buena Vida Estates, Inc.	640639722
Deford Charitable Trust, Herman	596841753
Kennedy Charitable Trust, William M.	596692270
Salvation Army Trust B	596748098
Williams Foundation, Inc., Albert Lynn	132836662
Georgia	
Bethany Home Trust	586075346
Mix Memorial Fund, Inc., Charles L.	580699008
Pebble Hill Foundation, Inc.	346525857
Tuttle Home, Newton	580566249
Hawaii	
Henriques Trust, Lucy K.	996002291
Lyman Charitable Trust, Orlando H.	996043763
Illinois	
Bane Charitable Trust, Earl M.	376188528
Barker Charitable Trust, Ernestine G.	376249141
Buehler Trust, Phoebe B.	370196790
Butterworth Memorial Trust, William	362255481
Coon Foundation, Owen L.	366066907
D & D Foundation	363195374
Field Trust, Clement V.	362157497
Harris Foundation, Stanley G.	366438478
Koehler Fund, John G.	376141953
Manaster - Dr. Charles H. Solomon Scholarship Fund, Abe and Esther	521244793
Mather Foundation Trust, Alonzo C.	366015440
Mather Trust, Alonzo Clark	366010112
Mitchell Foundation, John R. and Eleanor R.	376053100
Morton Arboretum	361505770
Perlman Family Foundation, Louis & Anita	362670190
Quarrie Charitable Fund	366646475
Quarrie Charitable Trust No. 2, William F., Mabel E., and Margaret K.	366646474
Seidenadel Charitable Trust	366791306

	E.I.N.
Society of Economic Geologists Foundation, Inc.	516020487
Ward Foundation, Alice M. & William M.	237311424
Whitman Trust, Jessie Collins	237423199
Zimmerman Foundation, William J.	421223262
Indiana	
Baber Foundation, Inc., Weisell	356024561
Bethesda Corporation	351401887
Blaffer Trust, Robert Lee	746060871
Bronstein Foundation No. 2, Sol & Arlene	356345774
Caldwell Memorial Home Trust, Jennie E.	350907305
Ellison Scholarship Fund, Harold	356375836
Ford Memorial Home, Charles	350985961
Indiana University Retirement Community, Inc.	310920220
Newland Testamentary Trust, Helen Gregory	310967148
Iowa	
Aliber Charitable Trust, Robert	426273581
Cole and Connie Belin Charitable Foundation, Marlin	421263748
Lacy Trust, W. Seymour	426051558
Shadle Memorial Fund, Webb	420746005
Kansas	
Butler County Historical Supply, Inc.	486120516
Gouldner Memorial Medical Foundation, R. M.	486258073
Justice Foundation, Walter E. and Velma G.	481004072
Wichita Home for the Aged	480554804
Kentucky	
English Charitable Trust, Fenton E.	376121328
Markey Trust for Bluegrass Boys Ranch, Inc., Lucille P.	592328292
Stitzel Trust f/b/o Louisville Protestant Altenheim, Florence	616026727
Louisiana	
Burden Foundation	726030712
McClure Fund, Albert N. & Hattie M.	726019978
Maine	
Carver Trust f/b/o Goodall Hospital, Helen E.	016044693
Knowles Trust B, Leonora H.	222789214
Maine Home for Boys	237119261
McKenney & Emery W. Booker Education Trust, Marion	016070365
Ross Trust Part I & II, Sylvia E.	016017314
Sunset Home of Waterville	010219135
Wardwell Home for Old Ladies of Saco & Biddeford	010213987
Maryland	
Ferguson Foundation, Inc., Alice	520694646
Reynolds Trust, Zachary Smith	526021749
Massachusetts	
American Friends of Maru a Pula School, Inc.	237449724
Babson Memorial, Inc., Isabel	046031813
Binney Charitable Foundation, Elizabeth Peter	046020266
Brandegee Charitable Foundation	042103930
Brooks Trust f/b/o Greater Boston Council on Alcoholism, Harold	046526806
DeLoura Family Trust, The	046460749
Domicilia, Inc.	042665097
Elliot Charitable Trust, John & Sarah C.	046282546
Fogg Trust, Horace T. Fogg, Isabella F. Fogg, Faulkner Fogg, and Helen L., The	112698718
Fraser Foundation, Richard M. & Helen T.	046566891
Harris Foundation, William H.	046197960
Heritage Plantation of Sandwich Fund	237259864
Holtzer Fund, Charles W.	046008252
Lynn Home for Elderly Persons	042400070
Maliotis Charitable Foundation 1981, Costas & Mary	042738800
McGillicuddy Charitable Trust, John T.	042642387
Merrimack Valley Textile Museum, Inc.	042276089
Newburyport Society for the Relief of Aged Men	042111219
Newburyport Society for the Relief of Aged Women	042121771
Peters Testamentary Trust, G. Gorham	046111827
Pinkham Memorial, Inc., Lydia E.	042104836
Raptelis Foundation, Demosthenis	046233953
Reed Charitable Trust	042603322

	E.I.N.
Sears Trust, Clara Endicott	046025576
Shaw Fund, Miriam	046497465
Smalley Foundation, Inc.	136225947
Stevens-Bennett Home, Inc.	042104803
Taylor Educational Foundation, Thomas & Charlotte Valentine, The	222571261
Tidd Home	042115502

Michigan

Akers Trust, Forrest H.	386066391
Avery Foundation, Charles Shirley	386218309
Edmore Trust, Glenn Curtis	386173942
Kiwanis of Michigan Foundation	381723513
Krasl Charitable Trust, George	386370529
MacCrone Trust, Edward E.	386043730
Schneider Trust for Village, Philip H.	386513806
Thompson Foundation, Mary	381359097
Whiting Auditorium Trust, James H.	386041292

Minnesota

Bell Testamentary Trust f/b/o University of Minnesota, James F.	416039114
Charlson Charitable Trust, Beryl W.	416242215
David Memorial Trust, John C. & Nettie V.	510159851
Hallett Charitable Trust	416211994
Hull Educational Foundation	416019516
Kennedy Memorial Fund Trust, Augustus H.	411328800
Long Prairie Housing Association, Inc.	411406191
Ozias Charitable Trust, Edward M.	416164912
Roberg Endowment Trust, Louis A.	416223072
South Washington County Senior And Handicapped Housing, Inc.	411349989
Yetter Charitable Trust, Berdie S.	237419768

Missouri

AJP Foundation	431420360
Blewett Trust, Scott	436018190
Blind Girls Home	430662450
Bohan Foundation, Ruth H.	436269867
Bonne Terre Hospital Association, Inc.	430188680
Burger Scholarship Foundation, Adeline and Edna L.	436189843
Dunn Memorial Trust, Thomas	436020367
Hall Library Trusts, Linda A.	440527122
Hedrick Trust, Minnie B.	446008725
Loose Million Dollar Charity Fund Trust, Jacob L.	446009244
Loose Trust, Ella C.	446009265
McQuigg Trust, Harry M.	436019661
McWilliams Memorial Hospital Trust	436062691
Noyes Testamentary Trust, Sarepta Ward	446013662
Policemen & Firemen Fund of St. Louis, Inc.	436032516
Sansone Trust B, Helen W.	436311833
Seay Foundation	436055549
Stoppe Trust, Lucy K.	431478917
Templin Trust, Lucinda	436106855
Tribble Trust, Andrew, Maxine & Carrie E.	436179211

Montana

Copulos Family Hospital Trust	816043540
Sweet Foundation, Lloyd D.	237131688

Nebraska

Spotts Trust, The	476126112

Nevada

Schooley Charitable Trust, Paul T. Schooley & Everette F.	886038983

New Hampshire

Britton Testamentary Trust, Arthur H.	026004800
Fitch Trust f/b/o Cheshire Health Foundation, Leon M. & Hazel F.	026061000
Fitch Trust f/b/o Elliot Hospital, Leon M. & Hazel F.	026061001
Friendship Fund, Inc. Trust f/b/o Institute of Current World Affairs	136045127
Gile Trust, Helen Blake	026003982
Gilman Trust, Oliver J. M.	020222133
Gregg, Jr. Family Foundation, Inc., Harry Alan	026012318
McIninch Scholarship Fund, The	026076262
Nashua Children's Association	020222162
Speare Foundation, Inc., Sceva	026011447
Taylor Home	020222149

New Jersey

Fellowship in Prayer, Inc.	135562408
Hersh Foundation, Inc., Dorothy B.	222280011
Leavitt Foundation, N. R.	226034106
Rahway Geriatrics Center, Inc.	222379197

New Mexico

La Vida Llena	850282570
Los Padrinos	850242722

New York

Alworth Trust f/b/o Marshall & Nellie Alworth Memorial Fund, Marshall	136041237
American Committee for Shenkar College in Israel, Inc.	237090228
Beth Abraham Housing Development Fund Company, Inc.	133067236
Bly Trust B, Halton D.	166154358
Bolton Fund, Inc., Frances P.	136069816
Bowen Charitable Fund, M. S. & W.	166273794
Carleton Charitable Trust f/b/o Columbia University, Christine S.	136843024
Cedar Fund, Inc.	136091737
College Development Foundation of Cortland, Inc.	160979814
Cornell Memorial Foundation, Joseph and Robert, The	133097502
D M Foundation, The	237345848
Duffy Foundation, George	146016445
Eckler Scholarship Trust, Leopold	222644263
Everett Charitable Trust, Fred M. and Ora H.	166018093
Eye Surgery Fund, Inc.	131992063
Faxton Street Home, Inc.	150539099
15 State Street Housing Trust	136860034
Fosburgh Foundation, Mary C.	136790979
Fund for European Scouting	136804976
Gilbert Memorial Trust, Fitch	136038276
Gleason Fund, Inc. Life Benefit Plan	166024331
Glorney Foundation, Inc., Corlette	136104151
Grenfell Association of America	136083942
Harcourt Foundation, Inc., Alfred, The	136084636
Harden Trust for Harrybrooke Park, Frank A.	136182462
Harned Trust Fund, Bedell Holmes	136839419
Hermitage Foundation Trust, The	136036378
Homan, Jr. Trust, B. H.	136741112
Huntington Charitable Trust f/b/o American Academy, Archer M.	136078583
Huntington Mariners Museum, Archer M.	136070709
Huntington Trust f/b/o American Academy and Institute of Arts and Letters and National Institute of Arts, Archer M.	136035643
Huyck Trust f/b/o the Edward Niles Huyck Foundation, Jessie van Antwerp	136047631
Hylas Charitable Foundation	133194063
Hyman Charitable Trust, Samuel M.	136761282
Isham Trust, Charles	136372804
Jacobs Foundation, Inc., Harry & Rose	136161740
Kade Fund in Memory of Max Kade, Annette	136754615
Kissam/Fordham Law Trust	136806139
Leland Trust for Charitable Purposes	136136775
M.E.E.T. Ophthalmology Foundation, Inc.	510243492
March Scholarship Fund, Clara A.	166119078
Marine Society of the City of New York	135643623
Melville Trust f/b/o Museums at Stony Brook, D. B.	133305823
Mohawk Homestead	150532222
Morgan Educational Fund, Urban	136750433
Morris Foundation u/w of Constance Lily Rothschild Morris, Constance	136058658
Moses Trust, Henry L.	136067865
Ocko Foundation, Inc., Rose	133006279
Oishei Appreciation Charitable Trust, John R.	166093037
Padula Foundation, Louis Paul and Christine	132905417
Peckham Trust f/b/o Chenago Valley Home, Mary M.	156017709
Perkins Gardens, Board of Trustees of	136056026
Pincus Foundation, Inc., Hannah Moisha	237032218

	E.I.N.
Poetry Society of America	136160421
Rare Breeds Survival Foundation of America	132909879
Schneiderman Foundation, Inc., Robert and Irwin	133422543
Schneier Charitable Trust, Saul	166229110
Selz Foundation, Inc.	133180806
Sheldon Trust f/b/o Ralph C. Sheldon Foundation, Isabella M.	136866947
Shields "A" Residuary Trust, Richard Tyner	136843700
Shubert Trust f/b/o Shubert Foundation, Lee	136260534
Smith Foundation, Flora Bernice	510181016
Smith Scholarship, Charles & Charlotte Bissell	146105261
South Fork Land Foundation, Inc.	237408436
Thompson Fund, William B.	136089682
Tinker 1957 Charitable Trust, Edward R.	136772877
Vanderbilt University Trust	136029309
Wallace Trust, DeWitt & Lila, The	133230554
Ward Charitable Trust, Justine B.	136728846
Watson Charitable Trust, Arthur K.	132989468
Wells Manor Housing Development Fund Corp.	112611902
Williams Home, Percy	131655266
Wolf, M.D. Scholarship Fund, Charles F.	141580597
Woodson Trust, Margaret C.	136072332
Yee Foundation, Inc., S. K.	133202047

North Carolina

Capel Charitable Trust	510160511
Davis Trust, James W.	566038479
Fassett Memorial Trust, Lucy T.	237357891
Fleshman-Pratt Foundation, Inc.	566063639
Foundation of Hope for Research & Treatment of Mental Illness	581654500
Morrison Charitable Trust	566093800
Myers Testamentary Trust f/b/o Mars Hill College, Elizabeth A.	566195036
Reddish Trust f/b/o South Mountain Industrial Institute, et al, Minnie Huffman	586151929

North Dakota

Merritt Memorial Trust, Sam and Bertha	237035116
Tisdale Foundation	450366901

Ohio

A.I.T. Foundation, Inc.	237026862
Abbott Home	314379421
American Electric Power System Educational Trust, The	237418083
Churches United for Senior Housing, Inc.	311036440
Clements Foundation, Vida S.	316095287
DeGenhart Paperweight and Glass Museum, Inc., The	310957101
Donahue Trust, Mary B.	346506072
Greene Charitable Trust, Helen Wade	346527172
Kling Trust, Louise	346841720
Kulas Trust No. 1, Elroy J.	346747423
Lehman Memorial Foundation, Carl, Ernest & Otto	346873806
Milligan Nursing Fund, Jane	346603468
Newcomb Fund, Helen D. and Adrian G.	346754483
Price Foundation, Harley C. & Mary Hoover	346510993
Ritter Trust, J. F. William	346555183
Schell Foundation, Charles E.	316019719
Shinnick Trust, William M.	316024875
Stambaugh Charitable Foundation, Arnold D. & Helen R., The	341327065
Toledo Community Foundation Donor Directed Pooled Fund	341243271
Weatherhead Estate Trust, Albert J.	346580925
Wexner Foundation, Leslie H.	311142480
Wolle Foundation Trust, Helen S.	346648972
Women's Philanthropic Union	340782268
Zartman Trust, Fred B. and Julia McC.	310601919

Oklahoma

Bartlett Foundation, Edward E. Bartlett & Helen Turner	736092250
Dobson Trust, Nellie	736131333
Grimes Foundation, Otha H.	731293858

Oregon

	E.I.N.
Brown Trust, E. C.	936019291
Carruth Foundation, Howard E.	930713792
McDowell-Catt Foundation	930437990
Morgan Fund for the Blind, J. R. & Emily	510192477
Sommer Memorial Lecture Fund, Ernest A., The	936019493
West Scholarship Fund, Merle S. & Emma J.	936160221

Pennsylvania

American Historical Truck Museum and Library	237240758
Baker Trust, Charles J.	236434249
Baumeister Reichard Trust Fund	232137301
Bell Trust, C. Herbert	236296503
Black Rock Retreat Association	231683475
Clamer Foundation, Guilliam H., The	236678246
Coulter Trust f/b/o Greensburg Recreation Board, William A.	256018848
Countess Detrampe Home for Unwanted Dogs	232020935
Elkins Fund, Lewis	236214962
England Trust, Elizabeth R.	236606334
Ephrata Recreation Center	231392955
Erdman Trust, Florence Waring	236225822
Feigler Trust, Ervin D.	236767052
Fetherston Foundation	231899347
Forrest Home, Edwin	231351240
Himmelstein Educational Trust	232111548
Home for Homeless Women	232256903
JGA Foundation	232326454
Knox Trust, Charles	236225502
Kratz Foundation, Jacob W.	236560409
Lacawac Sanctuary Foundation, Inc.	236419952
Lavino Foundation, Edwin M.	232032639
Lowengard Scholarship Foundation, Leon	236236909
McGillick Foundation, Francis Edward	251192205
Mercer Fonthill Museum, Trustees of the	231976299
Miller Trust, Edwill B.	236657558
Pennsylvania Society of the Sons of the Revolution	231353372
Presser Foundation, Theodore	237147687
Ressler Mill Foundation	236430663
Reyenthaler Memorial Home	236205492
Ross Loan Fund, The	236262609
Segui Residuary Trust, Bernardo J.	236494763
Vogeley T. Memorial Trust	256235851
Weller Foundation, Carl E. & Emily	222579082
West Foundation, Sara E. T.	236722334
Woods-Marchand Foundation, Mary M.	256018836

Rhode Island

Ballou Home for the Aged of Woonsocket, Rhode Island	050260671
Block Island Conservancy, Inc.	237226378

South Carolina

Arnold Memorial Foundation, Ben	576029371
Milliken Foundation, Inc., Seth M.	237213940
Sirrine Textile Foundation, Inc., J. E.	576025551

South Dakota

Dow Home, Inc., Baron & Emilie	466018386
McCrossan Foundation	460241590

Tennessee

Potter Trust, Valerie B.	581309898
Street Foundation, Gordon	620634450
Weir Trust, Joseph L.	626172822

Texas

Albaugh Trust, Ralph Buchanan	746041694
Boys Inc. of Dallas	751836904
Boys Inc. of Tarrant County	751828987
Brinton Educational and Charitable Trust, Frank & Ina	746036133
Bryce Trust No. 417, William	751682810
Burse Trust, Right Reverend Monsignor Henry and Julia Buchanan	742466542
Chandler Memorial Home	741143117
Clough Foundation	741686258
Collins Home for Women, Ben & Jane	750939908
Excellence in Education Foundation	751075163
Gething Memorial Trust, Margaret Allan	136600238

	E.I.N.
Gohlman Foundation, The	760162860
Hall Charitable Remainder Trust No. 7	756251306
Heard Foundation, Bessie	756035566
Heard-Craig Womens Club Trust	751362043
Hendrick Home for Children Trust	750827445
Imperial Palace Foundation - Dramatic Order Knights of Khorassa	520620506
Lanier Operating Foundation	237269729
Lux Trust, Dr. Konrad & Clara	746338117
McFaddin Ward House, Inc.	760074107
McNutt Memorial Foundation, V. H.	746035044
Miller Community Fund, Rudolph C.	741983753
Moor Children's Home, Lee	746033972
Navarro County Educational Foundation, Inc.	752227788
Newby Memorial Students Loan Fund	756013857
Newell Charitable Trust, W. P. & Dell Andrews	756059308
North Texas Higher Education Authority	237133739
Radford Trust, Rupert & Lillian	746320727
Ripley Foundation, Daniel and Edith	746049474
Slaughter Trust, Dick	756007584
Slick Memorial Trust for the Mind Science Foundation, Tom	746178406
Webre Foundation, Iris & Lloyd	760240169

Utah

Stewart Foundation, Donnell B. and Elizabeth Dee Shaw	876160658

Vermont

Barton Chambers Apartments, Inc.	237385650
Fletcher Farm Foundation, Inc.	036007183
Skinner Library, Mark	030184260

Virginia

	E.I.N.
American National Heritage Association, Inc.	510137948
Anderson Trust for Friendship Baptist Church, William W.	546131635
Armistead III Trust, Peter	526189264
Bustard Charitable Permanent Trust Fund, Elizabeth & James	546250970
Chastain Home for Gentlewomen	546044813
Peters Research Center for Parkinson's Disease and Disorders of the Central Nervous System Foundation, Harvey W.	541372833
Petersburg Home for Ladies, Inc.	540515720
Saint Andrew's Association	546039947
Via-Bradley College of Engineering Foundation	541402562

Washington

Cheney Foundation, Trust for the Ben B.	237215379
Egtvedt Charitable Trust, Clairmont L. and Evelyn S., The	916062228
Gehr Foundation, Emma C.	916279262
Irvine Testamentary Trust, Lizzie Brownell & John H.	916027040
Mattison Charitable Trust, Inez D.	237212646
Rainbow Lodge Retreat Center	911013034
Trimble Fund, George W.	916026531
Valle Scholarship Trust, Henrik A.	916233353
West Educational Fund, W. F. & Blanche E.	916101769
Wilson Foundation, John & Mary	237425273

West Virginia

Hood Memorial Trust Fund	556076900

Wisconsin

Amann Foundation	391269081
Brown-Wilcox Trustees Company, Inc., Brown-Wilcox Home for the Aged	390806176
Frank Family Memorial Scholarship Fund	396270979
Harmon Trust, Hester Ann	396035602
Nelson Trust, Victor and Mary D.	396184729
Xavier Foundation, Inc.	930847512

Wyoming

Cody Medical Foundation	836006491
Ivinson Memorial Home for Aged Ladies	830179773
Thorne-Rider Foundation	830203706
White Memorial Foundation, Ted and Marie	836018510

INDEXES

INDEX TO DONORS, OFFICERS, TRUSTEES

GEOGRAPHIC INDEX

Foundations in boldface type make grants on a national or regional basis; the others generally limit giving to the city or state in which they are located.

COLORADO

CONNECTICUT

DELAWARE

DISTRICT OF COLUMBIA

FLORIDA

GEORGIA

HAWAII

IDAHO

ILLINOIS

INDIANA

IOWA

KANSAS

KENTUCKY

LOUISIANA

MAINE

MARYLAND

MASSACHUSETTS

MICHIGAN

MINNESOTA

MISSISSIPPI

MISSOURI

MONTANA

NEBRASKA

NEVADA

NEW HAMPSHIRE

NEW JERSEY

NEW MEXICO

NEW YORK

OKLAHOMA

OREGON

PENNSYLVANIA

UTAH

VERMONT

VIRGINIA

WASHINGTON

WEST VIRGINIA

WISCONSIN

WYOMING

TYPES OF SUPPORT INDEX

Foundations in boldface type make grants on a national or regional basis; the others generally limit giving to the city or state in which they are located.

Annual campaigns: any organized effort by a nonprofit to secure gifts on an annual basis; also called annual appeals.

Building funds: money raised for construction of buildings; may be part of an organization's capital campaign.

Capital campaigns: a campaign, usually extending over a period of years, to raise substantial funds for enduring purposes, such as building or endowment funds.

Conferences and seminars: a grant to cover the expenses of holding a conference.

Consulting services: professional staff support provided by the foundation to a nonprofit to consult on a project of mutual interest or to evaluate services (not a cash grant).

Continuing support: a grant that is renewed on a regular basis.

Deficit financing: also known as debt reduction. A grant to reduce the recipient organization's indebtedness; frequently refers to mortgage payments.

Emergency funds: a one-time grant to cover immediate short-term funding needs on an emergency basis.

Employee matching gifts: a contribution to a charitable organization by a corporate employee which is matched by a similar contribution from the employer. Many corporations support employee matching gift programs in higher education to stimulate their employees to give to the college or university of their choice.

Employee-related scholarships: a scholarship program funded by a company-sponsored foundation usually for children of employees; programs are frequently administered by the National Merit Scholarship Corporation which is responsible for selection of scholars.

Endowment funds: a bequest or gift intended to be kept permanently and invested to provide income for continued support of an organization.

Equipment: a grant to purchase equipment, furnishings, or other materials.

Exchange programs: usually refers to funds for educational exchange programs for foreign students.

Fellowships: usually indicates funds awarded to educational institutions to support fellowship programs. A few foundations award fellowships directly to individuals.

General purposes: a grant made to further the general purpose or work of an organization, rather than for a specific purpose or project; also called unrestricted grants.

Grants to individuals: awards made directly by the foundation to individuals rather than to nonprofit organizations; includes aid to the needy. (See also 'Fellowships' and 'Student aid.')

In-kind gifts: a contribution of equipment, supplies, or other property as distinct from a monetary grant. Some organizations may also donate space or staff time as an in-kind contribution.

Internships: usually indicates funds awarded to an institution or organization to support an internship program rather than a grant to an individual.

Land acquisition: a grant to purchase real estate property.

Lectureships: usually indicates a grant to an educational institution to support a lectureship program.

Loans: temporary award of funds which usually must be repaid. (See also 'Program-related investments' and 'Student loans.')

Matching funds: a grant which is made to match funds provided by another donor. (See also 'Employee matching gifts.')

Operating budgets: a grant to cover the day-to-day personnel, administrative, and other expenses for an existing program or organization.

Professorships: usually indicates a grant to an educational institution to endow a professorship or chair.

Program-related investments: a loan made by a private foundation to profit-making or nonprofit organizations for a project related to the foundation's stated purpose and interests. Program-related investments are often made from a revolving fund; the foundation generally expects to receive its money back with interest which will then provide additional funds for loans to other organizations.

Publications: a grant to fund reports or other publications issued by a nonprofit resulting from research or projects of interest to the foundation.

Renovation projects: grants for renovating, remodeling, or rehabilitating property.

Research: usually indicates funds awarded to institutions to cover costs of investigations and clinical trials. Research grants for individuals are usually referred to as fellowships.

Scholarship funds: usually indicates a grant to an educational institution or organization to support a scholarship program, mainly for students at the undergraduate level. (See also 'Employee-related scholarships'; for scholarships paid to individuals, see 'Student aid.')

Seed money: a grant or contribution used to start a new project or organization. Seed grants may cover salaries and other operating expenses of a new project. Also known as 'start-up funds.'

Special projects: grants to support specific projects or programs as opposed to general purpose grants.

Student aid: assistance awarded directly to individuals in the form of educational grants or scholarships. (See also 'Employee-related scholarships.')

Student loans: assistance awarded directly to individuals in the form of educational loans.

Technical assistance: operational or management assistance given to nonprofit organizations; may include fundraising assistance, budgeting and financial planning, program planning, legal advice, marketing, and other aids to management. Assistance may be offered directly by a foundation staff member or in the form of a grant to pay for the services of an outside consultant.

Annual campaigns

Building funds

Capital campaigns

Conferences and seminars

Consulting services

Continuing support

Deficit financing

Emergency funds

Employee matching gifts

Employee-related scholarships

Endowment funds

Equipment

Exchange programs

Fellowships

General purposes

Grants to individuals

In-kind gifts

Internships

Land acquisition

Lectureships

Loans

Matching funds

Operating budgets

Professorships

Program-related investments

Publications

West Virginia: Kanawha 7406
Wisconsin: **Bradley 7433,** Evjue 7454, **Johnson 7478,** Kohler 7484, La Crosse 7488, Stackner 7544
Wyoming: Tonkin 7579

Renovation projects

Alabama: Sonat 59
Arizona: Arizona 70, First 76, Tucson 100, Whiteman 105
California: Ahmanson 144, **Amado 151, Baker 174,** Bright 221, Cowell 272, Crocker 275, **Doe 293,** Fairfield 317, Gellert 360, Gellert 361, Hedco 406, Herbst 411, Humboldt 431, Irvine 435, Jones 447, Keck 455, Koret 467, Marin 508, McConnell 524, Milken 535, Milken 537, Monterey 543, **Packard 584,** Parker 588, Parsons 589, Pasadena 592, Peninsula 599, Pratt 619, Sacramento 646, San Diego 648, Santa Barbara 653, Sonoma 702, Springhouse 706, Stafford 707, Stulsaft 722, Times 744, Tuohy 757, Valley 764, W.W.W. 773, Weingart 783, Wells 789
Colorado: Boettcher 817, Bonfils-Stanton 818, Denver 831, El Pomar 833, Gates 840, Johnson 853, Piton 877, Stone 888
Connecticut: Barnes 909, **Bingham's 913,** Bodenwein 916, **Community 929,** Gernon 959, Hartford 968, Hartford 969, Palmer 1014, **Panwy 1016,** Pequot 1018, Waterbury 1055
Delaware: Crystal 1082, **Fair 1087, Gurkha 1093, Raskob 1117**
District of Columbia: Fannie 1149, Fowler 1154, Graham 1164, **Loyola 1185,** Post 1198, Weir 1212
Florida: Beveridge 1243, Bush 1259, C.E. 1260, Center 1263, **Chatlos 1267,** Dade 1278, **Davis 1284,** Falk 1302, Foulds 1312, Friends' 1316, **Frueauff 1317,** Mayerson 1391, Mills 1403, Orlando 1420, Selby 1461
Georgia: Atlanta 1525, Atlanta 1526, Campbell 1544, Cox 1564, Day 1568, English 1578, Equifax 1579, Evans 1580, Georgia 1591, Glancy 1597, Illges 1611, Kuhrt 1615, Lee 1618, Marshall 1624, Murphy 1627, Porter 1638, Ships 1656, South 1657, Trust 1661, Woodruff 1678
Hawaii: Atherton 1684, Brewer 1687, Castle 1690, Cooke 1692, First 1694, Hawaii 1696, Hawaiian 1697, PRI 1705, Wilcox 1711
Idaho: Morrison 1724
Illinois: Beloit 1771, Borg-Warner 1787, **Brach 1793,** Champaign 1814, Chicago 1820, CLARCOR 1824, Coleman 1829, Continental 1832, Crown 1843, Grainger 1916, Haffner 1921, Harris 1925, Hermann 1938, McCormick 2016, Millard 2031, Nalco 2046, Northern 2053, OMC 2056, Pick 2067, Quaker 2082, Regenstein 2087, Rockford 2097, Upton 2179, USG 2180, Woods 2195
Indiana: Ball 2208, Ball 2209, Foellinger 2235, Fort 2236, Hayner 2244, Heritage 2245, Indianapolis 2256, Irwin-Sweeney-Miller 2258, Martin 2274, Miles 2281, Vevay-Switzerland 2319
Iowa: Bechtel 2331, Maytag 2355, Windsor 2382
Kansas: Baehr 2386, Beech 2391, DeVore 2400, Dreiling 2403, **Koch 2423,** Powell 2431, **Stauffer 2443,** Yellow 2448
Kentucky: Brown 2451, Gheens 2460, Robinson 2478, Vogt 2483
Louisiana: Baton 2488, Beaird 2490, Monroe 2526, Shreveport-Bossier 2539, Zigler 2552
Maine: Warren 2568
Maryland: Abell 2569, Baker 2573, Knott 2635, Macht 2645, Marshall 2646, Pearlstone 2665, USF&G 2697
Massachusetts: Alden 2713, Bank 2727, Blanchard 2739, Boston 2741, Boston 2743, Boston 2744, Boynton 2746, Campbell 2759, Chase 2767, Chase 2768, Codman 2774, Daniels 2790, Dexter 2798, Farnsworth 2815, Forte 2827, Fuller 2831, GenRad 2833, Henderson 2856, Heydt 2857, McCarthy 2912, Norton 2935, Parker 2943, Peabody 2944, Polaroid 2957, Prouty 2960, Ratshesky 2965, Riley 2971, State 3007, Stevens 3012, Stevens 3013, Stoddard 3014, Thompson 3028, Worcester 3054
Michigan: **Bauervic-Paisley 3066,** Dalton 3083, Dow 3102, Fremont 3123, **General 3128,** Grand 3137, Hudson-Webber 3153, Kennedy 3172, **Kresge 3174,** Lansing 3177, McGregor 3190, Merillat 3194, Midland 3198, Muskegon 3211, Northeast 3213, Sage 3231, Simpson 3243, Wickes 3284, Wilson 3288
Minnesota: Andersen 3303, Bigelow 3313, Bush 3317, **Deluxe 3338,** Duluth-Superior 3343, First 3351, Griggs 3362, Marbrook 3393, Mardag 3394, McKnight 3397, Ordean 3423, Red 3431, Saint Paul 3438, Weyerhaeuser 3461
Missouri: Anheuser-Busch 3484, Brown 3501, Community 3507, Green 3542, Hall 3544, Kansas 3560, Long 3572, Mathews 3581, Oppenstein 3602, Pendergast-Weyer 3605, Speas 3632, St. Louis 3634, **Sunnen 3641,** Union 3651
Montana: Montana 3672
Nebraska: Kiewit 3698, Omaha 3707, Phelps 3710
Nevada: First 3727, Wiegand 3740
New Hampshire: Hunt 3752, Mascoma 3759
New Jersey: **Allied-Signal 3775,** Campbell 3802, Harris 3850, Hyde 3860, Kirby 3880, Ohl 3922, Rippel 3935, Schering-Plough 3947, Snyder 3956, Turrell 3975, **Union 3976,** Victoria 3982, Westfield 3990
New Mexico: Carlsbad 4002, Maddox 4004, PNM 4006
New York: Achelis 4014, Albany's 4029, Alexander 4030, Allyn 4035, Astor 4062, **AT&T 4063,** Badgeley 4072, Barker 4086, Bayne 4097, **Booth 4139,** Buffalo 4164, Central 4196, Chautauqua 4201, Cowles 4260, Curtice-Burns/Pro-Fac 4275, Davenport-Hatch 4285, **Dillon 4313, Dorr 4325,** Emerson 4351, Evans 4360, French 4406, Gifford 4432, Glens 4443, Hackett 4517, Hayden 4541, Heckscher 4549, **Johnson 4623,** Jones 4625, Kaufmann 4651, Macdonald 4784, **Mayer 4825, McDonald 4835, Merrill 4853,** Milbank 4863, Morgan 4879, Northern 4935, O'Connor 4940, Raymond 5034, Reed 5042, Rochester 5077, **Ross 5103,** Schenectady 5140, Sheafer 5173, Snow 5210, Stern 5258, Stevens 5260, Sulzberger 5271, **Thorne 5296,** United 5323, Uris 5326, **Warhol 5351,** Weinberg 5372, Western 5385, Wikstrom 5396
North Carolina: Bryan 5456, Cannon 5460, Cumberland 5473, Daniels 5475, Dover 5481, Duke 5483, First 5493, Gaston 5495, Greensboro 5502, Kellenberger 5515, McAdenville 5531, Proctor 5551, Reynolds 5554, Rogers 5562, Smith 5567, Wachovia 5577, Western 5580
North Dakota: Fargo-Moorhead 5587
Ohio: Alms 5597, American 5601, Ashtabula 5607, Barr 5616, Beecher 5620, Beecher 5621, Beecher 5622, Beeghly 5623, **Bingham 5632,** Bruening 5642, Cincinnati 5655, Cleveland 5658, Columbus 5662, Columbus 5663, Coshocton 5667, Dayton 5675, Estabrook 5695, Fifth 5700, Finnegan 5702, Gund 5743, House 5764, Hynes 5771, Iddings 5772, Ingram 5774, Jergens 5780, Knight 5792, Kulas 5796, Mather 5815, Moerlein 5832, Molyneaux 5833, Montgomery 5835, Murch 5840, Murphy 5843, Nippert 5850, Ohio 5860, Ohio 5862, Prentiss 5877, Russell 5901, Schmidlapp 5911, Schottenstein 5913, Slemp 5932, Smith 5937, Stocker 5947, Stouffer 5948, Stranahan 5949, Toledo 5964, Troy 5969, Watson 5982, White 5991, Yassenoff 6000, Youngstown 6002
Oklahoma: **Broadhurst 6011,** Harris 6030, Historical 6032, Kerr 6038, Kerr 6039, Mabee 6044, McMahon 6047, **Noble 6051,** Occidental 6052, Phillips 6060
Oregon: Collins-McDonald 6097, Hunt 6109, Jackson 6110, Meyer 6118, Oregon 6120, Tektronix 6125, Walton 6129
Pennsylvania: **Air 6135,** Alcoa 6137, **Atochem 6149,** Beatty 6155, Beitel 6156, Bethlehem 6163, Consolidated 6198, Emergency 6224, Grundy 6263, Heinz 6276, Heinz 6277, Hillman 6283, Hillman 6284, Jennings 6304, Justus 6307, Justus 6308, Kline 6316, Lancaster 6321, McCune 6343, McLean 6349, Mellon 6355, Mellon 6357, 1957 6374, Penn 6382, **Pew 6384,** Phillips 6386, Pittsburgh 6391, Polk 6396, **Presser 6399,** Rider-Pool 6410, Scranton 6431, Smith 6445, Smith 6447, Stackpole-Hall 6458, Stockton 6467, Stott 6469, Trexler 6484, Union 6486, USX 6487, Wells 6497, **Whitaker 6503,** Widener 6505, Williams 6508
Puerto Rico: Puerto Rico 6519
Rhode Island: Champlin 6527, **Ford 6534,** Old 6550, Rhode Island 6554
South Carolina: Bailey 6571, Close 6579, Greenville 6585, Self 6605, Spartanburg 6609, Trident 6614
Tennessee: Benwood 6626, Chattanooga 6638, East 6646, Gherkin 6650, HCA 6656
Texas: Abilene 6709, Austin 6723, Brookshire 6749, Brown 6751, Carter 6763, Constantin 6782, Cullen 6793, Dallas 6794, Davis 6798, Doss 6809, Dougherty 6810, Ellwood 6821, Enron 6822, Fifth 6832, George 6846, Haas 6857, Harrington 6869, Hillcrest 6879, Hoblitzelle 6881, Johnson 6896, Kempner 6904, **Kleberg 6911,** Koehler 6916, Lightner 6925, Meadows 6958, Moody 6964, Munson 6972, **Oldham 6984,** Richardson 7017, Rockwell 7022, San Antonio 7028, **Shell 7043,** Simmons 7045, Straus 7060, Swalm 7068, Tarrant 7071, **Texas 7080,** Trull 7084, Turner 7085, Vaughan 7090, Waco 7094, Waggoner 7095, Wright 7127
Vermont: Lintilhac 7166
Virginia: Cabell 7182, **Gannett 7205,** Portsmouth 7258, Richmond 7265, Scott 7267, Seay 7268, Universal 7283, Washington 7285, Wheat 7286
Washington: Archibald 7293, Blue 7301, Johnston-Hanson 7328, Matlock 7340, McEachern 7341, New Horizon 7350, Norcliffe 7351, Robertson 7361, Seafirst 7364, Seattle 7365, Skinner 7368, Washington 7380, Weyerhaeuser 7386, Wharton 7387
West Virginia: Clay 7395, Daywood 7396, McDonough 7409
Wisconsin: **Bradley 7433,** Consolidated 7445, Cudahy 7448, Evinrude 7453, Gardner 7461, La Crosse 7488, McBeath 7500, Milwaukee 7506, Siebert 7541, Time 7548, Wisconsin 7563, Ziemann 7570

Research

Alabama: **Blount 9, Child 15,** Dixon 20, Dixon 21, **Gitenstein 30,** Hill 35, Meyer 44, Mitchell 47, Shook 55, Smith 58, Sonat 59
Alaska: Alaska 65
Arizona: Arizona 70, Cummings 72, First 76, Flinn 77, **Hermundslie 82, Kieckhefer 83,** Mulcahy 87, **Research 94,** Whiteman 105
Arkansas: Arkansas 109, **Nolan 121,** Ross 128
California: **Aequus 143,** Albertson 145, Allen 146, **Amado 151, American 152, Ameritec 154, Baker 174,** Bank 176, Baxter 183, Beckman 188, **C.S. 234,** California 239, **Carsey 246,** Christensen 254, Columbia 262, de Guigne 284, Diller 288, Drown 298, Drum 299, Early 303, **Eisenberg 311,** Erteszek 314, Factor 316, FHP 326, Flintridge 336, Fusenot 350, Gellert 360, Gellert 361, Gellert 362, **Getty 365,** Goldwyn 377, Haigh-Scatena 392, Haynes 405, **Hertz 412,** Hofmann 423, Holt 427, **Hoover 429,** Irwin 437, Jameson 441, Jewett 445, Johnson 446, **Kaiser 450,** Keck 455, Kirchgessner 462, Komes 466, Lewis 490, Lucas 497, M.E.G. 503, Margoes 506, Martin 511, Masserini 512, **Maxfield 515,** MCA 520, Mead 526, Milken 535, Milken 537, Monterey 543, Norris 568, Oxnard 579, **Packard 584,** Parker 588, Parsons 589, Pasadena 592, **Pfeiffer 605,** Pioneer 610, **Platt 611,** Powell 618, Pratt 619, **Preuss 620,** Rosenberg 638, Schmidt 663, Seaver 668, Shalan 678, Shoong 685, **Smith 696, Soiland 700, Stans 709,** Stein 714, Stern 715, Stulsaft 722, Thornton 740, Timken-Sturgis 745, Treadwell 754, Trust 756, Unocal 761, Valley 764, van Loben 766, Walker 775, **Warsh-Mott 777,** Washington 778, Wasserman 779, Weingart 783, Welk 787, **Wilbur 797,** Witter 801, Yorkin 804

Scholarship funds

Seed money

Special projects

Student aid

Student loans

Technical assistance

SUBJECT INDEX

Foundations in boldface type make grants on a national or regional basis; the others generally limit giving to the city or state in which they are located.

AIDS

Alcoholism

Animal welfare

Anthropology

Archaeology

Architecture

Arms control

Arts

Asia

Australia

Belgium

Biochemistry

Biological sciences

Biology

Business

Business education

Canada

Cancer

Caribbean

Catholic giving

Catholic welfare

Chemistry

Child development

Child welfare

Citizenship

Civic affairs

Civil rights

Community development

Community funds

Computer sciences

Conservation

Crime and law enforcement

Cultural programs

Dance

Delinquency

Denominational giving

Dentistry

Dermatology

Disadvantaged

Drug abuse

Ecology

Economics

Education

Education--building funds

Education--minorities

Education, early childhood

Educational associations

Educational research

Elementary education

Employment

Energy

Engineering

Environment

Europe

Family planning

Family services

Film

Fine arts

Foreign policy

France

Freedom

Government

Greece

Handicapped

Health

Health services

Heart disease

Heroism

Higher education

Historic preservation

History

Homeless

Hospices

Hospitals

Hospitals--building funds

Hotel administration

Housing

Human rights

Humanities

Hunger

Immigration

Insurance education

Intercultural relations

International affairs

International development

International law

International relief

International studies

Israel

Italy

Japan

Jewish giving

Jewish welfare

Journalism

Labor

Language and literature

Latin America

Law and justice

Leadership development

Legal education

Legal services

Leprosy

Libraries

Literacy

Marine sciences

Mathematics

Media and communications

Medical education

Medical research

Medical sciences

Mental health

Mexico

Middle East

Military personnel

Minorities

Museums

Music

Native Americans

Nursing

Nutrition

Pharmacy

Philippines

Physical sciences

Physics

Poland

Political science

Population studies

Portugal

Protestant giving

Protestant welfare

Psychiatry

Psychology

Public administration

Public affairs

Public policy

Race relations

Recreation

Rehabilitation

Religion

Religion--missionary programs

Religion, Christian

Religious schools

Religious welfare

Rural development

Safety

Schistosomiasis

Science and technology

Social sciences

Social services

Sociology

South Pacific

Southeast Asia

Southern Africa

Spain

Speech pathology

Theater

Theological education

Transportation

Turkey

Welfare, indigent individuals

Wildlife

Women

Youth

FOUNDATIONS NEW TO EDITION 13

The following foundations appear in this edition of *The Foundation Directory* but had not met criteria for inclusion in the 12th Edition. The entries for these foundations are highlighted with a star in the Descriptive Directory. They are included in all indexes.

Keelty Foundation, Inc., The, MD, 2629
Kellen Foundation, Inc., Anna Maria & Stephen, NY, 4656
Keller Foundation, Harry M., CA, 457
Kelley Foundation, Inc., IN, 2262
Kendall Foundation, Thomas and Miriam, The, CA, 458
Kennedy Family Foundation, Inc., Ethel & W. George, The, FL, 1363
Kennedy Foundation, Ethel, NY, 4660
Kennedy Foundation, Karen A. & Kevin W., NY, 4661
Kentucky Social Welfare Foundation, KY, 2468
Keren Alta Fiega Teitelbaum Fund, Inc., NY, 4663
Kervick Trust, Francis W., MA, 2886
Kest Family Foundation, Sol and Clara, The, CA, 460
Key Food Stores Foundation, Inc., NY, 4665
Kilcawley Fund, William H., OH, 5790
Killam Trust, Constance, MA, 2887
Killeshandra Foundation, PA, 6314
Killson Educational Foundation, Winifred & B. A., TX, 6906
Kilpatrick Educational Fund, Martin & Mary, IL, 1975
Kirschner Foundation, E. P. & Roberta L., OK, 6041
Kleinoder Foundation, Inc., Jack, NY, 4677
Knight Charitable Foundation, Norman, MA, 2890
Knight Foundation, William & Elsie, OH, 5793
Knight Fund, R. G. & E. M., IL, 1977
Koehring Foundation, NH, 3756
Kohl Charities, Inc., Herbert H., WI, 7483
Kohns Foundation, Inc., Robert Lee, NY, 4685
Koldyke Family Foundation, The, IL, 1980
Kolker Foundation, Inc., Fabian, MD, 2636
Kolschowsky Foundation, Inc., Gerald A. & Karen A., IL, 1981
Koochner Foundation, NY, 4687
Kopf Foundation, Elizabeth Christy, NY, 4689
Korean Association of New York, Inc., NY, 4690
Korn Foundation, Inc., Richard & Peggy, NY, 4691
Kornreich Foundation, Matthew R. & Susanne L., NY, 4692
Kornreich Foundation, Inc., Morton A. and Jo Anne, NY, 4693
Kramer Family Foundation, Inc., Harold and Adeline, The, NJ, 3884
Kramer Foundation, Inc., Selma & Raymond, NJ, 3885
Krause Charitable Foundation, Henry, KS, 2425
Krieger Charitable Trust, NY, 4701
Kroger Company Foundation, The, OH, 5795
Krueger Charitable Trust, William A., The, FL, 1370
KSM Foundation, NJ, 3886
Kucklinsky Foundation, Fred & Esther, NJ, 3887
Kugler Foundation, IL, 1985
Kugler Foundation, Inc., Michael J., NY, 4705
Kuhne Foundation Trust, Charles W., IN, 2266
Kupferberg Foundation, NY, 4707

Laband Foundation, Walter & Francine, CA, 471
Lancaster Lens, Inc., OH, 5798
Landau Family Foundation, IL, 1986
Lane Family Charitable Trust, CA, 473
Lane Foundation, Minnie & Bernard, VA, 7229
Langworthy Foundation, NJ, 3889
Larson Family Foundation, MI, 3178
Lassalle Fund, Inc., NY, 4719
Laughlin Trust, George A., WV, 7407
Leavens Foundation, The, NJ, 3895
Leavenworth Foundation, Elisha, CT, 992
Lebersfeld Family Charitable Foundation, NJ, 3896
LeBlond Foundation, OH, 5800
Leeds Foundation, Inc., The, NY, 4733
Lefteria Foundation, Inc., NY, 4736
Lehigh Portland Cement Company Charitable Trust, PA, 6327
Leonhardt Foundation, Inc., Dorothea L., The, NY, 4740
Lerman Educational Trust, Harry and Devera, TX, 6921
Lester Foundation, NJ, 3897
Levin Family Foundation, Donald, IL, 1992
Levin Foundation, Louis, NY, 4744
Levinson Foundation, Marilyn & Harry, IL, 1993
Levy Family Foundation, Joseph & Sarah, IL, 1994
Levy Foundation, Achille, CA, 487
Lewis Charitable Foundation, Inc., The, MA, 2898
Liberty Foundation, Inc., OK, 6042
Lichtenberg Foundation, William & Nora, DC, 1183
Lichterman-Loewenberg Foundation, TN, 6663
Lichtman Foundation, NJ, 3900
Lieb Foundation, Inc., David L., NY, 4754
Lighting Research Institute, Inc., NY, 4756
Lime Kiln Valley Foundation, Inc., MD, 2642
Lincoln Foundation, Inc., The, KY, 2472
Lindenbaum Charitable Foundation, Belda & Marcel, NJ, 3902
Linder Family Private Foundation Trust, FL, 1379
Lindler Foundation, George B. and Irene, TX, 6926
Linsey Foundation, Joseph M., MA, 2900
Lippman Family Foundation, Jerome, OH, 5804
Little River Foundation, VA, 7234
Livingston Foundation, Inc., Mollie Parnis, NY, 4770
Livingstone Charitable Foundation, Inc., Betty J. and J. Stanley, The, NC, 5525
Llagas Foundation, CA, 494
Loewenberg Foundation, Inc., NY, 4772
Longenbaugh Foundation, Gillson, TX, 6931
Lorber Foundation, The, NY, 4775
Lord Educational Fund, IL, 2001
Lost Tree Charitable Foundation, Inc., FL, 1381
Louis Foundation, Michael W., IL, 2002
Low Foundation, Inc., NY, 4778
Lowe Memorial Educational Fund, Mary Friese, MA, 2903
Lowry Charitable Foundation, Inc., Sumter and Ivilyn, The, FL, 1383
Lucas Foundation, Anthony Francis, VA, 7235
Luce Charitable Trust, Theodore, NY, 4780
Lund Foundation, CA, 498
Lurie Family Foundation, IL, 2004
Luse Foundation, W. P. & Bulah, TX, 6934
Lushing Family Foundation, Alfred, CA, 500
Luttrell Trust, TX, 6935

M.I.G. Foundation, The, TX, 6937
M/B Foundation, OH, 5807
MacKinnon Fund, Mary W., NY, 4787
MacLeod Stewardship Foundation, Inc., FL, 1385
Maddox Trust, Web, TX, 6939
Malcolm Foundation, David, TX, 6941
Maleh-Shalom Foundation, Inc., NY, 4795
Mann Charitable Foundation, Henry & Belle, IL, 2008
Marcus Family Charitable Trust, William M., MA, 2907
Mariposa Foundation, Inc., NY, 4804
Mark IV Industries Foundation, Inc., NY, 4805
Markel Charitable Trust, Pauline Yuells, NY, 4806
Marks Family Foundation, NY, 4808
Marnie Foundation, LA, 2524
Marshall Foundation, James Harper, The, NY, 4809
Marshall Fund, The, AZ, 85
Martin Trust, Joseph W., RI, 6547
Marx Foundation, Virginia & Leonard, NY, 4813
Mary Foundation, Inc., The, FL, 1389
Mascoma Savings Bank Foundation, NH, 3759
Masland Foundation, Charles H. & Annetta R., FL, 1390
Maslon Foundation, MN, 3395
Massachusetts Maternity & Foundling Hospital Corporation, MA, 2910
Massachusetts Society of the Cincinnati, MA, 2911
Matterhorn Foundation, Inc., The, OH, 5817
Mau Foundation, William K. H., HI, 1701
Maxwell Memorial Foundation, CA, 516
Mayer Foundation, Inc., Chaim, NY, 4824
Mayer Foundation, Robert and Beatrice, IL, 2014
Mayerson Foundation, Manuel D. & Rhoda, FL, 1391
McArthur Foundation, Inc., J. N., FL, 1392
McCall Foundation, Penny, NY, 4829
McCarthy Foundation, Mary A. and John M., NY, 4832
McComas Foundation, Sophia Byers, OR, 6116
McConnell Foundation, Robert Earll, FL, 1393
McCormack Foundation, The, OH, 5819
McCourtney Trust, Flora S., MO, 3583
McDonald & Company Securities Foundation, OH, 5820
McEnroe Foundation, John, NY, 4837
McHale Trust, Frank M., IN, 2276
McIninch Foundation, NH, 3760
McKnight Endowment Fund for Neuroscience, The, MN, 3396
McNamara Foundation, Robert S. and Margaret C., DC, 1190
Meadowdale Foundation, WA, 7343
Meadows Charitable Trust, NY, 4841
Meehan Foundation, Inc., William M. & Miriam F., NY, 4842
Mellam Family Foundation, NY, 4843
Melohn Chesed Fund, Joseph and Martha, NY, 4846
Memphis, Community Foundation of Greater, TN, 6676
Menlo Foundation, CA, 529
Merchants Bank Foundation, Inc., VT, 7167
Merkel Foundation, Inc., WI, 7502
Mermelstein Charitable Foundation, Henry and Louise, IL, 2026
Meshberg Foundation, Inc., Philip & Julia, The, FL, 1397
Metropolitan Health Council of Indianapolis, Inc., The, IN, 2279
Mette Foundation, Inc., MI, 3195
Meyer Educational Trust, Edward E., IN, 2280
Meyer Foundation, The, NY, 4860
Meyer Foundation, Inc., Bert & Mary, FL, 1400
Michaels Scholarship Fund, Frank J., PA, 6362
Microwave Associates Charitable Foundation, MA, 2920
Midwest Charitable Trust Number 7, WI, 7503
Mifflin Memorial Fund, George H. & Jane A., MA, 2922
Milan Foundation, Charles & Florence, MI, 3199
Milheim Foundation, CO, 864
Milken Family Foundation, The, CA, 535
Milken Family Medical Foundation, CA, 536
Milken Foundation, L. and S., CA, 537
Miller Charitable Foundation, Inc., Clyde & Betty, MI, 3200
Miller Charitable Trust, William, IL, 2032
Miller Foundation, Arjay R. & Frances F., CA, 539
Miller Foundation, Diane D., CA, 540
Miller Foundation, Earl B. & Loraine H., CA, 541
Miller Trust, Lila J., WA, 7346
Mirak Foundation, John, MA, 2924
Mitchell, Jr. Trust, Oscar, MN, 3408
Moerlein Foundation, Charles, OH, 5832
Molyneaux Foundation, OH, 5833
Monks Foundation, G. G., ME, 2561
Montana Community Foundation, MT, 3672
Monterey Peninsula Golf Foundation, CA, 544
Moore Family Foundation, CA, 546
Moores Foundation, The, TX, 6965
Moorman Charitable Trust, Pearl C., MO, 3595
Morrill Charitable Foundation, Inc., IN, 2285
Morris Foundation, Inc., Vera & Walter, AR, 118
Morrison Foundation, Ollege and Minnie, TX, 6967
Morrison Trust, Louise L., TX, 6968
Morse Family Foundation, MA, 2926
Moss Charitable Trust, Finis M., MO, 3597
Mount Vernon Mills Foundation, SC, 6597
MSI Foundation, MN, 3409
MSK Foundation, CA, 550
Mugar Foundation, MA, 2928
Mullins Foundation Trust, William O. & Louise H., TX, 6971
Muncie and Delaware County, Inc., Community Foundation of, The, IN, 2286
Murcott Charitable Trust, Charles & Constance, NY, 4895
Murdough Foundation, Thomas G. & Joy P., OH, 5841
Murphy Family Educational Foundation, The, OH, 5842
Murray, Sr. Educational Foundation, Lynne, TX, 6974
Musicians Club of America, NC, 5538
Musser Foundation, Warren V., PA, 6370
Mustard Seed Foundation, Inc., RI, 6548
Mustard Seed Foundation, Inc., VA, 7244
Myers Foundation, Inc., Israel & Mollie, The, MD, 2659

Nanney Foundation, Charles and Irene, NC, 5539
Nash Foundation, Inc., NH, 3761
Needle's Eye, Inc., The, FL, 1414
Neese Family Foundation, Inc., The, IL, 2048

Nelson Family Foundation, CA, 561
Nelson Foundation, Florence, CA, 562
Nelson Foundation, Grace S. & W. Linton, PA, 6371
Nesholm Family Foundation, WA, 7349
Nestor Foundation, Mary Margaret, PA, 6372
Neuhoff Charitable Trust, Joseph O., TX, 6980
Neuman-Publicker Trust, PA, 6373
Nevas Family Foundation, Inc., Leo, CT, 1008
New Cycle Foundation, NY, 4909
New England Biolabs Foundation, MA, 2931
New Hope Foundation, Inc., NY, 4910
New York Society for the Advancement of Cutaneous Biology and Medicine, Inc., CT, 1010
Newburyport Howard Benevolent Society, MA, 2932
Nichols Trust, MA, 2933
Nichoson Foundation, Ethel & Alexander, NY, 4925
Nicol Scholarship Foundation, Helen Kavanagh, FL, 1415
Nolan Foundation, Inc., Robert J., NY, 4928
Noland Memorial Foundation, VA, 7246
Norman/Nethercutt Foundation, Merle, CA, 567
Northeast Michigan Community Foundation, MI, 3213
Northrup II Fund Trust, Edwin D., OH, 5852
Norwottock Charitable Trust, MA, 2936
Numero-Steinfeldt Foundation, MN, 3417
Nutrasweet Company Charitable Trust, The, IL, 2054

O'Neill Charitable Trust, H. M., OH, 5857
O'Neill Foundation, Inc., William J. and Dorothy K., The, OH, 5858
O'Sullivan Children Foundation, Inc., The, NY, 4943
Oak Foundation, Inc., Calvin & Flavia, FL, 1417
Oak Foundation U.S.A., The, CA, 570
Ober Foundation, IN, 2292
Odyssey Partners Foundation, Inc., NY, 4946
Ogilvy Foundation, The, NY, 4949
Ohio National Foundation, The, OH, 5861
Old Kent Charitable Trust, MI, 3214
Olsten Foundation, Inc., William & Miriam, NY, 4954
Omaha Community Foundation, NE, 3707
Orenstein Foundation, Inc., Henry and Carolyn Sue, NJ, 3924
Oristano Foundation, The, DE, 1113
Oritt Foundation, Inc., Selma, FL, 1419
Oshman Foundation, TX, 6986
Osofsky Foundation, Meyer and Aileen, The, AZ, 88
Outagamie Charitable Foundation, Inc., WI, 7514
Overlock Family Foundation, NY, 4964
Ovitz Family Foundation, The, CA, 578

Pacific Endowment, The, CA, 580
Padnos Foundation, Louis & Helen, MI, 3216
Page Foundation, KS, 2430
Palm Beach Community Trust Fund, FL, 1422
Palmer Foundation, George M., MN, 3424
Palmer Fund, Francis Asbury, The, NY, 4970
Paloheimo Charitable Trust, CA, 586
Paragano Family Foundation, Inc., NJ, 3926
Park Foundation, Mary Barratt, SC, 6598
Parker Charitable Foundation, MA, 2942
Parker, Jr. Foundation, William A., GA, 1631
Parkersburg Community Foundation, WV, 7411
Parsons Foundation, Betty, NY, 4976
Paulson Foundation, Henry M. Paulson, Jr. & Wendy J., NY, 4979
Paxson Foundation, Lowell W., FL, 1427
Peacock Foundation, Inc., FL, 1428
Pearce Foundation, OH, 5866
Peerless Foundation, The, OH, 5867
Pendleton Memorial Fund, William L. & Ruth L., AZ, 91
Pepper Family Foundation, IL, 2061
Perlberg Foundation, Inc., Fred & Gertrude, NY, 4987
Perlman Foundation, Harold L., IL, 2064
Perrin Foundation, The, NY, 4989
Perry-Griffin Foundation, The, NC, 5545
Persephone Foundation, MN, 3425
Persis Hawaii Foundation, HI, 1704
Peterson Family Foundation, Inc., NC, 5546
Petrie Foundation, NJ, 3929
Pettit Foundation, Inc., Jane and Lloyd, WI, 7518
Pew Foundation, Mary I. & Robert C., MI, 3219
Philips Industries Foundation, OH, 5872
Phillips Charities, Inc., L. L., WI, 7519
Picotte Family Foundation Trust, NY, 4996
Piedmont Health City Foundation, Inc., SC, 6599
Pierce Trust, Frank, IA, 2361
Pine Street Foundation, NY, 4999
Pine Tree Foundation, PA, 6387
Pines Bridge Foundation, The, NY, 5000
Pinkert Charitable Foundation, IL, 2069
Pioneer Fund, Inc., CA, 610
Piper Foundation, Inc., PA, 6388
Pirelli Armstrong Foundation, Inc., CT, 1020
PMJ Foundation, MO, 3611
Polack Foundation, WA, 7356
Polk Bros. Fifty-Five Plus, IL, 2072
Polk County Community Foundation, Inc., NC, 5548
Poorvu Foundation, William J. & Lia G., MA, 2958
Pope Foundation, Inc., IL, 2075
Port Royal Foundation, Inc., NY, 5010
Porthouse Foundation, OH, 5875
Posnack Family Foundation of Hollywood, FL, 1435
Post Trust, Ralph B., NY, 5012
Potomac Foundation, The, VA, 7259
Powell Foundation, TX, 7006
Powers, Jr. Foundation, Inc., Elaine E. & Frank T., NY, 5014
Prentiss Foundation, James H., TN, 6681
PRI Foundation, HI, 1705
Pritzker Charitable Fund, The, IL, 2079
Progress Education Foundation, The, PA, 6400
Progress Foundation, PA, 6401
Prophet Sisters Foundation, The, IN, 2300
Putnam Prize Fund for the Promotion of Scholarship, William Lowell, MA, 2961

Quad City Osteopathic Foundation, IA, 2365
Quarton-McElroy-IRA Foundation, IA, 2366

Rabb Family Charitable Trust, Esther V. & Sidney R., MA, 2963
Ragland, Jr. Trust, Trent, NC, 5552
Rales Foundation, Norman R. Rales and Ruth, The, FL, 1440
Rank Charitable Trust, Ada & Helen, OH, 5881
Raper Foundation, Inc., Tom, IN, 2303
Ravitch Foundation, Inc., Richard, NY, 5033
Raymond Foundation, Inc., Robert, NY, 5035
Rebny Foundation, Inc., NY, 5039
Rechler Foundation, Inc., Morton & Beverley, NY, 5041
Redhill Foundation - Samuel & Jean Rothberg Family Charitable Trust, IL, 2086
Redies Foundation, Inc., Edward F., MI, 3227
Redmon Foundation, Inc., N. D. & Mary, TX, 7014
Redstone Charitable Foundation, Sumner M., MA, 2966
Regensburger Foundation, Elias & Hanna, TX, 7015
Reich Family Foundation, Henry S. and Anne S., DC, 1200
Reich Fund, The, NY, 5044
Reichmann Family Foundation, The, NY, 5046
Reinhart Memorial Scholarship Foundation, Floyd J., NY, 5047
Reinhold Foundation, Inc., Paul E. & Ida Klare, FL, 1442
Replogle Foundation, Luther I., IL, 2089
Resler Foundation, OH, 5889
Revere Foundation, Inc., The, FL, 1443
Reynolds Foundation, Eleanor T., The, TN, 6683
Rhodebeck Charitable Trust, NY, 5055
Rhoden Charitable Foundation, Elmer C., MO, 3617
Richards Foundation, Inc., Walter Alan, GA, 1643
Richardson Foundation, Frank E. and Nancy M., NY, 5059
Richenthal Foundation, NY, 5061
Riddle Charitable Foundation, J. P., NC, 5560
Rime Companies Charitable Foundation, The, AL, 52
Rincon Foundation, CA, 627
Ritchie Foundation, Mark and Nancy, IL, 2094
Ritter Charitable Trust, George W. & Mary F., OH, 5895
River Road Charitable Corporation, MA, 2972
Robbins Foundation, Inc., NY, 5071
Roberts Foundation, Edward R. & Rosalind S., NY, 5072
Robin Family Foundation, Albert A., IL, 2095
Robinson Foundation, The, TX, 7021
Robinson Foundation, James E., NY, 5073
Robinson Foundation for Hearing Disorders, Inc., CA, 633
Robson Foundation, La Nelle, AZ, 95
Rock Ledge Institute, Inc., CT, 1027
Rockford Community Trust, The, IL, 2097
Rocque Family Foundation, IL, 2098
Roehl Foundation, Inc., WI, 7528
Rogers Brothers Foundation, Inc., TX, 7023
Roosevelt Association, Theodore, The, NY, 5086
Rosen Foundation, Inc., Eli & Mae, CA, 636
Rosenau Foundation, Sidney R., PA, 6417
Rosenberg Charitable Foundation, Theodore, The, CA, 637
Rosenberg, Jr., Family Foundation, Louise and Claude, The, CA, 639
Rosenthal Foundation, Rose & Harry, FL, 1450
Ross Foundation, Inc., NY, 5101
Ross Foundation, Eric F., NJ, 3937
Ross Foundation, Irene Herbert & Harper Grant, NJ, 3938
Ross Foundation, Lyn & George M., NY, 5104
Ross Trust, Edith L. & H. Danforth, ME, 2563
Ross, Jr. Charitable Foundation, Inc., E. Burke, NJ, 3939
Rosse Family Charitable Foundation, Thomas A., MA, 2978
Roswell Foundation, Inc., Elizabeth B. and Arthur E., MD, 2675
Roth Foundation, Inc., Louis T., KY, 2479
Roxboro Foundation, Inc., GA, 1644
Royce Family Fund, Inc., NY, 5107
Rubenstein Foundation, Inc., Frank, NY, 5108
Rudd Foundation, Inc., KY, 2480
Rudolph Foundation, Inc., Jay B., FL, 1451
Rumbaugh Foundation, J. H. & F. H., FL, 1452
Russell Charitable Foundation, Adelia, AL, 53
RWK Foundation, OH, 5902

Saak Trust, Charles E., CA, 645
Sackler Foundation, Arthur M., NY, 5119
Sadinoff Family Foundation, NJ, 3942
Saibel Foundation, Inc., NJ, 3944
Salem Lutheran Foundation, OH, 5903
Salisbury Community Foundation, Inc., NC, 5564
Salmanson Family Foundation, Charles, The, RI, 6556
San Felipe del Rio, Inc., CA, 649
Santvoord Foundation, Inc., Peg, NY, 5130
Sarasota County Community Foundation, Inc., The, FL, 1457
Sargent Foundation, Newell B., WY, 7576
Sarofim Foundation, TX, 7031
Sattler Beneficial Trust, Daniel A. and Edna J., The, CA, 658
Saunders Charitable Foundation, Helen M., The, CT, 1032
Scarff Memorial Foundation, Stephen Edward, The, CA, 661
Schecter Private Foundation, Aaron & Martha, FL, 1459
Scheibler Jr. Trust, James A., TN, 6686
Schiff Foundation, Inc., IL, 2114
Schmeelk Foundation, Inc., Priscilla & Richard, NY, 5149
Schnurmacher Foundation, Inc., Adolph & Ruth, NY, 5150
Schoenstadt Family Foundation, IL, 2119
Schooler Family Foundation, The, OH, 5912
Schoonmaker Foundation, Lucy Kay, PA, 6427
Schoonmaker J-Sewkly Val Hospital Trust, PA, 6428
Schottenstein Foundation, Jerome & Saul, OH, 5913
Schrager Foundation, Philip, NE, 3714
Schwartz Foundation, Inc., Bernard & Irene, NY, 5154
Schwartz Foundation, Inc., Samuel & Bertha, NY, 5156
Schwartze Community Foundation, A. J., MO, 3621
Schwarz Foundation, NJ, 3952
Scudder Association, Inc., The, NY, 5161
Sea Coast Foundation, NY, 5162

Seasongood Good Government Foundation, Murray and Agnes, OH, 5917
Seaver Charitable Trust, Richard C., CA, 667
Segal Foundation, Inc., Hattie and Arnold, NJ, 3953
Segerstrom Foundation, The, CA, 674
Seidman Foundation, The, NY, 5164
Selig Foundation, The, GA, 1652
Servco Foundation, HI, 1707
Shandle Foundation, DE, 1120
Shapell Foundation, David and Fela, CA, 679
Shapell Foundation, Nathan & Lilly, CA, 680
Shapiro Charitable Foundation, Arthur & Bernice, MA, 2991
Sharp Foundation, NY, 5168
Sharpe Family Foundation, NY, 5170
Shattuck Charitable Trust, S.F., WI, 7540
Shaw Charitable Trust, Mary Elizabeth Dee, The, UT, 7157
Shawe Family Charitable Foundation, Inc., MD, 2682
Shaykin Family Foundation, NY, 5172
Shea Foundation, John & Dorothy, CA, 683
Sheaffer Memorial Foundation, Inc., W. A., IA, 2369
Shearman Foundation, Tom B. & Flora, The, LA, 2538
Shelton Foundation, The, NC, 5565
Shepherd Foundation, Inc., GA, 1655
Sherman Educational Fund, IN, 2309
Shimkin Foundation, The, NY, 5178
Shinn Foundation, Inc., George, NC, 5566
Shoemaker Trust for Shoemaker Scholarship Fund, Ray S., PA, 6437
Shook Trust, M. C., TX, 7044
Shughart, Thomson & Kilroy Charitable Foundation Trust, MO, 3625
Shulman Family Foundation, The, TN, 6690
Sibel Family Foundation, Inc., Hanan & Carole, MD, 2684
Sierra Pacific Foundation, CA, 688
Simmons Charitable Trust, The, OH, 5931
Simmons Family Foundation, R. P., PA, 6442
Simpson Foundation, John M., IL, 2135
Simpson Foundation, Joseph T. & Helen M., PA, 6444
Simpson Industries Fund, MI, 3244
Sims Foundation, Sy, NJ, 3955
Singer Foundation, Inc., Herbert & Nell, NY, 5187
Singer Fund, Inc., Louis P., NY, 5188
Sitt Family Foundation, Morris & Eddie, NY, 5190
Sitt 1986 Charitable Trust, Inc., Jack, The, NY, 5191
Skiers Injuries Charities Trust, NY, 5192
Sklarow Memorial Fund, Dr. Louis, NY, 5194
Slavik Foundation Charitable Trust, Joseph F. & Edna, MA, 3002
Smeal Foundation, Mary Jean & Frank P., NY, 5204
Smith Family Foundation, Charles E., VA, 7269
Smith Foundation, Inc., George Graham and Elizabeth Galloway, NY, 5205
Smith Foundation, Inc., McGregor, FL, 1464
Smith Foundation, Roy & Marianne, NY, 5206
Smith 1980 Charitable Trust, Kelvin, OH, 5936
Smysor Memorial Fund, Harry L. & John L., IL, 2140
Snee-Reinhardt Charitable Foundation, PA, 6450
Society for the Relief of Women & Children, NY, 5212
Sofaer Foundation, NY, 5213
Soforenko Foundation, Edwin S., RI, 6558
Solomon, Sarah M., IL, 2144
Solomon Foundation, Peter J. & Linda N., NY, 5217
Solow Foundation, Inc., Sheldon H., NY, 5219
Sonderling Foundation, Inc., The, FL, 1465
Sonnenblick Foundation, Inc., NY, 5221
Sonntag Foundation for Cancer Research, Christine and Alfred, IL, 2145
Sonoma County Foundation, The, CA, 702
Sorenson Family Foundation, Inc., CT, 1039
Soros Foundation-Hungary, Inc., The, NY, 5223
Sosnoff Foundation, Martin T., CT, 1041
South Dakota Community Foundation, SD, 6619
Spalding Health Care Trust, NC, 5568
Special People In Need, IL, 2147
Spektor Family Foundation, Inc., NY, 5224
Spencer Foundation, Galen & Ada Belle, CO, 885
Spencer Trust, John W., CA, 703
Spiegel Family Foundation, Abraham & Edita, CA, 704
Springfield Foundation, The, OH, 5940
Springhouse Foundation, CA, 706
St. Joe Foundation, Inc., FL, 1470

Standard Products Charitable Foundation, OH, 5941
Stanton Irrevocable Charitable Trust, Joan, The, NY, 5238
Starr Foundation, Anne & Jacob, NY, 5240
Stauffer Family Foundation, The, CO, 886
Stebbins Fund, Inc., The, NY, 5244
Stebens Charitable Foundation, Bertha, IA, 2372
Stein Foundation, Sidney J., PA, 6461
Steinbach Foundation, OR, 6123
Steinert Foundation, Albert & Marie, NY, 5252
Steinhardt Foundation, Judy and Michael, The, NJ, 3959
Stephens Foundation Trust, TN, 6693
Stern Family Foundation, Inc., Jane, NY, 5253
Stern Foundation, Inc., Gustav, NY, 5256
Stern Foundation, Helmut, The, MI, 3252
Stern Foundation, Marjorie & Michael, NY, 5259
Stern Foundation for the Arts, Richard J., MO, 3636
Sternberg Foundation, Erich, LA, 2542
Stevens Memorial Fund, Harley and Mertie, OR, 6124
Stewards Fund, The, NC, 5570
Stewart Foundation, Alexander, PA, 6466
Steyer Family Foundation, Inc., Stanley, NY, 5261
Stone Foundation, Inc., The, NY, 5262
Stone Trust, H. Chase, CO, 888
Stonestreet Trust, Eusebia S., TX, 7058
Straus Endowment Fund, Madeline B. & Henry H., IL, 2161
Strauss/Hanauer Memorial Fund, Inc., The, MD, 2688
Structured Employment/Economic Development Corporation, NY, 5268
Stuart, Jr. Foundation, Robert D., IL, 2162
Stumberg, Sr. Orphans, Crippled Children & Handicapped Persons Trust, H. E., TX, 7063
Subotnick Foundation, Stuart and Anita, The, NJ, 3963
Suden Scholarship Trust Fund, Rudy, MT, 3675
Sudler Charitable Trust, Samuel and Claire, The, NJ, 3964
Sulzle Foundation, Inc., Benjamin & Hedwig, NY, 5272
Summerlee Foundation, The, TX, 7065
Sundet Foundation, MN, 3446
Supino Foundation, David J., The, NY, 5275
Sussman Fund, Edna Bailey, NY, 5277
Sutton Family Foundation, Abraham, David & Solomon, NY, 5279
Sutton Foundation, The, NJ, 3966
Swasey Fund for Relief of Public School Teachers of Newburyport, Inc., The, MA, 3023
Sweatt Foundation, Charles B., MN, 3447
Swid Foundation, Stephen C. Swid and Nan G., NY, 5280
Szekely Foundation for American Volunteers, CA, 731

Tal Charitable Trust, The, NJ, 3967
Tamposi Foundation, Inc., The, NH, 3769
Tang Fund, The, NY, 5286
Tang Scholarship Foundation, Cyrus, IL, 2170
Taper Foundation, S. Mark, CA, 735
Tarnopol Foundation, Inc., Michael & Lynne, NY, 5287
Taveggia Mary Antonini Foundation, Charles, IL, 2171
Taylor Family Foundation, TX, 7074
Taylor Trust, Lydia M., OH, 5954
Templeton Foundation, John, TN, 6695
Ten-Ten Foundation, The, MO, 3646
Terry Foundation, The, TX, 7077
Teubert Charitable Trust, James H. and Alice, The, WV, 7415
Thendara Foundation, Inc., The, OH, 5957
Thermo Electron Foundation, Inc., MA, 3027
Thomas Trust, Adele M., NC, 5573
Thompson Trust, Mary Tabb & Clyde Berry, TX, 7081
Tilghman, Sr. Charitable Trust, Bell and Horace, The, VA, 7277
Timme Revocable Trust, Abigail S., CA, 746
Tinker Foundation, Grant A., The, CA, 747
Tipp City Foundation, OH, 5963
Torino Foundation, Francis P., CA, 748
Towbes Foundation, The, CA, 749
Tracy Scholarship Fund, Perry S. and Stella H., CA, 751
Trammell Foundation, The, TX, 7083
Traphagen, Jr. Fund, Ross E., NY, 5306
Trico Foundation, The, MI, 3265

Tripp Foundation, Inc., NY, 5309
Troubh Fund, Jean L. & Raymond S., NY, 5310
True Foundation, WY, 7580
True Trust, Henry A., OH, 5970
Tull Charitable Foundation, The, GA, 1662
Tulsa Foundation, OK, 6070
Tupancy-Harris Foundation of 1986, The, MA, 3033
Turner Fund, Inc., Ruth, NY, 5316

U.S. Oil/Schmidt Family Foundation, Inc., WI, 7550
Uihlein Foundation, Robert A., WI, 7551
Underhill Foundation, NY, 5318
United Counties Trust Foundation, NJ, 3978
USAA Trust, TX, 7087
Uvas Foundation, CA, 763

Valenti Charitable Foundation, IL, 2181
Valspar Foundation, The, MN, 3452
Van Houten Charitable Trust, Edward W. and Stella C., The, NJ, 3980
Van Waveren Foundation, Inc., Ann & Erlo, The, NY, 5331
Vanstrom Trust B., Andrew E., OR, 6128
Vero Beach Foundation for the Elderly, FL, 1492
Vevay-Switzerland County Foundation, Inc., IN, 2319
Vicksburg Hospital Medical Foundation, MS, 3480
Vidinha Charitable Trust, A. & E., HI, 1709
von Bulow Coma and Head Trauma Research Foundation, Sunny, The, NY, 5339

Waddell Ladies Home Association, The, OH, 5977
Wadsworth Memorial Fund, IL, 2183
Walker Foundation, Inc., Charles M., GA, 1663
Walker Wildlife Conservation Foundation, MS, 3482
Wall, Sr. Foundation, E. Craig, SC, 6615
Walter Foundation, Evelyn E., OH, 5980
Walters Family Foundation, Inc., The, NY, 5350
Waltom Foundation, Lillian, The, TX, 7099
Wardle Family Foundation, PA, 6493
Warren Benevolent Fund, Inc., MA, 3038
Warren Foundation, Virgil P., GA, 1665
Washington Research Institute, CA, 778
Wasily Family Foundation, Inc., The, NY, 5355
Wasmer Foundation, The, WA, 7382
Wasserman Foundation, Leo, MA, 3039
Waterloo Civic Foundation, IA, 2379
Waterman Foundation, Inc., The, FL, 1498
Wayne County, Indiana Foundation, Inc., IN, 2320
Weaver Foundation, Inc., NC, 5578
Webber Foundation, TX, 7102
Weber Foundation, Inc., Jacques, NY, 5360
Webster Foundation, TN, 6700
Weckbaugh Foundation, Inc., CO, 896
Weinberg Family Foundation, Judd A. & Marjorie, IL, 2188
Weinberg Foundation, Inc., Louis, NY, 5373
Weiner Foundation, M., NJ, 3988
Weininger Foundation, Inc., Richard and Gertrude, The, NY, 5375
Weiss Foundation, L. A., IL, 2189
Weiss Foundation, Stephen and Suzanne, The, NY, 5378
Weller Foundation, CT, 1056
Wellspring Mission Volunteers Foundation, KS, 2445
Wentworth Foundation, Inc., FL, 1502
West Foundation, GA, 1668
West Foundation, Inc., IN, 2321
West Foundation, Inc., LA, 2544
West Memorial Trust, Flossie E., KS, 2446
Westmark Charitable Foundation, CA, 791
Wexner Institutional Grants Program, Inc., OH, 5989
Whitaker Charitable Foundation, Lyndon C., MO, 3658
White Foundation, Inc., Harry R. & Rita, NY, 5387
White Fund, Inc., MA, 3048
Wickes Foundation, The, CA, 795
Wieland Family Foundation, Inc., John, GA, 1673
Wiener Foundation, Inc., Malcolm Hewitt, NY, 5394
Wiener Fund, Donald B., TN, 6703
Wiggins Memorial Trust, J. J., FL, 1505
Wight Foundation, Inc., The, NJ, 3993
Wilcox Foundation, Elsie H., HI, 1711
Willard Helping Fund, Cecilia Young, TX, 7114

FOUNDATION NAME INDEX